Who'sWho in the Midwest®

Published by Marquis Who's Who®

Titles in Print

Who's Who in America®
Who's Who in America Junior & Senior High School Version
Who Was Who in America®
Historical Volume (1607–1896)
Volume I (1897–1942)
Volume II (1943–1950)
Volume III (1951–1960)
Volume IV (1961–1968)
Volume V (1969–1973)
Volume VI (1974–1976)
Volume VII (1977–1981)
Volume VIII (1982–1985)
Volume IX (1985–1989)
Volume X (1989–1993)
Volume XI (1993–1996)
Index Volume (1607–1996)
Who's Who in the World®
Who's Who in the East®
Who's Who in the Midwest®
Who's Who in the South and Southwest®
Who's Who in the West®
Who's Who in American Education®
Who's Who in American Law®
Who's Who in American Nursing®
Who's Who of American Women®
Who's Who in Finance and Industry®
Who's Who in Medicine and Healthcare™
Who's Who in Science and Engineering®
Index to Marquis Who's Who® Publications
The *Official* ABMS Directory of Board Certified Medical Specialists®

Available on CD-ROM

The Complete Marquis Who's Who® on CD-ROM
ABMS Medical Specialists *PLUS*™

Who's Who in the Midwest®

1996~1997

SILVER 25TH EDITION

Including Illinois, Indiana, Iowa, Kansas, Michigan, Minnesota, Missouri, Nebraska, North Dakota, Ohio, South Dakota, and Wisconsin, and in Canada, Manitoba and western Ontario.

MARQUIS
Who'sWho®
121 Chanlon Road
New Providence, NJ 07974 U.S.A.

Who's Who in the Midwest®

Marquis Who's Who®

Published by Marquis Who's Who, a division of Reed Elsevier Inc.

Library of Congress Catalog Card Number 50-289
International Standard Book Number 0-8379-0726-8 (Classic Edition)
0-8379-0727-6 (Deluxe Edition)
International Standard Serial Number 0083-9787

Manufactured in the United States of America

Table of Contents

Preface ... vi

Board of Advisors ... vii

Standards of Admission ... viii

Key to Information ... ix

Table of Abbreviations ... x

Alphabetical Practices ... xvi

***Who's Who in the Midwest* Biographies** ... 1

Professional Index ... 715
- Agriculture ... 715
- Architecture and Design ... 715
- Arts
  - Literary ... 716
  - Performing ... 717
  - Visual ... 719
- Associations and Organizations ... 720
- Athletics ... 722
- Communications Media ... 723
- Education ... 726
- Engineering ... 733

Finance
- Banking Services ... 738
- Financial Services ... 739
- Insurance ... 742
- Investment Services ... 743
- Real Estate ... 745

Government
- Agency Administration ... 746
- Executive Administration ... 747
- Legislative Administration ... 749

Healthcare
- Dentistry ... 754
- Health Services ... 755
- Medicine ... 762

Humanities
- Liberal Studies ... 765
- Libraries ... 768
- Museums ... 769

Industry
- Manufacturing ... 770
- Service ... 774
- Trade ... 781
- Transportation ... 782
- Utilities, Energy, Resources ... 783

Law
- Judicial Administration ... 783
- Law Practice and Administration ... 784

Military ... 787

Religion ... 788

Science
- Life Science ... 789
- Mathematics and Computer Science ... 791
- Physical Science ... 793

Social Science ... 795

Preface

The Silver 25th Edition of *Who's Who in the Midwest* provides the latest biographical information on the men and women who are shaping the development and growth of midwestern North America. Such individuals are of decided reference value locally and, to an increasing degree, nationally.

The volume contains over 19,000 biographies of people working in Illinois, Indiana, Iowa, Kansas, Michigan, Minnesota, Missouri, Nebraska, North Dakota, Ohio, South Dakota, and Wisconsin in the United States, and from Manitoba and western Ontario in Canada. Some individuals listed are not residents of this region; however, the professional activities of these listees have been widely influential in the midwest.

The persons sketched in this volume represent virtually every important field of endeavor. Included are executives and officials in government, business, education, religion, the press, law, civic activities, and many other fields. Also included are leaders in the fields of science, healthcare, engineering, and notable people involved in the arts and cultural affairs.

Most Biographees have furnished their own data, thus ensuring a high degree of accuracy. As in previous editions, Biographees were given the opportunity to review prepublication proofs of their sketches. In some cases, where individuals of distinct reference value failed to supply information, Marquis staff members compiled the data through independent research. Such sketches are noted with an asterisk.

Also included in the Silver 25th Edition is a Professional Index, which groups Biographees professionally, and within profession, geographically. This reference tool will make it easy for interested readers to find Biographees in any given field or region.

The question is often asked, "How does one get into a Marquis Who's Who volume?" Name selection is based on one fundamental principle: reference value. Biographees in *Who's Who in the Midwest* can be classified within two basic categories: persons who are of regional reference importance to colleagues, librarians, researchers, scholars, the press, participants in business and civic affairs, and others with specific or general inquiry needs; and individuals of national interest who are also of such regional or local importance that their inclusion in the book is essential. Only those individuals deemed reference-worthy have sketches presented in a Marquis publication.

Marquis Who's Who editors exercise the utmost care in preparing each biographical sketch for publication. Occasionally, however, errors do occur. Users of this directory are requested to draw the attention of the publisher to any errors so that corrections can be made in a subsequent edition.

Board of Advisors

Marquis Who's Who gratefully acknowledges the following distinguished individuals who have made themselves available for review, evaluation, and general comment with regard to the publication of the Silver 25th Edition of *Who's Who in the Midwest.* The advisors have enhanced the reference value of this edition by the nomination of outstanding individuals for inclusion. However, the Board of Advisors, either collectively or individually, is in no way responsible for the final selection of names appearing in this volume, nor does the Board of Advisors bear responsibility for the accuracy or comprehensiveness of the biographical information or other material contained herein.

Steven C. Beering
President
Purdue University
West Lafayette, Indiana

Gwendolyn Brooks
Poet Laureate of Illinois
Publisher
The David Company

Charles C. Eldredge
Hall Distinguished Professor
of American Art
University of Kansas
Lawrence, Kansas

Homer W. Giles
Former Chairman
American Economic Foundation
Cleveland, Ohio

Andrew Leckey
Syndicated Investment Columnist
The Chicago Tribune
Financial Commentator
WLS-TV

Martin A. Massengale
President Emeritus
University of Nebraska
Lincoln, Nebraska

Wesley Jennings Matson
Dean Emeritus
Winona State University
Winona, Minnesota

Charles E. Stoltz
President, Owner
Charles E. Stoltz & Associates
Omaha, Nebraska

Marc F. Wilson
Director
The Nelson-Atkins Museum of Art
Kansas City, Missouri

Standards of Admission

The foremost consideration in selecting Biographees for *Who's Who in the Midwest* is the extent of an individual's reference interest. Such reference interest is judged on either of two factors: (1) the position of responsibility held, or (2) the level of achievement attained by the individual.

Admissions based on the factor of position include:

Members of the U.S. Congress

Federal judges

Governors of states covered by this volume

Premiers of Canadian provinces covered by this volume

State attorneys general

Judges of state and territorial courts of highest appellate jurisdiction

Mayors of major cities

Heads of major universities and colleges

Heads of leading philanthropic, educational, cultural, and scientific institutions and associations

Chief ecclesiastics of the principal religious denominations

Principal officers of national and international business

Others chosen because of incumbency or membership

Admission for individual achievement is based on qualitative criteria. To be selected, a person must have attained conspicuous achievement.

Key to Information

[1] WATTS, BENJAMIN GREENE, [2] lawyer; **[3]** b. May 21, 1935; **[4]** s. George and Sarah (Carson) W.; **[5]** m. Ellen Spencer, Sept. 12, 1960; **[6]** children: John Allen, Lucy Anne. **[7]** BS, Northwestern U., 1956; JD, U. Chgo., 1965. **[8]** Bar: Ill. 1965, U.S. Supreme Ct. 1980. **[9]** Mem. legal dept. Standard Publs. Corp., Chgo., 1965-73, asst. counsel, 1973-81, counsel, 1981-83; ptnr. Watts, Clayborn, Johnson & Miller, Oak Brook, Ill., 1983-85, sr. ptnr., 1985—; **[10]** lectr. Coll. of DuPage, 1970—. **[11]** Author: Legal Aspects of Educational Publishing, 1975, Copyright Legalities, 1990, Issues of Intellectual Property Law, 1996. **[12]** Chmn. Downers Grove (Ill.) chpt. ARC, 1982-83; active DuPage council Boy Scouts Am.; trustee Elmhurst (Ill.) Hist. Mus., 1972—; bd. dirs. Big Bros./Big Sisters DuPage County, 1994—. **[13]** Served to lt. USAF, 1959-61. **[14]** Recipient Outstanding Alumnus award Northwestern U., 1971. **[15]** Mem. ABA, Ill. Bar Assn., Chgo. Bar Assn., Am. Mgmt. Assn., Phi Delta Phi, Caxton Club, Tavern Club (Chgo.), Masons **[16]** Democrat. **[17]** Lutheran. **[18]** Home: 543 Farwell Ave Elmhurst IL 60126 **[19]** Office: Watts Clayborn Johnson & Miller 1428 Industrial Ct Oak Brook IL 60521

KEY

[1]	Name
[2]	Occupation
[3]	Vital statistics
[4]	Parents
[5]	Marriage
[6]	Children
[7]	Education
[8]	Professional certifications
[9]	Career
[10]	Career-related activities
[11]	Writings and creative works
[12]	Civic and political activities
[13]	Military
[14]	Awards and fellowships
[15]	Professional and association memberships, clubs, and lodges
[16]	Political affiliation
[17]	Religion
[18]	Home address
[19]	Office address

Table of Abbreviations

The following abbreviations and symbols are frequently used in this book.

*An asterisk following a sketch indicates that it was researched by the Marquis Who's Who editorial staff and has not been verified by the Biographee.
A Associate (used with academic degrees only)
AA, A.A. Associate in Arts, Associate of Arts
AAAL American Academy of Arts and Letters
AAAS American Association for the Advancement of Science
AACD American Association for Counseling and Development
AACN American Association of Critical Care Nurses
AAHA American Academy of Health Administrators
AAHP American Association of Hospital Planners
AAHPERD American Alliance for Health, Physical Education, Recreation, and Dance
AAS Associate of Applied Science
AASL American Association of School Librarians
AASPA American Association of School Personnel Administrators
AAU Amateur Athletic Union
AAUP American Association of University Professors
AAUW American Association of University Women
AB, A.B. Arts, Bachelor of
AB Alberta
ABA American Bar Association
ABC American Broadcasting Company
AC Air Corps
acad. academy, academic
acct. accountant
acctg. accounting
ACDA Arms Control and Disarmament Agency
ACHA American College of Hospital Administrators
ACLS Advanced Cardiac Life Support
ACLU American Civil Liberties Union
ACOG American College of Ob-Gyn
ACP American College of Physicians
ACS American College of Surgeons
ADA American Dental Association
a.d.c. aide-de-camp
adj. adjunct, adjutant
adj. gen. adjutant general
adm. admiral
adminstr. administrator
adminstrn. administration
adminstrv. administrative
ADN Associate's Degree in Nursing
ADP Automatic Data Processing
adv. advocate, advisory
advt. advertising
AE, A.E. Agricultural Engineer
A.E. and P. Ambassador Extraordinary and Plenipotentiary
AEC Atomic Energy Commission
aero. aeronautical, aeronautic
aerodyn. aerodynamic
AFB Air Force Base
AFL-CIO American Federation of Labor and Congress of Industrial Organizations
AFTRA American Federation of TV and Radio Artists
AFSCME American Federation of State, County and Municipal Employees
agr. agriculture
agrl. agricultural
agt. agent
AGVA American Guild of Variety Artists
agy. agency
A&I Agricultural and Industrial
AIA American Institute of Architects
AIAA American Institute of Aeronautics and Astronautics
AIChE American Institute of Chemical Engineers
AICPA American Institute of Certified Public Accountants
AID Agency for International Development
AIDS Acquired Immune Deficiency Syndrome
AIEE American Institute of Electrical Engineers
AIM American Institute of Management
AIME American Institute of Mining, Metallurgy, and Petroleum Engineers
AK Alaska
AL Alabama
ALA American Library Association
Ala. Alabama
alt. alternate
Alta. Alberta
A&M Agricultural and Mechanical
AM, A.M. Arts, Master of
Am. American, America
AMA American Medical Association
amb. ambassador
A.M.E. African Methodist Episcopal
Amtrak National Railroad Passenger Corporation
AMVETS American Veterans of World War II, Korea, Vietnam
ANA American Nurses Association
anat. anatomical
ANCC American Nurses Credentialing Center
ann. annual
ANTA American National Theatre and Academy
anthrop. anthropological
AP Associated Press
APA American Psychological Association
APGA American Personnel Guidance Association
APHA American Public Health Association
APO Army Post Office
apptd. appointed
Apr. April
apt. apartment
AR Arkansas
ARC American Red Cross
arch. architect
archeol. archeological
archtl. architectural
Ariz. Arizona
Ark. Arkansas
ArtsD, ArtsD. Arts, Doctor of
arty. artillery
AS American Samoa
AS Associate in Science
ASCAP American Society of Composers, Authors and Publishers
ASCD Association for Supervision and Curriculum Development
ASCE American Society of Civil Engineers
ASHRAE American Society of Heating, Refrigeration, and Air Conditioning Engineers
ASME American Society of Mechanical Engineers
ASNSA American Society for Nursing Service Administrators
ASPA American Society for Public Administration
ASPCA American Society for the Prevention of Cruelty to Animals
assn. association
assoc. associate
asst. assistant
ASTD American Society for Training and Development
ASTM American Society for Testing and Materials
astron. astronomical
astrophys. astrophysical
ATLA Association of Trial Lawyers of America
ATSC Air Technical Service Command
AT&T American Telephone & Telegraph Company
atty. attorney
Aug. August
AUS Army of the United States
aux. auxiliary
Ave. Avenue
AVMA American Veterinary Medical Association
AZ Arizona
AWHONN Association of Women's Health Obstetric and Neonatal Nurses

B. Bachelor
b. born
BA, B.A. Bachelor of Arts
BAgr, B.Agr. Bachelor of Agriculture
Balt. Baltimore
Bapt. Baptist
BArch, B.Arch. Bachelor of Architecture
BAS, B.A.S. Bachelor of Agricultural Science
BBA, B.B.A. Bachelor of Business Administration
BBB Better Business Bureau
BBC British Broadcasting Corporation

BC, B.C. British Columbia
BCE, B.C.E. Bachelor of Civil Engineering
BChir, B.Chir. Bachelor of Surgery
BCL, B.C.L. Bachelor of Civil Law
BCLS Basic Cardiac Life Support
BCS, B.C.S. Bachelor of Commercial Science
BD, B.D. Bachelor of Divinity
bd. board
BE, B.E. Bachelor of Education
BEE, B.E.E. Bachelor of Electrical Engineering
BFA, B.F.A. Bachelor of Fine Arts
bibl. biblical
bibliog. bibliographical
biog. biographical
biol. biological
BJ, B.J. Bachelor of Journalism
Bklyn. Brooklyn
BL, B.L. Bachelor of Letters
bldg. building
BLS, B.L.S. Bachelor of Library Science
BLS Basic Life Support
Blvd. Boulevard
BMI Broadcast Music, Inc.
BMW Bavarian Motor Works (Bayerische Motoren Werke)
bn. battalion
B.&O.R.R. Baltimore & Ohio Railroad
bot. botanical
BPE, B.P.E. Bachelor of Physical Education
BPhil, B.Phil. Bachelor of Philosophy
br. branch
BRE, B.R.E. Bachelor of Religious Education
brig. gen. brigadier general
Brit. British, Brittanica
Bros. Brothers
BS, B.S. Bachelor of Science
BSA, B.S.A. Bachelor of Agricultural Science
BSBA Bachelor of Science in Business Administration
BSChemE Bachelor of Science in Chemical Engineering
BSD, B.S.D. Bachelor of Didactic Science
BSEE Bachelor of Science in Electrical Engineering
BSN Bachelor of Science in Nursing
BST, B.S.T. Bachelor of Sacred Theology
BTh, B.Th. Bachelor of Theology
bull. bulletin
bur. bureau
bus. business
B.W.I. British West Indies

CA California
CAA Civil Aeronautics Administration
CAB Civil Aeronautics Board
CAD-CAM Computer Aided Design–Computer Aided Model
Calif. California
C.Am. Central America
Can. Canada, Canadian
CAP Civil Air Patrol
capt. captain
cardiol. cardiological
cardiovasc. cardiovascular
CARE Cooperative American Relief Everywhere
Cath. Catholic
cav. cavalry
CBC Canadian Broadcasting Company
CBI China, Burma, India Theatre of Operations
CBS Columbia Broadcasting Company
C.C. Community College
CCC Commodity Credit Corporation
CCNY City College of New York
CCRN Critical Care Registered Nurse
CCU Cardiac Care Unit
CD Civil Defense
CE, C.E. Corps of Engineers, Civil Engineer
CEN Certified Emergency Nurse
CENTO Central Treaty Organization
CEO chief executive officer
CERN European Organization of Nuclear Research
cert. certificate, certification, certified
CETA Comprehensive Employment Training Act
CFA Chartered Financial Analyst
CFL Canadian Football League
CFO chief financial officer
CFP Certified Financial Planner
ch. church
ChD, Ch.D. Doctor of Chemistry
chem. chemical
ChemE, Chem.E. Chemical Engineer
ChFC Chartered Financial Consultant
Chgo. Chicago
chirurg. chirurgical
chmn. chairman
chpt. chapter
CIA Central Intelligence Agency
Cin. Cincinnati
cir. circle, circuit
CLE Continuing Legal Education
Cleve. Cleveland
climatol. climatological
clin. clinical
clk. clerk
C.L.U. Chartered Life Underwriter
CM, C.M. Master in Surgery
CM Northern Mariana Islands
CMA Certified Medical Assistant
cmty. community
CNA Certified Nurse's Aide
CNOR Certified Nurse (Operating Room)
C.&N.W.Ry. Chicago & North Western Railway
CO Colorado
Co. Company
COF Catholic Order of Foresters
C. of C. Chamber of Commerce
col. colonel
coll. college
Colo. Colorado
com. committee
comd. commanded
comdg. commanding
comdr. commander
comdt. commandant
comm. communications
commd. commissioned
comml. commercial
commn. commission
commr. commissioner
compt. comptroller
condr. conductor
Conf. Conference
Congl. Congregational, Congressional
Conglist. Congregationalist
Conn. Connecticut
cons. consultant, consulting
consol. consolidated
constl. constitutional
constn. constitution
constrn. construction
contbd. contributed
contbg. contributing
contbn. contribution
contbr. contributor
contr. controller
Conv. Convention
COO chief operating officer
coop. cooperative
coord. coordinator
CORDS Civil Operations and Revolutionary Development Support
CORE Congress of Racial Equality
corp. corporation, corporate
corr. correspondent, corresponding, correspondence
C.&O.Ry. Chesapeake & Ohio Railway
coun. council
CPA Certified Public Accountant
CPCU Chartered Property and Casualty Underwriter
CPH, C.P.H. Certificate of Public Health
cpl. corporal
CPR Cardio-Pulmonary Resuscitation
C.P.Ry. Canadian Pacific Railway
CRT Cathode Ray Terminal
C.S. Christian Science
CSB, C.S.B. Bachelor of Christian Science
C.S.C. Civil Service Commission
CT Connecticut
ct. court
ctr. center
ctrl. central
CWS Chemical Warfare Service
C.Z. Canal Zone

D. Doctor
d. daughter
DAgr, D.Agr. Doctor of Agriculture
DAR Daughters of the American Revolution
dau. daughter
DAV Disabled American Veterans
DC, D.C. District of Columbia
DCL, D.C.L. Doctor of Civil Law
DCS, D.C.S. Doctor of Commercial Science
DD, D.D. Doctor of Divinity
DDS, D.D.S. Doctor of Dental Surgery
DE Delaware
Dec. December
dec. deceased
def. defense
Del. Delaware
del. delegate, delegation
Dem. Democrat, Democratic
DEng, D.Eng. Doctor of Engineering
denom. denomination, denominational
dep. deputy
dept. department
dermatol. dermatological
desc. descendant
devel. development, developmental
DFA, D.F.A. Doctor of Fine Arts
D.F.C. Distinguished Flying Cross
DHL, D.H.L. Doctor of Hebrew Literature
dir. director
dist. district
distbg. distributing
distbn. distribution
distbr. distributor
disting. distinguished
div. division, divinity, divorce
divsn. division
DLitt, D.Litt. Doctor of Literature
DMD, D.M.D. Doctor of Dental Medicine
DMS, D.M.S. Doctor of Medical Science
DO, D.O. Doctor of Osteopathy
docs. documents
DON Director of Nursing
DPH, D.P.H. Diploma in Public Health
DPhil, D.Phil. Doctor of Philosophy
D.R. Daughters of the Revolution
Dr. Drive, Doctor
DRE, D.R.E. Doctor of Religious Education
DrPH, Dr.P.H. Doctor of Public Health, Doctor of Public Hygiene
D.S.C. Distinguished Service Cross

DSc, D.Sc. Doctor of Science
DSChemE Doctor of Science in Chemical Engineering
D.S.M. Distinguished Service Medal
DST, D.S.T. Doctor of Sacred Theology
DTM, D.T.M. Doctor of Tropical Medicine
DVM, D.V.M. Doctor of Veterinary Medicine
DVS, D.V.S. Doctor of Veterinary Surgery

E, E. East
ea. eastern
E. and P. Extraordinary and Plenipotentiary
Eccles. Ecclesiastical
ecol. ecological
econ. economic
ECOSOC Economic and Social Council (of the UN)
ED, E.D. Doctor of Engineering
ed. educated
EdB, Ed.B. Bachelor of Education
EdD, Ed.D. Doctor of Education
edit. edition
editl. editorial
EdM, Ed.M. Master of Education
edn. education
ednl. educational
EDP Electronic Data Processing
EdS, Ed.S. Specialist in Education
EE, E.E. Electrical Engineer
E.E. and M.P. Envoy Extraordinary and Minister Plenipotentiary
EEC European Economic Community
EEG Electroencephalogram
EEO Equal Employment Opportunity
EEOC Equal Employment Opportunity Commission
E.Ger. German Democratic Republic
EKG Electrocardiogram
elec. electrical
electrochem. electrochemical
electrophys. electrophysical
elem. elementary
EM, E.M. Engineer of Mines
EMT Emergency Medical Technician
ency. encyclopedia
Eng. England
engr. engineer
engring. engineering
entomol. entomological
environ. environmental
EPA Environmental Protection Agency
epidemiol. epidemiological
Episc. Episcopalian
ERA Equal Rights Amendment
ERDA Energy Research and Development Administration
ESEA Elementary and Secondary Education Act
ESL English as Second Language
ESPN Entertainment and Sports Programming Network
ESSA Environmental Science Services Administration
ethnol. ethnological
ETO European Theatre of Operations
Evang. Evangelical
exam. examination, examining
Exch. Exchange
exec. executive
exhbn. exhibition
expdn. expedition
expn. exposition
expt. experiment
exptl. experimental
Expy. Expressway
Ext. Extension

F.A. Field Artillery
FAA Federal Aviation Administration
FAO Food and Agriculture Organization (of the UN)
FBA Federal Bar Association
FBI Federal Bureau of Investigation
FCA Farm Credit Administration
FCC Federal Communications Commission
FCDA Federal Civil Defense Administration
FDA Food and Drug Administration
FDIA Federal Deposit Insurance Administration
FDIC Federal Deposit Insurance Corporation
FE, F.E. Forest Engineer
FEA Federal Energy Administration
Feb. February
fed. federal
fedn. federation
FERC Federal Energy Regulatory Commission
fgn. foreign
FHA Federal Housing Administration
fin. financial, finance
FL Florida
Fl. Floor
Fla. Florida
FMC Federal Maritime Commission
FNP Family Nurse Practitioner
FOA Foreign Operations Administration
found. foundation
FPC Federal Power Commission
FPO Fleet Post Office
frat. fraternity
FRS Federal Reserve System
FSA Federal Security Agency
Ft. Fort
FTC Federal Trade Commission
Fwy. Freeway

G-1 (or other number) Division of General Staff
GA, Ga. Georgia
GAO General Accounting Office
gastroent. gastroenterological
GATE Gifted and Talented Educators
GATT General Agreement on Tariffs and Trade
GE General Electric Company
gen. general
geneal. genealogical
geod. geodetic
geog. geographic, geographical
geol. geological
geophys. geophysical
geriat. geriatrics
gerontol. gerontological
G.H.Q. General Headquarters
GM General Motors Corporation
GMAC General Motors Acceptance Corporation
G.N.Ry. Great Northern Railway
gov. governor
govt. government
govtl. governmental
GPO Government Printing Office
grad. graduate, graduated
GSA General Services Administration
Gt. Great
GTE General Telephone and ElectricCompany
GU Guam
gynecol. gynecological

HBO Home Box Office
hdqs. headquarters
HEW Department of Health, Education and Welfare
HHD, H.H.D. Doctor of Humanities
HHFA Housing and Home Finance Agency
HHS Department of Health and Human Services
HI Hawaii
hist. historical, historic
HM, H.M. Master of Humanities
HMO Health Maintenance Organization
homeo. homeopathic
hon. honorary, honorable
Ho. of Dels. House of Delegates
Ho. of Reps. House of Representatives
hort. horticultural
hosp. hospital
H.S. High School
HUD Department of Housing and Urban Development
Hwy. Highway
hydrog. hydrographic

IA Iowa
IAEA International Atomic Energy Agency
IATSE International Alliance of Theatrical and Stage Employees and Moving Picture Operators of the United States and Canada
IBM International Business Machines Corporation
IBRD International Bank for Reconstruction and Development
ICA International Cooperation Administration
ICC Interstate Commerce Commission
ICCE International Council for Computers in Education
ICU Intensive Care Unit
ID Idaho
IEEE Institute of Electrical and Electronics Engineers
IFC International Finance Corporation
IGY International Geophysical Year
IL Illinois
Ill. Illinois
illus. illustrated
ILO International Labor Organization
IMF International Monetary Fund
IN Indiana
Inc. Incorporated
Ind. Indiana
ind. independent
Indpls. Indianapolis
indsl. industrial
inf. infantry
info. information
ins. insurance
insp. inspector
insp. gen. inspector general
inst. institute
instl. institutional
instn. institution
instr. instructor
instrn. instruction
instrnl. instructional
internat. international
intro. introduction
IRE Institute of Radio Engineers
IRS Internal Revenue Service
ITT International Telephone & Telegraph Corporation

JAG Judge Advocate General
JAGC Judge Advocate General Corps
Jan. January
Jaycees Junior Chamber of Commerce
JB, J.B. Jurum Baccalaureus

JCB, J.C.B. Juris Canoni Baccalaureus
JCD, J.C.D. Juris Canonici Doctor, Juris Civilis Doctor
JCL, J.C.L. Juris Canonici Licentiatus
JD, J.D. Juris Doctor
jg. junior grade
jour. journal
jr. junior
JSD, J.S.D. Juris Scientiae Doctor
JUD, J.U.D. Juris Utriusque Doctor
jud. judicial

Kans. Kansas
K.C. Knights of Columbus
K.P. Knights of Pythias
KS Kansas
K.T. Knight Templar
KY, Ky. Kentucky

LA, La. Louisiana
L.A. Los Angeles
lab. laboratory
L.Am. Latin America
lang. language
laryngol. laryngological
LB Labrador
LDS Latter Day Saints
LDS Church Church of Jesus Christ of Latter Day Saints
lectr. lecturer
legis. legislation, legislative
LHD, L.H.D. Doctor of Humane Letters
L.I. Long Island
libr. librarian, library
lic. licensed, license
L.I.R.R. Long Island Railroad
lit. literature
litig. litigation
LittB, Litt.B. Bachelor of Letters
LittD, Litt.D. Doctor of Letters
LLB, LL.B. Bachelor of Laws
LLD, L.L.D. Doctor of Laws
LLM, L.L.M. Master of Laws
Ln. Lane
L.&N.R.R. Louisville & Nashville Railroad
LPGA Ladies Professional Golf Association
LPN Licensed Practical Nurse
LS, L.S. Library Science (in degree)
lt. lieutenant
Ltd. Limited
Luth. Lutheran
LWV League of Women Voters

M. Master
m. married
MA, M.A. Master of Arts
MA Massachusetts
MADD Mothers Against Drunk Driving
mag. magazine
MAgr, M.Agr. Master of Agriculture
maj. major
Man. Manitoba
Mar. March
MArch, M.Arch. Master in Architecture
Mass. Massachusetts
math. mathematics, mathematical
MATS Military Air Transport Service
MB, M.B. Bachelor of Medicine
MB Manitoba
MBA, M.B.A. Master of Business Administration
MBS Mutual Broadcasting System
M.C. Medical Corps
MCE, M.C.E. Master of Civil Engineering
mcht. merchant
mcpl. municipal
MCS, M.C.S. Master of Commercial Science
MD, M.D. Doctor of Medicine
MD, Md. Maryland
MDiv Master of Divinity
MDip, M.Dip. Master in Diplomacy
mdse. merchandise
MDV, M.D.V. Doctor of Veterinary Medicine
ME, M.E. Mechanical Engineer
ME Maine
M.E.Ch. Methodist Episcopal Church
mech. mechanical
MEd., M.Ed. Master of Education
med. medical
MEE, M.E.E. Master of Electrical Engineering
mem. member
meml. memorial
merc. mercantile
met. metropolitan
metall. metallurgical
MetE, Met.E. Metallurgical Engineer
meteorol. meteorological
Meth. Methodist
Mex. Mexico
MF, M.F. Master of Forestry
MFA, M.F.A. Master of Fine Arts
mfg. manufacturing
mfr. manufacturer
mgmt. management
mgr. manager
MHA, M.H.A. Master of Hospital Administration
M.I. Military Intelligence
MI Michigan
Mich. Michigan
micros. microscopic, microscopical
mid. middle
mil. military
Milw. Milwaukee
Min. Minister
mineral. mineralogical
Minn. Minnesota
MIS Management Information Systems
Miss. Mississippi
MIT Massachusetts Institute of Technology
mktg. marketing
ML, M.L. Master of Laws
MLA Modern Language Association
M.L.D. Magister Legnum Diplomatic
MLitt, M.Litt. Master of Literature, Master of Letters
MLS, M.L.S. Master of Library Science
MME, M.M.E. Master of Mechanical Engineering
MN Minnesota
mng. managing
MO, Mo. Missouri
moblzn. mobilization
Mont. Montana
MP Northern Mariana Islands
M.P. Member of Parliament
MPA Master of Public Administration
MPE, M.P.E. Master of Physical Education
MPH, M.P.H. Master of Public Health
MPhil, M.Phil. Master of Philosophy
MPL, M.P.L. Master of Patent Law
Mpls. Minneapolis
MRE, M.R.E. Master of Religious Education
MRI Magnetic Resonance Imaging
MS, M.S. Master of Science
MS, Ms. Mississippi
MSc, M.Sc. Master of Science
MSChemE Master of Science in Chemical Engineering
MSEE Master of Science in Electrical Engineering
MSF, M.S.F. Master of Science of Forestry
MSN Master of Science in Nursing
MST, M.S.T. Master of Sacred Theology
MSW, M.S.W. Master of Social Work
MT Montana
Mt. Mount
MTO Mediterranean Theatre of Operation
MTV Music Television
mus. museum, musical
MusB, Mus.B. Bachelor of Music
MusD, Mus.D. Doctor of Music
MusM, Mus.M. Master of Music
mut. mutual
MVP Most Valuable Player
mycol. mycological

N. North
NAACOG Nurses Association of the American College of Obstetricians and Gynecologists
NAACP National Association for the Advancement of Colored People
NACA National Advisory Committee for Aeronautics
NACDL National Association of Criminal Defense Lawyers
NACU National Association of Colleges and Universities
NAD National Academy of Design
NAE National Academy of Engineering, National Association of Educators
NAESP National Association of Elementary School Principals
NAFE National Association of Female Executives
N.Am. North America
NAM National Association of Manufacturers
NAMH National Association for Mental Health
NAPA National Association of Performing Artists
NARAS National Academy of Recording Arts and Sciences
NAREB National Association of Real Estate Boards
NARS National Archives and Record Service
NAS National Academy of Sciences
NASA National Aeronautics and Space Administration
NASP National Association of School Psychologists
NASW National Association of Social Workers
nat. national
NATAS National Academy of Television Arts and Sciences
NATO North Atlantic Treaty Organization
NATOUSA North African Theatre of Operations, United States Army
nav. navigation
NB, N.B. New Brunswick
NBA National Basketball Association
NBC National Broadcasting Company
NC, N.C. North Carolina
NCAA National College Athletic Association
NCCJ National Conference of Christians and Jews
ND, N.D. North Dakota
NDEA National Defense Education Act
NE Nebraska
NE, N.E. Northeast
NEA National Education Association
Nebr. Nebraska
NEH National Endowment for Humanities
neurol. neurological
Nev. Nevada
NF Newfoundland

NFL National Football League
Nfld. Newfoundland
NG National Guard
NH, N.H. New Hampshire
NHL National Hockey League
NIH National Institutes of Health
NIMH National Institute of Mental Health
NJ, N.J. New Jersey
NLRB National Labor Relations Board
NM New Mexico
N.Mex. New Mexico
No. Northern
NOAA National Oceanographic and Atmospheric Administration
NORAD North America Air Defense
Nov. November
NOW National Organization for Women
N.P.Ry. Northern Pacific Railway
nr. near
NRA National Rifle Association
NRC National Research Council
NS, N.S. Nova Scotia
NSC National Security Council
NSF National Science Foundation
NSTA National Science Teachers Association
NSW New South Wales
N.T. New Testament
NT Northwest Territories
nuc. nuclear
numis. numismatic
NV Nevada
NW, N.W. Northwest
N.W.T. Northwest Territories
NY, N.Y. New York
N.Y.C. New York City
NYU New York University
N.Z. New Zealand

OAS Organization of American States
ob-gyn obstetrics-gynecology
obs. observatory
obstet. obstetrical
occupl. occupational
oceanog. oceanographic
Oct. October
OD, O.D. Doctor of Optometry
OECD Organization for Economic Cooperation and Development
OEEC Organization of European Economic Cooperation
OEO Office of Economic Opportunity
ofcl. official
OH Ohio
OK Oklahoma
Okla. Oklahoma
ON Ontario
Ont. Ontario
oper. operating
ophthal. ophthalmological
ops. operations
OR Oregon
orch. orchestra
Oreg. Oregon
orgn. organization
orgnl. organizational
ornithol. ornithological
orthop. orthopedic
OSHA Occupational Safety and Health Administration
OSRD Office of Scientific Research and Development
OSS Office of Strategic Services
osteo. osteopathic
otol. otological
otolaryn. otolaryngological

PA, Pa. Pennsylvania
P.A. Professional Association
paleontol. paleontological
path. pathological
PBS Public Broadcasting System
P.C. Professional Corporation
PE Prince Edward Island
pediat. pediatrics
P.E.I. Prince Edward Island
PEN Poets, Playwrights, Editors, Essayists and Novelists (international association)
penol. penological
P.E.O. women's organization (full name not disclosed)
pers. personnel
pfc. private first class
PGA Professional Golfers' Association of America
PHA Public Housing Administration
pharm. pharmaceutical
PharmD, Pharm.D. Doctor of Pharmacy
PharmM, Pharm.M. Master of Pharmacy
PhB, Ph.B. Bachelor of Philosophy
PhD, Ph.D. Doctor of Philosophy
PhDChemE Doctor of Science in Chemical Engineering
PhM, Ph.M. Master of Philosophy
Phila. Philadelphia
philharm. philharmonic
philol. philological
philos. philosophical
photog. photographic
phys. physical
physiol. physiological
Pitts. Pittsburgh
Pk. Park
Pky. Parkway
Pl. Place
P.&L.E.R.R. Pittsburgh & Lake Erie Railroad
Plz. Plaza
PNP Pediatric Nurse Practitioner
P.O. Post Office
PO Box Post Office Box
polit. political
poly. polytechnic, polytechnical
PQ Province of Quebec
PR, P.R. Puerto Rico
prep. preparatory
pres. president
Presbyn. Presbyterian
presdl. presidential
prin. principal
procs. proceedings
prod. produced (play production)
prodn. production
prodr. producer
prof. professor
profl. professional
prog. progressive
propr. proprietor
pros. atty. prosecuting attorney
pro tem. pro tempore
PSRO Professional Services Review Organization
psychiat. psychiatric
psychol. psychological
PTA Parent-Teachers Association
ptnr. partner
PTO Pacific Theatre of Operations, Parent Teacher Organization
pub. publisher, publishing, published
pub. public
publ. publication
pvt. private

quar. quarterly
qm. quartermaster
Q.M.C. Quartermaster Corps
Que. Quebec

radiol. radiological
RAF Royal Air Force
RCA Radio Corporation of America
RCAF Royal Canadian Air Force
RD Rural Delivery
Rd. Road
R&D Research & Development
REA Rural Electrification Administration
rec. recording
ref. reformed
regt. regiment
regtl. regimental
rehab. rehabilitation
rels. relations
Rep. Republican
rep. representative
Res. Reserve
ret. retired
Rev. Reverend
rev. review, revised
RFC Reconstruction Finance Corporation
RFD Rural Free Delivery
rhinol. rhinological
RI, R.I. Rhode Island
RISD Rhode Island School of Design
Rlwy. Railway
Rm. Room
RN, R.N. Registered Nurse
roentgenol. roentgenological
ROTC Reserve Officers Training Corps
RR Rural Route
R.R. Railroad
rsch. research
rschr. researcher
Rt. Route

S. South
s. son
SAC Strategic Air Command
SAG Screen Actors Guild
SALT Strategic Arms Limitation Talks
S.Am. South America
san. sanitary
SAR Sons of the American Revolution
Sask. Saskatchewan
savs. savings
SB, S.B. Bachelor of Science
SBA Small Business Administration
SC, S.C. South Carolina
SCAP Supreme Command Allies Pacific
ScB, Sc.B. Bachelor of Science
SCD, S.C.D. Doctor of Commercial Science
ScD, Sc.D. Doctor of Science
sch. school
sci. science, scientific
SCLC Southern Christian Leadership Conference
SCV Sons of Confederate Veterans
SD, S.D. South Dakota
SE, S.E. Southeast
SEATO Southeast Asia Treaty Organization
SEC Securities and Exchange Commission
sec. secretary
sect. section
seismol. seismological
sem. seminary
Sept. September
s.g. senior grade
sgt. sergeant
SHAEF Supreme Headquarters Allied Expeditionary Forces
SHAPE Supreme Headquarters Allied Powers in Europe
S.I. Staten Island

S.J. Society of Jesus (Jesuit)
SJD Scientiae Juridicae Doctor
SK Saskatchewan
SM, S.M. Master of Science
SNP Society of Nursing Professionals
So. Southern
soc. society
sociol. sociological
S.P.Co. Southern Pacific Company
spkr. speaker
spl. special
splty. specialty
Sq. Square
S.R. Sons of the Revolution
sr. senior
SS Steamship
SSS Selective Service System
St. Saint, Street
sta. station
stats. statistics
statis. statistical
STB, S.T.B. Bachelor of Sacred Theology
stblzn. stabilization
STD, S.T.D. Doctor of Sacred Theology
std. standard
Ste. Suite
subs. subsidiary
SUNY State University of New York
supr. supervisor
supt. superintendent
surg. surgical
svc. service
SW, S.W. Southwest
sys. system

TAPPI Technical Association of the Pulp and Paper Industry
tb. tuberculosis
tchg. teaching
tchr. teacher
tech. technical, technology
technol. technological
tel. telephone
Tel. & Tel. Telephone & Telegraph
telecom. telecommunications
temp. temporary
Tenn. Tennessee
Ter. Territory
Ter. Terrace
TESOL Teachers of English to Speakers of Other Languages
Tex. Texas
ThD, Th.D. Doctor of Theology
theol. theological
ThM, Th.M. Master of Theology
TN Tennessee
tng. training
topog. topographical
trans. transaction, transferred
transl. translation, translated
transp. transportation
treas. treasurer
TT Trust Territory
TV television
TVA Tennessee Valley Authority
TWA Trans World Airlines
twp. township
TX Texas
typog. typographical

U. University
UAW United Auto Workers
UCLA University of California at Los Angeles
UDC United Daughters of the Confederacy
U.K. United Kingdom
UN United Nations
UNESCO United Nations Educational, Scientific and Cultural Organization
UNICEF United Nations International Children's Emergency Fund
univ. university
UNRRA United Nations Relief and Rehabilitation Administration
UPI United Press International
U.P.R.R. United Pacific Railroad
urol. urological
U.S. United States
U.S.A. United States of America
USAAF United States Army Air Force
USAF United States Air Force
USAFR United States Air Force Reserve
USAR United States Army Reserve
USCG United States Coast Guard
USCGR United States Coast Guard Reserve
USES United States Employment Service
USIA United States Information Agency
USMC United States Marine Corps
USMCR United States Marine Corps Reserve
USN United States Navy
USNG United States National Guard
USNR United States Naval Reserve
USO United Service Organizations
USPHS United States Public Health Service
USS United States Ship
USSR Union of the Soviet Socialist Republics
USTA United States Tennis Association
USV United States Volunteers
UT Utah

VA Veterans Administration
VA, Va. Virginia
vet. veteran, veterinary
VFW Veterans of Foreign Wars
VI, V.I. Virgin Islands
vice pres. vice president
vis. visiting
VISTA Volunteers in Service to America
VITA Volunteers in Technical Assistance
vocat. vocational
vol. volunteer, volume
v.p. vice president
vs. versus
VT, Vt. Vermont

W, W. West
WA Washington (state)
WAC Women's Army Corps
Wash. Washington (state)
WATS Wide Area Telecommunications Service
WAVES Women's Reserve, US Naval Reserve
WCTU Women's Christian Temperance Union
we. western
W. Ger. Germany, Federal Republic of
WHO World Health Organization
WI Wisconsin
W.I. West Indies
Wis. Wisconsin
WSB Wage Stabilization Board
WV West Virginia
W.Va. West Virginia
WWI World War I
WWII World War II
WY Wyoming
Wyo. Wyoming

YK Yukon Territory
YMCA Young Men's Christian Association
YMHA Young Men's Hebrew Association
YM & YWHA Young Men's and Young Women's Hebrew Association
yr. year
YT, Y.T. Yukon Territory
YWCA Young Women's Christian Association

zool. zoological

Alphabetical Practices

Names are arranged alphabetically according to the surnames, and under identical surnames according to the first given name. If both surname and first given name are identical, names are arranged alphabetically according to the second given name.

Surnames beginning with De, Des, Du, however capitalized or spaced, are recorded with the prefix preceding the surname and arranged alphabetically under the letter D.

Surnames beginning with Mac and Mc are arranged alphabetically under M.

Surnames beginning with Saint or St. appear after names that begin Sains, and are arranged according to the second part of the name, e.g. St. Clair before Saint Dennis.

Surnames beginning with Van, Von, or von are arranged alphabetically under the letter V.

Compound surnames are arranged according to the first member of the compound.

Many hyphenated Arabic names begin Al-, El-, or al-. These names are alphabetized according to each Biographee's designation of last name. Thus Al-Bahar, Neta may be listed either under Al- or under Bahar, depending on the preference of the listee.

Also, Arabic names have a variety of possible spellings when transposed to English. Spelling of these names is always based on the practice of the Biographee. Some Biographees use a Western form of word order, while others prefer the Arabic word sequence.

Similarly, Asian names may have no comma between family and given names, but some Biographees have chosen to add the comma. In each case, punctuation follows the preference of the Biographee.

Parentheses used in connection with a name indicate which part of the full name is usually deleted in common usage. Hence Chambers, E(lizabeth) Anne indicates that the usual form of the given name is E. Anne. In such a case, the parentheses are ignored in alphabetizing and the name would be arranged as Chambers, Elizabeth Anne. However, if the name is recorded Chambers, (Elizabeth) Anne, signifying that the entire name Elizabeth is not commonly used, the alphabetizing would be arranged as though the name were Chambers, Anne. If an entire middle or last name is enclosed in parentheses, that portion of the name is used in the alphabetical arrangement. Hence Chambers, Elizabeth (Anne) would be arranged as Chambers, Elizabeth Anne.

Where more than one spelling, word order, or name of an individual is frequently encountered, the sketch has been entered under the form preferred by the Biographee, with cross-references under alternate forms.

Who'sWho in the Midwest®

Biographies

AADNESEN, CHRISTOPHER, railroad company executive, consultant; b. Salt Lake City, Nov. 2, 1948; s. Grant C. and Helen Jay (Ray) A.; m. Helen Elizabeth Twelves, Aug. 14, 1973 (div. 1988); children: Aric Paul, Brian James, Nicholas Twelves; m. Betty Jean DeLeon, Aug. 19, 1988; children: Brooke Bingham, Brad Bingham. BA in English, U. Utah, 1971, MBA, 1973; PMD, Harvard U., 1990. Gen. mgr. and founder Thaddeus Duncan Co., Salt Lake City, 1968-72; divsn. supt. Western Pacific R.R., Sacramento, 1978-82; gen. supt. of transp. Mo. Pacific R.R., Spring, Tex., 1983-84; asst. gen. mgr. So. Region Union Pacific R.R., Spring, Tex., 1984-88; gen. dir. pers. svcs. Union Pacific R.R., Omaha, 1988-89, asst. v.p. ops. adminstrn., 1989-90, asst. v.p. employee devel. and involvement, 1990-91, sr. asst. v.p. field ops., 1992-93, sr. asst. v.p. transp., 1993-95, pres. captiol city group, pres. capitol city mgmt. assocs., 1996—; bd. dirs. Brownsville and Matamoros Bridge Co., Brownsville, Tex., 1992—. Campaign mgr. County Commr., Quincy, Calif., 1978. With USN, 1967-69. Mem. Am. Assn. R.R. Supts., Field Club of Omaha, Happy Hollow Country Club, Berry Creek Country Club, Greater Austin C. of C., Beta Theta Pi. Republican. Episcopalian. Home: 30205 Oak Tree Dr Georgetown TX 78628 Office: The Capitol City Group 2000 S Mays St Ste 303 Round Rock TX 78664

AANERUD, MELVIN BERNARD, government agency administrator; b. Spring Lake Park, Minn., Jan. 7, 1943; s. Bernard Melvin and Margaret Agnes (Beck) A.; BA, U. Minn., 1964; m. Kathleen Dipprey, Aug. 19, 1978; children: Adam Curtis, Eric Christopher. Prodn. analyst Honeywell, Inc., New Brighton, Minn., 1966-68; plant mgr. Ault, Inc., Mpls., 1968-71; gen. mgr. Mille Lacs Reservation Bus. Enterprise, Vineland, Minn., 1971-74; bus. devel. specialist SBA, Mpls., 1974-78; asst. dist. dir. SBA, Mpls., 1978-80, dep. dist. dir., 1980-85, portfolio mgr., 1986-94, asst. dist. dir., 1994—. Pres. Columbia Hts. Charter Commn., 1971-82; chmn. Minn. Minority Bus. Opportunity Com. 1976-79; treas. edn. adv. bd. McKinley Sch. Cmty., 1985—; chmn. park bd. Ham Lake, 1986—; coach North Metro Soccer, 1990-94; founding bd. mem. Anoka County Bus. Assn. Network; den leader, asst. pack leader, troup scoutmaster Boy Scouts Am., 1993—. Served with Signal Corps, AUS, 1964-66. Recipient Gold Key Man award Minn. Jaycees, 1971, 76, Silver Key, 1973; Columbia Heights Disting. Service award, 1970, Columbia Hgts. Outstanding Civil Servant award, 1970; named One of 10 Outstanding Young Minnesotans, 1978. Mem. Minn. Jaycees (dir. Minn. Jaycee Found. 1976-82), Columbia Heights Jaycees (nat. U.S. dir. 1972-73), Minn. Entrepreneurs Club (bd. dirs.), U. Minn. Alumni Assn., Toastmasters (treas., v.p. edn.), Mem. Democratic Farm Labor Party. Home: 15041 Fillmore St NE Anoka MN 55304-6107 Office: 100 N 6th St Minneapolis MN 55403-1505

AARSVOLD, OLE, state legislator; m. Marilyn Aarsvold; 3 children. BS, Maryville State U., U. N.D. Tchr., prin. secondary sch.; instr. Univ.; farmer; mem. N.D. Ho. of Reps. from 20th dist., 1989—; mem. Edn., Natural Resources, Joint Constl. Rev. Coms. N.D. Ho. of Reps.; bd. dirs. Farmers Union Oil Co., Clifco Energy. Bd. dirs. Trail County Econ. Devel. Commn.; clerk-treas. Greenfield (N.D.) Twp.; commr., v.p. N.D. Tchrs. Practices Commn.; field dir. No. Plains Indian Tchr. Corps. Recipient Outstanding Young Educator award, Outstanding Agriculturist award. Mem. Trail County Crop Improvement Assn. (past bd. dirs., past pres.), Trail County Farmers Union (bd. dirs.). Democrat. Address: RR 2 Box 12 Blanchard ND 58009*

ABADINSKY, HOWARD, criminal justice educator; b. N.Y.C., July 12, 1941; s. Benjamin and Ann (Kestenbaum) A.; m. Donna Rose Berman, June 24, 1967; children: Alisa Michele, Sandi Hether. BA, Queens Coll., 1963; MSW, Fordham U., 1970; PhD, NYU, 1983. Parole officer N.Y. State Div. Parole, N.Y.C., 1964-71, sr. parole officer, 1972-78; asst. prof. criminal justice Western Carolina U., Cullowhee, 1978-81; prof. St. Xavier U., Chgo., 1981—; inspector Sheriff's Office, Cook County, Ill., 1982-90; rsch. cons. Pres.'s Commn. on Organized Crime, 1985. Author: Probation and Parole: Theory and Practice, 1977, 5th edit., 1994; Social Service in Criminal Justice, 1978; Organized Crime, 1981, 4th edit., 1994; The Mafia in America: An Oral History, 1981; The Criminal Elite: Professional and Organized Crime, 1983; Discretionary Justice: An Introduction to the Use of Discretion in Criminal and Justice, 1984; Crime and Justice, 1986; Drug Abuse, 1989, 2d edit., 1993; Law and Justice, 1986, 3rd edit., 1995; Understanding Crime, 1996. Pres. Dist. 28 Sch. Bd., Queens, N.Y., 1970-75, Mem. Am. Soc. Criminology, Acad. Criminal Justice Scis., Internat. Assn. for Study of Organized Crime (founder 1984, pres. 1985-87). Jewish. Home: 433 W Briar Pl Chicago IL 60657-4752 Office: St Xavier U W 103 St Chicago IL 60655

ABATE, ANNE KATHERINE, librarian, consultant; b. Cleve., Mar. 10, 1958; d. Frank M. and Cecelia (Homic) Abate; m. George S. Maley, May 17, 1980. HAB with honors, Xavier U., Cin., 1980; MSLS, U. Ky., 1986; postgrad., Nova Southeastern U., Ft. Lauderdale, Fla., 1994—. Asst. dept. head Kenton County Pub. Libr., Covington, Ky., 1985-87; asst. dir. Lloyd Libr. and Mus., Cin., 1987-88; libr. Dinsmore & Shohl, Cin., 1988—; adv. bd. West Pub. Corp., Eagan, Minn., 1992-95. Contbr. articles to profl. jours.; cons./author video package: Managing Emerging Technologies, 1994. Mem. Spl. Librs. Assn. (chpt. pres. 1992-93, chair pub. rels. com. 1993-95), Am. Assn. of Law Librs., Ohio Regional Assn. Law Librs., Greater Cin. Area Law Librs. (convenor 1990-92), Beta Phi Mu. Roman Catholic. Office: Dinsmore and Shohl 255 E Fifth St Cincinnati OH 45202

ABBASI, TARIQ AFZAL, psychiatrist, educator; b. Hyderabad, India, Aug. 13, 1946; came to U.S., 1976, naturalized, 1983; s. Shujaat Ali and Salma Khatoon (Siddiqui) A.; m. Kashifa Khatoon, Nov. 10, 1972; children—Sameena, Omar, Osman. B.S., Madrasa-I-Aliya, Hyderabad, 1964; M.B.B.S., Osmania Med. Coll., Hyderabad, 1970; Diploma in Psychol. Medicine, St. John's Hosp., U. Sheffield (Eng.), 1976. Diplomate Am. Bd. Psychiatry and Neurology; diplomate in psychiatry Royal Coll. Physicians of Eng. Sr. house officer St. John's Hosp., Lincoln, Eng., 1972-73, registrar, 1973-76; resident in psychiatry Rutgers Med. Sch., Piscataway, N.J., 1976-79, chief resident, 1979, dir. adult in-patient services Community Mental Health Ctr., Rutgers Med. Sch., also asst. prof. psychiatry, 1979-82; staff psychiatrist Northville Regional Psychiat. Hosp. (Mich.), 1982-83, div. dir., 1983—; cons. psychiatrist Rahway State Prison (N.J.), 1979-82; clin. instr. psychiatry Wayne State U. Med. Sch., Detroit. Mem. Am. Psychiat. Assn., Mich. Psychiat. Soc. Office: Northville Regl Psychiat Hosp 41001 7 Mile Rd Northville MI 48167-2655 also: 33200 Dequindre Rd Ste 200 Sterling Heights MI 48310-5916 also: 999 Haynes St Ste 245 Birmingham MI 48009-6775

ABBATE, DEE, college administrator; b. Chgo., May 24, 1942; d. Carl John and Doris (Sbarbaro) Abbate-Auger; m. William F. Ruetsche, Sept. 5, 1964 (div. Mar. 1983); children: Laura M., William F. Jr., Jeffrey M. BA, Northeastern Ill. U., Chgo., 1983; MS, Nat. Coll. Edn., Evanston, Ill., 1986; EdD, No. Ill. U., DeKalb, 1995—. Exec. dir. Project REACH, Northbrook, Ill., 1978-83; human svcs. dir. River Forest (Ill.) Twp. Cmty. Ctr., 1983-85; asst. dir. Chgo. area Webster U., 1985-86; dir. Ft. Sheridan campus Columbia Coll., 1986-89, dir. Ill. br. campus, 1989-90, dir. Crystal Lake (Ill.) campus, 1990—; instr., adj. faculty Columbia Coll., Columbia, Mo., 1986—; chair Ill. River Corridor of Internat. Yr. of Youth Expdn., 1985; cons. Arden Shore Home for Boys, Spl. Edn. Dist. of Lake County, Ill., 1980-86; grad. student rep. Rsch. on Adult Edn. Bd., No. Ill. U., 1991. Author: Voices, Mirrors, Names and Dreams, 1995, (tng. manuals) REACH Instructor Manuals, 1983; editl. bd. Assn. for Exptl. Edn. Jour., 1980-85. Co-chair Com. to Elect Carol Moseley Braun Senator, McHenry County, Ill., 1992; bd. dirs. McHenry County Defenders, Woodstock, Ill., 1992-94; mem. Masthouse Com., Woodstock, 1993—; co-steward Cary Main St. Prairie, Nature Conservancy, 1990-93; cand. Cir. Ct. Clk., County of McHenry, 1992; mem. Masthouse Com. Gospel Music Singers. Mem. Endangered Species Coalition, Sierra Club (chmn. legis. com. 1982—). Office: Columbia Coll 8900 US Hwy 14 Crystal Lake IL 60012

ABBOTT, JAMES SAMUEL, marketing executive; b. Cleve., Nov. 19, 1918; s. James Samuel and Dorothy (Wilbor) A.; m. Mary Margaret Torrance, Oct. 13, 1957; 1 child, James Samuel. Student, Cornell U., 1941. Sales engr. Nat. Acme Co., Cleve., Chgo., 1945-63; chief sales engr. Nat. Acme Co., Cleve., 1963-67; sales mgr. Nat. Acme Co., 1967-69; mktg. mgr. Cleveland Twist Drill Co., Cleve., 1969-83; pres. James S. Abbott Consulting, Inc., Gates Mills, Ohio, 1983—. Contbr. articles to profl. jours. Mem. pk. bd. Village of Gates Mills, Ohio, 1979-86. Capt. USAF, 1941-45. Mem. Soc. Founders-Patriots (gov. 1968-69), Soc. Colonial Wars, Western Res. Hist. Soc., Clev. Mus. Natural History, U.S. Horse Cavalry Assn., Mayfield Country Club. Home: Hill Creek Ln Gates Mills OH 44040-9627

ABBOTT, JIM (JAMES ANTHONY ABBOTT), baseball player; b. Flint, Mich., Sept. 19, 1967. Grad., U. Mich. Pitcher Calif. Angels, Anaheim, 1989-92; former pitcher N.Y. Yankees; now with Chgo. White Sox; player U.S. Olympic Baseball Team, 1988, All-Star Team, 1991. Named to Coll. All-Am. Team The Sporting News, 1988. Office: Chgo White Sox 333 W 35th St Chicago IL 60616

ABBOTT, MARY ELAINE, photographer, lecturer, researcher; b. LaGrange, Ill., Apr. 23, 1922; d. Vergil and Goldie (Wright) Schwarzkopf; m. Harry Edward Abbott, Oct. 8, 1949; children: John Edward, Jane Ann. BA in English, Psychology, U. Iowa, 1944. With child welfare dept. Montgomery County Children's Home, Dayton, Ohio, 1944-47, Mich. Children's Inst., Ann Arbor, 1947-49; photographer, lectr., researcher, 1978—; researcher, lectr. in field. Documentary photography for regional history books, mags., calendars and brochures; commd. Taft Sculpture, Sculpture Jackson County; artistic dir. James Agee's Knoxville, Summer, 1915 Potter Ctr., Jackson Hillsdale Coll., 1996; Claire Allen Architecture for Mich. State Hist. Soc.; commd. by Jackson Historic Dist. Commn. and State Hist. Soc., Mich. Dance Assn.; hist. dist. commn. advisor Dance for the Handicapped, Savs. and Loan "40 Doors", Amitech, Jackson Alliance of Businessmen; works hung in various exhbns. and juried shows; photographs in many pvt., pub. and bus. collections; permanent commissions: Ella Sharp Mus., Jackson Symphony, St. Paul's Episcopal Ch., Carnegie Libr., others. Mem. Jr. League, Jackson Chorale, Nat. Trust for Hist. Preservation; panel participant on creative process Ella Sharp Mus.; advisor Jackson Hist. Commn. Lorado Taft Scholarship; tchr. Gt. Books, U. Chgo.; participant in enrichment for advanced children, also others; participant Save Outdoor Sculpture for Nat. Inst. Conservation Cultural Property, Smithsonian Instn. Recipient photography award Our Town Exhibit, Ella Sharp Mus., Hist. Trinity Ch., Detroit, Cert. of Honor, Spl. Recognitions Excellence Luth. Ctr. Assn.; Lorado Taft scholar. Mem. Internat. Platform Assn. (arts adv. bd., photography award, Juror's Choice in art exhibit, Inner Cir. Merit award 1993, 2d prize for photography 1994), Log Cabin Soc. Mich., Nat. Mus. Women in Arts, Arts Midwest, Kappa Alpha Theta. Republican. Episcopalian. Home and Office: 721 Oakridge Dr Jackson MI 49203-3914

ABDOO, RAYMOND THOMAS, preventive health consultant; b. Akron, Ohio, Sept. 28, 1944; s. Raymond A. and Florence Catherine (Haubert) A.; m. Sharon Lou Jones, Aug. 11, 1962; children: Joseph, Shari, Dianna, John, RaeLynn. Student, Sch. of Behavioral Sci., Phila., 1971, Sherwood Med. Intership Sch., St. Louis, 1972. Cert. counselor, tech. rep. Union committeeman Firestone Tire & Rubber, Akron, Ohio, 1965-67; policeman City of Akron, Akron, 1967-69; tech. med. rep. Sherwood Med., St. Louis, 1969-75; pvt. practice med. cons. Suffield, Ohio, 1975-83; pvt. practice wellness cons. Suffield, 1983-87; pres., cons. Physicians Wellness, Cuyahoga Falls, Ohio, 1987-89; chmn. Physicians Wellness Programs, Cuyahoga Falls, 1989—; mem. U.S. Admin. (pres. steering com. 1995, nat. dem. com. 1994); wellness advisor Ohio Sheriffs Assn. (analyst 1993-95); wellness advisor, mem. Buckeye Sheriffs Assn., 1993-96. Author: The Love Connections, 1976, Your Personal Experience, 1985 (Meta Physics Astro Physics award 1985), The Classic Wellness Program, 1987 (Pres. award 1993). Chmn. Concerned Citizens of Am., Cuyahoga Falls, 1990-95, pres. campaign advisor U.S. Dem. Party, Cuyahoga Falls, 1995, mem. Pub. Citizens Group, 1995. With U.S. Army, 1962-64. Mem. Fraternal Order of Police of Ohio, Inc. (wellness advisor, analyst 1994-95, booster 1992-96). Democrat. Roman Catholic.

ABEL, DONALD CLEMENT, philosophy educator; b. Pomeroy, Wash., June 26, 1948; s. Clement C. and Mary G. (Lammersen) A.; m. Diane S. Legomsky, Aug. 6, 1988. BA in Philosophy summa cum laude, Gonzaga U., 1971; MA in Philosophy, Tulane U., 1973; Licentiate in Philosophy, St. Michael's Inst., Spokane, Wash., 1975; MDiv summa cum laude, Loyola U., Chgo., 1979; PhD in Philosophy, Northwestern U., 1983. Instr. philosophy Gonzaga U., Spokane, Wash., 1973-75, Northwestern U., Evanston, Ill., 1981-83; editor Gt. Books Found., Chgo., 1983-84; asst. prof. philosophy St. Norbert Coll., De Pere, Wis., 1984-91, assoc. prof. philosophy, 1991—. Author: Freud on Instinct and Morality, 1989; editor: Theories of Human Nature, 1992, Fifty Readings in Philosophy, 1994; editor: Discourses: A Database of Philosophy Readings, 1994—. Dissertation Yr. fellow Northwestern U., 1981. Mem. Am. Philos. Assn., Am. Cath. Philos. Assn., Soc. for Ancient Greek Philosophy, Soc. for Philosophy and Psychology. Office: St Norbert Coll 100 Grant St De Pere WI 54115

ABEL, MARY, state legislator; m. Richard Abel; 1 child, Jason. BS, MSJ, Ohio U. Mem. Ohio Ho. of Reps., 1989—. Mem. adv. coun. exec. programs Capitol U.; bd. dirs. Big Bros.-Big Sisters. Mem. AAUW, LWV, Inst. Local Govt. Adminstrn. and Rural Devel. (mem. adv. com.), Delta Kappa Gamma. Democrat. Home: PO Box 113 Athens OH 45701-1480 Office: OH Ho of Reps State House Columbus OH 43215

ABEL HOROWITZ, MICHELLE SUSAN, advertising executive; b. Detroit, Mar. 31, 1950; d. Martin Louis and Phyllis (Berkowitz) A.; m. H. Jay Abel Horowitz, July 11, 1976; children—Jordan Michael, Stefanie Jennifer. Student Goucher Coll., 1967-70; B.A. in Econs., U. Mich., 1971; postgrad. in econs. U. Calif.-San Diego, 1973; M.A. in Econs., U. Detroit, 1974-76. Planning group supr. Hill Holliday Connors, Cosmopulos, Mass., 1976-78; econ. analyst Data Resources, Boston, 1978-79; v.p., media dir. Barkley & Evergreen, Southfield, Mich., 1979-80; v.p., dir. mktg. and media Yaffe/Berline, Southfield, Mich., 1980-82; exec. v.p., ptnr., corp. treas. Berline Group, Birmingham, Mich., 1982—; instr. Oakland U., Rochester, Mich., 1982; trustee, chairperson mktg. com. Harbinger Dance Co., Farmington, Mich., 1983—. Named Advt. Woman of Yr., Women's Ad Club Detroit, 1982. Mem. Adcraft Club Detroit, Women in Communications. Democrat. Jewish. Office: The Berline Group 31600 Telegraph Rd Ste 100 Franklin MI 48025-4371

ABELL, DONALD EUGENE, retired engineer, consultant; b. Pitcairn, Pa., Oct. 20, 1924; s. George Lester and Erma Rose (Coleman) A.; m. Geraldine Marie Sivori, Aug. 17, 1957; children: Lynn Marie, Peter Joseph. BSEE, Carnegie Inst. Tech., 1947; MBA, SUNY, Buffalo, 1961. Registered profl. engr., N.Y. Engring. mgr., product line mgr., ops. mgr., gen. mgr. Westinghouse, Buffalo, 1947-75; v.p. engring. Alvey, Inc., St. Louis, 1975-89; cons. Conveyor Equipment Mfr.'s Assn., 1990-93; mem. U.S. mission to Poland to evaluate Polish industry Ctrl. Inst. Labor Protection, Warsaw, 1976. Patentee for indsl. mfg. products and processes; contbr. articles to profl. publs. Mem. Kirk of the Hills Choir. Lt. (j.g.) USNR, 1943-46. Presbyterian. Home: 14241 Trailtop Dr Chesterfield MO 63017

ABELLA, JOSEPH FRANCISCO, electronics company executive; b. Buffalo, Nov. 27, 1943; s. Joseph and Gladys Monica (Croft) A.; m. Mary Elizabeth Grewe, Aug. 23, 1969; children: Jennifer, Joseph M., Corrine, Kathleen, Lauren. B in Elec. Engring., U. Detroit, 1969, M in Engring., 1969. Coop engr. Collins Radio Co., Cedar Rapids, Iowa, 1965-68; design engr. Magnavox Co., Ft. Wayne, Ind., 1969-74; project engr. Magnavox Govt. & Indsl. Electronics Co., Ft. Wayne, 1974-79, design engring. mgr., 1979-83; dir. passive sensors marine systems operation Magnavox Govt. & Indsl. Electonics Co., Ft. Wayne, 1983-87, dep. gen. mgr. marine systems operation, 1987-89, v.p. communications and info. mgmt., 1989-91; v.p. mfg. resource planning, program dir. Magnavox Electronics Systems Co., Ft. Wayne, 1991-94; v.p. sensor sys. Magnavox Electronics Sys. Co., Ft. Wayne, 1994—. With USN, 1961-64. Mem. IEEE, NSIA, AUSA, Magnavox Mgmt. Club (chmn. bd. 1989-90, pres. 1991-92), Tau Beta Pi, Eta Kappa Nu.

ABELLERA, THOMAS, JR., cartoonist; b. Washington, Oct. 16, 1947; s. Thomas and Ruth (Smallman) A. BA in Graphic Design, San Jose State U., 1973. Artist, designer Hallmark Cards, Kansas City, Mo., 1978-87; artist, cons. Kansas City, 1987—; writer, publisher Stochos Books, Kansas City, 1992—. Author: The Teachings of Don Von: A Turnkey Way of Knowledge, 1994.

ABELOV, STEPHEN LAWRENCE, uniform clothing company executive, consultant; b. N.Y.C., Apr. 1, 1923; s. Saul S. and Ethel (Esterman) A.; B.S., NYU, 1945, M.B.A., 1950; m. Phyllis S. Lichtenson, Nov. 18, 1945; children—Patricia C. (Mrs. Marvin Demoff), Gary M. Asst. div. mgr. Nat. Silver Co., N.Y., 1945; sales rep. Angelica Uniform Co., N.Y., 1945-50; asst. sales mgr., 1950-56, western regional mgr., Los Angeles, 1956-66, v.p. Angelica Uniform Co. of Calif., 1958-66, nat. v.p. sales, 1966-72, v.p. Angelica Corp. 1966-88, cons., 1988—, group v.p. mktg., 1972-80, exec. v.p., chief mktg. officer Angelica Uniform Group, 1980-88; vis. lectr. mktg. NYU Grad. Sch. Bus. Adminstrn. Vice comdr. Am. Legion; mem. vocational adv. bd. VA.; adv. bd. Woodcraft Rangers; bd. dirs. Univ. Temple. Served with USAF, 1942-44. Mem. Am. Assn. Contamination Control (dir.), Am. Soc. for Advancement Mgmt. (chpt. pres.), Am. Mktg. Assn., Health Industries Assn. Am. (dir.), Inst. Environ. Scis., various trade assns., St. Louis Coun. on World Affairs, Sales Execs. Club (bd. dirs.), NYU Alumni Assn., B'nai B'rith (past pres.), Coast Guard Aux. (Flotilla comdr.), Lake of the Ozarks Yachting Assn., Men's Club (exec. v.p.), Town Hall Club, NYU Club, Aqua Sierra Sportsmen Club, Moorings Yacht Club (v.p.), Phi Epsilon Pi (treas.). Contbr. articles to profl. jours. Home: 9821 Log Cabin Ct Saint Louis MO 63124-1133

ABER, JOHN IRWIN, humanities educator, researcher, fiction writer; b. Newark, Ohio, Apr. 15, 1951; s. Jesse Irwin and Helen Lucille (Lyle) A. BA, Otterbein Coll., 1973; MA, Ohio State U., Columbus, 1981, PhD, 1986. Tchr. English Washington Ct. House (Ohio) City Schs., 1976-81; coord. lang. arts dept. Stark County Schs., Louisville, Ohio, 1984-85; asst. prof. humanities Coll. of Mt. St. Joseph, Cin., 1986-91, assoc. prof. humanities, 1991—; cons. in field. Mem. Nat. Coun. Tchrs. of English, Conf. on Coll. Composition and Communication, Cin. Writers Project, Phi Kappa Phi. Office: Coll Mt St Joseph Dept Humanities 5701 Delhi Rd Cincinnati OH 45233-1672

ABER, SUSAN WARD, earth science educator; b. Halstead, Kans., May 6, 1955; d. Henry Allen and Marian Maxine (Buffington) Ward; m. James Sandusky Aber, June 5, 1977; children: Jeremy Ward Aber, Jay Thomas Aber. BS in Geology, U. Kans., 1977; postgrad., Emporia State U., 1995—. Needlecraft tchr. Creative Circle, Emporia, Kans., 1982-86; earth sci. tchr. Emporia State U., 1988—. Co-author: Petrographic Characteristics of Kansas Building Limestone, 1984, Introduction to Earth Science Lab, 1993; contbr. articles to profl. jours. Den leader Cub Scout pack Boy Scouts Am., Emporia, 1988-96; campus sponsor Presbyn. Student Orgn., Emporia State U. Mem. LWV Kans. (treas. 1987-89, v.p. 1989-91), LWV Emporia (sec. 1981-83), pres. 1983-85, 1991-93). Presbyterian. Home: 2002 Holiday Dr Emporia KS 66801-6120 Office: Emporia State U 12th & Commercial Emporia KS 66801

ABERLE, JAMES ROBERT, accounting executive; b. Deadwood, S.D., June 6, 1950; s. Wendelin Paul and Lorraine Shirley (Manning) A.; m. Cathie Christine Caropino, June 14, 1974; children: Laura Lyn, Melissa Ann, Natalie Kay, Edie Marie. BBA in Acctg., U. Notre Dame, 1972. Mgr. Dakota Ins. Planners, Lead, S.D., 1976; from metall. acct. to sr. acct. Homestake Mining Co., Lead, 1976-91, dir. acctg., 1991-92; chief acct., 1993—; govs. com. S.D. Blue Ribbon Workers Compensation Com., Pierre, S.D., 1991—, Employment People with Disabilities, Pierre, 1988—; chmn. bd. dirs. No. Hills. Gen. Hosp. City commr. City of Lead, 1978-82; mem. Lead-Deadwood Sch. Dist. Bd. Edn., 1988-94; bd. dirs., past pres. Lead-Deadwood C. of C., 1988-91; chmn. fin. com. No. Hills Gen. Hosp. Found., Deadwood, 1988-92. Capt. U.S. Army, 1972-76. Recipient Disting. Svc. award Lead-Deadwood Jaycees, 1985; named one of Outstanding Young Men. Am., 1981, Outstanding Sch. Bd. Mem. Lead-Deadwood Bd. Edn., 1992. Mem. Black Hills Officials Assn. (pres. 1985-86), S.D. Black Hills Officials Assn. (bd. dirs. 1985-92, regional coord.), Moose, Elks, Lead Country Club (pres. 1980), Notre Dame Club the Black Hills (senator 1990). Republican. Roman Catholic. Home: 415 Sunset Rd Lead SD 57754-2216 Office: Homestake Mining Co 630 E Summit St Lead SD 57754-1603

ABERNATHY, RANDY E., stockbroker; b. St. Louis, Nov. 22, 1948. BA, Webster U., Webster Groves, Mo., 1988. Owner, mgr. Pearl East Inc., Fairview Heights, Mo., 1974-82; stockbroker Thompson McKennan, N.Y.C., 1983-92, Prudential Securities Inc., Chesterfield, Mo., 1992—. Mem. Webster U. Alumni Assn. (exec. v.p. bd. dirs. 1993—), 95 Investment Club (pres. 1995—), Webster Groves Softball Club. Republican. Roman Catholic. Home: 5629 Eichelberger St Saint Louis MO 63109-2806 Office: Prudential Securities Inc 14528 S Outer 40 Dr Ste 333 Saint Louis MO 63017

ABERNETHY, IRENE MARGARET, county official; b. Ord, Nebr., Mar. 28, 1924; d. Glen Dayton and Margaret Lillian (Jones) Auble; m. Don R. Abernethy, Aug. 8, 1954 (dec. Nov. 1980); children: Jill Adele Abernethy Johnson, Ted Verne. BA cum laude, Hastings Coll., 1946; postgrad., U. Nebr., 1950-53. Tchr. Ord High Sch., 1946-50, Scottsbluff (Nebr.) High Sch., 1950-55, Grand Island (Nebr.) Sr. High Sch., 1961-62; mem. Hall County Bd. Suprs., Grand Island, 1979—, chair, 1984, 95. Vice chair Hall County Rep. Ctrl. Com., Grand Island, 1971-73; chair campaign Congresswoman Virginia Smith for Hall County, 1974-80; sr. v.p. Nebr. Rep. Founders Day, Lincoln, 1981; chair Gov.'s Juv. Justice Adv. Group, Lincoln, 1981-91; mem. Nebr. Commn. on Law Enforcement and Criminal Justice, Lincoln, 1970-91; bd. dirs. Head Start, 1979—, Hall County Leadership Tomorrow, 1990-94, Indsl. Found., 1991, College Park, 1991—, Community Help Ctr., 1991—, Family Violence Coalition, 1993—, Midland Area Agy. on Aging, 1993-95; adv. com. Region III Mental Health Adv.

Bd.; active Nat. Coalition State Juvenile Justice Adv. Groups, 1988-91, Partners in Community Planning, 1994—, Grand Island Area Edn. 2000; mem. task force on needs Heartland United Way. Named Woman of Yr., Grand Island Independent, 1980, Bus. and Profl. Woman, Grand Island, 1980, Beta Sigma Phi, 1982, Nebr. chpt. NASW, 1983; recipient Svc. to Mankind award Sertoma, 1994, recognition award PTA, 1988, Outstanding Cmty. Svc. award Rotary, 1985, Cmty. Leadership award Ak-Sar-Ben, 1995. Mem. LWV (local pres. 1962-64, state bd. dirs. 1965-69), AAUW (local pres. 1966-68, state bd. dirs. 1970-71), YWCA (local pres. 1974-75, Woman of Distinction award 1988). Republican. Methodist. Home: 707 S Blaine St Grand Island NE 68803-6146 Office: Hall County Adminstrn 121 S Pine St Grand Island NE 68801-6076

ABITZ, ANTHONY JOHN, test systems engineer, musician; b. Fond du Lac, Wis., Aug. 12, 1972; s. Dennis Norman and Sherry Lynn (Arndt) A. BS in Elec. Engring. Tech., Milw. Sch. Engring., 1994. Test sys. engr. Wells Mfg. Corp., Fond du Lac, Wis., 1992—. Named Nat. Dean's List. Mem. IEEE, Audio Engring. Soc., Tau Alpha Pi.

ABRAHAM, SPENCER, senator; b. Lansing, Mich., June 12, 1952. BA in Social Sci.and Polit. Sci., Mich. State U., 1974; JD, Harvard U., 1979. Asst. prof. law Thomas M. Cooley Law Sch., 1981-83; chmn. Mich. Republican Party, 1983-90; dep. chief of staff to Vice President Dan Quayle, 1990-91; co-chair Nat. Republican Congressional Com., 1991-93; of counsel Canfield, Paddock & Stone, 1993-94; U.S. senator from Mich., 1994—. Office: US Senate 245 Dirksen Senate Bldg Washington DC 20510-2203

ABRAHAMSON, DAVID STEPHEN RODLER, journalism educator, writer; b. Washington, May 7, 1947; s. Ernst Ludwig and Edith (Rodler) A.; m. Barbara Buzan, Aug. 8, 1980. BA in History, Johns Hopkins U., 1969; MJ, U. Calif., Berkeley, 1973; PhD in Am. Civilization, NYU, 1992. Assoc. editor Am. Boating mag., Lafayette, Calif., 1972-73; editor-in-chief AutoWeek mag., Reno, Nev., 1973; mng. editor Car and Driver mag., N.Y.C., 1973-77; ind. journalist, author, 1977—; mgmt. cons. Enfield Rsch./Editorial Cons., 1979—; adj. faculty U. N.H., Gorham, 1983-90, Sch. of Visual Arts, N.Y.C., 1986-88, Pratt Inst., N.Y.C., 1987-89; adj. asst. prof. NYU, 1988-90; adj. assoc. prof. NYU Mgmt. Inst. Ctr. for Pub., N.Y.C., 1991-94; assoc. prof., dir. mag. pub. project Northwestern U., 1994—; cons. AAAS, ABC, CBS, Chanticleer Press, Craim Comms., IDG Comms., Madison Ave. Pub., McGraw Hill, Mercedes Benz N.Am., Murdoch Mags., Oceanic Soc., Times Mirror Mags., Ziff Comms., numerous others. Author: The American Magazine: Research Perspectives and Prospects, 1995, Magazine-Made America: The Cultural Transformation of the Postwar Periodical, 1996; author numerous publs. and articles. Lt. U.S. Army, 1969-71. Recipient Ken Purdy award Internat. Motor Press Assn., 1978, faculty award NYU, 1992, Award for Excellence Ga. Mag. Assn., 1993; Univ. scholar NYU, 1991; Scripps Howard Found. scholar 1991-92; poynter tchg. fellow Poynter Inst. for Media Studies, St. Petersburg, Fla., 1993; NEH fellow CUNY, 1993. Mem. Assn. for Edn. In Journalism and Mass Comm., Am. Journalism Historians Assn., Am. Hist. Assn., Orgn. Am. Historians, Am. Studies Assn., History of Sci. Soc., Am. Soc. Journalists and Authors. Home: 2025 Sherman Ave Evanston IL 60201-3280 Office: Northwestern U Medill Sch Journalism 1845 Sheridan Rd Evanston IL 60208

ABRAMS, MAX, engineering executive; b. July 5, 1929. Student, Cowley County Tech. Sch., Arkansas City, Kans., 1949. Mech. designer Cessna Aircraft, Wichita, Kans., 1950-57, Space Craft, Dallas, 1958; ind. cons. Spring Machine, Wichita, 1960-70, cons. engr., pres., 1971—. Patentee on electric brake controls. Baptist.

ABRAMS, ROBERTA BUSKY, hospital administrator, nurse; b. Bklyn., Feb. 16, 1937; d. Albert H. and Gladys Busky; m. Robert L. Abrams, June 28, 1959 (div. 1977); children: Susan Abrams Federman, David B. BSN, U. Rochester, 1959; MA, Fairfield U., 1977. Asst. head nurse Jewish Hosp., Bklyn., 1959-60; instr. medicine/surgery Bklyn. Hosp., 1960-62, U. Rochester, N.Y., 1963-64; instr. ob-gyn Malden (Mass.) Hosp. Sch. Nursing, 1965-66; instr. prospective parents ARC, San Rafael, Calif., 1968-69; instr. ob-gyn SUNY, Farmingdale, 1970-71; instr. maternal/child health Stamford (Conn.) Hosp., 1971-75; clinician maternal/child health Lawrence Hosp., Bronxville, N.Y., 1975-78; asst. prof. nursing Ohio Wesleyan U., Delaware, 1981-84; dir. Elizabeth Blackwell Hosp. at Riverside Meth., Columbus, Ohio, 1978-86; dir. nursing Henry Ford Hosp., Detroit, 1986-87, assoc. adminstr. nursing, 1988-92; cons. Henry Ford Health Systems, Detroit, 1993—; cons. maternal/child nursing currents Ross Labs., 1984-94; cons. women's children's health Henry Ford Health Systems, 1993-94, cons. at large, 1994—; state coord. maternal/child health First Am. Home Care Co., 1994-96; co-dir. women's and children's health Arcadia Health Systems, 1996—; lectr. in field. Contbr. articles to profl. jours. Mem. NAACOG (vice-chmn. Ohio chpt. 1984-87), Am. Soc. Psychoprophylaxsis, Greater Detroit Orgn. Nurses Execs., LWV, Sigma Theta Tau. Home and Office: 32478 Dunford St Farmington Hills MI 48334-2724

ABRAMS, RONALD LAWRENCE, state legislator; b. Apr. 1952; m. Joanne Abrams; two children. BA, U. Minn.; JD, Harvard U. State rep. Dist. 45A Minn. Ho. of Reps., asst. minority leader, 1996—; atty., 1996—; mem. Fin. Instn. & Ins. Com., Gen. Legislation Com., Vet. Affairs & Elections Com., Rules & Legis. Adminstrn. Com., Ways & Means & Taxes Coms. Home: 209 State Office Bldg Saint Paul MN 55155-1201*

ABRAMS, SYLVIA FLECK, religious studies educator; b. Buffalo, Apr. 5, 1942; d. Abraham and Ann (Hanf) Fleck; m. Ronald M. Abrams, June 30, 1963; children—Ruth, Sharon. BA magna cum laude, Western Res. U., 1963, MA, 1964, PhD, 1988; BHL, Cleve. Coll. Jewish Studies, 1976, MHL, 1983; postgrad. U. Haifa, 1975, Yad Va Shem Summer Inst., Hebrew U., 1983. Hebrew tchr. The Temple, 1959-77, Hebrew coord., 1973-77; tchr. Beachwood H.S., 1964-66; tchr. Hebrew and social studies Agnon Sch., Cleve., 1975-77, social studies resource tchr., 1976-77; ednl. dir. Temple Emanu El, Cleve., 1977-85; asst. dir. Cleve. Bur. Jewish Edn., 1985-92, acting exec. v.p., 1993-94, exec. dir. ednl. svcs. Jewish Edn. Ctr. Cleve., 1994—; chmn. ednl. dirs. coun. Cleve. Bd. Jewish Edn., 1982-85. Appointed to Ohio Coun. Holocaust Edn., 1986. Recipient Elbert J. Benton award Western Res. U., 1963; Fred and Rose Rosenwasser Bible award Coll. Jewish Studies, 1974; Emmanuel Gamoran Meml. Curriculum award Nat. Assn. Temple Educator, 1978; Samuel Lipson Meml. award Coll. Jewish Studies, 1981 Bingham fellow Case Western Res. U., 1984-86. Mem. ASCD, Nat. Assn. Temple Educators (bd. dirs. 1984-88), Coun. Jewish Edn. (bd. dirs. 1991—, v.p. 1995, Bur. Dirs. fellow-sec./treas. 1995—), Coalition for Advancement of Jewish Edn. (bd. mem. at large 1989-93, chair 1996), Union Am. Hebrew Congregations (Israel curriculum task force), Cleve. Bur. Jewish Edn. (chmn. ednl. dirs. coun. 1982-85), Nat. Coun. Jewish Women (life), Phi Beta Kappa. Jewish. Club: Hadassah (life). Editor: You and Your Schools, 1972. Office: Jewish Edn Ctr of Cleve 2030 S Taylor Rd Cleveland OH 44118-2605

ABRAMSON, JANET CAROLYN, communicty college educator; b. Detroit, Apr. 4, 1942; d. Louis Morris and Anna Dorothy (Abrams) Schwartz; m. Paul Robert Abramson, Sept. 11, 1966; children: Lee Jacob, Heather Lyn. BA cum laude, Wayne State U., 1964; MA cum laude, U. Calif., Berkeley, 1967; postgrad., Mich. State U., 1967-74. Cert. secondary edn. tchr., Mich. Instr. Tripton's Sch. for Girls, London, 1966, Lansing (Mich.) Community Coll., 1976-87, 88—; editor, proofreader Mich. Edn. Assn., East Lansing, 1987; freelance researcher and editor, 1970—. Author of poetry. Bd. dirs. Health Cen., Lansing, 1970-72. Woodrow Wilson grad. fellow, 1964-65. Mem. NEA, Nat. Coun. Tchrs. English, Mich. Assn. for Higher Edn. Home: 2697 Linden Dr East Lansing MI 48823-3813

ABRATE, JAYNE ELYSE, language educator; b. Rochelle, Ill., Feb. 8, 1955; d. Burton E. and Pearl L. (Mitchell) Halsne; m. Serge Abrate, Aug. 18, 1979; children: Denis, Marc. BA, BFA, Ill. Wesleyan U., 1977; MA, Purdue U., 1980, PhD, 1983. Asst. Coll. d'Enseignement Secondaire Croix Crouge, Reims, France, 1977-78; tchg. asst. Purdue U., West Lafayette, Ind., 1979-83; instr. S.W. Mo. State U., Springfield, 1984; from asst. to assoc. prof. Drury Coll., Springfield, 1984-90; from lectr. to asst. prof. U. Mo., Rolla, 1990—; cons. Ednl. Testing Svc./Coll. Bd., 1987—; adj. prof. Southern Ill. U., Carbondale, 1996—. Contbr. articles to profl. jours. Mem. MLA, Am. Assn. Tchrs. of French (mem., editor Culture Commn. 1993—, mem., contbr. Telematics Commn. 1993—, Exploration Minitel Rsch. award 1993), Am. Coun. on Tchg. Fgn. Langs., Ctrl. States Adv. Coun. (editor Ctrl. States Conf. newsletter 1996—), Am. Coun. for Quebec Studies, Fgn. Lang. Assn. Mo. (regional rep. 1987-96), Ill. Coun. on the Tchg. Fgn. Langs., Pi Delta Phi (moderator 1984-90). Office: Southern Ill U Dept Fgn Langs Carbondale IL 62901

ABT, SYLVIA HEDY, dentist; b. Chgo., Oct. 7, 1957; d. Wendel Peter and Hedi Lucie (Wieder) A. Student, Loyola U., Chgo., 1975-77; cert. dental hygiene, Loyola U., Maywood, Ill., 1979, DDS, 1983. Registered dental hygienist. Dental asst. Office Dr. Baran and Dr. O'Neill, DDS, Chgo., 1977-78; dental hygienist Drs. Spiro, Sudakoff, Kadens, Weidman, DDS, Skokie, Ill., 1979-83, Dr. Laudando, DiFranco, Rosemont, Ill., 1980-83; gen. practice dentistry Chgo., 1983—. Vol. Community Health Rotations, VA Hosps., grammar schs., convalescent ctrs., mental health ctrs., Maywood, Ill. and Chgo., 1978-82. Recipient 1st Pl. award St. Apollonia Art Show Loyola U., 1982. Mem. ADA, PETA, Ill. Dental Soc., Chgo. Dental Soc., Loyola Dental Alumni Assn. (golf outing registration chmn. 1987, awards in golf and tennis 1987), Ill. Dentists 99th Club (legis. interest com.), Psi Omega (historian, editor Kappa chpt.). Office: 6509 W Higgins Ave Chicago IL 60656-2204

ABTS, GWYNETH HARTMANN, dietitian; b. Union, Ill., Oct. 31, 1923; d. William John and Olga Anna (Krause) Hartmann; m. Rufus Heath Jr., Apr. 6, 1942 (div. Dec. 1945); m. Harold Henry Abts, Feb. 14, 1948; children: Leigh, Michael, Patricia. BS, U. Ill., 1945; postgrad., U. Oreg., 1945-46, U. Ill., Elgin, 1957, No. Ill. U., 1966, 74, 82, 87. Registered dietitian, Ill. Clin. dietitian St. Joseph Hosp., Elgin, 1947; asst. dietitian French Hosp., San Francisco, 1948-50, Elgin State Hosp., 1950-58; dietary cons. Ill. Youth Commn., Springfield, 1958-70; food adminstr. Ill. Dept. of Corrections, Springfield, 1970-85; mem. Food and Nutrition Cou. on Govt. Commodities, Springfield, 1980-85; bd. dirs. Ill. Nutrition Assn., Urbana, 1983. Pres. PTO, Geneva, 1972. McHenry County Home Econ. scholar U. Ill., 1941-45. Mem. Am. Dietetic Assn. (citizens ambassador program to Australia and New Zealand), Fox Valley Home Economists, West Suburban Dietetic Assn., AAUW. Lutheran. Home: 1505 Dunstan Rd Geneva IL 60134-3327

ACCARDO, PHILLIP LOUIS, osteopath; b. Cheyenne, Wyo., Dec. 30, 1931; s. Louis J. and Lena (Benenate) A.; m. Glenda S. Huntsucker, June 4, 1976; children: Victoria Davis, Vincent, Joseph, Paul Landes, Paula Higber, Brett Trowbridge. BS, Rockhurst Coll., 1953; DO, U. Health Scis., Kansas City, Mo., 1959. cert. in family practice. Pvt. practice Indep, Mo., 1961—. Pres. alumni assn. Univ. Health Scis. Coll. Osteo. Medicine, 1972. Sgt. U.S. Army, 1953-55. Fellow Am. Coll. Osteo. Physicians, Am. Coll. Family Physicians; mem. Am. Osteo. Assn. (trustee), Mo. Assn. Osteo. Physicians and Surgeons (pres. 1976-77), Jackson County Osteo. Assn. (pres. 1967-68). Office: Indep Family Medicine 620 W 23rd Independence MO 64055

ACHGILL, RALPH KENNETH, retired research scientist; b. Indpls., June 17, 1938; s. Kenneth and Lois Ann (Philips) A.; m. Virginia Ann Swisher, July 21, 1956 (dec. Nov. 1992); children: Kenneth Edward, Douglas Alan, Kerry Wayne, Bridget Marie; m. Diane K. McCauley, Dec. 26, 1993. Student, Purdue U., 1956-60. Rsch. scientist Eli Lilly & Co., Indpls., 1956-93, internat. tech. coord., 1974-93; ret., 1993. Patentee in field. Mem. Masons (past master), Optimist Club (charter pres.). Republican. Home: PO Box 6508 Lafayette IN 47903-5408

ACKERMAN, JOHN C., state legislator; b. Morton, Ill., Nov. 23, 1933; m. Joann Ackerman; 4 children. Student, U. Ill. Ill. state rep. Dist. 89, 1979-82, 87—; mem. Agr., Urban Redevel., Econ. Devel., Elem. and Secondary Edn. and Pub. Utilities, Registration and Regulation Coms.; farmer. Address: 205 W Jefferson Morton IL 61550

ACKERMANN, RUSSELL ALBERT, manufacturing company executive; b. Cin., Aug. 14; s. Russell Albert and Jennie Agatha (Brockmeier) A.; m. Mildred Arlene Streicher, July 24, 1948; children: Layne Anne Seifert, Kristie Allison Clepper, Leslie Arlene Bickel. Student, U. Cin., 1944-47. Registered profl. engr., Ohio. Rsch. assoc. CHMR Rsch. Inst., Cin., 1947-54; adminstrv. svc. mgr. Cin. Milacron, 1954-76; mktg. mgr. Dresser Ind., Niagara Falls, N.Y., 1976-87; pres. Ackermann & Assoc., Cin., 1987-89; chmn. Internat. Abrasives Corp., Nashville, 1989-91, Ackermann & Assocs., Cin., 1991—; cons. Colonial Abrasives, Aberdeen, N.C., 1987-89; chmn. Greater Cin. Info. Svcs., Inc (d.b.a. Net Results), 1996. Author: Laboratory Techniques, 1954; contbr. numerous articles to profl. jours.; patentee grinding wheels. Mem. Rep. Cen. Com., 1960-65; mem. city coun., Madeira, Ohio, 1965-76; mem. regional coun. Boy Scouts Am., Cin., 1955-60, Econ. Dev. and Export Coun., Pinehurst, N.C., 1988. Mem. American Water Works Assoc., Water Pollution Control Fed., Grinding Wheel Inst. (committee mem. 1986-89), Abrasive Grain Assoc. (committee mem. 1976-86), Abrasive Eng. Soc. (dir.), Masons, Acacia Fraternity. Mem. United Ch. of Christ. Home: 1352 Rambling Hills Dr Cincinnati OH 45230-2359 Office: Ackermann & Assocs 2961 Madison Rd Cincinnati OH 45209-2027

ACKERSON, CHARLES STANLEY, minister, social worker; b. St. Louis, June 19, 1935; s. Charles Albert and Glenda Mae (Brown) A.; m. Carol Jean Stehlick, Aug. 18, 1957; children: Debra Lynn, Charles Mark, Heather Sue. AB, William Jewell Coll., 1957; MDiv, Colgate Rochester Div. Sch., 1961. Ordained to ministry Am. Bapt. Ch., 1961; lic. clin. social worker. Pastor, Glens Falls (N.Y.) Friends Meeting, 1961-65; assoc. pastor Delmar Bapt. Ch., St. Louis, 1965-68; resource dir. Block Ptnrship., St. Louis, 1968-71; group home dir. North Side YMCA, St. Louis, 1971-72; group home supr. St. Louis Juvenile Ct., 1973-74; program dir. Youth Opportunities Unltd., casework supr. St. Louis County Juvenile Ct., 1974-83; youth svcs. specialist St. Louis County Dept. Human Svcs., 1985-94; asst. dir. Gen. Protestant Children's Home, 1995—; instr. adminstrn. of justice and human svcs. Mo. Bapt. Coll., St. Louis, 1980—; asst. pastor St. Jordan's and St. John's United Chs. of Christ, 1976—; exhibit coord. Dog Mus., 1989-91; cons. Am. Youth Found., 1990—; mem. ordination coun. area V, Great Rivers region Am. Bapt. Chs. U.S.A., 1982-84; chmn. youth focus group Interfaith Ptnrship. Met. St. Louis, 1985-88; chmn. St. Louis Area Youth Svcs. Network, 1987-89. Chmn. group home com. Mo. Coun. on Criminal Justice, 1973-75; chmn. cts. and instns. subcom. Juvenile Delinquency Task Force for Gov. Mo. Action Plan for Pub. Safety, 1976. Mem. Nat. Coun. Juvenile and Family Ct. Judges, Mo. Juvenile Justice Assn. (v.p., chmn. tng. com.), Am. Correctional Assn., Nat. Audobon Soc., Smithsonian Instn. Assn., Cairn Terrier Club Am., Three Rivers Kennel Club of Mo. (past pres.), Mo. Conservation Fedn., Lambda Chi Alpha. Democrat. Baptist. Home: 1221 Havenhurst Rd Ballwin MO 63011-4402

ACTON, DAVID L(AWRENCE), automobile company executive; b. Detroit, Apr. 12, 1949; s. Lawrence E. and Johannah (Cassimatis) A.; m. Dianne Patience McNeill, Sept. 5, 1981; children: Andrew, Stephen, Amy. BME, Gen. Motors Inst., Flint, Mich., 1973; MBA, U. Mich., 1978. Assoc. engr. Hydra-matic div. GM, Ypsilanti, Mich., 1973-74, project engr., 1974-77, supr. indsl. engring., 1977-78, asst. supt. indsl. engring., 1978-81; asst. supt. progress tracking, quality and reliability GM, Detroit, 1981-83, sr. adminstr., 1983-85, mgr. program planning B-O-C- car group, 1985, program mgr. Allanté elec. test system, 1985-87; mgr. elec. design and processing Cadillac Motor Car Co., Detroit, 1987-91, mgr. electrical product systems, 1991-93; chief engr. elec./electronics Cadillac luxury car divsn. GM, Flint, Mich., 1993—. Mem. SAE. Office: Cadillac Luxury Car Divsn 4100 S Saginaw Mail Stop 2117 Flint MI 48557

ACUFF, JOHN THOMAS, technology educator; b. Decatur, Ill., Nov. 21, 1943; s. Dorothy Louise (Hewitt) A.; m. Linda L. Lief, Dec. 1964 (div. Oct. 1965); 1 child, Sherri Acuff; m. JoAnn D. Jeffries, July 2, 1982; children: Chris Wiseman, Monica Wiseman, Lynn Weichman. AAS in Indsl. Electronics, Black Hawk Coll., Moline, Ill., 1963; BS in Tech. Edn., Colo. State U., 1977; MS in Indsl. Engring. Tech., Western Ill. U., 1991. Apprentice, journeyman machinist Williams-White & Co., Moline, 1964-67; machinist Rock Island (Ill.) Arsenal, 1967-68, machinist CNC, 1971-73; svc. mgr. Sun Electric Corp., Mt. Joy, Iowa, 1970; tchr. Black Hawk Coll., 1973—; ind. cons., Moline, 1988—. Mem., sec. USCG Aux., Rock Island, 1986—; various offices U.S. Power Squadrons, Quad Cities area, Ill. and Iowa, 1974-86. With U.S. Army, 1968-70. Mem. Soc. Carbide Tooling Engrs. (faculty advisor). Office: Black Hawk Coll 6600 34th Ave Moline IL 61265

ACUFF, TODD W., stockbroker; b. Monett, Mo., Aug. 11, 1967. BS, U. Mo., 1989. Analyst Shearson, Lehman, Hutton, Kansas City, Mo., 1989-93; stockbroker PaineWebber, Kansas City, 1993—. Office: PaineWebber 4600 Madison Ave Ste 801 Kansas City MO 64112-3012

ADAMANY, DAVID WALTER, law and political science educator; b. Janesville, Wis., Sept. 23, 1936; s. Walter Joseph and Dora Marie (Mutter) A. AB, Harvard U., 1958, JD, 1961; MS, U. Wis., 1963, PhD in Polit. Sci., 1967; LLD (hon.), Adrian Coll., 1984; AAS (hon.), Schoolcraft Coll., 1986; D. Engring. (hon.), Mich. Tech. U., 1987. Bar: Wis. 1961. Spl. asst. to atty. gen. State of Wis., Madison, 1961-63, exec. pardon counsel, 1963; commr. Wis. Public Service Commn., 1963-65; instr. polit. sci. Wis. State U., Whitewater, 1965-67; asst. prof., then assoc. prof. Wesleyan U., Middletown, Conn., 1967-72; dean coll. Wesleyan U., 1969-71; assoc. prof., then prof. polit. sci. U. Wis., Madison, 1972-77; sec. of revenue State of Wis., 1974-76; v.p. acad. affairs, prof. Calif. State U., Long Beach, 1977-80, U. Md., College Park, 1980-82; prof. law and polit. sci. Wayne State U., Detroit, 1982—, pres., 1982—; chmn. Wis. Coun. Criminal Justice, 1973-75, Wis. Elections Bd., 1976-77; sec. Wis. Dept. Revenue, 1973-75; advisor to Gov. Patrick J. Lucey, State of Wis., 1972. Author: Financing Politics, 1969, Campaign Finance in America, 1972; co-author Borzoi Reader in American Politics, 1972, American Government: Democracy and Liberty in Balance, 1975, Political Money, 1975; editorial bd.: Social Sci. Quarterly, 1973—, State and Local Govt. Rev., 1974-80; contbr. articles to profl. jours. Mem. exec. com. Detroit Med. Ctr.; chmn. Mich. Bicentennial of U.S. Constrn. Commn., 1986-88; bd. dirs. Detroit Inst. Arts Founders Soc., 1983-92, Detroit Symphony Orch., 1983-89, Detroit Econ. Growth Corp., 1984-92, Mich. Cancer Found., New Detroit. Mem. ACLU, ABA (commn. on coll. and univ. legal studies 1992-95), Wis. Bar Assn., Am. Polit. Sci. Assn., Pres.'s Coun. State Univs. (chmn. 1986-88), Mich. Superconducting Super Collider Commn. (chmn. 1988-89), Can.-U.S. Fulbright Commn. (bd. dirs. 1993—), Nat. Adv. Com. on Institutional Quality and Integrity (U.S. dept. edn.). Democrat. Office: Wayne State U Office of Pres Detroit MI 48202

ADAMLE, KATHLEEN NORA DUFFY, oncological nurse; b. Cleve., Oct. 3, 1948; d. Joseph L. and Joan (Fierle) Duffy; m. Tony Adamle, July 14, 1969; children: Kelly Joan, Kerry Ruth. BS in Edn., Kent State U., 1971, BSN, 1983, postgrad., 1991—; MSN, U. Akron, 1989. Cert. advanced oncology nurse; RN, Ohio, Pa., Fla. Staff nurse oncology unit Akron (Ohio) City Hosp., 1983-87, telephone triage nurse family practice, 1987-89; oncology clin. nurse specialist Cancer Care Ctr. SMC Western Res. Care System, Youngstown, Ohio, 1989—; cons. in pediatric oncology; cons. Hospice of Youngstown; adj. faculty Kent State U. Sch. Nursing. Mem. Am. Heart Assn., Oncology Nursing Soc., Sigma Theta Tau. Home: 1111 Norwood St Kent OH 44240-3342

ADAMO, JOSEPH J., securities analyst; b. Cleve., Jan. 31, 1947. BS, BA, John Carroll U., 1969. Securities analyst A T Brod & Co. Inc., Cleve., 1970—. Office: A T Brod & Co Inc # 324 6505 Rockside Rd Cleveland OH 44131-2342

ADAMS, BEEJAY (MEREDITH ELISABETH JANE J. ADAMS), sales executive; b. Jefferson Banks, Mo., June 9, 1920; d. Alden Humphrey and Louise Marion (Banta) Seabury; m. Merlin Francis Adams, July 10, 1948 (dec. 1977); children; S(tephen) Kent, Mark Francis. AB, Bradley U., 1942. Svc. editor Peoria (Ill.) Jour. Star, 1942-46; women's program dir. Sta. WEEK-AM, Peoria, 1946-47; on air personality Sta. KSD-AM, St. Louis, 1948; lectr. Sch. Assembly Svc., Chgo., 1948-49; pres. M.F. Adams, Inc., Quincy, Ill., 1977-85; commodities broker Quincy, 1985-87; pres. MarKent, Inc., Quincy, 1975—; sec., treas. Miss. Belle Distbn. Co., Inc., Quincy, 1976—, v.p., treas., 1979—. Active Quincy Svc. League, 1949-57, local polit. campaigns, co-chmn. local presdl. campaigns, 1952-77; founder, past pres. Quincy Jr. Theatre, 1953-78; charter mem. Quincy Community Theatre; co-chmn. coll. fund drive Quincy Coll., 1988, chmn. 1989. Mem. Quincy C. of C., Adams County Red Cross Bd., Sales and Mktg. Execs. Club, Quincy Art Club, Atlantis Study Club, Quincy Country Club, Phi Beta Phi. Anglican. Home: 2303 Jersey St Quincy IL 62301-4343 Office: Miss Belle Distbn Co Inc PO Box 768 Quincy IL 62306-0768

ADAMS, GARY D., physical therapist; b. Arcadia, Calif., Aug. 30, 1962; s. David L. and Marilyn C. (Lang) A. BS in Health Sci. cum laude, Calif. State U., Northridge, 1985, cert. in phys. therapy, 1993; MBA, U. Kans., 1993. cert. phys. therapist, Calif., Kans. Mo. Staff phys. therapist Pleasant Valley Hosp., Camarillo, Calif., 1986-88, supr. phys. therapist, 1988-90; phys. therapist team leader Lawrence (Kans.) Meml. Hosp., 1990-93; regional clin. mgr. Associated Rehab. Svcs., Kansas City, 1993—. Mem. Am. Phys. Therapy Assn., Sierra Club, Kans. U. Alumni Assn. Office: Associated Rehab Svcs 5809 W 164th St Stilwell KS 66085

ADAMS, HENRY GEORGE, radiologist; b. Dallas, Oct. 25, 1947; s. Herbert Henry and Dale Evelyn (Jordan) A.; m. LuAnn Joyce Erickson, Aug. 25, 1979; children: Elyse Catherine, Lauren Jordan. BSEE, U. N.Mex., 1973, MSEE, 1974; MD, U. Nebr., 1980. Diplomate Am. Bd. Radiology. Surg. intern Naval Hosp., Oakland, Calif., 1980-81, resident in diagnostic radiology, 1982-85; fellow in magnetic resonance imaging U. Calif., San Diego, 1988-89; commd. ensign USN, 1973, advanced through grades to capt., 1991; chmn. dept. radiology USN, Camp Pendleton, Calif., 1986-88, USN NNMC, Bethesda, Md., 1989-92, Lakewood Hosp., 1992—; pres. Western Res. Radiology, Westlake, Ohio, 1994—. Author: Total Quality in Radiology, 1994; sci. reviewer Am. Jour. Roentgenology, 1989—. Mem. Am. Coll. Radiology (quality assurance com. mem. 1993—), Radiol. Soc. N.Am. Office: Lakewood Hosp 14519 Detroit Ave Lakewood OH 44107

ADAMS, JAMES ROBERT, medical organization sales professional; b. Kansas City, Mo., Dec. 4, 1946; s. James Watt and Helen Agnes (Cleary) A.; m. Mary Catherine Edwards, Mar. 27, 1971; children: Robert, Patrick. BA, Rockhurst Coll., 1970; AA in Respiratory Therapy, Penn Valley Community Coll., 1972; MA, Webster U., 1980. Registered respiratory therapist. Shift supr. Menorah Med. Ctr., Kansas City, 1970-73; asst. dir. respiratory therapy North Kansas City Meml. Hosp., 1973-77; dir. pulmonary lab. Truman Med. Ctr., Kansas City, 1977-80; clin. coordinator Nat. Med. Care, Merriam, Kans., 1980-85; br. mgr. Greene & Kellogg, Inc., Overland Park, Kans., 1985-87; sales rep. Nat. Med. Homecare (now Homedco of Kansas City), Lenexa, Kans., 1987—; cons. Sysco, Inc., Kansas City, 1978-79. Cubmaster local coun. Boy Scouts Am., Kansas City, 1984—. Republican. Roman Catholic. Home: 10417 Monroe Ave Kansas City MO 64137-1533

ADAMS, JILL ELAINE, legal educator; b. Durham, N.C., July 9, 1952; d. Elie Maynard and Phyllis Margaret (Stevenson) A.; m. Thomas Milton Alexander, July 2, 1983; children: Adam Hartley, Nathan Blake. BA with highest honors, U. N.C., 1974; MAT, U. Mass., 1978; JD summa cum laude, U. N.Mex., 1982. Bar: N.Mex. 1982, U.S. Dist. Ct. N.Mex. 1982, U.S. Ct. Appeals (10th cir.) 1984, Ill. 1986, U.S. Dist. Ct. (so. dist.) Ill. 1986, U.S. Ct. Appeals (7th cir.) 1986. Tchr. Albuquerque Indian Sch., 1976-77, Choctaw Cen. High Sch., Philadelphia, Miss., 1977-79; law clk. U.S. Dist. Ct. N.Mex., Albuquerque, 1982-84; assoc. Rodey, Dickason, Sloan, Akin & Robb, Albuquerque, 1984-86, Feirich, Schoen, Mager & Green, Carbondale, Ill., 1986-88; asst. prof. So. Ill. U., Carbondale, 1988-94, assoc. prof., 1994—; mem. So. Ill. dist. State of Ill. sect. Jud. Nominations Commn., U.S. Senate. Mem. ABA, Ill. State Bar Assn., Jackson County Bar Assn., Inn of Ct. (So. Ill. br.), Order of Coif. Democrat. Office: So Ill U Sch Law Carbondale IL 62901

ADAMS, JOHN CHARLES, electrical industry executive; b. E. Chgo., Ind., Nov. 20, 1931; s. Eber Clayton and Gertrude Mary (Lamb) A.; m. Joan Carol Reed, June 10, 1961; children: Amy, Robert, Susan. BSEE, Purdue U., 1954; MBA, U. Toledo, 1965. Registered profl. engr., Ill. Application engr. GE Lamp, Cleve., 1956-61, comml. & indsl. mktg., 1965-68, product mgr., 1968-70; supervisory dist. engr. GE Lamp, Chgo., 1961-65; dist. mgr. GE Lamp, St. Louis, 1970-73; dist. mgr. GE Lamp, Mpls., 1973-88, regional mgr., specifications, 1988-91; mgr., source Cooper Industry, Elk Grove Village, Ill., 1991-94; cons. Lite-Rite, Edina, Minn., 1994—. Contbr. articles to profl. jours. Conv. del. Rep. Party, Minn., 1982. Recipient Disting. Svc. award Chgo. Lighting Inst., 1969, Disting. Lighting award, 1972, Crime Prevention award Hennepin County Chief Assn., Mpls., 1991. Mem. Illuminating Engring. Soc. (regional v.p. 1991-94, sect. officer 1966, 72-76, lighting award 1988), Rotary. Methodist. Home: 4900 Larkspur Ln Edina MN 55435

ADAMS, JUANITA KAY (NITA ADAMS), public service administrator; b. Charleston, Ill., July 27, 1944; d. Charles Edward Gregory and Lois Juanita (Taylor) Wood; 1 child, April Lyn; m. Kenneth Roy Adams, Dec. 6, 1991 (div.). BA, Sangamon State U., 1980. Supr. fiscal mgmt. dept. adminstrn. svcs. State of Ill., Springfield, 1976-80, supr. gen. acctg. dept. commerce, 1980, supr. support svcs. dept. pub. health, 1980-84, audit mgr. dept. corrections, 1984-85, asst. chief of audit dept. pub. aid, 1985-94, asst. chief of audit dept. profl. regulation, 1994-96, pgm exec. adminstrv. svcs. profl. regulation, 1996—. Mem. NAFE, Assn. Info. Sys. Profls., Inst. Internal Auditors, Women in Mgmt., Capitol City Republican Women, Exec. Women in State Govt., Order of Eastern Star. Home: 2800 E Lake Shore Dr Springfield IL 62707-8912

ADAMS, KENT J., state legislator; m. Nancy Adams. BS, Manchester Coll.; MA, Ball State U.; EdD, Walden U. Trustee German Twp. Marshall County, 1978-88; spl. agt. FBI; Ind. state rep. Dist. 22, 1988-92; mem. pub. health, urban affairs and ways and means coms. Ind. Ho. Reps.; Ind. state senator Dist. 9, 1992—; mem. agrl. and small bus. edn. Ind. State Senate, environ. affairs coms., mem. Ind. state pension mgmt. oversight commn., gov.'s state adv. com. on child mental health; dir. fin. Warsaw Cmty. Sch.; state police trooper, pub. sch. adminstr.; pvt. cons. Dalton Foundries Inc.; mem. Warsaw Cmty. Develop Corp. Mem. Ind. Twp. Trustees Assn., Ind. Assn. Pub. Sch. Supts., Ins. Assn. Sch. Bus. Offcls., Bashor Home Bd. Home: 105 Beechwood Dr Bremen IN 46506-2206*

ADAMS, KRISTI KAY, association executive; b. St. Paul, Jan. 26, 1971; d. Fred James Adams and Valjeanne Rose Matson. BA, U. Minn., 1995. Mem. nat. bd. YWCA of the U.S.A., N.Y.C., chairwoman nat. student coun., 1992-94. Bd. dirs. U. Minn. YWCA, 1990-93. Mem. Democratic Farm Labor Party. Home: 72 Clarence Ave SE Minneapolis MN 55414-3528

ADAMS, LYNN, speech-language pathologist, educator; b. Coral Gables, Fla., Nov. 12, 1957; d. William A. and Georgia (Bonus) A. BS, Fla. State U., 1979, MS, 1980; PhD, U. Tenn., 1993. Speech pathologist Montgomery County Schs., Troy, N.C., 1980-84, Devel. Evaluation Ctr., Wadesboro, N.C., 1984-87; clin. supr. U. Tenn., Knoxville, 1988-92; asst. prof. S.W. Mo. State U., 1993—; cons. Project Access, Springfield, Mo., 1994—. Mem. Am. Speech and Hearing Assn., Mo. Speech and Hearing Assn., Autism Soc. Am. Democrat. Episcopalian. Home: 3371 E Sunset St # B Springfield MO 65804-3549 Office: SW Mo State U Dept Comm Disorders 901 S National Ave Springfield MO 65804-0027

ADAMS, PATRICIA LEE MINCKLER, program administrator; b. Kalamazoo, Apr. 25, 1945; d. Lyle Morris and Marian Louis (Caldwell) Minckler; children: Dorienne Rae, Michael Lyle. BA, Kalamazoo Coll., 1967. Tchr. O'Brien/Hackett H.S., Kalamazoo, 1967-70; pre-sentence investigator City of Kalamazoo 9th Ct., 1970-72; chief adminstr., dir. edn. Mich. Audubon Soc., Kalamazoo/Lansing, 1973-90; dir. River Ptnrs. program Forum for Kalamazoo County, Kalamazoo, 1991—; cons. Stryker Ctr., Kalamazoo, 1991—; dir. edn. program Kalamazoo Nature Ctr., 1985-91; chief adminstr. Mich. Audubon Soc., 1971-85; chief tchr./cons. sci. edn. and outdoor edn. ctr. constrn. Vicksburg Schs., 1992-95. Author, editor: Wildlife Rehabilitation Manual, 1990; organizer constrn. Kalamazoo River Trailway, 1991—. Chair Kalamazoo County Parks Commn., 1981-83; bd. dirs. Kalamazoo County Humane Soc., 1988-90; active in work with the homeless. Recipient Take Pride in Am. award State of Mich., 1991; Soil Conservation Svc. award USDA, 1990; Kellogg Found. grantee, 1992. Mem. Adventure Club of Gt. Lakes. Office: Forum for Kalamazoo County and Stryker Ctr 1327 Academy Kalamazoo MI 49006

ADAMS, PAUL STUART, corporate ergonomist; b. New Hampton, Iowa, Sept. 21, 1957; m. Cynthia Ruth Freel, Oct. 10, 1981. BS in Indsl. Engring., Iowa State U., 1980; MS in Indsl. Safety, Cen. Mo. State U., 1984; MS in Engring., U. Mich., 1988, PhD in Indsl. and Ops. Engring., 1993. Registered profl. engr. Mich.; cert. safety profl. Bd. of Cert. Safety Profls.; cert. prof. ergonomist. Loss prevention engr. Brass group Olin Corp., East Alton, Ill., 1981-85, sr. loss prevention engr. Winchester group, 1985-86; asst. prof. occupational safety Ill. State U., Normal, 1993-94; occupational health and safety process specialist, ergonomist Owens-Corning World Hdqs., Toledo, 1994—. Contbr. chpt. to book. Youth leader Ypsilanti (Mich.) Free Meth. Ch., 1989-91. U.S. Dept. Edn. Nat. Needs fellow, 1990-92. Mem. ASTM (mem. com. F23 on protective clothing), NSPE, Am. Soc. Safety Engrs., Am. Soc. for Engring. Edn., Human Factors and Ergonomics Soc. Office: Owens-Corning World Hdqs Fiberglas Tower T/11 Toledo OH 43659

ADAMS, PAULA, mechanical engineer; b. Rockledge, Ill., July 2, 1967. BS in Mech. Engring., Mich. Tech. U., 1989. Strength engr. McDonnell Douglas, St. Louis, 1989-93; mech. engr. The Antenna Co., Itasca, Ill., 1993—. Office: The Antenna Co 1100 Maplewood Dr Itasca IL 60143-3205

ADAMS, ROBERT JOE, real estate dealer, farmer; b. Goldsmith, Ind., Dec. 29, 1935; s. Verlie Everett and Gladys Lavone (Foster) A.; m. Lenora Snoderly, Sept. 10, 1964 (div. 1975); children: Lance Edward, Robin Ann, Eric Lynn; m. Cynthia Gay Adams, Dec. 16, 1976 (div. 1988); children: Hollie Jo, Dustin Shawn. Cert. real estate, Ind. U., Kokomo, 1987. Farmer Tipton, Ind., 1950—, Kelley Farms, Inc., Sharpsville, Ind., 1962-87; owner Eureka Log Home Dealer, Sharpsville, 1976—; sales person Nancy Burtch Realtors, Kokomo, Ind., 1987-89, Rinehart Realtors, Kokomo, 1989—; with C-21 Diamond Realty, Inc. (merged with Heartland Realtors); owner, operator Tipton County Farm Bur., Ind., 1950—; life ins. agt. A.L. Williams, Atlanta, 1985—; co-owner, sales assoc. Heartland Realtors, Kokomo, 1991—. With Res. Army Nat. Guard, 1958-66. Mem. NRA, Nat. Realtors Assn., Am. Quarter Horse Assn., Sml. Bus. Men Assn., Million Dollar Club (Sales awards 1991, 93). Republican. Methodist. Home: 300 N 5690 W Sharpsville IN 46068 Office: C-21 Diamond Realty Inc 3541 S Lafountain St Kokomo IN 46902-3804

ADAMS, WILLIAM JOHNSTON, financial and tax consultant; b. Detroit, Nov. 24, 1934; s. William Montgomery and Sara Emogene (Johnston) A.; m. Lynn Laviolette, Aug. 24, 1957 (div. Sept. 1976); 1 child, William David; m. Donna Wolcott, Apr. 24, 1977. BBA, U. Mich., 1957, MBA, 1958. CPA, Mich. Staff acct. Arthur Andersen & Co., Detroit, 1958-62, tax mgr., 1962-70, tax ptnr., 1970-90; corp. dir., 1990—; arbitrator Am. Arbitration Assn., 1994—; bd. dirs. Detroit Exec. Svc. Corps. Trustee, sec., treas., pres. Grosse Pointe (Mich.) Pub. Sch., 1969-72; chmn. Greater Detroit Fgn. Trade Zone, Inc., 1983—; mem. adv. bd. Paton Fund, 1988; bd. dirs. Civic Searchlight, Detroit, 1985—, 2d v.p., 1989-92, pres., 1992—; bd. dirs. Civic Inc., 1992. Named Outstanding Young Man of Yr. Grosse Pointe Jaycees, 1970; named to Pres.' Club U. Mich., Ann Arbor, 1975. Mem. AICPA, Mich. Assn. CPA's (Disting. Svc. award 1992), Tappan Soc., Detroit Regional Yachting Assn. (treas. 1993-94, rear commodore 1994, vice commodore 1995-96), Detroit Club, Detroit Boat Club (bd. dirs., treas. 1985-87, com. 1986), Detroit Yacht Club. Congregationalist. Home: 1453 Iroquois St Detroit MI 48214-2715

ADASKA, WAYNE SCOTT, geotechnical engineer; b. Chgo., Feb. 25, 1950; s. William and Blanche (Votava) A.; m. Michelle Helene Dobbe, Nov. 4, 1972; children: Scott, Joel, Allison Mae, Bridget Allison, Adam William. BS in Engring., U. Ill., Chgo., 1971. Registered profl. engr., Ill. Resident soil engr. Deleuw Cather Co., Chgo., 1971-72; sr. soil engr. Sargent & Lundy Engrs., Chgo., 1972-78; dir. pub. works Portland Cement Assn., Skokie, Ill., 1978—. Contbr. articles to profl. jours. Mem. ASTM (com. chair 1986—), Am. Concrete Inst. (com. chair 1989-95), Transp. Rsch. Bd. (com. chair 1986-87). Office: Portland Cement Assn 5420 Old Orchard Rd Skokie IL 60077-1060

ADCOCK, REBECCA LEIGH, educator; b. Wichita, Kans., Oct. 21, 1972; d. Thomas Dale and Rita Ellen (Behring) A.; divorced; 1 child, Samantha Ashlin Wilson. BS in Psychology, Baker U., 1995, BS in Mass Comm., 1995; MS in Early Childhood Spl. Edn., Kans. State U. Cert. tchr., Kans. Pub. rels. dir. Kans. Ju. Quarter Horse Assn., Canton, 1990-91; ops. mgr. KNBU-FM/Baker U., Baldwin City, Kans., 1992-93; asst. tchr. StoneHouse Child Care Ctr., Manhattan, Kans., 1995—; edn. coord. Pawnee Mental Health Svcs., Manhattan, 1995—. Mem. APA, Coun. for Exceptional Children, Nat. Assn. for Edn. Young Children (newsletter editor local affiliate), Assn. for Childhood Edn. Internat., Sigma Delta Chi, Phi Mu. Republican. Presbyn.

ADDUCCI, JOSEPH EDWARD, obstetrician, gynecologist; b. Chgo., Dec. 1, 1934; s. Dominee Edward and Harriet Evelyn (Kneppreth) A.; m. Mary Ann Tiertje, 1958; children—Christopher, Gregory, Steven, Jessica, Tobias. B.S., U. Ill., 1955; M.D., Loyola U., Chgo., 1959. Diplomate Am. Bd. Ob-Gyn., Nat. Bd. Med. Examiners. Intern Cook County Hosp, Chgo., 1959-60; resident in ob-gyn Mt. Carmel Hosp., Detroit, 1960-64; practice medicine specializing in obstetrics and gynecology Williston, N.D., 1966—; chief staff, chmn. obstetrics dept. Mercy Hosp., Williston; clin. prof. U. N.D. Med. Sch., 1973—; mem. gov. bd. Mercy Hosp. Cath. Health Corp. Mem. N.D. Bd. Med. Examiners, 1974—, past chmn.; project dir. Tri County Family Planning Svc.; past pres. Tri County Health Planning Coun.; mem. governing bd. Mercy Hosp., Williston, N.D. With Med. Corps, AUS, 1964-66. Fellow Am. Soc. Abdominal Surgeons, ACS (regent N.D. 1990—), Am. Coll. Obstetrics and Gynecologists (sect. chmn. N.D.), Internat. Coll. Surgeons (regent 1972-74, 88-89), Am. Fertility Soc., Am. Assn. Internat. Lazar Soc., Gynecol. Lataropists, N.D. Obstetricians and Gynecologists Soc. (pres. 1966, 76); mem. Am. Soc. for Colposcopy and Colpomicroscopy, Am. Soc. Cryosurgery, Am. Soc. Contemporary Medicine and Surgery, Am. Assn. Profl. Ob-Gyn., Pan Am. Med. Assn., Am. Coll. Surgeons (regent 1989—N.D.). Lodge: Elks. Home: 1717 Main St Williston ND 58801-4244 Office: Med Ctr Williston ND 58801

ADE, BARBARA JEAN, secondary education educator; b. Youngstown, Ohio, Nov. 6, 1951; d. Donald Eugene Sr. and Louise Ann (Bodnark) Kihm; m. Robert Randal Ade, Mar. 17, 1973. BS in Edn., Youngstown State U., 1975, MS in Edn., 1987. High sch. media specialist Springfield Local High Sch., New Middletown, Ohio, 1975—. Active Youngstown Area YWCA. Grad. Sch. scholar Youngstown State U., 1986-87; named Woman of the Yr., Youngstown Area YWCA, 1993. Mem. Ohio Ednl. Libr./Media Assn., Nat. Edn. Assn., Ohio Edn. Assn., Delta Kappa Gamma, Phi Delta Kappa. Democrat. Roman Catholic. Office: Springfield Local High Sch 11335 Youngstown Pittsburgh Rd New Middletown OH 44442-9738

ADE, LARRY B., investment executive; b. Abilene, Kans., Oct. 3, 1950. BA, Bethany Coll., 1972. Retail salesperson Midcon Investments, Wichita, Kans., 1976-84, Ransen & Co., Wichita, 1984-89, Steffel Nicholao Co., Wichita, 1989-93; investment exec. Paine Webber, Wichita, 1993—. Republican. Home: 860 English Ct Derby KS 67037-1307 Office: Paine Webber 4th Fl 100 N Broadway St Wichita KS 67202-2212

ADELBERG, ARNOLD MELVIN, mathematics educator, researcher; b. Bklyn., Mar. 17, 1936; s. David and Evelyn (Brass) A.; m. Harriet Diamond, June 30, 1962; children: Danielle Hamill, Erica. BA, Columbia U., 1956; MA, Princeton U., 1959, PhD, 1996. Instr. Columbia U., N.Y.C., 1959-62; instr., asst. prof., assoc. prof., prof. Grinnell (Iowa) Coll., 1962—, Myra Steele prof. math., 1991—; chair math. dept., sci. div. several times, chmn. faculty Grinnell Coll., 1974-76. Contbr. articles to profl. jours. Mem. Math. Assn. Am., Am. Math. Soc. Home: 1930 Manor Cir Grinnell IA 50112-1136 Office: Grinnell Coll Math Dept PO Box 805 Grinnell IA 50112-0805

ADELI, HOJJAT, engineer, educator, computer scientist; b. Langrood, Iran, June 3, 1950; came to U.S., 1974; s. Jafar and Mokarram (Soofi) A.; m. Nahid Dadmehr, Mar. 1979; children: Amir, Anahita, Mona, Cyrus Dean. MSCE summa cum laude, U. Teheran, Iran, 1973; PhD in Civil Engring. summa cum laude, Stanford U., 1976. Asst. prof. Northwestern U., Evanston, Ill., 1977; asst. prof. U. Teheran, 1978-81, assoc. prof., 1981-82; assoc. prof. U. Utah, Salt Lake City, 1982-83; assoc. prof. Ohio State U., Columbus, 1983-88, prof., 1988—, chmn. structures faculty, 1988-91, dir. Knowledge Engring. Lab., 1994—, exec. com., dept. civil/environ. engring., geometic sci., 1994-95; cons. Atomic Orgn. Iran, Teheran, 1978-79, Iran Ministry Housing, Teheran, 1970-82, U.S. Army Constrn. Engring. Rsch. Lab., 1988; keynote lectrs. in Italy, 1989, Mex., 1989, Japan, 1991, China, 1992, Can., 1992, Portugal, 1992, Germany, 1993, U.S., 1993, 95, Morocco, 1994, Singapore, 1994, Australia, 1995, Bulgaria, 1995, New Zealand, 1995, Bahrain, 1996; organizer of more than 80 lectrs. at more than 90 nat. and internat. confs. Author: Interactive Microcomputer-Aided Structural Steel Design, 1988; co-author: Expert Systems for Structural Design: A New Generation, 1988, Parallel Processing in Structural Engineering, 1993, Machine Learning-Neural Networks, Genetic Algorithms, and Fuzzy Systems, 1995; editor: Expert Systems in Construction and Structural Engineering, 1988, Microcomputer Knowledge-Based Expert Systems in Civil Engineering, 1988, Parallel and Distributed Processing in Structural Engineering, 1988, Knowledge Engineering, vols. 1 & 2, 1990, Supercomputing in Engineering Analysis, 1992, Parallel Processing in Computational Mechanics, 1992, Advances in Design Optimization, 1994; co-editor: Mechanics Computing in the 1990's and Beyond, vols. 1 & 2, 1991; editor-in-chief, founder Internat. Jour. Microcomputers in Civil Engring. Jour. Computer-Aided Civil & Infrastructure Engring, 1986—, Integrated Computer-Aided Engring., 1993—; editor-in-chief Heuristics: The Jour. of Knowledge Engring., 1991-93; assoc. editor Control Engring. Practice, 1993—, Jour. Artificial Neural Networks, 1995—; mem. editorial bd., editorial adv. bd. 25 sci. engring. jours. including Neural, Parallel, and Sci. Computations, 1993—, Parallel Algorithms and Applications, 1993—, Nanobiology-Jour. Rsch. Nanoscale Living Systems, 1993, Structural Engring. Review, 1989-91, Heuristic-Jour. Knowledge Engring., 1989-91, Engring. Analysis with Boundary Elements, 1987-92, Jour. of Condition Monitoring and Diagnostic Tech., 1990-92, Knowledge Based Systems, 1988—, ASCE Jour. of Aerospace Engring., 1989—, Internat. Jour. of Mini and Microcomputers, 1990—, Internat. Jour. of Imaging Systems and Tech., 1990—, Mechatronics, 1991—, Advances in Engring Software, 1991-95, Neurocomputing, 1991—, Jour. of Systems Engring., 1991—, Internat. Jour. of Construction Information Tech., 1992—, Chaos, Solitons and Fractals, 1991—, Structural Optimization, 1991—, Computer Applications in Engring. Edn., 1993—, Asian Jour. of Structural Engring., 1995—, Theory and Practice of Object Systems, 1995—, IASTED Control & Computers Jour., 1996—, Internat. Jour. Computational Intelligence and Organization, 1996—; contbr. over 260 publs. Recipient 1st degree medal of Knowledge Iran Ministry Higher Edn., 1973, Rsch. award NSF, USAF Flight Dynamics Lab., Cray Rsch., Inc., Bethlehem Steel Corp., Ohio Dept. Devel. Thomas edison Program, Am. Inst. Steel Constrn., Am. Iron and Steel Inst., U.S. Army Constrn. Engring. Rsch. Lab., Ohio Dept. Transp., Fed. Hwy. Adminstrn. Fellow World Lit. Acad.; mem. ASCE (mem. numerous coms. including aerospace structures and materials com. Aerospace divsn. 1986—, real time data acquisition com., 1988—, inelastic behavior com. engring. mechanics divsn. 1987—, com. on metrication, 1991—, advanced composite materials com. 1994—), IEEE Computer Soc. (mem. numerous coms. including compu94, pattern analysis and machine intelligence com. 1988-94, microprocessors and microcomputers com. 1988-95, distributed processing com. 1988-95, data base engring. com. 1993-95, software engring. com. 1993-95, sys. engring. 1993-95, robotics and automation com. 1993-95, design automation com. 1994-95, optical processing and switching com. 1994-95), AAAI, Assn. for Computing Machinery, Earthquake Engring. Rsch. Inst., Internat. Soc. for Structural and Multidisciplinary Optimization. Home: 1540 Picardae Ct Powell OH 43065-9791

ADELMAN, LYNN S., state legislator; b. Milw., Oct. 1, 1939; s. Albert B. and Edith Margoles Adelman; m. Elizabeth Halmbacher, 1976; children: Lisa, Mia. AB, Princeton U., 1961; LLB, Columbia U., 1965. State senator dist. 28 State of Wis., 1977—; chmn. judiciary and consumer affairs com. Wis. State Senate; pvt. practice as atty. Mem. Berlin Hist. Soc. Democrat. Office: 33725 Janesville Dr Mukwonago WI 53149-8909 also: State Senate State Capitol Madison WI 53702*

ADELMAN, PAMELA BERNICE KOZOLL, education educator; b. Milw., Dec. 26, 1945; d. Harry and Rebecca (Sharp) Kozoll; m. Steven H. Adelman, June 30, 1968; children: David, Robert. BS, U. Wis., Madison, 1967; MA, Northwestern U., 1972, PhD, 1982. Cert. tchr., Ill. Tchr. Peckham Jr. High Sch., Milw., 1967-68, Fairview Sch., Skokie, Ill., 1968-70; learning disabilities specialist Sch. Dist 28, Northbrook, Ill., 1971-77; instr., rsch. asst. Northwestern U., Evanston, Ill., 1977-80; lectr., asst. prof., then assoc. prof. Barat Coll., Lake Forest, Ill., 1977-90, prof. edn., 1990—, dir. learning opportunities program, 1985—; cons. Deerfield (Ill.) Pub. Schs., 1986-90; proposal reviewer State of N.J., Trenton, 1986-87; mem. Pres.'s Com. on Hiring of Disabled, 1990; mem. higher edn. adv. coun. State of Ill.; presenter at profl. confs. Co-author: Learning Disabilities, Graduate School, and Careers, 1990; co-editor: Success for College Students with Learning Disabilities, 1993; consulting editor Learning Disabilities Focus, 1989—, Jour. Developmental Edn., 1990—, Jour. of Postsecondary Edn. and Disabilities, 1991-93; contbr. articles to ednl. publs. Chair Sch. Dist. 107 Caucus, Highland Park, Ill., 1982; bd. dirs. Jewish Children's Bur., Chgo., 1985—, pres., 1994-96; co-author brochure for Ill. Dept. Human Rights, Chgo., 1986. Paul A. Witty fellow Northwestern U., 1978-80; grantee Lloyd A. Fry Found., 1985-86, Kraft Corp., Chgo., 1989, McDonald's Corp., Chgo., 1986. Mem. Coun. Exceptional Children, Learning Disabilities Assn. Am., Coun. Learning Disabilities, Orton Dyslexia Soc., Internat. Reading Assn., Asns. on Higher Edn. and Disabilities, Internat. Acad. for Rsch. in Learning Disabilities. Office: Barat Coll 700 E Westleigh Rd Lake Forest IL 60045-3263

ADELSON, BERNARD HENRY, physician; b. Tampa, Fla., Mar. 16, 1920; s. Edward H. and Esther (Hadesman) A.; m. Martha Stein, June 13, 1950; children: Duffie Ann, Edward H., David E. BS, Northwestern U., Evanston, Ill., 1942, PhD, 1946, MD, 1951. Diplomate Am. Bd. Internal Medicine. Intern Jackson Meml. Hosp., Miami, Fla., 1950-51; resident Evanston Hosp., 1951-53, Cook County Hosp., Chgo., 1953-54; prof. clin. medicine Northwestern U., Chgo., 1980—; assoc. chmn. dept. medicine Evanston Hosp., 1979—, dir. program on med. ethics, 1985—, chair instl. ethics com., 1989—. Capt. U.S. Army, 1955-57. Fellow AAAS, Am. Coll. Physicians (Clinician Laureate 1989, 90), Royal Soc. Medicine. Office: Evanston Hosp 2650 Ridge Ave Evanston IL 60201-1718

ADELSON, EDWARD, physicist, musician, lecturer; b. Bklyn., Aug. 19, 1934; s. Barnet and Sarah (Strongin) A.; m. Juliane A.W. Riedel, Aug. 5, 1961 (div. June, 1982); BA, N.Y.U., 1956; student (Woodrow Wilson fellow), Eastman Sch. of Music, 1956-57; MS, Ohio State U., 1965, PhD, 1974. Prin. physicist Battelle Mem. Inst., Columbus, Ohio, 1957-71; lectr. Ohio State U., Columbus, 1974-88, acad. program specialist, 1988—. Organist, choirmaster St. Alban's Episcopal Ch., Bexley, Ohio. Mem. Am. Phys. Soc., Am. Assn. Physics Tchrs., Am. Guild Organists, Phi Beta Kappa, Sigma Pi Sigma. Contbr. numerous articles to various profl. jours.; physics text cons. Home: 6384 Falkirk Pl Columbus OH 43229-2045 Office: Ohio State U Smith Lab Columbus OH 43210

ADENWALLA, MINOO, political science educator; b. Poona, India, Oct. 21, 1927; came to U.S., 1949; s. Dorab and Peroja (Boyce) A.; m. Mary June Hill, June 18, 1955 (dec. 1984); children: Elizabeth Shireen Kapadia, Sheila Anne Adenwalla. BA with honors, Bombay U., 1948; MS, Northwestern U., 1954, PhD, 1956. Teaching fellow, Wilson Coll. Bombay U., 1948-49; instr. Kenyon Coll., Gambier, Ohio, 1957-58; asst. prof. U. Mo., Columbia, 1958-59, Lawrence U., Appleton, Wis., 1959-62; assoc. prof. Lawrence U., Appleton, 1962-69, prof. polit. sci., 1969—, Mary Mortimer chair in liberal studies, 1989—; assoc. prof. Wesleyan U. summer sch., Middletown, Conn.; dir. Associated Colls. Midwest India Studies program in Pune, India, 1972, 76, 85. Contbr. articles to profl. jours. Recipient Howard Found. rsch. grant, 1962-63, Associated Colls. Midwest non-Western studies rsch. grant funded by Ford Found., 1967-68. Mem. Conf. on South Asia (program com. 1975, 85), Midwest Conf. on Asian Affairs (program chair 1964). Home: 222 N Union St Appleton WI 54911-5532 Office: Lawrence U PO Box 599 Appleton WI 54912-0599

ADICKES, SANDRA ELAINE, English language educator, writer; b. N.Y.C., July 14, 1933; d. August Ernst and Edythe Louise (Oberschlake) A.; 1 child, Delores, Sept. 16, 1966. BA, Douglass Coll., 1954; MA, CUNY, 1964; PhD, NYU, 1977. Asst. registrar NYU, 1954-55; sec. McCann Erickson, J. Walter Thompson Cos., N.Y.C., 1955-60; English tchr. N.Y.C. Bd. Edn., 1960-70, 1980-88; instr. edn. N.Y.C. Tech. Coll., 1970-72; asst. prof. English S.I. C.C., N.Y.C., 1972-77; dir. project chance Bklyn. Coll., 1977-80; from assoc. prof. to prof. English Winona State U., Minn., 1988—; cons. Antioch Coll. N.Y.C., 1970; guest tutor London U., 1979. Author: The Social Quest, 1991, Legends of Good Women, 1992; editor: By A Woman Writt, 1973; contbr. articles to profl. jours. Co-founder Tchrs'. Freedom Sch. Project, Miss., 1963-64, Tchrs'. Com. for Peace Vietnam, 1965-66. Named Woman of Yr. Nat. Assn. Negro Bus. Profl. Women, N.J., 1966. Mem. MLA, Midwest Modern Lang. Assn., Nat Coun. Tchrs. of English. Democrat. Home: 579 W 7th St Winona MN 55987-4226 Office: Winona State U Dept English Winona MN 55987

ADJEI, ALEX ASIEDU, internist, oncologist, pharmacologist; b. Kumasi, Ghana, Apr. 21, 1955; came to U.S., 1989; s. James Kwaku and Juliana (Owusua) A. MBChB, U. Ghana, 1982; PhD, U. Alta., Can., 1989. Diplomate Am. Bd. Internal Medicine. Med. officer Ghana Med. Sch., Accra, 1983-84; clin. rsch. fellow U. Alberta, Edmonton, Can., 1987-89; med. resident Howard U. Hosp., Washington, 1989-91, chief med. resident, 1991-92; sr. clin. fellow Oncology Clin. Ctr. Johns Hopkins Hosp., Balt., 1992-95; asst. prof. Mayo Med. Sch., Rochester, Minn., 1995—; mem. Grad. Student's Coun., Edmonton, 1984-86. Contbg. author book in field, 1988. Named Best Student, Ghana Med. Sch., 1979, Resident of Yr., D.C. Gen. Hosp., 1991; recipient Travel award Nat. Cancer Inst., Can., 1988, rsch. scholarship Alberta Heritage Found., Edmonton, 1985-89. Mem. AAAS, ACP, Am. Assn. Cancer Rsch., Am. Soc. Internal Medicine, Am. Soc. Hematology, N.Y. Acad. Scis. Home: 12443 White Bridge Ln NE Rochester MN 55906 Office: Mayo Clinic Div Med Oncology 200 First St SW Rochester MN 55905

ADKERSON, DONYA LYNN, clinical counselor; b. Mattoon, Ill., Oct. 5, 1959; d. Edwin Dwayne and Sonya Jeanne (Abernathie) Adkerson; m. George Anthony Ferguson, May 20, 1990; 1 child, Tiana Jo Berry. MA, So. Ill. U., Edwardsville, 1983. Outpatient dir. Children's Ctr. for Behavioral Devel., Centerville, Ill., 1983-90; pvt. practice psychotherapy Evaluation & Therapy Svc., Edwardsville, 1991-92; dir. Alternatives Counseling, Inc., 1993—; cons. St. Louis City Juvenile Ct., 1991-94, Covenant Children's Home, 1991-93. Co-author: Adult Sexual Offender Assessment Packet, 1994. Pres. Ill. Network for Mgmt. Abusive Sexuality, 1991; clin. mem. Assn. for Treatment of Sex Abusers, exec. bd., 1994—, mem. ethics and stds. com.; mem. Cmty. Coordinating Coun. Domestic Violence, 1996—; mem. Adolescent Perpetrator Network, 1987-95; exec. bd. Arts League Players Theatre, Edwardsville, 1986—; former chmn. Metro-East Task Force on Sexual Offenders. Mem. ACA, Ill. Counseling Assn., Ill. Mental Health Counselors Assn. Office: Alternatives Counseling 1 Mark Twain Plz Edwardsville IL 62025

ADKINS, FRED J., business director; b. Coeburn, Va., July 7, 1940; s. D. Martin and Gladys Lucille (Salyer) A.; children: Cynthia D., Carla E. Student, USAF Inst., 1960-62, Ohio State U., 1970-71, Catonsville C.C., 1990-92. Retail sales mgr. Western Auto Supply Co., Kansas City, Mo.; mgr. new bus. devel., sales and mktg., mgr. market devel. All Howe Co., 1980-92; dir. internat. bus. Ace Hardware Corp., Oak Brook, Ill., 1992—. Bd. dirs. Oriole Advocates-Balt. Orioles Baseball Club, 1977-90. With USAF, 1958-62. Named to Hon. Order Ky. Cols. Mem. Masons (officer Tuscan # 202 1968-73). Republican. Home: 39W259 Hilltop Dr Saint Charles IL 60175

ADLER, ANNE HERZBERG, counseling psychologist; b. San Antonio, June 23, 1941; d. Allen Forrest and Edna (Roberts) Herzberg; m. Stephen Charles Adler, Jan. 9, 1971; children: Rebecca Dawn, Eric Daniel. AB in Polit. Sci., Stanford U., 1963; MS in Psychol. Counseling, Calif. State U., San Jose, 1973. Counseling psychologist Anchorage Children's Ctr., 1973-75; grant applications reviewer Mt. Sinai Med. Ctr., N.Y.C., 1968-69; bus. officer Stanford (Calif.) Med. Sch., 1964-68. Mem. sch. bd. Moline (Ill.) Sch. Dist. No. 40, 1993—; mem. Child Abuse Coun., Moline, 1980-87, 89-94, pres., 1984; bd. dirs. PTA, Moline, 1979-93; radio reader for visually impaired Sta. WVIK-FM, Rock Island, Ill., 1989—.

ADLER, NAOMI SAMUEL, real estate counselor; b. N.Y.C., Sept. 30, 1931; d. Jacob Alexander and Madeline Samuel; m. Gerson Adler, Aug. 1, 1950; children: Don A., Samson Y., Nathan Tzvi, Eliyohu, Hillel M., Ezra, William Martin Selman, Zahava Sara. Student, 1945-50, John Carroll U., 1980-82. Real estate agt. B.O.D. Milliken, Cleveland Heights, Ohio, 1981-82, The Kenny Co., University Heights, Ohio, 1982-84, Century 21 Crysler-Kenny, Cleve., 1984-90; gen. mgr. Fialkoff Bungalow Colony Real Estate, Monticello, N.Y., 1981—; real estate counselor HKS Realty, Inc., Shaker Heights, Ohio, 1993-96; real estate counselor Realty One, Lyndhurst, Ohio, 1990-93. Bd. dirs. Monticello Bungalow Assn., Bur. Jewish Edn., Jewish Cmty. Fedn. Cleve.; child adv. Jewish Children's Foster Family, Jewish Day Nursery, Shaker Heights, 1970-93, Traditional Fund, Jewish Welfare, Hebrew Free Loan Assn., sec., 1992-94, treas., 1989-90; pres. Shorme Shabbas Sisterhood, 1978-82, N'shei Agudah Women, 1990-92, Hebrew Acad., Cleve., 1972-75, Union Orthodox Jewish Congregations, 1975-77, Mosdos Ohr Hatora Sch., 1977-80; founding charter mem., safety chairperson Chofetz Chaim Heritage Found., 1994—; vol. Chevra Kadisha Jewish Boriel Soc., 1963-86. Named Woman of Valor, Hebrew Acad., Woman of Yr., Beth Jacob High Sch. of Denver. Mem. Grad. Realtors Inst., Cleve. Area Bd. Realtors (RPAC com.), Nat. Assn. Parliamentarians, Post Office Adv. Home: 3595 Severn Rd Cleveland Heights OH 44118-1999 Office: Crysler Kenny Realty 4589 Mayfield Rd South Euclid OH 44121

ADLER, SEYMOUR JACK, social services administrator; b. Chicago, October 22, 1930; s. Michael L. and Sarah (Pasnick) A.; BS, Northwestern U., 1952; MA, U. Chgo., 1958; m. Barbara Fingold, Mar. 24, 1958; children: Susan Lynn Hoke, Karen Sandra Adler-Marder, Michelle Lauren Adler-Morrison. Caseworker, Cook County Dept. Pub. Aid, Chgo., 1955; juvenile officer Cook County Sheriff's Office, 1955-56; U.S. probation-parole officer U.S. Dist. Ct., Chgo., 1958-68; exec. dir. Youth Guidance, Chgo., 1968-73; dir. court svcs. Juvenile Ct. Cook County, Chgo., 1973-75; exec. dir. Methodist Youth Svcs., Chgo., 1975-85; program mgr. Dept. Social Svcs., Kenosha, Wis., 1985-91, dir. 1992-95, dir. Dept. Human Svcs., 1996—; mem. Ill. Law Enforcement Commn., 1969-72; instr. corrections program Chgo. State U., 1972-75; instr. Harper Coll., 1977, St. Joseph's Coll., 1978; case developer Nat. Ctr. on Instns. and Alternatives, 1985-86. Bd. dirs. Child Care Assn. Ill., 1979-84. Served to 1st lt. USMCR, 1952-55. Recipient Morris J. Wexler award Ill. Acad. Criminology, 1975, Meritorious Service award Chgo. City Colls., 1968. Mem. Ill. Acad. Criminology (pres. 1972), Nat. Assn. Social Workers (del. Assembly 1977, 79, 81, 84, 87, chmn. Chgo. dist. 1978-80, chmn. group for action planning childrens svcs. 1980-84, Disting. Svc. award Criminal Justice Coun. 1978 Ill. NASW 1978, chmn. population study group Kenosha Jail 1993-95, com. inquiry Wis. chpt. 1978-80), Ill. Probation, Parole and Correctional Assn., Internat. Half-way House Assn. (Ill. dir.), Alpha Kappa Delta, Tau Delta Phi. Contbr. articles to profl. jours. Home: 232 Grandview Ln Twin Lakes WI 53181-9572 Office: Kenosha Dept Human Svcs 714 52nd St Kenosha WI 53140-3426

ADLER, THOMAS PETER, English language educator, university official; b. Cleve., Jan. 3, 1943; s. Frederick Arnold and Catherine Suzanne (Casper) A.; m. Winifred Ruth Toohill, Aug. 10, 1968; children: Jeremy Peter, Christopher David. AB, Boston Coll., 1964, AM, 1966; PhD, U. Ill., 1970. Teaching fellow Boston Coll., Chestnut Hill, Mass., 1964-66; teaching asst. U. Ill., 1966-70; asst. prof. English Purdue U., West Lafayette, Ind., 1970-75, assoc. prof. English, 1975-83, asst. head English, 1979-82, prof. English, 1983—, assoc. dean grad. sch., 1984-88, assoc. dean liberal arts, 1988-95; interim dean liberal arts Purdue U., West Lafayette, 1995—. Author: Robert Anderson, 1978, Mirror on the Stage, 1987, The Moth and The Lantern, 1990, American Drama, 1940-60: A Critical History, 1994; co-author: The Writer's Choices, 1985; mem. editl. bd. Pinter Rev., 1987—, Studies in Am. Drama: 1940 to Present, 1988-95. Bd. dirs., treas. Montessori Sch. Greater Lafayette, West Lafayette, 1977-80; precinct committeeman Dem. Party, West Lafayette, 1983-89; bd. dirs. West Lafayette Pub. Libr., 1985-89, Greater Lafayette Mus. of Art, Lafayette, Ind., 1990—. Curriculum Devel. grantee NEH, 1990-91. Mem. Am. Drama and Theatre Soc. (bd. dirs. 1990—), Phi Beta Kappa. Roman Catholic. Home: 1001 Digby Rd Lafayette IN 47905-1106 Office: Purdue U Heavilon Hall West Lafayette IN 47907

ADLER, THOMAS WILLIAM, real estate executive; b. Rochester, N.Y., Dec. 21, 1940; s. Richard H. and Margaret (Freund) A.; m. Joann Seidenfeld, July 1, 1962; children: Peggy Lynn, Sally Ann, William Richard. BS, U. Wis., 1962. Salesman Cragin Lang Free Co., Cleve., 1962-65, Cragin Lang Free and Smythe, Cleve., 1965-67; ptnr. Cragin Lang Free & Smythe, Cleve., 1967-79, chmn. exec. com., 1975-79; prin. Adler Galvin Rogers, Cleve., 1979-86; pres. Grubb Ellis Instnl. Investment Group, 1988-90; chmn. The Hadley Group, Cleve., 1991; prin. Cleve. Real Estate Ptnrs., 1992—; pres. Clevetrust Realty Advisors, 1971-73, Nat. City Realty Corp., Cleve., 1973-75; trustee Nat. Assn. Real Estate Investment Trust, Washington, 1971-75; bd. dirs. Highwoods Properties, Inc., 1994—; vis. com. Sch. Bus. Cleve. State U. Author: Industrial Real Estate, 1971. Bd. dirs. Leadership Cleve., Am. Jewish Com., Jewish Cmty. Fedn. Cleve., Planned Parenthood of Cleve., Playhouse Sq. Found. Mem. Am. Soc. Real Estate Counselors (bd. govs.), Soc. Indsl. and Office Realtors (pres. 1990), Friends Shaker Sq., Union Club, Oakwood Club. Jewish. Home: 2851 Winthrop Rd Cleveland OH 44120-1825 Office: Cleve Real Estate Ptnrs 1801 E 9th St Ste 1700 Cleveland OH 44114-3103

ADOLF, MARY MCGINLEY, promotion and advertising executive; b. Lewellen, Nebr., July 23, 1955; d. John Patrick and Norma Louise (Olson) McGinley; m. John Raymond Adolf, Sept. 4, 1982. BS, U. Nebr., 1977, MS, 1980. Registered dietitian. Dir. foodsvcs. Okla. State U., Stillwater, 1977-79; dir. foodsvcs and retail programs Nat. Livestock and Meat Bd., Chgo., 1981-85; dir. foodsvc. programs and spl. events Beef Industry Coun., Chgo., 1985-90, v.p. promotion and advt., 1990—; exec. dir. consumer advt. and mktg. svcs. Nat. Cattlemen's Beef Assn., 1996—; owner, pres. Party Animals Catering, Hinsdale, Ill., 1988—. Contbr. articles to mags. Mem. speakers bur. Am. Heart Assn., Chgo., 1989—. Mem. Inst. Food Technologists (chmn. foodsvc. div. 1990), Home Economists in Bus. (chmn. Chgo. 1989-90), Dietitians in Communication (com. chair 1987), Am. Meat Sci. Assn., Internat. Foodsvc. Mfrs. Assn. Republican. Roman Catholic. Home: 56 Huntington Ct Burr Ridge IL 60521-6451 Office: Nat Cattlemen's Beef Assn 444 N Michigan Ave Chicago IL 60611-3903

ADRIAN, JOANNE DORIS, realtor; b. Chgo., Oct. 5, 1945; d. Charles Glen and Helen June (Witzke) Romke; m. Jeffrey Adrian, May 25, 1968 (div. Feb. 1971). BA, Augustana Coll., 1967; MDiv, Luth. Sch. Theology, 1987. Money market trader No. Trust Co., Chgo., 1969-71; v.p. 2d Dist. Securities, N.Y.C., 1972-76; adminstr. E.F. Hutton, N.Y.C., 1976-78; money market trader Smith Barney, N.Y.C., 1978-79; fin. analyst Texaco, Inc., White Plains, N.Y., 1979-83; pastor Trinity Luth. Ch., Pleasant Valley, Pa., 1988-91; realtor Prudential Country Heritage, Sycamore, Ill., 1993—; CEO, pres. Real Estate Adventures, Ltd., 1994—. Treas. Tenants Orgn., N.Y.C., 1979-83; ch. coun. St. Peter's Luth. Ch., N.Y.C., 1974-78; mem. Bread for the World, N.Y.C., Chgo., 1977-87, Ind. Voters of Ill., Chgo., 1986-88; treas. Christian Action Com., Pleasant Valley, Iowa, 1989-91; multicultural com. SE Iowa Synod, Iowa City, 1988-91. Mem. DeKalb Area Assn. Realtors (MLS com. 1995—), Women's Coun. Realtors, Home Buyers' Club (pres. 1994—). Lutheran. Office: Prudential Country Heritage 2900 DeKalb Ave Sycamore IL 60178

ADRIAN, RICHARD ROBERT, detective; b. N.Y.C., Aug. 14, 1951; s. Robert and Joan (Schmidt) Kieffer; m. Susan L. Gorsuch, Mar. 21, 1981; children: Ryan, Taylor. BA in Criminal Justice, U. Cin., 1979. Restaurant mgr. Maisonette Restaurant, Cin., 1973-74; detective Columbus (Ohio) Police Dept., 1979—; pres. The Aspen Group, Inc., Columbus, 1994—. Author: (book) Free Fire Zones: Urban Warfare USA, 1994, No-Cost Speeding!, 1995; patent for Cops N' Cars Sound Security Tape; creator: (map) The E Map, 1994. Mem. Nat. Tactical Officers Assn., Am. Soc. for Indsl. Security, Internat. Combat Martial Arts Assn. Office: The Aspen Group Inc 3000 B E Main St #179 Columbus OH 43209

ADRIANOPOLI, BARBARA CATHERINE, librarian; b. Fort Dodge, Iowa, January 27, 1943; d. Daniel Joseph and Mary Dolores (Coleman) Hogan; m. Carl David Adrianopoli, June 28, 1968; children: Carlin, Laurie. BS, Mundeline Coll., 1966; M.L.S., Rosary Coll., 1975. Tchr., Father Bertrand H.S., Memphis, 1966-68; caseworker Cook Dept. Pub. Aid Chgo., 1968; tchr. North Chicago Jr. H.S. (Ill.), 1968-70, Austin Middle Sch., Chgo., 1970-73; libr. Barrington Pub. Libr. (Ill.), 1976-79, Schaumburg Twp. Dist. Library (Ill.), 1979—; diversity com. N. Suburban/Suburban Libr. Systems, LaGrange, Ill., 1995—. Contbr. articles to jours. Mem. Com. Schaumburg Twp. Disabled, 1981—; historian Village of Hoffman Estates, 1986—; adv. com. Hoffman Estates Sister Cities, 1988-96; advisor Boy Scout Am. handicapped badge, Schaumburg Twp., 1981—; mem. adv. bd. Cmty. Nutrition Network, 1994—; organizer, mem. Northwest Corridor-St. Patrick's Day Parade com., 1986—; bd. dirs. Children's Mus. and Imaginasium, 1990-93; trainer A World of Difference Anti-Defamation League, 1995; speaker on library outreach svcs., 1995—; mem. Com. For Choices For Success-Seminars For Young Women, 1996—. Grantee Sears Community Project for Literacy; recipient Hoffman Estates Citizen of Yr. award VFW, 1995. Mem. ALA, Ill. Libr. Assn. Democrat. Roman Catholic. Home: 1105 Kingsdale Rd Schaumburg IL 60194-2378 Office: Schaumburg Twp Pub Libr 32 W Library Ln Schaumburg IL 60194-3421

ADROUNIE, V. HARRY, public health administrator, scientist, educator, environmentalist; b. Battle Creek, Mich., Apr. 29, 1915; s. Haroutune Asadour and Dorthy (Kalaidjian) A.; m. Emalea Riley, June, 1943 (div. Jan. 1980); children: Harry Michael, Vee Patrick; m. Agnes M. Slone, June 26, 1981. BS, St. Ambrose U., 1940, BA, 1959; MS in Environ. Health, Western States U. Profl. Studies, 1984, PhD Environ. Health, PhD in Pub. Health, 1984. Cert. Am. Bd. Indsl. Hygiene; registered sanitarian, Calif., Mich., Pa., N.C. Enlisted U.S. Army, 1941, commd. 2nd. lt., 1943; advanced through grades to lt. col. USAF, ret., 1968; tech. dir. ARA Environ. Svcs., 1968-70; dir. environ. health div. Chester County (Pa.) Health Dept., 1970-75, Berrien County (Mich.) Health Dept., 1975-78; prof. environ. health Sch. Pub. Health U. Hawaii, Manoa, 1978-80; dean, prof. Sch. Pub. Health, Western States U. Profl. Studies, Mo., 1980-83; ret., 1983; vis. prof. environ. and pub. health Am. U., Armenia, 1995; USAF rep. U.S. Interdepartmental Com. on Nutrition for Nat. Def., 1959-61; cons. Health Mobilization Program USPHS Surgeon Gen., 1961-62; mem. USAF Surgeon Gen.'s med. goodwill tour all S.Am. countries, 1960; chmn., vis. assoc. prof. dept. environ. health Am. U. Beirut, 1963-66, chmn. dept. environ. health, 1964-66; charter mem. RSH-UN Welfare Relief Agy. Pub. Health Examining Bd. for Mid. East, 1963-66, UNWRA cons., 1964-66; founder, coord. 1st and 2d Environ. Health Symposium of Mid. East, 1965-66; mem. Mich. Hazardous Waste Policy Com., 1990-91, Mich. Mustfa Fin. Policy Bd., 1994—; adj. instr., mem. adv. com. environ. health Ferris State Coll., Big Rapids, Mich., 1974-75, 77-78. Contbr. numerous articles to profl. jours.; author many manuals and tng. booklets for USAF and several books. Mem. environ. issues com. Bush for Pres. Campaign, Washington, 1988; co-chmn. Barry County (Mich.) Bush for Pres. Campaign, Barry County Abraham for U.S. Senate Campaign, 1994; chmn. Barry County Solid Waste Planning and Oversight com., 1981—; vice chmn. Hastings City Planning Commn., 1984—; mem., co-founder sci. adv. and policy bd. Mich. Ground Water Survey, Inc., 1983—, chmn., 1988-91; chmn. adv. coun. South Ctrl. Mich. Commn. on Aging, 1981-91; mem. UL Underwriters adv. coun. environ. and pub. health, 1996—; past adult leader Boy Scouts Am. Decorated Legion of Merit, USAF; named Alumnus of Yr., Hastings H.S., 1961; recipient Walter S. Mangold award Nat. Environ. Health Assn., 1963, spl. recognition Mich. Environ. Health Assn., 1980, Concerned Citizen award World Safety Orgn., 1992, Safety Person of World Safety Orgn., 1992, Safety Person of Yr. award World Safety Orgn., 1993. Mem. VFW (life), APHA (emeritus v.p., emeritus conf. 1993, pres.-elect 1994-95, pres. 1995-97), Mich. Assn. Local Environ. Health Adminstrs. (pres., founder 1976), Nat. Environ. Health Assn. (life, pres. 1961-62), Am. Acad. Sanitarians (diplomate), Assn. Mil. Surgeons U.S. (life), Internat. Pub. Health Soc. (charter-emeritus), Nat. Coun. Internat. Health, NRA (life, cert. rifle marksmanship instr.), World Safety Orgn. (bd. dirs. 1986-95, cert. bd. 1987—, editl. bd. 1988—), Mich. Environ. Health Assn. (pres. 1991-92), Air Force Assn., Am. Legion (comdr. 1989-90), Indonesian Environ. Health Assn. (co-founder), Lions, Elks (life), Moose, Kiwanis (pres. 1985-86). Home: 1905 N Broadway Hastings MI 49058-1056

ADUDDLE, LARRY STEVEN, marketing and sales executive, consultant; b. Miami Beach, Fla., Oct. 21, 1946; s. William Allen and Bernice Elizabeth (Newlon) A.; m. Susan Carol Dominiak, Nov. 27, 1982; 1 child, Melissa Sue. BBA, Lake Forest Coll., 1982; MBA, Lake Forest Sch. Mgmt., 1984. Supr. Rexnord, Inc., Milw., 1974-77, product mgr., 1977-79, sales mgr., 1979-81; mktg. mgr. V/R Wesson, Fansteel, Inc., Waukegan, Ill., 1981-82; v.p. Metropolymer Labs, Inc., Milw., 1983—, bd. dirs.; bd. dirs., treas. Metromark, Inc.; v.p., sec. Metropolymer Labs, Inc.; cons. in field, Milw., 1982-83. Patentee insert for drill stabilizers. vice chmn. United Fund Campaign, Milw., 1975; adv. Jr. Achievement, Milw., 1980. Served to capt. U.S. Army, 1965-69, Vietnam. Decorated Bronze Star. Mem. Reserve Officers Assn. (sec. 1977-78), Assn. Internat. Mktg. Execs. Republican. Lutheran. Home: 901 Golden Meadows Cir Nixa MO 65714-7957 Office: Metropolymer Labs Inc PO Box 1467 Nixa MO 65714-1467

ADULEWICZ, CASIMIR T., lawyer, court magistrate; b. Steubenville, Ohio, Aug. 11; s. Victor and Mary (Zuk) A.; m. Judith Lynn Beyer, Aug. 24, 1963 (div. Mar. 1994); children: Michael T., John C. BS, Ohio State U., 1960; JD, Ohio No. U., 1964. Bar: Ohio. Ct. magistrate. Home: 129 Brady Circle East Steubenville OH 43952-1464

ADZICK, SHIRLEY RAE, dentist; b. Mpls., Apr. 10, 1957; d. Gene Paul Shanus and Rosemary Therese (Leoni) Fruehling; m. George Norman Adzick, Dec. 22, 1979 (div. June 1983); 1 child, Anya Marie; m. John Daniel Butcher Jr., Oct. 17, 1986; 1 child, John Daniel III. BS, U. Minn., 1981, DDS with honors, 1985. Prin., founder Northstar Dental Clin. Ltd., Mpls., 1985—. Mem. ADA, Minn. Dental Assn., Am. Acad. Women Dentists, Minn. Women Dentists Study Club, Mpls. C. of C., Mpls. Athletic Club. Roman Catholic. Home: 2240 Sommer Gate Excelsior MN 55331-8800 Office: Pentagon Dental Group 4940 Viking Dr # 127 Edina MN 55435-5306

AEBI, IMOGENE MCDONOUGH, business educator; b. Washington, Pa., Jan. 31, 1933; d. John C. and Flora Elizabeth (Nicholl) McDonough; m. Charles J. Aebi, Aug. 5, 1955; children: Ruth Aebi McKinzie, Joy Aebi West, Mark Ellis, Mary Aebi Daughety. Student, Abilene Christian U., 1953-54; BS, Waynesburg Coll., 1955; MA, W.Va. U., 1980. Cert. tchr., Pa. Bus. tchr. Bentleyville (Pa.) High Sch., 1955-56, Stowe High Sch., McKees Rocks, Pa., 1956-58, Warren H.S., Vincent, Ohio, 1968-72; asst. prof. bus. Ohio Valley Coll., Parkersburg, W.Va., 1963-68, 72-87; instr. bus. Washington County Career Ctr., Marietta, Ohio, 1987—; presenter workshops on family rels., personal devel. Speaker various chpts. Child Conservation League, 1978—. Jennings scholar Ohio U., Athens, 1988-89. Mem. NEA, Nat. Bus. Edn. Assn., Am. Vocat. Assn., Ohio Edn. Assn., Stepping Stones Ohio Valley Coll. (pres. 1976-78). Republican. Mem. Ch. of Christ. Home: RR 1 Box 237 Vincent OH 45784-9730 Office: Washington County Career Ctr RR 2 Marietta OH 45750-9802

AELMORE, DONALD K., systems engineer; b. Greensburg, Kans., Aug. 25, 1952; s. Martin A. and Mary I. (Whalen) A.; m. Dorothy A. Hansen, Aug. 19, 1978; children; Timothy B., Jeffrey A., Matthew D. AA, Hutchinson Community Coll., 1973; BS, Pittsburg State Coll., 1976. Svc. engr. RCA Svc. Co., Chgo., 1976-78; design engr. NCR Corp., Dayton, Ohio, 1978-92; sys. engr. Mueller Industries, Wichita, Kans., 1992-95; dir. info. tech. Interex Computer Products, Wichita, 1995—; dir. Network Data Comm.- Mueller Industries, Wichita, 1992. Moderator Ctrl. Assn. of Kans. Okla. Conf. of United Ch. of Christ, Wichita, 1991-95. Mem. IEEE (tech. com. of computer comm.), Internat. Alliance Theatrical State Employees and Moving Picture Machine Operators. Home: 4278 Eagle Lake Ct Wichita KS 67220-1719 Office: Mueller Industries 2959 N Rock Rd Wichita KS 67226-1117

AFTERMAN, ALLAN B., accountant, educator, researcher, consultant; b. Chgo., Jan. 25, 1944; s. Joseph and Ruth Gertrude (Jacobson) A.; m. Joan Elaine Hoffman, Apr. 30, 1974; children: Debra, Lori, Julie, Robin. BBA, Roosevelt U., 1964; PhD, U. Birmingham, Eng., 1989. CPA, Calif. Asst. dir. securities exchange com. practices Alexander Grant & Co., Chgo., 1967-70; nat. staff mgr. Touche Ross & Co., Chgo., 1970-73; nat. tech. dir. Practice Devel. Inst., Chgo., 1977-82; acctg. prof. U. Ill., Chgo., 1983-88, dir. exec. edn.; mem. faculty grad. sch. bus. U. Chgo., 1992—; cons. to govts. Author: Accounting and Auditing Disclosure Manual, 1982, Compilation and Review, 1983, Accounting and Auditing Update, 1984, SEC Accounting and Reporting Update, 1985, GAAP Practice Manual, 1985 (best loosleaf bus. reference award profl. and scholastic divsn. Assn. Am. Pubs. 1985), Accounting and Tax Highlights, 1986, Handbook of SEC Accounting and Disclosure, 1987, Credit Analyst's Report, 1988, Financial Reporting and Disclosure Manual in the United Kingdom, 1989, Public Accounting Practice Manual, 1990, Governmental Accounting & Auditing Disclosure Manual, 1991, Nonprofit Accounting and Auditing Disclosure Manual, 1992, Auditing Standards and Practices in Poland, 1993, SEC Regulation of Public Companies, 1994, International Financial Accounting, Reporting & Analysis, 1994, U.S. Securities Regulation of Foreign Issuers, 1995. Mem. AICPA, Am. Acctg. Assn., Practicing Law Inst., N.Y. Soc. CPAs. Jewish. Home: 3900 Mission Hills Rd Apt 302 Northbrook IL 60062-5721 Office: 3330 Dundee Rd Ste N6 Northbrook IL 60062-2329

AGARWAL, GYAN CHAND, engineering educator; b. Bhagwanpur, India, Apr. 22, 1940; came to U.S., 1960; s. Hari Chand and Ramrati (Jindal) A.; m. Sadhna Garg, July 7, 1965; children: Monika, Mudita. BS, Agra U., India, 1957; BE with honors, U. Roorkee, India, 1960; MSEE, Purdue U., Ind., 1962, PhD, 1965. Lic. profl. engr. Ill., Wis. Asst. prof. engring. U. Ill., Chgo., 1965-69, assoc. prof. engring., 1969-73, prof. engring., 1973—, dir. grad. studies, 1975-79, 82-85, 91—; vis. prof. Rush Med. Coll., Chgo., 1976—; vis. prof. Indian Inst. Sci., Bangalore, 1971, Indian Inst. Tech., Kanpur, 1972; cons. FDA, Washington, 1979—; mem. study sect. NIH, 1990-94. Co-editor: Biomaterials, 1969; cons. editor Jour. Motor Behavior, 1981-93; assoc. editor IEEE Transactions on Biomed. Engring., 1988—, Jour. Electromyography and Kinesiology, 1994—; contbr. articles to profl. jours. U. Roorkee merit scholar, 1958-60; NSF, NIH, NASA, VA, Wright-Patterson AFB rsch. grantee. Fellow AIAAS, IEEE, Am. Inst. for Med. and Biol. Engring. (founding); mem. Soc. Neurosci., Sigma Xi, Phi Kappa Phi, Eta Kappa Nu. Home: 947 Lathrop Ave River Forest IL 60305-1448 Office: U Ill Coll Engring Dept Elec Engring 851 S Morgan St Rm 1120 SEO Chicago IL 60607-7053

AGARWAL, RAMESH KUMAR, aeronautical scientist, researcher, educator; b. Mainpuri, India, Jan. 4, 1947; came to U.S., 1968; s. Radhakishan and Parkashvati (Goel) A.; m. Sugita Goel, Oct. 26, 1976; children: Vivek, Gautam. BS, U. Allahabad, 1965; BTech, Indian Inst. Tech., 1968; MS, U. Minn., 1969; PhD, Stanford U., 1975. Rsch. assoc. NASA Ames Rsch. Ctr., Moffett Field, Calif., 1976-78; McDonnell Douglas fellow, program dir. McDonnell Douglas Aerospace, St. Louis, 1978-94; Bloomfield disting. prof., chair aerospace engring. Wichita (Kans.) State U., 1994—; affiliate prof. Washington U., St. Louis, 1986—. Contbr. over 100 articles to profl. jours. Fellow AIAA, AAAS, ASME; mem. Am. Phys. Soc., Am. Helicopter Soc., Sigma Xi. Office: Wichita State U Dept Aerospace Engring Wichita KS 67260-0044

AGARWAL, SUMAN KUMAR, editor; b. Bolpur, India, Jan. 21, 1945; came to U.S., 1980; s. Hari Prasad and Rukmini (Modi) A.; m. Uma Saraff, Oct. 22, 1974; children: Tripti, Samantha Rani. BSc with honors, Visva-Bharati, Santiniketan, India, 1966; MSc, Delhi U., India, 1971; PhD, U. Paris, 1975, DSc, 1979. Rsch. scholar Atomic Energy Commn. of France, Saclay, 1976-80; rsch. assoc. Purdue U., West Lafayette, Ind., 1980-82; sr. sci. info. analyst Chem. Abstracts Svc., Columbus, Ohio, 1982—; pres. Commodities Internat. Ltd. Inc., Columbus, Ohio, 1992—. Contbr. articles to profl. jours. Vol. Columbus Schs., 1984, 85, Ohio State U. TV, Columbus, 1986, 87, 88. Scholar Govt. of France, 1973-76. Mem. Am. Chem. Soc.

AGBETSIAFA, DOUGLAS KOFI, financial and management consultant; b. Anloga, Volta, Ghana; came to the U.S., 1976; s. Benjamin K. Agbetsiafa and Rebecca Afafa Agbakpe; m. Patricia Ann Williams. BS, U. Ghana, 1971, MS, 1975; MA, Western Ontario, 1976; PhD, U. Notre Dame, 1980. Secondary sch. tchr. Mininstry Edn., Accra, Ghana, 1966-68; instr. Univ. Western Ontario, London, 1973-75, Univ. Notre Dame, 1976-80; prof. econs., acad. senate pres. Ind. Univ., South Bend. Contbr. articles and revs. to profl. jours. Sec., treas. United Way St. Joe County, bd. dirs., 1987—; trustee Urban League, South Bend, 1988. Mem. Am. Econ. Assn. Am. Statis Assn., Internat. Bus. Assn., Western Econ. Internat., Midwest Econ. Assn., Midsouth Acad. Econs. and Fin. (bd. dirs.), Ind. Acad. Soc. Sci., Bus. Assn. Latin Am. Studies, Assn. for Global Bus. (program dir. 1993-94, v.p. program dir. 1995—), South Bend-Mishawaka C. of C. (bd. dirs., mem. minority bus. devel. task force), U. Notre Dame Alumni Assn. Home: 224 N Sunnyside Ave South Bend IN 46617-3332 Office: Ind U 1700 Mishawaka Ave South Bend IN 46615-1408

AGEE, DANIEL DAVID, mechanical engineer; b. St. Louis, Feb. 17, 1946; s. Vernon H. and Patricia M. (Newcomb) A.; m. Janice A. Honeberger, Aug. 26, 1972; children: Brian, Kevin. BS in Mech. Engring., U. Mo., Rolla, 1969. Chief engr. Williams Patent Crusher, St. Louis, 1975—. Mem. Eagles. Roman Catholic. Office: Williams Patent Crusher 813 Montgomery St Saint Louis MO 63102-1513

AGEE, DAVID E., stockbroker; b. Centralia, Ill., Aug. 4, 1958; s. Calvin B. and LuEllen (Heyduck) A.; m. Linda S. Berger, June 11, 1989. BS, So. Ill. U., Carbondale, 1980. Stockbroker Advest Inc., Centralia, Ill., 1981—. Chmn. Charitable Found., Centralia, 1982; mem. adv. Centralia Found., 1981, Centralia Fall Festival, Inc., 1992. Mem. Rotary, Moose. Republican. Office: Advest Inc 100 S Locust St PO Box 476 Centralia IL 62801

AGEE, JAMES G., state legislator. Mich. state rep. Dist. 92, 1993—. Address: PO Box 30014 Lansing MI 48909-7514*

AGGARWAL, RATTAN, electrical engineer; b. Punjab, India, Nov. 6, 1937; came to U.S., 1962; MSEE, U. Iowa, 1964. Engr. EPCO Products, Walkill, N.Y., 1988-92; magnetic design engr. Magnetek, Brownsville, Tex., 1992-94; product design engr. MTE Corp., Menomonee Falls, Wis., 1994—. Mem. IEEE. Office: MTE Corp W147n9525 Held Dr Menomonee Falls WI 53051-1640

AGICH, GEORGE JOHN, medical educator; b. Rochester, Pa., May 27, 1947; s. Charles Albert and Mary (Mikovich) A.; m. Mary Kate Fredriksen; 1 child, Nicholas Carl. BA in English and Philosophy cum laude, Duquesne U., 1969; MA in Philosophy, U. Tex., 1971, PhD in Philosophy, 1976. Prof. med. ethics and psychiatry So. Ill. U., Springfield, 1976—; dir. clin. ethics ctr. Meml. Med. Ctr., Springfield, Ill., 1994—, dir. ethics consultation svc., 1991—; vis. scholar history and philosophy of sci. Cambridge U., 1982-83; Paul Ruble Meml. lectr. Wayne State U., Detroit, 1987. Author: Autonomy and Long-Term Care, 1993; editor: Price of Health, 1986, Responsibility in Health Care, 1982. Bd. dirs. Friends of Lincoln Libr., Springfield. Recipient Nellie Westerman prize Am. Fedn. Clin. Rsch. Mem. Assn. for Advancement Philosophy and Psychiatry (pres. 1994—, founding fellow 1989—), Assn. Faculty in Med. Humanities (chairperson 1991-92), Am. Philos. Assn., Soc. Health and Human Values, Am. Soc. Law, Medicine, and Ethics, European Soc. Philosophy of Medicine and Health Care. Office: So Ill Univ Sch Medicine PO Box 19230 Springfield IL 62794-1113

AGIN, DENNIS MICHAEL, aircraft manufacturer, orthodontist educator; b. Cleve., Nov. 13, 1942; s. Henry E. and Mintsy (Gutterman) A.; m. karen Catone, May 20, 1984. Student, Toledo U., 1960-62; DDS, Western Res. U., 1966; postgrad., U. Rochester, 1966-67, 69-71, Ohio State U., 1988-91. Diplomate Am. Bd. Orthodontics; cert. flight instr. Instr. Case Western Res. U. Dental Sch., Cleve., 1972-84; clin. staff Cleve. VA Hosp., 1973-84; asst. prof. Ohio State U., Columbus, 1985-87; lectr. Columbus state Coll., 1993—; flight instr. Firebird Aviation, Middlefield, Ohio, 1980-84; flight advisor Exptl. Aircraft Assn., Oshkosh, Wis., 1994—; mfr. Heath Aircraft, Columbus, 1994—; bd. dirs. Heath Found., Columbus, 1994—. Lt. comdr. USNR, 1962-88, Viet Nam (1967-69). Decorated Ribbon of Combat Action, Nat. Defense medal, Vietnam Svc. medal (7 stars), Vietnam Cross of Gallantry with Palm, Vietnam Campaign medal. Mem. Nat. Flight Instrs.

Assn., Exptl. Aircraft Assn., VFW, Jewish War Vets., Kiwanis, Am. Mensa, Intertel, Alpha Epsilon Delta, Omicron Kappa Upsilon. Republican. Jewish. Home: 4460 Hayden Falls Dr Columbus OH 43221 Office: Heath Aerocraft Ltd 760 Clymer Rd H-208 Marysville OH 43040

AGINIAN, DIANA CAROL, child development specialist; b. Highland Park, Mich., June 7, 1944; d. Simon and Alice (Gurenlian) Tashjian; m. Richard Dicran Aginian, July 31, 1966; children: Dawn, Marla. BS, Mich. State U., 1966. Kindergarten tchr. Warren (Mich.) Woods Sch. Dist., 1966-69; substitute tchr. Southfield (Mich.) and Birmingham (Mich.) Sch. Dists., 1969-70, Beverly Hills (Mich.) Nursery Sch., 1974; cmty. sch. organizer Birmingham Sch. Dist., 1984—. Prodr. 15 programs for pub. cable TV, 1983-84. Mem. AAUW (bd. dirs. 1983), Jr. League Birmingham (sustainer, leadership team 1983, women's golf chmn. 9-hole group), Oakland Hills Country Club. Armenian Orthodox. Home: 835 Westwood Dr Birmingham MI 48009-1179

AGNO, JOHN G., management consultant; b. Gloversville, N.Y., Dec. 8, 1940; s. John G. and Margretta (Luff) Anagnostopulos; m. Lynn Airey Mar. 30, 1968 (div. Oct. 1979); children; J. Robert, Constance Blythe, Randy R.; m. Karen Clark Mikus, June 29, 1985; 1 stepchild, Luke Ravlin. BBA, U. Fla., 1962. Mktg. specialist Eastman Kodak Co., Rochester, N.Y., 1965-73; gen. mgr. sanitation appliance div. Thetford Corp., Ann Arbor, Mich., 1973-80; v.p. mktg. and adminstrn. Stirling Power Systems Corp. div. McDonnell Douglas Corp., Ann Arbor, 1980-87; pres. Signature, Inc., Ann Arbor, 1983—. Deacon First Presbyn. Ch., Ann Arbor; bd. dirs. Washtenaw United Way, 1991-95; bd. dirs. YMCA, 1995—. 1st lt. U.S. Army, 1963-65. Mem. ASTD, Recreational Vehicle Industry Assn. (chmn. mktg. commn. 1978-82, bd. dirs. 1981-83), Mich. Tech. Coun., Turnaround Mgmt. Assn., Ann Arbor C. of C., Am. Legion, Rotary. Republican. Home: 2222 Georgetown Blvd Ann Arbor MI 48105-1535 Office: Signature Inc PO Box 2086 Ann Arbor MI 48106-2086

AGOSTINI, STEPHEN JOSEPH, city budget director; b. N.Y.C., Nov. 15, 1960; s. Hector Francis and Nancy Mary (Murphy) A. BA, Harvard Coll., 1983; M in pub. policy, U. Calif., 1986. Spl. asst. to city mgr. City Oakland, Oakland, Calif., 1985-87; budget analyst Mayor's Office, San Jose, Calif., 1987-88; budget analyst Mayor's Office, San Francisco, 1988-90, co-budget dir., 1990-91; exec. policy and program analyst Port Authority of N.Y., N.J., N.Y., 1991-92; deputy budget dir. City Seattle, Seattle, Wash., 1992-94; budget dir. City Milw., Milw., Wis., 1994—; treas. S.E. Wis. Profl. Baseball Park Dist., 1995—. Contbr. articles to profl. jours. Bd. dirs. Latino Arts Bd., Inc., Milw., 1995—. Recipient scholarship N.Y. State Regents, 1978, League of United Latin Am. Citizens, 1978, Harvard Coll., 1978-83, fellowship U. Calif., 1984-86. Mem. Assn. Pub. Policy Analysis & Mgmt., Gov. Fin. Officers Assn. Office: City Milwaukee 200 E Wells St Rm 307 Milwaukee WI 53202

AGRANOFF, BERNARD WILLIAM, biochemist, educator; b. Detroit, June 26, 1926; s. William and Phyllis (Pelavin) A.; m. Raquel Betty Schwartz, Sept. 1, 1957; children: William, Adam. MD, Wayne State U., 1950; BS, U. Mich., 1954. Intern Robert Packer Hosp., Sayre, Pa., 1950-51; commd. surgeon USPHS, 1954-60; biochemist Nat. Inst. Neurol. Diseases and Blindness, NIH, Bethesda, Md., 1954-60; mem. faculty U. Mich., Ann Arbor, 1960—, prof. biochemistry, 1965—; R.W. Gerard prof. of neurosci. in psychiatry, 1991; rsch. biochemist Mental Health Rsch. Inst., 1960—, assoc. dir., 1977-83, dir. 1983-95, dir. neurosci. lab., 1983—; vis. scientist Max Planck Inst. Zellchemie, Munich, 1957-58, Nat. Inst. Med. Rsch., Mine Hill, Eng., 1974-75; Henry Russel lectr. U. Mich., 1987; cons. pharm. industry, govt. Contbr. articles to profl. jours. Fogart scholar-in-residence NIH, Bethesda, Md., 1989-95; named Mich. Scientist of Yr. Mus. of Sci., Lansing, 1992. Fellow Am. Coll. Neuropsychopharmacology; mem. Am. Soc. Biochemistry and Molecular Biology, Am. Chem. Soc., Inst. Medicine, Internat. Soc. Neurochemistry (treas. 1985-89, chmn. 1989-91), Am. Soc. Neurochemistry (pres. 1973-75). Home: 1942 Boulder Dr Ann Arbor MI 48104-4164 Office: U Mich Neurosci Lab 1103 E Huron St Ann Arbor MI 48104-1630

AGRUSS, NEIL STUART, cardiologist; b. Chgo., June 2, 1939; s. Meyer and Frances (Spector) A.; B.S., U. Ill., 1960, M.D., 1963; m. Teresa Marie Stafford; children—David, Lauren, Michael, Joshua, Susan. Intern, U. Ill. Hosp., Chgo., 1963-64, resident in internal medicine, 1964-65, 67-68; fellow in cardiology, Cin. Gen. Hosp., 1968-70, dir. coronary care unit, 1971-74, dir. echocardiography lab., 1972-74; dir. cardiac diagnostic labs., Central DuPage Hosp., Winfield, Ill., 1974—; asst. prof. medicine, U. Cin., 1970-74, Rush Med. Coll., 1976—. Chmn. coronary care com. Heart Assn. DuPage County, 1974-76; active Congregation Beth Shalom, Naperville, Ill. Served to capt. M.C. U.S. Army, 1965-67. Diplomate Am. Bd. Internal Medicine. Fellow ACP, Am. Coll. Cardiology, Am. Coll. Chest Physicians, Council Clin. Cardiology, Am. Heart Assn.; mem. AMA, DuPage County, Ill. State Med. Socs., Am. Fedn. Clin. Research, Chgo. Heart Assn. Author and co-author publs. in field. Office: 454 Pennsylvania Ave Glen Ellyn IL 60137-4402

AHERN, WILBERT HARRELL, history educator, academic administrator; b. Greenville, Ill., July 12, 1942; s. Alvin A. and Helen (Green) A.; m. Janet Louise Turbyne, Dec. 28, 1963; children: Alyson Louise, James Chapin. BA, Oberlin Coll., Ohio, 1963; MA, Northwestern U., Evanston, Ill., 1966, PhD, 1968. Asst. prof. U. Minn., Morris, 1967-70, assoc. prof., 1970-79; vis. assoc. prof. Northwestern U., Evanston, Ill., summer 1975; acting acad. dean U. Minn., Morris, 1978-79, fall 1992, prof., 1979—, chairperson divsn. social scis., 1987-95. Contbr. articles and book revs. to profl. jours. Mem., chairperson Minn. State Rev. Bd. for Hist. Preservation, St. Paul, 1983-92; chairperson DFL House Dist., 1984-92; mem. steering com. Bush Regional Collaboration in Faculty Devel., 1989-95, chairperson steering com. 1990-93. Fellow Newberry Libr., Chgo., 1974-75, Bush Sabbatical fellow, 1983-84, Summer Seminar NEH, 1988; grantee Am. Philos. Soc., 1983. Mem. Orgn. Am. Historians, Am. Hist. Assn., Am. Soc. Ethnohistory, World History Assn. Protestant. Home: RR 1 Box 173 Morris MN 56267-9719 Office: U of Minn 4th College Morris MN 56267

AHLER, KENNETH JAMES, physician; b. Meadryville, Ind., Aug. 4, 1940; s. James and Bernadine (Benner) A.; m. Margaret Ann Ahler, Aug. 24, 1963; children: Joh, Mary Margaret, James. AB in Biology magna cum laude, St. Joseph's Coll., Rensselaer, Ind., 1962; LLD (hon.), St. Joseph's Coll., 1988; MD, Ind. U., 1966. Diplomate Am. Bd. Family Practice. Intern St. Joseph's Hosp., South Bend, Ind., 1966-67, resident in gen. medicine, 1967-68; mem. med. staff Jasper County Hosp., Rensselaer, 1968—, George Ade Nursing Facility, Brook, Ind.; Med. dir. Rensselaer Care Ctr.; sr. assoc. Clinic of Family Practice, Ind. U. Sch. of Medicine, preceptor dept. family practice Ind. U. Sch. of Medicine; mem. gov.'s commn. Newborn Inborn Errors of Metabolism, 1978; asst. physician Boy Scouts Am. Nat. Jamboree at A.P. Hill, Va., 1985, and 89, chief physician subcamp 2, Nat. Jamboree, 1992; bd. dirs. 1st Am. Bank of Rensselaer; mem. utilization & quality assurance com. Arnett HMO, 1992, 93, 94. Mem. St. Augustine Cath. Ch., Rensselaer, exec. bd. Sagamore coun. Boy Scouts Am., pres. 1984-86; asst. scoutmaster Troop 409 Boy Scouts Am. Jamboree, Australia, 1988, v.p. program Area 4 Ctrl. Region Boy Scouts Am., 1987-94, mem. North Cen. region exec. bd.; trustee St. Joseph Coll. Rensselaer; chmn. bd. Jasper County Devel. Found., Inc.; coroner Jasper County, 1973-81, others. Fellow Am. Acad. Family Practice, Royal Soc. Medicine (London); mem. AMA, Am. Diabetes Assn. (profl. section), Ind. State Med. Assn. (disting.), Jasper County Med. Soc. (pres. 1987-88), Am. Geriatrics Soc., Am. Med. Dirs. Assn., Rotary (pres. Rensselaer chpt 1984-85), Knights of Columbus. Home: 703 Milroy St Rensselaer IN 47978-2756 Office: 1103 E Grace St Rensselaer IN 47978-3210

AHMAD, ANWAR, radiologist; b. Peshawar, Pakistan, Apr. 15, 1945; s. Shams and Amtulaziz (Lateef) A.; m. Amtur R. Hameed, May 20, 1970; children: Attiya, Ghazala, Iftekhar. FSc, Islamia Coll., Peshawar, 1962; MBBS, Khyber Med. Sch., Peshawar, 1968. Cert. Am. Bd. Radiology. Gen. practice medicine Govt. Pakistan, Peshawar, 1968-71; med. missionary Ahmadiyya Mission, Banjul, The Gambia, 1971-75; attending physician VA Hosp., Hines, Ill., 1975-85, Mercy Hosp., Benton Harbor, Mich., 1985—; clin. instr. Chgo. Med. Sch., North Chicago, Ill., 1978—; program dir. residency tng., VA Hosp., Hines, 1982-85. Pres. suburban chpt. Ahmadiyya Muslim Mission, Glen Ellyn, Ill., 1982-85. Mem. AMA, Am. Soc. Therapeutic Radiology and Oncology, Am. Soc. Clin. Oncology, Am. Coll. Radiology, Radiol. Soc. N.Am., Am. Endocurie Therapy Soc., European Soc. Therapeutic Radiology and Oncology, Am. Endocurietherapy Soc., Internat. Assn. Study of Lung Cancer. Home: 1515 Cardinal Dr Saint Joseph MI 49085-9748 Office: PO Box 273 Saint Joseph MI 49085-0273

AHONEN, ROBERT M., law educator; b. Warren, Ohio, Mar. 6, 1955; m. Denise Meehan, Nov. 15, 1980; children: Bryan, Cindy. BS in Acctg., U. Akron, 1976; MBA, Cleve. State U., 1980, JD, 1987. Bar: Ohio 1987; CPA, Ohio. Tax analyst LTV Steel Co., Inc., Cleve., 1977-85; tax atty., tax analyst BP Am., Cleve., 1985-93; adj. and vis. asst. prof. tax/law dept. acctg. and bus. law Cleve. State U., 1993-96; lead auditor, cons. Profit Retrieval Systems, Cleve., 1994-95; instr. David N. Myers Coll., Cleve., 1995; asst. prof. acctg., econs., bus dept. Mount Union Coll., Alliance, Ohio, 1996—; sr. tax specialist Ernst & Young, LLP, 1996—. Coach, asst. coach, helper YMCA T-Ball, Coach Pitch, and Soccer, Stow, Ohio, 1988-95; asst. cubmaster, den leader Cub Scouts, Stow, 1991-94; asst. scoutmaster Boy Scouts Am., Stow, 1994. Mem. AICPA, Cleve. Tax Club. Office: Mount Union Coll 1972 Clark Ave Alliance OH 44601

AHRENS, FRANKLIN ALFRED, veterinary pharmacology educator; b. Leigh, Nebr., Apr. 27, 1936; s. Alfred Henry and Agnes Elizabeth (Higgins) A.; m. Katherine Aldene Henning, May 8, 1960; children—Jeffrey, Gregory, Matthew, Kristin. D.V.M., Kans. State U., 1959; M.S., Cornell U., 1965, Ph.D., 1968. Instr. U. Minn.-St. Paul, 1959-60; asst. prof. pharmacology Coll. Vet. Medicine, Iowa State U., Ames, 1968-70; assoc. prof. pharmacology Coll. Vet. Medicine, Iowa State U., 1970-75, prof. pharmacology, 1975—, chmn. dept. vet. physiology and pharmacology, 1982-90. Served as capt. USAF, 1960-63, lt. col. Air N.G., 1971—. Recipient Norden Disting. Tchr. award Iowa State U., 1981; NIH spl. research fellow Cornell U., 1967-68. Mem. AVMA, N.Y. Acad. Scis., Assn. Mil. Surgeons U.S., Sigma Xi. Democrat. Lutheran. Office: Iowa State U Dept Vet Physiology & Pharmacology Ames IA 50011

AHRENS, JOYCE A., mechanical engineer; b. Greenville, Ohio, May 3, 1969. BSME summa cum laude, U. Dayton, 1994. Engr. PMI Food Equip. Group Tech., Troy, Ohio, 1994—.

AHRENS, STEVEN N(ORMAN), publisher; b. Grinnell, Iowa, Oct. 6, 1957; s. Richard Glenn and Virginia Rose (Turner) A.; m. Carla Lynn Davis, Nov. 18, 1975; children: Elizabeth, Jennifer, Stephanie, Alyssa. BS in Comm., S.W. Mo. State U., 1979. Editor Marshfield (Mo.) Mail, 1978-84; dir. publs. sec. state State of Mo., Jefferson City, 1985—; pres. DW Mktg., Jefferson City, 1992—. Del. Mo. Rep. Party, 1992; com. mem. United Way, Jefferson City, 1994—. Home: 1525 Timber Tr Jefferson City MO 65109 Office: Mo Sec of State PO Box 778 Jefferson City MO 65102

AIELESZUK, JAN, project engineer; b. 6Borek, Poland, Aug. 28, 1926; came to U.S., 1950; s. Kwaweryna and Antoni M.; m. Maria Skitek, Sept. 1, 1956; children: Elizabeth A., Anne M. B, U. Ill., 1960. Sr. project engr. Signode Corp., Glenview, Ill., 1960—. Patentee in field. Exec. pres. Polish Saturday Schs., Ill. With U.S. Army, 1951-53. Independent. Roman Catholic. Home: 5301 W Fletcher St Chicago IL 60641-4945

AIKEN, MICHAEL THOMAS, academic administrator; b. El Dorado, Ark., Aug. 20, 1932; s. William Floyd and Mary (Gibbs) A.; m. Catherine Comet, Mar. 28, 1969; 1 child, Caroline R. BA, U. Miss., 1954; MA, U. Mich., 1955, PhD, 1964. Asst. prof. U. Wis., Madison, 1963-67, assoc. prof., 1967-70, prof., 1970-84, assoc. dean coll. arts and scis., 1980-82; prof. U. Pa., Phila., 1984-93, dean sch. arts and scis., 1985-87, provost, 1987-93; chancellor U. Ill., Urbana, 1993—, Champaign/Urbana, 1993—. Author: (with others) The Dynamics of Idealism, 1971, Economic Failure, Alienation, and Extremism, 1968; editor: (with others) Complex Organizations: Critical Perspectives, 1981, The Structures of Community Power, 1970. Mem. Am. Sociol. Assn. (sec. 1986-89). Office: U Ill 320 Swanlund Adminstrn Bldg 601 E John St Urbana IL 61801

AIKEN, ROGER GEORGE, energy systems research analyst, educator; b. Feilding, N.Z., Jan. 12, 1933; came to U.S., 1973; s. Henry George and Muriel Christine A.; m. Susan Graham Hamilton, July 14, 1962 (div. 1980); children: Andrew Graham, David George; m. Connie Lynn Haugen, Feb. 19, 1983; 1 child, Julie Christine. BSc, U. Canterbury, Christchurch, N.Z., 1954, BE with honors, 1956, ME with distinction, 1958; postgrad. in mech. engring., U. Minn., 1973-83. Sci. officer physics and engring. labs., Dept. Sci. and Indsl. Research, Lower Hutt, N.Z., 1958-59; devel. engr. Collier and Beale Ltd., Wellington, N.Z., 1959-61; sr. sci. staff Hirst Research Centre, Brit. Gen. Electric Co., Wembley, England, 1961-65; mem. sci. staff Bell No. Research, Ottawa, Ont., Can., 1965-67; temporary engr. transmission dept. N.Z. Post Office, Wellington, 1968; research scientist, engr. Communications Research Centre, Can. Fed. Dept. Communications, Ottawa, Ont., 1968-73; research fellow Center for Studies of Phys. Environment, Inst. Tech., U. Minn., Mpls., 1974-76; energy research analyst research div. Minn. Energy Agy., St. Paul, 1976-78; research fellow Underground Space Ctr., U. Minn., Mpls., 1978-79, Bio Energy Coordinating Office, 1980, instr. energy, honors program Coll. Liberal Arts, 1982-83; prin. energy systems analyst Synergistic Design and Engring., Mpls., 1981-82; bldg. mgmt. systems analyst Honeywell, Inc., Mpls., 1982-83; tng. supr. MTS Systems Corp., Mpls., 1984-88; prin. Roger G. Aiken & Assocs., Falcon Heights, Minn., 1988—; exec. dir. Coon Rapids Regional Energy/Environ. Demonstration Project, 1996—; instr. physics and HVAC Dunwoody Inst., Mpls., 1990—, energy issues classes North Hennepin C.C., Anoka Ramsey C.C., 1994—. Contbr. articles to profl. jours. and meetings. Recipient Minn. Energy Design award 1979, Honeywell Futurist Competition award 1983. Coordinator Future Lifestyle Planners program U. Minn. YMCA, 1978-80; elder Bethany Presbyn. Ch., 1985-95; mem. edn. subcom. Mayor Latimer's Com. 100, 1979. Mem. IEEE, AIAA, Internat. Solar Energy Soc., Minn. Renewable Energy Soc. (chmn. policy com. 1978-79, treas. 1984-88), Minnesotans for Energy Efficient Economy, Twin Cities Energy Engrs. (treas. 1995—), Phi Kappa Phi. Clubs: U. Minn., YMCA. Home: 1589 Hollywood Ct Falcon Heights MN 55108-2130

AINSWORTH, JOHN H., state legislator; b. Sept. 21, 1940. State assemblyman dist. 4 State of Wis., 1990-92, state assemblyman dist. 6, 1993—; mem. agrl. adv. com. Wis. State Assmebly; dairy farmer. Mem. Shawano County Rep. Com. Mem. Shawno County Farm Bur. (former pres.). Republican. Office: W75 Soo Ln RR 1 Box 380 Shawano WI 54166-9788*

AINSWORTH, THOMAS C., seed company executive. Pres. Ainsworth Seed Co., Inc. Office: Ainsworth Seed Co Inc PO Box 153 Mason City IL 62664*

AITCHISON, ROBERT SNYDER, writer, publishing company executive; b. Colfax, Iowa, Aug. 18, 1913; s. Robert David and Lulu Adrian (Snyder) A.; m. Jeanne A. Popp, June 1950; children: Robert, Brooks, Brant. BS in Journalism, U. Ill., 1936. Reporter Lincoln (Ill.) Evening Courier, 1936-37; with advt. dept. Firestone Tire & Rubber Co., Akron, Ohio, 1937-41; dir. advt. Lindberg Engring. Co., Chgo., 1941-50; editor-in-chief Indsl. Mktg., Crain Communications Co., Chgo., 1950-54; v.p. Fensholt Advt., Chgo., 1954-70, chmn. bd. dirs., chief exec. officer, 1970-78; writer News-Voice newspapers, Sta. WNVR, various cities, Ill., 1979-91; pub., editor Educator Press, Lake Forest, Ill., 1986-90, Alcoholism Briefs, Deerfield, Ill., 1986—. Pub., editor Pun Am. Newsletter, 1989—; contbr. numerous articles to Indsl. Mktg. mag., also bus. stories to Chgo. Tribune, Chgo. Sun-Times. Bd. dirs. Irene Josselyn Clinic, Northfield, Ill., 1974-76; pres. Del Mar Woods Community, 1981-83. Lt. USNR, 1940-43. Mem. Chgo. Indsl. Advt. Assn. (bd. dirs. 1948-50), Chgo. Curling Club (Northbrook, Ill.), Pun Am. Club (co-founder 1986). Republican. Unitarian. Home and Office: 1165 Elmwood Pl Deerfield IL 60015-1209

AKCASU, AHMET ZIYAEDDIN, nuclear engineer, educator; b. Aydin, Turkey, Aug. 26, 1924; s. Osman Nuri and Faika (Egel) A.; m. Melahat Turksal, July 16, 1954; children: Nur, Feza, Aydin. B.S., M.S., Tech. U. Istanbul, 1948; Ph.D., U. Mich., 1963. Asst. prof., then assoc. prof. Tech. U. Istanbul, 1948-58; resident research asso. Argonne (Ill.) Nat. Lab., 1959-61; mem. faculty U. Mich., Ann Arbor, 1963—; prof. nuclear engring. U. Mich., 1968—. Leading author: Mathematical Methods in Nuclear Reactor Dynamics, 1971; contbr. articles on statis. physics, reactor dynamics, plasma physics and polymer solution dynamic to profl. jours. Recipient Glenn Murphy award Am. Soc. Engring. Edn., 1986, Alexander von Humboldt rsch. award for sr. U.S. scientist, 1991, sci. award Turkish Sci. and Tech. Rsch. Coun., 1992, Excellence in Rsch. award U. Mich. Coll. Engring., 1995. Fellow Am. Nuclear Soc., Am. Phys. Soc.; mem. Am. Chem. Soc., Turkish Phys. Soc., Sigma Xi. Home: 2820 Pebble Creek Dr Ann Arbor MI 48108-1728 Office: U Mich Dept Nuclear Engring Ann Arbor MI 48109

AKER, ALAN D., state legislator. Logging contractor Rapid City, S.D.; senator Senate of S.D., Pierre; mem. agr. and natural resources com., edn. and local govt. coms. S.D. State Senate.

AKHTAR, SALEEM, electrical engineer, consultant; b. Sahiwal, Punjab, Pakistan, Dec. 26, 1949; s. Siddique Ahmed and Aisha Begum; m. Ramona Lee Yonts, Mar. 29, 1974 (dec. 1978); 1 child, Roshi Ramona; m. Fakhera Yasmin, Dec. 24, 1990; children: Rukhsaar Aisha, Faraan Saleem. BSEE, U. Karachi, Pakistan, 1972; MSEE, Ill. Inst. Tech., 1990. Tech. mgr. Kohlberg Theatres Inc., Chgo., 1973-74; elec. test engr. J.B. Electronic Transformer Inc., Chgo., 1974-80; elec. engr. Bechtel Power Corp., Ann Arbor, Mich., 1980-84; elec. engr. Sargent & Lundy Engrs., Chgo., 1984-91, sr. engr., 1988-91, project engr., 1991—. Contbr. articles to profl. jours. Active Muslim Cmty. Ctr., Chgo., 1986—. Mem. IEEE (sr.), Power Engring. Soc. (sr.). Islam. Home: 3059 N Drake Ave Chicago IL 60618 Office: Sargent & Lundy Engrs 55 E Monroe St Chicago IL 60603

AKIN, W. TODD, state legislator; b. N.Y.C., July 5, 1947; m. Lulli Boe, 1971; six children. BS, Worchester Polytechnic Inst.; MDiv, Covenant Theol. Sem. Mo. State rep. Dist. 86; corp. mgr. Laclede Steel Co.; bus. mgr., educator; former mktg. profl. IBM Computer Systems; mem. energy and environ. com., judiciary com., higher edn. com. and edn. appropriations com. Officer Army Engrs. Office: 305 Conway Hill Rd Saint Louis MO 63141-7239*

AKINS, JACQUELINE VAN AUKEN, architect; b. Cleve., July 26, 1960; d. Richard Anthony Van Auken and Ann (McPolin) McGee; m. William D. Akins, Sept. 30, 1989; 1 child, Ashley Elizabeth. BArch, U. Notre Dame, 1983. Registered architect, Ohio. Project architect Ronald Sarstedt Architects, Cleve., 1983-87; dir. mktg., project mgr. Richard L. Bowen & Assocs., Cleve., 1987-92; prin. Van Auken Akins Architects, Cleve., Ohio, 1992—. Mem. AIA, NCCJ, Architects Soc. Ohio, Notre Dame Alumni Club. Roman Catholic. Office: Van Auken Akins Architects 27629 Chagrin Blvd Ste 205 Cleveland OH 44122

AKRE, BRIAN SCOTT, journalist; b. Long Beach, Calif., Sept. 7, 1957; s. Sidney Palmer and Virginia Barbara (Repzynski) A. BA in Journalism, Humboldt State U., 1980. Reporter Grants Pass (Oreg.) Daily Courier, 1980-83; reporter, editor AP, Portland, Oreg., 1983-88; corr. AP, Juneau, Alaska, 1988-94; bus. writer AP, Detroit, 1994—. Mem. Alaska Capital Corrs. Assn. (co-founder, pres. 1989), Alaska Press Club, Soc. Profl. Journalists, Investigative Reporters and Editors Inc. Office: 300 River Pl Ste 2400 Detroit MI 48207

AKRED, RONALD J., design engineer; b. St. Clair, Mich., July 26, 1935. AD, DeVry Tech. Inst., Chgo., 1959. Design engr. Baker Elec. Products, Memphis, Mich., 1970—. Patentee in electronics. With USN, 1953-57. Mem. IEEE. Office: Baker Elec Products 34775 Potter St Memphis MI 48041-4613

AKROP, PAUL GREGORY, ski area administrator; b. Deadwood, S.D., Sept. 24, 1949; s. Paul John and Genevieve A. (Duchene) A. BS, Black Hills State Coll., Spearfish, S.D., 1971. Snow ranger USDA Forest Svc., Deadwood, 1967-73; patrolman S.D. Hwy. Dept., Pierre, 1972-74; self employed Lead, S.D., 1980-85; asst. mgr. Black Hills Chair Lift Co., Lead, S.D., 1974-80, pres., gen.mgr., 1985—; gen.mgr. Terry Peak Ski Area, Lead. Trustee Terry Trojan Water Dist., Lead, 1986—. Roman Catholic. Office: Black Hills Chair Lift Co PO Box 774 Lead SD 57754

ALAM, MOHAMMAD SHOWKAT-UL, engineering educator; b. Chittagong, Bangladesh, June 14, 1961; came to the U.S., 1987; s. Bazlur Rahim and Noorjahan Begum Chowdhury; m. Sharmeen Aktar Banu Alam, Sept. 8, 1990; children: Shabab Farjad Alam, Shayan Bassam Alam. BSEE, Bangladesh U. Engring. & Tech., Dhaka, 1983, MSEE, 1985; MS in Computer Engring., Wayne State U., 1989; PhD in Elec. Engring., U. Dayton, 1992. Tchg. asst. Bangladesh U. Engring. and Tech., Dhaka, 1983-84, lectr., 1984-86, asst. prof., 1986-87; asst. engr. Bangladesh Atomic Energy Com., Dhaka, 1984; tchg. assoc. U. Tex., Arlington, 1988; tchg./rsch. asst. Wayne State U., Detroit, 1988-89; tchg. asst. Wright State U., Dayton, Ohio, 1990; rsch. asst. U. Dayton, Ohio, 1991-92; asst. prof. Purdue U., Fort Wayne, Ind., 1992—; mem. Bur. Rsch. Testing and Consultation Com., Bangladesh U. Engring. and Tech., Dhaka, 1986-87. Contbr. chpt. to book and articles to profl. jours. Pres. Bangladesh Student Assn., Dayton, 1990; mem. Bangladesh Assn. Ohio, Cin., 1990-92. Grad. Student fellow U. Dayton, Ohio, 1992; Excel Rsch. grantee Purdue Rsch. Found., West Lafayette, Ind., 1993-95. Mem. IEEE (sr.; sec. Ft. Wayne sect. 1994, v.p. 1994-95, pres. 1995—), Optical Soc. Am., Internat. Soc. Optical Engring., Am. Inst. Physics, Inst. Engrs. Bangladesh. Home: 5040 E Madiera Dr Fort Wayne IN 46815 Office: Purdue Univ Fort Wayne 2101 Coliseum Blvd East Fort Wayne IN 46805-1499

ALANEN, ARNOLD ROBERT, landscape architecture educator; b. Wadena, Minn., Aug. 1, 1941; s. William Jalmer and Ina Esther (Pursi) A.; m. Linda Kay Ronnerud, May 7, 1967; children: Maija Helene, Marit Ingrid. BA, U. Minn., 1963, MA, 1968, PhD, 1973; postgrad., U. Helsinki, 1968-69. Assoc. planner Community Planning and Design Assocs., Mpls., 1963-67; rsch. asst. dept. geography U. Minn., Mpls., 1967-68, teaching assoc., 1970-72; sr. planner Met. Coun. Twin Cities, St. Paul, 1969-70; instr. dept. geography Va. Poly. Inst. and State U., Blacksburg, 1972-74; asst. prof. dept. landscape architecture U. Wis., Madison, 1974-79, assoc. prof., 1979-84, prof., 1984—, chair, 1985-88; vis. rsch. prof. U. Helsinki, 1982, evaluator faculty of sci., 1989, Helsinki U. of Tech., 1993; advisor Finnish Ministry of Edn., 1992; evaluator faculty of social sci. U. of Joensuu, Finland, 1993; cons. and advisor Nat. Park Svc., Washington, 1980—, Minn. Hist. Soc., St. Paul, 1982—; cons. Norwegian Winter Olympics, 1991-92. Author: Nordic Environment: Historical and Contemporary Perspectives, 1995; co-author: Main Street Ready Made (Gambrinus prize 1988); co-editor Landscape Jour., 1982-89 (merit award 1984); contr. articles to profl. jours. Pres. Finnish-Am. Soc., Madison, 1984; program chair Ygdrasil Norwegian Lit. Soc., Madison, 1988-90; mem. coun. Bethel Luth. Ch., Madison, 1990-93. With Minn. Nat. Guard, 1963-68. Fulbright fellow U. Helsinki, 1968-69, W.K. Kellogg Found. fellow, 1980-83; recipient Outstanding Publ. award Minn. Hist. Soc., 1983, Excellence in Teaching award U. Wis. Alumni Assn., 1984. Mem. Finnish Geog. Soc., Alliance for Hist. Landscape Preservation (bd. dirs. 1989-96), Vernacular Arch. Forum, Assn. Am. Geographers, Am. Soc. City Planning and Regional Planning History, Coun. Educators in Landscape Architecture (spl. recognition award 1989). Democrat. Lutheran. Home: 1910 W Lawn Ave Madison WI 53711-2010 Office: U Wis Dept Landscape Architecture Dept Landscape Architecture Madison WI 53706

ALBAN, ROGER CHARLES, construction equipment distribution executive; b. Columbus, Ohio, Aug. 3, 1948; s. Charles Ellis and Alice Jacqueline (Hosfeld) A.; divorced; children: Allison Ann, Roger Charles II, Charles Michael. Student pub. schs. With Alban Equipment Co., Columbus, 1963—, sales mgr., 1972-75, gen. mgr., 1975-85, treas., 1978-85, v.p., 1980-85, pres. 1985—. Mem. Grandview Heights Bd. Edn., Columbus, 1978-85, pres., 1979, v.p., 1982, legis. liaison, 1978-79, 83-84, re-elected mem., 1992-93; elected Grandview Heights City Coun., 1986; mem. Met. Ednl. Coun., Columbus Area Leadership Program, 1982-83. Trustee Builders Exch. Benefit Trust, 1987—, chmn. 1996. Mem. Assoc. Equipment Distbrs. (lt. dir. region 6 1980, 85, 86, 88, dir. 1989-91, chmn. light equipment dist. com. 1985, chmn. sales and mktg. com. 1988, elected dir. region 6 1989-92), Ohio Sch. Bds. Assn. (all-ctrl. region bd. 1984), Bldg. Industry Assn. Ctrl. Ohio,

Am. Rental Assn., Builders Exch. Ctrl. Ohio (dir. 1990—, elected treas. 1996, 2nd v.p. 1996—), Am. Mgmt. Assn., Nat. Right To Work Com., Nat. Fedn. Ind. Bus., Ohio Equipment Distbrs. Assn. (dir. 1982, 84-91, pres. 1983), Roundtable, Mensa (chpt. exec. com. 1979-80), Rotary (elected Columbus dir. 1994), Downtown Columbus Club. Roman Catholic. Home: 827 Northwest Blvd Columbus OH 43212-3833 Office: 1825 McKinley Ave Columbus OH 43222-1003

ALBERS, SHERYL KAY, state legislator; b. Sauk County, Wis., Sept. 9, 1954; d. Marcus J. and Norma Anderson Gumz; m. James Albert Albers, 1978; 1 child, Joel Albert. BA, Ripon Coll., 1976. Dairy farmer. Publicity chmn. Sauk County Rep. Com., Wis., 1978-80, vice chmn., 1980-82, chmn., 1982-83, mem. exec. com.; exec. asst. dir. assembly Rep. Caucus Wis.; state assemblyman dist. 50 State of Wis., 1991—, mem. govt. export strategy com., chair assembly ins., securities and corp. policy com., mem. environ. resources com., mem. rural affairs com., mem. natural resources com., mem. colls. and univs. com., mem. state bldg. commn. Recipient Campbell award Sauk County Rep. Com., 1981, 90, Top 10 County award Wis. State Rep. Party, 1982, Pacesetter award Wis. Forage Coun., 1983, Bovay award Rep. Party Wis., 1990; named one of Outstanding Farmers Sauk County Farm Bur., 1982. Mem. Sauk County Farm Bur. (dir., treas. 1977-82), Agrl. Bus. Coun. Wis., LEPC Sauk County and Juneau County, Kiwanis. Republican. Home: 56896 Seeley Creek Rd Loganville WI 53943*

ALBERT, CHRISTINE LYNNETTE, accountant; b. Stillman Valley, Ill., May 21, 1965; d. Charles Ralph and June Ruth (Freeman) Peterson; m. James Howard Albert, May 28, 1988. AAS in Bus., Rock Valley Coll., 1986; BS in Acctg., Rockford Coll., 1992. CPA, Ill. Bookkeeper, supr. Harwood Aviation, Inc., Rockford, Ill., 1984-86; comml. lending credit analyst Bank One 1st Nat. Bank, Rockford, 1986-92; acct. Ringdahl's, Inc., Rockford, 1992-95; treas. analyst Woods Equipment Co., 1995—; owner, pres. CLA Fin. Svcs. Student mem. Coast Guard Aux., Ill., 1994; fundraiser Chgo. Children's Hosp., 1992-95. Mem. Ill. CPA Soc., Inst. Mgmt. Accts. (bd. dirs.), Golf League (treas.). Home: 7170 S Main St Rockford IL 61102-5114

ALBERT, DANIEL MYRON, ophthalmologist, educator; b. Newark, Dec. 19, 1936; s. Maurice I. and Flora Albert; m. Eleanor Kagle, June 26, 1960; children: B. Steven, Michael. B.S., Franklin and Marshall Coll., 1958; M.D., U. Pa., 1962; M.A. (hon.), Harvard U., 1976; D honoris causa, Louis Pasteur U., Strasbourg, 1992. Diplomate: Am. Bd. Ophthalmology. Intern Hosp. U. Pa., 1962-63, resident, 1963-66; surgeon USPHS, 1966-68; NIH spl. fellow in ophthalmic pathology Armed Forces Inst. Pathology, 1968-69; practice medicine specializing in ophthalmology; assoc. surgeon Mass. Eye and Ear Infirmary, 1976-86, surgeon, 1986-92, dir. David G. Cogan eye pathology lab., 1979-92, surgeon, 1986-92; asst. prof. ophthalmology Yale U. Sch. Medicine, 1969-70, assoc. prof., 1970-75, prof., 1975-76; prof. ophthalmic pathology Harvard U. Med. Sch., 1976-84, David G. Cogan prof. ophthalmology, 1984-92; Frederick Allison Davis prof., chmn. dept. ophthalmology U. Wis., Madison, 1992—. Author: (with Scheie) A History of Ophthalmology at the University of Pennsylvania, 1965, Textbook of Ophthalmology, 8th edit. 1969, 9th edit. 1977; author: Jaeger's Atlas of Ophthalmology, 1972, Foundations of Ophthalmology, 1979; (with Jacobiec) Atlas of Clinical Ophthalmology, 1996; (with Edwards) History of Ophthalmology, 1996; co-editor Principles and Practice of Ophthalmology, 1994; editor Archives of Ophthalmology, 1994—; contbr. articles to profl. jours. Recipient Friedenwald award, 1981, Von Sallmann award in vision and ophthalmology Internat. Conf. for Eye Rsch., 1988, award Humboldt Found., 1991, Mackenzie medal Scottish Ophthal. Soc., 1992, Jackson Meml. medal Am. Acad. Ophthalmology, 1996; William and Mary Greve scholar, 1978-79, scholar Alcon Rsch. Inst., 1984-85. Fellow ACS; mem. Am. Assn. Ophthalmic Pathology (Zimmerman medal 1993), Am. Acad. Ophthalmology (Jackson medal 1996). Jewish. Home: 1106 Wellesley Rd Madison WI 53705-2230 Office: U Wis Hosp and Clinics Dept Ophthalmology F4/334 600 Highland Ave Madison WI 53792-0001

ALBERT, GREGORY CHARLES, artist, book editor; b. Cin., Sept. 7, 1953; s. George Albert. BFA, No. Ky. U., 1976; MFA, U. Mont., 1978; MA in Art History, U. Cin., 1983. Instr. Art Acad. Cin., 1979—; lectr. Miami U., Oxford, Ohio, 1983-86; editor F&W Publs., Cin., 1986—, sr. editor, 1988—. Author: Drawing: You Can Do It, 1992. Home: 2843 Viki Ter Cincinnati OH 45211-7214 Office: F&W Publs 1507 Dana Ave Cincinnati OH 45207-1056

ALBERT, JANYCE LOUISE, business educator, banker; b. Toledo, July 27, 1932; d. Howard C. and Glenola Mae (Masters) Blessing; m. John R. Albert, Aug. 7, 1954; children: John R., James H. Student Ohio Wesleyan U., 1949-51; BA, Mich. State U., 1953; MS, Iowa State U., 1980. Asst. pers. mgr./tng. supr. Sears, Roebuck & Co., Toledo, 1953-56; tchr. adult edn. Tenafly Pub. Schs. (N.J.), 1966-70; pers. officer, tng. officer, tng. and edn. mgr. Iowa Dept. Transp., Ames, 1974-77; coll. recruiting coord. Rockwell Internat., Cedar Rapids, Iowa, 1977-79, engring. adminstrn. mgr., 1979-80; employee rels. and job evaluation analyst Phillips Petroleum Co., Bartlesville, Okla., 1980-81; v.p., dir. pers. Rep. Bancorp, Tulsa, 1981-83; sr. v.p. and dir. human resources First Nat. Bank, Rockford, Ill., 1983-94; dir. bus. divsn. Rock Valley Coll., Rockford, 1994—; advisor to Nat. Profl. Secs. Assn. Bd. dirs. Rocvale Children's Home., 1986—, pres., 1991-94; v.p. bd. dirs. United Way of Ames, 1976-77; mem. employee svc. comm., Rockford Pub. Schs., 1988-92; bd. dirs. Rockford Human Resources Community Action Program (bd. mem. of the year 1992), Womenspace Ctr., 1993-95, Riverside Cmty. Bank, 1995—; chairperson legis. com., Rockford Human Svcs. Dept.; chairperson Rockford State of Ill. Job Svcs. Employers Coun., 1990—; publicity chmn. Tenafly 300th Ann. Celebration, 1969; mem. task force Rockford Bd. Educators, 1993-94; mem. gala com. Janet Wattles Mental Health Ctr., 1990; bd. deacons Presbyn. Ch., Ames, 1972-75; mem. adv. coun. Rockford YWCA, bd. dirs., 1986; co-chmn. YWCA Leader Luncheon, 1986—; advisor Rockford chpt. ARC, 1991—; mem. Mayor's Task Force for Rockford Project Self-Sufficiency, 1986-89, chmn. adv. coun., 1991; chairperson info. and referral com. United Way of Rockford and Contact, 1994—, acct. exec. 1993—; bd. dirs. Rockford Symphony Orch., 1992-95, sec., 1994-95, Rockford Leadership Found., 1994—; dir. bus. divsn. Rock Valley Coll., Rockford, Ill., 1994—. Pres.'s scholar, 1951-53; recipient YWCA Kate O'Connor award for Women in Labor Force 1984, Athena award Rockford C. of C., 1991. Mem. Rockford Network (past chairperson 1985, 86), Rockford C. of C. (transp. com., human resources com., leadership program 1989, pres. club 1992-94), Rockford Pers. Assn. (co-chmn. programs 1985-86, adv. coun. 1983—), Am. Soc. Pers. Adminstrn., Employee Benefits Assn. No. Ill. (membership chmn.), Womenspace (bd. dirs. 1993-95), Rockford Personal and Profl. Power Coalition, P.E.O., Rockford Panhellenic Coun. (sec. 1992-93, treas. 1993-94, v.p., 1994-95, pres. 1995-96, Woman of Yr. award 1994), World Trade Coun. (bd. dirs. 1994—), Sigma Epsilon, Alpha Gamma Delta, Phi Kappa Phi. Home: 5587 Thunderidge Dr Rockford IL 61107-1756 Office: Rock Valley Coll Bus Divsn 3301 N Mulford Rd Rockford IL 61114-5640

ALBERTSON, K. THOMAS, environmental affairs executive. BS in Civil Engring., Iowa State U., 1980; MBA, St. Ambrose U., Davenport, Iowa, 1984. Registered profl. engr., Iowa, Ill. Mgr. transmission engring. Mid-Am. Energy Co., Davenport, Iowa, 1995—. Office: Mid-Am Energy Co 206 E 2nd St Davenport IA 52801

ALBRECHT, BEVERLY JEAN, special education educator; b. Dixon, Ill., Sept. 8, 1936; d. Harold Ivan Foster and Grace Gertrude Tracy Freed; m. Marvin Blackert Albrecht, Aug. 13, 1960; children: Bradley K., Brent D., Kimberly S. Albrecht Schluns. BS, Manchester Coll., North Manchester, Ind., 1958; MS, No. Ill. U., 1978. Cert. in elem. edn., educable mentally handicapped, learning disabled, supervision and early childhood edn., Ill. Kindergarten tchr. Sch. Dist. 300, Carpentersville, Ill, 1958-60; thcr. 5th grade Sch. Dist. 5, Sterling, Ill., 1960-61, 64-65, kindergarten tchr., 1962-64, substitute tchr., 1965-71; dir. nursery sch. Sterling YWCA, 1971-75; program dir. Ctr. for Human Devel., Sterling, 1975-76; family advocate Ill. Dept. Child and Family Svcs., Rock Falls, 1977-78; learning disablities and behavior disorders spl. edn. tchr. Sch. Dist. 289, Mendota, Ill., 1978-84, devel. pre-sch. tchr., 1984-89; clinician, case mgr., family preservation Sinnissippi Ctrs. Inc., Sterling, 1989—; replication specialist PEECH project U. Ill., Champaign, 1985-88; supervisory faculty Ill. State U., Normal, 1983-85, Ill. Valley C.C., Oglesby 1985-89. Host family Rock River Valley Internat. Fellowships, Sterling, 1975-92; chair coun. on edn. United Meth. Ch., Rock Falls, 1973-75, supt., tchr. ch. sch., 1968-88. Spl. Edn. fellow Ill. Office of Pub. Instrn., 1966; name grant honoree United Meth. Women, Rock Falls. Mem. NEA, Ill. Edn. Assn., Coun. for Exceptional Children. Republican. Home: 3254 Mineral Springs Rd Sterling IL 61081-4107

ALBRECHT, CHRIS EVAN, mechanical engineer; b. Champaign, Ill., Feb. 10, 1971. BSME, Milw. Sch. Engring., 1993. Design engr. Trison Machinery, Ltd., Milw., 1993—. Republican. Lutheran. Office: Trison Machinery Ltd 12020 W Ripley Ave Milwaukee WI 53226-3824

ALBRECHT, DIANE D., fundraiser; b. Portland, Oreg., Oct. 10, 1945; d. Earl and Vera (Rohm) Ode; m. Warren H. Albrecht, Feb. 10, 1967; children: Warren, Nikki. AA, Stephens Coll. Dir. devel. N.D. Easter Seals, Bismarck; dir., coord. N.D. C.A., Fargo; mem. advance team, v.p. Dan Quayle Office of V.P., Washington; fundraiser March of Dimes, Bismarck. Vol. N.D. Rep. Party, Bismarck. Mem. PEO. Lutheran.

ALBRECHT, EDWARD DANIEL, metals manufacturing company executive; b. Kewanee, Ill., Feb. 11, 1937; s. Edward Albert and Mary Jane (Horner) A.; BS in Metall. Engring., U. Ariz., 1959, MS, 1961, PhD, 1964, Metal. Engr. (hon.), 1973; m. Martha L. Fry, May 21, 1988; 1 child, Deborah J. Registered profl. engr., Calif. Rsch. metallurgist U. Calif. Los Alamos Lab., 1959-61; sr. physicist, project mgr. U. Calif. Lawrence Radiation Lab., Livermore, 1964-71; founder, pres. Metall. Innovations Inc., Pleasanton, Calif., 1969-71; chmn. bd., 1971-73; gen. mgr. Buehler Ltd. & Adolph I. Buehler, Inc., Lake Bluff, Ill., 1972, v.p., gen. mgr., 1973-76, chmn., pres., 1976-84, also dir.; pres. bd. dirs. Buehler-Met AG Basel, Switzerland, 1983-87; pres. Mowlem Tech. Inc., Lake Bluff, 1984-86; founder, pres., chief exec. officer, Buehler Internat. Inc., 1985-90, chmn., 1988-91, chmn. emeritus, 1991—; chmn. bd. Soiltest, Inc., Evanston, Ill., 1984-88, CPN Corp., Pacheco, Calif., 1984-89; bd. dirs. S.W. Steel, Inc., Tulsa, vice chmn., 1993-96, Gallery 10, Inc., Scottsdale, Ariz., 1988-94, Maxcor Mfg. Inc., Colorado Springs, Colo., 1990-92, Coal Gasification, Inc., Scottdale, Ariz., chmn. bd., 1986-87, 93—, Advanced Ceramic Rsch., Inc., Tucson, Ariz., 1995—; mem. indsl. adv. com. dept materials sci. and engring. U. Wash., 1993—; mem. alumni and indsl. rels. com. dept. aerospace and mech. engring. U. Ariz., 1996—. Bd. dirs. Danville (Calif.) Homeowners Inc., treas., 1966-68; trustee Lake Forest Acad.-Ferry Hall Prep Sch., 1977-81; mem. nat. adv. bd. Heard Mus. Anthropology, Phoenix, 1980-92, chmn., 1990-92, ex officio trustee, 1990-92, trustee, 1992—, v.p., 1995—, chmn. collections com., 1993—; trustee Millicent Rogers Mus., Taos, N.Mex., 1982-91, chmn. devel. com., 1983-85, hon. trustee, 1993. Recipient Alumni Citizenship award U. Ariz., 1982, Disting. Alumni Centennial medallion, 1989; NDEA fellow, 1959-62. Fellow Royal Micros. Soc. Eng. Mem. Am. Soc. Metals (chmn. Tucson 1961, fellow, 1976, disting. life mem. 1989); mem. Internat. Metallographic Soc. (v.p. 1971-73, 93-95, pres. 1973-75, 95—, dir. 1975-81, chmn. gen. tech. meeting San Francisco 1969, Chgo. 1972, Brighton, Eng., 1980, Albuquerque 1995, Pres's. award 1981, Henry Clifton Sorby award 1990), Deutsche Gesellschaft für Metallkunde, Inst. Materials, Eng., Sigma Gamm Epsilon, Delta Upsilon. Clubs: Chicago, Onwentsia (Lake Forest, Ill.), Desert Highlands, Paradise Valley (Ariz.), Quail Run (Santa Fe). Contbr. articles to profl. jours. Patentee in field. Office: Buehler Internat Inc PO Box 1 Lake Bluff IL 60044-0001

ALBRECHT, JOHN T., financial executive; b. Ann Arbor, Mich., Apr. 19, 1945. BS, U. Mich., 1967, MS, 1969. Lic. NASD, SCC, N.Y. Stock Exch. V.p. Saudi Arabia City Bank of N.Y., N.Y.C., 1969-79; family advisor Nat. Comml. Bank Saudi Arabia, Jeddah, 1979-83; v.p. Mfrs. Nat. Bank, Detroit, 1983-88, Dean Witter Reynolds, Detroit, 1988—. Bd. dirs. Christ's Episcopal Ch., Detroit. Office: Dean Witter Reynolds 17th Fl 333 W Fort St Detroit MI 48226-3134

ALBRECHT, SHARI FEIST, administrative law hearing officer; b. Lawrence, Kans., Mar. 9, 1959; d. Aaron Henry and Myrna Lee (Rumbaugh) Feist; m. Martin Kent Albrecht, Nov. 26, 1988; children: Claire Elizabeth, Amanda Leigh. BA in Spanish Lit., U. Kans., 1982; JD, Washburn U., 1984. Bar: Kans. 1984, U.S. Dist. Ct. Kans. 1984, U.S. Supreme Ct. 1988. Staff atty. Kans. Corp. Commn., Topeka, 1984-87; acting dir. conservation div. Kans. Corp. Commn., Wichita, 1987, dir. conservation div., 1987-91; acting gen. counsel Kans. Corp. Commn., Topeka, 1991; dep. dir. conservation div. Kans. Corp. Commn., Wichita, 1991; hearing officer Kans. Dept. Health and Environ., Topeka, 1993—; mem. Kans. delegation Interstate Oil Compact Commn., Oklahoma City, 1987-90, mem. regulatory practices com., 1988-90, horizontal drilling subcom., 1990. Author (manual) Kans. Ind. Oil and Gas Assn. Environ. Guide, 1991. Mem. Kans. Bar Assn. (Young Lawyers rep. 1987), Wichita Bar Assn., Supreme Ct. Hist. Soc., Women Attys. Assn. Office: Kans Dept Health Environ Ste 400 D Mills Bldg 109 SW 9th St Topeka KS 66612

ALBRECHT, THEODORE JOHN, conductor, music historian; b. Jamestown, N.Y., Sept. 24, 1945; s. Herman George and Margaret Ann (Sapper) A.; m. Carol Padgham, Aug. 16, 1976. BME, St. Mary's U., San Antonio, 1967; MM, North Tex. State U., 1969, PhD, 1975. Asst. prof. Appalachian State U., Boone, N.C., 1975-76; lectr. Case Western Res. U., Cleve., 1976-80; prof. Park Coll., Kansas City, Mo., 1980-92; music dir. Philharmonia of Greater Kansas City, 1980-92; prof. Kent (Ohio) State U., 1992—; music dir. German Concert Orch., Cleve., 1978-80; program annotator Kansas City Symphony, 1982-91. Condr. U.S. premieres of von Einem's Bruckner Dialog, 1982, Ludi Leopoldini, 1983 and Pfitzner's Symphony in C, Op. 46, 1984; first U.S. condr. to perform compete (9) Dvorak symphonies; editor: (with Thayer) Salieri; Rival of Mozart, 1989; translator (works by Weingartner) On Performing the Symphonies of Mozart, On Performing the Symphonies of Schubert and Schubert, 1987; translator-editor: Letters to Beethoven, 3 vols., 1996. Capt. U.S. Army, 1970-72. Recipient Excellence in Edn. award Northland C. of C., Kansas City, 1985. Mem. Am. Musicological Soc., Condrs.' Guild (asst. editor jour. 1987-91), Coll. Music Soc. (editor Symposium 1983-86), Am. Beethoven Soc. Home: 1635 Chadwick St Kent OH 44240-4409 Office: Kent State U Sch Music Kent OH 44242

ALBRECHT, WILLARD HAROLD, retired medical educator; b. Elkhart, Ind., June 12, 1926; s. Aaron J. and Kathrine R. (Hooley) A.; m. Mary Ann McMahn, Sept. 6, 1959; children: Sharon, Grace, Clara, John, Douglas. BA in Natural Sci., Goshen Coll., 1954; MD, Northwestern U., Chgo., 1958. Diplomate Am. Bd. Anesthesiology. Asst. dir. dept. anesthesiology Wishard Hosp., Indpls., 1963-93; asst. prof. Ind. U. Med. Sch., Indpls., 1969-93, asst. prof. emeritus, 1993—; v.p. Dryden Corp., Indpls., 1970-87; dir. Paoli (Ind.) Peaks-Ski, 1992—; dir. Global Gifts-Self Help, Indpls., 1994—. Contbr. articles to profl. jours. Home: 7400 Hollingsworth Indianapolis IN 46268

ALBRIGHT, DIANNE ELIZABETH, counseling educator; b. Phila., Dec. 20, 1944; d. William Henry Walters and Eleanor Florence (Astfalk) Walters Schmidt; m. Paul Robert Albright, June 1966 (div. Sept. 1973); children: Cherie Lynnette, Lisa Renee. BMus, Ea. Nazarene Coll., 1967; postgrad., Rivier Coll., 1978-79; MEd, Plymouth State U., 1990; PhD, Ohio U., 1994. Cert. tchr. music K-12, elem. K-6, guidance counselor, N.H., Mass., Conn.; lic. profl. clin. counselor, Ohio. Social worker Mass. Dept. Welfare, Dedham, 1968-70; sustitute tchr. Braintree/Quincy (Mass.) Pub. Schs., 1970-77; music tchr. Nashua (N.H.) Pub. Schs., 1976-80, classroom tchr., 1980-90; clin. counselor Backus Hosp., Norwich, Conn., 1990-91; sch. counselor Plainfield (Conn.) Pub. Schs., 1990-91; instr. Ohio U., Athens, 1991-94; asst. prof., coord. counselor edn. Cen. Mo. State U., 1994—; ednl. cons. IBM, Bedford, N.H., 1983-84; rsch. asst. NASA Mascot Project, Ohio U. Athens, 1992-93. Author: (booklet) Am. Counseling Assn., 1993; contbr. articles to profl. jours. Recipient scholarship grad. assn. Ohio. U., Athens, 1991-94, fellowship Chi Sigma Iota, 1992. Mem. ACA, Ohio Counseling Assn., Assn. for Humanistic Edn. and Devel. (editl. asst. 1992-94, sec.-elect 1993-94, sec. 1994-95, treas. 1996—, editl. bd. 1994—), Mo. Counseling Assn., Internat. Assn. Marriage and Family Counselors, Assn. for Counselor Edn. and Supervision, Am. Sch. Counselors Assn., Phi Delta Kappa, Phi Kappa Phi, Chi Sigma Iota (assoc. editor 1993-96, pres. Alpha chpt. Ohio U. 1992-93, Outstanding Chpt. award 1993). Home: 616 S Main St Apt 5 Warrensburg MO 64093-1550 Office: Central Mo State Univ Dept Pysch Warrensburg MO 64093

ALBRIGHT, MINDY SUE, college health and geriatrics nurse; b. Wooster, Ohio, June 29, 1955; d. Ernest Clyde and Miriam Jean (Leighty) Yates: m. Jerrold Arden Albright, Aug. 27, 1974; children: Franz, Emil, Ewen. Student, Kent State U., Canton, Ohio, 1973-74, Aultman Hosp. Sch. Nursing, Canton, 1973-75; AS with honors, North Cen. Tech. Coll., Mansfield, Ohio, 1986. RNC (coll. health nurse); cert. hynotherapist. Staff nurse Altercare of Millersburg, Ohio, 1986-87, Emerald Svcs., Lodi, Ohio, 1988—; supr. Good Shepherd Home, Ashland, Ohio, 1987-90; staff nurse Coll. of Wooster, 1988—; supr. Shady Lawn Nursing Home, Wooster, Ohio, 1990—; camp nurse Wooster Outdoor Ctr., Perrysville, Ohio, 1993—; owner Wellness Success Ctr., Wooster. Mem. Am. Coll. Health Assn., Ohio Coll. Health Assn. Home: 3441 Lattasburg Rd Wooster OH 44691-9223 Office: Coll of Wooster Hygeia Hall Wooster OH 44691

ALBRINCK, JAMES LOUIS, manufacturing company executive; b. Cin., July 21, 1943; s. Louis Joseph and Florence Virginia (Santel) A.; m. Susan Malloy, May 27, 1967; children: Amy Susan, Margaret Lynn. AS, SUNY, Albany, 1983. Prodn. schedule coord. Continental Can Co., Cin., 1967-69; mgr. staff svcs. Continental Can Co., Columbus, Ohio, 1970-75, Worthington, Ohio, 1975-80, Elwood, Ind., 1981-84; divsn. mgr. prodn. planning Continental Can Co., Milw., 1984-86; project mgr. Mfg. Resources Planning II Continental Can Co., Norwalk, Conn., 1986-90; corp. mgr. Statis. Process Control Crown Cork and Seal Co., Phila., 1990—. Councilman Village of Pickerington (Ohio), 1975-80, pres. coun., 1978-80. With U.S. Army, 1964-65. Fellow Am. Prodn. and Inventory Control Soc. (cert.); mem. Pickerington Jaycees (pres. 1976), Ozaukee Amateur Radio Club (v.p. 1992, pres. 1986). Roman Catholic. Home: 6616 Locksley Ln Cedarburg WI 53012-8845 Office: Crown Cork and Seal Co Ste 240 11925 W Lake Park Dr Milwaukee WI 53224

ALCORN, WALLACE ARTHUR, minister; b. Milw., Aug. 29, 1930; s. William Keith and Dora Mildred (Brazee) A.; m. Ann Margaret Carmichael, June 5, 1958; children: John Mark, Allison Alcorn-Oppedahl, Stephen Paul. Student, Marquette U., 1950; AB, Wheaton Coll., 1952; MDiv, Grand Rapids Bapt. Theol. Sem., 1959; AM, Wheaton Grad. Sch. Theology, 1959; postgrad., Mich. State U., 1959-60, U. Mich., 1960-61; ThM, Princeton Theol. Sem., 1965; PhD, NYU, 1974; cert. in clin. pastoral edn., Fitzsimons Army Med. Ctr., 1975; postgrad., U. Minn., 1980-81. Ordained to ministry Gen. Assn. Regular Bapt. Chs., 1957. Pastor Caddy Vista Bapt. Ch., Caldonia, Wis., 1955-57, Bloomfield Hills (Mich.) Bapt. Ch., 1960-61, Community Bapt. Ch. Shark River Hills, Neptune, N.J., 1961-67, 1st Bapt. Ch., Austin, Minn., 1976-83; prof. bible Moody Bible Inst., Chgo., 1967-73; assoc. prof. N.T. N.W. Bapt. Sem., Tacoma, 1974-76; affiliate chaplain Madigan Army Med. Ctr., Tacoma, 1974-76; police chaplain Tacoma, 1974-76, Austin, Minn., 1976—; prin. Wallace Alcorn Assocs., Austin, 1983—; pastoral counselor New Life Family Svcs., Rochester, Minn., 1987—; radio tchr. Moody Radio Network, 1968-74; radio commentator Sta. KTIS and Northwestern Coll. Network, 1987—; columnist Austin (Minn.) Daily Herald, 1993—; adj. faculty Austin C.C., 1994—; chmn. Minn. Assn. Regular Bapt. Chs., 1980-83; pres. Faith Acad., Fridley, Minn., 1986. Author: The Bible as Literature, 1965, Elijah, Prophet of God, 1972, The Life of Christ Visualized, 1973, Knowing and Using the Bible, 1975, Momentum, 1986; nat. editor Christian Life, 1956-59, Mil. Life, 1983-86; N.T. editor Living Bible Commentary, 1974-76; contbr. Wycliffe Bible Ency., 1974, Tyndale Family Bible Ency., 1976, New Commentary on the Whole Bible, 1990, The Book We Love, 1994; contbr. numerous articles to profl. jours. Mem. citizen's adv. coun. Neptune (N.J.) Bd. Edn., 1965-67; chair Austin Human Rights Commn., 1989—; mem. profl. adv. coun. Pub. Edn. Religion Studies Ctr., Wright State U., 1972-76; dir. 10th jud. dist. ethics com. League of Minn. Human Rights Commn.; dir. The Good News Hour, Austin, 1976-83. With USNR, 1947-52, U.S. Army, 1952-54, USAR, 1954-57, chaplain, col., 1957-90. Mem. Evang. Theol. Soc., Evang. Press Assn., Nat. Assn. Religious Broadcasters, Mil. Chaplains Assn. (pres. Chgo. chpt. 1970-74), hist. socs. Wis., Ohio, S.C. Home: 1010 7th Ave NW Austin MN 55912-2153 Office: PO Box 733 Austin MN 55912-0733

ALDAG, JEROME MARVIN, mechanical engineer, executive; b. Sheboygan, Wis., Nov. 19, 1929; s. Marvin Otto and Daisy B. (Jackson) A.; m. Sally Lou Mahnke, May 4, 1956 (dec. 1969); children: David, Heidi, Timothy, Jessica; m. Patricia Jean Schmidt, July 10, 1970. Student Wis. Engring. Sch., 1950-52. Registered profl. engr., Wis. Engr., Aldag Sheet Metal Works Inc. (name change to Aldag/Honold Mech., Inc.), Sheboygan, 1954-60, engr. in charge, 1960-68, pres., 1968—, chief exec. officer, chmn. bd. dir., 1991—; pres. Aldag Engring. Cons., Sheboygan, 1974—; chief exec. officer, chmn. bd. Lakeside Maintenance Inc., Manitowoc, Wis. Served with USNR, 1949-58. Mem. ASHRAE, Nat. Soc. Profl. Engrs., Air Pollution Bd. Republican. Lutheran. Club: Sheboygan Yacht Club, Pine Hills Country Club. Lodges: Elks, Kiwanis (pres. Lake Shore club 1985-86, lt. gov. div. II Wis./Upper Mich.). Avocations: skiing, yachting, hunting. Home: 645 Greentree Rd Kohler WI 53044-1459 Office: Aldag/Honold Mech Inc PO Box 1265 Sheboygan WI 53082-1265

ALDERMAN, ROBERT K., state legislator; b. Nov. 14, 1942; m. Susan M. Toycen. Student, Ind. U. Ind. state rep. Dist. 19, 1976-91, Dist. 83, 1991—; chmn. housing aged and aging com. Ind. Ho. Reps., Vet. Affairs com., pub. safety com., human affairs and interstate coop. coms., ranking minority mem., pub. policy com., ethics com., rules and legis. procedures com., local govt. com. Capt. Allen County Police Dept., Ft. Wayne. With U.S. Army Nat. Guard. Recipient Acad. Achievement award Ind. Law Enforcement Acad., 1971; named Top 10 Legislators Am. Nat. Assembly Govt. Employee, 1983. Republican. Home: 5715 Kroemer Rd Fort Wayne IN 46818-9328*

ALDRICH, ANN, federal judge; b. Providence, June 28, 1927; d. Allie C. and Ethel M. (Carrier) A.; m. Chester Aldrich, 1960 (dec.); children: Martin, William; children by previous marriage: James, Allen; m. John H. McAllister III, 1986. BA cum laude, Columbia U., 1948; LLB cum laude, NYU, 1950, LLM, 1964, JSD, 1967. Bar: D.C. bar, N.Y. bar 1952, Conn. bar 1966, Ohio bar 1973, Supreme Ct. bar 1956. Research asst. to mem. faculty N.Y. U. Sch. Law; atty. IBRD, 1952; atty., rsch. asst. Samuel Nakasian, Esq., Washington, 1952-53; mem. gen. counsel's staff FCC, Washington, 1953-60; U.S. del. to Internat. Radio Conf., Geneva, 1959; practicing atty. Darien, Conn., 1961-68; asso. prof. law Cleve. State U., 1968-71, prof., 1971-80; judge U.S. Dist. Ct. (no. dist.) Ohio, Cleveland, 1980—; bd. govs. Citizens' Communications Center, Inc., Washington; mem. litigation com.; guest lectr. Calif. Inst. Tech., Pasadena, summer 1971. Mem. Fed. Bar Assn., Nat. Assn. of Women Judges, Fed. Communications Bar Assn., Fed. Judge Assn. Episcopalian. Office: US Dist Ct 201 Superior Ave E Cleveland OH 44114-1201

ALDRICH, MICHAEL SHERMAN, neurologist, educator; b. Mpls., May 23, 1949; s. C. Knight and Julie H. (Murphy) A.; m. Leslie B. Aldrich, Oct. 20, 1985; children: Brian, Matthew, Jennifer. BA, Swarthmore (Pa.) Coll., 1970; MD, U. Va., 1980. Intern in internal medicine U. Mich., Ann Arbor, 1980-81, resident in neurology, 1981-84; fellow in sleep medicine Stanford (Calif.) U., 1984; fellow in neurophysiology U. Mich., Ann Arbor, 1984-85, instr. neurology, 1985-86, asst. prof. neurology, 1986-92, assoc. prof. neurology, 1992—, dir. sleep disorders ctr., 1985—; pres. Am. Bd. Sleep Medicine, Rochester, Minn., 1994—. Editor: Sleep Disorders, 1996, (CD-Rom) Neurobase-Sleep Disorders, 1994; mem. editl. bd. jour. Sleep, 1991—. Fellow Am. Sleep Disorders Assn. (adv. bd. 1987-91); mem. Am. Acad. Neurology. Office: U Mich Dept Neurology TC 1920-0316 Ann Arbor MI 48109

ALDRIDGE, SANDRA, civic volunteer; b. Iowa, Apr. 22, 1939; d. Maurice D. and Maureen M. (Bennett) Anderson; m. Guy E. Seymour, Jan. 8, 1960 (div. Oct. 1966); m. Victor E. Aldridge, Jr., Nov. 11, 1970; 1 child, Victor E. III. Student, Millikin U., Decatur, Ill., 1957-58. Pres. Crawford Sch. PTA, 1976-78, Terre Haute Lawyers Aux., 1979; pres., dir. Wabash Valley Assn. for Gifted and Talented Children, 1981-83, Vigo County Task Force for Alcohol and Drug Abuse, 1983-84; treas., dir. Union Hosp. Svc. League; bd. dirs. YWCA of Terre Haute, Inc., 1987-89; v.p., fin. chair, mem. exec. coun. Wabash Valley coun. Boy Scouts Am., Inc.; mem. Vigo County Tax Adjustment Bd., 1986-88; mem. Class IX Leadership Terre Haute, 1985; bd. trustees Vigo County Sch. Corp., Terre Haute, 1985—, v.p., 1992-93; active Children's Theatre, United Way of Wabash Valley. Mem. Ind. Assn. Gifted

Children, Swope Art Gallery, Vigo County Hist. Soc., Women's Dept. Club, Arts Illiana, Elks Women's Golf League. Democrat. Episcopalian. Home: 2929 Winthrop Rd Terre Haute IN 47802

ALESHIRE, RICHARD JOE, banker; b. Anthony, Kans., Feb. 18, 1947; s. Robert Allen and Alma Evelyn (Chesnut) A.; m. Janet Jean Bohrer, Apr. 30, 1977; children: Jeff Allen, Jennifer Anne. Student, Emporia (Kans.) State U., 1970. Tchr., coach Las Cruces (N.Mex.) High Sch., 1970-72; tennis tchr. Tennis Club of Albuquerque, 1972; loan officer Capitol Fed. Savs. and Loan, Overland Park, Kans., 1973-78; sr. v.p., area mgr. Capitol Fed. Savs. and Loan, Wichita, 1979—; exec. v.p. D.L. Mayor Realtors, Overland Park, 1978-79. Campaign chmn. United Way of Plains, Wichita, Kans., 1988, chmn. bd., 1990-91; chmn. Golden Rule award com. J.C. Penney, Wichita, 1989—; bd. dirs. St. Joseph Med. Ctr., 1991—, vice chmn., 1992-93; chmn. Via Christi Health Sys., , 1995. Mem. Wichita Real Estate Industry Coun. (chmn. 1988—), Wichita Area C. of C. (bd. dirs. 1993—, vice chmn. membership 1994,96), Rotary (v.p. East Wichita 1990-91, pres. 1991-92). Republican. Home: 1014 N Linden Cir Wichita KS 67206-4001 Office: Capitol Fed Savs and Loan 301 N Main St Ste 400 Wichita KS 67202-4804

ALEVIZOS, THOMAS JAMES, state representative, lawyer; b. Michigan City, Ind., Apr. 29, 1961; s. James O. and Vasso (Paras) A.; m. Cora Ann Castro, May 8, 1993. Bachelor, U. Mich., 1988; JD, Valparaiso U., 1988. Bar: Ind. 1988. Dep. pros. atty. LaPorte (Ind.) County Prosecutor, 1989-92; pvt. practice atty. Michigan City, 1988—; bd. dirs. LaPorte County Sheltered Workshop, Michigan City, Martin Luther King Ctr., Michigan City. Pres. city coun. Michigan City Common Coun., 1984-92; state rep. State of Ind., 1992—. Mem. ABA, Michigan City Bar Assn. (sec./treas. 1989—), Michigan City Exch. Club. Democrat. Greek Orthodox. Office: Thomas Alevizos PO Box 368 Michigan City IN 46361-0368

ALEWEL, TERESA FINE, university director; b. Mexico, Mo., Aug. 11, 1962; d. James Bruce and Geraldine Ann (Jarboe) Fine; m. Randy Allen Alewel, May 4, 1984; children: Paige Marie, Austin Allen, Kayla Anise. B of Ednl. Studies, U. Mo., 1984; MS, Cen. Mo. State U., 1990. Pers. cons. E.J. Ross & Assocs., Kansas City, Mo., 1984-85; adminstrv. asst. Cen. Mo. State U., Warrensburg, 1986, asst. dir., 1986-88, acting dir., 1988-90, dir., 1990—. Exec. bd. dirs. Totally Country Products Inc., 1986—; grad. Cmty. Leadership and Involvement Mean a Better Cmty., 1992, program com., 1993, bd. dirs., 1996—, fundraising chair 1996—; mem. bd. S.E. Elem. PTA. Recipient Hon. Recruiter award U.S. Army Recruiting, 1987, scholarship Mgmt. Inst., U. Richmond, Va., 1993; named Outstanding Young Women in Am., 1988. Mem. Assn. Sch., Coll. and Univ. Staffing (conf. planning com. 1995), Midwest Assn. Colls. and Employers (com. 1987—, conf. planning com. 1991, prospective mem. chair 1995—, mem. assembly governing bd. 1996—), Nat. Assn. Colls. and Employers, Human Resource Mgmt. Assn., Cen. Mo. State Univs. Pres.'s Soc., Warrensburg C. of C., U. Mo. Alumni Assn., Mo. Army Nat. Guard Women's Aux., Alpha Gamma Delta (chpt. advisor 1987-88, rush advisor 1986-88, faculty advisor 1988—). Republican. Roman Catholic. Home: 343 NE 51st Rd Warrensburg MO 64093-7490 Office: Cen Mo State U Union 302 Warrensburg MO 64093

ALEXA, WILLIAM E., state legislator; b. June 20, 1941; m. Joyce Ann Alexa. JD, Valparaiso U. Atty. Valparaiso Planning Commn. and Bd. Zoning Appeals, 1974; dep. and chief prosecuting atty. Porter County, 1975-79; pres. Valparaiso Park Bd.; Ind. state senator Dist. 5, 1988—; mem. labor, govt. and regulatory affairs, corrections Ind. State Senate, criminal and civil procedures and fin. coms., ranking minority mem., judiciary and pub. policy coms.; atty. Douglas, Alexa, Koeppen & Hurley. Bd. dirs. Porter county Assn. for Retarded Citizens, 1975-76; past pres. Valparaiso Park Bd.; mem. Thunderhouse Campus Ministry Ctr.; mem. United Way Budget and Allocation Com. Mem. Valparaiso Univ. Law Alumnae Assn., Porter County and Ind. State Bar Assn., Valparaiso C. of C. Democrat. Home: 14 Indiana Ave Valparaiso IN 46383-5634*

ALEXANDER, ANDREW JAMES, financial analyst; b. Bellaire, Ohio, Aug. 3, 1969; s. Daniel Richard Alexander. BSBA, Ohio State U., 1991. Rsch. analyst Prudential Securities, Wheeling, W.Va., 1992-93; fin. analyst 5B's Inc., Zanesville, Ohio, 1993—; MIS cons., Zanesville. Republican. Roman Catholic. Home: 6310 Carolina Rd Apt 14 Nashport OH 43830 Office: 5B's Inc 405 Moxahala Ave Zanesville OH 43701-4915

ALEXANDER, BARBARA LEAH SHAPIRO, clinical social worker; b. St. Louis, May 6, 1943; d. Harold Albert and Dorothy Miriam (Leifer) Shapiro; m. Richard E. Alexander. B in Music Edn., Washington U., St. Louis, 1964; postgrad., U. Ill., 1964-66; MSW, Smith Coll., 1970; postgrad., Inst. Psychoanalysis, Chgo., 1971-73, grad., child therapy program, 1976-80; cert. therapist Sex Dysfunction Clinic, Loyola U., Chgo., 1975. Diplomate in Clin. Social Work. Rsch. asst., NIMH grantee Smith Coll., 1968-70; probation officer Juvenile Ct. Cook County, Chgo., 1966-68, 70; therapist Madden Mental Health Ctr., Hines, Ill., 1970-72; supr., therapist, field instr. U. Chgo., U. Ill. Grad. Schs. Social Work; therapist Pritzker Children's Hosp., Chgo., 1972-82; therapist, cons., also pvt. practice, 1973—; pres. On Good Authority, 1992—; intern Divorce Conciliation Svc., Circuit Ct. Cook County, 1976-77. Contbr. articles to profl. jours. Bd. dirs., Grant Park Concerts Soc.; sec. Art Resources in Teaching. Recipient Sterling Achievement award Mu Phi Epsilon, 1964. Mem. Nat. Fed. Soc. for Clin. Social Work (chmn. 20th ann. conf., exec. bd.), Ill. Soc. Clin. Social Work (pres. 1986-90, bd. dirs., chmn. svcs. to mems. com., dir. pvt. practitioners' referral service), Assn. Child Psychotherapists, Amateur Chamber Music Players Assn., Jewish Geneal. Soc., Smith Coll. Alumni Assn. (bd. dirs., v.p. 1992-94). Home and Office: 6 Horizon Ln Galena IL 61036-9258

ALEXANDER, EUGENE J., medical imaging systems designer, research enginee; b. Chgo., Apr. 25, 1962; s. William Carson Alexander and Jeannine Mary (Schavone) Cardamore. BSEE, U. Ill., Chgo., 1991; MSEE, U. Ill., 1993, postgrad., 1993—. Rsch. technician Electro Diagnostic Instruments, Burbank, Calif., 1985-87; rsch. engr. 2 Rush Presbyn. Med. Ctr., Chgo., 1987—; engr. supr. Computerized Functional Testing, Chgo., 1991—; v.p. Greater Mid West Contractors, Berwyn, Ill., 1992—. Computer programmer: (software) Gaitlink Acquisition, 1993; designer (software) Gaitlink for Win 95, 1995. Cpl. U.S. Army, 1981-85. Fellow U.S. Dept. Edn., 1994; scholar Ill. State Commn., 1980; sr. scholar U. Ill., 1991. Mem. IEEE, Laser Soc., Electron Devices Soc., Robotics Soc., Biomed. Soc. Libertarian. Atheist. Office: Rush Presbyn Med Ctr 1653 W Congress Pkwy Chicago IL 60612

ALEXANDER, GRETA BELLE, parapsychologist; b. Manito, Ill., Feb. 5, 1932; d. Ernest A. and Hazel I. (Tackman) Beebe; m. Edward J. Alexander, Feb. 15, 1950 (dec. Sept. 3, 1976); children: Steven Edward, Rita Adele, Deborah Ann, Julie Bea, Cynthia June; m. Robert Edward Paice Sr., Jan. 8, 1978. Grad. high sch., Manito, 1950. Lectr. Bradley U., Peoria, 1973-75; instr. courses in meditation, self awareness, and other Fondulac, East Peoria, Ill., 1973-76; lectr. in field, 1976—; assisted police in homicides, 1974-95; lectr. Lincoln Land C.C., Springfield, Ill., 1975, Jaycees, Dem. Women of Spring Valley, 1990-91, numerous cmty. groups; participated in several rsch. projects; co-hosted or guested on numerous radio and TV shows. Author: Poetry from the Angles, 1994; editor: (newsletter) Letters from the Angels, 1995; host (t.v. show) Greta; appeared in (t.v. shows) Missing Rewards, Geraldo, Arthur C. Clark, Sighting, Psychic Detective, (series) Paranormal Borderline. Recipient Cert. of Recognition Crime Stoppers, Sangamon County, 1993, Cert. of Appreciation City of Bloomington, Ill., 1985, Village of Sherwood, Ill., 1993, Shabbona (Ill.) Fire Sch., 1991. Mem. Star of Hope Ctr. (founder, pres. 1977—), House of Hope (founder, pres. 1983-96), Internat. Assn. Counselors and Therapists, Ea. Star, Colona Fire Dept. (hon.), Virginia Beach (Va.) Police Dept. (hon.). Office: PO Box 621 Delavan IL 61734

ALEXANDER, JAMES MAX, lawyer; b. Detroit, May 1, 1948; s. Sidney L. and Marcia S. (Stern) A.; m. Lynn Metcalf, Sept. 5, 1982; 1 child, Scott R. BA, Miami U., Oxford, Ohio, 1970; JD, U. Detroit, 1973. Bar: Mich. 1973, U.S. Ct. Appeals (6th cir.) 1979. Assoc. Liberson & Crystal, Detroit, 1973-78, Schreiber, Alexander & Greer, Southfield, Mich., 1978-81, Papazian & Alexander, Brimingham, Mich., 1981-91; Foster, Swift, Collins & Smith, Farmington Hills, Mich., 1991—. Chmn. Oakland County Reps., Birmingham, 1988-94; mem. Bd. of State Canvassers, Lansing, Mich., 1991—; dir. detroit Jewish Cmty. Coun., Bloomfield, 1994—; co-chair Oakland County Exec. Ethics Com., Pontiac, 1993—. Mem. ABA, State Bar of Mich. (treas. alternative dispute resolution sec. 1994-95), Oakland County Bar Assn. (co-chair legis. com. 1993—, Fran Avadenka award 1992), Am. Arbitration Assn. (comml. arbitration adv. bd. 1988—). Office: Foster Swift Collins Smith 32300 Northwestern Hwy Farmington MI 48334-1567

ALEXANDER, JAMES WESLEY, surgeon, educator; b. El Dorado, Kans., May 23, 1934; s. Rossiter Wells and Merle Lydia Alexander; m. Maureen L. Strohofer; children: Joseph, Judith, Elizabeth, Randolph, John Charles, Lori, Molly. Student, Tex. Technol. Coll., 1951-53; MD, U. Tex., 1957; ScD, U. Cin., 1958-64; postgrad., U. Minn., 1966-67. Diplomate Am. Bd. Surgery, Am. Bd. Thoracic Surgery; lic. physician, Ohio. Intern Cin. Gen. Hosp., 1957-58; resident U. Cin.-Cin. Gen. Hosp., 1958-64; mem. faculty Coll. Medicine, U. Cin., 1962-64, 66—, prof. surgery, 1975—, dir. transplantation div., dept. surgery, 1967—, dir. surg. immunology lab., 1967—; dir. research Shriners Burns Inst., 1979-90; practice medicine and surgery Cin., 1966—; mem. staff U. Cin. Hosp., Bethesda Hosp., Cin. Children's Hosp., Christ Hosp., Good Samaritan Hosp., Jewish Hosp.; mem. study sect. NIH, 1983-87, 89-93, chmn., 1990-93. Author: (with R.A. Good) Fundamentals of Clinical Immunology, 1977; mem. editl. bd. Annals of Surgery, 1975—, Jour. Burn Care and Rehab., 1979—, Burns, Including Thermal Injury, 1985-92, Jour. Parenteral and Enteral Nutrition, 1991, Nutrition, 1991—, Transplantation Sci., 1991-94, Transplantatin, 1994—; contbr. over 600 articles to profl. jours. Served as capt. M.C., U.S. Army, 1964-66. Mem. AAAS, Am. Assn. for Surgery of Trauma, Am. Assn. Immunologists, Am. Burn Assn. (pres. 1984-85), ACS, Am. Soc. Transplant Surgeons (sec. 1985-87, pres. elect 1987-88, pres. 1988-89), Am. Soc. Parenteral and Enteral Nutrition, Am. Surg. Assn., Assn. for Acad. Surgery, Central Surg. Assn., Cin. Acad. Medicine, Cin. Curg. Soc., Halsted Soc., Immunocompromized Host Soc., Internat. Soc. for Burn Injuries, Internat. Soc. Surgery, Colombian Coll. Surgeons (hon.), Peruvian Acad. Surgery (hon.), St. Paul Surg. Soc. (hon.), Ohio Med. Assn., Soc. Univ. Surgeons, Surg. Biology Club, Surg. Infection Soc. (sec. 1981-84, pres.-elect 1985-86, pres. 1986-87), Tranplantation Soc., Shock Soc., Mont Reid Surg. Soc., Alpha Omega Alpha, Alpha Chi, Alpha Epsilon Delta, Phi Eta Sigma. Home: 2869 Grandin Rd Cincinnati OH 45208-3416 Office: U Cin Coll Medicine 231 Bethesda Ave Cincinnati OH 45267-0558

ALEXANDER, JEFFREY, performing company executive. Grad., New Eng. Conservatory of Music, Boston. Gen. mgr. Grapa Concerts, U.S.A., New York, 1980-82, Laredo Philharm. Orch., Laredo, Tex., 1982-84; dir. Cin. Symphony Orch., 1984-88, mgr., 1988-93, gen. mgr., 1993—; also gen. mgr. Cin. May Festival. Office: Cincinnati Symphony Orch 1241 Elm St Cincinnati OH 45210-2267

ALEXANDER, JOHN KURT, history educator; b. Vancouver, Wash., Oct. 25, 1941; s. Eugene Victor and Marta T. Alexander; m. June Granatir, Dec. 29, 1973. BS in Edn. with honors, Western Oreg. State Coll., Monmouth, 1964; MA in History, U. Chgo., 1965, PhD in History, 1973. Asst. prof. history U. Cin., 1969-75, assoc. prof., 1975-81, prof., 1981—. Author: Render Them Submissive, 1980, The Selling of the Constitutional Convention, 1990; assoc. editor Am. Nat. Biography, Oxford U. Press, Cary, N.C., 1989—; contbr. articles to profl. publs. Mem. Am. Hist. Assn., Orgn. Am. Historians, Hist. Soc. Pa., Pa. Hist. Soc., Ohio Acad. History, Soc. for Historians of Early Am. Republic. Home: 3410 Bishop St Cincinnati OH 45220 Office: Univ Cin Dept History ML 0373 Cincinnati OH 45221

ALEXANDER, JOSE, organic chemist; b. Eraviperur, Kerala, India, June 2, 1945; came to U.S., 1975; s. Ninan and Sosamma (Iype) A.; m. Susie Daniel; children: Jes, Jena. BSc, U. Kerala, India, 1966, MSc, 1968; PhD, Indian Inst. Sci., Bangalore, 1973. Postdoctoral fellow U. Oxford, Eng., 1973, U. Tokyo, 1974, U. Kans., Lawrence, 1975-79; rsch. fellow Interx, Merck & Co., Lawrence, 1979-87, sr. rsch. fellow, 1987-95; Contbr. 34 articles to profl. jours.; inventor 26 patents in drug delivery, medicinal chemistry. Recipient Ghose award Indian Inst. Sci., 1973; Japan Soc. for Promotion of Sci. fellow, 1974. Mem. Am. Chem. Soc. (divsns. of medicinal chemistry, organic chemistry). Home: 2908 Westdale Ct Lawrence KS 66049

ALEXANDER, KATHRYN E., mechanical engineer; b. Columbus, Ohio, July 18, 1960. BSME, Ohio State U., 1982, MSME, 1984. Staff engr. Plaskolite, Columbus, 1982-84; mech. engr. Battelle, Columbus, 1985—; design assembly instr. Boothroyd Dewhurst Inc. Patentee connector mate/de-mate tool. Mem. ASME (chmn. Ctrl. Ohio sect. 1988). Office: Battelle 505 King Ave Columbus OH 43201-2696

ALEXANDER, MARJORIE ANNE, artist, hand papermaker, consultant; b. Chgo., Apr. 16, 1928; d. Alexander and Nancy Rebecca (Cordrey) Roberts; m. Harold Harman Alexander, June 13, 1948; children: Jeffrey C., Cassandra J., Peter B., Timothy C., Patrick J. Student, Wilson Jr. Coll., 1946-47; MFA in Painting, U. Ill., 1968, MA in Art Edn., 1972. cert. tchr. K-12: Ill., Minn. Graphic artist Barry Martin Studio, Rumson, N.J., 1963-65; instr. painting, drawing U. YMCA, Champaign, Ill., 1968-72; teaching asst. U. Ill., Urbana, 1968-72, rsch. assoc., 1972-76; instr. art Champaign High Sch., 1973-75, Urbana High Sch., 1976-80, Concordia Acad., St. Paul, Minn., 1982-84, U. Minn., Mpls., 1984-87; design, housing and apparel artist in residence U. Minn., St. Paul, 1984-88; craft cons. and educator tech. asstance program USAID, OAS, U. Minn., Kingtson, Jamaica, 1986—; design cons. J.A.M. Corp., Mpls., 1988—; tech. cons. OAS, Kingston, 1990-91, Blandin Found. grantee, Minn., 1989—; rsch. and product devel. agrl. unilization rsch. inst., 1992-95; tech. cons. Zabbaleen Paper Project, Assn. for the Protection of the Environment, Cairo, 1993—. Works have appeared in over 20 solo shows, 1960—, over 19 invitational shows nationally and internationally, 1985—; co-author (book): Selected Papers, 1994; contbr. articles to profl. jours. Vestry mem. St. John's Episcopal Ch., Champaign, 1975-78, St. Matthew's Episcopal Ch., St. Paul, 1989—. Recipient Celebrity award Minn. State Fair, 1984, book First award 1986, Honorable mention 3rd Onn/Off Paper Nat., Wis., 1984; grantee Blandin Found. U. Minn., 1989-90, OAS, 1990-91, Agrl. Utilization Rsch. Inst. grantee, 1992-95. Mem. Nat. League Am. Penwomen (Minn. art chair 1990-94, state v.p. 1994—), Internat. Assn. Hand Papermakers and Paper Artists, Friends of Dard Hunter Paper Mus. (com. chair 1990—). Episcopalian. Home: Graybridge 3251 Fernwood St Arden Hills MN 55112

ALEXANDER, RALPH B(ERNARD), business executive, physicist; b. Leeds, Eng., Nov. 30, 1944. BS in Physics, U. Western Australia, 1967; PhD in Physics, Oxford U., Eng., 1971. Rsch. scientist Eng., Denmark, Australia, 1971-77; prof. phys. dept. Wayne State U., Detroit, 1977-84; pres. Ion Surface Tech., Clawson, Mich., 1985-91, R.B. Alexander & Assoc., Hunting Wd., Mich., 1992—; spkr. prof. soc. seminars, 84—; lectr. Surface Treatments for Wear and Corrosion, 96—. Contbr. articles to profl. jours. and trade mags. Mem. Böhmische Phys. Soc., Am. Phys. Soc., ASM Internat., Soc. of Mfg. Engnrs., Sigma Xi. Office: RB Alexander & Assocs 26028 Huntington Rd Huntington Woods MI 48070-1238

ALEXANDER, ROBERT LESTER, art historian, educator; b. N.Y.C., Mar. 23, 1920; s. Rex Grant and Ruth (Laird) A.; m. Margaret Ames, July 6, 1946; children: Margaret, Harriet. PhD, NYU, 1961. Instr. RISD, Providence, 1947-48; tutor Queens Coll., N.Y.C., 1949-51; instr. U. Pitts., Pitts., 1952-58; asst. prof. Pa. State U., University Park, 1958-61; vis. lectr. U. Iowa, Iowa City, 1961-63, assoc. prof. Art History, 1963-69, prof. Art History, 1969-87, prof. emeritus, 1987—; assoc. editor Archaeology, Cambridge, Mass., 1951-53; sr. editor The Papers of Robert Mills, Washington, 1984-89. Author (books) The Architecture of Maximilian Godefroy, 1974, The Sculpture and Sculptors of Yazilikaya, 1986. Sgt. U.S. Army, 1942-44. Samuels Fels fellow NYU, 1959-60, Am. Rsch. Inst. fellow, Turkey, 1965-66, NEH fellow, 1981-82. Mem. Soc. Archtl. Historians (bd. dirs. 1961-63), Coll. Art Assn., Archeol. Inst. Am., British Inst. Archaeology in Ankara. Home: 9 Forest Gln Iowa City IA 52245-1625

ALEXANDER, THOMAS STERN, immunologist; b. Detroit, Aug. 20, 1951; s. Sidney Louis and Marcia (Stern) A.; m. JoAnn McGettrick, Jan. 31, 1976; 1 child. BA, Northwestern U., 1973; MSc, Colo. State U., 1975; PhD, Kent State U., 1987. Lab mgr. Sch. Pub. Health, Harvard U., Boston, 1975-78; rsch. asst. Cleve. Clinic Found., 1978-79; rsch. assoc. Akron (Ohio) City Hosp., 1979-82; immunologist Summa Health System, 1982—. Treas. Harman Hills Homeowners Assn., Akron, 1990-94. Mem. AAAS, Assn. Med. Lab. Immunologists (treas. 1993-95), Am. Soc. Mibrobiology (chmn.-elect clin. and diagnostic immunology divsn. 1995-96, chmn. 1996—), Internat. Soc. Analytical Cytology. Office: Summa Health System 525 E Market St Akron OH 44304-1619

ALEXANDER, WILLIAM MARK, imaging company executive; b. Bowling Green, Ohio, June 6, 1950; m. Erin Alexander, Nov. 28, 1994; children from previous marriage: William Arthur, Preston Scott. BBA in Mktg. and Fin., Bowling Green U., 1972, MBA, 1976. Mgr. market devel. Doehler-Jarvis div. NL Industries, 1972-73, asst. div. mgr.tsales, 1973-74; sales rep. Kiemle-Hankins, 1974-77; mktg. specialist-new products Gould, Inc. subs. Nippon Mining, 1977-78, dist. sales mgr., 1978-79, regional sales mgr., 1979-81; various mgmt. and internat. assignments Gen. Electric Info. Svcs., 1981-91; mng. dir., exec. v.p. Asia ops. Gen. Electric Info. Svcs., Hong Kong, 1987-91; sr. v.p., gen. mgr. sys. group HSB Reliability Techs., Inc., 1991-94; pres., CEO worldwide imaging activities NBS Imaging Systems, Inc., Ft. Wayne, Ind., 1994—. Office: NBS Imaging Systems Inc 1530 Progress Rd Fort Wayne IN 46808-1181

ALEXANDROFF, MIRRON (MIKE ALEXANDROFF), academic administrator; b. Chgo., Mar. 3, 1923; s. Norman and Cherrie (Phillips) A.; m. Anna C. Avgerin, Dec. 22, 1947 (dec.); children: Niki Alexandroff Gray, Pam Alexandroff Eidenberg; m. Jane Ann Legnard, Jan. 27, 1962; 1 child, Norman. BA, Roosevelt U., 1947; MA, Columbia Coll., Chgo., 1948; D of Humane Letters (hon.), DePaul U., 1992. Pres. Columbia Coll., 1961-92, pres. emeritus, 1992—; chmn. Chgo. Met. Higher Edn. Coun., 1981-90; bd. dirs. Bank Bellwood, Ill. Adv. com. Chgo. Dept. Cultural Affairs, 1985-92; pres. Grant Park Cultural and Ednl. Cmty., 1985-92. Sgt. U.S. Army, 1942-45, PTO. Recipient Sydney R. Yates Advocacy award, 1991, Clarence Darrow award for leading svc. in cause of social justice, 1984, Louis Lerner award Ill. Pub. Action., 1992, Disting. Urban Fellow award Assn. Urban Univs. 1992, Outstanding Contbr. to Latin Am. TV award Mex. Nat. Assn. Broadcasters, 1980. Mem. Am. Assn. Urban Univs. (chmn. 1986-88), Fedn. Ind. Ill. Coll. and Univs. (exec. com. 1978-92). Home: 175 N Harbor Dr Chicago IL 60601-7344 Office: Columbia College 600 S Michigan Ave Chicago IL 60605-1901

ALFERMANN, GARY L., industrial designer; b. Washington, Mo., Nov. 19, 1958; s. Edmond J. and M. Dolores (Hanneken) A.; m. Christina G. Hinson, Sept. 13, 1986; children: Molly, Erin, Andrew Edmond, Abby Christine. A in Drafting and Design, East Ctrl. Coll., 1979. Machine designer Zero Mfg., Washington, 1978-81, Melton Machine and Control Co., Washington, 1981—; pres. Alfermann USA, Washington, 1994—; mem. adv. draft and design East Ctrl. Coll., Union, Mo. Patentee in field. Mem. Washington (Mo.) Jaycees, St. Francis Vorgia Cath. Ch., Washington, Gun Clubs, Washington. Home: 9 David Dr Washington MO 63090-1116 Office: Melton Machine & Control Co 1600 W Main St Washington MO 63090-1002

ALFONSI, WILLIAM E., interior designer, funeral industry consultant; b. Niles, Ohio, Jan. 27, 1923; s. Pacifico Tobia and Carmela (D'Angelo) A.; m. Adrell A. Alfonsi; children: Gary William, Pamela Jane, Scott Allan, Kevin Lawrence. Student, Miami U., Oxford, Ohio, 1942. Interior design asst. Carey W. Sims Inc., Cleve., 1946-47; interior designer Masticks, Inc., Cleve., 1947-49; dir. interior planning and decoating div. Superior Funeral Supply, Cleve., 1949-69; pres. Country Furniture Store, Inc., Kinsman, Ohio, 1969—, Custom Planned Funeral Interiors, Kinsman, Ohio, 1969—, William Alfonsi, Inc., Kinsman, Ohio, 1969—, Heritage Funeral Equipment, Kinsman, Ohio, 1969—. Designer, decorator homes in 15 states. Sgt. U.S. Army, 1942-45. Mem. Am. Assn. Cert. Interior Decorators, Am. Legion, VFW. Democrat. Methodist. Home: 9234 N Kingsville Rd Farmdale OH 44417-9750 Office: William Alfonsi Inc PO Box 77 Kinsman OH 44428-0077

ALFORD, JEFFREY W., university administrator; b. Providence, R.I., Oct. 2, 1947; s. Kenneth William and Lucille (Whitwam) A.; m. Gail Alford, Nov. 29, 1979; children: Jared, Kenneth G.; m. Terry Alford, Apr. 6, 1984. BS in Journalism, U. Fla., 1969. Edn. writer Palm Beach Post, West Palm Beach, Fla., 1971-74; asst. city editor Ft. Lauderdale (Fla.) News, 1974-76; rsch. editor U. Fla., Gainesville, 1976-79; assoc. dir. pub. info. Tex. A&M U., College Station, 1979-87; exec. dir. univ. rels. Ball State U., Muncie, Ind., 1987—; comm. cons. Taylor U., Upland, Ind., 1995. Contbr. articles to profl. jours. Elder Westminster Presbyn. Ch., Muncie, 1987—. Sgt. U.S. Army, 1969-71. Recipient William Hearst Prize for Editls. William R. Hearst Found., 1969, Fla. Sch. Bd. award United Tchrs. of Fla., 1974, Award of Excellence Internat. Assn. Bus. Communicators, 1993. Mem. Soc. of Profl. Journalists, Coun. for Advancement and Support of Edn. (Regional award for news writing 1986), Hoasier State Press Assn., Phi Gamma Delta. Resbyterian. Home: 4517 N Gishler Dr Muncie IN 47304 Office: Ball State U University Relations Muncie IN 47306

ALFREY, MARIAN ANTOINETTE, retired education educator; b. Crab Orchard, Nebr., Dec. 5, 1925; d. Rollin Milton and Emma Antoinette (Schultz) S.; m. David Homer, Aug. 10, 1947; children: Gary David, Judith Ann. BS, U. Nebr., Lincoln, 1968; MA, U. No. Iowa, Cedar Falls, 1972. Permanent Profl. Cert. Tchr. Louisville (Nebr.) Schs., 1945-46, Tecumseh (Nebr.) Schs., 1946-47, North Loup (Nebr.) Schs., 1949-51, Malvern (Iowa) Schs., 1951-52, Beatrice Schs., 1967-68, Waterloo (Iowa) Community Schs., 1968-89; active Waterloo Cmty. Schs., 1973-88. Mem. Covenant Hosp. Aux., 1989—, pres. Mem. NEA, Nebr. Congress PTA (hon. life). Republican. Methodist. Home: 3362 Mt Vernon Dr Waterloo IA 50701-4621

ALFT, E. C. (MIKE), columnist, retired secondary education educator; b. Chgo., July 13, 1925; s. E.C. and Miriam (Butler) A.; m. Frances Clark; children: Barbara, John, Michael, Susan. BA, Grinnell (Iowa) Coll., 1949; MA, Syracuse U., 1950; HHD, Judson Coll., Elgin, Ill., 1974. Tchr. Dundee (Ill.) H.S., 1950-52; tchr., dept. chmn. Elgin H.S., 1953-94, ret., 1994; columnist Elgin Courier-News, 1981—. Author: Elgin: An American History, 1984 (Superior Achievement award Ill. Hist. Soc.), Old Elgin: A Pictorial History, 1991, Elgin: Days Gone By, 1992. Councilman, City of Elgin, 1963-67, mayor, 1967-71; trustee Gail Borden Pub. Libr., Elgin, 1995—. John Hay fellow, 1958-59. Mem. Kiwanis, Phi Beta Kappa. Home: 1217 Mohawk Dr Elgin IL 60120

ALI, MOHAMMED, economics educator; b. Dire Dawa, Oromoland, Ethiopia, June 16, 1944; came to U.S., 1989; s. Ali and Asha (Musa) Diido. BA, Haile Selassie U., Addis Ababa, Ethiopia, 1967; advanced diploma, Cen. Sch. Planning and Stats., Warsaw, Poland, 1969, MA, 1970, PhD, 1983. Sr. economist Ministry of Commerce and Industry, Addis Ababa, 1970-71, Awash Valley Authority, Addis Ababa, 1971-73; instr. Addis Ababa U., 1975-78; head mktg. dept. Agrl. Inputs and Mktg. Svc., Addis Ababa, 1973-79; instr. Ethiopian Inst. Banking, Addis Ababa, 1975-78; assoc. prof. Inst. of Oriental Studies, Warsaw, 1984-88; vis. rsch. fellow Inst. of Ethnology, Berlin, 1989; vis. prof. U. Minn., Mpls., 1990—, St. Cloud (Minn.) State U., 1992—; cons. Ministry of Commerce and Industry, Addis Ababa, 1970-71, Ministry of Agr., Addis Ababa, 1971-73; dir. mktg. dept. Agrl. Inputs and Mktg., Addis Ababa, 1973-79. Co-author: Handbook of the Oromo Language, 1990; contbr. articles to profl. jours. SEED grantee U. Mich., 1992. Mem. African Studies Assn., Minn. Alliance for Global and Internat. Studies, French Soc. for Ethiopian Studies, Polish Econ. Soc., Oromo Studies Assn. (awards 1993, 94). Home: 2515 S 9th St Apt 1105 Minneapolis MN 55406-1036 Office: U Minn Inst Internat Studies 214 Social Studies Minneapolis MN 55455

ALIG, FRANK DOUGLAS STALNAKER, construction company executive; b. Indpls., Oct. 10, 1921; s. Clarence Schirmer and Marjory (Stalnaker) A.; m. Ann Bobbs, Oct. 22, 1949; children: Douglas, Helen, Barbara. Student, U. Mich., 1939-41; BS, Purdue U., 1948. Registered profl. engr., Ind. Project engr. Ind. State Hwy. Commn., Indpls., 1948; pres. Alig-Stark Constrn. Co., Inc., 1949-57, Frank S. Alig, Inc., 1957—; v.p., bd. dirs. Bo-Wit Products Corp., Edinburg, Ind.; CEO, bd. dirs. Home Stove Realty Co., Home Land Investment Co., Inc. With AUS, 1943-46. Mem. Dramatic Club, Lambs Club. Republican. Presbyterian.

ALKIRE, BETTY JO, artist, commercial real estate broker, marketing consultant; b. Kansas City, Mo., June 20, 1942; d. Robert Emmitt and Gladys Faye (Craigg) Sharp; m. Daniel Wayne Hedrick, Nov. 15, 1958 (div.); children—Diane Laurie, Lisa Kay, Brett, Darin, Julie; m. William Edgar Alkire, Sept. 23, 1975. Tchr. art Independence Adult Edn., Mo., 1967—; portrait artist Silver Dollar City Nat. Crafts Festival, 1971—; owner, operator portrait artist's concession Kansas City Worlds of Fun, 1972-96 ; tchr. pvt. art classes, 1970—; tchr., lectr. mktg. art U. Mo. Extension Program, 1982—; cons. mktg. and life-planning for artists; broker and cons. comml. investment real estate. Contbr. articles in field to various mags. Mem. Bur. of Tourism, Tri-Lakes Bd. of Realtors Edn. com., R.B. Bd. of Planning and Zoning; chmn. R.B. Park and Mus. Bd. Mem. Mo. Arts Council, Table Rock Art Guild, Independent Profl. Artists Assn. (pres. 1980—), Branson Mo. C. of C. (mem. leadership program). Methodist. Clubs: Rockaway Beach Ladies, Rockaway Beach Booster (Mo.). Avocations: local art and history, antiques, real estate. Home: Historic Taneywood Rockaway Beach MO 65740

ALLAIRE, GLORIA KAUN, Italian language educator; b. Reedsburg, Wis., Feb. 20, 1954; d. Robert W. and Arlowene Marie (Wolter) Kaun. MusB with honors, U. Wis., 1976, MA in Italian, 1986, PhD, 1993. Vis. lectr. in Italian lang. and lit. Univs. Mich. and Wis. Studies Abroad Program, Florence, Italy, 1987-88; grad. teaching asst. dept. French and Italian U. Wis., Madison, 1988-93, 84-87; vis. asst. prof. dept. modern langs. and linguistics Fla. State U., Tallahassee, 1993-94; vis. asst. prof. dept. modern langs. Ohio U., Athens, 1994—; Italian lang. tutor and translator, 1984—; Italian lang. coach Madison Opera, 1985-87. Author: The Chivalric Narratives of Andrea da Barberino; contbr. articles to profl. jours. Officer, newsletter editor Madison Opera Buffs, 1980-87. Fulbright grantee, 1990-91, Am. Philosophy Soc. grantee, 1996; summer fellow UCLA Ctr. for Medieval and Renaissance Studies, 1994, NEH Summer Inst., 1995. Mem. MLA, Am. Assn. Tchrs. Italian, Am. Assn. for Italian Studies, Medieval Acad. Am., Lyrica Soc., Soc. Rencesvals, ACTFL, Renaissance Soc. Am., Southeastern Renaissance Conf. Office: Ohio Univ Dept Modern Langs Ellis Hall 374 Athens OH 45701

ALLAN, ANN GOULD, library science educator; b. Youngstown, Ohio, Jan. 9, 1940; d. Charles Howard and Florilla (Tibbets) Gould; m. Aug. 17, 1963; children: Jennifer, Katherine, Matthew. BA, U. Mich., 1962; MLS, Simmons Coll., Boston, 1963; PhD in Libr. and Info Sci., Case Western Res. U., 1976. Bibliographer law sch. libr. U. Mich., Ann Arbor, 1963-64; bibliographer acquisitions dept. grad. libr. U. Mich., 1963-65; asst. head acquisitions Kent State U., Ohio, 1966-68; asst. univ. libr. Bierce Libr. U. Akron, Ohio, 1968-71; assoc. prof. libr. sci. Kent (Ohio) State U., 1975-93; prof. emeritus, libr. cons., 1993—; adv. com. State Libr. Catalog Com. for CD-ROM statewide catalog, Columbus, 1989. Contbr. articles to profl. jours.. Bd. dirs. Planned Parenthood of Medina-Summit-Portage Counties, Akron, 1988-90. Mem. Acad. Libr. Assn. Ohio (pres. 1982-82, Disting. Svc. award 1993), ALA, Assn. for Libr. and Info. Sci. Edn., Ohio Libr. Assn. (chmn. rsch. com. 1986-88), Jr. League, Garden Club Am. Home: 219 Ely Rd Akron OH 44313-4449

ALLDRITT, RICHARD, state legislator; m. Carmen Alldritt. Mem. Kans. Ho. of Reps., Topeka. Democrat. Home: 531 W 15th St Harper KS 67058-1512*

ALLEGRUCCI, DONALD LEE, state supreme court justice; b. Pittsburg, Kans., Sept. 19, 1936; s. Nello and Josephine Marie (Funaro) A.; m. Joyce Ann Thompson, Nov. 30, 1963; children: Scott David, Bowen Jay. AB, Pittsburg State U., 1959; JD, Washburn U., 1963. Bar: Kans. 1963. Asst. county atty. Butler County, El Dorado, Kans., 1963-67; state senator Kans. Legislature, Topeka, 1976-80; mem. Kans. Pub. Relations Bd., 1981-82; dist. judge Kans. 11th Jud. Dist., Pittsburg, 1982-87, adminstrv. judge, 1983-87; justice Kans. Supreme Ct., Topeka, 1987—; instr. Pittsburg State U., 1969-72; exec. dir. Mid-Kans. Community Action Program, Inc. Mem. Dem. State Com., 1974-80; candidate 5th Congl. Dist., 1978; past pres. Heart Assn.; bd. dirs. YMCA. Served with USAF, 1959-60. Mem. Kans. Bar Assn. Democrat. Office: US Supreme Ct Kans Jud Ctr 301 SW 10th Ave Topeka KS 66612-1502

ALLEN, ANNA MARIE, financial executive; b. Ft. Scott, Kans., Aug. 3, 1955; d. Harold Laverne and Dorothy Arlene Kirk; m. John Leroy Allen, Sept. 18, 1982. AA, Johnson County C.C., Overland Park, Kans., 1976; BSBA in Fin., Pittsburg (Kans.) State U., 1979; MBA in Internat. Bus., Ohio State U., 1995. CPA, Kans. Asst. teller supr. Kans. Nat. Bank & Trust, Prairie Village, 1975-77; bookkeeper Foodtown, Pittsburg, 1978-79; sr. v.p. tax GRA, Inc., Merriam, Kans., 1979-89, also bd. dirs.; sr. cons. Grant Thornton, Wichita, Kans., 1989-91; mgr. fin. ops. Legent Corp., Columbus, Ohio, 1991-94; asst. treas. CompuServe Inc., Columbus, 1994—. Mem. com. bd. Kansas City (Mo.) Ballet Guild, 1985-89; past mem. Jr. League Kans. City, Wichita Jr. League; bd. dirs. Jr. League, Columbus, Ohio; charter mem. Women's Resource Ctr., Johnson County bd. dirs., 1986-89. Mem. AICPA, AAUW (bd. dirs. Shawnee Mission, Kans chpt. 1979-89), Ctrl. Exchange, Ctrl. Ohio Treasury Mgmt. Assn., Treasury Mgmt. Assn., Am. Legion Aux., Sawmill Athletic Club, Phi Kappa Phi, Delta Mu Delta. Baptist.

ALLEN, BARBARA, state legislator. Atty.; mem. Kans. Ho. of Reps. Republican. Home: 8136 Rosewood Dr Shawnee Mission KS 66208-5008 Office: Kansas House of Representatives State Capitol Topeka KS 66612

ALLEN, JANET LOUISE, school system administrator; b. Cleve., Nov. 17, 1935; d. W. Paul and Clara (Townhill) A.; m. H. Paul Koepke, June 15, 1957 (div. 1978); children: Scott Paul, Sheryl Louise. BS, Syracuse U., 1957; MA, Wayne State U., 1971, PhD, 1976; postgrad., Ea. Mich. U., 1982, Wayne State U., 1989. Tchr. Grand Rapids, Mich., 1967-69; tchr. Birmingham (Mich.) Pub. Schs., 1969-77, dir. gifted edn., 1977-79; prin. Bingham Farms Sch., Birmingham, 1979-80; dept. head Derby Mid. Sch., Birmingham, 1980-81; prin. Twin Beach Sch., Walled Lake, Mich., 1981-87; dep. supt. Jackson (Mich.) Pub. Schs., 1988-90; supt. Three Rivers (Mich.) Community Schs., 1990-95, Willow Run Cmty. Schs., Ypsilanti, Mich., 1995—; adj. prof. Mich. State U., East Lansing, 1979-81, Eastern Mich. U., Ypsilanti, 11990, Western Mich. U., Kalamazoo, 1994. Contbr. articles to profl. jours. Apptd. mem. Three Rivers Indsl. Authority; mem. Three Rivers Family Coun., 1992-95, Three Rivers Human Rels. Commn., 1992-95. IDEA fellow Inst. Devel. Ednl. Activities, Appleton, Wis., 1992, 1994. Mem. Am. Assn. Sch. Adminstrs. (del. nat. conv. 1991—, leadership com. 1995—), Mich. Assn. Sch. Adminstrs. (chmn. ednl. leadership 1992-93, exec. bd. dirs. 1993—), Washtenaw County Supt. Assn., St. Joseph County Supt. Assn. (pres. 1991-93), Three Rivers c. of C., Rotary, Players, Phi Delta Kappa (pres. 1984-85). Home: 1732 S Grove Rd # 306 Ypsilanti MI 48198 Office: Willow Run Cmty Schs 2171 Michigan Ave Ypsilanti MI 48198

ALLEN, JANICE MANDABACH, interior designer, nurse, office manager, actress, model; b. Evanston, Ill., May 29, 1953; d. Paul John and Claudia Stroman (White) Mandabach; m. George Whitaker Allen, Apr. 26, 1980. Student, Syracuse U., 1971-72; BSN, Tex. Christian U., 1976. Nurse oper. rm., circulating nurse oper. rm. Northwestern Meml. Hosp., Chgo., 1976-78; model and actress Chgo., 1978-86, 94—; nurse, office mgr. George W. Allen, MD, Chgo., 1986—. Mem. Carlton Club, Sand Creek Country Club. Republican. Methodist. Home: 1503 Sand Creek Dr Chesterton IN 46304-9373 Office: George W Allen MD 150 E Huron St Chicago IL 60611-2912

ALLEN, LAYMAN EDWARD, law educator, research scientist; b. Turtle Creek, Pa., June 9, 1927; s. Layman Grant and Viola Iris (Williams) A.; m. Christine R. Patmore, Mar. 29, 1950 (dec.); children: Layman G., Patricia R.; m. Emily C. Hall, Oct. 3, 1981 (div. 1992); children: Phyllip A. Hall, Kelly C. Hall; m. Leslie A. Olson, June 10, 1995. Student, Washington and Jefferson Coll., 1945-46; AB, Princeton U., 1951; MPub. Admnstrn., Harvard U., 1952; LLB, Yale U., 1956. Bar: Conn. 1956. Fellow Ctr. for Advanced Study in Behavioral Scis., 1961-62; sr. fellow Yale Law Sch., 1956-57, lectr., 1957-58, instr., 1958-59, asst. prof., 1959-63, assoc. prof., 1963-66; assoc. prof. law U. Mich. Law Sch., Ann Arbor, 1966-71, prof., 1971—; rsch. scientist Mental Health Rsch. Inst., U. Mich., 1966—; cons. legal drafting Nat. Life Ins. Co., Mich. Blue Cross & Blue Shield (various law firms); quar. electronic data retrieval com. Am. Bar Assn.; ops. rsch. analyst McKinsey & Co.; orgn. and methods analyst Office of Sec. Air Force.; trustee Ctr. for Study of Responsive Law. Editor: Games and Simulations; author: WFF 'N PROOF: The Game of Modern Logic, 1961, latest rev. edit., 1973, (with Robin B.S. Brooks, Patricia A. James) Automatic Retrieval of Legal Literature: Why and How, 1962, WFF: The Beginner's Game of Modern Logic, 1962, latest rev. edit., 1973, EQUATIONS: The Game of Creative Mathematics, 1963, latest rev. edit., 1973, (with Mary E. Caldwell) Reflections of the Communications Sciences and Law: The Jurimetrics Conference, 1965, (with J. Ross and P. Kugel) QUERIES 'N THEORIES: The Game of Science and Language, 1970, latest rev. edit., 1973, (with F. Goodman, D. Humphrey and J. Ross), ON-WORDS: The Game of Word Structures, 1971, rev. edit., 1973; contbr. articles to profl. jours.; co-author/designer: (with J. Ross and C. Stratton) DIG Math; (with C. Saxon) Normalizer Clear Legal Drafting Program, 1986, MINT System for Generating Dynamically Multiple-Interpretation Legal Decision-Assistance Systems, 1991. With USNR, 1945-46. Mem. ABA (coun. sect. sci. and tech.), AAAS, ACLU, Assn. Symbolic Logic, Nat. Coun. Tchrs. Math. Democrat. Unitarian. Home: 2114 Vinewood Blvd Ann Arbor MI 48104 Office: U Mich Sch Law 625 S State St Ann Arbor MI 48109-1215

ALLEN, LEATRICE DELORICE, psychologist; b. Chgo., July 15, 1948; d. Burt and Mildred Floy (Taylor) Hawkins; m. Allen Moore, Jr., July 30, 1965 (div. Oct. 1975); children: Chandra, Valarie, Allen; m. Armstead Allen, May 11, 1978 (div. May 1987). AA in Bus. Edn., Olive Harvey Coll., Chgo., 1975; BA in Psychology cum laude, Chgo. State U., 1977; M.Clin. Psychology, Roosevelt U., 1980; MA in Health Care Adminstrn., Coll. St. Francis, Joliet, Ill., 1993. Clk., U.S. Post Office, Chgo., 1967-72; clin. therapist Bobby Wright Mental Health Ctr., Chgo., 1979-80; clin. therapist Community Mental Health Council, Chgo., 1980-83, assoc. dir., 1983—; cons. Edgewater Mental Health, Chgo., 1984—, Project Pride, Chgo., 1985—; victim services coordinator Community Mental Health Council, Chgo., 1986-87; mgr. youth family services Mile Square Health Ctr., Chgo., 1987-88; coord. Evang. Health Systems, Oakbrook, Ill., 1988-93; adminstr. Human Enrichment Devel. Assn., Hazel Crest, Ill., 1993—. Scholar Chgo. State U., 1976, Roosevelt U., 1978; fellow Menninger Found., 1985. Mem. Am. Profl. Soc. on Abuse of Children, Nat. Orgn. for Victim Assistance, Ill. Coalition Against Sexual Assault (del. 1985—), Soc. Traumatic Stress Studies (treatment innovations task force), Chgo. Sexual Assault Svcs. Network (vice-chair, bd. dirs.), Chgo. Coun. Fgn. Rels. Avocations: aerobics, reading, theatre, dining.

ALLEN, LEILANI ELEANOR, data processing executive; b. Rudesheim, Rhein, Fed. Republic Germany, Nov. 27, 1949; d. John Kaleiapu and Ilse Eva (Ritter) A. BA, San Francisco State U., 1971, MA, 1973; PhD, U. Conn., 1978. Sr. analyst VISA, U.S.A., San Mateo, Calif., 1978-81; asst. gen. mgr. Inst. for Info. Mgmt., Sunnyvale, Calif., 1981-85; pres. Knowledge Consortium, Oakland, Calif., 1985-87; sr. cons. Amdahl Corp., Sunnyvale, 1987-88; v.p. Aon Corp., Chgo., 1988-91; sr. v.p. PNC Mortgage Corp., Vernon Hills, Ill., 1991-95; dir. Tenex Consulting, Burlington, Mass., 1995—; chmn. No Cal Computer Measurement Group, San Francisco, 1982-84, chmn. MBA tech. com., 1994-95. Co-author: Management Handbook of Information Center and End User Computer, 1987, (survey) Strategic Planning for Info. Sys., 1987, (cartoon) Tech Tales; editor: Executive Perspectives on Info. Sys., 1985; contbr. articles to profl. jours.; columnist Software mag., 1991-94. Mem. NAFE, Mensa, Mortgage Bankers Assn. (chair tech. com.).

ALLEN, LEONARD BROWN, tax manager; b. Longmont, Colo., Sept. 5, 1932; s. Victor Brown and Anna Catherine (Cottrell) A.; m. Virginia Lee Harvey, May 27, 1960; children: Susan Ann, Denise Diane. BS, Colo. A&M Coll., 1954; MS, Colo. State U., 1967. CPA, Ill. Office mgr. Walco Distbg., Craig, Colo., 1962-65; teaching asst. Colo. State U., Ft. Collins, 1965-67; internal auditor Deere & Co., Moline, Ill., 1967-68, acct. consolidations dept., 1968-70, tax acct., 1970-73, mgr. state and local taxes, 1973—. Mem. stewardship and mission com. No. Assn. United Ch. of Christ, 1989-92, chmn., 1991-92. Capt. USAF, 1954-57, with USAFR, 1967. Mem. Ill. CPA Soc., Chgo. Tax Club (bd. dirs. 1986-88), Iowa Taxpayers Assn. (bd. dirs., chmn. 1991-93, mem. exec. com.), Taxpayers Fedn. Ill. (adv. com.), Wis. Mfrs. and Commerce Assn. (taxation com.), Ill. C. of C. (chmn. state and local tax com., tax com. 1991), Masons (master 1964-65). Republican. Mem. United Ch. of Christ. Home: 38 Crestview Dr Geneseo IL 61254-9528 Office: Deere & Co John Deere Rd Moline IL 61265-6785

ALLEN, LINDA GRAVES, hospital administrator; b. Indpls., Oct. 8, 1959; d. Charles Edward and Barbara Jean (Antle) Graves; m. William Allen, Nov. 16, 1985; children: Christine, Clarke, Jordan. BSN, U. Mo., 1981, MHA, 1995. RN, Mo.; cert. emergency nurse, Mo.; cert. instr. trauma nurse, advanced burn life support, cert. provider pediatric advanced cardiac and trauma/pediatric advanced life support, cert. trauma nurse specialist, cert. emergency nurse, advanced cardiac life support. Staff nurse level IV St. John's Mercy Med. Ctr., St. Louis, 1981-92; trauma coord. Barnes Hosp., St. Louis, 1992-96; re-engring. cons. Barnes Jewish Hosp., St. Louis, 1996—. Mem. AACN, Emergency Nurses Assn., Am. Trauma Soc., Am. Coll. Healthcare Execs., Soc. Trauma Nurses. Office: Barnes Hosp # 1 Barnes Plaza Saint Louis MO 63110

ALLEN, LOIS ARLENE HEIGHT (MRS. JAMES PIERPONT ALLEN), musician; b. Kenton, Ohio, Sept. 2, 1932; d. Robert Harold and Frances (Sims) Height; B.S., Ohio State U., 1954, M.A., 1958; m. James Pierpont Allen, June 14, 1953; children: Daniel Pierpont, Carole Elizabeth. Tchr. jr. and sr. high music, Upper Arlington H.S., Columbus, O., 1954-56; h.s. music supr., Westerville, Ohio, 1956-67; tchr. music Ohio State U. Sch., 1957-59; pvt. tchr. music, Columbus, 1960—; exec. dir. Battelle Scholars Program Trust Fund, 1983-86; ch. organist, choir dir. Mountview Bapt. Ch., Upper Arlington, Ohio, 1960-77; ednl. radio interviewer WOSU, 1970, 71, 72. Mem. Project Hope, Central Ohio, 1967-73; mem. sustaining bd. Maryhaven House for Alcoholic Women, 1969-73, 1st v.p.; mem. women's bd. Columbus Symphony, 1965-79, 1991, 92, 93, 94, bd. dirs., chmn. youth coun., 1965-68, pres.-elect. women's assn., 1973, chmn. edn. com., 1991—, pres., 1974-76; v.p. Am. Symphony Orch. League, 1987-88; organist, choir master The Ch. of St. Edwards, 1990-92; chmn. juried art competition Ctrl. Ohio Arts Festival, 1969, 70, chmn. fine and applied arts, 1971, gen. chmn. of festival, 1972; area chmn. United Appeals Franklin County, 1966-68, Heart drive, 1968-85; pres. Ohio State U. Soc. Friends Sch. Music, 1977-78; trustee Columbus Symphony Orch., 1973-81, Opera/Columbus, 1981-85; v.p. women's guild Opera/Columbus, 1986-94, pres., 1987-88; mem. vol. coun. Am. Symphony Orch. League, 1981—, v.p., 1983-84, mem. exec. com., 1986-88, mem. artistic affairs com., 1987-89, pres. 1987-88; organist, choir dir. North Congregational Ch., 1979-85; area leader Rep. party, 1966-68; mem. Mayor's Award Coun. Com., 1981-84; active Connexions, Columbus Literacy Coun.; bd. dirs., pres. Ohio Theatre Shop, 1995-96, Women's Bd. Columbus Mus. Art, 1991—. Mem. Am. Guild Organists, Choristers Guild Am., Fedn. Am. Bapt. Musicians, Center Sci. and Industry, Ohio State Hist. Soc., Ohio Orgn. Orchs. (treas. 1976-79, sec. 1979-82), Nat. Trust U.S.A., Mountview Bapt. Ch. (moderator 1996—), Rotory Club (Women of Yr. Upper Arlington Ohio 1995), Tau Beta Sigma, Delta Omicron, Kappa Delta (Ctrl. Ohio Woman of Yr. 1970). Mem. Order Eastern Star, White Shrine of Jerusalem. Clubs: Ohio State U. Alumnae of Franklin County (pres. 1962-64, 71-72). Home: 3355 Somerford Rd Columbus OH 43221-1436

ALLEN, LYNN ELIZABETH, foundation director; b. Louisville, Sept. 30, 1952; d. Mervyn E. and Elizabeth Ann (Whitler) A.; m. Jay Kirk Kittel, Apr. 29, 1978. BA in Social Work, U. Ky., 1974; M of Internat. Mgmt., U. Denver, 1992. Paralegal Sherman & Howard, Denver, 1978-82; asst. v.p. United Bank of Denver, 1982-87; dir. adminstrn. & devel. Colo. Springs (Colo.) Fine Arts Ctr., 1987-90; sr. cons. MIDAS Consulting Group, Denver, 1990-92; regional dir. CARE Found., Chgo., 1992—. Grant panelist Colo. Coun. on the Arts & Humanities, Denver, 1988-92. Mem. Chgo. Coun. on Fgn. Affairs, Alliance Francaise, Exec. Club. Office: CARE Found 70 E Lake St Chicago IL 60601

ALLEN, MARY LOUISE HOOK, physical education educator; b. Ironwood, Mich., July 18, 1930; d. Frank Eugene and Elsie Clara (Schneider) Hook; m. Dale Sanson Allen, June 30, 1955; children: Jack Eugene, Bradley Arthur. BS in Phys. Edn. cum laude, U. Mich., 1951; MA in Phys. Edn., U. Minn., 1970, postgrad., 1987—. Life teaching cert., coaching lic., Minn. Secondary edn. tchr. New Trier Twp. High Sch., Winnetka, Ill., 1951-55, Richfield (Minn.) Sch. Dist., 1955-59; teaching assoc. U. Minn., Mpls., 1969-70; part-time lectr. U. Minn., 1985-86; tchr. Bloomington (Minn.) Sch. Dist., 1961-85; adj. prof. Concordia Coll., St. Paul, Minn., 1987-92; officiator U.S. Synchro Minn. Assn., Minn. State High Sch. League, Pan-Am. Trials Swimming Co-Chair, others; past officiating bd. chmn. North Shore (Winnetka) Basketball/Volleyball, Ill. State Basketball com., others. Co-author: Soccer/Speedball Rule Book - Creative Game, 1952. Mem. Atonement Luth. Ch., Bloomington, 1956—; worker Dem. Party, Bloomington, 1988—; dir. Synchronized Swimming Camp, 1980-87. Recipient numerous athletic awards. Mem. AAHPERD (mem. com. 1949—), Minn. Assn. Health, Phys. Edn., Recreation and Dance (sec. 1982-83, pres.-elect 1984, pres. 1985, past pres. 1986, conv. chmn. 1984, 86, student confs. 1988-92), Synchronized Swim Coaches Assn. (state chmn. 1980-82), Athletic Fedn. Coll. Women (chmn. nat. conv. 1951), Phi Beta Kappa, Phi Kappa Phi, Mortarboard, Pi Lambda Theta, others. Home: 10312 Wentworth Ave Bloomington MN 55420-5249

ALLEN, MICHAEL D., investment broker; b. Atlantic, Iowa, May 19, 1957. Investment advisor IDS Fin., Mpls., 1980—; investment broker Norwest Investment, Atlantic, 1994—. Bd. dirs. Atlantic Park and Recreation, 1980—, Atlantic Golf and Country, 1994—. Mem. Elks. Republican. Lutheran. Home: PO Box 463 Atlantic IA 50022-0463 Office: Norwest Investment Svcs 600 Chestnut St Atlantic IA 50022-1451

ALLEN, MICHAEL KURT, municipal court judge; b. Weisbaden, Germany, Dec. 4, 1955; came to U.S., 1957; s. James Nathaniel and Jo Anne Rose (Franklin) A.; m. Lisa Conway, Dec. 18, 1982; children: Michael K. Allen Jr., Cora Lee Allen. AS in Law Enforcement, U. Cin., 1977, BS in Criminal Justice, 1980; JD, Ohio Northern U., 1983. Bar: Ohio 1984. Police officer City of Cin., Cin., 1978-80; asst. prosecuting atty. Preble County Prosecutor's Office, Eaton, Ohio, 1983-85, City of Cin., Cin., 1985-89; chief dep. Hamilton County Clk. of Cts., Cin., 1989-93; judge Hamilton County Mcpl. Ct., Cin., 1993—; founding chmn. Hamilton County Conservative Forum, Cin., 1991-93. Campaign chmn. Hamilton County Rep. Party, Cin., 1992. Capt. USAR, 1987—. Mem. Cin. Bar Assn., Ohio Bar Assn. Republican. Roman Catholic. Office: Hamilton County Mcpl Ct Rm 280 1000 Main St Cincinnati OH 45202

ALLEN, NORMAN LYNN, retail buyer; b. Kansas City, Mo., Dec. 28, 1934; s. Fountain Ridell and Mildred I. (Stultz) A. BA, Carleton Coll., 1956. Buyer Hallmark Cards, Inc., Kansas City, 1959—; mem. S.E.A.K., Zurich, 1963—, T.C.A., Strasburg, Pa., 1965—. Contbr. articles to mags. Republican. Home: 3612 N Walnut St Kansas City MO 64116-2705 Office: Hallmark Cards Inc 200 E 25th St Kansas City MO 64108-2509

ALLEN, STEPHEN D(EAN), pathologist, microbiologist; b. Linton, Ind., Sept. 8, 1943; s. Wilburn and Betty (Moffett) A.; m. Vally C. Autrey, June 17, 1964; children: Christopher D., Amy C. BA, Ind. U., 1965, MA, 1967; MD, Ind. U., Indpls., 1970. Diplomate Am. Bd. Pathology; cert. in anatomic and clin. pathology and med. microbiology. Intern in pathology Vanderbilt U. Hosp., Nashville, 1970-71; resident in pathology Vanderbilt U. Hosp., 1971-74; clin. asst. prof. pathology Emory U., Atlanta, 1974-77; asst. prof. clin. pathology Ind. U., Indpls., 1977-79; asst. prof. pathology Ind. U., 1979-81, assoc. prof. pathology, 1981-86, prof. pathology, 1986-92; prof. pathology and lab. medicine, 1992—; assoc. dir. div. clin. microbiology, dept. pathology Ind. U., 1977—, dir. grad. progam pathology, 1986—, sr. assoc. chmn. dept. pathology, 1990-91, dir. divsn. clin. microbiology dept. pathology/lab. medicine, 1992—; dir. disease control lab. divsn. Ind. State Dept. Health, 1994—. Co-author: Color Atlas of Diagnostic Microbiology, 4th edit. 1992, Introduction to Diagnostic Microbiology, 1994; contbr. articles to profl. jours. With USPHS, 1974-77. Fellow Coll. Am. Pathologists, Am. Acad. Microbiology, Am. Soc. Clin. Pathologists (coun. mem. microbiology 1983-89), Infectious Diseases Soc. Am., Soc. Sigma Xi; mem. Am. Bd. Pathology (trustee 1995—, chair microbiology test com., vice chair clin. pathology test com.), Masons (32d degreee), Shriners. Office: Ind U Hosp Rm 4430 550 N University Blvd Indianapolis IN 46202-5283

ALLEN, WAYDE P., manufacturing executive; b. Knox, Ind., Dec. 30, 1957. Student, Calif. State U., Northridge. Pres. U.S. R.R. Vest Corp., South Bend, Ind., 1989—. Office: US RR Vest Corp 108 N Main St Ste 805 South Bend IN 46601-1618

ALLEN, WILLIAM C., financial consultant; b. Monroe, La., July 27, 1939; s. Theodor H. and Alice (Cobb) A.; m. Susan Jantori, Oct. 9, 1977. BBA, Tulane U., 1961; MBA, La. State U., 1966. Credit mgr. Am. Can Co., various locations, 1967-76; fin. cons. Smith Barney Inc., Barrington, Ill., 1976—. Mem. Hist. Soc., 1985—. Lt. U.S. Army, 1962-63. Mem. Lions, Ducks Unltd. Republican. Episcopalian. Office: Smith Barney Inc # 105 101 Lions Dr Barrington IL 60010-3147

ALLEN, WILLIAM DALE, newspaper editor; b. Joplin, Mo., Aug. 16, 1938; s. William Longstaff and Freda Valera (Jones) A.; m. Barbara Bower, Aug. 26, 1960; children: Kendall Maria, Matthew Paul, Anna Elizabeth. AA in Arts, Mo. So. (formerly Joplin Jr. Coll.), 1959; BJ, U. Mo., 1961. Reporter Joplin Glove, 1957-59; news editor Newport (Ark.) Ind., 1961-63; asst. city editor, Carolinas editor, nat. editor Charlotte (N.C.) Observer, 1963-70; asst. mng. editor, assoc. mng. editor Phila. Inquirer, 1970-80; exec. editor Akron (Ohio) Beacon Jour., 1980-86, editor, 1986—. Juror Pulitzer Prize, 1986-87. With U.S. Army, 1956-57; sgt. USAR, 1957-74. Mem. Soc. Profl. Journalists. Methodist. Home: 700 Merriman Rd Akron OH 44303-1663 Office: Akron Beacon Jour 44 E Exchange St Akron OH 44328-0001

ALLEN-BOUSKA, REBECCA AUK, county official; b. Orlando, Fla., June 7, 1961; d. Donald Rae and Anneke (Schaafsma) Allen; m. Ronald D. Bouska, Dec. 10, 1988; children: Christopher J., Ronald D. Jr., Sara K., Phillip M. BA, Kans. State U., 1984; MPA, Wichita State U., 1987. Intern budget office City of Wichita, Kans., 1986; mgmt. analyst budget dept. County of Sedgwick, Wichita, 1986-87, sr. mgmt. analyst, 1987-88, info. svcs. supr., 1988-89, budget dir., 1989-95; fin. dir., 1995—. Mem. Am. Soc. Pub. Adminstrn. (pres. Wichita chpt. 1988), Forum Exec. Women, Govt. Fin. Officers Assn., Sigma Delta Pi, Phi Kappa Phi. Presbyterian. Home: 724 Fairway St Wichita KS 67212-4432 Office: Sedgwick County 525 N Main St Ste 823 Wichita KS 67203-3703

ALLERS, MARLENE ELAINE, legal administrator; b. Crosby, Minn., Dec. 29, 1931; d. Robert Prudent and Tressa Ida May (Hiller) Huard; m. Herbert Dodge Allers, Aug. 29, 1950 (dec. Aug. 1977); children: Melanie Lynn, Geoffrey Brian. B.S. in Math., U. Minn.-Mpls., 1966, BA in Acctg., 1968, MBA in Pers. and Fin. Mgmt., 1972. Bus. mgr., Earl Clinic, St. Paul, 1959-68, Lindquist & Vennum, Mpls., 1968-79, Stacker, Ravich & Simon, Mpls., 1979-82, Wagner, Johnston & Falconer, Ltd., Mpls., 1983-90; owner Minn. Express Process Servers, 1989—; lectr. Inst. of Continuing Legal Edn., Mpls., 1977. Recipient Outstanding Achievement award in Bus. Young Women's Christian Assn., Mpls., 1978. Mem. Minn. Legal Adminstrs. Assn., Mensa. Avocations: bridge, reading. Home: 608 Queen Ave S Minneapolis MN 55405-1968

ALLEY, THOMAS WILLIAM, physician; b. Anderson, Ind., Mar. 13, 1938; s. Harry Russell and Frances Ferree (Harvey) A.; m. Martha Lynn Elam, Oct. 18, 1975; children: Suzanne Jane, John Thomas, Sarah Elizabeth, Matthew David. BA in Chemistry, Ind. U., 1960, MD, 1963; Cert. Biblical Studies, Trinity Evangelical Divinity Sch., 1994. Diplomate Am. Bd. Internal Medicine. Intern Methodist Hosp., Indpls., 1963-64, resident internal medicine, 1964-65, 67-69, nephrology fellow, 1968-69; pvt. practice Indpls., 1969—; med. dir. Dialysis Inst. of Anderson, Ind., 1986—. Elder, Christian Ch., Indpls., 1990-94, 95—. Lt. USN, 1965-67. Fellow Am. Coll. Physicians; mem. Am. Soc. Nephrology, Am. Soc. Artificial Internal Organs, Am. Soc. Internal Medicine, Undersea Med. Soc., Christian Med. and Dental Soc., Nat. Kidney Found. Home: 8840 Mud Creek Rd Indianapolis IN 46256 Office: Nephrology and Internal Medicine Inc 1801 N Senate #355 Indianapolis IN 46202

ALLEY, TOM, state legislator; b. Bay County, Mich., Feb. 19, 1946; s. Frank Billy and Evelyn Ann (McHenry) A.; m. Joyce Marie Gildner, 1967; 1 child, Michael Thomas. BS, Ctrl. Mich. U., 1968, MA, 1975. State rep.

Mich. Ho. Reps., Dist. 103, 1978—; mem. dem. caucus, 1985-86, chmn. conservation, recreation & environ. com., mem. agrl. forestry & minerals, corps. & fin. & tourism, fisheries & Wildlife coms., Mich. Ho. Reps.; instr. Pinconning H.S., 1966-71, Ogemaw Hts. H.S., West Br., 1971-78. County coord. Frank Kelley for Senate, 1974, Sander Levin for Gov., 1974, donald Riegle for Senate, 1976; del. Dem. Nat. Conv., 1976; supr. Oegmaw (Mich.) Twp., 1977-78; chmn. Ogamae County Dem. Com.; mem. Mich. Stae Dem. Ctrl. Com.; mem.-at-large Mich. State Dem. Party. Recipient award for Outstanding Leadership & Contbr. to Recreation Cmty., Internat. Snowmobile Indsl. Assn. Mem. NRA, Lion, Moose, Eagles, Farm Bus., KC. (charter). Home: 920 W Wright St West Branch MI 48661-9309*

ALLI, RICHARD JAMES, SR., manufacturing executive; b. McKeesport, Pa., June 16, 1932; s. James and Elizabeth (Hallas) A.; m. Margaret Ann Coursin, Mar. 17. 1950 (div. Dec. 1973); children: Richard James Jr., Deborah Elaine, Stephen John; m. D. Joan Love, Sept. 17, 1976. Cer. in electronics, Devry Inst., 1962. Co-owner R&R Auto Trim, MCkeesport, 1962-68, Poolside Motel, Geneva-on-the-Lake, Ohio, 1966-96; structural steel insp. State of Ohio, 1968-79; pres. Pyramid 7 Corp., Warren, Ohio, 1979—; pres., chmn. bd., owner Corflex Internat., Inc., Warren, 1984—. V.p. Teenage Enterprises, Warren, 1979. Mem. KT, Shriners, Internat. Order of Merit. Republican. Home: 734 Kinsman St NW Warren OH 44483-3114 Office: Corflex Internat Inc PO Box 4324 Warren OH 44482-4324

ALLIN, CRAIG WILLARD, political science educator; b. Two Harbors, Minn., Oct. 3, 1946; s. Willard Stanton and Beverly Joy (Richmond) A.; m. Elizabeth Ann Sparks, Oct. 9, 1977. BA, Grinnell Coll., 1968; MA, Princeton U., 1970, PhD, 1976. Asst. prof. polit. sci. Cornell Coll., Mt. Vernon, Iowa, 1972-79, assoc. prof., 1979-85, chair dept., 1979-89, 95—, prof., 1985—; vis. asst. prof. Duke U., Durham, N.C., 1978. Author: Politics of Wilderness Preservation, 1982; editor, author: (with others) International Handbook of National Parks and Nature Reserves, 1990; contbr. articles to profl. jours. Park commr. City of Mt. Vernon, 1975-77; chief Lisbon-Mt. Vernon Ambulance Svc., 1976-87, bd. dirs. 1991—, pres. 1995—; planning and zoning commr. City of Lisbon (Iowa) 1979-82. Charles G. Osgood fellow Princeton (N.J.) U., 1969, Univ. House fellow Mellon Found. U. Iowa, Iowa City, 1983, Presdl. fellow Cornell Coll., Mt. Vernon, 1989. Mem. AAUP., Am. Polit. Sci. Assn., Phi Beta Kappa. Democrat. Home: 218 2nd Ave N Mount Vernon IA 52314-1303 Office: Cornell Coll 600 1st St W Mount Vernon IA 52314-1098

ALLINGTON, ROBERT WILLIAM, instrument company executive; b. Madison, Wis., Sept. 18, 1935; s. William B. and Norma Evelyn (Peterson) A.; m. Mary Lynn Kaylor, Sept. 4, 1976. BS, U. Nebr., 1959, MS, 1961, ScD (hon.), 1985. CEO, chmn. Isco, Inc., Lincoln, Nebr., 1961—. Inventor in field; contbr. numerous articles to profl. jours. Bd. dirs. League Human Dignity, Lincoln, 1981—, Nebr. Rsch. and Devel. Authority Lincoln, 1986-94, chmn., 1990-94; mem. Gov.'s Com. on Employment of the Handicapped, Lincoln, 1983; mem. Indsl. Adv. Bd., Dept. Chemistry, U. Nebr., 1988—; bd. dirs. Lincoln Cmty. Found. Inc., 1989-96; chmn. Nebr. EPSCOR Com., 1991—. Named Handicapped Nebraskan of the Yr., Gov. of Nebr., 1972, Outstanding Engring. Achievement Profl. Engrs., 1975, Nat. Small Bus. Person of the Yr., SBA, 1985, Exec. of the Yr., R&D Mag., 1991, U. of Nebr. Outstanding Alumnus, 1993; recipient Disting. Svc. award Kiwanis, 1978, Support of Rsch. award Sigma Xi, 1986. Mem. Am. Chem. Soc., Am. Inst. Chemists, IEEE, Instrument Soc. Am., Nat. Soc. Profl. Engrs., Analytical Instrument Assn. (bd. dirs. 1992-95), Univ. Club, The Club. Episcopalian. Office: Isco Inc 4700 Superior St Lincoln NE 68504-1328

ALLINSON, CARL, radiologist; b. New Haven, Feb. 20, 1912; s. Jacob Samuel and Sophie Allinson; m. Roze Bernstene Rapaport, Nov. 11, 1986; children: Arthur, Robert, Nancy, Jeffrey. BS, Yale U., 1932; PhD in Biochemistry, Boston U., 1938; MD, U. Ark., Little Rock, 1945. Diplomate Am. Bd. Radiology. Radiologist Franklin Hosp., Benton, Ill., 1957-75, A.G. Holley State Hosp., Lantana, Fla., 1981—; instr. physiology U. Ark. Sch. Medicine, Little Rock, 1940-45; instr. biochemistry La. State U., New Orleans, 1939-40. Rschr. in field; contbr. articles to profl. jours. Home: 619 Drexel Ave Glencoe IL 60022

ALLISON, DENNIS RAY, minister; b. Kansas City, Mo., July 24, 1953; s. Raymond Emmett and Edith Eleanor (Kistler) A.; m. Rebecca Jane Durham, May 27, 1953; children: Monica Michelle, Lauren Megan. AB, Ottawa U., 1980; MDiv, Princeton U., 1984. Ordained to ministry in Presbyn. Ch., 1984. Pastor White Oak Springs Presbyn. Ch., Butler, Pa., 1984-88, Northminster Presbyn. Ch., Pitts., 1988-94; sr. minister First Presbyn. Ch., Mansfield, Ohio, 1994—. Home: 399 S Trimble Rd Mansfield OH 44906-2938 Office: First Presbyn Ch 399 S Trimble Mansfield OH 44906-2938

ALLISON, ELLEN MAGDALEN, critical care nurse; b. Chgo., Mar. 5, 1952; d. Chester Ignatius and Helen Loretta (Simzek) Kosinski; m. Michael Patrick Allison, Apr. 19, 1986; 1 child, Molly Magdalen. AS, Moraine Valley C.C., Palos Hills, Ill., 1976; RN, Little Company of Mary Hosp., 1976; student, Coll. St. Francis, 1992—. RN, Ill.; cert. BLS, ACLS, PALS, pediatric EKLG, pediatric cardiology, pediatric ICU, IV therapy. Pediatric nurse Little Company of Mary Hosp., Evergreen Park, Ill., 1976-78, med. intensive care nurse, 1978-84; nurse, critical care resource pool Children's Meml. Hosp., Chgo., 1984-85, nurse pediatric intensive care, 1985-88; nurse pediatric intensive care Pro Nurse P.C., Chgo., 1988—; nurse pediatric intensive care Christ Hosp. and Med. Ctr., Oaklawn, Ill., 1990-91, nurse, MRI-radiology dept., 1992-93; neurol. and med. ICU nurse Hinsdale (Ill.) Hosp., 1993-95; pediatric ICU nurse Shriners Hosp. for Crippled Children, Chgo., 1995; pediatric nurse St. Francis Hosp., Blue Island, Ill., 1995—; pediatric ICU nurse Loyola Med. Ctr., Maywood, Ill., 1996—; ind. solo vocalist; handwriting analyst. Active St. Barnabas Folk Mass Group, Beverly Found. for Perfoming Arts.; mem. Brookfield Zoo Soc. Mem. Brookfield Zoo Soc., Little Company of Mary Nurse Alumni Assn., Polish Women's Civic Club, Beverly Hills Univ. Club, Polish Roman Catholic Union Am. Home: 8841 S Francisco Ave Evergreen Park IL 60805-1249

ALLISON, JAMES EDWARD, design engineer; b. Berwyn, Ill., Sept. 17, 1959; s. Jack and Carol A. AAS, Indian Hills C.C., Ottumwa, Iowa, 1980. Cert. machinist, tool and die maker. Design engr. Detroit Tool & Engring., Lebanon, Mo., 1980—. Coach, Little League Baseball, Lebanon. Baptist. Office: Detroit Tool & Engring 441 W Elm St Lebanon MO 65536-3523

ALLISON, SANDY, genealogist, appraiser, political consultant; b. Newburg, Mo., June 30, 1950; d. Jimmy James and A. Colleen (Bricker) Arthur; m. Lynn Leonard Allison, Oct. 3, 1969; children: Eric Lynn, Jason Wayne. Student, Columbia Coll., Rolla, Mo., North Ctrl. Jr. Coll., Clarksville, Tenn., East Ctrl. Coll., Union, Mo., U. Mo., Rolla. Sec./bookkeeper Biederman Furniture Store, Rolla, 1969-72; bookkeeper/clk. Rolla Auction Co.; degree State Farm Ins., Rolla, 1995; demonstrator, salesperson Roth Distbn., St. Louis; home inspector Allison Assn., Rolla; owner/designer Allison Residential Contr., Rolla; owner/acct. Flowers Unltd. Inc., Rolla; appraiser Stoltz Appraisal Co., Rolla, 1985-91; med. placement cons. Assoc. Svcs., Rolla, 1991-92; pub. adminstr. Phelps County, Rolla, 1992—; field dir. Carnahan for Gov. Campaign, St. Louis, 1991-92. Author/editor: Allison Book, 1995; editor, chmn. com.: The Phelps County Missouri Heritage, 1991. Dem. Nat. committeewoman for State of Mo., 1992—; 8th Dist. pres. Dem. Party, 1990-95; bd. dirs. Connect Mo., 1993-94; v.p., pres., bd. dirs. PHelps County Univ. Ext., 1989-95; chairwoman Phelps County Dem. Party; v.p., membership chair Jeffersonian Women's Group; mem. solid waste commn. Meramec Regional Planning Commn.; mem. Mothers Against Drunk Drivers. Named Dem. Outstanding Woman. Mem. Geneal. Soc. Mo. (pres., v.p., bd. dirs., State award 1992), Nat. Assn. Counties for Cmty. and Econ. Devel. (bd. dirs. 1992-93), Bus. and Profl. Women's Club (pres., legis. state chair 1991-94), Rolla Area C. of C., Phelps County Geneal. Soc. (founder, pres.), Toastmasters Internat., Nat. Assn. Real Estate Appraisers, Ind. Fee Appraisers Assn., Internat. Platform Assn., Alpha Sigma Alpha. Home and Office: 10095 County Road 5120 Rolla MO 65401-6162*

ALLISON, SANDY DIANE, public administrator; b. Rolla, Mo., June 30; d. Jimmy James Arthur and Colleen (Artis) Bricker; m. Lynn Leonard Allison, Oct. 3, 1969; children: Eric Lynn, Jason Wayne. Student, North Ctrl. Jr. Coll., East Ctrl. Coll.; BA in History/Govt., Columbia Coll., 1996, postgrad., 1996—. With Rolla Aviation Co., 1965-69, Bidermans Furniture Co., Rolla, 1969-73, State Farm Ins., Rolla, 1972-73, Roth Distbg. Co., St. Louis, 1976-79, Stoltz Appraisal Co., Rolla, 1985-91; founder, pres. Phelps County Geneal. Soc., Rolla, 1989-92; with Associated Svcs., Rolla, 1991—; polit. cons.; chmn., publ. staff Phelps County Heritage, Rolla, 1992-93; mem. U. Ext. Bd., Rolla, 1990-93, v.p., 1992-93, pres., 1993-94; polit. cons. Midwest Opinion Rsch. Enterprises. Active State Com. Women, 1989-92, South Dillon Twp. Com. Women, 1990—, Nat. Com. Women, 1992—; chair Phelps County Dem. com., 1990—; vice-chair Mo. State Geneal. Soc., 1990-93; pub. adminstr., Phelps County, 1992-93. Recipient Outstanding Work award State Geneal. Soc., 1992. Mem. MADD, Nat. Assn. of Counties for Comty. and Econ. Devel. (bd. dirs. 1992-93), Nat. Assn. Ind. Fee Appraisers, Mo. Fedn. Bus. and Profl. Women's State Legis. Chairwomen, Toastmaster Internat., Internat. Platform Assn., Phelps County Garden Club, Rolla Area C. of C., Alpha Sigma Lambda. Mem. Ch. of Christ. Home: 10095 County Road 5120 Rolla MO 65401-6162 Office: 4th and Elm St Rolla MO 65401-0055

ALLMAN, MARGARET ANN LOWRANCE, counselor; b. Carmel, Calif., June 2, 1938; d. Edward Walton and Rhoda Elizabeth (Patton) Lowrance; m. Jackie Howard Hamilton, Dec. 21, 1959 (div. May 1976); children: John Scott, David Lee, Dennis Lynn; m. Jack Fredrick Allman, Dec. 22, 1977; stepchildren: John Frederick, James Pau l, Jeffrey Lee. AA, Christian Coll., 1958; BA in Spanish, U. Mo., 1960, MEd, 1971, EdD, 1994. Tchr. Spanish Neosho (Mo.) H.S., 1961-62, asst. prin., 1974-77; florist Wallflower Shop and Greenhouse, Joplin, Mo., 1962-69; dean girls Joplin Sr. H.S., 1967-69; florist, bookkeeper Mueller's Garden Ctr., Columbia, Mo., 1969-71; instr. edn., asst. dean of students Columbia (Mo.) Coll., 1971-74; dir. guidance Am. Cmty. Sch., Buenos Aires, 1978-81; tchr. Spanish, psychology Ava (Mo.) H.S., 1982-84; tchr. Spanish, social studies McDonald County H.S., Anderson, Mo., 1984-88; counselor Mo. So. State Coll., Joplin, 1988—; mem. adv. bd. Adult Basic Edn., Joplin, 1992—; cons. Mo. So. State Coll., 1990—, mem. internat. task force, 1994—; presenter Ctr. for Applications of Psychol. Type Internat. Conf., 1996. Recipient William D. Phillips Music award 1st Christian Ch., Columbia, 1956. Mem. Mo. Sch. Counselor Assn., Southwest Mo. Sch. Counselor Assn. (sec. 1994—, v.p. 1992-94, mem. governing bd.). Home: 1214 Circle Dr Neosho MO 64850 Office: Mo So State Coll 3950 E Newman Rd Joplin MO 64850

ALM, ROGER RUSSELL, chemist; b. Kansas City, Mo., Nov. 19, 1945; s. Russell Arthur and Jean Grace (Frantz) A.; m. Laura Linnea Kiscaden, Oct. 14, 1983 (dec. June 1993); m. Lisa Monzel, May 7, 1995. BChemE, U. Minn., 1967; MS in Chemistry, Northwestern U., 1968. Adv. chemist Speciality Chems. divsn. 3M Co., St. Paul, 1968-72, sr. chemist, 1972-82, devel. specialist, 1982-93, patent liaison, 1993—; patent agt., 1995—. Contbr. articles to profl. jours. Singer 3M Male Chorus, St. Paul, 1970-85; bd. dirs., arranger Sundown, St. Paul, 1970-85; tutor sci. 3M Vol. Program, 1988—. Mem. Am. Chem. Soc., Alpha Chi Sigma (treas. 1982-84). Democrat. Unitarian Universalist. Home: 5187 Jamaca Ave N Lake Elmo MN 55042-9581 Office: 3M Co 3M Center Bldg 236-2B Saint Paul MN 55144-1000

ALMIRO, JACK J., stockbroker; b. Chgo., Jan. 25, 1943. Owner lumber co. Chgo., 1974-82; securities broker Merrill Lynch, Northbrook, Ill., 1984-91; stockbroker Prudential Securities, Deerfield, Ill., 1991—. Republican. Roman Catholic. Home: 125 Pine Tree Trl Deerfield IL 60015-1914 Office: Prudential Securities Inc # 100 500 Lake Cook Rd Deerfield IL 60015-4922

ALMONY, ROBERT ALLEN, JR., librarian, businessman; b. Charleston, W.Va., Oct. 14, 1945; s. Robert Allen and Margaret Elizabeth (Morrison) A.; m. Carol A. Krzeminski, May 6, 1972; children—Robby, Michael, Chandra, Rachel. A.A., Grossmont Coll., 1965; B.A., San Diego State U., 1968; M.L.S., U. Calif.-Berkeley, 1977. Sr. div. clk. San Diego State U. Library, 1965-68; acct. Calif. Tchrs. Fin. Services, Orange County, 1968-70, v.p., gen. mgr., 1971-76; research asst. library sch. U. Calif.-Berkeley, 1976-77; reference librarian Oberlin Coll. Library, Ohio, 1977-79; asst. dir. libraries U. Mo., Columbia, 1980—; owner Almony & Assocs. Tax and Fin. Planning, Columbia, 1980—; distbr. USA Today, Columbia, 1984-88; guest lectr. library budgeting; cons. library copy services; faculty coun. exec. bd., recorder Mo. U., 1994—. Contbr. articles to profl. jours. Treas. Bahai's of Columbia, 1982-86, 95—, sec., 1987-89, 93-95, chmn., 1989-93; coach Columbia Youth Soccer League, 1981-92; cubmaster Boy Scouts Am., Columbia, 1983-85; asst. scoutmaster, 1985-91, hon. warrior, Mic-O-Say, 1986—. Mem. ALA, Mo. Libr. Assn. (treas. 1996—), Assn. Coll. and Rsch. Librs. (exec. com. 1983-86), Libr. Adminstrn. and Mgmt. Assn. (chmn. mem. 1991-93, Outstanding Svc. award 1984), B & F Officers Group Libr. Adminstrn. amd Mgmt. (chmn. 1987-91), Nat. Commn. on Ednl. Stats. Integrated Post-Secondary Edn. Data System Acad. Librs. (coord. for Mo. 1992—), Mo. Assn. Coll. and Rsch. Librs. (vice chmn., chmn. 1982-84), Hickman Athletic Boosters (pres. 1991-94), Maplewood Barn Theatre (bd. dirs. 1993—, sec.), COE Coll. Parents (bd. dirs. 1993-95). Home: 301 Rothwell Dr Columbia MO 65203-0257 Office: U Mo 104 Ellis Libr Columbia MO 65201-5149

ALOISIO, MARIA THERESA, tax accountant; b. Chgo., July 11, 1960; d. Alfredo and Maria Rose (Altomari) Talarico. BS in Commerce, DePaul U., Chgo., 1982, MS in Taxation, 1988. CPA, Ill. Jr. tax acct. Harris Trust and Savs. Bank, Chgo., 1982-86, tax acct., 1986-87, sr. tax acct., 1988-89; tax supr. Aon Corp., Chgo., 1989-91; sr. tax cons. Arthur Andersen & Co., Chgo., 1991-92, experienced sr. tax cons., 1992-94, asst. tax mgr., 1994—. Mem. AICPA, Ill. Soc. CPAs.

ALOMAR, SANDY, JR. (SANTOS VELAZQUEZ ALOMAR), professional baseball player; b. Salinas, P.R., June 18, 1966. With San Diego Padres, 1988-89, Cleve. Indians, 1990—. Named Rookie of Yr. Baseball Writers' Assn. Am., 1990, Sporting News, 1990, named to Am. League All-Star team, 1990, 91; recipient Am. League Gold Glove award, 1990. Office: Cleve Indians Cleve Stadium 2401 Ontario St Cleveland OH 44115-4003*

ALONZI, LORETO PETER, finance executive; b. Evanston, Ill., Sept. 16, 1951; s. Saverio Joseph and Sheila Helen (McEnery) A.; m. Mary Rose Sievers; children: Loreto Peter III, Christopher Patrick, Nicholas Daniel. BA magna cum laude, Loyola U., Chgo., 1973; MA in Econs., U. Iowa, 1976, PhD in Econs., 1979. Asst. prof. econs. Bowling Green (Ohio) State U., 1978-80, Loyola U., Chgo., 1980-86; v.p. Sora Loan Corp., Chgo., 1986-87, pres., chief operating officer, 1988-90; sr. mgr. market devel. Chgo. Bd. Trade, 1991—; bd. dirs. Sora Loan Corp.; speaker Chgo. Bd. Trade, 1982-87, Commodities Edn. Inst., Iowa, 1987-88; adj. prof. econs., 1996. Contbr. articles to profl. jours. Recipient Teaching Rsch. Fellowship U. Iowa, Iowa City, 1973-77; named Tchr. of Yr. Alpha Lambda Delta, Bowling Green, 1981, Kemper Faculty Scholar, Loyola U., 1985. Mem. Internat. Wine and Food Soc. of Chgo., Am. Econ. Assn., Midwest Fin. Assn. (instl. dir.), Nat. Futures Assn. (mem. ednl./testing adv. com. 1994, 95), Ind. Fin. Assn. of Ill. (bd. dirs. 1987-90), Beta Gamma Sigma, Omicron Delta Epsilon. Home: 431 Greenleaf Ave Wilmette IL 60091-1911 Office: Chgo Bd Trade Market and Product Devel Lasalle At Jackson Chicago IL 60604

ALPERT, ANN SHARON, insurance claims examiner; b. Indpls., Feb. 24, 1938; d. Oscar and Adele Alpert. BS in Edn., Ind. U., 1959. Tchr. Indpls. Pub. Schs., 1959-60; libr. George Fry & Assocs., Chgo., 1960-62, DeLeuw, Cather & Co., Chgo., 1962-65, Arthur Young & Co., CPAs, Chgo., 1965-74; statis. asst. Sargent & Lundy, Chgo., 1974-81, computer liaison agt., 1981-83, tech. editor, 1983-87; sales assoc. Jewelmaster, Inc., Chgo., 1987-88; claims processor Benefit Trust Life Ins. Co., 1988-90; claims examiner Ft. Dearborn Life Ins. Co., 1990-91, sr. claims examiner, 1991—. Fellow Life Mgmt. Inst. (assoc. customer svc.); mem. Chgo. Claims Assn., Women in Workers' Compensation.

ALSBRO, DONALD EDGAR, health educator; b. Detroit, May 20, 1940; s. Oscar Edgar and Alice Eleanor (Roberts) A.; m. Sharon Marie Gildea, May 18, 1963; children: Laura Lynn, Steven Dieter, Alan Keith. BA, Western Mich. U., 1963; MA, Roosevelt U., 1973; MS, Ea. Mich. U., 1973; EdS, Western Mich. U., 1980; EdD, Wayne State U., 1988. Cert. health edn. specialist. Commd. 2d lt. U.S. Army, 1963, advanced through grades to col., 1989; instr. health Lake Michigan Coll., Benton Harbor, Mich., 1973-92; developer "Dump Your Plump" nat. worksite wellness program; bd. dirs. Rainbow Wellness, Benton Harbor. With USAR, 1972-94. Elected to Western Mich. U. ROTC Hall of Fame, 1991. Mem. AAHPERD, Mich. Coun. for Phys. Fitness and Health, Assn. for Mil. Surgeons. Republican. Methodist. Home: 942 Sierra Dr Benton Harbor MI 49022-3539

ALSBROOK, JAMES ELDRIDGE, journalist, educator; b. Kansas City, Mo., Nov. 28, 1913; s. Irving Adolphus and Elgeitha Dorothy (Stovall) A.; m. Brydie Rosetta Everett, June 6, 1942 (div. Dec. 1961); 1 child, James Eldridge Jr. BS, Kans. U., 1963, MS, 1964; PhD, U. Iowa, 1968. Reporter Kansas City (Kans.) Plaindealer, 1933-36; sports editor St. Louis Call, 1936-38; sports, theatricals editor Kansas City (Mo.) Call, 1938-40; copy editor, feature writer Afro-Am. Newspapers, Balt., 1940-42, 45-48; ghost writer Kansas City, Kans., 1948-61; reporter Courier-Jour., Louisville, 1963-65; dir. pub. rels. Cen. State U., Wilberforce, Ohio, 1968-71; prof. Cen. State U., Wilberforce, 1971-78; prof. Ohio U., Athens, 1978-84, prof. emeritus, 1984—; chain store owner, 1945-61; weekly columnist for 87 African-Am. newspapers, 1991—. Contbr. chpts. to books, and articles to profl. jours. With U.S. Army Signal Corps., Reserve, 1942-44. Mem. ASCAP, Assn. for Edn. in Journalism and Mass Comm., Nat. Assn. Black Journalists, Kappa Tau Alpha, Sigma Delta Chi. Home: 6844 Gura Rd Athens OH 45701-9636 Office: Ohio U 232 Scripps Hall Athens OH 45701

ALSOP, DONALD DOUGLAS, federal judge; b. Duluth, Minn., Aug. 28, 1927; s. Robert Alvin and Mathilda (Aaseng) A.; m. Jean Lois Tweeten, Aug. 16, 1952; children: David, Marcia, Robert. BS, U. Minn., 1950, LLB, 1952. Bar: Minn. 1952. Pvt. practice New Ulm, Minn.; ptnr. Gislason, Alsop, Dosland & Hunter, 1954-75; judge U.S. Dist. Ct. Minn., St. Paul, 1975—, chief dist. judge, 1985-92, sr. dist. judge, 1992—; mem. 8th cir. jud. coun., 1987-92, Jud. Conf. Com. to Implement Criminal Justice Act, 1979-87; mem. exec. com. Nat. Conf. Fed. Trial Judges, 1990-94. Chmn. Brown County (Minn.) Republican Com., 1960-64, 2d Congl. Dist. Rep. Com., 1968-72, Brown County chpt. ARC, 1968-74. Served with AUS, 1945-46. Mem. 8th Cir. Dist. Judges Assn. (pres. 1982-84), New Ulm C. of C. (pres. 1974-75), Order of Coif. Office: US Dist Ct 242 Fed Bldg 316 Robert St N Saint Paul MN 55101-1423

ALSOVER, WILLIAM C., securities company executive. BA, Mich. U., 1971. Stockbroker Fond Stock & Co., Grand Rapids, 1971-82; pres. Centennial Securities, Grand Rapids, 1982—. Office: Centennial Securities PO Box 6217 Grand Rapids MI 49516-6217

ALSPACH, DAVE D., financial consultant; b. Newark, Ohio, Mar. 15, 1959. BSBA, Ohio State U., 1981. V.p. ops. Mid-Ohio Coca-Cola, Newark, 1981-86; corp. cold drink mgr. Coca-Cola Bottling Co. Mich., Lansing, 1986-88; fin. cons. Smith Barney Inc., Columbus, Ohio, 1988—. Mem. bldg. com. Dublin Presbyn. Ch., Columbus, 1993—. Mem. Ohio C. of C., Newark Area C. of C., Rotary. Republican. Office: Smith Barney Inc 65 E State St Fl 20 Columbus OH 43215-4213

ALSPACH, DONN E., management company executive; b. Newark, Ohio, June 21, 1931; s. Harold C. and Mary Louise (Edwards) A.; m. Marilyn C. O'Donnell, June 14, 1953; 1 child, David D. BS in Edn., Ohio State U., 1953. Sales mgr. Newark (Ohio) Coca-Cola Bottling Co., 1956-62, exec. v.p., 1962-65; pres. Mid-Ohio Coca-Cola Bottling Co., various cities, 1965-86; pres., chief exec. officer, dir. SharonBrooke Mgmt. Co., Newark, 1987—. Bd. dirs. Licking County Airport Authority, Newark, 1983—, pres., 1987-88; bd. dirs., pres. Salvation Army. With USAF, 1953-56, U.S. and Europe. Recipient Disting. Svc. award Newark Jaycees, 1964-65, Outstanding Young Man of Yr. award, 1966. Mem. Moundbuilders Country Club, Rotary Internat. (pres. Newark chpt. 1977, dist. 6690 gov. 1988-89), Masons, Shriners, Elks. Presbyterian. Office: The Inn at Chestnut Hill 5055 Thompson Rd Columbus OH 43230-6336

ALSPAUGH, DALE WILLIAM, university administrator, aeronautics and astronautics educator; b. Dayton, Ohio, May 25, 1932; m. Marlowe Anne Alspaugh; 4 children. ME, U. Cin., 1955; MS in Engring. Scis., Purdue U., 1958, PhD in Engring. Scis., 1965. Profl. engr., Ohio. Project engr. GMC Frigidaire div., 1955-56, 59; instr. sch. aeronautics and astronautics & engring. Purdue U., West Lafayette, Ind., 1957-58, 59-64, asst. prof., 1964-68, assoc. prof., 1968-81; vice chancellor for acad. svcs., prof. Purdue U. North Cen. campus, Westville, Ind., 1981-82, acting chancellor, prof., 1982-84; chancellor, prof. aeronautics and astronautics Purdue U. North Cen. campus, Westville, 1984—; mem. numerous coms. Purdue U.; cons. Midwest Applied Sci. Corp., West Lafayette, 1959-66, Roper Corp., West Lafayette, 1972-73, Switzer div. Wallace Murray Corp., Indpls., 1972-73, Los Alamos (N.Mex.) Scientific Lab., 1977, U.S. Army MICOM, Huntsville, Ala., 1978-82, Campbell & Pryor Cons. Corp., Michigan City, Ind., 1984-86, Colsa, Inc., Huntsville, 1988; reviewer Applied Mechs. Rev., J. Franklin Inst., ASME Jour. Heat Transfer, Internat. Jour. Engring. Sci., also NSF rsch. proposals, various books; bd. dirs. Meml. Hosp. Michigan City, 1st Citizens Bank of Michigan City, Horizon Bancorp. Contbr. articles to profl. jours.; also numerous reports, papers, seminars. Mem. West Lafayette Bd. Sch. trustees, 1976-81, sec., 1976-77, v.p. 1977-78, pres. 1978-79; mem. West Lafayette Park & Recreation Bd., 1976-81, treas. 1979-80; mem. West Lafayette Sch. Bd. Negotiating Team, 1977-78, chief negotiator, 1978; mem. West Lafeyett Sch. Supt. screening Com., 1980-81; mem. West Lafayette Community Sch. Coun., 1970-73, pres., 1973; pres. Burtsfield PTA, 1970-71; supt. Covenant Presbyn. Ch. Sch., 1969-74; mem. West Lafayette Little League Bd., 1969-72; bd. dirs. N.W. Ind. Forum, 1983—, mem. subcom. on strategic planning, 1983-85, N.W. Ind. ednl. pub. TV consortium, 1984, subcom. on legis. affairs, 1985—, subcom. on hazardous materials, 1986-87, ednl. consortium, 1988—; mem. Barker Commn., 1986—; bd. dirs. Friends of Barker; mem. City of Valparaiso Ethics Commn., 1995—. Recipient grants NASA, Purdue Rsch. Found., Fund for Instructional Devel. & Innovative Teaching, Fund for Alternatives in Engring. Edn., U.S. Army MICOM. Mem. AIAA (coun. Cen. Ind. sect. 1969-71), Am. Soc. Engring. Edn. (space engring. com. 1970-78), Greater Valparaiso C. of C. (bd. dirs. 1985-90, chmn. div. on local & govtl. affairs 1987-88), Rotary. Office: Purdue U N Cen Campus Office of the Chancellor 1401 S US Highway 421 Westville IN 46391-9528

ALTCHULER, STEVEN IRA, psychiatry consultant, researcher; b. N.Y.C., Aug. 1, 1951; s. Murray and Lyn A. Altchuler; m. Debra A. Radack, Mar. 20, 1982; children: Joshua, Amy. BS, MIT, 1973, PhD, 1979; MD, Baylor Coll. Medicine, 1986. Nutritional physiologist NASA Johnson Space Ctr., Houston, 1978-82; cons. Tech., Inc., Houston, 1982-86; psychiatry cons. Mayo Clinic, Rochester, Minn., 1986—; med. dir. Mayo Psychiatry & Psychology Treatment Ctr., Rochester, 1993—; com. mem. Minn. Dept. Human Svcs., St. Paul, 1989-93; bd. dirs. Psychiatrists Mutual Ins. Co. Contbr. articles to profl. jours. Bd. dirs. Clear Lake Emergency Med. Corps., Houston, 1980-82; vol. Boy Scouts Am., Rochester, 1988—, exec. bd., v.p. Gamehaven coun., 1993—, nat. coun. mem., 1995—. Rock Sleyster fellow AMA, 1985, Laughlin fellow Am. Coll. Psychiatrists, 1990. Fellow Am. Sleep Disorders Assn.; mem. Am. Coll. Psychiatrists, Am. Psychiat. Assn. (Burroughs Wellcome fellow 1988, dir. purchasing group 1991—, assembly rep. 1989-90), Minn. Psychiat. Soc. (membership chmn. 1990-95, sec.-treas. 1993-95), Zumbro Valley Med. Soc. (ethics and religion com. 1988-95, exec. bd. 1994—). Office: Mayo Clinic 200 1st St SW Rochester MN 55905-0001

ALTER, JOHN, otolaryngologist, facial cosmetic surgeon, educator; b. Hoffgastein, Austria, Feb. 6, 1946; came to U.S., 1948; s. Irving Israel and Clara Klara (Scotchinsky) A.; m. Denise Mary Webber, Apr. 17, 1982; children: Andrea Leah, Geoffrey Ian, Carolyn Clare, Leslie Nicole. BS, Wayne State U., 1967; DO, Des Moines Coll. Osteo. Medicine and Surgery, 1971. Diplomate Am. Bd. Otolaryngology, Am. Bd. Osteo. Otolaryngology & Facial Cosmetic Surgery. Intern, Botsford Hosp., Farmington, Mich., 1971-72; resident in surgery Providence Hosp., Southfield, Mich., 1972-73; resident in otolaryngology, facial cosmetic surgery Wayne State U., Detroit, 1973-76; practice medicine specializing in otolaryngology and facial cosmetic surgery, Pontiac, Mich., 1976—, Henry Ford Hosp., West Bloomfield, Mich., 1981—; clin. instr. Wayne State U. Med. Ctr., also local hosps.; past chmn. dept. otolaryngology and ophthalmology Pontiac (Mich.) Gen. Hosp., Huron Valley Hosp., Milford, St. Joseph Mercy Hosp. Mem. Simon Weisenthal Found., Zionist Orgn. Am., Sierra Club (West Bloomfield, Mich.). Fellow Am. Acad. Otolaryngology, Am. Facial Plastic and Reconstructive Soc.,

Osteo. Coll. Ophthalmalogy and Otohinolaryngology, Am. Acad. Cosmetic Surgery; mem. Am. Osteo. Assn., Oakland County Osteo. Assn., Mich. Osteo. Assn. Physicians and Surgeons, Mich. Otolaryn. Jewish. Office: 7001 Orchard Lake Rd Ste 230 West Bloomfield MI 48322-3604 also: 4000 Highland Rd Ste 100 Waterford MI 48328-2163

ALTER, WILLIAM, state legislator; b. Iowa City, May 15, 1944; m. Merijo Robinson, 1963; children: Angela, William Brett. Student, Jefferson Coll. Law, Enforcement Tng. Ctr., 1982-84. mem. consumer protection com., employment com., security and fair practice com., fees and salaries com. Mos. State rep. Dist. 90; owner, mgr. sml. bus.; sales v.p. Nat. Co. Mem. NRA (life), Hist. Soc. and Rep. Club, Mo. Roundtable (founding mem.). Home: 1800 Gravois Rd High Ridge MO 63049-2610*

ALTHEIDE, PHYLLIS SAGE, computer scientist, software engineer; b. St. Louis, Apr. 13, 1963; d. Paul D. and Alvera Sage; m. Richard W. Altheide, Aug. 1984; 1 child, Martha Elizabeth. BS in Computer Sci., U. Mo., Rolla, 1985, MS in Computer Sci., 1992. GS-12 computer scientist U.S. Geol. Survey, Rolla, 1988—; lead developer SDTS Task Force, Rolla, 1990-95. Mem. IEEE Computer Soc. Lutheran.

ALTHOFF, J(AMES) L., construction company executive; b. McHenry, Ill., June 9, 1928; s. William H. and Eleanor M. (Smith) A.; m. Joan E. Andreen, June 18, 1949; children: Tim, Betsy, Kate, Tod, Patti, Jim Jr., Karyn. Grad., McHenry (Ill.) High Sch., 1947. Owner, pres. Althoff Gas Svc., McHenry, 1949-60, Fox Valley Propane, 1952-60, No. Equip. Corp., McHenry, 1958-72; CEO Althoff Industries, Crystal Lake, Ill., 1961—, Althoff & Assocs., McHenry, 1962—, Brookside Indsl., McHenry, 1991—; trustee Plumbers Welfare Fund, Chgo., 1972—; dir. McHenry Bank. Pres. McHenry High Sch. Bd. Edn., 1967-79, Fire Protection Dist., McHenry, 1964-92; chmn. bd. govs. Ill. Univs., 1980-91; commr. Ill. State Lottery, 1991—. Recipient award for outstanding leadership Chgo. State U., 1986, Leadership award No. Med. Ctr., McHenry, 1984, Ea. Ill. U., 1987. Mem. Contrs. Assn. No. Ill. (pres. 1969-72), Bradley Dads' Assn., Kiwanis. Home: 508 N Green St Mc Henry IL 60050-5684 Office: Althoff Industries 8001 S State Route 31 Crystal Lake IL 60014-8188

ALTICK, VIRNA LIZETTE, nurse; b. Guatemala, Mar. 27, 1969; came to U.S., 1979; d. Bernarda Torres. ADN, Kettering Coll. Med. Arts, 1991. RN, Ohio. Cardiothoracic care unit nurse Kettering (Ohio) Hosp., 1991—. Republican. Home: 412 E Dorothy Ln Kettering OH 45419-1801

ALTKORN, ROBERT IRA, research scientist; b. Chgo.; m. Diane L. Seidman. BA, Northwestern U., Evanston, Ill., 1979; PhD, Stanford (Calif.) U., 1984. Rsch. asst. prof. Northwestern U., 1987-90; rsch. scientist Chgo. Inst. of Neurosurgery and Neuroresearch, Chgo., 1988-90, Basic Industry Rsch. Lab./Northwestern U., 1990—. Mem. Am. Chem. Soc., Am. Electroplaters and Surface Finishers Soc., Soc. of Phot Optical Instrumentation Engrs. Office: BIRL/Northwestern U 1801 Maple Ave Evanston IL 60201-3135

ALTOMARI, MARK G., clinical psychologist; b. Ft. Monroe, Va., July 13, 1947; s. Guido and Mary Ann Altomari; m. Susan Alice Gross, Mar. 22, 1969; children: Alicia, Devin, Paul. BA, Villanova U., 1974; MA, West Chester State U., 1978; MS, Va. Poly. Inst. and State U., 1982, PhD, 1984. Lic. psychologist. Traffic hearing examiner Bur. Traffic Safety, Commonwealth of Pa., Harrisburg, 1973-78; behavioral specialist Community Svcs. Inc., Lancaster, Pa., 1977-78; counselor New River Valley Coun. on Alcoholism, Christiansburg, Va., 1981-82; psychology technician VA Med. Ctr., Salem, Va., 1981-82; case mgr. New River Valley Alcohol Safety Action Project, Christiansburg, 1982; clin. psychologist Va. Poly. Inst., Blacksburg, 1982-83; clin. psychology supr. Fulton (Mo.) State Hosp., 1984-86; pvt. practice clin. psychologist Columbia, Mo., 1986—; cons. Disability Determinations, Jefferson City, Mo., 1986—, Archdiocese of Jefferson City, 1987—, Fulton Police Dept., 1988—, Mo. State Hwy. Patrol, 1996—; cons. cert., forensic examiner Fulton State Hosp., 1986-; dir. of counseling William Woods Coll., Fulton, 1985—. Contbr. articles to profl. jours. Coach, mgr. Columbia Soccer Club, 1985; cons. Mo. Water Patrol, 1990—; fund raiser Clearview Neighborhood Assn., Columbia, 1990; assoc. chief justice Grad. Honor Ct.; pres. Strategy and Tactics Soc., Pottstown, Pa., 1975-80; dep. Pa. Athletic Commn., 1972. Senatorial scholar Commonwealth of Pa., 1971; rsch. co-grantee Gen. Motors, 1983. Mem. APA (divsn. clin. psychology, divsn. clin. hypnosis, psychology-law soc., neuropsychology divsn., divsn. psychologists in pub. svcs., divsn. pscyhologists in ind. practice), Mo. Psychol. Assn. Office: 916 N College Ave Columbia MO 65201-4784

ALUKAL, VARGHESE GEORGE, metallurgical engineer; b. Chengal, India, Jan. 3, 1945; came to U.S., 1967; s. Kunjipaulo and Elizabeth Lizy (Alapat) A. B in Tech., Indian Inst. Tech., Madras, 1965; MS, Marquette U., 1969; postgrad., Cornell U., 1969-72; MBA, Northwestern U., 1989. Cert. quality engr., quality auditor. Sci. pool officer Nat. Metall. Labs., Jamshedpur, India, 1973-74; metall. engr. Internat. Harvester Corp., Melrose Park, Ill., 1975; quality control mgr. Charles E. Larson & Sons, Chgo., 1976-85, tech. dir., 1985—, also bd. dirs.; lectr. metallurgy Calicut (India) Univ., 1965-67; adj. faculty Triton Coll., River Grove, Ill., 1984-85, MBA program North Park Coll., Chgo., 1993—; judge Ill. State Team Excellence award Ill. Mfrs. Assn., 1993; speaker Ill. Inst. Tech., Univ. Chgo., Mgmt. Devel. Inst., New Delhi, Internat. Forgemasters Conf., Spoleto,, Italy; inst. Affiliated Ednl. Cons., Harwood Heights, Ill., 1985—; cons. metallurgy, 1984—; quality cons., 1981—. Counselor Crossroads Student Ctr. U. Chgo., 1981—. Recipient Chgo. Assn. Tech. Socs. merit award, 1993. Mem. ASTM, Am. Mgmt. Assn., Am. Soc. Metals, Am. Soc. for Non-Destructive Testing, Am. Soc. Quality Control (dir. Tng. Inst. Chgo. 1990—, Dedicated Svc. award 1993, Joe Lisy Man of Yr. award 1988). Roman Catholic. Club: Toastmasters (adminstrv. v.p. Park Ridge chpt. 1986-87). Home: 1801 Courtland Ave Park Ridge IL 60068-5367 Office: Charles E Larson & Sons 2645 N Keeler Ave Chicago IL 60639-2133

ALVARADO, YOLANDA, journalist, editor, minority outreach consultant; b. Galveston, Tex., Sept. 27, 1943; d. Raymond G. Hernandez and Maria Luisa (Garcia) Vera; m. Sotero Ortega, Jr.; children: Rosario Alvarado, Yul Alvarado, Joseph Omar Alvarado. BA, Spring Arbor Coll., 1988. Editor, asst. mgr. El Renacimiento, Lansing, Mich., 1972-74; gen. assignment reporter Lansing State Jour., 1974-80, chief edn. writer, 1980-86, city hall reporter, 1986-87, copy editor, 1987—; minority media cons. to schs., colls. and cmty. groups, 1974—; coord. AMI/Oasis. Coordinator, editor: (booklet) Mental Illness: A Family Resource Guide, 1988, Greater Lansing Mental Health Task Force Report: the Wrap-Around Service Model, 1993. Coord. Midwest Hispanic Unity Conf., Mich. State U., 1990; founder, coord. Hispanic Women in the Network, 1988—; del. U.S.-Soviet Women's Summit, N.Y.C. and Washington, 1990; alumna Nat. Hispana Leadership Inst., 1989; mem. minority steering com. Nat. Alliance for Mentally Ill, 1989-90; ethnic del. to Soviet Union Dialogue on Diversity Conf., 1990; bd. dirs. Women for Meaningful Summits, 1991-94, Boy Scouts of Greater Lansing, 1992-93; coord. Hispanics in Journalism program Mich. State U., 1991—, coord. Mid-Mich. mental health task force, 1992—; corrd. Greater Lansing Health task force report, 1993. Recipient Disting. Svc. award Nat. Newspaper Guild, 1986, Sondra Berlin award for civil rights State Handicapper Assn. Pub. Employees, 1989, Diana award in comm. YWCA, 1985, Nat. Circle of Excellence award Soc. Profl. Journalists; named One of Am.'s Top 100 Hispanic Women in Comm., Hispanic U.S.A. mag., 1987; named to Mich. Women's Hall of Fame and Hist. Ctr., 1995. Mem. Nat. Assn. Hispanic Journalists, Nat. Newspaper Guild (past sec., v.p., pres. local 24, Nat. Disting. Svc. award 1986). Home: 16400 Upton Rd Lot 254 East Lansing MI 48823-9447

ALVAREZ, THOMAS, film and video producer, director; b. Ft. Wayne, Ind., Jan. 1, 1948; s. Raul and Felicitas (Vargas) A. Student, Ind.-Purdue U., 1965-69. Producer, dir. McGraw-Hill Broadcasting Co. Inc./WRTV Channel 6, Indpls., 1973-88; pres. The Alvarez Group Inc., Indpls., 1988—; freelance journalist Indpls. Star, Indpls. Monthly, Nuvo, Arts Inc., Ind. Bus. Mag., Indpls. New Times; bd. dirs. Dance Kaleidoscope, 1991-93; arts reporter Across Ind., WFYI-Channel 20, 1991-93, mem. adv. coun.; mem. cmty. adv. coun. Sta. WRTV, 1993—, Sta. WFYI-FM, 1991-93; assoc. telecom. faculty Ind. U. Indpls. Prodr., dir. (documentaries) A Portrait of La Gente, 1975, Dave Baker: A Medley, 1976, Concord Today, 1977, Nine Leaves on a Sprig: The Story of Madame C.J. Walker, 1977, Domestic Violence, 1977, 500 Miles: Yesterday and Today, 1979, Tuckaway, 1982, Under the Influence, 1983, Rag a Bop: A Memoir of Indianapolis Jazz, 1984, A Woman's Story, 1985, Indiana State Museum: Living the Legend, 1986, Indiana Repertory Theatre: The First Fifteen Years, 1986, Solid Gold Years, 1987; prod. James Dean & Me: Nineteenth Star, 1995, The Rythm Makers: A Chronicle of Indiana Jazz, 1996. Bd. dirs. Phoenix Theatre, Indpls., 1982-85, First Step Inc.,1 988-90, Ind. Film Soc., 1988-90, ARC, 1989, United Way Cen. Ind., Greater Indpls. Coun. on Alcoholism, 1993; founder, chair Festival of New Can. Cinema, 1988, 89; mem. Ind. Cares, Inc., 1991—; active Indpls. Men's Chorus; bd. dirs. Damien Ctr., 1996; mem. adv. com. Arts. Coun. Indpls., 1996. Recipient Casper award Community Svcs. Coun. Indpls., 1974, CEBA award of merit Advt. and Comm. to Black Communities Inc., 1981, Nat. Coun. on Family Rels. award, 1984, Arti award, 1991; fellow media arts, Ind. Arts Commn. Recipient Casper award Cmty. Svcs. Coun. Indpls., 1974, comm. excellence to black audiences award of merit Advt. and Comm. to Black Cmtys. Inc., 1981, award Nat. Coun. on Family Rels., 1984, Arti award, 1991; media arts fellow Ind. Arts Commn. Home: Apt 31 8650 Jaffa Ct West Dr Indianapolis IN 46260 Office: The Alvarez Group 1111 E 54th St # 112 Indianapolis IN 46220-3256

ALVES, ELIZABETH MARTHA HAGERTY, elementary education educator; b. Berea, Ky., May 23, 1946; d. Thomas and Dorothy F. (Van Winkle) Hagerty; m. James T. Alves, Apr. 23, 1990. BS in Edn., Bowling Green (Ohio) State U., 1968; MS in Edn., Lake Erie Coll., 1990. Tchr. grades 1-3 Euclid (Ohio) Bd. of Edn., 1968-96, retired, 1996. Mem. ASCD, NEA (bldg. rep.), Internat. Reading Assn., Ohio Edn. Assn., N.E. Ohio Edn. Assn., Euclid Tchrs. Assn. (tchr. liaison to PTA exec. bd., grade level lead tchr., advisor student coun., sch. newspaper and yearbook, Outstanding Euclid Tchr. award 1995).

AMAN, TERRY J., editor; b. Mpls., Mar. 11, 1970; s. Rupert James and Shirley Ethel Aman. BA in Mass Comm., Polit. Sci., U. N.D., 1993. Editor Bottineau (N.D.) Courant, 1993-96; reporter Devil Lake (N.D.) Jour., 1996—. Author: Developmental Economic Policy and the Third World, 1993. Mem. Bottineau (N.D.) Cmty. Theater, 1994-96. Mem. N.D. Newspaper Assn. (newspapers in edn. com. mem. 1994—, Hon. mention for agrl. reporting 1995). Democrat. Methodist. Office: Devils Lake Journal 516 4th St Devils Lake ND 58301

AMATANGELO, NICHOLAS S., financial printing company executive; b. Monessen, Pa., Feb. 12, 1935; s. Sylvester and Lucy Amatangelo; m. Kathleen Driscoll, May 16, 1964; children: Amy Kathleen, Holly Megan. BA, Duquesne U., 1957; MBA, U. Pitts., 1958. Indsl. engr. U.S. Steel Co., Pitts., 1959-61; indsl. engr. mgr. Anaconda Co., N.Y.C., 1961-63; product mktg. mgr. Xerox Corp., N.Y.C., 1965-68; dir. mktg. Macmillan Co., N.Y.C., 1968-70; dir. product planning Philco-Ford Corp., Phila., 1970-72; pres. Bowne of San Francisco, Inc., 1972-79, Bowne of Houston, Inc., 1979-87, Bowne of Chgo., Inc., 1983-96, Bowne of Detroit, Inc., 1987-96; instr. U. Pitts., 1959-61; asst. prof. Westchester Community Coll., N.Y.C., 1961-64, 70-72. Contbr. articles in field to profl. jours. Bd. dirs. San Francisco Boys Club, 1974-79, Boys Towns Italy, 1973-79, Alley Theatre, Houston, 1982-86, Roosevelt U., 1996—, faculty mem., 1996—; mem. president's coun. Houston Grand Opera, 1980-86; trustee Assn. Colls. of Ill., 1993—. With U.S. Army, 1958-59, 61-62. Mem. Printing Industries Am. (bd. dirs.), Am. Soc. Corp. Secs., Am. Mgmt. Assn. - Pres. Assn., Assn. Colls. of Ill. (bd. trustees), Exec. Club Chgo. (bd. dirs.), Econs. Club Chgo., Econs. Club Detroit, Union League Club (Chgo. chpt.), Duquesne U. Century Club (chmn. exec com.). Office: Bowne of Chgo 325 W Ohio St Chicago IL 60610-4109

AMATO, JOSEPH A., history educator; b. Detroit, Aug. 31, 1938; s. Joseph and Ethel May (Linsdau) A.; m. Catherine J. Bavolack, Aug. 6, 1966; children: Felice, Anthony, Adam, Ethel. BA in History, U. Mich., 1960; MA in History, U. Laval, Que., 1963; PhD in History, U. Rochester, 1970. Prof. history S.W. State U., Marshall, Minn., 1969—, dir. rural and regional studies, 1980-92. Pub. Crossing Press, Marshall, 1985-92; author: Mounier and Maritain: A French Catholic Understanding of the Modern World, 1975, Living or Dead?, Death Book, Fears, Consolation, Paradoxes and Contradictions, 1985, Guild and Gratitude: A Study of the Origins of Contemporary Conscience, When Father and Son Conspire, A Minnesota Farm Murder, 1988, Victims and Values: A History and a Theory of Suffering, 1990, Servants of the Land: God, Family and Farm, The Trinity of Belgian Economic Folkways in Southwestern Minnesota, 1990, A New College on the Prairie: The First Twenty-Five Years of Southwest State University, 1991, The Great Jerusalem Artichoke Circus: The Buying and Selling of the American Rural Dream, 1993, The Decline of Rural Minnesota, 1993, At the Headwaters: The 1993 Flood in Southwestern Minnesota-40 Photos and 40 Essays, 1995; editor and chief 20 small books on local, regional and rural history. Office: SW State U Dept History Regional Studies Dept Marshall MN 56258

AMATOS, BARBARA HANSEN, accounting executive; b. Toledo, Aug. 30, 1944; d. John Richard and Irene Emily (Greunke) Hansen; m. James David Mokren, Sept. 12, 1964 (div. Feb. 1974); children: Frederic Hansen Mokren, Jennifer Joy Mokren; m. David Michael Amatos, Dec. 27, 1975; 1 stepchild, Anthony Steven. Student, Capital U., 1962-64, Cen. Mich. U., 1965-66; BBA, Franklin U., 1979. CPA, Ohio; cert. fraud examiner, cert. govt. fin. mgr. Account clk. Buckeye Mart, Columbus, Ohio, 1971-73, SCOA Industries Inc., Columbus, 1973-75; payroll mgr. City of Columbus Auditor's Office, 1975-86; mgmt. adv. cons. State of Ohio Auditor's Office, Columbus, 1986-87, acctg. mgr., 1987-95; fiscal officer I Ohio Dept. Human Svcs., Columbus, 1995—; ptnr. McGuiness Amatos Properties, Amatos & Amatos, CPA's. Mem. AICPA, Assn. Govt. Accts. (regional v.p. 1996—, pres. 1993-94, exec. com. 1989-90, emerging issues task force), Assn. Cert. Fraud Examiners, Nat. Assn. Human Svcs. Fin. Officers, Greater Columbus Toastmasters (v.p. edn.). Office: Ohio Dept Human Svcs 30 E Broad St Columbus OH 43215

AMAWI, MOHAMMAD SA'DI, surgeon; b. Safad, Palestine, Apr. 10, 1946; came to U.S. 1971; s. Sa'di Mohammad and Fouzieh (Abudl Rahim) A.; m. Hala Aidi, July 11, 1970; children: Lana, Deana. MD, Damascus U., Syria, 1971. Diplomate Am. Bd. Surgery. Instr. gen. surgery U. Conn., Farmington, 1970-71, intern and resident in surgery, 1971-76; attending surgeon Western Plains Regional Hosp., Dodge City, Kans., 1976—; dir. Fidelity State Bank, Dodge City, 1989—. Fellow ACS (officer 1991—). Moslem. Home: 1904 Barham Blvd Dodge City KS 67801-2320 Office: Dodge City Med Ctr 2020 Central Ave Dodge City KS 67801-6411

AMBELANG, JOEL RAYMOND, social worker; b. Milw., Aug. 23, 1939; s. Raymond Frank and Clara Ottilie (Alft) A.; student Concordia Coll., Milw., 1953-59; B.S., Concordia Sr. Coll., Ft. Wayne, Ind., 1961; M.S. in Community Devel., U. Mo., 1971; Cert. ind. social worker, Wis.; m. Lois Jean Yarbrough, Aug. 15, 1964; children: Joel Mark, Kimi Lee, Elizabeth Jean. Chief officer juvenile ct. 11th Jud. Circuit Mo., St. Charles, 1968-74, dir. juvenile ct. services, 1974-76; dir., owner Counseling and Clin. Services, St. Charles, 1976-80; exec. dir. Luth. Family Services N.W. Ind., Inc., Merrillville, 1980-87; regional dir. Luth. Social Svc. of Tex., Austin, 1987-90; adminstr. Bair Found., Austin, 1991-92; dir. social work svc. prof. Concordia U. Wis., Mequon, 1992—; field instr., part-time asst. prof. dept. social work Valparaiso (Ind.) U., 1981-84; instr. sociology and adminstrn. of justice evening coll. Lindenwood Colls., St. Charles, 1975-80; co-founder Youth in Need, Inc., 1973, bd. dirs., 1974-78, pres., 1976-78; cons. Mo. Council on Criminal Justice, Juvenile Tech. Adv. Com., 1973-75; cons., tng. chmn. Mo. Juvenile Justice Assn., 1972-74; mem. St. Charles County Child Welfare Adv. Bd., St. Charles County Child Abuse Task Force; mem. U.S. Cycling Fedn.; chmn. Nat. Bicycle Safety Program, 1979-80; v.p. Adult Day Care Assn. Tex., 1987-89; bd. dirs. Austin Groups for the Elderly, 1988-90, Balance, Inc., 1994—. Recipient awards Nat. Dist. Attys. Assn., 1974, Nat. Council Juvenile Ct. Judges, 1979, Juvenile Ct. Services Adminstrn. Nat. Coll. Juvenile Justice, 1971; cert. advanced alcoholism counselor Mo. Dept. Mental Health. Mem. Acad. Cert. Social Workers, Nat. Council Juvenile and Family Ct. Judges, St. Charles Community Council (award 1978), Nat. Assn. Social Workers, Legal Services Eastern Mo. (adv. com.). Lutheran. Originator, host program Lean On Me, sta. KCLC-FM, 1973-80; participant seminars in field; designer, author courses of study in field. Home: 1009 Noridge Trl Port Washington WI 53074-1364 Office: Concordia U 12800 N Lakeshore Dr Mequon WI 53097

AMBROSE, THOMAS WILLIAM, broadcasting executive; b. Mpls., Feb. 11, 1946; s. Leo Joseph and Mary (Girling) A.; m. Kathryn Marie Murphy, June 28, 1969; 1 child, Timothy Thomas. BA, U. Minn., 1969. Announcer Sta. WCCO-TV, Mpls., 1969-73; program mgr. Sta. WCCO-FM, Mpls., 1973-82; ops. mgr. Sta. WAYL-FM, Mpls., 1982-84, Sta. KKSS, Mpls., 1982-84; v.p. MNN Radio Networks Inc, St. Paul, 1984-93; pres., chief operating officer, vice-chmn. bd. dirs. SportsAmerica Radio Network, Mpls.-St. Paul, 1993—. Mem. alumni bd. dirs. St. John's U., Collegeville, Minn., 1985--. Mem. Nat. Assn. State Radio Networks, AFTRA, Advt. Fedn. (bd. dirs. Mpls. 1984--), Alpha Epsilon Rho, Psi Upsilon. Republican. Roman Catholic. Home: 524 9th Ave SW Dyersville IA 52040-1774 Office: SportsAmerica Radio Network 1200 Field of Dreams Way Dyersville IA 52040-2599

AMBROSIUS, MARGERY MARZAHN, political scientist, educator; b. Des Moines, May 14, 1942; d. Wilbert Wesley and Mary Lucile (Warner) Marzahn; m. Lloyd Eugene Ambrosius, Aug. 24, 1963; children: Walter T., Paul W. AB in History, U. Ill., 1964, MA in History, 1967; MA in Polit. Sci., U. Nebr., 1984, PhD in Polit. Sci., 1986. Cert. in policy analysis and program evaluation. Asst. to dir. Ill. Hist. Survey, Urbana, 1965-67; interviewer Bur. Sociol. Rsch., Lincoln, Nebr., 1979, 80; rsch. asst., then teaching asst. U. Nebr., Lincoln, 1980, 81-85; asst. prof. Kans. State U., Manhattan, 1986-92, assoc. prof. polit. sci., 1992—. Bd. editors: Am. Politics Quar., Lincoln, 1989-92; contbr. articles to scholarly publs.; co-author monograph: Economic Development Districts, others. Coun. mem. Organized Sect. on State Politics and Policy, 1994—. Fling fellow U. Nebr., 1984-85. Mem. Am. Polit. Sci. Assn., Am. Soc. Pub. Adminstrn., Midwest Polit. Sci. Assn. (chair Brooks/Cole award com. 1992), So. Polit. Sci. Assn., Women's Caucus Polit. Scis., Soc. for Women in Pub. Adminstrn. Methodist. Office: Kans State U 226 Waters Hall Manhattan KS 66506-4030

AMENT, F. THOMAS, county government official; b. Milw., Nov. 17, 1937; s. Frank and Hildegard (Neubauer) A.; children: Christopher, Peter, Jennifer. BS in Bus. Adminstrn., Marquette U., 1959, JD, 1962. Atty. Milw., 1962-85; supr. Milw. County, 1968-92; chmn. Milw. County Bd., 1976-92; county exec. Milw. County, 1992—; chmn. intergovernment steering com. Nat. Assn. Counties Orgn., Washington, 1986—; bd. dirs. Milw. County Rsch. Pk., Milw., 1986-88. Contbr. to profl. jours. Mem. Milw. Zool. Soc., 1963—, Milw. County Hist. Soc., Milw., 1968—, Friends of the Museum, Milw., 1968—, Wis. State Del. to Soviet Union, 1988. Mem. ABA, Wis. Bar Assn., Wis. Counties Assn. (bd. dirs. 1977-92, pres. 1978-79), Nat. Assn. Counties (bd. dirs. 1979-82), AMVETS, Wis. County Execs. and Adminstrs. (pres. 1994—), Am. Legion, Marquette U. Alumni Assn. Democrat. Roman Catholic. Home: 315 N 95th St Apt 148 Milwaukee WI 53226-4457 Office: County Executive Rm 306 901 N 9th St Milwaukee WI 53233-1425

AMENT, RICHARD RAND, psychologist; b. Merrill, Wis., Aug. 5, 1950; s. Jacob John and Edith Jean (Selner) A.; m. Mary Elizabeth Beau, Aug. 5, 1978; children: Adrianne Beth, Jacob John III, Breanne Beau. BS, U. Wis., Eau Claire, 1972; MSEd, U. Wis., Stout of Menominee, 1974. Sch. psychologist Wausau (Wis.) Sch. Dist., 1974—; mem. profl. adv. bd. Children with Attention Deficit Disorders North Cen. Wis., 1991-92. V.p. Montessori Presch., Inc., Wausau, 1986, pres., 1987, 93-95; bd. dirs., 1992-94; treas. Marathon County Reps., Wausau, 1977—; campaign mgr. Kasten for Assembly, Wausau, 1982; Marathon County chmn. Gov. Thompson for Wis. campaign, 1990, 94; county chmn. Bush for Pres. campaign, 1992; mem. St. Michael's Cath. Ch., 1991-92; county coord. Vannes for Congress, 1992; bd. dirs. Citizens for Neighborhood Schs., 1991-94; parent adv. bd. Horace Mann Mid. Sch., 1994-95; treas. Friends of Judge Howard campaign, 1996, Jacobson for Assembly campaign, 1996. Mem. Wis. Sch. Psychologists Assn. (mem. exec. bd. 1983-85), Sch. Psychologists of Wis.'s North (v.p. 1976-77, 81-82, pres. 1983-85). Home: 1800 Forest Valley Rd Wausau WI 54403-2038 Office: Wausau Pub Schs 415 Seymour St Wausau WI 54403-6267

AMES, JANE IRENE, corporate controller; b. Lafayette, Ind., Aug. 27, 1950; d. John James and Adena Irene (Booker) Wilkerson; divorced; 1 child, Brian Dale. BS in Acctg., St. Joseph's Coll., Rensselaer, Ind., 1973; MBA, Ind. U., 1987. CPA. Intern Ernst & Ernst, Ft. Wayne, Indiana, 1972-73; staff acct. Coopers and Lybrand, Indpls., 1973-74; fin. analyst Westinghouse Electric Corp., Bloomington, Ind., 1974-78; mgr. fin. ops. G.D. Searle & Co., Skokie, Ill., 1979-84; dir. bus. affairs U. Ill., Chgo., 1984-87; corp. comptroller Munson Marine, Inc., Volo, Ill., 1987-90; corp. contr. Gold Standard Enterprises Inc./Computer Mktg. Inc., Lincolnwood, Ill., 1991-92; dir. fin. and pers. Acad. of Model Aeronautics, Inc., 1993-95; prof., contr. St. Joseph's Coll., Rensselaer, Ind., 1995—; affirmative action officer U. Ill., Chgo., 1984-86; mem. alumni bd. dirs. St. Joseph's Coll., 1991—; treas., bd. dirs. Ind. Credit Union League, Bloomington, 1976-78. Youth dir. Bethany Chapel Christian Ch., Fowler, Ind., 1968. Recipient Cert. Appreciation Outstanding Young Women of Am., 1985. Mem. Am. Inst. CPA's, Chgo. Council Fgn. Affairs. Republican. Home: 617 Dalton Pl Northbrook IL 60062-3905

AMES, JIMMY RAY, education educator; b. Oklahoma City, Feb. 19, 1951; s. Lester Ray and Joyce Elaine (Cox) A.; m. Annita Lyn White, Mar. 12, 1971; children: Michell Lynette, Trista Elaine, Jenny Lynn. BS, Southeastern Okla. State U., 1972, M Behavioral Studies, 1977; EdD, Okla. State U., 1982. Cert. tchr., Okla. Tchr. Tishomingo (Okla.) Pub. Schs., 1973-79; rsch. and teaching asst. Okla. State U., Stillwater, 1979-82; asst. prof. Bethany Coll., Santa Cruz, Calif., 1982-84; prof., dir. tchr. edn., dir. field experiences Southwestern Assemblies of God Coll., Waxahachie, Tex., 1984-92; assoc. prof. Evangel Coll., Springfield, Mo., 1992—; pres. Ellis County Tchr. Adv. Ctr., Waxahachie, 1990-92. Author, editor: Teacher Education: A Professional Approach, 1986, Writing Thematic Units, 1996; author study guides. Mem. Assn. Supervision and Curriculum Devel. Office: Evangel Coll 1111 N Glenstone Ave Springfield MO 65802-2125

AMICARELLI, ROBERT B., mechanical engineer; b. Cleve., Feb. 15, 1952. BS in Indsl. Edn., Miami U., Knoxford, Ohio, 1974. Tchr. Charles F. Brush H.S., S. Euclid, Ohio, 1974-78; mech. designer Methods Engr. Bakles Maberial Handling, Cleve., 1978-87; project engr. Accuspray, Cleve., 1987—. Mem. West Geauga Edn. Found., Chesterland, Ohio, 1995. Named Unrecognized Hero EDI, Cleve., 1993. Mem. West Geauga Recreation Coun., Soc. Mfg. of Engrs. Roman Catholic. Office: Accuspray 23350 Mercantile Rd Cleveland OH 44122-5921

AMIRIKIA, HASSAN, obstetrician-gynecologist; b. Tehran, Iran, Dec. 10, 1937; came to U.S., 1966; d. Ahmad and Showkat (Asgari) Cheftsaz; m. Mino Vassigh Amirikia, Apr. 4, 1964; children: Arezo, Omid. MD, Tehran U., 1964. Cert. Am. Bd. Ob-Gyn. Intern Cook County Hosp., Chgo., 1966-67; resident Wayne State U., Detroit, 1967-71, fellow, 1971-72; practice medicine specializing in infertility Detroit, 1972—; asst. prof. Wayne State U., Detroit, 1972—; dir. ob-gyn. tng. dept. family medicine Wayne State U., Detroit, Mich., 1979—; dir. infertility and reproductive endocrinology St. Joseph's Hosp., Pontiac, Mich., 1990-93; chief staff Hutzel Hosp. Detroit Med. Ctr., 1993—; researcher effects of androgens on the ovary. Contbr. articles to profl. jours. Fellow ACS, Am. Coll. Ob-Gyn (Mich. sect.), Royal Coll. Physicians and Surgeons, Wayne County Med. Soc. (pres. 1995-96). Home: 1435 Lone Pine Rd Bloomfield Hills MI 48302-2632 Office: 4727 St Antoine St Detroit MI 48201-1461 also: 29877 Telegraph Rd Southfield MI 48034-1332

AMLADI, PRASAD GANESH, management consulting executive, health care consultant, researcher; b. Mudhol, India, Sept. 12, 1941; came to U.S., 1967, naturalized, 1968; s. Ganesh L. and Sundari G. Amladi; m. Chitra G. Panje, Dec. 20, 1970; children: Amita, Amol. B in Engring. with honors, Indian Inst. Tech., Bombay, 1963; MS in Indsl. Engring., Ops. Rsch., Stanford U., 1968; MBA with high distinction U. Mich., 1975. Sr. rsch. engr. Ford Motor Co., Dearborn, Mich., 1968-75; mgr. strategic planning Mich. Consol. Gas Co., Detroit, 1975-78; mgr. planning services The Resources

Group, Bloomfield Hills, Mich., 1978-80; project mgr., sr. cons. Mediflex Systems Corp., Bloomfield Hills, 1980-85; mgr. strategic planning services Mersco Corp., Bloomfield Hills, 1985-86, mgr. corp. planning and rsch. Diversified Techs., Inc., New Hudson, Mich., 1986-87; mgr. planning and rsch. Blue Cross & Blue Shield of Mich., Detroit, 1987—. Contbr. papers to profl. publs. Recipient Kodama Meml. Gold medal, 1957; India Merit scholar Govt. of India, 1959-63, K.C. Mahindra scholar, 1967, R.D. Sethna Grad. scholar, 1968. Mem. Inst. Indsl. Engrs. (sr.), N.Am. Soc. Corp. Planning, Econ. Club Detroit, Beta Gamma Sigma. Office: Blue Cross Blue Shield of Mich # B526 27000 W Eleven Mile Rd Southfield MI 48034

AMMAR, RAYMOND GEORGE, physicist, educator; b. Kingston, Jamaica, July 15, 1932; came to U.S., 1961, naturalized, 1965; s. Elias George and Nellie (Khaleel) A.; m. Carroll Ikerd, June 17, 1961; children: Elizabeth, Robert (dec.), David. A.B., Harvard U., 1953; PhD., U. Chgo., 1959. Research assoc. Enrico Fermi Inst., U. Chgo., 1959-60; asst. prof. physics Northwestern U., Evanston, Ill., 1960-64; assoc. prof. Northwestern U., 1964-69; prof. physics U. Kans., Lawrence, 1969—; chmn. dept. physics and astronomy U. Kans., 1989—; (on sabbatical leave Fermilab and Deutsches Elektronen Synchrotron, 1984-85); cons. Argonne (Ill.) Nat. Lab., 1965-69, vis. scientist, 1971-72; vis. scientist Fermilab, Batavia, Ill., summers 1976-81, Deutsches Elektronen Synchroton, Hamburg, Germany, summers 1982-88, lab. of nuclear studies Cornell U., summers 1989—; project dir. NSF grant for rsch. in high energy physics, 1962—. Contbr. articles to sci. jours. Fellow Am. Phys. Soc.; mem. AAUP. Home: 1651 Hillcrest Rd Lawrence KS 66044-4525 Office: U Kans Dept Physics and Astronomy Lawrence KS 66045

AMMER, WILLIAM, retired judge; b. Circleville, Ohio, May 21, 1919; s. Moses S. and Mary (Schallas) A.; BS in Bus. Adminstrn., Ohio State U., 1941, JD, 1946. Admitted to Ohio bar, 1947; atty., examiner Ohio Indsl. Commn. Columbus, 1947-51; asst. atty. gen. State of Ohio, Columbus, 1951-52; practiced in Circleville, 1953-57, pros. atty. Pickaway County, Circleville, 1953-57, common pleas judge, 1957-95; ret. 1995; judge by assignment Supreme Ct. Ohio, 1995—; asst. city solicitor Circleville, 1955-57. Past pres. Pickaway County ARC, Am. Cancer Soc. Served with inf., AUS, 1942-46. Mem. ABA, Ohio Bar Assn. (chmn. criminal law com. 1964-67), Pickaway County Bar Assn. (pres. 1955-56), Ohio Common Pleas Judges Assn. (pres. 1968), Masons, K.T., Shriners, Kiwanis (Ohio dist. chmn., past lt. gov.). Methodist. Home: 141 Pleasant St Circleville OH 43113-1215 Office: Courthouse PO Box 87 Circleville OH 43113-0087

AMMERAAL, ROBERT NEAL, biochemist; b. Grand Rapids, Mich., Oct. 11, 1936; s. Cornelius and Janet (Kolenbrander) A.; m. Brenda Ferne Bysterveld, June 14, 1966; children: Audrey Jeanne, Bret Alan, Julia Marie Adamski. BA, Calvin Coll., 1958; PhD, Wayne State U., 1963. Rsch. assoc. U. Chgo., 1962-65; asst. prof. biochemistry U. Ill., Chgo., 1965-67; asst. prof. Trinity Christian Coll., Palos Heights, Ill., 1967-69; rsch. project leader Am. Maize-Products Co., Hammond, Ind., 1969-96. Inventor in field; contbr. articles to profl. jours. and books. Lay preacher Orland Park (Ill.) Christian Reformed Ch.; lay pastor Calvary Reformed Ch., Orland Park, 1990—. Fellow USPHS, 1963-65; cited for one of Top Ten Med. Discoveries by Time mag., 1966. Mem. AAAS, Am. Chem. Soc., N.Y. Acad. Sci. Republican. Mem. Reformed Ch. Am. Home: 11661 S Nagle Ave Worth IL 60482-2311 Office: Am Maize Products Co 1100 Indianapolis Blvd Hammond IN 46320-1019

AMMERMAN, CHARLES R., stockbroker; b. Detroit, Mar. 4, 1942. BS in Bus., Ctrl. Mich. U., 1964, MBA, 1967. Registered investment advisor. Corp. account and mktg. analyst Celanese Corp., Detroit, 1967-75; equity rep., v.p. Merrill Lynch, Louisville, 1979-90; stockbroker PaineWebber Inc., Birmingham, Mich., 1990—; instr. U. Louisville, 1968-72; bd. dirs. Devaney Svc. Corp., Birmingham. Mem. Cleveland Soc. Fin. Analysts (Mich., bd. dirs. 1985—).

AMOS, JAMES A., electrical engineer; b. Fort, Va., July 3, 1963. BSEE, U. Akron, 1986. Sys. engr. Diehold Inc., North Canton, Ohio, 1986-91; project engr. Quatech Inc., Akron, 1991—. Mem. IEEE.

AMOUR, JAN'ETTE ALICE, pet center owner; b. Elgin, Ill., July 2, 1957; d. Peter Jack and Gertrude Marie (Freudenburg) Buniatian. Student, Elgin C.C., 1980-82, 85, 93. Lic. med. technician, Ill.; lic. ins. agt., Ill., ordained minister Ministry of Salvation Ch., 1985. Groomer's asst. Bohanna Dog Salon, Elgin, Ill., 1969-74; owner Amour Dog Salon, Elgin, 1975-90; gen. contractor Rehabs., Elgin, 1985—; fin. cons. Primerica, De Kalb, Ill., 1987—; owner Hi I.Q. Kennels, Sycamore, Ill., 1988—, Amour Pet Ctr., Elgin, 1991—. Vol. DCFS work programs; donor ctr. for Larry Jones Ministries Feed the Children Programs, 1985—. Mem. Ill. Agrl. Assn., Assn. for Rsch. and Enlightenment, Theosophical Soc., Nat. Fedn. Ind. Bus., Internat. Platform Assn., Ill. Great Dane Club, Pet Industry Assn. Republican. Office: Amour Pet Ctr 561 N McLean Blvd Elgin IL 60123

AMSDEN, LUCIA LANDON, therapist, consultant; b. Kansas City, Mo., Nov. 9, 1941; d. Barney Williams; m. Timothy L. Amsden; children: Timothy, Matthew. BS in Edn., U. Mo., 1962; MSW, U. Kans., 1980. Cert. clin. social worker. Family therapist Crittenton Ctr., Kansas City, 1981-83; orgnl. cons. MBL Group, Kansas City, 1987-90; human rels. counselor Lucia W. Landon & Assocs., Kansas City, 1983-87; instr. Webster U., Kansas City, 1989; presenter seminars to assns. and corps. on Energy in the 90's: The Balancing Act; orgnl. cons. on teambuilding. Author: (curriculum/video series) The Taking Charge Series, 1989, (parenting curriculum) Blue Ribbon Parenting, 1987, The Energy Recharge Card, 1993; contbr. articles to profl. jours. Bd. dirs. Mid-Am. Assistance Coalition, Kansas City, 1989-94; prin. Family to Family Project for Homeless Families. Mem. Nat. Assn. Women's Health Profls., Am. Tng. and Devel. Assn., Greater Kansas City C. of C., Cen. Exch. Office: 8301 State Line Rd Ste 202 Kansas City MO 64114-2019

AMSTUTZ, RONALD, state legislator; m. Joanne Amstutz; children: Julianne, Jefferson. BA, Capitol U.; postgrad., Kent State U.; BA, Malone Coll.; postgrad., Goshen Coll. Mem. Ohio Ho. of Reps., Columbus, 1981—; now vice chmn. policy com. Mem. Orrville (Ohio) City Charter Commn., 1974-75; mayor City of Orrville, 1976-80; mem. Wayne County Rep. Exec. Com., past pres. and chmn.; bd. dirs. United Conservatives Ohio. Mem. Farm Bur., Am. Legis. Exch. Coun., Nat. Tax Payers Union Ohio, Orrville Jaycees (past pres. and chmn.), Rotary. Office: 2243 Friar Tuck Cir Wooster OH 44691-2023*

ANAGNOST, THEMIS JOHN, lawyer; b. Stadion, Arcadia, Greece, June 15, 1913; came to U.S. 1931; s. John and Maria (Psycoson) A.; m. Catherine C., Aug. 15, 1942 (dec. 1990); children: Maria (dec. 1992), Alexander Themis, James Anthony. AA, U. Chgo., 1935, BA, 1937, JD, Ill. Inst. Tech., 1941; LLM, John Marshall Law Sch., Chgo., 1942. With War Dept. Censorship, 1941-45; ptnr. Anagnost & Anagnost, Chgo., 1948—; instr. Berlitz Sch. Langs.; tutor Ill. Supreme Ct. Law Office Study Provision, 1944-48. Co-founder, past pres. and chmn. bd. The Beverly Farm Found. for Retarded Children; chmn. The Catherine Cook Anagnost Found.; past pres. Students Symphony Orgn. of Chgo.; fin. chmn. Chgo. Girl Scouts U.S.; candidate for Supreme Ct. Justice of Ill., Cook County, 1992, for Atty. Gen. of Ill., 1994. Mem. Hellenic Profl. Soc. Ill. (past pres.), Internat. House Alumni Assn. of U. Chgo. (past dir. and treas.), Panarcadian Fedn. Am. (past supreme legal advisor), Appellate Lawyers Assn. (life), West Suburban Bar Assn. (past v.p.), Women's Bar Assn. of Ill., Nat. Assn. Women Lawyers. Republican. Christian Ch. Office: Anagnost & Anagnost 30 N La Salle St Ste 3922 Chicago IL 60602-2507

ANAND, YOGINDRA NATH, civil engineer; b. Peshawar, India, Dec. 5, 1939; arrived in Canada, 1965; came to U.S., 1967.; m. Helga Tieves, 1970 (div. 1980); children: Lara, Martin; m. R. Pancharathna. MSCE, Wayne State U., 1968; D in Engring., U. Detroit, 1972. Registered profl. engr., Mich. Apprentice Stein, Chattertee and Polk, New Delhi, 1959-62; structural designer R. Reiser Co., New Delhi, 1962-65, Arthur G. McKee Co., Toronto, Ont., Can., 1965, Stelco, Hamilton, Ont., 1966; sr. project engr. Harley Ellington Co., Detroit, 1968-71; staff civil engr. Detroit Edison Co., 1972-95; adj. prof. structural design Lawrence Inst. Tech., 1974-84; pvt. practice cons. in computers and engring. Anand Enterprises. Editor: Seismic Experience Data, Nuclear and Other Plants, 1985, Structural Design, Cementitious Products and Case Histories, 1985. Mem. ASCE (pres. southeastern br. 1986-87), Am. Soc. Engrs. from India (pres. 1984-85), Am. Soc. Civil Engrs., Am. Concrete Inst., Engg Soc. of Detroit. Home and Office: 308 Longford Dr Rochester Hills MI 48309-2034

ANAPLE, ELSIE MAE, medical, surgical and geriatrics nurse; b. Urbana, Ohio, Apr. 22, 1932; d. Marion N. and Mae Irene (Newell) Bodey; div.; children: Glenn, Gretchen, Gloria, Giselle, Gregory, Gordon, Gary. BSN, Ohio State U., 1955. Cert. med.-surg. nurse. Night supr. Shriner's Burn Inst., Cin., 1971-73; clin. instr. med.-surg. Deaconess Hosp. Sch. Nursing, Cin., 1973-75; staff nurse Good Samaritan Hosp., Cin., 1960-92; clin. nurse, staff nurse Univ. Hosp.-U. Cin., 1984-95, asst. head nurse med. unit, 1992; ret., 1995; part-time nurse Mercy Hosp., Fairfield, Ohio, 1980—. Active Cin. chpt. ARC, Our Lady of Rosary Ch. Mem. ANA, Ohio Nurses Assn., S.W. Ohio Dist. Nurses Assn.

ANASTASIO, THOMAS JOSEPH, neuroscientist, educator, researcher; b. Washington, Dec. 7, 1958; s. Albert Thomas and Giovanna Grace (Russo) A.; m. Anne E. McKusick, Sept. 2, 1990; children: Albert Thomas, Grace Elizabeth. BS, McGill U., Montreal, Que., Can., 1980; PhD, U. Tex. Med. Br., Galveston, 1986. NASA fellow Vestibular Rsch. Facility, Moffett Field, Calif., 1982; predoctoral rsch. fellow U. Tex. Med. Br., Galveston, 1980-86; postdoctoral fellow Johns Hopkins U. Sch. Medicine, Balt., 1986-88; rsch. asst. prof. dept. otolaryngology U. So. Calif., L.A., 1988-91; asst. prof. dept. molecular and integrative physiology U. Ill., Urbana, 1991—; presenter seminars; reviewer Biological Cybernetics, others. Contbr. chpts. to books, numerous articles to peer-reviewed jours.; author abstracts. Mem. Internat. Brain Rsch. Orgn., Internat. Neural Network Soc., Soc. Neurosci. Home: 616 Bellerieve Dr Champaign IL 61821 Office: U Ill Beckman Inst 405 N Mathews Ave Urbana IL 61801-2325

ANCHETA, CAESAR PAUL, software developer; b. Manila, June 1, 1947; s. Carlos Fortunato and Rosalinda (Huliganga) A.; m. Ruth Segalman, June 1, 1969; children: Rebecca E., Amy L. BS in Physics, U. Tex., 1969; MS in Physics, UCLA, 1971. Mem. tech. staff Hughes Aircraft Co., Culver City, Calif., 1969-78; sr. staff engr. Fairchild Camera and Instrument, Simi Valley, Calif., 1978-82; software engr. Internat. Remote Imaging Systems, Chatsworth, Calif., 1982-84, Teradyne, Inc., Woodland Hills, Calif., 1984-86; sr. scientist Internat. Remote Imaging Systems, Chatsworth, 1986-88; rsch. scientist Teledyne Industries, Northridge, Calif., 1988-89; sr. systems engr. Hughes Aircraft Co., Long Beach, Calif., 1989-90; sr. software engr. GE, Milw., 1990-94; software devel. A&B Software, Brookfield, Wis., 1994—. Author: (publs.) Proceedings of the Society of Photo Optical Instrumentation Engineers, 1978, Proceedings of the International Test Conference, 1981. Mem. The Elfun Soc., Milw., 1992. Named New Elfun of Yr., Milw. chpt. The Elfun Soc., 1993; Hughes fellow Hughes Aircraft Co., 1969-71; Stevens scholar U. Tex., El Paso, 1965-68. Mem. AAAS.

ANDALAFTE, EDWARD ZIEGLER, mathematics educator; b. Springfield, Mo., Aug. 7, 1935; s. Edward E. and Ola M. (Ziegler) A. BS, S.W. Mo. State Coll., 1956; MS, U. Mo., Columbia, 1959, PhD, 1961. Assoc. prof. S.W. Mo. State Coll., Springfield, 1961-64; assoc. prof. U. Mo., St. Louis, 1964-85, prof. of math., 1985—, chmn. math. dept., 1990-91. Contbr. articles to Jour. of Geometry, Math. Nachrichlen. Mem. AAUP, Am. Math. Soc., Math. Assn. Am.

ANDELT, DAN ALLEN, welding technician; b. Crete, Nebr., Jan. 2, 1961; s. Marvin Louis and Rosemary Alberta (Murphy) A.; m. Carla Joy Murphey, Jan. 7, 1994; children: Nathan Allen, Danielle Marie. Mech. technician State of Nebr., Dorchester, 1983-92; welding technician Kawasaki Motors, Lincoln, Nebr., 1992—. Author/editor: U-Tune, 1993; inventor in field. Mem. Nebr. Corvette Assn. Home: 4226 Adams St Lincoln NE 68504

ANDERHUB, BETH MARIE, medical educator; b. St. Louis, Feb. 7, 1953; d. Anthony Pierre and Eleanor (Corich) A. A in Applied Sci., Forest Park C.C., St. Louis, 1974; BS in Radiologic Tech., U. Mo., 1975; MEd, St. Louis U., 1989, postgrad., 1989—. Cert. radiologic tech., nuclear medicine, abdominal sonography, ob-gyn sonography. Nuclear medicine and ultrasound technician VA Hosp., St. Louis, 1976-79; ultrasound technologist, sr. sonographer Deaconess Hosp., St. Louis, 1979-82, chief sonographer, 1982-83; assoc. prof., dir. ultrasound program St. Louis C.C., 1983—; chmn. accreditation com. Ultrasound Program, Englewood, Colo., 1990-95; v.p. Commn. on Accreditation for Allied Health Program, 1994-96; lectr., presenter programs in field confs., symposia, colls., univs. Author: Manual on Abdominal Sonography, 1983, General Sonography, 1994; contbr. articles to profl. jours. Fellow Soc. Diagnostic Med. Sonographers (chmn. edn. com. 1984-86, contbg. editor Jour. Diagnostic Med. Sonography 1984-89, bd. dirs. 1986-89, v.p. 1989-91, pres.-elect 1991-93, pres. 1993-95, treas. ednl. found. 1988-91, other coms.), Am. Soc. Radiologic Technologists (bd. dirs. 1982-85, task force modality del. roles 1988-89, rep. sonography summit 1988, chmn. ultrasound com. 1980, 82-85, others), Am. Inst. Ultrasound in Medicine, Mo. Soc. Radiologic Technologists (pres. 1979-80, pres. 4th dist. 1978-79). Home: 12449 Dawn Hill Dr Maryland Hts MO 63043-3636 Office: St Louis C C 5600 Oakland Ave Saint Louis MO 63110-1316

ANDERS, CLAUDIA DEE, occupational therapist; b. Buffalo, May 2, 1951; d. Walter Gregory and Helen (Cedizlo) A.; (div. 1983); 1 child, Andrew T. Kiko. BS in Occupational Therapy (high honors), Va. Commonwealth U., 1973; postgrad., Ashland (Ohio) Coll., 1984, Walsh (Ohio) Coll., 1985, Kent (Ohio) State U., 1988, 89, Colo. State U., 1991, 92. Lic. occupational therapist, Ohio; bd. cert. pediatric occupational therapist. With Children's Rehab. Ctr., Warren, Ohio, 1974-76; mem. transdisciplinary team Goodwill Rehab. Ctr., Canton, Ohio, 1976-78; pvt. practice, 1978-83; with Timken Mercy Med. Ctr., Canton, 1978-83; occupational therapist adult tng. team Stark County Bd. Mental Retardation, Canton, 1983-85; developer occupational therapy svcs. Stark County Local Schs., 1985-87; occupational therapist Lakewood (Ohio) City Schs., 1987-91; occupl. therapist, cons. Rehab Svcs. Inc., Seven Hills, Ohio, 1991—; occupl. therapist, supr. pediat. divn. Rehab. Svcs., Inc., Cleve., 1991; pvt. practice pediatric occupational therapy & rehab. svcs. Berea, Ohio, 1991—; seminar presenter State of Ohio Occupl. Therapy Conf., 1995; presenter all day workshop, Toledo, 1996. Vol. Nat. Park Svc., Cleve. Metroparks; sec. Rocky River Trailsiders, 1993-95. A. D. Williams scholar Va. Commonwealth U., 1972, 73. Mem. Am. Occupational Therapy Assn., Ohio Occupational Therapy Assn., Coun. for Exceptional Children, NDT, Inc. Home and Office: 237 Kraft St Berea OH 44017-1448

ANDERS, MAX EUGENE, author, speaker; b. Plymouth, Ind., Jan. 20, 1947; s. Orville Robert and Mae Elizabeth (Senff) A.; m. Margaret Louise Hargrove, Sept. 5, 1971. BA, Grace Coll., 1970; ThM, Dallas Theol. Sem., 1974; DMin, Western Conservative Bapt. Sem, 1978. Ordained to ministry Community Ch., 1981. Dean of students Ariz. Coll. of the Bible, Phoenix, 1974-77; minister Walk Through the Bible, Atlanta, 1977-81; pastor Grace Community Ch., Atlanta, 1981-86; pres. Trinity House Pubs., Atlanta, 1986-88; pastor Grace Covenant Ch., Austin, Tex., 1988-93; writer, spkr., 1993—. Author: Quietimes, 1988, 30 Days to Understanding the Bible, 1988, 30 Days to Understanding the Christian Life, 1989; co-author: 30 Days to Understanding Church History, 1991, Drawing Near, 1987, The Good Life, 1993, 30 Days to Understanding What Christians Believe, 1994, God: Knowing Our Creator, 1995, Jesus: Knowing Our Savior, 1995, The Holy Spirit: Knowing Our Helper, 1995, The Bible: Embracing God's Word, 1995, 21 Unbreakable Laws of Life, 1996, What You Need to Know About Prophecy, 1996, What You Need to Know About The Church, 1996. Named Outstanding Alumnus of Yr. Grace Coll., 1982. Home and Office: 411 Auditorium Blvd Winona Lake IN 46590

ANDERS, MICHEAL FRED, vocal music educator; b. Kountze, Tex., Nov. 20, 1954; s. Fred and Mae Bertie (Basar) A.; m. Denise Kay Reno, July 5, 1986; 2 chldn., Lucille Celeste, Martin Price. B.S. in Vocal Music Edn. with highest honors, Lamar U., Beaumont, Tex., 1976, M.M. in Music Lit. and Vocal Performance, 1979; postgrad. Ohio State U. Instr. music Port Arthur (Tex.) Ind. Sch. Dist., 1977; instr. choral and vocal music, music coordinator Silsbee (Tex.) Ind. Sch. Dist., 1977-81; minister of music Calvary Baptist Ch., Beaumont, 1981; prin. roles Beaumont Civic Opera, 1974-81; dir. choral activities, assoc. prof. music & chrmn. dept. Fine Arts, U. Findlay (Ohio) Coll., 1981—; choir dir. First Christian Ch., Findlay, 1983-87, Norcrest Presbyn. Ch., Findlay, 1988-93; mem. Cantari Singers, Columbus, Ohio, 1988-95; vocal recitalist. Mem. Interfaith Choral Soc., 1977-81, v.p., 1980-81, bd. dirs., 1978-81; mem. Beaumont Jr. Forum LUV Follies, 1977-81, Silsbee Bicentennial Musical Prodn. Co., 1976, Heidelburg Summer Theatre, 1983. Lamar U. Summer Opera Workshop, 1974-82, Ritz Players, Tiffin, Ohio, 1986—, Fort Findlay Playhouse, Findlay, Ohio, 1990—, Findlay Light Opera Co., 1995—, others. Recipient Cert. of Recognition for disting. achievement by a graduating senior Lamar U., 1976; Ohio State U. fellow, 1987-88. Mem. Opera Am., Nat. Opera Assn., Am. Choral Dirs. Assn., Am. Musicology Soc., Nat. Assn. Tchrs. Singing, Tex. Nat. Opera Assn., Cen. Opera Service, Music Educators Assn., Tex. Classroom Tchrs. Assn. Am. Choral Dirs. Assn., So. Bapt. Ch. Music Conf., Nat. Assn. Tchrs. of Singing, Coll. Music Soc., Music Libr. Assn., Sonneck Soc., Nat. Theatrical Honor Soc., Alpha Psi Omega, Phi Eta Sigma, Phi Kappa Phi. Appeared in My Fair Lady, 1776, Funny Girl, Kismet, George M, Once Upon a Mattress, The Best Little Whorehouse in Texas, The Most Happy Fellow, Trial by Jury, Fiddler on the Roof, Gianni Schicchi, Cavalleria Rusticana, Madama Butterfly, Der Zigeunerbaron, La Traviata, La Fille du Regiment, Amahl and the Night Visitors, Cinderella, Joseph and the Amazing Technicolor Dreamcoat; also solo appearances in maj. choral works; producer, mus. dir. No, No, Nanette, The Sound of Music, The King and I, South Pacific, 1776, A Funny Thing Happened on the Way to the Forum, Once Upon a Mattress, Of Thee I Sing, Call Me Madam, Follies, Brigadoon, Gypsy, The Music Man. Home: 712 Red Fox Rd Findlay OH 45840 Office: U Findlay 1000 N Main St Findlay OH 45840-3653

ANDERS, ROBERT JOSEPH, pharmaceutical company executive; b. Hammond, Ind., Dec. 29, 1956; s. Raymond L. and Josephine (Russell) A.; m. Mary Ellen Girardi, Sept. 1, 1984; children: Kurtis Robert, Justine Jolena, Christopher Joseph. BA in Biology and Chemistry, Ind. U., 1979; BS in Pharmacy with honors, U. Ill., Chgo., 1983, PharmD in Clin. Pharmacy with honors, 1985. Cardiovascular residency/fellowship U. Ill., Chgo., 1985-87; med. mgr. Squibb Pharms., Princeton, N.J., 1987-89; asst. dir. Bristol-Myers Squibb, Princeton, 1989-90; dir. cardiovascular clin. rsch. G.D. Searle, Skokie, Ill., 1991—. Contbr. articles to profl. jours. Mem. Am. Heart Assn., Am. Assn. Pharm. Scientists, Am. Coll. Clin. Pharmacy, Am. Soc. Hosp. Pharmacists, Vis. Scientists Assn. Pharm. Mfrs. Assn. (lectr), Am. Soc. Hypertension, Drug Info. Assn. Roman Catholic. Home: 140 Annapolis Dr Vernon Hills IL 60061-2051 Office: GD Searle 4901 Searle Pky # 3W Skokie IL 60077-2919

ANDERSEN, BERNARD M., stock broker; b. Lacombe, Alberta, Canada, June 29, 1951. Stock broker Paine Webber, Grand Rapids, Mich., 1992—. Baptist. Home: 545 East St Coopersville MI 49404 Office: Paine Webber 333 Bridge St NW Ste 1100 Grand Rapids MI 49504

ANDERSEN, BRIAN R., plant engineer; b. Harlan, Iowa, Dec. 5, 1961. BS, Iowa State U., 1987. Project engr. AFG Industries, Cinnamson, N.J., 1990-91, Johnson Controls, Middletown, Del., 1991-92; plant engr. Exide Corp., Manchester, Iowa, 1992—; mem. adv. bd. I.E.S. Utilities, 1995—. Mem. Ch. Coun., Manchester, Iowa. Office: Exide Corp S 10th St Manchester IA 52057

ANDERSEN, ELMER LEE, manufacturing and publishing executive, former governor of Minnesota; b. Chgo., June 17, 1909; s. Arne and Jennie (Johnson) A.; m. Eleanor Johnson, 1932; children: Anthony L., Julian L., Emily E. BBA, U. Minn., 1931; LLD (hon.), Macalester College, St. Paul, 1965; LHD, Carleton Coll., 1972; D of Mgmt. (hon.), U. Minn., 1984. With H.B. Fuller Co. (mfrs. indsl. adhesives), 1934—, sales mgr., 1937-41, pres., 1941-61, 63-71, chmn., 1961-63, 71-92, chief exec. officer, 1971-74, chmn. bd., 1974-92, bd. dirs., 1992—; dir. Davis Consol. Industries, Sydney, Australia, Prenor Group Ltd., Montreal, Que., 1972-76, Geo. A. Hormel & Co., Austin, 1971-75, First Trust Co., St. Paul, 1969-74; mem. Minn. Senate, 1949-58; gov. of Minn., 1961-63; pub. Princeton (Minn.) Union Eagle, 1976—, Sun Newspapers, 1978-84; chmn. bd. ECM Publishers, Princeton, Minn., 1987—. Campaign chmn. St. Paul Community Chest, 1959—; exec. com. Boy Scouts Am.; mem. Nat. Parks Centennial Commn., 1971, Gov.'s Voyageurs Nat. Park Adv. Commn., Select Com. on Minn. Jud. System; chmn. Minn. Constl. Study Commn.; Bd. dirs., pres. Child Welfare League Am., 1965-67; past pres. St. Paul Gallery and Sch. of Art; past trustee Augsburg Coll., Mpls.; pres. Charles A. Lindbergh Meml. Fund, 1978-88, chmn. 1986-88; regent U. Minn., 1967-75; chmn. bd., 1971-75; chmn. Bush Found., St. Paul; bd. dirs. Council on Founds., N.Y.C; chmn. U. Minn. Found.; chmn. bd. Alliss Found., 1982-88; mem. exec. council Minn. Hist. Soc. Decorated Order of Lion Finland; recipient Outstanding Achievement award U. Minn., 1959, award of merit Izaak Walton League, Silver Beaver award, Silver Antelope award Boy Scouts Am., Conservation award Mpls. C. of C., Taconite award Minn. chpt. Am. Inst. Mining Engrs., 1976, Nat. Phi Kappa Phi award U. Minn., 1977, Minn. Bus. Hall Fame award, 1977, Greatest Living St. Paulite award St. Paul C. of C., 1980, award Adhesive and Sealant Council, 1980, David Preus Leadership award, 1993, others. Fellow Morgan Library (N.Y.C); Mem. Adhesive Mfrs. Assn. Am. (past pres.), Voyageurs Nat. Park Assn. (past pres.), Minn. Hist. Soc. (exec. com., pres. 1966-70), Am. Antiquarian Soc. Republican. Lutheran. Clubs: Rotary (St. Paul) (past pres. St. Paul, past dist. gov.), Grolier, Univ. (N.Y.C.); Rowfant Club Cleve.; St. Paul Gavel (past pres.). Home and Office: 1483 Bussard Ct Saint Paul MN 55112-3628

ANDERSEN, HANS OLIVER, science and environmental education educator; b. Wisconsin Dells, Wis., Mar. 30, 1935; s. Henry Oliver and Ester Martha (Christensen) A.; m. Sandra Rae Johnston, Dec. 21, 1956; children: Scott Owen, Lynne Ellen, Barbara Leigh. BEd, U. Wis., Whitewater, 1959; MS, U. Mich., 1960; EdD, Ind. U., 1966. Tchr. biology Niles Twp. Community High Sch., Skokie, Ill., 1960-62, chmn. sci. dept., 1962-65; asst. prof., assoc. prof. sci. edn. Ind. U. Sch. Edn., Bloomington, 1966-74, assoc. prof., coord. sci. edn., 1973, prof., 1974—, dir. instrn. and curriculum, 1974-78; UNESCO sr. expert Inst. for Promotion Teaching Sci. and Tech., Bangkok, 1972, cons. on tchr. edn., 1972; cons. on environ. edn. U.S. Office Edn., Washington; cons. for AID, Inst. Edn. and Rsch., Lahore, Pakistan; vis. lectr. Macquarie U., North Ryde, NSW, Australia. Contbr. articles to profl. jours. Ind. U. Sch. edn. coord. and solicitor United Way; mem. precinct com. Indiana Creek Twp., Monroe County, Ind.; trustee, sec. Indian Creek Vol. Firefighters; mem. long range planning com. Corp. for Sci. and Tech. With U.S. Army, 1954-56. Recipient Disting. Teaching award Ind. U., 1973. Fellow AAAS; mem. Nat. Sci. Tchrs. Assn. (Carleton award for Disting. Nat. Leadership in Sci. Edn. 1992, pres. 1988-91), Assn. for Edn. Tchrs. Sci. (pres. 1979-81), Hoosier Assn. Sci. Tchrs. (Disting. Svc. award 1992, bd. dirs. 1975-78), Phi Delta Pi (treas. local chpt.), Phi Delta Kappa, Pi Lambda Theta (faculty advisor Iota chpt. 1989—). Democrat. Unitarian. Home: 4315 N Kinser Pike Bloomington IN 47404-9496 Office: Ind U Sch Edn Wright Edn Bldg 201 N Rose St Bloomington IN 47405-1005

ANDERSEN, HAROLD WAYNE, contributing editor, newspaper executive; b. Omaha, July 30, 1923; s. Andrew B. and Grace (Russell) A.; m. Marian Louise Battey, Apr. 19, 1952; children: David, Nancy. BS in Edn., U. Nebr., Lincoln, 1945; DHL (hon.), U. Nebr., Omaha, 1975; LHD (hon.), Dana Coll., 1983, Doane Coll., 1984; LLD (hon.), Creighton U., 1986; D of Internat. Communications, Bellevue Coll., 1986. Reporter Lincoln (Nebr.) Star, 1945-46; with Omaha World-Herald, 1946—, dir., 1964-95, pres., 1966-85, also bd. dirs., chmn. bd. dirs., pub., 1985-89, dir., 1964-95; dir. Raleigh (N.C.) News & Observer, 1976-94, Newspaper Advt. Bur., 1974-90; chmn. World Press Freedom Com., 1980-96; past chmn. Fed. Res. Bank, Kansas City (Mo.), 1977-79; bd. dirs. Williams Cos., dir. 1988-96, Am. Bus. Info. Past pres. United Arts/Omaha; past bd. govs. Ak-Sar-Ben; past chmn. U. Nebr. Found., past pres. Jr. Achievement Omaha; chmn. Nebr. Game and Pks. Found.; past sr. v.p. North Ctrl. Flyway, Ducks Unltd.; bd. dirs. Bellevue Coll. Found.; past bd. dirs. Creighton U.; trustee Nebr. Nature Conservancy. Recipient Disting. Journalist award U. Nebr. chpt. Kappa Tau Alpha, 1972, Americanism citation Henry Monsky lodge B'nai B'rith, 1972, Nebr. Builder award U. Nebr., Lincoln, 1976, Nat. Soc. Pks. Resources award, 1984, Comm. award Nat. Assn. Resource Dists., 1987, Casey award Inland Press Assn., 1989, Disting. Nebraskan award Nebr. Soc. Washington, 1989, Philanthropy Leadership award Heartland chpt. ARC, 1992, Humanitarian award NCCJ, 1993; named Omaha Health Citizen of Yr., 1986, Citizen of Yr., United Way of Midlands, 1987, Air Force Assn.,

1990; named to Nebr. Newspaper Hall of Fame, 1988. Mem. Newspaper Assn. of Am. (past chmn., dir.), Internat. Fedn. Newspapers Pubs. (past pres.), Nebr. Press Assn. (Master Editor-Pub. award 1979), Coun. Fgn. Rels., Omaha C. of C. (bd. dirs., chmn. 1987-88), Phi Beta Kappa, Phi Gamma Delta. Republican. Presbyterian. Home: 6545 Prairie Ave Omaha NE 68132-2747 Office: Am Bus Info 5711 S 86th Cir Omaha NE 68127-0347

ANDERSEN, HARRY EDWARD, oil equipment company executive; b. Omaha, Apr. 25, 1906; s. John Anton and Caroline (Ebbensgaard) A.; student pub. schs. and spl. courses, including Ohio State U., 1957, U. Okla., 1959; Ph.D. in Bus. Adminstrn. (hon.), Colo. State Christian Coll., 1972; m. Alma Theora Vawter, June 12, 1931; children—Jeanenne Dee (Mrs. Gaylord Fernstrom) and Maureen Lee (Mrs. Roger Podany) (twins), John Harry. Founder N.W. Service Sta. Equipment Co., Mpls., 1934, pres., treas., 1956—; owner Joint Ops. Co., real estate mgmt.; dir. Franklin Nat. Bank, Mpls. Spl. dep. sheriff Hennepin County, 1951—; hon. fire chief of Mpls., 1951—; pres. Washington Lake Improvement Assn., 1955. Mem. Shrine Directors Assn. (N.W. gov.), Nat. Assn. Oil Equipment Jobbers (pres. 1957-58, dir. 1954-56), C. of C., Upper Midwest Oil Mans Club. Lutheran. Mason (32deg., K.T., Shriner), Jester. Clubs: Viking (pres.), Engineers, Toastmasters, Minneapolis Athletic, Golden Valley Golf, Le Mirador Country (Lake Geneva, Switzerland). Home: 2766 W River Pky Minneapolis MN 55406-1840 Office: 1121 Jackson St NE Minneapolis MN 55413-1538

ANDERSEN, LARRY MICHAEL, county government official; b. Moline, Ill., June 26, 1944; s. Theodore Carl Andersen and Lodell May (James) Zimbelmann; m. Ethel Ruth Swaim, Apr. 28, 1967; children: Michael, Cory, John. BS, San Diego State U., 1967; student, U. Wis., 1992-95. Various positions Ill. Bell Telephone, Rock Island, 1967-79; asst. mgr. PBX Ill. Bell Telephone, Aurora, 1979-83; staff mgr. AT&T, Chgo., 1983-86; project mgr. data sys. AT&T, Schaumburg, Ill., 1986-89; comms. supr. McHenry County, Woodstock, Ill., 1989-91, mgr. bldg. ops., 1991—; self-employed comms. cons., Crystal Lake, Ill., 1990—. Mgr. Little League Baseball, Crystal Lake, 1988—; scoutmaster Boy Scouts Am., Crystal Lake, 1984-92; mem. Ams. with Disabilities Commn. McHenry County, 1992—. Served with USN, 1961-65, Asia. Mem. Assn. Energy Egnrs., Bldg. Owners and Mgrs. Assn., Lions Club. Republican. Mormon. Home: 744 Covington Cir Crystal Lake IL 60014 Office: McHenry County Govt 2200 N Seminary Ave Woodstock IL 60098

ANDERSEN, LEONARD CHRISTIAN, former state legislator, real estate investor; b. Waukegan, Ill., May 30, 1911; s. Lauritz Frederick and Meta Marie (Jacobsen) A.; BA, Huron (S.D.) Coll., 1933; MA, U. S.D., 1937; m. Charlotte O. Ritland, June 30, 1937; children: Karen (Mrs. Fred Schneider), Paul R., Charlene (Mrs. Kurt Olsson), Mark Luther. Tchr., Onida (S.D.) High Sch., 1934-35; dir. bus. tng. Waldorf Coll., Forest City, Iowa, 1935-39; ins. salesman, 1939-41; tchr. econs., current history Morningside Coll., Sioux City, Iowa, 1941-43; engaged in ins. and real estate, Sioux City, 1943-76; mem. Iowa Ho. of Reps. from Woodbury County, 1961-64, 66-71; mem. Iowa Senate from 26th Dist., 1972-76, chmn. rules and adminstrn. com. Former mem. Iowa Commn. on Aging; former mem. investment adv. bd. IPERS; former mem. cen. com. Woodbury County Reps., del. county, dist. and state convs.; former mem. Simpco Projects Rev. Com.; former pres., chmn. bd. Siouxland Rental Assn.; past mem. Sioux City Housing Appeals Bd., Siouxland Council on Alcoholism; bd. regents Augustana Coll., Sioux Falls, S.D., 12 yrs., now mem. Augustana Fellows; mem. Vision 20-20 com., Sioux City; past chmn. Morningside Luth. Ch.; active Rep. Party Campaign, 1996; mem. Human Rights Commn., Sioux City, del. to Evang. Luth. Ch. Dist. Conv., 1996. Mem. UN Assn. (past pres. Siouxland chpt.), Sioux City C. of C. (legis. com. 1986—). Lodges: Masons, Lions. Home and Office: 2525 Nebraska St Apt 113 Sioux City IA 51104-3508

ANDERSEN, NIELS TOFT, publisher, writer; b. Northampton, Mass., Apr. 1, 1922; s. Soren Toft and Myrtle Emily (Waite) A.; m. Edna Stoll Andersen, Dec. 21, 1945; children: Soren Toft Andersen, Beth Emily Andersen, Karen Meier. B in Fgn. Trade, Latin Am. Inst., N.Y.C., Chgo., 1948. Traffic dept. Ford Motor Internat., Jersey City, N.J., 1948-52; mgmt. trainee, 1952-55, sales mgmt., 1956-59; materials control mgmt. Valencia, Venezuela, 1959-62; prodn. control mgr., 1962-63; sys. analyst Ford Motor Internat., Newark, 1963-64; pub. Cedar Springs (Mich.) Clipper, 1964-76, Dalton (Mass.) News Record, 1976-80; sales mgr. Sun Cross, Pittsfield, Mass., 1980-82; campus dir. Jordan Coll. Energy Inst., Comstock Park, Mich., 1982-88; bd. mem., 1971-76, pres. 1983, Red Flannel Factory, Cedar Springs, Mich.; dir. C. of C., Cedar Springs, Mich., 1987-92; co-publisher Bugle, Cedar Springs, Mich., 1984—. Author: Sunrise Over Jordan, 1982; editor: Daily Diary of ANdrew McDonald Civil War, 1987; co-editor: Indian Legends of Michigan Indians, 1993. Mem. planning commn. City of Cedar Springs, Mich., 1984-95; mem. downtown devel. authority City of Cedar Springs, 1989—; editor Mich. Concord Coaliton Newsletter, Ada, Mich., 1995—. Sgt. U.S. Army, 1942-46. Recipient Pub. Servant Citizen of Yr. award Rotary, Lions, C. of C., Cedar Springs, Mich., 1976. Mem. Cedar Springs Hist. Soc., Cedar Springs Pub. Schs. Home: 136 South St Cedar Springs MI 49319 Office: The Bugle 136 South St Cedar Springs MI 49319

ANDERSEN, STEVE RICHARD, health care executive; b. Vermillion, S.D., Dec. 8, 1946; s. Elton Emil and Ruby Lee (Bagley) A.; m. Christie Joann Stater, June 14, 1969; children: Eric Steven, Amy Marie. AA in Natural Sci., Riverside City Coll., Calif., 1966; BS in Pharmacy, U. Pacific, 1970; MBA in Fin., Calif. State U., San Bernardino, 1982. Lic. pharmacist, Calif., Nev., Tex. Staff pharmacist Kaiser Found. Hosp., Sacramento, Calif., 1970-71, Riverside (Calif.) Gen. Hosp., 1971, St. Bernardine Med. Ctr., San Bernardino, Calif., 1971-74; dir. pharmacy svcs. St. Bernardine Med. Ctr., San Bernardino, 1974-82; dir. pharmacy svcs. Sisters of Charity Health Care System, Houston, 1982-85, dir. bus. devel., 1985-90, dir. planning and bus. devel., 1990-93; v.p. planning and strategic devel. Sisters of Charity of Leavenworth(Kans.)/Health Svcs. Corp., 1994—; bd. dirs. Primera Healthcare, L.L.C., St. James Cmty. Hosp.; pres. Caritas, Inc. Mgr. youth baseball, Spring, Tex., 1985; bd. dirs. Northland Cmty. Ch. Recipient Order of the Golden Sword, Am. Cancer Soc., San Bernardino, Calif., 1975. Mem. Am. Coll. Health Care Execs. (diplomate), Am. Soc. Hosp. Planners and Marketers. Office: Sisters of Charity of Leavenworth/Health Svc Corp 4200 S 4th St Leavenworth KS 66048-5054

ANDERSEN, THOMAS BURTON, engineer; b. Norfolk, Nebr., July 27, 1950; s. Burton Harding and Katherine Ann (Puschendorf) A.; m. Susan Elizabeth Steers, June 5, 1971 (div. Sept. 1989); children: Kristin Sue, Aimie Michelle; m. Jeanne Marie Roeder, Aug. 15, 1992. BSCE, S.D. State U., 1972, MSCE, 1973. Registered profl. engr., Iowa. Assoc. engr. Fitzsimons & Assocs., Valdosta, Ga., 1977-78, Ament Engring., Hiawatha, Iowa, 1983-86, Snyder & Assocs., Ankeny, Iowa, 1986-87; office mgr. Associated Engrs., Inc., Ft. Dodge, Iowa, 1978-83; engr., sanitarian Howard County, Cresco, Iowa, 1987—. Sec. Cresco Mcpl. Airport Com., 1988, Vernon Springs Conservation Assn., Cresco, 1988; spiritual chmn. Upper Iowa Kiwanis, Cresco, 1988; mem. United Meth. Ch. Choir, Cresco, 1987. Capt. USAF, 1973-77. Mem. Nat. County Engrs. Assn., Am. Water Works Assn., Iowa County Engrs. Assn., Water Environment Assn. Democrat. Home: 247 Red Maple Ave Cresco IA 52136 Office: Howard County Secondary Rd 137 N Elm St Cresco IA 52130

ANDERSEN, WAYNE R., federal judge; b. 1945; m. Sheila M. O'Brien. BA with honors, Harvard U., 1967; JD, U. Ill., 1970. Bar: Ill. 1970. Adminstrv. asst. to maj. leader Henry J. Hyde Ho. of Reps., Ill., 1970-72; assoc. Burditt & Calkins, Chgo., 1972-76, ptnr., 1976-80; dep. sec. state Ill., 1981-84; supervising judge traffic divsn. 1st Mcpl. Dist., 1989-91; dist. judge U.S. Dist. Ct. (no. dist.), Ill., 1991—. Contbr. articles to profl. jours. Interviewer schs. com. Harvard Club, Chgo.; dir. Rehab. Inst. Chgo. Mem. Chicago Bar Assn., Ill. Judges Assn., Fed. Judges Assn. Office: US Courthouse 219 S Dearborn St Chicago IL 60604-1702

ANDERSON, ALFRED JERRY, biostatistician; b. Mankato, Minn., June 18, 1942; s. Donald Harold and Emma Marie (Lee) A.; m. Jacquelyn M. Jensen, Mar. 15, 1974; children: Erik C., Kalle A. BS, Mankato State U., 1964, MA, 1966; MS, Vanderbilt U., 1972. Instr. maths. Northland Coll., Ashland, Wis., 1966-71; tng. fellowship Vanderbilt U., Nashville, 1971-72; biostatistician Med. Coll. Wis., Milw., 1972-87; biostatistician, cons. St. Luke's Med. Ctr., Milw., 1987—; bd. dirs. Badgerland Striders, Milw. Contbr. articles to Am. Heart Jour., Jour. Am. Med. Assn., Am. Jour. Epidemiology, European Heart Jour., Emergency Medicine, PACE. Race dir. Lombardi Run for Daylite, Menomonie Falls, Wis., 1993—. Fellow Am. Heart Assn. (coun. epidemiology, bd. govs. Wis. chpt. 1988-94); Am. Statis. Assn., Am. Coll. Epidemiology, Am. Soc. Quality Control, Soc. Epidemiologic Rsch. Office: St Lukes Med Ctr 2900 W Oklahoma Milwaukee WI 53215

ANDERSON, BOB, state legislator, business executive; b. Wadena, Minn., Jan. 16, 1932; s. Alfred Emmanuel and Frances Agnes (Hassler) A.; m. Janet Lynn Hemquist, Aug. 3, 1967. BBA, U. Miami, 1959; student, U.S. Army War Coll., 1996. Small businessman Minn., 1954—; mem. Minn. Ho. of Reps., 1976—, mem. House DFL Caucus Steering Com., 1993-94; mem. ways and means com., 1993—, chair human svcs. fin. divsn., 1985-86, chair health and housing fin. divsn., 1993-94, health and human svcs. com., 1995—, NCSL com. Agrl., 1985; vice chair, sec., mem. exec. com. Legis. Commn. on Waste Mgmt., 1980-96; dir. NCSL Found. for State Legislatures, 1987-93; past pres. Viking-Land USA. Past pres. Otter Tail Lake Property Owners Assn.; mem. Fergus Falls N.G. Citizens Com. With U.S. Army, 1952-54. Decorated D.S.M. Named Hon. Citizen, City of Winnipeg, Chief Author Glendalough State Pk., Fergus Falls Vets. Home, Prairie Wetlands Environ. Learning Ctr.; recipient Highroad Explorer award, Hon. Viking award, Svc. award Minn. Assn. Rehab. Facilities, West Cen. Emergency Med. Corp, Minn. Ambulance Assn., Nat. Fedn. Ind. Bus., Minn. Head Start Assn., Econ. Justice award MNCAP, Ctrs. For Ind. Living, Minn. Community Action award, Pub. Ofcl. Yr. award Minn. Nurses Assn., 1994, Food First Coalition award, 1995. Mem. Nat. Conf. State Legislatures (exec. com. 1986-88, commerce, labor and regulation com. 1991-94), Minn. Meat Processors Assn. (past pres.), Otter Tail County Hist. Soc., Am. Legion, VFW (Ladies Aux. Vet. of Yr. award 1994), Minn. Outdoor Heritage Caucus, Fergus Falls Fish and Game Club, Millerville Sportsmen Club, Evansville Sportsmen Club, Ottertail Rod and Gun Club, Knob Hill Sportsmen, Sons of Norway, Elks, Masons, Shriners. Democrat.

ANDERSON, BRUCE, state legislator; b. Mar. 12, 1950; m. Dottie Anderson; 5 children. AA, Willmar Tech. Coll. Bus courier; mem. from dist. 19B Minn. State Ho. of Reps., St. Paul, 1994—. Address: 7555 Meridian Cir Maple Grove MN 55430

ANDERSON, C. WILSON, JR., learning specialist; b. Cambridge, Mass., May 3, 1939; s. C. Wilson and K. Jane (Lee) A.; m. R. Pauline Anderson, June 12, 1962; children: Emily J., Jennifer L., Matthew W. BA, St. Olaf Coll., Northfield, Minn., 1961; postgrad., U. Minn., 1965-76; MAT, Augustana Coll., 1977. Tchr. Kenyon (Minn.) Pub. Schs., 1961-64, Robbinsdale (Minn.) Area Schs., 1964-89; learning disabilities specialist, tchr. educator Menninger Clinic, Topeka, Kans., 1989—. Author: Workbook of Resource Words 1, 2, 3, 1980, VAK-Tasks, 1987; author computer programs; author video: Homework and Learning Disabilities: A Common Sense Approach, 1990. Bd. dirs. Topeka Literacy Coun., 1991—; trustee Kildonan Sch., Amenia, N.Y., 1989—; coun. of advisors Pine Ridge Acad., Williston, Vt., 1990; adv. bd. Fairleigh-Dickinson U., Teaneck, N.J. Recipient Outstanding Leadership award Upper Midwest br. Orton Dyslexia Soc., 1980; named Gen. Educator of the Yr. Minn. Assn. for Children with Learning Disabilities, 1981. Office: Edn Cons of the Midwest Inc 2812 SW Osborn Rd Topeka KS 66614-2438

ANDERSON, CARLA LEE, psychologist; b. Edgeley, N.D., Nov. 26, 1930; d. Carl Erick and Ruth Johanna (Isaacson) Erickson; m. Wayne Perry Anderson, Dec. 22, 1952; children: Jerilyn, Debra, Rosalyn, Stephanie. BA, Jamestown Coll., 1952; MA, U. Del., 1964; MS, U. Mo., Columbia, 1977; PhD, U. Mo., 1978. Lic. psychologist, Mo. Tchr. Gilby (N.D.) High Sch., 1952-54, Moberly (Mo.) Jr. Coll., 1954-55, Hickman High Sch., Columbia, Mo., 1955-56; counseling intern U. Mo., Columbia, 1975-77; asst. prof. overseas counseling program Ball State U., Fed. Republic of Germany, 1979; psychologist Ctr. for Family & Individual Counseling, Columbia, 1979-96; pvt. practice Columbia, 1996—. Contbr. articles to profl. jours. Chair, bd. dirs. Unitarian-Universalist Ch., Columbia, 1985-86. Mem. Am. Psychol. Assn., Mo. Psychol. Assn., Mid-Mo. Network Women in Psychology (chair 1984-86). Home and Office: 1017 Prospect St Columbia MO 65203-2352

ANDERSON, CAROL JEAN, information systems executive; b. DeKalb, Ill., Aug. 8, 1946; d. Bernard George and Anna Maria (Bianchi) A.; m. John Ray Oltman, Sept. 25, 1971 (div. 1976). BA in Econs., Rosary Coll., River Forest, Ill., 1968; MA in Econs., DePaul U., 1971. Programmer Time, Inc., Chgo., 1968-71; programmer analyst Trailer Train Co., Chgo., 1972-73, sr. programmer analyst, 1973-74, systems analyst, 1974-76, sr. systems analyst, 1976, mgr. systems and programming, 1976-80, dir. systems devel., 1980-89, v.p., mgr. info. svcs., 1990-91; v.p. info. tech. TTX Co. (formerly Trailer Train Co.), Chgo., 1991—. Mem. Friends of Park, Chgo., 1983-85, Art Inst. Alliance, Chgo., 1986—; bd. dirs. Creative Children's Acad., 1991-95, vice chmn., 1993-95, mem. disting. women's adv. coun. Coll. of St. Catherine, 1991—. Mem. Women in Mgmt. (bd. dirs. Chgo. Loop chpt. 1984-89, pres. 1987-88, Woman of Achievement award 1991, nat. sec. 1988-89, nat. v.p. comm. 1989-90, Charlotte Danstrom Corp. award 1991), Soc. for Info. Mgmt. (chmn.-elect Chgo. chpt. 1993-94, chair 1994-95, past chair 1995-96, internat. v.p. mktg., sales and media rels. 1995—, Rosary coll. bd. trustees 1995—), Women's Transp. Assn. (treas. 1984-85, Women's Transp. Seminar, Chgo. Maritime Soc., Lincoln Park Conservation Assn., Sandburg Ski Club (treas. 1985-87), Lincoln Park Ski Club, Midwest Open Racing Fleet. Roman Catholic. Office: TTX Co 101 N Wacker Dr Chicago IL 60606-1718

ANDERSON, CAROL LEE, communications executive; b. Sharon, Pa., Nov. 5, 1943; d. James W. and Charlene Helen (Lang) Thomas; m. Duane A. Anderson, Dec. 16, 1978; children: Mark Powell, Steve Anderson. Student, Youngstown (Ohio) State U., 1961, Pa. State U., Sharon, 1964. Field mgr. Welcome Wagon Internat., Memphis, 1975-78; dir. Merrill Chase Gallery, Naperville, Ill., 1978-80; br. mgr. CONTEL/Executone, Burr Ridge, Ill., 1980-84; major mkt. account exec. Ill. Bell Comm., Westbrook, 1984-90; strategic account exec. govt. accounts Ameritech Custom Bus., Westbrook, Ill., 1990-93, account mgr. fed., mil. and civilian, 1993—. Mem. Internat. Orgn. Women in Telecommunications, Delta Chi Epsilon. Home: 213 Pfaff Dr Frankfort IL 60423-1624 Office: Ameritech Custom Bus Two Westbrook Corp Westchester IL 60154

ANDERSON, CAROLYN JOYCE, business development executive; b. Mishawaka, Ind., Mar. 14, 1947; d. Ebon Clayton and Maxine Ruth (Haag) Angel; m. Thomas Anderson (dec.); children: Charmien, Andrew, Paul. BS in Bus., Ind. U., 1978. CPA, Ind. Staff acct. Holdeman, Fulmer and Chiddister CPA's, Elkhart, Ind., 1974-78; comml. lender Midwest Commerce Bank, Elkhart, 1978-81; corp. controller Bivouac Industries, Inc., Vandalia, Mich., 1981-84; exec. dir. Small Bus. Devel. Ctr., South Bend, Ind., 1984—; developer, implementer Michiana Investment Network, 1986—, The Emerging Bus. Forum, 1992—. Bd. dirs. Davenport Coll., Grand Rapids, Mich., 1986-94; bd. dirs. The Montessori Acad., South Bend, 1994—, treas., 1995—; Ind. state judge Blue Chip Enterprise Initiative, 1990—; chmn. Small Bus. Week Awards, 1993—; co-chair Women's Econ. Summit, St. Mary's Coll., Notre Dame, Ind., 1993. Mem. Planned Parenthood (treas. 1987-90, pres. 1991-92), Kiwanis (sec. 1988-91, Disting. Svc. award 1989). Methodist. Office: Small Bus Devel Ctr 300 N Michigan St South Bend IN 46601-1239

ANDERSON, CHRIS GEORGE, stockbroker; b. Sparta, Mich., Feb. 7, 1951; s. Harold A. and Doris I. (Wallias) A.; m. Terresa Anne Grasiewicz, Sept. 1, 1972; chidlren: Eathon, April, Emily. BA in Bus. Adminstrn., U. Mich., 1973. Salesman Am. Hosp., Evingston, Ill., 1973-79; stockbroker Prudential Securities, Grand Rapids, Mich., 1979—. Mem. Internat. Retirement Planners, Am. Assn. Individual Investors, Western Mich. Assn. Retirement Planners. Republican. Lutheran. Home: 7501 Treeline Dr SE Grand Rapids MI 49546-7467 Office: Prudential Securities Inc Campan Sq 99 Monroe Ave NW Ste 101 Grand Rapids MI 49503-2639

ANDERSON, CLYDE BAILEY, musician, educator; b. Mpls., Dec. 23, 1934; s. Arthur William and Florence Pearl (Bailey) A.; m. Judith Dawn Johansen, Sept. 17, 1977. BS, U. Minn., 1957, MA, 1967, profl. cert. in tng. and devel., 1984. Cert. tchr., Minn. Tchr. music Hopkins (Minn.) Pub. Schs., 1967-85, Mpls. Pub. Schs., 1989—; profl. musician Mpls., 1953—; cons. Minn. Dept. Transp., 1988. Bd. dirs. Local Home Owners' Assn., Maple Grove, Minn., 1979-85. With U.S. Army, 1958-59. Mem. Music Educators Nat. Conf., Minn. Music Educators Assn., Am. String Tchrs. Assn., Assn. Childhood Edn. Internat., Am. Fedn. Musicians, Am. Fedn. Tchrs., Twin Cities Musicians Union (ofcl. 1978-85, 87—), Am. Legion, Evergreen Club, Phi Mu Alpha Sinfonia. Democrat. Home: 343 W Eagle Lake Dr Maple Grove MN 55369-5552 Office: Mpls Pub Schs 807 NE Broadway Minneapolis MN 55413-2332

ANDERSON, CYNTHIA LYNN, medical, surgical nurse; b. Kansas City, Mo., Aug. 4, 1959; d. Melvin Wesley and Laura Aileen (Pasley) Brewer; m. Robert Shawn Siemon, Aug. 12, 1985 (div. Mar. 1992); children: Colene Elizabeth, Christopher Daniel; m. Stephen James Anderson, Nov. 20, 1993. RN, Rsch. Med. Ctr., Kansas City, Mo., 1980. RN, Mo. Nurse neonatal ICU Rsch. Med. Ctr., Kansas City, 1980-83, nurse surgery dept., 1983-85, nurse open heart team, 1985-87, nurse trauma team, 1987-89, nurse open heart team, 1989—. Co-dir. Kid's Praise Club Westridge Christian Ch., 1993—, singer Voices of Joy, 1995—. Mem. Mo. Nurse Assn., Gospel Music Assn. Home: 13114 Winchester Grandview MO 64030 Office: Rsch Med Ctr 2316 E Meyer Blvd Kansas City MO 64132

ANDERSON, DALE C., scouting executive, travel consultant; b. Grinnell, Iowa, Sept. 13, 1953; s. Clifford Simon and Wilma Grace (Grunhaupt) A. AAS in Indsl. Mktg., Des Moines Area C.C., Ankeny, Iowa, 1973; BA in Comm. and Theatre, Cen. Coll., 1978. Asst. buyer Ardan Wholesaler, Des Moines, 1979; office mgr. Moingona Girl Scout Coun., Des Moines, 1979-82, dir. adminstrv. svcs., 1982-88, property/purchasing dir., 1988—; travel cons. Al Travel, Des Moines, 1989-90, First Tours, Des Moines, 1990—; camp visitor for camp accreditation State of Iowa, 1990—. Campaign co-chmn. Kellogg (Iowa) Community Chest, 1983-85, pub. rels. chmn., 1982; leader local club Jasper County 4-H, Kellogg, 1971-76, state leadership conf. del., 1971, nat. citizenship del., Washington, 1971, instr. county officers tng. sch. Jasper County, 1970-71, Jasper County v.p., 1970, state conv. del., Ames, Iowa, 1970, state counselor Des Moines Area 4-H, Madrid, Iowa, 1970; local club pres. Kellogg Club 4-H, 1970-71. Recipient State Leadership award Jasper County 4-H, 1970, named Outstanding 4-H'er of Yr., 1971; named Kellogg's Outstanding Citizen, 1983. Mem. Am. Camping Assn. (stds. chair for camp accreditation Iowa chpt. 1992-95, state of Iowa sec. 1996—), Iowa State Grange (lectr. 1983-85, 91-93, state youth com. 1981-82, Iowa state youth rep. 1976), Richland Grange (state del. 1980, 83, sec. 1980-84, steward 1970-73, 77-79, overseer 1973-77, youth chmn. 1973, 75-76). United Methodist. Office: 686 Hwy 224 S Kellogg IA 50135-8579

ANDERSON, DAMON ERNEST, lawyer; b. Minot, N.D., June 20, 1946; s. Melvin Ernest and Maxine I. (Spaulding) A.; m. Julie Kay Severson, Oct. 23, 1982; children: Joshua Daniel, Philip Kyle. BA, Dickinson State U., 1968; JD, U. N.D., 1974. Bar: N.D. 1974, Minn. 1981, U.S. Dist. Ct. N.D. 1974, U.S. Ct. Appeals (8th cir.) 1980, U.S. Supreme Ct. 1980. Pvt. practice Kessler and Anderson, Grand Forks, N.D., 1974-78, Grand Forks, N.D., 1978—; asst. state's atty. Grand Forks County, N.D., 1978—. Mem. divsnl. comdr. adv. coun. Salvation Army, Mpls., mem. Salvation Army local adv. bd., Grand Forks. Sgt. U.S. Army, 1968-70. Mem. Am. Legion, Masons. Lutheran. Office: 215A S 4th St Grand Forks ND 58206-5624

ANDERSON, DAVID, business executive; b. Princeton, Minn., Nov. 4, 1928; s. David and Ena Ruth Anderson; m. Carolyn M. Anderson, Apr. 3, 1953; children: Cheryl, Joni, Julie, Janice. Student, Minn. Sch. of Bus. V.p. sales Food Producers Inc., Mpls., 1950-72; pres., founder G.D. Anderson & Assoc., Mpls., 1972—; bd. dirs. Shrinners Hosp., Mpls., 1993—. Mem. Edina Masons, Shriners, York Rite, Zuhrah Shrine Temple (potentate 1992), S.W. Lions (pres.). Republican. Lutheran. Office: GD Anderson & Assoc 1623 South 5th St Hopkins MN 55343

ANDERSON, DAVID DANIEL, retired humanities educator, writer, editor; b. Lorain, Ohio, June 8, 1924; s. David and Nora Marie (Foster) A.; m. Patricia Ann Rittenhour, Feb. 1, 1953. B.S., Bowling Green State U., 1951, M.A., 1952; Ph.D., Mich. State U., 1960; D. Litt., Wittenberg U., 1986. From instr. to prof. dept. Am. thought and lang. to univ. disting. prof. Mich. State U., East Lansing, 1957-90; lectr. Am. Mus., Bath, Eng., 1980; editor U. Coll. Quar., 1971-80; Fulbright prof. U. Karachi, Pakistan, 1963-64; Am. del. to Internat. Fedn. Modern Langs. and Lit., 1969-93, Internat. Congress Orientalists, 1971-79, European Am. Studies Assn., 1994. Author: Sherwood Anderson, 1968 (Book Manuscript award 1961), Louis Bromfield, 1964, Critical Studies in American Literature, 1964, Sherwood Anderson's Winesburg, Ohio, 1967, Brand Whitlock, 1968, Abraham Lincoln, 1970, Suggestions for the Instructor, 1971, Robert Ingersoll, 1972, Woodrow Wilson, 1978, Ignatius Donnelly, 1980, William Jennings Bryan, 1981, Route two, Titus, Ohio, 1993, The Path in the Shadow, 1995; editor: The Black Experience, 1969, The Literary Works of Abraham Lincoln, 1970, Sunshine and Smoke: American Writers and the American Environment, 1971, (with others) The Dark and Tangled Path, 1971, Mid America, 1974, 2d edit., 1975, 3d edit., 1976, 4th edit., 1981, 9th edit., 1982, 10th edit., 1983, 11th edit., 1984, 12th edit., 1985, 13th edit., 1986, 14th edit., 1987, 15th edit., 1988, 16th edit., 1989, 17th edit., 1990, 18th edit., 1991, 19th edit., 1992, 20th edit., 1993, 21st edit., 1994, 22d edit., 1995, 23d edit., 1996, Sherwood Anderson: Dimensions of His Literary Art, 1976, Sherwood Anderson: The Writer at His Craft, 1979, Critical Essays on Sherwood Anderson, 1981, Michigan: A State Anthology, 1983; editor Midwestern Miscellany, 1974—; also numerous articles, essays, short stories, poems. Served with USN, 1942-45; with AUS, 1952-53. Decorated Silver Star, Purple Heart; recipient Disting. Alumnus award Bowling Green State U., 1976, Disting. Faculty award Mich. State U., 1974, Disting. Faculty award Mich. Assn. Governing Bds., 1988, Disting Research award Mich. State U., 1988. Mem. ASA, AAUP, MLA, Popular Culture Assn., Soc. Study Midwestern Lit. (founder, exec. sec., Disting. Service award 1982), Assn. Gen. and Liberal Edn. Am. Assn. Advancement Humanities. Club: University. Home: 6555 Lansdown Dr Dimondale MI 48821-9428 Office: Mich State U Dept Am Thought and Lang East Lansing MI 48824

ANDERSON, DAVID GARY, senior account executive; b. St. Paul, Sept. 25, 1963; s. Gary Arvid Anderson and Barb Jean (Springer) Zehoski; m. Julie Marie Anderson, Oct. 17, 1987. BA, St. Mary's Coll., Winona, Minn., 1987. Sales specialist United Healthcare, Minnetonka, Minn., 1987-88; mktg. cons. HMO Midwest, Blue Cross and Blue Shield Minn., Eagan, 1989—. Youth coach Hudson (Wis.) Hockey Assn., 1990—; mem. campaign com. Hudson United Way, 1991—. Recipient award Health Ins. Assn. Am., 1992, Life Underwriters Tng. Coun., 1993. Mem. Nat. Assn. Life Underwriters, Nat. Assn. Health Underwriters, Assn. Health Ins. Agts., Chippewa Valley Life Underwriters (health ins. com. 1992-95, sec., treas. 1993-94, pres. 1994-95, state dir. 1995-96), Hudson C. of C. (chmn. program com. 1990). Office: Atrium Health Plan Ste E 2215 Vine St Hudson WI 54016-5802

ANDERSON, DAVID GASKILL, JR., Spanish language educator; b. Tarboro, N.C., Feb. 21, 1945; s. David G. Sr. and Lucile (Gammon) A.; m. Jonetta Gentemann, Jan. 29, 1968; children: Allene Q., David III, James H., John G. AB, U. N.C., 1967; MA, Vanderbilt U., 1974, PhD, 1985. Instr. of langs. Union U., Tenn., 1975-76; instr. of Spanish Ouachita Bapt. U., Ark., 1976-85, asst. prof., 1985; asst. prof. fgn. langs. N.E. La. U., 1985-87; asst. prof. Spanish John Carroll U., Cleve., 1987-93, assoc. prof., 1993—, acting chmn. dept. classical and modern langs., 1996; tchg. fellow Vanderbilt U., 1983-84, NEH summer seminar on poetry, 1990; active East Asian Studies Adv. Com., John Carroll U., 1988-92, John Carroll U. Com. Rev. Core Curriculum, 1992-94; presenter in field. Author: On Elevating the Commonplace: A Structuralist Analysis of The Odas of Pablo Neruda, 1987; contbr. articles to profl. jours. vol. ESL Peace Corps, Colombia, 1968-70. Named Outstanding Young Men of Am., 1979. Mem. Am. Assn. U. Suprs. and Coords. Fgn. Lang. Programs, Am. Assn. Tchrs. Spanish and Portuguese, Modern Lang. Assn., Cleve. Diocesan Fgn. Lang. Assn. (bd. mem. 1988-93), Cleve. Assn., Phi Beta Kappa. Democrat. Home: 2573 Dysart Rd Cleveland OH 44118-4446 Office: John Carroll Univ Spanish Dept Cleveland OH 44118

ANDERSON, DAVID LOUIS, history educator; b. Pampa, Tex., Aug. 10, 1946; s. Benjamin Louis and Ruby Lucille (Baird) A.; m. Helen Esther

Fleischer, June 9, 1973; 1 child, Hope Mindy. BA cum laude, Rice U., Houston, 1968; MA, U. Va., 1972, PhD, 1974. Vis. asst. prof. of history U. Mont., Missoula, 1974-75, 76-77, Tex. Tech. U., Lubbock, 1975-76; asst. prof. of history Sam Houston State U., Huntsville, Tex., 1977-80; lectr. in history Calif. Polytechnic State U., San Luis Obispo, Calif., 1980-81; asst. prof. history U. Indpls., 1981-84, assoc. prof. history, 1984-90, prof. history, dept. chair, 1990—. Author: (book) Imperialism and Idealism, 1985, Trapped By Success: The Eisenhower Administration and Vietnam, 1991 (Robert H. Farrell Book prize Soc. for Historians of American Fgn. Rels. 1992), Shadow on the White House: Presidents and the Vietnam War, 1993. Sgt. U.S. Army, 1968-70. Named Ind. Prof. of the Yr. Coun. for Advancement and Support of Edn., 1991. Mem. Am. Hist. Assn., Orgn. of Am. Historians, Soc. for Historians of Am. Fgn. Rels. (coun. mem. 1995—). Office: U Indpls 1400 E Hanna Ave Indianapolis IN 46227

ANDERSON, DAVIN CHARLES, business representative, labor consultant; b. Mpls., July 26, 1955; s. Roland Lawrence Anderson and Merlyne (Aldrich) Bissell; m. Diane Elmshauser, Aug. 14, 1982; children: Kiersten Janel, Matilda Rae. Student, St. Cloud State U., Minn., 1973-76; BS, U. Minn., 1979. Technician Northwest Cinema, Mpls., 1976-78, Mann Cinemas, Mpls., 1978-81, Gen. Cinema Corp., Mpls., 1981—; account exec. Van Clemens & Co., Mpls., 1987—; sec. Assn. Entertainment Industries Unions, St. Paul, 1987—. Mem. AFL-CIO (del.), Internat Alliance Theatrical and Stage Employees (bus. rep. Local 219 1986—), Nat. Assn. Investors Clubs, Trades and Labor Council (del.), Cen. Labor Union Council (del.), Toastmasters. Lutheran. Home: 9941 Olive St NW Minneapolis MN 55433-5126

ANDERSON, DEBORAH KAY, physical therapist; b. Ft. Wayne, Ind., Mar. 1, 1963; d. Jack Lee and Sharon Kay (Williams) J.; m. John Richard Anderson, Aug. 25, 1984; children: Alicia Marie, Ashley Elizabeth, Jacob Richard. Student, U. Ill., 1981-83, No. Ill. U., 1983-84; BS in Phys. Therapy, Chgo. Med. Sch., 1986, MS in Phys. Therapy, 1992. Registered lic. phys. therapist, Ill. Staff phys. therapist Easter Seal Rehab. Ctr., Joliet, Ill., 1986-88, coord. phys. therapy, 1988-93, cons., 1993—; pvt. practice Naperville, Ill., 1993—. Religious edn. tchr. St. Raphael Ch., Naperville, 1994-95. Mem. Am. Phys. Therapy Assn., Neuro-Developmental Treatment Assn. (rsch. com.). Roman Catholic. Home and Office: 431 Aspen Ct Naperville IL 60540

ANDERSON, DONALD CARNEY, farmer; b. Holdrege, Nebr., Feb. 2, 1931; s. Walter A. and Anna Bell (Carney) A.; m. Mary Jean Niehaus, May 30, 1954; children: Stephen, Lynn, Mari Kay. BS, U. Nebr., 1953. Farmer Elm Creek, Nebr., 1956—; pres., bd. dirs. Holdrege Coop., 1975-81. Pres., bd. dirs. Phelps Meml. Health Ctr., Holdrege, Phelps Libr., Holdrege, 1969-79, Phelps-Gosper Ext., Holdrege, 1967-70. Served to 1st lt. U.S. Army, 1953-55. Mem. Nebr. Farm Bur. (state bd. 1991—), Crime Stoppers (pres. 1989-92), South Ctrl. Corn Growers (sec. 1986-87). Republican. United Methodist. Home: Rt 1 Box 45 Elm Creek NE 68836

ANDERSON, DOUGLAS CHARLES, juvenile probation administrator; b. Decatur, Ill., May 14, 1934; s. Douglas Burgess and Linnea Olga (Stone) A.; m. Virginia Susan Santucci, Sept. 20, 1965 (div. 1969). BA in Sociology, Cornell Coll., 1956; student, U. Chgo., 1956-58, Northwestern U. Sch. Law, 1965-68. Cert. social worker. Chief dep. probation officer Cook County Juvenile Ct., Chgo., 1958-95; tennis umpire Chog. Profl. Tennis Umpires Assn., 1970-75; archl. tour guide Irene Kreer & Assocs., Chgo., 1989—. Photographer, producer: (film) Wildlife of Africa, 1975, Zoos of the World, 1980; producer: (video) Chgo. River Tour, 1991. Naturalist Chgo. Audubon Soc., 1964—; bd. dirs. Abraham Lincoln Ctr., Chgo., 1987—, Hyde Park-Kenwood Community Conf., 1980-84; sec., bd. dirs. Hyde Park Co-op. Soc., 1986-96, Joanna C. Menge Meml. Fund, 1987—; scout master, merit badge counselor Chgo. Area Coun. Boy Scouts of Am., 1959—; docent tour guide Lincoln Park Zoological Gardens, 1971—, Chgo. Archl. Found., 1989—; vol. naturalist guide Chgo. Park Dist., 1974—; active Chgo. Gilbert & Sullivan Opera Co. Orch., 1960—, Northwestern U. Philharm. Orch., 1993—, Friends of the Parks. Recipient Outstanding Svc. award Chgo. Fedn. of Community Coms., 1965, Environ. Quality award U.S. Environ. Protection Agy., 1977, Chgo. Vol. of Week award Sta. WBBM-Radio, 1991, Vol. of Yr. award Hyde Park Neighborhood Club, 1992, Outstanding Svc. award Chgo. Arch. Found., 1994, 20-Yr. Outstanding Svc. award Friends of the Parks, 1994. Mem. Lincoln Park Zoo Docents (pres. 1980-82, 25-Yr. award 1996), Chgo. Audubon Soc. (pres. 1986-90, Outstanding Svc. award 1990), Hyde Park Hist. Soc. (bd. dirs. 1994—, Paul Cornell award 1980), Ill. Audubon Soc. (bd. dirs. 1974-78, 80-84, Svc. award 1984), Chgo. Acad. Scis., Chgo. Ornithological Soc. (pres. 1980-85), Soc. Archtl. Historians, Friends of the Parks (20-Yr. Outstanding Svc. award 1994), Chgo. Soc. Archtl. Historians. Democrat. Unitarian. Home: 5658 S Blackstone Ave Chicago IL 60637-1828

ANDERSON, ELIZABETH SECOR, philosopher, educator; b. Boston, Dec. 5, 1959. BA in Philosophy, Swarthmore Coll., 1981; AM in Philosophy, Harvard U., 1984, PhD in Philosophy, 1987. Instr. philosophy Swarthmore (Pa.) Coll., 1985-86; asst. prof. philosophy U. Mich., Ann Arbor, 1987-93, assoc. prof. philosophy and women's studies, 1993—, Arthur F. Thurnau prof., 1994. Author: Value in Ethics and Economics, 1993; contbr. articles to profl. jours. Inst. for Humanities fellow U. Mich., 1989-90. Mem. Am. Philos. Assn., Soc. for Analytic Feminism. Office: Univ Mich Dept Philosophy Ann Arbor MI 48109

ANDERSON, ELLEN RUTH, state senator; b. Gary, Ind., Nov. 25, 1959; d. John Ernest Anderson and Marion Jane (Reeves) Martin; m. Andrew J. Dawkins. BA in History, Carleton Coll., 1982; JD, U. Minn., 1986. Bar: Minn., 1987, U.S. Dist. Ct. Minn. 1988. Jud. law clk. Minn. Ct. Appeals, St. Paul, 1987-88; atty. Hennepin County Pub. Defender, Mpls., 1988-91; staff atty. Minn. Edn. Assn., St. Paul, 1991-92; state senator State of Minn., St. Paul, 1993—. Democrat. Office: State of Minn G27 State Capitol Saint Paul MN 55155-1002

ANDERSON, ERIC CHARLES, computer systems analyst, programmer; b. Barberton, Ohio, July 5, 1946; s. Harold Roy Anderson and Ethel May (Coolman) Burke; m. Ruta Ariihohoa Uy, July 7, 1976 (div. Jan. 1989); 1 child, Charles Ariihohoa Anderson. AAS in Hotel Mgmt., Tidewater C.C., 1981; BS in math., U. Akron, 1968, BS in physics, 1968. Physicist DOC NOAA Nat. Weather Svc., Washington, 1970; mathematician USN Civil Svc., Washington, 1971-73; mathematician USN Civil Svc., Norfolk, Va., 1973-79, computer specialist, 1979-82, computer sys. programmer, 1982-86, computer sys. analyst, 1986-88; ret.; internal cons. USN, Norfolk, 1976-88. Lt. USNR, 1968-75 (active duty 1968-69). Mem. IEEE (affiliate), Buckeye State Sheriff's Assn. (assoc.), Theosophi. Republican. Home: 166 Grand Ave Akron OH 44302

ANDERSON, FRANCES SWEM, nuclear medical technologist; b. Grand Rapids, Mich., Nov. 27, 1913; d. Frank Oscar and Carrie (Strang) Swem; m. Clarence A.F. Anderson, Apr. 9, 1934; children: Robert Curtis, Clarelyn Christine (Mrs. Roger L. Schmelling), Stanley Herbert. Student, Muskegon Sch. Bus., 1959-60; cert., Muskegon Community Coll., 1964; cert. adult edn. computer course, Fruitport Cmty. Schs., 1992. Registered nuclear med. technologist Am. Registry Radiol. Technologists. X-ray file clk., film librarian Hackley Hosp., Muskegon, Mich., 1957-59, radioisotope technologist and sec., 1959-65; nuclear med. technologist Butler Meml. Hosp., Muskegon Heights, Mich., 1966-70; nuclear med. technologist Mercy Hosp., Muskegon, 1970-79, ret., 1979. Mem. Muskegon Civic A Capella choir, 1932-39; mem. Mother-Tchr. Singers, PTA, Muskegon, 1941-48, treas. 1944-48; with Muskegon Civic Opera Assn., 1950-51; office vol. Alive '88 Crusade; mem. com. for 60th H.S. Class Reunion; mem. Sr. Harvest Day Com., Muskegon County, 1995; active Forest Park Covenant Ch., mem. choir, 1953-79, 83—, choir pres. 1992, 93, choir sec. 1963-69, Sunday Sch. tchr. 1954-75, supt. Sunday Sch., 1975-78, sec., treas. 1981-86, sec. 1991, 92, 93, mem. support team, sec. 1993, chmn. master planning coun., 1982; coord. centennial com. to 1981, ch. sec. 1982-84, 87, 91, 95-96, registrar vacation Bible sch. 1988, 89, 90. 91, treas., 1996; co-chmn. Jackson Hill Old Timer's Reunion, 1982, 83, 85. Mem. Am. Registry Radiologic Technologists, Soc. Nuclear Medicine (cert. nuclear medicine technologist). Home: 5757 Sternberg Rd Fruitport MI 49415-9740

ANDERSON, GEOFFREY ALLEN, retired lawyer; b. Chgo., Aug. 3, 1947; s. Roger Allen and Ruth (Teninga) A.; B.A. cum laude, Yale U., 1969; J.D., Columbia U., 1972. Bar: Ill. 1972. Assoc., Isham, Lincoln & Beale, Chgo., 1972-79, ptnr., 1980-81; ptnr. Reuben & Proctor, Chgo., 1981-85; dep. gen. counsel Tribune Co., Chgo., 1985-92; gen. counsel Chgo. Cubs, 1986-90, corp. counsel, 1991-92. Elder Fourth Presbyn Ch., Chgo., chmn. worship and music com., 1990-92, trustee, 1992-95, v.p. 1993-94; bd. dirs. The James Chorale, Chgo., 1993-96, chmn. program com., 1994-96. Recipient Citizenship award Am. Legion, 1965. Mem. Chgo. Bar Assn. (chmn. entertainment com. 1981-82, best performance award, 1977), Phi Delta Phi. Clubs: Yale (N.Y.C.).

ANDERSON, GERALDINE LOUISE, laboratory scientist; b. Mpls., July 7, 1941; d. George M. and Viola Julia-Mary (Abel) Havrilla; m. Henry Clifford Anderson, May 21, 1966; children: Bruce Henry, Julie Lynne. BS, U. Minn., 1963. Med. technologist Swedish Hosp., Mpls., 1963-68; hematology supr. Glenwood Hills Hosp. lab., Golden Valley, Minn., 1968-70; assoc. scientist dept. pediatrics U. Minn. Hosps., Mpls., 1970-74; instr. health occupations Hennepin Tech. Coll., Brooklyn Park, Minn., 1974—, St. Paul Tech. Vocat. Inst., 1978-81; rsch. med. technologist Miller Hosp., St. Paul, 1975-78; rsch. assoc. Children's and United Hosps., St. Paul, 1979-88; sr. lab. analyst Cascade Med. Inc., Eden Prairie, Minn., 1989-90; lab. mgr. VA Med. Ctr., Mpls., 1990; technical support scientist INCSTAR Corp., 1990-94; reg. affairs product analysis coord. Medtronic Neurological, Mpls., 1995; quality assurance documentation coord. Lectec Corp., Stillwater, MN., Minnetonka, Minn.; clin. rsch. monitor, Eli Lilly Rsch. Labs., Indpls., 1995—; mem. health occupations adv. com. Hennepin Tech. Ctrs., 1975-90, chairperson, 1978-79; mem. hematology slide edn. rev. bd. Am. Soc. Hematology, 1976—; mem. flow cytometry and clin. chemistry quality control subcoms. Nat. Com. for Clin. Lab. Standards, 1988-92; cons. FCM Specialists, 1989—. Mem. rev. bd. Clin. Lab. Sci., 1990-91, The Learning Laboratorian Series 1991; contbr. and presenter In Svc. Rev. in Clin. Lab. Sci., audio taped study program for ASMT, 1992; contbr. articles to profl. jours. Mem. Med. Lab. Tech. Polit. Action Com., 1978—; charter orgns. rep. troop #534 Boy Scouts Am., Viking Coun., 1988-90; resource person lab. careers Robbinsdale Sch. Dist., Minn., 1970-79; del. Crest View Home Assn., 1981—; mem. sci. and math. subcom. Minn. High Tech. Council, 1983-88, mem. Women Scientists Speakers Bur., 1989-92; observer UN 4th World Conf. on Women, Beijing, 1995. Recipient svc. awards and honors Omicron Sigma. Mem. AAAS, AAUW, NAFE (Twin Cities network), Am. Med. Writers Assn., Women in Com. Inc., Assn. Clin. Pharmacology, Soc. Tech. Comm., Nat. Assn. Women Cons., Inc., Minn. Emerging Med. Orgns., Minn. Soc. Med. Tech. (sec. 1969-71), Am. Soc. Profl. and Exec. Women, Am. Soc. Clin. Lab. Sci. (del. to ann. meetings 1972—, chmn. hematology sci. assembly 1977-79, nomination com. 1979-81, bd. dirs. 1985-88), Twin City Hosp. Assn. (speakers bur. 1968-70), Assn. Women in Sci., World Future Soc., Minn. Med. Tech. Alumni, Am. Soc. Hematology, Internat. Soc. Analytical Cytology, Great Lakes Internat. Flow Cytometry Assn. (charter mem. 1992), Sigma Delta Epsilon (corr. sec. Xi chpt. 1980-82, pres. 1982-84, membership com. 1990-92, nat. nominations chair 1991-92, nat. v.p. 1992-93, nat. pres.-elect 1993-94, nat. pres. 1994-95), Alpha Mu Tau. Lutheran. Office: FCM Specialists 8400-33 Pl N Minneapolis MN 55427

ANDERSON, GLEN ROBERT, federal official; b. Chgo., Apr. 20, 1952; s. Robert Frank Mares and Agnes Helen (Oftedahl) A.; m. Elaine Ruth Leonhard, July 20, 1990. BA, U. Wis., Stevens Point, 1988. Cert. secondary tchr., Wis. Store clk. Flexiforce Temporaries, Waupaca, Wis., 1989-90; security guard Am. Security Corp., St. Paul, Minn., 1990-91; claims rep. Social Security Adminstrn., St. Paul, 1991-96. Contbr. poetry: Am. Poetry Anthology, 1987, Best New Poets of 1987, Poetry of Life: A Treasury of Moments, 1987, Love's Greatest Treasures: Today's Poets Speak From the Heart, 1988, Contemporary Poets of America and Britain, 1992, National Library of Poetry: In the Desert Sun, 1994, Best Poems of 1995, Sparrow Grass Poetry Forum: Treasured Poems of America, 1995. Ind. candidate Minn. House Dist. 66A, 1996. With USN, 1971-73; with U.S. Army, 1974-82; with USAR, 1985-92. Lutheran.

ANDERSON, HARALD JENS, classical studies and languages educator; b. Boston, Mar. 17, 1967; s. Robin Lee and Judith Marian (Herring) A. BA, Coll. of William and Mary, 1989, U. Ky., 1991. Radio disk jockey Sta. WCWM-FM, Williamsburg, Va., 1986-89, classical music dir., 1988-89; fellowship scholar U. Ky., Lexington, 1989-91; tchg. asst. Ohio State U., Columbus, 1991—. Reviewer, commentator Valerian Mag., 1995. Named Travel fellow Mediterranean Soc. Am., 1990, fellow Univ. Bonn, Germany, 1996-97; grantee Ctr. for Medieval & Renaissance Studies, 1994; recipient Faculty Tchg. Recognition award Sphinx Honor Soc., 1995. Mem. Am. Philol. Assn., Nat. Speleological Soc., Internat. Plutarch Soc., Classical Assn. of the Mid. West and South. Office: Ohio State U Dept Classics 414 University Hall Columbus OH 43210

ANDERSON, IRVIN NEAL, state legislator; b. Internat. Falls, Minn., June 18, 1923; s. Albert Eugene and Agnes (Bodway) A.; m. Phyllis J. Peterson, 1945; children: Gregory M., Cynthia J. U. Minn., 1947. State rep. Dist. 3A Minn. Ho. of Reps., 1965—, majority leader, 1996—, spkr., 1994—; chmn. com. Rules & Legis. Adminstrn., 1973-82, 93—, Local Govt. & Met. Affairs, 1996—; mem. Labor-Mgmt. Rels., Regulated Industry & Energy, Taxes & Ways & Means Coms. Alt. del. Dem. Nat. Conv., 1976. Recipient Air medal, Asiatic Theater Ribbon. Mem. VFW, Am. Legion, KC, Moose. Office: 585 State Office Bldg Saint Paul MN 55155*

ANDERSON, JACK W., manufacturing engineer; b. Chgo., Feb. 10, 1947. BS in Indsl. Engring., U. Iowa, 1970. Mfg. engr. Square D Co., Columbia, Mo., 1977—. Mem. Optimus Club (past pres. 1988). Lutheran. Home: 5615 Pinehurst Ln Columbia MO 65202-2906 Office: Square D Co 4800 Paris Rd Columbia MO 65202-9396

ANDERSON, JAMES DONALD, mining company executive; b. Toledo, Oct. 31, 1935; s. Donald James and Erma Elizabeth (Dorfmeyer) A.; m. Norma Elvira Powers, Aug. 30, 1958; children: Scott David, Sharon Grace, Steven William. BS in Chemistry, Capital U., 1957; MS in Chemistry, Ohio U., 1957; MBA, St. Louis U., 1968; student, Stanford Exec. Program, 1979. Rsch. chemist rsch. and engring div. Monsanto, Dayton, Ohio, 1959-61; sr. rsch. chemist rsch. and devel. dept. Monsanto, St. Louis, 1961-68; asst. purchasing agt. Wm. G. Krummrich Plant Monsanto, Sauget, Ill., 1968; purchasing agt. Chemstrand Triangle Park Devel. Ctr. Monsanto, Durham, N.C., 1968-72; from raw materials mgr. to dir. corp. purchasing Monsanto, St. Louis, 1972-86; dir. purchasing and distbn. svcs. Monsanto Chem. Co., St. Louis, 1986-93; purchsing cons. J.D. Anderson and Assocs., 1993-94; dir. materials mgmt. Peabody Group, Mo., 1995—. Patentee in field; contbr. chpts. to books and articles to profl. jours. Bd. dirs. Jr. Achievement, St. Louis, 1982—. Mem. AAIM Mgmt. Assn. (purchasing exec. roundtable 1986—), Nat. Assn. Purchasing Mgmt., Nat. Petroleum Refiners Assn. (bd. dirs. 1980—, Petrochem. com. chmn. 1988-89), Am. Chem. Soc., Soc. Chem. Industry, S.W. Chem. Assn., Mo. Athletic Club.

ANDERSON, JAMES GEORGE, sociologist, educator; b. Balt., July 24, 1936; s. Clair Sherrill and Kathryn Ann (Plovanich) A.; m. Marilyn Anderson, 1984; children: Robin Marie, James Brian, Melissa Lee, Derek Clair. B.Engring. Scis. in Chem. Engring, Johns Hopkins U., 1957, M.S.E. in Ops. Research and Indsl. Engring, 1959, M.A.T. in Chemistry and Math., 1960, Ph.D. in Edn. and Sociology, 1964. Adminstrv. asst. to dean Eve. Coll., Johns Hopkins U., 1964-65, dir. div. engring., 1965-66; research prof. ednl. adminstrn. N.Mex. State U., 1966-70; mem. faculty Purdue U., 1970—, prof. sociology, 1974—; asst. dean for analytical studies Sch. Humanities, Social Sci. and Edn., 1975-78; assoc. dir. AIDS Rsch. Ctr., Purdue U., 1991—, co-dir. Rural Ctr. for Study and Promotion of HIV-STD Prevention, 1993—; adj. prof. med. sociology grad. med. edn. program Meth. Hosp. Ind., 1991—; dir. Social Rsch. Inst., Purdue U., 1995—; cons. in field. Author: Bureaucracy in Education, 1968; co-author: Use and Impact of Computers in Clinical Medicine, 1987, Simulation in Emergency Management and Engineering and Simulation in Health Care, 1991, Simulation in Health Care and Social Services, 1992, Simulation in the Health Sciences and Services, 1993, Simulation in the Health Sciences, 1994, Evaluating Health Care Information Systems: Methods and Applications, 1994, Health Sciences Physiological and Pharmacological Simulation Studies, 1995, Simulation in the Medical Sciences, 1996; guest editor spl. issue on simulation in health sci., Simulation, Apr. 1996; contbr. chpts. to books, articles to profl. jours. Mem. Am. Assn. for Med. Systems and Informatics Del. to the Peoples Republic of China, 1985; mem., citizens amb. People to People Med. Informatics Del. to Hungary and Russia, 1993. USPHS grantee; recipient award for outstanding paper Am. Assn. Med. Sys. and Informatics, 1983, Gov.'s award for Outstanding Contbns. to State of Ind., 1987, T. Hale New Investigators award Assn. Am. Med. Colls., 1988, Wyeth-Ayerst/William Campbell Felch, M.D. award Alliance for Continuing Med. Edn., 1995. Mem. AAUP, AAAS (rep. soc. for computer simulation biol. scis. sect. 1992—), Am. Sociol. Assn., Am. Pub. Health Assn., Am. Ednl. Rsch. Assn. (treas. spl. interest group 1969-71), Am. Med. Informatics Assn. (internat. affairs com. 1993—), Soc. Computer Simulation (assoc. v.p. simulation in health care 1992—), Internat. Network for Social Network Analysis, Internat. Soc. System Sci. in Health Care, Internat. Sociol. Assn., Social Sci. Computing Assn. (publ. com. 1991—). Office: Purdue U 1365 Winthrop E Stone Hall West Lafayette IN 47907-1365

ANDERSON, JANICE LEE ATOR, secondary education mathematics educator; b. LaSalle, Ill., Aug. 8, 1948; d. Glen Bertran and Josephine Mary (Urichko) Ator; m. Gene Vernon Hook, July 20, 1968 (dec. 1974); m. Robert John Anderson, May 11, 1979 (div. 1983); 1 child, Karen Lynn. AA, Ill. Valley Community Coll., 1968; BS in Edn., Minot State Coll., 1970. Cert. tchr., Ill. Tchr. reading Tonica (Ill.) Elem. Sch., 1970-71; tchr. math., sci. Tonica Jr. High Sch., 1971-80, Tonica High Sch., 1980; tchr. math. Bradley (Ill.)-Bourbonnais Community High Sch., 1983—; coach math. team Bradley-Bourbonnais Community High Sch., 1983—. Mem. NEA, Ill. Edn. Assn., Bradley-Bourbonnais Edn. Assn. (sec. 1990-93, treas. 1993—), Women of Moose. Democrat. Roman Catholic. Home: 904 Roosevelt Rd La Salle IL 61301-1405 Office: Bradley Bourbonnais Community High Sch 700 W North St Bradley IL 60915-1013

ANDERSON, JEFFREY LYNN, stone company executive; b. Rochester, Minn., Dec. 3, 1955; s. Rolland Mayo and Lenora A. (Damann) A.; m. Renee Elizabeth Stanley, Apr. 22, 1977; children: Cimarron, Chelsea, William. Student, Brigham Young U., 1976-80, BS in Indsl. Edn., 1989; AA in Bus. Adminstrn., Rochester C.C., 1978; postgrad., Winona State U., 1980-86. With Rochester Granite Co., 1985-90, owner, 1990—, gen. mgr., 1985—; bus. teller, bookkeeper Marquette Bank, Rochester, 1974-76; mgr., owner Anderson Memls., Austin, Minn., 1979—; owner Rochester Granite Co., 1990—, Cemetery Meml. Sales & Svcs., Owatonna, Minn., 1991—; pres. Anderson Memls. Inc., Austin, 1993—; trustee Monument Industry Edn. Found., 1987—. Designer, carver meml. art. Bishop LDS Ch. Mem. N.W. Monument Builders Assn. (pres. 1985-89), Monument Builders N.Am. (cert., v.p. 1990-92, pres. 1994, com. chmn. 1984-88, Archie L. Green award 1986, Grand prize expert divsn. 1987), Am. Inst. Commemorative Arts, Exch. Club. Republican. Home: 306 S Main St Austin MN 55912-4433 Office: Anderson Memls 106 4th St SW Austin MN 55912-3118 also: Rochester Granite Co 2843 S Broadway Rochester MN 55904-5517

ANDERSON, JERRY WILLIAM, JR., technical and business consulting executive, educator; b. Stow, Mass., Jan. 14, 1926; s. Jerry William and Heda Charlotte (Petersen) A. ; m. Joan Hukill Balyeat, Sept. 13, 1947; children: Katheleen, Diane. BS in Physics, U. Cin., 1949, PhD in Econs., 1976; MBA, Xavier U., 1959. Rsch. and test project engr. Wright-Patterson AFB, Ohio, 1949-53; project engr., electronics div. AVCO Corp., Cin., 1953-70, program mgr., 1970-73; program dir. Cin. Electronics Corp., 1973-78; pres. Anderson Industries Unltd., 1978—; chmn. dept. mgmt. and mgmt. info. svcs. Xavier U., 1980-89, prof. mgmt., 1989-94, prof. emeritus, 1994—; lectr. No. Ky. U., 1977-78; tech. adviser Cin. Tech. Coll., 1971-80. Contbr. articles on radar, lasers, infrared detection equipment, air pollution to govt. publs. and profl. jours.; author 3 books in field. Mem. Madeira (Ohio) City Planning Commn., 1962-80; founder, pres. Grassroots, Inc., 1964; active United Appeal, Heart Fund, Multiple Sclerosis Fund. With USNR, 1943-46. Named Man of Year, City of Madeira, 1964. Mem. Am. Mgmt. Assn., Assn. Energy Engrs. (charter), Internat. Acad. Mgmt. and Mktg., Assn. Cogeneration Engrs. (charter), Assn. Environ. Engrs. (charter), Am. Legion (past comdr.), Acad. Mgmt., Madeira Civic Assn. (past v.p.), Omicron Delta Epsilon. Republican. Home and Office: 7208 Sycamorehill Ln Cincinnati OH 45243-2101

ANDERSON, JOAN BALYEAT, religion educator, minister; b. Cin., Apr. 14, 1926; d. Hal Donal and Myrtle Skinner (Hukill) Balyeat; m. Jerry William Anderson, Jr., Sept. 13, 1947: children: Katheleen, Diane. AA, Stephens Coll., 1946. Ordained ministry, Ohio. Christian bible tchr. Cin., 1944—, pastoral advisor, 1964—; founder, sr. pastor, pres., dir., ruling elder Loving God "Complete Bible" Christian Ministries, Cin., 1988—; daily and Sunday radio pastor, bible tchr. and preacher throughout east and midwest, 1988—. Coord., collector Heart Fund, T.B., 1948-90; civic assn. officer and rep. of edn. com. to all Madeira Schs., 1960-62; co-founder, officer Grassroots, Inc., Cin., 1962-65; mem. U.S. Senate Adv. Com., Washington and Cin., 1987-88. Mem. Blue Book of Cin. Republican. Home: 7208 Sycamorehill Ln Cincinnati OH 45243 Office: Loving God Complete Bible Christian Ministries PO Box 43404 Cincinnati OH 45243

ANDERSON, JOHN MCNEILL, secondary education educator; b. Peoria, Ill., June 6, 1942; s. John Faris Anderson and Eugenia McNeill; m. Jeannette Elaine Kesser, Feb. 14, 1979; children: Samuel and Nicholas (twins), Benjamin. BA, Mankato State U., 1964; MEd, Nat. Coll. Edn., 1980. Cert. tchr. Tchr. Storden (Minn.) Consol. Sch. Dist., 1965-68, Mundelein (Ill.) Consol. Sch.. Dist., 1968—. Contbr. book revs. to libr. jour. Commn. mem. Plan Comm. Zoning Bd. of Appeals, Beach Park, Ill., 1986—. Mem. Nat. Assn. Profl. Educators, Nat. Audubon Assn., Ill. Edn. Assn. Republican. Episcopalian. Home: 10471 Pickford Ave Beach Park IL 60099-4223 Office: Mundelein H S 1350 W Hawley Mundelein IL 60060

ANDERSON, JOHN ROBERT, state agency administrator; b. Elgin, Ill., June 15, 1952; s. William Thomas Anderson and Helen Kathleen (Bowles) Burns; m. Barbara Rae Gerhart, Aug. 14, 1982; 1 child, Katie Arminda. BA in English, Ohio U., 1974. Asst. dept. mgr., dept. mgr. Ohio Bur. Employment Svcs., Columbus, 1988-92, benefits dept. mgr., 1992—; bd. dirs. Ohio Bur. Employee Credit Union, Columbus; mem. State of Ohio Quality Svc. Through Partnership, 1994—. Mem. Lancaster (Ohio) Sanderson Elem. Sch. PTO, 1995—. Mem. Alpha Phi Omega (nat. membership ext. chair 1994—, regional dir. 1988-94, sect. chair 1975-88, sec./treas. Delta Gamma chpt. 1984, chmn., chtp. pres. Workshop 1986-90, co-founder Region V Ducks 1988, Disting. Svc. key 1985, 87), Lancaster H.S. Alumni Band Assn., Inc. (pres. 1984-85). Office: Ohio Bur Employment Svcs 145 S Front St PO Box 1618 Columbus OH 43216

ANDERSON, JUDITH HELENA, English language educator; b. Worcester, Mass., Apr. 21, 1940; d. Oscar William and Beatrice Marguerite (Beaudry) A.; m. E. Talbot Donaldson, May 18, 1971 (dec. Apr. 1987). AB magna cum laude, Radcliffe Coll., 1961; MA, Yale U., 1962, PhD, 1965. Instr. English Cornell U., Ithaca, N.Y., 1964-66, asst. prof. English, 1966-72; vis. lectr. Coll. Seminar Program, Yale U., New Haven, 1973; vis. asst. prof. English U. Mich., Ann Arbor, 1973-74; assoc. prof. Ind. U., Bloomington, 1974-79, prof., 1979—, dir. grad. studies, 1986-90, 93, mem. governing bd. univ. Inst. for Advanced Study, 1983-85, 86-88; Morris W. Croll lectr. Gettysburg Coll., 1988, Kathleen Williams lectr., 1989, 95; dir. Folger Inst. Seminar, 1991. Author: The Growth of a Personal Voice, 1976, Biographical Truth, 1984, Words that Matter, 1996; editor: (with Elizabeth D. Kirk) Piers Plowman, 1990, (with Donald Cheney and David A. Richardson) Spenser's Life and the Subject of Biography, 1996; mem. editl. bd. Spenser Ency., 1979-90, Duquesne Studies in Lang. and Lit., 1976—, Spenser Studies, 1986—; mem. adv. bd. Textbase of Women Writers, Brown U., 1989—; contbr. articles on Renaissance lit. to profl. jours. Woodrow Wilson fellow, 1961-62, 63-64, NEH summer fellow and sr. rsch. fellow, 1979, 81-82, Dulin fellow Folger Libr., 1991; Huntington Libr. rsch. grantee, 1978, 95, vis. fellow, 1985-86, Mayers Found. fellow, 1990-91, Nat. Humanities Ctr. fellow, 1995-96; recipient Outstanding Scholar award Office of Women's Affairs Ind. U., 1996. Mem. MLA (mem. exec. com. Renaissance divsn. 1973-78, 86-90, del. to assembly 1991-93), AAUP, Spenser Soc. (pres. 1980, 88), Renaissance Soc. Am. (rep. for English to coun. 1991-93), Milton Soc., Shakespeare Assn., Phi Beta Kappa. Office: Ind U Dept English Bloomington IN 47405 Address: 1309 Arboretum Dr Chapel Hill NC 27514

ANDERSON, KARL STEPHEN, newspaper executive; b. Chgo., Nov. 10, 1933; s. Karl William and Eleanore (Grell) A.; m. Saralee Hegland, Nov. 5, 1977; children by previous marriage: Matthew, Douglas, Eric. BS in Editorial Journalism, U. Ill., 1955. Successively advt. mgr., asst. to pub., plant mgr. Pioneer Press, Oak Park and St. Charles, Ill., 1955-71; asst. to pub., then pub. Crescent Newspapers, Downers Grove, Ill., 1971-73; assoc. pub. and editor Chronicle Pub. Co., St. Charles, 1973-80; assoc. pub. Chgo. Daily Law Bull., 1981-88; dir. communications, editor Ill. State Bar Assn., 1988—; pres. Chgo. Pub. Rels. Forum. Trustee emeritus, Chi Psi Ednl. Trust; mem. steering com. Ill. Freedom Info. Coun.; bd. overseers Ctr. for Freedom of Info. Studies, Loyola U.; trustee Leo Sowerby Found. Recipient C.V. Amenoff award No. Ill. U. Dept. Journalism, 1976, Ill. State Bar Bd. of Govs. award, 1987, Coalition of Sub Bar Assns. Print Media Humanitarian award, 1987, Robert C. Preble, Jr. award Chi Psi, 1991, Asian-Am. Bar Media Sensitivity award, 1991, Liberty Bell award DuPage County Bar Assn., 1993, Glass Ceiling Busters award Assn. Women Lawyers, 1993, Disting. Svc. award Chgo. Vol. Legal Svcs. Found., 1993, Gratitude award Lawyers Assistance Program, 1993, Outstanding Achievement in Comm. award Justinian Soc., 1994, 3rd prize Nat. Libr. Poetry, 1995. Mem. Nat. Assn. Bar Execs., Baltic Bar Assn., Chgo. Legal Sec. Assn., Ill. Press Assn. (Will Loomis award 1977, 80), Kane County Bar Assn., DuPage Women Lawyers Assn., West Suburban Bar Assn., Bohemian Lawyers Assn., No. Ill. Newspaper Assn. (past pres.), Soc. Profl. Journalists, Headline Club (past pres.), Nordic Law Club, Nellie Fox Soc., Chi Psi. Home: 3180 N Lake Shore Dr Apt 14D Chicago IL 60657-4851 Office: 20 S Clark St Ste 900 Chicago IL 60603-1803

ANDERSON, KERRII B., construction company executive; b. 1957. BS, Elon Coll., 1978; MBA, Duke U., 1987. With Peat, Marwick, Mitchell & Co., Greensboro, N.C., 1978-84, RJ Reynolds Corp., Winston-Salem, N.C., 1984-85, Key Co., Greensboro, N.C., 1985-87; sr. v.p., CFO M/I Schottenstein Homes Inc., Columbus, 1987—. Office: M/I Schottenstein Homes Inc 41 S High St Ste 2410 Columbus OH 43215-6101*

ANDERSON, KIM ELIZABETH, health and fitness organization executive; b. Canton, OH, Oct. 29, 1960; d. Doyle Edward and Joan Elizabeth (Mayeros) Parcell; m. Mark Alan Anderson, Aug. 22, 1981; children: Kyle Edward, Nathan Alan. BA, Mount Union Coll., 1983. Cert. high sch. phys. edn. and bus. edn. tchr. Fitness instr. Scandinavian Health Spa, Canton, 1983-84, Goodyear Tire and Rubber, Akron, Ohio, 1984-86; youth sports dir. Canton YMCA, 1984-86; pres., owner IKEN Enterprises, Alliance, Ohio, 1987-94; adult fitness dir. Louisville (Ohio) YMCA, 1994—; instr. step aerobics Alliance YMCA, 1990-93; women's soccer coach Alliance High Sch., 1993-94. Mem. adv. bd. Am. Cancer Soc., Alliance, 1989-91, Ohio Edison Consumer Panel, Alliance, 1987-92; publicity chmn. Centennial Celebration Com., Alliance, 1989—; instr. ARC, Alliance, 1990-94; bd. dirs. Carnation Festival, Alliance, 1989-92; chmn. kick-off parade, 1990, 91; publicity chmn. Alliance Cmty. Hosp. follies, 1991; divsn. I coach Alliance Cmty. Youth Soccer Club, 1992, 93, 94, 95; bd. dirs., asst. treas. Liberty Elem. Sch. PTO, 1992-93. Mem. Alliance Jaycees (bd. dirs. 1986-87, v.p. 1987-90, Outstanding Community Project award 1986, Jaycee of Yr. award, 1987, Thoams CaSale award, 1989), Alliance C. of C. (bd. dirs., ways and means com. women's div., membership com. retail svc. div. 1991). Republican. Methodist. Office: Louisville YMCA 1421 S Nickelplate St Louisville OH 44641-2647

ANDERSON, LARRY LYNN, mechanical engineer; b. Torrington, Wyo., Apr. 18, 1945; s. Emerson G. and Dorthy J. (Ownbey) A.;m. Deirdre J. Knowlton, Aug. 29, 1965; children: Bonnie, Eric, Paul. BSME, U. Wyo., 1968. Rsch. engr. Outboard Marine Corp., Milw., 1968-79; farmer, rancher Wyo., 1979-89; mech. engr. Lockwood Corp., Gering, Nebr., 1989—. Copatentee punch press safety device. Mem. Soc. Automotive Engrs. Home: Rt 2 Box 297 Torrington WY 82240 Office: Lockwood Corp Hwy 92E Gering NE 69341

ANDERSON, LEO SHERIDAN, writer; b. Koochiching County, Minn., Oct. 31, 1924; s. Ray and Olga (Flatness) A.; m. Phyllis Ann Doherty, Jan. 3, 1953 (dec. June 1976); children: Kathleen, Thomas, Kristi, Elizabeth, Janet, Michael; m. Rebecca Carlton, Dec. 28, 1978 (div. Sept. 1991); children: Nicholas, David, Tedd, Amy. BA in Journalism, U. Minn., 1950. Newsman UPI, Milw., 1950-52; bur. mgr. UPI, Marion, Ill., 1953-55; mng. editor Indsl. Mktg. Mag., Chgo., 1955-64; editor Office Appliances Mag., Elmhurst, Ill., 1964-68, Telephony Mag., Chgo., 1968-80; exec. v.p., publ. Telephony Publ. Corp., Chgo., 1981-87; cons. Leo Sheridan Anderson Consulting, Gurnee, Ill., 1988-94; freelance writer, Gurnee, 1991—; Christmas tree farmer Fair Wind Farm, Pardeeville, Wis., 1991—. Author: Down the Mississippi, 1992, (short story) What is it, Daddy?, 1994, award. With U.S. Army, 1943-46, ETO. Recipient Editor of Best Single Issue of Trade Mag. award Am. Bus. Press, 1963. Mem. Ill. Writers Inc., Prairie State Canoeists, Lake Bluff Yacht Club (bd. dirs. 1988), Union League Club Chgo., Roadrunners Internat. Roman Catholic. Home and Office: 4484 Brighton Ct Gurnee IL 60031

ANDERSON, LINDA LEE, oncology nurse; b. Alpena, Mich., May 10, 1957; d. Roy James and Celia Jeanette (Swartzinski) A. ADN, Lake Superior State U., Sault Ste. Marie, Mich., 1977; BSN, Wayne State U., 1980; MS, U. Mich., 1988. Advanced oncology cert. nurse, cert. clin. nurse specialist. Staff nurse Alpena Gen. Hosp., 1977-79, U. Mich. Med. Ctr., Ann Arbor, 1980-81, Catherine McAuley Health Ctr., Ann Arbor, 1981-89; case mgr. Harper Hosp., Detroit Med. Ctr., Detroit, 1989-91; clin. nurse specialist McLaren Regional Med. Ctr., Flint, Mich., 1991-93; nurse practitioner Harper Hosp., Detroit Med. Ctr., Detroit, 1993-96, Oakwood Hosp. and Med. Ctr., Dearborn, Mich., 1996—. Mem. ANA, Oncology Nursing Soc. (sec. Detroit chpt. 1994-95), Ann Arbor Ski Club, Ann Arbor Bicycle Touring Soc., Farmington Single Profls. Democrat. Roman Catholic. Home: 21455 Green Hill Rd Apt 182 Farmington Hl MI 48335-4562 Office: Oakwood Hosp 18101 Oakwood Blvd Dearborn MI 48123

ANDERSON, LLOYD LEE, animal science educator; b. Nevada, Iowa, Nov. 18, 1933; s. Clarence and Carrie G. (Sampson) A.; m. Janice G. Peterson, Sept. 7, 1958 (dec. Dec. 1966); m. JaNelle R. Hall, June 15, 1970; children: Marc C., James R. Student, Simpson Coll., 1951-52, Iowa State U., 1952-53; BS in Animal Husbandry, Iowa State U., 1957, PhD in Animal Reproduction, 1961. NIH postdoctoral fellow Iowa State U., Ames, 1961-62, asst. prof., 1961-65, assoc. prof., 1965-71, prof. animal sci., 1971—, Charles F. Curtiss Disting. prof. agr., 1992—; Lalor Found. fellow Station de Recherches de Physiologie Animale, Institut National de Recherche Agronomique, Jouy-en-Josas, France, 1963-64; rschr. physiology of reprodn.; mem. reproductive biology study sect. NIH, 1984-88, Nat. Insts. Health Reviewers Res. (NRR), 1988-92; mem. peer rev. panel animal health spl. rsch. grants on beef and dairy cattle reproductive diseases USDA, 1986-88; Honor lectr. representing Iowa State U., Mid-Am. State Univs. Assn., 1989-90; mem. sustainable agrl. panel U.S. Dept. Agr., Agrl. Rsch. Svc., Nat. Program Staff to rev. rsch. projects, 1993; mem. Janice Peterson Anderson Excellence award and scholarship Coll. of Design, Iowa State U. Mem. editl. bd. Biology Reprodn., 1968-70, 86-90, Jour. Animal Sci., 1982-87, Animal Reprodn. Sci., 1978—, Inst. for Sci. Info. Atlas of Sci., 1987-90, Domestic Animal Endocrinology, 1992-95, Endocrinology, 1993—; contbr. articles to profl. jours. Mem. 4-H Club. With Constrn. Engrs., U.S. Army, 1953-55, Germany. USDA grantee, 1978—. Fellow AAAS, Am. Soc. Animal Sci. (hon. Animal Physiology and Endocrinology award 1988, Nat Pork Prodrs. Coun. Innovation award in basic rsch. 1993); mem. Endocrine Soc., Am. Physiol. Soc., Iowa Physiol. Soc., Am. Assn. Anatomists, Soc. for Study of Reprodn., Soc. for Exptl. Biology and Medicine (mem. coun. 1980-83), Brit. Soc. for Study of Fertility, Soc. for Neurosci., Am. Legion, VFW, Nat. Block and Bridle Club, Osborn Rsch. Club (chair 1994), Sigma Xi, Gamma Sigma Delta. Methodist. Home: 2812 Valley View Rd Ames IA 50014-4506 Office: Iowa State U Dept Animal Sci 11 Kildee Hall Ames IA 50011

ANDERSON, LOIS D., nursing administrator, mental health nurse; b. Fulton, Mo., July 7, 1929; d. John Henry and Flossie Margaret (Myers) Dye; m. Morris B. Anderson, Nov. 4, 1947 (dec.); children: Sheila Sesti, John Anderson. AS, St. Louis Community Coll., Florissant, Mo., 1981. RN, Mo.; cert. mental health and psychiat. nurse. Head nurse Fulton State Hosp., quality assurance coord., retired 1991. Named hon. Red Cross Nurse, 1988. Mem. ANA, Mo. Nurses Assn., Profl. Nurses Assn. (treas.).

ANDERSON, LORNA KATHRYN, government official; b. Harrisonville, Mo., May 9, 1942; d. Loran Francis and Mary Louise (Russell) Honley; m. Thomas Jerald Anderson, Mar. 5, 1962 (div. May 1991); children: Jerome William, Benjamin Joseph. Student, Cen. Mo. State U., 1960-62, postgrad., 1976-79; BA summa cum laude, U. No. Colo., 1972, postgrad., 1972; MPA, U. Mo., Kansas City, 1989. Dep. Cass County Recorder of Deeds, Harrisonville, 1966-68; coordinator abstract dept. Stewart Title Co., Greeley, Colo., 1972-73; benefit authorizer Social Security Adminstrn., Kansas City, Mo., 1973-77, recovery reviewer, 1977-80, claims authorizer, 1980-88, asst. module mgr. Mid-Am. Program Svc. Ctr., 1988-93, staff asst., 1993-94, module mgr., 1994—; asst. coordinator women's issues Local 1336 Am. Fedn. Govt. Employees, Kansas City, 1985-88. Mem. Community Coll. Support com., Blue Springs, Mo., 1984; dist. chmn. Am. Cancer Soc., Independence, Mo., 1982; committeewoman Dem. Ctrl. Com., Weld County, Colo., 1972; pres. Dem. Women's Club, Harrisonville, 1968; bd. dirs. 5th Congl. Dist. Dem. Women's Club, Kansas City, 1968. Mem. AAUW (v.p. Independence br. 1981-83, pres. 1983-85), Mensa, Mo. Fedn. Wome's Clubs, Sigma Sigma Sigma. Democrat. Home: 3924 Crackerneck Rd Independence MO 64055-3925 Office: Social Security Adminstrn Mid-Am Program Svc Ctr 601 E 12th St Kansas City MO 64106-2808

ANDERSON, MARK, state legislator. Operating engr.; mem. from dist. 9 S.D. State Ho. of Reps., Pierre, mem. local govt., retirement laws coms. Address: 301 E 5th Crooks SD 57020-9625

ANDERSON, MARK CURTIS, newspaper editor. Editor Shawnee Mission Star/The Kansas City Star, Overland Park, Kans. Office: The Kansas City Star 8455 College Blvd Overland Park KS 66210

ANDERSON, MAX ELLIOT, television and film production company executive; b. St. Charles, Ill., Nov. 3, 1946; s. Kenneth O. and Doris I. (Jones) A.; m. Claudia Lynd, Aug. 17, 1978; children: James Brightman, Sarah Lynd. BA in Psychology, Grace Coll., 1973; advt. rep., cameraman Ken Anderson Films, Warsaw, Ind., 1969-78; producer Q Media Group, Rockford, Ill., 1978-83, pres. Philip Lasz Gallery, Warsaw, 1973—, pres., owner The Market Place, Rockford, 1985—; producer, dir. Eagle Video, Rockford, 1986—; regional product distbr. Laney Honey, 1994—; producer promotional video W.A. Whitney (German translation), 1996. Producer: nat. TV spots for True Value Hardware, 1985—, 40th anniversary TV spots for Rockford Clin. (Raddy award 1992); nat. distbr. inspirational home video cassettes, 1985—; assoc. producer: Gospel at the Symphony, 1979; cinematographer: (film) Pilgrims Progress. Served with U.S. Army, 1967-69. Recipient Best Cinematographer award Christian Film Distbrs. Assn., 1978; 1st pl. award Video Internat. Tech. Video Assn., 1989, award for Sundstrand sales video, 1991, award for Woodward Gov. corporate video, 1991; Raddy Award of Excellence No. Ill. Advt Coun., 1989, 90, 1st place video award Hosp. Satellite Network, 1990. Mem. Internat. Christian Video Assn., Am. Beekeeper Assn., Christian Booksellers Assn. Republican. Mem. Evang. Free Ch. Home and Office: 4112 Marsh Ave Rockford IL 61114-6142

ANDERSON, MILTON ANDREW, chemical executive; b. Fond du Lac, Wis., Oct. 22, 1927; s. Andrew Andreas and Bertha Victoria (Almquist) A.; m. Dorothy Mae Verke, Nov. 27, 1954; children: Edward, Victoria. BS, U. Wis., Madison, 1954; MS in Mgmt., Lake Forest Coll., 1980. Registered profl. engr., Calif. Specification engr. Johns-Manville, Waukegan, Ill., 1955-59; supr. Johns-Manville, Waukegan, 1959-64, chemist, 1964-70, devel. engr., 1970-73; supr. Abbott Labs., North Chicago, 1973-74, quality engr., 1974-77, cons., auditing., 1977-81, mgr. rsch. auditing good lab. practices/good clin. practices, 1981-92; pres. Rsch. Compliance Svcs. Ltd., Lake Villa, Ill., 1992—. Author: GLP Quality Audit Manual, 1987, 2d edit., 1991, GLP Essentials, 1995. Pres. Millburn Elem. Sch. Bd., 1971-73. Lt. naval aviator, 1948-52. Mem. Soc. Quality Assurance, Am. Soc.. for Quality Control (chmn. Northea. Ill. sect. 1980-82, sect. bd. dirs. 1982—). Republican. Home and Office: Rsch Compliance Svcs Ltd 19176 W Grass Lake Rd Lake Villa IL 60046

ANDERSON, NANCY JANE, medical nurse; b. Harvey, Ill., July 13, 1957; d. Ernest Eugene and Ingrid Gertrude (Davig) A. AAS, Prarie State Coll., Chicago Heights, Ill., 1979; BA in Health Adminstrn., Gov's. State U., Univ. Park, Ill., 1995. Reg. profl. nurse. Staff nurse Oakforest (Ill.) Hosp., 1979-89; pres. Salam Enterprises, Monee, Ill., 1991-93; staff nurse LifeLink Corp., Bensenville, Ill., 1993—. Mem. Aglow Internat., Am. Hosp. Assn. (assoc.).

ANDERSON, PATRICIA ANN, home economics educator, family and consumer sciences educator; b. York, Nebr., Mar. 17, 1944; d. William G. and Ruth M. (Abrahams) Deremer; m. J. Roger Anderson, May 29, 1965; children: Lisa M., Craig D., Joel W., Leah J. BS in Vocat. Home Econs. Edn., Kearney State Coll., 1967. Home econs. tchr. Valley (Nebr.) Pub. Schs., 1967-79, Malcolm (Nebr.) Pub. Schs., 1979-94; family svc. asst. Minden (Nebr.) Head Start, 1994-95; lead tchr., cons. home econs. curriculum U. Nebr., Kearney, 1987—; extension asst. Buffalo County Coop. Extension, Kearney. Bd. dirs. Homestead Coun. Girl Scouts Am., Lincoln, 1992; mem. cmty. goals-bus. climate com. Village of Malcolm, 1992; active Minden Cmty. Improvement Program, 1994—. Mem. Nebr. Vocat. Home Econs. Tchrs. Assn. (pres. 1991-92), Nebr. Vocat. Assn. (home econs. rep. 1988—), Nat. Assn. Vocat. Home Econ. Tchrs. (legis. com 1991—), Malcolm Edn. Assn. (pres., v.p., sec., treas. 1980-84). Republican. Evangelical. Home: 342 N Hubbard Ave Minden NE 68959-1746 Office: Buffalo County Coop Extension 1400 E 34th Kearney NE 68847

ANDERSON, PHILIP VERNON, pastor; b. Tanzania, Aug. 29, 1928; came to U.S., 1941; s. George N. and Annette L. (Elmquist) A.; m. Joan Audrey Carlson, Sept. 15, 1951; children: Christine Swaskey, Karen, Carl, Janice, Erik. AB, Augustana Coll., Rock Island, Ill.; MDiv, Luth. Sch. Chgo., U. Chgo., 1962. Ordained to ministry, Luth. Ch., 1953. Pastor Faith Luth. Ch., Syosset, N.Y., 1953-60; chaplain Augustana Hosp., Chgo., 1962-64; pastor Augustana Luth. Ch., Chgo., 1964-70; dir. pastoral care Augustana Hosp., Chgo., 1970-89; pastor Nazareth Luth. Ch., Hazel Crest, Ill., 1989-90; chaplain Hospice Care/Chicagoland, Homewood, Ill., 1990-91; pastor Bethesda Luth. Ch., Chgo., 1990—; bereavement dir. VITAS—Innovative Hospice Care, Homewood, 1991-94; mgr. bereavement svcs. VITAS-Innovative Hospice Care, Chgo., 1994—; instr. pastoral care Luth. Sch. Theology, Chgo., 1972-82; instr. field work McCormick Theol. Sem., Chgo., 1972-82. Home: 5549 S Harper Ave Chicago IL 60637-1829 Office: VITAS Innovative Hospice 1424 E 53d St Ste 201 Chicago IL 60615

ANDERSON, RICHARD E., financial advisor; b. Rapid City, S.D., Apr. 11, 1951. BS, U. S.D., 1973; MS, U. St. Thomas, 1981. Fin. advisor Paine Webber, Mpls., 1975-83, Prudential Securities, Mpls., 1983-88; sr. v.p. Smith Barney Inc., Mpls., Minn., 1988—; bd. dirs. Chgo. Mktg. Exch., Future Adv. Bd., Dirs. Coun. Contbr. articles to mags. Mem. Eden Prairie Planning Commn., 1986-90. Mem. Elks. Roman Catholic. Office: Smith Barney Inc Ste 2600 333 S 7th St Minneapolis MN 55402

ANDERSON, ROBERT MARSHALL, bishop; b. S.I., N.Y., Dec. 18, 1933; s. Arthur Harold and Hazel Schneider A.; m. Mary Artemis Evans, Aug. 24, 1960; children: Martha, Elizabeth, Catherine, Thomas. BA, Colgate U., 1955; STB, Berkeley Div. Sch., 1961, DD (hon.), 1977; DD (hon.), Seabury Western Sem., 1978, Yale U., 1977. Ordained priest Episcopal Ch. Curate St. John's Ch., Stamford, Conn., 1961-63, vicar, 1963-67, assoc. rector, 1968-72; priest in charge Middle Haddan, Conn., 1963-67, rector, 1967-68; dean St. Mark's Cathedral, Salt Lake City, 1972-78; bishop Episcopal Diocese of Minn., Mpls., 1978-93; interim recotr Church of the Holy Spirit, Lake Forest, Ill., 1994-95; asst. bishop Diocese of L.A., 1995—. Served with U.S. Army. Danforth fellow, 1959-60. Mem. Berkeley Alumni Assn. (pres. 1972-76). Democrat. Clubs: Mpls, Minikahda. Office: Diocese of Minn 309 Clifton Ave Minneapolis MN 55403-3217

ANDERSON, ROY ALAN, chemical engineer; b. Freeport, Tex., Oct. 23, 1949; s. Roy Orville and Rose Louise (King) A.; m. Donna Carol Massey, May 27, 1978; children: Roy Brian, Laura Michelle. BS in Chem. Engring., U. Tex., 1973. Plant engr. Pennwalt Corp., Houston, 1975-78; environ. engr. Temple-Eastex, Diboll, Tex., 1978-80; project devel. engr. ARAMCO, Dhahran, Saudi Arabia, 1980-85; project engr. C&I Engring., Cin., 1985-87; pres. Tek-Arts, Loveland, Ohio, 1987-90; project mgr. Jacobs Engring., Cin., 1990-92; pres. TRACO INC, Loveland, 1992—; lectr. in field; pub. The Plant Engr., electronic mag. Author tech. manuals: Refinery Turnaround Manual, 1990, Engineering Administrative Procedures Manual, 1989, Fire and SAfety Procedures Manual, 1988. Computer cons. Children's Meeting House-Montessori Sch., Loveland, 1989; soccer coach Soccer Assn. for Youth, Loveland, 1992; discus/shotput coach ARAMCO Schs., Dhahran, 1985. Mem. AIChE, Project Mgmt. Inst. Office: TRACO INC 1049 Red Bird Rd Loveland OH 45140-7164

ANDERSON, RUDOLPH VALENTINO, JR., principal; b. Chgo., Apr. 4, 1953; s. Rudolph Valentino and Norma (Milsap) A.; m. Cecile Angela Partee, Sept. 8, 1984; children; Carisa, Rudi. BS, Western Ill. U., 1976, MA, 1977; PhD, So. Ill. U., 1988. Tchr. Chgo. Pub. Sch. Dist. 299, 1977-79, audiologist, 1979-86; spl. asst. Chgo. Bd. Edn., 1986-89; adminstr. spl. edn. Chgo. Pubs. Schs., 1989-90, mgr. lang. and cultural edn., 1990-95; prin. Sayre Lang. Acad., Chgo., 1992—; audiologist ONIT-Inc., Country Club Hills, Ill., 1980—. Chmn. adv. bd. spl. edn. dept. Northeastern Ill. U., 1990—. Recipient Meritorious Svc. in Edn. award Coppin Meml., 1984, Bell award Nat. Assn. Black Sch. Educators, 1991. Mem. Ill. Bd. Assitive Tech. (edn. com. 1990—), Coun. for Exceptional Children (adv. bd. publicity 1992—). Office: Sayre Land Acad 1850 N Newland Ave Chicago IL 60635-3305

ANDERSON, RUTH CARRINGTON, retired secondary education educator; b. Lake Hopatcong, N.J., Jan. 7, 1915; d. Harry Porter and Mary Lamberetta (Cook) Carrington; m. Lee Silas Anderson, Nov. 9, 1942 (dec. Dec. 1972); children: Lawrence Lee, Lynette G. Anderson Esposito, Leslie Carl. BA in English, Iowa State Tchrs. Coll., 1938; MS in Edn. and English, Western Ill. U., 1970; postgrad., U. Iowa, 1954, U. Ill., 1958. Cert. elem. tchr., Ill. Tchr. rural schs. Henry County, Ill., 1933-36; jr. high sch. tchr. Woodhull (Ill.) Grade Sch., 1936-42; interviewer U.S. Employment Svc., Galesburg, Ill., 1942-44; English, lit. and govt. tchr. Geneseo (Ill.) Jr. High Sch., 1952-76; ret., 1976; speaker in field; sr. svcs. planning com. Hammond Henry Hosp., Geneseo, Ill., 1992-93; co-chmn. tchr. welfare com. Geneseo Community Unit Dist. 228, 1975-76. Mem. Western Ill. Sr. Advocacy Coun., Kewanee, Ill., 1988-94, Rock Island Sr. Coun., 1988-94, Henry County Farm Bur.; pres Henry County Sr. Advocacy Coun., Geneseo, 1987-94, chmn. pub. info. meetings and programs, 1987-94, moderator Ill. legis. candidate forum, 1992; sec.-treas. Andover, Ill. Sr. Citizens, 1989—; mem. Henry County Sr. Citizens Bd., Kewanee, 1993—; del. to Ill. Conf. on Aging, Springfield, 1990; bd. dirs. Augustana Luth. Ch., Andover, 1989-95, chmn. congl. learning com.; edn. chmn. Augustana Luth. Ch. Women, 1985, mem. peace circle, 1965—; pianist United Meth. Ch., Woodhull, 1931-42; active Evang. Luth. Ch. Women. Mem. DAR, Ill. Ret. Tchrs. Assn. (life, legis. com. 1989-92), Am. Assn. Ret. Persons, Nat. Ret. Tchrs. Assn., Andover Hist. Assn. (life), Am. Legion Aux. (1st v.p. 1979—, pres. 1976-79), U. No. Iowa Alumni Assn., We. Ill. U. Alumni Assn., Kappa Delta Pi, Sigma Tau Delta. Home: PO Box 137 507 5th St Andover IL 61233-0137

ANDERSON, SANDRA FLORENCE, publishing executive; b. Chgo., Sept. 23, 1948; d. Theodore Budnik and Florence (Lehman) Eggert. BS in Edn., No. Ill. U., 1971; MBA with honors, Lake Forest Coll., 1989. Programmer Allstate Ins. Co., Northbrook, Ill., 1972-74; programming supr. Allstate Ins. Co., Northbrook, 1974-75; bus. systems analyst Abbott Labs., N. Chgo., Ill., 1975-78; credit support mgr. Trans Union Credit Info. Co., Chgo., 1978-79, product mgr., 1979-82; cons., pvt. practice Chgo., 1982-84; mgr. order completion Scott, Foresman & Co., Glenview, Ill., 1984-85; dir. customer support svcs. Scott, Foresman & Co., Glenview, 1985-88, dir. planning, client svcs., 1988-92; prin. bus. cons.-sales Landis & Gyr Powers, Buffalo Grove, Ill., 1993-94; dir. customer svc. ACCO USA, Wheeling, Ill., 1995—. Mem. fin. bd. St. Edna's Ch., Arlington Heights, Ill. Mem. Internat. Customer Svcs. Assn., Sales Automation Assn., Am. Soc. Quality Control. Office: ACCO USA 770 S ACCO Plz Wheeling IL 60090-9999

ANDERSON, STEPHEN DALE, lawyer; b. Omaha, Nebr., Sept. 3, 1950; s. O.J. and Francis Eileen (Callahan) A.; m. Helen N. Goodpaster, July 22, 1954; children: Emily Eileen, Susan Eleanor, Robert Bryan. BA, Grace Bible Inst., Omaha, 1972; MDiv, Trinity Evang. Div. Sch., Deerfield, Ill., 1975; JD, U. Chgo., 1980. Bar: N.Y. 1980, Nebr. 1983. Asst. dist. atty. King County, Bklyn., 1980-83; asst. U.S. atty. U.S. Atty. for Dist. of Nebr., Omaha, 1983-89; trial atty. Organized Crime and Racketeering Stake Force Dept. Justice, Chgo., 1989-90; asst. U.S. atty. U.S. Atty. for No. Dist. of Ill., Chgo., 1990—. Bd. dirs. Cabrini Green Legal Aid Clinic, Chgo., 1993—.

ANDERSON, STEPHEN FRANCIS, insurance company executive; b. Mattoon, Ill., Dec. 5, 1950; s. Francis J. and Juanita J. (Collings) A.; m. Mary Ann Pipek, Mar. 3, 1973; children: Matthew C., David S. BS in Bus, Ea. Ill. U., 1972. CLU; ChFC; CFP. Store mgr. Bush's IGA, Carrollton, Ill., 1972-76; agt. Country Co. Ins., Bloomington, Ill., 1976-80; agy. mgr. Country Co. Ins., Eureka, Ill., 1980-83, Woodstock, Ill., 1983-92; pres. Dreher Ins. Svcs., Oakbrook Terrace, Ill., 1992—; v.p. mktg. Dreher & Assocs., Oakbrook Terrace, Ill., 1994—; pres. Agy. Mgrs. Conf. Ill., 1987--. Bd. dirs. Untied Way of McHenry County, Crystal Lake, 1988—, treas., 1989-90, pres. 1992; v.p. McHenry County 4-H Found., Woodstock, 1984—. Mem. Gen. Agts. Mgrs. Conf. (Career Devel. award 1988, Nat. Mgmt. award 1989-92), McHenry County Life Underwriters (pres. 1988—), Ill. Life Underwriters (Railsplitter bd. 1989-93), Chgo. Soc. CFPs (bd. dirs. 1993—, v.p. 1994—), Chgo. Soc. CLU/ChFC, Crystal Lake C. of C. (bd. dirs.), Rotary (bd. dirs. Woodstock chpt.). Republican. Home: 7271 Foxfire Dr Crystal Lake IL 60012-1601 Office: Dreher Ins Svcs 1 Oakbrook Ter Ste 708 Villa Park IL 60181-4728

ANDERSON, THOMAS J., investment advisor; b. Muskegon, Mich., Mar. 3, 1953; m. Kay Lynn Bailey, Aug. 17, 1973; children: Thomas J. II, Nathan, Robert. BSE, U. Mich., 1975, MST, 1977. Investment advisor Andoves Securities, Muskegon, 1987-90, FSC Securities, Muskegon, 1990—. Contbr. articles to bus. mag. Republican. Mem. Covenant Church. Home: 720 Brookridge Dr Muskegon MI 49441 Office: FSC Securities Corp # 415 950 W Norton Ave Muskegon MI 49441-4184

ANDERSON, TIM, airport terminal executive. Dir. of airports Mpls. St. Paul Internat. Airport. Office: Mpls-St Paul Internat Airpo Lindbergh Terminal 4300 Glumack Dr Rm 325 Saint Paul MN 55111-3010

ANDERSON, TODD PETER, financial consultant; b. Mpls., Sept. 28, 1957. BA, Ariz. State U., Tempe, 1981. Fin. cons. Merrill Lynch, Edina, Minn., 1981—. Home: 6301 Ashcroft Ln Edina MN 55424-1731 Office: Merrill Lynch 3400 W 66th St Ste 190 Edina MN 55435-2109

ANDERSON, VERONICA L., financial consultant; b. Singapore, Mar. 7, 1950; came to U.S., 1983; MBA, St. Thomas Coll., Mpls., 1988. Fin. cons. Merrill Lynch, Edina, Minn., 1989—. Office: Merrill Lynch 3400 W 66th St Ste 190 Edina MN 55435-2109

ANDERSON, VINTON RANDOLPH, bishop; b. Somerset, Bermuda; came to U.S., 1947; m. Vivienne Louise Cholmondeley, 1952; children: Vinton Jr., Jeffrey, Carlton, Kenneth. BA, Wilberforce U., HHD (hon.), 1973; MDiv, Payne Theol. Sem., 1952; MA in Philosophy, Kans. U., 1962; postgrad., Yale U. Div. Sch.; DD (hon.), Paul Quinn Coll., Payne Theol. Sem., Temple Bible Coll., Interdenom. Theol. Sem., Eden Theol. Sem.; LHD (hon.), Morris Brown Coll., ITC Seminary, Eder Theol. Ordained to ministry A.M.E. Ch., 1952, bishop, 1972. Pastor various chs. in Kans. and Mo., 1952-72; presiding bishop A.M.E. Ch., Ala., 1972-76; presiding bishop, chief pastor A.M.E. Ch., Ohio, W.Va., Western Pa., 1976-84; dir. Office of Ecumenical Rels. and Devel. A.M.E. Ch., 1984-88, presiding bishop 5th Episcopal dist., 1988—; chmn. bd. dirs. Payne Theol. Sem., Xenia, Ohio; preacher, lectr. in Caribbean, Republic of South and West Africa, Middle East, Europe, South Pacific; del. World Meth. conf., Nairobi, Kenya, 1986; mem. exec. com. World Meth. Coun., 1981—, 1st v.p. N.Am. region; v.p. Consultation on Ch. Union; mem. Gen. Commn. Christian Unity and Interreligious Concern, United Meth. Ch.; pres. World Coun. Chs., 1991—, del. 7th assembly, moderator liaison com. of hist. black chs.; mem. governing bd., faith and order Nat. Coun. Chs.; charter mem., v.p. Congress Nat. Black Chs. Founder, editor Connector, info. publ.; editor A Syllabus for Celebrating the Bicentennial; contbr. articles to profl. jours. Mem. nat. adv.

com. on the black population 1990 U.S. Census; mem. Nat. Commn. on Sch./Community Role in Improving Adolescent Health; mem. nat. adv. bd. Schomburg Ctr. for Rsch. in Black Culture; immediate past chairperson bd. trustees Wilberforce U.; chairperson bd. dirs. Payne Theol. Sem. Recipient Ann. Religion award Ebony mag., 1988, Disting. Alumni Honoree award Nat. Assn. for Equal Opportunity in Higher Edn., 1991. Home: 22 W Sherwood Dr Overland MO 63114 Office: AME Ch 5th Episcopal Dist AMEC 4144 Lindell Blvd Ste 222 Saint Louis MO 63108-2932

ANDERSON, WALLACE, real estate executive; b. St. Louis, Dec. 5, 1929. AA, St. Louis Merameg Jr. Coll.; postgrad., Washington U. Rep. candidate for U.S. House, 1992, 96. With U.S. Army, 1950-52. Presbyterian. Office: 8061 Watson Rd Ste 119 Saint Louis MO 63119*

ANDERSON, WAYNE LEE, surgeon; b. Williston, N.D., May 25, 1953. AA, U. N.D., 1973, BS in psychology, 1975, MD, 1980. Diplomate Am. Bd. Surgery. Intern in family practice U. N.D., Grand Forks, 1980-81; resident in gen. surgery U. Nev., Reno, 1981-82, U. N.D., Grand Forks, 1982-86; asst. prof. dept. surgery U. N.D. Sch. Medicine, 1986-92; asst. chief surgical svc. VA Hosp., Fargo, N.D., 1986-92; asst. clin. prof. surgery U. N.D. Sch. Medicine, 1992—; attending staff Mercy Med. Ctr., Williston, N.D., 1994—; attending staff Trinity Hosp., Wolf Point, Mont., 1992-94, Belcourt PHS, Belcourt, N.D., 1986-92, courtesy staff United Hosps., Grand Forks, 1991-92; lectr in field; presentor at numerous confs. Contbr. articles to profl. jours. Medical records review com. VA Hosp., 1987-90, clinical lab. utilization com., 1987-91, STAMP program planning com., 1987, quality assurance com., 1987-89, environ. control com., 1986-92, rsch. and devel. com., 1987-89. Fellow Am. Coll. Surgeons, Am. Coll. Chest Physicians; mem. AMA, N.D. Medical Assn., Northeast Mont. Medical Soc., Northern Plains Vascular Soc., Am. Soc. Parenteral and Enteral Nutrition, Soc. Am. Gastrointestinal Endoscopic Surgeons, Soc. Laparoendoscopic Surgeons. Office: Craven-Hagen Clinic 1213 15th Ave W Williston ND 58801-3800

ANDERSON, WILLIAM EDWARD, electrical engineer; b. L.A., Apr. 29, 1942; s. Harold Lenard and Billie Lucille (McGuire) A.; m. Martha Cathrine Rastatter, Sept. 19, 1970 (div. 1986); children: John E., Robert W., Jeffrey P., Michael W.; m. Susan Elizabeth Cannon, July 27, 1990; 1 stepchild, Emily S. Terwilliger. BS in Applied Sci., Portland State U., 1972; MSEE, U. Portland, 1976; MBA, Xavier U., 1979. Registered profl. engr., Oreg., Ohio. Elec. engr. Leupold & Stevens, Portland, 1972-73, Sandwell Internat., Portland, Oreg., 1973—, C & I/Girdler, Louisville, 1977-78, Procter & Gamble Co., Cin., 1978—. With USN, 1964-69, Vietnam. Mem. IEEE, Am. Soc. for Quality Control. Office: Proctor & Gamble Winton Hill Tech Ctr 6105 Center Hill Ave Cincinnati OH 45224-1750

ANDERSON, WILLIAM GILCHRIST, physician, surgeon, educator; b. Americus, Ga., Dec. 12, 1927; s. John Daniel and Emma Jean (Gilchrist) A.; m. Norma Lee Dixon, Nov. 23, 1946; children: A. Laurita, W. Gilchrist, V. Jeanita, Frank, Darnita Dawn. BS, Ala. State Coll., 1949; DO, U. Osteo. Medicine, Des Moines, 1956; LHD (hon.), Ohio U., 1990, U. New Eng., 1992; DSc (hon.), W.Va. Sch. Osteopathic Medicin, 1993; LHD (hon.), U. Osteopathic Medicine, 1994; D of Pub. Svc., U. North Tex., 1995; DSc, Kirksville Coll., 1995. Diplomate Am. Coll. Osteopathic Surgeons. Intern Flint (Mich.) Osteo. Hosp., 1957; resident in gen. surgery Art Centre Hosp., Detroit, 1964-67; staff surgeon Art Centre Clin. Group, Detroit, 1967-71, Zieger Clin. Group, Detroit, 1971-74; sr. attending and consulting surgeon Detroit Surg. Assocs., 1974-84; chief med. officer, exec. v.p. Mich. Healthcare Corp., Detroit, 1984-86; dir. govtl. affairs Horizon Health System, Southfield, Mich., 1986-92; dir. med. edn. Riverview Hosp., Detroit, 1992—; dir. Citizens Trust Bank, Atlanta, 1975—; trustee U. Osteo. Medicine, Des Moines, 1974—; chmn. bd. dirs. Mich. Healthcare Corp., Detroit, 1978-84, Mich. Hosp. Centre, Detroit, 1977-84. Dir. YMCA, Detroit, 1971—; trustee Hartford Ch., Detroit, 1981—. Fellow Am. Osteo. Coll. Surgeons; mem. Am. Osteo. Assn. (pres. 1994-95, trustee 1981—). Home: 24535 N Carolina Southfield MI 48075 Office: Am Osteo Assn 142 E Ontario Chicago IL 60611

ANDERSON, WILLIAM JOHN, II, engineering and business management consultant; b. Randolph, Ohio, Dec. 2, 1924; s. Thomas Watt and Evelyn Alice (Phile) A.; m. Zelma Oleta Ashton, Sept. 8, 1946; 1 child, William John III. BSEE, Tri-State U., 1948; Cert. in Mgmt. Policy, U. So. Calif., L.A., 1963; Cert. in Western Mgmt., U. San Diego, 1978; Cert. in Advanced Mgmt., Claremont U., 1980. Mgr. field engr. Sylvania Elec., Emporium, Pa., 1950-53; sr. staff engr., pres. staff CBS Electronics, Danvers, Mass., 1953-56; regional mgr. Western CBS Electronics, L.A., 1956-61; dir. sales ops. TRW Electronics, Lawndale, Calif., 1956-61; cons. William Anderson Assocs., L.A., 1963-75; mktg. mgr. fiber optics Deutsch Electronics, El Segundo, Calif., 1975-80; mgr. mktg. programs TRW Electronics, Lawndale, 1980-85; sr. project engr. Hughes Electro-Optical, El Segundo, 1985-90; v.p. ops., cons. Master Distbrs., Santa Monica, Calif., 1990-94; systems design engr. Goodyear Aircraft, Akron, Ohio, 1948-50; mem. adv. bd. U. So. Calif., L.A., 1963-78, U. San Diego, 1978-90, Claremont U., 1986-88; lectr. in field. Author several books; contbr. articles to profl. jours. Mem. Planning Cmty. Econ. Devel., Portage County, Ohio, 1994-95; mem., campaigner Rep. Party, Portage County, 1994-95; mem. Kent City Charter Rev. Commn., 1995. Served with U.S. Army, 1943-45, PTO. Mem. IEEE, Nat. Def. Exec. Res., Masons, Kent Area C. of C. Home and Office: 426 Spaulding Dr Kent OH 44240

ANDERSON, WILLIAM ROY, machinist specialist; b. Trumbull County, Ohio, Aug. 14, 1939. Tool room die maintenance Perfection Steel Body, Galion, Ohio, 1961-85; pres. Anderson Art'y Artificers, Galion, 1983-86; machinist/toolmaker Minnich Mfg., Mansfield, Ohio, 1986-88; machinist Komatsu-Dresser, Galion, 1988-90; maintenance Hi-Stat Mfg. Co., Fabrication Dept., Lexington, Ohio, 1991—; advisor N.W.-Territorial Alliance, Chgo., 1979—. V.p. Code Environ. Group, Galion, 1989—. With USAF, 1957-61. Mem. U.S. Field Arty. Assn., Ohio Mil. Res. Baptist. Office: Hi Stat Mfg Fabrication Dept 345 Mill St Mansfield OH 44904-9573

ANDERT, JEFFREY NORMAN, clinical psychologist; b. Aberdeen, S.D., May 21, 1950; s. Norman Joseph and Irene Eleanor (Olson) A.; m. Diane Kay Dunham, May 29, 1971; Jason Ryan, Jonathan Erik, Justin Matthew. BA in Psychology, Augsburg Coll., 1971; MA in Psychology, Mankato (Minn.) State U., 1973; PhD in Psychology, U. So. Miss., 1976. Diplomate in Clin. Psychology Am. Bd. Profl. Psychology; lic. psychologist, Mich. Grad. asst. Mankato State U., Minn., 1972-73, U. So. Miss., Hattisburg, Miss., 1974-75; psychology intern Des Moines Child Guidance Ctr., Des Moines, 1975-76; clin. psychologist Battle Creek (Mich.) Child Guidance Clinic, 1976-80; pvt. practice Battle Creek, 1978—; pres., adminstrv. dir. Psychol. Cons. of Mich., P.C., Battle Creek, 1979—; administrv. dir. Chem. Dependency Resources, Battle Creek, 1982—; med. expert Office of Hearings and Appeals, Social Security Adminstrn., Lansing, Mich., 1986—. Contbr. articles to profl. jours. Pres., trustee Lakeview Pub. Sch. Dist., Battle Creek, 1991—; adult leader Boy Scouts Am., Battle Creek, 1988—. Disting. Svc. award, So. Cen. Mich. Substance Abuse Commn., Jackson, Mich., 1987. Fellow Acad. Clin. Psychology; mem. Assn. for the Advancement of Behavior Therapy, Am. Psychol. Assn., Mich. Psychol. Assn., Mich. Substance Abuse Program Dirs. Assn., South Cen. Mich. Substance Abuse Program Dirs. Assn. (pres. 1986-87). Lutheran. Home: 144 Waupakisco Bch Battle Creek MI 49015-3144 Office: Psychol Cons Mich PC 2518 Capital Ave SW Ste 2 Battle Creek MI 49015-4104

ANDERTON, JAMES FRANKLIN, IV, holdings company executive; b. Lansing, Mich., Aug. 2, 1943; s. James Franklin III and Florence Ethel (Bear) A.; m. Deborah Anne Garlock, Apr. 2, 1966 (div.); 1 child, James Franklin, V.; m. Denise Marie Thelen, July 6, 1985; 1 child, Sarah Elizabeth. BA, Hobart Coll., Geneva, N.Y., 1965; MBA, Cornell U, 1967. Controller Summit Steel Processing Corp., Lansing, 1967-69, exec. v.p., 1970, pres., 1971-90; pres. Processed Plastics Co., Ionia, Mich., 1986-90, Universal Steel Co. of Mich., Lansing, 1988-90; chmn., pres., chief exec. officer Summit Holdings Corp., Lansing, 1986—; pres. Inst. of Scrap Recycling Industries, Washington, 1982-83, bd. dirs.; v.p. Bur. Internat. de la Recuperation, Brussels, 1984-85; bd. dirs. Alpena (Mich.) Power Co., Fed. Forge Inc., Lansing, First of Am. Bank Ctrl. Lansing, First of Am. Bank Mich., Kalamazoo, Auto Owners Ins. Co., Lansing, ATHENA Found., Lansing, Capital Area Health Alliance, Lansing; mem. Mich. Resource Recovery Com., 1975-77, Mich. Job Devel. Authority, 1977-79. Pres. Lansing Met. Devel. Authority, 1971-72, Delta Twp. Econ. Devel. Authority, 1975-76; campaign chmn. Capital Area United Way, Lansing, 1976; chmn. Lansing Regional C. of C., 1977; chmn. Montessori Children's House, Lansing, 1982-85, St. Lawrence Hosp., Lansing, 1985-86, Capital Region Cmty. Found., Lansing, 1992-93; trustee Hobart and William Smith Colls., Geneva, N.Y., 1993—. Sgt. USNG, 1968-74. Mem. Country Club of Lansing. Republican. Episcopal. Home: 1700 Old Mill Rd East Lansing MI 48823-2158 Office: Summit Holdings Corp 1900 W Willow St Lansing MI 48917-1838

ANDRE, L. AUMUND, management consultant; b. Marquette, Kans., Dec. 21, 1916; s. Anders and Lillian Amanda (Johnson) A.; m. Elsie Viola (Nelson), June 1, 1941 (dec. Feb. 1986); children: Carolyn Aleda, Denise Ardis; m. Phyllis Jean Richter-Russo, Sept. 17, 1988. BS, CUNY, 1939; postgrad., Columbia U., 1940-41, George Williams Coll., 1947. Youth program dir. various YMCAs, N.Y.C., Syracuse, Chgo., 1939-51; exec. dir. YMCA Met. Chgo., 1951-65; sr. v.p. Cen. YMCA Coll., Chgo., 1965-80; pvt. practice cons. Chgo., 1980—; instr. Sch. Edn. Syracuse (N.Y.) U., 1941-44; adj. prof. George William Coll., Chgo., 1948-55; lectr. Northwestern U., Evanston, Ill., 1978-80. Author: So Now You Are a Fund Raiser, 1977, Boys and Dogs Have Right of Way, 1987; author poetry; contbr. articles to profl. jours. Mem. county com. Am. Labor Party, Syracuse, 1943; chmn. Northwest Community Coun., 1954-56, Citizens Com. to Establish Triton Coll., River Grove, Ill., 1962-64; advisor Ill. Atty. Gen. Commn. to Study Fund Raising Laws and Enforcement., 1980. Named Father of Year Chgo. Area Father's Day Coun., 1962; recipient Svc. to Youth award, Lincolnland Assn. Profl Dirs. (YMCA), 1977. Mem. Nat. Soc. Fund Raising Execs. (officer , dir. 1968-79, Founder's award 1980). Democrat. Lutheran. Office: 100 Forest Pl Apt 1250 Oak Park IL 60301-1141

ANDREA, JOSEPH F., state legislator; b. Kenosha, Wis., Nov. 29, 1927; m. Olivia Butteri, 1952; children: Alex, Martin, Thomas, Mary. Grad. high sch., 1946. Former employee telephone co.; former state rep. State of Wis., state senator dist. 22, 1984—. Former supr. County of Kenosha. Mem. Rosary Holy Name Soc. (past pres.). Democrat. Office: 2405 45th St Kenosha WI 53140-2626 also: State Senate State Capitol Madison WI 53702*

ANDREAS, DWAYNE ORVILLE, business executive; b. Worthington, Minn., Mar. 4, 1918; s. Reuben P. and Lydia (Stoltz) A.; m. Bertha Benedict, 1938 (div.); 1 dau., Sandra Ann Andreas McMurtie; m. Dorothy Inez Snyder, Dec. 21, 1947; children: TerryLynn, Michael D. Student, Wheaton (Ill.) Coll., 1935-36; hon. degree, Barry U. V.p., dir. Honeymead Products Co., Cedar Rapids, Iowa, 1936-46; chmn. bd., chief exec. officer Honeymead Products Co. (now Nat. City Bancorp.), Mankato, Minn., 1952-72; v.p. Cargill, Inc., Mpls., 1946-52; exec. v.p. Farmers Union Grain Terminal Assn., St. Paul, 1960-66; chmn. bd., chief exec. officer Archer-Daniels-Midland Co., Decatur, Ill., 1970—, also mem. exec. com., dir.; bd. dirs. Salomon, Inc., Hollinger Internat. Inc.; mem. Pres.'s Gen. Adv. Commn. of Fgn. Assistance Programs, 1965-68, Pres.'s Adv. Coun. on Mgmt. Improvement, 1969-73; chmn. Pres.'s Task Force on Internat. Pvt. Enterprise. Nat. bd. dirs. Boys' Club Am.; former chmn. U.S.-USSR Trade and Econ. Coun.; former chmn. Exec. Coun. on Fgn. Diplomats; trustee Hoover Inst. on War, Revolution and Peace; vice chmn. Woodrow Wilson Internat. Ctr. for Scholars; mem. Trilateral Commn.; chmn. Found. for Commemoration of the U.S. Constitution, 1986. Mem. Fgn. Policy Assn. N.Y. (dir.), Indian Creek Country Club (Miami Beach, Fla.), Blind Brook Country Club (Purchase, N.Y.), Economic of N.Y. (chmn.), Links, Knickerbocker, Friars (N.Y.C.).

ANDREASEN, BETHANY JAYNE, history educator; b. Milw., May 11, 1958; d. Norman Christian and Charlotte Louise (Buchanan) A. BA, U. Wis.-Eau Claire, 1980; MA, Cornell U., 1984, PhD, 1987. Asst. prof. S.W. Tex. State U., San Marcos, 1987-90, SUNY-Plattsburgh, 1990-91, Minot (N.D.) State U., 1991—. Mem. Women's Resource Ctr. (pres. 1992—), Orgn. Am. Historians, Am. Hist. Assn., Am. Studies Assn., Nat. Coun. for the Social Studies. Office: Minot State U Social Sci Divsn Minot ND 58707

ANDREASEN, JAMES HALLIS, state supreme court judge; b. Mpls., May 16, 1931; s. John A. and Alice M. Andreasen; m. Janet Andreasen, June 25, 1961 (dec. July 1985); children: Jon A., Amy E., Steven J.; m. Marilyn McGuire, May 17, 1987. BS in Commerce, U. Iowa, 1953, JD, 1958. Bar: Iowa 1958. Pvt. practice law Algona, Iowa, 1958-75; with Algona City Coun., 1961-68; judge 3d Jud. Dist. Ct., 1975-87, Supreme Ct. Iowa, Des Moines, 1987—. Lt. col. USAFR, 1954-75. Mem. ABA, Iowa State Bar Assn., Kossuth County Bar Assn. Republican. Methodist. Office: Supreme Ct Iowa St Capitol Bldg Des Moines IA 50319

ANDREASEN, NANCY COOVER, psychiatrist, educator; d. John A. Sr. and Pauline G. Coover; children: Robin, Susan. BA summa cum laude, U. Nebr., 1958, PhD, 1963; MA, Radcliffe Coll., 1959; MD, U. Iowa, 1970. Instr. English Nebr. Wesleyan Coll., 1960-61, U. Nebr., Lincoln, 1962-63; asst. prof. English U. Iowa, Iowa City, 1963-66; resident U. Iowa, 1970-73; asst. prof. psychiatry U. Iowa, Iowa City, 1973-77, assoc. prof., 1977-81, Andrew H. Woods prof. psychiatry, 1981—, dir. Mental Health Clin. Rsch. Ctr., 1987—; sr. cons. Northwick Pk. Hosp., London, 1983; acad. visitor Maudsley Hosp., London, 1986. Author: The Broken Brain, 1984, Introductory Psychiatry Textbook, 1991; editor: Can Schizophrenia be Localized to the Brain?, 1986, Brain Imaging: Applications in Psychiatry, 1988; book forum editor: Am. Jour. Psychiatry, 1988—, dep. editor, 1989-93, editor, 1993—. Woodrow Wilson fellow, 1958-59, Fulbright fellow Oxford U., London, 1959-60. Fellow Royal Coll. Physicians Surgeons Can. (hon.), Am. Psychiat. Assn., Am. Coll. Neuropharmacologists; mem. Am. Psychopathol. Assn. (pres. 1989-90), Inst. of Medicine of NAS. Office: U Iowa Hosps & Clinics 200 Hawkins Dr Iowa City IA 52242-1009

ANDREASEN, NIELS-ERIK ALBINUS, religious educator; b. Asminderod, Denmark, May 14, 1941; came to U.S., 1963; s. Caleb A. and Erna E. (Pedersen) A.; m. Demetra Lougani, Sept. 5, 1965; 1 child, Michael. BA, Newbold Coll., England, 1963; MA, Andrews U., Mich., 1965, BD, 1966; PhD, Vanderbilt U., 1971. From asst. to assoc. prof. Pacific Union Coll., Calif., 1970-75; vis. lectr. Avondale Coll., Australia, 1975-77; prof., dean of religion Loma Linda (Calif.) U., 1977-90; pres. Walla Walla (Wash.) Coll., 1990-94, Andrews (Mich.) U., 1994—. Author: The Old Testament Sabbath, 1972, Rest and Redemption, 1978, The Christian Use of Time, 1978. Mem. Soc. Bibl. Lit. Seventh Day Adventist. Office: Andrews University Office of the President Berrien Springs MI 49104

ANDREOFF, CHRISTOPHER ANDON, lawyer; b. Detroit, July 15, 1947; s. Andon Anastas and Mildred Dimitry (Kolinoff) A.; m. Nancy Anne Krochmal, Jan. 12, 1980; children: Alison Brianne, Lauren Kathleen. BA, Wayne State U., 1969; postgrad. in law Washington U., St. Louis, 1969-70; JD, U. Detroit, 1972. Bar: Mich. 1972, U.S. Dist. Ct. (ea. dist.) Mich. 1972, U.S. Ct. Appeals (6th cir.) 1974, Fla. 1978, U.S. Supreme Ct. 1980. Legal intern Wayne County Prosecutor's Office, Detroit, 1970-72; law clk. Wayne County Cir. Ct., Detroit, 1972-73; asst. U.S. atty. U.S. Dept. Justice, Detroit, 1973-80, asst. chief Criminal Div., U.S. Atty.'s Office, 1977-80, spl. atty. Organized Crime and Racketeering sect. U.S. Dept. Justice, 1980-84, dep. chief Detroit Organized Crime Strike Force, 1982-85, mem. narcotics adv. com. U.S. Dept. Justice, 1979-80; ptnr. Evans & Luptak, Detroit, 1985-93, Jaffe, Raitt, Heuer & Weiss, Detroit, 1995—; lectr. U.S. Atty. Gen. Advocacy Inst., 1984. Recipient numerous spl. commendations FBI, U.S. Drug Enforcement Adminstrn., U.S. Dept. Justice, U.S. Atty. Gen. Mem. ABA, Fed. Bar Assn. (speaker trial advocate and criminal law sect. Detroit 1983—, bd. dirs. 1989-91, chmn. criminal law sect. 1990-91), Mich. Bar Assn., Fla. Bar Assn., Nat Assn. Criminal Def. Lawyers, Detroit Bar Assn. Greek Orthodox. Home: 4661 Rivers Edge Dr Troy MI 48098-4161 Office: Jaffe Raitt Heuer & Weiss One Woodward Ave Ste 2400 Detroit MI 48226

ANDRESEN, GRACIELA VAZQUEZ, clinical psychologist; b. Santiago, Cuba, Dec. 11, 1952; d. Abelardo and Graciela (Diaz) Vazquez-Perez; m. Stephen Richard Andresen, Aug. 9, 1975; children: Elizabeth Nicole, Jennifer Michelle. BS, Ohio State U., 1977; MA, U. Ill., 1981, PhD, 1989. Lic. clin. psychologist. Tchr. psychology dept. U. Ill., Urbana, 1978-79, therapist intern, 1979-81, instr. psychology dept., 1984-85; rsch. instr. U. Ill. Coll. Medicine, Urbana, 1989-93; postdoctoral assoc. U. Ill., Urbana, 1989-90, psychotherapist Psychol. Svcs. Ctr., 1990-91; rsch. assoc. Carle Found. Hosp., 1989-95; psychotherapist, clin. psychologist Assocs. in Clin. Psychology, Champaign, Ill., 1991-93; grant reviewer Carle Found. Cancer Rsch. Com., Urbana, 1989-93. Contbr. articles to profl. jours. Bd. dirs. Jr. League of Champaign (Ill.)-Urbana, 1985-91, mem. Ill. State pub. affairs com. 85-87, pres. 1990-91; bd. dirs. Discovery Place Children's Mus., 1991-94, Am. Cancer Soc. 1992-96. Mem. APA, Ill. Psychol. Assn., Phi Kappa Phi. Office: Assocs in Clin Psychology 701 Devonshire Dr Champaign IL 61820-7337

ANDRESKI, RAYMOND JOHN, financial planner; b. Rahway, N.J., Aug. 4, 1946; s. Theodore R. and Jean A. (Birch) A.; m. Diane T. Bishoff, Dec. 31, 1968; children: Theresa R., Peter M., Laura M. Diploma, Agy. Mfrs. Tng. Coun., 1982; CFP, Coll. Fin. Planning, Denver, 1987; diploma in mgmt. tng., Purdue U., 1992. Sales mgr. The New England, Omaha, 1982—. Sgt. USMC, 1966-70. Recipient Regional Speaking award Toastmasters Internat., 1985. Mem. Nat. Assn. Life Underwriters (program chair 1981-94), C. of C. Office: The New England 9290 W Dodge Rd Ste 200 Omaha NE 68114

ANDREW, MARK HENRY, surgeon; b. Rural Summit, Wis., Oct. 20, 1954; s. Harry Wilmer and Genevieve Gladys (Trankle) A.; m. Marcia Kay Lemanski; children: Jessica Lynn, Brian Thomas, Benjamin David. BS, U. Wis., Platteville, 1976; MD, U. Wis., Madison, 1980. Diplomate Am. Bd. Surgery. Resident Southwest Mich. Area Health Edn. Ctr., Kalamazoo, 1980-85; gen. surgeon Vig-Gundersen Clinic, Viroqua, Wis., 1985-95, Vernon Meml. Hosp., Viroqua, 1996—; instr. advanced trauma life support ACS, 1985—; mem. rev. cons. Wis. Peer Rev. Orgn., Madison, 1987—. Chmn. Vernon County Dem. Party, Viroqua, 1988-90; treas. Com. Greater Western Wis., Viroqua, 1988-93; vice chmn. Vernon Area Fitness Wellness Assn., Viroqua, 1987—; mem. Viroqua Are Schs. Bd. Edn., 1994—, v.p., 1996—. Fellow Am. Coll. Surgeons; mem. AMA, Wis. Surg. Soc., State Med. Soc. Wis. (dir. 1992—, chmn. young physicians sect. 1991-92, vice chmn., bd. dirs. 1995—), Vernon County Med. Soc. (pres. 1988—). Home: PO Box 447 575 Prairiewind Way Viroqua WI 54665 Office: Vernon Meml Hosp 507 S Main St Viroqua WI 54665

ANDREWS, BETTYO, early childhood educator; b. Akron, Ohio, July 10, 1958; d. Jack and Betty Louise (Weaver) Manda; m. Tom W. Andrews, July 14, 1979; Laura R., Evan T., Neal I. Student, Friends U., 1976-78, Wichita Bible Coll., 1976-78, Kans. Newman Coll., 1978-79; A of Child Devel., Wichita Area Vocat. Tech. Coll, 1996. Tutor edn. lab. Kans. Newman Coll., Wichita, 1978-79; tchr. NAS Moffett Field, Mountainview, Calif., 1979-81, Andrews Home Day Care, Wichita, 1981—, St. Francis Regional Child Devel. Ctr., Wichita, 1992-93; cons. Sears Telecatalog, Wichita, 1990-93; aide Wichita Pub. Sch. System, 1991-92. Mem. PTO, Wichita, 1986-91, PTA, Wichita, 1992-94; leader, Girl Scouts Am., Wichita, 1986-87; tchr. Sunday sch. Four Square Ch., Wichita, 1981-85. Mem. Wichita Child Care Assn., Wichita Assn. Young Children. Home and Office: 5334 W Douglas Ave Wichita KS 67212-2450

ANDREWS, CAROLYN P., quality assurance professional; b. Memphis, June 23, 1941; d. Clarence Alfred and Lacoma P. (McLemore) Haugh; m. Larry Wayne Andrews, Sept. 6, 1957 (div. Aug. 1965); children: John W., Corey W., Troy W. BA in Bus. and Econs., Ill. Benedictine Coll., 1993. Mgr. quality assurance Amphenol Corp., Cicero, Ill., 1962-80; mgr. quality assurance and rels. Amphenol Corp., Broadview, Ill., 1980-85; mgr. quality assurance Chgo. Decal, 1985-86, Pyle-Nat., Chgo., 1986-93, John Gillen Co., Cicero, Ill., 1993-94; dir. quality Parkview Metal Products, Inc., Chgo., 1994-96; mgr. quality assurance The Phoenix Co. Chgo., 1996—. Mem. Am. Soc. for Quality Control (cert. quality engr., quality auditor, mgr., publicity chair Chgo. sect. 1988-90, vice-chair for program 1989-90, vice-chair for sect. affairs 1990-91, sect. chair 1991-92). Home: 25 Indian Trail Westmont IL 60559 Office: Phoenix Co Chgo Inc 555 E Pond Dr Wood Dale IL 60191

ANDREWS, ELEANOR DE LING, state education consultant; b. Battle Creek, Mich., Feb. 16, 1934; d. Byron Joseph and Vernice Beth (Boss) De Ling; m. Wesley Lynn Andrews, Sept., 1982; children: Robin Eric Dudley, Richard James Quendun. BS in Spl. Edn., Eastern Mich. U., 1960; MA in Anthropology, Ball State U., 1966; EdD, U. Mich., 1982. Cert. tchr., Mich. Teaching fellow archaeology lab., fieldwork asst. Ball State U., Muncie, Ind., 1984-95; ednl. cons. various sch. dists., Mich. Dept. Edn., 1966-70; ednl. staff cons. U. Microfilms Xerox Edn. Group, Ann Arbor, Mich., 1970-71; program dir. Mich. State Dept. Edn., Lansing, 1971-72; asst. prof. dept. social sci. Mich. Tech. U., Houghton, 1972-74; ednl. cons. Native Am. tribes and programs, 1974-76; program coord. bilingual edn. program Keweenaw Bay Tribal Ctr., Baraga, Mich., 1976-78; adminstrv. and ednl. cons., instr. Mich., 1978-82; acad. assoc. Native Am. Ednl. Svcs. Coll., Chgo., 1982-84; ednl. cons. adult extended learning svcs. Mich. Dept. Edn., 1984-90; cons. Andrews Cultural Resources, 1994—; coord. Family Employability Devel. Project Mich. Dept. Edn., 1985-91.

ANDREWS, EMMETT LYNN (RUSTY ANDREWS), promotional writer, consultant; b. Wichita, Kans., Nov. 15, 1954; s. Maurice Lynn Andrews and Ceola Marie (McAllister) Andrews-Jones; m. Jenne Sue Foster, June 21, 1974; children: Lyndsey Marie, Logan Lynn, Megan O'Neal. MS, Kans. State U., 1994; BS, Manhattan Christian Coll., 1976. Asst. news dir., announcer Manhattan (Kans.) Broadcasting Co., 1974-76; mem. prodn. crew, announcer Kans. State Network, Wichita, 1976-78; dir. pub. rels. Manhattan Christian Coll., 1978-81; owner, producer Andrews Multimedia, Manhattan, 1981-83; dir. annual giving, assoc. dir. $100,000,000 campaign Kans. State U. Found., Manhattan, 1983-91; v.p. Life Skills Inst., Manhattan, 1991-93; owner Rusty Andrews Cons., fundraising, polit., human sys. cons., Manhattan, 1991—; cons., writer polit. persons, Kans., 1990—; fundraising cons. numerous non-profit orgns., univs., hosps., Kans., Nebr., S.D., 1991—; pres. Heartland Christian Assn., Manhattan, 1991—. Bd. dirs. United Way Riley County, Manhattan, 1987-90; media advisor Kent Glasscock for State Rep. campaign, Manhattan, 1990—; media advisor, sales tax campaign Jobs for Manhattan, 1994, Ann Stevens for State Rep. campaign, Manhattan, 1994; vol. mental health provider ARC Disaster Relief, Manhattan, 1993; mem. leadership program class of 1990, Future Manhattan. Recipient 1st pl. award Coun. for Advancement and Support of Edn., 1986, 89, 90; scholar St. Mary Hosp. Aux., Manhattan, 1991, Helen C. Schutte scholar Kans. State U., 1993, human ecology scholar, 1994, Martha L. Dunlap scholar, 1995, Eva B. Potter scholar, 1996. Mem. Am. Assn. for Marriage and Family Therapy, Nat. Coun. on Family Rels., Kans. Assn. for Marriage and Family Therapy (bd. dirs.), Phi Kappa Phi, Kappa Omicron Nu (scholar Omicron Theta chpt. 1992). Republican. Home and Office: 757 Elling Dr Manhattan KS 66502-3635

ANDREWS, JAMES MACARTHUR, sales executive; b. Owatonna, Minn., Jan. 21, 1937; s. Harry and Lucille (MacArthur) A. Student, Mankato (Minn.) State U., 1957-58; AD, Dunwoody Inst., Mpls., 1960. Draftsman Electric Machinery & Mfg., Mpls., 1960-61; sales engr. The King Co., Owatonna, 1961—. Contbr. articles to profl. jours. Sgt. maj. Minn. N.G., 1956-89. Republican. Christian.

ANDREWS, JOHN GERARD, artist; b. Iowa City, Iowa, Dec. 29, 1960; s. Richard Vincent and Elisabeth Patricia Andrews; m. DeAnn Gay Jaworski, Aug. 16, 1986; children: Sarah Elizabeth, Luke Joseph, Samuel James. BFA, Creighton U., 1984; MA, U. Iowa, 1988, MFA, 1991. Exhibited works in one-man shows at Antiquarium, Omaha, 1985, Jewish Cmty. Ctr. Gallery, Omaha, 1984, U. Minn. Morris, The Print Club, Phila., 1993, Luther Coll., Decorah, Iowa, 1994, CSPS, Cedar Rapids, Iowa, Dartmouth Coll., Hanover, N.H., 1995; exhibited in group shows at Muscatine (Iowa) Art Ctr., 1988, 89, Hunterdon Art Ctr., Clinton, N.J., 1989, Knoxville (Tenn.) Mus. Art, 1989, Sioux City (Iowa) Art Ctr., 1991, Des Moines Art Ctr., 1991, 92, N.J. Ctr. for Visual Arts, Summit, 1991, Taipei Fine Arts Mus., 1992, Tex. Fine Arts Assn., 1992, 93, The Print Club, Pa., 1992, Sioux City (Iowa) Art Ctr., Skidmore Coll. (N.Y.), Bemis (Omaha), 1994, Davenport Mus., 1995, Des Moines Art Ctr., 1996; represented in collections at Taipei Fine Arts Mus., U. Iowa Print Archives, Phila. Mus. Art, Sioux City Art Ctr. Recipient various awards for art; Arts Midwest-NEA visual arts fellow, 1992. Home: PO Box 244 105 S Augusta Oxford IA 52322

ANDREWS, RICHARD VINCENT, physiologist, educator; b. Arapahoe, Nebr., Jan. 9, 1932; s. Wilber Vincent and Fern (Clawson) A.; m. Elizabeth

Williams, June 1, 1954 (dec. Dec. 1994); children: Thomas, William, Robert, Catherine, James, John. BS, Creighton U., 1958, MS, 1959; PhD, U. Iowa, 1963. Instr. biology Creighton U., Omaha, 1958-60; instr. physiology U. Iowa, 1960-63; asst. prof. Creighton U., 1963-65, assoc. prof., 1965-68, prof. physiology, 1968—, asst. med. dean, 1972-75, dean grad. studies, 1975-85, dean emeritus, 1995—; vis. prof. Naval Arctic Rsch. Lab., 1963-72, U. B.C., 1985-86, U. Tasmania, 1993-94; cons. VA, NSF, NRC, ARS; plenary speaker USSR Symposium on Environment, 1970, Internat. Soc. Biomet., 1972. Contbr. articles to profl. jours. Served with M.C. U.S. Army, 1951-54. NSF fellow, 1962-63; NSF-NIH-ONR-AINA grantee, 1963—. Fellow Explorers Club, Arctic Inst. N.Am.; mem. Am. Physiol. Soc., Am. Mammal Soc., Endocrine Soc., Soc. Exptl. Biology and Medicine, Internat. Soc. for Biometeorology, Sigma Xi. Office: 2500 California St Omaha NE 68131-1676

ANDREWS, RONALD KEITH, physician; b. Indpls., Feb. 12, 1949; s. Keith Lee and Geneva (Ross) A.; m. Barbara Ann Henriksen; children: Kristen, Erik, Kaari. AB, Ind. U., 1973, MD, 1978. Master scuba diver trainer. Intern, then resident Ind. U. Hosps., Bloomington, 1977-78; pvt. practice Greenfield, Ind., 1978—; sr. physician Ind. Law Enforcement Authorities; assoc. coord. Divers Alert Network; advisor Chgo. Police Dept. Marine Unit, Hamilton County Sheriff, Ind. Coun. of Emergency Response Teams, Ind. State Police, Indpls. Fire Dept., Jackson County Sheriff, Mich. State Police, Ont. Provincial Police, Shelby County Sheriff Ind. Dept. Natural Resources; instr. CMAS, N.A.U.I., Y.M.C.A.; diving cons. With USMC, 1967-69, Vietnam. Decorated Vietnamese Cross, Navy Achievement medal. Mem. A.A.F.P., Ind. State Med. Assn., Hancock County Med. Soc., Undersea Med. Soc., Nat. Assn. of Underwater Instrs., Profl. Assn. of Diving Instrs., World Underwater Fedn., Nat. YMCA Underater, B.S.A.C. Office: 1229 N State St Greenfield IN 46140

ANDREWS, RUTH KLASSEN, mediator, consultant; b. Chgo., Apr. 21, 1952; d. Otto Dyck and Helen Ruth (Bohn) Klassen; m. Jeff W. Andrews, May 6, 1978 (div. Apr. 1993); children: Alex, Simon, Marcus. BA, Columbia Coll., Chgo., 1978. Cert. in family mediation, Ind. Continuing Legal Edn. Forum. Adminstrv. asst. Elkhart (Ind.) County Prisoner and Comty. Together (PACT), 1983-85; devel. coord. Ctr. for Cmty. Justice, Elkhart, 1985-86, exec. dir., 1987-90; dir. St. Joseph County Victim Offender Reconciliation Program, South Bend, Ind., 1990-95; mediator, sentencing cons. Options for Conflict Resolution, Elkhart, 1990-95; co-dir. Golden Angels, Elkhart, 1995—. Filmmaker: Incumbent Mama, 1973 (Agfa Gevaert grant), Play, 1974; collaborator performance piece Bloodletters, 1994. Bd. dirs. Violence Intervention Project, Elkhart, 1992-95. Mem. Soc. Profls. in Dispute Resolution. Democrat. Office: Options for Conflict Resolution 429 S Main St Elkhart IN 46516

ANDREWS-KEENAN, PATRICIA J., public relations executive; b. New Orleans, July 19, 1954; d. James Clifton Andrews and Pearline (Henderson) Champman; m. Richard L. Andrews (div. Oct. 1993). BA, Grambling State U. Acct. rep. Mountain Bell, Denver; taxpayer svc. coord. IRS, Denver; pub. rels. coord. Ctr. Cable; cmty. rels. coord., mktg. mgr., dir. pub. affairs. Bd. dirs. Quad County Urban League, Ill., 1995—. fellow Walter Kartz Found., Oakland, Calif., 1988. Mem. Nat. Assn. Minorities in Cable (pres. Chgo. chpt. 1993-95, bd. dirs. 1995—), Women in Cable & Telecomm. (Betsey Magness fellowship 1993, bd. dirs. 1993—, nat. sec., 1995—), Pub. Rels. Soc. Am., Cable TV Pub. Affairs Soc., Aurora Rotary, Alpha Kappa Alpha. Democrat. Baptist. Office: Jones Intercable 1101 E Roosevelt Rd Wheaton IL 60187

ANDRIES, LINDA J., publishing director; b. Mpls., Jan. 27, 1962; d. Jame A. and Helen M. (Belsaas) A.; 1 child, Samantha Hogan. BBA, St. Norbert Coll., 1994. Account exec. Mid Continent Rsch., Mpls., 1984-85; regional mktg. mgr. Ency. Britannica, Chgo., 1985-92; exhibits mgr. Nordic Track, Mpls., 1992; dir. nat. mktg. Colliers Ency., N.Y.C., 1993; dir. strategic devel. and new channel devel. Ency. Britannica, Chgo., 1994—. Recipient Gov.'s commendation Minn. Gov.'s Office, 1990. Mem. Am. Mktg. Assn., Direct Mktg. Assn. Home: 1213 W Newport Ave Chicago IL 60657 Office: Ency Britannica 310 S Michigan Ave Chicago IL 60604

ANDRIST, JOHN M., state senator; b. Crosby, N.D., Aug. 1, 1931; s. Calvin L. and Lela G. (Revis) A.; m. Elaine G. Thvedt, June 17, 1951; children: Pamela, Paula, Steve, Stan, Penny. Senator N.D. State Senate, Crosby, 1993—. Mem. N.D. Newspaper Assn. (past pres.), Nat. Newspaper Assn. (N.D. state chmn. 1970-82, bd. dirs., representing Iowa, N.D., S.D., Minn. 1982-87, treas. 1988, v.p. 1989, pres. 1990), Crosby Bus. Builders (pres.), Crosby Jaycees (past pres.), N.D. Jaycees (state sec.), N.D. Profl. chpt. Soc. Profl. Journalists (past pres.). Presbyterian. Lodges: Kiwanis, Moose. Office: PO Box E Crosby ND 58730-0660

ANDRUS, THERESA KESTER, photojournalist, communications specialist; b. Manchester, Iowa, Aug. 2, 1953; d. Francis Alfred and Mary Veronica (Keegan) Kester; m. Douglas Burton Andrus, Dec. 23, 1978; children: Ian, Ross. AA in Applied Arts, Hawkeye Inst. Tech., 1975; BS summa cum laude, St. Cloud State U., 1992. Chief photographer Larson Publs., Osseo, Minn., 1978-86; reporter, photographer Monticello (Minn.) Times, 1992-94; comm. dir. Maple Lake (Minn.) Pub. Schs., 1994—. Photographer: (books) Full Circle Five, 1984, A Sampler of Women, 1984, Full Circle Seven, 1986. Ctrl. Minn. Mother's March chairperson March of Dimes, St. Cloud, 1988, Porch Light Night chairperson, 1988-91; gen. coord. for Centennial Playground, Maple Lake (Minn.) Schs., 1989-90, Blandin Cmty. Leadership Program, 1991-92; co-chairperson Irish Summer Fest, Maple Lake, 1992, 95, 96; mem. sch. bd. Mple Lake Schs., 1992-94. Recipient Maple Lake (Minn.) Disting. Svc. award, 1990, Mpls. Aquatennial Assn. Commodore's award, 1993, numerous state and nat. awards for photojournalism, 1980-95. Mem. Maple Lake (Minn.) Jaycees (v.p. for pub. rels. 1989-91, pres. 1991-92, chair bd., Jaycee of Yr. 1990), Phi Kappa Phi. Office: Maple Lake Pub Schs 200 State Hwy 55 E Maple Lake MN 55358

ANENE, JOHN ODIAKA, hospitality industry educator; b. Ubulu-Uku, Nigeria, Aug. 4, 1959; came to the U.S., 1982; s. John and Isabella (Obaya) A.; m. Kate Awele Utomi, Jan. 7, 1994. BS, Wiley Coll., 1985; MS, Fla. Internat. U., 1989. Asst. mgr. Ky. Fried Chicken, Marshall, Tex., 1984-85, Wyatt Cafeteria, Dallas, 1986; dir. hospitality mgmt. program Wiley Coll., Marshall, 1989-94; asst. prof. Ctrl. State U., Wilberforce, Ohio, 1994—. Contbr. articles to profl. jours. Named one of Outstanding Young Men Am., 1990; Louise McKinney Post-Secondary scholar, 1984. Mem. Travel and Tourism Rsch. Assn., CHRIE, Ohio CHRIE, Nat. Restaurant Assn., Nat. Coalition Black Meeting Planners. Home: 416 Bellbrook Ave # H Xenia OH 45385 Office: Ctrl State U 310 Smith Hall Wilberforce OH 45384

ANGELO, BRIAN GENE, electrical engineer; b. Warren, Ohio, May 9, 1968; s. Carl J. Angelo and Rebecca L. Lester. BSEE, Gen. Motors Inst., Flint, Mich., 1991. Application engr. GMC-Delphi-Packard Electric Sys., Warren, Ohio, 1986—; sr. project engr. power/signal distbn. sys. GMC-Delphi-Packard Electric Sys., Warren. Office: GMC Delphi-Packard PO Box 431 Warren OH 44486-0001

ANGERMAN, NEIL STANLEY, medical consultant; b. Entwistle, Alberta, Can., Jan. 21, 1944; came to U.S., 1973; s. Stanley John and Evelyn Grace A.; married June 6, 1972. BS with honors, U. Alberta, Edmonton, 1966, PhD, 1969; MD, U. Chgo., 1975. Diploamte Am. Bd. Ob/Gyn. Postdoctoral Oxford U., Eng., 1969-70; resident U. Chgo., 1975-79; postdoctoral Mayo Clinic, Rochester, Minn., 1979-82; pvt. practice Cleve., 1982-88; med. consultation Pearl Health Svcs., Inc., Cleve., 1988—. Contbr. articles to profl. jours. Recipient various sci. and med. awards, 1962-88. Mem. Am. Soc. Ob/Gyn. Office: Pearl Helth Sys Inc Ste 146 30799 Pine Tree Rd Pepper Pike OH 44124

ANGLE, MARGARET SUSAN, lawyer; b. Lincoln, Nebr., Feb. 20, 1948; d. John Charles and Catherine (Sellers) A. BA with distinction in Polit. Sci., U. Wis., Madison, 1970, MA in Scandinavian Studies (scholarship, NDEA fellow), 1972, JD cum laude, 1976. Bar: Wis. 1977, Minn. 1978. Law clk., Madison, Mpls., Chgo., 1974-76; law clk. U.S. Dist. Ct., Mpls., 1977-78; mem. firm Faegre & Bensen, Mpls., 1978-84; sr. atty., asst. gen. counsel, asst. sec. Nat. Car Rental System, Inc., Mpls., 1984-90; corp. sec. Car-Temps; CEO Angle & Assocs., Ltd., Eagan, Minn., 1990—, clients include Avis, Budget, Hertz, Nat. Car Rental Cos., 1990—. Note and comment editor U. Wis. Law Rev.; contbr. articles to profl. publs. Mem. ABA, Am. Car Rental Assn. (bd. dirs. 1987-90), Minn. Bar Assn., Wis. Bar Assn., Hennepin County Bar Assn., Alternative Dispute Resolution Com., Niños del Paraguay, Parents of Latin Am. Children, Order of Coif. Home: 4340 Fox Ridge Ct Saint Paul MN 55122-2257 Office: Angle & Assocs Ltd 1971 Seneca Rd Ste C Eagan MN 55122-1039

ANGLEMYER, ROMA KATHLEEN, elementary school educator; b. Wakarusa, Ind., Sept. 17, 1932; d. Wayne Douglas and Evelyn Virginia (Weldy) Wyman; m. Keith Alois Anglemyer, June 10, 1956; children: Debra Anglemyer McNally, Linda Anglemyer Stolley. BE, Goshen (Ind.) Coll., 1955; MA, St. Mary's Coll., Notre Dame, Ind., 1966. Lic. real estate rep. Tchr. Bremen (Ind.) Pub. Sch., 1955-59; tchr. Wa-Nee Schs., Nappanee, Ind., 1960-93, instr. enrichment classes, 1984-86; mem. adj. faculty, instr. Bethel Coll., Mishawaka, Ind., 1993; instr. mentally handicapped Concord Schs., Elkhart, Ind., 1967; instrl. asst. Coll. of the Gifted and Talented, Ind. U., Bloomington, 1984, Kids-on-Campus, Goshen Coll., 1985. Contbr. curriculum Wa-Nee Ind. History, 1980-86. Sponsor Wakarusa 4-H Clubs Elkhart County, 1974-76; pres. Progressive Homemakers, Elkhart County, 1984-85, Searchlight Club; sch. rep. Wa-Nee Sch. Reorgn. 25th Anniversary, Nappanee, 1987; mem. steering com. Gifted and Talented Program Wa-Nee, Nappanee, 1985-86, mem. curriculum devel. team for gifted and talented Elkhart Schs., 1984-86; mem. curriculum com. Wa-Nee Drug Awareness program, 1988—. Mem. NEA, Ind. State Tchrs. Assn., Wa-Nee Tchrs. Assn. (exec. mem. 1984-85), Wakarusa Tchrs. Assn. (pres. 1981-82), Wa-Nee Tchrs. Exec. Com., Elkhart County Reading Assn., Hoosier Assn. Sci. Tchrs., Inc., Pi Lambda Theta (membership chmn. No. Ind. 1985-87, pres. 1987-89, del., sec. Great Lakes Region II 1988-90, del. Biennial Coun. 1987, award com. 1987-89). Home: RR 1 Wakarusa IN 46573-9801

ANGUS, ROBERT CARLYLE, JR., health facility administrator; b. Grand Rapids, Mich., July 23, 1946; s. Robert Carlyle Sr. and Vicki I. (Weidman) Deiters; m. Elizabeth T. Angus, May 1990; children: Tamra, Robert M. BS, Donsbach U., Huntington Beach, Calif., 1985; PhD in Therapeutic Philosophy, World U., 1982. Registered cardiovascular technologist, pulmonary technologist, registered cardiology technologist, cert. respiratory therapy technician; lic. radiographer, respiratory care practitioner, hearing aid dispenser; cert. occupl. hearing conservationist. Dir. cardiopulmonary St. Mary's Hosp., Grand Rapids, Mich., 1970-74; Lectr. Muskegon (Mich.) Community Coll., 1974-76; dir. respiratory therapy Hackley Hosp., 1974-76; dir. cardiovascular, cardiopulmonary Am. Internat. Hosp., Zion, Ill., 1976-78; physician's asst. Dr. William J. Mauer; dir. med. svcs., clinic adminstr. Kingsley Med. Ctr., Arlington Heights, Ill., 1978-90; dir. med. diagnostics Celebration of Health Ctr., Inc., Bluffton, Ohio, 1990—; edn. cons. Brookhaven Med. Care Facility; lectr., advisor Muskegon Community Coll., 1974-76. Active Big Bros. Am., Muskegon, 1974-76. Mem. Nat. Bd. Cardiovascular Testing, Am. Cardiology Technologists Assn., Am. Assn. Respiratory Therapy, Nat. Soc. Cardiopulmonary Technologists, Coun. for Accreditation in Occupational Hearing Conservation, Clan MacInnes Soc.

ANIELLO, ANTHONY JOSEPH, information system executive; b. Hoboken, N.J., Aug. 24, 1941; s. Joseph Patrick and Louise (Gaetano) A.; m. Ann Elizabeth Brinkman, Aug. 10, 1963; children: Peter, Thomas, Catherine, Anthony. BS, St. Benedict's Coll., 1963; postgrad, Purdue U., 1963-64. Rsch. asst. Purdue U., West Lafayette, Ind., 1963-64; chemist Corn Products Co., Argo, Ill., 1964-65; programmer IBM Corp., Cocoa Beach, Fla., 1965-67; lead programmer Kennedy Space Ctr. Singer Corp., Link Div., 1967-69; section mgr. Control Data Corp., Arden Hills, Minn., 1969-75; asst. dir. U. Iowa Hosp. and Clinics, 1975-79; dir. U. Mo., 1979-85; assoc. v.p. U. Ill., Champaign, 1985—; mem. br. mgmt. adv. com. IBM, higher edn. adv. coun., IBM, 1994—. Mem. policy coun. Ill. Libr. Computing System Orgn. Grantee Ill. Bd. Higher Edn., 1987, Ill. State Libr., 1987—, NIH, 1963. Mem. Coll. and Univ. Systems Exch. Roman Catholic. Home: 2115 Mayfair Rd Champaign IL 61821-6477

ANJUR, SOWMYA SRIRAM, research scientist, educator; b. Ahmadi, Kuwait, Oct. 4, 1962; came to U.S. 1987; d. V.S. Krishna and Saraswathi (Venkitachalam) Moorthi; m. Sriram Padmanabhan Anjur, Aug. 22, 1991. BS in Biochemistry, Madras U., India, 1982; MS in Biochemistry, Bharathar U., India, 1984, MPhil in Biochemistry/Microbiology, 1986; PhD, Iowa State U., 1992. Biochemist ICCU, Modern Hosp., Salem, India, 1983-84; biochemist R&D Symbiotic Labs, Madras, India, 1984-85; chemistry lectr OCF High Sch., Madras, India, 1985-86; asst. prof. biochemistry Kongunadu Arts & Scis. Coll., Coimbatore, India, 1987; teaching asst. biology/zoology Iowa State U., Ames, 1987-92; lectr. U. Wis., Oshkosh, 1992; rsch. scientist Kimberly-Clark Corp., Neenah, Wis., 1993—; dietary cons. Hosp. Bd. Nutrition, Coimbatore, India, 1978-82; wastewater treatment cons. U. Madras, 1985-87, microbiology cons., 1984-86. Choreographer/performer solo Indian dance fundraisers: Bharathanatyam, 1979-82 (Best Dancer 1980, 81); dir. drama troupe: The Funsters, 1978-80. Group leader Nat. Adult Edn. Program, India, 1978-84; mgr. Nat. Svc. Scheme, India, 1978-84; team leader Community Social Svc. Projects, India, 1978-84; chief fundraiser Solo Bharathanatyam, 1979-82. Recipient Gold medal for proficiency Bharathiar U., India, 1984. Mem. IEEE, Soc. Engrs. in Medicine and Biology, Iowa Acad. Sci., Am. Soc. Animal Sci., Am. Dairy Sci. Assn., Soc. of Biol. Chemists (India), Am. Mensa, Gamma Sigma Delta. Home: 624 E Capitol Dr Appleton WI 54911-1209

ANKENBRAND, LARRY JOSEPH, physical education educator; b. Mt. Carmel, Ill., Jan. 5, 1935; s. William H. and Lorene (Wahler) A.; m. Maureen Kelly, Aug. 22, 1968; children: Laura, Eric, Jay, Ann. BS, Ea. Ill. U., 1959; MS, Ind. State U., 1966; PhD, U. Mo., 1972. Cert. in adminstrn. and spl. edn., Ill. Salesman Allyn & Bacon Inc., Chgo., 1962-64; tchr. Forrest Park Sch., Joliet, Ill., 1964-65, West View Sch., Romeoville, Ill., 1965-67; asst. prof. Chgo. State U., 1967-68; instr. U. Mo., Columbia, 1968-72; faculty assoc. Ill. State U., Normal, 1972-77; prof. phys. edn. Ea. Ill. U., Charleston, 1977—, chmn. dept., 1984-88, assoc. dean Coll. Health, Phys. Edn. and Recreation, 1989-91, dean, 1991-93, assoc. dean Coll. of Edn. and Profl. Studies, 1993—; cons. Ill. Bd. Edn., Springfield, 1982—; speaker in field. Meet dir. 9 Spl. Olympics, 1979—. With U.S. Army, 1958-62. Recipient Outstanding Tchr. award Ea. Ill. U., 1984. Mem. Am. Assn. Profl. Preparation in Health Phys. Edn. Recreation and Dance (pres. 1990-92, midwest chmn. 1984), Ill. Assn. Health Phys. Edn. Recreation and Dance (session chmn. 1968, 25th Anniversary award 1985, pres. 1989—), Panther Club, Trojan Boosters, P.E. Club, Univ. Club, KC, Moose, Elks. Republican. Roman Catholic. Home: 2418 Salem Rd Charleston IL 61920-4325 Office: Ea Ill U 210 Buzzard Charleston IL 61920

ANNING, ROBERT DOAN HOPKINS, brokerage company executive; b. Cin., Apr. 16, 1940; m. Sydney Ann Fish, July 6, 1963; children: Sydney M., Robert H., John H., Elizabeth M. BA, Trinity Coll., 1963. 1st v.p. investments Merrill Lynch Pvt. Client Group, 1967—. Bd. dirs. Convalescent Hosp. for Children, 1985—, chmn., 1988-94; bd. dirs. Children's Hosp. Cin., 1989—, Children's Hosp. Med. Ctr., 1990—, Cerebral Palsy Svcs. Ctr., United Cerebral Palsy Cin., 1994—, Cin. Parks Found., 1995—. Named one of All-Pro Stockbrokers Money mag., 1990, All-Star Brokers, 1994, Blue-Chip Brokers Town and Country mag., 1992, All-Star Brokers Money mag., 1995; named an All Star Broker, Money mag., Forecast 1996. Home: 25 Weebetook Ln Cincinnati OH 45208-3330

ANSELL, OSCAR WILLIAM, JR., data systems manager; b. Pana, Ill., Jan. 11, 1943; s. Oscar William Ansell and Mary M. (Milligan) Saries; m. Judith Kathleen Dunham, May 8, 1965 (div. Oct. 6, 1986); children: Oscar W. IV, Thomas Andrew, John Lewis, Peter James.; m. Susan Marie Lorscheider, Feb. 25, 1989; Timothy E. Scranton, Sarah Jane Scranton, Jesse Lee Scranton. AA, Springfield (Ill.) Coll., 1962; BA, U. Ill., 1964. Libr. asst. Ill. State Libr., Springfield, 1964-66; computer programmer, analyst Ill. Sec. of State, Springfield, 1966-75, mgr. photo drivers project, 1976-77, mgr. data base sect., 1977—; mem. subcom. Ill. State Libr. Title III, Springfield, 1972-76; chmn. data processing com. Ill. Libr. Assn., Chgo., 1972-74, Am. Assn. Motor Vehicle Adminstrs., Washington, 1973-74. Bd. dirs. Lincoln Libr. Bd., Springfield, 1972-77, Rolling Prarie Libr. System, Decatur, 1972-77; pres. Rolling Prarie Libr. System, Springfield, 1975-77. Home: 1837 Whittier Springfield IL 62704 Office: Ill Sec of State Office Data Processing Sect 2701 S Dirksen Pkwy Springfield IL 62703

ANSFIELD, RICHARD MORRY, home health services executive; b. Chgo., Oct. 28, 1957; s. Joseph Gilbert Ansfield and Paula Ann (Witzak) LaCesa. Student, East Tex. State U., 1975. Pres. Am.'s Disabled Homebound, Inc., Chgo., 1990—; adminstr. Jefferson Park Health Care Facility Ltd.; pres., exec. dir. Am.'s Disabled Children. Chmn. bd. commrs. North Maine Fire Protection Dist., Des Plaines, Ill.; past pres. Med. Habit Control Ctr. Named to Hon. Order of Ky. Cols. Mem. Ill. Fire and Police Commrs. Assn. Office: Ams Disabled Homebound 1216 N LaSalle Chicago IL 60610

ANSORGE, LUELLA M., retired association administrator; b. Manning, Iowa, Aug. 12, 1915; d. John Martin and Gertrud (Heinke) A. AB, Valparaiso U., 1938. Asst. sec. Western Securities Co., Omaha, 1940-83; reference chmn. U.S. Women's Curling Assn., Omaha. Lutheran. Home: 4114 N 53rd St Omaha NE 68104-2800

ANSPACH, ROBERT MICHAEL, lawyer; b. Tiffin, Ohio, Feb. 29, 1948; s. William Charles and Evelyn Helen (Smith) A.; m. Jane Evelyn Friedman, Oct. 29, 1983; children: Michael Robert, Robert Joseph, John William. BA, Cornell U., 1970, JD, 1973. Bar: Ohio 1973, U.S. Dist. Ct. (no. dist.) Ohio 1974, U.S. Ct. Appeals (6th cir.) 1976, U.S. Supreme Ct. 1976, U.S. Tax Ct. 1985. Assoc. Shumaker, Loop & Kendrick, Toledo, 1973-79, ptnr., 1979-83, mng. ptnr., 1984, adminstr. trial dept., 1985; founder, mng. ptnr. Robert M. Anspach Assocs., Toledo, 1986—. Co-author: Winning in Court—The Accountant's Role in Litigation, Arbitration and Dispute Resolution, 1986. Trustee Toledo Repertoire Theatre, 1993—, Boys and Girls Clubs Toledo, 1993—. Recipient award of merit Ohio Legal Ctr., 1986. Fellow Ohio State Bar Found.; mem. ABA, Ohio Bar Assn. (vice chmn. jud. adminstrn. and legal reform com. 1982, lawyer's assistance com. 1986—), Toledo Bar Assn., Nat. Assn. R.R. Trial Counsel, Def. Rsch. Inst. Home: 29640 Duxbury Ln Perrysburg OH 43551-3414 Office: 405 Madison Ave Ste 2100 Toledo OH 43604-1207

ANTENEN, ANN MARIE, restoration executive, consultant; b. Richmond, Va., May 19, 1925; d. Henry Aubrey and Emily Burwell (Boggs) Doyle; m. Jay F. Antenen, Sr., Dec. 26, 1951; children: Susan Doyle Antenen Kornhauser, Jay F. Jr. BS in Architecture, U. Cin., 1946. Market rschr. Procter & Gamble, Cin., 1946-48; sales & tng. assoc. Shillito's (now Lazarus), Cin., 1948-49; designer Dave Maxfield Sr., Architect, Oxford, Ohio, 1949-51; art tchr. YWCA, Hamilton, Ohio, 1959-71; pres. Ann Antenen-Restoration, Hamilton, 1980—; mem. Butler County Ct. House Restoration com., 1994—; bd. dirs. Ohio Hist. Soc., Elisha Morgan Farm Mansion Inc., 1995—. Author (quar. newspaper) Chaps News, 1984—. Mem. city coun. City of Hamilton, 1976-81, mayor, 1978-79; pres., mem. Hamilton Garden Club, 1959-81; nominating chmn. Butler County Alcoholism Coun., Hamilton, 1978—; Butler County chmn. Cin. Fine Arts Fund Dr., 1989-92. Recipient Award of Merit Miami Purchase Assn., Cin., 1984, 1st Pl. Hist. Preservation award, 1985. Mem. Citizens for Hist. and Preservation Svcs. (founder, pres. 1983—), Ohio Preservation Alliance (pres. 1992-95), Nat. Trust Hist. Preservation, Ohio Hist. Soc. (bd. dirs. 1995—). Democrat. Office: Ann Antenen Restoration Inc 365 S B St Hamilton OH 45013-3365

ANTHONY, DAVID, state legislator; b. Marquette, Mich., June 16, 1955; children: Courtney, Robbie. BA, No. Mich. U. State rep. Mich. Ho. Reps., Dist. 108, 1990—; co-chmn. agrl. & forestry coms., co-vice chmn. nil. & vets. affairs com., mem. judiciary, conservation, recreation & environ. & transp. coms., Mich. Ho. Reps. Regional rep. Sen. Carl Levin; mem. agrl. & forestry com. Nat. Conf. State Legis. Home: 314 S 3rd St # 1 Escanaba MI 49829-4016*

ANTHONY, KATHRYN HARRIET, architecture educator; b. N.Y.C., Sept. 11, 1955; d. Harry Antoniades and Anne (Skoufis) A.; m. Barry Daniel Riccio, May 24, 1980. AB in Psychology, U. Calif., Berkeley, 1976, PhD in Architecture, 1981. Rsch. promotion Kaplan/McLaughlin/Diaz Architects and Planners, San Francisco, 1980-81; vis. lectr. U. Calif., Berkeley, 1980-81, 82-83, San Francisco State U., 1981; assoc. prof. Calif. State Poly. U., Pomona, 1981-84; asst. prof. U. Ill., Urbana-Champaign, 1984-89, assoc. prof., 1989-96, chair bldg. rsch. coun., 1994—, prof. architecture, 1996—; guest lectr. numerous orgns., colls. and univs.; mem. numerous comms. Coll. of Fine and Applied Arts, Sch. Architecture, Housing Rsch. and Devel. Program, Dept. Landscape Architecture. Author: Design Juries on Trial: The Renaissance of the Design Studio, 1991; co-editor Jour. Archtl. Edn. 47:1, 1993; mem. editl. bd. Jour. Archtl. and Planning Rsch., 1989—, Jour. Archtl. Edn., 1990-95, Environ. and Behavior Jour., 1991—; reviewer Landscape Jour., 1990; contbr. articles to profl. jours; co-designer, co-prodr. (exhibit) Shattering the Glass Ceiling: The Role of Gender and Race in the Archtl. Profession, Nat. Conv. AIA, 1996. Recipient Creative Achievement award Assn. Collegiate Sch. Architecture, 1992, grant U.S. Army C.E.R.L., 1993, grant U. Ill., 1984, 87, 92, 93, 95, grant Graham Found., 1989-91, 93-96, grant Decatur Housing Authority, 1988, grant Upgrade Cos., Peoria, Ill., 1987, grant Nat. Endowment for Arts, 1986-87, grant L.A. County Community Devel. Commn., 1984, grant Calif. State U. and Colls., 1982, 83, summer grant U. Calif., Berkeley, 1980. Mem. AIA (Champaign Urbana sect.), Environ. Design Rsch. Assn. (bd. dirs. 1989-92, treas. 1990-92, co-editor Coming of Age: Proceedings of 21st Ann. Conf. 1990), Chgo. Women in Architecture, Women in Info. Tech. and Scholarship. Home: 309 W Pennsylvania Ave Urbana IL 61801-4918 Office: U Ill Sch Architecture 611 Taft Dr Champaign IL 61820-6922

ANTHONY-PEREZ, BOBBIE COTTON MURPHY, psychology educator, researcher; b. Macon, Ga., Nov. 15, 1923; d. Solomon Richard and Maude Alice (Lockett) Cotton; m. William Anthony, Aug. 22, 1959 (dec.); 1 child, Freida; m. Andrew Silviano Perez, June 20, 1979. BS, DePaul U., 1953, MS, 1954; MS, U. Ill., 1959; PhD, U. Chgo., 1967; MA, DePaul, 1975. Tchr. Chgo. Pub. Schs., 1954-68; math. coord. U. Chgo., 1965; prof. Chgo. State U., 1968-95, coord. Black Studies Program, 1982-83; with psychol. svcs. Chgo. Pub. Schs., 1971-72; rsch. coord. Urban Affairs Inst., Howard U., Washington, 1978; coordinator Higher Edn. Careers Counseling Campus Ministry, Ingleside Whitfield Parish, 1978-84, comms. chmn., 1991-92, 95; coord. Black Studies Chgo. State U., 1990-94. V.p. Community Affairs Chatham Bus. Assn., 1981-85, asst. sec., 1985-86, sec., 1986-87, directory com., 1987, 88; bus. rels. chmn. Chatham Avalon Park Cmty. Coun., 1984—, newsletter editor, 1993—; bd. dirs. United Meth. Found. at U. Chgo., 1980-84, Community Mental Health Council, Inc., 1979-83; pub. edn. chairperson Chatham Avalon Unit Am. Cancer Soc., 1977-88, 90—, pub. info. chairperson, 1988-94; pres. Aux. Chgo. Chpt. Tuskegee Airmen, Inc., 1994, 95. NSF fellow, 1957, 58, 59; recipient numerous awards religious, civic and ednl. instns. and assns. Mem. Am. Psychol. Assn., Internat. Assn. Applied Psychology, Internat. Assn. Cross-Cultural Psychology, Internat. Assn. Ednl. and Vocat. Guidance, Assn. Black Psychologists (pres. Chgo. chpt.), Chgo. Psychol. Assn., Nat. Council Tchrs. Math., Am. Ednl. Research Assn., Midwest Ednl. Research Assn., Am. Soc. Clin. Hypnosis, Midwestern Psychol. Assn. Methodist. Contbr. numerous articles to profl. jours. Office: Chgo State U Dept Psychology 9501 S King Dr Chicago IL 60628-1502

ANTICH, ROSE ANN, state legislator. Grad., Hammond Bus. Coll.; postgrad., Ind. U. N.W. Radio and TV personality, lectr. positive mental attitude and stress control, astrologist; mem. Ind. State Senate from 4th dist., 1991—. Mem. town coun., 1983-87. Democrat. Roman Catholic. Home: 5401 Lincoln St Merrillville IN 46410-1926 Office: Ind State House 200 W Washington St Indianapolis IN 46204-2728

ANTON, FRANK LELAND, insurance company executive; b. Mpls., Minn., Mar. 25, 1930; s. Arthur Fred and Gladys Mae (Miller) A.; m. Beverly Ann Johnson , June 11, 1955; children: Nancy Lynn, David Arthur. BA in journalism cum laude, U. of Minn., 1957. Editor Trane Co., LaCrosse, Wis., 1957-59; pub. rels. asst. Northwestern Nat. Life Ins., Mpls., 1959, editor, 1960-64, supr. field svcs., 1964-66, advt. mgr., 1966-74, advt./sales promotion dir., 1974-88, dir. convs./meetings, 1988—. Editor Kindley USAF Base Newspaper, Aquatennial Alumni Aqua Log; author various articles to profl. jours. Mpls. Aquatennial Assc. (pres.) 1986, Mpls. Community Coll Bd.

chmn., Mpls. Pub. Sch. Tchr. Recert. Comm. Chmn., sgt. USAF, 1950-54. Recipient Good Neighbor award WCCO, Mpls., 1986, Rosarians Honoree award, 1986, Flying Col. award Delta, 1990, Conv. Liaison Coun. Hall of Leaders award, 1994. Mem. Ins. Conf. Planners Assn. (pres. 1990-91), Life Ins. Communicators Assn. (pres. 1983-84, Lifetime Mem. award, Meritorious Svc. award 1992), Am. Coun. Life Ins. P.R., Mtg. Planners Internat., Soc. Incentive Travel Execs., Kiwanis, Admirals Club (grand admiral, past pres. and commodore). Lutheran. Home: 5712 Dupont Ave S Minneapolis MN 55419-1638 Office: Northwestern Nat Life 20 Washington Ave S Minneapolis MN 55401-1908

ANTONACCI, ANTHONY EUGENE, food corporation engineer; b. Sept. 21, 1949; s. Salvatore Natali and Odile Estella (Stanton) A.; m. Sherry Lee Kessler, Mar. 6, 1971; children: Don Warren, Lance Anthony. Student U.S. Air Force Acad., 1968-69; Assocs. in Sci., Forest Park Coll., St. Louis, 1971. Lic. power engr. Asst. supr. data processing ops. 1st Nat. Bank, St. Louis, 1969-71; engr. Installation and Service Engring. (Mech. and Nuclear) div. Gen. Electric Corp., St. Louis, 1971-76; engr. Anheuser-Busch Corp., St. Louis, 1976—; software author. Trustee, treas. Antonette Hills Trusteeship, Affton, Mo., 1976-80. Recipient Spl. Performance awards Gen. Electric Co., 1972, 74. Mem. Brewers and Maltsters Local 6 (del. 1982, 83), Nat. Aerospace Edn. Council, Apple Programmers and Developers Assn., Am. Legion. Republican. Roman Catholic. Avocations: classic auto restoration, music (trumpet). Home: 8971 Antonette Hills Dr Saint Louis MO 63123-6503

ANTONS, PAULINE MARIE, mathematics educator; b. Monticello, Iowa, Jan. 15, 1926; d. Henry and Eliza (Zimmerman) Tobiason; m. Richard William Antons, Aug. 13, 1950; children: Sharon Kay, Karen Lyn. BS, U. Dubuque, 1948. Cert. secondary tchr., Iowa. Tchr. math. Elkader (Iowa) Community Sch., 1948-50, Onslow (Iowa) Ind. Schs., 1950-60, Midland Community, Wyoming, 1960-90, Kirkwood Coll., Cedar Rapids, Iowa, 1982-90; mem. scholarship adv. bd. Jones County Health Assn., Anamosa, Iowa, 1983—. Treas. Evang. Luth. Ch. Women; v.p. Limestone Bluffs Resource Conservation and devel.; del. Iowa League. Recipient Pres. award for excellence, 1988, Friends of Math. award Iowa Coun. Tchrs. of Math., 1992; Pres.'s scholar U. Dubuque, 1945-48, NSF scholar Drake U., 1967, Clarke Coll., 1968, U. Iowa, 1969. Lutheran. Home and Office: 13481 105th Ave Center Junction IA 52212-9702

ANUTA, MICHAEL JOSEPH, lawyer; b. Pound, Wis., Feb. 4, 1901; s. Michael Anuta and Charlotte Zudnochowsky; m. Marianne M. Strelec; children: Mary Hope Milidonis, Nancy Ellen Beauchamp, Janet Grace Dalquist, Michael John, Karl Frederick. LLB, LaSalle Extension U., 1956; LLD (hon.), Alma Coll., 1960; BS (hon.), San Vicinte De Paul, Maracaibo, Venezuela, 1965. Bar: Mich. 1929, U.S. Supreme Ct. 1932, U.S. Dist. Ct. Mich., U.S. Dist. Ct. Wis., Bar of Interstate Commerce Commn. Traffic mgr. M&M Traffic Assn., Menominee, Mich., 1938-48; pros. atty. Menominee County, Menominee, 1938-48; mcpl. judge City of Menominee, 1958-68; reserve judge Menominee, 1929—. Author: East Prussians from Russia, 1979, Ships of our Ancestors, 1983, History of Rotary Clubs in Wisconsin-Michigan, 1993, Anuta Heritage Register, 1993. Dir., v.p. Mich. Children's Aid Soc.; active Boy Scouts Am., 1945—; moderator Synod Presbyn. Ch. Mich., 1953; chmn. Menominee County Def. Council, WWII, 1953. Lt. col. CAP, Mich. Recipient Silver Beaver award Boy Scouts Am., 1945, Silver Antelope, 1967, Disting. Svc. award community svc. Radio Sta. WAGN, 1963, Disting. citation, Govt. Legislature of Mich., 1989; named Man Yr. Menominee Area C. of C., 1971. Mem. ABA, State Bar Mich., Menominee County Bar Assn., Mich. Prosecuting Attys. Assn. (pres. 1945), Menominee County Hist. Soc. (pres. 1967-74, pres. emeritus), Am. Hist. Socs. Germans from Russia (dir. 1978-81), Hist. Soc. Mich. (dir. 1972-78, award merit 1980, Charles Follow award 1983), Am. Arbitrators Assn., Panel Arbitrators Res. Mich. Judge, Rotary (gov. dist. 1963-64, pres. 1934-35), Shriners, Masons (33 degree). Republican. Home and Office: 2847N 577 Menominee MI 49858

APARICIO, FRANCES RIVERA, Romance languages educator; b. Santurce, P.R., Dec. 11, 1955; d. Jorge A. and Vicky (Sierra) Rivera; m. H. Sunny Aparicio, Dec. 11, 1979 (dec. Jan. 1985); 1 child, Gabriela E.; m. Julio Cesar Guerrero, Sept. 26, 1990; 1 child, Camila M. BA, Ind. U., 1978; MA, Harvard U., 1980, PhD, 1983. Lectr., dir. Spanish for bilinguals Stanford U., Palo Alto, Calif., 1983-85; asst. prof., dir. Spanish for bilinguals U. Ariz., Tucson, 1985-90; assoc. prof. Romance langs. U. Mich., Ann Arbor, 1990—, acting co-dir. Latina-Latino studies, 1991-92; dir. U. Mich., 1995—. Author: Versiones, Interpretaciones, Creaciones, 1991; editor, translator: Song of Madness, 1985—; editor: Latino Voices, 1994—. Tchr. Ill. Migrant Coun., Aurora, 1989. Postdoctoral fellow Ford Found., 1987-88; rsch. grantee U. Mich., 1992. Mem. MLA (chmn. com. on ethnic lits. 1989-90), Am. Studies Assn., L.Am. Studies Assn. Office: U Mich Dept Romance Langs Ann Arbor MI 48109

APELBAUM, PHYLLIS L., delivery messenger service executive; b. Chgo., July 3, 1940; d. Harry Kelmanson and Evelyn Reiner Cohen; 1 child, Mark Apelbaum. Instr. Am. United Cab Co., Chgo., 1957-65; gen. mgr. City Bonded Messenger Svc., Chgo., 1960-74; founder, pres. Arrow Messenger Svc., Inc., Chgo., 1974—. 1st chair Affirmative Action Adv. Bd. of Chgo., 1991-92; chair Variety Club Children's Carnival, Chgo., 1990-94; mem. bicycle com. City of Chgo., 1992-95, parking task force, 1993-95; gov. Ill. Coun. on Econ. Edn., Chgo., 1995; mem. Lakefront SRO Adv. Bd., Chgo., 1989-94. Recipient Small Bus. Innovative Mgmt. award Bank of Am., 1994; named Entrepreneur of the Yr., Ernst & Young, 1992, Nat. Small Bus. Person of the Yr., Small Bus. Assn., 1990; named to Entrepreneurship Hall of Fame, U. Ill., Chgo., 1993. Mem. Messenger Courier Assn. of Am. (bd. dirs. 1989—), Messenger Svc. Assn. Ill. (co-founder, pres.), Network of Women Entrepreneurs (Entrepreneur Achievement award 1994), Nat. Assn. Women Bus. Owners, The Chgo. Network, Execs. Club of Chgo., Econ. Club of Chgo. Office: Arrow Messenger Svc Inc 1322 W Walton St Chicago IL 60622

APEL-BRUEGGEMAN, MYRNA L., entrepreneur; b. Cleve., July 19, 1942; d. Melvin Arthur and Merle Ruth (Hoffman) Rehlender; children: Timothy, Kristen, Michelle, Kim; m. Earl L. Brueggeman, May 7, 1994. BS in Edn., Kent State U., 1965, M. in Edn. Counseling, 1987. Cert. tchr., Ohio; lic. minister, Ohio. Owner, mgr. real estate investments Kent, Ohio; owner, founder IHS Counseling Ctr., Ravenna, Ohio; owner, mgr. Winning Edge, Kent, Ohio; founder, pres. IHS Sch. Personal Devel., Ravenna, Ohio; owner IHS Bookstore; co-owner Chapel on the Lakes. Mem. NAFE, Ohio Manufactured Housing Assn. (pres. We. Res. chpt.), Internat. Soc. Profl. Hypnotists, Sigma Epsilon, Chi Sigma Iota.

APOLINSKI, CASEY STANLEY, stockbroker; b. Chgo., Mar. 3, 1922. Stockbroker Wallston Co., Chgo., 1963-74, Cowen Co., Chgo., 1974-79, David Noyes & Co., Skokie, Ill., 1979—. Lt. col. USAF, 1942-62. Mem. VFW (comdr. 1974—), Lowrey Organ Club (chmn.), N.W. Ill. Computer Club. Republican. Roman Catholic. Home: 212 E Edgemont Ln Park Ridge IL 60068-2734 Office: David Noyes & Co 8707 Skokie Blvd Ste 100 Skokie IL 60077-2200

APOSTOLIDES, ANTHONY DEMETRIOS, economist, educator; b. Salonika, Greece; came to U.S., 1956; s. Demos Demetrios and Kalliopi (Papadourakis) A. BA with honors, U. Cin., 1965; MA, U. Pitts., 1966; PhD, U. Oxford, England, 1970. Economist The Conf. Bd., N.Y.C., 1972-74; assoc. econ. affairs officer UN, Geneva, Switzerland, 1975-78; economist Inst. Internat. Law Econ. Devel., Washington, 1978-79, Jack Faucett Assocs., Chevy Chase, Md., 1979-80; asst. prof., econs. Mary Washington Coll., Fredericksburg, Va., 1981-85; economist Ill Md. Dept. Health, Balt., 1985-88; asst. prof. Ind. U., South Bend, 1988—. Author: Overseas R & D by U.S. Multinationals, 1976, (with others) Energy Consumption in Manufacturing, 1974, (pamphlet) Public Health Services in Elkhart County, 1989. Capt. U.S. Army, 1970-72. Nu Tone Inc. scholar, Cin., 1962-65; Faculty Summer fellow, Ind. U., 1989. Mem. APHA, Am. Econ. Assn. Midwest Econ. Assn., Am. Assn. for Budget and Program Analysis, Hertford Soc., Omicron Delta Epsilon. Office: Ind U 1700 Mishawaka Ave South Bend IN 46615-1408

APPEL, JOHN C., investment company executive; b. 1948. Office: Dain Bosworth Inc 60 S 6th St Minneapolis MN 55402-4400*

APPEL, SUSAN KAY, architecture and art historian, educator; b. Toledo, July 7, 1946; d. Paul Herbert and Lucille Marie (Siewert) Bigley. BFA in Design, Bowling Green State U., 1968; MA in Art History, U. Iowa, 1972; PhD, U. Ill., 1990. Instr. Augustana Coll., Rock Island, Ill., 1974-76; asst. prof. Phillips U., Enid, Okla., 1976-79; vis. lectr. U. Ill., Urbana-Champaign, 1982-83; lectr., instr. dept. art Ill. State U., Normal, 1983-89, asst. prof. dept. art, 1989-92, assoc. prof. dept. art, 1992—; tenured, 1993; cons. archtl. historian City of Muscatine, Iowa, 1974, Environ. Rsch. Ctr., Iowa City, 1974-77, The Urbana (Ill.) Group, 1991-92; photographer, archtl. surveyor Iowa State Hist. Preservation Program, Iowa City, 1974; presenter in field; reader Edn. Testing Svc. Advanced Placement Exam in Art Hist., 1994, 95, 96. Contbr. chpts. to books and articles to profl. jours. Mem. hist. preservation com. Des Moines County Hist. Soc., Burlington, Iowa, 1973-74; evaluator Okla. Humanities Com., Oklahoma City, 1978-79; bd. dirs. Garfield County Hist. Soc., Enid, 1979-80; v.p., sec., bd. dirs. Preservation and Conservation Assn. Champaign (Ill.) county, 1991—, Ill. Hist. Sites Adv. Coun., 1993-95. Allerton Am. Traveling scholar Sch. of Architecture, U. Ill., Urbana, 1980; Rosann S. Berry fellow Soc. Archtl. Historians, 1985; univ. grantee Ill. State U., Normal, 1990-91, 92-93. Mem. Soc. for Indsl. Archeology (fellowship 1992-93, nomination com. 1993-96, chair 1995-96); mem. Coll. Art Assn., Landmark Preservation Coun. Ill., Midwest Art History Soc., Nat. Trust for Hist. Preservation, Soc. of Archtl. Historians, Vernacular Archtl. Forum, Women's Caucus for Art, Victorian Soc. in Am. Home: 307 N Garfield Ave Champaign IL 61821-2615 Office: Ill State Univ Dept Art 5620 Illinois State Univ Normal IL 61790-0001

APPIER, (ROBERT) KEVIN, professional baseball player; b. Lancaster, Calif., Dec. 6, 1967. Student, Fresno State U., Antelope Valley Coll. Pitcher Kansas City Royals, 1989—. Named Sporting News Rookie Pitcher of Yr., 1990. Office: Kansas City Royals PO Box 419969 Kansas City MO 64141-6969*

APPLEBY, R(OBERT) SCOTT, history educator; b. Shreveport, La., Dec. 3, 1956; s. John and Joanne (Jackson) A.; m. Margaret Calhoun; children: Benjamin, Paul, Clare, Tony. BA, U. Notre Dame, 1978; MA, U. Chgo., 1979, PhD, 1985. Asst. prof., chair dept. religious studies St. Xavier Coll., Chgo., 1985-87; rsch. assoc. U. Chgo., 1988-94; assoc. dir. The Fundamentalism Project Am. Acad. Arts and Scis., Chgo., 1988—; dir. Cushwa Ctr. for Study of Am. Catholicism U. Notre Dame, Ind., 1994—, assoc. prof. history, 1994—; cons. Lilly Endowment, 1994—, William Benton Broadcast Project, U. Chgo., 1989-92. Editor: (with Martin E. Marty) Fundamentalisms Observed, 1991. Mem. Am. Acad. Religion, Am. Hist. Assn., Am. Cath. Hist. Assn., Am. Soc. Ch. History, Coll. Theology Soc., Religious Rsch. Assn. (nominations com. 1993—). Office: U Notre Dame 614 Hesburgh Libr Notre Dame IN 46556

APPLEGATE, MALCOLM W., newspaper executive; b. Kansas City, Mo., Jan. 26, 1936; s. Paul W. and Florence E. (Moeller) A.; children: Kellie Kae, Paula Ann. BS, U. Kans., 1959; MA, U. Iowa, 1961. Reporter Salina (Kans.) Jour., 1959-61; news svc. asst. Ft. Hays State U., Hays, Kans., 1961-65; asst. dean dept. journalism U. Kans., Lawrence, 1965-69; mgr. recruiting and tng Gannett Co. Inc., Rochester, N.Y., 1969-71; editor, pub. Ithaca (N.Y.) Jour., 1971-75; pub. Lafayette (Ind.) Jour. & Courier, 1975-86, Lansing (Mich.) State Jour., 1986-90; pres., gen. mgr. Indpls. Newspapers, Inc., 1990—. Bd. dirs. Indpls. Downtown Inc., Goodwill Industries, Boys and Girls Clubs, 500 Festival. Mem. Newspaper Assn. Am., Inland Daily Press Assn. (pres.-elect), Soc. Profl. Journalists, Hoosier Press Assn., Greater Indpls. C. of C. (bd. dirs.), Kiwanis. Methodist. Home: 5830 E Fall Creek Pky North Dr Indianapolis IN 46226-1051 Office: Indpls Newspapers Inc 307 N Pennsylvania St Indianapolis IN 46204-1811

APPLEGATE, RANDALL GLENN, insurance executive; b. Hillsboro, Ohio, May 4, 1948; s. Cecil Douglas and Mary (Willman) A. BSBA, Ohio State U., ;1970, MBA, 1971. CLU; chartered fin. cons. Sec. Pub. Utilities Commn. of Ohio, Columbus, 1972-77; asst. v.p. Midland Mut. Life Ins., Columbus, 1978-82; assoc. gen. mgr. Manulife, Cleve., 1983-87; pres. Fin. Svcs. Mgmt., Hudson, Ohio, 1987-91, Data Plan Securities, Cleve., 1988-89, Life Ins. Mktg. Co., Beachwood, Ohio, 1991—. Office: Life Ins Mktg Co 6924 Stow Rd Hudson OH 44236-3241

APPS, JEROLD WILLARD, adult education educator; b. Wild Rose, Wis., July 25, 1934; s. Herman E. and Eleanor S. (Witt) A.; m. Ruth Ellen Olson, May 20, 1961; children: Susan, Steven, Jeffrey. BS, U. Wis., 1955, MS, 1957, PhD, 1967. Extension agt. U. Wis., Green Lake, 1957-60, Green Bay, 1960-62; asst. prof. U. Wis., Madison, 1962-67, assoc. prof., 1967-69, prof. adult and continuing edn., 1969-94; prof. emeritus, 1994—; vis. prof. N.C. State U., Raleigh, 1979, U. Guelph, Ont., Can., 1980, U. Alta., Can., 1982, 89, U. Man., Can., 1986, U. Victoria, Can., 1991, U. Alaska, 1995, No. Ill. U., 1996. Author: The Land Still Lives, 1970, How to Improve Adult Education in Your Church, 1972, Cabin in the Country, 1972, Toward a Working Philosophy of Adult Education, 1973, Ideas for Better Church Meetings, 1975, Barns of Wisconsin, 1977, rev. edit., 1995, Problems in Continuing Education, 1979, Spanish edit., 1983, Mills of Wisconsin and the Midwest, 1980, The Adult Learner on Campus: A Guide for Instructors and Administrators, 1981, Study Skills: For Adults Returning to School, 1981, Improving Your Writing Skills, 1982, Improving Practice in Continuing Education, 1985, Skiing into Wisconsin: A Celebration of Winter, 1985, Higher Education in a Learning Society, 1988, Study Skills for Today's College Student, 1990, Mastering the Teaching of Adults, 1991, Breweries of Wisconsin, 1992, Leadership for the Emerging Age, 1994, One-Room Country Schools, 1996. Capt. U.S. Army, 1956. Recipient Non=Fiction Book award of merit Wis. Hist. Soc., 1978, 81, 93, Wis. Idea award, 1994, Robert E. Gar Excellence in Lit. award, 1996; recognized for Outstanding Lit. Achievement, Wis. Libr. Assn. Mem. Am. Assn. Adult and Continuing Edn. (mem. exec. com. 1975-76, Rsch. to Practice award 1982), Commn. Profls. of Adult Edn. (pres. 1972-74), Wis. Acad. Scis., Arts and Letters (pres. 1987), Wis. Assn. Adult and Continuing Edn. (pres. 1969, Outstanding Adult Educator of Yr. award 1986), Wis. Coun. Writers (pres. 1978-80, Best Non-Fiction Book award 1977, Scholarly Book award 1988).

APSELOFF, MARILYN FAIN, English educator; b. Attleboro, Mass.; d. Arthur A. and Eva (Lubchansky) Fain; m. Stanford S. Apseloff, Nov. 21, 1956; children: Roy, Stan and Glen (twins), Lynn Susan. Student, Bryn Mawr Coll., 1952-54; BA, U. Cin., 1956, MA, 1957. From instr. to prof. English Kent (Ohio) State U., 1968—; adv. bd. mem. Parents' Choice, Waban, Mass., 1978—. Author: They Wrote for Children Too, 1989, Elizabeth George Speare, 1991; co-author: Nonsense Literature for Children, 1989 (award 1990); editor Children's Literature Assn. Quarterly, 1984-87. Grad. fellow U. Cin., 1956-57. Mem. MLA (session chair 1977, 78), Children's Literature Assn. (pres. 1979-80, dir. Harvard conf. 1978). Office: Kent State Univ English Dept Kent OH 44242

APTER, RONNIE SUSAN, English educator, translator; b. Hartford, Conn., June 4, 1943; d. Marvin and Rosalind Helen (Kenig) A.; m. Mark Norman Herman, June 18, 1967; children: Daniel A., Jeffry M. BA, Sarah Lawrence Coll., 1965; MA in English, NYU, 1967; PhD in English, Fordham U., 1980. Mem. English faculty Ctrl. Mich. U., Mt. Pleasant, 1986—; prof. Mich. U., Mt. Pleasant, 1996—. Author: Digging for the Treasure: Translation After Pound, 1984; co-author 16 opera translations; contbr. articles, poems and poetry translations to profl. jours. Recipient Thomas Wolfe Poetry award NYU, 1967, grant NEH, 1986. Mem. MLA (manuscript evaluator 1987—), Lyrica Soc. (pres. 1994—), Am. Lit. Translator's Assn. (exec. bd. 1986-89), Internat. Courtly Lit. Soc., Société Guilhem IX. Office: Ctrl Mich Univ Dept English Mount Pleasant MI 48859

ARABIA, PAUL, lawyer; b. Pittsburg, Kans., Mar. 28, 1938; s. John K. and Melva (Jones) A. B.A., Kans. State Coll.; J.D., Washburn U. Bar: Kans. 1966, U.S. Dist. Ct. Kans. 1966, U.S. Ct. Appeals (10th cir.) 1968. Ptnr., Fettis & Arabia, Wichita, 1968-74, Arabia & Wells, Wichita, 1974-78; pvt. practice, Wichita, 1978—. Program host Sta. KAKE-TV: Peoples Lawyer; TV host/producer: Legal Point. Mem. Kans. Bar Assn., Wichita Bar Assn. Office: PO Box 275 Wichita KS 67201-0275

ARAKAWA, KASUMI, physician, educator; b. Toyohashi, Japan, Feb. 19, 1926; came to U.S., 1954, naturalized, 1963; s. Masumi and Fayuko (Hattori) A.; m. Juen Hope Takahara, Aug. 27, 1956; children: Jane Riet, Kenneth Luke, Amy Kathryn. M.D., Tokyo Med. Coll., 1953; Ph.D., Showa U. Sch. Med., Tokyo, 1984. Diplomate: Am. Bd. Anesthesiology. Intern Iowa Meth. Hosp., Des Moines, 1954-56; resident U. Kans. Med. Ctr., Kansas City, 1956-58, instr. anesthesiology, 1961-64, asst. prof., 1964-71, assoc. prof., 1971-77, prof., 1977-94; prof. emeritus, 1994—; Arakawa Disting. prof. anesthesiology U. Kans. Med. Ctr., Kansas City, 1990, Kasumi Arakawa professorship, 1994, prof. emeritus, 1994—; clin. assoc. prof. U. Mo.-Kans. City Sch. Dentistry, 1973—; dir. Kansas City Health Care, Inc. Fulbright scholar, 1954; civilian cons. USAF. Recipient Outstanding Faculty award Student AMA, 1970. Fellow Am. Coll. Anesthesiology; mem. Assn. Univ. Anesthetists, Acad. Anesthesiology (pres. 1986-87), Japan-Am. Soc. Midwest (v.p. 1965, 71). Home: 6116 W 50th St Shawnee Mission KS 66202-1756 Office: Univ Med Ctr 3901 Rainbow Blvd Kansas City KS 66160-7197

ARANTES, JOSÉ CARLOS, industrial engineer, educator; b. Itamogi, Brazil, May 10, 1955; came to U.S., 1986; s. Antonio A. and Parizina (Marinzeck) A.; m. Nadia Maria Monti, July 26, 1986; 1 child, Ellen K. MSc in Indsl. Mgmt., Katholieke U. Leuven, Belgium, 1982; PhD in Indsl. Engring., U. Mich., 1991. Product engr. Kodak Co., Brazil, 1979-81; instr., cons. U. Campinas, Brazil, 1983-86; rsch. asst., teaching asst. U. Mich., Ann Arbor, 1987-90; asst. prof. U. Cin., 1991—; cons. Criminal Justice Task Force, Cin., 1992; co-founder, v.p. ImpEx Co. Author: Degeneracy in Gereralized Networks, 1990; contbr. to profl. jours. 2d lt. Brazilian armed forces, 1973-75. Grantee Westinghouse Environ., Cin., 1992, County of Hamilton, Cin., 1992, Fernald Environ. Mng. Co., Cin., 1993, 94. Mem. Sci. Rsch. Soc., Inst. Indsl. Engrs., Inst. Mgmt. Sci., Ops. Rsch. Soc. Am. Home: 6939 Lynnfield Ct Apt 143 Cincinnati OH 45243-1732 Office: U Cin Dept Engring Mail Location 116 Cincinnati OH 45221-0116

ARATA, LOUIS KENNETH, computer engineer; b. Cin., July 28, 1952; s. Louis Hobart and Lorraine Magdalen (Humbert) A.; m. Sandra Ellen Danzl, Dec. 22, 1973; children: Jennifer, Tamaran, Sean, Heather. BS in Biology summa cum laude, U. CIn., 1974, BS in Mech. Engring. summa cum laude, 1983, PhD in Computer Engring., 1992. Sales engr. Aramac Supply Co., Cin., 1975-81, programmer, analyst, 1981-86, system mgr., 1986-89; rsch. asst. U. Cin., 1989-92; prin. engr. Picker Internat., Cleve., 1993—. Mem. IEEE, Phi Beta Kappa. Roman Catholic. Home: 8211 Starburst Dr Mentor OH 44060-2320 Office: Picker Internat Nuc Medicine Divsn 595 Miner Rd Cleveland OH 44143

ARBUCKLE, MARJORIE ANN, real estate sales associate; b. Port Washington, Wis., July 9, 1954; d. Friedhelm and Marian June (Kassens) Cornils; m. Ward Kenneth Arbuckle Jr., July 7, 1973; children: Jennifer Marian, Fredrick Ward, Franklin Wilhelm, Jessica Martha, Francis Walter. Grad., Wis. Sch. Real Estate, Milw., 1990. Lic. real estate salesperson, Wis. Bookeeper, sec. Cornils Constrn., Cascade, Wis., 1970-91; sales assoc. C-21 Fairland Realty, Plymouth, Wis., 1987-91, office mgr., 1987-91; sales assoc. RE/MAX Universal Realty, Plymouth, Wis., 1991—, office mgr., 1993—. Sec. Cascade (Wis.) Firemans Auxillary, 1991—; cradle roll sec. Svc. & Fellowship, Adell, Wis., 1995. Named Vol./Citizens of the Yr., Cascade Elem. Sch., 1991, 1994 Exec. Club mem. North Ctrl. Region RE/MAX, 1994. Mem. Sheboygan County Bd. of Realtors, Nat. Assn. Realtors. Office: RE/MAX Universal Realty Inc 506 E Mill St Plymouth WI 53073

ARBUCKLE, PHILIP WAYNE, travel company executive; b. West Memphis, Ark., Feb. 9, 1954; s. Wayne C. and Betty Jo (Atkins) A.; m. Twila Downen. B.B.A., Mid-Am. Nazarene Coll., 1976, MBA, 1994; M.A., North Am. Sch. of Travel, 1979. Asst. to pres. Medco Inc., Overland Park, Kans., 1976-80; v.p. ops. Group Travel Service Ltd., Overland Park, 1980-84; dir. corp. communications Creative Travel Cons. Inc., Kansas City, Mo., 1984—; co-star TV show Posh Destinations, 1988-89; cons. travel Ozark Council of Govs., Jefferson City, Mo., 1983-84, Internat. Congress of Radiology, Kansas City, Kans., 1983—. Author: Paris for Little or Nothing, 1972, Handbook of Tour Management, 1988; producer, dir. TV show POSH Destinations, 1989-90. Mem. community development City of Olathe, Kans. 1982-83; mem. bi-centennial com. County of Johnson, Kansas, 1976. Mem. Am. Mgmt. Assn., Olathe C. of C. (community affairs com. 1983-84), Olathe Hist. Soc. Republican. Mem. Nazarene Ch. Club: Kansas City (Mo.) Friends of Art. Avocations: computers; genealogy; archaeology. Office: Creative Group Inc 4225 Baltimore Ave Kansas City MO 64111

ARBUCKLE, ROBERT DEAN, university administrator; b. New Kensington, Pa., Jan. 5, 1940; s. Roy Anthony and Connie (Santa Maria) A.; m. Lorraine C. Donati, Aug. 8, 1964; children: Lisa, Robert, Jeffrey. BS, Clarion State U., 1964; MA, Pa. State U., 1966, PhD, 1972. Teaching asst. Pa. State U., University Park, 1964-65, 66-67; from instr. to assoc. prof. Pa. State U., New Kensington, 1968—, assoc. dir. for acad. affairs, 1974-77, campus exec. officer, 1977-92; tchr. Burrell Sr. High Sch., Lower Burrell, Pa., 1965-66; asst. prof. history U. Pitts., 1967-68; pres. Lake Superior State U., Sault Sainte Marie, Mich., 1992—; bd. dirs. BIDCO of Mich., Internat. Bridge, River of History Mus. Author: John Nicholson, 1975; co-author: Pennsylvania History, 1983; contbr. articles to profl. jours. Trustee Allegheny Valley Hosp., Natrona Heights, Pa., 1990—; pres. New Kensington Area C. of C., 1985, Higher Edn. Coun. W. Pa., Pitts., 1982, United Way of Westmoreland County, 1984. Recipient Profl. of Yr. award Arnold Area C. of C., 1984, J. Harry Fisher Community Svc. award, C. of C. and area newspaper, 1984. Mem. Strongland Area C. of C. (bd. dirs.), Rotary (dist. gov. Pitts. area 1986-87, bd. dirs. New Kinsington club 1982-83, Sault Ste. Marie, Rotarian of Yr. 1982, Meritorious citation 1991, chair found.). Democrat. Roman Catholic. Home and Office: Lake Superior State U 803 N Campus Ct Sault Sainte Marie MI 49783-1617

ARCHABAL, NINA M(ARCHETTI), historical society director; b. Long Branch, N.J., Apr. 11, 1940; d. John William and Santina Matilda (Giuffre) Marchetti; m. John William Archabal, Aug. 8, 1964; 1 child, John Fidel. BA in Music History cum laude, Radcliffe Coll., 1962; MAT in Music History, Harvard U., 1963; PhD in Music History, U. Minn., 1979. Asst. dir. humanities art mus. U. Minn., Mpls., 1975-77; asst. supr. edn. div. Minn. Hist. Soc., St. Paul, 1977-78, dep. dir. for program mgmt., 1978-86, acting dir., 1986-87, dir., 1987—. Trustee, bd. dirs. Am. Folklife Ctr., Libr. of Congress, 1989—; bd. dirs. N.W. Area Found., 1989—, St. Paul Acad. and Summit Sch., 1993—; v.p. Friends of St. Paul Pub. Libr., 1983-93. NDEA fellow U. Minn., 1969-72, U. Minn. grad. fellow, 1974-75. Mem. Am. Assn. State and Local History (sec. 1986-88), Am. Assn. Mus. (v.p. 1991-94, chair bd. dirs. 1994-96). Office: Minn Hist Soc 345 Kellogg Blvd W Saint Paul MN 55102-1906

ARCHER, AMY T., marketing professional; b. Knob-Knoster, Mo., Aug. 16, 1963. BSEE, Gannon U., 1986; MBA, John Carroll U., 1993—. Product sys. control engr. Bailey Controls Co., Euclid, Ohio, 1986-89; product mktg. mgr. Allen Bradley Co., Cleve., 1989—. Mem. St. Paschal Baylon, Highland Heights, Ohio, 1969. Mem. IEEE.

ARCHER, DENNIS WAYNE, mayor, lawyer; b. Detroit, Jan. 1, 1942; s. Ernest James and Frances (Carroll) A.; m. Trudy Ann DunCombe, June 17, 1967; children: Dennis Wayne, Vincent DunCombe. BS, Western Mich. U., 1965; JD, Detroit Coll. Law, 1970; LLD (hon.), Western Mich. U., 1987, Detroit Coll. Law, 1988, U. Detroit, 1988, John Marshall Law Sch., 1991, Gonzaga U., 1991, U. Mich., 1994; D in Pub. Svc. (hon.), Ea. Mich. U., 1994. Bar: Mich. 1970. Tchr. spl. edn. Detroit Bd. Edn., 1965-70; assoc. Gragg & Gardner, 1970-71; ptnr. Hall, Stone, Allen, Archer & Glenn, P.C., 1971-73, Charfoos, Christensen & Archer, P.C., 1973-85; assoc. justice Mich. Supreme Ct., 1986-90; ptnr. Dickinson, Wright, Moon, Van Dusen & Freeman, Detroit, 1991-93; mayor City of Detroit, 1994—; assoc. prof. Detroit Coll. Law, 1972-78; adj. prof. Wayne State U. Law Sch., Detroit, 1984-85; mem. Mich. Bd. Ethics, 1979-83; mem. adv. bd. U.S. Conf. Mayors, 1994—; bd. dirs. Nat. Conf. Black Mayors, 1994—; mem. intergovtl. policy adv. com. U.S. Trade Rep. Contbr. articles to legal jours. Bd. dirs. Legal Aid and Defenders Assn., Detroit, 1980-82; co-chmn. Met. Detroit Community Coalition for Dems., 1979-80; bd. trustees Olivet Coll., 1991-93; active numerous local Dem. campaigns, 1970-85; host local pub. svc. radio programs. Named Most Respected Judge in Mich. Mich. Lawyers Weekly Jour., 1990. Mem. ABA (ho. dels. 1979-93, chmn. drafting com. 1986-88, com. on scope and correlation of work sect. officers liaison 1987-90, chmn. gen. practice sect. 1987-88, chair commn. on opportunities for minorities in the profession 1987-91, sect. legal edn. and admissions to the bar, coun. mem. 1989-95, task force on profl. skills instrn. 1989-91, task force on law schs. and the profession, Narrowing The Gap, 1989-91, chmn. spl. com. prepaid legal svcs. 1981-83, chmn. sect. officers conf. 1988-90, resource devel. coun. 1988-91, bd. editors ABA Jour. 1988-94, bd. editors The Practical Litigator 1989-94, chmn. rules and calendar com. 1990-92, state del. 1990-96), ATLA, Nat. Bar Assn. (pres. 1983-84), Am. Judicature Soc. (bd. dirs 1977-81), State Bar Mich. (pres. 1984-85), Wolverine Bar Assn. (pres. 1979-80), Detroit Bar Assn. (bd. dirs. 1973-75), Mich. Trial Lawyers Assn. (exec. bd. 1973-74), Econ. Club, Alpha Phi Alpha. Roman Catholic. Office: City of Detroit 1126 City-County Bldg Detroit MI 48226

ARCHER, LINDA L., disability specialist; b. Indiana, Pa., Mar. 28, 1948; d. Bernard Bernaun and Isabel (Emerick) Buterbaugh; m. Kenneth C. Archer, July 20, 1984. BSEd in Home Econs., Indiana U., Pa., 1970; postgrad., St. Paul Sch. Theology, Kansas City, Mo., 1991—. Disability authorizer Social Security Adminstrn., Balt., 1971-77, disability examiner, 1977-81; disability specialist Social Security Adminstrn., Kansas City, Mo., 1981—. Mem. Nat. Assn. Disability Examiners. Republican. Mem. Ch. of Christ.

ARCHIBALD, CHARLES ARNOLD, holding company executive; b. Louisville, Aug. 21, 1936; s. James Henry and Phyllis Maxine (Rice) A.; m. Rosa Jane Cusano, July 11, 1959; children: James Henry II (dec.), Diane Marie. BBA, U. Cin., 1959; postgrad., Xavier U., 1963-65. V.p., bd. dirs. J.H. Archibald Co., Cin., 1963-75; pres. J.H. Archibald Co., Springfield, Mo., 1975—; also chmn. bd. dirs. J.H. Archibald Co., Springfield; pres. C/D/R Assocs., Inc., Springfield, 1987—; ptnr. Bearcat Ltd., Springfield, 1995—; v.p. The Oasis, Inc., Southgate, Ky., 1963-73, Crawford Sales of So. Ohio, Cin., 1965-73, Mid-Western Bldg. Sys., Norwood, Ohio, 1968-73; ptnr. TGA Publ. Palm Springs, Calif., 1985—, The Graphic Arts Ctr., Cathedral City, Calif., 1985—, (all affiliates of J.H. Archibald Co.); chmn. bd. dirs. Eurocopter, S.A., Marbella, Spain, 1990—; pres. Eurocopter Svcs., Inc., Springfield, Mo. and Wilmington, Del.; bd. dirs. Archibald-Cowan-Ringer Comm., Inc., Springfield, Mo., Target Mktg., S.L., Madrid; bd. dirs. Barna Catering, S.L., Barcelona. Mem. Dem. Cen. Com., Hamilton County, Ohio, 1968-70. Served to lt. commdr. USN, 1959-62. Mem. Springfield C. of C., Tower Club, U. Cin. Alumni Assn., Pi Kappa Alpha (pres. local alumni chpt. 1980-90). Methodist. Home: 1224 W Highland St Springfield MO 65807-4626 Office: 3825 S Campbell Ste 166 Springfield MO 65807

AREKAPUDI, KUMAR VIJAYA VASANTHA, sanitarian, real estate agent; b. Angaluru, India, July 21, 1957; came to U.S., 1985, naturalized 1990; s. Rahgavendra Rao and Chandramma (Lingam) A.; m. Aruna Vallabhaneni, Sept. 4, 1988; 1 child, Raghava Chandra. BA, Osmania U., Hyderabad, India, 1984; MBA, Calif. Coast U., 1994. Patient transporter Ill. Masonic Med. Ctr., Chgo., 1985, psychiatric technician, 1985-88; communicable disease control investigator Chgo. Dept. Health, 1987-88, sanitarian, 1988-94; psychiatric technician Lincoln West Hosp., Chgo., 1988-91; real estate assoc. All Star Realty, Chgo., 1990; assoc. mgr. residential and comml. div. Century 21 Ben Garth Realty, Chgo., 1990-91; founder, pres., CEO Blue Planet Realty Inc., 1991—; sanitarian/team leader Mayor's Health and Sanitation Task Force for City of Chgo., 1994—. Chmn. Community Svcs. Indo Am. Dem. Orgn., Chgo., 1985-86, chmn. pub. relations, 1987-88; mem. 48th Ward Progressive Network, Chgo., 1985—; voting mem. Multiple Listing Svc. No. Ill., 1992—; signatary fair housing and equal opportunity with U.S. Dept. Housing and Urban Devel, opportunity pledged broker; active Ams. for Change, 1992—. Recipient Merit citation Indo-Am. Dem. Orgn., Chgo., 1985, Cert. of Recognition Mayor of City of Chgo. for Earth Day participation, Million Dollar Sales award Chgo. Assn. Realtors, 1991, Coop. Sales award N.W. Real Estate Bd., 1991, Man of Yr. medal honor ABI, 1994; named Man of Yr. 1986. Mem. Am. Fedn. State County Mcpl. Employees Union (pres. club), Congl. Network Team, Ill. Environ. Health Assn., Candlewick Lake Assn., Chgo. Assn. Realtors (voting mem. multiple listing svc. 1991—, leader comm. network team 1993, polit. affairs com., equal opportunity com. 1993), North Side Real Estate Bd. (Coop. Sales award 1991), N.W. Real Estate Bd. (Coop. Sales award 1991), N.W. Suburban Assn. Realtors (voting 1992-94), RNA, Euthanasia Club Ill., Real Estate Fin. Planners Inc. Hindu. Home and Office: 5770 N Ridge Ave Chicago IL 60660-3444

ARENDS, DAVID CHARLES, data processing administrator, educator; b. Highland Park, Mich., Mar. 13, 1952; s. Norman Walter and Erma Elizabeth (Hein) A.; m. Nancy Jean Hovey, Mar. 16, 1974 (div. Oct. 1978); m. Carol Emily Watson, June 20, 1981; children: Jason David, Sarah Emily. BS in Math., Mich. State U., 1974; BBA, U. Mich., Flint, 1978; MBA, Mich. State U., 1982. Programmer Genesee Intermediate Sch. Dist., Flint, 1974-77; systems analyst U. Mich., Flint, 1977-82, Merit Systems, Inc., Troy, Mich., 1982-85; systems analyst, cons. Sterling Software, N.Y.C., 1985-86; project leader Citizens Comml. and Savs. Bank, Flint, 1986-93; programming supr. FI-Serv, Inc., Flint, 1993—; owner PC Solutions of Grand Blanc (Mich.), Ind., 1992—; instr. Detroit Coll. Bus., Flint, 1984—. United Way loaned exec., Flint, 1991, 92; chmn. bd. fin. Faith Luth. Ch., Grand Blanc, 1983-88, elder, 1989-93. Republican. Office: PC Solutions of Grand Blanc PO Box 717 Grand Blanc MI 48439

ARENDS, MARK W., educator; b. Boston, Aug. 9, 1950; s. Jack and Margaret I. (Christianson) A.; m. Linda Sauber. BFA, No. Ill. U., 1975; MBA, U. Notre Dame, 1977. Prof. U. Ill., Urbana, 1980—. Author: Product Rendering, 1985, Presentation Sketching, 1990.

ARENDS, WENDELL LEONARD, apartment manager; b. Lennox, S.D., Aug. 18, 1922; s. Harm and Selina (Roberts) A.; children: Roger, Edith, Leonard (dec.). Grad. h.s., Hurley, S.D. Cook Nichol Plate Cafe, Sioux Falls, S.D., 1942; ambulance driver, EMT Beresford, S.D., 1961-93; farmer Beresford, 1946-62; mechanic Cotton Chevrolet, Beresford, 1962-65; svc. station owner Arends Champion, Beresford, 1965-79; truck driver Fountain Implement, Beresford, 1979-81, Union County Hwy. Dept., Alcester, S.D., 1982-85; county coroner Union County, S.D., 1989-92; mgr. Evergreen Squares Apts., Beresford, 1989—. Asst. leader Lincoln County 4-H, 1950-60; pres., sec. PTA, Beresford, 1950-60; mayor City of Beresford, 1970-72; pres. Beresford C. of C., 1968-69. Sgt. U.S. Army, 1942-45, 50-51. Decorated Bronze Star with two oak leaf clusters. Republican. Mem. Evangelical Ch. Home: 208 S 3rd St Beresford SD 57004-2102

ARENSON, DONALD LEWIS, consulting company executive; b. Chgo., June 15, 1926; s. Harvey Loeb and Ruth (Lazar) A.; m. Marcia G. Terman, Mar. 20, 1948; children: Gregory Keith, Michael Craig. Steven Lee. BS in Math., Ill. Inst. Tech., 1947, MS, 1950. Registered profl. engr., Ill. Rsch. engr. Armour Rsch. Found., Chgo., 1948-50; chief aerophysics Cook Elec. Co., Chgo., 1950-52; dir. Ex-Cel Devel. Lab., Chgo., 1952-57; asst. gen. mgr. Am. Machine and Foundry Co., Niles, Ill., 1957-63; v.p. Booz Allen Applied Rsch., Chgo., 1963-69; pres. BASYS Inc., Chgo., 1969-71; v.p. Chase Manhattan Cons. Co., N.Y.C., 1972-76; mng. dir. Mitsubishi Chase Manhattan Cons. Co., Tokyo, 1972-76; pres. Assoc. Cons. Internat. Corp., Evanston, Ill., 1976—; bd. dirs. Audio-Technica U.S., Inc. With USNR, 1944-46. Fellow AIAA (assoc.); mem. NSPE, Inst. Mgmt. Cons. (cert.), Union League (bd. dirs. 1990-95). Home: 7544 Karlov Ave Skokie IL 60076-3863 Office: Assoc Cons Internat Corp PO Box 447 Evanston IL 60204-0447

ARENZ, MARK WESLEY, video editor; b. Cleve., Jan. 27, 1970; s. Don L. and Sidney L. (Hamman) A.; m. Erin Doyle, Oct. 16, 1993. BA in Comm., DePauw U., 1992. Video editor Bennett Innovations, Indpls., 1992—; art. dir. The Scores Channel, Indpls., 1993. Mem. Phi Beta Kappa.

ARGABRIGHT, MELVIN SCOTT, retired conservation agronomist; b. Nemaha, Nebr., Dec. 21, 1927; s. Gilbert Scott and Clara Louise (Radspinner) A.; m. Dorthy Ann Dirks, Aug. 24, 1949; children: Norman Scott, Patrick Floyd, Virginia Louise, Diana Lee. BSc, U. Nebr., 1951. Dist. conservationist USDA Soil Conservation Svc., Murdo, S.D., 1956-60, Winner, S.D., 1960-68, Belle Fourche, S.D., 1968-70; area conservationist USDA Soil Conservation Svc., Mobridge, S.D., 1970-74; conservation agronomist USDA Soil Conservation Svc., Huron, S.D., 1974-77, state resource conservationist, 1977-80; conservation agronomist USDA Soil Conservation Svc., Lincoln, Nebr., 1980-92. Mem. Soil and Water Conservation Soc. (pres. S.D. chpt. 1979). Republican. Methodist.

ARIETI, DAVID FRANKLIN, environmental scientist, educator; b. N.Y.C., June 20, 1945; s. Silvano and Jane (Jaffe) A.; children: Aviva Jane Arieti, Amiel Silvan Arieti. BA, U. Denver, 1967; MS, L.I. U., 1974. Cert. in fiber counting. Waste coord. Assoc. Towns for Environ. Protection, Hadera, Israel, 1982-83; air sampler Anasbestics Co., Bridgeview, Ill., 1988-90; instr. Truman Coll., Chgo., 1981—; instr. environ. sci. Columbia Coll., Chgo., 1992—, Waubonsee C.C., Sugar Grove, Ill., 1991—, Oakton C.C., Des Plaines, Ill., 1987—; cons. to various orgns., 1980—. Mem. Am. Acad. Environ. Medicine, Men's Club of Congregation B'nai Zion, Chgo. Democrat. Jewish. Home: care Schwartz 5028 Fitch Skokie IL 60077

ARLINGHAUS, SANDRA JUDITH LACH, mathematical geographer, educator; b. Elmira, N.Y., Apr. 18, 1943; d. Donald Frederick and Alma Elizabeth (Satorius) Lach; m. William Charles Arlinghaus, Sept. 3, 1966; 1 child, William Edward. AB in Math., Vassar Coll., 1964; postgrad., U. Chgo., 1964-66, U. Toronto, Ont., Can., 1966-67, Wayne State U., 1968-70; MA in Geography, Wayne State U., 1976; PhD in Geography, U. Mich., 1977. Vis. instr. math. U. Ill., Chgo., 1966; vis. asst. prof. geography Ohio State U., Columbus, 1977-78, lectr. math., 1978-79; lectr. math. Loyola U., Chgo., 1979-81, asst. prof. math., 1981-82; lectr. math. and geography U. Mich., Dearborn and Ann Arbor, 1982-83; founding dir. Inst. Math. Geography, Ann Arbor, 1985—; guest lectr. U. Chgo., 1979, 87, U. Calif., 1979, Syracuse U., 1991, U. No. Iowa, 1991; guest lectr. U. Mich., Ann Arbor, 1983, 90-93, adj. prof. math. geography, population-environ. dynamics Sch. Natural Resources and Environ., 1994—, cons. Transp. Rsch. Inst., cons. Coll. Architecture, 1985-86, cons. Coll. Edn., 1992; cons. Cmty. Sys. Found., 1993—; prodr. Ann Arbor Cmty. Access TV, 1988-90; dir. spatial analysis divsn. Cmty. Systems Found., 1996—, dir. fellowship tng., 1996—. Author: Down the Mail Tubes: The Pressured Postal Era, 1853-1984, Essays on Mathematical Geography, 1986, Essays on Mathematical Geography-II, 1987, An Atlas of Steiner Networks, 1989, Essays on Mathematical Georgraphy-III, 1991; co-author: Population-Environment Dynamics, Sectors in Transition, 1992, Mathematical Geography and Global Art, 1986, Environmental Effects on Bus Durability, 1990, Fractals in Geography, 1993; founder, editor, co-author Solstice, 1990—, Image Interactive Atlases, Image Game Series, Image Discussion Papers, Internat. Soc. Spatial Scis., 1995—; author, editor-in-chief Practical Handbook of Curve Fitting, 1994; co-author, editor-in-chief Practical Handbook of Digital Mapping: Terms and Concepts, 1994; editor-in-chief Practical Handbook of Spatial Stats., 1995; editor internat. monograph series; reviewer Mathematical Reviews, 1992—; contbr. articles, book reviews to profl. jours. in field of geography, psychology, math., biology, history, philately. Planning commr. City of Ann Arbor, 1995—; bd. dirs., mem. chmn. Bromley Homeowners Assn., Ann Arbor, 1989-93, pres., 1990-93, 95—; bd. dirs. World Jr. Bridge Championships, Ann Arbor, 1990-91; bd. dirs. Dolfins Inc., 1993—; artist Math. Awareness Week, Lawrence Tech. U., 1988; mem. bd. trustees Cmty. Sys. Found., 1995—. Fellow Am. Geog. Soc. (rep. search com. for curator of collection in Golda Meir Libr. U. Wis.-Milw. Libr. 1993-94); mem. AAAS, Am. Math. Soc., Math. Assn. Am., Assn. Am. Geographers, Internat. Soc. Spatial Scis. (founder), N.Y. Acad. Scis., Engring. Soc. Detroit, Regional Sci. Assn. Office: Inst Math Geography 2790 Briarcliff St Ann Arbor MI 48105-1429 also: Sch Natural Resources U Mich Ann Arbor MI 48109

ARLINGHAUS, WILLIAM CHARLES, mathematics educator; b. Detroit, July 17, 1944; s. Francis Anthony and Blanche Therese (Stolinski) A.; m. Sandra Judith Lach, Sept. 3, 1966; 1 child, William Edward. BS summa cum laude, U. Detroit, 1964; PhD, Wayne State U., 1979. Mathematician GM Tech. Ctr., Warren, Mich., 1967-74; tchr. math. U. Detroit High Sch., 1974-75; lectr. Eastern Mich. U., 1975-77, Wayne State U., 1975-77; lectr. math. Ohio State U., Columbus, 1977-79; asst. prof. math. Loyola U., Chgo., 1979-83, U. Detroit, 1983-85; asst. prof. math., computer sci. Lawrence Technol. U., Southfield, Mich., 1985-90, assoc. prof., 1990-92, prof., 1992—, chair dept. math., computer sci., 1990—; vis. asst. prof. math. U. Mich., Dearborn, 1982-83; bus. mgr. Inst. Math. Geography, Ann Arbor, Mich., 1985—, adv. bd. for monograph series, 1985—. Author: The Classification of Minimal Graphs with Given Abelian Automorphism Group, 1985; mem. editl. bd. Solstice, 1990—; assoc. editor Handbook of Digital Mapping: Terms and Concepts, 1994, Practical Handbook of Curve Fitting, 1994, Practical Handbook of Spatial Statistics; contbr. articles to internat. profl. publs. Mem. pastoral coun. St. Thomas the Apostle Ch., Ann Arbor, 1990-93, v.p., 1991, pres. 1992, renovation and restoration com.; mem. local arrangements com. World Jr. Bridge Championship, 1991. Mem. Am. Math. Soc., Math. Assn. Am., N.Y. Acad. Scis., Assn. Am. Geographers, Am. Contract Bridge League (gold life master), Mich. Bridge Assn. (bd. dirs., tournament chmn. 1974, 87, 94, chmn. bd. dirs. 1976, 89, 96, pres. 1975, 88, 94), Alpha Sigma Nu. Roman Catholic. Home: 2790 Briarcliff St Ann Arbor MI 48105-1429 Office: Lawrence Technol Univ 21000 W 10 Mile Rd Southfield MI 48075-1051

ARMAGOST, ELSA GAFVERT, retired computer industry communications consultant; b. Duluth, Minn.; d. Axel Justus and Martina Emelia (Magnuson) Gafvert; m. Byron William Armagost, Dec. 8, 1945; children: David Byron, Laura Martina. Grad. with honors, Duluth Jr. Coll., 1936; BJ, U. Minn., 1938, postgrad. in pub. rels., bus. mgmt. and computer tech., 1965-81; PhD in Computer Commn. Cons. Sci. (hon.), Internat. U. Found. Freelance editor, Duluth, 1939-42; procedure editor and analyst U.S. Steel, Duluth, 1942-45; fashion advt. staff Dayton Co., Mpls., 1945-48; systems applications and documentation mgr. Control Data Corp., Mpls., 1969-74, promotion specialist, mktg. editor, 1974-76, corp. staff coord. info. on edn., 1976-78; instr. comm., publ. specialist, 1978-79; commn. cons. peripheral products group, 1979-83; industry comm. cons., 1983-88, ret., 1988; mem. steering com. U.S. Senatorial Bus. Adv. Bd., 1962-68; mem. U.S. Congl. Adv. Bd., 1958-62. V.p. Sewickley (Pa.) Valley Hosp. Aux.; bd. dirs. Sewickley Valley Mental Health Coun., LWV Pitts.; bd. dirs. publicity chmn. Sacred Arts Expo; mem. World Affairs Coun. radio program, Pitts. Recipient Medal of Merit Rep. Presdl. Task Force. Mem. AAUW (1st v.p. Caracas, Venezuela), Women in Communication (bd. dir. job mart), Marsh Pk. Condominium Assn. (bd. mem.), Toastmasters (Comm. award 1984), N. Ctrl. Deming Mgmt. Forum, Ctr. of the Am. Expt., Internat. Platform Assn., Friends of Mpls. Inst. Art., Walker Art Inst., Ceridian Corp. Retirees Assn. (bd. dirs.), Minn. Alumni Assn. (life), Am. Swedish Inst., Internat. Soc. Newspaper Editors, Phi Beta Nat. Profl. Arts Frat., Internat. Bible Study Fellowship. Nominated for Alumni Notable Achievement, U. Minn. Coll. Liberal Arts, 1995. Home and Office: 9500 Collegeview Rd Apt 312 Minneapolis MN 55437-2158

ARMBRECHT, MICHAEL RAY, accountant; b. Marshalltown, Iowa, Sept. 15, 1967; s. Kenneth Robert and Colene Rae (Bowman) A. BA, U. No. Iowa, 1990; MBA, U. Chgo., 1996. CPA, Iowa. Corp. fin. and systems auditor Honeywell Inc., Mpls., 1990-92; sr. factory asst. Honeywell Inc., Arlington Heights, Ill., 1992-94, sr. material specialist, 1994—. Mem. U. No. Iowa Alumni Assn. (bd. dirs., pres.-elect). Republican. Lutheran.

ARMENTROUT, MARY ELLEN, librarian; b. Akron, Ohio, Oct. 26, 1944; d. Joseph L. and Dorothy Charlotte (Draheim) A.; m. Bradford Ray Shambarger, Nov. 1, 1975 (div. Jan. 1980); 1 child, Marcella Shambarger. Diploma in French, U. Strasbourg, France, 1965; BA in Home Econs., Otterbein Coll., Westerville, Ohio, 1966; MLS, Ind. U., 1982. Asst. buyer Goldwater's, Phoenix, Ariz., 1966-68; kindergarten tchr. Tisor Schs., Phoenix, 1968-72; periodicals asst. Glendale (Ariz.) C.C., 1973-76; cataloguer Kendallville (Ind.) Pub. Libr., 1981-82; reference libr. Adrian (Mich.) Coll., 1982-87; periodicals libr. Otterbein Coll., Westerville, 1987-94, interlibr. loan libr., 1994—. Author: (newsletter) CINAHLNEWS, 1995, (jour.) Libr. Jour., 1995. Mem. libr. interest group Inniswood Metrogardens, Westerville, 1992—. Mem. Coun. Horticultural and Bot. Librs. Office: Otterbein Coll Courtright Meml Libr Westerville OH 43081

ARMES, WALTER SCOTT, vocational school administrator; b. Okmulgee, Okla., May 15, 1939; s. Ralph E. Armes; m. Jean Hopkins, June 5, 1965; children: Christina M., Rebecca J. BS in edn., Ohio No. U., 1960; MS, Ind. State U., Terre Haute, 1966; postgrad., Ohio State U. Cert. supt., prin., social studies tchr., Ohio. Tchr. social studies Holmes Liberty Sch. Dist., Bucyrus, Ohio, 1960-63, Painesville Twp. Schs., 1963-64, Weathersfield Twp. Sch. Dist., Mineral Ridge, Ohio, 1964-68, Eastland Career Ctr., Groveport, Ohio, 1968—; dir. Eastland Vocat. Sch. Dist., Groveport, 1968—; co-founder Franklin County Tchrs. Ctr. Vice chmn. Whitehall City Bd. Zoning and Bldg. Appeals. Mem. ASCD, Nat. Assn. Secondary Sch. Prins., Ohio Assn. Track and Field and Cross Country Ofcls., Track Registry Ctrl. Ohio, Ohio Sch. Bd. Assn., Ohio Assn. Secondary Sch. Adminstrs. (exec. bd.), Phi Delta Kappa (area coord.). Home: 4010 Etna St Columbus OH 43213-2317

ARMITAGE, KENNETH BARCLAY, biology educator, ecologist; b. Steubenville, Ohio, Apr. 18, 1925; s. Albert Kenneth and Virginia Ethel (Barclay) A.; m. Katie Lou Hart, June 5, 1953; children: Carol, Keith, Kevin. BS summa cum laude, Bethany Coll., W.Va., 1949; MS, U. Wis.-Madison, 1951, PhD, 1954. Instr. U. Wis.-Green Bay, 1954-55; instr. U. Wis.-Wausau, 1955-56; asst. prof. biology U. Kans., Lawrence, 1956-62, assoc. prof., 1962-66, prof., 1966-96, William J. Baumgartner disting. prof., 1987-96, chmn. dept. systematics & ecology, 1982-88, dir. environ. studies program, 1976-82, dir. exptl. and applied ecology program, 1974-94, prof. emeritus, 1996—; vis. prof. U. Modena, Italy, 1989; mem. com. examiners Grad. Record Exam. Biology Test, 1986-92, chmn., 1988-92; sr. investigator Rocky Mountain Biol. Lab., Gothic, Colo., 1962—, trustee, 1969-86, pres. bd. trustees, 1985-86. Author: (lab. manual) Investigations in General Biology, (with others) Principles of Modern Biology; contbr. articles to profl. jours.; mem. editl. bd.: Ethology, Ecology and Evolution, 1989—, Ibex Jour. Mountain Ecology, 1994—, Oecologia Montana, 1996—. Pres. Douglas County chpt. Zero Population Growth, 1969-71; bd. dirs. Children's Hour, Inc., Lawrence, 1969-70. Served with U.S. Army, 1943-46, ETO. Recipient Antarctic medal NSF, 1968, Edn. Service award U. Kans., 1979, Alumni Achievement award Bethany Coll., 1989. Fellow AAAS, Animal Behavior Soc.; mem. Am. Soc. Naturalists (treas. 1984-86), Am. Inst. Biol. Scis. (mem. task force for 90s), Ecol. Soc. Am., Am. Soc. Zoologists, Orgn. Biol. Field Stations (v.p. 1986-87, pres. 1988-89), Sigma Xi, Phi Beta Kappa, Beta Beta Beta, Gamma Sigma Kappa. Home: 505 Ohio St Lawrence KS 66044-2245 Office: Dept Systematics & Ecology Univ Kansas Lawrence KS 66045-2106

ARMITAGE, THOMAS EDWARD, library director; b. Torrington, Wyo., Dec. 11, 1946; s. Ross Eugene Armitage and Mary Kathleen (Donley) Wieland; m. Linda Lou Theisen, May 23, 1987; children: Anne, Nicholas, Rachel. AA in History, Santa Barbara (Calif.) C.C., 1971; BA in History, Kans. State U., Pittsburg, 1973; MLS, U. Mo., 1974. Asst. dir. Ottumwa (Iowa) Pub. Libr., 1975-77; libr. dir. Ft. Dodge (Iowa) Pub. Libr., 1977-86, Cedar Rapids (Iowa) Pub. Libr., 1987—. With USN, 1967-69. Mem. ALA, Iowa Libr. Assn., Iowa Urban Pub. Libr. Assn. (pres. 1990-91, sec. 1995-96), Linn County Libr. Assn. (v.p. 1993—), Linn County Libr. Consortium (sec. 1995—), Rotary, Greater Cedar Rapids C. of C. Office: Cedar Rapids Pub Libr 500 1st St SE Cedar Rapids IA 52401-2002

ARMOUR, JOHN M., management company executive; b. Memphis, Nov. 3, 1952; s. Mavrice K. and Flossie Louise (Stroupe) A.; m. Carol Ann Peaslee, Nov. 30, 1975; children: Andrea, John. BA, N. Park Coll., 1975. With maintenance dept. Dormeyer Industries, Chgo., 1970-72, line supr., 1972-74, exec. v.p., 1982-85, pres., 1985-88, CEO, owner, 1988—; plant mgr. Clayton Industries, Chgo., 1974-82. Bd. dirs. Park Ridge (Ill.) Youth Soccer, 1992. Office: Dormeyer Industries 6585 N Avondale Chicago IL 60631

ARMSTRONG, HART REID, minister, editor, publisher; b. St. Louis, May 11, 1912; s. Hart Champlin and Zora Lillian (Reid) A.; m. Iona Rhoda Mehl, Feb. 21, 1932; 1 son, Hart Reed. Grad. Life Bible Coll., 1931; A.B., Christian Temples U., 1936; Litt.D., Geneva Theol. Coll., 1967; D.D. (hon.) Central Sch. Religion, Surrey, Eng., 1972; Th.M., Central Christian Coll., 1968, Th.D., 1970; Ph.D. in Religion, Berean Christian Coll., 1980. Ordained to ministry Assembly of God, 1932; pastor, 1932-34; dean Bible Standard Coll., Eugene, Oreg., 1935-40; missionary, Indonesia, 1941-42; editor Open Bible Pubs., Des Moines, 1944-46, Gospel Pub. House, Springfield, Mo., 1947-53, Gospel Light Pubs., Glendale, Calif., 1954; crusade adminstr. Oral Roberts Assn., Tulsa, 1955-62; exec. dir. Assembly Homes, Inc., Glenwood, Minn., 1963-66; pres. Defenders Christian Faith, Kansas City, Mo., 1967-80; founder, pres., editor Christian Communications, Inc., Wichita, Kans., 1981—; editor Devotional Letter Monthly. Fellow London Royal Soc. Arts; mem. Nat. Sunday Sch. Assn., Pope County Hist. Soc., Sigma Delta Chi. Lodge: Rotary (past charter pres. Glenwood, Minn.). Author: To Those Who Are Left, 1950; You Should Know, 1951; The Rebel, 1967; The Beast, 1967; How Do I Pray, 1968; All Things for Life, 1969; What Will Happen to the United States, 1969; Impossible Events of Bible Prophecy, 1979; All You Need to Know about Bible Prophecy, 1980; Thoughts at Three Score and Ten, 1981; The A-B-C of Last Day Events, 1982, The World that Then Was, How Great Thou Art!, The Gospel of John--A Commentary, 1983, The True Site of the Temple of Solomon, The Holy Jerusalem, UFOs--Are They for Real, Petra--the Mysterious City, 1984, The Seven Churches of Revelation, Verses from the Heart, Katherine Beard--A Life Poured Out, 1985, Let Them Speak to You, The Primary Movers (3 sects.), Where is the Ark of the Covenant?, The Sacred Festivals of the Lord, 1989, Commentary on the Book of Revelation (vols. I-IV), 1992, Why Not?-Biography of Dr. Frank Lindquest, Glory to Come!, 1993, The Olivet Discourse, The Last Seven on Earth, The Story of God, 1994, When Is the Rapture? I Found the Ark, The Last Great Day of God Almighty, 1995, The Miracle Voyage of the Ghost Ship, Visions Yet Future in the Book of Daniel, 1996. Home: 6436 N Hillside St Wichita KS 67219-1805 Office: 6450 N Hillside Ave Wichita KS 67219

ARMSTRONG, LEONA MAY BOTTRELL, counselor; b. Rochester, Ill., Aug. 14, 1930; d. Vernon Sampson Bottrell and Leonia Ruth (Meeks) Cooper; m. Bryce Glenn Armstrong, June 11, 1950 (div. 1975); children: Steven Lee, Rebecca Sue, Paul Bryce, (twins) Kevin John and Brian Mark. BS, Ind. Ctrl. U., 1952; MS, U. Wis., 1967. Tchr. Dayton, Ohio, 1952-55; sch. counselor Oshkosh, Verona, West Allis, Wis., 1967-88; pvt. practice as counselor, astrologer, tchr. Milw., Wis., 1988—; Reiki master Reiki Healers Internat., 1992; guest spkr. in area of parapsychology and metaphysics U. Minn., U., Wis., Milw., other schs., 1980—; spkr. World Peace Program, Milw., 1987. Ecumenical spkr. United Ch. Women, 1966. Named Outstanding Sr. Woman, Philalethea Lit. Soc., 1952, one of Outstanding Personalities in Midwest, 1968. Mem. Nat. Coun. for Geocosmic Rsch. Home and Office: 2706 S 112th St Milwaukee WI 53227-3023

ARMSTRONG, REBECCA SUE, customer service representative; b. Clintonville, Wis., Oct. 2, 1956; d. Bryce Glen and Leona May (Bottrell) A.; m. Michael Lee O'Brien, Apr. 1, 1977 (div. July 13, 1983); children: John Joseph, Eric Michael. AAS, U. Wis. Ctrs., Waukesha, 1990; BS, Carroll Coll., 1992; MA, U. Wis., Milw., 1994. Sorter, computer operator 1st Am. Bank, Wausau, Wis., 1977-78; statis. coder Employers Ins. of Wausau, 1978-80; self employed R.S. Armstrong & Assocs., West Allis, Wis., 1985; supr. H&R Block, Wauwatosa, Wis., 1986-89; student ass. U. Wis.-Waukesha Ctr., 1988-89; adminstr. asst. RML Corp., Waukesha, 1989-93; asst. cartographer Cartographic Svcs. Lab., Milw., 1993; teaching asst. U. Wis. Milw., 1993-94; customer svc. rep. Ameritech, Waukesha, 1994—. Regional coord. Internat. Youth Exch., West Allis, 1982-86, regional contact, 1986—. Mem. North Am. Cartographic Info. Soc., Gamma Theta Upsilon Honor Soc., Delta Sigma Nu. Home: 10152 W Cleveland Ave West Allis WI 53227

ARMSTRONG, RICHARD D., transportation executive; b. Reedsburg, Wis., Oct. 18, 1943. BA in Anthropology, No. Ill. U., DeKalb, 1969; ABD in Anthropology, UCLA, 1972. Cert. practitioner ICC. Rate analyst Yellow Freight Sys., Kansas City, 1974-75; v.p. traffic Advance Transp., Milw., 1978-80; pres. Armstrong & Assoc., Stoughton, Wis., 1980—. Contbr. articles to profl. jours. Alderman, mem. The City of Stoughton, Wis., 1984-90. With U.S. Army, 1961-63. Mem. Nat. Classification Com., Assn. Transp. Practitioners. Office: Armstrong & Assoc 321 S Forrest St Stoughton WI 53589-2111

ARN, KENNETH DALE, physician, city official; b. Dayton, Ohio, July 19, 1921; s. Elmer R. and Minna Marie (Wannagat) A.; m. Vivien Rose Fontini, Sept. 24, 1966; children—Christine H. Hulme, Laura P. Hafstad, Kevin D., Kimmel R. B.A., Miami U., Oxford, Ohio, 1943; M.D., U. Mich., 1946. Intern Miami Valley Hosp., Dayton, Ohio, 1947-48; resident in pathology U. Mich., 1948-49, fellow in renal research, 1949-50; fellow in internal medicine Cleve. Clinic, 1950-52; pvt. practice specializing in internal medicine, pub. health and vocat. rehab. Dayton, 1952—; commr. of health City of Oakwood, Ohio, 1953—; assoc. clin. prof. medicine Wright State U., 1975—;

mem. staffs Kettering Med. Ctr., Dayton, Miami Valley Hosp.; adj. assoc. prof. edn. Wright State U.; field med. cons. Bur. Vocat. Rehab., 1958—, Bur. Svcs. to Blind, 1975—; med. dir. Ohio Rehab. Svcs. Commn., 1979-87; mem. Pres.'s Com. on Employment of Handicapped, 1971—; chmn. med. adv. com. Goodwill Industries, 1960-75, chmn. bd. trustees 1985-87, chmn. rehab. com. 1987—; mem., chmn. lay adv. com. vocat. edn. Dayton Pub. Schs., 1973-82; exec. com. Gov.'s Com. on Employment Handicapped; bd. dirs. Vis. Nurses Assn. Greater Dayton; chmn. profl. adv. com. Combined Gen. Health Dist. Montgomery County. Trustee Luth. Social Svc. of Miami Valley, 1982-88. Named City of Dayton's Outstanding Young Man, Jr. C. of C., 1957; 1 of 5 Outstanding Young Men of State, Ohio Jr. C. of C., 1958; Physician of Yr., Pres.'s Com. on Employment of Handicapped, 1971; Bishop's medal for meritorious service Miami U., 1972. Mem. AMA, Ohio Med. Assn., Montgomery County Med. Soc. (chmn. com. on diabetic detection 1955-65, chmn. polio com. 1954-58), Nat. Rehab. Assn., Am. Diabetes Assn., Am. Profl. Practice Assn., Am. Heart Assn., Am. Pub. Health Assn., Ohio Pub. Health Assn., Aerospace Med. Assn., Fraternal Order Police, Dayton Country Club, Kiwanis, Royal Order Jesters, Masons (past potentate), Shriners, K.T., Scottish Rite (33 deg.), Nu Sigma Nu, Sigma Chi. Lutheran. Home: 167 Lookout Dr Dayton OH 45409-2238 Office: 30 Park Ave Dayton OH 45419-3426

ARNDT, ROGER EDWARD ANTHONY, hydraulic engineer, educator; b. N.Y.C., May 25, 1935; s. Ernest Otto Paul and Olive (Walters) A.; m. Jane Elizabeth Pfund, Dec. 1, 1990; children from previous marriage: Larysa Tamara, Tanya Sofia. B.C.E., CCNY, 1960; S.M., M.I.T., 1962, Ph.D., 1967. Chemist Consol. Testing Labs., New Hyde Park, N.Y., 1956-57; jr. civil engr. N.Y.C. Dept. Public Works, 1960; rsch. engr. Allegheny Ballistics Lab., Cumberland, Md., 1962-63; sr. rsch. engr. Lockheed Calif. Corp., Burbank, 1963-64; assoc. prof. aerospace engring. Pa. State U., 1967-77; prof. hydromechanics, dir. St. Anthony Falls Hydraulic Labs., U. Minn., Mpls., 1977-93; prof. civil engring. U. Minn., 1977—; program dir. NSF, 1995—; mem. Gov.'s Commn. on Cold Weather Research; 1st Theodor Ranov disting. lectr. SUNY, Buffalo, 1979; cons. in field. Editor several books on fluid mechanics and hydropower; contbr. articles in field, chpts. in books; also spl. publs. mech. engring. Recipient George Taylor Tchg. award U. Minn., 1978, Lorenz G. Straub award, 1968, Fluids Engring. award ASME, 1993; NASA fellow, 1965-67. Fellow AIAA (assoc., Outstanding Faculty Adv. award 1971, 72, 73, 74l), ASME (Fluids Engring. award 1993); mem. Internat. Assn. Hydraulic Rsch., Acoustical Soc. Am., ASCE, ASTM, Am. Water Resources Assn., N.Y. Acad. Scis., Twin City Cloud 7 Club, Sigma Xi. Home: 6711 Pine Creek Ct McLean VA 22101 Office: NSF ENG/CTS Rm 525 4201 Wilson Blvd Arlington VA 22230

ARNELL, PAULA ANN YOUNGBERG, pathologist; b. Moline, Ill., Nov. 25, 1938; d. Paul Phillip and Mabel Eleanor (Arnell) Youngberg; B.A. summa cum laude, Augustana Coll., 1960; M.D., U. Iowa, 1964; m. Richard Anthony Arnell, June 28, 1969; children—Carla Ann, Paula Marie, Paul Anthony. Intern, St. Lukes-Mercy Hosp., Cedar Rapids, Iowa, 1964-65; resident pathology U. Iowa, Iowa City, 1965-68; chief resident State U. Iowa Hosp., Iowa City, 1968-69; pathologist, dir. labs. Luth. Hosp., Moline, Ill., 1970-89; dir. labs. United Med. Ctr., Moline, Ill., 1989—; mem. staffs Moline Pub. Hosp., Franciscan Hosp., Rock Island, Ill. Sec., Rock Island County Blood Bank, 1972-73, v.p., 1973-74; cons. Rock Island Tb Center, 1970-72; profl. del. Am. Cancer Soc., 1971-73; tchr. Luth. Hosp. Sch. Inhalation Therapy, Sch. Nursing, 1970-80 ; med. dir. Royal Neighbors of Am. Ins. Co., Rock Island; asso dir. Met. Med. Lab., Moline, Quad-Cities Pathologists Group Sch. of Med. Tech.; bd. dirs. Augustana Coll., 7th Street Realty Co., St. Katherine's and St. Mark's Sch.; bd. govs. Luth. Social Svcs. of Ill.; founder Quad Cities Regional Screening and Diagnostic Breast Ctr., 1984; gov. Ill. task Force Interrelationship of Luth. Ch. in Am. Instns., 1986-87; chmn. Task Force on Outdoor Ministries Ill. div. Cath. Ch. of Am., 1986-87. Pres. Rock Island County Cancer Soc., 1970-78; mem. alumni bd. Augustana Coll., Rock Island, 1972-75, bd. dirs., 1976-83, 87—, chmn. bd. dirs., 1977-83; sec. med. sect. Nat. Fraternal Congress, 1976-86; bd. dirs. Mississippi Valley Regional Blood Bank, 1973-87, Ill. div. Am. Cancer Soc., 1980-86; bd. govs. Luth. Social Services Ill., 1985-87—. Recipient Outstanding Alumni award Augustana Coll., 1986, Top Physician Pub. Svc. award Ill. State Med. Soc., 1989. Fellow Coll. Am. Pathologists (insp.), Am. Soc. Clin. Pathologists; cons. pathologist, ICON, 1981—; mem. Internat. Acad. Pathologists, Am. Assn. Cytologists, Am. Assn. Blood Banks, Am. Assn. Clin. Scientists, Am. Womans Med. Assn. (del. to China on nutrition 1986), AMA, Iowa Ill. med. socs., Ill. Pathologists Asso., Rock Island County Hist. Soc., Phi Beta Kappa, Beta Beta Beta. Home: 3904 7th Ave Rock Island IL 61201-2246 Office: Luth Hosp Luth Hosp 501 10th Ave Moline IL 61265

ARNELL, RICHARD ANTHONY, radiologist; b. Chgo., Aug. 21, 1938; s. Tony Frank and Mary Martha (Oberman) Yaki; BA (Younker Achievement scholar), Grinnell Coll., 1960; MD, U. Iowa, 1964; m. Paula Ann Youngberg, June 28, 1964; children: Carla Ann, Paula Marie, Paul Anthony. With Innc., 1968—, v.p., 1970-78, sec., 1978-90, pres., 1990—, trustee pension and profit plan, 1979—; pres. Moline Radiology Assocs., S.C., 1990-93, Advanced Radiology, S.C., 1993—; mem. staff Luth. Hosp., Moline, 1968-88, dir. continuing med. edn. program for physicians, 1979-83, bd. dirs., 1977-83; mem. staff Moline Pub. Hosp., 1968-88, Hammond-Henry Dist. Ill., Geneseo, Ill., United Med. Ctr., 1989-92, chmn. radiology dept. United Med. Ctr., 1989-92; mem. staff Trinity Med. Ctr., 1992, chmn. radiology dept., 1992-94, med. dir. radiology dept., 1992—; pres. Moline Radiology Assocs., Inc., 1990-93; pres. Advanced Radiology, S.C., 1993—; trustee Midstate Found. for Med. Care, 1975-79, exec. com., 1976-79; v.p. Quad City HMO Health Plan, 1979; clin. lectr. U. Iowa, 1980—; pres. med. staff, dir. Quad City MRI Inc., 1988-89; pres. Moline Mgmt. Assocs., Inc., 1990—; chmn. mng. com. Metro MRI Ctr., Ltd. Partnership. Supt. Sunday Ch. Sch. St. John's Luth. Ch., Rock Island, Ill., 1974-79, mem. ch. cabinet, 1975-76; del. Chs. United of Scott and Rock Island counties, Ill., 1977; mem. nat. exec. com. Augustana Coll., Rock Island, Ill., 1977-81; assoc. chmn. profl. div. United Way, 1985; bd. dirs. Luth. Hosp. Found., 1981-84, pres., 1982-84; bd. dirs. Quad Cities Health Care Resources, Inc., 1984-88 ; chmn. Luth. Health Care Found., 1984-88, chmn. United Health Care Found., 1989-91. Recipient David Theophillus trophy for outstanding athlete Grinnell Coll., 1960; diplomate Am. Bd. Radiology, Am. Bd. Nuclear Medicine. Mem. Am. Coll. Radiology, Ill. Radiol. Soc., Am. Coll. Nuclear Medicine, Soc. Nuclear Medicine, AMA, Ill. (ho. of dels. 1974-79), Rock Island County (exec. com. 1974-79, peer-rev. com. 1975-79), Iowa-Ill. Central (pres. 1978) med. socs., Central Ill. Med. Assn. (v.p. 1977, pres. 1978), Ind. Physicians Assn. Western Ill. (dir. 1984-86, v.p. 1985, pres. 1986), World Med. Assn., Am. Coll. Med. Imaging., Short Hills Country Club. Home: 3904 7th Ave Rock Island IL 61201-2246 Office: 1505 7th St Moline IL 61265-2918

ARNETT, CARROLL D., chemistry educator; b. Rowlesburg, W.Va., Aug. 22, 1946; s. Jerome C. and V. Maye (Fike) A.; m. Susan P. Crafton, June 20, 1970; children: Christopher S., Lindsay S. AB in Chemistry, Duke U., 1968; postgrad., Med. Coll. Va., 1968-69; PhD in Medicinal Chemistry, U. Md., 1976; postgrad., Duke U., 1976-79. Teaching asst. Med. Coll. Va., Richmond, 1968-69; chemistry assoc. Johns Hopkins Hosp., Balt., 1969-71; grad. asst. U. Md., Balt., 1971-75; rsch. assoc. Duke U. Med. Ctr., Durham, N.C., 1976-79; chemist Brookhaven Nat. Lab., Upton, N.Y., 1979-87; assoc. prof. psychiatry and behavioral scis. U. Wash., Seattle, 1988-91, adj. assoc. prof. radiology, 1988-91; assoc. prof. dept. radiology U. Minn., Mpls., 1991—; cons. in field. Contbr. articles to profl. jours.; patentee in field. Biomed. Research Support grantee, U. Wash., 1988. Mem. ACS, Soc. Neurosci., Soc. Nuclear Medicine, Sigma Xi, Rho Chi. Home: 351 Maple Island Rd Burnsville MN 55306-5523 Office: U Minn Dept Radiology PO Box 292 Minneapolis MN 55455-0292

ARNETT, JAMES EDWARD, retired insurance company executive, retired secondary school educator.; b. Gullett, Ky., Oct. 3, 1912; s. Haden and Josephine (Risner) A.; A.B., San Jose State Coll., 1947, M.A., 1955; Ed.S., Stanford, 1959; m. Helen Mae Vallish, Mar. 23, 1943. Tchr., prin. pub. schs., Salyersville, Ky., 1930-41; tchr., adminstr. pub. schs., Salinas, Calif., 1947-52; owner-mgr. Arnett Apts., Salinas, 1950-53; tchr., Innes High Sch., Akron, Ohio, 1953-73; owner-mgr. Arnett Apts., Akron, 1953-72; dir. Educator & Exec. Co., 1962-73, Educator and Exec. Insurers, 1957-76, Educator and Exec. Life Ins. Co., 1962-76, Great Am. of Dallas Fire and Casualty Co., 1974-76, Great Am. of Dallas Ins. Co., 1974-76, J.C. Penney Casualty Ins. Co., 1976; cons., 1976-77. Mem. county, state central coms. Democratic party, 1952. Served with AUS, 1942-45. Mem. NEA (life mem.; del. conv. 1957-65), Ohio (del. convs. 1957-73), Akron (1st v.p. 1964-65, parliamentarian 1965-72), edn. assns., San Jose State Coll., Stanford alumni assns., Phi Delta Kappa. Home: 691 Payne Ave Akron OH 44302-1347

ARNETT, LOUISE EVA, information records management executive; b. Cin., Sept. 8, 1945; d. Matthew Michael John Waldeck and Edith Louise (Reinholz) Driskell; m. Daniel L. Arnett, May 1, 1965; children: Matthew, Michael, John. Student, U. Cin., 1978-82, Thomas More, 1986—. Teller mgr. Tri State Savs., Cin., 1963-69; owner, operator Arnett's Hobby and Craft Shop, Inc., Erlanger, Ky., 1969-75; evening mgr. Wileswood Country Store, Greater Cin. Airport, Ky., 1975-78; records mgr. Federated Department Stores, Inc., Cin., 1978—. Commr. Tiger Cubs, Boy Scouts Am., Greater Cin., 1980-82; vol. Cin.'s 200th Birthday, 1988, Kenton County (Ky.) 150th Birthday, 1990; campaigner Kenton County Sch. Bd., 1987; booster alumna Dixie Band, Ft. Mitchell, Ky., 1986-92; vol. Tall Stacks, 1988, 92, 95, United Way and Cmty. Chest Greater Cin., 1994—, mem. corp. volunteerism coun., spl. projects liaison, 1994-96; vol. Cmty. Care Week, Nat. Vol. Week for the Elderly. Named for Meritorious Svc., Boy Scouts Am., 1979; recipient Order of the Heart, Boy Scouts Am., 1978. Mem. Assn. Records Mgrs. and Adminstrs. (dir. 1979-80, program chmn. 1980-81, v.p. 1983-84, pres. 1984-85, bd. dirs. Cin. chpt. 1986-92, chmn. bd. Cin. chpt. 1985, Membership award 1982, Mem. of Yr. 1980), Federated Ptnrs. in Time (volunteerism com.). Republican. Office: Federated Dept Stores Inc 7 W 7th St Cincinnati OH 45202-2405

ARNETT, STEVEN J., engineering manager; b. Kalamazoo, Sept. 19, 1960. BS in Elec. Engring., U. Mich., 1984; BS, Western Mich. U., 1991. Quality control test engr. Simmons Precision, Vergennes, Vt., 1986-88; cons. elec. engring. Portage, Mich., 1988-94; engring. mgr. Dunkley Internat., Kalamazoo, 1994—. Mem. Soc. Mfg. Engrs. Office: Dunkley Internat Inc 1910 Lake St Kalamazoo MI 49001-3274

ARNEY, RANDALL, artistic director. Artistic dir. Steppenwolf Theatre Co., Chgo. Office: Steppenwolf Theatre Co 1650 N Halsted St Chicago IL 60614-5518*

ARNHART, LARRY EUGENE, political science educator; b. Falfurrias, Tex., Jan. 13, 1949; s. Lawrence Edward andd Mary (Gaskill) A. BA, U. Dallas, 1971; MA, U. Chgo., 1974, PhD, 1977. Lectr. liberal arts U. Chgo., 1974-78; asst. prof. polit. sci. Rosary Coll., River Forest, Ill., 1978-79, Idaho State U., Pocatello, 1979-83; assoc. prof. No. Ill. U., DeKalb, 1983—. Author: Aristotle on Political Reasoning, 1981, Political Questions, 1987, Natural Right and Biology, 1997. Fellow NEH, 1988-89, rsch. fellow Earhart Found., 1992. Home: 1015 Ashley Dr De Kalb IL 60115-5210 Office: No Ill U Polit Sci Dept De Kalb IL 60115

ARNOLD, DANIEL DOUGLAS, financial consultant; b. Ft. Wayne, Ind., Sept. 30, 1959. BA, Ind. U., 1982. CPA. Acct. Coopers & Lybrand, Ft. Wayne, 1982-84; corp. controller Northhill Corp., Ft. Wayne, 1984-91; fin. cons. Smith Barney Inc., Ft. Wayne, 19916. Mem. AICPA (Personal Fin. Planner), Ind. CPA Soc. Office: Smith Barney Inc 1 Summit Sq 8th Fl Fort Wayne IN 46802

ARNOLD, DAVID ALAN, surgeon; b. Sioux City, Iowa, Apr. 10, 1946; s. Allen and Mary Jean (Harjehausen) A.; m. Lana Beth Carlson, Sept. 11, 1971; children: Chad, Carl, Wade, Craig. BS, Morningside Coll., 1968; DO, Kirksville Coll. Osteo. Med., 1972. Intern Osteo. Hosp. of Maine, Portland, 1972-73; emergency rm. physician Bridgton (Mass.) Community Hosp., 1973; sr. med. officer Naval Air Sta., S. Weymouth, Mass., 1974-76; sr. flight surgeon Naval Air Sta., S. Weymouth, 1974-76; resident Des Moines (Iowa) Gen. Hosp., 1976-78; pvt. practice gen. surgery Davenport, Iowa, 1980—; med. dir. Quad City Regional Wound Care Ctr., Davenport, Iowa, 1995—; chmn. dept. surgery Davenport Med. Ctr., 1996; AMCCOM flight surgeon Rock Island (Ill.) Arsenal, 1986; founder Midwest Hernia Inst., Davenport, 1980—. Capt. USNR, 1990-91, Desert Shield/Desert Storm. Decorated Commendation medal Iowa Nat. Guard, 1980, Meritorious Svc. medal U.S. Army, 1984; named Flight Surgon of Yr., U.S. Army, 1984. Mem. Am. Osteo. Assn., Am. Coll. Osteo. Surgeons, Am. Soc. Abdominal Surgeons, Iowa Med. Soc., Scott County Osteo. Soc., Scott County Med. Soc. Office: Ste 430 1351 W Central Park Davenport IA 52804 also: Quad City Regional Would Care Ctr 3801 N Marquette St Davenport IA 52806

ARNOLD, DAVID PAUL, sales professional; b. Pitts., May 11, 1942; s. Arthur and Elizabeth (Novak) A.; m. Patricia Arda Graham, Sept. 3, 1966; children: Nichelle, Bret, Janelle. BA in Bus., Ohio No. U., 1964; grad., Ohio State Inst. Fin., 1971. Sales engr. Reliance Electric, various cities, 1964-70; sales dir. Columbia Nat., Columbus, Ohio, 1970-73; owner Mint Lake Valley Lumber, Ashtabula, Ohio, 1973-76; v.p. sales Preformed Line Products, Cleve., 1976—. Founder, BOGSAT. Named to Hon. Order Ky. Cols. Mem. Am. Mgmt. Assn. Republican. Methodist. Home: 2221 Gageville Rd Ashtabula OH 44004-9636 Office: Preformed Line Products 660 Beta Dr Cleveland OH 44143-2319

ARNOLD, KATHLEEN MARY, nursing administrator, educator; b. East St. Louis, Mar. 3, 1949; d. George William Arnold and Rosemary (Meketa) Kerber. BS in Edn., So. Ill. U., 1971; ADN, Belleville (Ill.) Area Coll., 1979; MBA, Webster U., 1991. Lic. nurse Ill., Mo.; cert. emergency nurse, BLS, ACLS, Pre Hosp. Trauma Life Support, Trauma Nurse Core Course Provider, Trauma Nurse Core Course Instr., Trauma Nurse Specialist, Advanced Burn Life Support Provider, Flight Nurse Advanced Trauma Life Support. Staff RN Centreville Twp. Hosp., Centreville, Ill., 1979-81; staff RN St. Louis U. Hosp., 1981-82, RN liaison, 1989-91, dir. emergency nursing, 1991—; flight nurse Med. Air Rescue Corps, St. Louis, 1982-87, Area Rescue Consortium of Hosps., St. Louis, 1987-89; instr. St. Louis C.C., 1985—; bd. dirs. Crohn's and Colitis Found., St. Louis, 1990-91. Area med. svcs. coord. U.S. Olympic Festival, St. Louis, 1994, ESPN Extreme Games, Newport, R.I., 1995. Mem. Emergency Nurses Assn. Roman Catholic. Home: 2101 S 74th St Belleville IL 62223-3344 Office: St Louis U Hosp 3635 Vista Ave Saint Louis MO 63110-2539

ARNOLD, LINDA GAYLE, human resources executive; b. Columbia, Mo., Aug. 26, 1947; d. Lahmon Emery and Mary Lee (Bennett) Wren; m. Jerry Earl Arnold, Mar. 11, 1965; children: Lesley Arnold Siegfried, Bryce Jefferson. Student, U. Mo., Kansas City, 1965-66. Pricing coord. Gateway Sporting Goods, Kansas City, Mo., 1967-69; legal sec. Tull & Mayse, Columbia, Mo., 1969-74; profit sharing adminstr. McGraw-Edison, Columbia, Mo., 1978-81; dir. pers. Toastmaster Inc., Columbia, Mo., 1981-87, v.p. human resources, 1987—, corp. sec., 1992—. Bd. dirs. Columbia Area United Way, Mo. Women's Coun., 1993-95; bd. trustees Westminster Coll., Fulton, Mo., 1995—; chmn. adv. bd. dept. consumer and family econs. U. Mo. Mem. Soc. for Human Resource Mgmt. (Cen. Mo. chpt.), Women's Network (past pres.), Columbia C. of C., Mo. Found. Women's Resources (bd. dirs.). Baptist. Office: Toastmaster Inc 1801 N Stadium Blvd Columbia MO 65202-1330

ARNOLD, ROBERT JEFFREY, musician; b. San Marcos, Tex., Apr. 28, 1959. Student, U. North Tex., 1977-80, Baylor U., 1982-83. Concert pianist radio and TV, N.Am. and Europe, 1967—; exec. dir. Dallas Inst. Vocal Arts, 1988-89; exec. artistic dir. Lee County Opera, Giddings, Tex., 1989-92; accompanist, coach Opera Ensemble of San Antonio, 1994; voice tchr. and coach, Iowa City, 1995—, Chgo., 1995—. Recital debuts Carnegie Hall, N.Y.C., 1989, 95, St. Mary Magdalene Ch., Picton, Ont., 1993, Countess of Huntingdon Hall, Worcester, Eng., 1995. Mem. Nat. Assn. Tchrs. Singing, Organ Hist. Soc.

ARNOLD, SCOTT GREGORY, computer information systems specialist; b. Wabash, Ind., June 23, 1961; s. Don H. and Martha S. (Gregor) A. BS in Computer Sci., Ball State U., 1983; postgrad., St. Francis Coll., 1985, Ind. U./Purdue U., 1985, Ind. Vocat. Tech. Coll., 1985, Moraine Park Tech. Coll., 1987-89; student, Bus. and Econ. Inst., 1994-95. Programmer Slater Steel Corp., Ft. Wayne, Ind., 1983-85; programmer II N.Am. Van Lines, Ft. Wayne, 1985-86; programmer, analyst Speed Queen Co., Ripon, Wis., 1986-90, Direct Transit, Inc., Sioux City, Iowa, 1990; programming cons. Turille and Assocs., Omaha, 1991; programmer, analyst Warren Distbn., Inc., Omaha, 1991; programmer CMS-Tempro, South Bend, Ind., 1992; programmer, analyst Heaters Engring., Inc., North Webster, Ind., 1992; software support analyst NACCO Materials Handling Group, Inc., Danville, Ill., 1992—. Chmn. Circus Vegas, 1993—; bd. dirs. Jr. C. of C., 1985—, Riponfest, 1987-89, Springfest, 1992—, Internat. Mgmt. Coun., 1993—. Republican. Mem. Ch. of Christ. Home: 1024 Sunset Ridge Danville IL 61832

ARNOLD, STUART W., account executive; b. Decanter, Ill., Mar. 3, 1955. BA, Millikin U., Decatur, Ill., 1977. Account exec. Searson, Leaman Brather, Indpls., 1986-93, The Ohio Co., Indpls., 1993—. Republican. Methodist. Home: 4263 W Meadowvale Dr Bloomington IN 47404-9043 Office: The Ohio Co 251 E Ohio St Ste 150 Indianapolis IN 46204-2133

ARNSDORF, MORTON FRANK, cardiologist, educator; b. Chgo., Aug. 7, 1940; s. Selmar N. and Irmgard C. (Steinmann) A.; m. Mary Hunter Tower, Dec. 26, 1963 (div. 1982); m. Rosemary Crowley, Dec. 27, 1986. BA magna cum laude, Harvard U., 1962; MD, Columbia U., 1966. Diplomate Am. Bd. Internal Medicine. House staff officer U. Chgo., 1966-69; fellow cardiology Columbia-Presbyn. Med. Ctr., N.Y.C., 1969-71; asst. prof. medicine U. Chgo., 1973-79, assoc. prof., 1979-83, prof., 1983—, chief sect. cardiology, 1981-90; mem. pharmacology study sect. NIH, 1981-84. Contbr. articles to profl. jours. Maj. USAF, 1971-73. Recipient Rsch. Career Devel. award NIH, 1976-81; rsch. grantee Chgo. Heart Assn., 1976-78, NIH, 1977—, NIH Merit award, 1989—. Fellow ACP, Am. Coll. Cardiology (mem. editl. bd. JACC 1983-87, 90—, gov.-elect Ill. 1990-91, gov. Ill. 1991-94, pres. Ill. chpt. 1991-94, bd. gov. issues and concerns subcom. 1991-93, bd. gov. steering com. 1993-94, ad hoc com. quality assurance improvement initiative, sec. and trustee 1995, electrophysiology/electrocardiology/pacemaker com. 1994—); mem. Am. Heart Assn. (dir. 1981-83, chmn. exec. com. basic sci. coun. 1981-83, steering com. 1983-86, mem. rsch. program and evaluation com. 1989-91, assoc. editor circulation Rsch. 1986-91), Am. Heart Assn. Met. Chgo. (v.p. 1986, pres.-elect 1987-88, pres. 1988-89, bd. govs., chmn. rsch. coun. 1981, chmn. program coun. 1986-88), Am. Fedn. Clin. Rsch., Assn. Univ. Cardiologists, Ctrl. Soc. Clin. Rsch. (chmn. cardiovascular coun. 1986-87, sec.-treas. 1991-95), Assn. Profs. Cardiology (founding mem., bylaws com. 1989-90), Chgo. Cardiology Group (pres. 1990-92), Cardiac Electrophysiology Soc. (sec.-treas. 1984-86, pres. 1986-88). Club: Quadrangle. Office: U Chgo Hosps and Clinics Sect Cardiology MC 6080 5841 S Maryland Ave Chicago IL 60637-1463

ARNST, MIKE, mechanical design engineer; b. Ft. Benton, Mo., 1969. BSME, Mont. State U., Bozeman, 1992. Mech. engr. Boeing, Seattle, 1991-92, Midwest Conveyor, Kansas City, Kans., 1993—. Patentee in field. Mem. ASME.

ARORA, SWARNJIT SINGH, university administrator, economics educator; b. Sialkot, Punjab, India, Aug. 10, 1940; came to U.S., 1967; parents Uttam and Kartar (Kaur) S.; m. Nimmi K. Sindhu, July 28, 1974; children: Seema K., Deepa S. BSc with honors, Delhi (India) U., 1962, MA, 1964; MA, SUNY, Buffalo, 1970, PhD, 1971. Faculty rsch. fellow Nat. Bur. Econ. Rsch., Cambridge, Mass., 1972-73; assoc. prof. econs. U. Wis., Milw., 1978—, dir. Social Sci. Rsch. Facility, 1982—; vis. prof. So. Meth. U., Dallas, 1981-82, Justus Liebig U., Giessen, Fed. Republic Germany, summer 1990, U. Cambridge, Eng., 1989-90; cons. NSF, World Bank, Nat. Bur. Econ. Rsch. Contbr. articles to profl. jours. Mem. edn. bd. St. Roberts Sch., Milw., 1985-88; mem. steering com. Luth. Campus Ministry, Milw., 1987-88; sec. Sikh Religious Soc. Milw., 1986-88. Recipient rsch. awards Nat. Bur. Econ. Rsch., Cambridge, 1972-74, NSF, 1981-82, 89-90. Mem. Am. Econ. Assn., Econometric Soc., Regional Sci. Assn., Am. Statis. Assn. (bd. dirs. Milw. chpt. 1988-89). Democrat. Home: 2710 N Summit Ave Milwaukee WI 53211-3854 Office: U Milwaukee Soc Sci Rsch Facility Milwaukee WI 53211

ARPS, DAVID FOSTER, electronics engineer; b. Napoleon, Ohio, July 28, 1948; s. Fred B. and Melba Lavern (Harrison) A.; m. Vickie Lee Westrick, Mar. 19, 1982; children: Derek, Elizabeth. BS in Astronomy, Case Inst. Tech., 1970; MAT in Physics, Bowling Green State U., 1975; MS in Atmospheric Physics, U. Nev., Reno, 1977. Cert. secondary edn. and community coll. tchr. Astronomy instr. U. Toledo, Ohio, 1970; physics tchr. Napoleon (Ohio) High Sch., 1970-74; teaching asst. Bowling Green (Ohio) State U., 1974-75; rsch. fellow Desert Rsch. Inst., Reno, 1975-78; mech. engr., physicist Naval Air Warfare Ctr., Aircraft Div., Indpls., 1978-84, electronics engr., failure analyst, 1984—; astronomical rschr. Ritter Obs., U. Toledo, Ohio, 1970; solar radiation rschr. Desert Rsch. Inst., Reno, 1975-78. Mem. PTA, Mt. Comfort (Ind.) Elem., 1989-95; asst. coach Mt. Comfort (Ind.) Elem. Sports, 1992-95. Recipient Rsch. fellowships Desert Rsch. Inst., Reno, 1975-78. Mem. Ind. Astron. Soc., Sigma Pi Sigma. Methodist. Home: 7041 W Glendale Ln Greenfield IN 46140-9658 Office: Naval Air Warfare Ctr Aircraft Div 6000 E 21st St Indianapolis IN 46219-2189

ARRATHOON, LEIGH ADELAIDE, medievalist, editor, writer; b. N.Y.C., Nov. 30, 1942; d. Henry and Peggy Adelaide (Weed) A.; m. Raymond Arrathoon, June 10, 1967. Cours de Vacances at U. de Genève, Lausanne, Lille at Boulogne-sur-mer, 1961-63; AB in French and Spanish, Hunter Coll., 1963; MA in French, Stanford U., 1966, MA in Spanish, 1968; MA in Medieval French Lit., Princeton U., 1975, PhD in Medieval French Lit., 1975. Mem. UN Secretariat, N.Y.C., 1963-64; teaching asst., Stanford U., 1964-66; tchr. Spanish and French, Convent of Sacred Heart, Menlo Park, Calif., 1966-67; asst. prof. Spanish, Rider Coll., Trenton, N.J., 1970-71; pub. editor-in-chief Solaris Press, Troy, Idaho, 1975-80, Rochester, Mich., 1980-86; pres. Solaris Press II, 1986—; pres., advt./mktg. A.D. Images, Inc., 1986—; v.p. John J. Davio, Rochester, Mich.; pres. the Arrathoon-Davio Pub. Co. Scholar Centre d'Art Dramatique, 1957. Mem. MLA, Medieval Acad. Am., Courtly Lit. Soc., Sigma Delta Pi, Alpha Gamma Delta. Author: Woody Dicovers A New Kind of Tree: A Storybook to Color, 1996, The Man Who Changed the World: A Storybook to Color, 1996; contbg. editor: The Craft of Fiction: Essays in Medieval Poetics, 1984; editor, translator The Lady of Vergi, 1984; contbg. editor: Chaucer and the Craft of Fiction, 1986, numerous fictional short stories, articles to South Hill Gazette (weekly periodical), 1985-90. Office: PO Box 547 Rochester MI 48307

ARREOLA, PHILIP, police officer; b. Acambro, Oto, Mex., Feb. 4, 1940; came to U.S., 1943; s. Miguel Castro and Pauline (Szgiel) A.; m. Sandra Sauve, July 10, 1960; children: Richelle, Lisa, Gabrielle. BS with distinction, Wayne State U., 1974, JD, 1985; grad., FBI Nat. Acad., 1977, FBI Nat. Execs. Inst., 1990. Successively police cadet, patrolman, detective, sgt., lt., insp. Detroit Police Dept., 1960-76, comdr., 1976-87, ret., 1987; chief of police Port Huron (Mich.) Police Dept., 1987-89, Milw. Police Dept., 1989—. Chmn. Detroit Archdiocese Cath. Appeal, 1986; bd. dirs. Boys and Girls Club, Milw., 1991—; chair adv. com. Holton Youth Ctr., 1991—. Recipient medal for valor Detroit Police Dept., 1986; rsch. fellow Harvard U., 1970-71. Mem. ABA, Maj. Cities Chiefs Assn., Internat. Assn. Chiefs of Police, Police Athletic League (bd. dirs. 1990—), Hispanic Assn. Police Command Officers, Mich. Bar Assn. Office: Milw Police Dept 749 W State St Milwaukee WI 53233-1418

ARRINGTON, MICHAEL BROWNE, travel management company executive; b. Chgo., Mar. 24, 1943; s. W. Russell and Ruth Marian (Browne) A.; m. DeEtta Jane Watson, Dec. 15, 1966 (div. 1969); m. Trudi Jeanne Robertson, Dec. 4, 1971 (div. 1992); children: Jennifer Lorraine, Patrick Browne. AA, Kendall Coll., Evanston, Ill.; BA in Polit. Sci., U. Ill. Adminstrv. asst. to Senate Majority Leader State of Ill., Springfield, 1966-67; dir. pub. affairs Union League Club of Chgo., 1967-68; exec. dir. South Loop Improvement Orgn., Chgo., 1968-69; pres., chief exec. officer The Arrington Found., Chgo., 1979—, Arrington Travel Ctr., Inc., Chgo., 1969—; mem. bd. advisors Echols Internat. Travel and Hotel Schs., Inc., Chgo., 1970—; bd. dirs. Better Bus. Bur., Chgo.; mem. adv. bd. Classic Custom Vacations, Chgo. Conv. and Tourism Bur.; mem. Nat. White House Conf. Travel and Tourism, Preferred Hotels and Resorts Worldwide Travel Agt. Adv. Bd., Disting. Entrepreneurship Bd., U. Ill., Chgo. Bd. dirs. Robert R. McCormick Chgo. Boys & Girls Club, 1982—, Friends of Prentice Hosp., Chgo., 1986—, Access to Edn. Found., 1993. Cpl. USMC, 1962-64. Named to Outstanding Young Men of Am., The Outstanding Ams. Found., 1970, Who's Who in Chgo. Bus., Crain's Chgo. Bus. mag., 1989-96, finalist Entrepreneur of Yr. 1989, 90; recipient Excellence in Phys. Fitness award USMC, 1962, Man of Yr. Ill. Vietnam Vets. Leadership Program, 1993, Significant Contbn. to Dental Health award Ill. Dental Health Soc., 1967; inducted into Hall of Fame Nat. Assn. Trade and Tech. Schs., 1988, Entrepreneurship Hall of Fame, Chgo., 1994. Mem. Am. Soc. Travel Agts., World Pres.'s Orgn., Econ. Club of Chgo., Pacific Asia Travel Assn., Chgo. Club, Union League, Westmoreland Country Club, 100 Club Cook County, Chgo. Pres.'s Orgn., Travel Bus. Roundtable, Chief Execs. Orgn. Republican. Episcopalian. Office: Arrington Travel Ctr Inc 55 W Monroe St Ste 3800 Chicago IL 60603-5012

ARROYO, RODNEY LEE, city planning and transportation consultant; b. Miami, Fla., Dec. 31, 1958; s. Julian Avelino and Marilyn (Marsh) A.; m. Leslie Ponessa; children: Nicholas Julian, Anthony Eugene. BA cum laude, U. South Fla., 1980; M in city planning, Ga. Inst. Tech., 1982. Asst. dir. South Fla. Regional Planning Coun., Hollywood, Fla., 1982-86; sr. assoc. Barton Aschman Assocs., Inc., Southfield, Mich., 1986-89; v.p. Birchler Arroyo Assoc., Inc., Berkley, Mich., 1989—; founder and editor, Planning Mich. Magazine, 1988-91. Contbr. articles to profl. jours. Mem. Inst. Transp. Engrs. (sub. com. mem. 1986—), Am. Planning Assn. (Mich. exec. com. 1989-91), Am. Inst. Cert. Planners. Office: Birchler Arroyo Assocs Inc 3248 Greenfield Rd Berkley MI 48072

ARSENOVIC, ALEXANDER, physician; b. Beograd, Yugoslavia, Dec. 19, 1928; s. Ilija and Anna (Muk) A.; v. Vukosava Dokovic, Oct. 4, 1954; children: Ilija, Nanka Arsenovic Schneider. MD, U. Beograd, 1953. Diplomate Am. Bd. Family Practice, Am. Bd. Quality Assurance; lic. physician, Pa. Internist/infectologist Univ. Clinics, Beograd, 1954-58; specialist-infectologist, chief of clin. lab. Health Ctr. Vracar, Beograd, 1958-68; resident in family practice Edgewater Hosp., Chgo., 1969-70; internist VA Hosps., various locations, 1970-86; pvt. practice family practitioner and geriatrician Community Med. Ctr. of Burgettstown, Kansas City, Mo., 1986—. Fellow Am. Geriatrics Soc.; mem. Am. Acad. Family Practice. Home: 8207 NW Westside Dr Weatherby Lake MO 64152

ARTHUR, CHARLES GEMMELL, IV, accountant; b. St. Louis, Jan. 28, 1965; s. Charles Gemmell III and Mary Elizabeth (Senes) A.; m. Denise Renee Dougherty, June 13, 1987. BSBA in Acctg. and BS in Econs., S.E. Mo. State U., 1987; MBA in Internat. Studies, Lindenwood Coll., 1990. CPA. Fiscal analyst McDonnell Douglas Corp., St. Louis, 1987-90, sr. acct., 1990-93; sr. spl. acct., 1993—. Recipient U.S. Congl. Gold medal for svc., achievement and initiative, 1987. Mem. Mensa. Methodist. Home: 8750 North Ave Saint Louis MO 63114-4117

ARTHUR ESTNER, CHARTHEL, artistic director; b. L.A., Oct. 8, 1946; d. Charles Joseph and Thelma Katrina (Simonson) A.; m. Robert Marc Estner, Apr. 1, 1971; 1 child, Daniel Adam Estner. Prin. dancer Joffrey Ballet, N.Y.C., 1964-78; instr. Joffrey Workshop, San Antonio, 1981-92; co-dir. Summerfest Sch., Grand Rapids, Mich., 1983-88; artistic dir. Grand Rapids Ballet, 1988—. Office: Grand Rapids Ballet 233 E Fulton St Ste 126 Grand Rapids MI 49503-3200

ARTZT, EDWIN LEWIS, consumer products company executive; b. N.Y.C., Apr. 15, 1930; s. William and Ida A.; m. Ruth Nadine Martin, May 12, 1950; children—Wendy Anne, Karen Susan, William M., Laura Grace, Elizabeth Louise. B.J., U. Oreg., 1951. Account exec. Glasser Gailey Advt. Agy., L.A., 1952-53; with Procter & Gamble Co., Cin., 1953-75, brand mgr. advt. dept., 1956-58, asso. brand promotion mgr., 1958-60, brand promotion mgr., 1960, 62-65, copy mgr., 1960-62, advt. mgr. paper products div., 1965-68, mgr. products food div., 1968-69, v.p., 1969, v.p., acting mgr. coffee div., 1970, v.p., group exec., 1970-75, dir., 1972-75, 80-95, exec. v.p. then vice chmn., 1980-89; group v.p. Procter & Gamble Co., Europe, Belgium, 1975-80; pres. Procter & Gamble Internat., 1984-89, chmn., chief exec. officer, 1989-95; bd. dir. GTE Corp. Past chmn. residential div. United Appeal; past chmn. Public Library Capital Funds campaign; past dist. chmn. Capital Fund Raising dr. Boy Scouts Am., past leadership tng. chmn.; past chmn. advt. com. Sch. Tax Levy, County Govt. Issue; past trustee Kansas City Philharmonic, Nutrition Found., Boys' Clubs Greater Cin.; past bd. dirs. Kansas City Lyric Theater; past bd. govs. Kansas City Art Inst. Mem. Am. C. of C. Belgium (v.p.), Conf. Bd. Europe (adv. council), Internat. C. of C. (exec. com. U.S. council), Nat. Fgn. Trade Council. Clubs: Queen City (Cin.), Cin. Country (Cin.), Comml. (Cin.). Home: 9005 Cunningham Rd Cincinnati OH 45243-1503 Office: Procter & Gamble Co 1 Procter Gamble Plz Cincinnati OH 45202*

ARVIN, CHARLES STANFORD, librarian; b. Loogootee, Ind., Apr. 17, 1931; s. Leland Stanford and Mary Hope (Armstrong) A.; AB, Wayne State U., 1953, postgrad., 1956-57; MA in Libr. Sci., U. Mich. 1960. Asst. divisional Libr. U. Mich. Natural Sci. Libr., 1960-62; head reference Genesee County Libr., Flint, Mich., 1962-67, 77-83, head central services, 1967-77, head acquisitions, 1983-91; ret.. Served with AUS, 1953-56. Mem. Mich. Hist. Soc., Ind. Hist. Soc., Genesee County Hist. Soc., ACLU. Editor: Flint Geneal. Quar., 1981-95. Home: 702 W Oliver St Owosso MI 48867-2220

ASAAD, KOLLEEN JOYCE, special education educator; b. West Union, Iowa, July 13, 1941; d. Leonard Henry and Catherine Adelade (Bishop) Anfinson; children: Todd, Robin, Tara, Jason. BA in Elem. Edn., Upper Iowa U., 1961; MA in Spl. Edn. and Adminstrn., U. Cin., 1973. Elem. tchr. Fredericksburg (Iowa) Elem. Sch., 1961-62, Tyler Sch., Cedar Rapids, Iowa, 1962-64, Oasis Sch., 29 Palms, Calif., 1964-69, Longfellow Sch., Waterloo, Iowa, 1969-70; spl. edn. tchr. Fairview Sch., Cin., 1970-77; learning disabilities tchr. Lincoln Sch., Portsmouth, Ohio, 1977-78; dir. spl. edn. Vermilion Assn. for Spl. Edn., Danville, Ill., 1978-94; dir. edn. Swann Spl. Care Ctr., Champaign, Ill., 1994—; mem. Govtl. Rels. Com., Ill. Coun. for Exceptional Children, Jacksonville, Ill., 1992. Bd. mem. Crosspoints, Danville, Catlin Music Boosters, pres.; active Catlin Athletic Boosters. Named Best Adminstr., Regional Supt. of Schs., 1991. Mem. Coun. for Exceptional Children, Coun. for Adminstrs. of Spl. Edn., Ill. Adminstrs. of Spl. Edn., Assn. for Persons with Severe Handicaps, Exec. Club. Lutheran. Home: 122 Mapleleaf St Catlin IL 61817-9646 Office: Swann Spl Care Ctr 109 Kenwood Rd Champaign IL 61821-2905

ASADI, ASAD, mechanical engineer, educator; b. Shiraz, Fars, Iran, Jan. 28, 1946; came to U.S., 1971; s. Mohammad Asadzadeh-Fard and Bibi (Payravi) Payravi; m. Anita Murlene Wallace, Feb. 25, 1972; children: Soraya, Ali. BSME, U. Iowa, 1975, MS in Mech. Engring., 1976, MSEE, 1987. Indsl. supr. Isfahan (Iran) Steel Complex, 1968-69; dir. engring. St. Ambrose U., Davenport, Iowa, 1977-79; instr. engring. Scott Community Coll., Bettendorf, Iowa, 1981-83; mech. engr. Rock Island (Ill.) Arsenal, 1981-89; gen. engr., value engring. team leader Hdqrs. AMCCOM U.S. Army, Rock Island, Ill., 1989-90, asst. mgr., dep. value engring program for procurement and readiness directorate, 1990—. Mem. Scott County YMCA, Davenport, 1986. Recipient On the Spot award Dept. of the Army, 1987, Spl. Svc. award Dept. of the Army, 1987, Army Meritorious award, 1990. Mem. Fed. Mgrs. Assn., Soc. Automative Engrs., ASME, Soc. Am. Value Engrs., Am. Inst. Indsl. Engrs., Quad City Sci. and Engring. Coun. Office: Armament Munitions Command Us Army Amsmc Pdv Hdqr Rock Island IL 61299

ASBED, MONA H., healthcare administrator, university coordinator; b. Huntington, W.Va., Oct. 5, 1935; d. John Alfred and Esta Elma Houston; children: Steven, Jeffrey, Julie. BA, U. Mo., St. Louis, 1977, MEd, 1982. Lic. profl. counselor, clin. social worker, Mo. Coord. program alcohol and drug awareness Southern Ill. U., Edwardsville; sr. specialist substance abuse Cigna Health Plan-MCC subs., St. Louis; mgr. program CD treatment for women Normandy Osteopathic Hosp. South, St. Louis; family therapist Deaconess Hosp., St. Louis; pvt. practice; clin. supr. Personal Performance Cons., St. Louis; appeals coord. Medco Behavioral Care Systems, 1993-95; clin. mgr. People Resources, St. Louis, 1995—. Profl. mem. Nat. Coun. on Alcoholism and Drug Abuse. Mem. Am. Assn. Counseling and Devel., Coalition on Alcoholism and Other Chem. Dependencies (past pres., v.p.), MAAC (bd. dirs.), Chi Sigma Iota. Office: People Resources 10900 Manchester Rd Ste 201 Saint Louis MO 63122

ASBERRY, HENRY ANTHONY, vocational school educator; b. Ironton, Mo., Apr. 14, 1944; s. William Henry and Blanche (Ratliff) A.; m. Carol Sue Brewer, June 25, 1966; children: Karen Elizabeth, Amy Lynn. BS in Agriculture, U. Mo., 1969, MEd, 1975, postgrad., 1975-89. Cert. tchr., Mo. X-ray technician Crane Mfg., St. Louis, 1965; painter Columbia, Mo., 1965-66; trainee Farmer's Home Adminstrn., Columbia, Mo., 1968; yardman Columbia, Mo., 1966-69; vocat. agrl. inst. Mex. (Mo.) Pub. Sch., 1969-71, Doniphan (Mo.) Pub. Sch., 1971-76; vets. agrl. inst. Three Rivers Community Coll., Poplar Bluff, Mo., 1976-77; vocat. agrl. instr. West Plains (Mo.) R-7 Sch., 1977-92; welder, machinist instr. S.W. Mobil Systems, West Plains, 1992-93, R-7 Sch., West Plains, 1993—. Deacon First Bapt. Ch., West Plains, 1987—, Sunday Sch. dir., 1987—. With USN, 1963-65. Named Hon. State Farmer, Mo. Assn. Future Farmers of Am., 1980. Mem. Nat. Vocat. Agrl. Tchrs. Assn., Am. Vocat. Agril. Tchrs. Assn. (dist. pres. 1987, Disting. Svc. award 1983), Am. Vocat. Assn., Mo. Vocat. Assn., Mo. State Tchrs. Assn., West Plains Community Tchrs. Assn. (pres. 1987-88). Home: 4823 Marianna Dr West Plains MO 65775-5359

ASCH, SUSAN MCCLELLAN, pediatrician; b. Cleve., Dec. 31, 1945; d. William Alton and Alice Lonore (Heide) McClellan; m. Marc Asch, Sept. 10, 1966; children: Marc William, Sarah Susan, Rebecca Janney. AB, Oberlin (Ohio) Coll., 1967; MA, Mich. State U., 1968, PhD, 1975; MD, Case Western Res., 1977. Diplomate Nat. Bd. Med. Examiners, Am. Bd. Pediatrics (task force, sub-bd. emergency pediatrics 1987-93), Am. Bd. Emergency Pediatrics. Instr. sociology Mich. State U., East Lansing, 1971-73; resident in pediatrics Children's Nat. Med. Ctr., Washington, 1977-80; asst. to dir. Office for Med. Applications of Rsch. NIH, Bethesda, 1980-81; pvt. practice in pediatrics Millinocket (Maine) Regional Hosp., 1981-84; assoc. dir. emergency Akron (Ohio) Children's Hosp., 1984-87; asst. prof. pediatrics Northeastern Ohio U. Coll. Medicine, 1984-87; dir. emergency St. Paul Children's Hosp., 1987-91; asst. prof. pediatrics U. Minn., 1987-93, clin. assoc. prof., 1993-96; pvt. practice in pediatrics Stillwater (Minn.) Med. Group, 1992—; nat. faculty PALS Am. Heart Assn., Mpls., Dallas, 1987-94; mem. task force, sub-bd. emergency pediatrics Am. Bd. Pediatrics, 1987-93. Assoc. editor Pediatric Emergency Medicine, 1992, contbr., 1992, 96. State bd. dirs., affiliate faculty PALS Minn. affiliate Am. heart Assn., 1988-93, 96—; chairperson SIDS task force, Minn. Dept. Maternal and Child Health, St. Paul, 1990-92. Mem. Am. Acad. Pediatrics (nat. faculty advanced pediatric life support 1989—, exec. com. sect. on emergency pediatrics 1988-90, chair Minn. emergency pediatric com. 1989-91, Svc. commendation 1991), Minn. Med. Assn. (emergency svcs. com. 1990), Rotary Internat., Alpha Omega Alpha (Ohio chpt., Minn. chpt.). Democrat. Quaker. Home: 34 N Oaks Rd North Oaks MN 55127-6325 Office: Stillwater Med Group 921 Greeley St S Stillwater MN 55082-5935

ASCHAUER, CHARLES JOSEPH, JR., corporate director, former company executive; b. Decatur, Ill., July 23, 1928; s. Charles Joseph and Beulah Diehl (Kniple) A.; m. Elizabeth Claire Meagher, Apr. 28, 1962; children: Karen A. Vorwald, Thomas Arthur, Susan A. Baisley, Karl Andrew. B.B.A., Northwestern U., 1950; certificate internat. bus. adminstr., Centre d'Etudes Industrielles, Geneva, Switzerland, 1951. Prin. McKinsey & Co., Chgo., 1955-62; v.p. mktg. Mead Johnson Labs. div. Mead Johnson & Co., Evansville, Ind., 1962-67; v.p., pres. automotive group Maremont Corp., Chgo., 1967-70; v.p., group exec. Whittaker Corp., Los Angeles, 1970-71; v.p., pres. hosp. products div. Abbott Labs., North Chicago, Ill., 1971-76; v.p., group exec. Abbott Labs., 1976-79, exec. v.p., dir., 1979-89, ret., 1989; bd. dirs. Trustmark Ins. Co., Lake Forest, Ill., The Linc Group, Chgo., Rsch. Med. Corp., Salt Lake City, QLT Phototherapeutics Inc., Vancouver, Boston Sci. Corp., Watertown, Mass.; adv. bd. Shaw Med. Mgmt. Corp., San Francisco. Lt. Supply Corps, USNR, 1951-55. Mem. Univ. Club Chgo., Econs. Club Chgo., Sunset Ridge Country Club, Fairbanks Ranch Country Club.

ASCHER, CHRIS J., stockbroker; b. Mpls., Jan. 4, 1959; s. James L. and Geraldine (Magda) A. BA, Augsburg U., Mpls., 1981. Stockbroker Merrill Lynch, Edina, Minn., 1982-85, Dean Witter Reynolds, Bloomington, Minn., 1985—. Home: 10945 Sumter Ave S Bloomington MN 55438-2370 Office: Dean Witter Reynolds 8300 Norman Center Dr Ste 1150 Bloomington MN 55437-1027

ASCHER, JAMES JOHN, pharmaceutical executive; b. Kansas City, Mo., Oct. 2, 1928; s. Bordner Fredrick and Helen (Barron) A.; m. Mary Ellen Robitsch, Feb. 27, 1954; children: Jill Denise, James John, Christopher Bordner. Student, Bergen Jr. Coll., 1947-48, U. Kans., 1946-47, 49-51. Rep. B.F. Ascher & Co., Inc., Memphis, 1954-55; asst. to pres. B.F. Ascher & Co., Inc., Kansas City, Mo., 1956-57, v.p., 1958-64, pres., 1965—. Bd. dirs. Childrens Cardiac Ctr., 1964-70, pres., 1968-70; mem. cen. governing bd. Children's Mercy Hosp., 1968-80; bd. dirs. Jr. Achievement of Middle Am., 1970-90, pres., 1973-76, chmn., 1979-81; edn. chmn. Young Pres.'s Orgn. 6th Internat. Univ. for Pres., Athens, 1975. 1st. lt. inf., U.S. Army, 1951-53, Korea. Decorated Bronze Star, Combat Infantryman's Badge. Mem. VFW, Am. Mgmt. Assn. (pres.'s assn.), Kansas City C. of C., Pharm. Rsch. and Mfrs. Am., Drug, Chem. and Allied Trades Assn., World Pres.' Orgn., Nonprescription Drug Mfrs. Assn., Chief Execs. Orgn., Midwest Pharm. Advt. Club, Sales and Advt. Execs. Club, Lotos Club, N.Y. Athletic Club, Kansas City Club, Mercury Club, Indian Hills Country Club, Delta Chi. Home: 6706 Glenwood St Shawnee Mission KS 66204-1451 Office: 15501 W 109th St Lenexa KS 66219-1307

ASH, MAJOR MCKINLEY, JR., dentist, educator; b. Bellaire, Mich., Apr. 7, 1921; s. Major McKinley Sr. and Helen Marguerite (Early) A.; m. Fayola Foltz, Sept. 2, 1947; children: George McKinley, Carolyn Marguerite, Jeffrey LeRoy, Thomas Edward. BS, Mich. State U., 1947; DDS, Emory U., 1951; MS, U. Mich., 1954; Doctoris Medicine Honoris Causa, U. Bern, 1975. Instr. sch. dentistry Emory U., Atlanta, 1952-53; instr. U. Mich., Ann Arbor, 1953-56, asst. prof., 1956-59, assoc. prof., 1959-62, prof., 1962—, chmn. dept. occlusion, sch. dentistry, 1962-87, dir. stomatognathic physiology lab., sch. dentistry, 1969-87, dir. TMJ/oral facial pain clinic, sch. dentistry, 1983-87, Marcus L. Ward prof. dentistry, 1984-89, prof. emeritus, rsch. scientist emeritus, 1989—; cons. N.E. Regional Dental Bd., 1989—; vis. prof. U. Bern, 1989, U. Tex., San Antonio, 1990—; pres. Basic Sci. Bd., State of Mich., 1962-74; cons. over the counter drugs FDA, Washington, 1985-89. Author, co-author 54 textbooks, 1958—; editor 4 books; contbr. 171 articles to profl. jours. Served to tech. sgt. Signal Corps, US Army, 1942-45, ETO. Nat. Inst. Dental Research grantee, 1962-85. Fellow Am. Coll. Dentists, Internat. Coll. Dentists, European Soc. Craniomandibular Disorders; mem. AAAS, Am. Dental Assn. (cons. coun. on dental therapeutics 1982—, cons. coun. sci. affairs 1995—), N.Y. Acad. Scis., Washtenaw Dist. Dental Soc. (pres. 1963-64), Phi Kappa Phi. Presbyterian. Office: U of Mich Sch of Dentistry Ann Arbor MI 48109

ASH, MITCHELL GRAHAM, history educator; b. Mineola, N.Y., Sept. 26, 1948; s. Warren Howard and Carol Ann (Loeb) A.; m. Christiane Hartnack, Jan. 2, 1989. BA, Amherst Coll., 1970; AM, Harvard U., 1973, PhD, 1982; postgrad., Free U. Berlin, 1977-82. Rsch. assoc. Psychol. Inst., U. Mainz, Germany, 1982-84; asst. prof. history U. Iowa, Iowa City, 1984-89, assoc. prof., 1989—; vis. prof. U. Goettingen, Germany, 1992, U. Vienna, Austria, 1993; mem. editorial bd. Isis, Madison, Wis., 1991-94. Psychologie und Geschichte, Heidelberg, Germany, 1990—. Author: Gestalt Psychology in German Culture 1890-1967, 1995; editor: (wsith W.R. Woodward) The Problematic Science: Psychology in Nineteenth-Century Thought, 1982, (with U. Geuter) Geschichte der deutschen Psychologie im 20. Jahrhundert, 1985, (with Woodward) Psychology in Twentieth-Century Thought and Society, 1987, (with A. Soellner) Forced Migration and Scientific Change, 1996; gen. editor Cambridge Studies in the History of Psychology, 1988—; contbr. chpts. to books, articles to profl. jours. Bd. dirs. Iowa City Fgn. Rels. Coun., 1990—; mem. adv. bd. Iowa City Sci. Ctr., 1992—. Fulbright fellow, 1978-80, German Rsch. coun. postdoctoral fellow, 1982-84, NSF rsch. fellow, 1986-87, 95—, Inst. Advanced Study Berlin fellow, 1990-91; U. Iowa Faculty scholar, 1992-95. Mem. History of Sci. Soc., Am. Hist. Assn., Brit. Soc. History of Sci., Gesellschaft fuer Wissenschaftengeschichte (governing bd. 1996—), Internat. Soc. for History of Social and Behavioral Scis., Internat. Soc. for History of Psychoanalysis, Forum for History of Human Sci. (steering com. 1991-92, chair 1992—). Democrat. Jewish. Office: U Iowa Dept History W 616 Seashore Hall Iowa City IA 52242-1409

ASHBACHER, CHARLES DAVID, computer programmer, educator, mathematician; b. Fort Riley, Kans., Sept. 24, 1954; s. Rudolph Carl and Paula Louis (Enos) A.; m. Valencia Sue Ashbacher, Oct. 27, 1973 (div. May 1984); m. Mary L. Rhiner, Dec. 14, 1991 (div. Mar. 1994); 1 child, Katrina. AS, Kirkwood Community Coll., Cedar Rapids, Iowa, 1978; BS, Mount Mercy Coll., 1980. Instr. math. and computer sci. Mount Mercy Coll., Cedar Rapids, 1983-89; instr. computers Kirkwood C.C., Cedar Rapids, 1990—; rsch. programmer U. Iowa, Iowa City, 1990-92; rsch. scientist Decisionmark, Cedar Rapids, Iowa, 1993—; rev. panelist Math. and Computer Edn., Hicksville, N.Y., 1990—. Mem. editl. bd. Jour. Recreational Math., 1991, Recreational and Ednl. Computing, 1989—, Smarandache Nations, 1994—, An Introduction to the Smarandache Function, 1995; author: Collection of Problems On Smarandache Notions, 1996; PC software revs. editor, videotape revs. editor Math. and Computer Edn.; mem. editl. bd. contests in math. series; rev. panelist UMAP Jour. (Jour. Undergrad. Math. and Its Applications); contbr. articles to profl. jours.; editor of unsolved problems column of Smarandache Notions; editor of problems column of Smarandache Notions. Basketball coach YMCA, 1990—; judge local sci. fair; active local PTA. Mem. AAAS, IEEE, Am. Math. Soc., Am. Assn. Artificial Intelligence, Am. Math. Assn. Two-Yr. Colls. (mem. rev. panel Am. Math. Assn. Two-Yr. Colls. Rev. 1990—), Assn. Automated Reasoning, Assn. Computing Machinery, Math. Assn. Am., Fibonacci Assn. Home: 119 Northwood Dr Hiawatha IA 52233

ASHCROFT, JOHN DAVID, senator; b. Chgo., May 9, 1942; m. Janet Elise; children: Martha, Jay, Andrew. B cum laude, Yale U., 1964; JD, U. Chgo., 1967. Bar: Mo., U.S. Supreme Ct. Assoc. prof. S.W. Mo. State U., Springfield, 1967-72; pvt. practice Springfield, 1967-73; state auditor State of Mo., 1973-75, asst. atty. gen., 1975-77, atty. gen., 1977-84, gov., 1985-92; atty. Suelthaus and Kaplan P.C., 1993-94; U.S. senator from Mo., 1995—, mem. commerce, sci. and transp. coms., mem. fgn. rels. com., mem. labor and human resources com.; mem. Presdl. Adv. Coun. Intergovtl. Affairs; nat. chmn. Edn. Commn. States, 1987-88; chmn. Nat. Govs. Assn. Task Force on Coll. Quality, 1985, Nat. Govs. Assn. Task Force on Adult Literacy. Gospel singer: records include In the Spirit of Life and Liberty, The Gospel According to John; author: (with wife) College Law for Business, 7th, 8th, 9th, 10, 11th edits., It's the Law, 1979-91; contbr. articles to profl. jours. Chmn. Task Force on Adult Literacy, Task Force on College Quality Nat. Gov.'s Assn., 1991; chmn. Rep. Gov.'s Assn., 1990; co-chmn. Rep. Platform Com., 1992. Mem. ABA (ho. of dels.), Mo. Bar Assn., Cole County Bar Assn., Nat. Assn. Attys. Gen. (pres. 1980-81, chmn. budget com., exec. com., Wyman award 1983), Nat. Govs. Assn. (vice chmn. 1990, chmn. 1991-92, chmn. Pres.'s Commn. on Urban Families 1992). Republican. Mem. Assembly of God Ch. Office: 170 Russell Senat Bldg Washington DC 20510-2504*

ASHCROFT, RICHARD CARTER, controller; b. East Orange, N.J., Sept. 6, 1942; s. Herbert and Grace Alberta (Schwalb) A.; m. Gail P. Cook, Sept. 12, 1964 (div. May 1, 1981); children: Janet Lynn, Scott Carter; m. Marlene Ann Krueger, Jan. 23, 1982. BA in Econs., Grove City Coll., 1964; postgrad., U. Rochester, 1964-66. Asst. controller Schlegel Corp., Rochester, N.Y., 1972-73; adminstrv. mgr. Schlegel Tenn., Inc., Maryville, Tenn., 1973-74, controller, 1975-76, controller, asst. treas., 1977-79; group fin. dir. Schlegel U.K. Ltd., Leeds, Eng., 1979-80; corporate mgr. acctg. Schlegel Corp., Rochester, N.Y., 1980-83; controller, chief fin. officer Sugardale Foods, Inc., Canton, Ohio, 1983-86; pres., dir. Rotek, Inc., Aurora, Ohio, 1986-88; corporate controller Nesco, Inc., Cleve., 1988—; pres. Ashcroft Assocs. Inc., 1989—; also chmn., 1993—. Fin. chmn. St. Luke's Episc. Ch., Fairport, N.Y., 1983; chmn. Girls Clubs Am., Maryville, Tenn., 1978, treas., 1977. Mem. Prestwick Country Club (Uniontown, Ohio). Democrat. Methodist. Home: 98 Jefferson Dr Hudson OH 44236-2110

ASHE, REID, publishing executive; b. 1948. Student, MIT. With Tech. Rev., Boston, 1971-72; asst. editor Washington (N.C.) Daily News, 1972-73; reporter, editl. writer, editl. page editor Jackson (Tenn.) Sun, 1973-84, exec. editor, 1974-78, editor, pub., pres., 1978-84; gen. exec. Knight-Ridder Inc., 1984; CEO Viewdata Corp. (a subsidiary of Knight-Ridder Inc.), 1984-87; pres., pub. The Wichita (Kans.) Eagle, 1987—. Office: Wichita Eagle & Beacon Pub Co Box 820 825 E Douglas Ave Wichita KS 67202-3512*

ASHER, DONNA THOMPSON, psychiatric-mental health nurse; b. Kansas City, Mo., Aug. 29, 1933; d. William Volker and Frances Ellen (Todd) Thompson; 1 child, Janet Asher McKinney. RN, LPN, Kansas City Area Vo-Tech. Sch., Kans., 1989; student, Ft. Scott C.C., Paola, Kans., 1992-93, Sanford-Brown Coll., 1994. Cardiac catheterization technician Med. Ctr. U. Kans., 1953-57; lab. technician, chemistry lab. Greater Balt. Med. Ctr., rsch. asst., endocrinology and biochemistry lab. technician; practical nurse adult psychiat. unit U. Kans., Kansas City, 1989-91, Kans. State Sch. for the Blind, Kansas City, 1991-93; mem. alumni adv. bd. Kansas City Area Vo-Tech. Sch., 1990—. Home: 5315 W 95th Ter Shawnee Mission KS 66207-3209

ASHHURST, ANNA WAYNE, foreign language educator; b. Phila., Jan. 5, 1933; d. Astley Paston Cooper and Anne Pauline (Campbell) Ashhurst; m. Ronald G. Gerber, July 22, 1978. AB, Vassar Coll., 1954; MA, Middlebury Coll., 1956; PhD, U. Pitts., 1967. English tchr. Internat. Inst. Spain, Madrid, 1954-56; asst. prof. Juniata Coll., Huntingdon, Pa., 1961-63; asst. prof. Spanish dept. Franklin and Marshall Coll., Lancaster, Pa., 1968-74, acting chmn. Spanish dept., 1972, convenor, fgn. lang. council, 1972-74; assoc. prof. dept. modern fgn. langs. U. Mo., St. Louis, 1974-78. Author: La literatura hispano-americana en la crítica española, 1980. Mem. Welcome Wagon of Lancaster, Pa., 1968-70, 71-74. Fulbright-Hays grantee, Colombia, S.Am., summer 1963; Ford Humanities fellow, summer 1970; Mellon fellow, 1970-71. Mem. AAUW (pres. Ferguson-Florissant br. 1989-91, 95—, chmn. St. Louis area interbranch coun. 1992-94, chair environ. task force Mo. 1992-95), Internat. Inst. in Spain, Instituto Internacional de Literatura Iberoamericana, Am. Assn. Tchrs. Spanish and Portuguese. Home: 2105 Barcelona Dr Florissant MO 63033-2805

ASHING, ROBERT W., manufacturing company executive; b. Grinnell, Iowa, Aug. 28, 1967. AS, Marshalltown (Iowa) C.C., 1986. Pres. Ashing Machine Tool Co., Grinnell, 1986—. Office: Ashing Machine Tool Co RR 3 Box 215 Grinnell IA 50112-9344

ASHKIN, RAJASPERI MALIAPEN, marketing executive; b. Penang, Malaysia, Mar. 1, 1956; came to U.S., 1984; d. Maliapen A.M.N. (Annasamy) and Jayaletchemi (Chelliah) M.; m. Ronald Evan Ashkin, Nov. 25, 1984. BS in Forestry, U. Canterbury, 1978, D.B.A., 1979. Mktg. asst. Forest Rsch. Inst., Rotorua, Nw Zealand, 1978-79; mktg. officer Consulate Gen. India, Sydney, Australia, 1980-81; nat. mktg. coord. Estee Lauder Ltd., Sydney, 1981-84; assoc. buyer Brown Store Group, Terre Haute, Ind., 1984-85; mktg. mgr. A.T.C. Time Inc., Terre Haute, 1985-87; v.p. New Concepts Inc., Terre Haute, 1987-90; chief exec. officer, mng. dir. Excelsior Corp., Terre Haute, 1990—, also bd. dirs.; mktg. & advt. cons. in field; organizer Christmas Food Drive Salvation Army, Terre Haute, 1985-86; vol. reader Vigo County Pub. Libr. Literacy Program, 1989—. Mktg. com. Leadership Terre Haute, 1986-87; TV moderator Valley Point of View, Terre Haute, 1986—; bd. dirs. YWCA, Terre Haute, 1986—; internat. rels. chairperson Altrusa Club, Terre Haute, 1985-87; cake bake chairperson, on site rep. Century Club, YWCA, 1986. Recipient Letter of Commendation Ralph Davidson Time Inc., 1986, Nat. System Mktg. award A.T.C. Time Inc., 1986, Grand Prize HBO Summer Sales Campaign, 1986, Letter of Commendation Disney Channel, 1986, Outstanding Creative Contbrn. award, 1987, Tempo TV award, 1987; named to Scholastic Honor Soc. Pamarista Ind. State U., 1989, Literacy Grante Internat. Network for Women, 2000 Notable Am. Women Hall of Fame, A.B.I., 1990, Woman of Yr., A.B.I., 1990, Internat. Leaders in Achievement, IBC, 1990. Mem. NAFE, India Assn. Terre Haute, United Hebrew Congregation Terre Haute, Country Club of Terre Haute, M.V.P. Club Larry Bird, Altrusa Club of Terre Haute, YWCA, Leadership Terre Haute. Office: Excelsior Corp Ste 6012 505 N Lake Shore Dr Chicago IL 60611-3411

ASHKIN, RONALD EVAN, international executive; b. New Rochelle, N.Y., Apr. 5, 1957; s. Abraham and Arleen (Wollins) A.; m. Rajasperi Maliapen, Nov. 25, 1984. AB magna cum laude, Harvard U., 1977; MBA, Wharton Sch., U. Pa., 1982. Cert. fin. planner. V.p. Continental Chem. Corp., Terre Haute, Ind., 1978-83, pres., 1983-86; pres. New Concepts Inc., Terre Haute, 1987-90, Excelsior Corp., Terre Haute, 1990-92; dir. internat.

sales Gold Eagle Co., Chgo., 1992-95, v.p. internat., 1995—; dir. Internat. Sales Hydrosol Inc., Bridgeview, Ill., 1994—; adj. faculty Sch. Bus., Ind. State U., 1991-92. Moderator TV show, Terre Haute, 1985-86. Mem. Terre Haute sch. adv. com., 1984-86; bd. dirs. Glenn Civic Ctr., Terre Haute, 1985-88; mem. mktg. edn. curriculum study com. Ind. Dept. Edn. Group study exch. grantee Rotary Found., Sri Lanka and India, 1985-86; Harvard U. scholar, 1973-76; recipient Ill. Gov.'s Export award, 1995, 96. Mem. Leadership Terre Haute Alumni Assn. (chmn. 1986), Am. Prodn. and Inventory Control Soc. (local v.p. 1982-84, 86, local pres. 1985), Overseas Automotive coun., Automotive Exporters Coun. (v.p. 1994—, pres. 1995—), Jr. Achievement (vol. cons.), Toastmasters (local v.p. 1981-82), Phi Beta Kappa. Home: 505 N Lake Shore Dr Ste 6012 Chicago IL 60611-3411 Office: Gold Eagle Co 4400 S Kildare Ave Chicago IL 60632-4317

ASHLEY, LYNN, educator, consultant, administrator; b. Rock Island, Ill., Nov. 18, 1920; d. Francis Ford and Cleo Marguerite (Monahan) Haynes; m. Edward Messenger Ashley, Aug. 16, 1946; children: Edward Jr., Ann Rice, Rebecca Pocisk, William. BS in Social Psychology, Union Inst., Cin., 1978; MEd., U. Cin., 1979, EdD, 1985. Clk. Lumberman's Mutual Casualty Co., Chgo., 1940-41; account asst. Quaker Oats Co., Chgo., 1941-43; riveter Douglas Aircraft Co., Chgo., 1943-44; organizer, dir. Forest Park Youth Ctr., Forest Park, Ohio, 1967-73; staffing coord. Presbytery of Cin., 1973-78; grad. teaching asst. U. Cin., 1978-84; pres. Nat. Corrective Tng. Inst., Cin., 1979—; adj. faculty, mem. undergrad. studies bd. Union Inst., 1986—; cons. Hamilton County Probation Dept., Warren County Juvenile Ct., 1987—; field rep. Women in Mil. Svc. for Am.; trainer, cons. Allen County Juvenile Ct. Councilwoman City of Forest Park, 1981-85, organizer cmty. rels. coun., 1983; mem. Cin.-Harare, Zimbabwe Sister Cities Assn., 1989—; mem. Ohio Gov.'s Adv. Com. on Women Vets., 1993—. With WAC, 1944-46. Recipient in Recognition award Forest Park City Coun., 1985, In Appreciation award Union Inst., 1987, Recognition award AMVETS, U. Cin., 1993, award Commonwealth of Ky., 1989. Mem. Am. Corrections Assn., Nat. Assn. Corrective Tng. Affiliates (pres. 1987—), Women's Army Corp Vet. Assn., Assn. Family and Conciliatiion Cts., Am. Probation and Parole Assn. Office: Nat Corrective Tng Inst 811 Hanson Dr Forest Park OH 45240-1921

ASHTIANI, CYRUS NAKHAII, electrical engineer, automotive executive; b. Tehran, Central, Iran, Sept. 13, 1949; came to U.S., 1985; s. Joseph Nakhaii and Pari (Shahandeh) A.; m. Shohreh Vafaie, Sept. 15, 1975; 1 child, Cyamak. BSEE, U. Tehran, 1972; MSEE, McGill U., 1981, DEng, 1984. Sr. engr. Sundstrand Corp., Rockford, Ill., 1985-87; dir. engring. Ansoft Corp., Pitts., 1987-91; chief engr. Gen. Signal Corp., Goldsboro, N.C., 1991-93; cons. Megnatis Consulting, Mill Creek, Wash., 1993-95; project mgr. Chrysler corp., Madison Heights, Mich., 1995—. Recipient Harold Helm award McGill U., 1992, 93, summer award, 1993. Sr. mem. IEEE. Home: 2318 Dorchester #201 Troy MI 48084

ASHTON, ELIZABETH ANN, information industry manager; b. Washington, Jan. 16, 1947; d. Robert H. Snedeker and Harriett Leeds (DePriest) Miller; m. Terry E. Naylor, May 11, 1985. BA, UCLA, 1968; spl. cert., Keio U., Tokyo, 1970; MA, U. So. Calif., 1972, PhD, 1977. Japanese market mgr. System Devel. Corp., Santa Monica, Calif., 1977-81; sales mgr. Lexis-Nexis, Dayton, Ohio, 1981-90; product mgr. Lexis-Nexis, N.Y.C., 1991—. Mem. NAFE, NOW, UCLA Alumni Assn. Democrat. Congregationalist. Home: 9643 Bridlewood Trl Dayton OH 45458 Office: Lexis-Nexis PO Box 933 Dayton OH 45401-0933

ASMA, LAWRENCE FRANCIS, priest; b. Waukegan, Ill., Oct. 21, 1947; s. Francis Victor and Isabelle Amelia (Recktenwald) A. BA in English, U. Wis., Whitewater, 1969; MA in English, Ill. State U., 1974; MA in Scripture magna cum laude, De Andreis Sem., 1982, MDiv, 1983. Ordained priest Roman Cath. Chr., 1983. Dir. spritual formation Cardinal Glennon Coll., St. Louis, 1983-85, instr. theology dept., 1983-85; chaplain St. Vincent's Div. DePaul Health Ctr., St. Louis, 1985—; Bd. dirs. Rosati Stabilization Ctr., St. Louis, 1988-94; vice chmn. Rosati Stabilization Ctr., 1990-94. Local religious superior Congregation of the Mission, 1994—. With USNR, 1970-72, Vietnam. Mem. Assn. Mental Health Clergy (bd. cert.), Cath. Biblical Assn., Congreation of Mission, Sigma Tau Delta. Office: DePaul Health Center 12303 De Paul Dr Bridgeton MO 63044-2512

ASNER, MARIE A., musician, classical; b. St. Cloud, Minn., Feb. 28, 1948; d. Emil C. and Minnie A. (Anderson) Black; m. Aug. 18, 1973. BS, St. Cloud State U., 1972, MS, 1969; PhD, Columbia Pacific U., 1986. Supr. music Mpls. Sch. Sys., 1972-78; reviewer entertainment Jour. Herald, Shawnee, Kans., 1981—; reviewer entertainment Wed. Mag., Kansas City, Mo., 1989—; chmn. Trinity Fine Arts Com., Mission, Kans., 1992—. Composer (piano) Caroling with Bach, 1987; author (poetry collection) Secret Place, 1989, Man of Miracles, Man of Miracles II, Inquiring Mind, (with Rochelle Holt) The Tree of Life; adv. bd. mem. Kansas City Film Soc., Potpourri Publs., Prairie Village, Kans. Mem. Internat. Guild Women Writers, Am. Fedn. Musicians, Am. Guild Organists, Music Tchrs. Nat. Assn., Poets and Writers, Kansas City Music Tchrs. Assn. (publicity com.), Nationally Cert. Tchrs. Music. Home: 9000 W 82d Pl Shawnee Mission KS 66204-3511

ASPEN, MARVIN EDWARD, federal judge; b. Chgo., July 11, 1934; s. George Abraham and Helen (Adelson) A.; m. Susan Alona Tubbs, Dec. 18, 1966; children: Jennifer Marion, Jessica Maile, Andrew Joseph. BS in Sociology, Loyola Univ., 1956; JD, Northwestern U., 1958. Bar: Ill., 1958. Individual practice Chgo., 1958-59; draftsman joint com. to draft new Ill. criminal code Chgo. Bar Assn.-Ill. Bar Assn., 1959-60; asst. state's atty. Cook County, Ill., 1960-63; asst. corp. counsel City of Chgo., 1963-71; pvt. practice law, 1971; judge Cir. Ct. Cook County, Ill., 1971-79; judge U.S. Dist. Ct. (ea. dist.) Ill., Chgo., 1979-95, chief judge, 1995—; Edward Avery Harriman adj. prof. law Northwestern U. Law Sch.; chmn. new judges, recent devels. in criminal law, and evidence coms. Ill. Judicial Conf., adv. bdd. Inst. Criminal Justice, John Marshall Sch. Law; mem. Ill. Law Enforcement Commmn., Gov. Ill. Adv. Commn. Criminal Justice, Cook County Bd. Corrections; chmn. assoc. rules com. Ill. Supreme Ct., com. on ordinance violation problems; vice chmn. com. on pattern jury instrns. in criminal cases; lectr. at judicial confs. and trial advocacy programs nationally and internationally; planner, participant in legal seminars at numerous schools including Harvard U., Emory U., U. Fla., Oxford U. (Eng.), U. Bologna, Nuremberg (Germany) U., U. Cairo, Egypt, U. Zimbabwe, U. Malta, U. The Philippines, U. Madrid; mem. Georgetown U. Law Ctr. Project on Plea Bargaining in U.S., spl. faculty NITA advanced Trial Advocacy Program introducing Brit. trial techniques to experienced Am. litigators, spl. faculty of ABA designed to acquaint Scottish lawyers with modern litigation and tech.; frequent faculty mem. Nat. Judiciary Coll., Fed. Judicial Ctr., U. Nev. (Reno), Nat. Inst. for Trial Advocacy, Colo.; bd. dir. Fed. Judicial Ctr.; mem. Judicial Conf. Com. on Adminstrn. of the Bankruptcy System, Trial Bar Implementation Com. on Civility of the 7th Fed. Cir. Coauthor Criminal Law for the Layman-A Citizen's Guide, 2d edit., 1977, Criminal Evidence for the Police, 1972, Protective Security Law, 1983; contbr. over twodozen articles to legal publs. Past mem. vis. com. Northwestern U. Sch. Law, chmn. adv. com. for short courses (post law sch. ednl. program); mem. vis. com. U. Chgo. Law Sch.; organizer, past pres. Northwestern Univ. Sch. of Law chpt. Amincourt Program U.S. Judicial Conf; past mem. Cook County Bd. Corrections, John Howard Assn. With USAF, 1958-59. Recipient Nat. Ctr. Freedom of Info. Studies award, Ctr. for Pub. Resources award, Nat. Ctr. for Freedom of Info. Studies award, Merit award Northwestern U. Alumni Assn.; named Person of Yr. Chgo. Lawyer, 1995. Mem. ABA (bd. govs., mem. ho. of dels., past chmn. exec. com. Nat. Conf. Fed. Trial Judges, past mem. coun. sect. litigation, past chmn. coun. sect. criminal justice, past co-chmn. liaison jud. com. sect. litigation, mem. jury comprehension study com.), Judicature Soc. Ill. (past chmn. coms.), Chgo. Bar Assn. (bd. mgrs. 1978-79, chmn. criminal law com., bd. editors Chgo. Bar Record, mem. commn. on criminal justice. coms. on contiuning legal edn., devel. of law, civil disorder and others), Ill. State Bar Assn. (chmn. pub. rels., corrections, fair trial/fr ee press, criminal law coms., mem. others), Northwestern U. Law Alumni Assn. (p ast pres., Merit award). Office: US Dist Ct 1946 US Courthouse 219 S Dearborn St Chicago IL 60604-1702

ASSALEY, LEWIS A., investment company executive; b. Charleston, W.Va., Sept. 3, 1947. BS, U. Cin., 1971, MA, 1973, PhD, 1979. Vis. prof. Cin. Inst. Justice, 1974-82, Miami U., Oxford, Ohio, 1982-83; sr. v.p. Prudential Securities Inc., Cin., 1983—. Pres. bd. trustees Greek Orthodox Ch., Cin., 1983—; mem. adv. bd. Drake Planetarium, Cin. Mem. Smith Soc. Office: Prudential Securities Inc 525 Vine St Ste 1900 Cincinnati OH 45202-3124

ASSANIS, DENNIS N. (DIONISSIOS ASSANIS), mechanical engineering educator; b. Athens, Greece, Feb. 9, 1959; came to U.S., 1980; s. Nicholas and Kyriaki Assanis; m. Helen Stavrianos, Aug. 25, 1984; children: Nicholas, Dimitris. BSc in Marine Engring. with distinction, Newcastle U., U.K., 1980; SMME, SM in Naval Arch. Marine Engring., MIT, 1982, PhD in Power and Propulsion, 1985, SM in Mgmt., 1986. Asst. prof. mech. engring. U. Ill., Urbana-Champaign, 1985-90, assoc. prof. mech. engring., 1990-94; assoc. prof. Nat. Ctr. for Supercomputing Applications, 1992-94, head thermal scis./systems divsn., 1992-94; prof. mech. engring. U. Mich., Ann Arbor, 1994—, dir. program automotive engring., 1995—; part-time rsch. staff energy and environ. systems divsn. Argonne Nat. Lab., 1978—; cons. in field. Contbr. over 40 articles to profl. jours. and numerous conf. presentations. Univ. scholar, 1991-94, Athens Coll. Acad. scholar, 1967-77; recipient IBM Rsch. award, 1991, NSF Presdl. Young Investigator award, 1988-93, NSF Engring. Initiation award, 1987, NASA Cert. of Recognition for Creative Devel. of a Tech. Innovation, 1987; Lilly Endowment Teaching fellow, 1988. Mem. ASME (faculty advisor U. Ill. student sect. 1989-91, ASME/Pi Tau Sigma Gold Medal award 1990, Internal Combustion Engine Divsn. Speaker award 1993, 94), Soc. Automotive Engrs. (Ralph Teetor award 1987, Russell Springer Best Paper award 1991), Am. Soc. for Engring. Edn., Combustion Inst., Sigma Xi. Office: U Mich Dept Mech Engring & Applied Mechanics 325 WE Lay Automotive Lab Ann Arbor MI 48109-2121

ASTER, RUTH MARIE RHYDDERCH, business owner; b. Cleve., Aug. 15, 1939; d. Roy William and Ruth Marie (Teckmeyer) Rhydderch; m. Ferdinand Aster, Nov. 23, 1963; children: Anneliese Ruth Aster Wilt, Christian Josef Roy. Student, Cooper Sch. Art, 1956-57; BS, Kent State U., 1962. Art tchr. North Olmsted (Ohio) Jr. and High Sch., 1962; art dept. chmn. Andrews Sch. for Girls, Willoughby, Ohio, 1963-64; co-owner, treas. Aster Cabinet Shop, Chesterland, Ohio, 1963—; co-owner, v.p., treas. Ferdl Aster Ski Sch., Chesterland, 1964—; owner, v.p., sec., treas. Ferdl Aster Ski Shop, Chesterland, 1972—; owner, v.p., advt. designer, fashion buyer, tour advisor Ferdl Aster Sport Ctr., Chesterland, 1985—; chmn. region IV U.S. Ski Assn., Colorado Springs, Colo., 1980-84, Alpine ofcl., 1983-88; ski racing coach U.S. Ski Coaches Assn., Park City, Utah, 1980-89; adv. bd. First County Bank, Chesterland, 1992—; adv. coun. U.S. Postal Svc., Chesterland, 1993—. Exhibited paintings and photographs to various shows, 1963-93. Creator blind ski program Cleve. (Ohio) Sight Ctr., 1969; pres., trustee Chesterland (Ohio) Hist. Found., 1986—; chair, vice chair, commr. Chester Twp. Zoning Com., Chesterland, 1987—; life friend Friends of Geauga West Libr., 1989—. Mem. Internat. Platform Assn. (polit. ctrl. com.), Chesterland C. of C. (pres., v.p., treas., trustee, Bus. Person of Yr. 1993), Cmty. Improvement Corp. Geauga County (re-orgn. com., nominating com., trustee), North Ea. Ohio Ski Retailers Assn. (bd. mem. 1987—), Kent State U. (life mem.), Silver Reunion Com. (bd. mem., v.p.), Chi Omega, Alpha Psi Omega, Gamma Delta. Lutheran. Office: Ferdl Aster Ski Shop 8330 Mayfield Rd Chesterland OH 44026-2520

ATALLAH, SAMI, chemical engineer; b. Beit Jala, Palestine, May 7, 1931; came to U.S., 1950; BSChE, Lehigh U., 1953, MSChE, 1954; ChE, MIT, 1960. Registered profl. engr., Mass. Assoc. prof. Tufts U., Cambridge, Mass., 1957-67; sr. scientist Factory Mutual Rsch. Corp., Norwood, Mass., 1967-68; sr. cons. Arthur D. Little Inc., Cambridge, 1968-78; rsch. dir. Gas Rsch. Inst., Chgo., 1979-83; pres. Risk & Indsl. Safety Cons. Inc., Des Plaines, Ill., 1983—; rsch. assoc. Princeton (N.J.) U., 1956-57; mem. Nat. Rsch. Coun. Marine Bd. Control/Recovery Hydrocarbon Vapors from Ships and Barges, Washington, 1986-87. Author (with others): NFPA Fire Protection Handbook, 1986, 91; contbr. articles to profl. jours. Rsch. fellow, Fire Rsch. Station, Borehamwood, Eng., 1965-66. Fellow Am. Inst. Chem. Engrs.; mem. Am. Soc. Safety Engrs., Soc. Fire Protection Engrs. Office: Risk & Indsl Safety Cons 292 Howard Ave Des Plaines IL 60018-1906

ATASI, KHALIL ZIAD, engineering executive; b. Homs, Syria, July 29, 1951; came to U.S., 1976; s. Ziad K. and Lamia Faydi (Atasi) A.; m. Muna N. Malas, Aug. 12, 1976; children: Lamia, Samia, Hany. BS in Civil Engring., U. Damascus, 1974; postgrad., Am. U. Beirut, 1974-75; M of Sanitary Engring., U. Mich., 1977, PhD in Environ. Engring., 1982. Registered profl. engr., Mich.; diplomate Am. Acad. Environ. Engrs.; cert. in water and wastewater; cert. in hazardous waste mgmt.; cert. plant operator, class A. Sr. structural engr. Soilcons. Engring., Damascus, Syria, 1975-76; prof. environ. engring. Wayne State U., Detroit, 1983—; sr. assoc. engr. Detroit Water Sewerage Dept., 1983-86, head applied tech. evaluation sect., 1986-89; v.p. McNamee Advanced Tech. Inc., Ann Arbor, Mich., 1989-92, McNamee, Porter & Seeley, Inc., Ann Arbor, 1993—; engring. cons., Ann Arbor, 1978-82; adj. prof. Wayne State U. Coll. Engring., 1983—, DWSD prof. environ. engring., chair, 1988-89. Contbr. articles to profl. jours. Mem. ASCE (various exec. positions), Am. Water Works Assn., Am. Acad. Environ. Engrs., Internat. Assn. Water Pollution Rsch. Control (various coms. 1988—), Internat. Assn. Great Lakes Rsch., Water Environ. Fedn. (various exec. postions 1984—), Assn. Environ. Engring. Profs., Engring. Soc. Detroit, Hazardous Materials Control Resources Inst., Sigma Xi, Chi Epsilon. Home: 29510 Kings Point Ct Farmington MI 48331-2160 Office: McNamee Porter & Seeley Inc 3131 S State St Ann Arbor MI 48108-1623

ATKIN, HOWARD BARTH, physician; b. Mpls., May 22, 1949; s. Morris and Charlene (Benesovitz) A. AB, Northwestern U., 1971; MD, U. Minn., 1974. Diplomate Am. Bd. Internal Medicine, Am. Bd. Endocrinology and Metabolism. Resident in internal medicine U. Minn., Mpls., 1974-77; fellow in endocrinology U. Calif., Orange, 1977-79; physician Mpls. VA Hosp., 1993—. Mem. AMA, Minn. Med. Assn., Hennepin County Med. Assn. Office: PO Box 766 Hopkins MN 55343-0766

ATKINS, CLAYTON H., family physician, epidemiologist, educator; b. Beech Grove, Ind., Nov. 12, 1944; s. Amos H. Atkins and Edythe E. (Dale) Heneghan; m. Carole A. Kirlin, Aug. 2, 1974; children: Brenda M. Spencer, Craig N., Angela C. AB in Chemistry, Ind. U., Bloomington, 1965, MAT in Chemistry, 1967; MD, Ind. U., Indpls., 1969; BS summa cum laude in Math., Butler U., 1980. Diplomate Am. Bd. Family Practice. Rotating intern Meth. Hosp. Ind. Inc., Indpls., 1969-70; pvt. practice, Greenwood, Ind., 1970-94; mem. active staff family practice dept., 1970—; hosp. epidemiologist, mem. med. bd. dirs. and exec. mgmt. com. St. Francis Hosp. and Health Ctrs., Beech Grove, 1989—; pres. med. staff St. Francis Hosp. and Health Ctrs., Beech Grove, Ind., 1995, with, 1995—; mem. courtesy med. staff family practice dept. Cmty. Hosp. South, Indpls., 1970—; instr. NSF math. for high sch. tchrs. Ind. U., Bloomington, 1966-67; instr. microgiology Ind. Ctrl. Coll. (now U. Indpls.), 1968; adj. asst. prof. Butler U. Coll. Pharmacy, Indpls., 1991-95. With USAFR, 1971-77, 91— maj. med. corps. Fellow Am. Acad. Family Physicians; mem. AMA, Ind. Med. Assn., Inpls. Med. Soc., Assn. for Practitioners in Infection Control, Inc., Epidemiology, Inc., Soc. for Hosp. Epidemiology in Am., Math. Assn. Am., Sigma Xi, Phi Kappa Phi, Phi Delta Kappa, Alpha Epsilon Delta, Phi Lambda Upsilon, Phi Eta Sigma, Mu Alpha Theta. Home: 6506 Boulder Ct S Indianapolis IN 46217 Office: 100 N Madison Ave Ste 200 Greenwood IN 46142-3578

ATKINSON, JEFF JOHN FREDERICK, lawyer, educator, writer; b. Mpls., Nov. 12, 1948; s. Frederick Melville Atkinson and Patricia (Bauman) Atkinson Farnes; m. Janis Pressendo, Dec. 22, 1982; children: Tara, Abigail, Grant, Kelsey. BS, Northwestern U., 1974; JD summa cum laude, DePaul U., 1977. Bar: Ill. 1977, U.S. Ct. Appeals (7th cir.) 1977, U.S. Dist. Ct. (no. dist.) Ill. 1978, U.S. Supreme Ct. 1982. Editor, reporter various Chgo. area newspapers and radio stas., 1967-71; assoc., Jenner & Block, Chgo., 1977-80; pvt. practice, Evanston, Wilmette and Chgo., 1980—; vis. prof., instr. Loyola U. Law Sch., Chgo., 1982-91; lectr. DePaul U. Coll. Law, Chgo., 1991—. Author: Modern Child Custody Practice, (2 vols.) 1986; contbr. articles on criminal, family, constl. law, health law, and ethics to various publs. Mem. ABA (chmn. child custody com. 1983-84, 86-87, 89-92, mem. editoral bd. Family Advocate, 1988—, mem. publs. devel. bd. 1984-89, mem. task force on needs of children 1983-85, chmn. rsch. com., 1987-88, Merit awards 1984, 86-94), ACLU (bd. dirs. Ill. div. 1972-74), Ill. Bar Assn., Chgo. Bar Assn., Nat. Assn. Health Lawyers, Northwestern U. Coll. Alumni Assn. (v.p. 1987-89). Home: 3514 Riverside Dr Wilmette IL 60091-1050

ATKINSON, PATRICK JOHN, foundation executive, educator; b. Bismarck, N.D., Feb. 27, 1959; s. Myron Hilary Jr. and Marjory Lois (Barth) A. BSW, Moorhead (Minn.) State U., 1981, BA in Criminal Justice, 1981; postgrad., Proyecto Linguistico, Antigua, Guatemala, 1983, U. Mary, Bismarck, N.D., 1991. Exec. dir. for Guatemala Covenant Internat. Found., Antigua, 1983-89, exec. dir. for C.Am., 1986-89; exec. dir. for S.E. Asia Covenant Internat. Found., Singapore, 1989-90; exec.dir. The God's Child Project, Bismarck, 1990—. Author: Longest Road, 1992, Crazy Acts, 1992; photographer. Office: The God's Child Project PO Box 1573 Bismarck ND 58502

ATKINSON, RICHARD LEE, JR., internal medicine educator; b. Petersburg, Va., May 15, 1942; s. Richard Lee and Ruth (Scarborough) A.; m. Susan Stayner Hume, Aug. 13, 1966; children: Catherine Crane, Barbara Hill, Deborah Gildea. BA, VA Mil. Inst., 1964; MD, Med. Coll. Va., 1968. Liaison endocrinologist Vanderbilt U., Nashville, 1973-74; adj. asst. prof. UCLA, 1975-77; asst. prof. internal medicine U. Va. Sch. Medicine, Charlottesville, 1977-83; assoc. prof. internal medicine U. Calif., Davis, 1983-87; prof. internal medicine Ea. Va. Med. Sch., Norfolk, 1987-93; assoc. chief staff for rsch. VA Med. Ctr., Hampton, Va., 1987-93; prof. medicine, dir. nutritional scis. Beers-Murphy Clin. Nutrition Ctr. U. Wis., Madison, 1993—; mem. nutrition study sect. NIH, 1991-95, chair, 1993-95. Contbr. articles to profl. jours. Maj. U.S. Army, 1970-74. Mem. N.Am. Assn. Study Obesity (pres. 1990-91), Am. Soc. Clin. Nutrition (pub. info. com. 1988-91, membership com. 1986-90, pres. 1994-95), Am. Obesity Assn. (pres.). Home: 2132 Vintage Dr Fitchburg WI 53575-1928 Office: U Wis Nutritional Scis Bldg 1415 Linden Dr Madison WI 53706-1527

ATOJI, MASAO, physical chemist; b. Osaka, Japan, Dec. 21, 1925; came to U.S., 1951; naturalized U.S. citizen, 1961; s. Yoshinori and Kiyo (Matsushima) A.; m. Iris Noma, May 18, 1957; children: Naomi Jean, Cynthia Ann, David Masao. BS, Osaka U., 1948, PhD, 1956. Rsch. assoc. U. Minn., Mpls., 1951-56; asst. prof. Iowa State U., Ames, 1956-60; assoc. chemist Argonne (Ill.) Nat. Lab., 1960-69, sr. chemist, 1969-81; sr. staff chemist Litton Systems Inc., Morris Plains, N.J., 1981-83; sr. staff scientist Motorola, Schaumburg, Ill., 1984-87; rsch. scientist Northwestern U., Evanston, Ill., 1988-90; assoc. editor Chem. Abstracts Svc., Columbus, Ohio, 1990—. Contbr. over 200 articles to Jour. Chem. Physics, Acta Crystallographica, Solid State Communications, others. Fellow Am. Phys. Soc. (life); mem. AAAS, ASTM, Am. Chem. Soc., Am.Crystallographic Assn., Am. Assn. for Crystal Growth, Soc. for Applied Spectroscopy, Phys. Soc. Japan (life), Sigma Xi (life). Home: 702 86th Pl Downers Grove IL 60516-4951

ATTANASIO, JOHN BAPTIST, law educator; b. Jersey City, N.J., Oct. 19, 1954; s. Gaetano and Madeline (Germinario) A.; m. Kathleen Mary Spartana, Aug. 20, 1977; children: Thomas, Michael. BA, U. Va., 1976; JD, NYU, 1979; diploma in law, Oxford U., 1982; LLM, Yale U., 1985. Bar: Md. 1979, U.S. Dist. Ct. Md. 1980, U.S. Ct. Appeals (4th cir.) 1980, U.S. Supreme Ct. 1983. Pvt. practice Balt., 1979-81; vis. asst. prof. law U. Pitts., 1982-84; assoc. prof. law U. Notre Dame, Ind., 1985-88, prof. law, 1988-92; Regan dir. Kroc Inst. for Internat. Peace Studies, 1991-92; dean Sch. of Law St. Louis U., 1992—; bd. dirs. Legal Svcs. Ea. Mo. Co-author: Constitutional Law 1989. Chair adv. bd. Ctr. for Civil and Human Rights, 1990-92; mem. Fulbright awards area com., 1994—; bd. dirs. Legal Svcs. Ea. Mo., 1996—. Recipient Legal Teaching award Sch. of Law, NYU, 1994. Mem. Ctrl. States Law Sch. Assn. (v.p. 1992-94). Democrat. Roman Catholic. Office: Saint Louis U Sch Law 3700 Lindell Blvd Saint Louis MO 63108-3412

ATTARIAN, JOHN CHARLES, writer; b. Detroit, Nov. 25, 1956; s. Edward John and Edna Katharine (Heethuis) A. BA, U. Mich., 1978, PhD in Econs., 1984. Rsch. asst. Transp. Rsch. Inst. U. Mich., Ann Arbor, 1986-90; freelance writer, 1990—; ind. contractor instr. Ford Motor Co., Dearborn, Mich., 1992—. Contbr. numerous articles, essays, revs., to jours., mags., newspapers. Precinct del. Rep. Party, Ann Arbor, 1994-96. Mem. KC, Phi Beta Kappa. Roman Catholic. Home and Office: 213 N Thayer St # 1 Ann Arbor MI 48104

ATTERBERG, DOUGLAS KEITH, financial planner; b. Keokuk, Iowa, Feb. 7, 1945; s. Keith Conradt and Gracia Lou (Arnold) A.; m. Ann Katherine Stiens, May 8, 1982. BA, Grinnell Coll., 1967; MBA, U. Iowa, 1968. Office mgr. Keokuk Battery Co., 1972-85; treas. United Presbyn. Ch., Keokuk, 1976-85; docent Lee County Hist. Soc., Keokuk, 1988-90; acctg. mgr. Schuler Design Systems, Keokuk, 1991-92. Author: 125th Anniversary of Westminster, 1968, Samuel Miller: A Place in History, 1990, Galland Efforts, 1996. Mem. exec. bd. S.E. Iowa coun. Boy Scouts Am., 1976—, dist. chmn., 1993-94; mem. Lee County Rep. Ctrl. Com., 1984—; pres. Keokuk Child Day Care Ctr., 1986-88; mem. task forces and capital fund com. Presbytery of East Iowa, Iowa City, 1987-91, 93-95; trustee, treas. Keokuk Pub. Libr., 1988—; mem. Keokuk Planning Commn., 1990—; treas. Keokuk Cmty. Fine Arts Coun., 1991—; commr. assembly Synod of Lakes and Prairies, 1991, 93; mem. organizing com. Greater Keokuk Habitat for Humanity, 1993—, facilities com. Keokuk Mid. Sch., 1994—. Capt. USAF, 1968-72. Recipient Silver Beaver award S.E. Iowa coun. Boy Scouts Am., 1988. Mem. Lee County Hist. Soc. (pres. 1990-91), Order of Arrow (tribal coun. 1963—). Home: 507 Grand Ave Keokuk IA 52632-5003

ATTOH, SAMUEL ARYEETEY, geographer, educator, planner; b. Accra, Ghana, June 26, 1956; came to U.S., 1980; s. Samuel Aryeetey and Cecilia (Taylor) A.; m. Antoinette Yawa Alipui, Sept. 6, 1980; children: Annette, Annabelle, Stefan, Sasha. BA with honors, U. Ghana, Legon, Accra, 1977; MA, Carleton U., 1980; PhD, Boston U., 1988. Rsch. asst. U. Ghana, 1975-77; teaching fellow, rsch. fellow Carleton U., Ottawa, Ont., Can., 1978-80; teaching asst. Boston U., 1980-85, lectr. Met. Coll., 1985-86, instr., 1986-87; asst. prof. U. Toledo, 1987-92, assoc. prof. geography and planning, 1992—. Contbr. articles to profl. jours. Mem. Com. of 100 Housing Task Force, Toledo, 1989-91. Mem. Am. Inst. Cert. Planners, Assn. Am. Geographers (chair African splty. group 1994-96), Am. Planning Assn., Ohio Housing Rsch. Network, Mid-Continent Regional Sci. Assn., Urban Land Inst. (assoc.). Roman Catholic. Office: Univ Toledo Geography and Planning 2801 W Bancroft St Toledo OH 43606-3328

ATWATER, HORACE BREWSTER, JR., retired food company executive; b. Mpls., Apr. 19, 1931; s. Horace Brewster and Eleanor (Cook) A.; m. Martha Joan Clark, May 8, 1955; children—Elizabeth C., Mary M., John C., Joan P. AB, Princeton U., 1952; MBA, Stanford U., 1954. Divisional v.p., dir. mktg. Gen. Mills, Inc., Mpls., 1958-65, mktg. v.p., 1965-70, exec. v.p., 1970-76, chief operating officer, 1976-81, pres., 1977-82, chief exec. officer, 1981-95, chmn. bd., also dir., 1982-95; ret., 1995; bd. dirs. Merck & Co. Inc., GE; mem., sec. Internat. Coun. Morgan Guaranty Trust Co. Bd. dirs. Pub. Radio Internat., Walker Art Ctr.; trustee Mayo Found. Office: Gen Mills Inc PO Box 1113 1 General Mills Blvd Minneapolis MN 55440

ATWOOD, WILLIAM L., cost analyst, tax consultant; b. Liberty, Ky., Aug. 7, 1946; s. William L. Atwood and Mable Marie Cochran. Student, U.S. Mil. Inst., 1967; BS in Bus. Adminstrn., Wayne State U., 1973. appeared on numerous radio and TV shows about math. and the lottery. Author: The Lottery Solution, 1994, 96; creator (software) Lottery Solution—MATRA Method, 1994. With U.S. Army, 1966-69, Vietnam.

ATZMON, MICHAEL, materials scientist; b. Jerusalem, Israel, Oct. 15, 1956; came to U.S., 1980; s. David and Aliza (Weinstein) A.; m. Leslie Chandler, Aug. 1989; children: Amy Renee, Ethan Benjamin. BS, Hebrew U., Jerusalem, 1980; MS, Calif. Inst. Tech., 1982, PhD, 1986. Rsch. asst. Calif. Inst. Tech., Pasadena, 1981-85; rsch. fellow Harvard U., Cambridge, Mass., 1985-87; asst. prof. nuclear engring. U. Mich., Ann Arbor, 1987-93, assoc. prof. nuclear engring., 1993-94, assoc. prof. nuclear engring. and radiol. sci., materials sci. and engring., 1994—. Contbr. articles to Jour. Applied Physics, Jour. Materials Rsch., Physical Rev. Letters. Grantee U.S. Dept. Energy, 1988, NSF, 1989, 92. Mem. Am. Physical Soc., Materials

Rsch. Soc., Am. Nuclear Soc., Minerals, Metals, and Materials Soc. Office: U Mich 2355 Bonisteel Dr Ann Arbor MI 48109-2104

AUBURN, NORMAN PAUL, university president; b. Cin., May 22, 1905; s. Joseph and Huldah A.; m. Kathleen Montgomery, June 28, 1930 (dec. 1974); children: Ames Auburn Latta, Richard, Mark, David Bruce; m. Virginia Kirk, Jan. 4, 1977. AB, U. Cin., 1927, postgrad., 1927-28, 34-35, LL.D., 1952; LL.D., Parsons Coll., 1945, U. Liberia, 1959, U. Akron, 1971; D.Sc., U. Tulsa, 1957; Litt.D., Washburn U., 1961; L.H.D., Coll. of Wooster, 1963; D.C.L., Union Coll., 1979. Editor Cin. Constructor, 1928-33; asst. mgr. Asso. Gen. Contractors of Am., 1928-33; publicity mgr. Allied Constrn. Industries, 1930-33; exec. sec. U. Cin. Alumni Assn., 1933-36; editor Cin. Alumnus, 1929-36; asst. dir., asst. prof. Evening Coll., U. Cin., 1936-38; assoc. prof. U. Cin., 1938-40, acting dean, 1940-41, dean and prof., 1941-43, dean of univ. adminstrn., clk. bd. dirs., 1943-51, v.p., 1943-51, acting pres., 1949; exec. dir. U. Cin. Research Found., 1943-51; pres. U. Akron, 1951-71, pres. emeritus, cons., 1971—; acting pres. Council Fin. Aid to Edn., N.Y.C., 1957-58, bd. dirs., 1957-71; spl. asst. univ. relations AID, U.S. State Dept., 1965-66, cons., 1966—; cons. Acad. Ednl. Devel., Inc., N.Y.C., 1965-70, sr. v.p., dir. institutional ops., 1971-89, sr. v.p., emeritus, 1989—; acting pres. Poly. Inst., Bklyn., 1973, Stephens Coll., Columbia, Mo., 1974-75, Cedar Crest Coll., Allentown, Pa., 1977-78, Union Coll., Schenectady, N.Y., 1978-79; acting chancellor Union U., Albany, N.Y., 1978-79; sr. v.p., provost Widener U., Chester, Pa., 1979-82; acting pres. Salem Coll., W.Va., 1982-83, Lincoln U., Jefferson City, Mo., 1987-88; spl. asst. to pres. for planning W.Va. U., Morgantown, 1983-86; chmn. Univ. Council on Edn. for Pub. Responsibility, 1965-66; dir. Great Lakes Megalopolis Research Project, 1968-74; vice chmn. Am. Council Edn., 1963-64, dir., 1969-72; bd. dirs. First Fed. Savs. and Loan Assn., Akron, 1963, chmn., 1973—; bd. dirs. Charter One Fin., Cleve., 1988—, Charter One Bank, 1988—, 1st Nat. Bank Akron, emeritus; hon. pres. Lane Theol. Sem., Cin., 1990—. Contbr. articles to ednl. jours. Bd. dirs. Akron Gen. Hosp., U. Akron Devel. Fedn., 1967—; trustee Greater Akron Musical Assn., 1967—; trustee, sec. Lane Theol. Sem., Cin., 1945—, hon. pres., 1990—; trustee Ohio Coll. Assn., pres., 1960-61; mem. Air Force ROTC Adv. Panel to Dept. USAF, 1960-64; mem. exec. com. Ohio Research and Devel. Bd., 1962-65; pres. Herman Muehlstein Found., 1965—; mem. U. Cin. Endowment Fund Assn. Fellow AAAS; mem. Assn. Am. Colls. (vice chmn. commn. coll. adminstrn. 1965-68), Am. Soc. Engring. Edn., Am. Assn. State Colls. and Univs. (chmn. com. on internat. programs 1970-71), Assn. Univ. Evening Colls. (pres. 1944), Assn. Urban Univs. (pres. 1955-56, sec.-treas. 1956-65), Newcomen Soc., Cincinnatus Soc., Summit County Hist. Soc. (trustee 1975-80), Queen City Assn., Alpha Kappa Psi, Phi Alpha Delta, Lambda Chi Alpha, Omicron Delta Kappa, Scabbard and Blade. Presbyterian. Clubs: Rotary (pres. Cin. 1950-51, Akron 1958-59), Commonwealth (Cin.), Univ. (N.Y.C., Columbus, Ohio), City, Portage Country (Akron), Lago Mar Beach (Ft. Lauderdale, Fla.). Home: 2385 Covington Rd Akron OH 44313-4335 Office: U Akron Office Of Pres Emeritus Akron OH 44325

AUBYN, ROD, state legislator; m. Susan; 2 children. BS, U. N.D. Mem. N.D. Ho. of Reps., 1991-94, past mem. human svcs., vet. affairs., polit. subdivsn. coms., past mem. appropriations-human resources divsn. com., mem. appropriations com.; asst. dir. plant svcs. U. N.D. Bd. dirs. Med. Park, United Health Svcs., Valley Mental Health Assn. Mem. Optimist Club, Honor Club (pres.). Home: 1906 Willow Dr Grand Forks ND 58201-8111*

AUCOIN, PAUL, registrar, consultant; b. Port Arthur, Tex., July 30, 1945; s. Paul George Jr. and Gertrude (Blanchard) A.; m. Judith Ann Ford, Apr. 15, 1989; children: Ryan Paul, Grant Robert. BS, Nicholls State U., 1974, MBA, 1981. Record supr. Nicholls State U., Thibodaux, Calif., 1976-77, asst. registrar, 1977-80, assoc. registrar, 1980-88, dir. records and registration, 1988-90; dir. records Cornell U., Ithaca, N.Y., 1990-92; registrar U. Evansville (Ind.), 1992—. Editor Earthcare newsletter. Pres. Sealevel Striders, Thibodaux, La., 1981-90; exec. com. Finger Lakes Runners, Ithaca, N.Y., 1990-92; bd. dirs. Evansville Runners, 1995—; v.p. Nicholls Fed. Credit Union, Thibodaux, La., 1984-90. Mem. Am. Assn. Collegiate Registrars and Admissions Officers (mem. conf. news com. 1980, mem. records mgmt. and security com. 1991-94, mem. task force, editor The Academic Record and Transcript Guide 1994-95, mem. pubs. adv. bd. 1994-95, others), So. Assn. Collegiate Registrars and Admissions Officers, Coll. and Univ. Computer Users Assn., Am. Assn. Acad. Advisers. Office: U Evansville 1800 Lincoln Ave Evansville IN 47722

AUDLEY, BARBARA MARIE, adult education educator, university administrator; b. N.Y.C., Apr. 26, 1940; d. John and Elizabeth (Oxenhofer) Laub; m. Wilbur Edward Audley Jr., July 9, 1961; children: Amanda Jean, Victoria Elizabeth. BSBA magna cum laude, Calif. State U., Long Beach, 1972; D of Pub. Adminstrn., Nova Southeastern U., 1982. Adminstrv. asst. Sunset Internat. Petroleum Co., Beverly Hills, Calif., 1964-66; asst. acct. mgr. The Bowes Co., L.A., 1966-68; adminstrv. officer civic ctr. campus U. So. Calif., L.A., 1968-72; asst. dean extended programs and community svc. Calif. State U. Dominguez Hills, Carson, 1972-78; dir. div. lifelong learning and outreach summer session S.D. State U., Brookings, 1978-93, asst prof. edn., 1984-93, assoc. prof., 1993, mem. grad. faculty, 1992—; dir. continuing edn./extension U. Wis., River Falls, 1993—; pres. ops. bd. Wis. Overlay Network of Distance Edn., 1995-96. Contbr. articles to profl. jours. chair. city beautification com. City of Los Alamitos, Calif., 1966-68, chair parks and recreation com., 1968-74, councilmem. and vice mayor, 1974-78. Recipient Pres.'s award for Svc. in adult edn., 1991. Mem. ASTD, Nat. Univ. Continuing Edn. Assn., S.D. Assn. Lifelong Learning (pres. 1989-90, treas. 1990-95, Adult Educator of Yr. 1989), Mo. Valley Adult Edn. Assn. (sec. 1990-93, pres.-elect 1993, pres. 1994, Achievement award for S.D. 1989). Episcopalian.

AUDLEY, THOMAS JOSEPH, educational administrator, consultant; b. Kansas City, Kans., Dec. 10, 1939; s. Thomas J. and Mary E. (Quinlan) A.; m. Karen E. Hackbarth, May 20, 1967; children: Elizabeth E., Mary C., Ann T. BA, Rockhurst Coll., 1961; MA, Marquette U., 1964. Asst. to registrar Marquette U., Milw., 1964-65, dir. admission, 1965-74; dir. admission Rockhurst Coll., Kansas City, Mo., 1974-90; dir. campaign resources Rockhurst Coll., Kansas City, 1990-93; dir. prospect mgmt. Rockhurst Coll., 1993-95; dir. prospect and mgmt. Rockhurst Coll., Kansas City, Mo., 1993—; dir. admission Rsch. Coll. Nursing, Kansas City, 1985-90; dir. planned giving Rockhurst Coll., Kansas City, 1995—; cons. and mentor. Author: Interviewing Methods for Enrolling, Guiding and Retaining Students, 1991. Bd. regents Conception (Mo.) Sem. Coll., 1984-91; chair. Conf. Jesuit Admission Dirs., 1987-88. Mem. Am. Assn. Collegiate Registrars & Admissions Officers (publs. rev. panel 1990—), Mo. Assn. Coll. Admissions Counselors (profl. devel. chair 1984-87). Office: Rockhurst Coll 1100 Rockhurst Rd Kansas City MO 64110-2508

AUER, RON, state legislator; b. St. Louis, Jan. 24, 1950; s. Lawrence J. and Loretta B. Goettler A.; m. Ann Marie Hoelscher, 1980; children: Amanda Marie, Lindsey Marie, Neal Collins, Tracy Collins. BS, S.E. Mo. State U., 1972. Mo. State rep. Dist. 59, 1977—; educator, 1972-77, real estate and ins. agt., 1979—; staff, acct. Exec. Health Maintenance Orgn., 1983—. Office: 3120 S Compton Ave Saint Louis MO 63118-2110*

AUERBACH, MARSHALL JAY, lawyer; b. Chgo., Sept. 5, 1932; s. Samuel M. and Sadie (Miller) A.; m. Carole Landsberg, July 3, 1960; children—Keith Alan, Michael Ward. Student, U. Ill.; J.D., John Marshall Law Sch., 1955. Bar: Ill. 1955. Sole practice Evanston, Ill., 1955-72; ptnr. in charge matrimonial law sect. Jenner & Block, Chgo., 1972-80; mem. firm Marshall J. Auerbach & Assocs., Ltd., Chgo., 1980—; mem. faculty Ill. Inst. Continuing Legal Edn. Author: Illinois Marriage and Dissolution of Marriage Act, enacted into law, 1977; Historical and Practice Notes to Illinois Marriage and Dissolution of Marriage Act, 1980-88; contbr. chpts. to Family Law, Vol. 2. Fellow Am. Acad. Matrimonial Lawyers; mem. Ill. State Bar Assn. (chmn. family law sect. 1971-72), ABA (vice-chmn. family law sect. com. for liaison with tax sect. 1974-76). Home and Office: 180 N La Salle St Ste 2307 Chicago IL 60601-2703

AUFDERHEIDE, ARTHUR CARL, pathologist; b. New Ulm, Minn., Sept. 9, 1922; s. Herman John and Esther (Sannwald) A.; m. Mary Lillian Buryk, Jan. 26, 1946; children: Patricia Ann, Tom Paul, Walter Herman. MD, U. Minn., 1946; DSc (hon.), Coll. of St. Scholastica, 1983. Chief dept. pathology Mpls. VA Hosp., 1952-53, St. Mary's Hosp., Duluth, Minn., 1953-57; chief dept. pathology Sch. Medicine U. Minn., Duluth, 1970-87, dean Sch. Medicine, 1974-75, dir. paleobiology lab. Sch. Medicine, 1977—; rsch. cons. anthropology lab. U. Colombia, Bogota, 1989—, Pigorini Mus., Rome, 1988, Archeol. Mus. of Tenerife, Canary Islands, 1989-90; chmn. sci. com. Cronos Rsch Project, Santa Cruz, Tenerife, 1991—. Co-editor: Paleopathology, 1991; contbr. numerous articles to profl. publs. Chmn. civil com. to devel. a degree-granting med. sch., Duluth, 1988. Capt. U.S. Army, 1947-49. Mem. Paleopathology Assn., N.Y. Acad. Scis. Democrat. Lutheran. Home: 4711 Colorado St Duluth MN 55804-1512 Office: U Minn 10 University Dr Duluth MN 55812

AUFIERO, THOMAS XAVIER, cardiothoracic surgeon; b. Rockville Center, N.Y., Jan. 17, 1953; s. Xavier Thomas and Doris Le (Jung) A. BA, Haverford (Pa.) Coll., 1979; MD, Pa. State U., 1983. Assoc. prof. Ind. U., Indpls., 1995—; attending surgeon U. Ind. Med. Sch. Roederbush VAMC, Indpls., 1995—. Fellow ACS; mem. Soc. Thoracic Surgeons, Am. Soc. Artificial Organs, Pa. Assn. Thoracic Surgery, Soc. Critical Care Medicine, Alpha Omega Alpha. Office: Ind Med Ctr Sect Cardiothoracic Surg 545 Banhill Dr Rm 212 Indianapolis IN 46202

AUGUST, ROBERT WILLIAM, designer; b. Chgo., Mar. 31, 1944; s. Benjamin R. and Lillian (A.) A.; m. Lois J. Yoder, Feb. 19, 1977; children: Kristen J., Michael M. BA, L.I. U., 1970; MA, Nat.-Louis U., 1995. USNR, 1965-70; pres. Design Agy. Inc., Chgo., 1976-77; pres., chief exec. officer Expocom Inc., Elgin, Ill., 1977—. Elected to bd. edn. Sch. Dist. U-46, Elgin, 1989-93. Mem. North Suburban Assn. Commerce and Industry.

AUGUSTIN, KATHRYN MARY, financial advisor; b. Milw., Apr. 6, 1946; d. John Norbert and Berwyn (Burke) Augustin; m. Peter E. McAlpine, June 14, 1969 (div. 1984). BA, U. Mich., 1967, MBA, 1973. Sr. profit forecaster Ford Motor Co., Dearborn, Mich., 1973-77; asst. treas., asst. sec. RP Scherer Corp., Troy, Mich., 1977-81; lectr. bus. Wayne State U., Detroit, 1981-83; investment advisor A.G. Edwards, Bloomfield, Mich., 1983-85, Merrill Lynch, Rochester, Mich., 1985, First of Mich., Troy, 1992—; owner, fin. advisor August & Assocs., Lake Orion, Mich., 1985-92; part-time faculty Oakland U., Rochester, 1982-84, Walsh Coll., Troy, Mich. author/leader seminars in field; contbr. articles to profl. jours. Co-founder Mich. Libertarian Party. Mem. Nat. Assn. Accts. (cert.), Risk Assurance Mgmt. Soc., Orion Area C. of C. (bd. dirs. 1986-92). Office: First of Michigan 1719 W Big Beaver Rd Troy MI 48084-3510

AULD, FRANK, psychologist, educator; b. Denver, Aug. 9, 1923; s. Benjamin Franklin and Marion Leland (Evans) A.; m. Elinor James, June 29, 1946 (dec. June 1990); children—Mary, Robert, Margaret. A.B., Drew U., 1946; M.A., Yale U., 1948, Ph.D., 1950. Cert. psychologist, Mich., Ont. Instr. psychology Yale U., New Haven, 1950-52, asst. prof., 1952-59; asso. prof. Wayne State U., Detroit, 1959-61; prof. Wayne State U., 1961-67, dir. clin. psychology tng. program, 1960-66; prof. U. Detroit, 1967-70, dir. psychol. clinic, 1967-69; prof. U. Windsor, Ont., Can., 1970-91, prof. emeritus, 1992—; cons. in field. Author: Steps in Psychotherapy, 1953, Scoring Human Motives, 1959, Resolution of Inner Conflict, 1991; contbr. articles to profl. jours. Chmn. Dearborn (Mich.) Community Council, 1962; mem. adv. com. on coll. work Episcopal Diocese Mich., 1962-71. Recipient Alumni Achievement award Drew U., 1965. Fellow Am. Psychol. Assn. (evaluation com. 1961-66); mem. Can. Assn. U. Tchrs., Can., Mich. psychol. assns., Ont. Psychol. Assn. (edn. and tng. bd. 1976-91), Conn. State Psychol. Soc. (pres. 1958), Soc. Psychotherapy Research, Phi Beta Kappa, Sigma Xi. Home: 5436 Fairway Ct W West Bloomfield MI 48322-3463 Office: U Windsor, Dept Psychology, Windsor, ON Canada N9B 3P4

AULIE, RICHARD PAUL, science history educator; b. Chgo., May 17, 1926; s. Henry Martin and Thora Willa (Döderlein) A. Med. student, U. Ill., Chgo., 1945-46; BS, Wheaton Coll., 1948; MS, U. Minn., 1953; PhD, Yale U., 1968. Biology educator Northwestern Coll., Mpls., 1949-52, Habibia Coll., Kabul, Afghanistan, 1953, Am. Univ. at Cairo, Egypt, 1954-55, Bloom Twp. High Sch., Chicago Heights, Ill., 1955-61, Evanston (Ill.) Twp. High Sch., 1961-62; biology expert UNESCO U. Liberia, Monrovia, 1962-64; asst. prof. Chgo. State Coll., 1968-71; editor, writer Encyclopedia Brittanica, Chgo., 1971-72; educator natural sci. Loyola U., Chgo., 1972-76; sci. instr. Montay Coll., Chgo., 1992—; program chmn. Nat. Assn. Biology Tchrs., Chgo., 1971; organizer Creationism and Am. Culture Symposium, Chgo., 1982, Aids in Am. Soc., The Future of Food Prodn., 1988; mem. accreditation com. N. Ctrl. Assn., 1985; lectr. Am. Sci. Affiliation Conv., Wheaton, 1991. Contbr. articles to profl. jours. Vol. AIDS Com. Fourth Presbyn. Ch., Chgo., 1988-90; vol. meal deliverer Open Hand, 1989; participant NEH seminar on Islam and the sci. tradition in the Middle Ages, Columbia U., 1993. With USNR, 1943-45. USPHS fellow Yale U., 1964-68. Mem. Soc. for History of Discoveries, Soc. for History of Medicine in Chgo. Republican. Presbyterian.

AULT, SUSAN L., securities broker; b. Toledo, Ohio, Nov. 22, 1955. Assoc. Mktg., Tech. Owens Coll., Perrysburg, Pa., 1977. Registered sales asst. Bruce Wade & Co., Toledo, Ohio, 1977-79, Ohio Co., Columbus, Ohio, 1979-89, Advest, Columbus, 1990-92, McDonald & Co. Securities, Dublin, Ohio, 1992—. Republican. Home: 3100 Brightington Dr Dublin OH 43017-1796 Office: McDonald & Co Securities 6055 Tain Dr Dublin OH 43017-8560

AURAND, CLAY, state legislator; m. Gina Aurand. Mem. Kans. State Ho. of Reps. Dist. 109, 1995—.

AUSNEHMER, JOHN EDWARD, lawyer; b. Youngstown, Ohio, June 26, 1954; s. John Louis and Patricia Jean (Liguore) A.; m. Carole Marie Ausnehmer; children: Jill Ellen, Amber Layne. BS, Ohio State U., 1976; JD, U. Dayton, 1980. Bar: Ohio 1980, U.S. Dist. Ct. (no. dist.) Ohio 1981, U.S. Supreme Ct. 1984, U.S. Ct. Appeals (6th cir.) 1984. Law clk. Ohio Atty. Gen., Columbus, 1978, Green, Schiavoni, Murphy, Haines & Sgambati Co., L.P.A., 1978; assoc. Dickson Law Office, Petersburg, Ohio, 1979-85 ; sole practice, Youngstown, Ohio, 1984—; asst. prosecuting atty. Mahoning County, Ohio, 1986-89, 92—. Mem. Ohio Acad. Trial Lawyers, ABA, Ohio State Bar Assn., Mahoning County Bar Assn., Columbiana County Bar Assn., Phi Alpha Delta. Democrat. Roman Catholic. Club: Mahoning Valley Soccer (rep. 1982-84). Home: 51 S Shore Dr Youngstown OH 44512-5926 Office: PO Box 3965 721 Boardman-Poland Rd Youngstown OH 44513-3965

AUSTERLITZ, PAUL, ethnomusicologist, jazz musician; b. Helsinki, Finland, Aug. 26, 1957; came to the U.S., 1958; s. Robert and Sylvi Elise (Nevanlinne) A.; m. Karoll Josè Cortez, Jan. 8, 1992. BA, Bennington Coll., 1978; MA, Columbia U., 1984; 2d MA, Wesleyan U., Middletown, Conn., 1986, PhD, 1993. Instr. Hartford (Conn.) Camerata Conservatory, 1986; adj. prof. Hunter Coll., N.Y.C., 1990; vis. prof. U. Mich., Ann Arbor, 1993-94, vis. scholar, 1994-95; adj. prof. Bowling Green (Ohio) State U., 1994-95. Rsch. grantee Am.-Scandinavian Soc., N.Y., 1988, Predoctoral grantee Wenner-Gren Found., N.Y.C., 1990-91, 95; Fulbright scholar, Dominican Rep., 1996. Mem. Internat. Assn. for the Study Popular Music, Ctr. for Black Music, Soc. for Ethnomusicology (coun. 1984—). Home: 1011-1 Fountain St Ann Arbor MI 48103 Office: Univ Mich Burton Tower Ann Arbor MI 48109

AUSTIN, ALVIN EASTON, retired journalism educator; b. Grand Forks, N.D., July 17, 1909; s. Raymond Easton and Kathryn Veronica (Mayer) A.; m. Ellen Jane Megivern, June 4, 1946; children: Suellen, Heinrich, Sheila-Ann Lacy. BA, U. N.D., 1931; grad., Mil. Intelligence Ctr., 1944. Night city editor Grand Forks Herald, 1931-33, night editor, 1933-42, condr. Looking Around column, 1938-42, 46-57; asst. in journalism U. N.D., Grand Forks, 1940-42, prof., chair journalism dept., 1946-69, sr. prof. journalism, 1969-80, prof. journalism emeritus, 1980—; vis. prof. journalism U. Vt., Burlington, 1967; spl. assignment to Miami (Fla.) Herald, 1959, Burlington Free Press, 1957, 68, 69, Mpls. Star, 1962-72; rschr. Wall St. Jour., Chgo., 1957-58; pub. rels. cons. Garrison Conservancy Dist., Garrington, N.D., 1978-83. Author: Do You Belong in Journalism?, 1958, (with others) Modern Journalism, 1962, 100 Year History of Grand Forks Weldings, 1985; contbr. biographies to World Book Ency., 1995; editor 42 Dist. Dem. NPL Times, 1986—. Alderman Grand Forks City Coun., 1962-66, pres., 1964-66, chmn. bd. health, 1962-64. 1st lt. U.S. Army, 1942-46, PTO. Decorated Bronze Star; recipient Wells Key award Sigma Delta Chi, 1957, Nat. Journalism Educator of Yr. award Sigma Delta Chi, 1973, Sioux award U. N.D. Alumni Assn., 1983. Mem. VFW (life), Soc. Profl. Journalists (life), Am. Legion, KC. Democrat. Roman Catholic. Home: 525 N 25th St Grand Forks ND 58203

AUSTIN, DAN, state legislator; b. Mar. 16, 1967. BBA, U. N.D., 1989. Polit. dir. N.D. State Rep. Party, 1990-91; asst. to Majority Leader N.D. Senate, 1991; mem. N.D. Ho. of Reps. from 41st dist., 1993—; state trooper N.D. Hwy. Patrol, 1996—; bus. cons. Profiles, Inc. Trustee Fargo Dollars for Scholars; mem. N.D. Interagy. Coordinating Coun. Mem. Jaycees (Fargo chpt., Horizon award 1992), Fargo C. of C. Republican. Address: PO Box 9864 Fargo ND 58106*

AUSTIN, HARVEY B., financial consultant; b. Branard, Minn., Mar. 1, 1943. BA, Mankato (Minn.) State U., 1965. Stockbroker Regional Brokerage House, Mpls., 1971-73; fin. cons. Wordell & Reed, Mpls., 1973-88, Fin. Network Inc., Indpls., 1988—. With USN, 1962-64. Decorated Vietnam Svc. medal. Republican. Lutheran.

AUSTIN, RICHARD H., retired state official; b. Ala., May 6, 1913; s. Richard H. and Lelia (Hill) A.; m. Ida B. Dawson, Aug. 19, 1939; 1 child, Hazel. B.S., Detroit Inst. Tech., 1937; LL.D. (hon.), Detroit Coll. Bus., 1971, Mich. State U., 1985, U. Detroit, 1988, No. Mich. U., 1989. Pvt. practice accounting Detroit, 1941-71; auditor Wayne County, Mich., 1967-70; sec. of state Mich. Lansing, 1971-94; del. Mich. Constl. Conv., 1961-62. Bd. dirs. Harper Hosp., Detroit, Met. Detroit United Way, Community Found. SE Mich., Detroit Meml. Park Cemetery. Mem. AICPA, Mich. Assn. CPAs (Disting. Achievement award 1988). Democrat.

AUTHIER, GAIL JUDITH, preschool consultant; b. Detroit, July 26, 1943; d. Everett Bernie and Beatrice Lucy (Greenham) Curry; m. Gerald George Authier, June 26, 1965; children: Staci Lynn Authier Miserlian, James Bradley. BS, Ea. Mich. U., 1965; MA, Ctrl. Mich. U., 1977. Cert. elem. edn., mental impairment, learning disabled, presch. specialist. Kindergarten tchr. Waterford (Mich.) Pub. Schs., 1965-69; project coord. Alpena (Mich.) Pub. Schs., 1990-93; presch. cons., childfind coord. Alpena (Mich.)-Montmorency-Alcona Ednl. Svc. Dist., 1975—; v.p., bd. dirs. Cmty. Coordinated Child Care No. Mich., Alpena, 1990-94. Author manuals. Mem. Nat. Assn. Educators Young Children, Zonta Internat. Alpena (bd. dirs., sec., pres.). Lutheran. Home: 8329 Herron Rd Herron MI 49744 Office: Alpena-Montmoreny-Alcona Ednl Svc 2118 US 23 S Alpena MI 49707

AUTRY, CAROLYN, artist, art history educator; b. Dubuque, Iowa, Dec. 12, 1940; d. William Tilden and Vela (Laseman) A.; m. Peter Elloian, May 27, 1966; 1 dau., Cybele Justine. B.A., U. Iowa, 1963, M.F.A., 1965. Instr. art, art history Baldwin-Wallace Coll., Berea, Ohio, 1965-66; assoc. prof. art history dept. art Ctr. for Visual Arts, U. Toledo, 1966—; artist-in-residence Sch. Arts in France, Lacoste, 1984, 87, adj. instr. in printmaking, 1987. Exhbns. include San Francisco Mus. Art, 1973, Oakland Mus., 1975, Santa Barbara Mus., 1975, U. Mo., 1975, Ljubljana Internat. Biennial, 1975, 81, 87, Internationale Grafik Biennale, Frechen, W. Ger., 1976, Biella, Italy, 1976, Genoa, Italy, 1976, Leverkusen, Fed. Republic Germany, 1977, Phila. Mus. Art, 1980, Visual Arts Ctr., Anchorage, Alaska, 1980, U. Louisville, 1981, U. Dallas, 1981, Grunwald Ctr. Graphic Arts, UCLA, 1981, Ohio State U., 1982, Belle Arts & Graphic Inc., Nyack, N.Y., 1982, Mus. Arts and Scis., Macon, Ga., 1983, U. Tenn., Knoxville, 1983, Pratt Graphics Ctr., N.Y.C., 1983, Calif. State Coll., San Bernardino, 1983, Taipei Fine Arts Mus., 1983, 85, 87, 89, 91, 95, Museo Arte Contemporaneo, Ibiza, Spain, 1984, Drake U., 1985, Fla. State U., 1985, Am. Embassy Cultural Ctr., Belgrade, Yugoslavia, 1983, Irvine (Calif.) Fine Arts Ctr., 1986, Inter-graphic Internat., East Berlin, 1984, 87, Met. Mus. Art Ctr., Coral Gables, Fla., 1987, Fifth Internat. Graphic Exhbn., Catania, Italy, 1988, Korean Cultural Svc. Gallery, L.A., Walker Hill Gallery, Seoul, Korea, and Korean Embassy Cultural Ctr., Paris, 1989, Barbican Art Centre, London, Salford (Gt. Britain), Mus., Mead Gallery, U. Warwick, Coventry, Gt. Britain, Brighton and Poly. Gallery, Brighton, Gt. Britain, 1989, Internat. Exhbn. Prints, Kanagawa, Japan, 1989, 90, 95, Gallery Fine Arts Ctr. Seoul, 1989, Nat. Exhbn. Prints, Ringling Sch. Art and Design, Sarasota, Fla., 1990, Internat. Impact Art Festival, Kyoto City Mus., Japan, 1990, 91, 92, 93, 94, Ohio Drawing and Printmaking Invitational, Upper Arlington, 1991, Fondation Mona Bismarck, Paris, 1991, Fine Arts Assn. Gallery, Hanoi, Republic of Vietnam, 1991, Prints Internat., 1992, Silvermine Guild Arts Ctr., New Caanan, Conn., 1993, Taejon (Korea) Expo Graphic Art, 1993, Soc. Am. Graphic Artists 65th Nat., N.Y.C., 1993, Architecture in Contemporary Print Making, Boston Archtl. Ctr., 1994, Am. Inst. Architecture, Washington, 1994, U. N.H., 1995, Midwest Select, South Bend Regional Mus. of Art, Ind., 1994, Triton Mus., Santa Clara, Calif., 1995, Mansfield (Ohio) Art Ctr., 1995, numerous others; represented in permanent collections Libr. of Congress, Phila. Mus. Art, Worcester Art Mus., Mount Holyoke Coll., U. Colo., Bradley U., Calif. State U., San Diego, Ga. State U., U. S.D., U. N.D., U. Louisville, St. Lawrence U., U. Dallas, Hunterdon Art Ctr., Clinton, N.J., Fitchburg (Mass.) Mus., Duxbury (Mass.) Art Complex, Elvehjem Mus. Art U. Wis.-Madison, Inst. per la Cultura E L'Arte, Catania, Italy, Lakeview Mus. Arts and Scis., Peoria, Ill., Nat. Mus. Fine Arts, Hanoi. Recipient Ture Bengtz Meml. prize, 1981, Pennell award Libr. Congress, 1971, 75, Phila. Print Club awards, 1972, 75, 79, Wesleyan Coll. Internat. award of merit, 1980, Anne Steele Marsh award Hunterdon Art Ctr., Clinton, N.J., 1991, Bradley U. Nat. award, 1991, Friends of the Janet Turner Gallery Nat. Exhbn. award Chico State U., Calif., 1995; Ford Found. grantee, 1961-63, Ohio Arts Coun. grantee, 1979, 90, Yale-Norfolk Summer Sch. Art and Music scholar, 1962. Mem. Boston Printmakers (Louis Black award 1971), L.A. Printmakers Soc., Soc. Am. Graphic Artists (Jo Miller award 1985, Phillip Monteith award 1986), Calif. Soc. Printmakers, Coll. Art Assn. Am., The Print Club of Albany, N.Y. (Ledyard Logswell, Jr. Meml. prize 1995), Phi Beta Kappa. Address: 26114 W River Rd Perrysburg OH 43551-9128

AVED, BARRY, retail executive, consultant; b. Mpls., Mar. 27, 1943; s. Alick Leonard and Marna Claire (Sandon) A.; m. Marlys Sandra Drentlaw, Sept. 3, 1961; children: Andrea, Nicole Aved Badeau, Danielle, Rachelle. Grad. high sch., Mpls., 1961. Buyer Dayton Hudson Co., Mpls., 1963-72; v.p. Ltd. Stores, Columbus, Ohio, 1972-82; pres. Id, Inc., Green Bay, Wis., 1982-86; pres., CEO Brooks Fashion Stores, N.Y.C., 1986-89; pres. Ormond Stores, Inc., North Bergen, N.J., 1989-90; pres., CEO Lerner N.Y., N.Y.C., 1991-95; prin. Aved Cons., Lakeville, Minn., 1995—.

AVENDANO, NOEL JEROME, computerized machinist, inventor; b. Annecy, France, July 12, 1947; arrived in U.S., 1954; s. Pierre Laurent and Annie Francoise (Mondragon) A.; 1 child, Andrea. AA in Engring., Norwalk State Tech., Conn., 1995. Lab aide N.Y.C. Dept. Health, 1966-67; mechanic Mercedes Benz, Boulder, Colo., 1973; cabinet maker Arch. Woodworkers, Westport, Conn., 1979-82; CNC machinist Dickson Product Devel., Peoria, Ill., 1994—. Composer of Classical Works, 1971-96; inventor in field, 1992; contbr. articles to profl. jour. Recipient Full Tuition scholarship N.Y. State Regents, Albany, 1965; Named U.S. Hang Gliding Rep., Russia, 1994. Home: PO Box 6057 Peoria IL 61601-6057

AVERILL, BARRY WILLIAM, health insurance company executive; b. N.Y.C., May 14, 1938; s. William Patrick and Gertrude (Crowley) A.; m. Betsy Ross Lord, Oct. 15, 1962 (div. 1987); children: Barbara, Timothy, Christopher; m. Evelyn Flora Krauter, May 6, 1989. BS, U. Ky., 1966. Asst. dir. Univ. Health Svc. U. Ky., Lexington, 1964-66, asst. dean Coll. Medicine, 1966-67; asst. dir. Univ. Health Svc. U. Mass., Amherst, 1968-72, exec. dir. Univ. Health Svc., 1972-83; pres. Michael Reese Health Plan, Chgo., 1984-91; exec. dir. Humana Michael Reese HMO, Chgo., 1991-92; v.p. Humana Health Plans Ill., Chgo., 1992—; pres., bd. dirs. Am. Coll. Health Assn., Washington,1 974-79, Ill. HMO Assn., Chgo., 1985-92; treas., bd. dirs. Accreditation Assn. Ambulatory Health Care, Chgo., 1979-85; mem. Chgo. Health System Agy., Chgo., 1985-89. With U.S. Army, 1961-63. Recipient Hitchcock award Am. Coll. Health Assn., 1978. Mem. Group Health Assn. Am. (leadership group, com. chair 1987-94). Office: Humana Health Plans 2545 S King Dr Chicago IL 60616-2419

AVERY, DENNIS T., state legislator; b. Evansville, Ind., Sept. 28, 1946; m. Donna Avery; 1 child, Jessica. BS, U. Evansville, 1969. Ind. state rep. Dist. 75, 1974—; vice chmn. families, children and human affairs com. Ind. Ho. Reps., mem. environ. affairs, cities and towns, ways and means coms; bd. dirs. Evansville Ct. Appointed Spl. Adv. Program; mem. Juvenile Justice task force; mem. Ind. State CASA/GAL Project; pres. Hartford Supply Co.; bus. cons. in field; acct. exec. managed care Tristate Health Care Ptnrs. Mem. Vanderburgh County Dem. Club; chmn. Interstate Rail Passenger Compact. Mem. Youth Svc. Bur., Ind. Advocates Children, Evansville Youth Resources, Med. Sch. Adv. Coun. Address: 11400 Big Cynthiana Rd Evansville IN 47720-7308*

AVERY, MICHAEL T., state legislator; b. Newcastle, Wyo., Feb. 15, 1952; m. Candice Woebbecke, 1977; children: Brandon, Shawn. BS, U. Nebr. Mem. from dist. 3 Nebr. State Senate, Lincoln, 1992—, mem. appropriations com. on coms. Founder, bd. dirs. Gretna Area Devel. Corp. Mem. Am. Fisheries Soc., Nebr. Fisheries Soc. Office: Nebr State Senate State Capitol Rm 1101 Lincoln NE 68509*

AVERY, WILLIAM BARTON, broadcast executive; b. Washington, Sept. 17, 1946; s. William Barton and Cora Louise (Henry) A.; m. Linda Jean Chamberlain, Dec. 23, 1986; 1 child, William Blake. Student, Southwest Mo. State U., 1964-66. Anchor, news dir. KYTV-TV, Springfield, Mo., 1966-74; news dir. KELO-TV, Sioux Falls, S.D., 1974-76, KEVN-KIVV-TV, Rapid City, S.D., 1976-80; news dir. WNEM-TV, Saginaw, Mich., 1980-82, program mgr., 1982—; pres. AP Broadcasters Assn., Mo., 1968, Soc. Profl. Journalists, S.D., 1987; cons., speaker NATPE, Chgo., New Orleans, Washington, San Francisco. Contbr. articles to profl. publs. Pres. Pride of Saginaw, 1993, Saginaw County-Am. Cancer Soc., 1990; pres. bd. govs. Saginaw Bus.-Edn. Collaborative, 1991-92. Recipient Nat. Enterprise award AP, 1972, Internat. Film Festival award, N.Y.C., 1984. Mem. Internat. TV Program Execs., Radio and TV News Dirs. Assn. Presbyterian. Office: Sta WNEM-TV 107 N Franklin St Saginaw MI 48606

AVILA, ARTHUR JULIAN, metallurgical engineer; b. Hoboken, N.J., July 9, 1917; s. Michael Angel and Caroline Elizabeth (Bauman) A.; m. Mary Noreen DeMartino, Oct. 23, 1948; children: Susan Ekkebus, Philip, Stephen, John. BSCE, NYU, 1946; MS in Metallurgy, Stevens Inst. Tech., 1952. cert. profl. chem. and metall. cons., N.J. Prodn. engr. Western Electric Co., Kearny, N.J., 1943-57; sr. staff engr. Western Electric Co., Chgo., 1967-72; rsch. supr. W.E. Engring. Rsch. Ctr., Princeton, N.J., 1957-67; tech. dir. TRW Cinch, Chgo., Elk Grove, Ill., 1973-74; cons. Avila Engring. Svcs., Des Plaines, Ill., 1974—. Author: Production Pulse Plating, 1984; patentee in field. Commr. Cub Scouts, Middlesex, N.J. 1970; chmn. Boy Scouts Am., Middlesex, 1971-72; chmn. Cath. Youth Orgn. St. Mary's Parish, Flemington, N.J., 1960-65. Mem. Am. Soc. Metals, Am. Electroplaters Soc. Home and Office: 502 W Huntington Commons Rd Mount Prospect IL 60056-5278

AVISE, DONALD LEE, product engineering executive; b. Kansas City, Mo., Feb. 14, 1943. Student, U. Md., 1962-63. Draftsman, product engr. Rival Mfr., Kansas City, 1966-73; product engring. mgr. Dazey Corp., The New Century Air Ctr., Kans., 1973—. Patentee in field. With USAF, 1961-64. Mem. Mo. Yacht Club, VFW. Methodist. Home: R 19 Lake Lotawana MO 64086 Office: Dazey Corp 1 Dazey Cir New Century KS 66031

AVRIL, ELLEN BOWDRE, art museum curator, art historian, educator; b. Cin., Nov. 3, 1958; d. Ferdinand Ritter and Carol Bowdre (Hickman) A. BA, U. Kans., 1981, MA, 1983. Asst. instr. U. Kans., Lawrence, 1983; curatorial asst. Cin. Art Mus., 1983-85, asst. curator, 1985-88; instr. Sch. of Art U. Cin., 1992—; assoc. curator Far Ea. art Cin. Art Mus., 1988—. Contbr. articles to profl. jours. Recipient Exhbn. Planning grant NEH, 1993-95, Publ. grant Nat. Endowment for Arts, 1992-95. Mem. Assn. for Asian Studies, Coll. Art Assn., Oriental Ceramic Soc. London, Am. Assn. Mus., Midwest Mus. Conf. Office: Cin Art Mus Eden Park Dr Cincinnati OH 45202

AWE, CLARA, academic administrator; b. Lagos, Nigeria; d. Michael Okorie and Philomena (Ekeocha) Okorie; m. Olayimika Awe, June 24, 1978; children: Abiola, Bola. BS, Roosevelt U., Chgo., 1981; MS, 1983; D of Ednl. Adminstrn., No. Ill. U., DeKalb, 1995. Tng. specialist Truman Cmty. Coll., Chgo., 1986-87; adjunct prof. Northeastern U., Chgo., 1986-88; admissions counselor U. Ill., Chgo., 1991-92; sr. admissions counselor, 1991-92, 1992-93, asst. to dean, 1993; dir. urban health program Pharmacy, Chgo., 1993—; adjunct. asst. prof. U. Ill., Chgo., 1995—. Vol. Meals on Wheels, Chgo., 1994—; mentor Chgo., 1991—. Mem. AAUW, Ill. Concerned Blacks in Higher Edn., Assn. Black Women in Higher Edn., Am. Coun. on Edn. Nat. Identification, Am. Ednl. Rsch. Assn., Assn. for Study of Higher Edn., Beta Gamma Sigma. Home: 18058 Tarpon Ct Homewood IL 60430

AXELROD, BERNADETTE BONNER, television director, producer; b. Honolulu, Mar. 7, 1963; d. Horace Teddlie and Florence Ayson (Suyat) B. Student, Loyola Marymount U., 1981-82; BS in Broadcast Journalism, U. Ill., 1985. Prodn. asst. Sta. KITV-TV (ABC), Honolulu, 1984; studio technician Sta. WCIA-TV (CBS), Champaign, Ill., 1984; teaching asst. U. Ill., Champaign, 1984-85; programming coord. People's Choice TV, Rantoul, Ill., 1985; dir., tech. dir. Sta. WICS-TV (NBC), Springfield, Ill., 1985-89; producer, dir. Sta. KPLR-TV, St. Louis, 1989-90, Sta. WFLD-TV (Fox), Chgo., 1990-95, Sta., WLS (ABC), Chgo., 1995—; prodr. Children's Miracle Network Telethon, Springfield, 1988-89, dir., St. Louis, 1990; speaker St. Louis Sch. Partnership Program, 1990, U. Ill., Champaign, 1994; dir. Fox News Chgo., 1990; prodr., dir. A Sleek Preview, 1993, Bumper to Bumper, 1994. Recipient 3 Midwest Emmy award nominations, 1993, 2 nominations, 1994. Mem. NATAS, Dirs. Guild Am. (mem. East/Midwest coun. 1994—, Chgo. coordinating com. 1994—), Kappa Tau Alpha, Phi Kappa Phi. Roman Catholic. Office: WLS-ABC 190 N State St Chicago IL 60601

AXELROD, LEONARD, management consultant; b. Boston, Oct. 27, 1950; s. Morris and Doris S. A. BA, Ind. U., 1972; MPA, U. So. Calif., 1974; JD, Hamline U., 1982. Asst. dir. Ind. Jud. Ctr. Ind. U. Sch. Law, Indpls., 1974-76; cons. Booz, Allen & Hamilton, Washington, 1976-77; staff assoc. Nat. Ctr. State Cts., St. Paul, 1977-82; ptnr. Ct. Mgmt. Cons., Mpls., 1982-87; ptnr. Friedman, Farrar & Axelrod, Mpls., 1984-86; cons. Ctr. Jury Studies, Vienna, Va., 1979-82, Calif. Atty. Gen., 1972-73, Control Data Bus. Advisers, Mpls., 1982-88, prin. Ct. Mgmt. Concepts, Mpls.,1987-94; sec-treas. CMC Justice Svcs., Inc., 1994-96; v.p. Legal Rsch. Ctr., 1996—; . mem. presdl. search com. Hamline U., 1980-81. Author: North Dakota Bench Book, 1982; contbr. articles to profl. jours.; assoc. editor Law Rev. Digest, 1982. Mem. exec. bd. Am. Jewish Com., Mpls.-St. Paul, 1980; reporter Minn. Citizen Conf. on Cts., 1980; appointed to The Petrofund Bd., 1994. Samuel Miller scholar, 1981. Mem. ABA, ASPA, So. Calif. Soc. Pub. Adminstrn., Booz, Allen & Hamilton Alumni (pres. Minn. 1980), The Brandeis Soc. (exec. dir. Mpls. 1980), U. So. Calif. Midwest Alumni (exec. bd. Chgo. 1974), Phi Alpha Alpha, Phi Alpha Delta. Republican. Jewish.

AXFORD, ROY ARTHUR, nuclear engineering educator; b. Detroit, Aug. 26, 1928; s. Morgan and Charlotte (Donaldson) A.; m. Anne-Sofie Langfeldt Rasmussen, Apr. 1, 1954; children: Roy Arthur, Elizabeth Carole, Trevor Craig Charles. B.A., Williams Coll., 1952; B.S., Mass. Inst. Tech., 1952, M.S., 1955, Sc.D., 1958. Supr. theoretical physics group Atomics Internat., Canoga Park, Calif., 1958-60; assoc. prof. nuclear engring. Tex. A&M, 1960-62, prof., 1962-63; assoc. prof. nuclear engring. Northwestern U., 1963-66; assoc. prof. U. Ill., Urbana, 1966-68, prof., 1968—; cons. Los Alamos Nat. Lab., 1963—. Vice-chmn. Mass. Inst. Tech. Alumni Fund Drive, 1970-72, chmn., 1973-75; sustaining fellow MIT, 1984. Recipient cert. of recognition for excellence in undergrad. teaching U. Ill., 1979, 81; Everitt award for teaching excellence, 1985. Mem. ASME, Am. Nuclear Soc. (Excellence in Undergrad. Teaching award 1990, 95, Disting. faculty Alpha Nu Sigma 1991), SAR (sec.-treas. Piankeshaw chpt. 1975-81, v.p. chpt. 1982-3, pres. chpt. 1984-86), Kiwanis (charter life patron fellow 1992), Sigma Xi, Tau Beta Pi, Phi Kappa Phi. Home: 2017 S Cottage Grove Ave Urbana IL 61801-6353

AXT, RANDOLPH WILLIAM, volunteer municipal officer; b. Superior, Wis., Jan. 28, 1950; s. William Edward and Alice Cecelia (Claassen) A. BA in Social Studies, U. Ill., Urbana-Champaign, 1972; student, U. Wis., Superior, 1969—; MS in Edn., U. Wis., 1976; student, Wis. Indian Head Tech. Sch., Superior, 1968, Coll. of St. Scholastica, Duluth, Minn., 1984, U. Wis. Madison Extension. Cert. sec. elem. tchr., Ill., Wis., Minn. Tchr. elem. schs. Superior, Wis., 1975-78, libr. media audio visual ctr. coord. elem. schs., 1975-86; spl. capacity staff mem. Sch. Dist. of Superior, 1986-90, curriculum rev. task force mem., 1983-84, jr. Great Books tchr., 1986; recycling subcom. task force City of Superior, 1995—. Camp chmn. Douglas County Easter Seal Soc. of Wis., Superior, 1978—; bd. dirs. Wis. Coalition for Advocacy, Madison, 1978-82, Wis. Disability Coalition, 1980-81 ; Wis. alternate delagate White House Conf. of Handicapped Individuals, 1977; bd. trustees Superior Pub. Libr., 1991-94; active 1st Presbyn. Ch., Superior, 1995—; sec. Mayor's commn. on disabilities, 1990—. Mem. Cerebral Palsy Assn. of N.W. Wis. (bd. dirs. 1972—), U. Wis.-Superior Alumni Assn. (life, centennial subcom. 1992-93), U. Ill. Alumni Assn. (life), Phi Delta Kappa, Delta Sigma Omnicron. Democrat. Presbyterian. Home and Office: H.B. Sys Inc 802 17th Ave East Superior WI 54880-3466

AYADI, NAIDA ANITA, retired legislative assistant; b. Zephyrhills, Fla., Sept. 3, 1932; d. John Francis and Barbara Anita (Forbes) Hohenthaner; m. W. T. Walden Sr., Mar. 5, 1950; m. Emir Ayadi, Dec. 15, 1966 (div. 1972); children: William Thomas Jr., Barbara Jo, Carolyn S., Michael G., Steven C., Juanita N. Student, U. Md. Extension, Bitburg, Fed. Republic Germany, 1960; Student, Ventura (Calif.) Coll., 1963-64; student, Calif. Poly. Inst., 1964-65; BBA in Bus. & Admin., Travel & Tourism, Lansing C.C., 1993. Editorial asst. Ventura Star Free Press, 1963-64; supr. editorial proofreaders Telegram Tribune, San Luis Obispo, Calif., 1964-66; copy editor Pontiac (Mich.) Press (name now Oakland Press), 1966-67, Macomb Daily, Mt. Clemens, Mich., 1967-68; city editor Utica (Mich.) Sentinel, 1968-69; polit. reporter, acting mng. editor Community News, East Detroit, Mich., 1969-72; rsch. asst. Mich. Ho. Reps., Lansing, 1973-77, adminstrv. asst., 1977-91; instr. German lang. Lansing Sch. Dist., 1993-96; adminstrv. asst. Charles R. Green & Assocs., Lansing; pub. rels. coord., editor Mich. Paralyzed Vets. Am.; state sec. Ladies Aux. to VFW, 1996—. Author, editor: Investigative Report of Committee on Department of Licensing and Regulation, 1976; editor: Liederkranz Newsletter, 1993-96. Sec. 3d Dist. Dem. Com., Kalamazoo, 1979-84; sec. Eaton County (Mich.) Dem. Com., 1979-84, treas. 1984-89. Recipient Hon. Recruiter award USAF Recruiting Svc., 1983. Mem. Mich. Press Women (Woman of Achievement award 1983, pres. 1987-89), VFW Aux. (Meritorious Svc. award 1980, dist. pres. 1986-87), Am. Legion (Meritorious Svc. award 1980). Roman Catholic. Home: 1105 Eastfield Rd Lansing MI 48917-2347

AYEDUN, KEHINDE PETER, information systems executive; b. Lagos, Nigeria, Sept. 20, 1965; came to U.S., 1987; s. Joseph Olukayode and Aoka Olapeju (Ogun) A.; m. Faosatu Olubunmi Ogunnowo, July 27, 1990; 1 child, Folashade Olivia. U. Lagos, Nigeria, 1984-87, ITT Tech. Inst., Schaumburg, Ill., 1990-91. Programmer, cons. Sage Internat., Schaumburg, Ill., 1987-92; sys. adminstr. The Antenna Co., Itasca, Ill., 1992—; info. tech. cons. Algol Techs., Cary, Ill., 1994—. Mem. IEEE Computer Soc., Antenna Measurement Tech Assn., No. Ill. Deming Users Group. Office: The Antenna Co 1100 Maplewood Dr Itasca IL 60143

AYERS, JAMES CORDON, lawyer; b. Raleigh, N.C., Aug. 2, 1934; s. Edwin White and Laura Cordon (Stedman) A.; m. Leona Bell Weston, Aug. 1, 1965; children: Ashley Albert, Alan Andrew. BSBA, U. N.C., 1958; JD, Ohio State U., 1977. Bar: Ohio 1977, U.S. Dist. Ct. (fed. dist.) 1978, U.S. Ct. Appeals (6th cir.) 1983, U.S. Supreme Ct. 1992. Dist. sales mgr. Gen. Tel. Dir. Co., 1965-71; pres. Cols. Advt. co., 1971-74; sr. v.p. Assoc. Ind. Dir., 1972-74, exec. v.p. univ. dir., 1972-74; asst. atty. gen. workers' compensation sect. State of Ohio, Columbus, 1977-79; pvt. practice James C. Ayers Law Office, Columbus, 1979—; ind. hearing examiner Ohio Dept. Pub. Safety, 1993—; mem. Armed Forces Disciplinary Bd., N.C. 1960; bd. dirs. Post Exch., Camp Lejeune, 1960; summary ct. martial jurisdiction USMC Camp Lejeune, 1960. Chmn. Columbus County March of Dimes, 1961; pres. SBA; jud. panelist Ohio Mock Trial, 1995—. Recipient Dean's award, 1977. Mem. Internat. Law Soc. (co-founder 1976), Men's Golf Assn. (dir. 1990-92, treas. 1990-91, v.p. 1992), Scarlet and Gray (dir. 1988, v.p. 1989), Ohio Mock Trial (judicial panelist, 1995—), The Gang, Phi Delta Phi (Grad. of Yr.). Home: 3870 Lyon Dr Columbus OH 43220-4907 Office: 165 N High St Columbus OH 43215-2402

AYERS, JEFFREY DAVID, lawyer; b. Grant, Nebr., Nov. 30, 1960; s. William D. and Lela R. (Gilmore) A.; m. Shelly Jo Dodds, June 11, 1988. BS, Graceland Coll., 1982; MBA, JD, U. Iowa, 1985. Bar: Mo. 1985. Assoc. Stinson, Mag & Fizzell, Kansas City, Mo., 1985-88, Bryan, Cave, McPheeters & McRoberts, Kansas City, 1989-92; mem. Blackwell Sanders Matheny Weary & Lombardi L.C., Kansas City, Mo., 1992—; mayor City of Lake Tapawingo, Mo., 1993—. Trustee Little Blue Valley Sewer Dist., 1994-95. Democrat. Reorganized Ch. Latter-Day-Saints. Office: Blackwell Sanders Matheny Weary & Lombardi PC 2300 Main St Ste 1100 Kansas City MO 64108-2415

AYERS, RICHARD WAYNE, electrical company official; b. Atlanta, Aug. 23, 1945; s. Harold Richard and Martha Elizabeth (Vaughan) A.; BBA, Ga. State Coll., 1967; MBA, Ind. U., 1969; m. Nancy Katherine Martin, Aug. 9, 1969. Specialist mktg. communications research Gen. Electric Co., Schenectady, 1969-70, copywriter Lamp div., Cleve., 1970-73, supr., distbr. advt. and sales promotion, 1973-75, supr. comml. and indsl. promotional programs Gen. Electric Lighting Bus. Group, 1975-79, mgr. comml. and indsl. market distbr. and promotional programs, 1979-87, mgr. comml. and indsl. communications, 1987-91, mgr. mktg. comms., 1992—; lectr. in field. Author: Winning Through Promotion, 1987, 93, 96. Dir.-at-large Ga. Young Reps., 1966-67. Recipient Best Indsl. Promotion award Advt. Age, 1974, Incentive Showcase award Nat. Premium Sales Exec.Assn., 1975, 76, 87, 91, Gold Key award Nat. Assn. Incentive Mktg., 1976, 77, 87 Golden Key Communicators award Factory mag., 1976, Leader award Direct Mktg. Assn., 1983, Top Prize Am. Lighting Assn., 1988, Tower award Bus./Profl. Advt. Assn., 90, 91, 92, 95, Addy award Am. Advt. Assn., 1992. Mem. Elfun Soc., Blue Key, Delta Sigma Pi, Beta Gamma Sigma. Home: 26011 Lake Shore Blvd Apt 515 Cleveland OH 44132-1117 Office: Nela Park Bldg 307 Cleveland OH 44112

AYRES, JOHN T., marketing manager; b. Oak Park, Ill., Jan. 26, 1926; s. Thomas A. and Honore C. Ayres; m. Elizabeth Ayres; 1 child, Mary E. BS in Commerce, Loyola U., Chgo., 1950. Salesman St. Regis Paper Co., N.Y.C., 1950-60, Polymer Industries, Fairfield, Conn., 1960-70; mktg./sales mgr. De Soto Inc., DePlaines, Ill., 1970-76; mktg. mgr. Lustro Plastics Co., Evanston, Ill., 1976—; sec. Soc. Packaging Handling Engrs., N.Y.C., 1974-76. Pres. Longfellow and Cooper PTAs, 1974-80, Buffalo Grove (Ill.) Park Dist., 1978-82; commr. Buffalo Grove Youth Commn., 1980-82; trustee Wheeling Township, Arlington Heights, Ill., 1980-84, hwy. commr., 1984—; dep. committeeman Wheeling Township Rep. Orgn., 1988—. With U.S. Army, 1944-47. Named Rep. of Yr. Wheeling Township Rep. Orgn., 1991. Roman Catholic. Home: 377 Covington Ter Buffalo Grove IL 60089

AYRES, RALPH D., state legislator; b. Sept. 12, 1948. BS, Ind. U., 1970, MS, 1975. Coun. mem. Porter County, 1978-80; Ind. state rep. Dist. 4, 1980—; chmn. cts. and criminal code Ind. Ho. Reps., mem. environ. affairs and natural resources coms.; educator Duneland Sch. Corp. Bd. dirs. Chesterton Adult Learning Ctr. Named Outstanding Young Hoosier; recipient Elvis J. Stahr Outstanding Tchr. award. Mem. NEA, Ind. Tchrs. Assn., Phi Delta Kappa. Republican. Home: 520 Park Ave Chesterton IN 46304-2929*

AYRES, TED DEAN, lawyer, academic counsel; b. Hamilton, Mo., July 14, 1947; m. Marcia Sue Busselle; children: John Corbett, Jackson Frazer, Joseph Dean. BSBA, Cen. Mo. State Coll., 1969; JD, U. Mo., 1972. Bar: Mo. 1972, U.S. Dist. Ct. (we. dist.) Mo. 1972, U.S. Ct. Appeals (8th cir.) 1977, U.S. Supreme Ct. 1977, Colo. 1984, U.S. Ct. Appeals (10th cir.) 1984, U.S. Dist. Ct. Colo. 1984, Kans. 1987. Law clk. to presiding justice Mo. Supreme Ct., Jefferson City, 1972-73; ptnr. Stubbs & Ayres, Chillicothe, Mo., 1973-74; atty. Southwestern Bell Telephone Co., St. Louis, 1974-76; counsel U. Mo., Columbia, 1976-84; univ. counsel U. Colo., Boulder, 1984-86; gen. counsel Kans. Bd. Regents, Topeka, 1986-92, gen. counsel, dir. govtl. rels., 1992-96; acting pres. Pitts. State U., 1995; gen. counsel, assoc. to pres. Wichita State U., 1996—; adj. asst. prof. coll. bus. adminstrn. U. Colo., Denver, 1984-85, adj. assoc. prof., 1985-86; spl. asst. atty. gen. State of Colo., 1984-86, State of Kans., 1987—; presenter region II conf. Assn. Coll. Unions Internat., U. Mo., Rollas, 1983; speaker Soc. Colo. Archivists, U. Colo., Boulder, 1985; adj. prof. Washburn U., Topeka, 1990. Contbr. articles to profl. jours. Active adv. com. Boone County (Mo.) Cmty. Svcs.; mem. com. social concerns Mo. United Meth. Ch., 1979-81, supervisory com. Mothers' Morning Out program, 1980-84; adminstv. bd., com. on fin. and stewardship 1st United Meth. Ch., Topeka, 1989-91, family life coun., 1994-95; trustee Mid-Mo. chpt. Nat. Multiple Sclerosis Soc., 1981-84; mem. bd. mgrs. Topeka YMCA-Downtown Br., 1991-96, fedn. coun. Indian Guides program, 1988-91; treas. pack 175 Cub Scouts, 1990-95; bd. dirs. Innovative Tech. Enterprise Corp., 1991-94, S.W. Youth Athletic Assn., Inc., 1994-96, Topeka Zoo, 1995—. Curator scholar, 1969-70, Omar E. Robinson scholar, 1970-71, John M. Dalton Ednl. Trust scholar 1971-72. Mem. Mo. Bar Assn., Nat. Assn. Coll. and Univ. Attys. (chair southwestern region 1979-81, bd. dirs. 1985-88, various coms. 1979—, del. and presenter numerous continuing legal edn. workshops), Friends of Topeka Zoo, U. Mo. Alumni Assn. (life). Home: 2214 SW Brookfield St Topeka KS 66614-4236 Office: Wichita State U 201 Morrison Hall Wichita KS 67260-0001

BAADE, PAUL T., state legislator; b. Dec. 14, 1940; m. Carol Ann; children: Shondra, Lesli, Christopher; stepchildren: Kelley, Brent Allard. Grad. high sch., Mich. State rep. Mich. Ho. Reps., Dist. 91; vice chmn. tourism & recreation com., mem. agtl. forestry & transp. coms., Mich. Ho. Reps. Bd. dirs., sec. Printing Ind. Employment Credit Union; mem. Mona Shores Bus. Assn. Mem. NAACP, Pulaski Lodge, Am. Legion, Urban League, Trout Unltd. Home: 3131 Maple Grove Rd Muskegon MI 49441-4133*

BAAR, JOHN GREENFIELD, II, secondary school educator; b. New Haven, Sept. 10, 1952; s. William Henry and Katherine (Oie) B.; m. Janet Gail Hansa, July 9, 1988. BA, U. of the South, 1975; MS, U. Ill., Chgo., 1980; MEd, U. Ill., Urbana, 1991. Youth dir. Emmanuel Ch., La Grange, Ill., 1976-85; sci. instr. Evanston (Ill.) Twp. High Sch., 1980-81, Butler Sch., Oak Brook, Ill., 1981—; varsity basketball coach, 1981—, girls soccer coach, 1984—; cons. Dupage County Curriculum Com., Wheaton, Ill., 1990-91. Pres. Westchester (Ill.) Place Assn., 1988-91; advisor IMSA Leadership Conf., Aurora, Ill., 1990-91, Fermi Lab. Edn. Ctr., Batavia, Ill., 1990-92, DuPage Drug Edn. Com., Wheaton, Ill., 1988; v.p. Oak Brook Civic Assn., 1996—; mem. Oak Brook Police and Fire Commn., 1996—. Recipient Quest for Excellence in Chemistry award NSF, 1986, award of Excellence, Ill. Math. and Sci. Acad., 1991. Mem. AAAS, Ill. Sci. Tchrs. Assn., Nat. Sci. Tchrs. Assn., Ill. Coaching Assn., Oak Brook Edn. Assn. (region coun. 1989-91). Episcopalian. Home: 3 Brighton Ln Oak Brook IL 60521-2323 Office: Butler Sch 2801 York Rd Oak Brook IL 60521-2334

BABA, MARIETTA LYNN, business anthropologist, b. Flint, Mich., Nov. 9, 1949; d. David and Lillian (Joseph) Baba; m. David Smokler, Feb. 14, 1977 (div. 1982); 1 child, Alexia Baba Smokler; m. Ronald Delon Glotta, June 23, 1990. BA with highest distinction, Wayne State U., 1971, MA in Anthropology, 1973, PhD in Phys. Anthropology, 1975; MBA Mich. State U., 1994. Asst. prof. sci. and tech. Wayne State U., Detroit, Mich., 1975-80, assoc. prof. anthropology, 1980-88, prof., 1988—, spl. asst. to pres., 1980-82, econ. devel. officer, 1982-83, asst. provost, 1983-85; assoc. provost, 1985-89, dir. Internat. Programs and Interim Assoc. Dean of Grad. Sch., 1988-89, assoc. dean grad. sch., 1989-90, acting chair Dept. Anthropology, 1990-92; program dir. transformations to quality orgns., dir. social, behav. and econ. scis. NSF, 1994—; founder, corp. officer Applied Rsch. Teams Mich., Inc., Detroit, Intelligent Techs., Inc., Detroit; evolution researcher Wayne State U., 1975-82; cons. GM Rsch. Labs., 1988-92, Electronic Data Systems, 1990-93, McKinsey Global Inst., 1991; rsch. contractor GM/EDS, 1990—. With USAF, SBIR, 1992-94; lectr. nat. and internat. symposia, profl. confs. Contbr. numerous papers and abstracts to tech. jours; patentee in field. Bd. dirs. City-Univ. Consortium, Detroit, 1980-83; v.p. Neighborhood Svc. Orgn., Detroit, 1980-85; mem. State Rsch. Fund Feasibility Rev. Panel, 1982-94; mem. adv. panel on tech., innovation and U.S. trade U.S. Congl. Office Tech. Assessment, 1990-91, mem. panel on electronic enterprise, 1993-94; active Leadership Detroit Class IV, 1982-83; dir. Mich. Tech. Coun. (SE div.), 1984-85. Job Partnership Tng. Act grantee, 1981-90; NSF grantee, 1982, 84-85. Adv. editor for orgnl. anthropology American Anthropologist, 1990-93; Issued letters patent for method to map joint ventures and maps produced thereby. Fellow Am. Anthrop. Assn. (bd. dirs. 1986-88, exec. com. 1986-88, del. to the Internat. Union Anthrop. and Ethnol. Sci. 1990-94, chair global commn. anthropology, 1993—), Nat. Assn. Practice Anthropology (pres. 1986-88), Soc. Applied Anthropology, Phi Beta Kappa, Sigma Xi (Morton Fried award, 1991), Beta Gamma Sigma. Office: Wayne State U 137 MacKenzie Hall Detroit MI 48202

BABCOCK, CAROL BETH, postal carrier; b. Evansville, Ind., Apr. 1, 1952; d. John Wilson and Sarah Louise (Lukeman) Oberhausen; divorced; children: Cherie Ann, Roy Lewis Dickinson. Rural carrier U.S. Postal Svc., Evansville, Ind., 1976—. Author poems (Editors Choice award, Golden Poet award). Receptionist YWCA, Evansville, 1995—. Home: 516 E Jennings St Newburgh IN 47630-1441

BABCOCK, CHARLES WITTEN, JR., lawyer; b. Kansas City, Mo., Dec. 6, 1941; s. Charles W. and Esther L. (Marcy) B.; m. Sharon K. Chamberlain, June 26, 1976; children: David, William, Susan, Stephen. BA with honors, U. Mo., 1963; JD, Harvard U., 1966. Bar: Mo. 1966, Mich. 1971. Judge advocate USMC, various locations, 1966-69; assoc. Blackwell, Sanders, Kansas City, 1969-71; staff atty. Gen. Motors Corp., Detroit, 1971—. Contbr. articles to profl. jours. Nat. bd. dirs. Mothers Against Drunk Driving. Home: 917 Grand Marais St Grosse Pointe MI 48230-1867 Office: Gen Motors Corp PO Box 33122 Detroit MI 48232-5122

BABCOCK, MICHAEL WARD, economics educator; b. Bloomington, Ill., Dec. 10, 1944; s. Bruce W. and Virginia (Neeson) B.; BSBA, Drake U., 1967; M.A. in Econs., U. Ill., 1971, Ph.D. in Econs., 1973; m. Virginia Lee Brooks, Aug. 4, 1973; children: John, Karen. Teaching asst. U. Ill., Urbana, 1968, 71, research asst., 1972; prof. econs. Kans. State U., Manhattan, 1972—; cons. Santa Fe, Burlington Northern, and Union Pacific R.R., Brotherhood of Maintenence Way, United Transp. Union, Kans. Dept. Transp., Kans. Dept. Agr., U.S. Dept. Agr., Kans. Dept. Commerce. Contbr. articles to profl. jours., newspapers, mags. Apptd. to Govt. R.R. Working Group to Evaluate Class I R.R. Mergers, 1995. With U.S. Army, 1969-71. Fed. R.R. Adminstrn. grantee, 1976-78; U.S. Army C.E. grantee, 1978-79; USDA grantee, 1978-79, 80-82, 84-85; Kans. Dept. Agrl. grantee, 1987; Kans. Wheat Commn. grantee, 1989, 92, 93; Midwest Transp. Ctr. grantee, 1989, 92, 93; Kans. Dept. Transp. grantee, 1991—, Mid-Am. Transp. Ctr. grantee, 1995; recipient A.T. Kearney award Transp. Research Forum, 1987, 89, UPS Found. award, 1990, Edgar S. Bagley award Kans. State U., 1989, 93, Outstanding Rsch. in Agrl. Transp. award Burlington No. R.R., 1994. Mem. Am. Assn. Agrl. Economists, Missouri Valley Econ. Assn., Mid-Continent Regional Sci. Assn., So. Regional Sci. Assn., Nat. Assn. Bus. Economists, Transp. Research Forum, Transp. Rsch. Bd., Coun. Logistics Mgmt., So. Econs. Assn., Western Econs. Assn., Beta Gamma Sigma, Omicron Delta Epsilon. Club: Optimist. Home: 720 Harris Ave Manhattan KS 66502-3614 Office: Kans State U Dept Econs Manhattan KS 66506

BABCOCK, SCOTT V., stockbroker; b. Tucson, May 25, 1958. BS in Secondary Edn., U. Mo., 1980; MBA in Fin., Nat. U., San Diego, 1987. Lic. series 7, 63, 65 ins. Ops. mgr. Usco Distbn., P.R., 1989-90; stockbroker Merrill Lynch, Overland Park, Kans., 1990—. Mem. adv. coun. St. Joseph Hosp., Kansas City, Mo., 1992—; mem. Young Reps., Overland Park, 1992—. Capt. USMC, 1981-89. Republican. Baptist. Office: Merrill Lynch 10501 Metcalf Ave Overland Park KS 66212-1815

BABCOCK, WENDELL KEITH, religion educator; b. Mt. Morris, Mich., Nov. 21, 1925; s. George Dewey and Nettie (Miller) B.; m. Esther Marie Winger, Aug. 23, 1951; children: Timothy, Stephen. BA, Bob Jones U., Greenville, S.C., 1967; MA, PhD, Columbia Pacific U., San Rafael, Calif., 1984; PhD, World U., Benson, Ariz., 1987; LLD, London Inst. Applied Rsch., 1989; PhD, Australian Inst. Coord. Rsch., 1991; PhD Humanities, London Inst., 1992, PhD Music, 1991, LittD, 1992. Cert. min., S.C., Mich., Tenn. Pastor Free Bapt. Ch., Timmonsville, S.C., 1951-53; prof. Free Bapt. Coll., Nashville, Tenn., 1953-55, Grand Rapids (Mich.) Sch. Bible & Music,

1955-93; ret. Grand Rapids Sch. Bible (now Cornerstone Coll.), 1978-93, now assoc. dir. alumni, 1993—; chmn. gen. ministries Grand Rapids Sch. Bible, 1978—; chmn. Grand Rapids Corr. Sch., 1986-91; adj. prof. music Cornerstone Coll., 1993, assoc. dir. alumni. Composer: Songs in the Heavenlies, 1957, vol. 2, 1958; Everywhere You Go It's Christmas, 1970; arranger keyboard duets Favorite Hymn Duets, 1964; keyboard artist Sta. WFUR, 1956-57, Sound Assocs., 1961, 66, 70; author: Portraits of a Changing World, 1987, Great and Mighty Things (A History of Gull Lake), 1993, (poems) Glimpses of Worship, 1990; editor Grand Rapids Sch. Bible, 1960-94; contbr. poems Parnassus of World Poets, 1994. Organist religious stage prodns. Grand Rapids Civic Ctr., 1960-70, Gull Lake Conf., 1986—; asst. libr. Grand Rapids Sch., 1989-93. Mem. N.Y. Acad. Scis., World Wildlife Assn., Smithsonian Internat. Cultural Corr. Inst., Internat. Platform Assn., Internat. Poetry Soc., Olympoetry Soc., Internat. Biog. Ctr. (Cambridge, Eng.). Republican. Home: 3455 Williamson Ave NE Grand Rapids MI 49505-2612 Office: Cornerstone Coll 1001 E Beltline Ave NE Grand Rapids MI 49505-5803

BABJAK, RICHARD STEVEN, JR., financial counselor; b. Aurora, Ill., Nov. 13, 1963; s. Richard and Marilyn (Oros) B.; m. Margaret Saunders, Aug. 31, 1991. BA, North Cen. Coll., Naperville, Ill., 1985; MBA, Wayne State U., 1988. ChFC, CLU, RFC, CFS. Sales rep. Hilti, Inc., Detroit, 1985-86, territory salesman, 1987-88; nat. account mgr. Hilti, Inc., Chgo., 1988-89, OEM nat. account mgr., 1989-90; fin. cons. Cigna Fin., Chgo., 1990-91; fin. counselor Bedford Group, Northbrook, Ill., 1991-93; ptnr. Bedford Planning Group, Park Ridge, Ill., 1993—. Vol. event coord. Misericordia Home, Chgo., 1989—. Mem. Internat. Assn. Fin. Planners, Internat. Assn. Registered Fin. Cons., Northwestern Estate Planning Coun., Soc. Chartered Fin. Cons./CLU. Office: Bedford Planning Group 1550 N Northwest Hwy Ste 308 Park Ridge IL 60068-1460

BABU, SATRAM R., geriatric medical educator, researcher; came to U.S., 1988; BSc in Botany, Zoology and Chemistry, S.V. U., Tirupati, India, 1977, MSc in Environ. Biology, 1979, PhD in Heavy Metal Toxicology, 1985. Jr. rsch. fellow dept. zoology S.V. U., 1979-82, sr. rsch. fellow dept. zoology, 1982-85, postdoctoral fellow, 1985-88; srsch. assoc. dept. pharmacology Sch. Medicine So. Ill. U., Springfield, 1988-90; rsch. assoc. geriatric divsn. dept. internal medicine St. Louis U. Med. Sch. and VA Med. Ctr., 1990-93, rsch. asst. prof. geriatric divsn. dept. geriatric medicine, 1993—; presenter in field. Contbr. articles to profl. publs. Achievements include identification of several food contaminants in different processed foods and fruits; conducted pharmaco-kinetic studies of different drugs in small animal models; research on the mechanism of action of different cardinogens in vitro and in vivo systems; development of liver slice model to study pharmacokinetics of drugs which can be extrapolated directly to in vivo system; reported effects of heavy metal, chromium and its impacts on food chain in a highly poluted industrial area, effects of physostigmine trial drug for Alzheimers disease on neurotransimmter substances in different brain regions of rat which will help to develop the pretreatment does of the drug. Jr. rsch. fellow DST, 1979-80, SCIR, 1980-82, sr. rsch. fellow SCIR, 1982-84, rsch. assoc. fellow Dept. Energy, India, 1985-88. Mem. AAAS, Assn. Scientists of Indian Origin in Am., Inc., Indian Assn., Comparative Animal Physiology, Am. Assn. for Cancer Rsch., Inc. (assoc.). Home: 2095 Lennox Rd Apt 13 Cleveland Heights OH 44106-3299 Office: VA Med Ctr GRECC (11G-JB) Saint Louis MO 63125

BABULA, MARIA, software engineer; b. Toledo, Ohio, Nov. 12, 1966; d. Roman and Jane (Daly) B. BS in Computer Sci. and Engring., U. Toledo, Ohio, 1989. Engr. flight software systems NASA Lewis Rsch. Ctr., Cleve., 1990—. Mem. IEEE Computer Soc., Assn. Computing Machinery. Home: 688 Camden Ln Brunswick OH 44212 Office: NASA Lewis Rsch Ctr 21000 Brookpark Rd Cleveland OH 44135

BACEVICIUS, JOHN ANTHONY, V (JOHN BACE), communications executive; b. Chgo., Mar. 8, 1953; s. John Anthony IV and Mary Ann (Slazas) B.; m. Irene Joyce Rooney, Oct. 16, 1976; 1 child, John Anthony VI. BS in Psychology, Polit. Sci., Rockford Coll., 1975; MS in Journalism, Northwestern U., 1982; postgrad., The Union Inst. Accredited pub. rels. profl. Reporter, editor United Press Internat., Chgo., 1974-79; managing editor WCFL-AM, Mutual Broadcasting, Chgo., 1979-80; writer, editor WIND. Group W Westinghouse, Chgo., 1980-81; reporter, writer WBBM-AM, CBS News, Chgo., 1981-82; info. rep. IBM Field Communications, Chgo., 1982-84; staff info. rep. IBM ISG Hdqrs., Rye Brook, N.Y., 1985; sr. comms. specialist IBM Corp. Hdqrs., Armonk, N.Y., 1986-87, IBM Midwest Area Communication Svcs., Chgo., 1988-89; comms. advisor IBM Direct Mktg. Cons. Svcs., Chgo., 1990-91; pres. J.A. Bace Comms., Inc., 1991—; dir. mktg., rsch. and integrated comm. Technology Solutions Co., Chgo., 1995—; asst. prof. Northwestern U., Evanston, Ill., 1988-92; mgr. media rels. Zenith Data Systems, 1992-93. Nat. Sea Explorer Boy Scouts Am. Com., Irving, Tex., 1986—, recipient Quartermaster award, 1972, Silver Beaver award, 1990; Vigil honor, 1971. Gannett fellow, Northwestern U., 1981. Mem. NATAS, Pub. Rels. Soc. Am., Internat. Assn. Bus. Comms., U.S. Naval Inst., Publicity Club of Chgo., Soc. Profl. Journalists, Radio-TV News Dirs. Assn. Roman Catholic. Home: 252 W Washington Ave Lake Bluff IL 60044-2036 Office: Tech Solutions Co 205 N Michigan Ave Ste 15 Chicago IL 60601-5925

BACHANT, JOSEPH PETER, biologist; b. Clifton, N.J., July 8, 1937; s. Walter Strayer and Regina Gloria (Kruers) B.; m. Frances L. Trout, Nov. 25, 1959; children: Jeffrey Brian, Jennifer Jo. AAS in Forest Mgmt. Sci., Paul Smith's Coll., 1958; BS, W.Va. U., 1960; MS, Va. Poly. U., 1963. Grad. asst. Va. Poly. U., Blacksburg, 1961-63; forester U.S. Forest Svc., Littleton, N.H., 1963-65; supr. upland ecology res. Ohio Dept. Natural Resources, Delaware, Ohio, 1965-72; environ. coord. Mo. Dept. Conservation, Jefferson City, 1972-89, fisheries program coord., 1989—; adv. to river and stream com. Conservation Fedn. Mo., Jefferson City, 1989—; mem Blue Ribbon panel U.S. Fish and Wildlife Svc., Ft. Collins, Colo., 1978-80; dir. Mo. Stream Team, Jefferson City, 1989—; midwest rep. Urgan Rivers Coalition, Portland, Oreg., 1994—. Illustrator: Wildlife Mgmt. Techniques, 1963; contbr. articles to profl. jours. Recipient Izzak Walton Honor Roll award Izzak Walton League, 1993, Profl. Soil Conservationist award Soil Conservation Soc., 1993. Office: Mo Dept Conservation 2901 W Truman Blvd Jefferson City MO 65102

BACHMAN, FRANK A., financial advisor; b. Cin., Oct. 9, 1935. BSBA, Xavier U., 1957. Fin. advisor Dupont, Cin., E. F. Hutton, Cin., Shearson Lehman Bros., Cin., Smith Barney Inc., Cin. Active ch. activities, Cin. Capt. U.S. Army, 1957-59, 60-61. Mem. Rep. Club, Musketeer Club (bd. dirs.), All for One Club (co-founder). Roman Catholic. Office: Smith Barney Inc # 2300 Atrium 2 221 E 4th St Cincinnati OH 45202-4124

BACHMAN, NEAL KENYON, librarian; b. Iowa City, Aug. 10, 1950; s. Neal and Esther Elaine (Archer) B.; B.Mus. in Edn., U. Nebr., 1972, M.Ed., 1978. Tchr. instrumental and vocal music Osceola (Nebr.) Schs., 1972-73; band dir. Elkhorn (Nebr.) Public Schs., 1973-75; retail salesman Musicland, Lincoln, Nebr., 1975-76; media specialist Malcolm (Nebr.) Public Schs., 1978-83; librarian Clarinda (Iowa) High Sch., 1983-85, Eisenhower Sch., Fort Leavenworth Unified Schs., Kans., 1985-91; substitute tchr. Blue Valley Sch. Dist., Kans., 1991-92; substitute librarian Kansas City (Kans.) Pub. Library, 1992-94, libr. asst. U. Kansas Med. Ctr., 1993-94; libr. Atchison Cath. Elem. Sch., Kans., 1994-95; substitute tchr. Olathe (Kans.) Dist. Schs., 1995-96; coord. elem. libr. media Liberal Unified Schs., Kans.; vis. instr. U. Nebr.-Lincoln, 1982. Mem. Friends of Art, Nelson-Atkins Mus., Discovery Expedition, 1995. Recipient Malcolm Parent-Tchr. Orgn. cert. of recognition, 1981. Mem. ALA, Kans. Assn. Sch. Librs., Malcolm Edn. Assn. (pres. 1980-81), Nebr. Alumni Band (charter), Nebr. Ednl. Media Assn. (dir. 1982-83), Phi Delta Kappa. Contbr. articles to profl. jours. Home: 1320 B Sycamore St Liberal KS 67901

BACHMANN, DONNA GRACE, painter, art educator; b. Tulsa, Feb. 23, 1948; d. Theodore Hermann and Evelyn Grace (Trent) B.; m. Stanley Laurence Dresser, July 12, 1969 (div. 1996); 1 child, Eric Robert. BFA, Kansas City Art Inst., 1970; MA, U. Mo., 1978, MFA, 1995; $D. Adj. instr. art and art history various colls. and univs. Kansas City, 1978-86; chair, assoc. prof. art Park Coll., Parkville, Mo., 1986—; founder, dir. Campanella Gallery, Parkville, 1989—; treas. Women's Caucus for Art, 1979; asst. to muralist Eric Bransby in prodn. of Park Coll. mural, 1991. Co-editor: Women Artists: An Historical, Contemporary and Feminist Bibliography, 1978; artist mural in Libr. U. Mo., Kansas City, 1978; art critic New Art Examiner mag., 1986-90. Mem. Am. Fedn. Tchrs., Kansas City Artists Coalition (bd. dirs. 1986-88), Coll. Art Assn. Office: Park College 8700 NW River Park Dr Parkville MO 64152-4358

BACHMEIER, BRIAN ANTHONY, electrical engineer; b. Dickenson, N.D., Nov. 6, 1962; s. Marvin Anthony and Diane Mae (Tessier) B.; m. Sarah Jo Molldrem, Oct. 2, 1993. BSEE with honors, N.D. State U., 1985; MSEE, Purdue U., 1986. Registered profl. engr., Minn. Tchg. asst. Purdue U., West Lafayette, Ind., 1985-86; elec. engr. FMC Corp., Mpls., 1987-89, sr. elec. engr., 1989-92; sr. elec. engr. Aetrium, Inc., North St. Paul, 1992-96; sr. software engr. Survivalink Corp., Mpls., 1996—. Recipient 1st Team Acad. All-Am. Baseball Player award Coll. Sports Info. Dirs. of Am., 1984, 85. Mem. IEEE. Home: 4554 5th St NE Minneapolis MN 55421

BACK, ROBERT WYATT, investment executive, pharmaceutical company executive consultant; b. Omaha, Dec. 22, 1936; s. Albert Edward Jr. and Edith (Elliott) B.; m. Linaya Gail Hahn, Aug. 30, 1964; children: Christopher Frederick, Gregory Franklin. BA, Trinity Coll., 1958; postgrad. London Sch. Econs. and Polit. Sci., 1959-60, Harvard U., 1960-61; MA, Yale U., 1960. CLU, chartered fin. analyst, fin. cons. Head trader, security analyst Lincoln Nat. Life Ins. Co., Fort Wayne, Ind., 1964-69; sr. investment analyst Allstate Ins. Co., Northbrook, Ill., 1969-72; investment adv. acct. mgr. Brown Bros. Harriman & Co., Chgo., 1972-74; asst. v.p., investment analyst Harris Trust & Savs. Bank, 1974-82; v.p. instl. research Prescott Ball & Turben, 1982-83, Blunt, Ellis & Loewi, Inc., 1983-84; v.p. instl. equity sales Rodman & Renshaw, Inc., 1984-87; v.p. instnl. rsch. ins. Legg, Mason, Wood & Walker, Inc., 1987-89; mng. dir. instl. dept. J.E. Liss & Co., 1989-92; mng. dir. SNC Capital Mgmt., 1991—; mng. dir. Backfocus Cons. & Referrals, Wheaton, Ill., 1954—; mng. dir. investor pub. rels. CCR Assocs. Contbr. numerous articles to profl. jours. Mem. long-range planning com. Adlai Stevenson H.S., Prairie View, Ill., 1980-82; chmn. investments Ill. Police Pension Fund Assn., Chgo., 1985-87; pres. Buffalo Grove Police Pension Fund, 1973-90; deacon Presbyn. Ch; active Founding Coun. Nat. Edn. Access Fund, 1992; chmn. emeritus Biolipids Pharm. Corp., 1992; fund mgr. AIDS/HIV Select Fund, 1992—. Capt. USAFR, 1961-64. Woodrow Wilson fellow Yale U., 1958, English-Speaking Union fellow London Sch. Econs., 1959, Russian Research fellow Harvard U., 1960-61; subject of Superanalyst profile Crains Chgo. Bus., 1987. Fellow Fin. Analysts Fedn. (internat. del. 1974—), Assn. for Investment Mgmt. and Rsch.; mem. Inst. Chartered Fin. Analysts (sec., bd. dirs. Chgo. chpt. 1980-84), Am. Coll. CLUs and Chartered Fin. Cons. (bd. dirs. 1986-87), Yale Club Chgo. (bd. dirs. alumni assn. del. 1972—, coord. grad. and profl. alumni), Yale Club Fort Wayne (pres. 1964-69), Yale Club N.Y.C., Trinity Club (mem. exec. com. Chgo. chpt. 1987-90), Phi Beta Kappa, Pi Gamma Mu. Republican. Avocations: skiing, international travel. Home: 225 N Dorchester Ave Wheaton IL 60187-4707 Office: Backfocus Orgn 225 N Dorchester St Wheaton IL 60187-4707

BACKER, GRACIA YANCEY, state legislator; b. Jefferson City, Mo., Jan. 25, 1950; m. F. Mike Backer; 1 child, Justin. Student, S.W. Mo. State Coll. Mem. Mo. Ho. of Reps., 1983—. Active NAACP. Democrat. Baptist. Home: RR 2 Box 281 New Bloomfield MO 65063-9584 Office: Mo Ho of Reps State Capitol Building Jefferson City MO 65101-1556

BACKER, MARCELLA L., investment broker; b. Terre Haute, Ind., Aug. 8, 1968. BS in Acctg., St. Mary of Woods Coll., Terre Haute, 1990. Acct. Marsha Kelly CPA, Linton, Ind., 1990-91; acct., saleswoman Hometown USA, Bloomfield, Ind., 1991-94; investment broker J.J.B. Hilliard W.L. Lyons Inc., Jasper, Ind., 1994—. Roman Catholic. Office: JJB Hilliard WL Lyons Inc PO Box 770 269 US 231 Jasper IN 47546

BACKER, WILLIAM EARNEST, food products executive; b. Fulton, Mo., Dec. 3, 1922; s. William Earnest and Ida Lorraine (Smith) B.; m. Marjorie Jean Keller, Dec. 25, 1943; children: W. Dale, Vicki Lynn McDaniel, Carolyn Sue Cave. BA in Chemistry, Westminster Coll., 1943; postgrad., Wayne U., 1954. Chemistry lab. technician Delco Remy, Muncie, Ind., 1943-44; gen. mgr. Backer Potato Chip Co., Fulton, Mo., 1946-50, pres., chief exec. officer, 1957-88, chmn. of bd., 1988—; regional sales exec. A.P. Green Refractories, Mexico, Mo., 1950-51; salesman A.P. Green Refractories, Detroit, 1951-53; test engr. Ford Motor Co., Dearborn, Mich., 1953-57. Patentee M39-20mm Cannon components, package machine components. Pres. Fulton C. of C., 1977, also bd. dirs., chmn. planning and zoning; v.p. adminstrn./product sales Great Rivers coun. Boy Scouts Am., Columbia, Mo., 1980-92, also current trustee; chmn. bldg. and grounds Westminster Coll., Fulton, 1990-91; chmn. nominating com. Children's Hosp., Columbia; established Fulton Visitor Ctr./Collector Vehicle Mus., 1996. Lt. j.g. USN, 1944-46, PTO. Recipient Resolution, donation for bldg., Callaway County Commrs., Fulton, 1989, Disting. Eagle Scout award Nat. Eagle Scout Assn., 1995; named Disting. Indsl. Developer, Fulton Rotary, 1994. Mem. Kiwanis Internat. (lt. gov. Mo./Ark. divsns 1987-88), Fulton Kiwanis (pres. 1968, Kiwanian of Yr. 1984, 94). Republican. Presbyterian. Home: 2103 N Bluff St PO Box 128 Fulton MO 65251 Office: Backer Potato Chip Co One Industrial Rd Fulton MO 65251

BACKES, DAVID JAMES, communications educator; b. Milw., May 14, 1957; s. Gilbert Francis and Jeanne (Vogt) B.; m. Judith Kaye Miller, Aug. 26, 1978; children: Heidi, Timothy, Jennifer, Andrew. BS in Natural Resources, U. Wis., 1979, BS in Agrl. Journalism, 1982, MS in Agrl. Journalism, 1983, PhD in Mass Comm., 1988. Reporter Ely (Minn.) Echo, 1979-80, U. Wis. Coll.. Agrl. and Life Scis. News Svc., Madison, 1982-83; lectr. dept. agrl. journalism U. Wis., Madison, 1984-88; asst. prof. dept. mass comm. U. Wis., Milw., 1988-94, assoc. prof., 1994—, chair dept. mass comm., 1995-96. Author: Canoe Country: An Embattled Wilderness, 1991, The Wilderness Companion, 1992; contbr. articles to mags. and newspapers. Mem. adv. bd. Sigurd Olson Environ. Inst., Northland Coll., Ashland, Wis., 1994—. Recipient Nat. Writing award Outdoor Writers Assn. Am., 1982. Mem. Am. Soc. Environ. History, Forest History Soc. (Ralph W. Hidy award 1992), N.Am. Assn. for Environ. Edn. Office: U Wis PO Box 413 Milwaukee WI 53201-0413

BACKES, NANCY CONSTANCE, language educator; b. Petoskey, Mich., Apr. 25, 1949; d. Dale Meredith and Josephine Alvira (Pigeon) Switzer; m. Thomas John Backes, Apr. 19, 1969; 1 child, John-Thomas. BA, U. Wis., Eau Claire, 1971; MA, U. Wis., 1978, PhD, 1990. Cert. tchr. secondary edn., English, Wis. Asst. editor Country Beautiful, Waukesha, Wis., 1972-73; tchg. asst. U. Wis., Milw., 1977-78, 82-84; project asst. Ctr. for Improvement of Instrn., Milw., 1981-82; grants specialist U. Wis. Parkside, Kenosha, 1986-89; lectr. Marquette U., Milw., 1990-92, vis. asst. prof., 1992—. Author: Great Fires of America, 1973; contbr. chpts. in books. Mem. Modern Lang. Assn., Midwest Modern Lang. Assn. Home: 5943 N Berkeley Blvd Milwaukee WI 53217-4641

BACON, BETTY J., school administrator; b. Erie, Pa., June 22, 1938; d. Andrew Jackson and Betty Van Buren (Crawford) Nichols; m. Robert Sargent Bacon, June 8, 1968; 1 child, Julie Sargent Bacon. BA, U. Colo., 1962, MA, 1967; postgrad., Miami U., Oxford, Ohio, 1971-94. H.s. tchr. Rogers Hall, Lowell, Mass., 1963-66; elem. tchr. Broomfield (Colo.) Sch. Dist., 1967-68, Sacred Heart Sch., Boulder, Colo., 1968-71, Talawanda Sch. Dist., Oxford, Ohio, 1971-75, 81-82; tchr., adminstr. City of Oxford Pre-Sch., 1982—; leader workshops Butler County Tchr.'s Assn., Hamilton, Ohio, 1972, 74. Chmn. for drive for children's levy, Butler County Mental Health Bd., Hamilton, 1985; neighborhood dir. and troop leader Girl Scouts U.S., Oxford, 1982-91; v.p. Oxford Assn. for Ednl. Gifted, 1983-85; asst. coach Talawanda Girls Tennis Team, Oxford, 1993—; capt. mem. drive McCullough-Hyde Hosp. Aux., Oxford, 1985; mem. Faith Luth. Ch., 1972—. Named Oxford Citizen of Yr., City of Oxford coun., 1987, Outstanding Child Profl., Butler county Assn. Edn. Young Children, Hamilton, 1994; recipient Coun. Key award Great Rivers Girl Scouts, Cin., 1988. Mem. Ohio Tchrs. Assn., Alpha Omicron Pi, Phi Alpha Theta. Republican. Home: 411 Maxine Dr Oxford OH 45056 Office: City of Oxford 101 East High Oxford OH 45056

BACON, JOHN STUART, biochemical engineer; b. Washington, June 8, 1959; s. Edward Jennings and Martha Ora (Landefeld) B.; m. Julie Ann BlahniK, Oct. 1, 1994; 1 child, Ethan Edward. BS in Chemistry, U. Mich., 1982; MS in Chemical Engring., New Mex. State U., 1989. Student scientist NIH Lab. of Molecular Biology, Bethesda, Md., 1980; rsch. asst. U. Mich. Medical Sch., ANn Arbor, 1982-84; grad. asst. dept. of chemical engring. New Mex. State Univ., Las Cruces, 1984-87; process devel. engr. ChemGen Corp., Gaithersburg, Md., 1987-90; rsch. engr. Red Star Yeast Univ. Foods Corp., Milw., 1990-92, sr. rsch. engr., 1992-94, process engr., 1994—; adv. com. New Mex. grad. student, 1986-87; mem. Engrs. Coun., Las Cruces, 1987. Contbr. articles to profl. jours. Mem. Grand Jury Dona Ana County, Las Cruces, 1985. Mem. AICE, Am. Chem. Soc., Phi Kappa Phi, Soc. Omega Chi Epsilon. Home: N7673 State Road 175 Theresa WI 53091-9762 Office: Universal Foods Corp 433 E Michigan St Milwaukee WI 53202

BACUS, TERRENCE LEE, labor relations consultant; b. Vinton County, Ohio, Sept. 30, 1944; s. John E. and Margery A. (Jeffers) B.; m. Mary K. Kerr, July 11, 1964; children: Terrence L. Jr., Sherri D. BS in Indsl. Mgmt., Franklin U., 1975. Staff rep. AFSCME-AFL/CIO, Columbus, Ohio. Subchmn. Columbus Vets. Day Com., 1987-94, Armed Forces Day, Columbus, 1989; pres. Music Boosters, Canal Winchester, Ohio, 1983-84, Cmty. Labor Day Festival, Canel Winchester, 1985-86. Mem. Am. Soc. Pers. Adminstrs., Ohio Head Injury Assn. (exec. dir.), AMVETS, Am. Legion, Vietnam Vets. Am., (vets. svc. rep.), F&A Masons, Shriners, Order Ea. Star, Sigma Kappa Phi (nat. pres. 1974). Home: 240 Cherokee Ct N Canal Winchester OH 43110-1027

BACZENAS, PATRICK J., public relations professional; b. St. Louis, Dec. 19, 1955. BS in Comms., Ctrl. Mo. State U., Warrensburg, 1978. Coord. mktg. comms. St. Louis Blues Hockey Club, 1978-83; comms. coord. GTE, Wentsville, Mo., 1983-93; mgr. pub. rels. Thermadyne Industries, Inc., St. Louis, 1993—. Author articles. Mem. St. Charles Beautification, 1992—. Mem. Internat. Assn. Bus. Communicators, Internat. TV Assn. Roman Catholic. Office: Thermadyne Industries Inc 101 S Hanley Rd Saint Louis MO 63105-3406

BADAL, JAMES JESSEN, JR., writer, educator; b. Cleve., Feb. 9, 1943; s. James Jessen and Margaret Elizabeth (Boal) B. BA, Western Res. U., 1965, MA, 1967; PhD, Case Western Res. U., 1975. Classical music writer Cleve. After Dark, 1969-70; tchr. English Westminster Coll., New Wilmington, Pa., 1969-76, Ursuline Coll., Pepper Pike, Ohio, 1977-81; writer Cleve. Opera, 1977—; thcr. English and journalism Cuyahoga C.C., Cleve., 1981—; writer for Cleve. Edit., 1984-90, Fanfare, Tenafly, N.J., 1986-91; contbg. editor No. Ohio Live, Cleve., 1980-84. Author: Recording the Classics: Maewtros, Music and Technology, 1996, also articles. Home: 18000 Winslow Rd Shaker Heights OH 44122 Office: Cuyahoga CC 4250 Richmond Highland Hills OH 44122

BADALAMENT, ROBERT ANTHONY, urologic oncologist; b. Detroit, Mar. 20, 1954; s. Louis F. and Grace D. (Costello) B.; m. Providence F. Vitale, Nov. 9, 1980; children: Louis F., Peter P., Grace F. BS in Biology, So. Meth. U., 1976; MD, Emory U., 1980. Diplomate Am. Bd. Urology. Surg. intern Henry Ford Hosp., Detroit, 1980-81, surg. resident, 1981-82, urologic resident, 1982-85; fellow in urologic oncology Meml. Sloan Kettering Cancer Ctr., N.Y.C., 1985-87; asst. prof. Ohio State U., Columbus, 1987-92, assoc. prof., 1992-95, prof. Sch. Pub. Health, 1995—; mem. attending staff Arthur James Cancer Ctr., Columbus, 1990-95, Crittenton Hosp., Rochester Hills, Mich., 1995—. Contbr. chpt. to book, articles to profl. jours. Fellow ACS; mem. AMA, Am. Soc. Clin. Oncology, Soc. Univ. Urologists, Soc. Urologic Oncology, Soc. for Basic Urologic Rsch., Am. Cancer Soc. (bd. trustees Mich. divsn.). Office: Rochester Urology PC Ste 420 1135 W University Dr Rochester Hills MI 48307-1831

BADALAMENTI, ANTHONY, financial planner; b. St. Louis, Apr. 1, 1940; s. Sebastino and Grace (Orlando) B.; 1 child, Annette Marie. BS in Acctg., Washington U., 1970. CPA, Mo.; registered investment advisor. Staff acct. Fischer & Fischer, CPAs, St. Louis, 1959-63; acct. McDonnell Aircraft Corp., St. Louis, 1963-65; asst. chief acct. Dempsey Tegler, Inc., St. Louis, 1965-66; contr. Cummins Mo. Diesel, Inc., St. Louis, 1966-67; sr. acct. Elmer Fox & Co., CPAs, St. Louis, 1967-71; pvt. practice St. Louis, 1972-94; fin. planner Asset Builders Fin. Planners, St. Louis, 1995—; tchr. Meramec C.C., St. Louis, 1973-75. Mem. Mo. Soc. CPAs, Crestwood-Sunset Hills C. of C. (pres. 1980-81, Bus. Profl. Month award 1986), Rotary (pres. Crestwood-Sunset Hills chpt. 1982-83). Republican. Roman Catholic. Home: 1290 Enderbury Saint Louis MO 63125 Office: 8711 Watson Rd # 100 Saint Louis MO 63119-5100

BADER, RONALD L., advertising executive; b. 1931. With Amana (Iowa) Refrigeration, 1949-55, Gittens Co., Milw., 1955-60, Brady Co., Milw., 1961-70, Hoffman, York, Baker & Johnson, Milw., 1971-74; with Bader Rutter & Assocs., Inc., Brookfield, Wis., 1975—, now pres, sec., treas. Office: Bader Rutter & Assoc Inc Bishop's Wood Ctr 13555 Bishops Ct Ste 300 Brookfield WI 53005-6224*

BADERTSCHER, MARK ALLEN, vocational educator; b. Bluffton, Ohio, Oct. 9, 1964; s. Ronald Ray and Sharlee Gene (Burge) B. BS in Agr., Ohio State U., 1987. Agrl. edn. instr. Northmor Local Schs., Galion, Ohio, 1987-89, Northwestern Local Schs., Springfield, Ohio, 1989-91, Liberty-Benton Local Schs., Findlay, Ohio, 1991—; bd. dirs., mem. adv. bd. and sub-region coord. N.W. Ohio Regional Profl. Devel. Ctr., U. Findlay, 1992—. Deacon, consistory com., chmn. pastoral search com. St. Johns United Ch. of Christ. Mem. Am. Vocat. Assn., Nat. Vocat.-Agr. Tchrs. Assn., Am. Fedn. Tchrs., Ohio Vocat. Assn., Ohio Vocat.-Agr. Tchrs. Assn. (computer coord., Dist. 4 Outstanding Young Mem. of Yr. award 1992), Ohio Fedn. Tchrs., Liberty-Benton Tchrs. Assn., Hancock County Vocat.-Agr. Tchrs. Assn. (chmn.), Ohio State U. Alumni Assn. Republican. Home: 8632 County Road 84 Findlay OH 45840-9323 Office: Liberty-Benton High Sch 9050 W State Route 12 Findlay OH 45840-9304

BADO, KENNETH STEVE, automotive company administrator; b. Amherst, Ohio, Mar. 13, 1941; s. Steve and Hildegarde Paulene (Gutosky) B.; m. Linda Bonita Crabtree, May 30, 1962 (div. Oct. 1989); children: Bradley Steve, Cheryl Lynn Smith, John Robert; m. Polly Ann Steele, Nov. 28, 1989. Student, Ohio U., 1958-60, Lorain County Community Coll., 1960-62. Mfg. planning specialist Ford Motor Co., Lorain, Ohio, 1961—; farmer Henrietta, Ohio, 1972—; owner, mgr. The Galleon, Lorain, 1986—; leader Sub-System Group (Group Tng.), Lorain, 1987-92. Advisor Lorain County Steer Club (4-H), Lorain County, 1977-93, Henrietta Hazers Club (4-H), Lorain County, 1976-88. Mem. Am. Quarter Horse Assn., Ohio Quarter Horse Assn., Moose, Masons (32 degree), Scottish Rite Soc. Republican. Lutheran. Home: 12359 Baird Rd # 2 Oberlin OH 44074-9632 Office: The Galleon 4875 W Erie Ave Lorain OH 44053-1331

BADRA, ROBERT GEORGE, philosophy, religion and humanities educator; b. Lansing, Mich., Dec. 8, 1933; s. Razouk Anthony and Anna (Paul) B.; m. Maria Teresa Beer, Oct. 25, 1968 (div. 1973); m. Kristen Lillie Stuckey, Dec. 30, 1977; children: Rachal Jennifer, Danielle ElizabethJane. BA, Sacred Heart Sem., 1957; MA, Western Mich. U., 1968; MDiv, St. John's Provincial Sem., 1985. Ordained priest Roman Cath. Ch., 1961. Mem. faculty Kalamazoo Valley C.C., 1968—, prof. philosophy, religion and humanities, 1968—; adj. prof. Nazareth Coll., 1985-91, Siena Heights Coll., 1993—. Author: Meditations for Spiritual Misfits, 1983; columnist Western Mich. Cath., Grand Rapids, 1983-88. Bd. dirs. Kalamazoo Coun. for the Humanities, 1983-86, Van Buren Youth Camp, 1993-95. Recipient Edn. award Exxon, 1996; NEH grantee, 1991—, project dir., 1993—, Exxon Edn. Innovation award The Genetics Revolution, 1996. Mem. Assn. Religion and Intellectual Life. Office: Kalamazoo Valley CC PO Box 4070 Kalamazoo MI 49003-4070

BAER, JOHN RICHARD FREDERICK, lawyer; b. Melrose Park, Ill., Jan. 9, 1941; s. John Richard and Zena Edith (Ostreyko) B.; m. Linda Gail Chapman, Aug. 31, 1963; children—Brett Scott, Deborah Jill. BA, U. Ill., Champaign, 1963, JD, 1966. Bar: Ill. 1966, U.S. Dist. Ct. (no. dist.) Ill. 1967, U.S. Ct. Appeals (7th cir.) 1969, U.S. Ct. Appeals (D.C. cir.) 1975, U.S. Ct. Appeals (9th cir.) 1979, U.S. Supreme Ct. 1975. Assoc. Keck,

Mahin & Cate, Chgo., 1966-73, ptnr., 1974—; mem. Ill. Atty. Gen.'s Franchise adv. bd., 1992-94, 96—, chair 1996—. Mem editl. bd. U. Ill. Law Forum, 1964-65, asst. editor, 1965-66; contbg. editor: Commercial Liability Risk Management and Insurance, 1978; topics and articles editor Franchise Law Jour., 1995—. Mem. Plan Commn., Village of Deerfield (Ill.), 1976-79, chmn., 1978-79, mem. Home Rule Study Commn., 1974-75, mem. home rule implementation com., 1975-76. Mem. ABA (articles editor Franchise Law jour. 1995—), Internat. Franchise Assn. (legal/legis. com. 1990—), Inter-Pacific Bar Assn., Union Internat. des Avocats (sec., franchise commr. 1993-94, v.p. 1994—), Ill. Bar Assn. (competition dir. region 8 nat. moot ct. 1974, profl. ethics com. 1977-84, chmn. 1982-83, spl. com. on individual lawyers advt. 1981-83, profl. responsibility com. 1983-84, standing com. on liaison with atty. registration and disciplinary commn. 1989-93), Internat. Bar Assn. Office: 77 W Wacker Dr Fl 49 Chicago IL 60601-1634

BAER, SCOTT E., social worker; b. Honolulu, Oct. 2, 1954; s. Willis Equan and Mary Ann (Helenihi) B.; m. Arlene Frances Buss, May 8, 1982; children: Bryan S., Amy L., Alyssa M. AA in Biology, Belleville (Ill.) Coll., 1975; BA in Human Svcs., So. Ill. U., Edwardsville, 1977; MSW, St. Louis U., 1988. Cert. sch. social worker; lic. social worker, Ill. Farmer Trenton, Ill., 1972-77; child care worker Edgewood Children's Ctr., Webster Groves, Mo., 1977-79; mental health technician Belleville Mental Health, 1979-81; probation officer St. Clair County Ct. Svcs., Belleville, 1981-85; crisis intervention worker Children's Home and Aid Soc., Belleville, 1985-87; sch. social worker Belleville Alternative Night Sch., 1986—. Mem. gov.'s youth planning initiative Dept. Children and Family Svcs., East St. Louis, Ill., 1989—; adv. bd. Gateway Inc., Caseyville, Ill., 1992-95; mem. Leban Sch. Dist. #9 Bd. of Edn., 1993; vol. Big Bros./Big Sisters, Cahokia, Ill., 1975-77. Mem. NASW, Ill. Alternative Edn. Assn. (pres. 1994-95), MSW Student Assn. (treas. 1987-88). Democrat. United Ch. of Christ. Office: Belleville Alt Night Sch 2600 W Main Belleville IL 62223

BAER, WERNER, economist, educator; b. Offenbach, Ger., Dec. 14, 1931; came to U.S., 1945, naturalized, 1952; s. Richard and Grete (Herz) B. BA, Queens Coll., N.Y.C., 1953; MA, Harvard U., 1955, PhD, 1958; Doctor honoris causa, Fed. U. of Pernambuco, Brazil, 1988. Instr. Harvard U., 1958-61; asst. prof. Yale U., New Haven, 1961-65; asso. prof. Vanderbilt U., Nashville, 1965-69; prof. Vanderbilt U., 1969-74; prof. econs. U. Ill., Urbana, 1974—; vis. prof. U. São Paulo, Brazil, 1966-68, Vargas Found., Brazil, 1966-68; Rhodes fellow St. Antony's Coll., Oxford (Eng.) U., 1975. Author: The Brazilian Economy: Growth and Development, 4th edit., 1995, Privatization in Latin America, vol. 17, 1994; co-editor: Paying the Costs of Austerity in Latin America, 1989, U.S. Policies and the Latin American Economies, 1990, Latin America: The Crisis of the Eighties and the Opportunities of the Nineties, 1992, Latin America-Provalization, Property Rights and Deregulation, 1993. Decorated Order So. Cross (Brazil). Mem. Am. Econ. Assn., Latin Am. Studies Assn. Home: 1703 Devonshire Dr Champaign IL 61821-5901 Office: U Ill 1407 W Gregory Dr Urbana IL 61801-3606

BAERGA, CARLOS OBED ORTIZ, professional baseball player; b. San Juan, P.R., Nov. 4, 1968. With Cleve. Indians, 1989—; mem. Am. League All-Star Team, 1992-93. Named. to Am. League Silver Slugger Team, 1993-94. Office: Cleve Indians Cleve Stadium 2401 Ontario St Cleveland OH 44115-4003*

BAETZEL, TRACEY ALENE, information systems professional; b. Chgo., Apr. 6, 1954; d. Edward A. Baetzel and Harriette W. (Taylor) Miller. BA cum laude, U. Mich., 1976; MBA, Ea. Mich. U., 1983. Systems analyst U. Mich. Hosp., Ann Arbor, 1977-80; tech. support supr. Data Design, Ann Arbor, 1980-82; dir. info. systems Honigman/Miller, Detroit, 1983—; instr. Wayne State U., Detroit, 1989-91. Mem. Law Net (trade chmn. 1988-89, regional v.p. 1990-91, co-chmn. 1992-93). Unitarian. Office: Honigman Miller 2290 1st Nat Bldg Detroit MI 48226

BAGBY, MARVIN ORVILLE, chemist; b. Macomb, Ill., Sept. 27, 1932; s. Byron Orville and Geneva Floriene (Filbert) B.; m. Mary Jean Jennings, Aug. 31, 1957; children: Gary Lee, Gordon Eugene. BS, MS, Western Ill. U., 1957, LHD (hon.), 1992. With No. Regional Rsch. Ctr., USDA Agrl. Rsch. Svc., Peoria, Ill., 1957—, rsch. leader fibrous products rsch. unit, 1974-80; mgr. No. Agrl. Energy Ctr., 1980-85, also rsch. leader hydrocarbon plants and biomass rsch. unit, 1980-82, leader oil chem. rsch., 1985—; With National Ctr. for Agrl. Utilization Rsch. USDA Agrl. Rsch. Svc., Peoria, Ill., 1957—; cons. numerous spl. assignments govt. projects; team leader devel. process for making newsprint. Contbr. articles to profl. jours. Served with AUS, 1953-55. Recipient alunmi achievement award Western Ill. U., 1980, rsch. and devel. 100 award 1988, Am. Soybean Assn., hon. life membership award, 1993, domestic mktg. award 1990, ARS tech. transfer award 1990, award for excellence in tech. transfer Fed. Lab. Consortium, 1991, disting. svc. award U.S. Dept. Agriculture, 1992. Mem. AAAS, TAPPI, Am. Chem. Soc., Am. Oil Chemists Soc., N.Y. Acad. Sci., Am. Soc. Agrl. Engrs., Assn. for the Advancement Indsl. Crops. Methodist. Home: 209 S Louisiana Ave Morton IL 61550-2705 Office: 1815 N University St Peoria IL 61604-3902

BAGLEY, THOMAS STEVEN, private equity investor; b. Chgo., Oct. 25, 1952; s. James A. and Corinne M. (Catania) B.; m. Christine A. Elliott; 1 child, Derek Elliott Bagley. BA in Econs. cum laude, North Park Coll., Chgo., 1974; MBA in Fin., DePaul U., 1977. Mgr. contr. div. Continental Ill. Nat. Bank, Chgo., 1975-78, officer Cleve. Office, 1978-81, asst v.p. Corr. Banking, 1981, v.p. mgr. Ill. & Wisc., 1981-84; v.p. area mgr. of Midwest Area of Leveraged Capital Group Citicorp North Am., Inc., Chgo., 1984-88; founder, gen. ptnr. Pfingsten Ptnrs., Deerfield, Ill., 1989—; founder, gen. ptnr. Chgo. Assocs. Internat., 1988-89; bd. dirs. Woodall Pub. Group, Inc., Hallcrest, Inc., Huebcore Comm., Inc., Am. Acad. Suppliers, Inc., Park Foods, L.P. and Barjan Products, L.P. Recipient Blum Glover scholar for academic achievement in Bus. Adminstrn., 1973-74. Mem. Union League Club of Chgo., Conway Farms Golf Club, Lake Forest Club, Delta Mu Delta. Republican. Lutheran. Home: 1155 Ashlawn Dr Lake Forest IL 60045-1504 Office: Pfingsten Ptnrs Corporate 500 Centre 520 Lake Cook Rd Ste 375 Deerfield IL 60015-4926

BAGSTAD, KRISTIN KIM, nurse specialist, pediatric nurse practitioner; b. Salina, Kans., Nov. 11, 1954; d. Richard William and Barbara Bee (Billings) Fry; m. Brian D. Bagstad. Diploma in Nursing, St. Francis Hosp. Sch. Nursing, Wichita, Kans., 1975; BSN, Pitts. State U., 1979; MSN, U. Kans. Med. Ctr., 1987. cert. PNP. Staff nurse St. Francis Hosp., Wichita, Kans., 1975-76, charge nurse, 1976-78; staff nurse St. Joseph's Hosp., Kansas City, 1979-80, Wesley Med. Ctr., Wichita, Kans., 1981; charge nurse Wesley Med. Ctr., Wichita, Mo., 1981-82; nurse clin. Prime Health, Kansas City, 1982-87; clin. nurse specialist Children's Mercy Hosp., Kansas City, 1987-95; PNP Children's Mercy Hosp., Kansas City, Mo., 1995—; mem. affiliate faculty U. Mo., Kansas City, 1988—; mem. family ad. bd. Am. Lung Assn., Kansas City, 1987-94, mem. program com., 1992—; coord. Asthma Camp Western Mo., 1987—. Author, researcher: Erikson's Developmental Milestones in Relation to a Chronic Immune Deficiency Syndrome, 1992; contbr. articles to profl. jours. Vol. nurse Turner House Children's Clinic, Kansas City, Kans., 1991-92, bd. dirs. Turner House, 1992-95. Mem. ANA, Mo. Nurses Assn., Am. Acad. Allergy/Asthma/Immunology, Immunology Nurses Assn., Nsat. Assn. Pediat. Nurse Assocs. and Practitioners (Kansas City chpt.), Sigma Theta Tau. Episcopalian. Office: Children's Mercy Hosp 2401 Gillham Rd Kansas City MO 64108-4619

BAHADUR, B. N., business executive; b. Mysore, India, Nov. 6, 1945. MBA, Western Mich. U., 1973. Pres. Bahadur & Assocs., East Detroit, 1977-87; chmn. Accurate Boring Co., Fraser, Mich., 1984—; pres. Bahadur Balan & Kazerski Ltd., Southfield, Mich., 1987—; chmn. Accurate Fabricating, Roseville, Mich., 1990—. Treas. India League of Am., Detroit, 1993-94. Mem. Turn Around Mgmt. Assn., Comml. Law League of Am., Nat. Bankrupty Trustees Assn. Office: Bahadur Balan & Kazerski 300 Galleria Office Ctr Southfield MI 48034-4700

BAHR, SHEILA KAY, physician; b. Highland Park, Mich., June 2, 1956; d. Thomas Joseph and Catherine Mary (McCrohan) Bernhardt; m. Wayne Edward Bahr, June 19, 1981. BS, U. Mich., Dearborn, 1978; DO, Mich. State U., 1982. Diplomate Am. Osteo. Bd. of Internal Medicine. Intern Botsford Gen. Hosp., 1982-83, resident in internal medicine, 1983-86; staff physician Health Alliance Plan, Livonia, Mich., 1986-87; pvt. practice Farmington, 1987-95; physician Henry Ford Health Sys., 1996—; asst. clin. prof. Coll. Osteo. Medicine Mich. State U., 1991—. Regent's scholar U. Mich., 1974; named Physician Trainer of Yr., Garden City (Mich.) Osteo. Hosp., 1990. Fellow Am. Coll. Osteo. Internists; mem. Am. Osteo. Assn., Mich. Assn. Osteo. Physicians and Surgeons, Oakland County Osteo. Assn. Office: 9327 Telegraph Redford MI 48239

BAIK-KROMALIC, SUE S., metallurgical engineer; b. Seoul, Korea, June 21, 1965; came to U.S., 1968; d. Boo Sung Baik and Katherine Kim; m. Joseph Jay Kromalic, Dec. 14, 1991. BS in Metallurgical Engring., Ohio State U., Columbus, 1990. Project engr. Cummins Engine Co., Columbus, Ind, 1988-89; engring. staff, materials testing and devel. engr. Honda Am. Mfg., Inc., East Liberty, Ohio, 1990-92; trainer problem solving Honda Am., Inc., East Liberty, Ohio, 1992-93, new model project engr., 1993-94, leader tech. devel., 1994; prodn. planning ops. and control, 1994-95; engring. coord. mfg. ops. and cost control Honda of Am. Mfg., Inc., 1995—; guest speaker Ohio State U., Columbus, 1991—. Mem. ASM Internat. (awards chmn. 1992-94, sec. 1994, chpt. task force 1993-94, membership devel. com. 1994—, treas. 1994-96, chpt. coun. 1994—, chairperson 1996—). Roman Catholic. Office: Honda of Am Mfg Inc 11000 State Route 347 East Liberty OH 43319-9407

BAILEY, CHARLES WILLIAM, management consultant, researcher; b. Mpls., May 26, 1932; s. Charles Nelson and Ruth Elthleen (Brower) B.; m. Anne G. Stultz (div. 1979); children: Charles R., George L., Dana R., William W., Jonathan D., Margaret R. BBA in Indsl. Rels. and Psychology, U. Minn., 1955. Orgn. analyst Duluth Missabe & Iron Range Railway, 1958-60, supr. orgn. planning, 1960-67; dir. safety Duluth (Minn.) Missabe and Iron Range Ry., 1967-86; pres. Bailey and Assocs., Duluth, 1986—; cons. rail safety com. NRC, Washington, 1979-80; chmn. adv. com. masters program-indsl. safety U. Minn., 1976—. Author: Using Behavioral Techniques to Improve Safety Program Effectiveness, 1989; Inventor system for digital computer rec. of petroglyphs, 1991. Advisor Minn. Safety Coun., Mpls., 1982-86; bd. dirs., treas. Duluth Pub. Schs. Bd. of Edn., 1967-71. With U.S. Army, 1955-58, Korea. Mem. Nat. Safety Coun. (gen. chmn. r.r. sect. 1973-74), Assn. Am. R.R.s Washington (chmn. safety rsch. com. 1976-86), No. Lakes Archaeol. Soc. (sec., treas. 1988-91), Inst. for Study of Am. Cultures (researcher), Epigraphic Soc. (contbr.), Am. Rock Art Rsch. Assn., Kiwanis. Republican. Presbyterian. Office: Bailey and Assocs 530 N 40th Ave E Duluth MN 55804-2158

BAILEY, CHERYL, consulting company executive; b. Detroit, Aug. 21. V.p. HighEnergy Inc., St. Claire Shore, Mich., 1984-86; adminstrv. asst. Hoover Tool and Die, Warren, Mich., 1984-88; v.p. Tool Consulting Inc., Fraser, Mich., 1988—. Recipient Pres.'s Phys. Fitness award, 1993. Republican. Office: Tool Consulting Inc 33759 Groesbeck Hwy Fraser MI 48026-4207

BAILEY, ELLA JANE, academic librarian; b. Omaha, Aug. 26, 1940; d. William and Ann (Maguire) Dougherty; m. Leon St. Pierre Bailey, Aug. 10, 1969; 1 child, Cornelia Ann. BA in English, Duchesne Coll., Omaha, 1962; MA in LS, U. Denver, 1963. Govt. document libr. Omaha Pub. Libr., 1963; head interlibr. loan dept. U. Omaha, 1963-69; asst. br. libr. San Antonio Pub. Libr., 1969-70; sr. cataloging libr. Our Lady of the Lake Coll., San Antonio, 1970-73; audiovisual cataloger U. Nebr., Omaha, 1979-83, chair bibliog. access, 1984—. Recipient Disting. Svc. award Nebr. Libr. Assn., 1983. Home: 6328 Evans St Omaha NE 68104-3326 Office: U Nebr at Omaha 60th and Dodge St Omaha NE 68182-0726

BAILEY, JAMES C., financial consultant; b. Omaha, Aug. 31, 1956; m. Kanoengnit Bailey, Oct. 25, 1987; children: Bonita, James. BS in Criminal Justice, U. Nebr., 1979; MBA in Fin., Nat. U., San Diego, 1991. Lic. in ins. SEC. Commd. officer USMC, 1979, advanced through grades to maj.; ret., 1991; fin. cons. Merrill Lynch, Overland Park, Kans., 1992—. Maj. USMCR, 1991—. Methodist. Office: Merrill Lynch 10501 Metcalf Ave Overland Park KS 66212-1815

BAILEY, KRISTEN, legal assistant; b. Davenport, Iowa, Jan. 5, 1952; d. Donald Ray and Alta Llewellyn (Mandler) B. AS, Mo. So. State Coll., 1974; cert. paralegal studies, Rockhurst Coll., 1978. Legal sec. Ralph E. Baird, Lawyer, Joplin, Mo., 1972-75; legal asst. Benny J. Harding, Atty. at Law, Kansas City, Mo., 1976-87, Polsinelli, White, Vardeman & Shalton, Kansas City, 1988—; speaker in field. Vol. Heartland's Sch. Riding, Overland Park, Kans., 1988—; mem. Friends of the Zoo, Kansas City Mus. Assn. Winner Ark. and Iowa state championships, 3-gaited Pleasure Horse, Am. Saddlebred Pleasure Horse Assn., 1981; named Kansas City Legal Sec. of Yr., 1979. Mem. ATLA (paralegal mem. 1993-95), Kansas City Assn. Legal Assts. (bd. dirs. 1993-94), Kansas City Legal Sec. Assn. (bd. dirs. 1977-89, 92-93, pres. 1979-81, life mem.), Mid-Am. Saddle Horse Club (sec. 1981-83). Republican. Methodist. Office: Polsinelli White Vardeman & Shalton 700 W 47th St Ste 1000 Kansas City MO 64112-1805

BAILEY, MARIANNE THERESE, social service administrator; b. Evanston, Ill., Dec. 26, 1949; d. Eugene Thomas and Marguerite O'Brien B. Student, Sorbonne, Paris, 1970, San Francisco Coll. Women, 1967-69; BA, Barat Coll. of Sacred Heart, 1971; cert., U. Paris, Sorbonne, 1972; ancien élève, Ecole du Louvre, Paris, 1973-74. Cert. cmty. transp. mgr. Tchr. 2d and 3d grade Marymount Internat. Sch., Neuilly, France, 1971-72; dir. Ctr. Audio Visuel des Langues, Enghien, France, 1973-76; pre-sch. dir. P.L. Child Care Ctrs., Glenview, Ill., 1976-81; with dept. def. civilian Child Support Svcs., Ft. Sheridan, Ill., 1981-82; dir. tng. and spl. events N.W. Mcpl. Conf., Mt. Prospect, Ill., 1982-84; exec. dir. PRC Paratransit Svcs., Park Ridge, Ill., 1984—. Vice pres. N.W. Suburban chpt. Citizens with Disabilities; lobbyist disabled and sr. citizens State of Ill.; treas., exec. bd. Wheeling Twp. Rep. Org., 1988—; del. Rep. State Conv., Ill., 1994, 96; pres. N.W. Suburban Coun. for Cmty. Svcs., 1989-91; v.p. Twp. Ofcls. Ill. Disabled Advocacy, 1985-90, pres., 1990—; active Chgo. Area Transp. Study, 1984—, Gov.'s Task Force on Aging and Disability, 1987—, PACE-ADA Adv. Com., 1990—, Sage Sr. Advocacy Group, 1990—; mem. Twp. Ofcls. of Cook County, N.W. Suburban Regional Transp. Consortium, 1992—, Project Action II. steering com., 1995—. Mem. AAUW, ALTRUSA, Am. Pub. Transit Assn., Am. Pub. Works Assn., Ill. Paratransit Assn. (bd. dirs., sec. 1987-91), Ill. Assn. for Cmty. Transp. (bd. dirs.), Ill. Alliance Info. & Referral, Cmty. Transp. Assn. Am. (state del.), Lions Club (v.p. 1990-92, pres. 1992-93, Lion of the Yr. 1991-92, mem. bd. dirs. 1988-94, dist. diabetes awareness chmn. 1991-93), Pi Delta Phi. Roman Catholic. Home: 740 Weidner Rd Buffalo Grove IL 60089 Office: PRC Paratransit Svcs 1700 Ballard Rd Park Ridge IL 60068-1006

BAILEY, RICHARD R., technology development executive, consultant; b. Ashtabula, Ohio, Jan. 17, 1945; s. Robert Henry and Virgina Lee (Gray) B.; m. Joan Adelle Bednar, June 22, 1968; children: Chad Richard, Marnie Lynn. BS in indsl. mgmt., Baldwin Wallace Coll., 1968; MBA/MS in Stats., Case Western Res. U., 1973. Metall. engr. Republic Steel Corp., Cleve., 1968-72, mgr./asst. mgr. quality control, 1972-77; mgr. ops. rsch. and prod. sys. LTV Corp., Cleve., 1978-84, Dallas, 1978-84; prin. cons. Deloitte Haskins & Sells, N.Y., 1985-87; dir. McLouth Steel Corp., Trenton, Mich., 1988-91; prog. dir. tech. transfer Nat. Ctr. for Mfg., Ann Arbor, Mich., 1992-94; v.p./prin. Applied Mgmt. Tech., Inc., 1995—; cons. No. Telecom, 1986-87, Blue Cross/Blue Sheild of Mich., Detroit, 1986-87, Cytotherapeutics, Inc., Providence, 1995—, GM, Flint, Mich., 1995—. Mem. Soc. of Mfg. Engrs., Soc. Automotive Engrs. Home: 844 Medinah Dr Rochester Hills MI 48309

BAILEY, ROBERT EARL, environmental chemist, researcher; b. Washington, Jan. 19, 1938; s. Earl Belden and Margaret (Hickock) B.; m. Marcia Fisher, Jan. 26, 1963; children: Joanne, Linda. BS, Coll. William & Mary, 1959; PhD, U. Wis., 1965. Postdoctoral Victoria Univ., Wellington, New Zealand, 1965-67, Univ. Washington, Seattle, 1967-68; chemist The Dow Chem. Co., Midland, Mich., 1968-95; prin. Bailey Environ. Cons., Midland, 1995—. Contbr. articles to profl. jours. Mem. ASTM (coms. E47 and D20 1984—). Democrat. Office: Bailey Environ Cons 4115 Elm Ct Midland MI 48642-3502

BAILEY, ROBERT SHORT, lawyer; b. Bklyn., Oct. 17, 1931; s. Cecil Graham and Mildred (Short) B.; m. Doris Furlow, Aug. 29, 1953; children: Elizabeth Jane Goldentyer, Robert F., Barbara A. Jongbloed. A.B., Wesleyan U., Middletown, Conn., 1953; J.D., U. Chgo., 1956. Bar: Ill. 1965, U.S. Dist. Ct. D.C. 1956, U.S. Supreme Ct. 1960. Atty. U.S. Dept. Justice, criminal div., 1956-61; asst. U.S. atty. No. Dist. Ill., 1961-65; ptnr. LeFevour & Bailey, Oak Park, Ill., 1965-68; sole practice, Chgo., 1968—; mem. faculty Nat. Coll. Criminal Def. Lawyers, 1975-78; panel atty. Fed. Defender Program, 1965—. Mem. Nat. Assn. Criminal Def. Lawyers (legis. chmn. 1976-78). Home: 17 Timber Trl Streamwood IL 60107-1353 Office: 343 S Dearborn St Ste 1510 Chicago IL 60604-3813

BAILEY, SUSAN CAROL, commercial banking executive; b. Muskogee, Okla., Apr. 10, 1954; d. William E. and Lula M. (Holloway) Green; m. Wayne M. Bailey, Aug. 6, 1976; 1 child, Nathan W. BS in Fin., So. Ill. U., 1982, MBA, 1983. Tech. asst. ops. Marsh Stencil Machine Co., Belleville, Ill., 1973-85; loan officer Delmar Fin. Co., Belleville, 1985-86; asst. v.p., asst. br. mgr. Fidelity Fed. Savs. and Loan Assn., Fairview Heights, Ill., 1986; asst. v.p., br. mgr. Fidelity Fed. Savs. and Loan Assn., Belleville, 1986-87, v.p., br. mgr., 1987-89, v.p., br. mgr., Metro E. Deposit Acquisition & Fin. Svcs. officer, 1989-90; v.p., comml. loan officer, dir. mktg. Union Bank Ill., Swansea, 1991-96; v.p., comml. loan officer Bank of Alton, Ill., 1996—; fin. cons., Caseyville, Ill., 1985-86. Mem., treas. Belleville Welcome Wagon; mem. allocations bd. United Way Greater St. Louis; active leadership program Leadership Ctr. St. Louis, 1993-94, Civic Leader Tour, Scott AFB, 1994; chairperson teleparty St. Clair County Am. Heart Assn., 1995. Mem. St. Louis Fedn. Socs. for Coating Tech. (exec. com. 1980-85, chmn. edn. com. 1983-84), Belleville Bd. Realtors, Edwardsville-Collinsville Bd. Realtors, Women's Coun. Realtors, Homebuilders Assn., Belleville Econ. Progress (amb.), Belleville Postal Coun. (bd. dirs.), Ill. Bankers Assn., So. Ill. Network of Women (alliance rep., pres. 1991—), Fin. Women Internat., Noon Networking of Women, Fairview Hts. C. of C. (amb.), Swansea C. of C. (bd. dirs.), Rotary. Home: 710 Belleville Rd Caseyville IL 62232-1142 Office: Bank of Alton 1520 Washington Alton IL 62002

BAILEY, VAREL G., farmer; b. Wiota, Iowa, Aug. 5, 1940; s. Thomas W. and Iris A. (Heckman) B.; m. Jackie M. Scholl, oct. 21, 1962; children: Sue, Scot, Sara. BS, Iowa State U., 1962. Pres., mgr. Bailey Farms Inc., Anita, Iowa, 1966—; pres. BCD Assocs., Anita, Iowa, 1993—, Ag Producers Data Svc., Anita, Iowa, 1995—; agr. field rep. Congressman Greg Ganske, Des Moines, 1995—; speaker in field. Appeared in movie Gift of Harvest, 1979; comml. Farmer Ambassador, 1985. Chmn. Rep. Agy. Policy Coun., Dallas, 1984, Wallace Tech. Tranfer Found., Des Moines, 1988-90, Iowa High Tech. Coun., Des Moines, 1982-88; mem. USDA Export Program, Washington, 1985-87; bd. dirs. Iowa Internat. Devel. Found., Des Moines, 1990-94; candidate Agr. Sec., Des Moines, 1990; delegation leader People to People, China, 1995, Agr. in Transition, Hungary, Poland, Checkoslavakia, Germany, 1990. 1st lt. U.S. Army, 1963-65. Recipient Iowa Gov.'s Vol. award, Iowa Master Farmer award Wallaces Farmer, 1993, Agr. Excellence Pub. Svc. award Nat. Agr. Mktg. Assn. Mem. Am. Farm Bur. (county pres. 1973), Iowa Farm Bur. (Svc. to Agr. award 1985), Iowa Beef Improvement Assn. (pres. 1975), Iowa Corn Growers Assn., Nat. Corn Growers Assn. (pres. 1984-85), Farm Found. (bd. dirs. 1990-95), Nat. Agr. Forum (exec. coun. 1994—). Republican. Methodist. Home: RR1 Box 19 Anita IA 50020

BAILEY, WILLIAM ALVIN, retail executive, artist; b. Cozad, Nebr., Sept. 24, 1934; s. Vern and Esther D. (Rookstool) B.; m. Marilyn A. Kreutzer, Feb. 4, 1966; children: Michael, Traci, Troy. Rsch. Photographer Itek Corp., Boston, 1958-60; clk. Sporting Goods Retail Store, Lexington, Nebr., 1962-65; motorcycle dealer Lexington, Nebr., 1965-89, artist, 1980—; instr. Cen. Community Coll., Kearney, Nebr., 1985-87; chmn. Ducks Unlimited, Lexington, 1977. Photographer of numerous works. With USN, 1954-58. Mem. Affiliated Woodcarvers, Mid Am. Woodcarvers Assn., Art Club, Dawson County Hist., Elks, VFW. Republican. Lutheran. Home: 2000 E 13th St Lexington NE 68850-9573 Studio: Jeffrey Lake Brady NE 69123

BAILEY, WILLIAM W., state legislator, realtor; b. Mayfield, Ky., Aug. 1, 1948; m. Donna R. Bailey. BS, Murray State U., 1970; postgrad., Ind. U. City councilman Seymour, Ind., 1976-80; mayor Seymour, 1983-90; Ind. state rep. Dist. 66, 1990—; mem. com. rules and legis. procedures and human affairs com. Ind. Ho. Reps., ranking minority mem., local govt. com., chmn. cities and towns; mem. Ind. Job Tng. Coord. Coun.; chief offcl. So. Ctrl. Ind. Pvt. Industry Coun. Democrat. Home: 1137 Ernest Dr Seymour IN 47274-3100*

BAILLIE-DAVID, SONJA KIRSTEEN, controller; b. Lac Megantic, Quebec, Canada, Mar. 26, 1961; came to the U.S., 1964; d. Patrick Eugene and Erika (Bagdonowich) Baillie-David; m. Glenn Frank Skoff, Nov. 12, 1988; 1 child, Elaine Elise Skoff. AA, Joliet Jr. Coll., 1983; BBA, Coll. St. Francis, 1985; MBA in Entrepreneurship, DePaul U., 1992. CPA, Ill. Auditor Peat, Marwick Main, Chgo., 1985-87; auditor Ill. Tool Works, Chgo., 1987-88, fin. analyst, 1988-89; fin. systems project mgr. Ill. Tool Works, Glenview, Ill., 1989-94; controller U.S. Wire-Tie Systems, Woodridge, Ill., 1994—, Pennysaver Publs., Inc., Tinley Park, Ill., 1996—. Mem. Ill. CPA Soc., NAFE, Am. Mgmt. Assn. Roman Catholic. Office: Pennysaver Publs Inc 17746 Oak Park Ave Tinley Park IL 60477

BAISCH, STEVEN DALE, pediatric intensivist; b. Glendive, Mont., May 30, 1955; s. Maynard Jack and Edith Maxine (Milne) B.; children: Christopher, Rebecca. BA with honors, Jamestown Coll., 1977; Calculus fellow, Harvard U., 1975; MD, U. N.D., 1981. Pediatric resident U. N.D. Med. Ctr., 1981-84, asst. chief resident, 1983-84; ptnr., pres. Panhandle Pediatric Clinic, P.C., Scottsbluff, Nebr., 1984-88; pres. Region West Pediat. Svcs., P.C., Scottsbluff, 1988-91; fellow pediatric critical care medicine U. Minn., Mpls., 1991-94; attending staff in pediats. critical care Children's Hosp. of St. Paul, 1992—; attending staff in pediatric critical care Children's Health Care, Mpls. and St. Paul, 1994—; instr. pediats. U. Nebr. Med. Ctr., Omaha, 1984-91, med. dir. Camp Cosmos-Diabetic Camp, Scottsbluff, 1984-91; dir. Asthma Care Tng. Program, Scottsbluff, 1986-91. Outstanding fellow teaching award, 1993; U. Minn. fellow, 1991-94. Fellow Am. Acad. Pediatrics (PREP award 1990). Office: Children's Hosp St Paul Pediat Critical Care 345 Smith Ave N Saint Paul MN 55102-2369

BAISDEN, ELEANOR MARGUERITE, airline compensation executive, consultant; b. Bklyn., Nov. 7, 1935; d. Vernon McKee and Ethel Mildred (Cockle) Baisden. BA, Hofstra U., 1970. Clk., Trans World Airlines, N.Y.C., 1953-55, sec., 1955-64, compensation analyst, 1964-75, compensation mgr., 1975-85, dir. compensation and orgn. planning, 1985-88, dir. compensation and adminstrn., 1988—. Mem. Airline Personnel Dirs. Conf. (personnel com. 1984-85), Airline Tariff Pub. Co. (personnel com. 1978—), Nat. Fgn. Trade Council (compensation com. 1980-84), Internat. Personnel Assn. (co. rep. 1980-84), Mensa, Alpha Sigma Lambda (Scholar of Yr. 1965-66). Republican. Methodist. Club: Weatherby Lake Yacht (Mo.). Avocations: boating, swimming, piano, travel. Home: 7818 NW Scenic Dr Kansas City MO 64152-1643 Office: Trans World Airlines 11500 NW Ambassador Dr Kansas City MO 64153-1151

BAJARIA, HANS JAMNADAS, engineering and management consultant; b. Bombay, India, June 8, 1943; came to U.S., 1965; s. Jamnadas N. and Savitri J. Bajaria; m. Niranjana H. Asher, Aug. 8, 1968; children: Seema, Sona. BSEE, Gujarat U., Surat, India, 1964, BSME, 1965; MS, N.D. State U., 1966; PhD, Mich. Tech. U., 1972. Product design engr. Ford Motor Co., Dearborn, Mich., 1972-75; qualilty and reliability engr. Rockwell Internat., Detroit, 1975-78; assoc. prof. Lawrence Tech. Coll., Southfield, Mich., 1978-81; pres. Multiface, Inc., Garden City, Mich., 1978—. Mem. NSPE, Am. Soc. Quality Control (v.p. 1980-82, Man of Yr. award 1980, Grant award 1994), Soc. Mech. Engrs., Engring. Soc. Detroit (Gold award 1982), Nat. Spkrs. Bur. Home: 1345 Whitefield St Dearborn Heights MI 48127-3418 Office: Multiface Inc 6721 Merriman Rd Garden City MI 48135-1956

BAJOR, JAMES HENRY, musician, jazz pianist; b. Detroit, May 7, 1953; s. Henry Stanley and Irene (Hetmanski) B. Student, Wayne State U., 1976. Rec. artist Sugo Music, Half Moon Bay, Calif. Produced albums of own piano compositions: Awakening, 1987 (nominated for New Age solo acoustic Grammy award 1987), Gentle Images, 1988; appears regularly on radio and

TV programs. Mem. ASCAP, NARAS. Address: PO Box 81811 Rochester MI 48308-1811

BAKER, BARRY, broadcast executive; married. Student, Syracuse U. Former mktg. dir. Upstate Cablevision, Syracuse, N.Y.; former gen. mgr. Upstate Cablevision; co-owner Stas. WSOQ-FM and WEZG-FM; sta. mgr./gen. sales mgr. Sta. KMJQ-FM, Houston, 1977-79; v.p., gen. mgr. Sta. KMJQ-FM, St. Louis, 1979-83, Sta. KPLR-TV, St. Louis, 1983; sr. v.p., dir. broadcast div. Sta. KPLR-TV, Sta. KRBK-TV, Sacramento, Koplar Communications Ctr.; ceo River City Broadcasting, St Louis, MO, 1988S; guest lectr. Univ. Mo. Bd. dirs. Urban League, Asthma and Allergy Found., NAACP; mem. devel. bd. St. Louis Children's Hosp.; mem. adv. bd. Enterprise Bank, Jewish Community Assn. Mem. NATAS (bd. govs. St. Louis chpt.), St. Louis Radio Assn., Syracuse Ad Club. Office: River City Broadcasting 1212 Cole St Saint Louis MO 63106*

BAKER, BRUCE JAY, lawyer; b. Chgo., June 18, 1954; s. Kenneth and Beverly (Gould) B.; m. Lynn Sylvia Preece, July 18, 1976. Student, U. Leeds, Eng., 1974-75; BS, U. Ill., 1976; JD, Washington U., 1979. Bar: Ill. 1979, U.S. Dist. Ct. (no. dist.) Ill. 1984. Asst. atty. gen., antitrust div. State of Ill., Chgo., 1979-83; assoc. Mass, Miller & Josephson Ltd., Chgo., 1983-86; sr. counsel Discover Card Services Inc., Riverwoods, Ill., 1986-89; sr. legis. counsel Dean Witter Fin. Svcs. Group, Riverwoods, 1989-91; gen. counsel Ill. Commr. Banks and Trust Cos., Chgo., 1991-94; ptnr. Schiff Hardin & Waite, Chgo., 1994—. Contbr. articles to profl. jours. Registered lobbyist Ill. Legislature, Springfield, 1985-91, 94—. Named Ill. State scholar, 1972; recipient Am. Jurisprudence award (property) Washington, U., 1979. Mem. ABA (antitrust com., banking com.), Ill. State Bar Assn. (comml. banking and bankruptcy sect.), Chgo. Bar Assn. (fin. insts. com.), Ill. Bankers Assn. (legis. counsel 1985-86, gen. counsel 1994—, Disting. Bank Counsel award 1991). Office: Schiff Hardin & Waite 7200 Sears Tower Chicago IL 60606

BAKER, CHARLES B., publishing executive; b. Shaker Heights, Ohio, Oct. 11, 1935. BS, Mich. State U., 1957. Prin. A.T. Kearney, Cleve., 1973-82; pres. World Software, Chesterland, Ohio, 1982—; ptnr. Western Res. Assn., Cleve. Home: Echo Glen Gates Mills OH 44040

BAKER, CLARENCE ALBERT, SR., structural steel construction company executive; b. Kansas City, Kans., July 2, 1919; s. Earl Retting and Nancy Jefferson (Price) B.; m. Georgia Earlenen Wibberding (dec. Apr. 1957); children: Clarence Albert, Jorgeann Baker Hiebert; m. Marjorie Ellen Yoakum, Mar. 19, 1959 (dec. Feb. 1981); stepchildren: Robert Beale, Barbara Anne Stegner (Mrs. Robert T. Kenney II); m. 2d, Katherine V. Cochran, Nov. 6, 1982. Student, Kans. U., 1939-4, Finley Engring. Coll., 1937-39, Ohio State U., 1967, 69. With Kansas City (Kans.) Structural Steel Co., 1937-84, shop supt., 1959-68, v.p., plant mgr., 1968-73, v.p. plant ops., 1973-76, v.p. engring., 1976-84, dir., 1969-84. Curriculum adv. Kansas City (Mo.) Met. Jr. Coll., 1971-72, Kansas City Vocat. Tech. Sch., 1973-84 . Committeeman, Republican Party, 1970-72; chmn. City of Mission (Kans.) Rep. Party, 1970-72; councilman. City of Merriam (Kans.), 1957-59. Adv. bd. Wentworth Mil. Acad.; bd. dirs. Kansas City Jr. Achievement. With USNR, 1944-46. Mem. Am. Welding Soc. (pres. 1970-71, chmn. 1970-84, code com.), ASTM, Kans. Engring. Soc., Nat. Assn. Tax Profl. (enrolled agt. 1988—, IRS 1989—), Kans. City. C. of C., Masons. Home: 6635 Milhaven Dr Shawnee Mission KS 66202-4213 Office: 21st and Metropolitan Sts Kansas City KS 66106

BAKER, CLAUDE DOUGLAS, biology educator, researcher; b. El Dorado, Ark., Aug. 10, 1944; s. Claude Austin and Margaret Ester (Norman) B.; m. Karen Lee Sutterfield, Feb. 19, 1987; 1 child, Jessica Elizabeth. BS, U. Ark., 1966, MS, 1968; PhD, U. Louisville, 1972; postgrad., Fla. Atlantic U., 1985. Rsch. assoc. U. Ill., Champaign-Urbana, 1971-73; prof. biology Ind. U. S.E., New Albany, 1976—, preprofl. coord., 1994—; vis. scientist Ind. U., 1976—; selected spkr. Ind. Sci. Edn. Fund, Indpls., 1978-90; reviewer NSF, Washington, 1980-90; tchr. Ind. U./Aramco, Ras Tanura, Saudi Arabia, 1983. Contbr. chpts. to books, articles to profl. jours.; developer award winning field biology program, Fla., Hawaii, Belize. Tchr. extracurricular program Ind. U., 1976-90; co-dir. S.E. Regional Sci. Fair, New Albany, 1976-83. Mem. Ind. Acad. Sci., Fla. Acad. Sci., Fla. Audubon Soc., Nat. Soc. SAR, Pi Kappa Alpha. Democrat. Office: Ind U SE Dept of Biology 4201 Grant Line Rd New Albany IN 47150-2158

BAKER, DONALD, lawyer; b. Chgo., May 28, 1929; s. Russell and Elizabeth (Wallace) B.; m. Gisela S. Carli, Oct. 6, 1960; children: Caryna, Andrew, Russell. Student, Deep Springs Coll., Calif., 1947-49; J.D.S., U. Chgo., 1954. Bar: Ill. 1955, N.Y. 1964. Ptnr. Baker & McKenzie, Chgo., 1955-94, ret., 1994; sec., gen. counsel, bd. dirs. Air South, Inc., Columbia, S.C., 1994-95; bd. dirs. Trimedyne, Inc. Bd. dirs. exec. com. Mid-Am. Com., Chgo., 1980—. Mem. ABA, S.C. Bar Assn. Club: Michigan Shores (Wilmette, Ill.).

BAKER, ERNEST WALDO, JR., advertising executive; b. Sedalia, Mo., Oct. 20, 1926; s. Ernest Waldo and Sara Elizabeth (Staples) B.; m. Joan Elaine Bauman, Sept. 4, 1948; children: Robert E., Michael E. BJ, U. Mo., 1948; D in Bus. Sci., Cleary Coll., 1972. Copywriter Zimmer-Keller Advt. Agy., Detroit, 1948-51; account exec. Denman & Baker, Inc., Detroit, 1951-63; chmn. Baker, Abbs, Cunningham & Klepinger, Birmingham, Mich., 1964-90, DDB Needham Worldwide, Troy, Mich., 1990-93; exec. v.p. BBDO Detroit, 1993—. Bd. visitors Sch. Nursing, Oakland U., Rochester Hills, Mich., 1987—. With U.S. Army, 1944-45, PTO. Mem. Lansing Ad Club, Lansing City Club, Adcraft Club Detroit. Republican. Methodist. Office: BBDO Detroit 2600 W Big Beaver Rd Ste 500 Troy MI 48084-3337

BAKER, FRANK C. (BUZZ BAKER), advertising executive; m. Terry Baker; 1 child, Scott. BA in History and Econs., Harvard U., postgrad. With Fletcher/Mayo Assocs., St. Joseph, Mo., 1976-81; pres. & mng. dir. Cedar Rapids unit, dir. acct. mgmt. Creswel Munsell Fultz & Zirbel, Cedar Rapids, Iowa, 1981-90, pres., CEO, 1990—. Bd. dirs. United Way, Hugh O'Brien Found., March of Dimes, Young Parent's Network. Named to Ad Fed Hall of Fame, 1991. Mem. Nat. AgriMktg. Assn., Cedar Rapids Advt. Fedn. Office: Creswell Munsell Fultz & Zirbel PO Box 2879 Cedar Rapids IA 52406-2879*

BAKER, GILBERT JENS, management consultant; b. Clinton, Iowa, Nov. 15, 1946; s. Gilbert LeRoy and Jenis Marie (Willardsen) B.; m. Susan Diane Lettow, June 2, 1968; children: Courtenay, Kirstie, Gilbert, Geoffrey. Student, U. Iowa, 1965-68; BA, U. No. Iowa, 1970; postgrad., Mankato State U., 1971-72; BA in Acctg., Mt. St. Clare Coll., 1991. Tchr. History Lake Mills (Iowa) Community Schs., 1970-74; underwriter Am. Family Ins. Co., Madison, Wis., 1974-76; owner, dir. G. Baker Dist. Ins., Clinton, Iowa, 1976—, Gateway Vending Co., Clinton, 1977—, G.B. Systems Ltd., Clinton, 1979—, Bacor Ltd., Clinton, 1982—; bd. dirs. Gateway Home Health Care, Clinton, Clinton Area Devel. Corp., River City Ventures, Merc. Bank; mem. fin. com. Samaritan Health Systems, 1989—. Bd. dirs. River City Ventures, Clinton, 1987-88, 91, sec., 1987-88, Clinton Area Devel. Corp., 1991, v.p., 1994; trustee Mt. St. Clara Coll., Clinton, 1995—; mem. ctrl. com. Clinton County Rep. Com., 1986-88; v.p. Clinton County Gaming Commn.; pres. Clinton County Gaming Assn., 1993—; v.p. Gateway YMCA, 1988—. Mem. River City C. of C. (pres. 1986-87), Rotary (pres. 1988—), Clinton County Club (dir. 1988, pres.-elect., pres. 1990-91). Office: Bacor Ltd PO Box 3104 Clinton IA 52732-3104

BAKER, HARRISON SCOTT, computer consultant; b. Marion, Ohio, Mar. 12, 1950; s. Stanley Wallace and Starling (Dixon) B. BA, BS, Fla. State U., 1972, 80; MBA, Embry-Riddle Aeronaut. U., 1986. A&P rating, FAA; cert. product specialist, Microsoft; cert. computing technology, Computing Technology Industry Assn. Mgr. Vincent Auto Parts, Inc., Marathon, Fla., 1972-78; maintenance supr. Ea. Air Lines, Inc., Miami, 1980-92; computer cons. Upper Sandusky, Ohio, 1992—. Author: (books) Index to the Master Rolls of PA in War of 1812, 1995, Early Settlers of Wyandot County, 1995; indexer: (book), Obituaries in Upper Sandusky newspapers 1868-1911, 1994. Mem. SAR (pres. Hancock chpt. 1995-96), IEEE Computer Soc., Soc. War of 1812 (Ohio pres. 1996—), Sons of Union Vets. (camp sec. 1994—). Home: PO Box 411 Upper Sandusky OH 43351

BAKER, JACK SHERMAN, architect, designer, educator; b. Champaign, Ill., Aug. 8, 1920; s. Clyde Lee and Jane Cecilia (Walker) B. BA with honors, U Ill., 1943, MS, 1949; cert., N.Y. Beaux Art Inst. Design, 1943. Aero engr., designer Boeing Aircraft, Seattle, 1943-44; assoc. Atkins, Barrow & Lasswith, Champaign, 1947-50; pvt. practice architecture Champaign, 1947—; mem. faculty U. Ill., Urbana, 1947—, prof. architecture, 1950-90, acting prof. emeritus, 1990—; former mem. exec. com. Sch. Architecture, U. Ill.; hon. bd. dirs. Gerhart Music Festival, Guntersville, Ala., Stravinsky awards, Champaign, Conservatory of Cen. Ill.; hon. bd. dirs. Ruth Hindman Found., Huntsville, Ala.; dir., performer personal performance loft space for Interaction of the Arts and Architecture, 1960—; participant U. Ill. Exploring the Arts course (Act-NCEA award), 1970—; former mem. Chancellor's com. on graphic design and art acquisition and installation, former mem. adv. bd., designer of exhbn., Krannert Mus., U. Ill. Exhibitor water colors, arch. drawings, and photography; contbr. numerous jours. and profl. confs. Mem. U. Ill. Pres.'s Coun., U. Ill. Bronze Cir., 1986; mem. mus. bd. and affiliate World Heritage Mus.; former mem. adv. bd. Krannert Ctr. for Performing Arts, Assembly Hall U. Ill.; exhbn. designer World Heritage Mus., U. Ill. Served with U.S. Army, 1945-46, Italy, ETO. Recipient Excellence in Tchg. awards U. Ill., "prix d'Emulation Societe des Architectes Diplomes par le Gouvernment" Beaux-Arts medal, 1942, cert. for dedicated and disting. svc. Nat. AIA Com. on Environ. and Design, 1955, Decade of Achievmeent award World Heritage Mus., 1992, numerous other honors and design excellence awards in field. Fellow AIA (medal 1977, Excellence in Edn. award and medal IC/AIA 1989); mem. Ill. Coun./AIA, Soc. Archtl. Historians, Nat. Coun. Archtl. Registration Bds. (cert.), Gargoyle, Scarab, Cliff Dwellers Club (Chgo.), Nat. Resources Def. Coun., The Nature Conservancy, Alpha Rho Chi. Home: 71 1/2 E Chester St Champaign IL 61820-4149 Office: U Ill 117 Temple Hoyne Buell Hall 611 Taft Dr MC-621 Champaign IL 61820-6922

BAKER, JAMES EDWARD SPROUL, retired lawyer; b. Evanston, Ill., May 23, 1912; s. John Clark and Hester (Sproul) B.; m. Eleanor Lee Dodgson, Oct. 2, 1937 (dec. Sept. 1972); children: John Lee, Edward Graham (dec. Aug. 1988). A.B., Northwestern U., 1933, J.D., 1936. Bar: Ill. 1936, U.S. Supreme Ct. 1957. Practice in Chgo., 1936—; assoc. Sidley & Austin, and predecessors, 1936-48, ptnr., 1948-81; of counsel Sidley & Austin, 1981-93; lectr. Northwestern U. Law Sch., 1951-52; nat. chmn. Stanford U. Parents Com., 1970-75; mem. vis. com. Stanford Law Sch., 1976-79, 82-84, Northwestern U. Law Sch., 1980-89, DePaul U. Law Sch., 1982-87. Served to comdr. USNR, 1941-46. Fellow Am. Coll. Trial Lawyers (regent 1974-81, sec. 1977-79, pres. 1979-80); mem. ABA, Bar Assn. 7th Fed. Circuit, Ill. State Bar Assn., Chgo. Bar Assn., Soc. Trial Lawyers Ill., Northwestern U. Law Alumni Assn. (past pres.), Order of Coif, Phi Lambda Upsilon, Sigma Nu. Republican. Methodist. Clubs: John Evans (Northwestern U.) (chmn. 1982-85); University (Chgo.); John Henry Wigmore (past pres.); Midday (Chgo.), Legal (Chgo.), Law (Chgo.) (pres. 1983-85); Westmoreland Country (Wilmette, Ill.), Pauma Valley Country (Calif.). Home: 1300 N Lake Shore Dr Chicago IL 60610 Office: Sidley & Austin 1 First Nat Plz Chicago IL 60603

BAKER, JAMES KENDRICK, auto parts manufacturing company executive; b. Wabash, Ind., Dec. 21, 1931; s. Donald Dale and Edith (Swain) B.; m. Beverly Baker, Apr. 11, 1959; children—Betsy Ann, Dirk Emerson, Hugh Kendrick (dec.). A.B., DePauw U., 1953; M.B.A., Harvard U., 1958. Regional sales mgr. Arvinyl div. Arvin Industries, Inc., Columbus, Ind., 1958-60; gen. mgr., Arvinyl div. Arvin Industries, Inc., 1960-68, v.p., 1966-68, exec. v.p., 1968-81, pres., chief exec. officer, 1981-86; chmn., chief exec. officer Arvinyl div. Arvin Industries, Inc., 1986—, vice chmn. bd. dirs., 1996—; bd. dirs. INB Fin. Corp., CINergy, Cin., Ancast, Dayton, GEON, Cleve.; chmn. Space Industries, Washington, Tokheim, Ft. Wayne. Bd. dirs. Associated Colls. Ind., De Pauw U., vice chmn.; pres. Columbus Found. for Youth, 1965, United Way of Bartholomew County, 1979; bd. dirs. Vinyl-Metal Laminators Inst. div. Soc. for Plastics Industry, 1960—, pres., 1963-64; vice chmn. Ind. Rep. Conv., 1966; chmn. U.S. C. of C., 1990-91; trustee Inst. for Global Ethics; adv. bd. Kellogg Sch./Northwestern U.; founding chmn. Ind. Ctr. on Philanthropy; founding trustee New Am. Schs. Devel. Corp. Named Outstanding Boss C. of C., 1965; recipient Disting. Service award Ind. Jr. C. of C., 1966, Disting. Community Service award Columbus Area C. of C., 1983, Significant Sigma Chi award; named One of 5 Outstanding Young Men of Ind., 1966. Mem. Columbus C. of C. (bd. dirs.), Ind. C. of C. (bd. dirs.). Clubs: Rotary, DePauw University Alumni (pres. 1974), Harrison Lake Country. Home: Deer Crossing 12044 W State Rd 46 Columbus IN 47201-8726 Office: Arvin Industries Inc PO Box 3000 Columbus IN 47202-3000*

BAKER, JOHN EDWARD, cardiac biochemist, educator; b. London, Dec. 12, 1954; came to U.S., 1984; s. Edward D. and Florence I. (Dobson) B.; m. Mary E. Zurawski, Oct. 29, 1988; children: David J.. Elizabeth A. BSc, Poly. Wolverhampton, Eng., 1977; PhD, St. Thomas' Med. Sch., London, 1984. Sr. biochemist Cen. Pathology Labs., London, 1977-78; rsch. asst. St. Thomas' Hosp. Med. Sch., London, 1978-84; rsch. fellow Med. Coll. Wis., Milw., 1984-86, vis. prof., 1986-87, asst. prof. cardiothoracic surgery, 1987-92; assoc. prof., 1992—. Contbr. rsch. med. articles to profl. jours.; patentee method for sealing blood vessel puncture sites. Grantee NIH, 1989, 90, 93, Culpeper Found., 1987, Ronald McDonald Children's Charities, 1989, 91, Children's Hosp. Found., 1995. Mem. Am. Heart Assn. (mem. coun. on basic sci., mem. peer rev. rsch. com. Wis. affiliate 1989-93). Methodist. Office: Med Coll Wis 8701 W Watertown Plank Rd Milwaukee WI 53226-3548

BAKER, JOHN STEVENSON (MICHAEL DYREGROV), writer; b. Mpls., June 18, 1931; s. Everette Barrette and Ione May (Kadletz) B. BA cum laude, Pomona Coll., Claremont Colls., 1953; MD, U. Calif. at Berkeley and San Francisco, 1957. Writer, 1958—; book cataloger Walker Art Center, Mpls., 1958-59; editor, writer neurol. rsch. articles Louis E. Phillips Psychobiol. Rsch. Fund, Mpls., 1960-61. Contbr. articles and poetry to various publs. in Eng. and U.S.; author 65 pub. poems, 21 short essays and 10 sets of aphorisms. Donor numerous species of native plants and seeds to Minn. Landscape Arboretum, U.S. Nat. Arboretum and Arnold Arboretum, Harvard U., papers of LeRoi Jones and Hart Crane to Yale U., Brahms recs. to Bennington Coll., several others. Recipient Disting. Service award Minn. State Hort. Soc., 1976; Cert. of Appreciation U.S. Nat. Arboretum, 1978; property registered as a Minn. Natural Area Minn. chpt. Nature Conservancy, 1990. Mem. Nu Sigma Nu. Office: PO Box 16007 Minneapolis MN 55416-0007

BAKER, KENDALL L., academic administrator; b. Clearwater, Fla., Nov. 1, 1942; s. Robert B. and Anne E. Baker; m. Tobin Ratliff McGough, Apr. 12, 1981; children: Kraig, Kris, Shannon, Brian. BA with honors, U. Md., 1963; MA, Georgetown U., 1967, PhD, 1969. Instr., Dept. Polit. Sci. U. Wyo., Laramie, 1967-69, asst. prof., 1969-73, assoc. prof., 1973-77, prof., 1977-82, chmn., 1979-82, asst. v.p. for Acad. Affairs, 1976-77; dean, Coll. Arts & Scis., Bowling Green State U., Ohio, 1982-87; v.p., provost No. Ill. U., DeKalb, 1987-92; pres. U. N. D., 1992—; cons. on survey research to various agys. and polit. candidates, 1967—; panel chmn. Rocky Mt. Social Sci. Conv. 1973, We. Social Sci. Conv., 1975, Council Colls. Arts and Scis., 1983, 86; guest participant study trip to Fed. Republic of Germany, 1977; election observer Fed. Republic of Germany, 1980. Author: The Wyoming Legislature: Lawmakers, the Public, and the Press, 1973; (with R. Dalton and K. Hildebrandt) Germany Transformed: Political Culture and the New Politics, 1981; contbr. articles on polit. sci. to profl. jours. Coach Laramie Soccer Assn., 1978-81. Mem. Am. Polit. Sci. Assn. (chmn. panel ann. conv. 1983), Midwest Polit. Sci. Assn. (chmn. panel ann. conv. 1985, 86), Conf. Group on German Politcs (exec. com. 1984-87, co-editor newsletter 1985-91), Phi Kappa Phi, Omicron Delta Kappa, Pi Sigma Alpha. Home: Yale Dr Grand Forks ND 58201 Office: U ND Presidents Office Grand Forks ND 58202

BAKER, LOUIS W., lawyer; b. July 12, 1949. BS, U. Pa., 1971; MBA, George Washington U., 1976; JD, Loyola U., 1985. Bar: Ill. 1985. Cons./various gen. mgmt. positions, 1971-73; fin. mgr. Potomac Elec. Power, Washington, 1973-75; cons. FIN-ECON Inc., Washington, 1975-76; law and fin. exe . Whitman Corp., Chgo., 1976-92; pvt. practice, Chgo., 1992—. Office: 245 Waukegan Rd Northfield IL 60093

BAKER, MARK, television newscaster; b. Hannibal, Mo., Feb. 21, 1959; m. Jacqueline Christine Baker; 2 children. BA, U. Mo., 1981. Rep. candidate 17th dist. Ill. U.S. House of Reps., 1996. Methodist. Office: PO Box 5284 Quincy IL 62305*

BAKER, MARK CHRISTOPHER, computer engineer; b. Landstuhl, Germany, Oct. 28, 1961; s. Leander Arthur Jr. and Sue Ann (Kiefer) B. BS in Computer Sci., Purdue U., 1983, MS in Computer Sci., 1984. Grad. asst. Purdue U., West Lafayette, Ind., 1983-84; disting. mem. tech. staff Lucent Technologies, Lisle, Ill., 1984—. Vol. AFS Intercultural Programs, Lisle, 1990—. Mem. IEEE, Phi Beta Kappa. Office: AT&T Network Systems 2600 Warrenville Rd Lisle IL 60532-3640

BAKER, MARK EARLY, radiology educator; b. Pasadena, Calif., Mar. 2, 1953; s. William Edward and Virginia Markley (Voigtlander) B.; m. Deborah Lyn Saylor, Dec. 30, 1978; children: Rebekah Lyn, Jonathan Early. AB cum laude, Occidental Coll., 1974; student, U. Calif., Santa Barbara, 1970-71; MD cum laude, Loyola U., Chgo., 1978. Cert. in diagnostic radiology Am. Bd. Radiology. Intern internal medicine Loyola U. Affiliated Hosps., Maywood, Ill., 1978-79, resident internal medicine, 1979-80, resident radiology, 1980-83; fellow radiology Duke U. Med. Ctr., Durham, N.C., 1983-84, asst. prof. radiology, 1984-89, assoc. prof. radiology, 1989-94, chief section of abdominal imaging, 1992-94; head sect. abdominal imaging dept. radiology Cleve. Clinic Found., 1994—. Reviewer Am. Jour. Roentgenology, 1977, mem. editorial bd., 1979—; reviewer Radiology, 1977—; contbr. sci. papers and revs. to profl. jours.; co-author books. Clin. fellow Am. Cancer Soc., 1983; recipient Editor's Recognition award Radiology Jour., 1986-95. Mem. Am. Roentgen Ray Soc., Radiol. Soc. N.Am., Soc. Gastrointestinal Radiologists, Assn. Univ. Radiologists, AMA, Alpha Sigma Nu, Alpha Omega Alpha. Office: Cleveland Clinic Foundation Dept Radiology Hb6 9500 Euclid Ave Cleveland OH 44195-0001

BAKER, MARK JOSEPH, editor; b. Mpls., Aug. 12, 1953; s. Cyril Thomas and Dolores J. B.; m. Kay Marie Fritz, July 29, 1978; children: Molly Dee, Robert Richard, Patrick Cyril, Joseph Michael. BA, U. Minn., Mpls., 1975; BS in history, Mankato State U., Mankato, 1977. News editor Alexandria Newspapers, Alexandria, Minn., 1978-84; mng. editor Shawano Evening Leader, Shawano, Wis., 1984-87; editor Chippewa Herald-Telegram, Chippewa Falls, Wis., 1987-95; pub., editor Chippewa Herald, Chippewa Falls, 1995—; mem. Wis. AP exec. com., Milw. 1994-95. mem. Wis. AP exec. com., Milw., 1991-95. Chmn. fin. com. St. Joseph's Hosp. Cmty. Adv. Bd., Chippewa Falls, 1992—; pres. Chippewa Area United Way, 1996. Recipient Freedom of Info. award Minn. Soc. of Profl. Journalists, 1984. Mem. KC, Elks, Wis. Newspaper Assn. (best columnist 1992), Western Wis. Press Club, Chippewa Area C. of C. (bd. dirs. 1996—). Roman catholic. Office: Chippewa Herald 321 Frenette Dr PO Box 69 Chippewa Falls WI 54729

BAKER, MARY EVELYN, church librarian, retired academic librarian; b. Columbus, Ohio, May 8, 1912; d. Abram Jackson and Martha Maria (Dailey) Shoemaker; m. Richard Heinley Baker, Sept. 18, 1937 (dec.); children: Richard Shoemaker, David Guy. BA, Ohio State U., 1934; BS in Libr. Sci., Western Res. U., Cleve., 1935. Mem. staff libr. Ohio State U., Columbus, 1935-37, 38-44, 1955-74, part-time libr., 1955-66, adminstrv. asst., 1958, serial cataloger, 1958-67, asst. reviser, sr. cataloger, 1967-68, head serial div. catalog dept., 1968-71, head catalog dept., 1971-74; libr. com. First Congl. Ch., Columbus, 1950—, libr. co-chmn., 1962-65, 74-75, libr. chmn., 1976—; past mem. ALA, sec. serials sect., resources and tech. div., 1970-73. Den mother Boy Scouts Am., Columbus, 1953-58; libr. co-chmn. Friendship Village, Dublin, Ohio, 1981—. Mem. Ohioana Libr. Assn. (past chmn. various coms., life mem.), PEO, DAR (Indians com.), Ohio State Univ. Women's (past pres.), Agrl. Circle (past pres.), Franklin Co-Retired Tchrs. Assn. (life mem.), Ohio Retired Tchrs. Assn. (life mem.), Ohio State Alumni Assn. (life mem.), Polar Bear Alumni Assn. Columbus North H.S. (life), Alumni Assn. Univ. Sch. (life), Ohio State U. Retirees Assn. (life, bridge chmn. 1984—), Alumni Assn. Univ. Sch. (life), Polar Bear Alumni Assn. (life), Phi Mu (various offices alumni chpts.). Republican. Home: 6000 Riverside Dr Apt 233A Dublin OH 43017-1492

BAKER, R. KENT, entrepreneur; b. Indpls., May 24, 1954; s. Robert Earl and Bea Wilson (Green) B. BS in Chemistry/Physics magna cum laude, Ind. U., 1978. With Baker Machinery, Indpls., 1978-82; pres. CNC Systems Sales Inc., Indpls., 1982—, R. Kent Baker Racing Inc., Indpls., 1987—. Pres. Ind. Repertory Soc., 1989-91; bd. dirs. Ind. Repertory Theatre, 1989-91, Indpls. Police Dept. Drill Team, Indpls., 1989—, Herron Gallery, 1990—. Mem. SAR, Ind. Badminton Assn. (bd. dirs. 1990—), Indpls. Badminton Club (bd. dirs. 1990—), John Strange Alumni Assn. (chmn. bd. 1989—), Clan MacKay Soc. of U.S.A., Pioneers of Ky. Republican. Methodist. Office: CNC System Sales Inc 3004 E 56th St Ste A Indianapolis IN 46220-2946

BAKER, RICHARD LEE, book publishing company executive; b. Grand Rapids, Mich., July 27, 1935; s. Herman and Angeline (Sterkenberg) B.; m. Frances Leona Gesink, June 10, 1957; children: Dawn, Dwight, David, Daniel. Student, Calvin Coll., Grand Rapids, 1954-56. Pres. Baker Book House, Grand Rapids, 1957—. Bd. dirs. Christian Schs. Internat., 1981-86; pres. bd. dirs. Christian Schs. Internat. Found., 1988—. Mem. Christian Booksellers Assn. (bd. dirs. 1985-93), Evang. Christian Pubs. Assn. (bd. dirs. 1981-84). Republican. Mem. Christian Reformed Ch. Home: 2240 Shawnee Dr SE Grand Rapids MI 49506-5335 Office: Baker Book House PO Box 6285 Grand Rapids MI 49516-6285

BAKER, RICHARD SOUTHWORTH, lawyer; b. Lansing, Mich., Dec. 18, 1929; s. Paul Julius and Florence (Schmid) B.; m. Kathleen E. Yull, 1956 (dec. 1964); m. Marina J. Vidoli, 1965 (div. 1989); children: Garrick Richard, Lydia Joy. Student, DePauw U., 1947-49; A.B. cum laude, Harvard, 1951; J.D., U. Mich., 1954. Bar: Ohio 1957, U.S. Dist. Ct. (no. dist.) Ohio 1958, U.S. Tax Ct. 1960, U.S. Supreme Ct. 1971, U.S. Ct. Appeals (6th cir.) 1972. Since practiced in Toledo; mem. firm Fuller & Henry, and predecessors, 1956-91; pvt. practice Toledo, 1991—; Chmn. nat. com. region IV Mich. Law Sch. Fund, 1967-69, mem.-at-large, 1970-85. Bd. dirs. Asso. Harvard Alumni, 1970-73; mem. Epworth Assembly, Ludington, Mich.. Served with AUS, 1954-56. Fellow Am. Coll. Trial Lawyers; mem. ABA, Ohio Bar Assn., Toledo Bar Assn., Lawyer-Pilots Bar Assn., Toledo Club, Harvard Club (pres. Toledo chpt. 1968-77), Capital Club, Phi Delta Theta, Phi Delta Phi. Office: 2819 Falmouth Rd Toledo OH 43615-2215

BAKER, ROBIN NEIL, CAD operator; b. Rochester, Ind., Oct. 13, 1968; m. Kimberly A. Walters, July 31, 1993; 1 child, Kassandra Saleen. Grad. H.S., Tippecanoe Valley, Ind., 1987. CAD operator Airvac, Rochester, 1987—. Republican.

BAKER, RONALD PHILLIP, service company executive; b. Kansas City, Mo., Feb. 15, 1942; s. Harry and Ruth Sarah (Bornstein) B.; m. Marilyn Gitterman, Dec. 27, 1964 (div. Dec. 1993); children: Kevin, Corey; m. Dierdre Christensen, May 8, 1994. Student, U. Okla., 1960-63; BA in Sociology and Govt., U. Mo., Kansas City, 1965, postgrad., 1965. Acct. rep. Am. House and Window Cleaning Co., Kansas City, 1965-69; dist. ops. mgr. Am. Bldg. Services, Kansas City, 1969-72; pres. BG Maintenance Mgmt., Kansas City, 1972-86; chmn. bd. dirs. BGM Industries, Kansas City, 1987—. V.p. Jewish Community Ctr., Kansas City, 1985-88, pres., 1989-90; pres. Jewish Vocat. Svcs., Kansas City, 1979-81; bd. dirs. Beth Shalom Synagogue, Kansas City, 1985-89, Jewish Community Ctrs. Assn., 1989-93, exec. com., 1990-91; co-chmn. Jewish Fedn. Greater Kansas City, 1986-92, v.p., 1992-93; bd. dirs. Jewish Community Found. Greater Kansas City, 1991-94. Mem. Bldg. Svc. Contractors Assn. Internat. (bd. dirs., chmn. seminars, conv. speaker, pres. club 1981-93, mem. edn. com. 1981-90, chmn. edn. com. 1989—, info. ctrl. com. 1985-93, chmn. ann. conv. 1988, exec. com. 1988—, treas. 1989, v.p. 1990-92, pres. 1994, chmn. fin. com. 1990, mem. exec. com., chair strategic planning task force 1989-90), Bldg. Owners and Mgrs. Assn. Kansas City, Jewish Fedn. Kansas City (v.p. 1986-87, 91-93, Young Leadership award 1981), Menninger Found. (pres. Topeka chpt. 1986-95), Meadowbrook Country Club, Sigma Alpha Mu, Delta Sigma Pi. Republican. Office: BGM Industries 1225 E 18th St Kansas City MO 64108-1605

BAKER, ROSE ANN URDIALES, pediatric and mental health nurse; b. Akron, Ohio, July 4, 1947; d. Anthony Ramon and Anita Rita (Martinez) Urdiales; m. Robert Lee Baker, May 25, 1974. Diploma, Akron Gen. Hosp. Sch. Nursing, 1968; BSN, U. Akron, 1972; MSN, Kent State U., 1984. Staff nurse Fallsview Mental Health Ctr., Cuyahoga Falls, Ohio, 1968-71; staff nurse emergency rm. Akron Gen. Med. Ctr., 1971-75; staff nurse pediatrics ICU Children's Med. Ctr., Akron, 1975-76, supr. staff devel., 1976-90, coord. nursing rsch. com., 1988—, chair clin. practice com. continuing nursing edn., 1991—, sr. instr., 1990-94; continuing nursing edn. coord., 1994—; clin. specialist Vis. Nurse Svc., Akron, 1984—; mem. search com. for the dean Kent State U. Sch. Nursing, 1984. Campaign worker Mayoral Race, Akron, 1980; translator Internat. Inst., Akron, 1986—; mem. hispanic health com. Latin Am. Community, Akron, 1990—. Mem. Sigma Theta Tau. Democrat. Roman Catholic. Home: 625 Hickory St Akron OH 44303-2211 Office: Children's Med Ctr Nursing Edn 281 Locust St Akron OH 44302-1813 also: Vis Nurse Svc Summit County 1200 Mcarthur Dr Akron OH 44320-3902

BAKER, SAUL PHILLIP, geriatrician, cardiologist, internist; b. Cleve., Dec. 7, 1924; s. Barnet and Florence (Kleinman) B. B.S. in Physics, Case Inst. Tech., 1945; postgrad., Western Res. U., 1946-47; M.Sc. in Physiology, Ohio State U., 1949, M.D., 1953, Ph.D. in Physiology, 1957; J.D., Case Western Res. U., 1981. Intern Cleve. Met. Gen. Hosp., 1953-54; sr. asst. surgeon Gerontology Br. Nat. Heart Inst, NIH, now Gerontology Research Ctr., Nat. Inst. Aging, 1954-56; asst. vis. staff physician dept. medicine Balt. City Hosps. (now Francis Scott Key Hosp.) and Johns Hopkins Hosp., 1954-56; sr. asst. resident in internal medicine U. Chgo. Hosps., 1956-57; asst. prof. internal medicine Chgo. Med. Sch., 1957-62; assoc. prof. internal medicine Cook County Hosp. Grad. Sch. Medicine, Chgo., 1958-62; assoc. attending physician Cook County Hosp., 1957-62; practice medicine specializing in geriatrics, cardiology, internal medicine Cleve., 1962-70, 72-93, cons., 1993—; head dept. geriatrics St. Vincent Charity Hosp., Cleve., 1964-67; cons. internal medicine and cardiology Bur. Disability Determination, Old-Age and Survivors Ins., Social Security Adminstrn., 1963—; cons. internal medicine City of Cleve., 1964—; medicare med. cons. Gen. Am. Life Ins. Co., St. Louis, 1970-71; cons. internal medicine and cardiology Ohio Bur. Worker's Compensation, 1964—; cons. cardiovascular disease FAA, 1973—; cons. internal medicine and cardiology State of Ohio, 1974—. Contbr. articles to profl. and sci. jours. Mem. sci. coun. Northeastern Ohio affiliate Am. Heart Assn.; former mem. adv. com. Sr. Adult div. Jewish Community Ctr. Cleve.; mem. vis. com. colls. Case Western Res. U.; former mem. com. older people Fedn. Community Planning Cleve. Fellow AAAS, Am. Coll. Cardiology, Gerontol. Soc. Am. (former Ohio regent), Am. Geriatrics Soc., Cleve. Med. Library Assn. (life); mem. Am. Physiol. Soc., AMA, Ohio Med. Assn., N.Y. Acad. Scis., Chgo. Soc. Internal Medicine, Am. Fedn. Clin. Research, Soc. Exptl. Biology and Medicine, Am. Diabetes Assn., Diabetes Assn. Greater Cleve. (profl. sect.), Am. Heart Assn. (fellow council arteriosclerosis), Nat. Assn. Disability Examiners, Nat. Rehab. Assn., Am. Pub. Health Assn., Acad. Medicine Cleve., Internat. Soc. Cardiology (council epidemiology and prevention), Am. Soc. Law and Medicine, Sigma Xi, Phi Delta Epsilon, Sigma Alpha Mu (past pres. Cleve. alumni club). Club: Cleve. Clinical (past sec.). Lodges: Masons (32 degree), Shriners. Home: PO Box 24246 Cleveland OH 44124-0246

BAKER, SHERRY L., investment broker; b. Olney, Ill., Jan. 20, 1950. Pvt. practice; investment broker R. Rolland, Mt. Vernon, Ill., 1984-88, A.G. Edwards & Sons, Mt. Vernon, 1988—. Mem. Bus. and Profl. Women's Club, Centralia C. of C. Republican. Baptist. Office: AG Edwards & Sons Inc 3450 Broadway St # A Mount Vernon IL 62864-2270

BAKER, TERRY J., financial advisor; b. Lansing, Mich., Oct. 5, 1948. BA, Mich. State U., 1979. Self employed comml. artist Lansing, 1972-80; securities wholeszler oil and gas co., Denver, 1980-83; stockbroker, v.p. investments Dean Witter Reynolds, 1983—. Assoc. dir. Planes of Fame, Eden Prairie, Minn., 1991—; founding bd. dirs., chmn. bd., pres. Am. Aviation Heritage Found., Eden Prairie, 1995—. Republican. Home: 1451 W Minnehaha Pky Minneapolis MN 55409-2247 Office: Dean Witter Reynolds 8300 Norman Center Dr Ste 1150 Bloomington MN 55437-1027

BAKER, WALTER, III, bank executive; b. Ann Arbor, Mich., May 31, 1955; s. Walter Jr. and Maude Bragg (Dickson) B.; m. Janet Amy Bartak, May 12, 1984; 1 child, Walter IV. BA, Yale U., 1977; M in Mgmt., Northwestern U., 1986. Officer First Nat. Bank Louisville, 1977-80; asst. v.p. Union Planters Nat. Bank, Memphis, 1980-83; v.p. First Nat. Bank Chgo., 1983-92, Wachovia Bank, Winston-Salem, N.C., 1992-93, Continental Bank, Chgo., 1993-94, Bank of Am., Chgo., 1994; group v.p. ABN AMRO Bank Netherlands, Chgo., 1994—. Editl. advisor, columnist; contbr. articles to profl. jours. Mem. FCIB-NACM (adv. bd.), U.S. Coun. Internat. Banking (product mgmt. com.). Office: ABN-AMRO Bank Netherlands 135 S LaSalle St #760 Chicago IL 60674-9135

BAKER, WILBUR FRANCIS, retired state agency administrator; b. Grandview Heights, Ohio, Jan. 23, 1931; s. Edward F. and Elisabeth (Sibbald) B.; m. Jean Louise Warren, Mar. 27, 1954; children: Theresa A.F., Sandra L., Terrence A.F. BS, Ohio State U., 1959. Mortgage loan app. Panohio Mktg. Co., Columbus, Ohio, 1959-63; mortgage loan supr. Jefferson Standard Life Ins. Co., Columbus, 1963-67; comml. loan bgr. The Kissell Co., Columbus, 1967-69; administr. Bur. Appraisal Ohio Dept. Transpn., Columbus, 1989-91; 1st v.p. James A. Rhodes Mortgage Co., Columbus, 1972-73. Served with USN, 1948-52. John E. McCrahin scholar Ohio Assn. Real Estate Bd., 1957, 1958-59. Mem. Am. Inst. Real Estate Appraisers (chmn. legis. com. Ohio chpt. 1986—), Appraisal Inst., Disabled Am. Vets (trustee 1986), AMVETS (2d vice adj., trustee), Elks. Roman Catholic. Home: 16830 Krinn Unger Keck Rd Logan OH 43138-9050

BAKK, THOMAS, state legislator; b. June 8, 1954; 2 children. BBA, U. Minn., Duluth. Labor rep.; rep. Dist. 6A Minn. Ho. of reps., 1994—.

BAKKEN, DOUGLAS ADAIR, foundation executive; b. Breckenridge, Minn., Mar. 12, 1939; s. John and Marie (Folstad) B.; m. Jacquelyn Ann Nielsen, July 8, 1962; children: Amy Michelle, Wendy Kay. B.S., N.D. State U., 1961; cert. archives adminstrn., Am. U., 1966; M.A., in History, U. Nebr., 1967. Archivist Nebr. State Hist. Soc., Lincoln, 1966-67; assoc. archivist Cornell U., Ithaca, N.Y., 1967-71; archivist adminstr. Anheuser Busch Cos., St. Louis, 1971-77; dir. archives and library Henry Ford Mus., Dearborn, Mich., 1977-83; exec. dir. Ball Bros. Found., Muncie, Ind., 1983—; cons. history, archives, 1978—. Editor-in-chief: The Herald, Edison Inst., 1978-81. Bd. mem., officer Christian Ministries Delaware County, 1985—. Served to 1st lt. Intelligence Corps U.S. Army, 1962-64. Fellow Soc. Am. Archivists; mem. Hist. Soc. Mich. (v.p. 1982-83), Am. Assn. State and Local History, Nat. Automotive History Collection (trustee 1981—), Soc. Automotive Historians (dir. 1981-84), Ind. Donors Alliance (chmn., founding mem.). Republican. Lutheran. Home: 4801 N Everett Rd Muncie IN 47304-1092 Office: Ball Bros Found 222 S Mulberry St Muncie IN 47305-2802*

BAKKEN, HOWARD NORMAN, music educator, church musician; b. Luverne, Minn., Nov. 2, 1942; s. Obed Herman and Martha Ingeborg (Lunde) B.; m. May Ann Syzdek, June 29, 1968; children: Ethan Nathaniel, Emily Cooper. BA, Augustana Coll., 1964; MMus, Yale U., 1967; D of Musical Arts, U. Ill., 1975. Cert. music tchr., Ill. Organist, choirmaster St. Thomas's Episcopal Ch., New Haven, 1966-69; instr. music Guilford (Conn.) Pub. Schs., 1967-69; teaching asst. U. Ill., Urbana, 1969-71; organist, choirmaster St. Mark's Episcopal Ch., Geneva, Ill., 1971-80; music dir. The Little Home Ch., Wayne, Ill., 1980-87; accompanist Elgin (Ill.) Choral Union, 1981—; musical dir. Waubonsee Children's Theater, Sugar Grove, Ill., 1989—; organist, choirmaster St. Charles Episcopal Ch., 1987—; instr. music Geneva Pub. Schs., 1971—; vis. lectr. Judson Coll., Elgin, 1983-90; organist Chgo. Symphony Chorus, 1987-93, Do-It-Yourself Messiah, Chgo., 1981—; freelance keyboard performer, 1975—; tchr. keyboard, St. Charles, 1971—. Mem. NEA, Ill. Edn. Assn., Am. Guild Organists (dean), Music Educators Nat. Conf., Fox Valley Arts Coun., Geneva Acad. Found. (tchr. rep. 1992—). Episcopalian. Home: 18 Whittington Course St Charles IL 60174 Office: Geneva Mid Sch 1415 Viking Dr Geneva IL 60134

BALALE, AMELIA, physical therapist; b. Cleveland, Nov. 22, 1954; d. Michael and Stella (Bymakos) B.; m. David Eugene Armstrong, Aug. 21, 1983; children: Athena, Dana. BS, Ohio State U., 1976, MS, 1980. Lic. phys. therapist, Ohio; cert. phys. therapy educator, Ohio. Phys. therapist Franklin County Bd. Mental Retardation/Devel. Disabilities, Columbus, Ohio, 1976-77, Colerain Sch., Columbus, Ohio, 1977-80; phys. therapy dir. D.T. Watson Rehab. Hosp. for Children, Sewickley, Pa., 1980-81; phys. therapist Broadmoor Sch., Mentor, Ohio, 1981-83; phys. therapy dir. Health Hill Hosp., Cleveland, 1983-84; phys. therapy cons. Lake County Bd. Mental Retardation/Devel. Disabilities, Mentor, 1984-94; phy. therapist East Shore Ctr., Mentor Pub. Schs., 1994—; guest lectr. Ohio State U., 1976-80, Cleve. State U., 1981-94, clin. tchr., 1981—. Neighborhood liaison Am. Cancer Soc., Cleve., 1994-96. Mem. Am. Phys. Therapy Assn. (pediat. sect. 1976-95), Neurodevelopmental Treatment Assn. Democrat. Greek Orthodox. Home: 17414 Harland Ave Cleveland OH 44119

BALANOFF, CLEMENT, real estate agent; b. Chgo., Apr. 14, 1953; m. Virginia Balanoff; 2 children. Student, Ripon Coll., 1971-73. Mem. Ill. House, 1989-95; Dem. candidate U.S. House, 1994, 96. Home: 11128 S Avenue D Chicago IL 60617-6846 Office: Balanoff for Congress 10100 S Ewing Ave Chicago IL 60617*

BALBACH, BENJAMIN S., stockbroker; b. Grand Rapids, Mich., Mar. 18, 1960; s. Joseph and Ester (Van Stencil) B. BA, Ctrl. Mich. U., Mt. Pleasant, 1984—. Rschr. Am. Internat., N.Y.C., 1984-86; ins. broker Frank B. Hall, Grand Rapids, Mich., 1986-88; stockbroker Smith Barney, Grand Rapids, 1989—. Office: Smith Barney Inc 99 Monroe Ave NW Ste 200 Grand Rapids MI 49503-2639

BALBACH, GEORGE CHARLES, technology company executive; b. Waukegan, Ill., June 29, 1931; s. George Jacob and Martha Patterson (Shewmaker) B.; m. Elaine Barbara Davis, Dec. 15; children: Vanessa Anne, Melissa Lynn, George F. BS in Econs., U. Pa., 1953. Asst. controller Hills McCanna, Chgo., 1955-58; dir. mktg. Imperial-Eastman, Chgo., 1958-68; exec. v.p. Keltec, Inc., Elkhart, Ind., 1968-70; pres., CEO Hubbell Corp., Mundelien, Ill., 1970-74; pres., CEO, owner ASI Techs., Inc., Milw., 1974—. Inventor in field. Mem. Internat. Assn. Refrigerated Warehouses, Refrigeration Rsch. Found., Exec. Com. (adv. bd. 1991). Republican. Presbyterian. Home: 321 W Onwentsia Rd Lake Forest IL 60045-2828 Office: ASI Techs Inc 5848 N 95th Ct Milwaukee WI 53225-2613

BALDASSARI, JEFFREY JOHN, lawyer; b. Chgo., Jan. 16, 1963; s. Fred John and Rosemary (Spinello) B. BS in Acctg., Miami U., 1985; JD, Case Western Res. U., 1988. CPA, Ohio; Bar: Ohio 1988, U.S. Tax Ct. 1989, U.S. Ct. Appeals (6th cir.) 1989. Assoc. Burke, Haber & Berick, Cleve., 1988-90, Baker & Hostetler, Cleve., 1990-95; v.p., gen. counsel The Taylor Chair Co., 1995—; instr. Becker CPA Rev. Course, Cleve., 1988—. Mem. Ohio Venture Assn. (trustee), Lakewood Hist. Soc. Republican. Roman Catholic. Home: 1296 Arlington Rd Lakewood OH 44107-1042 Office: The Taylor Chair Co 75 Taylor St Bedford OH 44146

BALDER, JAMES ELLSWORTH, infosystems specialist; b. Foley, Minn.; s. Ellsworth Edward and Alvina Mary (Rau) B.; m. Alberta M. Milton, Oct. 20, 1956; children: Cindy, James W., Timothy W., Rene Ann, Richard E. Student, U. Minn., 1956-57. Lead programmer Honeywell, Mpls., 1954-60; data processing mgr. North Am. Life and Casualty, Mpls., 1961-66; ops. mgr. Pullman, Inc., Hammond, Ind., 1966-69; operations mgr. Sci. Computers Inc., Mpls., 1969-76; v.p. ops. Warrington Assocs., Hopkins, Minn., 1977-86; v.p. mgmt. info. systems Dataserv, Inc., Eden Prairie, Minn., 1986-89; v.p. ops. Image Integration Inc., Eden Prairie, Minn., 1990-91; tech. svc. rep. Digital Solutions, Inc., Bloomington, Minn., 1992-95; ret., 1995; systems cons. Computer Related Mpls., 1956-93. With U.S. Army, 1951-54. Mem. Data Processing Mgrs. Assn. Republican. Roman Catholic.

BALDUS, ALVIN J., state legislator; b. Apr. 26, 1926; married; 5 children. AA, Austin Jr. Coll. Former rep. dist. 3 State of Wis., state assemblyman, 1966-72; mem. U.S. House Reps. Washington, 1974-78; state assemblyman dist. 29 State of Wis., 1988—; pub. rels. cons. Decorated Bronze star. Mem. VFW. Democrat. Address: 631 Grandview Ct Menomonie WI 54751-1753*

BALDWIN, ALLAN OLIVER, information scientist, higher education executive; b. Chgo., Apr. 10, 1948; s. Albert Oliver and Virginia Josephine (Stack) B.; m. Suzanne Balasty, Nov. 28, 1969 (div.); m. Janice Louise DiVito, Jan. 25, 1992; children: Steven, Jennifer, Jeremy, Matthew, Katherine. BS, U. Ill., Chgo., 1969; MBA, Keller Grad. Sch. Mgmt., 1982. Asst. systems mgr. U. Ill., Chgo., 1970-76, asst. dir. info. systems svcs., 1976-79, dir. hosp. info. svcs., 1979-86; dir. systems devel. Loyola U. Chgo., Maywood, Ill., 1986-88, asst. v.p. info. systems, 1988-90, acting v.p. info. tech., 1990-92, v.p. info. tech., 1992—. Chmn. parent human rels. com. Oak Park (Ill.)-River Forest High Sch., 1991. Mem. Coll. and Univ. Systems Engrs., Healthcare Info. Mgmt. Systems Soc., Med. Info. System Assn. Home: 1100 N East Ave Oak Park IL 60302-1230 Office: Loyola Univ Chicago 2160 S 1st Ave Bldg 201 Maywood IL 60153-3304

BALDWIN, GEORGE KOEHLER, retail executive; b. Cedar Rapids, Iowa, Nov. 17, 1919; s. Nathan and Ada Lillian (Koehler) B. BBA, State U. Iowa, 1942. Office mgr., mgr. Wapsie Valley Creamery, Cedar Rapids, 1946-60; treas., head payroll, accounts payable, sales audit depts. Armstrong's, Inc., Cedar Rapids, 1960-87, also dir.; treas. Armstrong's of Dubuque (Iowa), 1982-87, also dir.; ret., 1987; mem. adv. com. Firstar Club Firstar Bank, Cedar Rapids, 1991-93; also theatre organist. Mem. Cedar Rapids Performing Arts Commn.; bd. dirs., pres. Cedar Rapids Community Concert Assn.; sec., treas., asst. conductor. El Kahir Shrine Band of Cedar Rapids; chmn. adminstrv. bd. Trinity United Meth. Ch., 1987-92, head usher and worship com. chmn.; apptd. by mayor to Cedar Rapids Mcpl. Band Commn., 1994. With U.S. Army, 1942-46, ETO. Decorated Bronze Star medal; named hon. Ky. col.; George K. Baldwin day proclamation in his honor, Mayor of Cedar Rapids, Apr. 16, 1987; composed and copyrighted for band Kinnick Stadium band march, 1992. Mem. Cedar Rapids Consumer Credit Assn. (pres. 1968-69), Am. Theatre Organ Soc. (dir., treas. Cedar Rapids chpt.), Am. Legion, VFW, Rotary, Masons, Shriners (past pres. uniformed units), Rotary Svc. Club (chmn. fellowship com., sgt. of arms), State U. Iowa President's Club. Methodist. Home: 1017 F Ave NW Cedar Rapids IA 52405-2724

BALDWIN, HELAINE RAE, clinical psychologist; b. Fond du Lac, Wis., Oct. 16, 1940; d. Raymond Edward and Bertha Helen (Schorer) Schrank; m. Keith R. Baldwin, Sept. 21, 1963; children: Laura, Steven, Jennifer. BS, U. Wis., 1962; MA, Roosevelt U., 1987; D in Psychology, Forest Inst., 1991. Lic. Psychologist, Ill. Clin. psychologist PsyCare, Schaumburg, Ill., 1990-93, Complete Psychol. Care, Hoffman Estates, Ill., 1993—. Mem. APA, Ill. Psychol. Assn., Chgo. Psychol. Assn., Am. Assn. of Christian Counselors. Office: Complete Psychol Care Ste 140 2200 W Higgins Rd Hoffman IL 60195

BALDWIN, JAMES ALLEN, librarian, researcher; b. Utica, N.Y., July 28, 1944; s. Allen C. and Margaret C. (Lafferty) B.; m. Rosalie A. Vermette, Jan. 2, 1982. AB, Cath. U. Am., 1966; MA, U. Tex., 1971; MLS, Ind. U., 1985. Lectr. U. Akron, Ohio, 1972-73; instr. U. Calif., Davis, 1973-74, Bowling Green (Ohio) State U., 1976-79; asst. prof. Ind. U.-Purdue U., Inpls., 1979-84; assoc. libr., head dept. acquisitions Ind. U. - Purdue U., Inpls., 1985—; field researcher Nat. Geog. Soc., Papua New Guinea, 1975-76. Mem. Editorial bd. Jour. of Cultural Geography, 1991—; contbr. articles to profl. jours. Mem. ALA, AAAS, Am. Name Soc., Ohio Valley Group Tech. Svcs. Libr. (treas. 1990-91), Assn. Am. Geographers, Sierra Club, Sigma Xi, Gamma Theta Upsilon, Beta Phi Mu. Democrat. Roman Catholic. Home: 1845 Weslynn Dr Indianapolis IN 46208-3057 Office: Ind U - Purdue U Librs 755 W Michigan St Indianapolis IN 46202-5195

BALDWIN, JAMES GORDON, stockbroker; b. Detroit, May 10, 1929. BA in Humanities, Kans. State U., 1951, postgrad., 1951-54. Dir. Sta. WIBW-TV, Topeka, 1954-55; sr. sales rep. Addressograph Corp., Cleve., 1955-62; agt. Nat. Life Ins., Topeka, 1962-67; gen. agt. Am. Home Life Ins., Topeka, 1968-70; regional mgr. Trend Carpet Mills, Rome, Ga., 1970-72; owner, mgr. wholesale carpet co., Topeka, 1970-74, dept. and furniture store, Topeka, 1976-82; stockbroker Thomson-McKennin, Topeka, 1986-90, Paine Webber, Topeka, 1990—. Mem. Nat. Topeka Rep. Com., 1982—. With N.G., 1948-50. Episcopalian. Office: Paine Webber 634 S Kansas Ave Topeka KS 66603-3804

BALDWIN, JEFFREY KENTON, lawyer, educator; b. Palestine, Ill., Aug. 8, 1954; s. Howard Keith and Annabelle Lee (Kirts) B.; m. Patricia Ann Mathews, Aug. 23, 1975; children: Matthew, Katy, Timothy, Philip R. BS summa cum laude, Ball State U., 1976; JD cum laude, Ind. U., 1979. Bar: Ind. 1979, U.S. Dist. Ct. (so. dist.) Ind. 1979, U.S. Ct. Appeals (7th cir.) 1979, U.S. Dist. Ct. (no. dist.) Ind. 1984. Mem. majority leader's staff Ind. Senate, Indpls., 1976; instr. Beer Sch. Real Estate, Indpls., 1977-78, Am. Inst. Paralegal Studies, Indpls., 1987—; dep. Office Atty. Gen., Indpls., 1979-81; mng. ptnr. Baldwin & Baldwin, Danville, Ind., 1979—; agt. Nat. Attys. Title Assurance Fund, Vevay, Ind., 1983—; officer, bd. dirs. Baldwin Realty, Inc., Danville; conf. participant White House Conf. on Small Bus. (Ind. meeting 1994), congl. appointee, 1995. Organizer, Hendricks County Young Republicans, 1972; sec. Hendricks County Rep. Com., 1978-84; bd. dirs. Hendricks County Assn. for Retarded Citizens, Danville, 1982-86; cons. Hendricks County Right for Life, Brownsburg, Ind., 1984—; mem. philanthropy adv. com. Ball State U., Muncie, Ind., 1987—; judge Hendricks County unit Am. Cancer Soc., 1987; coordinator region 2 Young Leaders for Mutz, Indpls., 1987-88; cubmaster WaPaPh dist. Boy Scouts Am., 1988, S.M.E. chmn., 1988-89; steering com. Ind. Lawyers Bush/Quayle; founder, chmn. Christians for Positive Reform; candidate for Congress 7th Congl. Dist. of Ind. Recipient Presdl. award of honor Danville Jaycees, 1980; named hon. sec. State Ind., 1980. Mem. ABA, Ind. Bar Assn., Hendricks County Bar Assn., Indpls. Bar Assn., Internat. Platform Assn., Nat. Assn. Realtors, Ind. Assn. Realtors, Met. Indpls. Bd. Realtors (Hendricks County div.), Danville C. of C. (sec. 1986), Moot Ct. Soc., Blue Key, Phi Sec. Methodist. Home: PO Box 63 Danville IN 46122-0063 Office: 67 N Cross St PO Box 63 Danville IN 46122

BALDWIN, JOHN CHARLES, surgeon, researcher; b. Ft. Worth, Sept. 23, 1948; s. Charles Leon and Anabel (West) B.; m. Christine Janet Stewart, Mar. 31, 1973; children: Alistair Edward Stewart, John Benjamin West, Andrew Christian William. BA summa cum laude, Harvard U., 1971; MD, Stanford U., 1975; MA Privatim (hon.), Yale U., 1989. Diplomate Am. Bd. Internal Medicine, Am. Bd. Surgery, Am. Bd. Thoracic Surgery. Fellow in medicine Harvard Med. Sch., Boston, 1975-77, fellow in surgery, resident in surgery, 1977-81; resident in surgery Mass. Gen. Hosp., 1977-81; resident in cardiothoracic surgery Stanford (Calif.) U., 1981-82, chief resident cardiothoracic surgery, 1983, asst. prof., 1984-87; dir. heart-lung transplantation, transplant rsch. lab. Stanford U., 1986-87; prof. surgery and chief cardiothoracic surgery Yale U., New Haven, 1988-94; cardiothoracic-surgeon-in chief Yale-New Haven Hosp.; DeBakey/Bard prof., chmn. Baylor Coll. Medicine, Houston, 1994—; sr. attending physician, chief surg. svcs. Meth. Hosp., Houston, 1994—; sr. attending physician, surgeon in chief Ben Taub Gen. Hosp., Houston, 1994; dir. multi-organ transplant ctr. Meth. Hosp./Baylor U., Houston; dir. thoracic surgery residency program Coll. Medicine Baylor U., Houston; dir. thoracic surgery residency program Yale-New Haven Hosp., 1988-94; vis. lectr. Yale U., bd. permanent officers, 1988-94; cons. gen. thoracic surgery Waterbury (Conn.) Hosp. health Ctr., 1988-94; bd. dirs. United Network Organ Sharing, 1984-87; mem. clin. rsch. com. ad hoc rsch. grant rev. Cystic Fibrosis Found.; trustee New Eng. Organ Bank, 1988; mem. solid organ transplant com. Blue Cross & Blue Shield of Conn., 1990—; mem. sci. adv. bd. Alexion Pharms., Inc., 1991-94; bd. dirs. Baylor Coll. medicine Healthcare, Inc.; mem. adv. bd. Donate Life Found.; mem. exec. faculty Baylor Coll. of Medicine, pres.'s coun.; bd. dirs. New England chpt. Transplant Recipients Internat. Orgn., 1992-94. Co-editor: Thoracic Surgery, Oxford Textbook of Surgery, 1989—; editor: Cardiac Surgery: Principles and Techniques, 1994; assoc. editor Jour. Applied Cardiology, 1985-92; editorial bd. Jour. Thoracic and Cardiovascular Surgery, 1990—, Transplantation, 1990—, Transplantation Sci., 1992—, Andromeda Interactive Ltd., The Cardiovasc. System Interactive Teaching Program, 1993—; contbr. numerous articles and book chpts. in field. Mem. Harvard Club Schs. Com., Harvard Coll. Fund, Harvard U. Undergrad. Admissions Interview Com.; fellow Timothy Dwight Coll. Yale U., Yale U. Art Gallery Assocs.; mem. appointments and promotions com. Sch. Medicine, Yale U., 1991—, clin. scis. bldg. planning com., 1990—; bd. dirs. Neighborhood Music Sch. New Haven., 1989-92; bd. overseers Harvard U., 1995—; bd. permanent officers Yale U., 1988-94. John Harvard scholar, 1969, 70, Wendell scholar Harvard U., 1969, Rhodes scholar Oxford U., Alumni scholar Stanford Sch. Medicine, 1974 ; medalist Gothenburg (Sweden) Thoracic Soc., 1985; recipient Medaille de la Ville de Bordeaux French Thoracic Soc., 1987, travelling lectureship, 1988, Master Tchr. award Cardiovascular Revs. & Reports, 1990; travelling fellow Australia and New Zealand chpt., ACS, 1989; traveling lectureship, 1989. Fellow ACP, ACS, Royal Coll. Surgeons (Eng., traveling lectr. 1989), Am. Coll. Angiology, Am. Coll. Cardiology (mem. transplantation com. 1991—, chmn. task force cardiac donor procurement Bethesda Conf. 1992), Am. Coll. Surgeons (bd. govs. 1993—), Am. Coll. Chest Physicians, Mass. Med. Soc.; mem. AMA, AAAS, Am. Assn. Thoracic Surgery (mem. com. grad. edn. thoracic surgery 1992—, Evarts A. Graham Meml. Traveling Fellowship com. 1993—), Am. Soc. Transplant Surgeons (com. on heart transplantation 1986—, adv. com. in issues 1989—, chmn. subcom. on heart transplantation, physician payment reform commn. 1989—), Nat. Heart, Lung and Blood Inst. (cons. divsn. extramural affairs rev. br. 1990—), Assn. Acad. Surgery, Am. Physiol. Soc., Am. Heart Assn. (mem. rsch. grant pe—, coun. circulation, cert. of appreciation for outstanding svc. 1986), Am. Surg. Assn., Am. Thoracic Soc., Am. Soc. Artificial Internal Organs, Am. Soc. Extracorporeal Tech., Am. Assn. Lab. Animal Sci., Am. Organ Transplant Assn., Am. Venous Forum, Internat. Soc. Heart and Lung Transplantation (chmn. program com. 1988), Internat. Assn. Cardiac Biol. Implants, Internat. Fedn. Surg. Colls., Internat. Soc. Cardiovasc. Surgery, Internat. Soc. Cardio-Thoracic Surgeons, Internat. Soc. for Heart Rsch. (mem. Am. sect.), Internat. Soc. for Artificial Organs, Mediterranean Assn. for Cardiology and Cardiac Surgery, New Century Soc., Thoracic Surgery Found. for Rsch. and Edn., Norman E. Shumway Surg. Soc., New Eng. Surg. Soc., Pan Am. Med. Assn. (coun. on organ transplantation), North Am. Soc. Pacing and Electrophysiology, Societe Internat. de Chirurgie, Royal Soc. Medicine, Soc. Univ. Surgeons, Thoracic Surgery Dirs. Assn. (chmn. curriculum com. transplantation 1993), Transplantation Soc., Assn. Alumni of Magdalen Coll. Oxford U., Assn. Rhodes Scholars, Acad. Surg. Rsch., Assn. Surg. Edn., Assn. Program Dirs. in Surgery, Conn. Thoracic Soc., Harris County Med. Soc., Calif. Med. Assn., Calif. Thoracic Soc., Calif. Thoracic Soc. Respiratory Care Assembly, No. Calif. Cystic Fibrosis Found., So. Calif. Transplant Soc., Conn. Med. Soc., Conn. Soc. Am. Bd. Surgeons, Mass. Med. Soc., N.Y. Soc. Thoracic Surgery, New Haven County Med. Soc., Harvard Med. Alumni Assn. (assoc.), Physicians' Assn. New Haven County, Soc. Crit. Care Medicine, Soc. Thoracic Surgeons, Southeastern Surg. Congress, Southern Surg. Assn., Southwestern Surg. Congress, Tex. Surg. Soc., Halsted Soc., Houston Surg. Soc. Soc. for Organ Sharing, United Network for Organ Sharing, San Francisco Surg. Soc., Santa Clara Med. Soc., Stanford Med. Alumni Assn., Stanford Club Conn., Harvard Clubs San Francisco, Peninsula, N.Y.C., So. Conn., Houston, Boston, Mory's Assn., New Haven Lawn Club, Inner Quad Stanford U., The Hasty Pudding Club - Inst. 1770, Quinnipiack Club, Yale Club New Haven, Forum World Affairs, Ambs. Roundtable, Oxford Soc., Phi Beta Kappa, others. Office: Dept Surgery One Baylor Plz Houston TX 77030

BALDWIN, M(ARY) KAREN, marketing professional, editor; b. Oak Park, Ill., Dec. 10, 1965; d. Vernon Lawrence Barg and M. Diane (Gasper) Marston; m. Michael Patrick Baldwin, July 7, 1990. BA in Communications, DePauw U., 1988. CFP. Co-editor Cenflo, Inc., Chgo., 1988-91; pub. rels. coord. Smith, Bucklin & Assocs., Chgo., 1991; asst. mktg. dir. Precast/Prestressed Concrete Inst., Chgo., 1992—; freelance editor Baldwin Fin. Sys., Northbrook, Ill., 1990-91, Village of Oak Park (Ill.) Citizen Involvement Com., 1994—. Allocations com. mem. Oak Park and River Forest Community Chest, 1989. Office: Precast Concrete Institute 175 W Jackson Blvd Chicago IL 60604-2601

BALDWIN, ROBERT THOMAS, school superintendent; b. Peoria, Ill., Mar. 21, 1943; s. Harold Earl and Hazel (Burns) B.; m Cynthia Ann Johnson, Jan. 22, 1966; children: Mark, Ann. BS in Edn., Western Ill. U., 1965; MA in Adminstrn., Bradley U., Peoria, 1972; postgrad., Nat. Louis U.,

Evanston, Ill., 1991-93. Tchr. Carbon Cliff (Ill.) Schs., 1965-66; prin./tchr. Peoria Sch. Dist. 150, 1966-91; supt. Rosemont (Ill.) Sch. Dist. 78, 1991—. Mem. Ill. Assn. Supervision and Curriculum Devel., Leyden Supts. Orgn. (pres. 1990), Ill. Reading Coun., Nat. Assn. Elem. Sch. Prins., Ill. Prins. Assn., Rosemont Lions, Phi Delta Kappa. Lutheran. Home: 10018 Devon Rosemont IL 60018 Office: Rosemont Sch Dist 78 6101 N Ruby Rosemont IL 60018

BALDWIN, SUSAN OLIN, lawyer; b. Battle Creek, Mich., Sept. 1, 1954; d. Thomas Franklin and Gloria Joan (Skidmore) Olin; m. James Patric Baldwin, Sept. 15, 1979; children: Christopher Mark, David James. BA, Miami U., Ohio, 1976; JD, U. Cin., 1979. Bar: Ohio 1979, Mich. 1984. Assoc. editor Am. Legal Pub. Co., Cin., 1979-80; corp. atty. Hosp. Care Corp., Cin., 1980-84; legal counsel Peak Health Plan, Cin., 1984; assoc. Cook & Goetz, P.C., Bloomfield Hills, Mich., 1984-91; assoc. Pringle & Assocs., P.C., Farmington Hills, Mich., 1991-94; dir. Calhoun County Econ. Devel. Forum, Battle Creek, 1994—; mem. steering com. Ctr. Workforce Excellence, 1994—; mem. bd. dirs. BC/Cal/Kal Inland Port Devel. Corp., The Forum for Kalamazoo County, 1995—. Contbr. articles to profl. jours. Pres. Hunter's Green Homeowner's Assn., Independence, Ky., 1982-83; charter mem. Young Reps., Ashland, Ohio, 1972; chairwoman Safety Town Cmty. Project, 1993-95; v.p. fin. Jr. League Battle Creek, 1996—; key communicator, Minges Brook PTA, 1993—, treas., 1994-96. Mem. ABA, State Bar Mich., Ohio State Bar, Am. Businesswomen's Assn. (v.p. 1980-81, editor 1980), Alpha Lambda Delta, Phi Alpha Delta. Club: Birmingham Evening Newcomers (treas. 1986-87, pres. 1988). Office: 164 W Hamilton Ln Battle Creek MI 49015-4030

BALDWIN, TAMMY, state legislator; b. Madison, Wis., Feb. 11, 1962. BA, Smith Coll.; JD, U. Wis. Former pvt. practice as atty. Former supr. Dane County; mem. Nat. Women's Polit. Caucus, 1993—; state assemblywoman dist. 78 State of Wis., 1993—. Mem. NOW, ACLU, Wis. State Bar Assn., Internat. Network Lesbian and Gay Ofcls. Democrat. Home: 525 Riverside Dr Madison WI 53704-5529*

BALE, JAMES FRANKLIN, JR., pediatric neurologist; b. Kalamazoo, Mich., Jan. 11, 1949; s. James F. and Marilyn J. Bale; m. Martha Jens, Oct. 12, 1974; children: Zachary, Jeffrey, Margaret. BS in Zoology, U. Mich., 1971, MD, 1975. Diplomate Nat. Bd. Med. Examiners, Am. Bd. Pediatrics, Am. Bd. Psychiatry and Neurology. Intern then resident in pediatrics U. Utah, Salt Lake City, 1975-77, resident in neurology, 1977-80, fellow in infectious diseases, 1980-81; fellow in neurovirology VA Med. Ctr.-U. Calif., San Francisco, 1981-82; asst. prof. U. Iowa Coll. Medicine, Iowa City, 1982-85, assoc. prof., 1985-90, prof., 1990—; examiner Am. Bd. Psychiatry and Neurology, 1986—. Author: Infections in Children, 1986, 2d edit., 1994; contbr. chpts. to Cytomegalovirus Infections, 1991. Mem. Child Neurology Soc. (ethics com. 1990—), Soc. Pediatric Rsch., Am. Acad. Neurology, Am. Acad. Pediatrics, Am. Pediatric Soc. Office: U Iowa Dept Pediatrics 2504 Jcp Univ Hospital Iowa City IA 52242

BALES, EDWARD WAGNER, manufacturing executive; b. Chgo., Jan. 30, 1939; s. Edward Joseph and Esther (Wagner) B.; m. Barbara LaVarre, Nov. 26, 1960; children: Edward Joseph, Karen Mary, Kathryn Mary, Timothy Joseph. BEE, Ill. Inst. Tech., 1960; MBA, U. Chgo., 1969. Elec. engr. Motorola, Inc., Chgo., 1963-69, sales mgr., 1969-80, mgr. mktg. and client services, 1980-85, dir. ops., chief of staff, 1985-90, dir. edn., external systems, 1990—. Mem. editorial bd. U.S. Gen. Acct. Office Jour. Mem. edn. coun. NSF; mem. edn. com. Nat. conf. Bd.; vice chmn. edn. com. Bus. Industry Adv. Coun. to Orgn. Econ. Corp. and Devel.; pres. Mary Seat of Wisdom Ch. Bd., Park Ridge, Ill., 1980-83; bd. trustees Nat. Sch. Bd. Found. Lt. USN, 1960-63. Mem. Nat. Alliance of Bus. (mem. edn. com., bus./policy com.). Republican. Roman Catholic. Office: Motorola Inc 1303 E Algonquin Rd Schaumburg IL 60196-4041

BALES, JERRY F., state legislator; m. Teresa Bales. Student, Ind. U. Ind. state rep. Dist. 60, 1976—; mem. cities and towns com., pub. health com. Ind. Ho. Reps., mem. cts. fin. inst. and ways and means com.; pres. J.F. Bales & Assoc., H&B Mfg.; mem. Love Catering and Northside Exch.; mem. Northside Exch.; pres. P&F Advt. Active Big Bro.-Big Sister. Home: PO Box 115 Bloomington IN 47402-0115*

BALFOUR, DANNY LEE, public administration educator, consultant; b. St. Joseph, Mich., Aug. 6, 1955; s. Wendell Herbert Balfour and Margaret Ann (Dorgelo) Nickel; m. Mayumi Ito, Oct. 9, 1987; 1 child, Trevor. BA, Mich. State U., 1977; PhD, Fla. State U., 1990. Sr. assoc. Fla. Ctr. for Productivity Improvement, Tallahassee, Fla. Ctr. for Pub. Mgmt., Tallahassee, 1986-90; asst. prof. U. Akron, Ohio, 1990-95, assoc. prof., 1995-96, coord. MPA program, 1993-96; dir., assoc. prof. Sch. of Pub. Adminstrn. Grand Valley State U., Grand Rapids, Mich., 1996—; cons. Ohio Ctr. for Family Devel., Columbus, 1991-95, Fla. Alcohol and Drug Abuse Assn., Tallahassee, 1988-90. Mng. editor Jour. Pub. Adminstrn. Edn.; contbr. articles to profl. jours. and books. Rsch. fellow Ctr. for Urban Studies, 1990-96. Mem. USTA, ASPA, Acad. Mgmt., Phi Kappa Phi, Pi Alpha Alpha. Office: Grand Valley State Univ Sch of Pub Adminstrn 25 Commerce SW Ste 300 Grand Rapids MI 49503

BALGEMAN, RICHARD VERNON, radiology administrator, alcoholism counselor; b. Berwyn, Ill., Dec. 25, 1929; s. Vernon Ernest and Regina Marie (Fitzgerald) B.; m. Wauneta Frances Laird, Nov. 15, 1952; children: Marcia, Kathleen, Barbara, Daniel. Radiology technician, Cook County Grad. Sch. of Med., 1951; BA in Health Svc., Governor State U., 1976, MA in Sci., 1978. Cert. technologist. Radiology adminstr. Manteno (Ill.) Mental Health Ctr., 1951-84; adminstrv. asst. bus. office Shapiro Devel. Ctr., Kankakee, Ill., 1984-88; with St. James Hosp., Chicago Heights, Ill., 1990—. Inventor DuPont Cronex Tech. Aid, 1965. Village trustee Village of Manteno, 1969-72, chmn. planning commn., 1985-93; pres. Village View TV, Channel 10. With USNG, 1948-56. Gov.'s award Ill. Dept. Mental Health, Manteno, 1971. Mem. Am. Legion, Moose, Rotary. Roman Catholic. Home: 555 Park St Manteno IL 60950-1045

BALGEMANN, LEE ALAN, photographer; b. Oak Park, Ill., Jan. 5, 1946; s. Ralph Ewald and Edna Myfanwy (Owen) B.; m. Linda Rae Bredehorn, June 19, 1971; children: Bryan, Brad. BA in English, Knox Coll., 1968. Photo editor AP, Chgo., 1968-81; pres. Lee Balgemann Photographics, River Forest, Ill., 1981—. Bd. dirs. Youth Svc. Project, Chgo., 1990-95. Mem. ASMP (bd. dirs. 1994-95), ASMP Chgo./Midwest (bd. dirs. 1983-95, pres. 1987-88), NPPA, CPPA, IPPA. Home and Office: 725 Monroe River Forest IL 60305

BALL, DARRELL WAYNE, construction company executive, consultant; b. Hardinsburg, Ky., Mar. 13, 1960; s. Burman Ballard and Fannie Lee (Hylton) B.; m. Brenda Gayle Robbins, Aug. 26, 1978 (div. Nov. 1983); m. Christine Marie Joshu, Mar. 14, 1986; 1 child, Samantha Katlyn. BS, Western Ky. U., 1983. Jr. engr. Ky. Dept. Transp., Frankfort, 1978-80, Warren County Water Dist., Bowling Green, Ky., 1980-83; estimator J.A. Tobin Constrn. Co., Kansas City, Kans., 1983-84; estimator Tomahawk Constrn. Co., Kansas City, 1984-85, project mgr., 1985-88, constrn. mgr., 1988-91, v.p., 1991-92; v.p. Ball Constrn., Inc., 1992-94; pres. Ball Construction, Inc., 1994—. Named Contractor of 1985 Omaha dist. U.S. Army C.E., 1986, Real Property Maintenance Acquisition Contractor of 1987, 1988. Mem. Soc. Am. Mil. Engrs., Am. Concrete Inst., Assn. Gen. Contractors (C.E. com.), Airplane Owners and Pilots Assn. Republican. Home: 8058 Lakeview Ave Shawnee Mission KS 66219-1826 Office: Ball Construction Inc PO Box 15103 Shawnee Mission KS 66285-5103

BALL, ELIZABETH SUZETTE, home health care-coronary care nurse; b. Lima, Ohio, Sept. 9, 1955; d. Jackie Alden and Beverly Irene (Nebergall) Mason; m. Thomas John Ball, July 21, 1973; children: Thomas John II, James David, Anna Elizabeth. AD, Lima Tech. Coll., 1983. Staff nurse coronary observation unit Lima Meml. Hosp., 1984-92, home health care RN, 1992—, asst. intake coord. for home health care, 1994—; mem., RN Nursing Care Com., Lima, 1991—; unit rep. Lima Meml. Hosp., 1988-92. Mem. Profl. Nursing Assn., Ohio Nursing Assn. (cert. appreciation 1989-91). Democrat. Mem. Ch. of God. Home: 1130 W High St Lima OH 45805-2725 Office: Lima Meml Hosp Home Health Care 1001 Bellefontaine Ave Lima OH 45804-2800

BALL, JASON JOSEPH, plant manager; b. Mpls., Mar. 30, 1962; s. Adolph Francis and Marie Delia (Cota) B. BChemE, U. Minn. Inst. Technology, 1985; cert. hazardous materials mgmt., U. Calif., Irvine, 1987; MBA, Ind. U., 1991. Safety, environ., project engr. Cargill Inc., L.A., 1985-86, maintenance mgr., 1986-87; engring. mgr. Cargill Inc., Chicago Heights, Ill., 1987-88, prodn. mgr., 1988-91, asst. plant mgr., 1991-93; plant mgr. McWhorter Technologies, Chicago Heights, 1993—. Achievements include discovery of process of treating wastewater from synthetic resin manufacturing with salt, resulting in a 50% cost savings. Mem. AIChE, Chgo. Soc. for Coatings Technology, Nat. Fire Protection Assn., Southland C. of C. Republican. Roman Catholic. Office: McWhorter Technologies Inc 374 E Joe Orr Rd Chicago Heights IL 60411

BALL, JERRY LEE, professional football player; b. Beaumont, Tex., Dec. 15, 1964. Student, So. Meth. U. Nosetackle Detroit Lions, 1987-93, Cleveland Browns, 1993, L. A. Raiders, 1994—. Voted to Pro Bowl, 1989, 90, 91. Office: Los Angeles Raiders 332 Center St El Segundo CA 90245-4047*

BALL, KENNETH LEON, manufacturing company executive, organizational development consultant; b. N.Y.C., Aug. 11, 1932; s. Oscar and Elvira (Klein) B.; m. Patricia Ann Whitley; children: David B., Dana K. BA, Antioch Coll., Yellow Springs, Ohio, 1954; PhD, Washington U., St. Louis, 1958. Lic. psychologist, Mo. Gen. mgr. Pacific Coast div. Orchard Corp. Am., 1960-62; indsl. rels. dir. Orchard Corp. Am., St. Louis, 1963-64; v.p. indsl. rels. Orchard Corp. Am., 1965-66, v.p., dir., 1967-72, exec. v.p., dir., 1972-75, pres., dir., 1976-88; pres. Orchard Decorative Products div. Borden, Inc., St. Louis, 1988-92, Ken Ball Mgmt. Resources, St. Louis, 1993—; adj. prof. Washington U., 1978-79. Contbg. author: Humanizing Organizational Behavior, 1976, Making Organizatios Humane and Productive, 1981; contbr. articles to publs. Trust Antioch U., 1980-85, 89—; dir. Met. Employment and Rehab. Svc., St. Louis, 1975—, chair, 1985-86; dir. St. Louis chpt. Young Audiences, 1990, Narcotic Svc. Coun., 1976. Human Rels. Rsch. Found. fellow, 1955-58. Mem. APA, Mo. Psychol. Assn., St. Louis Psychol. Assn., Acad. Mgmt., Soc. Psychologists in Mgmt. (dir. 1989—, pres. 1992-93). Home: 9875 Northbridge Rd Saint Louis MO 63124-1025 Office: Ken Ball Mgmt Resources 1750 S Brentwood Blvd Ste 453 Saint Louis MO 63144-1340

BALL, LOUIS ALVIN, insurance company executive; b. Kansas City, Mo., Oct. 25, 1921; s. George Rhodom and Frances Mariam (Beals) B.; B.A. in Bus. Adminstrn., Kans. State U., 1947; m. Norma Jane Laudenberger, Jan. 17, 1947. Asst. purchasing agt. Kansas City (Mo.) br. Ford Motor Co., 1942-46; with Farm Bur. Mut. Ins. Co., Inc., Manhattan, Kans., 1947—, claims underwriting mgr., 1956-61, systems and procedures mgr., 1961—, asst. sec., 1977-81, corp. sec., 1981-90, ret., 1990—. Mem. Nat. Assn. Ind. Insurers, Conf. Casualty Cos., Assn. Systems Mgmt. (Internat. Merit award 1971, Internat. Achievement award 1978, Kansas City chpt. Merit award 1970, Kansas City chpt. Diamond Merit award 1977, chmn. ann. conf. 1982). Club: Manhattan Country. Home: 1101 Pioneer Ln Manhattan KS 66502-4624

BALL, MICHAEL RAY, sociologist, educator; b. Munich, Mar. 4, 1950; came to U.S., 1951; m. Elizabeth Ann Peterson, Aug. 31, 1971. AA, Cotner Sch. Religion, 1976; BA in Photography, U. Nebr., 1983, MA in Sociology, 1985, PhD in Sociology, 1989. Asst. mgr. Lincoln (Nebr.) Camera Repair, 1971-83; instr. U. Nebr., Lincoln, 1984-89, grad. teaching fellow, 1983-89, Alice Frost Howard fellow, 1988; instr. U. Nebr., Omaha, 1988; sr. lectr. Beijing Tchrs.' Coll., 1989-90; asst. prof. sociology U. Wis., Superior, 1990-94, chair sociology and social work, coord. women's studies, 1991-94, coord. sociology, 1990—, assoc. prof., 1994—; cons. Internat. Tng. Ctr. on Erosion and Sedimentation, Beijing, 1989-90; mem. Planning & Zoning Commn., Village of Lake Nebagamon, Wis., 1994—. Author: Social Problems, 1989, Criminology, 1990, Professional Wrestling as Ritual Drama in American Popular Culture, 199o, Proresu Shakai-Gaku, 1993; assoc. editor: Wis. Sociologist, 1992-93; co-editor Jour. of Race, Sex, and Class, 1993-94. Active Nebraskans for Peace, Lincoln, 1970-76, bd. dirs., 1976; co-founder, pres. Native Am. Leadership Found., Lincoln, 1983-89; mem. Twin Ports Race Task Force, Superior,1 992. Recipient Jean R. Faulkner Art award Sheldon Art Gallery, Lincoln, 1983, cert. of recognition Gov. Bob Kerry, State of Nebr., 1983, Cloward and Ohlin award Soc. for Study of Social Problems, 1987, Max Lavine award for scholarly contbns. to social concerns, U. Wis., 1994. Mem. AAUP, Am. Sociol. Assn., Assn. for Advancement of Policy, Rsch. and Devel. in 3d World, Assn. U. Wis. Profls. Rsch. Com. (campus del. 1995, 96), Assn. Humanist Sociology. So. Poverty Law Ctr. (leadership coun.), Global Awareness Soc. Internat., Midwest Sociol. Soc. (Don Martindale award 1987), Wis. Sociol. Assn. Home: 7051 S East Lake Blvd Lake Nebagamon WI 54849-9109 Office: Univ Wis-Superior Dept History Politics & Soc Superior WI 54880

BALL, OWEN KEITH, JR., lawyer; b. Louisville, Feb. 19, 1950; s. Owen Keith and Martha Katherine (Guntherberg) B.; m. Shirley Marie Galinski, Sept. 16, 1972. BSCE, U. Kans., 1972, JD, 1980. Bar: Mo. 1980, U.S. Dist. Ct. (we. dist.) Mo. 1980, Kans. 1988, U.S. Dist. Ct., Kans., 1988. Ptnr. Smith, Gill, Fisher & Butts P.C., Kansas City, Mo., 1980-87; pvt. practice as a loan broker Lawrence, 1987-88, pvt. practice, 1988-91; legal counsel Marian Merrell Dow Inc., Kansas City, Mo., 1991-92; corp. counsel Marion Merrell Dow Inc., Kansas City, Mo., 1992-95, Hoechst Marion Roussel, Inc., kansas City, Mo., 1995—. Mem. staff Hyatt Regency Hotel com. to investigate safety of the Hyatt Regency Hotel, Kansas City C. of C., 1981. Lt. USN, 1972-77. Mem. Am. Corp. Counsel Assn., Am. Mensa, Mo. Bar Assn., Kansas City Met. Bar Assn. Office: 10236 Marion Park Dr Kansas City MO 64137-1405

BALL, RICHARD EVERETT, sociology educator; b. Pasadena, Calif., Oct. 31, 1937; s. Floyd Richard and Ruby Pauline (Wrest) B.; m. Charlotte Ann Wicks, Dec. 28, 1962; children: Jonathan, Graham. BA, Calif. State U., Long Beach, 1961; MA, U. Fla., 1975, PhD, 1980. Asst. prof. Livingston (Ala.) U., 1978-79; asst. prof., assoc. prof. Ferris State U., Big Rapids, Mich., 1980-90, prof. sociology, 1990—; vis. asst. prof. Erskine Coll., Due West, S.C., 1977-78; Fulbright lectr. Coun. Internat. Exch. Scholars, U. Tokyo, Keio U., Tsuda Coll., Japan, 1993-94. Contbr. articles to profl. jours. Lt. (j.g.) USNR, 1961-64. Mem. So. Sociol. Soc., So. Sociol. Soc., Mich. Sociol. Assn. (pres. 1986-87, v.p. 1985-86, sec./treas. 1991-96), Alpha Kappa Delta. Office: Ferris State U Dept Social Scis Big Rapids MI 49307

BALL, VIRGINIA B., investor; b. Jacksonville, Tex., Jan. 1; d. John A. and DeLouise (McClelland) Beall; m. Edmund F. Ball, June 28, 1952; children: Robert, Nancy. Student, Lon Morris Jr. Coll., 1936-37; AB, Baylor U., 1940; grad. student, Tex. Christian U., 1942-43, Ball State U., 1952-54; HHD (hon.), Wabash Coll., 1975; hon. degree, Ball State U., 1986; Hon. degree, Keuka Coll., 1994. V.p. Muncie (Ind.) Airport, Inc., 1992—, B.B.S. Properties, Muncie, 1992—; trustee, chmn. Nat. Wildlife Fed. Endowment, Washington, 1980-93. Bd. dirs. Minnetrista Cultural Found., Muncie Ind. Com. Humanities, 1973-79; former mem. adv. bd. Connor Prairie Settlement, Fishers, Ind., Ind. Youth Inst., Indpls., Interlochen (Mich.) Ctr. for Arts, Muncie Children's Mus., Human Genetics and Engring. Lab., Ball State U., Muncie. Recipient Civic award Woman of Influence, Muncie, 1980; Old Main Tower award Baylor U., 1981, Sagamore of Wabash award Gov. of Ind., Indpls., 1984, Baylor Woman of Merit award Omicron Delta Kappa, 1989, Distinction award Ind. Humanities Coun., Indpls., 1990, VIVA award Muncie C. of C., Rotary Club, 1993, Huckins medal Baylor U.; named Disting. Alumni, Lon Morris Jr. Coll., 1983. Mem. The Ninety-nines, Explorer's Club, Soc. Woman Geographers, Internat. Woman's Forum, Rotary Club. Republican. Home: 1707 W Riverside Ave Muncie IN 47303-3548 Office: Ball Assocs PO Box 1408 222 S Mulberry St Muncie IN 47308

BALL, WILLIAM JAMES, pediatrician; b. Charleston, S.C., Apr. 16, 1910; s. Elias and Mary (Cain) B.; BS, U. of South, 1930; MD, Med. Coll. S.C., 1934; m. Doris Hallowell Mason, July 9, 1938. Intern, Roper Hosp., Charleston, 1934-35; resident dept. pediatrics U. Chgo. Clinics, 1935-37; instr. pediatrics Med. Coll. S.C., 1938-42; practice medicine specializing in pediatrics, Charleston, 1938-42, Northwest Clinic, Minot N.D., 1946-51, Aurora, Ill., 1951-70; physician student Health Svc. No. Ill. U., 1970-72; mem. staff Copley Meml., Mercy Ctr. Health Care Svcs.; assoc. prof. Sch. Nursing, No. Ill. U., 1971-72. Mem. Bd. Health, Aurora, Ill., 1958-62; pediatrician, divsn. svcs. for crippled children U. Ill., 1952-86; pediatric cons. sch. dists. 129 and 131, Aurora, 1972-85, DeKalb County Spl. Edn. Assn., 1972-81, Sch. Assn. Spl. Edn. Dupage County, 1980-83, Mooseheart, Ill., 1970-83, Northwestern Ill. Assn. Handicapped Children; chmn. adv. com. Kane County Health Dept., 1986-95; pres. Kane County sub-area coun. Health Sys. Agy., Kane, Lake, McHenry Counties, 1977-78, sec., 1978-79. Served as capt. M.C., AUS, 1942-46; maj., 1946 to col., 1963, ret. 1970. Diplomate Am. Bd. Pediatrics. Recipient Golden Apple award Ill. Sch. Dist. 129, 1983, Shimkus award Aurora Vis. Nurses Assn., 1993. Fellow Royal Soc. Health, Am. Acad. Pediatrics; mem. AMA, Kane County Med. Soc. (pres. 1962), Am. Heart Assn., Am. Sch. Health Assn., Am. Cancer Soc., Am. Pub. Health Assn., Juvenile Protective Assn. of Aurora , The Ret. Officers Assn. (west suburban Chgo. chpt.), Phi Beta Kappa, Phi Chi, Pi Kappa Phi. Rotarian. Address: 433 S Commonwealth Ave Aurora IL 60506-5439

BALLA, (FERENC) BULCSU, hospital manager, clinical engineer; b. Budapest, Hungary, Feb. 23, 1934; came to U.S., 1977; naturalized, 1982; s. Jozsef and Maria (Balogh) B.; m. Gloria Male, Sept. 15, 1986. Diploma in Electronic Tech., MUM 13 Tech. Coll., Budapest, 1961; BSEE, KKMF Tech. Coll., Budapest, 1967. Electronic technician Orion TV-Radio Co., Budapest, 1959-63; dir. electronic instrument and customer service dept. HTSZ Co., Budapest, 1963-72; mgr. electronic instrument service dept. HIKI Co., Budapest, 1972-74; tech. mgr. GELKA Co., Budapest, 1974-76; clin. engr., mgr. clin. engring. Ill. Masonic Med. Ctr., Chgo., 1979—. With Hungarian Armed Forces, 1954-56. Mem. Assn. for the Advancement of Med. Instrumentation (cert. biomed. equipment technician 1982, cert. clin. engr. 1985). Republican. Buddhist. Home: PO Box 486 Lake Zurich IL 60047-0486 Office: Ill Masonic Med Ctr 836 W Wellington Ave Chicago IL 60657-5147

BALLANCE, JOHN D., financial associate; b. Leonard, Mo., Mar. 13, 1947; s. Billy Lee and Gladys Raydene (Davidson) B.; m. Cynthia L. Snell, Feb. 10, 1978; children: Scott A., Erika N. BS, William Jewel Coll., Liberty, Mo., 1969. Farm owner Leonard; fin. advisor Pvt. Ledger, Curtsville, Mo., 1984-89; fin. assoc. Edward D. Jones & Co., Quincy, Ill., 1989—; bd. dirs. Quincy (Ill.) Kuan's, 1989—, Gym City, Quincy, 1994—. Mem. Masons, Shriners. Democrat. Home: 3518 The Courts of West U Quincy IL 62301 Office: Edward D Jones & Co 2 State And 8th Plz Quincy IL 62301-4960

BALLARD, BARBARA W., state legislator; m. Albert L. Ballard. Rep. dist. 44 State of Kansas, 1993—; adminstr., dir. U. Kans. Democrat. Home: 1532 Alvamar Dr Lawrence KS 66047-1605 Office: U Kans Emily Taylor Women's Ctr 115 Strong Hall Lawrence KS 66045-7501

BALLARD, CHARLIE, state legislator. Mem. Mo. Ho. of Reps., Jefferson City. Republican.

BALLARD, DANIEL JOSEPH, risk manager; b. Chicopee Falls, Mass., May 18, 1954; s. Herbert A. and Jean L. (Crowley) B.; m. Cathy Cameron, Sept. 4, 1974 (div. July 1976); m. Barbara J. Corley, Aug. 15, 1981; children: Toni K. Arneson, Mike P. AS, Belleville Area Coll., 1975; student, DePaul U., 1992-95. CPCU; Assoc. in Risk Mgmt., Ins. Inst. Am. Real estate appraiser, br. mgr. First Fed. Savs. and Loan, Mascoutah, Ill., 1975-77; claims adjuster Economy Fire & Casualty Co., Freeport, Ill., 1977; unit underwriting mgr. Economy Fire & Casualty Co., Freeport, 1978-79; mktg. rep. N.H. Ins. Group, Springfield, Ill., 1979; divsn. personal lines mgr. N.H. Ins. Group, Ft. Collins, Colo., 1979-81; regional product mgr. Home Ins. Co., Chgo., 1981-83; regional sales mgr. Automated Ins. Resource Sys., Naperville, Ill., 1983-84; underwriting mgr., risk mgmt. Talman Ins. Svcs., Chgo., 1985-90; asst. v.p. risk mgmt. AMA, Chgo., 1990—. Asst. scoutmaster, dir. Boy Scouts Am., Naperville, 1984-88; coord. Hesed House, Aurora, Ill., 1989-95. Mem. CPCU Soc. (com. chair 1992-95), Risk and Ins. Mgmt. Soc. (risk employee benefit expo com. dir. 1988-95). Roman Catholic. Office: AMA 200 N LaSalle St Chicago IL 60601

BALLBACH, PHILIP THORNTON, political consultant; b. Lansing, Mich., May 22, 1939; s. Nathan Anthony and Thelma Frances (Bowes) B. BA, Mich. State U., 1960; student, U. Mich., 1960-61; MA, Mich. State U., 1967. Social worker State of Mich., Corunna, 1961-64; legis. aide State Rep. H. James Starr, Lansing, Mich., 1964-67; exec. asst. State Atty. Gen.'s Dept., Lansing, Mich., 1967-81; county commr. Ingham County, Mason, Mich., 1980-93. Pub., Lansing This Weekend, 1963-64, The Gooseneck Tidings, 1977. Coord. Greater Lansing Assn. for Cmty. Edn., 1961-66; mem. Lansing Bd. Election Canvassers, 1965-69; dir. Cmty. Mental Health Bd., Lansing, 1977-96; treas. Zolton Ferency for Gov. Com., 1977-83; county liaison Eastside Neighborhood Orgn., Lansing, 1980-93; commr. Tri-County Regional Planning Com., Lansing, 1981-84; chairperson Ingham Cnty Emergency Planning Com., Mason, Mich., 1988-93; campaign dir. Citizens for Pub. Recycling, Lansing, 1990; treas. People Achieving Legis. Power, 1992-95; campaign coord. Citizens for a Better Lansing, 1993-96. Recipient Achievement award Nat. Assn. Counties, 1986. Mem. Mich. Assn. Counties, Mich. Assn. Community Mental Health Bds. Democrat. Home: 312 Leslie St Lansing MI 48912-2723

BALLENGER, HURLEY RENÉ, electrical engineer; b. Jacksonville, Ill., Nov. 26, 1946; s. Leonard Hurley and Katherine Natalie (Daniel) B.; m. Sandra Ann Rubley, Dec. 9, 1986. Student, Ill. Coll., 1964-65, 75. Technician electronics div. Hughs Aircraft, Inc., Tucson, 1973; maintenance supr. Fiatallis N.Am., Springfield, Ill., 1973-75, project engr., 1975-83, plant engr., 1983-86; tech. advisor CNC/CAM Fiatallis Europe, Lecce, Italy, 1986-87; plant engr. Illini Tech., Inc., Springfield, Ill., 1988, plant and mfg. engr., 1988—. Mem. career adv. bd. Lincoln Land Community Coll., Springfield, 1983-85. Served to staff sgt. USAF, 1965-72, Vietnam. Lutheran. Office: Illini Tech Inc 3430 Constitution Dr Springfield IL 62707-9402

BALLENTINE, WILLIAM ANDREW, stockbroker; b. Chgo., Nov. 27, 1951. BS, Northeastern U., 1985. Stockbroker Schelter Rock, Deerfield, Ill., 1987-89, Dean Witter, Riverwoods, Ill., 1989-90, Alliance Capital Inc., Lake Zurich, Ill., 1990-96; pres., CEO, owner Ballentine & Bauer Investments, Barrington, Ill., 1996—. Republican. Roman Catholic. Home: 9209 Jasmine Way # C Fox River Grove IL 60021-1341 Office: 800 Hart Rd Ste 109 Barrington IL 60010

BALLOU, JOHN DENNIS, state legislator. Grad., Shawnee Mission North H.S., Kans., 1975. Plasterer, 1979-83; owner Ballou Plastering Inc., 1984-95; mem. Kans. State Ho. of Reps. Dist. 43, 1995—; owner, operator Ballou, Weeks & Assocs., Inc. Home Inspections, 1996—.

BALLOWE, JAMES, English educator, author; b. Carbondale, Ill., Nov. 28, 1933; s. Frank Charles and Wilma Ruth (Maynard) B.; children: Jeffrey, Mary; m. Ruth Ganchiff. BA, Millikin U., 1954; MA, U. Ill., 1956, PhD, 1963. Tchr. pub. schs. Decatur, Ill., 1954-55; grad. asst. U. Ill., 1955-61; asst. prof. English Millikin U., 1961-63; mem. faculty dept. English Bradley U., Peoria, Ill., 1963—, prof., chmn., 1971-74, dean Grad. Sch., 1974-86, assoc. provost, 1979-86, dean communications and fine arts, 1986-90; chmn. Commn. Instns. Higher Edn., North Central Assn., 1985-86. Author: poetry The Coal Miners, 1979; editor: George Santayana's America, 1967, Anglo-Welsh Poetry, 1989. Mem. Ill. Arts Coun., 1975-83, Ill. State Mus.Bd., 1977—. Recipient Poetry award Ill. Arts Coun., 1975, 78, Creative Nonfiction award Ill. Arts Coun., 1993. Mem. Ill. Assn. Grad. Schs. (pres. 1979-80), Midwestern Assn. Grad. Schs. (pres. 1978-79). Office: Bradley U 1501 W Bradley Ave Peoria IL 61625-0001

BALOG, RITA JEAN, librarian; b. Ashtabula, Ohio, Sept. 24, 1930; d. Frederick Carroll and Marguerite Ethel (White) Grady; m. Richard Francis Balog, Oct. 16, 1949; children: Rebecca Kay, Richard Francis Jr., Ronald Frank, Robert Henry. AA, Kent State U., 1977, BA in Gen. Studies, 1978, MLS, 1980. Clk., typist Harbor Pub. Libr., Ashtabula, 1973-75, children's libr., 1975-80; libr., dir. Harbor-Topky Meml. Libr., Ashtabula, 1980—; vol. libr. Thomas Jefferson Elem. Sch., Harbor Spl. Sch., Ashtabula, 1972-75. Sec., mem. Ashtabula Archtl. Restoration and Rev. Bd., 1975—; vol. leader

Lake River coun. Girl Scouts U.S., Niles, 1958-73, mem. nominating com., 1989-91, bd. dirs., 1991-95, child camp dir.; trustee Coun. Ashtabula County Librs., chair, 1994—. Mem. ALA, AAUW, Ohio Libr. Assn., N.E. Ohio Libr. Assn. (regional adv. bd. 1984-86), Coun. Ashtabula County Librs. (pres. 1985-86), Ashtabula Area Mus. and Hist. Soc. (trustee 1992—), Zonta (pres. 1987-89). Democrat. Office: Harbor Topky Meml Libr 1633 Walnut Blvd Ashtabula OH 44004-2814

BALON, RICHARD, psychiatrist, educator; b. Olomouc, Czechoslovakia, Oct. 11, 1951; s. Ota and Marie (Sindylek) B.; m. Helena Rachel Zador, July 24, 1976. MD, U. Karlova, Prague, Czechoslovakia, 1976. Diplomate Am. Bd. Psychiatry and Neurology; bd. cert. in psychiatry in Czechoslovakia. Resident in psychiatry and clin. rsch. Psychiat. Rsch. Inst., Prague, 1978-81; resident in psychiatry Lafayette Clinic, Detroit, 1983-87; asst. prof. Wayne State U., Detroit, 1987-90, assoc. prof., 1990-96, prof., 1996—; dir. jr. med. students program in psychiatry Wayne State U., Detroit, 1989-92, dir. med. student edn. psychiatry, 1993—; staff psychiatrist Lafayette Clinic, Detroit, 1987-92, pres. med. staff, 1990-92; co-chair Mich. Tech. Adv. Rsch. com., 1991—. Contbr. chpts to books and articles to profl. jours. Recipient Travel fellowship award Am. Coll. Neuropsychopharmacology, 1987. Fellow Am. Psychiat. Assn. (1st ann. Nancy C.A. Roeske award 1991); mem. AMA, Internat. Soc. Psychoneuroendocrinology, Am. Assn. Suicidology, Soc. Biol. Psychiatry, Collegium Internat. Neuro-Psychopharmacologicum, Assn. Dirs. of Med. Student Edn. in Psychiatry, Am. Coll. Psychiatrists. Office: Univ Psychiat Ctr 2751 E Jefferson Ave Ste 200 Detroit MI 48207-4100

BALSON, CHRIS P., stockbroker, financial planner; b. Warren, Ohio, Feb. 10, 1968. B of Polit. Sci. and Econs., Kent State U., 1991. Asst. mgr. I.T.T., Cleve., 1991-93; stockbroker, fin. planner Dean Witter Reynolds, Westlake, Ohio, 1993—. Republican. Methodist. Office: Dean Witter Reynolds Gemini Towers 1991 Crocker Rd Westlake OH 44145-1962

BALTER, ALAN, conductor, music director. Music dir. Memphis Symphony Orch., Akron Symphony Orch.

BALTHASER, LINDA IRENE, academic administrator; b. Kokomo, Ind., Feb. 25, 1939; d. Earl Isaac and Evelyn Pauline (Troyer) Showalter; B.S. magna cum laude, Ind. Central U., 1961; M.S., Ind. U., 1962; m. Kenneth James Balthaser, June 1, 1963. Tchr. bus. edn. Southport High Sch., Indpls., 1962-63; sec., adminstrv. sec. Office of Pres., Ind. U., Bloomington, 1963-66; with Ind. U.-Purdue U., Fort Wayne, Ind., 1969—, asst. to dean arts and letters, 1970-86, asst. dean arts and letters, 1986-87; asst. dean arts and scis., 1987—, founding co-dir. Weekend Coll., 1979-80. Bd. dirs. Associated Chs. Fort Wayne, 1980. Ind. Conf. N. Evang. United Brethren Ch. scholar, 1957-61. Recipient Women of Achievement award YWCA, 1990. Mem. Fort Wayne-Allen County Hist. Assn., Embassy Theatre Found., Fort Wayne Mus. Art, Fort Wayne Zool. Soc., Nat. Assn. Women Edn., Am. Assn. Univ. Adminstrs., Internat. Platform Assn., AAUW (trustee 1995—, Nat. grantee Fort Wayne br. 1995), Delta Pi Epsilon, Phi Alpha Epsilon, Alpha Chi, Kappa Delta Pi, Phi Kappa Phi, Mensa. Mem. United Ch. of Christ (trustee 1994—). Club: Univ. Women's (pres. 1967-68). Home: 2917 Hazelwood Ave Fort Wayne IN 46805-2403 Office: 2101 E Coliseum Blvd Fort Wayne IN 46805-1499

BALTHIS, BILL W., state legislator; b. Edgemond, Ind., Aug. 18, 1939; m. Jody Balthis; 5 children. Ill. state rep. Dist. 79, 1991—; mem. Consumer Protection, Aging, Fin. Inst., Human Svcs. Appropriations, Transp. and Motor Vehicles Coms. Mayor, Village of Lansing. Address: 3232 Ridge Rd Lansing IL 60438*

BALTZ, RICHARD ARTHUR, chemical engineer; b. Red Bud, Ill., Aug. 1, 1959; s. Arthur A. and Arlou M. (McDonald) B. BS in Chem. Engring., U. Mo., Rolla, 1981. Process design engr. corp. engring. dept. Monsanto, St. Louis, 1981-83; process engr. Nitro Plant Monsanto, Nitro, W.Va., 1983-89; process engring. specialist W.G. Krummrich Plant Monsanto, Sauget, Ill., 1989--. Mem. Am. Inst. Chem. Engrs. Roman Catholic. Home: 3749 Huntington Valley Dr Apt J Saint Louis MO 63129-2267 Office: Monsanto Co 500 Monsanto Ave Sauget IL 62206-1198

BALTZER, KIMBERLY LENORE, civil engineer, consultant; b. Quincy, Ill., Nov. 10, 1964; d. George Washington and Verna Marie (Goodwin) B. Student engring., N.E. Mo. State U., 1982-84; BS in Engring. Mgmt., U. Mo., Rolla, 1986, MS in Engring. Mgmt., 1988. Cert. engr.-in-tng.; registered LPA II AC inspector State of Kans. Engring. aide Ill. Dept. Transport, Quincy, 1985; tech. engr. Poepping, Stone, Bach & Assocs., Quincy, 1986, 87; civil engr. Torres Cons. Engrs., Kansas City, 1989-90; asst. city engr. City of Leavenworth (Kans.), Kans., 1990—. Mem. choir Cen. Bapt. Ch., Quincy, 198l—. Pres.'s hon. scholar N.E. Mo. State U., 1982; named Outstanding Coll. Students of Am. and Disting. Am. High Sch. Students. Mem. Am. Pub. Works Assn., Rainbow for Girls (life majority mem., officer 1978-84), Kappa Mu Epsilon. Home: 35379 187th St Leavenworth KS 66048

BALZEKAS, STANLEY, JR., museum director; b. Chgo., Oct. 8, 1924; s. Stanley and Emily B.; (widower); children—Stanley, III, Robert, Carole Rene. B.S., DePaul U., Chgo., 1950, M.A., 1951. Pres. Balzekas Mus. Lithuanian Culture, Chgo., 1966—, Balzekas Motor Sales, Chgo., 1952—. Trustee Lincoln Acad., Cath. Charities, Ukrainian Inst. Modern Art, Am.-Lithuanian Coun.; chmn. Sister Cities/Chgo.-Vilnius Friendship Com.; mem. Human Rels. Commn. Chgo.; mem. adv. bd. Chgo. Cultural Affairs. Served with AUS, 1942-45. Decorated 3d degree order Grand Duke Gediminas (Lithuania), Bronze Star; recipinet Wigilia medal Polish Geneal. Soc. Am. Mem. Ethnic Cultural Preservation Coun. (pres. 1977—), Press Club (Chgo.), Literary Club (Chgo.), City Club (Chgo., ethnic chmn.), Exec. Club (Chgo.). Office: 4030 S Archer Ave Chicago IL 60632-1140

BAMBERGER, DAVID, opera executive; b. Albany, N.Y., Oct. 14, 1940; s. Bernard J. and Ethel K. Bamberger; m. Carola Beral, June 8, 1965; 1 son, Steven B. B.A., Swarthmore Coll., 1962; postgrad., U. Paris, 1961, Yale U., 1963. Mem. directing staff N.Y.C. Opera, 1966-70; guest dir. Nat. Opera Chile, 1970, Cin. Opera, 1968, Augusta Opera (Ga.), 1970, Pitts. Opera, 1971, 76, 81, Columbus Opera (Ohio); gen. dir. Cleve. Opera, 1976—; artistic dir. Toledo Opera Assn., 1983-85. Bd. dirs. Opera Am., Nat. Alliance Musical Theater Producers. Author Jewish history textbooks; contbr. articles to Opera News. Office: Cleveland Opera 1422 Euclid Ave Ste 1052 Cleveland OH 44115-2001*

BAMBERGER, RUTH, educator; b. Newport, Ky., Aug. 18, 1937. BS, Spalding Coll., 1966; MA, Ohio State U., 1968, PhD, 1973. Dem. candidate for U.S. House 7th Dist., Mo., 1996. Roman Catholic. Office: PO Box 4149 Springfield MO 65808*

BAMBRICK, JAMES JOSEPH, labor economist, labor relations executive; b. N.Y.C., Apr. 26, 1917; s. James Joseph and Mae (Murphy) B.; m. Margaret Mary Donlan, June 26, 1948; children: Patricia Bambrick Benek, Thomas G., Mary Alice Bambrick Schneider, Kathleen, James Joseph Jr. BS, NYU, 1940, MBA, 1942; BS, U.S. Mcht. Marine Acad., 1946. Exec. dir. Labor Bur., N.Y.C., 1940-42; personnel dir. Allegheny Airlines, Wilmington, Del., 1942-44; mgr. labor relations research The Conf. Bd., N.Y.C., 1947-58; corp. labor economist Standard Oil Co., Cleve., 1958-81; exec. dir. Labor Econ. Inst., Cleveland Heights, Ohio, 1981—; mem. bus. adv. council U.S. Bur. Labor Stats., Washington, 1971—, chmn. wages and indsl. relations com., 1980-85; instr. NYU, 1946-53, John Carroll U., University Heights, Ohio, 1968-71; lectr. Cleve. State U., 1963-68. Author: Preparing for Collective Bargaining, 1959, Handbook of Modern Personnel Administration, 1972; contbr. chpts. to The Foreman/Supervisor's Handbook, 1984; contbr. articles to profl. jours. Chmn. Ohio Rep. Fin. Com., Cuyahoga County, Cleve., 1966—; pres. Cath. Interracial Council, Cleve., 1965-68, bd. dirs. 1969—; v.p. Navy League of U.S., Cleve., 1984—. Served to lt. USNR, 1944-46. Named Hibernian Man of the Yr. Ancient Order of Hibernians, 1974. Fellow Soc. for Advancement of Mgmt. (pres. 1955-58); mem. Am. Econ. Assn., Indsl. Relations Research Assn., U.S. Mcht. Marine Acad. Alumni Assn. (pres., bd. dirs. N.E. Ohio, 1965—). Republican. Clubs: City (Cleve.) (trustee 1972-75, v.p. Forum Found. 1981—). Lodge: K.C.

BANACH, ART JOHN, graphic artist; b. Chgo., May 22, 1931; s. Vincent and Anna (Zajac) B. Grad. Art. Inst. of Chgo., 1955; pupil painting studies Mr. Melin, Chgo.; m. Loretta A. Nolan, Oct. 15, 1966; children: Heather Anne, Lynnea Joan. Owner, dir. Art J. Banach Studios, 1949—, cartoon syndicate for newspapers, house organs and advt. functions, 1954—, owner and operater advt. agy., 1954-56, feature news and picture syndicate, distbn. U.S. and fgn. countries. Dir. Speculators S Fund. Recipient award 1st Easter Seal contest Ill. Assn. Crippled, Inc., 1949. Chgo. Pub. Sch. Art Soc. Scholar. Mem. Artist's Guild Chgo., Am Mgmt. Assn., Chgo. Assn. of Commerce and Industry, Chgo. Federated Advt. Club, Am. Mktg. Assn., Internat. Platform Assn., Chgo. Advt. Club, Chgo. Soc. Communicating Arts, Am. Ctr. For Design, Chgo. Calligraphy Collective, Columbia Yacht Club, Advt. Execs. Club, Art Dirs. Club (Chgo.). Home: 1076 Leahy Cir E Des Plaines IL 60016-6050

BANAS, JOHN STANLEY, obstetrician, gynecologist; b. Chgo., May 27, 1955; s. Edward Thomas and Stephanie Victoria (Gatz) B.; m. Kerry Jeanine Keenan, June 7, 1981; children: Melissa, Kevin, Daniel, Amanda. BS in Biology cum laude, Loyola U., Chgo., 1977; MD, Loyola U., Maywood, Ill., 1981; bd. eligible obstetrics and gynecology, SUNY, Buffalo, 1985. Diplomate Am. Bd. Ob-Gyn. Obstetrician-gynecologist Associated Obstetrics and Gynecology Inc., Ft. Wayne, Ind., 1985, Affiliated Obstetrics and Gynecology, Inc., Ft. Wayne, 1986-88, Kurten Med. Group, Racine, Wis., 1988-90, United Trinity Med Ctr., Moline, Ill., 1990—. Fellow Am. Coll. Obstetricians and Gynecologists; mem. AMA, Ill. State Med. Soc., Rock Island County Med. Soc. Roman Catholic. Home: 2130 Nathan Ct Bettendorf IA 52722-2100 Office: Trinity Med Ctr 501 10th Ave Moline IL 61265-1217

BANASZYNSKI, JACQUELINE MARIE, newspaper reporter; b. Green Bay, Wis., Apr. 17, 1952; d. Eugene Francis and Ethel Marie (McGillivray) B. BA in Journalism, Marquette U., 1974. Reporter intern Wall St. Jour., Boston, 1973; reporter fellow Indpls. Star, 1974; staff reporter Janesville (Wis.) Gazette, 1974-75, Duluth (Minn.) News Tribune, 1976-78, Eugene (Oreg.) Register-Guard, 1978-80, Mpls. Star and Tribune, 1981-83; became staff reporter St. Paul Pioneer Press Dispatch, 1984; now environment editor The Oregonian, Portland; adj. instr. Coll. of St. Thomas, St. Paul, 1986. Recipient Gene O'Brien Excellence in Journalism award Minn. Press Club, 1985, Disting. Svc. award Gen. News Soc. Profl. Journalists, 1987, Sweepstakes award, 1987, Pulitzer prize, 1988, Dag Hammerskjöld award Physicians Assn. for AIDS Care, 1988, Outstanding Achievement award Melpomene Inst., 1988, Minn. AP award, 1988, Best Sports Event Story award Nat. AP Sports Editors, 1988. Mem. Internat. Newspaper Guild. Office: The Oregonian 1320 SW Broadway Portland OR 97201-3469*

BANCROFT, RANDY CECIL, electrical engineer; b. Belmond, Iowa, Sept. 24, 1957; s. Donald Edward Bancroft and Cora Lee (White) Sizer. BEE, Iowa State U., 1983; MEE, U. Colo., 1992. Assoc. engr. Lockheed Calif. Co., Burbank, 1983-85; design engr. Martin Marietta Denver Astronautics, 1985-89, Ball Comms. Systems Divsn., Broomfield, Colo., 1989-90; mem. tech. staff Thompson Consumer Electronics, Indpls., 1993—. Author: Understanding Electromagnetic Scattering Using the Moment Method, 1996; contbr. articles to profl. jours. Mem. bd. dirs. Rocky Mountain Skeptics, Boulder, 1987-92. Home: 7339 A Jessman Rd S Dr Indianapolis IN 46256

BAND, JORDAN CLIFFORD, lawyer; b. Cleve., Aug. 15, 1923; s. Samuel Melville and Helen Rita (Krause) B.; m. Alice Jeanne Glickson, Apr. 27, 1946; children: Terril R., Stefanie Band Allweiss, Claudia Band McCord. Student, U. Ala., 1943-44; BBA, Case Western Res. U., 1947, LLB, 1948. Bar: Ohio 1948, U.S. Dist. Ct. (no. dist.) Ohio 1948. Assoc. Ulmer & Berne, Cleve., 1948-56, ptnr., 1956-94, ret., 1994—; bd. dirs. numerous cos. Chmn. Greater Cleve. Conf. on Religion and Race, 1964-66, Greater Cleve. Project, 1978-81; nat. chmn. Nat. Jewish Community Rels. Adv. Coun., N.Y.C., 1967-70; presiding officer Cleve. Community Rels. Bd., 1970-90; nat. vice chmn. Am. Jewish Com., 1976-79; legal counsel Jewish Community Fedn. Cleve., 1984-87, also trustee, officer numerous civic and non-profit orgns. Recipient Kane Leadership award Jewish Community Fedn., 1961, Bronze medal, 1978, Cert. of Appreciation, City of Cleve., 1970-88, Cert. of REcognition, Ohio Senate, 1987. Mem. ABA, Ohio Bar Assn., Cuyahoga County Bar Assn., Cleve. Bar Assn., Order of Coif. Democrat. Office: Ulmer & Berne 1300 E 9th St Cleveland OH 44114-1503

BANDER, THOMAS SAMUEL, dentist; b. Grand Rapids, Mich., Mar. 3, 1924; s. Samuel and Jennie (David) B.; m. DoLores Abraham, Sept. 7, 1947; children: Samuel T., Jacquelyn Marie. AS, Grand Rapids Jr. Coll., 1944; DDS, U. Mich., 1948. Pvt. practice dentistry Grand Rapids, Mich., 1948—. Pres. St. Nicholas Orthodox Ch., Grand Rapids, 1965. Served with U.S. Army, 1941-44, to capt. USAF, 1955-57. Fellow Am. Coll. Dentists, Internat. Coll. of Dentists, ADA, Acad. Operative Dentistry; mem. West Mich. Dental Soc. (pres. 1978), Mich. Dental Assn. (chmn. sci. program 1977-78), Kent County Dental Soc. (pres. 1965), Cascade Hills Country Club. Republican. Eastern Orthodox. Home: 616 Manhattan Rd SE Grand Rapids MI 49506-2077 Office: 2426 Burton St SE Grand Rapids MI 49546-4806

BANE, BRADLEY LEWIS, marketing account executive; b. De Moines, Feb. 17, 1967; s. James Julian and Marylin Lee (Vansant) B.; m. Cheryl Elizabeth Quick, Apr. 16, 1994. BBA in mktg., U. Iowa, 1989; MBA in mktg., econs., Ind. U., 1992. Coding supr. Rabin Rsch. Co., Chgo., 1992-93, project supr., 1993-94; mktg. project dir. NFO Rsch., Inc., Chgo., 1994-95, mktg. account exec., 1995—. Editor MBA Jour., 1991-92. Mem. Am. Mktg. Assn. Republican. Office: NFO Rsch Inc 500 w Monroe Ste 2710 Chicago IL 60661

BANERJEE, PRASHANT, industrial engineering educator; b. Calcutta, West Bengal, India, Apr. 15, 1962; came to U.S., 1986; s. Prabhat K. and Bani Banerjee; m. Madhumita Banerjee, Dec. 11, 1987; children: Jay, Ann. BSME, Indian Inst. Tech., Kanpur, India, 1984; MS in Indsl. Engring., Purdue U., 1987, PhD, 1990. Indsl. engr. Tata Steel Co., Jamshedpur, India, 1984-85; rsch. scientist Engring. Rsch. Ctr. Intelligent Mfg. Systems, Purdue U., West Lafayette, Ind., 1986-90; asst. prof. U. Ill., Chgo., 1990—; cons. Kraft Cheese Co., Noblesville, Ind., 1988, Caterpillar Inc., Peoria, Ill., 1992, Motorola Inc., 1994, Ford Motor Co., 1994. Author: Automation and Control of Manufacturing Systems, 1991, Object-oriented Technology in Manufacturing, 1992; contbr. articles to profl. jours. Equipment grantee Digital Equipment Corp., 1990, NSF rsch. grantee, 1992, 95, Nat. Inst. Standards and Tech. rsch. grantee, 1995. Mem. ASME, Inst. Indsl. Engrs., Inst. Mgmt. Scis., Soc. Mfg. Engrs. Home: 197 Brookwood Ln W Bolingbrook IL 60440-5508 Office: Univ Ill Engring Dept Chicago IL 60607-7022

BANIAK, SHEILA MARY, accountant; b. Chgo., Feb. 26, 1953; d. DeLoy N. and Ann (Pasko) Slade; m. Mark A. Baniak, Oct. 7, 1972 (div. Feb. 1994); 1 child, Heather Ann. Assocs. in Acctg., Oakton Community Coll., 1986; student, Roosevelt U., 1986—; MBA, North Park Coll., Chgo., 1995. Cert. enrolled agt. IRS; accredited tax adviser Accreditation Coun. Accountancy and Taxation. Owner, mgr. Baniak and Assocs., Park Ridge, Ill., 1984—; acct. Otto & Snyder, Park Ridge, 1984-87; spl. projects coordinator, supplemental instr. Oakton Community Coll., Des Plaines, Ill., 1986—; acctg. computer instr. Oakton Community Coll., Des Plaines, 1987—; adm. mem. acctg. Oakton C.C., Des Plaines, 1986—, cons., mem. Edn. Found., 1986—; instr. Ray Coll. Design, 1987—, dir. evening sch., 1994, fin. aid officer, Chgo. and Woodfield, 1994; mem. rsch. bd. advisors Am. Biog. Inst., Inc., 1988; tchr. fin. mgmt., retail math., bus. math., bus. computers, strategic retail mgmt. and econs.; part time coll. instr. commerce dept. Northwestern Bus. Coll., 1995—; asst. to interim fin. dir. Art Inst. Ill., 1995—. Author: A Small Business Collection Cycle Primer for Accountants, 1985, The Mathematics of Business, 1989. Ill. CPA Soc. scholar, 1984, Roosevelt U. scholar, 1986, Nat. Assn. Accts. scholar, 1985. Mem. Nat. Assn. Accts. (dir. community responsibility suburban Chgo. chpt. 1986—, speaker 1988, dir. profl. devel. seminars 1988, dir. communications 1989—), Nat. Assn. Tax Practitioners, Nat. Assn. Enrolled Agts., Ill. Soc. Enrolled Agts. (pres.; pres. N.W. Chgo. chpt. 1992, chmn. edn. 1990—). Home: 5718 W Cullom Ave Chicago IL 60634-1718

BANICH, MARIE THERESE, neuropsychologist; b. N.Y.C., Aug. 6, 1957; d. John and Serafina (Fiore) B. BA, Tufts U., 1978; PhD, U. Chgo., 1985. Asst. prof. dept. psychology U. Ill., Urbana, 1985-91, assoc. prof., 1991—; leader cognitive neurosci. group Beckman Inst. U. Ill., Urbana, 1989—. Mem. editl. bd. Laterality, 1995—. Beckman fellow Ctr. for Advanced Study, 1989. Mem. Internat. Neuropsychol. Soc., Psychonomics Soc., Cognitive Neurosci. Soc., Am. Psychol. Soc. Office: U Ill Dept Psychology 603 E Daniel St Champaign IL 61820

BANIS, ROBERT JOSEPH, pharmaceutical company executive, educator; b. N.Y.C., Oct. 26, 1943; s. Vincent Nicholas and Roberta Irma (Shwedo) B.; m. Lois Elaine Polson, Jan. 25, 1970; children: Andrea Berit, Lauren Nicole. BS in Sci. Edn., Cornell U., 1967; MS in Animal Nutrition, Purdue U., 1969; PhD in Biochemistry, N.C. State U., 1973; MBA in Mktg. and Fin. with honors, U. Chgo., 1982. Cert. mgmt. acct. NIH postdoctoral fellow Harvard U., Cambridge, Mass., 1973-75; sr. rsch. scientist Armour Pharm. Co., Kankakee, Ill., 1975-79, tech. mgr. biochems. and parenterals, 1979-81, mgr. biochem. and pharm. devel., 1981-83; rsch. group leader health care div. Monsanto Co., St. Louis, 1983-85, mgr. rsch. ops. and fin. planning, 1985-86, mgr. rsch. ops. and fin. planning, Searle R&D Div., 1986-88, dir. ops. and fin., 1988-94; pres. 21st Century Stewardship Inc., St. Louis, 1994—; prin. Banis & Assocs., St. Louis, 1994—; mem. adj. faculty Vincennes U., St. Louis, 1994, Webster U., St. Louis, 1995—; instr. St. Louis C.C., St. Louis, 1994—; adj. asst. bus. prof. U. Mo., St. Louis, 1987-92, adj. assoc. prof., full-time lectr., 1992—. Contbg. author: COMPUTE!'s Second Book of VIC, 1983, The Science of Meat and Meat Products, 3d edit., 1987; contbr. articles to profl. jours., chpts. to books. Co-chmn. Searle-St. Louis divsn. United Way campaign, 1988-89, chmn., 1989-90, allocations panel vol. Greater St. Louis area, 1991-95, loaned exec. fundraisers, 1993, torchlight spkr., 1993-94; vol. St. John's Mercy Med. Ctr., 1992—; pres., chmn. bd. Burns Recovered Support Group, Inc., 1993-96; mgmt. cons. United Way Mgmt. Assistance Ctr., 1994—; regional coord. The Phoenix Soc., 1993; gen. chmn. World Burn Congress VII, 1995. Recipient Vol. of Yr. award Trinity Luth. Ch., 1991, United Way Star Communicator award, 1993, 94. Mem. AAAS, Am. Chem. Soc., Inst. Mgmt. Accts. (St. Louis chpt. dir. civic activities, assoc. dir. CMA rev. course 1993-95), Inst. for Ops. Rsch. and Mgmt. Scis. (sec. Gateway chpt. 1993-94, v.p./pres.-elect 1994-95, pres. 1995-96), Am. Burn Assn., Phi Lambda Upsilon, Beta Gamma Sigma.

BANJAC, JOYCE ANNETTE, entrepreneur, business educator; b. Cleve., June 10, 1957; d. Lossie Jackson and Mavis Bernice (Lovett) Kilpatrick; m. Bob Banjac, Oct. 18,1980; children: Brian, Jenna. BA in Bus. and Econs., Baldwin-Wallace Coll., Berea, Ky., 1983, MBA, 1987. Project dir. Cardinal Bank, Cleve., 1984-86; prof. bus. Tri-C Coll., Parma, Ohio, 1987—; CEO Bus. Smarts Inc., Broadview Heights, Ohio, 1990—; mem. adv. com. Cuyahoga Cmty., Parma, 1987—; mem. bus. adv. coun. Becksville (Ohio) H.S., 1992-93. Author: Silent Weapon, 1995. Founder Cmty. Awareness of Sch. Issues, Cleve., 1992; active PTA, Rep. Club, Indpendence. Recipient Appreciation award C. of C., 1990. Mem. Coun. of Small Enterprises, Cleve. World Trade. Republican.

BANK, HARVEY L., biologist; b. Bklyn., Feb. 13, 1943; s. Myron and Ruth (Lefkowitz) B.; m. Ellen S. Shield (div.); children: Daniel, Laura, Michael. BA, Hunter Coll., 1965; PhD, Oak Ridge Nat. Labs., 1971. Assoc. prof. Med. U. S.C., Charleston, 1973-90; exec. dir. Beacon Light Ctr., Sedona, Ariz., 1990-92; co-dir. Ctr. for Pranic Restoration, Springfield, Ohio, 1992—. Author several book chpts.; mem. editl. bd. Crybiology Soc., 1983—; contbr. 75 articles to profl. jours.; patentee in field. Smith Klein & French fellow, 1973-74. Mem. Sigma Xi (pres. 1979-80). Home: 1330 E High St Springfield OH 45505-1126

BANKER, WILLIAM G., financial consultant; b. Lafayette, Ind., Oct. 9, 1962. BA in Comms., Purdue U., 1985. Cellular phone salesman MCI, Mpls., 1985; fin. cons. Smith Barney Inc., Lafayette, 1985—. Republican.

BANKHEAD, CHARLA MARIE, bank officer; b. Moberly, Mo., July 7, 1950; d. Charles James and Ruth (Flud) Rockett; married; children: L.C. Bankhead II, Chanda Rose lee. Student, Moberly Area C.C. Procurement coord. Higbee (Mo.) Savs. Bank; customer svc. coord. Union State Bank, San Antonio; with Credit Dept. City Bank and Trust Co., Moberly; adminstrv. asst. Heilig-Meyers Co., Moberly. Mem. Randolph County Red Cross; mayor City of Higbee; trustee Higbee Meth. Ch. Named Woman of Yr. Am. Bus. Women, 1984. Mem. ABWA (pres.), Order of Ea. Star (past matron), VFW (ladies pres., 1994—). Democrat. Methodist. Home: Rt 1 Box 168 Higbee MO 65257 Office: 1720 Crete St Ste A Moberly MO 65270

BANKS, J.B., state legislator; b. Hermondale, Mo., Mar. 13, 1926; m. Anita Banks. BS, Lincoln U. Mortgage banker; Mo. State sen. dist. 5, 1985—; senate majority leader; mem. Mo. State Dem. Com. Mem. Masons. Office: 1442A N Grand Blvd Saint Louis MO 63106-1331 also: State Senate State Capitol Building Jefferson City MO 65101-1556*

BANKS, LOIS MICHELLE, nurse; b. Columbus, Ohio, Apr. 2, 1963; d. Arthur Martin and Druenetta Valerice (Smith) Martin Broadnax; m. Donald Steward, June 23, 1984 (div. Nov., 1989); children: Charlton Horton Jr., Candace Steward, Michael Steward; m. Joseph Persimon Banks; 1 child, Ashley. LPN, Mich. Infant tchr. Cradle-n-Crayon, Worthington, Ohio, 1983-85; LPN, nurse Health Ptnrs. Inc., Southfield, Mich., 1994—; owner, operator Uniquely Reading, Detroit, 1991—. Author: Learn your ABC's God's Way, 1991; author posters. Home: 19751 Mark Twain Detroit MI 48235

BANKS, MICHAEL ALAN, freelance writer; b. Princeton, Ind., Mar. 21, 1951; s. James Luther and Valera Sue (Galloway) B.; children: Susan, Michael. Student, U. Cin., 1970-71. Cert. vocat. instr., Ohio. Field engr. BMI, Cin., 1975-83; freelance writer Milford, Ohio, 1983—; adj. lectr. U. Cin., 1985-91. Author: The Odysseus Solution, 1985, The Modem Reference, 1992, CompuServe for Windows, 1995, numerous non-fiction books and novels. Troop leader Boy Scouts Am., Goshen, Ohio, 1986; precinct chmn. Rep. Ctrl. Com., Goshen, 1986-90. With USAF, 1972. Mem. Sci. Fiction Writers Am. (chair online com. 1989-92), Computer Press Assn., Am. Soc. Journalists and Authors, Am. Legion, Masons, Scottish Rite. Lutheran. Home and Office: PO Box 312 Milford OH 45150

BANOWETZ, ARLEEN FRANCES, entrepreneur, educator; b. Bronx, N.Y.. BSBA, Kans. Newman Coll., 1983; MBA, Wichita State U., 1986. Asst. dir. Ctr. for Entrepreneurship Wichita State U., 1986—; cons. Banowetz Consultants, Wichita, 1988—. Office: Wichita State Univ Ctr for Entrepreneurship 1845 Fairmount Wichita KS 67260-0147

BANTON, STEPHEN CHANDLER, lawyer; b. St. Louis; s. William Conwell and Ruth (Chandler) B. AB, Bowdoin Coll., 1969; JD, Washington U., St. Louis, 1973, MBA, 1974. Bar: Mo. 1973, U.S. Dist. Ct. (ea. and we. dists.) Mo. 1973. Asst. pros. atty. St. Louis County, 1973-75; sole practice Clayton, Mo., 1975-83; ptnr. Quinn, Ground & Banton, Manchester, Mo., 1983—. Exploring chmn. St. Louis council Midland Dist. Scouts, 1975-77; pres. Am. Youth Hostels Ozarks area, 1976-80; bd. trustees St. Louis Art Mus., 1985-94. Served with USMC. Recipient Leadership award Lafayette Community Assn., 1983, Service award The Meramec Palisades Community Assn., 1985, Service award Profl. Remodeling Assn., 1985, Service award St. Louis Symphony Orch., 1985. Mem. ABA, Mo. Bar Assn., St. Louis County Bar Assn., Bar Assn. Met. St. Louis, Assn. Trial Lawyers Am., St. Louis County League of C. of C. (pres. 1978), West Port C. of C. (bd. dirs. 1978-81, Service award 1983). Republican. Club: Toastmasters (Clayton) (adminstrv. v.p.). Lodge: Lions (pres. 1977). Home: 929 Saint Paul Rd Ballwin MO 63021-6061 Office: Quinn Ground & Banton 14611 Manchester Rd Ballwin MO 63011-3757

BAPTIST, ERROL CHRISTOPHER, pediatrician, educator; b. Colombo, Sri Lanka, Feb. 24, 1945; came to U.S., 1974; s. Egerton Cuthbert and Hyacinth Margaret (Colombo) B.; MB, BS, Faculty of Medicine, U. Ceylon, 1969; m. Christine Rosemary Francke, Aug. 7, 1976; children: Lauren Marianne, Erik Christopher. Intern, Colombo Gen. Hosp. and Children's Hosp., Colombo, Sri Lanka, 1969-70; resident house officer Dist. Hosp., Gampola, Sri Lanka, 1970-71; resident house officer Base Hosp., Kegalle, Sri Lanka, 1971-74; family practitioner, Marawila, Sri Lanka, 1974; resident physician in pediatrics Coll. Medicine and Dentistry N.J., Newark, 1975-77; practice medicine specializing in pediatrics, Rockford, Ill., 1977—; asst. prof. pediatrics U. Ill. Coll. Medicine, Rockford, 1977—, assoc. prof., 1994—; chmn. dept. pediatrics St. Anthony Med. Ctr., Rockford, 1986—. Recipient 9 Raymond B. Allen Instructorship awards U. Ill. Diplomate Am. Bd. Pediatrics. Fellow Am. Acad. Pediatrics; mem. So. Med. Assn. Roman Catholic. Home: 5112 Parliament Pl Rockford IL 61107-5066 Office: Mulford Village Office Park 461 N Mulford Rd Rockford IL 61107-5165

BARABTARLO, GENNADY ALEXIS, foreign literature and language educator, writer; b. Moscow, USSR, Feb. 15, 1949; came to U.S., 1980; s. Alexander and Maria (Zelvyansky) B.; m. Alla Patricia Toshchakov, Aug. 24, 1968; 1 child, Maria Elizabeth. BA, MA, U. Moscow, 1972; PhD, U. Ill., 1985. Sr. rsch. fellow Pushkin Lit. Mus., Moscow, 1971-76, vice provost for rsch., 1976-78; asst. prof. Russian U. Mo., Columbia, 1984-90, assoc. prof., 1990-94, prof. Russian, 1994—, chmn. dept., 1995—. Author: Phantom of Fact, 1989, Aerial View: Essays on Nabokov's Art and Metaphysics, 1993; editor, author: Small Alpine Form, 1992; contbr. more than 20 articles to profl. jours. Recipient Acad. grant Aaron Schoenfeld Found., 1980-82, Travel grant Am. Coun. Learned Socs., 1990, Travel grant NEH, 1991, Rsch. grant U. Mo., 1990, Rsch. grant IREX, 1995, Rsch. grant MAUI, 1995, Rsch. grant DAAD, 1996. Mem. Am. Assn. for Advancement of Slavic Studies, Vladimir Nabokov Rsch. Soc. Pres. 1992-94). Russian Orthodox. Office: U Missouri German and Russian Studies 451 GCB Columbia MO 65211

BARANOWSKI, EDWIN MICHAEL, lawyer; b. Utica, N.Y., Jan. 26, 1947; s. Edwin Joseph and Mary Jane (Ostrouch) B.; m. Shelley Osmun, Dec. 27, 1969. BA, Hamilton Coll., 1968; JD, U. Va., 1971. Bar: N.Y. 1972, Ohio 1982. Assoc. Kenyon & Kenyon, N.Y.C., 1971-81; counsel Porter Wright Morris & Arthur, Columbus, Ohio, 1981-83, ptnr., chmn. intellectual property law sect., 1983—; v.p. Plaskolite, Inc., Columbus, 1981-82; mem. adv. bd. for program in law and tech. U. Dayton Sch. of Law. Mem. Rep. Nat. Com., 1975—. Patentee of 7 patents in wheelchair accessibility devices. Mem. ABA (co-author, editor Preliminary Injunctions in Patent Litigation 1981, Comparative and False Advertising Under 15 U.S.C. Section 1125(a)- A Five Year Review 1994), Assn. Bar City N.Y., Columbus Intellectual Property Law Assn. (past pres.), Hamilton Coll. Ctrl. Ohio Alumni Assn. (pres. 1990—, alumni leadership coun. 1992—), Ohio Rails-to-Trails Conservancy (bd. dirs. 1989-95), St. Michael's Lancers (hon.), Rocky Fork Hunt and Country Club, Breakers Club, Chi Psi. Home: 75 Marrus Dr Gahanna OH 43230-2154 Office: Porter Wright Morris & Arthur 41 S High St Columbus OH 43215-6101

BARANOWSKI, SHELLEY OSMUN, history educator; b. Columbus, Ohio, June 14, 1946; d. Robert Reynar and Ann (Stoneman) Osmun; m. Edwin Michael, Dec. 27, 1969. BA, Wells Coll., 1968; MA, Princeton U., 1978, PhD, 1980. Instr. Ohio State U., Columbus, 1984; asst. prof. dept. history U. Akron, Ohio, 1989-91, assoc. prof., 1991-95, prof., 1995—; vis. asst. prof. Kenyon Coll., 1985-89. Author: The Confessing Church, 1986, The Sanctity of Rural Life, 1995; contbr. articles to profl. jours. ACLS Aid grantee, 1989; NEH fellow, 1984-85. Home: 75 Marrus Dr Gahanna OH 43230-2154 Office: U Akron Dept History Akron OH 44325

BARANSKI, DENNIS ANTHONY, diversified corporation executive; b. Buffalo, Oct. 25, 1950; s. Joseph Anthony and Florence (Manka) B.; m. Linda Diane Catron, Mar. 30, 1970; children: Joseph Eugene, John Anthony, Damien Alexander. B.A. in Psychology, Washburn U., 1972, J.D., 1978. Chmn., Barancorp., Topeka, Kans., 1974—, Solartech Energy and Research Corp., Topeka, 1981—, No. Cross Co., Topeka, 1983—. Mem. No. Cross Soc. (chmn., founder 1983). Roman Catholic. Clubs: London (chmn., founder 1975), Polecat Athletic. Office: Northern Cross Co Rt 1 Lecompton KS 66050

BARANY, JAMES WALTER, industrial engineering educator; b. South Bend, Ind., Aug. 24, 1930; s. Emery Peter and Rose Anne (Kovacsics) B.; m. Judith Ann Flanigan, Aug. 6, 1960 (div. 1982); 1 child, Cynthia. BSME, Notre Dame U., 1953; MS in Indsl. Engring., Purdue U., 1958, PhD, 1961. Prodn. worker Studebaker Corp., 1949-52; prodn. liaison engr. Bendix Aviation Corp., 1955-56; mem. faculty Sch. Indsl. Engring. Purdue U., West Lafayette, Ind., 1958—, now prof., assoc. head indsl. engring. Sch. Indsl. Engring.; cons. Taiwan Productivity Ctr., Western Electric, Gleason Gear Works, Am. Oil Co., Timken Co. Served with U.S. Army, 1954-55. Recipient Best Counselor award Purdue U., 1978, Best Engring. Tchr. award, 1983, 89, Outstanding Indsl. Engring. Tchr. award, 1983, 87, 89, Outstanding Tchr. award Purdue U., 1989, Marion Scott Faculty Exemplary Character award Purdue U., 1993; NSF and Easter Seal Found. rsch. grantee, 1961, 63, 64, 65. Mem. Inst. Indsl. Engring. (life, Fellows award 1982, Disting. Educator award 1989, Disting. Svc. award 1992, Cert. of Svc. Appreciation 1994), Soc. Mfg. Engr., Am. Soc. Engring. Edn., Methods Time Measurement Rsch. Assn., Human Factors Soc., Order of Engr., Sigma Xi, Alpha Pi Mu, Tau Beta Pi (Eminent Engr. award 1982). Home: 101 Andrew Pl Apt 201 West Lafayette IN 47906-3928 Office: Purdue U Dept Indsl Engring West Lafayette IN 47907-1287

BARB, CYNTHIA MARIE, mathematics educator; b. Akron, Ohio, Nov. 18, 1962; d. Gene and Mary Barb. BS in Math. magna cum laude, U. Akron, 1985, BS in Statistics, 1985, cert. in Secondary Edn., 1985-86, MS in Math., 1990; postgrad., Kent State U., 1995. Cert. 7-12 tchr., Ohio. Grad. teaching asst. U. Akron, 1985-86; long term substitute Tallmadge (Ohio) City Schs., 1987-88, Stow (Ohio) City Schs., 1988-89; instr. math. U. Akron, 1989-90, Kent State U. Stark Regional Campus, Canton, Ohio, 1990—; spkr. on math. edn. Contbr., referee articles to profl. jours. Acad. scholar U. Akron, 1985-86. Mem. Am. Ednl. Rsch. Assn., Math. Assn. Am., Nat. Coun. Tchrs. Math., Ohio Coun. Tchrs. Math., Phi Sigma Alpha, Alpha Lambda Delta. Office: Kent State U Stark Regional Campus 6000 Frank Ave NW Canton OH 44720-7548

BARBATIS, GRETCHEN LYNDA, telecommunications educator; b. Albert Lea, Minn., Feb. 28, 1943; d. Lawrence Theodore and Aileen Leone (Putnam) Schoen; m. Nicholas Barbatis, Aug. 28, 1966 (div. 1973); children: Patrick Eliot, Matthew Eugene; m. Martin Wong, 1991. BA, U. Minn., 1965, MA, 1975, PhD, 1979. Asst. prof. U. Nebr., Omaha, 1975-78, Middle Tenn. State U., Murfreesboro, 1978-79; assoc. prof. dept. telecomms. Mich. State U., East Lansing, 1979—. Producer-dir. video It Speaks for Itself, 1994. Media cons. Gull Lake Quality Orgn., Hickory Corners, Mich. 1993-95. U.S. Dept. Edn. fellow, 1982; CIC acad. leadership fellow, 1992. Mem. Speech Comm. Assn. (div. chair 1984-85). Office: Mich State U Dept Telecomms East Lansing MI 48824

BARBE, BETTY CATHERINE, financial analyst; b. Chgo., Dec. 24, 1930; d. Norbert Lambert and Helen Weishaar; m. Edward William, Aug. 8, 1953; children: Leonard Walter, Roger Andrew. Student, U. Toledo, 1970, 85. Acct. Gorr Printing, Allstate Ins., Muntz TV, Chgo., 1947-53; hostess Welcome Wagon Internat., Maumee, Ohio, 1965-70; v.p. sec., cost acctg. Craftmaster, Toledo, 1970-72; sec., estimator Grinnell Fire Protection, Toledo, 1972-73; exec. sec., payroll Crow, Inc. Aviation, 1973-77; asst. city clk., payroll City of Perrysburg, 1977-83, tax adminstr., 1983—. Vol. George Bush campaign candidates, 1978—; v.p. bd. Zepf Comty. Mental Health, Toledo, 1986-87; reader for Sight Ctr.; mem. Women Alive! Coalition, 1987—, Nat. Women's Polit. Caucus, 1987—, MADD, 1987—, YWCA, Perrysburg Arts Coun.; mem. Lourdes Coll. Aux., 1990. Honoree Maumee Valley coun. Girl Scouts U.S., 1990; named Woman of Yr., Bus. and Profl. Women Black Swamp Region II. Mem. Internat. Inst., Nat. Fedn. Bds. and Profl. Women, Key to the Sea Bus. and Profl. Womens Orgn. (pres. 1982-83, 83-84), Maumee Bus. and Profl. Women (pres. 1995-96, 96—), Maumee Valley Toastmasters (pres. 1989—, area gov.), Toledo Opera Soc. Assn., Two Toledos (sec., 1st v.p.), Christ Child Soc., Maumee C. of C. (sec.), Samagama Club, Zonta II (treas.), Rotary (Paul Harris fellow). Republican. Roman Catholic. Home: 724 W Wayne St Maumee OH 43537-1923 Office: City of Perrysburg 201 W Indiana Ave Perrysburg OH 43551-1525

BARBER, CHARLES TURNER, political science educator; b. Washington, Aug. 30, 1941; s. Charles Turner and Vera Hess (Nolt) B.; m. Billie Kathleen Jaco, June 16, 1968 (div. 1976); children: Gretchen, Katrina; m. Sandra Powell Anderson, Apr. 18, 1978 (div. 1987); m. Carolyn Louise Roth, Aug. 4, 1991. BA cum laude, W.Va. Wesleyan Coll., 1963; MA, Am. U., 1965; PhD, The Am. U., 1967. Asst. prof. polit. sci. East Tenn. State U., Johnson City, 1967-71; asst. prof. polit. sci. Ind. State U., Evansville, 1971-75, assoc. prof., 1975-83; prof. U. So. Ind., Evansville, 1983—, chmn. dept. polit. sci., 1986—; rep. Truman Scholarship Found., Washington, 1975-90; editl. cons. Prentice Hall, 1987, West Pub., 1990, 94, 95, Houghton-Mifflin, 1991, Harcourt, Brace, Jovanovich, 1992, Wadsworth, 1993; faculty sponsor Polit. Sci. Club U. So. Ind., 1988—; bd. dirs. Ind. Cons. Internat. programs, 1987—; dep. dir. Ind. Com. for U.S.-Arab Rels., 1989—, U. Mich. Inst. on Islam, 1989, Internat. Faculty Devel. Seminar, Maastricht, The Netherlands, 1994. Contbr. articles to profl. jours. Chmn. UN Day Evansville, 1980; moderator deacons 1st Presbyn. Ch., Evansville, 1982-85; judge coord. oratorical contest Am. Legion, Evansville, 1987-93; active All-Star Conv. and Visitors Bur., Evansville, 1987; candidate sch. bd. Evanville-Vanderburgh Sch. Corp., 1990. Recipient Group Study Exchange award Rotary Found., India, 1975-76, Faculty Enrichment award Can. Embassy, 1987, Summer Seminar award NEH, 1977; Malone fellow, 1987, 92. Mem. Am. Coun. Québec Studies, Internat. Polit. Sci. Assn., Acad. Coun. on the UN Sys., Internat. Studies Assn., Ind. Acad. Social Scis., Am. Polit. Sci. Assn., Western Polit. Sci. Assn., Soc. for Utopian Studies, Communal Studies Assn. Friends of Mesker Park Zoo. Democrat. Presbyterian. Home: 10801 S Woodside Dr Evansville IN 47712-8422 Office: U So Ind 8600 University Blvd Evansville IN 47712-3534

BARBER, EARL EUGENE, consulting firm executive; b. Dayton, Ohio, Dec. 8, 1939; s. Earl Garnet and Mary Helen (Brown) B.; m. Sandra Kay Reese, Mar. 11, 1960; children: Steven, Amy, Dana. BS, Ball State U., 1963; MDiv., Asbury Theol. Sem., Wilmore, Ky., 1977. Tchr. Muncie (Ind.) Community Schs, 1963-65; exec. mem. Gen. Motors, Muncie, 1965-73; pres. Barber Electric, Wilmore, 1973-77; sr. pastor Calvary Temple, Plainview, Tex., 1977-79; exec. Borg Warner Corp., Muncie, 1979-84; chief ops. officer Barber Cons. Resources, Muncie, 1984—. Author: Statistical Process Control for the Worker, 1985, Statistical Process Control: The Basic Tools, 1986, Understanding SPC for Short Production Runs, 1990. Mem Mayor's Task Force, Muncie 1980. Mem. Am. Soc. Quality Control (Ptnrs. award for quality 1989, sustaining mem.), Delaware County Ministerial Assn., Epsilon Pi Tau. Republican. Methodist. Office: Barber Cons Resources Inc 4900 N Wheeling Ave Muncie IN 47304-5843

BARBER, EDWARD BRUCE, medical products executive; b. Chgo., Mar. 11, 1937; s. Edward Vanrennsaler and Alice (Reinertsen) B.; m. Louise Joy Griebler, May 23, 1964. BS, Lake Forst (Ill.) Coll., 1957; MBA, U. Chgo., 1958. Market rsch. cons. Container Corp. of Am., Chgo., 1959-61; pres. Christiansen & Barber Assoc. Ltd., Chgo., 1961—; chmn., CEO Odyssey Travel Ltd., Chgo., 1974—; founder, chmn. M.E. Team, Inc., South Plainfield, N.J., 1980—, also bd. dirs.; pres. Colts Necks Farms, Inc. 1990—; cons. Lab. Supply Co., Louisville, 1990—, Graham-Field Surg., Inc., Hauppage, N.Y., 1990—; ptnr. Wynne Med./Statco Med., 1996—, Sci. Supply Co., Schiller Park, Ill., 1990—; bd. dirs. Golden Eagle Travel, Huntington Beach, Calif. Mem. Internat. Assn. of Travel Agys., Health Industries Distbr. Assn., Masons. Republican. Lutheran. Office: Christiansen Barber Assocs Ste 310 6800 W Raven St Chicago IL 60631-2586

BARBER, HUGH PHILIP, engineering executive; b. Charleston, W.Va., July 18, 1936; s. Hugh Philip and Goldie Grace (Dieterle) B.; m. Sally Marguerite Sherer, June 20, 1959; children: Gregory Philip, Suzanne Lynn Barber Stone, Brian Lee. BS in Engring. Physics, Ohio State U., 1959; MS in Adminstrn., Ctrl. Mich. U., 1993. Registered profl. engr., Ohio. Prin. physicist Battelle Meml. Inst., Columbus, Ohio, 1962-68; sr. project engr. Grimes Aerospace, Urbana, Ohio, 1968-79; plant equipment designer Internat. Harvester, Springfield, Ohio, 1979-83, maintenance supr., 1983-85; control systems supr. Navistar Internat. (formerly Internat. Harvester), Springfield, 1985-89, sr. mfg. engr., 1989-93, paint process mgr., 1993—. Contbr. articles to profl. jours.; patentee aircraft light invention. Bd. trustees Family Svc. Agy., Springfield, 1991-93. Lt. USN, 1954-62. Presbyterian. Home: 1806 Audubon Park Dr Springfield OH 45504 Office: Navistar Internat 6125 Urbana Rd Springfield OH 45501

BARBER, KIMBERLY LISANBY, elementary education educator; b. Oak Park, Ill., Sept. 3, 1955; d. Donald Ross Lisanby and Mary (MacInnes) Walker; m. Gary F. Barber, Aug. 6, 1977; children: Kati Jean, Kari Elizabeth. AA, Moraine Valley Community Coll., 1975; BA cum laude, North Cen. Coll., 1977; postgrad., Roosevelt U., Chgo.; MSEd summa cum laude, No. Ill. U., 1991, postgrad., 1993—. Cert. tchr., Ill. Tchr. kindergarten Horizon Day Care, Northbrook, Ill.; dir. Mom's Day Out/Des Plaines (Ill.) United Meth. Ch., Mom-Tots/Des Plaines United Meth. Ch.; tchr., gifted edn. coord., asst. prin., grantwriter Ohio (Ill.) Cmty. Consol. Grade Sch. Co-author: Small, Rural, Broke and Gifted. Edn. cons., insvc. tng., chair div. human rights Bd. of Ch. and Soc., United Meth. Ch.; conf. coord. Christian Social Involvement.

BARBI, JOSEF WALTER, engineering, manufacturing and export companies executive; b. Melk, Noe, Austria, Sept. 26, 1949; s. Walter and Hermine (Mayr) B.; m. Yolanda Kathy Rojas, Aug. 29, 1981; 1 child, Anna Katherina. Student, U. Saskatoon, Sask., Can., 1974, Kans. State U., 1982. Mech. engr. Zizala Metalwarenfabriken, Melk, 1963-65, Austrian Farmers Coop., Pochlarn, Austria, 1970-72; area mgr. Internat. Systems & Controls Corp., Regina, Sask., Can., 1974-75; mng. dir. Bakem Agro-Indsl. C.A., Caracas, Venezuela; gen. mgr. Intercon. Agro Indsl. Devel. Inc., Hialeah, Fla., 1977-81; internat. mktg. mgr. MEC Co., Kans., 1982-84; adviser internat. ops. Calif. Pellet Mill Co., I.R., San Francisco, 1984-91; CEO ASIMA Corp., Independence, Kans., 1984—; pres. Internat. Nutrition Techs., Independence, 1987—, Engineered Systems & Equipment, Inc., Caney, Kans., 1988—; cons. govts. of Venezuela, 1976-77, fish farm coops., Europe, 1987; speaker at internat. profl. confs. Contbr. articles to profl. jours. Bd. dirs. Internat. Independence C.C., 1987-89, Jr. Achievement, Independence, 1987-90. Mem. World Aquaculture Soc., Am. Feed Industries Assn. (bd. dirs. 1993—), C. of C., Rotary Internat. Home: RR 4 Box 194E Independence KS 67301-9169

BARBOUR, CLAUDE MARIE, minister; b. Brussels, Oct. 2, 1935; came to U.S., 1969; Diploma d'État d'Infirmières, École d'Infirmières, Paris, 1956; diploma d'Études Religieuses, Faculté Libre de Théolog, Paris, 1958; MST, N.Y. Theol. Sem., 1970; DST, Garrett Evang. Theol. Sem., 1973. Ordained to ministry Presbyn. Ch., 1974. Youth counselor Young Women's Christian Assn., Geneva, 1959-61, Edinburgh, 1965-67; missionary Paris Evang. Missionary Soc., So. Africa, 1962-64; deaconess Ch. of Scotland, Edinburgh, 1967-69; from asst. to assoc. pastor First United Presbyn. Ch., Gary, Ind., 1974-80; from asst. to assoc. prof. Cath. Theol. Union, Chgo., 1976-86, prof., 1986—; prof. McCormick Theol. Sem., Chgo., 1990-96; founder, dir. Shalom Ministries and Community, Chgo., 1975—; parish assoc. First Presbyn. Ch., Evanston, Ill., 1983—. World Coun. Chs. scholar, Geneva, 1969, United Presbyn. Ch. Commn. on Ecumenical Mission and Rels., N.Y., 1972; recipient Laskey award United Meth. Ch. Womens Div. the Bd. Global Ministries, N.Y., 1972, Civic award Ind. Women's Coun., 1976, Challenge of Peace award Chgo. Ctr. for Peace Studies, 1991, Martin P. Wolf O.F.M. award Justice, Peace and Integrity of Creation Coun. of the English-Speaking Conf. of the Order of Friars Minor, 1996. Mem. AAUW, Internat. Assn. for Mission Studies, Nat. Assn. Presbyn. Clergywomen, Am. Soc. Missiology, Assn. Prof. Mission, Midwest Fellowship Prof. Mission, Assn. Presbyn. in Cross-Cultural Mission. Home: 1649 E 50th St Apt 21A Chicago IL 60615-6109 Office: Catholic Theological Union 5401 S Cornell Ave Chicago IL 60615-5698

BARCEY, HAROLD EDWARD DEAN (HAL BARCEY), real estate counselor; b. Flint, Mich., Sept. 11, 1949; s. Glen Edward and Joyce Paulene (Dean) B.; children: Allen, David, Richard, Jackson, Joseph, Chris, Andrew, Steve. BA, U. Fla., 1971, postgrad., 1971-76. Cert. residential mktg. specialist, cert. residential brokerage mgr., cert. residential appraiser, cert. buyer rep. Activist, lectr., fundraiser various environ. orgns. and projects, Fla., Ga., 1970-75; advt. mgr., salesman Towne & Suburban Realty, Salem, Ohio, 1977-87; broker-mgr. Seasons Real Estate Counselors, Salem, 1987—; Artist "Man in Balance with Nature" symbol, 1969. Campaign worker McCarty for Pres., Youngstown, 1967; bd. dirs. adult edn. program Alachua County, Fla., 1969; bd. dirs. Balance Fund Found., Balt., 1970-73, Good Earthkeeping, Inc., Gainesville, Fla., 1971-73; del. Conf. on Population Explosion and the Devel. Profl., Airlie, Va., 1969; solicitor LifeBanc of Ohio, Salem, 1989—; campaign worker Morris Udall for Pres., Gainesville, 1975. Named for Outstanding Citizen Contbn., Village of Canfield, Ohio, 1967. Mem. Nat. Assn. Realtors, Am. Assn. Cert. Appraiser, Realtors Nat. Mktg. Inst., Alpha Gamma Sigma. Democrat. Roman Catholic. Home and Office: 1288 W Perry St Salem OH 44460-3550

BARCIA, JAMES A., congressman; b. Bay City, Mich., Feb. 25, 1952. Student Saginaw Valley State Coll., 1974. Staff asst. to U.S. Senator Philip Hart, 1971; community service coordinator Mich. Community Blood Ctr., Bay City, 1974-75; adminstrv. asst. to State Representative Donald Albosta, 1975-76; mem. Ho. of Reps. from 101st Mich. Dist., 1977-82, mem. edn. com., 1977-82, mem. joint legis. sub-com. higher edn., 1979-82, chmn. pub. works com., 1979-82; majority whip, 1979-82; mem. Mich. Senate, 1983-92; mem. 103rd Congress from 5th Mich. dist., 1993—; mem. UAW Local 688, 1970-71, Saginaw Valley Coll. Bd. Control, 1973-74. Active Mus. of Great Lakes, Bay City YMCA. Recipient Disting. Service award Saginaw Valley State Coll. Alumni Assn., 1977, Outstanding Community Service award B.A.S.I.S. Corp., 1978, Mich. Jaycees Top Five I.M.P.A.C.T. award, 1979, Spanish Speaking Council Community Involvement award, 1979, Chicano-Latino Substance Abuse Program award, 1979; elected to Bay City Central Hall of Fame, 1981. Mem. Bay Area C. of C., Mich. United Conservation Clubs, VFW Nat. Home (life), Nat. Rifle Assn., Mich. Assn. Osteopathic Physicians and Surgeons (hon. lay mem.), Bay City Jaycees (Disting. Service award 1982). Lodges: Elks, Eagles. Home: 915 E Harbor View Bay City MI 48706

BARCUS, MARY EVELYN, primary school educator; b. Peru, Ind., Apr. 3, 1938; d. Arthur Gibson and Mildred (Neher) Shull; m. Robert Gene Barcus, Aug. 9, 1959; children: Jennifer Sue, Debra Lynn. BS, Manchester Coll., 1960; MA, Ball State U., 1964. Kindergarten tchr. Miami Elem. Sch., Wabash, Ind., 1960-64; elem. tchr. Crooked Creek Sch., Indpls., 1964-72; preschool tchr. Second Presbyn. Preschool, Indpls., 1980-85, Speedway Coop., Indpls., 1985-86; tchr. asst. St. Monica Cath. Sch., Indpls., 1990; preschool tchr., fun club tchr. Arthur Jordan YMCA, Indpls.; preschool tchr. Indpls. (Ind.) Children's Mus., 1979—; docent sch. tours Children's Mus., Indpls., 1987—; interpreter at Indpls. children's mus.; facilitator Systematic Tng. Effective Parenting, Indpls. Writer: (children's songs) Piggback Songs for Infants and Toddlers, 1985, Piggyback Songs in Praise of God, 1986; editor elem. sch. newspaper; producer (with others) weekly show for cable TV. Profl. vol., libr. helper in local sch. systems; office helper North Cen. High Sch.; served on PTOs in various capacities; mem. Crossroads Guild, Parents Day Out of St. Luke's Meth. Ch., mem. ch. bd., Two's Tchr. Early Childhood Ctr.; Sun. sch./vacation ch. sch. tchr.; bd. dirs. Manchester Coll. Parents Assn. Mem. AAUW (charter, sec.), NEA (life), Ind. Assn. Edn. Young Children (state conf. com.), Pi Lambda Theta. Democrat. Mem. Church of Brethren. Home: 2230 Brewster Rd Indianapolis IN 46260-1521

BARCUS, ROBERT GENE, educational association administrator; b. Monticello, Ind., Oct. 22, 1937; s. Harold Eugene and Marjorie Irene (Dilling) B.; BPE (Alumni scholar 1957), Purdue U., 1959; MA, Ball State U., 1963; postgrad. Ind. U., summer 1966; supts. license Butler U., 1967; m. Mary Evelyn Shull, Aug. 9, 1959; children: Jennifer Sue, Debra Lynn. Tchr., coach Wabash (Ind.) Jr. H.S., 1959-63; tchr. Wabash H.S., 1963-64; tchr., coach North Central H.S., Indpls., 1964-65; salary cons. Ind. State Tchrs. Assn., Indpls., 1965-67, asst. dir. rsch., 1967-68, dir. spl. services, 1968-70, exec. asst., 1971-72, adminstrv. asst., 1972-73, asst. exec. dir. spl. services and tchr. rights, 1973-82, asst. exec. dir. adminstrn., personnel and governance, 1982-85, asst. exec. dir. labor rels. and adminstrn., 1985-93, assoc. exec. dir. labor rels and adminstrn., 1993—. Mem. NEA, Wabash City (past pres.), Washington Twp. (past pres.) tchrs. assns., Kappa Delta Pi, Pi Delta Kappa. Mem. Ch. of the Brethren (clk. 1966-74, chmn. 1979-83, 87, 92—). Clubs: Indpls. Press, Columbia, Ind. Schoolmen's. Home: 2230 Brewster Rd Indianapolis IN 46260-1521 Office: 150 W Market St Indianapolis IN 46204-2875

BARCUS, WILLIAM ARTHUR, manufacturing engineer; b. June 9, 1945. BSEE, Ohio Tech. Inst. Elec. design engr. Jeffrey Mining & Machinery, Columbus, Ohio, 1972-83; prodn. engr. Dynamic Telecom Syss., Columbus, Ohio, 1983-84; mgr. internat. tech. Liebert Corp., Columbus, Ohio, 1984—. Office: Liebert Corp 1050 Dearborn Dr Columbus OH 43085-1544

BARDEN, ROBERT CHRISTOPHER, psychologist, educator, lawyer; b. Richmond, Va., June 7, 1954; s. Elliott Hatcher and Jane Elizabeth Cole (Ferris) B.; m. Robin Jones, Nov. 14, 1987. BA summa cum laude, U. Minn., 1976, PhD in Clin. Psychology, 1982; postgrad., U. Calif., Berkeley, 1977; JD cum laude, Harvard U., 1992. Lic. consulting psychologist, Minn., Tex. Project asst. NSF, 1978-79; intern in psychology VA Med. Ctr., Stanford Med. Ctr., Palo Alto, Calif., 1979-80; dir. psychology Internat. Craniofacial Surg. Inst., Dallas, 1980-87; corp., litigation, family and health law atty. Lindquist and Vennum, Mpls., 1992—; asst. prof. psychology So. Meth. U., Dallas, 1980-84; asst. prof., dir. child clin. psychology U. Utah, Salt Lake City, 1984-87, rsch. faculty dept. surgery, 1987-93; vis. faculty, asst. prof. psychology Gustavus Adolphus Coll., St. Peter, Minn., 1988; pres. Optimal Performance Sys., Inc., Cambridge, 1989—; mem. Minn. Bd. Psychology, 1993—; adj. prof. law U. Minn. Law Sch.; cons. in field. Consulting editor Devel. Psychology, 1989; contbr. to profl. publs. Project dir. ch. cmty. svc. projects, Mpls. and Cambridge, 1988—; mem. Minn. Bd. Psychology, 1993—, Higher Edn. Coordinating Bd., 1993-94; rep. Minn. Sixth Congl. Dist. Fellow NSF 1978, NIMH 1976, 77; Recipient Young Scholar award Found. for Child Devel., faculty scholar award W.T. Grant Found. 1987-89. Mem. ABA, APA, Soc. for Rsch. in Child Devel., Internat. Soc. Clin. Hypnosis, Harvard Law Sch. Soc. Law and Medicine, Lowell House Commons Rm. Harvard U., Nat.Assn. for Consumer Protection in Mental Health Practices (pres. 1995—), Sigma Xi, Phi Beta Kappa. Office: RC Barden & Assocs 4025 Quaker Lane N Plymouth MN 55441-1637

BARDEN, ROLAND EUGENE, university administrator; b. Powers Lake, N.D., Sept. 11, 1942; s. Harry S. and Sena (Furness) B.; m. Carolyn Jane, Nov. 25, 1967; children: Carl, Janine, Ann. BS, U. N.D., 1964; MS, U. Wis., 1966, PhD, 1969. Postdoctoral fellow Case Western Res. U., Cleve., 1969-71; prof. U. Wyo., Laramie, 1971-89, dept. head, 1980-83, assoc. dean, 1983-84, assoc. provost, 1984-89; v.p. acad. affairs Moorhead (Minn.) State U., 1989-94, pres., 1994—; cons./evaluator North Ctrl. Assn. Schs. and Colls., Chgo., 1988—; commr. Tri Coll. U., 1989-94, dir. 1994—. Contbr. articles to profl. jours. Recipient Rsch. Career Devel. award NIH, 1976-80. Mem. Am. Chem. Soc., Am. Soc. Biochem. Molecular Biology. Office: Moorhead State U Off of Acad Affairs Moorhead MN 56563

BARDIS, PANOS DEMETRIOS, sociologist, social philosopher, historian, author, editor, poet, educator; b. Lefcohori, Arcadia, Greece, Sept. 24, 1924; came to U.S., 1948; s. Demetrios George and Kali (Christopoulos) B.; m. Donna Jean Decker, Dec. 26, 1964; children: Byron Galen, Jason Dante. Attended, Panteios U., Athens, Greece, 1945-47; BA magna cum laude in Sociology and Polit. Sci., Bethany (W.Va.) Coll., 1950; MA in Sociology and Edn., Notre Dame U., 1953; PhD in Sociology, Psychology and Anthropology, Purdue U., 1955; postgrad., U. Toledo, 1994—. Instr. to assoc. prof. sociology Albion (Mich.) Coll., 1955-59; assoc. prof. sociology U. Toledo, 1959-62, prof. sociology, 1963—; sec., treas. World Student Relief, Athens, 1946-48; mem. adv. bd. New World Communications, 1980—; U.S. rep. Internat. Congress Social Scis., Spain, 1965, 66, 71, Italy, 1969; participant World Congress Sociology, France, 1966, Italy, 1969, Bulgaria, 1970, Can., 1974, Sweden, 1978, Inst. Internat. de Sociologie, Italy, 1969, Venezuela, 1972, Algeria, 1974, Portugal, 1980, Inst. Sociology of Religion, Italy, 1969, Internat. Sci. Congress, Greece, 1973, 77, Internat. Conf. Unity Scis., annually, 1976—, Internat. Conf. Sociology of Religion, France, 1977, Lausanne, Switzerland, 1981, London, 1983, Louvain, Belgium, 1985, Inst. Internat. Conf. on Love and Attraction, Swansea, Wales, 1977, Internat. Seminar on Philosophy and Religion, P.R., 1978, 79, Acapulco, Mex., 1980, 81, Athens, Greece, 1985, Inst. Internat. Conf. World Peace, Taipei, Taiwan, 1980, Geneva, 1985, London, 1989, Seoul, Korea, 1991, Internat. Seminar Marxist Theory, 1981, World Peace Acad. Conf., 1979-89, Internat. Conf. on the Family, Seoul, 1991, Democritus U. Internat. Conf. on History of Edn., Thrace, Greece, 1991, Internat. Conf. on Futurism, Seoul, 1992, numerous others; speaker keynote address Internat. Conf. Peace and Apartheid, Johannesburg, 1986; lectr. Japan, Korea, Taiwan, 1980, 87, 88, 91; lectr. Internat. Conf. on Peace, Seoul, South Korea, 1992; mem. acad. adv. bd. Georgetown U. Inst., 1981—; sci. dir. Tng. and Rsch. Inst., Athens, 1992—; sponsoring editor Mellen U. Press, 1993—; advanced doctorate advisor and faculty resource history of sci., social philosophy, poetry, sociology, classics, linguistics Mellen U., 1993—; lectr. Ireland, Italy, Slovenia, Switzerland, France, Germany, Luxembourg, Austria, Greece. Author: (novel) Ivan and Artemis, 1957, (books) The Family in Changing Civilizations, 1967, 69, Encyclopedia of Campus Unrest, 1971, Studies in Marriage and the Family, 1975, 78, History of the Family, 1975, The Future of the Greek Language in The United States, 1976, History of Thanatology, 1981, Atlas of Human Reproductive Anatomy, 1983, Evolution of the Family in the West, 1983, Global Marriage and Family Customs, 1983, Nine Oriental Muses, 1983, Dictionary of Quotations in Sociology, 1985; A Cosmic Whirl of Melodies (poems by Bardis, articles by others), 1985, Marriage and Family: Continuity, Change and Adjustment, 1988, South Africa and the Marxist Movement: A Study in Double Standards, 1989, The Theater of Epidaurus and the Mysterious Vanishing Vases, 1990, (poems) The Silent Dr. X, 1990, Ode to Orion: An Epic Poem in Twenty Rhapsodies, 1995, The Dance of the Muses: A Guide to Lasting Poetry, 1995; editor: (with Man Das) The Family in Asia, 1978, 79, (with others) Poetry Americas, 1982, Cronus in the Eternal City: Scientific, Social, and Philosophical Aspects of Time in Ancient Rome, New Edition with a Comment, 1995; poet: Cicadas: The Tragic Troubadours, Sea Symphonies, Boze Narodzenie (Kulikowski Spl. award Gusto Press, 1981, Internat. Lachian Poetry prize, 1981) and numerous others; essayist: First English translation of Archimedes' lost work On Balances, numerous others; columnist Greek News, Athens; translator numerous poems and essays; editor: Social Sci., 1959-81, book rev. editor, 1963-81; assoc. editor Indian Sociol. Bull, 1965-71, Indian Psychol. Bull, 1965—, Revistituto de Ciencias Sociales, Spain, 1965—, Internat. Jour. Sociology of Family, 1970—, Internat. Jour. Contemporary Sociology, 1971—, Jour. Polit. and Mil. Sociology, 1972—, Jour. Marriage and the Family, 1975-78, Ocarina, 1987—, Humboldt Jour. of Social Rels., 1989—; book rev. editor Internat. Rev. History and Polit. Sci, India, 1966—; asst. Am. editor: book rev. editor Indian Jour. Social Research, 1965—; adv. editor: book rev. editor S. African Jour. Sociology, 1971—, Revue Internationale de Sociologie, 1995, Synthesis: The Interdisciplinary Jour. Sociology, 1973-74; Am. editor: book rev. editor Sociology Internat, India, 1967—; mem. editorial bd.: book rev. editor Darshana Internat, India, 1965—; Jour. Edn, India, 1965—, Sociologia Religiosa, Italy, 1966—; co-editor: Internat. Rev. Sociology, 1970—, book review editor 1995—, Internat. Rev. Modern Sociology, 1972—; linguistic cons., assoc. editor Nauka dla Pokoju (Poland), 1990—; assoc. and book rev. editor, columnist Napa Funny Pages, 1990—, Bard Bardis's Barbs, 1991—; editorial cons. Soc. and Culture, 1972—, Coll. Jour. Edn, 1973—; adv. editor: Sociol. Inquiry, 1981—, Jour. Sociol. Studies, 1979—; editorial adv. Am. Biog. Inst, 1980—; assoc. editor, book rev. editor: Sociol. Perspectives, 1981—; contbg. editor Indian Writer, 1989—; editor, book rev. editor Internat. Social Sci. Rev., 1982—; editor-in-chief, book rev. editor Internat. Jour. World Peace, column An Arcadian Voice Greek News, Athens 1995; lit. pseudonyms, inventions and shows include The Silent Dr. X, The Mysterious Bard, Agora, Arcadian Echoes, Bard Bardis's Barbs, Da Vinci Demon, numerous others; composer more than 20 songs for mandolin including Ode to Wallenberg; constructed 25 statis. scales used internationally measuring attitudes and knowledge; inventor in field. Trustee Marriage Mus., N.Y.C., 1969—; chmn. crime reduction com. of Commn. Cmty. Devel., Toledo, 1967-68; chief internat. bd. and mem. gov. body World U., 1981—; bd. advisors Internat. Mid. East Alliance; sci. dir. Tng. and Rsch. Innovations Inst., Athens, 1992—. Recipient Couphos prize Anglo-Am.-Hellenic Bur. Edn., 1949, Seminario de Investigacion Historica y Arqueologica award Mus. de Historia, Barcelona, Spain, 1967, Hoosier Challenger Poetry prize, 1983, Disting. Educator award Am. Hellenic Edn. Progressive Assn., 1987, Melina Mercoure Internat. Poetry prize, 1995, several poetry prizes and awards; named Ohio Author of Yr. Ohioana Libr. Assn., 1986; discovered "ditoxon" in geometry; honored for lecture tour in Orient and for contbns. to world peace in spl. tea ceremony, prayers and religious svc. in Kaguraden Ceremony Hall for Sacred Music and Dance, Nanku, the inner shrine of Sun Goddess Amaterasu-Omikami, Jingu Grand Shrines, Ise, Japan, 1988. Fellow AAAS, Am. Sociol. Assn. (membership com. 1966-71), Internat. Inst. Arts and Letters (life), Inst. Internat. de Sociologie (chmn. membership com. 1970— , coord. for U.S.A. 1974—, exec. com. 1982—), World Acad. Scholars, Internat. Poets Acad. (Internat. Eminent Poet award 1987); mem. AAUP, Nat. Coun. Family Rels., Ohio Coun. Family Rels., Global Congress World Religions, Internat. Sociol. Assn. (rsch. coms. on social change 1972—, sociology of edn. 1972—, family sociology 1974—), Profs. World Peace Acad. (co-founder), Conf. Internat. de Sociologie de la Religion, N. Ctrl. Sociol. Assn., Inst. Mediterranean Affairs (adv. coun. 1968—), Internat. Personnel Rsch. (hon. advisor 1971—), Royal Asiatic Soc., Internat. Sci. Commn. on Family, Am. Soc. Neo-Hellenic Studies (bd. advisers 1969—), Hellenic Profl. Assn. of America Internat., Group for Study Sociolinguistics, N.Y. Acad. Scis., Nat. Acad. Econs. and Polit. Sci. (bd. dirs. 1959—), Nat. Writers Club, Nat. Assn. Standard Med. Vocabulary (cons. 1963—), Midwest Sociol. Soc., Inst. Study Plural Socs. (hon. asso.), Internat. Assn. Family Sociology, Modern Greek Soc., Nat. Soc. Lit. and Arts, Acad. Am. Poetoets, World Poetry Soc. Intercontinental, World Alliance For Civil Rights, Prague Soc. for Social Rsch. (Czechoslovakia), Sigma Xi, Alpha Kappa Delta, Pi Gamma Mu (ann. regional, nat., internat. confs. 1959—, plaque for editl. contbns. 1994), Phi Kappa Phi, Kappa Delta Pi. Home: 2533 Orkney Dr Toledo OH 43606 Office: U Toledo Bancroft St Toledo OH 43606

BARE, JAMES RANDOLPH, minister; b. San Francisco, Apr. 1, 1957; s. Joseph Edward and Meta Rose (Bramer) B; m. Carolyn Louise Grable, May 31, 1980; children: Alexander Joseph, Timothy James Richland. AB in History, U. Calif., Berkeley, 1979; MDiv in Bibl. Studies, Fuller Theol. Sem., 1990. Ordained to ministry Presbyn. Ch. Campus min. InterVarsity Christian fellowship, Madison, Wis., 1980-82, area dir., 1982-88, nat. dir. of grad. student ministry, 1988—; pastor Bethany Presbyn. Ch., Mpls., 1992—. Mem. Marcy-Holmes Neighborhood Assn. Mem. Phi Sigma Kappa. Office: Inter Var Christian Fell 501 Oak St SE Minneapolis MN 55414

BARE, LOIS KIEFFABER, college director; b. Kansas City, Kans., Jan. 23, 1942; m. James J. Bare, Sept. 22, 1962; children: Rebecca Suzanne, Elizabeth Anne, Joseph Eric. BA, Goshen Coll., 1979. Adminstrv. asst. Ch. World Series, Elkhart, Ind., 1980-82, dir. info. svcs., 1982-87; dir. alumni rels. Goshen (Ind.) Coll., 1987—, assoc. dir. coll. rels., 1989-92, dir. constituency rels., 1992—, chair of congregation, 1993-96; dir. study svc. term in Dominican Republic Goshen Coll., 1991-92. Contbr. articles to mags. Vol. Elkhart Jazz Festival, 1988-89. Mem. LWV (fundraiser chair for Soviet women's visit 1990), Coun. for Advancement and Support of Edn., Women for Meaningful Summits.

BARENBOIM, DANIEL, conductor, pianist; b. Buenos Aires, Nov. 15, 1942; s. Enrique and Aida (Schuster) B.; m. Jacqueline DuPre, June 15, 1967 (dec.); m. Elena Bashkirova, Nov. 28, 1988; 2 children. Student, Mozarteum, Salzburg, Austria, Accademia Chigiana, Siena, Italy; grad., Santa Cecilia Acad., Rome, 1956. Music dir. Chgo. Symphony Orch., 1991—. Debut with Israel Philharm. Orch., 1953, Royal Philharm. Orch., Eng., 1953, debut as pianist, Carnegie Hall, N.Y.C., 1957, Berlin Philharm. Orch., 1963, N.Y. Philharm. Orch., 1964, 1st U.S. solo recital, N.Y.C., 1958, as pianist performed in N.Am., South Am., Europe, Soviet Union, Australia, New Zealand, Near East; condr., 1962—, conducted English Chamber Orch., London Symphony Orch., Israel Philharm. Orch., N.Y. Philharm. Orch., Phila. Symphony, Boston Symphony, Chgo. Symphony Orch., others; mus. dir., Orchestre de Paris, 1975-89, Chgo. Symphony Orch., 1991—, Staatsoper Berlin, 1992—; artistic adviser, Israel Festival, 1971-74, over 100 recordings as pianist and condr.; debut as pianist at age 7, Buenos Aires. Recipient Beethoven medal, 1958; Harriet Cohen Paderewski Centenary prize, 1963, Legion of Honor, France, 1987. Office: 29 rue de la Coulouvreniere, 1204 Geneva Switzerland also: Chgo Symphony Orch 220 S Michigan Ave Chicago IL 60604-2508

BAREOFF, KATHY See **ZOUBAREFF, OLGA KATARINA**

BARGER, RALPH THOMAS, consulting executive; b. Peoria, Ill., Jan. 15, 1943; s. Louray and Margret (Kesten) B.; m. Barbara L. Claude, Oct. 30, 1963 (div. Aug. 1971); children: Scott Thomas, Michael Bruce. BA in Mgmt., Sangamon State U., Springfield, Ill., 1990. Account customer engr. IBM, Peoria, 1967-94; pres., CEO Spl. Events and Cons., Chillicothe, Ill., 1995—; advisor Chillicothe Summer Theater, 1994—. Alderman 3d Ward, City of Chillicothe. Mem. Nat. Ctr. for Non Profit Bds., N.Am. Fishing Club, Chillicothe C. of C. (treas. 1993—, Mem. of Yr. 1993). Home: 1166 Sugar Loaf Rd Winona MN 55987-1409

BARGER, RICHARD B., communications consultant; b. Marshall, Mo., Dec. 9, 1946; s. Harry D. Barger and Barbara Lee (Houston) Moore; m. Rita Sue Hamlin, Apr. 1, 1969. BS in Agrl., U. Mo., 1969, MS in Agrl. Econs., 1970; M of Liberal Arts, Baker U., 1982. Mgr. Edenvale Farms, Malta Bend, Mo., 1972-74; econ. analyst Cargill, Inc., Minnetonka, Minn., 1974-75; editl. asst. Sosland Publ., Kansas City, Mo., 1975-77; sr. editor Commodity New Svcs., Inc., Leawood, Kans., 1977-79; mng. editor, pub. rels. divsn. Fletcher/Mayo/Assocs., Inc., St. Joseph, Mo., 1979-82; comms. cons. Barger Cons., Kansas City, Mo., 1982—. Contbr. articles to profl. jours. Judge Kansas City Spirit Awards, 1982; arbitrator Better Bus. Bur., Kansas City, 1986—; divsn. coord. IABC Internat. Gold Quill Competition, Kansas City, 1992, 94. 1st. lt. USAF, 1970-72. Mem. U. Mo. Alumni Assn. (chmn. rules com. 1987-92), Mo. Alumni Assn. (bd. dirs. Kansas City chpt. 1988—), Gifted Assn. of Mo. (parliamentarian 1990—), Mo. Sch. Pub. Rels. Assn. (treas. 1994-95), Internat. Assn. of Bus. Communications (accreditation chair Kansas City chpt. 1993—, Incredible Vol. award 1994), Pub. Rels. Soc. of Am. (greater Kansas City chpt.), Mo. Sch. Pub. Rels. Assn. (treas. 1994-95), Kans. Sch. Pub. Rels. Assn. (joint conf. com. 1994), Am. Legion, Mensa. United Methodist. Home and Office: Barger Cons 1156 Queen's Pl Kansas City MO 64131-3264

BARIFF, MARTIN LOUIS, information systems educator, consultant; b. Chgo., Jan. 26, 1944; s. George and Mae (Goldberg) B. BS in Acctg., U. Ill., 1966, MA in Acctg., 1967, PhD in Acctg., 1973. CPA, Chgo. Asst. prof. acctg. and decision scis. Wharton Sch., Phila., 1973-78; vis. asst. prof. acctg. U. Chgo., 1978-79; assoc. prof. acctg. and mgmt. info. decision systems Case Western Res. U., Cleve., 1979-83; Coleman Found. assoc. prof. info. mgmt., dir. Ctr. for Rsch. on Impacts of Info. Systems, Ill. Inst. Tech., Chgo., 1983—; cons. in field, N.Y.C., Phila., Washington, 1976—; exec. v.p. EDP Auditors Found., 1979-80; program chmn. Internat. Conf. Info. Systems, Phila., 1980. Contbr. articles to profl. jours. Bd. dirs. Community Accts. Inc. of Phila., 1974-75. Mem. AICPAs, Am. Acctg. Assn. (chmn. acctg., behavior and orgns. sect. 1987-88), Assn. Computing Machinery (sec. Spl. Interest Group on Security, Auditing and Control 1981-85), Soc. Info. Mgmt. (treas. Chgo. chpt. 1988-90, 95-96), Internat. Engrng. Consortium (bd. dirs. ednl. overseers 1991—), Inst. Mgmt. Sci. Jewish. Office: Ill Inst Tech 565 W Adams St Ste 422 Chicago IL 60661-3601

BARILLEAUX, RYAN J., politcal science educator; b. Lafayette, La., June 15, 1957; s. Ira C. and Joanna (Beyt) B.; m. Marilyn Wasick, May 23, 1981; children: Gerard, Madeleine, Christine, Paul, Thomas, Michael. BA summa cum laude, U. Southwestern La., 1979; MA, U. Tex., 1980, DPhil, 1983. Asst. prof. polit. sci. U. Tex., El Paso, 1983-87; assoc. prof. Miami U., Oxford, Ohio, 1987-95, prof., 1995—; steering com. mem. Presidency Rsch. Group, Washington, 1993-95. Author: The President and Foreign Affairs, 1985, The Post-Modern Presidency, 1988, The President as World Leader, 1991, Leadership and the Bush Presidency, 1993, American Government in Action, 1995; contbr. articles to profl. jours. Intern/aide Sen. J. Bennett Johnston, Washington, 1977-78. Salvatori fellow Heritage Found., Washington, 1994-95. Mem. Am. Polit. Sci. Assn. (com. chmn. 1994), Soc. Cath. Soc. Scientists, Ctr. Study Presidency. Roman Catholic. Office: Miami U Dept Polit Sci Oxford OH 45056

BARISH, LAWRENCE STEPHEN, nonpartisan legislative staff administrator; b. Bklyn., Nov. 30, 1945; s. Louis C. and Anna (Sanders) B.; m. Sharon Lee Shapiro, July 2, 1967; 1 child, Lauren. BS in Polit. sci., U. Wis.-Madison, Wis., 1967; MA in Govt., U. Ariz., 1970. Legis. analyst Legis. Reference Bur., Madison, Wis., 1971-87, dir. of Reference and libr. svcs., 1987—; chmn. rsch., comm. staff sec. Nat. Conf. State Legislatures, Denver, 1995—; redistricting cons. Wis. Legis. and Local Govt. units, 1980—. Editor State Almanac, 1987—; contbr. articles to profl. jours. Home: 1429 W Skyline Dr Madison WI 53705 Office: Wis Legis Reference Bur 100 N Hamilton St Madison WI 53703

BARKAN, SANDRA LYNN, dean, literature educator; b. Chgo., Dec. 26, 1941; d. Joseph P. and Florence P. (Podersky) Hackman; m. Joel David Barkan, Sept. 9, 1962; children: Bronwyn Michelle, Joshua Manuel. AB in French with honors, Cornell U., 1963; MA in French, UCLA, 1964; PhD in Comparative Lit., U. Iowa, 1984. Lectr. comparative culture U. Calif., Irvine, 1970-72; lectr. dep. edn. U. Dar es Salaam, Tanzania, 1973-74; asst. dir. honors program U. Iowa, Iowa City, 1983-87, assoc. dir. honors program, 1987-92, acting dir. honors program, 1989, 92, exec. dir. honors program, 1992-95, asst. dean grad. coll., 1995—; vis. asst. prof. comparative lit. U. Iowa, Iowa City, 1985-88, 90, adj. asst. prof. comparative lit., 1991—; convener CIC Honors Adminstrs., Champaign, Ill., 1992-94; nat. selection com. Truman Found., Washington, 1994. Editor: African Literatures: Retrospectives and Perspectives, 1985; contbr. articles to profl. jours. Mem. MLA, Midwest MLA, Am. Comparative Lit. Assn., African Lit. Assn. (treas. 1989-93, v.p. 1996—), African Studies Assn. (conf. sect. head 1995), Iowa City Fgn. Rels. Coun. Democrat. Home: 833 River St Iowa City IA 52246 Office: Univ Iowa Grad Coll Gilmore Hall Iowa City IA 52246

BARKEMA, DAVID VICTOR, secondary education educator; b. Grand Rapids, Mich., Feb. 11, 1940; s. Frank and Grace Rebecca (Redman) b.; m. Diane Wilma Lemery, Dec. 24, 1960 (div. Mar. 1983); children: Susan Diane Barkema Andrews, Robert David; m. Marianna Penton Merizon, Sept. 2, 1983; children: Stephanie Merizon Worden, John Merizon. AB in English/Edn., Ctrl. Mich. U., 1962; MSW, Grand Valley State U., 1981. Cert. tchr., Mich. Tchr. White Cloud (Mich.) Pub. Schs., 1962; tchr. secondary lang. arts Grand Rapids Pub. Schs., 1962—. Mem. Grand Rapids Edn. Assn. (treas. 1967-68, v.p. 1968-70, pres. 1970-72). Home: 3984 Keeweenaw NE Grand Rapids MI 49505

BARKEN, BERNARD ALLEN, lawyer; b. St. Louis, July 20, 1924; s. Gottlieb and Hattie E. (Rubin) B.; m. Jocelyn Moss Kopman, Sept. 1, 1948; children: Thomas L., Dale Susan. JD, Washington U., 1947. Bar: Mo. 1947, U.S. Dist. Ct. (ea. dist.) Mo. 1947, U.S. Tax Ct. 1966, U.S. Ct. Appeals (8th cir.) 1954, U.S. Ct. appeals 2d cir.) 1985, U.S. Supreme Ct. 1984. Sole practice St. Louis, 1947-80; ptnr. Shifrin & Treiman, St. Louis, 1980-88; pres. Bernard A. Barken, P.C., St. Louis, 1988-91; ptnr. Barken & Bakewell, St. Louis, 1991—. Served with USAAF, 1943-44. Mem. ABA, Bar Assn. Met. St. Louis (v.p. 1958, chmn. young lawyers 1953). Jewish. Home: 30 Vouga Ln Saint Louis MO 63131-2628 Office: 8182 Maryland Ave Fl 4 Saint Louis MO 63105-3786

BARKER, BARBARA, real estate professional; b. Pulaski, Tenn., July 18, 1938; d. Dan and Anna (Butler) Ingram; m. Emmet Barker, Nov. 25, 1960; children: Melanie, Lynn, Harvey, Dan. BS, U. Tenn., 1960. Home economist Knoxville (Tenn.) Utilities Bd.; tchr. Arlington High Sch., Arlington Heights, Ill.; pres. Barbara Barker and Assocs., Brownsville, Tenn., Deerfield (Ill.) Ptnrs.; also owner, mgr. Re/Max Deerfield; broker, assoc. Re/Max Premier Properties, Lake Forest, Ill. Exec. bd., treas. Arden Shore Sch.; elder Presbyn. Ch. Mem. Nat. Assn. Realtors, Ill. Assn. Realtors, Women's Coun. Realtors (pres. 1993-94, exec. bd.), North Shore Bd. Realtors, Tenn. Home Econs. Assn. (v.p.). Home: 1050 Meadowbrook Ln Deerfield IL 60015-3459 Office: 990 S Waukegan Rd Lake Forest IL 60045-2655

BARKER, BRENT CLARK, stockbroker; b. Newton, Kans., June 7, 1964. BSBA, Kansas State U., 1987. Stockbroker Cohig & Assocs., Seattle, 1990-94, PaineWebber, Wichita, Kans., 1994-96, Intrust Bank Investment Svcs., Wichita, 1996—. Mem. Am. Cancer Soc., Wichita. Republican. Methodist. Home: 306 Rosewood Hesston KS 67062 Office: 105 N Main Wichita KS 67201

BARKER, DONALD J., health facility administrator; b. Cin., May 10, 1953. BA, Xavier U., 1975, MA in Hosp. Adminstrn., 1977. Asst. v.p. human resources Middletown (Ohio) Hosp., 1977-83; v.p. Health Svc. Rev. of Ohio, 1983—; mem. Queen City Case Mgmt. Physiatric Svcs. for Disadvantaged, Cin., 1993—. Mem. AMCRA, Cin. Banker Club. Republican. Roman Catholic. Office: Health Svc Rev Ohio 6730 Roosevelt Ave Franklin OH 45005-5724

BARKER, GARY LELAND, mining company executive; b. Madison, W.Va., Dec. 18, 1942; s. Woodrow Harry and Cressie Mae (Mullins) B.; m. Carol Jean Barker, May 23, 1964; children: Gary Jr., Sally Lynn. Student, W.Va. Tech. Inst., 1963-64, W.Va. U., 1964-65. Chief elec. and maint. supr. So. Appalachian Coal Co., Montgomery, W.Va., 1965-70; maint. supt. Energy Devel. Co., Hanna, Wyo., 1970-74, Mid-Continent Coal & Coke Co., Carbondale, Colo., 1974-76; maint. supt. U.S. Fuel Co., Hiawatha, Utah, 1976-79, gen. mine supt., 1979-83; v.p., gen. mgr. Carpentertown Coal & Coke Co., Templeton, Pa., 1983-89; pres., gen. mgr. U.S. Fuel Co., Hiawatha, 1989-91; pres. Arava Natural Resources Co., Wichita, Kans., 1991—; pres., dir. Bayard Mining Corp., Silver City, N.Mex., 1990-92, Amwest Exploration Co., Hanover, N.Mex., 1990-92, Canco Oil & Gas Ltd., Calgary, Alta., 1990-92; pres., CEO, dir. Alaska Gold Co., Nome, 1990-92. With U.S. Army, 1959-63. Mem. AIME, Utah Mining Assn., Rocky Mountain Mining Assn., Am. Mgmt. Assn. Republican. Home: 763 N 500 E Price UT 84501-2121

BARKER, JUDY, foundation executive; b. Burlington, N.C., Feb. 5, 1941; d. Thelma Ferguson; children: Lesa, Lori. Student, Ohio State U., Franklin U.; HHD, Xavier U., 1986. Administrv. asst. Children's Hosp., Columbus, Ohio, 1963-68, Mount Carmel Hosps., Inc., Columbus, 1969-72; administr. Borden Found., Borden, Inc., Columbus, 1973-75, exec. dir., 1975-83, dir. civic affairs, 1977-79, pres., 1983—, v.p. social responsibility, 1979—; Bd. dirs. Ohio State U. Hosps.; mem. Columbus Commn. on Ethics and Values; mem. adv. bd. Ohio State U. Sch. Home Econs.; mem. found. ctr. adv. nat. Nat. Directory Corp. Giving; active N.Y. Contbns. Adv. Group; mem. corp. adv. bd. Philanthropic Adv. Svc.; bd. dirs. Coun. Better Bus. Bur. Found., Greater Columbus Art Coun.; mem. Afro.-Am. adv. bd. Columbus Mus. Art. Bd. dirs. Pub./Pvt. Ventures, Ohio State U. Hosps., Columbus Commn. on Ethics and Values; mem. Sch. Home Econs. adv. bd. Ohio State U.; mem found. ctr. adv. bd. nat. Directory Corporate Giving; active N.Y. Contributions Adv. Group; mem. corp. adv. com. Philanthropic Adv. Svc.; mem., bd. dirs. Coun. Better Bus. Bur. Founds., Greater Columbus Arts Coun.; mem. Afro-Am. adv. bd. Columbus Mus. of Art; bd. dirs Columbus Airport Authority. Recipient award to women achievers YWCA, 1982, 84, 91, named Woman of Yr. YMCA Columbus, Ohio; recipient cmty. svc. award United Negro Coll. Fund, 1981. Office: Borden Inc 1620 E Broad St Columbus OH 43203

BARKER, KEITH RENE, investment banker; b. Elkhart, Ind., July 28, 1928; s. Clifford C. and Edith (Hausmna) B.; AB, Wabash Coll, 1950; MBA, Ind. U., 1952; children by previous marriage: Bruce C., Lynn K.; m. Elizabeth S. Arrington, Nov. 24, 1965; 1 child, Jennifer Scott. Sales rep. Fulton, Reid & Co., Inc., Ft. Wayne, Ind., 1951-55, office, 1955-59, asst. v.p., 1960, v.p., 1960, dir., 1961, asst. sales mgr., 1963, sales mgr., 1964, dir. Ind. ops.; sr. v.p. Fulton, Reid & Co., 1966-75; pres., chief exec. officer Fulton, Reid & Staples, Inc., 1975-77; ptnr. William C. Roney & Co., 1977-79; exec. com. Cascade Industries, Inc.; assoc. A.G. Edwards & Sons, Inc., 1984-89, v.p. investments, 1989—; dir. Fulton, Reid & Staples, Inc., Craft House Corp., Nobility Homes, Inc. Pres. Historic Ft. Wayne, Inc.; cons. to Mus. Historic Ft. Wayne; nominee, trustee Ohio Hist. Soc.; mem. Smithsonian Assocs.; bd. dirs. Ft. Wayne YMCA, 1963-64. Lt. USNR, 1952-55. Recipient Achievement certificate Inst. Investment Banking, U. Pa., 1959. Mem. Ft. Wayne Hist. Soc. (v.p.), Alliance Française, VFW (past comdr.), Co. Mil. Historians, Cleve. Grays, Am. Soc. Arms Collectors, 1st Cleve. Cavalry Assn., Nat. Assn. Securities Dealers (bus. conduct com.), Masons, Phi Beta Kappa. Episcopalian. Clubs: Beaver Creek Hunt, Cleve. Athletic, Rockwell Springs, Hill and Dale. Home: 14722 Windsor Castle Ln Strongsville OH 44136-8783 Office: AG Edwards & Sons Inc King James Office Park 24651 Center Ridge Rd Westlake OH 44145

BARKER, LINDA K., state legislator. Rep. S.D. State Ho. Reps. Dist. 13, mem. commerce and taxation coms. Home: 2016 S Pendar Ln Sioux Falls SD 57105-3023 Office: SD House of Reps State Capitol Pierre SD 57501*

BARKER, MARY KATHERINE, retired nurse; b. Roxana, Ill., Feb. 1, 1921; m. Willard H. Barker, May 26, 1962 (dec. Aug. 1986). BS in Nursing, Washington U., St. Louis, 1952, MS in Nursing, 1956; diploma in nursing, Alton Meml. Hosp. Sch. Nursing, Ill., 1942. Surg. instr., assoc. nursing svc. adminstr. St. Catherine Hosp., East Chicago, Ind.; asst. prof. So. Ill. U., Carbondale; staff nurse, instr., asst. dir. Sch. Nursing Alton Meml. Hosp.; now ret., 1972-81, ret., 1981. Lt. col. nurse corps AUS, 1942-56, 72-81. Mem. ANA, AAUW, Am. Orgn. Nurse Execs., Res. Officers Assn. U.S. (life), Nat. League for Nursing.

BARKER, NANCY LEPARD, university official; b. Owosso, Mich., Jan. 22, 1936; d. Cecil L. and Mary Elizabeth (Stuart) Lepard; m. J. Daniel Cline, June 6, 1956 (div. 1971); m. R. William Barker, Nov. 18, 1972; children: Mary Georgia Harker, Mark L. Cline, Richard E., Daniel P., Melissa B. Van Arsdel, John C. Cline, Helen Grace Garrett, Wiley D., James G. BSc, U. Mich., Ann Arbor, 1957. Spl. edn. instr. Univ. Hosp. U. Mich., Ann Arbor, 1958-61; v.p. Med. Educator, Chgo., 1967-69; asst. to chmn., dir. careers for women Northwood U., Midland, Mich., 1970-77, asst. prof., chmn. dept. fashion mktg. and merchandising, 1972-77, dir. arts programs and external affairs, 1972-77, v.p., 1978—; cons. and lectr. in field; bd. dirs. First of Am. Bank Corp. Co-author: (children's books) Wendy Well Series, 1970-72; contbr. chpts. to books, articles to profl. jours. Advisor Mich. Child Study Assn., 1972—; chmn. Matrix: Midland Festival, 1978; bd. dirs. Nat. Coun. of Women, 1971—, pres., 1983-85, chmn. centennial com., 1988; bd. dirs. Concerned Citizens for the Arts, Mich., Family and Children's Svcs., Internat. Coun. Women, Paris. Recipient Hon. award Ukrainian Nat. Women's League, 1983, Disting. Woman award Northwood U., 1970, Outstanding Young Woman award Jr. C. of C., 1974; named one of Outstanding Young Women in U.S. and Mich., 1974; nominee (2) Mich. Women's Hall of Fame. Mem. Internat. Coun. Women (bd. dirs. Paris 1991—), The Fashion Group, Internat. Furnishings and Design Assn. (pres. Mich. chpt. 1974-77), Mich. Women's Studies Assn. (founding mem.), Midland Art Coun. (pres. 2 terms, 25th Anniversary award), Internat. Women's Forum, Mich. Women's Forum, Contemporary Rev. Club, Midland County Lawyers' Wives, Zonta, Phi Beta Kappa, Phi Kappa Phi, Alpha Lambda Delta, Phi Lambda Theta, Phi Gamma Nu, Delta Delta Delta. Republican. Episcopalian. Home: 209 Revere St Midland MI 48640-4255 Office: Northwood U Off of VP Midland MI 48640-2398

BARKER, VERLYN LLOYD, retired minister, educator; b. Auburn, Nebr., July 25, 1931; s. Jack Lloyd and Olive Clara (Bollman) B. AB, Doane Coll., 1952, DD, 1977; BD, Yale U., 1956, STM, 1960; postgrad., U. Chgo., 1960-61; PhD, St. Louis U., 1970. Ordained to ministry United Ch. of Christ, 1956. Instr. history, chaplain Doane Coll., Crete, Nebr., 1954-55; pastor U. Nebr., 1956-59; sec. ministry higher edn. United Ch. Bd. Homeland Ministries, N.Y.C., 1991-96; ret. United Ch. Bd. Homeland Ministries, Cleve., 1996. Author: Health and Human Values: A Ministry of Theological Inquiry and Moral Discourse, 1987; editor: The Church and the Public School, 1980, Science, Technology and the Christian Faith, 1990; contbg. author: Campus Ministry, 1964; mem. editorial adv. com. Jour. Current Social Issues; contbr. articles to various publs. Pres. United Ministries in Higher Edn., N.Y.C., 1971-77. Mem. AAAS, ACLU, Am. Assn. Higher Edn., Am. Studies Assn., Acad. Polit. Sci., Am. Acad. Polit. and Social Sci., Soc. Health and Human Values, Doane Coll. Alumni Assn. (pres. 1957-58), Nat. Assn. for Sci., Tech. and Soc., Yale Club.

BARKHAUSEN, DAVID N., state legislator; b. Lake Forest, Ill., Jan. 31, 1950; m. Susan; 2 children. BA with high honors, Princeton U., 1972; grad. magna cum laude, Woodrow Wilson Sch. Pub. Affairs; JD, So. Ill. U. Asst. atty. gen. State of Ill.; mem. Ill. State Ho. of Reps., 1981-83; mem. dist. 30 Ill. State Senate, 1983—; minority spokesman, judiciary com., mem. fin. and credit regulations, ins. pension and lic. activities, elections and reappointment, judiciary II and legis. reference bur. com., also atty., also ins. agt. Office: 714 E Prospect Ave Lake Bluff IL 60044-2620 also: State Senate State Capital Springfield IL 62706 Address: 273 Market Sq Lake Forest IL 60045*

BARKLEY, FRED L., mechanical engineer; b. Salem, Ohio, May 22, 1959. A in Mech. Engring., Youngstown State U., 1991, postgrad., 1991. Proposal engr. Electric Furnace Co., Salem, Ohio, 1987—. Office: Electric Furnace Co 435 W Wilson St Salem OH 44460

BARKLEY, JOHN RICHARD, physicist; b. Oswego, N.Y., Aug. 22, 1938; s. John Wesley and Helen Y. (Marsden) B.; married; children: John Timothy, Jeanne Marie, Brenda Ann. BS, LeMoyne Coll., Syracuse, N.Y., 1960; MS, Ohio U., 1963, PhD, 1966. Rsch. physicist E.I. DuPont, Wilmington, Del., 1966-81; sr. rsch. assoc. E.I. DuPont, Circleville, Ohio, 1981—; R&D for Mylar polyester films DuPont, Circleville, 1981—. Office: DuPont Films PO Box 89 Circleville OH 43113

BARKS, HORACE BUSHNELL, publisher, editor; b. St. Louis, July 13, 1921; s. Horace Bushnell Jr. and Cordie (Sherrow) B.; m. Elsie Dickson, June 14, 1947; children: Elizabeth, Kate, Joe, Barbara, Bill. AB, Westminster Coll., 1942; MSJ, Northwestern U., 1947. Editor Grocer's Digest, Chgo., 1947-54; pres. Barks Publs., Inc., St. Louis, 1955-66, Chgo., 1967—; editor, pub. Elec. Apparatus Mag., Chgo., 1964—. Contbr. articles to profl. jours. Lt. USNR, 1942-46, reserve duty, 1946-68, ret. lt. comdr. Inducted into Chgo. Journalism Hall of Fame, 1995. Mem. Am. Bus. Press (dir. 1973-76), Chgo. Headline Club, Soc. Profl. Journalists (pres. 1981-82). Episcopalian. Office: Barks Pub Inc 400 N Michigan Ave Chicago IL 60611-4198

BARKSDALE, CHARLES MADSEN, psychoneuroendocrinologist; b. San Diego, June 20, 1947; s. Madsen Lewis and Esther Elizabeth (La Force) B. BA in Chemistry and Math., U. Calif. San Diego, 1970; MS in Biochemistry, Columbia Pacific U., 1982, PhD in Chemistry, 1983. Rsch. assoc. U. Calif. San Diego, U. Hosp., 1970-76; rsch. scientist Diagnostics Products, Inc., La Jolla, Calif., 1976-77; sr. rsch. assoc. Hyland Diagnostics, Costa Mesa, Calif., 1977-81; NIH postdoctoral fellow U. Wis., Madison, 1981-84, rsch. assoc. dept. psychiatry, 1984-86, rsch. scientist, 1986-88; rsch. assoc. pharmacokinetics and drug metabolism Parke-Davis Pharm. Rsch., Ann Arbor, Mich., 1988—; Contbr. articles to numerous profl. jours. Recipient NIH Postdoctoral Rsch. fellowship U. Wis., 1983. Fellow Royal Entomol. Soc. of London; mem. Internat. Soc. for Psychoneuroendocrinology, The Endocrine Soc., Soc. Adolescent Medicine, The Neurosci. Soc., Calif. Acad. Scis. (hon. life). Office: Parke-Davis 2800 Plymouth Rd Ann Arbor MI 48105-2430

BARLEY, BARBARA ANN, accountant; b. Sewickley, Pa., June 19, 1954; d. William Stephen and Maude Adel (Wilt) B. BS in Math., BA in Bus. magna cum laude, Westminster Coll., 1976. CPA, Ohio, Wis. Staff acct. Price Waterhouse & Co., Pitts., 1976-78; internal auditor Federated Dept. Stores, Inc., Cin., 1978-79; gen. ledger mgr. Formica Corp., Cin., 1980-81; staff acct. Bethesda Hosp., Cin., 1981-82; acctg. mgr. Madison Area Assn. for Retarded Citizens Devel. Ctrs. Corp., Madison, Wis., 1982-88; dir. fin. Retardation Facilities Devel. Found., Inc., Madison, Wis., 1988—; treas. Integrated Community Work, Inc., Madison, 1989-90. Treas. Access to Cmty. Svcs., Inc., 1988—; mem. Environ. Def. Fund, 1986—; treas. Peace Project Inc., Madison, 1985-95; coms. Wis. Nuclear Weapons Freeze Campaign, Madison, 1985-86, Madison nuclear free zone com., Madison, 1986. Mem. AICPA, ACLU, Wis. Inst. CPAs, Amnesty Internat., Sierra Club, Kappa Mu Epsilon, Omicron Delta Epsilon, Delta Sigma Rho-Tau Kappa Alpha, Omicron Delta Kappa. Unitarian. Home: 101 Femrite Dr #107 Madison WI 53716 Office: Retardation Facilities Devel Found Inc 2875 Fish Hatchery Rd Madison WI 53713-3120

BARLOW, FRANKLIN SACKETT, sales executive, consultant; b. Hudson, Ohio, Jan. 18, 1912; s. Henry Case and Flora Isabel (Sackett) B. m. Mary Elizabeth Irvin, June 29, 1940; children: Byron Irvin, Donald Sackett, Hester Elizabeth. Student, Coll. of Wooster, Ohio, 1930-32; AB, Kent (Ohio) State U., 1935. Internat. sales mgr. Harris-Intertype Corp., Cleve., 1947-74; pvt. practice cons. Hudson, Ohio, 1974-90. Author: booklet Reminiscences of a Hudson Ohio Farm Boy, 1983. Councilman Village of Hudson City Coun., 1975-78. 2d lt. (inf.) U.S. Army, 1942-45, ETO. Decorated Bronze Star. Mem. Cleve. World Trade Assn. (life bd. dirs. 1959-62), Internat. Execs. Club, Hudson Heritage (bd. dirs. 1965-68, 88-91), Rotary (sec. Hudson 1980-90), Masons (master 1950-51). Republican. Congregationalist. Home: 200 Laurel Lake Dr W-314 Hudson OH 44236

BARLOW, HOWARD C., social services administrator; b. Badger, S.D., Mar. 12, 1936; s. Barlow Jens and Stella M. (Jordet) B.; m. Dorothy Ann Holm; children: Nancy Jo Farnham, Laurie Ann, David Alan. Student, Huron (S.D.) Coll. Salesperson Pierce Co., Fargo, N.D., 1970-78; pres. Fine Print, Inc., Fargo, 1978-86; v.p. resource devel. Lutheran Social Svcs. N.D., Fargo, 1986—; pres. Barlow Mgmt. Inc., Fargo, 1992—. Congregation chmn. Peace Lutheran Ch., 1980-82; bd. dirs. Vols. for Cmty. Svc., Fargo, 1979-81. Recipient vol. action award N.D. Coord. Vol. Svcs., 1982. Mem. Nat. Assn. Fund Raising Execs., Red River Valley Estate Planning Coun., Fargo C. of C., Planned Giving Ptnrs., Optimist Internat. (dist. gov. 1986-87, dist. sec.-treas. 1991-92, named outstanding lt. gov. 1984). Home: 1214 Elm St N Fargo ND 58102 Office: Lutheran Social Svcs ND 1325 S 11th St Fargo ND 58103

BARLOW, JOHN LESLIE ROBERT, physician; b. Skipton, Yorkshire, Eng., May 6, 1926; came to U.S., 1966; s. John and Louise Baker (Pollok) B.; m. Johnnie M. Barlow; children: Louise Claire, Donal Patrick, Mary Teresa, Margaret Anne, Catherine Jayne Maria. B.A., Cambridge U., 1947, M.B., B.Chir., 1950. Resident in gen. medicine, gen. surgery, ob-gyn. South West Eng., 1950-56; practice medicine South West Eng., 1956-66; with internat. div. Abbott Labs., North Chicago, 1966-77, med. dir., 1974-77; dir. clin. research Merrell Dow Pharms., Cin., 1976-88; pvt. practice cons., Cin., 1988—, ret., 1988. Mem. Brit. Med. Assn., Am. Soc. Clin. Pharmacology and Therapeutics.

BARLOW, THOMAS REED, broadcast executive; b. Coldwater, Mich., Sept. 7, 1952; s. Max W. Houck and Janet (Newth) Barlow; m. Susan J. Faull, May 18, 1974; children: Lara C., Daniel C. BA, Western Mich. U., 1974; MS (hon.), Boston U., 1978. Sales assoc. Zales Jewelers, Kalamazoo, Mich., 1974-76, Shaws Jewelers, Lansing, Mich., 1976-78; mem. sales mgmt. staff Jacobson Stores, Grand Rapids, Mich., 1978-82; broadcasting/sales rep. WMIQ/WIMK, Iron Mountain, Mich., 1982-88; program dir., operation dir. WJNR-FM/Hitz 101, Iron Mountain, 1988-93; sales svcs. dir., sales/mktg. cons. and creative svcs. dir. Midwest Family Broadcasting Group, 1993—; mgr. Midwest Family Affiliate Stas. WCMM-WTIQ, 1996—; cons. Radio Without a Net Prodns., Iron Mountain, 1991—. Active child protection/children's rights issues, 1989—; mem. World Radio Monitor, 1973-80. Recipient Spl. Tribute, State of Mich., 1986, 92. Mem. Mich. Assn. Broadcasters.

BARMAN, SUSAN MARIE, physiologist; b. Joliet, Ill., Aug. 28, 1949; d. Vernon Rutherford and Shirley Marie (Shea) B. BS in Biology, Loyola U., Chgo., 1971; PhD in Physiology, Loyola U., 1976. From research assoc. to asst. prof. Mich. State U., East Lansing, 1975-84, assoc. prof., 1984-94, prof., 1994—; sci. cons. NIH, Bethesda, Md., 1981, 83—. Contbr. articles to profl. jours. Recipient Merit award NIH Heart, Lung, Blood Inst., 1995—. Mem. Soc. for Neuroscience, American Physiological Soc., AAAS. Democrat. Roman Catholic. Office: Mich State U Dept Pharmacology East Lansing MI 48824

BARMETTLER, JOSEPH JOHN, lawyer; b. Omaha, Sept. 10, 1933; s. William Thomas and Dorothy Lucy (Flynn) B.; m. Jeanne Waller, June 21, 1958; children: Joseph Jr., Gregory, Richard, Katie, Peggy, Timothy, Michael. BSC, Creighton U., 1956, JD, 1959. Bar: Nebr. 1959, U.S. Dist. Ct. Nebr. 1959, U.S. Ct. Appeals (8th cir.) 1963, U.S. Ct. Claims 1963. Assoc. Fitzgerald, Hamer, Brown & Leahy, Omaha, 1959-64; ptnr. Fitzgerald, Schorr, Barmettler & Brennan, Omaha, 1964—, CEO, 1988—; gen. counsel Metro. Community Coll., Omaha, 1974—, Village of Boys Town, Nebr., 1991—, City of La Vista, Nebr., 1963—. Mem. devel. coun. Omaha Legal Aid Soc., 1989—; pres.'s coun. Creighton U., Omaha, 1990—. Fellow Nebr. Bar Found.; mem. Nebr. Bar Assn. (chmn. ways, means and planning com. 1993-94, ho. of dels. 1986—, chmn. budget and adminstrn. com. 1993-94), Omaha Bar Assn., Omaha Downtown Rotary (dir. 1986-89, Paul Harris fellow). Republican. Office: Fitzgerald Schorr Barmettler & Brennan PC 1000 Woodmen Tower Omaha NE 68102

BARNA, KENNETH JAMES, design engineer; b. Medina, Ohio, Nov. 16, 1954; s. Ruben Gene and Alice Jean (Stefan) B.; m. Debra Ann Komin, Aug. 3, 1987. Student, Case We. Res. U., 1972-75, Cleve. State U., 1976-92. Prodn. mgr. New Era Products, Inc., Cleve., 1975-80, design engr., 1980-84, engring. mgr., 1984-90, gen. mgr., 1990—. Patentee in field. Adult leader Youth/Adult com. Unitarian Ch., Ohio-Meadville Dist., 1987-91. Mem. Wilderness Soc., Sierra Club, Sigma Alpha Mu. Office: New Era Products Inc 6305 Barberton Ave Cleveland OH 44102-5427

BARNARD, ALLEN DONALD, lawyer; b. Williston, N.D., Feb. 22, 1944; s. Donald J. and Ruth E. (Franklin) B.; m. Andra Lynn Lebsock, Nov. 24, 1962; children: Alana, Aaron. BA in Social Scis., U. N.D., 1965; JD, U. Notre Dame, 1968. Bar: Minn. 1968, U.S. Dist. Ct. Minn. 1968, U.S. Ct. Appeals (8th cir.) 1971, U.S. Supreme Ct. 1973. Assoc. Best & Flanagan, Mpls., 1968-72, ptnr., 1972—, mng. ptnr., 1991-93; city atty. City of Golden Valley, Minn., 1988—, housing and redevel. authority atty., 1978—. Mem. ABA, Assn. Trial Lawyers, Minn. Trial Lawyers Assn., Hennepin County Bar Assn., Mpls. Athletic Club, Madeline Island Yacht Club (dir. 1991—). Office: Best & Flanagan 4000 First Bank Pl 601 2nd Ave S Minneapolis MN 55402-4303

BARNARD, ANN WATSON, retired academic administrator, educator, writer; b. Kansas City, Mo., Feb. 17, 1930; d. Howard Dale and Gladys (Conklin) Watson; (div. 1959); children: Faith, John. BA in English, U. Kansas City, 1950, MA in English, 1952; PhD in Humanities, U. Mo., Kansas City, 1963. Tchr. English Blackburn Coll., Carlinville, Ill., 1960-93, chair dept. English, 1964-93, prof. emerita, 1993—; chair humanities div. Blackburn Coll., 1979-85, coll. marshal, 1989-93. Author poetry; contbr. articles to profl. jours. Mme. Common Cause, Defenders of Wildlife. Blackburn Coll. grantee, 1987-90. Mem. Assn. for Can. Studies in the U.S., Am. Studies Assn., Modern Lang. Assn., Nat. Coun. Tchrs. of English, AAUW, NOW. Democrat. Episcopalian.

BARNARD, JAMES H., technical service representative; b. Ft. Worth, Feb. 15, 1959; s. James Montgomery and Lucille Marie (Rebedoux) B. Grad. high sch., 1977. Supr. Stroehmann Bakeries, Williamsport, Pa., 1978-84, supt., 1984-86; mfg. mgr. Arnold Foods, Greenwich, Conn., 1986-88; tech. svcs. rep. J.R. Short Milling Co., Chgo., 1988—. Mem. Inst. Food Technologists, Am. Soc. Bakery Engrs. Home: 351 Eddington Ave Harrisburg PA 17111 Office: JR Short Milling Co 500 W Madison St Chicago IL 60606

BARNARD, JOHN, history educator; b. Wichita, Kans., Nov. 5, 1932; s. Hugh Blake and Ora Bea (Burford) B.; m. Joan Pennock, Aug. 31, 1953; children: Bruce W., Elizabeth Orr, Stephen B. AB, Oberlin Coll., 1955; MA, U. Chgo., 1957, PhD, 1964. Instr. Ohio State U., Columbus, 1960-64; prof. Oakland U., Rochester, Mich., 1964—. Author: Oberlin College 1866-1917, 1969, Walter Reuther, 1983; editor: Children and Youth, 1970-74. Rsch. fellow Charles Warren Ctr., Harvard U., 1967-69, fellow NEH, 1971, rsch. resident/fellow Rockefeller Found., Wayne State U., 1990-91. Mem. AAUP, Am. Hist. Assn., Orgn. Am. Historians. Home: 3248 Woodside Ct Bloomfield Hills MI 48304-2575 Office: Dept History Oakland U Rochester MI 48309

BARNARD, JOHN KENT, engineering executive; b. Cleve., May 7, 1940. B, Case Inst. Tech., 1962; MBA, SUNY, Buffalo, 1967. Co-founder Progressive Equipment Co., Erie, Pa., 1972-79; pres. Systems Specialist, Erie, Pa., 1979-81; v.p. Vita-Mix Corp., Cleve., 1981—. Holder 8 patents in field. Republican. Office: Vita Mix Corp 8615 Usher Rd Cleveland OH 44138-2103

BARNARD, MARCUS, machinist, poet, writer; b. Lincoln County, Ky., May 19, 1938; s. Samuel J. and Vivian C. (Osborne) B.; m. Phyllis A. Kirts, May 18, 1958; children: Melvin, Vivian, Marcia. Machinist Dodge Reliance Divsn. Rockwell Automation, Columbus, Ind., 1965—. Author: Poems, Stories Vol. I, 1990, Poems, Songs and Stories Vol. II, 1995. Mem. IAM Machinists, Hoosier Beemers (dir. 1987-90). Democrat. Roman Catholic. Home: 8632 W 2d St Kurtz IN 47249 Office: PO Box 53 Kurtz IN 47249

BARNARD, MORTON JOHN, lawyer; b. Chgo., Mar. 22, 1905; s. Julius and Martha (Wittman) B.; m. Eleanor Spivak, Aug. 16, 1936; 1 child, James W. PhB, U. Chgo., 1926, JD, 1927. Bar: Ill. 1927, U.S. Supreme Ct. 1949, U.S. Ct. Mil. Appeals 1954, U.S. Dist. Ct. (no. dist.) Ill., U.S. Ct. Appeals (7th cir.). Ptnr. Barnard and Barnard, Chgo., 1934-41, 46-84, Foss, Schuman, Drake & Barnard, Chgo., 1985-88; ptnr. Gottlieb & Schwartz, Chgo., 1989-90, of counsel, 1990-93; of counsel Miller, Shakman, Hamilton, Kurtzon & Schlifke, Chgo., 1993—; adj. prof. John Marshall Law Sch., Chgo., 1947-64; pres. Ill. State Bar Assn., 1971-72; lectr. in field. Author: Contested Estates, 1985, 93; contbr. articles to profl. jours. Life mem. Chgo. Hist. Soc. Lt. col. U.S. Army, 1942-46. Recipient Certs. of Appreciation Ill. State Bar Assn., 1972, Chgo. Bar Assn., 1986, Bd. Govs.' award Ill. State Bar Assn., 1988, Austin Fleming Disting. Svc. award Chgo. Estate Planning Coun., 1993, Addis E. Hull award Ill. Inst. for Continuing Legal Edn., 1996. Fellow Am. Coll. Trust and Estate Counsel (bd. regents 1968-74), Am. Bar Found., Ill. Bar Found., Chgo. Bar Found.; mem. Union League Club (Chgo.). Republican. Office: Miller Shakman et al 208 S La Salle St Ste 1100 Chicago IL 60604-1101

BARNELLO, MICHAEL DAVID, investment company executive; b. Shrieveport, La., Aug. 26, 1965; s. Anthony Angelo and Mary Jo (McDonough) B. BS, Cornell U. Asset mgr. Vons Realty Ptnrs., Chgo., asst. v.p., v.p.; v.p. Strategic Realty Advisors, Inc., Chgo. Mem. Hospitality Asset Mgrs. Assn. (cert.). Roman Catholic. Office: Strategic Realty Advisors Inc 8700 W Bryn Mawr Chicago IL 60631

BARNER, BRUCE MONROE, state agency administrator; b. Delaware, Ohio, Jan. 16, 1951; s. Charles Ray and Annabel (Monroe) B. BA in Philosophy with honors, Muskingum Coll., 1973; postgrad., Cleve. State U., 1975-77. Adminstrv. researcher Dept. Pub. Safety State of Ohio, Columbus, 1980—; fatal crash analyst Nat. Hwy. Traffic Safety Adminstrn., Washington, 1982-83, 85, Nat. Accident Sampling System, 1983; researcher study on motorcycle/moped crash trends, 1985, study on driving edn. in Ohio, 1987, study on semi-truck crash trends, 1986, 87, 88, study on child safety seat usage in Ohio, 1989, study on driver errors in serious heavy truck crashes in Ohio, 1989, studies on shoulder belt usage by roadway functional class in Ohio, 1991, 92, 93, 94, study on fatal crash involvement of repeat DWI offenders in Ohio, 1991-93. Contbr. articles to profl. jours. Cofounder Ohio Safety Belt Coalition, 1983-84; adminstrv. rschr. gov.'s motor carrier adv. com. State of Ohio, 1986-90, adminstrv. rschr. Ohio hwy. safety elderly driver task force, 1990, DWI task force, 1992, 93; advisor Safety Mgmt. Sys., 1994, 95. Mem. Internat. Platform Assn., Assn. Advancement Automotive Medicine, Planetary Soc., World Future Soc., Nat. Space Soc., Saved by the Belt Club. Presbyterian. HOME: PO Box 510 Galloway OH 43119 Office: State Ohio Dept Pub Safety 240 Parsons Ave Columbus OH 43215-5331

BARNER, HENDRICK BOYER, cardiovascular surgeon; b. Seattle, Wash., Feb. 23, 1933; s. Henry Adolph and Billie Elizabeth (Halvorsen) B.; m. Mechthild Brigitta Boehnke, Mar. 6, 1961; children: Boyer Hendrick, Bjorn Oluf, Bela Mattis. BS, U. Wash., 1954, MD, 1957. Instr. U. Rochester, N.Y., 1964-65; prof. of surgery St. Louis U., 1966-91, Albert Einstein Coll. Medicine, Bronx, N.Y., 1991-93, Washington U., St. Louis, 1993—. Editl. bd. Annals of Thoracic Surgery, 1989—, Jour. Cardiovascular Surgery, 1989—, Eur Cardiovascular Surgery, 1994—, Internat. Jour. Angiol., 1993—; contbg. author 21 book chpts.; contbr. articles to profl. jours. Capt. USNR, 1955-91. Recipient Honors Achievement award Angiology Rsch. Found., 1967-68. Mem. Am. Surg. Assn., Soc. Thoracic Surgeons (editl. bd. 1989—), Am. Assn. Thoracic Surgery, So. Thoracic Surg. Assn. (sec./treas. 1989-94), Am. Coll. Surgery, European Assn. Cardiovascular Surgery (editl. bd. 1994—). Home: 39 Portland Pl Saint Louis MO 63108 Office: Ste 211 11125 Dunn Rd Saint Louis MO 63136

BARNES, DAVID, engineering executive; b. Ripley, Tenn., Mar. 15, 1949. BS, U. Tenn., 1971. Dealer cons. Trane Co., Columbus, Ohio, 1971-74, mgr., 1980—; v.p. engring. Columbus Worthington Trane, Columbus, 1974-80. Coach youth sports; vol. sch. activites, Jaycees. Named Coach of Yr., U.S. Youth Soccer Assn., Jaycee of Yr., Worthington Jaycees. Methodist. Office: Trane Co 2550 Corporate Exchange Dr Columbus OH 43231-1660

BARNES, DON A., business executive; b. Dodge City, Kans., May 17, 1937. BSBA, Kans. State Coll., 1961. Field mgr. Ford Motor Co., Kansas City, Mo., 1961-67; sr. account exec. Carlson Mktg. Group, Mpls., 1967-94; v.p. Excellence in Motivation, Inc., Bloomington, Ill., 1994—. Performing vol. Brokaw Follies, Bloomington, 1980—; mem. Young Men's Club, Bloomington, 1985—. With USN, 1954-57. Scholarship Okla. City U., 1958. Republican. Methodist. Office: Excellence in Motivation 2310 E Oakland Ave Ste 2B Bloomington IL 61701-5865

BARNES, EARNEST E., engineering executive; b. Sheridan, Ind., Dec. 22, 1944. Processing engr. mgr. Biddle Precision Products, Sheridan, 1963—. Coach, umpire, Little League. Office: Biddle Precision Products 701 S Main St Sheridan IN 46069-1340

BARNES, ERNIE L., fundraiser; b. Grenada, Miss., Nov. 26, 1952; s. H.L. Jr. and Ann (Gresham) B.; m. Paula Shoaf, Sept. 12, 1980; children: Joshua Paul, Courtney Renae. BS, Miss. State U., 1974. Hog buyer Bryan Foods, West Point, Miss., 1974-75; sales rep. The Upjohn Co., San Antonio, 1975-76; S.E. field rep. Am. Yorkshire Club, West Lafayette, Ind., 1976-81; CEO Am. Landrace Assn., West Lafayette, 1981-86; dir. resource devel. Nat. Pork Producers, Des Moines, 1986—; mem. bd. Louisville and Nat. Barrow Shows, Austin, Minn., 1981-86; mem. Earlham (Iowa) Agr. Com.; mem. Nat. Future Farmers Am. Swine Proefficiency Team, 1986-95. Editor Am. Landrace and Purebred Picture, 1981-86. Mem. agr. com. Des Moines Agr. Coun., 1987; coach 5th/6th grade basketball, Earlham, 1993-95; coord. JC 4th of July Baseball Tourney, Earlham, 1995. Mem. Nat. Agrl. Mktg. (program chmn./Agr. Day chair 1986-95, mem. bd. 1992-94, Gureilla Mktg. award 1993), Nat. Pork Producers (exec. com. 1983-86, Team award 1991), Nat. Assn. Swine Records (sec. 1981-86), Miss. Block and Bridle Alumni (pres. 1984), Nat. Pedigreed Livestock Coun. (mem. bd. 1983-86). Baptist. Home: 2094 350th St Adel IA 50003 Office: Nat Pork Producers Coun 1776 NW 114th St Clive IA 50325

BARNES, JAMES A., state legislator; b. Kansas City, Mo., Dec. 4, 1951; s. Cecil H. and Doris E. (Rawlings) B.; m. Kathleen Ann Hale, 1977; children: Jacqueline Celeste, Jenna Elise. BA, Rockhurst Coll., 1975; MA, Webster Coll., 1982. Rschr. Cmty. Attitude Rsch. Group, Inc., 1977; rsch. economist Mo. Coun. Econ. Devel., 1978; mem. Mo. Ho. of Reps., Jefferson City, 1979—, former majority floor leader. Committeeman Brooking Twp. Dem. Com., Raytown, Mo., 1978—; bd. govs. Park Lane Hosp., Cmty. Mental Health Ctr.; hon. bd. dirs. Rockhurst Coll., Webster Coll.; active Boy Scouts Am. Recipient Disting. Svc. award Raytown Jaycees, 1980. Mem. Raytown C. of C., Masons, Rotary, Alpha Sima Nu, Phi Theta Kappa, Phi Sigma Tau.

BARNES, JAMES L., financial consultant; b. Columbus, Ohio, June 15, 1947. BA in Sci. and Bus., Ohio State U., 1971. Fin. cons. Merrill Lynch, Dublin, Ohio, 1977—. Sponsor Dublin H.S. Young Profl. Assn., 1993—. Maj. USAF and Coast Guard Res., 1969-83. Mem. Air Field Village Country Club, Chmn.'s Club (Merrill Lynch). Republican. Episcopalian. Home: 235 Indian Run Dr Dublin OH 43017-2184 Office: Merrill Lynch 555 Metro Pl N Ste 550 Dublin OH 43017-1375

BARNES, LAHNA HARRIS, water treatment company owner; b. New Albany, Ind., May 23, 1947; d. Robert and Catherine (Edwards) H. AA, U. Louisville, Louisville, Ky., 1969. Cert. real estate broker, accredited crisis counselor, paralegal. Property mgr. various cos., Jeffersonville, Ind. and Louisville, 1966-76, 78-80, 81-83; sales agt. Century 21, Clarksville, Ind., 1978-83; sales broker Bass & Weisberg Realtors, Jeffersonville, Ind., 1980-81; owner Superior Typing Svc., Jeffersonville, Ind., 1983-89, 91—, Barnes Realty Mgt., Jeffersonville, Ind., 1983-85; corp. sec. Water Energizers Inc., Jeffersonville, Ind., 1983-90; v.p. Water Energizers Inc., Jeffersonville, 1991-92, 94—, co-owner, bd. dirs., 1992—; property mgr. Gardenside Terrace Coop., 1992-93. Author numerous poems; contbr. articles to local newspapers. Active Right To Life, New Albany, 1990—, Realtors Polit. Action Com., 1980-83, NFIB, 1986—, Equal Housing Commn., 1980-83; counselor Ctr. for Lay Ministries, New Albany, Ind., 1972-75; coord. Perot Petition Com. for Clark County, 1992; presdl. elector, Ind., 1992; vol. Earth Day '96, 1996; mem. Rainforest Action Network, 1996—; coord. USA Make A Difference Day, 1995; vol. ARC, 1995—. Mem. SCLC (charter mem. So. Ind. chpt., bd. dirs. 1992-94, social justice com. 1992-93, editor The Voice of Freedom newsletter 1992-94), Assn. Water Technologies. Office: Water Energizers Inc 3008 Middle Rd Jeffersonville IN 47130-5500

BARNES, RICHARD GEORGE, physicist, educator; b. Milw., Dec. 19, 1922; s. George Richard and Irma (Ott) B.; m. Mildred A. Jachens, Sept. 9, 1950; children: Jeffrey R., David G., Christina E., Douglas A. B.A., U. Wis., 1948; M.A., Dartmouth Coll., 1949; Ph.D., Harvard U., 1952. Teaching fellow Harvard, 1950-52; asst. prof. U. Del., 1952-55, asso. prof., 1955-56; asso. prof. Iowa State U., 1956-60, prof., 1960-88, chmn. dept. physics, 1971-75, prof. emeritus, 1988—; sr. physicist Ames Lab., U.S. Dept. Energy, 1960-88; chief physics div. Ames Lab., AEC, 1971-75; vis. rsch. prof. Calif. Inst. Tech., 1962-63; guest prof. Tech. U. Darmstadt, Germany, 1975-76; vis. prof. Cornell U., 1982-83; program dir. solid state physics NSF, 1988-89, condensed matter physics NSF, 1995; chmn. Metal Hydrides Gordon Rsch. Conf., 1987. Served with USAAF, 1942-43; C.E. AUS, 1944-46. Recipient U.S. Sr. Scientist award Alexander von Humboldt Found., 1975-76. Fellow Am. Phys. Soc. Home: 8 Lockwood Dr Kennebunk ME 04043-2244 Office: Iowa State U Physics Dept Ames IA 50011

BARNES, ROBERT F., agronomist; b. Estherville, Iowa, Feb. 6, 1933; s. Chester Arthur and Pearl Adella (Stoelting) B.; m. Bettye Jeanne Burrell, June 25, 1955; children: Bradley R., Rebecca L. Reinalda, Roberta K. Nixon, Brian L. AA, Estherville Jr. Coll., 1953; BS, Iowa State U., 1957; MS, Rutgers U., 1959; PhD, Purdue U., 1963. Rsch. agronomist USDA-Agrl. Rsch. Svc., West Lafayette, Ind., 1959-70; lab. dir. USDA-Agrl. Rsch. Svc., University Park, Pa., 1970-75; staff scientist nat. program staff USDA-Agrl. Rsch. Svc., Beltsville, Md., 1975-79; assoc. dep. adminstr. So. region USDA-Agrl. Rsch. Svc., New Orleans, 1979-84, dep. adminstr. So. region, 1984-86; exec. v.p. Am. Soc. of Agronomy, Madison, Wis., 1986—, also fellow; asst. prof. Purdue U., West Lafayette, 1963-66; assoc. prof. Pa. State U., University Park, 1966-70, adj. prof., 1970-75; adj. prof. agronomy U. Wis., Madison, 1986—; pres. Internat. Grassland Congress, Lexington, Ky., 1981. Editor: Forages, 1995; contbr. articles to profl. jours. With U.S. Army, 1953-55, Germany. Recipient H.S. Stubbs Meml. Lecture award Tropical Grassland Soc., Brisbane, Australia, 1984, Henry A. Wallace award Iowa State U., 1991. Fellow AAAS, Crop Sci. Soc. Am. (pres. 1984-85); mem. Am. Forage and Grassland Coun. (medallion 1981), Grazing Lands Forum (pres. 1986-87), Forage and Grassland Found. (pres. 1993—). Office: Am Soc of Agronomy 677 S Segoe Rd Madison WI 53711-1048

BARNES, ROBERT VINCENT, elementary and secondary school art educator; b. Flint, Mich., May 27, 1948; s. Albert J. and Mary Elizabeth (Morey) B.; m. Sandra E. Mathews-Barnes, Dec. 20, 1986; 1 child, Kathryn R. BA, Adrian Coll., 1970; postgrad., U. Mich., 1973-75, Cen. Mich. U., 1976-80, Getty Ctr. Edn. Arts, Cin. Art Mus., Cranbrook Acad. Art, Marygrove Coll., 1995—. Cert. tchr. art grades kindergarten through 12, Mich. Tchr. art Flushing (Mich.) Community Schs., 1971—; instr. Flint Inst. Arts, 1975-76; tchr. genealogy adult edn. program Mott C.C., Flushing, Fenton and Grand Blanc, Mich., 1976-84. Author: Flushing Area Families, 1981, Fenton Area Families, 1984; editor Flint Geneal. Quar., 1981. Past pres. Flint Geneal. Soc., Fenton Hist. Soc.; bd. dirs., past pres. Flushing Area Hist. Soc.; pres. Fenton Mus. Bd., 1984-86; chmn. Fenton 150th Com., 1984; co-chmn. Fenton Civic Com. for New Mus., 1985-86; com. mem. Genesee County Sesquicentennial, Flint, 1986; exhibiting mem. Left Bank Gallery, Grand Blanc Arts Guild. Recipient 1st prize Flushing Art Fair, Flushing Jr. Women's League, 1975, 78, Orren Hart award Flushing Area Hist. Soc., 1983. Mem. NEA, Mich. Edn. Assn., Nat. Art Edn. Assn.,

Mich. Art Edn. Assn., Flushing Edn. Assn., Ohio Geneal. Soc., Ohio Hist. Soc., Jaycees (Flushing chpt.). Methodist. Office: Springview Elem Sch 2033 Springview Dr Flushing MI 48433-1447

BARNES, ROSEMARY LOIS, minister; b. Grand Rapids, Mich., Sept. 17, 1946; d. Floyd Herman and Cora Agnes (Beukema) Herms; m. Louis Herbert Adams, Feb. 22, 1969 (div. Oct. 1976); 1 child, Louis Herbert Jr.; m. Robert Jearold Barnes, Oct. 8, 1976. BA, Calvin Coll., 1968. Ordained to ministry Home Ministry Fellowship, 1980; cert. social worker. Group worker Kent County Juvenile Ct., Grand Rapids, Mich., 1966-68; tchr. Sheldon Elem. Sch., Grand Rapids, 1968-69; social worker Kent Dept. Social Services, Grand Rapids, 1969-75, 75-84; tchr., mission worker Emmanuel House, San Diego, 1975; co-pastor, founder River of Life Ministries, Grand Rapids, 1980—; instr. Gt. Lakes Inst. Bible Studies, Grand Rapids, 1988; tchr., founder River of Life Sch. Christian Leadership, Grand Rapids, 1981—; v.p. Aglow, Grand Rapids, 1982-83; sec., treas. Western Mich. Full Gospel Ministers Fellowship, Grand Rapids, 1984-85; mem. bd. chaplains Dunes Correctional Facility, Saugatuck, Mich., 1986-91; coord. 1988 Washington for Jesus March, One Nation Under God, Inc.; co-pastor Gun Lake River of Life, 1988; prof. Great Lakes Inst., 1988; county coord. Grand Rapids Full Gospel Ministers Fellowship, 1990-92; co-pastor Defiance, Ohio River of Life, 1992-93. Participant TV show Ask the Pastor, 1993—; dir., producer TV show River Reflections, 1994—; Mich. women's coord. Let The Redeemed of the Lord Say So, 1994; sponsor Grand Rapids cable TV Jewish Jewels, 1995—. Bd. dirs. Alcohol Incentive Ladder, Grand Rapids, 1979. Participant TV show Ask the Pastor, 1993—, Michigan Alive, 1994—; dir., prodr. TV show River Reflections, 1994-95; Mich. women's coord. Let The Redeemed of the Lord Say So, 1994; sponsor Grand Rapids cable TV Jewish Jewels, 1995—. Mem. Women in Leadership. Democrat. Mem. Ind. Charismatic Ch.

BARNES, STEVEN LEE, certified public accountant; b. Columbus, Ohio, July 1, 1950; s. Leroy S. and Betty Lou (Hedges) B.; 1 child, Tracey Lynne. BS in Bus., Acctg., Franklin U., 1973. CPA, Ohio. Staff acct. Knospe & Barnes, Columbus, Ohio, 1973-85; pres. Barnes, Barnes & Assocs., Inc., Columbus, Ohio, 1985—; pres. Advanced Practice Mgmt., Inc., Columbus, 1985—, Midwest Med. Practice Concepts, Inc., Columbus, 1985—; lectr. numerous assns. including Dept. Medicine Ohio U., Grant Hosp., Riverside Hosp., Doctors Hosp. Contbr. articles to profl. jours. Active Salem Village Civic Assn., Columbus, 1975-82, Olentangy Highlands Civic Assn., Worthington, Ohio, 1982-88; treas. NW Meth. Ch., Columbus, 1986-87, bd. dirs., 1986-90. Mem. Pub. Accts. Soc. Ohio (treas. 1979-81, v.p. 1981-83, pres. 1983-84, vice chmn. 1984-85, chmn. 1985-86, mem. long range planning com. 1985-90, continuing edn. com. 1975, chmn. accountancy law awareness com. 1987-88, Disting. Svc. award 1986, chmn. legis. com. 1990—), Med. Group Mgmt. Assn., Nat. Soc. Pub. Accts., Ohio Soc. CPAs, OSCPA (bd. mem.), OSCPA Govtl. Affairs Coun., Masons. Office: Barnes Barnes & Assocs Inc 29 W 3rd Ave # 8160 Columbus OH 43201-3208

BARNES, VANESSA SUMMERS, state legislator; m. Nicholas T. Barnes. Grad., Mid-Am. Coll. Funeral Svcs. State rep., mem. aged & aging, pub. policy, ethics, vet. affairs & urban affairs coms., chmn. interstate coop. com. Ind. Ho. of Reps., Indpls., 1991—; funeral dir. Summers Funeral Chapel. Named one of Top Ladies of Distinction. Mem. Alpha Kappa Alpha, Alpha Mu Omega. Democrat. Office: Ind Ho of Reps State Capitol Indianapolis IN 46204

BARNES-BRUCE, MARY HANFORD, English language educator. BA in English, U. Tex., Arlington, 1965; MA in English, So. Meth. U., 1968; PhD in English, Ariz. State U., 1986. Cert. secondary tchr., Tex., Tenn.; cert. C.C. instr., Ariz. Tchr. L.D. Bell High Sch., Hurst, Tex., 1965-66; instr. Memphis State U., 1968-69, 75, Tex. Southmost Jr. Coll., Brownsville, 1969-73; tchr. St. Mary's Episcopal Sch., Memphis, 1975-76; instr. Phoenix C.C. Dist., 1978-83; tchr. Seton Cath. Sch., Chandler, Ariz., 1982; instr. Ariz. State U., Tempe, 1979-85; tchr. Ecole Normale Supérieure, U. Yaoundé, YaoundÉ, Cameroon, 1988-90; prof. Monmouth (Ill.) Coll., 1985—, U. Zimbabwe, Harare, 1995; freelance editor MacMillan Pub., Mesa, Ariz., 1985, Parker-Thomas Design, Mesa, 1985, Mountain West Nuclear Rsch., Tempe, 1983, Luce Printing Co., Mesa, 1981; Assoc. Colls. of Midwest dir. to ACM Program in Zimbabwe, 1995, rep. to ACM Program to Tanzania. Author: Holding to the Light, 1991; contbr. poetry and prose to numerous publs. Mem. Warren County Writers' Assn., Monmouth, 1990—, The Fortnightly, Monmouth, 1990—, Al-Anon, Monmouth, 1986—, Am. Sch. of Yaounde, 1988-90; vol. Crisis Ctr., Memphis, 1976, Mercy Hosp. Brownsville, 1971-72, Buchanan Art Ctr., Monmouth, 1993, 94; mem. Jr. League, Brownsville, 1970, steering com. Associated Colls. Midwest Com. on Women's Concerns, Chgo., 1987-88; Fulbright Assn. liaison officer Monmouth Coll., 1992-94. Named to the Acad. of Am. Poets, 1993; winner nat. Flume Poetry Contest, 1990; Fulbright sr. scholar Ecole Normale Supérieure, Yaounde, 1988-90. Mem. AAUP (exec. bd. Monmouth 1986-88), MLA, Internat. Friends of Lit. (Haifa, Israel). Roman Catholic. Home: 511 E Boston Ave Monmouth IL 61462-1859 Office: Monmouth Coll 700 W Broadway Monmouth IL 61462-1533

BARNETT, EDGAR ALLAN, real estate executive; b. Chgo., Jan. 15, 1937; s. Edgar Allan and Ruth Leontine (Lindrose) B.; m. Judith Park, Jan. 1, 1938; children: David Scott, Peter Allan. BS, Drake U., Des Moines, 1958. Ptnr. The Whiston Group, Chgo., 1965-78; v.p. Fuller Comml. Co., Chgo., 1978-80; sr. v.p. Paine/Wetzel Assocs., Inc., Chgo., 1980—; dir. Edville Bankcorp, Inc., Villa Park, Ill., Villa Park Trust and Savs. Bank. Chmn. Fire and Police Commn., Villa Park, 1977, Plan Commn., Villa Park, 1971; mem. Zoning Bd. Appeals, DuPage County, Ill., 1979-86. Recipient Oreon E. Scott Meml. award Drake U., 1958. Mem. Nat. Assn. Realtors, Assn. Indsl. Brokers of Chgo., Comml. Investment Real Estate Inst., CCIM (Ill. chpt. dir. 1980—), Jaycees (chpt. pres. 1965). Republican. Home: 609 W Willow St Chicago IL 60614 Office: Paine/Wetzel Assocs Inc 8700 W Bryn Mawr Ave Chicago IL 60631

BARNETT, MARGARET EDWINA, nephrologist, researcher; b. Ft. Benning, Ga., July 28, 1949; d. Eddie Lee and Margaret Thomas (Herndon) B. BS magna cum laude with distinction in Zoology, Ohio State U., 1969; MD, Johns Hopkins U., 1973; PhD in Cellular and Molecular Biology, Case Western Res. U., 1984; postgrad. Purdue U., 1992. Med. technologist blood bank Johns Hopkins Hosp., Balt., 1971-73; intern Greater Balt. Med. Ctr., Towson, Md., 1973-74; med. resident Cleve. Clinic Ednl. Found., 1974-75, Univ. Hosps. Cleve., 1975-76; nephrology fellow, 1976-78, med. teaching fellow, 1978-84; nephrology rounding physician Cmty. Dialysis Ctr., Cleve. and Mentor, Ohio, 1978-83; rsch. assoc. Case Western Res. U., Cleve., 1978-79, 83-84; physician emergency medicine Huron Regional Urgent Care Ctrs., Inc., Cleve., 1983-84; preceptor renal correlation conf., Case Western Res. Sch. Medicine, 1980-81, lectr. anatomy and histology 1979-83; asst. prof. medicine/nephrology Milton S. Hershey Med. Ctr. Pa. State U., Hershey, 1984-87, acting chief renal and electrolyte divsn., 1985, dir. peritoneal, 1986-87, assoc. dir. hypertension, 1986-87; pvt. practice medicine specializing in nephrology and hypertension Arnett Clinic, Lafayette, Ind., 1987-93; dir. outpatient dialysis St. Elizabeth Hosp. Med. Ctr., Lafayette; clin. assoc. faculty of Lafayette Ctr. Sch. Medicine Ind. U., 1987-93; clin. asst. prof. of medicine, Ind. U. Sch. Medicine, 1989-94, pharmacology clin. preceptor Purdue U., 1988-93; spl. guest lectr. hypertension Drug Cos., Ill., Ind., S.D., Ky., Ohio, Pa., 1988-94, Calif., 1995; assoc. dean rsch. and grad. studies Sch. Allied Health Scis. Ind. U., 1993-94, vis. prof. medicine dept. health info. adminstrn. Allied Health Scis., Ind., U., 1994; dir. dialysis svcs. King/Drew Med. Ctr., L.A., 1994—; asst. prof. medicine Charles R. Drew U., 1994—, asst. dir. nephrology fellowship program, 1995—; vis. prof. medicine dept. physical therapy Nat. Inst. Fitness and Sport, Ind. U., 1993-94; faculty mem. Nat. Bur. Info. on Coronary Heart Disease Risk, 1991-94, mem. cardiorenal subcom., 1995—; rep. rsch. and grad. studies alumni adv. coun. Ohio State U., 1990-93. Del. in nephrology and hypertension citizen amb. program People to People Internat. to Russia, Belarus and Lithuania, 1994, Chinese Med. Assn. 80th Anniversary, Beijing, 1995, active, 1994—. Scholar GM, Leo Yassinoff, Alpha Epsilon Delta, Beanie Drake, Am. Heart Assn., 1977; recipient NIH-Nat. Rsch. Svc. award, 1979-82; Ohio div. Am. Heart Assn. grantee, 1980-81; Ohio Kidney Found. grantee, 1977-78; Pres.'s Scholarship award, 1967-69; AMA Physician Recognition award, 1984-87, various medals for slalom racing. Fellow ACP; mem. John Hopkins Med. and Surg. Soc., AMA (physician rsch. evaluation panel 1981-83), Internat. Soc. of Nephrology, Assn. Black Cardiologists, Inc., Am. Soc. Hypertension, Nat. Kidney Found., Am. Acad. Med. Acupuncture (assoc.), World Tae Kwon Do Fedn., Seoul, Korea, Mensa, Am. Film Inst., Phi Beta Kappa, Alpha Epsilon Delta, Alpha Kappa Alpha. Democrat. Avocations: slalom racing, Tae Kwon Do (2d degree black belt). Office: King/Drew Med Ctr 12021 S Wilmington Ave 1140 W Michigan St Los Angeles CA 90059

BARNETT, MARILYN, advertising agency executive; b. Detroit; d. Henry and Kate (Boesky) Schiff; BA, Wayne State U.; children: Rhona, Ken. Founder, part-owner, pres. Mars Advt. Co., Southfield, Mich. Bd. dirs. Mich. Strategic Fund. Named Outstanding Retail Woman of Yr., Outstanding Retail Mktg. Exec. Mem. AFTRA (dir.), SAG, Exec. Women Am., Am. Women in Radio & TV (Top Agy. Mgmt. award, Outstanding Woman of Yr.), Internat. Women Forum, Women's Forum Club, Com. of 200, Women's Econ. Club (Ad Woman of Yr.), Adcraft. Office: MARS Advt 24209 Northwestern Hwy Southfield MI 48075-2551 also: MARS Advt Co 6671 W Sunset Blvd Ste 1591 Los Angeles CA 90028-7123

BARNETT, MARILYN DOAN, secondary education business educator; b. Trafalgar, Ind., Jan. 14, 1934; d. Roscoe James and Nellie Margaret (Betts) Doan; m. Joe A. Barnett, Mar. 23, 1952; 1 child, Michael Shayne. BS, Ball State U., 1965, MA, 1972. Cert. bus. tchr., Ind. Vocat. bus. tchr. John H. Hinds Area Vocat. Sch., Elwood, Ind., 1966-72; bus. tchr. Elwood Community High Sch., 1973-91, chair bus. dept., 1979-89; sponsor Future Bus. Leaders Am., Elwood, 1973-91. Mem. YMCA; vol. Meals on Wheels, Elwood. Mem. NEA, Ind. State Tchrs. Assn., Ind. Bus. Edn. Assn., Elwood Classroom Tchrs. Assn., Delta Kappa Gamma, Pi Omega Pi, Delta Pi Epsilon. Mem. Disciples of Christ Ch. Home: 9416 N Meadowlark Ln Elwood IN 46036

BARNETT, MARK WILLIAM, state attorney general; b. Sioux Falls, S.D., Sept. 6, 1954; s. Thomas C. and Dorothy Ann (Lievrance) B.; m. Deborah Ann Barnett, July 14, 1979. BS in Govt., U. S.D., 1976, JD, 1978. Bar: S.D. Pvt. practice law Sioux Falls, 1978-80; asst. atty. gen. State of S.D., Pierre, 1980-83, spl. prosecutor, 1984-90, atty. gen., 1990—; ptnr. Schmidt, Schroyer, Colwill and Barnett, Pierre, 1984-90; mem. S.D. Law Enforcement Tng. Commn., 1987—; mem. S.D. Bar Commn., 1986-88, 89-92, S.D. Corrections Commn., 1987. Bd. dirs. D.A.R.E., S.D. drug prevention prog., 1987—. Mem. S.D. Bar Assn. (pres. young lawyers' sect. 1985), Am. Judicature Soc. (nat. bd. dirs. 1984-88), State's Atty. Assn. (bd. dirs. 1987-90). Republican. Office: Office Atty Gen 500 E Capitol Ave Pierre SD 57501-5070*

BARNETT, MELINDA MONTGOMERY, counselor, psychology educator; b. Austin, Tex., Oct. 30, 1948; d. Bert Lamar and La Verne (Barton) Gentry; m. William Arnold Barnett, Sept. 1, 1991; children: Kimberly Taylor, Alicia Montgomery. BA in psychology, U. Tex., Austin, 1978; MEd, Southwest Tex. State U., 1980, specialists degree in sch. psychology, 1990. Therapist Tex. Sch. for Blind, Austin, 1978-79; unit counselor Austin State School, 1979-80; case mgr. Pilot Parents Program, Austin, 1988-89; sch. psychology intern Austin Sch. Dist., 1990, Balconies Sch. Dist., Travis County, Tex., 1990; assoc. clin. psychologist Travis State Sch., Austin, 1991; counselor, psychology instr. Belleville (Ill.) Area Coll., 1992—; telephone counselor Travis County Mental Health Hotline, Austin, 1979. Vol. coord. United Action for Elderly, Austin, 1985-88, Belleville Area Coll, 1992; sponsor Friends of Musk Ox, Alaska, 1994—. Mem. Am. Counseling Assn., Assn. Specialists in Group Work, Am. Mental Health Counselor Assn., People for Ethical Treatment of Animals, The Nature Conservatory, Psi Chi and Phi Kappa Phi honor societies. Home: 11030 Wellsley Ct Saint Louis MO 63146 Office: Belleville Area Coll 4950 Maryville Rd Granite City IL 62040

BARNETT, REX, state legislator. Mem. from dist. 4 Mo. State Ho. of Reps. Address: 708 W Lincoln Rm 116-A1 Maryville MO 64468

BARNETTE, JOSEPH D., JR., bank holding company executive; b. 1939. BA, Wabash Coll., 1961; MBA, Ind. U., 1968; postgrad., Rutgers U., 1972. With Am. Fletcher Nat. Bank & Trust, Indpls., 1962-69, 82—; pres., chief operating officer Am. Fletcher Nat. Bank & Trust, now Banc One, Indpls., NA subs. Banc One Corp., Indpls., 1982—, Banc One Ind. Corp. subs. Banc One Corp., Indpls., 1987—; sr. v.p., then pres., chief exec. officer First Nat. Bank, Evanston, Ill., 1969-76; pres., chief exec. officer Lakeview Trust and Savs. Bank, Chgo., 1976-81. Office: Banc One Ind Corp 101 Monument Cir Indianapolis IN 46277 also: Lake View Trust & Savs Bank 3201 N Ashland Ave Chicago IL 60657-2107 also: 100 E Broad St Columbus OH 43215-3607

BARNEY, EILEEN K., stockbroker; b. Grand Rapids, Mich., July 26, 1947. Assoc., Grand Rapids C.C., 1984. Sales asst. Robert Baird, Grand Rapids, 1977—. Office: Robert W Baird & Co Inc 333 Bridge St NW Ste 1000 Grand Rapids MI 49504-5356

BARNHART, BRUCE A., JR., stockbroker; b. Ann Arbor, Mich., Jan. 15, 1960; s. Bruce A. and Marcia A. (Bulliss) B.; m. Margaret Ford, June 8, 1985; children: Ally, Caley, Crosby. BA, Northwestern U., 1982, MS, 1984. Reporter Sta. WWMT-TV, Grand Rapids, Mich., 1984-87; stockbroker Edward D. Jones & Co., St. Louis, 1987-89, A.G. Edwards & Sons Inc., St. Louis, 1989—. Recipient award for best fin. reporting series Internat. Assn. Fin. Planning, 1992. Mem. Northwestern U. Alumni Assn., Algonquin Country Club. Republican. Roman Catholic. Home: 12320 Dunmorr Dr Saint Louis MO 63131-3832 Office: AG Edwards & Sons Inc 1 City Ctr Ste 1300 Saint Louis MO 63101-1893

BARNHILL, JEAN ELIZABETH, office manager, personnel officer; b. Slinger, Wis., Apr. 21, 1952; d. Robert G. and Irma C. (Kurtz) Mayer; m. Theodore A. Barnhill, June 30, 1973 (div.); 1 child, Meagan Ann. With Dept. Vocat. Rehab., State of Minn., St. Paul, 1970-80; adminstrv. sec. Children's Hosp., Milw., 1980-81; office mgr., pers. officer Legis. Auditor, State of Minn., Milw., 1981—. Mem. Amery (Wis.) Pub. Schs. Bd. of Edn., 1989—, pres., 1995—. Mem. Indianhead Miniature Horse Club (v.p. 1994-95, newsletter editor 1995). Home: 398 95th St Clear Lake WI 54005

BARNHOUSE, LILLIAN MAY PALMER, retired medical surgical nurse, researcher, civic worker; b. Canton, Ohio, Sept. 26, 1918; d. Frank Barnard and Jenny Mildred (Leggett) Shear; m. Arnold Barnhouse, June 26, 1940; 1 child, James Wilson. Diploma, Aultman Hosp. Sch. Nursing, Canton, 1939. RN, Ohio, obstetrics specialty. Supr., 1943-44; nurse physician's office Canton, Ohio, 1943-49; ind. critical care nursing local hosps., 1953-68. Instr., blood bank worker ARC, 1940-70; mem. Rep. Nat Com., 1980—; vol. genetic researcher, 1972—; vol. in community. Mem. Ohio Nurses Assn. (past v.p., past chmn. dist. legis. com.), First Families of Ohio, Ladies Oriental Shrine.

BARNICK, HELEN, retired judicial clerk; b. Max, N.D., Mar. 24, 1925; d. John K. and Stacy (Kankovsky) B. BS in Music Edn. cum laude, Minot State Coll., 1954; postgrad., Am. Conservatory of Music, Chgo., 1975-76. With Epton, Bohling & Druth, Chgo., 1968-69; sec. Wildman, Harrold, Allen & Dixon, Chgo., 1969-75; part-time assignments for temporary agy. Chgo., 1975-77; sec. Friedman & Koven, Chgo., 1977-78; with Lawrence, Lawrence, Kamin & Saunders, Chgo., 1978-81; sec. Hinshaw, Culbertson et al., Chgo., 1982; sec. to magistrate judge U.S. Dist. Ct. (we. dist.) Wis., Madison, 1985-91; dep. clk., case adminstr. U.S. Bankruptcy Ct. (we. dist.) Wis., Madison, 1992-94; ret., 1994. Mem. chancel choir 1st Bapt. Ch., Mpls.; mem. choir, dir. sr. high choir Moody Ch., Chgo.; mem. chancel choir Fourth Presbyn. Ch., Chgo., Covenant Presbyn. Ch., Madison; dir. chancel choir 1st Bapt. Ch., Minot, N.D.; bd. dirs., sec.-treas. Peppertree at Tamarack Owners Assn., Inc., Wisconsin Dells, Wis.; mem. Festival Choir, Madison. Mem. Christian Bus. and Profl. Women (chmn.), Bus. and Profl. Women Assn., Sigma Sigma Sigma. Home: 7364 Old Sauk Rd Madison WI 53717-1213

BARNUM, SALLY J., librarian; b. Patterson Heights, Pa., Apr. 20, 1949; d. Forrest E. and Gladys A. (Currey) Justis; m. Terry M. Barnum, June 4, 1969; 1 child, Leah. BA, Adrian Coll., 1969; MLS, Rosary Coll., 1971. Cataloger, transp. libr. Northwestern U., Evanston, Ill., 1971-77; dir. libr./records United Way/Crusade of Mercy, Chgo., 1977—. Office: United Way Crusade of Mercy 560 W Lake St Chicago IL 60661

BARR, DIXIE LOU, geriatrics nurse; b. Butler, Ohio, Mar. 11, 1934; d. Gerald Edward and Aldine Marie (Barre) Beam; children: Daniel, Dennis, Denise. Lic. practical nurse, Timken-Mercy Hosp., Canton, Ohio, 1971; ADN, Walsh Coll., Canton, 1990. Charge nurse Wyandot County Nursing Home, 1994-95; DON Atwood Manor, Galion, Ohio, 1995—. Home: 855 S Hazel St Apt 4 Upper Sandusky OH 43351-9409 Office: Atwood Manor Nursing Ctr 347 W Atwood St Galion OH 44833

BARR, GINGER, business owner, former state legislator; b. Kansas City, Mo., Dec. 4, 1947; d. W.M. and Ann (Armstrong) Barr; m. Edwin P. Carpenter, Jan. 2, 1984. BS, Baker U., Baldwin, Kans., 1969. Tchr. secondary edn., 1969-71; cemetery mgmt. Topeka Cemetery, Kans., 1971-76, Maplewood/Meml. Lawn Cemeteries, 1973-80, v.p., Graceland/Fairlawn Cemeteries, Decatur, Ill., 1976-94, pres., 1994—. Rep. Kans. State Legislature, 1983-91, vice chmn. fed. and state affairs com., 1987-89, chmn., 1989-91; pres. Crifter Care Co., 1987—; bd. dirs. World Topeka Famous Zoo, 1986-91, Humane Soc., Topeka, 1983-87, Shawnee County Mainstream Coalition, edn. chmn, 1995—; mem. Jr. League, Topeka, 1985; trustee Baker U., 1986-90; v.p. Topeka Blood Bank, 1991-93, pres., 1992, 93; active Auburn Community Action Project, 1993. Mem. Am. Cemetery Assn. (dir. 1980-82, sec. 1980-83), Kans. Cemetery Assn. (pres. 1979-80), Kans. Young Reps. (chmn. 1977-79), Ill. Cemetery Assn. (bd. dirs. 1994-95, v.p. 1995, pres. 1996). Republican. Home: 9421 SW Hoch Rd Auburn KS 66402-9664

BARR, JAMES, IV, publishing executive, book; b. Ames, Iowa, July 4, 1962; s. James III and Joan (Benning) B.; m. Linda S. Barr; children: Kaitlin H., James V. BS in Acctg., Miami U., Oxford, Ohio, 1984; MBA, U. Chgo., 1990. CPA, Ill. Sr. acct. Ernst & Whinney, Chgo., 1984-87; v.p. internal audit Rodman & Renshaw, Inc., Chgo., 1987-89, v.p., asst. to chmn., 1989-90; mgr. corp. fin. consulting Ernst & Young, Chgo., 1990-92; v.p. strategic planning and analysis Ency. Britannica, Chgo., 1992—. Mem. Union League Club Chgo. Office: Ency Britannica 310 S Michigan Ave Chicago IL 60604

BARR, MARLENE JOY, volunteer; b. Grosse Pointe Farms, Mich., Feb. 25, 1935; d. Max John and Viola Christina (Funke) Bielenberg; m. John Monte Barr, Dec. 17, 1954; children: John Monte Jr., Karl Alexander, Elizabeth Marie Letter. Student, Mex. City Coll., 1955; BA, Mich. State U., 1956; MA, Ea. Mich. U., 1959. Cert. elem. edn. Tchr. A.G. Erickson Sch., Ypsilanti, Mich., 1956-66; chair 5th grade tchrs., sec. curriculum coun. Ypsilanti Pub. Schs., 1961-66; receptionist Barr, Anhut, and Assoc., P.C., Ann Arbor, Mich., 1989-95; vol. Thrift Shop Assn. of Ypsilanti, 1969—; block coord. Ypsilanti Recycling, 1990—; bookkeeper, 1996—. Mem. Fletcher Sch. Adv. Coun., 1980-81, Ann Arbor Power Squadron, 1965—; mem. chancel choir Emmanuel Luth. Ch., 1980—, youth coord., 1983-89, sec. youth standing com. , 1983-89, ch. coun. 1986-90, endowment com. sec. 1995—; v.p. Thrift Shop Assn. Ypsilanti, 1979-81, pres. 1981-83, scheduling chmn. 1993—; bd. dirs. Ypsilanti Cmty. Choir, 1984—; asst. leader Girl Scouts U.S., 1978-81; sec. troop 290 Boy Scouts Am., 1989-95; rm. mother Fletcher Elem. Sch. Ypsilanti, 1982-83, High/scope Ednl. Rsch. Found. Endowment Bd., 1993-96. Mem. AAUW (life), chmn. gourmet arts study group 1968—), Ann Arbor Women's City Club (chmn. ways and means com. 1995—), Friends of the Ypsilanti Dist. Libr., Depot Town Assn., Law Wives of Washtenaw County (editor 1970-72), Ladies Lit. Club (corr. sec. 1976-78), sec. bd. trustees 1982-86, v.p. 1986-90, pres. 1990-92, treas., bd. trustees 1992—), Chandler Birthday Club (treas. 1990), Ypsilanti Hist. Soc. (life) (P.E.O., chaplain 1991-93), Ann Arbor Power Squadron of U.S. Power Squadron, Ann Arbor Bike Touring Soc. (co-chair One Hell of a Ride 1995), Alpha Delta Kappa (pres. Beta Zeta chpt. 1965-68, historian 1986-88, pres. area X pres. coun. Mich. ADK chpt. 1966-68). Lutheran. Home: 1200 Whittier Rd Ypsilanti MI 48197-2152 Office: Barr Anhut and Assoc PC 105 Pearl St Ypsilanti MI 48197

BARR, RICHARD GARY, radiologist, chemist; b. Youngstown, Ohio, May 25, 1956; s. Frank W. and Minnie (Fognini) B. BS, Ohio State U., 1978; PhD, Mich. State U., 1981; MD, Case-Western Res. U., 1985. Diplomate Am. Bd. Radiology. Intern Univ. Hosps. of Cleve., 1985-86; resident in diagnostic radiology Cleve. Clinic Found., 1986-90; adj. instr. dept. biochemistry Case Western Res. U., Cleve., 1986-91; clin. instr. radiology U. Calif., San Francisco, 1990-91; fellow U. Calif.-San Francisco Gen. Hosp., 1990-91; adj. rsch. radiologist U. Calif., San Francisco, 1991—; dir. ultrasound and computed tomography St. Elizabeth's Med. Ctr., Youngstown, Ohio, 1991—; assoc. prof. radiology Coll. Medicine Northeastern Ohio U., 1996—; adj. asst. prof. chemistry Youngstown (Ohio) State U. Contbr. articles to profl. publs. Mem. Am. Coll. Radiology, Am. Inst. Chemists', Am. Inst. Ultrasound in Medicine, Soc. Magnetic Resonance in Medicine, Radiol. Soc. N.Am., Soc. Radiologists in Ultrasound. Home: 671 Robinson Rd Campbell OH 44405-2029 Office: Dept Radiology St Elizabeth Med Ctr 1044 Belmont Ave Youngstown OH 44504-1006

BARR, SANFORD LEE, dentist; b. Chgo., Jan. 18, 1952; s. Mike and Bernice (Kaplan) B.; m. Randy Joyce Briskman, Dec. 24, 1973; children: Shelby Paige, Blake Jared, Taylor Ashley. BS, U. Ill., 1972; DDS, Northwestern U., 1976. Resident gen. practice VA Hosp., Chgo., 1976-77; gen. practice dentistry Chgo., 1977—; attending dentist Rush Med. Coll., Chgo., 1977—; asst. prof. Presbyn.-St. Luke's Hosp., Chgo., 1977—, Northwestern U. Sch. Dentistry, Chgo., 1977-83; cons. VA Hosp., Chgo., 1978—. Mem. adv. bd. Homehealth of Ill. Chgo., 1984—. Fellow Acad. Gen. Dentistry, Acad. Facial Aesthetics; mem. ADA, Acad. Hosp. Dentistry, Chgo. Dental Soc., Alpha Omega (treas. 1984, pres. elect 1988), Tau Delta Phi. Jewish. Lodge: B'nai B'rith (v.p. Chgo. chpt. 1984—). Home: 632 Dauphine Ct Northbrook IL 60062-2256 Office: 25 E Washington St Chicago IL 60602

BARR, WILLIAM CRAWFORD, manufacturing company executive; b. Omaha, Sept. 26, 1944; s. Bradley and Barbara Louise (Kinsler) B.; m. Donna Lea Ingram, Apr. 8, 1989. BS in Feed Tech., Kans. State U., 1967. Salesperson Bradley Barr & Co., Kansas City, Mo., 1967-68; ptnr. C. Bradley Barr & Assocs., Overland Park, Kans., 1970-73; pres. Bill Barr & Co., Inc., Overland Park, 1974—. Bd. dirs. Big Bros./Big Sisters of Kansas City, Mo., 1991—. With U.S. Army Intelligence, 1968-70. Mem. Am. Feed Industries Assn. (exec. bd. dirs. 1992—, sec. ingredient suppliers exec. coun. 1994—), Nat. Feed Ingredients Assn. (bd. dirs. 1987-91), Kansas Feed Mfg. Assn. (pres. 1975-76), Kansas City Feed Club (pres. 1977-78). Office: Bill Barr & Co Inc # 101 8725 Rosehill Rd Lenexa KS 66215

BARRADA, AMR, psychotherapist; b. Cairo, Oct. 9, 1938; came to U.S., 1962; s. Hassan and Makarem (Wassef) B.; 1 child from previous marriage, Mona Mae. BA in English, Cairo U., 1959; MA in English, Am. U., Cairo, 1963; PhD in English, U. Minn., 1970; MA in Psychology, Fielding Inst., Santa Barbara, Calif., 1991. Teaching asst. Cairo U., 1959-62; teaching assoc. U. Minn., Mpls., 1963-70; asst. prof. Williams Coll., Williamstown, Mass., 1970-74; fgn. student counselor 916 Vo-Tech., Mahtomedi, Minn., 1975-78; asst. therpaist Ctr. for Behavior Therapy, Mpls., 1979-82; psychotherapist Abbott-Northwestern Hosp., Mpls., 1982—. Author: Embracing the Fear, 1994. Mem. APA, Minn. Psychol. Assn., Anxiety Disorders Assn. Am. Home: 1920 E 86th St # 126 Bloomintong MN 55425-2127 Office: Abbott-Northwestern Hosp 800 E 28th St Minneapolis MN 55407

BARRAT-GORDON, RENE, social worker; b. Utica, N.Y., May 9, 1955; d. Joseph and Helen (Korman) B.; m. Armand Grunberger, July 9, 1979 (div. Feb. 1990); 1 child, Monique Jacqueline; m. Lawrence Gordon, June 23, 1991; 1 child, Jenna Michelle. Student, Miami U., Oxford, Ohio, 1973-75; BSW, Ohio State U., 1976; M Social Sci. Adminstrn., Case Western Res. U., 1979. Lic. ind. social worker, Ohio. Social worker neurosurg and trauma units Cleve. Met. Gen. Hosp., 1979-87; social worker neuro-oncology unit Cleve. Clin. Found., 1987-93, social worker out-patient oncology, 1993—; adj. prof. Case We. Res. U. Sch. Applied Social Sci., Cleve., 1980—, instr. continuing edn., 1988; active Cleve. Area Head Injury Found., 1980-90; cons., Cleve., 1987-89. Contbr. articles to profl. jours. Vice pres. Pioneer Women, Cleve., 1985-87, fundraiser, 1986-88. Bruce H. Stewart fellow, 1994-95. Mem. NASW (chmn. practice and knowledge com. 1983-85), Acad. Cert. Social Workers, Nat. Orgn. Oncology Social Work. Home: 2155

Halcyon Rd Beachwood OH 44122-1301 Office: Cleveland Clinic Found 9500 Euclid Ave Cleveland OH 44195-0001

BARRESI, FRANK M., investment broker; b. St. Louis, July 11, 1953; s. Joseph J. and Dorothy M. (Swayze) B.; m. Stephanie Samuals. BA, U. Mo., 1976. Broker Dean Whitter, Chesterfield, Mo., 1983-87, Payne Webber, Chesterfield, 1987-92; investment broker Prudential Securities Inc., Chesterfield, 1992—. Mem. New Covenant Ch. Home: 15506 Cloverich Dr Chesterfield MO 63017 Office: Prudential Securities Inc 14528 S Outer 40 Chesterfield MO 63017-5743

BARRETT, ALFRED H., electrical engineer; b. N.Y.C., Mar. 4, 1941. BSEE, Worcester (Mass.) Poly. Inst., 1963, MSEE, 1965; PhD, U. R.I., 1970. From elec. engr. to staff engr. Delco Electronics, Kokomo, Ind., 1970—; ind. cons., Kokomo, 1985—. Patentee in field. Mem. Sigma Xi.

BARRETT, CAROLYN HERNLY, paralegal; b. Geneva, Ill., Jan. 17, 1954; d. Wayne Francis and Genevieve (Moyer) Hernly; m. Bradley Clayton Barrett, June 20, 1976; children: Heather Hernly, Lance Clayton, Colin Courtney. Grad., Moser Bus. Coll., 1975; BS in Bus. Mgmt., Nat.-Louis U., 1996. Legal sec. Rathje, Woodward, Dyer & Burt, Wheaton, Ill., 1975-77; paralegal Chadwell, Kayser, Ruggles, McGee & Hastings, Chgo., 1978-80, Patrick James Perretti, Glen Ellyn, Ill., 1992-94, 96—. Pres. Forest Glen PTA, Glen Ellyn, 1988-90; mem. Rep. Senatorial Innter Cir., Washington, 1991—, Nat. Trust for Hist. Preservation; chair ways and means com. Glen Ellyn Hist. Soc., 3d v.p., 1992—. Recipient Medal of Freedom, Rep. Senatorial Inner Cir., 1994. Mem. DAR, Nat. Fedn. Rep. Women, Women in Arts (charter). Presbyterian. Home: 675 N Main St Glen Ellyn IL 60137-4045

BARRETT, FREDERICK CHARLES, engineering executive; b. Chgo., Apr. 1, 1949; s. Robert D. and Phyllis S. (Paul) B.; m. Wendy Lynn Freyer; 1 child, Richard. BSEE, Iowa State U., 1972; MBA with high honors, Lake Forest Grad. Sch. Mgmt., 1988. Registered profl. engr., Ill.; cert. Novell engr., 1995. Project. engr. Motorola, Inc., Schaumburg, Ill., 1972-76; sales rep. Computer Automation, Inc., Elk Grove Village, Ill., 1976-77; product engr. Entron Controls, Inc., Carol Stream, Ill., 1977-79; staff engr. AM Multigraphics, Mt. Prospect, Ill., 1979-81; sr. engr. Extel Corp., Northbrook, Ill., 1981-84; staff engr. Bell & Howell Co., Lincolnwood, Ill., 1984-88; dir. engr. Associated Rsch., Inc., Lake Bluff, Ill., 1988-94; pres. Project Works, Inc., Vernon Hills, Ill., 1994—; instr. Coll. Lake County, Grayslake, Ill., 1984. Patentee in field. Eugene Hotchkiss scholar Lake Forest Grad. Sch. Mgmt., 1988. Mem. IEEE. Office: Proejct Works Inc Ste 330 262 Hawthorn Village Common Vernon Hills IL 60061

BARRETT, JAMES ALLAN, photographer, author, lyricist, business owner; b. St. Louis, Oct. 9, 1942; s. James Roscoe amd Gwendolyn (Roberts) B.; m. Albertine Carter; 1 child, Mary Moore; 4 stepchildren. Grad. high school, Denver, 1963. Case worker St. Louis Juvenile Ct. and Detention Ctr., 1971-77; bus operator Bi-State Transit, St. Louis, 1979-81; mail sorter U.S. Post Office, St. Louis, 1982-90; prin., photographer Barrett of Beverly Hills ... 90210, 1990—; prin. J. Allan Barrett Group, St. Louis, 1991—; photographer Little Richard, 1990, Mayor of City of St. Louis, 1993, Pres. Bill Clinton, 1994, Million Man March, 1995. Author: (autobiography) Not An Average Guy, 1985, Writing for Profit and Thinking for Success, 1990, Reforming The Juvenile Corruption System, 1993, The People's Own Story, 1994. Democrat. Office: Barrett of Beverly Hills 90210 PO Box 15704 Beverly Hills CA 90210

BARRETT, JAMES ROBERT, history educator, writer; b. Chgo., June 14, 1950; s. Thomas Eugene and Catherine Marie (Ellis) B.; m. Jane May Wong, Aug. 14, 1971; 1 child, Sean Eugene. AB in History with honors, U. Ill., Chgo., 1972; MA in Comparative Labor History, U. Warwick, Coventry, Eng., 1974; PhD in History, U. Pitts., 1981. Asst. prof. history N.C. State U., Raleigh, 1981-84; prof. U. Ill., Urbana, 1984—, assoc. chair dept. history, 1988-90, 91-93; mem. exec. com. Union of Profl. Employees, Champaign, Ill., 1985—, pres., 1994—. Author: Work and Community in the Jungle, 1987 (Ill. State Hist. Soc. book award, 1988); co-author: Steve Nelson, American Radical, 1981; editor: The Jungle, 1988. Univ. scholar U. Ill., 1990-93; Lloyd Lewis fellow Newberry Libr., Chgo., 1990-91. Mem. Am. Hist. Assn., Orgn. Am. Historians, Ill. State Hist. Soc. (bd. dirs. 1989-92), Marho-The Radical Historians Assn. Socialist. Roman Catholic. Office: U Ill Dept History 810 S Wright St Urbana IL 61801-1447

BARRETT, JEFFREY SCOTT, real estate company executive; b. Elgin, Ill., Dec. 12, 1949; s. Charles Clayton and Dorothy Grace (Smith) B.; m. Mary Ferriss Vincent, July 24, 1971; children: Elizabeth Towne, Chad Brayton. BS, Drake U., 1971. Loan officer, v.p. Greenebaum Mortgage Co., Chgo., 1971-76; with CB Comml. Real Estate Group, Chgo., 1976—, real estate fin. officer, sales mgr., v.p., resident mgr.; 1st v.p., resident mgr. CB Comml. Real Estate Group; sr. v.p., sr. mng. officer CB Comml. Real Estate Group, Chgo. Mem. Chgo. Real Estate Coun. (pres. 1982), Chgo. Office Leasing Brokers Assn. (sec. 1992), Meadow Club, Chgo. Soc. of Clubs, Glen Oak County Club. Republican. Presbyterian. Home: 1114 Irving St Wheaton IL 60187-3843 Office: CB Comml Real Estate Group 1900 E Golf Rd Schaumburg IL 60173-5834

BARRETT, MARILYN WOODY, nursing administrator, educator, business consultant; b. Portsmouth, Va., Dec. 1, 1949; married; children. BSN, U. Md., Balt., 1972; MA, Cen. Mich. U., 1982; MPA, U. So. Calif., L.A., 1985, D of Pub. Adminstrn., 1986. RN, Md., Va. Assoc. prof. pub. adminstrn. Cen. Mich. U., Mt. Pleasant, 1986—; cons.; bd. dirs. The Nursing Spectrum, 1991—. Lt. col. USAR, ret. Mem. ANA (cert. in nursing adminstrn.), Phi Kappa Phi, Sigma Theta Tau.

BARRETT, MICHAEL JOHN, anesthesiologist; b. Milw., Feb. 27, 1954; s. Walter Joseph and Valerie Clara (Wisniewski) Baclawski; m. Joan Marie Rowley, May 28, 1983; children: Michael J. Jr., Jessica Marie, Monica Jane. BS in math. with honors, U. Wis., 1974; MD, Med. Coll. Wis., 1981. Diplomate Am. Bd. Anesthesiology, Nat. Bd. Medicine and Surgery, Nat. Bd. Med. Examiners, Am. Acad. Pain Mgmt., Am. Bd. Anesthesiology Pain Mgmt. Intern Med. Coll. Wis. Affiliated Hosps., Milw., 1981, resident in anesthesiology, 1982-84; dir. anesthesiology Putnam Community Hosp., Palatka, Fla., 1984-92, dir. Putnam Pain Ctr., 1985-92; pres. Putnam Anesthesia Assocs., Palatka, 1985-92; staff anesthesiologist St. Vincent Med. Ctr., Toledo, 1992—, dir. Pain Mgmt. Ctr., 1995—. Bd. dirs. Round Lake Park Homeowners Assn., Palatka, 1986-88. Walter Zeit fellow; recipient St. Vincents Physician Excellence award, 1996. Mem. AMA, Internat. Anesthesia Rsch. Soc., Am. Soc. Anesthesiologists, Am. Soc. Regional Anesthesiologists, Ohio Med. Assn., Acad. Medicine of Toledo and Lucas County, Ohio Soc. Anesthesiologists, Putnam County Med. Soc. (pres. 1989-91), Phi Beta Kappa, Phi Kappa Phi. Republican. Roman Catholic. Home: 8646 Plum Hollow Pt Holland OH 43528-8487 Office: Assoc Anesthesiologists 2409 Cherry St Ste 4 Toledo OH 43608-2600

BARRETT, THOMAS M., congressman; b. Milwaukee, Wis., Dec. 8, 1953; m. Kristine Barrett; children: Thomas John, Anne Elizabeth. BA in Economics, U. Wis., 1976, JD with honors, 1980. Atty. Smith & O'Neill, Milw., 1982-84; mem. Wis. State Assembly, 1984-89, Wis. State Senate from 5th Dist., 1989-92, 103rd Congress from 5th Wis. dist., Washington, D.C., 1993—; chmn. Com. on Elections, 1987, Com. on Health, 1988-89, Devel. Disabilities Law Legislative Coun. Com., 1988, Long Term Health Care Ins. Legislative Coun. Com., 1988; chmn. Trial Court System Funding Legislative Coun. Com., 1990; mem. Banking & Fin. Svcs. Com., Govt. Reform & Oversight Com. Bd. dirs. Sojourner Truth House, Shalom High Sch., Transcenter Home for Youth. Recipient Circle of Friends award Milw. Advocates for Retarded Citizens, 1989, Health Leadership award State Med. Soc., Govt. Leadership award Rehab. for Wis.; named to Clean Sixteen list for environ. voting record by Wis. Environ. Decade, 1987, 89, 90. Mem. Wis. Bar Assn., Phi Beta Kappa. Office: US Ho Reps 1224 Longworth Washington DC 20515-4905

BARRETT, WILLIAM E., congressman; b. Lexington, Nebr., Feb. 9, 1929; s. Harold O. and Helen Stuckey B.; m. Elsie L. Carlson, 1952; children: William C., Elizabeth A., David H., Jane M. AB, Hastings (Nebr.) Coll., 1951; grad., Nebr. Realtors Inst. Cert. real estate broker, Nebr. Admissions counselor Hastings Coll., 1952-54, asst. dir. admissions, 1954-56; ptnr. Barrett Agy., Lexington, 1956-59; pres. Barrett-Housel & Assocs., Inc., 1970-90; former pres. Dawson County Young Rep.; del. Rep. Co. Conv., from 1958; mem. Nebr. Rep. State Exec. Com., 1964-66; chmn., formerly mem. Rep. Nat. Com., state coord. Mobilization of Rep. Enterprise Programs, 1965-66; del. Rep. Nat. Conv., 1968; mem. Nebr. State Legislature, 1979-90, speaker, 1987-90; mem. 102nd-103rd Congresses from 3rd Nebr. Dist., 1991—; work in campaigns for various rep. candidate, 1960; officer Barrett-Housel & Assocs., Inc., 1969—; dir. Farmers State Bank; chmn. Ag. subcom. on Gen. Farm Commodities; mem. Econ. & Ednl. Opportunity Com. Trustee, cofounder Nebr. Real Estate Polit. Edn. Com.; elder First Presbyn. Ch., Lexington; moderator Presbytery of Platte, 1972-73, chmn. gen. coun., 1973, mem. staff nominating com. Synod of Lakes and Prairies, from 1973. With USN, 1951-52. Named Legislator of Yr. Nat. Rep. Legislators Assn., 1990. Mem. Nebr. Assn. Ins. Agts., Nat. Assn. Ins. Agts., Dawson Co. Bd. Realtors, Nebr. Assn. Realtors, Nat. Assn. Realtors, Nebr. Jaycees (named one of three outstanding young men of Nebr. 1962), Rotary (Lexington). Office: Offices of House Mems US Ho of Reps 1213 Longworth Washington DC 20515

BARRIE, LEE JOHN, address management systems specialist; b. Sleepy Eye, Minn., Apr. 17, 1950; s. Meddie Jerome and Regina G. (Van Dromme) B.; m. Francine Marie Schiro, July 4, 1970; children: Krista Marie, Bradley Mitchell. Letter carrier U.S. Postal Svc., Rockford, Ill., 1970—; advisor, bd. dirs. Rockford Postal Employees Credit Union, 1994—. Author: Fantasy and Science Fiction Index, 1988. Mem. Nat. Assn. Postal Carriers (computer cons. 1993-95, treas. 1983-87, trustee 1971-83), Nat. Assn. Postal Suprs. Democrat. Roman Catholic.

BARRIGER, JOHN WALKER, IV, transportation executive; b. St. Louis, Aug. 3, 1927; s. John Walker and Elizabeth Chambers (Thatcher) B.; m. Evelyn Dobson, Dec. 29, 1955; children: John Walker V, Catherine Brundige. BS, MIT, 1949; CT, Yale U., 1950. With Santa Fe Ry., 1950-68, 70-83, GTE Sylvania Info. Systems, 1968-70, Santa Fe Pacific Corp., 1983-85, Venango River Corp and Chgo. Mo. and Western Ry., 1986-90; v.p. Derson Group Ltd., 1990—. Trustee John W. Barriger III Nat. R.R. Libr., St. Louis; bd. dirs. St. Louis Merc. Libr. Served with USN, 1946. Recipient Bronze Beaver award MIT, 1975. Mem. Am. Assn. R.R. Supts., Am. Ry. Engring. Assn., Ry. Planning Officers Assn., Roadmasters and B&B Assn., Transp. Rsch. Forum, Western Ry. Club, Newcomen Soc., MIT Alumni Assn., Econ. Club. Chgo., Exec. Club Chgo., MIT Club Chgo., Kenilworth Club, Union League Chgo., Sheridan Shores Yacht Club, Delta Kappa Epsilon. Republican. Roman Catholic. Home: 155 Melrose Ave Kenilworth IL 60043-1248 Office: 332 S Michigan Ave Ste 700 Chicago IL 60604-4303

BARRINGTON, RODNEY CRAIG, financial executive; b. Chgo., Dec. 8, 1953; s. John David and Anna (Harris) B.; m. Paula Spivey, June 1993. Student, Northwestern U., 1974-78. Vice pres. NAC subs. Walter E. Heller Co., Chgo., 1972-84; v.p., mgr. IFC Corp., Chgo., 1984-86; v.p., gen. mgr. asset base loan div. Oak Brook (Ill.) Bank, 1986-87; v.p. NBD Bus. Fin., Inc., Highland Park, Ill., 1987-88; v.p., dir. The Randolph Group, Inc., Chgo., 1988-89; mng. dir., prin. Stonebridge Capital Group, Chgo., 1989—. Office: Stonebridge Capital Group 150 N Wacker Dr Chicago IL 60606-1611

BARRON, D. DOUGLAS, engineering executive; b. Anderson, Ind., Apr. 5, 1942. BS, GM Inst., 1965; MS, Rensaelar Poly. Inst., 1966. Registered profl. engr., Ind. Mgr. product engring. Delco Remy, Anderson, 1960—. Vol., bd. dirs. Jr. Achievement; chmn. adminstrv. bd. local church. Mem. SME, Optimists Club.

BARRON, ROBERTA, human resources management consultant; b. N.Y.C., May 11, 1940; d. Irv and Roslyn (Engerow) Yellin; m. Harold S. Barron, Nov. 17, 1963; children: Lawrence Ira, Jean Louise. Student, UCLA, 1960-61; BA, Conn. Coll., 1962; MSIR, Loyola U., Chgo., 1987. Corp. pub. dept. staff Time Inc., N.Y.C., 1962-64; pub. relations cons., 1965-87; cons. Exec. Assets, Chgo., 1987-88, Barron Assocs., Chgo., 1988—. Mem. IAOP, Women's Athletic Club. Office: 180 E Pearson St Chicago IL 60611-2130

BARROW, GEOFFREY RIDLEY, Spanish language educator; b. Wallasey, Cheshire, Eng., Jan. 23, 1944; s. John and Beryl Freda Pomfrett (Darbyshire) B.; m. Arleen May Zanetto, May 31, 1969; children: Catherine, Anne Mary, John William. BA, Leeds U., U.K., 1966; AM, Brown U., Providence, 1968, PhD, 1971. Lectr. U. Madrid, Colegio Mayor, 1964-65; instr. Brown U., Providence, 1968-70; mem. faculty Columbia U., N.Y.C., 1971-79, Ripon (Wis.) Coll., 1979-83; univ. grants resource person Purdue U. Calumet Campus, Hammond, Ind., 1985-88; dept. head dept. fgn. langs. Purdue U. Calumet Campus, Hammond, 1983-89, prof. Spanish, 1988—; cons. Chgo. area businesses, 1979—; project dir. U.S. Dept. Edn. Title II grant/demo and exemplary programs, 1985-86; lang. tester State of Ill., 1988—; mem. fgn. lang. adv. coun. State of Ind., 1986-90. Author: Satiric Vision of Blas de Otero, 1988; contbr. articles and trans. to nat. and internat. profl. jours. Skipper Sea Explorers, Boy Scouts Am., Ind. Harbor Ship 1, 1991-94. Brown U. fellow, 1966-68, 70-71, Columbia U. Chamberlain fellow, 1976, Lilly Open Faculty fellow Lilly Endowment, 1991-92. Mem. Internat. Assn. Hispanists, Assn. Hispanists Gt. Britain and No. Ireland, Ind. Sailing Assn. (commodore 1990—), USCG Aux. (hon.). Home: 9136 Crestwood Ct Munster IN 46321-4100

BARROW, ROGER G., securities company executive; b. Centralia, Ill., July 23, 1952; s. James C. and Mertle M. (Garner) B.; m. Cindy J. Grisham, May 24, 1974; children: Michael, Amanda. AA, Cascasky Coll., Centralia, 1993. Mgr. Prudential Securities, Centralia, 1987—. Sgt. USAF, 1971-75. Mem. Life Underwriters, Rotary. Baptist. Home: 35 Cessna Dr Centralia IL 62801-6510 Office: Prudential Securities Inc 1303 N Elm St PO Box 573 Centralia IL 62801

BARROWS, SCOTT THORN, medical illustrator; b. Chgo., June 14, 1952; s. Glendon L. and Mabel R. (Thorn) B.; m. Jo L. Barrows, Feb. 23, 1974; children: Carrie L., Justin T., Lauren E. BS with honors, U. Ill. Med. Ctr., 1976; postgrad., U. Tex. S.W. Med. Ctr., 1976-83. Cert. med. illustrator. Media producer Luth. Gen. Hosp., Park Ridge, Ill., 1974-76; asst. prof. U. Tex. S.W. Med. Ctr., Dallas, 1976-83; med. art dir. Hamilton, Carver & Lee, Chgo., 1983-84; Cl asst. prof. U. Ill. at Chgo. Med. Ctr., 1983—; pres. Med. Art Assocs., Lisle, Naperville, Ill., 1978—, Dallas, 1978—; bd. dirs. Lisle Found. Edn. Excellence; designer Chgo. White Sox Uniform, 1991; creator/developer Aging Photos of Missing Children, 1985; med. illustrator Am. Acad. of Orthopaedic Surg., Rosemont, Ill., 1993—. Illustrator: Prac. Colon Surgery, 1992 (Best Illustration book 1992); artist mural Edward Hosp., 1993. Bd. dirs. Citizens Adv. Coun. Bd. Edn., Lisle, 1991-93. Named Outstanding Alumnus U. Ill. Chgo., 1988; recipient Elmer Friman award HeSCA, 1978, Gold medal N.Y. Advt. Club, 1988, Comeback of Yr. Nat. Found. Illeitis and Colitis, 1987. Fellow Assn. of Med. Illustrators (bd. govs.); mem. U. Ill. Alumni Assn. (life mem., bd. dirs. 1990-92), Ill. State Univ. Parents Assn., Nat. Right To Life Assn., U. Ill. at Chgo. Alumni Assn. (bd. dirs. 1988-90, 92-94). Republican. Home and office: Med Art Assocs 5182 Cypress Ct Lisle IL 60532

BARRY, AILEEN ELLA (ALISA BARRY), poet, songwriter, retired practical nurse; b. Jamesport, Mo., Aug. 22, 1918; d. George Thomas and Elsie Mae (Barnett) Swaithes; m. Ralph W. DeVaul, Sept. 6, 1941 (div. Oct. 1952); 1 child, Jimmie Martin DeVaul; m. David Walter Barry, Feb. 17, 1958. Student, Kansas City Bus. Sch. Contbr. poetry to Desert Mag., Boy's Life, Hamilton Advocate; writer of Country Western and Southern Gospel songs. Mem. Top Records Songwriters Assn., Nat. Trust for Historic Preservation. Democrat. Home: 265 S 8th St Breckenridge MO 64625 also: Box 124 Breckenridge MO 64625

BARRY, BERT, language educator; b. St. Louis, Mar. 11, 1954; s. Robert Adrian Jr. and Tam (Benoist) B.; m. Elizabeth Marie Lottes, May 19, 1989; children: Katherine Curry, Kevin Hunt. BA, Washington U., St. Louis, 1976, MA, 1980; PhD, St. Louis U., 1995. Cert. tchr. English, German. Tchr. Wilson Sch., St. Louis, 1973-77, Annunciation Sch., St. Louis, 1977-81; instr. Fontbonne Coll., St. Louis, 1981-85, Meramec C.C., St. Louis, 1982—; asst. prof., coord. internat. students Fontbonne Coll., St. Louis, 1985—; grant coord. Higher Edn. Ctr., St. Louis, 1991, chair, 1991-92. Active Transport 2000 Can., Montreal, 1978—. Mem. NAFSA Assn. Internat. Educators, Am. Assn. Tchrs. German, MLA, Amnesty Internat., Greenpeace, Nat. Assn. R.R. Passengers. Roman Catholic. Home: 1520 Andrew Dr Saint Louis MO 63122-1704 Office: Fontbonne Coll 6800 Wydown Saint Louis MO 63105

BARRY, DONALD LEE, investment broker; b. Ft. Gordon, Ga., Sept. 1, 1953; s. C. Donald and Della (Newman) B.; m. Peggy Summerfield, Aug. 8, 1980 (div. June 1983); m. Lora Fankhauser, Oct. 6, 1990. Student, Wichita State U., 1974-1981. Lic. stocks and commodity trader, life ins. agt. Instr. Cyr's Driving Sch., Wichita, Kans., 1974-78, v.p., 1978-81; investment broker A.G. Edwards & Sons, Wichita, 1981-85, v.p. investments, 1985-96, sr. v.p. investments, 1996—; chmn.,coun. mem. A.G. Edwards & Sons, 1990. Bd. dris. Wichita Pub. libr., 1980, 93—, treas., 1981-83; bd. dirs. Interfaith Ministries Exec. Com., Wichita, 1983—, St. Francis Hosp. Found., 1991-95, Wichita chpt. NCCJ, 1991, Via Christi Hosp. Found., 1996—; bd. dirs. Goodwill Industries, 1994—, treas., 1995—. Recipient Outstanding Citizen award Interfaith Ministries, 1991. Mem. Am. Mensa Ltd., Internat. Assn. for Fin. Planners, Rotary Internat., Wichita Com. on Fgn. Rels. Republican. Episcopalian. Home: 7715 Oneida Ct Wichita KS 67206-3850 Office: AG Edwards & Sons 201 N Main St Wichita KS 67202-1500

BARRY, JAMES P(OTVIN), writer, editor; b. Alton, Ill., Oct. 23, 1918; s. Paul Augustine and Elder (Potvin) B.; m. Anne Elizabeth Jackson, Apr. 16, 1966. BA cum laude, Ohio State U., 1940. Commd. 2d. lt. Arty. U.S. Army, 1940, advanced through grades to col., served ETO, 1944-46; adviser to Turkish Army, 1951-53; detailed Army Gen. Staff, Washington, 1953-56; ret., 1966; adminstr. Capital U., Columbus, Ohio, 1967-71; freelance writer, editor Columbus, 1971-77; dir. Ohioana Library Assn., 1977-88; editor Ohioana Quar., 1977-88; sr. editor Inland Seas, 1984—; photographer, documentary and book illustrator, 1968—. Author: Georgian Bay: The Sixth Great Lake, 1968, 3rd edit., 1995, The Battle of Lake Erie, 1970, Bloody Kansas, 1972, The Noble Experiment, 1972, The Fate of the Lakes, 1972, The Louisiana Purchase, 1973, Henry Ford and Mass Production, 1973, Ships of the Great Lakes, 1973, rev. edit., 1996 (Dolphin Book Club selection), The Berlin Olympics, 1975, The Great Lakes: A First Book, 1976, Wrecks and Rescues of the Great Lakes, 1981 (Dolphin Book Club selection), Georgian Bay: An Illustrated History, 1992, Old Forts of the Great Lakes, 1994, also booklet on Lake Erie for Ohio EPA, 1980; contbr. articles to mags. and jours.; over 300 photographs accepted for permanent collection Inst. Gt. Lakes sch. Recipient award Am. Soc. State and Local History, 1974, Nonfiction History award Soc. Midland Authors, 1982; named Gt. Lakes Historian of Yr., Marine Hist. Soc. Detroit, 1995. Mem. Internat. Assn. Gt. Lakes Rsch., Assn. Gt. Lakes Maritime History, Gt. Lakes Hist. Soc., Marine Hist. Soc., Ohio Hist. Soc., World Ship Soc., Royal Can. Yacht Club, Columbus Country Club, Univ. Club, Phi Beta Kappa. Home: 353 Fairway Blvd Columbus OH 43213-2507

BARRY, JAMES RONALD, account executive; b. Mar. 26, 1955. BS, Grand Valley State U., Allendale, Mich., 1978. With TV News, Dover, Del., Battle Creek, Mich., Harrisburg, Pa.; investment rep. Dean Witter Reynolds, Harrisburg, Pa., 1991-93, Keystone Brokerage, Harrisburg, 1993-94; account exec. FMB Investments, Zeeland, Mich., 1994—. With Grand Valley U. Found., Allendale, Mich., 1986—. Recipient Cmty. Svc. award UCP of Del., Wilmington, 1988, Del. State Edn. Assn. Bell Sch. award, Dover, 1988, 89, TV Prodr. Emmy winning newscast Phila. chpt., TV Arts & Scis., 1989. Mem. Wyomming Rotary. Republican. Home: 11303 Ruralview Dr Holland MI 49424-9574 Office: FMB Investments 101 E Main St Zeeland MI 49464

BARSAN, ROBERT BLAKE, dentist; b. Akron, Ohio, Apr. 7, 1948; s. Emil O. and Letitia (Dobrin) B.; m. Cheryl Lee Adams, Dec. 16, 1972; children: Erin Lee, Kathleen Letitia. BS, U. Cin., 1970; DDS, Ohio State U., 1974. Resident U. Chgo., 1976; gen. practice dentistry Cuyahoga Falls, Ohio, 1976—. Contbr. editor Modern Dental mag., 1984-89. Fellow Acad. Gen. Dentistry; mem. ADA (chmn. CPR 1984-90), Am. Endodontic Soc., Akron Gnathological Soc. (pres. 1986), Am. Acad. Cosmetic Dentistry, Fedn. Dentaire Internat., Canton Akron Cleve. Orthodontic Study Club (pres. 1994). Home: 3084 Silver Lake Blvd Silver Lake OH 44224-3033 Office: 330 Stow Ave Cuyahoga Falls OH 44221-2516

BARSUK, SIDNEY ALAN, fundraising executive; b. Batavia, N.Y., June 22, 1941; s. Max and Nellie (Greenberg) B.; m. Maxene Frances Soloway, Aug. 19, 1967; children: Peter Scott, Jeffrey Howard. BS, Rochester Inst. Tech., 1969, MBA, 1971. Cert. fundraising exec. Acting devel. dir. Rochester (N.Y.) Inst. Tech., 1969-72, spl. asst. to v.p., 1971-72; dir. devel. Upper Iowa Coll., Fayette, 1972-73; regional devel. officer Northwood Inst., Midland, Mich., 1973-75; asst. v.p. devel. Jackson Park Hosp., Chgo., 1975-80, v.p. resource devel., 1980-90. v.p. devel. St. Francis Hosp. and Health Ctr., Blue Island, Ill., 1990-92; v.p. Brakeley, John Paul Jones, Inc., Stamford, Conn., 1992-94; bus., mktg. & mgmt. instr. Roosevelt U., Nat. Louis U., Chgo., 1994—; dir. devel. Five Hosp. Program, Chgo., 1995—. Chmn. Citizens Referendum Com., Homewood, Ill., 1980; mem. Homewood Sch. Dist. 153 Bd., 1980-93, chmn. property and fin. com., 1982—; chmn. South Shore Revitalization Ctr., Chgo., 1980; vice-chmn. Rosenblum Boys Club, Chgo., 1980-84, chmn., 1984-88; mem. Homewood Cultural Arts Com., 1986-89; bd. dirs. South Shore YMCA, 1984-90. Named Outstanding Young Person, Chgo.-Southend Jaycees, Chgo., 1977. Mem. Nat. Soc. Fund Raising Execs. (dir., mem. exec. com. 1977-82), Nat. Assn. Hosp. Devel. (legislative chmn. 1983—), South Shore C. of C. (pres. 1978-79), Cosmopolitan C. of C. (vice chmn. 1986-90), Rotary. Republican. Jewish. Home: 18612 Carpenter St Homewood IL 60430-3536

BARTELAK, CHRIS, vice president; b. Aug. 19, 1963. V.p. Plant Support and Evaluation, Inc., New Berlin, Wis., 1990—. Republican. Office: Plant Support & Evaluation 2921 S 160th St New Berlin WI 53151-3605

BARTELEME, VINCENT P., design engineer; b. Fond du Lac, Wis., Sept. 13, 1970. Assoc. in Design, A.I.T., 1993. Design engr. Waukesha (Wis.) Cutting Tools, 1993—. Office: Waukesha Cutting Tools 1111 Sentry Dr Waukesha WI 53186-5965

BARTELL, SCOTT EUGENE, psychotherapist, social worker; b. Mpls., Aug. 27, 1948; s. Kenneth Eugene and Arloine Janet (Smith) B.; m. Candace Kristine Gilles-Brown, Mar. 15, 1968 (div. Dec. 1973). Cert. of attendance, U. Oslo, Norway, 1973; BA in Speech, Comm. and Theatre, U. Minn., 1973, MSW, 1986. Cert. social worker; lic. ind. clin. social worker; diplomate in clin. social work. Grad. intern Project Remand, St. Paul, 1976-77, Walk-In Counseling Ctr., Mpls., 1977-78; cmty. edn. coord. The Men's Ctr., Mpls., 1978; mental health worker Ross (Calif.) Hosp., 1979-81; tour guide, publicity writer Robert Mondari Winevy, Oakville, Calif., 1979-81; cmty. mental health worker Hennepin County Mental Health Divsn., Mpls., 1982-84; psychiat. social worker Fairview-Southdale Hosp., Edina, Minn., 1984-85, Metro Med. Ctr., Mpls., 1986-88; psychotherapist, supr. Family Svc. Inc., St. Paul, 1988—; cons. Prog. in Human Sexuality, U. Minn., Mpls., 1975—, YES/NEON, Mpls., 1985-90; dir., founder, bd. chair The Men's Ctr., Mpls., 1976—; counselor, supr., cons. Walk-In Counseling Ctr., Mpls., 1977—. Author, editor The Men's Resource Directory, 1979; author (food column) City Pages Weekly Newspaper, 1982; contbr. articles to profl. jours. Soloist Highland Piper Ann. May Day Parade, Mpls., 1978—, Ann. Minn. Marathon Race, Mpls., 1982-92, Ann. AIDS Walk, Mpls., 1982—. Recipient Cmty. Svc. award WICC, Mpls., 1989. Mem. NASW, Sex Info. Edn. Coun. U.S., Minn. Soc. for Clin. Hypnosis, Mensa Minn. Home: 4510 Blaisdell Ave S Minneapolis MN 55409 Office: Children's Svc 414 S 8th St Minneapolis MN 55404

BARTELS, JEAN ELLEN, nursing educator; b. Two Rivers, Wis., July 15, 1949; m. Terry D. Bartels, Aug. 14, 1971; children: Justin Dean, Ashlee Jill. Diploma, Columbia Hosp. Sch. Nursing, 1970; BS in Nursing with honors, Alverno Coll., 1981; MS in Nursing, Marquette U., 1983; PhD in Nursing, U. Wis., 1990. Staff nurse ICU Columbia Hosp., Milw., 1970-83; prof. of nursing Alverno Coll., Milw., 1990—. Contbr. articles to profl. jours. Mem. ANA, AACN (bd. dirs.), Internat. Soc. for Sci. Study Subjectivity, NLN, Midwest Nursing Rsch. Soc., Am. Assn. Collegiate Schs.

Nursing, Sigma Theta Tau, Phi Kappa Phi. Home: N24w22623 Meadowood Ln Waukesha WI 53186-8822 Office: Alverno Coll PO Box 343922 Milwaukee WI 53234-3922

BARTELS, ROBERT EDWIN, aerospace engineer; b. Des Moines, May 24, 1955; s. Everett M. and Iola J. (Van Wyck) B. BS, Iowa State U., 1977; MDiv cum laude, N.W. Baptist Sem., Tacoma, Wash., 1983; MS, Iowa State U., 1992, PhD, 1994. Sr. engr. Boeing Comml. Airplane Co., Seattle, 1984-87; teaching asst. Iowa State U., Ames, 1987-92; grad. rsch. fellow NASA Iowa State U., 1992-94; NRC rsch. assoc. NASA Langley Rsch. Ctr., Hampton, Va., 1994—. Recipient Grad. Student Tchg. Excellence award Iowa State U., 1991. Mem. AIAA (sr.), Phi Kappa Phi. Home: 6212 Auburn Ln Hampton VA 23666

BARTELS, SUSAN HERDMAN, art educator, artist; b. Yonkers, N.Y., May 29, 1941; d. Raymond Charles and Ellen (Saunders) Herdman; m. John C. Barker, June 12, 1965 (div. July 1984); children: Jennifer, Carrie, John; m. Robert John Bartels, Apr. 7, 1990. BFA, Alfred U., 1963; MA, U. Iowa, 1965. Art educator Muscatine (Iowa) Pub. Schs., 1965-66, Iowa City Pub. Schs., 1966-67, Regina High Sch., Iowa City, 1967-68; artist, owner Custom Stained Glass, Bettendorf, Iowa, 1979-84, Herdman Photographic Archive (formerly Native Images), Bettendorf, Iowa, 1992—; art educator Davenport (Iowa) Cmty. Schs., 1985—. Group shows include Drake U., Des Moines, 1984, U. Iowa, Iowa City, 1987, 91, Davenport Mus. Art, 1987, Quad City Arts Coun., Rock Island, Ill., 1987, Whispering Winds Gallery, Iowa City, 1991, Quincy (Ill.) Art Ctr., 1992, Walton Art Ctr., Fayetteville, Ark., 1992, 93, Alias Gallery, Atlanta, 1992, Ga. Tech., Atlanta, 1992, Lincoln (Colo.) Art Ctr., 1992, 93, Davenport Mus. Art, 1992, Mus. Anthropology U. Calif., Chico, 1992, Red Mesa Art Gallery, Gallup, N.Mex., 1992, Putnam County Arts Coun., Mahopac, N.Y., 1992, Near Northwest Arts Coun., Chgo., 1993, North Platte Valley Art Guild, Scottsbluff, Nebr., 1993, U. Iowa, 1993, Chautaugua Art Assn. Galleries, 1993, Greater Harrisburg (Pa.) Arts Coun., 1993, 94, Fla. Soc. Fine Arts, Miami, Fla., 1993, Columbia Arts Ctr., Vancouver, Wash., 1993, Eiteljorg Mus. Am. Indian and Western Art, Indpls., 1994, Maude Kerns Art Center, Eugene, Oreg., 1994, Soc. Contemporary Photography, Kansas City, 1994, Mus. Northwest Colo., Craig, 1994, Fuller Mus. Art, Brockton, Mass., 1994, Perry House Galleries (Silver medal), Alexandria, Va., 1995, No. Colo. Artists Assn., Fort Collins, Colo., 1996, Photo Nat. 96 (2nd place award), Mo., 1996, Oscar Howe Art Ctr., S. Dakota, 1996; permanent collections include Am. Indian Art Ctr., Chgo., Mus. Anthropology U. Calif., Chico., Deere and Co., Moline, Ill, Eiteljorg Mus. Native Am. & Western Art, EverColor Corp., El Dorado Hills, Calif., Heard Mus. Libr. & Archives, Phoenix. Mem. Nat. Mus. Am. Indian, Nat. Mus. Women in Arts, Davenport Indian Parent Adv. Com., 1991-95. Recipient Best of Show award Quad City Arts Coun., 1987, Best of Photography Ann. Photographers Forum Mag., 1993, others; grantee Iowa Arts Coun., 1995. Mem. Iowa Alliance for Arts Edn., Quad City League of Native Ams. Home: 3303 Oxford Dr Bettendorf IA 52722-2667

BARTELSMEYER, LINDA, state legislator. Mem. Mo. Ho. of Reps., Jefferson City. Republican.

BARTH, CHARLES FREDRIK, aerospace engineer; b. Cleve., Nov. 5, 1935; s. Henry Alphons and Margaret N. (Pleasnick) B. BS, Fenn Coll., 1965; MS, Case Western Reserve U., 1969, PhD, 1971. Lab. technician to dept. mgr. TRW Materials & Mfg. Tech. Ctr., Cleve., 1957-86; dir. Textron Materials & Mfg. Tech. Ctr., Cleve., 1986-91; dir. new products devel. Advanced Fabrications div. Barnes Aerospace, Lansing, Mich., 1991-94; dir. mfg. learning ctr. Cleve. Advanced Mfg. Program, 1995—; cons. Brush-Wellman, Cleve., 1982, Union Carbide, Buffalo, 1980, NACI, Annapolis, Md., 1994-95. Contbr. articles to profl. jours. Patents in field. Republican. Home: 451 Vineyard Dr #201 Broadview Heights OH 44147-3332

BARTH, ROLF FREDERICK, pathologist, educator; b. N.Y.C., Apr. 4, 1937; s. Rolf L. and Josephine Barth; m. Christine Ferguson, Oct. 30, 1965; children: Suzie, Alison, Rolf, Christofer. AB, Cornell U., 1959; MD, Columbia U., 1964. Diplomate Am. Bd. Pathology. Surg. intern Columbia-Presbyn. Med. Ctr., N.Y.C., 1964-65; postdoctoral fellow Karolinska Inst., Stockholm, 1965-66; rsch. assoc. Nat. Inst. Allergy and Infectious Diseases, NIH, Bethesda, Md., 1966-68; resident pathology br. Nat. Cancer Inst., 1966-68, Nat. Inst. Health, 1968-70; Prof. dept. pathology and oncology U. Kans. Med. Ctr., Kansas City, 1970-77; clin. prof. dept. pathology Med. Coll. Wis. and U. Wis., Madison, 1977-79; prof. dept. pathology Ohio State U., Columbus, 1979—. Contbr. articles to profl. jours. Sr. asst. surgeon USPHS, 1966-70, inactive Res., 1970—. Grantee, Am. Cancer Soc., Dept. Energy, NIH. Mem. Am. Assn. Exptl. Pathology, Am. Assn. Immunologists, Am. Assn. Cancer Rsch., Internat. Soc. for Neutron Capture Therapy, Sigma Xi, Phi Kappa Phi. Office: Ohio State U Dept Pathology 165 Hamilton Hall 1645 Neil Ave Columbus OH 43210-1218

BARTH, TAMI SUE, food products company executive; b. Norfolk, Nebr., Dec. 25, 1962; d. Dale and Bonita (Stork) B. BS, Wayne (Nebr.) State Coll., 1986. Account rep. Richman Gordman, Omaha, 1987-91; promotion specialist II, ConAgra Frozen Foods, Omaha, 1991—. Home: 3005 S 126th Plz Apt 5 Omaha NE 68144-3838 Office: ConAgra Frozen Foods 5 ConAgra Dr Omaha NE 68102-5094

BARTH, WILLIAM R., editor; b. Paris, Ill., Sept. 5, 1951; s. Raymond C. and Peggy A. (Scott) B.; m. Janice E. Reynolds, Jan. 13, 1953; children; Traci, William K., John W. B of Journalism, So. Ill. U., 1973. Assoc. editor Bus. Rsch. bur., Carbondale, Ill., 1972, editor, 1973; reporter Charleston (Ill.) Times-Carrier, 1973-76; city editor Beloit (Wis.) Daily News, 1977-80, mng. editor, 1980-94, editor, 1994—. Bd. dirs. United Way, Beloit, 1992-95, Beloit Boys Club, 1980-95; founding bd. dirs. Crime Stoppers, 1982. Home: 749 Patriots Way Rockton IL 61072 Office: Beloit Daily News 149 State St Beloit WI 53511

BARTHOLD, CLEMENTINE B., retired judge; b. Odessa, Russia, Jan. 11, 1921; came to U.S., 1925; d. Joseph Anton and Magdalene (Richter) Schwan; m. Edward Brendel Barthold, July 5, 1941 (dec.); children: Judith Anne Barthold DeSimone, John Edward. Student Aberdeen Bus. Coll., 1940; BGS, Ind. U. Southeast, 1978; JD, Ind. U.-Indpls., 1980. Bar: Ind. 1980, U.S. Dist. Ct. (so. dist.) Ind., 1980. Sec. and asst. to mgr. Clark County C. of C. (Ind.), 1959-60; chief probation officer Clark Circuit Ct. and Superior Cts., Jeffersonville, 1960-72; rsch. cons. Pub. Action Correctional Effort, Clark and Floyd Counties, 1972-75; instl. parole officer Ind. Women's Prison, Indpls., 1975-80; atty. State of Ind., 1980-83; judge Clark Superior Ct. No. 1, Jeffersonville, 1983-95, ret., 1995. Active in developing and implementing juvenile delinquency prevention and alternative programs, group counseling for juvenile delinquents and restitution programs. Recipient Good Govt. award Jeffersonville Jaycees, 1966, Good Citizenship award, 1967; Wonder Woman award, 1984, Robert J. Kinsey award, 1986, Sagamore of Wabash award, 1986, Outstanding Cmty. Svc. award Social Concerns League, Jeffersonville, 1966, Disting. Svc. award, Outstanding Contbn. to Field of Correction award, Women of Achievement award, Jeff BPW Appreciation award, Juvenile Justice award, Disting. Contemporary Women in History award, Disting. Leadership award, Women of Achievement award 1982-83, Appreciation award VIPO, 1983, Children and Youth Recognition award 1984, Gov's Exemplary award, 1985, 88, 89, 92, Commitment to Youth award 1987, Warren W. Martin award, 1973, 87, Outstanding Child Advocacy in Ind. award, 1987, Community Svc. award, 1988, Orgnl. Renewal award, 1988, Parents Without Ptnrs. award, 1989, Ind. Youth Investment award, 1992, Excellence in Pub. Info. & Edn. award, 1992. Mem. Ind. Bar Assn., Clark County Bar Assn., Ind. Correctional Assn. (pres. 1971, Disting. Service award 1967, 85), Ind. Judges Assn., Nat. and Ind. Juvenile and Family Ct. Judges (bd. dirs.), Ind. Juvenile Justice Task Force, Ind. U. Alumni Assn., Howard Steamboat Mus., LWV, Bus. and Profl. Women's Club, Ladies Elks Aux. Democrat. Roman Catholic. Home: 948 E 7th St Jeffersonville IN 47130-4106

BARTHOLOME, WILLIAM GIBSON, pediatrician, educator; b. Helena, Mont., Feb. 19, 1944; s. William Franklin and Virginia Marie (Gibson) B.; m. Marita O'Rourke, July 29, 1967 (div. 1991); children: Bridget, Sheila, Claire; m. Pamela Roffol Dobies, Jan. 15, 1995. AB, Rockhurst Coll., 1965; MD, U. Kans., 1969. Diplomate Am. Bd. Pediatrics. Intern, resident Johns Hopkins Hosp., Balt., 1969-72; fellow in med. ethics Harvard U., Cambridge, Mass., 1974-76; asst. prof., then assoc. prof. pediatrics U. Tex. Health Sci. Ctr., Houston, 1976-83; adj. prof. ethics U. Ill. Med. Sch., Chgo., 1983-86; assoc. prof. pediatrics, history and philosophy of medicine U. Kans. Med. Ctr., Kansas City, 1986-93, prof., 1993—; cons. Joseph P. Kennedy, Jr. Found., Washington, 1972-78; bd. dirs. U. Tex. Med. Sch., Houston, 1979-83, acting med. dir. March of Dimes program, 1979-83; pediatric med. ethicist Luth. Gen. Hosp., Park Ridge, Ill., 1983-86; presenter at profl. confs. Bd. dirs. Houston Assn. Retarded Citizens, 1977-79, Glencoe (Ill.) Pub. Libr., 1985-86; mem. Kans. Com. for Humanities, Topeka, 1986-91. Maj. USAF, 1972-74. Mem. Am. Soc. Law and Medicine, Soc. Health and Human Values, Am. Acad. Pediatrics (com. on bioethics 1981-87, task force on infant bioethics 1984-85, nat. media spokesperson on pediatric ethics), Alpha Omega Alpha, Alpha Sigma Nu. Home: 6106 Walnut Kansas City MO 64113 Office: Univ Kans Med Ctr 3901 Rainbow Blvd Kansas City KS 66160-7311

BARTHOLOMEW, DONALD DEKLE, engineering executive, inventor; b. Atlanta, Aug. 2, 1929; s. Rudolph A. and Rubye C. (Delke) B.; m. Paula Hagood; children: John Marshall, Barbara Ann, Deborah Paige, Sandra Dianne. Student in Physics, Ga. Inst. Tech., 1946-48, 55-58. Lic. worldwide. Owner Happy Cottons and Jalopy Jungleland, Atlanta, 1946-48, Beach Hotel Supply, Miami Beach, Fla., 1949-50; engr. Sperry Microwave Electronics, Clearwater, Fla., 1958-61; v.p., owner Draft Pak, Inc., Tampa, Fla., 1961-65, Merit Plastics, Inc., East Canton, Ohio, 1966-79; pres., owner Modern Tech., Inc., Marine City, Mich., 1979—; owner, officer and dir. various internat. mfg. companies, 1981—. Patentee in field of indsl. applications. Mem. Soc. Automotive Engrs., Soc. Plastics Engrs. (dir. 1982), Soc. Mfg. Engrs., Holiday Isles Jr. C. of C. (founding dir.). Republican.

BARTHOLOW, GEORGE WILLIAM, psychiatrist; b. Yale, Iowa, June 17, 1955; s. Harry Clifford and Marjorie Virginia (Wilson) B.; m. Beverly N. Nelson, June 17, 1955; children: Jeanne, Deborah, Bruce. BS, State U. Iowa, Iowa City, 1951, MD, 1955. Lic. psychiatry, Iowa, Nebr.; diplomate Am. Bd. Psychiatry and Neurology. Intern Wayne County Gen. Hosp., Eloise, Mich., 1955-56; chief psychiatry VA Hosp., Omaha, 1962-90; clin. dir. Norfolk (Nebr.) Regional Ctr., 1991—; prof. U. Nebr., Omaha, 1961—, Creighton U., Omaha, 1977—; cons. VA, Omaha, 1992—, Luth. family Svc., Omaha, 1993—. Lt. comdr. USN, 1959-61. Fellow APA (rep. 1972—); mem. Nebr. Psychiatric Soc. (pres. 1995—), Nebr. Med. Assn. Home: 721 N 57th St Omaha NE 68132 Office: Norfolk Regional Ctr 1700 N Victory Rd Norfolk NE 68701

BARTLETT, ALICE BRAND, psychotherapist, educator, dean, researcher; b. Carrollton, Mo., Oct. 27, 1950; d. Daniel Arthur and Nellie May (Farmer) Brand; m. Thomas Sidney Bartlett, Aug. 12, 1989. BA, U. Mo., 1972, MLS, 1973; postgrad., Topeka Inst. Psychoanalysis, 1979-96. Dir. libr. Mo. Inst. Psychiatry, St. Louis, 1973-74; chief libr. Menninger Clinic, Topeka, 1975—, psychotherapist, 1984—, assoc. dean info./media Karl Menninger Sch. Psychiatry, 1988—, E. Greenwood prof., 1990—; prin. investigator Child and Family Ctr. Menninger Clinic, 1995—; prin. investigator Child and Family Study Ctr., 1995—; cons. C.F. Menninger Meml. Hosp., Topeka, 1987—; bd. dirs., asst. treas. Psychoanalytic Rsch. Consortium, N.Y.C. and Topeka, 1989-95. Contbr. articles to profl. publs. Interfuture scholar, 1971-72. Mem. Am. Psychoanalytic Assn. (chair libr. com. 1991—, Liddle grantee 1985), Med. Libr. Assn. (co-chair ethics com. 1985-87), Topeka Psychoanalytic Soc. (recorder 1983-86, program chair 1993—). Office: Menninger Clinic 5800 SW 6th Ave Topeka KS 66606-9604

BARTLETT, FRANK WALTER, university administrator; b. Sioux Falls, S.D., Sept. 14, 1961; s. James R. and Barbara (Ochs) B. BA, U. S.D., 1984; MEd, Temple U., 1994. Hall dir. S.E. Mo. State U., Cape Girardeau, 1984-87; resident dir. Humboldt State U., Arcata, Calif., 1987-89; asst. to dir. of housing So. Conn. State U., New Haven, 1989-90; area coord. Temple U., Phila., 1990-94; dir. residential life Maryville U., St. Louis, 1994—; com. mem. Housing Ops. & Svcs., Mid-Atlantic Coll. & Univ. Housing Officers, 1992—. Mem. Nat. Assn. Student Pers. Adminstrs. (profl. affiliate 1986—), Assn. Coll. Pers. Adminstrs., Assn. Coll. and Univ. Housing Officers. Office: Maryville Univ AC-JHP 13550 Conway Rd Saint Louis MO 63141

BARTLETT, GERALD LLOYD, pathologist, medical educator, researcher; b. Portland, Oreg., July 24, 1939; s. Lloyd Llewellyn and Clarice (Fenton) B.; m. Kerry Judyth Bush, July 10, 1965; children: Jonathan, Kevin, Kathryn. BA in French and Chemistry, Seattle Pacific U., 1961; MD, U. Washington, 1966; PhD in Pathology, U. Pa., 1972. Rsch. assoc. Inst. for Cancer Rsch., Phila., 1966-70; staff assoc. Nat. Cancer Inst., Bethesda, 1970-72; from asst. prof. pathology to prof. Hershey (Pa.) Med. Ctr. Pa. State U., 1972-89; prof., chair pathology U. Ill. Coll. Medicine, Peoria, 1989—; cons. Nat. Cancer Inst., 1972-78, 81, 85, 90, 91, Transplantation (a jour.), 1973-79, Nat. Inst. for Dental Rsch., 1971-77, Bur. of Mines, 1984, Nat. Bd. Med. Examiners, 1995-97. Contbr. 56 articles and reports to Sci., Jour. Nat. Cancer Inst., Internat. Jour. Cancer, others. Recipient Rsch. Career Devel. award Nat. Cancer Inst., 1973-79, rsch. grantee, 1973-76, rsch. contract, 1973-80; rsch. grantee U.S Bur. Mines, 1983-89. Mem. AAAS, Am. Assn. Immunologists, Group for Rsch. in Pathology Edn., Am. Assn. for Cancer Rsch., Am. Soc. Investigative Pathologists, Assn. Pathology Chairs. Evang. Mennonite. Office: U Ill Coll Medicine PO Box 1649 Peoria IL 61656-1649

BARTLETT, PAUL DANA, JR., agribusiness executive; b. Kansas City, Mo., Sept. 16, 1919; s. Paul D. and Alice May (Hiestand) B.; m. Joan Jenkins, May 14, 1949; children—J. Alison Bartlett Jager, Marilyn Bartlett Hebenstreit, Paul Dana III, Frederick Jenkins. BA, Yale U., 1941. Chmn. Bartlett and Co., Kansas City, Mo., 1961-77; pres., chmn. bd. Bartlett and Co. (formerly Bartlett Agri Enterprises, Inc.), Kansas City, 1977—; chrm., dir. Bartlett and Co.; bd. dir. United Mo. Bank, United Mo. Bancshares. Lt. USN, 1942-46. Office: Bartlett and Company 4800 Main St Ste 600 Kansas City MO 64112-2509

BARTLETT, PETER GREENOUGH, engineering company executive; b. Manchester, N.H., Apr. 22, 1930; s. Richard Cilley and Dorothy (Pillsbury) B.; Ph.B., Northwestern U., 1955; m. Jeanne Eddes, July 8, 1954 (dec. 1980); children: Peter G., Marta, Lauren, Karla, Richard E.; m. Kathleen Organ, July 21, 1984. Engr., Westinghouse Electric Co., Balt., 1955-58; mgr. mil. communications Motorola, Inc., Chgo., 1958-60; pres. Bartlett Labs., Inc., Indpls., 1960-63; assoc. prof. elec. engring. U. S.C., Columbia, 1963-64; dir. research Eagle Signal Co., Davenport, Iowa, 1964-67; div. mgr. Struthers-Dunn, Inc., Bettendorf, Iowa, 1967-74; pres. Automation Systems, Inc., Eldridge, Iowa, 1974-89; pres., chmn. Cybertronics, Inc., Davenport, 1989—. Mem. IEEE. Republican. Presbyterian. Patentee in field. Home and Office: 2336 E 11th St Davenport IA 52803-3701 Office: Cybertronics Inc Davenport IA 52803

BARTLETT, ROBERT WILLIAM, lawyer, publishing executive; b. Chgo., Nov. 11, 1941; s. Robert C. and Rita E. Bartlett; m. Mary Lou Holtzman, Mar. 8, 1988. AB, Stanford U., 1963; LLB, U. Va., 1966. Bar: Ill. 1966. Assoc. counsel U.S. League Savs. Instns., Chgo., 1970-77, assoc. gen. counsel, editor legal bull., 1977-81, sr. v.p., 1981-91; mng. editor bus. and fin. team group Commerce Clearing House, Riverwoods, Ill., 1991—. Mem. ABA (mem. com. on savs. instns. 1973--). Roman Catholic. Home: 8 Anglican Ln Lincolnshire IL 60069 Office: Commerce Clearing House 2700 Lake Cook Rd Deerfield IL 60015-3867

BARTLETT, ROGER DANFORTH, engineering executive; b. Brentwood, Mo., Dec. 19, 1949; s. Robert Danforth and Margaret Elizabeth (Gruber) B.; m. Cynthia A. Adkins, July 1, 1978; children: Rex Danforth, Ryan Andrew, Megan Leigh. BSEE, Bradley U., 1971. Engr., Revomat, Parkville, Mo., 1971-72; div. engr. Am. Multi-Cinema, Inc., Kansas City, Mo., 1972-75, project mgr., 1975-78, assoc. dir. corp. engring., 1978-82, dir. corp. engring., 1982-85; dir. constrn. Commonwealth Theatres, Inc., 1985-87, dir. purchasing/tech. svcs., 1987-88; dir. midwest constr. United Artist Theatre Cir., 1988-89; pres. Bartlett & Assocs., Inc., 1989—. Mem. IEEE, SMPTE, Constrn. Specifications Inst. Home and office: 8701 W 72nd St Shawnee Mission KS 66204-1132

BARTMESS, JOSEPH PELL, financial consultant; b. Kennett, Mo., Nov. 30, 1958; m. Erin O'Flaherty, June 11, 1983; children: J.P., Leah. BSBA, U. Mo., 1981; MBA, St. Louis U., 1987. Banker Centerre Bank Corp., St. Louis, 1981-86, Mercantile Bank Corp., St. Louis, 1987-90; fin. cons. Merrill Lynch, Chesterfield, Mo., 1990—. Mem. youth leadership coun. Manchester (Mo.) United Meth. Ch., 1985—. Mem. Kennett C. of C., Chesterfield Rotary. Home: 16421 Hollister Crossing Dr Ellisville MO 63011 Office: Merrill Lynch 16100 N Outer 40 PO Box 4369 Chesterfield MO 63006

BARTOL, JON R., stockbroker; b. Marquette, Mich., Sept. 28, 1956. BS, No. Mich. U., 1982. Stockbroker, sr. fin. cons. Merrill Lynch, Green Bay, Wis., 1986—. Mem. U.S. Power Squadron, Corvettes of the Bay, Optimist Club Green Bay, Green Bay Boat Club. Republican. Office: Merrill Lynch 225 S Monroe Ave Green Bay WI 54301-4011

BARTON, EDWARD READ, educator; b. Kalamazoo, Mich., May 10, 1938; s. Clare A. and Caroline (Read) B. BS, Mich. State U., 1960; MPA, Cornell U., 1964, JD, 1964; MA, Mich. State U., 1993. Pres. Edward Read Barton P.C., Allegan, Mich., 1967-89; v.p. sales, treas. Diamond Tool Co., South Haven, Mich., 1989-90; exec. mgr. Consortium for Belizean Devel. Inc., Washington, 1990-92; adj. instr. Oakland Community Coll., 1990-92; adj. curator Changing Men Collection Spl. Collections, Mich. State U. Libr., 1990—; dir. West Mich. Men's Ctr., 1990—, pres., 1990-91. Mem. Allegan County Agrl. Assn. (life), Mich. Jaycees (area coord., life mem. senate 1990-91), FarmHouse (pres. Mich. assn. 1986-91, pres. Found. Coun. 1988—). Home: 920 Miller Rd Plainwell MI 49080-1053

BARTON, FLORIN EDWARD, retired social services administrator; b. Springfield, Ill., Oct. 4, 1912; s. Roland I. and Rose Ella (Jouett) B.; m. Vivian Gertrude Vancil, Apr. 11, 1937; children: Judith Lee Williamson, JoAnn Steffens. Dist. dir. Muscular Dystrophy Assn., Springfield, 1968-71; regional coord. Muscular Dystrophy Assn., St. Louis, 1971-77; cons. Cardiac Pulmonary Recussitation Telethon WCIA-TV, Champaign, 1977-79; dir. info. svc. on aging Ill. Presbyn. Home, Springfield, 1979-93; ret., 1993; mem. Presbytery Great Rivers Task Force on Aging, Peoria, Ill., 1981-91; pres. Springfield Ministry Coun., 1986-89. Author: (booklet) Manual to Assist Congregations in their Ministry to the Elderly, 1981; editor The Informer quar. periodical, 1971-91. Sec. DeMolay Legion of Honor, Springfield, 1976-91; fin. officer Contact Ministries, Springfield, 1983-86; mem. Ill. State DeMolay Found., Collinsville, 1985-91. Mem. Masons. Presbyterian. Home: 2525 S 5th St Springfield IL 62703-3801

BARTON, JANICE SWEENY, chemistry educator; b. Trenton, N.J., Mar. 22, 1939; d. Laurence U. and Lillian Mae (Fletcher) S.; m. Keith M. Barton, Dec. 20, 1967. BS, Butler U., 1962; PhD, Fla. State U., 1970. Postdoctoral fellow Johns Hopkins U., Balt., 1970-72; asst. prof. chemistry East Tex. State U., Commerce, 1972-78, Tex. Woman's U., Denton, 1978-81; assoc. prof. Washburn U., Topeka, 1982-88, prof., 1988—, chair chemistry dept., 1992—; mem. undergrad. faculty enhancement panel NSF, Washington, 1990; mem. NSF instr. lab. improvement panel, 1992, 96. Contbr. articles to profl. jours. Active Household Hazardous Waste Collection, Topeka, 1991, Solid Waste Task Force, Shawnee County, Kans., 1990; mem. vol. com. YWCA, Topeka, 1984-87. Rsch. grantee Petroleum Rsch. Fund, Topeka, 1984-86, NIH, Topeka, 1985-88; instrument grantee NSF, Topeka, 1986, 95. Mem. Am. Chem. Soc. (sec. Dallas-Ft. Worth sect. 1981-82), Kans. Acad. Sci. (pres.-elect 1991, pres. 1992), Biophys. Soc., Sigma Xi (pres. TWU club 1980-81), Iota Sigma Pi (mem.-at-large coord. 1987-93). Home: 3401 SW Oak Pky Topeka KS 66614-3218 Office: Washburn U Dept Chemistry Topeka KS 66621

BARTOSZEK, JOSEPH EDWARD, environmental specialist; b. Chicopee, Mass., Feb. 27, 1952; s. Walter Joseph and Madonna Elizabeth (Haan) B.; m. Lila Diane Pizarro, Aug. 20, 1977. AS, Holyoke Community Coll., 1972; BS, Westfield State Coll., 1974; MS, No. Ariz. U., 1976. Animal health technician animal and plant health inspection svc., veterinary svcs. USDA, Waltham, Mass., 1977-79; chem. dir. Ultramotive Corp., Bethel, Vt., 1980-83, v.p. rsch. and devel., 1983-89, nat. mgr. marine products, 1987-89; pres. Tundico Inc., Tunbridge, Vt., 1987-91; environ. biologist spl. studies and surveillance unit Agy. Natural Resources, Montpelier, Vt., 1989-91; environmentalist Guernsey County Health Dept., Cambridge, Ohio, 1991-93; environ. specialist Ohio Environ. Protection Agy., Dayton, 1993—; cons. Scheindel Assocs., Randolph Center, Vt., 1984-89; sanitarian Guernsey County Health Dept., Cambridge, Ohio. Patentee pressurized barrier package in U.S. and fgn. countries. Sec. Tunbridge Planning Commn., 1987-88, chmn. 1988-91; sanitarian Guernsey County Health Dept., Cambridge, Ohio, 1991-93. Mem. Chem. Spltys. Mfrs. Assn. (small bus. subcom. 1987-89). Unitarian. Office: Tundico Inc 755 Meadowview Dr Dayton OH 45459-2918 also: Ohio Environ Protection Agy 401 E 5th St Dayton OH 45402-2911

BARTSCHERER, THOMAS L., scholar; b. N.Y.C., Feb. 7, 1969; s. Joseph and Rita B. BA, U. Pa., 1991. Laborer Kelly Masonry Corp., N.Y.C., 1991-92; bldg. adminstr. U. Pa., Phila., 1992-93; adminstrv. dir. Dawson Consultants, Inc., Chgo., 1993-94; scholar Com. on Social Thought U. Chgo., 1993—; editorial asst. U. Chgo. Press, 1994—; bd. dirs. Galahpogas Theatre, Weehawken, N.J., Cleve., 1992—; mem. editorial adv. bd. Madrugada Publs., San Francisco, 1993-95. Author: (monograph) Søren Kierkegaard, 1991, (poetry) Madrugada, 1994. Recipient Burr Book award U. Pa., 1991. Fellow Com. on Social Thought, Phi Beta Kappa. Home: 1520 E 59th St Chicago IL 60637

BARTTER, BRIT JEFFREY, investment banker; b. Berea, Ohio, Dec. 27, 1949; s. Lynn Martin Bartter and Scharlie Ellen (Watson) Handlan; m. Marilyn McCullough, Aug. 25, 1973; children: Bryndl Lynn and Blake McCullough (twins). AB in Econs., Duke U., 1972; MS in Fin., Cornell U., 1976, PhD in Fin., 1977. Asst. prof. computer sci. Grad. Sch. Bus. Cornell U., Ithaca, N.Y., 1976; asst. prof. fin. Grad. Sch. Mgmt. Kellogg Grad. Sch. Mgmt., Northwestern U., Evanston, Ill., 1977-79; assoc., then v.p. Merrill Lynch Capital Markets, Chgo., 1979-83; v.p. The First Boston Corp., Chgo., 1983-87, dir., 1988-89, mng. dir., 1989-94; mng. dir. Merrill, Lynch Investment Banking, Chgo., 1995—; bd. dirs. Coun. for Young Profls., Chgo., 1985-87. Contbr. articles to Jour. of Fin., Fin. Mgmt. Bd. dirs. Cornell Coun. Chgo., 1987-88, Duke Campaign Chgo., 1987-88; mem. governing bd. Chgo. Symphony Orch. Mem. Econ. Club Chgo., Northwestern U. Assocs., Glen View Golf Club, Chgo. Club. Home: 221 Apple Tree Rd Winnetka IL 60093-3703 Office: Merrill Lynch Investment Bkng 5500 Sears Tower Chicago IL 60606

BARTTER, MARTHA ANN, English language educator; b. Oakland, Calif., Dec. 15, 1932; d. Lewis Walter and Ethel Davis (Putnam) Taylor; m. Robert B. Bartter, Aug. 22, 1951 (dec. Oct. 1976); children: Carol L. Bartter Lowy, Bradley D., Barbara A., Kenneth R.; m. C.A. Hilgartner, Jan. 17, 1986. BS, U. Rochester, 1975, MA, 1979, PhD, 1986. Instr. English U. Rochester, N.Y., 1979-84; asst. prof. Monroe Community Coll., Rochester, 1982; instr. English Rochester Inst. Tech., 1983; asst. prof. Ohio State U., Marion, 1985-92; assoc. prof. Truman State U., 1992—; cons. Hilgartner & Assocs., Kirksville, 1982—. Author: The Way to Ground Zero, 1988; contbr. articles to acad. jours. Treas. Internat. Assn. for the Fantastic In the Arts, 1995-98; bd. dirs. Heritage Trails Coun. Girl Scouts U.S.A., 1988-92. Lilly Endowment teaching fellow, 1988-89. Mem. Nat. Coun. Tchrs. English (judge 1990, 91, 92), LWV, Altrusa (chmn. internat. affairs Marion 1987-90). Office: Truman State U Dept Lang & Lit 310 McClain Hall Kirksville MO 63501

BARTUNEK, JAMES SCOTT, psychiatrist; b. Flint, Mich., Oct. 20, 1962; s. Steven James and Frances Annabelle (Peters) B.; m. Carol Lynn Tobis, Feb. 26, 1994; 1 child, Rebecca. BS, U. Mich., Flint, 1985; MD, Wayne State U., 1989. Resident in psychiatry Sinai Hosp. Detroit, 1989-92; mem. staff Crittenton Hosp., Rochester, Mich., 1993—. Mem. Am. Psychiat. Assn., Founder's Soc. Detroit Inst. Arts, U. Mich. Club, Wayne State U. Med. Alumni Club. Home: 3541 Hidden Forest Ct Orion MI 48359 Office: 1460 Walton Blvd Ste 215 Rochester Hills MI 48309-1779

BARTZ, PAUL ALAN, editor; b. Shawano, Wis., May 1, 1948; s. Kurt Wolfgang and Lucile (Vogel) B.; m. Bonnie Jo Bruhn, May 29, 1971. BA, Concordia Sr. Coll., Ft. Wayne, Ind., 1973; MDiv, Concordia Theol. Seminary, 1977. Pastor St. Stephens Luth. Ch., Braham, Minn., 1977-81, St.

John's Luth. Ch., Rush City, Minn., 1977-81; sec. Bible-Sci. Assn., Mpls., 1978-80; editor Bible-Sci. Assn., 1981—, radio host, 1987—, communication dir., 1989-91; chmn. planning coun. Luth. Coun. on Biblical Inerrancy, St. Paul, 1988-89. Author: Luther on Evolution, 1977, Letting God Create Your Day, 1989, 91, 92, 93; editor sci. books. Mem. Internat. Platform Assn., Nat. Writer's Club. Office: Bible-Sci Assn 9920 Zilla St NW Minneapolis MN 55433-5476

BARUA, JAYANTA LAL, stockbroker; b. Nagaon, India, Oct. 29, 1951; came to U.S., 1981; BA in History, Gowahati U., India, 1977; MBA in Fin., St. Francis Coll., Ft. Wayne, Ind., 1984. Lic. series 7 Nat. Assn. Securities Dealers. Mktg. mgr. Bahr Inc., Ft. Wayne, 1985-87; stockbroker Smith Barney Inc., Ft. Wayne, 1988—. Hindu. Home: 1728 Whitewater Ct Fort Wayne IN 46825-5971 Office: Smith Barney Inc One Summit Sq 8th Fl Fort Wayne IN 46802

BARZYDLO, ARNOLD JAMES, electronics technician; b. Lincoln, Nebr., May 20, 1958; s. Walter Chester and Evelyn Irene (Wilson) B. Electronics technician Versatec, Santa Clara, Calif., 1980-82; mfg. support/machine tool repair technician Isco, Inc., Lincoln, 1982—; computer hardware cons., Lincoln, 1992-95. Author: Time and Geometry:..., 1982, 89, 90, 93; writer, prodr. video Mirrors, Strings and Manifolds: The Gemoetry of Everything, 1994. Treas. Abate of Nebr., Lincoln, 1994-95. Sgt. USAF, 1976-80. Home: 5640 Francis St Lincoln NE 68505

BASEL, MARGARET MARY, management consultant; b. Milw., Jan. 29, 1956. BSN, Vanderbilt U., 1978. RN, Ohio. Pub. health nurse Milw. Health Dept., 1981-83; med. floor nurse St. Joseph Hosp., Milw., 1978-81; v.p. Libensmittel Cons. Co., Fostoria, Ohio, 1984—; part-time nurse Fostoria Cmty. Hosp., 1992-93. Active Ohio Child Conservation League, Fostoria. Roman Catholic. Office: Lebensmittel Cons Co 10760 W Sneca County Rd 18 Fostoria OH 44830

BASFORD, JAMES ORLANDO, container manufacturing company executive; b. Akron, Ohio, Apr. 17, 1931; s. Napoleon Orlando and Hazel Martha (Fersner) B.; m. Mary Eleanor Hagmeyer, Mar. 16, 1957; children: Jeffrey James, Gregory Robert, Lisa Jean. Student, Kent State U., 1949-51, 55-58. Asst. sales mgr. San Hygene Mfg. Co., Akron, 1958-60; gen. sales mgr. Adjusta Post Mfg., Akron, 1960-64; area sales mgr. Gaylord Container, Columbus, Ohio, 1964-74; v.p. Buckeye Container Co., Wooster, Ohio, 1974-78, pres., 1978-95, chmn. bd. dirs., 1995—; bd. dirs. United Telephone of Ohio, Mansfield, Wayne County Nat. Bank, Wooster. Bd. dirs. Boys Village, Smithville, Ohio, 1985—; chmn. Wayne County Econ. Devel. Commn., 1995. With USAF, 1951-54, Korea. Mem. Wooster C. of C. (bd. dirs. 1977-80). Republican. Lutheran. Club: Wooster Country (pres. 1981-83). Lodge: Rotary (bd. dirs. Wooster club 1978-81). Home: 1097 Greens View Dr Wooster OH 44691-2659 Office: Buckeye Corrugated Container PO Box 16 Wooster OH 44691-0016

BASHIRI, IRAJ, Central Asian studies educator; b. Behabahan, Iran, July 31, 1940; came to U.S., 1966; s. Muhammad and Robab Bashiri; m. Carol L. Sayers, Apr. 18, 1968; children: Mariam, Manuchehr, Mehrdad. BA cum laude, Pahlavi U., Shiraz, Iran, 1963; MA, U. Mich., 1968, PhD, 1972. Coord., tchr. Peace Corps, Brattleboro, Vt., 1967-68; asst. prof. Iranian studies U. Minn., Mpls., 1972-77, coord. Middle East studies program, 1975-77, assoc. prof. Iranian studies, 1977-87, acting chair South Asian studies, 1981, assoc. chair Russian and Eastern European studies, 1987-90, acting chair Russian and Eastern European studies, 1990-91, assoc. prof. Cen. Asian studies, 1987-96, prof. Ctrl. Asian studies, 1996—; assoc. prof. Iranian studies U. Tex., Austin, 1982; mem. rev. bd. Internat. Rsch. and Exchs. Bd. for Tajikistan, Princeton, N.J., 1991—; editor bilingual series Mazda Pub., Encino, Calif., 1985-90; mem. selection com. MacArthur Found., Mpls., 1990-91, mem. internat. seminar, 1990. Author: Fiction of Sadeq Hedayat, 1984, Firdowsi's Shahname: 1000 Years After, 1994; editor: The Pearl Cannon, 1986; contbr. articles, essays to profl. publs. Internat. edn. travel grantee U. Minn., 1990-92; IREX resident scholar, Tajikistan, 1993-94. Fellow Middle East Studies Assn.; mem. Am. Inst. Iranian Studies (trustee 1975-79), Assn. for Cen. Asian Studies, Assn. Advancement Cen. Asian Rsch. (chair devel. com. 1990—), Am. Assn. Tchrs. of Slavic and Eastern European Langs. Home: 518 8th St SE Minneapolis MN 55414-1208

BASKE, C. ALAN, manufacturing company executive; b. Detroit, Apr. 19, 1927; s. Clarence A. and Alice Loraine (Severance) B.; m. Shirley Ann Duckworth, Feb. 24, 1945; children: Nance, Roger, Douglas, Brian. Radio officer, USCG Hoffmann Island, Bklyn., 1944. Radio officer U.S. Maritime Svc., Atlantic, Pacific, Caribbean, 1944-45; owner/mgr. Alan's Auto Svc., Dearborn, Mich., 1946; svc. parts mgr. Detherage-McDonald Auto Sales, Dearborn, Mich., 1946-48; field sales agt. Sun Electric Corp., Detroit/Jackson, 1948; asst. dir. Sun Electric Corp., Chgo., 1948-53; mfg. rep. Valley Bearing, Chgo., 1953-74, owner/pres., 1974-86; cons. Libertyville, Ill., 1986—. Advisor Boy Scouts Am. troop 80, Libertyville, 1954-65; vestryman St. Lawrence Ch., Libertyville, 1958-66; bd. dirs. Libertyville/Freemont High Sch. Dist., 1962-64; chmn. Condell Hosp., 1968-72, 84-86, bd. dirs., 1963-72, 77-86; trustee Lake Forest (Ill.) Acad., 1969-75; pres. Waukegan (Ill.) Symphony Chorus, 1984-88; founding mem. Coll. Lake County Found., pres., 1975-82. Mem. Libertyville Country Side Assn. (bd. dirs./officer), Island Goat Sailing Soc., Waukegan Power Squadron (life), Waukegan Yacht Club (dir., past commodore), Libertyville Boat Club (founder dir.). Republican. Episcopalian. Home and Office: 15252 W Oak Spring Rd Libertyville IL 60048-1620

BASLER, THEODORE EUGENE, poet; b. St. Louis, Nov. 15, 1955; s. Robert Charles and Theresa Mary Ann (Gerard) B.; m. Mary Denise Bakameyer, Sept. 19, 1981; children: John Theodore, Luke John, Maria Claire, Emily Caroline. Grad. high sch. Automotive Svc. Excellence master cert. mechanic. Mechanic various small garages, Florissant, Mo., 1976-93, Clark and Son Mobil, Florissant, 1993—. Author: Brush with Heaven, 1995. Home: 1009 Pinecone Trail Dr Florissant MO 63031

BASOLO, FRED, chemistry educator; b. Coello, Ill., Feb. 11, 1920; s. John and Catherine (Marino) B.; m. Mary P. Nutley, June 14, 1947; children: Mary Catherine, Freddie, Margaret-Ann, Elizabeth Rose. BE, So. Ill. U., 1940, DSc (hon.), 1984; MS, U. Ill., 1942, PhD in Inorganic Chemistry, 1943; LLD (hon.), U. Turin, 1988. Rsch. chemist Rohm & Haas Chem. Co., Phila., 1943-46; mem. faculty Northwestern U., Evanston, Ill., 1946—, prof. chemistry, 1958—, Morrison prof. chemistry, 1980-90, chmn. dept. chemistry, 1969-72; Charles E. and Emma H. Morrison prof. emeritus Nortwestern U., Evanston, Ill., 1990—; guest lectr. NSF summer insts.; chmn. bd. trustees Gordon Rsch. Conf., 1976; pres. Inorganic Syntheses, Inc., 1979-81; mem. bd. chem. scis. and tech. NRC-Nat. Acad. Scis.; adv. bd. Who's Who in Am., 1983; cons. in field. Author: (with R.G. Pearson) Mechanisms of Inorganic Reactions, 1958, (with R.C. Johnson) Coordination Chemistry, 1964; assoc. editor Chem. Revs., 1960-65, Inorganica Chemica Acta, 1967—, Inorganica Chemica Acta Letters, 1977—; editorial bd. Jour. Inorganic and Nuclear Chemistry, 1959—, Jour. Molecular Catalysis, Chem. Revs.; co-editor Catalysis, Transition Metal Chemistry; editor Inorganic Syntheses XVI; contbr. articles to profl. jours. Recipient Ballar medal, 1972, So. Ill. U. Alumni Achievement award, 1974, Dwyer medal, 1976, James Flack Norris award for Outstanding Achievement in Teaching of Chemistry, 1981, Oesper Meml. award, 1983, IX Century medal Bologna U., 1988, Mosher award, 1990, Padova U. medal, 1991, Chinese Chem. Soc. medal, 1991, G.C. Pimental award, 1992, Chemical Pioneer award, 1992, Gold medal Am. Inst. Chemists, 1993, Joseph Chatt medal Royal Soc. Chemistry, 1996; Guggenheim fellow, 1954-55; NSF fellow, 1961-62; NATO sr. scientist fellow Italy, 1981; Sr. Humboldt fellow, 1992. Fellow NAS, AAAS (chmn. chemistry sect. 1979), Am. Acad. Arts and Scis.; mem. Am. Chem. Soc. (asst. editor jour. 1961-64, chmn. divsn. inorganic chemistry 1970, pres. 1983, bd. dirs. 1982-84, award for rsch. in inorganic chemistry 1964, Disting. Svc. award in inorganic chemistry 1975, N.E. regional award 1971, award in chem. edn. 1992, Chem. Pioneer award 1992, Gold Medal award 1993, Willard Gibbs medal 1996), Chem. Soc. London, Italian Chem. Soc. (hon.), Acad. Nat. dei Lincei (Italy), Sigma Xi (Monie A. Ferst medal 1992), Phi Lambda Upsilon, Alpha Chi Sigma, Phi Kappa Phi, Kappa Delta Phi, Phi Lambda Theta (hon.). Office: Northwestern U Chemistry Dept 2145 Sheridan Rd Evanston IL 60201-2926

BASOM, ANN MARIE, Russian language and literature educator; b. Eau Claire, Wis., Feb. 6, 1960; d. John F. and Mary Ann (Kinnick) Haines; m. Kenneth E. Basom, Aug. 25, 1984; children: Edward, Erik, Kyle. BA in Russian, U. Minn., 1980; MA in Slavic Langs., U. Wis., 1982, PhD, 1987. Asst. prof. Russian Middlebury (Vt.) Coll., 1987-93; asst. prof. Russian U. No. Iowa, Cedar Falls, 1993-96, assoc. prof. Russian, 1996—. Mem. editorial bd. The Silver Age of Russian Culture, 1994—; author articles. Internat. Rsch. and Exchs. Bd. grantee, Leningrad/Moscow, 1985-86; Fulbright grantee, 1985-86, Social Sci. Rsch. Coun. grantee, 1986-87. Mem. MLA, Am. Assn. Tchrs. Slavic and East European Langs., Am. Coun. Tchrs. Russian, Am. Assn. for Advancement of Slavic Studies, Am. Coun. on Teaching of Fgn. Langs., N.E. MLA, Rocky Mountain MLA. Office: U No Iowa Dept Modern Langs Cedar Falls IA 50614

BASS, STEVEN CRAIG, computer science educator; b. Indpls., July 29, 1943; s. Leland Ellsworth and Isabelle Frances (Ross) B.; m. Sara Ann Hiday, Sept. 4, 1965 (div. Apr. 1988); children: Leland Kai, Marshall Lynn; m. Kevyn Anne Salsburg, Jan. 2, 1989. BSEE, Purdue U., 1966, MSEE, 1968, PhD in Elec. Engring., 1971. Prof. elec. engring. Purdue U., Lafayette, Ind., 1971-88; prof. elec. and computer engring. George Mason U., Fairfax, Va., 1988-91; prin. engr. Mitre Corp., McLean, Va., 1988-89; prof. computer sci. and engring., chmn. dept. U. Notre Dame, Notre Dame, Ind., 1991—; cons. Magnovox Co., Ft. Wayne, Ind., 1971-73, Admiral Corp., Chgo., 1973-76, Kimball Internat., Jasper, Ind., 1978-84, Tektronix Corp., Wilsonville, Oreg., 1987-88. contbr. over 25 articles to profl. jours., delievered over 35 papers at sci. confs. Rescue officer Stockwell (Ind.) Vol. Fire Dept., 1985-88. Recipient numerous grants from NSF, USAF, IBM, Mitre Corp., others. Fellow IEEE (v.p. circuits and sys. soc. 1981, 91-93, mem. audio engring. soc.); mem. Tau Beta Pi. Roman Catholic. Office: U Notre Dame Dept Computer Sci & Engring 384 Fitzpatrick Hl Engrng Notre Dame IN 46556-5637

BASSI, SUZANNE H., volunteer; b. Santa Ana, Calif., Feb. 26, 1945; d. David Gould and Marian (Matthews) H.; Roger Joseph Bassi, Aug. 25, 1973; children: Carrie, Steven, Gregory. BA, Rosary Coll., River Forest, Ill., 1966; MA in Teaching, U. Ill., Champaign, 1973. Tchr. Resurreciton H.S., Chgo., 1966-67, Provisco Twp. H.S., Hillside, Ill., 1967-76; hoe day care operator Palatine, Ill., 1980-84; mem. bd. Palatine Elem. Sch. Dist. # 15, 1987-95. Rep. candidate for state rep. dist. 54, Ill.; vice chmn. Ed-Red, Park Ridge, Ill., 1993, chmn., 1994—; legis. chmn. IASB North Cook divsn., Lombard, Ill., 1994—; vol. Gary Skoien for Congress, Palatine, 1994. Named Those Whoe Excel, Ill. State Bd. Edn., 1992. Mem. League Women Voters (bd. dirs., legis. chair), YMCA, Palatine Rep. Women's Orgn., PTA (bd. dirs.). Republican. Roman Catholic. Home: 959 Carolyn Dr Palatine IL 60067-5982

BAST, ROSE ANN, biology educator; b. Cuba, Mo., Sept. 10, 1934; d. George Lester and Berenice Anna (Daehn) B. BS cum laude, Notre Dame Coll., St. Louis, 1960; MS, U. Okla., 1963, PhD, 1966. Cert. secondary sci. tchr, Mo.; joined Sch. Sisters of Notre Dame, 1954. Elem. sch. tchr. Ill. and Iowa, 1954-58; secondary sci. tchr. Sacred Heart High Sch., New Orleans, 1958-61; grad. teaching asst. U. Okla., Norman, 1961-63; assoc. prof. biology Notre Dame Coll., 1966-77, Mt. Mary Coll., Milw., 1977—; postdoctoral rsch. U. Tenn., Memphis, 1990-91. Reviewer: Cell Biology, 1984, Human Physiology, 1995; contbr. articles to profl. jours. Mem. AAAS, Am. Inst. Biol. Sci., N.Y. Acad. Sci., Beta Beta Beta (advisor Mount Mary Coll. chpt. 1977-94, Wis. state rep. 1987-91, dist. dir. 1991—), Sigma Xi, Phi Sigma Soc. Office: Mt Mary Coll 2900 N Menomonee River Pky Milwaukee WI 53222-4545

BASTIN, CATHERINE JEAN, elementary education educator; b. San Diego, Feb. 27, 1965; d. Daniel Carter and Beverly Jean (Boesinger) Harlan; m. Richard Dale Bastin, June 13, 1987; 1 child, Maggie Marie. BA, Hanover Coll., 1987; MS, Ind. U., 1991. Cert. elem. tchr., Ind. Tchr. grade 4 Centerton Elem. Sch., Martinsville, Ind., 1987—, computer coord., 1990—; Author: The Parent Involvement Program, 1991. Fund raiser Fall Foliage Festival, Martinsville, 1992—. Speaker, role model Girl Scouts Am., Ctrl. Ind., 1995; mem. Crohn & Colitis Found., 1993—. Grantee Edn. Found., Martinsville, 1992-94, South Ctrl. Solid Waste Dist., Plainfield, 1995. Mem. Cmty. Concerts Assn. (bd. dirs. 1995—), Morgan Co. Rodders Assn. (founder, pub. rels. chmn., sec. 1993—). Home: 610 Edna Ave Martinsville IN 46151 Office: Centerton Elem Sch 6075 High St Martinsville IN 46151

BASTO, LA DONNA JOAN, business administrator; b. Mpls., July 22, 1933; d. Mayland and Irene (Bennett) Bussart; m. Ronald Martin Basto, June 5, 1952; children: Patricia Ann, Richard Martin, Judith Renee. Bookkeeper various cos., Wichita, Kans., 1964-74; office mgr. William F. Hurst Co., Inc., Wichita, 1974-92, v.p., 1993—. Trustee AMS Found, 1993—. Mem. Adminstrv. Mgmt. Soc. (bus. expo chmn. 1984-86, exec. v.p. 1985-86, pres. 1986-87, asst. area dir., 1987-89, chmn. strategic planning com. 1987—, nominating com. 1988—, internat. dir. 1989-91, internat. pres.-elect 1992-93, internat. v.p. area/chpt. ops. 1991—, bd. dirs. 1994—, found. trustee 1993-94, internat. mebership com. 1988-89, Achievement award 1985, Cert. Appreciation 1986, Disting. Svc. award 1993). Republican. Presbyterian. Office: Wm F Hurst Co Inc PO Box 771069 Wichita KS 67277-1069

BASTOKY, BRUCE MICHAEL, human resources executive; b. Cleve., June 15, 1953. Student, Cuyahoga Community Coll., 1971-73, U. Akron, 1984-85. Personnel/tng. adminstr. The May Co., Cleve., 1974-77; cons. Roth Young, Cleve., 1978-80; dir. human resources The Lawson Co., Cuyahoga Falls, Ohio, 1980-86, Cardinal Industries, Columbus, Ohio, 1986-89; pres. January Mgmt. Group, Columbus, 1989—; mem. strategic planning bd. Profl. Secs. Internat., 1989. Author: Supervisor's Guide, 1985, Sixty Minute Mastery, 1987, Property Management First Aid Kit, 1988, The January Report, 1989, The Human Resources Executive's Guide to Mergers and Acquistions, 1989, Executvie Development: At The Crossroads, 1990, The Board of Director: A Peek Behind the Boardroom Doors, 1990, Human Resources and The Quest for Corporate Quality, 1992, Selecting the Chief Executive Officer, 1993; producer films-videos The Visitor, 1984, Deli Heros, 1985. Mem. Youth Motivation Task Force, Akron, Ohio, 1983-86; officer Pvt. Industry Council, Akron, 1983-86. Recipient Silver Quill for Script-writing award Internat. Assn. Bus. Communicators, 1985, Best Film/Video Series award Nat. Assn. Convenience Stores, 1985, Exec. of Yr. award Profl. Secs. Internat., 1987. Mem. Soc. for Human Resources Mgmt. (bd. dirs. 1985-86), Am. Soc. Tng. and Devel., Internat. Assn. of Corp. and Profl. Recruiters. Office: Jan Mgmt Group 5503 E Briardale Ln Dublin OH 43016

BATCHA, JAY P., investments broker; b. Austin, Tex., Jan. 29, 1962. BA, Alma (Mich.) Coll., 1984. Investment broker First of Mich. Corp., Traverse City, 1985—. Contbr. articles to trade mags. and newspapers. Vol. Boys and Girls Clubs, Traverse City, 1992; fundraiser, vol. Habitat for Humanity, Traverse City, 1993. Methodist. Office: First of Mich Corp 10850 E Traverse Hwy Traverse City MI 49684-1315

BATCHELDER, ALICE M., federal judge; b. 1944; m. William G. Batchelder III; children: William G. IV, Elisabeth. BA, Ohio Wesleyan U., 1964; JD, Akron U., 1971; LLM, U. Va., 1988. Tchr. Plain Local Sch. Dist., Franklin County, Ohio, 1965-66, Jones Jr. High Sch., 1966-67, Buckeye High Sch., Medina County, 1967-68; assoc. Williams & Batchelder, Medina, Ohio, 1971-83; judge U.S. Bankruptcy Ct., Ohio, 1983-85, U.S. Dist. Ct. (no. dist.) Ohio, Cleve., 1985-91, U.S. Ct. of Appeals (6th cir.), Cleveland, 1991—. Mem. ABA, Fed. Judge's Assn., Medina County Bar Assn. Office: 807 E Washington St Ste 200 Medina OH 44256-3330

BATCHELDER, ANNE STUART, former publisher, political party official; b. Lake Forest, Ill., Jan. 11, 1920; d. Robert Douglas and Harriet (McClure) Stuart; m. Clifton Brooks Batchelder, May 26, 1945; children: Edward, Anne Stuart, Mary Clifton, Lucia Brooks. Student Lake Forest Coll., 1941-43. Clubmobile driver ARC, Eng., Belgium, France, Holland and Germany, 1943-45; pub., editor Douglas County Gazette, 1970-75, 79-90; bd. dirs. Firstier Bank Omaha; dir., treas. U.S. Checkbook Com. Mem. Rep. Ctrl. Com. Nebr., 1955-62, 70-83, vice chmn. Ctrl. Com., 1959-64, chmn., 1975-79, mem. fin. com., 1957-64; chmn. women's sect. Douglas County Rep. Fin. Com., 1995, vice chmn. com., 1958-60; v.p. Omaha Woman's Rep. Club, 1957-58, pres., 1959-60; alt. del. Nat. Conv., 1956, 72, del., 1980, 84, 88; mem. Rep. Nat. Com. for Nebr., 1964-70; asst. chmn. Douglas County Rep. Ctrl. Com., 1971-74; 1st v.p. Nebr. Fedn. Rep. Women, 1971-72, pres., 1972-74; chmn. Nebr. Rep. Com., 1975-79; chmn. fundraising com. Nat. Fedn. Rep. Women, 1981-93, vice chmn., 1994-96, chmn., 1996—; mem. Nebr. State Bldg. Commn., 1979-83; Rep. candidate for lt. gov., 1974. Sr. v.p. Nebr. Founders Day, 1958; bd. dirs. YWCA, 1983-89, Omaha Libr. Found., 1991—; past trustee Brownell Hall, Vis. Nurse Assn., Omaha Libr. Found.; past pres. Nebr. chpt. Freedoms Found. at Valley Forge; chmn. fin. George Bush for Pres., Nebr., 1987-88; apptd. Kennedy Ctr. Performing Arts, 1989, 94, Pres.' Adv. Com. on the Arts, 1990—; mem. Nebr. Rep. State Fin. Com., 1990, Nat. Fin. Com. Bush-Quayle, 1992; active Omaha Meth. Hosp. Found., Brownell-Talbot Sch. Found. Elected to Nebr. Rep. Hall of Fame, 1984. Mayflower Soc., Colonial Dames, P.E.O., Nat. League Pen Women Omaha Country, Omaha. Presbyterian (trustee). Home: 6875 State St Omaha NE 68152-1633

BATE, BRIAN R., psychologist; b. Cleve., July 4, 1940; s. Paul A. and Claire N. B.; children: Jennifer A., Julia L. BA in English, Western Res. U., 1963, MS in Psychology, 1965; PhD in Psychology, Case Western Res. U., 1972. Lic. psychologist, Ohio. Instr. Cuyahoga Community Coll., Parma, Ohio, 1969, from asst. prof. to prof. of psychology, 1970—; pvt. practice Cleve., 1972—. Contbr. articles to profl. jours. Nat. Merit Scholar Princeton U., 1958-61, Western Res. U., 1962-63; USPHS fellow, 1963-67. Mem. APA, Am. Fedn. Musicians, Gestalt inst. of Cleve., Nat. Register Health Svc. Providers in Psychology (cert.), Edelweiss Ski Club, Cleve. Buddhist Temple. Home and Office: 6511 Mill Rd Cleveland OH 44141-1560

BATEMAN, C. BARRY, airport terminal executive. Airport dir. Gen. Mitchell Internat. Airport, Milw. Office: Gen Mitchell Internat Airport 5300 S Howell Ave Milwaukee WI 53207-6156

BATEMAN, ROCKLIN (ROCKY), state legislator; m. Nancy Jo Bateman; 2 children. Diploma, Bismark State Coll. Farmer and rancher; mem. N.D. Ho. of Reps. from 31st dist., 1991—; mem. Appropriations, Edn. and Environ. Coms. N.D. Ho. of Reps. Mem. N.D. Stockmen's Assn. (bd. dirs.), Nat. Cattlemen's Assn. Republican. Address: RR 1 Box 87 New Salem ND 58563*

BATEMAN, SAMUEL T., state legislator, insurance agency executive; b. Cin., June 11, 1936; s. Samuel T. and Marjorie (Wilkenson) B.; m. Barbara Lee Kane, 1958; children: Tim, Richard, Christopher. Student, U. Cin., 1958-60. Owner, mgr. Sam Bateman Ins. Agy., Milford, Ohio, 1958-80; v.p. Harding Ins. Agy., Milford, 1980-84, Tri-County Ins. Agy., Milford, 1984—, C. Edward Lovins Ins., Milford, 1984—; mem. Ohio Ho. of Reps., Columbus, 1984—. Mem. Clermont-Milford Sch. Bd., 1974-84; bd. dirs. Cin. Area chpt. ARC, Salvation Army Clermont County. Named Legislator with Best Interest of Children, 1987; named to Hall of Fame, Milford H.S., 1985, 86. Mem. Milford Area C. of C. (Outstanding Citizen award 1978), Clermont County C. of C., Clermont County Farm Bur., Clermont County Ind. Ins. Agts., Kiwanis. Republican. Home: PO Box 214 Milford OH 45150-0214*

BATES, DALLAS KELVIN, chemistry educator; b. Hillsdale, Mich., Oct. 17, 1949; s. Albert Jerome and Iva G. (Speakman) B.; m. Carol Ann Wilcox, June 19, 1971; 1 child, Caleb Allan. BS, Mich. Tech. U., 1971; PhD, U. Idaho, 1975. Asst. prof. of chemistry Mich. Technol. U., Houghton, 1975-78, assoc. prof., 1978-95, prof., 1995—, asst. head dept. of chemistry, 1985-90. Co-editor: Organic Electronic Spectral Data, vols. 1-3, 1977—. Mem. AAAS, Am. Chem. Soc., Internat. Soc. Heterocyclic Chemistry, Sigma Xi. Office: Mich Technol U Dept Chemistry 1400 Townsend Dr Houghton MI 49931-1200

BATES, DAVID ALLEN, municipal administrator; b. Goshen, Ind., Sept. 24, 1948. BS, Ball State U., Muncie, Ind., 1971; MPA, Western Mich. U., 1991. Cert. in wastewater ops., Ind. Pre-treatment dir. City of Elkhart (Ind.) Wastewater, 1983-89; environ. compliance adminstr. City of Goshen (Ind.) Utilities, 1989—. Pres. Household Hazardous Waste Com., Elkhart County, 1993-95. Mem. Water Environment Fedn. Home: 1328 Haughey Dr Union City MI 49094 Office: City of Goshen 1000 W Wilden Ave Goshen IN 46526

BATES, GERALD EARL, bishop; b. Caldwell, Ohio, Sept. 12, 1933; s. Earl and Lillian Inez (Merritt) B.; m. Marlene Rachel Parsons, Aug. 21, 1954; children: David Earl. William Randall, Elizabeth Ann. AA, Spring Arbor Coll., 1953; AB, Greenville Coll., 1955; MDiv, Asbury Theol. Sem., 1958; ThM, Western Theol. Sem., 1964; PhD, Mich. State U., 1975; DD (hon.), Roberts Wesleyan Coll., 1986. Missionary with Gen. Missionary Bd. Free Meth. Ch. of N.Am., Winona Lake, Ind., 1957-85; area adminstrv. asst. for Cen. Africa Free Meth. Ch. of N.Am., 1973-85; bishop Free Meth. Ch. of N.Am., Indpls., 1985—. Author: Soul Afire, 1981, 2d edit., 1993; chmn. bd. editors: Book of Discipline, 1985. Trustee Ctrl. Coll., Asbury Theol. Sem., Wilmore, Kay., Spring Arbor Coll.; chmn., bd. dirs. Free Meth. Ch. of N.Am.; bd. dirs. India Missionary Tng. Bd., Wesley Internat. Bible Coll., Nigeria; pres. bd. dirs. Free Meth. World Fellowship, 1989-95. Recipient Alumnus of Yr. award Spring Arbor Coll., 1974, Goodwill Amb. award Noble County C. of C., 1988, Alumnus of Yr. award Asbury Theol. Sem., 1991. Mem. Phi Kappa Phi. Republican. Home: 6715 Oak Lake Dr Indianapolis IN 46214-2038 Office: PO Box 535002 Indianapolis IN 46253-5002

BATES, JOHN ROBERT, government agency administrator; b. New Castle, Ind., May 3, 1947; s. Robert Edward and Theda Mavis (Edwards) B.; m. Jacqueline Lou Parady, May 13, 1985; 1 child, Jeremy Richard. BS in Bus. Mgmt., Ind. U., 1979. Loan servicing specialist U.S. SBA, Indpls., 1972-77, loan processing specialist, 1977-79, disaster br. mgr., 1979, liquidation loan specialist, 1979-81, chief liquidation div., 1981-86, acting asst. dir. mgmt. assistance, 1983, asst. dist. dir. fin., 1986—, asst. dir. for econ. devel., 1994—, pub. info. officer, 1988—; mem. Gov.'s Task Force on Small Bus., Indpls., 1988-90; participant Gov.'s Conf. Small Bus., Indpls., 1989, Ind. Econ. Devel. Congress., 1988, Ind. White House Conf. on Small Bus., 1986; editor, author SBA News, 1988—. Bd. dirs. Pike Youth Soccer Club, Inc. Mem. Ind. U. Alumni Assn., Ind. U. Sch. Bus. Dean's Assn., Phi Sigma Kappa. Office: US SBA 429 N Pennsylvania St Indianapolis IN 46204-1873

BATES, MARGARET HELENA, special education educator; b. Irvington, N.J., Jan. 27, 1943; d. Marcel Bogstahl and Helena Christina (Yarosczynsky) Bogstahl; divorced; children: Robert Crew, Diane Carlyle. BA, Coll. Steubenville, 1966; MS, St. Cloud State U., 1982. Cert. tchr. English, spl. edn., emotionally/behaviorally disorders and learning disabilities, Minn. Tchr. Ind. Sch. Dist. # 742, St. Cloud, 1976—. Adv. bd. Minn. Acad. Excellence Found., St. Paul., 1993-94; state coun. chair Minn. Edn. Assn., 1993—; co-chair. St. Cloud Edn. Assn., 1979-84; sec. Audubon Soc., 1992—; historian Stearns County Theatrical Co., 1992, 93, 94; bd. dirs. The New Tradition Theatre Co., 1988-89. Grantee Bremer Found., 1991, incentive grantee Ind. Sch. Dist. 742. Mem. Coun. for Exceptional Children, Minn. Coun. Children with Behavior Disorders, Minn. Educators of Children with Emotional Disorders, Delta Kappa Gamma (1st v.p. 1994—). Home: 825 17th Ave S Saint Cloud MN 56301-5234 Office: Area Learning Ctr 809 12th St N Saint Cloud MN 56303-2847

BATES, MILTON J., English language educator; b. Warrensburg, Mo., June 4, 1945; s. Milton F. and Helen (Harter) B.; m. Elizabeth J. Kwapy, May 6, 1972; children: Jeremy A., Elizabeth S. BA, St. Louis U., 1968; MA, U. Calif., Berkeley, 1972, PhD, 1977. Asst. prof. Williams Coll., Williamstown, Mass., 1975-81; asst. prof. English Marquette U., Milw., 1981-86, assoc. prof. English, 1986-91, prof. English, 1991—; rsch. fellow Am. Coun. Learned Socs., 1980, 86, NEH, 1985, Guggenheim Found., 1989. Author: Wallace Stevens: A Mythology of Self, 1985 (Notable Book of Yr. N.Y. Times Book Rev. 1985), The Wars We Took to Vietnam: Cultural Conflict and Storytelling, 1996; editor: Sur Plusieurs Beaux Subjects: Wallace Steven's Commonplace Book, 1989, Opus Posthumous (Wallace Stevens), 1989. Sgt. U.S.. Army, 1969-71, Vietnam. Kent fellow Danforth Found., 1973. Mem. MLA (exec. com. 20th Century Am. lit., 1986-90), Wallace Stevens Soc. (adv. bd. 1990—), Vietnam Vets. Am., Sierra Club. Home: 8114 W

Chestnut St Wauwatosa WI 53213-2508 Office: Marquette U Dept English Milwaukee WI 53233

BATLIVALA, ROBERT BOMI D., oil company executive, economics educator; b. Bombay, India, Feb. 17, 1940; came to U.S., 1962, naturalized, 1968; s. Dean Shaw and Rose (Engineer) B.; m. Carole Gretchen Feustel, May 9, 1964; children: Amy, Dina. BS in Geology, Chemistry, St. Xavier Coll., Bombay, Ind., 1960; MBA in Bus., Econs., Loyola U., Chgo., 1970; PHD in Bus., Econs., Ill. Inst. Tech., 1971; post-doctoral studies, U. Chgo., 1972-73. Rsch. chemist Reynolds Metals Co., McCook, Ill., 1962-64; from sales engr. to staff dir. econs. Amoco Corp., Chgo., 1964-1988, dir. antitrust econs., 1988-93; dir. regulatory econs., 1993—; adj. prof. bus. and econs. Rosary Coll., River Forest, Ill., 1976—, Graduate Sch. Bus., 1986—; bd. dirs. Pvt. Bancorp, Inc., Chgo. Contbr. articles to profl. jours., 1971-78. Bd. dirs. Ctr. for Conflict Resolution, 1990—. Recipient Stuart Tuition scholarship, Ill. Inst. Tech., 1970-71, Recognition award Rosary Coll. Grad. Sch. Bus. Alumni Assn., River Forest, 1986. Mem. ABA (assoc.), Nat. Assn. Mfrs. (corp. fin., mgmt. & competition com., regulation, transp. com. 1980—), Am. Econ. Assn., Assn. of Energy Economists, Loyola U. Grad. Bus. Alumni Assn. (pres., sr. v.p. 1971-73, Disting. Alumni award 1975), Oak Park Country Club. Home: 1106 Keystone Ave River Forest IL 60305-1326 Office: Amoco Corp 200 E Randolph St Chicago IL 60601-6436

BATORY, RONALD LOUIS, transportation executive; b. Detroit, Jan. 25, 1950; s. Louis Frank and Bonita Faye (Hall) B.; m. Barbara Ellen Berger, Apr. 19, 1975; 1 child, Erin Faye. BA, Adrian Coll., 1971; MA, Eastern Mich. U., 1975. With Detroit, Toledo & Ironton R.R., 1971-81; adminstrn. asst. to v.p. ops. Dearborn, Mich., 1972-75; asst. engr. track Flat Rock, Mich., 1975-76; mgr. indsl. engr. Dearborn, 1976-77, dir. material procurement and planning, 1977-81; with Grand Trunk Western R.R., 1981-87; transp. supr. Pontiac, Mich., 1981-82; trainmaster Toledo, 1982-84; terminal mgr. Chgo., 1984-86, dist. mgr. ops, 1986-87; dir. transp. planning Detroit, 1987; v.p., gen. mgr. Chgo. Mo. & Western Rlwy., Springfield, Ill., 1987-89; asst. mgr. ea. region So. Pacific Transp., Lisle, Ill., 1989-92, gen. mgr. Midwest region, 1992-94; pres. The Belt Railway Co. of Chgo., 1994—; bd. dirs. Kansas City Terminal Rlwy., Terminal Railroad Assn. St. Louis. Author: Purchasing Perspective, 1979, Econs. of Planning, 1980. Mem. The R.R. Tie Assn., Am. Rlwy. Engr. Assn., Ry. Ops. Officers, Inc., Am. Assn. R.R. Supts. (bd. dirs.), Fairlane Club, Union League Club of Chgo., Oak Brook Bath and Tennis Club. Republican. Methodist. Home: 4 Mockingbird Ln Oak Brook IL 60521-1725 Office: Belt Railway Co Chgo 6900 S Central Ave Chicago IL 60638-6312

BATRA, ROMESH CHANDER, engineering mechanics educator, researcher; b. Dherowal, Panjab, India, Aug. 16, 1947; came to U.S., 1969; s. Amir Chand and Dewki Bai (Dhamija) B.; m. Manju Dhamija, June 26, 1972; children: Monica, Meenakshi. BSME, Panjabi U., Patiala, India, 1968; MASc, U. Waterloo, Ont., Can., 1969; PhD, Johns Hopkins U., 1972. Postdoctoral rsch. assoc. Johns Hopkins U., Balt., 1972-73; rsch. assoc. McMaster U., Hamilton, Ont., 1973-74; asst. prof. U. Ala., Tuscaloosa, 1976-77; asst. prof. engring. mechanics U. Mo., Rolla, 1974-76, assoc. prof., 1977-81, prof., 1981-94; Clifton C. Garvin prof. Va. Polytech. Inst. & State U., Blacksburg, 1994—. Mem. editl. bd. Internat. Jour. Plasticity, 1989—, Continuum Mechanics and Thermodynamics, 1993—, Internat. Jour. Engring. Design and Analysis, 1992—, Computational Mechanics, 1994—; editor: Mathematics and Mechanics of Solids, 1995—; reviewer for various jours. in field; contbr. numerous articles to profl. jours. Grantee NSF, 1980-83, 87—, Army Rsch. Office, 1985—, Office of Naval Rsch., 1994—; recipient Halliburton Excellence award U. Mo., 1986, Faculty Excellence award, 1987-93, Fellow Mems. award Am. Soc. Engring. Edn., 1992, Alexander von Humboldt award for sr. scientists, 1992, Jai Krishna award Indian Geotech. Soc., 1994, Outstanding Teaching award U. Mo., 1989; inducted into Hopkins Soc. Scholars, 1993. Fellow ASME (chair elasticity com. 1995—, co-editor symposium procs. 1991, 94, 95, assoc. editor Jour. Engring. Materials and Tech. 1996—), Am. Acad. Mechanics, Am. Soc. Engring. Edn. (Centennial award 1993); mem. Soc. for Natural Philosophy (treas. 1987-89, editor meeting procs. 1981), Soc. Rheology, Soc. Engring. Sci. (bd. dirs. 1991—, editor meeting procs. 1982, symposium procs. 1995, pres. 1996), Midwestern Mechanics Conf. (editor procs. 1991, co-editor procs. 1996). Office: Va Polytech Inst & State U Dept Engring Sci & Mechanic 220 Norris Hall Blacksburg VA 24061-0219

BATT, NICK, property and investment executive; b. Defiance, Ohio, May 6, 1952; s. Dan and Zenith (Dreher) B.; BS, Purdue U., 1972; JD, U. Toledo, 1976. Asst. prosecutor Lucas County, Toledo, 1976-80, civil div. chief, 1980-83; village atty., Village of Holland, Ohio, 1980-91; law dir. City of Oregon, Ohio, 1984-91; spl. counsel State of Ohio, 1983-93; pres. Property & Mgmt. Connection, Inc., Toledo, 1993—. Mem. Maumee Valley Girl Scout Coun., Toledo, 1977-80; bd. mem. Bd. Community Rels., Toledo, 1975-76; mem. Lucas County Dem. Exec. Com., 1981-83. Named One of Toledo's Outstanding Young Men, Toledo Jaycees, 1979. Mem. KC, Elks. Democrat. Roman Catholic. Office: 1732 Arlington Ave Toledo OH 43609

BATTANI, NANCY LEE, rehabilitation nurse; b. Romeo, Mich., Mar. 23, 1934; d. George F. Jersey; m. Paul F. Battani, June 2, 1956; 1 child, Mary Ann. Diploma, Deaconess Hosp. Sch. Nursing, 1955; BSN, Wayne State U., 1983; MS, Cen. Mich. U., 1989. Supr. Oakland Gen. Hosp., Madison Hgts., Mich., 1964-72; dir. nursing Cambridge Nursing Ctr., Madison Hgts., Mich., 1975-76; asst. dir. nursing Rehab. Inst., Detroit, 1976-88, Orchard Hills Nursing Ctr., Pontiac, Mich., 1989—; bd. dirs. Detroit Med. Ctr. Adv. Bd., 1985-88. Contbr. articles to profl. jours. Mem. Guardian Angels Alter Soc., Clawson, Mich., 1966—; instr. ARC, Detroit, 1978—; mem. Am. Legion Aux., Detroit, 1980—. Recipient Svc. award ARC, 1983, honoree Nat. Disting. Svc. Registry; named Golden Key scholar Wayne State U., 1983. Mem. Assn. Rehab. Nurses (cert.), Congress Rehab. Medicine, Mich. League for Nursing, Wayne State U. Alumni Assn., Women of Wayne State U., Wayne State U. Alumni Coll. Nursing, Sigma Theta Tau.

BATTLE, GREGORY, operations research analyst; b. Nashville, N.C., Mar. 24, 1955; s. Roger and Viola May B. BS, Morehouse Coll., 1977; DPhil, Washington U., St. Louis, 1995. Rsch. assoc. Nat. Ctr. Atmospheric Rsch., Boulder, 1976; rsch. asst. Fermi Nat. Accelerator Lab., Batavia, Ill., 1977; adminstrv. asst. IBM, Charlotte, 1978; sorter operator Fulton Nat. Bank, Atlanta, 1979; occupational rsch. analyst Ga. Career Info. Systems, Atlanta, 1980; mathematician, statistician Naval Personnel Rsch. & Devel. Ctr., San Diego, 1982-83; geodesist Defense Mapping Agy. Aerospace Ctr., St. Louis, 1984-87; ops. rsch. analyst Aviation-Troop Commd., St. Louis, 1987—; lectr. in field. Author of poems. Mem. Am. Math. Soc., Toastmasters, Kappa Alpha Psi, Phi Beta Kappa, Sigma Pi Sigma, Pi Mu Epsilon, Beta Kappa Chi. Baptist. Home: 5617 Enright Ave #302 Saint Louis MO 63112 Office: PEO Aviation 4300 Goodfellow Blvd Saint Louis MO 63120

BATTLE, JOE DAVID, engineer; b. Montgomery, Ala., Apr. 11, 1958; s. Marvin Andrew and Mary Della (Reynolds) B.; m. Margaret Carol Gillum, Jan. 18, 1980; children: Chloe Christine, John Edward. BS in Civil Engring. Tech., U. Ala., 1981. Coop. engr. Harbert Internat., Birmingham, Ala., 1977-78, B,E&K Inc., Birmingham, 1979-80; estimator Campbell & Assocs., Tuscaloosa, Ala., 1980-81; project coord. Pitts.-Desmoines Corp., Birmingham, 1981-83; staff project engr. VA, Dublin, Ga., 1983-85; asst. chief engr. VA, Indpls., 1985-88, chief engr., 1988—. Mem. Fed. Exec. Assn., Am. Soc. Hosp. Engrs. Baptist. Lodge: Lions. Office: VA Med Ctr 1481 W 10th St Indianapolis IN 46202-2803

BATTO, BERNARD FRANK, religious studies educator; b. Bandera, Tex., Jan. 16, 1941; s. Raymond Howard and Agatha Frances (Mazurek) B.; m. Teresa Ann Becker, Aug. 17, 1967; children: Rachel Ann, Nathan Frank, Amos Becker, Jeremiah Paul, Sarah Frances. BA, MaryKnoll Coll., 1963; PhD, Johns Hopkins U., 1972. Asst. prof. Old Testament Mount St. Mary's Sem., Emmitsburg, Md., 1971-75; asst. prof. religion Williamette U., Salem, Oreg., 1975-79; assoc. prof. theology U. Dallas, Irving, Tex., 1979-86; from assoc. prof. to prof. religion DePauw U., Greencastle, Ind., 1987—. Author: Women at Mari, 1974, Slaying the Dragon, 1992; co-editor: Biblical Canon in Comparative Perspective, 1992; contbr. articles to profl. jours.; assoc. editor: Cath. Bibl. Quar., 1988-90, book rev. editor, 1990-95. Rsch. grantee NEH, 1975; Summer seminar fellow Yale U., 1990. Mem. Cath. Bibl. Assn. Am., Soc. Bibl. Lit. (pres. S.W. region 1985-86), Am. Oriental Soc., Am. Schs. Oriental Rsch. Roman Catholic. Home: 636 E Seminary St Greencastle IN 46135 Office: DePauw U 102D Harrison Hall Greencastle IN 46135

BAUER, ARTHUR ADOLPH, metallurgical engineer; b. N.Y.C., Mar. 5, 1925; s. John Stephen and Eldrieda Louise (Weisenberger) B.; m. Katharina Ruth Meszkat, June 15, 1947; children: Gary L., Stephen J., Faith E. BS, Columbia U., 1950, MS, 1952. Registered profl. engr., Ohio. Metall. engr. Battelle Meml. Inst., Columbus, Ohio, 1952-56, asst. div. chief, 1956-62, cons., 1962-67, rsch. leader, 1967-78, project mgr., 1978-87; project mgr. A.A. Bauer, Cons., Columbus, Ohio, 1987—; U.S. rep. to German Fast-Breeder Project, Karlsruhe, Fed. Republic of Germany, 1964-67, U.S. waste mgmt. rep. Fed. Republic of Germany, Braunschweig, 1980-82. Author: Constitutional Diagrams of Uranium and Thorium Alloys, 1958; contbr. over 60 articles to scholarly and profl. jours. Cpl. U.S. Army, 1943-46, ETO. Mem. Am. Nuclear Soc., Am. Soc. for Metals, Masons, Sertoma (pres. Tri-Village chpt. 1968—), Columbus Maennerchor, Tau Beta Pi. Republican. Lutheran. Home and Office: 3171 Kingstree Ct Dublin OH 43017-2202

BAUER, BURNETT PATRICK, state legislator; b. LaPorte, Ind., May 25, 1944; s. Burnett Calix and Helen (Cryan) B.; m. Karen Bella, 1980; children: Bartholomew, Meagan, Maureen. BA, U. Notre Dame, 1966; postgrad., Miami U., 1966-68; MS, Ind. U. Ind. state rep. Dist. 7, 1970-91, Dist. 6, 1991—; asst. minority leader, 1977, 83; ranking minority leader Ind. Ho. Reps., 1984-89, chmn., ways and means, 1989, ranking minority mem., state budget com., 1989; tchr. Muessel Jr. H.S., South Bend, Ind., 1968-74, Madison Jr. H.S., 1974-75, Dickinson Jr. H.S., 1976-78, Washington H.S.; asst. to supt. South Bend Cmty. Sch. Corp. Recipient Legis. award EPA Region V, 1976. Mem. K.C., Am. Fedn. Tchrs., Ind. State Tchrs. Assn. Home: 1307 Sunnymede Ave South Bend IN 46615-1017*

BAUER, CHRIS MICHAEL, banker; b. Milw., Sept. 2, 1948; s. Heinz Gerald and Maria (Weber) B.; m. Susan Marie Branton, June 28, 1969. BBA, U. Wis., 1970; MBA, Marquette U., 1976. Mgmt. trainee 1st Wis. Nat. Bank, Milw., 1970-72, spl. enterprise officer, 1972-74, asst. mgr., 1974-75; v.p. 1st Wis.-Racine, 1976-78; pres. 1st Wis.-Brookfield, 1978-84; 1st v.p. Firstar Corp. (formerly 1st Wis. Corp.), Milw., 1984-86, sr. v.p., 1986-89; pres., COO Firstar Bank Milw. (formerly 1st Wis. Nat. Bank), Milw., 1989-91; chmn., CEO Firstar Bank Milw. (formerly 1st Wis. Nat. Bank), 1991—, also bd. dirs. Bd. dirs. St. Luke's Med. Ctr., Milw., U. Wis.-Milw. Found., Milw. Pub. Libr. Found., Milw. World Festival Inc., Next Door Found., Siebert Lutheran Found., AAA Mich.; mem. Greater Milw. Com. Mem. Bankers Roundtable, Milw. Country Club, Univ. Club, Westmoor Country Club. Lutheran. Office: Firstar Bank Milw 777 E Wisconsin Ave Milwaukee WI 53202-5302

BAUER, GERARD JOSEPH, municipal administrator; b. Belleville, Ill., Sept. 9, 1954; s. Alphone A. and Henrietta F. Bauer. BA in Psychology and Speech Communications, Kans. U., 1976; MBA, Sangamon State U., 1990. Planning technician S.W. Ill. Met. Planning Commn., Collinsville, 1977, City of Fairview Heights, Ill., 1977-79; community rels. specialist City of Decatur, Ill., 1979-83; community rels. coord. City of Decatur, 1983-87, risk mgr., 1987—. Bd. dirs. Shemamo Girl Scout Coun. Mem. Risk and Ins. Mgmt. Soc. (cert. assoc. risk mgr., sec. Ctrl. Ill. chpt. 1992-93, v.p. 1994-95, pres. 1996—), Pub. Risk Mgmt. Assn., Decatur Bus. Health Roundtable, Kiwanis Club (bd. dirs. 1993-95), Decatur Leadership Inst. Alumni Assn., Kans. U. Alumni Assn., KC, Phi Beta Kappa. Roman Catholic.

BAUER, JOHN HARRY, physician; b. Phila., Apr. 15, 1943; s. LaVerne N. and Antoinette E. (Black) B.; m. Barbar Gruger, June 18, 1966; childrne: Holly Anne, Daniel John. BA cum laude, SUNY, Buffalo, 1965; MD, Jefferson Med. Coll. Phila., 1969. Diplomate Am. Bd. Internal Medicine. Intern then resident Ind. U. Med. Ctr. and Hosps., 1969-71, fellow, 1974-75; staff physician Harry S. Truman Meml. Vets. Hosp., Columbia, Mo., 1975-85, rsch. assoc., 1979-81, chief med. svc., 1993-95, acting chief of staff, 1994-95, chief of staff, 1995—; asst. prof. medicine U. Mo., Columbia, 1975-79, assoc. prof., 1979-87, prof. medicine, 1987—, dir. clin. rsch. unit, 1991-95, assoc. chmn., 1993-95, assoc. dean, 1995—. Mem. editorial bd. jours. Cardiovascular Drugs and Therapy, Blood Pressure, Hypertension: Index and Revs., Current Opinion in Nephrology and Hypertension, Hypertension; reveiwer jours.; contbr. numerous articles to profl. jours. Med. officer USNR, 1971-73. Decorated Navy Achievement medal. Fellow ACP, Am. Heart Assn. (coun. high blood pressure rsch.); mem. Am. Fedn. Clin. Rsch., Am. soc. Nephrology, Am. Soc. Hypertinsion, Mo. found. Med. Rsch. (bd. dirs. 1994—), Nat. Kidney Found. (coun. dialysis and transplantation 1983—), Assn. VA Chiefs of Staff, Phi Beta Kappa, Sigma Xi. Office: Harry S Truman Meml Vets Hosp 800 Hospital Dr Columbia MO 65201

BAUER, KURT W., civil engineer; b. Milw., Aug. 25, 1929; BS in Civil Engring., Marquette U., 1951; MS, U. Wis., 1955, PhD, 1961. Registered profl. engr., registered land surveyor, Wis. City planner City of South Milwaukee, Wis., 1953-55; instr. civil engring. U. Wis., Madison, 1955-56, Ford Found. rsch. fellow, 1960-61; assoc. civil engr. H.C. Webster & Son, Milw., 1956-59; chief current planning City of Madison, 1959-60; dir. Southeastern Wis. Regional Planning Commn., Milw., 1961—; surveyor Milw. County, 1984—. Contbr. numerous papers to profl. jours. Served to lt. col. USAF, 1953—. Fellow ASCE (editor Manual Practice on Engring. Surveying); mem. Am. Inst. Cert. Planners, Am. Congress on Surveying and Mapping, Am. Pub. Works Assn., Inst. Mcpl. Engring., Transp. Research Bd., Sci. Adv. Bd., Internat. Joint Commn. on Gt. Lakes. Lutheran. Office: Southeastern Wis Regional Planning Commn 916 N East Ave Waukesha WI 53186-4808

BAUER, MARK TIMOTHY, electrical engineer; b. Beatrice, Nebr., Oct. 3, 1957; s. John A. and Fran (Bohner) B.; m. Toni Kay DeWitt, Dec. 27, 1991; 1 child, Josh. BS in Computer Sci., U. Nebr. Lincoln, 1980; MSEE, 1989. Elec. engr. Lester Elec. of Nebr., 1981—. Office: Lester Electrical of Nebr 625 W A St Lincoln NE 68522-1706

BAUER, PETER HEINZ, engineering educator; b. Bamberg, Germany, June 17, 1959; came to U.S., 1984; s. Konrad and Maria (Hohner) B.; m. Sabine Schweizer, June 13, 1992; children: Lisa, Stephen. Diploma, Tech. U., Munich, 1984; PhD, U. Miami, 1988. Engr. Siemens, Munich, 1984; from tchg. and rsch. asst. to lectr. U. Miami, 1985-88; asst. prof. U. Notre Dame, Ind., 1988-94, assoc. prof., 1994—. Contbr. chpts. to books. Recipient Tech. Innovator award NASA, 1984; grantee NASA, NSF, Clark Components, office of Naval Rsch., 1990-95. Mem. IEEE (sr. mem.), Soc. Automotive Engrs. Roman Catholic. Office: Univ Notre Dame Fitzpatrick Hall of Engring Notre Dame IN 46556

BAUER, ROBERT ALAN, engineering geologist; b. Chgo., Jan. 19, 1952; s. Stanley John and Gladys (Triskosko) B.; m. Wendy Louise Shields, Feb. 12, 1977; 1 child, Kathryn Ruth. BS in Geol. Sci., U. Ill., Chgo., 1976; MS in Engring Geology, U. Ill., 1983. Geologist McHenry County Planning Commn., Woodstock, Ill., 1976; geologist Ill. State Geol. Survey, Champaign, Ill., 1976-88, head engring. geology sect., 1988—. Contbr. articles to profl. jours. Tech. mgr. Ill. Mine Subsidence Rsch. Program, Champaign, 1984-91, dir. 1991-93. Mem. AIME (Soc. Mining Engrs. div.), Internat. Soc. Rock Mechanics, Am. Underground Space Assn., Assn. Engring. Geologists (Douglas R. Piteau Outstanding Young Mem. awar 1987, chmn. rock mechanics com. 1986—). Office: Ill State Geol Survey 615 E Peabody Dr Champaign IL 61820-6918

BAUER, WILLIAM JOSEPH, federal judge; b. Chgo., Sept. 15, 1926; s. William Francis and Lucille (Gleason) B.; m. Mary Nicol, Jan. 28, 1950; children—Patricia, Linda. A.B., Elmhurst Coll., 1949, LLD, 1969; JD, DePaul U., 1952, LLD (hon.), 1993; John Marshall Law Sch., 1987; LLD (hon.), Roosevelt U., 1994. Bar: Ill. 1951. Ptnr. Erlenborn, Bauer & Hotte, Elmhurst, Ill., 1953-64; asst. state's atty. Du Page County, Ill., 1952-56; 1st asst. state's atty., 1956-58, state's atty., 1959-64; judge 18th Jud. Cir. Ct., 1964-70; U.S. dist. atty. No. Ill. Chgo., 1970-71; judge U.S. Dist. Ct. (no. dist.), Chgo., 1971-75; judge U.S. Ct. Appeals (7th cir.), 1975-86, chief judge, 1986-93; instr. bus. law Elmhurst Coll., 1952-59; adj. prof. law DePaul U., 1978-91; former mem. Ill. Supreme Ct. Com. on Pattern Criminal Jury Instrns.; chmn. Fed. Criminal Jury Instrn. Com. 7th Cir. Trustee Elmhurst Coll., 1979—, De Paul U., 1984—, DuPage Meml. Hosp.; bd. advisors Mercy Hosp. Served with AUS, 1945-47. Mem. ABA, Ill. Bar Assn., Du Page County Bar Assn. (past pres.), Chgo. Bar Assn., Fed. Bar Assn. (former bd. dirs.). Roman Catholic. Clubs: Union League, Law, Legal (Chgo.). Office: US Ct Appeals 219 S Dearborn St Ste 2754 Chicago IL 60604-1803

BAUERLY, RONALD JOHN, marketing educator; b. Monroe, Wis., Oct. 31, 1953; s. Jack Leroy and Josephine (Wiegel) B.; m. Robin Rochelle Kramer, Aug. 8, 1981; children: Shannon Marie, Thomas Joseph. BBA, U. Iowa, 1975, MBA, 1977; DBA, Southern Ill. U., Carbondale, 1989. Asst. mgr. K-Mart Corp., Racine, Wis., 1977-78; instr. Metropolitan Tech. Community Coll., Omaha, 1978, Loras Coll., Dubuque, Iowa, 1979-81, Northwest Mo. State U., Maryville, 1981-82; asst. prof. Brescia Coll., Owensboro, Ky., 1983-86; asst. prof. mktg. Western Ill. U., Macomb, 1987-91, assoc. prof., 1991-96, prof., 1996—. Editor Jour. of Contemporary Business Issues; contbr. articles to jours. Mem. Am. Acad. Advt., Am. Mktg. Assn., Assn. for Consumer Rsch., Acad. Mktg. Sci., Phi Kappa Phi, Beta Gamma Sigma. Office: Western Ill U 424 Stipes Macomb IL 61455

BAUER-TOMICH, FAITH E., programmer, analyst; b. Columbus, Ohio, June 1, 1957; d. Arthur A. and Katharina R. (Meszkat) Bauer; m. Edward T. Tomich, Sept. 8, 1979; children: Katharina A., Edward B. BS, Ohio State U., 1979, MBA, 1981. Budget analyst Ohio State U., Columbus, 1981-83; asst. to dean Cleve. State U., 1984-85; collegewide registrar Ivy Tech., Indpls., 1985-91, SIS project chmn., 1988-91; sec.-treas. Classic Concrete, Inc., 1991—; sys. analyst Marian Coll., Indpls., 1991—, coll. coun., 1993-96. Vestrywoman, Sunday sch. tchr., reader St. Christopher's Episcopal Ch., Carmel, Ind., 1990—. Mem. Ind. Assn. Instl. Rsch. (treas. 1994—), Ind. Assn. for Women in Edn. (treas. 1989-94, sec. 1995—), Ind. Coun. on Continuing Edn. (newsletter editor 1988-91), Nat. SIS Users Assn. (adv. com. student records 1989-90), Ind. Assn. Collegiate Registrars (data sys. com. 1989-90), Ind. Info. Assocs. User Group (chair). Home: 15110 Goodtime Ct Carmel IN 46032-1035 Office: Marian Coll 3200 Cold Spring Rd Indianapolis IN 46222-1997

BAUGH, JOYCE A., political science educator; b. Charleston, S.C., July 19, 1959; d. Jeff and Ella Mae (Jones) B.; m. Roger D. Hatch, Nov. 23, 1989. BA, Clemson U., 1981; MA, Kent State U., 1983, PhD, 1989. Asst. prof. polit. sci. Ctrl. Mich. U., Mt. Pleasant, 1988-94, assoc. prof., 1994—, chairperson dept. polit. sci., 1995—. Contbr. articles to profl. jours. Bd. dirs. Women's Aid Svc., Mt. Pleasant, 1990—, sec., 1991-92. Harry S. Truman scholar, 1979. Mem. Am. Polit. Sci. Assn., Midwest Polit. Sci. Assn., Nat. Conf. Black Polit. Scientists, Midwest Women's Caucus for Polit. Sci., (sec. 1990-91). Office: Ctrl Mich U Dept Polit Sci Mount Pleasant MI 48859

BAUGHMAN, GEORGE WASHINGTON, III, retired university official, financial consultant; b. Pitts., July 7, 1937; s. George W. and Cecile M. (Lytel) B.; m. Sandra Anne Johnson, June 21, 1987; 1 child, Lynn. BS in Psychology, Ohio State U., 1959, MBA, 1961, postgrad., 1961-63. Pres., Advanced Research Assos., Worthington, Ohio, 1960—; asst. instr. fin. Ohio State U., Columbus, 1961-63, research assoc., office of controller, 1964-66, dir. data processing, 1966-68, 70-72, dir. adminstrv. research, 1966-72, asso. to acad. v.p., 1968-70, exec. dir. univ. budget, 1970-72, dir. spl. projects, office of pres., 1972-88, ret., 1988; chmn. bd. Hosp. Audiences, Inc., 1974-80; spl. advisor Ohio Super Computer Ctr., 1989—; bd. dirs. Consortium for Higher Software Support, Inc., La Marquise, Inc., Halliday Techs., Inc., Sleep Medicine Internat., Inc., Sleep Medicine Rsch. Found., Duramed. Pharm. Inc., Alarm Ctr. Internat., Forerunner Corp., Implementation Assocs., Inc., 1995—, Greek Island Ltd., 1996—. Founding bd. dirs. Coll. and U. Machine Records Conf., 1971-73; bd. dirs. Uniplan Environ. Groups, Inc., 1970-73, chmn., 1971-73, Eagle Exhibit Systems, Inc., 1993—; chmn. Franklin County (Ohio) Rep. Demographics and Voter Analysis Com., 1975-80; active Ohio State Dental Bd., 1980-85, Gov.'s Export Council, 1982-83, Gov.'s Tech. Task Force, 1982-83. Am. Council on Edn. grantee, 1976-77; Nat. Assn. Coll. and Univ. Bus. Officers grantee, 1977-79; NSF grantee, 1980-86; Reisman fellow, 1962. Mem. Press Club Ohio, Coll. and Univ. Systems Exchange, AAAS, World Future Soc., Phi Alpha Kappa, Delta Tau Delta. Republican. Presbyterian. Author: (with D.H. Baker) Writing to People, 1963; (with R.W. Brady) University Program Budgeting, 1968, Administrative Data Processing, 1975; contbr. articles to profl. publs. Home: 833 Lake Shore Dr Columbus OH 43235-1289 Office: 1224 Kinnear Rd Columbus OH 43212-1154

BAUGHMAN, JENNIFER JANE, automotive executive; b. Youngstown, Ohio, Dec. 14, 1967; d. Gail William and Mary Linda (McCoy) B. B Bus./Mgmt., Temple U., 1990, MBA, 1994. Tng. mgr. environ. scis. Marriott Corp., Phila., 1990-94; zone mgr. Ford Motor Co., Detroit, 1994—. Mem. NAFE, Temple Owl Club, Pi Sigma Epsilon. Presbyterian. Home: 5040 Heather Dr Dearborn MI 48126-2878

BAUGHMAN, LEONORA KNOBLOCK, lawyer; b. Bad Axe, Mich., Mar. 21, 1956; d. Lewie L. and Jannette A. (Krajenka) K.; m. Jene W. Baughman, Dec. 5, 1981; children: Wesley J. and Adrianne J. Student, Cen. Mich. U., 1973-75; AB, U. Mich., 1977; JD, U. Notre Dame, 1981. Bar: Mich. 1981, U.S. Dist. Ct. (ea. dist.) Mich. 1982. Assoc. Foster, Swift, Collins & Coey, P.C., Lansing, Mich., 1981-86; staff atty. Chrysler Fin. Corp., Troy, Mich., 1987—. Mem. ABA, Mich. Bar Assn., Nat. Assn. Women Lawyers, Am. Bankruptcy Inst., State Bar Mich. (sec. bus. law sect., speaker 4th ann. comml. law seminar). Office: Chrysler Financial Corp 27777 Franklin Rd Southfield MI 48034

BAUGHMAN, R(OBERT) PATRICK, lawyer; b. Zanesville, Ohio, Nov. 18, 1938; s. Robert G. and Kathryn E. B.; m. Joyce Hall, June 17, 1959; 1 dau., Patricia. B.S., Ohio State U., 1960, J.D., 1963. Bar: Ohio 1963. Assoc. firm Sindell & Sindell, Cleve., 1964-71, Jones, Day, Reavis & Pogue, Cleve., 1972-73; asst. atty. gen. State of Ohio, Columbus, 1971-72; pres., prin. firm Baughman & Assocs., Cleve., 1973—. Mem. ABA, Ohio Bar Assn., Cuyahoga County Bar Assn., Nat. Council Self-Insurers, Internat. Assn. Indsl. Accident Bds. and Commns., Internat. Platform Assn. Episcopalian. Club: Columbia Hills Country. Office: 55 Public Sq Cleveland OH 44113-1901

BAUGHMAN, RUSSELL GEORGE, chemical educator, researcher; b. Washington, Dec. 7, 1946; s. Merle Eugene Baughman and Flora Marie (Kohl) Olson; m. Deborah Kim Dye, June 21, 1969; 1 child, Steven Matthew. AB, William Jewell Coll., 1968; PhD, Iowa State U., 1977. Asst. prof. Northeast Mo. State U., Kirksville, Mo., 1977-84, assoc. prof., 1984-92; prof. Truman State U. (formerly Northeast Mo. State U.), Kirksville, 1992—. Contbr. articles to profl. jours. Staff sgt. USAF, 1969-73. Mem. Am. Chem. Soc. (Outstanding Chemistry Prof. award N.E. Mo. State U. 1978), Am. Crystallographic Assn., Mo. Acad. Sci. (co-chmn. chemistry 1987-88), Sigma Xi. Lutheran. Office: Truman State U Div Sci Kirksville MO 63501

BAUKNECHT, BARBARA BELLE, educator; b. Gleason, Wis., Apr. 21, 1933; d. William John and Jessie Marie (Fox) Beyer; m. Ross Eugene Bauknecht, Aug. 11, 1956; children: JoDee Ann Moran, Shelley Marie Courter, Wanda Jean Pace, Todd Randall. Tchr. cert., Lincoln County Normal, Merrill, Wis., 1953; BS, U. Wis., Stevens Point, 1964, M, 1974. Lic. tchr. grades 1-8, reading tchr. K-12, reading specialist K-12. Tchr. grades 5 and 6 Crandon, Wis., 1953-57; tchr. grades 7 and 8 Elcho, Wis., 1957-59; pub. libr. Three Lakes, Wis., 1963-66; tchr. Title 1, reading tchr. Three Lakes, 1966-74, tchr., reading specialist, 1974—; retired, 1995; tchr., founder Story Hour - Presch. Program, Three Lakes and Sugar Camp, Wis., 1964—; reading coord. Three Lakes Sch. Dist., Three Lakes and Sugar Camp, 1978—; tchr. grades 4, 5, 6, 7, 8 Sch. Dist., Crandon and Elcho, Wis., 1957-59; mem., chmn. Read Com. Three Lakes Dist., 1978—. Co-founder Ecumenical Vaction Bible Sch., 1978—; chmn. bd. Ed U. Demmer Meml. Libr., Three Lakes, 1989—; Sunday sch. supt. Union Congl. Ch., Three Lakes, 1977—, moderator, 1988—; local organizer, leader Campfire Girls, 1970-75. Recipient Ind. Celebrate Lit. award Headwaters Reading Coun., Rhinelander, Wis., 1990; Kohl Scholarship/Fellowship CESA Dist. Winner, 1992. Congregationalist. Mem. Ch. of Christ. Home: 6653 Schoenfeldt Rd

Three Lakes WI 54562-9703 Office: Sch Dist Three Lakes PO Box 280 Three Lakes WI 54562-0280

BAUM, JONATHAN EDWARD, investment banker; b. Kansas City, Mo., Sept. 25, 1960; s. G. Kenneth and Jean (Berkely) B.; m. Sarah Ruth Henshaw, Aug. 20, 1988; 3 children. BS in Fin., Kans. State U., 1983; MBA, U. Chgo., 1987. Fin. analyst Salomon Bros., Inc., N.Y.C., 1983-85, assoc., 1987-90, v.p., 1990-94; exec. v.p. George K. Baum & Co., Kansas City, 1991-94, chmn., CEO, 1994—, also bd. dirs./exec. com. Bd. dirs. Am. Royal Horse Show, Kansas City, 1991—, Heartland's Sch. of Riding, Overland Park, Kans., 1991—, Kansas City Area Devel. Coun., 1993—, Kansas State U. Found., 1994—, Greater Kansas City C. of C., 1995—, Civic Coun. of Kansas City, 1996—. Home: 3600 W 64th Mission Hills KS 66208 Office: George K Baum & Co 120 W 12th St Kansas City MO 64105-1902

BAUMAN, AARON A., project engineer; b. Rittman, Ohio, Oct. 4, 1963. BSEE, U. Akron, 1987. Design engr. Keithley Instruments, Cleve., 1987-90; comm. engr. Telxon, Akron, 1990-92; project engr. Quatech Inc., Akron, 1992—. Mem. Tau Beta Pi, Eta Kappa Nu. Republican. Home: 52 Washington Ave Rittman OH 44270-1041 Office: Quatech Inc 662 Wolf Ledges Pky Akron OH 44311-1511

BAUMAN, ANDREW WILLIAM, author; b. Cheyenne Wells, Colo., June 27, 1972; s. William Franklin and Diana Margaret (Bussen) B. Author, pub.: Forest of Doubt, 1995; author: (poem) The Calm Tree, 1995.

BAUMAN, JOSEPH WESLEY, steel company executive; b. Knoxville, Iowa, Mar. 20, 1961; s. Richard Warren and Barbara Jane (Sims) B.; m. Kathy Lynn Haney, Aug. 30, 1980. BS in Elec. Engring., U. Mo., Rolla, 1995. Security sys. installer/technician Protective Security Systems, Independence, Mo., 1980-85; journeyman electrician, elec. constrn. supr. AVM Electric Constrn., Raytown, Mo., 1985-90; mgmt. trainee Cargill, North Star Steel Co., Monroe, Mich., 1995—. Recipient scholarships and grant. Mem. IEEE. Home: 1326 Frank Dr Monroe MI 48162

BAUMAN, KENNETH A., investment company executive; b. Holland, Mich., Feb. 9, 1957. BA, Hope Coll., Holland, 1979. Sales mgr. ODL, Zeeland, Mich., 1983-94; investment officer Robert W. Barid & Co. Inc., Grand Rapids, Mich., 1994—. Mem. Grand Rapids Country Club. Republican. Mem. Reformed Ch. Home: 3521 Tripoli Ct SE Grand Rapids MI 49546-7270 Office: Robert W Baird & Co Inc 333 Bridge St NW Ste 1000 Grand Rapids MI 49504-5356

BAUMAN, ROBERT GENE, architect; b. St. Paul, Feb. 11, 1945; s. Willis E. and Mildred C. (Rogholt) B.; (div.). Student, Boston Archtl. Ctr., 1976. Designer Ferland Corp., Pawtucket, R.I., 1970-74; project architect Med. Bldg. Designers, Newport, R.I., 1974-76, Continental Telephone Co., St. Paul, 1979-81, 3M Co., 1981-83, FMC Corp., 1983-84, Johnson, Sheldon & Sorensen, 1984-86, Eldon Morrison Architects, White Bear Lake, Minn., 1986-89, Buetow Architects, St. Paul, 1989; architect KKE Architects, Mpls., 1990; sr. project coord. ATS&R Architects, Golden Valley, Minn., 1990-91; prin. R. Bauman Designs, Inver Grove Heights, Minn., 1992-94; dir. prodn. Dennis Batty & Assocs., Mpls., 1994—; cons. Inver Grove Heights Fire Dept., 1976-79. With Seabees, USN, 1966-69, Vietnam.

BAUMAN, SUSAN JOAN MAYER, lawyer; b. N.Y.C., Mar. 2, 1945; d. Curt H. J. and Carola (Rosenau) Mayer; m. Ellis A. Bauman, Dec. 29, 1968. BS, U. Wis., 1965, JD, MS, 1981; MS, U. Chgo., 1966. Bar: Wis. 1981, U.S. Dist. Ct. (we. dist.) Wis. 1981, U.S. Ct. Appeals (7th cir.) 1983, U.S. Dist. Ct. (ea. dist.) Wis. 1985. Tchr. Madison (Wis.) Pub. Sch., 1970-78; research asst. U. Wis. Law Sch., Madison, 1981; ptnr. Thomas, Parsons, Schaefer & Bauman, Madison, 1981-84; sole practice Madison, 1984-85; ptnr. Bauman & Massing, Madison, 1985-87; pvt. practice, Madison, 1987—. Alderman Madison Common Coun., 1985—, coun. pres., 1989-90; commr. equal opportunities com. City of Madison, 1985-89; mem. Econ. Devel. Commn., 1986-87, chmn. human resources com., 1987-90, mem. affirmative action com., 1988-93; mem. Cmty. Action Commn., 1988—, pres., 1991—; mem. Pub. Health Commn., 1991—, Monona Terr. Conv. and Cmty. Ctr. Bd., 1993—; pres. South Madison Health and Family Ctr., Inc., 1993—. Mem. Wis. Bar Assn., Dane County Bar Assn., Wis. Indsl. Rels. Alumni Assn. (pres. 1985-86), Madison Civics Club. Democrat. Home: 4809 Hillview Ter Madison WI 53711-1201 Office: Bauman Law Offices 312 E Wilson St Madison WI 53703-3427

BAUMANN, CAROL EDLER, political science educator; b. Plymouth, Wis., Aug. 11, 1932; d. Clarence Henry and Beulah Hanetta (Weinhold) E.; m. Richard Joseph Baumann, Feb. 28, 1959; children: Dawn Carol, Wendy Katherine. BA in Internat. Rels., U. Wis., 1954; PhD in Internat. Rels., London Sch. Econs./Polit. Sci., 1957. Chmn. Internat. Rels. Major U. Wis., Milw., 1962-79; dep. asst. sec. Bur. of Intelligence and Rsch./Dept. of State, Washington, 1979-81; prof. U. Wis., Milw., 1972-95, dir. internat. studies and programs, 1982-88, emeritus, 1995—; dir. Inst. of World Affairs, Milw., 1964—. Author: Program Planning About World Affairs, 1991, The Diplomatic Kidnappings, 1973; editor: Europe in NATO: Deterrence, Defense, and Arms Control, 1987, Western Europe: What Path to Integration?, 1967. Active Gov.'s Commn. on the UN, 1964-79, 82-89; dem. candidate 9th Congl. Dist., 1968; mem. World Affairs Coun. of Milw., 1964-75. Named Marshall scholar, 1954-57; recipient Pub. Svc. Achievement award Common Cause in Wis., 1991. Mem. Atlantic Coun. of U.S. (edn. com., bd. dirs.), China Coun. of Asia Soc., Coun. on Fgn. Rels., Fgn. Policy Assn. (bd. dirs. 1990—, editl. adv. com. 1977-79, 82-88), Nat. Coun. World Affairs Orgns. (pres. 1977-79, bd. dirs. 1992-96), UN Assn. of USA (bd. dirs. 1977-79, 82-89), Soc. for Citizen Edn. in world Affairs (pres. 1977-79), Com. on Atlantic Studies, Internat. Studies Assn., Phi Kappa Phi, Phi Beta Kappa. Democrat. Lutheran. Home: W 6248 Lake Ellen Dr Cascade WI 53011 Office: U Wis Milw Inst of World Affairs PO Box 413 Milwaukee WI 53201

BAUMANN, DANIEL E., newspaper executive; b. Milw., Apr. 10, 1937; s. Herbert F. and Agnes V. (Byrne) B.; m. Karen R. Weinkauf, Apr, 29, 1961; children: James W., Jennifer R., Colin D. BJ, U. Wis., 1958, MA in Polit. Sci., 1962, Cert. in Russian Area Studies, 1962. Reporter South Milwaukee (Wis.) Voice Jour., 1958-59, East St. Louis (Ill.) Jour., 1959-60; pub. relations rep. Credit Union Nat. Assn., Washington, 1962-64; reporter Paddock Publs., Inc., Arlington Heights, Ill., 1964-66, mng. editor, 1966-68, exec. editor, 1968-70, editor and pub. Paddock Circle newspapers, 1970-75, v.p., editor, 1975-83, sr. v.p., gen. mgr., editor, 1983-86, pres., editor, 1986-90, dir., 1986—; pres., chief operating officer Paddock Publs., Inc., Arlington Heights, 1990—. Mem. High Tech. Corridors Coun., Palatine, Ill., 1986—; bd. dirs. Greater Woodfield Conv. and Visitors Bur., Schaumburg, Ill., 1985-93. With USNR. Recipient William Alan White award U. Kans., 1976. Mem. Newspaper Assn. Am., Am. Soc. Newspaper Editors, Internat. Newspaper Advt. and Mktg. Execs., Soc. Profl. Journalists, Chgo. Headline Club (Peter Lisagor award 1983), Chgo. Assn. Dir. Mktg., Sigma Delta Chi. Office: Paddock Publs Daily Herald 217 W Campbell St # 280 Arlington Heights IL 60005-1411*

BAUMANN, GREGORY WILLIAM, physician, consultant; b. Detroit, June 20, 1947; s. Alfred Louis Baumann and Marian (Bartholomew) Martens. BS, U. Mich., 1968, MD cum laude, 1972, MA in Telecom. Arts, 1993. Diplomate Am. Bd. Emergency Medicine. Intern Albert Einstein Coll. Medicine, Bronx Mcpl. Dept. Surgery, 1972-73; resident in neurology U. Mich., 1973-74; staff physician Foote Hosp., Jackson, Mich., 1974—, chmn. emergency med. dept., 1979-89, med. dir. emergency med. svcs. project, 1981-86, dir. ambulatory care, 1982-90; pres. Abcedarian Prodns., Inc., Ann Arbor, Mich.; cons. emergency med. svcs., Jackson, 1982—; mem. adv. life support tech. com. Mich. Dept. Pub. Health, Lansing, 1985-87; med. dir. Mich. Internat. Speedway, Bklyn., 1986—; chief med. examiner Jackson County, 1986-88; med. dir. Cleve. Indy Car Grand Prix. Bd. dirs. Hospice of Jackson, 1984-88; med. dir. Nazareth (Pa.) Speedway, 1987—. Recipient Merit award March of Dimes, 1970; rsch. grantee U. Mich. Med. Sch., 1972. Mem. AMA, Mich. Med. Soc., Jackson County Med. Soc., Kappa Tau Alpha. Lutheran. Office: PO Box 1086 Ann Arbor MI 48106-1086

BAUMANN, MARK H., business executive; b. Grand Island, Nebr., Dec. 24, 1956. BS in Edn., U. Nebr., 1982. With sales dept. Info. Systems, Omaha, 1982-89; pres. Mark H. Baumann Inc., Omaha, 1989—. Republican. Roman Catholic. Office: 348 N 76th St Omaha NE 68114-3681

BAUMBERGER, STEVEN BRUCE, management consultant; b. Chgo., Feb. 8, 1967; s. Bruce George and Nancy (Rinker) B. BS in Engring., Duke U., 1989. Staff cons. Andersen Cons., Chgo., 1989-91, sr. cons., 1991-94, mgr., 1994—; alumni rels. and recruiting liaison Duke U./Andersen Cons., Chgo., 1993—. Active Natural Ties, Evanston, Ill., 1992—. Republican. Presbyterian. Home: 3828 N Kenmore Ave # 1 Chicago IL 60613-2916 Office: Andersen Cons 33 W Monroe St Chicago IL 60603

BAUMGARDT, ARDEN CHARLES, insurance company executive; b. Racine, Wis., Jan. 14, 1941; children: Andy, Amy. BA in Bus. Adminstrn., U. Wis., 1963. CPCU. Casualty underwriter Wausau Ins. Cos., Indpls., 1964-66; casualty underwriter, sales rep. Wausau Ins. Cos., River Forest, Ill., 1966-69; nat. accounts underwriter Wausau Ins. Cos., Wausau, Wis., 1969-70, dir. product mgmt. and liability underwriting, 1970-74; mgr. casualty underwriting Wausau Ins. Cos., Detroit, 1974-76; mgr. regional casualty underwriting Wausau Ins. Cos., Chgo., 1976-83, asst. v.p. casualty underwriting, 1983-85, v.p. casualty underwriting, 1985-94, v.p. risk mgmt. accounts, 1994—. Home: 1210 Pine St Wausau WI 54401-4247 Office: Wausau Ins Cos 2000 Westwood Dr Wausau WI 54401-7802

BAUMGART, JAMES RAYMOND, state legislator; b. Dec. 22, 1938; 1 child. BA, U. Wis., Stevens Point. State assemblyman dist. 26 State of Wis., 1990—; outdoor writer. Mem. Sheboygan County Izaak Walton League (pres.). Democrat. Home: 1337A Carl Ave Sheboygan WI 53081-2583*

BAUMGARTEN, ELIAS, philosopher, educator; b. N.Y.C., July 15, 1945; s. Gabriel and Selma (Stanislavsky) B. AB, Brandeis U., 1967; MA, Northwestern U., 1971, PhD, 1975. Assoc. prof. philosophy U. Mich., Dearborn, 1980—; cons. med. ethics U. Mich. Med. Ctr., Ann Arbor, 1986—; rsch. assoc. Ctr. for Middle East and North African Studies, U. Mich., Ann Arbor, 1989—. Contbr. articles to learned publs. Mem. Jewish Peace Lobby. Mem. ACLU, Am. Philos. Assn., Concerned Philosophers for Peace, Sierra Club. Democrat. Jewish. Office: Univ Mich Dearborn Dept Humanities 4901 Evergreen Rd Dearborn MI 48128-2406

BAUMGARTNER, REUBEN ALBERT, retired school administrator; b. Pearl City, Ill., Dec. 30, 1912; s. Albert Centennial and Laura Anna (Hummermeir) B.; m. Arleigh Camille Mears, June 27, 1942 (dec. Aug. 1969); 1 child, Richard. BA, U. Ill., 1934, MA, 1935; postgrad., U. Iowa, 1938, 41, 55. Math. instr. Polo (Ill.) High Sch., 1935-38, N.D. State U., Fargo, 1938-40; dept. head, math. instr. Freeport (Ill.) High Sch., 1940-56; dir. adult edn. Freeport Pub. Schs., 1949-55; prin. Freeport High Sch., 1956-72; curriculum dir. Freeport Pub. Schs., 1972-77. Contbr. articles to profl. jours. State coord. 55 Alive/Mature Driving, Ill., 1985-88; pres. Stephenson County Sr. Ctr., Freeport, 1975-77; mem. Sec. of State Sr. Adv. Com., Ill., 1985-88. Lt. USN, 1942-46. Mem. Kiwanis (pres. 1954-55, lt. gov. 1975-76). Presbyterian. Home: 1729 W Parkview Dr Freeport IL 61032-4661

BAUNACH, BRUCE NELSON, marketing professional; b. Toledo, June 20, 1945; s. Roy Jacob and Juanita (May) B.; m. Dorothy Champion Baunach, May 23, 1970; children: Emily, Elizabeth. BA in Econ., Wittenberg U., Springfield, Ohio, 1968; MBA, Case Western Reserve U., Cleve., 1987. Dir. Internat. SIS Cawneer Inc., Harrisonburg, Va., 1975-80; mgr. Mktg. Crawford Fitting Co., Cleve., 1980-88; v.p. SIS and Mktg. Lumitex Inc., Cleve., 1988—. Contbr. articles to profl. jours. Capt. USAF, 1968-73, Vietnam. Recipient 3 Disting. Flying Crosses with oak leaf cluster. Mem. John Knox Presbyn., Mason 32nd degree, Soc. Auto Engrs. Office: Lumitex Inc 8443 Dow Cir Cleveland OH 44136-1759

BAUR, BOB, company executive; b. Cin., Apr. 20, 1954. V.p. Triumph Magna Mixer, Cin. With U.S. Army, 1973-76. Republican. Roman Catholic.

BAUSCH, MICHAEL GEORGE, clergyman; b. Milw., Oct. 6, 1949; s. George Elwyn and Marilyn Naomi Bausch; m. Catherine Ann Carlson, Apr. 24, 1950; children: Anica, Brianna. BS, Carroll Coll., Waukesha, Wis., 1971; MDiv, Pacific Sch. Religion, Berkeley, Calif., 1974. Ordained to ministry United Ch. of Christ, 1974. Conf. youth coord. Cal-Nev. Conf. United Meth. Ch., San Francisco, 1974-78; writer, cons. San Francisco, 1978-79; minister Williams Bay (Wis.) United Ch. of Christ, 1979-87, Union Congl. Ch., Waupun, Wis., 1987—; dir. United Ch. Christ Bd. for World Ministries, N.Y.C., 1975-81; commr. United Ministries Higher Edn., Madison, Wis., 1983-87; dir. United Ch. Camps, Inc., Madison, 1987-95. Editor: Everflowing Streams, 1981; contbr. to The Minister's Annual, 1987, 88, 89, 90; contbr. articles to ministry publs. Co-founder Williams Bay Recycling Ctr., 1981; chairperson Lakeland Hosp. Chaplaincy Staff, Elkhorn, Wis., 1981-87; bd. dirs. Cmty. Action Rock/Walworth Counties, Wis., 1982-85; mem. med. ethics com. Waupun Meml. Hosp., 1991-94; pres. Waupun Pub. Libr. Bd., 1991—. Named Outstanding Young Man of Yr. Lake Geneva Jaycees, 1982. Office: Union Congl Ch 125 Beaver Dam St Waupun WI 53963-1861

BAUTISTA, MARIETA PASCUAL, psychiatrist; b. Manila, Apr. 10, 1947; came to U.S., 1974; d. Amado and Amparo (Pascual) B. BS, U. Santo Tomas, 1966, MD, 1971. Diplomate Am. Bd. Psychiatry and Neurology with subspecialty in child and adolescent psychiatry (bd. examiner). Intern Meriden (Conn.)-Wallingford Hosp., 1974-75; resident psychiatry Fairfield Hills Hosp., Newtown, Conn., 1975-78; resident child psychiatry Lafayette Clinic, Detroit, 1978-79, Fairlawn Ctr., Pontiac, Mich., 1979-81; staff psychiatrist/unit chief Birchwood Hall Fairlawn Ctr., Pontiac, 1981-85, dir. young adolescent div., 1985-87; dir. gen. psychiatry tng. program Fairlawn Ctr., Mich. State U./Wayne State U., Pontiac, 1987—; dep. dir. in charge residency tng. program Wayne State U./Fairlawn Ctr.; dir. div. grad. edn. and tng. and dir. pre-adolescent div. Fairlawn Ctr., Wayne State U., Pontiac, 1991—; asst. prof. psychiatry Wayne State U., Detroit, 1992—; chief admission/ cts. Clinton Valley Ctr., Pontiac, 1995—; cons. in field; supr. Residents in Tng., 1989—, cons. Oakland Intermediate Sch. Dist.; instr. dept. psychiatry Mich. State U., 1980-81, assoc. clin. prof. dept. psychiatry, 1983—. Recipient Five Yr. Svc. award State of Mich., Ten. Yr. Svc. award State of Mich. Mem. Am. Acad. Child and Adolescent Psychiatry, Mich. Coun. Child Psychiatry, Philippine Med. Assn. Mich., U. Santo Tomas Med. Assn. Midwest, Am. Assn. Dirs. Psychiat. Residency Tng. Roman Catholic. Home: 4046 Hanover Ct West Bloomfield MI 48323-1815 Office: Clinton Valley Center 140 Elizabeth Lake Rd Pontiac MI 48341-1007

BAUTZ, JEFFREY EMERSON, mechanical engineer, educator, researcher; b. Milw., Apr. 13, 1966; s. Thomas W. and Dona J. (Emerson) B.; m. Heather Sienkiewicz. BS in Math. and Engring. Mechanics, U. Wis., 1988, MS in Engring. Mechanics, 1989; postgrad., Stanford U., 1992—. Devel. engr. McDonnell Douglas Corp., St. Louis, 1989-90; rsch. engr. GE, Milw., 1990-91; engring. project mgr., cons. on finite element method GM & Body Structure Design, Detroit, 1991—; instr. engring. mechanics U. Wis., Madison, 1988-89; instr. indsl. tech. and math. Macomb C.C., Warren, Mich., 1992—; part-time engring. cons. Patentee in field. Mem. Am. Soc. Body Engrs., Engring. Soc. Detroit. Home: 50405 Bellaire Chesterfield MI 48047 Office: GM Advanced Tech Vehicles PO Box 7083 1986 Technology Dr Troy MI 48007

BAVER, ROY LANE, retired protection services official, consultant; b. Dayton, Ohio, Sept. 20, 1942; s. Paul Vincent and Winifred (Korn) B.; m. Sandra Jean Stephen, Oct. 7, 1967; children: Dawn Maria, Denise Michele, Diana Melissa. AAS, Sinclair C.C., Dayton, 1979; BA in Urban Affairs, Wright State U., Dayton, 1985. Cert. state fire safety inspector, class IV automatic sprinkler inspector, fire inspector level I, sr. fire inspector, paramedic, CPR/first aid instr. Mechanic Casey's Union Oil, Centerville, Ohio, 1967-70; sales rep. Hauer Music, Dayton, Ohio, 1970-73; dep. fire marshal Washington Twp. Fire Dept., Centerville, 1973-96; ret., 1996; cons., RLB Consulting, Centerville, 1989—. Served in U.S. Army, 1964-66. Mem. Bldg. Ofcls. and Code Adminstrs. Internat., S.W. Ohio Fire Safety Coun., Ohio Bldg. Ofcls. Assn. (Fire Ofcl. of Yr. 1993-94), Ohio Assn. Profl. Fire Fighters, Washington Twp. Fire Fighters Assn., Internat. Assn. Fire Fighters, Masons, Scottish Rite, Shriners, Order Ea. Star, Centerville HighTwelve Club, Internat. Shrine Clown Assn., Great Lakes Shrine Clown Unit Assn., Wright State Alumni Assn., City of Centerville Sister City Com. Assoc., Phi Theta Kappa, Phi Alpha Alpha. Lutheran. Home: 145 Boyce Rd Centerville OH 45458-2475

BAVIN, LYNDA ANN, tutor, mentor; b. Yokohama, Japan, Dec. 4, 1947; came to U.S., 1948; d. Norman J. and Ann (Hulecka) Harner; m. Ric Lee Bavin, June 16, 1973; 1 child, Stefoni Ann. Student, St. Francis Coll., 1965-67, Ind. U., 1968-69; BA in English and Psychology, Lourdes Coll., 1996. chair Bowling Green (Ohio) Study Group, 1995; head Olympic of Mind Group, Waterville, Ohio, 1982. Chmn. Young Dem. for Robert Kennedy, South Bend, Ind., 1967-68; publicity chmn. Toledo Area Assn. Gifted Children, 1986-87. Mem. Elks, Planetary Soc., Smithsonian Inst., Stone Oak Bridge League, KC (Lady of Columbus 1978).

BAXTER, ELAINE, state government official; b. Chgo., Jan. 16, 1933; d. Clarence Arthur and Margaret (Clark) Bland; m. Harry Youngs Baxter, Oct. 2, 1954; children: Katherine, Harry, John. BA, U. Ill., 1954; teaching cert., Iowa Wesleyan Coll., 1970; MS, U. Iowa, 1978. History tchr. Burlington (Iowa) High Sch., 1971-72; mem. Burlington City Coun., 1973-75; sr. liaison officer U.S. Dept. HUD, Washington, 1979-81; state rep. Iowa Ho. Reps., Des Moines, 1982-86; sec. state State of Iowa, Des Moines, 1987—. Nat. co-chmn. Dukakis-Bentsen campaign, 1988; del. Dem. Nat. Conv., Atlanta, 1988, mem. at large Dem. Nat. Com.; mem. Exec. Coun. and Voter Registration Commn.; chair State Records Commn., State Ins. Commn., Iowa; internat. del. Nat. Dem. Inst. for Internat. Affairs to Paraguay, 1989; hon. res. chair Iowa chpt. Am. Heart Assn., 1989. Recipient RJR Nabisco Fellowship to Sr. Execs. in State and Local Govt., J.F. Kennedy Sch. Govt., Harvard U., 1988. Nat. co-chmn. Dukakis-Bentsen campaign, 1988; del. Dem. Nat. Conv., Atlanta, 1988, mem.-at-large Dem. Nat. Com.; mem. Exec. Coun. and Voter Registration Commn.; chair State Records Commn., State Ins. Commn., Iowa; internat. del. Nat. Dem. Inst. for Internat. Affairs to Paraguay, 1989; hon. res. chair Iowa chpt. Am. Heart Assn., 1989; candidate Iowa 3d Congl. Dist., 1992. Home: 1016 N 4th St Burlington IA 52601-4803 Office: State House Des Moines IA 50319*

BAXTER, HOWARD H., lawyer; b. Cleve., July 31, 1931; s. Harold H. and Bessie (Bovee) B.; m. Ona Mae Miller, June 25, 1955; children: Kevin, Douglas, John, Susan. BS, Iowa State Coll., 1953; JD, Case Western Res. U., 1956. Bar: Ohio 1956, D.C. 1982; U.S. Dist. Ct. (no. dist.) Ohio 1962, U.S. Ct. Appeals (3rd cir.) 1978, U.S. Supreme Ct. 1978, U.S. Ct. Appeals (fed. cir.) 1982. Assoc. McNeal & Schick, Cleve., 1956-60; group counsel Harris Corp., Cleve., 1960-76; sec., gen. counsel Molins USA Inc., Richmond, Va., 1976-79; v.p., gen. counsel The Langston Co., Inc., Cherry Hill, N.J., 1976-79, Cuyahoga County Hosp. System, Cleve., 1979-81; v.p., sec., gen. counsel Macey Machine Co., Inc., Cleve., 1981-88, exec. v.p., 1988-91; ptnr. Kasdan & Baxter Co., Cleve., 1992—. Chmn. zoning com. Lakewood (Ohio) Rep. Club, 1959-60; vestry, sr. warden St. Stephens Episcopal Ch., Beverly, N.J., 1977-79, Lakewood, 1981—, Ch. of the Ascension, Lakewood. Mem. NRA, Ohio State Bar Assn., Cleve. Bar Assn., Great Lakes Hist. Soc. (vice chmn. 1981-88, exec. v.p. 1968-76, trustee 1968—, chmn. exec. com. 1982-94), Ohio Gun Collectors Assn., Inc., Edgewater Yacht Club. Home: 18107 Clifton Rd Lakewood OH 44107-1024 Office: Kasdan & Baxter Superior Bldg 815 Superior Ave E Ste 1920 Cleveland OH 44114-2701

BAXTER, SUSAN JOHNSON, medical sales consultant; b. Washington, June 25, 1965; d. David Pierce and Barbara Ann (Green) Johnson; m. Stephen Padraic Baxter, May 19, 1990. BS in Dietetics, James Madison U., 1987; MS in Nutrition, Pa. State U., 1989; MBA, U. Richmond, 1994. Registered dietitian. Mgr. territory sales N.Am. Lab. Co., Indpls., 1989-91; healthcare mktg. specialist Unifax Corp., Roanoke, Va., 1992-93; med. sales cons. Procter & Gamble, Cin., 1994—. Mem. Am. Dietetic Assn., Am. Mktg. Assn. Home: 11417 Old Ivy Home Pl Richmond VA 23233 Office: Procter & Gamble Cincinnati OH

BAY, SUSAN LOUISE, critical care nurse; b. Ottumwa, Iowa, Sept. 18, 1946; d. Stanley Leo and Emily Ella (Newlin) B. Diploma, St. Joseph Sch. Nursing, Ottumwa, Iowa, 1967; BSN, N.E. Mo. State U., Kirksville, 1971. RN, Nebr.; CEN; cert. BLS, ACLS. Staff nurse St. Joseph Hosp., Ottumwa, Iowa, 1967-71, Omaha VA Hosp., 1971-74; dir. nursing emergency dept. Immanuel Med. Ctr., Omaha, 1974-79, staff nurse-emergency dept., 1979—. Vol. mission to India, 1983. Mem. Emergency Nurses Assn., Disciplined Order of Christ (Nashville chpt.). Republican. Presbyterian.

BAY, THOMAS ROBERT, clinical social worker; b. St. Clair, Mich., Mar. 19, 1965; s. Edwin Henry and Lois Jean (Olson) B.; m. Sharon Lynn Stutzman, July 30, 1988. AA, Mid Mich. C.C., Harrison, 1985; BS, Western Mich. U., 1987, MSW, 1990. Registered social worker, Mich. Laborer, 1995—; bd. dirs. Kalamazoo County Cmty. Mental Health, Kalamazoo. Mem. NASW, Nat. Alliance to End Homelessness, Nat. Alliance for the Menatlly Ill. Democrat.

BAYER, GARY RICHARD, advertising executive; b. St. Louis, Mar. 15, 1941; s. Kenneth Joseph and Ruth Margarite (Johnson) B.; m. Jeanette Marie Stis, July 13, 1963; children: Gregory Scott, Keith Russell, Kristen Holly. BA, Washington U., 1963. Copywriter Adult Edn. Council of Greater St. Louis, St. Louis, 1962, D'Arcy Advt. Co., St. Louis, 1963-67; from v.p. creative dir. to sr. v.p. exec. creative dir. D'Arcy MacManus & Masius, St. Louis, 1968-80; pres. Adcom. div. Quaker Oats Co., Chgo., 1980-85; pres., chief ops. officer Backer & Spielvogel Chgo., Inc., Chgo., 1985-87; chmn., CEO, chief creative officer Bayer Bess Vanderwarker Advt., Chgo., 1987—. Vice chmn. Vols. Am., Ill. Mem. Am. Assn. Advt. Agys. (gov.-at-large 1988—, sec.-treas. bd. dirs. 1991-92, bd. dirs. 1993—, pres., vice chair Ill. bd. govs.), Chgo. Advt. Fedn. (pres. 1990-93), Am. Advt. Fedn. (Hall of Fame judge 1994-95), Univ. Club, Met. Club, Phi Beta Kappa, Omicron Delta Kappa. Republican. Home: 1010 E Illinois Rd Lake Forest IL 60045-2410 Office: Bayer Bess Vanderwarker 225 N Michigan Ave Ste 1900 Chicago IL 60601-7601*

BAYH, EVAN, governor; b. Terre Haute, Ind., Dec. 26, 1955; s. Birch Evans Jr. and Marvella (Hern) B.; married. BS in Bus. Econs., Ind. U., 1978; JD, U. Va., 1981. Atty. Bingham, Summers, Welsh & Spilman; sec. of state State of Ind., Indpls., 1987-89, gov., 1989—; chmn. State Recount Commn. & Corp. Law com.; mem. Nat. Edn. Goals Panel & Nat. Assessment Edn. Panel; chmn. Edn. Commn. States; vice chmn. Nat. Govs. Assn. Task Force Workforce Devel. Democrat. Office: Office of Gov 206 State House Indianapolis IN 46204*

BAYLESS, ROMAINE BELLE, physician, educator; b. Chillicothe, Ohio, Aug. 26, 1945; d. Irvin and Lillian (Glassco) B.; m. Earl Sylvester Sherard Jr., Apr. 2, 1982 (dec. July 1983); m. Christopher Charles Thomas, Aug. 25, 1990. BS, Ohio U., 1967; MD, Ohio State U., 1978. Computer programmer Mead Corp., Chillicothe, 1965-66; systems engr. IBM Corp., Columbus, Ohio, 1966-74; intern and resident in ob-gyn Case-Western Res. U., Cleve., 1978-82; lt. commd., staff physician U.S. Navy Hosp., Agana, Guam, 1982-84; instr., research assoc. Yale U., New Haven, 1985-86; asst. prof. clin. ob-gyn U. Ill., Peoria, 1987-92, assoc. prof. clin. ob-gyn., 1992-93; clin. asst. prof. ob-gyn., 1993—; mem. gov. bd. Heartland Community Health Clinic, 1991—; mem. minority recruitment adv. com. Ill. Ctrl. Coll., 1992—. Author: (with others) Clinical Obstetrics and Gynecology, 1987, Decision Making in Infertility, 1988. Bd. dirs. Tri-County Urban League, Peoria, 1987—, Peoria Area Community Found., 1990—. Fellow Am. Coll. Ob-Gyn.; mem. Am. Soc. Reproductive Medicine, Am. Inst. Ultrasound in Medicine, Nat. Med. Assn., Am. Assn. Gynecologic Laparoscopists, Peoria Gynecol. Soc., Nat. Coun. Negro Women, Alpha Kappa Alpha (Nu Pi Omega chpt.). Baptist. Home: 9821 N Thousand Oaks Ct Peoria IL 61615-4312 Office: Fert & Repro Ctr of Ctrl Ill 214 NE Glen Oak Ave Ste 606 Peoria IL 61603-4309

BAYLOR, ELISABETH ANNE, retired foreign language educator; b. Weissenau, Germany, Dec. 31, 1906; came to U.S., 1907; d. Aristide Marie and Anna (Oppiller) Barbou; m. Murray Baylor, Sept. 1, 1937 (dec. June 1992); children: Denis Aristide, Michael George, Stephen Murray. BA,

Augustana Coll., Rock Island, Ill., 1928; MA, U. Iowa, 1930, PhD, 1936; Diploma, Sorbonne, Paris, 1928. Instr. French U. Iowa, Iowa City, 1928-37; prof. French and art Penn Coll., Oskaloosa, Iowa, 1938-41; asst. prof. French Knox Coll., Galesburg, Ill., 1950-51, 60-70; pvt. French tchr. Galesburg, 1972-87. Mem. Alpha Sigma Epsilon, Sigma Alpha Iota. Home: 1187 N Cherry St Galesburg IL 61401

BAZANT, ZDENEK PAVEL, structural engineering educator, scientist, consultant; b. Prague, Czechoslovakia, Dec. 10, 1937; came to U.S., 1968, naturalized, 1976; s. Zdenek and Stepanka (Curikova) B.; m. Iva Marie Krasna, Sept. 27, 1967; children: Martin Zdenek, Eva Stephanie. Civil Engr., Tech. U., Prague, 1960; Ph.D. in Mechanics, Czechoslovak Acad. Sci., 1963; postgrad. diploma in theoretical physics, Charles U., Prague, 1966; hon. doctorate, Czech Tech. U., Prague, 1991. Registered structural engr., Ill. Scientist, adj. prof. Bldg. Research Inst., Tech. U., Prague, 1963-67; docent habilitation Tech. U., Prague, Czechoslovakia, 1967; vis. research engr. Centre d'Étude et de Recherche du Bâtiment et des Travaux Publics, Paris, 1967, U. Toronto, 1967-68, U. Calif., Berkeley, 1969; assoc. prof. civil engring. Northwestern U., Evanston, Ill., 1969-73, prof., 1973-90, Walter P. Murphy prof., 1990—, coordinator structural engring. program, 1974-78, 92—; founding dir. Ctr. for Concrete and Geomaterials, 1981-86; cons. Sargent & Lundy Engrs., Chgo., 1973-77, ARgonne Nat. Lab., 1974—, Oak Ridge Nat. Lan., 1975-82, Babcock & Wilcox, 1978-80, Sandia Labs., Albuquerque, 1979-80, Portland Cement Assn., Skokie, 1980-82, Ont. Hydro, Toronto, 1980-84, U.S. Forest Products Lab., Madison, Wis., 1981-83, W.R. Grace & Co., 1982—; vis. prof. Royal Inst. Tech., Stockholm, 1977, Politechnico di Milano, 1982, Swiss Fed. Inst. Tech., Lausanne, 1983, Tech. U. Munichen, 1990, ENS de Cachan, France, 1992; vis. scholar U. Calif.-Berkeley, 1978, Calif. Inst. Tech., 1979, ETH, Zurich, Switzerland, 1983, U. Capetown, South Africa, 1984, U. Adelaide, Australia, 1985, U. Tokyo, 1996; mem. coms. Nat. Acad. Engring., 1977—; patentee in field. Author: Creep of Concrete in Structural Analysis, 1966, (with others) Analysis of Concrete Structures by Finite Element Method, 1978, Inelasticity and Failure of Concrete, 1979, Creep and Shrinkage in Concrete Structures, 1982, Mechanics of Geomaterials, 1985; Stability of Structures: Elastic, Inelastic, Fracture and Damage Theories, 1991; editor in chief Jour. Engring. Mechanics, 1989—; regional editor Internat. Jour. Fracture, 1991—; assoc. editor Applied Mechanics Rev., 1987—; mem. editorial bd. Cement and Concrete Research Internat. Jour, 1970—, Internat. Jour. Numerical and Analytical Methods in Geomechanics, 1979—, Solid Mechanics Archives, 1980-91, Materials and Structures, 1981—, Jour. Probabilistic Mechanics, 1986—, Engring. Computations, 1987—, Internat. Jour. Numerical Methods in Engring., 1989—, Ingenieur-Archiv, 1990—, Nuclear Engring. and Design, 1990—; contbr. (with others) numerous articles to profl. jours. Grantee NSF, 1970—, ERDA, 1975-77, AFOSR, 1975—, Los Alamos Sci. Lab., 1978-80. EPRI, 1980—, ONR, 1990—; Ford Found. fellow, 1967-68, Guggenheim fellow, 1978-79, Kajima Found. fellow U. Tokyo, 1987, NATO fellow, Paris, 1988, JSPS fellow U. Tokyo, 1995-96; recipient Best Engring. Book of Yr. award Soc. Am. Pubs., 1992, Outstanding New Citizen award Chgo. Citizenship Coun., 1976, IR100 award, 1982, A. von Humboldt award, 1990. Fellow ASME, Am. Acad. Mechanics (founder), ASCE (chmn. com. properties of materials 1976-78, 82-84, editor in chief Jour. Engring. Mechanics 1989—, chmn. EMD programs com. 1989-91, Walter L. Huber rsch. prize 1976, T.Y. Lin Prestressed Concrete award 1977, Newmark medal 1996), Am. Concrete Inst. (chmn. fracture mechanics com. 1985—), Internat. Union Testing and Rsch. Labs. Materials Structures, Internat. Union Rsch. Lab Materials Structures (chmn. com. on creep, gold medal 1975); mem. NAE, Internat. Assn. Structural Mechanics Reactor Tech. (coord. concrete structures divsn.), ASTM (mem. concrete com.), Prestressed Concrete Inst., Am. Ceramic Soc., Internat. Assn. Soil Mech. Found. Engring., Internat. Assn. Bridge and Structural Engring., Soc. Exptl. Mechanics, Soc. Engring. Sci. (past pres., Prager medal 1996), Am. Soc. Engring. Edn., Bldg. Rsch. Inst. Spain (hon., Torroja Goldech Soc. Civil Engring. (hon.), Czech Soc. Mechanics (award of merit 1993), Structural Engrs. Assn. Ill. (Meritorious Paper award 1992), Nat. Skiing Assn., U.S. Olympic Soc., Centennial Tennis Club, Kenilworth Sailing Club. Home: 707 Roslyn Ter Evanston IL 60201-1721 Office: Northwestern Univ Dept Civil Engring Evanston IL 60201

BAZANY, LE ROY FRANCIS, manufacturing company executive, controller; b. Chgo., Sept. 29, 1932; s. Steven and Florence Corrine (Rybski) B.; m. Frances Ann Armstrong, Oct. 20, 1956; children: Mark, Karen, Gregory, Timothy, Kimberly, Kristin. BS, U. Notre Dame, 1954. Auditor Arthur Andersen & Co., Chgo., 1956-58; internal auditor Am. Photocopy Equipment Co., Chgo., 1958-59, acctg. mgr., chief acct., 1960-64, contr., 1965-68, v.p. fin., treas., 1968-74; v.p. fin., treas. Fed. Sign and Signal Corp., 1974-75; v.p. fin. and adminstn. Quasar Electronics Co., Franklin Park, Ill., 1975-79; contr. Bemis Co. Inc., Mpls., 1979-82, v.p., contr., 1982—. Fin. advisor Project Pride in Living, Inc., Mpls., 1982—, bd. dirs., 1982-85. With U.S. Army, 1954-56. Mem. Fin. Execs. Inst., Mpls. Club, KC (Excelsior, Minn.). Republican. Roman Catholic. Office: Bemis Co Inc 222 S 9th St Ste 2300 Minneapolis MN 55402-3363

BAZAZ, MOHAMMED S., accounting educator; b. Yazd, Iran, Nov. 4, 1949; came to U.S., 1977; s. Ghasem and Nosrat (Pourkeramati) B.; married; children: Ehsan, Hamed. BS in Acctg., N.I.O.C. Coll. of Faculty, Tehran, 1973, M Accountancy, 1974; PhD, U. Okla., 1985. Instr. acctg. Babolsar U., Iran, 1973-77; controller RitaCi, Tehran, 1974-77; asst. prof. U. Tehran, 1985-86, U. Windsor, Can., 1986-87; assoc. prof. Oakland U., Rochester, Mich., 1987—. Recipient fellowships Oakland U., Rochester, Mich., 1992, Ministry of Edn., Tehran, 1977-81, U. Okla., Norman, 1981-84. Home: 283 Tanglewood Dr Rochester Hills MI 48309 Office: Oakland Univ Rochester MI 48309

BEACH, DAVID DUNCAN, naval architect; b. New Haven, Conn., May 1, 1918; s. David Duncan and Helen (Gibson) B.; m. Helen Elizabeth Fisher, July 22, 1943; 1 child, David Duncan. Student, U. Mich., 1935-40; Diplomate, Westlawn Inst., Stamford, Conn., 1980. Registered profl. engr., D.C. Naval architect Higgins Boats Corp., New Orleans, 1955-58, Outboard Marine Corp., Waukegan, Ill., 1958-60, McCulloch Corp., L.A., 1960-62, Owens Yachts (Brunswick Corp.), Balt., 1962-66, Nat. Marine Mfrs. Assn., Chgo., 1966-94; ret., 1994; cons. F.A.O. of UN, Rome, 1971-72, Nat. Marine Mfg. Assocs. Fellow Royal Instn. Naval Architects; mem. Soc. Naval Architects and Marine Engrs. (life), Soc. Sml. Crafts Designers (v.p. 1982-96). Office: Nat Marine Mfg Assocs Amoco Bldg #5100 200 E Randolph Chicago IL 60601-6528

BEAL, WANDA ELNORA, psychologist, writer; b. Flint, Mich.; d. Glenn R. and Nettie (Capron) R.; m. Howard William Beal (div. Feb. 1980); children: Wesley William, Patrice Annette, Cynthia Joan; m. Raymond Mileur, Aug. 30, 1992. BA in Art Edn. and Psychology, Southwest State U., 1977; MS in Psychology, MS Art Therapy, Emporia State U., 1980; PsyD, Forest Inst. Profl. Psychology, 1995. Writer Denver Post, 1956-70; artist, designer Wanda's Designs, Limon, Colo., 1970-80; psychologist Menard (Ill.) Psychiat. Ctr., 1980-95, Chester (Ill.) Mental Health, Menard, Ill., 1995—; freelance writer, Limon, 1960-80; mem. Denver chpt. Fashion Group, 1970-80. Pres. Nat. League Am. Pen Women, 1969, art dir., 1968; bd. dirs. Am. Lung Assn., 1965-70, Colo. chpt. ARC, 1965-70. Mem. Am. Correctional Assn., Am. Assn. Correctional Psychologists, Am. Art Therapy Assn. (registered 1981), Mo. Psychol. Assn., Ozark Psychol. Assn., St. Louis Network for Women Psychologists. Methodist. Office: Chester Mental Health PO Box 56 Chester IL 62259-0056

BEALL, CYNTHIA, anthropologist, educator; b. Urbana, Ill., Aug. 21, 1949; d. John Wood and J. Alene (Beachler) B. BA in Biology, U. Pa., 1970; MA in Anthropology, Pa. State U., 1972, PhD in Anthropology, 1976. Asst. prof. Case Western Res. U., Cleve., 1976-82, assoc. prof. of anthropology, 1982-87, prof. anthropology, 1987—. Co-editor Jour. of Cross-Cultural Gerontology, 1986-95; contbr. articles to profl. jours. Active Internat. Rsch. Exch. Program, 1990, 91. Rsch. grantee NSF, 1981, 83, 86, 87, 93, 94, 95, Am. Fedn. for Aging. Rsch., 1983, 86, Nat. Geog. Soc., 1983, 86-87, 93, 95; Nat. Program for Advanced Study and Rsch. in China fellow NAS, 1986-87. Mem. AAAS, U.S. Nat. Acad. Scis., Am. Anthrop. Assn., Am. Assn. Phys. Anthropology (exec. com. 1989-92), Human Biology Coun. (exec. com. 1989-92, pres. 1992-94), Soc. for Study Human Biology, Assn. for Anthropology and Gerontology. Office: Case Western Res U Dept Anthropology 238 Mather Memorial Bldg Cleveland OH 44106-2699

BEALL, WARE THOMPSON, JR. (TOM BEALL), industrial sales and marketing executive; b. Savannah, Ga., June 24, 1940; s. Ware Thompson and Elise (Trowell) B.; m. Inez Todd, Oct. 22, 1960; children: John Keith, Renée Beall Boucher. AA, Armstrong Coll. of Savannah, 1964; BS in Electron Physics and Math., La. State U., 1966; MS in Engring. Mgmt. & Mktg., Milw. Sch. Engring., 1983. Rsch. physicist Linde div. Union Carbide Corp., Indpls., 1966-69; sr. rsch. physicist Linde div. Union Carbide Corp., Tarrytown, N.Y., 1969-75; regional sales engring. rep. Linde div. Union Carbide Corp., Milw., 1975-81, sales rep., 1981-84, sr. sales rep., 1984-85; Midwestern sales-dist. mgr., sales engr. L-Tec Welding & Cutting Systems, Florence, S.C., 1985-88; indsl. account exec. Indpls. Power & Light, 1988-93, electrotech. devel. dir., 1993—; assoc. Electric Power Rsch. Inst., 1988—, utility adviser Ctr. Materials Prodn., 1989—, founding adv. com. affiliate mem. program, 1990—, mem. customer sys. divsn. task force, 1994, utility adviser Foundry Office, 1994—; grad. lectr. Milw. Sch. Engring., 1981-88. Author: Planning for Survival and Growth of a Small Business, 1983; contbr. articles to scholarly jours. Elected precinct com. chmn. Indpls. Reps., 1967-69; appointed pres. Eagle Creek Rep. Club, Indpls., 1968; vice chmn. Cherry Hill Homeowners Assn., Yorktown Heights, N.Y., 1970-71; com. chmn. vol. Yorktown Heights Fire Dept. troop Boy Scouts of Am., 1971-75, asst. scoutmaster, 1974-75; speaker Wis. Assn. Vocat. and Adult Edn., Madison, 1977. With USN, 1959-63. Recipient Champion award Electric Power Rsch. Inst., 1993, R & D 100 award Indsl. Rsch. and Devel. mag., 1993. Mem. Am. Soc. for Metals, Am. Welding Soc. (seminar leader 1977-88), Am. Foundrymen's Soc., Inc., Soc. Mfg. Engrs., Sales and Mktg. Execs. Milw., Electric League Ind., Great Lakes Power Assn. Republican. Methodist. Club: Toastmasters (local exec. v.p. 1967-68).

BEAM, CLARENCE ARLEN, federal judge; b. Stapleton, Nebr., Jan. 14, 1930; s. Clarence Wilson and Cecile Mary (Harvey) B.; m. Betty Lou Fletcher, July 22, 1951; children—Randal, James, Thomas, Bradley, Gregory. BS, U. Nebr., 1951, JD, 1965. Feature writer Nebr. Farmer Mag., Lincoln, 1951; with sales dept. Steckley Seed Co., Mount Sterling, Ill., 1954-58, advt. mgr., 1958-63; ptnr. Knudsen, Berkheimer, Beam, et al, Lincoln, 1965-82; judge U.S. Dist. Ct. Nebr., Omaha, 1982-86, chief judge, 1986-87; cir. judge U.S. Ct. Appeals (8th cir.), 1987—; mem. com. on lawyer discipline Nebr. Supreme Ct., 1974-82; mem. Conf. Commrs. on Uniform State Laws, 1979—, chmn. Nebr. sect., 1980-82; mem. jud. conf. com. on ct. and jud. security, 1989-93, chmn., 1992-93. Contbr. articles to profl. jours. Mem. Nebr. Rep. Cen. Com., 1970-78. Capt. U.S. Army, 1951-53, Korea. Regents scholar U. Nebr., Lincoln, 1947, Roscoe Pound scholar U. Nebr., Lincoln, 1964. Mem. Nebr. State Bar Assn. Office: US Ct Appeals 8th Cir 435 Federal Bldg 100 Centennial Mall N Lincoln NE 68508-3803

BEAN, ATHERTON, food company executive; b. New Prague, Minn., Sept. 14, 1910; s. Francis Atherton and Bertha Juanita (Boynton) B.; m. Winifred E. Wollaeger, June 26, 1934; children: Douglas Atherton, Bruce William. Student, Blake Sch.; A.B. summa cum laude, Carleton Coll., 1931; B.A. (Rhodes scholar), Oxford U., 1934; postgrad., Harvard Sch. Bus. Adminstrn., 1931-32. With Upjohn Co., Dallas, 1934-36, duPont Co., Wilmington, Del., 1936-37; price exec. OPA, Washington, 1942-43; joined Internat. Milling Co. (co. name changed to Internat. Multifoods), Mpls., 1937, exec. v.p., 1944-55, pres., 1955-64, chmn., chief exec., 1964-68, chmn. exec. com., 1968-84; chmn. bd. 9th dist. Fed. Res. Bank, 1961-65; dir. First Bank Mpls., 1946-60, 66-76, Bus. Internat., 1969-83. Trustee Mpls. Soc. Fine Arts, 1964-78, chmn. bd., 1975-76, vice chmn. bd., 1969-75, 76-78; trustee Mayo Found., Rochester, 1964-78, chmn. bd., 1969-76; trustee Carleton Coll., Northfield, Minn., 1944-85, chmn. bd., 1961-68; trustee Mpls. Found., 1961-80, Sci. Mus. Minn., 1972-80; bd. dirs. Nat. Bur. Econ. Research, 1970-79; apptd. by Pres. Nixon to Spl. Task Force on Econ. Growth, 1969, to Presdl. Commn. on Fin. Structure and Regulation, 1970. Served as civilian spl. br. M.I., 1943-44. Office: 4900 IDS Ctr 80 S 8th St Minneapolis MN 55402-2226*

BEAN, GLEN ATHERTON, entrepreneur; b. Mpls., Aug. 30, 1962; s. Douglas Atherton Bean and Eleanor Green (Caswell) Nolan; m. Mary Catherine Slingsby, June 16, 1990. BS, Ariz. State U., 1988. Promotion specialist John Deere & Co., Waterloo, Iowa, 1987; regional mgr. Elliott Meat Co., Duluth, Minn., 1989-90; gen. ptnr. No. Star Food Brokerage, Savage, Minn., 1990-92; pres. Hunter Holdings, Ltd., Savage, 1993—; dir. McGab Agribusiness Scholar., Ariz. State Univ., 1989—. Media coord. U.S. Olympic Festival, Mpls. 1990; vol. Multiple Sclerosis Soc., 1989—; founder Ariz. State Univ. Agribus. Speakers Bur., 1987; bd. mem. alumni assn. Phoenix County Day Sch., Phoenix, 1983-89; guarantor Minn. Orch. Mem. Nat. Cattlemens Assn., Ariz. Cattle Growers Assn., Clan MacBean in N.Am., Universidad Iberoamericana (assoc.), Ducks Unlimited (publicity chmn. Phoenix 1986-88, dinner chmn. Burnsville 1990, 91, zone chmn. 1992—), Trout Unlimited, T.C. Pub. TV, Mustang Club Am., Sigma Nu. Republican. Episcopal. Office: Hunter Holdings Ltd PO Box 276 Savage MN 55378-0276

BEAN, KIMBERLY SUE, information system specialist; b. Franklin, Nebr., Aug. 29, 1957; d. Jerry Allen Bean and Carol Jean (Dallmann) Bean Bennett. BA magna cum laude, Towson State U., 1979, BS, 1979. Latin Am. sales mgr. Chesapeake Internat. Svcs. Co., Balt., 1978-83, Internat. Mgmt. Svcs. Inc., Lincoln, Nebr., 1983-86; internat product devel. mgr. First Data Infosource, Omaha, 1987-88, regional sales rep., 1989-92, nat. account exec., 1992-94, bus. unit mgr., sales mgr., 1995—; owner Magna Charters, Inc., Omaha, 1991—. Vol. Kerry for Senate Com., Omaha, 1991-92. Mem. FDC Womens Network, Jr. League Omaha (Outstanding Vol. of Yr. award 1993). Home: 1517 N 123d St Omaha NE 68154

BEARD, MICHAEL CARL, linguist, educator; b. Cambridge, Eng., Sept. 27, 1956; came to U.S., 1959; s. William Arthur Jr. and Barbara Lee (Cathey) Appleton; m. Barbara Loraine Gipson, May 6, 1978; children: Elaine Denise, Pamela Jean. BS, Southwestern Coll., 1979; MA, Western Sem., Oreg., 1982, Wayne State U., 1996. Ordained to Ministry, Baptist Ch. Pastor Sacramento St. Bapt. Ch., Portland, 1981-82, Haley Bapt. Ch., Boring, Oreg., 1983-84; adminstr. Golf Links Acad., Tucson, 1984-86; cons., speaker Profl. Strategies Group, Inkster, Mich., 1986, Profl. Resume Service, Sterling Heights, Mich., 1986-88; corp. communications officer Genesis Internat. Corp., Farmington Hills, Mich., 1988-90; dir. mktg. comm. Mortgage Corp. Am., 1990-93; dir. comm. svcs., prof. William Tyndale Coll., Farmington Hills, 1993-94; adj. prof. Wayne State U., 1995—. Republican. Office: Wayne State Univ 51 West Warren Ave Detroit MI 48202

BEARDSLEE, DANIEL BAIN, venture capitalist, educator; b. Flint, Mich., Mar. 25, 1960; s. Kelly Bain and Joyce Ann (Adamson) B.; m. Susan Helen Mousseau, Mar. 12, 1983. BSME, GM Inst., 1983; MS in Mgmt., MIT, 1986. Computer systems engr. AC Spark Plug div. GM, Flint, 1983-84; cons. Arthur D. Little, Inc., Cambridge, Mass., 1985-86; v.p. fin. and adminstrn. Data to Info., Troy, Mich., 1986-87; asst. to pres. Demery Mgmt. Group, Birmingham, Mich., 1987-89, v.p., 1989-95; pres. Coll. Pk. Industries, Inc., Fraser, Mich., 1996—; lectr. Oakland U., Rochester, Mich., 1987-89, Walsh Coll., Troy, Mich., 1990-91; adj. faculty Macomb Cmty. Coll., Warren, Mich., 1988; v.p. Southeastern Mich. Venture Group, 1990-91, pres., 1991-95, chmn., 1995—. Mem. Inventor's Coun. of Mich., Southeastern Mich. Venture Group, Mich. Tech. Council. Home: 32324 Nestlewood St Farmington Hills MI 48334-2738 Office: Coll Pk Industries Inc 1705 Helvo Fraser MI 48026

BEASLEY, CARLTON M., investment advisor; b. Chgo., Jan. 5, 1967. BA, Augustana Coll., Rock Island, Ill., 1988. Investment advisor McLaughlin, Piven, Vogel, Chgo., 1990-91, Hamilton Investments, Chgo., 1991-93, Rodman & Renchal, Chgo., 1993-94, Prudential Securities Inc., Deerfield, Ill., 1994—. Mem. Jazz United (bd. dirs. 1995—). Office: Prudential Securities Inc 500 Lake Cook Rd Ste 100 Deerfield IL 60015-4922

BEASLEY, JAMES GEORGE, civil engineer; b. Cin., Apr. 27; s. John Henry and Harriet Francis (Copas) B.; m. Alta Mae Farrell, Aug. 15, 1970. BSCE, Ohio State U., 1972, MS, 1973; cert., CE Hydrologic Engring. Ctr., 1974. Profl. engr., Ohio; lic. profl. surveyor, Ohio. Teaching assoc., rsch. assoc. Ohio State U., Columbus, 1971-72, 73; hydraulic engr. Ohio Dept. Natural Resources, 1973-74, engr.-in-charge, 1974-75; dep. engr. Brown County Hwy. Dept., Georgetown, Ohio, 1975-79; county engr. County of Brown, Georgetown, 1981—; vice chmn. Dist. 15 Ohio Pub. Works Com., 1988-89, chmn., 1989-90. Adviser Hamersville (Ohio) 4-H Club, 1979-84; del. Dem. State Conv., 1980. Capt. U.S. Army, 1972-80. Mem. Am. Pub. Works Assn., Profl. Land Surveyors Ohio (pres. S.W. chpt. 1982), Nat. Assn. County Engrs., County Engrs. Assn. Ohio, Am. Pub. Works Assn., Am. Rd. and Transp. Builders Assn., Ohio Valley Antique Machinery Assn., Ohio Farmers' Union, Am. Legion (conservation officer Georgetown chpt.), Brown County Hist. Soc., Vietnam Vets. Assn., Brown County Dem. Club (pres. 1981), Kiwanis (pres. Russellvlle chpt. 1984), Lions. Office: Brown County Engr County Fairgrounds Georgetown OH 45121

BEASLEY, VAL RICHARD, veterinarian educator; b. Indpls., Nov. 2, 1948; s. Robert Eugene and Doris Jean (Sallee) B.; m. Victoria Jeanne Nahas, Jan. 25, 1971; children: Lelah Augusta, Livia Amber. DVM, Purdue U., 1972; PhD, U. Ill., 1984. Diplomate Am. Bd. Vet. Toxicology. Vet. clinician Asbury Pk. Animal Hosp., Neptune, N.J., 1972-74; owner, pres. Old Troy Pike Vet. Clinic, Dayton, Ohio, 1974-78; rsch. assoc. U. Ill. Coll. Vet. Medicine, Urbana, 1978-83, asst. prof., 1983-89, assoc. prof., 1989-96, prof., 1996—; toxicology cons. in field; dir. ENVIROVET Program, Duluth, Minn., 1991—; contract prof. Univ. Pisa, Facolta di Medicina Veterinaria, 1991, 93; cons. Thai Min. Edn. on future of toxicology in vet. medicine. Editor, author: Trichothecene Mycotoxicosis, Pathophysiologic Effects, 1989, Veterinary Clinics of North America, 1989; contbr. articles to profl. jours. Mem. U. Ill. Senate, Urbana, 1991-93, USDA Team on Fungal Contaminants of Food, China, 1989; co-chair FASEB Summer Rsch. Conf. on Natural Toxins, 1988; chair AAVCT-FDA-USDA Symposium on Natural Toxicants in Animal Feeds, 1989. Recipient Beecham award for Rsch. Excellence, U. Ill., 1990; Fulbright scholar, Kenya, 1997. Fellow Am. Acad. Vet. and Comparative Toxicology (pres. 1989-91), Am. Assn. Vet. Lab. Diagnosticians, Soc. Toxicology (founder officer vet. specialty sect.). Office: U Ill Coll Vet Medicine Dept Vet Bioscis 2001 S Lincoln Ave Urbana IL 61801-6178

BEAT, ANDREW JAMES, mechanical engineer; b. Rugby, Eng., Jan. 25, 1963; came to U.S., 1969; Assoc. Mech. Engring., U. Toledo, Ohio, 1990, B Engring. Tech., 1994. Structural design technician Poggemeyer Design Group, Bowling Green, Ohio, 1988-89; mech. engr. Toledo Engring. Co., Inc., 1989—. Roman Catholic. Office: Toledo Engring Co Inc 3400 Executive Pkwy Toledo OH 43606

BEAT, GREGORY J., technology facility administrator; b. Macomb, Ill., May 25, 1956; s. Arthur Albert and Rose Ann (Sullivan) B. BS, Western Ill., 1978; MS in Edn., Ea. Ill., 1979; MBA, U. Iowa, 1985. Dir. housing and student activities King's Coll., Wilkes-Barre, Pa., 1979-80; coord. resident edn. Slippery Rock (Pa.) U., 1981-83; bus. mgr. U. Iowa, Iowa City, 1983-85; info. ctr. mgr. Greyhound Lines, Phoenix, Dallas, Des Moines, 1986-89; asst. v.p. info. svcs. Merchants Nat. Bank, Cedar Rapids, Iowa, 1989-91; systems support mgr. Mercy Hosp., Iowa City, 1992-93, dir. info. systems, 1994-95; mgr. Ctr. for Technology Enablement Ernsy & Young LLP, Chgo., 1995—. Cmty. rep. Iowa Pub. TV Network, Johnston, 1989-95. Mem. IEEE, Health Info. Mgmt. Mgrs. Soc., Assn. Computing Machinery, Eastern. Iowa Case Mgmt Assn. (program/membership com. 1989—). Office: Ernst & Young LLP 233 S Wacker Dr Chicago IL 60606

BEATTY, CONNY DAVINROY, lawyer; b. Belleville, Ill., July 28, 1959; d. William Thomas and Kay (Schuck) Davinroy; m. Daniel Patrick Beatty, Aug. 23, 1986; children: Robert Daniel, Alexandria Marie. BA cum laude, Monmouth Coll., 1981; JD cum laude, St. Louis U., 1987, MBA, 1987. Bar: Mo. 1987, U.S. Dist. Ct. (ea. dist.) 1987, Ill. 1988, U.S. Dist. Ct. (so. dist.) 1988. Assoc. Thompson Coburn (formerly Thompson & Mitchell), St. Louis, 1987-95; ptnr. Thompson Coburn, St. Louis, 1996—. Mem. vol. lawyer program Legal Svcs. Ea. Mo.; bd. dirs. Belleville Area unit Ill. divsn. Am. Cancer Soc.; alumni bd. dirs. Monmouth Coll.; mem. Millstadt Cmty. Band. Recipient Disting. Young Alumni award Monmouth Coll., 1995. Mem. ABA, Mo. Bar Assn., Ill. Bar Assn., Bar Assn. Met. St. Louis, Healthcare Fin. Mgmt. Assn. (advanced mem.), Pi Beta Phi. Home: 11 Coronation Dr Millstadt IL 62260-1809 Office: Thompson Coburn Ste 3400 One Mercantile Ctr Saint Louis MO 63101

BEATTY, FRANCES, civic worker; b. Chgo., Apr. 17, 1940; d. Pasquale and Rose (Brunetti) Calomeni; m. Robert Alfred Beatty, Aug. 24, 1963; children: Bradford, Roxanna. BA, Northwestern U., 196l; MA, U. Chgo., 1967. Tchr. math. Proviso West High Sch., Hillside, Ill., 196l-66. Active Oak Brook Dist. 53 Sch. Bd., 1979-85; mem. women's bd. Field Mus. Natural History, Chgo., 1985—, mem. founders coun., 1988—, treas. women's bd., 1991-93; mem. governing bd. Chgo. Symphony, 1985-92; trustee Chgo. Symphony Orch., 1992—; mem. women's bd. Ravinia Festival, Highland Park, Ill., 1987—, Northwestern U., Evanston, Ill., U. Chgo.; mem. coun. Wellness House, Hinsdale, Ill., 1994. Mem. Alumnae of Northwestern U. (pres. 1996—), Women's Athletic Club Chgo. (3d v.p. 1985-87, 1st v.p. 1992-94, pres. 1994-96), John Evans Club.

BEATTY, GROVER DOUGLAS, stockbroker; b. Little Rock, Feb. 16, 1952; m. Cheryl Christine Kiecksee, Dec. 1, 1979. BSBA, Lincoln U., Jefferson City, Mo., 1977, MS in Bus. and Fin., 1983. Lic. security dealer Nat. Assn. Securities Dealers. Auditor Mo. Div. Employment Security, Jefferson City, 1979-82; stockbroker Scherck Stein & Franc, Inc., Jefferson City, 1983-86; stockbroker Stifel Nicolaus & Co., Jefferson City, 1986—, mem. president's coun., 1991—; instr. Lincoln U., 1981-94; apptd. Stifel Nicolaus Brokers Adv. Com., 1996. Fin. chmn. 9th Dist. Ross Perot Campaign. Republican. Baptist. Office: Stifel Nicolaus & Co 222 Madison St Jefferson City MO 65101-3230

BEATTY, JUDY IOLA SPENCER, educational specialist; b. McAllen, Tex., Oct. 12, 1954; d. Wayne Ellsworth and Vivian Ruth (Comer) S.; m. Terry L. Beatty, Mar. 21, 1976; children: Amanda Marie, Emily Renee, Matthew Spencer. Student, Iowa Ctrl. C.C., 1973-75. Field exec., newsletter editor Midland Empire Girl Scout Coun. U.S., St. Joseph, Mo., 1988—, tng. program specialist, 1993—. Bd. dirs. United Meth. Ch., Parnell, Mo. Mem. ASTD, Assn. Girl Scout Exec. Staff. Office: Midland Empire Girl Scout Coun US 1702 Buckingham St Saint Joseph MO 64506-3605

BEATTY, OTTO, JR., state legislator, lawyer; m. Joyce Beatty; children: Otto III, Laural. BA, Howard U.; JD with honors, Ohio State U. Bar: Ohio. Ptnr. Beatty & Roseboro, Columbus; mem. Ohio Ho. of Reps., Columbus, 1980—; mem. pub. utilities com., vice chmn. civil and comml. law com., mem. judiciary and criminal justice com., state govt. com., fin. instns. com., set-aside rev. bd., ct. reorgn. com., state penitentiary devel. commn.; pres. Otto Beatty Jr. LPA Co., Otto Beatty Jr. & Assocs., real estate developers. Recipient Cmty. Svc. award Ohio Minority Bus. Assn., Outstanding Svc. award Franklin County Children's Svcs., award Black C. of C., Ea. Union Missionary Bapt. Assn., Ohio Assn. Real Estate Brokers, Pioneer award Ohio Equal Opportunities Ctr., 1992. Mem. ABA, Ohio Bar Assn. (lectr., Leadership award 1992), Columbus Bar Assn., Franklin County Trial Lawyers Assn. (past pres.), Nat. Conf. Black Lawyers, Nat. Inst. Justice, Black Elected Dems. Ohio, Robert B. Elliott Law Club (past pres.),. Home: 2344 Woodward Ave Columbus OH 43219-2127*

BEATTY, ROBERT MICHAEL, neurosurgeon; b. Anaconda, Mont., Aug. 13, 1952; s. Martin Thomas and Ann Celeste (Milkovich) B.; m. Shelley Melinda Smith, Apr. 19, 1978; children: Jennifer, Becca, B.J. BS, Stanford U., 1974; MD, U. Utah, 1978. Diplomate Am. Bd. Neurosurgeons. Intern then resident Peter Bent Brigham, Boston, 1978-84; resident in neurol. surgery Mass. Gen. Hosp., Boston, 1979-82; pvt. practice Kansas City, Kans., 1984—; 'em. staff Bethany Med. Ctr., Providence-St. Margaret Health Ctr., St. Luke's Hosp. Kansas City; chief neurol. surgery Children's Mercy Hosp.; assoc. clin. prof. neurosurgery U. Mo., Kansas City. Contbr. articles to profl. jours. Mem. bd. Spina Bifida Found. Fellow ACS, Am. Stroke Coun.; mem. Am. Assn. Neurol. Surgeons, Mo. Neurosurg. Soc., Kansas City Neurology and Neurosurg. Soc., Met. Med. Soc., Rocky Mountain Neurol. Surgeons, Congress Neurol. Surgeons. Office: 8919 Parallel Pkwy # 455 Kansas City KS 66112

BEATTY, WILLIAM LOUIS, federal judge; b. Mendota, Ill., Sept. 4, 1925; s. Raphael H. and Teresa A. (Collins) B.; m. Dorothy Jeanne Starnes, June 12, 1948; children: William S., Steven M., Thomas D., Mary C. Student, Washington U., St. Louis, 1945-47; LL.B., St. Louis U., 1950. Bar: Ill. 1950. Gen. practice law Granite City, 1950-68; circuit judge 3d Jud. Circuit Ill., 1968-79; U.S. dist. judge So. Dist. Ill., 1979—. Served with AUS, 1943-45. Mem. Madison County Bar Assn., Tri-City Bar Assn. Roman Catholic. Office: US Dist Ct Rm 377 750 Missouri Ave East Saint Louis IL 62201

BEATY, HARRY NELSON, internist, educator, university dean; b. Brookfield, Mo., June 25, 1932; s. William Harry and Agnes Marie (Walton) B.; m. Georgia Kay Luther, July 30, 1955; children: Christopher, Kara Lynn. Student, U. Wash., 1950-54, M.D., 1958. Intern in medicine U. Minn., Mpls., 1958-59; resident in medicine U. Wash., Seattle, 1962-63; NIH fellow in medicine and biochemistry, 1963-65; instr. medicine U. Wash., 1965-67, asst. prof., 1967-71, assoc. prof., 1971-75, prof., 1975-77; prof., chmn. dept. medicine U. Vt., Burlington, 1977-83; prof., dean Med. Sch. Northwestern U., Chgo., 1983—; head infectious diseases Harborview Med. Ctr., Seattle, 1968-73; med. dir. Providence Med. Ctr., Seattle, 1973-77; chief med. service Med. Ctr. Hosp. Vt. Burlington, 1977-83; investigator Howard Hughes Med. Inst., 1965-66; bd. dirs. Becton, Dickinson & Co. Contbr. articles on infectious disease to med. to profl. jours., chpts. to med. textbooks. Served to lt. USN, 1959-63. Fellow ACP (sec. treas. Wash. chpt. 1975-76); mem. Assn. Profs. Medicine (chmn. task force manpower needs 1980-83), Infectious Diseases Soc. Am. (councillor 1979-82), Am. Soc. Clin. Investigation, Assn. Am. Med. Colls. (coun. deans adminstrv. bd., exec. coun. 1989—), Alpha Omega Alpha. Office: Northwestern U Med Sch 303 E Chicago Ave Chicago IL 60611-3008 also: Northwestern U 633 Clark St Evanston IL 60208-0001

BEAUBIEN, RICHARD FROMM, transportation executive; b. Edmonton, Alta., Can., Mar. 17; s. Richard Parker and Edith Mildred (Fromm) B.; m. Mary Jo Dooley, June 15, 1974; children: Richard, James, Marie. AB, U. Mich., 1967, BSCE, 1967, MSCE, 1968. Registered profl. engr., Mich., Ill., Calif. Hwy. engr. Fed. Hwy. Adminstrn., Washington, 1968-73; chief engr. Reid, Cool & Michalski, Inc., Southfield, Mich., 1973-75; dir. transp. City of Troy, Mich., 1975-89, Hubbell, Roth & Clark, Inc., Bloomfield Hills, Mich., 1989—; chmn. Triangle Bldg. Fund, Troy, 1991—. Contbr. articles to profl. jours. Transp. adv. coun. S.E. Mich. Coun. Govts., Detroit, 1976—. Fellow (ASCE (pres. 1993-94), Inst. Transport Engrs. (internat. bd. dirs. 1985-87, v.p. 1989, internat. pres. 1990); mem. Mich. Soc. Profl. Engrs. (bd. dirs. 1987-88, Engr. of Yr. award 1987), Internat. Right-of-Way Assn., Transp. Rsch. Bd., Pontiac Yacht Club (commodore 1988), Triangle Frat. (nat. pres. 1976-77). Republican. Episcopalian. Home: 1685 Ross Dr Troy MI 48084-1401 Office: Hubbell Roth & Clark Inc 555 Hulet Dr Bloomfield Hills MI 48302-0360

BEAUCHAMP, JANN A., information scientist, educator; b. Chgo., Dec. 7, 1931; d. Albert A. Sr. and Cornelia M. (Harrison) Cox; m. James A. Beauchamp, Oct. 16, 1954; children: David A., Carol S., Marcia E. AA, Triton Coll., 1974; BA in Bus. Adminstrn., Rosary Coll., 1980, MBA, 1984. Adminstrv. asst. St. John Luth. Sch., Forest Park, Ill., 1985-86; sec. mktg. LyphoMed, Inc., Rosemont, Ill., 1986-87; adj. faculty Data Processing and Computer Info. Sys. Depts. Triton Coll., River Grove, Ill., 1987—; adminstr. purchasing and payroll E.J. Brach Corp., Chgo., 1987-94; bd. dirs. Proviso Family Svcs., Westchester, Ill., 1977—, Disting. Svc. award, 1979-80, Leadership award, 1985-87; apptd. to Fifth Annual Conf. in Commemoration of Natl. Community Education Day "Celebrating Partnerships", Triton Coll., River Grove, Ill., 1996. Mem. sch. bd. Dist. 209, Proviso H.S., Maywood, Ill., 1992—; village trustee Village of Bellwood, Ill., 1995—; bd. dirs. St. John Luth. Ch., Forest Park, Ill.; chair Proviso Edn. Partnership, 1995—. Recipient Fred Hampton Scholarship Fund Image award, 1991, Cmty. Support Svcs., Inc. award for Svc. to Persons with Mental Disabilities, 1989-92. Mem. NAFE, AAUW, Chgo. Computer Soc., Ill. Assn. Sch. Bds. Home: 1025 24th Ave Bellwood IL 60104

BEAUCHAMP, THOMAS EVAN, retired military officer; b. Castlewood, Va., Oct. 30, 1934; s. Irving A. and Sarah (Thomas) B.; m. Bobbe Jean Johnson, July 10, 1954; children: Amanda Kae, Ida Annette, Evan Alonzo. B in Gen. Studies, U. Nebr., Omaha, 1972; MA, Webster Coll., 1981. Lic. comml. pilot. Joined as pvt. U.S. Army, 1954, commd. 2d lt., 1959, advanced through grades to col., 1984, ret., 1989; command exec. officer 123X Army Res. CMP, Ft. Harrison, Ind., 1983-95; sch. comdr. 4160th USARF Sch., Kingsbury, Ind., 1986-89; comdr. 123d Support Group USARC, Ft. Harrison, 1984-86. Decorated Legion of Merit, D.F.C. (3), Bronze star (2), Purple Heart, Air medal (39).

BEAUDETTE, ROBERT LEE, transportation and logistics consultant; b. White City, Kans., May 28, 1943; s. Axle John and Beatrice A. (Beaudette) Olson; m. Beverly Ann Robell, May 14, 1971; children: Jason M., Sara Ann. A in Commerce, Henry Ford U., 1975; postgrad., U. Mich., 1986. Traffic mgr. Detroit Stoker Co., Monroe, Mich., 1981-83; chief exec. officer Timely Air Freight, Romulus, Mich., 1985, v.p. spl. projects, 1986-88; dir. logistics Wolverine Transp. Group, Wayne, Mich., 1988-89; ptnr. IBM bus. Chuck Schubert & Assocs. Inc., 1989; transp. agt., logistics cons. IBM, 1989—, mktg. dir., 1992-95; cons. Multiplex Systems, Wyandotte, Mich., 1985—. Served to sgt. U.S. Army, 1960-66. Mem. The Packaging Inst. (profl.), Am. Legion, FOP (sec.), Vietnam Vets. Am., Delta Nu Alpha (pres. chpt. 92 1991—). Republican. Roman Catholic. Lodges: Fraternal Order Police (pres. 1988), KC. Home: 2050 22nd St Wyandotte MI 48192-3838 Office: IBM Detroit Metro HX4 18000 W 9 Mile Rd PO Box 698 Southfield MI 48037

BEAUDOIN, ROBERT LAWRENCE, small business owner; b. Newberry, Mich., Nov. 22, 1933; s. Leo Joseph and Edith Wilhelmina (Graunstadt) B.; m. Margaret Cecelia Linck, June 20, 1953; children: Eugene Robert, Kathleen Therese, Annette Marie, Suzanne Margaret. Student, Marquette U., 1952-53. With Fisher plant GM, 1953; dock hand State of Mich., St. Ignace, 1953; sch. bus driver Engadine (Mich.) Consol. Schs., 1957; owner, operator Beaudoin's Texaco, Beaudoin's Cafe, Naubinway, Mich., 1956-82, Beaudoin's Cafe and Marathon, Naubinway, 1982-83, Beaudoin's Cafe, Naubinway, 1956—; bd. dirs. Naubinway Mchts. Inc., 1985—. Mem. Naubinway July 4th Com., 1954—; past mem. Naubinway Port commn., Garfield Twp. Planning and Zoning Commn.; vol. fireman Garfield Twp. Fire Dept., Naubinway, 1980-94; mem. recreation com. Garfield Twp. Bd., Engadine, 1983; support fellow N.G. and Res., support mem. U.S. Army Recruiting Main Sta., Detroit; mem. USAF Ground Observer Corp. Recipient Cert. of Appreciation, U.S. Army Recruiting Main Sta., Detroit, 1971, Statement of Support, N.G. and Res., 1976. Mem. Internat. Platform Assn., West Mackinac C. of C., Nat. Fedn. Ind. Bus. (mem. adv. bd. 1971—, 20 Yr. award 1985), Hiawatha Sportsmans Club (mem. bd. govs. Engadine 1965-67, 89-95), Engadine Trap Shooting Club, KC (grand knight 1979-83, mem. coun. 7472 Naubiway membership and program, dir. East Marquette diocese 1984-88, dist. dep. 1988-92, supreme coun. dist. dep. 1988-92, state dir. coun. activities 1992-94, dep. grand knight coun. 7492 1995), Lions (3rd v.p. Engadine club 1970-71). Roman Catholic. Home: PO Box 143 Naubinway MI 49762-0143 Office: Beaudoins Cafe PO Box 143 US Hwy 2 Naubinway MI 49762

BEAUPRE, LAWRENCE KENNETH, newspaper editor; b. Kankakee, Ill., Nov. 1, 1944; s. Kenneth Louis and Rita (Blanchette) B.; m. Judith Ann Haverfield, Dec. 6, 1969 (div. 1994); children: Rebecca Ann, Peter Lawrence; m. Laurie M. Burgener, July 9, 1994; children: Alexandra, Laura. BS in Communications, U. Ill., 1966, MS in Journalism, 1968. Reporter Times-Union, Rochester, N.Y., 1968-72; asst. city editor Times-Union, 1972-74, city editor, ops., 1974-77, exec. city editor, 1977-79, asst. mng. editor, 1979-80, mng. editor, 1980-84; exec. editor, v.p. Westchester Rockland Newspapers, White Plains, N.Y., 1984-92; editor, v.p. Cin. Enquirer, 1992—; lectr. Am. Press Inst., Reston, Va., 1982—. With U.S. Army, 1969-71. Mem. Soc. Profl. Journalists (pres. Rochester chpt. 1983), Am. Soc. Newspaper Editors, N.Y. State AP Assn. (pres. 1984), AP Mng. Editors (pres. 1995). Office: Cincinnati Enquirer 312 Elm St Cincinnati OH 45202

BEAVER, ROBERT ALLEN, school system administrator; b. Knoxville, Iowa, Feb. 2, 1941; s. Herbert Cecil and Arlys Jean (Cummins) B; m. Margo Ann Keil, May 23, 1962; children: Kristopher, Kevin. BA, Simpson Coll., 1967; MS, Ill. State U., 1968; cert. in Adminstrn., No. Ill. U., 1972. Tchr. Glenbard East High Sch., Lombard, Ill., 1968-73; prin. Platteville (Wis.) High Sch., 1973-76; dist. adminstr. Black Hawk Sch. Dist., South Wayne, Wis., 1976-85, Adams-Friendship Area Schs., Adams, Wis., 1985—; bd. dirs. Mid-State Tech. Coll., pres. 1995—. With USAF, 1961-65. Named Citizen of Yr., Adams-Friendship C. of C., 1990, Adminstr. of Yr., Wis. Assn. Sch. Adminstrs., 1995-96; recipient Friend of Youth award Wis. Assn. Sch. Couns., 1993. Mem. Wis. Assn. Dist. Adminstrs. (bd. dirs. 1990-94), Adams-Friendship C. of C. (pres. 1990-91), Lions. Methodist. Home: 1926 13th Dr Friendship WI 53934-9200 Office: Adams-Friendship Area Schs 420 N Main PO Box # 346 Adams WI 53910

BECCHETTI, FREDERICK DANIEL, physicist, educator; b. Mpls., Mar. 3, 1943; s. Frederick Daniel and Olga Maxine Becchetti. B.S., U. Minn., 1965, M.S., 1968, Ph.D., 1969. Research assoc. Niels Bohr Inst., Copenhagen, 1969-71; research assoc. Lawrence Berkeley Lab., Calif., 1971-73; asst. prof. U. Mich., Ann Arbor, 1973-76; assoc. prof. U. Mich., 1976-82, prof. physics, 1982—. Contbr. articles to profl. jours. NSF fellow, 1970-71. Mem. IEEE, Am. Phys. Soc., Am. Assn. Physics Tchrs. Democrat. Roman Catholic. Office: Dept Physics Randall Lab Univ Mich Ann Arbor MI 48109-1120

BECHERER, HANS WALTER, agricultural equipment manufacturing executive; b. Detroit, Apr. 19, 1935; s. Max and Mariele (Specht) B.; m. Michele Beigbeder, Nov. 28, 1959; children: Maxime, Vanessa. BA, Trinity Coll., Hartford, Conn., 1957; postgrad., Munich U., 1958; MBA, Harvard U., 1962. Exec. asst. office of chmn. Deere & Co., Moline, Ill., 1966-69; gen. mgr. John Deere Export, Mannheim, Germany, 1969-73; dir. export mktg. Deere & Co., Moline, 1973-77, v.p., 1977-83, sr. v.p., 1983-86, exec. v.p., 1986-87, pres., 1987-90, chief oper. officer, 1987-89, chief exec. officer, 1989—, chmn., 1990—, also bd. dirs.; bd. dirs. Schering-Plough Corp., Allied Signal Inc., 1991—; mem. industry sector adv. com. U.S. Dept. Commerce, 1975-81; mem. Bus. Roundtable, 1989—; mem. adv. com. Chase Manhattan Bank Internat., 1990—; trustee Com. for Econ. Devel., 1990—. Trustee St. Katherine's/St. Mark's Sch., Bettendorf, Iowa, 1983—. 1st lt. USAF, 1958-60. Mem. Coun. on Fgn. Rels., The Bus. Coun., Conf. Bd., Equipment Mfgs. Inst. (bd. dirs. 1987-90), Chgo. Club, Rock Island (Ill.) Arsenal Golf Club. Republican. Roman Catholic. Home: 788 25th Avenue Ct Moline IL 61265-5132 Office: Deere & Co John Deere Rd Moline IL 61265

BECHERER, JOSEPH PAUL, art educator; b. Canton, Ohio, Apr. 9, 1965; s. Joanne Marie (Zugcic) B.; m. Lisa Anne Peters, Sept. 1, 1965; 1 child, Joseph Roland. BFA in Art History/Studio, Ohio U., 1983-87, MFA in Art History, 1987-89; postgrad., Ind. U., 1989—. Asst. dir. edn. Fort Wayne Mus. of Art, 1988-89; curator of art/artifacts Kinsey Inst., Bloomington, Ind., 1989-90; asst. prof. art Ohio U., Athens, 1990-91; asst. prof. art Grand Rapids C.C., 1991—, chair art dept., 1994—; art history/humanities cons. Prentice Hall, 1994—; curatorial cons. Grand Rapids Art Mus., 1992—. Author: Instructor's Manual to Stokstad's Art History, 1995, Selections From Kinsey Inst., 1990; co-author: Guide to 20th Century Landscape Painting, 1992. Cultural advisor Internat. Com. City of Grand Rapids, 1992—. Rsch. grantee Mich. Humanities Coun., 1994, Van Andel Found., 1996, Profl. Devel. grantee Grand Rapids C.C., 1991-94; Perugia fellow City of Grand Rapids, 1994. Mem. Coll. Art Assn., Am. Assn. of Museums, Sons of Italy. Home: 441 Briarwood Grand Rapids MI 49506 Office: Grand Rapids CC 143 Bostwick NE Grand Rapids MI 49503

BECK, DARIN ERIC, family business owner; b. Lincoln, Nebr., July 5, 1963; s. Robert Wendell Beck and Patricia Jane (King) Smith; m. Catherine Denise Garlich, Oct. 7, 1987; children: Travis, Brittany. Grad., Marshalltown, Iowa. Pres., CEO Beck Enterprises, Marshalltown, 1982-84, Beck-Tech, Inc., Cedar Falls, Iowa, 1986—, Midnite Magic Inc., Waterloo, Iowa, 1992—, Jokers Inc., Cedar Falls, Iowa, 1994—; v.p., CEO Bolliver T's Inc., Cedar Falls, 1993-94; pres., CEO Image Brokers Inc., Cedar Falls, 1993—, Pre Press Internat., Cedar Falls, 1992—; cons. Trendsetters, Inc., Cedar Falls, 1994-95, Core Tech, Inc., Racine, Wis., 1993%. Vice pres. State Assn. Beverage Retail Establishments, Waterloo/Cedar Falls, 1991; mem. Boy Scouts Am. Recipient Order of Arrow Boy Scouts Am., 1980. Republican. Office: Beck-Tech Inc 2915 McClain Dr Cedar Falls IA 50613

BECK, DONALD W., stockbroker; b. Fargo, N.D., Mar. 25, 1952. BA in Edn., N.D. State U., 1975. Dir. recreation City of Wahpeton, N.D., 1975-80; stockbroker PaineWebber Inc., Grand Forks, N.D., 1980-82, Dain Bosworth Inc., Fargo, 1982—. Republican. Lutheran.

BECK, E. LEE, writer; b. Ft. Wayne, Ind., Aug. 8, 1960; m. Lora Boblitt, Oct. 1, 1988; 2 children. BA, Purdue U., 1984. Publicist Auburn (Ind.)-Cord-Duesenberg Mus., 1987-89; staff writer Amos Press, Sidney, Ohio, 1989-91; writer Piqua, Ohio, 1991—. Author: Auburn/Cord: The History of the Auburn Automobile Company, 1996; feature editor monthly articles Car Collector; contbr. articles to Classic Auto Restorer. Mem. Soc. Automotive Historians, Soc. Profl. Journalists.

BECK, EDWARD THOMAS, electrical engineer; b. West Bend, Wis., Apr. 1, 1944. A in Elec. Engring., Milw. (Wis.) Sch. Engring., 1986. Devel. engr. RTE Corp., Waukesha, Wis., 1979-88; test tech. engr. GE, New Berlin, Wis., 1988-90; devel. engr. Thor Tech. Corp., Menomonee Falls, Wis., 1990—. Staff sgt. USAF, 1966-70. Office: Thor Tech Corp N56w13605 Silver Spring Dr Menomonee Falls WI 53051-6127

BECK, FRANCES JOSEPHINE MOTTEY (MRS. JOHN MATTHEW BECK), secondary education educator; b. Eleanora, Pa., July 12, 1918; d. George F. and Mary (Wisnieski) Mottey; B.S., Ind. State Tchrs. Coll., 1939; M.A., U. Chgo., 1955, Ph.D., 1980; m. John Matthew Beck, Aug. 23, 1941. Jr. visitor Pa. Dept. Pub. Assistance, 1940-41; asst. to the sec. dept. edn. U. Chgo., 1952-58, asst. sec., 1958, asst. dean of students Grad. Sch. Edn., 1958-75; asst. to dean Sch. Edn., De Paul U., Chgo., 1975-79, asst. prof., 1979-82; reading tchr. Bontemps Pub. Sch., Chgo., 1982-85, Chgo. Pub. Sch., 1982—; reading instr. Central YMCA, Chgo., 1958-61. Bd. dirs. Reading is Fundamental, Chgo., 1979—. Recipient Aquin Guild award, 1990, Educator of Yr. award Phi Delta Kappa, 1993. Mem. Internat. Reading Assn., Chgo. Area Reading Assn. (dir. 1980-85), Delta Kappa Gamma. Pi Lambda Theta (nat. v.p. 1966-70, 1st v.p. 1971-74, pres. Chgo. area chpt. 1987-91), Sigma Sigma Sigma. Co-author: Extending Reading Skills, 1976; contbr. articles to profl. jours. Home and Office: 5832 S Stony Island Ave Chicago IL 60637-2025

BECK, IRENE CLARE, educational consultant, writer; b. N.Y.C., Dec. 18, 1944; d. James E. and Helen (Carroll) Clare; m. William J. Beck, Aug. 9, 1986; children: Daniel, James Chesire. BA, St. Mary's Coll., 1966; MA, Fairfield U., 1977; EdD, U. Rochester, 1982. Cert. tchr., N.Y. Tchr. Elem. Sch., N.Y.C., 1966-68, Montessori Acad. N.Y., Bklyn., 1968-73; faculty Housatonic Community Coll., Bridgeport, Conn., 1975-77, Nazareth Coll., Rochester, N.Y., 1977-83; faculty dir. Sheppard Pratt Nat. Ctr. Human Devel., Balt., 1983-91; exec. dir. William & Irene Beck Found., 1987—; cons. Headstart Programs, Rochester, 1980-83, Family Day Care Tng., Rochester, 1980-83; presenter workshops and seminars. Author: Expect Respect, Let Me Tell You (manuals), (No Hang Ups (telephone audiotape), 1987, In Tune With Teens (booklet), 1990; weekly news col. Parents and Teens, 1987-90; freelance writer, 1986—; contbr. articles to profl. jours. Mem. AAUW (chair equity task force Ill. chpt.), PTA, Assn. Childhood Edn. Internat. Home: 424-F W Armitage Ave Chicago IL 60614

BECK, JEAN MARIE See WIK, JEAN MARIE

BECK, JOAN WAGNER, journalist; b. Clinton, Iowa, Sept. 5, 1923; d. Roscoe Charles and Mildred (Noel) Wagner; m. Ernest William Beck, Sept. 9, 1945; children—Christopher, Melinda. B.J. cum laude, Northwestern U., 1945, M.S. in Journalism, 1947. Radio script writer O.W.I. Voice of Am., 1945-46; copy writer Marshall Field & Co., 1947-50; feature writer Chgo. Tribune, 1950-61, writer syndicated column about young people, 1956-61, syndicated column about children, 1961-72, editor daily features sect., 1972-75, mem. editorial bd., 1975-92; syndicated editorial page columnist, 1974—. Author: How to Raise a Brighter Child, 1967, (with Dr. Virginia Apgar) Is My Baby All Right?, 1973, Effective Parenting, 1976, Best Beginnings, 1983. Hon. chmn. Mother's March of Met. Chgo. chpt. Nat. Found. March of Dimes, 1970-75; trustee Ill. Children's Home and Aid Soc., 1971-92, life trustee, 1992—; mem. Women's Bd. Northwestern U. Coun. of 100, 1993—. Recipient AP award for best newspaper feature series award Ill., 1964, best feature, 1966, best columns, 1983, 84, Alumni Merit award Northwestern U., 1965, Alumnae award, 1977, Nat. award of Achievement Alpha Chi Omega, 1966, 1st pl. award Penny-U. Mo., 1973, Lisagor award dor editorials, 1982, 88, 91, and commentary, 1994, UPI Ill. award for editorial writing, 1984, commentary award Am. Soc. Newspaper Editors, 1994; named to Chgo. Journalism Hall of Fame, 1994. Mem. Chgo. Network, Chgo. Headline Club, Alpha Chi Omega. Methodist. Office: Chicago Tribune 435 N Michigan Ave Chicago IL 60611-4001

BECK, JULES KARROLL, technical writer; b. Mpls., May 10, 1944; s. Harry Lowell and Evelyn (Karroll) B.; m. Karen Jeanette Ostenso, Mar. 23, 1967 (div. Mar. 1981); 1 child, Kevin Karroll; m. Ann Marie Kelly, Sept. 21, 1986. Student, U. Chgo., 1962-65; BA, U. Minn., 1967, MSW, 1972. Lic. social worker, Minn. Tech. writer Century Design, Hopkins, Minn., 1983-84, 86-88; pres. Gambit Publ., Inc., St. Louis Park, Minn., 1989—; tech. writer H.C. Yoh Co., St. Paul, 1989-90; assoc. dir. Hispanos en Minn., St. Paul, 1993-94; tech. writer Strom Engring., Minnetonka, Minn., 1994; info. systems cons. McGladrey & Pullen LLP, St. Paul, 1994-95; tech. writer Writing Assistance, Inc., Plymouth, Minn., 1995; dir. comm. 3rd Dimension Systems, St. Louis Park, Minn., 1996—; project adminstr. Mpls. Pub. Schs., 1972-82; H.S. tchr. Ind. Sch. Dist. 38, South Shore, S.D., 1969-70; chmn. Northside Agencies, Inc., Mpls., 1974-75, 82-83, vice-chmn. 1981, sec., 1976-80. Contbr. articles to profl. jours. Vol. Peace Corps, Potosi, Bolivia, 1967-69; chmn. Human Rights Commn., St. Louis Park, 1993-95; v.p. Minn. ACLU, Mpls., 1995, pres., 1996, bd. dirs. 1993—; media dir. 44th Dist. Dem. Party, St. Louis Park, 1993-95; pres. Kiwanis North Mpls., 1982-83, v.p. 1980-82; bd. dirs. Camden Area Cmty Concerns Coun., 1982-83. Recipient Commendation award City of Mpls., 1979, 82, 4th Precinct Police Citizens Adv. Coun., Mpls., 1982, Cert. Appreciation City of St. Louis Park, 1995. Mem. Freelance Communicator Network, Latin Am. Philatelic Soc. (chmn. expertization com., dir. n. area), Am. Philatelic Soc. Office: Gambit Publ Inc 3007 Cavell Ave S Saint Louis Park MN 55426

BECK, PAUL ADAMS, metallurgist, educator; b. Budapest, Hungary, Feb. 5, 1908; came to U.S., 1928, naturalized, 1945; s. Philip O. and Laura (Bardos) B.; children—Paul John, Philip Odon. MS, Mich. Coll. Mining and Tech., 1929; ME, Royal Hungarian U. Tech. Scis., 1931; Dr.Min. (hon.), Leoben Inst. Tech., 1979; DSc (hon.), U. Ill., 1991. Metallurgist Am. Smelting & Refining Co., Perth Amboy, N.J., 1937-41; chief metallurgist Beryllium Corp., Reading, Pa., 1941-42; supt. metall. lab. Cleve. Graphite Bronze Co., 1942-45; faculty U. Notre Dame, 1945-51, prof. metallurgy, 1949-51, head dept. metallurgy, 1950-51; research prof. phys. metallurgy U. Ill., 1951-76, prof. emeritus, 1976—. Contbr. to: The Physics of Powder Metallurgy, 1951, Metal Interfaces, 1952, The Sorby Centennial Symposium on the History of Metallurgy, 1963, Recrystallization, Grain Growth and Textures, 1966, Phase Stability in Metals and Alloys, 1966, Order-Disorder Transformations in Alloys, 1974, Noble Metal Alloys, 1986; Editor: Theory of Alloy Phases, 1956, Electronic Structure and Alloy Chemistry of Transition Elements, 1963; co-editor: Magnetic and Inelastic Scattering of Neutrons by Metals, 1968, Magnetism In Alloys, 1972. Recipient U.S. Scientist award Humboldt Found., 1978, Heyn Meml. award German Metall. Soc., 1980. Fellow Metall. Soc. of AIME (Mathewson Gold Medal award 1952, ann. lectr. 1971, Hume-Rothery award 1974), Am. Soc. Metals (Sauveur Achievement award 1976), Am. Phys. Soc., Hungarian Phys. Soc. (hon.); mem. Nat. Acad. Enging. Office: Univ of Illinois Dept of Materials Science 1304 W Green St Urbana IL 61801-2920

BECK, RICHARD EUGENE, JR., bank officer, educator, reserve police officer,; b. Ft. Wayne, Ind., Feb. 24, 1952; s. Richard Eugene Sr. and Sally Elizabeth (Patterson) B.; m. Susan Kay Goodwin Farrell, Sept. 2, 1972 (div. Jan. 1981); children: Beth Ann Marie, Brandon Michael; m. Sylvia Lynn Pease, Sept. 9, 1989. BS in Edn., Ball State U., 1974; MSM, Ind. Wesleyan U., 1987. With Ft. Wayne (Ind.) Nat. Bank, 1975—, loan collection, 1975, collection mgr., loan officer, br. bank asst. mgr., br. bank mgr., bank trainer, loan dept. mgr., pvt. banking officer; tchr. Concordia Internat. U., 1989—, vis. instr., 1995—; cons. in field, 1990—. Contbr. articles to jour. in field. Police officer res. Allen County Police Dept., Ft. Wayne, 1974—; chmn. bd. dirs.Consumer Credit Counseling of NE Ind., Ft. Wayne, 1987—; pres. bd. dirs. Allen County Police Reserve, Inc., Ft. Wayne, 1995. Named Officer of Yr., Allen County Police Res., Ft. Wayne, Ind., 1980. Mem. BBB N.E. Ind. (Ft. Wayne chpt. bd. dirs., 1987—), Summit Club. Republican. Office: Fort Wayne National Bank 110 W Berry St Fort Wayne IN 46802

BECK, ROBERT LEE, bookstore owner; b. Chgo., Apr. 9, 1921; s. Harvey Beck and Edith (Blitch) Eichelberg; m. Anna Nadine Wood, May 20, 1947; children: Linda Olson, Philip S. Grad. high sch., Chgo. Mgr. Faulkner's Ednl. Books, Chgo., 1945-55; owner Beck's Book Stores, Chgo., 1955—. Served with U.S. Coast Guard. Mem. Nat. Assn. Coll. Stores. Office: Beck's Book Stores Inc 4520 N Broadway St Chicago IL 60640-5602

BECK, STEVEN ROY, design engineer; b. Omaha, May 24, 1965. AA in Drafting, U. Nebr., 1989; AA in Tool and Die, 1989. Mech. designer TIC engr. York Mfg., Nebr., 1990-92, MFS York, Grand Island, Nebr., 1992—. Patentee: Lid opener for hopper bin, 1994. Leader Boy Scouts Pack 102, Central City, Nebr., 1994—. Mem. Soc. Mech. Engrs. Republican. Home: 2015 11th St Central City NE 68826-1008 Office: MFS York 2928 E US Highway 30 Grand Island NE 68801-8318

BECKER, BETTIE GERALDINE, artist; b. Peoria, Ill., Sept. 22, 1918; d. Harry Seymour and Magdalene Matilda (Hiller) B.; m. Lionel William Wathall, Nov. 10, 1945; children: Heather Lynn (dec.), Jeffrey Lee. BFA cum laude, U. Ill., Urbana, 1940; postgrad. Art Inst. Chgo., 1942-45, Art Student's League, 1946, Ill. Inst. tech., 1948. Dept. artist Liberty Mut. Ins. Co., Chgo., 1941-43; with Palenskie-Young Studio, 1943-46; free lance illustrator N.Y. Times, Chgo. Tribune, Saturday Rev. Lit., 1948-50; co-owner, operator Pangaea Gallery/Studio, Fish Creek, Wis.; pvt. tutor, tchr. studio classes. Exhibited one-man show Crossroads Gallery, Art Inst. Chgo., 1973; exhibited group shows including Critics' Choice show Art Rental Sales Gallery Art Inst. Chgo., 1972, Evanston-North Shore exhbns., 1964, 65, Chgo. Soc. Artists, 1967, 71, Union League, 1967, 72, Women in Art, Appleton (Wis.) Gallery Art, Milw. Art Mus., 1986, Neville Pub. Mus., Green Bay, Wis., 1987, Valperine Gallery, Madison, Wis. 1989, 92, Wis. Arts Gallery, Allouez, 1990, 94, North Cen. Coll., Naperville, Ill., 1991, Neville Mus., Green Bay, Wis., 1990, 91, 95-96, Art Works Gallery, Green Bay, 1992, 94, Tria II Gallery, Fish Creek, Wis., Oesterle Gallery, N. Ctrl. Coll., Naperville, 1993, Neville Mus., Green Bay, 1993-94, Rabbi Joseph L. Baron Mus., Milw., 1994, Beacon St. Gallery, Chgo., 1995, Paint Box Gallery, Ephraiph, Wis., 1995—, Oldtown Gallery, Chgo., 1995, William Bonifas Fine Arts Ctr., Escanaba, Mich., 1996; represented in permanent collection Witte Meml. Mus., San Antonio, Miller Art Ctr., Stugeon Bay, Wis., Neville Mus., Green Bay, Wis.; executed mural (with F. Wiater) Talbot Lab. U. Ill., Urbana, 1940; contbr. articles and illustrations to mags. and newspapers. Active Campfire Girls, Chgo., 1968, 70; art chmn., mem. exec. bd. local PTA, 1959-60; active various art festivals, 1967—. Mem. Chgo. Soc. Artists (rec. sec. 1968-77, print and drawing show), Wis. Arts Coun., N.E. Wis. Arts Coun. (bd. dir.), Alumni Assn. Art Inst. Chgo., Door County Art League, Wis. Women in the Arts, Soc. Exptl. Artists. Republican. Mem. Unity Ch. Home: 46 E Pine St Sturgeon Bay WI 54235-2726

BECKER, BRUCE CARL, II, physician, educator; b. Chgo., Sept. 8, 1948; s. Carl Max and Lillian (Podzamsky) B. BS in Aero. and Astron. Engring., U. Ill., 1970; MSME, Colo. State U., 1972; postgrad. Wright State U., 1973-74; MD, Chgo. Med. Sch., 1978; MS in Health Svcs. Adminstrn., Coll. St. Francis, Joliet, Ill., 1984; Diploma in Spanish, U. Chgo., 1988; Diploma in Polish, Coll. of Du Page, 1989. Diplomate Am. Bd. Med. Mgmt. Resident in surgery U. N.C.-Chapel Hill, 1978-79, in family practice St. Mary of Nazareth Hosp. Ctr., Chgo., 1979-81, chmn., program dir. dept. family practice, 1985-90; clin. instr. Chgo. Med. Sch., 1982, affiliate instr., 1982-83, asst. prof., 1983, vice chmn. dept. family medicine, 1983-91; asst. dir. med. edn. St. Mary of Nazareth Hosp. Ctr., Chgo., 1981-82, dir. family practice residency, 1983-90, chief Family Practice Ctr., 1983-85, chmn. dept. family practice, 1985-90, med. dir. Home Health Svc., 1985—, med. dir. HMO-Ill., 1985—, mem. fin. com. governing bd., 1987-91, planning and devel. com. governing bd., 1990—, v.p. med. affairs, 1989—; mem. adv. com. family practice residency Ill. Dept. Health, 1991—. Contbr. articles to profl. jours. Mem. editorial rev. bd. Postgrad. Medicine, 1987-89. Mem. Pub. Health Svc. Adv. Network Dept. Health & Human Svcs., 1990-91; bd. dirs. Inn Care of Am. Midwest Region, 1991—; mem. dinner com. Ill. chpt. Lupus Found. Am., 1991. Capt., USAF, 1970-75. Recipient Literary Key award St. Mary of Nazareth Hosp. Ctr., 1981, 85. Fellow Am. Acad. Family Physicians (rep. to accreditation rev. com. for physician assts. 1989-94, chmn. 1991-93), Am. Coll. Physician Execs., Am. Coll. Health Care Execs.; mem. AMA, Ill. Acad. Family Physicians (commn. on internal affairs 1986, commn. pub. and govt. policy 1987-89, chmn. 1989-90, bd. dirs. 1988-92, chmn. pub. rels. and info. com. 1988-92, state rep. family practice res. act com. 1990-92, vice speaker, 1991-92), Soc. Tchrs. of Family Medicine, Assn. Am. Med. Colls., Alliance Continuing Med. Edn., Am. Coll. Occupl. Medicine, Am. Acad. Med. Adminstrs., Chgo. Med. Soc. (councilor for Chgo. Med. Sch. 1986-91, alt. councilor for Chgo. Med. Sch. 1991-95, physicians stress ad hoc com. 1989-90, vice chmn. 1990-91, adv. com. on pub. health policy 1990—, presdl. adv. com. 1991—), Ill. State Med. Soc. (coun. on edn. and manpower 1986-96, chmn. com. on CME activities 1991-96, chmn. subcom. physican placement and practice issues 1986-90, third party payment and processes com. IAFP rep. 1990-92), Phi Delta Epsilon. Roman Catholic.

BECKER, DAVID JOSEPH, geologist; b. Omaha, Nebr., Aug. 24, 1959; s. Joseph Peter and Stella (Erickson) B.; m. Lynne Holley, July 6, 1984. BS in Geology, U. Nebr., Omaha, 1981; MS in Geophysics, So. Meth. U., Dallas, 1985. Registered profl. geologist, Tenn.; cert. profl. geologist. Geologist U.S. Army C.E., Omaha, 1984—. Contbr. articles to profl. jours. Mem. Am. Geophys. Union, Geol. Soc. Am., Am. Assn. Petroleum Geologists, Nebr. Geol. Soc. (pres.). Democrat. Roman Catholic. Home: 9160 Manderson St Omaha NE 68134 Office: US Army Corps of Engrs 12565 W Center Rd Omaha NE 68144-3869

BECKER, GARY STANLEY, economist, educator; b. Pottsville, Pa., Dec. 2, 1930; s. Louis William and Anna (Siskind) B.; m. Doria Slote, Sept. 19, 1954 (dec.); children: Judith Sarah, Catherine Jean; m. Guity Nashat, Oct. 31, 1979; children: Michael Claffey, Cyrus Claffey. AB summa cum laude, Princeton U., 1951, PhD (hon.), 1991; AM, U. Chgo., 1953, PhD, 1955; PhD (hon.), Hebrew U., Jerusalem, 1985, Knox Coll., 1985, U. Ill., Chgo., 1988, SUNY, 1990, U. Palermo, Buenos Aires, 1993, Columbia U., 1993, Warsaw (Poland) Sch. Econs., 1995, U. Econs., Prague, Czech Republic, 1995, U. Miami, 1995, U. Rochester, 1995. Asst. prof. U. Chgo., 1954-57; from asst. prof. to assoc. prof. Columbia U., N.Y.C., 1957-60, prof. econs., 1960-68, Arthur Lehman prof. econs., 1968-70; Univ. prof. U. Chgo., 1970-83, Univ. prof. econs. and sociology, 1983—, chmn. dept. econs., 1984-85; Ford Found. vis. prof. econs. U. Chgo., 1969-70; assoc. Econs. Rsch. Ctr. Nat. Opinion Rsch. Ctr., Chgo., 1980—; mem. domestic adv. bd. Hoover Instn., Stanford, Calif., 1973-90, sr. fellow, 1990—; mem. acad. adv. bd. Am. Enterprise Inst., 1987-90; rsch. policy advisor Ctr. for Econ. Analysis Human Behavior Nat. Bur. Econ. Rsch., 1972-78, mem. and sr. research assoc., 1957-79; assoc. mem. Inst. Fiscal and Monetary Policy, Ministry of Japan, 1988—. Author: The Economics of Discrimination, 1957, Human Capital, 1964, 3d edit., 1993, Japanese transl., 1975, Spanish trans., 1985, Human Capital and the Personal Distribution of Income: An Analytical Approach, 1967, Economic Theory, 1971, Japanese transl., 1976, (with Gilbert Ghez) The Allocation of Time and Goods Over the Life Cycle, 1975, The Economic Approach to Human Behavior, 1976, German trans., 1982, Polish transl., 1990, Chinese transl., 1993, A Treatise on the Family, 1981, expanded edit., 1991, Spanish transl., 1987, Chinese transl., 1988, Accounting for Tastes, 1996, The Economics of Life, 1996; editor: Essays in Labor Economics in Honor of H. Gregg Lewis, 1976; co-editor: (with William M. Landes) Essays in the Economics of Crime and Punishment, 1974; columnist, Bus. Week, 1985—; contbr. articles to profl. jours. Recipient W.S. Woytinsky award U. Mich., 1967, Profl. Achievement award U. Chgo. Alumni Assn., 1968, Frank E. Seidman Disting. award in Polit. Economy, 1985, Merit award NIH, 1986, John R. Commons award Omicron Delta Epsilon, 1987, Nobel prize in Econ. Scis., 1992. Fellow Am. Statis. Assn., Econometric Soc., Am. Acad. Arts and Scis., Am. Econ. Assn. (Disting., v.p. 1974, pres. 1987, John Bates Clark medal 1967); mem. NAS, NAE (founding mem., v.p. 1965-67), Am. Philos. Soc., Internat. Union for Scientific Study Population, Mont Pelerin Soc. (exec. bd. dirs. 1985—, v.p. 1989-90, pres. 1990-92), Western Econ. Assn. (pres. 1996-97), Phi Beta Kappa. Office: U Chgo Dept Econs 1126 E 59th St Chicago IL 60637-1580

BECKER, GERALD ARTHUR, publisher; b. Elyria, Ohio, Sept. 29, 1941; s. Louis A. and Eleanor (Phillipson) B.; m. Ryna L. Trope, Nov. 27, 1965; children: David, Adam. BS in Journalism, Ohio U., 1963. Asst. to pub. Penton Publ., Inc., Cleve., 1964-69; editorial dir. CRC Press, Cleve., 1969-77; v.p., assoc. pub. Oster Communications, Chgo., 1977-84; pub. Commodity Perspective div. Knight Ridder, Inc., Chgo., 1984-91, Commodity Research Bur. div. Knight Ridder, Inc., N.Y.C., 1984-91; sr. v.p. Commodity News Services, Inc., Chgo., 1984-91; pub. fin. publishing group Knight-Ridder, Inc., 1991-93; v.p. mktg. Knight-Ridder Fin. Americas, Chgo., 1993-94; v.p. global product mktg.-commodities Knight-Ridder Fin., Inc., Chgo., 1995-96; pres. The Insight Group, Inc., Arlington Heights, Ill., 1996—. Served with USCGR, 1963-69. Mem. Futures Industry Assn. (pres., sec. mktg. div.). Home: 3270 N Windsor Dr Arlington Heights IL 60004-1615 Office: The Insight Group Inc 3270 N Windsor Dr Arlington Heights IL 60004

BECKER, JOHN J., state legislator; m. Jean Becker. BS, Purdue U.; MA, Ball State U. Tchr. Paul Harding H.S.; mem. Ind. State Ho. of Reps. Dist. 80, mem. aged and aging com., mem. families, children and human affairs com., mem. natural resources com., vice chmn. edn. com. Mem. Nat. State Tchrs. Math., K. of C.

BECKER, KAREN ANN, academic program director; b. Willoughby, Ohio, Apr. 9, 1963; d. William Herbert and Janet Mae (Wilkins) B. BA in English and Speech, Allegheny Coll., 1985, MEd, 1986; postgrad., Baldwin-Wallace Coll., 1987-88; PhD, Ohio State U., 1993. Cert. tchr. English and speech provisional, Ohio. Student asst. Allegheny Coll., Meadville, Pa., 1981-85; high sch. tchr. North Royalton (Ohio) City Schs., 1985-87, substitute tchr., 1987-88; instr., researcher Townsend Learning Ctr., Chagrin Falls, Ohio, 1987-90; cognitive interventionist Excellence in Learning, Upper Arlington, Ohio, 1990; rsch. asst. Nat. Assn. Secondary Sch. Prins., Va., 1990; grad. teaching assoc. Ohio State U., Columbus, 1988-93; upper sch. tchr., dir. Learning Unltd. Internat. Schs. Inc.-Village Acad., Powell, Ohio, 1994—; adj. faculty Columbus State C.C., 1989—, Capitul U., 1994—, Franklin U., 1995—, Otterbein U., 1996—; instr. and cons. Learning 20/20 and Kids in Coll., 1993—. Rsch. author: Word Atlas, 1988. Mem. ASCD, Phi Kappa Phi. Home: 208 W Como Ave Columbus OH 43202-1039 Office: 284 S Liberty St Powell OH 43065

BECKER, LANSON, engineering executive; b. Kalamazoo, Mich., Feb. 10, 1941; s. Ellis and Elizabeth May (Coville) B.; m. Linda Diane Schuyler, June 1, 1963; children: Timothy Ray, Matthew Jay, Lanson Tyler. BS, Western Mich. U., 1963, MBA in Fin., 1978. Layout draftsman Argonne Nat. Labs., Lemont, Ill., 1963, Hydreco Co. div. Gen. Signal Corp., Kalamazoo, Mich., 1963-65; from asst. project engr. to v.p. engring. Hydreco Co. div. Gen. Signal Corp., Kalamazoo, 1965-87; engr. in pharm. mfg. The Upjohn Co., Kalamazoo, 1987-90, mgr. pharm. mfg. engring., 1990-92; mgr. facilities engring. The Uphohn Co., 1992-96; project mgr. Pharmacia & Upjohn, Kalamazoo, 1996—. Patentee hydraulics (6). Chmn. Cub Scouts Am., Galesburg, Mich., 1975-83; mem., then chmn. Galesburg City Planning Commn., 1965-75. Mem. Soc. Mfg. Engrs., Soc. Automotive Engrs. (remote controls and steering subcom. 1966-87), Nat. Fluid Power Assn. (T3.5 valve sect., 1967-87, Standards Devel. award 1986). Methodist. Home: 12505 Ft Custer Dr Galesburg MI 49053-9660

BECKER, LEE BERNARD, journalism educator; b. Covington, Ky., June 25, 1948; s. Bernard G. and Helen (Bertram) B.; m. C. Ann Hollifield, May 14, 1988; 1 child, Jessica Elizabeth. BA, U. Ky., 1969, MA, 1971; PhD, U. Wis., 1974. Reporter Cin. Enquirer, 1969-70; asst. prof. Syracuse (N.Y.) U., 1974-77; prof. Ohio State U., Columbus, 1977—. Co-author: Training and Hiring of Journalists, 1987; co-editor: Coping With Plenty, 1989. Named Fulbright Prof., German-Fulbright Commn., 1981, 91-92. Office: Ohio State U Sch of Journalism 242 W 18th Ave Columbus OH 43210-1107

BECKER, MARY JULIA, secondary education educator, author; b. Akron, Ohio, Aug. 29, 1928; d. Nick and Mary (Krieger) Lengyel; m. Samuel Becker, Dec. 3, 1953 (dec. May 1954); 1 child, Samuella Rebecca. BS, U. Akron, 1962, MS, 1965; postgrad. U. London, Cambridge U., Oxford U., U. New Delhi, U. Moscow. Sec. B.F. Goodrich Co., Akron, 1948-50, Goodyear Tire & Rubber Co., Akron, 1954-56; draftswoman Ohio Bell Telephone Co., Akron, 1950-51; tchr. Akron Pub. Schs., 1958—; counselor West Jr. High Sch., Akron, 1964-67. Editor: Shoestring Anthology; guest editor Ohio Reading Tchr., Columbus, 1983; writer Ohio Survey Tests 1962-63, adv. editor TV Creative Writing Series Sta. WVIZ; contbr. articles to mags., newspapers, profl. jours. Vol. Ohio Ballet, 1983; pres. Hadassah, 1985-86, 1991-92; v.p. College Club; teaching Children's Literature at Kent State. Recipient Martha Holden Jennings Master Tchr. award Kent State U., 1978, Tchr. of Week award Scholastic mag., N.Y.C., 1981; nominated Rita Dove award, 1990. Mem. AAUW, Ohio Press Women, Ohio Profl. Writers, Akron Storytelling League, Women in Communications, Women's History Bd., Akron Assn. Childhood Edn. (pres. 1960-61), Canton Writers Guild (editor Short Stories), Internat. Reading Assn., Soc. of Children's Book Writers, Akron Manuscript Club, Windows of the World Story League of Akron, Ohio Speakers Bur., Ohio Published Authors League, Nat. League Am. Pen Women, Literary Singles, Kappa Delta Gamma. Clubs: Toastmasters, College (v.p. 1993-94), Press (Akron). Lodge: B'nai B'rith, Hadassah (pres. Lilah chpt. 1992-93). Home: 1894 Evergreen Ave Akron OH 44301-2957

BECKER, RALPH LEONARD, psychologist; b. Cin., July 15, 1927; s. Morris and Sarah Ruth B.; m. Evelyn Zeifman, Aug. 15, 1976. BA in Sci., Ohio State U., 1958, BS in Edn., 1960, MA in Psychology, 1961, PhD in Psychology, 1979. Lic. psychologist, Ohio; cert. counselor, Ohio. Spl. tchr. Columbus (Ohio) City Schs., 1962-64; staff psychologist Ohio Dept. Mental Retardation/Devel. Disabilities, Columbus, 1964-68, research scientist, 1968-72, research assoc., 1972-82; research dir. Elbern Pubs., Columbus, 1982—. Author: Reading-Free Vocational Interest Inventory, 1981, rev. edit. 1988, Occupational Title List, 1984, rev. edit. 1992, Becker Work Adjustment Profile, 1989; contbr. articles to profl. jours. Grantee State of Ohio, 1966, 67, U.S. Office of Edn., 1968. Fellow Am. Assn. on Mental Retardation; mem. Coun. for Exceptional Children, Ohio Psychol. Assn., Ohio State Alumni Assn., Am. Psychol. Assn. Office: Elbern Publs PO Box 09497 Columbus OH 43209-0497

BECKER, ROBERT ALLEN, data processing executive; b. Chgo., June 27, 1942; s. Sig Herman and Dorothy (Shaw) B.; m. Babs Lee Hefter, Dec. 24, 1964; children: David, Edie. BS in Indsl. Mgmt., Purdue U., 1964. Programmer analyst Standard Oil Co. (Amoco), Chgo., 1964-67; programmer analyst R.R. Donnelley & Sons, Chgo., 1967-68, project leader, 1968-71, supr. computer ops., 1971-72, supr. tech. svcs., 1972-79; mgr. data. ctr. ops. Chic Merc. Exch., Chgo., 1979-82; dir. info. resources Richard D. Irwin, Homewood, Ill., 1982-87; dir. system svcs. Holy Cross Health System, South Bend, Ind., 1987-89; dir. info. systems and communications Elkhart (Ind.) Gen. Hosp., 1989-92; dir. info. systems Mt. Sinai Hosp. Med. Ctr., Chgo, 1992—, Schwab Rehab. Hosp., Chgo, 1993—; instr., Thornton Community Coll., South Holland, Ill., 1970-71, Prairie State Coll., Chicago Heights, Ill., 1982-87. Asst. cub master, Boy Scouts Am., Homewood, Ill., 1976; mgr. Homewood Little League. Mem. Guide Internat. (bd. dirs. 1971-80), Computer Ops. Mgmt. Assn., Data Processing Mgmt. Assn (bd. dirs. 1984-88, pres. Calumet chpt. 1987-88, Indivual Performance award 1988), Soc. Info. Mgmt., Healthcare Info. and Mgmt. Sys. Soc. (sec.-treas. region III med. users software exchange), Purdue Club (bd. dirs. 1987, treas. 1989—), Alpha Epsilon Pi. Home: 12996 Pierce Ct Crown Point IN 46307-9255 Office: Mt Sinai Hosp Med Ctr California 15th Chicago IL 60608

BECKER, ROBERT JEROME, allergist, health care consultant; b. Milw., May 29, 1922; s. Jacob and Sarah (Saxe) B.; m. June Granof, June 25, 1950; children: Scott M., Jill Becker Wilson, Jon G. BS, U. Wis., Milw., 1943; MD, Med. Coll. Wis., 1949. Intern Michael Reese Hosp., Chgo., 1949-50; resident in internal medicine VA Hosp., Wood, Wis., 1950-53; resident in allergy Roosevelt Hosp., N.Y.C., 1955-56; pvt. practice specializing in allergy Joliet, Ill., 1956-82; founder, chmn. HealthCare COMPARE, 1982-90, chmn. emeritus, bd. dirs., 1990—; cons. health care utilization co., 1982-90; founder, pres. Becker Cons. Corp., 1990—; founder, chmn. Healthcare Communications Mgmt. Corp., 1990-93; med. dir. Quad river Found. Med. Care, 1976-84; pres. Am. Assn. Profl. Stds. Rev. Orgns., 1980-82; exec. v.p. Joint Coll. Allergy and Immunology, 1978-86; mem. adv. coun. Nat. Inst. Environ. Health Scis., 1984-88; bd. dirs. GMIS, Allerx, Am. Psych Sys.; chmn. Utilization Rev. Accreditation Commn., 1991-94, bd. dirs., 1994-96. Author articles in field. Pres. bd. edn. Joliet Twp. High Sch. Dist. 204, 1969-70, 75-76; mem. bus. adv. com. U. Ill. Sch. Bus., Chgo., 1987—. Recipient Clemens von Pirquet award Georgetown U. Internat. Interdisciplinary Ctr. Immunology, 1978; named Entrepreneur of Yr. Arthur Young/Venture Mag., 1988. Fellow ACP, Am. Acad. Allergy, Am. Coll. Allergists (pres. 1987), Am. Coll. Chest Physicians; mem. Ill. Soc. Internal Medicine (pres. 1984-86), Asthma and Allergy Assn. Am. (bd. dirs. 1987—), Asthma and Allergy Found. Am. (bd. dirs. 1990-94), Am. Managed Care and Rev. Assn. (bd. dirs. 1989-95), Am. Assn. Preferred Providers Assn. (bd. dirs. 1989—), Utilization Rev. Accreditation Commn. (chair 1991-94, bd. dirs. 1991—), Am. Assn. Preferred Provider Orgns. (bd. dirs. 1988-93), Am. Psychiat. Systems (bd. dirs. 1994—), Alpha Omega Alpha, Alpha Sigma Nu. Home: 2036 Intracoastal Dr Fort Lauderdale FL 33305-3636 Office: 1 Tower Ln Ste 1140 Villa Park IL 60181-4625

BECKER, ROBERT JOSEPH, database consultant, computer science specialist, database software developer and educator; b. Grand Rapids, Mich., Apr. 22, 1946; s. Leon Joseph and Alfreda Mary (O'Rielly) B.; m. Kathleen Zbikowski, Jan. 16, 1970; children: Steven, Michael, Kimberly, John. BS in Computer Sci., Mich. State U., 1970. Computer sci. specialist Wolverine World Wide, Rockford, Mich., 1970-73; data base adminstr. Foremost Ins. Co., Grand Rapids, 1973-80, with data base, data communications, 1980-86, mgr. data base adminstrn., 1986-88, cons. of tech. directions, 1988—; keynote data base performance speaker U.S. and European Software AG Confs., 1973—; tchr. computer basics to elem. sch. students, 1988-93. Editor (data base products) Software Ag Connections, 1987—, author performance courses, 1993—; contbr. articles to profl. jours. Community edn. instr., Wyoming, Mich., 1974-80; vol. examiner FCC, Grand Rapids, 1975-85; vol. religious edn. instr., 1980—. Mem. Software AG Internat. Users Group (cert., chmn. performance spl. interest group 1978—, tech. rep. 1983-85, data base products rep. 1987—, chmn. data base future directions 1989—, comm. and client-server software rep. 1994—, best presentation award 1978, 82, best speaker award 1979), Am. Radio Relay League, Nat. Train Collectors Assn. Republican. Roman Catholic. Home: 4560 Bremer St SW Grandville MI 49418-2238 Office: ISSC/Foremost Ins Co PO Box 1233 Grand Rapids MI 49501-1233

BECKER, THEODORE MICHAELSON, lawyer; b. Chgo., Feb. 18, 1949; s. Michael and Hazel Becker; m. Tamara B. Kaplan, June 11, 1983; children: Adam Michael, Alex Jordan, Ian David. AB summa cum laude, Washington U., St. Louis, 1970; MA in Sociology, Northwestern U., 1972, JD summa cum laude, 1974, PhD in Sociology, 1981. Bar: Ill. 1975, U.S. Dist. Ct. (no. and so. dist.) Ill. 1975, U.S. Ct. Appeals (7th and 10th cirs.) 1975, U.S. Ct. Appeals (9th cir.) 1976, U.S. Supreme Ct. 1978, U.S. Dist. Ct. (cen. dist.) Ill. 1979, U.S. Dist. Ct. (no. dist. trial bar) Ill. 1982, U.S. Ct. Appeals (Fed. cir.) 1983. Russell Sage fellow, instr. Yale U., New Haven, 1974-75; pvt. practice Chgo., 1975—. Contbr. articles to books and profl. jours. Mem. ABA, Ill. Bar Assn., Chgo. Bar Assn., Phi Beta Kappa, Order of Coif. Office: Becker Assocs 19 S La Salle St Ste 1500 Chicago IL 60603-1401

BECKER, VANETA G., state representative; b. Alton, Ill., Oct. 7, 1949; m. Andrew C. Guarino. Attended, U. Evansville. Rep. dist. 75 State of Ind., 1981-91, rep. dist. 78, 1991—, ranking minority leader, 1991—; mem. pub. health & cities & towns coms.; mem. asst. minority caucus State of Ind.; realtor Don Cox & Assoc.; mem. bd. dirs. Albion Fellows Bacon Ctr., Patchwork Cent. Recipient Legis. Excellence award United Mine Workers, 1989; named Legislator of the Yr. Ind. Primary Health Care Assn., 1990. Mem. Nat. Assn. Realtors, Ind. Primary Health Care Assn., Evansville Zool. Soc., A Network of Evansville Women, Leadership Evansville, Crisis Prevention Nursery. Republican. Methodist. Home: 420 E Buena Vista Rd Evansville IN 47711-2720 Office: Ind Ho of Reps State Capitol Indianapolis IN 46204

BECKER, WALTER HEINRICH, vocational educator, planner; b. St. Louis, Mar. 20, 1939; s. Anthon and Maria (Fleischman) B.; m. Ayse Nur Alpyoruk, Aug. 3, 1971; children: Volkan P., Kirstal S. BS, S.E. Mo. State U., 1963; MS, U. Mo., Columbia, 1969; PhD, St. Louis U., 1978; MS, Fontbonne Coll., 1989. Cert. tchr. Secondary tchr. Sch. Dist. of Hancock Pl., Lemay, Mo., 1963-64, Mascoutah (Ill.) Sch. Dist., 1964-65, U.S. Dept. of Def., Japan, Turkey, Philippines, 1965-70; vocat. edn. supr. Mo. Divsn. of Mental Health, Farmington, Mo., 1971-79; program analyst Arabian Am. Oil Co., Dhahran, Saudi Arabia, 1979-80, planning and programs analyst, 1981-85; vocat. edn. supr. Mo. Dept. of Corrections, Jefferson City, 1990-93.

BECKETT, THEODORE CHARLES, lawyer; b. Boonville, Mo., May 6, 1929; s. Theodore Cooper and Gladys (Watson) B.; m. Daysie Margaret Cornwall, 1950; children: Elizabeth Gayle, Theodore Cornwall, Margaret Lynn, William Harrison, Anne Marie. B.S., U. Mo., Columbia, 1950, J.D., 1957. Bar: Mo. 1957. Since practiced in Kansas City; mem. firm Beckett, Lolli & Bartunek; instr. polit. sci. U. Mo., Columbia, 1956-57; asst. atty. gen. State of Mo., 1961-64. Former mem. bd. dirs. Kansas City Civic Ballet; mem. City Plan Commn., Kansas City, 1976-80; mem. bd. curators U. Mo., 1995—. 1st lt. U.S. Army, 1950-53. Mem. Am., Mo., Kansas City bar assns., Lawyers Assn. Kansas City, Newcomen Soc. N.Am., SAR, Order of Coif, Sigma Nu, Phi Alpha Delta. Presbyterian. Clubs: Kansas City (Kansas City, Mo.), Blue Hills Country (Kansas City, Mo.). Office: Beckett Lolli & Bartunek 1400 Commerce Trust Bldg 922 Walnut St Kansas City MO 64106-1809

BECKETT, THEODORE CORNWALL, lawyer; b. Heidelberg, Fed. Republic of Germany, Nov. 21, 1952; (parents Am. Citizens); s. Theodore Charles and Daysie Margaret (Cornwall) B.; m. Patricia Anne McKelvy, June 18, 1983; children: Anna Kathleen, Kerry Christine, Cooper Charles. BA, U. Mo., 1975, JD, 1978. Bar: Mo. 1978, U.S. Dist. Ct. (we. dist.) Mo. 1978. Ptnr. Beckett & Hensley L.C., Kansas City, Mo., 1994—. Bd. dirs. Kans. Spl. Olympics, 1979-84, legal advisor, 1984—, Kans. City Metro Spl. Olympics, 1993—. Mem. ABA, Mo. Bar Assn., Kansas City Bar Assn., Mo. Assn. Trial Attys., Assn. Trial Lawyers Am., Kansas City Club, Carriage Club, Beta Theta Pi. Democrat. Presbyterian. Office: Beckett & Hensley LC PO Box 13185 610 Commerce Tower Kansas City MO 64199

BECKHOLT, ALICE, public health nurse; b. N.Y.C., Aug. 7, 1941; d. Julius and Mary (Katz) Kalkow; m. Richard H. Polakoff, Aug. 12, 1962 (div. 1984); children: Katherine, Michael, Matthew; m. Kenneth Eugene Beckholt, Feb. 3, 1990. BA, Syracuse U., 1962; ADN, El Centro Coll., 1977; BSN, U. Tex., Arlington, 1980; MS, Tex. Women's U., 1988. RN, Tex., Ohio. Staff nurse, outpatient mgr. Irving (Tex.) Cmty. Hosp., 1977-86; staff nurse Meth. Hosp., Dallas, 1986-89, U. Tex. S.W. Med. Ctr., Dallas, 1989-90; pediat. home care nurse various agys., Columbus, Ohio, 1990-94; pub. health nurse and nurse clinician Columbus (Ohio) Bd. Health, 1994—. Sec., 2nd v.p., 1st v.p., pres. Am. Cancer Soc., 1971-76, bd. dirs. Irving, Tex., 1971-90, BSE instr., nurse's com., 1990—, triple touch coord., 1991—, BSE faculty, 1986-90; vol., auction subchair Sta. KERA-TV, Dallas, 1972-84; CPR instr. Am. Heart Assn., 1984—. Recipient Outstanding Svc. award Am. Cancer Soc. Columbus chpt., 1992-93; named Outstanding Vol., Am. Cancer Soc., Irving, Tex., 1973, 74, 76. Mem. Nat. Assn. Neonatal Nurses, Ohio Pub. Health Assn., Sigma Theta Tau. Home: 2605 Brookwood Rd Columbus OH 43209 Office: Columbus Dept Health 181 Washington Blvd Columbus OH 43215

BECKMAN, MELISSA ANN, insurance account executive; b. Harvard, Ill., May 1, 1964; d. Richard William and Nancy Clair (Fullmer) Mueller; m. Joseph Anthony Beckman, Nov. 4, 1989. BA, U. Wis., 1986. Casualty underwriter Liberty Mut. Ins., Chgo., 1986-87, Northwestern Nat. Ins., Milw., 1987-90; sales devel. rep. Aetna Life and Casualty, Milw., 1990-96, account exec., 1996—. Republican. Episcopalian.

BECKMAN, TRACY, state legislator; b. Jan. 7, 1945; m. Janel Beckman; five children. Senator Dist. 26, Minn. State Senate, 1986—; mgr., Owatonna Canning Co., 1996—; cons., 1996—. vice-chmn. Econ. Devel. & Housing com., edn. com.; mem. Agrl. & Rural Devel. Com., Crime Prevention Com., Edn. Com., Edn. Funding Divsn., Fin. Com. & Govt. Ops. & Reform Com.; chmn. Crime Prevention Fin. Divsn., Joing Claims Divsn. Address: PO Box 37 Bricelyn MN 56014-0037 also: State Senate State Capital Building Saint Paul MN 55155-1606*

BECKMANN, ROBERT DEAN, JR., real estate broker; b. Indpls., Oct. 12, 1941; m. Cynthia Stebbing Lewis, Nov. 27, 1965 (div. Mar. 1975). BA Polit. Sci. cum laude, Hanover Coll., 1963; MA Polit. Sci. cum laude, Georgetown U., 1965. Polit. writer UPI, Washington, 1964-65; exec. dir. Greater Indpls. Rep. Fin. Com., 1965-68; adminstrv. asst. mayor office Richard G. Lugar, Indpls., 1968-72; exec. dir. Greater Indpls. Progress Com., 1972-73; broker F.C. Tucker Co., Inc., Indpls., 1973-93; broker, cons., 1993—; reporter, polit. writer UPI, Washington, 1964-66; producer, writer, on-air host PBS Channel 20 Indiana Arts, Indpls., 1982-88. Bd. dirs. Riley Area Revitalization Program, Indpls., Metro Indpls. Pub. Broadcasting, Inc., Greater Indpls. Progress Com., Dance Kaleidoscope; local organizing com. mem. Pan Am. Games, 1987; chmn. Pan Am. Arts Festival, 1987; chmn. bd. Festival Music Soc., 1972-74, Indpls. Art League, 1987-88; bd. dirs. Arts Coun. Indpls., pres., 1988-90; bd. dirs. Ind. Repertory Theatre, treas., 1974-75, 86-87. Recipient Alumni Achievement award Hanover Coll., 1971, Arti award Arts Coun. Indpls., 1990. Mem. Nat. Assn. Realtors, Ind. Assn. Realtors, Metro. Indpls. Bd. Realtors, Penrod Soc. (bd. dirs.). Presbyterian. Home and Office: 415 Massachusetts Ave Indianapolis IN 46204-1501

BECKMEYER, HENRY ERNEST, anesthesiologist, medical educator; b. Cape Girardeau, Mo., Apr. 13, 1939; s. Henry Ernest Jr. and Margaret Gertrude (Link) B.; m. Virginia Hobson; children: Henry, James, Martha, Leigh, Hillary, Nicole. BA, Mich. State U., 1961; DO, U. Health Scis., 1965. Diplomate Am. Bd. Med. Examiners, Am. Osteo. Bd. Anesthesiology, Am. Acad. Pain Mgmt. Chief physician migrant worker program and op. head start Sheridan (Mich.) Community Hosp., 1967-69; resident in anesthesia Bi-County Community Hosp./DOH Corp., Detroit, 1969-71, chief resident, 1968-69; staff anesthesiologist Detroit Osteo. Hosp./BCCH, 1971-75; founding chmn. dept. anesthesia Humana Hosp. of the Palm Beaches, West Palm Beach, Fla., 1975-79; assoc. prof. Mich. State U., East Lansing, 1979-88, prof. anesthesia, 1988—, chmn. dept. osteo. medicine, 1985—; chief staff Mich. State U. Health Facilities, 1988-90, chmn. med. staff exec. and steering coms., 1988-90; chmn. of anesthesia St. Lawrence Hosp., Lansing, Mich., 1984-90, adminstrv. dir. dept. anesthesia, 1994—; chief of staff Sheridan Community Hosp., 1968-69; mem. adminstrv. coun. Mich. State U., 1988—, mem. acad. coun., 1992—, mem. faculty coun., 1992—, mem. clin. practice bd., bd. dirs. sports medicine; mem. internal mgmt. com. Mich. Ctr. for Rural Health; cons. Ministry Health, Belize C.A., 1993—; amb. Midwestern Univ. Consortium Internat. Activities, 1993; program chmn. Am. Russian Med. Exch., 1993—; bd. dirs. Belize Med. Partnership. Speaker Sta. WKAR, Mich. State U.; bd. dirs. Boy Scouts Am., W. Bloomfield, Mich., 1973-74, Palm Beach Mental Health, 1977-79, Care Choices HMO, Lansing, 1987-88. Fellow Am. Coll. Osteo. Anesthesiologists; mem. Am. Osteo. Coll. Anesthesiology (chmn. commn. on colls. 1988-89, cert. anesthesiology 1976), Soc. Critical Care Medicine, Internat. Anesthesiology Rsch. Soc., Am. Coll. Physician Execs., Am. Osteo. Assn. (spkr.), Am. Acad. Pain Mgmt. (cert. 1991), Am. Arbitration Assn., Mich. Pain Soc., Mich. Peer Rev. Orgn., Am. Soc. Regional Anesthesia, Soc. Security Disability Evaluation, Univ. Club, Phi Beta Delta. Republican. Office: Mich State U West Fee Hall East Lansing MI 48824

BECKNER, JEFFERY EDWARD, periodical editor; b. East Chgo., Ind., Nov. 17, 1960; s. David Edward and Betty Lou (Beck) B. BA in English Composition, DePauw U., 1983; MFA, U. Iowa, 1985. Supr. Beckner Painting Co., Inc., St. Louis, 1985-89; account exec. Multimedia Co. Inc., St. Louis, 1989; editor Finan Pub. Co. Inc., St. Louis, 1990—. Home: 1955 Hunting Lake Ct Saint Louis MO 63122 Office: 8730 Big Bend Blvd Saint Louis MO 63119

BECKWITH, CATHERINE S., veterinarian; b. St. Louis, Apr. 8, 1958; d. John P. Sr. and Dolores A. Beckwith. BA in Germanic Langs. and Lit., U. Ill., 1981, BS in Biology, 1981, BS in Vet. Med. with hons., 1984, DVM with honors, 1986. Assoc. vet. Cen. Hosp. for Animals, Carterville, Ill., 1986-87, Coble Animal Hosp., Springfield, Ill., 1987-91, Northgate Pet Clinic, Decatur, Ill., 1991-92; postdoctoral fellow in lab. animal medicine U. Mo., Columbia, 1992—. Contbr. articles to profl. jours. Fulbright grantee Tech. U., Munich, 1981. Mem. Am. Assn. for Lab. Animal Sci., Am. Soc. for Lab. Animal Practitioners, Am. Vet. Med. Assn., Phi Zeta. Home: 1457 S Sonora Dr Columbia MD 65201 Office: U Mo Coll Vet Med Vet Path W213 Vet Med Bldg 1600 E Rollins Rd Columbia MO 65211

BECKWITH, JOHN ADAMS, school superintendent; b. Howell, Mich., July 16, 1942; s. Ford D. M. and Avis M. (Brown) B.; m. B. Joanne Bird, June 17, 1967; children: Tammie, Michael, Kellie. BA, Cen. Mich. U., 1965; MA, U. Mich., 1967, PhD, 1970. Tchr. Flint (Mich.) Community Schs., 1965-68; prin. Lincolnwood (Ill.) Sch. Dist. 74, 1970-72, asst. supt., 1972-75; supt. Toluca (Ill.) Community Unit #2, 1975-77; prin., supt. Kenilworth (Ill.) Sch. Dist. #38, 1977-94; assoc. prof. Northeastern Ill. U., 1995—; chmn. No. Suburban Coop. Benefit Trust, Winnetka, 1990-95. Co-author: Inside the Management Team, 1973. Elder Westminster Presbyn. Ch., Skokie, Ill., 1972-75; pres. Rotary Club, Toluca, 1977; chair Lake Forest (Ill.) Gorton Cmty. Ctr., 1990-94, North Cook Ednl. Svc. Region, 1993-94; bd. dirs. Ill. Curling Assn. Mem. ASCD, Am. Assn. Sch. Adminstrs., Am. Assn. Sch. Bus. Officials, Phi Delta Kappa. Office: Northeastern Ill Univ 5550 N St Louis Ave Chicago IL 60625-4699

BECKWITH, LARRY EDWARD, mechanical engineer; b. Pierre, S.D., Oct. 21, 1943; s. Charles Edward and Junebelle Ann (Robley) B.; m. AnhTuyet Thi Pham, Mar. 3, 1970. BSME, S.D. Sch. Mines Tech., Rapid City, 1966. Mil. engring. officer USACE, 1967-69; from mech. engr. to ptnr. Dunham Assocs., Bloomington, Minn., 1966—; bd. dirs. Beckwith Hardware, Inc., Presho, S.D., 1977-92. State chmn. S.D. Coll. Reps., 1965-66; mem. Rep. Nat. Com., 1994—; bd. govs. Walden Assn., 1994—. Cpt. U.S. Army, 1967-69, Viet Nam. Recipient bronze star U.S. Army, 1968, w/oak leaf cluster, 1969. Mem. VFW, Am. Legion. Office: Dunham Assocs Inc Ste 500 8200 Normandale Blvd Bloomington MN 55437

BEDELL, S. CLARK, stockbroker; b. Bell Plaine, Kans., Nov. 2, 1922. Agt. Prudential Life Ins., Wichita, Kans., 1956-86; stockbroker Profl. Investors Svcs., Arkansas City, Kans., 1987—. Mem. Lions, Masons, Shriners. Presbyterian. Office: Profl Investors Svcs 117 W 5th Ave Arkansas City KS 67005-2627

BEDFORD, EMMETT GRUNER, retired professor; b. Columbia, Mo., Oct. 30, 1922; S. John Stephen and Irma (Gruner) B.; m. Frances Murray Bedford, Sept. 17, 1924; children: Eric Douglas, Monte Scott, Shelley Bedford Miller. AB, U. Mo., Columbia, 1947, BJ, 1947; postgrad, U. Md., College Park, 1963; MA, So. Ill. U., Carbondale, 1967, Phd, 1970. Copy editor Salt Lake Tribune, Salt Lake City, 1947-48; reporter St. Joseph Gazette, St. Joseph, Mo., 1948-49; asst. mng. editor Congressional Quarterly, Washington, 1949-54; asst. city editor Washington Post, Washington, 1954-55; asst. chief of copy desk Evening Star, Washington, 1955-63; instr. in journalism So. Ill. U., Carbondale, Ill., 1963-65; prof. of English U. Wisc. Parkside, Kenosha, Wis., 1970-87. Editor: A Concordance to the Poems of Alexander Pope, 2 volumes, 1974. 2nd lt. U.S. Army, 1943-45. Mem. MLA, Nat. Press Club. Soc. Profl. Journalists, Am. Soc. for 18th Century Studies, Midwestern Soc. for 18th Century Studies, (Samuel) Johnson Soc. of Ctrl. Region, Am. Mensa, Sons of the Revolution, Order of Descendants of Ancient Planters. Independent. Episcopalian. Home: 1654 College Ave Racine WI 53404

BEDNAREK, JANET ROSE, history educator; b. Omaha, Oct. 14, 1959; d. John Louis and Corinne Janet (Ryan) Daly; m. Michael Henry Bednarek, Mar. 23, 1991. BA, Creighton U., 1981, MA, 1983; PhD, U. Pitts., 1987. Historian USAF, Washington, 1989-92, Dayton, Ohio, 1992; asst. prof. history U. Dayton, 1992—. Author: The Changing Image of the City, 1992, also articles. Mellon fellow, 1985-87, U. Dayton rsch. fellow, 1993, 94. Mem. Orgn. Am. Historians, Am. Hist. Assn., Urban History Assn., Aircraft Owners and Pilots Assn. Roman Catholic. Home: 7507 James Bradford Dr Centerville OH 45459 Office: U Dayton Dept History 300 College Park Dayton OH 45469

BEDNARZ, SHIRLEY DIANE, publishing company executive; b. Wis. Rapids, Wis., Sept. 15, 1946; d. Stewart Fausch and Marge (Lyons) Peterson; m. Timothy F. Bednarz, Aug. 14, 1989. B in Edn., U. Wis., Stevens Point, 1974, M in Profl. Devel. magna cum laude, 1981; PhD in Bus. Adminstrn., Pacific Western U., 1994. Tchr. Wis. Rapids Pub. Schs., 1974-90; ret., 1990; CEO Bednarz Bus. Strategies, Stevens Point, Wis., 1990—; pres., owner Menagerie Pet Ctr., Wis. Rapids, 1977-90. Mem. NAFE, Nat. Assn. Univ. Women. Home and Office: Bednarz Bus Strategies 2025 Main St Stevens Point WI 54481-3019

BEDNARZ, SUSAN CLARE, educational administrator; b. Omaha, Aug. 9, 1955; d. Michael Francis and Theresa Ann (Kosuth) B. EdB magna cum laude, U. Nebr., 1977, MS in Elem. Edn., 1982. Tchr. St. Peter and St. Paul Sch., Omaha, 1977-78, Miller Park Pub. Schs., Omaha, 1978-79, St. Bernadette Sch., Bellevue, Nebr., 1979-86, St. Columbkille Sch., Papillion, Nebr., 1986-88, St. Stanislaus Sch., 1988-89; dir. edn. Sylvan Learning Ctr., Omaha, 1989-90, part-time tchr., 1989—; devel. kindergarten tchr. Millard Pub. Schs., 1990—; advisor Archdiocesan Kindergarten Tchrs., Omaha, 1987—. Organist St. Francis Assisi Ch., 1990—. Mem. AAUW, Nat. Orgn. Edn. Young Children, Delta Kappa Gamma Soc., Young Adult Singles Club. Democrat. Roman Catholic. Home: 4507 S 34th St Omaha NE 68107-1439

BEDOUN, EDDIE AMAD, electrical engineer; b. Dearborn, Mich., Jan. 7, 1958; s. Harrison A. and Laura M. (Abbas) B.; m. Deborah Ranee; children: Erick, Jason, Ryan, Deanna. BSEE, Wayne State U., Detroit, 1980. Dynomometer test technician Ford Motor Co., Dearborn, 1978-80, instrumentation engr., 1980-84; project engr. Horiba Instruments, Inc., Ann Arbor, Mich., 1984-86; sr. project engr. Eaton Corp., Southfield, Mich., 1986—. Bd. mem. Islamic Ctr. Am., Detroit, 1984—. Mem. Instrumentation Soc. Am., Engring. Soc. Detroit. Home: 1368 Wagon Wheel Rd Canton MI 48188-1159 Office: Eaton Corp 26201 Northwestern Hwy Southfield MI 48076-3926

BEEKMAN, LLOYD GEORGE, retired education educator; b. Holland, Mich., Dec. 15, 1927; s. Russell A. Alger and Fannie (Breuker) B.; m. Lillian Richards, June 19, 1978 (dec. Dec. 1989); m. Roberta Fay Simons, Aug. 19, 1991; children: David, Sandra Moore. AB, Hope Coll., 1953; MA, U. Mich., 1959, 1968. Tchr. Social Studies Mt. Clemens (Mich.) H.S., 1955-57, Fruitport (Mich.) Cmty. Schs., 1957-60; counselor H.S. Cherry Creek Pub. Schs., Englewood, Colo., 1963-64; study hall supr. Grand Rapids (Mich.) South H.S., 1964-65; job corps counselor Marsing (Idaho) Job Corps Ctr., 1964-65; job corps activities dir. Clam Lake (Wis.) Job Corps Ctr., 1965; EMI tchr. Oakridge Pub. Schs., Muskegon, Mich., 1965-86; sch. bd. trustee Grand Haven (Mich.) Bd. Edn., 1992; pres. Oakridge Tchrs. Club, Muskegon, Mich., 1968-69; bd. mem. Grand Haven (Mich. Recreation Bd., 1992—; judge VFW Post 2326 Essay Contest, 1987—. V.p. Grand Haven (Mich.) Bowling Assn., 1968-87. Cpl. USAF, 1946-49. Recipient All Conf. Football award Mich. Southwestern Conf., Grand Haven, 1945, Mich. Intercollegiate Athletic Assn., Hope Coll., 1950-52, Master's Champion Grand Haven (Mich.) Bowling Assn., 1976-79; named Capt. Hope Coll. Football Team, 1952. Mem. VFW, Mich. Edn. Assn., Mich. Assn. Sch. Bds. Democrat. Home: 13618 Fawn Ln Grand Haven MI 49417 Office: Grand Haven School Board 1415 Beech Tree St Grand Haven MI 49417

BEELER, DONALD DARYL, retail executive; b. Hettinger, N.D., Nov. 13, 1935; s. Earl Aaron and LaVera Grace (Krause) B.; m. Laurice Marianne Fish, May 23, 1954; children: Jillayne Marianne, Jacalyn Faye, Donald Earl. Grad. high sch., Lemmon, S.D. Owner, operator Lemmon (S.D.) Recreation, 1954-55; owner D&M Gifts, Lemmon, 1956-57; mgr. trainee to store mgr. Snyder Drug Stores, Inc., Hopkins, Minn., 1964-67, dist. mgr. to dir. of franchise ops., 1967-77, v.p. franchise ops. to v.p. gen. mgr., 1977-82, sr. v.p., gen. mgr., 1982, pres., 1982-86, chmn., pres., chief exec. officer, 1986-94, chmn., CEO, 1994—; bd. dirs. Minn. Bus. Partnership. Bd. dirs. Variety Club Children's Hosp., U. Minn., 1991—, "Brauns", 1992—; mem. U.S. Olympic Com., Minn., 1986—; vis. exec. United Fund, Mpls., 1988, sect. chmn., 1989; pres. Food, Drug and Liquor Coun., City of Hope, Mpls., 1984-87; exec. coun., 1987—. Served with U.S. Army, 1957-64. Recipient Spirit of Life award City of Hope, 1984. Mem. Nat. Assn. of Chain Drug Stores (bd. dirs. 1990—), So. Drug Stores Assn., Am. Found. Pharm. Edn. (bd. dirs.), Minnetonka Country Club (bd. govs. 1988—, v.p. 1991, pres. 1992). Republican. Presbyterian. Home: 5357 Ashcroft Rd Minnetonka MN 55345 Office: Snyders Drug Stores Inc 14525 Hwy 7 Hopkins MN 55345-3734

BEEM, JOHN KELLY, mathematician, educator; b. Detroit, Jan. 24, 1942; s. William Richard and June Ellen (Kelly) B.; m. Eloise Masako Yamamoto, Mar. 24, 1964; 1 child, Thomas Kelly. A.B. in Math., U. So. Calif., 1963, M.A. in Math., 1965, Ph.D. in Math., 1968. Asst. prof. math. U. Mo., Columbia, 1968-71, assoc. prof., 1971-79, prof., 1979—. Author: (with P. Y. Woo) Doubly Timelike Surfaces, 1969, (with P. E. Ehrlich) Global Lorentzian Geometry, 1981, (with P.E. Ehrlich and K.L. Easley), 2d edit., 96; condr. research in differential geometry and gen. relativity. Recipient Kemper Tchg. award, 1996; NSF fellow, 1965, 68. Mem. Math. Assn. Am., Am. Math. Soc., Phi Beta Kappa. Home: 5204 E Tayside Cir Columbia MO 65203-5191

BEEMAN, JOHN SANDERS, lawyer; b. Indpls., May 21, 1945; m. Cynthia S. Olczak, Dec. 27, 1969; children: Kristin M., Melissa K., Lindsey E. BS in Bus. Adminstrn., Ball State U., 1968-71, MS, 1971-74; JD cum laude, Ind. U., Indpls., 1974. Law clk, rsch. atty. Ind. Ct. Appeals, Indpls., 1974-75; assoc. Harrison, Moberly & Gaston, Indpls., 1975-78; ptnr. Harrison & Moberly, Indpls., 1975-95, sr. ptnr., 1981-83, mng. ptnr., 1983-94; dep. pros. officer Marin County Prosecutions Office, Indpls., 1973-74, 78-82; gen. coun. United Home Life Ins., Greenwood, Ind., 1986—; 11th dist. dir. Ind. State Bar Assn. Young Lawyers, Indpls., 1981.

BEEMAN, TERRY, stockbroker; b. Concordia, Kans., Aug. 29, 1950; m. Nancy Beeman; 2 children. BS in Animal Sci. and Bus., Kans. State U., 1977. Asst. mgr. Country Elevator, Washington, Kans., 1977-81; stockbroker B.C. Christopher Securities, Topeka, 1981—. Mem. Topeka Conv. and Tourism Bd., 1985—. With U.S. Army, 1970-73. Recipient award Topeka Conv. and Tourism Bd. Mem. Topeka C. of C., Rotary. Office: BC Christopher Securities 534 S Kansas Ave Topeka KS 66603-3406

BEERING, STEVEN CLAUS, academic administrator, medical educator; b. Berlin, Germany, Aug. 20, 1932; came to U.S., 1948, naturalized, 1953; s. Steven and Alice (Friedrichs) B.; m. Catherine Jane Pickering, Dec. 27, 1956; children: Peter, David, John. BS summa cum laude, U. Pitts., 1954, MD, 1958; DSc (hon.), Ind. Cen. U., 1983, U. Evansville (Ind.), 1984, Ramapo Coll., 1986, Anderson Coll., 1987; ScD (hon.), Ind. U., 1988; LLD (hon.), Hanover Coll., 1986. Intern Walter Reed Gen. Hosp., Washington, 1958-59; resident Wilford Hall Med. Center, San Antonio, Tex., 1959-62, chief internal medicine, edn. coordinator, 1967-69; prof. medicine Ind. U. Sch. Medicine, Indpls., 1969—, asst. dean, 1969-70, assoc. dean, dir. postgrad. edn., 1970-74, dir. statewide med. edn. system, 1970-83, dean, 1974-83; chief exec. officer Ind. U. Med. Center, Indpls., 1974-83; pres. Purdue U. and Purdue U. Research Found., West Lafayette, Ind., 1983—; prof. pharmacology and toxicology Purdue U.; bd. dirs. Arvin Industries, Eli Lilly Co., NIPSCO Industries, Am. United Life, CALSPAN SRL Corp.; cons. Indpsl. VA Hosp., St. Vincent Hosp.; chmn. Ind. Commn. Med. Edn., 1973-83, Med. Edn. Bd. Ind., 1974-83, Liaison Com. on Med. Edn., 1976-81. Contbr. articles to sci. jours. Sec. Ind. Atty. Gen.'s Trust., 1974-83; regent Nat. Library Medicine, 1987-91; mem. Lafayette Community Council. Served to lt. col. M.C. USAF, 1957-69. Fellow ACP, Royal Soc. Medicine; mem. Am. Fedn. Clin. Rsch., Am. Diabetes Assn., Endocrine Soc., Assn. Am. Med. Colls. (chmn. 1982-83), Coun. Med. Deans (chmn. 1980-81), Assn. Am. Univs. (chair 1995-96), Nat. Acad. Sci. Inst. of Medicine, Ind. Acad., Indpls. Athletic Club, Columbia Club, Skyline Club, Woodstock Club, Meridian Hills Club, Phi Beta Kappa, Sigma Xi, Alpha Omega Alpha, Phi Rho Sigma (U.S. v.p. 1976-85). Presbyterian (elder). Home: 500 McCormick Rd West Lafayette IN 47906-4911 Office: Purdue U Office of Pres Rm 200 1031 Hovde Hall West Lafayette IN 47907-1031*

BEERLINE, KURT ALAN, sociology educator; b. Bakersfield, Calif., Oct. 26, 1960; s. Glenn Edwin and Beverly Jean (Stopher) B.; m. Kathryn Marie Vastine, Aug. 19, 1984; children: Marc Judson, Michael Glenn, Jaron Montana. BA, San Diego State U., 1983, MA, 1986; PhD, U. Tex., 1992. Mission coord. Hope Chapel, Austin, 1987-90; instr. Austin Community Coll., 1986-90; asst. prof. sociology Evangel Coll., Springfield, Mo., 1990-96; total quality cons. Breakthrough Performance, 1996—; cons. Citywide Rsch., Springfield, 1992—; social rsch. dir. Human Svc. Ctr., Evangel Coll., 1992—. Coord., dir. Austin Perspectives on World Missions, 1987; chmn. Springfield March for Jesus, 1991—. Mem. Am. Sociol. Assn., Soc. for Study of Social Problems, Soc. for Sci. Study of Religion. Home: 1473 N Clay Ave Springfield MO 65802-1947 Office: Evangel Coll Behavioral Scis Dept 1111 N Glenstone Ave Springfield MO 65802-2125

BEERMANN, ALLEN J., former state official; b. Sioux City, Iowa, Jan. 14, 1940. B.A., Midland Lutheran Coll., Fremont, Nebr., 1962; J.D., Creighton U., Omaha, 1965; LLD (hon.), Midland Luth. Coll., 1995. Bar: Nebr. 1965. Legal counsel, adminstrv. asst. to sec. state State of Nebr., 1965-67, dep. sec. state, 1967-71; sec. of state, 1971-95; mem. Fed. Election Commn. adv. panel. Bd. dirs. Nebr. Land Found.; exec. bd. Cornhusker coun. Boy Scouts Am. Lt. col. U.S. Army, ret. Recipient Disting. Svc. plaque Omaha Legal Aid Soc., 1964, Silver Beaver award Boy Scouts Am., 1979; named Outstanding Young Man Lincoln Jaycees, 1975, Outstanding Young Man Nebr. Jaycees, 1975. Mem. ABA, Nat. Assn. Secs. State (pres. 1976-77), Nebr. Bar Assn. (exec. dir. 1995—), Nebr. Press Assn., Am. Legion (fed. election commn. adv. panel, Cert. Appreciation). Lutheran. Office: Nebr Press Assn 1120 K St Lincoln NE 68508

BEERS, ROBERT B., project manager; b. Evansville, Ind., Nov. 13, 1948. B, U. Toledo, 1971. Design engr. RCW Peterson, Toledo, 1983-87; product engr. Champion Spark Plug, Toledo, 1987-89; project mgr. Ort Tool & Die Corp., Erie, Mich., 1989—. Mem. ASME. Office: Cor Tool & Die Corp 6555 S Dixie Hwy Erie MI 48133-9658

BEERS, V(ICTOR) GILBERT, publishing executive; b. Sidell, Ill., May 6, 1928; s. Ernest S. and Jean (Bloomer) B.; m. Arlisle Felten, Aug. 26, 1950; children: Kathleen, Douglas, Ronald, Janice, Cynthia. A.B., Wheaton Coll., 1950; M.R.E., No. Baptist Sem., 1953, M.Div., 1954, Th.M., 1955, Th.D., 1960; Ph.D., Northwestern U., 1963. Prof. No. Baptist Sem., Chgo., 1954-57; editor Sr. High Publs., David C. Cook Pub. Co., Elgin, Ill., 1957-59, exec. editor, 1959-61, editorial dir., 1961-67; pres. Books for Living Inc., Elgin, 1967—; editor Christianity Today, 1982-85, sr. editor, 1985-87; pres. Scripture Press Publs. Inc., Wheaton, Ill., 1990-96, Scripture Press Ministries, 1990—. Author: more than 100 books, including: Family Bible Libr., 10 vols., 1971, The Book of Life, 23 vols., 1980. Bd. dirs. Christian Camps Inc., N.Y., Wheaton (Ill.) Youth Symphony, 1961-63, pres. 1962-63; trustee Wheaton Coll., 1975-92, Scripture Press Inc., 1973—. Home: 11N720 Rohrssen Rd Elgin IL 60120-9801 Office: Scripture Press Pubs Inc 1825 College Ave Wheaton IL 60187-4480

BEESLEY, DONALD E., securities company executive; b. Charlevoix, Mich., July 7, 1949. Lic. series 7 Nat. Assn. Securities Dealers. Investment advisor Am. Field Mktg., Grand Rapids, Mich., 1978-86; v.p. Centennial Securities, Grand Rapids, 1986—. Office: Centennial Securities 3075 Charlevoix Dr SE Grand Rapids MI 49546-7035

BEETHAM, CHRIS D., stockbroker; b. Columbus, Ohio, Mar. 25, 1970. Student, Ohio State U., 1989-91. With lawn care co., Columbus, 1986-88; stockbroker Corna Co. Investment Securities, Columbus, 1992—; lectr. investment seminars. Republican. Presbyterian. Office: Corna Co Investment Securities 5302 McKitrick Blvd Columbus OH 43235-7366

BEETS, F. LEE, retired insurance company executive; b. Paola, Kans., Apr. 2, 1922; s. William Francis and Nellie (Bryan) B.; B.B.A., Tulane U., 1945; postgrad. Harvard U., 1945, evening sch. U. Kansas City, Rockhurst Coll.; m. Dorothy Loraine Shelton, June 20, 1945; children—Randall Lee, Pamela Lee. Sr. accountant Lunsford Barnes & Co., Kansas City, Mo., 1946-49; v.p., gen. mgr. Viking Refrigerators, 1949-53; v.p., sec.-treas. Equipment Finance Co., 1949-53; exec. v.p., treas., gen. mgr. T.H. Mastin & Co., Consol. Underwriters, Mo. Gen. Ins. Co., Plan-O-Pay, Inc., Mid-Am. Data Co., B O L Assos., Inc., 1953-69; founder, chmn. bd., chief exec. officer Fin. Guardian Group, Inc., and subs., 1969-84; exec. v.p., gen. mgr. Consol. Ins. Service, Inc., ret. 1991. Served with USNR, 1942-45. CPA, CPCU. Mem. AICPA, Soc. CPCU, Pi Kappa Alpha, Sigma Tau Gamma, Phi Mu Alpha Sinfonia. Home: 16 Le Mans Ct Shawnee Mission KS 66208-5208

BEGALKA, TIMOTHY PAUL, horticulturist; b. Clear Lake, S.D., Feb. 19, 1960; s. Leon Royal and Elizabeth Louise (Junas) B. BS, S.D. State U., 1982. Cert. nurseryman, S.D. Nursery mgr. Sodak Gardens, Clear Lake, S.D., 1982—. Actor Clear Lake Cmty. Playhouse, 1977-93; pro-life activist Operation Rescue, 1988—, Rescue the Perishing, Sioux Falls, S.D., 1989—; county committeeman S.D. Rep. Party, 1990-93, sec.-treas., 1993—; sec. Trinity Ch., Wis. Luth. Synod, 1991-94; pres. Deul County Right to Life, 1989-91; mem. Nat. Right to Work Com.; mgr. Sodak Softball Team, 1985-91. Mem. S.D. Nurserymen's Assn. (dir. 1989-95), S.D. Hort. Soc. (dir. 1985—), Clear Lake Comml. Club, Deul County FFA Alumni (treas. 1988—), S.D. Farmhouse. Republican. Home and Office: Sodak Gardens RR 1 Box 181 Clear Lake SD 57226-9454

BEGGS, CAROL EDWARD, state legislator; m. Betty Beggs. Retailer; mem. Kans. State Ho. of Reps. Dist. 71, 1995—.

BEGNOCHE, R. TERRY, environmental engineer; b. Detroit, May 5, 1950. AS, Schoolcraft C.C., 1978; BS in Environ. Sci., U. Mich., 1981. Gen. mgr., tech. dir. Great Lakes Environ. Svcs., Warren, Mich., 1981-88; mgr. environ. svcs. W.W. Engring. and Sci., Livonia, Mich., 1988-93; v.p. Stock Environment Ltd., Detroit, 1993—; tchr., lectr. Oakland U., Rochester, Mich., 1993—. Underwater photographer Great Lakes Shipwreck Hist. Soc., Sault Ste. Marie, Mich., 1985—. Mem. Mich. Assn. Environ. Profls. (past pres. 1987-88). Home: 28475 Wildwood Trl Farmington Hl MI 48336-2164 Office: Stock Environment Ltd 10900 Harper Ave Detroit MI 48213-3364

BEHLAR, PATRICIA ANN, political science educator; b. New Orleans, Jan. 16, 1939; d. James Edward and Maude Albertine (Davis) B. BA, U. New Orleans, 1966; MA, La. State U., 1968, PhD, 1974. Instr. Northwestern State U. of La., Natchitoches, 1971-72; instr. Pan Am. U., Edinburg, Tex., 1974-76; asst. prof. Pan Am. U., Edinburg, 1976-77, U. Ark., Pine Bluff, 1977-84; asst. prof. Pittsburg (Kans.) State U., 1986-92, assoc. prof., 1992—; mem. U. Ark. Pine Bluff Winthrop Rockefeller lectures steering com., 1980-82; referee Ark. Polit. Sci. Jour., 1983-84; alt., edit. com. Univ. Press of Kans., 1991-93; mem., edit. com. Univ. Press of Kans., 1993-95; book rev. editor, The Midwest Quarterly, 1994—. Audio reader for the blind, Pittsburg, 1992. Recipient La. State U. fellowship, 1970-71. Mem. Am. Polit. Sci. Assn., Sou. Polit. Sci. Assn., Kans. Polit. Sci. Assn., Southwestern Social Sci. Assn., Phi Kappa Phi. Democrat. Roman Catholic. Home: 508 Hobson Dr Pittsburg KS 66762-6315 Office: Pittsburg State U Dept Social Sci Pittsburg KS 66762

BEHLING, CHARLES FREDERICK, psychology educator; b. St. George, S.C., Sept. 8, 1940; s. John Henry and Floy (Owings) B.; m. Jennifer Crocker; children: John Charles, Andrew Crocker. BA, U. S.C., 1962, MA, 1964; MA, Vanderbilt U., 1966, PhD, 1969. Asst. dean of students U. S.C., Columbia, 1962-63; asst. state news editor The State Newspaper, Columbia, 1963-64; asst. prof. psychology Lake Forest (Ill.) Coll., 1968-74; assoc. prof Lake Forest Coll., 1974-88, chmn. dept., 1977-84; pvt. practice psychotherapy Lake Bluff, Ill., 1970-88, Buffalo, 1988-95; clin. assoc. prof. SUNY, Buffalo, 1988-95; dir. of undergraduate studies, 1989-95; adj. prof. U. Mich., Ann Arbor, 1995—; dir. intergroup rels., conflict and cmty., 1995—. Contbr. articles to profl. jours. Bd. dirs. Nat. Abortion Rights Action League, Planned Parenthood; mem. long-range planning com. Lake Bluff Bd. Edn. Named Outstanding Prof., Underground Guide to Colls., 1971, Birnbaum Guide, 1992, Outstanding Tchr., Lake Forest Coll., 1981, SUNY, Buffalo, 1991; NASA fellow. Mem. Am. Psychol. Assn., Soc. Psychol. Study of Social Issues, Assn. Humanistic Psychology, AAUP, Univ. S.C. Alumni Assn., Psi Chi, Sigma Delta Chi. Democrat. Home: 1325 Wynnstone Dr Ann Arbor MI 48105 Office: U Mich Dept Psychology Ann Arbor MI 48109

BEHM, JOHN ROBERT, physician; b. Marietta, Ohio, Dec. 13, 1953; s. Russell C. and Jean M. (Styles) B.; m. Lori Grace Smith, June 21, 1975 (div. Aug. 1976); m. Leslie Merrill Hallstead, Aug. 21, 1977. BS in Biology, Heidelberg Coll., 1976; DO, Mich. State U., 1990, cert. in secondary edn., 1983. Diplomate Am. Bd. Osteo. Family Physicians, Am. Acad. Family Practice. Grad. asst. dept. biophysics Mich. State U., 1977-78, rschr. dept. entomology, 1979-83, med. technician animal health diagnostic lab., 1983-84, rsch. technician plant rsch. lab., 1984-85; intern in osteo. medicine Lansing (Mich.) Gen. Hosp., 1990-91; resident Sparrow Family Practice, Lansing, 1991-93, chief resident, 1992-93; shift physician Mason (Mich.) Urgent Care Ctr., Delta Med. ctrs., Lansing area, Mich., 1991-93. V.p. Lansing Area Commodore Club, 1984; mem. exec. bd. Clerical Tech. Union, Mich. State U., 1982-83. Mem. AMA, Am. Osteo. Assn., Am. Acad. Family Practice. Democrat. Mennonite. Home: PO Box 947 Okemos MI 48805-0947 Office: Perry Family Practice 3337 Britton Rd Perry MI 48872-9706

BEHM, KEN W., manufacturing executive; b. Grayslake, Ill., May 26, 1938. AD, Coll. Lake County. Plant supt. Onsrud Cutter Mfg., Libertyville, Ill., 1956-72; co-owner Fore Tool, Mundelein, Ill., 1972—. Vil. local ch. fundraisers, 1975—. Sgt. Air Nat. Guard, 1955-62. Mem. TMW. Roman Catholic.

BEHNER, ELTON DALE, dentist; b. Oberlin, Ohio, Sept. 6, 1952; s. Wayne Edwin and Velma Jean (Sevison) B.; m. Brenda Kay Crabtree, Aug. 18, 1974 (div. July 1982); m. Annette Lynn Brunst, Oct. 27, 1984: children: Nicolas, Ryan, Tadd. Student, Andrews U., 1971-74; BS, Loma Linda U., 1976; DDS, Ind. U., 1984. Dipolmate Am. Bd. Dental Examiners. Staff technologist clin. lab. Loma Linda (Calif.) U. Hosp., 1976-77, rsch. technologist, 1977-79; sr. technologist Ind. U. Hosp., Indpls., 1982-84; asst. prof. sch. dentistry Ind. U., Indpls.; grad. residency Ind. U. Med. Ctr., Indpls., 1984; owner Lakewood Dental Group, 1985—; coord., cons. dental svc. Am. Surgery Ctr., Indpls., 1987—; active mem. staff dental svc. Wishard Meml. Hosp., Indpls. Fellow Acad. Gen. Dentistry; mem. ADA, Ind. Dental Assn., Indpls. Dist. Dental Soc. Office: Lakewood Dental Group 5987 E 71st St Ste 103 Indianapolis IN 46220-4049

BEHNING, ROBERT W., state legislator; b. Indpls., Jan. 18, 1954; m. Rosalie Dix; children: Nathan, Grant. BS, Ind. U., 1976. Vice ward chmn. Wayne Twp., Ind.; vol. Crane for Congrl. campaign; precinct committeeman Decatur; registered and polling coord. Decatur Twp., 1991; mem. Eagle Creek GOP, Wayne Twp. GOP; 2nd v.p. Decatur Twp. GOP; Ind. state rep. Dist. 91, 1992—; mem. com. and econ. devel., labor and employment, 1993—, govt. affairs com., 1993—; chmn. elections and apportionment com. Ind. Ho. Reps.; with L.S. Ayres & Co., Indpls., 1971-73, Great A&P Tea Co., 1973-84; co-owner Plants, Posies and Accents, Inpls., 1977-81; owner Berkshire Florist, Indpls., 1981—; bd. dirs. Multi Svc. Ctr. Mem. Decatur Twp. Civic Coun.; past pres. Luth. Laymen's League No 6. Mem. Nat. Fedn. Ind. Bus., Teleflora Golden Dove Club, Allied Florist Assn. (past dir.). Republican. Home: 3315 S Tibbs Ave Indianapolis IN 46221-2270*

BEHR, SUSANNA MARIE, language professional, music educator; b. Superior, Wis., Oct. 26, 1969; d. Michael Ross and Joanna Marie (Allen) B. BA in English and Music, Hamline U., St. Paul, 1991; MusM, Southern Meth. U., Dallas, 1993. Instr. English as 2nd Lang. Eglish Link Lang. Sch., Prague, Czech Republic, 1993-95; instr. of Music Konos Acad. Prague, 1993-94; instr. English as 2nd Lang. Ctr. for English Lang. Tng.- Ind. U., Bloomington, 1996—. Recipient Internat. PEO Scholar award PEO Women's Ednl. Orgn., 1992-93, Mu Phi Epsilon Musicological Rsch. Contest 1st

Place, 1992. Mem. Am. Assn. for Advancement of Slavic Studies, Am. Musicological Soc., Ind. Assn. Tchr's. of English to Speakers of Other Langs., Nat. Assn. Tchrs. Czech. Office: Ind Univ Ctr for English Lang Training Memorial Hall 313 Bloomington IN 47405

BEHRENDT, DAVID FROGNER, journalist; b. Stevens Point, Wis., May 25, 1935; s. Allen Charles and Vivian (Frogner) B.; m. Mary Ann Weber, Feb. 4, 1961; children: Lynne, Liza, Sarah. BS, U. Wis., 1957, MS, 1960. Reporter Decatur (Ill.) Review, 1957-58; reporter Milw. Jour., 1960-70, copy editor, 1970-71, editorial writer, 1971-84, editorial page editor, 1984-95; Crossroads sect. editor Milw. Jour. Sentinel, 1995—. Home: 1928 Hillside Ct Delafield WI 53018-2302 Office: The Milwaukee Jour Sentinel PO Box 371 Milwaukee WI 53201-0661

BEHRENDT, MARY ANN WEBER, marketing consultant; b. Manitowoc, Wis., Oct. 18, 1938; d. Daniel Edward and Sylvia M. (Schneck) Weber; m. David F. Behrendt, Feb. 4, 1961; children: Lynne, Liza, Sarah. BS, U. Wis., 1960, MA, 1980. Dir. pub. rels. and fund devel. Great Blue Heron Girl Scouts, Waukesha, Wis., 1981-86; dir. devel. Girl Scouts Milw., Milw., 1986-91; dir. client devel., client svcs. Growth Design Corp., Milw., 1991—. Mem., officer Kettle Moraine Sch. Bd., Wales, Wis., 1978-84; dir. Waukesha Area Arts Alliance, 1994—. Mem. Nat. Soc. Fund Raising Execs. Office: Growth Design Corp 828 N Broadway Milwaukee WI 53202

BEHRENS, DANIEL ECKERT, newspaper editor, lawyer; b. Lancaster, Ohio, June 8, 1943; s. Winfield Eckert and Mary Elizabeth (Gaumer) B.; m. Melanie Ann Tharp, June 24, 1967; children: Michael David, Kevin John. BA, Miami U., Oxford, Ohio, 1965; JD, Ohio State U., 1968. Assoc. atty. Coleman & McKinley Law Firm, Marysville, Ohio, 1969-74; bus. mgr. Marysville (Ohio) Jour.-Tribune, 1969-74, editor, 1974—; pres. Marysville Newspapers, Inc., 1995—; mem. adv. bd. Huntington Nat. Bank, Marysville, 1987—; pres. bd. Marysville Newspapers, Inc., 1995—. Trustee United Way of Union County, Marysville, 1987-95. Mem. Ohio Bar Assn., Union County Bar Assn., Am. Soc. Newspaper Editors, Am. Legion, Elks (exalted ruler 1995-96, Elk Hall of Fame award 1992). Lutheran. Office: Marysville Jour-Tribune 207 N Main St PO Box 226 Marysville OH 43040

BEHRENS, MARC, electrical engineer; b. Grinnell, Iowa, Apr. 7, 1959. BSET in Indsl. Tech., U. No. Iowa, Cedar Falls, 1985. Designer Enomoy Forms Des Moines, 1985; programmer Centerline Co., 1986-90; designer Allied Signal, Olathe, Kans., 1990, Garmin Corp., Shawnee Mission, Kans., 1990—.

BEIDEMAN, RONALD PAUL, chiropractor, college dean; b. Norristown, Pa., Mar. 22, 1926; s. Jonas Paul and Bertha May (Cane) B.; student Temple U., 1948; D. Chiropractic, Nat. Coll. Chiropractic, Chgo., 1952; postgrad. Wheaton Coll.; B.A., Lewis U., 1976; m. Lorraine Marian Barrett, Aug. 19, 1950 (dec.); children—Ronald Paul, J. Kirk; m. 2d, Peggy Ann Bartlett, May 31, 1980. Dir. dept. diagnosis Nat. Coll. Chiropractic, Chgo., 1952-66, sr. tenured prof., 1963—, registrar, 1966-78, dean admissions and records, 1973-88, ofcl. coll. historian, 1987—; dean of records 1988-94, coll. archivist, 1994—; exam. physician Chgo. Gen. Health Service, 1954-65; lectr. in field; pvt. practice chiropractic Chgo., 1954—; mem. nat. profl. standards rev. council, Health Care Financing Adminstrn., HHS, 1982; prof. Nat.-Lincoln Sch. Postgrad. Edn., 1964—; accrediting evaluator Council on Chiropractic Edn., 1978—, mem. task force panels on admissions Commn. on Accreditation, 1980, 84—; accrediting evaluator Western Assn. Schs. and Colls., 1985. Served with USAAF, 1944-46. Fellow Internat. Coll. Chiropractors (faculty); mem. Nat. Coll. Chiropractic (corp. sec. 1972-94), Nat. Bd. Chiropractic Examiners (chmn. test com. 1967-69), Ill., Chgo. chiropractic socs., Am. Chiropractic Assn. (vet. affairs com. 1979-81), Am. Legion (post comdr. 1957-58), Am., Ill. assns. Collegiate Registrars and Admissions Officers, Ill. Assn. Student Financial Aid Adminstrs., Nat. Assn. Coll. Admissions Counselors, Sigma Phi Kappa (grand chancellor), Lambda Phi Delta. Author: In The Making of a Profession: The National College of Chiropractic 1906-1981, 1995; contbr. articles to profl. publs. Office: 200 E Roosevelt Rd Lombard IL 60148-4539

BEIDER, ANDREW MICHAEL, insurance agent; b. Detroit, Aug. 15, 1951; s. Morris and Shirley Harriet (Greenspan) B.; m. Libby Arlene Rogoff, June 13, 1976; children: Marla Aviva, Rachel Fay, Shoshana Mae. BA in History, Wayne State U.; MBA, U. Mich., 1983. CLU. Tchr. Detroit Bd Edn., 1971-75; ins. agt. Minn. Mut. Life, Southfield, Mich., 1975-79, Southfield, 1980-83; sr. v.p. Smith Barney Shearson, Detroit, 1984—. Pub. Broker World, 1989—. Mem. Deans Com. Wayne State U., 1972. Named to top 10 list Crains Bus. Detroit, 1985, 86, 87, 88, 89, top 10 list Fin. Planning on Wall St., 1995. Mem. Oakland County Life Underwriters Assn. (v.p. 1983-84), Nat. Assn. Life Underwriters, Million Dollar Round Table, Top of the Million Dollar Round Table, Met. Chess Assn. (bd. dirs. 1972-85). Republican. Jewish. Home: 5425 Whitehall Cir West Bloomfield MI 48323-3461 Office: Smith Barney Shearson 600 Renaissance Ctr Ste 1800 Detroit MI 48243-1705

BEIGHT, JANICE MARIE, interior designer; b. Toledo, Oct. 9, 1947; d. Clyde Harding and Ida Belle (Ragland) McCluskey; m. Daryll Russell, Aug. 29, 1991; children: Stephen C., Scott J. BA in Interior Design, Chgo. U., 1974. Pres. Interiors by Janice, Poland, Ohio, 1974—; fin. planner Primerica Fin. Svcs.; real estate investor. Contbr. poems to Women of West Minster, 1980, Angels and Friends Cookbook, 1980, 91. Mem. NAFE, Internat. Platform Assn., Angels of Easter Seal, Am. Lung Assn., Am. Cancer Soc. Republican. Mem. Ch. of Christ.

BEIGL, WILLIAM, physician, naturopath, hypnotist, acupuncturist, consultant; b. Chgo., July 9, 1950; s. William C. Beigl and Mary Tomlinson; m. Mavis Johnson, Aug. 5, 1977. BA in Elem. Edn., U. South Fla., 1971; D of Natural Medicine, Acad. Sci. of Man, Sussex, Eng., 1979. Founder "You Too Can Choose Happiness" System, 1975; pvt. practice hypnotherapy Chgo., 1977—, pvt. practice naturopathic medicine, acupuncture and oriental natural medicine, 1979—; mem. rsch. team Donsbach U., 1980; chief rschr. disease prevention B.P.H. Corp.; bd. dirs. Mid-West Hypnosis Conv.; cons. in field; 1st syndicated hypnosis columnist, 1982; CEO Bill Beigl Enterprises, Inc., 1992, World Hypnosis Orgn., Inc., 1992; guest presenter Paramedics 25th Anniversary Celebration, Phila., 1993, (with Lee Ramsey) Blair Cheese Fest, 1994; devised lowered casino game tables; expert witness on hypnosis Cook County Ct. Sys. Editor, pub. Portage Park News, 1980; originator Paramedic System, 1968 (honored by Pres. Johnson 1968, Pres. Nixon 1969, Pres. Reagan 1985); responsible for Ramped Curbs, Braille Markings on Elevators and Monuments, Handicapped Parking Space, Licence Plates and Pub. Accessibility for Wheelchairs, Lowered Casino Gaming Tables; author: Adventures in Hypnosis, 1990, 2d edit., 1991; contbg. author: Think & Grow Breasts, 1994; contbr. articles on natural healing and hypnosis to newspapers and mags.; patentee in field. Assoc. bd. mgrs. Robert R. McCormick chpt. Chgo. Boy's Club, 1975; mem. trauma unit Operation Desert Storm, 1991; vol. with Hurricane Andrew victims, 1992, Mississippi River flood victims, 1993, summer Centennial Olympics physician, Atlanta, 1996; bd. dirs. Kids Internat., 1996. Recipient award Congressman Sidney Yates, 1971, Disease Prevention award Better Positive Health Found., 1979, Pen and Quill award Nat. Bd. for Hypnotherapy and Hypnotic Anesthesiology, 1991, Excellence award Honeywell, 1994; named Chicagoan of Yr., Mayor Richard J. Daley, 1968, Chgo. Cath. of Yr., Cardinal John Cody, 1968, Illinoisan of Yr., Gov. Richard B. Ogilvie, 1968, One of 10 Outstanding Young Citizens, Chgo. Jaycees, 1980, Inspirational Mind of Four Profl. Championship Sports Teams, 1983-84, Citizen of Week, Sta. WBBM, 1984; appeared in Ripley's Believe It Or Not, 1984; honored by Gov. James R. Thompson, 1985, U.S. Senator Charles H. Percy, 1986; featured on CBS-TV Portrait Series, 1985, Cablevision's Good Neighbors, 1987; inducted into Internat. Hypnosis Hall of Fame, 1989. Mem. Internat. Naturopathic Assn. (cert., Naturopathic Physician Yr. 1985), Nat. Assn. Naturopathic Physicians (cert.), Nat. Guild Hypnotists (cert.), Assn. Advance Ethical Hypnosis (cert., past v.p., past sec. Ill. chpt., bd. dirs. 1986, participant the biggest hypnosis conv. 1988, co-chmn. world's largest and friendliest 1987-88, 89), World Hypnosis Orgn. (cert.), Am. Naturopathic Assn., Am. Soc. Clin. Hypnosis, Minn. Assn. Naturopathic Physicians (cert.), Hemlock Soc., Chgo. Meml. Assn., Boys Clubs Am. (life, Boy of Yr. 1968), Hospice, Midwest Pain Soc., Pain Clinic Physicians. Lodge: Moose. Office: 2521 W Montrose Ave Chicago IL 60618-1505

BEISECKER, ANALEE ELIZABETH, medical sociology educator, researcher; b. Evergreen Park, Ill., Aug. 9, 1943; d. Maurice Edward and Analee (Hill) Burns; m. Thomas David Beisecker, July 25, 1964; children: David Wayne, Randall Thomas. BA, U. Kans., 1964; MA, U. Wis., 1966, PhD, 1986. Health specialist Nat. Ctr. Extension Gerontology, Kansas City, Mo., 1987-88; asst. prof. allied health U. Kans. Med. Ctr., Kansas City, 1988-90, assoc. prof. preventive medicine, 1990—; assoc. dir. Cancer Inst., Kansas City, 1991—; dir. edn. Alzheimer's Disease Ctr. U. Kans. Med. Ctr., Kansas City, 1991-96. Contbr. articles to profl. jours., chpts. to books. Sec.-treas. Baldwin Recreation Commn., Baldwin City, Kans., 1980-86; bd. dirs. Kaw Valley coun. Girl Scouts U.S.A., 1989-92; pres. Baldwin Community Arts Coun., 1990-92. Rsch. grantee Alzheimer's Assn., 1990, Nat. Inst. Aging, 1991, 94, 95, Speas Found., 1993, Nat. Cancer Inst., 1993. Mem. APHA, Am. Acad. Physician and Patient, Gerontol. Soc. Am., Alpha Phi (bd. dirs. Found. 1980-86). Home: 351 E 1950 Rd Baldwin City KS 66006 Office: U Kans Med Ctr 3901 Rainbow Blvd Kansas City KS 66160-0001

BEITLER, STEPHEN SETH, retail company executive; b. N.Y.C., Oct. 1, 1956; s. Stanley Samuel and Arline (Mandell) B.; m. Deborah Joy Gottlieb, Jan. 16, 1982; children: Grace Jacqueline, Elinore Meredith. BA, cert. of Asian Study, Am. U. Sch. Internat. Studies, Washington, 1977; postgrad., U. Chgo., 1977-78; MS, Def. Intelligence Coll., 1986. Legis. aide U.S. Ho. of Reps., Washington, 1975-77; commd. 2d lt. U.S. Army, 1977, advanced through grades to maj., 1989; intelligence briefing officer to Sec. Def. and Chmn. Joint Chiefs of Staff, Washington, 1984-86; asst. to asst. sec. of def. Office Sec. Def., Washington, 1987-88; asst. to undersec. of def. Office of Sec. of Def., Washington, 1988-89; resigned U.S. Army, 1989; mgr. ops. devel. Helene Curtis, Inc., Chgo., 1989-90, corp. mgr. strategy and devel., 1990-92, dir. strategy and devel., 1993; nat. mgr. operational planning and info. Sears Merchandise Group, Hoffman Estates, Ill., 1993-95, sr. dir. fin. processes and systems, 1995—; comdr. 305th psychol. ops. bn. USAR, Arlington Heights, Ill., 1992—; cons. MGA, Inc., Chgo., 1985—; founding chmn. Conf. Bd. Coun. Competitive Analysis. Contbg. author: The Military Intelligence Community, 1986; contbr. articles to profl. publs. Vol. Bus. Vols. for the Arts, Chgo., 1991-94. Lt. col. USAR. Decorated Green Beret for valor and svc. Fellow Inter-univ. Seminar on Armed Forces and Soc., Soc. Competitive Intelligence Profls. (bd. dirs. 1991-94); mem. Spl. Forces Club, Army and Navy Club. Home: 378 Delta Ln Highland Park IL 60035-5204 Office: Sears Roebuck & Co D/768S B5-283B 3333 Beverly Rd Hoffman Estates IL 60179-0001

BEKKEDAHL, BRAD DOUGLAS, dentist; b. Williston, N.D., Nov. 23, 1957; s. Oliver Lawrence Jr. and Gudrun Joan (Sundby) B. BA, Jamestown (N.D.) Coll., 1979; BS, U. Minn., 1982, DDS, 1984. Gen. practice dentistry Williston, 1984—; chmn. dental staff Mercy Med. Ctr., 1991-93. Scoutmaster Boy Scouts Am., Williston, 1984-86; mem. pastoral com. Gloria Dei Luth. Ch., Williston, 1986-88, mem. coun., 1993—, congregation pres., 1995; pres. Am. Legion Drum and Bugle Corps, Williston, 1986; edn. officer Luth. Brotherhood br. 8334, 1989-93; mem. exec. com. Raymond Family Cmty. Ctr., 1988—; bd. dirs. Williston Pard, 1988-96, pres. 1988-92; commr. Williston, 1996—. Mem. ADA, N.D. Dental Assn., N.W. Dist. Dental Assn., Williston Dental Soc. (sec.-treas.), N.D. Amateur Hockey Assn. (v.p. 1990—, cmty. rep., pres. 1986-90, pres. 1993—). Republican. Home: 2501 13th Ave W Williston ND 58801-3225 Office: PO Box 2443 2204 2d Ave W Williston ND 58801

BEKKEN, JAMES MALCOLM, district judge; b. Grand Forks, N.D., July 15, 1948; s. Ralph W. and ElizabethG. (Nolan) B.; m. Sandra Erban, July 16, 1970; children: Scott, Aaron, Stephanie. BS in Edn., U. N.D., 1970, JD, 1977. Bar: N.D. 1977, U.S. Dist. Ct. N.D. 1979. Tchr. Proctor (Minn.) Pub. Schs., 1970-71, Grand Forks Pub. Schs., 1971-74; ptnr. Hovey & Bekken, New Rockford, N.D., 1977-83; county judge Eddy, Benson, Foster & Wells Counties, New Rockford, 1983-94; dist. judge Southeast Judicial Dist. Eddy County Courthouse, New Rockford, 1994—; mem. Jud. Standards Com., chair subcom. on jud. conduct, 1987-88; mem. N.D. Jud. Conduct Commn., Bismarck, 1988—, Atty. Gen.'s Domestic Violence Response Task Force, Bismarck, 1990-91. Bd. dirs. Heart of Dakota Coalition for Health, New Rockford, 1989—; past pres. 4th Corp., New Rockford. Mem. Jud. Conf. (exec. com. 1987-90), County Judges Assn. (pres. 1988), Dist. Judges Assn. (treas. 1995), Kiwanis Internat. (gov. Minn.-Dakotas dist. 1991-92). Lutheran. Office: Dist Judge Eddy County Courthouse PO Box 32 New Rockford ND 58356-0032

BELAGAJE, RAMA M., molecular biologist; b. Belagaje, Karnataka, India, May 9, 1942; came to U.S. 1967; s. Subraya and Shankary (Shastry) B.; m. Nalini Kirumakki, Jan. 25, 1973; children: Samir, Sudhir. BSc, Mysore U., India, 1962; MSc, Banaras Hindu U., India, 1965; MS, NYU, 1970, PhD, 1971. Instr. St. Philomena's Coll., Puttur, India, 1962-63; rsch. fellow Indian Inst. Sci., Bangalore, 1965-67; teaching fellow NYU, N.Y.C., 1971-72; rsch. assoc. MIT, Cambridge, 1972-79; rsch. scientist Eli Lilly & Co., Indpls., 1979—. Patentee in field. Treas. India Assn. Indpls., 1987; adminstr., chmn. India Community Ctr., Indpls., 1988; pres. Havyaka Assn. of Am., Indpls., 1989; chmn. Geeta Mandal, Indpls., 1986; vol. Boy Scouts Am., Indpls., 1992. Recipient Padma Shri award Govt. of India, 1977, Founders' Day award NYU, 1972, Gold medal Banaras Hindu U., 1965. Mem. AAAS, Am. Chem. Soc., N.Y. Acad. Sci., Acad. Gen. Edn. India. Hindu. Home: 7821 Mohawk Ln Indianapolis IN 46260-3339 Office: Eli Lilly & Co Dept MC625 Lilly Corp Ctr Indianapolis IN 46285

BELANGER, WILLIAM V., JR., state legislator; b. Mpls., Oct. 18, 1928; m. Lois Jean Winistorfer, 1953; seven children. St. Thomas Coll., 1948-50. With Honeywell Def. Sys., 1951-90, ret., 1990; mem. Minn. Senate Dist. 41, 1980—; mem. Commerce & Consumer Protection com., Crime Prevention com., Rules & Adminstrn., Taxes & Tax Laws Com., Transp. & Pub. Transit Com. Res. U.S. Army, 1947; active duty, 1950; cpl. U.S. Army, 1951, 3rd Infantry Divsn. Office: 10716 Beard Ave S Minneapolis MN 55431-3616 also: State Senate State Capital Building Saint Paul MN 55155-1606*

BELATTI, RICHARD G., state legislator; m. Marilyn Belatti; four children. Student, Coll. St. Thomas, U. S.D., Creighton U., Mayo Grad. Sch. Former senator S.D. State Senate Dist. 13, former vice chmn. health and human svc. com., former mem. taxation com., transp. com.; rep. S.D. State Ho. Reps. Dist. 8, mem. health and human svc. and judiciary coms. Home: 940 N Division Ave Madison SD 57042*

BELCHAK, FRANK ROBERT, computer technologist; b. Chgo., June 21, 1943; s. Paul and Marion (Vrba) B. BS, Roosevelt U., 1969; MBA, Ill. Inst. Tech., 1990. Computer tech. capacity planner, systems developer, dealer support analyst Navistar Internat. Corp., Oakbrook Terrace, Ill., 1969—, also mgr., sales mktg. tng., mem. council future employee recognition program, mem. good govt. com.; chief fin. officer, systems. cons. Innovative Software Solutions, Inc., Lombard, Ill. Mem. keystone council John G. Shedd Aquarium. Recipient Gen. Robert E. Wood Citizenship award, 1965. Mem. Computer Measurement Group, Assn. Individual Investors, Art Inst. Chgo., Chgo. Zool. Soc., Edward J. Sparling Soc., Keystone Coun., Internat. Platform Assn., Ill. High Sch. Athletic Assn. Roman Catholic. Office: Navistar Internat Corp 1901 S Meyers Rd Villa Park IL 60181

BELCHER, LA JEUNE, automotive parts company executive; b. Chgo., Nov. 16, 1960; d. Lewis Albert and Dorthy (Brandon) B. BA, Northwestern U., 1982; postgrad., Am. Inst. of Banking, 1983-84. Notary pub.; securities lic.; ins. lic., Ill. Securities processor Am. Nat. Bank, Chgo., 1983, divisional asst., 1983-84; mgmt. trainee Toyota Motor Distbrs., Carol Stream, Ill., 1984-85, dist. parts mgr., 1985-90, sr. customer rels. adminstr., 1990—; fin. rep. Waddell and Reed, 1992; founder Crystal Clear Concepts; fin. rep. Waddell and Reed, 1992; rep. to Japan-U.S. Toyota Dealer Meeting, Tokyo, 1985; owner Crystal Clear Concepts. Author: (booklet) The Cutting Edge: 127 Tips to Improve Your Professional Image. Mem. alumni admissions coun. Northwestern U., Evanston, Ill.; bd. dirs. Boys and Girls Club; comty. docent Art Inst. Chgo. Mem. NAFE, NAACP, Northwestern Club Chgo., Toastmasters (edn. v.p. 1988, 94, 95, advt. v.p. 1989, pres. 1990-93), Delta Sigma Theta. Home: 1212 S Michigan Ave Chicago IL 60605-2416 Office: Toyota Motor Distbrs 2350 Sequoia Dr Aurora IL 60506-6211

BELCHER, MAX, social services administrator; b. East Lynn, W.Va., Mar. 16, 1942; s. George H. and Ella D. (Dickerson) B.; children: Kipling, Babbette, Andrew, Raleigh, Perry. BA, Berea (Ky.) Coll., 1969; ThM, Toledo Bible Coll., 1972; ThD, Toledo Theol. Sem., 1973; MA, Liberty (Va.) U., 1994; DD, LLD (hon.), Internat. Free Prof. Episc. U., London, 1966; PhD, U. San Jose, 1996. From caseworker to dist. mgr. Mich. Dept. Social Svcs., Flint, 1964—, dist. mgr., 1992—; faculty dept. psychology Baker Coll., Flint, 1987—. Bd. dirs. Consortium on Child Abuse and Neglect, Flint, 1993—. Recipient Cert. of Merit in Youth Employment, Genesee Intermediate Sch. Dist., 1979, Cert. of Appreciation, Health Care Access Project, 1990. Mem. Am. Counseling Assn., Ky. Counseling Assn., Am. Assn. Christian Counselors, Intercollegiate Studies Inst. (faculty advocate). Home: 9421 Macafee Rd Montrose MI 48457 Office: Mich Dept Social Svcs 125 E Union St Flint MI 48502

BELCHER-REDEBAUGH-LEVI, CAROLINE LOUISE, nursing home administrator, nurse; b. Dixon, Ill., May 23, 1910; d. Charles R. and May Caroline (Barnes) Kreger; m. Richard E. Belcher, Nov. 24, 1934 (dec. 1964); children: Richard Charles (dec.), Mary; m. Charles H. Redebaugh, Dec. 3, 1966 (dec. 1979); m. Paul Levi, July 20, 1985 (dec. Sept. 1993). R.N., Katherine Shaw Bethea Sch. Nursing, 1930. Nurse, various hosps., 1930-49; adminstr. Orchard Glen Nursing Home, Dixon, Ill., 1949-76; coordinator Sr. Action Ctr., Springfield, Ill., 1977-87; charter mem. Ill. Nursing Home Adminstrs. Licensure Bd., 1970-76; mem. Sauk Valley Community Coll. Found., Dixon, Ill., 1988, adv. com. for sr. programs, 1988, chmn. ball com., 1989-90, Co Coun. on Aging, 1988, various adv. coms. advocating for srs. Contbr. articles to profl. jours. Mem. nat. adv. com., del. White House Conf. on Aging, 1961-81; v.p. Ill. Joint Council to Improve Health Care for Aged, 1953, pres., 1954; chair Sec. State George Ryan Adv. Com. Health Maintenance, 1991; charter mem. bd. dirs. Lee County Vol. Care Ctr., 1994, Free Health Clinic. Mem. Capitol City Rep. Women (v.p. 1983-90), Lee County Rep. Women, State Council on Aging, Am. Coll. Nursing Home Adminstrs. (charter, edn. com., pres.), Am. Nursing Home Assn. (v.p. 1953), Ill. Nurses Assn. (bd. dirs.), Ill. Nursing Home Adminstrs (charter), Sr. Illinoisian's Hall of Fame (charter). Home: 1420 Eustace Dr Dixon IL 61021-1742

BELDEN, KAREN SCHEIRING, shop owner, realtor; b. Canton, Ohio, Oct. 28, 1942; d. Norwood Edward and Della Doris (Bowser) Scheiring; m. William H. Belden Jr., Aug. 22, 1964; children: William H. III, Brian Scheiring. BS, Bowling Green State U., 1964. Elem tchr. Lakewood (Ohio) Pub. Schs., 1960-61; retail store owner Easterdays, Canton, Ohio, 1982—; realtor Prudential DeHoff, North Canton, Ohio, 1995—; mem. adv. bd. Society/Key Corp., Canton; trustee Citizens Savs., Canton; bd. dirs. Civesta Corp., Canton, Citizens Nat. Bank, Akron/Canton, First Merit, Akron. Editor: National Football Hall of Fame Cookbook, 1990. Mem. state ctrl. com. Rep. Party, 1992-94; chmn. Nat. Football Hall of Fame Festival, Canton, 1995; trustee Ohio Fedn. Ind. Colls., 1994—, Stark Tech. Coll., 1993—, Mt. Union Coll., 1993—; vice chmn. Ednl. Enhancement Project, 1990—. Named Alumnus of Yr., Bowling Green State U., 1987, Woman of the Yr., Jr. League, 1987. Mem. Canton Regional C. of C. (pres. 1994), Rotary Club of Canton. Roman Catholic. Office: Easterday's Gift & Flora 821 S Main St North Canton OH 44720

BELFORD, VIRGINIA HELEN WISDOM, freelance writer; b. Waynesville, Mo., Oct. 20, 1948; d. David Glen and Beverly Jean (Prescott) Wisdom; m. Scott Lee Belford, Oct. 14, 1974; children: Scott J., Elizabeth (dec.). BA with honors, U. Ill., Chgo., 1972; postgrad., Garrett-Evang. Theol. Sem., 1988—. Primary teaching cert. Am. Montessori Soc. Tchr. Chatham County Schs., Savannah, Ga., 1973-74, Montessori Sch., Crown Point, Ind., 1974-75, Will County (Ill.) Pub. Schs., 1978-80; juvenile writer Pioneer Press, Wheaton, Ill., 1984-85; freelance writer Naperville, Ill., 1985-89; with Garrett Evang. Theol. Sem., Evanston, Ill., 1989—; camp dir. Opportunity Ctr., Teutopolis, Ill., summer 1976; instr. Learning Exchange, Evanston, Ill., 1975-76; adult edn. tutor Coll. of DuPage, Glen Ellyn, Ill., 1985-87. Organizer Chgo. Peace Coun., 1969-72; newsletter Women's Club, 1980-85; workshop leader Heifer Project Internat., Chgo., 1986-88; co-chmn. Women in Ministry, Garrett-Evang. Theol. Sem., 1989—. Recipient 1st place for poetry Ill. Federated Women's Club, 1982; Hoosier scholar, 1966, James scholar, 1969-72, Ga. Harkness scholar, 1991. Mem. NOW (v.p. of action DuPage chpt. 1993), Global Educators No. Ill. (charter, bd. dirs. 1988—), AAUW (internat. chmn. Naperville 1986-88, R & P grantee 1989-90), Ducks Unltd. Methodist. Home: 1517 Marquette Ave Naperville IL 60565-1739

BELFOUR, ED, professional hockey player; b. Carman, Man., Can., Apr. 21, 1965. Student, U. N.D. Goalie Chgo. Blackhawks; mem. NCAA All-Am. West second team, 1986-87, tournament team, 1986-87, WCHA All-Star first team 1986-87; player NHL All-Star game, 1992-93. Recipient Vezina trophy, 1990-91, 92-93, Calder Meml. trophy, 90-91, William M. Jennings trophy, 90-91, 92-93, Trico Goaltender award, 1990-91; co-recipient Garry F. Longman Meml. trophy, 1987-88; named Rookie of the Year, 1990-91, Sporting News All-Star 2nd team, 1992-93, NCAA All-Am. Second Team, 1986-87, NHL All-Rookie Team, 1990-91, NHL All-Star First Team, 1990-91, 92-93. Office: Chgo Blackhawks 1901 W Madison St Chicago IL 60612-2620*

BELIN, DAVID WILLIAM, lawyer; b. Washington, June 20, 1928; s. Louis I. and Esther (Klass) B.; m. Constance Newman, Sept. 14, 1952 (dec. June 1980); children: Jonathan L., James M., Joy E., Thomas R., Laura R.; m. Barbara Hauben Ross, May 2, 1992. BA, U. Mich., 1951, MBA, 1953, JD, 1954. Bar: Iowa 1954. Ptnr. Herrick & Langdon, 1955-62, Herrick, Langdon, Sandblom & Belin, 1962-66; sr. ptnr. Herrick, Langdon, Belin, Harris, Langdon & Helmick, 1966-78, Belin Harris Lamson McCormick, Des Moines, 1978—; trustee Kemper Mut. Funds; bd. dirs. Outdoor Techs. Group; counsel Pres.'s Commn. on the Assassination of President Kennedy (Warren Commn.), 1964; exec. dir. Commn. on CIA Activities within the U.S. (Rockefeller Commn.), 1975; mem. Pres.'s Com. on Arts and the Humanities, 1984-90. Author: November 22, 1963: You Are the Jury, 1973, Final Disclosure: The Full Truth About the Assassination of President Kennedy, 1988, Leaving Money Wisely: Creative Estate Planning for Middle- and Upper-Income Americans for the 1990s, 1990. Bd. dirs. Des Moines Cmty. Drama Assn., 1961-64, Des Moines Symphony, 1968-70; mem. adv. bd. Nat. Assn. Gifted Children, 1993—; pres. Ams. for Gifted and Talented Edn., 1996—. Served with AUS, 1946-47. Recipient Henry M. Bates Meml. award U. Mich. Law Sch., Brotherhood award NCCJ, 1978; hon. orator U. Mich., 1950. Mem. Soc. Barristers, Michigamua Club, Order of Coif, Phi Beta Kappa Assocs., Phi Beta Kappa, Phi Kappa Phi, Delta Sigma Rho, Beta Alpha Psi. Home: 1705 Plaza Cir Windsor Heights IA 50322

BELL, BAILLIS F., airport terminal executive. Budget analyst City of Wichita, Kans., 1970-75; dir. Wichita Airport Authority, Kans., 1975—. Office: Witchita Airport Authority 2173 Air Cargo Rd Wichita KS 67209-1958

BELL, BRIAN, manufacturing engineer; b. Detroit, Mich., Nov. 5, 1953. AS, McComb Coll., 1977. Project engr. Craft Inds., Shelby Twp., Mich., 1984-91, Utica Enterpises, Inc., Shelby Twp., 1991—. Co-commissoner Baseball Club. Republican. Office: Utica Enterprises Inc 13231 23 Mile Rd Shelby Township MI 48315-2713

BELL, CHARLES EUGENE, JR., industrial engineer; b. N.Y.C., Dec. 13, 1932; s. Charles Edward and Constance Elizabeth (Verbelia) B.; B. Engring., Johns Hopkins U., 1954, M.S. in Engring., 1959; m. Doris R. Clifton, Jan. 14, 1967; 1 son, Scott Charles Bell. Indsl. engr. Signode Corp., Balt., 1957-61, asst. to plant mgr., 1961-63, plant engr., 1963-64, div. indsl. engr., Glenview, Ill., 1964-69, asst. to div. mgr., 1969-76, engring. mgr., 1976-93; cons., 1993—; host committeeman Internat. Indsl. Engring. Conf., Chgo., 1984, 92. Served with U.S. Army, 1955-57. Registered profl. engr., Calif. Mem. Am. Inst. Indsl. Engrs. (pres. 1981), Indsl. Mgmt. Club Central Md. (pres. 1964), Nat. Soc. Profl. Engrs., Ill. Soc. Profl. Engrs., Soc. Plastics Engrs. Republican. Roman Catholic. Home: 1021 W Old Mill Rd Lake Forest IL 60045-3749

BELL, DAVID CURTIS, manufacturing company executive; b. St. Paul, Nov. 5, 1953; s. Dwain Curtis and Aurel Lorna (Waknitz) B.; m. Lee Ellen Wandersee, Feb. 12, 1982; B.A. summa cum laude with honors, Concordia Coll., 1975; postgrad. Am. U., 1973. Prodn. asst. Pako Photo, Mpls., 1975; sales rep. Pako Corp., Chgo. and ea. Wis., 1976-79; venture plant sales mgr. Pako Corp., Mpls., 1979-83; mktg. dir. system sales Multi-Arc (now Multi-Arc Sci. Coatings) div. Andal Corp., St. Paul, 1983-89, program mgr. nat. accounts, mgr. system sales, 1989, pres. Excel Inc., 1993-94, pres. ElectroPhysics, Inc., 1994—; bd. dirs. Bell Mfg. & Services, Inc., Mpls. Ltd. Mem. Internat. Machine Tool Assn. (selected speaker 1986), Soc. Mfg. Engrs. (conf. speaker 1989), North Side Jaycees (officer 1976-78), New Hope Jaycees (pres. 1981-82), C-400 Club, Kinship Club Greater Mpls. (bd. dirs. 1988-92), Kiwanis Office: 1400 Marshall St NE Minneapolis MN 55413

BELL, DOROTHY FRANCES, nurse, educator; b. Milw.; m. Daniel J. Bell, 1970; 5 children. BS, Coll. St. Teresa, Winona, Minn., 1969; postgrad., U. Md., 1969-70; MS, Winona State U., 1973. RN, Minn. Staff nurse pediatrics U. Md. Hosp., Balt., 1969-70; staff nurse psychiatry St. Marys Hosp., Rochester, Minn., 1970-71, staff nurse pediatrics, pediatric ICU, 1974-75; instr. pub. health Coll. St. Teresa, Rochester, 1971-73; mem. nursing edn. staff Rochester Meth. Hosp., 1977-85, staff devel./continuing edn. coord., 1985-91; nursing edn. specialist Mayo Found., Rochester, 1991—. Editorial bd. Jour. Nursing Staff Devel., 1991—; contbr. articles to profl. publs. Vol. Rochester Parochial Schs., 1980—, Am. Cancer Soc., Rochester, 1989, 91, 92; mem. Rochester Ctrl. Cath. Sch. Bd. Edn., 1994—, treas., 1995—. Mem. ANA (at-large exec. com., coun. continuing edn. and staff devel.), APHA, Nursing Continuing Edn. Consortium S.E. Minn. (sec.-treas. 1987-91, pres. 1994-95, chmn. 1993-95), Minn. Nurses Assn. (vice chmn. continuing edn. approval program 1993-95, chmn. 1995—), Nat. Nursing Staff Devel. Orgn. (charter), Sigma Theta Tau (charter Kappa Mu chpt, sec. 1989-91). Republican.

BELL, HARRY EDWARD, quality consulting company executive; b. Jamaica, N.Y., Aug. 28, 1947; s. Harry Edward and Margaret Florence (Ketcham) B.; m. Rosann Branciforte, Sept. 2, 1967; children: Michael Harry, Brian Scott. BS in Chemistry, CCNY, 1970, MA in Organic Chemistry, 1975. Sr. chemist NL Industries, Inc., West Caldwell, N.J., 1970-73; sales svc. chemist Alcan Ingot & Powders, Union, N.J., 1973-74; tech. mgr. pigments Alcan Ingot & Powders, 1974-75, tech. mgr. div., 1975-84; corp. spc coordinator Alcan Aluminum Corp., Cleve., 1984-85; mgr. productivity Alcan Rolled Products Co., Cleve., 1985-90; pres. Quality Resources Internat., Hudson, Ohio, 1987—; bd. dirs., cons. Branch Cons., E. Brunswick, N.J., 1978-82. Contbr. articles to profl. jours.; patentee in field. Pratt Inst. Tech. art scholar, 1961; NSF geophysics scholar, 1963. Mem. ACS, ASTM (chmn. D1 subcom. metallic pigments 1979-83), Assn. for Quality and Participation, Am. Soc. for Quality Control, Aluminum Assn. (chmn. pigments and powders tech. com. 1979-83). Office: Quality Resources Internat PO Box 426 Hudson OH 44236-0426

BELL, HOWARD WESLEY, JR., educational administrator; b. Phila., Mar. 12, 1948; s. Howard Wesley and Elva (Glenn) B.; m. Sheila Trice, June 7, 1971; children: Mayet, Annora, William. BS in Aerospace Engring., Princeton U., 1970; M in Pub. Policy, Harvard U., 1973; MS in Mgmt. Sci., MIT, 1973. Computer analyst Fed. Res. Bank Boston, 1972-73; comml. loan officer State St. Bank & Trust Co., Boston, 1973-77; v.p. devel. and syndication Landura Corp. of Southeast, Nashville, 1977-80; pres., owner Tenn. Power Mgmt. Co., Inc., Nashville, 1981; v.p. fin. and budget Fisk U., Nashville, 1981-83; v.p. adminstrv. svc. and info. technologies, adj. prof. U. Cin., 1983—. Mem. adv. bd. Cin. Salvation Army, 1985-91; vice chmn. bd. dirs. WCET-TV Cin., 1987-90, chmn., 1990-92, emeritus, 1992—; bd. dirs. Cin. Ballet, 1993—, Am. Pub. TV Stations, 1994—; mem. building bridges to jobs com. Cin. Youth Collaborative, 1988-91; co-sponsor Minority Enterprise Devel. Week recognition, Cin., 1988-93; chmn. fin. com. Roselawn Luth. Ch., 1988. Mem. Urban League (life), NAACP, Assn. for Managing and Using Info. Resources in Higher Edn. (nominations and elections com. 1995—), Am. Mgmt. Assn., Nat. Assn. Coll. and Univ. Bus. Officers, Ctrl. Assn. Coll. and Univ. Bus. Officers, Assn. Black Princeton Alumni (treas. 1972-75), Princeton Alumni Assn. So. Ohio, Black Male Coalition, Rotary, Sigma Pi Phi. Office: U Cin P O Box 210630 Cincinnati OH 45221-0630

BELL, JASON CAMERON, accountant; b. Danville, Ill., Dec. 14, 1963; s. Lamont Bell and Marion (Turner) Butler; m. Yolanda Scott, June 19, 1992; children: Maurice, Ricky Scott, Marcus Bell. BS, Fla. A&M U., 1987; postgrad., Ill. Inst. Tech. CPA, Ill. Dir. after-sch. program Frontline Outreach, Orlando, Fla., 1987-88; acct. Washington, Pittman & McKeever, Chgo., 1989-91; acct., founder J. Cameron Bell & Assocs., Chgo., 1991—; founder East Oak Jewelry, 1994—, Ednl. Resources, 1995—. Bd. dirs. Black Ensemble Theatre Co., Chgo., 1991-93, Phoebe's Place Sr. Ctr., Chgo., 1994—. Named one of Outstanding Young Men Am., 1990. Mem. AICPA, Nat. Assn. Black Accts. (Outstanding Svc. award Chgo. chpt. 1990, 92), Ill. CPA Soc. Office: J Cameron Bell & Assocs 1226 W 112th St Chicago IL 60643-4502

BELL, JEANETTE LOIS, state legislator; b. Milw., Sept. 2, 1941; d. Harold Arthur and Luella Ruth (Block) Jeske; m. Chester Robert Bell Jr., 1962; children: Chester R. III, Colleen M., Edith L. BA, U. Wis., Milw., 1988. State assemblywoman dist. 22 State of Wis., 1982-92, state assemblywoman dist. 15, 1993—; chairwoman ways and means com. Wis. State Assembly. Active child abuse prevention program. Recipient Clean 16 Environment award, Child Abuse Prevention award. Mem. LWV. Home: 1415 S 60th St Milwaukee WI 53214-5159*

BELL, LAURA JEANE, retired nurse; b. Chgo., Mar. 11, 1922; d. Harold Elwood and Mary Etta (Sprague) Downey; m. David Hoge Bell, Feb. 2l, l943; children: David, Roy, Thomas, John, Ruth, Keith, Mary, Richard, Howard. AA, Blackburn Coll., 194l; diploma in nursing, St. Elizabeths Hosp., Washington, 1946; BS in Nursing, Washington U., St. Louis, 1962; MS in Edn., St. Louis U., 1969. RN, Mo. Relief supr. St. Vincent's Hosp., St. Louis, 1949-58; staff asst. head nurse, head nurse Barnes Hosp., St. Louis, l958-6l, instr., coord. Sch. Nursing, 1962-67; instr. Jefferson Barracks VA Hosp., St. Louis, 1967-70, asst. chief nursing svc. for edn., 1970-7l; instr. Jefferson Barracks div. St. Louis VA Med. Ctr., 197l-73, med. supr. John Cochran div., 1973-8l, supr. ambulatory care Jefferson Barracks div., 198l-84; ret., 1984. Dist. rep. intercultural programs Am. Field Svc., St. Louis, 1983-91; rec. sec. Overland (Mo.) Hist. Soc., 1988-89, pres., 1990-92; pres. United Meth. Women, Stephan Meml. Ch., Charlack, Mo., 1988-92; mem. Women's Polit. Caucus, St. Louis, 1987—; v.p. St. Louis North Dist. United Meth. Women, 1992-95; sec. Mo. Ch. Women United, 1992-95, pres., 1996—; chair Commn. on Status and Role of Women, Mo. East Conf., U. Mo., 1992—; bd. dirs. Wesley Found., St. Louis, 1992—; pres. Met. St. Louis Ch. Women United, 1993—. Recipient Alumni Achievement award Blackburn Coll., 1995; named Fed. Employee of Yr., Fed. Exec. Bd., 1970. Mem. ANA (accreditation com. cen. region 1984-88), Mo. League for Nursing (pres. 1978-80, chmn. bylaws 1985-92), Mo. Nurses Assn. (continuing edn. and bylaws com., chmn. nominating com., 3d dist. 1988, regional bd. dirs. 1988-90, Pres.'s award 1989), Mo. Student Nurses Assn. (hon., scholarship named in her honor 1982). Home: 2418 Oakland Ave Saint Louis MO 63114-5016

BELL, ROBERT HOLMES, federal judge; b. Lansing, Mich., Apr. 19, 1944; s. Preston C. and Eileen (Holmes) B.; m. Helen Mortensen, June 28, 1968; children: Robert Holmes Jr., Ruth Eileen, Jonathan Neil. BA, Wheaton Coll., 1966; JD, Wayne State U., 1969. Bar: Mich. 1970, U.S. Dist. Ct. (we. dist.) Mich. 1970. Asst. prosecutor Ingham County Prosecutor's Office, Lansing, Mich., 1969-72; state dist. judge Mich. State Cts., 1973-78; state cir. judge Mich. State Cts., Mason, 1979-87; judge U.S. Dist. Ct. Mich., Grand Rapids, Mich., 1987—. Office: US Dist Ct 416 Fed Bldg 110 Michigan St NW Grand Rapids MI 49503-2313

BELL, SAMUEL H., federal judge; b. Rochester, N.Y., Dec. 31, 1925; s. Samuel H. and Marie C. (Williams) B.; m. Joyce Elaine Shaw, 1948 (dec.): children: Henry W., Steven D.; m. Jennie Lee McCall, 1983. BA, Coll. Wooster, 1947; JD, U. Akron, 1952. Practice law Cuyahoga Falls, Ohio, 1956-68; asst. pros. atty. Summit County, Ohio, 1956-58; judge Cuyahoga Falls Mcpl. Ct., Ohio, 1968-73, Ct. of Common Pleas, Akron, Ohio, 1973-77, Ohio Ct. Appeals, 9th Jud. Dist., Akron, 1977-82, U.S. Dist. Ct. (no. dist.) Ohio, Akron, 1982—; adj. prof., mem. adv. bd. U. Akron Sch. Law, trustee Dean's club; bd. dirs. Jos. R. Miller Found. Co-author: Federal Practice Guide 6th Cir., 1996. Recipient Disting. Alumni award U. Akron, 1988, St. Thomas More award, 1987. Fellow Akron Bar Found. (trustee 1989-94, pres. 1993-94); mem. Fed. Bar Assn., Ohio Bar Assn., Akron Bar Assn., Fed. Judges Assn. (bd. dirs.), Akron U. Sch. Law Alumni Assn. (Disting. Alumni award 1983), Charles F. Scanlon Akron Inn Ct. (pres. 1990-92), Ohio Hist. Soc., Supreme Ct. Hist. Soc., Akron City Club, Masons, Phi Alpha Delta. Republican. Presbyterian. Office: US Dist Ct 526 Fed Bldg & US Courthouse 2 S Main St Akron OH 44308-1813

BELL, SUE A., financial services company executive; b. Marquette, Mich., Feb. 22, 1952. V.p. Bell Fin. Svcs., Ishpeming, Mich., 1983—. Chairperson Wesley United Meth. Coun. on Ministries, Ishpening, Mich., 1992—. Office: Dennis Bell & Assocs 219 S Main St Ishpeming MI 49849-2018

BELL, SUSAN JANE, nurse; b. Columbus, Ohio, July 24, 1946; d. Donald Richard Bell and Martha Jane (McDowell) Nichols; m. Robert Earlin Ward, Oct. 24, 1964 (div. 1984); children: Duane Allen Ward, Melissa Jane Ward, Bryan Thomas Ward. Degree in nursing, Columbus Sch. Practical Nursing, 1986; ADRN, Columbus State C.C., 1989; student, Franklin U., 1993—. RN, Ohio; cert. CPR; notary pub., Ohio. Nurse's asst. Riverside Meth. Hosp., Columbus, 1970-80, Norworth Convalescent Ctr., Columbus, 1980-86; lic. practical nurse, charge nurse Heartland Thurber Care Ctr., Columbus, 1986-89; staff nurse Am. Nursing Care, Columbus, 1989—; medicare home visitation, staffing and pvt. duty nurse Telemed, Columbus, 1989—; asst. head nurse Northland Terr., Columbus, 1989; supr. Elmington Manor, Columbus, 1989; staff nurse cardiac step down unit Grant Hosp., Columbus, 1989-92; nurse med. ICU, CCU and pediatric ICU, 1992-93; charge nurse critical/skilled unit First Cmty. Village Health Care Ctr., Columbus, 1992-95; pres. Bell Mktg. Distbrs., pvt. duty ALS ventilator patients Med. Pers. Poole; regional claims rep. Fed. Resources Group. Rev. Am. Fellowship Ch. Mem. NAFE, Internat. Clergy Assn., World Wildlife Fund.

BELL, WILSON TOWNSEND, banker; b. St. Louis, Feb. 24, 1934; s. Francis James and Dorothy Mae (Townsend) B.; m. Marilyn Joan Weber, June 29, 1957. BA, Vanderbilt U., 1955; grad., Stonier Grad. Sch. Banking, 1968. Cert. comml. lender. Salesperson Wagner Elec. Corp., St. Louis, 1957-59; asst. v.p. Bank of St. Louis, 1959-67; v.p. Boatment's Nat. Bank, St. Louis, 1967-72; pres. Big Bend Bank, Webster Groves, Mo., 1972-82; v.p. Boatment's Nat. Bank, St. Louis, 1982-89, Mega Bank of St. Louis County, Town & Country, Mo., 1989-92, UMB Bank of St. Louis, N.A., 1992—. Bd. dirs. Dance St. Louis; mem. pres.'s coun. Repertory Theatre of St. Louis. 1st lt. U.S. Army, 1955-57. Mem. Bank Mgmt. Assn. (past pres.), Am. Inst. Banking (St. Louis chpt. past pres.), Robert Morris Assocs. (St. Louis chpt. past pres.), Webster Grove C. of C. (past pres.), St. Louis Vanderbilt Club (past pres.), Rotary, Tuscan Lodge #360, St. Louis Soc. Sons of the Revolution (past pres.), Tenn. Soc. St. Louis (past pres.). Office: UMB Bank of St Louis NA 12050 Dorsett Rd Maryland Heights MO 63043-2404

BELL-JACKSON, MARIANNE JEANNE, elementary education educator; b. Chgo., Feb. 13, 1944; d. David Vincent and Jeanne Elizabeth Bell; m. Michael Ross Jackson, Aug. 12, 1989; m. Roscoe Edward Mitchell; 1 child, Atala-Nicole; m. Jerry Alan Levy. B Art History, U. Chgo., 1967; M Elem. Edn., U. Wis., Platteville, 1985. Lic. tchr. 1st - 8th grades. Sec. The Filter People, Chgo., 1960-66; office mgr. U. Chgo. Maroon, 1966-68; asst. program dir. Emerson & Taylor House Community Ctrs., Chgo., 1968-71; child advocate Lawndale Day Care Ctr., Chgo., 1971-73; potter, owner Burnt Earth Pottery, Hollandale, Wis., 1973-85; tchr. Madison (Wis.) Met. Sch. Dist., 1985—; cons. Ednl. Devel. Ctr., Newton, Mass., 1991-92; Search for Extra Terrestrial Intelligence pilot program tchr., 1993-94; resource agt. Am. Astron. Soc., 1994—. Author: Model for a 4th Grade Curriculum, 1990 (with Larry Johns) Proposal for Construction of an Effigy Mound, 1990, The Swan Twins, ColoranDraw 1, 1995; contbr. to Poetry Out of Wisconsin, 1982; inventor ColoranDraw Books, 1995. Recipient 1st pl. for pottery, 1st pl. for hand painted ceramics Cambridge (Wis.) Art Fair, 1979; named to Golden Apple Club Madison Met. Sch. Dist., 1993. Mem. Madison Tchrs. Inc., Wis. Earth Sci. Tchrs., Greenpeace, Amnesty Internat., People for Ethical Treatment of Animals. Lutheran Buddhist. Home: 6251 Portage Rd De Forest WI 53532-2900 Office: Madison Met Sch Dist Lake View Elem 1802 Tennyson Ln Madison WI 53704-2323

BELLA, EUGENE ALAN, health systems company official; b. South Bend, Ind., Feb. 7, 1953; s. Albert Edward and Suzanne Theresa (Pietrzak) B.; m. Judy Ann Mark, Nov. 19, 1978. BA, Ind. U., 1976. Owner, founder Bella Buttons, South Bend, 1978—; computer oper. On-Line Data, Inc., Mishawaka, Ind., 1981-84; dispatcher Whiteford Trucklines, Inc., South Bend, 1984-88; caseworker Ind. Dept. Pub. Welfare, Elkhart, 1990-94; assoc. tech. support specialist Holy Cross Health Sys. Corp., South Bend, 1995—. Pub. handbook Space Primer, 1973; editor, pub. monthly periodical The Grand Tour, 1978-81. Campaign vol. local, state and nat. polit. campaigns, 1968—. Democrat. Office: Bella Buttons PO Box 1953 South Bend IN 46634-1953

BELLAMY, GAIL ANNE GHETIA, magazine editor, author, speaker; b. Lakewood, Ohio, Dec. 19, 1949; f. George and Janice Arlene (Fleming) Ghetia; m. Stephen Paul Bellamy, Nov. 17, 1990. BA, Ohio U., 1971; postgrad., Case Western Res. U., 1971. Sr. editor Restaurant Hospitality mag., Cleve., 1980—; contbg. columnist Cleve. Free Times newspaper, 1992—; workshop presenter Dept. Cmty. Svcs., Cleve., 1993—, Lakeland C,ty. Edn., Mentor, Ohio, 1993—; online dining columnist Am. Online, 1995—. Author: Design Spirits, 1995; author chpts. to books; contbr. articles to profl. jours. Vol. lectr. Write-on Cleve!, 1993—; vol. examiner Am. Radio Relay League, 1994—. Recipient Communicators award/Merit cert. Women in Comm., 1993. Mem. Am. Soc. Bus. Press Editors (1st Place/Editl. Ctrl. Region Competition award 1994), Am. Inst. Wine & Food, Am. Radio Relay League, Internat. Foodservice Editl. Coun. (bd. dirs. 1994-95, pres. 1996), Soc. Profl. Journalists, Poets' League Greater Cleve., Women's Foodservice Forum.

BELLAMY, JOAN ELIZABETH, psychologist, consultant; b. Hutchinson, Kans., Jan. 20, 1935; d. Portel Arthur and Elizabeth S. (Linscheid) Guyer; m. Bruce M. Bellamy, 1957; children: Portel, Ruth E., Jennifer, John J. BS, Kans. State U., 1957; MS, U. Kans., 1971; EdS in Marriage and Family Therapy, Wichita State U., 1981; PhD, Massey U., Palmerston North, New Zealand, 1990. Cert. marriage and family therapist. Tchr. U.S. Dept. Edn. Group, Croix Chapeau, France, 1959-62; counselor human rels. pub. schs. Arlington, Va., 1967-76; psychologist Mental Health Ctr., Hutchinson, 1977-81, Taranaki Base Hosp., New Plymouth, New Zealand, 1982-85, Taranaki Psychology, New Plymouth, 1984-87; assoc. prof. Laredo (Tex.) State U., 1987-89; psychologist Horizons Mental Health Ctr., Hutchinson, 1989-90, Alder Psychology, Hutchinson, 1989—; coord. peer counseling USD 308, Hutchinson, 1990—; exec. dir. drug and alcohol treatment program Skylights, Inc., Hutchinson; exec. dir. Skylights Drug and Alcohol Treatment Facility, Hutchinson, 1993-94; presenter S.W. Psychol. Conf., Austin, 1992. Author: Stress in Families, 1989; mem. editorial staff Crisis Intervention pamphlet, 1990. Pres. bd. dirs. Unitarian Ch. Group, Hutchinson, 1989-92; bd. dirs. Heritage Festival, Hutchinson, 1990; pres. parents inc. Twin Oaks Boys Home, Hutchinson, 1991-92; sponsor Octagon Club of Hutchinson High Sch., 1991-92; mem. AIDS Task Force of Reno County. Kans. State Div. Drug and Alcohol grantee, 1990, United Meth. Health Min. grantee, 1992; recipient Mental Health Contbn. award State Mental Health Assn., 1991. Mem. APA, Am. Assn. Marriage and Family Therapists, Nat. Peer Helpers Assn., Kans. Peer Helpers Assn. (pres. 1991-92), Optimist Club of Hutchinson, Phi Delta Kappa, Delta Kappa Gamma. Mem. Unitarian Ch. Home: 100 E 12th Ave Hutchinson KS 67501-1421 Office: Skylights Inc 5 E 14th Ave Hutchinson KS 67502

BELLE, ALBERT JOJUAN, professional baseball player; b. Shreveport, La., Aug. 25, 1966. Student, La. State U. With Cleve. Indians, 1987—. Player Am. League All-Star Game, 1993-96; ranked 1st in Am. League for runs batted in, 1993; named to Am. League Silver Slugger Team, 1993-95, Sporting News Am. League All-Star Team, 1993-94; named Player of Yr. Sporting News, 1995. Office: Cleve Indians Jacobs Field 2401 Ontario St Cleveland OH 44115-4003*

BELLER, DOUG, engineering manager; b. Muncie, Ind., Jan. 17, 1952; s. Clarence L. and Marjorie E. Beller; children: Christopher A., Brandon D. Student, Ind. Vocat.-Tech. Coll., South Bend, Ind. U., South Bend, Ancilla Coll. Engring. mgr. Fulton Industries, Inc., Rochester, Ind., 1978-84, 88—, Kingston Products, Kokomo, Ind., 1984-88. Big br. Big Bros./Big Sisters, Rochetser, 1994—. With U.S. Army, 1971-72. Mem. Soc. Mfg. Engrs., Elks. Office: Fulton Industries Inc PO Box 290 Rochester IN 46975-0290

BELLER, LUANNE EVELYN, accountant; b. Ft. Dodge, Iowa, Feb. 5, 1950; d. Gerald L. and Evelyn E. (Liston) Heyl; m. Stephen M. Beller, June 28, 1970; children: Clancy D., Corby L. BA, Oreg. State U., 1977; MBA, Rochester Inst. Tech., 1981. CPA, Ill. Plant acct. DuBois Plastic Products, Avon, N.Y., 1977-79; coll. acct. SUNY, Geneseo, 1979-81; gen. acctg. supr. M&M/Mars, Inc., Cleveland, Tenn., 1981-83, Hackettstown, N.J., 1983-84; sales rep. M&M/Mars, Inc., Jacksonville, Ill., 1984-86, terr. sales supr., 1986-88; gen. acctg. coord. Kal Kan Foods, Inc., Columbus, Ohio, 1988-90, fin. info. coord., 1990-92, gen. acctg. supr., 1992—. Vol. Girl Scouts Am., Jacksonville, 1985-88, Bexley, Ohio, 1988—; mem. edn. com., mem. sound control com. Bexley United Meth. Ch., 1989—. Mem. Phi Kappa Phi, Beta Gamma Sigma, Beta Alpha Psi. Democrat.

BELLER, STEPHEN MARK, university administrator; b. Chgo., Aug. 14, 1948; s. I.E. and De Vera (Jameson) B.; m. Luanne Evelyn Heyl, June 28, 1970; children: Clancy Dee, Corby Lu. BS, U. Ill., 1970; MS, Western Ill. U., 1972; PhD, Oregon State U., 1977. Asst. head ed. Awards of Rotary Found., Evanston, Ill., 1972-73; asst. dean of students SUNY, Geneseo, N.Y., 1977-81; dean of student svcs. Tenn. Wesleyan Coll., Athens, 1981-83, MacMurray Coll., Jacksonville, Ill., 1984-88, Capital U., Columbus, Ohio, 1988—. Mem. Nat. Assn. Student Pers. Adminstrs., Am. Coll. Personnel Assn., Assn. of Student Jud. Affairs, Ohio Coll. Pers. Assn., Phi Kappa Phi, Phi Delta Kappa. Methodist. Home: 2474 Seneca Park Pl Bexley OH 43209 Office: Capital U 2199 E Main St Columbus OH 43209

BELLES, CHRISTINE FUGIEL, office administration educator; b. Hamtramck, Mich., Sept. 6, 1945; d. Ted and Theresa (Ellman) Fugiel; m. Duane Allen Belles, Aug. 10, 1973; children: Douglas, Michael. BA, Mich. State U., 1967, MA, 1970. Clk. Warren Schs. Credit Union, Centerline, Mich., 1963; sec. to dean of students Mich. State U., East Lansing, 1964-67, Consumers Power Co., East Detroit, 1964-65; key punch oper. Fisher Body div. GMC, Warren, Mich., 1966, sec., 1967, 69; legal sec. Rollins, Genser and White, Detroit, 1974; tchr. Lakeview High Sch., St. Clair Shores, Mich., 1967-73; prof. bus. info. sys. Macomb Community Coll., Warren, 1973—, cert. profl. sec., 1974—, prof. bus. info. syss.; exam. proctor Profl. Secs. Internat., 1983-89. Recipient Excellence in Teaching award, 1993. Mem. Nat. Bus. Edn. Assn., Delta Pi Epsilon, Pi Omega Pi. Office: Macomb Community Coll 14500 E 12 Mile Rd Warren MI 48093-3870

BELLOW, SAUL C., writer; b. Lachine, Que., Can., June 10, 1915; s. Abraham and Liza (Gordin) B.; m. Anita Goshkin, 1937 (div.); 1 child, Gregory; m. Alexandra Tschacbasov, 1956 (div); 1 child, Adam; m. Susan Glassman, 1961 (div.); 1 child, Daniel; m. Alexandra Ionesco Tuleca, 1974 (div.); m. Janis Freedman, Sept., 1989. Student, U. Chgo., 1933-35; BS, Northwestern U., 1937, LittD, 1962; LittD, Bard Coll., 1962, NYU, 1970, Harvard U., 1972, Yale U., 1972, McGill U., 1973, Brandeis U., 1974, Hebrew Union Coll.-Jewish Inst. Religion, 1976, Trinity Coll., Dublin, Ireland, 1976. Instr. Pestalozzi-Froebel Tchrs. Coll., Chgo., 1938-42; mem. editl. dept. "Great Books" project Ency. Brit., Inc., Chgo., 1943-46; mem. English dept. U. Minn., Mpls., 1946, asst. prof., 1948-49, assoc. prof. English, 1954-59; vis. lectr. NYU, 1950-52; creative writing fellow Princeton (N.J.) U., 1952-53; faculty mem. Bard Coll., Annandale-on-Hudson, N.Y., 1953-54; vis. prof. English U. P.R., Rio Piedras, 1961; celebrity in residence U. Chgo., 1962, Grunier Disting. Svcs. prof., 1962—, mem. com. on social thought, 1962—, chmn. com. on social thought, 1970-76; Tanner lectr. Oxford U., Romanes lectr., 1990. Author: (novels) Dangling Man, 1944, The Victim, 1947, The Adventures of Augie March, 1953 (Nat. Book award 1954), Seize the Day, 1956, Henderson the Rain King, 1959, Herzog, 1964 (Prix Internat. de Litterature 1965, Nat. Book award 1964, Soc. Midland Authors Fiction award 1976), Mr. Sammler's Planet, 1970 (Nat. Book award 1970), Humboldt's Gift, 1975 (Pulitzer prize for fiction 1976), The Dean's December, 1982, More Die of Heartbreak, 1986, A Theft, 1989, The Bellarosa Connection, 1989, It All Adds Up: From the Dim Past to the Uncertain Future, 1994; (short stories) Mosby's Memoirs, and Other Stories, 1968, Him with His Foot in His Mouth, and Other Stories, 1984, Something to Remember Me By: Three Tales, 1991, Occasional Pieces, 1993; (plays) The Wrecker, 1954, The Last Analysis, 1964, Under the Weather, 1966; (autobiography) To Jerusalem and Back: A Personal Account, 1976; contbr. fiction to Esquire and lit. quars.; criticisms appear in New Leader, others; short story to Atlantic's 125th Anniversary Edit., 1982. Decorated Croix de Chevalier, France, 1968, Comdr. Legion of Honour, France, 1983, Comdr. Order of Arts and Letters, France, 1985; Guggenheim fellow, 1948, Neil Gunn Internat. fellow, 1977; Nat. Inst. Arts and Letters grantee, 1952, Ford Found. grantee, 1959-61; recipient O. Henry prize for The Gonzaga Manuscripts, 1956, for A Silver Dish, 1980, Friends of Lit. Fiction award, 1960, James L. Dow award, 1964, Jewish Heritage award B'nai B'rith, 1968, Formentor prize, 1970, Nobel prize for lit., 1976, Gold medal Am. Acad. Arts and Letters, 1977, Brandeis U. Creative Arts award, 1978, Medal of Honor for lit. Nat. Arts Club, 1978, Malaparte Lit. award, 1984, Premio Scanno Lit. award Italy, 1988, Nat. Medal of Arts, 1988, Lifetime Achievement award Nat. Book Award, 1990. Mem. Am. Acad. Arts and Scis. (Emerson-Thoreau medal 1977).

BELLUS, PETER A., engineer; b. Norwalk, Conn., Feb. 8, 1952. BS, Lehigh U., 1974; PhD in Chemistry, U. Ill., 1980. Rsch. specialist 3M Co., St. Paul, 1979-88; adv. engr. Westinghouse Electric, Minnetonka, Minn., 1988—. Patentee in field. Cub Scout den leader Boy Scouts Am., Eden Prairie, Minn., 1994—. Mem. SAMPE, Am. Chem. Soc. Office: Westinghouse Electric Co 10950 Bren Rd E Minnetonka MN 55343-4413

BELMONTE, FRANCES ROSE, pastoral studies educator; b. Bklyn., Nov. 30, 1941; d. Thomas Eugene and Dominica Anne (Chimento) B. BA, Siena Coll., 1967; MA, U. Dayton, 1971; PhD, Boston Coll., 1980. Internat. reciprocal clin. cert. in addictions counseling. Tchr. jr. and sr. h.s. Cath. schs., Memphis and Louisville, 1961-68; in-svc. for faculties 15 schs., Boston and N.Y., 1970-72; instr. grad. and undergrad. colls. and sems., Memphis and Boston, 1971-81; resident theologian Diocese of Memphis, 1975-81; assoc. grad. faculty Loyola U., Chgo., 1982-90; ind. provider addictions svcs. Chgo., 1986-92; asst. prof. pastoral studies Loyola U., Chgo., 1990—; cons. in addictions recovery Congregations of Women Religious Cath. Schs., 1981-90; cons. in prevention programs Cath. schs. Archdiocese of Chgo., 1985; cons. Vila Serena Treatment Ctrs., Rio de Janeiro and Sao Paulo, Brazil, 1989-93; theol. cons. to pres. Dominican Sisters, St. Catharine, Ky., 1980-84; clin. affiliate Cornel U. Employee Devel. Ctr., 1990—. Author: (study materials) Reconciliation, 1976; contbr. articles to mags. and jours.; weekly columnist, page editor: (newspaper) Common Sense, 1976-81. Bd. dirs., pres. Dehon House, Chgo., 1989-92, educator, counselor, 1987-91; bd. dirs. Nat. Coalition of Am. Nuns, 1983-85. Doctoral fellow Boston Coll., 1972-75; tchg. assistantship U. Dayton, 1969, 70. Mem. AAUW, Nat. Assn. Women in Cath. Higher Edn., Ill. Alcohol and Other Drug Profl. Assn., Am. Acad. Religion, Coll. Theology Soc. (convenor women and religion 1993—). Roman Catholic. Office: Loyola U Chgo Chicago IL 60626

BELOW, ROBERT CLAUDE, music educator; b. Louisville, Jan. 3, 1934; s. Claude M. and Rose (Hohmann) B.; m. Barbara Anne Rule, Dec. 27, 1955; children: Alison, Andrew. MusB, U. Louisville, 1954, MusM, 1958; konzertdiplom, Hochschule für Musik, Cologne, Germany, 1960. Asst. prof. U. Calif., Davis, 1958-64; prof. Lawrence U., Appleton, Wis., 1964-96, prof. emeritus, 1996—; pianist solo and concerto performances, U.S., Europe, Latin Am., 1952—. Composer mus. works, 1952—, music published Augsburg, Concordia, Nat. Cello Inst., Latham Music Enterprises; contbr. articles to profl. jours. With U.S. Army, 1955-57. Named U. Louisville Alumnus of Yr., 1993. Home: 1730 E Melody Ln Appleton WI 54915-8945 Office: Lawrence U PO Box 599 Appleton WI 54912-0599

BELTER, WESLEY R., state legislator; b. Fargo, N.D., Apr. 18, 1945; s. Wesley R. and Rachel (Dimmer) B.; m. Judy Grauman; children: Michael,

Matthew, Mark. BS, MS, N.D. State U., 1970. Farmer; mem. N.D. Ho. of Reps. from 22d dist., 1985—; mem. Fin. and Taxation Com. N.D. Ho. of Reps., chmn. Transp. Com. Mem. drug adv. bd. Leonard Sch. Major N.D. Air Nat. Guard. Mem. Am. Legion, N.D. Stockmen's Assn., Lions (pres.), Farm Bur. Republican. Address: 15287 47th St SE Leonard ND 58052*

BELTZ, GEORGE ALLEN, retired company executive; b. Oak Park, Ill., Feb. 15, 1933; d. George Heinrich and Helen (Allen) B.; m. Merry Belle Kercher, Oct. 14, 1955; children: Jennifer, Sharon, Gregory. BA, Lawrence U., 1954. Various mktg. positions Amoco, 1958-92; coord. jobber rels. Amoco, Chgo., 1992; v.p. program devel. Bunker & Bunker Corp., Waltham, Mass., 1993-95; ret., 1995. State del. Rep. Party, 1980. Capt. USAF, 1955-58. Home: 12985 Duner Point Ln Minocqua WI 54548

BELZ, MARK, lawyer; b. Marshalltown, Iowa, July 19, 1943; s. Max Victor and Jean (Franzenburg) B.; m. Linda Cole, July 24, 1965; children: Aaron Sanderson, Jane Evangelyn. BA, Covenant Coll., Lookout Mountain, Ga., 1965; JD, U. Iowa, Iowa City, 1970; MDiv, Covenant Theol. Sem., St. Louis, 1981. Bar: Iowa 1970, Mo. 1976. Ptnr. Rosenberger, Peterson, Conway & Belz, Muscatine, Iowa, 1970-72, Keyes & Crawford, Cedar Rapids, Iowa, 1972-78, Belz & Belz, St. Louis, 1983-87; prin. Belz & Beckemeier, P.C., St. Louis, 1987-94, Belz & Jones, P.C., Clayton, Mo., 1995—. Author: Suffer the Little Children, 1989. Bd. dirs. Westminster Acad., 1977-85, Covenant Coll., 1972-81, Cono Christian Sch., 1993—, Mercy H.S., 1995—; moderator Presbyn. Ch. Am., Atlanta, 1991-92, mem. standing jud. com., 1989—. Named Alumnus of Yr., Covenant Coll., 1989. Republican. Office: Belz & Jones PC 7777 Bonhomme Ave Ste 1710 Clayton MO 63105-1911

BEMBRIDGE, JOHN ANTHONY, newspaper editor; b. Halifax, N.s., Can., Aug. 12, 1937; s. John Thomas and Mary Elizabeth (Schneider) B.; m. Carolyn Elizabeth Naugle, Dec. 27, 1958; children: Anthony Adam, Joel Thomas. Reporter Halifax (N.S.) Herald, 1953-58; reporter London (Ont.) Free Press, Can., 1958, copy editor, copy desk chief, asst. mng. editor, 1958-89, mng. editor, 1989, exec. editor, 1992—. Office: The London Free Press, 369 York St, London, ON Canada N6A 4G1*

BENDER, DARRELL G., state legislator. Former mayor; senator S.D. State Senate Dist. 23, mem. appropriations and legis. procedure coms. Home: 1509 Kennedy Memorial Dr Mobridge SD 57601-1020*

BENDER, JANET PINES, artist; b. Chgo., June 14, 1934; d. Nathan and Hana (Leff) Pines; m. Irwin Robert Bender, Feb. 25, 1966. BS, U. Wis., 1955; MA, Northwestern U., 1956; postgrad., U. Ill./Loyola U., Chgo., 1955-56, Tyler Sch. Fine Arts, Phila., 1957. One-woman shows include One Ill. Ctr., Chgo., 1979, 87, Olive Hyde Gallery, Fremont, Calif., 1980, 81, N.A.M.E. Gallery, Chgo., 1982, W.A.R.M. Gallery, Mpls., 1984, A.R.C. Gallery, Chgo., 1985, 87, 89, 94, 96, R.H. Love Galleries, Chgo., 1989, 92, Soho 20 Gallery, N.Y.C., 1990, Galerie Thea Fischer-Reinhardt, West Berlin, Germany, 1990. R.H. Love Contemporary Gallery, Chgo., 1992, 96; exhibited in group shows at Mus. Sci. & Industry, Chgo., 1995, Gallery 750, Sacramento, 1996, Women's Nat. Art Gallery, Washington, 1995, Rockford (Ill.) Art Mus., 1994, U. Wis. Art Gallery, Madison, Amos Enos Gallery, N.Y.C., 1993, Tonali Gallery, Mexico City, 1992, Renaissance Soc., Chgo., 1986, Ill. State Mus., 1983, 72nd Newport (R.I.) Nat. Exhbn., 1983, Chautauqua Nat. Exhbn., 1981, Zolla Leiberman Gallery, Chgo., 1980; represented in permanent collections at Young & Rubicam, Chgo., Brown-Forman Corp., Louisville, Nugent Wenckus Corp., Chgo., Louis Zahn Drug Co., Melrose Park, Ill, Fuller Comml. Brokerage Co., Chgo., Dynamark Inc., Chgo., Aabott Distbn., Miami, Art Beasley Inc., San Diego, Siegel, Denberg, Vanasco, Shivkovsky, Moses and Shoenstadt, Chgo., Altschuler, Melvoin & Glassner, Chgo., Shafer, Meltzer & Lewis Assocs., Wilmette, Ill., Schiff, Hardin & Waite, Chgo. Bd. dirs. A.R.C. Gallery, Chgo., 1984—; juror IAFA Awards, 1993. Recipient Ill. Arts Coun. Project Completion grants, 1979, 81-82, Visual Arts Fellowship grant Ill. Arts Coun., 1983; fellow Northwestern U., 1955-56. Mem. NAFE, Women's Caucus for Art, Mus. Contemporary Art, Art Inst. Chgo., Chgo. Artist Coalition, Ill. Arts Alliance, Mus. Modern Art (N.Y.), Met. Mus. Art (N.Y.), Coll. Art Assn., Peace Mus., Ill. State Gallery, Com. for Artist Rights (organizing com. 1988), Oriental Art Soc., Siam House, Pi Lambda. Studio: 2001 N Elston Ave Chicago IL 60614-3901

BENDER, JOHN CHARLES, library director; b. Williamsport, Pa., June 15, 1937; s. John Henry and Loraine Emily (Mathies) B.; m. Jane Ellen Hoose, June 25, 1966; children: Laura Ann, Megan Jane, Heather Marie, John Garth. BA, Maryknoll Coll., Glen Ellyn, Ill., 1960; MLS, Cath. U., 1965. Libr. adult svcs. Akron-Summit County Pub. Libr., Akron, 1965-68, head info. dept., 1968-70; dir. Salem (Ohio) Pub. Libr., 1970-73, Taylor Meml. Pub. Libr., Cuyahoga Falls, Ohio, 1973—; pres. Young Librs. Assn., Akron, 1967; mem. Libr. Tech. Bd. Akron U., 1985-90. Mem. Ohio Libr. Coun. (chmn. various coms. 1965—), C. of C., Cuyahoga Falls (pres. 1977, Citizen of Yr. 1979), Kiwanis Internat. (pres. ctrl. Cuyahoga Falls Chpt 1978, lt. gov. Ohio 1982, Disting. lt. gov. 1983). Roman Catholic. Office: Taylor Meml Pub Libr 2015 3rd St Cuyahoga Falls OH 44221

BENDER, JOHN R., state legislator; b. Pitts., Dec. 14, 1938; s. John R. and Ruth (Brown) B.; m. Cookie Bender, 1963 (dec. Dec. 12, 1993); children: Jay, Jennifer. BS, U. Pitts., 1960, MA, 1962, PhD in Higher Edn., 1969. Dir. residence halls, 1960-61, 63-65; admissions asst. Pa. State U., 1961-62; adminstr. Ohio Ho. of Reps., Columbus, 1960-87; counselor Lorain County C. C., 1970-87; outreach counselor, 1987-93; mem. Ohio Ho. of Reps. Columbus, 1993—. Mem. Elyria (Ohio) City Coun., 1984-89, 91-93, Elyria Planning Commn., 1984, Health Svc. Agy., 1991-92; bd. dirs. Lorain Internat. Assn.; mem. Lorain County Sr. Citizens Bd. Named Treas. of Yr., Nat. Assn. Campus Activities, 1984, 87, Nat. Environ. award Izaak Walton League, 1988. Mem. Western Res. Civil War Round Table, Urban League, Lorain County C. of C., KC, Phi Delta Kappa (Hall of Fame award 1988), Omicron Delta Kappa, Sigma Chi. Democrat. Home: 645 Georgetown Ave Elyria OH 44035-3051*

BENDER, LARRY WAYNE, vocational educator; b. Indpls., May 23, 1942; s. Wayne Crawford and Margaret Dell (Ramer) B.; m. Barbara Agnes Kroll, Aug. 26, 1967; children: Anissa Gayle, Timothy Alan. BS in Indsl. Edn., Purdue U., 1967, MS in Indsl. Edn., 1972. Tchr. South Newton Sch. Corp., Kentland, Ind., 1967-81; tchr. tech. edn. Franklin (Ind.) Community Schs., 1981—. Mem. Internat. Tech. Edn. Assn. (Outstanding Program of Yr. award 1987), Tech. Educators of Ind. (Meritorious Tchr. award 1987), Transformations Project. Episcopalian. Home: 4215 N Graham Rd Whiteland IN 46184-9732 Office: Custer Baker Middle Sch 101 West St Rd 44 Franklin IN 46131-1659

BENDER, ROBERT KEITH, actuary; b. Chgo., May 28, 1947; s. David Greg and Mildred Leone (Fredricks) B.; m. Virginia Best, July 19, 1969; children: Victoria Ruth, Christopher Keith. BS in Physics, No. Ill. U., 1969; MS in Physics, U. Ill., Chgo., 1971, PhD in Physics, 1976. Cert. secondary sch. tchr., Ill. Grad. tchg. asst. U. Ill., Chgo., 1970-75; math./sci. tchr. Prospect H.S., Mount Prospect, Ill., 1975-80; with actuarial dept. Lumbermen's Mut. Casualty Co., Long Grove, Ill., 1980-92; asst. actuary Kemper Reins. Co., Long Grove, 1992—. Contbr. articles to profl. jours. Deacon Hickory Hills (Ill.) Presbyn. Ch., 1970-73. Fellow Casualty Actuarial Soc. (mem. com. on rev. of papers 1991—, mem. actuarial exam. com. 1991-92); mem. Am. Acad. Actuaries, Am. Assn. Physics Tchrs. Home: 411 W Hackberry Dr Arlington Heights IL 60004

BENDER, VIRGINIA BEST, computer science educator; b. Rockford, Ill., Feb. 10, 1945; d. Oscar Sheldon and Genevieve Best; m. Robert Keith Bender, July 19, 1969; children: Victoria Ruth, Christopher Keith. BS in Chemistry, Math., No. Ill. U., 1967; postgrad., U. of Ill. Coll. of Med., 1967-69; MBA, Loyola U., Chgo., 1973. Cert. computer profl. Sr. systems rep. Burroughs Corp., Chgo., 1969-73; systems analyst Marshall Field & Co., Chgo., 1973-74; project leader Fed. Home Loan Bank, Chgo., 1974-76; sr. systems analyst United Air Lines, Elk Grove Village, Ill., 1976-78; supr. Kemper Group, Long Grove, Ill., 1978-82; prof. computer info. sys., coord. computer info. sys. William Rainey Harper Coll., Palatine, Ill., 1982—; spkr. Midwest Computer Conf., DeKalb, Ill., 1988, moderator, 1991; exch. prof. Maricopa C.C., Mesa, Ariz., 1990, rsch. sabbatical, 1993; spkr. conf. info. tech. League for Innovation, Kansas City, Mo., 1995; steering com. Midwest Computer Conf., 1995—. Nation chief YMCA mother-dau. group Indian Maidens, Des Plaines, 1982-83. Named Tchr. of the Month Burroughs Corp., Chgo, 1972. Mem. Inst. Certification Computer Profls. (life), Ill. Assn. of Data Processing Instrs., No. Ill. Computer Soc., Bay Area Multimedia Coll. Consortium, No. Ill. Alumni Assn. (life). Methodist. Home: 411 W Hackberry Dr Arlington Heights IL 60004-1938 Office: William Rainey Harper Coll 1200 W Algonquin Rd Palatine IL 60067-7373

BENEDEK, JOHN JOSEPH, accountant, city official; b. Chgo., Aug. 13, 1949; s. Julius Benedek and Margaret Mary (Mahoney) O'Connor. BS, Ill. Inst. Tech., 1971. Jr., then sr. clk. Chgo. Bd. Edn., summers 1968-70; spl. svc. teller Highland Community Bank, Chgo., 1971-72; sr. clk. Compt.'s Office, Compt.'s Office City of Chgo., 1972-73; acct. technician City of Chgo., 1973; acct. I Compt.'s Office City of Chgo., 1973-80; acct. II water collection divsn. City of Chgo., 1980-81, acct. III water collection divsn., 1981-93, acct. IV water collection divsn., 1993—. Mem. 13th Ward Dem. Orgn., Chgo., 1971—; instr. swimming, lifeguarding, CPR and standard first aid ARC. Recipient ARC Cert. of Recognition for extraordinary personal action, 1992. Mem. Hon. Order Ky. Cols., Cath. Alumni Clubs Internat. (treas. 1980-82, v.p. midwest region 1985-87, 2d v.p. 1987-88, 1st v.p. 1988-89, pres. 1989-90), Cath. Alumni Club Chgo. (v.p. 1977, 78, 79, treas. 1983-84, pres. 1985, 93, Cath. Alumni Clubber of Yr. award 1983, 85, Leo H.S. Alumni v.p. 1996-97).

BENESH, JAMES L., manufacturing engineer; b. Springfield, Minn., Oct. 12, 1955. AS, Winona, Minn., 1986. Tool maker Winona Corp., 1977-86, mfg. engr., 1986-92; mfg. engr. Dumore Corp., Mauston, Wis., 1992—. With USMC, 1974-76. Office: Dumore Corp 1030 Veterans St Mauston WI 53948-9314

BENFORD, ROSA WRIGHT, special education administrator; b. Belvedere, S.C., Aug. 8, 1945; d. Charlie and Alice (Robinson) Wright; divorced; children: D'Artagnan Dordain C., D'Angelice R. BA, Morris Coll., 1970; MEd, Marygrove Coll., 1986. Cert. elem. tchr., learning disabilities tchr. cons., supervisor spl. edn. 7th grade tchr. River Rouge (Mich.) Bd. Edn., 1970-71, relief tchr., 1971-72, 6th grade tchr., 1973-74, pre-sch. tchr., 1974-75, 3rd and 4th grade tchr., 1975-82, 2nd and 3rd grade tchr., 1983-84, learning disabilities resource room tchr., 1984-86, learning specialist, 1987-91, academic specialist, 1991-93, supr. spl. edn., 1993—; sec. River Rouge Edn. Assn., 1987-92; mem. Youth Assistance Program, River Rouge, 1988—. corr. sec. UCRR, River Rouge, 1994, camp dir., summer 1994; mem. NAACP, River Rouge, 1994. Grantee River Rouge Fed. Grant, 1992. Baptist. Home: 267 Beechwood River Rouge MI 48218 Office: River Rouge Bd Edn 1411 Coolidge River Rouge MI 48218

BENGHIAT, RUSSELL, advertising agency executive; b. N.Y.C., July 10, 1948; s. Isaac and Pearl (Feld) B.; m. Nancy Felman, Nov. 8, 1987; children: Joshua Laurence, Gabriel William. BA in English Lit., Swarthmore Coll., 1970; MS in Advt., U. Ill., 1972. Copywriter Kight, Cowman, Abram, Columbus, Ohio, 1972-73; assoc. creative dir. Johnson & Dean, Grand Rapids, Mich., 1973-76; mktg. analyst FTC, Cleve., 1976-81; v.p. Nicholes & Benghiat Advt., Cleve., 1981-83; pres. Benghiat Advt. and Mktg., Inc., Cleve., 1983—. Pres. bd. dirs. Cleve. Dancers, 1983; del. Dem. Nat. Convention, San Francisco, 1984. Recipient Nat. Addy award Am. Advt. Fedn., 1974. Mem. Greater Cleve. Growth Assn. (com. chmn., COSE Vol. of Month 1989). Office: 3628 Walnut Hills Ave Ste 200 Cleveland OH 44122-4484

BENHAM, LELIA, small business owner, social/political activist; b. Cartersville, Ga., July 15, 1945; d. Emory and Nellie Pearl (Carson) Benham; m. Larry L. Mabins, Jan. 15, 1966 (div. 1970); children: Gary K., Margo L., Berrie E. Student, North Cen. Tech. Coll., Mansfield, Ohio, 1981-83, 91—, Mansfield Bus. Coll., 1964-66, 84-85. Bookkeeper/sec. M-R-M Cmty. Action Program, 1970-72; with The Tappan Co., 1972-81; sec./bookkeeper daycare ctr. Mansfield Opportunities Industrialization Ctr., 1983-84; office svcs. contractor FSC Ednl., Inc., Mansfield, 1988-89; sales asst. Hill's Dept. Store, Mansfield, 1988-90; pres./dir. Benham & Co., Mansfield, 1988—; ind. sales distbr. Shaklee Products, 1985-86; home health habilitation aide, waiver/supportive living provider Ohio Dept. Mental Retardation and Developmentally Disabled, 1992—, Richland Newhope Ctr., Mansfield, 1992—; nurse asst. Mansfield Meml. Geriatric Ctr., 1994; nat. and internat. cons. in field. Editor Richland NOW News, 1985-87, 91-92. Cand. Mansfield Sch. Bd. and City Coun., 1987, 89, 91; founding mem. adv. bd., bd. dirs. Litter Prevention and Recycling/KAB (Mid-Ohio Clean Scene), 1982-96; v.p., founding treas. Sister Cities Assn., Mansfield, 1986-94; active various charitable orgns.; mem. Ohio Women Inc.; bd. dirs. Canton Regional Transit Authority, 1989-96, Cleve. Sch. Bd., 1989-93, Ohio Dept. Adminstrv. Svcs. Minority Bus. Enterprise, 1989-96, others; adv. bd. mem. Keep Yourself Alive, 1992, 93. Recipient 10 billboard advt. awards Cleve. Regional Transit Authority Community Minority Taskforce, 1991, Keeper of the Flame Proclamation award Ohio Sec. of State, 1990, award AFrican Am. Women Agenda of Ohio,. 1991, others. Mem. NOW (Richland County founder, pres. 1985-96, Scholarship award 1987, task force chair state bd. racial and ethnic diversity 1993—), NAACP (Ohio rep. to state orgns. 1989—, Pres.'s award 1982, Cmty. award 1988). Democrat. Ch. of God in Christ. Home and Office: Benham & Co 166 Western Ave Mansfield OH 44906

BENINSON, JOSEPH, dermatologist; b. Bklyn., Apr. 17, 1918; s. Isadore and Ida (Kopalof) B.; m. Eleanor Stolmack, 1946 (dec. Mar. 1966); children: Maureen Elena, Ellen Lynn, Ilene Lee, Fern Alison; m. Evelyne Marte Holschauer, July 17, 1977; children: Jonathan Adam Mathew, Jennifer Alexandra. BS in Zoology, Tex. A&M, 1944, DVM, 1947; MD, U. Tex., 1951. Diplomate Am. Bd. Dermatology. Resident in dermatology U. Tex. Sch. Medicine, 1952-53; resident in dermatology Henry Ford Hosp., 1953-55, assoc. in dermatology, 1955—; clin. assoc. prof. dept. dermatology U. Mich. Med. Sch., 1978—; dir. Leg Ulcer Clinic, Henry Ford Hosp., Dermatology Peripheral Vascular Sect., physician advisor; lectr., speaker in field. Contbg. author to books; mem. editl. bd. Angiology, Vascular Medicine, Internat. Coll. Angiology, Jour. of Disability; contbr. over 75 articles to profl. jours. Achievements include research in the field of angiology in pressure gradient therapy. Served with USAF, 1942-46. Recipient Golden Eagle award The Coun. on Internat. Non-theatrical Events, 1979, grants NIH, 1985-86, 87-88; Nat. Pres.'s award Am. Coll. Angiology, 1989. Mem. AMA, Am. Acad. Dermatology, Soc. Investigative Dermatology, Mich. Dermatol. Soc., Am. Coll. Angiology (v.p.), Brazilian Coll. Angiology (hon.), Wayne County Med. Soc., Internat. Soc. Lymphology (Nat. Pres.'s award 1984), N.Am. Soc. Lymphology, Internat. Coll. Angiology (hon., v.p.), Henry Ford Hosp. Med. Assn. (Disting. Career award 1990). Home: 975 Stuyvessant Rd Bloomfield Hills MI 48301 Office: Henry Ford Hosp Dept Dermatology 2799 W Grand Blvd Detroit MI 48202

BENJAMIN, ANN WOMER, state legislator; m. to David M. Benjamin; children: Katherine, Johanna. BA magna cum laude, Vandberbilt U., 1975; JD, Case Western Reserve U., 1978. Bar: Ohio. Assoc. Arter & Hadden, Cleve.; mem. Ohio Ho. Reps., Columbus; adj. prof. law Case Western Reserve U., Cleve. Producer: Aurora (Ohio) Comty. Theatre; contbr. articles to Estate Planning. Trustee, advocate Broadway Sch. Music and Arts; former chmn. Aurora (Ohio) Civil Svc. Commn. Mem. Ohio Bar Assn., Cleve. Bar Assn., Portage County Bar Assn., Phi Beta Kappa. Office: Ohio Ho Reps Ohio State Bldg. Columbus OH 43215

BENJAMIN, JANICE YUKON, small business owner; b. Kansas City, Mo., Aug. 12, 1951; d. Stanley and Frances (Weneck) Yukon; m. Bert Lyon Benjamin, June 14, 1975; children: Brett David, Blair Yukon. AS, Bradford Coll., 1971; BA, Newcomb Coll., 1973; MA, U. Mo., 1978. Tchr. secondary, dept. chmn. Shawnee Mission (Kans.) Sch. Dist., 1973-80; career counselor Career Mgmt. Ctr., Kansas City, 1980-82, pres., owner, 1982—; ptnr. Career Mgmt. Press, Kansas City, 1983—, The MBL Human Resources Cons. Group, 1989-91. Contbr. articles to profl. jours.; co-author career planning book. Bd. dirs. Cmty. Jr. League, Kansas City, 1988-89, v.p., 1989-90, pres.-elect, 1990-91, pres., 1991-92; bd. dirs. Menorah Med. Ctr., Kansas City, 1995—, Menorah Med. Ctr. Aux., 1984— (auditor, 1990-92, v.p., 1994-96), Women's Found. Greater Kansas City, 1991-96 (chmn. bd. dev., 1993-95), Kansas City Friends of Alvin Ailey, 1992-94 (co-chmn. planning com. adv. bd., 1994—), Ctrl. Exch., Kansas City, 1988-90; mem. adv. bd. women's coun. U. Mo. Kansas City, 1988-89; initiator, sponsor Kansas City Youth Vol. Svc. awards United Way, 1989-90, adv. com. Heart of Am. United Way, 1994—; mem. Promise Project Steering Com., Kansas City Consensus, 1994—, co-chmn. Youth Declaration. Recipient Miss T.E.E.N. Encouraging Excellence award, 1990; named One of 25 Up and Comers award Jr. Achievement of Mid. Am., 1994. Mem. Am. Counseling Assn., Heart of Am. Relocation Coun. (bd. dirs.), K.C. Employment Mgrs. Assn. Republican. Jewish. Office: Career Mgmt Ctr 8301 State Line Rd # 202 Kansas City MO 64114-2019

BENLON, LISA L., state legislator; b. July 9, 1953; m. Randal, July 9, 1953; 2 children. Student, Johnson County C.C. Councilman City of Shawnee, 1988-91; rep. dist. 17 State of Kans., 1991—; mgr. acctg. office. Home: 7303 Earnshaw St Shawnee KS 66216-3505 Office: Kans Ho of Reps State Capitol Topeka KS 66612

BENNANE, MICHAEL J., state legislator; b. Detroit, Jan. 27, 1945; s. John M. and Harriet (Fortner) B.; m. Julie Ann Potter, 1968 (div.). BA, Wayne State U., 1970. State rep. Mich. Ho. Reps., Dist. 1, 1977-94, Mich. Ho. Reps., Dist. 14, 1995—; assoc. spkr. pro tem., 1985-88, chmn. pub. health com., mem. judiciary & labor, taxation & housing & urban affairs coms., Mich. Ho. Reps.; tchr. Christ the King Sch., Detroit, 1968-69; tchr., footbal lcoach St. Agatha H.S., 1969-74; ins. estate planner N.Am. Life Assurance Co., 1975-76. transp. coord. Kennedy for Pres., 1972; state press. coord. McGovern for Pres., 1972; field coord. Reuther for Cong., 1974; mem. Emerson Cmty Homwowners Orgn., 17th Dist. Dems., Northwest Cmty. Orgn. Recipient Coach of Yr. award, Detroit News, 1969. Mem. NAACP, Common Cause. Home: 23750 Fenkell St # B116 Detroit MI 48223-1482*

BENNETT, ARLIE JOYCE, clinical social worker; b. Central Lake, Mich., Nov. 22, 1921; d. Charles Herbert and Bernice Evelyn (Miller) B. Student, Alma (Mich.) Coll., 1946-48; BA, U. Mich., 1950, MSW, 1955. Cert. social worker, Mich.; diplomate Am. Bd. Examiners in Clin. Social Work. Social worker Ypsilanti (Mich.) State Hosp., 1950-54; staff social worker Kalamazoo Child Guidance Clinic, 1955-67, chief social worker, 1967-71; clin. social worker State Tech. Inst. Rehab. Ctr., Plainwell, Mich., 1971-90; pvt. practice, Kalamazoo, 1991-92; field instr. Western Mich. U. Sch. Social Work, Kalamazoo, 1971-90. Author: Pie Is in the Eye of the Beholder, 1980, War and Memory, 1991; also articles. Bd. dirs. Youth Opportunities Unltd., Kalamazoo, 1968—. Tech. sgt. WAC, AUS, 1944-46, ETO. Mem. NASW (past chmn. and officer), AAUW (legis. chmn. Kalamazoo br. 1985-89, 93-95, pres. 1991-93), Acad. Cert. Social Workers, Mensa (local coord. 1990—), Loners Am. (pres. Mich. chpt. 1990-92), U. Mich. Alumnae Club (past pres. and officer). Home: 1110 W Maple St Kalamazoo MI 49008-1846 Office: Crosstown Counselling Ctr 1223 S Park St Kalamazoo MI 49001-5607

BENNETT, BRUCE W., construction company executive, civil engineer; b. St. Joseph, Mo., Dec. 24, 1930; s. Bruce W. and Laura Louella (Clark) B.; m. Barbara Gail Haase, July 26, 1957; children: Stacy Suzanne, Bruce W. B.S. in Civil Engring., U. So. Calif., 1954. Project mgr. George A. Fuller & Co., Chgo., 1956-61; contract mgr. Huber, Hunt & Nichols, Indpls., 1961-70, v.p., 1970-82, exec. v.p., 1982-84, pres., 1984-95, ret., 1995; pres. Hunt Corp., 1988-95, bd. dirs. Served to capt. USAF, 1954-57. Mem. Archimedes Circle, David Wilson Assocs., Newcomen Soc. Republican. Clubs: Indpls. Athletic, Skyline (Indpls.). Home: 8181 Horseshoe Bend Ln Las Vegas NV 89133 Address: 8181 Horseshoe Bend Ln Las Vegas NV 89113

BENNETT, CHARLOTTE ANNE, library director, educator; b. Washington, Feb. 21, 1946; d. Carl William and Maureen Eloise (Gustafson) Hannemann; m. Michael John Bennett, Aug. 31, 1968; children: Andrew Michael, Jacob Earl. AA, Montgomery Coll., Takoma Park, Md., 1967; BA in Psychology, Western Md. Coll., Westminster, 1968; student, U. Louisville, 1970, Ind. U., 1991-92. VISTA vol. Utah Migrant Coun., Salt Lake City, 1969-70; ESL instr. English Lang. Svcs., 1970-72; houseparent Ft. Wayne (Ind.) Children's Home, 1973-74; recruiter ACTION, Peace Corps, VISTA, Indpls., 1974-75; bank teller Springs Valley Bank, West Baden, Ind., 1976-78; 4-H program asst. Orange County Extension, Paoli, Ind., 1989-92; tchr. aide Paris (Ill.) Head Start, 1992-93; dir. Kansas (Ill.) Cmty. Meml. Libr., 1993—; ESL instr. Dist. 95 Schs., Paris, 1995—. Active Boy Scouts Am., various locations, 1986-94; v.p., sec., treas. PTA, French Lick, Ind., 1983-87; chair Cmty. Outreach Com., Paris, 1995—; Sunday sch. tchr. First Christian Ch., Paris, 1995—. Democrat. Office: Kansas Cmty Meml Libr PO Box 319 Kansas IL 61933

BENNETT, CHUCK WILLIAM, stockbroker; b. Grand Rapids, Mich., Sept. 1, 1942. BBA, Western Mich. U., Kalamazoo, 1964. Asst. v.p. investments Mich. Nat. Bank, Grand Rapids, 1965-72; stockbroker Roney & Co., Grand Rapids, 1972—. Chmn. bd. May Freebead Hosp. & Ctr. Rehab. Ctr., Grand Rapids, 1987—. With USAF Res., 1963-69. Office: Roney & Co 405 Water Bldg 161 Ottawa Ave NW Grand Rapids MI 49503-2701

BENNETT, CYNTHIA ANN FORSYTHE, software engineer; b. Lorain, Ohio, Nov. 16, 1963; d. Mark Edward and Mary Ann (Nöecker) Forsythe; m. John Anthony Bennett, Oct. 12, 1991; 1 child, Mary Ann. BS in Engring., Ohio State U., 1987. Programmer/analyst Univ. Systems, Columbus, Ohio, 1986-88; sr. engr. ABB-Impell Corp., Lincolnshire, Ill., 1988-91; prin. engr. Baxter Internat., Round Lake, Ill., 1991—. Patentee in field. Mem. IEEE, IEEE Computer Soc., Assn. for Computing Machinery. Roman Catholic. Office: Baxter Internat Rte 120 and Wilson Rd Round Lake IL 60073

BENNETT, DONALD CHARLES, JR., insurance and finance executive; b. Houston, Sept. 27, 1956. BBA, U. Wis., 1978; M in Mgmt., Northwestern U., 1993. CPA, Ill. Sr. auditor Arthur Andersen & Co., Chgo., 1978-81; asst. treas., asst. sec. Mark Controls Corp., Skokie, Ill., 1981-91; v.p., treas. Ednl. and Institutional Ins. Adminstrs. Inc., Chgo., 1991—. Treas. bd. dirs. Am. Youth Hostels, Chgo., 1990—. Mem. AICPA, Ill. CPA, Risk and Ins. Mgmt. Soc. Presbyterian. Office: Ednl and Instnl Admn Inc 10 S Riverside Plz Ste 1844 Chicago IL 60606-3801

BENNETT, ELIZABETH ANN, elementary education educator, music specialist; b. Toledo, Ohio, Apr. 16, 1967; d. David Lee and Barbara Catherine (Upp) B. B in music edn., U. Mich., 1989; M in music, Ark. State U., 1992. Sec., rep. Wiards Orchards, Ypsilanti, Mich., 1989; substitute tchr. Ann Arbor (Mich.) Pub. Schs., 1990; teaching asst. Ark. State U., Jonesboro, Ark., 1990-92; music tchr. Toledo Pub. Schs., 1992—; pres. Ark. State U. grad. coun., Jonesboro, 1991-92. Tchr. Worldwide Ch. of God, 1994—. Mem. Speech and Leadership Training Club (sec. 1994—). Home: 1046 Branleigh Dr Toledo OH 43612-1717

BENNETT, JON, state legislator. Mem. Ho. of Reps., Jefferson City. Republican.

BENNETT, LOREN, state legislator; b. Jan. 17, 1951. Grad., Schoolcraft Coll. Clk. Canton Twp., Mich.; senator Mich. State Dist. 8, 1995—; chmn. natural resources and environ. affairs com. Mich. State Senate, vice chair fin. svc. com., local, urban & state affairs com. Address: PO Box 30036 Lansing MI 48909-7536

BENNETT, MARGARET AIROLA, lawyer; b. San Francisco, July 20, 1950; d. Virgil Raymond and Caroline (Maccoun) Airola; m. Eugene Le Brun Bennett, Mar. 1, 1980; children: Scott, Brad, Elizabeth. AB cum laude, U. Calif., Berkeley, 1972; JD, U. San Francisco and Loyola U., 1976. Bar: Ill.1976, U.S. Dist. Ct. (no. dist.) Ill. 1977, U.S. Ct. Appeals (7th cir.) 1983. Intern Cook County State's Atty.'s Office, Chgo., 1975-76; assoc. Dunlap, Thompson & Boyd, Ltd., Libertyville, Ill., 1977-79; ptnr. Bennett & Bennett, Ltd., Oak Brook, Ill., 1980—; atty. rep. McDonald's Corp., Oak Brook, 1982—, County of DuPage, Wheaton, Ill., 1990-95. Counsel fo DuPage Ill. Fair and Exposition Authority, County of DuPage, 1991-95, co-chmn. next generation com.; mem. devel. coun. Good Samaritan Hosp., 1988-92. Mem. DuPage County Bar Assn. (chmn. real estate law com. 1994-95, Cert. of Appreciation 1989, chmn. profl. responsibility com. 1996—), Ill. State Bar Assn. (cert. of Appreciation 1990), Womens Bar Assn. DuPage County, Evang. Health Found. (bd. sponsors 1988-92). Republican. Roman

Catholic. Home: 11 Lochinvar Ln Oak Brook IL 60521-1612 Office: Bennett and Bennett Ltd 720 Enterprise Dr Hinsdale IL 60521

BENNETT, PAMELA GALE, computer scientist, knowledge engineer; b. L.A., Oct. 6, 1938; d. Jerome Laurence Ehrlich and Babette Virginia (Kline) Maples; m. Bennie Dale Bennett (div. Dec. 1988); children: Hilary Gale Bennett Graff, Heather Bennett Cibula. BA in Edn., Calif. State U., L.A., 1961; MA in Ednl. Philosophy, Calif. State U., Dominguez Hills, 1974; MS in Computer Sci., U. Oreg., 1987. Elem. sch. tchr. L.A. Sch. Dist., 1960-63; adult edn. tch. Torrance (Calif.) Unified Sch. Dist., 1966-68; pvt. sch. dir., owner The Learning Tree, Palos Verdes, Calif., 1969-79; pvt. sch. dir. Temple Beth Shalom, Santa Ana, Calif., 1980-81; part-time tchr. Josephine County Sch. Dist., Grants Pass, Oreg., 1982-83; sr. instr. Tandy Computer Ctrs., Eugene, Oreg., summer 1985; grad. teaching fellow U. Oreg., Eugene, 1984-87; computer scientist BDM, Dayton, Ohio, 1987-88; knowledge engr. EDS, Troy, Mich., 1989—; founder The Learning Tree Preschools, 1969. Contbr. articles to profl. jours. Founder Bapt. Athletic Fellowship, Palos Verdes, 1970; mem. Mich. Sr. Olympic Volleyball Team, 1995. Mem. Am. Sailing Inst., Spl. Interest Group in Artifical Intelligence. Home: 2735 W Avon Rd Rochester Hls MI 48309-2340 Office: EDS 750 Tower Dr MS-5321 Troy MI 48098

BENNETT, PAUL LEWIS, retired educator, writer; b. Gnadenhutten, Ohio, Jan. 10, 1921; s. John Emerson and Mary Eva (Gehring) B.; m. Martha Jeanne Leonhart, Dec. 31, 1941; children: Charles Kirby, William David. BA with highest honors, Ohio U., 1942; AM, Harvard U., 1947. Instr. Samuel Adams Sch. Social Studies, Boston, 1945-46, U. Maine, Orono, 1946-47; tchg. asst. Harvard U., Cambridge, Mass., 1945-46; from instr. to assoc. prof. Denison U., Granville, Ohio, 1947-86, Lorena Woodrow Burke prof. English, 1978-86, dir. writing program, 1953-82, chmn. English dept., 1957-60, poet-in-residence, 1986—; writing cons. Owens-Corning Fiberglas Corp., Newark, Ohio, 1957-60, Aerospace Labs., Granville, Ohio, 1964-67, Ohio Arts Coun., Columbus, 1978-81, Ohio Bd. Regents, Columbus, 1985-86; profl. gardener and orchardist, 1947-90. Author: (fiction) Robbery on the Highway, 1961, The Living Things, 1975, Follow the River, 1987, (poetry) A Strange Affinity, 1975, The Eye of Reason, 1976; contbr. articles to N.Y. Times Mag., Jour. Am. Folklore, others; film writer Russell R. Benson Prodns., Indpls., 1957-80. Lt. (j.g.) USNR, 1942-45. Writing fellow Nat. Endowment Arts, 1973-74; recipient Significant Achievement award Ohio U., Athens, 1992. Mem. AAUP, Phi Beta Kappa. Home: 1281 Burg St Granville OH 43023 Office: Denison U English Dept Granville OH 43023

BENNETT, RENÉE HOTARD, theology educator; b. New Orleans, July 11, 1942; d. Francis Hotard and Leonie (Evans) Galatoire; m. Kenneth John Bennett, Mar. 10, 1962; children: Marianne Bennett Droulia, Elizabeth Bennett Sheerin, Charles Evans. BA, Tulane U.; MA, St. Louis U., PhD, 1995. English lit. tchr. Metairie Park County Day Sch., 1962-66; adj. prof. theology St. Louis U., 1993—. Contbr. articles to profl. jours. Mem. Internat. Lit. Soc., Am. Soc. Church History, Tex. Medieval Assn., Theta Alpha Kappa (award for religious and theol. studies 1995). Roman Catholic. Office: St Louis U Dept Theol Study 221 N Grand Saint Louis MO 63103

BENNETT, RICHARD CARL, social worker; b. Eau Claire, Wis., July 25, 1933; s. Ira Anthony and Marion Rhoda (Johnson) B.; BA, Hamline U., St. Paul, 1955; MS, George Williams Coll., 1957; MS (Lou Hougttellian fellow, Am. Lutheran Ch. fellow), U. Chgo., 1962; postgrad. Loyola U., Chgo., Roosevelt U., Chgo., Forest Inst., Chgo., Coll. Fin. Planning, Denver, Columbia Pacific U., 1990—; grad. in computer sci. Nat. Radio Inst.,1985, grad. in computerized acctg., 1988; grad. Ind. Family Mediation Tng., 1992; PhD Clayton Sch, Birmingham, Ala.; Diplomate Am. Bd. of Examiners in Clin. Social Work. m. Patricia Ann Work, Oct. 27, 1972; children: Matthew, Elizabeth, Kimberly, Timothy. Caseworker, Rock County Welfare Dept., Janesville, Wis., 1957-61; area dir. Luth. Family Service Oreg., Eugene, 1962-67; exec. dir. Family Service Travelers Aid, Fort Worth, 1967-70; mgr. agy. ops. Tarrant County United Way, Fort Worth, 1970-73; mile coord. Hands Accross Am., 1986, coord. Porter County Share Food, 1986-87; exec. dir. Luth. Family Service N.W. Ind., Merrillville, 1973-80; exec. v.p. Listening Inc., 1979—; exec. dir. Inst. for Family Life Porter County, 1982-93; CEO Environtech, 1988-94; cons. Ind. sentencing; lectr. Calumet Coll., Hammond, Ind., 1988-94, Purdue U., Westville, 1991-94, adult edu. instr, Indiana U., coord. of telecourses Calumet Coll., 1989-91; cons. Support Group Adult Attention Deficit Disorder, 1992. Apptd. by gov. Ind. Social Work and Marriage and Family Therapist Cert. Bd., 1991; host TV show Life's Dimensions, 1985-90; cons. internat. bd. Parents without Ptnrs.; cons. numerous social agys. With USAR, 1958-62. Mem. Nat. Assn. Social Workers (dir. Ind. chpt.), Acad. Cert. Social Workers (diplomate in clin. social work), Assn. Marriage and Family Therapists, Nat. Orgn. Forensic Social Workers, Ind. Pub. Defender Coun., Assn. Family and Conciliatory Cts. Author: Second Opinion: A Holistic Approach to Treating Adults with ADD, 1994, Reversing Attention Deficit Disorder, 1996; author divorce mgmt. materials and newspaper column, profl. manuals; pub. Step Families and Beyond, 1979—; editor: The Business of Social Work, 1983-84, ADD-Up Bi-monthly Newsletter dor ADD-Adults. Home and Office: 8716 Pine Ave Gary IN 46403-1441

BENNETT, RODGER W., stockbroker; b. Kirksville, Mo., Nov. 11, 1955. Student, U. Mo., 1973-77. Lic. stockbroker N.Y. Stock Exch. Mag. salesman, 1977-82; stockbroker Edward D. Jones & Co., Trenton, Mo., 1982—. Mem. Rotary. Baptist. Home: PO Box 68 Trenton MO 64683-0068 Office: Edward D Jones & Co 404 E 9th St Trenton MO 64683-2207

BENNETT, SHARON KAY, music educator; b. West Jefferson, Ohio; d. Harold Stewart and Dorothy Eleanor (McKinley) B. BMus, Eastman Sch. Music, 1960, MMus, 1962. Asst. prof. Univ. Iowa, Iowa City, 1980-84, Capital U., Columbus, Ohio, 1992—; adj. lectr. Otterbein Coll., Westerville, Ohio, 1986-87, Capital U., 1985-92; resident coloratura Nurnberg (Germany) Opera, 1970-73, Hamburg (Germany) State Opera, 1973-76; resident guest artist Scottish Opera, Glasgow, 1976-77; presenter symposium. Author: 40 Vocalises, 1993, Class Voice Simplified, 1994. Recipient 1st place award Iowa Symphony competition, 1981; named to Women of Achievement, YWCA, 1986; Rockefeller Found. grantee, N.Y.C., 1966-68; Old Gold fellow U. Iowa, Iowa City, N.Y. and Paris; Capital U. faculty devel. grantee, 1995. Mem. Nat. Assn. Tchrs. of Singing, Opera Am., Coll. Music Soc. (mem. nat. com. women, music, and gender), Sigma Alpha Iota (sec. 1985-87). Home: 2877 Astor Ave Columbus OH 43209-2626

BENNETT, TERRY ALLEN, technical services consultant; b. Natrona Heights, Pa., Nov. 28, 1946; s. Clifton Owen and Betty Louise (Young) B.; m. Constance Lucille Capine, Sept. 3, 1977; 1 child, Casey. B, Pa. State U., 1981. Automotive engr. P.P.G. Industries, Pitts., 1968-86; supr. mfg. prodn. Viracon, Owatona, Minn., 1986-89; dir. quality & engring. Premier Auto-Glass Corp., Lancaster, Ohio, 1989-94; dir. tech. svcs. GPAX Internat., Inc., Columbus, Ohio, 1994—. Patentee in field. Big bro. Big Bros./Big Sisters, 1987—. With U.S. Army, 1964-67.

BENNETT, THOMAS MITCHELL, secondary education educator; b. Lexington, Ky., Jan. 20, 1945; s. Frank Mitchell and Edith Marie (Thurman) B. BS, So. Ill. U., 1967, MS in Edn., 1971; postgrad., Fordham U., 1986, U. Pa., Phila., 1987. Cert. tchr., Mo., Ill. Tchr. social studies Hazelwood Sch. Dist., Florissant, Mo., 1970—; dir. pep club and cheerleaders Hazelwood West High Sch., 1976-95; v.p., bd. dirs. Heritage House Tchr. Retirement Ctr., St. Louis, 1981-90. V.p. Florissant Twp. Dem. Club, 1984-85; chmn. Florissant City Bi-Centennial of Constitution, 1987-91; v.p. Florissant Cable Commn., 1989-94; mem. St. Louis Region Tchr.'s Acad., 1996-97. Sgt. U.S. Army, 1968-70, Vietnam. Thomas Jefferson fellow NEH, 1986. Mem. NEA (resolutions com. 1981-86, bd. dirs. Mo. 1979-85, pres. Hazelwood 1986-88), Nat. Coun. Social Studies (ethics com. 1978-80), Mo. Coun. Social Studies, Phi Delta Kappa. Democrat. Baptist. Home: 1085 St Matthew Dr Florissant MO 63031-7738 Office: Hazelwood Sch Dist 1 Wildcat Ln Hazelwood MO 63042-1180

BENNETT, WILLIAM NEAL, forensic toxicologist, researcher; b. Kalamazoo, Feb. 10, 1959; s. Neal Ervin and Mary Janette (Muche) B. BS in Biology, U. Miami, 1981, BS in Marine Sci., 1981; MS in Zoology, U. Wis., Milw., 1984, PhD in Biology, 1989. Merchandiser Pepsi Cola, Houston, 1981, Coca Cola, Houston, 1981-82; tchr., rschr. U. Wis., Milw., 1982-89; technologist Bayshore Clin. Labs., Brown Deer, Wis., 1989-90, supr., 1990-91, asst. dir. toxicology, 1991—. Author: Plankton Regulation Dynamics, 1993; contbr. articles to profl. jours. Recipient James B. Anthony award U. Wis., 1984. Mem. AAAS, Golden Key, Sigma Xi. Office: Bayshore Clin Labs 4555 W Schroeder Dr Brown Deer WI 53223

BENNINGTON, BARRY ALLAN, judge; b. St. Louis, Jan. 27, 1941; s. Hugh and Jessie Lorraine (Long) B.; m. Jane K. Wiles, June 8, 1966 (div. Apr. 1983); children: Wendy, Valerie; m. Lynette Sue Hargett, Aug. 19, 1983; stepchildren: Eric, Mandi. BSBA, U. Kansas, 1963, JD, 1967. Bar: Kans. 1967, U.S. Dist. Ct. (fed. dist.) Kans. 1967. Ptnr. Shields & Bennington, St. John, Kans., 1967-83; county atty. Stafford County, St. John, 1970-74; dist. judge 20th Jud. Dist. Ct., State of Kans., 1983—; adm. judge, 1996—. Mem. Kans. Bar Assn. (bd. govs.), Kans. Dist. Judges' Assn. (bd. dirs.). Office: Dist Ct 215 N Broadway Saint John KS 67576

BENNINGTON, JERRY WILLIAM, medical technologist, technical consultant; b. LaCrosse, Wis., Oct. 15, 1942; s. Russell J. and Helenmary (Albitz) B.; m. Patricia A. Bennington, Nov. 20, 1970; children: Celeste, Nathan, Jerry W. ASD, U. Wis., Marshfield, 1979; BS, U. Wis., Superior, 1988; MBA, City U., Bellevue, Wash., 1993. Supr. chemistry Bio-Test Labs., Northbrook, Ill., 1964-68; supr. 2d shift Sherman Hosp., Elgin, Ill., 1968-72; supr. 24-hour lab. Marshfield (Wis.) Clinic, 1972-88, tech. cons., 1988—. Alderman from 5th dist. City of Marshfield, 1988—, pres. City Coun., 1990—; pres. sch. bd. Columbus H.S., Marshfield, 1985-93; chmn. univ. commn. U. Wis., Marshfield, 1988—. Mem. Nat. Certifying Agy., Am. Med. Technologists Assn. (nat. treas. 1987-88, nat. v.p. 1989-91, nat. pres. 1991-93, Order of Golden Microscope 1988, Exceptional Merit award 1984), Clin. Lab. Mgmt. Assn., KC. Roman Catholic. Home: 1413 S Adams Ave Marshfield WI 54449 Office: Marshfield Clinic 1000 North Oak Ave Marshfield WI 54449

BENSELER, DAVID PRICE, foreign language educator; b. Balt., Jan. 10, 1940; s. Ernest Parr and Ellen Hood Escar (Turnbaugh) B.; m. Suzanne Shelton, May 25, 1985; children: James Declan, Derek Justin. BA, West Wash. U., 1964; MA, U. Oreg., 1966, PhD, 1971. Prof. german, dept. chair Ohio State U., 1977-85; chair dept. modern langs and lits. Case Western Reserve U., 1991—, Louis D. Beaumont U. Prof. Humanities, 1991—; disting. vis. prof. fgn. langs. U.S. Mil. Acad., West Point, N.Y., 1987-88, N.Mex. State U., Las Cruces, 1989; mem. numerous coms. Case Western Res. U., U.S. Naval Acad., U. Akron, Ohio State U., Wash. State U., Ind. U., Emory U., U. Md., U. Cin., U. Wis., Pa. State U., U. Va., U. Mich., various others; lectr., panel mem., workshop condr., cons. in field. Author: (with Renate A. Schulz) Intensive Foreign Language Courses; editor 29 books, bibliographies, jours.; contbr. chpts. to books and articles to profl. jours. With USN, 1958-60. Recipient Bundesverdienstkreuz I. Klasse Pres. Fed. Republic Germany, 1985, Army Commendation medal for disting. civilian svc. U.S. Mil. Acad., 1988; Lilly Found. Faculty Renewal fellow, Stanford U., 1975, Fullbright Graduate fellow, 1967-68, NDEA fellow, U. Oreg., 1964-67; various other grants, fellowships, scholarships. Mem. TESOL, Am. Assn. Applied Linguistics, Am. Assn. Tchrs. of German, Am. Assn. Univ. Profs., Am. Goethe Soc., German Studies Assn., Ohio Fgn. Lang. Assn., Phi Sigma Iota, Sigma Kappa Phi, Delta Phi Alpha. Office: Case Western Res U Dept Modern Langs and Lit Cleveland OH 44106-7118

BENSLEY, BARBARA L., investment broker; b. Traverse City, Mich., Sept. 26, 1954; m. John Gillen, Mar. 5, 1988; 1 child, Jeffrey Kulis. Investment broker A.G. Edwards & Sons Inc., Traverse City, 1984—. Bd. dirs. Grand Travese United Way, Traverse City, 1986—, Leadership Grand Traverse, 1994—. Republican. Methodist. Office: AG Edwards & Sons Inc Delta Ctr 415 Munson Ave Traverse City MI 49686-3059

BENSON, JANET ELIZABETH, transportation finance executive; b. Ewell, Eng., Apr. 1, 1954; came to U.S., 1981; d. James Gillies and Jean Muriel (Waugh) B. BA with honors, U. London, 1976; MBA, U. Pa., 1983. Econ. cons. Rendel Palmer & Tritton Econ. Studies, London, 1976-81; fin. analyst Morgan Guaranty Trust Co., London, 1982; fin. analyst Am. Airlines, Dallas, 1983-85, contr., 1985; v.p. fin. Am. Airlines Direct Mktg. Corp., Dallas, 1986; dir. reservations ops. Eastern Airlines, Inc., Miami, 1987-89; mng. dir. fin. planning Internat. div. Am. Airlines, Dallas, 1989-92; gen. mgr. Am. Airlines, Cin., 1992-94; mng. dir. airport svcs. Am. Airlines, Dallas, 1994-95; sr. dir. ground ops. Airborne Express, Wilmington, Ohio, 1995—. English Speaking Union scholar London, 1981, Teagle scholar Exxon Corp, 1982. Mem. Ch. Eng. Club: Thames Rowing (London). Home: 15 E Maple Ave Covington KY 41011-2615 Office: ABX Air Inc Airborne Air Park 145 Hunter Dr Wilmington OH 45177-9390

BENSON, JOANNE, lieutenant governor of Minnesota; b. Jan. 4, 1943; m. Robert Benson; 2 children. BS, St. Cloud State U. Mem. Minn. Senate, St. Paul, 1991-94; lt. gov. State of Minn., St. Paul, 1994—. Office: State Capitol Rm 130 Saint Paul MN 55155

BENSON, JOHN ALLEN, mathematics educator; b. Chgo., Nov. 16, 1945; s. Randolph John and Calista May (Long) B.; m. Lynn Elizabeth Tupy, June 2, 1968; children: Bradley, Brian, Kathryn. BA, Luther Coll., 1967; MAT, Vanderbilt U., 1969. Tchr., math. Frederick Douglass High Sch., Atlanta, 1968-69, Evanston (Ill.) Township High Sch., 1969—, North Suburban Talent Srch., Niles, Ill., 1972-77, Harper Jr. Coll., Schaumburg, Ill., 1974-75, Midwest Talent Srch. Northwestrn U., Evanston, 1976—; pres. North Suburban Math. League, Evanston, 1977—; reader, Advanced Placement Calculus, Princeton, N.J., 1987—; question writer Math Counts. Author: (textbooks) Algebra 1, 1991, Algebra 2, 1991, Gateways to Algebra and Geometry, 1993. Recipient Ill. Presdl. award, 1987, Disting. Svc. award Luther Coll., 1992, Lola May award for leadership in math. edn., 1993; Tandy Tech. scholar, 1991, Edith May Sliffe award, 1994. Mem. Nat. Coun. Tchrs. Math., NEA, Nat. Assn. Supervisors MAth., Math Assn. Am., Ill. Coun. Tchrs. Math., Ill. Edn. Assn., Met. Math Club, Met. Maths. Club of Chgo. (pres. 1995-96). Lutheran. Office: Evanston H S 1600 Dodge Ave Evanston IL 60201-3449

BENSON, JOHN BRADY, investment company executive; b. Amana, Iowa, Nov. 8, 1933; m. Kathleen Fadell, May 19, 1962; children: John B., Thomas F., Michael, David. BA, U. Minn., 1955. Sr. v.p. Dean Witter Reynolds, Bloomington, Minn., 1958—. Capt. USAR, 1956-64. Republican. Roman Catholic. Home: 4901 Bruce Ave Edina MN 55424-1113 Office: Dean Witter Reynolds 8300 Norman Center Dr Ste 1150 Bloomington MN 55437-1027

BENSON, JOHN EARL, construction executive; b. Chgo., July 20, 1931; s. Benjamin Albert and Vivian (Ericsson) B.; m. Carolyn B. Liegler, July 3, 1954; 1 child, Lynn Ann Benson Heunisch. BA in Geology and Geography, Beloit Coll., 1953; student, Chgo. Tech., 1956, U. Chgo., 1964-65. V.p. CA Tharnstrom & Co., Skokie, Ill., 1956-71; v.p., ptnr. Andy Nyquist Contractors, Chgo., 1971-76; prin. John E Benson, Ltd., Island Lake, Ill., 1976—; v.p. Jon Constrn., Inc., Lincolwood, Ill., 1977-78, Thorleif Larsen & Son, Inc., Itaska, Ill., 1978-90; project mgr. Met. Structures, Chgo., 1980-91. Contbr. articles to profl. jours. Vice-chmn. Chgo. Com. for Hi Rise Bldgs., 1991; mem. ch. coun. Edgebrook Luth. Ch., Chgo., North Side coun. Boy Scouts Am., Chgo. With U.S. Army, 1953-55. Mem. Beloit Coll. Alumni Assn., Am. Legion, Ground Hogs, Masons, Shriners, Lions. Lutheran. Home and Office: 3517 Highland Dr Island Lake IL 60042-9497

BENSON, JOSEPH FRED, journalist, legal historian; b. St. Louis, Dec. 14, 1953; s. Max and Addie Marie (Klein) B.; m. Lynn Walker, July 31, 1993 (div. 1995). AA, St. Louis C.C., 1974; AB cum laude, St. Louis U., 1976, AM, 1977, JD, 1985. Legal historian, archivist Cir. Ct. St. Louis County, Clayton, Mo., 1978-85; columnist St. Louis Daily Record and St. Louis Countian, 1987—, spl. corres., 1989—, editorial writer, 1990—; asst. law libr. St. Louis County Ct. House Law Libr., 1979-85; adj. instr. Am. history Harris-Stowe State Tchr.'s Coll., St. Louis, 1987; rsch. cons. law firm David C. Godfrey, Clayton, 1981—, Zwibelman, Edelman & Godfrey, Clayton, 1989-95; friend of the ct. 21st cir. Cir. Ct. St. Louis County, Mo., 1993-94; instr. Am. history Van Buren (Mo.) R-1 Pub. Schs., 1994-95; instr. Am. history and Am. govt. East Carter County R-II Pub. Schs., Ellsinore, Mo., 1995, U. City (Mo.) High Sch., 1995—. Author newspaper column Law In History, 1987—; contbr. articles on internat. law to profl. jours. Judge St. Louis County Bd. Elections, Clayton, 1978-84, supr., 82-84; incorporator Hist. Soc. St. Louis County, 1978, exec. dir., asst. sec., 1979-87, comm. Bicentential U.S. Constn., 1983-91. Sam. A. Kessler Meml. scholar, 1981, Project '87: Bicentennial scholar, 1985-91; faculty fellow St. Louis U., 1983, 84. Mem. Supreme Ct. Hist. Soc., B'nai B'rith, Rotary, Phi Alpha Theta, Phi Theta Kappa. Democrat. Jewish. Home: 7812 Delmar Blvd University City MO 63130-3711

BENSON, LINDA KAY, Modern China and Inner Asia educator, researcher; b. Aberdeen, S.D., June 11, 1947; d. Bennie Gerald and Margaret (Westby) B.; m. David R. Maines, 1995. BS, No. State U., 1968; MPhil, U. Hong Kong, 1976; PhD, U. Leeds, Eng., 1986. Teaching asst. polit. sci. U. Hong Kong, 1974-76; from asst. prof. to assoc. prof. Nat. Chengchi U., Taipei, Taiwan, Republic of China, 1981-88; vis. prof. U. Miami, Fla., 1988-89; asst. prof. Oakland U., Rochester, Mich., 1989-92, assoc. prof., 1992-96; prof. Oakland U., Rochester, 1996—; panelist and panel organizer, various confs. on Asia. Author: (book) The Ili Rebellion: The Moslem Challenge to Chinese Authority in Xinjiang 1944-1949, 1990; co-author, co-editor (book) The Kazaks of China: Essays on an Ethnic Minority, 1988; contbr. articles and book revs. to profl. publs. NEH fellow, 1988, 94, fellow Oakland U., 1989, 96. Mem. AAUP, Am. Oriental Soc., Assn. Asian Studies, Am. Hist. Assn. Office: Oakland U Rochester MI 48309-4401

BENSON, MOSES, JR., military education specialist; b. Jackson, Miss., May 31, 1943; s. Moses and Lydia M. (Weathersby) B.; m. Lauree White. BS in Edn., Chgo. State U., 1971, MS in Edn., Guidance and Counseling, 1975. Cert. tchr., counselor, Ill. Tchr. Chgo. Bd. Edn., 1971-75; employment security specialist Ill. Dept. Employment Security, Chgo., 1975-85; substitute tchr. Sch. Dist. 144, Sch. Dist. 147, Markham and Harvey, Ill., 1985-86; guidance counselor Army Edn. Ctr., Ft. Sheridan, Ill., 1987-91; edn. specialist Navy Recruiting Processing Sta., Milw., 1991—; presenter seminars, workshops on career devel. Staff sgt. USAF, 1967-70, Vietnam. Mem. ACA, Assn. Humanistic Edn. Devel., Assn. Multicultural Counseling Devel., Mil. Educators Counselors Assn., Grant Park Concert Soc., DAV (Commanders Club), Am. Legion. Home: PO Box 7759 Chicago IL 60680-7759 Office: Navy Processing Station Ste 650 310 W Wisconsin Ave Milwaukee WI 53203-2280

BENSON, ROBERT S., investment broker; b. Iowa City, July 27, 1949. BBA in Mktg., U. Iowa, 1974. Computer salesman IBM, Cedar Rapids, Iowa, 1974-77; investment broker Norwest Investment Svcs. Inc., Galesburg, Ill., 1992—. Mem. Lions. Republican.

BENSON, STEPHEN HAROLD, automotive executive; b. Portland, Oreg., July 30, 1943; s. Harold Eugene and Emily Helen Marie (Carlson) B.; m. Jane Ann Olson, Aug. 23, 1964; children: Kristin Elizabeth, Gordon Bror. BS, Southern Oreg. Coll., 1966. Regional svc. mgr. Nissan Motor Corp., Memphis, 1974-83; tech. svc. mgr. Mercedes-Benz N.Am., Chgo., 1983-86; dir. fixed ops. Kenwood Dealer Group, Cin., 1986—; cons. Great Oaks Vocat. Sch., Cin., 1990, 93-96. Capt. USAF, 1967-71. Mem. NRA, Soc. Auto. Engrs. (assoc.), Master Technician Auto. Svc. Excellence. Republican. Episcopalian. Home: 700 Cedarhill Dr Cincinnati OH 45246-1408 Office: Kenwood Dealer Group 9610 Montgomery Rd Cincinnati OH 45242-7206

BENTLEY, ROSEANN, educational consultant, state senator; b. Joplin, Mo., Apr. 22, 1936; d. Lincoln John and Marcella (Donahue) Knauer; m. John D. Bentley, Apr. 12, 1958; children: Jeffrey, Christopher, Melissa, Jonathan. BS in Edn., U. Mo., 1958. Tchr. U.S. Army Schs., Okinawa, Japan, 1959-60, West Phila. (Pa.) Schs., 1961-63, Madison (Wis.) Pre-sch., 1966-67; mem. local sch. bd. Springfield (Mo.) Pub. Schs., 1974-83; mem. state sch. bd. Mo. Dept. Edn., Jefferson City, 1983-92; bd. mem. Lit. Investment for Tomorrow, St. Louis, Nat. Parents as Tchrs. Bd., St. Louis, Nat. Coun. for Accreditation on Tchr. Edn.; task force mem. Right From the Start, 1989. Pres. Springfield Sch. Bd., 1981, 82, Community Found., 1986-87, Mo. State Bd. Edn., 1988, 89, Nat. Assn. State Bds. Edn., Washington, 1990, United Way of Ozarks, 1992; co-chmn. Code Blue: Uniting for Healthier Youth, 1990. Named Mo. Gifted Educator of Yr., Gifted Assn. Mo., Jefferson City, 1990; recipient Mary Harriman award Assn. of Jr. Leagues Internat., N.Y.C., 1992. Mem. Springfield C. of C., Jr. League of Springfield (pres. 1976), Pi Beta Phi. Home: 1500 E Meadowmere St Springfield MO 65804-0244

BENTON, W. DUANE, judge; b. Springfield, Mo., Sept. 8, 1950; s. William Max and Patricia F. (Nicholson) B.; m. Sandra Snyder, Nov. 15, 1980; children: Megan Blair, William Grant. BA in Polit. Sci. summa cum laude, Northwestern U., 1972; JD, Yale U., 1975; MBA in Accounting, Memphis State U., 1979; student Inst. Jud. Adminstrn., NYU, 1992; LLD (hon.), Ctrl. Mo. State U., 1994; LLM, U. Va., 1995. CPA, Mo. Bar: Mo. 1975. Commd. USN, 1972, advanced through grades to capt.; judge advocate USN, Memphis, 1975-79; chief of staff for Congressman Wendell Bailey, Washington, 1980-82; pvt. practice Jefferson City, Mo., 1983-89; dir. revenue Mo. Dept. of Revenue, Jefferson City, 1989-91; judge Mo. Supreme Ct., Jefferson City, 1991—. Contbr. articles to profl. jours.; mng. editor Yale Law Jour., 1974-75. Chmn. Multistate Tax Commn. Washington, 1990-91; chmn. Mo. State Employees Retirement System, Jefferson City, 1989-93; regent Ctrl. Mo. State U., 1987-89; dir. Coun. for Drug Free Youth, Jefferson City, 1989—; mem. Mo. Mil. Adv. Com., 1989-91; mem. Mo. Commn. Intergovernmental Coop., Jefferson City, 1989-91; trustee, deacon 1st Bapt. Ch., Jefferson City. Danforth fellow JFK Sch. Govt. Harvard U., 1990. Mem. ABA (tax com. 1975—), Mo. Bar Assn. (tax com. 1975—), AICPA (tax com. 1983—), Mo. Soc. CPA's (tax com. 1983—), Navy League, Mil. Order of World Wars, Vietnam Vets of Am., VFW, Am. Legion, Phi Beta Kappa, Beta Gamma Sigma, Rotary (sgt. at arms 1990—). Baptist. Lt. USN, 1975-80. Capt. JAGC USNR. Office: Supreme Court PO Box 150 Jefferson City MO 65102-0150

BENTON-BORGHI, BEATRICE HOPE, educational consultant, author, publisher; b. San Antonio, Nov. 7, 1946; d. Donald Francis and Beatrice Hope (Peche) Benton; BA in Chemistry, North Adams State Coll., 1968; MEd, Boston U., 1972; m. Peter T. Borghi, Aug. 12, 1980; children: Kathryn Benton Borghi, Sarah Benton Borghi. Tchr. chemistry Cathedral H.S., Springfield, Mass., 1968-69; tchr. sci. and history Munich (W.Ger.) Am. H.S., 1969-70; tchr. English, Tokyo, Japan, 1970-71; tchr. chemistry and sci. Marlborough (Mass.) H.S., 1971-80; project dir., adminstr. ESEA, Marlborough Pub. Schs., 1976-77; CEO, pres., chmn. bd. dirs. Open Minds, Inc., 1996—; project dir., proposal writer Title III, Title IX, U.S. Dept. Edn., 1975-76, 76-77; evaluation team New Eng. Assn. Schs. and Colls., 1974, 78; mem. regional dept. edn. com., 1977-78; ednl. cons., lectr., 1978—. Author: Project ABC (Access By Computer), 1991, Alternative Funding/Recycling Project, 1991, Down the Aisle, 1996, Best Friends, 1996, A Thousand Lights, 1996, Whoa, Nellie!, 1996. Energy conservation rep. Marlborough's Overall Econ. Devel. Com., 1976; mem. strategic planning com. Upper Arlington Sch., Ohio, 1994; chmn. Marlborough's Energy Conservation Task Force, 1975; dir. Walk for Mankind, 1972; sec. Group Action for Marlborough Environment, 1975-76; bd. dirs. Girls Club, Marlborough, 1979; pres. Sisters, Inc., 1979-83, dba Open Minds, 1995. Mem. AAUW, Council for Exceptional Children, Nat. Women's Health Network. Home: 2449 Edington Rd Columbus OH 43221-3047 Office: Open Minds Inc PO Box 21325 Columbus OH 43221-0325

BENZ, JOHN CHARLES, county clerk; b. Appleton, Wis., Feb. 24, 1943; s. Herbert G. and Erna A. (Eichsteadt) B.; m. Judy L. Benz, Oct. 12, 1943; children: Tori L. Benz-Hillstrom, Amanda M. Grad. high sch. Regional warehouse mgr. Miller Electric Mfg. Co., Phila., 1969-72; distbn. mgr. Miller Electric Mfg. Co., Appleton, Wis., 1972-81, Curwood divsn. Bemis Inc., Oshkosh, Wis., 1982-92; county clk. Waushara County, Wautoma, Wis., 1992—. Chmn. Waushara County Rep. Club, Wautoma, 1985-88; twp. chmn., clk. Dakota Town bd., Wautoma, 1985-95; pres. sch. bd. Wautoma Area Sch. Bd., 1989—; bd. dirs. mem. fin. com. Peace Luth. Ch., Wautoma, 1983-89. Mem. Am. Welding Soc. (chmn. 1978-80), Ctrl. Wis. Pub. Purchasing Assn. (sec.-treas. 1992-96), Wis. County Clks. Assn., Wis. County Constnl. Officers Assn., Delta Nu Alpha, Rotary. Office: Waushara County Courthouse PO Box 488 Wautoma WI 54982

BENZEL, KATHRYN NOWICKI, English language educator; b. Toledo, Sept. 27, 1947; d. Casimir William and Kathryn Lorraine (Miller) Nowicki; m. Michael Arnold Benzel, Oct. 7, 1973; 1 child, Blake Conrad. BE, U. Toledo, 1969, MA, 1971; PhD, U. Ill., 1987. Instr. English Bowling Green (Ohio) State U., 1971-75, Idaho State U., Pocatello, 1975-79; prof. English U. Nebr., Kearney, 1987—, dir. English grad. studies, 1995—. Co-author: The Little English Workbook, 1984, 45 Ideas for Teaching Writing, 1985; co-editor: Images of the Self as Female, 1992; contbr. articles to profl. jours. Office: U Nebr English Dept Kearney NE 68849

BENZIES, BONNIE JEANNE, clinical and industrial psychologist; b. Chgo., May 3, 1943; d. Roy Benzies and Margaret Lucille (Hernly) Benzies-Sorensen. BS, MacMurray Coll., 1965; MS, Ill. Inst. Tech., 1971, PhD, 1980. Cert. nat./internat. cert. alcohol and other drug abuse counselor; cert. alcohol, tobacco and other drug abuse preventionist; diplomate, bd. cert. forensic examiner diplomate. Statistician, psychologist State of Ill., Chgo., 1966-73; psychologist State of Ill., Manteno, 1976-82; pub. svc. adminstr. State of Ill., Elgin, 1988—; psychologist Ingalls Meml. Hosp., Harvey, Ill., 1982-84, Cook County Juvenile Ct., Chgo., 1987-88; pvt. practice Chgo., Hanover Park, Palatine, Ill., 1984—; cons., trainer PREVENTION PLUS of Palatine, 1994—; grad. tchg. asst. Ill. Inst. Tech., Chgo., 1973-74; mem. staff Hoffman Estates Med. Ctr., Woodland Hosp., Hoffman Estates. Co-author psychol. test: Time Questionnaire, 1979. Mem. Nat. Task Force on Depressive Disorders, 1991—; mem. Statewide Subcom. on Mentally Ill Substance Abuser, 1991-93. MacMurray scholar, 1961-65, Am. Legion scholar, 1963-64; recipient Achievement award in addictions counseling Loop Coll., 1986. Mem. APA, Am. Assn. Christian Counselors, Am. Bd. Forensic Examiners, Chgo. Assn. for Psychoanalytic Psychology, Employee Assistance Profls. Assn., Christian Assn. Psychol. Studies, Internat. Critical Incident Stress Found., Inc., Palatine C. of C. Home and Office: Prevention Plus of Palatine 1531 E Anderson Dr Palatine IL 60067-4101

BENZING, BRUCE M., mechanical engineer; b. Pitts., Mar. 31, 1953. BSME, U. Cin., 1990. Mech. engr. OPW Engineered Sys., Mason, Ohio, 1990-92; product devel. engr. Hydro Sys., Cin., 1992—. Patentee in field. Office: Hydro Systems Co 2798 Round Bottom Rd Cincinnati OH 45244

BENZLE, CURTIS MUNHALL, artist, art educator; b. Lakewood, Ohio, Apr. 20, 1949; s. Arthur George and Martha (Munhall) B; m. Suzan Scianamblo, Feb. 6, 1972 (div. 1995); children: Elliott, Kyle, Marisa. Student, Hillsdale Coll., 1967-69; BFA, Ohio State U., 1972; post-grad., Rochester Inst. Tech., 1973; MA, No. Ill. U., 1978. Owner, mgr. Oz Crafts, Hilton Head, S.C., 1973-76, Benzle Porcelain Co., Columbus, Ohio, 1980-93, Benzle Applied Arts, Hilliard, Ohio, 1988—; owner Creative Spirit Workshop; interim dir. Ohio Designer Craftsmen; owner Creative Spirit Workshop; mng. dir. Ohio Designer Craftsmen, 1996—; instr. U. S.C., Beaufort, 1978-79, Savannah (Ga.) Coll. Art and Design, 1982—; pres. Japan-USA Esch. Exhbn., 1988-92; bd. overseers Am. Craft Assn., 1991—, chmn., 1994-95; bd. trustees Am. Crafts Coun., 1992. One-man show U. S.C., 1979, Indpls. Mus. Art, 1984, Lawrence Gallery, Portland, Oreg., 1986, Running Ridge Gallery, Santa Fe, 1986, Akasaka/Green Gallery, Tokyo, 1987, 90, Zanesville Art Ctr., 1988, Swidler Gallery, 1990, Tsukushi Gallery, Kitakyushu, Japan, 1991, also others; exhibited in numerous group shows, 1971—, including Smithsonian Instn., 1980, 83, Suntory Art Mus., Tokyo, 1984, Cermaic Nat. Everson Mus., Syracuse, 1988, Internat. Competition of Ceramics, Mino, Japan, 1989; represented in numerous permanent collections, including Smithsonian Instn., Everson Mus. Art, Los Angeles County Mus. Art, Cleve. Mus. Art., White House Collection Contemporary Craft. Mem. Ohio Citizens Com. for Arts, 1986—. Nat. Endowment for Arts fellow, 1980, Ohio Arts Coun. fellow, 1981, 83, 84, 86, 88, Greater Columbus Arts Coun. fellow, 1987. Mem. Am. Crafts Coun. (bd. overseers 1991—, trustee 1992—), Nat. Coun. on Edn. in Ceramic Art, Ohio Designer Craftsmen (bd. dirs. 1984—, pres. 1985-87). Republican.

BEPKO, GERALD LEWIS, university administrator, law educator, lecturer, consultant, lawyer; b. Chgo., Apr. 21, 1940; s. Lewis V. and Geraldine S. (Bernath) B.; m. Jean B. Cougnenc, Feb. 24, 1968; children: Gerald Lewis Jr., Arminda B. B.S., No. Ill. U., 1962; J.D., Ill. Inst. Tech.-Chgo. Kent Coll. Law, 1965; LL.M., Yale U., 1972. Bar: Ill. 1965, U.S. Supreme Ct. 1968, Ind. 1973. Assoc. Ehrlich, Bundesen, Friedman & Ross, Chgo., 1965; spl. agt. FBI, 1965-69; asst. prof. law Ill. Inst. Tech.-Chgo. Kent Coll. Law, 1969-71; prof. Ind. U.-Indpls., 1972-86, assoc. dean acad. affairs, 1979-81, dean, 1981-86, v.p. Ind. U., 1986—; vis. prof. Ind. U.-Bloomington, summers 1976, 77, 78, 80, U. Ill., 1976-77, Ohio State U., 1978-79; cons. and reporter Fed. Jud. Ctr.; bd. dirs., First Ind. Bank/Corp., 1988—, Ind. Energy Inc. & Ind. Gas Co., Inc., 1989—, USA Group and USA Funds, 1996—; Circle Income Shares, Inc., 1992—; mem. Conf. Commrs. on Uniform State Laws, 1982, Permanent Editl. Bd. for the Uniform Comml. Code, 1993—; vice chair Ind. Lobby Registration Commn., 1992-96, chair, 1996—. Indpls. Chgo. Title and Trust Co. Found. scholar, 1962-65; Ford Urban law fellow, 1971-72. Fellow Am. Bar Found., Ind. State Bar, Indpls. Bar Found.; mem. ABA, Ind. State Bar Assn., Indpls. Bar Assn. Methodist. Club: Country of Indpls. Lodge: Rotary. Author: (with Boshkoff) Sum and Substance of Secured Transactions, 1981; contbr. articles on comml. law to profl. jours. Office: Ind U 355 Lansing St Indianapolis IN 46202-2815

BERCHTOLD, MERRILL E., engineering executive, retired; b. Cin., Sept. 30, 1931. BS, U. Cin., 1960. Engrng. supr. Cin. Milacron, 1961-94, ret., 1994. Patentee hydraulic circuits. Mem. zoning bd. of appeals City of Loveland, Ohio. With U.S. Army, 1950-52, Korea. Republican. Methodist. Home: 2100 W Loveland Ave Loveland OH 45140-7179

BERDICH, VERA, artist, educator; b. Chgo., Jan. 18, 1915; d. Adolph and Agnes (Koncel) B. BFA, Sch. of Art Inst., Chgo., 1946; PhD in Fine Arts, Elmhurst Coll., Chgo., 1977. Prof. Sch. of Art Inst. Art Inst. Chgo., 1947-79, artist, prof. emeritus Sch. of Art Inst., 1933—. One person shows include Chgo. Cultural Ctr.; represented in permanent collections Smithsonian Instn., Art Inst. Chgo. Recipient Frank G. Logan medal for painting Art Inst. Chgo., 1977. Mem. Arts Club Chgo. Democrat. Home: 3126 N Christiana Chicago IL 60618-6819

BERENDI, ERLINDA BAYAUA, surgeon; b. Santiago, Isabela, The Philippines, Oct. 31, 1947; came to U.S., 1972; d. Jeremias Carreon and Amanda (Florentin) Bayaua; m. S. Alexander Berendi, Jan. 2, 1981. BS, U. Santo Tomas, Manila, 1966, MD, 1971. Med. dir. Great Pacific Life Ins. Co., Manila, 1971-72; intern, resident Michael Reese Hosp., Chgo., 1973-77; pres., physician, surgeon Consultative Exams., Inc., Chgo., 1980—; med. dir. Intracorp. Med. Rev. Svcs., Arlington Heights, Ill., 1987-89; pres. Finnegan's Choice, Inc., Chgo., 1985—; med. cons. Dept. Health and Human Svcs., Chgo., 1977-83, State of Ill., Dept. Rehab. Svcs., Chgo., 1981—; acting chmn. med. quality rev. com. Bur. of Program Integrity, Ill. Dept. Pub. Aid, Chgo., 1977—; physician cons. Comprehensive Health Svcs, Inc., Chgo., 1978-79; chief med. cons. U.S. R.R. Retirement Bd., 1981—. Mem. AMA, Am. Acad. Family Physicians, Nat. Assn. Disability Examiners, N.Y. Acad. Scis. Home: 6666 Tower Circle Dr Lincolnwood IL 60646 Office: Consultative Exams Inc 55 E Washington St Ste 2101 Chicago IL 60602-2202

BERES, MICHAEL JOHN, project manager; b. Gary, Ind., June 26, 1950; s. Edward Kenneth and Joan Marie (Petrovich) B.; m. Susan Eileen Heminger, Oct. 26, 1973; children: Amanda Eileen, Matthew James. AAS, Purdue U., 1972, BS, 1973. Registered profl. engr., Ill. Estimator, field engr. J.M. Foster, Inc., Gary, 1973-74; civil engr. Brown & Root, Inc., Oakbrook, Ill., 1974-76; field piping engr. Dedelow, Inc., Gary, 1977; plant facilities engr. Reynolds Metals Co., McCook, Ill., 1977-88; constrn. mgr. midwest region Waste Mgmt. of N. Am., Inc., Westchester, Ill., 1988-91; project supt. Exec. Constrn., Inc., Downers Grove, Ill., 1992—; pres. Beres Engrng., Downers Grove, 1993—; v.p. White-Whitfield & Assocs., Downers Grove, 1993—; plant engr. Heinemann's Bakeries, Inc., 1995—. Team leader Dupage County Pub. Action to Deliver Shelter, Downers Grove, Ill., 1983-92. Recipient Cert. of Recognition Gov. James R. Thompson. Roman Catholic. Club: Waste Mgmt., Inc. Midwest Region Golf League (pres. 1989-90), Reynolds Golf League (McCook, pres. 1981-87). Home and Office: 4210 Highland Ave Downers Grove IL 60515-2133

BERES, WILLIAM PHILIP, physics educator; b. Peabody, Mass., Jan. 8, 1936; s. Solomon Alvin and Rachel (Cooper) B.; m. Mary J. Chinn, June 19, 1966; children: Deborah, Sharon, Ben David. BS, MIT, 1959, PhD, 1964. Physicist GCA Corp., 1964; rsch. assoc. U. Md., 1964-66; asst. prof. Duke U., Durham, N.C., 1966-69; assoc. prof. physics Wayne State U., Detroit, 1969-75, prof., 1975—, assoc. chmn., 1991—; participant Latin Am. Sch. Physics, Mexico City, summer 1965; vis. prof. nuclear theory Lawrence Radiation Lab., Berkeley, Calif., summer 1967; Fulbright lectr. Hebrew U., Jerusalem, 1977-78. Contbr. numerous publs. to physics jours. Mem. Am. Phys. Soc., Am. Assn. Physics Tchrs. Office: Wayne State U Dept Physics Detroit MI 48202

BEREUTER, DOUGLAS KENT, congressman; b. York, Nebr., Oct. 6, 1939; s. Rupert Wesley and Evelyn Gladys (Tonn) B.; m. Louise Meyer, June 1, 1962; children: Eric David, Kirk Daniel. BA, U. Nebr., 1961; M in City Planning, Harvard U., 1966, MPA, 1973. Urban planner HUD, San Francisco, 1965-66; dir. div. state and urban affairs Nebr. Dept. Econ. Devel., 1967-68, state planning dir., 1968-70; coord. fed.-state relations Nebr. State Govt., 1967-70, urban planning cons., 1971-78; assoc. prof. U. Nebr., Kans. State U., 1971-78; mem. Nebr. Legislature, 1974-78, 96th-104th Congresses from 1st Nebr. Dist., 1979—; mem. com. on banking and fin. svcs., vice chmn. internat. rels. com., chmn. Asia-Pacific subcom.; mem. Nebr. State Crime Commn., 1969-71; chmn. standing com. on urban devel. Nat. Conf. State Legislatures, 1977-78; mem. Nat. Agrl. Export Commn., 1985-86. Served as officer U.S. Army, 1963-65. Mem. Am. Planning Assn., Phi Beta Kappa, Sigma Xi. Republican. Lutheran. Office: Ho of Reps 2348 Rayburn Ofc Bldg Washington DC 20515

BERG, CHARLES A., state legislator; b. Oct. 15, 1927; m. Carol Berg; seven children. Ctrl. Sch. Agriculture. Senator Dist. 13 Minn. State Senate, 1973-74, 81—; farmer, 1996—; chmn. Gaming Regulation Com.; mem. Agrl. & Rural Devel., Environ. & Natural Resources Com., Rules & Adminstrn. Com. Office: General Delivery Chokio MN 56221-9999 also: State Senate State Capital Building Saint Paul MN 55155-1606*

BERG, DONALD JAMES, sociologist, educator; b. St. James, Minn., May 9, 1935; s. Robert Edwin and Clementine (Freking) B.; m. Nancy K. James, Aug. 12, 1976 (div. 1989); 1 child, Philip. BA in Sociology, U. Minn., 1958; BS in Social Studies, Mankato State U., 1967, MS in Sociology, 1969; post-grad., U. Nebr., 1970, Washington U., 1973, U. Tenn., 1978-79. Social worker St. Louis County Govt., Duluth, Minn., 1964-65; tchr. Lakeshore Sr. High Sch., Benton Harbor, Mich., 1967-68; sociologist, educator Iowa Western C.C., Council Bluffs, 1969-72, Southeast Mo. State U., Cape Girardeau, 1972—; producer sociol. and anthrop. convs. Contbr. articles to profl. publs. Bd. dirs. Cape Girardeau Coun. on Aging, 1986-88; bd. dirs. Cape Girardeau Civic Ctr., 1982-88, pres. bd. dirs., 1985. Capt. USAF, 1959-62. Mem. AAUP, Am. Sociol. Assn., North Cen. Sociol. Assn., Midwest Sociol. Soc., Mo. State Sociol. Assn. Democrat. Roman Catholic. Office: Southeast Mo State U Dept Sociology 1 University Plz Cape Girardeau MO 63701-4710

BERG, DONALD W., investment company executive; b. Mpls., July 29, 1930. BS, U. Minn., Mpls., 1954. Dist. mgr. Am. Greeting, Grand Rapids, Mich., 1955-67; broker mgr. E. F. Hutton, Grand Rapids, 1967-76; broker Payne Webb, Grand Rapids, 1976-80; br. mgr., v.p. First of Mich. Corp., Grand Rapids, 1980—. Mem. Better Bus. Bur. Home: 1729 Fountainview Ct SE Caledonia MI 49316-9100 Office: First of Mich Corp 300 Ottawa Ave NW Ste 150 Grand Rapids MI 49503-2305

BERG, EVELYNNE MARIE, geography educator; b. Chgo.; d. Clarence Martin and Mildred Berg; BS with honors, U. Ill., 1954; MA, Northwestern U., 1959. Geography editor Am. Peoples Ency., Chgo., 1955-57; social studies tchr. Hammond (Ind.) Tech.-Vocat. High Sch., 1958-59; geography tchr. Carl Schurz High Sch., Chgo., 1960-66; faculty geography Morton Coll., Cicero, Ill., 1966-95. Asst. leader Cicero coun. Girl Scouts U.S.A., 1951-53; Fulbright scholar, Brazil, 1964; NSF scholar, 1963, 65, 71-72; NDEA fellow, 1968-69; fellow Faculty Inst. S. and S.E. Asia, 1980; NEH scholar DePaul U., 1984; recipient award Ill. Geog. Soc., 1977. Fellow Nat. Coun. Geog. Edn. (state coord. 1973-74, exec. bd. 1973-77); mem. Nat., Ill. (sec.-treas. 1968-69, sec. 1969-70, v.p. 1970-71, pres. 1971-72), Am. Overseas Educators (sec. Ill. chpt. 1974-76, v.p. chpt. 1977-78), AAUW (Chgo. br. rec. sec. 1963-65), Assn. Am. Geographers, Ill., Acad. Sci., AAAS (scholar 1973-74), Ill. Coun. Social Studies, Geol. Soc. Am. (membership chair Morton Coll. chpt.), Ill. C.C. Faculty Assn. (v.p. membership and del. affairs 1982-84), Des Plaines Valley Geol. Soc., Fulbright Assn., Sierra Club, Sigma Xi, Gamma Theta Upsilon, Delta Kappa Gamma (pres. Gamma Omicron chpt. 1988-90, parliamentarian 1990-94, membership chair 1992-94, nominations chair. 1994-95), Des Plaines Valley Geological Soc. Clubs: Oak Park Bus. Profl. Women's Club (pres. 1995), 19th-Century Women's Club, Order Eastern Star, Bus. and Profl. Women's (Acting pres. 1980-81, parliamentarian 1989-90). Contbr. to profl. jours. Home: 3924 N Pioneer Ave Chicago IL 60634-2050

BERG, JEAN STEWART, consultant; b. Vancouver, B.C., Feb. 16, 1934; d. Campbell and Grace (Callander) Stewart; m. B. Richard Berg, Apr. 7, 1956; children: Scott Richard, Gregory Stewart. BA, U. So. Calif., 1955; MA, Eden Theol. Seminary, St. Louis, 1983. Program dir. YMCA, South Pasadena, Calif., 1955-56, 60-63, YWCA, Lowell, Mass., 1956-57; exec. dir. YWCA County Br., St. Louis, 1969-71; asst. dir. St. Louis County Housing Authority, 1977-81; assoc. dir. Bus. Devel. Ctr. U. Mo., St. Louis, 1981-82; exec. dir. Joint Community Ministries, St. Louis, 1982-84; minister for parish life 1st Presbyn. Ch., Ferguson, Mo., 1984-90; cons. various orgns., Mo., 1990—; Outreach dir. Religious Coalition Abortion Rights, 1991, exec. dir. 1992—; chair Mo. State Coord. Com. Internat. Women's Yr., 1977-78. Author: The Justice Church, 1986, God & Caesar: One Loyalty or Two, 1990; producer, host (TV program) Steeple and People, 1987—. Candidate U.S. Congr. 9th Dist., Mo., 1976; bd. dirs. St. Louis/Georgetown, Guyana Sister City Orgn., 1990, UN Assn., St. Louis, 1988-91, Wellspring Found., St. Louis, 1989—; bd. dirs., past pres. Friends of Peace Studies, U. Mo., Columbia, 1985-90; leader Nat. Coun. Chs. ecumenical study tour, USSR, 1988; mem. Leadership St. Louis, 1978. Recipient Advancement of Women's Equality award Mo. Women's Network, 1988, Sentinel Signal award St. Louis Sentinel newspaper, 1989. Mem. Nat. Conf. Christians & Jews, Confluence St. Louis (co-chair task force). Democrat. Mem. Ch. of Christ. Home: 7103 Waterman Ave Saint Louis MO 63130-4326

BERG, MARY JAYLENE, pharmacy educator, researcher; b. Fargo, N.D., Nov. 7, 1950; d. Ordean Kenneth and Anna Margaret (Skramstad) B. BS in Pharmacy, N.D. State U., 1974; PharmD, U. Ky., 1978. Lic. pharmacist, N.D., Ky., Iowa. Fellow in pharmacokinetics Millard Fillmore Hosp./SUNY, Buffalo, 1978-79; asst. prof. U. Iowa, Iowa City, 1980-85, assoc. prof., 1985-95, prof., 1995—; with dept. clin. rsch., clin. pharmacology/pharmacokinetics F. Hoffmann-La Roche, Ltd., Basel, Switzerland, 1992; mem. adv. com. rsch. on women's health NIH, 1995—. Reviewer Cin. Pharmacy, 1984—, Epilepsia, 1987—; editor: Internat. Leadership Symposium, The Role of Women in Pharmacy, 1990, Pharmacy World Congress '91; Women-A Force in Pharmacy Symposium, 1992, Gender-Related Health Issues, 1996; contbr. articles to Drug Intelligence & Clin. Pharmacy, New Eng. Jour. of Medicine, Jour. Forensic Scis., Therapeutic Drug Monitoring, Epilepsia. Advisor Kappa Epislon, Iowa City, 1980-94; pres. Mortar Bd. Alumnae, Iowa City, 1986-88. NIH grantee, 1984, Nat. Insts. on Drug Abuse grantee, 1986; recipient Career Achievement award Kappa Epsilon, 1985. Mem. Am. Assn. Pharm. Scientists, Am. Soc. Hosp. Phrmacists (chair spl. interest group of clin. pharmacokinetics 1987-89), Am. Epilepsy Soc., Am. Pharm. Assn., Internat. Forum for Women in Pharmacy (U.S. contact), Fedn. Internat. Pharmaceutique (del. World Health Assembly 1992), Leadership Internat., Women in Pharmacy (bd. dirs. 1991—), Sigma Xi, Rho Chi, Kappa Epsilon, Phi Beta Delta. Lutheran. Office: U Iowa Coll of Pharmacy Iowa City IA 52242

BERG, MELODY G., author; b. Grand Rapids, Mich., May 25, 1945; d. William Edward and Margaret Elizabeth (Stephen) Danthuma; m. Harvey Berg, Sept. 14, 1969; children: Natasha Lynn, Justin Luther. Grad. h.s., Grand Rapids. Author: Round By the Point, 1990, A Safe Harbor, 1993; dir. (play) Death-Resurrection, 1990-91, 92-93, Beggar Lady, 1992-93. Mem. Seventh-Day-Adventist. Home: 4145 Joan Dr Dorr MI 49323

BERG, RICHARD C., stockbroker; b. St. Louis, Mar. 28, 1956. BSBA, U. Mo., 1978. Stockbroker Shearson, St. Louis, 1987-90, Prudential Securities Inc., Chesterfield, Mo., 1990—. Home: 99 Meadowbrook Country Club Est Ballwin MO 63011-1601 Office: Prudential Securities Inc 14528 S Outer 40 Chesterfield MO 63017-5743

BERG, RICK ALAN, state legislator, real estate investor; b. Maddock, N.D., Aug. 16, 1959; s. Bert R. and Francie (Brink) B.; m. Tracy Jane Martin, Sept. 19, 1987. BS in Agrl. Econ., N.D. State U., 1981. Cert. comml. investment mem. Mem. N.D. Ho. of Reps., Fargo, 1984—, Rep. caucus chmn., 1990-92, speaker, 1992-94; chmn. IBL com. Industry Bus. and Labor, Fargo. Mem. Farmhouse Frat. (bd. dirs., pres. 1990-94). Lutheran. Home: 6437 13th St N Fargo ND 58102

BERG, STANTON ONEAL, firearms and ballistics consultant; b. Barron, Wis., June 14, 1928; s. Thomas C. and Ellen Florence (Nedland) Silbaugh; m. June K. Rolstad, Aug. 16, 1952; children: David M., Daniel L., Susan E., Julie L. Student U. Wis., 1949-50; LLB, LaSalle Extension U., 1951; post-grad. U. Minn., 1960-69. Diplomate Am. Bd. Forensic Examiners. Claim rep. State Farm Ins. Co., Mpls., Hibbing and Duluth, Minn., 1952-57, claim supt., 1957-66, divisional claim supt., 1966-70; firearms cons., Mpls., 1961—; regional mgr. State Farm Fire and Casualty Co., St. Paul, 1970-84; bd. dirs. Am. Bd. Forensic Firearm and Tool Mark Examiners, 1980—; instr. home firearms safety, Mpls., 1975—; cons. to Sporting Arms and Ammunition Mfrs. Inst., 1974—; internat. lectr. on forensic ballistics. Adv. bd. Milton Helpern Internat. Ctr. for Forensic Scis., 1975—; mem. bd. cons. Inst. Applied Sci., Chgo., 1974—; cons. for re-exam. of ballistics evidence in Robert Kennedy assasination/Sirhan case Superior Ct. L.A., 1975; ct. expert witness in most state cts., Mil. Gen. Ct. Martial and U.S. Dist. Cts., and the Supreme Ct. of Ontario, Can.; mem. Nat. Forensic Ctr., 1979—, internat. study group in forensic scis., 1985—; chmn. internat. symposiums on forensic ballistics, Edinburgh, Scotland, 1972, Zurich, Switzerland, 1975, Bergen, Norway, 1981, Dusseldorf, Germany, 1993. With CIC, RA, 1948-52. Fellow Am. Acad. Forensic Sci., Am. Coll. Forensic Examiners (life, bd. cert. forensic examiner and diplomate); mem. ASTM, Assn. of Firearm and Tool Mark Examiners (exec. council 1970-71, charter mem., life mem., Disting. Mem. and Key Man award 1972, exam. and standards com. 1975-76, spl. honors award 1976, nat. peer group on cert. of firearms examiners 1978—, fellow of the coll.), Forensic Sci. Soc., Internat. Assn. Forensic Scis., Internat. Assn. for Identification (mem. firearms subcom. of sci. and practice com. 1961-74, 86-96, chmn. firearm subcom. 1964-66, 69-70, 91-95, lab. rsch. and techniques subcom. 1980-81, life and disting. mem. 1947—, life charter mem. Minn. dvsn. 1963—), Internat. Wound Ballistics Assn. (full mem.), Western Conf. Criminal and Civil Problems (sci. adv. com.), Am. Legion, Army Counter-Intelligence Corp. Vets. Assn., Browning Arms Collectors Assn. (life 1988—), Am. Ordnance Assn. (life), NRA (life mem. 1957—), Minn. Weapons Collectors, Internat. Cartridge Collectors Assns. (life mem.), Internat. Reference Orgn. Forensic Medicine and Scis, Internat. Assn. Bloodstain Pattern Analysts, Assn. Firearms and Toolmark Examiners (editorial com. AFTE jour. 1989-92), Am. Nat. Standards Inst., Am. Soc. Testing and Materials (criminalistics subcom. 1989—, non powder guns subcom 1990—, paintball guns & sys. subcom. 1994—). Contbg. editor Am. Rifleman mag., 1973-84; mem. editorial bd. Internat. Microform Jour. Legal Medicine and Forensic Scis., 1979—, Am. Jour. Forensic Medicine and Pathology, 1979-91; contbr. articles on firearms and forensic ballistics to profl. publs. Address: 6025 Gardena Ln NE Minneapolis MN 55432-5840

BERGEN, MARTHA STEAGALL, religious educator; b. Reidsville, N.C., May 28, 1954; d. George Wade Steagall and Blanche Smith (Vaughn) Carter; m. Robert Dale Bergen, Dec. 28, 1979; 1 child, Wesley Wade Bergen. BA, Gardner-Webb Coll., 1976; MDiv, Southwestern Bapt. Theol. Sem., 1979, MRE, 1982, PhD, 1994. Editorial asst. Southwestern Jour. of Theology, Fort Worth, Tex., 1981-86; asst. prof. dept. Christian studies Hannibal-LaGrange Coll., 1990—; adj. prof. Hannibal-LaGrange Coll, 1987-90; seminar and conf. leader in field. Editor (booklets) Computerizing Your Ministry Series, 1989-91; contbr. articles to profl. publs. Mem. Mo. Bapt. Religious Edn. Assn. (sec.-treas. 1992-95, pres.-elect 1995-96), So. Bapt. Religious Edn. Assn., So. Bapt. In-Svc. Guidance, N.Am. Profs. Christian Edn. Office: Hannibal-LaGrange Coll 2800 Palmyra Rd Hannibal MO 63401-1940

BERGER, EDMOND LOUIS, theoretical physicist; b. Salem, Mass., Dec. 5, 1939; s. Edmond Antonio and Ethel Mary (Brown) B.; m. Susan Katherine Teffner, Sept. 5, 1964; children—Bruce, Catherine, Stephen. B.S., MIT, 1961; Ph.D., Princeton U., 1965. Asst. prof. dept. physics Dartmouth Coll., Hanover, N.H., 1965-68; research assoc. Lawrence Berkeley Lab.-U. Calif., Berkeley, 1968-69; physicist Argonne Nat. (Ill.) Lab., 1969-72, sr. theoretical physicist, theory group leader high energy physics div., 1974—; staff scientist CERN, Geneva, 1972-74, 83-84, 92-93; vis. prof. Stanford U., 1978-79; mem. physics adv. com. Fermi Nat. Accelerator Lab., 1980-84; mem. high energy and nuclear physics adv. com. Brookhaven Nat. Lab., 1985—; mem. high energy physics adv. panel U.S. Dept. Energy, 1990-94; dir. Snowmass summer study on high energy physics, 1990. Contbr. articles to profl. jours. NSF fellow, 1961-65; recipient Disting. Performance award U. of Chgo., 1987. Fellow Am. Phys. Soc. (chmn. exec. com. divsn. particles and fields 1990, mem. com. on mtgs. 1990—, chmn. 1994-96). Home: 5711 Dearborn Pky Downers Grove IL 60516-1430 Office: Argonne Nat Lab High Energy Physics Dv Argonne IL 60439

BERGER, HARRIS MERLE, ethnomusicologist, educator; b. Albany, N.Y., Feb. 16, 1966; s. Charles and Judith (Nisoff) B.; m. Giovanna Patrizia Del Negro, Feb. 1, 1993. BA, Wesleyan U., Middletown, Conn., 1988; MA, Ind. U., 1991, PhD, 1995. Instr. Ind. U., Bloomington, 1994; auditory cognition rschr. Sound/Video Analysis and Instrn. Lab., Ind. U. Bloomington, 1995; asst. prof. music Tex. A&M U., 1996—; adj. prof. U. Indpls., 1996; ethnomusicology cons. Donna Lawrence Prodns., Louisville, 1994, Portia Maultsby Rsch., Bloomington, 1991. Composer, performer jazz composition Flying: A Evening of Contemporary Jazz, 1984. Jacob K. Javitz fellow U.S. Dept. Edn., 1989-92. Mem. Soc. for Ethnomusicology (founder popular music sect. 1996), Am. Anthrop. Assn., Am. Folklore Soc. Office: Music Program Tex A&M Univ College Station TX 77843

BERGER, JAMES (HANK), business broker; b. Lakewood, Ohio, July 27, 1951; s. James Henry and Joan Marie (Wertz) B.; m. Rochelle Anne Kiehl, Apr. 29, 1977; children: Justin Henry, Max Albert. Degree, Cooper Sch. Art, 1972. Owner H.M.S. Titanic Art Studio, Cleve., 1971-73; mgr. various rock groups Cleve., 1972-73; exec. producer TV show Music Your'e My Mother, 1975-76; owner Club Roundtable, Cleve., 1976, Deja Vu, Cleve., 1977-78, Club Traxx, Hanks Cafe, Cleve., 1976-88, Club Metropolis, 1988-90; Club U41A; owner Berger Bus. Brokerage, Rocky River, Ohio, 1990—; owned and marketed sections of original Hollywood (Calif.) Sign, 1980-82; owner The Probe-Disco, Hollywood, 1983-85; cons. in field. Author screen play When The Music's Over, 1980. Coach Rocky River Little League, 1990-93, Rocky River Recreation, 1994-95. With USN, 1969-71, Vietnam. Recipient High Pope of Pub. Rels., The Ch. of Sub Genius, 1983; named 78 Most Ineresting People Cleve., Cleve. mag., 1978; Club Probe voted # 1 disco So. Calif. D.J. Assn., 1984; featured in People mag., 1979, 80. Republican. Roman Catholic. Home and Office: 24446 Lake Rd Bay Village OH 44140

BERGER, JERRY ALLEN, museum director; b. Buffalo, Wyo., Oct. 8, 1943. BA in Psychology, U. Wyo., 1965, BA in Art, 1971, MA in Art History, 1972. Curator collections U. Wyo. Art Mus., Laramie, 1972-88, asst. dir., 1980-83, 87-88, acting dir., 1984-86; dir. Springfield (Mo.) Art Mus., 1988—. Office: Springfield Art Mus 111 E Brookside Dr Springfield MO 65807-1829

BERGER, MICHAEL E., financial consultant; b. Phila., Aug. 24, 1959. B of Nutrition Sci., Pa. State U., 1981; postgrad., U. Ill., 1982. Owner Berger Enterprises, Champaign, Ill., 1982-92; fin. cons. Merrill Lynch, Peoria, Ill., 1992—. Jewish.

BERGER, MILES LEE, land economist; b. Chgo., Aug. 9, 1930; s. Albert E. and Dorothy (Ginsberg) B.; student Brown U., 1948-50; m. Sally Eileen Diamond, Aug. 27, 1955; children—Albert E., Elizabeth Ann. Engaged in real estate appraisal, research and devel., econs. fields, 1950—; mng. chmn.

bd. Berger Fin. Services Corp., Chgo., 1950—; chmn. bd. Mid-Am. Appraisal & Research Corp., Chgo., 1959-80) also dir.; chmn. bd. Real Estate Services Corp., 1969—; vice chmn. bd., trustee Heitman Fin. Services Ltd., 1970—; prin. econ. cons. Columbia Nat. Bank, Chgo., 1965—; dir. Evans Inc.; trustee Heitman Mortgage Investors. Commr., chmn. Chgo. Plan Commn., 1980—; cons. city Chgo. on Ill. Central Air Rights, 1967—; trustee Latin Sch. Chgo., 1967-73, treas., 1953-55, bd. dirs. Latin Sch. Found.; bd. dirs. Albert E. Berger Found. Mem. Am. Inst. Real Estate Appraisers, Soc. Real Estate Appraisers, Soc. Real Estate Counselors, Am. Right-of-Way Assn., Nat. Assn. Housing and Redevel. Ofcls., Nat. Tax Assn., Internat. Assn. Assessing Officers, Lambda Alpha. Jewish (trustee synagogue). Office: Heitman Financial LTD 180 N La Salle St Chicago IL 60601

BERGERE, CARLETON MALLORY, contractor; b. Brookline, Mass., Apr. 4, 1919; s. Jason J. and Anna Lillian B.; student Burdett Bus. Coll., 1938, Babsons Sch. Bus., 1940; m. Jean J. Pach, Oct. 1, 1950. Self-employed contractor, Chgo., 1949-57; pres. Permanent Bldg. Supply Co., Inc., Chgo., 1957-62, Gt. No. Bldg. Products, Inc., Chgo., 1962-67, C.M. Bergere Co., Inc., Chgo., 1967—. Served with USN, 1944. Named Man of Yr., Profl. Remodelers Assn. Greater Chgo., 1978. Nat. Assn. Remodeling Industry (pres. Greater Chicagoland chpt., exec. dir., reg. v.p. 1991-95, President's awd. 1990, Professional awd. 1992), Chgo. Assn. Commerce and Industry (indsl. devel. com.), Better Bus. Bur. Met. Chgo., Industry Trade Practice Com. on Home Improvement (chmn., bd. dirs. 1992—), Nat. Panel Consumer Arbitrators. Club: Exec. (Chgo.). Address: 175 E Delaware Pl Chicago IL 60611-1731

BERGESON, JAMES, advertising executive. Pres., COO Colle and McVoy Inc., Mpls. Office: Colle & McVoy Inc 8500 Mormandale Lake Blvd Minneapolis MN 55437*

BERGGREN, JEAN FRANCES REDDELL, psychiatrist, educator; children: Kirsten, Nathan. BA cum laude, Radcliffe Coll., 1962; MD, We. Res. U., 1966; postgrad., Gestalt Inst. Cleve., 1969-72. Diplomate Am. Bd. Psychiatry and Neurology. Intern pediatrics Cleve. Met. Gen. Hosp., 1967-68; resident psychiatry U. Hosps. Cleve., 1968-69, Fairhill Mental Health Ctr., Cleve., 1970-72; asst. clin. prof. psychiatry Case We. Res. U., Cleve., 1972—; staff physician Mt. Sinai Med. Ctr., Cleve., 1982—; mem. faculty Gestalt Inst., Cleve., 1979-90. Bd. dirs. Cleve. Heights Cmty. Congress, 1975-78. Mem. AMA, Am. Psychiatric Assn., Acad. Psychosomatic Medicine, Soc. Health and Human Values, Cleve. Acad. Medicine, Cleve. Psychiatric Soc. Democrat. Mem. Soc. of Friends. Office: Mt Sinai Health Care Sys One Mount Sinai Dr Cleveland OH 44106

BERGGREN, JERRY LEE, architect, consultant; b. Grand Island, Nebr., Apr. 14, 1948; s. Theodore Harold and Georgia (Isaac) B.; m. Kathleen Kay Peetzke, Jan. 2, 1971; children: Scott Ryan, Stephen Eric. BArch, Kans. State U., 1971. Registered architect, Nebr., Iowa. Designer, chief plans expert Urban Renewal Agy., Kansas City, Kans., 1971-73; project architect Davis Fenton Stange Darling, Lincoln, Nebr., 1973-77; prin. Hull & Berggren Architects, Lincoln, 1977, Jerry L. Berggren, AIA Architect & Assocs., Lincoln, 1977-87, Berggren & Woll Architects, Lincoln, 1987—. Mem. bldg. com. St. Marks United Meth. Ch., Lincoln, 1985-95, White Hall Family Resource Ctr., Lincoln, 1991—; commr. Hist. Preservation Commn.; mem. Nebr. Energy Coun.; bd. dirs. Nebr. Preservation Coun., pres., 1996. Recipient Lincoln Jour. Community award Lincoln Jour. Newspaper, 1984; grantee Nebr. Energy Office, 1987. Mem. AIA (com. hist. resources 1985—, chmn. 1996, PIA adv. coun. vice chair 1996), Assn. for Preservation Tech., Nat. Trust for Hist. Preservation, Nebr. chpt. AIA, Nebr. State Hist. Soc. Office: 206 S 13th St Lincoln NE 68508-2004

BERGGREN, TERRY K., financial executive; b. St. Paul, Dec. 25, 1958; s. Edmund W. and Margaret G. Berggren; children: Preston, Morgan, Eden. Student, Brown Inst., Mpls., 1977. With Peter Boo Advt. Agy., St. Paul; loan officer Town & Country Bank, St. Paul, 1977-81; corp. loss prevention mgr. G.E. Capital Corp., Kansas City, Kans., 1982-94; dir. bus. devel. GE Capital Credit Svcs., Lenexa, Kans., 1994—. Mem. Internat. Assn. Credit Card Investigators (bd. dirs. 1989—, bd. advisors 1989—), Consumer Credit Cons. (bd. dirs. 1992—), Toastmasters. Office: GE Capital 7905 Quivira Rd Lenexa KS 66215-2732

BERGHOETTER, ANTHONY C., stockbroker; b. Red Bud, Ill., July 11, 1954. Salesman Spicer Chevy Olds, Neosho, Mo., 1983-87; stockbroker IDS Fin. Svcs., Neosho, 1987-90; stockbroker, br. mgr. Advest, Hartford, Conn., 1990-93; mng. exec. Royal Alliance Assocs., Neosho, 1993—. Advisor Turnaround Ranch, Joplin, Mo., 1994—. Mem. Newton County Hist. Soc., Rotary (sgt.-at-arms Neosho 1992—), KC. Roman Catholic. Office: Royal Alliance Assocs PO Box 527 Neosho MO 64850-0527

BERGHOLZ, GEORGE FREDERICK, activity therapist; b. Chgo., May 13, 1963; s. Bernard III and Soburnnessa (Ali) B. BFA, Sch. of Art Inst., Chgo., 1986, MAAT, 1987; MAAT, Rush-Presbyn-St Lukes MedCtr., Chgo, 1987; student, Young Artist Studios, Chgo., 1979. Coll. work study asst. to head of reader svcs. Sch. of the Art Inst. Libr., Chgo., 1981-87; gen. graphic design asst. Yeaton Svcs., Chgo., 1987-88; art therapy activity therapist, fitness ctr. cons. James C. King Home, Evanston, Ill., 1988-91; art therapy activity therapist Presbyn. Home, Evanston, 1990; dir. Recreation Therapy Dept. C.P.C Old Orchard, Evanston, Streamwood, 1995—; activities dir. Convalescent Ctr. of Honolulu, 1996—; pres. St. Luke's Rush Day Sch., 1992—, art educator, recreational therapist, art therapist, 1992-94, mental health worker, child psychiatrist, 1993—, 4 Kellogg mental health worker, 1992—; activity dir. for adminstr. Old Orchard Hosp., Skokie, 1994—; print model Suzanne Johnson A Plus Talent, 1992; model for on camera, off camera, radio comml. fashion print and runway Talent Plus, Inc., St. Louis, 1993—; model for Act One, Green and Green, Miami; exclusive model David & Lee, Chgo., 1995; print model Centro, St. Louis, 1994—, Kathy Muller, Honolulu, 1996—; ADR model and talent comml. print film, Honolulu, 1996—. Gynmastic instr. Bernard Horwich Jewish Community Ctr., Chgo., 1986-87, acrosport performer, 1986-87. Mem. Am. Art Therapist Assn., Ill. Art Therapy Assn., Soc. of Art Inst. Alumni Assn. Home: Mailbox 77 445 Seaside Ave Ste 1018 Honolulu HI 96815 Office: Convalescent Ctr of Honolulu 1900 Bachelor St Honolulu HI 96817

BERG-JOHNSON, KAREN ANN, photographer, art educator; b. Mpls., Sept. 25, 1959; d. Wallace Edgar and sylvia June (Schyman) Berg; m. Jay Timothy Johnson, May 20, 1983; children: Christina Berg, Caroline Paige. BFA, U. Minn., 1981, MFA, 1984. Instr., chair photography dept. Art Ctr. of Minn., Crystal Bay, 1982-84; teaching asst. studio art dept. U. Minn., Mpls., 1983; instr. of art Bethel Coll., St. Paul, 1984-87, asst. prof., 1988-92, assoc. prof., 1992—, chairperson art dept., 1994—; juror mus. workers show Katherine Nash Gallery, U. Minn., 1989, chair adv. com., 1981-83. One woman show include Honors Gallery, U. Minn., 1981, Art Ctr. of Minn., Crystal Bay, 1983, Katherine Nash Gallery, 1983, Jewish Community Ctr., Mpls., 1984; exhibited in group shows at Studio Arts Gallery U. Minn., Mpls., 1980, 84, Katherine Nash Gallery, 1981, 88, Coffman Gallery 1, 1982-83, U. Art Mus., 1987, NA Gallery, Northfield, Minn., 1983, Art Ctr. of Minn., Crystal Bay, 1984, Daedalus Gallery, Mpls., 1984, 310 Arts Gallery, Mpls., 1984, Wall St. Gallery, St. Paul, 1984, B Square One Gallery, Mpls., 1984, Eugene Johnson Gallery of Art Bethel Coll., St. Paul, 1984-87, Minn. State Fair, St. Paul, 1986, Mpls. Inst. of Arts, 1986, Sioux City (Iowa) Art Ctr., 1987, Pinder Gallery, N.Y.C., 1987, Foundry Gallery Washington, 1987, San Diego Art Inst., 1987, Mpls. Coll. Arts and Design Gallery, 1988, Mid Hudson Arts and Sci. Ctr., Poughkeepsie, N.Y., 1988, N.J. Ctr. for Visual Arts, Summitt, 1989, Forum Gallery, Mpls., 1989, Miami Expo '89, Fla., 1989, Cen. Mo. State U. Art Ctr. Gallery, Warrensburg, 1990, Jewish Community Ctr. of Houston, 1990, W.A.R.M. Gallery, Mpls., 1990, Phipps Ctr. for Arts, Hudson, Wis., 1990, Laguna Gloria Art Mus., Austin, Tex., 1991, Barrett House Galleries, Poughkeepsie, N.Y., 1991, ARC Gallery, Chgo., 1991, Pleiades Gallery, N.Y.C., 1991, Univ. Gallery U. Del., 1992, Downey Mus. Art, Calif., 1992, Mus. Without Walls, Internat., Bemus Point, N.Y., 1993, New England Fine Art Inst., Boston, 1993, The Phipps Ctr. for Arts, Hudson, Wis., 1993, 94, New Gallery S.D. Sch. Mines and Tech., Rapid City; numerous others. U. Minn. grantee, 1981-83; recipient Juror's award Leedy Voulkos Art Ctr., 1991, Artist's Choice award Phipps Ctr. for Arts, 1990, Juror's award N.J. Ctr. for Visual Arts, 1989, NA Gallery, 1983, Purchase award Univ. Art Mus., 1987. Mem. Soc. for Photographic Edn. Home: 3688 Woodland Trl Saint Paul MN 55123-2406 Office: Bethel Coll Art Dept 3900 Bethel Dr Saint Paul MN 55112-6902

BERGLUND, KIM ANNE, investment company executive; b. Milw., Aug. 24, 1957; d. Kenneth John Raufmann and Marlene A. (Schafer) Preiss; m. Wallace L. Berglund, May 26, 1989; 1 child, Kelsey. Ops. mgr. Kidder Peabody, Milw., 1981-86; bus. devel. specialist Merrill Lynch, Milw., 1986-88, 92-94; asst. portfolio mgr. Prudential Securities, Milw., 1988-92; adminstr. GS Squared Securities, Milw., 1994; bus. devel. specialist Charles Schwab & Co., Milw., 1994—. Recipient Citizenship award West Allis Police Dept., West Milwaukee, Wis., 1993. Home: 6030 N Hyacinth Ln Glendale WI 53217-4421 Office: Charles Schwab & Co Inc 411 E Wisconsin Ave Milwaukee WI 53202-4409

BERGMAN, JERRY RAE, science educator; b. Detroit, May 30, 1946; s. Ernest R. and Irene (Buck) B.; m. Marie Fox, June 20, 1970; children: Aeron, Mishalea; m. Dianne Haldiman, Dec. 28, 1985. BS, Wayne State U., 1969, MEd, 1971, PhD, 1976; MA, Bowling Green State U., 1986; PhD, Columbia Pacific U., 1992. Prof. Bowling Green State U., Bowling Green, Ohio, 1973-80, U. Toledo, Toledo, Ohio, 1981-86, Northwest Coll., Archbold, Ohio, 1987—; dir. Soc. for Study of Male Psychology and Physiology, Montpelier, Ohio, 1974—. Author 20 books and monographs; contbr. articles to profl. jours. Fellow Am. Sci. Affiliation; mem. AAAS, Am. Chem. Soc., Am. Inst. Physics. Office: Northwest State Cmty Coll 22-600 S R 34 Rt 1 Archbold OH 43502

BERGMAN, JOHN H., fire department administrator; b. Kansas City, Mo., Oct. 6, 1943; s. J.H. and Lorene C. (Felten) B.; m. Sharron J. Cole, Aug. 3, 1963; children: Jeffrey, Michael, Stacy. AA, Kansas City (Kans.) C.C., 1987; BA in Pub. Adminstrn., Park Coll., 1981. Fire fighter Kansas City (Kans.) Fire Dept., 1969-74, fire apparatus op., 1974-84, fire capt., 1984-90, bn. chief, 1990-91, asst. fire marshal, 1991-92, fire chief, 1992—; project mgr. Underground Code Symposium, Kansas City, 1993; adj. instr. Nat. Fire Acad., 1994, curriculum com., 1994. Prodr. (TV series) Fire Forum, 1987. Chmn. Community Correction Bd., Wyandotte County, Kansas, 1986-92; bd. dirs. El Centro, Wyandotte County, 1993—; ward capt. Wyandotte County Dem. Com., 1978-92. Harvard fellow J.F.K. Sch. Govt., 1994. Fellow Congl. Fire Inst.; mem. Internat. Assn. Fire Chiefs, Nat. Fire Protection Assn. (chmn. subterranean spaces life safety tech. com. 1994), Metro Chiefs Fire Assn., Soc. Exec. Fire Officers. Roman Catholic.

BERGMAN, ROBERT PAUL, museum administrator, art historian, educator, lecturer; b. Bayonne, N.J., May 17, 1945; s. Abe and Ethel (Leitner) B.; m. Marcelle Posnak, June 30, 1971, 1 child, Maggie. B.A., Rutgers U., 1966; M.F.A., Princeton U., 1969, Ph.D., 1972; DHL (hon.), U. Balt., 1993; DFA (hon.), Md. Inst. Coll. of Art, 1993, Baldwin-Wallace Coll., 1995. Asst prof. history of art U. Rochester, N.Y., 1971-72; asst. prof. history of art Princeton U., N.J., 1972-76; assoc. prof. Harvard U., Cambridge, 1976-81; dir. Walters Art Gallery, Balt., 1981-93, Cleve. Mus. Art, 1993—; vis. instr. Lincoln U., fall 1968; adj. prof. Johns Hopkins U., Balt., 1981-93, Case Western Res. U., 1993—. Author: The Salerno Ivories, 1980; cons. editor: Art Bull.; contbr. articles and revs. in art field. Vol. various mayoral and gubernatorial coms., Balt., Cleve.; fundraiser for various causes. Guggenheim fellow; Dumbarton Oaks fellow; Fulbright fellow; Henry Rutgers scholar. Fellow Am. Acad. in Rome; mem. AAUP, Am. Assn. Mus. (chmn. bd. dirs.), Assn. Art Mus. Dirs. (trustee, pres.), Coll. Art Assn., Internat. Ctr. of Medeval Art (bd. dirs.), Soc. Archtl. Historians, Medieval Acad. Am., Am. Arts Alliance (bd. dirs., treas., chmn.), Phi Beta Kappa. Office: The Cleve Mus of Art 11150 East Blvd Cleveland OH 44106-1711

BERGMANN, LINDA J., marketing professional; b. Milw., Jan. 3, 1955; d. Gordon Walter and Ann Leona (Mueller) Bertschy; m. Myron George Bergmann, June 30, 1984. BS, U. Wis., Milw., 1977. Translator Allis-Chalmers Power Systems, Milw., 1978-82; payroll coord. Utility Power Corp., Milw., 1982-84; mktg. adminstr. Utility Power/Siemens Power Corp., Bradenton, Fla., 1984-92; mgr., mktg. comms. Siemens Power Corp., Milw., 1992—. Contbr. articles to profl. jours. Mem. Dem. Leadership Coun., Washington, 1991—, Manatee County Exec. Com., Bradenton, 1990-92. Mem. Am. Mktg. Assn., Ecology Assn. New Berlin (sec. 1994-95, pres. 1996—), Phi Beta Kappa. Lutheran. Home: 16275 W Crescent Dr New Berlin WI 53151 Office: Siemens Power Corp 1040 S 70th St Milwaukee WI 53214

BERGQUIST, GENE ALFRED, farmer, rancher; b. Paynesville, Minn., Aug. 5, 1927; s. Albin and Viola (Heinrich) B.; m. Ann Dorothy Corwin, Aug. 2, 1958; children: Wayne A., Viola M. Grad. high sch., Rhame, N.D. Self-employed farmer-rancher Rhame, 1948—; Slope County commr. Amidon, N.D., 1982—; bd. dirs. Rhame, N.D. Cenex, 1970-82; bd. dirs. Harper Twp. Rhame; com. mem. Slope County Agrl. Stabilization and Conservation Svc.-USDA Commn., Amidon, 1968-84. Bd. dirs. Rhame Rural Fire Dept., 1976—, Bowman-Slope Social Svc. Bd., Bowman, N.D., 1991—, Deep Creek Twp., 1958-64, Richland Center Twp. Bd., 1952-57; elder Lyle Presbyn. Ch.; youth leader 4-H Slope County, 1950-57. Mem. N.D. Assn. Counties. Presbyterian. Office: Courthouse Amidon ND 58620

BERGREN, LINDA JEAN, stockbroker; b. Kenosha, Wis., July 30, 1946. BAS, U. Wis., 1971. Tchr. Madison (Wis.) Sch. Sys., 1971-81; stockbroker Gordon Flash Co., Madison, 1981-88, Robert Baird, Madison, 1988-94, Dean Witter Reynolds, Madison, 1994—. Pres. YMCA, Church of Christ ch. Democrat. Office: Dean Witter Reynolds # 412 6510 Grand Teton Plz # 412 Madison WI 53719-1029

BERGSTROM, TERRY LEE, research analyst; b. Detroit, May 30, 1952; s. Leslie E. and Marie C. (Montjoy) B.; m. Patti Gallion, July 25, 1987. BS in Polit. Sci., No. Mich. U., Marquette, 1974, MPA, 1986. Rsch. analyst Mich. Legis. Svc. Bur., Lansing, 1986—. Author: (booklets) Get Involved in Local Government, 1991, Schools of Choice, 1992, 94, others. Mem. Am. Soc. for Pub. Adminstrn., Phi Alpha Theta, Phi Kappa Phi.

BERGTHOLD, RICHARD LEE, engineering administrator; b. Hannibal, Mo., Jan. 20, 1960. Engring.mgr. Perry (Mo.) Machine Die Inc., 1978—. Mem. Odd Fellows (vice grand 1995). Baptist.

BERK, HARLAN JOSEPH, numismatist, writer, antiquarian; b. Joliet, Ill., June 7, 1942; s. Sammy and Ruth (Press) B.; m. Ellen Landman, Sept. 20, 1966 (div. 1978); children: Aaron R., Shanna L.; m. Pamela Margaret Blade, June 22, 1982; 1 child, Sammy. Student, U. Ill., 1960-64. Vice pres. New Star Jewelers, Joliet, 1964-85; pres. Harlan J. Berk Ltd., Joliet, 1964, Chgo.; bd. dirs. OLICON Imaging Systems, Inc., Louisville; lectr., treas. N.Y. Internat. Numis. Conv.; Am. rep. Numismatica Ars Classica, Zurich. Author: Roman Gold Coins, 1985, Eastern Roman Successors, 1987, Roman Gold Coins of the Medieval World 383-1453 A.D. (Robert Friedberg award 1987), Eastern Roman Successors of the Sestertius; columnist World Coin News, 1989—, What's Old (Best Fgn. Column Numismatic Literary Guild, 1989, 90, 91, 92). Mem. exec. com. World Heritage Mus., Champaign, Ill., 1988—. Mem. Internat. Assn. Profl. Numismatists (pub. rels. for Am.), Profl. Numismatist Guild (edn. chmn., bd. dirs.), Am. Numismatists Assn. (dealer liaison com.). Democrat. Jewish. Office: 31 N Clark St Chicago IL 60602-2806

BERKE, AMY TURNER, health science association administrator; b. Cleve., Oct. 27, 1942; d. Elliott L. and Evelyn (Silverman) Glicksberg; m. Donald Alan Turner, Dec. 16, 1962 (div. 1979); children: Matthew, Kelli; m. Joseph Jerold Berke, June 21, 1981; children: Richard, Rachel, Jason. Student, Ohio State U., 1960-63; BS, Wayne State U., 1965, MA, 1966. Tchr. Waterford (Mich.) Sch. System, 1965-67; v.p. Apt. Referral Service, Oak Park, Mich., 1970-73; instr. Detroit Coll. Bus., Dearborn, Mich., 1975-79; exec. dir. Detroit Neurosurgical Found., 1979—. Past bd. dirs. Internat. Mus. Surg. Sci., Friends of Belle Isle; bd. dirs. Goodwill Industries Found., Alliance for Safer Greater Detroit; mem. Citizens Adv. Wayne County Youth; commr., vice chair Detroit Recreation Adv. Commn.; commr. Youth Sports and Recreation Commn. Mem. Coun. Mich. Founds. Host Com., Project Pride Detroit C. of C., Wayne State U. Alumni Club, Ohio State U. Alumni Club. Office: Detroit Neurosurg Found 8900 E Jefferson Ste 1117 Detroit MI 48214-2961

BERKENSTADT, JAMES ALLAN, lawyer; b. Chgo., June 26, 1956; s. Edward Jules and Lois Marion (Solomon) B.; m. Holly Lynn Cremer, Aug. 3, 1985; children: Rebecca, Bradley. BA, Northwestern U., 1978; JD, So. Ill. U., 1981. Bar: Ill., Wis. Litigation atty. Pollina & Phelan, Chgo., 1982-85; legal cons. to security dept. Chgo. Cubs Nat. League Ball Club, Chgo., 1982-84; litigation atty. Axley & Brynelson, Madison, Wis., 1986-87; v.p., corporate counsel The Wisconsin Cheeseman, Inc., Madison, 1987—. Author: Black Market Beatles: The Story Behing The Lost Recordings, The Making of Nirvana's Nevermind; prodr. The Beatle Tapes CD, The Best of the Big Bands CD; contbr. articles to jours. Bd. dirs. Cremer Charitable Found., Madison, 1989—. Mem. NARAS, Maple Bluff Country Club. Office: The Wisconsin Cheeseman Inc 301 Broadway Dr Sun Prairie WI 53590-1742

BERKMAN, DAVE, mass communications educator; b. Bklyn., May 6, 1934; s. Henry and Edna (Berkowitz) B.; m. Gloria Scnap, June 1953 (div. May 1963); 1 child, Linda; m. Jo Castellucci, Dec. 1989 (div. Nov. 1989); 1 child, Andrea Lemke. BA cum laude, L.I. U., 1955; MS, Syracuse U., 1956; EdD, NYU, 1963. Prodr., dir. Sta. WHIZ-TV, Zanesville, Ohio, 1956-57, Sta. WTVS, Wayne State U., Detroit, 1957-59; dir. pub. rels. and edn. Dist. 65 AFL-CIO, N.Y.C., 1963-64; asst. prof. comm. Nassau C.C., SUNY, Garden City, 1964-65, Kingsborough C.C., CUNY, Bklyn., 1965-67; sr. media sys. specialist pub. divsn. Xerox Corp., N.Y.C. and Stamford, Conn., 1967-70; assoc. prof. mass comm. Am. U., Washington, 1970-71; program mgr. ESSA-TV, U.S. Office Edn., HEW, Washington, 1971-79; asst. dean telecom. Newhouse Sch., Syracuse (N.Y.) U., 1979-83; prof. mass comm. U. Wis., Milw., 1983—; v.p., chmn. bd. dirs. Alternative Publs., Inc., Milw.; mem. minority affairs task force Corp. for Pub. Broadcasting, 1977-79. Media columnist Shepherd Express, Milw., 1989—; host call-in/interview program Media Talk, Wis. Pub. Radio Network, 1993—; mem. editl. bd. TV Quar., NATAS, 1983—; contbr. over 125 articles to various publs. Active ACLU, 1957—, mem. Conn. state bd., 1968-70, mem. Wis. state bd., 1988-89. Sole non-minority recipient Minority Pub. Broadcasting Achievements award Nat. Assn. Ednl. Broadcasters, 1979. Mem. Broadcast Edn. Assn., Soc. Profl. Journalists (bd. dirs. Milw. chpt. 1984-85). Home: 2555 N Lake Dr Milwaukee WI 53211 Office: Univ Wis Dept Mass Comm Box 413 Milwaukee WI 53201

BERLINGER, NORMAN THOMAS, physician, author; b. Detroit, Sept. 16, 1944; s. Stanley Edmund and Bernice (Glinka) B.; m. Patricia Ann Cybert, June 17, 1968; 1 child, Michael. BS, U. Mich., 1966, MD, 1970; PhD, U. Minn., 1978. Diplomate Am. Bd. Otolaryngology. Intern Henry Ford Hosp., Detroit, 1970-71; resident U. Minn. Hosps., 1971-73, 77-79; assoc. scientist Sloan-Kettering Inst. for Cancer Rsch., N.Y.C., 1973-77; instr. U. Minn. Med. Sch., Mpls., 1977-79; asst. prof. Uniformed Svcs. U. Health Scis., Bethesda, Md., 1979-81; surgeon, clin. br. NIH, Bethesda, 1979-81; assoc. prof. U. Minn. Med. Sch., 1981-88; surgeon Oakdale ENT, P.A., Mpls., 1988—; cons. FMC, Phila., 1986-88; advisor for marine mammals Minn. Zoo, Apple Valley, 1986-88. Contbr. numerous articles to textbooks, articles to profl. jours. and lay periodicals. Comdr. USNR, 1979-81. Grantee NIH, 1973-81, Am. Otological Soc., 1986-88; Nat. Cancer Inst. rsch. fellow, 1974-77. Fellow Am. Acad. Otolaryngology (Meritorious Svc. award 1987); mem. Assn. for Rsch. in Otolaryngology, Phi Rho Sigma. Office: 2855 Campus Dr Ste 630 Plymouth MN 55441

BERMAN, ARTHUR LEONARD, state senator; b. Chgo., May 4, 1935; s. Morris and Jean (Glast) B.; m. Barbara Dombeck; children: Adam, Marcy Padorr. B.S. in Commerce and Law, U. Ill., 1956; J.D., Northwestern U., 1958. Bar: Ill., 1958. Pvt. practice, Chgo.; ptnr. White, White & Berman, Chartered, 1958-74, Maragos, Richter, Berman, Russell & White, Chartered, 1974-81, Chatz, Berman, Maragos, Haber & Fagel, 1981-82, Berman, Fagel, Haber, Maragos & Abrams, 1982-86, Karlin & Fleisher, 1986—; spl. atty. Bur. Liquidations, Ill. Dept. Ins., 1962-67; spl. asst. atty. gen. Ill., 1967-68; mem. Ill. Ho. of Reps., 1969-76, Ill. Senate, 1977—. Bd. dirs. Zionist Orgn. Chgo.; mem. Rogers Park, Edgewater, Northtown communtiy councils. Pres., 50th Ward Young Dems., 1956-60; v.p. Cook County Young Dems., 1956-60, 50th Ward Regular Dem. Orgn., 1955—; exec. bd. Dem. Party, Evanston, Ill., 1973—. Bd. dirs. Bernard Horwich Jewish Community Center, High Ridge YMCA; bd. govs. State of Israel Bonds. Mem. ABA, Ill. Bar Assn., Chgo. Bar Assn. (bd. mgrs. 1976-77), Decalogue Soc. Lawyers (bd. mgrs. 1988—), Nat. Assn. Jewish Legislators (pres. 1987-89), Am. Trial Lawyers Assn., John Howard Assn., Common Cause, Northwestern U. Alumni Assn., U. Ill. Alumni Assn., Phi Epsilon Pi, Tau Epsilon Rho. Office: 7344 N Western Ave Chicago IL 60645-1814

BERMAN, HOWARD ALLEN, rabbi; b. Paterson, N.J., June 21, 1949; s. Bernard and Elaine (Geller) B. BA, U. Cin., 1972; BA in Hebrew Letters, Hebrew Union Coll., 1973, MA in Hebrew Letters, 1974. Ordained rabbi, 1974. Asst. rabbi Temple Emanu-El, N.Y.C., 1974-79; assoc. rabbi Temple Beth Israel, Hartford, Conn., 1979-81; sr. rabbi Chgo. Sinai Congregation, 1982—; vis. prof. Luth. Sch. Theology, Chgo., 1988—. Contbr. to World Book Ency. Year Book, 1984-93. V.p. Hyde Park Interfaith Coun., Chgo., 1988-91; mem. Chgo. Nuclear Free Zone City Commn., 1987—; mem. adv. coun. Ctr. for Ethics and Corp. Policy, 1987-90; mem. met. task force Parliament of World Religions; mem. steering com. Interfaith Response to AIDS; mem., bd. dirs. Planned Parenthood of Chgo. Mem. Central Conf. Am. Rabbis, Chgo. Assn. Reform Rabbis, Caxton Club, Pilgrim Soc. Office: Sinai Temple 5350 S South Shore Dr Chicago IL 60615-5708

BERMAN, MAXINE, state legislator; b. Mich., Apr. 17, 1946. BA, U. Mich., 1968. State rep. Mich. Ho. Reps., Dist. 64, 1982-94, Mich. Ho. Reps., Dist. 36, 1995—; chmn. elec. com., vice chmn. consumers com., mem. appropriations com., Mich. Ho. Reps.; tchr. English Oak Parj H.S., 1968-78; pub. rels., freelance writing & cmty. rsch., 1978-82; mem. Mich. Job Tng. Coord. Coun.; mem. Jewish Vocat. Svc.; bd. dirs. telecommunications adv. com. Lawrence Inst. Tech. Mem. exec. bd. 17th Dist. & Oakland County Dem. Com., Mich. Dem. Women's Caucus; chmn. Mich. Women's Campaign Fund, 1989; mem. Mich. Dem. Agrl. Party. Recipient Wonder Woman award Women's Survival Ctr., Catalyst award Nat. Assn. Women Bus. Owners. Mem. NOW, NAACP, LWV, Nat. Coun. Jewish Women, Detroit Women's Forum, Gray Panthers. Home: 24213 Evergreen Rd Southfield MI 48075-5558 Office: Mich State Senate State Capitol Lansing MI 48909*

BERMAN-HAMMER, SUSAN, public relations executive; b. Buffalo, Sept. 12, 1950; d. Leonard and Judith H. (Goldenberg) Berman; m. Tony Hammer, Aug. 17, 1975; 1 child, Erik Jason. BA, Northwestern U., 1972, MS in Journalism, 1975. Pub. info. asst. Sta. WBBM-TV, Chgo., 1972; news asst. exec. trailer Dem. Nat. Conv. ABC-TV News, Miami, Fla., 1972; writer Chgo. Conv. and Visitors Bur., 1973-75; Washington corr. Sta. WYEN, Des Plaines, Ill., 1975; sr. v.p. Herbert H. Rozoff Assocs., Inc., Chgo., 1976-82; pres., owner Susan L. Berman Assocs., Inc., Deerfield, Ill., 1982—; v.p. corp. communications Sheldon Good & Co., Chgo., 1988-89; chairperson Chgo. Communications/10, a consortium in field, 1982-83. Asst. regional dir. Nat. Movement for Student Vote, Chgo., 1972; bd. dirs. Chgo. Women in Broadcasting, 1972-76, Younger Set Jewish Fedn., Dallas, 1985-87; trustee North Shore Sch. Dist. 112 Found., 1995—; mem. North Shore Sch. Dist. 112 Caucus, 1995, also sec., mem. exec. bd.; Edgewood Sch. PTO liaison to North Shore Sch. Dist. 112, 1995—, also safety co-chair; founder, chair steering com. Safe Home Program North Shore Sch. Dists. 112 & 109, 1994—; Sherwood Sch. PTO liaison to North Shore Sch. Dist. 112 & CIC Legis. Com., Highland Park, Ill., 1994-95; mem. young women's exec. bd., v.p. cmty. devel., co-chair Trendsetter luncheon, co-chair Insights com., nominating com. Shalom Chgo. com., mem. campaign cabinet Jewish United Fund Chgo., 1991-96; bd. dirs. nat. women's com. North Shore chpt. Brandeis U., 1991-93; exec. bd., v.p. programming, reenrollment and membership, nominating com. Tamarisk chpt. ORT, Deerfield, Ill., 1990-95; chair comm. com. North Shore Congregation Israel, Glencoe, Ill., 1993-94; spokesperson and co-leader Parents Against Proposed Annexation of Deerfield subdivsns. from North Shore Sch. Dist. 112 into Deerfield Sch. Dist. 109, 1993-94. Recipient Recognition award City Coun. of Highland Park, Ill. Mem. North Shore Congregation, Israel, Northwestern U. Alumni Club,

Alpha Lambda Delta, Multiplex, Chgo. Soc. Clubs. Office: 9 Tamarisk Ln Deerfield IL 60015-5075

BERN, SCOTT E., stockbroker; b. Chgo., Oct. 29, 1963. BA, U. Wis., 1987. Stockbroker Thompson McKinnen, Milw., 1988-89, Smith Barney, Milw., 1989—. Helper O Group Homes for Retarded Adults, Milw., 1995—.

BERNADETTA, SISTER MARIA, special education educator; b. Chgo., Apr. 25, 1925; d. Anthony and Maria Grace (Rizzo) Beninato. Student, Pestolozzi Frobel Coll., 1967-70; cert. tchr., DePaul U., 1985; degree in spl. edn., Nat.-Louis U., 1990. Joined Queen of Peace Order, Roman Cath. Ch., 1945. Sec. bishop Sacred Heart Ch., Chgo., 1965-89, catechism tchr., 1967; founder, tchr., adminstr. Little Sisters Sch., Chgo., 1970-90; founder, spl. edn. tchr., adminstr. St. Bernadette's Sch., Chgo., 1991—; mistress of novices Queen of Peace Order, 1972-82, rev. mother superior, 1985—; pres. St. Bernadette's Corp.; mem. Case Rsch. Com. Organist Sacred Heart Ch., 1955. Mem. ASCD, Nat. Assn. Pvt. Sch. for Exceptional Children, Ill. Coun. for Exceptional Children, Ill. Affiliation of Pvt. Sch. for Exceptional Children, Ill. Coun. for Behavioral Disorders. Office: Saint Bernadette's Sch 3550 W Peterson Ave Chicago IL 60659-3214

BERNARD, FRANK CHARLES, lawyer; b. Chgo., June 21, 1908; s. Albert and Melanie (Frank) B.; m. Lillian Sturman, Sept. 11, 1938 (dec. Aug. 1972); children: James W., Patricia B. Haber; m. Jenice A Hecht, July 15, 1973. PhB, U. chgo., 1928, JD cum laude, 1930. Bar: Ill. 1930. Assoc. Sonnenschein Nath & Rosenthal, Chgo., 1930-49; ptnr. Sonnenschein Carlin Nath & Rosenthal (name now Sonnenschein Nath & Rosenthal), Chgo., 1949—. Contbr. articles on real estate law to profl. jours. Mem. Zoning Bd. Appeals, City of Highland Park, Ill., 1966-84. Mem. ABA, Ill. State Bar Assn. (chmn. real estate law sect. 1971-72), Chgo. Bar Assn. (chmn. real property law com. 1954-56), Am. Coll. Real Estate Lawyers. Home: 1220 Park Ave W Apt 135 Highland Park IL 60035-2241 Office: Sonnenschein Nath & Rosenthal 8000 Sears Tower 233 S Wacker Dr Chicago IL 60606-6306

BERNARDELLI, KATHY LOUISE, critical care nurse; b. Detroit, Apr. 29, 1957; d. James J. and Helen Marie (Lesniowski) B. BSN, Wayne State U., 1980; postgrad., Cen. Mich. U., 1990—. RN, Mich.; cert. ACLS, critical care nurse. Staff nurse intermediate care PCHA Heritage Hosp., Taylor, Mich., 1980-81,, 1981-86, asst. head nurse intermediate care, 1986-88; asst. head nurse CCU, Oakwood Hosp., Dearborn, Mich., 1988-90; head nurse critical care unit Saratoga Community Hosp., Detroit, 1990-91; nurse mgr. spl. care unit ICU/critical care unit Heritage Hosp., Dearborn, 1991-95; nurse Vivra Renal Care, 1996—. mem. AACN, Soc. Critical Care Medicine.

BERNARDI, JAMES EDWARD, retail executive, real estate investor and developer; b. Highland Park, Ill., July 26, 1946; s. Irving D. and Nell D. (Dimmitt) B.; m. Michelle DiCarlo, June 12, 1976; children: Jamie Elizabeth, Michael James. BA, North Park Coll., 1969. Cert. real esate agt. Tchr., coach Carmel High Sch., Mundelein, Ill., 1969-75; gen. mgr. and officer Armanetti Liquors, Mundelein, 1976—; gen. ptnr. Hawthorn Lanes, Vernon Hills, Ill., 1989-91; real estate agt., Century 21; owner, pres. and CEO LaSalle Nail Care Products Line. Mem. Com. Bus. Devel. Commn., Mundelein, ARC, Mundelein; Officiated Ill. High Sch. Basketball Championship Series since 1975. Recipient George Young award for contbns. to football officiating NFL Ofcls. Assn. Mem. Ill. H.S. Assn. (ofcl. 1969—), No. Ofcls. Assn. (past pres., bd. dirs.), Suburban Basketball Ofcls. Assn. (chmn.) Rotary (pres. Mundelein chpt. 1992-93), Libertyville, Mundelein, Vernon Hills C. of C. (bd. dirs. 1993-96). Roman Catholic. Home: 1330 Kurtis Ln Lake Forest IL 60045-4305 Office: Armanetti Liquors 425 Townline Rd Mundelein IL 60060-4413

BERNARDIN, JOSEPH LOUIS CARDINAL, archbishop, university chancellor; b. Columbia, S.C., Apr. 2, 1928; s. Joseph and Maria M. (Simion) B. AB in Philosophy, St. Mary's Sem., Balt., 1948; MA in Edn., Cath. U. Am., 1952. Ordained priest Roman Catholic Ch., 1952; asst. pastor Diocese of Charleston, S.C., 1952-54; vice chancellor Diocese of Charleston, 1954-56, chancellor, 1956-66, vicar gen., 1962-66, diocesan consultor, 1962-66, adminstr., 1964-65; aux. bishop Atlanta, 1966-68; pastor Christ the King Cathedral, 1966-68; sec., mem. exec. com. Nat. Conf. Cath. Bishops-U.S. Cath. Conf., gen. sec., 1968-72, pres., 1974-77; archbishop of Cin., 1972-82, Chgo., 1982—; chancellor U. St. Mary of the Lake, Mundelein (Ill.) Seminary; mem. Congregation for Bishops, 1973-78; del., mem. permanent coun. World Synod of Bishops, 1974, 77, 80, 83, 87, 90, 94; mem. Coll. of Cardinals, 1983—, Pontifical Commn. for Revision Code Canon Law, 1983, Congregation for Evangelization of Peoples, 1983-88, Congregation for Sacraments and Divine Worship, 1984—, Coun. for Promoting Christian Unity, 1984—; chmn. ad hoc com. on war and peace Nat. Conf. Cath. Bishops, 1983, chmn. ad hoc com. to assess the moral status of deterrence, 1985-88, chmn. com. for pro-life activities, 1983-89, chmn. com. for marriage and family life 1990-93, chmn. ad hoc com. on structure and function of conf. with U.S. Cath. Conf. Author: Prayer in Our Time, 1973, Let the Children Come to Me: A Guide for the Religious Education of Children, 1976, Called to Serve, Called to Lead: Reflections on the Ministerial Priesthood, 1981, It Is Christ We Preach, 1982, Our Communion, Our Peace, Our Promise, 1984, Christ Lives in Me, 1985, In Service of One Another, 1985, Guidelines on Access to the Sacraments of Initiation and Reconcilation for Developmentally Disabled Persons, 1985, The Challenges We Face Together: Reflections on Selected Questions for Archdiocesan Religious Educators, 1986, A Challenge and A Responsibility: A Pastoral Statement on the Church's Response to the AIDS Crisis, 1986, Growing in Wisdom, Age and Grace: A Guide for Parents in the Religious Education of Their Children, 1988, The Consistent Ethic of Life, 1988, Come Holy Spirit: A Pastoral Statement on the Catholic Charismatic Renewal, 1988, The Family Gathered Here Before You: A Pastoral Letter on the Church, 1989, The Parish in the Contemporary Church, 1992, The Call to Service: Pastoral Statement on the Permanent Diaconate, 1993, A Sign of Hope: A Pastoral Letter on Healthcare, 1995. Mem. adv. coun. Am. Revolution Bicentennial, 1975-76, Pres.'s Adv. Com. on Refugees, 1975, pres.'s nat. adv. coun. U. S.C., 1979-90; mem. bd. trustees Cath. U. Am., 1973-81, 89-93, chmn. bd., 1985-88. Recipient Albert Einstein Internat. Peace prize, 1983; named to S.C. Hall of Fame, 1988. Mem. Nat. Cath. Edn. Assn. (chmn. bd. 1978-81), Religious Alliance Against Pornography (founding mem., vice chmn.), Cath. Charities USA Nat. Devel. Task Force. Home: 1555 N State Pky Chicago IL 60610-1613 Office: Archdiocese of Chgo PO Box 1979 Chicago IL 60690-1979

BERNARD-STEVENS, DAVID F., state legislator; b. Gothenburg, Nebr., June 23, 1951; m. Janet E., 1978; children: David, Matthew. Student, Wesleyan U., Lincoln, 1969-71, Am. U., 1971-72; BA, U. Nebr., 1974. H.S. tchr. Nebr.; staff mem. Cozad (Nebr.) Newspaper, Nebr., 1960-68; mem. assembly line Monroe Auto Equipment, Cozad, 1969; asst. common carrier coord. Nebr. Consol. Comms. Corp., 1973-74; instr. Am. and world history North Platte (Nebr.) Pub. Sch. Dist., 1976-78; instr. internat. rels., econs. and Am. govt. Papillon/La Vista Pub. Sch., 1978-85, chmn. dept. social studies, 1978-85; mem. from dist. 42 Nebr. State Senate, Lincoln, 1988—, mem. cm. on coms., vice appropriations and intergovtl. coop. com.; mem. Health, Edn. and Humsn Svc. Adv. Bd. Midwestern Legis. Conf.; apptd. to Nebr. Com. for Distbn. of Fed. and State Block Grants, 1993—; asst. press. liaison to U.s. Senate, 1971-73. Named Nebr. Tchr. of Yr., 1982, One of Top Four Tchrs. in Nation, Nat. Sch. Orcls. Assn., 1983; recipient Outstanding Cmty. Svc. award C. of C., 1983, Honorarium for Acad. Excellence Papillon/La Vista Challenge Com., 1984, Outstanding emergency Svc. award North Platte CAP, 1985. Office: Nebr State Senate State Capitol Rm 1016 Lincoln NE 68509*

BERNATH, OTTO NICOLAUS, physician; b. Budapest, Apr. 4, 1932; came to U.S., 1956; s. Eugene Bernath and Etelka Nagy; m. Melinda Helen Hiripi, Sept. 8, 1956; children: Linda, Juliet. MD, U. Med. Scis., Budapest, 1956. Diplomate Am. Acad. Family Practice. Intern, then resident Barberton Citizens Hosp., 1959-62; physician Mogadore, Ohio, 1962-92; instr. N.E. Ohio Med. U., 1976—. Fellow Am. Acad. Family Practice.

BERNATOWICZ, FRANK ALLEN, management consultant, expert witness; b. Chgo., Nov. 3, 1954; s. Chester and Pauline (Maciula) B.; m. Kathleen Ann Carlson, Apr. 29, 1978; children: Amy Elizabeth, Laura Ann. BSEE, U. Ill., 1976; MBA in Fin., Loyola U., Chgo., 1981, postgrad in acctg., 1982-84. Registered profl. engr., Ill.; CPA, Ill. Engr. Commonwealth Edison Co., Chgo., 1976-79, gen. engr., 1979-82, prin. engr., 1982-84; sr. cons. Brenner Group, Chgo., 1984-85; supr. Ernst & Young (formerly Ernst & Whinney), Chgo., 1985, mgr., 1985-86; sr. mgr. Ernst & Young, Chgo., 1986-88, ptnr., 1989-96; prin. J. Alix & Assoc., Chgo., 1996—; Speaker in field. Active retreat St. Barnabas Ch., Chgo., 1986—, fundraising com., 1986—; mem. bd. regents Mercy Boys Home, 1990—. Mem. AICPA, Ill. Soc. CPAs (committeeman 1985-87), Project Mgmt. Inst., Nat. Soc. Profl. Engrs., Builders Assn. Chgo. (committeeman 1988—), Chgo. Soc. Clubs (Met.), Chgo. Bldg. Congress. Home: 10422 S Oakley Ave Chicago IL 60643-2506 Office: Ernst and Young 233 S Wacker Dr Chicago IL 60606-6306

BERNBERG, MICHAEL NATHAN, consulting company executive; b. Chgo., Feb. 12, 1953; s. Fred A. and Doris F. Bernberg; 1 child, Henry. BA in History, U. Ill., 1974; MBA in Mktg. and Fin., U. Ill., Chgo., 1982. Sales rep. Cadillac Plastics & Chems., Detroit, 1975-78; ter. mgr. Am. Cyanamid, Wayne, N.J., 1978-85; dir. mktg. and sales Am. Weco Corp., Elk Grov, Ill., 1985-87; pres. M. Bernberg Cons. Assocs., Des Plaines, Ill., 1987-93; CEO, A. Marks & Assoc., Wheeling, Ill., 1993—. Contbr. articles to mags. and national and regional publs. Mem. Am. Mktg. Assn. (exec.), Midwest Soc. Profl. Cons. Office: Ste 450 395 E Dundee Rd Wheeling IL 60090

BERNEIS, KENNETH STANLEY, physician, educator; b. Bloomington, Ind., Dec. 25, 1951; s. Hans Ludwig and Regina (Fischhoff) B.; m. Karen Lou Sachs, Nov. 23, 1975; children: Erica, Erin, Ellen, Elaina, Elyse. B.S., U. Mich., 1973, M.D., 1977. Diplomate Am. Bd. Family Practice; cert. geriatrics. Intern-resident Bronson Hosp., and Borgess Med. Ctr., 1977-80; practice family medicine, Ostego, Mich., 1980—; pres., owner Ostego Family Physicians, P.C., 1981—; clin. instr. Mich. State U., 1980—; preceptor Southwestern Mich. Area Health Edn. Ctr., 1980—; chief of staff Pipp Community Hosp., 1982-85, vice-chief of staff, 1985-86, chief of staff 1986—, chief ob-gyn, 1985—, chief pharmacy and therapeutics, 1984—; chief quality assurance Mirnet Research Network, 1981—, mem. steering com., 1982—; med. dir. Bronson Healthcare Group Nursing Homes. Mem. AMA, NRA, Am. Geriatrics Soc. (cert.), Am. Acad. Family Physicians. Home: 131 N Sunset St Plainwell MI 49080-1296 Office: 900 Dix St Otsego MI 49078-1563 also: 1576 Main St Martin MI 49070

BERNHAGEN, LILLIAN FLICKINGER, school health consultant; b. Cleve., Oct. 1, 1916; d. Norman Henry and Bertha May (Rogers) Flickinger; m. Ralph John Bernhagen, Sept. 2, 1940; children: Ralph, Janet Elizabeth Darling, Penelope Anne Braat. Student, Ohio Wesleyan U., 1934-37; B.S., R.N., Ohio State U., 1940, M.A., 1958; postgrad., LaVerne Coll., 1972-73. Cert. health edn. specialist. Asst. dir. Kiwanis Health Camp for Underprivileged Children, Steubenville, Ohio, summer 1940; asst. dir. nurses Jefferson Davis Hosp., Houston, 1940-41; ARC instr. Ohio State U., 1943, 63, elem. edn. lectr., 1970; dir. health services Worthington (Ohio) City Schs., 1951-76; health edn. instr. Ohio State U., 1976-77; spl. cons. venereal disease and sex edn. Ohio Dept. Health, 1976-82; sch. health cons., 1976—; vice chmn. medicine/edn. com. on sch. and coll. health AMA, 1976-78, chmn., 1978-80. Author: Sex Education: Understanding Growth and Social Development, 1968, What A Miracle You Are-Boys, 1968, 3d rev. edit., 1986, What A Miracle You Are-Girls, 1968, 3d rev. edit., 1986, Toward a Reverence for Life, 1971, Personality, Sexuality and Stereotyping, 1974, (with others) Growth Patterns and Sex Education: A Suggested Curriculum Guide K-12, 1967; contbr. articles to profl. jours., mags. Bd. dirs. Hearing and Speech Ctr. of Columbus and Franklin County, 1954-57, sec., 1957; mem. nat. adv. com. Nat. Ctr. for Health Edn., 1978-82; sec.-tres. Ohio Wesleyan U. Class of 38, 1968-78, 83-88; bd. dirs. V.D. Hotline Columbus and Franklin County, 1974-87, bd. expansion chmn., 1978-85, pres., 1985-86; mem. profl. adv. com. Ptnrs. Home Health Inc., 1991—; mem. Worthington Hist. Soc., Doll Docent, 1982—; mem King Ave. United Meth. Ch., 1938—; mem. choir, 1950—, pres., 1961-63, pastor/parish rels. com., 1985-88, bd. trustees, 1989-92, adminstrv. coun., 1992—, edn. commn., 1982-85, nominations and pers., 1992-94; treas. Franklin County Women's Golf Tournament, 1992. Recipient Centennial award Ohio State U., 1970, Outstanding Alumna award Ohio State U. Sch. Nursing, 1964, Disting. Service award Mich. Sch. Nurses Assn., 1972, hon. mention La Sertoma Internat. Woman of Yr., 1972. Fellow Am. Sch. Health Assn. (v.p. 1974, pres. 1976, governing coun. 1973-88, chmn. health guidance in sex edn. com. 1963-67, 71-77, chmn. sr. adv. coun. 1983-89, Disting. Service award 1969, Howe award 1979, cert. of merit, 1985, mem. awards com. 1986-89, mem. hist. com. 1989—), Am. Pub. Health Assn. (chmn. com. on urban health problems 1972); mem. NEA (life, ret.), Sex Edn. and Info. Coun. of U.S., Worthington Edn. Assn. (v.p. 1961-62, Tchr. of Year 1972-73), Cen. Ohio Tchrs. Assn. (chmn. sch. health svcs. sect. 1963), Ohio State U. Women's Golf Assn. (chmn. 1973, parliamentarian 1988—), Ohio Wesleyan U. Alumni Assn. (chmn. alumni recognition com. 1994-95, bd. dirs. 1989-95, chmn. bylaws revision com. 1991—, mem. orgn. com. 1994-95), Columbus Women's Dist. Golf Assn. (treas. 1985, sec. 1987, v.p. 1989, pres. 1990, adv. bd. 1991-95, parliamentarian 1996—), Columbus Computer Soc., Chi Omega (pres. Columbus Alumnae chpt. 1947-49, fin. adv. Ohio Wesleyan U. 1964-76, Outstanding Alumna of Yr. State of Ohio 1986), Pi Lambda Theta (citation award 1971, mem. program com. 1986-89, chmn. by laws revision com. 1990—, parliamentarian), Sigma Theta Tau, Phi Delta Kappa. Clubs: Monnett, Worthington Women's. Home and Office: 5916 Linworth Rd Worthington OH 43085-3357

BERNHARDT-KABISCH, ERNEST KARL-HEINZ, English and comparative literature educator; b. Chemnitz, Germany, Nov. 15, 1934; came to U.S., 1955; s. Karl-Heinz and Brunhild Anna Bertha (Kabisch) Bernhardt; m. Eva Carolyn Dessau, Sept. 1, 1956; 1 child, Ethan Karl. BA, U. Calif., Berkeley, 1957, MA, 1959, PhD, 1962. Instr. Ind. U., Bloomington, 1962-64, asst. prof., 1964-68, assoc. prof., 1968-80, prof., 1980—; dir. Living Learning Ctr., Ind. U., Bloomington, 1977-90, resident dir. Overseas Study Program, Hamburg, Germany, 1990-91, 94-95. Author: Robert Southey, 1977, Begegnungen mit Erda, 1991; co-editor: Yearbook of Comparative and General Literature, 1977-90; contbr. articles to profl. jours. Mem. AAUP, Am. Comparative Lit. Assn., Modern Lang. Assn., Oesterreichischer Alpenverein. Democrat. Home: 616 S Jordan Ave Bloomington IN 47401-5122 Office: Dept English Ind Univ Bloomington IN 47405

BERNING, ROBERT WILLIAM, librarian; b. Carroll, Iowa, Dec. 2, 1949; s. Norbert John and Marjorie Lavine (Miller) B. BSE, Northwest Mo. State U., 1972; MLS, Emporia State U., 1974. Cert. pub. libr., Iowa. Sch. libr. Mount Ayr (Iowa) Cmty. Schs., 1974-76, Wall Lake (Iowa) Cmty. Schs., 1977-79, West Point (Nebr.) Pub. Schs., 1979-81; dir. Dubuque County Libr., Farley, Iowa, 1981-82; sch. libr. HLV Cmty. Schs., Victor, Iowa, 1982-84; dir. Carlisle (Iowa) Pub. Libr., 1985—; adv. bd. mem. State Libr. Iowa, Des Moines, 1987, 89, Ctrl. Iowa Regional Libr., Clive, 1992-94. Rep. Lanning Bequest com. City of Carlisle, 1995—. Mem. ALA, KC, Iowa Libr. Assn. (govtl. affairs com. 1988-91), Iowa Small Libr. Assn. (sec. 1985-87), Carlisle Lion's Club, Carlisle C. of C. (libr. rep. 1990—). Roman Catholic. Office: Carlisle Pub Libr 135 School St PO Box S Carlisle IA 50047

BERNSTEIN, EVA GOULD, retired elementary education educator, reading specialist; b. Milw., Nov. 25, 1918; d. Nathan and Lena Fried Gould; m. E. Ace Bernstein (dec.); children: Marcy B. Lichtig, Lynn C. Arriale. BS in Elem. Edn., State Tchrs. Coll., Milw., 1940; MS in Reading, U. Wis., Milw., 1970. Tchr. S.S. Jr. High, Sheboygan, Wis., 1940-42, Greendale (Wis.) Pub. Schs., 1947-49; reading specialist Milw. Pub. Schs., 1970-79; with Lake Worth (Fla.) Schs., 1989—. Docent Milw. Art Mus., 1987—. Mem. AAUW (coll. women's club, leader, mem. book group 1989—), Nat. Coun. Jewish Women (v.p. pub. affairs 1950-54), Hadassah (v.p. Am. affairs 1951-53), Pi Lambda Theta (v.p. conv. tours chair, v.p. U. Wis.-Milw. chpt. 1976-78). Jewish.

BERNSTEIN, JEFFREY ALAN, pharmacist, mathematician, computer scientist; b. Dec. 28, 1959; s. Jack L. and Jean B. (Gruenke) B.; m. Paula E. Ringer, July 10, 1982; children: Sara A., Benjamin P. BS in Pharmacy, Ohio No. U., 1982; MS in math., Youngstown State U., 1995; postgrad., Kent State U. Registered pharmacist, Md., Pa., Ohio. Pharmacist, store mgr. People's Drug Stores, Inc., Prince Georges County, Md., 1982-87; pharmacist, owner Laurel (Md.) Park Pharmacy, 1987-88; pharmacist, mgr. Phar-Mor, Inc., Youngstown, Ohio, 1988-90; staff pharmacist St. Elizabeth's Hosp. Med. Ctr., Youngstown, 1990-91, Conva-Med Pharm., Inc., Youngstown, 1991-92; owner, ptnr. Med-Pack, Inc., Youngstown, 1992-94, Rite-Aid, Inc., 1992-95; prof. Kent State U., Salem, Ohio, 1995—. Mem. Logos Sys. Assocs., Poland, Ohio, 1989, mem. steering com., 1992—. Mem. Assn. for Computing Machinery. Home: 31 Nesbitt St Poland OH 44514-3737 Office: Kent State Univ 2491 State Rte 45 S Salem OH 44460-9412

BERNSTEIN, LEROY G., state legislator; m. Kathleen Bernstein; 4 children. Pres., owner Valley Movers, Inc.; mem. N.D. Ho. of Reps. from 45th dist., 1989—; vice chmn. Transp. Com. N.D. Ho. of Reps., mem. Indsl. Appropriations Com, Govt. Ops., Bus. and Labor Com. Mem. DAV, KC, U.S. C. of C., Am. Legion, Eagles. Republican. Address: 1333 N 10th St Fargo ND 58103*

BERNSTEIN, MARK D., theater director. Grad., U. Pa. Gen. mgr. Phila. Drama Guild; instr. financial mgmt. Nonprofit Arts Inst., Drexel U.; instr. Nonprofit Mgmt. Ctr., Wash. U.; mng. dir. The Repertory Theatre of St. Louis; mem. nat. negotiating com. League of Resident Theatres; mem. citizens adv. panel Mo. Regional Arts Commission. mem. membership com. Greater Phila. Cultural Alliance. Office: Repertory Theatre St Louis PO Box 191730 Saint Louis MO 63119-7730*

BERNSTEIN, NEIL SANFORD, mechanical engineer, consultant; b. Burbank, Calif., July 5, 1952; s. Charles M. and Phyllis (Ammer) B.; m. Aliza D. Acker, Sept. 4, 1979; children: Oren S., Michal, Asaf, Omri. BSME, Ben-Gurion U. of the Negev, Beer Sheva, Israel, 1985, MSME, 1989; PhD in Applied Math. and Computers, Cranfield (Eng.) U., 1996. Draftsman various firms, L.A., 1969-71, Vidar Corp., Mountain View, Calif., 1972; mem. Kibbutz Kfar Haruv, South Golan Heights, Israel, 1973-82; engr. Israel Aircraft Industries, Beer Sheva, 1984-86; rsch. asst. Ben-Gurion U. of the Negev, 1983-89; lectr. Cranfield Inst. Tech., 1989-92; mgr. Cumming Engine Co., Columbus, Ind., 1992-93; pvt. practice design and manufacture automation cons. Columbus, 1994-96; sr. info. technologist Product Data Integration Techs., Inc., Long Beach, Calif., 1996—. Author papers in field. Achievements include research on representation model for dimensions and tolerances in mechanical design, model for validity analysis of dimensions and tolerances in mechanical design, mathematical model for datum systems in mechanical design. ESL tutor, Palo Alto, Calif., 1970-71; scoutmaster Israel Scouts, Beer Sheva, 1980-81; chmn. Extended Day Care Program, Omer, Israel, 1988-89, Music for Youth Parents, Columbus, 1995; vol. Kibbutz Movement, Israel, 1972-73. Cpl. Israel Def. Forces, 1974-76. Nat. Merit scholar, 1970-71; recipient Family of Yr. award City of Columbus, 1993. Mem. ASME, IEEE, Am. Soc. Quality Control, Soc. Mfg. Engrs., Assn. Computing Machinery. Jewish.

BERNSTEIN, ROBERT, advertising executive; m. Phyliss Bernstein; children: Steven, David, Susan. Grad., U. Okla., 1960. With Potts Woodbury Advt., 1962-64; founder Bernstein-Rein, Kansas City, Mo., 1964—, pres, CEO; bd. dirs., chmn. Mark Twain Bank Kansas City. Active Youth Vol. Corps, Epilepsy Found., Heart Am. Shakespeare Festival, Met. Luth. Ministry, STOP Violence Coalition, Children's Pl., Children's Mercy Hosp., Genesis Sch., Ronald McDonald Houses, Variety Club Kansas City; pres. Starlight Theatre Assn.; bd. dirs. Kansas City Art Inst. Recipient Spirit of Kansas City award, 1991, Hy Vile Cmty. Svc. award, 1995, Advt. Profl. of Yr. award Am. Advt. Fedn., 1995, Manking award Cystic Fibrosis award, 1995. Mem. Am. Assn. Advt. Agys., Nat. Assn. Broadcasters. Office: Bernstein-Rein Advt Inc 4600 Madison Ave #1500 Kansas City MO 64112-1277

BERON, GAIL LASKEY, real estate analyst, consultant, appraiser; b. Detroit, Nov. 13, 1943; d. Charles Jack Laskey and Florence B. (Rosenthal) Eisenberg; divorced; children: Monty Charles, Bryan David. Cert. real estate analyst, Mich. Chief/staff appraiser Ft. Wayne Mortgage Co., Birmingham, Mich., 1973-75; pvt. practice fee appraiser S.C., Iowa, Mich., 1976-80; pres. The Beron Co., Southfield, Mich., 1980—; cons. ptnr. Real Estate Counseling Group Conn., Storrs, 1983—, Real Estate Counseling Group Am., prin., 1984—; lectr. real estate confs. Recipient M. William Donnally award Mortgage Bankers Assn. Am., 1975. Mem. Appraisal Inst. (nat. faculty 1991—), Soc. Real Estate Appraisers (bd. dirs. Detroit chpt. 1980-82, nat. faculty 1983-91), Am. Inst. Real Estate Appraisers (bd. dirs. Detroit chpt. 1982-86, nat. faculty 1984-91), Nat. Assn. Realtors, Detroit Bd. Realtors, Southfield Bd. Realtors, Women Brokers Assn. (treas. Southfield chpt. 1981-83), Young Mortgage Bankers (bd. dirs. 1974-75), B'nai B'rith. Home: 7008 Bridge Way West Bloomfield MI 48322-3527 Office: Beron Co 17228 Westhampton Rd Southfield MI 48075-4351

BERRETH, MICHELLE RENÉE, medical surgical nurse; b. Mass., Feb. 15, 1961; m. Tim Berreth, Nov. 13, 1982; 1 child, Dustin. Diploma, St. Luke's Sch. Nursing, Sioux City, Ia., 1982. Cert. ACLS, NALS, Trauma Nurse Core; RN intravenous. ICU staff nurse Marian Health Ctr., Sioux City, 1985; staff nurse CCU McKennan Hosp., Sioux Falls, S.D., 1983-84; I.V. therapy supr., staff nurse Hawarden (Iowa) Community Hosp., 1985-95; patient care coord. Option Care, Hawarden, Iowa, 1995—. Editorial Reviewer Jour. of Intravenous Nursing. Mem. Intravenous Nursing Soc. (past pres. Siouxland chpt., dist. leader Nat. Coun. Edn. 1994—). Office: Option Care 611 9th St Hawarden IA 51023

BERREY, ROBERT WILSON, III, judge, lawyer; b. Kansas City, Mo., Dec. 6, 1929; s. Robert Wilson and Elizabeth (Hudson) B.; AB, William Jewell Coll., 1950; MA, U. S.D., 1952; LLB, Kansas City U., 1955; LLM, U. Mo. at Kansas City, 1972; grad. Trial Judges Coll., U. Nev., 1972; postgrad. Ariz. State U., U. Nev.; m. Katharine Rollins Wilcoxson, Sept. 5, 1950; children: Robert Wilson IV, Mary Jane, John Lind. Admitted to Mo. bar, 1955, Kans. bar, 1955, since practiced in Kansas City; assoc. mem. firm Shugert and Thomson, 1955-56, Clark, Krings & Bredehoft, 1957-61, Terry and Welton, 1961-62; judge 4th Dist. Magistrate Ct., Jackson County, Mo., 1962-79; assoc. cir. judge 16th Jud. Cir. Ct., Jackson County, Mo., 1979-81, cir. judge, 1981-83, mem. mgmt.-exec. com., 1979-83; judge Mo. Ct. Appeals-Western Dist., Kansas City, 1983—, chief judge, 1994, chmn. rules com. 1990-91, mem., 1993-95, conf. sec. 1992-93, mem. security com., 1992-94; mem. Supreme Ct. Com. to Draft Rules and Procedures for Mo.'s Small Claims Ct., 1976-86. Vol. legal cons. Psychiat. Receiving Ctr. Del. Atlantic Coun. Young Polit. Leaders, Oxford, Eng., 1965; Kansas City rep. to President's National Conference on Crime Control; del.-at-large White House Conf. Aging, 1972; former pack chmn. Cub Scouts Am.; counselor, com. mem. Boy Scouts Am., sponsor Eagle Scouts; vice chmn. water fowl com. Mo. Conservation Fedn., 1968-69, chmn. water fowl com., 1971-73; v.p. Cook PTA, 1967-68; mem. cts. and judiciary com. Mo. bar, 1969-73; mem. Midwest region adv. com. Nat. Park Svc., 1973-78, chmn., 1973-78; mem. Mo. State Judicial Planning Commn., 1977; chmn. Senatorial Redistricting Com., Mo., 1991; bd. dirs., founder Kansas City Open Space Found., 1976. Regional dir. Young Rep. Nat. Fedn., 1957-59, gen. counsel, 1959-61, nat. vice-chmn.; chmn. Mo. Young Rep. Fedn., 1960, nat. committeeman, 1959-60, 61-64; Mo. alternate at large Republican Nat. Conv., 1960, asst. gen. counsel, 1964, del. state and dist. convs., 1960, 64, 68. Bd. dirs. Naturalization Coun., Kansas City, pres., 1973—, Native Sons of Kansas City, 1987—, chmn. long range planning com., 1992, 1st v.p., 1994, pres., 1995; trustee Kansas City Mus., 1972-73, Hyman Brand Hebrew Acad., 1983—; trustee Woods Meml. Christian Ch., 1988—, chmn. deacon, 1988-91, elder 1991-94, 96—; del. gen. assembly Disciples of Christ, 1991, 93; chmn. trustees, 1992-95; chmn. property Rockhurst Coll., 1991-96, chmn. strategic and bldg. planning com., 1995, hon. life dir. Rockhurst Coll.,Mem. Mo. Bar (Disting. Service award 1973, agr. law com., com. council 1980-81), Kansas City Bar Assn., Urban League (past exec. com., dir.), S.A.R., Kansas City Mus. Natural Sci. Soc. (charter), Tex. Longhorn Breeders Assn. (life), Am. Royal (bd. of govs.), Am. Forestry Assn. (life), Mo. Longhorn Breeders Assn. (life), Mo. Farm Bur., Scottish Rite (hon. life provost, marshall 1993), Clay County Lodge (life, Mo. Marshall 1993, jr. warden 1994, sr. warden 1995, worshipful master 1995—), Shrine, Ararat Temple (life, provost), DeMolay Legion Honor (life), Alpha Phi Omega, Delta Theta Phi (life, Toast 1990), Pi Gamma Mu, Tau Kappa Epsilon (Hall of Fame 1986), Nat. Soc. Son of the Am. Revolution (law commendation medal, 1995). Clubs: Waldo Optimist (v.p. 1967-68); Ducks Unltd. (life, nat. trustee 1986-89, state trustee/nat. del. 1992, 94, nat. special projects com. 1990-95, trustee emeriti 1993, life sponsor U.S., Can., Mex., state coun. 1985—, Sportsman of Yr. 1985, Conservation Svc. award 1992, Absentee Conservation Farmer Lubbock County Soil and

Water Conservation Dist. 1994), The Explorers, Kansas City Club, Hartwell Hunt Club (dir. 1994-95), U. Club Kansas City, J Club, William Jewell Coll. Home: RR 2 Box 1078 Excelsior Springs MO 64024-9402 also: RR 2 Battle Lake MN 56515-9802 Office: Mo Ct Appeals Bldg 1300 Oak St Kansas City MO 64106-2904

BERRY, BEVERLY A., real estate investment executive; b. Wayne County, Ohio, Aug. 3, 1939; d. Arleigh Lester and Mabel Bell (Weltmer) Cooper; m. David P. Berry, June 9, 1957; children: Wesley, Tamala, Stephanie. Student, Akron U., 1976-78. Cert. real estate broker, residential specialist, Ohio. Sec., asst. underwriter Westfield Ins. Cos., Westfield Center, Ohio, 1957-69; office mgr., sec. of bd. Johnson Mfg. Co., West Salem, Ohio, 1972-76; prin. acct. Johnson Mfg. Co., West Salem, 1974-76; real estate agt. Gerspacher Realty, Lodi, Ohio, 1976-79, Rickel Realty, Lodi, 1979-82; pres., owner Bev Berry Ins. Agy., Inc., Lodi, 1982-90, Bev Berry Realty, Inc., Auction Co., Lodi, 1982—; mem. of Bus. Option Adv. Com. at Wayne Gen. and Tech. Coll., U. Akron, 1989-90. Mem. Nat. Assn. Real Estate Appraisers, Profl. Ins. Agt. Assn., Women's Coun. Realtors, Realtors Polit. Action Com. (life), Medina County Bd. Realtors (sec. 1986-87, bd. dirs. 1982-86, sec., trustee 1991, Broker of Yr. 1986, Sales Achievement award 1981, Realtor of Yr. 1991), Wayne County Bd. Realtors, Ashland County Bd. Realtors, Lodi C. of C., Medina C. of C., Ruritan. Lutheran. Office: PO Box 131 Lodi OH 44254-0131

BERRY, CHARLENE HELEN, librarian, musician; b. Highland Pk., Mich., Jan. 4, 1947; d. Harold Terry and Mattie Lou (Colvin) B. BSE, Wayne U., 1964-68, MA, 1969-70, MLS, 1971-74; postgrad., Howard Sch. Broadcast Arts, 1992. Ordained music minister. Libr. asst. Wayne State U., Detroit, 1970-74; libr. serials cataloger SUNY, Stony Brook, 1975-79; cataloger Madonna U., Livonia, Mich., 1980—; organist various area chs., Detroit, 1981—, 1st Ch. of Christ, Wyandotte, Mich., 1986—; music min. Gospel Light House Ministries, Detroit, 1991—; scholar, performer, tchr. hammer dulcimer, 1986—; libr. cons. Superior Twp. (Mich.) Libr. Bd., 1989-91; host Charlene Berry's Dulcimer World, Sta. WCAR, Garden City, Mich., WALE, Providence, R.I. Composer: Dulcimer Delights, 1991, marches, waltzes, free compositions and solo symphony, 1993, Dulcimer Praise, 1993, Fruits of the Spirit, 1993; solo recs.: Traditional Dulcimer, 1989, Christmas Dulcimer, 1989, Sacred Dulcimer, 1990, Dulcimer Fun, 1991, Dulcimer Praise, 1993, Fruits of the Spirit, 1993, Dulcimer Americana, 1995; (video) Hammering the Hammer Dulcimer, 1994. Pres. Libr. Staff Assn., SUNY, 1978-79; ch. libr. Ch. Bds. Coms., Long Island, Detroit, 1975—; bd. dirs. Livonia Symphony Soc.; performing artist Mich. Touring Arts Agy., 1994-96. Recipient Performance award Silver Springs Dulciner Soc., 1988, 89, 90, Interat. Order of Merit, ASCAP; named Internat. Woman of Yr., 1992-93, Most Admired Woman of Decade. Fellow Internat. Biographical Assn. (life). Am. Biographical Inst. (Woman of Yr. 1993); mem. AAUW, ALA, NAFE, Am. Biographical Rsch. Assn. (hon. dep. gov.), Bus. and Profl. Women, Am. Soc. of Notaries, Am. Fedn. Musicians, Am. Guild Organists (bd. dirs. 1985-88), Plymouth C. of C., Luth. Ch. Musicians Guild, Order Ea. Star, Kappa Delta Pi. Home and Office: Dulcimer Evente 49614 Oak Dr Lot 67 Plymouth MI 48170-2353

BERRY, HENRY GORDON, physicist, educator; b. Huddersfield, Eng., July 25, 1940; came to U.S., 1962; s. Henry Vernon and Lucy Yates Potts; m. Mary Hynes, Dec. 26, 1968; children: Geb, Sebastien, Nicolas, Daniel. BA, Oxford U., Eng., 1962; MS, U. Wis., 1963, PhD, 1968. Postdoctoral fellow U. Ariz., Tucson, 1968-69; guest researcher The Rsch. Inst., Stockholm, 1969-70; asst. prof. physics U. Lyon, France, 1970-72, U. Chgo., 1972-79; vis. scientist then scientist Argonne (Ill.) Nat. Lab., 1974-87, sr. scientist, 1987-94; prof. physics U. Notre Dame, Ind., 1994—; adj. prof. U. Ill., Chgo., 1987-94; acting dir. Acad. Math. and Sci. Tchrs., Chgo., 1990-91. Editor 8 conf. proceedings; contbr. more than 150 articles to physics jours. Bd. dirs. Little League Baseball, Hyde Park-Kenwood, 1977-81; bd. dirs. Ancona Montessori Sch., Chgo., 1982-87, bd. pres., 1984-86; organizer parents' demonstration to end tchrs. strike, Chgo., 1987; co-chair Concerned Parent Network-Believe in Pub. Schs., Chgo., 1987-88; bd. dirs. Citizens Schs. Com., 1987-91, bd. pres., 1988-91; cmty. mem. Bret Harte Elem. Sch. local sch. coun., 1991-93. Fellow Am. Phys. Soc. (atomic, molecular and optical physics div., program com. 1984-86, publs. com. 1987-89, chair organizing com. ann. meeting, Chgo. 1992); mem. Acad. Sci. (NRC measurements and standards com. 1988-91). Home: 917 W Washington Ave South Bend IN 46601-1436 Office: U Notre Dame Dept Physics Notre Dame IN 46556

BERRY, J(AMES) CHRISTOPHER, journalist, radio station executive; b. Decatur, Ill., Aug. 11, 1960; s. Richard Lyman and Phyllis Lee (Phipps) B.; m. Cynthia Ann Till, Sept. 5, 1982; children: James Christopher Jr., Nicholas Andrew. BA, U. Miss., 1981. Prodr. Sta. WHBQ-TV, Memphis, 1981-82; news editor Sta. KNX, CBS, L.A., 1982-86; exec. prodr. CBS Radio News Svc., Washington, 1986-87; asst. news dir. Sta. WBBM, CBS, Chgo., 1987-90, dir. news and programming, 1990—; profl. advisor dept. journalism U. Miss., Oxford, 1988—; mem. journalism adv. com. U. Nebr., 1995—. Committeeman Nat. Freedom of Info. Ctr., Chgo., 1990—; bd. dirs. Wreath of Hope Charity, Chgo., 1990—. Recipient Angel award Religion in Media, L.A., 1985. Mem. Radio and TV News Dirs. Assn. (Edward R. Murrow award 1991, Freedom of Info. award 1993), Soc. Profl. Journalists, Ill. News Broadcasters Assn., Writers Guild Am., Chgo. Headline Club (bd. dirs. 1990-95, Peter Lisagor award 1990). Presbyterian. Home: 9451 Crawford Ave Evanston IL 60203-1317 Office: Sta WBBM 630 N Mcclurg Ct Chicago IL 60611-3007

BERRY, JAMES FREDERICK, lawyer, biology educator; b. Washington, Dec. 22, 1947; s. James Frederick and Joyce (Drummond) B.; children: Jennifer, Andrea L. BS, Fla. State U., 1970, MS, 1973; PhD, U. Utah, 1978; JD, Chgo.-Kent Law Sch., 1990. Bar: Fla. 1990, Ill. 1991, U.S. Dist. Ct. (mid. dist.) Fla. 1991, U.S. Dist. Ct. (no. dist.) Ill. 1991, U.S. Ct. Appeals (11th cir.) 1991. Teaching asst. Fla. State U., Tallahassee, 1969-73; chemist Fla. Dept. Agr., Tallahassee, 1973-74; teaching fellow U. Utah, Salt Lake City, 1974-78; rsch. assoc. Carnegie Mus., Pitts., 1983—; prof. biology Elmhurst (Ill.) Coll., 1978—; assoc. Burke, Bosselman & Weaver, Chgo., 1990-93; cons. ENCAP, Inc., DeKalb, Ill., 1983-84; rsch. asst. IIT Chgo.-Kent Law Sch., 1989-90; instr. law Am. Planning Assn., Chgo., 1992-94; adj. prof. Stuart Sch. Bus., Ill. Inst. Tech., 1995—. Contbr. articles to profl. jours. Bd. trustees Chgo. String Ensemble, 1989-94. Rsch. grantee U.S. Fish and Wildlife Svc., Washington, 1983-85, Elmhurst Coll., 1979-86. Mem. ABA, Ill. State Bar Assn., Sigma Xi, Phi Kappa Phi. Roman Catholic. Office: Elmhurst Coll 190 Prospect Ave Elmhurst IL 60126-3271

BERRY, MICHAEL JOHN, author, medical/dental management consultant; b. Waynesville, Mo., Dec. 30, 1957; s. John Patrick and Gloria Mae (Flynn) B.; m. Mary Ellen Larson, Oct. 31, 1981; children: Justin Michael, Amy Leah, Jessica Ann, Allison Marie. Student, U. Md., 1982-83, Ind. U., 1979-80, Purdue U., 1976-79. Med. and dental mgmt. cons. Monticello, Ind.; adv. cons. Health Care Info. Network, Monticello; ind. sub-contr./writer Am. Med. News (AMA), Chgo., 1992—; condr. seminars and table clinics in field. Author: Collections Made Easy, 1991, Reality Check (fiction), 1995; contbr. numerous articles to profl. jours.; book reviewer Chgo. Medicine, 1992, Health Care Fin. Mgmt., 1994. Ch. adv. bd. on fin. Yeoman (Ind) United Meth. Ch., 1988-91. Home and Office: 602 Canary Ln Monticello IN 47960

BERRY, PHILLIP REID, flexible staffing executive; b. Owensboro, Ky., Apr. 4, 1950; s. Patrick Henry and Dorothy Lee (Best) B.; m. Linda Mae Harm, July 28, 1973; children: Patricia Brooke, Phillip Benjamin. BA in Psychology, Western Ky. U., 1972. Dir. Otis Bowen Ctr. for Human Svcs., Warsaw, Ind., 1982-84; exec. dir. Fourth Freedom Forum, Goshen, Ind., 1984-88; pres. Nagao-Berry Internat., Goshen, Ind., 1988—. Chmn. strategic planning com. Jaycees Internat., Coral Gables, Fla., 1989-91 (world pres., 1987). With USAR, 1972-78. Recipient Don Cavalli Meml. award U.S. Jaycees, Tulsa, 1984-85; Rep. of China Order of Merit #30. Mem. Jr. Chamber Internat., Kiwanis Internat., Lambda Chi Alpha. Republican. Office: Interim Personnel 508 S Green River Rd Evansville IN 47715

BERRY, RICHARD STEPHEN, chemist; b. Denver, Apr. 9, 1931; s. Morris and Ethel (Alpert) B.; m. Carla Lamport Friedman, Sept. 4, 1955; children: Andrea, Denise, Eric. AB, Harvard U., 1952, AM, 1954, PhD, 1956. Instr. chemistry Harvard U., 1956-57, U. Mich., 1957-60; asst. prof. Yale U., 1960-64; assoc. prof. U. Chgo., 1964-67, prof., 1967—, James Franck Disting. Svc. prof., 1989—; Arthur D. Little prof. MIT, 1968; Phillips lectr. Haverford Coll., 1968; Lôwdin lectr. Uppsala U, 1989; cons. Avco-Everett Research Labs., 1964-83, Argonne Nat. Lab., 1976—, Oak Ridge Nat. Labs., 1978-81, Los Alamos Sci. Lab., 1975—, mem. adv. com. theory; vis. prof. U. Copenhagen, 1967, 79; mem. adv. panel for chemistry NSF, 1971-73; mem. rev. com. radiol. and environ. research div. Argonne Nat. Lab., 1970-76; mem. evaluation panel measures for air quality Nat. Bur. Standards; mem. numerical data adv. bd. NRC, 1978-86, chmn., 1981-86; mem. steering com. panel on environ. monitoring, mem. com. on atomic and molecular sci., 1984-89, com. on chem. scis. NAS-NRC, 1977-79; mem. adv. panel on health of sci. and tech. enterprise, mem. adv. panel on nat. labs. Office Tech. Assessment; mem. adv. bd. Environ. Health Resource Center, Inst. for Theoretical Physics, Santa Barbara, 1989-91; mem. vis. com. div. applied physics Harvard U., 1977-81; mem. adv. panel dept. chemistry Princeton U., 1978-81; Hinshelwood lectr. Oxford U., 1980; prof. associé U. Paris-Sud, 1979-80; Newton Abraham prof. Oxford U., 1986-87; Phi Beta Kappa lectr. 1989-90; Welch Symposium lectr., 1995; pres. Telluride Summer Rsch. Ctr., 1989-93; chmn. NRC com. Internat. Exch. Sci. Info., 1994—. Author: Understanding Energy, 1991; co-author: TOSCA, The Total Social Cost of Fossil and Nuclear Power, 1979, Physical Chemistry, 1980; assoc. editor: Jour. Chem. Physics, 1971-74, Accounts Chem. Rsch., 1975-90, Revs. Modern Physics, 1983-95, Phys. Rev. A, 1986-92; bd. dirs. Bull. Atomic Scientists, 1974-83; adv. editor: Resources and Energy, 1978-92; contbr. articles to profl. jours. Alfred P. Sloan fellow, 1962-66; Guggenheim fellow, 1972-73; MacArthur prize fellow, 1983; Humboldt Rsch. awardee, 1993. Fellow AAAS (chmn. chemistry sect. 1993-94), Am. Phys. Soc. (coun. 1993-95, publs. oversight com. 1996—, chmn. few-body sys. topical group 1994-95), Japan Soc. Promotion of Scis., Am. Acad. Arts and Scis. (v.p. 1987-90, 95—); mem. NAS, Am. Chem. Soc., Nat. Coun. Lawyers and Scientists, Royal Danish Acad. Arts and Letters (fgn.), Sigma Xi (nat. lectr. 1976-77).

BERRY, ROBERTA MILDRED, civic worker; b. Medinah, Ill., Feb. 27, 1926; d. Judson Stewart and Anna Doretha (Neddermeyer) Lawrence; m. Moses Berry, June 29, 1948; children: Scott, Mark. B.Mus., Cornell Coll., 1948. Choir dir. Presbyterian, Methodist Chs., Cedar Rapids, Iowa, 1949-71; tchr. assoc. Cedar Rapids Cmty. Schs., 1963-73; dir. Pioneer Village, Cedar Rapids, 1982-83; dir. Linn Cmty. Food Bank, Cedar Rapids, 1983—; pres. Chs. United, Cedar Rapids, 1984-85, v.p. Iowa state bd., 1994—; orginator Grade Sch. Picture Lady Program, Cedar Rapids, 1968-69; pres. Seminole Valley Farm, Cedar Rapids, 1980-81; pres. Ch. Women United, Cedar Rapids, 1985-86, also bd. dirs., editor newsletter for Iowa State. Bd. dirs. YWCA, Cedar Rapids, 1970-72, Cedar Rapids Symphony Guild, 1983-88, Iowa Rails to Trails, Cedar Rapids, 1983-88; pres. Methwick Manor Aux., Cedar Rapids, 1985; sec. Council on Aging, Cedar Rapids, 1984-85; rep. Civic Newcomers, 1986-93; pres. Cedar Rapids Area Peace Network Guide; Guide Brucemore Hist. Home, 1982—. Mem. UN Assn. (Iowa state bd. 1993—, Linn County pres. 1996—). Clubs: Beethoven (pres. 1964-65), College (pres. 1965-66), PEO (pres. 1982-83), Demolay Mothers Aux (pres. 1974-75), Postal Workers Aux (pres. 1974-75) (Cedar Rapids). Avocations: oil painting, needlework, tennis, biking. Home: 1118 Maplewood Dr NE Cedar Rapids IA 52402-4710

BERRY, WILLIAM MARTIN, financial consultant; b. Chgo., June 21, 1920; s. William John and Mary Frances (Martin) B.; m. Julia McIntire Vail, Dec. 19, 1972; children: William E., Mary P., Peter D. BS, St. Mary's Univ., 1941; MA, DePaul U., 1949. Divsn. contr. Hughes Aircraft Co., Culver City, Calif., 1950-55; div. contr. TRW, Redondo Beach, Calif., 1955-58; mgr. mgmt. cons. dept. Peat, Marwick, Mitchell and Co., L.A., 1958-61; v.p. Litton Industries Inc., Beverly Hills, Calif., 1961-74; chmn., CEO NN Corp., Milw., 1974-80; chmn. Northwestern Nat. Ins. Group, 1981-84; bd. dirs. PK Tool & Die Mfg. Co., Chgo. Bd. dirs. Columbia Hosp., Milw., 1976—, Milw. Assn. Commerce, 1976-81, Milw. Symphony Orch., 1974-81, United Performing Arts Fund., Milw., 1977-81. With U.S. Army, 1941-46. Mem. Fin. Execs. Inst., Milw. Club, Milw. Country Club, Univ. Club. Home and Office: 13800 N Birchwood Ln Mequon WI 53097-1702

BERRYMAN, JAMES, state legislator; b. Feb. 17, 1947; m. Susan; children: Steve, Eric, Julie. Student, Adrian Coll., 1965-69. State senator Mich. State Senate, Dist. 17, 1990—; asst. minority whip, 1993, majority floor leader, 1995—, mem. tech. & energy, fin. svc., agrl. & forestry coms., Mich. State Senate. Mem. Adrian (Mich.) City Planning Commn., 1978-81; mem. Adrian City Commn., 1979-85; mayor City of Adrian, 1985; mem. Govs. Health Occupations Coun., 1989—. Mem. Mich. Assn. Mayors (pres. 1987—). Home: 380 S Scott St Adrian MI 49221-3126*

BERTCH, KAREN ELIZABETH, pharmacist, educator; b. Waterloo, Iowa, Feb. 4, 1958; d. William Eugene and Norma Elizabeth (Becker) B. Student pre-pharmacy, U. Nebr., 1979, PharmD with honors, 1982. Resident U. Ky., Lexington, 1982-84; clin. pharmacist U. Ill. Hosp., Chgo., 1984-89; clin. asst. prof. U. Ill. Coll. Pharmacy, Chgo., 1984-91; clin. pharmacist Humana Hosp./Michael Reese, Chgo., 1989-91; clin. assoc. prof. U. Ill. Coll. Pharmacy, 1991—; pharmacy mgr. HMSS, Inc., Elmhurst, Ill., 1991-94; pharmacy supr. Coram Healthcare, Mt. Prospect, Ill., 1994—; vis. clin. pharmacy coord. Derbyshire Royal Infirmary, Derby, England, 1989; edit. advisor, author Medi-Span, Inc., Indpls., 1990—. Mem. Am. Coll. Clin. Pharmacy (sect. editor pharmacotherapy self-assessment program 1991—), Am. Soc. Cons. Pharmacists, Am. Soc. Health-Sys. Pharmacists (chmn. specialty practice group on nutrition support 1991-92), Am. Soc. Parenteral and Enteral Nutrition (pharmacist com. 1991-93), Chgo. Area Soc. Parenteral and Enteral Nutrition (program planning, bd. dirs. 1990-94, 96, sec. 1994-95), Ill. Coll. Clin. Pharmacy (sec.-treas. 1994-95), Ill. Coun. Hosp. Pharmacists. Roman Catholic. Office: Coram Healthcare Ste 500 1471 Business Center Dr Mount Prospect IL 60056

BERTELLI, MONTY RAY, state official; b. Centerville, Iowa, Aug. 2, 1948; s. Raymond and Betty J. (Sorrell) B.; m. Adrienne Ann Crowley, June 14, 1984 (dec.); children: Mikaila Susan, Blair Margaret, Zachary Raymond. BSBA, Drake U., 1970, JD, 1975. Bar: Iowa. Law clk. Iowa Dept. Transp., Des Moines, 1974; citizens aide Office of Iowa Ombudsman, Des Moines, 1974; adminstrv. aide Iowa Senate, Des Moines, 1974; rsch. asst., legal counsel Iowa Ho. Rep., Des Moines, 1975-76; pres. Ray Bertelli Sons, Inc., 1976-83; assoc. Humphreys and Assocs., 1983-85; pvt. practice, 1985-88; adminstrv. officer Legal Svcs. div., asst. to chief counsel Kans. Dept. Human Resources, Topeka, 1988-95; dep. and chief of staff Iowa Sec. of State, Des Moines, 1995—. Mem. Omicron Delta Kappa, Phi Alpha Delta. Republican. Home: 1201 Office Park Rd # 501 West Des Moines IA 50265 Office: Iowa Sec of State Hoover Bldg Des Moines IA 50319

BERTELSON, ROBERT CALVIN, chemical company executive, research chemist; b. Milw., Nov. 5, 1931; s. Edward and Ida Clara (Ruskin) B.; m. Mary Lee Johnson, Jan. 21, 1960; children—Thomas Edward, Kenneth Andrew. B.S. in Chemistry, U. Wis.-Madison, 1952; Ph.D., MIT, 1957. Sr. research chemist NCR Corp., Dayton, Ohio, 1957-73; sr. research assoc. NSF, Wright-Patterson, Ohio, 1972-74; pres. ChromaChems. Inc., Dayton, 1974—. Contbr. articles to profl. jours., also book chpts. Patentee in field. Served with U.S. Army, 1957-60. Fellow Am. Inst. Chemists; mem. Am. Chem. Soc., AAAS, N.Y. Acad. Scis., Soc. for Imaging Sci. and Tech., Internat. Union of Pure and Applied Chemistry, European Photochemistry Assn., InterAm. Photochem. Soc., Sigma Xi. Avocation: music. Office: Chroma Chems Inc PO Box 20273 Dayton OH 45420-0273

BERTHELSEN, JOHN ROBERT, printing company executive; b. Albert Lea, Minn., July 23, 1954; s. Robert Eugene and Erna Catherine (Petersen) B.; m. Debra Denise Peterson, June 29, 1974 (div. Oct. 1990); children: Angela Marie, Derek John; m. Kay A. Richards, April 29, 1995. Student public schs., cert. graphic arts exec., NAPL Mgmt. Inst., 1993. Albert Lea, Minn. Prodn. worker Arrow Printing Co., Albert Lea, 1972-73; journeyman Munson Printing Co., Red Wing, Minn., 1973-75; prep. foreman O'Connor Printing Co., Sioux Falls, S.D., 1975-76; preparation supr. Modern Press Inc., Sioux Falls, 1976-79; gen. mgr. Suttle Press, Inc., Waunakee, Wis., 1979-82, pres., 1982—. Dir. Nat. Scholarship Trust Fund, 1994—. Recipient 1st place Nat. Skill Olympics (printing), Vocat. Indsl. Clubs Am., 1972, Gold award best managed printing co. Nat. Assn. Printers and Lithographers, 1983, 87, 88, named to Hall of Fame, 1990; recipient Silver award Mgmt. Plus Program Nat. Assn. Printers and Lithographers, 1986. Mem. Madison Craftsmen (pres. 1983-85, named Craftsman of the Yr. 1987), Nat. Assn. Printers and Lithographers (bd. dirs. 1992—), Internat. Assn. Printing House Craftsmen (gov. 6th dist. 1985-87, internat. treas. 1987-89, v.p. 1989-91, internat. pres. 1991-92), Wis. State Coun. on Printing (dir. 1988-90), Soderstrom Soc. Office: Suttle Press Inc 1000 Uniek St PO Box 370 Waunakee WI 53597

BERTHOFF, ROWLAND TAPPAN, historian, educator; b. Toledo, Sept. 20, 1921; s. Nathaniel and Helen (Tappan) B.; m. Tirzah Margaret Park, Aug. 5, 1954; children: Thomas Arthur, Margaret Olivia, Andrew Warner, Clarissa Helen. A.B., Oberlin Coll., 1942; A.M., Harvard U., 1947, Ph.D., 1952. Instr. Princeton U., 1953-57, asst. prof., 1957-62; assoc. prof. Washington U., St. Louis, 1962-65; prof. Washington U., 1965-92, chmn. history dept., 1968-74, 81-82, William Eliot Smith prof. history, 1974-92, prof. emeritus, 1992—; Fulbright lectr. U. Edinburgh, 1965-66. Author: British Immigrants in Industrial America, 1790-1950, 1953, An Unsettled People, Social Order and Disorder in American History, 1971, contbg. author: Small Business in American Life, 1980, Harvard Ency. of American Ethnic Groups, 1980; contbr. articles to profl. jours. Served to 1st lt., inf. AUS, 1942-46. Recipient Green-Ramsdell award So. Hist. Assn., 1988. Mem. So. Hist. Assn. Home: 7195 Washington Ave Saint Louis MO 63130-4313

BERTRAM, JOE, SR., state legislator; b. July 3, 1954; s. Clarence A. and Viola (Gruber) B.; m. Mary Lee Imdieke, 1977; three children. Student, Cloud Area Vocat. Tech. Inst., 1974-75, St. Cloud State U., 1978-79; Bemidji State U. Staff asst. 6th Congl. Dist. Minn. Ho. of Reps., 1976-80; state senator Dist. 14 Minn. State Senate, 1980—; family farmer, 1996—; chmn. Agrl. & Rural Devel. Com.; mem. Vet. & Gen. Legis. & Pub. Gaming Com., Local & Urban Govt. Com., Rules & Adminstrn. Com., Taxes & Tax Laws Com. Recipient Vol. Fireman award Paynesville Vol. Fire Dept., Lions Internat. award for efforts on behalf of Lions in Minn. Senate, Disting. Civilian Svc. award; named one of ten Outstanding Young Minnesotans. Mem. Cystic Fibrosis Found., Citizens for Ednl. Freedom, Jaycees, KC, Farmers Union. Office: 887 Flanders Dr Paynesville MN 56362-2011 also: State Senate State Capital Building Saint Paul MN 55155-1606*

BERTRAM, MICHAEL WAYNE, secondary education educator; b. Princeton, Ind., Jan. 24, 1945; s. Leroy Victor and Lela Mae (Redman) B.; m. Bonnie Lee Holmes, Aug. 21, 1985; 1 child, John. BS, U. Indpls., 1967; MS, U. Wyo., 1972; MA, U. Evansville, 1975. Cert. secondary math. and physics tchr., Ind. Tchr. math. and physics South Gibson Sch. Corp., Ft. Branch, Ind., 1967—, chmn. math. dept., 1974—; athletic dir. Gibson So. High Sch., 1977-79. Recipient cert. of merit Ind. Acad. Competitions for Excellence, 1988, 95, 96; grantee NSF, 1971. Mem. Nat. Coun. Tchrs. Math., Math. Assn. Am., Am. Assn. Physics Tchrs. Methodist. Home: RR 1 Box 197 Fort Branch IN 47648-9717 Office: Gibson So High Sch RR 1 Box 496 Fort Branch IN 47648-9776

BERTSCH, FRANK HENRY, furniture manufacturing company executive; b. Mpls., Oct. 2, 1925; s. Herbert Thomas and Eleanor Emma (Tuscany) B.; m. Rita Bertsch, Nov. 7, 1987; children: Jeffrey T., Steven H., Carolyn T. BS in Mech. Engring, Northwestern U., 1947; D of Law (hon.), U. Dubuque, 1992. With Flexsteel Industries, Inc., Dubuque, Iowa, 1947—, plant engr., 1947-49, plant mgr., 1949-53, v.p., dir. design and devel., 1953-58, pres., 1958-85, chmn bd., chief exec. officer, 1985-90, chmn. exec. com., 1990—; bd. dirs. Retirement Investment Corp., Am. Trust and Savs. Bank, Dubuque, CyCare Systems Inc. Bd. dirs. U. Dubuque, Four Mounds Found. With USNR, 1944-46. Recipient Disting. Svc. award Dubuque C. of C., 1964, Man Behind the Boy award Dubuque Boys Club, 1969, Bronze Merit award Jr. Achievement of Am., 1995. Mem. Am. Legion, Dubuque Golf and Country Club, Desert Mountain Club (Scottsdale), Thunder Hills Country Club (Peosta, Iowa). Presbyterian (elder, trustee). Office: Flexsteel Industries Inc Brunswick Indsl Block PO Box 877 Dubuque IA 52004-0877

BERVEN, NORMAN LEE, counselor, psychologist, educator; b. Des Moines, May 14, 1945; s. Arthur N. and Ruth N. (Sharp) B.; m. Estella Stone, Oct. 11, 1969; 1 child, Jennifer. BS, U. Iowa, 1967, MA, 1969; PhD, U. Wis., 1973. Lic. Psychologist; cert. rehab. counselor, profl. counselor. Rehab. counselor San Mateo County Mental Health Svc., San Mateo, Calif., 1969-71; rsch. assoc. Internat. Ctr. for Disabled, N.Y.C., 1973-75; asst. prof. counseling and spl. svcs. Seton Hall U., South Orange, N.J., 1975-76; asst. prof. to prof. rehab. psychology, program chair U. Wis., Madison, 1976—; cons. to univ., govt. and pvt. non-profit programs. Editor: Rehab. Counseling Bull., 1985-92, assoc. editor, 1982-85, editorial bd., 1980-82, 92—; editorial bd. Rehab. Psychology, 1981—, Vocat. Evaluation and Work Adjustment Bull., 1980—, Assessment in Rehab. and Exceptionality, 1992—; contbr. articles to profl. jours., chpts. to books. Grantee U.S. Dept. Edn., 1986-89, 89-92, 90-93, 92-95, 93—, 95—, Spencer Found., 1981-82, Wis. Alumni Rsch. Found., 1979-80. Fellow APA (rehab., counseling and evaluation, measurement and stats. divsn.); mem. ACA (rsch. award 1986), Am. Rehab. Counseling Assn. (bd. dirs. N.J. chpt. 1975-76, disting. profl. award 1990, rsch. award 1981, 84, 86, 92-93, 95), Nat. Rehab. Counseling Assn. (bd. dirs. Wis. chpt. 1981-83, Meritorious Svc. award 1992, Calif. chpt. 1971), Nat. Rehab. Assn. (bd. dirs. S.W. Wis. chpt., 1980—, San Mateo chpt. 1969-71, grad. lit. award 1968), Assn. for Counselor Edn. and Supervision, Assn. for Assessment in Counseling, Assn. for Specialists in Group Work, Vocat. Evaluation and Work Adjustment Assn. Home: 10 Southwick Cir Madison WI 53717-1415 Office: U Wis Madison Rehab Psychology 432 N Murray St Madison WI 53706-1407

BERVIG, V. ARLEEN HAALAND, clergyperson, music teacher; b. Woden, Iowa, Sept. 29, 1925; d. Clarence Selmer and Mary (Yost) Haaland; m. Arthur Leonard Bervig, June 9, 1946 (div. Aug. 1977); children: Ronald Arthur, Gregory Dean, David Allen. Student, King's Coll., New Castle, Del., 1944-45; BA in English magna cum laude, Bemidji (Minn.) State U., 1991; student, Oxford (Eng.) U., 1991. Cert. lay pastor Lutheran Ch. Am. Chair/liaison Ch. Women United, Mpls., 1970-75, dir. ecumenical seminars, 1972-75; pres. Am. Luth. Ch. Women, Mpls., 1973-74; personnel adminstr. Charmilles/Andrews, Hopkins, Minn., 1980-81; bd. regents Oak Grove Luth. H.S., Fargo, N.D., 1980-85, campus chaplain, 1986-88; with ELCA, N.D., 1986-88; pastor First Lutheran, Akeley, Minn., 1982-85, Our Savior/Zion Parish, Federal Dam/Boy River, Minn., 1992-95, Bethlehem, Backus, Minn., 1995-96; pres. Ministerial Assn., Park Rapids, Minn., 1984-85; mem. interdisciplinary team Hospice, St. Joseph's Hosp., Park Rapids, 1984-85; synod rep. Minn. Coun. Chs., Mpls., 1991-96; mem. Pastor's Cluster Group, 1993-95. Author: Color Coded, 1996; contbr. articles to newspapers. Mem. joint religious legis. coalition Minn. Coun. Chs., St. Paul, 1991-96; mem. Minn. Citizens Organized Acting Together, St. Paul, 1990-96; dir. Cmty. Choirs, 1980-93. Recipient grants in field. Mem. Smithsonian Assocs., Wilson Ctr. Assocs. Home: 500 Riverside Ave Apt 217 Park Rapids MN 56470

BERZAC, CARY J., investment broker, educator; b. Detroit, Dec. 2, 1947. BA in Edn., Ea. Mich. U., 1971. Various mgmt. positions KMart, various locations, 1971-77; investment broker A.G. Edwards & Sons Inc., Bloomfield Hills, Mich., 1977—; adj. prof. Oakland C.C., Farmington Hills, Mich., 1979—. Republican. Office: AG Edwards & Sons Inc PO Box 3025 1471 S Woodward Ave Bloomfield Hills MI 48302

BESER, ROBERTA RUTH (BOBBIE BESER), physical therapy company executive; b. Lewiston, Maine, July 31, 1947; d. Joseph and Eileen (Barron) Friedman; m. Joel Grand, 1969; m. Donald Beser, Aug. 1975 (div. Nov. 1987); children: Daniel Grand, James Beser. BS in Phys. Therapy, Boston U., 1969. Phys. therapist in pvt. practice Southfield, Mich., 1971-87; phys. therapist N. Oakland Phys. Therapist, Waterford, Mich., 1987-89; dir. phys. therapy Orthopedic Rehab., Southfield, 1989-91; phys. therapist, dir. mktg. Corcoran Phys. Therapy, Chgo., 1993; pres. U.S. Med. Placements, Chgo., 1992—, Therapists Inc., Chgo., 1992—; lectr. on incontinence to sr. groups, Ill. Contbr. articles to newspapers and profl. jours. Mem. Am. Phys. Therapy Assn., Ill. Phys. Therapy Assn. Office: US Med Placements Inc 325 W Huron Ste 508 Chicago IL 60610

BESPALEC, DALE ANTHONY, clinical psychologist; b. Waukegan, Ill., Sept. 21, 1951; s. Anthony Frank Bespalec and Mildred B. (Glogovsky) Etolen; m. Marylou B. Bartholomae, June 23, 1973; 1 child, Christine

Marie. BS magna cum laude with honors, Loyola U., 1973, MA, 1975, PhD, 1978. Lic. psychologist, Ill., Wis. Staff cons. psychologist Behavior and Mgmt. Cons., Inc., Milw., 1977-79; instr. U. Wis.-Parkside, Racine, 1979; staff psychologist St. Michael Hosp. Mental Health Ctr., Milw., 1979-86, mgr. outpatient, 1986-90; pvt. practice Milw., 1979-88; clinical prof. Wis. Sch. Profl. Psychology, Milw., 1985—, dir. clin. tng., 1990-92; mgr. mental health program Community Meml. Hosp., Menomonee Falls, Wis., 1992—; clin. instr. Med. Coll. Wis., Milw., 1981—; coord. Wis. Psychol. Assn. Diaster Response Team. Contbr. articles to profl. jours. Past v.p. internal devel. Grafton Jaycees; past mem. bd. dirs United Way Ozaukee County; vol. ARC, chair mental health function; active Riveredge Nature Ctr. Fellow NIMH, USPH, 1973-74. Mem. APA, Wis. Psychol. Assn. (mem. adv. coun. 1994—), Milw. Area Psychologist Assn. (pres. 1994—). Roman Catholic. Office: Cmty Meml Hosp Mental Health Ctr, PO Box 408 W180N8085 Town Hall Rd Menomonee Falls WI 53052-0408

BESSLER, ELECTA L., securities company executive, councilwoman; b. Indpls., Oct. 23, 1948. BA, Ball State U., Muncie, Ind., 1970. Ltd. ptnr. Edward D. Jones & Co., Batesville, Ind., 1984—. Mem. Batesville City Coun., 1992—; trustee 2d Ch. of Christ Scientist, Cin., 1994—. Mem. Batesville C. of C., Beta Sigma Phi. Republican. Home: 32 Ash Hill Ct Batesville IN 47006-9253 Office: Edward D Jones & Co 111 S Main St Batesville IN 47006-1344

BEST, JEFFREY DEAN, electronics technician; b. Champaign, Ill., Dec. 31, 1954; s. Winston and G. Rose (Partridge) B.; m. Doris Marie Frisse, 1975. AA, SUNY, Albany, 1981. Cert. journeyman electronics technician. Store mgr., electronics technician Bally's Aladdin's Castle, Champaign, 1982-84, Spaceport/Adventure Properties, Champaign, 1985-86, Jolly Time/Pocket Change, West Bend, Wis., 1988-91, Circus/AAA, West Bend, 1991-96; indsl. electrician QuadGraphics, Hartford, Wis., 1996—; comm technician Carpenter Tech., Hartford, Wis., 1996—; real estate agt. Glynn Realty/Coldwell Banker, Slinger, Wis., 1992; real estate broker Homestead Realty, Milw., 1993; owner Doc Best VCR Svc., Jackson, Wis., 1993—; ptnr. Best Vending Co., Jackson, 1996—. Columnist Star Tech Jour., 1991. Active Jackson Jaycees, 1992-93, pres., 1993; mem. Zool. Soc. Milw. county, 1991—; vol., adult leader Mil. Explorer Post, Boy Scouts Am., Hartford, 1995—. With U.S. Army, 1977-81, 86-88. Mem. Internat. Soc. Cert. Electronics Technicians, Profl. Assn. Diving Instr. (divemaster). Roman Catholic. Home & Office: Doc Best VCR Svc N168W21700 Main St Lot 120 Jackson WI 53037-9644

BESTEHORN, UTE WILTRUD, retired librarian; b. Cologne, Germany, Nov. 6, 1930; came to U.S., 1930; d. Henry Hugo and Wiltrud Lucie (Vincentz) B. BA, U. Cin., 1954, BEd, 1955, MEd, 1958; MS in Library Sci., Western Res. U. (now Case-Western Res. U.), 1961. Tchr. Cutter Jr. High Sch., Cin., 1955-57; tchr., supr. libr. Felicity (Ohio) Franklin Sr. High Sch., 1959-60; with libr. sci. dept. Pub. Libr. Cin. and Hamilton County, 1961-78, with libr. info. desk, 1978-91; ret., 1991; textbook selection com., Felicity-Franklin Sr. High Sch., 1959-60; supr. Health Alcove Sci. Dept. and annual health lectures, Cin. Pub. Library, 1972-77. Book reviewer Library Jour., 1972-77; author and inventor Rainbow 40 marble game, 1971, Condominium game, 1976; patentee indexed packaging and stacking device, 1973, mobile packaging and stacking device, 1974. Mem. Clifton Town Meeting, 1988—; mem. Bookfest 90 com. Pub. Libr. Cin. and Hamilton County. Recipient Cert. of Merit and Appreciation Pub. Library of Cin., 1986. Mem. Cin. Chpt. Spl. Libraries Assn. (archivist 1963-64, 65-70, editor Queen City Gazette bull. 1964-69), Pub. Library Staff Assn. (exec. bd., activities com. 1965, welfare com. 1966, recipient Golden Book 25 yr. service pin, 1986), Friends of the Library, Greater Cin. Calligraphers Guild (reviewer New Letters pub. 1986-88), Delta Phi Alpha (nat. German hon. 1951). Republican. Mem. United Ch. of Christ. Home: 3330 Morrison Ave Cincinnati OH 45220-1440

BETANCOURT, CINDY ALYCE, music educator; b. Huntington, N.Y., May 24, 1964; d. Charles Victor and Lillian Irene (Hutka) B. MusB, Juilliard Sch. Music, 1986, MusM, 1987. Instr. music Ball State U., Muncie, Ind., 1990—; violist Muncie Symphony Orch., 1987—, Marion (Ind.) Philharm. Orch., 1988—; instr. music Huntington (Ind.) Coll., 1990-92, Ind. Wesleyan U., Marion, 1992-95, Taylor U., Upland, Ind., 1993—; founder, dir. East Ctrl. Ind. Debut Orch., Muncie, 1987—, Ball State Summer String Clinic, Muncie, 1992—. Office: Ball State Univ 2000 W University Muncie IN 47306

BETHKE, JESSE, non-profit organization executive; b. Robbinsdale, Minn., Jan. 31, 1961; s. Jack Arthur and Irene Maria (Gomez) B.; m. Raquel Ortencia Cervantes-Bethke, Nov. 12, 1983. BA, U. Minn., 1983; M in mgmt. and adminstrn., Metro. State U., 1987. Cert. completion Minn. exec. program Carlson Sch. Mgmt., U. Minn., 1993. Interim exec. dir. Insituto Arte Y Cultura, Mpls., 1982-84; asst. dir. INROADS/Mpls.-St. Paul, 1984-87; sr. campaign divsn. dir. United Way Mpls. Area, 1987-89; sr. bus. cons. Metro. Econ. Devel. Assn., Mpls., 1989-91; dir. fin. devel. Am. Red Cross, Greater Mpls. Area Chpt., 1991-95; exec. dir. Chicanos Latinos Unidos en Servicio, Inc. Bd. dirs. Internat. Inst. Minn., St. Paul, 1989-91. Recipient Presdl. Scholarship award Am. Nat. Red Cross, Washington, 1993. Mem. Inst. Mgmt. Cons. (assoc.), Assn. MBA Execs., Rotary. Roman Catholic. Office: Am Red Cross 220 S Robert St Ste 103 Saint Paul MN 55107

BETINIS, EMANUEL JAMES, physics and mathematics educator; b. Oak Park, Ill., Oct. 31, 1927; s. James Emanuel and Ioanna Helen (Kallas) B.; children: Demetrios, Joanna, Markos. BS in Chemistry and Math., Northwestern U., 1950; MS in Applied Math., U. Ill., 1952; MS in Physics, U. Chgo., 1979. Aerodynamicist Northrop Aviation, Hawthorne, Calif., 1953-54; theoretical reactor physicist Atomics Internat., Canoga Park, Calif., 1954-57; applied sci. rep. IBM, Chgo., 1957-61; math. cons. Math. Cons. Svc., Chgo., 1961-81; adj. prof. math. and physics IIT, Roosevelt U., Chgo., 1981-88; mathematician Batelle Meml. Labs., Willowbrook, Ill., 1988-89; asst. prof. physics Elmhurst (Ill.) Coll., 1990—. Contbr. articles to Jour. Geophys. Rsch., Jour. Brit. Interplanetary Soc., Hadronic Jour., Matrix, Lensor Soc. Great Britain. Mem. PTO. With U.S. Army, 1946-47. Fellow Brit. Interplanetary Soc.; mem. Am. Nuclear Soc., Sigma Pi Sigma, Pi Mu Epsilon. Republican. Orthodox. Office: Elmhurst Coll Dept Physics Box 47 190 Prospect Ave Elmhurst IL 60126-3271

BETSINGER, PEGGY ANN, oncological nurse; b. St. Charles, Mo., Dec. 11, 1939; d. Edward and Dorothy (Brockgrietens) Oelklaus; m. Richard Betsinger, Mar. 17, 1964 (div. Mar. 1986); children: Bryon, Alicia. Diploma, St. John's Hosp. Sch. Nursing, St. Louis U., St. Louis, 1960; student, U. Colo., Colorado Springs, 1973, St. Joseph Coll., 1985. RN, Ohio, Mo.; cert. oncology-chemotherapy nurse. Charge nurse oncology unit Grandview Hosp., Dayton, 1976-81; asst. dir. nurses Alta Nursing Home, Dayton, Ohio, 1982-86; nurse oncology unit De Paul Hosp., St. Louis, 1986—. Vol. nurse ARC, 1971-74. Capt. Nurse Corps, USAF, 1961-64. Mem. Oncology Nursing Soc.

BETTAC, TERESA FORSYTHE, secondary education educator; b. Columbus, Ohio, Mar. 18, 1948; d. Darius Hugh and Opal Virginia (Marshall) Forsythe; m. John Bettac, Sept. 12, 1967; 1 child, Adam Christopher. BS, Ohio State U., 1972; MS, Ashland U., 1983. Tchr. Ohio elem. edn. 1-8, Ohio gifted edn. K-12. Tchr. 7th and 8th grade sci., math. London (Ohio) Pub. Schs., 1972-79; tchr. 7th grade sci. Delaware (Ohio) City Schs., 1979-87, tchr. 6th, 7th, 8th grade advanced sci., 1987—; bd. dirs. Forest Park Christian Sch., Columbus, 1994—. Sunday sch. tchr. North Ch. Christ in Christian Union, Columbus, supt. Recipient gov.'s award Ohio Acad. Sci., 1986-94, Jerry Acker outstanding tchr. award, 1991, 94, Battelle award for profl. devel., 1990-91, OHAUS-NSTA award for innovations in middle level sci. tching., 1991-92. Mem. Ohio Assn. for Gifted Children, Nat. Sci. Tchrs. Assn., Nat. Mid. Sch. Tchrs. Assn., Phi Sigma, Pi Lambda. Home: 755 Bering Ct Westerville OH 43081 Office: Willis Mid Sch 74 W William St Delaware OH 43015

BETTENDORF, JAMES BERNARD, minister, church association administrator; b. Jackson, Mich., Oct. 22, 1933; s. Bernard Anthony and Kathryn Marie (Vaughan) B. BA, Sacred Heart Sem., 1955; postgrad. U. Detroit, 1956, U. Notre Dame, 1957, Cath. U. of Am., 1958; STB, St. John Sem., 1959; MA, Western Mich. U., 1970; D Ministry, St. Mary Coll., Balt., 1989. Ordained priest Roman Cath. Ch., 1959. Assoc. pastor Holy Trinity Ch., Fowler, Mich., 1959-60, St. Phillip Ch., Battle Creek, Mich., 1960-63, Sacred Heart Ch., Flint, 1963-66; dir. Flint Newman Ctr., Flint Cath. Info. Ctr., Mich., 1966—; pastor Good Shepherd Ch., Montrose, Mich., 1983-91, St. Leo Ch., Flint, Mich, 1991—. Mem. Cmty. Coalition, Flint, 1968—; exec. bd. Tall Pine coun. Boy Scouts Am.; mem. exec. bd. ARC, 1991—; trustee C.S. Mott Community Coll., 1987—, chmn. bd. trustees, 1989-91; pres. Flint Neighborhood Improvement and Preservation Project. Mem. Lansing Cath. Campus Ministry Assn. (diocesan bd. dirs. 1971-86), Mich. Cath. Campus Ministry Assn., Cath. Campus Ministry Assn. (recipient Charles Forsyth award 1983). Home: 1802 E Court St Flint MI 48503-5344 Office: Flint Newman Ctr 609 E 5th Ave Flint MI 48503-1503

BETTENHAUSEN, BRAD LEE, treasurer, auditor; b. Joliet, Ill., Apr. 2, 1958; s. Robert Theodore and Enid Colleen (Mink) B. BS in Acctg. cum laude, No. Ill. U., 1980. CPA, Ill.; cert. Ill. mcpl. treas.; cert. mcpl. fin. adminstr. Audit and acctg. supr. KPMG Main Hurdman, Chgo., 1980-84; audit and acctg. mgr. Evans Olson & Co., CPAs, Itasca, Ill., 1984-87; treas., fin. dir. Village of Tinley Park, Ill., 1984—; auditor/owner Brad L. Bettenhausen, CPA, Tinley Park, 1987—. Mem. Tinley Park Hist. Preservation Commn.; officer Kimberly Heights Homeowners Assn., Tinley Park, 1989-93; trustee Kimberly Heights Sanitary Dist., 1992—. Named Outstanding Civic Leader Tinley Park C. of C., 1990. Mem. AICPAs, Ill. Soc. CPAs, Govt. Fin. Officers Assn., Ill. Govt. Fin. Officers Assn., Mcpl. Treas. Assn., Ill. Mcpl. Treas. Assn. (bd. dirs. 1989—, pres. 1992), Tinley Park Hist. Soc. (life, pres. 1988—). Office: Village of Tinley Park 16250 Oak Park Ave Tinley Park IL 60477-1628

BETTERMAN, KAREN, travel management consultant; b. Chicago Heights, Ill., July 31, 1951. BS with highest honors, U. Ill., 1973. Ops. mgr. C.U.C. Internat., Chgo., 1985-88; client svc. dir. IVI Travel, Northbrook, Ill., 1988-91; travel mgmt. cons. Runzheimer Internat., Rochester, Wis., 1991—. Mem. Nat. Bus. Travel Assn. Office: Runzheimer Park Rochester WI 53167

BETTERMANN, HILDA, state legislator; b. Oct. 22, 1942; m. William; two children. U. Minn., St. Cloud U., Moorhead U., Hamline U. Rep. Dist. 10B Minn. State Ho. of Reps., 1991—, asst. minority leader, 1996—; instr. Alexandria Tech. Coll., 1996—; mem. Commerce Com., Econ. Devel. Com., Labor Mgmt. Rels., Agrl. & Higher Edn. Fin. Divsn. Coms. Mem. NEA, Minn. Edn. Assn., Am. Vocat. Assn., Minn. Vocat. Assn., Minn. Sec. Assn., Nat. Sec. Assn. Office: Minn Ho of Reps State Capital Building Saint Paul MN 55155-1606*

BETTS, NORA LINDEN, kennel owner; b. Toledo, July 31, 1961; d. Bryan Jesse and Patricia Lynn (Sullivan) Wilkerson; m. Jeffrey Allen Betts, Mar. 15, 1985; 1 child, Bryan Jeffrey. Student, Davis Bus. Coll., 1980-81, 81-83, Cornell U., 1991. Cert. small animal dietitian/nutritionist, cert. animal behaviorist/psychologist. Kennel supr. Karnik Inn of Toledo, Holland, Ohio, 1989-90; vet. technician Trilby Animal Hosp., Toledo, 1989-90; kennel mgr. Pampered Pet Petel, Erie, Mich., 1983-89, kennel owner, 1990—. Contbr. articles to profl. newsletters. Speaker in field Bedford Pub. Schs., Lambertville, Mich., 1989, 90, 91, 92, Monroe (Mich.) County Libr. System, 1992; active Nat. Audubon Soc., 1993—, Defenders of Wildlife, 1991—, World Wildlife Fund, 1992—, Maumee Valley Save-A-Pet, 1992—. Mem. ASPCA, Nat. Humane Edn. Assn., People for the Ethical Treatment of Animals, Am. Boarding Kennels Assn. (cert. kennel technician, cons. 1990—), Nat. Fedn. Ind. Bus., Nat. Dog Groomers Assn., Toledo Vet. Med. Assn., Humane Soc. Monroe. Methodist. Office: Pampered Pet Petel 7190 Dixie Hwy Erie MI 48133-9660

BETZ, HANS DIETER, theology educator; b. Lemgo, Lippe, Germany, May 21, 1931; came to U.S., 1963, naturalized, 1973; s. Ludwig and Gertrude (Vietor) B.; m. Christel Hella Wagner, Nov. 10, 1958; children: Martin, Ludwig, Arnold. Student, Kirchliche Hochschule, Bethel, Fed. Republic Germany, 1951-52, U. Mainz, Fed. Republic Germany, 1952-55, 56-58, Westminster Coll, Cambridge, Eng., 1955-56; Doctor Theologiae, U. Mainz, Fed. Republic Germany, 1957; Habilitation, U. Mainz, 1966. Pastor Evangelical Ch., Rhineland, Fed. Republic Germany, 1961-63; from asst. prof. to prof. Sch. Theology, Claremont Grad. Sch., Calif., 1963-78; prof. N.T. and early Christian lit. U. Chgo., 1978—, Shailer Mathews prof., 1989—, chmn. dept. N.T. and early Christian lit., 1985-94. Author, editor numerous books and articles in German and English, 1959—. Recipient Humboldt Rsch. prize, 1986; Lady Davis fellow Hebrew U., Jerusalem, Israel, 1990, Sackler scholar Tel Aviv U., 1995; NEH rsch. grantee, 1970-83, Am. Assn. Theol. Schs. grantee, 1977, 84. Mem. Soc. Bibl. Lit. (pres. 1996—), Studiorum Novi Testamenti Societas, Chgo. Soc. Bibl. Rsch. (pres. 1983-84). Office: U Chgo 1025 E 58th St Chicago IL 60637-1509

BETZ, RONALD PHILIP, pharmacist; b. Chgo., Nov. 26, 1933; s. David Robert and Olga Marie (Martinson) B.; BS, U. Ill., 1955; MPA, Roosevelt U., 1987; m. Rose Marie Marella, May 18, 1963; children: David Christian, Christopher Peter. Asst. dir. of pharmacy U. Ill., Chgo., 1959-62; dir. pharmacy Mt. Sinai Hosp., Chgo., 1962—; pres. Pharmacy Systems, Inc., 1982-89; teaching assoc. Coll. of Pharmacy, U. Ill., Chgo., 1977-88; adj. clin. asst. prof. pharmacy, U. Ill., 1988—; pres. Pharmacy Svc. and Systems, 1972-81; dir. Ill. Coop. Health Data Systems, 1976-80. Bd. dirs. Howard/Paulina Redevel. Corp., 1983-92 . With U.S. Army, 1956-58. Mem. Am. Soc. Hosp. Pharmacists, Ill. Pharm. Assn. (pres. 1975), Ill. Acad. Preceptors in Pharmacy (pres. 1972), No. Ill. Soc. Hosp. Pharmacists (pres. 1966), Kappa Psi. Democrat. Lutheran. Contbr. articles in field to profl. jours. Home: 1021 Sussex Dr Northbrook IL 60062 Office: 2750 W 15th Pl Chicago IL 60608-1704

BETZOLD, DONALD RICHARD, state senator; b. Mpls., Aug. 27, 1950; s. Donald A. and Georgiana (Beauchamp) B.; m. Leesa Marie Simonson, Aug. 11, 1989; 1 child, Ben Anthony. BA, U. Minn., 1972; JD, Hamline U., 1979. Bar: Minn. 1979. Atty. Brooklyn Center, Minn., 1980—; state senator State of Minn., St. Paul, 1993—. Lt. col. USAR. Mem. Minn. State Bar Assn. (chair bar media com. 1987-90). Roman Catholic. Home: 6150 Briardale Ct NE Fridley MN 55432-5210 Office: Minn State Senate 624 Capitol Blvd Saint Paul MN 55103-1836

BEUC, RUDOLPH, JR., architect, real estate broker; b. St. Louis, Nov. 7, 1931; s. Rudolph M. and Lillian Ann (Rethemeyer) B.; B.Arch., Washington U., St. Louis, 1955; m. Mildred Hild, Jan. 25, 1968; children: Rudolph III, Ralph M. Archtl. draftsman Bank Bldg. & Equipment Corp. Am., St. Louis, 1950, Hammond & Gorlock, architects, St. Louis, 1957-58; designer Schwarz & Van Hoefen, architects, St. Louis, 1958; architect George E. Berg Architects, St. Louis, 1958-60; architect R. Beuc, Architects, Inc., St. Louis, 1960—, pres., 1960—, also dir.; pres., dir. Hilterdevco, Inc., St. Louis, 1964—; Dir. pub. works Peerless Park, 1967—; deacon Webster Groves Presbyn. Ch. Served with AUS, 1955-57. Mem. AIA, Soc. Am. Registered Architects, Mo. Council Architects, Mo. Assn. Bldg. Ofcls. and Inspectors, Council of Am. Bldg. Officials, Bldg. Officials Code Adminstrs., NCARB, Am. Legion (past comdr.), ODD Fellows Lodge. Clubs: Mason, Lion (past pres.); Order Eastern Star, DeMolay, High Twelve (past state pres.), Scottish Rite, Washington University, Westborough Country. Home: 138 W Glendale Rd Saint Louis MO 63119-4060 Office: 142 W Glendale Rd Saint Louis MO 63119-4060

BEUTER, RICHARD WILLIAM, accountant; b. Iowa City, Iowa, Dec. 21, 1942; s. Eugene Richard and Marietta (Lehman) B.; m. Kathleen Louise Jedlicka, June 5, 1965; children: Matthew Jon, Brian Michael. BBA, U. Iowa, 1965. Staff acct. Coopers & Lybrand, South Bend, Ind., 1965-66; staff acct. Coopers & Lybrand, Des Moines, 1966-74, ptnr., 1974-78; ptnr. Coopers & Lybrand, Indpls., 1978—. Mem. Am. Inst. CPA's (trial bd. Region 7 1987—), Ind. CPA Soc. (ethics com. 1979-82), Hosp. Fin. Mgmt. Assn., Ins. Acctg. Statis. Assn., Crooked Stick Golf Club (Carmel, Ind.), Skyline Club. Roman Catholic. Office: Coopers & Lybrand 2900 1 American Sq PO Box 82002 Indianapolis IN 46282

BEUTLER, ARTHUR JULIUS, manufacturing company executive; b. LaCrosse, Wis., Sept. 2, 1924; s. Arthur Julius and Augusta Henrietta (Dobe) B.; m. Carolee Yvonne Crawford, Dec. 28, 1952; 1 child, Karen Elizabeth. BSEE, U. Wis., 1948, Grad. in EE, 1968. Registered profl. engr., Wis. Trainee inventor program Gen. Electric Co., Schenectady, N.Y., 1948-51; devel. engr. Gen. Electric Co., Milw., 1951-59, project engr., 1959-61, sr. engr., 1961-64; chief engr. Dings Magnetic Separator Co., Milw., 1964-67; pres., owner Creative Engring. Assocs., Inc., Greendale, Wis., 1967-72, 88—; v.p. mfg. Gettys Mfg. Co., Racine, Wis., 1972-79, v.p. internat., 1979-81; v.p. tech. planning div. motion control div. Gould, Inc. (formerly Gettys Mfg. Co.), Racine, 1981-88; cons. engr. mfg. control systems, robotics. Patentee elec. controls. Served with U.S. Army, 1943-46, PTO. Mem. IEEE (sr., chpt. chmn. 1969-72), NSPE, Soc. Mfg. Engrs. (cert.), Tau Beta Pi, Eta Kappa Nu.

BEUTLER, CHRISTOPHER JOHN, state legislator; b. Omaha, Nov. 14, 1944; s. John E. and Dorothy M. (Lanning) B.; m. Patty Hershey, 1967; children: Alexa, Erica, Mikahla, Samuel. BA, Yale U., 1966; JD, U. Nebr., 1973. Tchr. Peace Corps, Turkey, 1966-67; rschr. Nebr. Crime Commn., 1972-73; assoc. Cline, Williams, Wright, Johnson & Oldfather, Lincoln, 1973-78; pvt. practice, 1978—; mem. from dist. 28 Nebr. State Senate, Lincoln, 1978-86, 90, chmn. judiciary com., 1983-84, mem. natural resources com., mem. rules com., com. on coms., edn. com. Named to Benson H.S. Hall of Fame, 1984. Mem. Nebr. Bar Assn., Lincoln Bar Assn., Nebr. Art Assn., Kiwanis (mem. exec. com. 1976), Beta Theta Phi. Office: Nebr State Senate State Capitol Rm 1210 Lincoln NE 68509*

BEUTLER, FREDERICK JOSEPH, information scientist; b. Berlin, Oct. 3, 1926; came to U.S., 1936, naturalized, 1943; s. Alfred David and Kaethe (Italiener) B.; m. Suzanne Armstrong, Jan. 5, 1969; children—Arthur David, Kathryn Ruth, Michael Ernest. S.B., Mass. Inst. Tech., 1949, S.M., 1951; Ph.D., Calif. Inst. Tech., 1957. Mem. faculty U. Mich., Ann Arbor, 1957—, prof. info. and control engring., 1963-90, prof. emeritus, 1990—, chmn. computer info. and control engring., 1970-71, 77-90, chmn. grad. elect. engring. systems program, 1985-90; vis. prof. Calif. Inst. Tech., 1967-68; vis. scholar U. Calif. at Berkeley, 1964-65. Editorial cons. Math. Rev., 1965-67, 75-88; contbr. articles to profl. jours. and books. Bd. dirs. Ann Arbor Civic Theatre, 1976-78, 91-94. With AUS, 1945-46. NSF rsch. grantee, 1971-75, 76-81, 92-94, Air Force Office Sci. Rsch. grantee, 1970-74, 75-80; NASA grantee, 1959-69. Fellow IEEE (life); mem. Soc. Indsl. and Applied Math (coun. 1969-74, mng. editor Jour. Applied Math. 1970-75, editor, 1984-90, editor Rev. 1967-70), Am. Math. Soc., Inst. Math. Stats., Am. Arbitration Assn., Barton Boat Club, Racquet Club of Ann Arbor. Office: Elec Engr and Comp Sci Bldg Univ Michigan Ann Arbor MI 48109-2122

BEVAN, ROBERT LEWIS, lawyer; b. Springfield, Mo., Mar. 23, 1928; s. Gene Walter and Blanche Omega (Woods) B.; m. Ronice Diane Gartin, Jan 25, 1977; children: Matthew Gene, Lisa Ann. AB, U. Mo., 1950; LLB, U. Kansas City, 1957. Bar: Mo. 1957, D.C. 1969. Adminstrv. asst. U.S. Senator T. Hennings Jr., Washington, 1957-60; legis. asst. U.S. Senator E.V. Long, Washington, 1960-69; sr. govt. relations counsel Am. Bankers Assn., Washington, 1970-84; ptnr. Hopkins & Sutter, Washington, 1984-95; cons. atty. Stinson, Mag and Fizzell, Kansas City, Mo., 1995—. Ghost author: The Intruders, 1967; contbg. editor U.S. Banker, 1985-88. Fieldman Dem. Nat. Com., 1968. Served with U.S. Army, 1946-47, 1951-53. Mem. ABA (bus. law sect., chmn. banking law com. 1988-92), Echequer Club. Office: 4545 Wornall Rd # 805 Kansas City MO 64111

BEVINGTON, TERRY PAUL, professional baseball manager; b. Akron, Ohio, July 27, 1966; m. Cyndi Lochard; 1 child, Cortney. Grad., Santa Monica (Calif.) H.S. Baseball player N.Y. Yankees, 1974-80; mgr. midwest league Milw. Brewers, Burlington, 1981-82; mgr. Calif. league Milw. Brewers, Stockton, 1983-85; mgr. AAA league, Pacific Coast league Milw. Brewers, Vancouver, B.C., Can., 1986; mgr. AAA league Milw. Brewers, Denver, 1987; minor league mgr. no. divsn. Chgo. White Sox, Vancouver, 1987-94; 3d base coach Chgo. White Sox, 1988-94, team mgr., 1995—; mem. N.Y. Penn All-Star Team, 1975.

BEYER, JANE MAGDALYN, governmental management consultant; b. Milw., Mar. 8, 1959; d. George Joseph and Evelyn Augusta (Grams) B. BA with honors, U. Wis., Milw., 1982; MA, U. Wis., Madison, 1986. Personnel policy specialist Wis. Dept. Ind., Labor and Human Rels., Madison, 1984-86; fiscal and policy analyst Wis. Legis. Fiscal Bur., Madison, 1986-89; sr. budget and mgmt. analyst Dept. Adminstrn., Budget and Mgmt. Div., City of Milw., 1989, budget and mgmt. team supr., 1989-94; govtl. mgmt. cons. Virchow, Krause and Co., Madison, 1995—; intern Sen. William Proxmire, Milw., 1981; dir. Univ. Legal Clinic, Milw., 1979-82. Pres. Young Women's Caucus/Nat. Women's Pilot. Caucus, Dane County, Wis., 1985-86; com. mem. Milw. Lakefront Festival, 1993—, Am. Legion Aux. Am. Legion Aux. scholar, 1981; recipient Exceptional Performance award Legis. Fiscal Bur., State of Wis., 1987. Fellow Robert M. LaFollette Inst.; mem. LaFollette Inst. Alumni Assn., U. Wis.-Milw. Alumni Assn. (mortar bd. 1993—), Wis. Women's Network (bd. dirs., exec. com. 1991-93), Mortar Bd., Phi Eta Sigma, Pi Sigma Alpha. Home: 4809 Lien Rd Apt 208 Madison WI 53704 Office: Virchow Krause & Co 4600 American Pky Madison WI 53704

BEYER, MARY EDEL, primary education educator; b. Winona, Minn., July 16, 1932; d. Edmund Aloysious and Gertrude Cecilia (Knopick) Edel; m. Agrene Lester Beyer, June 7, 1958 (dec. Aug. 1985); children: Jason Edel Beyer, Trudy Edel Beyer, Gerard Edel Beyer, Jeremy Edel Beyer. AS in edn., Winona State U., 1952, BS, 1967, MS, 1978. Cert. elem. education tchr. Tchr. 1st grade Dodge Ctr. (Minn.) Sch., 1952-55; tchr. 1st grade, kindergarten Dist. 857, Lewiston, Minn., 1955-63; tchr. kindergarten Dist. 861, Winona, 1968-95, Stockton (Minn.) Sch., 1966-70; tchr. Rollingstone Elem. Sch., 1970-95; sch. del. Minn. Edn. Effective Program, 1987-95; pres. Winona Dist. 861 Reading Com. Contbr. to Poland Today Pol-Am. Jour., 1993; celebrity reader Children's Books Reading on the mall, 1990-95; photographer, writer School News Winona Post, 1985-95; freelance writer. Spencer, cadet mem. USO Group, Winona, 1950-52; leader Girl Scouts-Boy Scouts, 1952-70; mem. Sweet Adelines, 1978—, lead singer Hiawatha Valley Sweet Adelines, sec. 1994-95. Recipient Pres.'s award Lakeside St. Machines, Winona, 1992, Disting. Svc. award, 1993, Diamond award 4-H Club, Winona, 1995; named Master Knitter Extension Office, Winona, 1985. Mem. PTA (pres.), Minn. Reading Assn. (del. 1985-95), Polish Heritage Soc. (sec.), Am. Legion Aux., Knights Columbus (4th degree lady). County Hist. Soc., Winona Athletic Club, C. of C. (bus. edn. intern 1995). Home: 260 W Broadway Winona MN 55987

BEYER, ROBERT EDWARD, retired biochemist, educator; b. Englewood, N.J., Feb. 20, 1928; s. Edward I. and Rebecca H. (Lewis) B.; m. Boon Neo Juliana Ong, Aug. 24, 1991. BS, U. Conn., 1950, MS, 1951; PhD, Brown U., 1954. USPHS postdoctoral fellow U. Stockholm, 1954-56; asst. prof. Sch. Medicine Tufts U., 1956-62; asst. prof. enzyme chemistry Inst. Enzyme Rsch. U. Wis., 1962-65; prof. biology U. Mich, Ann Arbor, 1965-93; ret. U. Mich., Ann Arbor, 1994; vis. prof. dept. neurology U. Calif., San Francisco, 1973-74; vis. prof. dept. biochemistry U. Stockholm, 1985-86; vis. scientist biomed. ctr. U. Uppsala, Sweden, 1994; vis. scientist dept. biochemistry U. Bologna, Italy, 1995. Sr. Rsch. fellow NIH, 1958-60, Fogarty Sr. Internat. fellow, 1985-86; recipient Rsch. Career Devel. award NIH, 1960-65. Office: 1615 Traver Rd Ann Arbor MI 48105-1737

BEYERCHEN, ALAN DUANE, historian; b. Mt. Clemens, Mich., May 14, 1945; s. Albert Ray and Eleanor Evelyn (Sexton) B. BA, U. Calif., Santa Barbara, 1967, MA, 1968, PhD, 1973. Asst. prof. U. Fla., Gainesville, 1976-78; assoc. prof. Ohio State U., Columbus, 1978—, rsch. assoc. Mershon Ctr., 1980—. Author: Scientists Under Hitler, 1977, translations in Japanese, 1979, German, 1980, Italian, 1981, Dutch, 1982, Turkish, 1985. 1st lt. U.S. Army, 1974-75, capt., 1976. Recipient Postdoctoral Teaching award Eli Lilly Endowment, 1977-78, Scholar's award NSF, 1985; fellow Guggenheim Found., 1983-84, Nat. Humanities Ctr., 1984. Fellow AAAS (com. on sci. freedom and responsibility 1988-92); mem. Am. Hist. Assn., Conf. Group for Ctrl. European History, German Studies Assn., History of Sci. Soc. (editl. adv. bd. 1985-91). Office: Ohio State U History Dept 230 W 17th Ave Columbus OH 43210-1311

BEYERS, CATHERINE MEYER, media specialist; b. Chgo., May 29, 1947; d. Warren and Lois (Anderson) Meyer; m. Richard Duane Beyers, Feb. 17, 1970; children: Lois Jean, James Matthew, Mary Catherine. BS, U. Ill., 1969; MS, U. Wis., LaCrosse, Wis., 1986. Tchr. Montgomery County

Schs., Rockville, Md., 1969-70, Smith Valley Sch., LaCrosse, Wis., 1970-73; tchr. Spence Elem. Sch., LaCrosse, Wis., 1983-84, libr. media dir., 1984-92; libr. media dir. So. Bluffs Elem. Sch., LaCrosse, Wis., 1992—; cons. in field. Recipient Kohl Found. fellowship, 1991, John Cotton Dana award ALA, 1991, Tchr. of Yr. award Sch. Dist. LaCrosse, 1991, Venture grants LaCrosse Edn. Found., 1986, 91, 93, WEMA grant, 1995, J. Sparkman fellowship in tech. tng., 1996; named Educator of Yr. Phi Delta Kappa, 1990, Disting. Alumni U. Ill. Coll. Edn., 1996. Mem. ALA, Wis. Ednl. Media Assn. (MediaDir. of Yr. award 1995), Wis. Libr. Assn., Midwest Wis. Reading Coun. (Reading Tchr. of Yr. 1994), Am. Assn. Sch. Librs. (Sch. Libr. Media Program of Yr. award 1995). Office: So Bluffs Elem Sch 4010 Sunnyside Dr La Crosse WI 54601-2251

BHALLA, DEEPAK KUMAR, cell biologist, toxicologist, educator; b. Kasauli, India, Aug. 31, 1946; s. Khazan Chand and Shyama Bhalla; 1 child, Neel. BS, Punjab U., India, 1968, MS, 1969; PhD, Howard U., Washington, 1976. Postdoctoral fellow Harvard U., Boston, 1976-79; asst. rsch. cell biologist U. Calif., San Francisco, 1979-82; asst. prof. U. Calif., Irvine, 1982-86, assoc. prof., 1986-95; assoc. prof. Wayne State U., Detroit, 1995—; speaker in field. Contbr. articles and revs. to profl. jours. NIH grantee, 1985-88, 88—, Calif. Air Resources Bd. grantee, 1990—. Mem. AAAS, Am. Thoracic Soc., Am. Soc. Cell Biology, Soc. Toxicology. Office: OEHS-Sch Pharmacy 628 Shapero Hall Wayne State Univ Detroit MI 48202

BHARATH, RAMACHANDRAN, decision sciences educator; b. Madras, Tamilnadu, India, Jan. 7, 1935; came to U.S., 1976; s. Thiagaraja Sadasiva and Sarojini (Rangaswami) Ramachandran. BSc, Madras (India) U., 1954, BL, 1960; M.Sc., London Sch. Econs., 1967; PhD, Simon Fraser U., 1976. Mem. Indian Adminstrv. Svc. Govt. of India, 1957-71; vis. asst. prof. U. Mass., Amherst, 1976-77; asst. prof. No. Mich. U., Marquette, 1977-78, assoc. prof., 1978-82, prof., 1982—. Author: Introduction to Prolog, 1986, Prolog: Sophisticated Applications, 1989, Computers and Graph Theory, 1991, (with J. Drosen) Neural Network Computing, 1994; contbr. articles to profl. jours. Recipient Disting. Faculty award Mich. Assn. Governing Bds. of Schs. & Colls., 1987; Fulbright scholar Fulbright Found., 1988-89. Mem. Inst. Ops. Rsch. & Mgmt. Scis., Soc. Am., Decision Scis. Inst., Brit. Computer Soc.

BHARGAVA, HEMENDRA NATH, pharmacologist, educator; b. Delhi, India, Sept. 30, 1942; m. Shakti Bhargava. B in Pharmacy, Banaras Hindu U., India, 1963, PharmM, 1965; PhD, U. Calif., San Francisco, 1969. Postdoctoral fellow U. Calif. Med. Sch., San Francisco, 1969-72, rsch. pharmacologist, 1972-74, lectr., 1974-75; asst. prof. pharmacology U. Ill. Med. Ctr., Chgo., 1975-78, assoc. prof., 1978-81, prof. pharmacology, 1981—; reviewer grants from NSF, Nat. Inst. on Drug Abuse, Ont. Mental Health Found (Can.). Contbr. over 520 articles to profl. jours., chpts. to books; reviewer manuscripts from 18 nat. and internat. jours. of pharmacology and neurosci. Recipient Madan Mohan Malviya prize Banaras Hindu U., 1963, Gold medal, 1965, Sr. Neurosci Rsch. Achievement award, 1991 and Rsch. Scientist Devel. award NIH, 1992—, Golden Apple award, 1980, Pride of India Gold medal, 1991, Mother India Internat. award, 1994; named to Chgo. Tribune's Tempo All-Prof. Team Acad. Champions, 1993; rsch. grantee NIH, Am. Heart Assn., Ill. Dept. Mental Health. Fellow Internat. Peptide Soc.; mem. Am. Soc. for Pharmacology and Exptl. Therapeutics, Am. Heart Assn. Met. Chgo., Am.. Assn. Coll. of Pharmacy, Indian Acad. Neurosci., Soc. for Neurosci., Internat. Narcotic Rsch. Club. Office: U Ill at Chgo M/C 865 833 S Wood St Chicago IL 60612-7229

BHORE, JAY NARAYAN, psychiatrist; b. Kavalapur, Bombay, India, Sept. 12, 1915; came to U.S. 1958; s. Narayan Suleman and Chandra (Nandrekar) B.; m. Mary Elizabeth Singleton, June 17, 1960. BS, Govt. Coll., India, 1939; M.B.B.S., BJJ Med. Coll., India, 1943; MD, Northwestern U., Chgo., 1967. Med. officer Student Health Ctr., Bishop Coll., Calcutta, India, 1947-51; resident physician Jubar Sanatorium, Simla Hills, India, 1951-53; resident diseases of chest Mcpl. T.B. Sanatorium, Chgo., 1958-60; fellow neurology/psychiatry Northwestern U. Med. Sch., Chgo., 1960-61; rotating intern Augustana Hosp., Chgo., 1962; resident in psychiatry St. Joseph Hosp., London, Ont., Can., 1964-65, Northwestern U., Chgo., 1965-67; staff psychiatrist Downey (Ill.) VA Hosp., 1968-71, West Side VA Hosp., Chgo., 1970-73, VA Hosp., Woods, Wis., 1973; pvt. practice psychiatry Milw., 1974—; founder, pres. Rev. N.S. Bhore Meml., Kavalapur, India, 1975; pres. Rev. N.S. Bhore Mem. Evang. Assocs., Milw., 1976. Founder Free Pub. Libr., Kavalapur, 1980, Med. Clinic Day Care Ctr., Kavalapur, 1981, Chandra Hosp., Kavalapur, 1990. Mem. APA, AMA, Wis. Psychiat. Assn., Christian Med. Dental Soc., Am. Assn. Physicians from India. Presbyterian. Home and Office: 1543 N Prospect Ave Milwaukee WI 53202-2367

BIANCHI, ROBERT GEORGE, retired pharmacologist; b. Chgo., Mar. 20, 1925; s. Anthony and Ann (Lazzarotto) B.; m. Shirley S. Kluesing, Apr. 24, 1948; children: Bruce, Beth Ann, Craig, Glenn. BS, Franklin and Marshall Coll., 1945. Sr. technologist G.D. Searle & Co., Skokie, Ill., 1946-53, jr. biologist, 1953-60, jr. investigator, 1960-68, rsch. investigator, 1968-88; sr. rsch. investigator G.D. Searle & Co., Skokie, 1988-95; ret., 1995. Author: Use of Experimental Peptic Ulcer Models for Drug Screening, 1971; contbr. 50 rsch. articles to profl. jours. Mem. Sch. Bd. Dist. 71, Niles, Ill., 1970—. Mem. AAAS, Am. Soc. for Pharmacology and Exptl. Therapeutics (assoc.), Gastrointestinal Rsch. Group, Niles Hist. Soc., Holy Name Soc., KC, Sigma Xi. Republican. Roman Catholic. Home: 8336 N Caldwell Ave Niles IL 60714-2602

BIANCO, DON CHRISTOPHER, civil servant; b. Steubenville, Ohio, Sept. 26, 1947; s. Dominic Joseph and Anna Mary (Buonaguro) B.; m. Sally Ann Bungart, Dec. 7, 1968 (div. Jan. 1980); 1 child, Celia Z.; m. Cynthia Irene Kuceyski, June 16, 1984. Student, Miami U., Oxford, Ohio, 1965-67; BS in Edn., Ohio State U., 1973. Adminstrv. asst. Ohio Dept. Transp., Columbus, 1973-75; investigator Ohio Div. Consumer Protection, Columbus, 1975-76, Ohio Div. Real Estate, Columbus, 1976; investigator Ohio Div. Unclaimed Funds, Columbus, 1976-82, chief investigator, 1982—. Home: 127 Brevoort Rd Columbus OH 43214-3823 Office: Ohio Dept Commerce 77 S High St Columbus OH 43266-0545

BIANCO, JOSEPH PETER, securities salesperson; b. N.Y.C., May 28, 1956. BA, Overland Coll., 1978; PhD, Yale U., 1984; MBA, Washington U., St. Louis, 1990. Assoc. prof. romance studies Washington U., 1984-88; securities salesperson A. G. Edwards & Sons Inc., St. Louis, 1990—. Contbr. articles to profl. jours. Bd. dirs. corp. partnership com. St. Louis Art Mus., 1993—; tour guide for mus. Recipient Henry Parish award France, 1981; scholar in bus. Washington U., 1988. Mem. St. Louis Yale Club. Home: 12800 Mason Manor Rd Saint Louis MO 63141-7352 Office: A G Edwards & Sons Inc Ste 1 City Ctr Ste Saint Louis MO 63101-1893

BIAR, JEFFERY KEN, data processing executive; b. Dayton, Ohio, Feb. 27, 1958; s. Homer J. and Martha A. (Constance) B. BS in Computer Sci., Wright State U., Dayton, 1980, MS in Computer Sci., 1981. CAD mgr. NCR, Dayton, 1980-89; dir. engring. Ceecom/Dayton, 1989-93; owner/pres. Kettering Color Graphics, Dayton, 1993—. Office: Kettering Color Graphics PO Box 292804 Dayton OH 45429-8804

BIBB, JAMES RICHARD, sales executive; b. Sturgis, Mich., Apr. 16, 1952; s. James Elmer and Melva Jean (Wiser) B.; m. Debra Sue Kuhn, July 27, 1974; children: Erika, Ryan, Evan. Student, Glen Oaks Community Coll., 1971. V.p., gen. mgr. Michiana Oil Co., Howe, Ind., 1975-87; stock broker IDS Am. Express, South Bend, Ind., 1987-88; sales mgr. Larry James VW & Mazda, Sturgis, 1988-90; gen. and sales mgr. Larry Engel Ford Sales Inc., Sturgis, Mich., 1990-91, Vicksburg (Mich.) Chrysler, Plymouth, Dodge, Jeep & Eagle, 1991-92; asst. new truck sales mgr., Isuzu sales mgr. Don Seelye Ford, Isuzu Inc., Kalamazoo, Mich., 1992-94; sales mgr. South Ctrl. U.S. Quadr Mfg., Inc., White Pigeon, Mich., 1994—. Notary pub., Mich., 1989. Mem. Mich. Auto Dealers Assn., Mich. Notary Assn., Mazda Guild (Gold award 1990), Volkswagon Guild (Gold award 1990), Ford Master Sales Guild (Gold award 1989). Home: 411 E South St Sturgis MI 49091-2264

BIBBS, LONA CAROL, educational program administrator; b. Chgo., Jan. 6, 1948; d. Willie P. and Canara (Graham) Cooley; m. Guy L Bibbs, Sept. 6, 1970; children: Lona Demetria, Guy Lee III. BA, Bradley U., 1970; MS, Northeastern U., 1975; postgrad., Loyola U., Chgo. Children's dir. Carver Community Ctr., Peoria, Ill., 1968-70, med. ctr. supr., 1970-72; tchr. Chgo. Bd. Edn., 1972-75, guidance counselor, 1975-85, sr. counselor, chmn. guidance dept., 1985-89; asst. dir. summer transition program Northeastern Ill. U., 1989—; facilitator Bur. of Vocat. and Technol., Chgo., 1985—, program chmn. Dist. 31 Coll. Fair, Chgo. 1986-87; counselor articulation bd. DePaul U. Coach NAACP ACT-So Program, Chgo., 1986—, Midwest Community Council. Chgo., 1988; mem. individualized student career plan task force Ill. State Bd. Edn.; mem. The Nat. Disting. Svc. Registry. Recipient Outstanding Vocat. Articulation Facilitator Chgo. Bd. of Ed. Bur. of Vocat. and Technol. Edn. Awds. Chair Ill. Sch. Counselors Assn., Connections 2000 award Ill. State Bd. Edn. Mem. ACA, ASCD, AAUW, NAFE, Aux. to Chgo. Dental Soc., Caux Ill. Assn. Counseling and Devel., Sec. Sch. Counselors Coun. (pres. 1987), Nat. Coun. Negro Women, Nat. Hook-up of Black Women Inc. (v.p.), Loyola U. Leadership and Policy Studies Assn. (sec.), Nat. Bd. Cert. Counselors, Inst. for Athletes in Edn., Dental Wives of Chgo. (pres.), Am. Vocational Assn., Ill. Vocational Assn., Ill. Assn. Supervision & Curriculum Devel. Democrat.

BIBBY, JOHN FRANKLIN, political science educator, writer; b. LaCrosse, Wis., Aug. 26, 1934; s. Joseph Winder and Mildred May (Franklin) B.; m. Lucile Helen Hanson, Aug. 16, 1958; children: John F. Jr., Peter Mark. BS, U. Wis., LaCrosse, 1956; MA, U. Ill., 1957; PhD, U. Wis., 1963. Fellow in govt. Brookings Inst., Washington, 1961-62; asst. prof. U. Wis., Milw., 1962-63, assoc. prof., 1966-72, prof. polit. sci., 1972—; asst. prof. No. Ill. U., DeKalb, 1963-65; adminstrv. asst. to chmn. Rep. Nat. Com., Washington, 1965-66; exec. dir. Ho. Rep. Conf. U.S. Ho. Reps., Washington, 1969-70; dir. congress study Am. Enterprise Inst., Washington, 1979-86; lectr. U.S. Info. Agy., Eng., Belgium, Germany, Japan, Austria, Australia, 1981, 83, 88, 92. Author: Party Organization in American Politics, 1984, Parties, Politics and Elections in America, 1987, 3d edit., 1996, Governing by Consent, 1st edit., 1992, 2d edit. 1995; contbr. articles to profl. jours. Alt. del. Rep. Nat. Conv., Kansas City, 1976, Dallas, 1984, New Orleans, 1988; exec. dir. Platform Com. Rep. Nat. Conv., Kansas City, 1976; vice-chmn. Rep. Party Wis., Madison, 1977-85. Mem. Am. Polit. Sci. Assn. (trustee, devel. bd. 1994—, chmn. polit. orgns. & parties field 1995—, Best Pub. Paper), Pi Sigma Alpha (pres.-elect 1995-96). Presbyterian. Office: U Wis Dept Polit Sci PO Box 413 Milwaukee WI 53201

BIBEAU, DENNIS I., electrical engineer; b. St. Paul, Oct. 10, 1962. BS in Elec. Engring., N.D. State U., Fargo, 1985. Elec. engr. Printware, Eagan, Minn., 1989-93, Carl Zeiss Inc., Brooklyn Park, Minn., 1993-94, Digital Biometrics Inc., Minnetonka, Minn., 1994—. Office: Digital Biometrics Inc 5600 Rowland Rd Minnetonka MN 55343-4315

BIBER, ALLAN, mechanical engineer; b. Kennedy Township, Pa., Feb. 17, 1958; s. Nikolem J. and Susan (Yalch) B. BSME, U. Akron, 1991. Mgr. Bibers Garage, Pitts., 1976-92; design engr. Therm-o-Disc Inc., Mansfield, Ohio, 1992—. Roman Catholic. Office: Therm-o-Disc Inc 1320 S Main St Mansfield OH 44907-2516

BICKEL, MARVIN DEAN, printing director state house of representatives; b. Syracuse, Mo., June 19, 1943; s. Jacob and Mattie Elizabeth (Moad) Bickel; div. July, 1983; 1 child, Elizabeth Ann. Student, Lincoln Univ. Printing dir. Mo. Ho. of Reps., Jefferson City, Mo. Named Ky. Colonel State of Ky., 1991. Mem. Nat. State Printing Asssn. Home: 117 S Ventura # 6 Jefferson City MO 65109 Office: Mo Ho of Reps Printing Dept B 21 State Capital Jefferson City MO 65101

BICKETT, RICHARD JOSEPH, retired elementary school principal, elementary education educator; b. Cin., May 29, 1922; s. Richard Alexander and Katherine Henrietta (Schook) B.; m. Shirley Ann Schmidt, Dec. 26, 1945; children: Diane, Timothy, Joan, Paula, Blase, Laura. B.S. in Edn., U. Cin., 1948, M.S. in Edn., 1954. Tchr. jr. high Ohio City (Ohio) Sch., 1948-51; tchr. 5th grade Deer Park (Ohio) Sch., 1951-52; tchr. 4th-6th grade Raschig Sch., Cinn., 1952-57; asst. prin. Fairview Sch., Cin., 1957-60; prin. Guilford Sch., Cin., 1960-61, Peaslee Sch., Cin., 1961-75, Chase Sch., Cin., 1975-77. Sch. bus. driver severely handicapped children Settle Svc., Cin., 1977-87; counselor Boy Scouts Am. Merit Badges, Madisonville and Mariemont, Ohio, 1952-62; chmn. bd. of edn. St. John's Sch., Deer Park, Ohio, 1963-65, St. Vincent's Peace and Justice Com., Kenwood, Ohio, 1983-87; legis. adv. Archdiocese Cin. Social Action, 1987—. Lt. (j.g.) USN, 1943-46, PTO. Named Outstanding Title I Prin., Cin. Parent Adv. Coun., 1973-74. Mem. Eastside Discussion Club, Cornerstone Homesource Regional Loan Fund (treas., 1990-95), Global Edn. Assocs., Common Cause. Democrat. Roman Catholic.

BICKFORD, JAMES ALLAN, electrical engineer, consultant; b. Bay Village, Ohio, Oct. 15, 1960; s. Allan Leroy and Patricia Ann Bickford; m. Debra Jean Bickford, June 18, 1983; children: Christopher, Matthew, Stephen. BSEE, U. Toledo, 1983. Registered profl. engr., Ohio. Elec. engr. Newport News (Va.) Shipbldg., 1983-85, Morrison Knudsen Corp., Cleve., 1985—. Mem. IEEE, North Ridgeville Radio Assn. Office: Morrison Knudsen Corp 1500 W 3d St Cleveland OH 44113

BICKLEIN, JOHN P., resource specialist; b. St. Louis, Aug. 21, 1941. Resource specialist Watlow Electric Co., St. Louis, 1972—. Republican. Office: Watson Electric Co 12001 Lackland Rd Saint Louis MO 63146-4001

BICKNELL, BRIAN KEITH, dentist; b. Orlando, Fla., Mar. 8, 1957; s. Keith Arthur and Mary Lou (Papish) B.; m. Gina Rose Smajo; children: Michael Brian, Daniel Keith. BS, U. Notre Dame, 1979, U. Ill., Chgo., 1981; DDS, U. Ill., Chgo., 1983. Practice gen. dentistry Batavia, Ill., 1984—. Fellow Acad. Gen. Dentistry; mem. ADA, Ill. State Dental Soc., Fox River Valley Dental Soc. Roman Catholic. Home: 594 N Van Nortwick St Batavia IL 60510-1119 Office: 109 E Wilson St Batavia IL 60510-2658

BIDDINGER, DAVID LEE, financial consultant; b. Indpls., Sept. 29, 1945. BS, No. Ariz. U., Flagstaff, 1968; MBA, Ind. U., 1970. V.p., mgr. Am. Fletcher, Indpls., 1970-78; fin. cons. City Securities, Indpls., 1978-79, Merrill Lynch, Ft. Wayne, Ind., 1979-89, Smith Barney Inc., Ft. Wayne, 1989—; dir. Wall St. Properties Holders, Syracuse, Ind., 1993. Home: 8116 E Quiet Harbor Dr Syracuse IN 46567-7523 Office: Smith Barney Inc 1 Summit Sq 8th Fl Fort Wayne IN 46802

BIDELMAN, WILLIAM PENDRY, astronomer, educator; b. L.A., Sept. 25, 1918; s. William Pendry and Dolores (De Remer) B.; m. Verna Pearl Shirk, June 19, 1940; children: Lana Louise Stone, Linda Elizabeth Holden, Bille Jean Little, Barbara Jo Talley. Student, U. N.D., 1936-37; SB, Harvard, 1940; PhD, U. Chgo., 1943. Physicist Aberdeen Proving Ground, Md., 1943-45; instr., then asst. prof. astronomy Yerkes Obs., U. Chgo., 1945-53; asst. astronomer, then. assoc. astronomer Lick Obs., U. Calif., 1953-62; prof. U. Mich., 1962-69, U. Tex. at Austin, 1969-70; prof. Case Western Res. U., Cleve., 1970-86, prof. emeritus, 1986—; chmn. dept., dir. Warner and Swasey Obs., 1970-75; mem. adv. panel on astronomy NSF, 1959-62; mem. NRC adv. com. on astronomy Office Naval Rsch., 1964-67. Contbr. articles to profl. jours. Mem. Am. Astron. Soc. (councilor 1959-62, participant vis. prof. program 1961-65), Astron. Soc. Pacific (editor publs. 1956-61), Internat. Astron. Union (mem. commns. 29, 45, pres. 1964-67), Phi Beta Kappa. Presbyterian. Home: 3171 Chelsea Dr Cleveland OH 44118-1256 Office: Case Western Res U Dept Astronomy 10900 Euclid Ave Cleveland OH 44106-1712

BIEBEL, CURT FRED, JR., dentist; b. St. Louis, Dec. 7, 1947; s. Curt F. and Jewell (Frank) B.; children: Betheny Doreen, Brendon Matthew. AB in Psychology, U. Mo., Columbia, 1970; DDS, U. Mo., Kansas City, 1974. Assoc. dentist Louis R. Nolan, Inc., St. Louis, 1976-79; gen. practice dentistry Chesterfield, Mo., 1979—. Capt. USAF, 1974-76. Mem. ADA, Greater St. Louis Dental Soc., Chgo. Dental Soc., Country Club of St. Albans, Forest Park Handball Assn., St. Louis Hinder Club. Office: 14378 Wood Lake Dr Chesterfield MO 63017-5714

BIEGEL, DAVID ELI, social worker, educator; b. N.Y.C., July 3, 1946; s. Jack and Estelle (Lentin) B.; B.A., CCNY, 1967; M.S.W., U. Md., 1970, Ph.D., 1982; m. Margaret S. Smoot, Jan. 31, 1976; 1 child, Geoffrey S. Field coordinator United Farm Workers, AFL-CIO, Balt., 1971; exec. dir. Junction, Inc., Westminster, Md., 1971-72; dir. office planning and program devel. Catholic Charities, Balt., 1973-76; center asso., dir. neighborhood and family services project for U. So. Calif., Washington Public Affairs Center, 1976-80; asst. prof. social work U. Pitts., 1980-85, assoc. prof., 1985-86; Henry L. Zucker Prof. social work practice, prof. sociology Mandel Sch. Applied Social Scis., Case Western Reserve Univ., 1987—, co-dir. Ctr. for Practice Innovations, 1991—; co-dir. Cuyahoga County Community Mental Health Rsch. Inst., Mandel Sch. Applied Social Sci. Case Western Reserve Univ., 1994—. cons. Vol. VISTA, Raton, N.Mex. and Balt., 1967-70; active Big Bros. Am., Balt., 1974-77. N.Y. State Incentive scholar, 1963-64; VISTA Fellows Program fellow, 1968-70. Fellow Gerontol. Soc. Am.; mem. APHA, Acad. Cert. Social Workers, Am. Orthopsychiat. Assn., Council Social Work Edn., Nat. Assn. Social Workers. Democrat. Jewish. Co-editor: Innovations in Practice and Service Delivery with Vulnerable Populations Series, Family Caregiving Applications Series; contbr. articles to profl. jours., books; co-author 10 books.

BIEHL, FRANCIS WALTER, consulting engineer; b. Menomonee, Mich., Nov. 20, 1928; s. Walter Bernard and Florence Mary (Vickman) B.; m. Clara A. Diedrich, Sept. 30, 1950; children: Thomas, Steven, Marna. BS in Mech. Engring., Marquette U., 1950; MS in Mech. Engring., Wayne University, Detroit, 1953. Registered profl. engr., Wis., Ill, structural engr., Ill., architect, Wis., sanitarian, Wis.; nat. cert. in engring.; cert. safety profl., fire and arson investigator, plumbing engr., bldg. code insp., dwelling code insp., elec. insp. Mgmt. trainee Detroit Transmission Div. GMC, 1950-51; mech. engr. Giffels & Valet Inc., Detroit, 1952-53; design engr. V.K. Boynton, Milw., 1953-60; pres. Biehl Engring., Inc., Menomonee Falls, Wis., 1960—; auto cons. Better Bus. Bur. Leader Boy Scouts Am., 1959—; mem. bldg. com. Girl Scouts U.S.A., 1977-78; instr. ARC, 1975-85; mem. Wis. Bldg. Code Adv. Com., 1980—, Wis. Amusement Adv. Com., 1978—, Internat. Exec. Svc. Corps, Guatemala, 1988, Engring. Ministries Internat., Haiti, 1990, Keyna, 1994. Mem. ASTM (slip resistance com. 1985—), Am. Soc. Plumbins Engrs., Am. Soc. Safety Engrs., Wis. Environ. Health Assn., Internat. Assn. Arson Investigators, Nat. Fire Protection Assn., Internat. Assn. Elec. Insps., Human Fractures Soc., Nat. Inst. Bldg. Sci. (consultative coun. 1992—, numerous tech. coms.). Roman Catholic. Home and Office: N66W12659 Ravine Dr Menomonee Falls WI 53051-5260

BIEK, RICHARD WILLIAM, physician; b. Chgo., Nov. 16, 1931; s. Frederick John and Irmadell Lucille (Vielehr) B.; m. Joan Elaine Siedschlag, Aug. 30, 1953 (div. 1979); children: Christi Lynn, David Andre; m. Gail Wilson Shively, Jan. 10, 1981; 1 stepchild, Heather Jeanne Shively; 1 adopted child, Bryant Telford Shively. BA, U. Dubuque, 1953; BS in medicine, U. Ill., 1955, MD, 1957; MPH, U. Minn., 1969. Missionary physician supt. United Ch. Bd. for World Ministries, Worawora, Ghana, Africa, 1958-69; area health officer, bur. dir. Staff Wis. Div. Health, Madison, 1969-77; supt., dir. City of Milw. Health Dept., 1977-85; physician, infection control State Ill. Elgin Mental Health Ctr, 1985-88; pres. Ultimate Medicine Corp., W. Allis, Wis., 1984-88; deputy commr. Chgo. Health Dept., 1988-92; med. adviser Cook County Dept. Pub. Health, 1992—; chair Immunize Wis., Madison 1977-84. Editor: Lowdown on High Blood Pressure 1984; contbr. articles to profl. jours. 1975. With Ill. Army N.G., 1988-90. Recipient Distinguished Leaders in Health Care award 1978. Fellow Am. Coll. Preventive Medicine; mem. AMA, World Med. Assn., Wis. Soc. Preventive Medicine (pres. 1979-84), Assn. Tchrs. Preventive Medicine. Office: Cook County Dept Pub Health 1010 Lake St Oak Park IL 60301-1147

BIELFELDT, DENNIS C., investment broker; b. Hammond, Ind., Apr. 7, 1946. BS in Econs., Marquette U., 1968; M of Fin., Ind. U., Gary, 1984. Tchr. St. Thomas Moore Jr. H.S., Munster, Ind., 1968-71; v.p., trust officer Mercantile Nat. Bank of Ind., Hammond, 1971-81; v.p. 1st Bank of Whiting, Whiting, Ind., 1981-87; investment broker Kemper Securities, Highland, Ind., 1987-94, Roney & Co., Munster, Ind., 1994—. Coach, mgr. Munster Little League, 1982-90, Munster Babe Ruth League, 1982-90; athletic dir. St. Thomas Moore Sch., Munster, 1987-92; mem. adv. bd. Gary Diocese, 1992—. Mem. Scherville Rotary Club (bd. dirs. 1985—). Roman Catholic. Home: 10418 Marlou Dr Munster IN 46321-4353 Office: Roney & Co 900 Ridge Rd #R Munster IN 46321-1722

BIELFELT, TERRY JAMES, manufacturing engineer; b. Boone, Iowa, June 26, 1955. B, U. Nebr., 1987. Layout engr. Union Pacific R.R., Omaha, 1978-89; project engr. Road Railer, Chicago Heights, Ill., 1989-91; chief engr. Fairmont (Minn.) Tamper, 1991—. Coach little league, baseball and basketball, Chicago Heights, 1980's. With U.S. Army, 1973-78. Mem. Nat. Truck Assn., Am. Legion, Soc. Automotive Engrs., Elks. Home: 2636 Albion Ave Fairmont MN 56031-3307 Office: Fairmont Temper 415 N Main St Fairmont MN 56031-1837

BIELKE, PATRICIA ANNE, psychologist; b. Bay Shore, N.Y., May 11, 1949; d. Lawrence Curtis and Marcella Elizabeth (Maize) Widdoes; m. Stephen Roy Bielke, July 10, 1971; children: Eric, Christine. BA, Carleton Coll., 1971; PhD, U. Minn., 1979. Lic. psychologist, Wis. Rsch. asst. Nat. Inst. Mental Health, Washington, 1972-74; sch. psychologist Roseville Pub. Schs., St. Paul, 1978-79; psychologist Southeastern Wis. Med. and Social Svcs., Milw., 1979-93; staff psychologist Elmbrook Meml. Hosp., 1986—; pvt. practice Brookfield, Wis., 1991—; Lic. psychologist, Wis.; cert. marriage & family therapist. Bd. dirs. LWV, Brookfield, 1984-88, Elmbrook Sch. Bd., 1989—. Mem. APA, Am. Assn. Marriage and Family Therapists. Home: 17455 Bedford Dr Brookfield WI 53045-1301 Office: 17000 W North Ave Brookfield WI 53005-4423

BIEMAN, LEONARD H., director vision engineering; b. Detroit, Jan. 27, 1947. BA, Wayne State U., 1970, MA, 1974, PhD, 1976. Dir. sensor ctr. Indsl. Tech. Inst., Ann Arbor, 1986-91; mgr. Air Gge, La Vonia, Mich., 1991-94; dir. vision engring. Medar, Farmington, Mich., 1994—. Inventor: patents in optical measurement. Recipient Circle of Excellence award Phontonics Mag., R&D 100 award R&D Mag. Mem. Optical Soc. Am., Automated Imaging Assn. (bd. dirs.). Office: Medar 38700 Grand River Ave Farmington MI 48335-1521

BIENEN, HENRY SAMUEL, political science educator, university executive; b. N.Y.C., May 5, 1939; s. Mitchell Richard and Pearl (Witty) B.; m. Leigh Buchanan, Apr. 28, 1961; children: Laura, Claire, Leslie. B.A. with honors, Cornell U., 1960; M.A., U. Chgo., 1962, Ph.D., 1966. Asst. prof. politics U. Chgo., 1965-66; asst. prof. politics & internat. affairs Princeton (N.J.) U., 1966-70, assoc. prof., 1970-72, prof., 1972-95, William Stewart Tod prof. politics and internat. affairs, 1981, James S. McDonnell Disting. Univ. prof., 1985, dir. Ctr. Internat. Studies, 1985-92, chair dept. politics, 1973-76, dir. African studies progrm, 1977-78, 83-84, dir. rsch. Woodrow Wilson Sch. Pub. & Internat. Affairs, 1979-82, dean; pres. Northwestern U., Evanston, Ill., 1995—; mem. exec. com. Inter-Univ. Seminar on Armed Forces and Soc., 1970; cons. U.S. State Dept., 1972—, Nat. Security Council, 1978-79, World Bank, 1981-89, CIA, 1982-89, Hambrecht & Quist Investment Co., Boeing Corp., Econ Corp., Enserch Corp., Ford Found., Rockefeller Found., John D. and Catherine T. MacArthur Found.; nat. co-dir. Movement for a New Congress, 1970-71; mem. Inst. for Advanced Study, 1982-83; vis. prof. Makerere Coll., Kampala, Uganda, 1963-65, Univ. Coll., Nairobi, Kenya, 1968-69, Univ. Ibadan, 1972-73. Editor: World Politics, 1970-74, 78—; author: Tanzania: Party Transformation and Economic Development, 1967, 70, Kenya: The Politics of Participation and Control, 1974, Violence and Social Change, 1968, Armies and Parties in Africa, 1978, Political Conflict and Economic Change in Nigeria, 1984. Grantee Rockefeller Found., 1968-69, 72-73; Nat. Def. Title IV fellow, 1960-63, Rockefeller Found. fellow, 1979; Seeger fellow, 1989. Mem. Am. Polit. Sci. Assn., Council on Fgn. Relations. Office: Northwestern U Office of Pres 633 Clark St Evanston IL 60208-1230*

BIERS, WILLIAM RICHARD, classical studies educator; b. Brussels, Oct. 29, 1938; came to the U.S., 1940; s. Howard and Constance (Herzog) B.; m. Jane Carol Chitty, Aug. 13, 1966; 1 child, Katherine Laura. BA, Brown U., 1961; PhD, U. Pa., 1968. Sec. Am. Sch. Classical Studies, Athens, 1964-68; asst. prof. U. Mo., Columbia, 1968-72, assoc. prof., 1972-81, dept. chmn.,

1973-77, 77-80, prof. classical archaeology, 1981—; exec. com. Am. Sch. Classical Studies, 1990-94, mng. com., 1972—. Author: The Archaeology of Greece, 1980, 2d edit., 1996, Art, Artefacts and Chronology in Classical Archaeology, 1992; co-author: Lost Scents: Investigations of Corinthian "Plastic" Vases by Gas Chromatography-Mass Spectrometry, 1994; editor, co-editor 3 additional books; contbr. more than 40 articles to profl. jours. Recipient sr. rsch. fellowship Fulbright Found. Portugal, 1982, Faculty Rsch. award Golden Key Honor Soc. Mo., 1987, Parker Vis. Scholar award Brown U., 1982, 96, Elizabeth Whitehead vis. professorship Am. Sch. Classical Studies, 1980-90; Noted scholar U. British Columbia, 1996. Mem. AAUP, Archaeol. Inst. Am. (various coms. 1976—, pres. local soc. 1978-80, 86-88, 90-92, governing bd. Nat. Inst. 1983-88), Midwest Art History Soc. Office: U Mo Dept Art History Archeology 109 Pickard Hall Columbia MO 65211

BIERSCHBACH, DOUG, state legislator. Rep. S.D. State Ho. Reps. Dist. 6, mem. commerce and local govt. coms. Home: RR 2 Box 21D De Smet SD 57231-9802*

BIERWIRTH, HENRY CHRISTIAN, history educator; b. Hawardin, Iowa, June 14, 1950; s. Henry Christian and Eldora Fay (Eliason) B.; m. Donna Kay Huston, Jan. 8, 1974 (div. 1984); 1 child, Martha Jada; m. Johanna Catherina Marr, Mar. 20, 1987. BA, U. Minn., 1975; MA, U. Colo., 1987; PhD, U. Wis., 1994. Graphic artist various publs., Mpls., Denver, 1977-89; instr. history Hawkeye C.C., Waterloo, Iowa, 1994—. Fulbright fellow Bd. Fgn. Scholarship, 1992. Mem. African Studies Assn. Home: 9421 Gibson Rd Hudson IA 50643 Office: Hawkeye CC PO Box 8015 Waterloo IA 50704

BIESTEK, JOHN PAUL, lawyer; b. Chgo., May 28, 1935; s. John P. and Selma (Glick) B.; m. Elizabeth Mary Frer, Dec. 31, 1956; children—Scott, Becky. B.S., Loyola U., Chgo., 1957, J.D., 1964. Bar: Ill. 1964, U.S. dist ct. (no. dist.) Ill. 1964. Sr. ptnr. Biestek & Facchini, Chgo., 1965-74; founding ptnr. John P. Biestek & Assocs., Ltd., Arlington Heights, Ill., 1974—. Atty. Wheeling Twp. Republican. Orgn., 1978, fin. chmn., 1982-84; founder, chmn. Arlington Heights Econ. Devel. Commn., 1983-84. Mem. NW Suburban Bar Assn. (pres. 1977-78), Arlington Heights C. of C. (pres. 1982-84, dir. and atty., 1972-86, 91-95, award Extraordinary Commitment and Leadership 1984), Bridgeview C. of C. (pres. 1969). Roman Catholic. Clubs: Rolling Green Country (sec. 1978-81, atty. 1980-84, 90-95). Lodge: Rotary (sec. Arlington Heights chpt. 1987—). Home: 1314 Dunheath Dr Barrington IL 60010-5245 Office: 115 N Arlington Heights Rd Arlington Heights IL 60004-6033

BIFFER, JAMES LEWIS, nuclear training manager; b. Saratoga Springs, N.Y., Mar. 27, 1950; s. George Richard and Marion Patricia (Millis) B.; m. Ava Marsha Messinger, Aug. 25, 1973; 1 child, Sabrina Dawn. BS in Nuclear Engring., Rensselaer Poly. Inst., 1972, ME of Nuclear Engring., 1976, PhD in Nuclear Sci. & Engring., 1977. Sr. engr. Combustion Engring., Inc., Windsor, Conn., 1977-81, cons. engr., 1981-84, sr. cons. engr., 1984-92; v.p. reactor engring. Tetra Engring. Group, Simsbury, Conn., 1992-94; sr. cons. engr. Consumers Power Co., Covert, Mich., 1994-95, mgr. nuclear tng., 1995—; nat. spkr. U.S. Com. on Energy Awareness, Washington, 1980—; mem. adv. bd. Nat. Energy Edn. Found., Washington, 1981—; founder, mem. Conn. Voice of Energy, Bloomfield, 1978-92. Mem., vice-chair Bloomfield Bd. Edn., 1985-93. Mem. Am. Nuclear Soc., Scientists and Engrs. for Secure Engr. Republican. Office: Palisades Nuclear Power Plt 27780 Blue Star Memorial Hy Covert MI 49043

BIGELOW, DANIEL JAMES, aerospace executive; b. Harrisville, Pa., Mar. 26, 1935; s. Raymond James and Hilda Irene (Graham) B.; m. Elizabeth Jane Allison, Sept. 10, 1955; 1 child, Allison Jane. BFA in Art Advt., Kent (Ohio) State U., 1957; MA in Edn., La. Tech. U., 1974; MS in Polit. Sci., Auburn U., 1986; MS, Air U., 1987; postgrad., Ohio State U., 1989—. Commd. 2d lt. USAF, 1957, advanced through grades to col., 1979, ret., 1987; combat pilot 167 combat missions Vietnam; air attaché to Soviet Union, 1983-85; dir. Soviet program Air War Coll. Air U., Ala., 1985-87; gen. mgr. aerospace divsn. Modern Techs. Corp., Dayton, Ohio, 1987—. Contbr. articles to profl. jours.; author, editor: Soviet Studies, 1986-88. Decorated Legion of Merit with one oak leaf cluster, DFC, 14 Air medals, Def. Superior medal. Mem. Acad. Polit. Sci., Air Rescue Assn., Air Force Assn., Am. Def. Preparedness Assn., Discussion Club Dayton, Internat. Platform Assn., F-86 Sabre Pilots' Assn., B-52 Stratofortress Assn., The Ret. Officers' Assn., Order Daedalians, Shriners. Presbyterian. Home: 2537 Indian Wells Trl Xenia OH 45385-9373

BIGGERSTAFF, RANDY LEE, medical products executive, sports medicine rehabilitation consultant; b. Buffalo, Feb. 13, 1951; s. Dever Poole and Mary Martha (Smith) B.; m. Sue Ann Knobeloch, Nov. 26, 1977; children: Nicholas Lee, Amy Elizabeth. BS, U. Mo., 1973; MS in Health Mgmt., Lindenwood Coll., 1995. Dist. athletic tng. tchr. Granite City (Ill.) Community Sch. Dist., 1973-77; athletic trainer St. Louis Hummers, Profl. Softball Team, Valley Park, Mo., 1978-79; founder-ptnr., clinic dir. St. Louis Sports Medicine Clinic, Chesterfield, Mo., 1977-82; founder, clin. dir. Iowa Orthopedic Sports Medicine Clinic, Urbandale, 1982-84; clinic dir. St. Louis Orthopedic Sports Medicine Clinic, Chesterfield, 1984-86; ptnr., v.p. St. Louis Rehab. Sports Clinic, Crystal City, Mo., 1986-88; adminstr., regional dir. St. Louis Orthopedic Sports Medicine Clinic, Chesterfield, 1989-90; coord., trainer, cons. St. Luke's Hosp., Chesterfield, 1990-92; v.p. D. P. Biggs Cons. Ltd., Inc., 1992-93; pres. Phoenix Sports Med. Systems, St. Louis, 1993—; cons. Brentwood & Creve Coeur Skating, St. Louis, 1986—, Gateway Athletics, St. Louis, 1984—; med. coord. Show-Me-Bowl, St. Louis, 1979-82, Summer Biathalon Series, Essex Junction, Vt., 1989—. Contbr. articles to profl. jours. Sec. bd. overseers Lindenwood Coll., St. Charles, Mo., 1992-93, vice chmn., 1993-95, chair, 1995—, bd. dirs., 1995—. Inducted to Mo. Sports Medicine Hall of Fame, 1995. Mem. Nat. Athletic Trainers Assn. (cert., clin. corp. com.), Mo. Athletic Trainer Assn. (registered, chair Hall of Fame com. 1991-94), Mid-Am. Athletic Trainers Assn. (treas.). Methodist. Home: 82 Shirecreek Ct Saint Charles MO 63303-5432 Office: Phoenix Sports Med Systems 13357 Olive St Rd Chesterfield MO 63017

BIGGERT, JUDITH BORG, lawyer, state representative; b. Chgo., Aug. 15, 1937; d. Alvin Andrew and Marjorie Virginia (Mailler) Borg; m. Rody Patterson Biggert, Sept. 21, 1963; children: Courtney Ray, Alison Mailler, Rody Patterson, Adrienne Taylor. B.A., Stanford U., 1959; J.D., Northwestern U., 1963. Bar: Ill. 1963, Law clk. to presiding justice U.S. Ct. Appeals (7th cir.), Chgo., 1963-64; sole practice, Hinsdale, Ill., 1964—; rep. Ill. Gen. Assembly, 1993—; minority spokesperson 81st Dist. Judiciary I Com., 1993-94. Mem. bd. editors Law Rev., Northwestern U. Sch. Law, 1961-63. Pres., bd. dirs. Hinsdale Twp. High Sch. Dist. 86 Bd. Edn., 1983-85, 78-85; pres. Jr. League Chgo., 1976-78, treas., bd. bd. mgrs., 1966—; chmn. Hinsdale Antiques Show, 1980; pres. Oak Sch. PTA, Hinsdale, 1976-78; pres.-treas. Chgo. jr. bd. Travelers Aid Soc., 1965-70; Sunday sch. tchr. Grace Episcopal Ch., Hinsdale, 1978-80, 82-85; chair, treas., 2d v.p., bd. dirs. Vis. Nurses Assn. Chgo., 1978. Recipient Servian award Jr. aux. U. Chgo. Cancer Research Found. Mem. ABA, Ill. Bar Assn., Du Page Assn. Women Lawyers, Coalition Women Legislators. Republican. Home: 6301 S Cass Ave Westmont IL 60559-3276*

BIGGINS, ROBERT A., state legislator; b. Oak Park, Ill., Oct. 20, 1946; m. Judy Biggins; children: Jennifer, Kevin. BA, Northeastern Ill. U., 1969. Assessor Addison Twp., Ill., 1973-77; Ill. state rep. Dist. 78; mem. Gen. Svcs., Consumer Protection, Fin. Insts. and Revenue Coms.; tchr. Mannheim Jr. H.S., Northlake, Ill., 1969, Daniel Webster Elem. Sch., Chgo., 1970-73; property tax cons., Chgo., 1977-81; ptnr. Property Assessment Advisors, Inc., 1981—, exec. v.p. Bd. dirs. Suburban Bank Elmhurst, 1975—, chmn., 1983-84; chmn. Bank of Bellwood, 1981-85; mem. Elmhurst Gardens Homeowners Assn. (past pres.), Edison Sch. PTA (past pres.). Recipient award Internat. Assn. Assessing Officers, 1990. Mem. DuPage County Assessors Assn. (legis. liaison 1975-76, pres. 1976), Inst. Property Taxation (cert.). Address: 2012-H Stratton Bldg Springfield IL 62706*

BIGHAM, DARREL EUGENE, history educator; b. Harrisburg, Pa., Aug. 12, 1942; s. Paul D. and Ethel B.; BA, Messiah Coll., 1964; postgrad. Harvard Div. Sch., 1964-65; PhD, U. Kans., 1970; m. Mary Elizabeth Hitchcock, Sept. 23, 1965; children: Matthew, Elizabeth. Asst. prof. history U. So. Ind., Evansville, 1970-75, assoc. prof., 1975-81, prof., 1981—. dir. Hist. So. Ind. Project, 1986—. Exec. dir. Leadership Evansville, 1976-79; chmn. Evansville Bicentennial Coun., 1974-77; bd. dirs. Evansville Mus., 1972—, sec., 1977-78, pres., 1979-81; trustee Evansville Vanderburgh County Pub. Libr., 1971-80; bd. dirs. Met. Evansville Progress Commn., 1981-85, chmn., 1983-85; bd. dirs. Evansville Arts and Edn. Coun., 1982-86, pres., 1984-85; pres. Vol. Action Ctr., 1983-85; bd. dirs. Conrad Baker Found., 1971-85, Planned Parenthood S.W. Ind., 1978-79; chmn. 175th Anniversary Com. City of Evansville, 1985-87; dir. Hist. So. Ind. Project, 1986—. Rockefeller Bros. Theol. fellow, 1964-65; NDEA fellow, 1965-68. Mem. Soc. Ind. Archivists (dir. 1972-75, pres. 1977-79), Am. Hist. Assn., Orgn. Am. Historians, Ind. Assn. Historians (chair hist. edn. com. 1994—), Ind. Hist. Soc., Vanderburgh County Hist. Soc. (pres. 1981-84, 93—). Mem. United Ch. of Christ. Author: We Ask Only a Fair Trial, 1987, An Evansville Album, 1988; contbr. articles to scholarly jours. Home: 8215 Kuebler Rd Evansville IN 47720-7427 Office: U So Ind Dept History Evansville IN 47712

BIGLEY, NANCY JANE, microbiology educator; b. Sewickley, Pa., Feb. 1, 1932; d. William Howard and Frances Jane (Engle) B. B.S., Pa. State U., 1953; M.Sc., Ohio State U., 1955, Ph.D., 1957. Research assoc. Ohio State U., 1957-65, asst. prof. immunology, 1965-68, assoc. prof., 1968-69; assoc. prof. U. Health Sci. Chgo. Med. Sch., 1969-72, prof., 1972-76; prof dept. microbiology and immunology Wright State U., Dayton, Ohio, 1976—; chmn. dept. Wright State U., 1976-86, also program dir. Author: Immunologic Fundamentals, 1975, 2d edit., 1981; mem. editorial bd.: Infection and Immunity, 1977-80. NIH grantee, 1970-76, Am. Heart Assn. grantee, 1994-97. Mem. Am. Assn. Immunologists, AAAS, Reticuloendothel Soc., Am. Soc. Microbiology, Am. Acad. Microbiology, Sigma Xi. Presbyterian. Home: 1427 Ticonderoga Ct Beavercreek OH 45434-6944 Office: Wright State U 021 M&M Bldg Colonel Glenn Hwy Dayton OH 45435

BIKE, WILLIAM STANLEY, fundraiser, writer; b. Chgo., Apr. 9, 1957; s. William F. and Jean A. (Smolen) B.; m. Anne M. Nordhaus, May 10, 1986. BA in Polit. Sci., DePaul U., Chgo., 1979. Publ. prodn. asst. Bus. Ins. Mag., Chgo., 1979-81; editor-in-chief Oak Park (Ill.) News, 1981; assoc. editor Dental Products Report, Skokie, Ill., 1982-84; dir. publs. Loyola U., Chgo., 1984-93, U. Chgo., 1993-95; assoc. dir. advancement U. Ill. at Chgo. Coll. Dentistry, 1995—; v.p. ANB Comms., Chgo., 1993—; v.p. The Near West Gazette Pub. Co., Chgo., 1983—. Chief media plan com. Dem. leadership for the 21st Century, Chgo., 1992-96; mem. Ill. Environ. Coun., Springfield, 1993—, 20/20 Vision, Washington, 1991—. Recipient DePaul Newswriting awards, 1977-79, Bronze award Internat. Mercury Competition, 1990, The Peter Lisagor award for exemplary journalism Chgo. Headline Club, 1993, 95, Conroyd Outstanding Employee award Loyola U., 1993, Nat. Apex award of excellence for feature writing, 1991. Mem. Quadrangle Club, Am. Assn. Polit. Cons. Democrat. Roman Catholic. Home: 3632 N Central Park Ave Chicago IL 60618 Office: U Ill at Chgo 801 S Paulina MC 621 Chicago IL 60612

BILANDIC, MICHAEL A., state supreme court justice, former mayor; b. Chgo., Feb. 13, 1923; s. Matthew and Domenica (Lebedina) B.; m. Heather Morgan, July 15, 1977; 1 son, Michael Morgan. JD, DePaul U., 1948. Bar: Ill. 1949. Master in chancery Cir. Ct. Cook County, Ill., 1964-67; spl. asst. to atty. gen., 1965-68; ptnr. Anixter, Bilandic & Pigott and predecessors, Chgo., 1963-77; acting mayor Chgo., 1976, mayor, 1977-79; ptnr. Bilandic, Neistein, Richman, Hauslinger and Young, Chgo., 1979-84; justice Ill. Appellate Ct., 1984-90, Ill. Supreme Ct., 1990—. Mem. Chgo. City Coun., 1969-76, chmn. com. on environ. control, 1970-74, chmn. fin. com., 1974-76. 1st lt. USMC, 1942-46. Mem. Am., Ill., Chgo. bar assns., Cath. Lawyers Guild. Democrat. Roman Catholic. Office: 160 N La Salle St 20th Flr Chicago IL 60601-3103

BILDER, JAMES GERARD, marketing manager; b. Blue Island, Ill., Sept. 21, 1958; s. Michael Charles and Mary Francis (Fairfield) B.; m. Bernadette Josephine Bauman, July 11, 1981; children: Joanne, Janet, Jacqueline, James. BA in Journalism, Lewis U., 1981; M in Indsl. Rels., Loyola U., Chgo., 1986. Dir. pub. rels. Healthstop, Lyons, Ill., 1981-82; specialty mgr. Bristol-Myers Squibb, Evansville, Ind., 1982—. Mem. Worth (Ill.) Village Bd. Trustees, 1991-93; sec. Worth Libr. Bd. Trustees, 1983-89; sec. Worth Libr. Bd. Trustees, 1983-89, pres., 1989-92; village pres. Worth, 1993—; mem. Worth Bd. Edn., 1985-91, v.p., 1989-91; sec. Worth Planning and Zoning Commn., 1983-91; bd. dirs. PACE; alt. del. Rep. Nat. Conv., Detroit, 1980. Mem. Pub. Rels. Soc. Am., KC (4th degree). Republican. Roman Catholic. Home: 10701 S Nashville Ave Worth IL 60482-1616

BILDERBACK, GEORGE GARRISON, III, human services manager; b. Portsmouth, Ohio, Jan. 11, 1964; s. George Garrison Jr. and Jane (Rhodes) B. BSBA in Mgmt. and Fin., Ohio No. U., 1986; student, Franklin U., 1995—. Gen. mgr. Ohio No. U. (WONU Radio), Ada, 1985; customer svc. specialist Nationwide Life Ins. Co., Columbus, Ohio, 1986-87, licensing and commn. specialist, 1987-88; rsch. analyst Wausau Ins. Co., Columbus, 1988-89; sr. mktg. specialist Nationwide Life Ins. Co., Columbus, Ohio, 1989-92; regional mktg. dir. Nationwide Life Ins. Co., Portsmouth, N.H., 1992; registered rep. MML Investors Svcs., Inc., West Worthington, Ohio, 1993-94; jr. ptnr. Moyer Fin. Group, West Worthington, 1993-94; investment exec. Hamilton Investments Inc., Columbus, 1994-95; co-case mgr. Recovery Assistance, Inc., Westerville, Ohio, 1995-96; counselor Harding Hosp., Worthington, Ohio, 1996—. Dir. local club Civitan Internat., Columbus, 1989-91, 1st v.p. programs, 1991-92, pres., 1994-95, immediate past pres., 1995—. Mem. Employee Assistance Student Assn., Employee Assistance Profl. Assn. (pres. 1996—, newsletter editor So. Ohio chpt. 1996—). Republican. Episcopalian. Home: PO Box 340112 Columbus OH 43234-0112 Office: Harding Hosp 445 E Dublin Granville Rd Worthington OH 43085

BILES, JANICE MARIE, journalist; b. Ft. Scott, Kans., Aug. 21, 1952; d. Lloyd Martin Jr. and Bertha Florence (Koch) B. BA in Edn., Pitts. State U., 1974, M in Counselor Edn., 1977. English/journalism tchr. Jayhawk-Linn H.S., Mound City, Kans., 1974-76; ednl. cons. Joplin (Mo.) Regional Ctr. for Devel. Disabilities, 1977-80; learning disabilities tchr. Louisburg (Kans.) Mid. and H.S., 1980-84; news editor, reporter Louisburg Herald, 1983-84; features editor, reporter Pittsburg (Kans.) Morning Sun, 1984-88; assoc. editor, reporter Hutchinson (Kans.) News, 1988-95; arts editor Lawrence (Kans.) Jour.-World, 1995—; Coord. Kans. Press Women/Kans. Scholastic Pres Assn. H.S. Journalism Contest, 1994—;. Co-chmn., advisory bd. New Beginnings Homeless Shelter, Hutchinson, 1991-94; vol. Dillon Nature Ctr., Hutchinson, 1993-94. Named Outstanding Alumna Ft. Scott C. C., 1995; recipient Community Svc. award Kans. Assoc. Press Mng. Editors, 1988, Media award Kans. Nurses Assn., Assn. Retarded Citizens, Pittsburg, 1990; named hon. resident, Elm Acres Youth Homes, Pittsburg, 1989, others. Mem. Soc. Newspaper Design, Soc. Profl. Journalists, Nat. Fedn. Press Women (recipient numerous awards for reporting and editing 1988-96), Kans. Press Women (bd. dirs. 1994-95, Sweepstakes award 1988, 89, 93, 96, first runner-up 1991, 95, 2nd runner-up 1987, 90, numerous other awards). Democrat.

BILHEIMER, ROBERT WILLIAM, metal processing company executive; b. Bethlehem, Pa., Sept. 7, 1956; s. Willard Henry and Jeanne Lois (Herman) B.; m. Mary Ann Ardoline, May 29, 1982 (div. 1985); m. Laurie Jeanne Moore; children: Andrew Robert, Stephen John, Sarah Elizabeth. BSBA magna cum laude, Gettysburg Coll., 1978; MBA, Lehigh U., 1982. Claims rep. Aetna Life and Casualty Co., Allentown, Pa., 1978-80; state govt. affairs asst. Bethlehem (Pa.) Steel Corp., 1981-85, state govt. affairs rep., 1985-90; sr. pub. affairs rep. Bethelehem (Pa.) Steel Corp., 1990-92; dir. pub. affairs Burns Harbor Divsn., Chesterton, Ind., 1992—. Bd. dirs. Duneland C. of C., 1992, Leadership N.W. Ind., 1994, Ind. Mfrs. Assn. Polit. Action Com., 1994; mem. N.W. Ind. Regional Planning Commn. Air Quality Adv. Commn., 1992, Porter County Solid Waste Mgmt. Dist. adv. com., 1993; chmn. Ind. Mfrs. Assn. Pub. Affairs Com. Mem. Phi Beta Kappa, Phi Alpha Theta, Pi Lambda Sigma. Republican. Methodist. Home: 1106 Burlington Beach Rd Valparaiso IN 46383-2079 Office: Burns Harbor Divsn PO Box 248 Chesterton IN 46304-0248

BILLARD, WILLIAM THOMAS, insurance company executive; b. Peru, Ill., May 14, 1946; s. George Max and Mildred Jean (Kincheski) B.; m. Janice Kay Metcalfe, Aug. 29, 1970; children: Rachelle Lynn, Kimberly Dawn, Bethany Kaye. AA, Ill. Valley Community Coll., 1966; BS in Actuarial Sci., U. Ill., 1969. Asst. mgr. group actuarial CNA Ins. Co., Chgo., 1969-75; dir. actuarial svcs. Delta Dental Plan of Mich., Lansing, 1975-79, v.p., actuary, 1979—; chmn. actuarial com. Delta Dental Plans Assn., Chgo., 1976-80, 84-89; cons. Delta Dental Plans in Ark., Ind., Kans., Mass., Ohio, Okla., Tenn., Va., Wis., 1986—. Contbr. articles to profl. publs. Pres. Great Lakes Gymnastics Booster Club, Lansing, 1981-82; coach Okemos (Mich.) Athletic Klub, 1982-89; worker Habitat for Humanity, Lansing-Kalamazoo, 1986—; elder Presbyn. Ch., Okemos, 1987-90; trustee, mem. sch. bd. Lansing Christian Schs., 1992-95, pres., 1994-95. Mem. Am. Acad. Actuaries, Mich. Actuarial Soc., West Mich. Actuarial Club (pres. 1988—), Walnut Hills Country Club. Home: 3901 Highwood Pl Okemos MI 48864-3790 Office: Delta Dental Plan of Mich PO Box 30416 Lansing MI 48909-7916

BILLER, GERALDINE POLLACK, curator; b. Milw., Apr. 4, 1933; d. Sidney Samuel and Frieda (Eisenberg) Pollack; m. Joel Wilson Biller, May 1, 1955; children: Sydney Ellen, Andrew John, Charles Benjamin. BS, Northwestern U., 1955; MA, U. Wis., 1991. Tchr. art Va. Sch. System, 1955-56, Internat. Sch., The Hague, The Netherlands, 1959-62; adminstr. internat. rels. program Georgetown U., Washington, 1973-75; freelance graphic designer Washington, Milw., 1978-86; art historian, curator Milw. Art Mus., 1988—. Mem. Wis. State Dem. Adminstrv. Com., 1992-93; v.p. women's divsn. cmty. planning com. Milw. Jewish Fedn., 1986-90; pres. bd. dirs. Jewish Family Svcs., Milw., 1991-94. Home: 4716 N Wilshire Rd Milwaukee WI 53211-1262

BILLIG, ETEL JEWEL, theater director, actress; b. N.Y.C., Dec. 16, 1932; d. Anthony and Martha Rebecca (Klebansky) Papa; m. Steven S. Billig, Dec. 23, 1956; children: Curt Adam, Jonathan Roark. BS, NYU, 1953, MA, 1955; student, Herbert Berghof Studio, N.Y.C., 1955-56. Cert. elem. and high sch. tchr. Actress Washington Square Players, N.Y.C., 1950-55, Dukes Oak Theatre, Cooperstown, N.Y., 1955, Triple Cities Playhouse, Binghampton, N.Y., 1956, Candlelight Dinner Playhouse, Summit, Ill., 1970, 73, 77, 79, 90; mng. dir. Theatre 31, Park Forest, Ill., 1971-73; asst. mgr. Westroads Dinner Theatre, Omaha, 1973-76; mng. dir., actress Forum Theatre, 1973, 94, Ill. Theatre Ctr., Park Forest, 1976—, Goodman Theatre, Chgo., 1967, 95, Ct. Theatre, 1990, Wisdom Bridge Theatre, 1991; dir. drama Rich Cen. High Sch., Olympia Fields, Ill., 1978-86; mng. dir., actress Forum Theatre, 1994; del. League of Chgo. Theatres Russian Exchange to Soviet Union, 1989; actress Drury Lane, Oak Brook, Ill.; cons. and lectr. in field. Appeared in films including the Dollmaker, Running Scared, Straight Talk, (TV series) Hawaiian Heat, Missing Persons, Untouchables. V.p. Nat. Coun. Jewish Women, Park Forest, 1968-70; sec. Community Arts Coun., Park Forest, 1984-86; pres. Southland Regional Arts Coun., 1986-92. Recipient Risk Taking award NOW, 1982; grantee Nebr. Arts Coun., 1975, Ill. Arts Coun., 1995, 96. Mem. Am. Fedn. TV and Radio Artists, Actors' Equity Assn., Screen Actors Guild, League Chgo. Theatres, Ill. Arts Coun. Theatre Panel, Producers Assn. Chgo. Area Theatre (sec. 1988-89), Park Forest Rotary (bd. dirs. 1988—). Office: Ill Theatre Ctr 400A Lakewood Blvd Park Forest IL 60466-1641

BILLINGS, STEVEN ALLEN, municipal official; b. Fort Belvoir, VA, Feb. 16, 1953; s. Charles Harvey and Zita Marie (Olinger) B.; m. Charlene Elizabeth Farmer, Oct. 4, 1986; 1 child, Rebecca Elizabeth. AA, Maple Woods C.C., Kansas City, Mo., 1972; BS, Ctrl. Mo. State, 1974; MS, Wichita State U., 1982. Comm. officer Riverside Police Dept., Mo., 1970,73; police dispatcher Ctrl. Mo. State U., 1974-75; various positions Kansas City (Mo.) Mcpl. Govt., 1975-80; safety and investigative officer Kansas City Area, 1980-84; from mgr. safety and instrn. dept. to supt. Kansas City (Mo.) Transp. Authority, 1984-92; dir. Parking and Transit Utility, Sheboygan, Wis., 1992—; bd. dirs. Transit Mut. Ins. Corp., Appleton, Wis.; commr. Wis. Ins. Mut. TransitCommn., 1992—. Active transp. tech. comm., Sheboygan Metro planning orgn., 1992—. Mem. Am. Soc. Indsl. Security, Wis. Urban Transit Assn. (chmn. joint efforts), Sheboygan C. of C. (transp. com.). Methodist. Office: Parking and Transit Utility 608 S Commerce St Sheboygan WI 53081

BILLINGSLY, Z. DWIGHT, investment consultant, city assessor aide, financial analyst; b. St. Louis, Sept. 25, 1954; m. Marilyn Maxwell. BA, Yale U., 1976; MBA, Harvard U., 1978. Dep. comptroller City of St. Louis, 1988-93. Dem. candidate 1st dist. Mo. U.S. House Reps., 1990; sought Dem. nom. U.S. House of Reps., 1994. Mem. African Methodist Episcopal Ch. Office: Billingsly For Congress PO Box 1679 Saint Louis MO 63188*

BILLION, JOHN JOSEPH, orthopedic surgeon, state representative; b. Sioux Falls, S.D., Mar. 4, 1939; s. Henry Alphonse and Evelyn Margaret (Heinz) B.; div.; children: Matthew, Suzanne, John, James, Jane; m. Deborah Wagner, Mar. 22, 1980; children: Timothy, Allyson. BA, Loras Coll., 1960; MD, Stritch-Loyola U., 1964. Diplomate Am. Bd. Orthopedic Surgery. Resident orthopedics St. Francis Hosp., Peoria, Ill., 1964-69; orthopedic surgeon Sioux Falls, 1971-96; state rep. State of S.D., 1992—. Elected to S.D. Ho. Reps., 1992, re-elect. 1994. Maj. USAF, 1969-71. Fellow Am. Acad. Orthopedic Surgeons. Democrat.

BINDER, MADELINE DOTTI, counselor; b. Chgo., Oct. 7, 1942; d. Martin and Anne (Sweet) Binder; children: Mark Nathan, Marla Susan. BEd, Nat. Coll. Edn., 1964, MS, 1972, MS in Human Svcs.-Counseling, 1993. Tchr., Rochester Schs. (Minn.), 1963-64, Orange County Schs., Orlando, Fla., 1967-68; reading cons. Palatine Schs. (Ill.), 1972-73; instr. Parent Effective Tng., Wilmette, Ill., 1974-76, tchr. Effectiveness Tng., 1974-76; pres. Profls. Diversified, Wilmette, Ill., 1976-89; remedial and enrichment reading tchr. Waukegan (Ill.) Pub. Schs., 1986; pres. Lifeline, 1989-90; mgmt. cons. World Wide Diamonds Assn., Schaumburg, Ill., 1979-89, Artistic Color, Dallas, 1983-87; Pearl direct distbr. Amway Corp., Ada, Mich., 1976-94; exec. distbr. NU Skin, 1992; distbr. Emerald-Starlight Internat., 1994—; psychotherapist, 1993—. Author: Organic Gardening, 1975, The Go-Getters Planner, 1986, Singles Guide to Chicagoland, 1995. Leader, Camp Fire Girls, Evanston, Ill., 1963, 75. Recipient Ednl. Scholarship, Nat. Coll. Edn., 1971. Mem. Phi Delta Kappa, Alpha Delta Omega. Jewish.

BINDERNAGEL, JACKIE MARIE, finance executive; b. Cleve., June 19, 1955. Student, Cuyahoga C.C. Office mgr. Adams Automatic, Cleve., 1980-83; v.p. finance Edward J. Keating Mgmt. Agy., Cleve., 1983—. Active Human Rights Campaign Fund, Washington, 1994—. Democrat. Mem. United Ch. Christ. Office: Edward J Keating Mgmt Agy 812 Huron Rd Cleveland OH 44115

BINDLEY, ALBIN, IV, financial consultant; b. Niagara Falls, N.Y., June 2, 1939; s. Albin III and Rosaley (Harshbarger) B.; m. Ursala Debska, June 6, 1990; children: Albin V, Jennifer, Melanie, Celeste. BS, Pa. State U., 1966. Dist. salesman Std. Oil Ohio, Cleve., 1967-76; dir. market planning Am. Motors, South Bend, Ind., 1976-83; fin. cons. Smith Barney, South Bend, 1983—; bd. mem. Rochester Funds, N.Y.C., 1993—. With USN, 1960-64. Recipient Pres. Freedom award, Washington, 1956. Republican. Episcopalian. Home: 2005 Poppy Ct Mishawaka IN 46544-6758 Office: Smith Barney Inc 211 W Washington St Ste 2300 South Bend IN 46601-1708

BINDLEY, WILLIAM EDWARD, pharmaceutical executive; b. Terre Haute, Ind., Oct. 6, 1940; s. William F. and Gertrude (Lynch) B.; children: William Franklin, Blair Scott, Sally Ann. BS, Purdue U., 1961; grad. wholesale mgmt. program, Stanford U., 1966. Asst. treas. Controls Co. Am., Melrose Park, Ill., 1962-65; vice-chmn. E.H. Bindley & Co., Terre Haute, 1965-68; pres., chmn. bd., CEO Bindley Western Industries, Inc., Indpls., 1968—; Scholl scholarship guest lectr. Loyola U., Chgo., 1982; guest lectr. Young Pres. Orgn., Palm Springs, Calif. and Dallas, 1981, 82, 84, Ctr. for Entrepreneurs, Indpls., 1983, Purdue U., West Lafayette, Ind., De Pauw U., Greencastle, Ind., disting. lectr. Georgetown U., Washington, 1989—, mem. adv. bd.; bd. dirs. Key Bank NA, Cleve., Shoe Carnival, Inc.; former owner basketball team Ind. Pacers. State dir. Bus. for Reagan-Bush, Washington and Indpls., 1980; trustee Marian Coll., Indpls., Indpls. United Way, St. Vincent Hosp., Indpls.; bd. dirs. Indpls. Entrepreneurship Acad., Nat. Entrepreneurship Found., U.S. Ski Team, chmn. fin., exec. com. mem.; mem. adv. bd. Rose Hulman Inst. Tech.; mem. pres.'s coun. Purdue U., dean's adv. bd. Named Hon. Ky. Col., 1980, Sagamore of the Wabash, Gov. Orr, State of Ind., 1989, Entrepreneur of Yr., State of Ind., 1992. Mem. Young Pres.

Orgn. (area dir., chmn. 1982, award 1983), Nat. Wholesale Druggists Assn. (dir. 1981-84, Svc. award 1984), Purdue U. Alumni Assn. (life), Woodstock Club, Meridian Hills Countryn Club. Republican. Roman Catholic. Office: Bindley Western Industries Inc 10333 N Meridian St Indianapolis IN 46290-9999

BINGHAM, RICHARD DONNELLY, journal editor, director, educator; b. Orange, N.J., Oct. 27, 1937; s. Seymour Potter and Helen Barbara (Donnelly) B.; children from previous marriage: Connie Elizabeth, Paul Douglas; m. Claire L. Felbinger. BBA, Boston U., 1959; MAPA, U. Okla., 1971, PhD, 1973. Asst. prof. Marquette U., Milw., 1973-76; asst. prof. U. Wis., Milw., 1975-77, assoc. prof., 1977-84, dir. Urban Rsch. Ctr., 1982-86, prof., 1984-88; editor Econ. Devel. Quar., Cleve., 1985-94, founding editor, 1994—; dir. MS and PhD programs Cleve. State U., 1993—; mem. editl. bd. Urban Affairs Quar., 1978-80, 89-92, The Urban Interest, 1979-82, Rsch. in Urban Policy, 1982—, State and Local Govt. Rev., 1984-87; program analyst HUD, Washington. Author: State and Local Government in an Urban Society, 1986, Evaluation in Practice, 1989, State and Local Government in a Changing Society, 1991, Managing Local Government, 1991; editor: Urban Economic Development, 1984, The Homeless Contemporary Society, 1987, Economic Restructuring of the American Midwest, 1990, Financing Economic Development, 1990, Theories of Local Economic Development, 1993; contbr. articles to profl. jours. With USAF, 1959-70. Recipient numerous grants from govt. orgns. and agencies. Mem. Am. Econ. Assn., Am. Pol. Sci. Assn., Southwestern Social Sci. Assn., Am. Soc. Pub. Adminstrn., Policy Studies Assn. Office: Cleve State U Coll Urban Affairs Cleveland OH 44115

BINKLEY, JONATHAN ANDREW, secondary education educator, government educator; b. Princeton, Ill., Dec. 18, 1940; s. Carl Victor and Catherine Madie (Willson) B.; m. Barbara Ann Meyers, June 6, 1964; children: Tregg Jonathan, Trent Stephen. AB, U. Findlay, Ohio, 1963; MA, U. Toledo, 1966; EdS, Eastern Mich. U., 1970. Film mounter Eastman Kodak Co., Findlay, 1960-61; stock processor Kroger's, Scheck's and Joseph's Super Markets, Findlay, Toledo, 1961-65; tchr. Donnell Jr. High Findlay Pub. Schs., 1963-64, Romulus (Mich.) Jr. High Sch., 1965-66, Romulus High Sch., 1966-67; instr. in govt. Whitmer High Sch., Washington Local Schs., Toledo, 1967—; sales assoc. Apple Creek Realty, Toledo, 1979-84, Dew Realty Co., 1987-89; instr. in polit. processes Cmty. and Tech. Coll., U. Toledo, 1983, 93-94; faculty advisor Whitmer High Sch. Pub. Forum Club, 1981—; bd. dirs. NWOEA (Northwest Ohio Education Association), 1977-82, 93-96. Author: (with others) A History of the Ohio Conference, 1986; contbr. articles to profl. jours.; patentee lawn furniture weights. patentee lawn furniture weights. Pres. State of Ohio Conf. Chs. of God, Findlay, 1984-86, 90-91, v.p., 1982-84, 91-92; chmn. bd. dirs. Home Acres Cmty. Ch., 1982-85, 94-97. Mem. NEA (del. to nat. convs. 1979-80, 83-84, 88-96, nat. chair NEA Rep. Educators' Caucus 1995-97, nat. treas. 1993-95). Republican. Home: 1786 Bucklew Dr Toledo OH 43613-2310 Office: Whitmer H S 5601 Clegg Dr Toledo OH 43613-2022

BINNING, WILLIAM CHARLES, political scientist, educator; b. Boston, Mar. 8, 1944; s. Kenneth William and Josephine Agnes (Crotty) B.; BA in Politics, St. Anselm's Coll., 1966; PhD in Govt. and Internat. Relations (NDEA fellow), U. Notre Dame, 1970; m. Maureen G. Fannon, Nov. 26, 1966; children: Patrick, Catherine. Asst. prof. polit. sci. Youngstown (Ohio) State U., 1970-77, asso. prof., chmn. polit. sci., 1977-84, prof., 1984—; project dir. NSF, 1978-79, grant evaluator, 1979; part-time staff Office of Gov. G. Voinovich, Ohio, 1991—. Trustee Internat. Inst., Youngstown, 1972-80, Children and Family Services Bd., Mahoning County, 1977-81; vice chmn. Mahoning County Republican Central Com., 1973-74, chmn., 1980-88; del. Rep. Nat. Com., 1984, 88, 96; chmn. Mahoning County Rep. Exec. Com., 1980-88; mem. Mahoning County Bd. Elections, 1980-90; bd. dirs. Youngstown Area Urban League, 1993—. Mem. Am. Polit. Sci. Assn., Am. Soc. Pub. Adminstrn., Midwest Polit. Sci. Assn., AAU. Office: Dept Polit Sci Youngstown State U 410 Wick Ave Youngstown OH 44555-0001

BINSFELD, CONNIE BERUBE, lieutenant governor; b. Munising, Mich., Apr. 18, 1924; d. Omer J. and Elsie (Constance) Berube; B.S., Siena Heights Coll., 1945, D.H.L. (hon.), 1977; postgrad. Wayne State U., 1966-67; m. John E. Binsfeld, July 19, 1947; children—John T., Gregory, Susan, Paul, Michael. County commr., Leelanau County, Mich., 1970-74; mem. Mich. Ho. of Reps., 1974-82, asst. rep. leader, 1979-81; del. Nat. Conv., 1980, 88, 92; mem. Mich. Senate, 1982-90, asst. rep. leader, 1979, 81; lt. gov. State of Mich., 1990—. Mem. adv. bd. Nat. Park System. Named Mich. Mother of Year, Mich. Mothers Com., 1977; Northwestern Mich. Coll. fellow. Mem. Nat. Council State Legislators, LWV, Siena Heights Coll. Alumnae Assn. Republican. Roman Catholic. Home: RR 2 Maple City MI 49664-9802 Office: Office of Lt Gov State Capitol Bldg PO Box 30026 Lansing MI 48909*

BIOK, ASPI K., mechanical engineer; b. Bombay, India, Nov. 3, 1956. MSME, Wichita (Kans.) State U., 1986. Sr. engr. Greenway Electric, Wichita, 1986—. Office: Greenway Electric 1424 N Mosley St Wichita KS 67214-1340

BIONDI, LAWRENCE, university administrator, priest; b. Chgo., Dec. 15, 1938; s. Hugo and Albertina (Marchetti) B. B.A., Loyola U., Chgo., 1962, Ph.L., 1964, M.Div., 1971, S.T.L., 1971; M.S., Georgetown U., 1966, Ph.D. in Socioloinguistics, 1975. Ordained priest Roman Cath. Ch., 1970. Joined Soc. Jesus; asst. prof. sociolinguistics Loyola U., Chgo., 1974-79, assoc. prof., 1979-81, prof., 1982-87, dean Coll. Arts and Scis., 1980-87; pres. St. Louis U., 1987—. Author: The Italian-American Child: His Sociolinguistic Acculturation, 1975, Poland's Solidarity Movement, 1984; editor: Poland's Church-State Relations in the 1980s, 1980, Spain's Church-State Relations, 1982. Trustee Xavier U., 1981-87, Loyola Coll., Balt., 1988-94, Santa Clara U., 1988—, Kenrick-Glennon Sem., 1988-94, St. Louis U., 1982—, Loyola U., Chgo., 1988—; bd. dirs. Epilepsy Found. Am., 1985-95, Civic Progress, St. Louis, 1987—, Regional Commerce and Growth Assn., 1987—, Mo. Bot. Gardens, 1987—, St. Louis Zoo, 1994, St. Louis Symphony, 1994, Harry S. Truman Inst. for Nat. and Internat. Affairs, 1987—. Mellon grantee, 1974, 75, 76, 82. Mem. Linguistic Soc. Am., MLA, Am. Anthrop. Assn. Office: St Louis U 221 N Grand Blvd Saint Louis MO 63103-2006

BIPPUS, DAVID PAUL, manufacturing company executive; b. Evansville, Ind., Nov. 29, 1949; s. James Paul and Mary Louise (Elder) B.; m. Kohnne Susann Heikens, Aug. 28, 1971; 1 child, Laura. BS, Iowa State U., 1971; MBA with honors, Boston U., 1975. Cert. CPCU. Tech. mgr. Ill. Dept. Transp., Springfield, 1976; asst. dir. planning Horace Mann Ins. Co., Springfield, 1976-79; mgr. fin. planning Hydro-Transmission div. Sundstrand Corp., Ames, Iowa, 1979-82; controller Hydraulics div. Sundstrand Corp., Rockford, Ill., 1982-84; v.p. fin., sec., treas. Suntec Industries, Inc., Rockford, 1984-89, v.p. ops., sec., treas., 1989-94; corp. controller Reliant Industries, Inc., Rock Falls, Ill., 1994, CFO, 1995—; instr. Lincoln Land Community Coll., Springfield, 1976-78. Bd. dirs. New Am. Theater, Rockford, 1991—, pres., 1993-95; bd. dirs. Parents for Gifted Edn., Rockford, 1989-91; bd. dirs. Rockford Civic New Comers, 1982-85; mem. Story County Planning and Zoning Commn. 1st lt. U.S. Army, 1972-76. Mem. Fin. Exec. Inst. (bd. dirs. local chpt. 1989—, pres. 1993-94), Soc. of CPCU's, Nat. Assn. Accts., Am. Legion. Republican. Home: 9640 N Blaine Dr Byron IL 61010-9101 Office: Reliant Industries Inc 201 E 2nd St Rock Falls IL 61071-1362

BIR, MICHELLE MARIE, sales executive; b. Canandaigua, N.Y., June 29, 1965; d. Thomas A. and Carol A. (Genecco) B. BS in Econs., Wells Coll., 1987. Merchandiser Bratt-Foster, Syracuse, N.Y., 1988-89; sales exec. 110 Winner Eastman-Kodak Co., Cape Girardeau, Mo., 1989-95; retail rep. Hallmark Cards, Inc., St. Louis, 1995—. Mem., starter Make-A-Wish Found., Cape Girardeau, 1989. Mem. Am. Women's Econ. Devel. Assn., Cape Girardeau Jaycees. Democrat. Roman Catholic. Home: 518 N Sprigg St Cape Girardeau MO 63701 Office: Eastman Kodak Co 5609 K Hunters Valley Ct Saint Louis MO 63129

BIRCH, JOHN EDWARD, JR., publisher, retired military officer; b. Hinsdale, Ill., Sept. 12, 1953; s. John Edward Birch and Terrie Roberta (Hollowed) Munder; m. Jennifer Young Jang, April 25, 1980; 1 child, Teri Lea. BA in psychology, DePaul U., Chicago, 1975. Maj. U.S. Army, 1975-95; pres. Selective Publishing, Inc., Oakbrook, Ill., 1995—; bd. dirs. Hammacher-Schlemmer Inst., Chgo. Author: M.S. Anthology, 1993, M.S. Anthology II, 1995; editor-in-chief M.S. Magazine, 1993—. Vol. Stu Wesbury for U.S. Congress, Westmont, Ill., 1992. Mem. Am. Legion, Masons, Elks, VFW. Libertarian. Office: Selective Publishing Inc 209 W Lake 4th Fl Chicago IL 60661

BIRCHBAUER, MICHAEL A., business executive; b. Milw., Dec. 9, 1955. BS in Computer Sci., LaCrasse U., 1979. V.p. Smith, Birchbauer & Assocs., New Berlin, Wis., 1989—. Office: 3033 S 128th St New Berlin WI 53151-4071

BIRD, HARRIE WALDO, JR., psychiatrist, educator; b. Detroit, Sept. 21, 1917; s. Harrie Waldo and Ann Josephine (Tossy) B.; m. Della Mae Clemmer, Jan. 4, 1943; children: Harrie Waldo, Kathleen Bird Steinhour, Deborah Bird Hall, Mark Henry, Matthew Alexius, Liza George-Aidan Browning. AB, Yale U., 1939; postgrad., U. Mich. Med. Sch., 1939-41; MD, Harvard U., 1943. Intern Phila. Gen. Hosp., 1943-44; resident Menninger Sch. Psychiatry, Topeka, 1946-48; chief infirmary sect. Winter VA Hosp., Topeka, 1946; psychiatrist Adult Psychiat. Clinic, Detroit, 1949, acting dir., 1950; psychiat. cons. Mich. Epilepsy Center, Detroit, 1950-55; clin. instr. psychiatry Wayne State U., Detroit, 1952-55; assoc. prof. psychiatry U. Chgo., 1955-56; asso. prof. psychiatry U. Mich., Ann Arbor, 1956-63; asst. dean Med Sch., 1959-61; prof. psychiatry, assoc. dean St. Louis U.-Sch. Medicine, 1965-68, clin. prof., 1970-95, clin. prof. emeritus, 1995, dir. The Family Psychiat. Ctr., 1972-93; ret., 1993, prof. emeritus, 1995—; lectr., cons. in field. Bd. dirs. Mich. Epilepsy Ctr., 1956-63, Wayne County Mental Health Soc., 1956-63, Mich. Epilepsy Assn., 1956-63, El Paso Mental Health Assn., 1969-70, Cranbrook Sch., 1961-63. With M.C., AUS, 1944-46. Recipient Mental Health Inst. award St. John's U., 1966. Fellow Am. Psychiat. Assn. (life); mem. AMA, Am. Family Therapy Assn. (charter), Group for Advancement of Psychiatry, Mo. Med. Soc. (hon.), St. Louis Met. Med. Soc. (life), Ea. Mo. Psychiat. Soc., Phi Beta Kappa.

BIRD, MATTHEW ALEXIUS, horticulturist, consultant; b. Ann Arbor, Mich., May 5, 1957; s. H. Waldo and Della Mae (Clemmer) B.; m. Suzann Miller, Apr. 16, 1988; 1 child, Hillary Clemmer. AAS in Horticulture, St. Louis Community Coll., 1979. Interior horticulturist Exotica Plants, St. Louis, 1976-81; v.p. Townscape Maintenance, Inc., St. Louis, 1982-88; owner, pres. Diversifolia, Inc., St. Louis, 1988—, Down Under Aquatics, St. Louis, 1992—. Sponsor to foliage Clean Air Coun. Recipient Best Project award Interiorscape mag., 1987-96, Grand Winner award, 1990. Mem. Am. Landscape Contractors Am. (cert.). Home: 116 Slocum Ave Saint Louis MO 63119-2254 Office: Diversifolia Inc 1227-29 Hanley Indsl Ct Saint Louis MO 63144-1911 also: Down Under Aquatics 1227-29 Hanley Indsl Ct Saint Louis MO 63144-1911

BIRD, PHILLIP CRAIG, mortgage company executive; b. Harlan, Iowa, Feb. 22, 1947; s. Victor T. and Dorothy Ann (Book) B.; m. Jane Ann Wilwerding, Aug. 1, 1970; children: Andrea, Sheri, Kelley. Student, U. Nebr., Omaha, 1969-72, Ottawa U., Kansas City, Mo., 1981-82. Lic. real estate broker, Mo. Asst. sec. Iowa Securities, Omaha, 1971-72; asst. v.p. Banco Mortgage Co., Omaha, 1974-75; v.p., br. mgr. Banco Mortgage Co., Denver, 1975-76; v.p. Banco Mortgage Co., Overland Park, Kans., 1976-79; v.p., br. mgr. Norwest Mortgage, Overland Park, 1979-84; pres. Newport Fin., Kansas City and Overland Park, 1984-87; v.p. 1st Interstate Mortgage, Kansas City, 1987-91; asset mktg. specialist RTC, 1991-94; dir. comml. lending Regional Investment, 1994—. Served with U.S. Army, 1966-68. Mem. Nat. Assn. of Indsl. and Office Parks (v.p., sec. 1982-83, bd. dirs. 1984-85, newsletter editor 1982), Comml. Investment div. Johnson County Bd. Realtors (bd. dirs. 1985-87). Republican. Roman Catholic. Club: Milburn Golf & Country Club.

BIRD, ROBERT BYRON, chemical engineering educator, author; b. Bryan, Tex., Feb. 5, 1924; s. Byron and Ethel (Antrim) B. Student, U. Md., 1941-43; B.S. in Chem. Engring., U. Ill., 1947; Ph.D. in Chemistry, U. Wis., 1950; postdoctoral fellow, U. Amsterdam, 1950-51; DEng (hon.), Lehigh U., 1972, Washington U., 1973, Tech. U. Delft, Holland, 1977, Colo. Sch. Mines, 1986, Kyoto U., 1996; Sc.D. (hon.), Clarkson U., 1980; ScD (hon.), The Technion U., Israel, 1993; D in engring. sci. (hon.), Eidgenössische Tech. Hochschule, Zürich, Switzerland, 1994; DrEngring (hon.), Kyoto (Japan) U., 1996. Asst. prof. chemistry Cornell U., 1952-53, Debye lectr., 1973, Julian C. Smith lectr., 1988; research chemist DuPont Exptl. Sta., summer 1953; mem. faculty U. Wis., 1951-52, 53-57, prof. chem. engring., 1957-92, C.F. Burgess distinguished prof. chem. engring., 1968-72, John D. MacArthur prof., 1982-92, Vilas research prof., 1972-92, chmn. dept., 1964-68; emeritus prof., 1992—; Burgers prof. Technische Univ. Delft, The Netherlands, 1994; vis. prof. U. Calif., Berkeley, 1977, Univ. Catholique de Louvain, Belgium, 1994; D. L. Katz lectr. U. Mich., 1971; W. N. Lacey lectr. Calif. Inst. Tech., 1974; K. Wohl Meml. lectr. U. Del., 1977; W. K. Lewis lectr. MIT, 1982; R. H. Wilhelm lectr., Princeton U., 1991, G. N. Lewis lectr. U. Calif., Berkeley, 1993; lectr. Lectures in Sci. Humble Oil Co., 1959, 61, 64, 66; lecture tour Am. Chem. Soc., 1958, 75, Canadian Inst. Chemistry, 1961, 65; cons. to industry, 1965-90; mem. adv. panel engring. sci. divsn. NSF, 1961-64. Author: (with others) Molecular Theory of Gases and Liquids, 2d printing, 1964, Transport Phenomena, 53 printing, 1996, Spanish edit., 1965, Czech edit., 1966, Italian edit., 1970, Russian edit., 1974, Chinese edit., 1990, Een Goed Begin: A Contemporary Dutch Reader, 1963, 2d edit., 1971, Comprehending Technical Japanese, 1975, Chinese edit., 1985, Dynamics of Polymeric Liquids Vol. 1, Fluid Mechanics, Vol. 2, Kinetic Theory, 1977, 2d edit., 1987, Reading Dutch: Fifteen Annotated Stories from the Low Countries, 1985, Basic Technical Japanese, 1990, Technical Japanese Supplements: Polymer Science and Engineering, 1995; also numerous rsch. publs.; Am. editor (with others) Applied Sci. Rsch., 1969-86, 89—; mem. adv. bd. Indsl. and Engring. Chemistry, 1970-72; mem. editl. bd. Jour. Non-Newtonian Fluid Mechanics, 1975—. Served to 1st lt. AUS, 1943-46. Decorated Bronze Star; Fulbright fellow, Holland, 1950, Guggenheim fellow, 1958; Fulbright lectr., 1958, Japan, 1962-63, Sarajevo, Yugoslavia, 1972; recipient Curtis McGraw award Am. Assn. Engring. Edn., 1959, Westinghouse award, 1960, Corcoran award, 1987, Centennial Medallion, 1993, Nat. Medal Sci., 1987. Fellow AIChE (William H. Walker award 1962, Profl. Progress award 1965, Warren K. Lewis award 1974, Founders award 1989, Inst. Lect. award 1992), Am. Phys. Soc., Am. Acad. Arts and Scis.; mem. NAS, NAE, Am. Acad. Mechanics, N.Y. Acad. Scis., Wis. Acad. Scis., Arts and Letters, Am. Assn. Netherlandic Studies, Am. Chem. Soc. (chmn. Wis. sect. 1966, unrestricted rsch. grant Petroleum Rsch. Fund 1963), Soc. Rheology, Royal Dutch Acad. Scis. (fgn.), Royal Belgian Acad. Scis. (fgn.), Soc. Chem. Engrs. Japan (hon.), Phi Beta Kappa, Sigma Xi (v.p. Wis. sect. 1959-60), Tau Beta Pi, Alpha Chi Sigma, Phi Kappa Phi, Omicron Delta Kappa, Sigma Tau. Office: U Wis Dept Chem Engring 3004 Engring Hall 1415 Engineering Dr Madison WI 53706-1691

BIRD, THOMAS JOSEPH, retired microbiologist, environmental consultant; b. Scranton, Pa., Nov. 15, 1927; s. Carl Patrick and Mary (Collins) B.; m Ann Dorothy Gaughan, Sept. 6, 1952; children: Mary Lourdes Pekron, Patricia Wiezien, Michelle Pelsor, Laureen Carini, Sharon R., Karen Merlazeau. BS, U. Scranton, Pa., 1951; MS, U. Pa., 1954, PhD, 1956. Instr. microbiology Northwestern Med. Sch., Chgo., 1954-58; asst. prof. microbiology Loyola U. Med. Sch., Chgo., 1958-65; adj. prof. Chgo. Med. Sch., 1965-70; chief microbiology Hines (Ill.) VA Hosp., 1965-88. With U.S. Army, 1946-47. Retired Col. U.S. Army Res. Fellow Am. Acad. Microbiology; mem. Am. Soc. Microbiology (mem. coun. 1965-66), Ill. Soc. Microbiology (pres. 1964), Soc. Gen. Microbiology, Ill. Acad. Sci., N.Y. Acad. Sci.

BIRDSALL, ARTHUR ANTHONY, chemical executive; b. Oneonta, N.Y., Feb. 28, 1947; s. Charles Albert and Mary (Danzi) B.; m. Jane Elaine Fink, Jan. 28, 1967; children: Robert, Thomas, William. AAS in Chemistry, Erie County Tech. Inst., 1966; BS in Chemistry, Saginaw Valley Coll., 1969. Applications engr. Dow Corning Corp., Midland, Mich., 1966-70; product devel. chemist Dow Corning Corp., Elizabethtown, Ky., 1970-71, quality reliability engr., 1971-73; quality assurance supr. Dow Corning Corp., Chgo., 1973-75; product devel. specialist Dow Corning Corp., Midland, Mich., 1975-77; pilot plant mgr. Dow Corning Corp., Freeland, Mich., 1977-80; quality mgr., govt. relations coordinator Dow Corning Ophthalmics, Inc. div. Dow Corning Corp., Cosa Mesa, Calif., 1980; quality mgr., govt. relations coordinator Dow Corning Ophthalmics, Inc. div. Dow Corning Corp., Midland, 1980-82, mgr. quality/regulatory affairs, 1982-85; corp. mgr. product stewardship Dow Corning Corp., Midland, Mich., 1985-88, program chmn. Dow Corning health environ. and safety bd., 1986-91, mem. Dow Corning product liability issue mgmt. com., 1988-91, mgr. product stewardship, safety and regulatory compliance, 1988-91; European dir. health, environment and regulatory affairs Dow Corning Corp., 1991—; European dir. health, environ. and regulatory affairs; mem. Dow Corning Europe Environment, Health and Safety Coun., 1992—; cons. ophthalmic device regulations Dow Corning Corp., Midland, 1985; bd. dirs. Contact Lens Inst., also vice-chmn. bd. dirs., 1983-84, treas., 1984-85; chmn. pro-tem ophthalmic device com. Health Industry Mfrs. Assn., Washington, 1982-84, mem. Product Safety Mgmt. Forum; mem. Chem. Industry Dirs. Exch., Material Safety Data Sheet, Electronic Date Interchange Std. Coms., 1986-91; mem. environ, health and safety com. Am. C. of C. in Belgium, 1991—; mem. mgmt. bd. Centre European des Silicones, 1991—. Co-inventor silicone resins for optical devices, 1977; contbr. articles to profl. jours.; patentee in field. Chmn. Cub Scout Pack com., Midland, 1979; treas. local Parent Tchr. Orgn., Midland, 1977, v.p., 1978, pres., 1979; tchr. Cath. Youth Coun., Midland, 1985; bd. dirs. Blessed Sacrament Sch., 1986-87, mem. edn. commn., 1986-88; mem. adv. bd. Midlan County United Way Citizen, 1990-91. Contbr. recipient I.R. 100 award silicone contact lens devel., 1982. Mem. Am. Soc. Quality Control, Regulatory Affairs Profl. Soc., Am. C. of C. in Belgium (environ., health and safety com. 1991—), Ctr. European des Silicones (environ. com. 1991-94, bd. dirs. 1994—). Republican. Roman Catholic. Office: Dow Corning Corp Internat Mail Stop Eh601 Midland MI 48686

BIRDSONG, EMIL ARDELL, psychologist; b. Detroit, Feb. 23, 1943; s. Emil Ardell and Ruby Carolyn (Weaks) B.; m. Beatrice Lee Johnson, Sept. 12, 1981. BA in Psychology, U. Mich., Dearborn, 1968; MA in Psychology, Merrill Palmer Inst., 1981; Psy. S Clin. Edn., Ctr. Humanistic Studies, Detroit, 1988; PhD of Clin. Psychology, Union Inst., Cin., 1994. Lic. psychologist, Mich. Spl. edn. educator Wolf Mid. Sch., Centerline, Mich., 1987-88; intern psychology Ypsilanti (Mich.) Psychiat. Hosp., 1988-90; psychologist Detroit, 1994—; grant writer Law Enforcement Assist Act, Mich. With U.S. Army, 1968-70. Named Ky. Col. Gov. of Ky., 1993. Mem. APA, Am. Psychology Soc., Mich. Psychol. Assn., U. Mich. Alumni Assn. (bd. govs., bd. dirs. 1972-73). Democrat. Lutheran. Home: 12001 Lakepointe Detroit MI 48224 Office: Employment Detroit Central City Cmty Mental Health 10 Peterboro Detroit MI 48201

BIRKETT, CYNTHIA ANNE, theater company executive; b. Kansas City, Mo., Oct. 31, 1960; d. Alan Kendal and Barbara Jean (Burnett) B. Student, Baker U., 1979-80. Dance instr., receptionist, office mgr., sales rep. Nina Molleson Overland Park (Kans.) Sch. of Dance, 1972-80; mgr., instr. Kinetics Fitness Ctr., Evanston and Chgo., 1980-85; asst. to Lea Darwin Giordano Dance Ctr., Evanston, 1980-82; ptnr., owner Kinetic's Fitness/Portess Med. Ctr., Chgo., 1984-85; dir. ops. Ctr. Theater Ensemble, Chgo., 1985—; works with numerous actors, Chgo., 1990-92. Fundraiser UNICEF, Kansas City and Chgo., 1969-91, Salvation Army, Chgo., 1980-85; mem. Overland Park Christian Ch., 1969-80. Recipient Oli award Artists/Peers and Colleagues Theater Adminstrs., 1991. Mem. DAR, Nat. Geographic Soc., Smithsonian Inst.

BIRMELE, RAYMOND ELSWORTH, small business owner; b. Watervliet, Mich., Oct. 16, 1948; s. Marvin E. and Mary Ann (Bodine) B.; m. DiAnn M. Birmele, June 7, 1970; children: Andrea, Candace. AAS, Ferris State Coll., 1968. Gen. foreman Auto Specialties Mfg., Hartford, Mich., 1979-80, prodn. supt., 1980-81; owner, pres. Pro Slot Mfg., Hartford, 1981-85, Fantom Racing Enterprises, Hartford, 1980—; founder Fantom Computer Systems, divsn. Fantom Racing Enterprises, Hartford, 1992, Cyber Solutions Inc., 1995; designer engring. cons. Race Car Rsch. Co., Hartford, 1968-75, N.Am. Oil Co., Schaumburg, 1973-74; cons. Racer Products, Inc., Livermore, Calif., 1984-87; deisgner, mfr. only 100% Am.-made radio control car motor, 1988. Served with USN, 1968-70, Vietnam. Mem. Nat. Fedn. Small Bus. Methodist. Home: 101 Washington St Hartford MI 49057-1165 Office: Fantom Racing Enterprises PO Box 216 Hartford MI 49057-0216

BIRMINGHAM, WILLIAM JOSEPH, lawyer; b. Lynbrook, N.Y., Aug. 7, 1923; s. Daniel Joseph and Mary Elizabeth (Tighe) B.; m. Helen Elizabeth Roche, July 23, 1955; children: Deirdre, Patrick, Maureen, Kathleen, Brian. ME, Stevens Inst. Tech., 1944; MBA, Harvard U., 1948; JD, DePaul U., Chgo., 1953. Bar: Ill. 1953, U.S. Patent and Trademark Office, 1955, U.S. Dist. Ct. (no. dist.) Ill. 1960, U.S. Supreme Ct. 1961, U.S. Ct. Appeals (7th cir.) 1962, U.S. Ct. Appeals (3d cir.) 1968, U.S. Ct. Appeals (D.C. cir.) 1973, U.S. Ct. Mil. Appeals 1973, U.S. Ct. Appeals (fed. cir.) 1982, U.S. Ct. Claims 1986; registered profl. engr., Ill., Ind. Chem. engr. Standard Oil Co. Ind., Chgo., 1948-53, patent atty., 1953-59; assoc. Neuman, Williams, Anderson & Olson, Chgo., 1959-60, ptnr., 1961-91, Leydig, Voit & Mayer, Ltd., Chgo., 1991-93, of counsel, 1994—. Served to capt. USNR, 1942-75. Mem. ABA, ASME, Fed. Cir. Bar Assn., Am. Intellectual Property Law Assn., Intellectual Property Law Assn. Chgo. Home: 233 Pine St Deerfield IL 60015-4853 Office: Leydig Voit & Mayer Ltd Two Prudential Plz Ste 4900 Chicago IL 60601-6780

BIRR, LARRY GALE, software systems designer; b. Mankato, Minn., May 29, 1954; s. Orin Carl and Dorladyne Faye (Gilberts) B. BS in Econs., Fin., Mankato State U., 1977; computer programming cert., Brown Inst., 1983. cert. profl. Microsoft. With data processing support Farmland Industries, Kansas City, Mo., 1980-81; systems analyst S.J. Groves & Sons, Plymouth, Minn., 1983-85, Harrison Western Corp., Golden, Colo., 1986-87; project leader S.J. Groves & Sons, Plymouth, 1987-89; v.p. H & B Advantage, Maple Grove, Minn., 1989—; computer system designer, cons. Balfour Beatty, Miami, Fla., 1990-91. Mem. ACLU, Mpls., Amnesty Internat., Oxfam Am., Boston, Mpls. Inst. of Arts. Democrat. Home: 4624 Cedar Lake Rd S # 8 Minneapolis MN 55416-3727 Office: H & B Advantage 9199 Harbor Ln N Maple Grove MN 55369-8864

BIRRER, HOLLI ILEEN, public relations executive; b. El Paso, Tex., Oct. 8, 1954; d. Robert and Gail Flora Birrer; m. Duane Howard Salls, Jan. 1, 1983; 1 child. Grad. high sch., Cleve. Asst. dir. alumni rels. Case Western Res. U., Cleve., 1974-76, dir. spl. programs, 1976-77; asst. dir. Rapid Recovery, Inc., Cleve., 1977-79; exec. dir. CleanLand, Ohio, Cleve., 1979-82; dir. mktg. Tower City Ctr., Cleve., 1982-89, v.p. pub. rels., 1989-91; dir. media rels. Cleve. Clinic Found., 1991—. Exec. producer: (film documentary) Tower City Center, 1990 (Emmy nomination). Bd. dirs. WomenSpace, Cleve., 1992, New Cleve. Campaign, 1989—, CleanLand Ohio, 1982—; mem. alumni Leadership Cleve. Class of 1990, 1990—; mem. Bicentennial Events Com., 1993—; chmn. healthcare sect. Cleve. Convention and Visitors Bur., 1993—; publicity chmn. United Negro Coll. Fund of Cleve., 1993—. Recipient Outstanding Pub. Rels. award Arthur W. Page Soc., 1990, MacEachern award for Mgmt. Excellence, 1993, Communicators award and cert. of merit Women in Comm., Inc., 1993, 1995 Internat. Health & Med. Film Festival award. Mem. Pub. Rels. Soc. Am. (accredited, cert. of commendation Silver Anvil program 1993), The Press Club. Office: Cleve Clinic Found 9500 Euclid Ave # K2 Cleveland OH 44195-0001

BIRSCHBACH, JOHN PETER, manufacturing engineer; b. Fond Du Lac, Wis., Apr. 27, 1953; s. Franklin A. and Cathrine (Thelen) B.; m. Alice M. Anderson, Oct. 18, 1975; children: Heather M., Sabrina L. Cert. tool and die, MPTC, Fond du Lac, 1978, degree in indsl. engring., 1980. Mfg. engr. Mercury Marine, Fond du Lac. Chairperson Blue Line Figure Skating, Fond du Lac, 1990-94; bd. dirs. Blue Line Club, Fond du Lac, 1991—, sec., 1994—; gov. Fond de Vettes, Fond du Lac, 1981-86. Recipient Membership Involvement award Area Safety Coun., 1995. Home: W 5801 Maplewood Dr Fond Du Lac WI 54935 Office: Mercury Marine 660 S Hickory St Fond Du Lac WI 54935

BIRZER, RICHARD, engineer; b. Ness City, Kans., Mar. 31, 1934. B, Kans. State U., 1956; M, U. Kans., 1966. Sr. product engr. Faribanks Morse, Kansas City, Kans., 1963-67; rsch. engr. Westinghouse Rsch. Labs., Churchill Birrough, Pa., 1967-69; chief engr. ITT Bell & Gossett, Morton Grove, Ill., 1969—. Patentee in field. Webloe den leader Boy Scouts Am. Mem. ASRAE. Home: 1517 Churchill Rd Schaumburg IL 60195-3225

BISCHOFF, JANET E., city government business analyst; b. Milw.. BBA, Concordia U., Milw., 1975; cert. pub. adminstrn., U. Wis., Milw., 1989. City govt. mgr. City of Milw. Mem. NAFE, Am. Mgmt. Assn., Milw. Mcpl. Engring. Assn. (treas.). Office: City of Milw 841 N Broadway Rm 311 Milwaukee WI 53202-3613

BISCOTTI, MATTHEW LOUIS, landscape nursery wholesaler, publisher; b. Euclid, Ohio, Oct. 25, 1946; s. Matthew Eli and Louise (Antonacci) B.; m. Margo Lynn Bell, Dec. 21, 1968; children: Matthew Lincoln, Margaret Louise. BS, Cornell U., 1968. Tchr. Conneaut (Ohio) City Schs., 1969-72; mgr. Am. Garden Products, Hamilton, Miss., 1973-79, Charleston, S.C., 1979-81; mgr. Amfac Nurseries, Fallbrook, Calif., 1981-83; mgr., owner Ridge Manor Nurseries, Madison, Ohio, 1984—, Sunrise Pub. Co., Austinburg, Ohio, 1991—. Author: Borzoi Books for Sportsmen, 1992, American Sporting Book Series, 1994. Republican. Lutheran. Home: 481 Rt 45 S Austinburg OH 44010 Office: Ridge Manor Nurseries 7925 N Ridge Madison OH 44057

BISHAI, YOUSEF B., medical administrator; b. Egypt, Nov. 9, 1929; arrived in U.S., 1956; s. Basta Bishai; m. Turid Eileen Bishai; 3 children. MD, Cairo U., 1954; postgrad., Wayne State U., 1960, McGill U., Montreal, Can., 1960-63. Chief dept. ob-gyn. Holy Cross Hosp., Macomb Hosp.; cons. to hosps. Fulbright scholar, 1956. Mem. Grosse Pointe Yacht Club. Republican. Home: 105 Lakeshore Grosse Pointe MI 48236-3761 Office: 28043 Hoover Warren MI 48093

BISHOP, DAVID T., state legislator; b. Mar. 29; m. Bea Bishop; 5 children. JD, Cornell U.; MPA, Harvard U. Pvt. practice law; rep. Dist. 30B Minn. Ho. of reps., 1983—, mem. appropriations com., ethics and judiciary coms., mem. ways and means com., capitol investment com., mem. econ. devel., internat. trade coms., mem. tech. and econ. devel. divsn. coms.

BISHOP, ELIZABETH SHREVE, psychologist; b. Ann Arbor, Mich., Nov. 18, 1951; d. William Warner Jr. and Mary Fairfax (Shreve) B. AB, U. Mich., 1972; MA, Ohio State U., 1973, PhD, 1976. Lic. psychologist, Mich. Psychologist Franklin County Program for the Mentally Retarded, Columbus, Ohio, 1974, WC Mental Health, Willmar, Minn., 1977-83; chief psychologist Battle Creek (Mich.) Child Guidance Ctr., 1981; dir. psychometrics Meridian Profl. Psychol. Cons., East Lansing, Mich., 1983-92; pres. Arbor Psychol. Cons., Ann Arbor, 1991—. Troop leader Girl Scouts U.S.A., Minn., Mich., Ohio, 1971-87, trainer, 1993—. Assoc. Univ. London Inst. Edn., 1976. Fellow Am. Orthopsychiat. Assn.; mem. APA, AAUW, Mich. Psychol. Assn., Mich. Women Psychologists, Coun. for Exceptional Children (local pres. 1977-78), Internat. Coun. Psychologists, Internat. Sch. Psychology Assn., LWV (Willmar v.p. 1989-91). Home: 1612 Morton Ave Ann Arbor MI 48104-4441 Office: Arbor Psychol Cons 1565 Eastover Pl Ann Arbor MI 48104-6316

BISHOP, JAMES FRANCIS, lawyer; b. Oak Park, Ill., Aug. 25, 1940; s. George H. and Helen E. (Newcomb) B.; children: Christopher J., Pamela J., Jennifer Lynn. BS, St. Joseph's Coll., Rensselaer, Ind., 1963; JD, Chgo. Kent Coll., 1966. Bar: Ill. 1966, Nev. 1989. Trust officer Am. Nat. Bank & Trust Co., Chgo., 1964-67; assoc. Gould & Ratner, Chgo., 1967-73; ptnr. Bishop & Callas, Crystal Lake, Ill., 1973—. Trustee McHenry County Easter Seal Soc., Woodstock, Ill., 1974—; vice chmn. McHenry County Sch. Dist. reorganization com., Woodstock, 1985-87, McHenry County Ducks Unltd., Crystal Lake, 1976-89; bd. dirs. McHenry (Ill.) Hosp. 1980-82;. Mem. Nat. Solid Waste Assn. Mgmt. (mem. legis. com. 1988), Govt. Refuse Collection and Disposal Assn. (mem. legis. com. 1986-88), McHenry County Bar Assn., Ill. State Bar Assn., Clark County Bar Assn., State of Nev. Bar Assn. Office: Bishop & Callas 550 W Woodstock St Crystal Lake IL 60014-3425

BISHOP, LINDA DILENE, lawyer, small business owner; b. La Grange, Ill., Dec. 21, 1961; d. James William and Margaret Ann Bishop. BA, U. Colo., 1985, JD, 1987. Bar: Colo., 1988, Ill., 1989, Fla., 1990, Fed. Ct. (no. dist. Ill.) 1992, (cen. dist. Ill.) 1994; cert. travel cons., real estate broker, mediator. Dep. dist. atty. Colorado Springs (Colo.) Dist. Atty., 1987-89, Jefferson County Dist. Atty., Golden, Colo., 1989-91; owner, pres. Bishop and Bishop, Oak Brook, Ill., 1991—, Great Lakes Installation Co., Oak Brook, 1991—, Bishop Travel Ctr., Oak Brook, 1992—; analyst draft codes for ea. Europe Ctrl. & East European Law Initiative, Washington, 1993, 94, 95. Mem. Colo. Bar Assn., Ill. Bar Assn., Fla. Bar Assn., Assn. Retail Travel Agts., Pacific Assn. Travel Agts., Internat. Forum Travel and Tourism. Republican. Home: 716 S Stough Hinsdale IL 60521-4412 Office: Bishop and Bishop 1111 W 22d St Ste C-40 Oak Brook IL 60521-1940

BISHOP, MARC W., investment broker; b. Lafayette, Ind., May 26, 1957. BS, Fair State U., Big Rapids, Mich., 1980. Sales rep. Durmabalic, Kalamazoo, 1980-84, Chesterdon Corp., Traverse City, Mich., 1984-86; banquet coord. Grand Traverse Resort, Traverse City, 1983-86; stockbroker A.G. Edwards & Sons Inc., Holland, Mich., 1986—. Mem. Holland Exch. Club. Republican. Roman Catholic. Office: AG Edwards & Sons Inc PO Box 1169 355 Settlers Rd Holland MI 49422

BISHOP, OLIVER RICHARD, state official; b. El Dorado, Kans., Dec. 5, 1928; s. Oliver Harrison and Hazel May (Garabrandt) B.; m. Fuyo Oyake, Aug. 14, 1959; children: Lisa Naomi, Rachel Eri. BS in Pub. Adminstrn. magna cum laude, U. So. Calif., 1963; MS in Econs cum laude, U. S.D., 1971. Cert. planner, office automation profl., assisted housing mgr.; lic. steam engr., Ohio. Commd. 2d lt. USAF, 1956, advanced through grades to maj., 1966, ret., 1971; city mgr. City of Slater, Mo., 1971-73, City of Highland, Ill., 1973-76, City of Napoleon, Ohio, 1976-77; village mgr. Village of Westmont, Ill., 1977-85; revenue and fiscal advisor State of Ill., Chgo., 1985—; planning cons. Bishop's Cons. Services, Westmont. 1985—. Precinct committeeman Rep. Ctrl. com., Dupage County, Ill., 1987-88; candidate for County Bd. Dupage County Dist. 3, 1988; com. chmn. Westmont Planning Commn., 1986-95; bd. dirs. T.E.A.C.H., Inc., I-Care, Inc. Mem. IEEE, Internat. City Mgmt. Assn., Am. Planning Assn., Am. Inst. Cert. Planners, Govt. Fin. Officers Assn., Office Automation Soc. Internat., Mensa, Intertel, Elks, Masons, Shriners, Pi Sigma Alpha, Omicron Delta Epsilon (pres. Lambda chpt.). Mem. Ch. of Christ. Home: 645 Newport Ave Westmont IL 60559-1220 Office: Ill Dept Commerce and Community Affairs 100 W Randolph St Ste 3400 Chicago IL 60601-3219

BISHOP, RUTH ANN, coloratura soprano, voice educator; b. Homewood, Ill., Feb. 21, 1942; d. George Bernard and Grace Mildred (Hoke) Riddle; m. John Allen Reinhardt, June 9, 1962 (div. 1975); children: Laura, Jonathon; m. Merrill Edward Bishop, Aug. 16, 1975; stepchildren: Mark, Lynn. BS in Music Edn., U. Ill., 1962; M of Music in Voice, Cath. U. Am., 1972; postgrad., U. Md., 1975. Music tchr. Prince Georges County (Md.) Schs., 1963-71, Yamaha Music Co., College Park, Md., 1971-73; voice tchr. Prince Georges Community Coll., Largo, Md., 1972-75, U. Md., College Park, 1975; profl. lectr. voice Chgo. Mus. Coll. Roosevelt U., 1977-82; tchr. voice McHenry County Coll., Crystal Lake, Ill., 1978—, Elgin (Ill.) Community Coll., 1981—; pvt. voice tchr. Crystal Lake, 1975—; dir. music Epworth United Meth. Ch., Elgin, 1984-86, Cherub choir 1st Congl. Ch., Crystal Lake, 1986-88; mem. Camerata Singers, Lake Forest, 1988, Arts Chorale of Elgin Choral Union; performer, vocal dir. Woodstock (Ill.) Mus. Theatre Co., 1983—; soprano soloist Internat. Band Festival, Besana Brianza, Italy, 1993. soprano soloist, Oratorio- The Psalms of David, 1986, opera, The Light of the Eye, 1985-86, Children's Day at the Opera, Washington, 1972, U.S. Navy Band, The White House, 1969; soloist with Crystal Lake Community Choir and Band, 1987—, First Congl. Ch., 1975—, others. Ill. State scholar, 1959. Mem. Nat. Assn. Tchrs. Singing (chpt. rec. sec. 1984-86, bd. mem. Chgo. chpt. 1995-96), Sigma Alpha Iota, Pi Kappa Lambda, Kappa Delta. Republican. United Ch. of Christ. Home: 951 Cambridge Ln Crystal Lake IL 60014-7608 Office: Elgin Community Coll Dept Music 1700 Spartan Dr Elgin IL 60123-7189

BISINGER, JERRY H., investment representative; b. Burlington, Iowa, July 21, 1950. BSBA, N.E. Mo. State U., 1983. Traffic mgr. Conifer Corp., Burlington, 1983-86; investment rep. Edward D. Jones & Co., Sparta, Wis., 1986—. Mem. Kiwanis (past sec./treas. 1989-92, past pres. 1992-93). Republican. Roman Catholic. Home: 1012 S Fairway Dr Sparta WI 54656-1445 Office: Edward D Jones & Co PO Box 168 Sparta WI 54656-0168

BISSELL, WILLIAM W., financial consultant; b. Springfield, Ill., July 16, 1926; s. Grant C. and Kathereen (Rutherford) B.; m. Elizabeth Balch, Apr. 23, 1949; children: Katherine, Nancy, Ann. BS, Pa. State U., 1948. Cert. Fin. Mgr. Dir. mktg. Miles Lab., Elkhart, Ind., 1967-82; v.p. fin. cons. Merrill Lynch, South Bend, Ind., 1982—. Lt. USNR, 1951-52, Korea. Mem. Rotary Internat. Republican. Episcopalian. Office: Merrill Lynch 404 Columbia St South Bend IN 46601-2355

BISSEN, DALE M., electronics engineer; b. Harlan, Iowa, Oct. 15, 1963. BS in Elec. Engring. Tech., DeVry Inst. Tech., Kansas City, Mo., 1985. Sys. engr. Boeing Mil. Airplanes, Wichita, Kans., 1986-90; elec. engr., sys. engr. Aero Systems Engring., St. Paul, 1990—. Republican. Roman Catholic. Office: Aero Systems Engring 358 Fillmore Ave E Saint Paul MN 55107-1204

BISSETT, BARBARA ANNE, steel distribution company executive; b. Cleve., Sept. 27, 1950; d. George Jr. and Helen (Kirkwood) B.; m. Kerry Mark Kitchen, Oct. 6, 1979; children: Mark Jeffrey, Lauren Brooke. BFA, U. Denver, 1974. Inside sales rep. Bissett Steel Co., Cleve., 1977-78, inside sales mgr., 1978-80, v.p., 1980-88, pres., 1988—; mentor strategic planning course Greater Cleve. Growth Assn., 1987-95. Bd. dirs. Greater Cleve. Growth Assn. Govt. Affairs, 1994—; trustee Enterprise Devel., Inc., 1994—. Mem. Am. Soc. Metals, Steel Svc. Ctr. Inst. (v.p. programming young leadership forum 1989, pres. 1991-93, bd. dirs. No. ohio chpt., v.p. 1994), Coun. Smaller Enterprises (leadership coun. 1989—, bd. dirs. 1990—, first vice chair 1996), Assn. Women in Metals Indusries, Steel Svc. Ctr. Inst. (pres. N. Ohio chpt. 1995—), Cleve. Yacht Club, Women's City Club. Republican. Presbyterian. Home: 1994 Coes Post Run Cleveland OH 44145-2059 Office: 9005 Bank St Cleveland OH 44125-3425

BISSINGER, MARK CHRISTIAN, lawyer; b. Steubenville, Ohio, June 4, 1957; s. Emerson Melvin and Nancy (Osbun) B.; m. Julie Furber, Sept. 28, 1985; 1 child, Lucas Christian Bissinger. BS in Civil Engring., Purdue U., 1979; JD, U. Cin., 1983. Bar: Ohio 1983, U.S. Dist. Ct. (so. dist.) Ohio 1983, U.S. Ct. Appeals (6th cir.), Ky. 1993. Assoc. Dinsmore & Shohl, Cin., 1983-90, ptnr., 1990—; speaker Ohio Continuing Legal Edn., Cin., 1990—; lectr. Nat. Bus. Inst., 1990—. Pres. Ctr. for Comprehensive Alcoholism Treatment, Cin., 1989-92; bd. mem. Community Operation Devel. Inc., Cin., 1991—, Five Mile Chapel Soc., Cin., 1989—. Named Order of Coif, Cin., 1983. Mem. Cin. Bar Assn., Ohio Bar Assn., ABA. Office: Dinsmore & Stohl 255 E 5th St Cincinnati OH 45202-4700

BISSLER, RICHARD THOMAS, mortician; b. Ravenna, Ohio, Nov. 23, 1953; s. Richard Samuel and Ruth Marion (Cowan) B.; m. Jane H. Vair, Aug. 23, 1975; children: Stephanie Ann, Carlie Jane. BS in Mortuary Sci., U. Minn., 1976; grad., Nat. Found. Funeral Svc. Mgmt., 1983. Lic. funeral dir. and embalmer Ohio; cert. crematory operator Cremation Assn. N.Am. Funeral svc. asst. Bissler & Sons Funeral Home, Kent, Ohio, 1970-74, mortician, 1976—, corp. sec., 1983-86, corp. sec.-treas., 1986-88, pres., 1988—; bd. dirs. Home Savs. Bank, Kent. Trustee Kent Free Libr., 1986—, St. Patrick's Sch. Endowment Fund, 1994, Nat. Selected Morticians Ins. Trust, 1995—; past bd. dirs., pres. Portage County A.C.S., Kent; past treas. NEO-SIDS Found., Akron, Ohio, 1990; mem. adult edn. adv. com. Kent City Schs.; steering com. Portage County Hospice; devel. com. United Christian Ministries, 1996—; mem. Vision 2000 com. City of Kent; mem. Kent Bus. and Edn. adv. com. Recipient Disting. Svc. award Kent Jaycees, 1986. Mem. Nat. Funeral Dirs. Assn., Ohio Embalmers Assn., Ohio Funeral Dirs. Assn., Nat. Selected Morticians (meeting chair 1989), Funeral Ethics Assn., Kent Area C. of C. (dir. 1985-89, Outstanding Bus. Person award 1992), Order of the Golden Rule, Kent Rotary (dir. 1991-93, pres. 1995-96), K.C. Republican. Roman Catholic. Office: Bissler & Sons Funeral Home 628 W Main St Kent OH 44240-2212

BITONDO, MICHAEL LEONARD, pollution control professional; b. L.A., Oct. 26, 1953; s. Domenic and Delphine May (Dicola) B.; m. Evie Lou Bolgos, Aug. 10, 1985. BS, Ea. Mich. U., 1975. Chemist bearing div. NSK Corp., Ann Arbor, Mich., 1976-89; environ. quality analyst Mich. Dept. Environ. Quality, Lansing, 1989—, Amway Distbr., Pinckney, Mich., 1991—. Bd. dirs. Hamburg Twp. Environ. Review Bd., 1986-88; trustee Hamburg Twp. Govt., 1988-92; fellowship com. chair Shalom Luth. Ch. Coun., Pinckney, Mich., 1994—. Mem. Wilderness Soc., Bass Anglers Sportsman Soc., Practical Sportsman, Mercedes Benz Club of Am., North Am. Fishing Club, Livingston County Wildlife and Conservation Club, Sierra Club, Audubon Soc., Natural Resources Def. Coun., Moose (gov. Brighton lodge 1994-96). Republican. Office: Mich Dept Environ Quality PO Box 30273 Lansing MI 48909

BITSCH, RICHARD, electrical engineer; b. St. Louis, Aug. 1, 1937; s. Philip and Ida M. (Kassel) B.; m. Diane Claire Schulte, June 8, 1963; children: Dale, Carol, Brenda. A in Computer Electronics, Washington U., A in Elec. Tech., BSEE. Head engr. Emerson Electric, St. Louis, 1955—. Patentee in field. Active St. Marks Luth. Ch., Eureka, Mo.; merit badge counselor Boy Scouts Am., St. Louis, 1967—. With U.S. Army, 1960-62. Mem. Emerson Engrs. Club.

BITTNER, MARVIN JOEL, physician, educator; b. Lincoln, Nebr., Apr. 3, 1950; s. Morris Baer and Clarissa Louise (Hollander) B. SB, U. Chgo., 1972; MD, Harvard U., 1976. House officer dept. internal medicine U. Mich., Ann Arbor, 1976-79; fellow in infectious diseases U. Minn. Med. Sch., Mpls., 1979-81; asst. prof. med. microbiology and medicine Creighton U. Sch. Medicine, Omaha, 1981-91, assoc. prof., 1991—; assoc. prof. U. Nebr. Med. Ctr., Omaha, 1992—; staff physician VA Med. Ctr., Omaha, 1981—; physician travel clinic Douglas County Health Dept., Omaha, 1985—. Contbr. articles to Am. Jour. Infection Control, Archives Internal Medicine, Am. Jour. Medicine, Infection Control, Hosp. Practice, Jour Antimicrobial Chemotherapy, Clin. Infectious Diseases. Tng. fellow Venereal Disease Rsch. Fund., Am. Social Health Assn., 1980-81. Fellow ACP; mem. Infectious Disease Soc. Am., Sigma Xi (assoc.). Office: VA Med Ctr 111 D 4101 Woolworth Ave #8W Omaha NE 68105-1873

BIVEN, JAMES R., mechanical engineer; b. Bloomington, Ill., 1955. A. Petroleum Tech., BS in Engring. Tech., Okla. State U., 1982. Prodn. engr. Day Zimmerman, Parsons, Kans., 1988-89; chief engr. Catalytic Inc. Group, Independence, Kans., 1989-94; mech. engr. Comstock-Castle Stove Co., Quincy, Ill., 1994—. Maj. U.S. Army, 1985-87, USAR, 1987—.

BIVENS, PAULA SUE, journalist; b. Anderson, Ind., Oct. 21, 1946; d. Forrest Nile and Nadine Elizabeth (Wilson) Starr; m. Ray Arnold Bivens, Dec. 23, 1966 (div. Aug. 1975); 1 child, John Andrew. BS, Ball State U., 1968. Tchr. Frankton (Ind.) H.S., 1971-74; staff reporter Anderson Daily Bull., 1969-71, assoc. news editor, 1974-80, city editor, 1980-86; city editor The Herald Bull., Anderson, 1986-95, copy chief, staff trainer, 1995—. Bd. dirs. YWCA, 1991—, East Ctrl. Ind. Food Bank, Anderson, 1993—; mem. Madison County Child Sexual Abuse Task Force, Anderson, 1990—; mem. Mayor's Commn. on Domestic Violence, Anderson, 1994—; mem. adv. bd. St. John's Home Health Care and Hospice, Anderson, 1995—; mem. Anderson Leadership Acad., 1995-96. Named Young Career Woman, Bus. and Profl. Women Anderson, 1971, Woman of Achievement, YWCA, 1996; named to Outstanding Young Women of Am., 1972. Mem. Soroptimist Internat. (past pres.), Soc. Profl. Journalists. Office: The Herald Bulletin PO Box 1090 Anderson IN 46015

BIXLER, SANDRA DIANE, elementary education educator; b. Greencastle, Ind., Sept. 4, 1968; d. Jack Dempsey and Lyndall Dale (Haltom) Bixler.$D. Mark Lewis Priest, Aug. 15, 1987. BA in Elem. Edn., DePauw U., Greencastle, 1992; postgrad., Ind. U.-Purdue U. at Indpls., 1994—. Tchr. Cloverdale (Ind.) Sch. Corp., 1993—. Mem. Phi Beta Kappa, Kappa Delta Pi. Republican. Methodist.

BJERK, KEITH A., stock brokerage executive, home builder; b. Grand Forks, N.D., May 16, 1947. Student, U. N.D., 1967-68; BA in Econs., U. Minn., 1973. Sales mgr. Nat. Steel Svc. Ctr., Mpls., 1973-75; regionala salesman Personal Sportswear, N.Y.C., 1975-80, White Stag Sportswear, Portland, Oreg., 1980-86; v.p., stockbroker Piper-Jaffray Inc., Grand Forks, 1986—. 2d class petty officer USN, 1965-67, Vietnam. Mem. Grand Forks Country Club. Republican. Lutheran. Office: Piper Jafray Inc PO Box 5549 319 Demers Ave Grand Forks ND 58206

BJERKAAS, CARLTON LEE, technology services company senior scientist; b. Fergus Falls, Minn., Apr. 17, 1948; s. Jay Oscar and Anna Marie (Bangert) B.; m. Estrella Maria Calingasan, Nov. 18, 1971; children: Kristopher Scott, Eric Stefan, Todd Philip. BS, U. N.D., 1970; MS, MIT, 1977; MPA, Auburn U., Montgomery, Ala., 1983. Commd. 2d lt. USAF, 1970, advanced through grades to col., 1992; weather forecaster Weather Detachment, Homestead AFB, Fla., 1971-73; flight examiner Weather Reconnaissance Squadron, Andersen AFB, Guam, 1973-75; radar rsch. meteorologist A.F. Geophysics Lab., Hanscom AFB, Mass., 1976-82; chief support br. operational requirements & testing Hdqrs. Mil. Airlift Command, Scott AFB, Ill., 1983-85; chief aerospace environ. requirements Hdqrs. A.F. Systems Command, Andrews AFB, Md., 1985-87; comdr. Weather Detachment, Lajes Field, Azores, Portugal, 1987-89; asst. chief of staff Hdqrs. Air Weather Svc., Scott AFB, 1989-91, dir. resource mgmt., 1991-92, dir. program mgmt., integration, 1992-94; dir. sys. and comm., 1994-95, dir. tech., plans and programs, 1995—, sr. scientist, 1995—. Contbr. articles to profl. jours. Com. chmn. Boy Scouts Am., O'Fallon, Ill., 1991-92; coach, referee youth sports, O'Fallon, 1989—; chmn. Sch. Bd., Lajes Field Azores, 1988-89; mem. Sch. Dist. Com., Lajes Field Azores, 1987. Fellow Am. Meteorol. Soc.; mem. AAAS, ASPA, N.Y. Acad. Scis., Acad. Polit. Sci., Air Weather Assn., Air Lift and Tanker Assn., Phi Beta Kappa, Sigma Xi, Phi Eta Sigma, Pi Alpha Alpha. Methodist. Office: Science Applications Internat Corp 619 W Highway 50 O'Fallon IL 62269

BLAAUW, RUSSELL WAYNE, legislative liaison; b. Chgo., July 20, 1944; s. John Joseph and Bernice (Rabusch) B.; m. M. Bernadette Lynch, June 20, 1981. B.A. So. Ill. U., 1968, M.S., 1974. Legis. budget analyst Ill. Ho. of Reps., Springfield, 1972-77; legis. fiscal analyst La. Legis. Fiscal Office, Baton Rouge, 1977-78; exec. dir. Commn. on Welfare Law Revision, Springfield, 1978-80; assoc. dir. Washington office, Ill. Legislature, 1980-81; legis liaison Dept. Mental Health Devel. Disabilities, Springfield, 1981-87, bur. chief, 1987-88; legis. liaison Dept. Children and Family Svcs., 1988—; forester Instituto Internacional, San Jose, Costa Rica, 1988; cons. Ill. Council on Nutrition, Springfield, 1980, Legis. Adv. Commn. on Welfare, Springfield, 1975-77; speaker-panelist Nat. Legal Services Corp., Kansas City, Mo., 1977. Vol. Big Brother/Big Sister of Sangamon County, Springfield, 1979-78, bd. dirs. 1979-80; vol. Family Court East Baton Rouge Parish, 1978-79; co-dir. Elem. Ed. Tutoring Program, Springfield, 1976-77. Avocations: traveling; photography; skiing; canoeing; running. Home: 1778 Old Chatham Rd Springfield IL 62704-3202 Office: Ill Dept Mental Health & Devel Disabilities 401 S Spring St Springfield IL 62706

BLACK, DAVID DELAINE, investment consultant; b. Cin., Mar. 3, 1926; s. Robert L. Blcak and Anna (McNaughton) Smith; m. Maralyn Anderson (dec.); m. Polly P. Black, Oct. 7, 1967 (dec. Apr. 1996); children: Peter, Susan, Robert, Dorothy, James, Evelyn. BS in Engring. with honors, Princeton U., 1949; MBA, Harvard U., 1951. Mgr. co. planning Cin. Millacron, Cin., 1952-77; owner Planning Counsel, Cin., 1977-84; sr. v.p. Gradison div. McDonald & Co., Cin., 1984—. Vice chmn. bd. The Children's Hosp., Cin., 1985—; chmn. bd. WCET-TV 48, Cin., 1980-83; pres. Cincinnatus Assn., 1966-67, Agnes and Murray Seasongord Good Govt. Found., 1994-95; chmn. Children's Hosp. Found., 1993—; treas. Planned Parenthood Assn. Cin., 1986. Mem. Rotray (bd dirs. 1992-95, treas. Cin. Rotary Found. 1993-94). Office: Gradison 580 Walnut St Cincinnati OH 45202-3110

BLACK, DENISE LOUISE, secondary school educator; b. Ft. Sill, Okla., Apr. 16, 1950; d. Nelson Arthur and Virginia Mary (Smith) Taber; AA, C.C. of Allegheny County, Boyce campus, 1970; BS, Slippery Rock State Coll., 1972; MA, Eastern Mich. U., 1978; m. Robert Paul Black, Aug. 12, 1972; children: Paula Ann, Jennifer Lea. Adult edn. tchr. ecology and physiology Huron Valley Schs., Milford, Mich., 1973-74; tchr. gen. biology and earth sci. Howell (Mich.) Public Schs., 1974-75; adult edn. tchr. life sci. Holly (Mich.) Area Schs., 1978-80, Hartland (Mich.) Consol. Schs., 1978-86; tchr. biology Walled Lake (Mich.) Consol. Schs., 1988—, Hartland (Mich.) Consolidates Schs., 1990—. Coach, Milford Youth Athletic Assn., 1973-85; leader 4-H Club; Huron Valley Horse Com.; youth advisor Mich. State Rabbit Breeders Assn., 1990-92. Cert. guidance and counselor. Mem. Nat. Assn. Biology Tchrs., Mich. Assn. Biology Tchrs., Mich. Adult Curriculum Connection (bd. dirs.), Mich. Sci. Tchrs. Assn., Beta Beta Beta, Phi Kappa Phi, Phi Theta Kappa. Methodist. Home: 2576 Shady Ln Milford MI 48381-1438

BLACK, DOUGLAS D., lumber company executive; b. Glasgow, Mont., Feb. 22, 1961; s. Gordon Grant Pierce and Arlene Catharine (Brown) B.; m. Dawn Black; children: Ginger Gabrielle, D. Vincent. Student, Lawrence Tech. U., 1979-82. Lic. residential builder, Mich. Systems designer Simplicity Engring., Durand, Mich., 1978-79; designer Wolverine-Badger Structures, Holt, Mich., 1982-83, SANKAY Corp., Dansville, Mich., 1982-83; v.p., constrn. mgr. TCM, Inc., Mason, Mich., 1983-84; pres. Crescent Homes, Inc., Fenton, Mich., 1991-96; sales exec. Glasers Lumber Co., Vernon, Mich., 1990-92; gen. mgr., 1992—; cons. in field. Artwork pub. in Am. Artists: Leading Contemporaries, 1990. Acad. Hons. scholar, Lawrence Tech., 1979. Mem. Shiawassee Arts Coun., Toastmasters, Rotary Internat., Fenton C. of C. (amb. 1993, 94). Republican.

BLACK, JACINTH BAUBLITZ, clinical social worker; b. Corpus Christi, Tex., Feb. 17, 1944; m. Donald James Baublitz, Oct. 26, 1968 (div. June 1979); children: Jessica Ruth, Stefanie Elizabeth; m. Robert Drummond Black, Mar. 14, 1987. BA, Sam Houston U., 1965; MSW, Boston Coll., 1972; postgrad., Am. Assn. Sex Educators, Counselors and Therapists, Washington, 1976-77; advanced studies with Maxie Maultsby Jr., U. Ky., 1980. Cert. Acad. Social Workers, 1976; lic. social worker and marriage and family therapist, Mich.; diplomate Acad. Social Workers, 1988; nat. bd. cert. clin. hypnotherapist, 1995. Tchr. English and Spanish Brazosport Schs., Freeport, Tex., 1965-67; caseworker Harris County Child Welfare Unit, Houston, 1967-69; vocat. counselor Mass. Employment Security, Lowell, 1969-70; family therapist Cath. Family Service, Saginaw, Mich., 1973-75; contractual clin. social worker Midland-Gladwin Community Mental Health Ctr., 1975-80; pvt. practice clin. social work Midland, Mich., 1975—; adj. prof. psychology Northwood Inst., 1982-85; cons., lectr., speaker various profl. and lay orgns. Author: Relationshift, 1983, A Singles Guide to Tight Spots and Tricky Situations, 1986; newspaper advice columnist Bay Area Rev., 1985-89. Bd. dirs. Big Sisters Am., Inc., Midland, 1978-80; mem. bd. mgrs. Midland County Hist. Soc., 1996—. Mem. NASW. Episcopalian. Home: 4553 S Saginaw Rd Midland MI 48640-8554 Office: PO Box 2227 Midland MI 48641-2227

BLACK, LARRY DAVID, library director; b. Section, Ala., Mar. 3, 1949; s. Haskin Byron and Mima Jean (Holcomb) B.; m. Mary Frances Patterson, Aug. 29, 1971; 1 child, Amy Susan. BA in History & Polit. Sci., U. Ala., 1971, MLS, 1972; M in Pub. Adminstrn., Ohio State U., 1981. Asst. dir. Bedsole Library Mobile (Ala.) Coll., 1972-73; dir. Baldwin County Libr. System, Summerdale, Ala., 1973-76; dir. libr. svc. Troy State U., Bay Minette, Ala., 1976-77; dir. main libr. Columbus Met. Libr., Ohio, 1977-83, asst. exec. dir., 1983-84, exec. dir., 1984—. Mem. ALA, Pub. Libr. Assn., Ohio Libr. Assn., Libr. Adminstrn., Am. Soc. Pub. Adminstrs. Democrat. Club: Cen. Ohio Corvette (Columbus). Home: 7381 Seeds Rd Orient OH 43146-9608 Office: Columbus Met Libr 96 S Grant Ave Columbus OH 43215-4702

BLACK, PAUL D., health facility administrator; b. Flint, Mich., Nov. 5, 1951. BS, Ctrl. Mich. U., 1974; M in Mgmt., Aquinas Coll., 1989. Life and health ins. agt., Mich. With adj. faculty Grand Rapids (Mich.) Jr. Coll., 1976-79; athletic dir. Grand Rapids Metro YMCA, 1979-84; owner, pres. PD Black Enterprises Inc., Allendale, Mich., 1984—; v.p. Project Health Muskegon, Mich., 1993—. Active Allendale Bd. Edn., 1988—. Mem. NALU.

BLACK, ROBERT DURWARD, television producer; b. Flint, Mich., June 6, 1952; s. Joseph Perrin and Lois Jane (Hamilton) B. BA, Wheaton (Ill.) Coll., 1974; cert. bus. adminstrn., U. Ill., Chgo., 1991. Pres., producer weekly ecumenical TV broadcast Chgo. Sunday Evening Club, 1987—. Office: Chgo Sunday Evening Club 200 N Michigan Ave Chicago IL 60601-5909

BLACK, SPENCER, state legislator; b. N.Y.C., May 25, 1950; married. BA, SUNY, Stony Brook, 1972; MS, U. Wis., 1980, MA, 1981. State assemblyman dist. 77 State of Wis., 1984—. Edn. curator Wis. State Hist. Soc. Democrat. Address: 5742 Elder Pl Madison WI 53705-2516*

BLACK, STEPHEN P., small business owner; b. Rapid City, S.D., Dec. 22, 1949; s. Robert Lee and Jaqueline Ann (Brown) B.; m. Cynthia Ann Thomas, Nov. 29, 1969; children: Stephanie, Byron. AA, Hutchinson Tech. Coll.; BS, Upper Iowa U., 1974. Testing specialist quality assurance Pitts. Des Moines Steel, 1974-77; founder, pres. Quad City Testing Lab., Inc., Davenport, Iowa, 1977—; advisor N.E. C.C., 1990-92. Mem. Am. Soc. Nondestructive Testing (bd. dirs. 1996—), Davenport C. of C. Republican. Office: Quad City Testing Lab Inc 21112 Scott Park Rd Davenport IA 52804

BLACK, VIRGINIA MORROW, writer; b. Glassport, Pa., July 1, 1926; d. Bernard James and Anna Bernice (Ashton) Morrow; m. Anthony R. Black, July 23, 1949; children: Stephanie Ann, Robert Joseph, Mary Kay, Bernard Morrow. BA, Seton Hill Coll., 1948; postgrad., U. Pitts., 1949, Ind. U., South Bend, 1965. Cert. tchr., Ind. Tchr. Pierre Navarre Sch., South Bend, 1952-53, John Adams High Sch., South Bend, 1966-68, St. Joseph High Sch., South Bend, Ind., 1968-70, Marian High Sch., Mishawaka, 1972-78, Washington High Sch., South Bend, 1978-85. Author: Tackling Notre Dame, 1986; author: (plays) Dilemma with Emma, 1989, Bed-Time Story, 1989, Dust to Dust, 1990, While Stands the Colosseum, 1990; contbr. articles to Christian and tchr. mags. Pres. St. Joseph County Right to Life, South Bend, 1982-83; vol. St. Vincent de Paul Soc., South Bend, 1980—; precinct committeeman Rep. Party, 1980-91; active Emmaus Group for Mentally Handicapped, South Bend, 1988—; Repl Congl. candidate 3d Dist. Ind., 1974. Named Guardian of Yr. Logan Sch., South Bend, 1990. Mem. Assn. Ind. Retired Tchrs. Republican. Roman Catholic. Home: 53546 Elmhurst St South Bend IN 46637-5201

BLACK, WILLIAM B., state legislator; b. Danville, Ill., Nov. 11, 1941; m. Sharon Black; 2 children. BA, William Jewel Coll.; MA, Ea. Ill. U.; postgrad., Ill. State U. Ill. state rep. Dist. 105, 1986—; spokesman Econ. Devel. Com., mem. Edn. Com., Transp. and Motor Vehicles Com., Urban Redevel. Com., Elem. and Secondary Com., Human Svc. Com.; educator and adminstr. Address: Rm 300 9 E Fairchild Danville IL 61832*

BLACKBURN, MICHAEL D., design engineer; b. Medina, Ohio, Jan. 24, 1951. A in Electronic Tech., U. Akron, 1972. Sr. design engr. Novar Controls Corp., Barberton, Ohio, 1981—. Mem. Parma (Ohio) Luth. Ch., 1986—, ch. coun. mem., 1989-91, pres. 1991-94. Mem. Great Lakes Chpt. PCAD Group. Home: 2406 Grovewood Ave Parma OH 44134-1904 Office: Novar Controls Corp 24 Brown St Barberton OH 44203-2315

BLACKBURN, PAMELA M., medical surgical nurse; b. Fitchburg, Mass., Sept. 12, 1948; d. Paul E. and Eugenia K. (Marsh) Gastonguay. ADN, Mt. Wachusett Community Coll., Gardner, Mass., 1975. RN, Mass., Tex. Charge nurse Leominster (Mass.) Hosp.; travel nurse Cross Country Nurses, Ga., La., Mass., Fla., Tex., Ariz.; charge nurse diabetes ctr., travel nurse Beaumont (Tex.) Med.-Surg. Hosp.; asst. dir. nursing Seymour (Mo.) Healthcare Inc.; nurse community home health Douglas County Health Dept., Ava, Mo.

BLACKFAN, CYRUS LINTON, specialty chemicals company executive; b. Phila., Sept. 10, 1935; s. Cyrus Linton and Ethel Carrel (Hobensack) B.; m. Barbara Lee Hance, Dec. 17, 1960; children: Barbara May, John Cyrus, David Lyle. B.S., Lafayette Coll., 1957; postgrad. Northwestern U., 1973, MIT, 1982. Sales engr. Union Carbide, N.Y.C., Cleve., 1957-66; product mgr. B.F. Goodrich, Cleve., 1967-72, mgr. new products, 1972-74, mgr. corp. planning, Akron, Ohio, 1974-75, dir. planning, Cleve., 1977-78, v.p. mktg., Akron, 1978-80, v.p., gen. mgr., 1980-82; pres. Chemionics Corp., Tallmadge, Ohio, 1982—, chief exec. officer, 1992—. Mem. Akron Regional Development Bd., 1982—. Served to 1st lt. U.S. Army, 1957-59. Mem. Burning Ridge Club. Republican. Presbyterian. Contbr. articles to profl. jours.

BLACKFORD, JASON COLLIER, lawyer; b. Findlay, Ohio, Oct. 30, 1938; s. Emerson Miller and Isabel (Collier) B.; m. Jane Edith Howells; children: Thomas, Melinda. BA, Denison U., 1960; LLB, Yale U., 1963. Bar: Ohio 1964, U.S. Dist. Ct. (no. dist.) Ohio 1966, U.S. Ct. Appeals (10th cir.) 1974, U.S. Ct. Appeals (6th cir.) 1985, U.S. Supreme Ct. 1985. Assoc. Weston, Hurd, Fallon, Paisley & Howley, Cleve., 1964-69, ptnr., 1969—; adj. prof. Cleve. Marshall Sch. of Law. Author: Ohio Corporation Law and Practice, 2 vols., Organizing an Ohio Corporation, Business Organizations; editor: Ohio Legal Form. Mem. Fairmount Presbyn. Ch. 1st lt. USAR, 1963-69. Mem. Ohio Bar Assn. (corp. law com. 1969—), Cleve. Bar Assn. (trustee 1978-81), Am. Arbitration Assn. (comml. and securities panel, chmn. regional adv. coun., nat. securities com.). Office: Weston Hurd Fallon Paisley & Howley 2500 Terminal Towers Cleveland OH 44113

BLACKIE, SPENCER DAVID, physical therapist, administrator; b. Endicott, N.Y., Sept. 27, 1946; s. Norman and June (Spencer) B.; m. Bonnie Jean Randall Moulton, June 11, 1967 (div. Apr. 1985); children: Rhonda, Randy, Brenda; m. Sharon Joan Clingman, May 10, 1986; children: Kristen, Sean, Alex. BS, Loma Linda U., 1968; MA, U. So. Calif., 1973; MS, Boston U., 1980. Cert. in manual therapy, clin. specialist in orthop. phys. therapy. Clin. dir. Loma Linda (Calif.) U. Med. Ctr., 1972-74; dir. rehab. svcs. New Eng. Meml. Hosp., Stoneham, Mass., 1974-84, Mt. Carmel Hosp., Colville, Wash., 1984-92, Regina Med. Ctr., Hastings, Minn., 1992—. Mem. Pool Com., Hastings, 1994; chmn. Parks and Recreation Bd., Colville, 1991-92. Capt. U.S. Army, 1969-71. Cmty. Fitness grantee Perrier Mineral Waters, Stoneham, 1978; decorated U.S. Army commendation medal. Mem. Am. Phys. Therapy Assn., Am. Occupational Therapy Assn., Minn. and Wis. Occupational Therapy Assn., Rotary Internat. Seventh-Day Adventist. Office: Regina Med Ctr 1175 Nininger Rd Hastings MN 55033

BLACKMAN, EDWIN JACKSON, software engineer; b. Pulaski, Tenn., Nov. 19, 1947; s. Alley J. and Martha (Williams) B.; m. Nancy Kamin, Mar. 11, 1982 (div. Mar., 1990); m. Michelle Fautz, May 25, 1990. AA, Martin Coll., Pulaski, Tenn., 1972; BS, Tenn. Tech. U., 1974. State auditor State of Tenn., Nashville, 1974-76; internal auditor Firestone Tire & Rubber Co., Akron, Ohio, 1976-79; mgr. internal audit Leewards Creative Crafts, Elgin, Ill., 1979-81; acct. mgr. Mgmt. Sci. Am., Oakbrook, Ill., 1981-85; sales cons. Mgmt. Sci. Am., Oakbrook, 1985-88, sr. mktg. rep., 1988-90; customer svc. mgr. Dun & Bradstreet Software, Columbus, Ohio, 1990-92, acct. exec., 1993-94; sr. application sales rep. Oracle Corp., Columbus, 1994-96; acct. exec. Gt. Plains Software, 1996—. With U.S. Navy, 1966-70, Vietnam. Mem. Moose, Young Ams. for Freedom, Elks, Exchange Club. Methodist. Home: 13824 Bainwick Dr NW Pickerington OH 43147-8722

BLACKMAN, JEANNE A., policy advisor; b. Decatur, Ill., Sept. 23, 1943; d. Robert Russell and Elizabeth Irene (DeWolfe) Shulke; m. Gary L. Blackman, Apr. 16, 1963 (div. Aug. 1983); children: Jeffrey Lynn, Stephanie Sue; m. Bill Weitekamp, Nov. 21, 1995. BS Elem. Edn., Ind. U., 1965; MS in Edn. Adminstrn., Eastern Ill. U., 1979. Cert. tchr. and administr.; lic. real estate salesperson. Elem. tchr. Taylorville (Ill.) Community Sch. Dist., 1965-86; real estate salesperson Craggs-Adams Realtors, Taylorville, 1985-87; adminstrv. asst. to chief of staff Ill. Dept. of Aging, Springfield, 1986-87, consumer adv., 1987-89; lobbyist Ill. Guardianship and Advocacy Commn., Springfield, 1989-95; policy advisor Office of the Atty. Gen., Springfield, Ill., 1995—; pres. Taylorville Edn. Assn., 1983-85; mem. adv. coun. Gov.'s Rehab., Springfield, 1987—; chmn. Springfield Civil Svc. Commn., 1995—. Co-founder, treas. Ill. Vol. Optometry Svcs. to Humanity, Taylorville, 1976—; pres. Capitol City Rep. Women's Club, 1988—; pres. Women in Mgmt., 1989—, pres.-elect, 1990; fundraiser, chairperson Ill. Women's Polit. Caucus, Springfield, 1985—; pres. Am. Field Svc. Student Exch. Program, Taylorville, 1985-87; bd. dirs. LWV Springfield chpt., 1984—; pres. bd. dirs. Mental Health Ctrs. Ctrl. Ill., 1994—; trustee Lincolnland C.C., 1989, vice chair 1992-93, chmn. 93-94; pres. Ill. C.C. Trustees Assn., 1992; mem. Mayor's Commn. Internat. Visitors; chmn. Springfield (Ill.) Civil Svc. Commn., 1995—. Mem. AAUW (edn. chairperson Taylorville chpt. 1985—), DAR, Sister Cities Assn. Springfield, Ill. Women in Govt. (bd. dirs. 1988—, v.p. 1990—), Women's Legis. Network, Ill. Fedn. Rep. Women (v.p., bd. dirs. 1988—, ways and means com. 1987—, world affairs coun. 1990—), Greater Springfield C. of C., Rotary, Delta Delta Delta. Presbyterian. Home: 19 Washington Pl Springfield IL 62702-4634 Office: Office of the Atty Gen 500 S 2nd St Springfield IL 62706

BLACKMAR, CHARLES BLAKEY, state supreme court justice; b. Kansas City, Mo., Apr. 19, 1922; s. Charles Maxwell and Eleanor (Blakey) B.; m. Ellen Day Bonnifield, July 18, 1943 (dec. 1983); children: Charles A. (dec.), Thomas J., Lucy E. Blackmar Alpaugh, Elizabeth S., George B.; m. Jeanne Stephens Lee, Oct. 5, 1984. AB summa cum laude, Princeton U., 1942; JD, U. Mich., 1948; LLD (hon.), St. Louis U., 1991. Bar: Mo. 1948. Pvt. practice law Kansas City; ptnr. Swanson, Midgley, Jones, Blackmar & Eager, and predecessors, 1952-66; profl. lectr. U. Mo. at Kansas City, 1949-58; prof. law St. Louis U., 1966-82, prof. emeritus; judge Supreme Ct. Mo., 1982-89, 1991—, chief justice, 1989-91, sr. status, 1992; spl. asst. atty. gen. Mo., 1969-77, labor arbitrator, active sr. judge, 1992—; chmn. Fair Pub. Accommodations Commn. Kansas City, 1964-66; mem. Commn. Human Rels. Kansas City, 1965-66. Author: (with Volz and others) Missouri Practice, 1953, West's Federal Practice Manual, 1957, 71, (with Devitt) Federal Jury Practice and Instructions, 1970, 3d edit., 1977, (with Devitt, Wolff and O'Malley) 4th edit., 1988-92; contbr. numerous articles on probate and corp. law to profl. publs. Mem. Jackson County Rep. Com., 1952-58; mem. Mo. Rep. Com., 1956-58. 1st lt., inf. AUS, 1943-46. Decorated Silver Star, Purple Heart. Mem. Am. Law Inst., Nat. Acad. Arbitrators, Mo. Bar (spl. lectr. insts.), Disciples Peace Fellowship, Scribes (pres. 1986-87), Order of Coif, Phi Beta Kappa. Mem. Disciples of Christ Ch. Home: 612 Hobbs Rd Jefferson City MO 65109-1075 Office: PO Box 916 Moberly MO 65270-0916

BLACKSTAD, LARRY ROGER, county official; b. Winnebago, Minn., July 13, 1948; s. Milton S. and Geneva C. (Lindquist) B.; m. Rita Eckman, Aug. 26, 1972; children: Erik, Thorin. BS, Mankato State U., 1970, MA, 1975. Campus planner U. Minn., Mpls., 1970-73; planner Hennepin County, Mpls., 1973-75, community devel. mgr., 1975-94; comty. work dir. County of Hennepin, Minn., 1995—; cons. Zack Johnson Assocs., St. Paul, 1976-79, Urbananlysis, Bloomington, Minn., 1987-89. Vice chmn. Metro. Housing Authority, St. Paul, 1988—; chmn. Minnetonka Housing Authority, 1976-83, Minnetonka Park Bd., 1985—, Minnetonka Hopkins Recreation Bd., 1985—; bd. dirs. Ridgedale YMCA, Minnetonka, 1992—. Recipient Scott Howell Plumber award Ridgedale YMCA, Minnetonka, 1992, Nat. Assn. Counties Excellence award 1996; named Leadershp fellow TwinWest C. of C., 1992. Mem. Minn. Recreation and Parks Assn. (sect. chmn. 1992—, Citizen Leadership award 1992), Nat. Assn. County Community Devel. Dirs. (pres. 1985-86, bd. dirs. 1989-90, community and econ. devel. steering com. 1984—). Lutheran. Home: 13409 Preston Rd Minnetonka MN 55305-2726 Office: Hennepin County First Level South Govt Ctr 300 S 6th St Minneapolis MN 55487-0012

BLACKWELL, JOHN, polymers scientist, educator; b. Oughtibridge, Sheffield, Eng., Jan. 15, 1942; came to U.S., 1967; s. Leonard and Vera (Brook) B.; m. Susan Margaret Crawshaw, Aug. 5, 1965; children: Martin Jonathan, Helen Elizabeth. B.Sc. in Chemistry, U. Leeds, Eng., 1963, Ph.D. in Biophysics, 1967. Postdoctoral fellow SUNY-Syracuse Coll. Forestry, 1967-69; vis. asst. prof. Case Western Res. U., Cleve., 1969-70; asst. prof. Case Western Res. U., 1970-74, asso. prof., 1974-77, prof. macromolecular sci., 1977—; chmn. dept., 1985-95; F. Alex Nason prof., 1991—; vis. prof. Kennedy Inst. Rheumatology, London, 1975, Centre National de Recherche Scientifique, Grenoble, France, 1977, U. Frieburg, Fed. Republic Germany, 1982; chmn. Gordon Conf. on Liquid Crystalline Polymers, 1992; cons. in field. Author: (with A.G. Walton) Biopolymers, 1973; mem. editorial bd. Macromolecules, 1989-92; adv. bd. Jour. Macromolecular Sci.-Physics, 1986—; internat. adv. bd. Acta Polymerica, 1992—; contbr. articles to profl. jours. Recipient award for disting. achievement Fiber Soc., 1981, Sr. Scientist award Alexander von Humboldt Found., Max Planck Inst. for Polymer Rsch., Mainz, Fed. Republic Germany, 1991, Rsch. Career Devel. award, 1973-77; grantee NSF, 1970—, NIH, 1970—, Dept. Def., 1976-82. Fellow Am. Phys. Soc. (exec. com. divsn. high polymer physics 1986-90, vice chmn. 1987-88, chmn. 1988-89); mem. Am Chem. Soc., Am. Crystallography Soc. (chmn. fiber diffraction spl. interest group 1993-94), Biophys. Soc. (chmn. biopolymer subgroup 1975-76), Fiber Soc. Episcopalian. Home: 2951 Attleboro Rd Cleveland OH 44120-1815 Office: Case Western Res U Dept Macromolecular Sci Cleveland OH 44106-7202

BLACKWELL, THOMAS T., leadership educator, consultant; b. Jackson, Mich., Aug. 8, 1948; s. Thomas and Maria (Joyner) B. BA, Spring Arbor Coll., 1973; MA, Ea. Mich. U., 1976, Ea. Mich. U., 1978; PhD, Golden State U., 1986. Dept. chair Willow Community, Ypsilanti, Mich., 1973—; instr. Washtenaw C.C., Ypsilanti, 1984—, Wayne County C.C., Taylor, Mich., 1988-89; cons. basketball team Ea. Mich. U., Ypsilanti, 1986—; pres. IMPEL, Ypsilanti, 1978—, chmn. bd. dirs., 1992. Author: Hierarchy of Achievement, 1990, Junior High-Good Grief, 1991, Grow By Thinking Successfully, 1992, The Quest for Certainty, 1992, Increasing your OE, 1993, Restructuring: Methods and Models, 1995. Fundraising chair Meals on Wheels, Ypsilanti, 1990. Mem. Profl. Speakers Assn. Mich. (exec. bd. 1984-88), Mich. Coun. Social Studies (awards chair 1980), Ypsilanti Area Jaycees (leadership chair 1980), Ypsilanti Minority Bus. Owners (human resources com. 1988). Home and Office: IMPEL 1122 Lori St Ypsilanti MI 48198-6294

BLADES, HORATIO BENEDICT (BENNIE BLADES), professional football player; b. Ft. Lauderdale, Fla., Sept. 3, 1966. Student, Miami U., Fla. Safety Detroit Lions, 1988—. Voted to Pro Bowl, 1991; The Sporting News Coll. All-American Team 1986-87, Co-winner Jim Thorpe award, 1987. Office: Detroit Lions 1200 Featherstone Rd Pontiac MI 48342-1938*

BLAESER, KIMBERLY MARIE, English and comparative literature educator; b. Billings, Mont.; d. Anthony Peter and Marlene Dawn (Antell) B.; m. Leonard Joseph Wardzala, Aug. 17, 1985; 1 child, Gavin Leonard. BA, Coll. of St. Benedict, 1977; MA in English, U. Notre Dame, 1982, PhD in English, 1990. Reporter, photographer Thief River Falls (Minn.) Times, 1977-79; teaching fellow U. Notre Dame, Ind., 1981-84; info. systems staff U. Notre Dame, 1983; reporter Daily Courier News, Elgin, Ill., 1986-87; lectr. U. Wis., Milw., 1987-88, instr., 1988-90, asst. prof. English and comparative lit., 1990-94; assoc. prof., 1995—; mem. Native Am. Lit. Prize Com., 1988-91; vis. asst. prof. Am. Studies, U. Notre Dame, Ind., 1990; mem. gov. bd. Native Am. Internat. Prize in Lit., 1991-94. Author: (poetry) Trailing You, 1994; contbr. articles, fiction and poetry to jours. and collections. Bd. dirs. Ind. Indian Relief, Inc., 1983-84; edn. adv. com. Friends of the Fox River, Ill., 1990-92. Recipient Francis C. Allen fellowship Darcy McNickle Ctr. for the History of the Am. Indian, The Newberry Libr., 1985, fellowship Ctr. for Twentieth Century Studies, U. Wis., Milw., 1993-94, Rsch. award Inst. on Race and Ethnicity, U. Wis., 1992, First Book Poetry award Native Writers Cir. of the Ams., 1993; trantee Zahm Rsch. Travel, U. Notre Dame, 1987; George Miller Am. Indian scholar Squaw Valley Cmty. of Writers, 1994. Mem. Am. Studies Assn., Modern Lang. Assn., Assn. Studies in Am. Indian Lit. Home: 2431 Partridge Woods Ct Burlington WI 53105-9098 Office: Univ Wis Milw Dept English PO Box 413 Milwaukee WI 53201-0413

BLAGOJEVICH, ROD R., state legislator. Student, N.W. U., Pepperdine U. Former asst. state atty. Cook County, Ill.; Ill. state rep. Dist. 33; pvt. practice atty. Dem. Cand. for U.U. House 5th Dist. I.L., 1996. Address: 2072 L Stratton Bldg Springfield IL 62706*

BLAIN, ALEXANDER, III, surgeon, educator; b. Detroit, Mar. 9, 1918; s. Alexander William and Ruby (Johnson) B.; m. Josephine Woodbury Bowen, May 3, 1941; children—Helen Bowen, Alexander IV, Bruce Scott Murray, Josephine Johnson; m. Mary E. Mains, 1968. B.A., Wayne U., 1940, M.D., 1943; M.S. in Surgery, U. Mich., 1948. Diplomate Am. Bd. Surgery. House officer, Halsted fellow in surgery Johns Hopkins U., 1943-46; resident surgeon U. Hosp., Ann Arbor, Mich., 1946-50; instr. surgery U. Mich., 1950-57; chief surgeon 14th Field Hosp., Bad Kreuznach, Fed. Republic Germany; clin. assoc. prof. surgery Wayne State U., 1962-87; surgeon-in-chief Alexander Blain Hosp., Detroit, 1953-78; cons. surgeon Highland Park Gen. Hosp, St. Josephs's Hosp., Blain Clinic, Ostego Meml. Hosp., Gaylord, Mich.; med. dir. The Budd Co., 1977-82; staff periop. St. John Hosp., 1988-92; med. cons. bd. 67 adjudication VA, 1990—; pres. Met. Detroit Family Svc. Assn., 1962-63, Detroit Mus. Soc., 1961-62; staff Harper Hosp., Detroit Deaconess Hosp.; surgeon Detroit Urban Indian Health Ctr., 1982-90. Author: (with F.A. Coller) Indications For and Results of Splenectomy, 1950, Prismatic Papers and an Ode, 1968, Prismatic Haiku Poems (Remembered Voices), 1973, (poems) Shu Shu Ga, 2d edit., 1983, Clackshant, 1982; contbr. numerous articles to surg. jours.; editorial bd. Rev. Surgery, 1959-79. Mem. Detroit Zool. Park Commn., 1974-82, pres., 1978-82; trustee Alexander Blain Hosp., 1942-67, Ostego Meml. Hosp. Found., Gaylord, Mich., 1976—; bd. dirs. Detroit Zool. Soc., 1972-75, 82—; pres. W.J. Stapleton Found. Health Edn., 1978-84. Served as lt. M.C., AUS, 1942-44, maj., 1955-57. Recipient Wayne State U. Med. Alumni award, 1968. Fellow ACS, N.Y. Acad. Scis.; mem. Internat. Cardiovascular Soc., F.A. Coller Surg. Soc., Am. Fedn. for Clin. Rsch., Cranbrook Inst. Sci., Soc. Vascular Surgery, Am. Thyroid Assn., Soc. Internat. de Chirugie, Mich. Med. Soc. (chmn. surg. sect. 1963), Assn. Clin. Surgery, Pan-Pacific Surg. Assn., Acad. Am. Poets, Am. Poetry Assn., Mich. Poetry Soc., Acad. of Surgery of Detroit, Coun. of Wayne County Med. Soc., Nu Sigma Nu, Phi Gamma Delta. Clubs: Grosse Pointe (fleet surgeon 1986-89), Otsego, Prismatic (pres. 1967), Detroit Racquet (pres. 1976-80), Cardio-Vascular Surgeons (pres. 1961-62), Acanthus, Waweatonong (pres. 1978), Circumnavigators, Witenagemote. Home: 8 Stratford Pl Grosse Pointe MI 48230-1907 Office: VA 477 Michigan Ave Detroit MI 48226-2523

BLAINE, G. JAMES, III, electronic radiology administrator, educator; b. St. Louis, Oct. 6, 1937; m. Beverly A. Blair, July 1, 1961. BSEE, Washington U., 1959, MSEE, 1961, DSc, 1974. Systems engr. EMR, Sarasota, Fla., 1960-67; rsch. asst. Biomed. Computer Lab. Washington U. Sch. Medicine, St. Louis, 1967-74; asst. dir. Washington U. Sch. Medicine, 1974-80, assoc. dir., 1980-92; mem. tech. staff Hewlett Packard Labs., Palo Alto, Calif., 1984; dir. Electronic Radiology Lab. Washington U. Med. Sch., St. Louis, 1987—. Mem. IEEE (sr.), Tau Beta Pi, Sigma Xi, Eta Kappa Nu. Office: Mallinckrodt Inst Radiology 510 S Kingshighway Saint Louis MO 63110

BLAIR, CLAY C., real estate developer; b. Joplin, Mo., Feb. 22, 1944. BS, U. Kans., 1965, EdD, 1969; MBA, U. Ind., 1966. Pres. Clay Blair Svcs. Assn., Shawnee Mission, Kans., 1966—. Chmn. Nat. Alumni Adv. Bd., Lawrence, Kans., 1991—. Office: 5904 Martway St Shawnee Mission KS 66202-3337

BLAIR, HOWARD S., business executive; b. Chgo., Oct. 28, 1956. BS in Fin. and Acctg., No. Ill. U., 1978. Project mgr. Met. Structures, Chgo., 1981-85; v.p., ptnr. Devel. Resources Inc., Chgo., 1985—; real estate cons. Chgo. Title and Trust Co., 1985—, Chgo. Mercantile Exch., Chgo., 1985—, Stone Container Corp., Chgo., 1985—, Sara-Lee, Chgo., 1985—. Contbr. articles to profl. jours. Office: Devel Resources Inc 439 N Wells St Chicago IL 60610-4512

BLAIR, JOHN RAYMOND, educational psychology educator; b. Brazil, Ind., Oct. 6, 1942; s. Raymond and Fama K. (Rissler) B.; m. Susan M. Blair, June 25, 1977; children: Jason, Alissa, Kelsey. BS, Ind. U., 1964, MS, 1966; PhD, U. Mich., 1970. Cert. counselor in substance abuse, Mich. Psychologist Muscatatuck State Hosp., Butlerville, Ind., 1966; asst. prof. Ea. Mich. U., Ypsilanti, 1970-76, assoc. prof., 1976-82, prof. ednl. psychology, 1982—; vis. scholar U. Mich., Ann Arbor, 1980, 93—, U. Notre Dame, Ind., 1992-96; vis. prof. Ind. U., Bloomington, 1995-96; mem. adv. bd. Ea. Mich. U. Alcohol and Other Drug Program, 1993-95, Inst. for Study of Children and Families, Ypsilanti, 1979-92; bd. dirs. Mich. Coun. on Family Rels., East Lansing, 1979-87. Assoc. editor Family Rels., 1979-86; contbr. articles to profl. jours. Trustee Saugatuck-Douglas (Mich.) Dist. Libr., 1995—. Mem. APA, Midwest Assn. Tchrs. Ednl. Psychology, Mich. Acad. Sci. Arts and Letters (chair psychology sect. 1985-86, instnl. rep. 1986—, vice chair religion sect. 1995-96, co-chair edn. sect. 1996—). Benedictine Oblate. Home: 874 Campbell Rd Saugatuck MI 49453-0748 Office: Ea Mich U 234 Boone Hall Ypsilanti MI 48197

BLAIR, LACHLAN FERGUSON, urban planner, educator; b. Lakewood, Ohio, Sept. 6, 1919; s. Neil Ferguson and Rebecca Henderson (Gunn) B.; m. Mary Anne Novotny, Dec. 12, 1942; children: Douglas MacLachlan, Marilyn Ruth. Student, Cleve. Sch. Arch., Western Res. U., 1936-40; B. City Planning, MIT, 1949. Archtl. designer various firms Cleve., 1940-43; sr. planner Providence City Plan Commn., 1949-51; chief state planning div. R.I. Devel. Council, 1952-56; pres. Blair Assocs., Planning Cons., Providence, Syracuse, N.Y., Washington, 1957-66; assoc. prof. urban planning U. Ill., Urbana, 1966-70; prof. urban and regional planning U. Ill., 1970-88, prof. emeritus urban and regional planning, 1988—; pres. The Urbana Group Inc., planning cons., 1986—; Mem. Ill. Hist. Sites Adv. Council, 1969-77, 1984-86; chmn. Urbana Plan Commn., 1973-80; mem. Champaign County Regional Planning Commn., 1974-86. Editor: Cape Cod 1980, 1962, College Hill: A Demonstration of Historic Area Renewal, 1959, 67, The Distinctive Architecture of Willemstad, 1961. Mem. hon. bd. Landmarks Preservation Coun. Ill., 1989—; governing bd. Ill. Heritage Assn., 1991—, treas., 1994—. Recipient Disting. Ill. Preservationist award Landmarks Preservation Coun. Ill., 1991; EPA Public adminstrn. fellow, 1972-73. Mem. Am. Inst. Cert. Planners (past pres. New Eng. and Ill. chpts., gov.), Am. Planning Assn. (Disting. Profl. Planner award Ill. chpt. 1989), Ptnrs. for Livable Communities, Nat. Trust Hist. Preservation, Preservation Action, Tau Beta Pi. Democrat. Unitarian. Home and Office: 506 W Illinois St Urbana IL 61801-3928

BLAIR, MARGARET BAYLOR (MEG SCHOOLFIELD), emergency nurse; b. Honolulu, May 8, 1959; d. Marvin Smith and Baylor Doris (Hale) Blair; m. Lloyd Michael Schoolfield, May 29, 1982. BA in Lit., U. Nebr., 1981; BSN, Creighton U., 1982; MSN, U. Nebr. Med. Ctr., 1992. Staff nurse telemetry U. Nebr. Med. Ctr., Omaha, 1982-89, staff nurse emergency dept., 1989—, clin. instr. Coll. Nursing, 1995—. Mem. ANA (cert. med./surg.), AACCN, Nebr. Nurses Assn., Emergency Nurses Assn. (cert. emergency nursing), Sigma Theta Tau (Iota Tau chpt.). Democrat.

BLAIR, VIRGINIA ANN, public relations executive; b. Kansas City, Mo., Dec. 20, 1925; d. Paul Lowe and Lou Etta (Cooley) Smith; m. James Leon Grant, Sept. 3, 1943 (dec. July 1944); m. Warden Tannahill Blair, Jr., Nov. 7, 1947; children: Janet, Warden Tannahill, III. BS in Speech, Northwestern U., 1948. Free-lance writer, Chgo., 1959-69; writer, editor Smith, Bucklin & Assocs., Inc., Chgo., 1969-72, account mgr., 1972-79, account supr., 1979-80, dir. pub. relations, 1980-85; pres. GB Pub. Rels., 1985—; judge U.S. Indsl. Film Festival, 1974, 75; instr. Writer's Workshop, Evanston, Ill., 1978; dir. Northwestern U. Libr. Coun., 1978-91, dir. alumnae bd., 1986—, John Evans Club bd., 1990—. Emmy nominee Nat. Acad. TV Arts & Scis., 1963; recipient Service award Northwestern U., 1978, Creative Excellence award U.S. Indsl. Film Festival, 1976, Gold Leaf merit cert. Family Circle mag. and Food Coun. Am., 1977. Mem. Pub. Rels. Soc. Am. (counselors acad.), Am. Advt. Fedn. (lt. gov. Ill. 6th dist.), Women's Advt. Club Chgo. (pres.), Publicity Club Chgo., Nat. Acad. TV Arts & Scis., John Evans Club (bd. dirs.), Woman's Club Evanston (pres.), Zeta Phi Eta (Svc. award 1978, 93), Alpha Gamma Delta, Philanthropic and Ednl. Orgn. (Ill. chpt. pres.. dist. pres.). Author dramas (produced on CBS): Jeanne D'Arc: The Trial, 1961; Cordon of Fear, 1961; Reflection, 1961; If I Should Die, 1963; 3-act children's play: Children of Courage, 1967. Home and Office: 463 Highcrest Dr Wilmette IL 60091-2357

BLAIR, WILLIAM DAVID, mathematics educator; b. Balt., Apr. 20, 1943; s. William Thomas and Frances Thelma (Brooks) B.; m. Kathleen Graves McMullen, June 19, 1965; children: Carla, Stephanie. BA, Johns Hopkins U., Balt., 1965; PhD, U. Md., 1971. Asst. prof. No. Ill. U., DeKalb, 1971-76, assoc. prof., 1976-85, prof., chmn. dept. math. sci., 1985—. Author: (with J.A. Beachy) Abstract Algebra, 1990. Mem. Am. Math. Soc., London Math. Soc., Math. Assn. Am., Sigma Xi. Home: 308 Augusta Ave De Kalb

IL 60115-3109 Office: No Ill U Dept Math Sci Dept Math Sci De Kalb IL 60115

BLAIR, WILLIAM TRAVIS (BUD BLAIR), retired organization executive; b. Canton, Ohio, Dec. 17, 1925; s. George Neely and Helen Irene (Travis) B.; m. Eleanor I. Reid, Mar. 16, 1954; children: Carol Blair Oliver, Timothy R., Anne T. Blair Sisson, Linda Blair Hall. B.A., Ohio Wesleyan U., 1950; grad., Advance Mgmt. Inst. for Assn. Execs., Mich. State U., 1964. Sales rep. Columbus (Ohio) Coated Fabrics, 1950-57; assoc. dir. legis. affairs Ohio C. of C., Columbus, 1958-61, dir. indsl. devel., 1961-77, dir. social legis., 1963-77, dir. legis. affairs, 1973-77, exec. v.p., 1977-80, pres., 1980-87, life dir., 1987—; sec., mem. exec. com. Ohio Med. Indemnity, Inc., Worthington, 1966-79; pres. Gt. Lakes Indsl. Devel. Coun., 1971. Chmn. bd. mgmt. Ctrl. YMCA. Columbus, 1974; bd. trustees Ctr. of Sci. and Industry, 1962—; mem. Gov.'s Adv. Coun. on Internat. Trade, 1970-74, Gov.'s Devel. Adv. Coun., 1977-82, Gov.'s Adv. Coun. on Labor/Mgmt. Cooperation, 1984-87, Gov.'s Trade Mission to China, 1979; exec. dir. Ohio Small Bus. and Entrepreneurship Coun., 1993-94; elder Overbrook Presbyn. Ch., Columbus. With USCG, 1943-46. Mem. Ohio Commodores (charter), Coun. State C. of C. (sec. treas. 1978, vice chmn. 1979, mem. exec. com., chmn. 1980-82), Ohio Trade Assn. Execs. (dir. 1979-82), SAR, C. of C. Execs. of Ohio (dir. 1978), Ohio Wesleyan U. Alumni Assn. (v.p.), Jazz Arts Group (bd. dirs. 1989-92), University Club (bd. dirs. 1980-83, v.p. 1982-83), Columbus Athletic Club, York Golf Club, Rotary, Masons, Phi Mu Alpha, Phi Kappa Psi. Presbyterian (Elder). Home: 138 W Cooke Rd Columbus OH 43214-3022 Office: Ohio State C of C 230 E Town St Columbus OH 43215-0159

BLAKE, DARLENE EVELYN, political worker, consultant, educator, author; b. Rockford, Iowa, Feb. 26, 1947; d. Forest Kenneth and Violet Evelyn (Fisher) Kuhlemeier; m. Joel Franklin Blake, May 1, 1975 (dec. Jan. 1989); 1 child, Alexander Joel. AA, North Iowa Area Community Coll., Mason City, 1967; BS, Mankato (Minn.) State Coll., 1969; MS, Mankato (Minn.) State U., 1975. Cert. profl. tchr., Iowa; registered art therapist. Tchr. Bishop Whipple Sch., Faribault, Minn., 1970-72; art therapist C.B. Wilson Ctr., Faribault, 1972-76, Sedgwick County Dept. Mental Health, Wichita, Kans., 1976-79; cons. Batten, Batten, Hudson & Swab, Des Moines, 1979-81; pres. J.F. Blake Co., Inc., Des Moines, 1990—; polit. cons. to Alexander Haig for Pres., 1987-88; mgmt. tng. specialist Comms. Data Svcs., Inc., Des Moines, 1988-90, exec. mgr. customer svc. spl. interest fulfillment div., 1990-92; mem. nat. adv. bd. Alexander Haig for Pres., 1987-88; cert. cons. assoc. Drake, Beam, Morin, Inc., Des Moines, 1993—. Exhibited in one-woman show at local libr., 1970. Mem. U.S. Selective Svc. Bd. 26 and 27, Polk County, Iowa, 1981—; sustaining mem. Rep. Nat. Com.; Rep. cand. Polk County Treas., Des Moines, 1982; chmn. Polk County Rep. Party, 1985-88; commr. Des Moines Commn. Human Rights and Job Discrimination, 1984-89; mem. Martin Luther King Scholarship Com., 1986-88; mem. Iowa State Bd. Psychology Examiners, 1983-90; mem. 5th Dist. Jud. Nominating Commn., 1990-96. Mem. Am. Art Therapy Assn., Iowa Art Therapy Assn. (pres. elect 1984-85, founder), Des Moines Garden Club (pres. 1984-85), Polk County Rep. Women (pres. elect 1983-85). Lutheran. Home and Office: 3815 SW 30th St Des Moines IA 50321-2050

BLAKE, FRANK BURGAY, librarian, writer; b. N.Y.C., Feb. 10, 1924; s. Francis Gilman and Marguerite (Burgay) B.; B.S., U. Minn., 1947; B.S. in Med. Record Library Sci., St. Louis U., 1948; M.S., N.Y. U., 1951; diploma Air U., 1960; postgrad. Cornell U., N.Y.C., 1962; m. Filomena Yolanda Ciaccio, Dec. 15, 1962; children—Anthony Francis, Robert Burgay. Staff U.S. Army Hosp., Ft. Ord, Calif., 1964-65; med. record librarian County of Tulare, Visalia, Calif., 1966-69, Winnebago (Wis.) Mental Health Inst., 1970-81; preceptor U. Minn. ind. study program in mental health adminstrn., 1977; exec. dir. Medica, Inc., Tulare, Calif., 1968-70. 1968-70; cons. Brown County Mental Health Center, Green Bay, Wis., 1971-76; cons. Med. record program evaluation Herzing Insts., Inc., Milw., 1971-73, Interboro Gen. Hosp., Bklyn., 1949-50; with Kings County Hosp. Ctr., Bklyn., 1949-54, Met. Hosp., N.Y., 1954-55, VA Hosp., N.Y.C., 1956-58, 2500th USAF Hosp., Mitchel AFB, Hempstead, N.Y., 1958-60, St. Francis Hosp., Bronx, N.Y., 1960-63, Rahway (N.J.) Hosp., 1963-64, Bur. Correctional Health Svcs., Madison, Wis., 1981-82, Clovis (Calif.) Meml. Hosp., 1969-70, and many others; mem. med. stenographer program, 1971-72; bd. advisers med. record technician program Moraine Park Tech. Inst., Fond du Lac, Wis., 1974-78, bd. dirs. Oshkosh Com. on Aging, 1988—; sec. Coalition Wis. Aging Groups, 1990-92. Mem. AARP (pres. Winnebago chpt. 450, vice-chmn. Wis. state legislative com., 1993-95, work force cons. 1991-93, health care am. speaker 1993—, award for Health Care Am. Forums, 1993-94, Leadership award 1994, Meritorious Svc. award 1995), Am. Assn. Med. Records Librs., AAAS, Coalition of Wis. Aging Groups (state sec. 1990), Am. Pub. Health Assn., Am. Mgmt. Assn., Internat. Platform Assn., Northeastern Assn. Med. Record Librarians (v.p. 1970-71). Author: Medical Terminology Source Book, 1983; An Instruction Manual for the Problem Oriented Medical Record in Correctional Institutions, 1984. Contbr. articles to profl. jours. Home: 110 Cimarron Ct # B Oshkosh WI 54901-7218 Office: PO Box 1581 Oshkosh WI 54902-1581

BLAKE, GEORGE ROWELL, newspaper executive; b. Chgo., Dec. 4, 1945; s. Robert John and June (Grace) B.; m. Mary Catherine Softcheck, Dec. 27, 1969. BS in Econs., Wheeling Coll., 1967. Reporter Herald News, Joliet, Ill., 1967-73; copy editor Times-Union, Rochester, N.Y., 1973; mng. editor Pacific Daily News, Agana, Guam, 1973-76; corr. Gannett News Service, Washington, 1977; exec. editor News-Press, Fort Myers, Fla., 1977-80; editor, v.p. Cin. Enquirer, 1980-94, v.p. cmty. affairs, 1994—. Bd. dirs. Neediest Kids of All, Cin., Free Store Food Bank, Cin., 1986—, United Food and Clothing Dr., Cin.; mem. Task Force on Minorities in Newspaper Bus. Recipient Disting. Alumni award Wheeling Coll., 1981. Mem. AP Mng. Editors Assn. (bd. dirs. 1980-86), Am. Soc. Newspaper Editors, Coldstream Country Club, Cin. Club, Cin. Athletic Club. Roman Catholic. Office: Cin Enquirer Inc PO Box 141239 Cincinnati OH 45250-1239*

BLAKE, JOHN EMERSON, youth organization administrator; b. Kansas City, Kans., Sept. 30, 1961; s. John Emerson Jr. and Dail Denise (Brown) B.; m. Terri Denise Smith, Apr. 14, 1984; children: Brandon Conner, Benjamin Robert. BS, Baker U., 1983, MBA, 1992. Spl. rep. Overland Park (Kans.) C. of C., 1983; exploring exec. Heart of Am. Coun. Boy Scouts Am., Kansas City, Mo., 1983-85; dist. exec. HOAC Boy Scouts of Am., Kansas City, Mo., 1985, sr. dist. exec., 1988-91, dist. dir., 1991-94; field dir. Sioux Coun. Boy Scouts of Am., Sioux Falls, S.D., 1994-95; field dir. Viking Coun., Mpls., 1995—. Mem. alumni bd. Baker U. Named Outstanding Man of Am. Jaycees, 1984, 85, 88, 92. Mem. Masons, Abdallah Shrine, Delta Tau Delta (chpt. advisor 1985-92, Alumni award 1988, Outstanding Alumni award 1995). Republican. Methodist. Home: 11011 Quebec Ave N Champlin MN 55316 Office: Boy Scouts of Am 5300 Glenwood Minneapolis MN 55422

BLAKE, PHILIP EDWARD, newspaper executive; b. Evanston, Ill., Nov. 7, 1944; s. Thomas Matthew and Louise Frances (Penning) B.; m. Katherine Ward Dower, Sept. 3, 1974; children: Matthew, Edward, Daniel. BA, Brown U., 1966; M in Fin., Northwestern U., 1979. Asst. controller Littelfuse Inc., Des Plaines, Ill., 1975-79; controller Madison (Wis.) Newspapers Inc., 1979-83, gen. mgr., 1983-86; pub. The Missoulian, Missoula, Mont., 1986—; group exec. Lee Enterprises Western Newspapers, 1990-95; pub. Wis. State Jour., 1993—; pres. Madison (Wis.) Newspapers, Inc., 1993—; pres. Audience Info. Measurement Systems, Inc., 1986—; bd. dirs. NAPP Systems Inc., Madison Newspapers Inc. Mem. Future Madison. Served to lt. j.g. USN, 1966-69. Mem. Madison Area C. of C., Madison Repertory Theater. Office: Wis State Jour 1901 Fish Hatchery Rd Madison WI 53713

BLAKE, WILLIAM HENRY, credit and public relations consultant; b. Jasonville, Ind., Feb. 18, 1913; s. Straude and Cora (Pope) B.; m. Helen Elizabeth Platt, Jan. 2, 1937 (dec. Feb. 1990); children: William Henry, Allen Howard. Student, Knox Coll., 1932-35; BS, U. Ill., 1936, MS, 1941, postgrad., 1946; student, NYU, 1950-51, Am. U., 1955-56, 1958; grad., Columbia U. Grad. Sch. Consumer Credit, 1956, Northeastern Inst., Yale U., 1957. Tchr. Champaign (Ill.) Pub. Schs., 1936-41; exec. sec. Ill. Soc. CPAs, Chgo., 1941-44; dean men, assoc. prof. bus. adminstrn. Catawba Coll., 1947-51; dir. rsch. Nat. Consumer Fin. Assn., Washington, 1954-59; exec. v.p. Internat. Consumer Credit Assn., St. Louis, 1959-78; pres. Consumer Trends Inc., also Blake Enterprises, cons., 1978—; cons. Decatur Consumer Credit Assn., 1979-88; adminstr. Soc. Cert. Consumer Credit Execs., 1961-78. Author: Good Things of Life on Credit, 1960, rev., 1975, How to Use Consumer Credit Wisely, 1963, rev., 1975, Home Study Courses in Credit and Collections, 1968, Human Relations, 1969, Communications, 1970, Retail Credit and Collections, rev., 1974, Adminstrative Office Management, 1972, Consumer Credit Management, 1974; pub.: Consumer Trends Newsletter. Mem. pres.'s adv. cabinet Southeastern U.; adviser Office Edn. Assn.; chmn. public relations com. Ill. Heart Assn., 1979-85; bd. dirs. Salvation Army, Decatur, 1979—; mem. fund raising com. Sch. Edn., U. Ill., 1979-84; chmn. bd. trustees Alta Deana div. University City, 1970-73, congressional liaison, 1959-78; trustee Internat. Consumer Credit Assn. Ins. Trust and Retirement Program, 1960-78; mem. Session Westminster Presbyn. Ch., Decatur, 1971-84, fin. con., 1981-84, 89-92. trustee. 1981-84 ; apptd. by mayor to Decatur Aging Adv. Commn., 1991-94. Served to lt. USNR, 1944-47; lt. comdr. 1951-54, ret. Named Man of Yr., Mo. Consumer Credit Assn., 1977; recipient Knox Coll. Scroll of Honor, Knox-Lombard 50 Yr. Club, Galesburg, 1991, Alumni Achievement award Knox Coll., 1994. Mem. Credit Grantors Assn. Can. (bd. dirs. 1959-72), U.S. C. of C. (mem. banking and currency com. 1968-71, mem. trade assn. com. 1964-67), Am. Soc. Assn. Execs. (bd. dirs. 1965-66), Pub. Rels. Soc. Am. (chpt. sec.-treas. 1979-85), Internat. Platform Assn., Washington Trade Assn. Execs., Am. Pub. Rels. Assn. (nat. treas. 1960-61, chpt. pres. 1958-59), U. Ill. Alumni Assn., Press Club St. Louis, Capitol Hill Club (Washington), Exchequer Club (Washington), Rotary (pres. Decatur chpt. 1985-86, Paul Harris fellow 1984), Phi Sigma Kappa. Republican. Home: 5 Edgewood Ct Decatur IL 62522-1860

BLAN, KENNITH WILLIAM, JR., lawyer; b. Detroit, Dec. 15, 1946; s. Kennith William and Sarah Shirley (Shane) B.; 1 child, Noah Winton; m. Lyndy R. Ervin, Sept. 1, 1995. BS, U. Ill., 1968, JD, 1971. Bar: Ill. 1972, U.S. Supreme Ct. 1978. With Office State's Atty., Vermilion County, Ill., 1971-72; atty. Chgo. Title & Trust Co., 1972; assoc. Graham, Meyer, Young, Welsch & Maton, Chgo., Springfield and Danville, Ill., 1972-74; pvt. practice law, Danville, 1975—; spl. asst. atty. gen. Ill., 1974-76; atty. City of Georgetown, Ill., 1985-92, Village of Belgium, Ill., 1987-89, Village of Westville, Ill., 1988-91. Author chpt. to book. Chmn. Vermilion County Young Rep. Club, 1975-77; founding sponsor Civil Justice Found. Mem. Christian Businessmen's Com., Christian Legal Soc. Capt. CAP. Mem. ABA, ATLA, Ill. Bar Assn., Vermilion County Bar Assn., Lawyer-Pilots Bar Assn., Ill. Trial Lawyers Assn. (bd. advocates), Ind. Trial Lawyers Assn., Am. Soc. Law and Medicine, Christian Legal Soc., Gideons Internat., Aircraft Owners and Pilots Assn., Elks. Office: PO Box 1995 Danville IL 61834-1995

BLANCHARD, JAMES ARTHUR, engineer and computer systems specialist; b. Evanston, Ill., Oct. 26, 1949; s. Arthur Knights and Verna Eloise (LeMann) B.; m. Debra Kathleen Smith, July 10, 1976; children: Andrew, Charles, Kenneth. BSCE, Northwestern U., 1972; MBA, U. Chgo., 1987. Registered profl. engr., Ill. Trainee DeLeuw, Cather and Co., Chgo., 1969-72; trainee Chgo. Transit Authority, 1972-74, procedural analyst, 1974-78, supt. capital program support, 1978-90, dir. capital program support, 1990-92, mgr. tech. support, 1992—; mem. Chgo. Area Transp. Study Unified Work Program com., 1981. Bd. dirs. Morton Grove (Ill.) Baseball Assn., 1991—; mem. St. Martha's Parents Assn., Morton Grove, 1985—. Mem. Mensa, Beta Gamma Sigma. Roman Catholic. Office: Chgo Transit Authority PO Box 3555 Chicago IL 60654-0555

BLANCK, LORRAINE THERESA, industrial engineer; b. Jefferson City, Mo., Aug. 4, 1957; d. Bernard Henry and Marcella Regina (Boeckmann) Schwartze; m. Richard Joseph Blanck, Jr., Aug. 31, 1990; children: Richard Joseph III, Joshua Henry. BS in Indsl. Engring., U. Mo., Columbia, 1979, MS in Indsl. Engring., 1984. Indsl. engr. Square D, Columbia, 1979-86, sr. indsl. engr., 1986-87, mfg. engr., 1987-88, cost acct./analyst, 1988-89, indsl. engring. mgr., 1989-90; mktg. fin. analyst Square D, Lexington, Ky., 1990-91; mgr. material svcs. St. Elizabeth Community Health Ctr., Lincoln, Nebr., 1991-93. Vol. St. Teresa's Thrift Shop, Lincoln, 1991-92. Mem. Inst. Indsl. Engrs. (sr., v.p. 1986-87). Roman Catholic. Home: 7015 Rockingham Dr SW Cedar Rapids IA 52404-8007

BLAND, MARY GRAVES, state legislator; b. Kansas City, Mo., Jan. 24, 1936. Student, Ottawa U., Penn Valley Coll., Pioneer C.C., Weaver Sch. Real Estate. Mo. State rep. Dist. 43; community specialist Lan Clearance for Redevel., Kansas City, 1971-79; vice-chmn. human rights and resources com.; free-lance community cons., 1979—; exec. bd. Freedom, Inc. Active Mayor's Neighborhood Coun. on Crime Prevention; mem. S.E. Neighborhood Coalition, U.S. Commn. on Civil Rights; active Niles Home for Children. Home: 6135 Indiana Ave Kansas City MO 64130-4458 Office: Miss State Senate State Capitol Building Jefferson City MO 65101-1556*

BLANK, REBECCA MARGARET, economist; b. Columbia, Mo., Sept. 19, 1955; d. Oscar Vel and Vernie (Backhaus) B.; m. Johannes Kuttner, 1994; 1 child, Emily. BS, U. Minn., 1976; PhD, MIT, 1983. Cons. Data Resources, Inc., Chgo., 1976-79; asst. prof. econs. Princeton U., 1983-89; assoc. prof. econs. Northwestern U., Chgo., 1989-94, prof. econs., 1994—; sr. staff economist Coun. of Econ. Advisors, Washington, 1989-90. Contbr. articles to profl. jours. Vis. Professorships for Women, 1988-89; Sloan Found. fellow, 1982-83; recipient Jr. Faculty Teaching award Princeton U., 1985, David Kershaw award Assn. Pub. Policy Analysis and Mgmt., 1993. Mem. Nat. Bur. Econ. Rsch., Am. Econs. Assn., Assn. of Pub. Policy Analysis and Mgmt., Indsl. Rels. Rsch. Assn. United Ch. of Christ.

BLANKENBURG, PHILLIP B., investment broker; b. Decatur, Ill., June 5, 1940. BSBA, Millikin U., 1962. Registered prin. Project coord. Rand McNally, Decatur, Ill., 1965-66; clk. Taber & Co., Decatur, 1966-70; stockbroker A. G. Edwards & Sons Inc., Champaign, Ill., 1970—. Dir. Kirby Hosp., Monticello, Ill., 1987—; mayor City of Monticello, 1981-89; dir. Red Cross, Piot County, 1992—. With U.S. Army, 1962-65. Republican. Lutheran.

BLANTON, LINDA GAYLE, counselor, former educator; b. Rockford, Ill., Mar. 15, 1940; d. Clyde Martin and Agatha (Happe) Christiansen; m. Paul Edward Blanton, Aug. 6, 1972; 1 child, Diane Renee Hayes; 1 stepchild, Linda Jean DeLawder. BS in Edn./Music Supervision, Wittenberg U., Springfield, Ohio, 1962; MEd, Wright State U., 1968, MS in Mental Health Counseling, 1990. Lic. social worker; lic. profl. counselor; cert. tchr. elem. music; cert. in reading supervision; cert. elem. prin.; nat. cert. counselor. Tchr. elem. music Northmont Schs., Englewood, Ohio, 1962-63; instr. Wittenberg U., 1967-68; elem. tchr. New Carlisle (Ohio) Bethel Local Schs., 1963-69; instr. Wright State U., Dayton, Ohio, 1970-75; supr. fed. edn., tchr. Ohio Vets. Children's Home, Xenia, 1969-86; psychology asst., cognitive specialist Rehab Continuum, Cin., 1990—. Developer elem. materials. Youth leader, fin. sec. First Luth. Ch., Xenia, 1979-89; vol. Greene Meml. Hosp., Xenia, 1986—, Children's Med. Ctr., Dayton, 1990—; CROP organizer Xenia Area Assn. Chs., 1990; active Greater Xenia Habitat for Humanity, 1991—. Recipient Outstanding Paper on Alzheimers Disease, Profl. and Sci. Ohio Conf. on Aging, Ohio Network Ednl. Cons. in the Field of Aging, Ohio Rsch. Coun. on Aging, 1995. Mem. ASCD, ACA, Ohio Mental Health Counselors Assn., Ohio Ret. Tchrs. Assn., Greene County Ret. Tchrs. Assn., Internat. Soc. for Study of Multiple Personality and Dissociation, Ohio Wander Freunde and Xenia Peg Legs (corr. sec. 1989-92, membership chairperson 1991—, v.p. 1992-96, pres. 1996), Ohio Rsch. Coun. on Aging, Miami Valley Counseling Assn., Sigma Alpha Iota (v.p. 1966-67), Delta Kappa Gamma (v.p. 1976-78, pres. 1978-80, sec. 1988-90), Phi Delta Kappa. Lutheran. Home: 92 Kinsey Rd Xenia OH 45385-1537

BLASDEL, BETH L., plant and engineering manager; b. Hamiton, Ohio, Mar. 4, 1965. B, Purdue U., Inpdls., 1989. Registered engr.-in-tng., Ind. Mech. engr. Naval Weapons Support Ctr., Crane, Ind., 1989-90; quality and assembly engr. Cummins Engine Co., Columbus, Ind., 1990; plant mgr. Blasdel Enterprises, Greensburg, Ind., 1991—. Mem. ASME, SAE. Office: Blasdel Enterprises Inc PO Box 260 Greensburg IN 47240-0260

BLASKO, MONICA LEE, investment company executive; b. Mishawaka, Ind., Apr. 2, 1968. Reservationist Jamison Inn, South Bend, Ind., 1989-92; desk mgr. asst. Health & Life Style Ctr., South Bend, 1988-93; asst. fin. cons. Norwest Investment Sch., South Bend, 1992-94; asst. mgr. Merrill Lynch, South Bend, 1994—. Active United Way, South Bend. Roman Catholic. Office: Merrill Lynch 404 S Columbia St PO Box 4013 South Bend IN 46699

BLAU, ANDREW P., project engineer; b. Akron, Ohio, July 19, 1960. BS, Cleve. State U., 1982, MS, 1986. Mech. engr. Gould Inc. OSD, Cleve., 1982-85; design engr. Caterpillar Indsl. Inc., Mentor, Ohio, 1985-90; project engr. MTD Products, Cleve., 1990—. Patentee in field. Past coach ladies softball. Recipient 3rd place award ASME. Mem. SAE.

BLAUSEY, JEANNE MARTHA, accountant, financial systems analyst; b. Toledo, Ohio, Aug. 21, 1958; d. Richard Herman and Dorothy Lucille (Flury) B. A in Bus. Tech. summa cum laude, Tiffin U., 1978; BA summa cum laude, Siena Heights Coll., 1983; MA, George Washington U., 1990. Acct. The Prestolite Co., Toledo, 1978-83, SCA Svcs., Inc., Boston, 1983-84; enlisted USN, 1984, advanced through grades to lt., 1991; data processor USN, Norfolk, Va., 1984-89; systems analyst Electronic Data Systems, Detroit, 1990; plant acct. Prestolite Electric, Inc., Dearborn Heights, Mich., 1990; fin. systems analyst USN, Bethesda, Md., 1991-94; cons. acctg. software Solomon Software, Findlay, Ohio, 1994-95; sys. bus. analyst Omnicare Health Plan, Detroit, 1995—; adj. prof. acctg. Univ. Md., College Park, 1991-92. Lt. USNR, 1996—. Mem. Inst. Mgmt. Accts., Am. Legion, Info. Systems Audit and Control Assn. Republican. Roman Catholic.

BLAUT, JAMES MORRIS, geography educator; b. N.Y.C., Oct. 20, 1927; s. Samuel Joseph and Theresa Ellen (Henschel) B.; m. América Sorrentini, Apr. 2, 1963; 1 child, Gini. PhB, U. Chgo., 1947, BSc, 1950; MSc, La. State U., 1954, PhD, 1958. Instr. U. Malaya, Singapore, 1951-53; instr. Yale U., New Haven, 1956-58, asst. prof., 1958-61; prof., dir. OAS Caribbean Grad. Program U. Puerto Rico, San Juan, 1961-63; rsch. cons. Govt. Venezuela, Ciudad, Guayana, 1963-65; dir. Caribbean Rsch. Inst. Coll. of V.I., St. Thomas, 1964-66; prof. Clark U., Worcester, Mass., 1966-71, U. Ill., Chgo., 1971-96; tech. adv. Planning Bd. UNESCO, OAS, Dominican Rep., 1961-65. Author: The National Question: Decolonizing the Theory of Nationalism, 1987, Fourteen Ninety-Two, 1992, The Colonizers Model of the World, 1993; co-author: Aspectos de la Cuostión Nacional en P.R., 1988. With U.S. Army, 1954-56. Rsch. grantee U.S. Office Edn., Washington, 1966-72, NSF, Washington, 1963, 95. Mem. Assn. Am. Geographers, Nat. Coun. Geog. Edn., Am. Anthrop. Assn. Office: U Ill 1007 W Harrison St Chicago IL 60607-7138

BLAYLOCK, JIM L., gas industry business executive; b. Miami, Okla., Aug. 11, 1947. Grad., high sch., 1965. Owner, originator Blaylock Diesel Svc., Baxter Springs, Kans., 1979—. With U.S. Army, 1966-68, Vietnam. Mem. World Trade Ctr. Republican. Office: Blaylock Diesel Svc Inc 3100 Military Ave Baxter Springs KS 66713

BLECHA, CLARENCE ORVILLE, physical therapist, retired; b. Narka, Kans., June 3, 1917; s. Albert and Maggie Theresa (Sistek) B.; m. Esther Amelia Mintz, Sept. 11, 1947; children: Kathryn Ann Manus, Jane Clare Plumhoff, Kae Lynn. Grad., State Normal Indsl. Coll., Ellendale, N.D., 1949; BS in Phys. Therapy, U. Kans., 1951. Lic. phys. therapist, N.D., Minn.; cert. phys. therapist, Am. Registry Phys. Therapy, Kans. Chief phys. therapist Grand Forks (N.D.) Clinic, 1951-82, St. Michael's Hosp., Grand Forks, 1954-69, Deaconess Hosp., Grand Forks, 1952-55; staff phys. therapist Med. Ctr. Rehab. Ctr., Grand Forks, 1983-84; advisor Dial-a-Ride Svc., Grand Forks, 1987—. Mem. adv. bd. Grand Forks Master Chorale, 1992—; mem., bd. dirs. Grand Forks Symphony, 1989-92. With U.S. Army, 1941-45. Mem. Am. Phys. Therapy Assn. (life, founder, first pres. N.D. chpt. 1953-54, Outstanding Svc. award 1980), 164th Inf. Assn., Sertoma Club (Keith Moon award 1980, Sertoman of Yr. 1976, Outstanding Sec. award 1983, Clarence Blecha Speech and Hearing award named in honor 1992). Republican. Lutheran. Home: 4582 Belmont Rd Grand Forks ND 58201

BLECK, THOMAS FRANK, architect; b. Waukegan, Ill., Aug. 13, 1929; s. Henry Bernard and Edna (Kilbert) B.; m. Virginia Eleanore Pavlik, June 16, 1951; children: Thomas G., James H., Catherine Bleck Muschler, Marilynn Bleck Cobbs, Robert F., Susan M. Gibbs, Linda M. Mai, John W., Charles D. BS in Archtl. Engring., U. Ill., 1951. Lic. architect, Ill., Wis., N.J., Tex., Mass. Pvt. practice architecture Waukegan, 1956—; cons. Six Flaggs Corp., Ocean Spray Cranberries Inc. prin. works include mcpl. bldgs., librs., fire stas., chs., schs. Mem. AIA, Nat. Council Archtl. Registration Bds. Republican. Roman Catholic. Home: 10330 W Yorkhouse Rd Waukegan IL 60087-2402 Office: 1321 Glen Rock Ave Waukegan IL 60085-6231

BLECK, VIRGINIA ELEANORE, illustrator; b. Waukegan, Ill., Dec. 22, 1929; d. George William and Eugenia (Van Honder) Pavlik; m. Thomas Frank Bleck, June 16, 1951; children: Thomas G., James H., Catherine Bleck-Muschler, Marilynn Bleck-Cobbs, Robert F., Susan M. Bleck-Gibbs, Linda Bleck-Mai, John W., Charles D. U. Ill. Art Inst. Chgo., 1947-50, Student, 1947-50. Free lance artist Waukegan, 1950-86; artist Merrill-Chase Galleries, Chgo., 1972-77, Hallmark Cards Inc., Kansas City, Mo., 1977—; owner, operator Bleck Tree Farms, Waukegan, Green Oaks and Grayslake, Ill., 1972—. Republican. Roman Catholic. Home and Office: 10330 W Yorkhouse Rd Waukegan IL 60087-2402

BLEGEN, JOHN CLIFFORD, library administrator; b. Chgo., June 14, 1942; s. Harold S. and Thelma C. (Berge) B.; m. Rachel E. Diamond, Dec. 16, 1967; children: Michael Louis, Theodore Charles. AB, Bowdoin Coll., 1964; PhD, Johns Hopkins U., 1973; MSLS, Cath. U. Am., 1979. Instr. Romance lang. SUNY, Binghamton, 1968-73; reference libr. Enoch Pratt Free Libr., Balt., 1974-79, sr. adminstrv. asst., 1979-82, asst. dir., 1982-88; dir. Glenview (Ill.) Pub. Libr., 1989—; cons. St. Paul Pub. Libr., 1994, Lake Forest (Ill.) Pub. Libr., 1994-95, Cooperative Computer Svcs., Arlington Heights, Ill., 1994-95. Contbr. articles and revs. to profl. jours. Active Glenview Values Project, 1991—, co-chair, 1993-95; bd. dirs. Youth Svcs. Glenview, 1991-92. Mem. ALA, Pub. Libr. Assn. (chair com. 1980—), Info. Futures Inst., Rotary (pres. Glenview club 1994, 96). Office: Glenview Pub Libr 1930 Glenview Rd Glenview IL 60025

BLEIWEIS, JEFFREY I., lawyer; b. Chgo.. BA, Brandeis U., 1975; JD, Boston Coll., 1979. V.p. C.J.A. & Assocs., Chgo., 1994—.

BLESCH, K(ATHY) SUZANN, small business owner; b. Evansville, Ind., Dec. 14, 1951; d. Robert Lee McBride and E. Jean (Oliver) Schumacher; m. Larry J. Blesch, Aug. 17, 1974; children: Nicholas R., Spencer A., Clayton W. Grad. Grad. Realtors Inst., Ind. U., 1979; cert. residential specialist, Nat. Assn. Realtors, 1980. Waitress, hostess Skyway & Pete's, Evansville, Ind., 1971-73; operator, asst. mgr. Stecklers T.A.S., Evansville, 1969-71; salesperson, broker Midwest Realty, Evansville, 1973-78; broker, owner Blesch Realty, Evansville, 1978-80; broker, salesperson Brand Realty, Evansville, 1980-83; owner, operator Nick Nackery Pl., Evansville, 1985—. Bd. dirs. Hope of Evansville, 1976-79. Mem. Nat. Costumers Assn. Home and Office: 201 E Virginia St Evansville IN 47711-5529

BLESSING, LOUIS W., JR., state legislator, lawyer; b. Cin., Oct. 9, 1948; s. Louis W. and Rita (Robers) B.; m. Linda Lameier, 1973; children: Billy, Alex. BBA, U. Cin., 1970; JD, No. Ky. U., 1976. Bar: Ohio. practice law, Cin.; mem. Ohio Ho. of Reps., Columbus, 1983—; common pleas referee Hamilton County, Cin., 1980-82. Trustee Colerain Twp., 1979-82. Named Legislator of Yr., Hamilton County Twp. Assn., 1983, Watchdog of Treasury, 1988, 90. Mem. Cin. Bar Assn., Hamilton County Trustees and Clks. Assn., Phi Kappa Theta. Republican. Home: 3153 McGill Rd Cincinnati OH 45251-3111*

BLETTNER, JAMES DONALD, engineering company executive; b. Indpls., May 8, 1924; s. Joseph Anthony Blettner and Dorothea C. (Daum) Linville; m. Margaret P. Falkenroth, Aug. 22, 1948; 1 child, Dale Thomas. BEE, Purdue U., 1949. Registered profl. engr., Ind. Prodn. engr. Brown Rubber Co., Lafayette, Ind., 1949-52; tooling engr. Brown Rubber Co., Lafayette, 1952-55, head research div., 1955-58; supt. job shop Leaman Machines, Lafayette, 1958-60; pres. Blettner Engring. Co., Fairland, Ind., 1961—. Patentee in field. Elder St. James Luth. Ch., Lafayette, 1983-85. Served with USAF, 1943-46. Republican. Club: Power Squadron Stuart (Fla.). Home: PO Box 155 4719 S Main St Buck Creek IN 47924-9999

BLEVINS, DALE GLENN, agronomy educator; b. Ozark, Mo., Aug. 29, 1943; s. Vernon Henry and Edna Gertrude (Payne) B.; m. Brenda Jo Graves,

Aug. 27, 1967; 1 child, Jeremy. BS in Chemistry, S.W. Mo. State U., 1965; MS in Soils, U. Mo., 1967; PhD in Plant Physiology, U. Ky., 1972. Postdoctoral fellow botany dept. Oreg. State U., Corvallis, Oreg., 1972-74; asst. prof. botany U. Md., College Park, 1974-78; assoc. prof. agronomy dept. U. Mo., Columbia, 1978—, prof. Mem. Am. Soc. Plant Physiology, Am. Soc. Agronomy, Crop Sci. Soc. Am. Office: Univ Mo Dept Agronomy I-87 Agriculture Columbia MO 65211

BLEVINS, JACK LOUIS, hardware and software development consultant; b. Dayton, Ohio, Feb. 27, 1947; m. Susan Ellen Burns, June 7, 1969; 1 child, Melissa Anne. BS, U. Ill., 1970, MSEE, 1971. Design engr. Sangamo Electric, Springfield, Ill., 1968-72; sr. design engr. Sys. Tech. Assocs., Falls Church, Va., 1973-74; sr. programmer McAuto, St. Louis, 1975-78; sys. programmer Monsanto, St. Louis, 1978; mgr. comms. Modcomp, Ft. Lauderdale, Fla., 1979-80; mgr. Unix devel. Gould SEL, Ft. Lauderdale, 1981-83; dir. engring. Ctrl. Data, Champaign, Ill., 1984-89; sr. programmer GCOM, Urbana, Ill., 1989-92; hardware and software devel. cons. Mahomet, Ill., 1992—; software cons. U. Ill. Football, Champaign, 1989—. Columnist Super Micro, 1987-89. Bd. dirs. Mahomet Area Youth Activities Assn., 1993-94. Mem. Lions Club (sec. 1987—). Republican. Christian. Office: PO Box 800 Mahomet IL 61853

BLEY, ANN, program analyst; b. N.Y.C., July 12, 1954; d. Albert Vincent and Autilia (Eliseo) Rizzo; m. Elmer Raymond Bley; 1 child, Shannon Kathryn Bley. BA cum laude, U. Mich., 1976; MBA cum laude, Boston U., 1978. Mgmt. analyst U.S. Army Tank-Auto. Command Force Devel. Div., Warren, Mich., 1979-85; Program, Budget analyst PM Abrams Tank Systems, Warren, Mich., 1985-91; program analyst PM Combat Mobility Sys., PEO, Armored Sys. Modernization, Warren, Mich., 1991—. Contributed to professional publications. Protegee to Dep. Asst. Sec. Plans, Programs, Policy Dept. of Army, 1995-96; registration chair Mich. Women's Vote 96. Mem. Federally Employed women (chpt. pres. 1995-97, Nat. award for compliance activities 1993), Nat. Tng. Program (chair 1985), Am. Soc. Mil. Comptrs., Performance Mgmt. Assn., Beta Gamma Sigma, business honors soc. Home: 31080 Mckinney Dr Franklin MI 48025-1313 Office: US Army Tank Auto Command PM Combat Mobility Veh SFAE-ASM-CV-M Warren MI 48397-5000

BLEY, MARGALO ANNE, social worker; b. Pitts., Mar. 19, 1936; d. James Charles and Dorothy Elizabeth (Laughlin) B.; adopted children: James, Kim, Mindy, Scott, Andrew, Heather. BA, Mich. State U., 1957; MSW, Wayne State U., 1965. Lic. marriage and family therapist. Elem. tchr. Hazel Park (Mich.) Schs., 1957-60, sch. social worker, 1960-64; family social worker Children's Aid and Family Svc., Warren, Mich., 1964-68; sch. social worker Warren Consol. Schs., 1968-71, Charlevoix (Mich.)-Emmet Ind. Sch. Dist., 1971-90; dir., social worker Bay Area Counseling, Harbor Springs, Mich., 1990—; dir., program mgr. Families First, 1991—. Mem. NASW (pres. Macomb County chpt. 1966-68),Mich. Assn. Sch. Social Workers (sec. Region G. 1988-90, Sch.Social Worker of Yr. award 1990), Acad.Cert.Social Workers. Mem. Family of Christ Ch. Home: 162 Misha Mokwa Dr Harbor Springs MI 49740-9417 Office: Bay Area Counseling 8484 M 119 Harbor Springs MI 49740-9595

BLEZNICK, SUSAN RISA, writer, journalist; b. State College, Pa., Aug. 9, 1958; d. Donald W. and Rozlyn (Burakoff) B. Grad. cum laude, Walnut Hills H.S., Cin., 1976; BA, NYU, 1981; MS, Ohio U. B.W. Scripps Sch. Journalism, 1988. Daily newspaper reporter Athens (Ohio) Messenger, 1988; newspaper reporter Sandusky (Ohio) Reporter, 1988-89; news editor, editorial asst. McGraw-Hill Archtl. Record Mag., N.Y.C., 1989-91; writer WGTE Pub. TV, Toledo, 1991-93; exec. editor Montage Mag., Toledo, 1993; TV series project dir. Bowling Green (Ohio) State U./WBGU-TV, 1994-95; writer self-employed, Toledo, 1991—; pub. rels. cons. Toledo Bar Assn., 1993-94, writer for electronic and print media, video script writer. Author: Media Coverage of Jackson Pollock, An Abstract Expressionist Painter, 1988 (Ohio U. masters thesis); contbr. articles to nat. and regional mags., alumni mags.: U. Mich., NYU, Ohio U., Bowling Green State U.; newspapers: Ann Arbor (Mich.) News, The Post, Cin.; also newsletters for Toledo C. of C., Toledo Bar Assn., WGTE pub. TV. Vol. TV WBGU, 1993, Fox, 1996, Toledo. Recipient Crystal Award Women in Comms., 1993. Mem. Kappa Tau Alpha. Home: 1954 Princeton Dr Toledo OH 43614

BLICKENSDERFER, PETER WILLIAM, analytical chemist, retired chemistry educator; b. Cin., Nov. 28, 1932; s. Robert and Mildred (Schmalhorst) B.; m. Mary Virginia Scott, June 9, 1956; children: Sally Ann, Mary Jo, Lynn Allis, Elizabeth Lea. BA, Coll. of Wooster, 1954; PhD, U. Mo., 1963. Instr. U. Mo., Rolla, 1961-62; assoc. rsch. chemist Whirlpool Corp., St. Joseph, Mich., 1962-65; asst. prof. chemistry U. Wis., Kenosha, 1965-66; assoc. prof. chemistry Kearney (Nebr.) State Coll., 1966-70; sr. rsch. scientist Whirlpool Corp., Benton Harbor, Mich., 1970-71; assoc. prof. chemistry U. Nebr., Kearney, 1971-75, chmn. dept. chemistry, 1972-75, 87-91, prof. chemistry, 1976-95; owner, mgr. Platte Valley Testing Lab., Kearney, 1972-78; mgr. Kearney State Coll. Analytical Svc. Lab., 1978-95. Local leader Amnesty Internat., Kearney, 1988—. With U.S. Army, 1954-56. Mem. Am. Chem. Soc., Sigma Xi. Home: 1202 W 31st St Kearney NE 68847-3367

BLIEK, ELDON MAURICE, real estate company officer, consultant; b. Wisconsin Rapids, Wis., Nov. 25, 1945; s. Martin Jacob and Tena (Anema) B.; m. Marilyn Yff, Aug. 16, 1969 (div. June 1982); children: Bradley, Gregory, Bryan; m. Alice Luretta. BS, U. Wis., 1966; BA, Calvin Coll., 1968; MBA, Western Mich. U., 1973. Cert. state appraiser Mich. Instr. Calvin Coll., Grand Rapids, Mich., 1968-72; asst. controller Ore Ida Foods, Boise, Idaho, 1972-74; dir. adminstrn. Pine Rest Hosp., Grand Rapids, 1974-80; mgr. C/I Divsn. Greenridge Realty, Grand Rapids, 1980-86; pres. Westdale Comml. Indsl. Co., Grand Rapids, 1986-89; v.p., owner Prime Devel. Co., Grand Rapids, 1989—; pres. Pinnacle Real Estate Mgmt. Co., 1995—; sr. instr. Comml. Indsl. Real Estate Inst., Chgo., 1987—. Contbr. articles to profl. jours. Bd. dirs., sec. Kentwood (Mich.) Econ. Devel. Corp., 1984; bd. dirs., pres. Cascade Thornapple Assn., 1986-89; bd. dirs. Grand Rapids Opportunity Indsl. Ctr., 1978-80; mem. Gerald R. Ford Mus. Com., Grand Rapids, 1981. Fellow Soc. Disting. Real Estate Profls.; mem. Comml. Indsl. Real Estate Inst., Nat. Assn. Realtors (spl. achievement award 1981-86), Mich. Assn. Realtors (chmn.-elect comml. indsl. group 1993, chmn. 1994), Grand Rapids C. of C. (Leadership award 1983), Wyoming C. of C., Realtors Polit. Action Com. (life), Island Club of Hilton Head (bd. dirs., treas. 1990-94), Hilton Head Yacht Club. Republican. Mem. Reformed Ch. Am. Office: Prime Devel Co 660 Cascade West Pky SE Grand Rapids MI 49546-2147

BLIM, RICHARD DON, pediatrician; b. Kansas City, Mo., Nov. 8, 1927; s. Miles G. and Latha Mae (Daniels) B.; m. Myrle Rae Blim, Apr. 12, 1952; children: Richard David, Carol Rae, John Miles. B.A., U. Kans., 1949, M.D., 1953. Diplomate: Am. Bd. Pediatrics. Intern U. Kans., 1953-54, resident in pediatrics, 1954-56; practice medicine specializing in pediatrics; pres. Pediatric Assocs., Kansas City, Mo., 1956-89; dir. med. affairs St. Lukes Hosp., Kansas City, 1989—; Peter T. Bohan lectr. U. Kans., Kansas City, 1978; Max Seham lectr. U. Minn., Mpls., 1982; mem. editorial bd. Mo. Medicine, 1978-92, Pediatric Annals, 1982-92, Pediatric News, 1983-92. Bd. dirs. Marillac Spl. Sch. for Children, 1976-79 . Served to sgt. U.S. Army, 1946-48, PTO. Named Outstanding Med. Alumnus U. Kans. Sch. Medicine, 1978; recipient Clifford G. Grulee award, 1984. Fellow Am. Acad. Pediatrics (pres. 1980-81, exec. bd. 1973-80, chmn. Mo. chpt. 1964-67); mem. AMA, Inst. Medicine of NAS, Jackson County Med. Soc. (pres. 1976), S.W. Pediatric Assn. (pres. Kansas City 1963), Mo. Med. Assn., Coun. Med. Specialties Soc. (rep., exec. bd. 1974-80), Kans. U. Med. Alumni (pres. 1973), Loch Lloyd Club, Alpha Omega Alpha. Republican. Presbyterian. Home: 304 W 172d St Belton MO 64012-9758 Office: St Lukes Hosp 44th Wornall Kansas City MO 64111

BLISS, GEORGE N., chief engineer; b. Jamaica Plain, Mass., Mar. 16, 1922. BA, Cornell U., 1942. Chief engr. Diamond Automation, Farmington, Mich., 1956—; Inventor both elec. and mech. patents. Mem. Amateur Theater Group. Home: 7455 Franklin Ct Bloomfield Hills MI 48301-3564 Office: Diamond Automation 23400 Haggerty Rd Farmington MI 48335-2613

BLITT, RITA LEA, artist; b. Kansas City, Mo., Sept. 7, 1931; d. Herman Stanley and Dorothy Edith (Sofnas) Copaken; m. Irwin Joseph Blitt, Apr. 18, 1951; 1 child, Chela Connie. Student, U. Ill., 1948-50; BA, Kansas City U., 1952; postgrad., Kansas City Art Inst., 1952-54. Freelance painter, sculptor Leawood, Kans., 1958—. One-woman exhbns. include Unitarian Gallery, Kansas City, Mo., 1965, Spectrum Gallery, N.Y.C., 1969, Angerer Gallery, Kansas City, Mo., 1974, Battle Creek (Mich.) Civic Art Ctr., 1975, Harkness Gallery, N.Y.C., 1977, Martin Schweig Gallery, St. Louis, 1977, Gargoyle Gallery, Aspen, Colo., 1978, Tumbling Waters Mus., Montgomery, Ala., 1978, St. Louis U., 1980, Leedy-Voulkos Gallery, Kansas City, Mo., 1987, Joy Horwich Gallery, Chgo., 1987, Goldman Gallery, Haifa, Israel, 1989, Bet Shmuel, Jerusalem, 1989, Goldman Kraft Gallery, Chgo., 1990, Singapore Nat. Mus., 1991, Albrecht-Kemper Mus., St. Joseph, Mo., 1991, Aspen (Colo.) Inst., 1992, Foothills Art Ctr., Golden, Colo., 1992, Mackey Gallery, Denver, 1992, U. Ill., Urbana, 1994, Kennedy Mus.-U. Ohio, Athens, 1994, Krasl Art Ctr., St. Joseph, Mich., 1994, Baker U., Baldwin, Kans., 1995, Ctrl. Exch., Kansas City, Mo., 1995, Atchison (Kans.) Muchnik Gallery, 1996; group exhbns. include Kansas City (Mo.) Mus., 1959, Ringling Mus., Sarasota, Fla., 1967, Springfield (Mo.) Mus., 1967, Joslyn Mus., Omaha, 1972, Doug Drake Gallery, Kansas City, 1975, Conry Gallery, Kansas City, Mo., 1976, Cyvia Gallery, New Haven, 1977, Gargoyle Gallery, Aspen, Colo., 1979, Putney Gallery, Aspen, 1979, Carrefour Gallery, N.Y.C., 1979, Elaine Benson Gallery, Bridgehampton, N.Y., 1980, Tall Grass Fine Arts Gallery, Kansas City, Mo., 1980, 81, Art and Design Gallery, N.Y.C., 1982, Winter Manhattan (Kans.), Streker, Gallery, 1983, Joanne Lyons Gallery, Aspen, 1984, Banaker Gallery, 1987, 88, Andrea Ross Gallery, Santa Monica, Calif., 1990, LA 90, L.A., 1990, Eva Cohon, Chgo., 1995, Obere Galerie, Berlin, 1995, Din Deutsches Inst., Berlin, 1995, many others; permanent collections include Albrecht-Kemper Mus., St. Joseph, Mo., Ga. Inst. Tech., JFK Libr., Cambridge, Mass., Kennedy Mus. Ohio U., Athens, Nat. Mus. Singapore, Skirball Mus., L.A., Spertus Mus., Chgo., Kansas City (Mo.) Children's Mus., Kennedy Mus., Ohio U., Ga. Tech. Ctr. for the Arts, and other numerous pvt. and pub. collections; sculptures in numerous pub. places. Mem. Soc. Fellow The Nelson Gallery Found., The Aspen Inst.; bd. dirs. Trio Found.; mem. The Stop Violence Coalition. Mem. Internat. Sculpture Ctr., Kansas City Artists Coalition. Office: 8900 State Line Rd Ste 333 Leawood KS 66206-1936

BLOCH, ANDREA LYNN, physical therapist; b. Cleve., Nov. 25, 1952; d. Sanford and Nadalane Lee (Benchell) B. BA in Zoology, Miami U., Oxford, Ohio, 1974; MA in Allied Health Scis., Kent State U., 1975; Cert. in Phys. Therapy, Ohio State U., 1977. Lic. phys. therapist, Ohio; bd. cert. orthopedic clin. specialist. Asst. dir. phys. therapy The Mt. Sinai Med. Ctr., Cleve., 1977-86; dir. rehab. therapy svcs. Marymount Hosp., Garfield Heights, Ohio, 1986-88; pres., owner Bloch Phys. Therapy, Inc., University Heights, Ohio, 1988—; speaker Arthritis Found.; speaker in field; mem. Ohio Occupl. Therapy, Phys. Therapy and Athletic Trainers Bd., 1994—. Editor newsletter Cleve. Phys. Therapy Orthopedic Study Group, 1989-91; contbr. articles to profl. jours. Chmn. essay-poster contest University Heights Meml. Day Parade, 1985-91; mem. coun.-at-large City of University Heights. Mem. AAPHERD, NAFE, Am. Phys. Therapy Assn. (reimbursement chmn. N.E. dist. Ohio 1992—), Am. Back Soc., Am. Soc. Profl. and Exec. Women, Ohio Phys. Therapy Assn., Delta Zeta Eastside Alumnae (program chmn. 1985-87, ways and means com. 1987-88, v.p. 1988-90, pres. 1990-92), Delta Zeta Province Alumnae (bd. dirs. Ohio V-N 1991-94, Outstanding Province V Alumna award 1992), Eta Sigma Gamma. Office: 2195 Warrensville Center Rd University Heights OH 44118-3155

BLOCH, ANTHONY MICHAEL, mathematician, educator; b. Johannesburg, Republic South Africa, Feb. 28, 1955; s. Harry and Mary Elizabeth (Gotlop) B.; m. Sheila Janet Hurwitz, Dec. 30, 1984; 1 child, Mitchell Keith. BS with honors, U. Witwatersrand, Johannesburg, 1978; MS, Calif. Inst. Tech., 1979; M of Philosophy, Cambridge U., England, 1981; PhD, Harvard U., 1985. Teaching fellow Harvard U., Cambridge, Mass., 1982-84; T.H. Hildebrandt research asst. prof. math. U. Mich., Ann Arbor, 1985-88; research fellow Math Sci. Inst. Cornell U., Ithaca, N.Y., 1988-89; asst. prof. math. Ohio State U., Columbus, 1988-92, assoc. prof. math., 1992-95; assoc. prof. math. U. Mich., Ann Arbor, 1994—. Contbr. articles to scholarly jours. Recipient Presdl. Young Investigator award, 1991; NSF grantee, 1987—; Guggenheim fellow, 1996-97. Mem. IEEE, Am. Math. Soc., Soc. Indsl. and Applied Math.

BLOCK, ALLAN JAMES, communications executive; b. Oct. 1, 1954; s. Paul Jr. and Marjorie (McNab) B. BA, U. Pa., 1977. Coord. electronic tech. planning Toledo Blade Co., 1981-83, dir. electronic planning, 1984-85; dir. mktg. Buckeye Cablevision Inc., Toledo, 1985-87; v.p. cablevision and TV Blade Communications, Inc., Toledo, 1987-88, exec. v.p., 1989, mem., chief exec. com., co-CEO, 1989—, vice chmn. bd., 1990—; pres. Blade Cablevision Co., 1987—, Blade Broadcasting Co., 1987—; bd. dirs. Toledo Blade Co., Blade Communications, Inc., P.G. Pub. Co., other cable and broadcasting cos. Bd. dirs. C-SPAN, 1991—; trustee Med. Coll. Ohio, 1991—. Mem. Toledo Club, Met. Club (N.Y.C.), Penn Club (N.Y.C.). Home: 2200 Scottwood Ave Toledo OH 43620-1101 Office: Blade Communications Inc 541 N Superior St Toledo OH 43660-1000

BLOCK, CAROLYN REBECCA, criminologist, researcher; b. Columbus, Ohio, July 8, 1943; d. Charles Hamilton and Marjorie Kraft (Morrison) Britt; m. Richard L. Block, June 30, 1966; children: Daniel, Devora. BA, Ohio State U., 1965; MA, U. Chgo., 1968, PhD, 1975. Lectr. Loyola U., Chgo., 1968-77; cons. Ministry Justice, The Netherlands, 1985-86; sr. rsch. analyst Ill. Criminal Justice Info. Authority, Chgo., 1976—; co-founder, coord. Homicide Rsch. Working Group, 1991—. Author: Homicide in Chicago, 1987, Initiation and Continuation of a Criminal Career in the Netherlands, 1991; editor: (3 vols.) Questions and Answers in Letal and Nonlethal Violence, 1993, 94, 95, Crime Analysis Through Computer Mapping, 1995; developer software STAC (Spatial and Temporal Analysis of Crime), TSPAT (Time Series Pattern Description); contbr. articles to profl. jours. Mem. Needs Assessment Com. United Way Chgo., 1988-94; mem. planning com. Chgo. Assembly Cook County, 1992-93. Recipient Excellence in Analysis award Justice, Rsch., and Stats. Assn., 1986, Hans Mattick award for outstanding contbns. to rsch. in criminology Ill. Acad. Criminology, 1990. Mem. Am. Soc. Criminology (program planning com. 1984, 92). Office: Ill Criminal Justice Info Authority 120 S Riverside Plz Chicago IL 60606-3913

BLOCK, MARYLAINE, librarian; b. Wichita, Kans., Nov. 8, 1943; d. Scott Clark and Merle (Ewan) Bagby; m. Robert Paul Block, Aug. 27, 1966 (div. 1982); 1 child, Brian Friedrichsen. BS in English Edn., Northwestern U., 1965; MA in Am. Civilization, U. Iowa, 1968, MA in Libr. Sci., 1977. Ref. libr. St. Ambrose Coll., Davenport, Iowa, 1977-79; assoc. dir. McMullen Libr. St. Ambrose Coll. (now St. Ambrose U.), Davenport, Iowa, 1979—. Reviewer Libr. Jour., 1981—; co-author: 20th Century Romance and Gothic Writers, 1982; columnist (internet) My Word's Worth, BookBytes, Web Site: Where the Wild Things Are, Librarians Guide to the Best Information on the Net. Democrat. Office: St Ambrose Univ Libr 518 W Locust St Davenport IA 52803-2829

BLOCK, WILLIAM K., JR., newspaper executive; b. New Haven, Nov. 28, 1944; s. William and Maxine (Horton) B.; m. Carol Pauline Zurheide, Aug. 1, 1970; children: Diana, Nancy, Katherine. BA, Trinity Coll., Hartford, Conn., 1967; JD, Washington and Lee U., 1972. Bar: Pa., U.S. Supreme Ct. Staff mem. Red Bank (N.J.) Register and Toledo Blade, 1972-77; advtg. mgr. Red Bank (N.J.) Register, Shrewsbury, N.J., 1977-79, sales mgr., 1979-80; Red Bank (N.J.) Register; dir. ops. Toledo Blade Co., 1983-84, v.p. ops., 1984-86, v.p., gen. mgr., 1986-87, pres., 1987—, co-pub., 1990—; co-pub. Pitts. Post Gazette, 1990—; v.p. Blade Communications, Inc., Toledo, 1987-88, pres., 1989—. V.p. Toledo Sesquicentennial Commn., 1986-87; bd. dirs. Toledo Mus. Art, Toledo Symphony, Maumee Valley Hist. Soc., Ohio Newspaper Assn., Inland Press Assn.; pres. Read for Literacy, Inc. With U.S. Army, 1968-70, Vietnam. Mem. Toledo Country Club, Toledo Club. Office: Blade Communications Inc 541 N Superior St Toledo OH 43660-1000

BLOCKINGER, JAMES ANSON, superintendent of schools; b. Ravenna, Ohio, Apr. 7, 1945; s. Robert John and Florence (McCully) B.; m. Johanna Mary Phillips, June 27, 1970; children: Todd Andrew, Beth Ann, James Fitzgerald. BA, Kent State U., 1968, MEd, 1971; Ed.S., No. Ill. U., 1986, EdD, 1990. Cert. gen. adminstrv. (supt.'s endorsement), Ill. Tchr. Crestwood Schs., Mantua, Ohio, 1968-72, Work Experience/Career Exploration program coord., 1972-73; Work Experience/Career Exploration program coord. Nordonia Hills Sch. Dist., Northfield, Ohio, 1973-74, asst. prin., 1974-77; dean of students Zion-Benton High Sch. Dist. # 126, Zion, Ill., 1978-82; prin. Alden-Hebron Dist. 19, Hebron, Ill., 1982-87, McHenry (Ill.) Elem. Dist. 15, 1987-89; supt. Millburn C.C. Sch. Dist., Wadsworth, Ill., 1989-95, Morton Grove (Ill.) Sch. Dist. 70, 1995—; trainer Ill. Adminstrs.' Acad., Grayslake, 1991-95, assoc. mem., 1988; presenter Ill. Prins. Assn., St. Charles, 1990, instrnl. leader, 1989; presenter N. Ill. U. Soc. Edn. Adminstrs., DeKalb, 1990. Contbr. articles to profl. jours. Organist Bethel Luth. Ch., Gurnee, Ill., 1991—. Mem. ASCD, Ill. Assn. Sch. Adminstrs., McHenry County Curriculum Coun. (pres. 1985-87), Supts. Roundtable Study Club of No. Ill. Home: 4814 Dorothy Ct Waukegan IL 60087-1866 Office: Morton Grove Dist 70 6200 W Lake St Morton Grove IL 60053

BLOEMER, ROSEMARY CELESTE, bookkeeper; b. St. Louis, Jan. 26, 1930; d. Edward J. and Leslie F. (McCreary) Walsh; m. Edward H. Bloemer, Sept. 4, 1948; children: Stephen, Diane, Janet. Cert. in court reporting, Bayside Coll., San Francisco, 1948; student, U. Mo., St. Louis, 1949-51, 83. Teller Roosevelt Savs. & Loan, 1967; income tax sec. Boatmen's Nat. Bank, St. Louis, 1968-73; sec. psychology dept. Washington U., St. Louis, 1978; beverages contr. Chase-Park Plaza Hotel, St. Louis, 1977-81; owner Bloemer Tax Svc., St. Louis, 1975—; legal sec. Lickhalter Law Office, St. Louis, 1970-88, Law Office of James K. Steitz, St. Louis, 1981-83; bookkeeper, tax advisor Mo. Hwy. Patrol Assn., Inc., St. Louis, 1981-83; bookkeeper, tax acct. Mo. State Hwy. Patrol Civilian Employees Assn., St. Louis, 1983-92; acct. Clarion Hotel, St. Louis, 1986, Bel-Air Hilton Inn, St. Louis, 1984-85; consignment standard stock machine screws, contr. accounts receivable Consol. Aluminum Co., 1973-75; sec. to 5 fin. specialists Cmty. Devel. Agy., St. Louis, 1980-81; tax preparer H&R Block, 1991-95; mem. team of reporters Price Waterhouse, 1990-96. Arbitrator, shopper, speaker Better Bus. Bur. St. Louis, 1980—; sec. to pres. Bd. Higher Edn., Christian Ch., 1975-77; vol. in choir Shrine of St. Joseph, St. Louis. Mem. Nat. Soc. Tax Profls., Nat. Assn. Tax Practitioners, Am. Soc. Notaries; Internat. Platform Assn. Roman Catholic. Home and Office: 1435 Trampe Ave Saint Louis MO 63138-2541

BLOMBERG, GORAN ERNST DANIEL, biologist; b. Tidaholm, Sweden, July 27, 1941; came to U.S., 1952; s. Ernst Harald Natan and Karin Josefina (Åsberg) B. BS, U. Minn., St. Paul, 1965; MS, Colo. State U., 1969; PhD, Mich. State U., 1990. Forester's aide No. Forest Inventory Div., Stockholm, 1962; lab. tech. asst. U. Minn., Mpls., 1965; biol. technician U.S. Fish and Wildlife Svc., Denver, 1969-71; crocodile biologist Peace Corps, Gaborone, Botswana, 1974-76; grad. teaching asst. Mich. State U., East Lansing, 1977-79; instr. biology Lansing (Mich.) Community Coll., 1979-87, tutor in biology, 1987-94, lab. technician, 1995—. Asst. mng. editor The Jack-Pine Warbler, 1987-90; contbr. The Atlas of Breeding Birds of Michigan, 1991, also articles to sci. jours., 10 book revs. Head children's nature program Capitol Area Audubon Soc., Lansing, 1981-93. Recipient faculty publ. recognition cert. Lansing Community Coll., 1989, 90. Mem. World Wildlife Fund, Wildlife Soc. (charter Mich. chpt.), Nature Conservancy, Nat. Audubon Soc. (Mich. chpt. bd. dirs. 1986-92). Pentecostal.

BLOMQUIST-STANBERY, RUTH ELLEN, computer services company owner, elementary education educator; b. Chgo., Feb. 12, 1949; d. Roy Theodore Sr. and Ruth Theresa (Johnson) Blomquist; m. Donald Loran Stanbery, Aug. 16, 1985; children: Elyn Nicole Blomquist, Dena Terese Blomquist, Lukas Brock Theodor Stanbery. BA, Elmhurst (Ill.) Coll., 1979; MA, No. Ill. U.; postgrad., Nat. Coll. Edn., Evanston, Ill. Sec., real estate and comml. mortgage First Nat. Bank of Chgo., 1972-73; substitute tchr. DuPage County (Ill.) Schs., 1979-82; tchr., adminstr. DuPage Alt. Elem. Sch., Downers Grove, Ill., 1979-82; with Jewel Foods, Lombard, Ill., 1982-83; office and factory worker Frank's Office Svcs., St. Charles, Ill., 1984-85; in sales and distbn. Homes Mag., Downers Grove, 1987-88; youth counselor Job Tng. Partnership Act, Ogle County, Rochelle, Ill., 1990; in prodn. Del Monte Corp., DeKalb, Ill., 1985-91; on-line prodn. coord. and facilitator The Suter Co., Sycamore, Ill., 1991-93; owner, CEO Stanbery Computer Svcs., Rochelle, Ill., 1994—. Contbr. articles to profl. jours. Mem. AAUW, ASCD, Ill. Edn. Assn., Nat. Coun. Tchrs. English, Order Ea. Star, Job's Daus., Phi Delta Kappa, Omicron Delta Kappa, Kappa Delta Epsilon. Congregationalist. Home: PO Box 55 Malta IL 60150-0055 Office: Stanbery Computer Svcs 508 N 2d St Box 546 Rochelle IL 61068

BLOOM, DAVID L., tool and die designer; b. South Bend, Ind., May 31, 1960; s. Leo William and Deloras (Wawrzynsczk) B. AS in Die Design, Acme Inst. Tech., 1988. Plant mgr., tool and die designer Contour Tool & Die Inc., South Bend, 1978—. Mem. Soc. Mech. Engrs. Roman Catholic. Office: Contour Tool & Die Inc 416 W Calvert St South Bend IN 46613-2104

BLOOM, ERIC ANDREW, financial services company executive; b. Chgo., Feb. 8, 1965; s. Philip Martin and Sybil Joy (Stone) B.; m. Donna Marie Meyer, Nov. 24, 1991; 1 child, Ryan Alexander. BA in Econs., Ind. U., 1987. Ind. trader Chgo. Merc. Exch., 1987-88; v.p. Sentinel Mgmt. Group, Chgo., 1988-92, pres., CEO, 1992—. Mem. Managed Futures Assn. (mem. audit com. 1995—, membership com.), European Managed Futures Assn. Republican. Jewish. Office: Sentinel Mgmt Group Inc 10 S Riverside Plz 21st Fl Chicago IL 60606

BLOOM, JAMES EDWARD, commodity trading and financial executive; b. Milw., Aug. 24, 1941; s. Edward Harry and Clarina Louise (Hoppe) B. Cert. in radiology tech., Columbia Hosp., 1963; AA in Edn. with honors, Milw. Area Tech. Coll., 1964; BBA in Sales and Mktg. with honors, Concordia U., 1968, BBA in Bus. Mgmt. with honors, 1968; postgrad., Marquette U., 1969-72. Radiologic technologist Columbia Hosp., Milw., 1963-69; asst. adminstr. Bel Air Convalescent Ctr., Inc., Milw., 1969-70; asst. mktg. mgr. Champion Internat. Inc., Milw., 1970-72, human resources mgr., safety and tng. dir., 1972-75; corp. dir. indsl. rels. Weyenburg Shoe Mfg. Co., Milw., 1975; gen. mgr. Aqua Spray, Inc., Milw., 1976; mgmt. cons. Bloom & Assocs., Milw., 1976—; pres. M.F.C., Milw., 1985—; internat. agt. Superior Coffee and Foods divsn. Sara Lee Corp., Milw., 1991—; internat. and U.S. rep. Al-Sabah Internat., Safat, Kuwait, 1992—; internat. agt. Moti Enterprises Internat., 1992—, Protea Diamond Corp. (site holders: DeBeers Cons. Mines), 1992—; internat. disting. agent Al-Ewan Med. Establishment, 1993—, Kingdom Saudi Arabia, 1993—, Pharmacal, 1993, Hovercraft Am., 1993—, Mico Farms, Malaysia, 1993—, Steenberg Homes, 1994—, Lemke Seed Farms, Inc., 1994—, Xiangtan Fgn. Econ. Rels. and Trade Corp. China, 1994—, Greg Orchards and Produce, Inc., 1994—, Heileman Brewing Co., 1994—, Holsum Foods, 1994—, Manipal Printers and Pubs. Ltd., India, 1994—; Portea site holder DeBeers Mines Ltd, ComDisco, Inc., 1993—; internat. Distbn. agent Polfa Tarchomin, S.A., Poland, B.B.M. Internat. S.A., De C.V., Mexico, 1995—, Valezzi, S.A. De C.V., Mexico, 1996; guest lectr. mgmt. Milw. Area Tech. Coll., 1974-75, Marquette U., Milw., 1975, U. Milw.-Wis., 1975; advisor bus. devel. State Wis., 1978—. Mem. ASTD, Am. Mgmt. Assn., Indsl. Rels. Rsch. Assn., Am. Soc. for Human Resource Mgmt., Am. Soc. Safety Engrs., Assn. for Corp. Growth, Am. Soc. Radiologic Technologists. Home: 8060 N Navajo Rd Fox Point WI 53217-2726 Office: MFC 1 Park Plz Milwaukee WI 53202

BLOOMBERG, TERRY, early childhood education administrator; b. St. Louis, July 18, 1938; d. Herbert Valentine Goldwasser and Ruth (Ferer) Kopman; m. Gordon Richard Bloomberg, June 29, 1958; children: Jayne Bloomberg Langsam, Judy, Jill, Jacqui. BS in Edn. (with highest honors), Northwestern U., 1959; MA in Teaching, Webster Coll., St. Louis, 1978; A.G.C., Webster Coll., 1979. Cert. elem. educator, Mo. Tchr. elem. Washington Sch., Elmhurst, Ill., 1959-60, Dielman Sch., Ladue, Mo., 1960-61; early childhood tchr. Lucky Lane Nursery Sch., St. Louis, 1969-77; tchr. in parent-toddler and parent-infant program Clayton (Mo.) Early Childhood Program, 1977-80; early childhood specialist Child Day Care Assn., St. Louis, 1982-85; exec. dir. Developmental Child Care, Inc., St. Louis, 1983—; regional cons. Project Construct-Mo. Early Childhood Curriculum and Assessment Project, 1988. Pres. Am. Jewish Com., 1989-91, sec. 1986-89, v.p. 1982-86, bd. dirs. 1979-82; bd. dirs. Govt. Rels. Office for Mo. Jewish Fedns., 1990; St. Louis contact Action for Children's TV, 1975—; bd. dirs. Metro Theater Circus, 1975-89, Jewish Fedn. of St. Louis, 1983-88, 90-93, v.p. planning, 1993-96, v.p. allocations, 1996—; bd. mem., study group leader Brandeis Univ. Nat. Women's Com., St. Louis, 1968-74; mem. Congregation Temple Israel, 1961—; dir. consumer affairs Nat. Coun. Jewish Women, 1978-79. Recipient Outstanding Svc. award Midwest Assn. Edn. Young Children, 1989, The Love of Children award St. Louis Assn. for Edn. Young Children, 1991, Woman of Valor award Bus. and Profl. Women of Jewish Fedn. St. Louis, 1993, Netzach award Am. Jewish Com., 1993, Early Childhood and Parent Edn. Disting. Svc. award Mo. Dept. Elem. and Secondary Edn., 1995. Mem. Assn. for Edn. Young Children (Outstanding Svc. award 1986). Democrat. Jewish. Home: 47 Frontenac Estates Dr Saint Louis MO 63131-2615 Office: Devel Child Care 1211 Tamm Ave Saint Louis MO 63139-3442

BLOOMINGDALE, TERESA BURROWES, writer, lecturer; b. St. Joseph, Mo., July 26, 1930; d. Arthur Victor and Helen (Cooney) Burrowes; m. A. Lee Bloomingdale Jr., July 2, 1955; children—A. Lee, John, Michael, James, Mary, Dan, Peg, Ann, Tim, Patrick. Columnist, Omaha Metro, 1972-77, Our Sunday Visitor, 1973-83, Omaha Sun, 1976-78; contbg. editor McCall's mag., N.Y.C., 1982-84; lectr. Keedick Lecture Bur., N.Y.C., 1983—. Author: I Should Have Seen It Coming When the Rabbit Died, 1979; Up a Family Tree, 1981; Murphy Must Have Been a Mother, 1982; Life Is What Happens When You're Making Other Plans, 1984; Sense and Momsense, 1986. Recipient Disting. Alumna award Duchese Alumnae Assn., 1983. Mem. Assoc. Alumnae of Sacred Heart, Children of Mary Sodality, Authors Guild, Nebr. Writers Guild, Catholic League for Religious and Civil Rights, Alpha Sigma Nu. Republican. Roman Catholic. Clubs: St. Joseph Women's Press (Mo.); Omaha Press. Office: Julian Bach Literary Agy 747 Julian Bach Literary A # 3 New York NY 10017

BLOSER, DIETER, radiologist; b. Yugoslavia, Aug. 17, 1944; came to U.S., 1947, naturalized, 1954; s. Peter and Eva Helen Bloser; A.B., Princeton U., 1966; M.D., Case Western Res. U., 1970; m. Deborah Pierce Forbes, Nov. 25, 1967; children—Peter Forbes, Timothy Philip. Intern dept. medicine U. Hosps. of Cleve., 1970-71, resident in radiology, 1971-72, 74-76, chief resident, 1975-76; practice medicine specializing in radiology, Parma, Ohio, 1976—; mem. staff Parma Community Gen. Hosp., 1976—, chief nuclear medicine, 1977—, chief radiology, 1984—; pres. Parma Radiologic Assocs, Inc., 1990—. Gen. Hosp. Bd. dirs. Cleve. chpt. Juvenile Diabetes Found., 1986-90; active Am. Diabetes Assn., 1985—; trustee Case Western Reserve U. Sch. Med Alumni Assn., 1985-89. Served to lt. comdr. USN, 1972-74. Diplomate Am. Bd. Radiology. Mem. Am. Coll. Radiology, Radiol. Soc. N. Am., Ohio Radiol. Soc., Cleve. Radiol. Soc. (pres.-elect 1986-87, pres. 1987-88), Am. Inst. Ultrasound in Medicine, Cleve. Acad. Medicine, AMA, Ohio Med. Assn., Princeton Alumni Assn. (schs. com.), Phi Beta Kappa, Alpha Omega Alpha. Lutheran. Office: Parma Community Hosps 7007 Powers Blvd Cleveland OH 44129-5437

BLOUNT, MICHAEL EUGENE, lawyer; b. Camden, N.J., July 9, 1949; s. Floyd Eugene and Dorothy Alice (Geyer) Durham; m. Janice Lynn Brown, Aug. 22, 1969; children: Kirsten Marie, Gretchen Elizabeth. BA, U. Tex., 1971; JD, U. Houston, 1974. Bar: Tex. 1974, Ill. 1980, D.C. 1981, U.S. Ct. Appeals (D.C. cir.) 1978, U.S. Ct. Mil. Appeals 1975, U.S. Supreme Ct. 1977. Atty. advisor Office of Gen. Counsel SEC, Washington, 1977-78, legal asst. to chmn., 1978-79; assoc. Gardner, Carton & Douglas, Chgo., 1980-84; ptnr. Arnstein, Gluck, Lehr, Barron & Milligan, Chgo., 1984-86, Seyfarth, Shaw, Fairweather & Geraldson, Chgo., 1987—; trustee Assn. Securities Exchange Commn. Alumni. Served as lt. JAGC, USN, 1974-77. Mem. ABA (fed. regulation of securities com.), Chgo. Bar Assn., Order of Barons, Phi Alpha Delta (chpt. treas. 1973.), Univ. Club (Chgo.). Home: 1432 S Highland Ave Arlington Heights IL 60005-3662 Office: Seyfarth Shaw Fairweather & Geraldson 55 E Monroe St Ste 4200 Chicago IL 60603-5803

BLOVITS, LARRY JOHN, retired art educator; b. Detroit, Oct. 19, 1936; s. George Edward and Audrey (Codde) B.; m. Jean Curtis; children: Laurie, Lisa, Jay, Jack, Greg; m. Joyce Elaine Dreyer, Nov. 17, 1978 (div. 1992). BFA, Wayne State U., Detroit, 1964, MFA, 1966. Clk. U.S. P.O., Royal Oak, Mich., 1958-64; grad. teaching asst. Wayne State U., Detroit, 1964-66, adj. instr., 1966-67; adj. instr. U. Detroit, 1966-67, Macomb County Community Coll., Warren, Mich., 1966-67; instr. Europe program Providence Coll., 1971, 73, 75,77; instr. No. Mich. U., Marquette, 1966-67; prof. art Aquinas Coll., Grand Rapids, Mich., 1967-93, retired, 1993; visual arts advisor Mich. Coun. Arts, 1976-81, mem. in artist-in-schs. pool, 1977-81, artist in residence, 1977-78; vis. artist Henry Ford Community Coll., Dearborn, Mich., 1972, Montcalm Community Coll., Sidney, Mich., 1982, 83, Mich. Tech. U., Houghton, 1989; artist in residence Lowell (Mich.) Middle Schs., 1984, Forest Hills Middle Schs., Grand Rapids, 1987, St. Jude Elem., Grand Rapids, 1989. One-man shows include Aquinas Coll., Grand Rapids, 1993; solo exhbns. include Grand Rapids Art Mus., 1977, City Art Gallery, Grand Rapids, 1984, Farmhouse Gallery, Montcalm C.C., Sidney, 1985, Arnold Klein Gallery, Royal Oak, Mich., 1985, 88, Aquinas Coll., 1986, Muskegon (Mich.) Mus. Art, 1988; group shows include Krasl Art Ctr., St. Joseph, Mich., 1987, Canyon Gallery, Riudoso, N.Mex., 1987, Soc. Pastellistes de France Internat. Exhbn. Pastells, Lille, 1987, 33d Knickerbocker Artists NMat., N.Y.C., 1983; author: Pastel forthe Serious Beginner, 1996; cover artist, featured Pastel Interpretations, North Light Books, 1993; featured artist in several books. With U.S. Army, 1954-57. Grantee Mich. Coun. Arts, 1980, 83, Nat. Endowment for Arts, 1983, Aquinas Coll., 1988; recipient art awards Kans. Pastel Soc., Met. Portrait Soc., Internat. Exhbns. Pastels, Pen and Brush Gallery, 1989, 90, Am. Artist mag., 1990, Nat. Portrait Seminar, Atlanta, 1991, 93, others; named Master Pastelist, 1993. Mem. Pastel Soc. Am., Am. Portrait Soc. (co-chmn. edn. com.), Kans. Pastel Soc., Oil Pastel Assn., Midwest Pastel Soc., Am. Soc. Portrait Artists, Salmagundi Club, Knickerbocker Artists. Home and Studio: 0-1835 Luce St SW Grand Rapids MI 49544-9503

BLUE, ANITA FAE, nurse; b. Webster City, Ia., Apr. 15, 1967; d. Veryl D. and Linda (Sollie) B. BSN, Morningside Coll., Sioux City, Iowa, 1989. RN, S.D.; cert. BCLS. Intern Meth. Hosp., Rochester, Minn., 1988; critical care unit nurse Marian Health Ctr., Sioux City, Iowa, 1989; mental health nurse St. Lukes Regional Med. Ctr., Sioux City, Iowa, 1991; charge nurse children, adolescent, adult, geriatric Psychiat. units Charter Hosp. of Sioux Falls, S.D., 1992-95; psychiat. nurse S.D.'s Children's Specialty Clinics, Sioux Falls, 1995—; charge nurse child-adolescent psyciat. unit McKennan Hosp., Sioux Falls, 1995—, charge nurse child, adolescent psychiatry unit, 1995—; mem. nursing practice coun., 1992, charting by exception com., 1992; presenter insvc. concerning IV therapy to staff RN's on mental health unit, 1992.

BLUE, NELSON CLAYTON, civil engineer; b. Mt. Vernon, Ohio, Jan. 28, 1945; s. Waldo Clayton and Florence Irene (Conard) B.; m. Ella Mae Farley, Sept. 24, 1966; children: Angela, Barbara. BSCE, Ohio State U., 1968. Registered profl. engr., profl. surveyor, Ohio. From engr. in tng. to traffic engr. Ohio Dept. Transp., Columbus, 1968-90, engr. field maintenance, 1990—; land surveyor, Newark, Ohio, 1973-75. Mem. Ohio Soc. Profl. Engrs., Sertoma Internat. (dist. gov.), Masons (past master Licking Lodge #291 1988). Republican. Presbyterian. Home: 566 N Washington St Utica OH 43080

BLUE, ROBERT LEE, secondary education educator; b. Columbiaville, Mich., Apr. 23, 1920; s. Arthur Floyd and Elma (Ellis) B.; BA, Mich. State U., 1941; MA, U. Mich., 1952; m. Dorothy L. Seward, July 15, 1961. Tchr., Chesaning (Mich.) H.S., 1941-42, 45-57; prin. Ricker Jr. H.S., Saginaw, Mich., 1957-59, Buena Vista H.S., Saginaw, 1960-69; asst. prof. secondary edn. Central Mich. U., Mt. Pleasant, 1969—. Bd. dirs. Hartley Edn. Nature Camp, 1957-69; pres. Saginaw County Assn. Ret. Sch. Pers., Mich. Assn. Ret. Sch. Pers. (chmn. awards com., Disting. Svc. award 1995). With U.S. Army, 1942-45. Decorated Bronze Star. Mem. NEA (life), Mich. Edn. Assn., Assn. Tchr. Educators, Mich. Assn. Tchr. Educators, Nat. Assn. Secondary Sch. Prins., Mich. Assn. Secondary Sch. Prins., Mich. PTA (hon. life), Am. Legion, Mich. Hist. Soc., Saginaw County Hist. Soc., Lapeer County Hist. Soc., Optomist, Pit and Balcony, Masons, Phi Delta Kappa. Republican. Methodist. Author: Footsteps Into The Past, A History of Columbiaville, 1979, also articles. Home: 1437 Lathrup Ave Saginaw MI 48603-4787 Office: 3037 Davenport Ave Saginaw MI 48602-3652

BLUESTEIN, PAUL HAROLD, management engineer; b. Cin., June 14, 1923; s. Norman and Eunice D. (Schullman) B.; m. Joan Ruth Straus, May 17, 1943; children: Alice Sue Bluestein Greenbaum, Judith Ann. B.S., Carnegie Inst. Tech., 1946, B.Engring. in Mgmt. Engring., 1946; M.B.A., Xavier U., 1973, MA in Humanities, 1992. Registered profl. engr., Ohio. Time study engr. Lodge & Shipley Co., 1946-47; adminstrv. engr. Randall Co., 1947-52; partner Paul H. Bluestein & Co. (mgmt. cons.), 1952—, Seinsheimer-Bluestein Mgmt. Services, 1964-70; gen. mgr. Baker Refrigeration Co., 1953-56; pres., dir. Tabor Mfg. Co., 1953-54, Bluejay Corp., 1954—, Blatt & Ludwig Corp., 1954-57, Jason Industries, Inc., 1954-57, Hamilton-York Corp., 1954-57, Earle Hardware Mfg. Co., 1955-57, Hermas Machine Co., 1956—, Panel Machine Co., Ermet Products Corp., 1957-86, Tyco Labs., Inc., 1968-69, All-Tech Industries, 1968; gen. mgr. Hafleigh & Co., 1959-60; sr. v.p., gen. mgr. McCauley Ind. Corp., 1959-60; gen. mgr. Am. Art Works div. Rapid-Am. Corp., 1960-63; sec.-treas., dir. Liberty Baking Co., 1964-65; pres. Duguesne Baking Co., 1964-65, Goddard Bakers, Inc., 1964-65; pub. Merger and Acquisition Digest, 1962-69; partner Companhia Engenheiros Indsl. Bluestein Do Brasil, 1970-84; v.p., gen. mgr. Famco Machine div. Worden-Allen Co., 1974-75; exec. v.p., gen. mgr. Peck, Stow & Wilcox Co., Inc., 1976-77; mem. Joint Engring. Mgmt. Conf. Com., 1971-78. Com. mem. Cin. Art Mus. With AUS, 1943-46. Mem. ASME, Internat. Inst. Indsl. Engrs., Am. Soc. Engring. Mgmt., C.I.O.S.-World Council Mgmt. (dir., 1982-87). Home and Office: 3420 Section Rd Amberley Village Cincinnati OH 45237

BLUHM, GENE ELWOOD, trade journal editor and publisher; b. Cleve., June 6, 1920; s. Elmer Karl and Helga (Johansen) B.; m. Florence Ethel Slingo, Oct. 6, 1942; children: Gary Gene, Judy Edith. Student, Western Res. U., Cleve., 1948; real estate cert., Cleve. C.C., 1978. Lic. realtor, Ohio. Reporter Cleve. Press, 1939-41; radio broadcaster WHK, WERE, WJW, others, Cleve., 1948-70; editor Properties Mag., Cleve., 1947—, pub., 1989—; mem. pub. rels. com. Midtown Corridor, Cleve., 1980's. Editor: Polka Parade, 1951; editor, pub.: My Confidential Golf Progress Book, 1973; author series Properties Mag., 1963; contbr. articles to profl. jours. Councilman Mayfield Village, Ohio, 1970s; cubmaster Cub Scout Pack 139, Hillcrest Area, Cleve., 1950s; organizer Indian Guide and Indian Princess Tribes Hillcrest YMCA, Lyndhurst, Ohio, 1950s-60s; program chmn. Mayfield Twp. Hist. Soc., Hillcrest Area, 1980s. Master 1st sgt. USAF, 1942-45. Mem. Cleve. Area Bd. Realtors (pub. rels. com. 1970s, chmn. Spkrs. Bur. 1970s, chmn. Pres. Ball 1970s, Affiliate of Yr.), Soc. Profl. Journalists, Press Club, Masons (chaplain). Office: Properties Mag 4900 Euclid Ave Cleveland OH 44103

BLUHM, MYRON DEAN, sales professional; b. St. Joseph, Ill., Dec. 7, 1934; s. Lorenz E. and Etta (Sieberns) B.; m. Lucinda Ann Meade, June 27, 1954; children: Kathie S. Alblinger, Mitchell D., Beth A.Russell. Student, Ill. Comml. Coll., 1954, Dale Carnegie U., 1966. Franchise sales mgmt. Mr. Steak Embers & Char Steak, Urbana, Ill., 1966-71; sales mgr. McCurdy Seed, Fremont, Iowa, 1974-86, Crow's Seed, Milford, Ill., 1986-94, Sams/Hockaday Ins., Decatur, Ill., 1994—. Named Agt. of the Year life Ins. Co. 1962, Gen. Mgr. of the Year, 1963, Shaklee Sales Coord., 1973—. Mem. Jaycees, Moose, Lions. Lutheran. Home: 207 S West Union St Monticello IL 61856-1041 Office: Sams Hockaday & Assocs 120 W Prairie Ave Decatur IL 62523-1219

BLUHM, NEIL GARY, real estate company executive; b. 1938; married. B.S., U. Ill.; J.D., Northwestern U. Bar: Ill. Ptnr. firm Mayer, Brown & Platt, Chgo., 1962-70; pres. JMB Realty Corp., Chgo., from 1970; pres., trustee JMB Realty Trust, Chgo., 1972—. Office: Urban Shopping Ctrs Inc 900 N Michigan Ave Chicago IL 60611-1542

BLUM, MICHAEL, aerospace engineer; b. Harrison, Ohio, Dec. 12, 1968. Degree in aerospace engring., U. Ohio, 1992. Aerospace engr. Carr Tool, Cin., 1993—.

BLUME, PAUL CHIAPPE, lawyer; b. Omaha, Oct. 11, 1929; s. Herman Alexander and Marie (Simoni) B.; m. Mary Lou Higgins, June 28, 1958; children—Nancy, Julia, Paul II, William. B.S. in Commerce, Loyola U., Chgo., also J.D. Bar: Ill. 1957. Legal sect. mgr. Aldens Inc., 1957-58; assoc. Lord, Bissell & Brook, 1959-63, of counsel, 1983—; v.p., gen. counsel Nat. Assn. Ind. Insurers, Des Plaines, Ill., 1963-83, Ill. Ins. Info. Svc., 1987—, Ill. Ins. Conf., Chgo., 1986—; pres. Ins. Briefs, Inc., 1984—. Served to capt. U.S. Army, 1951-53. Mem. ABA, Ill. State Bar Assn., Chgo. Bar Assn., Internat. Assn. Ins. Counsel, Fedn. Ins. Counsel, Ill. Def. Counsel. Club: Turnberry Country (Crystal Lake, Ill.). Office: 115 S La Salle St Chicago IL 60603

BLUMENSHINE, MAHLON, banker; b. Washington, Ill., May 11, 1928; s. Mahlon and Mabel Mae (Schick) B.; m. Carolyn Sue Longden, June 26, 1960; children: J. Wesley, Bradley Ward, Blake Alan. Standard Banking degree, So. Ill. U., 1967; Grad. Banking degree, U. Wis., 1974. V.p. Community Bank, East Peoria, Ill., 1956-75; pres., trust officer Sunnyland Bank, Washington, Ill., 1975—; also bd. dirs. Sunnyland Bank. Alderman City of Washington, Ill., 1979-83; treas. Dist. 50 Schs., Washington, 1983-87; past chmn. Easter Seal Drive, Heart Fund Drive, Cancer Fund Drive. Served as cpl. U.S. Army, 1950-52. Mem. Am. Inst. Banking (pres. cen. Ill. chpt. 1957-58), Washington C. of C., Am. Legion, VFW. Republican. Methodist. Lodge: Kiwanis. Home: 910 Hampton Rd Washington IL 61571-1258 Office: Sunnyland Bank Box 99 Washington IL 61571

BLUMHAGEN, JEANNE BOURLAND, pediatrician, emergency physician; b. Seattle, July 6, 1923; d. Harry McClelland and Lillian (Held) Bourland; m. Rex Vernon Blumhagen, Dec. 23, 1943; children: Dan William, Susan Carol, Wendy Ann, Karyn Lee. BS, U. Ill., 1948, MD, 1949. Diplomate Am. Bd. Pediatrics, Am. Bd. Emergency Medicine; cert. ACLS. Contract physician Feds Creek (Ky.) United Mines Workers, 1949-51; dir. pediatrics, staff physician Madera (Calif.) County Hosp., 1953-56; asst. dir. pub. health for maternal and child health Madera County Health Dept., 1956, acting dir. pub. health, 1957, dir. pub. health, 1957-59; pvt. practice, 1959-60; embassy med. officer U.S. Embassy, Dept. State, Kabul, Afghanistan, 1960-65; gen. practice rotating resident Tulare (Calif.) County Hosp., 1965, resident pediatrics, 1977-78; pediatrician Shanta Bhawwan Hosp., Kathmandu, Nepal, 1973; asst. clin. prof. population scis. and internat. health U. Ill., Chgo., 1972-77; emergency dept. physician Delnor Hosp., St. Charles, Ill., 1978-86; staff physician Ctrl. Dupage Hosp. Urgent Care Ctr., 1984-89; co-internat. med. advisor, health care cons. INTERSERVE and Blumhagen Med. Svcs., Nicosia, Cyprus, 1989—; vis. prof. internat. health U. Ill. Grad. Divsn. Pub. Health, Med. Ctr., Chgo., 1975; cons., instr. Sch. Midwifery, Frontier Nursing Svc., Hyden, Ky., 1951; cons. Merced County Hosp.; asst. to dir. MAP Afghanistan Project BMMF Internat., Upper Darby, Pa., 1966-72, program dir., 1972-73; vis. prof. internat. health U. Ill. Grad. Sch. Pub. Health, Med. Ctr., Chgo., 1975; cons. rural health care APHA, 1977; owner Cons. in Rural Health Care Delivery; lectr. Econs. of Republics of Former Soviet Union, Wheaton Coll. Author: The Hazarajat Project: Family Health Care, A Rural Health Care Delivery Scheme, 1974. Bd. trustees Wheaton (Ill.) Coll., 1981—; bd. dirs., cons. Westside Holistic Family Ctr., 1981-89; bd. dirs. Ctrl. Asia Devel. Agy., 1992—; bd. dirs. Women of the World, Washington, 1995—, chmn. bd. dirs., 1995—; tchr. courses for Sunday schs. and ch. groups. Mem. APHA, Dupage County Med. Soc. Home: 28W575 Diversey Pky West Chicago IL 60185

BLUNCK, KLAIRE DARLENE, nurse; b. Oconomowoc, Wis., May 3, 1954; d. Wynn F. and Frances Lavern (Bartlein) Kemnitz; m. William Randel Blunck, Aug. 11, 1973; children: Jacob William, Joseph Randel. AD, Milw. Area Tech. Coll., 1974; BSN, Carroll Coll., 1992. Cert. CPR, neonatal resusitation and pitocin adminstrn., lactation educator, pediat. emergency care nurse; cert. inpatient obstet. nurse Nat. Cert. Corp. for Ob-gyn. and Neonatal Specialities. Staff nurse, home visit nurse post partum Meml. Hosp., Oconomowoc, head quality improvement ob-gyn. unit. Vol. spkr. March of Dimes; pres. ch. women Dr. Martin Luth. Ch., Oconomowoc, 1994, 95. Laureate Group scholar.

BLUNT, ROY D., state official; b. Niangua, Mo., Jan. 10, 1950; s. Leroy and Neva (Letterman) B.; m. E. Roseann Ray; children: Matthew Roy, Amy Roseann, Andrew Benjamin. BA, S.W. Bapt. U., 1970; MA, S.W. Mo. State U., 1972. Tchr. Marshfield (Mo.) High Sch., 1970-73; instr. Drury Coll., Springfield, Mo., 1973-82; clk. Greene County, Springfield, 1973-85; sec. of state State of Mo., Jefferson City, 1985—; mem. Fed. Election Commn. Adv. Panel; del. Atlantic Treaty Assn. Conf., 1987. Author: (with others) Missouri Election Procedures: A Layman's Guide, 1977; Voting Rights Guide for the Handicapped. Chmn. Mo. Housing Devel. Commn., Kansas City, 1981, Rep. State Conv., Springfield, 1980; chmn. Gov.'s Adv. Coun. on Literacy; co-chmn. Mo. Opportunity 2000 Commn., 1985-87; Rep. candidate for lt. gov. of Mo., 1980; active local ARC, Muscular Dystrophy Assn., others. Named One of 10 Outstanding Young Americans U.S. Jaycees, 1986, Springfield's Outstanding Young Man Jaycees, 1980, Mo.'s Outstanding Young Civic Leader, 1981. Mem. Nat. Assn. Secs. of State (chmn. voter registration and edn. com., sec., v.p. 1990). Am. Coun. Young Polit. Leaders. Baptist. Lodges: Kiwanis, Masons. Office: Sec of State 208 State Capitol Bldg Jefferson City MO 65102*

BLURTON, KEITH FREDERICK, chemist; b. Grays, Essex, Eng., Apr. 11, 1940; came to U.S. 1966; s. Frederick and Phyllis (Green) B.; m. Patricia Mary Kendrick, Aug. 19, 1966; 1 child, Heather. BSc, U. Southampton, Eng., 1961; PhD, U. Southampton, 1966. Supr. Leesona Corp., Great Neck, N.Y., 1966-68; rsch. dir. Energetics Sci., Inc., Elmsford, N.Y., 1968-76; dir. energy conversion/storage Inst. Gas Tech., Chgo., 1976-80; v.p. PCK Tech. div. Kollmorgen Corp., Melville, N.Y., 1980-86; gen. mgr. Ctr. for Innovative Tech., Herndon, Va., 1986-93; pres. Merra, Ann Arbor, Mich., 1993—. Contbr. articles to profl. jours.; patentee in field. Mem. Electrochem. Soc., Am. Chem. Soc., Royal Soc. Chemistry, AAAS. Home: 30700 Ivy Glen Ct Bingham Farms MI 48025-4624 Office: Merra PO Box 130500 Ann Arbor MI 48113-0500

BLYTH, ANN MARIE, secondary education educator; b. Sharon, Pa., June 18, 1949; d. Chester Stanley and Mary Clara (Romian) Kacerski; m. Lynn Allan Blyth, June 26, 1976 (dec. June 1983); 1 stepchild, Breton Alan Blyth; 1 child, Amanda Lynn. BS in Edn., Kent (Ohio) State U., 1971; postgrad., Loyola U., New Orleans, 1973-74; MS in Teaching, John Carroll U., 1978. Cert. comprehensive sci., maths. and physics tchr., Ohio. Jr. high math. tchr. New Philadelphia ((Ohio) Bd. of Edn., 1971-72; high sch. sci. and math. tchr. Hubbard (Ohio) Exempted Village Bd. of Edn., 1972-76, Painesville (Ohio) City Local Bd. Edn., 1976—; instr. math. Morton Salt, Painesville, 1979-80; part-time faculty Lake Erie Coll., 1992. Mem. Adv. Bd. Western Res. br. Am. Lung Assn. of Ohio, Painesville, 1986-89, sec, 1988-89, Northeastern br., Youngstown, Ohio, 1989—; judge state level Nat. Pre-teen and Pre-Teen Petite Pageants, 1990. Martha Holden Jennings Found. scholar, 1984-85; named Tchr. of the Yr., Harvey High Sch. Key Club, 1981-82. Mem. NEA, Ohio Edn. Assn., Northeastern Ohio Edn. Assn., Painesville City Tchrs. Assn., Am. Assn. Physics Tchrs., Nat. Sci. Tchrs. Assn., Cleve. Regional Coun. of Sci. Tchrs., Sci. Edn. Coun. of Ohio. Democrat. Episcopalian. Home: 8545 Willow Ln Chardon OH 44024-9231 Office: Thomas W Harvey High Sch 167 W Washington St Painesville OH 44077-3328

BOAL, MARCIA ANNE RILEY, clinical social worker, administrator; b. Carthage, Mo., Sept. 29, 1944; d. William Joseph and Thelma P. (Simpson) Riley; m. David W. Boal, Aug. 12, 1967; children: Adam J. W., Aaron D. Boal. BA, U. Kans., 1966, MSW, 1981. Lic. clin. social worker. Child therapist Gillis Home for Children, Kansas City, Mo., 1981; social worker Leavenworth (Kans.) County Spl. Edn. Cooperative, 1981-84; sch. social worker, dir. health and social svcs. Kans. State Sch. for the Blind, Kansas City, Kans., 1984—; pvt. practice adoption counseling and workshops, 1981—; field instr. Sch. of Social Welfare, Kans. U., 1986—. Author: Surviving Kids, 1983, Teaching Social Skills to Blind and Visually Impaired Children, 1987. Nat. networking chmn. Jr. League Kansas City, 1977-81; bd. dirs. Wyandotte House Ind, 1973-81, Kans. Action For Children, Topeka, 1981, Gov.'s Commn. on Parent Edn., Topeka, 1984—, Lake of the Forest, 1994— (sec.). Named Kans. Sch. Social Worker of Yr., 1989. Mem. Council Exceptional Children, Nat. Assn. Social Workers, Kans. Assn. Sch. Social Workers, Am. Orthopsychiat. Assn., Kans. Conf. Social Welfare, R.P. Found., Phi Kappa Phi. Home: Lake Of The Frst Bonner Springs KS 66012 Office: Kans St Sch for Blind and Handi 1100 State Ave Kansas City KS 66102-4411

BOARMAN, MARJORIE RUTH, manufacturing company executive, consultant; b. Lakeland, Fla., Apr. 14, 1953; d. Hugh Francis and Nancy Addair (McCracken) Roberts; m. Edward F. Moore, June 28, 1975 (div. 1986); children: Kulani Anne, Brittany Elizabeth; m. James Louis Boarman, Feb. 5, 1987; 1 child, Joshua; stepchildren: Steven, Christina, Paulette. BS in Edn., Fla. State U., 1975; MEd, U. Hawaii/Manoa, 1978. Cert. tchr., Fla., Mo. Substitute tchr. KCCA Preschs., Honolulu, 1975; tchr. Hickam Day Care Ctr., Hickam AFB, Hawaii, 1975-77; tchr., sales rep. Grolier Interstate Inc., Honolulu, 1977; tchr. Kiddie Kollege Presch., Hickam AFB, 1977-79, Our Lady of Sorrows Schs., St. Louis, 1979-80; program dir. Clayton (Mo.) YWCA, 1981-82; cons. Parent Talk Svcs., Phoenix, 1983-85; tchr. Polk County Schs., Polk City, Fla., 1986-89; co-owner Boarman Built Inc., Green Ridge, Mo., 1989—. Co-creator: Bon Voyage board game, 1992. V.p. Green Ridge 2000 Team, 1995—; leader, coord. Camp Fire Boys and Girls, Lakeland, 1988—; bd. dirs. Boswell PTA, Auburndale, 1991-92. Mem. NAFE, Auburndale C. of C. (bd. dirs. 1991-92), Green Ridge C. of C. (bd. dirs. 1994-96), Sedalia Bus. and Profl. Women (2nd v.p. membership chmn. 1994-95, 1st v.p. issues mgmt. chmn. 1995-96, pres.-elect 1996-97, State Individual Devel. award), Kappa Delta Pi. Republican. Pentecostal. Home and Office: Boarman Built Inc PO Box 145 Green Ridge MO 65332-0145

BOATRIGHT, MATT, state legislator. Mem. Mo. Ho. of Reps., Jefferson City. Republican.

BOBBITT, RONALD ALBERT, lawyer; b. Chgo., Dec. 23, 1953; s. Booker T. and Clara M. Bobbitt; married; 2 children. BS, U. Ill., 1976; JD, Antioch U., 1979. Bar: Ill. 1979, U.S. Dist. Ct. (no. dist.) Ill. 1979, U.S. Ct. Appeals (7th cir.) 1979. Clk. to adminstrv. asst. to chief justice, 1978; sr. ptnr. Bobbitt & Assocs., Chgo., 1979—. Mem. NAACP, Chgo., 1990. Recipient Key to City Mayor's Office, Birmingham, 1980, Goodwill Community Svc. award Chgo. Heights, Ill., 1981. Mem. ABA, Nat. Bar Assn., Nat. Bus. Execs., Nat. Urban League, Chgo. Bar Assn., Cook County Bar Assn., Psi Chi, Phi Eta Sigma. Office: Bobbitt & Assocs 155 N Michigan Ave Chicago IL 60601-7511

BOBCO, WILLIAM DAVID, JR., consulting engineering company executive; b. Chgo., Aug. 11, 1946; s. William David and Eleanor Josephine (Dvojack) B.; m. Donna Domenica DiFrancesca, Sept. 13, 1969; 1 child, Christina Marie. BS in Engring., U. Ill., Chgo., 1969; MBA in Prodn. Mgmt., U. Chgo., 1983. Prodn. mgr. Am. Can Co., Maywood, Ill., 1972-73; with Footlik & Assocs., Evanston, Ill., 1973—; exec. v.p. Footlik & Assocs., Evanston, 1986—; mem. indsl. adv. bd. U. Ill. Coll. Engring., Chgo., 1992—, chmn. alumni devel. com., 1991-95, mem. dean selection com., 1994. Vol. Art Inst. of Chgo., 1983-84; mem. facilities and grounds com. St. Giles Parish, 1995—; com. mem. U. Ill. Chgo. Pier 50th Anniversary, 1996. Capt. U.S. Army, 1969-72, Vietnam. Mem. ASME (bd. dirs. Chgo. sect. 1984—, vice chmn. 1991, newsletter editor 1987—, chmn. Chgo. sect. 1992-94, region VI rep. to A World in Motion K-12 tng. program, SAE (co-sponsor 1993), Engring. Alumni Assn. U. Ill. chgo. (pres. 1984-88, bd. dirs. 1975—), U. Ill. Alumni Assn. (bd. dirs. 1985-91, nominating com. 1991, Loyalty award 1988, Constituent Leadership award 1991, Disting. Svc. award 1994). Roman Catholic. Office: Footlik & Assocs 2521 Gross Point Rd Evanston IL 60201-4928

BOBE, HENRY DALE, pharmaceutical executive; b. Vincennes, Ind., July 2, 1952; s. Bruce Edward and Helen Louise (Atkinson) B.; m. Connie Faye McCoy, June 29, 1974; children: Brooke Michelle, Jason Ryan, Ashley Elizabeth. AS, Vincennes U., 1972; BS, Purdue U., 1976. Tech. rep. Shell Chem.-A.H., Vincennes, Ind., 1977-79; asst. regional mgr. Diamond Shamrock Animal Health, Cleve., 1980-81; mgr. comml. devel. Diamond Shamrock-A.H., Cleve., 1981-82, mgr. R&D, 1983-84; gen. mgr. SDS Biotech, Painesville, Ohio, 1984-85; pres. Fermenta Animal Health, Cleve., 1985-86; pres., COO Fermenta Animal Health, Kansas City, Mo., 1986-90, pres., CEO, 1991—; pres. Tech. Am. Corp. Inc., St. Joseph, Mo., 1986-88; bd. dirs. Named Outstanding Alumni Vincennes U., 1990. Mem. Purdue U. Alumni Assn. (life), Vincennes U. Alumni Assn. (life), Pres. Coun. Purdue U. Republican. Home: 9637 N Bradford Ave Kansas City MO 64154-1723

Office: Fermenta Animal Health 10150 N Exec Hills Blvd Kansas City MO 64153-2314

BOBENHOUSE, NELLIE YATES, insurance company executive; b. Spickard, Mo., May 3, 1936; d. Joseph Howard and Nellie Elizabeth (Tuttle) Yates; m. Lewis L. Griffin, Apr. 22, 1956 (div. Jan. 1964); 1 child, Elizabeth Anne Griffin Schafer; m. Robert A. Bobenhouse, Aug. 28, 1965. Student, St. Joseph (Mo.) Jr. Coll., 1955, Grandview Coll., 1980. Sec. News-Press & Gazette, St. Joseph, 1954-56; sec., bookkeeper Wilson's Locker & Ins., Spickard, Mo., 1956-60, Oyler's Locker, Spickard, 1960-64; sec. Equitable of Iowa Agy., Des Moines, 1964-68, agy. office supr., 1968-94. City clk. City of Spickard, 1959-60; support group leader, co-founder Chronic Fatigue Syndrome Soc., Des Moines, 1988—; bd. dirs. Iowa Chronic Fatigue Syndrome/CFIDS Assn., Cedar Rapids, 1991; mem. Des Moines Women's Club, 1994—, Urbandale Garden Club, 1994—. Fellow Life Mgmt. Inst.; mem. Ins. Women Des Moines (com. chmn. 1975), P. Buckley Moss Soc., Beta Sigma Phi (sec.-treas. 1958-60, Woman of Yr. 1959). Republican. Disciple of Christ. Home: 905 59th St West Des Moines IA 50266-7516

BOBIER, BILL, state legislator; m. PAtrice; children: Jason, Meagon. State rep. Mich. Ho. Reps., Dist. 101, 1991—; mem. appropriations com., vice chair agrl., natural resources & corrections subcoms. & gen. govt. subcom., Mich. Ho. Reps.; co-founder Ferry Truck Farmers; operator Earthscpae Cons. Home: RR1 4220 Loop Rd Hesperia MI 49421*

BOBINS, NORMAN R., banker. Vice chmn. Exch. Nat. Bank Chgo., 1969-90; formerly vice chmn. LaSalle Nat. Bank, Chgo.; now pres., ceo LaSalle Nat Bank, Chgo. Office: LaSalle Nat Bank 135 S La Salle St Chicago IL 60603-3402

BOCHNAK, MARY LOUISE, financial consultant; b. Mpls., Mar. 16, 1951; d. George Paul and Madeline Ann (Mengelkoch) B. BS, U. Minn., 1972, MBA, 1976, PhD, 1982. Sr. rsch. analyst Minn. Dept. Revenue, St. Paul, 1977; instr. U. Minn., Mpls., 1975-80, cons., 1975-78; asst. prof. fin., bus. adminstrn., real estate acctg. Coll. St. Thomas, St. Paul, 1980-86; fin. cons. Mpls., 1986—; assoc. prof., chair mgmt. & econs. dept. Hamline U., Mpls., 1990—; cons. Von Kuster & Assocs, Mpls., 1978-80. Contbr. articles to profl. jours. Treas. Turning Point Inc., Mpls., 1984-88, Lowry Hill Residents Inc., Mpls., 1984-89, Manor Homes Lowry Hill, 1980-84, Bridge for Runaway Youth Inc., Mpls., 1977-80. Corp. assoc. fellow, U. Minn., 1975. Mem. Am. Fin. Assn., Am. Real Estate and Urban Econs. Assn.

BOCK, ANGELA MARIE, librarian; b. Cape Girardeau, Mo., Mar. 12, 1939; d. Byron Ford and Bonnie Marie (Farquhar) Dormeyer; m. Ralph Garland Bock, June 24, 1961; children: Julie Anne, Karen Lynnette Bock. BSEd., U. Mo., 1961. Cert. libr. K-12, Mo. Libr. Pattonville Sch. Dist., St. Louis County, Mo., 1961-62; libr. Orchard Farm Sch. Dist., St. Charles, Mo., 1971—, dept. chmn., 1985—, chmn. North Ctrl. Accreditation Commn., 1985-87; com. mem. Mo. Sch. Libr. Evaluation, Jefferson City, 1984; mem. evaluation team for Bayless Sch. Dist. and N.W. Sch. Dist., North Ctrl. Accreditation Commn., Mo., 1980, 85. Sponsor Youth in Govt., St. Charles, 1981—; libr. 1st United Meth. Ch., St. Charles, 1969-74, dir. Vacation Ch. Sch., 1967-68. Recipient Svc. award YMCA, St. Charles, 1988. Mem. Mo. Sch. Librs., Mo. Assn. Ednl. Tech., St. Louis Suburban Librs., St. Louis Area Sch. Libr. Suprs. (sec. 1992—), Phi Delta Kappa (historian 1989-90), Delta Delta Delta (group pres. 1963-68), Kappa Epsilon Alpha, Sigma Epsilon Sigma, Pi Lambda Theta. Republican. Home: 5 Sussex Ct Saint Charles MO 63301-1114 Office: Orchard Farm HS 2165 Highway V Saint Charles MO 63301-6004

BOCK, PETER ERNEST, state legislator; b. Milw., Dec. 12, 1948; s. Peter R. and Thelma J. (Miron) B. BA, U. Wis., Milw., 1977. Former parcel delivery worker; state assemblyman dist. 7 Wis. State Assembly, 1987—; chmn. environ. resources com. Wis. State Assembly, 1993—, mem. health, natural resources, labor and job tng., state affairs, urban and local affairs coms. Chmn. Milw. County Dem. Com., 1985-86. *

BOCKELMAN, JOHN RICHARD, lawyer; b. Chgo., Aug. 8, 1925; s. Carl August and Mary (Ritchie) B. Student, U. Wis., 1943-44, Northwestern U., 1944-45, Harvard U., 1945, U. Hawaii, 1946; BSBA, Northwestern U., 1946; MA in Econs., U. Chgo., 1949, JD, 1951. Bar: Ill. 1951. Atty.-advisor Chgo. ops. office AEC, 1951-52; asso. firm Schradzke, Gould & Ratner, Chgo., 1952-57, Brown, Dashow & Langeluttig, Chgo., 1957-59, Antonow & Weissbourd, Chgo., 1959-61; partner firm Burton, Isaacs, Bockelman & Miller, Chgo., 1961-69; pvt. practice Chgo., 1970—; prof. bus. law Ill. Inst. Tech., Chgo., 1950-82; lectr. econs. DePaul U., Chgo., 1952-53; bd. dirs., v.p. Beale Travel Svc., Inc., Chgo., Internat. Travel Concepts, Inc., LaJolla, Calif.; v.p. sec. Del Mar (Calif.) Gallery, Inc., D.M. Gallery, La Jolla; bd. dirs., sec. Arlington Engring. Co.; bd. dirs., v.p., Universal Distbrs., Inc. Pres. 1212 Lake Shore Dr. Condo Assn., Chgo., Near North Assn. of Condo Pres., Chgo., Park Row Community Assn., San Diego. Served with USNR, 1943-46. Mem. ABA, Ill. Bar Assn., Chgo. Bar Assn., Cath. Lawyers Guild Chgo., Lake Point Tower Club, Barclay Ltd. Club, Whitehall Club, Internat. Club, Anvil Club (East Dundee, Ill.), Univ. Club (San Diego), Phi Delta Theta. Home: 1212 N Lake Shore Dr Chicago IL 60610-2371 Office: 104 S Michigan Ave Ste 808 Chicago IL 60603-5906

BOCKSERMAN, ROBERT JULIAN, chemist; b. St. Louis, Dec. 20, 1929; s. Max Louis and Bertha Anna (Kremen) B.; m. Clarice K. Kreisman, June 9, 1957; children: Michael Jay, Joyce Ellen, Carol Beth. BSc, U. Mo., 1952, MSc, 1955. Chemist Sealtest Corp., Peoria, Ill., 1955-56; prodn. mgr. Allan Drug Co., St. Louis, 1957-59; rsch. chemist Monsanto Co., St. Louis, 1960-65; purchasing agt. Monsanto Co., Sauget, Ill., 1966-67; founder, pres. Pharma-Tech Industries, Inc., Union, Mo., 1967-84; tech. dir. Overlock-Howe Consulting Group, St. Louis, 1984-85; founder, pres. Conatech Consulting Group, Chesterfield, Mo., 1985—; sec., mem. industry packaging adv. com. Sch. of Engring., U. Mo., Rolla, 1979—; adj. prof. dept. food sci./nutrition U. Mo., Columbia; adj. prof. dept. engring. mgmt. U. Mo., Rolla; vis. lectr. U. Mo., Clayton, Northwestern U., Evanston, Ill., and various programs. Tech. reviewer Jour. Inst. of Packaging Profls., Jour. Packaging Tech., Mo. Waste Control Scholarship Grants and Research, Medical Device and Diagnostic Industry Jour., Medical Plastics and Biomaterials Publication. (editorial adv. bd.). Mem. Mo. Waste Control Coalition; mem. stormwater engring. com. City of Creve Coeur, Mo. With U.S. Army, 1952-54, Korea. SBIR grantee. Mem. ASTM, Cons. Packaging Engring. Coun., Inst. Packaging Profls., Am. Technion Soc., Inst. Food Technologists Arrangements (St. Louis), Nat. Forensic Ctr., Teltech Resource Network, Am. Chem. Soc., Am. Plastics Coun., Mo. Acad. Scis., N.Y. Acad. Sci., Sigma Xi. Home: 54 Morwood Ln Creve Coeur MO 63141-7621 Office: Conatech Cons Group 287 N Lindbergh Blvd Creve Coeur MO 63141-7849

BODEM, BEVERLY A., state legislator; b. Wis., Feb. 22, 1940; m. Denise Bodem; 3 children. Student, U. Wis. State rep. Mich. Ho. Reps., Dist. 109, 1991—; mem. tourism & recreation com., co-chair econ. devel. com., conservation, environ. & great lakes com. & pub. health com., chair task force tourism, mem. task force sr. policy, Mich. Ho. Reps. Mem. Club Alpena, Lions. Home: 121 E White St Alpena MI 49707-3831 Office: Mich Ho of Reps State Capitol Lansing MI 48909*

BODENSTAB, JOHNNA LYNN, nursing educator; b. Kansas City, Mo., June 11, 1963; d. Gerald and Christine (Ferguson) Meyer; m. Todd Andrew Bodenstab, Aug. 7, 1983; children: Lindsey Nicole, Tyler Andrew. BSN, Rockhurst Coll., 1985; MSN, U. Mo., Kansas City, 1992; grad. post-masters program, U. Mo., Columbia, 1996. CCRN, Mo.; cert. ACLS instr. Staff nurse cardiac intermediate care Rsch. Med. Ctr., Kansas City, 1985-90, nurse recruiter, 1990; adj. clin. resource assoc. Rsch. Coll. Nursing, Kansas City, 1990-91, asst. prof., 1991—. Mem. AACN, ANA, Rsch. Coll. Nursing Honor Soc. Lutheran. Office: Rsch Coll Nursing 2300 E Meyer Blvd Kansas City MO 64132-1136

BODIKER, RICHARD WILLIAM, SR., state legislator; b. Richmond, Ind., Aug. 17, 1936; m. Nancy Bodiker; 7 children. Student, Ball State U., Ind U. East. Mem. Richmond Common Coun., 1983-86; Ind. state rep. Dist. 56, 1986—; mem. commerce com., utility regulatory flexibility com., interstate coop com. and econ. devel. and govt. affairs com.; mem. Ind. Ho. of Reps., Richmond Power and Light, 1983-86; with Dana Engine Products. Mem. Richmond Evening Optimist, Richmond/Wayne County C. of C., Cambridge City C. of C. Home: 1710 Capri Ln Richmond IN 47374-1504 Office: State House Rm 336 Indianapolis IN 46204*

BODINE, LAURENCE, lawyer, editor, marketer; b. Kissimmee, Fla., Nov. 4, 1950; s. Cornelius and Tatiana (Krupenin) B.; 1 child, Theodore Laurence. Student, Universitat Munchen, Munich, Germany, 1970-71; BA, Amherst Coll., 1972; JD, Seton Hall U., 1981. Bar: Wis. 1981, U.S. Dist. Ct. (we. dist.) Wis. 1981. Reporter The Star-Ledger, Newark, 1973-76, N.Y. Daily News, N.Y.C., 1976-78; reporter, asst. editor Nat. Law Jour., N.Y.C., 1978-81; assoc. Stafford, Rieser, Rosenbaum & Hansen, Madison, Wis., 1982; assoc. editor ABA Jour., Chgo., 1982-85, editor, pub., 1986-89; pub. Lawyers Alert, 1989-91; dir. communications Sidley & Austin, Chgo., 1991—; panelist SNAP Pubs. Mgmt. Conf., Washington, 1988-89, 91-93, Folio Mag. Pub. Week, 1988-89, 91; legal malpractice columnist Ill. Legal Times, 1995-96. Co-author: Trial Manual for Proving Hedonic Damages, 1992, author supplement, 1995; mng. editor newsletter The Legal View, 1991-96; law columnist Mag. Week, 1989-92; profl. responsibility columnist Lawyers Weekly U.S.A., 1993—. Recipient Media award N.J. Bar Assn., 1977, Enterprise award N.J. Press Assn., 1977, 78, Extended Deadline award Sigma Delta Chi, 1977, Editorial Excellence award Am. Soc. Bus. Press Editors, 1983, 87, Writing award Soc. Nat. Assn. Pubs., 1983, Most Improved Mag. award Soc. Nat. Assn. Pubs., 1986, Nat. Gold Circle award Am. Soc. Assn. Execs., 1988. Mem. ABA (chmn. United Way campaign 1985, panelist gen. practice sect. 1991), Nat. Law Firm Mktg. Assn. (bd. dirs. Chgo. chpt. 1995). Office: Sidley & Austin One First National Plz Chicago IL 60603

BODINE, RONALD JESSE, pilot; b. Kansas City, Kans., May 9, 1961; s. James J. and Rita B. (Effertz) B.; m. Honey I. Costello, June 29, 1985; children: J.R. Allen, Rachel Irene. BS in Aeronautical Engring., USAF Acad., 1983. Commd. 2d lt. USAF, 1983, advanced through grades to capt.; student pilot 80 TFW, Wichita Falls, Tex., 1983-84; F-15 pilot/instr. 12 TFS, Kadena AB, Okinawa, Japan, 1985-88; OV-10 pilot instr. 27 TASS, George AB, Calif., 1988-90; flight engr. B 727 American Airlines, Dallas/Ft. Worth, 1990-91; 1st officer F-100 Am. Airlines, Dallas-Ft. Worth, 1991-96, 1st officer S-80, 1996—. Roman Catholic. Home: 1732 Tudor Ln Liberty MO 64068

BOEDIGHEIMER, SCOTT MICHAEL, accountant; b. St. Cloud, Minn., Sept. 18, 1966; s. Michael Lawrence and Sue Ann Boedigheimer; m. Cari Ann Kallio, Aug. 25, 1990. BS, St. John's U., Collegeville, Minn., 1988. CPA. Acct. Larson, Allen, Weishair & Co., St. Cloud, Minn., 1989-92; fin. mgr. Receivables Control Corp., Mpls., 1992; mgr., acct. Larson, Allen, Weishair & Co., Mpls., 1992—. Mem. St. Cloud C. of C. (chair 1990, chair Colls. and Univ. div. 1990-91), Twin West C. of C. (chair entrepreneur of yr. award com. 1996). Office: Larson Allen Weishair & Co 200 S 6th St Ste 1000 Minneapolis MN 55402-1411

BOEHM, JAMES, state legislator; m. Pat Boehm. Mem. N.D. Ho. of Reps. from 31st dist., 1991—; vice chmn. Edn. Com. N.D. Ho. of Reps., mem. Transp. Com. Mem. Sch. Bd. Mem. KC, Future Farmers Am. (hon. state farmer), Elks, Moose, Eagles. Republican. Address: Rte 1 Box 83 Mandan ND 58554*

BOEHM, MICHAEL J., electrical engineer; b. Pitts., Feb. 28, 1966. BSEE, U. Pitts., 1980. Project engr. GMC Packard Electric, Warren, Ohio, 1991—. Office: GMC Packard Electric PO Box 431 Warren OH 44486-0001

BOEHM, ROBERT KENNETH, telecommunications consultant; b. St. Louis, Aug. 26, 1925; s. James Richard Boehm and Della Ann Barrett Perkins; m. Martha L. Barker, Dec. 13, 1951 (dec. 1957); children: Robert Jr., Michael; m. Shirley Annette Huffman, Oct. 12, 1958; children: Mark, Brenda, Christopher. Student, E.O.C.E., LaGrande, Oreg., 1943-44. Sales rep. Philco Distbrs., St. Louis, 1948-54; regional sales mgr. Bendix Corp., St. Louis, 1955-57, Stromberg Carlson, Miami, Fla., 1958-60; sales mgr. Stromberg Carlson, N.Y.C., 1961-66; pres. Rent-A-Cruise of Am., div. Bangor Punta Corp., Florence, Ala., 1967-73; prin. Crescent Hotel, Eureka Springs, Ark., 1973-76; various positions in real estate devel. and investment R. Boehm Real Estate Devel., 1976-81; pres. Compute-A-Call Long Distance Svc., Springfield, Mo., 1982-90, Robert Boehm & Assocs., Springfield, Mo., 1991—, Springfield Fin. Ctr., 1991—, Nutrition Prescription Svc., Springfield, 1992—, Worldwide Telcard Corp., Branson, Mo., 1995—. Aviation cadet USAAF, 1943-46. Mem. Masons. Assemblies of God. Home: 350 Hammons Pky Springfield MO 65806 OfficeY: Springfield Fin Ctr 350 Hammons Pkwy Springfield MO 65806

BOEHM, TONI GEORGENE, seminary dean, nurse; b. New Kensington, Pa., Dec. 28, 1946; d. Sylvio Chipoletti and Eula Gene (Smittle) Fox; m. Raymond Stawinski, Dec. 11, 1965 (div. Sept. 1978); 1 child, Michelle Stawinski Ivy; m. Jay Thomas Boehm, Apr. 28, 1983; children: Jonathon, Kimberly, Allison Cole, Amanda. Diploma, Allegheny Valley Sch. Nursing, Natrona Heights, Pa., 1967; family nurse practitioner cert., U. Kans., 1976; BA in Edn., Ottawa (Kans.) U., 1978; MSN, U. Mo., Kansas City, 1981; grad., Unity Sch. of Christianity, Unity Village, Mo., 1989. Ordained to ministry Assn. of Unity Chs.; cert. occupl. health nurse. Nurse Allegheny Valley Hosp., Natrona Heights, 1967-74; head nurse, dir. nursing Truman Med. Ctr., Kansas City, Mo., 1974-78; mgr. med. Hallmark Card Inc., Kansas City, Mo., 1978-85; sr. staff specialist ANA, Kansas City, Mo., 1985-87; dean of adminstrn. Unity Sch. Christianity, 1987—; nat. spkr. and freelance writer for ministry and self-unfoldment. Author: The Spiritual Intrapreneur, 1996. Mem. nat. steering com. for fundraising Unity Sch. of Christianity; mem. women's coun. U. Mo. Recipient scholarships. Mem. ANA, NCCJ, Mo. Nurses Assn. (bd. dirs. 1975-85), U. Mo. Sch. Nursing Alumni Assn., Assn. Unity Chs. (urban curriculum com. 1987—, ministerial edn. com. 1987—, field licensing com. 1990). Republican. Home: 430 N Winnebago Dr Lake Winnebago MO 64034-9321 Office: Unity Sch Christianity Lees Summit MO 64065

BOEHNER, JOHN A., congressman; b. Reading, Ohio, Nov. 17, 1949; m. Deborah Gunlack, 1973; children: Lindsay M., Tricia A. BS, Xavier U., 1977. Pres. Nucite Sales, Inc.; mem. Ohio Ho. of Reps., 1984-90, 102nd-103rd Congresses from 8th Ohio dist., Washington, D.C., 1991—; gen. dep. whip Rep. Ho. Leadership; vice chair Nat. Rep. Congl. Com.; chmn. Ho. Rep. Conf. Com.; mem. Ag. Com., Ho. Oversight Com. Active Ohio Farm Bur.; chmn. Conservative Opportunity Soc. Mem. KC, Cin., Dayton, Middletown C. of C. Roman Catholic. Republican. Office: US Ho of Reps 1011 Longworth Washington DC 20515-3508*

BOEKHOLDER, THERESA MARIE, geriatrics nurse; b. Ft. Smith, Ark., Jan. 20, 1938; d. Paul John and Rose Marie (Roll) Wewers; m. William Henry Boekholder, Apr. 23, 1960; children: Deborah Joan, William Joseph. Diploma, St. Edward Hosp. Sch. Nursing, 1959. Obstet. nurse St. Edward Mercy Hosp., Ft. Smith, 1959-60, St. Joseph Mercy Hosp., Dubuque, Iowa, 1960, St. Joseph Hosp., Elgin, Ill., 1961, St. Francis Hosp., Freeport, Ill., 1962-65; head nurse post operative Freeport Meml. Hosp., 1966-67, supr. P.M., 1967-68; office nurse, internist Dr. D.J. Chang, Freeport, 1968-85; geriatrics nurse St. Joseph Home for the Aged, Freeport, 1985-94, asst. dir. nursing, 1994—; home assess nurse Hospice of N.W. Ill., Freeport, 1986-94. Pres. Am. Heart Assn., Freeport, 1980-82; blood pressure screener Am. Heart Assn., Freeport, 1982-94. Recipient People of Northwest Ill. award, 1990. Roman Catholic.

BOELENS, PATRICIA ANN, accountant, nurse; b. Grinnell, Iowa, May 21, 1943; d. Harold Willis and Mary Louise (Phipps) Andes; m. William Carl Laubengayer, Aug. 15, 1963; children: Karl E., Kevin E.; m. Francis Raymond Boelens, Sept. 19, 1992; stepchildren: Kristina M., Kirk M. Diploma in nursing, St. Lukes Hosp., Cedar Rapids, Iowa, 1965; BSN, Coe Coll., 1976; AAS in Acctg. Tech., Kirkwood C.C., Cedar Rapids, 1987. Staff nurse Cedar Rapids, 1974-77; dir. nursing North Brook Manor Care Ctr., Cedar Rapids, 1977-78; staff nurse Linn County Pub. Health, Cedar Rapids, 1979-81; staff acct. Jean E. Kruse, CPA, Cedar Rapids, 1987-88; office mgr. Gordon Mollman, PA, Cedar Rapids, 1988-89; staff acct. Cindy Davis & Assocs., Moline, Ill., 1990-93, Watts & Assocs., Moline, Ill., 1993-94, AAA Iowa, Bettendorf, 1994-95, On With Life, Inc., Ankeny, Iowa, 1996—; spkr. continuing edn. workshops for various orgns., 1977-79; Iowa Nurses Assn. rep. Iowa Health Sys. Agy., Iowa City, 1979-83. Chair vol. adv. com. Linn County Coun. on Aging, Cedar Rapids, 1978-81. Nominee Nurse of Yr., Jour. Gerontol. Nursing, 1978. Mem. ANA (Iowa del. 1982), Iowa Nurses Assn. (continuing edn. rev. panel 1976-78, 3d v.p. 1978-80), Inst. Mgmt. Accts. (treas. Illowa chpt. 1992-94), Nat. Assn. Tax Practitioners, Kiwanis (com. chair Moline chpt. 1991-94), Phi Theta Kappa, Sigma Theta Tau. Home: 209 13th St SW Altoona IA 50009-2403 Office: On With Life Inc 715 SW Ankeny Rd Ankeny IA 50021

BOELMAN, KIM BRIAN, electrical design engineer; b. Grand Rapids, Mich., Apr. 10, 1954. AS, No. Iowa C.C., 1974. Electronic specialist Bourns Inc., Ames, Iowa, 1977-90; elec. design engr. Ryko Mfg., Grimes, Iowa, 1990—. Mem. Elks. Office: Ryko Mfg 11600 NW 54th Ave Grimes IA 50111

BOELZ, THOMAS LEONARD, furniture retail executive; b. St. Cloud, Minn., Sept. 15, 1935; s. Lawrence John and Priscilla Angeline (Jackson) B. Grad. high sch., St. Cloud, Minn., 1953. Driver Concrete Industry, St. Cloud, Minn., 1953-77; owner Thomas Park Antiques, Clear Lake, Minn., 1977—. mem. Clear Lake City Council, 1979— Clear Lake Planning Commn., 1980—; del. Sherburne County High Task Force, Becker, Minn., 1985—; bd. dirs. Sherburne County Hist. Soc., Becker, 1980-86. Served to sgt. Minn. N.G., 1956-64. Mem. Am. Legion, Carriage Assn. Am., Whip Wheels Carriage and Driving Soc., Horn'N Hame Horse Club (Sauk Rapids, Minn.), No. Minn. Draft Horse Club (Princeton). Republican. Roman Catholic. Home: 607 Center St Clear Lake MN 55319-9468

BOERSMA, MARK, data processing executive; b. Omaha, Nebr., Feb. 6, 1964. BA in Fin., No. Ill. U., 1987. V.p. sales Prefered Mortgage Assn., Downers Grove, Ill., 1988-92; pres. Synergy Solutions Inc., Warrenville, Ill., 1992—. Office: Synergy Solutions Inc 29w150 Butterfield Rd Warrenville IL 60555-2804

BOERTJE, STANLEY BENJAMIN, retired zoology educator; b. Pella, Iowa, Aug. 1, 1930; s. Paul and Hattie (Spoelman) B.; div.; children: Judith Karen, Gregory Irwin, Rodney Dean, Julie Beth, Kevin Jay, Eric Lyle. AB in Secondary Edn., Calvin Coll., Grand Rapids, Mich., 1951; MS in Zoology, State U. Iowa, 1957; PhD in Zoology, Iowa State U., 1966. Lic. tchr. secondary edn., Iowa. Prin., tchr. Prairie City (Iowa) Christian Sch., 1951-52; tchr., coach Pella (Iowa) Christian High Sch., 1954-60; instr., assoc. prof. Dordt Coll., Sioux Center, Iowa, 1960-67; assoc., prof. Midwestern Coll., Denison, Iowa, 1967-70; prof. zoology So. U. New Orleans, 1970-94; Contbr. articles to profl. jours. With U.S. Army, 1952-54. NSF fellow Iowa State U., Ames, 1964-65, NIH fellow Tulane U. Med. Ctr., New Orleans, 1982-84. Mem. La. Acad. Scis. Republican. Lutheran. Home: 12 220 Land's End Ln SE Bemidji MN 56601

BOESCH, DEBORAH ANN, elementary education educator; b. Wenatchee, Wash., Aug. 13, 1948; d. Lloyd Wilbur and Julia Marie (Cernickey) B. BS, No. Ill. U., 1970, MS in Edn., 1977. Cert. elem. tchr., Ill. Tchr. Edgar Allan Poe Sch., Arlington Heights, Ill., 1971-85, Henry Wadsworth Longfellow Sch., Buffalo Grove, Ill., 1985—. Mem. ASCD, NEA, Ill. Edn.Assn., Assn. for Childhood Edn. Internat. Home: 1937 N Coldspring Rd Arlington Heights IL 60004-7242 Office: Longfellow Sch 501 N Arlington Heights Rd Buffalo Grove IL 60089-1607

BOESE, KATHLEEN CAROL, principal; b. Quincy, Ill., Dec. 25, 1942; d. Earl Washburn McCune and Elizabeth Marie (Hall) Mosley; m. Charles Boese; children: Trudi, Heather. BS in Elem. Edn., Western Ill. U., 1965; MS in Elem. Edn., No. Ill. U., 1972, administrv. type 75 cert., 1983; Cert. Reading Specialist, Nat. Coll. Edn., 1986. Tchr. Fox Lake (Ill.) Schs., 1965-68; Title I remedial reading tchr. Grant Reading Co-op, Fox Lake, 1972-81; 3d grade tchr. Gavin Dist. #37, Ingleside, Ill., 1981-87; prin. Washington Sch., Harvard, Ill., 1987—; prekindergarten dir./coord. Harvard Sch. Dist. # 50. Editor (newsletter) Harvard Educator. Sec., treas. pres., trustee Fox Lake Library Dist. Master Ill. Adminstrs. Acad.; mem. SCIRA, Internat. Reading Assn. (suburban coun.), Ill. Prins. Assn., Adminstrs. and Reading Spl. Interest Coun., Chgo. Assn. for Edn. of Young Children, Scottish Cultural Soc. (Elgin), Order Eastern Star (past matron Grayslake chpt. 1972), Kappa Delta Gamma Soc., Pi Delta Epsilon. Republican. Home: 7418 Garfield St Harvard IL 60033-1746 Office: Harvard Sch Dist #50 Washington Sch 305 S Hutchinson St Harvard IL 60033-2718

BOESEL, MILTON CHARLES, JR., lawyer, business executive; b. Toledo, July 12, 1928; s. Milton Charles and Florence (Fitzgerald) B.; m. Lucy Laughlin Mather, Mar. 25, 1961; children: Elizabeth Boesel Sagges, Charles Mather, Andrew Fitzgerald. B.A., Yale, 1950; LL.B., Harvard, 1953. Bar: Ohio 1953, Mich. 1953. Of counsel firm Ritter, Robinson, McCready & James, Toledo, 1956—; chmn., bd. dirs. Michabo, Inc.; bd. dirs. Fifth Third Bancorp, Fifth Third Bank of Northwestern Ohio. Lt. USNR, 1953-56. Episcopalian. Clubs: Toledo Country; Leland Country (Mich.). Sawgrass Country (Fla.). Home: 5520 S Citation Rd Toledo OH 43615-2154 Office: 405 Madison Ave Toledo OH 43604-1207

BOETTCHER, PHIL G., industrial service executive; b. Wausau, Wis., June 26, 1942. B, U. Wis., 1964. Tchr. secondary sch. Black River Falls, Wis., 1964-68; head mfg. Quality Machine Sales, Wausau, Wis., 1971-84; owner Indsl. Svc., Schofield, Wis., 1985—. Office: Indsl Svc & Machine PO Box 20 Schofield WI 54476-0020

BOGART, CAROL LYNN, small business owner, freelance reporter, video producer, radio personality; b. Lakewood, Ohio, Mar. 9, 1949; d. Lloyd William and Evelyn Mary (Overmyer) B.; 1 child, Michael Lloyd. BLS, Bowling Green State U., 1973; grad., Nat. Theater Conservatory, Denver, 1992. Reporter, anchor WNEP-TV, Scranton, Pa., 1975-76; reporter WXIA-TV, Atlanta, 1976-79; reporter, fill-in morning anchor WLS-TV, Chgo., 1979-82; anchor, reporter KMGH-TV, Denver, 1982-89; media cons., video producer, voice-over and on-camera talent Bogart Inc., Denver, 1989-93; freelance reporter WOTO-WUAB-TV, Cleve., 1995-96; radio host WTTF Radio, Tiffin, Ohio, 1996—; field producer, writer WUAB and WOIO-TV, Cleve., 1996—; guest speaker various schs. and univs., Denver, 1982-93, Cleve. 1994—. Mem. Greater Cleve. Growth Assn., Coun. of Sml. Enterprises; vol. Odyssey of the Mind coach, pet therapy, grief counseling. Mem. AFTRA, SAG, Nat. Assn. Broadcast Engrs. and Techs. Presbyterian.

BOGART, KEITH CHARLES, neurologist; b. Lorain, Ohio, Apr. 12, 1936; s. Lloyd William and Evelyn (Overmyer) B.; m. B. Diane Seigel, June 8, 1967; children: Keith Charles Jr., Catherine Michelle; m. Alice Craib, July 21, 1976; 1 child, Matthew William. BA, Ohio State U., 1958, MD, 1961. Diplomate Am. Bd. Psychiatry and Neurology, Am. Bd. Qualification in EEG. Asst. prof. neurology U. Wis., Madison, 1968-69, Creighton U., Omaha, Nebr., 1975-78; chmn. neurology Gunderson Clinic, Lacrosse, Wis., 1969-75; clin. neurologist Mansfield (Ohio) Neurology, Inc., 1978—; med. dir. rehab. unit Mansfield Gen. Hosp., 1988-91; cons. neurology VA Hosp., Omaha, 1977-78. Bd. dirs. Boy Scouts Am., Mansfield, 1986. Served to lt. comdr. USPHS, 1963-65. Fellow Am. Acad. Neurology, Am. EEG Soc. (mem. lab. accreditation bd. 1984-87); mem. AMA (Physician's Recognition awad 1969, 72, 77, 82, 86, 87, 88, 91, 94), Cen. Assn. EEGers (pres. 1977-78), Nebr. Epilepsy League (pres. 1976-78), Wis. Med. Soc. (chmn. neurology sect. 1975), Wis. Neurol. Soc. (pres. 1973), Richland County Med. Soc. (pres. 1988, sec.-treas. 1986—), Knights of Magic (pres. 1986-87, Magician of Yr. 1984, 85, 86), Internat. Brotherhood Magicians (v.p. ter. 1986-91, Presdl. Citation 1988), Inner Magic Circle (assoc.), Internat. Platform Assn., Rotary. Home: 730 Woodhill Rd Mansfield OH 44907-1540 Office: Mansfield Neurology Inc 222 Marion Ave Mansfield OH 44903-2138

BOGDON, GLENDON JOSEPH, orthodontist; b. Green Bay, Wis., Sept. 23, 1935; s. Joseph Frank and Anne Marie (Jacklin) B.; m. Susanne Ellen Daley, Aug. 8, 1959; 1 child, Amy Sue. BS, St. Norbert Coll., DePere, Wis., 1957; DDS, Marquette U., 1971, MS in Clin. Dentistry, 1973. Officer IRS, Chgo., 1958; social worker Cath. Welfare Bur., Milw., 1958-59; tchr. secondary sch. Door County Schs., Brussels, Wis., 1959-67; practice dentistry specializing in orthodontics Milw., 1973—; pres. So. Orthodontic Services,

Milw., 1986—. Writer fitness column Cath. Herald; contbr. articles to profl. jours.; patentee in field. Served with U.S. Army, 1957-58. Mem. Greater Milw. Dental Assn. (Continuing Edn. award 1971-73), Wis. Dental Assn. (Continuing Edn. award 1971-74, 79-81, ADA (Continuing Edn. award 1976-78), Royal Soc. Health, Wis. Soc. Orthodontists, Midwestern Soc. Orthodontists, Am. Assn. Orthodontists, Spitfire Soc., Am. Running and Fitness Assn. Democrat. Roman Catholic. Office: 3044 S 92nd St Milwaukee WI 53227-3678

BOGDONOFF, MAURICE LAMBERT, physician; b. Chgo., May 11, 1926; s. Harry A. and Mary Ivy (Grogan) B.; m. Diana Edith Rauschkolb, June 29, 1956; children: Vivian, Gregory, Audrey. BS, Tufts U., 1948; MD, Yale U., 1952. Intern U. Ill. Rsch. and Edn. Hosp., Chgo., 1952-53; resident in internal medicine Boston City Hosp., 1953-54; resident in radiology Columbia-Presbyn. Med. Ctr., N.Y., 1955-57; asst. prof. to assoc. prof. radiology to prof. U. Ill., Chgo., 1958-69; attending radiologist Rush-Presbyn.-St. Luke's Med. Ctr., Chgo., pres. med. staff, 1975-77; prof. radiology and medicine Rush Med. Coll., Chgo., 1970-88, 1969-88, prof. emeritus, 1988—; cons. Argonne (Ill.) Nat. Lab., 1963-88; cons., health dir. Canal Zone Panama, 1973-80; vis. lectr. nuclear power engring. Maine Maritime Acad., 1989. Contbr. articles to profl. jours. Pres. Wheaton (Ill.) Dist. 36 Sch. Bd.,1964-67; bd. visitors Coll. of DuPage Radio and TV Sys., Glen Ellyn, Ill., 1987-94. With USN, 1944-46. Fellow Am. Coll. Radiology, Inst. Medicine, also others; mem. Chgo. Lit. Club. Republican. Home: 203 W Willow Ave Wheaton IL 60187-5238

BOGETT, WILLIAM R., accident reconstructionist and safety engineer; b. Hinsdale, Ill., Nov. 22, 1937; s. A. Merle Bogett and Patricia (Pier) Jackson; m. Darlene Paasche, Apr. 27, 1957; children: Suzanne Marie Bogett Wegener, Jacqueline Denise Bogett Wentzel. LLB, LaSalle Ext. U., Chgo., 1970; MSE, Calif. Coast U., 1984, PhD in Engring., 1986. Registered profl. engr., Ill., Calif., Wis.; cert. Accreditation Commn. for Traffic Accident Reconstructionists. Project engr. Electro-Motive divsn. GMC, LaGrange, Ill., 1966-68, sr. project engr., 1968-81, staff analysis engr., 1981-86, supr. product litigation & safety, 1986-91; prin. TBX Assocs., Inc., Downers Grove, Ill., 1991—. Co-author tech. papers. Mem. NSPE, Soc. Automotive Engrs. (chmn. advanced tech. com. 1993—), Sys. Safety Soc. (sr.), Soc. Accident Reconstructionists. Office: TBX Assocs Inc 915 Burlington Ave Ste 915E Downers Grove IL 60515-4730

BOGGESS, THOMAS PHILLIP, III, graphics arts company executive; b. Greenville, Ky., Jan. 22, 1921; s. William C. and Gertrude Lucille (Lumpkins) B.; grad. high sch.; m. Ann Marie Mossner, Sept. 1, 1942; children—Thomas Phillip IV, Nancy L. Vice-pres. Alfred Mossner Co., Chgo., 1945-70, pres., chief exec. officer, 1970—, also dir.; treas., dir. Blue Printers Supply Corp., Chgo. Chmn. zoning bd. of appeals, Village of River Forest, Ill., 1950—; mem., past bd. dirs. Westchester (Ill.) Bible Ch. Served with USNR, 1942-45. Decorated Purple Heart, Bronze Star (5). Mem. Blue Print Club of Chgo. (pres. 1957-62), Disabled Am. Vets. Club: Oak Park Country. Home: 335 Gale Ave River Forest IL 60305-2015 Office: 137 N Wabash Ave Chicago IL 60602-1910

BOGGS, JOHN ROBERT, JR., minister, writer; b. Bremen, Ga., Apr. 13, 1922; s. Wesley and Lola Gertrude (Posey) B.; m. Doris Maxine Ratcliff, July 10, 1943; children: Robert Earl, Betty Ann, Carol Jeanine, Barbara Jo. BA, Wilmington Coll., 1945; MDiv, Asbury Theol. Sem., Wilmore, Ky., 1949. Ordained Meth. Ch., 1950. Pastor United Meth. Ch., Beach, N.D., North Ind. Conf., Ft. Wayne, various cities. Author: I'll Move Over—The Story of a Great Love, 1994; prodr.: (edn. video) Feeding & Dental Hygiene, 1995. Elder Meth. ch.; seminar leader for Alzheimer's Disease edn. Republican. Office: Boggs Books PO Box 122 Warsaw IN 46580

BOGGS, JOHN STEVEN, sales and development executive; b. Indpls., Apr. 7, 1960; s. William Joseph and Bernadine Ann (Hague) B.; m. Vicky Swank, May 2, 1981. BS, U. Indpls., 1982. Press room machinist Farm Fans, Inc., Indpls, 1978-79; delivery work to inside office help Cen. Pub. Co., Indpls, 1979-81; outside and inside salesperson Mutual Pipe and Supply Co., Indpls., 1982-94; councilman City of Greenwood, 1988-95; pres. Greenwood City Coun., 1991; sales and bus. devel. S.R. Jacobs and Assocs., Indpls., 1994—; pres. Lofts of Valle Vista Homeowners Assn., Greenwood, 1985-88. Vol. Reagan/Bush re-election, Indpls., 1984; Rep. precinct committeeman, 1987-95; Greenwood Rep. City chair, 1995; chmn. Johnson County Solid Waste Mgmt. Dist., 1991-95; chmn. bd. trustees University Hts. United Meth. Ch., Indpls. Mem. Nat. League Cities, Ind. Assn. Cities and Towns. Office: SR Jacobs and Assocs Ste 220 10585 N Meridian St Indianapolis IN 46290-1067

BOGGS, ROBERT J., state senator; m. Judie Sylak; children: Larissa, Kelly, Kristin. BS, Am. U., 1969; postgrad., Youngstown State U.; MPA, Kent State U. Mem. Ohio Ho. of Reps., Columbus, former chmn. edn. com. and edn. rev. com.; mem. Ohio Senate Ohio Ho. of Reps., 1983—; ranking minority mem. energy and natural resources com., mem. state and local govt. com., hwys. and transp. com., minority leader; mem. adj. faculty U. San Francisco, McLaren Coll. Bus. Co-chmn. Ohio Lake Erie Shore Area Redevel. Task Force; chmn. Ohio High Speed Rail Authority; mem. transp. and comm. com., mem. econ. devel. com. Nat. Conf. State Legislators. Recipient Disting. Svc. award Gt. Lakes Commn., Ohio Sea Grant Program, Ohio Environ. Coun., Western Res. Conservation Club, Ohio County Treas. Assn., Lake County Trustees and Clks. Assn., Elem. Adminstrs. Assn., Ohio Assn. Secondary Adminstrs. Mem. Ohio Trustees and Clks. Assn. (assoc.), Am. High Speed Rail Assn. (bd. dirs.), Farm Bur., Sierra Club, Omicron Delta Kappa. Democrat. Office: 2281 Morning Pt Rock Creek OH 44084-9654 also: State Senate State Capital Columbus OH 43215*

BOGGS, ROSS A., JR., state legislator, dairy farmer; m. Eleanor Boggs; children: Robin, Leslie, Suzanne, Shelley. Student, Kent State U. Dairy farmer, Andover, Ohio; mem. Ohio Ho. of Reps., Columbus, 1985—; vice chmn. elecric and township com., mem. agr. and natural resources com., fin. and appropriations com., pub. utilities com., ways and means com., high speed rail task force and Ohio Rail Authority com., chmn. select com. to study effects of fed. cutbacks on local govt. and select com. on child abuse and juvenile justice, commerce and labor com. Named Legislator of Yr., Airplane Owners and Pilots Assn., 1987, Conservation Legislator of Yr., League Ohio Sportsmen, 1988, Outstanding Legislator, Pub. Children's Svc., 1988; recipient President's award Ohio Youth Svc. Assn., 1990. Mem. Ashtabula Clks. and Trustees Assn., Farm Bur., Ohio Farmers Union, Elks. Democrat. Home: 4779 State Route 7 Andover OH 44003-9663*

BOGINA, AUGUST, JR., state senator; b. Girard, Kans., Sept. 13, 1927; s. August and Mary (Blazic) B.; B.S., Engring., Kans. State U., 1950; m. Nancy L. Pock, 1988; children: Kathleen A., August III, Michael E., Mark A., Kathleen R., Korey A. Owner, Bogina & Assocs., Lenexa, Kans., 1962-70; pres. Bogina Cons. Engrs., 1970-; partner Bogina Petroleum Engineers, 1983—; mem. Kans. Ho. of Reps., 1974-80, Kans. Senate, 1980—. Precinct committeeman Kans. Republican party, 1970-74, chmn. city com., 1972-74. Served with U.S. Army, 1946-48. Registered profl. engr., Kans., Mo., Colo., Okla.; registered land surveyor Kans., Mo. Mem. Nat., Mo. socs. profl. engrs., Kans. Engring. Soc., Kans. Soc. Land Surveyors, Mo. Registered Land Surveyors. Roman Catholic. Office: 12510 W 62nd Ter Ste 109 Shawnee Mission KS 66216-1869 also: State Senate State Capitol Topeka KS 66612

BOGLE, JOEANN ROSE, florist; b. St. Louis County, Mo., July 27, 1934; d. Albert Ray and Lillian Ann (Wilson) Weston; m. J.W. Bogle, Oct. 31, 1956; children: Jerome Alan, Janice Kim Bogle Bohr. Cert. in practical nursing, Lincoln Inst., Chgo., 1954; student, Pope Pius Early Childhood Inst, 1984; cert. in flower arranging, Lifetime Career Schs., 1988. Office mgr. Monumental Life Ins. Co., St. Louis, 1952-57; co-owner, flower arranger Only Yours-Silk Wedding Flowers, St. Louis, 1985—. Active Hazelwood Schs. PTA, 1963-75; den leader, pack leader St. Louis area Boy Scouts Am., 1965-69; cons., sec., troop leader St. Louis area Girl Scouts U.S., 1967-80; dir. concession stands Hazelwood Khoury League, 1966-71; coord., tchr. Our Lady of Mercy Ch., Hazelwood, 1966—, dir. ch. flowers, 1984—; active Archdiocesan Deanery Councillor Coun., St. Louis, 1981—; active support dogs for handicapped, Humane Soc., St. Louis, 1979—. Mem. MADD, K.C. Ladies Aux., Our Lady of Mercy Women's Coun. Home: 946 Chula Dr Hazelwood MO 63042-1207

BOGNAR, BOTOND, architecture educator; b. Budapest, Hungary, Feb. 28, 1944; came to U.S., 1979; s. Istvan and Amalia (Toth) B.; m. Concepcion V. Borromeo, Aug. 15, 1975; children: Balazs, Zsolt, Balint. BArch, Budapest Tech. U., 1968, MArch, 1972; postgrad., Tokyo Inst. Tech., 1973-75; MA in Architecture and Urban Planning, UCLA, 1981. Archtl. designer Közti, Budapest, 1968-72, prin. designer/architect-in-charge, 1972-77; designer Design System Archtl. Office, Tokyo, 1978; from asst. prof. to assoc. prof. U. Ill., Urbana, 1981-90, prof. architecture, 1990—, univ. scholar, 1986; endowed chair professorship Rsch. Ctr. for Advanced Sci. and Tech. in Urban Design, Tokyo U., 1993; guest speaker, lectr. ednl. and profl. orgns., U.S. and worldwide locations, 1980—; mem. Ctr. for East Asian and Pacific Studies, U. Ill. Author: Japanese Architecture of Today, 1979 (award), Contemporary Japanese Architecture, 1985 (award), The New Japanese Architecture, 1990 (award), The Japan Guide, 1995 (award), Togo Murano: Master Architect of Japan, 1996 (award); (with others) Nikken Sekkei 1990-91: Building Modern Japan, 1990 (award); editor: (monograph) Minoru Takeyama, 1995, (spl. feature issue) Jour. Archtl. Design, 1988, 92, Architecture and Urbanism, 1990; corr. (jour.) Architecture and Urbanism, Tokyo, 1976—; contbr. numerous articles to internat. jours.; contbr. chpts. to books. Graham Found. fellow, Chgo., 1985, Social Sci. Rsch. Coun. fellow, N.Y., 1988, Asian Cultural Coun. fellow, N.Y., 1995; recipient Togo Murano: Master Architect of Japan award, 1996. Mem. AIA (assoc.), Assn. for Asian Studies, Soc. for Phenomenology and Human Scis., Hungarian Inst. Architects, Phi Kappa Phi. Office: U Ill Sch Architecture 611 Taft Dr Champaign IL 61820-6921

BOGNER, JAMES M., electrical engineer; b. Washington, Oct. 25, 1944. BS in Elec. Engring., U. Calif., Berkeley, 1974. Sys. engr. Global Marine, Houston, 1977-85; design engr. Delco Electronics, Santa Barbara, Calif., 1974-77, 85-93; adv. project engr. Delco Electronics, Kokomo, Ind., 1993—. Patentee in field. With U.S. Army, 1965-67, Viet Nam. Mem. IEEE. Republican.

BOGUE, ERIC H., state legislator, lawyer. Bar: S.D. Lawyer pvt. practice, Dupree, S.D.; mem. S.D. Ho. of Reps., Pierre; mem. judiciary and tax coms. S.D. Ho. of Reps.

BOHAN, RUTH LOUISE, art educator; b. Galesburg, Ill., Dec. 27, 1946; d. John Lynch and Ethel Margaret (Gillmor) B. BA, U. Ill., 1969; MA, U. Md., 1972, PhD, 1980. Rsch. assoc. Yale U. Art Gallery, New Haven, 1979-80; Mellon fellow Washington U., St. Louis, 1980-81; asst. prof. art U. Mo., St. Louis, 1981-87, assoc. prof., 1987—; chairperson U. Mo., St. Louis, 1995—. Author: The Société Anonyme's Brooklyn Exhibition: Katherine Dreier and Modernism in America, 1982; contbg. editor: The Société Anonyme Collection and The Dreier Bequest at Yale University: A Catalogue Raisonné, 1984; also articles. Grantee Smithsonian Instn., 1975-76, 87, NEH, 1984, J. Paul Getty Trust, 1985-86. Mem. MLA, Am. Studies Assn., Coll. Art Assn., Mid-Am. Am. Studies Assn., Midwest Art History Soc. Office: U Missouri Dept Art and Art History 8001 Natural Bridge Rd Saint Louis MO 63121-4401

BOHATA, EMIL ANTON, rancher; b. Sept. 10, 1918; s. Frank and Mary Frances (Vodraska) B.; m. Ruth Joan Fletcher, July 14, 1963; children: Ruth Marie, Robert Anton. Student, S.W. Tex. State U., 1942-43. Lifelong rancher Brookville, Kans., 1935-42, 1945—. Trustee United Meth. Ch., Carneiro, Kans., 1970-88, chmn. bd., 1988-89; treas. Carneiro Twp., 1975-88. With U.S. Army, 1944-46. Recipient Fred Astaire Bronze, Silver and Gold Dance trophies Fred Astaire Dance Studio, Salina, Kans., 1960-62. Mem. Ellsworth County Farm Bur., Kans. Livestock Assn., Polled Hereford Assn., Kans. Livestock Assn., Friends Marymount Coll., Arts Series Soc., Salina Art Ctr., Am. Legion. Republican. Methodist. Home and Office: 765 27th Rd Brookville KS 67425-9508

BOHLING-PHILIPPI, VICKI DEE, family educator; b. Lincoln, Nebr., June 28, 1964; d. L.O. and Fern Elaine (Hoops) Bohling; m. Timothy J. Philippi; 2 children: Alec John, Gabriel Grace. BA, U. Nebr., 1986, MEd, 1988. Undergraduate acad. advisor U. Nebr., Lincoln, 1984-86, grad. rsch. asst., 1986-88; dir. for leadership devel. and student activities Doane Coll., Crete, Nebr., 1988-91, asst. dean of students, 1991-92; dir. Christian edn. Faith Luth. Ch., Forest Lake, Minn., 1993-96; parent educator Forest Lake Sch. Dist., 1996—; mem. Chancellor's Commn. on Status of Women U. Nebr., 1987-88. Named one of Outstanding Young Women Am., 1991. Mem. Nat. Assn. Student Pers. Adminstr., Am. Coll. Pers. Assn., Nat. Assn. Campus Activities (ednl. sessions coord. 1988-89, membership coord. 1991), Jaycees (bd. dirs. 1989-90, v.p. 1990-91), Tri-County Youth and Family Partnership (co-chair). Democrat. Lutheran.

BOHLKE, ARDYCE, state legislator; b. Omaha, Nov. 2, 1943; m. Jan Bohlke, 1967; children: Jon Jr., Jason. BS, U. Nebr., 1965. Mem. from dist. 33 Nebr. State Senate, Lincoln, 1992—, mem. com. on coms., natural resources and rules coms., vice chair edn. com. Past pres. Hastings Bd. Edn., Hastings YWCA. Mem. LWV (past pres.), Bus. and Profl. Women, Rotary. Office: Nebr State Senate State Capitol Rm 1120 Lincoln NE 68509*

BOHN, CHARLOTTE GALITZ, real estate executive; b. Chgo., Aug. 7, 1930; d. Chester Charles and Sarah Madelyn (McCarthy) B; m. Robert Allan Galitz, Nov. 25, 1955; children: Charles Robert, Thomas Allan, Madelyn Clare, (div. Sept. 1965). Student, Northwestern U., 1955, City Coll., Chgo., 1989. Lic. real estate salesperson, N.C. Lab. tech. Kraft Foods Rsch. Lab., Glenview, Ill., 1950-56; researcher data processing control Kemper Ins. Co., Chgo., 1967-70; jr. acct. Tractor Supply Co., Chgo., 1970-75; real estate salesman MGM Realty Co., Chgo., 1975-81, 85-88, Prime Realty, 1989—; broker Bohn Real Estate Agy, Raleigh, N.C., 1981-85; founder, pres. Pvt. Rsch., Chgo., 1985—; researcher zoning map City of Raleigh, 1980-81; bd. dirs. Off-Campus Writers Workshop. Contbr. various rsch. projects and sci. proposals. Vol. Chgo. Boys' Club; treas. churchwomen of St. Mary's, Crystal Lake, Ill.; vol. lifeguard Easter Seal Soc.-Multiple Sclerosis, Raleigh, 1983-84, PTA, 1967-77; bd. dirs. Off-Campus Writer's Workshop; chair grammar sch. 50th reunion, 1994; scholarship judge Mensa, Chgo., 1995, 96. Recipient Adviser Emblem of Merit award Jr. Achievement, 1955. Mem. AAAS, Smithsonian Inst. (assoc.), Nat. Trust Hist. Preservation, Raleigh C. of C., Jaycee Aux. (restaurant mgr.), Chgo. N. Side Realty Bd., Nat. Geog. Soc., Wilson Ctr. Assn., Mensa (nominating), Am. Assn. Ret. Persons, Irish Am. Heritage Ctr., Libr. Congress (assoc. charter). Roman Catholic. Home: 6126 W Roscoe St Chicago IL 60634 Office: Private Rsch 6126 W Roscoe St Chicago IL 60634-4145

BOHNE, JEANETTE KATHRYN, mathematics and science educator; b. Quincy, Ill., June 7, 1936; d. Anton Henry and Hilda Wilhelminia (Ohnemus) B. BA, Ursuline Coll., Louisville, 1961; MA, St. Louis U., 1962. Cert. math. and chemistry tchr., N.D., Ill., Mo. Math. tchr. Ryan High Sch., Minot, N.D., 1962-66, Althoff Cath. High Sch., Belleville, Ill., 1966-72, St. Francis Borgia High Sch., Washington, Mo., 1974-77; math. tchr. St. Louis Pub. Schs., 1977—, head dept. math., 1977-85; speaker in field. Treas. Welcome Wagon Club, Washington, 1974-76; pres. Bus. and Profl. Women's Club, Washington, 1978-79; active Animal Protective Assn., Zoo Friends of St. Louis Zoo, S.W. Garden Neighborhood Assn., S.W. Garden Neighborhood Assn. Mobile Patrol. Mem. AAUW, NEA, Mo. State Tchrs. Assn., St. Louis Tchrs. Union, Nat. Coun. Tchrs. Math., Math. Educators Group St. Louis, Mo. Coun. Tchrs. Math., St. Louis Sci. Ctr., Urban Math. Collaborative St. Louis, Math. Assn. Am. Home: PO Box 2252 Saint Louis MO 63109-0252 Office: St Louis Pub Schs 911 Locust St Saint Louis MO 63101-1401

BOHNENKAMPER, KATHERINE ELIZABETH, library science educator; b. Wichita, July 20, 1955; d. William Eugene and Emily Jane (Yount) Miller; m. David Allen Bohnenkamper, May 29, 1994. BS in Edn., Emporia State U., 1977; MEd, Wichita State U., 1981; MA, Kans. State U., 1988; MLS, Emporia State U., 1990. Tchr. high sch. Brown County Pub. Schs., Horton, Kans., 1978-79; substitute tchr. Wichita Pub. Schs., 1979-81, 86-90, tchr. jr. high sch., 1981-86; libr. Kans State Hist. Soc., Topeka, 1990-91; asst. prof. libr. sci. Drury Coll., Springfield, Mo., 1991—. Instr. 1st aide & CPR ARC, Wichita and Springfield, 1976—. Recipient Arnie H. Richards Meml. scholar, 1990. Mem. Mo. Libr. Assn. (officer-reference coun. 1995—), Springfield Area Libr. Assn. (v.p. 1995—), DAR (chpt. historian 1982-84, 94—), Order of Ea. Star. Presbyterian. Home: 1022 E Greenwood Springfield MO 65807 Office: FW Olin Libr Drury Coll 900 N Benton Springfield MO 65802

BOIMAN, DONNA RAE, artist, art academy executive; b. Columbus, Ohio, Jan. 13, 1946; d. George Brandle and Donna Rae (Rockwell) Hall; m. David Charles Boiman, Dec. 8, 1973 (div. Aug. 1990). BS in Pharmacy, Ohio State U., 1969; student, Columbus Coll. Art & Design, 1979-83. Registered pharmacist, Ohio. Pharmacist, mgr. various retail stores, Cleve., 1970-73, Columbus, 1973-77; owner L'Artiste, Reynoldsburg, Ohio, 1977-81; pres. Cen. Ohio Art Acad., Reynoldsburg, 1981-90, Art Acad. Ctrl. Ohio, Reynoldsburg, 1990—; owner Big Red Designs, Reynoldsburg, 1989—; pub. rels. mgr. Freedom Farm Equestrian Ctr., Pataskala, Ohio, 1991—; cons. to Mayor City of Reynoldsburg, 1986-87; ptnr. Broken Horse, Inc. Represented in permanent collections including Collector's Gallery Columbus Mus. Art, Gallery 200, Columbus Art Exch., The Huntington Collection, Dean Witter Reynolds Collection, Zanesville Art Ctr., Mt. Carmel East Hosp., Columbus, Corp. 2005, Radisson Hotels, Mich. and Ohio, Fifth 3d Bank, Bexley, Ohio, On Line Computer Libr., Dublin, Ohio; author: Anatomy Made Easy: Draw, Color and Learn, Anatomy and Structure: A Guide for Young Artists, 1988. Recipient John Lennon Meml. Award for the Arts, Internat. Art Challenge com., 1987. Mem. Pa. Soc. Watercolorists, Nat. Soc. Layerists in Multimedia, Columbus Art League, Cen. Ohio Watercolor Soc. (pres. 1983-84), Am. Quarter Horse Assn., Ohio Quarter Horse Assn., Allied Artists of Am. (assoc.), Licking County Art Assn., Nat. Wildlife Fedn., Ohio State U. Alumni Assn., Ohio State U. Pharmacy Alumni Assn. (charter), Mid-Ohio Dressage Assn., U.S. Dressage Fedn., Ohio Arabian Horse Assn., Internat. Arabian Horse Assn., Arabian Sport Assn., Inc. Office: Art Acad of Cen Ohio 7297 E Main St Reynoldsburg OH 43068-2105

BOKA, STEVEN WAYNE, building and zoning administrator; b. Ankara, Turkey, July 19, 1952; came to U.S., 1952; s. Stanley Duane and Virginia Rose (Lorenz) B.; m. Diane Lynn, July 26, 1975; children: Jeremy Michael, Brian Steven. Sgt. U.S. Army, 1971-74; chem. worker 3M Chem. Divsn., Cordova, Ill., 1974-75; asst. city planner City of Clinton, Iowa, 1975-76, cmty. devel. dir., 1976-77; bldg. and zoning adminstr. City of Muscatine, Iowa, 1977—; city rep. Zoning Bd. of Adjustment, New Constrn. Adv., Appeals Bd. Housing Code, Bd. of Appeals, Elec. Licensing, Bd. Health, Plumbing Code Bd. Appeals, Muscatine, 1977—, ex-officio mem., 1977—. Pres., supt. adv. coun. L&M Sch. Dist., Letts, Iowa, 1991-93. Recipient Soldier of God award U.S. Army, 1973. Fellow Am. Legion. Republican. Roman Catholic. Home: 6708 51st St S Muscatine IA 52761-1001 Office: City of Muscatine 215 Sycamore Muscatine IA 52761-3899

BOLAN, RICHARD STUART, urban planner, educator, researcher; b. Salem, Mass., Dec. 11, 1927; s. Robert Stuart and Mildred Elizabeth (Fay) B.; m. Elizabeth Ann Murphy, Sept. 4, 1954 (dec. 1977); 1 child, Geoffrey Stuart; m. Margaret Mary Altschul, Mar. 30, 1978 (div. May 1983); m. Nancy Jane Johnston, Dec. 19, 1987. B of Engring., Yale U., 1954; M of City and Regional Planning, MIT, 1956; PhD, NYU, 1974. Planner Providence Redevel. Authority, 1956-57, Planning and Renewal Assocs., Cambridge, Mass., 1957-58; prin. planner Boston City Planning Bd., 1958-60; dir. renewal planning Boston Redevel. Authority, 1960-62; dir. planning Boston Regional Transp. Study, 1962-64; asst. to dir. Joint Ctr. for Urban Studies of MIT and Harvard, Cambridge, 1964-67; prof. Boston Coll., Chestnut Hill, Mass., 1967-85; prof. urban planning U. Minn., Mpls., 1985—. Editor: Planning Metropolitan Boston, 1967; co-author: Urban Planning and Politics, 1975; co-editor workshop procs., 1991; contbr. articles to profl. jours. Vol. United Way, Mpls., 1986—; bd. dirs. Minn. Jobs with Peace, Mpls., 1989-96. Sgt. USAF, 1945-47, 50-51. Mem. Am. Planning Assn., Am. Inst. Cert. Planners, Assn. Collegiate Schs. of Planning (sec.-treas. 1989-93), Am. Soc. Pub. Adminstrn. Democrat. Unitarian. Home: 2833 E Lake Of The Isles Pky Minneapolis MN 55408-1055 Office: U Minn Humphrey Inst Pub Affairs Minneapolis MN 55455

BOLAND, EDMUND P., lawyer; b. Evergreen Park, Ill., Jan. 24, 1942; s. Edmund V. and Dorothy G. (Sullivan) B.; m. Luellen M. Moore, Apr. 19, 1969; children: Bridget, Peter, Anne, Andrew, James. BA in Polit. Sci., St. Procopius Coll. (now known as Ill. Benedictine Coll.), 1964; JD, Loyola U., Chgo., 1967. Atty. Carey, Filter, White & Boland, Chgo., 1967—; bd. dirs. Borse Industries, Inc., Willowbrook, Ill. Trustee Village North Barrington, Ill., 1985-93, 95—. Mem. ABA, Ill. State Bar Assn., Chgo. Bar Assn., Union League Club. Roman Catholic. Office: Carey Filter White & Boland 33 W Jackson Blvd Chicago IL 60604

BOLAND, MICHAEL JOSEPH, state legislator; b. Davenport, Iowa, Aug. 20, 1942; s. Francis Charles and Opal (Waites) B.; m. Mary Rose Lavorato, 1967; children: Susan, Barbara Ann. BA, Upper Iowa U., Fayette, 1967; MSE, Henderson State U., Arkadelphia, 1972. Del. County and Iowa State Conv., 1970; East Moline chmn. and 36th legis. dist. chmn. Polit. Action Coms. for Edn., 1974-75; mem. Bicentennial Com.; del. Ill. State Dem. Conv., 1978; alt. del. Dem. Nat. Mid-Term Conf., 1978; del. Dem. Nat. Conv., 1980; Ill. state rep., 1994—; coord. West Ill. Coalition for Polit. Honesty's Legis. Cutback Amendments; mem. United Twp. H.S. Bd. Edn., 1984-85; former pres. Citizens Utility Bd., Ill.civ. Nat. bd. dirs. UN Reform Campaign Com.; libr. bd. trustees, East Moline, Ill., 1975-79. Named one of 11 Who Made a Difference in Ill., Chgo. Tribune Sunday Mag. Mem. LWV (mem. govt. com. 1980-81), Ill. Coalition Polit. Honesty (bd. dirs. 1987), Consumers and Taxpayers Together (founding mem.). Address: 3440 3d St East Moline IL 61244

BOLAND, RAYMOND JAMES, bishop; b. Tipperary, Ireland, Feb. 8, 1932; came to U.S., 1957; Ed., Nat. U. Ireland and All Hallows Sem., Dublin. Ordained priest Roman Cath. Ch., Dublin, 1957. Vicar gen., chancellor of Washington archdiocese; ordained bishop Birmingham, Ala., 1988-93; transferred as bishop Kansas City, St. Joseph, Mo., 1993—. Address: PO Box 419037 Kansas City MO 64141-6037

BOLAÑOS, ANITA MARIE, lawyer; b. Berwyn, Ill., Apr. 20, 1964; d. Jose M. and Anita Marie (Loycano) Bolaños. AB, U. Mich., 1986; JD, DePaul U., 1989. Bar: Ill. 1990. Assoc. Schiller DuCanto & Fleck, Chgo., 1990—. Mem. ABA, Ill. Bar Assn. Roman Catholic. Office: Schiller DuCanto & Fleck 200 N La Salle St Ste 2700 Chicago IL 60601-1014

BOLCOM, WILLIAM ELDEN, musician, composer, educator, pianist; b. Seattle, May 26, 1938; s. Robert Samuel and Virginia (Lauermann) B.; m. Fay Levine, Dec. 23, 1963 (div. 1967); m. Katherine Agee Ling, June 8, 1968 (div. 1969); m. Joan Clair Morris, Nov. 28, 1975. BA, U. Wash., 1958; MA, Mills Coll., 1961; postgrad., Paris Conservatoire de Musique, 1959-61, 64-65; D of Mus. Art, Stanford U., 1964; studies with, Berthe Poncy Jacobson, 1949-58; D of Music (hon.), San Francisco Conservatory, 1994; studies with, John Verrall, 1951-58, Leland Smith, 1961-64, Darius Milhaud, 1957-61, George Rochberg, 1966; D of Mus. (hon.), Albion Coll., 1995. Acting asst. prof. music dept. U. Wash., Seattle, 1965-66; lectr., asst. prof. music Queens Coll., CUNY, Flushing, 1966-68; vis. critic music theater Drama Sch., Yale U., 1968-69; composer in residence Theater Arts Program, NYU, N.Y.C., 1969-71; asst. prof. U. Mich. Sch. Music, Ann Arbor, 1973-78, assoc. prof., 1973-77, prof., 1977-83, Ross Lee Finney disting. prof. composition, 1983—; mem. jury Nat. Endowment for Arts, 1976-77, 84, 85. Composer: 5 symphonies, 1957, 64, 79, 86, 89, String Quartets 1-8, 1950-65, String Quartet #9 (Novella), 1972, String Quartet #10, 1988, Décalage for cello and piano, 1961-62, Fantasy-Sonata for piano, 1960-62, Concertante for Flute, Oboe, Violin, and Orch, 1960, opera Dynamite Tonite, 1960-61, rev., 1966, Octet, 1962, Concerto-Serenade for Violin and Strings, 1964, 12 Etudes for Piano, 1959-66, Fives, Double Concerto for Violin, Piano and Strings, 1966, Morning and Evening Poems, Cantata, 1966, Session for Chamber Ensemble, 1965, Session II for violin and viola, 1966, Session III for clarinet, violin, cello, piano, percussion, 1967, Session IV for chamber ensemble, 1967, Black Host for organ, percussion and taped sounds, 1967, Piano Rags, 1967-74, opera Greatshot, 1967-69, Praeludium for vibraphone and organ, 1969, Dark Music for timpani and cello, 1969, Duets for Quintet, 1970, Unpopular

Songs, 1970, Hydraulis for organ, 1971, Commedia for chamber orch, 1971, Whisper Moon, chamber ensemble, 1971, Frescoes for two pianists, 1971, Seasons for solo guitar, 1974, Open House, cycle on poems by Roethke, 1975, Piano Concerto, 1975-76, Piano Quartet, 1976, Revelation Studies for Carillon, 1976, Mysteries for Organ, 1976, Songs of Innocence, 1982, score for stage works Puntila (Brecht), 1977, Man is Man (Brecht), 1978, Beggar's Opera (posthumous collaboration with Darius Milhaud), 1978, Violin Sonatas, 1956, 78, 92, 94, 12 Gospel Preludes for Organ, 1978-79, 81, 84, Humoresk for organ and orch., 1979, Brass Quintet, 1980, 12 Cabaret Songs, 1978-83, Aubade for Oboe and Piano, 1982, Songs of Innocence and of Experience (Blake), 1956-82, Violin Concerto in D, 1983, Lilith (saxophone, piano), 1984, Fantasia Concertante, 1985, Abendmusik, 1977, Little Suite of Dances in E flat for clarinet and piano, 1984, Orphée-Sérénade, 1984, Fantasia Concertante for viola, cello and orch., 1985, Capriccio for Violoncello and Piano, 1985, orchestral dance suite Seattle Slew, 1985-86, 12 New Etudes for Piano, 1977-86 (recipient Pulitzer Prize, 1988), Spring Concertino for Oboe and Chamber Orch., 1986-87, Five Fold Five for woodwind quintet and piano, 1987; Clarinet Concerto, 1988; (musical) Casino Paradise (libretto Arnold Weinstein), 1986-92, Fairy Tales for viola, cello, bass, 1988, Sonata for Violoncello and Piano, 1989, (song cycle on Am. women poets) I Will Breathe a Mountain, 1990, The Mask (chorus and piano), 1990, Recuerdos for two pianos, 1991, opera McTeague (libretto A. Weinstein and R. Altman), 1990-92, Lyric Concerto for flute and orch., 1993, Trio for clarinet, violin and piano, 1993, Sonata for 2 pianos, 1993, Suite for play Broken Glass by Arthur Miller, 1994, Let Evening Come (soprano, viola, piano), 1994, A Whitman Triptych, (mezzo and orchestra), 1995, GAEA Concertos 1-3 for Left Hand and Orch., 1995, Second Piano Quartet, 1995; pianist in recs: (with Gerard Schwarz) Cornet Favorites, (with Clifford Jackson, baritone) An Evening with Henry Russell, (with mezzo-soprano Joan Morris) Songs of Leiber and Stoller, (with Joan Morris and Max Morath) These Charming People, (with Joan Morris) The Girl on the Magazine Cover, (with Joan Morris) Songs of Irving Berlin, (with Joan Morris and Lucy Simon) The Rodgers and Hart Album, (with Joan Morris and Max Morath) More Rodgers and Hart, (with Joan Morris) Silver Linings (anthology of Jerome Kern), Blue Skies (anthology of Irving Berlin), Black Max (Bolcom cabaret songs with A. Weinstein poetry), Lime Jello: An American Cabaret, Night & Day (anthology of Cole Porter), Let's Do It, (with Sergiu Luca) Works for Violin and Piano (by Bolcom), After the Ball (with Joan Morris), Vaudeville, Songs by Ira and George Gershwin, (with Eubie Blake) Wild About Eubie, (with J.M. and Clifford Jackson) Who Shall Rule This American Nation: Songs of Henry Clay Work, (with Joan Morris and Robert White) Orchids in the Moonlight (songs of Vincent Youmans); recs. Bolcom's 4th Symphony (Grammy nominee 1987), Violin Concerto 5th Symphony, Fantasia Concertante (Am. Composers Orch.), 10th String Quartet (Stanford String Quartet), 1st and 3rd Symphonies, Seattle Slew Suite (Louisville Orch.), Orphée-Sérénade (Grammy nominee 1994), others; solo recordings include Heliotrope Bouquet, Pastimes and Piano Rags, Bolcom Plays His Own Rags, Piano Music of George Gershwin, Piano Music of Darius Milhaud, Bolcom: 12 Etudes, Euphonic Sounds (Scott Joplin anthology); author: (with Robert Kimball) Reminiscing with Sissle and Blake, 1973, Trouble in the Music World, 1988; editor book of essays: The Aesthetics of Survival by George Rochberg; contbr. to Grove's Dictionary, 6th edit; contbg. editor: Annals of Scholarship. Recipient Kurt Weill award, 1962, William and Noma Copley award, 1960, Marc Blitzstein Award for Excellence Am. Acad. Arts and Letters, 1965, N.Y. State Council award, 1971, Nat. Endowment for Arts award, 1974, 75, Koussevitzky Found. award, 1974, 93, Henry Russel award, 1977, Arts Council Mich. award, 1986, Gov.'s Mich. Artist award, 1987, Pulitzer Prize in Music, 1988, Citation of Merit U. Mich. Sch. Music Alumni Assn., 1989, Disting. Achievement award U. Wash., 1993, Alfred I. Du Pont award, 1994; Guggenheim Found. fellow, 1964, 68; Rockefeller Found. grantee, 1965, 69-70. Mem. Am. Acad. Arts and Letters, Am. Music Ctr., Am. Composer Alliance, Am. Repertory Theatre (bd. dirs.), Grant Pk. Concerts Chgo. (bd. dirs.), Charles Ives Soc. (bd. dirs.), Century Club, Delta Omicron (nat. patron), Azazels. Home: 3080 Whitmore Lake Rd Ann Arbor MI 48105-9649 Office: U Mich Sch Music 1339 Moore Hall Ann Arbor MI 48109-2085

BOLDA, DANIEL J., electrical engineer; b. Milw., May 29, 1966. BSEE, Marquette U., 1989. Engring. coop. Philips Circuit Assemblies, Milw., 1987-89; sr. devel. engr. Allen Bradley Co., Milw., 1989—. Patentee fuse and suppression circuits. Vol. Milw. Rescue Mission, 1992-95. Office: Allen Bradley Co Indsl Controls Dept 1201 S 2nd St Milwaukee WI 53204-2410

BOLDT, OSCAR CHARLES, construction company executive; b. Appleton, Wis., Apr. 20, 1924; s. Oscar John and Dorothy A. (Bartmann) B.; m. Patricia Hamar, July 9, 1949; children: Charles, Thomas, Margaret. BSCE, U. Wis., 1948. Pres. O.J. Boldt Constrn. Co., Appleton, 1950-79, CEO, chmn. bd. dirs., 1979-84; chmn. bd. dirs. The Boldt Group Inc., Appleton, 1984—; sec. W.S. Patterson Co., 1963-89, also bd. dirs.; bd. dirs. M&I Bank, Midwest Express Airlines, Galleher Hardwood Co., L.A., W.S. Patterson. Chmn. bd. dirs. Cmty. Found. for Fox Valley Region, 1991-93; pres. Appleton YMCA, 1955-57, Appleton Meml. Hosp., 1975-76; bd. dirs. United Health, United Health Wis.; co-chmn. fund drive Fox Cities United Way, 1994. 2d lt. USAAF, 1943-45. Recipient Disting. Svc. award Appleton Jaycees, 1960, Disting. Engr. award U. Wis., 1985, Walter Rugland Cmty. Svc. award, 1988, Master Entrepreneur award Ernst and Young, 1991, Renaissance award, 1991, Regent's award St. Olaf's Coll., 1993, N.E. Wis.'s Sales amd Mktg. Mag. Exec. of Yr. award, 1994; Paul Harris fellow, 1979. Mem. Appleton Area C. of C. (pres. 1967), Appleton Rotary (pres. 1975-76, Vocat. Svc. award 1977, Paul Harris fellow), Riverview Country Club (pres. 1968-69). Republican. Presbyterian. Home: 1715 W Reid Dr Appleton WI 54914-5175 Office: The Boldt Group Inc PO Box 373 2525 N Roemer Rd Appleton WI 54912

BOLE, GILES G., physician, researcher, medical educator; b. Battle Creek, Mich., July 28, 1928; s. Giles Gerald, Sr. and Kittie Belle B.; children—David Giles, Elizabeth Ann. B.S., U. Mich., Ann Arbor, 1949, M.D., 1953. Diplomate Am. Bd. Internal Medicine. Resident in internal medicine U. Mich., Ann Arbor, 1953-56, fellow rheumatology Rackham arthritis research unit, 1958-61, asst. prof. internal medicine, 1961-64, assoc. prof. internal medicine, 1964-70, prof. internal medicine, 1970—; physician-in-charge Rackham Arthritis Research Unit, Ann Arbor, 1971-86, chief rheumatology div., 1976-86; assoc. dean clin. affairs, sr. assoc. dean Med. Sch. U. Mich., Ann Arbor, 1986-88, exec. assoc. dean Med. Sch., 1988-90, interim dean Med. Sch., 1990-91, dean Med. Sch., 1991—; dir. U. Mich. Arthritis Ctr., Ann Arbor, 1977-86; bd. govs. Am. Bd. Internal Medicine, 1979-83, chmn. rheumatology com., 1979-83. dir. U. Mich. Arthritis Ctr., Ann Arbor, 1977-86; bd. govs. Am. Bd. Internal Medicine, 1979-83, chmn. rheumatology com., 1979-83; mem. physician payment rev. commn. Office Tech. Assessment, U.S. Congress. Capt. M.C., USAF, 1956-58. Recipient Borden Academic Achievement award U. Mich., 1953; Postdoctoral Research fellow Arthritis Found., 1961-63. Mem. Am. Fed. Clin. Rsch. (chmn. Midwest sect. 1967-68), Cen. Soc. Clin. Rsch. (pres. 1976-77), Am. Rheumatism Assn. (pres. 1980-81). Home: 6015 W Ellsworth Rd Ann Arbor MI 48103-9609 Office: U Mich Med Sch M7324 Med Sci I 1301 Catherine St Ann Arbor MI 48109-0624

BOLENDER, TODD, choreographer; b. Canton, Ohio, 1914. Student, Hanya Holm, N.Y.C.; enrolled, Sch. American Ballet, N.Y.C., 1936. Joined Lincoln Kirstein's Ballet Caravan, 1937; formed Am. Concert Ballet; choreographed 1st ballet, 1943; also danced with Ballet Theatre, 1944 and Ballet Russe de Monte Carlo, 1945, joined Ballet Soc., 1946; prin. dancer N.Y.C. Ballet, 1948-61; dir. ballet cos. of opera houses of Cologne and Frankfurt; numerous nat. and internat. freelance choreography assignments, 1952-80; artistic dir. State Ballet of Mo., Kansas City, 1981—. Recipient Mo. Arts Coun. awrd, 1987, W.F. Yates for disting. svc. William Jewell Coll., 1995. Office: State Ballet Mo 706 W 42nd St Kansas City MO 64111-3120

BOLEY, ROBERT WILLIAM, clergyman, educator; b. Normal, Ill., July 6, 1923; s. Arthur William and Gail (Washburn) B.; m. Emily Ruth McRae, Aug.26, 1950; children: Arthur, John, Sandra Kitts, William. AB, Cornell Coll., Mt. Vernon, Iowa, 1948; MDiv, Boston U., 1951; DMin, Hamna Sch. Theology, Springfield, Ohio, 1976. Ordained to ministry Meth. Ch., 1951. Pastor United Meth. Ch., Monmouth, Iowa, 1946-48, Assumption, Ill., 1951-55; assoc. pastor First United Meth. Ch., Champaign, Ill., 1955-58, Strathmoor United Meth. Ch., Detroit, 1958-61; pastor Beverly Hills United Meth. Ch., Birmingham, Mich., 1961-70, Redford United Meth. Ch., Detroit, 1970-74, First United Meth. Ch., Adrian, Mich., 1974-82, 92—, Grosse Pointe United Meth. Ch., Grosse Pointe Farms, Mich., 1982-89; adj. prof. mgmt. Siena Hts. Coll., Adrian, 1979-82; adj. prof. religion Adrian Coll., 1989-91; adj. prof. philosophy Jackson (Mich.) C.C., 1993. Pres. Children/Family Svcs. of Mich., Okemos, 1993-95, Family and Child Svcs. of Lenawee, Adrian, 1993-95. Served with U.S. Army, 1943-46, PTO. Mem. Civitan Club (v.p. 1992). Home: 1368 Fairlane Dr Adrian MI 49221 Office: First United Meth Ch 1245 W Maple Ave Adrian MI 49221

BOLGER, DAVID P., bank executive; b. Aug. 23, 1957. BS in Acctg./Fin., Marquette U., 1979; MM in Fin., Northwestern U., 1980. Credit analyst Am. Nat. Bank & Trust Co., Chgo., 1980-82, comml. banking officer, 1982-89, sr. v.p., CFO, 1989-92, exec. v.p., 1992-93, exec. v.p., treas., 1993-94, pres., 1996—. Bd. dirs. Mercy Hosp. & Med. Ctr., Impulse Theatre Co., Fist Non-Profit Ins. Co.; active United Way/Crusade of Mercy. Mem. Chgo. Hist. Soc., Execs. Club Chgo., Robert Morris Asscos. Office: Am Nat Bank & Trust Co 33 N La Salle St Chicago IL 60690*

BOLLA, ROBERT IRVING, biology educator; b. Dansville, N.Y., Aug. 18, 1943; s. John A. and Thelma A. (Lawrence) B.; m. Terese F. Mandel, Sept. 4, 1966; children: Jennifer A., Stephen A. BS, SUNY, Buffalo, 1961; MS, U. Mass., 1965, PhD, 1970. Prof. biology U. Mo., St. Louis, 1976-88; prof., chmn. biology St. Louis U., 1988—; rsch. scientist Forestry & Forest Products Rsch. Inst., Tsukuba, Japan, 1988. Assoc. editor Jour. Nematology, 1988-94; contbr. more than 60 articles to profl. jours. Rsch. grantee USDA, 1986-93, Mo. Soybean Merchandising Coun., 1991-99. Mem. AAAS, Am. Aging Assn., Am. Soc. Microbiology, Japanese Soc. Nematologists (editorial bd.),. Euroepan Soc. Nematologists, Russian Soc. Nematologists, Soc. Nematologists, Sigma Xi. Office: St Louis U Dept Biology Saint Louis MO 63103-2010

BOLLENBACHER, HERBERT KENNETH, steel company official; b. Wilkinsburg, Pa., Apr. 16, 1933; s. Curtis W. and Ebba M. (Frendberg) B.; m. Nancy Jane Cercena, June 29, 1957; children: Mary E., Kenneth E. AB, U. Pitts., 1960, MEd, 1963. Cert. safety profl. Staff asst. tng. J & L Steel Co., Pitts., 1963-66; mgr. tng., devel. and accident prevention Textron Corp., Pitts., 1966-72; supr. safety Copperweld Steel Co., Warren, Ohio, 1972-75, mgr. safety, security, 1975-78, mgr. human resources conservation, 1978-94; exec. v.p. Charles Mgmt., Inc., 1994—; mem. adj. faculty Pa. State U. Served with U.S. Army, 1954-56. Mem. Am. Soc. Safety Engrs. (past pres. Ohio-Pa. chpt., Ohio Safety Profl. of Yr. 1983-84, 92-93), Ohio Soc. Safety Engrs. (state chaplain), Am. Iron and Steel Inst. (chmn. safety task force), Mfrs. Assn. Eastern Ohio and Western Pa. (safety chmn. 12 yrs.; safety profl. of yr. award 1984, coordinator Ohio seat belt coalition 1986, Gov.'s spl. recognition award), Gov.'s Traffic Safety Coun., 1989, Trumbull Camp Gideons Internat. (past pres.), Ohio Gideons (area coordinator, membership cabinet), Rotary (Paul Harris fellow, pres., benefactor, Ideal of Svc. in Workplace award), Boy Scouts Am. (western reserve coun., loss prevention com.). Presbyterian (elder). Author suprs. monthly discussion guide, article for tech. publ. Avocations: softball; volleyball; reading. Office: Charles Mgmt Inc 25200 Miles Rd Cleveland OH 44146-1321

BOLLINGER, ROBERT B., process engineer; b. Columbus, Ohio, Nov. 16, 1966. BS in Chem. Engring., U. Buffalo, 1989. Process engr. Babcock & Wilcox Co., Barberton, Ohio, 1990—.

BOLT, EUNICE MILDRED DEVRIES, artist; b. Clifton, N.J., Oct. 31, 1926; d. Lambert H. and Cora (Martin) DeVries; m. Maurice L. Bolt (dec. Nov. 1989); children: Macyn Bolt, Tamsen Bolt Clark, Valerie Martin Bolt Wegner. Grad., Pratt Inst. Art & Design, Bklyn., 1949; BA, Calvin Coll., 1952; MA, Western Mich. U., 1973. Book illustrator Fideler Pubs., Grand Rapids, Mich., 1952-53, Zondervan Pub. Co., Grand Rapids, Mich., 1953-56; prof. Calvin Coll., Grand Rapids, Mich., 1962-67, Grand Rapids C.C., 1968-91; represented by Corporate Portfolios and Bergsma Gallery, Grand Rapids, Rental/Sales Gallery of Grand Rapids Art Mus.; internat. art study tours coord. and guide, 1978—; fine art exhbn. juror, 1987—; lectr. art history, 1991—, presenter watercolor workshops, 1991—. Exhibited in group shows at Grand Rapids Art Mus., Kalamazoo Inst. Art, U. Mich. Schlusser Gallery, Pitts. Ctr. for the Arts, Westmoreland Mus. Art, Detroit Inst. Art. Home and Studio: 2421 Breton Rd SE Grand Rapids MI 49546-5627

BOLT, JOHN, theology educator; b. Grrotegast, Groningen, The Netherlands, Oct. 7, 1947; s. Berend and Hielkje (Piers) B.; m. Ruth Ann Bolt, Sept. 16, 1971; children: Michelle Joy, David Michael, Justin Matthew. BSc, Calvin Coll., Grand Rapids, Mich., 1970; BD, Calvin Theol. Seminary, Grand Rapids, Mich., 1973, ThM, 1977; PhD, U. St. Michael's Coll., Toronto, Ontario, Can., 1982. Clergyman Christian Reformed Ch., Kelowna, Penticton, B.C., 1973-76; instr. theology and religion Calvin Coll., 1980-82; prof. religion and theology Redemer Coll., Ancaster, Ontario, Can., 1982-89; prof. theology Calvin Theol. Seminary, Grand Rapids, 1989—; assoc. minister Immanuel Christian Reformed Ch., Hamilton, Ontario, 1982-89, Plymouth Heights Christian Reformed Ch., Grand Rapids, 1989—. Author: Christian and Reformed Today, 1984, The Christian Story and The Christian School, 1994; editor and contbr.: Orthodoxy and Orthopraxis, 1986; translator: Calvinist Trinitarianism and Theocentric Politics, 1989. Calvin Theol. Seminary scholar, 1976-78; Can. Coun. fellow, 1978-80; Pew Evang. scholars grantee, 1996-97. Mem. Calvin Studies Soc. Home: 1830 Lotus SE Grand Rapids MI 49506 Office: Calvin Theol Seminary 3233 Burton SE Grand Rapids MI 49546

BOLTE, RICHARD ALAN, transportation executive; b. Brooklyn, N.Y., Dec. 16, 1945; s. Henry Fredrick and Anna Marie (Knickerbocker) B.; m. Joan Ellen Parker, Aug. 19, 1967; children: Jennifer Jean, Brian Richard. BSCE, Clarkson Coll., 1967; MECE, Rensselaer Poly. Inst., 1970. Registered profl. engr., N.Y., Wis. Asst. rlwy., hwy. coord. W.Va. Dept Hwys., Charleston, 1967; transp. analyst N.Y. State Dept. Transp., Albany, 1968-73; sr. transp. planner Fairfax County Planning, Va., 1973-75; county traffic engr. Monroe County Dep. Pub. Works, Rochester, N.Y., 1975-84; dir. transp. Waukesha County Transp. Dept., Wis., 1984—; exec. cabinet mem. Waukesha County, 1991—, mem. County Traffic Safety Bd., 1984—. Chief Wales Fire Dept., Wis., 1995. Recipient Award of Excellence Wis. Asphalt Paving Assn., 1994. Mem. ASCE, Am. Pub. Works Assn., Nat. Assn. County Engrs., Inst. Transp. Engrs. Office: Waukesha County Transp Dept 1320 Pewaukee Rd Waukesha WI 53188

BONACINA, MARIA PAOLA, computer science educator; b. Milan, Italy, Oct. 28, 1963; d. Alessandro and Annita (Fusari) B. Laurea in Computer Sci. cum laude, U. Degli Studi, Milan, 1986, Dottorato di Ricerca in Computer Sci., 1991; PhD in Computer Sci., SUNY, Stony Brook, 1992. Postdoctoral scholar Inria Lorraine & Crin, Nancy, France, 1993; asst. prof. computer sci. U. Iowa, Iowa City, 1993—; mem. program com. Internat. Symposium on Parallel Symbolic Computation, Linz, Austria, 1994; mem. organizing com. Internat. Conf. on Rewrite Techniques and Applications, Como, Italy, 1991. Contbr. articles to profl. jours. U. Degli Studi-Milan fellow, 1991, Human Capital and Mobility Programme of the European Union fellow, 1993, U. Iowa Old Gold fellow, 1994, GE Found. Faculty fellow, 1994. Mem. European Assn. Theoretical Computer Sci., Assn. for Automated Reasoning.

BONAVENTURA, LEO MARK, gynecologist, educator; b. East Chicago, Ill., Aug. 1, 1945; s. Angelo Peter and Wanda D. (Kelleher) B.; student Marquette U., 1963-66; M.D., Ind. U., 1970; married; children—Leo Mark, Dena Anne, Angela Lorena, Nicole Palmira, Leah Michelle, Adam Xavier. Intern in surgery, Cook County Hosp., Chgo., 1970-71; resident in ob-gyn., Ind. U. Hosps., 1973-76, fellow in reproductive endocrinology and infertility, 1976-78; asst. prof. ob-gyn., Ind. U., 1976—, asst. head sect. reproductive endocrinology and infertility, 1978-80, head sect., 1980-81. Served with USN attached to USMC, 1971-73. Named Intern of Yr., Cook County Hosp., 1971. Diplomate Am. Bd. Obstetrics and Gynecology, Am. Bd. Reproductive Endocrinology and Infertility. Mem. Central Assn. Ob-Gyn., Am. Coll. Obstetricians and Gynecologists, Am. Fertility Soc., Can. Fertility Soc., Soc. Reproductive Endocrinologists, Soc. Reproductive Surgeons. Roman Catholic. Contbr. articles to profl. jours. Office: 8091 Township Line Rd Indianapolis IN 46260-2495

BOND, CHRISTOPHER SAMUEL (KIT BOND), senator, lawyer; b. St. Louis, Mar. 6, 1939; s. Arthur D. and Elizabeth (Green) B.; 1 child, Samuel Reid. BA with honors, Princeton U., 1960; LLB, U. Va., 1963. Bar: Mo. 1963, U.S. Supreme Ct. 1967. Law clk. to presiding chief justice U.S. Ct. of Appeals (5th cir.), Atlanta, 1963-64; assoc. Covington & Burling, Washington, 1965-67; pvt. practice law Mexico, Mo., 1968; asst. atty. gen., chief counsel consumer protection div. State of Mo., 1969-70, gov., 1973-77, 81-85; auditor, 1971-73; ptnr. Gage & Tucker, Kansas City, 1985-87; U.S. senator from Mo., 1987—, chmn. small bus. com. 104th Congress; pres. Gt. Plains Legal Found., Kansas City, Mo., 1977-80; chmn. Rep. Gov.'s Assn., Midwestern Gov.'s Conf., chmn. con. on econ. and community devel., 1981-83, chmn. con. on energy and environment, 1983-84. Republican. Presbyterian. Office: US Senate 293 Russell Senate Bldg Washington DC 20510

BOND, LORA, retired biology educator; b. Bryan, Tex., May 17, 1917; d. J. David and Leila (McGregor) B. BA, U. Tenn., 1938; MA, Wellesley Coll., 1941; PhD, U. Wis., 1945. Acting instr. botany U. Tenn., Knoxville, 1943; mem. faculty Drury Coll., Springfield, Mo., 1943-45, 48-82; instr. botany Wellesley Coll., 1945-48; prof. biology emeritus Drury Coll., Springfield, 1982—. Mem. AAAS, Am. Inst. Biol. Scis., Bot. Soc. Am., Mo. Acad. Sci., Assn. S.E. Biologists, Sigma Xi. Home: 1512 N Washington Ave Springfield MO 65803-2849 Office: Drury Coll 900 N Benton Ave Springfield MO 65802-3712

BOND, RICHARD LEE, lawyer, state senator; b. Kansas City, Kans., Sept. 18, 1935; s. Clarence Ivy and Florine (Hardison) B.; m. Sue S. Sedgwick, Aug. 23, 1958; children: Mark, Amy. BA, U. Kans., 1957, JD, 1960. City atty. Overland Park, Kans., 1960-62; adminstrv. asst. to Congressman Robert Ellsworth, Washington, 1961-66, Congressman Larry Winn, Washington, 1967-85, Congressman Jan Meyers, Washington, 1986; chmn. bd. dirs. Home State Bank, Kansas City, 1983-94; ptnr. Bennett, Lytle, Wetzler et al, Prairie Village, Kans., 1986-89; senator State of Kans., Topeka, 1985—; vice chmn. Guaranty Bank and Bancshares, Kansas City, Kans., 1995—. Republican. Presbyterian. Home: 9823 Nall Ave Shawnee Mission KS 66207-2915

BONDIE, RICHARD ANTHONY, financial executive; b. Wyandotte, Mich., Sept. 29, 1943. BA in Psychology/Pers. Mgmt., Wayne State U., 1970, MBA in Mgmt., 1971. Pres. Independence One Mortgage Corp., Southfield, Mich., 1985-90, Bondie Fin. Group, Bingham Farms, Mich., 1990—; cons. in field. Asst. scout master Boy Scouts Am., Bloomfield Hills, 1988—. With USAF, 1962-66. Mem. Am. Soc. Chartered Life Underwriters, Mortgage Builders Assn. Am. Office: 32400 Telegraph Rd Ste 100 Bingham Farms MI 48025-2459

BONDOW, BRUCE A., electrical engineer; b. Neenah, Wis., Mar. 12, 1945. BS in Elec. Engring., U. Wis., 1967; MBA in Bus. Mgmt., U. St. Thomas, St. Paul, 1982. Registered profl. engr., Minn. Design engr. Allis Chalmers Mfg. Co., Milw., 1967-72; dir. mktg. Electric Machinery Mfg. Co., Mpls., 1972-86; chief elec. engr. AmClude Engineered Products, St. Paul, 1987—. Contbr. articles to profl. jours. Mem. Environ. Quality Commn., City of Fridley, Minn., 1982—, vice chair, 1992—. Mem. IEEE, Minn. Soc. Profl. Engrs. (Seven Wonders of Engring. award 1990). Home: 6616 Central Ave Fridley MN 55432 Office: AmClyde Engineered Products 240 E Plato Blvd Saint Paul MN 55107-1609

BONER, DONALD LESLIE, information systems executive; b. Lawton, Okla., June 3, 1944; s. Jessie Edward and Violet (Cravens) B.; m. Carol Ann Stevens, Oct. 25, 1966 (div. June, 1973); children: Freda L., Donald R.; m. Suellen Jackson, Dec. 1, 1973. Student, Area Vocat. Tech. Sch., Nashville, Tenn., 1967, Tenn. Inst. Broadcasting, Nashville, 1969; AS, Ind. Vocat. Tech. Coll., Indpls., 1983. Acting dir. Near East Side Community Orgn., Indpls., 1971-74; sgt. Marion County Sheriff's Dept., Indpls., 1975-76; acquisition mgr. Colonial Discount, Indpls., 1977-80; community organizer Christamore House, Indpls., 1978-79; pres., co-founder Smoner Investment Co., Indpls., 1979-80; sgt. Pinkerton, Inc., Indpls., 1980-82; computer programmer Group VI Marketing, Indpls., 1982-83; product and programming mgr. Mktg. Resources Plus, Indpls., 1983—; freelance programmer Programmers Guild, Indpls., 1980-82. Author: 5 computer games, 1980-82. Mem. adv. com. Purdue U. Dept. of Computer Tech. Industry; dcampaign coord. Small Claims Ct. judge, Indpls., 1974; mem. Dem. precinct com., Indpls., 1974-78. Recipient Caspar award Community Svc. Coun., Indpls., 1972, first prize for winemaking, Ind. State Fair, 1975. Mem. Nat. Assn. for Computing Machinery (bd. dirs. cen. Ind. chpt. 1986-87, vice chmn. 1987-88, chmn. 1988-89), Indpls. Computer Soc., IEEE Computer Soc., Cellar Master Club (treas. Indpls. 1975-91). Home: 516 E 15th St Indianapolis IN 46202-2634 Office: Mktg Resources Plus VNU Bus Info Sys Inc 151 N Delaware St Ste 1750 Indianapolis IN 46204-2503

BONFIELD, ARTHUR EARL, lawyer, educator; b. N.Y.C., May 12, 1936; s. Louis and Rose (Lesser) B.; m. Doris Harfenist, June 10, 1958; 1 child, Lauren. BA, Bklyn. Coll., 1956; JD, Yale U., 1960, LLM, 1961, postgrad. (sr. fellow), 1961-62. Bar: Conn. 1961, Iowa 1966. Asst. prof. U. Iowa Law Sch., 1962-65, assoc. prof., 1965-66, prof., 1966-69, Law Sch. Found. prof., 1969-72, John Murray prof., 1972—, assoc. dean for research, 1985—; summer vis. prof. law U. Mich., 1970, U. Tenn., 1972, U. N.C., 1974, Hofstra U., 1977, Lewis and Clark U., 1984; gen. counsel spl. joint com. state adminstrv. procedure act Iowa Gen. Assembly, 1974-75; spl. counsel adminstrv. procedure exec. br. State of Iowa, 1975; chmn. com. constl. law Nat. Conf. Bar Examiners Multi-State Bar Exam, 1977—; reporter 1981 Model State Adminstrv. Procedure Act, Nat. Conf. Commrs. Uniform State Laws, 1979-81; cons. Ark. State Constl. Conf., 1980; chmn. Iowa Gov.'s Com. State Pub. Records Law, 1983; Iowa commr. Nat. Conf. Commrs. on Uniform State Laws, 1984—; chmn. Iowa Gov.'s Task Force on Uniform Adminstrv. Rules, 1985-92. Prin. draftsman Iowa Civil Rights Act, 1965, Iowa Fair Housing Act, 1967, Iowa Adminstrv. Procedure Act, 1974, Iowa Open Meetings Act, 1978, Iowa Civil Rights Act, 1978, Amendments to Iowa Public Records Law, 1984; author: State Administrative Rule Making, 1986, State and Federal Administrative Law, 1989; contbr. numerous articles to law jours. Recipient Outstanding Service to Civil Liberties award Iowa Civil Liberties Union, 1974, Hancher Finkbine Outstanding Faculty Mem. award U. Iowa, 1980, Faculty Excellence award Iowa Bd. Regents, 1995, Outstanding Law Sch. Tchg. award U. Iowa, 1996; named Frederick Klocksiem fellow Aspen Inst. Humanistic Studies, summer 1978. Mem. ABA (chmn. divsn. state adminstrv. law 1976-80, coun. 1980-84, chmn. 1987-88, sect. admiminstrv. law and regulatory practice), Am. Law Inst., Iowa State Bar Assn., (chmn. com. adminstrv. law 1971-85, coun. sect. adminstrv. law 1990-93, 94—, reportr and mem. task force on state adminstrv. law reform 1994-96, Pres.'s award for outstanding svc. to bar and public 1996), Adminstrv. Conf. U.S. (cons. 1968-76, mem. 1990-95), Am. Coun. Learned Soc., Assn. Am. Law Schs. (del. 1984-94). Home: 206 Mahaska Dr Iowa City IA 52246-1606 Office: U Iowa Law Sch Iowa City IA 52242

BONHAM, RUSSELL AUBREY, chemistry educator; b. San Jose, Calif., Dec. 10, 1931; s. Russell Aubrey and Margaret Florence (Wallace) B.; m. Miriam Anne Dye, Mar. 23, 1957; children: Frances, Margaret, Anne. BA, Whittier Coll., 1954; PhD, Iowa State U., 1958. Instr. Ind. U., Bloomington, 1958-60; postdoctoral fellow Naval Rsch. Lab., 1960; asst. prof. math. U. Md., 1960; asst. prof. chemistry Ind. U., Bloomington, 1960-63, assoc. prof., 1963-65, prof. chemistry, 1965-95; rsch. prof. chemistry Ill. Inst. Tech., Chgo., Ill., 1995—. Co-author: High Energy Electron Scattering, 1974; mem. editorial bd.: The Jour. of the Brazilian Chem. Soc., 1989—; contbr. over 175 articles and papers to profl. jours. Recipient Fulbright fellowship U. Tokyo, 1964-65, Guggenheim fellowship, 1964-65, Humboldt prize, 1977, 81, grant NSF, 1993—. Fellow Am. Phys. Soc., AAAS; mem. Am. Phys. Soc., Am. Crystallographic Assn., Am. Chem. Soc., Sigma Xi. Office: Ill Inst Tech Dept Biol Chem Phys Scis 3101 S Dearborn Chicago IL 60616

BONIOR, DAVID EDWARD, congressman; b. Detroit, June 6, 1945; s. Edward John and Irene (Gaverluk) B.; children: Julie, Andy. BA, U. Iowa, 1967; MA in History, Chapman Coll., Calif., 1972. Mem. Mich. Ho. of Reps., 1973-77, 95th-103rd Congresses from 12th (now 10th) Mich. Dist., 1977—; mem. com. on rules, House Majority Whip, 1991—. Author: The Vietnam Veteran: A History of Neglect, 1984. Served in USAF, 1968-72. Democrat. Roman Catholic. Office: US Ho of Reps 2207 Rayburn Bldg Washington DC 20515-0005

BONKOWSKI, RONALD LAWRENCE, mayor; b. Detroit, June 6, 1938; s. Lawrence and Estelle (Nowakowski) B.; m. Christine Van Simaeys, Oct. 1958; children: Robert, Lori, Mark, Lisa. Student, Walsh Inst. Acctg., 1957-58; BBA, U. Detroit, 1969; postgrad., Mich. State U. Acct. Gen. Motors Corp., 1960-66; budget analyst, indsl. engr. Chrysler Corp., 1966-69; indsl. engr. LTV Aerospace, 1968-69; dist. sales mgr. Sales Follow Up Corp., 1969-71; fin. officer Macomb County (Mich.) Pub. Works, 1971-85; mayor City of Warren, Mich., 1985-95. Councilman City of Warren, 1969-70, 79-85; commr. Macomb County Commn., 1971; past sec., past chmn. Warren Bd. Appeals; past chmn. Warren Bldg. Com.; trustee Macomb Cmty. Coll., treas., 1977-79; bd. dirs. Bi-County Hosp. With U.S. Army, 1958-60. Mem. VFW (Polish Legion), Am.-Polish Century Club, Alhambra. Office: Office of the Mayor 29500 Van Dyke Ave Warren MI 48093-2304

BONNER, DENNIS, state legislator. Mem. Mo. Ho. of Reps., Jefferson City. Democrat.

BONNER, HELEN WARD, English language and literature educator; b. Richmond, Calif., May 25, 1930; d. Eugene Edward and Nevelyn (Henderson) Ward; m. William J. Bonner, Apr. 12, 1958 (div. 1970); children: Steven J., Mark E. MA, Calif. State U., Sacramento, 1972; PhD, Ohio U., 1982. Prof. English various C.C., Calif., 1974-75, 82-88, El Paso (Tex.) C.C., 1975-80, Bemidji (Minn.) State U., 1988—; speaker in field. Author: The Laid Daughter, 1995; (screenplay) Jeanette Rankin Story, 1985; (short stories) Forum, Wellspring, Thema (Best short story award 1980); (commentaries) Sta. KCRB, 1990—; editor Dust and Fire; Womens Stories, 1990—. Grantee Bush Found., 1993, faculty Bemidji State U., 1994. Mem. Beginning Experience, A Course in Miracles, Bemidji State U. Assn. (senator, faculty). Office: Bemidji State U Dept English Bemidji MN 56601

BONNER, HERBERT DWIGHT, construction management educator; b. Lakewood, Ohio, Sept. 5, 1942; s. Herbert C. and Ruth (H.) B.; m. Marilyn Anne Seidel, Sept. 18, 1965. BArch, Ohio State U., 1969, MArch, 1971. Registered architect, Ohio. Tng. engr. H.K. Ferguson Co., Cleve., 1961-62, U.S. Steel Corp., Cleve., 1962-64, Hausman Steel Corp., Grandview, Ohio, 1964-65; tng. architect Kellam & Foley Architects, Columbus, Ohio, 1965-68; rsch. assoc. bldg. rsch. lab. Ohio State U., Columbus, Ohio, 1968-71, asst. prof., 1971-74; prof. Columbus State C.C., 1974-95; owner Bonner Constrn. Svcs., Sugar Grove, Ohio, 1971—; cons. Aubon Ednl. Svcs., Columbus, 1980-85; adj. faculty mem. Caiptal U., Columbus, 1986-95; exec. dir. Associated Two Yr. Sch. Constrn., Edmonds, Wash., 1989-95. Author: Building Plans and Working Drawings, 1981; editor: Scheduling Construction Projects, 1984, Construction Equipment Operators, 1992; contbr. articles to profl. jours. Trustee Am. Coun. for Constrn. Edn., Monroe, La., 1990-95. Recipient Disting. Svc. award Assn. Bus. and Profl. Women, 1982, Nat. Assn. Women in Constrn., 1984; grantee Dept. of Def., 1970-71, 1st Community Village, 1974, Owens Corning Fiberglass, 1981-82. Mem. AIA, Am. Inst. Constructors, Ohio Horeman's Coun., Tenn. Walking Horse Beaders and Exhibitors Assn., Mid-Ohio Walking Horse Assn., Hocking County Trail Blazers. Office: Bonner Constrn Svcs PO Box 340 Sugar Grove OH 43155-0340

BONNESON, MARY ELISABETH, psychotherapist; b. Milw., Aug. 3, 1961; d. Garland W. and Marilyn Adah (Giese) B. BA summa cum laude, Marquette U., 1983; MS in Clin. Psychology, Purdue U., 1986. Cert. Advanced Practice Social Worker; nat. cert. counselor. Teaching asst. psychology dept. Purdue U., West Lafayette, Ind., 1984-85; rsch. asst. Purdue U., West Lafayette, 1985-86; clin. assoc. Purdue Pschol. Svcs. Ctr., West Lafayette, 1986; clinic counselor Weight Loss Clinics of Wis., Wauwatosa, 1988-91; psychotherapist Family Care Psychol. Svcs., Wauwatosa, 1993—. Contbg. author: Jour. Consulting and Clin. Psychology, 1987, Avoiding Tragedy, 1996, Our Family Together, 1996. Mem. Arthritis Found. Reader's Adv. Panel. Recipient Davis Found. Grant for Disabled, Brookfield E. High Sch., Brookfield, Wis., 1979; scholar Marquette U., 1979-82. Mem. ACA, AACC, APA (assoc.), Am. Mental Health Counselor's Assn., Phi Beta Kappa, Phi Kappa Phi. Evangelical Christian.

BONNOCINI, PAUL M., stockbroker; b. Royal Oak, Mich., Jan. 5, 1963; s. Leonard Paul and Sandra Roseann (Morone) B.; m. Maude Rieder, Oct. 5, 1991; 1 child, Melina. BA, Ctrl. Mich. U., Mt. Pleasant, 1986, Saginaw State U., University Center, Mich., 1986. Consumer lender Old Kent Bank, Traverse City, Mich., 1987-90; stockbroker Prudential Securities, Traverse City, 1990-94, Roney & Co., Traverse City, 1994—. Contbr. articles to profl. jours. Mem. Rep. Coun., Traverse City, 1984—. Mem. Grand Traverse Resort Country Club, Elks. Republican. Roman Catholic. Office: Roney & Co 522 E Front St PO Box 926 Traverse City MI 49685

BONUTTI, KARL BORROMEO, retired economics educator; b. Gorica, Slovenia, Feb. 3, 1928; s. Anton and Maria (Lovec) B.; m. Hermina Rijavec; children: Alex, Henry, Magda, Peter, Boris, Miriam. MA in Polit. Sci. and Econs., U. Fribourg, Switzerland, 1950, PhD in Social Economy, 1969; MA in Econs., Case-Western Res. U., 1957. Instr., then asst. prof. econs. & sociology Notre Dame Coll., South Euclid, Ohio, 1959-65; instr. econs. Cleve. State U., 1966-69, asst. prof. econs., 1967-69, assoc. prof. econs., 1969-76, prof. econs., 1977-94, prof. emeritus, 1995—; coord. ethnic studies Cleve. State U., 1976-94; vis. prof. econs. U. Ljubljana, Slovenia, 1990-94; vis. prof. mgmt. U. Maribor, Slovenia, 1994-95; lectr.- cons. Office of Edn. City of Cleve., 1970-78; mgr. edn. City of Cleve., 1970-79; editor monographs in field. Pres., mem. exec. com. Internat. Svcs. Ctr., Cleve., 1970-95; lectr.-cons. Office of Edn. City of Cleve., 1970-79; editor monographs in field; hon. consul Republic of Slovenia, 1992—. Decorated knight, Republic of Italy; recipient Catholic Interracial award Cath. Diocese of Cleve., 1961. Mem. Slovenian-Am. Heritage Found. (pres. 1983, award 1993). Roman Catholic. Home: 29399 Shaker Blvd Pepper Pike OH 44124 Office: Consulate of Slovenia 1111 Chester Ave Cleveland OH 44114

BONZELAAR, GREGORY SCOTT, accountant; b. Zeeland, Mich., Aug. 6, 1966; s. Willis Jay and Mary Lou (Beek) B.; m. Rachelle Lee Bennett, Dec. 14, 1991. BBA, Grand Valley State U., Allendale, Mich., 1988. Enrolled agt. IRS; accredited tax advisor, accountant; registered investment advisor agent, H.D. Vest Adv. Svcs., Inc.; resident agent-accident, health, life, State of Mich. Acct. Clinton Hop & Co., Inc., Grandville, 1988-93; acct./investment advisor Burlingame Fin. Svcs., Wyoming, Mich., 1993-95; acct., investment advisor Bonzelaar Fin. Svcs., Hudsonville, Mich., 1996—; contr. Burlingame Garage Inc., Wyoming, 1993-95. Mem. Ind. Accts. Assn. of Mich. Republican. Office: Bonzelaar Fin Svcs Ste A 3680 Chicago Dr Hudsonville MI 49426

BOODEN, THEODORE, dean; b. Chgo., Sept. 17, 1936; s. Hyman and Gertrude (Rubenzik) B.; m. Betty B. Katz, June 28, 1959; children: Michael R., Stewart K., Rebecca E. BS, Roosevelt U., 1960; MS, Northwestern U., 1962; DPhil, Fla. State U., 1968. From instr. to assoc. prof. The Chgo. Med. Sch., 1970-91, prof., 1991—; site sec. Liaison Com. Med. Edn., Chgo. and Washington. Office: FUHS/CMS 3333 Green Bay Rd North Chicago IL 60064

BOOK, WILLIAM JOSEPH, manufacturing executive; b. Council Bluffs, Iowa, Feb. 20, 1942; s. Leo William and Marie Ann (Korth) B.; m. Phyllis Theresa Kurzak, Nov. 25, 1962 (div. 1983); children: Gregory, Gary, Carolyn, Janet; m. Marjorie Schuler, Sep. 21, 1985. BSEE, U. Minn., 1973. Registered profl. engr., Minn. Evaluation engr. Honeywell Inc., Mpls., 1966-74; dist. mgr. Bussmann Mfg. co., Mpls., 1974-77; sales mgr. Lakeland Engring. Equipment Co., Mpls., 1977-78; mktg. mgr. Onan Corp., Mpls., 1978-85; chief exec. officer Ainslie Co., Mpls., 1985—. Home: 309 Westwood Dr S Minneapolis MN 55416-3362 Office: Ainslie Co 2909 Wayzata Blvd Minneapolis MN 55405

BOOKBINDER, KEITH J., financial planner; b. Providence, R.I., July 30, 1953. BS, Loyola U., 1975; MBA, No. Ill. U., 1977. Registered investment advisor. Pres. Bookbinder & Assocs. Inc., Cin., 1982—, Harbour Fin. Group, Blue Ash, Ohio, 1988—. Head fin. com. City Coun., Montgomery, Ohio, 1989-93. Republican. Office: Harbour Fin Group 9900 Carver Rd Ste 104 Blue Ash OH 45242

BOOKS, JOY ANN, human resource professional; b. Muncie, Ind., Apr. 1, 1937; d. Carl Thomas and Dorothy Elmina (Benson) Miller; m. Charles Edward Books, June 18, 1960 (div. 1981); children: C. Randall, Michele Ann. BS, Ball State U., 1960, student, 1963, 64, 74; student, Ind. U., 1955-57. Tchr. Petroleum (Ind.) High Sch., 1960-63, Daleville (Ind.) High Sch., 1964; sec. Wayne High Sch., Ft. Wayne, Ind., 1971-74; substitute tchr. Ft. Wayne Community Schs., 1974-76; counselor, job developer Comprehensive Employment & Tng. Act/Job Works, Ft. Wayne, 1977-88; employment specialist human resource dept. City of Ft. Wayne, 1988—; mem. faculty Ind.-Purdue U., Ft. Wayne, 1976; adv. bd. Ind. Tech. Coll., Ft. Wayne, 1987—. Pres. PTA, Ft. Wayne H.S., 1981-83. Mem. N.E. Ind. Human Resource Assn., Soc. Human Resource Mgmt., Arts United Greater Ft. Wayne, Ball State U. Alumni Assn., Alexia Woman's Club (past pres., v.p., sec., treas.), Ft. Wayne Rep. Club. Presbyterian. Home: # 131 2102 Ardmore Ave Fort Wayne IN 46802-4843 Office: City of Fort Wayne Rm 380 One Main St Fort Wayne IN 46802

BOONE, DOROTHY MAE, county official; b. Gordon, Nebr., May 29, 1919; d. C.H. and Ethel Mae (Lewis) Perkins; m. M.H. Boone Oct. 2, 1943 (dec. Sept. 1954). AA, Iowa Western Community Coll., Council Bluffs, 1977; grad., Am. Legion Officers Sch., Indpls., 1973. Notary pub., Iowa. Nat. VA accredited svc. rep. Office Gen. Counsel, Washington, 1976—; exec. sec., adminstrv. asst., adminstrv. sec. Pottawattamie County Veterans' Affairs Commn., Council Bluffs, Iowa; dir. Veteran Affairs Commn., Pottawattamie County, 1987-92; profl. svc. officer DAV, 1989—; mem. local bd. SSS, Washington, 1980—; mem., chair Harrison, Shelby and Pottawattamie counties Shelby and Pottawattamie counties SSS, 1981—. Recipient Cert. of Appreciation Kiwanis, 1985, VA Nat. Svc. Officers award, 1960, SSS, 1991, commendation DAV, 1987, County Svc. award Nat. VA, 1986, 92, Woman of Yr. award Am. Biol. Inst., 1993, Rep. Congl. Order Liberty, 1993, Internat. Order Merit award, 1994, Rep. Nat. Congl. Order of Freedom, 1995; named Most Admired Woman of Decade Am. Biog. Inst. Home: 1320 N 21st St Council Bluffs IA 51501-0909

BOONE, RICHARD RAY, psychologist, naval officer; b. Gallipolis, Ohio, Sept. 14, 1954; s. Ray and Betty Gean (Medley) B.; m. Maria Ann Hanson, May 30, 1981; children: Ryan Eliot, William Tyler, Olivia Nicole. BA in Psychology summa cum laude, Ohio U., 1977; student, U. Ala., 1978-82; MA, Biola U., 1991, PhD, 1993. Lic. psychologist, Ohio, N.C. Intern clin. psychology Nat. Naval Med. Ctr., Bethesda, Md., 1982-83; staff psychologist USN Naval Hosp., Jacksonville, Fla., 1983-88, USN Naval Hosp. Camp Lejeune, Jacksonville, N.C., 1988-90; sch. cons. and counselor La Puente (Calif.) Unified Sch. Dist., 1991-92; staff therapist Ingleside Psychiatric Hosp., Rosemond, Calif., 1992-93; med. staff, instr. Holzer Med. Ctr., Gallipolis, Ohio, 1994—; clin. psychologist Holzer Clinic, Gallipolis, Ohio, 1993—; cons., therapist Work Hardening Program, Gallipolis, 1994—, cons. psychologist RehabCare, Incorporated. Warden St. Peter's Episcopal Ch., Gallipolis, 1995. With USNR, 1982—. Mem. APA (psychoanalysis, milit. psychology, psychology and religion, psychotherapy, clin. psychology),Ohio Psychol. Assn. (treatment provider, colleague assistance program), N.C. Psychol. Assn., Phi Beta Kappa, Phi Kappa Phi, Pi Gamma Mu. Anglican. Home: 204 Chris Ln Gallipolis OH 45631 Office: Holzer Clinic Psychology Svc 90 Jackson Pike Gallipolis OH 45631

BOOR, MYRON VERNON, psychologist, educator; b. Wadena, Minn., Dec. 21, 1942; s. Vernon LeRoy and Rosella Katharine (Eckhoff) B. BS, U. Iowa, 1965; MA, So. Ill. U., 1967, PhD, 1970; MS, U. Pitts., 1981. Lic. psychologist, Kans., Mo. Research psychologist Milw. County Mental Health Ctr., 1970-72; asst. prof. clin. psychologist Ft. Hays State U., Hays, Kans., 1972-76; assoc. prof. Ft. Hays State U., Hays, 1976-79; NIMH postdoctoral fellow in psychiat. epidemiology U. Pitts., Western Psychiat. Inst. and Clinic, 1979-81; research psychologist R.I. Hosp. and Butler Hosp., Providence, 1981-84; clin. psychologist Newman Meml. County Hosp., Emporia, Kans., 1985-93, Heartland Health Sys., St. Joseph, Mo., 1994—; clin. psychologist Ft. Hays State U., 1972-79; asst. prof. psychiatry and human behavior Brown U., Providence, 1981-84; adj. faculty Emporia State U., 1985-94. Contbr. articles to profl. jours. U.S. Pub. Health Service fellow, 1965-67, NIMH fellow 1979-81. Mem. Am. Psychol. Assn., Soc. for Psychol. Study of Social Issues, Internat. Soc. for Study of Multiple Personalities (charter). Office: Heartland Health Sys 801 Faraon St Saint Joseph MO 64501-1868

BOOTE, TERRY J., engineering manager; b. Detroit, May 9, 1946. Chief engr. Etronic, Detroit, 1965-86; project engr. Air Gage, Lavonia, Mich., 1987-92; engring. mgr. Dearborn Gage Co., Garden City, Mich., 1992—. Coach Little LEague Soccer, Hockey and Baseball. With U.S. Army, 1965-69. Office: Dearborn Gage Co 32330 Ford Rd Garden City MI 48135-1507

BOOTH, ALAN RUNDLETT, history educator; b. Manchester, N.H., Mar. 20, 1934; s. Robert Plues and Lois (Rundlett) B.; m. Beatrice Edgcomb, June 23, 1956 (div. June 1978); children: Thomas E., Samuel R., Holly; m. Margaret Zoller, Aug. 6, 1988; 1 child, Grace Marie. AB, Dartmouth Coll., 1956; MA, Boston U., 1962, PhD, 1964. Asst. prof. history Ohio U., Athens, 1964-68, assoc. prof. history, 1968-73, prof. history, 1973—, Hamilton/Baker & Hostetler prof. humanities, 1994—; manuscript cons. Jour. of Devel. Areas, Kalamazoo, 1965-95, Internat. Jour. African Historical Studies, 1970-95, African Econ. History, Mpls., 1980-95; Fulbright lectr. Swaziland, 1980-81, 89-90. Author: The United States Experience in South Africa, 1976, Swaziland: Tradition and Change in a Southern African Kingdom, 1983; contbr. articles to profl. jours. Lt. USNR, 1956-60. Fulbright lectr., Basutoland, 1965-66, Swaziland, 1980-81, 89-90. Mem. Ohio Acad. History (exec. com. 1994-95), African Studies Assn. Democrat. Roman Catholic. Home: 6 Northwood Dr Athens OH 45701 Office: Ohio U Dept History Bentley Hall 56 Athens OH 45701

BOOTH, DOUGLAS ALAN, news director; b. St. Louis, June 13, 1956; s. Robert William and Elaine Lucille (Fifield) B.; m. Christine Marie Wieland, July 27, 1979; children: Jessica, Kimberly. Student, St. Louis U., 1973-74, Ctrl. Meth. U., Fayette, Mo., 1975-76. Announcer WRIN-AM 1560, Rensselaer, Ind., 1979, WJCK-FM 97.7, Rensselaer, 1979-80; ops. mgr. WRIN-AM 1560, WLQI-FM 97.7, Rensselaer, 1980-83; sta. mgr. WLQI-FM 97.7, Rensselaer, 1982-83; news dir. WDDD-AM 810 and FM 107.3, Marion, Ill., 1983-88; campaign mgr. Kelly for Congress, Carbondale, Ill., 1988; news dir. WFXV-TV30, WAUR-AM, WSPY-FM, Aurora and Plano, Ill., 1988—. Bd. mem. Marion (Ill.) City Libr. Bd., 1986-88; vice-chmn. Fox Valley Freeway Citizen's Adv. Com., South Region, Aurora, 1991-92; bd. mem. East Aurora Bd. Edn., 1991—. Mem. Radio-TV News Dirs. Assn., Ill. News Broadcasters, Rensselaer Jaycees (treas. 1982-83). Republican. Methodist. Home: 1347B Park Dr Montgomery IL 60538-1866 Office: 1 Broadcast Ctr Plano IL 60545-9667

BOOTH, JAMES ALBERT, engineer; b. Salem, Ohio, Dec. 14, 1946; s. Kenneth Bishop and Helen Elizabeth (Kelly) B.; m. Anita Jean Willford, Aug. 10, 1974; children: Jennifer Lynn, Stephen Andrew. BS, Bowling Green (Ohio) State U., 1968, MS in Physics, 1973; MS in Nuclear Engring., Ohio State U., 1974; MS in Engring. Mgmt., U. Dayton, Ohio, 1983. Registered profl. engr., Ohio. Sr. research engr. Monsanto Research Corp., Dayton, 1974-81, mgr. engring. design, 1981-84; group leader non-destructive testing Monsanto Research Corp., Miamisburg, Ohio, 1984-86, group leader quality engring., 1986-88; quality engring. mgr. E G and G Mound Applied Techs., Miamisburg, 1988-89, group leader material tech., 1989-92; program mgr. Decommissioning and Decontamination, 1993—. Served as sgt. U.S. Army, 1969-71, Vietnam. Mem. ASME, Am. Soc. for Non-Destructive Testing (chmn. Dayton sect. 1994-95), Am. Soc. for Quality Control (cert. quality engr., quality auditor, quality mgr., sr.) Project Mgmt. Inst. (cert. quality project mgr.). Methodist. Home: 3141 Westview Dr Beavercreek OH 45434-6039 Office: E G and G Mound Applied Techs PO Box 3000 Miamisburg OH 45343-3000

BOOTH, JODY SHELTON, educational executive director; b. Norton, Kans., Aug. 4, 1944; d. James Pratt and Rita Merle (Thompson) Shelton. BA, Ottawa U., 1967; MEd, Emporia State U., 1977; EdD, Kans. U., 1991. Tchr. Belvoir Elem. Sch., Topeka, 1967-68, Ctrl. Elem. Sch., Olathe, Kans., 1968-77; prin. Westview Elem. Sch., Olathe, Kans., 1977-80, Tomahawk Elem. Sch., Olathe, Kans., 1980-88; exec. dir. human resources Olathe Dist. Schs., 1988—; cons. Master Tchr., Manhattan, Kans., 1981-86; adj. prof. Emporia (Kans.) State U., 1990—; chair North Ctrl. Edn. Team, 1984; mem. adv. coun. Sch. Edn., Kans. U., Lawrence, 1992—; mem. com. Five Yr. Tech. Plan, Olathe, 1991—. Contbr. articles to profl. jours. Recipient Outstanding Jayne award Jaycees, 1972, Outstanding Young Woman Kans., 1980. Mem. NAESP (Nat. Disting. Prin. award 1987-88), AASPA (affiliate), Kans. Career Devel. and Placement Assn., Kans. Assn. Elem. Sch. Prins. (pres., Nat. Disting. Prin. award 1987-88, Olathe C. of C., United Sch. Adminstrs. (bd. dirs.), Optimist. Home: 11546 S Brentwood Dr Olathe KS 66061-9388 Office: Olathe Dist Schs 1005 S Pitt St Olathe KS 66061-5242

BOOTH, SARA DANIEL, editor; b. Greensboro, N.C., May 8, 1964; d. John Latham and Patricia (Daniel) B.; m. Gary Albero Panetta, Oct. 14, 1989. BS in Journalism, Northwestern U., 1986. Freelance writer Evanston, Ill., 1986-87; feature writer, then news editor, tourism mag. editor The Mountaineer, Waynesville, N.C., 1987-89; copy editor Herald-Whig, Quincy, Ill., 1990-91; reporter The Observer, Peoria, Ill., 1992; writer Dynamics Graphics, 1992-95; editor-in-chief Step-by-Step Electronic Design mag., 1995—. Recipient awards for feature articles, series, columns, N.C. Press Assn., 1988, 89; named for best of typography Ill. Cen. Coll. design show, 1992. Democrat. Episcopalian. Home: 501 W Maywood Ave Peoria IL 61604-2837

BOOTSMA, GREG D., financial consultant; b. Belflower, Calif., Oct. 12, 1962; s. Kenneth Bernard and Marybeth (Devires) B.; m. Julie R. Deyoung, Aug. 20, 1983; children: Jessica, Grace. BS, Grand Valley State U., Allendale, Mich., 1986. Account exec. Smith Barney, Grand Rapids, Mich., 1986-90; v.p. sales and mktg. Market Pl. Media, Grand Rapids, 1990-94; fin. cons. The Ohio Co., Grand Rapids, 1994—. Treas. Ford br. Kellogsville Schs., Kentwood, Mich., 1994—. Mem. Grand Rapids C. of C. (mem. com. 1995). Republican. Mem. Christian Reformed Ch. Home: 4700 Brooklyn Ave SE Kentwood MI 49508-4514 Office: The Ohio Co 4843 Cascade Rd SE Grand Rapids MI 49546-3781

BOOZ, GRETCHEN ARLENE, marketing executive; b. Boone, Iowa, Nov. 24, 1933; d. David Gerald and Katherine Bevridge (Hardie) Berg; m. Donald Rollett Booz, Sept. 3, 1960; children: Kendra Sue (dec.), Joseph David, Katherine Sue. AA, Graceland Coll., 1955. Med. asst. Robert A. Hayne M.D., Des Moines, 1955-61; mktg. services mgr. Herald Pub. House, Independence, Mo., 1975—. Author: (book) Kendra, 1979. Mem. Citizens Adv. Bd., Blue Springs, Mo., 1979-91, Independence Mayor's Christmas Concert Com., 1987-91; bd. dirs. Comprehensive Mental Health, 1981-83, Child Placement Svcs., Independence, 1987-94, Hope House, Inc., Independence, 1987-91, Ctr. for Profl. Devel. and Life-long Learning, Inc., 1995-96; trustee Graceland Coll., Lamoni, Iowa, 1984-96. Mem. Leadership Edn. Action Devel. (L.E.A.D.), Independence C. of C. (diplomat, Outstanding Mem. award 1981). Republican. Mem. Reorganized Ch. Jesus Christ Latter Day Saints. Home: 1200 Crestview Dr Blue Springs MO 64014-2312 Office: Herald Pub House 3225 S Noland Rd Independence MO 64055-1317

BOOZELL, MARK ELDON, state legislative affairs executive; b. Mason City, Iowa, Mar. 4, 1955; s. Eldon Dwayne Boozell and Betty Jean (Gordon) Kruger; m. Susan Elizabeth Abelt, Nov. 26, 1977; children: Kari Elizabeth, Lindsay Patricia. BA, Augustana Coll., 1977. Budget analyst rep. staff Ill. Ho. of Reps., Springfield, 1977-78, dep. dir. rep. staff, 1978-80; legis. liaison Ill. Dept. Transp., Springfield, 1980-83; dir. legis. affairs Ill. Sec. State, Springfield, 1983—. Named one of Outstanding Young Men Am., 1980. Republican. Lutheran. Home: 78 Stony Creek Dr Chatham IL 62629-1551 Office: Sec of States Dept of Legis Affairs 476 Centennial Bldg Springfield IL 62756

BORAZ, ROBERT ALAN, dentist, surgery and pediatrics educator; b. St. Louis, Apr. 13, 1951; s. Herbert Sigmund and Pearl Yetta (Garber) B.; m. Janet Ruth Knie, Jan. 3, 1981; children: Jonathan Daniel, Katharine Elizabeth. Student, U. Mo., 1969-72, DDS, 1975, postgrad., 1975-77. Resident Children's Mercy Hosp., Kansas City, Mo., 1975-77; dir. dental svc. U. Kans. Med. Ctr., Kansas City, 1977—, prof. surgery, 1984—; assoc. prof. U. Mo. Dental Sch., Kansas City, 1977—, chief dentistry Children's Rehab. Unit, Kansas City, 1977—; assoc. dir. Sutherland Inst. Facial Rehab., Kansas City, 1984—; specialty examiner Mo. Dental Bd., Jefferson City, Mo., 1987—. Contbr. articles to profl. jours. Mem. Gov.'s Task Force on Hemophilia, Topeka, 1984-86; mem. prof. edn. com. Am. Cancer Soc., Topeka, 1987—; mem. regional bd. Easter Seal Soc., Greater Kansas City, 1979-82; trustee Am. Soc. of Dentistry for Children, 1989-96. Fellow Am. Coll. Dentists, Internat. Coll. Dentists, Am. Acad. Pediatric Dentistry (component pres. 1984—, trustee 1991-94, parliamentarian 1994-96, sec.-treas. 1996—), Am. Soc. Dentistry for Children (Kans. pres. 1988—, bd. trustees 1989—, Cert. of Merit 1976), Am. Assn. Hosp. Dentists, Acad. Dentistry for the Handicapped; mem. ADA, S.W. Soc. Pediatric Dentistry (v.p. 1988-89, pres.-elect 1992, pres. 1992-93), Alpha Omega (local pres. 1973-75), Omicron Kappa Upsilon. Office: U Kans Med Ctr 3901 Rainbow Blvd Kansas City KS 66160-0001

BORDENKIRCHER, JOHN J., investment represenative; b. Springfield, Ill., Oct. 29, 1949. BA, Bradley U., 1981. Indsl. engr. Internat. Harvester Co., Canton, Ill., 1972-81; investment rep. Edward D. Jones & Co., Jacksonville, Ill., 1982—. Mem. Elks. Home: 856 W 8th St Jacksonville IL 62650

BOREL, STEVEN JAMES, lawyer; b. Kansas City, Mo., Nov. 12, 1947; s. Mark and Margaret (Gibson) B.; m. Nancy Jean Dunnaway, Aug. 31, 1967; children: Lindsay Kay, Emily Jean, Amy Lynn. BSBA, Pitts. State U., 1969; JD, U. Mo., Kansas City, 1972. Bar: Mo. 1972, Kans. 1989. Assoc. Stubbs, Epstein & Mann, Kansas City, 1972-79; pvt. practice Kansas City, 1979—. Rsch. editor U. Mo.-Kansas City Law Rev., 1971-72. Capt. U.S. Army, 1969-74. Mem. ATLA, Mo. Assn. Trial Attys., Kans. Trial Lawyers Assn., Kansas City Met. Bar Assn. (chmn. workers' compensation com. 1991-93). Office: Borel & Assocs 1101 Walnut St Ste 900 Kansas City MO 64106-2122

BORELLI, GEORGE LOUIS, psychologist; b. N.Y., June 13, 1926; s. Anthony and Mary (Morano) B.; m. Carol Jean Jeffers, June 3, 1953; children: Jeff, Lisa, Scott, Michael. AA, Champlain Coll., 1948; BA, Kent Sate U., 1950, MA, 1951; PhD, Ohio State Coll., 1960. lic. psychologist, Ohio, Fla. Chief psychologist Sunny Acres T.B. Hosp., Cleve., 1949-51; psychology intern Cleve. State Hosp., 1955-57; chief psychologist Ohio State T.B. Hosp., Columbus, 1955-57, Columbus State Hosp., 1957-62; pvt. practice clin. psychology, dir. Ohio, 1962-73; cons. psychologist Columbus Psychol. Svc., 1973—; asst. prof. psychiatry Ohio State U., Columbus, 1975-79; cons. AT&T, Columbus, 1989-94, GM Fisher Guide, 1989—, Ohio State B.V.R., 1960—. Author: Wizard of Imp, 1994, Role Simulation; A Collection of Pop Psych. Articles, The Boogaloo Pirates, (plays) Jwel in the Sword, 1995, Love Child, 1995, Unit Nine, 1995, also numerous popular psychology articles. Served with U.S.N., 1944-46. Mem. Am. Psychol. Assn. (clin. program chair), Ohio Psychol. Assn. (pres. cen. chpt.). Office: Columbus Psychol Svc Inc 24 E Weber Rd Columbus OH 43202

BORELLI, MARIO, mathematics educator, program director; b. Quarrata, Pistoia, Italy, Sept. 7, 1934; came to U.S., 1956; s. Casimiro and Emilia (Belardi) B.; m. Angela A. Colón, Dec. 26, 1958; 1 child, Mario R. BSc Scuola Normale Superiore, U. Pisa, Italy, 1956; PhD in Math., Ind. U., 1961; trainee, Inst. Retraining Computer Sci., 1985, 86. Instr. Ind. U., Bloomington, 1959-61, asst. prof., 1963-65; from lectr. to asst. prof. U. B.C., Vancouver, Can., 1961-63; asst. prof. U. Notre Dame, Ind., 1965-70, assoc. prof., program dir., 1971—, assoc. chmn. math. dept., 1984-88; vis. prof. Univ. Católica del Perú, Lima, 1967; Faculty fellow Harvard U., 1968; instr. NSF Summer Inst. U. Notre Dame, 1968-70, project co-dir., 1970-73, program dir., 1974-79. Contbr. articles to profl. jours. Fulbright fellow, 1956, NSF Profl. Devel. grantee, Dartmouth Coll., 1977. Mem. NAACP, Am. Math Assn., Am. Math Soc., Nat. Coun. Ednl. Opportunity Assn., Midwest Assn. Ednl. Opportunity Prog. Pers. Roman Catholic. Office: Univ Notre Dame 236 Security Notre Dame IN 46556

BOREN, DONNA, primary school educator; b. Huntington, W.Va., July 25, 1937; d. Vess C. and Oma M. (Sullivan) McCally; m. Larry R. Boren, Nov. 19, 1977; children: Kyle Purpura, Kevin Purpura, David (dec.), Jeff, Steve. AA, Shawnee State U., Portsmouth, Ohio, 1989; student, Miami U., 1955-56, Eastern Ky. U., 1956-57, Ohio State U., Ohio U., 1988. Tchr. First Nat. Bank, Dayton, Ohio, 1962-66; clk. Vandalia (Ohio) Pre-Sch., 1971-72; income tax preparer City of Portsmouth, 1976-78; tchr. Johnson's Pre-Sch., Portsmouth, 1974-76, 79-93; clk. 1st Presbyn. Pre-sch., Portsmouth, Ohio, 1993-94; tchr., asst. dir. 1st Presbyn. Pre-sch., Portsmouth, 1994—. Numerous civic actitivies. Home: 4190 Timber Ln Des Moines IA 50317

BOREN, STEPHEN DARWIN, medical director; b. Chgo., Nov. 15, 1946; s. Harry Lion and Charlotte Pearl (Levinson) B.; m. Louise M. Sinsko, Dec. 15, 1973; children: Nancy Elizabeth, David Michal. MBA, Northwestern U., 1987; MD, U. Ill., Chgo., 1970. Cert. Am. Bd. Emergency Medicine. Intern U. Ill. Hosps., 1970-71; resident Tufts-New England Med. Ctr., 1974-75, Med. Coll. Wis., 1978-80; med. dir. emergency medicine Humana Hosp., Hoffman Estates, Ill., 1983, St. Catherine's Hosp., Kenosha, Wis., 1984-90; chief staff St. Catherine's Hosp., Kenosha, 1989; developer, med. dir. Kenosha (Wis.) Indsl. Clinic, 1990; asst. prof. emergency medicine U. Ill., Chgo., 1990—; med. dir. CNA Ins., Chgo., 1991-95, Maxicare Health Plans of M.W., Chgo., 1995—; med. dir. St. Catherine's IPA, Kenosha, 1987-89. contbr. articles to profl. jours. Mem., del. Sch. Bd. Caucus, Wilmette, Ill., 1990. Capt. U.S. Army, 1971-73, Korea. Named Friend of the Residents, Med. Coll. Wis., Kenosha, 1989. Fellow Am. Bd. Emergency Medicine; mem. AMA, Am. Coll. Emergency Physicians, Am. Acad. Ins. Medicine, Ill. Med. Assn., Chgo. Med. Soc., Ind. Physicians Assn., Soc. Am. Baseball Rsch. Home: 932 Ashland Wilmette IL 60091 Office: CNA Ins Co CNA Plaza Chicago IL 60685

BORENSTEIN, HOWARD A., stockbroker; b. Mpls., July 21, 1959; m. Shari Weinenstein, Feb. 20, 1984; children: Peretz, Chim, Maier, Baroch. Degree in fin., Northeastern Ill. U., 1983. Stockbroker David A. Noyes & Co., Skokie, Ill., 1983—. Bd. dirs. Yesh McDoll Thuh, Chgo., 1992—, Ill. Good of Israel, Chgo., 1994—. Republican. Jewish. Office: David A Noyes & Co Ste #100 8707 Skokie Blvd Skokie IL 60077-2200

BORG, RUTH I., in-home nursing care provider; b. Chgo., Mar. 29, 1934; d. Axel Gunner and Charlotte (Benston) B. Diploma, West Suburban Sch. Nursing, 1956; tchr.'s degree, Chgo. Conservatory, 1958; BSN, Alverno Coll., 1981. Staff nurse Boath Meml. Hosp., Chgo.; head nurse psychiatry, head nurse long-term medicine VA North Chgo. Med. Ctr.; staff nurse, night supr. intermediate care VA Clement Zabiocki Med. Ctr., Milw.; pool nurse, in-home nursing care provider Milw. County Mental Health Complex. Contbr. 2 articles to profl. jours.

BORGER, MICHAEL HINTON IVERS, osteopathic physician, educator; b. Kirksville, Mo., Nov. 10, 1951; s. Donald L. Borger and Dorothy M. Hinton. BA in Sociology, U. Akron, 1974; DO, Coll. Osteo. Medicine and Surgery, Des Moines, 1977. Diplomate Nat. Bd. Examiners in Osteo. Medicine and Surgery; ordained elder Presbyn. Ch., 1969. Rotating extern Youngstown (Ohio) Osteo. Hosp., 1976; extern in family medicine Dietz Diagnostic Clinic, Des Moines, 1977; rotating intern South Bend (Ind.) Osteo. Hosp. (now Michiana Community Hosp), 1977-78, active staff, 1978-79, assoc. staff, 1979-82; pvt. practice Nappanee, Ind., 1978-; mem. staff Elkhart (Ind.) Gen. Hosp., 1978—, Goshen Gen. Hosp., 1981—; clin. asst. prof. gen. practice Kirksville (Mo.) Coll. Osteo. Medicine, 1990-93; apptd. clin. preceptor Kansas City U. of Health Scis. Coll. of Osteo. Medicine, 1993—; asst. clin. prof. family practice Kansas City U. of Health Scis. Coll. of Osteo. Medicine, Kansas City, 1995—; Nappanee, Ind., 1993—; assoc. manuscript reviewer Jour. Respiratory Diseases, 1986-88, Jour. Musculoskeletal Medicine, 1989—; pres. Northwood Profl. Assocs., Inc., 1995—. Bd. dirs. Nappanee chpt. Families in Action, 1980-82; bd. dirs., chmn. Mission and Svcs. Commn., 1st Mennonite Ch., Nappanee, 1984-90, chmn. pastoral search com., 1989-90; mem. screening com. for elem. prin. Wa-Nee Sch. Dist., 1988; med. advisor United Presbyn. Ch. Nursery Sch., Nappanee, 1995—. Recipient Physician of Yr. award Ind. Assn. Emergency Med. Technicians, 1981, Good Citizens award Tower Savs., 1982, 1st degree black belt Tae Kwon Do, 1988, Tae Kwon Do Student of Yr. award, Hong's USA Tae Kwon Do, 1988; Burroughs-Wellcome Osteo rsch. fellow, 1980-81. Mem. Am. Osteo. Assn., Ind. Assn. Osteo. Physicians and Surgeons, Am. Acad. Applied Osteopathy, Nat. Honor Soc., Masons (3d degree), York Rite. Home: 353 N Hartman St Nappanee IN 46550-1417

BORGMAN, JAMES MARK, editorial cartoonist; b. Cin., Feb. 24, 1954; s. James Robert and Florence Marian (Maly) B.; m. Lynn Goodwin, Aug. 20, 1977. B.A., Kenyon Coll., 1976. Editorial cartoonist Cin. Enquirer, 1976—, King Features Syndicate, 1980—; contbr. to Newsweek Broadcasting's Cartoon-A-Torial (animated editorial cartoon feature), 1978-81. Author: (collection of editorial cartoons) Smorgasborgman, 1982, The Great Communicator, 1985, The Mood of America, 1986, Jim Borgman's Cincinnati, 1992. Recipient Sigma Delta Chi award, 1978, 95, Thomas Nast prize, 1980, 2d prize for editorial cartooning Internat. Salon Cartoons of Montreal, 1981, Ohio's Gov.'s award, 1990, Pulitzer Prize for editorial cartooning, 1991, Nat. Headliner award, 1991, Reuben award for outstanding cartooning of yr., 1993. Mem. Am. Assn. Editorial Cartoonists, Nat. Cartoonists Soc. (Best Editorial Cartoonist award 1987, 88, 89). Office: 312 Elm St Cincinnati OH 45202-2739

BORGMANN, CONNIE SUE, advertising and public relations executive; b. Norfolk, Nebr., Mar. 20, 1963; d. James Elmer and Rita Marie (Vecera) Sukup; m. Donald Robert Borgmann, Mar. 20, 1982 (div. July 1987); children: Nicole, Megan, Danielle. BA, Doane Coll., 1985. Graphics specialist Miller & Paine Dept. Stores, Lincoln, Nebr., 1985-86; prodn. supr. United Phone Book Advertisers, Lincoln, 1986-89; composition proofer Peed Corp., Lincoln, 1989-90; advt. & pub. rels. dir. daVinci's Restaurants, Lincoln, 1990—; cons. Mary Kay Cosmetics Inc., Dallas, 1988—; freelance designer, Lincoln, 1985—; phone book prodn. cons., Lincoln, 1985-86. Mem. Advt. Fedn. Lincoln (Addy award 1991, 92, bd. dirs.), Doan Coll. Alumni Assn., Cathedral Home Sch. Assn. Roman Catholic. Home: 2601 S 41st St Lincoln NE 68506-2513 Office: daVinci's Restaurants 1431 S 33rd St Lincoln NE 68506-1002

BORGMANN, NORMA LEE, school superintendent; b. Belleville, Ill., Sept. 9, 1948; d. William Henry and Loraine Anna (Wolff) B. BA, Greenville Coll., 1970, BS, 1973; MS in Edn., So. Ill. U., 1979, EdS in Adminstrn., 1994. Cert. adminstr., tchr., Ill. Tchr. elem. edn. Patoka (Ill.) Community Unit # 100, 1971-90, tchr. jr. high sch., adminstrv. asst., 1990-91, tchr. jr. high sch., prin., 1991-92, prin. K-12, 1992-94, supt., 1994—. Author: (cookbook) Our Family Favorites, 1987; compiler: (cookbook) Cookin' with DuBois Center Auxiliary, 1983. Recipient Human Svcs. award Ill. Edn. Assn., 1984. Mem. Ill. Assn. Sch. Adminstrs., Am. Camping Assn., Ill. Women Adminstrs., Pakota Cmty. Edn. Assn. (sec.-treas. 1977-79, v.p. 1979-81, pres. 1981-83), Beta Sigma Phi (pres. Delta chpt. 1993-94, 4 Mem. of Yr. awards). Mem. United Ch. of Christ. Home: 502 E Bond Ave Patoka IL 62875-1037 Office: Patoka Cmty Unit #100 1220 Kinoka Rd Patoka IL 62875-1300

BORGO, JOHN L., marketing executive; b. Pitts., Apr. 1, 1949; s. John B. and Elizabeth Borgo; m. Linda Ann Vitunic, Dec. 22, 1972; children: Monica, Lisa, Amy, John, Megan. BS, Pa. State U., 1971. Sales trainee Dow Chem. Co., Baton Rouge, 1972; acct. specialist Dow Chem. Co., Phila., 1973; broker sales mgr. Dow Chem. Co., Buffalo, 1974-78; consumer promotion mgr. Dow Chem. Co., Indpls., 1978; brand mgr. Dow Brands, Indpls., 1979-85; dist. sales mgr. Dow Brands, Chgo., 1985-88; dir. sales Dow Brands, Indpls., 1988-89, group mktg. mgr., 1989-93, dir. consumer comm., 1993-95, dir. mktg., 1995—. Basketball coach Cath. Youth Orgn., Indpls., 1988-90, football coach, 1991. Republican. Roman Catholic. Home: 13641 Wood Mill Ct Carmel IN 46032-9211 Office: Dow Brands 9750 Zionsville Rd Zionsville IN 46077-8755

BORK, KENNARD BAKER, geology educator; b. Kalamazoo, Oct. 13, 1940; s. Meinhard John and Glenda Davis (Baker) B.; m. Katherine Camille Odell, Dec. 29, 1963; 1 child, Robert Odell. BA, DePauw U., 1962; MA, Ind. U., 1964, PhD, 1967. Asst. prof. geology Denison U., Granville, Ohio, 1966-71, assoc. prof., 1971-77, prof., 1977-90, Alumni prof., 1990—, dir. Jan. term, 1969-72; cons. univ. systems, Pa., Mass., Ind. Author: Cracking Rocks and Defending Democracy: Kirtley F. Mother (1888-1978), 1994; editor inaugural issue Earth Scis. History, 1982; contbr. articles to profl. jours. Recipient Best Paper of Yr. award Ohio Acad. Sci., 1982. Fellow Geol. Soc. Am.; mem. AAAS, History of Earth Scis. Soc. (exec. sec. 1987-93), History Sci. Soc., French Com. on History Geology, Internat. Commn. on History Geology (corr.), Sigma Xi. Home: 324 Mt Parnassus Dr Granville OH 43023-1002 Office: Denison U Dept Geology/Geography Dept Geology Geography Granville OH 43023

BORK, TRICIA, athletics association administrator; b. Hutchinson, Kans., Dec. 18, 1953; d. William Samuel and Julia Ellen (Karrigan) B. BS in Jounalism, U. Kans., 1976. Writer, editor trade mag. Golf Course Superintendents Assn. Am., Lawrence, Kans., 1976-78; publs. editor Nat. Collegiate Athletic Assn., Overland Park, Kans., 1978-81; asst. dir. championships NCAA, Overland Park, 1981-82, dir. women's championships, 1982-88, asst. exec. dir. championships, 1988-92, group exec. dir. championships, 1992—; Mem. bd. dirs. Women's Basketball Hall of Fame, 1993—, Honda Awards, 1994—. Mem. Nat. Assn. Collegiate Women Athletics Adminstrs. Democrat. Roman Catholic. Home: 2020 West 48th Terrace Mission Woods KS 66205

BORN, JAMES E., art educator, sculptor; b. Toledo, Nov. 16, 1934; s. Elmer Arthur and Dorthy (Halstead) B.; m. Donna Jones; children: Karl, Anna Born Ross, Thomas, Christopher, Tanya. BA, Toledo U., 1959; MFA, U. Iowa, 1962. Grad. teaching asst. U. Iowa, Iowa City, 1964-65; asst. prof. Calif. State U., Arcata, 1962-65, Calif. Western U., San Diego, 1965-67, Calif. State U., Turlock, 1967-69; prof. art Cen. Mich. U., Mt. Pleasant, 1969—. Bronze sculptures exhibited in group and one-man shows; represented in permanent collections Outdoor Sculpture Exhibit, Southfield, Mich., 1991; exhibited in one-man show Gallery Abbott Kinney, Venice, Calif., 1992, Mich. Competition, Birmingham, Bloomfield Art Ctr., 1992, Commn. Trans World Airlines, L.A. Airport, Watercolor Paintings, All Calif., San Diego Mus. of Art, 1995, Mich. Exhibition, Mt. Clemens, Mich., Art Mus., 1993-95, Mich. Art Exhibition, Saginaw Art Mus., 1993-94. Recipient honor award Battle Creek Art Mus., 1982, 1st award sculpture Ball State U., 1982, grand award S.W. Ark. Art Mus., 1982, 1st award sculpture Mt. Clemens Art Mus., 1989, sculpture award Saginaw Art Mus., 1992. Home: 502 S University Ave Mount Pleasant MI 48858-3150 Office: Cen Mich U Art Dept Mount Pleasant MI 48859

BORNS, ROBERT AARON, real estate developer; b. Gary, Ind., Oct. 24, 1935; s. Irving Jonah and Sylvia (Mackoff) B.; m. Sandra Solotkin, Mar. 30, 1958; children: Stephanie, Elizabeth, Emily. BS, Ind. U., 1957, hon. degree U. Indpls., 1987. Account exec. Reynolds & Co., Chgo., 1957-59, Francis I. duPont Co., Indpls., 1960; owner, operator Borns & Co., Indpls., 1960-63; chmn. Borns Mgmt. Corp., Indpls., 1963—; bd. dirs. Indpls. Water Co., IWC Resources Corp., Heritage Ptnrs. Mgmt. Corp., Indpls. Power and Light Co., Mid Am. Capital Resources Corp.; dir. Standard Mgmt. Corp. Bd. dirs. Indpls. Mus. of Art-Life, IPALCO Enterprises, Indpls. Symphony Orch.; mem. bd. vis. Borns Jewish Studies Program, Ind. U.; past bd. dirs. Indpls. Children's Mus. U.; past trustee St. Vincents Hosp. Found., Marian Coll.; bd. adv. Indpls. Com. on Fgn. Relations, St. Vincents Hosp. Recipient Enterprise award Indpls. Bus. Jour., 1982, Peace award State of Israel, 1979. Mem. Confrerie des Chevaliers du Tastevin, Econ. Club (bd. dirs.). Jewish. Office: Borns Mgmt Corp 200 S Meridian St Indianapolis IN 46225-1076

BORNSTEIN, JEFFREY VICTOR, marketing executive; b. Bklyn., June 25, 1950; s. Adolph and Thelma (Helfenbein) B.; m. Sheila Abby Dombek, June 3, 1972; children: Gregory, Todd, Taryn. BSChemE, Poly. Inst. Bklyn., 1971; MBA, Fairleigh Dickinson U., 1977. Prodn. supr. Hoffman-La Roche Inc., Nutley, N.J., 1971-74, mktg. mgr., 1974-79; cons. Booz, Allen & Hamilton, Florham Park, N.J., 1979-80; mgr., market rsch. & comml. devel. A.E. Staley Mfg. Co., Decatur, Ill., 1980-83, gen. mgr. polymerizable products dept., 1983-85, group mgr. tech. transfer, 1986-87; pres. A.E. Staley Mfg. Co., Decatur, 1987-88, JUB Assocs. Mgmt. Cons., Decatur, 1988—; v.p., mktg. Fully Compounded Plastics, Inc., Decatur, 1988-93. Mem. Decatur YMCA Mktg. Bd. Mem. Soc. Plastics Engrs., Comml. Devel. Assn., Chem. Mktg. Rsch. Assn. Home: 411 Woodhill Dr Decatur IL 62521-5541 Office: JVB Assocs 411 Woodhill Dr Decatur IL 62521

BOROCHIN, EUGENE, mechanical engineer; b. Saratov, Russia, Jan. 21, 1947; came to U.S., 1994; Mech. Engr., Aircraft Tech. Sch., 1965; M in Theoretical Mechanics, U. Saratov, Russia, 1971. Computer programmer Rsch. Inst., Saratov, Russia, 1971-86, Tantal, Saratov, Russia, 1986-94; engr. TEH Pilliod, Swanton, Ohio, 1994—; cons. in field, Saratov, Russia. Contbr. articles to profl. jours. in Russia. Recipient 18 Yr. Svc. award Rsch. Inst., Saratov, 1986. Office: Teh Pilliod Co 302 Church St Swanton OH 43558-1017

BOROTA, TIMOTHY DOUGLAS, stockbroker; b. Kewanee, Ill., Apr. 26, 1956. Stockbroker Edward D. Jones & Co., Baraboo, Wis., 1982—. Coach Baraboo Boys Basketball Team, 1994—. Mem. Baraboo C. of C. (mem. amb. club), Kiwanis (past pres. 1983—), Country Club Baraboo (dir. 1987-90. Office: Edward D Jones & Co 406 Broadway St Baraboo WI 53913-2413

BOROVOY, MARC ALLEN, podiatrist; b. Detroit, Oct. 22, 1960; s. Mathew and Joyce Francis (Weisman) B.; m. Michele Lynn Flusty, Oct. 23, 1983; children: Danielle, Brandon. Student, Wayne State U., 1978-81; D. Podiatric Medicine, Ohio Coll. Podiatric Medicine, 1985. Diplomate Am. Bd. Podiatric Sugery, Am. Bd. Quality Assurance and Utilization Rev. Resident Straith Hosp., Southfield, Mich., 1985-86; podiatrist Associated Podiatrists, Oak Park, Mich., 1986—; chief dept. podiatric surgery Providence Hosp., Southfield, Mich. Contbr. articles to profl. jours. Mem. exec. bd. Congregation Bnai Moshe, West Bloomfield, Mich., 1989—. Fellow Am. Coll. Foot Surgeons; mem. APHA, Am. Diabetes Assn., Mich. Podiatric Med. Assn. (exec. sec. 1986-89, chmn. pub. rels. 1988—, v.p. 1990-91, pres.-elect 1992-93, pres. 1993-95). Office: Associated Podiatrists 25725 Coolidge Hwy Oak Park MI 48237-1307 also: 47601 Grand River Ave Ste B-230 Novi MI 48374-1233

BOROW, RANDY, accountant; b. LaGrange, Ill., Jan. 20, 1966. Rep. candidate 7th dist. Ill. U.S. House of Reps., 1996. Roman Catholic. Office: 8909 W Cermar Rd North Riverside IL 60546*

BORROR, DONALD A., construction company executive; b. 1929. Grad., Ohio State Univ., Columbus, Ohio State Univ. Sch. of Law, Columbus. With Summer & Co. Inc., Columbus, Ohio, 1956-71; with The Borror Corp. (now Borror Realty Co.), Dublin, Ohio, 1971—, pres., 1976-82, chmn., 1977—; chmn. bd. dirs. The Borror Corp. (now Borror Realty Co.), Dublin, 1994—. With USAF. Office: Borror Realty Co PO Box 7166 5501 Frantz Rd Dublin OH 43017-7502

BORROR, DOUGLAS G., construction company executive; b. 1955. Grad., Ohio State U., 1977. With Huntington Nat. Bank, Columbus, 1977-79; with Borror Corp. (now Borror Realty Co.), Dublin, Ohio, 1979—, pres., CEO, COO, 1994—. Office: Borror Corp 5501 Frantz Rd Dublin OH 43017-7502*

BORSICK, MARLIN LESTER, data processing executive; b. Norwalk, Ohio, Feb. 16, 1953; s. Lester Charles and Delores Arlene (Yutzy) B.; m. Deborah Jean Taylor, May 6, 1988; 1 child, Tegan Marie. BA in Polit. Sci., Ohio State U., 1975; MBA, Ashland U. (formerly Ashland Coll.), 1987. Asst. mgr. F.W. Woolworth, Fremont, Ohio, 1978-81, K-Mart Enterprises, Marion, Ohio, 1982; v.p. MBA Systems Automation, Columbus, Ohio, 1982-83; v.p., dir., founder CBM Automated Systems (name now Babbage-Simmel/And Assocs.), Columbus, 1983-88; dir., chmn. bd., pres. Coastalan, Inc. (formerly Coastal Marine Info. Svcs., Inc.), Huron, Ohio, 1988—; cons. Compu Bus Co. (acquired by CBM Systems), Norwalk 1986-87. Chmn. Firelands coun. Boy Scouts Am., 1987-88. Maj. Ohio Mil. Res., 1991—. Mem. Local Area Network Dealers Assn. (pres. Ohio chpt. 1990-93, program chmn. and sec.-treas. 1987-89, contbg. editor The Network Report, chpt. adv. coun. 1991-93), State Def. Force Assn. U.S., Ohio Mil. Res. Assn., Assn. of U.S. Army (v.p. Firelands chpt.), Erie County C. of C.

BORST, LAWRENCE MARION, state legislator; b. Champaign County, Ohio, July 16, 1927; s. Lawrence M. and Mary (Waldeck) B.; m. Eldoris Borst; children: Philip, Elizabeth, David. DVM, Ohio State U. Mem. Ind. State Reps., 1966-68; del. Rep. Nat. Conv., 1968—; mem. state tax and financing policy com., mem. funds mgmt. oversight com.; chmn. fin. taxation com. Ind. State Senate Dist. 36, 1968—, ranking mem. pensions and labor com., ethics com. ins., fin. inst. and transp. coms., interstate coop coms.; chmn. Ind. budget com. Office: 4994 Hayes St Gary IN 46408-4354 Home: 1725 Remington Dr Indianapolis IN 46227-8307*

BORTKO, EDWARD JOSEPH, municipal official, retired utilities executive; b. Kansas City, Kans., May 15, 1929; s. Peter and Josephine (Siwicki) B.; m. Delores Ann Yonevich, Nov. 26, 1955; children: John Alexander, Mary Josephine. BSBA with honors, Rockhurst Coll., 1960; MBA, U. Mo., 1965. Investigator Retail Credit Co., Kansas City, Mo., 1947-51; elec. clk. GM, Kansas City, Kans., 1951-53; sr. methods analyst William Bros. Pipeline Co., Kansas City, Mo., 1955-66; systems mgr. Black, Sivalls & Bryson, Inc., Kansas City, Mo., 1966-67; dir. systems devel. Yellow Freight System, Kansas City, Mo., 1967-70; systems mgr. Certainteed Products Corp., Kansas City, Kans., 1970-75; banking analyst Commerce Bancshares, Kansas City, Mo., 1975; ret. Bd. Pub. Utilities, Kansas City, Kans., 1975-92, 1992; tchr. mgmt. subjects U. Kans. Extension, 1960-67, Am. Inst. Banking, 1960-67, Rockhurst Coll., 1960-67; mem. Data and Analysis Task Force Mid-Am. Regional Coun., Kansas City, Mo., 1980-81; mem. comm. subcom. S.W. Power Pool, Little Rock, 1988-93. Trustee Polish Am. Citizens Club, Kansas City, Kans., 1977-81, fin. sec., 1982-87, v.p., 1988-93; mem. adv. bd YMCA, 1991-94, co-chair Invest-In-Youth Campaign, 1991-93, 96; mem. allocations com. United Way, 1988-92; mem. Assn. Systems Mgmt., 1965-92. Recipient Internat. Merit award Assn. Systems Mgmt., 1976, Achievement award, 1982, Disting. Svc. award, 1988, Diamond Merit award, 1989. Mem. Am. Pub. Power Assn. (vice chmn. info. system sect. 1988-89, chmn. 1989-90), Am. Assn. Ret. Persons (tax aide coord. 1993—, tax instr. 1994—, tax instr. coord. 1995—), Rockhurst Coll. Alumni Assn. (dir. 1961), Johnson County C.C. Brown and Gold Club, Am. Legion 408 Soc., Optimists (gov. Kans. dist. 1988-89, exec. bd. 1987-91, Kans. rep. to internat. found. 1992-93), Serra Club (trustee Kansas City, Kans. chpt. 1993-94, v.p. 1994-95), Pub. Utilities Ret. Club (bd. dirs., v.p. 1995-96, pres. 1996—), Kans. Acad. Decathlon Assn. (bd. trustees 1994—). Democrat. Roman Catholic. Home: 10101 W 89th Ter Shawnee Mission KS 66212-4669

BORTON, ALAN WAYNE, electrical engineer; b. Richland Center, Wis., Oct. 26, 1962; s. Edward Wayne and Barbara Ann (Gillingham) B.; m. Kelly Dawn Felton, May 25, 1985; children: Benjamin E., Zackary A. BSEE, U. Wis., Platteville, 1987. Elec. engr. Kornacki & Assocs., Inc., New Berlin, Wis., 1987-94, v.p. engring., 1994—. Mem. IEEE. Home: 1960 Cliff Alex Ct N Waukesha WI 53186 Office: Kornacki & Assocs Inc 2835 S Moorland Rd New Berlin WI 53151

BORTON, JERRY LEE, head religious order; b. Montpelier, Ohio, Oct. 1, 1959; s. Kenneth Virgil and Eleanor Louise (Newman) B. BS in Christian Edn., Cin. Bible Coll., 1983, postgrad., 1989—. Founder, dir., min. to persons with disabilities Power Ministries, Inc., Clarksville, Ind., 1983—. Contbg. author: Reaching Out to Special People, 1989, Special Ministries/Caring Churches, 1988, Networks, 1993, Key to Christian Education, 1988, Christian Standard, 1985—. Bd. dirs. Spl. Needs Adv. Coun., Clarksville, 1989-90, South Ind. Assn. Handicapped, Clarksville, 1988-90; mem. coun. N.W. Ohio Crisis Pregnancy Ctr., 1985-87; v.p. Right to Life, Williams County, Ind., 1985-87. Named one of Outstanding Young Men Am., 1987. Mem. Christian Coun. on Persons with Disabilities (bd. dirs. 1991—), Greater Louisville Christian Mins.' Assn. Home: 2110 Lombardy # 119 Clarksville IN 47129 Office: Power Ministries 1732 Thames Dr PO Box 2730 Clarksville IN 47131

BORYSEWICZ, MARY LOUISE, editor; b. Chgo.; d. Thomas J. and Mabel E. (Zeien) O'Farrell m. Daniel S. Borysewicz, June 11, 1955; children: Mary Adele, Stephen Francis, Paul Barnabas. BA, Mundelein Coll., 1970; postgrad. in English lit., U. Ill, 1970-71; grad. exec. program, U. Chgo., 1981-82. Editor sci. publs. AMA, Chgo., 1971-73; exec. mng. editor Am. Jour. Ophthalmology, Chgo., 1973-95; asst. sec., treas Ophthalmic Pub. Co., 1985-95; guest lectr. U. Chgo. Med. Sch., 1979, Harvard U. Med. Sch., 1978, Northwestern U. Med. Sch., 1979, Am. Acad. Ophthalmology, 1976, 81. Editor: Ophthalmology Principles and Concepts, 8th edit., 1996; contbr. articles to sci. publs. Active vol. svcs. Art Inst. Chgo. Mem. Am. Soc. Profl. and Exec. Women, Coun. Biol. Editors (bd. dirs. 1988-91, mem. fin. com. 1985-88, mem. teller com. 1992-95), Internat. Fedn. Sci. Editors.

BOS, NORMAN CALVIN, retired orthopaedic surgeon; b. Chgo., Nov. 4, 1924; s. Nonna Calvin and Jean (Adams) B.; m. Gladys Sullivan, Aug. 23, 1946; children: Norman Calvin II, Robert Scott, Steven John. BS, U. Ill., Chgo., 1945, MD, 1947. Diplomate Am. Bd. Orthopaedic Surgery. Intern Cook County Hosp., Chgo., 1947-49; pvt. practice Kewanee, Ill., 1951-53; pvt. practice orthopaedic surgery Hutchinson, Kans., 1960-90; mem. staff Hutchinson Orthopaedic Clinic, 1960-76, Hutchinson Clinic, P.A., 1976-90; ret., 1990. Capt. U.S. Army, 1943-46, 49-51; maj. USAF, 1953-60. Fellow Am. Acad. Orthopaedic Surgeons (bd. councilors 1980-86); mem. AMA Kans. Orthopaedic Soc., Mid-Cen. States Orthopaedic Soc., Kans. Med. Soc., Rotary, Am. Legion. Republican. Home: 2606 N Van Buren St Hutchinson KS 67502-2016

BOSCH, DONNA, home health nurse administrator; b. Emmons County, N.D., Sept. 26, 1945; d. Peter and Rose (Ternes) Silbernagel; m. Frank Bosch, June 5, 1965; children: Lynette, Darrin, Wade. BSN, Mary Coll., 1967; MSN, U. Mary, Bismarck, N.D., 1988. RN, N.D.; cert. in community health, 1986, 91. Instr. Mary Coll., Bismarck; EPS coord. Bismarck Burleigh Nursing Svc., home health nurse; home care coord., exec. dir. Home Med. Resources, Bismarck; task force Medicare. N.D. Nurses Assn. grantee. Mem. ANA, N.D. Pub. Health Assn., N.D. Home Health Assn. (pres.), Cath. Daus. Am., Sigma Theta Tau. Home: 4885 Wildrose Cres Bismarck ND 58501-8975

BOSCH, JOHN ALBERT, manufacturing executive, consultant; b. Buffalo, Mar. 14, 1929; s. Carl Edwin and Elizabeth (Babson) B.; m. Marna Eline Kunstmann, July 10, 1954; children: Corinne Ida, Carl Martin, Kenneth Paul, Christopher John. BS in Agrl. Engring., Pa. State U., 1951. Dir. engring., gen. mgr. Gen. Electric, Lynn, Mass. and Binghamton, N.Y., 1953-82; pres. Sheffield Measurement, Dayton, Ohio, 1982-93; rsch. assoc. Nat. Inst. Standards and Tech., 1993-95; chmn., CEO Commander Aero Inc., Xenia, Ohio, 1985—; bd. dirs. Leland Electrosystems, Inc., Vandalia, Ohio, Shaw Aero Devices, Inc., Ft. Myers, Fla. Editor: Coordinate Measuring Machines and Systems, 1995. Trustee Nat. Aviation Hall of Fame, 1985—; group chmn. United Way, Dayton, 1986; vice chmn. Joint Labor Mgmt. Coun., 1988; bd. dirs. Air Force Mus. Found., 1996—. 1st lt. USAF, 1951-53. Fellow Am. Soc. Aerospace Engring. (assoc.); mem. Soc. Automotive Engrs. (sr.), Soc. Mfg. Engrs. (sr.), Rotary.

BOSCO, JAY WILLIAM, optometrist; b. Bay City, Mich., May 6, 1951; s. Frank Carl and Jeanette (Frontiera) B.; m. Mary Lou Roth, Jan. 22, 1972; children: Angela, Jason, Andrea. BS, Saginaw Valley State Coll., 1977; OD, Ill. Coll. Optometry, 1982. Pvt. practice optometry Bay City, Mich., 1982-83; dir. vision care services Blue Care Network of East Mich., Saginaw, 1983—. Served with USAF, 1969-73. Mem. Am. Optometric Assn., Mich. Optometric Assn., Beta Sigma Kappa. Roman Catholic. Lodge: Lions (chmn. Site-Mobile, Bay City, 1984—). Home: 1382 N Wagner Rd Essexville MI 48732-9532 Office: Blue Care Network East Mich 4200 Fashion Square Blvd Saginaw MI 48603-1247

BOSEKER, BARBARA JEAN, education educator; b. Milw., Dec. 2, 1944; d. Edward Herbert and Alice Margaret (Maas) B.; student U. Nigeria, Nsukka, 1966; BS (hon.) in Secondary Edn. (Elks Nat. and State Youth scholar), U. Wis., Milw., 1968; MA in Anthropology (Ford Found. fellow 1968-69, NDEA fellow 1970-71), U. Wis., Madison, 1971, PhD in Edn. (NDEA fellow), 1978; m. Dale Leslie Sutcliffe, Aug. 8, 1975. Chemistry lab. technician Allen-Bradley Corp., Milw., 1963; coordinator Neighborhood Youth Corps, Madison, 1970; program devel. specialist Tchr. Corps, Madison, 1976-77; asst. prof. edn. Occidental Coll., 1978-80, Moorhead State U., 1980-86, assoc. prof., 1986-90, prof., 1990-95, Winona State U., 1995—;

cons. Inst. Latin Am. Studies, U. Tex., Austin, 1980. Grant writer Fargo-Moorhead (N.D.) Indian Center, 1980; evaluator Indian edn. grant Fargo Pub. Schs., 1985-90. Cert. intermediate and secondary English tchr., Wis. Mem. NEA, Minn. Edn. Assn., Nat. Women's Studies Assn., Mortar Bd., Phi Kappa Phi, Pi Lambda Theta, Kappa Delta Pi, Sigma Tau Delta, Sigma Epsilon Sigma. Democrat. Christian Scientist. Contbr. articles to profl. jours. Home: 1535 W 5th St Apt 303 Winona MN 55987 Office: Winona State U Winona MN 55987

BOSETTI, EUGENE R., supervising engineer; b. Detroit, Mar. 5, 1934. BS, Lawrence Tech. Inst., Detroit, 1955. Supr. elec. equipment Detroit Edison, 1973-77, supervising engr., 1977—. Vol. local election; chmn., adminstr. local ch. With U.S. Army, 1957. Mem. IEEE. Republican. Roman Catholic.

BOSKO, LEE DOUGLAS, investment representative; b. Mansfield, Ohio, Dec. 27, 1954; m. Jane Wilson; children: Shelby Leigh, Whitney Anne, Derek Wilson. BA, Ohio U., 1978. Lic. pilot. Mktg. mgr. Seagram Distiller, Casper, Wyo., 1985-87; brokerage mgr. Golden Rule Ins., Casper, 1987-89; investment rep. Edward Jones, Holland, Mich., 1989—. Vol. host HCTV-Pub. Access TV, 1991. Bd. dirs. Holland Chorale, 1990—, Am. Heart Assn., 1994—; mem. United Way Campaign, 1995; mem. most wanted com. Am. Cancer Soc., 1994-95; mem. leadership team Am., Family Hope, 1994; mem. search com. Macatawa Area/Future Coordinating Coun., 1995. Mem. Holland C. of C. (bd. dirs. 1990—). Republican. Office: Edward Jones 246 River Ave Holland MI 49422

BOSLEY, WARREN GUY, pediatrician; b. Palisade, Nebr., Jan. 1, 1922; s. Charles M. and Verna M. (Gruver) B.; m. Alleen Finney, May 20, 1944; children: Michael, Barbara, Matthew, Timothy, David, John. AB, U. Nebr., 1942, MD, 1944. Diplomate Am. Bd. Pediatrics. Intern Johns Hopkins Hosp., Balt., 1944-45; resident in pediatrics Babies Hosp., N.Y.C., 1948-50; pvt. practice Grand Island, Nebr., 1950-91; med. dir. substance abuse unit Hastings (Nebr.) Regional Ctr., 1991—; mem. Am. Bd. Pediatrics, Chapel Hill, N.C., 1981-92, Medicaid Adv. Commn. Nebr., Lincoln, 1988-91, Nebr. State Bd. Health, Lincoln, 1968-71, 77-80. Author: (chpt.) Medical Liability in Pediatrics, 1988, 90. Pres. Bd. Edn., Grand Island, 1973-74, mem., 1959-93; mem. Libr. Bd., Grand Island, 1966-80, Friends of Librs. U. Nebr., Lincoln, 1989—, Friends of Librs. U. Nebr. Coll. Medicine, Omaha, 1978—. Mem. AMA, Am. Acad. Pediatrics (chmn. coun. on pediatric practice 1981-84, chpt. chmn.'s forum 1981-83), Nebr. Med. Assn. (pres. 1975-76), Phi Beta Kappa, Sigma Xi, Alpha Omega Alpha. Home: 1515 W First St Grand Island NE 68801

BOSMA, BRIAN CHARLES, state legislator; b. Indpls., Oct. 31, 1957; s. Charles Edward and Margaret Hagge Bosma; m. Cheryl Lyn Hollingsworth, 1982. BSE, Purdue U., 1981; JD, Ind. U., 1984. Precinct committeeman Marian County Rep. Ctrl. Com., Ind., 1983-86, ward vice chmn., 1987—; legis. and congrl. liaison Ind. State Dept. Edn., 1985-86; Ind. state rep. Dist. 50, 1986-91, Dist. 88, 1991—; ranking mem. com., mem. ways and means com. Ind. Ho. Reps., mem. elections and apportionment, environ. affairs and natural resources coms.; environ. engr. Ind. State Bd. Health, 1981-83; assoc. editor Ind. U. Law Rev., 1983-84, 1983-84; atty. Bingham, Summers, Welch & Spilman, Indpls., 1984-85, Kroger, Gardis & Regas, 1986—. Recipient Commencement Spkr. award Ind. U. Law Sch., 1984, Lacy Exec. Leadership award Indpls. C. of C., 1986; named Outstanding Freshman Legislator Ind. Broadcasters Assn. Mem. ABA, Ind. Bar Assn., Indpls. Bar Assn. (Pres. Spl. award 1984), Ind. Environ. Policy Commn., Assn. Retarded Citizens Trust (adv. bd.), Nat. Rep. Lawyers Assn., Lawrence C. of C., Beta Sigma Psi, Phi Delta Phi. Republican. Home: 8971 Bay Breeze Ln Indianapolis IN 46236-8568*

BOSS, EDWARD HERMAN, JR., banker, economist, fiscal advisor; b. Oak Park, Ill., Mar. 12, 1938; s. Edward H. and Lorraine (Hoffman) B. BA, Albion Coll., 1960; MBA, Columbia U., 1962. V.p., sr. fin. economist Continental Bank, Chgo., 1962-90; chief econ. Econ. and Fiscal Commn. Ill. State Legislature, Springfield, 1991—; cons. economist Bankers Monthly Mag., N.Y.C., 1980—; advisor Sch. Profl. Mgmt., Albion (Mich.) Coll., 1988—. Fellow Nat. Assn. Bus. Economists (pres. Chgo. chpt. 1969, bd. dirs. 1975-78). Home: 517 E Monroe St Apt H Springfield IL 62701-1523 Office: Ill State Legislature 703 Stratton Bldg Springfield IL 62706-9999

BOSS, JUDITH CAROL, writer, consultant; b. Mpls., Nov. 26, 1935; d. David Robert and Florence Eleanor (Weisner) Alford; m. James McCarthy, Apr. 21, 1956 (dec. Aug. 19, 1969); children: Kevin, Kathleen, Michael, Mary, James; m. W. Andrew Boss, July 10, 1971; (div. Dec., 1982). BS, U. Minn., Mpls., 1960. Dir. Montgomery (Minn.) State Bank, 1978-81; v.p. Continuum Minn., Inc., Mpls, 1982, pres., 1983; advisor Kids for Saving Earth, Mpls, 1991-92; speaker, local, nat. and internat. levels. at ednl. instns., librs., on TV and radio. Author: (books) In Silence They Return, 1974, A Garden of Joy, 1976, A Cosmic Connection I, II, III, IV, 1995, Dying to Live, 1995; (screen play) Covenant, 1995; also poetry, and contbr. articles to popular mags.

BOST, MIKE, state legislator. Ill. state rep., 1995—. Office: 300 E Main Carbondale IL 62901

BOSTIAN, HARRY EDWARD, chemical engineer; b. Lewisburg, Pa., Jan. 16, 1933; s. Harry Edward Sr. and Florence Anne (Musser) B.; m. Marion E. Maurer, July 30, 1955. BS, Bucknell U., 1954; M in Chem. Enging., Rensselaer Poly. Inst., 1956; PhD, Iowa State U., 1959. Registered profl. engr., N.J. Asst. prof. U. N.H., Durham, 1959-61; engr. Exxon Research, Baton Rouge and Florham Park, N.J., 1961-65; assoc. prof. U. Miss., Oxford, 1965-70; sr. chem. engr., rsch. program mgr. U.S. EPA, Cin., 1970-94; chem. and environ. enging. cons., 1994—; cons., reviewer environ. topics, 1975—; mem. task forces, mem. work groups on environ. control and regulation U.S. EPA and Water Environ. Fedn., 1987-94. Mem. editl. bd. Process Safety and Environ. Protection, Transactions of Inst. Chem. Engrs., Eng., Part B, 1990-94; contbr. articles to profl. jours., meetings and symposia. NSF grantee, 1969-70, U.S. Dept. Agr. grantee, 1969-70. Mem. AAAS, Am. Inst. Chem. Engrs., Sigma Xi, Tau Beta Pi, Alpha Chi Sigma. Home and Office: 6001 Bagdad Dr Cincinnati OH 45230-1302

BOSTIC, JAMES H., design engineer; b. Mt. Vernon, Ohio, Feb. 11, 1951. A in Drafting Tech., Franklin U., 1972, BSME, 1980. Project engr. Gorman-Rupp Industries, Bellville, Ohio, 1982-88; design engr.SOHA divsn. Dana Corp., Fredericktown, Ohio, 1990—. Coach Fredericktown (Ohio) Area Soccer League, 1984-91. Home: P O Box 320 Fredericktown OH 43019

BOSTICK, WILLIAM ALLISON, museum administrator; b. Marengo, Ill., Feb. 21, 1913; s. William Frederick and Alice Mabellian (Johnson) B.; m. Mary Jane Moore Barbey, June 14, 1942; children: Beatrice Annette Barbey, Christopher Barbey. BS in Graphic Comm. Mgmt., Carnegie Inst. Tech., 1934; MA in Graphic Arts History, Wayne State U., 1954. Field rep. NRA Graphic Arts Code Authority, Detroit, 1934-35; typographer Detroit Typesetting Co., 1935-36; advt. designer Evans, Winter, Hebb, Inc., Detroit, 1936-38; prop. Comml. Art Studio, Detroit, 1939-40; city supr. printing City of Detroit, 1940-41, 46; adminstr., sec. Detroit Inst. Arts, 1946-76; prop. La Stampa Calligrafica, Bingham Farms, Mich., 1970—; bd. trustees mem. Detroit Inst. Arts Founders Soc., 1988—, exec. sec., 1946-58, chmn. antiquaries, 1988—. Author: A Guide to the Guarding of Cultural Property, 1977; author, illustrator: England Under GI's Reign, 1946, Calligraphy for Kids, 1991, Back to the Second Basic R—'Ritin', 1996; co-author: The Amphibious Sketch, 1944; designer, illustrator: The Mysteries of Blair House, 1948. Lt. USN, 1942-45; designed landing chart/maps for invasions of Sicily and Normandy. Mem. Scarab Club Detroit (bd. dirs., pres. 1962-63, Gold medal 1963, 68, 80), Internat. Torch Club Detroit and Windsor (pres. 1956-57), L'Alliance Francaise de Detroit (pres. 1972-73, bd. dirs.), Prismatic Club Detroit, Antiquaries of Detroit Inst. Arts (chmn. 1988-95), Skyline Club, Mich. Water Color Soc. (pres. 1946-47), Mich. Assn. Calligraphers, Delta Tau Delta. Republican. Home: 23350 Old Orchard Trl Bingham Farms MI 48025

BOSTON, GARRY, state legislator; b. Oct. 1, 1936; m. Jeanette Fox. Student, El Dorado Jr. Coll., Emporia State Coll. Mem. Kans. Ho. of Reps., Topeka, 1991—; ins. agent.; owner Gen. Ins. Agy. Mem. Profl. Ins. Agents Assn., Harvey County Builders Assn., Newton C. of C. Republican. Home: 14 Circle Dr Newton KS 67114-1329*

BOSTWICK, CYNTHIA, lawyer; b. South Haven, Mich., Sept. 7, 1956; d. Frank Allen Bostwick and Joan Beverly (Gemeinhardt) Walker. AB in English and Econs., Smith Coll., 1978; JD, Wayne State U., 1987. Bar: Mich. 1987, U.S. Dist. Ct. (ea. dist.) Mich. 1987. Paralegal Mich. Legal Svcs., Detroit, 1983-87; rsch. asst. sch. of law Wayne State U., Detroit, 1985-87; staff atty. Legal Assistance St. Clair County, Port Huron, Mich., 1986-92; assoc. Zick and Swegles, P.C., Marysville, Mich., 1989-92; pvt. practice Port Huron, 1992—; instr. criminal justice St. Clair County C.C., Port Huron, 1992—; mem. Criminal Justice Adv. Bd., Port Huron, 1990—; bd. dirs. Lakeshore Legal Svcs., Mt. Clemens, Mich. Bd. dirs. Ctr. for Human Resources, Port Huron, 1994—, v.p., 1995—; bd. dirs. Pathway Shelter Home, Port Huron, 1992—; v.p. Attys. for Animals, Marshall, Mich., 1992—; local counsel Fund for Animals, N.Y.C., 1993—; elder St. Martin Luth. Ch., Port Huron, 1994—; precinct del. Dem. Ctrl. Com., Port Huron, 1991—. Mem. Mich. State Bar Assn., St. Clair County Bar Assn. (Pro Bono awrd 1991), Blue Water Women Lawyers Assn. (sec. 1991-93), Criminal Def. Attys. Mich. Office: Ste #571 511 Fort St Port Huron MI 48060

BOSWAY, MICHAEL E., securities broker; b. Columbus, Ga., Sept. 15, 1958. BA, U. Dayton, 1980; MBA, Ohio State U., 1981. Broker City Securities, Indpls., 1982—. Office: City Securities Corp 8900 Keystone Crossing Indianapolis IN 46240-2146

BOSWELL, LARRY RAY, electronics company executive; b. Greencastle, Ind., Dec. 14, 1940; s. John Ernest and Thelma Ruth (Williams) B.; m. Sandra Jean Rains, Jan. 19, 1963; children: Tina Marie, Cynthia Kay, Brian Tad. BA, Ind. U., 1988; MBA, Marion Coll., 1990. Ordained to ministry Soc. of Friends, 1967. With R.R. Donnelly & Sons, Crawfordsville, Ind., 1962-65; analyst, researcher Delco Electronics, Kokomo, Ind., 1965—; minister Soc. of Friends Ch., West Middleton, Ind., 1967—. Contbr. articles to profl. jours. Bd. dirs. Love Haven Home, Jamestown, Tenn., 1972—, Pathway div. Ind. U., Kokomo, 1990—; mem. Pres.'s League of Underwriters Union Sem., Westfield, Ind., 1985—. Cooper fellow Earlham Sch. of Religion, 1994. Mem. Am. Philatelic Soc., Ind. Council Chs., Howard County Council Chs., No. Postal History Soc. (pres. 1976-84), Western Ind. Folklore Soc. (pres. 1980-84), Alpha Chi. Club: Quaker Men (pres. 1984—). Home: 100 W 7971 S Fairmount IN 46928-1928 Office: Little Ridge Friends Church 1731 West 1050 Fairmount IN 46928

BOSWELL, LEONARD L., state senator; b. Harrison County, Mo., Jan. 10, 1934; s. Melvin and Margaret B.; m. Dody Boswell; 3 children. BA in Bus. Adminstrn., Graceland Coll. Commd. 2d lt. U.S. Army; advanced through grades to lt. col. U.S. Army, Vietnam, Germany, Portugal; state senator Iowa, 1984—; pres. Iowa Senate, 1993—; grain, livestock farmer Decatur County, 1976—. Past pres., bd. dirs. local Coop. Elevator, Lamoni. Decorated two Disting. Flying Crosses, Soldiers medal, two Bronze Stars. Mem. VFW, Am. Legion, Cattleman's Assn., Lamoni Lions Club. Office: RR 1 Box 130 Davis City IA 50065-9756 also: State Senate State Capitol Des Moines IA 50319

BOSWELL, MARK VANCE, physician; b. Portland, Oreg., Mar. 30, 1951; s. Vance Robert and Darlene Ann (Desjardins) B.; m. Barbara Piazza, Jan. 31, 1990; children: Jonathan, Erin. BS, Portland State U., 1975; PhD, Case Western Res. U., 1982, MD, 1984. Diplomate Am. Bd. Anesthesiology. Dir. pain mgmt. svcs. dept. anesthesiology U. Hosp., Cleve., 1990-96; assoc. prof. anesthesiology, 1996—; asst. prof. anesthesiology U. Ariz., 1988-90, Case Western Res. U., 1990—. Author: Principles of Anesthesiology, 1995. Mem. AMA, AAAS, Am. Soc. Anesthesiologists, Internat. Assn. for Study of Pain. Office: U Hosps Dept Anesthesiology 11100 Euclid Ave Cleveland OH 44106

BOSWELL, NATHALIE SPENCE, speech pathologist; b. Cleve., May 9, 1924; d. Harrison Morton and Nathalie Muriel (Clem) Spence; student Skidmore Coll, 1941-42; MusB in Edn., Northwestern U., 1945; MA, Western Res. U., 1961; m. June 15, 1946; children: Louis Keith, Donna Spence, Deborah Anne. Speech therapist Highland View Hosp., Cleve., 1961-64; speech pathologist Cleve. VA Hosp., 1964-87 ; chmn. Equal Employment Opportunity Counselors, 1969-74, Fed. Women Speakers Bur., 1968-87, Fed. Career Info. Program, 1970-72, Fed. Coll. Rels. Coun., 1970-74, Fed. Exec. Bd., 1972-73; adj. instr. Case Western Res. U., 1982-87; mem. adv. coun. sch. electromedicine scis., City U. Los Angeles, 1985; mem. adv. bd. Nat. Inst. Electromedicine Info., 1985; trustee, cons. Donna Spence Boswell Massther, 1992—. Mem. Cleve. Orch. Chorus, 1969-82; vol. Seamen's Svc., 1976—; patron Police Athletic League; mem. Citizen Adv. Com on Solid Waste, Cleveland Heights Ohio, 1989-94. Endowed Tuba Chair, Cleve. Orch., 1983. Recipient Performance award Equal Employment Opportunities, 1973; Quality Increase award, 1980; others; lic. speech pathologist, Ohio. Mem. Am. Speech and Hearing Assn. (cert. clin. competence), Ohio Speech and Hearing Assn., Aphasiology Assn. Ohio, Chi Omega Alumni Assn., Musical Arts Assn., Western Res. Hist. Soc., Cleve. Mus. Natural History (vol. 1988—), Cleve. Mus. Art, Smithsonian Assns., Nat. Wildlife Fedn., Audubon Soc., Nat. Trust Hist. Preservation, Am. Heritage Soc. Mem. Ch. Reorganized Latter-Day Saints. Author: Guidelines for EEO Counselors in their Training Program, 1973; prin. author: Laryngectomy-Orientation for Patients and Families, 1981; contbr., asst. editor: Am. Jour. Electromedicine, 1984. Home: 2946 Berkshire Rd Cleveland OH 44118-2444

BOSWORTH, JEFFREY WILLSON, insurance company manager, computer systems specialist; b. Sayre, Pa., Dec. 5, 1948; s. Joseph Reinhart and Jean Margaret (Willson) B.; m. Marianne Bosworth. Student, Pa. State U., 1966-68; AA in Communications, Harrisburg Area Community Coll., 1973; BS in Pub. Communications, Syracuse U., 1975. Comml. underwriter Nationwide Ins. Co., Syracuse, N.Y., 1975-78; mktg. rep. Ins. Co. N.Am., Lemoyne, Pa., 1978-80; systems analyst Nationwide Ins. Co., Columbus, Ohio, 1980-83; office mgr., fin. analyst Nationwide Ins. Co., Columbus, 1983-84, spl. projects analyst, 1984-85, systems programming mgr., 1985—; cons. computer programming Altair Four Software, Columbus, 1983—. Author: (software product) PCSecure, 1986, FXFER, 1988, AREACALC, 1989, Ind. Tgn. Plan DB (ITP) Navy, 1991, NAVLOG, 1995. Mem. Civic Action Program, Columbus, 1980—. With USN, 1968-72 (Vietnam); with Res., 1980—. Mem. Am. Mgmt. Assn. Republican. Office: Nationwide Ins Co 1 Nationwide Plz Columbus OH 43215-2220

BOTTENS, RONALD GENE, minister; b. Jacksonville, Ill., Jan. 30, 1939; s. Wilbur K. and Fern E. Bottens; children: Marissa R., Bethany D. Henry, Tirzeh N. BA, Lincoln (Ill.) Christian Coll., 1962. Min. Ctrl. Christian Ch., Browning, Ill., 1960-62, Literberry (Ill.) Chrisitan Ch., 1962-66, Brighton (Ill.) Christian Ch., 1966-69, Milton (Ill.) Christian Ch., 1969-73, Community Chrisitan Ch., Alton, Ill., 1973-83; instr. sales rep. Mutual of N.Y., 1983-91; ins. sales broker, 1991—; min. West Alton (Mo.) Community Ch., 1989—; camp dean Miss. Valley Christian Svc. Camp, 1970-73, Mac-Gomery Christian Svc. Camp, 1967-68, 74-82. Camp staff Lake Sprinfield Christian Assembly, LaMoine Christian Svc. Camp, 1960—; camp bd. dirs. Mac-Gomery Christian Svc. Camp, 1973-83; steering com. new ch. Jacksonville, Ill., 1965-66; active various ch. activities; coord. West Alton Restorationists, 1994-95. Home: 815 Douglas St Alton IL 62002 Office: PO Box 248 119 St Charles St West Alton MO 63386

BOTTI, ALDO E., lawyer; b. Bklyn., Dec. 27, 1936; s. Ettore and Filomena (DeLucio) B.; m. Sheila Higgins, Aug. 4, 1967; children: Michael, Joseph, Mark, Sarah, Elizabeth, John. BA, Rockhurst Coll., 1962; JD, St. Louis U., 1965. Bar: Ill. 1966, U.S. Dist. Ct. (no. and so. dists.) Ill. 1967, U.S. Supreme Ct. 1973, U.S. Ct. Appeals (7th cir.) 1979. Assoc. Frank Glazer & William O'Brien, Chgo., 1966-69; asst. state's atty. DuPage County, Wheaton, Ill., 1969-71, pub. defender, 1971-72; sr. ptnr. Botti, Marinaccio & DeLongis, Ltd., Oak Brook, Ill., 1972—; atty. Village of Villa Park, 1985-88; gen. counsel Ill. State Crime Commn. Mem. Opera Theatre Ill., 1981-84; bd. dirs. Cmty. House, Hinsdale, Ill., 1988-91, mid-Am. chpt. ARC, 1991-94; chmn. bd. dirs. Hinsdale Cmty. Svcs., 1972-73; elected chmn. DuPage County, 1990-94; pres. Metro. Counties Coun., 1991-93. Served in U.S. Army, 1955-58. Mem. ABA, Ill. Bar Assn., Chgo. Bar Assn., DuPage County Bar Assn. (chmn. speakers bur. 1975-78, chmn. pub. relations 1973-75, gen. counsel 1988-89), Am. Judicature Soc., Assn. Trial Lawyers Am. Republican. Roman Catholic. Club: Butterfield Country (Oak Brook). Office: Botti Marinaccio & DeLongis 720 Enterprise Dr Oak Brook Mall IL 60521

BOTTOMS, ROBERT GARVIN, academic administrator; b. Birmingham, Ala., June 28, 1944; s. Dalton Garvin and Mary Inez (Cruce) B.; m. Gwendolynn Jean Vickers, June 14, 1968; children: David Timothy, Leslie Clair. BA, Birmingham So. U., 1966; BD, Emory U., 1969; D Ministry, Vanderbilt U., 1972. Chaplain Birmingham (Ala.) So. Coll., 1973-74, asst. to pres., 1974-75; asst. dean, asst. prof. church and ministry Vanderbilt U., Nashville, 1975-78; v.p. for univ. rels. DePauw U., Greencastle, Ind., 1978-79, exec. v.p. external rels., 1979-83, exec. v.p. of the univ., 1983-86, acting pres., 1985, pres., 1986—; cons. on theol. edn. The Lilly Endowment, Indpls., 1979-82; cons. Luth. So. Sem., Columbia, S.C., 1979-80, Fund for Theol. Edn., N.Y.C., 1981-82, Arthur Vining Davis Found., Jacksonville, Fla., 1978-79; Am. Ctr. for Internat. Leadership organizer Edn. Policy Commn. U.S.-USSR Emerging Leaders Summit, Phila., 1988; chmn. audit com. Centel Cable TV Co., Oak Brook, Ill, 1987-89, also bd. dirs. Author: Lessons in Financial Management, 1981-82. Chmn. com. on ch. and coll. Episcopal Diocese Ind., 1979-84; mem. bd. visitors Vanderbilt U., 1980—; bd. dirs. Joyce Found., 1994—. Mem. NCAA (coun. 1989-95, subcom. eligibility appeals), Nat. Coun. Chs. (governing bd. 1985-91), Nat. Assn. Ind. Colls. and Univs. (task force on increasing the participation of minorities in ind. higher edn. 1989—), Nat. Assn. Schs. and Colls. United Meth. Ch. (bd. dirs. 1987-90), Am. Coun. Edn. (commn. on women in higher edn. 1990—), Ind. Colls. of Ind. (bd. dirs. 1987—, exec. com. 1991—), Ind. Colls. of Ind. Found. (bd. dirs. 1987—, nominating com. 1990—), Great Lakes Colls. Assn. (bd. dirs. 1987—, chair 1994—), Columbia Club (Indpls.), Univ. Club of N.Y.C., Cosmos Club (Washington), Chgo. Club. Home: 125 Wood St Greencastle IN 46135-1829 Office: DePauw Univ Office of Pres Greencastle IN 46135

BOTTORFF, JAMES, state legislator; b. Jeffersonville, Ind., July 28, 1944; m. Charlene Bottorff; children: Christopher, Robert. Student, Ind. U. Treas. Clark County, 1979-86, assessor, 1987-90; mem. Ind. State Rep. Dist. 71, 1990—; chmn. govt. affairs com., mem. com. and econ. devel. Ind. Ho. of Reps., county and twp. fin. inst. and natural resource coms.; chmn. Clark County Dem. Ctrl. Com.; real estate appraiser. chmn. Clark County Dem. Men's Club. Mem. Elks, Moose, Eagles, Farm Bur. Home: 2413 E Highway 62 Jeffersonville IN 47130-6003*

BOTTS, ELIZABETH DORIS, newspaper editor; b. Chgo., Feb. 2, 1956; d. Lambert Spottswood and Lee (Carman) Botts. Student, U. Chgo., 1972-76; MA, Am. U., 1985; postgrad, Poynter Inst., 1985. Copy clk. Chgo. Tribune, 1974-75; editorial asst. Bull. Atomic Scientists, Chgo., 1977-78; news editor Pointer-Ecomonist Newspapers, Lansing, Ill., 1978-79; assoc. editor Hyde Park Herald, Chgo., 1979-84; assoc. ctrl. Ill. editor Decatur (Ill.) Herald and Rev., 1986-87; wire editor Daily Southtown Economist, Chgo., 1987; assoc. met. editor Chgo. Tribune, 1987—. Mem. Soc. Profl. Journalists, Chgo. Headline Club, Kappa Tau Alpha. Office: Chicago Tribune 435 N Michigan Ave Chicago IL 60611-4001

BOUCHARD, JAMES PAUL, steel manufacturing sales executive; b. Kansas City, Kans., May 2, 1961; s. Robert Clayton and Helen (Clancy) B.; m. Carolyn Keegan, July 19, 1986. BBA, Loyola U., Chgo., 1984. Asst. to dist. mgr. Inland Steel Co., Chgo., 1983-85; sales rep. Denver br. Westinghouse Electric, 1985-87, U.S. Steel (divsn. USX Corp.), Milw., 1987-91; Midwest area sr. rep. U.S. Steel (divsn. USX Corp.), Oak Brook, Ill., 1987-94, resident mgr., 1994—; bd. dirs. Edgecom LLC, Clarendon Hills, Ill., U.S. Recovery, Hinsdale, Ill. Co-inventor patented light weight concrete, 1983. Mem. Evans Scholars Found., Japan Am. Soc. Chgo. Mem. Japan Am. Soc. Chgo., Loyola U. Alumni Assn., U. San Diego Alumni Assn. (scholar), Chgo. Dist. Golf Assn., Edgewood Valley Country Club. Republican. Roman Catholic. Office: 2021 Spring Rd Ste 700 Oak Brook IL 60521-1862

BOUCHARD, MICHAEL J., state legislator; b. Flint, Mich., Apr. 12, 1956; s, Donald A. and Doris (Sams) B.; m. Pamela Johnson, 1988; 1 child, Makayla Kathryn. BA, Mich. State U., 1979; grad., Mich. Law Enforcement Ctr. Police officer Bloomfield Twp. (Mich.), 1977-78; pub. safety officer Beverly Hills (Mich.), 1978-88; pres. TACT, Inc., 1986-91; pres, founder Beverly Hills Gourmet Yogurt & Ice Cream, 1989-91; state rep. Mich. Ho. Reps.; state senator Mich. State Senate, Dist. 13; chair fin. svc., vice chair families, mental & health & human svcs., mem. tech. & energy, asst. majority leader, Mich. State Senate. del. Mich. State Rep. Conv., 1984-91; coun. mem. Village of Beverly Hills, 1986-90, pres., 1989-90; treas. 18th Dist. Rep. Com., 1989-91; chmn. Oakland County Rep. Campaign Com., 1990; mem. Oakland County Young Reps.; bd. dirs. Birmingham/Bloomfield Cultural Com. Recipient Leadership award Am. Cancer Humanitarian Com., Outstanding Svc. award March of Dimes, Legis. of Yr. award Police Officers Assn. Mich., Humanitarian award Arab-Am. & Chaldcan Coun., Birmingham Bro. Rice Disting. Alumnus award. Mem. Birmingham/Bloomfield C. of C. (bd. dirs.). Home: 344 Fairfax St Birmingham MI 48009-1275*

BOUCHARD, PHILIPPE OVIDE, career officer; b. Salem, Mass., Mar. 25, 1932; s. Raymond Emile and Alma Aurore (Beaulieu) B.; m. Carol Ann Mitchell, June 21, 1958; children: Michael, Suzanne, David, Donald. BS in Enging., U.S. Mil. Acad., 1955; MS in Aero. Enging., U. Okla., 1963. Cert. flight instr. Commd. pilot USAF, 1955; advanced through grades to brig. gen., 1986; dir. Ctr. for Artificial Intelligence Applications, Dayton, Ohio, 1987-92; v.p. enging. Universal Tech. Corp., Beavercreek, Ohio, 1992-94, pres., CEO, 1995—; asst. v.p. rsch. Wright State U., Dayton, 1986-88. Pres. Miami Valley Rsch. Inst., Dayton, 1988-92; v.p. fin. Air Force Inst. Tech. Found., 1986-93; bd. dirs. Enging. Sci. Found., Dayton; chmn. fund raising Nightingale House Assn., 1990-93. Pres. Miami Valley Rsch. Inst., Dayton, 1988—; v.p. fin. Air Force Inst. Tech. Found., 1989—; bd. dirs. Enging. Sci. Found., Dayton; chmn. fund raising Nightingale House Assn., 1990—. Decorated D.S.M., D.F.C., Legion of Merit, Air medal. Mem. AIAA, Am. Def. Preparedness Assn. (bd. dirs.), Engrs. Club Dayton (bd. govs. 1988-92, pres. 1989-90). Republican. Roman Catholic. Home: 270 Scarlett Dr Beavercreek OH 45434-6241

BOUCHER, BILL, state legislator. Mo. State rep. dist. 48. Home: 11320 Sunnyslope Dr Kansas City MO 64134-3148*

BOUCHER, MERLE, state legislator; m. Susan Boucher; 4 children. AA, N.D. State U.; BS, Mayville (N.D.) State U. Mem. N.D. Ho. of Reps. from 9th dist., 1991—; farmer; mem. Human Svcs. and Agr. Coms. N.D. Ho. of Reps. Mem. Rolette Cmty. Improvement Inc., Rolette Jobs Auth. Mem. N.D. Edn. Assns. Democrat. Office: ND Ho of Reps State Capitol Bismarck ND 58505*

BOUDREAU, LYNDA, state legislator; b. Mar. 9, 1952; m. Jim Boudreau; 3 children. Family health aide Rice County Pub. Health; rep. Dist. 25B Minn. Ho. of Reps., 1994—.

BOUDREAU, ROBERT JAMES, nuclear medicine physician, researcher; b. Lethbridge, Alta., Can., Dec. 27, 1950; came to U.S., 1983; s. George Joseph Boudreau and Eleanor Joyce (Dalzell) Hamilton; m. Francine Suzanne Archambault, Jan. 16, 1982. BSc with highest honors, U. Sask., Saskatoon, Can., 1972; PhD, U. B.C., Vancouver, Can., 1975; MD, U. Calgary (Alta.), 1978. Diplomate Am. Bd. Nuclear Medicine. Resident in diagnostic radiology and nuclear medicine McGill U., Montreal, Que., Can., 1978-82; asst. prof. U. Minn., Mpls., 1983-87, assoc. prof., 1987-93, prof., 1993—, dir. grad. studies dept. radiology, 1987-91, dir. nuclear medicine divsn., 1987—. Author book chpts.; contbr. articles to profl. jours. Recipient Gold Key award Soc. Chem. Industry, 1972, Soc. Clin. Investigation Young Investigator award, 1978; Can. Heart Found. Med. Scientist fellow, 1976-78. Fellow Royal Coll. Physicians; mem. Am. Heart Assn., Am. Coll. Nuclear Physicians, Assn. Univ. Radiologists, Soc. Chiefs of Acad. Nuclear Medicine Sects. (treas. 1989-93), Soc. Nuclear Medicine (edn. and tng. com. 1983-91, trustee 1994-95, bd. govs. ctrl. chpt. 1989—, treas. 1992-94, pres. 1994-95),

Radiol. Soc. N.Am., Am. Coll. Radiology. Office: U Minn PO Box 292 UMHC 420 Delaware St SE Minneapolis MN 55455

BOUGALIS, KATHERINE G., medical surgical nurse, educator; b. Naupaktos, Greece, May 23, 1940; d. Dimitrios and Eleftheria (Mamalougas) Papadimitriou; m. George Bougalis, Feb. 19, 1961; children: Nickolas, Joanne, James, John. AD, Arrowhead Community Coll., Hibbing, Minn., 1971; BS in Community Svc., Bemidji (Minn.) State U., 1985; BA in Nursing, Coll. St. Scholastica, Duluth, Minn., 1986, MA in Nursing, 1987. Cert. in med.-surg. nursing, community health. Asst. head. nurse Mesabi Regional Med. Ctr., Hibbing, adminstr., supr., patient care facilitator; educator Hibbing Community Coll. Mem. ANA, AAUW, Minn. Nurses Assn., Sigma Theta Tau.

BOULDIN, HEIDI G., company executive; b. Milw., July 11, 1966. BA in Journalism, Ohio State U., 1989. V.p. Daniel R. Barry and Assoc., Columbus, Ohio, 1992—. Lutheran.

BOULOS, EDWARD NASHED, transportation specialist; b. Damanhour, Egypt, May 19, 1941; came to U.S., 1979; s. Nashed Boulos and Lila (Habib) Georgy; m. Mervet Saleh, Aug. 31, 1967; children: Nermine E., Yasmine E. BS in Chemistry and Physics, Cairo U., 1963; MS in Solid State Sci., Am. U., Cairo, 1966; PhD in Ceramic Engring., U. Mo., 1970. Supr., cons. Ministry of Industry, Cairo, 1963-79; assoc. prof. Am. U., Cairo, 1972-79; vis. prof. Cath. U. Am., Washington, 1979-81; sr. scientist Anchor Hocking Co., Lancaster, Ohio, 1981-84; team leader Ford Motor Co., Dearborn, Mich., 1984—; cons. USAF, Boston, 1984-89; liaison bd. mem. Alfred (N.Y.) U., 1985—, chmn.-elect, 1992. Co-editor: Advances in the Fusion of Glass, 1988, PAC RIM Glass and Optical Materials Issues, 2 vols., 1994; contbr. articles on glass tech. to profl. jours.; patentee in field. NSF rsch. grantee, 1967-71, 72-79. Fellow Am. Ceramic Soc. (chair Glass and Optical Materials Div., 1996-97); mem. ASTM, Materials Rsch. Soc., Deutsche Glastechnische Gesellschaft, Sigma Xi. Office: Ford Motor Co Glass Divsn 15000 N Commerce Dr Dearborn MI 48120-1225

BOULTON, EDWIN CHARLES, retired bishop; b. St. Joseph, Mo., Apr. 15, 1928; s. Glen Elwood and Elsa Adina Elizabeth (Person) B.; m. Betty Ann Fisher, July 17, 1949; children—Ann Lisa, Charles Mitchell, James Clay, Melanie Beth. A.B., William Jewell Coll., 1950; MDiv,Duke U., 1953; DD, Iowa Wesleyan Coll., 1974, Rust Coll., 1982, Dakota Wesleyan U., 1985, Mt. Union Coll., 1989, Baldwin-Wallace Coll., 1994; DHL, Simpson Coll., 1980, Westmar Coll., 1984. Ordained to ministry Meth. Ch., 1953; pastor chs., West End-Vass, N.C., 1953, Republic Community, Iowa, 1954-57, Pocahontas, Iowa, 1957-64, Bettendorf, Iowa, 1964-70; dist. supt., Dubuque, Iowa, 1970-73; adminstrv. asst. to bishop, Des Moines, 1973-80, bishop of Dakotas Area, Fargo, N.D., 1980-88; bishop of Ohio East Area, 1988-96, ret., 1996; bd. dirs. World Meth. Coun. Named Disting. Alumnus, Duke U. Div. Sch., 1980. Office: The United Meth Ch 8800 Cleveland Ave NW Canton OH 44720-4564

BOUNDS, NANCY, modeling and talent company executive; b. Rodney, Ark.; d. William Thomas and Mary Jane (Fields) Southard; m. Robert S. Bounds, 1960 (div. 1965); 1 child, Ronnie Jean; m. Mark Curtis Sconce, Nov. 28, 1972. Exec. dir. Internat. Fashion/Modeling Assn., N.Y.C., 1978; founding pres. Internat. Talent and Model Schs. Assn., N.Y.C., 1979-80; pres. Nancy Bounds Internat., Omaha, 1959—. Contbr. articles to profl. jours. Producer TV Heart Fund Auction, 1965; dir., choreographer fashion show N.Y. fashion editors, 1989, Czechoslovakian Model Search, Prague, 1991. Chairperson Douglas/Sarpy County Heart Assn., Omaha, 1966, 73-74. Recipient Nat. Tchr.'s award MiLady Pub. Co., 1965, Outstanding Service award Mayor of Omaha, 1984, Uta Halee Girls Village, 1983-87, March of Dimes service award, 1977, 84, Toys for Tots service award, 1986, Muscular Dystrophy citation of merit, 1982; named Best of Omaha, 1988-92, Woman of Distinction YWCA, 1992, 93, 94, 95; Nancy Bounds Day proclaimed by City of Omaha, 1994. Avocations: reading, painting, travel, golf, tournament bridge. Home: 4803 Davenport St Omaha NE 68132-3108 Office: 11915 Pierce Plz Omaha NE 68144

BOURDELAIS, ALFRED ARTHUR, social services administrator; b. Lawrence, Mass., Oct. 3, 1936; s. Alfred Edmund and Lillian (Mildred) B.; m. Marlene Bourdelais, May 6, 1962; children: Shawn, Cerise. BS, Merrimack Coll., North Andover, Mass., 1958; Master City Planner, U. Calif., Berkeley, 1976. Exec. dir. Model Cities Program City of Manchester, N.H., 1969-75; program officer City of Grand Rapids, Mich., 1975-79; dean, adminstr. Highland C.C., Freeport, Ill., 1979-86; neighborhood devel. coord. City of Rockford, Ill., 1986-87; exec. dean Ivy Tech., Valparaiso, Ind., 1987-89; cons. Freeport Bus. Cons., Valparaiso, 1989-91; assoc. dir. adminstrn. The Caring Pl., Inc., Hobart, Ind., 1991—. Author: Speed Reading for Adults, 1971, Computer Literacy, 1973; contbr. articles to newspapers and profl. jours. Pres. bd. CAP, Freeport, 1983. Mem. Merrimack Coll. Alumni (pres. 1973), Kiwanis Club of Freeport (pres. 1985). Republican. Roman Catholic. Home: 1208 Peachtree Dr Valparaiso IN 46383-4026 Office: The Caring Pl Inc 511 Randle St Valparaiso IN 46383-2677

BOUSFIELD, JAMES EUSTACE, industrial engineer; b. Bar Harbor, Maine, June 1, 1937; s. Neal D. and Elizabeth R. (Beckett) B.; m. Eula Jane Morris, Feb. 4, 1961; children: Elizabeth Jane, William H. BCE, U. Maine, 1959. Registered profl. engr., Ohio. Maintnance engr. Delphi: Packard Electric Syss., Warren, Ohio, 1959-60; plant layout engr., new plant installation engr. Packard Electric Div. GM, Warren, Ohio, 1960-75, system design and installation engr., 1975-77, spl. project, system design engr., 1977—, sr. engr. spl. projects, material handling engr., 1975—; designed, fabricated or ordered material handling systems, 1975—. Unit commr. Warren Coun. Boy Scouts Am., 1976—. Sgt. USNG, 1955-63. Scouter of Yr. award 1981. Mem. Nat. Soc. Profl. Engrs. Republican. Episcopalian. Home: 526 Towson Dr NW Warren OH 44483-1737 Office: Packard Electric Div PO Box 431 Warren OH 44486-0431

BOUSON, BROOKS, English educator; b. Washington, Pa.; m. Roberts Bouson Jr. BA, U. Ill., Chgo.; PhD, Loyola U., 1979. Asst. prof. English Mundelein Coll., Chgo., 1980-86, assoc. prof., 1986-91; assoc. prof. Loyola U., Chgo., 1991—. Author: Brutal Choreographies: Oppositional Strategies and Narrative Design in the Novels of Margaret Atwood, 1993, The Empathic Reader: A Study of the Narcissistic Character and the Drama of the Self, 1989; contbr. articles to profl. jours. and chpts. to books. Edmund J. James scholar U. Ill. Mem. Margaret Atwood Soc., Toni Morrison Soc., MLA, Midwest MLA, Women's Caucus, Phi Kappa Phi, Alpha Sigma Nu. Office: Loyola U Chgo Dept English-Crown Ctr 6525 N Sheridan Rd Chicago IL 60626

BOUTELLE, EDWARD W., industrial designer; b. Elkhorn, Wis., Feb. 26, 1946. AS, Gateway Tech. Coll., Kanosho, Wis., 1966. Chief designer Sta-Rite Industries, Inc., Delavan, Wis., 1966—. Mem. adv. bd. Gateway Tech. Coll., Kanosho; vol. chmn. Park and Recreation Commn. With U.S. Army, 1969-70. Office: Sta-Rite Industries Inc 293 Wright St Delevan WI 53115

BOVARY, THOMAS DEAN, design draftsman; b. Nashville, Ill., Jan. 2, 1968. Student, Belleville (Ill.) C.C., 1983; AAS, Kaskaskia C.C., Centralia, Ill., 1990. Draftsman Prollex Inc., Edwardsville, Ill., 1989-90; design draftsman Emerson Electric, St. Louis, 1990—. Baptist. Office: Emerson Electric Mail Sta 8496 8100 W Florissant Ave # 3 Saint Louis MO 63136-1417

BOVÉE, WARREN GILLES, retired journalism educator; b. Billings, Mont., Jan. 2, 1922; s. Claire L. and Ida (Gilles) B.; m. Gladys Helen Rose, Aug. 2, 1947; children: Priscilla, Christopher, David, John, Paul. BA cum laude, Marquette U., 1947, MA, 1949; postgrad., Columbia U., 1949-53. Instr. English and Journalism Coll. of New Rochelle, N.Y., 1948-53; asst. prof. Journalism Marquette U., Milw., 1953-59, assoc. prof., 1959-64, prof., 1964-90, prof. emeritus, 1991—; dir. grad. programs Marquette U. Coll. Journalism, Milw., 1970-77, asst. dean, 1975-77, acting dean, 1971-72, 77-78, chair dept. Journalism, 1988-89; bd. dirs. Cath. Renaissance Soc., Milw., 1950-53. Author: Research Materials, 1956, Magazine Editor-Writer Relationship; editor The By-Lines Awards, 1995; contbr. articles to various publs. Dir. Wis. Freedom of Info. Ctr., Milw., 1979-86, Artist Series at the Pabst, 1978-87; bd. dirs. Sta. WUWM-FM, 1981-87, Bradley Inst. for Democracy, 1989-90. 1st lt. U.S. Army Air Corps, 1942-45, CBI. Mag. Pubs. Assn. fellow, 1963, Nat. Conf. Editorial Writers rsch. grantee, 1980, Atlantic Ctr. for the Arts assoc. grantee, 1987; recipient Andrew Hamilton award Marquette U., 1961. Mem. AAUP (pres. Marquette U. chpt. 1962-63), Quarter Century Club (pres. 1988-89), Nat. Conf. Editl. Writers (life, exec. bd. 1983-85, dir.), Milw. Press Club, Soc. Profl. Journalists. Democrat. Roman Catholic. Home: 527 N Story Pky Milwaukee WI 53208-3668 Office: Marquette U Brooks Hall Ste #200 Milwaukee WI 53233

BOVEN, DAVID L., investment company executive; b. Fremont, Mich., Apr. 12, 1941; m. Heide M. Meister, Nov. 27, 1965; 1 child, Morrey. BA, U. Mich., 1964; MA, Ea. Mich. U., 1967. Owner, mgr. Windmill Investments, Muskegon, Mich., 1974-80; v.p. investments PaineWebber, Muskegon, 1980-88, Robert W. Baird & Co. Inc., Muskegon, 1988—. With N.G., 1967. Office: Robert W Baird & Co Inc PO Box 89 200 Terrace Plz Muskegon MI 49443

BOVICH, EDWARD PHILIP, marketing educator, consultant; b. Pitts., May 11, 1959; s. Edward Hugh and Michela B. BBA, U. Mich., 1981, MA, 1983, PhD, 1987. Rsch. assoc. DDB Needham Worldwide Advt., Chgo., 1984-85, rsch. supr., 1985-87; staff cons. Frank Lynn & Assocs. Cons., Chgo., 1987-88, mng. cons., 1988-90; dir. mktg. Hughes Network Systems div. Hughes Aircraft, San Diego, 1990-94; vis. asst. prof. U. Mich. Grad. Sch. Bus. Adminstrn., Ann Arbor, 1994—; mktg. and telecomms. cons., Ann Arbor, 1994—; v.p. bd. dirs. Univ. Cellar Bookstore, Ann Arbor, 1980-81. Mem. Am. Mktg. Assn.

BOW, SING TZE, engineer, educator; b. Kwangtong, People's Rep. of China, Oct. 3, 1924; s. Shi-yun and Rui-Lien (Chang) B.; m. Xia Fang Wang, July 20, 1957; 1 child, Nai-jun. BSEE, Chiao Tung U., 1947; MS in Elec. Engring., U. Wash., 1952; PhD in Elec. Engring., Northwestern U., 1956; postgrad., Gen. Electric Co., 1949-50. Lic. profl. engr. Rsch. engr. Delta Star Electric Co., Chgo., 1955-56; rsch. prof., lab. dir. Academia Sinica, People's Rep. of China, 1956-81, 83-84; prof. elec. engring. Pa. State U., University Park, 1981-83, 84-87; prof. elec. engring., computer engring. Shanghai Jiao Tong U., People's Rep. of China, 1979—; prof., chair elec. engring., lab. dir. Northern Ill. U., DeKalb, 1987—. Author: Optimal Operation and Control of Power System, 1965, Pattern Recognition-Application to Large Data-Set Problems, 1984, Pattern Recognition and Image Preprocessing, 1992; contbr. articles to profl. jours. Grantee Academia Sinica 1958-81, Digital Equipment Corp. 1984-88, Ideal Industries 1987-90, CTS Knights Div. 1989-90, Dekalb Genetics, Inc. 1990—. Mem. IEEE (sr. mem.), Internat. Soc. Photo-Optical Instrumentation Engrs., Internat. Pattern Recognition Soc., Classification Soc. North Am., Internat. Neural Network Soc., Edit. Bd. Elec. Engring. Electronics Series, Marcel Dekker, Chinese Soc. Space Rsch. (v.p. 1979-86), Chinese Soc. Astronautics (chmn. remote sensing technique com. 1979-86), Shanghai Assn. Automation (exec. bd. 1979—), Eta Kappa Nu, Pi Mu Epsilon, Sigma Xi. Home: 467 W Hillcrest Dr De Kalb IL 60115-2377 Office: No Ill U Dept Elec Engring De Kalb IL 60115

BOWELL, WILLIAM DAVID, SR., cruise and excursion company executive; b. St. Paul, Feb. 14, 1921; s. Ralph Raymond and Leone C. (Padelford) B.; m. 1946; children: William D., Shelley Ann Bowell Kosmo, Beth Ann Myers. BA, Macalester Coll., 1949, postgrad. in journalism, 1952. Curator Minn. State Hist. Soc., St. Paul, 1949-51; liaison engr. Studebaker Corp., South Bend, Ind., 1952-55; account exec. Edwards & Deutsch Litho, Chgo., 1956-61; exec. v.p. United Sci., St. Paul, 1962-69; pres. Miller Farms, St. Paul, 1969-70, Stillwater Tug & Salvage, Minn., 1969-76; founder, pres. Padelford Packet Boat Co., Inc., St. Paul, 1970—; founder, co-pub. United Airline Mainliner Mag., 1956; co-pub. Oldsmobile Rocket Circle mag., 1956; co-pub. Holiday Inns Am. mag., 1956. Patentee binaural earphone, 1958. Grand marshall Aquatennial Boat Parade, St. Paul/Mpls., 1972, East Side Parade, St. Paul, 1979; bd. dirs. Metroland, St. Paul, 1972-84, St. Paul Riverfront Commn., West Side Neighborhood House, Minn. Transp. Mus.; founder Nat. Rivermen's Hall of Fame, Dubuque, Iowa. Served with Paratroopers, U.S. Army, 1942-45; ETO. Decorated Bronze Star, Purple Heart; recipient award for top tourist attraction Gov. Minn., 1972, Outstanding Contbns. John Bickel award Nat. Rivers Hall of Fame, 1991, Lifetime Achievement award, 1995, Contbn. to State commendation Gov. Minn., 1995, Contbn. to City Mayor St. Paul, 1995. Mem. Sons and Daus. Pioneer Rivermen, Am. Sternwheel Assn., Nat. Passenger Vessel Assn. (pres. 1970-77, Founders award 1996), Minn. Hist. Soc. (life), Ramsey County Hist. Soc. (dir. 1984). Home: 3540 James Ave S Minneapolis MN 55408-3327 Office: Padelford Packet Boat Co Inc Harriet Island Saint Paul MN 55107

BOWEN, GILBERT WILLARD, minister; b. Muskegon, Mich., Dec. 30, 1931; s. Bruce Oliver and Beatrice Lillian (Sibley) B.; m. Marlene Mary Michell, July 31, 1954; children: Kathryn Leigh, Mark Kevin, Stephen James. BA, Wheaton Coll., 1955; MDiv, McCormick Theol. Sem., 1957, PhD in Ministry, 1976; cert., Ctr. for Religion and Psychotherapy, 1976; DLL (hon.), Nat. Coll. Edn., 1987. Ordained to ministry Presbyn. Ch., 1956. Minister 1st United Presbyn. Ch., Blue Earth, Minn., 1956-63, Faith United Presbyn. Ch., Tinley Park, Ill., 1963-65, Community Presbyn. Ch., Mt. Prospect, Ill., 1965-70, Kenilworth (Ill.) Union Ch., 1970—; exchange minister Johanneskirche, Neuwied, Fed. Republic Germany, 1961-62; pres. bd. Ctr. for Religion and Psychotherapy; bd. dirs. McCormick Theol. Sem., Chgo., Anatolia Coll., Thessaloniki, Greece, Presbyn. Home, Evanston. Mem. adv. com. North Shore Sr. Ctr., Winnetka, Ill.; bd. dirs. Hospice of North Shore, Wilmette, Ill., Shelter for Battered Women, Evanston; chmn. Instl. Rev. Bd., Evanston. Mem. Am. Assn. Pastoral Counselors, Acad. Parish Clergy, Am. Waldensian Aid Soc. Republican. Club: Indian Hill. Home: 909 Westerfield Dr Wilmette IL 60091-1810 Office: Kenilworth Union Ch 211 Kenilworth Ave Kenilworth IL 60043-1242

BOWEN, RICHARD LEE, architect; b. Canton, Ohio, Nov. 1, 1935; s. Raymond Leed and Lillian E. (White) B.; m. Robin Herrington (div. Mar. 1989); children: Richard Lee, David Herrington, Laurel Ann, Sean Andrew, Scott Edward; m. Gail Audrey Morofka, Mar. 25, 1990; children: Tabitha Erin, Colin Leed. BA, Case Western Res. U., 1959. Registered architect 50 states, D.C., P.R., Eng., Can., Australia, Nat. Coun. Archtl. Registration Bds., Archtl. Registration Coun. U.K. Founder, pres. Richard L. Bowen & Assocs. Inc., archtl. engrs. and planners, Cleve., Richard L. Bowen & Assocs. Inc., Cleve., 1963—, Richard L. Bowen, Inc., Cleve., 1976—; pres. Enerwaste, Inc., 1992—; mng. ptnr. ComDel, 1970; pres. Richard L. Bowen & Assocs. of Fla., Pompano Beach, 1969—. Prin. works include Western Campus, Cuyahoga C.C., Akron State Office Bldg., West Jr. High Sch., Cleve. Cen. Police Hdqs., Cleve. Hopkins Internat. Airport, FAA Regional Office Bldg., classroom and libr. bulds. Ashtabula Campus, Kent State U., Wade Park VA Hosp., Westerly Sewage Treatment Facility for Cuyahoga Regional Sewer Authority, Cuyahoa C.C. Manpower Skills Ctr. for Ohio; also others. Mem. Leadership Cleve.; mem. exec. com. Cuyahoga County Rep. Com., Cleve., 1963—; trustee St. Luke's Hosp. Assn., Cleve. Internat. Air Show. Recipient energy conservation design award Fla. Power Winter Garden Shopping Ctr., 1986, merit award Cleve. Restoration Soc., 1992. Mem. AIA (design award of excellence 1976, award 1979), Architects Soc. Ohio (honor award 1988), Nat. Assn. Indsl. and Office Parks (awards 1985, 89), Royal Archtl. Inst. Can., Royal Inst. Brit. Architects, Am. Soc. Ch. Architecture, Soc. Archtl. Historians, Guild for Religious Architecture, Internat. Coun. Shopping Ctrs., Constrn. Specifications Inst., Bldg. Ofcls. Coun. Am., Am. Assn. Planners, Urban Land Inst., Am. Arbitration Assn., Rowfant Club, Cat Cay Club, Ft. Lauderdale Yacht Club, Useppa Island Club, Phi Gamma Delta, also others. Home: 2824 Eaton Rd Shaker Heights OH 44122-2514 Office: 13000 Shaker Blvd Cleveland OH 44120-2063

BOWER, BARBARA JEAN, nurse; b. Akron, Ohio, Aug. 25, 1942; d. William Howard and Maxine (Goodykoontz) Sturm; m. Howard Bower, Aug. 25, 1961 (dec. 1989); children: Nancy, Janet; m. Richard Chavez, Dec. 24, 1993. BA, Elmhurst Coll., 1974, postgrad., 1987—; diploma, Evang. Sch. Nursing, 1970; PhD, U. Chgo., 1993. RN. Supr. nursing Med. Ctr.; nurse critical care Loyola U., Maywood, Ill., 1970-78, Med. Staffing Services, Oak Park, Ill., 1978-84; pres. Heart Care Unltd., Oakbrook, Ill., 1982—; one of first ind. nurse contractors in Ill. Creator ednl. programs for cardiac patients, families, 1971—. Stephen min. Christ Ch. of Oak Brook, Ill. Mem. AAUW, Am. Nurses Assn., Am. Assn. Critical Care Nurses, Am. Heart Assn., Elmhurst Coll. Alumni Assn. Home: 3203 York Rd Oak Brook IL 60521-2312 Office: Heart Care Unltd PC Oak Brook IL 60521

BOWER, GLEN LANDIS, lawyer; b. Highland, Ill., Jan. 16, 1949; s. Ray Landis and Evelyn Ferne (Ragland) B. BA, So. Ill. U., 1971; JD with honors, Ill. Inst. Tech., 1974. Bar: Ill. 1974, U.S. Ct. Mil. Appeals 1975, U.S. Ct. Appeals (7th cir.) 1976, U.S. Dist Ct. (so. dist.) Ill. 1977, U.S. Dist. Ct. (cen. dist.) Ill. 1992, U.S. Supreme Ct. 1978, U.S. Tax Ct. 1984, U.S. Ct. Claims 1986, U.S. Dist. Ct. (no. dist.) Ill. 1994, U.S. Ct. Veterans Appeals 1995. Sole practice Effingham, Ill., 1974-83; prosecutor Effingham County, Ill., 1976-79; mem. Ill. House of Reps., Springfield, 1979-83; asst. dir., gen. counsel Ill. Dept. Revenue, Springfield, Ill., 1983-90; Presdl.' appointed chmn. U.S. Railroad Retirement Bd., Chgo., 1990—; liaison mem. Adminstrv. Conf. of U.S., 1991-95; mem. Nat. Adv. Com. for Juvenile Justice and Delinquency Prevention, Washington, 1976-80, U.S. Econ. Adv. Bd. of U.S. Dept. Commerce, Washington, 1981-85, Ill. Gen. Assembly State Adv. Com. on Cir. Ct. Fin., Springfield, 1984; mem. Revenue Bd. Appeals, Chgo., 1985-87, chmn., 1986-87; mem. Com. of 50 on Ill. Constn., 1987-88; active Am. Coun. Young Polit. Leaders to China, 1988. Co-editor: Handbook on State Taxation, 1991; contbr. articles to profl. jours. Alt. del. Rep. Nat. Conv., Miami Beach, Fla., 1972, Rep. Nat. Conv., New Orleans, 1988, Rep. Nat. Conv. Houston, 1992; vice chmn. Effingham County Rep. Ctrl. Com., Ill., 1976-90; bd. dirs. Dana-Thomas House Found., Springfield, Ill., 1989-90, So. Ill. U. at Carbondale Found., 1993—, pres.'s coun.; trustee McKendree Coll., Lebanon, Ill., 1978-81; chmn. State of Ill. Organ and Tissue Donors Adv. Bd., 1993—. Lt. col. USAFR, 1974—. Recipient The Univ. Disting. Svc. award, 1971, Recognition citation Am. Legion, 1980, Outstanding Svc. cert. to tchg. profession Ill. Edn. Assn., 1981, Disting. Svc. award Am. Vets., 1980, 82, Presdl. citation Navy League U.S., 1981, Constitution award Mus. of Our Nat. Heritage, 1988, Silver Good Citizenship medal Ill. Soc. SAR, 1990, Profl. Achievement award Ill. Inst. Tech., 1993, Friend of History award Ill. State Hist. Soc., 1994, Alumni Achievement award So. Ill. U., 1994; named Outstanding Freshman Legislator, Ill. Edn. Assn., 1980, Legislator of Yr., Ill. Assn. Rehab. Socs., 1981, 82, One of 10 Dels. to China, Am. Coun. Young Polit. Leaders, 1988. Fellow Ill. Bar Found. (life), Am. Bar Found. (life); mem. ABA (adminstrv. practice com. of taxation sect., ct. procedure com., mem. exec. com. nat. assn. state tax bar sects., employment taxes com. 1990), Fed. Bar Assn., Fed. Cir. Bar Assn., Rep. Nat. Lawyers Assn., Ill. State Bar Assn. (sec. state taxation sect. coun. 1987-88, vice-chair 1988-89, chair 1989-90, labor law sect. coun. 1976-77, sect. coun. on employee benefits 1991—), Effingham County Bar Assn. (sec. 1976-77, pres. 1983-84), Chgo. Bar Assn., Nat. Assn. Tax Adminstrs. (vice chmn. attys. sect. 1985-86, 88-89, chmn. 1986-88), Nat. Conf. Spl. Ct. Judges, Effingham County Old Settlers Assn. (pres., bd. dirs. 1983-86), Ill. State Hist. Soc., (v.p. 1979-81, bd. dirs. exec. com. 1983-86, Ralph C. Francis award 1967), Effingham Regional Hist. Soc., Small Bus. Adminstrn. Adv. Coun. (bd. dirs. 1973-77), Effingham County Mental Health Assn. (pub. affairs com. 1977-78), U.S. Capitol Hist. Soc. (charter), Abraham Lincoln Assn., Capitol Hill Club, Army and Navy Club Washington D.C., U.S. Supreme Ct. Hist. Soc., The Nat. Sojourners, Burgesses of Colonial Williamsburg (charter), Am. coun. of Young Political leaders, Art Institute of Chgo., Smithsonian Assocs., So. Ill. U. Carbondale Found. (bd. dirs. 1993—), Field Mus. of Natural History, So. Ill. Univ. Alumni Assn. (life), Am. Legion, Res. Officers Assn., Judge Advs. Assn., Air Force Assn., Shriners, Kiwanis (pres. 1977-78), Sons of Am. Revolution, Phi Alpha Delta (dist. justice Cen. Ill. and Ind. 1988-92). Methodist. Home: 1 E Scott Unit 799 Chicago IL 60610-2348 Office: U S Railroad Retirement Bd 844 N Rush St Ste 804 Chicago IL 60611-2092

BOWER, KENNETH FRANCIS, electrical engineer; b. Fostoria, Ohio, June 16, 1942; s. Carl Albert and Carmia June (Butzier) B.; m. Vicki Marie Lambert, Feb. 14, 1975; children: Candi Marie, Jillian June, Brett Kenneth, Michael Courtland, Daniel David. BSEE, Purdue U., 1965. Registered profl. engr., Ohio, Fla. Aerospace engr. NASA Manned Spacecraft Ops., Kennedy Space Center, Fla., 1965-67, NASA Unmanned Launch Ops., Kennedy Space Center, 1967-73; systems engr. Cin. Electronics, 1973-76; programmer AMF, Vandalia, Ohio, 1976-77, Access Corp., Cin., 1977-78; mgr. GTE Compact, Cin., Anaheim, Calif., 1978-81; cons. Telos Cons. Svcs., Hughes Aerospace, Irvine, Calif., 1982-83, Telos Fed. Systems, Jet Propulsion Lab., Pasadena, Calif., 1983-86; lead engr. GE Aircraft Engines, Cin., 1987-93; propr. software cons. bus. Quality Used Profls., 1993—; pres. Quality Used Profls., Inc., 1996—, also chmn. bd. dirs.; v.p., bd. dirs. Gedanken Systems, Inc., Cin. Patentee in field. Bd. trustees First Ch. of God, Rubidoux, Calif., 1982-83, 86. Named Father of Yr. First Ch. of God, Cin., 1978. Mem. Mensa (local sec. 1963-83), Purdue Alumnus, Clermont County C. of C. Democrat. Home: 248 Seton Ct Batavia OH 45103-3285 Office: PO Box 97 Batavia OH 45103-0097

BOWER, MICHAEL L., clergyman; b. Altus, Okla., May 15, 1958; s. Robert Francis and Glenda Pauline (Blackburn) B.; m. Beatrice Anne Byrd, Nov. 4, 1977; children: Rachel Anne, Jonathan Michael Lynn. Student, Tex. Tech. U., 1974, U. Tex., Arlington, 1975; student in theology, Tex. Bible Coll., Houston, 1976. Evangelist United Pentecostal Ch., St. Louis, 1977-85; asst. pastor Apostolic World Ctr., Ft. Worth, Tex., 1985-88; missionary United Pentecostal Ch., Korea, 1988; seminar tchr. United Pentecostal Ch., St. Louis, 1989-90; pioneer home missionary United Pentecostal Ch., Chgo., 1990-93; sr. pastor New Hope Worship Ctr., Ft. Wayne, Ind., 1993—. Judge, Rep. Party, Ft. Wayne, 1993-94; attache Navajo Indian Tribe, Gallup, N.Mex., 1980-81; chamber chaplain Ft. Worth Greater C. of C., 1985-88. Apostolic Ch. Office: New Hope Worship Ctr 9019 Stellhorn Rd Fort Wayne IN 46815

BOWER, ROBERT HEWITT, surgeon, educator, researcher; b. Omaha, Aug. 20, 1949; s. John Walter and Dorothy May (Sibert) B.; m. Debra Lea Goettsche, July 4, 1980; children: Timothy Conrad, Michael Harvey, Emily Frances. BA, Grinnell Coll., 1971; MD, U. Nebr., 1975. Diplomate Nat. Bd. Med. Examiners, Am. Bd. Surgery (dir. 1995—). Intern, U. Nebr., 1975-76, resident in surgery, 1976-80, chief resident, 1979-80; clin. and rsch. fellow U. Cin., 1980-81; asst. prof. surgery, 1981-85; dir. dept. parenteral and enteral nutrition U. Hosp., 1981—, assoc. prof. surgery, 1985-95, prof. surgery, 1995—, dir. surg. residency, 1986—, vice chmn. edn., 1995—; chief surgery svc. Cin. VA Med. Ctr., 1994—; pres., trustee, chmn. bd. trustees Vocal Arts Ensemble of Cin. Fellow ACS; mem. Cen. Surg. Assn., Am. Coll. Nutrition, Soc. Am. Gastrointestinal Endoscopic Surgeons, Assn. Acad. Surgery, Am. Soc. Parenteral and Enteral Nutrition, Ohio Med. Assn., Surg. Infection Soc., Acad. Medicine Cin., Soc. Univ. Surgeons, Soc. Surgery of Alimentary Tract, Cin. Surg. Soc. Presbyterian, Surg. Infection Soc. Contbr. articles to profl. jours., chpts. to books. Office: Cin VA Med Ctr 3200 Vine St Cincinnati OH 45220-2213

BOWER, RONALD EDWARD, insurance agency owner; b. Coal City, W.Va., Sept. 3, 1944; s. Dodd and Sadie G. (Farley) B.; m. Eileen M. O'Donnell, Dec. 10, 1954; 1 child, John David. Advanced tchrs. cert., Mt. Vernon Bible Coll., 1968; councellor selling cert., Larry Wilson, 1974; effective tng. cert., Richland County Juvenile Ct., 1976. Ordained to ministry Openm Bible Std. Chs., 1992, Full Gospel Lighthouse, 1994; notary pub., Ohio. Agent Allstate Ins. Co., Hudson, Ohio, 1974-80; pastor Foursquare Gospel Ch., Galion, Ohio, 1972-74; chaplain asst. Mansfield (Ohio) Reformatory, 1974-79; radio pastor 7 states Ron Bower Faith for Deliverance Hour, Mansfield, 1973-79; dir. Bower Farm Group Home, Mansfield, 1972-79; evangelist Ron E. Bower Evangelist Assn., Mansfield, 1972-80; tchr. adults 1st Assembly of God, Louisville, 1987-90; with Bible class Ron Bower Evangelistic, Girard, Ohio, 1989-90; owner, pres. Ron E. Bower Ins. Agy. Inc., Canton, Ohio, 1980—; trainer ins. Farmers Ins. Group, Canton, 1981-85; Bible tchr. Manfield Reformatory, 1974-79. Author: Children's Bread, 1973. Bd. dirs. Lay Leadership Internat., Canton, 1986-87; pastor Full Gospel Ch., Perry, N.Y., 1968-71; mem. steering com. Mt. Vernon (Ohio) Bible Coll., 1974-75; v.p. student body, pres. mission club, 1964-68; min. Full Gospel Lighthouse Inc., Canton, 1994—, tchr. adult Sunday sch.; mem. steering com. Ohio Youth Commn.-Group Home Panel, Columbus, 1974-79; Senica youth dir. N.Y. dist. Foursquare Gospel Chs., 1968-71. Recipient Svc. to Youth award Ohio Youth Commn., State of Ohio, 1974, Top Hatter award Preferred Risk Mut. Ins. Co., Des Moines, 1986—, Honor Ring award Allstate Ins. Co., Hudson, Ohio, Go for the Gold award Western Res. Mut., 1995. Mem. Am. Assn. Christian Counsellors, Full Gospel Men's Internat. Fellowship (v.p. Galion chpt. 1976, song leader). Republican. Foursquare Gospel. Home: 1122 Birchtree St NE Louisville OH

44641-2104 Office: Ron E Bower Ins Agy Inc 4636 Tuscarawas St W Canton OH 44708-5339

BOWERS, CARLTON LEROY, secondary school educator; b. Bronx, N.Y., Nov. 26, 1961; s. Harold E. and Catherine (Koppenhaver) B.; m. Carolyn S. Warner, Oct. 19, 1985 (div. Oct. 1995); children: Timothy Owen, Jonathan Robert. BA, Johns Hopkins U., 1984; MS, U. Dayton, 1992. Workshop supr. Echoing Hills Village, Inc., Warsaw, Ohio, 1984-86, program dir., QMRP, 1986-87; sci. and math. tchr. Bethel H.S., Tipp City, Ohio, 1989-95, Milton-Union H.S., West Milton, Ohio, 1995—; adult basic literacy edn. instr. Upper Valley Joint Vocat. Sch., Piqua, Ohio, 1990—. Ohio EPA grantee, 1992, Bethel Local Schs. 21st Century grantee, 1991-94. Office: Milton-Union Exempted Village HS 221 S Jefferson St West Milton OH 45383

BOWERS, FRANK DANA, botany educator; b. Fayetteville, Ark., Mar. 21, 1936; s. Frank M. and Bess Ann (McDonald) B.; m. Donna Jaye Olsen, Mar. 18, 1967. B.S., Southwest Mo. State U., 1966; M.S., U. Tenn., 1968, Ph.D., 1972. Asst. curator herbarium U. Tenn.-Knoxville, 1968-72; research assoc., 1973-75; asst. prof. biology, U. Wis.-Stevens Point, 1975-80, assoc. prof., 1980-86, prof., 1986—. Contbr. articles to profl. jours. Mem. Am. Bryological and Lichenological Soc. (sec.-treas. 1978-80), Am. Soc. Plant Taxonomists, Soc. Econ. Botany, Sigma Xi, Phi Kappa Phi. Baptist. Avocations: fishing, camping, painting. Home: 848 Oak Ridge Ln Stevens Point WI 54481-3330 Office: U Wis Biology Dept Stevens Point WI 54481

BOWLBY, RICHARD ERIC, retired computer systems analyst; b. Detroit, Aug. 17, 1939; s. Garner Milton and Florence Marie (Russell) B.; m. Gwendoline Joyce Coldwell, Apr. 29, 1967. B.A., Wayne State U., 1962. With Ford Motor Co., Detroit, 1962-65, 66-94, now computer systems analyst, ret. 1994; pres. 1300 Lafayette East-Coop., Inc., 1981-82. Mem. Antiquaries, Friends Detroit Pub. Library, Friends Orch. Hall. Club: Founders Soc. (Detroit).

BOWLES, FRANK WILLIAM, JR., health facility administrator; b. Lakewood, Ohio, Nov. 7, 1956; s. Frank William and Iris Mae (Davenport) B.; m. Brenda Sue McAlister Francis, Aug. 21, 1981 (div. Mar. 1993); children: Frank William III, Erin Elizabeth; m. Monica Pena, Jan. 17, 1994; 1 child, Geoffrey Colin. BS in Mgmt., Purdue U., 1984; MBA, Ind. Wesleyan U., 1992. Bus. mgr. Lafayette (Ind.) Eye Ctr., 1987-90; practice adminstr. Fisher-Swale Eye Ctr., Kankakee, Ill., 1990-93, Richmond (Ind.) Eye Ctr., 1993—. Mem. sch. buddy program Richmond Cmty. Schs., 1995. Mem. Am. Coll. Med. Practice Execs., Am. Soc. Ophthalmic Adminstrs., Richmond Pers. Assn., Richmond Area Mgmt. Assn., Elks. Republican. Methodist. Office: Richmond Eye Ctr 1900 Chester Blvd Richmond IN 47374

BOWLES, JOHN L., industrial designer; b. Reading, Pa., Oct. 19, 1944; s. Charles W.D. and Mary A. (Kershner) B.; m. Susan A., Arnold, Dec. 1, 1970; children: Gregory, Amanda. BS in Math., Muhlenberg Coll., 1966. Resident mgr. Bethlehem (Pa.) Steel Corp., 1966-83; pres., CEO N. Am. Wire Products, Salon, Ohio, 1983-90; v.p. Am. Spring Wire Corp., Bedford Heights, Ohio, 1990-92, Bowles Enterprises, Inc., Pepper Pike, Ohio, 1992—; 1st v.p. Wire Assn. Internat., Guildford, Conn., 1983—; treas., bd. dirs. Am. Wire Producers Assn., Washington, 1985-92. Bd. govs. Meth. Ch., Pepper Pike, Ohio, 1990-93; commr. Boy Scouts of Am., Cleve., 1987-90. Mem. ASTM (com. mem. 1988—), Wire Assn. Internat. (1st v.p. exec. com. 1983—), Kiwanis Internat. Home: 2875 Chatham Rd Pepper Pike OH 44124

BOWLING, NANCY JEANNE, bank executive; b. Pitts., Mar. 22, 1952; d. Joseph and Anna Gross; married; 1 child, Jamie Jo. Student, U. Pitts., 1970-74. Regional v.p. 1st Ind. Bank, Indpls., 1984—. Sec. Tri County Mental Health, Indpls., 1989—. Home: 6359 Cherbourg Dr Indianapolis IN 46220

BOWMAN, BILL, state legislator; m. Karen Bowman; 3 children. BS, Dickinson State U. Auctioneer, owner farm implement dealership Bowman; state senator dist. 39, 1991—; mem. human svcs. com.; chmn. agr. com. N.D. State Senate. Recipient Bronze award Vigortone Premix Sales. Mem. N.D. Stockmen's Assn., N.D. Wheat Growers Assn., N.D. Implement Dealers Assn., Rotary. Republican. Home: RR 2 Box 227 Bowman ND 58623-9753*

BOWMAN, ELIZABETH SUE, psychiatrist, educator; b. Roanoke, Va., Mar. 9, 1954; d. Edward David and Mildred Lenora (Miller) B.; m. Philip Meredith Coons, Sept. 5, 1981. BS, Purdue U., 1976; MD, Ind. U., Indpls., 1980; STM summa cum laude, Christian Theol. Sem., Indpls., 1987. Resident in psychiatry sch. of medicine Ind. U., 1980-84, chief resident sch. of medicine, 1984, asst. prof. sch. of medicine, 1984-93; asst. dir. inpatient psychiatry dept. Ind. U. Hosp., 1984-90; assoc. prof. Ind. U., 1993—; staff psychiatrist Indpls. VA Hosp., 1986-89. Contbr. articles to med. jours. Fellow Am. Psychiat. Assn., Am. Med. Women's Assn., Assn. Women Psychiatrists, Ind. Psychiat. Soc. (sec. 1985-86, editor newsletter 1985-88, pres.-elect 1992, pres. 1993), Internat. Soc. for Study of Dissociation (treas. 1992-94, pres.-elect 1995, pres. 1996). Methodist. Office: Ind U Clin Bldg 291 541 Clinical Dr Indianapolis IN 46202

BOWMAN, GEORGE ARTHUR, JR., judge; b. Milw., Dec. 1, 1917; s. George Arthur and Edna Oral (Hunter) B.; m. Rose Mary Thorpe, Aug. 8, 1947 (dec. 1980); children: George A. III, Daniel Andrew. Student, U. Wis., 1936-39; JD, Marquette U., 1943. Bar: Wis. 1943, U.S. Supreme Ct. 1943. Asst. dist. atty. Milw. County, 1947-48, children's ct. judge, 1967-72; asst. city atty. City of Milw., 1948-67; adminstrv. law judge Office of Hearing and Appeals Social Security Adminstrn. Dept. HHS, Chgo., 1973—; appointed Pres.'s Task Force, Law Enforcement Assistance Adminstrn., 1972; former counsel Milw. Police Dept.; advisor Nat. Council of Juvenile Ct. Judges, Nat. Conv., Atlanta; chmn. conv. com. Nat. Council of Juvenile Ct. Judges, Milw., 1972; chmn. State Task Force on Juvenile Delinquency, 1970-71; legis. com. Wis. Bd. Juvenile Ct. Judges, 1970-71; former mem. numerous legis. coms., Milw.; pioneered Legal Defender System in Children's Ct.; lecturer, Marquette U. Co-author: LEAA Uniform Standards for Police Departments, 1973 (Pres.'s citation). Bd. dirs. Am. Indian Info. and Action Group, Inc. "Project Phoenix", Juneau Acad.; chmn. Milw. County Rep. Party, 1961-62; active supporter numerous community juvenile programs, including Milw. Boys' Club, St. Joseph's Home for Children, Mt. Mary Coll. Proglram for Truant and Delinquent Girls, Operation Outreach, others; Social Security judge. With USN, 1943-46. Recipient Continious Svc. award Office of Hearings and Appeals Soc. Security Adminstr., 1991. Mem. Fed. Assn. Adminstrv. Law Judges, Assn. Office of Hearing and Appeals Adminstrv. Law Judges, Wis. State Bar Assn., Milw. Bar. Assn., Nat. Council Juvenile Ct. Judges, Am. Judicature Soc., Nat. Council of Sr. Citizens, Inc., Internat. Juvenile Officers Assn., Am. Legion (former post comdr.), Nat. Probate Judges Assn., New Trier Rep. Orgn., Committeeman's Club, Hawthorne Turf Club, Sigma Alpha Epsilon. Roman Catholic. Home: 2824 Orchard Ln Wilmette IL 60091-2144 Office: Social Security Adminstrn Office of Hearing & Appeals DHSS 200 W Adams St Bldg 510 Chicago IL 60606-5217

BOWMAN, JOHN EZRA, human resources executive; b. Columbia, Pa., Oct. 8, 1947; s. Ezra Alva and Jane Margret (Belknap) B.; m. Helen Elaine Palmer, Dec. 14, 1968 (div. July 1981); children: Heather Jane, Howard Thomas; m. Connie Jo Howard, July 24, 1982; 1 child, Audrea Leigh Hess. BS in Math., Calif. State U., Pomona, 1970. Mgmt. trainee Pacific Mut. Ins. Co., Newport Beach, Calif., 1970-72; personnel rels. officer Security Pacific Nat. Bank, L.A., 1972-74; personnel adminstr. Litton Industries Mellonics Div., Canoga Park, Calif., 1974-75, mgr. adminstr., 1975-77; compensation adminstr. Ctrl. Soya, Ft. Wayne, Ind., 1977-79; mgr. compensation Eckrich, Ft. Wayne, Ind., 1979-85; mgr. benefits N.Am. Van Lines, Inc., Ft. Wayne, Ind., 1985, dir. compensation and benefits, 1986-93, v.p. human resources, 1994—. Mem. bd. trustees East Allen County (Ind.) Schs., 1992—; mem. bd. dirs. Sci. Ctrl., Ft. Wayne, 1995—; v.p. allocations div. United Way of Allen County, Ft. Wayne, 1981-91. Republican. Methodist. Home: 10231 Garman Rd Leo IN 46765 Office: NAm Van Lines Inc 5001 US Hwy 30 W Fort Wayne IN 46818

BOWMAN, PASCO MIDDLETON, II, federal judge; b. Timberville, Va., Dec. 20, 1933; s. Pasco Middleton and Katherine (Lohr) B.; m. Ruth Elaine Bowman, July 12, 1958; children: Ann Katherine, Helen Middleton, Benjamin Garber. BA, Bridgewater Coll., 1955; JD, NYU, 1958; LLM, U. Va., 1986; LLD (hon.), Bridgewater Coll., 1988. Bar: N.Y. 1958, Ga. 1965, Mo. 1980. Assoc. firm Cravath, Swaine & Moore, N.Y.C., 1958-61, 62-64; asst. prof. law U. Ga., 1964-65, assoc. prof., 1965-69, prof., 1969-70; prof. Wake Forest U., 1970-78, dean, 1970-78; vis. prof. U. Va., 1978-79; prof., dean U. Mo., Kansas City, 1979-83; judge U.S. Ct. Appeals (8th cir.), Kansas City, MO., 1983—. Mng. editor: NYU Law Rev, 1957-58; Reporter, chief draftsman: Georgia Corporation Code, 1965-68. Served to col. USAR, 1959-84. Fulbright scholar London Sch. Econs. and Polit. Sci., 1961-62, Root-Tilden scholar, 1955-58. Mem. N.Y. Bar, Ga. Bar, Mo. Bar. Office: US Ct Appeals 8th Circuit 819 US Courthouse 811 Grand Blvd Kansas City MO 64106-1904

BOWMAN, SCOTTY, professional hockey coach; b. Montreal, Que., Can., Sept. 18, 1933; s. John and Jane Thomson (Scott) B.; m. Suella Belle Chitty, Aug. 16, 1969; children—Alicia Jean, David Scott, Stanley Glen, Nancy Elizabeth and Robert Gordon (twins). Student, Sir George Williams Bus. Sch., 1954. Scout exec. Club de Hockey Canadien, Montreal, 1956-66; coach Club de Hockey Canadien, 1971-79; coach, gen. mgr. St. Louis Blues Hockey Club, 1966-71; coach, gen. mgr., dir. hockey ops. Buffalo Sabres Hockey Club, 1979-86; TV analyst Hockey Night in Can., 1987-90; dir. player devel. Pitts. Penguins Hockey Club, 1990-91, interim head coach, 1991-92, head coach, 1992-93; head coach Detroit Red Wings Hockey Club, 1993—, dir. player pers., 1993—. Recipient Jack Adams award, 1977; named NHL Exec. of Yr. Sporting News, 1979-80; inducted in the Hockey Hall of Fame, 1991. Office: Detroit Red Wings Joe Louis Arena 600 Civic Center Dr Detroit MI 48226*

BOWMAN, STEPHEN D., stockbroker; b. Grand Rapids, Mich., Nov. 1, 1958. BA, Alma Coll., 1980. Stockbroker Paine Webber, Grand Rapids, 1981-85, A G Edwards & Sons, Grand Rapids, 1985—. Vol. Comty. Sch. Dist., Grand Rapids, 1994—. Mem. Orchard Hills Sports Club. Republican. Home: 2405 Elmwood Dr SE Grand Rapids MI 49506-4216 Office: A G Edwards & Sons Inc # 100 50 Monroe Ave NW # 100 Grand Rapids MI 49503-2643

BOWMAN-RANDALL, GAYLE DARLENE, equal employment specialist, writer; b. Tallahassee, Mar. 5, 1964; d. Ollie Monroe and Gaynelle Annette (Sharpe) Bowman; m. David Keith Randall, Feb. 14, 1992; 1 child, Sterling Noelle. BS in Mktg., Hampton U., 1986. Admissions counselor Hampton U., 1984-87; equal employment specialist U.S. Dept. Def., Warren, Mich., 1987—; owner Diversified Writing and Bus. Svcs., Oak Park, Mich., 1989—. Author poetry and children's books. Mem. NAFE, Internat. Women's Writing Guild, Nat. Writers Assn., Alpha Kappa Alpha. Democrat. Presbyterian.

BOWYER, JAMES LOUIS, forester educator; b. Shorewood, Wis., Dec. 18, 1942; s. Raymond Herbert and Jean Virginia (Bennington) B.; m. Ruth Ann Baker, Aug. 22, 1964; children: Kimberly, Jeffrey. BS in Forest Mgmt., Okla. State U., 1964; MS in Forest Products, Mich. State U., 1965; PhD in Wood Sci. & Tech., U. Minn., 1972. Economist Forestry Scis. Lab. U.S. Forest Svc., Princeton, W.Va., 1966; prof. forest products Dept. Forest Products U. Minn., St. Paul, 1973—, head Dept. Forest Products, 1984-95, dir. forest products mgmt. devel. inst., 1995—; sci. adv. Temperate Forest Found., Beaverton, Oreg., 1990—; pvt. cons. in field; external examiner cum assessor U. Portanian Malaysia, Selangor, 1993-95; bd. dirs. Tropical Forest Found., Alexandria, Va. Author: (book) Introduction to Frest Products and Wood Science, 1st edit., 1982, 2nd edit., 1989, 3rd edit., 1996; contbr. over 120 articles to profl. jours. Lt.(j.g.) USN, 1966-69. Recipient J.C. Ryan Outstanding Svc. award for Contbns. to the Forestry Profession, Minn. Dept. of Natural Resources, 1993, Disting. Svc. award Forest Products Frat. of Mpls., 1994. Fellow Internat. Acad. Wood Sci.; mem. Soc. Wood Sci. and Tech. (pres. 1987-88), Minn. Forestry Assn., Internat. Acad. Wood Anatomists, Soc. Am. Foresters, Forest Porducts Soc. (pres. 1993-94). Office: U Minn Dept of Forest Products 2004 Folwell Ave Saint Paul MN 55108

BOX, ROBERT ALLEN, minister; b. Kansas City, Mo., July 15, 1937; s. Otic Cecil and Lois Irene (Davis) B.; married, June 24, 1966; children: Melinda June, Juliette Anne, Tamara Louise. BA, Ottawa U., 1964; BD, Ctrl. Bapt. Theol. Sem., 1967; DMin, Midwest Bapt. Theol. Sem., 1977. Ordained to ministry Am. Baptist Chs., 1967. Pastor First Bapt. Ch., Alden, Kans., 1967-70; sr. pastor Victory Hills Bapt. Ch., Kansas City, Kans., 1970-78; sr. pastor First Bapt. Ch., Wyandotte, Mich., 1978-82, Galesburg, Ill., 1982-88, Augusta, Kans., 1988—; adj. prof. Butler County C.C., El Dorado, Kans., 1995; bd. dirs. Ctrl. Bapt. Cem., Kansas City, 1976-79; bd. dirs. Ctrl. region Am. Bapt. Ch., 1972-78, 89-93, Mich. region, 1979-82, Gt. Rivers region, 1984-88; tour dir. to Israel, Gt. Britain, china, Europe. Contbr. articles to devotional book and newspapers. Chmn. Human Rights Commn., Galesburg, 1986-88; police chaplain Augusta Safety Dept., 1995—. Mem. Internat. Conf. Police Chaplains, ABC Chaplains, ABC Colloquium, Rotary Club (v.p. 1982-88), Optimist Club (bd. dirs. 1989-93). Home: 1524 State St Augusta KS 67010 Office: First Bapt Ch 1501 State St Augusta KS 67010

BOX, THOMAS MORGAN, management consultant, educator; b. Cleve., July 12, 1937; s. Bert William and Margaret Kathryn (Williams) B.; m. Barbara Jean Grden, Nov. 25, 1961; children: Anne Louise, Valerie Morgan, Thomas Morgan. BS in Math., U. Tulsa, 1977, MBA, 1979, PhD, Okla. State, 1988. Mgr. prodn. and inventory Kirby Bldg. Systems, Houston, 1968-69; v.p., div. mgr. Riverside Industries, Tulsa, 1969-72; v.p. ops. Braden Steel, Tulsa, 1972-80; sr. v.p. Southwest Tube Mfg., Tulsa, 1980-84; ptnr. Webb Shirley and Box, Tulsa, 1984-86; ptnr. H&B Assocs., 1986—; asst. prof. U. Tulsa, 1984-89; dir. Small Bus. Inst. Pitts. State U., 1990—. Vol. United Way, 1977, Walk for Mankind, 1978. Served with USMC, 1956-59. Nat. Merit Scholar, 1955; John Huntington Fund. grantee, 1956. Mem. Am. Mktg. Assn. (bd. dirs Tulsa Chpt.), Am. Prodn. & Inventory Control Soc., Am. Soc. Quality Control, Acad. of Mgmt. Roman Catholic. Condr. research in field. Home: 4304 E 83rd St Tulsa OK 74137-1815 Office: Pitts State Univ 110 Kelce Pittsburg KS 66762

BOYATZIS, RICHARD ELEFTHERIOS, academic administrator; b. N.Y.C., Oct. 1, 1946; s. Kyriakos Eleftherios and Sophia (Glacous) B.; m. Sandra Scott, Sept. 17, 1977. BS in Aero. & Astronautic, MIT, 1968; MA in Social Psychology, Harvard U., 1970, PhD, 1973. Engr. Northrop/Norair, Los Angeles, 1966-67; pvt. practice cons. Boston, 1967-72; consulting psychologist Veterans Adminstrn. Hosp., Brockton, Mass., 1970-72; dir. research McBer and Co., Boston, 1972-76, pres., chief exec. officer, 1976-87; assoc. prof. dept. organizational behavior Case Western Reserve Univ., Cleve., 1987-90, prof. leadership and adult devel., 1990—, chair dept. orgnl. behavior, 1996—, assoc. dean exec. edn., 1996—; dir., trustee Coun. for Adult Exptl. Learning, Chgo., 1989-95, Grad. Mgmt. Admissions Coun., 1995—. Author: The Competent Manager, 1982; co-author: Innovations in Professional Education: Steps on a Journey from Teaching to Learning, 1995. Mem. Instrnl. Systems Assn. (pres. 1987-89, v.p. 1985-87, 89-91), Am. Psychol. Assn., Acad. Mgmt. Office: Case Western Res Univ Weatherhead Sch Mgmt 10900 Euclid Ave Cleveland OH 44106-7235

BOYCE, DANIEL HOBBS, financial planning company executive; b. Flint, Mich., Oct. 19, 1953; s. James Edward and Alice Marilyn (Hobbs) B.; m. Suzanne Kay Williams; children: Kenneth C., Geoffrey A., Stephen J. BA, U. Mich., 1974, MA, 1979. Cert. fin. planner; cert. investment mgmt. cons. Rep. Mut. Svc. Corp., Detroit, 1982-87; br. mgr. Investment Mgmt. & Rsch. Inc., Atlanta, 1987—; treas., chief fin. officer Ctr. Fin. Planning Inc., Southfield, Mich., 1988-90; v.p. Southworth, Boyce & McFawn Planning Corp., Troy, Mich., 1982-85; owner, fin. planner Daniel H. Boyce Fin. Adv. Svcs., Birmingham, Mich., 1985-88; mem. adj. faculty Coll. Fin. Planning, Denver, 1985-90; mem. adv. coun. cert. program in personel fin. planning Oakland U., Rochester, Mich., 1987—; edn. cons. Nat. Ctr. for Fin. Edn., Denver, 1985—. Bi-weekly columnist Money Matters, Legal News newsletter, 1984-86; monthly columnist Personal Fin. for suburban Detroit newspaper chain, 1987-93. Mem. Internat. Assn. Fin. Planning (bd. dirs. S.E. Mich. chpt. 1984-87, 89-91), Inst. for Investment Mgmt. Cons., Internat. Soc. Cert. Employee Benefit Specialists, Detroit Soc. Inst. CFPs (pres. 1986-87, chmn. 1987-88), Detroit Chamber Winds (bd. dirs., pres. 1995—). Office: Ctr Fin Planning Inc 26211 Central Park Blvd Ste 604 Southfield MI 48076-4164

BOYCE, MARK STEPHEN, ecology educator; b. Yankton, S.D., May 24, 1950; s. John Harold and Mirriam (Dahl) B.; m. Jaren Jeanette Evers, May 29, 1971 (dec. 1981); 1 child, Cody James; m. Evelyn Hunter Merrill, July 31, 1987; 1 child, Aaron LaVon. BS, Iowa State U., 1972; MS, U. Alaska, 1974; MPhil, Yale U., 1975, PhD, 1977. Instr. U. Wyo., Laramie, 1976-77, asst. prof. Zoology, 1977-81, assoc. prof. Zoology, 1981-87, vis. prof. Math., 1984-85, prof. Zoology and Physiology, 1987-93, dir. Nat. Park Rsch. Ctr., 1989-92; Vallier chair ecology, disting. prof. U. Wis., Stevens Point, 1993—; postdoctoral fellow Oxford (Eng.) U., 1982-83. Author: The Jackson Elk Herd, 1989; editor: North American Elk, 1979, Evolution of Life Histories of Mammals, 1988, The Greater Yellowstone Ecosystem, 1991; assoc. editor: IMA Jour. Math. Applied Biology and Medicine, 1986-94, Ecologia Montana, 1991—; editor-in-chief Jour. Wildlife Mgmt., 1995—; contbr. articles to profl. jours. Recipient Outstanding Achievement award U. Alaska, 1974; Frederick Vanderbilt fellow Yale U., 1976, Fulbright fellow, India, 1991; exch. scholar NAS, Poland, 1982. Mem. Am. Soc. Naturalists, Am. Soc. Mammalogists, Brit. Ecol. Soc., Ecol. Soc. Am., Wildlife Soc., Sigma Xi (Faculty Scholar award 1994), Gamma Sigma Delta. Home: 2208 County Rd P Stevens Point WI 54481 Office: Coll Natural Resources Univ Wis Stevens Point WI 54481-3897

BOYD, ADELINE SMITH, art history educator; b. St. Louis, Nov. 10, 1910; d. Luther Ely and Salees (Kennard) Smith; m. Ingram F. Boyd Jr., Oct. 6, 1931; children: Sally, Stephen, Anne, Louise. Student, John Burroughs Sch., St. Louis, 1921-28, Vassar Coll., Poughkeepsie, N.Y., 1929, 30; BA, Washington U., St. Louis, 1942. Mem. of edn. dept. St. Louis Art Mus., 1959-64; mem. Asian studies dept. Washington U., St. Louis, 1964-70, dept. Chinese and Japanese, 1970-90; founding mem. Friend's of St. Louis Art Mus., 1940—. Bd. pres. Edgewood Childrens Ctr., St. Louis, 1943-44; bd. dirs. Little Symphony, St. Louis, 1956—; citizens com. Honer Phillips Hosp., St. Louis, Adv. com., City Plan Commn. Mem. Phi Beta Kappa.

BOYD, ARTHUR BERNETTE, JR., surgeon, clergyman, beverage company executive; b. Durham, N.C., June 29, 1947; s. Arthur Bernette and Mammie Lee (Chalmers) B.; m. Delphine Victoria Huffman, Mar. 14, 1981; children: Arthur III, Vicki. BA, Fla. A&M Univ., 1969; postgrad., NYU, 1970; MD, Meharry Med. Coll., 1978. Cert. ATLS instr., PALS. Intern in surgery Howard Univ. Hosp., Washington, 1978-80; resident and chief resident in surgery St. Luke's Hosp., Cleve., 1981-84; fellow in liver transplant U. Pitts., 1984-85; chief adminstrv. fellow trauma/surg. critical care R.A. Cowley Shock Trauma Ctr., U. Md. Med. Sys., Cali, Colombia, 1993-94; clin. instr. surgery, sr. fellow, traumatologist R.A. Cowley Shock Trauma Ctr., U. Md. Med. Sys., Baltimore County, 1994—; co-traumatologist Prince George Cmty. Hosp., Cheverly, Md., 1994-95; chief surgeon, pres. Phoenix Med. Surgical Svc., Inc., Cleve., Carribean, 1986—; clin. instr. surgery, sr. trauma fellow Shock Trauma Ctr. U. Md. Med. Ctr., Balt., 1995-96; pres., CEO Motown Beverage Co. of Ohio, Cleve., 1988—, Towne Club Internat. of Ohio, Inc., Cleve., 1988—; chief adminstrv. fellow in trauma/crit. care R.A. Cowley Shock Trauma Ctr./U. Md. Med. Systems, 1993-94, clin. instr., sr. trauma rsch. fellow, 1994-95; sr. trauma fellow, clin. instr. Shock Trauma Ctr./U. Md., 1995; adj. prof. Anatomy and Physiology Cuyhoga C.C., Cleve., 1988—; cons. surgeon other hosps. and physicians, Cleve., 1988—. Inventor: wheelchair with mechanism to raise or lower left or right buttocks of person, hemostat that carries two sutures, synthetic covering with zipper to cover bowel when abdomen unable to be closed after surgery. Vol. Cleve. Community Action Against Addiction, 1987-88; mentor Case Western U. Inner City Program, Cleve., 1988—. Fellow ACS (assoc.), Internat. Coll. Surgeons; mem. AAAS, AMA, N.Y. Acad. Scis., Nat. Med. Assn. (mentor 1990—), Ohio State Med. Soc., Cleve. Surg. Soc., Nat. Assn. Small Bus. Owners, Internat. Assn. Small Bus. Owners, Greater Cleve. Urban League, Masons, Omega Psi Phi, Alpha Phi Omega. Democrat. Methodist. Home and Office: Motown Beverage Co 22462 Westchester Rd Shaker Heights OH 44122-4863

BOYD, BARBARA, state legislator; m. Robert Boyd; 1 child, Janine. BS, St. Paul's Coll., 1965. Mem. Ohio Ho. of Reps., Columbus, 1992—. Named Officer of Yr. No. Ohio Police Benevolent Assn., 1989; recipient Black Women's History award, 1992. Mem. LWV, Delta Sigma Theta.

BOYD, BEVERLY, English literature educator; b. Bklyn., Mar. 27, 1925; d. James Gray and Elspeth Kathleen (Mossop) B. BA, Bklyn. Coll., 1946; MA, Columbia U., 1948, PhD, 1955. Instr. English Bklyn. Coll., N.Y.C., 1947, U. Tex., Austin, 1955-57; prof. English Radford (Va.) Coll., 1957-62; from asst. prof. to prof. English U. Kans., Lawrence, 1962—. Author: The Middle English Miracles of the Virgin, 1963, Chaucer and the Liturgy, 1967, Chaucer and the Medieval Book, 1973, Chaucer According to William Caxton, 1978, (verse) Philippine's Windows, 1988; contbr. chpts. to books. Recipient Disting. Alumna award Bklyn. Coll., 1979; Guggenheim fellow, 1969; Huntington Libr. fellow, 1960, 75. Office: U Kans Dept of English Lawrence KS 66045

BOYD, MARY DEXTER, newspaper editor; b. Columbus, Ga., Feb. 5, 1913; d. Charles Amory and Lydia Cook (Folwell) Dexter; m. Francis William Boyd, Jr., Sept. 1, 1934 (dec. July 1972); children—Robert Alexander, Richard Dexter, Mary Frances Boyd Logback, Elizabeth Folwell Boyd James. Student Agnes Scott Coll., 1930-31; B.S., Kans. State U., 1934. Cert. tchr., Kans. Tchr., Kensington High Sch., Kans., 1934-35; asst. editor Jewell County Record, Mankato, Kans., 1940-72, editor, 1972-91; ret. 1991. Mem. Comml. Devel. Assn., Mankato, 1972-91 , Mankato Endowment Assn., 1972—, Housing Authority City of Mankato, 1975—, Jewell County Fair Bd., 1980—. Mem. Kans. Press Assn., Kans. Press Women, Omicron Nu, Kappa Alpha, Xo Chi Omega (v.p. 1932-33). Clubs: Modern Minerva (pres. 1939-40), Desire Tobey Sears, DAR, P.E.O.. Home: 405 S Center St Mankato KS 66956-2507

BOYD, RICHARD LYN, secondary school educator; b. Edmore, Mich., Jan. 2, 1953; s. Clinton Adelina and Mildred (Camp) B.; m. Debra Lyn, Mar. 6, 1982. BS, Cen. Mich. U., 1975; MS, Ind. U., Ft. Wayne, 1980. Tchr./coach Garrett Keyser Butler Schs., Garrett, Ind., 1975-85; tchr./coach DeKalb Cen. Schs., Waterloo, Ind., 1985-90, computer coord., 1990—, track, football coach, 1985—; asst. coach Ind. All-Star Track and Field team, 1991-93, head coach, 1994. Sponsor Fellowship of Christian Athletes. Named Coach of the Yr. Auburn Evening Star, 1991, 92, Northeast Hoosier Conf., 1991. Mem. Ind. Coaches of Track and Cross Country (sectional rep. 1991-93), Ind. State Tchrs. Assn., Ind. Computer Educators Assn., Ind. High Sch. Football Coaches Assn.

BOYD, ROBERT COTTON, English language educator; b. Little Rock, Sept. 20, 1938; s. Robert Hampton and Jessie Leigh (Cotton) B.; m. Katherine Lenore Rock, Jan. 3, 1964; children: Robert Rock, Katherine Anne, Elizabeth Leigh. BA, U. Ark., 1965; postgrad., U. Hamburg, Fed. Republic of Germany, 1965-66; MA, U. Ark., 1967; PhD, Ind. U., 1989. Instr. English Ind. State U., Terre Haute, 1966-70; prof. English St. Louis Community Coll., 1970—, asst. chair english dept., 1993—; editor Webster Review, 1992-96; theater critic Sta. KWMU-FM, St. Louis, 1980-94, Sta. KDHX, St. Louis, 1995—. Mem. editl. bd. Gateway Heritage mag., 1996—. Mem. St. Louis-Lyon Sister Cities Com., 1988—, treas., 1993-96; pres. Kirkwood chpt. Am. Field Svc., 1986-87. Recipient Guy Owen Poetry prize So. Poetry Rev., 1991, Poetry award Mo. Writers' Week, 1995. Mem. Nat. Coun. Tchrs. English, Conf. on Coll. Composition and Comm. Democrat. Unitarian. Home: 804 Lisakay Dr Saint Louis MO 63122-3128 Office: St Louis Community Coll 11333 Big Bend Blvd Saint Louis MO 63122-5720

BOYD, STEVEN R., stockbroker; b. Ainsworth, Nebr., July 14, 1950. BS, U. Nebr., 1972. Stockbroker Perkins Smart & Co. (formerly Brown Church Securities), Wichita, Kans., 1973—. Mem. Masons, Jesters. Republican. Methodist. Office: Perkins Smart & Co. 400 S Broadway St Wichita KS 67202-3910

BOYD, WILLARD LEE, museum administrator, educator, lawyer, professor; b. St. Paul, Mar. 29, 1927; s. Willard Lee and Frances L. (Collins) B.; m.

Susan Kuehn, Aug. 28, 1954; children: Elizabeth Kuehn, Willard Lee, Thomas Henry. BS in Law, U. Minn., 1949, LLB, 1951; LLM, U. Mich., 1952, SJD, 1962. Bar: Minn. 1951, Iowa 1958. Assoc. Dorsey & Whitney, Mpls., 1952-54; from instr. to prof. law U. Iowa, Iowa City, 1954-64, assoc. dean Law Sch., 1964, v.p. acad. affairs, 1964-69, pres., 1969-81, pres. emeritus, 1981—; pres. The Field Mus., Chgo., 1981-96, pres. emeritus, 1996—; chmn. Nat. Mus. Scis. Bd., 1988-96. Bd. dirs. Am. Coun. on Arts, Ill. Arts Coun., Northwestern Meml. Hosp.; mem. adv. bd. Cabrini-Green Legal Aid Clinic, Chgo. Dept. Cultural Affairs; chmn. Nat. Mus. Svcs. Bd., Ctr. for Rsch. Librs., Chgo.; past mem. adv. bd. Met. Opera; past adv. com. Getty Ctr. for Edn. in Arts, Ill. Humanities Coun. Recipient Charles Frankel prize Nat. Endowment for Humanities, 1989. Mem. ABA (mem. sect. legal edn. and admission to bar chmn. 1980-81, coun. mem. 1975-82, com. social labor and indsl. legislations 1963-65, chmn. 1965-66, chmn. coun. of sect. on legal edn. and admission), Am. Assn. Univs. (chmn.), Nat. Commn. Accrediting (pres.), Nat. Coun. on Arts, Iowa Bar Assn. Home: 3800 N Lake Shore Dr Apt 3A Chicago IL 60613-3313 Office: Field Mus Natural History Roosevelt Rd at Lakeshore Dr Chicago IL 60605

BOYER, DON RAYMOND, biology educator; b. Lexington, Okla., Mar. 31, 1929; s. Raymond Henry and Mary Nash (Connolly) B.; m. Phyllis Ann Richardson, Dec. 29, 1959 (div. Aug. 1981); children: Brian T., Barry R., Heather Ann. BS, U. Okla., 1950, MS, 1953; PhD, Tulane U., 1958. Instr. dept. zoology Tulane U., New Orleans, 1958; from asst. prof. to prof. biology Washburn U., Topeka, 1958—. Contbr. articles to profl. jours. 1st lt. arty. U.S. Army, 1950-52, Korea. NIH rsch. grantee, 1960-68. Mem. AAAS, Am. Soc. Ichthyologists and Herpetologists. Office: Washburn U 17th and College Sts Topeka KS 66621

BOYER, KENNETH DUNCAN, economics educator; b. N.Y.C., June 30, 1948; s. Carl Benjamin and Marjorie (Nice) B.; m. Suzanne Patricia Tainter, Aug. 1, 1981; children: Elizabeth, Margaret, Mark. BA, Amherst Coll., 1970; MA, U. Mich., 1972, PhD, 1975. Asst. prof. econs. Mich. State U., East Lansing, 1975-79, assoc. prof. econs., 1979-84, prof. econs., 1984—; mem. commn. to study freight transport NAS Transp. Rsch. Bd., Washington, 1993-95; prof. Sino-Am. Econs. Tng. Ctr., Shanghai, China, 1988. Author: Principles of Transportation Economics, 1996; editor: Economic Regulation, 1981. Mem. Am. Econs. Assn. Home: 711 Amherst Ave Ann Arbor MI 48105 Office: Michigan State Univ Dept Economics Marshall Hall East Lansing MI 48824-1058

BOYER, KEVIN GARY, marketing professional; b. Salt Lake City, Jan. 22, 1963; s. Carl J. and Kathryn (Dean) B. BS, Weber State U., 1986; MS, U. Oreg., 1988. Pres. Comm. Mgmt., Inc., Wilmette, Ill., 1990—; adminstr. Promotional Products Assn. Chgo., 1993—; adminstr. Chgo. Chpt. ASTD, 1994—. Vol. Stop AIDS Chgo., 1989-91, Art Inst. Chgo., 1989-91, Gerber-Hart Libr., Chgo., 1989—; pres. Grad. Student Assn./Northwestern U., 1988-90; mem. Ill. Gay and Lesbian Task Force; pres. Gerber/Hart Gay and Lesbian Libr. and Archives, Chgo., 1994-95, bd. dirs., 1993-94, 96—; bd. dirs. Gay/Lesbian/Straight Tchrs. Network, N.Y.C., 1996—. Nat. Debate Champion, Cross Examination Debate Assn., Ogden, Utah, 1985. Mem. U. Oreg. Alumni Assn. (bd. dirs. Chgo. chpt. 1989-92), YMCA Youth Gov.'s Assn., Nat. Assn. Grad./Profl. Students (bd. dirs. 1988-89, exec. dir. 1990—), Chgo. Area Gay and Lesbian C. of C. (co-chair 1996—). Democrat. Office: Communication Mgmt Inc 825 Green Bay Rd Ste 270 Wilmette IL 60091-2500

BOYER, NICODEMUS ELIJAH, organic-polymer chemist, consultant; b. Daugavpils, Latgale, Latvia, June 1, 1925; came to U.S., 1949; s. Aloizs and Elvira Adele (Buchholtz) Bojars; married. BS in Natural Scis., U. Göttingen, Germany, 1949; PhD in Chemistry, U. Ill., 1955; postgrad., Princeton U., 1955-56. Sch. chemist Hooker Chem. Corp., Niagara Falls, N.Y., 1956-61; project leader, lectr. Ill. Inst. Tech., Chgo., 1961-63; rsch. fellow Borg-Warner Chems., Washington, 1964-76; sr. staff mem. Raychem Corp., Menlo Park, Calif., 1976-78; asst. prof. Ind. State U., Terre Haute, 1978-80; sr. rsch. assoc. PPG Industries, Chgo., 1980-88; sr. cons. Delta Sci. Cons., Parkersburg, W.Va., 1988-92, Three Rivers, Mich., 1992—; lectr. evening sch. U. Buffalo, 1958-60; prof. Glen Oaks Coll., Centreville, Mich., 1995-96. Vol. abstractor Chem. Abstracts Svc., Columbus, Ohio, 1958-71; editor Cosmology Technikas Apskats, Montreal, Que., Can., 1987-93; author: Organophosphorus Chemistry, Vol. 1, 1957, Vol. 2, 1959, Radiation Chemistry: Monomers and Polymers, 1977, A New Theory of Cosmology, 1983, The Physics of Creation, 2 vols., 1990, Fire Retardants: A Review and Selected Patents, 1991, Cosmogony, 1992; contbr. over 70 articles to profl. jours.; 180 chemistry patents. Founding mem. Latvian Cath. Students' Assn., Germany, 1946-64; vice chmn. Latvian Acad. Soc. Valdemarija, Ill., Calif., Mich., 1964—; mem. Rep. Presdl. Task Force, 1989-93. With U.S. Army, 1945. Internat. Refugee Orgn. scholar U. Göttingen, 1946-49, Nat. Cath. Welfare Conf. scholar U. Ill., 1949-51; recipient Quality Control & Safety award PPG Industries Inc., 1987. Mem. AAAS, Am. Chem. Soc., N.Y. Acad. Scis. (life), Latvian Acad. Scis., U. Ill. Alumni Assn., Phi Lambda Upsilon, Sigma Xi. Republican. Roman Catholic. Office: Delta Sci Cons PO Box 312 Three Rivers MI 49093-0312

BOYER, RICHARD WAKEFIELD, stockbroker; b. Kansas City, Kans., May 8, 1954. BA, U. Kans., 1977. Stock assn. v.p. Kidder, Peabody, Kansas City, Mo., 1981-94; account v.p. Paine Webber, Kansas City, 1994—. Author quar. newsletter. Republican.

BOYER, ROBERT LEWIS, photographer; b. Wooster, Ohio, Oct. 6, 1953; s. Lloyd Leroy and Margaret White (Anderson) B.; m. Debra Joy Kramer, July 10, 1988; 1 child, Theodore Lee. AAS, U. Akron, 1980, Rochester Inst. Tech., 1981; BFA, Rochester Inst. Tech., 1982. Sr. photographer The Reuben Group, Cleve., 1983—. Recipient 1st place color photography award Wayne County Ctr. for Arts, Wooster, 1978, Merit award "Rose Show", Cleve. Soc. Communicating Arts, Cleve., 1988, Svc. award Wayne Coll., U. Akron, Orrville, Ohio, 1975. Mem. Am. Soc. Media Photographers (bd. mem., sec. 1994-95 Ohio North Coast chpt.). Home: 203 James Cir Avon Lake OH 44012-1533 Office: The Reuben Group 2215 Saint Clair Ave NE Cleveland OH 44114-4046

BOYERS, JANETH MAUREE, interior designer; b. Wauseon, Ohio, Nov. 15, 1931; d. Ralph Harry Monroe and Fern Amanda (Nofziger) Slagle; m. Jerry Lee Boyers, Mar. 29, 1953; children: J.C., Nadine Magee, Matthew. Student, LaSalle U., Chgo., 1976-77. Sec. City Loan & Savings Co., Wauseon, Ohio, 1949-55; contr. Boyers Constrn. Co., Wauseon, Ohio, 1971-83; pvt. practice Wauseon, Ohio, 1983—; cons. Home Enterprises, Inc., 1982—, Interior Design firm. Dir. Community Choirs. Mem. Allied Am. Soc. of Interior Designers. Republican. Office: Home Enterprises Inc PO Box 209 Wauseon OH 43567-0209

BOYKE, PAUL WILLIAM, association executive; b. Chgo., Oct. 31, 1940; s. John Thomas and Gertrude (Barlick) B.; m. Virginia Louise Polk, Aug. 6, 1967; children: Laura E., Suzanne B. BSBA, Elmhurst (Ill.) Coll., 1967; MBA, Northwestern U., 1972. CPA, Ill., Minn. Staff acct. Price Waterhouse & Co., Chgo., 1967-71; v.p., contr. Am. Hosp. Supply Co., Evanston, Ill., 1971-77; v.p. ops. Patterson Dental Co., Bloomington, Minn., 1977-85; chief operating officer Oppenheimer Wolff & Donnelly, Mpls., 1985-93; sr. v.p. for fin. and adminstrn. Am. Hosp. Assn., Chgo., 1993—; chmn. Am. Hosp. Assn. Svcs. Inc., Chgo., 1993—; bd. dirs. Am. Hosp. Svcs. Inc., Am. Hosp. Publ. Inc., Am. Hosp. Ins. Resources Inc. and Am. Hosp. Assn. Investment Funds. Bd. advisors Internat. Bus. Ctr., St. Cloud (Minn.) State U.; bd. dirs. Village Ranch. Mem. AICPA, Fin. Execs. Inst., Minn. Soc. CPAs, Healthcare Fin. Mgmt. Assn., The Execs. Club of Chgo. Republican. Home: 260 Aberdeen Dr Barrington Hills IL 60010 Office: Am Hosp Assn 1 N Franklin St Chicago IL 60606-3421

BOYKIN, NANCY MERRITT, academic administrator; b. Washington, Mar. 20; d. Matthew and Mary Gertrude (White) Merritt; m. Ulysses Wilhelm Boykin, Apr. 17, 1965 (dec. 1987); 1 child by previous marriage, Taunya Lovell Banks. BS, D.C. Tchrs. Coll.; MA, Howard U., MSW, 1965; PhD, U. Mich., 1976. Employee rels. counselor Office Chief of Fin., U.S. Army, Washington; adminstrv. asst. to Civilian Aide to Sec. of Def., Washington; policewoman Met. Police Dept., Washington; social worker Dept. Pub. Welfare, Washington; adminstrv. asst. to dir. Active Community Teams, Inc., Detroit, 1965-66; dir. continuing edn. for girls program Detroit Pub. Schs., 1966-87; ednl. cons. and community outreach coord. New Health Ctr., Livonia, Mich., 1988-90; cons U.S. Dept. Edn., 1982; presdl. appointee Nat. Adv. Coun. on Extension and Continuing Edn., 1973-80. Contbr. articles to profl. jours. Mem. Mich. Bd. Examiners of Social Workers, 1978-83; mem. Mich. Rep. Com., 1975-80, 83—; presdl. appointee to nat. adv. bd. C.C. of Air Force, 1984—; gov.'s appointee Mich. Youth Adv. Com., 1984-87, Commn. on Svcs. to Aging, 1992—; sec. 1st Rep. Dist., 1973-77; mem. Nat. Black Republicans., 1972—. Named Educator of Yr., Nat. Black Women's Polit. Leadership Caucus, 1981, Hon. Lt. Col. Aide De Camp in Ala. Militia, Gov. Wallace, 1986; recipient Disting. Contbn. placque Pres.'s Nat. Adv. Com., 1973-80, Spirit of Detroit award, 1979, Meritorious Svc. plaque, Air Force Bd. Vis., 1986, Superior Svc. to USAF Enlisted Pers. plaque, Air Force Bd. Vis., 1986, Nat. Kool Achiever's award in Edn. Brown and Williams Tobacco Co., 1987, Outstanding Contbns. to Community award Assn. Black Judges Mich., 1988-90, Community Svc. award YWCA, 1992, plaque for Svc. on Bd. Dirs., Lula Belle Stewart Ctr., Inc., 1994, Pioneer award Frederick Douglas Soc., 1994, others; The Nancy Boykin Continuing Edn. Ctr. named in her honor Detroit Pub. Sch. Bd., 1993; honored by Spl. Legis. Tribute for advocacy of comprehensive edn. for student parents, State of Mich., 1993. Mem. Profl. Women's Network, Nat. Assn. Supervision and Curriculum Devel., Detroit Orgn. of Sch. Adminstrs., Nat. Assn. Black Sch. Educators, Detroit Assn. Univ. Mich. Women, Sch. Edn. Alumni Assn. Wayne State U. (bd. govs.), U. Mich. Alumnae Assn., Mich. Assn. Concerned with Sch. Age Parents (founding mem., past pres., Recognition award, 1986, Outstanding Svc. award 1993), Phi Delta Kappa (U. of M. chpt.), Eta Phi Beta (Outstanding Profl. Woman award 1992), Alpha Kappa Alpha. Home and Office: 17224 Fairfield St Detroit MI 48221-3084

BOYKO, CHRISTOPHER ALLAN, lawyer, judge; b. Cleve., Oct. 10, 1954; s. Andrew and Eva Dorothy (Zepko) B.; m. Roberta Ann Gentile, May 29, 1981; children: Philip, Ashley. B in Polit. Sci. cum laude, Mt. Union Coll., 1976; JD, Cleve. Marshall Coll. Law, 1979. Bar: Ohio 1979, U.S. Dist. Ct. (no. dist.) Ohio 1979, Fla. 1985, U.S. Tax Ct. 1986. Prin. Boyko & Boyko, Parma, Ohio, 1979—; asst. prosecutor City of Parma, 1981-87, dir. of law, 1987-93; gen. counsel Mural & Sons, Inc., 1983, C & D Truck Service & Equipment, Inc., 1986—, Bethel Temple, 1987—; sec., gen. counsel Charles Schulz Bldg. Co. Inc., Cleve., 1986—; exec. v.p., gen. counsel copy Am., Inc., 1993-94; judge Parma Mcpl. Court, 1993; ptnr. Boyko & Boyko, Attys., Parma, 1994—; judge Ct. Common Pleas, Cuyahoga County, Ohio, 1996—; exec. v.p., gen. counsel, bd. dirs. Copy Am., Inc., 1994; guardian ad litem Juvenile Ct., 1979—; legal advisor spl. weapons and tactics divsn. City of Parma Police Dept., 1984—; gen. counsel Indsl. Surface Sealer, Inc., 1985—; chief counsel S.W. Enforcement Bur., 1991—. Active Citizens League of Greater Cleve., 1985—; ctrl. committeeman Dem. Party, Parma, 1984-87; mem. exec. com. County Dem. Party, 1992—; mem. Parma Drug Task Force, 1987—; mem. adv. com. Paradale Children's Svcs., 1991—. Mem. ABA, Fla. Bar Assn., Ohio Bar Assn., Cleve. Bar Assn., Parma Bar Assn. (pres., trustee) Ukrainian Bar Assn., Internat. Platform Assn., Cuyahoga County Police Chief Assn. (assoc.), Narcotics Law Officers Assn., Cleve. Am. Mid. Eastern Orgn., Mt. Union Coll. Alumni Assn., Cleve. Marshall Law Sch. Alumni Assn., Elks. Byzantine Catholic. Home: 5291 Huntington Reserve Dr Parma OH 44134-6172 Office: Justice Ctr 1200 Ontario St Cleveland OH 44113

BOYLAN, BRIAN RICHARD, author, producer, photographer, director, literary agent; b. Chgo., Dec. 11, 1936, s. Francis Thomas and Mary Catherine (Kane) B.; children: Rebecca, Gregory, Ingrid. Student Loyola U., 1954-58; DD, Universal Ch., 1969. CEO Otitis Media Literary Agy., exec. prodr. OTM Prodns., audio-video prodr. Media Medica. Editor Jour. AMA, Med. World News, Modern Medicine, 1956-77; author: The New Heart, 1969, Infidelity, 1971, The Legal Rights of Women, 1973, Benedict Arnold: The Dark Eagle, 1973, A Hack in a Hurry, 1980, Final Trace, 1983 ; works include 15 books, 3 plays, 3 screenplays; book reviewer, critic 1952—; photographer, 1962—; theatre dir., 1970—; directed works include 31 plays, videotapes and films. Home: 1926 Dupont Ave S Minneapolis MN 55403-3035

BOYLE, BRADLEY CHARLES, civil engineer; b. St. Paul, Dec. 18, 1959; s. Fosten Annett and Beverly Ann (Rehbein) B.; m. Dana Satenick Ramezzano, Aug. 20, 1983. BSCE, U. Minn., 1984, MBA, 1995. Rsch. asst., environ. engring. dept. U. Minn., Mpls., 1984-85; project mgr. Ramsey Engring. Co., St. Paul, 1985-87, N.W. Airlines, Inc., St. Paul, 1987-91; mktg. dir. M.A. Mortenson Co., Mpls., 1991-93; market devel. dir. Image Sensing Sys., Inc., St. Paul, 1995—. Mem. ASCE, Am. Soc. Metals, U. Minn. Alumni Assn., Minn. Surveyors and Engrs. Soc., Chi Epsilon, Beta Gamma Sigma. Republican. Episcopalian. Home: 1565 Tamberwood Tr Woodbury MN 55125 Office: Image Sensing Sys Inc Ste 500 1600 University Ave W Saint Paul MN 55104

BOYLE, FRANK JAMES, state legislator; b. Phillips, Wis., Feb. 20, 1945; s. Frank and Mary Boyle; m. Kate Boyle; children: Annie, Patrick. BA, U. Wis., 1967. Former bldg. contractor and constrn. worker. Mgmt. commr. Douling Lake, Wis., 1976—; former county supr. Douglas County Bd.; state assemblyman dist. 73 State of Wis., 1986—; sec. Douglas County Dem. Com.; pres. Tri-Lake Civic Club; v.p. Summit Vol. Fire Dept. Mem. Am. Legion. Home: RR 1 Box 175 Superior WI 54880-9730*

BOYLE, GLEN A., business executive; b. Milw., Wis., Dec. 2, 1961. Law clk. State of Calif., San Francisco, 1986-88; mgr. Cost Care, Inc., Huntington Beach, Calif., 1988-90; pres. Midwest Comp Review Svcs., Racine, Wis., 1990—. Roman Catholic. Office: Midwest Comp Review Svcs P O Box 81365 Racine WI 53408-7956

BOYLE, KAMMER, management psychologist; b. New Orleans, June 17, 1946; d. Benjamin Franklin and Ethel Clair (Kammer) B.; m. Edward Turner Barfield, July 23, 1966 (div. 1975); children: Darren Barfield, Meloe Barfield. BS in Mgmt., magna cum laude, U. West Fla., 1976; PhD in Indsl./Organizational Psychology, U. Tenn., 1982. Lic. psychologist, Ohio, Tenn. Pvt. practice mgmt. psychology, Knoxville, 1978-81; teaching and research asst. U. Tenn., Knoxville, 1977-81; mgmt. trainer U.S. State Dept., Washington, 1978; cons. PRADCO, Cleve., 1982-83; pres., cons. Mgmt. and Assessment Services, Inc., Cleve., 1983—; pres. Kammer Investment Co., Cleve., 1989-91. Mem. editl. rev. bd. Jour. of Managerial Issues; author and presenter ann. Conf. APA, 1980, Southeastern Psychol. Conf., 1979, ann. Conf. Soc. Indsl./Orgnl. Psychologists, 1987, ann. conf. Am. Soc. Tng. & Devel., 1988. Mem. Jr. League Am., Pensacola, Fla., 1970-75; treas. Bar Aux., Pensacola, 1971. Recipient Capital Gifts Stipend, U. Tenn., 1976-80; Walter Bonham fellow, 1980-81. Mem. APA, Cleve. Psychol. Assn., Orgn. Devel. Inst., Acad. of Mgmt., Soc. Advancement Mgmt. (pres. 1974-75), Am. Soc. Tng. & Devel. (chpt. rep. career devel. 1984-86), Cleve. Psychol. Assn. (bd. dirs. 1987-88), Real Estate Investor's Assn. (Cleve., trustee/sec. 1992-94), Mensa. Office: Kammer Investment Co Inc PO Box 24460 Cleveland OH 44124

BOYLE, RICHARD EDWARD, lawyer; b. Westville, Ill., Mar. 27, 1937; s. Kelley George and Florence (Weisert) B.; m. Janet E. Peskar, Nov. 22, 1968; children: Kevin, Douglas, Leslie. BA, U. Ill., 1959, LLB, 1961. Bar: Ill. 1962, Mo. 1985, U.S. Dist. Ct. (so. dist.) Ill. 1962, U.S. Dist. Ct. (cen. dist.) Ill. 1962, U.S. Dist. Ct. (ea. dist.) Mo. 1991, U.S. Ct. Appeals (7th cir.) 1975, U.S. Supreme Ct. 1985. Assoc. Costello, Wiechert, Roberts & Gundlach, 1962-68; ptnr. Gundlach, Lee, Eggmann, Boyle & Roessler, Belleville, Ill., 1968—. With USAFR. Fellow Am. Coll. Trial Lawyers (mem. Adv. Group Civil Justice Reform Act 1990—), Am. Bar Found.; mem. Nat. Assn. R.R. Trial Counsel (pres. 1991-92), St. Clair County Bar Assn. (pres. 1979-80). Home: 13 Oak Knoll Pl Belleville IL 62223-1817 Office: Gundlach Lee Eggmann Boyle & Roessler Box 23560 5000 W Main St Belleville IL 62223-0560

BOYNTON, IRVIN PARKER, educational administrator; b. Chgo., Mar. 27, 1937; s. Ben Lynn and Elizabeth (Katterjohn) B.; m. Alyce Jane Coyle, Sept. 3, 1964; children: Gregory Allen, Cathy Lynn, Julie Marie, Michael Irvin, Jonathan David. BA, Ohio Wesleyan U., 1959; BS, U. Akron, 1964; MEd, Wayne State U., 1968; counseling endorsement, Siena Heights Coll., 1988. Cert. tchr., Ohio, Mich. Spl. edn. tchr., acting prin. Sagamore Hills Children's Psychiat. Hosp., Cleve., 1961-64; spl. edn. tchr. Fairlawn Ctr., Pontiac, Mich., 1964-68, Walled Lake (Mich.) High Sch., 1968-71; asst. prin. Oakland Tech. Ctr./Southwest Campus, Wixom, Mich., 1971—; mem. spl. needs guideline com. Mich. Dept. Edn., Lansing, 1973-78; keynote speaker Utah Secondary Conf., Salt Lake City, 1978; evaluator North Cen. Accreditation Assn., Waterford, Mich., 1971-73; adv. com. State Tech.Instn. and Rehab. Ctr., Plainwell, Mich., 1978-85. Pres. Roger Campbell Ministries, Waterford, 1987—. Cited as exemplary spl. needs program U. Wis. Mem. ASCD, Am. Vocat. Assn., Mich. Occupational Edn. Assn., Mich. Occupational Spl. Needs Assn. (Outstanding Spl. Needs Educator), Nat. Assn. Vocat. Spl. Needs Personnel (Outstanding Spl. Needs Program 1975), Phi Delta Kappa. Republican. Home: 4901 Juniper Dr Commerce Township MI 48382-1545 Office: Oakland Tech Ctr 1000 Beck Rd Wixom MI 48393-1862

BOYSEN, MELICENT PEARL, finance company executive; b. Houston, Dec. 1, 1943; d. William Thomas and Mildred Pearl (Walker) Richardson; m. Stephen M. Boysen, Sept. 10, 1961 (dec. 1973); children: Marshella, Stephanie, Stephen. Student, Cen. Mo. State, 1973-75. Owner, pres. Boysen Enterprises, Kansas City, Mo., 1973-93; fin. cons., underwriter New Eng. Life Ins. Co., Kansas City, 1978-81; owner, pres. Boysen Agri-Svcs., Kansas City, 1984-94; pres. Boysen & Assocs., Inc., Kansas City, 1987—; stockholder, pres. Am. Crumb Rubber, Inc., Kansas City, 1996—; cons. San Luis Rey (Calif.) Tribal Water Authority, Wind River (Wyo.) Reservation, Cheyenne River (S.D.) Sioux, Iroquois Nations (N.Y.), 1983—; founding bd. dirs. , pres. Am. Indian Youth Orgn., Visible Horizons, 1987—. Founding bd. dirs. Rose Brooks Ctr. Battered Women, Kansas City, 1979-87, treas., 1979-81; exec. dir. The Flame Spirit Run, 1992; citationist, 1993; pres. Vol. Action Awards Program. Recipient Women of Conscience award Panel Am. Women of Greater Kansas City. Mem. Internat. Fin. Planners Assn., Internat. Agri-Bus. Assn., DAR, Kans. C. of C. and Industry, Kansas City C. of C. Methodist. Office: Boysen & Assocs 1130 Westport Rd Kansas City MO 64111

BOZARTH, PHILIP HOWARD, mechanical engineer; b. Lawrence, Kans., May 25, 1947; s. Fred G. and Virginia (Farris) B. BS in Aerospace Engring., U. Kans., 1969, MS in Engring. Mgmt., 1990. Registered profl. engr. Mo. Structural engr. Cesna Aircraft, Wichita, Kans., 1969-71; project engr. Pitman Mfg., Grandview, Mo., 1971-75, Allis Chalmers, Independence, Mo., 1975-84; sr. project engr. Broderson, Lenexa, Kans., 1985—. Office: Broderson Mfg Corp 14741 W 106th St Lenexa KS 66215-2015

BOZEMAN, THEODORE D., religion educator; b. Gainesville, Fla., Jan. 27, 1942; s. Simuel Bozeman and Kathleen Ford; m. Hannelore Bozeman, July 29, 1973. BA, Eckerd Coll., 1964; BD, Union Theol. Sem., N.Y.C., 1968; ThM, Union Sem., Richmond, Va., 1970; PhD, Duke U., 1974. Prof. U. Iowa, 1974—. Author: Protestants in an Age of Science, 1977, To Live Ancient Lives, 1988. NEH fellow, 1982, 95; recipient James Henley Thornwell award Presbyn. Hist. Assn., 1975. Mem. Am. Soc. Ch. History, Orgn. Am. Historians, So. Hist. Assn. Office: U Iowa Sch Religion Iowa City IA 52242

BRACE, JOHN MICHAEL, osteopathic physician, otolaryngologist; b. Ashtabula, Ohio, Feb. 16, 1942; s. Mark Stanley and Eunice Ann (Vettel) B.; m. Sandra Mae Peterson, Nov. 6, 1981; children: Amanda K., John M. BA, Gannon U., 1964; DO, Kansas City Coll. Osteo. Medic, 1969; postgrad., U. London Inst. Laryngology; Diplomate Am. B. Diplomate Am. Bd. Otolaryngology, Am. Bd. Plastic Surgery. Intern Bay Village, Ohio, 1969-70; resident in otolaryngology Okla. Osteo. Hosp., Tulsa, 1970-73, mem. staff, 1973; mem. staff Ashtabula (Ohio) County Med. Ctr., 1974—, pres. med. staff, 1982-86; mem. staff Northeastern Ohio Osteo. Hosp., Madison, 1974—. Mem. exec. com. Am. Cancer Soc. Bd., 1978; bd. dirs. Family Services Agy., 1978; pres. Mental Health 648 Bd., 1982; med. cons. Red Cross Safety Service Com. 1984; mem. Civic Devel. Corp., 1986; trustee Ashtabula County Cath. Endowment Found. Contbr. articles to profl. jours. Recipient citation for life saving, swimming and rescue, city of Ashtabula, 1966. Fellow Osteo. Coll. Otolaryngology and Ophthalmology; mem. Acad. 11 Ohio Osteo. Assn. (v.p. 1988), Am. Osteo. Assn., Ohio Osteo. Assn., Northeastern Ohio Otorhinolaryngology Club. Democrat. Roman Catholic. Office: 2334 Lake Ave Ashtabula OH 44004-3440

BRACHMAN, JUDITH Y., federal official; b. Columbus, Ohio, Aug. 1, 1938; married; 3 children. BA, Harvard U., 1961; MA, Ohio State U., 1977. Dep. chief Housing and Econ. Devel. Planning Bd. State of Ohio, Columbus, 1977-78, adminstr. State Clearinghouse, 1978-82; field mgr. U.S. Dept. Housing and Urban Devel., Columbus, 1983—; acting regional adminstr. midwest region, 1984-85; asst. sec. Fair Housing and Equal Opportunity, Washington, 1987—. Office: HUD-Fair Housing & Equal Opportunity 451 7th St SW Washington DC 20410-0001

BRACHMAN, RICHARD JOHN, II, financial services consultant; b. Madison, Wis., Oct. 30, 1951; s. Richard John and Joan Katherine (Harrington) B.; m. Connie Beth Ten Haken, May 14, 1977; children: Samantha Joan, Richard John. BS, U. Wis., 1974. With The Rural Cos., Madison, 1975-83; v.p. CBI Ins. Svcs., Inc., Middleton, Wis., 1983-84; exec. v.p. CBI Ins. Svcs., Inc., 1984-85, pres., 1985-87; sr. v.p. Valley Bank Ins., Madison, 1987-94; pres. Community Life Ins. Co., div. Valley Bancorporation, Madison, 1987-94; owner, v.p., dir. Lexlawn, Inc., Lexington, Ky., 1993—; pres., CEO The Brachman Group, Madison, 1994—; bd. dirs. Ins. Svcs. Inc., Community Life Ins. Co., Madison, Career Mgmt. Group. Mem. parish coun. Our Lady Queen of Peace Ch., Madison, 1989—; bd. dirs. U. Wis. Meml. Union. Mem. U. Wis. Alumni Assn. (bd. dirs. 1988—, Spark Plug award 1987), KC, Mendota Gridiron Club (bd. dirs.). Roman Catholic. Home & Office: 1217 Tramore Trl Madison WI 53717-1054

BRACKENRIDGE, ROBERT L., state legislator; b. Douglas, Mich., Nov. 7, 1941; s. Robert E. and Ethel (Ekdahl) B.; m. Susan Wotila, 1965; children: Dean R., Julie M. BA, Kalamazoo Coll., 1963; MA, U. Mich., 1968. County clk., 1987-90; state rep. Mich. Ho. Reps., Dist. 79, 1990—; mem. tax policy, tourism & revreation coms., chair local govt. com., Mich. Ho. Reps.; educator, v.p. Edn. Svc., Inc., Mich., 1970-87. Mem. Mich. State Ctrl. Com., 1981-82; chmn. Berrien County Rep. Exec. Com., 1982-83. Mem. Rotary. Home: Brakenridge 2211 Wilson Ct Saint Joseph MI 49085-1833*

BRACKETT, EDWARD BOONE, III, orthopedic surgeon; b. Fort Worth, Jan. 5, 1936; s. Edward Boone and Bessie Lee (Hudgins) B.; student Tex. Tech. Coll., 1957; MD, Baylor U., 1961; JD, Ill. Inst. Tech., 1993; Bar: Ill. 1993; m. Jean Elliott, July 11, 1959; children: Bess E., Geoffrey, Elliott Mencken, Edward Boone IV, Anneke Gail; m. Andrea Inman, 1992; 1 child, Amelia. Intern, Cook County Hosp., Chgo., 1961-62; resident Northwestern U., Chgo., 1962-66; practice medicine specializing in orthopedic surgery, Oak Park, Ill., 1966—, Westgate Orthopaedics Ltd., Oak Park, 1969—; mem. staff Loyola U., Oak Park Hosp., Loretto Hosp., Hinsdale Hosp., Gottlieb Hosp., Westlake Hosp., Rush Med. Sch.; chmn. dept. orthopedics West Suburban Hosp., pres. med. staff, 1982-84 ; clin. assoc. prof. orthopedics Loyola U.; chmn. bd. Chgo. Loop Mediclinic, 1973-75; cons. orthopedic surgery City Svc. Oil Co., 1970. Guarantor, Lyric Opera Chgo., 1971-84; guest condr. Chgo. Symphony Orch., 1979 gov. mem. 1992, Chgo. Chamber Orch., 1980; trustee Music of the Baroque; nat. patron Met. Opera Co., N.Y.C.; mem. humanities adv. council Triton Coll., 1983-84; charter mem. vis. com. Northwestern U. Sch. Music, 1982—; chmn. Friends of WFMT, Inc. Served as lt. comdr. USNR, 1967-69; Vietnam. Recipient Outstanding Tchr. award Dept. Orthopedic Surgery, West Suburban Hosp., 1978, 79. Diplomate Am. Bd. Orthopedic Surgery, Am. Bd. Neurol. Orthopedic Surgeons. Fellow A.C.S., Am. Acad. Orthopedic Surgeons, Inst. of Medicine of Chgo., Am. Acad. Neurol. and Orthopedic Surgeons, Am. Assn. for Hand Surgery, Internat. Coll. Surgeons; mem. Am. Trauma Soc. (founder), Royal Soc. Medicine, Ill. Orthopedic Soc., Chgo. Orthopedic Soc., AMA, Chgo. Med. Soc. (alt. councilor, chmn. ethical rels. com., mem. book rev. panel), Clin. Orthopedic Soc. (chmn. membership com., libr. historian, 1994), Internat. Platform Assn., Civil War Round Table, Friends Chgo. Symphony Orch. (governing mem.), Chgo. Chamber Orch. Assn. (dir.v.p.), Symphonia Musicale (dir.), Sigma Alpha Epsilon, Phi Eta Sigma, Phi Chi, Alpha Epsilon Delta, Phi Alpha Delta. Cons. orthopedic editor Jour. Indsl. Medicine, 1966-67; mem. editl. bd. Jour. Clin. Orthopedics. Cert. flight instr. single and multi engine land, single engine sea and airline transport pilot, designated med. examiner, FAA. Home: 25333 W State Rte 60 Grayslake IL 60030-9542 Office: 1125 Westgate St Oak Park IL 60301-1007

BRACKETT-BURGETTE, EILEEN YANN, healthcare administrator; b. Louisville, Mar. 23, 1947; d. George William Jr. and Elizabeth Marie (Peters) Yann; divorced; children: Dana Gerald Brackett, Anthony Jeffrey Burgetta. RN, Binghamton State Hosp., N.Y.; BS, Coll. St. Francis, Joliet, Ill. RN; cert. psychiat./mental health nurse; cert. alcoholism counselor. Nurse Binghamton Psychiat. Ctr., 1968-70, head nurse, 1970-79; supr. Parkview Hosp., Ft. Wayne, Ind., 1979-81, mgr., 1981-88, dir., 1988-89, div. dir., 1989—; mem. program adv. com. Ivy Tech. Coll. Bd. dirs. PCI, Ft. Wayne, 1990—, Rudisill Neighborhood Assn., Ft. Wayne, 1991-95, Georgetown Little League, Ft. Wayne, 1984-86. Named among Women of Achievement, YWCA, 1993. Mem. Ind. Soc. for Respiratory Care. Home: 1697 Bayview Dr Fort Wayne IN 46815 Office: Parkview Hosp 2200 Randallia Dr Fort Wayne IN 46805

BRACKMAN, EDWARD DENNIS, engineer; b. Cin., Ohio, June 7, 1995. A in Drafting Design Tech., Sinclair C. Cl, Sinclair, Ohio, 1984—. Engr. Fred D. Pfening Co., Columbus, 1990—. coor. boys' basketball St. Matthew Athletic Assn., Gahanna, Ohio, 1993—. Roman Catholic. Office: Fred D Pfening Co 1075 W 5th St Columbus OH 43212-2629

BRADBURY, DANIEL JOSEPH, library administrator; b. Kansas City, Kans., Dec. 7, 1945; m. Mary F. Callaghan, May 10, 1967 (div. 1987); children—Patricia, Tracy, Amanda, Anthony, Sean, m. Jobeth Baile Cannady, Nov. 23, 1988. B.A. in English, U. Mo., Kansas City, 1971; M.L.S., Emporia State U., 1972; LittD, Baker U., 1992. Assoc. dir. extension service Waco-McLennan Library, Tex., 1972-74; library dir. Rolling Hills Consol. Library, St. Joseph, Mo., 1974-77, Janesville Pub. Library, Wis., 1977-83; dir. leisure services City of Janesville, 1982-83; library dir. Kansas City Pub. Library, Mo., 1983—; interim exec. dir. Kansas City Sch. Dist., Mo., 1985; faculty Baylor U., Waco, 1973-74; participant Gov.'s Conf. on Library and Info. Sci., Wis., 1979; mem. council Kansas City Metro Library Network, 1984—, pres., 1987, mem. coordinating bd. for higher edn. library adv. com., 1984—, chmn., 1986-87, pres. 1991—; bd. dirs. Greater Kansas City Coun. Philantrophy. Bd. dirs. Arrowhead Library System, Janesville, 1978-83, Mid-Town Troost Assn., Kansas City, St. John's Sch., Janesville, 1980-83, Pub. Sch. Retirement Fund, Kansas City, 1995—. Named Libr. of Yr. Libr. Jour., N.Y.C., 1991; recipient Disting. Grad. award Emporia State U., 1985, Cornerstone award Kansas City Econ. Devel. Corp., 1988; Hon. Doctorate, Baker U., 1991. Mem. ALA (various offices 1972—), Am. Soc. Pub. Adminstrs. (bd. dirs. Kansas City chpt. 1994—), Mo. Libr. Assn. (legis. chmn. 1984-85), Libr. Adminstrn. and Mgmt. Assn. (sec. 1983-85), Wis. Libr. Assn. (pres. 1982). Roman Catholic. Lodge: Rotary. Home: 3318 Karnes Blvd Kansas City MO 64111-3628 Office: Kansas City Pub Libr 311 E 12th St Kansas City MO 64106-2412

BRADDOM, RANDALL L., physician, medical educator; b. Monarch, Va., Oct. 29, 1942; s. Audy Lee and Ruth Janet Braddom; m. Carolyn Lentz; children: Eric C., Steven R., Karen L. BA, DePauw U., 1964; MD, Ohio State U., 1968, MS, 1971. Diplomate Am. Bd. Electrodiagnostic Medicine, Am. Bd. Phys. Medicine and Rehab. Rotating intern Mt. Carmel Hosp., Columbus, Ohio, 1968-69; resident in phys. medicine and rehab. Ohio State Univ. Hosps., Columbus, 1969-72; physiatrist, electromyographer Rancocas Valley Hosp., Willingboro, N.J., 1972-74, Phila. Naval Med. Ctr., 1972-74; asst. prof. phys. medicine and rehab. U. Cin., 1974-75, assoc. prof., dir. phys. medicine and rehab., 1975-81; med. dir. phys. med. and rehab. St. Francis-St. George Hosp., Cin., 1987-89, Providence Hosp., Cin., 1982-89; assoc. prof., dep. chmn. rehab. medicine Temple U., Phila., 1989-91; chmn. rehab. medicine Albert Einstein Hosp., Phila., 1989-91; v.p. med. affairs Moss Rehab. Hosp., Phila., 1989-91; practitioner Rehab. Assocs., Indpls., 1991—; med. dir. Hook Rehab. Ctr., Indpls., 1991—; prof., chmn. phys. medicine and rehab. Ind. U. Sch. Medicine, Indpls., 1991—; cons. physiatrist Albert Einstein Med. Ctr. N., Phila., 1973; clin. instr. rehab. medicine Thomas Jefferson Coll. Med., Phila., 1972-74; assoc. in medicine Jewish Hosp., Cin., 1974-89; cons. phys. medicine and rehab. VA Hosp., Cin., 1975-81; dir. phys. med. and rehab. U. Hosps., U. Cin., 1975-81; assoc. clin. prof. phys. med. Ohio State U., Columbus, 1984—; clin. assoc. prof. phys. medicine and rehab. U. Cin., Coll. Medicine, 1982-89; cons. St. Francis Hosp., Indpls., 1991—; phys. med. and rehab. svc. chief Wishard Meml. Hosp., Indpls., 1991—; dir. phys. medicine and rehab. svc. Richard Roudebush VA Hosp., Indpls., 1991—; presenter Internat. Rehab. Fedn., Montreal, 1968, U. Wash., Seattle, 1972, Thomas Jefferson U. Med. Coll., Phila., 1974, 75, 76, Santa Clara Valley Med. Ctr., San Jose, Calif., 1976, Ohio State U., 1976, Nat. Paraplegia Found., 1977, Am. Acad. Orthopaedic Surgery, New Orleans, 1977, Jewish Hosp., Cin., 1977, Rehab. Inst. Chgo., 1982, 84, Am. Assn. Electromyography and Electrodiagnosis, Toronto, 1984, Las Vegas, 1985, Pitts., 1985, Ky. Family Practice Assn. Symposium, Covington, 1984, Am. Heart Assn., Cin., 1984, Ohio State U. Coll. Medicine, Salt Fork, 1985, Am. Acad. Phys. Medicine and Rehab., Kansas City, 1985, Nat. Spinal Cord Injury Assn., Cin., 1985, Am. Rehab. Edn. Network, Pitts., 1985; presenter in field; vis. prof. Dept. Phys. Medicine and Rehab. U. Ark., 1992, U. Ky. Dept Phys. Medicine and Rehab., 1992, Dept. Internal Medicine Dvsn. Phys. Medicine & Rehab. La. State U. Sch. Medicine, New Orleans, La., 1994, Baylor Coll. Medicine Dept. Physical Medicine & Rehab., 1994, N.J. Sch. Medicine and Dentistry Dept. P.M. & R., lectr. in field; Licht lectr. Dept. Phys. Medicine & Rehab. U. Minn., 1993. Author: (with others) Physical Medicine & Rehabilitation Review, 1980; editor: Sports Medicine and Rehabilitation: A Sport-Scientific Approach, 1994; contbr. articles to profl. jours. Founder, med. dir. ECCO Family Health Ctr., Inc., Columbus, 1970-72; bd. dirs. Nat. Paraplegia Found., 1975-80; med. adviser Easter Seals Soc. Southwestern Ohio, 1980-82; asst. scoutmaster Troop 291, Boy Scouts Am., 1982-84; chmn. Citizens for Our Schs. Tax Levy Campaign, Forest Hills Sch. Dist., Cin., 1985; trustee Total Living Concepts, Inc., Cin., 1977-85, Disability Svcs. Group, Inc., Cin., 1985-89; bd. examiners The Henry B. Betts award, 1991—. Lt. comdr. USNR, 1972-74. Recipient Kiwanis Club Citizenship award, Dayton, 1960, Rsch. award Am. Paralyzed Vets. Assn., 1968, Am. Therapeutic Soc., 1968, Landacre Soc. award Ohio State U., 1978, Sidney Licht Lectureship Ohio State U., 1985, Alumni Achievement award Ohio State U., 1993, Sidney Licht Lectureship U. Minn., 1993, Randy Braddom award U. Cin. Coll. Medicine, 1989; named Man of Yr. Columbus Citizen-Jour., 1970, Landerwerlen award Muscular Dystrophy Found. Ind., 1m. Am. Coll. Phys. Execs., Indpls. Med. Soc., Ind. Soc. Phys. Med. and Rehab., Nat. Stroke Assn., Am. Kinesiotherapy Assn. (mem. adv. bd. 1993—), Am. Acad. Phys. Med. and Rehab. (med. edn. com. 1983-86, membership recruitment group 1987, career brochure devel. group 1987, joint annual meeting planning subcom. 1987-88, chairperson continuing med. edn. subcom. 1982-86, sci. program com. 1982-86, mktg. and comms. com. 1987—, chairperson med. edn. com. 1986-88, sec. bd. govs. 1988-90, third-mem.-at-large 1990-91, 2nd mem.-at-large 1991-92, 1st mem.-at-large 1992-93, chair awards com. 1992-93, v.p. 1994-95, fin. com. 1994-95, chair annual meeting task force 1994-95, pres. elect 1994-95)), Am. Assn. Electrodiagnostic Medicine (com. on edn. 1974-76, exam. com. 1975-76, liaision to assn. of acad. physiatrists 1988, chairperson courses com. 1986-89, pres.-elect 1989-90, bd. dirs. 1989—, pres. 1990-91, immediate past pres.-chairperson long-range planning com. 1991-92, chmn. long range planning com. 1991-92, alt. del. AMA House of Dels. 1993-95, nominating com. 1993-94, chairperson 1994-95), Am. Congress of Rehab. Medicine, Am. Assn. Electrodiagnostic Medicine, Assn. Acad. Physiatrists, Ohio State Med. Alumni Assn., AMA, Am. Bd. Electrodiagnostic Medicine (bd. dirs. 1994, long-range planning com. 1994), Am. Kinesiotherapy Assn. (adv. bd. 1993—), Cin. Soc. of Phys. Medicine and Rehab. (pres., founder 1987-88), Internat. Med. Med. Assn. (U.S. counselor 1986-95). Office: Rehab Assocs 1400 N Ritter #351 Indianapolis IN 46219

BRADEN, WILLIAM LOU, non-profit agency manager; b. Altadena, Calif., Apr. 11, 1944; s. Laurence Orel and Dorothy (Parker) B.; m. June Yates, Mar. 29, 1969; children: Christopher L., Gregory W. BS, Miami U., Oxford, Ohio, 1966. Asst. dir. safety ARC, San Francisco, 1970-72; dir. disaster ARC, San Rafael, Calif., 1972-73, dir. safety and health, 1973-74; mgr. chpt. ARC, Pomona, Calif., 1974-80; asst. div. mgr. ARC, L.A., 1980-81, mgr. chpt., 1981-86; chief exec. officer Mid-Am. chpt. ARC, Chgo., 1986—; coordinating chpt. mgr. ARC, Ill., 1992—; prof. designation mgmt. UCLA, 1977. Pres., bd. dirs. Shelter Partnership, L.A., 1985-86; mem. United Way Rsch. Commn., 1985-86, FEMA, L.A.; mem. parents com. Troop 55 Boy Scouts Am., 1987-93; founding dir. Vol. Action Ctr., Pomona, 1977-82; mem. Gov.'s Earthquake Preparedness Task Force, 1989-90; mem. State of Ill. Emergency Ops. Task Force, 1993-95; mgr. spectator 1st aid svcs. 1984 Olympic Games; founding bd. dirs., exec. com. Life Source, 1987—, sec., 1987-89; founding dir. Ill. State Rels. Commn. ARC, 1990—, mem. svc. delivery 21 nat. commn., 1988-91; mem. Points of Light Found., Washington, D.C., 1991—; mem. Paradigm Project, Washington, 1995—, mem. program com., 1995—; mem. comm. agy. rels. task force United Way, 1993-95; mem. lt. gov.'s adv. coun. vol. action, 1992-94; mem. Ill. Cmty. Svc. Commn., 1994—; mem. Ill. State Bar Assn., mem. dist. 34 Edn. Found. adv. coun., 1992-95, vice chair exec. com., 1995-96. Named one of Outstanding Young Men in Am., 1980; recipient Community Svc. award City of Pomona, 1980. Mem. Am. Mgmt. Assn., Am. Soc. Agy. Execs., Corp. Responsibility Group, Chgo. Exec. Club, Calif. ARC Execs. Assn. (pres. 1984-85), Soc. Non-Profit Orgns., Pomona Jaycees, Chgo. Soc. Agy. Execs., Coun. Ill. Non-Profit Orgns., Chgo. Execs. Club, Met. Club, Rotary (bd. dirs. Pomona chpt. 1976-80, bd. dirs. Glenview, Ill. chpt. 1988-92, v.p. 1990-91, pres.-elect 1991-92, chair Polio Plus USA Com. 1995-96). Republican. Methodist. Home: 1034 Highland Ln Glenview IL 60025-2540 Office: Mid Am Chpt ARC 43 E Ohio St Chicago IL 60611-2744

BRADFORD, CHRISTINA, newspaper editor; b. Dec. 23, 1942; d. J. Robert and Lesley (Jones) Merrill; m. Alan Bradford, Sept. 24, 1966 (div. 1973). AA, Stephens Coll., Columbia, Mo., 1962; BS in Journalism, U. Mo.-Columbia, 1964. Asst. city editor Detroit Free Press, 1975-80; asst. mng. editor Democrat and Chronicle, Rochester, N.Y., 1980-82, mng. editor, 1982-86; mng. editor/news Detroit News, 1986-89, mng. editor, 1989—. Mem. AP Mng. Editors, Am. Soc. Newspaper Editors, Detroit Athletic Club. Home: 208 Main Sail Ct Detroit MI 48207-5008 Office: Detroit News 615 W Lafayette Blvd Detroit MI 48226-3124*

BRADING, CHARLES RICHARD, state representative; b. Lima, Ohio, Feb. 19, 1935; s. Richard H. Brading; m. Sandra Berry, June 26, 1963; children: William, Sarah, Amanda. BS in Pharmacy, Ohio No. U., 1957. From employee to owner Rhine and Brading Pharmacy, Wapakoneta, Ohio, 1958-92; state rep. State of Ohio, Columbus, 1991—. Bd. dirs. Wapakoneta Indsl. Devel. Inc.; mem. Wapakoneta City Coun., 1964-66, pres. 1974-75, 86-88; mayor of Wapakoneta, 1988-91. With U.S. Army, 1958-59, 61-62. Recipient Disting. Svc. award Wapakoneta Area Jaycee, 1965, Bowl of Hygeia award 1973, Retailer of Yr. 1978, Outstanding Achievement in Profession of Pharmacy award Merck, Sharp & Dohme 1991, Significant Contbn. to Profession of Pharmacy Beal award 1992, Alumni award Ohio No. U., 1993. Mem. Am. Pharm. Assn., Nat. Assn. Retail Druggists, Nat. Assn. Bds. of Pharmacy, Ohio State Pharm. Assn. (chmn. legis. com. 1971, chmn. bd. Pharmacy Replacement com. 1985), No. Ohio Pharm. Assn. (pres. 1969), Ohio State Bd. Pharmacy (apptd. 1976-84, pres. 1979-80), Wapakoneta C. of C., Auglaize County Hist. Soc., Elks, Eagles, Am. Legion, Masons, Shriners, Rotary Club (pres. 1971, Paul Harris fellow). Republican. Home: 808 Glynwood Rd Wapakoneta OH 45895-1125

BRADLEY, CLAIBORNE SHELDON, stockbroker; b. Hartford, Conn., Apr. 21, 1926. BS, Naval Acad., 1948. Stockbroker Paine Webber, Deerfield, Ill., 1979-92, Prudential Securities, Deerfield, 1992—; trustee, vice-chmn. Naval Acad. Alumni Assn., 1990—. Capt. USN, 1948-78. Mem. Chgo. Curling Club. Republican. Episcopalian. Office: Prudential Securities Inc 500 Lake Cook Rd Ste 100 Deerfield IL 60015-4922

BRADLEY, FRAN, state legislator; b. June 13, 1942; m. Mary Bradley; 4 children. Engr. IBM; rep. Dist. 30A Minn. Ho. of Reps., 1994—.

BRADLEY, JOAN ELLEN, biology educator; b. Troy, N.Y., Sept. 30, 1952; d. Norman Haight and Bessie Clara (Parry) Yarter; m. John Jerome Bradley, June 15, 1975; children: Lauren Marissa, Rachel Marilynne. BA in Biology, Hartwick Coll., 1974; postgrad., Ohio State U., 1989—. Substitute tchr. Stillwater (N.Y.) High Sch., 1974-76; sec., bookkeeper Allen Ins. Agy., Bangor, Maine, 1976-77, Killarney's Restaurant, Bangor, 1977-78; lectr. Ohio State U., Mansfield, 1985—; naturalist Ketch Kamp Summer Camp, Shelby, Ohio, 1994. Sci. instr., leader Black Fork Sailors, 1994-95; sec. bd. dirs. Friends of Stone Lab., Columbus, Ohio, 1993—; hon. chmn. Daffodil Days Am. Cancer Soc., Shelby, 1991; mem. SeaGrant Dir.'s Adv. Com., Columbus, 1996—. Recipient Svc. award Hartwick Coll., 1970. Mem. N.Am. Benthological Soc., Am. Soc. Ichythyologists and Herpetologists, Beta Beta Beta. Office: Ohio State U 1609 University Dr Mansfield OH 44906

BRADLEY, JOHN MICHAEL, English language educator, writer; b. Bklyn., Sept. 26, 1950; s. Thomas John and Mary Caroline (Xidas) B.; m. Jana Patrice Brubaker; 1 child from previous marriage, Jesse. BA in History, U. Minn., 1973, BA in English, 1977; MA in English, Colo. State U., 1981; MFA in Creative Writing, Bowling Green State U., 1989. Teaching fellow Bowling Green (Ohio) State U., 1987-89, instr., 1989-91; instr. English No. Ill. U., DeKalb, 1992—. Author: A-E-I-O-U, 1981, All for Blanca, 1988, Love-in-Idleness, 1989 (Washington prize), The New Wine Dreaming in the Vat, 1993; editor: Atomic Ghost: Poets Respond to the Nuclear Age, 1995, To Dance with Uranium, 1996. Nat. Endowment for Arts fellow, 1988. Mem. MLA, Nat. Coun. Tchrs. English, Amnesty Internat., Assoc. Writing Programs. Home: 504 Sycamore Rd De Kalb IL 60115-3425 Office: No Ill U English Dept 215 Reavis Hall De Kalb IL 60115-3084

BRADLEY, KIM ALEXANDRA, sales and marketing specialist; b. Glen Cove, N.Y., Aug. 27, 1955; d. Harold William and Helen Doris (Rosenthal) Shepard; m. Gary Morgan Bradley, Oct. 2, 1982; children: Hunter Morgan, Parker Davis, Preston Carter. BS, U. Ill., 1977. Media estimator Lee King & Ptnrs., Chgo., 1977-78; asst. buyer Grey North Advt., Chgo., 1978; broadcast negotiator J. Walter Thompson, Chgo., 1978-80; acct. exec. Katz Communications, Inc., Chgo., 1980-84, sales mgr., 1984-88, v.p. sales mgr., 1988-93; prin., pres. The Encore Group, Inc., Chgo., 1993; pres., owner Bradley Mktg. Group, Lake Forest, Ill., 1993—. Mem. mktg. com., bd. dirs. Child Abuse Prevention Svcs.; alliance mem. Art Inst. of Chgo.; vol. Infant Welfare Soc.; aux. bd. dirs. Juvenile Protection Assn. Mem. Am. Mgmt. Assn., Inst. Mgmt. Cons., Am. Mktg. Assn., Broadcast Advt. Club (bd. dirs., v.p., exec. v.p., pres., chair for Child Abuse Prevention Svcs. chairity com.). Home: 30 Barnswallow Ln Lake Forest IL 60045-2984

BRADLEY, LEON CHARLES, musician, consultant; b. Battle Creek, Mich., Sept. 8, 1938; s. Leon Harvey and Sigrid Pearl (Anderson) B.; m. Mary Elizabeth, Dec. 23, 1968; children: Kyle Newman, Shannon Sigrid, Karl Norman, Charles Nathan. BA, Mich. State U., 1961, MM Brass Specialist, 1967; postgrad. U. Okla., summer 1974, U. Wis., summer 1975. Band dir. Owosso-St. Paul, Mich., 1958-61, Hopkins (Mich.) Pub. Schs., 1961-62, Cedar Springs (Mich.) Pub. Schs., 1962-65; grad. asst. music theory-aural harmony Mich. State U., East Lansing, 1965-67; asst. prof. asst. dir. bands Minot (N.D.) State Coll., 1967-69; assoc. prof. instrumental music & music edn., dir. bands Coll. of the Ozarks, Point Lookout, Mo., 1969-93, dept. chmn., 1987-89, ret., 1993; clinician low brass instruments Selmer, Inc., 1979—; condr., performer Xian Conservatory of Music, China, 1995—. Performed with Springfield (Mo.) Symphony Orch., 1969-72, 81—, Springfield Regional Opera Orch., 1981—, Branson Brass Quintet, 1982—, Coll. of the Ozarks, others; originator, instr. brass ensembles and lessons Am. Concert Band, 1996—. Dir. Abou Ben Adhem Shrine Band, 1978-80. Contbr. articles to profl. jours. Mem. Coll. Band Dir.'s Nat. Assn. (nat. chmn. Sacred Wind Music commn.), Music Educators Nat. Conf., Internat. Assn. Jazz Educators, Nat. Assn. Wind & Percussion Instrs. (new music reviewer, assn. jour. 1968-71), Mo. Music Edn. Assn., Mo. Bandmasters Assn., Am. Fedn. Musicians (local 150), Ducks Unltd. (mem. com. 1978-81, chmn., 1981), Phi Mu Alpha (life), Phi Beta Mu. Episcopalian. Lodges: Masons, Lions (pres. 1983-84). Home: 119 South Dr Branson MO 65616-3708

BRADLEY, MARILYNNE GAIL, advertising executive, advertising educator; b. Rockford, Ill., Apr. 12, 1938; d. Sherwin S. and Lillian (Leopold) Gersten; m. Charles S. Bradley, 1959 (div. Dec., 1994); children: Suzanne, Scott. BFA, Washington U., 1960; MAT, Webster U., St. Louis, 1975; MFA, Syracuse U., 1981; postgrad., St. Louis Tchrs. Acad., 1990. With Essayons Studio, St. Louis, 1968-69; tchr. Webster Groves (Mo.) H.S., 1970—; instr. Webster Coll., Webster Groves, 1973-82, U. Mo., 1980—, St. Louis U., 1978—, Washington U., St. Louis, 1984-87; sec. Mo. Art Edn., State of Mo., 1986-87; mem. Tchrs. Acad. 1990-92. Author, illustrator: Arpens and Acres, 1976, Packets on Parade, 1980; illustrator: St. Louis Silhouettes, 1977; editor: (videos) 12 Water Color Lessons, 1987, Techniques of American Watercolor, 1990, The Santa Fe Trail Series, 1993, Over Gauguin's Shoulder, 1994, Aboriginal Art Techniques, 1994, City of Century Homes, 1995, Australian Dreamings, 1996. Bd. govs. Webster Groves Hist. Soc., 1965-72, 94—; mem. St. Louis Philharm. Soc., 1956-72; commr. City of Webster Groves, 1995—. Named Tchr. of Yr., 1987. Mem. So. Watercolor Soc. (sec. 1978-80), St. Louis Woman Artists, St. Louis Artist Guild (sec. 1985-86, pres. 1989-92, Disting. Woman 1987, v.p. pres.'s coun. 1995—), Monday Club (chmn. 1979-83).

BRADLEY, SISTER MYRA JAMES, health science facility executive; b. Cin., Feb. 1, 1924; d. John Joseph and Mary (McMannus) B. BS in Edn., Atheneum Ohio, 1950; BS in Nursing, Mt. St. Joseph Hosp., 1954; MHA, St. Louis U., 1959; LHD (hon.), Coll. Mt. St. Joseph, Cin., 1993; HHD (hon.), Xavier U., 1993. RN, Ohio. Mem. faculty U. Dayton, Ohio, 1955-57, Good Samaritan Hosp., Dayton, 1955-57; asst. adminstr. St. Mary-Corwin Hosp., Pueblo, Colo., 1960; adminstr. St. Joseph Hosp., Mt. Clemens, Mich., 1960-65; pres., chief exec. officer Penrose Hosp., Colorado Springs, Colo., 1965-90, Penrose-St. Francis Cath. Healthcare, Colorado Springs, Colo., 1987-91; pres., CEO Good Samaritan Hosp., Cin., 1991—. Recipient Bus. Citizen of Yr. award Colo. Springs C. of C., 1990, Disting. Svc. award U. Colo., 1983, Civic Princeps award Regis Coll., Colorado Springs, 1984, Elizabeth Ann Seton nursing award for excellence dept. nursing Penrose Hosp. and Penrose Community Hosp., 1987, Sword of Hope Am. Cancer Soc., 1988; named woman of Distinction Soroptimist Internat., 1988. Mem. Cath. Hosp. Assn., Am. Hosp. Assn., Colo. Hosp. Assn. (trustee), Nat. Coun. Community Hosps. (trustee), Am. Coll. Hosp. Adminstrs., Healthcare Forum (trustee), Downtown Rotary Club. Office: Good Samaritan Hosp 375 Dixmyth Ave Cincinnati OH 45220-2475

BRADLEY, STUART COLLINS, investment representative; b. Ann Arbor, Mich., Mar. 22, 1943. BS, Ctrl. Mich. U., 1966; MBA, So. Ill. U., 1976. Investment rep. Edward Jones, Marquette, Mich., 1993—. Bd. advisors, v.p. Marquette Cmty. Found.; commr. City of Marquette. Col. USAF, 1966-92. Mem. Kiwanis, Econs. Club (bd. dirs.). Office: Edward Jones PO Box 147 106 W Ridge St Marquette MI 49855

BRADLEY, THOMAS, state legislator; m. Mary Jane Bradley. Mem. Kans. Ho. of Reps., Topeka. Republican. Home: 2412 SW Eveningside Dr Topeka KS 66614-1312*

BRADLEY, THOMAS MICHAEL, school system administrator; b. Peoria, Ill., Feb. 22, 1946; s. Thomas Marshall and Waneta Jean (Kinsall) B.; m. Janet Marie Blech, Jan. 28, 1968; children: Angela Michelle, Adam Todd. BA, Bradley U., 1968, MA, 1975; EdD, Ill. State U., 1983. Cert. tchr., bus. ofcl., adminstr., supt., Ill. Tchr. social studies Pekin (Ill.) High Sch., 1968-83, dir. instrn., 1983-88; supt. of sch. Pinckneyville (Ill.) Community High Sch., 1988-92, O'Fallon (Ill.) Twp. High Sch., 1992—; bd. dirs. Belleville Area Spl. Edn. Dist., St. Clair County Regional Delivery Sys. for Vocat. Edn.; pres. St. Clair County Scholarship Trust. Contbr. papers to profl. publs. Elder Presbyn. Ch. USA, Ill. Synod, 1970—; mem. Pinckneyville C. of C.,1 988-92. Mem. Am. Assn. Sch. Pers. Adminstrs., Am. Assn. Sch. Adminstrs., Ill. Assn. Sch. Adminstrs., Rotary Internat., Phi Delta Kappa, Pi Sigma Alpha. Home: 305 Aladar Dr O'Fallon IL 62269 Office: O Fallon Twp High Sch 600 Smiley St O Fallon IL 62269

BRADLEY, WILLIAM STEVEN, art museum director; b. Salina, Kans., Aug. 20, 1949; s. William Bernard and Jane Ray (Gebhart) B; m. Kathryn Mann, Mar. 18, 1972; children: Kate, Christina, Megan, Emma, Drew. BA, U. Colo., 1971; MA, Northwestern U., 1974, PhD, 1981. Instr. Wells Coll., Aurora, N.Y., 1979-81; curator, asst. prof. Tex. Tech. U. and Mus., Lubbock, Tex., 1982-85; chief curator San Antonio Mus. Art, 1985-86; dir. Alexandria (La.) Mus. Art, 1987-92, Davenport (Iowa) Mus. Art, 1992—; vis. lectr. Cornell U., Ithaca, N.Y., 1980-81; cons. Am. Assn. Mus., Washington, 1989—. Author: Emil Nolde, 1986; editor: (catalog) Elemore Morgan, 1992, Emery Clark, 1989; reviewer Inst. Mus. Svcs., 1985-90. V.p. La. Assn. Mus., Baton Rouge, 1988, 90. Office: Davenport Mus Art 1737 W 12th St Davenport IA 52804-3547

BRADNA, JOANNE JUSTICE, manufacturer's representative; b. Evergreen Park, Ill., May 1, 1952; d. John George and Virginia Dorothy (Breault) Justice; m. William Charles Bradna, Aug. 20, 1972; children: Trevor William, Cameron Jon. Student, North Cen. Coll., Naperville, Ill., 1970-72; BS, Northwestern U., 1974; MS, U. Ill., Chgo., 1981. Med. technologist Northwestern U. Med. Sch., Chgo., 1974-76, Good Samaritan Hosp., Downers Grove, Ill., 1977-78; instr. med. lab. scis. U. Ill., Chgo., 1976-81, asst. prof., 1984-89, clin. coord., 1984-89, admissions coord., 1988-89; tech. sales rep. Analytab Products, Plainview, N.Y., 1981-84; owner, mgr. Rochelle Sci., mfr.'s reps. lab. equipment and supplies, Oak Brook, Ill., 1989—; ednl. cons. Hinsdale (Ill.) Hosp., 1979-80; mem. adv. com. Moraine Valley C.C., Palos Hills, Ill., 1982-92. Contbr. articles and abstracts to profl. jours. V.p. St. Isaac Jogues Home Sch. Assn., 1990-91, pres., 1991-92; mem. youth commn. St. Isaac Jogues Ch., Hinsdale, 1986-90, mem. edn. commn., 1988-92; bd. dirs. Care and Counseling Ctr., Downers Grove, Ill., 1993-95, treas., 1994-95; treas. Hinsdale Jr. Women's Club, 1983-85, 88-89, pres., 1985-86; 3d v.p. 5th dist. Ill. Fedn. Women's Clubs, 1986-88, treas., 1988-90; mem. alumni bd. U. Ill. Coll. Assoc. Health Professions, 1992—, v.p. alumni bd., 1993-95. Recipient Outstanding Mem. award Hinsdale Jr. Woman's Club, 1981, 82, lifetime svc. award 5th-6th Dist. Jr. Orgn., 1990, Ill. Fedn. Women's Club, 1990, Heart of Gold citation United Way, 1994. Mem. Am. Soc. Clin. Pathologists, Am. Soc. Med. Technologists (cert. of appreciation 1977), Chgo. Soc. Med. Technologists (bd. dirs. 1977-80, cert. of recognition 1978-80), Am. Soc. Microbiology, Ill. Soc. Microbiology (sec. 1981-83, bd. dirs. 1985-87, 92-94, nominations com. 1987-89, tellers com. 1994-95, pres.-elect 1995-96, Tanner Shaughnessy merit award 1992), Ill. Med. Technologists Assn. (cert. of recognition 1978, 79), South Ctrl. Assn. Clin. Microbiology. Roman Catholic. Office: Rochelle Sci PO Box 3274 Hinsdale IL 60522-3274

BRADSHAW, BILLY DEAN, retail executive; b. Decatur, Ill., June 25, 1940; s. Lester H. and Gertrude (Davis) B.; children: Deborah, Amanda. Grad., Lakeview High Sch., Decatur, Ill., 1959. Retail div. supr. Schnepps Assocs., Decatur, 1964-74; store mgr. Firestone Tire & Rubber Co., Decatur, 1975—. Coach Decatur's Boys Baseball, 1965-69. With USAF, 1960-64. Mem. Am. Motorcyclist Assn., Tennessee-Squire, Am. Legion. Home: 24 Lake Grove Clb Decatur IL 62521-2321 Office: Firestone Store 2605 N 22nd St Decatur IL 62526-4745

BRADSHAW, JEAN PAUL, II, lawyer; b. May 12, 1956; married; children: Andrew, Stephanie. BJ, JD, U. Mo., 1981. Bar: Mo. 1981, U.S. Dist. Ct. (we. dist.) Mo. 1982, U.S. Dist. Ct. (so. dist.) Ill. 1988, U.S. Ct. Appeals (8th cir.) 1986, U.S. Supreme Ct. 1987. Assoc. Neale, Newman, Bradshaw & Freeman, Springfield, Mo., 1981-87, ptnr., 1987-89; U.S. atty. we. dist. Mo. U.S. Dept. Justice, Kansas City, 1989-93; of counsel Lathrop & Gage, Kansas City, 1993—; named Spl. Asst. Atty. Gen. State of Mo., 1985-89; mem., chmn. elect U.S. Atty. Gen.'s adv. com., office mgmt. and budget subcom., sentencing guidelines subcom. Chmn. Greene County Rep. cen. com., 1988-89; pres. Mo. Assn. Reps., 1986-87; bd. dirs. Greene County TARGET, 1984-89; mem. com. on resolutions, family and community issues and del. 1988 Rep. Nat. Conv.; mem. platform com. Mo. Reps., 1988; chmn. Greene County campaign McNary for Gov., 1984, co-chmn. congl. dist. Dole for Pres., 1988, regional chmn. Danforth for Senate, 1988, co-chmn. 7th congl. dist. Webster for Atty. Gen., 1988; county chmn. U. Mo.-Columbia Alumni Assn., 1985-87; bd. dirs. Springfield Profl. Baseball Assn., Inc.; past mem. Mo. Adv. Coun. for Comprehensive Psychiat. Svcs., former bd. dirs. Ozarks Coun. Boy Scouts Am. Named Outstanding Recent Grad. U. Mo.-Columbia Sch. Law, 1991. Mem. ABA, Mo. Bar Assn., Kansas City Met. Bar Assn., U. Mo.-Columbia Law Sch. Alumni Assn. (v.p. 1988-89, pres. 1990-91), Law Soc. U. Mo.-Columbia Law Sch. Office: 2345 Grand Blvd Ste 2800 Kansas City MO 64108-2625

BRADSHAW, LAURENCE JAMES, artist, educator; b. St. Paul, Kans., Sept. 21, 1945; s. James Lawrence and Pauline Marie (Nunnink) B.; BFA, Pittsburg (Kans.) State U., 1967, MA, 1971; MFA, Ohio U., Athens, 1973.

Designer, Union Oil Co., Honolulu, summer 1967; with script dept. CBS-TV, Hollywood, Calif., 1967-69; with prodn. dept. Writers Service, Hollywood, 1969; advt. mgr. J.C. Penney Co., Pittsburg, 1970-71; grad. asst. Pittsburg State U., 1970-71; teaching asst. Ohio U., 1971-73; instr. Akron (Ohio) Art Inst., summer 1973; prof. art U. Nebr., Omaha, 1973-90, dir. univ. galleries, 1974-76; visual arts rep., designer Met. Arts Council, Omaha, 1976; art dir. Akron City Scholarship Program, 1973; juror various art exhbns., 1974—; one-man exhbns. include U. Nebr., 1974, Pitts. State U., 1974, 77, Barton County C.C., Great Bend, Kans., 1987, Peru (Nebr.) State Coll., 1987; group exhbns. include Museo Nazionale dell' Accademia Italia, 1983, Centre Internat. D'Art Contemporian, Paris, 1985, Esta Robinson Gallery, N.Y.C., 1982, Paul VI Inst. Arts, Washington, 1988, numerous others. Mem. ednl. adv. bd. Collegiate Press, Cath. Artists of 90s; nat. bd. advisors Am. Biog. Inst., 1985, Internat. Religious Arts Program, 1987—. Recipient Spl. award Internat. Platform Assn., 1981, Sardinian Regional prize Internat. Invitational Biennial, Calgari, Italy, 1984, Honorable Mention award Internat. Evelyn Royce Gallery, Fall River Mills, Calif., 1995, First Place award Marxhausen Art Gallery, 1995; named Outstanding Young Alumnus Pitts. State U., 1982; recipient Gold medal for artistic merit Internat. Parliament, Salsamaggiore, Italy, 1983. Mem. Visual Artists & Galleries Assn. Office: U Nebr 327 Fine Arts Bldg Omaha NE 68182-0011

BRADSHAW, MARY FENTON, government executive secretary; b. Peoria, Ill., Mar. 14, 1933; d. Hugh and Theresa (Byers) Gill; m. Paul Gareth Bradshaw, June 7, 1951; children: Rick Paul, Lorraine Kay Bradshaw Lulay. Grad. high sch., Peoria. Sec. to dist. mgr. Marchant Calculators (later SCM Corp.), Peoria, 1961-66; office clk., typist Peoria Twp. Relief Office, 1967-73; acct. McGladry, Hansen & Dunn, Peoria, 1973-74; budget and fiscal clk.-typist Regional Office, Agrl. Rsch. Svc., USDA, Peoria, 1974-76, sec. to regional inf. officer, 1976-83, supr. stenographer pool No. Regional Rsch. Ctr., 1984; sec. to rsch. leader Nat. Ctr. for Agrl. Rsch. Svc. Nat. Ctr. for Agrl. Util. Rsch., Peoria, 1984—. Recipient Sustained Superior Performance award Agrl. Rsch. Svc., USDA, 1991, 92,93, also others. Republican. Presbyterian. Home: 305 W Lakeland Rd Morton IL 61550-1407 Office: USDA Agrl Rsch Svc NCAUR 1815 N University St Peoria IL 61604-3902

BRADSHAW, PHILIP E., farmer, consultant; b. Quincy, Ill., Apr. 13, 1939; s. Thomas Frederick and Lois (Sweeting) B.; m. Linda L. Bradburn, July 2, 1961; children: Cindy, Lisa, Todd. BS in Edn., Western Ill. U., Macomb, 1961. Life ins. and mut. funds agt. Investors Security, Chgo., 1961-63; self employed farmer Bradshaw Frams, Griggsville, Ill., 1963—; nat. and internat. cons. Brierly Investments, New Zealand, 1989—; chmn. Griggsville Bancshares Inc., 1993; chmn. bd. Farmers Nat. Bank, Griggsville, 1991-94. Chmn. bd. Illini Cmty. Hosp., Pittsfield, 1978-80; co-chmn. Farmers for Bush Com., 1992. With USAR, 1962-68. Mem. Pittsfield Rotary (chmn. Farmers Night, bd. dirs. 1995—), Livestock Conservation inst. (bd. dirs.), Nat. Pork Producers Assn., Ill. Port Producers Assn. (pres. 1971-74), Am. Farm Bur., Am. Farm Bur., others. Republican. Home: RR 1 Box 133 Griggsville IL 62340

BRADSHAW, WILLIAM DAVID, insurance company executive; b. Barnett, Mo., Jan. 23, 1928; s. Ivor Eugene and Susan Pearl (Tipton) B.; m. Dorothy Louise Weir, Aug. 26, 1951; children—Deborah Bradshaw Dangos, Jane. BS in Chemistry and Physics, Central Mo. State Coll., 1950; BS in Medicine, U. Mo., 1952; M.D., U. Kans., 1954. Diplomate Am. Bd. Family Practice, Am. Coll. Physician Execs., Am. Bd. Quality Assurance and Utilization Rev. Physicians, Am. Coll. Utilization Rev. Physicians. Rotating intern U. Kans. Med. Ctr., Kansas City, Kans., 1954-55; gen. practice medicine Clinton, Mo., 1955-76; assoc. prof. family and community medicine U. Mo., Columbia, 1976-88; dir. continuing med. edn. U. Mo., 1976-83, dean Sch. of Medicine, 1983-86, dean emeritus, 1988—; pres. Mo. Patient Care Rev. Found., 1987-88; v.p. Blue Cross and Blue Shield of Kansas City, Mo., 1988—; dean emeritus sch. medicine, 1988—; coroner Henry County, Mo., 1955-59; med. examiner FAA, 1960-88. Mayor, City of Clinton, Mo., 1962-66. Recipient Disting. award of Merit Mo. Acad. Family Practice, 1986. Fellow Am. Coll. Physician Execs.; mem. AMA, Am. Acad. Family Physicians, Mo. State Medicine Soc. (award of merit 1987), Met. Med. Soc. of Greater Kansas City, Rotary. Democrat. Mem. Christian Ch. Office: Blue Cross/Blue Shield 2301 Main St Kansas City MO 64108-2423

BRADT, REXFORD HALE, chemical engineer; b. Versailles, Ind., Oct. 17, 1908; s. Fletcher Hale and Mary Elizabeth (Peak) B.; m. Mabel Geraldine Enos, Sept. 16, 1932 (dec. May 1990); children: Dale Rexford, Constance L., Douglas Hale, Gregory G., Geryce, Camille; m. Joanna Dickey Ferguson, May 23, 1991. BA, Ind. U., 1930; postgrad., U. Wis., 1930-32. Registered profl. engr., Ill. Chemist Nicolet Paper Co., De Pere, Wis., 1935-37; chief chemist Fox River Paper Co., Appleton, Wis., 1937-40; head chemist Oak Ordinance, Illiopolis, Ill., 1941; div. group leader Metallurgical Labs. U. Chgo., Chgo., Oak Ridge, 1942-45; pvt. practice cons. chemist, engr. Chgo., 1946-50; pres., v.p. dir. rsch. Fiberfil Corp., Warsaw, Ind., 1951-60; pres., chief exec. officer Materials Rsch. Inc., Warsaw, 1960—. Recipient fellowship U. Wis., 1930-32. Mem. Am. Chem. Soc., Soc. Plastic Engrs., Phi Lambda Upsilon (hon.). Republican. Presbyterian. Office: Materials Rsch Inc PO Box 1216 Warsaw IN 46581-1216

BRADWAY, KEITH EMERSON, research scientist, retired; b. Indpls., Dec. 31, 1926; s. Donald Daniel and Nelle Viola (Strode) B.; m. Rita Dymphina Godschalx, Sept. 9, 1950; children: Daniel, Patricia, Thomas, Barbara. BSChE, Purdue U., 1948; MS, Lawrence U., 1950, PhD, 1953. Asst. to rsch. dir. Camp Corp., Franklin, Va., 1953-56; supt. process engring. Union Camp Corp., Franklin, Va., 1956-60, supt. process control, 1960-62; rsch. scientist Union Camp Corp., Lawrenceville, N.J., 1962-80, sr. rsch. scientist, 1980-91; ret., 1991. Contbr. articles to profl. jours.; patentee in field. Pres. Pine Knoll Civic Assn., Lawrenceville, 1977-78. Home: 8044 N State Rd 135 Morgantown IN 46160

BRADY, CATHERINE RAWSON, software company executive; b. Bloomington, Ill., Oct. 15, 1959; d. Norman Earl and Barbara (Stewart) Rawson; m. Patrick K. Brady, June 13, 1990; children: Ian A., Madeline K. BS in econs., Ill. Benedictine Coll., 1981; MS in fin., No. Ill. U., 1985. Futures trader Chgo., 1984-90; co-founder, exec. Teledata Solutions, Wheaton, Downers Grove, Ill., 1990—; adj. faculty Elmhurst (Ill.) Coll., 1989-92; faculty mem. Keller Grad. Sch., Schaumburg, Ill., 1989-91. Author: New York Institute of Finance Guide to Investing, 1991. Pres. Greater DuPage Meld's Young Moms, Glen Ellyn, Ill., 1992-93; bd. dirs. 1989-93. Mem. Chgo. Software Assn. Office: Teledata Solutions Inc. 2901 Finley Rd Ste 107 Downers Grove IL 60515

BRADY, MARY SUE, nutrition and dietetics educator; b. Sedalia, Mo., Mar. 29, 1945; d. H. Wesley and K. Virginia (McGaw) Steele; m. Paul L. Brady, Sept. 2, 1967; 1 child, Chad W. BA, Marian Coll., Indpls., 1968; MS, Ind. U., Indpls., 1970, DMSc, 1987. Registered dietitian; cert. specialist in pediatric nutrition. Pediatric dietitian J.W. Riley Hosp. Children, Ind. U. Sch. Medicine, Indpls., 1970-75, acting dir. pediatric nutrition, 1975-78, 80-82, neonatal dietitian, 1978-80, dir. pediatric nutrition, 1982-96; asst. prof. Ind. U. Sch. Medicine, Indpls., 1975-88, assoc. prof., 1988-96, prof. 1996—. Contbr. articles to Jour. of Am. Dietetic Assn., Pediatric Pulmonology, Jour. of Pediatrics. Fellow Am. Dietetic Assn. (mem. jour. bd. 1988-94, Excellence in Practice of Clin. Nutrition award 1991, PNPG Outstanding Mem. of Yr. 1994); mem. Sigma Xi. Office: JW Riley Hosp for Children 702 Barnhill Dr Rm 3747 Indianapolis IN 46202-5200

BRADY, MICHAEL CAMERON, investment consultant; b. Michigan City, Ind., Jan. 28, 1957; s. Robert John and Patricia Ann (Moon) B.; m. Lisa Lee Blauvelt, June 25, 1983; children: Meagan Lee, Cameron Matthew, Collin Patrick. BSBA, Ohio State U., 1979; MBA, Cleve. State U., 1981. Cert. fin. planner; registered investment advisor. Vice pres. Nat. City Bank, Cleve., 1979-87; mng. dir. Brady, Foley & Co., Inc., Cleve., 1987-89, McCollum Fin. Svcs., Cleve., 1989-92; pres. Chapel Hill Advisors, Inc., Cleve., 1992—; mng. dir. Brady & Co., Inc., Cleve., 1983-92; pres., registered prin. Chapel Hill Securities, Inc., Cleve., 1992—. Mem. exec. bd. Greater Cleve. coun. Boy Scouts Am., 1989—, Greater Cleve. chpt. ARC, 1988-89; v.p. Olmsted Falls Bd. Edn., 1992-95, pres., 1995. Recipient Silver Beaver award Nat. Coun. Boy Scouts Am., 1995. Mem. Inst. Cert. Fin. Planners, Estate Planning Coun. Cleve., Newcomen Soc. U.S., Edgewater Yacht Club, Cleve. Athletic Club. Roman Catholic. Home: 8348 Old Post Rd Olmsted Falls OH 44138-1871 Office: Chapel Hill Advisors Inc 4859 Dover Center Rd Ste 11 North Olmsted OH 44070-3189

BRADY, MICHAEL JOSEPH, municipal official; b. Chgo., Oct. 22, 1947; s. Joseph Paul and Kathryn (Desh) B.; m. Dolilynn Kipp, Dec. 30, 1972; children: Kelly, Kevin, Molly, Mara. BA in Liberal Arts, Marquette U., Milw., 1969. Pre-sch. tchr., organizer VISTA, St. Thomas Islands, 1969-70; tchr. St. James Catholic Sch., Mequon, Wis., 1970-71; dir. children's programs Next Door Found., Milw., 1971-76; staff dir. Congressman Henbry s. Reuss, Milw., 1976-82; supr. cmty. rels. Wis. Electric Power Co., Milw., 1982-89; dir. housing and neighborhood devel. City of Milw., 1989-92, dir. cmty. block grant adminstr., 1992—. Mem. Jobs with Peace, Milw., 1980—, Irish Fest Bd., Milw., 1981—, Trinity Dance, Milw., 1990—; bd. dirs. Parkside Housing Coop., Milw., 1984-88, Westside Conservation Corp., Milw., 1978-88; trustee St. Rose Parish, Milw., 1994—; vol. numerous polit. campaigns, 1976—. Mem. Westside Bike Club (founder). Democrat. Roman Catholic. Office: City of Milw 200 E Wells Milwaukee WI 53208

BRADY, WILLIAM E., state legislator; m. Nancy Brady; children: Katie, William, Duncan. Grad., Ill. Wesleyan U., 1983. Founder, pres., oper. officer Brady Weaver Realtors/Better Homes & Gardens, 1984—, Brady Property Mgmt., 1984—; co-founder, sec. Brady & Assocs. Constrn. & Devel., 1986—; pres. Decade 200 Mortgage Svcs., Inc., 1991—; mem. from 88th dist. Ill. Ho. of Reps. Bd. dirs. YMCA, 1990—; v.p. bd. dirs. Ctrl. Cath. H.S. Found., 1980-94; mem. Rep. Ctrl. Com., 1986—; active in polit. campaigns of Ed Madigan and Jim Edgar. Mem. Bloomington/Normal Assn. Realtors (bd. dirs. 1990—), Bloomington/Normal Homebuilders Assn., McLean County Young Reps. (bd. dirs. 1986—), McLean County C. ofC. (bd. dirs. 1987-90, sec. 1990-91). Home: 3 Jill Ct Bloomington IL 61701-2011*

BRADY, WILLIAM ROBERT, state legislator; b. Parsons, Kans., May 25, 1956; s. William Frances and Mary (Hemmer) B.; m. Nancy Brady. AA, Labette Cmty. Coll., 1975; BA, Pitts. State U., 1977, MS, 1981. Former atty. Maloney, Hedman & Assocs.; mem. Kans. Ho. of Reps., Topeka, 1981-90, mem. edn. com., agenda chmn., house leader; U.S. senator from Kans., 1991—; owner, floral and greenhouse. Active Patrick's Parish Coun.; bd. dirs. Youth Coun. Shelter. Mem. Parsons C. of C., Lions, Rotary (Citizenship scholar 1974—, Parsons, Kans.). Democrat. Address: 319 Crestview Dr Parsons KS 67357-3513*

BRAGG, MICHAEL ELLIS, lawyer, insurance company executive; b. Holdrege, Nebr., Oct. 6, 1947; s. Lionel C. and Frances E. (Klinginsmith) B.; m. Nancy Jo Aabel, Jan. 19, 1980; children: Brian Michael, Kyle Christopher, Jeffrey Douglas. BA, U. Nebr., 1971, JD, 1975. Bar: Alaska 1976, Nebr. 1976. CLU, ChFC, CPCU. Assoc. White & Jones, Anchorage, 1976-77; field rep. State Farm Ins., Anchorage, 1977-79; atty. corp. law dept. State Farm Ins., Bloomington, Ill., 1979-81, sr. atty., 1981-84, asst. counsel, 1984-86, counsel, 1986-88; asst. v.p., counsel gen. claims dept. State Farm Fire and Casualty Co., Bloomington, 1988-94; v.p., counsel, gen. claims dept. State Farm Ins. Cos., Bloomington, Ill., 1994—; lectr., contbr. legal seminars. Contbr. and editor of articles to legal and ins. jours. Bd. dirs. Friends of Arts, Bloomington, 1984-85; pres. McLean County Crime Detection Network, 1988-95. With USNG, 1970-76. Mem. ABA (various offices tort and ins. practices sect. including chmn. ins. coverage litigation com. 1991-92, vice chmn. property ins. law com. 1986-91), Am. Corp. Counsel Assn., Def. Rsch. Inst., Fedn. Ins. and Corp. Counsel (chair industry coop. sect. 1995—), Crestwicke Country Club. Republican. Unitarian. Office: State Farm Ins Cos One State Farm Plz A-4 Bloomington IL 61710

BRAGG, RICHARD CHRISTOPHER, electrical design engineer; b. Pasadena, Tex., June 1, 1967; s. Phillip Mead and LaDawn Kay (Rowland) B. Student, Indian Area Capitol Vo-Tech., Muskogee, Okla., 1983-85, Tulsa Jr. Coll., 1985-88; AAS, Purdue U., 1989, BS, 1992. With Tex. Ea. Products Pipeline, Seymour, Ind., 1990; intern 3M Co., St. Paul, 1990, 91, design engr., 1992—. Mem. IEEE, 3M Downhill Ski Club. Office: 3M Co 3M Center Bldg 518-1-1 Saint Paul MN 55144-1000

BRAHAM, DELPHINE DORIS, government accountant; b. L'Anse, Mich., Mar. 16, 1946; d. Richard Andrew and Viola Mary (Niemi) Aho; m. John Emerson Braham, Sept. 23, 1967 (div. Dec. 1987); children: Tammy, Debra, John Jr. BS summa cum laude, Drury Coll., 1983; M in Mgmt., Webster U., St. Louis, 1986. Bookkeeper, Community Mental Health Ctr., Marquette, Mich., 1966-68; credit clk. Remington Rand, Marietta, Ohio, 1971-72; acctg. technician St. Joseph's Hosp., Parkersburg, W.Va., 1972-74; material mgr. U.S. Army, Ft. Leonard Wood, Mo., 1982-86, accountant, 1986-92; acct. Dept. Defense Indpls., 1992—; instr., adj. faculty Columbia Coll., 1987-92, Park Coll., 1988-92. Leader Girls Scouts U.S., Williamstown, W.Va., 1972-74, Hanau, Germany, 1977-79. Mem. AAUW (treas. Waynesville br. 1986-90), NAFE, Assn. Govt. Accts., Am. Soc. Mil. Comptrs., Waynesville Bus. and Profl. Women's Orgn. Home: PO Box 16234 Indianapolis IN 46216-0234

BRAHMBHATT, SUDHIRKUMAR, chemical company executive; b. Dabhoi, Gujarat, India, Apr. 4, 1951; came to U.S., 1973; s. Ramanlal Kalidas and Kamalaben Motilal Barot Brahmbhatt; m. Ashaben Amarsingh, May 22, 1977; children: Tejal Sudhirkumar, Nisha Sudhirkumar. B in Chem. Engring., Nadiad Inst. Tech., India, 1973; M in Chem. Engring., Steven Inst. Tech., 1975; MBA in Internat. Mgmt. and Mktg., Fairleigh Dickinson U., 1982; PhD in Chem. Engring., Kennedy Western U., 1991. Rsch. asst. Stevens Inst. Tech., Hoboken, N.J., 1975-77; chem. engr. Exxon Co. U.S.A., Linden, N.J., 1977-79; sr. process engr. Air Products and Chemicals, Inc., Allentown, Pa., 1979-84; applications engr. MG Industries div. of Hoechst, Valley Forge, Pa., 1984-87, sr. project engr., 1987-89, mgr. chems. group, 1989-92, head R&D dept., 1992—; owner Ashutej Co., Trexlertown, Pa., 1982-84; pres., founder Bal Vihar Sch., St. Louis, 1992—. Patentee in environ. and chem. engring. fields; contbr. articles to profl. jours. Dir., host radio program Music of India, WMUH, Allentown, 1981-91, KDHX, St. Louis, 1992—; pres. Exxon Volleyball League, Linden, 1978-79; pres. Bal Vihar Assn., Hindu Temple Soc., Allentown, Pa., 1989-91; founder, pres. Bal Vihar (Children's Ethnic Sch.) of St. Louis, 1992—. Recipient Merit cert. Poly-Olefins Industries Ltd., Bombay, India, 1972. Mem. AIChE, TAPPI, Am. Powder Metallurgy Inst. (chmn. Phila. sec. 1987-88), Am. Chem. Soc., Am. Ceramic Soc., Am. Soc. Metals. Home: 1700 Countrytop Ct Glencoe MO 63038-1446 Office: MG Industries #6 Research Park Dr Saint Charles MO 63304

BRAILSFORD, ALAN DAVID, physicist; b. Mansfield, Eng., Apr. 3, 1930; came to U.S., 1956; s. William and Laura Emily (Heath) B.; m. Yvonne Josephine Perkins, Dec. 12, 1952; children: Amanda Jane, Melanie Dee, Gavin Joseph. BSc, U. Birmingham, Eng., 1953, PhD, 1956, DSc, 1992. Postdoctoral fellow Bell Tel. Labs., Murray Hill, N.J., 1956-57; mem. Rsch. Staff and Ford Motor Co., Dearborn, Mich., 1957-71; rsch. scientist, mgr. physics dept. Ford Motor Co., Dearborn, 1973-95; prof. rsch. fellow Harwell Lab., Oxfordshire, Eng., 1971-73; cons. Oak Ridge (Tenn.) Nat. Lab., 1975—. Contbr. over 100 articles to scholarly and profl. jours. Elder Presbyn. Ch., Dearborn, 1975, Cpl. U.K. Army, 1949-50. Fellow ASM Internat., Am. Phys. Soc., Inst. Physics; mem. Materials Rsch. Soc. Home: 1212 Beechmont St Dearborn MI 48124-1573

BRAM, ISABELLE MARY RICKEY MCDONOUGH (MRS. JOHN BRAM), civic worker; b. Oskaloosa, Ia., Apr. 4; d. Lindsey Vinton and Heddy (Lundee) Rickey; B.A. in Govt., George Washington U., 1947, postgrad., 1947-49; m. Dayle C. McDonough, Jan. 20, 1949; m. 2d, John G. Bram, Nov. 24, 1980. Dep. tax assessor and collector Aransas Pass Ind. Sch. Dist., 1939-41; sec. to city atty., Aransas Pass, Tex., 1939-41; info. specialist U.S. Dept. State, Washington, 1942-48. Treas. Mo. Fedn. Women's Clubs, Inc., 1964-66, 2d v.p., 1966-68, 1st v.p., 1968-70, pres., 1970-72; bd. dirs. Gen. Fedn. Women's Clubs. Mem. steering com. Citizens Com. for Conservation; mem. exec. com. Missourians for Clean Water. Pres., DeKalb County Women's Democratic Club, 1964. Bd. dirs. DeKalb County Pub. Library, pres., 1966; bd. dirs. Mo. Girls Town Found.; dir. DeKalb County Little Theater Inc. Mem. AAUW, Nat. League Am. Pen Women, DeKalb County Hist. Soc., Internat. Platform Assn., Law Soc. U. Mo., Jefferson Club of U. Mo., Zeta Tau Alpha, Phi Delta Delta, Phi Delta Gamma. Democrat. Episcopalian. Mem. Order Eastern Star. Clubs: Tri Arts, Shakespeare, Wimodausis, Gavel, Ledgers, Jefferson. Editor: Mo. Clubwoman mag. Home: Sloan and Cherry Sts PO Box 156 Maysville MO 64469

BRAMAN, HEATHER RUTH, technical writer, editor, consultant, antiques dealer; b. Wilmington, Ohio, Apr. 27, 1934; d. William Barnett and Violet Ruth (Davis) Hansford; m. Barr Oliver Braman, June 29, 1957 (div.); children: Sean Robert, Heather Paige. BA, Hiram Coll., 1956; postgrad., Sinclair Community Coll., Dayton, Ohio, 1977-85, Wright State U., Dayton, 1986. Pers. clk. USAF, Wright-Patterson AFB, Ohio, 1956, specifications editor, 1956-57, publs. editor, writer, 1957-63; vol. Children's Med. Ctr., 1963-67, Dayton Pubs. Schs., 1969-87; tchr. Gloria Dei Montessori Sch., Dayton, 1973-77; asst. mgr., acctg. mgr., mgr. tennis club USAF, Wright-Patterson AFB, Ohio, 1977-81; tech. writer Miclin, Inc., Alpha, Ohio, 1982, Indsl. Design Concepts, Dayton, 1982-83; tech. writer, cons. Belcan Corp., Cin., 1984—; owner Chimney Sweep Antiques Shoppe, Arcanum, Ohio, 1991—; real estate investor. Founder, bd. dirs. Trotwood (Ohio) Women's Open Tennis Tournament, 1976-81; mem. Harrison Twp. Parks Bd., 1980-82; ballpersons coord. Dayton Pro Tennis Classic, 1977-80; pres. Dayton Tennis Commn., 1978-80; mem. parents exec. com. Hiram (Ohio) Coll., 1985—; ct.-appointed Spl. Advocate/Guardian Ad Litem (CASA GAL), 1988—; tutor English as a second lang. citizenship classes, 1991—. Mem. NOW, NAACP, Dayton Pub. Schs. Orgns., Dayton Tennis Umpires Assn., Mothers Against Drunk Drivers., AARP, WWF, HALT, Sigil of Phi Sigma. Democrat. Mem. Soc. Friends. Home: 320 Elm Hill Dr Dayton OH 45415-2943 Office: Belcan Corp 10200 Anderson Way Cincinnati OH 45242-4700

BRAMLETT, LONNIE L., JR., airline towing company executive; b. Pontotoc, Miss., Mar. 16, 1943; s. Lonnie and Iola (Lunn) B.; m. Judith C. Bramlett, Nov. 21, 1967; 1 child, Brian Scott. Grad. high sch., Thaxton, Miss. Pres. UAW Local 333, Chgo., 1964-66; mgr. J & R Machinery Co., Cal Park, Ill., 1966-68; pres. J & R Towing, Orland Park, Ill., 1968-79, Airline Towing, Orland Park, 1981-88; owner Chgo. Tow Truck Equipment Co., Cal Park, 1979-88, Pine Acres Estate Subdiv., Orland Park, 1987-88, Airline Limo-ser, Orland Park, 1988—; CEO Airline Towing Inc. With U.S. Army, 1961-62. Mem. Profl. Towing and Recovery Operators Ill. (pres.), Towing and Recreation Assn. Am., Interstate Towing Assn., Towing Assn. Ill. Republican. Baptist.

BRAMWELL, MARVEL LYNNETTE, nurse, social worker; b. Durango, Colo., Aug. 13, 1947; d. Floyd Lewis and Virginia Jenny (Amyx) B. Diploma in lic. practical nursing, Durango Sch. Practical Nursing, 1968; AD in Nursing, Mt. Hood Community Coll., 1972; BS in Nursing, BS in Gen. Studies cum laude, So. Oreg. State Coll., 1980; cert. edn. grad. sch. social work, U. Utah, 1987, cert. counselor alcohol, drug abuse, 1988, MSW, 1992; M in Social Work, 1992. RN, Utah, Oreg., Ind.; cert. social worker, Utah, Ind.; cert. clin. social worker, Ind. Staff nurse Monument Valley (Utah) Seventh Day Adventist Mission Hosp., 1973-74, La Plata Community Hosp., 1974-75; health coordinator Tri County Head Start Program, 1974-75; nurse therapist, team leader Portland Adventist Med. Ctr., 1975-78; staff nurse Indian Health Service Hosp., 1980-81; coordinator village health services North Slope Borough Health and Social Service Agy., 1981-83; nurse, supr. aides Bonneville Health Care Agy., 1984-85; staff nurse Latter Day Saints Adolescent Psychiat. Unit, 1985-86; coordinator adolescent nursing CPC Olympus View Hosp., 1986-87, 91; charge and staff nurse adult psychiatry U. Utah, 1987-88; nurse MSW Community Nursing Svc., Salt Lake City, 1989-90; with Community Nursing Svc. and Hosp., Clearfield, Utah, 1993-94; med. social worker Meth. Home Health, Indpls., 1994—; assisted with design and constrn. 6 high tech. health clinics in Ala. Arctic, 1982-83; psychiat. nurse specialist Community Nursing Svc. Contbr. articles to profl. jours. Active Mothers Against Drunk Driving, Program U. Alaska Rural Edn., 1981-83. Recipient Cert. Appreciation Barrow (Alaska) Lion's Club, 1983, U.S. Census Bur., Colo., 1970. Mem. NOW, Nat. Assn. Social Workers, Assn. Women Sci. Home: 925 N Alabama St Indianapolis IN 46202-3318

BRANCEL, BEN, state assemblymen; m. Gail Brancel; children: Micheleen, Tod, Brandon. Degree, U. Wis., Platteville. Mem. State Assembly, 1986—; mem. joint fin. com., gov.'s coun. on trouism, legis. coun., legis. audit com., joint com. on employment rels., state claims bd. Former mem. Portage Sch. Bd.; former chmn. Town of Douglas. Mem. Wis. Dairies Coop., Marquette County Farm Bur., Marquette Holstein Assn., World Dairy Authority. Office: PO Box 8952 Madison WI 53708-8952

BRANCH, EDGAR MARQUESS, American literature researcher, writer; b. Chgo., Mar. 21, 1913; s. Raymond Sydney and Marian (Marquess) B.; m. Mary Josephine Emerson, Apr. 29, 1939; children: Sydney Elizabeth, Robert Marquess, Marian Emerson. BA, Beloit Coll., 1934; MA, U. Chgo., 1938; PhD, U. Iowa, 1941. Instr. in English Miami U., Oxford, Ohio, 1941-43, asst. to assoc. prof. of English, 1943-57; vis. assoc. prof. U. Mo., Columbia, 1950; prof. English Miami U., 1957-64, chmn. English dept., 1959-64, rsch. prof. English, 1964-78, assoc. in Am. lit., 1978-95; lit. executor James T. Farrell estate, 1977—; cons. Mark Twain Home Found., Hannibal, Mo., 1992—; presenter in field. Author: The Literary Apprenticeship of Mark Twain, 1950, James T. Farrell, 1971, 1993; editor: Mark Twain's Early Tales and Sketches, Vol. 1, 1979 (Nancy Dasher Book award 1981), Roughing It, by Mark Twain, 1993 (MLA Dist. Scholarly Edit.);and many other books on Twain and Farrell; contbr. articles to profl. jours. Sr. rshc. fellow NEH, 1971-72, 76-77; Guggenheim fellow 1978-79; recipient Disting. Svc. Citation award Beloit coll., Wis., 1979, Lifetime Achievement award Mark Twain Circle Am., 1992, Midameric award Soc. Study Midwestern Lit., 1994. Ohioana Pegasus award Ohioana Libr. Assn., 1996; namesake Edgar M. Branch Sem. Rm., Bachelor Hall, Miami U., authorized by Miami U. bd. trustees, 1978. Mem. MLA, Am. Lit. Assn., Mark Twain Circle, James T. Farrell Soc. (pres., 1987-95), Soc. for Study of Midwestern Lit., Phi Beta Kappa, Beta Theta Pi. Home: 4810 Bonham Rd Oxford OH 45056

BRAND, GROVER JUNIOR, retired state agricultural official; b. Stark City, Mo., July 5, 1930; s. Grover Cleveland and Ada Neomi (Evans) B.; m. Juanita Sue Warden, Aug. 30, 1952 (div. Oct. 1968); children: Ellen E., Teresa L., Lisa S. B Liberal Studies, U. Okla., 1970. Cert. profl. purchasing agent. Mgr. Crest Drive-In Commonwealth Theatres, Joplin, Mo., 1952-58; buyer Eagle-Picher Ind., Joplin, 1958-65, purchasing mgr., 1965-73; project coord. Atlas Industries, Oswego, Kans., 1973-78; warehouse examiner Kans. State Grain Inspection, Topeka, 1979-92. Recipient 6th pl. award Nat. Amateur Typing Contest, 1948. Mem. Nat. Assn. Purchasing Mgrs. (chmn. value techniques com. 1972-73). Home: PO Box 207 Oswego KS 67356-0207

BRAND, MYLES, academic administrator; b. N.Y.C., May 17, 1942; s. Irving Philip and Shirley (Berger) B.; m. Wendy Hoffman (div. 1976); 1 child: Joshua; m. Margaret Zeglin, 1978. BS, Rensselaer Poly. Inst., 1964, PhD (hon.), 1991; PhD, U. Rochester, 1967. Asst. prof. philosophy U. Pitts., 1967-72; from assoc. prof. to prof., dept. chmn. U. Ill., Chgo., 1972-81; prof., dept. head U. Ariz., Tucson, 1981-83; dir. cognitive sci. program U. Ariz., 1982-85; dean, social & behavioral scis. U. Ariz., Tucson, 1983-86; provost, v.p. acad. affairs Ohio State U., Columbus, 1986-89; pres. U. Oreg., Eugene, 1989-94, Ind. U., Bloomington, 1994—. Author: Intending and Acting, 1984; editor: The Nature of Human Action, 1970, The Nature of Causation, 1976, Action Theory, 1976. Bd. dirs. Ariz. Humanities Coun., 1984-85, Am. Coun. on Edn., Washington, 1992—. Recipient research award NEH, 1974, 79. Mem. Am. Philos. Assn., Phi Kappa Phi. Office: Ind Univ Bryan Hall 200 Bloomington IN 47405

BRAND, STEPHEN, research associate; b. N.Y.C., June 16, 1955; s. George Albert and Florence Alice (Yates) B. BA with honors, Oxford U., Eng., 1976; MA, UCLA, 1978; PhD, U. Ill., 1992. Rsch. assoc. Family Impact Seminar, Washington, 1983-84; rsch. assoc. U. Ill., Urbana, 1991—, instr., 1984-85, rsch. program coord., 1988-91; freelance statistician Urbana, 1986-88. Contbr. articles to profl. jours. Policy com. Head Start, Champaign, Ill., 1995—; adv. bd. dirs. Self-Help Ctr., Champaign, 1995—; bd. dirs. Champaign County Bd., 1992-94; mem. Champaign County Mental Health Bd., 1992-94; treas. Champaign County Dems., 1994—. Mem. APA, APHA, Soc. Rsch. Child Devel., Soc. Rsch. Adolescence. Home: 805 S Cottage Grove Urbana IL 61801 Office: U Ill 1002 W Nevada Urbana IL 61801

BRAND, STEVE AARON, lawyer; b. St. Paul, Sept. 5, 1948; s. Allen A. and Shirley Mae (Mintz) B.; m. Gail Idele Greenspoon, Oct. 9, 1977. BA, U. Minn., 1970; JD, U. Chgo., 1973. Bar: Minn. 1973, U.S. Dist. Ct. Minn. 1974, U.S. Supreme Ct. 1977. Assoc. Briggs & Morgan, St. Paul, 1973-78, ptnr. 1978-91; ptnr. Robins, Kaplan, Miller & Ciresi, 1991—. Pres. Jewish Vocat. Svc., 1981-84, Mt. Zion Hebrew Congregation, 1985-87. Mem. ABA, Minn. Bar Assn. (chmn. probate and trust law sect. 1984-85), Hebrew Union Coll.-Jewish Inst. Religion (bd. overseers 1987—), Am. Coll. Trust and Estate Counsel (Minn. chair 1991-96), Phi Beta Kappa, B'nai Brith. Democrat. Home: 1907 Hampshire Ave Saint Paul MN 55116-2401 Office: Robins Kaplan Miller & Ciresi 2800 LaSalle Plz 800 Lasalle Ave Minneapolis MN 55402-2006

BRANDABUR, JOSEPH HUBERT, pathologist; b. Cleve., July 20, 1937; s. John Joseph and Genevieve Mary (O'Harra) B.; m. Margaret L. Dewhurst, Dec. 30, 1961; children: Michael, Kathleen, Joseph, Timothy. BS in Chemistry with honors, Xavier U., 1959; MD, St. Louis U., 1963. Diplomate Am. Bd. Pathology, Am. Bd. Nuclear Medicine, Am. Bd. Forensic Examiners. Internship St. Mary's Hosp., Huntington, W.Va., 1963-64; resident in pathology U. Wis., Madison, 1968; advanced through grades to maj. U.S. Army, 1964-72; dir. labs. Mercy Hosp., Hamilton and Fairfield, Ohio, 1968—; pres., chief exec. officer Pathologists, Inc., Hamilton, 1968—. Fellow Am. Coll. Pathologists, Am. Soc. Clin. Pathologists; mem. Am. Coll. Nuclear Physicians, Ohio Soc. Pathologists (bd. govs.), Cin. Soc. Pathologists (past pres.), Rotary (past pres., Paul Harris fellow). Republican. Irish Catholic. Home: 1556 New Rd Hamilton OH 45013-9217 Office: Pathologists Inc 100 Riverfront Plz Hamilton OH 45011-2780

BRANDELL, JERROLD R., psychotherapist, educator; b. Chgo., Oct. 13, 1952; s. Jules and Edna B. (Honoroff) B.; m. Esther R. Teich, Aug. 30, 1980; children: Andrea Elizabeth, Joseph Wolf. BA, U. Ill., Chgo., 1975; MSSW, U. Wis., 1977; PhD, U. Chgo., 1982. Diplomate Am. Bd. Examiners in Social Work; lic. ind. social worker. Psychotherapist Bklyn. Psychiat. Ctrs., 1977-78, Youth and Family Counseling, Libertyville, Ill., 1981-83; Edith Abbott doctoral teaching fellow U. Chgo. Sch. Social Svc. Adminstrn., 1981-82; assoc. prof. Mich. State U. Sch. Social Work, East Lansing, 1983-88; assoc. prof. Boston U. Sch. Social Work, 1988-92, program coord. postgrad. program in advanced child and adolescent psychotherapy; assoc. prof. Sch. of Social Work, chmn. mental health prog. Wayne State U., Detroit, 1992—; clin. cons. Framingham (Mass.) Pub. Schs., 1989-91; sr. staff Grand Ledge (Mich.) Counseling Ctr., 1984-88. Editor: Jour. Analytic Social Work, 1990—, (books) Countertransference in Psychotherapy with Children and Adolescents, 1992, Narration and Therapeutic Action, 1996, Theory and Practice in Clinical Social Work, 1996; contbr. articles to profl. jours. Fellow Am. Orthopsychiat. Assn.; mem. Soc. for Clin. and Exptl. Hypnosis, Nat. Membership Com. on Psychoanalysis, Mich. Psychoanalytic Coun., Nat. Assn. Social Workers.

BRANDEMUEHL, DAVID A., state legislator; b. Dec. 7, 1931. Student, U. Wis. State assemblyman dist. 49 State of Wis., 1986—; mem. transp. project com. and legis. coun. farm safety com.; farmer. Former mem. local sch. bd.; pres. Regional CESA. Office: 13081 Pine Rd Fennimore WI 53809-9619*

BRANDON, CALVIN CORNELIUS, biology educator; b. Balt., Nov. 30, 1938; s. Thomas and Mary Magelina Brandon; m. Mae R. Brandon, Mar. 26, 1964; children: Calvin Jr., Wanda, Michael. BS, Morgan State U., 1962; MA, Nat. Coll. of Edn., Evanston, Ill., 1984. Tchr. Praie State Coll., Chgo., 1969-71, 77-79; tchr. Sch. Dist. # 169, Ford Heights, Ill., 1969—, trainer, 1980-83, asst. prin., 1971-79; dir. Cmty. Econ. Devel. Assn., Chicago Heights, 1974-79; rsch. asst. U. Chgo., 1965-69; coord. Md. State Mental Health Hosp., Sykesville, 1964-65. Campaign mgr. Ind. Voter of Ill., Park Forest, Ill., 1970. Served with USMCR, 1962-69. Recipient grant NIH, 1968. Mem. Nat. Alliance of Sci. Tchrs., Nat. Coll. Edn. Alumnae, Ill. Edn. Assn., Hoosier Assn. Sci. Tchrs. Democrat. Baptist. Home: 28 Braeburn Dr Park Forest IL 60466

BRANDON, RONALD ARTHUR, zoology educator; b. Mount Pleasant, Mich., Dec. 3, 1933; s. Donald Vance Brandon and Ruth (Myers) Price; m. Doris Marie Huston, Sept. 16, 1954; children: Connie Joanne Klimek, Elizabeth Marie Ritter, Jennifer Ruth Radtke. BS, Ohio Univ., 1956, MS, 1958; PhD, U. Ill., 1962. Asst. prof. U. Ala., Tuscaloosa, Ala., 1962-63; asst. prof. zoology So. Ill. U., Carbondale, 1963-67, assoc. prof., 1967-74, prof., 1974—, chmn. dept. zoology, 1980-87; affiliate profl. scientist Ill. Natural History Survey Ctr. for Biodiversity, Champaign, Ill., 1993—. Index editor (jour.) Herpetologica, Herpetological Monographs, 1986—; contbr. over 100 articles to profl. jours., two chpts. to books and almost a dozen contract reports. Recipient Kaplan Rsch. award So. Ill. Univ. Carbondale, Soc. Sigma Xi, 1980; grantee NSF, U.S. Fish and Wildlife, Ill. Dept. Conservation, Ill. Endangered Species Protection Bd. and others. Fellow AAAS, Herpetologists' League (v.p. 1982-83, pres. 1984-85); mem. Soc. Study of Amphibious Reptiles (chmn. 1970), many other profl. orgns. Home: 209 Hewitt St Carbondale IL 62901 Office: So Ill U at Carbondale Dept Zoology Carbondale IL 62901-6501

BRANDT, DAVID DEAN, accountant, financial planner; b. Estherville, Iowa, Feb. 4, 1947; s. Floyd August and Evelyn Ruth (Littell) B.; m. Ruth Dorothea Adams, Aug. 25, 1968; children: Lesley Marie, Jonathan Dean. BA, U. No. Iowa, 1969. CPA, S.D., Iowa; cert. fin. planner, S.D. Staff acct. McGladrey, Hansen, Dunn & Co., Clinton, Iowa, 1969-73, supr., mgr., 1973-75; ptnr. Wohlenberg, Gage and Co., Sioux Falls, S.D., 1975-80; mng. ptnr. La Follette, Jansa, Brandt & Co., Sioux Falls, 1980—. Mem. Sioux Falls Pub. Sch. Dist. Sch. Bd., 1977-82; treas. Asbury United Meth. Ch., Sioux Falls, 1982—; bd. dirs. Sioux Falls Vol. and Info. Ctr., 1982-88, Sioux Falls Area Jr. Achievement, 1984-88, Sioux Falls Literacy Coun., 1986—; pres. bd. dirs. Vol. and Info. Ctr., 1987-88; chair S.D. affiliate Am. Diabetes Assn., 1993—. Mem. AICPA (coun. 1987-88), S.D. Soc. CPAs (bd. dirs. 1982-84, pres.-elect 1986-87, pres. 1987-88), Iowa Soc. CPAs, Nat. Assn. Accts. (pres. Sioux Falls chpt. 1981-82), Internat. Bd. Standards and Practices for Cert. Fin. Planners, Continental Assn. CPA Firms (acctg. and auditing com. 1978-80), Kiwanis (pres. Downtown Sioux Falls Club 1989-90). Republican. Methodist. Home: 4209 Glenview Rd Sioux Falls SD 57103-4932 Office: LaFollette Jansa Brandt & Co 622 S Minnesota Ave Sioux Falls SD 57104-4825

BRANDT, JOHN ASHWORTH, fuel company executive; b. Chgo., Oct. 3, 1950; s. William W. and Joan V. (Ashworth) B.; m. Debbie M. Fico, June 2, 1984; children: Briana Ashley, Bryan Ashworth. Student, U. Colo., 1969-72. Mgr. co. accounts Lincoln Wood Commodities, Chgo., 1972-74; pres. Lafayette Coal Co., Burr Ridge, Ill., 1974—, Hoosier King Coal Co., 1993—; pres. Chgo. Coal Shippers, 1984—; pres. Hoosier King Coal Co.; dir. Muliganeers Non-Profit Orgn. Office: Lafayette Coal Co 200 S Frontage Rd Ste 310 Hinsdale IL 60521-6917

BRANDT, JOHN EDWARD, human services administrator; b. Mason City, Iowa, July 31, 1946; s. Edward Floyd and Sarah Elizabeth (Holdcroft) B.; m. Karen Maurine Hilleman, July 30, 1977. Student, St. Olaf Coll., 1964-66; BA in History, U. Iowa, 1968, JD, 1971, MBA, 1973. Evaluation specialist/legal analyst Integrated Svcs. Project, Des Moines, 1973-77; coord. planning and grants Linn County Health Ctr., Cedar Rapids, Iowa, 1977-86; exec. dir. Linn County Dept. Human Resources Mgmt., Cedar Rapids, 1986—; bd. dirs. Hawkeye Area Cmty. Action Program, Cedar Rapids, 1986—, Linn County Fed. Emergency Mgmt. Agy. for Emergency Food and Shelter Program, Cedar Rapids, 1988—; mem. adv. coun. Heritage Area Agy. on Aging, Cedar Rapids, 1986-93; mem. grant com. United Way Time Ltd., Cedar Rapids, 1988—; mem. Linn County Foresight 2020 Cmty. Planning, 1994—; chmn. Mental Health Planning Com., Cedar Rapids, 1989—, Linn County Tng. Com., 1993—, Patch Grant Adv. Com., Cedar Rapids, 1991—; active State Decategorization Projects Com., 1991—, Sixth Jud. Dist. Ct. Ordered Svc. Planning Com., 1991—; co-chmn. AmeriCorp I Can Regional Bd., 1994—; chmn. exec. com. Linn County Decategorization Project, 1991—; others. Contbr. articles to profl. jours. Mem. adv. coun. Jr. League Cedar Rapids Community, 1986-89; mem. Linn County Emergency Ops. Ctr. for Duane Arnold Nuclear Plant Evacuation Plan, Cedar Rapids, 1987—; chmn. St. Paul's Meth. Ch. Outreach Task Force, 1987-89, Neighborhood Chs. Task Force, 1989-93; docent Herbert Hoover Mus., 1990—. Recipient award 6th Jud. Dist. Dept. Correctional Svcs., Cedar Rapids, 1985. Mem. Herbert Hoover Presdl. Libr. Assn., Iowa State Hist. Soc., Iowa Club Linn County, Family Resource Ctr. Devel. Assn. (chmn.), Phi Alpha Delta. Office: Linn County Dept Human Resources Mgmt 305 2nd Ave SE Cedar Rapids IA 52401-1215

BRANDT, PETER A., company executive; b. Mpls., Sept. 2, 1939. V.p., gen. mgr. No. Plastics, Inc., St. Paul, 1970-75; regional sales mgr. Monogram Industries, Redondo Beach, Calif., 1975-78; pres. Lakeland Trading Co., St. Paul, 1978—;. Contbr. articles to bus. mags. Coach Highland Youth Hockey Assn., Highland Park, Minn., 1973-78; recreation dir. Linwood Park Recreation Assn., St. Paul, 1962-70. Office: Lakeland Trading Co 1676 Miss River Blvd S Saint Paul MN 55116

BRANDT, RICHARD BOOKER, former philosophy educator; b. Wilmington, Ohio, Oct. 17, 1910; s. Henry and Clara Belle (Guyatt) B.; m. Mary Elizabeth Harris, June 19, 1937 (div. Oct. 1968); children: Richard Charles and Karen Elizabeth. AB, Denison U., 1930, LHD (hon.), 1977; BA, Cambridge U., 1933; Burney student; Stanton student, Trinity Coll., Cambridge, 1933-35; student, Tuebingen U., Germany, 1934-35; Ph.D., Yale, 1936. Mem. faculty Swarthmore (Pa.) Coll., 1937-64, successively instr., asst. prof., asso. prof., 1937-52, prof., 1952-64, chmn. dept. philosophy and religion, McDowell prof., 1957-64; prof., chmn. dept. philosophy U. Mich., Ann Arbor, 1964-77; Sellars Collegiate prof. U. Mich., 1978-81; assoc. Center for Philosophy and Public Affairs, U. Md., 1980-81; vis. prof. Fla. State U., 1982, Georgetown U. Law Ctr., 1982-83, U. Calif., Irvine, 1990. Author: The Philosophy of Schleiermacher, 1941, Hopi Ethics: A Theoretical Analysis, 1954, Ethical Theory, 1959, Value and Obligation, 1961, A Theory of the Good and the Right, 1979, Morality, Utilitarianism and Rights, 1992; also articles in profl. publs. Guggenheim fellow, 1944-45; fellow Center for Advanced Study in Behavioral Scis., 1969-70; sr. fellow Nat. Endowment for Humanities, 1971-72; John Locke lectr. Oxford U., 1973-74. Mem. AAUP, Am. Philos. Assn. (exec. com. Eastern div. 1951-54, v.p. 1965, pres. Western div. 1969-70), Am. Soc. Polit. and Legal Philosophy (pres. 1965-66), Soc. for Philosophy and Psychology (pres. 1979), Am. Acad. Arts and Scis., Phi Beta Kappa. Office: U Mich Dept Philosophy Ann Arbor MI 48109

BRANDT, WILLIAM ARTHUR, JR., consulting executive; b. Chgo., Sept. 5, 1949; s. William Arthur and Joan Virginia (Ashworth) B.; m. Patrice Bugelas, Jan. 19, 1980; children: Katherine Ashworth, William George, Joan Patrice, John Peter. BA with honors, St. Louis U., 1971; MA, U. Chgo., 1972, postgrad., 1972-74. Asst. to pres. Pyro Mining Co., Chgo., 1972-74; commentator Sta. WBBM-AM, Chgo., 1977; with Melaniphy & Assocs., Inc., Chgo., 1975-76; pres., cons. Devel. Specialists, Inc., Chgo., 1976—; mem. adv. bd. Sociol. Abstracts, Inc., San Diego, 1979-83. Contbr. articles to profl. jours. Trustee Fenwick H.S., 1991-94, Comml. Law League of Am., Internat. Coun. Shopping Ctrs., Nat. Assn. Bankruptcy Trustees, Ill. Sociol. Assn., Midwest Sociol. Soc., Urban Land Inst. LaVerne Noyes scholar, 1971-74. Mem. Am. Bankruptcy Inst. (bd. dirs.), Am. Sociol. Assn., Monroe Club, Amelia Island Plantation Club, Union League Club Chgo., City Club of Miami. Democrat. Roman Catholic. Home: 1000 Venetian Way Unit 702 Miami FL 33139 also: Amelia Island Plantation 6518 Beachwood Rd Amelia Island FL 32034-9103 also: 1134 Sheridan Rd Winnetka IL 60093-1538 also: 182 Temple Ave Apt 24 Old Orchard Beach ME 04064-1265 Office: Three First Nat Plz Ste 2300 Chicago IL 60602 also: 200 S Biscayne Blvd Ste 900 Miami FL 33131-2321 also: Devonshire House, 146 Bishopsgate, London EC2M 4JX, England also: Wells Fargo Ctr 333 S Grand Ave Ste 2010 Los Angeles CA 90071-1524 also: Two Oliver St 5th Fl Boston MA 02109-4901

BRANDT, WILLIAM EDMUND, school system administrator; b. York, Nebr., Jan. 10, 1936; s. Arthur and Erna Marie (Pliefke) B.; m. Carol Ann Eikhoff, Dec. 27, 1958; children: Lori dawn, Dirk Allen, Jody Lynn. AA, St. John's Coll., Winfield, Kans., 1955; BS, Concordia Coll., 1958; MS, So. Ill. U., 1967, PhD, 1976. Prin., tchr. Bethlehem Luth. Sch., Ferrin, Ill., 1958-61, St. Paul Luth. Sch., Hamel, Ill., 1961-67; grad. asst. So. Ill. U., Carbondale, 1967-69; counselor Perryville (Mo.) Pub. Schs., 1969-78; supr. Mo. Dept. Elem. and Secondary Edn., Jefferson City, 1978—; supr. and cons. for guidance and placement programs in Mo., 1978—; supr. vocat. funded guidance and placement spl. projects in Mo., 1978—; R & D rel. to Mo. spl. need, guidance and placement, 1978—; dir. rsch. studies on evaluation Ctrs. for At-Risk Youth, Mo.; co-developer of a system of stds., local plan format and handbook for guidance and placement programs in area vocat.-tech. schs. statewide; developer funding formula for vocat. schs. Contbr. articles to profl. jours. Mem. Am. Vocat. Assn., Mo. Placement Assn. (advisor 1988—), Mo. Vocat. Assn., Mo. Sch. Counselors Assn. Home: 915 Ihler Rd Jefferson City MO 65109-0647 Office: Mo Dept Elem and Secondary Edn PO Box 480 Jefferson City MO 65102-0480

BRANDT, WILLIAM EDWARD, surgeon, consultant; b. Fort Wayne, Ind., Oct. 29, 1925; s. Diedrich Henry and Grace Ellen (Rohrer) B.; children: Sandra Kay, Susan Marie, William Henry, Michael Edward. BS in Anatomy and Physiology, Ind. U., Indpls., 1948, MD, 1951. Diplomate Am. Bd. Surgery. Intern Milw. County Gen. Hosp., 1951-52; resident in surger Dayton (Ohio) VA Hosp., 1952-56; surgeon Linville Clinic, Columbia City, Ind., 1956-59; pvt. practice Fort Wayne, Ind., 1959—; cons. VA, Fort Wayne, 1960—, H.H.S., Fort Wayne, 1980—. With U.S. Army, 1944-46. Fellow ACP; mem. KC (trustee 1961-65). Home: 6708 Mallard Cove Pl Fort Wayne IN 46804

BRANDYS, VINCENT WALTER, JR., optometrist, consultant; b. Hammond, Ind., May 15, 1963; s. Vincent Walter and Diane Marie (Pachura) B.; m. Sherry Chrishop, July 8, 1989; children: Nicole Diane, Matthew Vincent. BS, DePaul U., 1985; BS, PhD, Ill. Coll. Optometry, 1990. Lic. optometrist, Ill. Ohio, Tex., Wis. Owner Family Eyecare of Bartlett, Ill., 1991—; cons. United Vision Assocs., Hoffman Estates, Ill., 1995; sec., treas. Ill. Optometric Assn., Springfield, 1995; dir. profl. rels. PRN Consulting, St. Charles, Ill., 1994—. Mem. Bartlett C. of C., Lions. Office: Family Eyecare of Bartlett 110 S Oak Ste D Bartlett IL 60103

BRANN, DONALD TREASURER, manufacturing executive; b. Mt. Vernon, N.Y., Apr. 22, 1929; s. Mark Benjamin and Beatrice Elizabeth (Treasurer) B.; m. Joan Louise Stieb, June 23, 1951 (div. 1970); children: Duane, Joy, Daryl, Jan, Dale, Dennis; m. Margaret Peggy Ann Allen, Oct. 9, 1971. Grad. high sch., Carmel, N.Y. With Pontiac (Mich.) Motor Div., 1949-50; cabinet maker Rochester (Mich.) Cabinets, 1950-51, GEO F. Robertson Co., Romeo, Mich., 1951-53; draftsman Pontiac Millwork Co., Rubin Assocs., Pontiac, 1954; sales engr., v.p. Detroit Partition Co., 1954-67; owner, pres., chief exec. officer Don Brann Assocs., Inc., Oak Park, Mich., 1967—; owner, pres. Advance Mill & Cabinet, Oak Park, 1972—. Inventor Modular Pole Supported Desk. Candidate Rochester Hills City Coun., 1987. Sgt. USAF, 1946-49. Mem. Constrn. Assn. Mich., Detroit Execs. Assn. (bd. dirs. 1985-89, 94—), Constrn. Specifications Inst., Acad. MODEL Aeronautics, Birmingham Optimist Club (pres. 1978-79), Detroit Athletic Club, Lake Shore Sail Club (commodore 1978-79). Office: Don Brann Assocs Inc 21840 Wyoming Pl Oak Park MI 48237-3112

BRANN, EDWARD R(OMMEL), editor; b. Rostock, Mecklenburg, Germany, May 20, 1920; s. Guenther O.R. and Lilli (Appel) B.; came to U.S., 1938, naturalized, 1966; BA, Berea Coll., 1945; MA, U. Chgo., 1946; postgrad. U. Wis., 1948-56; m. Helen Louise Sweet, Dec. 9, 1948; children: Johannes Weidler, Paul George. Asst. membership sec. central YMCA, Chgo., 1946-48; asst. editor Credit Union Mag., Madison, Wis., 1955-65; dir. hist. projects, asst. dir. publs. CUNA Internat., Inc., Madison, 1965-70, staff historian, 1958-65; asst. dir. publs. Credit Union Nat. Assn., Inc., Madison, 1970-72, 83-84, asst. dir. communications, 1973-83, sr. editor Credit Union mag., 1973-84, coordinator Innovative Ideas Center, 1980-84; contbg. editor Credit Union Exec. mag., 1982-84; dir. hist. projects World Council of Credit Unions, Inc., 1970-79, dir. European relations, 1972-83. Active ARC, various coms. Dane County chpt., vol. cons., 1984—. Recipient Christo et Ecclesiae award Concordia Coll., Milw., 1968, Distinguished Alumnus award Berea Coll., 1977, Risser award Dane County chpt. ARC, 1983; named Ky. col. Mem. Am. Hist. Assn., NEA. Lutheran. Contbr. articles to profl. jours. Home: PO Box 383 Madison WI 53701-0383 Office: PO Box 5905 Madison WI 53705

BRANNIGAN, LAWRENCE HARLAN, chemist, educator; b. Hastings, Nebr., Mar. 18, 1939; s. Earl Joseph and Olinda Catherine (Walker) B.; m. Joan Dianne Rockwell, Aug. 29, 1965; children: Susan, Lisa. BS, U. Nebr., 1963, MS, 1966; PhD, Vanderbilt U., 1969. Postdoctoral rsch. assoc. U. Ariz., Tucson, 1970-71; vis. prof. chemistry U. Ga., Athens, 1971-72; postdoctoral rsch. fellow Vanderbilt U., Nashville, 1972-74; sr. rsch. scientist Monsanto Co., St. Louis, 1974-94; adj. prof. chemistry St. Louis Coll. Pharmacy, 1994—; cons. Monsanto/Searle, St. Louis, 1994. Contbr. articles to profl. jours. Foster parent Mo. Dept. Family Svcs., St. Louis, 1994-95. Mem. AAAS, Am. Chem. Soc. (award chmn.), Am. Chemometrics Soc. (charter), Am. QSAR Soc. Democrat. Home: 9411 Cimarron Ct Olivette MO 63132 Office: Saint Louis Coll Pharmacy 4588 Parkview Pl Saint Louis MO 63110

BRANNON, RONALD ROY, minister; b. Aberdeen, S.D., Apr. 16, 1928; s. Walter Carlos and Mary Erma (Snyder) B.; m. Rosalee Vernela Carry, July 20, 1949; children: Rhonda Lee Storer, Rodney Vaughn, Randall Roy. BA, Bartlesville Wesleyan Coll., Okla., 1950; DD, Southern Wesleyan U., 1987. Ordained to ministry Wesleyan Ch., 1951. Pastor Heber Wesleyan Ch., Miltonvale, Kans., 1949-52, First Wesleyan Ch., Wichita, Kans., 1952-68; dist. supt. Kans. Dist. of the Wesleyan Ch., Miltonvale, 1968-83; gen. sec. Internat. Ctr.-The Wesleyan Ch. Hdqtrs., Indpls., 1982—; co-founder, coord. police chaplaincy, Wichita. Trustee/sec. bd. dirs. Miltonvale Wesleyan Coll., 1967-72, Bartlesville Wesleyan Coll., 1968-84, Ctrl. Wesleyan Coll., 1984-92; chair bd. dirs. Hephzibah Children's Home, 1982—, mem., sec. 1983-92; bd. dirs. Wesleyan Investment Found., 1983—. Mem. Nat. Assn. Evangelicals (bd. dirs. 1970-72), Christian Holiness Assn. (treas. 1984-88). Republican. Home: 1412 N Marlin Dr Marion IN 46952-1536 Office: The Internat Ctr TWC 6060 Castleway West Dr Indianapolis IN 46250-1969

BRANSCUM, CHRISTINE MARIA, delivery service executive; b. Wichita, Kans., Oct. 8, 1951; d. George Phillip Hephner and Lela Mae Eitel; m. David Lee Ware, July 4, 1972 (div.); stepchildren: Anthony David, Geoffery Joseph; m. Bruce Duane Branscum, Sept. 1, 1983 (div.); 1 stepchild, J. Cody. BA in Human Resource Mgmt., Friends U., Wichita, 1987; MBA, U. Phoenix, 1994. Indsl. engr. United Parcel Svc., Lenexa, Kans., 1983-87; ops. supr. United Parcel Svc., Wichita, 1987-89; human resource supr. United Parcel Svc., Lenexa, 1989-91, deployment mgr. dist. strategic systems, 1991-92; ops. mgr. United Parcel Svc., Wichita, 1992—. Mem. NOW, Hist. Preservation Alliance, Wichita Blues Soc., Sierra Club. Office: United Parcel Svc 3003 S West St Wichita KS 67217

BRANSON, STEPHANIE RITA, English language educator, literary critic; b. LaCrosse, Wis., Oct. 3, 1953; d. John Raymond and Mary Angela (Pinion) Harry; m. Thomas Patrick Branson, Aug. 16, 1975 (div. Mar. 1987). BA, U. Wis., 1975; MA in French, Tufts U., 1979; PhD in Modern Letters, U. Tulsa, 1990. Cert. secondary edn. tchr., Mass., Ind. Tchg. asst. Purdue U., W. Lafayette, Ind., 1979-81, U. Tulsa, 1985-90; prof. English U. Wis., Platteville, 1990—. Contbr. literary criticism to jours. Treas. Platteville Arts Bd., 1991-93. Scholarly Improvement Achievement grantee U. Wis., 1994; undergrad. teaching improvement coun. fellow, 1991-92. Mem. Midwest Modern Lang. Assn., Wis. Coun. Tchrs. English. Office: U Wis 1 University Plaza Platteville WI 53818-3012

BRANSTAD, TERRY EDWARD, governor, lawyer; b. Leland, Iowa, Nov. 17, 1946; s. Edward Arnold and Rita (Garl) B.; m. Christine Ann Johnson, June 17, 1972; children: Eric, Allison, Marcus. BA, U. Iowa, 1969; JD, Drake U., 1974. Bar: Iowa. Sr. ptnr. firm Branstad-Schwarm, Lake Mills, Iowa, until 1982; farmer Lake Mills; mem. Iowa Ho. of Reps., 1973-78; lt. gov. State of Iowa, 1979-82, gov., 1983—; Bd. dirs. Am. Legion of Iowa Found. With U.S. Army, 1969. Mem. Nat. Govs. Assn. (past chmn.), Midwestern Govs. Assn., Am. Legion, Farm Bur. Republican. Roman Catholic. Lodges: Lions, KC. Office: Office of Gov State Capital Des Moines IA 50319

BRANTLY, LAURA J., physical therapist; b. Houston, June 26, 1961; d. Robert T. and Betty J. (Wilson) B. BS in Phys. Therapy, U. N.D., 1983. Sr. phys. therapist Curative Rehab. Svcs., Milw., 1983—. Recipient M.P. Murray Award for Excellence in Clin. Practice, Wis. Phys. Therapy Assn. Mem. Am. Phys. Therapy Assn. (cert. in neurologic phys. therapy). Presbyterian. Home: W160 N10587 Fieldstone Pass Germantown WI 53022

BRASHEAR, DIANE LEE, marital and sex therapist; b. Parkersburg, W.Va., July 21, 1933; d. Ralph Elijah and Dorothea Esther (McDade) Blake; m. Richard Evers Brashear, Aug. 31, 1956; children: Allison, Meredith Kay. BS in Social Adminstrn., Ohio State U., 1955, MSW, 1957; PhD, Purdue U., 1971. Diplomate Am. Bd. Sexology. Chief social worker Ind. Sch. for Blind, Indpls., 1965-68; asst. prof. social work Ind. U., Indpls., 1970-72; dir. Brashear Ctr., Inc., Indpls., 1972-84; news reporter marriage & family coun. Sta. WTHR-TV, Indpls., 1980—; assoc. prof. ob-gyn and psychiatry Ind. U. Sch. Medicine, Indpls., 1984—; vis. prof. Purdue U., West Lafayette, Ind., 1971-72; bd. dirs. Alan Guttmacher Inst., National, 1985-93. Author: Social Worker as Sex Educator, 1977; editor Indpls. Mo., 1975-91; contbr. articles, book chpts. and video tapes. Pres. Planned Parenthood Greater Indpls., 1985-87; bd. dirs. Planned Parenthood Fedn. Am., 1983-88, 91-93; vice chmn. Greater Indpls. Progress Cmty., 1989-92, United Way, Indpls., 1989—; pres. Cmty. Svc. Coun., Indpls., 1989-91; chair adv. bd. Women's Fund Indpls. Found. Recipient Pauline Selby award, Big Sisters Greater Indpls., 1986, Leadership award YWCA, Ind., 1986, Disting. Svc. award Planned Parenthood Cen. Ind., 1991. Mem. Am. Assn. Marriage and Family, Am. Coll. Ob/Gyn., Soc. Sci. Study Sex, Soc. Sex Therapy & Rsch. Office: Ind U Blvd #2440 550 University Indianapolis IN 46202-5270

BRASHEAR, KERMIT ALLEN, II, lawyer; b. Crawford, Nebr., Mar. 16, 1944; s. Kermit A. and Marguerite (Pokorny) B.; m. Susan Wolf (div.); 1 child, Kermit A. III; m. Kathleen K. Wellman, Aug. 9, 1971; children: Kurth A., Kord A. BA, U. Nebr., 1966, JD, 1969. Bar: Nebr. 1969, U.S. Dist. Ct. Nebr. 1969, U.S. Ct. Appeals (8th cir.) 1976, U.S. Supreme Ct. 1976, U.S. Ct. Appeals (10th cir.) 1982, U.S. Tax Ct. 1982, U.S. Dist. Ct. (ea. dist.) Mich. 1987. Ptnr. Nelson & Harding, Omaha, 1969-88, Heron, Burchette et al., Omaha, 1989, Brashear & Ginn, Omaha, 1990—; spl. asst. atty. gen. State of Nebr., 1977-90. Mem. Republican Nat. Com., 1983-85; chmn. Nebr. Republican Party, 1983-85; candidate Republican Gubernatorial Nomination, Nebr., 1986. Lutheran. Office: Brashear & Ginn 1623 Farnam 800 American Charter Ctr Omaha NE 68102

BRASHEAR, ROBERT MARION, retired education educator, consultant; b. Memphis, Jan. 10, 1929; s. Paschal Merlin and Mary Lucile (Lewis) B.; m. Eula Fern Thigpen, Nov. 25, 1952. BS, U. Memphis, 1951; MRE, Southwestern Sem., Ft. Worth, 1956; MEd, Tex. Christian U., 1962; PhD, U. Tex., 1969. Cert. secondary tchr., Tex. Design draftsman Gen. Dynamics, Ft. Worth, 1956-60; math. tchr. Ft. Worth Ind. Sch. Dist., 1960-69; prof. edn., profl. devel. Western Mich. U., Kalamazoo, 1969-90, retired, 1991; cons. Mich. Emergency Med. Transport, Kalamazoo, 1989—, Western Mich. U. Faculty and Students, 1970—, Nursing divsn. Wayne State U., 1972—, Nazareth Coll. Faculty Adminstrn., 1970—, Union Univ., 1992—. Co-author several rsch. articles. Fund raiser Arthritis Found., Kalamazoo, 1991; bd. dirs., treas. West Tenn. Regional Inter-Faith Assn.; chmn. R & D com., mem. adv. coun. Jackson (Tenn.) Ctr. for Adult Reading Enhancement; mem. bd. dirs. Youth Town. Mem. ASCD, Am. Ednl. Rsch. Assn., Mich. Acad. Sci., Arts and Letters. Baptist. Home: 76 Alta Vista Dr Jackson TN 38305-3142 Office: Western Mich U Kalamazoo MI 49008-3899

BRASIC, GREGORY LEE, financial administrator; b. Grand Rapids, Mich., Sept. 3, 1961; s. Karl Harold and Shirley Devra (Shinneldecker) B.; m. Lori Ann Saltman, June 8, 1986; children: Logan Alexander, Linden Saltman. BS, Mich. State U., 1984. Rsch. chemist Standard Oil Co., Naperville, Ill., 1984; data processing mgr. LeMatic Inc., Jackson, Mich., 1984-94, fin. contr., 1989-94, dir. MIS/fin., 1994—; owner Brasic Computer Svcs., Lansing, Mich., 1988-90; cons. Plassman and Assocs., Albion, Mich., 1988-91, Ecosystems Cons., Coventry, Conn., 1988-89, Eastminster Community Concerns, East Lansing, Mich., 1988-91, Adtech, Inc., Jackson, 1988-91, Sud-Z Cleaners, Hillsdale, Mich., 1988-91, Design Phase, Grand Rapids, 1989, Fluid Aire, Jackson, State of Mich. Dept. Edn., 1989, Barry Saltman Al Spanuolo, 1990-91; supplemental instr. Jackson C.C., 1987-89, adv. com., 1988-91, chmn., 1989. Mem. Soc. Mfg. Engrs., Am. Soc. Bakery Engrs. Home: 1527 Spencer St Lansing MI 48915-1269

BRASSEUR, JAMES WALTER, physician assistant, health care administrator; b. Ypsilanti, Mich., Oct. 7, 1949; s. James Walter Heffington and Barbara Caroline (Geddis) B.; m. Linda Marie Arrigoni, Aug. 16, 1970; children: Wendy, Victoria, Paul. BS, U. Neb., 1978; MA, Ctrl. Mich. U., 1980. Dir. health svcs. Alma (Mich.) Coll., 1982-87; physician asst. coord. Sparta (Mich.) Health Ctr., 1987-88; physician asst. Westside Med. Assocs., Grand Rapids, Mich., 1989-90; head med. dept. USN, Port Hueneme, Calif., 1990-91; physician asst. Carson City (Mich.) Hosp., 1991-93, Dr. John Hildebrandt, Ionia, Mich., 1993-95; physician asst./clinics mgr. Gratiot Cmty. Hosp., Alma, Mich., 1995-96, Stanton (Mich.) Care, 1996—; expert domestic violence Nat. Spkr.'s Bur., N.Y.C., 1994—; mgmt. cons., Stanton, 1984—. Contbr. articles to profl. jours. Sec. Zoning Bd. of Appeals, Pine Township, Montcalm County, Mich., 1989—. Lt. comdr. USNR, 1969—. Fellow Am. Acad. Physician Assts., Mich. Acad. Physician Assts. (com. chair 1990-95, lectr. domestic violence 1995), Naval Assn. Physician Assts. (dir. 1994—); mem. Naval Res. Assn.

BRATER, ELIZABETH, state legislator; b. Boston, Apr. 12, 1951. BA, U. Pa., MA. City councilwoman City of Ann Arbor, 1988-91, mayor, 1991-93; state rep. Mich. Ho. Reps., Dist. 53, 1995—; mem. conservations, environ. & great lakes, higher edn. & mental health coms., Mich. Ho. Reps. Home: PO Box 7955 Ann Arbor MI 48107-1406*

BRATNOBER, PATRICIA RAY, artist; b. Duluth, Minn., Jan. 30, 1925; d. Philip Lacey and Berenice (Steuerwald) Ray; m. Harry L. Bratnober Jr., July 2, 1948 (dec. July 1978); children: Philip, John, Jane, Sarah. BA, Wellesley Coll., 1946; postgrad., U. Minn., 1952-65; MFA, U. Guanajuato, Mex., 1977. Lectr. SW State U., Marshall, Minn., 1976-77; tchr., Split Rock Program U. Minn., Duluth, 1987, 91; lectr. U. Minn., Mpls., 1980; tchr. Art Ctr. Minn., Wayzata, 1985-86, WARM Gallery Mentor Program, Mpls., 1986. One-woman shows include Mpls. Coll. Art and Design, 1283, Tweed Mus., Duluth, 1983, Benedicta Art Ctr., St. Cloud, Minn., 1985, Pindar Gallery, N.Y.C., 1988, Forum Gallery, Mpls., 1990; exhibited in group shows at WARM Gallery, Mpls., 1984, Artbanque Gallery, Mpls., 1986, Am. Watercolor Soc., 1987, Nat. Watercolor Soc., 1991, Pa. Watercolor Soc., 1992; represented in permanent collections Minn. Cmty. Devel. Agy., Tweed Mus., Evansville, Ind. Mus. of Art, 1988. Founder S.W. Minn. Arts Humanities Coun., 1969-78; trustee Parents for Integrated Edn., St. Paul, 1965-68, Mpls. Coll. Art and Design, 1978-91; bd. dirs. Jerome Found., St. Paul, 1979-90; chmn. bd. dirs. Jungle Theater, Mpls., 1993. Recipient Ann. Nat. Brotherhood award NCCJ, St. Paul, 1967, Mayor's award Twin Cities Mayors, 1985, First award painting Minn. State Fair, 1978, First award Great River Rd. Show, Minn. Mus. Art, 1967, 2d award watercolor painting Minn. State Fair, 1991, Purchase award Nat. Watercolor Soc., 1991, Mems. award Pa. Watercolor Soc., 1993. Democrat. Unitarian. Home and Studio: 2420 Stevens Ave Minneapolis MN 55404-3529

BRATTAIN, ARLENE JANE CLARK, interior designer; b. Phila., July 27, 1938; d. Franklin Corning Clark and Nora May Robertson; children: Kathy, Kurt, Karen, David. Cert. in interior design, N.Y. Sch. Interior Design, 1975; BS, U. Minn., 1986. Exec. United Way, Mpls., 1980; interior designer AB Interiors, Minnetonka, Minn., 1982—; pvt. practice color analyst, Minnetonka, 1984—; cons. showroom Rollin B. Child Tile, Plymouth, Minn., 1985; interior designer Room & Bd. Stores, Minnetonka, 1985-86. Designer Window Fashions mag., 1988—, Am. Soc. Interior Designers Showcase Home, 1987, Showcase Home for March of Dimes, 1988, Showcase Vignette, 1989. Trainer dist. Camp Fire Girls, Minnetonka, 1967-78; trainer, leader Boy Scouts Am., Mpls., 1967-80; pres. PTA, Minnetonka, 1970; pres. Music Boosters, Minnetonka, 1976-84. Recipient Silver Fawn award Boy Scouts Am., 1973. Mem. Am. Soc. Interior Designers (profl.), Internat. Furnishings and Design Assn. (exec. 1988—), Nat. Trust for Hist. Preservation, Mensa.

BRAUDE, MICHAEL, commodity exchange executive; b. Chgo., Mar. 6, 1936; s. Sheldon and Nan B.; m. Linda Rae Miller, Aug. 20, 1961; children—Peter, Adam. B.S., U. Mo., 1957; M.S., Columbia U., 1958. Vice pres. Commerce Bank, Kansas City, Mo., 1960-73; vice pres. Mercantile Bank, Kansas City, Mo., 1966-73; exec. v.p. Am. Bank, Kansas City, Mo., 1973-84; pres., CEO Kansas City Bd. Trade, Mo., 1984—; bd. dirs. Country Club Bank, Kansas City, Mo., Midwest Grain Products, Inc., Atchison, Kans. Author: Managing Your Money, 1975, also 12 childrens books. Pres. Metr. Community Coll. Found., Kansas City, Mo., 1982-84; mayor City of Mission Woods, Kans., 1982-84. Mem. Futures Industry Assn., Nat. Futures Assn. (bd. dirs.), Nat. Grain Trade Coun. (bd. dirs., immediate past chmn.), U. Mo. Alumni Assn. (bd. dirs. 1985-87). Jewish. Home: 5319 Mission Woods Ter Shawnee Mission KS 66205-2013 Office: Kansas City Board of Trade 4800 Main St Ste 303 Kansas City MO 64112-2506

BRAUER, DONALD GEORGE, land developer, planning consultant, engineer; b. Clinton, Iowa, Nov. 24, 1929; s. Alvin P. and Mildred R. (King) B.; m. Borghild G. Erickson, June 16, 1956; children: Mark Daniel, Sonta Kay Milstead, Susan Brauer Mickelberg. AA, Clinton (Iowa) Jr. Coll., 1949; BS in Civil Engring., Iowa State U., 1951; MAPA, U. Minn., 1959. Registered profl. engr., Minn. Project engr. Pitts.-Des Moines Steel Co., Des Moines, Iowa, 1953-55; rsch. asst. U. Minn. League of Cities, Mpls., 1955-56; asst. city mgr. City of Edina, Minn., 1956-60; chief engr. Harrison, Brauer, Rippel, Inc., Edina, 1960-64; pres., founder Brauer & Assocs., Inc., Eden Prarie, Minn., 1964-80, The Brauer Group, Inc., Edina, 1980—; bd. dirs. Cmty. Bank Group, Eden Prairie, J. Vogal Water Co., Mpls., Disti-Pure, Inc., Fridley, Minn., Mgmt. Medicine Found., Excelsior, Minn., Freshwater Found., Wayzata, Minn., past chair, 1993-94. Contbr. articles to profl. jours. Bd. dirs. Minn. Recreation and Park Assn., 1975, mem. 1975—; founder Rotary Club of Eden Prarie, 1975; chmn. Ebenezer Found., Mpls., 1980-85; founder, bd. dirs. Ctr. for Conflict Resolution, Mpls., 1980-84. Recipient Sue Tinker award Am. Camping Assn., Mpls., 1982, Svc. award Internat. Exec. Svc. Corp., Stamford, Conn., 1989, 92. Fellow ASCE; mem. Nat. Soc. Profl. Engrs., Rotary Club Edna (pres. 1964, 65, Paul Harris fellow 1975), World Future Soc., Humphrey Inst. Alumni Assn., Minn. Soc. Landscape Architects (hon.), Nat. Golf Found., Flagship Athletic Club (founder). Republican. Lutheran. Home: 6116 Parnell Ave Edina MN 55424-1742 Office: Solid Waste Integrated Systems 4300 Baker Rd Minnetonka MN 55343

BRAUER, DREW SEAN, sales executive; b. Belleville, Ill., Nov. 15, 1962; s. Eugene Henry and Mary Ann (Eschmann) B.; m. Debra Jo Wolfersberger, Aug. 3, 1991; children: Hannah Marie, Conrad Nicholas. AAS in Mktg. Mgmt., Belleville (Ill.) Area Coll., 1993. Salesman Carpet Mart, Belleville, 1982-94, Beeaulieu Carpet and Rug Mills, Dalton, Ill., 1994—. Home and Office: 3216 W Blvd Belleville IL 62221

BRAUER, FRED GÜNTHER, mathematics educator; b. Königsberg, Germany, Feb. 3, 1932; came to U.S., 1960; s. Richard D. and Ilse (Karger) B.; m. Esther Luterman, June 22, 1958; children: David, Deborah, Michael. B.A., U. Toronto, 1952; S.M., Mass. Inst. Tech., 1953, Ph.D., 1956. Instr. U. Chgo., 1956-58; lectr., then asst. prof. U. B.C., 1958-60; mem. faculty U. Wis., Madison, 1960—; prof. math. U. Wis., 1966—. Author: (with J.A. Nohel) Ordinary Differential Equations: A First Course, 1967, 2d edit., 1973, Elementary Differential Equations: Principles, Problems, Solutions, 1968, Problems and Solutions in Ordinary Differential Equations, 1968, Qualitative Theory of Ordinary Differential Equitions, 1969, reprinted, 1989, Introduction to Differential Equations with Applications, 1986, (with J.A. Nohel & H. Schneider) Linear Mathematics, 1970, Introduction to Differential Equations with Applications, 1986. Mem. Am. Math. Soc. (asso. editor Proc. 1971-74), Math. Assn. Am., Canadian Math. Congress, Soc. Indsl. and Applied Math., Soc. Math. Biology, Can. Soc. Theoretical Biology, Soc. for Theoretical Biology, Sigma Xi. Home: 5113 Coney Weston Pl Madison WI 53711-1105

BRAUER, ROBERT E., retired bankruptcy judge; b. Staunton, Ill., Apr. 7, 1923; s. Louis H. and Alma E. (Oettel) B.; m. Constance Faye McMichael, Jan. 11, 1945 (div. 1972); m. Billie G. Baker, July 26, 1974. BA, Washington U., St. Louis, 1949, LLB, 1951. Bar: Mo. Assoc. Mattingly, Boas & Richards, St. Louis, 1951-53; asst. U.S. Atty. Eastern Dist. Mo., St. Louis, 1953-60; assoc., ptnr. Rassieur, Long & Yawitz, St. Louis, 1960-61; referee in bankruptcy, U.S. bankruptcy judge U.S. Cts. Ea. and We. Dists. Mo., 1961-86. 2d lt. USAF, 1942-46. Mem. Mo. Bar Assn., St. Louis Bar Assn., Comml. Law League Am., Assn. Bankruptcy Judges, Order of Coif. Home: 9853 Mockingbird Hill Bonne Terre MO 63628

BRAUN, MICHAEL D., electrical engineer; b. Cin., Nov. 12, 1954. A in Electro-Mech., Cin. State U., 1975. Elec. engr. Cin. (Ohio) Milacron, 1981-89, Gold Crown Machinery, Cin., 1990—; advisor UL, 1990, Robot Industry Advisor, 1990. Patentee in field. Roman Catholic. Office: Gold Crown Machinery 4201 Malsbary Rd Cincinnati OH 45242-5509

BRAUN, MICHAEL P., stockbroker; b. Grand Rapids, Mich., Feb. 14, 1965. B Fin., Ariz. State U., 1988. Stockbroker PaineWebber Inc., Grand Rapids, 1989—. Active various charitable orgns. Republican. Roman Catholic. Office: PaineWebber Inc 333 Bridge St NW Ste 1100 Grand Rapids MI 49504-5356

BRAUN, ROBERT ALEXANDER, retired psychiatrist; b. Chemnitz, Germany, Dec. 14, 1910; came to U.S., 1939, naturalized, 1946; s. Leo and Bertha (Eisenschiml) B.; m. Gertrud E. Mittler, 1946; children: Eleanor, Ronald. MD, U. Vienna (Austria), 1937. Intern, William McKinley Meml. Hosp., Trenton, N.J., 1940-41; resident in psychiatry Rochester (Minn.) State Hosp., 1950-51, staff psychiatrist, 1951-56; resident in psychiatry Lafayette Clinic, Detroit, 1956-58; staff psychiatrist, clin. dir. Clinton Valley Center (formerly Pontiac State Hosp.), Pontiac, Mich., 1958-63, dir. Oakland Div., 1963-80; pvt. practice psychiatry, 1980-95; med. dir. Jensen Counseling Ctrs., Farmington Hills, Mich., 1984-95; ret. from practicing psychiatry, 1996; clin. assoc. prof. dept. psychiatry Mich. State U., 1969-80. Contbr. chpt. And So We Must Remember: Holocaust Memories, 1992. Life fellow Am. Psychiat. Assn.

BRAUN, ROBERT C., airport executive. Airport dir. Detroit Met. Airport, 1990—. Office: LC Smith Terminal-Mezz Detroit Met Wayne County Airport Detroit MI 48242

BRAUN, ROBERT CLARE, retired association and advertising executive; b. Indpls., July 18, 1928; s. Ewald Elsworth and Lila (Inman) B.; B.S. in Journalism-Advt., Butler U., 1950; postgrad. Ind. U., 1957, 66. Reporter, Northside Topics Newspaper, Indpls., 1949, advt. mgr., 1950; asst. mgr. Clarence E. Crippen Printing Co., Indpls., 1951; corp. sec. Auto-Imports, Ltd., Indpls., 1952-53; pres. O. R. Brown Paper Co., Indpls., 1953-69; pres., chief exec. officer Robert C. Braun Advt. Agy., 1959-70, Zimmer Engraving Inc., Indpls., 1964-69; former chmn. bd. O. R. Brown Paper Co., Zimmer Engraving, Inc.; advt. cons. Rolls-Royce Motor Cars, 1957-59; exec. dir., chief exec. officer Historic Landmarks Found., Ind., 1969-73; exec. v.p., Purchasing Mgmt. Assn. Indpls., 1974-85; cen. dist. coordinator Ind. Regional Minority Supplier Devel. Council, 1985-88; pres. A.P.S. Industries, Inc., 1979—; nat. pres. Associated Purchasing Publs., 1981-85; gen. mgr. Midwest Indsl. Show, 1974-85, Midwest Office Systems and Equipment Show, 1974-85, Grand Valley Indsl. Show, 1974-85, Evansville Indsl. Show, 1982-85, Ind. Bus. Opportunity Fair, 1985-88. Chmn., Citizens' Adv. Com. to Marion County Met. Planning Dept., 1963; pres. museum com. Indpls. Fire Dept., 1966-76; mem. adv. com. Historic Preservation Commn. Marion County, 1967-73; Midwestern artifacts cons. to curator of White House, Washington, 1971-73; mem., chmn. Mayor's Contract Compliance Adv. Bd., 1977-91; mem. Mayor's Subcom. for Indpls. Stadium, 1981-83; adv. bd., exec. com. Inpls. Office Equal Opportunity 1982—; mem. Ind. Minority Bus. Opportunity Council, 1985-88; mem. Met. Mus. Art, Indpls. Mus. Art. Bd. dirs. Historic Landmarks Found. Ind., 1960-69; dir., sec. Ind. Arthritis and Rheumatism Found., 1960-67, pres., 1969, dir., 1970-90, hon. lifetime dir., 1992—, dir. Asso. Patient Services, 1976-91, dir. emeritus, 1992; pres. Amanda Wasson Meml. Found., 1961-72, Huggler-Ault Meml. Trust, 1961-72. Recipient Meritorious Service award St. Jude's Police League, 1961; citation for meritorious service Am. Legion Police Post 56, 1962; Tafflinger-Holiday Park appreciation award, 1973; Nat. Vol. Service Citation, Arthritis Found., 1979; Margaret Egan Meml. award Ind. Arthritis Found., 1980; Indpls. Profl. Fire Fighters meritorious service award, 1982. Mem. Marion County Hist. Soc. (dir. 1964—, pres. 1965-69, 74-76, 1st v.p. 1979), Am. Guild Organists (mem. Indpls. chpt., charter mem. Franklin Coll. br.), Indpls. Humane Soc., Ind. Museum Soc. (treas., dir. 1967-74), Internat. Fire Buff Assos., Indpls. Second Alarm Fire Buffs (sec.-treas. 1967, pres. 1969), Ind. Hist. Soc., Nat. Hist. Soc., Nat. Trust Historic Preservation, Smithsonian Assn., Friends of Cast Iron Architecture, Soc. Archtl. Historians, Am. Heritage Soc., N.A.P.M. Editors Group (nat. sec. 1979-81, nat. chmn./pres. 1981-84), Am. Assn. State and Local History, Decorative Arts Soc. Indpls., Ind. Soc. Assn. Execs., Nat. Assn. Purchasing Mgmt. (W.L. Beckham internat. pub. relations award 1983), Purchasing Mgmt. Assn. Indpls. (dir. 1974—), Victorian Soc. Am. (nat. sec. 1971-74), Lambda Chi Alpha, Alpha Delta Sigma, Sigma Delta Chi, Tau Kappa Alpha. Club: Indpls. Press, Rolls-Royce Owners. Author: The Mr. Eli Lilly that I Knew, 1977. Editor: Historic Landmarks News, 1969-74; Hoosier Purchasor mag., 1974-85, I.R.M.S.D.C. News, 1985-88. Contbr. articles to profl. jours. Home: 1415 W 52nd St Indianapolis IN 46208-2316

BRAUN, WARREN D., church administrator, social activist; b. Eden, Wis., June 12, 1934; s. George Henry and Elizabeth Mary (Smith) B.; m. Sharon Lee Davis; children: David, Timothy, Amy. BS in Polit. Sci., Baronette U., 1956; MS in History, U. Wis., Milw., 1970. Tchr., coach Waukesha (Wis.) Meml. H.S., 1956-60, Pius XI H.S., Milw., 1960-68; alderman City of Milw., 1968-76; state senator State of Wis., 1976-83; adminstr. Archdiocese of Milw., 1983—. With U.S. Army, 1956-63. Home: 4904 W Woodlawn Ct Milwaukee WI 53208 Office: Social Concerns Office Box 07912 Milwaukee WI 53207-0912

BRAUNSDORF, JAMES ALLEN, physics educator; b. South Bend, Ind., Apr. 13, 1938; s. Walter Louis and Ruth Harriet (Tuttle) B.; m. Donna Lou Munson, June 10, 1960; children: Kevin Scott, Allen Keith, Walter James. AB in Physics, De Pauw U., 1960; MS in Math., Purdue U., 1965. Cert. secondary tchr., Ind. Tchr. physics Greencastle Schs., 1960-62, Mishawaka (Ind.) Sch., 1962-1—; tax preparer, Mishawaka, 1967—; adj. lectr. Ind. U., South Bend, 1981-89. Pres. Beiger Heritage Corp., Mishawaka, 1981-86. Mem. NEA, Ind. State Tchrs. Assn., Am. Assn. Physics Tchrs. (Ind. Disting. Physics Tchr. 1984), Nat. Sci. Tchrs. Assn., Mishawaka Edn. Assn. (pres. 1970-74), Phi Beta Kappa. Methodist. Home: 449 Edgewater Dr Mishawaka IN 46545-6909

BRAUNSTEIN, ETHAN MALCOLM, skeletal radiologist, paleopathologist; b. Chgo., June 16, 1945. BA, Dartmouth Coll., 1967; MD, Northwestern U., Chgo., 1970. Instr. radiology U. Mich., Ann Arbor, 1976-81, assoc. prof., 1983-87; asst. prof. radiology Harvard U., Cambridge, Mass., 1981-83; prof. Ind. U., Indpls., 1987—; adj. prof. anthropology Ind. U., Indpsl., 1990—. Contbr. numerous articles to profl. jours. and chpts. to books. Bd. dirs. Kelsey Mus. of Archeology, Ann Arbor, 1983-87. Mem. Internat. Skeletal Soc., Am. Assn. Physical Anthropologists, Radiologic Soc. N.Am., Assn. Univ. Radiologists. Office: Ind U Hosps Dept Radiology Indianapolis IN 46202

BRAWNER, GENE E., financial executive; b. Iowa City, Jan. 3, 1933. BA in Sociology, U. Iowa, 1955. Broker L. C. Berindson, Iowa City, 1959; v.p. resident mgr. White Co., Iowa City, 1959-69; v.p. Stifel-Nicolaus & Co., 1969-75; v.p. resident mgr. Dain Bosworth Inc., Iowa City, 1975—. 1st lt. USAF, 1955-59. Mem. Noontime Kiwanis (bd. dirs. 1992-95). Republican. Lutheran. Office: Dain Bosworth Inc 112 S Dubuque St Iowa City IA 52240-4009

BRAY, JOAN, state legislator; b. Sept. 16, 1945; m. Carl Hoagland; 2 children. BA, Southwestern U.; MEd, U. Mass. Former tchr., journalist, former dist. dir. for Congresswoman Joan Kelly Horn; mem. Mo. Ho. of Reps. Bd. dirs. Citizens for Modern Transit. Flemming fellow, 1995. Mem. PTO, Nat. Womens Polit. Caucus. Democrat. Home: 7120 Washington Ave Saint Louis MO 63130-4312 Office: Mo Ho of Reps State Capitol Bldg Rm 411 Jefferson City MO 65101-6806

BRAY, RALPH, physics educator; b. Moghilev, Bylorussia, U.S.S.R., Sept. 11, 1921; s. Harry and Pauline (Ginzberg) B.; m. Felice Sandra Tannenbaum, Feb. 1, 1948; children: Stephen, Peter, Sharon. BA, Bklyn. Coll., 1942; MS, Purdue U., W. Lafayette, Ind., 1945, PhD, 1949. Instr. Purdue U., W. Lafayette, 1945-50, asst. prof. physics, 1950-57, assoc. prof., 1957-65, prof., 1965-88, prof. emeritus, 1989—; vis. prof. Becton Ctr., Yale U., New Haven, 1970, Christ Ch./Oxford U., Eng., 1969-70, Hebrew U., Jerusalem, 1978; NRC fellow Tech. U. Delft, Holland, 1951-52; vis. scientist Gen. Atomics Rsch. Lab., LaJolla, Calif., 1960-61; cons. in field. Contbr. numerous articles to profl. jours.; editorial bd. Jour. Applied Physics, 1967-69. Recipient Vis. Scientist award Japan Soc. for Promotion of Sci., 1977, von Humboldt Sr. Scientist award Max Planck Inst., Stuttgart, 1985-86; Guggenheim fellow, 1969-70. Fellow Am. Phys. Soc.; mem. Sigma Xi, Sigma Pi Sigma. Home: 322 Hollowood Dr West Lafayette IN 47906-2146 Office: Purdue Univ Dept of Physics West Lafayette IN 47907

BRAY, RICHARD D., state legislator; m. Maurine Bray; 3 children. AB, Ind. U., JD. Precinct committeeman; prosecuting atty. Morgan County, 1959-70; chmn. state wages adjustment bd., 1973-74; mem. Ind. State Rep. Dist. 47, 1974-90; mem. county and twp. com. Ind. Ho. of Reps., mem. govt. affairs com., co-chmn. cts. com.; mem. corrections com. Ind. State Senate Dist. 37, 1992—; criminal and civil procedures com., elections com., elections com., agrl. and small bus. com.; ranking mem. judiciary com. Ind. State Ho. Reps. Pres. Sheriff Merit Bd., 1971-74. Mem. Masons, Scottish Rite, Shriners, Elks, Moose. Home: 210 E Morgan St Martinsville IN 46151-1545*

BRAYAK, THOMAS LEE, concrete and gravel company executive; b. Escanaba, Mich., Jan. 20, 1948; s. Thomas F. and Jeanette E. (Peterson) B.; m. Rosemary E. Murzello, May 3, 1975; 1 child, Tamara. BS in Physics, Mich. Tech. U., 1970. Foreman Bichler Paving Co., Escanaba, 1967-70; tchr. U.S. Peace Corps, Orissa, India, 1971-73; instr. in math. and physics Bay Denoc C.C., Escanaba, 1974-89, heavy equipment operator, 1974-79, v.p., 1979—; pres. Delta County Builders Exch., Escanaba, 1992-94; treas. Upper Peninsula Builders Exch., Escanaba, 1993-95. Bd. dirs. Bay De Noc Chroal Soc., Escanaba, 1975—. Office: Bichler Gravel & Concrete PO Box 263 Escanaba MI 49829

BRAZIL, JOHN RUSSELL, academic administrator; b. Los Angeles, Mar. 5, 1946; s. Burton R. and Helen Frances (Douglas) B.; m. Janice Hosking; children: Adrian, Morgan;. AB, Stanford U., 1968; MPhil, Yale U., 1972, PhD, 1975. Coordinator Am. studies program San Jose (Calif.) State U., 1976-79, assoc. prof., prof., 1979-84, spl. asst. to acad. v.p., 1979-81, exec. asst. to pres., 1981-83, assoc. acad. v.p., 1983, acad. v.p., 1983-84; pres. Southeastern Mass. U., North Dartmouth, 1984-92, Bradley U., 1992—; chmn. S.E. Mass. Partnership, 1988-92; exec. dir. Sourisseau Acad. State and Local History, San Jose, 1977-79; cons. Calif. Coun. for Humanities in Pub. Policy, 1976-78, NEH; chmn. Coun. of Pub. Pres.'s and Chancellors, Mass., 1986-87; hon. adv. bd. SHARE, Inc., 1986-92; mem. Am. Coun. Edn., 1984—; bd. dirs. Cilcorp, Inc., First of Am. Bank, Ill. N.A., Meth. Med. Ctr., NAICU; exec. com. FIICU, 1992—. Contbr. articles on Twain, London, Sterling, Bierce, the 1920's, numerous book revs. Bd. dirs. Mass. Ctr. for Excellence in Marine Sci., 1986-92; mem. Fall River Regional Task Force, 1984-92; com. mem. SEMTECH, Mass., 1984-92; trustee Greater New Bedford Indsl. Found., 1984-92; mem. Charlton Meml. Hosp., 1985-92; pres. S.E. Mass. U. Found., 1985-92. Fulbright Sr. scholar, U. Sydney, 1980; Phi Kappa Phi Disting. Faculty Achievement award, San Jose State U., 1984; S&H Found. lectureship grant. Mem. NCAA (Pres.'s Commn. 1987-92, chair Walter Byers scholarship com. 1991—), Am. Assn. State Colls. and Univs., Am. Studies Assn., Am. Assn. Higher Edn., New Bedford C. of C. (bd. dirs. 1984-88), No. Calif. Am. Studies Assn. (exec. bd. 1978-80), Soc. Advancement of Mgmt. (adv. rev. bd. 1991-92), Fall River C. of C. (bd. dirs. 1984-87), Peoria Country Club, Creve Coeur Club, Ill. Valley Yacht Club, Univ. Club Chgo., Phi Beta Kappa, Phi Kappa Phi, Omicron Delta Kappa. Democrat. Office: Bradley Univ Office of President Peoria IL 61625

BREARLEY, HARRINGTON COOPER, JR., computer science educator; b. Greenville, S.C., Jan. 17, 1926; s. Harrington Cooper and Margaret Douglas (Marion) B.; m. Mary Jo Bradford, Dec. 28, 1957; children: Ann, William, Caroline. BEE, Ga. Inst. Tech., 1946; MS, U. Ill., 1950, PhD, 1954. Mem. tech. staff Bell Telephone Labs., Burlington, N.C., 1947-49; engr. GE Co., Syracuse, N.Y., 1953-59; rsch. asst. prof. U. Ill., Urbana, 1959-65; assoc. prof. Iowa State U., Ames, 1965-77, prof., 1977—; cons. Coll. Bd./Edn. Testing Svc., Trenton, N.J., Clemson, S.C., 1984, 86, 88, 89, 90. Author: Introduction to Assembler Language for the IBM System 360/370, 1974; contbr. article to profl. jourl. Treas., other officers County Dem. Com., Ames; pres. bd. Ames Visiting Nurse Assn., 1981-84. Ensign USNR. Fellow U.S. Atomic Energy Commn., 1952-54. Mem. IEEE (chair ctrl. Iowa sect. 1976-77, vice chair 1975-76, sec.-treas. 1974-75, life), IEEE Computer Soc. (sec., editor, edn. bd. 1980-88). Presbyterian. Home: 1537 Linden Dr Ames IA 50010 Office: Iowa State U Computer Sci Dept Ames IA 50011

BREAUX, BILLIE J., state legislator. BS, W.Va. State U.; MS, Ind. U. Tchr. Indpl. Pub. Sch.; mem. legis. appropriations and elections Ind. State Senate Dist. 34, 1990—, mem. natural resources, pensions and labor coms., mem. corrections, cime and civil program com., mem. health and environ. affairs com. and pub. policy com. Mem. Indpls. Edn. Assn. (past pres.), Friends of Urban League (pres.), Indpls. Urban League, State Tchrs. Assn. *

BRECHNITZ, JAN G., investment consultant; b. St. Louis, Feb. 5, 1935. BA, Princeton U., 1957. Investment cons. Kemper Securities Inc., Belleville, Ill., 1962—. Mem. St. Clair Country Club. Republican. Office: Everen Securities Inc PO Box 488 23 Public Sq Ste 404 Belleville IL 62222

BREDAR, MARCIA ANN, lawyer; b. Des Moines, Jan. 29, 1953; d. Vincent Leo and Teresa (Peter) B. BA, Creighton U., 1974, JD, 1977. Bar: Nebr. 1977. Law clk. Nebr. Supreme Ct., Lincoln, Nebr., 1977-78; asst. gen. counsel Mut. of Omaha, 1978—; 1st v.p., counsel Mutual of Omaha, 1995—, v.p., sr. counsel, 1996—; legal rsch. instr. Creighton U. Sch. Law, Omaha, 1980-85. Pres. Worknet Exec. Bd., 1995, 96; bd. dirs. Gt. Plains coun. Girl Scouts U.S., 1989-92, nominating chair, 1992; mem. St. Leo Parish Coun., 1989—, pres., 1990-92, facilitator for RCIA, 1993; vol. Emergency Pregnancy Svc., 1985—. Named Woman of Achievement, Gt. Plains Girl Scouts, 1987, Dist. Disabled Person Yr., Pilot Club, 1985, Outstanding Omahan, Jaycees, 1988; recipient Nat. Cath. Edn. Merit award, 1995, Creighton U. Alumni Merit award Coll. Arts & Scis., 1995. Mem. Nebr. Bar Assn., Omaha Bar Assn., Nebr. Polio Survivors Assn. (bd. dirs. 1985-92, pres. 1991-92). Roman Catholic. Office: Mut of Omaha Omaha Plz Omaha NE 68175

BREDECK, MARTIN JAMES, clergyman, theology educator; b. St. Louis, Nov. 5, 1933; s. Joseph Francis and Kathleen Mary (Downes) B. AB, St. Louis U., 1957, MA, 1958; PhD, Cath. U. Am., 1977. Joined Soc. of Jesus, 1951, ordained priest Roman Catholic Ch., 1964. Instr. DeSales Coll., Hyattsville, Md., 1967-68, St. Joseph's U., Phila., 1971-74; from instr. to asst. prof. Mt. St. Mary's Coll., L.A., 1976-78; asst. prof. theology Rockhurst Coll., Kansas City, Mo., 1978-81, assoc. prof., 1981-89, prof., 1989—, chmn. divsn. philosophy and theology, 1982-85; chmn. Rockhurst Libr. Bd., Kansas City, 1988-93. Author: Imperfect Apostles, 1988; editor: Memoir of Felix Verrydt, S.J., 1994, Autobiography of Walter H. Hill, S.J., 1994. Mem. AAUP (exec. com. Mo. state conf., Disting. Svc. award 1995), Am. Acad. Religion, Coll. Theology Soc. Democrat. Office: Rockhurst Coll 1100 Rockhurst Rd Kansas City MO 64110

BREDT, CHARLES FRANKLIN, lumber and timber executive; b. Cleve., June 12, 1952; s. Jack Bourquoin and Helen (Collins) B.; m. Victoria Elizabeth Jackson, Sept. 23, 1978; 1 child, Victoria Lynn. BS in Agr., Ohio State U., 1974. Salesman C.S. Interiors, Cleve., 1974-77; sales mgr. C.S. Supply, Cleve., 1977-81; gen. mgr. No. Ohio Lumber & Timber, Cleve., 1982-85, v.p., gen. mgr., 1986—. Mem. design rev. com. City of Cleve., 1991—. Mem. Ohio Lumbermans Assn. (rep. to nominating com. of Nat. Lumber and Bldg. Material Dealers Assn. 1992, bd. dirs. 1996—), Lumber Club (bd. dirs. 1987—, pres. 1989), Flats Oxbow Assn. (bd. dirs. 1990—, vice chmn. 1993—), Cleve. Yachting Club (bd. dirs. 1988-94, officer 1991-94, Sailor of Yr. 1986, Yachtsman of Yr. 1994), Rotary (bd. dirs. 1995—, Paul Harris fellow 1992). Office: No Ohio Lumber & Timber 1895 Carter Rd Cleveland OH 44113-2401

BREE, ALANNA FLATH, medical researcher; b. Highland, Ill., Dec. 17, 1971; d. Allen victor and Shirley Ann (Donnelly) Flath. BS in Biology magna cum laude, S.W. Mo. State U., 1994. Lab. and teaching asst. S.W. Mo. State U., Springfield, 1991-93, rsch. asst. microbiology, 1993-94; med. rsch. lab. dir. Washington U. Sch. Medicine, St. Louis, 1994—; new student liasion So. Ill. U. Sch. Medicine, Springfield, 1995-96. Contbr. articles to profl. jours. Vol. St. John's Hosp., Springfield, 1993; Sundacy sch. tchr. Redeemer Luth. Ch., St. Louis, 1994-95. State of Ill. scholar, 1995. Mem. AMA, Acad. Am. Family Physicians, Am. Med. Students Assn., Sangmon County Med. Soc., Beta Beta Beta (v.p., treas. 1990-94), Sigma Kappa (pres. 1991-94, Officer of Yr. award 1994). Lutheran.

BREE, MARLIN DUANE, publisher, author; b. Norfolk, Nebr., May 16, 1933; s. George F. and Luile Bree; m. Loris Bree; 1 child, William Marlin. BA, cert. in journalism, U. Nebr., 1955. Mng. editor Davidson Pub. Co., 1958-61; editor Greater Mpls. mag., 1962-63; pub. rels. specialist Blue Shield, 1964-67; editor Sunday Mag., Star and Tribune, Mpls., 1968-72; columnist Corp. Report, Mpls., 1973-77; publs. cons., 1978-83; co-founder, ptnr., editorial dir. Marlor Press, Inc., St. Paul, 1983-91, co-owner, pub., 1992—; chmn. Midwest Book Awards, St. Paul, 1992. Author: In the Teeth of the Northeaster: A Solo Voyage on Lake Superior, 1988, Call of the North Wind: Voyages and Adventures on Lake Superior, 1996; co-author: Alone Against the Atlantic, 1981; contbr. No. Breezes mag., 1992—. Dir. comm. Mpls. Bicentennial Celebration, 1976. With U.S. Army, 1955-57. Mem. Pubs. Mktg. Assn., Midwest Ind. Pubs. Assn. (pres. Mpls. 1984, named publisher of yr. 1994). Office: Marlor Press Inc 4304 Brigadoon Dr Saint Paul MN 55126-3100

BREED, EILEEN JUDITH, small business owner; b. Chgo., Sept. 18, 1945; d. John Joseph and Helen Agatha (Hoy) Kennedy; m. Harvey Breed, Feb. 3, 1973; 1 child, Diana Marie Parks. BA, Northeastern Ill. U., 1966, MA, 1976, postgrad., 1980-81; postgrad., Nat. Coll. Edn., 1981, 83, No. Ill. U., 1987—. Tchr. Canty Elem. Sch., Chgo., 1967-76; tchr. St. Raymond's Sch., Mt. Prospect, Ill., 1976-78; pvt. practice diagnosis and remediation learning disabilities, cons. spl. edn., Des Plaines, Ill., 1976-78; prin. Angel Town Pvt. Sch., Des Plaines, 1978-79; tutoring, coop. work tng. coordinator Nipper Sch., Des Plaines, 1979-86; tchr. acad. resources Oak Terr. Sch., Highwood, Ill., 1986-87; vocat. coord. North and West regions Sch. Assn. Spl. Edn. Du Page County, Roselle, Ill., 1987-89; prin. Sch. Assns. Spl. Edn./Du Page N. Alternative Sch., 1989-91, Aura Extended Day Sch., 1990-91; asst. prin. Stratford Jr. High Sch., Bloomingdale, Ill., 1991-94; founder, pres. Handy Ma'ams, Inc., Saugatuck, Mich., 1994—; tchr. parent-edn. classes; cons. in field to pvt. schs., various groups and agys. Past chmn. Smiles Campaign. Mem. NAFE, TRADE Industries (parent group),, Holland C. of C., Saugatuck-Douglas Hist. Soc., Lakeshore Garden Club. Home & Office: 3480 64th St Saugatuck MI 49453-9706

BREEDLOVE, JIMMIE DALE, JR., elementary education educator; b. Pekin, Ill., Jan. 18, 1958; s. Jimmie Dale Sr. and Kay Maria (Goodin) B. BA in Elem. Edn. magna cum laude, Eureka (Ill.) Coll., 1980; postgrad., No. Ill. U., Pekin. Cert. elem. tchr. K-9, high sch. tchr. 6-12. Homebound instr., learning resource room aide Lewistown (Ill.) Community High Sch., 1980-81; elem. tchr. San Jose (Ill.) Community Unit Sch. Dist. 122, 1981-89, Illini Cen. Community Unit Sch. Dist. 189, 1989—; geography curriculum, developer; sch. librarian, gifted/talented instr. San Jose Grade Sch. Dir. choir, mem. worship com. San Jose United Meth. Ch. Mem. NEA, Internat. Reading Assn., Ill. Edn. Assn., Illini Cen. Edn. Assn., Alpha Chi. Office: Illini Central Grade Sch Mason City IL 62664

BREEN, KATHERINE ANNE, speech and language pathologist; b. Chgo., Oct. 31, 1948; d. Robert Stephen and Gertrude Catherine (Bader) Breen; B.S., Northwestern U., 1970; M.A. (U.S. Rehab. Services trainee), U. Mo., Columbia, 1971. Speech/lang. pathologist Fulton (Mo.) pub. schs., 1971-73; co-dir. Easter Seal Speech Clinic, Jefferson City, Mo., summers 1972, 73; speech/lang. pathologist Shawnee Mission (Kans.) pub. schs., 1973-96; staff St. Joseph's Hosp., Kansas City, Mo., 1978-81, Midwest Rehab. Ctr., Kansas City, 1985; pvt. practice speech therapy; cons. East Central Mo. Mental Health Center; guest lectr. Fontbonne Coll., St. Louis. Clin. certification in speech pathology. Mem. Am., Kans. speech and hearing assns., NEA, Mo. State Tchrs. Assn., Kansas City Alumni Assn. of Northwestern U. (dir. alumni admissions council, Outstanding Leadership award for work on alumni admissions council 1981, Svc. award, 1991), Friends of Art Nelson/Atkins Art Gallery and Museum (vol.), Nat. Trust Hist. Preservation, Kansas City Hist. Found., Zeta Phi Eta. Methodist. Home: 6865 W 51st Ter Apt 1C Shawnee Mission KS 66202-1576

BREESE, THOMAS ROBERT, investigative firm executive, investor; b. Iowa City, Feb. 7, 1941; s. Edwin Eugene and Marlys Arlovene (Gillespie) B.; m. Holly Sue Hann, June 27, 1964; children: Eric Edwin, Chad Stuart. BS in mech. engring., U. Iowa, 1963. Lic. Pvt. Investigator; cert. Notary Pub. Pres. The Breese Co., Inc., Iowa City, 1980—; co-owner Southtown Properties, LC, Iowa City, 1987—, Third-Party Svcs, LC, Iowa City, 1994—. Bd. dirs. Mercy Hosp., Iowa City, 1983-92, pres. Iowa City Jaycees (local outstanding pres. 1968), dir. C. of C., 1979-81, dir. United Way, 1975, coun. mem. City U. Heights, 1975-80. Capt. USNR, 1965—. Mem. Naval Res. Assn., Res. Officers Assn., Iowa City Apartment Owners Assn., Iowa Assn. Pvt. Investigators, Rotary. Republican. Methodist. Office: Third Party Svc LC 611 Southgate Ave Iowa City IA 52244

BREHM, JACK WILLIAMS, social psychologist, educator; b. Rockwell City, Iowa, Jan. 16, 1928; s. Carl and Charlotte (Williams) B. AB, Harvard Coll., 1952; PhD, U. Minn., 1955. Rsch. asst. Yale U., New Haven, Conn., 1955-57, asst. prof., 1957-58; asst. to prof. Duke U., Durham, N.C., 1958-75; prof. U. Kans., Lawrence, 1975—; mem. exec. com. Soc. Experimental Social Psychology, 1975-79, chair exec. com., 1977-78. Author: A Theory of Psychological Reactance, 1966; co-author Explorations in Cognitive Dissonance, 1962, Perspectives on Cognitive Dissonance, 1976, Psychological Reactance: A Theory of Freedom and Control, 1981. Mem. AAAS, APA, Am. Psychol. Soc., Soc. for Exptl. Social Psychology. Office: U Kans Psychology Dept Lawrence KS 66045

BREHM, WILLIAM ALLEN, JR., urban planner; b. Neenah, Wis., Jan. 18, 1945; s. William Allen and Katharine (Gilbert) B.; B.A., Lawrence U., 1967; M.U.P. (Richard King Mellon fellow 1967-68), Mich. State U., 1973; m. Patricia Lee Kelley, Dec. 30, 1967; children: Laura Kelley, William Hunt, Katharine Ann. Dir. planning Charter Twp. of Meridian (Mich.), 1969-72; v.p., treas. Planning Cons. Services, Inc., Lansing, Mich., 1972-76; dir. planning Manson, Jackson, Kane, Architects, Inc., Lansing, 1974-76; dir. planning and devel. City of Appleton (Wis.), 1976-90, exec. dir. Redevel. Authority, 1979-90; pres. Community Devel. Systems, Appleton, 1990—; owner Brehm Real Estate, 1991—; mem. Wis. State Hist. Soc., 1978—, Outagamie Hist. Soc., 1980—, bd. dirs. 1993, v.p., 1995. Trustee, Charter Twp. of Meridan, 1972-74, supr., 1974-76; dist. chmn. Boy Scouts Am., 1979-81; bd. dirs. Pub. Art Found., 1985-91, Houdini Hist. Ctr., 1995—; bd. supr. Outagamie County, 1988—. Awarded Cert. Nat. Recognition Community Devel. Excellence HUD, 1986. Lic. real estate broker, Wis. Mem. Am. Inst. Cert. Planners, Am. Planning Assn., Nat. Assn. Realtors, Nat. Trust Historic Preservation, Assn. Wis. Planners (treas. 1977-79, pres. 1981-82), Soc. Am. Magicians, Houdini Club Wis., Internat. Brotherhood Magicians, Realtors Assn. Northeast Wis., Delta Tau Delta. Mem. United Ch. of Christ. Club: Rotary (pres. 1991-92). Home: 716 S Fidelis St Appleton WI 54915-3559 Office: PO Box 1502 Appleton WI 54913

BREIMYER, HAROLD FREDERICK, agricultural economist; b. Ft. Recovery, Ohio, Apr. 13, 1914; s. Fred Christian and Ella Anna Margaret (Schulz) B.; m. Rachel Eudora Styles, Dec. 13, 1941; 1 child, Frederick Styles. B.S., Ohio State U., 1934, M.S., 1935; Ph.D., Am. U., 1960. Staff economist Agrl. Adjustment Adminstrn., 1936-39, Bur. Agrl. Econs., 1939-53, Agrl. Mktg. Service, 1954-59, 61-66, Council Econ. Advisers, 1959-61; mem. faculty U. Mo., Columbia, 1966-84; prof. agrl. econs. U. Mo., 1966-84, extension economist, 1968-84; vis. Anderson scholar Ohio State U., 1985; teaching assoc. U. Mo., 1986—. Author: Individual Freedom and the Economic Organization of Agriculture, 1965, Economics of the Product Markets of Agriculture, 1976, Farm Policy: 13 Essays, 1977, Over-fulfilled Expectations: A Life and an Era in Rural America, 1991. Mem. Montgomery County (Md.) Bd. Edn., 1959-62, pres., 1961; pres. Columbia Council Chs., 1974-76. Served with USNR, 1942-45. Recipient Superior Service award Dept. Agr., 1954, 59, Centennial award Coll. Agr. and Home Econs., Ohio State U., 1970, Faculty-Alumni award U. Mo., 1975, Thomas Jefferson award U. Mo., 1983. Fellow Am. Agrl. Econs. Assn. (pres. 1969); mem. Internat. Assn. Agrl. Economists. Democrat. Methodist. Club: Lions. Home: 1616 Princeton Dr Columbia MO 65203-1852 Office: U Mo 214 Mumford Dr Columbia MO 65211

BREINER, SANDER JAMES, psychiatry educator, psychoanalyst; b. Fiume, Italy, July 12, 1925; (parents Am. citizens); s. Alfred and Margaret (Steiner) B.; m. Beatrice Marsha Oboler, Mar. 18, 1951; children: Linda Marie, Myles Steven, Robert Ethan. BS, U. Ill., 1948; MB, MD, Chgo. Med. Sch., 1953. Diplomate Nat. Bd. Med. Examiners, Am. Bd. Psychiatry and Neurology, Nat. Bd. of Accreditation in Psychoanalysis. Asst. prof. psychiatry Wayne State U., Detroit, 1957—; assoc. prof. Mich. State U., East Lansing, 1970—; attending staff, mem. psychiatry dept. Harper Grace Hosp., Detroit, 1960—; attending psychiatry dept. William Beaumont Hosp., Royal Oak, Mich., 1968—; cons. depts. ob-gyn., surgery and medicine Harper Grace Hosp., 1960—; cons. dept. ob-gyn. William Beaumont Hosp., 1982—; cons. in marital/sexual problems; tng./surpervising analyst Mich. Psychoanalytic Coun.; trustee Nat. Bd. Accreditation in Psychoanalysis. Author: Slaughter of the Innocents: Child Abuse Through the Ages and Today, 1990; contbr. more than 70 articles to profl. jours. Cons. Detroit Commn. on Children and Youth, 1957-62; cons. bd. edn. Detroit, Garden City and Bloomfield Hills, 1957-71. With inf. U.S. Army, 1943-45, ETO. Fellow Am. Psychiat. Assn., Am. Soc. Psychoanalytic Physicians; mem. AMA, AAAS, Psychosmatic Medicine, N.Y. Acad. Sci., Internat. Assn. for Psychohistory, Mich. Soc. for Psychoanalytic Psychology, Mich. Psychoanapytic Coun., Tng. and Supervising Psychoanalyst. Democrat. Home: 7410 Franklin Rd Bloomfield Hills MI 48301-3610 Office: 31811 Middlebelt Rd Ste 203 Farmington Hills MI 48334-2368

BREIPOHL, WALTER EUGENE, real estate broker; b. Ottawa, Ill., Mar. 24, 1953; s. Eugene E. and Margaret L. (Hughes) B. BS, Loyola U., Chgo., 1974. Real estate broker and devel. Breipohl Co., Ottawa, 1975—; bd. dirs. No. Ill. Devel. Corp., Union Bank Holding Co., Ottawa, Union Bank, Ottawa. Bd. dirs. Greater Ottawa, Inc., 1984—, Main Street U.S.A. Program, Ottawa, 1991-93, Cmty. Hosp. of Ottawa Found., 1994—; chmn. Econ. Devel. Commn., Ottawa, 1985-88; trustee Cmty. Hosp. Ottawa, 1986-89. Mem. Illini Valley Assn. Realtors (sec.-treas. 1983-85, President's award 1985), No. Ill. Comml. Assn. Realtors, Ill. Assn. Realtors, Nat. Assn. Realtors, Nat. Assn. Real Estate Appraisers, Nat. Assn. Home Builders, Ottawa Area C. of C. and Industry (chmn. bd. dirs. 1988), Ill. C. of C., Internat. Club (Chgo.), Boat Club, Union League Club (Chgo.), Elks, KC. Republican. Roman Catholic. Home and Office: PO Box 1039 Ottawa IL 61350-6039

BREITLOW, JOHN RICHARD, retired speech communication educator; b. Chgo., Jan. 17, 1932; s. Carl Gottfried and Lillian Louise (Damm) B.; m. Penelope Crawford, Mar. 22, 1958; children: Stanton Hopkins, Carla Grace Breitlow Antoff. BA, St. Olaf Coll., 1953; AMS, U. Minn., 1957, MA, 1970, PhD, 1972. Cert. mortician, Minn., 1959-92. Mortician, 1959-68, educator, 1960-92. Wine columnist, 1979—. Intelligence officer USAR, 1953-87; col. USAR, 1977-87. Decorated CDR-Outstanding Unit/USAR Meritorious Svc. medal Dept. Army, Washington, 1983-84, Legion of Merit U.S. Army Command and Gen. Staff Coll., Ft. Leavenworth, Kans., 1987. Home and Office: PO Box 328 Winona MN 55987-0328

BREKKE, GAIL LOUISE, broadcasting administrator; b. Fargo, N.D., Dec. 9, 1949; d. Curtis Eugene Sr. and Geraldine Ann (Hughes) B.; m. Harold E. Protter (div. 1991). BS in Edn., U. N.D., 1971; AA in Retailing, Lucerne, Switzerland, 1972; MA, Webster Coll., 1981. News reporter WXIX-TV, Cin., 1973-74; news reporter KPLR-TV, St. Louis, 1974-75, in sales, 1975-77, sales mgr., 1977-80; gen. mgr. KRBK-TV, Sacramento, 1980-83, WNOL-TV, New Orleans, 1983-86, WGBO-TV, Chgo., 1986-87, KITN-TV, Mpls., 1987-93, WBNE, New Haven, 1996—; chair, mem. exec. bd. Pavek Mus. Broadcasting, Mpls., 1990—; owner, pres. Black Diamond Communications Inc., 1994—. mem. Nat. Alumni Leadership Coun., U. N.D., 1992. Mem. Minn. Broadcasters Assn. (pres. 1991—), Advt. Fedn. Minn. (bd. dirs. 1993—), Women in Cable & Telecom. Midwest (bd. dirs. 1993—).

BREMNER, JOHN MCCOLL, agronomy and biochemistry educator; b. Dumbarton, Scotland, Jan. 18, 1922; came to U.S., 1959; s. Archibald Donaldson and Sarah Kennedy (McColl) B.; m. Eleanor Mary Williams, Sept. 30, 1950; children: Stuart, Carol. BS, Glasgow U., 1944, DSc, 1987; PhD, U. London, 1948, DSc, 1959. With chemistry dept. Rothamsted Exptl. Sta., Harpenden, Eng., 1945-59; assoc. prof. Iowa State U., Ames, 1959-61, prof. agronomy and biochemistry, 1961—, C.F. Curtiss disting. prof. agriculture, prof. agronomy, biochemistry, 1975—; tech. expert IAEA, Austria, 1964-65, Yugoslavia, 1964-65. Author or co-author over 300 publs. including 30 chpts in sci. monographs. Recipient Outstanding Research award First Miss. Corp., 1979, Alexander Von Humboldt award Alexander Von Humboldt Found., Fed. Republic of Germany, 1982, Gov.'s Sci. medal State of Iowa, 1983, Harvey Wiley award U.S. Assn. Ofcl. Analytical Chemists, 1984, Spencer award Am. Chem. Soc., 1987, Burlington No. Found. Faculty Achievement award for Research, Gamma Sigma Delta award of merit for disting. service to agriculture, Regents award for faculty excellence, 1992, Award for Advancement of Agrl. & Food Chemistry, Am. Chem. Soc.; fellow Rockefeller Found., 1957, Guggenheim Found., 1968. Fellow AAAS, Am. Acad. Microbiology, Am. Soc. Agronomy (Agronomic Rsch. award 1985, Environ. Quality Rsch. award 1990), Soil Sci. Soc. Am. (Achievement award 1967, Bouyoucos Disting. Career award 1982, Disting. Svc. award 1993), Iowa Acad. Sci. (disting.); mem. NAS, Am. Soc. Microbiology, Brit. Soc. Soil Sci., Internat. Soil Sci. Soc., Phi Kappa Phi, Sigma Xi, Gamma Sigma Delta. Home: 2028 Pinehurst Dr Ames IA 50014-4561 Office: Iowa State U Dept Agronomy Ames IA 50011

BREMNER, JOSEPH P., management consultant; b. Chgo., June 28, 1947; s. John M. and Dorothy J. (Gibson) B.; m. Linda C. Hanlon, July 10, 1971; children: Ryan, Christine, Maureen. JD, Loyola U., 1972. Asst. v.p. 1st Wis. Trust Co., Milw., 1974-79; v.p., COO Mgmt. Contents, Northbrook, Ill., 1979-84; pres. Database Devel., Milw., 1984—; bd. dirs. Chem. Abstracts Svc., Columbus, Ohio. Author: Guide to Database Distribution, 1994, Database Distribution, 1987; contbr. chpt. to CD-ROM II Optical Publishing, 1986. Pres. Future Milw., 1979-80; chmn. A Better Chance, Shorewood, Wis., 1977-78. Recipient Alumni award for outstanding leadership and scholastic achievement Loyola U. Law Sch. Alumni Assn., 1972. Mem. Info. Industry Assn. (chmn. proprietary rights com. 1990-92), ABA (chmn. subcom. on database registration 1993—). Office: Database Devel 2703 E Newton Ave Milwaukee WI 53211

BRENEMAN, DEBRA LYNN, dermatologist, educator; b. Spirit Lake, Iowa, Jan. 17, 1955; d. Walter Edward and Mildred Mathilda (Bonde) Johnson; m. John Charles Breneman, May 30, 1981; children: Christopher John, Kevin Michael, Alyssa Nicole, Nathan Andrew. BS, Iowa State U., 1977; MD, U. Iowa, 1981. Intern, Butterworth Hosp., Grand Rapids, Mich., 1981-82; resident in dermatology U. Cin., 1982-85, instr. dermatology, 1985-86, asst. prof., 1986-91, assoc. prof. dermatology, 1991—, dir. div. dermatopharmacology, 1985—; staff physician U. Cin. Med. Ctr., 1985—; staff physician VA Med. Ctr., Cin., 1985-91, cons. physician, 1992—; cons. physician Children's Hosp. Med. Ctr., Cin., 1986—. Contbr. articles to profl. jours. Fellow Am. Acad. Dermatology; mem. Midwestern Congress Dermatol. Socs., Ohio Dermatol. Assn., Cin. Dermatol. Soc., Phi Beta Kappa, Phi Kappa Phi, Alpha Lambda Delta. Office: U Cin Dept Dermatology 234 Goodman St # 523 Cincinnati OH 45267-2364

BRENINGSTALL, GALEN NATLEY, physician; b. Denver, Jan. 18, 1951; s. Natley Russell and Ruth Irene (Emrich) B.; m. Debi Glick; children: Jeremy, David, Nechama, Joseph, Elisha, David Herron, Aviva Herron. BA, St. John's Coll., Santa Fe, 1973; MD, U. Tex. Med. Br., Galveston, 1979. Diplomate Am. Bd. Psychiatry & Neurology, Am. Bd. Pediatrics. Resident in pediatrics U. Minn. Hosps., 1979-81, fellow in pediatric neurology, 1981-84; asst. prof. pediatrics & neurology Temple U. Sch. Medicine, Phila., 1984-87; attending staff physician St. Christopher's Hosp. for Children, Phila., 1984-87; pediatric neurologist Park Nicollet Med. Ctr., Mpls., 1987—; attending staff physician Mpls. Children's Med. Ctr., 1987—; cons. Albert Einstein Med. Ctr. No. Divsn., Phila., 1984-87, Meth. Hosp., Mpls., 1987—, Abbott Northwestern Hosp., Mpls., 1987—. Contbr. numerous articles to profl. jours., chpts. to books. Mem. Am. Acad. Neurology, Child Neurology Soc. Jewish. Office: Park Nicollet Med Ctr Pediatric Subspecialties 910 E 26th St Ste 325 Minneapolis MN 55404-4549

BRENNAN, DONALD GEORGE, university dean, research administrator; b. St. Louis, Sept. 9, 1945; s. James Loughlin and Genevieve Theresa (Trigg) B.; m. Martha Kennedy; children: Laura, Erin, Kate, Emily. BS, St. Louis U., 1967, MA, 1969; PhD in Comm. Disorders, U. Okla., 1974. Lic. speech pathologist; cert. tchr., Mo.; cert. clin. competence in speech pathology. Speech-lang. pathologist Mo. Crippled Children's Svc., 1967, St. John's Mercy Med. Ctr., 1967; cons. speech-lang. pathologist Ctrl. Ala. Rehab. Ctr., 1969-71; from asst. prof. to assoc. prof. comm. disorders St. Louis U., 1975-86, prof., 1986—, chair dept. comm. disorders, 1981-88, dean Grad. Sch., univ. rsch. adminstr., 1988—; adj. prof. Ctrl. Inst. for Deaf, Washington U., St. Louis, 1980—; mem. Coun. Grad. Schs., 1988—, Midwest Assn. Grad. Schs., 1988—, Am. Assn. Grad. Schs. in Cath. Colls./Univs., 1988—, others; presenter in field. Contbr. numerous articles to profl. jours. Bd. dirs. Spl. Edn. Enrichment Found., 1991-92. Capt. USAF, 1968-71. Grantee U.S. Office of Edn., 1976—, U.S. Office of Spl. Edn., 1984-88, others. Mem. Am. Speech-Lang.-Hearing Assn. (com. on doctoral edn. 1989-90, site visitor edn. standards bd. 1989—), Mo. Speech-Lang.-Hearing Assn. (exec. bd. 1983-89), Speech and Hearing Assn. of Greater St. Louis (pres. 1976-77, exec. bd. 1975-78, chair com. on fin. 1978), Am. Coun. on Edn., Am. Assn. for Higher Edn., Soc. Rsch. Adminstrs., Nat. Coun. for Univ. Rsch. Adminstrs. Office: St Louis U 3663 Lindell Blvd Saint Louis MO 63103

BRENNAN, EDWARD A., merchandising, insurance and real estate executive; b. Chgo., Jan. 16, 1934; s. Edward and Margaret (Bourget) B.; m. Lois Lyon, June 11, 1955; children: Edward J., Cynthia Walls, Sharon Lisnow, Donald A., John L., Linda Thode. BS, Marquette U., 1955. With Sears, Roebuck and Co., 1956—; exec. v.p. So. terr. Sears, Roebuck and Co., Atlanta, 1977-80; pres. merchandise group Sears, Roebuck and Co., Chgo., 1980-81, chmn., CEO merchandise group, 1981-84, corp. pres., COO merchandise group, 1984-86, chmn., CEO, 1986—; bd. dirs. Minn. Mining & Mfg. Co., Sears, Roebuck and Co., AMR Corp., Dean Witter, Discover & Co., Allstate Corp. Chmn. bd. trustees Marquette U.; trustee De Paul U., Rush-Presbyn.-St. Luke's Med. Ctr. Mem. Bus. Roundtable, Bus. Coun. Office: Sears Roebuck and Co 233 S Wacker Dr Chicago IL 60684*

BRENNAN, MATTHEW CANNON, English literature educator, poet; b. Richmond Heights, Mo., Jan. 18, 1955; s. William Joseph and Suzanne (Simon) B.; m. Laura Lee Fredendall, Aug. 13, 1977 (div. June 1987); 1 child, Daniel William; m. Beverley Simms, May 21, 1994. AB, Grinnell Coll., 1977; MA, U. Minn., Mpls., 1980, PhD, 1984. Editor Golle and Holmes Fin. Learning, Minnetonka, Minn., 1982-84; vis. asst. prof. U. Minn., Mpls., 1984-85; asst. prof. Ind. State U., Terre Haute, 1985-88, assoc. prof., 1988-92, prof. English, 1992—. Author: (poetry) Seeing in the Dark: Poems, 1993, The Music of Exile: Poems, 1994, (exhbn. catalogs) Wordsworth, Turner and Romantic Landscape, 1987, Is Poetry a Visual Art?, 1993. Ind. Arts Commn. fellow, 1994; Univ. Rsch. grantee Ind. State U., Terre Haute, 1991, Univ. Arts grantee, 1993; named to Acad. Am. Poets, U. Minn., Mpls., 1979, 80, 84. Mem. MLA, Wordsworth-Coleridge Assn., Inst. Evolutionary Psychology, Phi Beta Kappa, Phi Kappa Phi. Home: 1013 Maple Ave Terre Haute IN 47804-2936 Office: Ind State U Dept English Terre Haute IN 47809

BRENNAN, ROBERT WALTER, association executive; s. Walter R. and Grace A. (Mason) B.; m. Mary J. Engler, June 15, 1962; children: Barbara, Susan (twins). BS, U. Wis., 1957. Tchr., coach Waukesha (Wis.) High Sch., 1960-63; track coach U. Wis., Madison, 1963-71; exec. asst. to mayor City of Madison, 1971-73; pres. Greater Madison C. of C., Madison, 1973—. Mem. adv. council U. Wis.-Madison Sch. Edn., 1984—; mem. Madison Urban League, 1971—; bd. dirs. Cherokee Park, Inc., Wis. Nordic Sports Found., Very Spl. Arts, Wis. Named Madison's Favorite Son, 1971. Mem. Wis. Alumni Assn. (pres. 1985-86, chmn. bd. 1986-87), "W" Club (life, cert. of merit), Theta Delta Chi. Home: 5514 Comanche Way Madison WI 53704-1026 Office: Greater Madison C of C 2114 N Sherman Ave Madison WI 53704-3969

BRENNAN, RUTH ANNE, arts administrator; b. Sioux Falls, S.D., Oct. 8, 1932; d. William D. and Loucille (Seibel) Howalt; m. James Brennan, Nov. 17, 1956 (dec. Jan. 1986). BA in Sociology, U. S.D., 1954. Tchr. Edison Jr. H.S., Sioux Falls, S.D., 1954-55; registrar/vets. advisor U. Colo.-Denver Ext., 1955-56; arts-staff writer Rapid City (S.D.) Jour., 1968-83; exec. dir. Rapid City Arts Coun., 1983—; mem. Historic Preservation Commn., Rapid City, S.D., 1987—; bd. mem. S.D. Arts Coun., 1988—, Arts Midwest, Mpls., 1991-96; arts cons. plannind/bd. devel. South Dakotans for Arts, Deadwood, 1994—. Author: Missouri River, 1991, Glorious Adornment, 1992, New Eyes, 1993. Pres. Black Hills Playhouse, Rapid City, 1993-94, bd. dirs.; bd. dirs. Black Hills Heritage Festival, 1988—; bd. dirs. Rapid City Concert Assn., 1970—. Recipient I Can Soar award Boys Club, Rapid City, 1982. Mem. Assn. S.D. Museums, Nat. Assembly Local Arts Agys., Am. Assn. Museums, PEO (pres. 1964-66), Rapid City C. of C. (chair beautification com. 1989-90, Rushmore Honors award 1994). Home: 1121 St Chares Rapid City SD 57701 Office: Rapid City Arts Coun 713 7th St Rapid City SD 57701

BRENNAN, T. CASEY, writer; b. Port Huron, Mich., Aug. 11, 1948; s. William James and Mildred Alice (Goodrich) B. Free-lance writer Avoca, Mich., 1969—. Author: (comic book) Vampirella of Drakulon No. 1, Jan. 1996; contbr. articles and poetry to profl. pubs. Leader of campaign to ban smoking portrayals in comic books and other children'spubs. Subject hon. resolution Mich. State Legislature, 1987, Calif. State Assembly, 1989, honored with T. Casey Brennan Month in Fla., State of Fla. and City of MiamiBeach, Jan. 1989, States of Ariz. and Ark., Jan. 1990. Mem. Mensa. Democrat. Roman Catholic.

BRENNAN, WILLIAM J., information industry financial executive; b. Watertown, Wis., Oct. 31, 1950; s. Eugene H. and Jean (Dolan) B.; m. Kathy G. Pillsbury, Nov. 6, 1971; children: Erin K., Kerry E. BBA, U. Wis., 1977; MBA, Marquette U., 1984. Auditor, sr. auditor Grant, Thornton, CPAs, Milw., 1977-79; internal auditor Wis. Bell, Inc., Milw., 1980-81, staff mgr. taxes, 1981-82, staff mgr. ops. and corp. acctg., 1982-86, dist. mgr. regulatory-separations, 1986-90, dist. mgr. regulatory-long range planning, 1990-91, comptroller, 1992-93; v.p. fin., contr. Ameritech Info. Industry Svcs., Chgo., 1993—; bd. dirs. Quantum Control Sys. LLC, Chgo. Bd. dirs. Florentine Opera Co., Milw., 1992-93; mem. allocations com. United Way, Waukesha, Wis., 1990-92. Recipient Gov.'s award for Bravery, State of Wis., 1967, Merit award VFW, 1968. Mem. AICPA, Wis. Inst. CPAs, Conf. Bd. (Coun. of CFOs), Met. Milw. Assn. Commerce (legis. com. 1992-93). Republican. Roman Catholic. Home: 2809 Federal Ct Crystal Lake IL 60012 Office: Ameritech Info Ind Svcs 350 N Orleans 3d Fl Chicago IL 60654

BRENNEMAN, HUGH WARREN, JR., judge; b. Lansing, Mich., July 4, 1945; s. Hugh Warren and Irma June (Redman) B.; m. Catherine Sheperd; children: Justin Scott, Ross Edward. BA, Alma Coll., 1967; JD, U. Mich., 1970. Bar: Mich. 1970, D.C. 1975, U.S. Dist. Ct. (we. dist.) Mich. 1974, U.S. Dist. Ct. Md. 1973, U.S. Ct. Mil. Appeals 1971, U.S. Ct. Appeals (6th cir.) 1976, U.S. Ct. Appeals (D.C. cir.) 1981, U.S. Supreme Ct. 1980. Law clk. Mich. 30th Jud. Cir., Lansing, 1970-71; asst. U.S. atty. Dept. Justice, Grand Rapids, Mich., 1974-77; assoc. Bergstrom, Slykhouse & Shaw, P.C., Grand Rapids, 1977-80; U.S. magistrate judge U.S. Dist. Ct. (wc. dist.) Mich., Grand Rapids, 1980—. Instr. Western Mich. U., Grand Valley State U., 1989-92; mem. exec. bd. West Michigan Shores coun. Boy Scouts Am., 1984-87, 88-92, adv. coun., 1987-88, 93—, v.p., 1988-92; mem. Grand Rapids Hist. Commn, 1991—, pres., 1995; dir. Community Reconciliation Ctr., 1991. Capt. JAGC, U.S. Army, 1971-74. Fellow Mich. State Bar Found.; mem. State Bar Mich. (rep. assembly 1984-90), D.C. Bar Assn., Fed. Bar Assn. (pres. Western Mich. chpt. 1979-80, nat. del. 1980-84), Grand Rapids Bar Assn. (chmn. U.S. Constn. Bicentennial com., co-chmn. Law Day 1991), Fed. Magistrate Judges Assn., Am. Inns of Ct. (master of bench Grand

Rapids chpt.), Phi Delta Phi, Omicron Delta Kappa. Congregationalist. Clubs: Peninsular, Rotary (past pres., Charities Found. of Grand Rapids v.p.), Econ. of Grand Rapids (past bd. dirs.). Office: 580 Fed Bldg Grand Rapids MI 49503

BRENNEMAN, JAMES ALDEN, biology educator; b. Elida, Ohio, Aug. 26, 1943; s. William Oral and Mabel Esther (Smith) B.; m. Sandra Kay Schrock, Aug. 5, 1967; children: Kerry, Kent. BA, Goshen (Ind.) Coll., 1965; MS, W.Va. U., 1967; PhD, La. State U., 1970. Prof. biology U. Evansville, Ind., 1970—; cons. Ind. Poison Control, Indpls. Mem. AAAS, Am. Inst. Biol. Scis., Nat. Audubon Soc., Nat. Assn. Biology Tchrs., Mycol. Soc. Am., N.Am. Mycol. Assn., Population Reference Bur., Midwestern Coll. Biology Tchrs. Assn., Ind. Acad. Scis., Sigma Xi. Home: 4033 Count Fleet Dr Newburgh IN 47630-2261 Office: U Evansville 1800 Lincoln Ave Evansville IN 47722-0001

BRENNEMAN, JON E., marketing executive; b. Topeka, Kans., Dec. 11, 1962; s. James Christian and Mary Virginia (Ussery) B.; m. Julianna G. Rappard Brenneman, June 13, 1987. BS in Bus. Administrn., U. Kans., 1985. Provisional dist. mgr. First Investors Corp., Prairie Village, Kans., 1985-87; v.p. Brennco Mktg., Inc., Kansas City, 1987—; mem. Am. Express Travel Mktg. and Advt. Task Force, 1995—. Mem. Kansas City Lacrosse Club (pres. 1993—), Great Plain Lacrosse League (bd. dirs. 1993—). Republican. Roman Catholic. Office: Brennco Mktg Inc 11130 Holmes St Kansas City MO 64131-3625

BRENNER, DAVID MCCASKIE, botanist; b. Washington, May 16, 1957; s. Edgar Hirsh and Phyllis (Rudstrom) B.; m. Anne Kimber; 1 child, Iris Linnea Kimber, Dec. 4, 1994. BA in Botany, Antioch Coll., Yellow Springs, Ohio, 1980; MA in Geography, U. Oreg., 1986. Curator North Cen. Plant Intro. Sta. Iowa State U., Ames, Iowa, 1989—. Editor Legacy, Amaranth Inst., 1990. Office: Iowa State U Plant Introd Sta Ames IA 50011

BRENNER, DEAN ELLIOTT, medical oncology and pharmacology educator; b. Phila., Sept. 24, 1949. AB, U. Pa., 1971; MD, Hahnemann U., 1974. Diplomate Am. Bd. Internal Medicine, Am. Bd. Med. Oncology. Resident in medicine Pa. State U. Hershey Med. Ctr., 1974-77; clin. assoc. Nat. Cancer Inst. NIH and Balt. Cancer Rsch. Ctr., 1977-80, expert, 1980-81; asst. prof. medicine Vanderbilt U., Nashville, 1981-86; rsch. clinician Roswell Park Meml. Inst., Buffalo, 1986-89; assoc. prof. SUNY, Buffalo, 1987-89; assoc. prof. medicine and pharmacology U. Mich., Ann Arbor, 1989-92; chief sect. of hematology/oncology Dept. Veterans Affairs Medical Ctr., Ann Arbor, 1992-96; dir. Cancer Prevention Program, U. Mich. Cancer Ctr., 1996—; mem. adv. bd. on oncologics FDA, Rockville, Md., 1987-91; mem. Cancer Clin. Investigation Rev. Com., NCI, 1992—; reviewer jour. articles. Recipient Jr. Clin. Faculty award Am. Cancer Soc., 1982, Career Devel. award VA, 1984; rsch. grantee VA, 1984, 94, Nat. Cancer Inst., 1988, 92, 94, 95, 96, Am. Cancer Soc., 1993. Fellow ACP; mem. Am. Assn. for Cancer Rsch., Am. Soc. Clin. Oncology, Southwestern Oncology Group. Office: U Mich Med Sch 100 Simpson 102 Observatory Ann Arbor MI 48109-0724

BRENNER, STEPHEN MARK, marketing professional; b. Chgo., Feb. 14, 1948; s. Paul and Marcella (Zenner) B. BA, Drake U., 1969. Sales exec. Brenner Casket Co., Chgo., 1971-80; asst. mktg. mgr. Reliable Corp., Chgo., 1980-84; mailing list specialist Foote Cone and Belding Direct Mktg., Chgo., 1985-92; pres. Brenner Assocs., Chgo., 1993—. Pres. Condominium Assn., Chgo., 1983-84. With USAR, 1969-71. Mem. Direct Mktg. Assn. (Echo award 1985), Chgo. Assn. Direct Mktg., Am. Mgmt. Assn., Olympin Collectors Club. Home: 2333 N Geneva Ter Apt 3C Chicago IL 60614-3346

BRENT, RUTH STUMPE, design educator, researcher, educator; b. Washington, Mo., Sept. 11, 1951; d. Clarence Frank and Dorothy May (Horstick) Stumpe; m. Edward Everett Brent, Jr., May 14, 1972; children: Jessica Elizabeth, Jonathan Edward. BS cum laude, U. Mo., 1972; MA, U. Minn., 1974, PhD, 1978. Cert. of qualification Nat. Coun. Interior Design Qualification. Postdoctoral fellow in socio-clin. geriatrics NIMH, 1978-79; asst. prof. U. Mo., Columbia, 1981-86, assoc. prof. design, 1986-92, prof., 1992—, acting dept. chair, 1984-85, chair environ. design dept., 1985—; project dir. Adminstrn. on Aging Grant, 1979-81; v.p. Idea Works, Inc., Columbia, 1981—. Co-author: (computer software) Home-Safe-Home, 1989; co-editor: Popular American Housing, 1995; contbr. articles to profl. jours. Active Mayor's Task Force, Columbia Low-Income Housing, 1984-85; mem. Main St. adv. coun. dept. econ. devel. State of Mo., 1989-90; regional chairperson dists. 84 and 85 United Way, Columbia, 1989, 90; mem. adv. bd. Pub. Housing Authority, Columbia, 1984-85; chairperson North Cen. Region-54 Agrl. Expt. Sta. Rsch., 1989-91; mem. Columbia Regional Home Health and Hospice Adv. Bd., Columbia Regional Hosp., 1993—. Grantee Adminstrn. on Aging, 1979-81, VA, 1981, Am. Home Econs. Assn., 1981-82, 2 Joel Polsky Found. Interior Design Rsch. grantee, 1986, 87; recipient Fulbright award Chinese History and Culture, 1988, exch. faculty award Prince of Sonkla U., Thailand, 1990, Chonnam U., Korea, 1992; Fulbright fellow to Morocco and Tunisia, 1993. Mem. Am. Home Econs. Assn. (chmn. art/design sect. 1984-87, New Achievers award 1987), Am. Assn. Housing Educators, Am. Soc. Interior Designers (allied mem., chmn. position papers com. 1988-90, Presdl. citation 1990), Interior Design Educators Coun., Nat. Coun. for Interior Design (cert.), Environ. Design Rsch. Assn., Illuminating Engring. Soc. (participant workshop for tchrs.), Gerontol. Assn., Mo. Fulbright Alumni Assn. (membership chmn. 1989-90, v.p. 1990-92, pres. 1992-94), Univ. Club Inc. (pres. 1991-92, bd. dirs., sec. 1993-95, U. Mo. faculty alumni award 1992), Gamma Sigma Delta (pres. 1992-93), Omicron Nu, Phi Upsilon Omicron. Home: 100 W Briarwood Ln Columbia MO 65203-1678 Office: U Mo 137 Stanley Hall Columbia MO 65211

BRENZ, GARY JAY, publishing executive; b. Belvidere, Ill., Dec. 21, 1945; s. Gerald J. and Shirley W. (Berg) B.; m. Elaine E. Swanson, Jan. 9, 1969; 1 child, Graham Jofrei. BS in Art, U. Wis., Platteville, 1969; MA in Teaching, Beloit Coll., 1979. Asst. to city mgr. City of Beloit (Wis.), 1970-71; adminstrv. asst. Wis. Dept. Justice, Madison, 1971-76; graphic designer The Design Group, Madison, 1976-78; mgr. Sand End Inc., Madison, 1980-85; owner Arclight/Midwest Books, Stoughton, Wis., 1985—; cons. Arlington Nat. Cemetery, Vietnam War Meml. Bd. Hist. Rsch. Unit, Washington, 1989—. Author: (reference book) Military Insignia of the Republic of South Vietnam, 1979; designer, author: (promotional program book) U.N. Public Promotion, 1971. Mem. local spiritual assembly Baha'i Cmty., Beloit, Wis., 1970-72; mem. local spiritual assembly Baha'i Cmty., Stoughton, Wis., 1973-79, 90-92, dist. tchg. com., 1973-76; exec. dir. Stoughton Housing Authority, 1975-79; asst. scoutmaster Troop 164, Boy Scouts Am., Stoughton, 1988—; sec. Bus. Improvement Dist., Stoughton, 1992-93. With USNR, 1969-70, Vietnam. Recipient Amos Alonzo Stagg medal, 1964. Mem. Rotary Club Stoughton (bd. dirs. 1991-93, sec. 1993—). Office: Arclight/Midwest Books 111 E Main St Stoughton WI 53589-1720

BRERETON, CHARLAINE PHYLLIS, company administrator; b. Lodi, Wis., Jan. 11, 1939. BA in Elem. Edn., U. Wis., Platteville, 1964. Cert. property and casualty ins. agt., Wis. V.p. Maple Knoll Corp., Lodi, 1980—; sec./treas. United Network, Madison, Wis., 1992—. Chairperson Town of Lodi, 1989—, Columbia County Towns Assn., Portage, 1991—; exec. dir. Assn. Retarded Citizens, Columbia County, 1983-86; supr. county bd. Columbia County, Portage, Wis., 1992—. Named one of Outstanding Young Women Am., 1971, Outstanding Young Leader, 1971. Mem. Rotary, Lodi C. of C. (1st exec. dir. 1986-89). Republican. Methodist.

BRESCIA, WILLIAM FRED, JR., development officer; b. Chgo., Nov. 4, 1947; s. William Fred and Katy Ruth (Phillips) B.; m. Jimmie D. Harrington, July 17, 1985; children: Rahka R., Misty Dawn, Christopher. BA in Drama & Speech, Wartburg Coll., 1970; MS in Curriculum & Instrn., U. Wis., 1973. Curriculum specialist Miss. Bd. of Choctaw Indians, Phila., Miss., 1974-75; dir. Follow Through Program Miss. Bd. of Choctaw Indians, Phila., 1975-76; curriculum coord. United Indians of All Tribes, Seattle, 1976-78, dir. cmty. edn. svc., 1978-81; dir. R & D Miss. Bd. of Choctaw Indians, Phila., 1982-87; mgr. sch. restructuring conf. Ind. U., Bloomington, 1990, devel. officer, 1990—; edn. cons. ORBIS, Washington, 1989-94. Editor: (book) Mentoring Guide for Community College, 1995; contbr. articles to profl. jours. Bd. dirs. Internat. Mentoring Assn., Kalamazoo, Mich., 1990—, Cmty. Svc. Coun., Bloomington, 1991-93; com. chair Coalition of Alternative Cmty. Schs., 1990-93; pres. Ind. U. Am. Indian Students Assn., Bloomington, 1990-91. Recipient Constance Dorothea Weinman Nat. scholarship, 1988, 89, Tchr. Tng. scholarship Apple Ctr., 1985, Instrnl. Technology award Ind. U., 1988; named Cmty. Mem. of Month., Cmty. Svc. Coun., 1991. Mem. Nat. Indian Edn. Assn., Nat. Soc. for Performance & Instrn., Coun. for Advancement & Support of Edn. (listserv mgr. 1990—), Internat. Mentoring Assn. (com. chair 1990-93, bd. dirs. 1995). Methodist. Office: Ind U 501 N Morton Ste 109B Bloomington IN 47404

BRESKE, ROGER M., state legislator; b. Nov. 8, 1938. Grad. high sch. Former tavern owner; state senator dist. 12 State of Wis., 1990—. Mem. Tavern League Wis. (former pres.), Nat. Lic. Beverage Assn. (v.p.). Office: 8800 State Highway 29 Eland WI 54427-9409*

BRESLAUER, SUZANNE EISEN, public relations consultant; b. N.Y.C., Dec. 28, 1938. BA, NYU, 1959; MA, Webster U., St. Louis, 1986. Tchr. Beth Jacob Acad., Malden, Mass., 1959-61, NYC Pub. Schs., 1961-65; coord. Jewish Community Ctrs. Assn., St. Louis, 1970-75; media buyer and planner GGH&M Advt., St. Louis, 1976-81; counselor Reproductive Health Svcs., St. Louis, 1982-84; dir. Transitions, Inc., St. Louis, 1984-87; exec. dir. Women's Resource Ctr., St. Louis, 1987-89; pres. Rsch./Response, Inc., St. Louis, 1990—; mem. adv. com. St. Louis Job Corps, 1988-90; cons. Planned Parenthood St. Louis Region, 1990-91, bd. dirs.; membership co-chmn. Coun. Vol. Dirs., St. Louis, 1990-92. Mem. task force Confluence, St. Louis, 1988-91; bd. dirs. Coro Midwestern Ctr., St. Louis, 1988-91; panel mem. United Way Greater St. Louis, 1990—; pres. The Women's Consortium, St. Louis, 1991-93, Grace Hilll Child Devel. Bd., 1993-94; pres. Mo. Religious Coalition for Reproductive Choice, 1994-96; bd. dirs. Reproductive Health Svcs., 1994-96. Mem. Nat. Coun. Jewish Women (bd. dirs. 1990—), Women in Leadership Alumnae (bd. dirs., pres. 1988-90), Older Women's League (bd. dirs. 1994—, pres. 1996—). Home and Office: Rsch/Response Inc 11152 Crickett Hill Dr Saint Louis MO 63146-4902

BRESNAHAN, ROGER JIANG, humanities educator, researcher; b. Chicopee, Mass., July 1, 1943. BA, Boston Coll., 1967; MA, NYU, 1968; PhD, U. Mass., 1974. Asst. prof. humanities Voorhees Coll., Denmark, S.C., 1974-78; prof. Am. thought & lang. Mich. State U., East Lansing, Mich., 1978—. Editor: In Time of Hesitation, 1981, Conversations with Filipino Writers, 1990, Angles of Vision, 1992. Mem. Coll. English Assn. (assoc. exec. sec. 1979-82), Assn. for Asian Studies, Filipino Studies Group (exec. sec. 1993-95), Soc. for Study Midwestern Lit. (corr. sec./treas. 1980—). Office: Dept Am Thought and Lang Mich State U East Lansing MI 48824-1033

BRESSLER, JOSHUA DREW, construction executive; b. Chgo., May 24, 1961; s. Leonard Martin and Mary Jane (Bare) B.; m. Kelly Leigh Dolezal, Apr. 9, 1988; children: Nathan Alexander, Corey Benjamin. BS, Hobart Coll., 1983; MBA, Lindenwood Coll., 1993. Sales rep. Williams Scotsman, Arlington Heights, Ill., 1986-89; br. mgr. Williams Scotsman, St. Charles, Mo., 1989-93, West Chicago, Ill., 1993—. Mem. Home Builders Assn., Assn. Gen. Contractors. Home: 78 Forest Ave Glen Ellyn IL 60137

BRETT, GEORGE HOWARD, baseball executive, former professional baseball player; b. Glen Dale, W.Va., May 15, 1953; s. Jack Francis and Ethel (Hansen) B. Student, Longview C.C., Mo., El Camino Coll., Torrance, Calif. Former third baseman Kansas City (Mo.) Royals Profl. Baseball Team, v.p. baseball ops. Named Am. League batting champion, 1976, 80, 90, Am. League Most Valuable Player, 1980; player Am. League All-Star Game, 1976-88. Address: care Kansas City Royals PO Box 419969 Kansas City MO 64141-6969*

BRETZ, KELLY JEAN RYDEL, actuary; b. Wadena, Minn., Oct. 30, 1962; d. Edmund Leroy and Glenyce Clara (Andrie) B.; m. Daniel Mark Bretz Rydel. BA in Math., Moorhead State U., 1984. Completed Assn. for Investment Mgmt. and Rsch. chartered fin. analyst level 1. Asst. actuary Northwestern Nat. Life Ins. Co., Mpls., 1984-92; assoc. actuary TMG Life Ins. Co., Fargo, N.D., 1993-94, MSI Life Ins. Co., Arden Hills, Minn., 1994; assoc. actuary MidAm. Mut. Life Ins. Co., Roseville, Minn., 1994-95, sr. staff actuary, 1995—; assoc. actuary Fortis Fin. Group, 1995-96; grader Soc. Actuaries' Exam 220, 1992, 93. Contbr. articles to co. jours. Organizer blood drive Mpls. Blood Bank, 1992; meal deliverer Meals on Wheels, Fargo, 1993; meal server Sharing and Caring Hands, Mpls., 1992. Fellow Soc. Actuaries (mem. fin. and investment mgmt. practice edn. com.); mem. Am. Acad. Actuaries, Twin Cities Actuarial Club, Whitewater Investment Club, Life Ins. Mktg. and Rsch. Assn. (fin. mktg. and svcs. com. 1993). Office: Fortis Fin Group 500 Bielenberg Dr Woodbury MN 55125

BRETZ, RONALD JAMES, lawyer; b. Detroit, Nov. 11, 1951; s. James Louis and Nancy Kathleen (Murphy) B.; m. Leslie Jane Lucas, June 13, 1973; children: Jeffrey, Elissa, Sarah. BA, Mich. State U., 1973; JD, Wayne (Mich.) State U., 1976. Bar: Mich. 1976, U.S. Supreme Ct 1985. Asst. defender Appellate Defender Office State of Mich., Lansing, 1977-96; lectr. Mich. Appellate Assigned Counsel System, Lansing, 1985, 88; lectr. Cooley Law Sch., Lansing, 1985-90, adj. prof., 1991-96, vis. prof. 1996—; bd. dirs. Legal Aid Ctrl. Mich., 1987-93, pres. bd., 1991-93. Mem. adv. com. Community Alternatives Program, Lansing, 1984-85; bd. dirs. Legal Aid Cen. Mich., 1987—, sec., 1988, v.p., 1990. Mem. Nat. Lawyers Guild (pres. Lansing chpt. 1985-86, sec. 1986-87), U.S. Supreme Ct. Bar Assn., State Bar Assn. Mich. (com. standard criminal jury instrns. 1988—), Criminal Def. Attys. Mich. (lectr. 1982, Outstanding Criminal Def. Work award 1986). Office: Thomas M Cooley Law Sch 217 S Capital Ave Lansing MI 48901

BRETZ, WILLIAM FRANKLIN, retired elementary and secondary education educator; b. Urbana, Ill., May 30, 1937; s. William Franklin and Lois Evelyn (Scheffler) B. AA, Springfield (Ill.) Coll., 1957; BA, Ill. Coll., 1959; MA, Georgetown U., 1972. Cert. tchr., Ill. Chief page Ill. Senate, Springfield, 1957-63; tchr. history Lanphier High Sch., Springfield, 1964-78; tchr. history Benjamin Franklin Sch., Springfield, 1979—, chmn. social sci. dept., 1989-94; ret., 1994; staff mem. U.S. Ho. of Reps., Washington, 1975; site interpreter Lincoln's Tomb, Springfield, 1988—. Mem. Animal Protective League, Springfield. Univ. scholar Georgetown U., 1959-60. Mem. NEA, Ill. Edn. Assn., Springfield Edn. Assn., Ctr. for French Colonial Studies in Ill., Nat. Trust for Hist. Preservation, U.S. Capitol Hist. Soc. Home: 2325 S Park Ave Springfield IL 62704-4354

BREU, GEORGE, accountant; b. Milw., May 8, 1954; s. George and Grace (Rossmaier) B.; m. Nancy Lee Roblee, June 6, 1987; children: Michael G., Lisa A. BBA in Acctg. cum laude, U. Wis., Milw., 1976. CPA, Wis. Audit staff Reilly, Penner & Benton, Milw., 1976-78; tax mgr. Radke, Schlesner & Wernecke, S.C., Milw., 1978-88; contr. Megal Devel. and Constrn. Corp., Milw., 1988—. Treas. Elmbrook Hist. Soc., Brookfield, Wis., 1981-83. Mem. Am. Inst. CPA's (tax div.), Wis. Inst. CPA's, U. Wis. Milw. Tax Assn., Germany Philatelic Soc. (treas. Milw. chpt. 1978—), U. Wis. Milw. Philatelic Soc. (founder, treas. 1972-81), Milw. Philatelic Soc. Inc. (corp. registered agt. 1986—), U. Wis. Milw. Alumni Assn., Beta Gamma Sigma, Phi Eta Sigma. Republican. Roman Catholic. Home: 15840 Fieldbrook Dr Brookfield WI 53005-1419 Office: Megal Devel Corp 12650 W Lisbon Rd Brookfield WI 53005-1825

BREUER BACULIS, DIANA RUTH, community relations executive, business owner; b. Burlington, Iowa, Mar. 14, 1949; d. William H. and Dorothy M. (Nelson) B.; m. George J. Baculis, Aug. 9, 1986; 1 child, Kimera L. BS in Journalism, U. Iowa, 1981. Advt. sales mgr. Sta. KNIA of Leighton Enterprises, Knoxville, Iowa, 1976-80; sr. staff asst. community rels. dept. Mercy Hosp., Cedar Rapids, Iowa, 1982-88; dir. community rels. dept. Cedar Rapids Pub. Libr., 1988—. Treas. fundraising Iowa Women's Polit. Caucus, Johnson County, 1973-75; v.p. Des Moines chpt. Am. Women in Radio and TV, 1975-79. Recipient John Cotton Dana award ALA, 1989, Mktg. Excellence award Iowa Libr. Friends, 1988, 90, EPIC Salute award Wmen in Communications, Inc., 1991, 92, L. Percy award Libr. Pub. Rels. Coun., 1992. Mem. Pub. Rels. Soc. Am. (bd. dirs. 1988-93, accredited 1991, pres. Cedar Valley chpt. 1993), Downtown Promotion Com. Cedar Rapids (bd. dirs. Winterfest 1992—), Friends of Cedar Rapids Libr., U. Iowa Alumni Assn., Beta Sigma Phi. Office: Cedar Rapids Pub Libr 500 1st St SE Cedar Rapids IA 52401-2002

BREUKER, JOHN, private school educator; b. Muskegon, Mich., Dec. 19, 1938; s. John and Cornelia (Heemstra) B.; m. Christine Louise Garvelink, Aug. 15, 1964; children: John Patrick, Jamieson David. AB, Calvin Coll., Grand Rapids, Mich., 1960; MA, U. Mich., 1964, U. Iowa, 1967; postgrad., Ohio State U., 1968-73. Tchr. Latin, Grand Rapids Christian High Sch., 1960-65; teaching asst. U. Iowa, Iowa City, 1965-67; asst. prof. classics Ashland (Ohio) Coll., 1967-72; tchr. Latin, Western Res. Acad., Hudson, Ohio, 1972—; exam. reader Ednl. Testing Svc., Princeton, N.J., 1984, 87, 94; mem. faculty NEH Inst., Oxford, Ohio, 1986. Trustee Calvin Coll. and Sem., 1982-88. Grantee U. Iowa, 1965-67; Fulbright-Hays fellow, Rome, 1968; summer fellow Classical Assn. Mid. West and South, Ohio Classical Conf. Am. Classical League, Cumae, Sicily, Italy, 1988. Mem. Classical Assn. Midwest and South (state v.p. 1991-95, regional v.p. 1995—, Outstanding V.P. award 1992), Ohio Classical Conf. (treas. 1969-72, 2d v.p. 1986, 1st v.p. 1987, pres. 1988), Vergilian Soc. (trustee 1996—), Am. Classical League (summer fellow 1988, 93), Classical Soc. Am. Acad. in Rome. Home: 73 Hudson St Hudson OH 44236-2915 Office: Western Res Acad 115 College St Hudson OH 44236

BREUNIG, CHARLES, historian, educator; b. Indpls.; s. Leroy Clinton and Lydia (Latham) B.; m. Elizabeth Douglas Horton, Aug. 27, 1955; children: Thomas H., Charles L., Martha W. BA, Harvard U., 1942, MA, 1947, PhD, 1953; MA (hon.), Lawrence U., 1986. Instr. Wesleyan U., Middletown, Conn., 1953-55; from asst. prof. to prof. Lawrence U., Appleton, 1955-86, prof. emeritus, 1986—. Author: The Age of Revolution and Reaction 1789-1850, 1970, 2d edit., 1977, A Great and Good Work: A History of Lawrence University 1847-64, 1994. With U.S. Army, 1942-45, ETO. Fulbright fellow, 1950-51. Mem. AAUP, Am. Hist. Assn., Soc. French Hist. Studies. Office: Lawrence Univ Appleton WI 54911

BREWER, DANIEL F., engineer; b. Akron, Ohio, Dec. 23, 1964. BS in Mech. Tech., U. Akron, 1987. Project engr. Carg Corp., Tallmadge, Ohio, 1989-92, Kent (Ohio) Air Tools, 1992-94, Extrusion Svcs. Inc., Akron, 1994—. Mem. ASME, NSPE. Office: ESI Extrusion Svcs Inc 850 Moe Dr Akron OH 44310-2517

BREWER, DONALD LOUIS, school superintendent; b. Carbondale, Ill., Nov. 28, 1938; s. Louis Wiliam and Merline Ruth Brewer; m. Wilna Jean Turnage, May 13, 1961; children: Donna Jean Brewer Sanders, Clay Thomas. BS in Edn., So. Ill. U., 1960, MS, 1961. Tchr., coach Alexander County Cen. High Sch., Tamms, Ill., 1961-63; tchr., athletic dir. Egyptian Unit Schs., Olive Branch, Ill., 1963-64; tchr., athletic dir., elem. prin., high sch. asst. prin. Murphysboro (Ill.) Unit Schs., 1964-87; regional supr. Jackson and Perry Counties, Murphysboro, 1987—. Weekly columnist Murphysboro Am., 1982-91. Trustee John A. Logal Coll., Carterville, Ill., 1972—, chmn., 1975-76, 81-87, 93-96; mem. So. Ill. Airport Authority, Carbondale, 1977-86; mem. Mruphysboro Park Bd., 1972—. Elected to Ill. Amateur Softball Assn. Hall of Fame, 1979. Mem. NEA, Assn. Regional Supts., Ill. Athletic Dirs. Assn., Ednl. Coun. of 100, Phi Delta Kappa. Democrat. Methodist. Home: 25 Westwood Ln Murphysboro IL 62966-3004 Office: Jackson County Courthouse Regional Supt Schs Murphysboro IL 62966

BREWER, DONALDEE, mechanical engineer; b. Andrew County, Mo., Nov. 26, 1932. BS in Mech. Engring., Finlay Engring. Coll., 1952. Engr. Cessna Air, Witcha, Kans., 1957, Vornado, Witcha, 1958, FMC Corp., San Jose, Calif., 1958-60, Martin Marietta, Denver, 1960-64, Corning, Charleroi, Pa., 1965-66, Collins, Cedar Rapids, Iowa, 1967-69, Bandag Inc., Muscatine, Iowa, 1970—. Patentee in field. Staff sgt. USAF, 1952-56. Republican. Office: Bandag Inc 6500 49th St S Muscatine IA 52761-1162

BREWER, LINGG, state legislator; b. Oct. 13, 1944. BA, Mich. State U.; postgrad., Calif. State U., L.A. Rep. Mich. State Dist. 68, 1995—; edn. com. Mich. Ho. Reps., higher edn. com., local govt. com. Address: 2129 Dean Ave Holt MI 48842

BREWER, MARTHA M., hotel executive; b. Oakley, Kans., Feb. 5, 1954; d. Joe Edward and Norma L. (McKean) Darnall; m. Jerald N. Zerr, Aug. 11, 1972 (div. Mar. 1987); children: Austin Ross Zerr, Jill Dawn Zerr; m. Kenneth A. Brewer, Nov. 20, 1987; 1 child, Bryan David. From room attendant to asst. gen. mgr. Ramada, Colby, Kans., 1979-92; gen. mgr. Ramada, Colby, 1992—. V.p. Tourism Bd., Colby, 1993-95, pres., 1995—; leader Girl Scouts U.S., Colby, 1989—, 4-H, Russell Springs, Kans., 1973-79. Mem. Epsilon Chi. Republican. Office: Ramada 1950 S Range Colby KS 67701

BREWER, PAUL ALAN, biologist; b. Taylorville, Ill., May 28, 1956; s. Earl Allen and Lula F. (Nemeyer) B.; m. Katharyn Ewing, Oct. 26, 1985. BS in Biology, U. Ill., 1978; MS, Ea. Ill. U., 1985. Rsch. biologist Ill. Nat. History Survey, Champaign, 1979-86; wildlife biologist Ill. Dept. Conservation, Springfield, 1986—. Asst. chief Lincoln Fire Protection Dist., Charleston, Ill., 1988—. Mem. Wildlife Soc. (Continuing Edn. award 1992, cert. wildlife biologist, nominations chmn. Ill. chpt., pres. 1990-91, bd. dirs. 1987-90), Nature Conservancy, Nat. Fire Protection Assn. (Wildland Fire Mgmt. sect., Fire Svc. sect.), Ill. State Acad. Sci., Ill. Soc. Fire Svc. Instrs., U. Ill. Alumni Assn. (life), Sigma Xi, Phi Sigma (award 1982). Office: Ill Dept Conservation RR 2 Box 108 Charleston IL 61920-9401

BREWER, RICHARD LYNN, psychology educator; b. Jackson, Mich., Dec. 18, 1953; s. John Robert and Roberta Marie (Grubb) B.; m. Marcia Ellen Pote, Aug. 2, 1985 (div. Jan. 1990); children: Kristin, Kara, Evan; m. Paula Faye Abel, July 1, 1992. BA in Psychology and Religion, S.W. Bapt. U., Bolivar, Mo., 1978; MA in Psychology, Wheaton (Ill.) Coll., 1981; D Psychology, Forest Inst., Springfield, Mo., 1991. Lic. clin psychologist; cert. health svcs. provider; Medicaid certified. Psychotherapist Quad-County Counseling Ctr., Princeton, Ill., 1981-82; assoc. prof. psychology, chair dept. behavioral scis. S.W. Bapt. U., 1982—, mem. grad. faculty, 1992—, chair dept. behavioral scis., 1995; psychotherapist, counselor, cons. Family Inst. Ozarks, Bolivar, 1986—. Mem. APA, Mo. Psychol. Assn., Psi Chi. Baptist. Office: SW Bapt U 1600 University Ave Bolivar MO 65613-2559

BREWER, ROSE MARIE, sociologist, educator; b. Tulsa, Okla., Oct. 30, 1947; d. Wilson Bill and Cloviece (Stroud) B.; m. Walter Griffin; 1 child, Sundiata. BA, Northeastern Coll., Tahlequah, Okla., 1969; MA, Ind. U., 1971, PhD, 1976; postgrad., U. Chgo., 1981-83. Vis. lectr. Rice U., Houston, 1974-77; asst. prof. U. Tex., Austin, 1977-80, 1983-86; postdoctoral fellow U. Chgo., 1981-83; asst. prof. U. Minn., Mpls., 1986-89, assoc. prof., 1989—, chair Afro-Am. and African studies, 1992—; disting. vis. prof. Miami U. of Ohio, 1996. Editor: Bridges of Power, 1990; contbr. articles and revs. to profl. jours.; assoc. editor: Signs, 1991—. Recipient Morse-Alumn Teaching Excellence award, 1993; CIC leadership fellow, 1993-94. Mem. Soc. for Study of Social Problems (v.p. 1991-92), Midwest Sociol. Soc. (bd. dirs. 1990-92), Sociologists for Women in Soc. (chair discrimination com. 1992—, Feminist lectureship in social change 1995).

BREY, JAMES ARNOLD, geography and geology educator; b. Manitowoc, Wis., Mar. 7, 1950; s. Arnold George and Shirley Ann (Rusboldt) B.; m. Celeste Ann Lehrer, Nov. 12, 1979; children: Catrine, Mireille, Gabrielle. AA, U. Wis., Sheboygan, 1970; BA, U. Wis., 1972, MS, 1974, PhD, 1985. Bus. mgr. I.A.T.S.E. Local 251, Madison, 1974-78; theatre tech. Am. Multi-Cinema, Madison, 1976-79; co. rep. Crisp Co., Realtors, St. Petersburg, Fla., 1979; supr. Site Selection Cons., Tampa, Fla., 1979-81; theatre tech. Madison 20th Century Theatre, 1981-83; lectr. geography/geology, 1982-90; counselor U. Wis., Fond du Lac, 1983-84; dir. student svcs. U. Wis. Ctrs. PREP Program, Fond du Lac, 1984-90; assoc. prof. geography and geology U. Wis., Menasha, 1990—; chair campus steering com. U. Wis., 1994-95, chair campus budget com., 1995—; cons. Ice Age Nat. Sci. Rsch., Madison, 1972-74, U. Cons. in Corrections, Chilton, 1990—; cons./geologist Ledgeview Nature Ctr., Chilton, 1984—. Author field guide: Field Guide to the Glacial History and Geology of the Kettle Moraine, 1973; contbr. articles to profl. jours. Mem. Calumet County Local Emergency Planning Com., Chilton, 1990—; v.p. Calumet Nature Studies, Inc., Chilton, 1987-89, pres., 1989-91, chmn. tower com., 1988-93; bd. dirs. Wee Friends Childcare Ctr., Chilton, 1987-89. Recipient Disting. Svc. award Calumet Nature Studies, Inc., 1992, Cutting Edge Tchg. award Rotary Club, 1994; grantee U.

Wis. Ctrs., 1991—, Kaplan tchg. fellow, 1993. Mem. AAAS, Assn. Am. Geographers, Wis. Land Info. Assn., Correctional Edn. Assn. Democrat. Unitarian Universalist. Home: 419 N Madison St Chilton WI 53014-1252 Office: Univ Wis Ctr-Fox Valley PO Box 8002 1478 Midway Rd Menasha WI 54952-1224

BREYMAIER, CHRISTINE A., investment company executive; b. Cin., Aug. 1, 1961; m. Michael Breymaier; 1 child, Jack. BS in Mktg., Ohio State U., 1983. Lic. series 7, 63 and 64 Nat. Assn. Securities Dealers. Agt. Esser Ins., Naperville, Ill., 1984-85; ins. agt. VanDuran & Howell, Columbus, Ohio, 1985-86; investment rep. Bank One, Milford, Ohio, 1986-88, Ameritrust, Cin., 1989, Starbank, Columbus, 1989-90; stockbroker, v.p. Huntington Investment Co., Columbus, 1990—. Mem. children's bd. Womens Hosp., Columbus, 1991—. Republican. Roman Catholic. Office: Huntington Investment Co 41 S High St Columbus OH 43287

BREZENE, GEORGE S., systems analyst; b. East Chicago, Ind., Nov. 5, 1946; s. Mike and Mary Jane (Bukvich) V. BS in Math., St. Joseph's Coll., Rensselaer, Inc., 1968; BS in Computer Info. Systems, Calumet Coll., Hammond, Ind., 1986. Systems engr. IBM Corp., Hammond, 1968-72; owner, operator Bubba's Corner, Whiting, Ind., 1972-76, Kennedy Park Liquors, Hammond, 1977-86; cons. Computer People, Inc., 1987; staff systems analyst Inland Steel Co., East Chicago, Ind., 1987—. Bd. dirs. Sch. Bd., City of Whiting, 1989-95, pres., 1991-92; chmn. March of Dimes, 1980-82. Mem. Elks (Elk of Yr. 1982). Home: 2010 Indianapolis Blvd Whiting IN 46394-1951 Office: 3210 Watling St East Chicago IN 46312-1716

BRIAN, PATRICIA ANN, social services administrator; b. Sioux Falls, S.D.; d. Lawrence Alexander and Ethelyn Lucille (Milaney) Dumas; children: Robert Milling III, Courtney Dumas. BS, Northwestern U., 1959; postgrad., So. Ill. U., 1982. Cert. instr. human potential, parent effectiveness tng., rational behavior theory. Tchr. Belleville (Ill.) Pub. Schs., 1963-76; instr., project dir., dir. spl. svcs. ctr. Belleville Area Coll., 1977—; cons. Ill. Bd. Edn., 1978—, Ill. C.C. Bd., 1985—; presenter seminars. Author, editor: (resource books) Help for Addictive Diseases, 1988, Out of the Darkness: Arresting Rape, 1988, Survival Study Skills, 1989, Values Clarification, 1979, Attitudes and Communications, 1986. Bd. dirs. So. Ill. Network for Women, Parents in Action, Living Independently Now Ctr., Care and Counseling Social Svcs., Metro East, Ill., Pregnant Teen Svcs., Job Track, 1991—; mem. mayoral steering com. Belleville's 175th Birthday, 1989, co-chmn. Celebration Ball, 1989. Recipient Bright Idea award Ill. Coun. C.C. Adminstrs., 1994. Mem. Nat. Assn. Vocat. Edn. Spl. Needs Pers., Ill. Assn. Vocat. Edn. Spl. Needs Pers. (pres. 1994, Person of Yr. 1990), Ill. Vocat. Assn. (bd. dirs. 1993-94, ho. of dels. mem. 1993-96, Outstanding Programming in Cmty. and Coll. Alcohol Awareness award 1988). Office: Belleville Area Coll 2500 Carlyle Ave Belleville IL 62221-5859

BRICK, SHIRLEY JEAN, rehabilitation nurse; b. Des Moines, Feb. 6, 1954; d. Leo J. and Margaret I. (Powers) B. BSN, U. Nebr., 1976. Cert. in rehab. nursing and case mgmt. Rehab. staff nurse Immanuel Med. Ctr., Omaha, 1976-80, rehab. team leader, 1980-82, rehab. health care facilitator, 1982-88, rehab. charge nurse, 1988-91; nurse case mgr. Hines and Assocs., Inc., Omaha, 1991-93; med. case mgr. Mutual of Omaha, 1993-96; case mgmt. specialist Blue Cross Blue Shield Nebr., Omaha, 1996—; lectr. numerous Omaha area workshops, 1982-90. Mem. ANA, Nebr. Nurses Assn., Assn. Rehab. Nurses (cert.), Case Mgmt. Soc. Am. (bd. dirs. Nebr. chpt. 1994-95), U. Nebr. Alumni Assn. (bd. dirs. 1990-92), Sigma Theta Tau. Democrat. Roman Catholic. Home: 10604 Hartman Ave Omaha NE 68134-1242 Office: Blue Cross Blue Shield Nebr 7261 Mercy Rd Omaha NE 68180-0001

BRICKER, GERALD WAYNE, marketing executive; b. York, Pa., Dec. 21, 1947; s. Wayne Gilbert Bricker and Grace Fern (Quickel) Geisler; m. Linda Lee Desenberg, June 21, 1969; children: Kristin Lorraine, Scott Michael. BSME, Drexel U., 1970; MBA, No. Ill. U., 1976. Jr. product engr. Borg-Warner Corp., Ithaca, N.Y., 1970-71; product engr. Borg-Warner Corp., Aurora, Ill., 1971-72; with Maremont Corp., Chgo., 1972-86, dir. sales div., 1981-84, V.P. sales div., 1984-86; dir. mtkg. Intelligent Controls, Inc., Novi, Mich., 1986-90, v.p. mktg., 1990-93; v.p. products group Intelligent Controls, Inc., Novi, 1993-95; mktg. mgr. Pierburg Instruments, Inc., Clinton Twp., Mich., 1995—. Pres. Gethsemane Luth. Ch., Berkley, Mich., 1979-80, Cana Luth. Ch., Berkley, 1980-91, chmn. audit com., 1991—; chmn. Homeless Warming Ctr. Task Force, 1996; chmn. scout troop Boy Scouts Am., Southfield, Mich., 1988-90; chmn. fund raising Southfield-Lathrup Music Boosters, Lathrup Village, Mich., 1989-90. Mem. Soc. Automotive Engrs. (assoc.), U.S. Golf Assn., Drexel U. Alumni of Mich. (b. dirs. 1990—), Lambda Chi Alpha, Pi Tau Sigma, Beta Gamma Sigma. Home: 47765 Lake View Ct Northville MI 48167-8503 Office: Piersburg Instruments Inc 33939 Harper Ave Clinton Township MI 48035

BRICKLEY, JAMES H., state supreme court justice; b. Flint, Mich., Nov. 15, 1928; s. J. Harry and Marie E. (Fischer) B.; 6 children. B.A., U. Detroit, 1951, LL.B., 1954, Ph.D. (hon.), 1977; LL.M., NYU, 1957; Ph.D. (hon.), Spring Arbor Coll., 1975, Detroit Coll. Bus., 1975, Ferris State Coll., Big Rapids, Mich., 1980, Saginaw Valley State Coll., University Center, Mich., 1980, Detroit Coll. Law, 1981. Bar: Mich. 1954. Spl. agent FBI, Washington, 1954-58; sole practice law Detroit, 1959-62; mem. Detroit City Council, 1962-67, pres. pro tem, 1966-67; chief asst. prosecutor Wayne County, Detroit, 1967-69; U.S. atty. U.S. Dist. Ct. (ea. dist.), Detroit, 1969-70; lt. gov. State of Mich., Lansing, 1971-74, 79-82; justice Supreme Ct. of Mich., Lansing, 1982—; pres. Eastern Mich. U., Ypsilanti, 1975-78; lectr., adj. prof. U. Detroit, Wayne State U., U. Mich., Ann Arbor, Cooley Law Sch., 1958-73. Mem. Mich. Bar Assn., ABA, Inst. Jud. Adminstrn. Republican. Roman Catholic. Office: Supreme Ct Mich PO Box 30052 Lansing MI 48909-7552

BRICKNER, BRUCE, food products executive; b. 1943. BBA, De Pauw U., 1965; JD, U. Mich., 1968. Law clk. U.S. Dist. Ct., 1968-70; ptnr. Sidley & Austin, Chgo., 1970-75; with DeKalb (Ill.) Corp., 1975—, v.p., 1976, group v.p., 1980, exec. v.p., dir., 1980, pres., 1986-90, CEO, chmn. bd., 1988—; CEO, chmn. bd. DeKalb Energy Co., DeKalb Swine Breekers Inc. Office: DeKalb Swine Breeders Inc 3100 Sycamore Rd De Kalb IL 60115*

BRICKNER, PAUL, administrative law judge; b. N.Y.C., Aug. 7, 1940; s. Julius and Mollie (Gibelman) B. BA, U. Richmond, 1962; JD, Case Western Res. U., 1966; LLM, Cleve. State U., 1983. Bar: Ohio 1966, Va. 1967, U.S. Dist. Ct. (so. dist.) Ohio 1968, (no. dist.) Ohio 1971, U.S. Ct. Appeals (6th cir.) 1972, U.S. Army Ct. Criminal Appeals 1985, U.S. Ct. Mil. Appeals 1983, U.S. Supreme Ct. 1982. Intern IRS, 1963; atty. advisor NASA, Cleve., 1966; asst. U.S. atty. Columbus, Ohio, 1968-69, Cleve., 1972-76; atty.-inspector Ohio Div. Securities, Columbus, 1969-70; city prosecutor Cleveland Heights, Ohio, 1971-72, Cleve., 1970-71, 77-78; pvt. practice Painesville, Ohio, 1976-77; gen. counsel Ohio Lottery Commn., Cleve., 1978-81; adminstrv. law judge Social Security Adminstrn. Office Hearings & Appeals, Cleve., 1981—; instr. Lakeland C.C., Kirtland, Ohio, 1977-79, Notre Dame Coll., South Euclid, Ohio, 1986; adj. faculty U. Akron Sch. Law, 1987—, Cleve. State U. Coll. Law, 1989-91; pres. Ohio State Bd. Edn., 1989-90, v.p. 1987-88, mem. 1983-91; v.p. Ohio Acad. Sci. Centennial Commissionary, 1991; mem. Commn. on Edn. Improvement, 1989-90, Willoughby-East Lake City Bd. Edn., 1994—. Contbr. articles to profl. jours. Rep. candidate for Lake County pros. atty., 1976. Capt. U.S. Army, 1966-68; col. JAGC Res., 1969-95. Recipient Letter Commendation, FBI, 1975. Mem. ABA (jud. adminstrn. divsn.), Fed. Bar Assn., Va. State Bar Assn., Lake County Bar Assn., Bar Assn. Greater Cleve., Ashtabula County Bar Assn., Nat. Sch. Bds. Assn., Am. Soc. for Legal History, Supreme Ct. Hist. Soc., Am. Legion, Ducks Unltd., Masons (temple lodge #28), Nat. Sojourners, Fraternal Order of Police Assocs., The Club at Soc. Ctr. Jewish.

BRIDEWELL, DAVID ALEXANDER, lawyer; b. Forrest City, Ark., Dec. 8, 1909; s. Alexander Carver and Martha Elizabeth (Hatcher) B.; m. Mary Frances Badger, May 21, 1949; children: Jonathan Lee (dec.), Alexander Hunt. AB, U. South, 1931; MA, Princeton U., 1932; JD, George Washington U., 1938. Bar: Ark. 1933, D.C. 1938, Ill. 1940, U.S. Supreme Ct. 1940. Assoc. Mann & Mann, Forrest City, Ark., 1932; dist. atty. Home Owners Loan Corp., Jonesboro, Ark., 1933-34, Fed. Home Loan Bank Bd., Washington, 1935-40; ptnr. Russell & Bridewell, Chgo., 1940-85, Righeimer, Martin, Bridewell & Ciquino, Chgo., 1985-88; counsel Spindell & Kemp, Chgo., 1988-90, Lewis, Overbeck & Furman, Chgo., 1990-93, DeWolfe, Poynton & Stevens, Chgo., 1993—; bd. dirs. First Bank & Trust Co., Palatine, Ill., Kankakee (Ill.) Fed. Savs. Bank; lectr. Northwestern U., 1946-70; arbitrator Cir. Ct. Cook County, 1990—; counsel 1st Fed. Savs and Loan Assn. Chgo., 1960-85, 2d Fed. Savs. and Loan Assn. Chgo., 1945—. Author: History of Federal Home Loan Bank Board and Its Agencies, 1935, Bridewell on Credit Unions, 3d edit., 1945, Bridewell on Bailments, Liens and Pledges, 1973; editor: Selected Illinois Statutes, 1947; A Lawyer's Guide to Retirement, 2d edit., 1994, Reverse Mortgages and Other Senior Income and Housing Options, 1995. Chancellor Christ Episcopal Ch., Winnetka, Ill., 1960-75. Capt. JAGD, U.S. claims commr., U.S. Army, 1943-45, ETO. Mem. ABA (bus. law sect. 1965—, chmn. savs. and loan comm. 1965-70, coun. 1970-75, sr. lawyer divsn. coun. 1985—), Ill. Bar Assn. (chmn. savs. and loan com. 1980-85), Chgo. Bar Assn. (chmn. sr. lawyer com. 1985-87), Univ. Club Chgo. (chmn. lit. and arts com. 1980-85), Kappa Sigma. Republican. Episcopalian. Home: 789 Burr Ave Winnetka IL 60093-1802 Office: 135 S LaSalle St Ste 1943 Chicago IL 60603-4301

BRIED, LYNNDON HERMAN, manufacturing engineer; b. Rockford, Ill., June 6, 1941. Applications engr. Sundstrand, Rockford, 1964-82; chief engr. Daley Inc., Rockford, 1982-87, Fibro Inc., Rockford, 1987—. Chmn. com. Boy Scouts Am., Rockford, ill., 1992—. Office: Fibro Inc PO Box 5924 139 Harrison Ave Rockford IL 61125-5924

BRIGGS, ADA JANE, emergency nurse; b. Lakin, Kans., July 20, 1942; d. Stephen Dale and Thelma L. (Rider) Frazee; m. Joe F. Briggs, Nov. 20, 1978; children: Mike, Dana, Dale. ADN, Dodge City Community Coll., Dodge City, Kans., 1985; BSN magna cum laude, Ft. Hays State U., 1990. Cert. ACLS, CEN, PALS Am. Heart Assn., trauma nurse core course provider. Staff nurse St. Catherine Hosp., Garden City, Kans., 1985-86, charge nurse, 1986-93; staff nurse Western Plains Regional Hosp., 1994—. Mem. Emergency Nurses Assn. (cert.). Home: PO Box 41 Cimarron KS 67835-0041 Office: We Plains Regional Hosp 3001 Ave A Dodge City KS 67801

BRIGGS, FRANCES ELAINE, nursing adminstrator; b. Great Falls, Mont.; d. Samuel Edward and Elaine Blanche (Bailey) Straub; m. Kenneth E. Briggs; children: Michael, Stephen. BSN, U. Wash., Seattle, 1957; MSN, U. Portland, 1979. Pub. health nurse Seattle King County Health Dept., 1957-61, 66-70; instr. Shoreline C.C., Seattle, 1970-71, Chemeketa C.C., Salem, Oreg., 1972-79; asst. prof. Corpus Christi (Tex.) State U., 1979-80, Sangamon State U., Springfield, Ill., 1980-81; assoc. prof. MacMurray Coll., Jacksonville, Ill., 1981-84; dir. nursing South Suburban Coll., South Holland, Ill., 1984-91; dir. nursing edn., asst. divsnl. dir. Oak Forest (Ill.) Hosp., 1991-94; dir. nursing Kent State U., Ashtabula, Ohio, 1994—. Mem. ANA (bd. dirs. Ashtabula County chpt.), AAUW, Nat. League Nursing, Assoc. Degree Edn. Adminstrs. (Ohio coun.), Sigma Theta Tau, Phi Kappa Phi. Home: 6740 Sanborn Rd Ashtabula OH 44004

BRIGGS, JAMES STEMEN, JR., association executive; b. Columbia City, Ind., Aug. 5, 1937; s. James Stemen and Crystal Bonetha (LaRue) B.; m. Mary Ann Poffenberger, Apr. 7, 1960; children: Andrew Robert, Michael Allen. Student, Ind. U., 1958-59, DePauw U., 1955-57. Announcer WKAM Radio, Goshen, Ind., 1957-59, 62, WONE Radio, Dayton, Ohio, 1963-64; news anchor, news dir. WING Radio, Dayton, 1964-83; acct. exec. Image Mktg. Svcs., Dayton, 1983-84; v.p. ATA, Inc., Dayton, 1984-87; writer Dayton, 1965-87; exec. dir. Dayton Area Heart and Cancer Assn., 1987—; bd. dirs., mem. exec. com. UCC, Indpls., 1986-91; bd. dirs. Aviation Trail, Inc., 1983-90. Author more than 100 audiovisual scripts, 1965-87. Bd. dirs. FROC Neighborhood Priority Bd., Dayton, 1972-75. With U.S. Army, 1959-62, Korea. Mem. Comus Club (pres. 1984—), Rotary Club, Assn. Execs. of United Way (sec., treas. 1987—). Republican. United Methodist. Home: 170 Glenburn Dr Dayton OH 45459 Office: Dayton Area Heart & Cancer Assn 120 Zeigler St Dayton OH 45402

BRIGGS, JANET MARIE LOUISE, nurse practitioner; b. Pitts., June 11, 1951. Cert. family med. nurse practitioner. Staff nurse neonatal ICU Univ. Hosps. Cleve., 1972-73; staff nurse gen pediatrics Mt. Sinai Hosp. Cleve., 1973-76; head nurse health svc. Mt. Sinai Med. Ctr., Cleve., 1976-82; grad. rsch. asst. Case Western Res. U., Cleve., 1983-84; dir. nursing Ashtabula County Health Dept., Jefferson, Ohio, 1984-85; staff nurse, dir. nursing insvc., coord., clin. nurse specialist, coord. infection control Meml. Hosp. Geneva, Ohio, 1985-87; nurse practitioner, unit mgr. Parkside Health Mgmt. Corp., Toledo, 1986-87; nurse practitioner ambulatory surgery. Met. Gen. Hosp., Cleve., 1987; nurse practitioner domiciliary homeless program VA Med. Ctr., Cleve., 1987-91, clin. nurse specialist, nurse practioner AIDS team, 1991—; project dir., chmn. Child and Family Health Svc. Grant, Ashtabula County, Ohio, 1984-85; cons. case mgmt. head injuries subcom. Gov.'s Task Force, Ohio, 1988; nurse practitioner Free Clinic, Cleve., 1988—; mem. ethics com. VA Med. Ctr., 1989—; adj. clin. faculty Kent. State U., 1993—; investigator multiple clinically based AIDS rsch. projects. Lectr., group leader Hitchcock House, Cleve., 1981-83. Recipient Fed. Exec. Bd. award, 1995, Hearts and Hands award, Sec. Vet. Affairs, 1995; grantee Fed. Facility Based HIV/AIDS Edn. Demonstration, 1991, Fed. Facility HIV/AIDS Edn. Rsch., 1992, 93, Dept. Vet. Affairs. Mem. Frances Payne Bolton Sch. Nursing Alumni Assn. (bd. dirs.), Sigma Theta Tau. Roman Catholic.

BRIGGS, LESLIE RAY, mechanical engineer; b. Knoxville, Iowa, Dec. 18, 1944; s. Raymond Edward and Doris Geraldine (Wallace) B.; m. m. Donna Lou Van Dyke, July 1, 1967 (div. July 1990); children: Douglas William, Rebecca Lynn; m. Janis A. Vezzoso, Dec. 27, 1990. AS in Mech. Tech., Iowa State Tech. Inst., Ames, 1966; BSME cum laude, U. Evansville, 1986. Registered profl. engr., Iowa. Engring asst. Alcoa, Davenport, Iowa, 1966-79; tech. asst. Alcoa, Newburgh, Ind., 1979-85, tech. specialist, 1985-86, mech. engr., 1986-93, sr. mech. engr., 1993—. Mem. NSPE, Phi Beta Chi. Republican. Baptist. Lodge: Masons. Home: 1408 Parkside Dr Evansville IN 47714-2752 Office: Alcoa Warrick Ops PO Box 10 Newburgh IN 47629-0010

BRIGGS, ROBERT HENRY, infosystems specialist; b. Elk River, Minn., Apr. 25, 1937; s. Archie Elwin and Charlotte Lorette (Rand) B.; m. Jacqueline Hascoet, Apr. 20, 1963; children: Thomas Henry, Terence Gregory. BA in Bus., U. Wash., 1960. Indsl. engr. Boeing Co., Seattle, 1962-66; with 3M, St. Paul, 1966—, catalog analyst, 1966-68, sr. file control coordinator, 1968-74, advanced analyst, 1974-80, sr. analyst, 1980-85, lead analyst, 1985-96; supr. 3M, 1996—. Mem. cmty. edn. adv. coun. South Washington County (Minn.) Schs., 1977-94, chmn., 1981-83, 88-89; with Cottage Grove (Minn.) Parks and Recreation Commn., 1974-80, chmn., 1978; mem. Internat. Inst. Minn., St. Paul, 1982—; treas. Twin Cities Area Camera Club Coun., 1993; pres. 3M Camera Club, 1995—; v.p. South Washington County Schs. Edn. Found., 1995—. Mem. Data Adminstrn. Mgmt. Assn., Cottage Grove Jaycees (bd. dirs. 1972-73). Lutheran. Home: 8369 80th St S Cottage Grove MN 55016-2019 Office: 3M 3M Ctr Saint Paul MN 55144-1000

BRIGHTON, MARCELLA ANN, academic administrator; b. Detroit, Mar. 9, 1964; d. Leonard R. and Marjory J. (Chantler) Nautsch. BA, U. Mich., 1986; MBA, Ea. Mich. U., 1994. Mgr. office Housing divsn. U. Mich., Ann Arbor, 1987-89, adminstrv. asst. Sch. Nursing, 1989-91, adminstrv. asst II, 1991-93, adminstrv. asst II Coll. Engring., 1993-94, adminstrv. assoc. I, 1994-95, adminstrv. assoc. I Sch. Info., 1995—; cons. in field. Regents scholar, 1982, State of Mich. scholar, 1982. Mem. U. Mich. Alumni Soc. Office: U Mich Sch Info 550 E University Rm 304-C Ann Arbor MI 48109

BRILL, ALAN RICHARD, entrepreneur; b. Evansville, Ind., July 5, 1942; s. Gregory and Bernice Lucille (Froman) B.; AB, DePauw U., 1964; MBA, Harvard U., 1968; m. Bonnie Faye Phillips, May 26, 1973; children: Jennifer Leigh, Katherine Anne, Alison Elizabeth. Mgmt. cons. Peace Corps, Ecuador, 1964-66; sr. acct., cons. Arthur Young & Co., N.Y.C., 1968-71; v.p. ops. Charter Med. Mgmt. Co., Inc. and v.p.-controller Hosp. Investors, Atlanta, 1972-73; v.p., treas., dir. Worrell Newspapers, Inc., and Worrell Broadcasting Inc., Charlottesville, Va., 1973-79; pres. Brill Assos., Evansville, Ind., 1979—, Brill Media Co., Inc., Evansville, 1980—. Mem. AICPA, N.Y. State Soc. CPAs, Inst. Newspaper Contrs. and Fin. Officers, Evansville C. of C. (bd. dirs.), The Alliance: A Forum of Chairman and Presidents. Republican. Methodist. Clubs: Farmington Country (Charlottesville), Safari Internat. Home: 211 E Jennings St Newburgh IN 47630-1434 Office: Brill Media Co Inc PO Box 3353 Evansville IN 47732-3353

BRILL, DONALD MAXIM, educator, writer, researcher; b. Elk Mound, Wis., Sept. 8, 1922; s. John James and Grace Darling (Mayo) B.; m. Meredith Joy Wright, June 25, 1955; children: John Richard, Rebecca Jean, Linda Marie, Susan Elizabeth. BS, Stout State U., 1947; MA, U. Minn., 1949; PhD, U. Wis., 1972. Tchr. Mpls. Pub. Schs., 1949-50, Eau Claire (Wis.) Pub. Schs., 1950, Chippewa Valley Tech. Coll., 1951-58; supr. Wis. Tech. Colls., Madison, 1958-65; coord. Great Cities Program for Sch. Improvement Rsch. Coun., Chgo., 1965-67; supr. rsch. Wis. Tech. Colls., Madison, 1967-70, asst. state dir., 1970-83; ret., 1986; adj. prof. U. Wis., Stout, 1983-86. Mem. state com. for employment support of Guard and Res., 1983-86; mem. Eau Claire Dist. Sch. Bd., 1989-92; bd. dirs. Fourth Dimension, Inc., WHEM-FM; candidate 3d Congl. Dist., Wis., 1994. With U.S. Army, 1942-45, ETO. Mem. DAV, VFW, SAR, Am. Vocat. Assn. (life). Republican. Baptist. Home: 316 Hudson St Eau Claire WI 54703-5447

BRILLIANT, HOWARD MICHAEL, aeronautical engineer; b. Balt., Aug. 15, 1945; s. Benjamin and Anne Gertrude (Grodnitzky) B.; m. Arleen H. Blatt, Oct. 22, 1978; children: Rachelle I., Amy A. BSME, U. Pitts., 1966; MS in Aero Engring., U. Mich., 1967, PhD, 1971. Registered profl. engr., Colo. Commd. 2d lt. USAF, 1970, advanced through grades to col.; ret., 1994; project engr. Aero Propulsion Lab., Wright Patterson AFB, Ohio, 1970-75; instr. to assoc. prof. USAF Acad., Colo., 1975-80; project officer, group and br. chief Air Force Weapons Lab., Kirtland AFB, N.Mex., 1980-84; program mgr., dir. acquisition support Dep. for Propulsion, Wright Patterson AFB, 1984-86; chief spl. projects office Aero Propulsion Lab., Wright Patterson AFB, 1986-89; MIDS program mgr. JTIDS Joint Program Office, Hanscom AFB, Mass., 1989-90, dir. systems engring., 1990-91; dep. dir. Aero Propulsion and Power Directorate Wright Lab., Wright Patterson AFB, 1991-94; engring. and mgmt. cons. Dayton, Ohio, 1994-95; cons. heat transfer and fluid mechanics engr. GE Aircraft Engines, Cin., 1995—; cons. NASA Dryden Flight Rsch. Ctr., Edwards AFB, Calif., 1976-78; adj. prof. mech. and materials engring. Wright State U., Dayton, 1992—, mech. and aerospace engring., U. Dayton, 1995—. Contbr. articles to profl. jours.; co-author 2 vol. tech. report: Integral Rocket-Ramjet Component Evaluation Program, 1975. Decorated Air Force Commendation medal, 3 Air Force Meritorious Svc. medals, 1 Def. Meritorious Svc. medal, 1 Legion of Merit medal; recipient Sci. Achievement award Air Force Sys. Command, 1973. Assoc. fellow AIAA; mem. ASME, Am. Soc. Engring. Edn., Sigma Xi.

BRILLSON, CATHERINE GRAF, marketing professional; b. Akron, Ohio, Oct. 5, 1948; d. Joseph Palmer and Martha (Berry) Graf; m. Michael I. Brillson, Aug. 17, 1975 (div. Dec. 1994); 1 child, Leila. BA cum laude, U. Mo., 1970; postgrad., U. Chgo., 1972-74. Dir. comm. Heidrick & Struggles Inc., Chgo., 1970-74, KPMG Peat Marwick-Midwest, Chgo., 1974-79; mgr.-industry comm. Arthur Andersen & Co., Chgo., 1979-80; pres. The Brillson Found., Chgo., 1981-89; pres./prodr. The Synesthetic Network, Michigan City, Ind., 1989-91; chief marketing exec. Dieckmann & Assocs., Chgo., 1991—; mem. nat. adv. bd. Coalition for Creative Orgns., Chgo., 1989-93; v.p. Chgo. Pub. Rels. Clinic. Mem. The Executives Club (chmn. internat. comm. 1992-95). Office: Dieckmann & Assocs 180 N Stetson # 5555 Chicago IL 60601

BRINEGAR, ELIZABETH ANNE, critical care nurse, educator; b. Ottumwa, Iowa, Apr. 26, 1949; d. H.M. and Dorothy Jean (Fitzgerald) Thompson; children: Holly, Adam. ADN, Indian Hills Community Coll., Ottumwa, 1971, AA, 1982; BSN cum laude, N.E. Mo. State U., 1983; MS in Nursing, U. Mo., Columbia, 1994. Cert. critical care nurse;cert. ACLS. CCU and emergency room nurse St. Joseph's Hosp., Ottumwa, 1971-87, pub. health nurse Wapello County, Ottumwa, 1981-88; nursing resource pool Ottumwa Regional Health Ctr., 1988-91; instr. nursing Indian Hills Community Coll., 1987-91; clin. supr. med. ICU, U. Mo., Columbia, 1991—; tchg. asst. MS RN clin. specialist/family nurse practitioner U. Mo. Sch. Nursing; geriatric nurse practitioner, 1995. Mem. AACN. Home: 5620 Waterfront Dr N Columbia MO 65202-9056

BRINER, JOSEPH LEE, banker; b. Cin., Apr. 29, 1964; s. William W. and Norma (Stone) B.; m. Carolyn L. Bell, Dec. 20, 1986; children: Alexandra Elizabeth, Samantha Bell. BA, Denison U., 1985; MBA, Case Western Res. U., 1991. Mem. mgmt. tng. program Bank One, Cleve., N.A., 1985-86, adminstrv. asst., 1986-87; asst. mgr. Nat. City Bank, Cleve., 1987-88, credit analyst, 1988, br. mgr./comml. loan officer, 1989-90, sales mgr., 1990-91; fin. advisor Am. Express Fin. Advisors, Inc., Cleve., 1991-95; pvt. banking and investing officer, asst. v.p. Key Pvt. Bank, a KeyCorp Bank, Cleve., 1995—. Episcopalian. Home: 17670 Plum Creek Trail Bainbridge OH 44023 Office: Key Corp Key Pvt Bank 5915 Landerbrook Dr Ste 310 Mayfield Heights OH 44124

BRINK, JOHN WILLIAM, finance corporation executive; b. Chgo., July 14, 1945; s. M.W. and Alice L. (Nelson) B.; m. Cynthia Hollowell, Jan. 2, 1982; children: Bethany, Peter, Gwendolyn, Courtney. BBA, U. Wis., 1967; MBA, West Tex. State U., 1970. Comml. lending officer Huntington Nat. Bank of Columbus, Ohio, 1970-72; asst. treas. Peabody Internat., Galion, Ohio, 1972-75; v.p., treas. Avis, Inc., Garden City, N.Y., 1975-82, Savin Corp., Valhalla, N.Y., 1983; A.G. Becker Paribas, N.Y.C., 1983-84, U.S. Surg. Corp., Norwalk, Conn., 1984; pres. Treasury Adv. Corp., Pound Ridge, N.Y., 1985-86; exec. v.p., treas., CFO, Green Tree Fin. Corp., Inc., St. Paul, 1986—; mem. faculty Franklin U. Gen. Evening Coll., Columbus, 1971-75. Served with AUS, 1968-70. Mem. Fin. Execs. Inst. (pres. twin cities chpt.), Hazeltine Nat. Golf Club. Office: Green Tree Fin Corp 345 Saint Peter St Saint Paul MN 55102-1637

BRINK, MARION FRANCIS, trade association administrator; b. Golden Eagle, Ill., Nov. 20, 1932; s. Anton Frank and Agnes Gertrude B. B.S., U. Ill., 1955, M.S., 1958; Ph.D., U. Mo., 1961. Research biologist U.S. Naval Radiol. Def. Lab., San Francisco, 1961-62; assoc. dir. div. nutrition research Nat. Dairy Council, Chgo., 1962-65, dir. div. nutrition research, 1965-70; pres. Nat. Dairy Council, Rosemont, Ill., 1970-85; exec. v.p. ops. United Dairy Industry Assn., Rosemont, 1985-88, chief exec. officer, 1988-91; vice chmn. human nutrition adv. com. USDA, 1980-81. Contbr. articles to prof. jours. Recipient citation of merit U. Mo. Alumni Assn. Mem. Am. Inst. Nutrition, Am. Soc. Clin. Nutrition, Am. Dietetic Assn. (assoc.), Dairy Shrine Club, Soc. for Nutrition Edn., Nutrition Today Soc., Chgo. Nutrition Assn., Alpha Tau Alpha, Gamma Sigma Delta. Home: 444 Highcrest Dr Wilmette IL 60091-2358

BRINK, NORMA S., performing arts educator, actress; b. Grand Rapids, Mich., Sept. 26, 1928; d. Henry and Helen M. (Seamon) S.; m. Edward H. Brink Jr., Nov. 11, 1950 (div. Oct. 1965); children: John, Mary Teresa, Edward H. III. BA, Western Mich. U., 1949, MA, 1968. Tchr., adminstr. Grand Rapids Pub. Schs., 1949-86; adj. prof. performing arts Davenport Coll., Grand Rapids, 1986—; condr. comm. workshops for bus. Davenport Entrepreneurial Ctr.; tchr. adult acting Grand Rapids Civic Theatre. Actress profl. theater, radio and TV appearances, numerous cmty. theatre prodns., 1950—. Founder, life bd. dirs. Cmty. Cir. Theatre, Grand Rapids, 1955—; bd. dirs. Kent County Humane Soc., Actors Theatre; vol., past bd. dirs. Grand Rapids Civic Theatre; active LWV; vol. Am. Cancer Soc. Recipient Grand Rapids Arts Coun. award, 1985, other arts awards; named Grand Rapids Vol. of Yr., 1972. Mem. Western Mich. Jazz Soc., French Soc. Home: 3835 Villa Montee Dr SE Grand Rapids MI 49512-1835

BRINKER, GARY D., engineering executive; b. Toledo, Ohio, Nov. 30, 1940. BS, MIT, 1962; MS, Cornell U., 1963; PhD, Calif. Inst. Tech., 1969. Devel. engr. McMaster Engring., Toledo, 1970-76; dir. system engring. Glasstech Inc., Perrysburg, Ohio, 1976—; past mem. tech. adv. com. Edison Industrials Systems Ctr. Office: Glasstech Inc 995 4th St Perrysburg OH 43551-4369

BRINKER, LEE J., manufacturing company executive; b. Beloit, Kans., Dec. 21, 1951. BSME, Kans. State U., 1973. Engr. Kent Engring., Tippton, Kans., 1973-77; engr. to pres. Kan Am Industries, Inc., Beloit, Kans., 1978—. Office: Kan Am Industries 1600 W 8th St Beloit KS 67420

BRINKLEY, JAMES WILEY, industrial designer, bioengineering consultant; b. Portsmouth, Ohio, Aug. 5, 1935; s. Wiley Homer and Dorothy Marie (Pryfogle) B.; m. Carol Marie Malpiedi, Oct. 15, 1961; children: Christine Marie, Leslie Ann, Linda Suzanne, Susan Jennifer. BS in Indsl. Design Engring., Ohio State U., 1958. Designer protective equipment Air Force Aerospace Med. Rsch. Lab., Wright-Patterson AFB, Ohio, 1958-60, biodynamist, 1960-70, br. chief, 1970-88, div. dir., 1988-91, dir. crew systems Armstrong Lab., 1991—. Contbg. author: Foundations of Space Biology and Medicine, 1975, Fundamentals of Aerospace Medicine, 1985; contbr. articles to Aviation, Space and Environ. Medicine, Jour. Trauma, SAFE Jour. Recipient Outstanding Engr. of Yr. award City of Dayton and 9 engring. socs., 1967, Meritorious Svc. medal Air Force Systems Command, 1968, Pub. Svc. award GEICO, 1981, Exceptional Civilian Svc. award USAF, 1986. Fellow Aerospace Med. Assn. (Eric Liljencrantz award 1983, John Paul Stapp award 1995); sr. mem. AIAA, Internat. Soc. for Fall Protection, SAFE Assn. (Outstanding Leadership award 1992). Home: 2244 Brookpark Dr Dayton OH 45440-2615 Office: Armstrong Lab (AL/CF) Wright Patterson AFB OH 45433-7901

BRINKLEY, WILLIAM JOHN, secondary education educator; b. Shawneetown, Ill., Dec. 8, 1925; s. William Henry and Frances (Leath) B.; m. Venita J. Schwarm, Aug. 7, 1988; BS, U. Ill., 1945. Tchr. high sch., Mc Leansboro, Ill., 1945—, high sch. coord. vocations, 1968—; owner Brinkley Interiors and Galleries, antique porcelain, Mc Leansboro. Mem. editorial bd. Schroeders Antique Guide, 1979—; adv. bd. Ill. Edn. Coun., 1967—; mem. Pres.'s Com. 100, 1968; mem. Hamilton County Bicentennial Com.; chmn. rehab. com. McCoy Meml. Libr. and Hamilton County Hist. Soc. Bldg.; mem. Friends of Mus., Mitchell Mus., Mt. Vernon, Ill., 1978-84; mem. adv. coun. Hamilton-Jefferson County Comprehensive Svcs., Ill., 1991—; mem. Hamilton County Rep. Com., 1950-68; bd. trustees Trade Industries, 1994—; deacon Presbyn. Ch., 1995. Recipient Tchr. of Year award U. Ill. Edn. Dept., 1963; Disting. Svc. award Vocat. Edn., 1981; Merit award Gov. Ill. 1964; Disting. Svc. award Future Farmers Am., 1967, Thor Agr. award outstanding svc., 1972, FAA disting. svc. award, 1968; George Washington medal honor Freedoms Found. Am., 1966, 69; Outstanding Vocat. Edn. award Ill. State Vocat. Edn. Svc., 1981; Presbyn. Svc. award, 1984. Mem. NEA, Ill. Edn. Assn., Hamilton County (pres. 1970), Gallatin County Hist. Socs., Nat., Ill. Assn. Vocat. Agr. Tchrs. (Tchr. of Tchrs.), Rend Lake Symphony Soc., Arts and Humanities Soc., SAR (bd. govs. Ill., state chmn. constructive citizenship com.), Hamilton County Hist. Soc. (pres. 1994—), Cedarhurst Dinner Theater Club, Hereditary Register of U.S., Phi Beta Kappa, Delta Sigma Phi. Lodges: Masons, Kiwanis, Elks, Lions, Rotary (charter mem., bd. dirs. 1986). Home: 401 S Washington St Mc Leansboro IL 62859-1235 Office: 200 S Pearl St Mc Leansboro IL 62859-1157

BRINKMAN, ELMER PAUL, insurance sales agent, county commissioner; b. Sibley, Iowa, Oct. 28, 1946; s. Gerald Arthur and Jeannette (Pap) B.; m. Barbara Jean Miller, Feb. 7, 1971; children: Donna S., Paula J., Kendra C., Kayla N. BA, Dakota Wesleyan U., Mitchell, S.D., 1969; MDiv, Iliff Sch. Theology, Denver, 1972. Ordained minister Methodist Ch., 1972. Pastor Leola-Frederick U. Meth. Ch., Leola, S.D., 1972-74; assoc. pastor 1st United Meth. Ch., Watertown, S.D., 1974-77; spl. agt. Northwestern Mut. Life Ins. Co., Watertown, 1977—; county commr. Codington County, Watertown, 1985—; pres. Watertown Area Life Underwriters, 1985-86; trustee S.D. Retirement System, Pierre, 1991—. Pres. Human Svc. Agy., Watertown, 1986; mem. Local Govt. Study Com., Pierre, 1988-92. Mem. Mem. Watertown Area C. of C. (pres. 1989-90), S.D. Assn. County Commrs. (pres. 1990-91), Rotary Club of Watertown (pres. 1983-84, Paul Harris fellow 1987). Republican. Home: 1212 7th Ave NE Watertown SD 57201-1913 Office: Northwestern Mut Life Ste 119 420 4th St NE Watertown SD 57201

BRINKMAN, JOYCE ELAINE, state legislator; b. Louisville, Oct. 4, 1944; d. Jess Weber and Marie (French) Hopewell; children: Shane, Muffett. BA in History, Hanover Coll. Lic. real estate agt., Ind. Engrossing and enrolling clk. Ind. State Senate, Indpls., 1973, legis. asst., 1974-75; mem. Ind. Ho. Reps, Indpls., 1985—; committeewoman Pike Twp., Indpls., 1973-76; field representative Rep. Nat. Com., Indpls., 1976; mem. City-County Council, Indpls., 1976-83; realtor F.C. Tucker, Indpls., 1979—; exec. dir. Near North Devel. Corp., Indpls., 1983-85. Named Female Young Rep. of Yr. Ind. Young Reps., 1974. Mem. Marion County Council Rep. Women (v.p. 1974-76, pres. 1976-88), Hendricks County Rep. Women's Club, Nat. Bd. Realtors, Metro Indpls. Bd. Realtors. Methodist. Home: 5276 Deer Creek Dr Indianapolis IN 46254-3557

BRISBANE, ARTHUR SEWARD, newspaper editor; b. N.Y.C., Sept. 30, 1950; s. Seward Scatcherd and Doris Mae (Fauser) B.; m. Jo Ellen Hull, Oct. 16, 1982; children: Allison Faith, Madeline Mariah, Laura Calista. AB, Harvard Coll., 1973. Child care worker McLean Hosp., Belmont, Mass., 1973-74; pvt. practice musician, 1974-76; reporter Glen Cove (N.Y.) Guardian, 1976-77; reporter Kansas City (Mo.) Star & Times, 1977-79, columnist, 1979-84; reporter Washington Post, 1984-87, asst. city editor, 1987-89; columnist Kansas City Star, 1990-92, editor, v.p., 1992—. Author: Arthur Brisbane's Kansas City, 1982. Mem. Am. Soc. Newspaper Editors. Office: The Kansas City Star 1729 Grand Blvd Kansas City MO 64108-1413

BRISBEN, JOSEPH D., investment broker; b. Enid, Okla., Feb. 27, 1941; s. John James and Olive Jane (Quinn) B.; m. Lind Jean Henry, June 27, 1964 (div. Jan. 1972); children: Erin Jane Meyers, Amy Jean, Adam Joseph; m. Melinda Eleanor Young Tully, July 7, 1974 (div. July, 1995); 1 child, Graham Young Brisben. BA in English, U. Chgo., 1969; MA, Drake U., 1976; postgrad., U. Iowa, 1979, 80. CFP, Colo. Reporter City News Bur. of Chgo., 1964-65; reporter, copy reader Chgo. Tribune, 1965-67; staff writer pub. info. U. Chgo., 1967-69, asst. dir. pub. info., 1969-70; asst. dir. univ. rels. Drake U., Des Moines, 1970-73, assoc. dir. univs. rels., 1973-77; assoc. dir. pub. info. U. Iowa, Iowa City, 1977-83; registered rep. Securities Corp. of Iowa, Cedar Rapids, 1983-92, v.p. investments, 1992—; columnist Iowa City Mag., 1993—; reporter, commentator WSUI Info. Radio, Iowa City, 1990—; farmer Brisben Farms, Pond Creek, Okla., 1966—; musician, singer Back Porch Swing, Iowa City, 1992-95. Religious svcs. chair, social action Unitiarian-Universalist Soc., Iowa City, 1977—; steering com. Health People 2000, Iowa City, 1992—; alumni student search com. U. Chgo., 1989—. Mem. Nat. Assn. CFP, Greater Iowa City C. of C. (econ. devel. com. 1985—). Democrat. Office: Securities Corp of Iowa 2000 Second Ave SE Cedar Rapids IA 52406

BRITT, RONALD LEROY, manufacturing company executive; b. Abilene, Kans., Mar. 1, 1935; s. Elvin Elbert and Lona Helen (Conn) B.; B.S.M.E., Wichita State U., 1963; m. Judith Ann Salter, June 29, 1957; children—Brett Gavin, Mark Damon, Melissa Ann. Product engr. to product planner Hotpoint div. Gen. Electric Co., Chgo., 1963-68; product planner Norge Co., Chgo., 1968; product mgr., asst. dir. engring. Leigh Products Inc., Coopersville, Mich., 1968-74; mgr. rsch. and devel. Miami Carey div. Jim Walter Corp., Monroe, Ohio, 1974-84; sr. v.p. mfg. and engring. div. SICO, Belvedere Co., Belvidere, Ill., 1984—; industry rep. for electric fans Underwriters Labs. Active, Boy Scouts Am., 1970-73, PTA, 1973-78; exec. adviser Jr. Achievement, 1984-85, Boone County chmn., 1986-88; bd. dirs. YMCA, Belvidere, 1990-96, vice chmn., chmn. fin. com., 1991, v.p., 1992; dir. on adv. bd. St. Joseph Hosp., 1990-95, chmn. long range planning com., 1991; bd. dirs. Boone County Dist. # 100 Edn. Found., 1991-95. Served with U.S. Army, 1958-60. Recipient Inventor's award Gen. Electric Co., 1967. Mem. ASME, Home Ventilation Inst. (engring. com. 1975-84), Belvidere C. of C. (bd. dirs. 1986-89). Republican. Congregationalist. Clubs: Free Blown Glassblowing, Northern Ill. Corvette, Carnival and Art Glass Collectors. Lodge: Rotary. Patentee in field. Home: 1628 Riverside Rd Belvidere IL 61008-8655 Office: 1 Belvidere Blvd Belvidere IL 61008-8594

BRITTAIN, DAVID LAWRENCE, marketing executive; b. Rahway, N.J., Dec. 30, 1944; s. Sidney Sager and Lydia (Leber) B. married, July 22, 1972; children: Sean David, Carrie Colleen, Lance Lee. Project mgr., mgr. engring., mktg. devel. mgr. Busch, Virginia Beach, Va., 1983-92; tech. and mktg. dir. Becker Pumps Corp., Akron, 1992—; com. mem. Nat. Fire Protection Assn., Boston, 1988—; owner Indsl. Publications of Ohio. With USAF, 1965-69. Mem. Am. Soc. Health Engring., Soc. Plastics Engrs.

BRITTEN, JAMES LEO, SR., assessor; b. Somerville, Tenn., Feb. 19, 1943; s. Lucy B. (Kyle) Britten; married; children: James Leo Jr., Barbara. BS, Lane Coll., Jackson, Tenn., 1959. Cert. tchr., Ill. Assessor City of Chgo. Dept. of Transp., 1963—. Mem. Masons. Home: 1103 E 93d St Chicago IL 60619

BRITTEN, WILLIAM HARRY, editor, publisher; b. Zearing, Iowa, Aug. 25, 1921; s. Harry William and Gertrude Alice (Lehman) B. BA, Western Union Coll., 1943; student Iowa State Coll., summer 1942; MA, State U. Iowa, 1948. Reporter, Worcester (Mass.) Telegram, 1948-55; landscaper John F. Keenen, Leicester, Mass., 1956; sales dept. clk. Reed & Prince Mfg. Co., Worcester, 1957-63, inventory control clk., 1964, chief expeditor, 1965; state editor Marshalltown (Ia.) Times-Republican, 1965-66, staff writer, 1966-67; news editor Denison (Ia.) Bull. and Rev., 1967-68; city editor Boone News Republican, 1968; editor, pub., owner The Tri-County News, Zearing, 1968--89, editor emeritus, 1990—; editor, pub. Hubbard (Iowa) Rev., 1969-72; Sec., Young Men's Republican Club, Worcester, 1957; corr. sec. Young People's Rep. Club, 1958; mem. Ward 8 Rep. Com., Worcester, 1960-65; Rep. candidate Mass. state legislature, 1960; ward chmn. to elect Edward W. Brooke atty. gen. Mass., 1962, 64; bd. dirs. Story County Cancer Soc., 1976-81; chmn. Story County, Lincoln Twp. Reps., 1992, 94; active Ch. of Christ, United Meth. Ch. Served with AUS, 1943-45. Mem. Iowa Newspaper Assn., Nat. Newspaper Assn., Am. Fedn. Arts., Am. Legion (post comdr. 1982-83), Westmar Coll., U. Iowa Alumni Assns. Home: 416 S Pearl St Zearing IA 50278-0156 Office: Main St Zearing IA 50278

BRITTIN, MARIE ELEANOR, communications, psychology, speech and hearing science educator; b. Wichita, Kans.; d. F. E. and A. M. Brittin. BS, Northwestern U.; MA, U. Iowa; PhD, Northwestern U. Lic. speech pathologist Ohio, Wash. Instr. U. Wis., Madison, 1950-53; coord. comm. disorders Tacoma Pub. Schs., 1956-64; dir. speech and hearing Coll. Edn. Ohio State U., Columbus, 1964-73, assoc. prof. speech and hearing sci., 1973-89; cons. Kent (Wash.) Pub. Schs., 1991; chair Chauncey D. Leake award for excellence in pharmacology, 1978-90; elected mem. compensation and benefits com. Ohio State U., 1985-89; adj. faculty comm. U. Wash., 1994—; pvt. cons. in field; presenter comm. seminars. Editor: Ohio Jour. Speech and Hearing, 1984-85. Pres., com. chair Zonta Internat., Tacoma, Columbus. Fellow Am. Speech-Lang.-Hearing Assn. (legis. coun. 1989, 90, 91, site visitor 1982-84, Ace award 1986); mem. APA, Internat. Assn. Logopedics and Phoniatrics (presenter), AAAS, Nat. Aphasia Assn., PEO, Christian Med. and Dental Soc., Ohio State U. Faculty Women's Club (pres. 1966-67), Pi Lambda Theta (pub. adv. bd. 1983-85), Delta Kappa Gamma (pres. Alpha Tau chpt. 1964). Home: 1220 7th Ave SW Puyallup WA 98371-6759 Office: Ohio State U Speech and Hearing Sci 1070 Carmack Rd Columbus OH 43210-1002

BRITTON, DENNIS A., newspaper editor, newspaper executive; b. Santa Barbara, 1940; m. Theresa Romero Britton; children: Robert, Patrick, Anne. Attended, San Jose State U. Joined L.A. Times, 1966, various positions, including copy editor, reporter, news editor, asst. nat. editor, nat. editor, 1977-83, then dep. mng. editor; now editor Chgo. Sun-Times, 1989—, also exec. v.p. Mem. Nat. Assn. Hispanic Journalists. Office: Chgo Sun Times 401 N Wabash Ave Chicago IL 60611-3532*

BRITTON, DUNCAN A., stockbroker; b. Du Quoin, Ill., Oct. 21, 1952. Stockbroker IM Simon & Co., De Quoin, 1981-87, 1st Gateway Securities, De Quoin, 1987—. Mem. Elks. Office: 1st Gateway Securities PO Box 445 221 E Main St Du Quoin IL 62832

BRITTON, SAM, state legislator; m. to Kaye Britton; 1 child, Samuel. BS, U. Cin. Real estate agt. Britton and Assocs., Cin.; treas. Avondale Redevelop. Corp., Cin.; mem. Ohio Ho. of Reps., Columbus. mem. adv. bd. Cin. Comty. Devel. Mem. NAACP (life), Madisonville Comty. Coun. (past pres.), Cin. Area Bd. Realtors, Ohio Assn. Realtors (trustee), Black Male Coaliton, Kappa Alpha Psi. Office: Ohio Ho of Reps Ohio State Bldg Columbus OH 43215

BROACH, DAVID, state legislator. Mem. Mo. Ho. of Reps., Jefferson City. Republican.

BROADBENT, JEFFREY PRAED, sociology educator; b. Chgo., Mar. 2, 1944; s. William Robert Broadbent and Marjorie Praed Anderson; m. Gretchen Brickett Priest (div. 1990); children: Leafye Brickett, Eben North. BA, U. Calif., Berkeley, 1974; MA, Harvard U., 1975, PhD, 1982. Asst. prof. sociology SUNY, Plattsburgh, 1981-83; jr. fellow Soc. Fellow, U. Mich., Ann Arbor, 1983-86; rsch. scientist Ctr. for Japanese Studies, U. Mich., Ann Arbor, 1983-86; asst. prof. sociology U. Mich., Ann Arbor, 1983-86, U. Minn., Mpls., 1986—. Author: Comparing Policy Networks, Environmental Politics in Japan; contbr. articles to profl. jours. NSF fellow, 1974-77, 89-90; Fulbright fellow, 1978-80, 88-90. Mem. Am. Sociol. Assn., Assn. for Asian Studies. Office: Univ of Minn Dept Sociology 267 19th Ave S Minneapolis MN 55455-0499

BROADWELL, TONJA JOANN, computer analyst; b. Cambridge, Nebr., Aug. 20, 1961; d. Byron Brunswick and Darlene JoAnn (Krauss) McBee; m. Gregory Clay Rothfuss, Apr. 6, 1983 (div. Jan. 1987); m. Douglas Franklin Broadwell, June 1, 1996. AS, Cen. C.C., Grand Island, 1990; BS, Bellevue U., 1991; MA, GWU, 1996. Clk., cashier Kinman Chevrolet-Cadillac, Grand Island, 1977-80; receptionist, keypuncher Cen. C.C., 1980, keypunch operator, 1980-82, computer operator, 1982, programmer, 1982-86, analyst, programmer, 1986—; adj. instr. Cen. C.C., 1988—; trainer, cons. Datatel, Inc., 1994—; hardware cons. Cook & Doyle, P.C., Lexington, Nebr., 1987; staff exch. Postsecondary Internat. Network, Durham Coll., Oshawa, Ont., Can., 1991. Precinct chair Proposed Civic Ctr. Supporters, Grand Island, 1989; bd. dirs. Leadership Tomorrow, Grand Island, 1990-93, Ctrl. Nebr. Coun. on Alcoholism, Grand Island, 1992—, v.p., 1993, pres., 1994—; divsn. chair United Way, Grand Island, 1990-94; co-chair Grand Island Task Force, 1993—; bd. dirs. Heartland United Way, 1996—. Mem. Grand Island Jaycees (v.p. cmty. devel. 1989, pres. 1990, Jaycee of Yr. 1988), Bus. and Profl. Women (Young Careerist 1991), Am. Assn. Women in Cmty. Colls. (v.p. 1993, pres. 1994), Info. Tech. Com. Office: Cen Community Coll 3134 W US Highway 34 Grand Island NE 68801-7279

BROCK, CHARLES MARQUIS, lawyer; b. Watseka, Ill., Oct. 8, 1941; s. Glen Westgate and Muriel Lucile (Bubeck) B.; m. Elizabeth Bonilla, Dec. 17, 1966; children: Henry Christopher, Anna Melissa. AB cum laude, Princeton U., 1963; JD, Georgetown U., 1968; MBA, U. Chgo., 1974. Bar: Ill. 1969, U.S. Dist. Ct. (no. dist.) Ill. 1969. Asst. trust counsel Continental Ill. Nat. Bank, Chgo., 1968-74; regional counsel Latin Am., Can. Abbott Labs., Abbott Park, Ill., 1974-77, regional counsel, Europe, Africa and Middle East, 1977-81, div. counsel domestic legal ops., 1981-88, assoc. gen. counsel internat. legal ops., asst. sec., 1989-92, divsnl. v.p., assoc. gen. counsel, asst. sec., 1992—. Served with Inter-Am. Def. Coll., U.S. Army, 1964-66. Mem. ABA, Chgo. Bar Assn., Mich. Shores Club, Phi Beta Kappa. Republican. Home: 1473 Asbury Ave Winnetka IL 60093-1467 Office: Abbott Labs One Abbott Park Rd Abbott Park IL 60064

BROCKA, BRUCE, editor, educator, software engineer; b. Davenport, Iowa, Nov. 1, 1959; s. Donald H. and Daisy Ann (Robertson) B.; m. M. Suzanne St. Ledger, Mar. 17, 1984; children: Melinda Athena, Bennett Paul. BS, St. Ambrose U., 1981; MS, U. Iowa, 1984. Instr. Army Mgmt. Engring. Coll., Rock Island, Ill., 1984-90; exec. editor, assoc. pub. Exec. Scis. Inst., Davenport, 1986—. Editor: Quality Control and Applied Statistics, 1987—, Operations Research/Management Science, 1987—, Automation in Quality Assurance, 1988, Biostatistica, 1990—, Quality Management, 1992; contbr. articles on sci. tech. to profl. jours. Ptnr. Preservation Group Partnership, Davenport, 1985—. Republican. Home and Office: 1005 Mississippi Ave Davenport IA 52803-3938

BROCKA, M. SUZANNE, controller; b. Moline, Ill., May 25, 1960; d. Paul Edmund and Therese Clemence (Fleischman) St. Ledger; m. Bruce Brocka, Mar. 17, 1984; children: Melinda Athena, Bennett Paul. BA in Acctg., St. Ambrose U., Davenport, Iowa, 1981; postgrad., Teikyo-Marycrest U., Davenport, Iowa, 1984-86. CPA, Ill. Acct. Iowa-Ill. Gas and Elec. Co., Davenport, 1981-86; acctg. supr. Frank E. Basil/Gen. Dynamics, Rock Island, Ill., 1986-87, mgr. fin., 1988-90, mgr. fin./contracts, 1990-91; controller City of Davenport, 1991—; cons. Frank E. Basil Inc., Washington, 1990-91, Rocky Mountain Metals Inc., Raton, N.Mex., 1994—, Exec. Scis. Inst., Davenport, Iowa, 1987—. Author: Quality Management, 1992. Bd. dirs. Scott County Historic Preservation Soc., Davenport, 1985-88. Mem. Am. Mgmt. Assn., Fin. Mgmt. Assn., Am. Econ. Assn., Govt. Fin. Officers Assn., Alpha Chi. Home: 1005 Mississippi Ave Davenport IA 52803-3938 Office: City of Davenport 226 W 4th St Davenport IA 52801-1308

BROCKERT, DAVID JOSEPH, food products executive; b. Globe, Ariz., Dec. 11, 1955; s. David Joseph and Mary Alta (Moe) B.; m. Mary Agnes Foesch, May 17, 1980; 1 child, Lauren Nicole. AA, Madison Area Tech. Coll., 1978. Donut maker Donuts Unltd., Madison, Wis., 1975-93; baker Triggs Bakery, Madison, 1993-94, Colonial Bakery, Madison, 1994—. Roman Catholic. Home: 4622 Academy Dr Madison WI 53716

BROCKET, JUDITH ANN, elementary education mathematics educator; b. Muscatine, Iowa, Feb. 3, 1942; d. Kenneth McKay and Dorothy Pearl (Stewart) Uebe; m. Raymond Gene Brocket, July 28, 1963; 1 son, Jamie. AA, Muscatine Jr. Coll., 1962; BA, Parsons Coll., 1965; grad., Children's Inst. of Lit., 1987. Cert. tchr., Iowa. Swim instr. for handicapped ARC, Burlington, IA, 1965; 3d grade tchr. Burlington Community Sch. Dist., 1965-68, 5th grade tchr., 1970-80, chpt. I math. tchr., 1980—; 4th grade tchr. West Burlington (Iowa) Community Sch. Dist., 1968-70; presenter in field; mem. North Cen. Accreditation Com., 1984-87; mem. Lit. Mag. Com., 1988—. Contbr. articles to profl. publs.; author math. workbooks, curriculum guide. Pres. Burlington PTA, 1981-82, treas., 1988-89; mem., spokesperson Burlington Sch. Dist. Adv. Com., 1980—; mem. Burlington Parent Adv. Com., 1980—; nom. coun. Messiah Lutheran Ch. Recipient cert. of merit U.S. Dept. Edn., 1987; Fed. Govt. grantee, 1983, 84. Mem. NEA, Iowa State Edn. Assn., Burlington Edn. Assn., Burlington Art Guild. Democrat. Lutheran. Home: 13084 115th St Burlington IA 52601-8705

BROCKHAUS, DONALD, engineer; b. Humphrey, Nebr., July 17, 1932. BS, U. Nebr., 1959. Registered profl. engr., Nebr., S.D., Ohio, Minn. Engring. mgr., chief engr. Stormor Inc., Fremont, Nebr., 1976-87; sr. project engr. Behlen Mfg. Co., Columbus, Nebr., 1959-76, chief estimator, 1988—. Patentee for grain drying components. With U.S. Army, 1952-54, Korea. Mem. NSPE. Office: Behlen Mfg Co PO Box 569 Columbus NE 68602-0569

BROCKHAUS, ROBERT HEROLD, SR., business educator, consultant; b. St. Louis, Apr. 18, 1940; s. Herold August and Leona M (Stutzke) B.; m. Joyce Patricia Dees, June 13, 1970; children: Cheryl Lynn, Robert Herold. BS in Mech. Engring., U. Mo.-Rolla, 1962; MSIA, Purdue U., 1966; PhD, Washington U., St. Louis, 1976. Mgr. Ralston-Purina, St. Louis, 1962-69; pres. Progressive Mgmt. Enterprises, Ltd., St. Louis, 1969—; asst. prof. mgmt. sci. St. Louis U., 1972-78, assoc. prof., 1978-84, prof., 1984—, Coleman Found. Chair in Entrepreneurship, 1991—; dir. Small Bus. Inst., St. Louis U., 1976-86, Inst. Entrpreneurial Studies, 1987-90; treas. CORO Found., 1987-92; exec. dir. Jefferson Smurfit Ctr. for Entrepreneurial Studies, 1990—; 1st. v.p. Mo. Inventor's Assn., 1988-94; state adminstr. Mo. Small Bus. Devel. Ctrs., St. Louis, 1982-86, state dir., 1987-89; Schoen prof. entrepreneurship Baylor U., 1981; McAninch prof. entrepreneurship Kans. State U., 1985-87, vis. scholar S. Cross U., Australia, 1995; del. White House Conf. Small Bus., 1986, 95. Co-author: Encyclopedia of Entrepreneurship, 1982; Building A Better You, 1982; Nursing Concepts for Health Promotion, 1979, Art and Science of Enterpreneurship, 1985, Entrepreneurship in the 1990's, 1991, The State of the Art of Entrepreneurialship, 1992; editor Journal of Consulting, 1988-90; co-editor: Frontiers of Entrepreneurship Research, 1990, Advances in Entrepreneurship, Firm Emergence and Growth, 1993, 95; editor Family Bus. Rev., 1993—; also contbr. articles to profl. jours. Bd. dirs. City Venture, St. Louis, 1982-86; del. White House Conf. on Small Bus., 1986, 95; v.p. United Ch. of Christ, 1991-92, pres., 1992-93; chairperson troop 25 Boy Scout Am., 1990-93. Recipient Outstanding Svc. award BSA, 1994; Fulbright fellow, U. Waikato, N.Z., 1985. Fellow Internat. Coun. for Small Bus. (sr. v.p. 1981-83, internat. pres. 1983-84, bd. dirs. 1983, v.p. 1986, exec. dir. 1987—), Nat. Small Bus. Inst. Dirs. Assn. (nat. v.p. 1980-82, 96—, nat. pres. 1982-83), U.S. Assn. for Small Bus. Entrepreneurship; mem. Assn. Collegiate Entrepreneurs (internat. bd. dirs., exec. com. 1991-93, recipient outstanding entrepreneurship educator award, 1992), Acad. Mgmt. (nat. program chmn. 1977-78, exec. com. 1993-95), Inventors' Assn. St. Louis (bd. dirs. 1989-94, 1st v.p. 1991), Family Firm Inst. (internat. conf. chair, 1995), Fenton Jaycees (treas.), Exec. Club (St. Louis, moderator 1973-86), Pi Kappa Alpha (dist. pres. 1969-74, faculty adv. 1990—, recipient disting. svc. award 1972, bd. dir. endowment found. nat. coun. for youth and relgion, 1994—). Avocations: swimming, sailing, camping. Home: 10000 Hilltop Dr Saint Louis MO 63128-1512

BROCKMAN, DAVID DEAN, psychoanalyst, psychiatrist; b. Greer, S.C., Aug. 4, 1922; s. Hiram LeRoy and Flora Grace (Witt) B.; m. Martha Ann Rinebolt, June 28, 1950; children: Pamela Ann Brockman Cevallos, Sherrill Ruth Reed, David Dean Jr. BS in Biology, Furman U., 1943; MD with honors, Med. Coll. S.C., 1946. Diplomate Am. Bd. Psychiatry and Neurology; lic. psychiatrist, S.C., Ill. Intern in pathology Duke Hosp., Durham, N.C., 1946-47, resident in psychiatry, 1947-48; from resident to staff mem. North Shore Health Resort, Winnetka, Ill., 1950-52; from asst. in psychiatry to instr. U. Chgo. Clinics/U. Chgo. Med. Sch., 1952-54; asst. prof., acting chmn. psychiatry dept. U. Chgo., 1954-55; pvt. practice Chgo., 1955—; from clin. asst. prof. to clin. prof. psychiatry U. Ill., 1956-90; clin. prof. psychiatry U. Chgo., 1994—; bd. regents Am. Bd. Psychoanalysts; faculty Inst. for Psychoanalysis, Chgo., 1971, 78-90, tng. and supervising analyst, 1973—, psychoanalytic edn. coun., 1978-90, progression com., 1978-81, chmn. examination subcom., 1978-83, geographic com., 1981-83, chmn. geographic com. 1983-90, chmn. media award com., 1984-90, ethics com. 1987-88, chmn. Harris award com., 1989-90, editorial com., 1990; adj. staff mem. Michael Reese Hosp., 1989—; presenter, lectr. in field. Editor: (newsletter) The Am. Coll. Psychoanalysts, 1990, Bulletin The Inst. Psychoanalysis Chgo., 1990; contbr. articles to profl. jours. Capt. U.S. Army, 1948-50, Japan. Fellow Am. Soc. for Adolescent Psychiatry (life), Am. Coll. Psychoanalysis (v.p. 1992-93, pres.-elect 1993, pres. 1994-95, chmn. arrangement com. 1987—), Am. Psychiat. Assn., Am. Coll. Psychiatrists (life); mem. AMA (Physicians Recognition award 1984-90), Internat. Psychoanalytic Assn., Am. Psychoanalytic Assn. (cert.), Ill. Psychiat. Soc., Ill. Med. Soc., Chgo. Psychoanalytic Soc. (assoc.), Chgo. Med. Soc., Chgo. Soc. Adolescent Psychiatry (exec. com. 1987-89), Alpha Epsilon Delta, Pi Kappa Phi, Phi Rho Sigma, Alpha Omega Alpha. Office: Inst for Psychoanalysis 1030 Kenilworth Ln Glenview IL 60025-1918 also: Inst for Psychoanalysis 180 N Michigan Ave Chicago IL 60601

BROCKMEIER, MATTHEW GEORGE, arts administrator; b. Chgo., Feb. 14, 1955; s. Warren Gustav and Virginia Elliene (Selke) B.; m. Darinka Dimitrijevic, May 28, 1977 (div. 1984). BA, Lawrence U., 1976. Inventory mgmt. Parker Hannifin, Niles, Ill., 1976-89; exec. dir. Chgo. Music Alliance, 1989—; spl. lectr. Chgo. Mus. Coll.-Roosevelt U., 1990—; bd. dirs. Burgundian Consort, Oak Park, Ill., pres., 1982-90; panelist City Arts/Dept. Cultural Affairs, Chgo., 1991-92; panelist Chgo. Artists Internat., Chgo. Dept. Cultural Affairs, 1995, panelist Cmty. Arts Assistance Music Panel, 1996; mem. Evanston (Ill.) Arts Coun. Music Panel, 1995, Ill. Arts Coun. Symphonies and Ensembles Panel, 1994, Oak Park Area Arts Coun. Arts I Panel, 1994; coord. com. Ill. Coalition for Music Edn., 1992—. Bd. dirs. Comty. Support Svcs., Inc., Brookfield, Ill., 1992—, pres., 1994-96; com. mem. Comty. Edn. and Advocacy for Disabilities, Brookfield, 1990-94; mem. consumer and family adv. coun. Ill. Dept. Mental Health & Devel. Disabilities, 1995—. Mem. Family Support Adv. Coun., Legis. Com. Ill. Arts Alliance. Home: 220 S Ridgeland Ave Oak Park IL 60302-3226 Office: Chgo Music Alliance Ste #819 410 S Michigan Ave Ste 819 Chicago IL 60605-1402

BROD, CATHERINE MARIE, college director; b. Aurora, Ill., Sept. 16, 1959; d. Harold Keith and Arlene Ruth (Peterson) Feltz; m. Michael Nicholas Brod, Aug. 13, 1983; children: Ryan Michael, Kelsey Taylor. BA in Comm., Ea. Ill. U., 1981, MA in Comm., 1986. Grad. asst. Ea. Ill. U., Charleston, 1982-83; acct. exec. B&G Enterprises, Inc., Champaign, Ill., 1984-85; program coord., program dir. U. Ill., Chgo., 1985-91, exec. dir. Ill. Eye Found., 1991-95; assoc. exec. dir. Cancer Treatmet Rsch. Found., Arlington Heights, Ill., 1995—; exec. dir. Internat. Soc. Refractive Keratoplasty, Chgo., 1989-93, mng. editor newsletter, 1989—. Health concerns chair Christus Victor Luth. Ch. Mem. Acad. for Health Svcs. Mktg., Nat. Sch. Pub. Rels. Assn.,Coun. for Advancement and Support of Edn. (2 Silver medals 1993, 2 Bronze medals 1994), Med. Group Mgmt. Assn., Jaycees (v.p. 1987), Assn. for Health Care Philanthropy, Nat. Soc. Fund Raising Execs. Home: 1223 Montego Ct Elk Grove Village IL 60007-7132 Office: Cancer Treatment Rsch Found 3455 Salt Creek Ln Arlington Heights IL

BRODERICK, B. MICHAEL, state legislator, banker. Banker Canton, S.D.; mem. S.D. Ho. of Reps., Pierre, S.D.; mem. agr., nat. resources and transp. coms. S.D. Ho. of Reps.

BRODIE, MARK STANLEY, electrophysiologist, pharmacologist; b. Chgo., Aug. 23, 1957; s. Warne and Evelyn Margaret (Ryczkowski) B.; m. Sara Ellen Appel Shefner, Feb. 23, 1985. BA, Northwestern U., 1979; PhD, U. Ill., Chgo., 1984. Postdoctoral fellow U. Colo., Denver, 1984-86; rsch. scientist Abbott Labs., Abbott Park, Ill., 1986-90; rsch. asst. prof. U. Ill., Chgo., 1990—; vis. prof. Belgrade (Yugoslavia) U., 1989. Mem. Am. Soc. Pharmacology and Exptl. Therapeutics. Roman Catholic. Office: Univ of Ill Dept Physiology M/C 901 835 S Wolcott Rm E-202 Chicago IL 60612-7342

BRODKEY, ROBERT STANLEY, chemical engineering educator; b. L.A., Sept. 14, 1928; s. Harold R. and Clara (Goldman) B.; m. Martha Mahr, Dec. 22, 1958 (div. Nov. 1971); 1 son, Philip Arthur; m. Carolyn Patch, Dec. 6, 1975. A.A., San Francisco City Coll., 1948; B.Chemistry with highest honors, U. Calif.-Berkeley, 1950, M.S. in Chem. Engring, 1950; Ph.D. in Chem. Engring. (Gulf Oil fellow), U. Wis., 1952. Research chem. engr. Esso Research & Engring. Co., Linden, N.J., 1952-56; research chem. engr. Esso Standard Oil Co., Bayway, N.J., 1956-57; asst. prof. chem. engring. Ohio State U., Columbus, 1957-60; assoc. prof. Ohio State U., 1960-64, prof., 1964-92, prof. emeritus, 1992—; cons. on turbulent motion, mixing kinetics, rheology, 2-phase flow, fluid dynamics, image processing and analysis; expository lectr. GAMM Conf., 1975; vis. prof. Japan Soc. Promotion Sci., 1978; Clyde chair engring. U. Utah, fall 1994. Author: Transport Phemomena, A Unified Approach, 1988, The Phenomena of Fluid Motions, 1967; editor: Turbulence in Mixing Operations, 1975; contbr. articles to profl. jours.; patentee in field. Recipient Outstanding Paper of Yr. award Can. Jour. Chem. Engring., 1970; NATO sr. fellow in sci. Max Planck Institut für Strömungsforschung, Göttingen, Fed. Republic Germany, 1972; Alexander Von Humboldt Found. sr. U.S. scientist award, 1975, 83; sr. rsch. award Coll. Engring. Ohio State U., 1983, 86; Disting. Sr. Rsch. award Am. Soc. Engring. Edn., 1985; Chem. Engr. lectureship award Am. Soc. Engring. Edn., 1986; North Am. Mixing Forum award, 1994. Fellow AAAS, AIChE, Am. Phys. Soc., Am. Inst. Chemists; mem. Am. Chem. Soc., Am. Acad. Mech., Soc. Engring. Sci., Soc. Rheology, Sigma Xi, Phi Lambda Upsilon, Alpha Gamma Sigma, Phi Beta Delta. Office: Ohio St Univ 140 W 19th Ave Columbus OH 43210-1110

BRODRICK, NANCY ANN, human resources specialist; b. Dayton, Ohio, Feb. 19, 1944; d. Everett Cidric and Justine Emaline (Myers) B. BS in Edn., U. Cin., 1966; M in Counseling, Xavier U., 1981, postgrad. With Globe Industries, Dayton, 1962-63; accounts receivable clk. AIA, Washington, 1964; math. tchr. Cin. Bd. Edn., 1966-68; math. instr. Army Edn. Ctr., Ft. Sill, Ohio, 1969; math. tchr. Oak Hills Bd. Edn., Cin., 1970-71, 74-79; comml. real estate and bus. brokerage cons. Cin., 1982-85; with Theodore Mayer & Bros. Realtor, Cin., 1985-87, Investment Real Estate Svcs., Dayton, 1987-89; ind. mktg. cons. Greyhound Package Express, Cin., 1989-90; ind. human resource devel. cons. Cin., 1990—; presenter various workshops and seminars; holistic trainer and cons. Chairperson Arty Party Summerfair, 1982, judging and screening com., 1981; guest speaker Hyde Park Meth. Ch., 1983; chairperson fundraising art auction Meadowland Art Sch., 1984; chairperson screening and judging com. Hyde Park Art Show, 1983, 84, co-chairperson, 1985; vol. English tchr. Traveler's Aid Inst., 1985, 86. Mem. Alternative Health Group Cin. (co-chairperson program com. 1991), Cin. Womens Network, Soroptimists (chairperson ways and means com. 1986), Inst. Noetic Scis. (area coord. Cin. chpt. 1994-96).

BRODSKY, WILLIAM J., futures options exchange executive; b. N.Y.C., 1944. Student, Syracuse U., 1965, JD, 1968. Bar: N.Y. 1969, Ill. 1985. Atty. Model, Roland & Co., 1968-74; with Am. Stock Exch., 1974-82, exec. v.p. ops., 1979-82; exec. v.p., COO Chgo. Merc. Exch., 1982-85, pres., CEO, 1985—; bd. dirs. Chgo. Merc. Exch.; adv. mem. internat. capital mktgs. adv. com. Fed. Res. Bank N.Y.; mem. adv. coun. J.L. Kellogg Grad. Sch. Mgmt. Bd. visitors Northwestern U. Law Sch.; bd. dirs. Northwestern Meml. Corp.; trustee Syracuse U., Ill. Inst. Tech.; mem. midwest regional adv. bd. Inst. Internat. Edn. Mem. N.Y. State Bar Assn., Ill. Bar Assn., Swiss Commodities Futures and Options Assn. (bd. dirs.), Internat. Futures and Commodities Inst. (Geneva, bd. dirs.), Nat. Futures Assn. (bd. dirs.), Ill. Coun. on Econ. Edn. (bd. dirs.), Chicagoland C. of C., Econ. Club Chgo., Comml. Club Chgo. Office: Chgo Merc Exch 30 S Wacker Dr Chicago IL 60606-7402

BRODY, ROBERT, dermatologist; b. Cleve., June 15, 1948; s. Melvin and Nancy Elizabeth Brody; m. Mary Ann Conn, July 23, 1988; children: Ian Hamilton Conn, Hartley Messing Conn, Matthew Grant Hutchinson. AB with distinction, Stanford U., 1970; MD, U. Mich., 1974. Intern in internal medicine, Cleve. Clinic, 1974-75, resident in dermatology, 1975-78; practice medicine specializing in dermatology, Cleve., 1978—; staff physician Kaiser-Permanente Med. Center, 1978-82, mem. profl. edn. com., 1978-82, chmn., 1980-82, also sec. exec. com., 1980; pvt. practice, 1982—; asst. clin. prof. Case Western Res. U. Med. Sch., 1978-80, 83—, clin. instr., 1980-83, dermatology dept. rep. to gen. faculty, 1980-82; asst. physician Univ. Hosps. Cleve., 1979—. Sec., Cleve. Play House Men's Com., 1979-82; mem. ann. fund com. Stanford U., 1978—, regional co-chmn., 1981-82. Diplomate Am. Bd. Dermatology. Mem. Am. Acad. Dermatology, Cleve. Acad. Medicine. Contbr. articles to med. jours. Club: Cleve. Skating, Rowfant. Home: 2870 Glengary Rd Cleveland OH 44120-1731 Office: 3461 Warrensville Center Rd Cleveland OH 44122-5227

BROECKER, SHERRY, state legislator; b. Feb. 14, 1951; m. Jerry Broecker; 3 children. Student, U. Minn. Self-employed custom picture framer; rep. Dist. 53B Minn. Ho. of Reps., 1994—.

BROKAW, KATHRYN LOUISE ZIMMER, municipal finance administrator; b. Cin., Aug. 27, 1946; d. Paul Francis and Bess Louise (Kennedy) Zimmer; m. Carlton Walter Brokaw, May 15, 1965; children: Jeremy Clayton, Melanie Kay. BS summa cum laude in Mktg., U. Cin., 1990. Cert. mcpl. fin. adminstr. Sec. Kelly Svcs., Cin., 1965, Magna Am. Corp., Evendale, Ohio, 1965-66; sec. Randall div. Randall Co., Cin., 1966-69, exec. sec. Hall Mack div., 1969-71; exec. sec. Multi-Pak div. Internat. Paper, Cin., 1971-73; customer svc. rep. Sears, Roebuck & Co., Springdale, Ohio, 1977-82; dep. clk. Village of Greenhills, Ohio, 1980-85, dir. fin., 1985—. Trustee Greenhills Civic Found., 1980-85; coord. Christmas Crib Dedication, Greenhills, 1985-87; master of ceremony Arbor Day, Village of Greenhills, 1985-86; voter registrar Hamilton County, Ohio, 1985—. Mem. Mcpl. Treas.' U.S.A. and Can. (cert. mcpl. fin. adminstr. 1995), Ohio Mcpl. Fin. Officers, Govt. Fin. Officers Assn., Southwestern Ohio Tax Adminstrs. Assn. (corr. sec. 1986-88, rec. sec. 1988-90, chmn. 1992-94; spkr., panelist 1990—), Greater Cin. Fin. Officers (charter, chmn. 1988-90, rec. sec. 1990—), Village Voices (chmn. 1990-94, former sec. 1990—, membership chmn., publicity chmn., historian, wedding liaison, music chmn.), Alpha Sigma Lambda, Delta Mu Delta, Delta Tau Kappa. Office: Village of Greenhills 11000 Winton Rd Cincinnati OH 45218-1106

BROKKE, CATHERINE JULIET, mission executive; b. Mpls., Dec. 25, 1926; d. Emil John and Alma (Brye) Eliason; m. Harold Joseph Brokke, Sept. 9, 1949; 1 child, Daniel. Diploma in nursing, Luth. Deaconess Hosp., Mpls., 1947; student, Concordia Coll., Moorhead, Minn., 1948-49, Bethany Coll. Missions, Mpls., 1949-51. RN, Minn. Sch. and occupational nurse Bethany Fellowship, Mpls., 1951-75; missions sec. Bethany Fellowship Missions, Mpls., 1963-86, dir., 1986—; instr. Bethany Coll. Missions, 1950-88; bd. dirs. STEM Ministries, 1995—. Mng. editor Message of Cross, 1990—; composer hymns. Organist Bethany Missionary Ch., Bloomington, Minn., 1956-89. Mem. Evang. Fellowship of Mission Agys. (trustee 1987-93), Evang. Missions Info. Svc. (bd. dirs. 1994—). Office: Bethany Fellowship Missions 6820 Auto Club Rd Bloomington MN 55438-2413

BROMELMEIER, GALE MARIE, retired nursing association administrator; b. Sherwood, N.Y., Aug. 28, 1936; d. James and Julia Tabor (Otis) Fiorenzo; m. John Henry Bromelmeier, July 26, 1958; children: Mary Anne, Martha Louise, Matthew Otis. BSN, Western Res. U., 1959, MSN, 1979. RN, Ohio. Staff nurse Univ. Hosps. Cleve.; exec. dir. Greater Cleve. Nurses Assn.; dir. govtl. affairs Vis. Nurse Assn. Cleve., 1993-95. Mem. ANA, Am. Soc. Assn. Execs. (cert. assn. exec. for life), Ohio Nurses Assn. (chmn. heritage com. 1987-89, chmn. PAC 1995), Sigma Theta Tau. Home: # PH07 2250 Par Ln Willoughby Hills OH 44094

BROMM, CURT, state legislator; b. Oakland, Nebr., Mar. 19, 1945; m. Vicki Nodlinski, 1968; children: Jason, Jenefer, John, Jina, Jaron. Student, U. Nebr. Past county atty. Saunders County; mem. from dist. 23 Nebr. State Senate, Lincoln, 1992—, mem. bus. and labor com., mem. natural resources and urban affairs com., vice chmn. rules com. Chmn. bd. dirs. Saunders County Sch. Reorgn. Bd.; mem., pres. Wahoo Pub. Sch. Bd. Mem. Nebr. State Bar Assn. Office: Nebr State Senate State Capitol Rm 1017 Lincoln NE 68509*

BROOK, DANIEL T., mechanical engineer; b. Burlington, Wis., Nov. 27, 1964. BSME, Milw. Sch. Engring., 1986. Mech. engr. Newport News (Va.) Ship Building, 1987-90, D & L Mfg., Menomonee Falls, Wis., 1992—; project engr. Rite-Hite, Cudahy Brown Deer, Wis., 1990-92. Mem. Am. Welding Soc. Republican. Roman Catholic. Office: D&L Mfg Co PO Box 630 Menomonee Falls WI 53052-0630

BROOK, SUSAN G., state agency administrator, horse farmer; b. N.Y.C., Dec. 7, 1949; d. Alvin Ira and Sally (Behar) Greenberg. BA, Northwestern U., 1971; MA in Child Devel. and Pub. Adminstrn., Mich. State U., 1975. Community rep. Office Child Devel. HEW, Chgo., 1971-72; program asst. office of pres. OEO, Chgo., 1972-73; exec. coord. Mich. 4-C Coun. Mich. Dept. Mgmt. and Budget, Lansing, 1973-80; adminstr. office interagy. transp. coordination Mich. Dept. Transp., Lansing, 1980-83; adminstr. freight svcs. and safety Bur. Urban and Pub. Transp., Mich. Dept. Transp., Lansing, 1983—; chairperson legis. com. Mich. Coun. Family Rels., Lansing, 1976-77; mem. coalition on children and youth, Lansing, 1976-80; co-chairperson Mich. White House Conf. on Families, Lansing, 1979-80, gov's liaison Internat. Yr of the Child, Lansing, 1978-79; guest lectr. Mich. State U., East Lansing, 1976, Davenport Coll., 1985; inst. Lansing Community Coll., 1978; mem. curriculum devel. adv. com. Lansing community coll., 1979-80. Advisor neighborhood health clinic, Chgo., 1969; youth group advisor Shaare Tikvah Congregation, Chgo., 1967-71; campaign treas. city council candidate, East Lansing, Mich., 1981. Mem. ASPCA, Am. Morgan Horse Assn., Am. Donkey and Mule Soc., Nat. Assn. Edn. Young Children, Nat. Assn. State Dirs. Child Devel., Nat. Conf. State Ry. Ofcls., Am. Horse Shows Assn., Mich. Horse Show Assn., Mich. Justin Morgan Horse Assn., Mich. Morgan Horse Breeders Futurity, Mich. Assn. Edn. Young Children (hon.), Mich. Farm Bur., Capital Area Humane Soc., Calif. Marine Mammal Ctr., Gt. Lakes Miniature Horse Club, Ingham County Farm Bur., Soc. Women in Transp., Women in State Govt., Animal Protection Inst., Am. Miniature Horse Assn., Australian Shepherd Club Am., Hadassah. Office: Mich Dept Transp 425 W Ottawa St Lansing MI 48933-1532

BROOKER, THOMAS KIMBALL, oil company executive; b. L.A., Oct. 1, 1939; s.Robert Elton and Sally Burton Harrison (Smith) B.; m. Nancy Belle Neumann, 1966; children: Thomas Kimball Jr., Isobel, Vanessa. BA in French Lit., Yale U., 1961; MBA, Harvard U., 1968; MA in Art History, U. Chgo., 1989, PhD in Art History, 1996. Assoc. in corp. fin. Morgan Stanley & Co., Inc., N.Y.C., 1968-73, v.p., 1973-75, mng. dir., 1976-88; head Chgo. office Morgan Stanley & Co., Inc., 1978-88; pres. Barbara Oil Co., Chgo., 1989—, also bd. dirs.; bd. dirs. Arthur J. Gallagher & Co., Zenith Electronics Corp., Miami Corp., Cutler Oil & Gas Corp.; bd. govs. Midwest Stock Exch., 1980-88, vice chmn., 1986-88. Chmn. vis. com. libr. U. Chgo., mem. vis. com. music dept.; mem., chmn. com. on libr. Yale U. President's Coun., 1980-84; bd. dirs. Lyric Opera Chgo., Alliance Francaise Chgo.; vice chmn., trustee Newberry Libr.; chmn. com. on libr. Yale U., 1980-84; trustee Yale Libr. Assocs., chmn., 1976-79; trustee Pierpont Morgan Libr.; bd. govs. John Carter Brown Libr.; mem. adv. com. Bibliotheca Wittockiana, Brussels. Lt. USN, 1962-66. Recipient Sir Thomas More medal U. San Francisco, 1992; assoc. fellow Saybrook Coll., Yale U. Mem. Adminstrv. Coun. (v.p.), Assn. Internat. de Bibliophilie, Coun. Am. Bibliog. Soc., Bandar-Log, Caxton Club, Chgo. Club, Comml. Club, Econ. Club, River Club (N.Y.C.), Knickerbocker Club (N.Y.C.), Grolier Club (N.Y.C.), The Casino, Saddle and Cycle Club, Edgartown (Mass.) Yacht Club, The Reading Room (Edgartown), Quadrangle Club, Racquet Club, Rockaway Hunt Club, Wayfarers Club. Home: 1500 N Lake Shore Dr Chicago IL 60610-1624 Office: Barbara Oil Co 1 First Nat Plz Ste 2656 Chicago IL 60603

BROOKS, GWENDOLYN, writer, poet; b. Topeka, June 7, 1917; d. David Anderson and Keziah Corinne (Wims) B.; m. Henry L. Blakely, Sept. 17, 1939; children: Henry L., Nora. Grad., Wilson Jr. Coll., Chgo., 1936; L.H.D., Columbia Coll., 1964. Instr. poetry Columbia Coll., Chgo., Northeastern Ill. State Coll., Chgo.; mem. Ill. Arts Council; cons. in poetry Library of Congress, 1985-86; Jefferson lectr., 1994. Author: (poetry) A Street in Bronzeville, 1945, Annie Allen, 1949 (Pulitzer prize 1950), Maud Martha: (novel) Bronzeville Boys and Girls, 1953; (for children) The Bean Eaters, 1956; poetry, 1960, Selected Poems, 1963, In the Mecca, 1968, Riot, 1969, Family Pictures, 1970, Aloneness, 1971, To Disembark, 1981; (autobiography) Report From Part One, 1972, The Tiger Who Wore White Gloves, 1974, Beckonings, 1975, Primer for Blacks, 1980, Young Poets' Primer, 1981, Very Young Poets, 1983, The Near-Johannesburg Boy, 1986, Blacks, 1987, Gottschalk and the Grande Tarantelle, 1988, Winnie, 1988, Children Coming Home, 1991, Report From Part Two, 1995. Named one of 10 Women of Yr. Mademoiselle mag., 1945; recipient Creative Writing award Am. Acad. Arts and Letters, 1946, Aninsfield-Wolf award, 1969, Essence award, 1988, Frost medal Poetry Soc. Am., 1989, Lifetime Achievement award Nat. Endowment for the Arts, 1989, Soc. for Lit. award U. Thessaloniki, Athens, Greece, 1990, Aiken-Taylor award, 1992, Jefferson lectr. award NEH, 1994, Nat. Book Found. medal for lifetime achievement, 1994, Am. Book award Gwendolyn Brooks Jr. H.S., 1995, Nat. medal of arts, 1995; Guggenheim fellow, 1946, 47; named poet laureate of Ill., 1968; inducted into Nat. Women's Hall of Fame, 1988; Gwendolyn Brooks chair in Black Lit. and Creative Writing established in her honor Chgo. State U., 1990; The Gwendolyn Brooks Ctr. established, 1992; Gwendolyn Brooks Elem. Sch. named in her honor, Aurora, Ill., 1995. Mem. Soc. Midland Authors. Home: 5530 S South Shore Dr Apt 2A Chicago IL 60637-1921

BROOKS, JOSEPH W., stockbroker; b. Murry City, Ohio, May 2, 1949. BA, Hiram (Ohio) Coll., 1973. V.p., gen. mgr. Mills Nisan, Willobey, Ohio, 1977-88; gen. mgr. sales Marshall Ford, Mayfield Heights, Ohio, 1988-94; stockbroker Merrill Lynch, Cleve., 1994—. Staff sgt. USMC, 1968-69, Vietnam. Republican. Home: 8006 Buckthorn Dr Mentor OH 44060-7449 Office: Merrill Lynch 1375 E 9th St Ste 10 Cleveland OH 44114-1724

BROOKS, KENNETH JOHN, electrical estimator, music engineer; b. Toledo, June 24, 1963; s. James Francis and Mary Lillian (Gilbert) B. A in Gen. Studies, Lima (Ohio) Tech. Coll., 1985. Owner, ptnr. Rosewood Music, Findlay, Ohio, 1985; sales mgr. House of Hindenach, Findlay, Ohio, 1986; purchasing project mgr. Brooks Electric, Findlay, Ohio, 1987-91; journeyman, inside wireman Advantage Enterprises, Toledo, 1992, estimator, project mgr., 1992—; beta testing cons. Trade Svc. Corp., Torrence, Calif., 1990-95, McCormick Sys., Phoenix, 1990-95. Composer: The Day Will Come, 1990. Mem. parish coun. St. Mary's Ch., Bluffton, Ohio, 1984-93. Mem. Findlay Area Plant Engrs. Republican. Roman Catholic. Home: 110 E Nicholas St Arlington OH 45814 Office: Advantage Enterprises 5030 Advantage Dr Toledo OH 43612

BROOKS, PATRICIA SCOTT, principal; b. St. Louis, July 19, 1949; d. John Edward and Doris Louise (Webb) Scott; m. John Robert Brooks, May 22, 1986; 1 child, Ollie. BS, W.Va. State Coll., 1971; MA, Marshall U., 1974; adminstrv. cert., Ind. U., 1990. Cert. tchr., Ind. Tchr. spl. edn. Huntington (W.Va.) State Hosp., 1971; tchr. elem. edn. Kanawha County Sch., Charleston, W.Va., 1971-78; tchr. elem. edn. Washington Twp., Indpls., 1979-82, tchr. mid. sch., 1982-90, adminstrv. intern, 1989-90, asst. coord., 1990, 92, asst. prin., 1990-93; prin. Pike Twp., Indpls., 1993—; participant Ind. U. Tchr. as a Decision Maker Program, Bloomington, 1989; mem. Human Rels. Com., Indpls., 1996; presenter U.S. Dept. Edn. Active Urban League, Indpls., 1990—. Recipient Tchr. Spotlight award Topics Newspaper, 1983; named one of 100 Outstanding Black Women in State of Ind., Nat. Coun. Negro Women, 1990; Danforth fellow Ind. U., 1989. Mem. Ind. Assn. for Elem. and Mid. Sch. Prins., Phi Delta Kappa, Delta Sigma Theta. Methodist. Home: 2711 Pomona Ct Indianapolis IN 46268-1248

BROOKS, PHILLIP, advertising executive; b. 1955. With Affiliate of Excellence Co., Mpls., 1976—, now pres.; with Excellence Co., Mpls. Office: Excellence Co 2601 E Hennepin Ave Minneapolis MN 55413

BROOKS, RANDY MARK, technical communication educator, computer publishing consultant; b. Hutchingson, Kansas, June 18, 1954; s. William Dean and Grace Margaret (Andrews) B.; m. Shirley Kay Burchett, April 6, 1974; children: Alan, Arik, Jessica. BA in English, Ball State U., 1975; MA in English, Purdue U., 1977, PhD in English, 1991. Asst. dir. devel. writing Purdue U., West Lafayette, Ind., 1977-81, staff humanities library, 1982-87, grad. instr. English, 1987-90; dir. writing major Millikin U., Decatur, Ill., 1990—; book design and publishing staff Brooks Books, Decatur, Ill., 1976—; computer curriculum design cons. U. Tenn., Knoxville, 1993-94; police commn. skills testing cons. City of Decatur Police Dept., 1994—; info. kiosk designer Cmtys. in Partnership, 1994—. Editor: (book) Midwest Haiku Anthology, 1992 (Merit award Haiku Soc. Am. 1993); developer, programmer (online hypermedia software) Font Tutorial, 1991, (computer touch screen kiosk) Answer Machine, 1995 (HSAC award 1995). Recipient Computer Classroom Devel. grant George I. Alden Trust, 1991; Outstanding Prof. award Zeta Tau Alpha Sorority, 1993, Edn. Volunteerism award Decatur Clean Cmty. System, 1994. Mem. Am. Computing Machinery, Nat. Coun. Tchrs. of English, Haiku Soc. of Am., Assn. of Tchrs. of Tech. Writings, Soc. for Tech. Communication, Optimist Club. Mem. Christian Disciples of Christ Ch. Office: Millikin U 1184 W Main Decatur IL 62522

BROOKS, ROGER, state legislator. Rep. S.D. State Ho. Reps. Dist. 10, mem. agr. and natural resources and edn. coms.; computer cons. Home: 1800 Sylvan Cir Brandon SD 57005-1518*

BROSZ, DON, state legislator, retired educator. Sales mgr. Procter & Gamble Dist. Co.; mem. S.D. Ho. of Reps., Pierre; mem. edn. and judiciary coms. S.D. Ho. of Reps.

BROTHEN, JEFFREY PETER, theatre, speech educator; b. St. Paul, Sept. 14, 1948; s. Harvey Tamnes and Kathleen Marie B.; 1 child, Christine Nicole. BA in Speech and Theatre, Sioux Falls Coll., 1972; MFA in Theatre, U. Houston, 1974; postgrad., U. N.D., 1979-83, U. Bergen, Norway, summer 1980; PhD in Theatre, Fla. State U., 1993. Instr. dept. speech and theatre arts Ea. Ky. U., 1974-78; adj. instr. dept. speech U. N.D., 1979-80, 86; teaching asst. Sch. of Theatre, Fla. State U., 1989-92; faculty speech and theatre Hibbing (Minn.) C.C., 1993-94; traffic/continuity mgr., classical announcer KFJM Pub. Radio, Grand Forks, N.D., 1985-89; judge, critic Ea. Ky. U. Film Festival, 1977. Actor 36 prodns. including School for Scandal, Desire Under the Elms, Masks of Angels, Pantagleize, Dracula, Angel Street, Bye Bye Birdie, The Sandbox, Fashion, Francesca da Rimini, Gentlemen Prefer Blonds, The Mad Woman of Chaillot, As You Life It; dir. plays: You're A Good Man Charlie Brown, 1994, Fables for Friends, 1993, Medea, 1978, 74, Story Theatre, 1977, The Prisoner of Second Avenue, 1976, Dark of the Moon, 1975, And Miss Reardon Drinks a Little, 1974, A Study in Color, 1972, Postage Due, 1971, Siren's Song, 1971, Hello Out There, 1970. Fla. State U. dissertation fellow, 1992-93; Saastad scholar, 1980, U. Houston Drama Dept. scholar, 1973-74, Sioux Falls Coll. Speech and Drama Dept. scholar, 1971-72; Scandinavian Cultural Ctr. grantee, 1980; recipient Purple Feather award Sioux Falls Coll., 1971. Mem. Assn. for Theatre in Higher Edn., Internat. Phenomenological Soc., Ibsen Soc. of Am., Paideia Group, Norwegian-Am. Hist. Assn. Home: 6531 S 139th Circle Omaha NE 68137

BROTZKE, GERALD F., manufacturing company executive; b. Troy, Mich., Sept. 22, 1946. BS, Wayne State U., 1970. Pres. Scorpion Mfg., Alpena, Mich., 1985-89, Premium Mold Enterprises Inc., Madison Heights, Mich., 1989—. Patentee in tooling and automotive field. Mem. Rotary Club. Home: 3955 Cheyenne Ct Oxford MI 48370-2915

BROUGHTON, BEVERLY JANE, construction executive; b. Detroit, Oct. 8, 1927; d. Donald John and Ida Mae (Coller) Garpow; m. Howard Millar Trerice, Jan. 3, 1953 (div. Mar. 1974); children: Howard Owen, Bruce Whitney. BA, Wayne U., 1949, cert. in teaching, 1951. Free-lance lectr., 1951-54; ins. agt. Donald Garpow Agy., Detroit, 1954-64; ptnr. Mobile Office Equipment Co., Detroit, 1979-85; owner, pres. Best Mobile Office/Modulars, Waterford, Mich., 1985—. Acrylic art represented in pvt. collections. Alt. del. Mich. Reps., Grand Rapids, 1984. Mem. Nat. Assn. for Self-Employed, NAFE, Constrn. Assn. Mich. Christian Scientist. Office: Best Mobile Office Modulars 4080 Dixie Hwy Waterford MI 48329-4277

BROUHARD, BEN HERMAN, pediatric nephrologist; b. Indpls., Oct. 30, 1946; s. Edgar Elton and Emma Jean (Pevler) B.; m. Julia Ranney, June 12, 1970; 1 child, Katherine Jean. BA, Wabash Coll., 1968; MD, Ind. U., Indpls., 1972. Diplomate Am. Bd. Pediatrics, Am. Bd. Pediatric Nephrology. Resident Duke U., Durham, N.C., 1972-74; fellow U. Tex., Galveston, 1974-76, asst. prof., 1976-79, assoc. prof., 1979-83, prof., 1983-88; dir. rsch., dept. pediatrics Cleve. Clinic Found., 1988—; bd. mem. Am. Jour. Disorders of Children, Chgo., 1981-91, Diabetes Care, Richmond, Va., 1989-92, Kidney Found. Ohio, Cleve., 1988—; mem. NIH site visit, Bethesda, Md., 1988. Author: Diabetes Mellitus in Childhood and Adolescence; editor Clin. Pediatrics, 1990—; contbr. articles to profl. jours. Grantee NIH, Am. Heart Assn., Kidney Found., Juvenile Diabetes Found. Mem. Soc. Pediatric Rsch., Am. Pediatric Soc., So. Soc. Clin. Investigation, Midwest Soc. Pediatric Rsch., Phi Beta Kappa, Sigma Xi, Alpha Omega Alpha. Office: Cleve Clinic Found Dept Pediatrics A120 9500 Euclid Ave Cleveland OH 44195-0001

BROUILLARD, WILLIAM CRAIG, artist, art educator; b. Madison, Wis., Sept. 8, 1947; s. Clair Lavern and Johnettee Brouillard. BA in Art Edn., State U. Wis., 1969; MFA, SUNY, Alfredy, 1976. Asst. prof. East Tenn. State U., Johnson City, 1979-80; resident craftsman Pen land (N.C.) Sch., 1976-79; assoc. prof. Cleve. Inst. Art, 1980—; resident craftsman Archy Bray Found., Helena, Mont. summer 1983; resident artist Watershed Ctr. for Arts, North Edgecomb, Maine, summer 1987; vis. artist summer program R.I. Sch. Design, Providence, 1987, N.Y. State Coll. Ceramics, Alfred (N.Y.) U., 1976, 80, 86; instr. summer program Cleve. Inst. Art, 1982, 84; vis. artist, instr. spring and fall concentrations Pen land Sch., 1979-80; lectr. and workshop leader in field. Exhibited in group shows The Works Gallery, Phila., 1991, Am. Craft Mus., N.Y.C., 1991, Cleve. Ctr. for Contemporary Art, 1991, Cheltenham (Pa.) Ctr. for Arts, 1992, Mansfield (Ohio) Art Ctr., 1992, Cleve. State U. Art Gallery, 1993, Dayton (Ohio) Visual Arts Ctr., 1993, Artworks Gallery, Seattle, 1993, Ohio Craft Mus., Columbus, 1994, Duncan Gallery, Stetson U., DeLand, Fla., 1994, Craft Alliance Gallery, St. Louis, 1995, Ariana Gallery, Royal Oak, 1995, others; represented in permanent collections Detroit Mus. Art, Cleve. Mus. Art, Millard Collection, St. Louis, Sinker Collection, Detroit, U. So. Ill., Ohio Designer Craftsmen, Alfred U., Kaiser Hosps. of Cleve., others; works published in Am. Ceramics mag., Studio Potter mag., Craft Horizons, Ceramics Monthly, others. Recipient Design award Am. Craft Mus., 1987; summer work and travel grantee Art Park, 1980, Lily Faculty Enrichment grantee Cleve. Inst. Art, 1983, 87, Summer Incentive grantee Cleve. Inst. Art, 1986, 88, 89, travel grantee Cleve. Inst. Art, 1991. Mem. AAUP, Nat. Conf. for Edn. in Ceramic Arts, Ohio Designer Craftsmen (Excellence in Design award 1992), Arts Orgn. Home: 1011 Literary Rd Cleveland OH 44113 Office: Cleve Inst Art 11141 East Blvd Cleveland OH 44106 Studio: 2662 W 14th St Cleveland OH 44113

BROUWER, JOHN J., engineer; b. Chgo., July 27, 1939. B, Purdue U., 1961, M, 1975. Tool designer Interlake Steel Corp, Riverdale, Ill., 1965-68; product engr. Maremount Corp., HArvey, Ill., 1968-73; asst. chief engr. Panduft Corp., Tinley Park, Ill., 1973—. Home: 161 Ridgewood Ln Dyer IN 46311-2169

BROWDER, CHARLES BARCLAY, sales executive; b. New Haven, Conn., Dec. 13, 1955; s. Charles Barclay and Elsie Louise (Brown) B.; m. Anita Koeppel, June 23, 1989. BSME, Northeastern U., 1978. Asst. sales engr. Westinghouse Electric, Framingham, Mass., 1978-81; sales rep. Wesco, Peoria, Ill., 1981-83; sales mgr. Chevrolet Motor Divsn., Peoria, 1983; dist. sales mgr. Chevrolet Motor Divsn., Rochester, Minn., 1983; asst. sales engr. Westinghouse Electric, Peoria, 1983-87; sales application engr. Allen-Bradley Co., Peoria, 1987-91; sr. sales engr. Square D Co., Peoria, 1991—; adv. bd. mem. Ill. Tech. Acad., Peoria, 1995—, mentor com. mem., 1994-95, chmn. workplace com., 1995—. Pres. Woodside Creek Condo Assn., Peoria, 1995—. Mem. Peoria C. of C. Home: 6440 N Allen Rd Unit 58 Peoria IL 61614 Office: Square D Co 331 Fulton St #325 Peoria IL 61602

BROWDER, OLIN LORRAINE, legal educator; b. Urbana, Ill., Dec. 19, 1913; s. Olin Lorraine and Nellie (Taylor) B.; m. Edna Olive Forsythe, Sept. 9, 1939; children: Ann Browder Sorensen, Catherine Browder Morris, John. A.B., U. Ill., 1935, LL.B., 1937; S.J.D., U. Mich., 1941. Bar: Ill. 1939. Practiced in Chgo., 1938-39; asst. prof. bus. law U. Ala., 1939-41; asst. prof. law U. Tenn., 1941-42; mem. legal dept. TVA, 1942-43; spl. agt. FBI, 1943-45; prof. law U. Okla., 1946-53, U. Mich., Ann Arbor, 1953-79; James V. Campbell prof. law U. Mich., 1979-84, prof. emeritus, 1984—. Author: (with others) American Law of Property, 1953, (with L.W. Waggoner) Family Property Transactions, 1965, 3d edit., 1980, (with R. A. Cunningham, G.S. Nelson, W.B. Stoebuck, D.A. Whitman) Basic Property Law, 1966, 5th edit., 1989, (with L. W. Waggoner and R. V. Wellman) Palmer's Cases on Trusts and Succession, 4th edit., 1983. Mem. Am. Bar Assn., Order of Coif, Phi Beta Kappa, Beta Theta Phi, Phi Alpha Delta, Phi Kappa Phi. Home: 1520 Edinborough Rd Ann Arbor MI 48104-4128

BROWER, JAMES CALVIN, graphic artist, painter; b. Clarksburg, W.Va., Dec. 30, 1914; s. Leroy Cooper and Margaret Wood (Watkins) B.; m. Elsie Margaret Day, Sept. 19, 1936; children: James Lawrence, Sandra Joan, Margaret, Linda Ann, Beth. Grad. high sch., Charleston, W.Va., 1932. Pvt. practice Huntington, W.Va., 1933-43, Toledo, 1952—; ptnr., art dir. Brower, Brownsberger and Burda, Toledo, 1944-51; dir. art and design Meeks Heit Pub. Co., 1992—. Illustrator: Education for Sexuality, 1970, Human Sexuality, 1982, Education for Sexuality and HIV/AIDS, 1993. Recipient Pres. award Okla. Watercolor Soc., 1987, Past Pres. award San Diego Watercolor Soc. Internat. Exhbn., 1989. Mem. Ohio Watercolor Soc. (bd. dirs. 1986-92, publicity chmn. 1986-92, Gold medal 1984, Charles Burchfield Meml. award 1991, Exhbn. award 1992), Northwestern Ohio Water Color Soc. (pres. 1983-84), Nat. Water Color Soc. (Artist's Mag./Liquitex award 1990), Ky. Watercolor Soc. (artist mem.), Ga. Watercolor Soc. (Gold award Nat. Exhbn. 1990), Toledo Fedn. Art Soc. (pres. 1987-88), Tile Club Toledo. Republican. Presbyterian. Home and Office: 2222 Grecourt Dr Toledo OH 43615-2918

BROWER, WADE MICHAEL, stockbroker; b. Papillion, Nebr., Mar. 26, 1968; s. Dennis Allan and Joy Margaret (Updegraff) B.; m. Rhonda Marie Gaul, June 30, 1990; 1 child, Brenden. BS, U. S.D., 1990. Registered prin., Iowa. Stockbroker Payne-Webber, Sioux City, Iowa, 1989-92; chmn. bd. dirs. Brower Investments, Retirement & Svc., Inc., Sioux City, 1993—. Chmn. fin. 1st Luth. Ch., Sioux City, 1993. Mem. Sioux City C. of C., Rotary, Jaycees, Siouxland Hinder Club (treas. 1993), Kid's Care Club (bd. dirs. 1994), Elks. Republican. Lutheran. Office: Brower Investments Retirement & Svc Inc PO Box 3437 4th and Jackson Sioux City IA 51102

BROWN, ALAN CRAWFORD, lawyer; b. Rockford, Ill., May 12, 1956; s. Gerald Crawford and Jane Ella (Herzberger) B.; m. Judy Ellen Bourn, Dec. 28, 1978, child, Parker Crawford. BA magna cum laude, Miami U., Oxford, Ohio, 1978; JD with honors, U. Chgo., 1981. Bar: Ill. 1981, U.S. Dist. Ct. (no. dist.) Ill. 1981, U.S. Tax Ct. 1986. Assoc. Kirkland & Ellis, Chgo., 1981-87; sr. assoc. Coffield Ungaretti Harris & Slavin, Chgo., 1987-89; ptnr. McDermott, Will & Emery, Chgo., 1989—. Deacon Northminster Presbyn Ch., Evanston, Ill., 1989-92. Apiarist Chgo. Botanic Garden, Glencoe, Ill., 1988—. Mem. Order of Coif, Chgo. Estate Planning Council, Phi Beta Kappa. Club: Univ. (Chgo.). Office: McDermott Will & Emery 227 W Monroe St Chicago IL 60606-5096

BROWN, ARNOLD, physical therapy consultant; b. N.Y.C., Apr. 8, 1930; s. Murray and Tessie Brown; m. Alice L. Kahn, July 31, 1955; 1 child, Alan. BS in Edn., Panzer Coll., 1951; cert. in phys. therapy, Columbia U., 1952; MA in Psychology, Ball State U., 1972. Lic. phys. therapist, Ind. Staff phys. therapist VA Hosp., East Orange, N.J., 1954-55; sr. phys. therapist Cerebral Palsy Clinic, Union City, N.J., 1955-56; chief phys. therapist Mobility, Inc., New Rochelle, N.Y., 1956-57, Inland Steel Co. Hosp., East Chicago, Ind., 1957-67, Ball Meml. Hosp., Muncie, Ind., 1967-84; dir. phys. therapy Profl. Med. Svc., Clay County, Ind., 1984-86, St. Anthony Hosp., Michigan City, Ind., 1986-93; ret., 1993, cons. physical therapy, 1993—; cons. Lake County Assn. Retarded Children, Gary, Ind., 1963-67; insvc. instr. Ball Meml., St. Anthony Hosp., 1967-93; adj. clin. prof. phys. therapy Andrews U., Berrien County, Mich., 1987-93; clin. supr. student affiliations Ball State U., 1975-83, clin. instr., 1981-83; mem. adv. bd. Visiting Nurse Assn., Muncie, 1972-78. Author: Physiological and Psychological Considerations in Management of Stroke, 1976; author/instr.: Orientation to Physical Therapy, 1979, Body Mechanics, 1987(videotapes); contbr. to profl. jours. Bd. dirs. Nat. Multiple Sclerosis Soc., 1974-77, Easter Seal Soc., Muncie, 1976-78. With U.S. Army, 1952-54. Recipient Vocat. Dirs. award A.K. Smith Career Ctr., Michigan City, 1993. Mem. Am. Phys. Therapy Assn. (mgmt. sect.). Home: 2 Buckingham Ct Apt 2 Michigan City IN 46360

BROWN, ARNOLD HARRIS, professional athlete management executive; b. N.Y.C., July 8, 1930; s. Samuel S. and Etta (Levine) B.; m. Rachel White, Mar. 23, 1956 (div. 1983); children: Laura, Elizabeth, Joanne; m. Donna Jean Stauffer, June 14, 1987; children: Sarah, Jessica. BS in Econs., U. Pa., 1951; JD, Yale U., 1956. CPA, Calif., Mo.; bar: Calif. 1958. Ptnr. Arthur Andersen & Co., Kansas City, Mo., 1956-87; sr. v.p. George K. Baum & Co., Kansas City, Mo., 1987-90; pres. Assured Mgmt. Co., Westwood, Kans., 1990—; chmn. tax inst., Ariz. State U., Phoenix, 1971-72. Bd. dirs. Ctr. for Mgmt. Assistance, 1985—, Pub. Sta. KCPT-TV, Kansas City, 1989-93; treas., bd. dirs. Phoenix Symphony Assn., 1970-73; chmn. bd. dirs. Menorah Med. Ctr., Kansas City, 1989-93; bd. dirs. Jewish Heritage Found., Kansas City Symphony Assn. Mem. AICPA, Mo. Soc. CPAs, Ariz. Soc. CPAs (pres. 1971-72), Nat. Assn. Mental Health (treas., nat. bd. dirs. 1970-76), Fin. Exec. Inst., Oakwood Country Club, Overland Park Racket Club, Woodside Tennis Club. Office: Assured Mgmt Co 1901 W 47th Pl Ste 200 Shawnee Mission KS 66205-1834

BROWN, ARNOLD M., state legislator. Rep. S.D. State Ho. Reps. Dist. 7, mem. health and human svc. and transp. coms. Home: 1718 Teton Pass Brookings SD 57006-3626*

BROWN, AUTRY, psychology educator, clergyman; b. Watson, Okla., May 1, 1924; s. Solon Lemley and Bessie Jane (Wilhelm) B.; m. Opal Irene Landers, Sept.5, 1942; children: Juanice, Rebecca, Steven, Deborah. BA, Eastern N.M. U., 1950; M of Div., New Orleans Bapt. Theol. Sem., 1955, MRE, 1956, EdD, 1968; postgrad., Colo. State U., 1970, Southwest Mo. State U., 1985. Ordained to ministry Bapt. Ch., 1942. Pastor Bookcliff Bapt. Ch., Grand Junction, Colo., 1957-61, Carrollton Ave. Bapt. Ch., New Orleans, 1962-64, Immanuel Bapt. Ch., Ft. Collins, Colo., 1964-72; asst. prof. psychology Mo. Bapt. U., St. Louis, 1972-74; asst. prof. psychology Southwest Bapt. U., Bolivar, Mo., 1974-76, prof. psychology, 1978-89, dir. counseling services, 1978-89; disting. prof. psychology, 1989—; cons. family ministry Colo. Bapt. Gen. Conv., Denver, 1976-78. Author: Church Family Life Conference Guidebook, 1973; contbr. books, profl. jour. Recipient Spl. Services award Bd. Trustees New Orleans Bapt. Theol. Sem., 1972. Mem. Am. Assn. Marriage and Family Therapy, Mo. Assn. Marriage and Family Therapy (Spl. Service award 1984, treas. state exec. bd. 1979-83), Ozark Assn. Marriage and Family Therapy (pres. 1985-86), Mo. Assn. Counseling and Devel., Fellows Menniger Found. Lodge: Optimists (Community Service award 1972). Home: 1223 Woodland Cir Bolivar MO 65613-3351 Office: Christian Tng Inst 1223 Woodland Cir Bolivar MO 65613-3351

BROWN, BOB OLIVER, retired manufacturing company executive; b. Ft. Dodge, Iowa, June 5, 1929; s. Frank Arthur and Winona (Thietje) B.; m. JoAnn Louise Brown, Sept. 7, 1963 (div. Oct. 1989); children: Scott, Douglas. BSBA, U. Omaha, 1950; MS, U. Ill., 1951. CPA, Mo. Auditor Price Waterhouse, St. Louis, 1954-58, E A Rothaus, St. Louis, 1958-62; treas. Hazell Machine, St. Louis, 1962-64, Troug Nichols, Kansas City, Mo., 1964-66; v.p. Unitog Co., Kansas City, 1966-94; ret., 1994. Capt. USMC, 1951-54, Korea. Mem. AICPA, Mo. Soc. CPA, Tax Execs. Inst., Smithsonian Assocs., VFW, Am. Legion, Kansas City C. of C. Republican. Episcopalian. Home: 527 S 36th Ct Omaha NE 68105

BROWN, BOYD ALEX, physicist, educator; b. Columbus, Ohio, July 21, 1948; s. Frank L. and E. Catherine (Chenoweth) B.; m. Mary J. Hohenstein, July 21, 1984; children: Elizabeth Lorraine, Mark Alexander. BA in Physics, Ohio State U., 1970; MS in Physics, SUNY, Stony Brook, 1971, PhD in Physics, 1974. Research fellow Japan Soc. for the Promotion of Sci., Tokyo, 1974-75; research assoc. Mich. State U., East Lansing, 1975-78; research officer Oxford U., Eng., 1978-82; assoc. prof. physics Mich. State U., East Lansing, 1982-90, prof. physics, 1990—. Contbr. more than 200 articles to physics jours. Humboldt sr. rsch. fellow, 1991—. Fellow Am. Phys. Soc.; mem. The Am. Phys. Soc., Sigma Pi Sigma. Office: Mich State U Cyclotron Lab East Lansing MI 48824

BROWN, BRUCE HARDING, naval officer; b. Gary, Ind., Nov. 27, 1954; s. Russell Harding and Dorothy Jane (Schaeffer) B.; m. Laurie Marshall McPhillips, Sept. 12, 1981; children: Brendan Harding, Colin Campbell. Student, Cambridge U., 1975; BA in Polit. Sci., Ind. U., 1977; MA in Mgmt., Nat. U., San Diego, 1988. Counselor Lake County Juvenile Ctr., Crown Point, Ind., 1978; commd. ensign USN, 1979, advanced through grades to lt. comdr., 1989; comm. officer USS St. Louis, San Diego, 1980-83; 1st lt. USS Jouett, San Diego, 1983-85; exec. officer Spl. Boat Unit 13, Coronado, Calif., 1985-89; asst. officer in charge USS Alamo, San Diego, 1989-90; 1st lt. USS Tuscaloosa, San Diego, 1990-92; commdg. officer Naval and Marine Corps Res. Ctr., South Bend, Ind., 1992-94; engr. CSX Corp., Garrett, Ind., 1995-96; co. ofcl. CSX Corp., Plymouth, Mich., 1996—; lectr. U. Notre Dame, South Bend, 1992. Coord. Navy Relief Soc., San Diego, 1989, Combined Fed. Campaign, South Bend, 1992; asst. scoutmaster Boy Scouts Am., 1992. Mem. Naval Res. Assn. (life), U.S. Naval Inst., Masons, Shrine. Republican. Methodist. Home: 15345 Old Bedford Trl Mishawaka IN 46545-1517 Office: CSX Corp 500 Junction St Plymouth MI 48170

BROWN, CAMERON, insurance company consultant; b. Chgo., Sept. 29, 1914; s. George Frederic and Irene (Larmon) B.; m. Dorothea Fruechtenicht, May 10, 1947 (div. Feb. 1965); children: Reid L., Deborah Sue; m. Jean McGrew, Dec. 22, 1965; 1 dau., Sophia Lyn. A.B., U. Ill., 1937; grad., Indsl. Coll. Armed Forces, 1941. Vice pres. R. B. Jones & Sons, Inc., 1938-41; dir. Geo. F. Brown & Sons, Inc., Chgo., 1947-79; v.p. Geo. F. Brown & Sons, Inc., 1947-50, exec. v.p., 1950-53, pres., 1953-64, chmn., chief exec. officer, 1964-76; dir. Interstate Nat. Corp., 1968-79, pres., 1968-74, chmn., 1970-76; dir. Nat. Student Mktg. Corp., 1970-79, pres., 1970-72, chmn., 1970-75; dir. Interstate Fire & Casualty Co., 1952-79, exec. v.p., 1953-56, pres., 1956-74, chmn., 1970-76; dir. Chgo. Ins. Co., 1957-79, pres., 1957-74, chmn., 1970-76; dir. Interstate Reins. Corp., 1957-79; pres. Cameron Brown Ltd., 1976—; underwriting mem. Lloyd's of London, 1971-95; sec., dir. Ill. Ins. Info. Svc., 1967-76. Contbg. author: Property and Liability Handbook, 1965. Pres. Chgo. area Planned Parenthood Assn., 1969-72; bd. dirs. Planned Parenthood Fedn. Am., 1976-79; active John Evans Club, Northwestern U., U. Ill., Pres.'s Club, U. Ill. Found., U. Chgo. Pres.'s Club. Lt. col. Gen. Staff Corps AUS, 1941-45. Decorated Bronze Star with oak leaf cluster. Mem. Lloyd's Broker Assn. (chmn. 1959-60), Nat. Assn. Ind. Insurers (bd. govs. 1961-77). Ill. St. Andrews Soc., Internat. Wine and Food Soc. (Chgo.), Surplus Line Brokers Assn. (chmn. 1954), Confrerie des Chevaliers du Tastevin (officer-comdr. Chgo. and L.A.), Commanderie de Bordeaux (Maitre emeritus at Chgo., Santa Barbara, bd. govs. 1973—), Conseiller de Bordeaux, Santa Barbara Wine and Food Soc., Chgo. Club, Exec. Club (dir. 1969-73, 1st v.p. 1970-71), Econ. Club, Mid-Am. Club, Casino Club Chgo., Army-Navy Country Club, Old Elm Club, Shoreacres Club, Onwentsia Club, Pine Valley Golf Club, Birnam Wood Golf Club, The Valley Club, Hon. Co. Edinburgh Golfers, Royal and Ancient Golf Club St. Andrews, Psi Upsilon. Home: 1400 N Green Bay Rd Lake Forest IL 60045-1110 also: 2004 Sandy Pl Santa Barbara CA 93108-2226

BROWN, CARL E., stockbroker; b. Alexandria, Ind., Dec. 8, 1923. BS, Internat. Bus. Coll., Ft. Wayne, Ind., 1949. Acct. Neff Engring. Co., Ft. Wayne, 1966-79; stockbroker Rooney & Co., Detroit, 1979-88, Van Guard Capital, San Diego, 1988-89, Am. Investment Svcs., Ft. Wayne, 1990—. Sgt. USAF, 1942-45, 50. Mem. Northside Optimists Club (pres. 1994), Foremans Club Ft. Wayne (pres. 1965). Republican. Lutheran. Office: Am Investment Svcs PO Box 15505 5005 Woodmark Ct Fort Wayne IN 46885

BROWN, CHARLES EARL, lawyer; b. Columbus, Ohio, June 6, 1919; s. Anderson and Ruth (Keeran) B.; m. Mary Elizabeth Hiett, May 23, 1959; children: Douglas Charles, Rebecca Ruth. A.B., Ohio Wesleyan U., 1941; J.D., U. Mich., 1949. Bar: Ohio 1949. Pvt. practice Toledo; assoc. Zachman, Boxell, Bebout & Torbet, 1950-53, ptnr. Brown, Schlageter, Craig & Shindler (and predecessors), 1953-90, of counsel, 1991—; chmn. bd., dir. Maumee Fabrics Co.; chmn. steering and exec. coms. Auto Trim Wholesalers div. Automotive Service Industry Assn., 1960-68. Lucas County Rep. Exec. Com., 1968-92. Capt. AUS, 1941-46; col. Res. ret. Decorated Bronze Star; recipient John J. Pershing award U.S. Army Command and Gen. Staff Coll., 1963. Fellow Am. Bar Found. (state chmn. 1978-84), Ohio State Bar Found. (trustee 1987-92), Am. Coll. Trust and Estate Counsel; mem. ABA, Ohio Bar Assn. (bd. govs. real property sect. 1953-76, coun. of dels. 1973-84, exec. com. 1984-87), Toledo Bar Assn. (past mem. exec. com.), Sixth Cir. Jud. Conf. (life), Toledo Area C. of C. (past trustee, com. chmn.), Res. Officers Assn., Assn. U.S. Army, Phi Beta Kappa. Congregationalist (past chmn. trustees). Lodge: Masons (32 deg.). Home: 3758 Brookside Rd Toledo OH 43606-2614 Office: 1200 Edison Plaza 300 Madison Ave Toledo OH 43604-1556

BROWN, CHARLIE, state representative; b. Williston, S.C., Mar. 8, 1938; m. Angela Baker; 1 child, Charlisa. BS, Cheyney U.; MPA, Ind. U. Founder Mayor Hatcher's Youth Found., Gary, Ind.; CEO Gary (Ind.) Cmty. Mental Health Ctr.; risk mgr. City of Gary; state rep. dist. 3 Ind. House of Reps., 1982—, chmn. pub. health com., local govt. com., environ. affairs com., ins. and corp. com., family and children com., ranking minority mem. pub. health com.; bd. dirs. Lake County Hosp. Bldg. Authority; cons. mgmt. and health; mem. Med. Ctr. of Gary, Nat. Civil Rights Mus. and Hall Fame & Benson & Taylor Ensemble Co. Mayor Hatcher's Youth Found., Gary. Mem. Gary Frontiers Svc. Club, Black Minority Health Adv. Coun., Nat. Black Caucus State Legislators, Interagency Coun. on Black and Minority Health. Democrat. Home: 9439 Lake Shore Dr Gary IN 46403-1609*

BROWN, CHUCK, state legislator; b. Apr. 5, 1951; m. Rebecca Brown; four children. Southwest State U., Brown Inst. State rep. Dist. 13A Minn. Ho. of Reps., 1984—; auctioneer, 1996—; chnn. Appropriations Com.; mem. Edn. Judiciary & Transp. Coms.; vice-chmn. Edn.-Higher Edn. Fin. Divsn. Com.; mem. Local Govt. & Met. Affairs Com. Home: 569 State Office Bldg Saint Paul MN 55155*

BROWN, D. ROBIN, elementary educator; b. Cleve., Oct. 31, 1949; d. William Michael and Darla G. (Carlson) Linsenmann; m. Ross H. Brown, Aug. 21, 1971. BA cum laude, W.Va. Wesleyan U., 1971; MA, Ashland U., 1988, postgrad., 1988-90; postgrad., Ohio State U., 1989-90. Cert. elem. tchr., Ohio, W.Va. Tchr. Lost Creek Elem. Sch., Clarksburg, W.Va., 1971-72, Leesburg (Va.) Middle Sch., 1972-75, Northmoor Elem. Sch., Dayton, Ohio, 1975-79, Jonathan Alder Local Schs., Plain City, Ohio, 1979—. Active TWIG # 158, Columbus, Ohio, 1990—, Salvation Army, Columbus, 1990—, Worthington Hills Women's Club, Columbus, 1985—. Recipient Sci. award Exxon, 1974. Mem. Internat. Reading Assn., Reading Recovery, Kappa Delta Pi, Sigma Eta Sigma, Pi Gamma Mu, Tri Beta. Home: 825 Highview Dr West Worthington OH 43235-1232 Office: Jonathan Alder Local Schs 4331 Kilbury Huber Rd Plain City OH 43064-9064

BROWN, DANIEL, independent art consultant, critic, writer; b. Cin., Nov. 4, 1946; s. Sidney H. and Genevieve Florence (Elbaum) B.; m. Ellen Neveloff, May 24, 1970; m. Jane Felson, Sept. 14, 1980; stepchildren: Christopher Minton, Andrew Daniel Brown. AB cum laude, Middlebury Coll., 1968; AM, U. Mich., 1970; postgrad. Princeton U., 1971-72, Union Inst., 1993—. Dir. cultural events U. Cin., 1972, spl. asst. to pres., 1973; v.p., corp. sec. Brockton Shoe Trimming Co., Cin., 1974—; instr. Art Acad. Cin., 1980—, Art Acad. Cin., 1988—; prin. Daniel Brown, Inc., Cin. and Columbus, 1990; panel leader, mem. Midwest Coll. Art Assn. Conv., 1995; curator KZF Gallery, Cin., 1987-94; co-curator Katz and Dawgs Gallery, 1989-90; art critic Cin. Mag., 1980-83, Cin. Herald, 1992, Cin. Art Acad. Newsletter, Provincetown Arts, 1988-90, The Cin. Herald, 1992-94, Everybody's News, 1993-94; commentator Sta. WKRC-TV, Cin., art and movie critic Sta. WCPO-TV, Cin., 1986; art critic USA Arts, The Cin. Herald, 1992-94; arts editor, essayist Cin. City Beat, 1994-95; guest lectr. dept. fine arts and dept. psychiatry U. Cin., 1990, lectr. English and art history, 1993—; guest lectr. dept. fine arts U. Ky., 1990—; guest curator New Art from Academe: An Overview The Cen. Exchange, Kansas City, Mo., 1988, Figure It Out! inaugural exhibition Katz and Dawgs Gallery, Columbus, Ohio, 1988, Lyrical Abstractions, 1989, Design of the Future, 1989, Contemporary Landscape Kencabco Co., Cin., 1988, A Critic's Choice: Art of the '90's, No. Ky. U., 1989, Katz and Dawgs Decorative Arts: Wave of the Future, 1989, The Arts Consortium, 1991-92, co-chmn. fine arts com., 1990-94; guest curator The African-Am. Mus. at Union Terminal, 1991-92, 93-94, The Arts Consortium, 1991-92, 93-94,, Aronoff Ctr. Arts, 1995—, Cuba Now Carnegie Arts Ctr., 1996; guest co-curator Cincinnati Yesterday and Today Tangeman Fine Arts Gallery U. Cin., 1987, guest curator, 1988; frequent guest lectr. on arts; permanent curator The KZF Art Gallery, Cin., 1987-94; guest co-curator The Artist at Mid-Career A Dialogue Between Columbus and Cin., 1989-90; curator for exhbns. at Liberties Restaurant, Cin., 1990-93, Fifth Third Bank, Cin., 1991-92; curator African-Am. Mus., 1992, 93, African Am. Artists, 1994; guest spkr. Arts Consortium, 1994; guest critic dept. painting and drawing U. Cin., 1993—; corr. editor: Dialogue Mag., 1986, 94—, art reviewer 1983—; lead editorialist: The Arts Consortium Newsletter, 1992; monthly editorialist Antenna Newspaper, 1995—; author: David Bumbeck: The Romantic Classicist, 1989, Tom Bacher: High Tech American Impressionist, 1989, The Universe Watching: The Art of Nancy Fletcher Cassell, 1990, John Stewart: A Retrospective, 1991, Bukang Kim: Journey to the East, 1992, Hustlers, 1992, 93, The Evolution of Form, Bukang Kim: A Retrospective, 1995; columnist Art Acad. News, 1990-94; monthly guest columnist The Cin. Post, 1991, The Downtowner, 1991—; occasional columnist, 1991—; monthly columnist Everybody's News, 1994-95; editor Antenna Arts mag., 1996—. Mem. exhbns. com. Contemporary Arts Ctr.; sec., bd. dirs. Mercantile Library, 1985-91, treas. 1986, chmn. programs com., 1987—, Young Wing; trustee Contemporary Arts Ctr. 1984-87, co-chmn. artists adv. bd., 1987, Vocal Arts Ensemble, 1984, Enjoy the Arts, 1985-88, v.p. 1986; mem. bd. advisors Cin. Artists Group Effort, 1986-88; guest curator Carnegie Arts Ctr., Covington, Ky., 1986—; juror art competitions Cin. and Columbus, Ohio, 1986-87; mem. citizens' adv. com. Art Acad. of Cin., 1989—, trustee, 1991—; trustee Art Acad. cin Coop. Gallery, 1990—; co-chmn. fine art com. The Arts Consortium, Cin., 1990—, curator, 1991—; sole juror Art Acad. Alumni Juried Exhbn., 1992; trustee UMOJA Artists' Group, 1994—. Recipient The Critic's Purse award Dialogue mag., 1985. Mem. Shoe and Leather Club, Two-Ten Nat. Found., Internat. Platform Assn., Internat. Soc. Art Critics, Univ. Club (art com. 1990-91, guest curator 1992). Home: 2200Cincinnati OH 45206-2824

BROWN, DAVID PAUL, finance educator; b. Sedro Woolley, Wash., June 25, 1953; s. Paul Asa and Mary Margaret (Dostert) B.; m. Claudia Conroy, Oct. 8, 1983; children: Heather, Michael, Courtney. Student, Coll. of Idaho, 1971-73; BA, U. Wash., 1977; PhD, Stanford U., 1984. Asst. prof. fin. Ind. U., Bloomington, 1984-89, assoc. prof., 1991—; vis. asst. prof. MIT, Boston, 1989-90. Contbr. articles to profl. jours. Bd. dirs. treas. Shelter, Inc., Bloomington, 1992-95. Mem. Am. Fin. Assn., We. Fin. Assn., Econometric Soc. Office: Ind U Sch Bus 10th and Fee Ln Bloomington IN 47405

BROWN, DAVID ROBERT, pharmacologist; b. Johnson City, N.Y., Oct. 1, 1954; s. Robert William and Lois M. (Kinley) B.; m. Laura Jeanne Mauro, Aug. 27, 1988. BA in Biology/Psychology, U. Rochester, 1976; PhD in Pharmacology, Emory U., 1981; Mini-MBA Cert., U. St. Thomas, St. Paul. Postdoctoral fellow U. Chgo., 1981-84; asst. prof. U. Minn., St. Paul, 1984-89, assoc. prof., 1989—; vis. prof. U. Naples, Italy, 1991; vis. rsch. investigator U. Mich., Ann Arbor, 1991-93; specific field editor Jour. Pharmacology and Exptl. Therapeutics, 1992—. Editor: Handbook of Experimental Pharmacology, vol. 106, 1993; contbr. more than 80 articles to profl. jours. Bd. dirs. Chamber Music Soc. Minn., 1994—. Nat. Rsch. Svc. Award Sr. fellow NIH, 1992; recipient Norden Disting. Vet. Teaching award, 1994. Mem. AAAS, Am. Soc. Pharmacology Exptl. Therapeutics, Soc. for Neurosci., Gastroenterology Rsch. Group, Chamber Music Soc. Minn. (bd. dirs. and publicity coord.). Office: U Minn Dept Vet PathoBiology 1988 Fitch Ave Saint Paul MN 55108-6009

BROWN, DEBRA LYNN, financial analyst, accountant, consultant; b. Badd Constadt, Germany, Feb. 25, 1959; (parents Am. citizens); d. Robert D. and Roberta I. (Rosenstengel) Stevens; m. Thomas A. Brown, June 12, 1976 (div. Mar. 1988); children: Christopner J., Steven R. AA, St. Louis C.C., 1990; BSBA in Acctg., U. Mo., St. Louis, 1994. Fin. aid asst. St. Louis C.C., 1988-89; accounts receivable clk. Dr. Sam Hawatmeh, St. Louis, 1989-90; fiscal accounts Dept. Vet. Affairs, St. Louis, 1990-91, acct., technician, 1991-94; fin. analyst-budgets McDonnell Douglas Aerospace, St. Louis, 1994-95, sr. fin. analyst program integration, precision assembly, electrical, missiles, 1995—; cons., fin. matters William Tell Enterprises, Natchez, Miss., Gibson & Martin, Starkville, Miss. Student govt. v.p. St. Louis C.C., Forest Park, 1988-89. Mem. Am. Student Assn. Jr. Tech. and C.C.'s (bd. dirs. 1989-90), Mo. Assn. Cmty.-Jr. Colls. (bd. dirs. 1989-90). Home: 6 Mill Brooke Ct Saint Peters MO 63376

BROWN, DON G., mechanical engineer; b. College Corner, Ohio, Nov. 6, 1932. Grad. high sch., College Corner, Ohio, 1950. Design craftsman OPW, Cin., 1960-65, Sheffer Hydraulic, Cin., 1965-70, Mercury Instruments, Cin., 1970-75, Ellis and Watts, Batavia, Ohio, 1976-91, Engineered Environments, Inc., West Chester, Ohio, 1995—. With USN, 1951-55. Office: Engineered Environments 9826 Crescent Park Dr West Chester OH 45069

BROWN, DONNA KAY, executive; b. Ellwood City, Pa., Apr. 12, 1950; d. Robert Sullivan and Donna Lee (Fehl) Bango; m. Martin E. Brown, June 5, 1981; stepchildren: Kevin, Wayne. BS in Edn., Slippery Rock State U., 1972, MA in Edn., 1976; PhD in Orgn. Devel. and Personnel, Kent State U., 1984. Tchr. spl. edn. Greenville (Pa.) Schs., 1972-76; ednl. cons. Fulton County Bd. Edn., Wauseon, Ohio, 1978-85; prin., asst. supr. Swanton (Ohio) Bd. Edn., 1985-87; owner, pres., sr. cons. Oak Wood Assocs., Grand Rapids, Ohio, 1987—. Co-author: The Executive Nurse, . Teaching fellow Kent (Ohio) State U., 1976-78. Mem. Deming Users Study Group (mentor 1993—).

BROWN, FREEZELL, JR., private school educator; b. Indpls., Aug. 19, 1957; s. Freezell Brown and Alice Samuel; m. Barbara Weir, June 11, 1988. BA in Religion, Carroll Coll., Waukesha, Wis., 1979; MA in Religious Edn., Christian Theol. Sem., Indpls., 1984; M. Theol. Studies in Social Ethics, Garrett-Evang. Theol. Sem., 1988; postgrad., Ind. U.-Purdue, U. Indpls.; postgrad. in edn., Walden U. Consecrated diaconal minister United Methodist Ch., 1985. Youth dir. YMCA, Waukesha, 1980-81; minister with youth N. United Meth. Ch., Indpls., 1983, min. with youth and community, 1984-87; program coord. Crooked Creek Multi-Svc. Ctr., 1990-91; instr. PSI Inst. of Indpls., Indpls., 1991; trainer Training, Inc., 1991-92; tchr. religion and English, coord. diversity concerns Brebeuf Prep. Sch., Indpls., 1992-95; dir. diversity Brebeuf Prep Sch., Indpls., 1995—; mem. com. Religion and Race So. Ind. Conf. United Meth. Ch., alt. com. investigation; mem. adv. bd. Metro. Adv. Ministry, Butler U. Campus Ministry, Indpls.; bd. dirs. Ind. Writer's Ctr. Contbr. book revs. to Christian Century, Christian Ministry; editor Connections newsletter. Mem. neighborhood adv. bd. Indpls. Children's Mus.; mem. profl. adv. bd. Buchanan Counseling Ctr.; mem. adv. bd. Coll. Ave. Youth Behavior Acad.; mem. Christian Educators Fellowship of United Meth. Ch.; program coord. Crooked Creek Multi-Svc. Ctr., 1990; bd. dirs. The Writers' Ctr. of Indpls. Mem. Nat. Coun. Tchrs. English, So. Poverty Law Ctr., Ind. Interreligious Commn. on Human Equality. Democrat. Home: 6466 Robinsrock Dr Indianapolis IN 46268-4057

BROWN, GEORGE E., judge, educator; b. Hammond, Ind., July 27, 1947; s. George E. and Violet M. (Matlon) B.; m. Patricia A. Schneider, June 6, 1970; children: Janet M., Elizabeth A. BS, Ball State U., 1969; JD, DePaul U., 1974. Bar: Ind. 1974, Ill. 1974, U.S. Dist. Ct. (no. dist.) Ind. 1979, U.S. Supreme Ct. 1977, U.S. Tax Ct. 1977. Pvt. practice LaGrange & Lake Counties, Ind., 1974-84; judge LaGrange County Ct., 1984-87, LaGrange Superior Ct., 1988—; part-time chief dep. prosecutor LaGrange County, 1975-77; adj. faculty Tri-State U., Angola, Ind., 1991—. Mem. ABA, Ind. State Bar Assn. (com. on legal edn., com. on written pub.), LaGrange County Bar Assn. (pres. 1978), Ind. Judges Assn., LaGrange Rotary (past dir.). Office: Lagrange Superior Ct Courthouse Lagrange IN 46761

BROWN, GORDON A., financial stockbroker; b. Mpls., Oct. 15, 1941; s. Gordon A. Sr. and Deloris M. (Schur) B.; m. Margarie Ann Shae, Aug. 13, 1960; children: Kevin, Lisa. With Prudential Ins. Co., Bloomington, Minn., 1968-73; sales rep. Capp Homes, Mpls., 1973-78, Martin Homes, Mpls., 1979-83; stockbroker Dean Whitter Reynolds, Bloomington, Minn., 1983-89, Fin. Network Investment Corp., Edina, Minn., 1989—. With U.S. Army, 1966-68. Democrat. Lutheran. Home and Office: 5040 Windsor Ave Edina MN 55436-2441

BROWN, GRANT C., state legislator; m. Linda Brown. Farmer, state rep. dist. 36, 1991—; chmn. constrn. rev. com., 1993—; vice chmn. joint constrn. rev. com.; mem. fin. and taxation com. N.D. Ho. Reps. Sec. Ch. Trust Fund. Recipient Outstanding Young Men Am. award, 1970. Mem. County Farm Bur. (pres.), Stockmen's Legion, Masons (past master), Elks. Republican. Home: HC 1 Box 69 Dunn Center ND 58626-9782*

BROWN, HAROLD, aerospace engineer; b. N.Y., Mar. 11, 1930; s. Herman Abraham and Gertrude (Koppel) B.; m. Elaine Milner Cohen, June 14, 1953; children: Betsy Deborah Blumenthal, Alan Jack, Natalie Ellen Dennis, Beverly Sue Lesser, Dina Louise. BSME, Newark Coll. of Engring., Newark, 1951. Registered profl. engr., Ohio. Performance engr. GE Aircraft Engines, Cin., 1951-59; mgr. mission analysis GE Nuclear Power, Cin., 1959-65, GE Advanced Nuclear Sys., Valley Forge, Penn., 1965-68; mgr. aerothermo sys. GE Aircraft Engines, Cin., 1968-82, mgr. advanced controls, 1982-93; mgr. advanced sys. Grey Fox Techn., Cin., 1994—; chmn. performance design bd. GE Aircraft Engines, 1977-84; bd. of advisors U. Cin. elec. engring. dept., 1988-92. Author: (with others) Space Power Systems Engineering, 1966; contbr. articles to profl. jours. Home: 11 Diplomat Dr Cincinnati OH 45215

BROWN, HARRIET, state legislator. Mo. State rep. Dist. 13, 1993—. Home: PO Box 486 Wentzville MO 63385 Office: Mo Ho of Reps State Capitol Building Jefferson City MO 65101-1556*

BROWN, HERBERT CHARLES, chemistry educator; b. London, May 22, 1912; came to U.S., 1914; s. Charles and Pearl (Gorinstein) B.; m. Sarah Baylen, Feb. 6, 1937; 1 son, Charles Allan. AS, Wright Jr. Coll., Chgo., 1935; BS, U. Chgo., 1936, PhD, 1938, DSc (hon.), 1968; hon. doctorate, Wayne State U., 1980, Lebanon Valley Coll., 1980, L.I. U., 1980, Hebrew U. Jerusalem, 1980, Pontificia Universidad de Chile, 1980, Purdue U., 1980; hon. doctorates, U. Wales, 1981, U. Paris, 1982, Butler U., 1982, Ball State U., 1985. Asst. chemistry U. Chgo., 1936-38, Eli Lilly post-doctorate research fellow, 1938-39, instr., 1939-43; asst. prof. chemistry Wayne U., 1943-46, assoc. prof., 1946-47; prof. inorganic chemistry Purdue U., 1947-59, Richard B. Wetherill prof. chemistry, 1959, Richard B. Wetherill research prof., 1960-78, emeritus, 1978—; vis. prof. U. Calif. at L.A., 1951, Ohio State U., 1952, U. Mexico, 1954, U. Calif. at Berkeley, 1957, U. Colo., 1958, U. Heidelberg, 1963, State U. N.Y. at Stonybrook, 1966, U. Calif. at Santa Barbara, 1967, Hebrew U., Jerusalem, 1969, U. Wales, Swansea, 1973, U. Cape Town, S. Africa, 1974, U. Calif., San Diego, 1979; Harrison Howe lectr., 1953, Friend E. Clark lectr., 1953, Freud-McCormack lectr., 1954, Centenary lectr., Eng., 1955, Thomas W. Talley lectr., 1956, Falk-Plaut lectr., 1957, Julius Stieglitz lectr., 1958, Max Tishler lectr., 1958, Kekule-Couper Centenary lectr., 1958, E. C. Franklin lectr., 1960, Ira Remsen lectr., 1961, Edgar Fahs Smith lectr., 1962, Seydel-Wooley lectr., 1966, Baker lectr., 1969, Benjamin Rush lectr., 1971, Chem. Soc. lectr., Australia, 1972, Armes lectr., 1973, Henry Gilman lectr., 1975, others; hon. prof. Organomet Chem., Chinese Acad. Scis., 1994; chem. cons. to indsl. corps; researcher in phys., organic and inorganic chemistry relating chem. behavior to molecular structure, selective reductions, hydroboration and chemistry of organoboranes. Author: Hydroboration, 1962, Boranes in Organic Chemistry, 1972, Organic Synthesis via Boranes, 1975, The Nonclassical Ion Problem, 1977, (with A. W. Pelter and K. Smith) Borane Reagents, 1988; contbr. articles to chem. jours. Bd. govs. Hebrew U., 1969-90; co-dir. war rsch. projects U. Chgo. for U.S. Army, Nat. Def. Rsch.Com., Manhattan Project, 1940-43. Decorated Order of the Rising Sun, Gold and Silver Star (Japan); recipient Purdue Sigma Xi rsch. award, 1951, Nichols medal, 1959, award Am. Chem. Soc., 1960, S.O.C.M.A. medal, 1960, H.N. McCoy award, 1965, Linus Pauling medal, 1968, Nat. Medal of Sci., 1969, Roger Adams medal, 1971, Charles Frederick Chandler medal, 1973, Chem. Pioneer award, 1975, CUNY medal for sci. achievement, 1976 Elliott Cresson medal, 1978, C.K. Ingold medal, 1978, Nobel prize in chemistry, 1979, Priestley medal, 1981, Perkin medal, 1982, Gold medal award Am. Int. Chemists, 1985, G.M. Kosolapoff medal, 1987, NAS award in chem. scis., 1987; Hon. fellow U. Wales Swansca, 1994. Fellow AAAS, Royal Soc. Chemistry (hon.), Indian Nat. Sci. Acad. (fgn.); mem. NAS, Am. Acad. arts and Sci., Am. Chem. Soc. (chmn. Purdue sect. 1955-56, Oesper award Cin. sect. 1990), Chem. Soc. Japan (hon.), Pharm. Soc. Japan (hon.), Ind. Acad Sci., Chinese Acad. Sci. (hon. prof. 1994), Phi Beta Kappa, Sigma Xi, Alpha Chi Sigma, Phi Lambda Upsilon (hon.). Office: Purdue U Dept Chemistry West Lafayette IN 47907*

BROWN, JACK EDWARD, investment counselor; b. Lansing, Mich., Nov. 11, 1950. BA, No. Mich. U., 1973. Owner, mgr. Hayward Ins., Wilmington, Mich., 1973-83; investment counselor E.F. Hutton, Muskegon, Mich., 1983-89, Robert Baird & Co. Inc., Muskegon, 1989—. Contbr. articles to various publs. Mem. adv. bd. YMCA Parkwood, East Lansing, Mich., 1975—; past deacon, treas. Ferry Meml. Reformed Ch., Montague, Mich., 1987—; mem. Big Bros. and Big Sisters, Child Abuse Coun. Muskegon County. Mem. Masons. Office: Robert W. Baird & Co Inc PO Box 89 200 Terrace Plz Muskegon MI 49443

BROWN, JAMES ALLISON, anthropology educator; b. Evanston, Ill., Jan. 16, 1934; s. Richard Paul and Olive (Harris) B.; m. Constance Margaret Kimball, Aug. 5, 1967 (div. 1975); m. Judith Quinn Drick Toland, Oct. 1, 1978 (div. 1981); 1 child, Douglas Alfred Kimball. AB, U. Chgo., 1954, MA, 1958, PhD, 1965. Asst. prof. Anthropology and Computer Inst. Stovall Mus. Okla., 1965-66; asst. prof. dept. anthropology and computer instrn. soc. sci. rsch. Mich. State U., 1966-69, assoc. prof., 1967-71, rsch. assoc., 1967-71; assoc. prof. dept. anthropology Northwestern U., Evanston, Ill., 1971-79, prof., 1979—, chair, 1989-95; rsch. assoc. Field Mus. Natural History, Chgo., 1989—; editor Ill. Archaeol. Survey, Urbana, 1966-78, bd. dirs., 1978-85, 88-91, pres., 1991-93; vis. fellow Clare Hall Coll., Cambridge, 1987-88, life fellow, 1989—; advisor dir. registration and edn. State of Ill., 1977, NSF, NEH, Nat. Geographic Soc., AAAS, Time-Life Books, Readers Digest Books, Smithsonian Press, U. Chgo. Press; scientific advisor on redesign Mus. of Ocmulgee Nat. Monument, Macon, Ga., 1978-80. Author: (with others) Pre-Columbia Shell Engravings from Craig Mound at Spiro, Oklahoma, Vols. 1-6, 1975-83, Ancient Art of the American Woodland Indians, 1985; author: Aboriginal Cultural Adaptations in the Midwestern Prairies, 1991, The Spiro Ceremonial Center, 1996; editor: Essays on Archaeological Typology, 1982, Archaic Hunters and Gatherers in the American Midwest, 1983, Prehistoric Hunters and Gatherers: The Emergency of Cultural Complexity, 1985. Sec. Found. for Ill. Archaeology/Ctr. for Am. Archaeology, 1973-83, bd. dirs., 1973—, mem. exec. com., 1984—; mem. Ill. and Mich. Canal Nat. Heritage Corridor Commn., 1985-87; bd. dirs. Ill. State Mus., 1985—, chmn. bd., 1995—; bd. dirs. Mississippi Valley Archaeol. Ctr., 1986—. With U.S. Army, 1957-59. Grantee NSF, 1970, 72, 74, 77, 87, Nat. Park Svc., 1980, 86, Ill. Dept. Transp., 1978, Ill. Historic Preservation Agy., 1980, 85, 86, Am. Philos. Soc., 1973, Wenner-Gren Found., 1974; fellow NEH. Fellow AAAS, Am. Anthrop. Assn.; mem. Current Anthropology (assoc.). Home: 734 Noyes St Apt L3 Evanston IL 60201-2843 Office: Northwestern U Dept Anthropology 1810 Hinman Ave Evanston IL 60208-0809

BROWN, JAMES MONTGOMERY, retired English language and literature educator, academic administrator; b. Dallas, May 21, 1921; divorced; 4 children. Student, Tex. Christian U., 1938-39; BA in Chemistry, Rice U., 1942; MS in Meteorology, Calif. Inst. Tech., 1943; MA in English, State U. Iowa, 1948; postgrad., Kenyon Sch. English, 1948; PhD in English, State U. Iowa, 1951. Chemist Pan Am. Oil Co., 1942; assoc. prof. English Ea. Mont. Coll. Edn., Billings, 1950-54; assoc. prof., then prof. North Tex. State U., Denton, 1954-60, prof. English and Bus. Adminstrn., 1960-62, prof. English, 1962-63; tech. publs. specialist Gen. Dynamics, Ft. Worth, 1963-65; prof. English lang. and lit. So. Ill. U., Edwardsville, 1965-89, asst. to v.p. acad. affairs, 1966-68, various adminstrv. positions, 1968-70, prof. emeritus, 1989—, chancellor; chief bd. staff of bd. trustees So. Ill. U., 1970-74; gen. sec. So. Ill. U. Sys., 1974-79, acting chancellor, 1979, 86, vice chancellor, 1979-86, 86-89, vice chancellor emeritus, 1989-91, chancellor, 1991-95, chancellor emeritus, 1995—. Author: Casebook for Technical Writers, 1961, Introductory Technical Writing, 1962, Cases for Business Communications, 1962; author short stories; contbr. articles to profl. jours. Capt. U.S. Army, 1942-46.

BROWN, JAMES W., mechanical engineer; b. St. Louis, Oct. 5, 1965; s. Oscar W. and Dorothy M. (Hays) B.; m. Joella L. Shay, Sept. 4, 1993. BS in Mech. Engring., U. Mo., Rolla, 1989, postgrad., 1994—. Design engr. McDonnell Douglas, St. Louis, 1989-93; project engr. Star Mfg. Internat., St. Louis, 1993—. Patentee injection molded part. Home: 379 Beckley Pl Saint Charles MO 63304-1030 Office: Star Mfg Internat 9325 Olive Blvd Saint Louis MO 63132

BROWN, JAMES WARD, mathematician, educator, author; b. Phila., Jan. 15, 1934; s. George Harold and Julia Elizabeth (Ward) B.; m. Jacqueline Read, Sept. 3, 1957; children: Scott Cameron, Gordon Elliot. AB, Harvard U., 1955; MA, U. Mich., 1958, Ph.D. (Inst. Sci and Tech. predoctoral fellow), 1964. Asst. prof. math. U. Mich., Dearborn, 1964-66, assoc. prof., 1968-71, prof., 1971—, acting chmn. dept., 1974, 85; asst. prof. Oberlin Coll., 1966-68; editorial cons. Math. Rev., 1970-85; dir. NSF Grant, 1969. Author: (with R.V. Churchill) Complex Variables and Applications, 6th edit., 1996, Internat. Student edit., 1974, Japanese edit., 1995, Spanish edit., 1978, Arabic edit., 1983, Chinese edit., 1985, Korean edit., 1992, Greek edit., 1993, Fourier Series and Boundary Value Problems, 5th edit., 1993, internat. student edit., 1993, Japanese edit., 1980; contbr. articles to U.S. and fgn. sci. jours. Recipient Disting. Faculty award U. Mich.-Dearborn, 1976, Disting. Faculty award Mich. Assn. Governing Bds. Colls. and Univs., 1983. Mem. Am. Math. Soc., Research Club of U. Mich., Sigma Xi. Home: 1710 Morton Ave Ann Arbor MI 48104-4522 Office: 4901 Evergreen Rd Dearborn MI 48128-1491

BROWN, JASON R., stockbroker; b. Mpls., July 1, 1968. BA, St. Cloud (Minn.) State U., 1990. Stockbroker John Kenard, Mpls., 1992-94, R.J. Steichen & Co. Inc., Bloomington, Minn., 1994—. Republican. Lutheran. Office: 7900 Xerxes Ave S Ste 830 Bloomington MN 55431-1122

BROWN, JEFFREY DOUGLAS, historic preservation administrator; b. Sandusky, Ohio, Aug. 14, 1951; s. Carl Frank Jr. and Marion Elizabeth (Butts) B.; m. Susan Lynn Douglas, June 16, 1973; children: Laura Elizabeth, Craig David. BA magna cum laude, Muskingum Coll., New Concord, Ohio, 1973; MA, Kent State U., 1979. Fed. prof. cert. in prehistoric archaeology and history. Mgmt. trainee, credit analyst Harter Bank & Trust Co., Canton, Ohio, 1973-74; preservation officer Kent State U., New Philadelphia, Ohio, 1976-81; cons. Kent State. U./U.S. Army C.E., New Philadelphia, 1981-82; regional coord. Ohio Historic Preservation Office, Columbus, 1982—; cons. in field, 1978-82. Author: The Tower Site and Ohio Monongahela, 1981, Meyers Lake Revisited, 1985, Meters Lake: A Second Look, 1988, Meyers Lake Park Remembered, 1993, The Lake Terminal Railroad 1895-1995, 1996; also articles. Trustee Wm. McKinley Mental Health Soc., Massillon, Ohio, 1989-94, Stark Preservation Alliance, Canton, 1983-89, 91-93, Canton Palace Theatre Assn., 1985-87, Dennison (Ohio) R.R. Depot Mus., 1993-95; chmn. adminstrv. bd. Bolivar (Ohio) United Meth. Ch., 1992. Recipient Outstanding Achievement award Ohio Assn. Hist. Socs. and Museums, 1994; grantee Kent State U., 1975, Ohio Archaeol. Coun., 1985. Mem. Soc. for Hist. Archaeology, Ohio Archaeol. Coun. (various coms. and ad hoc coms., cert. prin. investigator), Nat. Trust for Historic Preservation, Nature Conservancy, Gt. Lakes Hist. Soc., Soc. for Pa. Archaeology, Am. Farmland Trust, Ry. and Locomotive Hist. Soc., Lake Erie Islands Hist. Soc. Home: PO Box 104 10787 Northwood Ave Bolivar OH 44612 Office: Ohio Historic Preservation 201 3rd St NE Canton OH 44702-1231

BROWN, JEFFREY SHERMAN, electrical engineer; b. Gary, Ind., Dec. 26, 1964; s. Sherman William and Jean Sophie (Marcoff) B.; m. Melinda Sue Follman, July 28, 1990. BSEE, Purdue U., 1987. Registered profl. engr., Ind., Ohio, Mich., N.J. Jr. engr. The Port Authority of N.Y. and N.J., N.Y.C., 1988-89, asst. engr., 1989-90, assoc. engr., 1990-91; elec. engr. Hoisington Engrs. Ltd., Princeton, 1991-94; engr. 3 3 Cole Assocs., Inc., South Bend, Ind., 1994-96; dept. mgr. elec. engring. 3 Cole Assocs., Inc., South Bend, 1996—. Mem. IEEE, Illuminating Engring. Soc. N.Am. Republican. Roman Catholic. Home: 15321 Stony Run Trail Granger IN 46530 Office: Cole Assocs Inc 2211 E Jefferson Blvd South Bend IN 46615

BROWN, JOHN ALLIN, test pilot educator; b. Kettering, Northamptonshire, Eng., Apr. 15, 1947; came to U.S., 1985; s. Roy Sancton and Nancy (Shellard) B.; m. Bronwen Mary Davies, Sept. 9, 1967 (div. Jan. 1982); children: Geraint John, Alun Rhys; m. Paula Elaine Ludlam, Feb. 22, 1982. Cert., #1 Radio Sch. RAF, Locking, Somerset, Eng., 1966, Basic Flying RAF, Leeming, Yorkshire, Eng., 1968, Advanced Flying RAF, Oakington, Cambridge, Eng., 1968, Empire Test Pilot Sch., Boscombe Down, Wiltshire, Eng., 1978. Enlisted RAF, 1963; copilot No. 214 Squadron, Marham, Norfolk, Eng., 1969-71, pilot, 1971-75; pilot, refueling instr. No. 55 Squadron RAF, Marham, 1975-78; test pilot B Squadron Aeroplane and Armament Experimental Establishment RAF, Boscombe Down, 1978-79, sr. pilot, 1979-83; ret. RAF, Boscombe Down, 1985; sr. test pilot instr. Nat. Test Pilot Sch., Mojave, Calif., 1985-88; flt. simulator test pilot Northwest Airlines, St. Paul, Minn., 1988-93, mgr. crew resource mgmt., 1993-95, mgr. flt. tech. programs, 1995—; adminstr. Internat. Air Tattoo, Greenham Common, Eng., 1984. Assoc. fellow Soc. Exptl. Test Pilots. Home: 3101 Country Wood Dr Burnsville MN 55337-3439 Office: Northwest Airlines Dept N7420 5101 NW Dr Saint Paul MN 55111-3027

BROWN, JOHN CHARLES, stockbroker; b. Norton, Kans., Sept. 4, 1954; m. Anne Brown, July 2, 1977; children: Matthew, Ed, Elizabeth. BA in Radio and TV, U. Kans., 1976. Mgr. Brown's Clothing Store, Manhattan, Kans., 1976-86; stockbroker Stifel Nicolaus & Co., Manhattan, 1986—. Roman Catholic.

BROWN, JOHN J., financial services company executive; b. Vinita, Okla., May 10, 1946; s. Johny H. and Mary Jo (Reece) B.; m. Donna J. Hayward, Mar. 11, 1966; children: Soncee, John H. Student, S.W. Mo. State U., 1964, Drury Coll., 1964-67, Cen. Bible Coll., 1977. Mktg. dir. HQ Corp., Springfield, Mo., 1977-80; v.p. Internat. Ch. Bus. Mgmt. Corp., Springfield, 1980-82; pres. North Capital Resource Corp., Springfield, 1982—; cons. John Brown Assocs., Springfield, 1970-77. Author: Church Financing for the '80s, revised '90s, 1985. Mem. Evangel Coll. Coun., Springfield, 1984-87, Nat. Rep. Com. (sustaining), 1985-87. Recipient Outstanding Achievement award Alyeska Svc. Orgn., 1975, 76, Outstanding Contbn. award Royal Heritage Soc., 1983; Paul Harris fellow Rotary Internat., 1984. Mem. Am. Mgmt. Assn., CEOs Assn., Assn. Ch. Financing Profls. (pres. 1987-89), Rotary. Mem. Assemblies of God Ch. Home: 5949 S Thetford Rd Springfield MO 65804-5227 Office: Northern Capital Resource Capital Ctr 2115 S Brentwood Blvd Springfield MO 65804-2538

BROWN, KAREN RIMA, orchestra manager, Spanish language educator; b. N.Y.C., Apr. 26, 1943; d. Alexander and Leona (Rosenfeld) Jaffe; m. Russell Vernon Brown, Aug. 13, 1966; children: Stephanie Leona and Gregory Russell. BA, Colby Coll., 1965; MA, U. Wis., 1966. Teaching asst. U. Wis., Madison, 1965-66; instr. Spanish U. Wis., Janesville, 1966-68, Baraboo, 1968-70, Eau Claire, 1970-71; instr. Spanish Ohio U., Zanesville, 1978—; mgr. Southeastern Ohio Symphony, New Concord, 1977—; lectr. Spanish Muskingum Coll., New Concord, 1984; mem., music panelist Ohio Arts Coun., Columbus, 1979-83, 90-93; pres. S.E. Ohio Regional Arts Coun., Zanesville, 1978-80. Bd. dirs. Muskingum County Visitors and Conv. Bur., Zanesville, 1987-90, bd. sec., 1989-90; bd. dirs. Assn. of Two Toledos, 1984-87, Ohio Citizens Com. for Arts, Canton, 1979-84; regional coord. Ohio Citizens for the Arts, 1995—. Mem. Am. Assn. Tchrs. Spanish and Portuguese, Ohio Valley Fgn. Lang. Assn., Bus. and Profl. Women, Phi Beta Kappa, Phi Sigma Iota, Sigma Delta Pi (hon.). Democrat. Office: Southeastern Ohio Sym Orch PO Box 42 New Concord OH 43762-0042

BROWN, KATHRYN LISBETH, secondary education educator; b. Cleve., June 22, 1948; d. Henry Walter and Muriel Ann (Sindelar) Mahowski; m. Gary A. Brown, Sept. 27, 1974 (div. June 1988); 1 child, Sarah G. AA, Cuyahoga C.C., 1970; BA, U. Akron, 1988. Cert secondary educator, Ohio. Tchr. English and journalism Medina (Ohio) City Schs., 1989—. Coach Cheerleaders of Medina H.S., 1989—; advisor Medinamite Mag., 1994-95, Jr. Class, 1991, Vol. Opportunities for Teens, 1993-94. Mem. Mensa. Home: 500 Pine St Medina OH 44256 Office: Medina H S 777 E Union St Medina OH 44256

BROWN, KENNETH HACKMAN, economics educator; b. St. Louis, Aug. 4, 1968; s. William Brown and Roberta E. (Hackman) Hornbeak; m. Traci L. Schloss, Aug 28, 1993. BS in Bus. Adminstrn., St. Louis Univ., 1990; MS in Econs., U. Ill., 1992, PhD in Econs., 1994. Econ. analyst Southwestern Bell Corp., St. Louis, 1989-90; tchg. asst. U. Ill., Champaign, 1991-92, rsch. asst., 1992-94; asst. prof. U. No. Iowa, Cedar Falls, 1994—; cons. Waterloo, Iowa, Sports Commn., 1994-95. Recipient fellowship U. Ill., 1990, dissertation fellowship, Robert Harbeson Meml. Found., Champaign, 1993. Mem. Am. Econ. Assn. Office: Univ Northern Iowa Dept Econs Cedar Falls IA 50614-0129

BROWN, LAURENCE DAVID, retired bishop; b. Fargo, N.D., Feb. 16, 1926; s. John Nicolai and Ada Amelia (Johnson) B.; m. Virginia Ann Allen, Sept. 6, 1950; children: Patricia Ann, Julia Louise, Claudia Ruth. BS, U. Minn., 1946; BA, Concordia Coll., 1948; M of Theology, Luther Theol. Sem., 1951. Ordained to ministry Evang. Luth. Ch., 1951. Pastor Our Savior's Luth. Ch., New Ulm, Minn., 1951-55; nat. assoc. youth dir. Evang. Luth. Ch., Mpls., 1955-60; nat. youth dir. Am. Luth. Ch., Mpls., 1960-68; instn. dir. Tchr. Tng., U. Minn., Mpls., 1968-69; exec. dir. Freedom from Hunger Found., Washington, 1969-73; sr. pastor St. Paul Luth. Ch., Waverly, Iowa, 1973-79; bishop Iowa Dist. Am. Luth. Ch., Des Moines, 1979-89, N.E. Iowa Synod, Evang. Luth. Ch. in Am., Waverly, 1989-92; prof. religion Wartburg Coll., Waverly, Iowa, 1992-93; interim sr. pastor Calvary Luth. Ch., Mpls., 1996—; bd. regents Luther Coll., Decorah, Iowa, 1989-92, Wartburg Coll., 1988-92, Wartburg Theol. Sem., Dubuque, Iowa, 1988-91, Self-Help, Inc., 1989-94. Author: Take Care: A Guide for Responsible Living, 1983; contbr. articles to profl. jours. Lt. USN, 1943-46. Lutheran. Home: 1200 On the Mall # 215 Minneapolis MN 55403

BROWN, LAWRENCE ALAN, geography educator; b. Erie, Pa., Nov. 22, 1935; s. George and Anna Mildred (Baker) B.; m. Angelika Renate Gerbes, July 28, 1967 (div. 1974); 1 child, Arnika Rachael. BS, U. Pa., 1958; MA, Northwestern U., 1963, PhD, 1966. CPA, Pa., Ohio. Asst. prof. dept. geography U. Iowa, Iowa City, 1965-68; assoc. prof. Ohio State U., Columbus, 1968-71, prof., 1971-96, chairperson dept. geography, 1995—, disting. univ. prof., 1996—. Author: Diffusion Dynamics, 1968, Diffusion Processes and Location, 1968, Innovation Diffusion, 1981, Place, Migration and Development in the Third World, 1991; mem. editorial bd. various profl. publs.; contbr. articles to profl. jours. Guggenheim fellow, 1985. Mem. Assn. Am. Geographers (nat. councillor 1978-81, v.p. 1995-96, pres. 1996—, Honors award 1983), Population Assn. Am., Regional Sci. Assn. (v.p. 1988-89, pres. 1995-96), Internat. Union for Sci. Study of Population, Internat. Geog. Union. Democrat. Jewish. Home: 140 Erie Rd Columbus OH 43214-3615 Office: Ohio State Univ Dept Geography 154 N Oval Mall Columbus OH 43210-1330

BROWN, LINDA DIANE, women's health nurse; b. Havre, Mont., Jan. 23, 1956; d. Vernon Leroy and Shirley Mae (Sennard) Lindell; m. Eric Edward Brown, Sept. 30, 1979; children: Adam Jacob, Reid Edward, Katherine Elizabeth. BS, Iowa State U., 1978; BSN, Grand View Coll., 1985; MSN, U. Nebr., 1995. RN, Iowa; Neonatal Individualized Devel. Care and Assessment Program, reliability infant developmental specialist, Iowa. Neonatal staff nurse Mercy Hosp. Med. Ctr., Des Moines, 1986-92, air and ground transport nurse (neonatal), 1988-94, advanced clin. specialist, 1991-94; pvt. practice nurse Des Moines, 1993-96; project Ladders in Nursing Careers coord. Iowa Hosp. Assn., Des Moines, 1994—; mem. Iowa Birth Defects Inst., Iowa Dept. Pub. Health, Des Moines, 1993—, mem. neonatal hearing screening com., 1994-95; cons. Iowa Protection and Advocacy, Des Moines, 1993—; guest spkr. in field. Exec. prodr. (videos) Sometimes Miracles Hide....Dispelling The Stereotype, 1993, Katie's Story-A Child's Story of Full Inclusion, 1993. PTA pres. S.E. Polk Cmty. Schs., Altoona, 1990-92, guest lectr. cultural diversity teenage sexuality, 1992—, mem. human growth and devel. com., 1992; jr. high youth leader Rising Sun Ch. of Christ, Des Moines, 1994—. Mem. ANA, Iowa Nursing Assn. (dist. del. 1994—, bd. dirs. 1996), Sigma Theta Tau. Republican. Home: 408 25th Ave SW Altoona IA 50009-1526

BROWN, LOMAS, JR., professional football player; b. Miami, Fla., Mar. 30, 1963. Student, U. Fla. Offensive tackle Detroit Lions, 1985—. Founder Lomas Brown, Jr. Found., 1991. Played in Pro Bowl, 1990-93; named tackle The Sporting News All-America team, 1984, offensive tackle The Sporting News All-Pro team, 1992. Office: Detroit Lions 1200 Featherstone Rd Pontiac MI 48342-1938*

BROWN, LYNETTE RALYA, journalist, publicist; b. Beloit, Wis., Dec. 15, 1926; d. Lynn Louis and Ethel Clara (Meeker) Ralya; m. Donald Adair Brown, Jr., Dec. 20, 1947; children: Donald Adair III, Alison Laura, Julia Carol. BA in Journalism, Mich. State U., 1948; MA in Journalism, Michigan State U., 1985; MA in Mass Comm., Wayne State U., 1983. Actress, publicist Grand Traverse Playhouse, Traverse City, Mich., 1946 (summer), N.Y. Summer Playhouse, Mackinac Island, Mich., 1947 (summer); writer WILS Radio, Lansing, Mich., 1947-48; writer, performer WJBK Radio, TV, Detroit, 1948-49; editor Denby Ctr. News, Detroit, 1949-51; freelance writer Oakland County, Mich., 1952-78; editor Henry Ford Mus., Dearborn, Mich., 1979-81; writer, reporter Legal Advertiser Newspaper, Detroit, 1983-85; publicist Bloomfield (Mich.) and Birmingham (Mich.) Pub. Librs., 1986-89; freelance writer, publicist Lynette Brown Comm., Birmingham, Mich., 1989—. Columnist: (newspaper) At the Libraries, 1986-89. Probation sponsor Dist. Ct. Mich., 1960-70; publicist Oakland County Vol. Bur., 1979-82; leader sr. high/jr. high youth group Drayton Ave. Presbyn. Ch., Oakland County, 1952-54, 62-66, Pine Hill Congl. Ch., Oakland County, 1968-71, Northbrook Presbyn. Ch., Oakland County, 1976-77; polit. campaign worker Rep. candidates and non-partisan jud. candidates, 1952—; Cub Scout leader Royal Oak Emerson Sch., Oakland County, 1961-64; Girl Scout troop leader Bloomfield Twp. Meadow Lake Sch., Oakland County, 1966-71. Mem. AAUW (chair women's issues, pub. info. dir. 1995—), Oakland County C. of C. (Athena award 1995). Home and Office: 6120 Westmoor Rd Bloomfield Hills MI 48301

BROWN, MARGARET ANN, international human resources executive; b. Woodstock, Ill., July 12, 1954; d. Walter Nicholas and Phyllis Marian (Cervenka) B. BA in Bus. Mgmt., Mundelein Coll., 1985. Cert. compensation profl. With Baxter Healthcare Corp., 1974-89; exec. compensation mgr. Baxter Healthcare Corp., Deerfield, Ill., 1983-85; internat. compensation and benefit dir. Baxter World Trade Group, Deerfield and Brussels, 1986-89; corp. internat. human resources mgr. FMC Corp., Chgo., 1989-92; sr. mgr. internat. compensation and benefits SaraLee Corp., Chgo., 1992—; speaker, lectr. in field. Mem. Chgo. Coun. Fgn. Rels.; bd. dirs. Internat. Visitors Ctr., Chgo.; mem. bus. and profl. assn. Chgo. Symphony Orch. Bus. and Profl. Women's Assn. scholar, 1972. Mem. Human Resources Mgmt. Assn. Chgo. (chmn. internat. com. 1988-90), Mgmt. Compensation Svcs. Internat. (steering com. 1988—), Internat. Pers. Assn., Pacific Area Pers. Assn., Latin Am. Pers. Assn., Am. Compensation Assn., Chgo. Compensation Assn., Alliance Francaise, The Art Inst. of Chgo., The Arts Club of Chgo., Lincoln Park Zool. Soc., Japan/Am. Soc. (Chgo.), City Club Chgo. Roman Catholic. Office: Sara Lee Corp Three First National Pla Chicago IL 60602

BROWN, MARK LESLIE, biomedical scientist; b. Normal, Ill., Jan. 8, 1955; s. Francis Robert and Helen Elizabeth (Tucker) B.; m. Lydia Anne Huttar, Sept. 3, 1977; children: Nathan, Daniel, Stephen (dec.), Jacob, Philip. AB magna cum laude, Hope Coll., 1977; MS, U. Mich., 1978, PhD, 1994. Digital design engr. Prime Computer, Framingham, Mass., 1978-80; mem. tech. staff Bell Labs., Naperville, Ill., 1980-83; asst. prof. Hope Coll., Holland, Mich., 1983-85; prin. scientist Donnelly Corp., Holland, Mich., 1985-89; rsch. scientist Medtronic, Mpls., 1994—. Contbr. articles to profl. jours. Bd. pres. Infant Day Care Ctr., Holland, 1988-89; coach youth baseball, soccer and wrestling Ann Arbor Recreation, 1989-94; mem. vestry Grace Episcopal Ch., Holland, 1987-89; mem. sch. curriculum com. Holland Pub. Sch., 1987-89. Mem. IEEE, Soc. for Ind. and Applied Math., Biomed. Engring. Soc., Mortar Bd., Phi Beta Kappa. Home: 10 Buffalo Rd North Oaks MN 55127 Office: Medtronic Inc 7000 Central Ave NE Minneapolis MN 55432

BROWN, MARY CARNEY, former state representative; b. Midland, Mich., Aug. 18, 1935; d. Sheldon and Wilma Carney; m. Donald J. Brown; children: Linda, Jeff, Jim. Student, Albion Coll., 1953-55; AB in Recreation, Syracuse U., 1957, MS in Phys. Edn., 1961. Tchr. various cos., camps and colls.; asst. prof. dept. phys. edn. for women Western Mich. U., 1965-76; state rep. State of Mich., 1975-9; mem. legis. coms. Civil Rights and Women's Issues, Conservation, Environ. and the Great lakes, Human Svcs. and Children, Taxation; chmn. Ins. Com., Air Quality Subcom.; chair House Dem. Caucus, 1983-94. Mem. Friends of Kal-Haven Trail, Kalamazoo Womens Network; bd. dirs. Jobs for Mich. Grads., 1982-89; pres. Kalamazoo Area LWV, 1969-73, lobbyist, state bd. dirs., 1973-74; chairperson Kalamazoo County Dem. Party, 1975-76; founding mem. Kalamazoo Environ. Coun., 1991—; charter mem. Kalamazoo Nature Ctr.; mem. citizens adv. com. KRPH, 1987—; century club mem. Mich. Dem. Party, com. to assess need for constl. conv., 1977, co-chair policy com., 1986; spokesperson Mich. Dem. Women's Caucus, 1978-79,. Named Outstanding Freshman Legislator, State Capitol Bur. Booth newspapers, 1977, one of 10 Top Legislators, Detroit News poll, 1977, 79, Legislator of Yr., Mich. Assn. Children's Alliances, 1985, Woman of the Yr. NOW, 1982, Legislator of the Yr. Mich. Township Assn., 1989, Conservationist of the Yr. Sierra Club, 1990; recipient Cert. of Appreciation, Kalamazoo Alcohol and Drug Abuse Coun., Cert. of Svc. with distinction Assn. Student Govt. Western Mich. U., 1980; honored by Women Lawyers Assn. Mich., 1980, Community Svc. award Eagles Aerie 526 Kalamazoo, Cert. of Appreciation, County Rd. Assn. Mich., 1983, Woman of Achievement award Kalamazoo YWCA, 1993, The Brown Jacobs Equality in Edn. award Mich. NOW, 1994, Outstand Pub. Svc. award Planned Parenthood of Kalamazoo, 1994, Lifetime Achievement award Sierra Club, 1994. Mem. AAUW (co-winner Outstanding Mich. Legislator 1982), ACLU, Am. Camping Assn. (bd. dirs. Mich. sect. 1972-76, 80-82), ACLU. Home: 1624 Grand Ave Kalamazoo MI 49006-4419 also: Mich State Ho of Reps State Capitol Lansing MI 48909

BROWN, MARY ELLEN, educator; b. Shreveport, La.; d. Albert Emery and Mary Ruth (Laughlin) B.; children: Kevin Randall, Colin Louis, Eleanor Sean, Christopher Jonathan. BA, U. Southwestern La., 1969; MA, U. South Fla., 1975, U. Iowa, 1985; PhD, Murdoch U., 1991. Lectr. Edith Cowan U., Perth, Australia, 1985-88; asst. prof. SUNY, Brockport, 1988-92, U. Mo., Columbia, 1992—. Author: Television and Women's Culture, 1990, Soap Opera and Women's Talk, 1994. Office: Dept Comm 115 Switzler Hall Columbia MO 65211

BROWN, MARY SUE, library administrator; b. Fon du Lac, Wis., Mar. 15, 1941; d. Nicholas and Julia Susannah Miller; m. Timothy Woods Ross, Feb. 10, 1962 (div. 1973); children: Patrick Nelson Ross, Susannah Catherine Ross; m. Stanley Brown, Mar. 15, 1973. BA, North Ctrl. Coll., Naperville, Ill., 1975; MLS, Rosary Coll., 1979. Reference libr. Elmhurst (Ill.) Pub. Libr., 1978-81, head of reference, 1978-86; libr. adminstr. Woodridge (Ill.) Pub. Libr., 1986—; chair stds. Ill. Pub. Librs. Com., 1993-95. Trustee Coll. DuPage, Glen Ellyn, Ill., 1993—. Mem. Ill. Libr. Assn. (exec. bd. dirs. 1993—), Beta Phi Mu. Democrat. Home: 1 S 750 Milton Glen Ellyn IL 60137 Office: Woodridge Pub Libr 3 Plaza Dr Woodridge IL 60517-5014

BROWN, MICHAEL H., freelance writer; b. Montgomery, Ala., Sept. 11, 1942; m. Lani Maisterra; 9 children. AA, Palomar Coll., 1987-88; postgrad., Southwest Mo. State U., 1992. Dem. candidate for U.S. House, 1994, 96. With U.S. Army, 1960-64. Office: PO Box 4884 Springfield MO 65808*

BROWN, MICHAEL RICHARD, minister; b. Columbus, Ohio, Mar. 2, 1959; s. Cornelius Paul Brown and Pearl Elizabeth (Baker) Buck; m. Christine Elaine Stanley, Aug. 23, 1980; 1 child, Stephanie Nicole. BA in Bible and Religion, Huntington Coll., 1981, M in Ministry, 1983, postgrad., 1984. Ordained to ministry Ch. of United Brethren in Christ, 1983. Minister Monroe (Ind.) United Brethren Ch., 1982-89, Franklin United Brethern Ch., New Albany, Ohio, 1989—. Dir. Adams County Soccer Clinic, Decatur, Ind., 1984-85; chmn. Adams County Child Protection Team, Decatur, 1985; v.p. Adams County Energy Assistance Inc., 1986; mem. Hoosiers for Better Schs., A-Plus Program; soccer coach New Albany Mid. Sch., 1989-91. Named one of Outstanding Young Men of Am., 1985. Mem. New Albany Ministerial Assn. (v.p. 1994, pres. 1991, 94, conf. supt. Columbus dist. 1995-97). Republican. Home: 6695 Albanyview Rd Westerville OH 43081-9236 Office: Franklin United Brethren Ch 7171 Central College Rd New Albany OH 43054-9742

BROWN, MORTON LINDON, securities company executive; b. Nashville, Feb. 1, 1946. BA, Vanderbilt U.; MBA, Washington U., St. Louis, 1975. Prin. Edward D. Jones & Co., St. Louis, 1975—. Sgt. U.S. Army, 1968-74. Mem. St. Louis Fin. Soc. (bd. dirs.). Office: Edward D Jones & Co 12555 Manchester Rd Saint Louis MO 63131

BROWN, NANCY MCINTIRE, academic administrator; b. Alexandria, La., Aug. 1, 1965; d. Robert and Janet (Hauser) McIntire; m. James Roger Brown, Jan. 2, 1988. BS in Journalism, U. Wis., 1987; MS, U. Notre Dame, 1995. Automobile sales Eversole Motors, Inc., La Crosse, Wis., 1988; asst. dir. admissions Winona (Minn.) State U., 1989-95; dir. ann. fund and planned giving Marian Coll., Fond du Lac, Wis., 1995; head coach cheer and stunt team Winona (Minn.) State U.; advisor to Delta Phi Epsilon (WSU chpt.), 1992-95, Sigma Omega Sigma (Marian chpt.), 1996—. Mem. comm. coun. Fond du Lac Assn. Commerce. Mem. NAFE, AAUW, Nat. Soc. Fundraising Execs., Women Mgmt., U. Wis. Alumni Assn. U. Notre Dame Alumni Assn. Roman Catholic. Office: Marian Coll 45 S National Ave Fond Du Lac WI 54935

BROWN, OLEN RAY, medical microbiology research educator; b. Hastings, Okla., Aug. 18, 1935; s. Willis Edward and Rosa Nell (Fulton) B.; m. Pollyana June King, Aug. 30, 1958; children: Barbara Kathryn, Diana Carol, David Gregory. BS in Lab. Tech., Okla. U., 1958, MS in Bacteriology, 1960, PhD in Microbiology, 1964. Diplomate Am. Bd. Toxicology, Am. Bd. Forensic Examiners. Instr. Sch. Medicine, U. Mo., Columbia, 1964-65, asst. prof., 1965-70, assoc. prof., 1970-77, prof. dept. molecular microbiology and immunology, 1981—; joint appointments, prof. depts. microbiology and biomed. scis. Coll. Vet. Medicine, U. Mo., 1977—, prof. biomed. scis., 1987—; guest lectr. Ross U., St. Kitts, W.I., 1984, 88; asst. dir. Dalton Rsch. Ctr., U. Mo., 1974-78, Dalton rsch. investigator grad. sch., 1968—; grant peer reviewer for program projects SCOR and Superfund grants NIH, 1979, Nat. Inst. Environ. Health Scis., Dept. Commerce, EPA, 1986, 90-96, Am. Inst. Biol. Scis. for Dept. Def.; cons. drug abuse policy office White House, 1982, Immunol. Vaccines, Inc., Columbia, 1984—, Lab. Support, Inc., Chgo., 1988-89, Ea. Rsch. Group, Lexington, Mass., 1991—, Teltech, Mpls., 1992—, Scis. Internat., Inc., Alexandria, Va.; judge top 100 products for 1996, Rsch. and Devel. Mag. Author: Laboratory Manual for Veterinary Microbiology, 1973, The Expert Witness: A Manual for Attorneys and Professionals Under Contract; co-author: elem. and advanced lab. manuals for med. microbiology, 2 vols., 1978, 79; contbr. Progress in Clinical Research, Vol. 21, 1978, 79, Oxygen, 5th Internat. Hyperbaric Conf., Vols. I, II, 1974, 79, numerous articles to profl. jours.; book and film critic AAAS, Washington, 1986—; item preparer Am. Coll. Test, Med. Coll. Admissions Test, 1981—; mem. editorial staff Biomed. Letters, 1981—; responder Sci. and Math. Helpline for Mus. Sci. Discovery, Harrisburg, Pa., 1996—, reviewer profl. jours. Track and field ofcl. U. Mo. and Big Eight Conf., Columbia, 1979-86. Investigative rsch. grantee Office Naval Rsch., Dept. Def., 1968-81, NIH, 1976-88, NIEHS, 1981-94, 95—, USAID, 1983-86, Nat. Inst. Dental Health Scis., 1989-92. Fellow Am. Inst. Chemists (cert. chemistry and chem engring., profl. program bd. 1989-90, sd com. chemistry and environ. concerns); mem. Top One Percent Soc., Soc. Toxicology, Internat. Soc. Study Xenobiotics, Am. Chem. Soc., Am. Heart Assn., Internat. Soc. Exposure Analysts, Nat. Space Soc., Oxygen Soc., Columbia Track Club (sec.-treas. 1979-82). Office: U Mo Dalton Rsch Ctr Columbia MO 65211

BROWN, PAM, state legislator. Senator State of Nebraska, Lincoln, 1995—.

BROWN, PAUL EDMONDSON, lawyer; b. Van Buren County, Iowa, Dec. 24, 1915; s. William Allen and Margaret (Edmondson) B.; m. Lorraine Hill, Jan. 9, 1944; 1 child, Scott. BA, U. Iowa, 1938, JD with distinction, 1941. Bar: Iowa 1941, U.S. Supreme Ct. 1966. Ptnr., Mahoney, Brown, Mahoney, Boone, Iowa, 1946-52; v.p., counsel Bankers Life Co., Des Moines, 1952-80, now prin. fin. group; pres. Iowa Life Ins. Assn., Des Moines, 1980-85; of counsel Grefe & Sidney, Des Moines, 1980-84, Davis, Hockensberg, Wine, Brown, Koehn, Shors, Des Moines, 1984-91; pvt. practice, 1991—; atty. County of Boone, Iowa, 1948-52. With U.S. Army, 1942-46, to col. USAR, 1946-70. Named Outstanding Young Man of Iowa, Iowa State Jr. C. of C., 1948. Mem. ABA, Fed. Bar Assn., Iowa Bar Assn., Polk County Bar Assn., Assn. Life Ins. Counsel, U. Iowa Alumni Assn. (mem. Pres.' Club and various coms.), Civil War Roundtable, Downtown Des Moines Kiwanis Club (pres. 1961). Republican. Congregationalist. Home and Office: 5804 Harwood Dr Des Moines IA 50312-1206

BROWN, PAUL SHERMAN, lawyer; b. St. Louis, June 26, 1921; s. Paul Michael and Norma (Sherman) B.; m. Ann Wilson, Feb. 7, 1959; 1 son, Paul S. BS in Commerce, St. Louis U., 1943, JD cum laude, 1951. Bar: Mo. 1951, U.S. Dist. Ct. (ea. dist.) Mo. 1951, U.S. Ct. Appeals (8th cir.) 1951, U.S. Supreme Ct. 1966. Shareholder, Brown & James , P.C., St. Louis, 1980—; instr. St. Louis U. Night Law Sch., 1978—; lectr. in field. Mem. St. Louis Amateur Athletic Assn. (dir. 1974-76, pres. 1976-78); mem. com. on civil pattern jury instructions, Mo. Supreme Ct. Fellow Am. Coll. Trial Lawyers, Internat. Acad. Trial Lawyers, Internat. Soc. Barristers; mem. ABA (vice-chmn. com. consumer products liability 1977-78), Mo. Bar Assn. (bd. govs. 1963-67), Am. Bd. Trial Advocates, Lawyers Assn. St. Louis, Bar Assn. Met. St. Louis (pres. 1970-71), Am. Judicature Soc., Order of Woolsack, Alpha Sigma Nu. Roman Catholic. Contbr. numerous articles to profl. jours. Home: 7331 Kingsbury Blvd Saint Louis MO 63130-4143 Office: Brown & James 705 Olive St Ste 1100 Saint Louis MO 63101-2213

BROWN, PHILIP EDWARD, geology educator; b. St. Louis, July 12, 1952; s. David H. and Barbara (Illingworth) B.; m. Kristine A. Larson, July 20, 1974; children: Jason, Peter, Karin. BA, Carleton Coll., Northfield, Minn., 1974; MS, U. Mich., 1976, PhD, 1980. Postdoctoral rschr. U.S. Geologic Survey, Reston, Va., 1980-81; asst. prof. U. Wis., Madison, 1981-87, assoc. prof., 1987-92, prof. geology, 1992—; rsch. fellow U. Western Australia, 1992—. Fellow Soc. Econ. Geologists, Geol. Assn. Can., Mineral. Soc. Am. (assoc. editor 1990-94); mem. Am. Geophys. Union, Sigma Xi. Office: U Wis 1215 W Dayton St Madison WI 53706-1600

BROWN, RHODERICK EDMISTON, biochemistry researcher, educator; b. Hendersonville, N.C., Apr. 7, 1953; s. Rhoderick Edmiston and Jane Patterson (Servais) B.; m. Laura Strippel Brown, Sept. 12, 1981; children: Caroline Finley, Christopher Hamilton. AB in Chemistry and Zoology, U. N.C., 1975; PhD in Biochemistry, Wake Forest U., 1981. Rsch. assoc. dept. biochemistry U. Va., Charlottesville, 1981-86; asst. prof. Hormel Inst., U. Minn., Austin, 1986-92, assoc. prof., 1993—; grad. faculty dept. biochemistry/molecular biology Mayo Grad. Sch., Mayo Clinic, Rochester, Minn., 1989—. Mem. editl. bd. Chemistry and Physics of Lipids, 1996—; contbr. articles to profl. jours., chpt. to book. Mem. AAAS, Am. Heart Assn. (coun. on basic rsch.), Am. Soc. Cell Biology, Biophys. Soc., Microscopy Soc. Am., Minn. Acad. Scis. Office: U Minn Hormel Inst 801 16th Ave NE Austin MN 55912-3679

BROWN, RHONDA MARIE, secondary education educator; b. Clinton, Ind., Dec. 1, 1955; d. Jack Raymond and Wilma Lee (Graham) Moretto; m. Richard Thomas Tapp, Mar. 26, 1976 (div. June 1993); 1 child, Thomas Matthew Tapp; m. Thomas Wayne Brown, Feb. 14, 1995; 1 child, Mikayla Marie. AS, U. Evansville; BS, U. So. Ind., 1992; MEd, Wesleyan U., Marion, Ind., 1995. Cert. tchr., Ind. Sci. tchr. Mater Dei H.S., Evansville, Ind., 1992-95, McGary Mid. Sch., Evansville, Ind., 1995—. Roman Catholic. Home: 6288 Indian Dr Newburgh IN 47630

BROWN, RICHARD E., state legislator. Gen. agt. Sioux Falls, S.D.; mem. S.D. Ho. of Reps., Pierre; mem. edn. and taxation coms., S.D. Ho. of Reps.

BROWN, RICHARD HARRIS, financial executive; b. New Brunswick, N.J., June 3, 1947; s. Harris Ransford and Winifred (Clelland) B.; Christine Demler, Sept. 27, 1969; children: Ryan, Allison. BS in Communications, Ohio U., 1969. Comml. rep. Ohio Bell, Columbus, 1969-71, comml. mgr., 1971-74; dist. comml. mgr. Ohio Bell, Toledo and Cleve., 1974-80; div. mgr. Ohio Bell, Cleve., 1980-81; v.p. engring. & ops. United Telephone System, Inc. subs. United Telecommunications, Inc., Westwood, Kans., 1981-82; v.p. ops. United Telephone Co. of Midwest, Overland Park, Kans., 1982-83; v.p., COO United Telephone Co. of Fla., Apopka, 1983-87; sr. v.p. human resources & adminstrn. United Telecommunications, Inc., Shawnee Mission, Kans., 1987, sr. v.p. ops., 1987-89, exec. v.p., chief info. & planning officer, 1989; vice chmn., bd. dirs. Ameritech, 1993-95, Chgo., 1993-95; pres., CEO H&R Block, Inc., Kansas City, Mo., 1995—; bd. dirs. Pharmacia and Upjohn Inc., London. Trustee, vice-chmn. Ohio U. Found., Athens, 1989—; vice chmn. Chgo. United Way Campaign, 1994. With USNG, 1969-74. Named Outstanding Alumnus, Coll. of Interpersonal Comms., Ohio U., 1988. Mem. Chgo. Club, Shoreacres Country Club, Coml. Club, Econ. Club, Northwestern U. Assocs. Execs. Club. Office: H&R Block Inc 4410 Main St Kansas City MO 64111

BROWN, RICHARD LAWRENCE, lawyer; b. Evansville, Ind., Dec. 8, 1932; s. William S. and Mildred (Tenbarge) B.; m. Alice Rae Costello, June 14, 1957; children: Richard, Catherine, Vanessa, Mary, James. AA, Vincennes U., 1953; BA, Ind. State U., 1957; JD, Ind. U., 1960. Bar: Ind., 1960, U.S. dist. ct. (so. dist.) Ind., 1961, U.S. Ct. Apls. (7th cir.), 1972, U.S. Sup. Ct., 1972. Mng. ptnr. Butler, Brown, Hahn and Little, and predecessor firms, Indpls., 1961-85; mng. ptnr. Butler, Brown and Blythe, Indpls., 1985-92, of counsel, 1992-94; city atty. City of Beech Grove, Ind., 1967—; pvt. practice Beech Grove, Ind., 1992—; of counsel Blythe & Ost, Indpls., 1994—; sec., treas. Internat. Bus. Inst., Dayton, Ohio, 1987--, Internat. Pub. Inst., Dayton, 1987--; bd. dirs. Vincennes U. Found. Editor: Indiana Municipal Lawyers Assn. Newsletter, 1985—. Chmn. bd. zoning appeals small cities and towns Marion County, Ind., 1965-66; gen. counsel Habitat for Humanity Greater Indpls., 1985-95; parish chmn. St. Jude's Ch. With U.S. Army, 1953-55. Fellow Indpls. Bar Assn.; mem. ABA, Ind. Bar Assn., Ind. Mcpls. Lawyers Assn. (co-editor newsletter, bd. dirs., pres. 1987-88), Vincennes U. Alumni Assn. (pres., bd. dirs. 1990-92), KC, Delta Theta Phi. Roman Catholic. Office: 1820 Main St Beech Grove IN 46107-1418

BROWN, RICK ROBERT, mechanical engineer; b. Lincoln, Nebr., Aug. 12, 1954; s. Scott Robert and Clarice LaVern (Freye) B.; m. Kerry Lynn Erhman, Oct. 20, 1979; children: Crystalyne, Vicki, Stephanie, Kimberly. BSME, U. Nebr., 1977. Registered profl. engr., Nebr. V.p., engr. Brownie Mfg. Co., Inc., Waverly, Nebr., 1977—. Scoutmaster Boy Scouts Am., Waverley, 1986-88, troop com. mem., 1990-95. Mem. ASME (sec. Nebr. sect. 1988-95). Republican. Mem. Assemblies of God. Office: Brownie Mfg Co Inc PO Box 446 Waverly NE 68462-0446

BROWN, ROBERT SAMUEL, administrative assistant; b. Westfield, Mass., Oct. 4, 1968; s. Robert Thomas and Roslyn Judith (Kapner) B. BA, Keene (N.H.) State Coll., 1990; MA, Ind. State U., 1992. Teaching asst. Ind. State U., Terre Haute, 1990-92; adminstrv. asst., predoctoral Ind. U., Bloomington, 1992—. Editl. intern Quarterly Jour. of Speech, 1992-96. Mem. Ctrl. States Speech Assn. (asst. to exec. sec. 1991-93). Office: Ind U Dept Speech Comm 809 E 7th St Bloomington IN 47805

BROWN, ROGER WILLIAM, manufacturer's representative, real estate developer; b. Lansing, Mich., Feb. 25, 1940; s. Gustave Adolph and Beulah Alice (Bates) B.; m. Janet Rose Neiman, Apr. 16, 1977. BA, Denison U., 1961; commerce diploma, U. Birmingham, Eng., 1962; MBA, U. Chgo., 1966. Instr. Dept. Econs. Denison U., Granville, Ohio, 1966-67; lectr. Dept. Econs. Ohio State U., Columbus, 1966-67; cons. Boston Cons. Group, Boston and London, 1967-69; mgr. mktg. services Graflex div. Singer Co., Rochester, N.Y., 1969-70; v.p. Gustave Brown and Assoc., Inc., Oak Brook, Ill., 1970-87; pres. Roger Brown and Assoc., Inc., Elburn, Ill., 1987—. Author: Study to Learn, 1965; contbr. articles on USAF programmed instrn., econs, corp. strategy. Mem. land use com. Campton Twp., Kane County, Ill., 1978-81. Served to 1st lt. USAF, 1962-65. Mem. Omicron Delta Epsilon, Rho Beta Chi, Omicron Delta Kappa. Republican. Methodist. Clubs: Upton Country (Jamaica), Runaway Bay Country (Jamaica). Home: 4n654 Anderson Rd Elburn IL 60119-0420 also: Tranquillity PO Box 224, Ocho Rios Jamaica Office: PO Box 420 Elburn IL 60119-0420

BROWN, ROY ELDRIDGE, lawyer; b. Urbana, Ohio, Oct. 27, 1967; s. Clarence J. and Joyce (Eldridge) B. BA, U. Va., 1989, MA, 1994; JD, Ohio State U., 1994. Bar: Ohio 1995. Law clk. to presiding judge Charles R. Richey U.S. Dist. Ct. D.C., 1994; assoc. Vorys, Sater, Seymour & Pease, Columbus, Ohio, 1995—; Offensive lineman N.Y. Fottball Giants, East Rutherford, n.J., 1990; bd. dirs. Brown Pub. Co., Cin. Mgr. camppaign Snyder for Senate, Hillsboro, Ohio, 1992. Recipient 2d Team AP All-Am. Offensive Guard award Associated Press, 1989, 1st Team All-ACC Offensive Guard award ACC Sportswriters & Assoc. Press, 1988, 89, 1st Team All-ACC Academic Offensive Guard award Atlantic Coast Conf., 1986, 88, 89. Office: Vorys Sater Seymour & Pease 52 E Gay St Columbus OH 43216-1008

BROWN, SAMUEL, JR., accountant; b. Hartford, Conn., Nov. 11, 1961; s. Samuel Brown Sr. and Sharon Elizabeth (Robinson) Haskins. BA, St. Leo Coll., 1983; MBA, Golden Gate U., 1985. Cert. fraud examiner. Enlisted USAF, 1979, advanced through grades to capt. Mem. Am. Soc. Mil. Comptrs., Nat. Assn. Black Accts., Masons, Kappa Alpha Psi. Baptist. Home: 414 Red Haw Rd Dayton OH 45405

BROWN, SANDRA LEE, educational consultant, watercolorist; b. Chgo., July 9, 1943; d. Arthur Willard and Erma Emily (Lange) Boettcher; m. Ronald Gregory Brown, June 21, 1983; 1 child, Jon Michael. BA in Art and Edn., N.E. Ill. U., 1966; postgrad., No. Ill. U. Cert. K-9 tchr., Ill. Travel agt. Weiss Travel Bur., Chgo., 1959-66; tchr. Chgo. Sch. System, 1966-68; tchr. Schaumburg (Ill.) Sch. Dist. 54, 1968-94, creator coord. peer mentoring program for 1st-yr. tchrs., 1992-96; cons./dir. Yardstick Ednl. Svcs., Monroe, Wis., 1994—; mem. adv. bd. Peer Coaching and Mentoring Network, Chgo. suburban region, 1992—; peer cons. Sch. Dist. 54, 1988-94. Exhibited in group shows Court House Gallery, Woodstock, Ill., Millburn (Ill.) Gallery, Gallerie Stefanie, Chgo. Campaign chmn. for mayoral candidate, Grayslake, Ill., 1989; campaign chmn. for trustee Citizens for Responsible Govt., Grayslake, 1991. Mem. Lakes Region Watercolor Guild, Delta Kappa Gamma (chmn. women in arts Gamma chpt. Ill. 1992-94, Alpha Mu chpt. 1995—). Home: PO Box 416 Monroe WI 53566 Office: Yardstick Ednl Svcs PO Box 416 Monroe WI 53566

BROWN, SHARON GAIL, company executive, consultant; b. Chgo., Dec. 25, 1941; d. Otto and Pauline (Lauer) Schumacher; B in Gen. Studies, Roosevelt U.; m. Robert B. Ringo, Aug. 2, 1984; 1 dau. by previous marriage, Susan Ann. Info. analyst Internat. Minerals & Chems., Northbrook, Ill., 1966-71, programmer analyst, 1971-74; programmer analyst Procon Internat. Inc. subs. UOP Inc., Des Plaines, Ill., 1974-76, systems analyst, 1976-77, project leader, 1977-78; mgr. adminstrv. services, 1978-82; spl. cons. to pres. IPS Internat., Ltd., 1982-83; spl. cons. to pres. CEI Supply Co. div. Sigma-Chapman, Inc., 1984-87, ptnr. and co-founder Brown, Ringo & Assocs., 1987—; data processing cons. Mem. Buffalo Grove (Ill.) Youth Commn., 1978-82; mem. adv. com. UOP Polit. Action Com., 1979-82; Mem. Rep. Senatorial Com. Inner Circle. Mem. Am. Mgmt. Assn., Chgo. Council on Fgn. Rels., Lake Forest-Lake Bluff Hist. Soc. Home: 90 Atteridge Rd Lake Forest IL 60045-1713

BROWN, SHERROD, congressman, former state official; b. Mansfield, Ohio, Nov. 9, 1952; s. Charles G. and Emily (Campbell) B.; children: Emily, Elizabeth. B.A., Yale U., 1974; M.A. in Edn., Ohio State U., 1979, M.A. in Pub. Adminstrn., 1981. Mem. Ohio Ho. of Reps., Mansfield, 1975-82; Sec. of State State of Ohio, Columbus, 1983-91; mem. 103rd-104th Congresses from 13th Ohio dist., Washington, 1993—; instr. Ohio State U., Mansfiled, 1978-79; com. mem. commerce, subcom. health and environment, subcom. commerce, trade and hazardous waste, internat. relations com., subcom. on Asia and the Pacific. Active India Caucus. Recipient Eagle Scout Am. 1966, Friend of Edn. award, 1978. Mem. Nat. Assn. Secs. State. Democrat. Lutheran. Office: US Ho of Reps 1019 Longworth HOB Washington DC 20515-3513

BROWN, SHIRLEY JEAN, funeral home director, owner; b. Ft. Scott, Kans., Mar. 14, 1947; d. Roy Otto and Betty Louise (Briggs) Bruce; m. Steven D. Brown, Jan. 28, 1967 (div. Mar. 1987); children: Scot D., Shane B. BS in Edn., Polit. Sci., Kans. U., 1976. Lic. funeral dir. Jr. H.S. tchr. Lawrence (Kans.) Pub. Schs., 1969-71; adult edn. tchr. Johnson County C.C., Overland Park, Kans., 1973-76; funeral dir. Bruce Funeral Home, Gardner, Kans., 1976—; mem. adv. bd. First Kans. Bank and Trust, Gardner, 1994, Johnson County Vocat. Sch., Olathe, Kans., 1980. Mem. sch. bd., officer Gardner Sch. Dist., 1976—; bd. dirs. Kans. Assn. Sch. Bds., Tokepka, 1980-88, S.W. Johnson County Econ., Gardner, 1994. Named Woman of Yr., Beta Sigma Phi, 1985, Kans. Funeral Dir. of Yr., S.W. Morticians, 1995. Mem. Nat. Funeral Dirs. Assn. (govtl. affairs com.), Kans. Funeral Dirs. Assn. (dist. 2 pres. 1983, dir. 1984-89, sec. to pres.-elect 1989-93, pres. 1994—), Gardner Cemetery Assn. (bd. dirs. 1990), Gardner Study Club (pres. 1974), Gardner C. of C. (pres. 1989, Citizen of Yr. 1994), DAR. Republican. Presbyterian. Office: Bruce Funeral Home Inc PO Box 192 106 S Center Gardner KS 66030

BROWN, STEVEN MICHAEL, engineering physicist, acoustician; b. N.Y.C., Dec. 3, 1944; s. Raphael and Olga (Sacharoff) B.; m. Carol Lynn Swanson, 1969; children: Alycia, Daniel. BA, Johns Hopkins U., 1966, MA, 1969, PhD, 1972. Physicist U.S. Naval Research Lab., Washington, 1966-70; rsch. assoc., instr. physics Johns Hopkins U., Balt., 1966-72; rsch. resident and sci. sec. Ctr. Theoretical Studies, U. Miami, Fla., 1972-73; dir. quality control AMSCO, Inc., Warren, Pa., 1973; sr. rsch. scientist Armstrong World Industries, Lancaster, Pa., 1973-86; prin. engr. Steelcase, Grand Rapids, Mich., 1986-94; sr. prin. engr., 1994—. Sci. sec., co-editor: Fundamental Interactions in Physics, 1973; contbr. articles to profl. jours. Active local sch. dist., 1979—. NSF fellow, 1966, NASA fellow, 1966-69. Fellow Acoustical Soc. Am. (tech. com. archtl. acoustics 1979—, TCAA fellowship subcom. 1985—, sec. 1987-89, chmn. 1989-92, mem. long range planning com. 1989-92); mem. IEEE, Am. Phys. Soc., ASTM (com. sec. 1980-85, vice chmn. 1986-92, Wallace Waterfall award, 1994), Inst. Noise Control Engring. (dir. 1995—), Am. Assn. Physics Tchrs., Am. Physical Soc., Phi Beta Kappa, Sigma Xi, Omicron Delta Kappa. Home: 599 Rookway Dr SE Grand Rapids MI 49546-9607 Office: Steelcase Inc Grand Rapids MI 49501

BROWN, STUART G., city administrator; b. Patterson, N.J., Mar. 21, 1963; s. Robert H. and Frida A. (Trajtman) B.; m. Nancy A. Zimmerman, June 24, 1994. BA in Polit. Sci., Rutgers Coll., 1985; MPA, U. Cin., 1993. Camp dir. Camp Tesah, Bridgewater, N.J., 1981-85; store mgr. U.S. Gen. Tools, Eatontown, N.J., 1985-86; tchg. asst. U. Cin., Cin., 1986-88; mgmt. analyst City of Cin., Cin., 1988-91, devel. officer, 1992—; coord. task force Convention Ctr. Expansion, Cin., 1994-95. Mem. adv. bd. Am. Jewish Com., Cin., 1993—, Hoxworth Blood Ctr., Cin., 1994—; vol. Childrens Hosp., Cin., 1994—. Mem. ASPA. Jewish. Home: 513 Elizabeth St Cincinnati OH 45203 Office: Dept Econ Devel City of Cin 805 Central Ave Ste 710 Cincinnati OH 45202

BROWN, THOMAS, history educator; b. N.Y.C., Mar. 8, 1954; s. William Robert and Helen (Dobrovich) B. BA, Bklyn. Coll., 1975; MA, Columbia

U., 1976, MPhil, 1978, PhD, 1981. Instr. history U. Ga., Athens, 1988-89; asst. to assoc. prof. history U. Detroit Mercy, 1989—. Author: Politics and Statesmanship, 1985, JFK: History of an Image, 1988; contbr. articles to profl. jours. Recipient Bancroft Dissertation award Columbia U., 1981; Travelto Collections grantee NEH, 1990; Peterson fellow Am. Antiquarian Soc., 1990. Mem. Am. Hist. Soc., Orgn. Am. Historians, Soc. Historians of the Early Republic. Office: Univ of Detroit Mercy 4001 W McNichols Rd Detroit MI 48219

BROWN, TIMOTHY CLARK, engineer; b. Tacoma, Feb. 4, 1948. Student, Ind. Inst. Tech., 1966-68, BSEE, 1972. Project engr. Motorola, Schaumburg, Ill., 1974-79; tech. staff Cin. (Ohio) Elec. Inc., 1979-83; sr. engr. Cin. (Ohio) Microwave, 1983-86; engring. mgr. Satcom Dept., Cin. (Ohio) Electronics, 1986-89; sr. engr., project mgr. R.L. Drake Co., Franklin, Ohio, 1989-96. Rep. precinct exec. Hamilton County Ctrl. Com., Cin., 1994-95, twp. Rep. chmn., exec. com., 1996—. With USN, 1968-72, Vietnam. Lutheran. Home: 11945 Deerhorn Dr Cincinnati OH 45240-1513

BROWN, TIMOTHY N., state legislator. BA, Ill. Wesleyan U.; MD, U. Ill. Physician Crawfordsville (Ind.) Family Care; rep. Dist. 41 Ind. Ho. of Reps., mem. fin. inst., ins., corp. and small bus. coms., pub. safety com., vice chmn. pub. health com.; asst. clin. prof. medicine Ind. U. Mem. Ind. State Med. Assn. Office: Crosby Heafey Roach & May Ste #2580 333 Bush St Ste 2580 San Francisco CA 94104-2806*

BROWN, TRACY ELIZABETH, elementary education educator; b. Kansas City, Mo., Nov. 7, 1966; d. Ronald James Brown and Elizabeth James (Hoffman) Dolton. AA, Stephens Coll., Columbia, Mo., 1987, BS, 1989; MEd, Lesley Coll., Cambridge, Mass., 1996. Elem. tchr. Columbia Pub. Schs., 1990—. Mem. Inernat. Reading Assn., Nat. Coun. Tchrs. Math., Mo. State Tchrs. Assn., Mo. Coun. Tchrs. Math. Office: ColumbiaPub Schs Parkade Elem 111 Parlade Blvd Columbia MO 65202

BROWN, VINCENT D., lawyer; b. Trenton, Nebr., Nov. 1, 1935; s. Joseph Gilbert and Alma Elmira (Schmidt) B.; m. Arlyss E. Spence Welch, Apr. 3, 1965 (div. 1991); children: Jeffrey M. Brown, Julie M. Brown. BS, U. Nebr., 1958, LLB, JD, 1960. Commd. lt. col. USAF, 1960; assoc. Healey Wilson & Barlow, Lincoln, 1960-61; asst. city atty. City of Lincoln, 1962-67; asst. clk. Nebr. Legislature, Lincoln, 1968-69, clk., 1969-78; exec. dir. Nebr. Petroleum Coun., Lincoln, 1978—; sec. First Sec. Nat. Bank, 1989-93. Pres. Nebraskaland Found., Lincoln, 1990-92, treas., 1992—; treas. Nebr. Hwy. Users Coalition, 1984—. Mem. Am. Soc. Assn. Execs. (cert. assn. exec.), Air Force Assn. Republican. Office: Nebr Petroleum Coun 301 S 13th St Lincoln NE 68508

BROWN, WESLEY ERNEST, federal judge; b. Hutchinson, Kans., June 22, 1907; s. Morrison H. H. and Julia (Wesley) B.; m. Mary A. Miller, Nov. 30, 1934 (dec.); children: Wesley Miller, Loy B. Wiley; m. Thadene N. Moore. Student, Kans. U., 1925-28; LLB, Kansas City Law Sch., 1933. Bar: Kans. 1933, Mo. 1933. Practiced in Hutchinson, 1933-58; county atty. Reno County, Kans., 1935-39; referee in bankruptcy U.S. Dist. Ct. Kans., 1958-62, judge, 1962-79, sr. judge, 1979—; apptd. Temporary Emergency Ct. of Appeals of U.S., 1980-93; dir. Nat. Assn. Referees in Bankruptcy, 1959-62; mem. bankruptcy divsn. Jud. Conf., 1963-70; mem. Jud. Conf., U.s., 1976-79. With USN, 1944-46. Mem. ABA, Kans. Bar Assn. (exec. council 1950-62, pres. 1964-65), Reno County Bar Assn. (pres. 1947), Wichita Bar Assn., S.W. Bar Kan., Delta Theta Phi. Office: US Dist Ct 423 US Courthouse 401 N Market St Wichita KS 67202-2000

BROWN, WILLIAM MORGAN, manufacturing executive; b. Clearwater, Fla., July 5, 1944; s. Hamlin L. and Mildred (Rogers) B.; m. Sandra Lou McPherson, Dec. 23, 1967; children: Ronald E., Craig A. BS in Indsl. Engring., Clemson U., 1966; MS in Indsl. and Sys. Engring., Ohio U., 1969. Registered profl. engr., Wis. Ops. mgr. Lennox Industries, Lima, Ohio, 1983-85; mgr. engring. Nicholson File Cooper Industries, Cullman, Ala., 1985-92; mgr. ops. Cooper Industries, Greenville, Miss., 1992; dir. mfg. engring. Sauder Woodworking, Archbold, Ohio, 1993—; chmn. Indsl. Engring. Adv. Bd. Clemson (S.C.) U., 1983—; mgmt. cons. Arrow Truline, Archbold, 1994—. Author: Changeovers - How to Reduce Them, 1995. Mem. Inst. Indsl. Engrs. (sr.), Am. Mgmt. Assn. Home: PO Box 193 Archbold OH 43502

BROWN, WYATT W., utilities executive; b. Woodsville, N.H., Feb. 5, 1947; s. Earl and Hilda (Gould) B.; m. Mary J. Sweeney, July 29, 1967; children: Jennifer, Rebecca. BSEE cum laude, U. N.H., 1971; MBA, Northeastern U., 1975. Various staff positions Pub. Svc. Co. N.H., Manchester, 1971-83, mgr. energy mgmt., 1983-87, mgr. system planning, 1987-93, mgr. conservatio, 1993-94; dir. demand side mgmt. Am. Electric Power, Columbus, Ohio, 1994, dir. key accounts, 1995, dir. market planning, 1996—. Mem. IEEE, Tau Beta Pi. Home: 21 Ridgewood Dr Bow NH 03304-3509 Office: Am Electric Power Svc Corp 1 Riverside Plz Columbus OH 43215

BROWN-CHAPPELL, BETTY L., social worker, educator; b. San Francisco, Nov. 25, 1946; d. Benjamin Franklin and Clara Lucille (Williams) Brown; m. Michael James Chappell, Oct. 1, 1975; children: Michael Jahi, Aisha Ebony. BA, U. Mich., 1969, MSW, 1971; PhD, U. Chgo., 1991. Social caseworker Detroit Health Dept., 1971; cmty. svc. asst. Commn. on Cmty. Rels., Detroit, 1971-73; adminstrv. asst. Sr. Citizens Dept., Detroit, 1973-77; asst. dir. Walter Reuther Sr. Citizens Ctrs., Detroit, 1977-79; vis. instr., rsch. assoc. U. Ill. Chgo., 1979-80; coord. acad. adv., assoc. prof. Northeastern Ill. U., Chgo., 1980-84; asst. dean U. Chgo., 1984-89; field coord. Ill. State U., Normal, 1990-92; asst. prof. U. Mich., Ann Arbor, 1992—; mgmt. cons. United Tenants Speak, Detroit, 1994; ednl. cons. C.O.T.S., Detroit, 1994. Contbr. articles to profl. jours. Fellow U. Mich., 1991-92, Ill. Consortium on Edn. Opportunity, 1989-90, Delta Sigma Theta, 1988, Ctr. Urban Rsch. and Policy Studies, 1987; recipient Citation Acad. All-Am., 1988, Detroit Bd. Edn., 1975, Cert. Appreciation City Detroit Mayor's Office and Sr. Citizens Dept., 1976, Resolution of Merit Mich. State Rep., Jackie Vaughn, 1975. Mem. Nat. Assn. Black Social Workers (steering com. 1975-79, v.p. Detroit chpt. 1974-75). Office: Univ Mich 1065 Frieze Bldg Ann Arbor MI 48109-1285

BROWNE, ALDIS JEROME, JR., real estate broker; b. Chgo., Mar. 21, 1912; s. Aldis J. and Elizabeth (Cunningham) B.; m. Bertha Erminger, Oct. 22, 1938; children: Aldis J. III, Howell E., John Kenneth. BA, Yale U., 1935. V.p., dir. Browne & Storch Inc., and predecessors, Chgo., 1935-81, dir., 1961-81; cons. Quinlan & Tyson, Evanston, Ill., 1981-84; sr. real estate broker L.J. Sheridan Co., 1985—. Bd. dirs. English Speaking Union, Civic Fedn., Mil. Order World Wars; chmn. Bldg. Rev. Bd. Lake Forest; vestryman, St. James Episcopalian Ch., 1947-60; trustee, Old People's Home, Chgo.; bd. dirs. Key West Art and Hist. Soc. Capt. USNR. Mem. Chgo. (dir.), Ill., N. Side Chgo. real estate bds., Nat. Realtors Assn., Order Founders and Patriots (gov. Ill. chpt.), Soc. Colonial Wars (gov. Ill. chpt.), Order St. Lazarus, Mil. Order World Wars (past comdr. Chgo. br.), Mil. Order Loyal Legion, Chgo. Art Inst. (governing life), Navy League (past dir.). Republican. Clubs: Chgo., Tavern, Army Navy Washington, Masons.

BROWNE, DALLAS, anthropology educator; b. Chgo., Oct. 9, 1944; s. William Eldridge and Ann (Sherman) B.; m. Imelda M. Siedentopf, Apr. 8, 1972; children—Eldridge, La Salle, Hubert, William. B.A., Northeastern U., 1966; M.A., U. Ill., 1971, Ph.D., 1983. Asst. prof. Wabash Coll., Crawfordsville, Ind., 1981-82, Colby Coll., Waterville, Maine, 1982-86, York Coll., Jamaica, N.Y., 1986—; cons. evaluation Kenya Govt., 1975; UNICEF Ford Found. fellow, 1971, fellow Inst. Study Racism, 1980, Ctr. Polit. Studies and Inst. Social Research, 1984. Mem. Am. Anthropol. Assn., Soc. Urban Anthropology, Assn. Black Anthropologists (rep. east coast 1983—), New Eng. Black Studies (sec. 1984—). Avocation: building models of famous inventions. Office: Dept Anthropology S Ill U Edwardsville Edwardsville IL 62026

BROWNFIELD, WILLIAM HARRY, real estate appraiser; b. Mason City, Ill., Sept. 1, 1926; s. Jed Hayes and Anna Lena (Thompson) B.; m. Margaret Ann Morris, Mar. 27, 1948 (dec. May 1995); children: Gary Lee, Larry Curtis, Michael Kevin, Gregory Bryant, William Mark. Student, Bradley U., Peoria, Ill., Ill. Ctrl. Coll. Cert. real estate appraiser. Decorator Bergners, Peoria, 1948-52; interior decorator Fay Fabrics, Peoria, 1952-54; mgr. drapery Block & Kuhl Co., Peoria, 1954-58; merchandise mgr. Ackemann's, Elgin, Ill., 1958-68, K-Mart, Peoria, 1968-71; v.p. Ill. Ctrl. Realty, East Peoria, 1971-88; sales mgr. Brownfield Home Bldrs., East Peoria, 1971-88; real estate appraiser East Peoria, 1975—; chauffeur Riverview Retirement, East Peoria, 1988—. Home and Office: 1110 Massachusetts Ave Washington IL 61571

BROWNSON, E. RAMONA LIDSTONE BRADY, secretary; b. Big Sandy, Mont., May 13, 1930; d. Elmer Gordon and Ethel Mercy (Kuhl) Lidstone; m. William Chauvin Brady, Oct. 10, 1949 (div. 1976); children: William Kim Brady, Colleen Kay Brady, Scott Patrick C. Brady; m. Elwyn James Brownson, Nov. 14, 1980. AS with dept. distinction, No. Mont. Coll., 1976, BA with dept. distinction, 1977. Owner/operator Pep's Bar & Bowling Lanes, Big Sandy, 1954-76; guidance sec./registrar Havre (Mont.) High Sch., 1976-77; sec. to asst. supt. Havre Pub. Schs., 1977-78; sec./bookkeeper Bear Paw Devel. Corp., Havre, 1978-79; new accts./vault cash teller Great Am. Savings Bank, Havre, 1979-88; sec. to ombudsman U. Nebr., Lincoln, 1989-92, receptionist, sec. dept. human resources, 1992—. Active Dems. Hill County, Mont., 1977-88, Nebr., 1988—; polit. precinct committeewoman Hill County, Mont., 1980-88; life mem. P.E.I. Hist. Soc., Can., Lidstone Soc., Plymouth, Eng.; charter mem. Big Sandy, Mont. Hist. Soc. Recipient Toastmasters' Internat. Speechcraft cert., 1979; No. Mont. Coll. scholar, 1949-50, 75-76. Mem. AAUW (internat. affairs chair 1986-88, booksale co-chair 1986), AARP, Nat. Assn. Edn. Office Pers., Cert. Ednl. Office Employee (cert. 1993), Nebr. Ednl. Office Pers., U. Nebr. Office Pers. (membership chair 1991-92), No. Mont. Coll. Alumni, Lincoln Lancaster County Geneal. Soc., Assinboine Geneal. Soc. (charter), Irish/Scotch Soc., Eagles Aux. Lodge, VFW Aux., Am. Legion Aux., The Westerners. Home: 2205 Southwood Pl Lincoln NE 68512-1375 Office: U Nebr Dept Human Resources 407 Administrn Bldg Lincoln NE 68588-0438

BROWNSTEIN, GLORIA, physical therapist; b. N.Y.C., June 2, 1933; d. Samuel Ahren and Ada Rachael Applebaum; m. Byron Brownstein, Nov. 20, 1966 (div. Dec. 1970). BS, U. Pa., 1954; diploma, Maryville Coll., St. Louis, 1972. RN, Mo.; cert. phys. therapist, Mo. Cons. long term care facilities, St. Louis, 1960-70, 75-85; pres. Profl. Therapy Providers, St. Louis, 1985—. Mem. Toastmasters. Home: 955 N Spoedl Saint Louis MO 63146

BROYHILL, ROY FRANKLIN, manufacturing executive; b. Sioux City, Iowa, June 20, 1919; s. George Franklin and Effie (Motes) B.; BBA, U. Nebr., 1940; m. Arline W. Stewart, Jan. 30, 1943; children: Lynn Diann (dec.), Craig G., Kent Bryan, Bryce Alan. Trainee mgr. Montgomery Ward Co., 1940; semi-sr. acct. L. H. Keightley, 1941-42; chief accountant Army Exchange Service, Sioux City, 1942-46; chmn. Broyhill Co., 1946-88, dir., 1988—; pres., dir. Star Printing & Pub. Co., South Sioux City, 1949-94, ret. 1994, chmn., bd. dir., 1994—; pres. Broyhill Corp., 1953-92, dir. 1992—, chmn., 1953—; v.p. Broyhill Mfg. Co., 1978-87, pres., 1953-92, dir., 1992—; pres., chmn. bd. Broyhill Inc.; ret. dir. 1st Nat. Bank, Sioux City. Mem. U.S.A. Exec. Res.; past mem. Nebr. dist. adv. council SBA. Mayor of Dakota City, 1951-53; mem. Nebr. Republican Central Com., 1954-56. Past mem. local sch. bd. Trustee U. Nebr. Found. Served with AUS, 1940-41. Mem. Farm Equipment Mfrs. Assn. (past dir., pres. 1971-72), Atokad Racing Assn. (past dir.), N.A.M., U.S., South Sioux City chambers commerce, Nebr. C. of C. (dir. 1972-73), Alumni Assn. U. Nebr. (past dir.), Trustee Found. U. Nebr., Am. Legion (life), Beta Theta Pi, Alpha Kappa Psi. Presbyn. (elder). Clubs: U. Nebr. Chancellor's. Lodges: Masons (Shrine). Home: 1610 Broadway Box 454 Dakota City NE 68731 also: 2185 Ibis Isle Rd # 12 Palm Beach FL 33480-5355 also: 16746 Inner Ln Box 9318 Spirit Lake IA 51360 Office: Broyhill Co N Market Sq Dakota City NE 68731

BROYLES, GLADYS BENITES, psychologist, hypnotherapist, counselor; b. Lima, Peru, June 3, 1959; came to U.S., 1982; d. Ernesto and Gladys Cayetana (Herrera) Benites; m. Spencer Barry Broyles, Apr. 21, 1984. Grad., Mater Admirabilis School, Lima, 1975; degree in teaching English, Inst. Cultural Peruano N.Am., Lima, 1975; student, U. Catholica del Peru, Lima, 1974-77, 76-78, Inst. Italiano de Cultura, Lima, 1976-77; B Gen. Psychology, Inca Garcilaso de La Vega U., Lima, 1982. QMRP Mental Health Profl. Audiologist, psychologist, translator Centro Peruano de Audicion y Lenguaje, Monterrico Lima, Peru, 1983-84; counselor Cen. Inst. for Deaf, St. Louis, 1984; substitute tchr. Archdioceses of St. Louis Cath. Schs., 1984-85; reservations and spl. svcs. sec., front desk rep. Rodeway Inn, St. Louis, 1985; front desk rep. Northwest Inn, St. Louis, 1985; counselor for mentally retarded and developmentally delayed Magdala Found., St. Louis, 1985-86; qualified mental retardation profl. Bellefontaine Habilitation Ctr., Dept. Mental Health, St. Louis, 1986-88; behavior coach Judevine Ctr. for Autism, St. Louis, 1988—, program mgr., 1991—; clin. caseworker asst. II St. Louis Mental Health Ctr., Dept. Mental Health, 1991; owner The Peruvian Image; founder Gladys Broyles Assn. Homes for Mentally Ill Individuals; instr. CPR and 1sat aid, ARC; pers. asst. British Consulate Ofcl. in Lima, Peru, 1976; reservations mgr. Paracas Hotel, Lima, 1975; organizer Hosp. Mental Bravo Chico, Lima, 1979-80; founder Centro Medico Lince, Lima, 1979-82, Centro Medico Pucallpa, Peru, 1978-82, Centro Peruano Audicion y Lenguaje, Lima, 1983-84. Mem. Alliance Mentally Ill, PACER, IACT. Roman Catholic. Home: 9835 Portage Dr Saint Louis MO 63136-5313 Office: Judevine Ctr for Autism 5161 Washington Pl Saint Louis MO 63108-1114

BROZEK, JEFFREY MICHAEL, research engineer; b. Summit, N.J., Mar. 29, 1969; s. Robert John and Charlotte (Perkins) B.; m. Susan Carol Seyfert, June 6, 1992. BS in elec. engring., Purdue U., 1991; MS, U. Wis., 1993. Engring. aide Nippes Profl. Assocs., Holmdel, N.J., 1989, engring. tech., 1990; applications engr. Caterpillar, Inc., Lafayette, Ind., 1991-92; rsch. engr. Milw. Electric Tool Corp., Brookfield, 1993—. Mem. IEEE-Power Engring. Soc., IEEE-Power Electronics Soc., IEEE-Industry Applications Soc., IEEE-Indsl. Electrics Soc., Christian Coalition. Republican. Office: Milw Electric Tool Corp 13135 West Lisbon Rd Brookfield WI 53005

BRUBAKER, EDWIN SILVANUS, local government consultant; b. Eaton, Ohio, Jan. 9, 1934; s. Silvanus and Lillian (Ozias) B.; m. Patricia L. Cooper, June 14, 1958 (dec. Oct. 24, 1988); children: Charles, Jayne Brubaker Black, Jeffrey; m. Shirley Phares, Jan. 19, 1996. MPA, U. Dayton, 1978. Farmer Brubaker Farms, Eaton, 1958-87; county commr. Preble County, Eaton, 1969-84; cons. PAR, Inc., Cin., 1985-87; asst. prof. cmty. devel. and local govt. Ohio State U., Columbus, 1987-92; cons. state and local govt. Brubaker Consulting, Eaton, 1992—; mem. Cmty. Action Agy., Dayton Area, 1992—; mem. Housing Task Force, Eaton, 1994—; cons. Cmty. Improvement Corp., Eaton, 1994-95, bd. dirs. 1994—. Author: (bulletin) Local Govt. Structure and Fin., 1992; consulting author: County Commissioners' Association of Ohio Handbook, 1994; author: (booklet) Preble County Profile, 1995. Mem. Rep. Ctrl. Com., Eaton, 1991—; chmn. Eaton Planning Bd., 1992-95, Health Dept. Levy, Eaton, 1994, Miami Valley Regional Planning, Dayton, 1972, 73, 74. Served to cpl. U.S. Army, 1955--57. Mem. Nat. Assn. Regional Couns. (bd. dirs. 1975-78), Eaton C. of C. (chmn. 1994), Eaton-Preble County C. of C. (exec. dir. 1996—), Jaycees (Eaton pres. 1966-67, Disting. Svc. award 1967), Rotary (Eaton pres. 1977), Eaton Country Club, Preble County Farm Bur., Victoria Theatre Assn. Mem. United Ch. of Christ. Home and Office: 211 S Beech St # 201 Eaton OH 45320

BRUBAKER, JAMES CLARK, construction executive; b. Normal, Ill., Mar. 22, 1947; s. Walter Clark and Vernie Helen (Rubenaker) B.; m. Celeste Renee Rohling, Jan. 16, 1971; children: Elizabeth, Andrew. BS in Communications, U. Ill., 1969. Sales mgr. Proctor & Gamble, Chgo., 1969-71, Johnson & Johnson, St. Louis, 1971-74; v.p. sales Omega Sports, St. Louis, 1976-79; exec. v.p. Thomas Constrn., St. Louis, 1982-89; chief exec. officer Permastone, Inc., St. Louis, 1987-90; pres. Encore Enterprises, Inc., St. Louis, 1987—; bd. dirs. Constrn. Industry Arbitration and Mediation. Dir. Grace Ch. of Mid-Mo., Columbia, 1986-89; bd. dirs. Citadel Christian Sch., 1992—. Mem. Profl. Remodeler's Assn. (bd. dirs. 1988-93). Republican. Fundamentalist. Home: 3411 Erman Dr Bridgeton MO 63044-3073 Office: Encore Enterprises Inc 2222 Schuetz Rd Ste 212 Saint Louis MO 63146-3422

BRUCE, PETER WAYNE, lawyer, insurance company executive; b. Rome, N.Y., July 12, 1945; s. G. Wayne and Helen A. (Hibling) B.; m. Joan M. McCabe, Sept. 20, 1969; children: Allison, Steven. B.A., U. Wis., 1967; J.D., U. Chgo., 1970; postgrad., Harvard Bus. Sch., 1986. Bar: Wis. 1970. Atty. Northwestern Mut. Life Ins. Co., Milw., 1970-74, asst. gen. counsel, 1974-80, gen. counsel, sec., 1980—; v.p. Northwestern Mut. Life Ins. Co., 1983-87, sr. v.p., gen. counsel, sec., 1987-90, sr. v.p. ins. ops., 1990-95; exec. v.p. Ins. Ops. & Adminstrn., chief compliance officer, 1995—; past mem., com. corp. law depts. ABA. Former chmn. Alverno Coll., Curative Rehab. Ctr., former mem. Shorewood Civic Improvement Found.; bd. dirs. Alverno Coll. Badger Meter Found., St. Mary's Hill Hosp., Curative Found. (chair); mem. Village of Shorewood (Wis.); mem. Village Shorewood Cmty. Devel. Assn.; former mem. Planning and Devel. Commn. Mem. Wis. Bar Assn., Milw. Bar Assn., Am. Law Inst. Office: Northwestern Mut Life Ins Co 720 E Wisconsin Ave Milwaukee WI 53202-4703

BRUCE, WILLA MARIE, education educator; b. Huntington, W.Va., Aug. 22, 1938; d. Frank Hance and Inez Marie (Lunsford) Smallwood; m. Robert B. Bruce, July 31, 1960 (dec. Oct. 1978); children: Joseph, Robert, George; m. James Walton Blackburn, Aug. 1, 1985. BA, Marshall U., 1960; MA, W. Va. Coll. Grad. Studies, 1978, MPA, 1981; PhD, Va. Poly Inst. & State U., 1985. Social worker W.Va. Dept. Welfare, Welch, 1968-71; social svc. supr. W.Va. Dept. Welfare, Charleston, 1971-73; from asst. dir. social svc. to pub. safety coord. Charleston (W.Va.) Housing Authority, 1973-81; from instr. to dir. upward bound talent search Va. Poly Inst. & State U., Blacksburg, 1981-85; asst. prof. U. Nebr., Omaha, 1985-90, assoc. prof., 1990-93, prof., 1993—; cons. and presenter in field. Author: Problem Employee Management, 1990; co-author: Managing Dual Career Couples, 1991, Balancing Job Satisfaction and Performance, 1992; co-editor Mediating Environmental Conflicts: Theory and Practice, 1995; mem. editl. bd. Pub. Voices, Pub. Adminstrn. Rev.; book review editor Pub. Integrity Ann. U. Nebr. fellow. Fellow Ctr. for Gt. Plains Studies: mem. Am. Soc. for Pub. Adminstrn. (nat. chair sect. for women, 1991-92, nat. chair com. on ethics, 1992-93, midwest rep. to nat. coun. 1991-94, nat. chair task force on sexual harrassment), Internat. Inst. Mcpl. Clks. (ednl. com. 1991-92). Democrat. Episc. Office: Univ Nebr Dept Pub Adminstrn Annex # 27 Omaha NE 68182

BRUCKEN, LOIS GILBERT, volunteer; b. Parkersburg, W.Va., July 7, 1936; d. Rowland and Lula (Herdman) Gilbert; m. Robert Matthew Brucken, June 30, 1960; children: Nancy, Elizabeth, Rowland, Gilbert. BA, Marietta Coll., 1958. Bd. trustees Cleve. Internat. Program, 1978-84; pres. Shaker Heights (Ohio) PTA Coun., 1981-82; bds. trustees Cleve. Coun. on World Affairs, 1982-84; co-chmn. Shaker Heights Sch. Levy, 1983; pres. Shaker Heights Libr. Bd. Trustees, 1985-87, Plymouth Ch. Shaker Heights, 1988-90; v.p. Cleve. Bd. Edn. Adult Adv. Com., 1989-90; trustee Cleve. Soc. for the Blind, 1979—, St. Luke's Hosp., Cleve., 1995—; v.p. bd. trustees Shaker Family Ctr., 1993—. Mem. Alpha Psi Omega, Pi Kappa Delta. Republican. Home: 18210 Fernway Rd Shaker Heights OH 44122-3434

BRUCKEN, NANCY ELIZABETH, systems analyst; b. Cleve., Aug. 8, 1961; d. Robert Matthew and Lois Rowland (Gilbert) B. BS, Marietta Coll., 1983; MS, U. Mich., 1985. Statistician Mich. Bell, Detroit, 1985-89; programmer/analyst Mich. Bell, Southfield, 1989-91; systems analyst Warner-Lambert Co., Ann Arbor, Mich., 1991-93, sr. systems analyst, 1993—. Co-chairperson Mich. Bell SAS Users Group, Southfield, 1987-91. Presdl. Honor scholar Marietta Coll., 1979-83, Ohio Acad. scholar State of Ohio, 1979-83; named Outstanding Female Athlete, Corp. Sports Battle, Detroit, 1990. Mem. Am. Statis. Assn., Assn. for Computing Machinery, Mich. SAS Users Group. Office: Parke Davis Pharm Rsch Div 2800 Plymouth Rd Ann Arbor MI 48105-2430

BRUCKNER, JOHN JOSEPH, patent lawyer, materials engineer; b. Bronxville, N.Y., Jan. 13, 1960; s. John H. and Judith B. (Egan) B. AA, Union County Coll., 1986; BS, Rutgers U., 1989; postgrad., U. Va., 1989-90; JD, George Mason U., 1994; MS, U. Wis., 1996; postgrad., Argonne Nat. Lab., 1995—. Student technician Ctr. for Ceramic Rsch., Piscataway, N.J., 1988-89; patent examiner U.S. Patent and Trademark Office, Arlington, Va., 1989-92; patent agt. Wegner, Cantor, Mueller & Player, Washington, 1992-94; patent atty. Niles & Niles, Milw., 1994—. Mem. Materials Rsch. Soc., Am. Ceramic Soc., Am. Intellectual Property Law Assn.

BRUEGGEMAN, TIMOTHY ALAN, investment broker; b. Alton, Ill., Mar. 10, 1968; m. Catherine M. Hentrich, Nov. 6, 1993. BA, So. Ill. State U., 1991. Sales rep. Bus. Products, St. Louis, 1991-93; investment broker A.G. Edwards & Sons Inc., Alton, 1993—. Mem. East End Bus. Assn., Jaycees. Republican. Roman Catholic. Home: 3108 Edwards St Alton IL 62002-4058 Office: A G Edwards & Sons Inc 215 E Center Dr Alton IL 62002-5931

BRUEGMANN, ROBERT, architectural historian, educator; b. Chgo., May 21, 1948; s. Karl A. and Margaret (Cartwright) B. BA, Principia Coll., Elsah, Ill., 1970; PhD, U. Pa., 1976. Historian Hist. Am. Bldgs. Survey, Nat. Park Svc., various locations, 1973-78; lectr. Phila. C.C., 1975-76, Phila. Coll. Art, 1976-77; asst. prof. archtl. history U. Ill. at Chgo., 1977-83, assoc. prof., 1983-93; prof., 1993—. Author: Benicia: Portrait of an Early California Town, 1980, Holabird & Root: An Illustrated Catalog of Works, 1991 (Wittenborn award 1991); contbr. articles to profl. jours. Fellow Inst. of Humanities at U. Ill., Chgo., 1992, Temple Hoyne Buell Ctr., Columbia U., 1989, Graham Found., Chgo., 1985, Nat. Endowment for Humanities, 1983-84. Mem. Soc. Archtl. Historians, Coll. Art Assn., Chgo. Archtl. Found., Chgo. Archtl. Club (bd. dirs. 1989-92). Home: 1815 N Orchard St # 7 Chicago IL 60614-5136 Office: U Ill Art History Dept M/C 201 935 W Harrison Chicago IL 60607

BRUGAM, RICHARD BLAIR, biology educator; b. Phila., Dec. 23, 1946; s. Richard Jerrom and Margaret Suzanne (Blair) B.; m. Ella Suzanne Oren, Aug. 1, 1970; children: Amy Susann, Matthew Richard. BA in Biology, Lehigh U., 1968; M of Philosophy, Yale U., 1974, PhD in Biology, 1975. Rsch. assoc. Limnol. Rsch. Ctr. U. Minn., Mpls., 1975-78; asst. prof. So. Ill. U., Edwardsville, 1978-84, assoc. prof., 1984-90, prof., 1990—; vis. scholar U. Wash., Seattle, 1984-85. Contbr. articles to Ecology, Archiv fur Hydrobiologie. Sgt. U.S. Army, 1969-72. Recipient J. Willard Gibbs prize Yale U., 1968; grad. fellowship NSF, 1968. Mem. AAAS, Ecol. Soc. Am., Am. Soc. Limnology and Oceanography, Ill. Acad. Scis., Phi Beta Kappa, Sigma Xi (grant 1973). Home: 1400 Lantz Ct Edwardsville IL 62025-3901 Office: So Ill U PO Box 1651 Edwardsville IL 62026-1594

BRUGLER, ALAN ROBERT, economic analyst; b. Sharon, Pa., Feb. 12, 1954; s. Robert Edward and Ruth Elinor (Weller) B.; m. Nancy Ann Lesiecki, June 14, 1980; children: Alexandra Marie, Zachary Alan. BS with honors, MS, Ohio State U., 1976. Orgn. dir. Richland/Crawford/Morrow Co. Farm Burs., Mansfield, Ohio, 1976-78; market analyst Ohio Farm Bur., Columbus, 1978-83; dir. market info. svcs. Ohio Farm Bur. Fedn., Columbus, 1983-92; sr. analyst Data Transmission Network, Omaha, 1992—; v.p. 1st Charter Credit Union, Delaware, Ohio, 1991-92; exec. sec. Ohio Corn Growers Assn., Columbus, 1978-81; treas., bd. dirs. LDAB Software Inc., Columbus, 1984-91. Editor newsletters Agri-Map, 1978-86, Townshead Tidings, 1980-83; designer computer software Option Master, 1984. Contbg. economist econ. adv. coun. Ohio Office Budget and Mgmt., 1983-92; pres. FH/PM Homeowners Assn., 1993-94; active Sanitary and Improvement Dist. 291 Bd., 1994—, chmn., 1995-97. Recipient Young Profl. Achievement award Ohio State U., 1988. Mem. Ohio State U. Alumni Assn. (life), Varsity O Assn., Alpha Zeta (v.p., pres. alumni Columbus 1983-87), Gamma Sigma Delta. Republican. Home: 15711 Howard St Omaha NE 68118-2107 Office: Data Transmission Network 9110 W Dodge Rd Omaha NE 68114-3306

BRULE, THOMAS RAYMOND, franchise executive, lawyer; b. Rochester, N.Y., Feb. 18, 1954; s. Raymond and Barbara (Ann) B.; m. Sonia Lynn Doll, Feb. 12, 1983; children: Adam Thomas, Ryan Daniel, Justin Robert. BS, Ind. U., Pa., 1976; MBA, U. Ky., 1977; JD, U. Louisville, 1980. Bar: Ky., 1980, U.S. Dist. Ct. (we. dist.) Ky., 1980, U.S. Dist. Ct. (cen. dist.) Ill., 1983, U.S. Dist. Ct. (no. dist.) Ohio 1993, U.S. Ct. Appeals (6th cir.) 1985. Pvt. practice Louisville, 1980-83; franchise counsel Kentucky Fried Chicken, Louisville, 1983-85, dir. franchise svcs., 1985-87, dir. franchise adminstrn., 1987-89, sr. dir. franchise adminstrn., 1989-90, sr. dir. franchise devel., 1990-92; sr. v.p., gen. counsel Physicians Weight Loss Ctr. of Am., Diet Ctr. Worldwide Inc., Akron, 1992—; lectr. U. Louisville, 1980-89. Trustee Ind. U., Pa., 1975-76. Mem. ABA, Ky. Bar Assn., Ohio State Bar Assn. Republican. Home: 80 Berkshire Park Dr Chagrin Falls OH

44022-3500 Office: Diet Ctr Worldwide 395 Springside Dr Akron OH 44333-4512

BRULLO, ROBERT ANGELO, chemical company executive; b. Chgo., Aug. 20, 1948; s. Ralph V. and Vicky M. (Santapa) B.; m. Kathleen M. Peltier, Feb. 27, 1993; children: Jennifer, Amy, Dawn. BSChemE, Ill. Inst. Tech., 1970; MBA, U. St. Thomas, 1976. Sr. analyst corp. mktg. 3M Co., St. Paul, 1977-78, supr. market devel. comml. chems. div., 1978-80; sr. account rep. comml. chems. div. 3M Co., Detroit, 1980-82; mgr. market devel. comml. chems. div. 3M Co., St. Paul, 1982-86, global mktg. mgr. indsl. chem. products div., 1986-88, global bus. mgr. indsl. chem. products div., 1988-92, dept. gen. mgr. specialty fluoropolymers dept., 1993-96; pres. dyneon LLC 3M/Hoechst JV, 1996—. Patentee in field. Mem. Rubber Mfrs. Assn., Am. Chem. Soc. (bd. dirs. rubber div. area 1986-88), Twin Cities Rubber Group (sec. 1979-80), Soc. Plastics Industry (fluoropolymers div.). Lutheran. Home: 1387 Belmont Dr Woodbury MN 55125-2381 Office: 3M Co 3M Ctr Bldg 220-10E-10 Saint Paul MN 55144

BRULOTTE, RICHARD, librarian; b. Middleboro, Mass., Feb. 4, 1949; s. Ernest and Cecile Marianne (Beaulieu) B.; m. Carol Joyce Everett, Feb. 17, 1973; children: Jennifer Anne, Sarah Lynne, Carrie Elizabeth, Phillip Douglas. BA in History, Bridgewater State Coll., 1971; MEd, Boston Coll., 1975. Cert. tchr., Ohio, Mass., N.Y. 2nd libr. Apponequet Regional Jr./Sr. H.S., Lakeville, Mass., 1971-72; media specialist George R. Austin Mid. Sch., Lakeville, 1972-76; dir. Learning Materials Ctr. Rutherford B. Hayes H.S., Delaware, Ohio, 1976—; trustee Lakeville Pub. Libr., 1971-75. Mem. Ohio Ednl. Libr. Media Assn. Home: 292 West Fountain Ave Delaware OH 43015 Office: Rutherford B Hayes H S 289 Euclid Ave Delaware OH 43015

BRUMAGHIM, PAUL, small business owner; b. Gloversville, N.Y., June 26, 1926; s. William and Lydia (Slack) B.; children: Sheryl A. Petersen, Todd. Grad., Real Estate Inst., Peoria, Ill. Staff. sgt. USAF, U.S.A., 1944-52; with acctg. sales Nat. Cash Register Co., Danville, Ill., 1952-57; v.p. sales mgr. Danville Community Homes, 1957-62; real estate sales Montgomery Realty Co., Danville, 1962-64; owner-realtor ins. appraiser Brumaghim Real Estate, Danville, 1964—. Pres. bd. dirs. YMCA, Danville, 1968; chmn. bd. Vermillion County Red Cross, Danville, 1970-91. Recipient House Resolution 885 award House of Rep., Springfield, Ill., 1980, Hall of Fame award ARC, Shelter Ins. Co., Danville, 1987. Mem. NAREA (pres. ctrl. Ill. divsn. 1995-96), Danville Area Bd. Realtors (pres. 1978, 81, Realtor Yr. 198)), Ill. State Bd. Realtors (dist. v.p., Danville Life Underwriters pres. 1987—), Danville Archtl. Control Bd., First Ill. Credit Union (bd. dirs.), Am. Legion, Elks, Kiwanis (pres. 1967, lt. gov. 1970). Republican. Office: Brumaghim Real Estate 408 Sheridan PO Box 753 Danville IL 61834-0753

BRUMBACK, CHARLES TIEDTKE, retired newpaper executive; b. Toledo, Sept. 27, 1928; s. John Sanford and Frances Hannah (Tiedtke) B.; m. Mary Louise Howe, July 7, 1951; children: Charles Tiedtke Jr., Anne Meyer, Wesley W., Ellen Allen. BA in Econs., Princeton U., 1950; postgrad., U. Toledo, 1953-54. CPA, Ohio, Fla. With Arthur Young & Co., CPAs, 1950-57; bus. mgr., v.p., treas., pres., CEO Sentinel Star Co. subs. Tribune Co., Orlando, Fla., 1957-81; pres., CEO Chgo. Tribune subs. Tribune Co., 1981-88, pres., COO, 1988-90; CEO Tribune Co., 1990-95; chmn. Chgo. Tribune subs. Tribune Co., 1993-95; also bd. dirs. Tribune Co., Chgo.; bd. dirs. Avid Technology, Inc.; chmn., bd. dirs. Robert R. McCormick Tribune Found. Life trustee Northwestern U.; trustee Culver Ednl. Found., Chgo. Symphony Orch., Chgo. Hist. Soc., Northwestern Meml. Hosp., chmn., 1987-90; chmn. Northwestern Healthcare Network, 1994—. 1st lt. U.S. Army, 1951-53. Decorated Bronze star. Mem. AICPA, Fla. Press Assn. (treas. 1969-76, pres. 1980, bd. dirs.), Am. Newspaper Pubs. Assn. (bd. dirs., treas. 1991-92), Newspaper Assn. Am. (bd. dirs., sec., 1992-93, vice chmn. 1993-94, chmn. 1994-95), Comml. Club Chgo., Chgo. Club, Tavern Club. Home: 1500 N Lake Shore Dr Chicago IL 60610-1624 Office: Tribune Co 435 N Michigan Ave Chicago IL 60611-4001

BRUMFIELD, STEVEN JACK, business executive; b. Royal Oak, Mich., June 18, 1951; m. Jane E.; children: Sara, Betsy, Katie, Natalie. BS, Ctrl. Mich. U., 1976. Plant mgr. Plasti-Fiber, Ithaca, Mich., 1976-79, Brown City, Mich., 1979-85; v.p., gen. mgr. Elicon, Madison Hts., Mich., 1985-95; pres. Sidler Inc., Madison Hts., Mich., 1995—. Author: (computer software) Management Consulting. Past pres. Rotary, Brown City. Mem. Automotive Soc. Quality Engring. Office: Sidler Inc 1155 E Whitcomb Ave Madison Heights MI 48071-1414

BRUMMEL, MARK JOSEPH, magazine editor; b. Chgo., Oct. 28, 1933; s. Anthony William and Mary (Helmreich) B. BA, Cath. U. Am., 1956, STL, 1961, MSLS, 1964. Joined Order of Claretians, Roman Cath. Ch., 1952; ordained priest Order of Caretians, Roman Cath. Ch., 1960; librarian, tchr. St. Jude Sem., Momence, Ill., 1961-70; asso. editor U.S. Cath. mag., Chgo., 1971-72; editor U.S. Cath. Mag., 1970—; dir. St. Jude League, Chgo., 1970—; bd. dirs. Eastern Province Claretians, 8th Day Ctr., Ill. Cath. Conf.; pres., bd. dirs. Claretian Med. Ctr., 1980-95. Editor Today mag., 1970-71; contbr. article to publ. Chmn. bd. Eighth Day Ctr. for Justice, Chgo., 1988-92, Claretian Med. Ctr., Chgo., 1979-95; bd. dirs. Assn. of Chgo. Priests, 1994-96; mem. Ill. Cath. Conf., 1993-96. Mem. Cath. Press Assn. (v.p. 1985-87, St. Francis De Sales award 1996), Associated Ch. Press. Home: 3200 E 91st St Chicago IL 60617-4408 Office: US Cath 205 W Monroe St Chicago IL 60606-5001

BRUMMER, MARY D., administrative assistant; b. St. Cloud, Minn., June 23, 1943. With Silker Studios, Little Falls, Minn., 1975-88; adminstrv. asst. Trans Global Tours, Bloomington, Minn., 1988-90, R.J. Steichen & Co. Inc., Bloomington, 1990—. Roman Catholic. Home: 14620 Garrett Ave Apt 201 Apple Valley MN 55124-8430 Office: 7900 Xerxes Ave S Ste 830 Bloomington MN 55431-1122

BRUMMET, SHAUNA RENEA, molecular biologist; b. Columbus, Ind., Oct. 4, 1955; d. Basil Roscoe and Vera Louise (Tracy) B.; m. Jeffrey Alan Skinner, July 29, 1978. BS in Microbiology, Purdue U., 1978; MS in Chemistry, U. Akron, 1983, PhD in Chemistry, 1987. Instr. Notre Dame Coll. Ohio, Cleve., 1986; post-doctoral scientist Ohio Agrl. R&D Ctr., Wooster, 1987-88; assoc. scientist R&D Amersham Life Sci., Inc. formerly U.S. Biochem. Corp., Cleve., 1988-90; scientist, dir. custom svcs. U.S. Biochem. Corp., Cleve., 1990-93; mgr. Molecular Biology Quality Assurance, 1992-95; prin. scientist R&D, 1995—. Contbr. chpts. to books and articles to profl. jours. Contbr. Humane Soc. Greater Akron, 1988—, Purdue All-Am. Band, 1979—. Mem. Am. Chem. Soc., AAAS, Ohio Acad. Sci., Medina Kennel Club (corr. sec. 1989-90, achievement award 1984-92), Western Res. Kennel Club (achievement award 1991, 92, 93, 94), Samoyed Club Am., Emerald Necklace Samoyed Club (sec. 1988-90), Iota Sigma Psi. Republican. Home: 3850 S Medina Line Rd Wadsworth OH 44281-8758 Office: Amersham Life Sci Inc 26111 Miles Rd Cleveland OH 44128-5933

BRUNDAGE, JAMES ARTHUR, historian, educator; b. Lincoln, Nebr., Feb. 5, 1929; s. Frank L. and Anna (Morrissey) B.; m. Victoria Claire Conlin, 1979 (div.); children: James Arthur, Brigitte, Gregory C., David B., Thomas T., Ann Kristin. B.A., U. Nebr., 1950, M.A., 1951; Ph.D., Fordham U., 1955. Instr. Fordham U., 1953-57; asst. prof. U. Wis. Milw., 1957-60, assoc. prof., 1960-65, prof., 1965-89, emeritus, 1989—, chmn. dept. history, 1972-76; Ahmanson Murphy Disting. prof. history/courtesy prof. law U. Kans., Lawrence, 1989—; vis. fellow Clare Hall Cambridge U., 1977-78, life mem. 1985—; Catedratico visitante U. Madrid, 1967-68; postdoctoral research at Cambridge U., Munich U., Innsbruck, Rome, and Madrid. Author: The Chronicle of Henry of Livonia, 1961, The Crusades: A Documentary Survey, 1962, Medieval Canon Law and the Crusader, 1969, Richard Lion Heart: A Biography, 1974, Sexual Practices and the Medieval Church (with Vern L. Bullough), 1985, Law, Sex, and Christian Society in Medieval Europe, 1987, The Crusades, Holy War and Canon Law, 1991, Sex, Law and Marriage in the Middle Ages, 1993, Medieval Canon Law, 1995; contbr. articles to profl. jours.; assoc. editor: Jour. Medieval History. Guggenheim fellow, 1964-65; Fulbright grant to Spain, 1967-68; NEH fellow Newberry Library, Chgo., 1983-84. Fellow Royal Hist. Soc., Medieval Acad. Am.; mem. Am. Hist. Assn., Am. Catholic Hist. Assn. (pres. 1985), Mediaeval Acad. Am. (council), AAUP (past chpt. pres.), Selden Soc. Democrat. Home: 1102 Sunset Dr Lawrence KS 66044-4548 Office: U Kans 2018 Wescoe Hall Lawrence KS 66045-2130

BRUNDAGE, VICTORIA CONLIN, past psychotherapist, social worker; b. Omaha, Nov. 28, 1944; d. Frank Dixon and Marcia (McCumsey) Conlin. BA, U. Wis., 1967, MSW, 1983; MA, U. Toronto, 1969, PhD, 1973. Psychotherapist Family Svc. Milw., Milw. Psychiat. Hosp., Group Health, Inc., Mpls., DCCCA Ctr., Lawrence, Kans.; presenter in field. Contbr. articles to publs. Mem. NASW, Am. Assn. for Marriage and Family Therapy (Grad. Student Rsch. award), Wis. Assn. for Marriage and Family Therapy (bd. dirs. 1985-86). Home: 333 Wartburg Pl Dubuque IA 52003-7769

BRUNE, LESTER HUGO, American history educator; b. Reading, Ohio, Jan. 14, 1926; s. Frederick Gustave and Marie (Bueker) B.; m. Joan Loretta Herzfeld, Oct. 21, 1950. AB, Elmhurst Coll., 1948; MA, Bradley U., 1950; PhD, U. Rochester, 1959. Instr. Morris-Harvey Coll., Charleston, W.Va., 1950-53; fellow Am. history U. Rochester (N.Y.), 1953-56; prof. Am. history Bradley U., Peoria, Ill., 1956—, Ogelsby chair Am. heritage, 1988; Dir. Bradley Berlin Seminar, 1980—. Author: Origins of American National Security Policy, 1900-1941, 1981, Chronological History of U.S. Foreign Relations Since 1776, 2 vols., 1985, Missile Crisis of October 1962, 1985, The Reagan Era, vol. 3 of Chronological History, 1991, Guide to Bibliography of America and Indochina's Three Wars Since 1945, 1991, America and the Iraqi Crisis: 1990-92, 1993, Korean War: Handbook of Literature and Research, 1996; contbr. articles to profl. jours. Fellow Harry S. Truman Inst., Independence, Mo., 1982, Air Force Hist. Libr., Maxwell AFB, Ala., 1984. Mem. Soc. for Historians of Am. Fgn. Rels., Am. Hist. Assn., Phi Delta Kappa. Home: 2921 W Winterberry Ln Peoria IL 61604-1831 Office: Bradley U History Dept Peoria IL 61625

BRUNING, DAVID HALL, astronomer; b. Elgin, Ill., May 7, 1952; m. Kathryn Wenham, Dec. 27, 1973. BS, U. Ariz., 1973; MS, U. Colo., 1977; PhD, N.Mex. State U., 1981. Sci. programmer Lockheed Electronics, Las Cruces, N.Mex., 1977-78; postdoctoral fellow Mt. Wilson Observatory, Pasadena, Calif., 1981-84; asst. astronomer Inst. for Astronomy, Honolulu, 1984-85; asst. prof. U. Louisville, 1985-91; Astronomy Mag. Waukesha, Waukesha, Wis., 1991-96, cons. editor, 1996—; webmaster Kalmbach Pub. Co., 1996—. Co-author: Online Astronomy Student, 1996; contbr.: Voyages Through the Universe, 1996; contbr. articles to Solar Physics, Astrophys. Jour., Publs. of Astron. Soc. of the Pacific. Mem. Internat. Astron. Union, Astron. Soc. of the Pacific, Am. Astron. Soc., Phi Kappa Phi. Office: Astronomy PO Box 1612 Waukesha WI 53187-1612

BRUNKEN, GERALD WALTER, SR., manufacturing company executive; b. Oak Park, Ill., May 31, 1938; s. Walter Richard and Elenore (Troost) B.; m. Louise Nunziato, June 29, 1968; children: Gerald Jr., Patrick. BS, Lincoln Coll., 1958; BA in Econs., Baker U., 1961. Br. coord. A.M. Castle, Franklin Park, Ill., 1961-62; sales rep. Proviso West Realty, Berkley, Ill., 1962-65; CEO Addison (Ill.) Machine Engring., 1965—, CEO, pres., 1995—; pres. Sci. Tube Inc., Addison, 1971-95. One man show, Addison, 1971; contbr. articles to profl. jours. Cub master Boy Scouts Am., Addison, 1976-78; athletic dir. St. Philip the Apostle Sch., Addison, 1982-84; pres. Driscoll Cath. High Booster Club, 1985-86. Mem. Fabricating Mfrs. Assn. (speaker, panelist), Am. Tube Assn. (speaker, panelist), Ducks Unlimited (treas. Salt Creek chpt. 1982-90, zone chmn. State of Ill. 1990—, Spl. Projects awards 1987, 88, 89, 90), KC. Roman Catholic. Home: 4444 N Ann Ct Addison IL 60101

BRUNKHORST, ROBERT JOHN, computer programmer, analyst; b. Waverly, Iowa, Dec. 5, 1965; s. John Blaine and Edna C. (Atkins) B.; m. Kris Nielsen, Sept. 12, 1992; 1 child, Karalynn Kristine. BS in Computer Sci., Loras Coll., 1989. Computer programmer Century Cos. Am., Waverly, 1990—; press intern Sen. Charles Grassley, Washington, fall 1986. State rep. State of Iowa, 1992—; organizer Solid Waste Adv. Com., Waverly, 1990—; active Boy Scouts Am., N.E. Iowa, 1982—. Mem. Jaycees, Farm Bur. Home: 419 3rd Ave SW Waverly IA 50677-3114 Office: Century Cos Am Waverly IA 50677

BRUNNER, CHARLOTTE MARIE, civil engineer; b. Chgo., May 3, 1956; d. Robert Anthony and Mary Therese (Gonwa) Einweck; m. Gerald Keith Brunner, July 28, 1979. BSCEE, U. Wis., 1978. Registered profl. engr., Wis. Civil engr. City of Waukesha, Wis., 1978—. Mem. Inst. Transp. Engrs. (affiliate), Nat. Soc. Profl. Engrs., Wis. Parking Assn. Office: City of Waukesha 130 Delafield St Waukesha WI 53188-3616

BRUNNER, ELDON JOHN, mechanical engineer, consultant; b. Reddick, Ill., Mar. 31, 1923; s. George Adam and Laura Minnie (Oberlin) B.; m. Gladys Eleanor Dassow, July 9, 1945; children: Roger Lee, Betty Jane. BSME, U. Ill., 1949, MSME, 1950. Registered profl. engr., N.J. Test engr. nuclear lab. Gen. Dynamics, Ft. Worth, 1956-64; ops. mgr. Gen. Atomic, Idaho Falls, Idaho, 1964-67; project officer Idaho ops. office U.S. AEC, Idaho Falls, 1967-68; reactor inspector U.S. AEC, Glen Ellyn, Ill., 1968-71; br. chief U.S. NRC, King of Prussia, Pa., 1971-82, tech. asst., 1982-83; cons. EG & G Tech. Svcs., Idaho Falls, 1986-91. Co-author flight simulator specifications, 1954, navigation simulator specifications, 1955. Pres. Reddick Ambulance Svc., Inc., 1985—; mem. Reddick Sch. Bd., 1984-87; mem. Kankakee County Mutual Fire Ins. Bd., Kankakee, Ill., 1984-88. Lt. col. U.S. Army, 1943-47, ETO. Mem. Am. Nuclear Soc. (chair Del. sect. 1982-83). Home: 19754 W Route 17 Reddick IL 60961-8113

BRUNO, JAMES DAVID, financial consultant; b. Detroit, July 1, 1952. BA, Mich. State U., 1974; JD, Boston Coll., Newton, Mass., 1978. Fin. cons. Merrill Lynch, Farmington Hills, Mich., 1982-92, Smith Barney Inc., Traverse City, Mich., 1992—. Mem. Mich. State Bar Assn. Home: 473 Peninsula Knolls Ln Traverse City MI 49686 Office: Smith Barney Inc 300 Grandview Pk PO Box 1330 Traverse City MI 49685

BRUNO-STANLEY, MELINDA ANN, technology facilitator; b. Topeka, Aug. 19, 1963; d. Louis Daniel and Shirley Ann (Kowalski) Bruno; m. Douglas Howard Stanley, July 17, 1992. BBA, Washburn U., 1987; postgrad., Kans. State U., 1994—. Multi br. mgr. Columbia Savs., Topeka, 1987-90; mktg. cons. IBM, Topeka, 1990-92; tech. facilitator Unified Sch. Dist. 437 Auburn Washington, Topeka, 1992—; edn. cons., 1993—. Mem. ASCD, Internat. Tech. in Edn. Assn. Roman Catholic. Office: Unified Sch Dist 437 5928 SW 53 Topeka KS 66610

BRUNS, BILLY LEE, consulting electrical engineer; b. St. Louis, Nov. 21, 1925; s. Henry Lee and Violet Jean (Williams) B.; B.A., Washington U., St. Louis, 1949, postgrad. Sch. Engring., 1959-62; EE, ICS, Scranton, Pa., 1954; m. Lillian Colleen Mobley, Sept. 6, 1947; children—Holly Rene, Kerry Alan, Barry Lee, Terrence William. Supt., engr., estimator Schneider Electric Co., St. Louis, 1950-54, Ledbetter Electric Co., 1954-57; tchr. indsl. electricity St. Louis Bd. Edn., 1957-71; pres. B.L. Bruns & Assos., cons. engrs., St. Louis, 1963-72; v.p., chief engr. Hosp. Bldg. & Equipment Co., St. Louis, 1972-76; pres., prin. B. L. Bruns & Assos. cons. engrs., St. Louis, 1976—; tchr. elec. engring. U. Mo. St. Louis extension, 1975-76. Mem. Mo. Adv. Council on Vocat. Edn., 1969-76, chmn., 1975-76; leader Explorer post Boy Scouts Am., 1950-57. Served with AUS, 1944-46: PTO, Okinawa. Decorated Purple Heart. Registered profl. engr., Mo., Ill., Wash., Fla., La., Wis., Minn., N.Y., N.C., Iowa, Pa., Miss., Ind., Ala., Ga., Va., R.I. Mem. Nat. Soc. Profl. Engrs., Mo. Soc. Profl. Engrs., Profl. Engrs. in Pvt. Practice, Am. Soc. Heating, Refrigeration and Air Conditioning Engrs., Illuminating Engrs. Soc., Am. Mgmt. Assn., Nat. Fire Protection Assn. (health care div., archtl./engr. div.), Masons. Baptist. Tech. editor The National Electrical Code and Blueprint Reading, Am. Tech. Soc., 1959-65. Home: 1243 Hobson Dr Saint Louis MO 63135-1422 Office: 400 Brookes Dr Ste 203 Hazelwood MO 63042-2745

BRUNS, PAMELA JANE, marketing and public relations consultant; b. Hamilton, Ohio, Sept. 27, 1953. AA, Miami U., Oxford, Ohio, 1973; BA, Wright State U., Dayton, Ohio, 1981, MS in Econs., 1983. Chief devel. officer Fisk U., Nashville, 1984-86, Cumberland Valley Girl Scouts, Nashville, 1986-88; v.p. institutional advancement Franklin U., Columbus, Ohio, 1988-92; asst. dir. Dayton Art Inst., 1992-96; pres. Contbn. Strategies Inc., Dayton, 1996—. Mem. Ohio Mus. Assn., 1996; bd. trustees Dayton Visual Arts Ctr., 1996—, Greater Dayton Humane Soc., 1996—. Recipient Woodrow Wilson Found. fellowship, Princeton, N.J., 1984. Mem. Nat. Soc. Fundraising Execs. Office: Contbn Strategies Inc 101 Bluegate Circle Ste 3 Dayton OH 45429

BRUNS, ROBERT FREDERICK, JR., pharmacologist; b. St. Louis, June 4, 1950; s. Robert Frederick and Ila May (Goodpaster) B.; m. Eucaris Lucila Juvinao, Oct. 20, 1979 (div. Jan. 1992); children: Erica I., Robert Frederick III, William H., Nicholas E., Kenneth P. Student, New Coll., Sarasota, Fla., 1968-69; AB, Washington U., St. Louis, 1972; PhD, U. Calif., San Diego, 1978. Rsch. fellow NIH, Bethesda, Md., 1978-81; postdoctoral fellow Johns Hopkins U., Balt., 1978-81; sr. scientist Warner Lambert/Parke-Davis, Ann Arbor, Mich., 1981-88; rsch. scientist Eli Lilly & Co., Indpls., 1988-95, sr. rsch. scientist, 1996—. NSF grad. fellow, 1972. Mem. Am. Soc. for Pharmacology and Exptl. Therapeutics, Am. Soc. for Biochemistry and Molecular Biology, Soc. for Neurosci. Office: Eli Lilly & Co Lilly Corp Ctr Indianapolis IN 46285

BRUNSDALE, MITZI LOUISA MALLARIAN, English language educator, book critic; b. Fargo, N.D., May 16, 1939; d. Gregory Starn and Phyllis (Grobe) Mallarian; BS with honors (Nat. Merit scholar), N.D. State U., 1959, MS, 1961; postgrad. Ind. U., 1959-60; PhD (Danforth fellow), U. N.D., 1976; m. John Edward Brunsdale, Dec. 2, 1961; children: Margaret Louisa, Jean Ellen and Maureen Lois (twins). Departmental tchr. N.D. State U., 1958-59, grad. asst., 1960-61, instr. English and French, 1961; grad. asst. Ind. U., 1959-60; book critic Houston Post, 1971-85; book reviewer Chgo. Tribune, 1987—, The Armchair Detective, 1995—, Publishers Weekly, 1996—; state sec., treas. N.D. Am. Coun. on Edn./Nat. Identification Program Bd.; instr. English, Mayville (N.D.) State Coll., 1975-76, asst. prof., 1976-78, assoc. prof., 1978-83, prof., 1983—. Author Sigrid Undset: Chronicler of Norway, 1988, Dorothy L. Sayers: Solving The Mystery of Wickedness, 1991, James Joyce: The Short Fiction, 1993, James Herriot, 1996. Sec., 20th Dist. N.D. Republican Party, 1963-70; chmn. N.D. Humanities Council, 1980, 81-82; grant rev. panelist Nat. Endowment for Humanities; corr. sec. N.D. Fedn. Rep. Women, 1990-92. Mem. MLA, D.H. Lawrence Soc. Am., James Joyce Soc., Phi Kappa Phi, Sigma Alpha Iota, Kappa Alpha Theta. Republican. Contbr. articles to profl. jours. and reference encys. Home: RR 1 Box 9 Mayville ND 58257-9706 Office: Mayville State Coll Dept English Mayville ND 58257

BRUNST-MAY, LOIS, accounting & association management firm executive; b. Columbus, Ohio, Sept. 18, 1944; d. Edwin Charles and Carolyn Howard (Reedy) Brunst; m. Joseph Manuel Miguez, Sept. 18, 1966 (div. Nov. 1976); children: Joseph Anthony, Thad Elliot; m. George Gordon May, June 13, 1987. BS in Edn., Ea. Ill. U., 1965. CPA, Ill. Tchr. math. Flossmoor (Ill.) Sch. Dist. 161, 1965-68; from staff acct. to mgr. tax dept. Wilkes, Besterfield & Co., Ltd., Olympia Fields, Ill., 1974-79; compt. The Old Mountain Co., Chgo., 1979-86, Intercraft Industries Inc., Chgo., 1986-87; asst. Office of Pres., Duchossois Industries Inc., Elmhurst, Ill., 1987-91; COO Burnison, Martello & Assocs., Inc., Chgo., 1991-93; owner Lois Brunst May CPA, Homewood, Ill., 1993—; instr. Northwestern U., Chgo., Evanston, Ill., 1985-87; assn. mgmt. co. pres., CEO Hutchison Group, Ltd., Homewood, Ill., 1994—. Bd. dirs. Family Svc. Ctrs. South Cook County, Matteson, Ill., 1984-91, 92—, Cultural Arts Ctr. Found., Homewood, Ill., 1989-92. Mem. AICPA, Ill. CPA, Am. Woman's Soc. CPA (past pres.). Office: Hutchison Group Ltd 1820 Ridge Rd Homewood IL 60430

BRUNSVOLD, JOEL DEAN, state legislator, educator; b. Mason City, Iowa, Feb. 26, 1942; s. Burnell Raymond and Esther Agusta (Geilendeld) B.; m. Barbara Louise Bashaw, Feb. 22, 1964; children: Timothy, Theodore. BA, Augustana Coll., 1964; student, Black Hawk Coll., Western Ill. Univ. Tchr. Sherrard (Ill.) Cmty. Unit # 200, 1969-83; mem. Ho. of Reps., Rock Island, Ill., 1982—. Trustee, Milan, Ill., 1973-77, mayor, 1977-83. Mem. NEA, Ill. Edn. Assn., C. of C., Ducks Unlimited, Pheasants Forever, Phi Omega Phi. Democrat. Lutheran. Home: 1212 Hilltop Dr Milan IL 61264 Office: House of Reps 303 18th St Rock Island IL 61201

BRUS, WAYNE O., engineer; b. Carroll, Iowa, Jan. 20, 1941. B of Arch. Engring., Iowa State U., 1964. Cert. data processing. Sr. engr., data processing mgr. Green Constrn. Co., Des Moines, 1965-77; engr., software developer Davis Cons., Inc., Ankeny, Iowa, 1977—; instr. Des Moines Area C.C., Ankeny, 1968-74. Office: Davis Cons Inc 110 SE Grant St Ste 103 Ankeny IA 50021-3143

BRUSKI, PAUL STEVEN, marketing executive; b. Kansas City, Mo., Mar. 10, 1949; s. Paul and Elizabeth Ann (Cravens) B.; m. Mary Margaret Williams, May 3, 1980. BS in Journalism, U. Berlin, 1972. With engring. mgmt. Storage Tech. Corp., Louisville, Colo., 1973-77; dir. tech. svcs. Internat. Mktg. Communications, Denver, 1977-79; ptnr. Flack and Bruski Advt., Denver, 1979-80; pvt. practice advt. cons. Schenectady, N.Y., 1981-82; dir. tech. Services D. J. Moore Advt., Guilderland, N.Y., 1983-84; dir. mktg. Enable Software, Inc., Ballston Lake, N.Y., 1984-86; dir. corp. commnications Innovative Software Inc., Lenexa, Kans., 1986-89, Informix Software, Inc. (formerly Innovative Software, Inc.), Lenexa, 1988-89; pres. Market Rels. Cons., Olathe, Kans., 1989—, Am. Ednl. Resources, Inc., Olathe, Kans., 1989-91, MRC Cos., Olathe, 1992—; dir. Corp. Comms. & Spl. Sys. sect. Long Data Sys., Inc., Lenexa, Kans., 1992-96; v.p. mktg. and sales Visual Applications, Inc., Kansas City, Mo., 1996—; cons. publ. Brodock Press Inc., Utica, N.Y., 1983-86; computer cons. and free-lance journalist, 1974—. Author: Collected Works, 1977. With U.S. Army, 1968-72. Mem. Pub. Rels. Soc. Am. (accredited, Prism award 1989). Office: Market Rels Cons 15404 W 152nd St Ste F Olathe KS 66062-3085

BRUSKY, LINDA L., middle school mathematics and science educator; b. Chgo., Sept. 22, 1948; d. Ervin and Elizabeth (Martinek) Lange; m. George F. Brusky, Mar. 13, 1971. BA in Elem. Edn., Northeastern Ill. State Coll., Chgo., 1970. Cert. tchr. K-9, Ill. Tchr. St. Mary of the Angels Sch., Chgo., 1970—, tchr. jr. high sch. math. and sci., 1987-93, tchr. mid. sch. math., 1993—. Charter mem. Statue of Liberty Ellis Island Found., Inc., N.Y.C., 1985—; site coord. Joyce Found. Magnet Summer Sch., 1991, DeWitt-Wallace/Readers Digest Found. Magnet Ctr. Summer Sch., 1992. Recipient Cardinal Bernadin Tchr. Achievement award 1992; Joyce Found. scholar, 1987-91. Fellow Nat. Assn. Watch and Clock Collectors; mem. Nat. Coun. Tchrs. Math., Nat. Cath. Edn. Assn. (Disting. Grad. award 1995), Ill. Coun. Tchrs. Math., Assn. for Supervision and Curriculum Devel., Psi Chi. Roman Catholic. Office: St Mary of the Angels Sch 1810 N Hermitage Ave Chicago IL 60622-1101

BRY, JEFFREY ALLEN, auditor; b. Mpls., Nov. 27, 1949; s. Allen Parnell and Alvina Clarice (Olson) B.; m. Marjorie Ann Kittridge, Dec. 4, 1971; children: Jeffrey Allen Jr., Nathan Andrew. BA in Acctg., Fin., Augsburg Coll., 1972; MA in Mgmt., Webster U., 1976. lic. pub. acct., Minn.; nat. cert. cost analyst. Cost acct. tank automotive command U.S. Dept. of Army, Warren, Mich., 1975-76; super. field auditor office insp. gen. office adult svcs. HHS, St. Paul, 1976—. Co-chair Valley Park Homeowners Assn., Lakeville, Minn., 1989—; spokesperson various citizen task forces; appointee Lakeville Strategic Growth Mgmt. Task Force; ch. lay reader. With U.S. Army, 1972-74. Mem. Assn. Govt. Accts. (vol. tax preparer for underprivileged filers), Soc. Cost Estimating and Analysis, Big Apple Toastmasters (pres. 1986). Lutheran. Home: 16170 Garner Ave W Rosemount MN 55068-1059 Office: HHS Audit Svcs 375 Jackson St Saint Paul MN 55101-1810

BRYAN, DAVID ALAN, physicist, researcher, engineer; b. Austin, Tex., July 29, 1946; s. William C. and Virginia S. (Vedder) B.; m. Jo Ann Grossman, Aug. 3, 1974; children: Kenna, Kimberlee, Benjamin, Joshua, Josiah. BA in Physics, Rice U., 1968; MS in Physics, U. Mo., 1973, PhD in Physics, 1976. Grad. rsch. asst. U. Mo., Rolla, 1971-76; tech. specialist McDonnell Douglas Elec. Systems Co., St. Louis, 1976-89; rsch. engr. Laser Diode, Inc., Earth City, Mo., 1989-93; engring. specialist 3M Electronic Products Div., Columbia, Mo., 1993—. Reviewer Applied Physics Letters, 1989—, Jour. Applied Physics, 1989—, Jour. Quantum Electronics, 1989; contbr. over 30 articles to profl. jours. including Procs. of SPIE, Optics Letters, Jour. Applied Physics, Jour. Optical Soc. Am., Optical Engring. Lt. USNR, 1968-71. Mem. Optical Soc. Am., Internat. Laser Communications Soc. (charter). Mem. Christian Ch. Office: 3M Electronic Products Divsn Electronics Products Divsn PO Box 1228 Columbia MO 65205

BRYAN, JAMES TIMOTHY, state trooper; b. Coffeyville, Kans., Jan. 28, 1967; s. James Bicknell and Lee Donna (Gibson) B.; m. Janette Rae Swearingen, Aug. 3, 1991. Grad., State Police Acad., Salina, Kans., 1990; AS, Mo. Western U., 1992, BS, 1992. DUI svc. officer City of Wichita (Kans.) Police Dept., 1988-89; state trooper/K-9 handler Kans. Hwy. Patrol, Wichita, Kans., 1989—. Mem. Am. Assn. State Troopers, Kans. State Troopers Assn., Kans. Peace Officers Assn., Police Marksman Assn., Kans. Intelligence Assn., Kans. Narcotics Officers Assn. Methodist. Office: Kans Hwy Patrol 3200 E 45th St N Wichita KS 67220-1432

BRYAN, JEAN MARIE WEHMUELLER, nurse; b. St. Louis, Aug. 10, 1964; d. Harold Leroy and Rose Marie (Mauer) Wehmuelle; m. Michael Thomas Bryan; children: Emily, Dennis. ADN, St. Louis C.C., 1984; BSN cum laude, U. Mo., St. Louis, 1986. RN, Mo. Libr. asst. St. Louis County Libr., 1980-86; charge nurse Southgate Care Ctr., St. Louis, 1985-86; charge/staff nurse Incarnate World Hosp., St. Louis, 1986-88, Alexian Bros. Hosp., St. Louis, 1988-89, Compre Health, Inc., St. Louis, 1989-91; office nurse to pvt. practice physician St. Louis, 1991—; owner Stained Glass Classics Studio, 1992—. Republican. Lutheran. Home: 200 Martigney Dr Saint Louis MO 63129

BRYAN, JEFFREY J., financial consultant; b. Ft. Wayne, Ind., Oct. 8, 1962. Fin. cons. Blinder Robinson, Chgo., 1986-89, Smith Barney Inc., Ft. Wayne, Ind., 1989—; bd. mem. Arins House, Ft. Wayne, 1993—; adv. bd. fund raiser Bishop Lours H.S., Ft. Wayne, 1992—. Contbr. articles to profl. jours. Recipient Commitment and Dedication award Hutton, L.A., 1990. Roman Catholic. Office: Smith Barney Inc 1 Summit Sq 8th Fl Fort Wayne IN 46802

BRYAN, JOAN MARIE, consumer products executive; b. Silver Spring, Md., July 19, 1963; d. John Leland and Sarah Emilie (Barton) B. BS in Mktg. magna cum laude, U. Colo., 1985; MBA, Cornell U., 1992. Sales intern Sheraton Carlton Hotel, Washington, 1982; devel. assoc. intern KBDI-TV, Broomfield, Colo., 1983-84; campus rep. Columbia Pictures, Boulder, Colo., 1984; asst. group merchandiser Montgomery Ward, Thornton, Colo., 1985-86, group merchandiser, 1986-88; ops. mgr. Montgomery Ward, Boulder, 1988-89, Aurora, Colo., 1989-90; rsch. asst. Cornell U., Ithaca, N.Y., 1991; brand asst. Procter & Gamble, Cin., 1992-93, asst. brand mgr., 1993-95, brand mgr., 1995-96; mktg. mgr. Hasbro Toy Group, 1996—. Admissions interviewer Cornell U., 1991—; mentor Cin. Youth Collaborative, 1992—; respite care provider Spl. Children's Ctr., Ithaca, N.Y., 1991-92; vol. stroke and head injury ward Mapleton Rehab. Ctr., Boulder, 1989-90.

BRYAN, JOHN HENRY, food and consumer products company executive; b. West Point, Miss., 1936. BA in Econs. and Bus. Adminstrn, Rhodes Coll., Memphis, 1958. Joined Bryan Foods, 1960; with Sara Lee Corp. (formerly known as Consol. Food Corp.), Chgo., 1960—; from exec. v.p. to pres. Sara Lee Corp. (formerly known as Consol Food Corp.), Chgo., 1974, chief exec. officer, 1975—, chmn. bd., 1976—, also bd. dirs.; bd. dirs. Gen. Motors Corp., Amoco Corp., 1st Chgo. Corp., 1st Nat. Bank Chgo. Chmn. bus. adv. coun. Chgo. Urban League; bd. govs. Nat. Women's Econ. Alliance, Chgo.; trustee, vice-chmn., exec. com. U. Chgo., Rush-Presbyn.-St. Luke's Med. Ctr.; trustee Com. Econ. Devel.; trustee, treas. Art Inst. Chgo.; chmn. Catalyst; bd. dirs. Bus. Com. for Arts; chmn. Chgo. com. Chgo. Coun. on Fgn. Rels.; mem. trustee's coun. Nat. Gallery Art, Washington; mem. pres.'s com. on the arts and humanities; dir. bus. com. for the arts. Decorated Legion of Honor (France), Order of Orange Nassau (The Netherlands), Order of Lincoln Medallion; recipient Nat. Humanitarian award NCCJ, William H. Albers award Food Mktg. Inst., Man of Yr. award Harvard Bus. Sch. Club Chgo.; named Exec. Yr. Crain's Chgo. Bus., 1992, Jr. Achievement Chgo. Bus. Hall of Fame, 1992, Miss. Hall of Fame, 1992. Mem. Grocery Mfrs. Assn. (sr., past. chmn. bd.), Bus. Coun., Bus. Roundtable. Office: Sara Lee Corp 3 1st Nat Plz 70 W Madison St Chicago IL 60602-4205*

BRYAN, LESLIE AULLS, JR., military officer, university professor; b. Syracuse, N.Y., Mar. 1, 1933; s. Leslie Aulls and Gertrude C. (Gelder) B.; m. Peggy Ann Hoover, Oct. 8, 1955; children: Deborah, Rebecca, Cynthia, William. BA, U. Ill., 1955; MBA, Syracuse U., 1966; PhD, Purdue U., 1978. Commd. 2nd lt. USAF, 1955, advanced through grades to major, 1966, ret., 1976; assoc. prof. occupational safety and health Purdue U., West Lafayette, Ind., 1977—. Mem. sch. bd. Tippecanoe Sch. Corp., Lafayette, Ind., 1986-94; bd. dirs. Pub. Sch. Found., 1988-92. Mem. Am. Soc. Safety Engrs., Air Force Assn. Mem. LDS Ch. Home: 2134 Robin Hood Ln West Lafayette IN 47906-5027 Office: Purdue U Knoy Hall of Tech West Lafayette IN 47907

BRYAN, NORMAN E., dentist; b. South Bend, Ind., Jan. 20, 1947; s. Norman E. and Frances (Kuhn) B.; m. Constance C. Cook, Feb. 23, 1974 (div. Apr. 1985); m. Linda Markley, Dec. 31, 1986; 1 child, Noelle. AB, Ind. U., 1969; DDS, Ind. U. Purdue U., Indpls., 1973. Sr. dentist Downtown Dental Svcs., Elkhart, Ind., 1973—; specialist Temporomandibular Joint Disfunction. Author: Canine Endodontics, 1982. Mem. ADA, Ind. Dental Assn., Elkhart Dental Assn. (pres. 1976-77, 84-86), Am. Acad. Head, Neck and Facial Pain, Great Lakes Cruising Club (Chgo.), Elcona Country Club, Great Lakes Cruising Club (Chgo.). Republican. Office: 505 Vistula St Elkhart IN 46516-2809

BRYAN, SHIRLEY WINIFRED, education educator; b. Gary, Ind., June 12, 1916; d. Louis Ashel and Winifred Alvina (Harner) B. AB, U. Chgo., 1937; MSEd, Ind. U., 1951; MA in Social Scis., Syracuse U., 1967. Tchr. Gary (Ind.) Community Schs., 1937-43, 47-80; mem. Ind. Bd. Spl. Edn. Appeals, 1986-88, Ind. State Bd. Edn., 1976-84; moderator Ind. Edn. Employee Rels. Bd., 1984-86. Mem. Crown Point (Ind.) Bd. Sch. Trustees, 1988-94; state coord. AARP 55-Alive Mature Driving Program, 1992-94. Mem. Am. Legion, Internat. Platform Assn., Naval Res. Assn., Ind. Retired Tchrs. Assn. (bd. dirs. 1987-92), Lake County Retired Tchrs. Assn., Eastern Star, Delta Kappa Gamma (pres. 1969-71). Christian Scientist. Home: 3910 106th Ln Crown Point IN 46307

BRYAN, WAYNE, producer. Producing dir. Music Theatre of Wichita, Kans. Office: Music Theatre of Wichita 225 W Douglas Ave Ste 202 Wichita KS 67202-3100

BRYANT, CHRISTOPHER ALAN, elementary education educator; b. Marshaltown, Iowa, May 11, 1963; s. Robert Charles and Kay Marie (Babcock) B. BA, U. Chgo., 1985; MST, U. Wis., Whitewater, 1994. Tchr. Antioch (Ill.) Dist. #34, 1987—. Coach soccer, basketball. Home: PO Box 132 Camp Lake WI 53109 Office: Antioch Upper Grade Sch 800 Highview Dr Antioch WI 60002

BRYANT, JAMES HAMILTON, III, health care executive; b. Vincennes, Ind., July 8, 1949; s. James H. Jr. and Barbara Jean (Reininga) B.; m. Susan Carol Dillon, Jan. 26, 1974; 1 child, Matthew. BS in Indsl. Engring., Purdue U., 1971; MBA, U. Dayton, 1977. Plant mgr. O.M. Scott & Sons Inc., Marysville, Ohio, 1974-78; sr. dir. distbn. Pepsico Foodsvc., Wichita, Kans., 1978-85; v.p. distbn. Limited, Inc., Columbus, Ohio, 1985-88; sr. v.p. ops. Carter Hawley Hale Inc., L.A., 1988-91; pres. Caremark Prescription Svc., Lincolnshire, Ill., 1991-94, Caremark Health Mgmt. Svc., Northbrook, Ill., 1994—; bd. dirs. Technology Assessment Group. Sgt. U.S. Army, 1971-77. Mem. Purdue Alumni Soc. Home: 67 Mallard Ln Lake Forest IL 60045 Office: Caremark Internat 2211 Sanders Rd Northbrook IL 60062

BRYANT, JAMES PATRICK, medical technologist; b. Monroe, Mich., Jan. 21, 1961; s. James Everett Bryant and Shirley Mae (Patterson) Poniedzialek; m. Tammy Lynn Klungler, Sept. 12, 1992 (div. Feb. 4, 1994). Assocs., Ctrl. Mich. U., 1981; Bachelor's USAF, Dayton U., 1986. Cert. ophthalmic technician. Med. lab. technologist Dr. Shear Family Practice, Dayton, Ohio, 1986-87; ophthalmology technician Joint Commd. Allied Health Personnel In Ophthalmology, St. Paul, 1989—. Sgt. USAF, 1982-86. Mem. Mich. Ophthalmology Peasonal Soc., The Gold Tones. Democrat. Home: 222 N Liberty Belleville MI 48111

BRYANT, LESTER R., surgeon, educator; b. Louisville, Sept. 8, 1930; s. L.R. and Pearl Bryant; m. Linda H. Fletcher; children—Leslie Bond, Lance Bryant. B.S. with high distinction, U. Ky., 1951; M.D., U. Cin., 1955, D.Sc. in Surgery, 1962. Diplomate: Am. Bd. Surgery., Am. Bd. Thoracic Surgery. Intern Cin. Gen. Hosp., 1955-56, asst. resident in surgery, 1956-61, chief resident in surgery, 1961-62; fellow in physiology Baylor U. Coll. Medicine, 1961; mem. faculty U. Ky. Coll. Medicine, 1962-73, prof., 1969-73, chief div. cardiothoracic surgery, 1967-73, vice chmn. dept. surgery, 1972-73; prof. surgery, chief sect. thoracic and cardiovascular surgery La. State U., 1973-77; prof., chmn. dept. surgery East Tenn. State U. Coll. Medicine, Johnson City, 1977-85; cons. VA Hosp., Johnson City, 1977-85; attending staff Med. Center Hosp., Johnson City, 1978-85; v.p. health scis., dean Sch. Medicine, Marshall U., Huntington, WV, 1985-88; dean Med. Sch., U. Mo., 1989—; chmn. Surg. Merit Rev. Bd, VA, 1972-76; mem. anesthetic and life support drugs adv. com. HEW, Pub. Health Svc., FDA, Washington, 1975-80; mem. rsch. com. Tenn. affiliate Am. Heart Assn., 1978-80; vis. prof. U. Hong Kong, 1968; mem. spl. med. adv. group Dept. Vets. Affairs, 1993—. Contbr. articles to med. jours. Fellow A.C.S., Am. Heart Assn.; mem. Am. Assn. Thoracic Surgery, Am. Surg. Assn., Am. Coll. Chest Physicians, Central Surg. Assn., Soc. Thoracic Surgeons, Soc. Surg. Chmn., Soc. Univ. Surgeons, So. Surg. Assn., So. Thoracic Surg. Assn., U. Cin. Grad. Surg. Soc., Phi Beta Kappa, Alpha Omega Alpha, Pi Kappa Epsilon. Office: U Mo Columbia Sch Medicine MA 204 Medical Scis Bldg Columbia MO 65212

BRYANT, PAUL EVERETT, civil engineer, city engineer; b. Sewickley, Pa., June 20, 1957; s. Everett Paul and Mary Emma (Casasanta) B.; m. Kathleen Mary Ververs, Aug 2, 1986; children: Michael Paul, Valerie Sloane. BS in Civil Engring., W. Va. U., 1990. Engring. technician Consoer Townsend Assocs., Chgo., 1981-82; quality control inspector Baldwin Assocs., Clinton, Ill., 1982-84; resident dir. U. Wis., Platteville, 1984-88; engring. technician Triad Engring., Inc., Morgantown, W. Va., 1988-90; site rep. Strand Assocs., Madison, Wis., 1990; engring. technician City of Wheaton, Ill., 1978-80; project engr. City of Wheaton, 1990—. Mem. ASCE (affiliate), Am. Pub. Works Assn. Republican. Mem. Christian and Missionary Alliance. Home: 514 Inca Blvd. Carol Stream IL 60188 Office: City of Wheaton 303 W. Wesley St Wheaton IL 60187

BRYANT, WILLIAM, mechanical engineer; b. Milw., Feb. 5, 1960. BSME, Marquette U., 1982. Project engr. Champion Pheematic, Montgomery, Ala., 1983-85; engr. Campbell Hausfeld, Harrison, Ohio, 1986—. Office: Campbell Hausfeld 100 Production Dr Harrison OH 45030-1477

BRYANT, WILLIAM M., state legislator; m. Mary Carol Bryant. DVM, Kans. State U., 1968. Mem. Kans. Ho. of Reps., Topeka, 1985—; vet. and farmer. Republican. Home: 1884 Quivira Rd Washington KS 66968-9316*

BRZOSKA, MICHAEL JEROME, industrial manufacturing corporation executive; b. Detroit, Oct. 5, 1940; s. William Michael and Stella (Bardyga) B.; m. Nancy Brzoska, Aug. 8, 1959; childen: Michael, Shelley, Kathleen. B in Indsl. Engr. and Mgmt., Detroit Coll. Applied Sci., 1967. Mgr. prodn. Clipper Industries, Roseville, Mich., 1963-72; v.p. BJR, Madison Heights, Mich., 1973-78; pres. Bachan, Windsor, Ont., 1978-83, ACR Industries, Roseville, Mich., 1983-84, Chardam Gear Co., Sterling Heights, Mich., 1984—. Mem. Soc. Mech. Engring. Office: Chardam Gear Co 40810 Brentwood Dr Sterling Heights MI 48310-2213

BUB, ALEXANDER DAVID, acoustical engineer; b. Milw., Oct. 19, 1949; s. Alex Robert and Rose (Monafo) B.; m. Kay Lynn Johannes, Jan. 5, 1982; 1 child, David. AAS in Electronic Communications, Milw. Sch. Engring., 1969, postgrad., 1993—; BA in Econs., History and Anthropology, U. Wis., Milw., 1976. Nuclear weapons specialist USAF, 1969-73; with Harley Davidson, Inc., Milw., 1977—, project coord., 1986—, with powertrain devel. group, 1993—. U.S. nat. champion 410 Superbike, 1979, Mexican champion 750 Prodn. and Open Superbike, 1980, Midwest champion Supertwins and Formula Twins, 1985, 86, 87. Mem. Acoustical Soc. Am. (guest speaker conf. 1990, 92), Soc. Automotive Engrs., Western/Eastern Roadracing Assn., Am. Motorcyclist Assn. Home: W 4802 Knuth Rd Random Lake WI 53075-1355 Office: Harley Davidson Inc 3700 W Juneau Ave Milwaukee WI 53208-2818

BUBASH, PATRICIA JANE, special education educator; b. St. Louis; d. Emil John and Anne Marie (Candrl) B. BA in Deaf Edn., Fontbonne Coll., 1974; postgrad., St. Louis U., 1975-76, U. Mo., Columbia, 1982-84, U. Mo., St. Louis, 1984; MA in Edn., Washington U., 1996. Life cert. K-12 tchr. of deaf, learning disabilities, emotional and behavior disorders, K-8 elem. tchr., Mo. Tchr. of deaf Spl. Sch. Dist. St. Louis County, 1974—; mem. curriculum devel. action com. Drug Free Schs.; com. mem. Drug Edn. Task Force. Mem. Jr. League St. Louis, 1989—; mem. bd. jr. divsn. St. Louis Symphony Soc., co-chmn. membership, 1991-92, 92-93; co-chmn. Gypsy Caravan Vols., St. Louis, 1991, 92-93; leader Boy Scouts Am., 1984—, Explorer Scouts, 1990, Girl Scouts U.S.A., 1984—, Just Say No Club, 1987—; mem. dance St. Louis Bravo, 1991—; mem. Step Up St. Louis, 1991—; active Alliance Francaise; mem. St. Louis-Lyon Sister Cities, Inc. Named Tchr. of Month, Spl. Sch. Dist. St. Louis County, 1987; recipient Spl. Needs Tchr. award for Classroom Boy Scouts Am., 1989, 96. Mem. Coun. for Exceptional Children, Mo. Edn. Assn., Alexander Graham Bell Assn. for Deaf, Coun. Edn. of Deaf, St. Louis Ski Club, Brentwood Figure Skating Club. Roman Catholic. Office: Spl Sch Dist St Louis County 12110 Clayton Rd Saint Louis MO 63131-2516

BUCHANAN, BRYANT W., research biologist; b. Jackson, Miss., July 1, 1960; s. Wayne S. and Dorothy J. (Tyson) B.; m. Sharon E. Wise, Aug. 15, 1992. BS in Zoology, U. So. Miss., 1986; MS in Biology, U. Southwestern La., 1988, PhD in Ecology and Evolutionaary Biology, 1993. Doctoral fellow, bd. regents U. Southwestern La., Lafayette, 1988-92; Pratt postdoctoral fellowship Mont. Lake Biol. Sta., U. Va., Pembroke, 1993; tchg. assoc. U. Mo., Columbia, 1993—. Author: (with others) Experimental Animal in Biomedical Research, 1994; contbr. articles to profl. jours. Recipient Rsch. award Scientific Rsch. Soc. of Sigma Xi, 1992. Mem. Am. Soc. of Naturalists, Soc. for the Study of Evolution, Animal Behavior Soc., Internat. Soc. for Behavioral Ecology, Herpetologists League (Award for Grad. Rsch. 1993), Am. Soc. of Ichthyologists and Herpetologists, Soc. for the Study of Amphibians and Reptiles, Phi Kappa Phi. Office: Divsn of Biol Scis Tucker Hall U Mo Columbia MO 65211

BUCHANAN, DAVID HAMILTON, chemistry educator; b. Indiana, Pa., July 4, 1942; s. Edward H. and Annabel (Kunkle) B.; m. Susanna Forbes, June 13, 1967; children: Jeannette, Rebecca. BS in Chemistry, Case Inst. Tech., 1964; PhD in Chemistry, U. Wis., 1969. NIH predoctoral fellow U. Wis., Madison, 1966-68; NIH postdoctoral fellow U. Calif., Berkeley, 1969-71; from asst. to prof. Eastern Ill. U., Charleston, 1971—, acting grad. dean, 1983-84, dept. chmn. chemistry, 1989—; vis. sci. SRI Internat., Inc., Menlo Park, Calif., 1978-79; cons. environ. law sect. coun. Ill. Bar Assn., 1986-89. Contbr. articles to profl. jours. Mem. Am. Chem. Soc. (sec. fuel chemistry div. 1990-92). Office: Ea Ill U Dept Chemistry Charleston IL 61920-3099

BUCHANAN, MARY ELLA, nurse; b. Hot Springs, Ark., July 19, 1950; d. Robert Glynn and Georgia Catherine (Dobson) B.; BS in Nursing, Vanderbilt U., 1972; MS, U. Tenn., 1974. Staff nurse Met. Health Dept., Nashville, 1972-73; commd. lt. Nurse Corps, U.S. Army, 1973, advanced through grades to maj., 1983; ambulatory care nurse clinician Family Practice Clinic, Ft. Belvoir, Va., 1974-76, Robinson Barracks Army Health Clinic, Stuttgart, Germany, 1976-77, 5th Gen. Hosp., 1977-79, Acad. Health Scis., Ft. Sam Houston, Tex., 1979-80; ambulatory care nurse clinician Walter Reed Army Med. Center, Washington, 1980-81, nurse researcher Nursing Rsch. Svc., 1980-82, Nurse Ward 72, 1982-84; head nurse Ward 4A Irwin Army Cmty. Hosp., Ft. Riley, Kans., 1984-85, evening and night supr., 1985-86, coord. infection control, quality assurance, 1986-87; infection control cons. 18th MEDCOM, Seoul, 1988, infection control officer Silas B. Hays Army Cmty. Hosp., Ft. Ord, Calif., 1989-91, nurse epidemiologist Preventive Medicine Svc., Ft. Riley, Kans., 1991-95, chief epidemiology and disease control, 1995—; quality care cons. Manhattan, Ks., 1990—. Mem. ANA (cert. family nurse clinician, div. community health), APHA, Assn. for Profls. in Infection Control and Epidemiology (cert.), Sigma Theta Tau. Methodist. Clubs: Smithsonian Assocs. Home: 2010 Anderson Ave Manhattan KS 66502-3606 Office: USA MEDDAC Preventive Medicine Sv Fort Riley KS 66442

BUCHANAN, RICHARD KENT, electronics company executive; b. Schenectady, Sept. 10, 1951; s. Richard Linton and Jeanette (Dunn) B.; m. Diane Carolyn Laffler, Oct. 14, 1984; 1 child, Lindsay Sarah. BSEE, USAF Acad., 1973; MBA, Harvard U., 1980. Commd. 2d lt. USAF, 1973, advanced through grades to capt., 1976; resigned, 1978; mgmt. cons. Bain and Co., Boston, 1979-82; corp. dir. strategy Gen. Instrument Corp., N.Y.C., 1982-84; mgr. strategic planning GE Med. Systems Group, Milw., 1984-86, mgr. mktg. magnetic resonance, 1986-87, product gen. mgr. magnetic resonance bus. unit, 1987-89; dir. strategic mktg. Motorola Communications Sector, Schaumburg, Ill., 1989-91; dir. internat. networks svcs. Motorola Land Mobile Sector, Schaumburg, Ill., 1991-94; v.p., gen. mgr. Am. Parts Divsn., Motorola, Schaumburg, Ill., 1994—. Contbr. numerous articles on time div. multiple access comm. systems to profl. jours. Scholar NSF, 1968. Mem. IEEE, N.Y. Acad. Scis. Republican. Home: 1076 Aberdeen Rd Inverness IL 60067-4313 Office: Motorola 1313 E Algonquin Rd Schaumburg IL 60196-4041

BUCHANAN, WILLIAM MURRAY, consulting actuary; b. Valley Junction, Iowa, Apr. 14, 1935; s. William Murray and Margaret Ann (Kehoe) B.; m. Jean Marie West, Aug. 20, 1955; children: Belinda Jean, Jennifer Sue, William Murray, Timothy John. BBA, Drake U., 1957. Actuarial assoc. Western and Southern Life Ins. Co., Cin., 1957-61; cons. actuary Nelson & Warren, Kansas City, Mo., 1961-65, Buchanan & Lewis, Dallas and Kansas City, Mo., 1966-76; pres. Knickerbocker Life Group, Austin, Tex., 1976-79; cons. actuary Buchanan & Assocs., Overland Park, Kans., 1979—; chmn., owner Unified Life Ins. Co., 1986—. Editor, commentator taped info. service Exec. Info. Service, 1981-83. Fellow Soc. Actuaries, Conf. of Consulting Actuaries; mem. Am. Acad. Actuaries. Roman Catholic. Home: 15904 Meadow Ln Shawnee Mission KS 66224-9741 Office: Buchanan and Assocs 7201 W 129th St Ste 300 Overland Park KS 66213

BUCHBINDER-GREEN, BARBARA JOYCE, art and architectural historian; b. Bronx, N.Y., Dec. 23, 1944; d. Michael and Esther Buchbinder; m. Raymond Jerome Green, Dec. 18, 1970. BA cum laude, Vanderbilt U., 1965; PhD, Northwestern U., 1974. Teaching asst. Northwestern U., Evanston, Ill., 1967-68; lectr. Northwestern U., Chgo., 1975; freelance researcher and writer Evanston, 1977—; editor GreenAssoc. Architects, Inc., Evanston, 1979—; cons. nomination forms Nat. Register of Historic Places, 1983—; mem. architecture adv. com. Mus. Sci. and Industry, Chgo., 1980-86; trustee Evanston Hist. Soc., 1986-92, pres., 1988-90, mem. house walk com. 1981-83, 88-90, chmn., 1988-90, mem. restoration planning com., 1980-91, editor newsletter TimeLines, 1989-92. Author: Lucy Fitch Perkins, 1984, Evanston: A Pictorial History, 1989; editor, compiler Evanstoniana, 1984; guest curator "Lucy Fitch Perkins" exhibit, 1983-84, "Photographs from Evanstoniana" exhibit, 1984-87; pub. photographer: Evanstoniana, 1984, Evanston: A Pictorial History, 1989, Victorian Details, 1990; history editor Chgo. Yacht Club Blinker, 1993-95; editor Cruising Sail Fleet, 1993—; contbr. articles to profl. jours. Founding mem. Preservation League Evanston, 1982; commr. Evanston Preservation Commn., 1981-89, chmn. preservations awards com., 1983-84, mem. evaln. com., 1978-92, chmn., 1985-89; mem. Citizen's Avd. Com. on Pub. Pl. Names, 1989-92; bd. dirs. Dewey Cmty. Conf., 1981-84, mem. exec. com., 1981-82, rec. sec., 1982-83. Univ. fellow Northwestern U., 1968-69, Dissertation Year fellow, 1969-70; Vanderbilt U. scholar, 1962-65. Mem. Victorian Soc. in Am. (bd. dirs. Chgo. chpt. 1978-81), Chgo. Architecture Found. Aux. Bd. (sec. 1990-91, exec. com. 1990-92, v.p. for cmty. affairs 1991-92), Archtl. Soc. Art Inst. Chgo., Soc. Archtl. Historians, Women's Archtl. League (v.p. 1980-82), Chgo. Maritime Soc., Nat. Turst for Hist. Preservation, Howard Van Doren Shaw Soc., Tibetan Terrier Club, Am. Cliff Dwellers Club. Home and Office: 1026 Michigan Ave Evanston IL 60202-1436

BUCHELE, WESLEY FISHER, retired agricultural engineering educator; b. Cedar Vale, Kans., Mar. 18, 1920; s. Charles John and Bessie (Fisher) B.; m. Mary Wanda Jagger, June 12, 1945; children: Rod, Marybeth, Sheron, Steven. BS, Kans. State U., 1943; MS, U. Ark., 1951; PhD, Iowa State U., 1954. Registered profl. engr., Iowa, Calif. Jr. engr. John Deere Tractor Works, Waterloo, Iowa, 1946-48; asst. prof. U. Ark., Fayetteville, 1948-51; agrl. engr. USDA, Ames, Iowa, 1954-56; assoc. prof. Mich. State U., East Lansing, 1956-63; prof. Iowa State U., Ames, 1963-89, prof. emeritus, 1989—; vis. prof. U. Ghana, Legon, 1968-69, Beijing Agrl. Engring. U., 1983-84; vis. scientist Commonwealth Sci. and Indsl. Rsch. Orgn., Australia, Internat. Inst., Tropical Agr., Ibadan, Nigeria, 1979-80, Internat. Rice Rsch. Inst., Manila, 1991-92; cons. engr. Detroit Arsenal, Ordnance Corps, Waterways Exptl. Sta., Corps of Engrs., U.S. Steel Corp., GM, Detroit, 1974-76; bd. dirs. Farm Safety 4 Just Kids, Earlham, Iowa, Self-Help, Inc., Waverly, Iowa, JAC Tractor Co. Author 18 books; inventor 23 patents. Mem. Ames Energy Com., 1974-75; advisor Living History Farm, Urbandale, Iowa, 1965—, bd. govs., 1984—. Maj. U.S. Army, 1943-46, PTO; maj. Ordnance Corps, USAR, 1946-69, ret. Named Eminent Engr., Iowa Engring. Soc., 1989. Fellow Am. Soc. Agrl. Engrs. (bd. dirs. 1978-80, McCormick-Case award 1988), Nat. Inst. Agrl. Engrs.; mem. AAAS, Soc. Automotive Engrs., Am. Soc. Agronomy (mem. com. 1961-65), Steel Ring, Internat. Assn. Mechanization of Field Experiments (v.p. 1964-93), Internat. Platform Assn., Osborne Club, Toastmasters. Home and Office: 239 Parkridge Cir Ames IA 50014-3645

BUCHHOLZ, MARY, computer systems administrator; b. Laporte, Ind., Dec. 13, 1945; d. Frank Henry and Ruth Marie (Schwind) Stockhausen; m. Ronald Lewis Buchholz, May 20, 1972; children: Lauren Robert, Geoffrey Alan. BS, U. Milw., 1970. Newsletter editor Saint Maria Goretti, Madison, 1985-91; music compositor A-R Editions, Middleton, Wis., 1989-91; computer systems adminstr. Victor Allen's Coffee, Madison, 1991-94, payroll mgr., 1991-94; acct. asst. Williams, Young & Assocs., Madison, 1994; software support Softmart, Madison, 1994—; computer sys. adminstr. Investment Realty Svcs., Ripple Mgmt., Madison; edn. com., Wis. Hosp. Assn., Madison, 1995—; testing microsoft software, Microsoft, Madison, 1994—; total quality training, Victor Allens Coffee, 1993-94. Editor: Saint Maria Gorette Yearbook, 1988-92. Adult leader, treas. Cub Scouts 4 Lakes Coun., Madison, 1982-89, Boy Scouts Am., 1985-93; asst. scoutmaster, 1985-93; mem. Orchard Ridge Cmty. Club, Madison, 1974—. Mem. Math. Honorary Soc., Madison Pers. Computer Users Group. Roman Catholic. Home: 4925 Knox Ln Madison WI 53711 Office: Ripple Mgmt 3800 Regent St Madison WI 53705

BUCHKO, AARON ANTHONY, management educator; b. Lakewood, Ohio, June 7, 1956; s. Walter B. and Blanche Martha (Vaida) B.; m. Kathleen Jo Hughbanks, May 23, 1981. AAS, Grand Rapids (Mich.) Jr. Coll., 1975; BS, Ferris State U., 1977; MBA, Bradley U., 1983; PhD, Mich. State U., 1990. Sales rep. ABC Records & Tapes, Grand Rapids, 1977-78, Lieberman Enterprises, Peoria, Ill., 1978-79; mktg. rep. Johnson & Johnson, Inc., Peoria, 1979; asst. mktg. mgr. Foster & Gallagher, Inc., Peoria, 1979-83; mktg. dir. PJS Publ., Peoria, 1983-84; grad. asst. Mich. State U., East Lansing, 1984-89; assoc. prof. mgmt. Bradley U., Peoria, 1989—; cons. in field. Co-author: Field Casework: Methods for Consulting to Small and Startup Businesses, 1996; contbr. articles to profl. jours., textbooks. Mem. River City Athletic Club, Beta Gamma Sigma, Sigma Iota Epsilon, Delta Tau Delta. Lutheran. Home: 1719 W Tiffany Ct Peoria IL 61614-1721 Office: Bradley University 326 Baker Hall Peoria IL 61625

BUCHNER, DANIEL RICHARD, electrical engineer, defense contractor; b. Chgo., July 29, 1963; s. Richard Ernest Buchner and Madeline Katherine Genisio Light; m. Jamie Jo Henry, Apr. 13, 1991. BSEE, Christian Bros. U., 1985; MSEE, U. Mo., Rolla, 1994. Cert. engr.-in-tng. Engring. asst. Owens Engring. Co., Jackson, Tenn., 1984; assoc. engr. McDonnell Douglas Corp., St. Louis, 1985-86, engr. electronics, 1986-91; journeyman engr. Sci. Applications Internat. Corp., St. Ann, Mo., 1991-92; asst. staff mem. BDM Internat., Inc., Fairview Heights, Ill., 1992-93; journeyman engr. CAS, Inc., St. Ann, 1993-94, sr. analyst, 1994—. Mem. men's retreat com. Florissant (Mo.) Ch. Christ, 1994—; vol. Bush Reelection Campaign com., Creve Coeur, Mo., 1992. Recipient Appreciation award St. Louis Sci. Olympiad, 1989, Appreciation letter Ecumenical Housing Project, 1990, Appreciation letter pres. of CAS, 1995. Mem. IEEE (aerospace electronics soc.), Armed Forces Comm. and Electronics Assn., Assn. Old Crows (acting bd. dirs.

1994—), U. Mo. Alumni Assn., Christian Bros. U. Alumni Assn. (reunion com. 1985), Tau Kappa Epsilon Alumni Assn. Home: 744 Baltic Dr Florissant MO 63031-1404 Office: CAS Inc 500 Northwest Plz Ste 700 Saint Ann MO 63074-2222

BUCHSIEB, WALTER CHARLES, orthodontist; b. Columbus, Ohio, Aug. 30, 1929; s. Walter William and Emma Marie (Held) B.; BA, Ohio State U., 1951, DDS, 1955, MS, 1960; m. Betty Lou Risch, June 19, 1955; children: Walter Charles II, Christine Ann. Pvt. practice dentistry specializing in orthodontics, Dayton, Ohio, 1959-93; cons. orthodontist Miami Valley Hosp., Childrens Med. Ctr., Dayton; asst. prof. dept. orthodontics Ohio State U. Coll. Dentistry, 1984-93, clinic dir., 1993—. Mem. fin. and program com. United Health Found., 1971-73; mem. dean's adv. com. Ohio State U. Coll. Dentistry; bd. dirs. Hearing and Speech Ctr., 1968-82, 2d v.p., 1976-78, pres., 1978-79; orthodontic advisor Ohio Dept. Health Bur. Crippled Children's Services, 1983-84. Capt. AUS, 1955-58. Fellow Am. Coll. Dentists (pres. Ohio sect. 1988); mem. ADA (alt. del. 1968, del. 1991, coun. on ann. sessions and internat. rels. 1984-88), Am. Assn. Dental Schs., Am. Cleft Palate Assn., Am. Assn. Dental Schs., Internat. Assn. Dental Rsch., Ohio Dental Assn. (sec. coun. legis. 1969-78, v.p. 1978-79, pres.-elect 1979-80, pres. 1980-81, polit. action com. 1987—, Coun. on Constn. and Bi Laws 1988-92, Achievement award 1989), Am. Coll. Dentists (pres. Ohio sect. 1988), Dayton Dental Soc. (pres. 1970-71), Am. Bd. Orthodontics, Great Lakes Soc. Orthodontists (sec.-treas. 1972-75, pres. 1977-78), Internat. Coll. Dentists, Am. Assn. Orthodontists (chmn. council legis. 1976, speaker of house 1982-85, ad hoc com. to revise by-laws, coun. on govtl. affairs, 1988—, recipient James E. Brophy Dist. Svc. award 1992, bd. mem. political action com.), Pierre Fauchard Acad., Coll. of Diplomats Am. Bd. Orthodontics (pres. 1990-91), Ohio State U. Alumni Assn. (advocates group), Delta Upsilon, Psi Omega. Republican. Lutheran (elder 1965-68, v.p. 1974). Clubs: Masons, Rotary (pres. 1973-74, Paul Harris fellow). Home: 4145 Mumford Ct Columbus OH 43220-4435 Office: Ohio State U Orthodontics Dept 305 W 12th Ave Columbus OH 43210-1249

BUCHWALD, CARYL EDWARD, geology educator, environmental consultant, educational consultant; b. Medford, Mass., Oct. 15, 1937; s. Charles Edward and Frances (Van Ormer) B.; m. Cynthia Morgan Greene, Aug. 21, 1959; children—Charles E., Julia G., Adam R. B.S., Union Coll., 1960; M.S., Syracuse U., 1963; Ph.D., U. Kans., 1966. Postdoctoral fellow McMaster U., Hamilton, Ont., Can., 1966-67; asst. prof. geology Carleton Coll., Northfield, Minn., 1967-71, assoc. prof., 1971-77, prof. geology, 1977—, Lloyd McBride prof. environ. studies, 1984—, coll. naturalist, 1977-86; also dir. nat. history program; cons. in field. Fellow Geol. Soc. Am. Office: Carleton Coll Geology Dept Northfield MN 55057

BUCHWALD, KURT A., mechanical engineer; b. Springfield, Ohio, Jan. 26, 1965. BA in Geology, Denison U., 1987; MSME, Ohio No. U., 1990. Design engr. Ariel Corp., Mt. Vernon, Ohio, 1991—. Office: Ariel Corp 35 Blackjack Rd Mount Vernon OH 43050-9480

BUCHWEITZ, JOHN E., stockbroker; b. Detroit, Feb. 21, 1949; s. Harvey C. and Mary Buchweitz; m. Norma J. Smith, Dec. 21, 1969; children: Bonnie J., John Philip. BA, John Carroll U., Unviersity Heights, Ohio, 1984. Gen. mgr., stockbroker Roney & Co., Muskegon, Mich., 1987—. With USAF, 1967-87. Mem. Lions (treas. 1989—). Baptist. Office: Roney & Co PO Box 156 Muskegon MI 49443-0156

BUCHY, JIM, state legislator, packing company executive; b. Greenville, Ohio, Sept. 24, 2940; s. George Jacob and Amba (Armbruster) B.; m. Sharon Lynn Steinvall, 1965; children: Kathryn, John. BS, Wittenberg U., 1962. Pres. Charles G. Buchy Packing Co., Greenville, 1977—; mem. Ohio Ho. of Reps., Columbus, 1983—. Mem. Greenville Bd. Edn., 1980-82; dist. del. Rep. Nat. Conf.; mem. Darke County (Ohio) Rep. Exec. Com.; chmn. Darke Econ. Found., 1977-82; bd. dirs. Greenville Indsl. Park; past pres. Darke County Rep. Men's Club. Mem. Darke County C. of C., Rotary, Phi Mu Delta. Home: 281 Dogwood Dr Greenville OH 45331-2807*

BUCINSKI, JANICE KAY, secondary education educator; b. Poplar Bluff, Mo., Mar. 24, 1952; d. John Wiley and Sylvia (Brown) Smith; 1 child, Wesley Alexander. BA in History and Edn., U. Ark., 1974; MS in Edn., Ea. Ill. U., 1991. Lic. tchr., Ill., Mo. Social studies tchr. Bryant (Ark.) H.S., 1974-77, Meml. H.S., Evansville, Ind., 1981-82; market support rep. Van Ausdall and Farrar, Evansville, Ind., 1983-86; adminstrv. asst. Farm Credit Svcs., Effingham, Ill., 1986-87; social studies tchr. Effingham H.S., 1987-92, Cmty. H.S. Dist. # 218, Oak Lawn, Ill., 1992—; girl's track and field coach Effingham H.S., 1989-92; asst. girl's cross-country coach Eisenhower H.S., Blue Island, Ill., 1992; yearbook advisor Polaris Sch., Oak Lawn, 1993—. Active Friends of the Libr., Art Inst. Chgo., Chgo. Hist. Soc. Mem. NEA, Ill. Edn. Assn., Aircraft Owners and Pilots Assn., Internat. Women's Pilot Assn., Phi Delta Kappa. Home: 15150 Quail Hollow Dr # 3-n Orland Park IL 60462-4045

BUCK, DAVID DOUGLAS, historian; b. Denver, Dec. 31, 1936; s. Douglas H. and Mildred (Meyer) B.; m. Diane Maxine Ratty, Aug. 12, 1964; children: Douglas S., Andrew D. BA, Stanford U., 1958, PhD, 1972; MA, Harvard U., 1960. Dir. Inter-Univ. Program Chinese Lang. Study, Taipei, Taiwan, 1971-72; asst. prof. U. Wis., Milw., 1972-78, assoc. prof., 1978-88, prof., 1988—; assoc. dir. Joint Ctr. Internat. Studies U. Wis. and Marquette U., 1991—. Author: Urban Change in China, 1978; contbg. author: The Several Worlds of Pearl Buck, 1994; editor: Jour. Asian Studies, 1990-95, Recent Chinese Studies of the Boxer Movement, 1987. Dir. Wis. China Coun., Milw., 1976-82; bd. dirs. Literary Soc. Milw. Pub. Libr., 1991—; pres. Buck Found., 1986—. Lt. jr. grade USN, 1960-64. Mem. Assn. Asian Studies (bd. dirs. 1990-95), Nat. Com. U.S. China Rels., Am. Hist. Assn. Democrat. Episcopalian. Home: 3559 N Summit Ave Milwaukee WI 53211-2661 Office: Dept History 290 Holton Hall Milwaukee WI 53201

BUCK, EARL WAYNE, insurance investigator, private detective; b. La Porte City, Iowa, Jan. 15, 1939; s. Edwin Earl and Uleta Pearl (Purdy) B.; m. Maxine E. Parker, Oct. 19, 1969; children: Brian, Douglas. LLB, La Salle U., 1969. Asst. mgr. Chgo. br. Atwell, Vogel & Sterling, Scarsdale, N.Y., 1965-70; pvt. detective, Sioux City, Iowa, 1968-74; mgr. Milw. br. Atwell, Vogel & Sterling, Scarsdale, N.Y., 1970; sr. auditor Comml. Union Ins. Co., Chgo., 1970-74; police chief McHenry Shores (Ill.) Police Dept., 1973-79; self-employed ins. investigator McHenry, Ill., 1980-88, Rapid City, S.D., 1988—; owner Corral Motel, Rapid City, 1988—; liquor liability investigator for various ins. cos., 1980-88; farm owner, 1986-96. Chmn. McHenry Shores (Ill.) Zoning Commn., 1972, Police Support Subcom., C. of C. Pub. Safety Com.; key contact Help Abolish Legal Tyranny; active Rapid City Police Res., 1989-90, North Rapid Civic Assn., 1991-94, pres., chmn. bd., 1993-94; active Pennington County Air Quality Bd., 1990-93, chmn., 1992-93. With U.S. Army, 1957-61. Recipient Police Meritorius Service award Vill. of McHenry Shores, 1979. Mem. Midwest Inst. Auditors Assn., McHenry County Police Chief's Assn., Rapid City Police Officers Assn., Rapid City Area Hospitality Assn., Rapid City Area C. of C. (safety com. 1989-91), S.D. Innkeepers Assn., Black Hills Badlands & Lakes Assn., Rapid City Humane Soc., Old West Trail Assn., NRA, Moose. Republican. Lutheran.

BUCK, JAMES RUSSELL, state legislator; m. Judith Ann Buck. BA, BS, MBA, Ind. Wesleyan Coll. Mem. Ind. State Ho. of Reps. Dist. 38, mem. commerce & econ. devel., ins., corp. & small bus. coms., mem. roads and transp. com., vice-chmn. labor and employment com. Mem. Nat. Assn. Realtors, Ind. Assn. Realtors, Kokomo Bd. Realtors.

BUCK, ROSEMARY A., linguistics educator; b. Fort Dix, N.J., Dec. 27, 1953; d. Arthur C. Buck and Christiane M. (Bouffier) Sweeney; m. David Alan Jay, May 14, 1990. BA in English summa cum laude, W.Va. U., 1975, MA in French magna cum laude, 1978; M in Internat. Mgmt., Am. Grad. Sch. Internat. Mgmt., Glendale, Ariz., 1979; PhD in linguistics, Northwestern U., Evanston, Ill., 1993. With internat. mktg. Ency. Britannica Edn. Corp., Chgo., 1979-82; with fin. mgmt. Fed. Res. Bank, Chgo., 1982-87; lectr. bus. comm. Roosevelt U., Chgo., 1987; sr. teaching fellow Northwestern U., 1987-92, lectr. Coll. Arts & Scis. linguistics dept. & writing prog., 1992-94; asst. prof. English, lang., and linguistics Ea. Ill. U., Charleston, 1994—. Bd. trustees Hindsboro (Ill.) City Coun.; bd. dirs. Ea. Ill. U. Women's Resource Ctr., 1996—. Mem. MLA (sec. linguistic approaches divsn. 1996), Linguistic Soc. Am., Nat. Coun. Tchrs. English, Am. Assn. Applied Linguistics, Phi Beta Kappa (v.p. alumni assn. 1996—), Phi Delta Phi, Phi Kappa Phi. Office: Eastern Ill Univ English Dept Charleston IL 61920

BUCKELLEW, WILLIAM FRANKLIN, retired education educator; b. Georgetown, Ill., June 10, 1928; s. Frank and Verla (Haworth) B.; m. Lois Soliah, Apr. 9, 1952; children: Michael, Mark, Jon. BS, N.D. State U., 1953; MS, U. Ill., 1954; EdD, U. Ark., 1968. Cert. tchr., coach, Ill. Tchr., coach Kanakaee (Ill.) Pub. Schs., 1954-56; athletic dir. Lake Park High Sch., Medinah, Ill., 1956-62; asst. prof. phys. edn. Ea. Ill. U., Charleston, 1962-68, assoc. prof. teaching, rsch. and kinesiology, 1968-70, prof., chmn. dept. phys. edn., 1970-77, coord. grad. program dept. health, phys. edn. and recreation, 1977-88, acting dean Coll. Health, Phys. Edn. and Recreation, 1986-88, adviser to postgrad. students Coll. Edn., 1988-93; ret., 1993; mem. com. on assessment Ill. Office Edn., Springfield, 1973-75, com. on competency-based tchr. edn. program, 1975-78; ednl. cons. to Ill. sch. dists., 1960-82; cons., evaluator Nat. Coun. Accreditation of Tchr. Edn., 1973, 85; speaker, rsch. cons. Asian Phys. Edn. and Sport Rsch. Assn., Kaoshiung, Taiwan, 1984; chmn. Ill. Athletic Coaching Cert. Program, 1985-86; presenter at profl. confs. Contbr. articles to Ill. Jour. Health, Phys. Edn. and Recreation, Asian Jour. Phys. Edn., others. With USAF, 1946-49. Mem. NEA, AAHPERD, Ill. Assn. Health, Phys. Edn., Recreation and Dance, N.Am. Soc. Psychology of Sport and Phys. Edn., Ill. Edn. Assn., Ill. Assn. Higher Edn., Fishing Tackle Collectors Ill., Nat. Fishing Lure Collectors Club, Masons, Scottish Rite, Shriners, Phi Epsilon Kappa, Phi Delta Kappa, Sigma Alpha Epsilon. Methodist. Home: 1602 Shaffer Pl Charleston IL 61920-3163

BUCKEYE, DONALD ANDREW, mathematics educator; b. Lakewood, Ohio, Mar. 12, 1930; s. Andrew M. and Betty (Wagner) B.; m. Nancy R. O'Neill, June 16, 1962; children: Pamela Jean, Karen Ann. BS in Edn., Ashland U., 1953; MAT, Ind. U., 1961, EdD, 1968. Tchr. math. Norwalk (Ohio) Pub. Schs., 1953-54, 56-64, A.E. Ctr., Sendai, Japan, 1954-56; instr. math. Ohio State U., Lakewood, 1964-66; grad. asst. math. Ind. U., Bloomington, 1966-68; instr. math. Cleary Coll., Ypsilanti, Mich., 1968-72; prof. math. Ea. Mich. U., Ypsilanti, 1968—; cons. in field. Author: Couldburst of Math Activity, 1990 (3 vols.), Problem Solving Using Computers (3 vols.), 1989, Problem Solving Using Bingo Chips (2 vols.), 1994; author booklets: Lab Activities in Math., 1971-81; contbr. articles to profl. jours. With U.S. Army, 1954-56. Mem. Nat. Coun. Tchrs. Math., Math. Assn Am., Mich. Coun. Tchrs. Math. (Cert. of Recognition 1990), Detroit Coun. of Tchrs. Math., Cleve. Coun. Tchrs. Math. (pres. 1963), Phi Delta Kappa. Office: Ea Mich Univ Dept Math Ypsilanti MI 48197

BUCKHOLTZ, KENNETH ROBERT, electrical engineer; b. Elyria, Ohio, Jan. 18, 1971; s. Robert Charles and Janice Marie (Sadowski) B. BSEE, GMI Engring. and Mgmt. Inst., Flint, Mich., 1994. Mfg. engr. GM Delphi Chassis, Dayton, Ohio, 1989—. Mem. IEEE, IEEE Controly System Soc., IEEE Robotics Soc., Soc. for Indsl. and Applied Math. (mem. control and sys. theory group). Roman Catholic. Home: 7025 Woodcroft Dr Englewood OH 45322 Office: GM Delphi Chassis 2000 Forrer Blvd Dayton OH 45420

BUCKLE, FREDERICK TARIFERO, international holding company executive, political and business intelligence analyst; b. Accra, Ghana, Nov. 17, 1949; s. Festus Kofi Buckle and Clara Anyema Korley; 1 child, Nicole Ohenewa. MBA, PhD in Internat. Relations. Pres., chief exec. officer, chmn. Buckle Internat. Aktiengesellschaft; pres. Tarifero and Tazewell, Inc.; chmn. Lafayette Internat. Bank; bd. dirs. Oxicron Systems Corp., N.J., U.S. Pub. Corp., Chgo., Internat. Investments and Devel. Corp., Transglobal Investment and Devel. Corp., Bermuda, Selwyn Corp., N.Y.C., Richmond Computer Software Corp., Los Angeles. Author: The Logic of Laissez Faire, 1974, Third World and the Economic Supply Process, 1981, Strategic Balance in the Nuclear Age, 1981, Financial Privacy in the World of Computers, 1983, Industrial Espionage, 1984. Named Hon. Consul Gen. Republic of Maldives, 1983-85. Fellow Internat. Strategic Studies Inst.; mem. Chgo. Assn. Commerce, Assn. Internat. Financiers, Mortgage Bankers Assn. Office: Buckle Internat Inc 211 S Clark St PO Box 2522 Chicago IL 60690

BUCKLEY, GAIL GEARY, health administrator; b. Providence, Jan. 18, 1951; d. Thomas Francis and Marianne (Stauble) Geary; m. Glenn William Buckley, Feb. 5, 1972 (div. Aug. 1988); children: Eric W., Aaron W. BA, U. R.I., 1972; MS in Health Adminstrn., U. Colo., 1983. Admintrv. asst. Yale-New Haven Hosp., 1973-78, Rose Med. Ctr., Denver, 1978-81; staff analyst Colo. Dept. Health, Denver, 1982; mgr. utilization Blue Cross/Blue Shield Co., Cheyenne, Wyo., 1984-85; health services coordinator ConnectiCare, Inc., Hartford, Conn., 1985-86; data adminstr. ConnectiCare, Inc., Hartford, 1986-87, sysrems coordinator, 1987-88, mgr. mgmt. info. systems, 1988-91; dir. MIS CliniCare Inc., Rockford, Ill., 1992—.

BUCKLEY, JOHN JOSEPH, obstetrician, gynecologist; b. Youngstown, Ohio, Jan. 21, 1930; s. John Joseph and Rosalie Catherine (Singler) B.; m. Anne Theresa Finnerty, Apr. 24, 1954; children: John, Joy, Colleen, Mollie. BS in Biology cum laude, Holy Cross Coll., 1952; MD, Ohio State U., 1959. Staff St. Elizabeth Med. Ctr., Youngstown, Ohio, 1963—, chief ob-gyn., 1977-80, chief of staff, 1986—; practice medicine specializing in ob-gyn. Youngstown, Ohio, 1963—; asst. prof. Northeastern Ohio Coll. Medicine, Rootstown, 1980—. co-founder Right to Life, Youngstown, 1970. Served to lt. USN, 1952-55, with res. MC, 1959-63. Fellow Am. Coll. Ob-Gyn; mem. AMA, Ohio Med. Assn., Mahoning County Med. Assn., Youngstown Soc. Ob-Gyns., Alpha Omega Alpha. Democrat. Roman Catholic. Clubs: Youngstown Country, Cotillion. Home: 1337 Stonington Dr Youngstown OH 44505-1657 Office: 935 Trailwood Dr Youngstown OH 44512-5008

BUCKLEY, JOHN JOSEPH, JR., health care executive; b. Evanston, Ill., Oct. 5, 1944; s. John Joseph and Mary Ruth (Smith) B.; m. Sarah Amelia Puceloski, May 16, 1970; children—Ruth Mary, Patricia Kimberly, John Joseph III. A.B., Kenyon Coll., 1966; M.B.A., George Washington U., 1969. Asst. adminstr. Maricopa County Gen. Hosp., Phoenix, 1969-71; asst. adminstr. St. Joseph's Hosp. and Med. Ctr., Phoenix, 1971-74, assoc. adminstr., 1974-76, v.p., 1976-79, pres., 1984-88; pres. St. Anthony's Hosp., Amarillo, Tex., 1979-84, St. Anthony's Devel. Corp., Amarillo, 1982-84; chief operating officer Harrington Cancer Ctr., Amarillo, 1982-84; sr. v.p. Mercy Health System, Cin., 1988-91; pres. So. Ill. Healthcare Enterprises, Carbondale, Ill., 1992—. Active Amarillo Alliance of Cmty. Svc. Execs., Amarillo Area Acad. Health Ctr. Corp., Amarillo Area Hosp. Home Care, Amarillo Found. Health and Sci., Panhandle chpt. Tex. Soc. to Prevent Blindness, Amarillo Jr. League, Children's Oncology Svcs. of Tex. Panhandle; Amarillo diocesan coord. health affairs; mem. adminstrv. com. Amarillo; pres. Mercy Svcs. Corp., 1984-88; bd. dirs. Greater Phoenix Affordable Health Care Found., 1984-88; trustee Kenyon Coll., Gambier, Ohio, 1991-95. Fellow Am. Coll. Healthcare Execs. (regent Ariz. 1984-88); mem. Tex. Hosp. Assn. (trustee 1983-84), Ill. Hosp. Assn. (trustee 1995—), Cath. Health Assn. U.S. (bd. dirs., svcs. com., trustee 1985-91), Ariz. Kidney Found., Ariz. Hosp. Assn. Republican. Roman Catholic. Office: So Ill Health Care Enterprises PO Box 3988 Carbondale IL 62902-3988

BUCKNER, WILLIAM CLAIBORNE, real estate broker; b. Ft. Leavenworth, Kans., June 29, 1926; s. Simon Bolivar Jr. and Adele (Blanc) B.; m. Virginia Jordan Lester, May 15, 1932; children: Simon Bolivar IV, Peter Ridenour, Robert Lester. BS in Engring., U.S. Mil. Acad., 1948. Cert. real estate broker, cert. comml. investment mem. Sales engr. Gustin Bacon Mfg., Kansas City, Tulsa, Mo., Okla., 1955-65; exec. v.p. Keystone Chem. Co., North Kansas City, Mo., 1965-66; chmn., chief exec. officer Alexander Electronics Inc., Kansas City, 1967-72; broker Jones & Co. Realtors, Kansas City, 1973-81; broker, treas. Kerr & Co. Realtors, Kansas City, 1982-87; owner, operator Buckner Realty, Westwood, Kans., 1988—. Pres. S.W. Area Edn. Coun., Kansas City, 1972-73; active Citizens Assn., Kansas City, 1969-92. Capt. U.S. Army, 1948-54. Mem. Univ. Club, Carriage Club, Kansas City, Mo. chpt. CCIMs (pres. 1982), S.R. Mo. (pres. 1987), Rotary, Comml. Brokers Assn. Kansas City (pres. 1990-92). Republican. Episcopalian. Home: 6526 Pennsylvania Ave Kansas City MO 64113-1819 Office: Buckner Realty 1900 W 47th Pl Ste 230 Westwood KS 66205-1801

BUCY, MICHAEL RAY, firefighter; b. McKeesport, Pa., Apr. 2, 1965; s. Leah R. (Graft) Nemec; m. Kimberly K. Potter, Aug. 5, 1989; 1 child, Jordan Michael. BS in Mgmt., Ball State U., 1987. Cert. master fire instr., Ind. Program dir. WDSO-FM, Chesterton, Ind., 1979-83; residence asst. Ball State U., Muncie, Ind., 1984-87; emergency med. technician Delaware County Emergency Med. Svcs., Muncie, 1987-89, Jay County Emergency Med. Svcs., Portland, Ind., 1987-89, Albany (Ind.) Emergency Med. Svcs., 1987-89; firefighter, emergency med. technician Portage Fire Dept., 1989—; telecommunicator Valparaiso (Ind.) U. Police, 1991—; Haz-Mat gechnician Porter County, Valparaiso, 1991—; owner, instr. Emergency Media Svcs., Valparaiso, 1992—. Contbr. photos to various fire svc. mags. Vol., Union Twp. Fire Dept., Wheeler, Ind., 1989—. Mem. IAFF Local 3151 (sec.). Office: Emergency Medical Svcs 505 Sunshine Dr Valparaiso IN 45383

BUCZAK, DOUGLAS CHESTER, financial advisor, lawyer; b. Detroit, Feb. 6, 1949; s. Chester and Rose Marie (Czech) B. BA in English, U. Mich., 1971; JD, U. Detroit, 1975. Bar: Mich. 1975. Pvt. practice Lansing, Mich., 1978-80; bus. cons. Dynamic Learning Systems, Farmington Hills, Mich., 1981-82; fin. planner Pacific Fin. Cos., Farmington Hills, 1982-86, Pacific Fin. Group, Birmingham, 1986—; pres. Pacific Adv. Svcs., Inc., 1986—. Fin. columnist Detroit Legal News, 1992-94. Mem. Mich. Bar Assn., Internat. Assn. Fin. Planning (bd. dirs., editor newsletter S.E. Mich. chpt. 1987-88, v.p. 1990-91), Optimist Club Farmington Hills (pres. 1984-85), Sigma Phi Epsilon (pres. alumni bd. Ann Arbor, Mich. 1983-93). Home: 6426 Heritage West Bloomfield MI 48322-1336 Office: Pacific Fin Group 380 N Woodward Ave Ste 126 Birmingham MI 48009-5347

BUDAK, MARY KAY, state legislator; b. Phila.; m. Michael S. Budak, 1953; children: Kathy Budak Norred, Michael S. III, Patricia A. Budak Jones. Student, Temple U., 1950-51, Purdue U., 1968, 80. Owner, mgr. Budak Memls. Inc., 1960-81; sec. to campaign coord. Michigan City Mayor Campaign, Ind., 1966-79; mem. Ind. Ho. of Reps., 1980—, mem. various coms., ranking majority mem. judiciary com., former ranking Rep. mem. family and children com., asst. Rep. whip. Pres. Miss Ind. Scholar Pageant, 1970-74, former mem. exec. bd.; mem. exec. bd. Michiana Sheltered Workshop, 1981-86, Parents & Friends of Handicapped; asst. Rep. WAIP; bd. dirs. Stepping Stone for Spousal Abuse. Named Outstanding Woman in Politics, 1982, Outstanding Legislator, Fraternal Order Police and State Employees, 1983. Mem. LWV, LaPorte County Grange, LaPorte GOP Women's Club (v.p. 1979-81), Bus. & Profl. Women's Club, LaPorte Rep. Women's Club, LaPorte Homemakers Ext. Club, VFW Aux., Kiwanis. Roman Catholic. Home: 5144 N Pawnee Trl La Porte IN 46350-8261 Office: State House State Capital Indianapolis IN 46204

BUDD, ELAINE, social worker; b. Pitts., Dec. 26, 1923; d. Jacob and Bessie (Cohen) L.; m. William Budd, June 8, 1952 (div. Mar. 1984); children: Jonathan, Sandra. BS in Social Sci. with highest honors, Carnegie Mellon U., 1944; postgrad., Wayne State U., 1944; MSW, U. Pitts., 1948. Lic. ind. clin. social worker, Minn. Social worker various orgns. and agys., 1948-58; rsch. asst. NIMH, Bethesda, Md., 1959-60; with dept. selection and evaluation U.S. Peace Corps, Washington, 1961-62; dir. social work careers Dept. Human Svcs., State Minn., St. Paul, 1964-65, dir. adoption recruitment, dir. human svcs., 1965-69; faculty Sch. Social Work, Univ. Minn., Mpls., 1971-73; mgmt. analyst Hennepin County Affirmative Action, Mpls., 1973-74; developer and dir. family life enrichment svcs. Jewish Family and Children's Svc., Mpls., 1974-78; sr. social worker Hennepin County Dept. Community Svcs., Mpls., 1982—; pvt. practice Mpls., 1990—; counselor and group facilitator Chrysalis Ctr. for Women, Mpls., 1979-82; presenter at internat. conf.; invited to teach in Israel. Activist Kennedy for Pres., Washington, 1960, Peace Corps, Washington, 1960, Anti-Nuclear Movement, Minn., 1965—; union grievance chairperson, Chgo., 1950; mem. Simon Wiesenthal Ctr., CARE. Recipient Outstanding and Innovative Svc. award Nat. Assn. County Orgns., 1988, Spl. Honors Citation County Commrs. Hennepin County, 1992. Mem. Minn. Bd. Social Work, Amnesty Internat., Mus. of Tolerance, Walker Art Ctr., Hadassah, Holocaust Mus., Phi Kappa Phi, Pi Delta Epsilon. Home: 111 Marquette Ave Apt 2102 Minneapolis MN 55401-2032

BUDD, JIM, communications manager; b. Austin, Minn.; s. Stanley James and Margaret (Deutschman) B. Student, Austin State Jr. Coll. Head of CCTV dept. Northwest Camera Svc., Mpls., 1971-72; head of video svc. dept., engring., TV studio and video svc. dept. ops. Internat. Communications Svcs., Mpls., 1972-73; talent scout coord. and video cons. Wag Arts Prodns.-Talent Agy., Mpls., 1972-75; electronics dept. svc. mgr. Gordon Electric Co., Austin, 1975-78; operational ptnr. in design and mfr. of projection TV consoles with McAllister Trading Co. and ABC Electronics, Austin, 1979-84; video systems specialist The Electronics Warehouse, Inc., Rochester, Minn., 1984-85; engr., video dir., mgr. ABC Electronics & Video, Austin, 1985—; producer, dir. N.W. TV-Prodns., Austin, 1986—; systems design cons. in field. Script author, narrator of documentary videofilm: "Celebration of Hmong New Year"--Laos, 1991; producer: (video) Big Isl. Rendezvous, 1995. Videographer Summerset Theatre Group Austin Cmty. Coll., 1987; prodn. fund vol. PBS Sta. KSMQ-TV, Austin, 1984, 88-95. Mem. Am. Film Inst., Am. Legion, Comm. Computer Club. Roman Catholic. Office: N W TV Prodns/ABC Electronics 1008 5th Ave NW Austin MN 55912-2114

BUDKE, CAMILLA EUNICE, secondary education educator; b. Diller, Nebr., Nov. 9, 1928; d. Rudolph Elmer and Abbie Lena (Zarybnicky) Hubka; m. Larry Francis Budke, Sept. 13, 1952 (dec. June 1993); children: Laurie, Mary, David, Mark. BA cum laude, Duchesne Coll., Omaha, 1950; MS summa cum laude, Kans. State U., 1978, reading specialist, 1980. Tchr. English/history pub. schs., Blue Springs, Nebr., 1950-51; tchr. English/history Junction City, Kans., 1951-52, Marysville, Kans., 1969-73; tchr. English/reading Unified Sch. Dist. 383, Manhattan, Kans., 1974-91, substitute tchr., 1991—. Mem. Parent and Sch. Involvement Com., Manhattan, Kans., 1988-90. Mem. AAUW, NEA (bldg. rep. 1986-90), Internat. Reading Assn., Riley County Hist. Soc., Kans. Tchrs. English, Atheneum, Cath. Daus., United Nations (Manhattan Flint Hill chpt.), Alumnae of Sacred Heart, Delta Kappa Gamma, Kappa Gamma Pi. Democrat. Roman Catholic. Home: 1312 Nichols St Manhattan KS 66503

BUDNY, JAMES CHARLES, federal agency administrator; b. Dearborn, Mich., Aug. 11, 1948; s. William B. and Marion Catherine (Jazdzewski) B.; m. Maureen Anne Taylor, July 9, 1970; 1 child, Andrea. BBA, Ea. Mich. U., 1970; JD, Detroit Coll. Law, 1981. Revenue agent IRS, Dearborn, 1972-75; employee plans specialist IRS, Detroit, 1975-79, appeals officer, 1979-87, assoc. chief, 1987—, regional appeals employee plans coord., 1990-95; sec. Cass Plaza Corp., Grosse Ile, Mich., 1980—; acting chief Cleve. Appeals Office IRS, 1995; v.p. Cass Plaza Corp., Grosse Ile, Mich., 1983-90, pres., 1990—, also bd. dirs. Sec. Indsl. Park Promotion Com., Grosse Ile, 1986-91; asst. registrar Grosse Ile Youth Recreation Assn. for Football, 1991-92. Mem. Nat. Assn. Accts., Ea. Mich. U. Alumni Assn., Detroit Coll. Law Alumni Assn., Metro Detroit Alumni (Senate bd. govs. 1994—), Delta Theta Phi. Roman Catholic. Office: IRS Appeals Office 477 Michigan Ave Rm 470 Detroit MI 48226-2518 also: Cass Plz Corp PO Box 412 Grosse Ile MI 48138-0412

BUDRY, JOHN FRANCIS, mortgage banker, investment real estate broker; b. Grosse Pointe Farms, Mich., Aug. 13, 1966; s. Edwin Gary and Elizabeth Rose (Tocco) B.; m. Cynthia Beth Ruskin, June 28, 1992. BS in Econs., Mich. State U., 1990. Comml.-investment real estate broker Thomas A. Duke Co., Farmington Hills, Mich., 1990-91; asst. v.p. Rock Fin. Corp., Bingham Farms, Mich., 1991-95, FNMA/FHLMC and non-conforming mortgage banker, 1991—; nat. sales mgr. S.N.A.P. Corp. Ptnrs./Wholesale Mortgage Banking & Trust, Bloomfield Hills, Mich., 1995—. Mem. Rochester (Mich.) Bd. Realtors, Nat. Assn. Realtors, Mortgage Bankers Assn. Am. Republican. Roman Catholic. Home: 22 Hillstone Ct Columbia SC 29212

BUDZAK, KATHRYN SUE (MRS. ARTHUR BUDZAK), physician; b. Racine, Wis., May 6, 1940; d. Raymond Philip and Emma Kathryn (Sorensen) Myer; student Stephens Coll., 1957-58, Luther Coll., 1958-59; BS with honors, U. Wis. at Milw., 1962; MD, U. Wis., 1969; m. Arthur Budzak, Dec. 21, 1961; children: Ann Elizabeth, Lynn Marie. Intern, Madison (Wis.) Gen. Hosp., 1969-70; emergency physician, emergency suite St. Mary's Hosp., Madison, 1971-75; urgent care physician Dean Clinic, Madison, 1975-95; contract rsch. Dean Found., 1991—. Recipient Disting. Alumnae award Stephens Coll., 1979; named to Washington Park H.S. Hall of Fame, 1985. Mem. AMA, Am. Acad. Family Physicians, Wis. Acad. Family Physicians (pres. south ctrl. chpt. 1979-81), Wis. Med. Soc., Dane County Med. Soc., Am. Med. Women's Assn. (sponsor U. Wis. student br., pres. 1989-95), Wis. Med. Alumni Assn. (bd. dirs. 1979-82, pres. 1983-84, sec.-treas. 1994—), Wagon Trail Condo Assn. (dir., treas. 1990—, pres. 1993-95), Sigma Sigma Sigma. Presbyterian. Home: 6110 Davenport Dr Madison WI 53711-2446 Office: 1313 Fish Hatchery Rd Madison WI 53715-1911

BUECHEL, WILLIAM BENJAMIN, lawyer; b. Wichita, Kans., July 27, 1926; s. Donald William and Bonnie S. (Priddy) B.; m. Theresa Marie Girard, Nov. 3, 1955; children: Sarah Ann, Julia Elaine. Student U. Wichita, 1947-49; BS, U. Kans., 1951, LLB, 1954. Bar: Kans., 1954, U.S. dist. ct. (Kans.), 1954. Sole practice, Concordia, Kans., 1954-56; stockholder Paulsen, Buechel, Swenson, Uri & Brewer, Chartered, and predecessors, Concordia, 1971-75, sec.-treas., 1975-77, pres., 1977-92, of counsel, 1992—; bd. dirs. County Bank & Trust, Concordia, 1971-92, Cloud County Community Coll. Found., 1983-89, trust and adminstrn. com. Citizens Nat. Bank, 1992—. Mem. ABA, Kan. Bar Assn. (exec. council 1966-68, chmn. adv. sect. profl. ethics com. 1974-76), Cloud County Bar Assn. (pres. 1984-86). Republican. Methodist. Clubs: Concordia Country, Elks, Moose, Rotary (pres. 1969-70).

BUECHLER, BRADLEY BRUCE, plastic processing company executive, accountant; b. St. Louis, Dec. 5, 1948; s. Phillip Earl and Mildred M. (Braun) B.; m. Stephanie A. Walker, June 20, 1969; children: Sheila, Lisa, Brian. BSBA, U. Mo., St. Louis, 1971. CPA, Mo. Audit mgr. Arthur Andersen & Co., St. Louis, 1971-81; corp. controller Spartech Corp., St. Louis, 1981-83, exec. v.p., COO, 1984-87, pres., COO, 1987-91, pres., CEO, 1991—. Bd. regents St. Louis U., 1994—; mem. corp. bd. St. Joseph Inst. for the Deaf, 1995—. With Mo. Army N.G., 1969-75. Mem. AICPA, Soc. Plastics Industry (chmn. sheet prodrs. divsn., bd. dirs. 1993-95). Methodist. Office: Spartech Corp 7733 Forsyth Blvd Ste 1450 Clayton MO 63105-1817

BUEHLER, EVELYN JUDY, poet; b. Chgo.; d. Marzell William and Ida Mae Rubbia (Fields) Regulus; m. Henry Eric Buehler, Aug. 23, 1985; children: Ashley Leonard, Evelyn Judy. Student, Loop Coll., Chgo. Contbr. poetry to Today's Greatest Poems, Our Twentieth Century's Greatest Poems, Our World's Best Loved Poems, Our World's Most Beloved Poems, Night Skies in Winter, Am. Poetry Anthology, Best New Poets of 1987, Poems That Will Live Forever, The Best Poems of the 90's, Whispers in the Wind, Outstanding Poets of 1994, The Songs of Poetry, At Day's End, A Writer's Season, The Best Writers of 1995, Worldly Thoughts, Lyrics of Poetry, The Best Poems of 1995, others. Mem. Internat. Soc. Poets (life). Democrat. Baptist. Home: 5658 S Normal Blvd Chicago IL 60621

BUELOW, GEORGE JOHN, musicologist, educator; b. Chgo., Mar. 31, 1929; s. George J. and Florence (Cook) B. Mus.B., Chgo. Mus. Coll., 1950, Mus.M., 1951; postgrad., U. Hamburg, Germany, 1953-54; Ph.D., N.Y. U., 1961. Instr. music history Chgo. Conservatory, 1959-61; from asst. prof. to asso. prof. musicology U. Calif., Riverside, 1961-68; prof., chmn. dept. music U. Ky., 1968-69; prof., dir. grad. program in music Rutgers U., New Brunswick, N.J., 1969-77; prof. musicology Ind. U., 1977—; mem. Commn. Mixte Internat. Inventory Musical Sources; co-chmn. Internat. Johann Mattheson Symposium, Wolfenbüttel, Fed. Republic Germany, 1981. Author: Thorough-bass Accompaniment According to J.D. Heinichen, 1966, 3d edit., 1992, Johann Mattheson's Opera, Cleopatra, in Das Erbe deutscher Musik, vol. 69, 1975, The Ariadne auf Naxos by Hofmannsthal and Strauss, 1975, Man and Music: The Late Baroque, vol. 4, 1993; Am. editor: ACTA Musicologica, 1967-86; editor: Coll. Music Soc.'s Symposium, 1970-71; mem. exec. com. The New Grove Dictionary of Music and Musicians, 1971-80; editor: UMI Research Press Studies in Musicology, 1977-89; mem. nat. adv. bd. Die Musik in Geschichte und Gegenwart, 1990—; contbr. articles profl. jours; co-editor: New Mattheson Studies, 1983. Mem. German nat. screening com. Fulbright-Hays Program, 1993—. Guggenheim fellow, 1967, Rutgers Rsch. Coun. fellow, 1974-75; Fulbright scholar Germany, 1954-55; Festa musicologica: Essays in Honor of George J. Buelow, 1995. Mem. Am. Musicol. Soc., Internt. Musicol. Socs. (mem. direktorium 1987—), Royal Mus. Assn., Gesellschaft fur Musikforschung, Am. Bach Soc. (pres. bd. dirs. 1987—), Am. Handel Soc. (v.p., bd. dirs. 1989-94). Home: 2935 N Bankers Dr Bloomington IN 47408-1021 Office: Ind U Sch Music Bloomington IN 47405

BUELSING, JEFF, mechanical engineer; b. Cin., Jan. 16, 1962. Degree in mech. engring., U. Cin., 1991. Project engr. Alba Mfg., Cin., 1991—. Office: Alba Mfg 19 Kiesland Ct Hamilton OH 45015-1375

BUERKI, ROBERT ARMIN, pharmacy educator; b. Madison, Wis., Nov. 15, 1939; s. Robert Arthur and Gail Genevieve (Banks) B.; m. Sara Jane Adams, Sept. 3, 1956 (div. Aug. 1978); m. Leslie Jean Stein, Apr. 25, 1979; 1 child, Robin Arthur. BS in Pharmacy, U. Wis., 1963, MS in Pharmacy, 1967; PhD in Edn., Ohio State U., 1972; MA in History, Wright State U., 1988. Registered pharmacist, Wis., Ohio. Instr. Coll. Pharmacy Ohio State U., Columbus, 1965-72, asst. prof., 1972-77, assoc. prof., 1977—; exec. sec. Coun. Ohio Colls. Pharmacy, Columbus, 1966-78, series editor, 1976—; hist. cons. Ohio Hist. Soc., Columbus, 1984—. Author: Historical Perspective, Continuing Education in Pharmacy, 1987, Pharmaceutical Education in 19th Century Ohio, 1995; co-author: Rho Chi Society, 1988, History of Dosage Forms, 1992, Ethical Responsibility in Pharmacy Practice, 1994; editor: Jour. Pharmacy Teaching, 1993—; contbg. editor: Pharmacy in History, 1984—. Fellow Am. Coll. Apothecaries; mem. Am. Assn. Coll. Pharmacy (chmn. sect. on continuing profl. edn. 1977-79), Am. Inst. Hist. Pharmacy (pres. 1983-85, Cert. of Commendation 1987), Am. Pharm. Assn., Am. Assn. History of Medicine, History of Sci. Soc., Sigma Xi, Phi Delta Kappa, Phi Lambda Sigma, Phi Alpha Theta, Rho Chi (pres. 1976-78, Disting. Svc. award 1972, 85). Democrat. Jewish. Home: 4093 Chico Ct Springfield OH 45502-9709 Office: Ohio State U Coll Pharmacy 500 W 12th Ave Columbus OH 43210-1214

BUESCHEL, RICHARD MARTIN, writer; b. Chgo., Dec. 26, 1926; s. Martin William and Helen Gloria (Kernacs) B.; m. Helen Marian Snyder, Nov. 24, 1951; children: Stacey Brooks McDonald, Megan Conley Conaty. AS, Wright Jr. Coll., Chgo., 1949; BA, Ill. Coll., 1951. Cert. bus. communicator. Traffic mgr. Henri, Hurst & McDonald, Chgo., 1951-52; copywriter Wallace-Ferry-Hanly Co., Chgo., 1952-55; jr. account exec. Erwin Wasey & Co., Chgo., 1955-57; account exec. Erwin, Wasey, Ruthrauff & Ryan, Chgo., 1957-59; pres. Waldie and Briggs, Inc., Chgo., 1959-75; exec. v.p. Ladd, Wells, Presba Inc., Chgo., 1976-79; sr. account exec. Zylke & Assocs., Northbrook, Ill., 1979-89; v.p. W. M. Shanahan, Inc., Chgo., 1990-95. Author: Hien, 1966, Communist Chinese Airpower, 1968, Aircam Fighters Series, 8 vols., 1970-71, Aircam Bombers Series, 4 vols., 1972-73, Illustrated Guide to Collectible Slot Machines, 4 vols., 1978-88, Illustrated Guide to Trade Stimulators, 2 vols., 1979-92, Pinball 1: 1775-1931, 1988, Saloon, 1989, Jennings Slot Machines, 1992, Aracade 1: 1876-1905, 1993, Trade 2, 1993, Coin-Ops on Location, 1993, Mills Consoles, 1994, Payout Dice Machines, 1994, Zero-Sen, 1995, Collector's Guide to Vintage Coin Machines, 1995, Hayabusa, 1995, Big Head "Lollipop Scales," 1995, Lemons, Cherries, and Bell-Fruit Gum, 1995, Arcade Sport Games, 1996, Shoki, 1996, Encyclopedia of Pinball 1930-1933, vol. 1, 1996; editor: Air Progress, 1965-68, Air Combat, 1968-73, Classic Amusements, 1992-94, Coin-Op Classics, 1994—; histr. editor The Coinslot, 1973-94; columnist Antique Week, Coin Machines, 1991—. Mem. Authors Guild, Author's League Am., Soc. for History Tech., Am. Assn. for State and Local History, Bus. Mktg. Assn. (pres. Chgo. chpt. 1965-67). Home and Office: 414 N Prospect Manor Ave Mount Prospect IL 60056-2046

BUESCHER, THOMAS PAUL, labor market analyst; b. Cleve., May 16, 1949; s. Victor Paul and Geraldine Juel (Durkin) B.; m. Pamela Ann Piscitotta, Jan. 29, 1977; 1 child, Brittany Beth. BBA, Kent State U., 1975. Auditor Ohio Bur. Employment Svcs., Cleve., 1978-83, labor market analyst, 1983—; guest instr. for exec. MBA program Cleve. State U.; chmn. bd. Ohio Indsl. Tng. Program Greater Cleve. Author: (analysis report for nat. league of cities) Demographic Analysis of the Targeted Job Tax Credit program for Cleve., 1985. Mem. allocations panel Fedn. of Cath. Cmty. Svcs., 1987-92; mem. Local Welfare Reform Panel for Congress, 1987, Cleve. area Gov.'s Regional Econ. Adv. Bd., 1992—, Cleve. Area Devel. Corp. Bd., 1994—; mem. consortium to develop a nat. inst. Labor Market Info.; chmn. Initiative V task force, mem. adv. com. Cleve. Pub. Schs., 1988—;. Mem. Internat. Assn. Pers. in Employment Security (Ohio pres. 1988, internat. v.p. 1993-94, award of merit 1989, inducted into Hall of Fame 1990, internat. pres.-elect 1994-95, internat. pres. 1995—). Democrat. Home: 464 Calverton Pl Brunswick OH 44212-1820 Office: Ohio Bur Employment Svc 5739 Chevrolet Blvd Cleveland OH 44130-1414

BUFFO, WILLIAM JOSEPH, mortgage company executive, consultant; b. Berwyn, Ill., Oct. 17, 1947; s. William Joseph B. Sr.; m. Jane Ann Thuesen, Aug 30, 1975; 1 child, William Joseph III. BS in Mktg., U. Wis., 1975. Registered realtor, Wis., lic. mortgage broker, Wis. Salesman foods divsn. Coca-cola, Milw., 1975-80; owner Buffo Floral & Gifts, Inc., Madison, Wis., 1977-83, Am. Fin. Corp. Wis., Madison, 1980-83; br. mgr. M & I Mortgage Co., Inc., Madison, 1983-84; mem. bd. dirs. Buffo Mortgage Co., Inc., Madison, 1983—, pres., 1984—; pres. Metro Mortgage Co., Inc., Madison, 1986—, Mo., 1986—; bd. dirs. Exch. Club, Madison, Wis., 1981—; ptnr. Star Investments, Madison, 1984—, Snapshots, 1986-93; mem. adv. bd. WHEDA, 1994—. Mem. Citizens Against Govt. Waste, D.C., 1990—. With USN, 1967-71. Mem. Nat. Assn. Mortgage Brokers, Wis. Mortgage Brokers Assn., Wis. Builders Assn., Wis. Realtors Assn., Greater Madison Bd. Realtors Inc., Madison Area Builders Assn., Blackhawk Country Club, Sigma Chi. Roman Catholic. Home: 401 N Gammon Rd Madison WI 53717 Office: Metro Mortgage Co Inc 6657 Odana Rd Madison WI 53719

BUFFTON, DEBORAH DARLENE, history educator; b. Valley City, N.D., Nov. 24, 1958; d. William George and Catherine Edith (Matthews) B. BA, Ithaca Coll., 1979; MA, Binghamton U., 1981; PhD, U. Wis., 1987. Teaching asst. Binghamton (N.Y.) U., 1979-81, U. Wis., Madison, 1983-84, 86-87; asst. prof. U. Wis., LaCrosse, 1987-90, assoc. prof. history, 1990—, dir. history fair, 1989-93. Co-editor: A Gathering of Voices on the Asian American Experience, 1994; contbr. articles to profl. publs. Mem. exec. com. Wis. Inst., 1993—, exec. dir., 1995—. Recipient Bourse Chateaubriand, French Govt., 1984-85; U. Wis.-LaCrosse rsch. grantee, 1990; U. Wis. System teaching fellow, 1994—; Disting. faculty scholar Wis. Inst., 1993. Mem. Am. History Assn., Am. Hist. Assn., Assn. Asian Scholars, French History Soc., Western Soc. French History, Amnesty Internat. Office: U Wis History Dept 401 North Hall La Crosse WI 54601

BUFKA, JOHN ANDREW, sales executive; b. St. Louis, Apr. 8, 1958; s. Vernon Andrew and LaVerne Lee (Houston) B.; m. Terri Lea Fudge, Oct. 4, 1986. BS in Bus. Mgmt., Maryville Coll., 1987. Scheduler Shillington Box Co., St. Louis, 1978-81, customer service rep., 1981-84, sales rep., 1984; sales exec. Boxes, Inc., St. Louis, 1991—. Mem. Am. Ind. Corrugated Convertors, The Legends Country Club, Delta Epsilon Sigma.

BUGBEE, E. EUGENE, farmer, stockman; b. Republican City, Nebr., July 17, 1957; s. Raymond Haskell and Marjorie Lucille (Kendall) B.; m. Raylene Kay Tegtman, July 30, 1983; children: Amanda, Ross, Abby. BS in Bus. Mgmt., Ft. Hays State U., 1979. Farmer, stockman Phillipsburg, Kans., 1979—; bd. dirs. Phillipsburg Co-op Assn. Mem. sch. bd. United Sch. Dist. # 325, Phillipsburg, 1993—; mem. Rural Fire Bd., Phillipsburg, 1991—; mem. Ext. Coun., Phillipsburg, 1985, 86; trustee Glenwood Twp., Phillipsburg, 1979—. Recipient award Soil Conservation Svc., 1991. Republican. Lutheran. Home and Office: RR 1 Box 143 Republican City NE 68971

BUGGEY, LESLEY JOANNE, education educator, consultant; b. Mpls., July 25, 1938; d. Leslie Francis and Blanche (Moore) B. BS, Macalester Coll., 1960; MEd, U. Wash., Seattle, 1968; PhD, U. Wash., 1971. Cert. elem. tchr., Minn. Tchr. elem. Mpls. Pub. Schs., 1960-71; co-dir. Social Studies Svc. Ctr., St. Paul, 1971-73; lectr. in edn. Stanford (Calif.) U., 1973-74; ednl. cons., author, tchr., lectr. in edn. U. Minn., Mpls., 1974—; cons. in field. Speaker various orgns. Mem. ASCD, Nat. Coun. Geographic Edn. (past bd. dirs.), Nat. Coun. Social Studies (nat. com. mem.), Minn. Coun. for Social Studies. Presbyterian. Home: 2800 W 44th St Minneapolis MN 55410-1557 Office: Univ Minn Education Dept Minneapolis MN 55455

BUGIELSKI, ROBERT JOSEPH, state legislator; b. Chgo., June 5, 1947; s. Edward Leon and Lottie Regina (Ptak) B.; m. Dona Rosalie Obrzut, Aug. 2, 1980. BS in Bus. Edn., Chgo. State U., 1971. Tchr. Weber High Sch., Chgo., 1971-83; asst. athletic dir., 1973-78; dir. devel. Weber High Sch., Chgo., 1974-83, adminstrv. bd. dirs., 1975-83; rep. Ill. Gen. Assembly, Chgo., 1987—. Named Legislator of Yr. Am. Legis. Exch. Coun., 1991. Democrat. Roman Catholic. Office: 6839 W Belmont Ave Chicago IL 60634

BUHL, WILLIAM CHRISTIAN, circuit court judge; b. Port Huron, Mich., Sept. 8, 1942; s. Lloyd Frank and Rosamond (Davidson) B.; m. Leslie Jean Baxter, June 24, 1967; children: Kelly Ann, William Christian, Shannon Marie, Courtney Jean, Dana Ambre, Micah Sun Chul, Shea Tristan, Tyson Sung Jung, Ginia Alexandria, Tyne Kyung Ja, Sherline Hannah, Amanda Brooke, Farah Rosamond, Christian Noah. BA in History, U. Mich., 1964, JD, 1967. Asst. prosecuting atty. Van Buren County, Paw Paw, Mich., 1968; prosecuting atty. Van Buren County, Paw Paw, 1969-74, 7th dist. ct. judge, 1974-88, 36th cir. ct. judge, 1989—. Columnist: The Gavel Rap, The Deckerville Recorder, 1989-93. Presbyterian. Office: Van Buren County Circuit Ct 212 Paw Paw MI 49709

BUHNER, BYRON BEVIS, health science facility administrator; b. Hammond, Ind., Feb. 19, 1950; s. John Colin and Betty (Bevis) B.; children: Zachery Aaron, Rebecca Davis. AB in Comm., Ind. U., 1976, MS in Human Resource Devel., 1981. Adminstr. Ind. U., Indpls., 1976-77, instr. evaluator sch. nursing, 1981-82; tng. specialist Ayr-Way, Target Stores, Indpls., 1977-81; assoc. exec. dir. Cen. Ind. Regional Blood Ctr., Indpls., 1984-88, pres., chief exec. officer, 1988—; founding mem. Blood Ctrs. Ins. Exch., Risk Retention Group, 1993, chmn. bd. dirs., 1993—; adminstr. Blood Rsch. and Edn. Foundn. of Ind., Inc., Indpls., 1985-89, bd. mem., 1989-94. Producer: Multi-Image film, Focus on Transition, 1981, A Manager's Perspective, 1981; photographer: Sound, Slide program, Wearable - Arts '81. Trustee Coun. Cmty. Blood Ctrs., 1986—, chmn. purchasing com., 1988-92, chmn. fin. com., treas., 1992-94, v.p., 1994-96, pres.-elect, 1996, chmn. group svcs. com., chmn. long-range planning com. Fellow Am. Acad. Healthcare Execs.; mem. Ind. U. Alumni Assn. (bd. dirs. 1983-88), Am. Assn. Blood Banks, Ind. Assn. Blood Banks (bd. dirs. 1988-91), Kiwanis. Home: 11362 Bayhill Way Indianapolis IN 46236-9233 Office: Cen Ind Regional Blood Ctr 3450 N Meridian St Indianapolis IN 46208-4437

BUHR, CRAIG ALLEN, geotechnical engineer; b. Waterloo, Iowa, Feb. 25, 1953; s. Edwin Louis and Glenna Lucile (Bliss) B.; m. Ellen Kae Ledet, Nov. 26, 1977; children: Douglas Karl, Erin Christine, Christopher Allen. BS in Civil Engring., Iowa State U., 1976; MS, U. Kans., 1981. Registered profl. engr., Mo., Kans., Fla., Md., Ill., Colo., Mich., Iowa, Va., ohio, N.Y., Calif. Mgr. geotech. engring. dept. Burns & McDonnell Engring., Kansas City, Mo., 1976—. Contbr. articles to profl. jours.; presenter in field. Active Lee's Summit Christian Ch. Mem. NSPE, ASCE, Internat. Soc. Soil Mechs. and Found. Engring., Assn. Engring. Firms Practicing in Geoscis., Chi Epsilon. Home: 316 SE Williamsburg Cir Lees Summit MO 64063-3621

BUHR, FLORENCE D., county official; b. Strahan, Iowa, Apr. 7, 1933; d. Earnest G. and May (Brott) Wederquist; m. Glenn E. Buhr, 1955; children: Barbara, Lori Lynn, David. BA, U. No. Iowa, 1954. Precinct chair Polk County Dem. Ctrl. Com., Iowa, 1974-79; clerk, sec. Iowa Ho. Reps., 1974-79, 81-82; rep. dist. 85 State of Iowa, 1983-90, asst. majority leader Ho. Reps., 1985-90; state senator Iowa State Senate, 1991-95, asst. majority leader, 1992-95; Polk County supr. Des Moines, 1995—. Democrat. Presbyterian. Home and Office: 4127 30th St Des Moines IA 50310-5946

BUI, TY VAN, computer programmer, systems analyst; b. Cai Tau Ha, Sadec, Vietnam, Dec. 7, 1959; came to U.S., 1988; s. Tu Van and Nhung Thi (Ha) B.; m. CamVan Nguyen, Feb. 15, 1986; 1 child, Quoc Trung Dinh. BS in Secondary Edn., Edn. Coll., Vietnam, 1980; BS in Computer Sci. and Applied Math., U. Wis., Oshkosh, 1992. Tchr. math. Cao Lanh (Vietnam) High Sch., 1980-82; tchr. physics Sadec High Sch., 1982-84; chief comm. sect. UN High Commn. for Refugees, The Philippines, 1986-87; computer programmer Wis. Dept. Revenue, Madison, 1990, systems analyst, 1991; cons. computer lab. U. Wis., 1990-92, computer programming cons. English dept., 1992; computer programmer, cons. Kag Labs. Internat., Inc., Oshkosh, 1992; sr. programmer analyst Northwestern Mut. Life Ins., Milw., 1993—; software engr. Mgmt. Control System, 1991; programmer An Invention or Idea Generating Program, 1992. Mem. Assn. for Computing Machinery, Math. Assn. Am., Alpha Lambda Delta. Home: 7046 W Evans Dr Franklin WI 53132

BUISMAN, V. WAYNE, safety engineer; b. York, N.D., Mar. 18, 1941; s. Victor and Helen M. (Johnson) B.; children: Allen, Donald, Nicholaas. BA/BS, U. N.D., 1969; MS, U. Idaho, 1991, Cen. Mo. State U., 1993. CSP; registered profl. engr., Mass. Compliance officer U.S. Dept. of Labor (OSHA), Phila., 1971-75; safety engr. U.D. Dept. Energy, Idaho Falls, Idaho, 1975—. With USN, 1960. Mem. Am. Soc. Safety Engrs. Mem. LDS. Home: PO Box 245 Harris MN 55032

BUKALA, ALEXANDER E., engineering administrator; b. Chgo., Oct. 9, 1940. Chief engr. Littlefuse, Inc., Des Plaines, Ill., 1983-90, mgr. automotive, 1990-93, mgr. engring., 1993—. Patentee in field. Mem. SAE (adv. bd. 1982-93). Republican. Roman Catholic. Home: 1340 Marble Hill Dr Lake Zurich IL 60047-1744

BUKAR, MARGARET WITTY, physician assistant, healthcare administrator, civic leader; b. Evanston, Ill., June 21, 1950; d. LeRoy and Catherine Ann (Conrad) Witty; m. Gregory Bryce Bukar, June 5, 1971 (dec. 1989); children: Michael Bryce, Caroline Nicole. BS, DePaul U., 1972, MBA, 1981; MS, Finch U. Health Scis., 1996. Staff med. technologist The Evanston (Ill.) Hosp., 1972-75, immunopathology lab. supr., 1975-77, lab. mgr., 1977-84, dir. lab. adminstrn., 1984-85; bookkeeper Ronald Knox Montessori Sch., Wilmette, Ill., 1986-87; beauty cons. Mary Kay Cosmetics, 1990—; sec. Northwestern U., Evanston, 1991-94; physician asst. Women's Med. Group, P.C., Skokie-Evanston, Ill., 1996—. Den leader Cub Scouts, Boy Scouts Am., Wilmette, 1985-87, den leader coach, 1987-88; active PTA of St. Francis Xavier Sch., 1985—, chair rummage sale, 1987-88, scouting coord., 1991-92, mem. sch. bd., 1986-87, sec. 1988-89, vice chmn., 1989-90; eucharistic min. sick St. Francis Xavier Ch., 1990—, liturgical song leader, 1993—; troup co-leader, song leader Girl Scouts Am., 1992—. Recipient Emily Withrow Stebbins award Evanston Hosp., 1985. Mem. NAFE, Am. Soc. Clin. Pathologists, Am. Acad. Physician Assts., Ill. Acad. Physician Assts., Wilmette Hist. Soc., Elms Social Club (pres. 1992). Avocations: knitting, interior design, reading.

BUKER, ELOISE ANN, political science educator; b. Jan. 3, 1941; d. Thomas R. and Eloise L.; m. Robert Cahill. BA in English, Capital U., 1963; MA in Polit. Sci., U. Hawaii, 1978, PhD in Polit. Sci., 1981. Dir. internat. studies Gonzaga U., Spokane, Wash., 1985-88, co-dir. women's studies, 1988-91; asst. prof. polit. sci. Gonzaga U., Spokane, 1981-88, assoc. prof. polit. sci., 1988-91; dir. women's studies program U. Utah, Salt Lake City, 1991-93, assoc. prof. polit. sci., 1991-93; dir. women's studies Denison U., Granville, Ohio, 1993-95, prof. polit. sci. & women's studies, 1993—, assoc. prof. women's studies, 1993—. Author: Politics Through A Looking Glass: Understanding Political Cultures Through a Strucutralist Interpretation of Narratives, 1987 (Jesuit Nat. Book award 1987), Taking Parts: Ingredients for Leadership, Participation and Empowerment, 1994. Mem. various tasks forces; active cmty. orgns. for women's edn. Mem. Am. Polit. Scis. Assn. (awar 1989), Western Polit. Sci. Assn., Nat. Women's Studies Assn., N.W. Women's Studies Assn., Midwestern Polit. Sci. Assn., Alpha Sigma Nu. Office: Denison U 106 Fellows Hall Granville OH 43023

BUKHARI, AFTAB ALI, computer company executive; b. Shujabad, Multan, Pakistan, Nov. 7, 1959; s. Syed-Muhammad Ali-Shah and Hafeeza-Begum (Gilani) B. BSc in Physics and Math., Govt. Coll., Multan, 1979; MBA in Fin., U. Multan, 1983; LLB, U. Law Coll., Multan, 1985; MS in Computer Engring., Wayne State U., 1987. Mgr. Ice Factory, Shjabad, Pakistan, 1977-78; rsch. asst. U. Multan, 1982; project engr. Bukhari Electric Concern, Lahore, Pakistan, 1988-90; pres., CEO The 786 Co., Detroit, 1991—; dir. Internat. Bus. Advisors, Detroit, 1991—; cons. Cost Reductions Cons., Bloomfield Hills, Mich., 1993—, Mich. Telecomm. Assocs., Bloomfield Hills, 1994—; lectr. computer info. sys. Lewis Coll. of Bus., Detroit, 1994—, mem. curriculum revision com., 1994.Co. Leader Boy Scouts, Shujabad, 1970-74, Rover Scouts, Multan, 1980-82; capt. Pakistan U. Hockey Team, 1982-84, Friends Field Hockey Club, Detroit, 1986-88. Merit scholar Higher Edn., U. Multan, 1981-83. Mem. IEEE, Computer Soc. of IEEE, MBA Execs., Instrument Soc. Am., Engring. Soc. Detroit (cmty. amb. 1993-94). Islam. Address: PO Box 10263 Detroit MI 48210-0263 Office: The 786 Co 3434 Michigan Ave Detroit MI 48216-1041

BUKONDA, NGOYI K. ZACHARIE, health care management educator; b. Lubumbashi, Shaba, Zaire, Feb. 14, 1951; came to U.S., 1987; s. Munyuka Kalambayi and Tumba (Tshileo) Marie; m. Muyumba Kapinga Agnes, Aug. 29, 1975; children: Munyuka Ngoyi, Muyumba Ngoyi, Kalambayi Ngoyi, Tshileo Ngoyi, Kashala Ngoyi, Ntumba Ngoyi Gloria. BS in Health Systems Mgmt., U. Kinshasa, Zaire, 1981; Diploma in Teaching, U. Zaire, 1983; MPH, U. Minn. Sch. Pub. Health, 1989; PhD, U. Minn., 1994. Hosp. adminstr. Gen. Hosp., Bukavu, Zaire, 1975-76; chief of bur. Ministry of Health Zaire, Kinshasa, 1981-83, chief of div., 1983-87; health planner Sanru B.P. 3355 Kinshasa, Kinshasa, 1987; asst. prof. Inst. Superieur de Techniques Medicales, Kinshasa, 1981-87; grad. fellow African Am. Inst., N.Y.C., 1987-94; grad. teaching asst. Grad. Program in Social & Adminstrv. Pharmacy, Mpls., 1991-94; asst. prof. health care mgmt. So. Ill. U., Carbondale, 1994—; acad. sec. Inst. Superieur de Techniques Medicales, Kinshasa, 1983-86. Recipient Afgrad fellowship African Am. Inst., 1987, Melendy Grad. fellowship Coll. of Pharmacy, 1991; grantee Mac Arthur Interdisciplinary Program on Peace Internat., 1991; named Hon. Citizen of Louisville, 1986. Mem. Am. Pub. Health Assn., Am. Pharmacy Assn., Assn. des Adminstrs. Gestionnaires (pres. 1981-87). Roman Catholic. Home: 803 S Glenview Dr Carbondale IL 62901 Office: So Ill U Dept Health Care Profession Mail Box 6615 Carbondale IL 62901

BUKOWCZYK, JOHN JOSEPH, history educator, consultant, writer, lecturer; b. Perth Amboy, N.J., June 16, 1950. BA, Northwestern U., 1972; AM, Harvard U., 1973, PhD, 1980. Vis. instr. Conn. Coll., New London, 1978-79, vis. asst. prof., 1979-80; from asst. prof. to assoc. prof. history Wayne State U., Detroit, 1980-92, prof., 1992—, rsch. grant, 1987-88. Author: And My Children Did Not Know Me: A History of the Polish-Americans, 1987; co-editor: Detroit Images: Photographs of the Renaissance City, 1989; editor: Polish Americans and Their History: Community, Culture, and Politics, 1996. Sec. to corp. Preservation Detroit, 1984-86. Recipient McCormick prize N.J. Hist. Commn., 1985, award for acad. achievement Probus Club, Detroit, 1985. Mem. Am. Hist. Assn. (co-recipient William Gilbert award for best article in tchg.), Orgn. Am. Historians, Social Sci. History Assn. (nominating com. 1985-87), Nat. Coun. on Pub. History, Oral History Assn., Urban History Assn., Immigration History Soc. (exec. bd. 1988-91), Polish Am. Hist. Assn. (nat. pres. 1990-92, co-recipient Halecki prize for best book 1987, Haiman award 1994). Office: Wayne State U History Dept 3094 Faculty/Adminstrn Bldg Detroit MI 48202

BUKOWSKI, DANIEL JOSEPH, portfolio manager; b. Milw., May 6, 1963; s. Ronald R. Bukowski and Emilie K. (Plevak) Velzka. BA, U. Chgo., 1984, MBA, 1986; postgrad., Chgo. Theol. Sem., 1992—. Portfolio mgr. Morgan Stanley Asset Mgmt., Chgo., 1984-88; quantitative analyst IDS Fin. Svcs., Mpls., 1988-89; sr. v.p., dir. quantitative rsch. Zurich Kemper Investments, Chgo., 1989—. Treas. Uhlich Children's Home, Chgo., 1991—; bd. dirs. Chgo. quantitative Alliance, 1993—. Mem. Phi Beta Kappa, Beta Gamma Sigma. Office: Kemper Fin Svcs 120 S La Salle St Chicago IL 60603-3402

BULL, BARRY LEONARD, education educator; b. Billings, Mont., Aug. 29, 1947; s. Arthur Clyde and Marjorie Fern (Grenier) B.; m. Irene Sue Ruderman, Dec. 16, 1971; children: Alan G., Ethan S. BA in English cum laude, Yale U., 1969; MA in English, U. Va., 1970; MA in Teaching, U. Idaho, 1972; PhD in Philosophy of Edn., Cornell U., 1979. Cert. standard secondary English tchr., Idaho; cert. secondary English, social studies, chemistry tchr., Mass.; cert. continuing elem. and secondary tchr., Wash. Tchr. English and social studies Tottenham Tech. Sch., Braybrook, Victoria, Australia, 1972-74; mem. profl. staff in evaluation, planning and stats. Idaho Dept. Edn., Boise, 1974-76; cons. curriculum com. for K-12 social studies Ithaca (N.Y.) City Sch. System, 1978-79; asst. prof. edn. Wellesley (Mass.) Coll., 1979-84; policy assoc. acad. program unit Wash. Coun. for Post-secondary Edn., Olympia, 1984-85; instrnl. program specialist 2 Office Supt. Pub. Instrn., Olympia, 1985-86; assoc., asst. prof. dept. ednl. founds. U. Hawaii at Manoa, Honolulu, 1986-89; assoc. prof. dept. ednl. policy and adminstrn. U. Minn., Mpls., 1989-90; assoc. prof. dept. ednl. leadership and policy studies Ind. U., Bloomington, 1990-95; prof., chair dept. ednl leadership and policy studies Indiana U., Bloomington, 1995—; dir. Ind. Edn. Policy Ctr., Bloomington, 1992—; presenter in field, 1976—; guest manuscript reviewer Jour. Tchr. Edn., 1990; mem. rev. bd. Ednl. Theory, 1985-89; mem. adv. com. on edn. for gifted and talented Wellesley Pub. Sch. Dist., 1979-80; mem. profl. edn. adv. com. Wash. Bd. Edn., 1984-85; mem. adv. com. on schs. of choice Hawaii Bd. Edn., 1989; numerous others. Mem. editorial bd. Ednl. Theory, 1987-89; contbr. articles to profl. jours. Francis I. Dupont fellow U. Va., 1969-70, Edn. Professions Devel. Act fellow U. Idaho, 1971-72, grad. fellow Cornell U., 1976-78, Allen Seymour Olstead fellow Cornell U., 1978-79, fellow Am. Coun. Learned Socs., 1982-83, Wellesley Ctr. for Rsch. on Women, 1983-84. Fellow Philosophy of Edn. Soc. (program com. 1982, membership com. 1984-85, resolutions com. 1986-87, exec. bd. 1995-97); mem. Am. Ednl. Rsch. Assn. (proposal reivewer divsn. G, 1984-86, 88, 89), Am. Ednl. Studies Assn. (program com. 1982). Home: 2505 E Rechter Rd Bloomington IN 47401-6170 Office: Ind U Edn # 4232 Bloomington IN 47405

BULLARD, WILLIS CLARE, JR., state legislator; b. Detroit, July 12, 1943; s. Willis C. and Virginia Katherine (Gilmore) B.; children: Willis C. III, Melissa Ann. AB, U. Mich., 1965; JD, Detroit Coll. Law, 1971. Bar: Mich. 1971. Practice of law Detroit, 1971-77, Troy, Mich., 1977-80, Milford, Mich., 1983—; supr. Highland Twp., Mich., 1980-82; mem. Mich. Ho. of Reps., 1983—; asst. Rep. caucus chmn., 1983-84, asst. Rep. floor leader, 1985-88, chmn. House Rep. campaign, 1987-90; chmn. House taxation com., 1993—; chmn. task force Midwestern Legis. Conf. Coun. State Govts., 1985-86; mediator cir. and dist. cts., 1988—. Bd. dirs. Dunham Lake Property Owners Assn., 1975-78, treas., 1975-76, pres., 1976-78; mem. Dunham Lake Civic Com., 1982-87; trustee Highland Twp., 1978-80, mem. zoning bd. appeals, 1979. Named Legislator of Yr. Mich. Twp. Assn., 1984. Mem. Oakland County Bar Assn., State Bar Mich., Oakland County Assn. Twp. Suprs. (sec.-treas. 1981), Michigamua. Clubs: U. Mich. of Greater Detroit, Highland Republican, Highland Men's (sec. 1979, pres. 1980). Home: 1843 Wixom Trail Milford MI 48381-1563 Office: State Capitol Lansing MI 48909

BULLER, GARY W., investment broker; b. Brookings, S.D., Nov. 9, 1952. BS in Agrl. Engring., S.D. State U., 1977, MS. Cert. EIT sect. 7. Dir. mem. svcs. Assn. Ill. Elec. Corp., Springfield, Ill., 1978-81; computer applications specialist U. Ill., Springfield, 1982-84; indsl. sales mgr. Ill. Power Co., Decatur, Ill., 1984-89; investment broker A. G. Edwards & Sons Inc., Champaign, Ill., 1989—. Mem. Am. Soc. Agrl. Engrs. (fin. com. 1992—), Ill. Farm Electrification (pres. 1981), Rotary, Champaign C. of C. Office: A G Edwards & Sons Inc PO Box 950 100 Trade Centre Champaign IL 61824

BULLOCK, DAVID L., stockbroker; b. Whiteland, Ind., Aug. 2, 1949. BA in Econs., U. Indpls., 1973. Pres. Bargersville (Ind.) Fed., 1973-92; stockbroker City Securities Corp., Bloomington, Ind., 1992—. Mem. Rotary. Mem. Christian Ch. (Disciples of Christ). Office: City Securities Corp 513 S Woodcrest Dr Bloomington IN 47401-5335

BULLOCK, JOHN DAVID, ophthalmic surgeon; b. Cin., July 31, 1943; s. Joseph Craven and Emilie Helen (Woide) B.; m. Gretchen Hageman, June 25, 1966; children: John David Jr., Katherine Ann, Richard Joseph. AB, Dartmouth Coll., 1965, BMS, 1966; MD, Harvard U., 1968; postgrad. Armed Forces Inst. Pathology, 1970; MS in Microbiology and Immunology, Wright State U., 1982. Diplomate Am. Bd. Ophthalmology. Intern, asst. in medicine Washington U., St. Louis, 1968-69; resident in ophthalmology and plastic surgery Yale U., 1971-74, clin. instr. ophthalmology, 1974; Heed fellow U. Calif., San Francisco, 1974-75; Orbital fellow Mayo Clinic, Rochester, Minn., 1975; clin. instr. ophthalmology Stanford (Calif.) U., 1974-75, U. Cin. Coll. Medicine, 1976-79; assoc. prof. plastic surgery, microbiology and immunology, Wright State U. Sch. Medicine, 1975-84, prof. ophthalmology and plastic surgery, 1986—, chmn. dept. ophthalmology, 1984—; asst. clin. prof. ophthalmology Ohio State U. Sch. Medicine, 1981-85; lectr. law and medicine U. Dayton Law Sch., 1981—; practice medicine specializing in ophthalmic surgery, Dayton, Ohio; mem. staff Miami Valley Hosp., Children's Med. Ctr., Kettering Med. Ctr., St. Elizabeth Hosp., Good Samaritan Hosp., Sycamore Med. Ctr. Mem. editl. bd. Jour. Ophthalmic Plastic & Reconstructive Surgery; also articles. Trustee Children's Med. Ctr., Dayton, 1977-80; bd. dirs. Lions Eye Bank W. Cen. Ohio, 1982—. Served to lt. M.C., USNR, 1969-71. Recipient numerous profl. awards. Fellow Am. Acad. Facial Plastic and Reconstructive Surgery, Am. Acad. Pediatrics, Am. Bd. Forensic Examiners; mem. AAUP, Internat. Soc. Ophthalmic Pathology, European Soc. Ophthalmic Plastic & Reconstrucive Surgery, Cogan Ophthalmic Hist. Soc., R. Townley Paton Soc., Am. Acad. Forensic Scis., N.Am. Neuro-Ophthalmology Soc., Am. Coll. Legal Medicine, Def. Rsch. Inst., Assn. Advancement Automotive Medicine, Am. Assn. Ophthalmology, Am. Acad. Ophthalmology, ACS, AMA, Am. Coll. Cryosurgery, Am. Soc. Ophthalmic Plastic and Reconstructive Surgery, Am. Assn. Pediatric Ophthalmology and Strabismus, Assn. for Research Vision and Ophthalmology, Keratorefractive Soc., Am. Soc. Ophthalmic Ultrasound, Am. Intraocular Implant Soc., Orbit Soc., Internat. Soc. Orbital Disorders, Internat. Corneal Soc., Internat. Neuro-Ophthalmology Soc., Castroviejo Soc., Frank Walsh Soc., Soc. Heed Fellows, Ocular Microbiology and Immunology Group, Soc. of Geriatric Ophthalmology, Internat. Oculoplastic Soc., Am. Soc. Microbiology, Am. Soc. Laser Medicine and Surgery, Am. Ophthal. Soc., Soc. Eye Surgeons, Soc. Cosmetic Surgeons, Am. Soc. Law and Medicine, Am. Assn. Ophthalmic Pathologists, Theobald Soc., Sigma Xi. Clubs: Dayton Country, Dayton Racquet, Miami Valley Hunt and Polo. Home: 1155 Ridgeway Rd Dayton OH 45419-3032

BULLOCK, JUDY ROESKE, human resources executive, certified public accountant; b. Monroe, Mich., Sept. 10, 1957; d. Ivan Kenneth and Nell Elizabeth (Giles) Roseke; m. Charles C. Bullock, Jr., Feb. 17, 1991; children: Charles Christopher Bullock, Catherine Christina Bullock. BA in Acctg., U. South Fla., 1982; ChFC, Am. Coll., 1987; postgrad., Keller, 1994—. ChFC, AICPA/PFS; CPA, Fla., Mo., SPHR (Sr. Profl. Human Res.). Sr. tax specialist KPMG Peat Marwick, Tampa, Fla., 1982-84; tax/tech. design dir. CIGNA Fin. Svcs., Tampa, 1984-87; sr. mgr. tax/exec. fin. svcs. Price Waterhouse, Tampa, St. Louis, 1987-93; mgr. compensation unit, exec. compensation practice leader, exec. benefits practice leader, sr. cons. Towers Perrin, St. Louis, 1994-95; dir. exec. compensation & benefits Deere & Co., Moline, Ill., 1995—; artist Innovative Solutions, Moline, 1991—. Loaned exec. United Way, Tampa, 1989. Mem. AICPA, Am. Compensation Assn., Am. Soc. CLU/ChFC, Mo. Soc. CPAs (mem. personal fin. svcs. com. 1993, mem. investment com. 1994, dir. programs exec. compensation mgmt. coun. conf. bd. 1996), Soc. Human Resource Mgmt. Republican. Roman Catholic. Home: 3850 35th Avenue Ct Moline IL 61265 Office: Deere & Co John Deere Rd Moline IL 61265

BUMPUS, TERRY KEITH, bank officer; b. Mt. Vernon, Ohio, Jan. 14, 1958; s. R. Leroy and Juanita J. (Miller) B.; m. Debra D. Spellman, July 27, 1980; children: Nicholas, Lindsey, Emily, Collin. BS in Govt. and Pub. Adminstrn., David Lipscomb U., 1980. Teller Ctrl. Ohio Fed. Savs. and Loan, Columbus, Ohio, 1980-81; asst. br. mgr. Dollar Savs. Assn., Columbus, 1981-82, br. mgr., 1983-84; br. mgr. Equitable Fed. Savs. and Loan Assn., Lancaster, Ohio, 1983, County Savs. Bank, Pataskala, Ohio, 1984-85; asst. sec. First Fed. Savs. and Loan Assn., Centerburg, Ohio, 1985—; treas. Ctrl. Ohio Retirement Adminstrs., Columbus, 1990. Treas. and coach Centerburg Little League Assn., 1990—; mem. Centerburg Planning Commn., 1989-93; deacon Pataskala (Ohio) Ch. of Christ, 1987-89, Spring Rd. Ch. of Christ, Westerville, Ohio, 1991—. Republican. Home: 25 Jerry Ave PO Box 708 Centerburg OH 43011-0708

BUNCE, JAYNE, interior designer; b. Harvey, Ill., Oct. 13, 1956. BFA with highest honors, Internat. Acad. Design, Chgo., 1994. Sys. analyst Control Data Corp., Chgo., 1980-87, London, England, 1982-83; sr. computer cons. Spectrum Group, Oakbrook, Ill., 1987-91; owner Jayne Bunce Design, Northfield, Ill., 1991—; instr. Internat. Acad. Design, Chgo., 1994—; bd. dirs. Internat. Furnishing and Design Assn., Chgo., 1995—; student rep. ASID, Chgo., 1993-94. Exec. com. Chgo. Baseball Cancer Charities, 1986—. Republican. Presbyterian. Office: Jayne Bunce Design 21 Landmark Ct Northfield IL 60093-3452

BUNCH, R. DIANA, stockbroker; b. Hannibal, Mo., Dec. 10, 1956. Stockbroker Edward D. Jones & Co., Hannibal, 1988-94, Smith Barney Inc., Quincy, Ill., 1994—. Mem. Hannibal Arts Coun., 1994—. Mem. Hannibal C. of C. Presbyterian. Home: 2 Homestead Hannibal MO 63401-2705 Office: Smith Barney Inc 418 Maine St Quincy IL 62301-3930

BUNDALO, MILAN RICHARD, management consultant; b. Olde Barton Village, Wis., Jan. 18, 1951; s. Emil and Mary Alice (Baumgartner) B.; children: Sarah Ann, Melissa Ann. BA magna cum laude, Dominican Coll., Racine, Wis., 1973; MS in Bus., Cardinal Stritch Coll., Milw., 1984; postgrad., U. Wis., 1982. Mktg. corres. Kyle Corp., Milw., 1973-74; purchasing agt. McGraw Edison, Milw., 1974-76, prodn. control mgr., 1976-78, purchasing mgr., 1978-80, mgr. procurement and inventory control, 1980-83; materials mgr. Cooper Power Systems, Milw., 1983—. Contbr. articles to profl. jours. Assoc. mem. United Performing Arts Fund, Milw., 1988; mem. Citizens Amb. Program, 1990. Mem. Nat. Assn. Purchasing Mgrs (cert.), Am. Prodn. and Inventory Control Soc. (cert.), Nat. Mgmt. Assn., Cooper Profl. Devel. Assn. (dir. 1985-87), Rsch. Inst. Am. (assoc.), MRA Inst. of Mgmt., Milw. Assn. Purchasing Mgrs., Cardinal Stritch Alumni Assn. Roman Catholic.

BUNDY, BLAKELY FETRIDGE, early childhood educator, advocate; b. Chgo., Aug. 31, 1944; d. William Harrison and Bonnie Jean (Clark) Fetridge; m. Harvey Hollister Bundy III, Aug. 20, 1966; children: H. Hollister IV, Clark Harrison, Elizabeth Lowell, Reed Fetridge. BA cum laude, Wheaton Coll., Mass., 1966; MEd, Nat.-Louis U., 1985. Tchr. Norwich (Vt.) Kindergarten, 1966-67, Willow Wood Pre-Sch., Winnetka, Ill., 1983-93, bd. dirs., 1972-81, adv. bd., 1981-83, 93—; bd. dirs. North Ave. Day Nursery, Chgo., 1970-76, Ill. Family-to-Family Child Care Initiative, 1994-95; exec. dir. Winnetka Alliance for Early Childhood, 1989—; accreditation system validator Nat. Acad. Early Childhood Programs, Washington, 1986—; mem. pres.'s commn. Wheaton Coll., Norton, Mass., 1987—; trustee Brooks Sch., North Andover, Mass., 1993—; cons. editor Nat. Assn. Edn. Young Children, 1991-94. Author pamphlets: What an Executive Should Know About Industry Sponsored Day Care, 1984, What an Executive Should Know About Child Care Services, 1985, Winnetka Alliance for Early Childhood, 1990, 94, Week of the Young Child, 1993, Reaching for Quality in Illinois, 1992; contbr. articles to Chgo. Tribune, Redbook, Glamour mags., Early Childhood News, Dartnell Inst. Bus. Rsch. Jour., Child Care Ctr. Mag., Chgo. Sun-Times, Day Care and Early Education, Young Children, other publs. Mem. United Rep. Fund, Chgo., 1968-85; active N.E. Ill. coun. Boy Scouts Am., 1976-80, 85-88, Ill. Shore Coun. Girl Scouts U.S., 1981-89, World Found. for Girls Guides and Girl Scouts Friends of Our Cabaña Com., Cuernavaca, Mexico, 1986-94. Mem. Nat. Assn. for the Edn. Young Children (photographer publs.), World Assn. Girl Guides and Girl Scouts, Ill. Soc. Early Childhood Profls. (bd. dirs. 1993—, editor newsletter), Chgo. Assn. Edn. Young Children (steering com. Near North Suburban chpt. 1986—, commn. on salaries and working conditions, 1988-92, comm. adv. com. 1989-92, bd. dirs. 1992-96, co-chair pub. rels. com. 1992—, chair accreditation project mgmt. com. 1994—), Olive Baden-Powell Soc. (London). Episcopalian. Clubs: Indian Hill (Winnetka); Stevensville (Mich.) Yacht; Ocean Reef (Key Largo, Fla.). Avocations: golf, sailing. Office: Winnetka Alliance for Early Childhood 1235 Oak St Winnetka IL 60093-2168

BUNGE, MARCIA JOANN, religious studies educator; b. Dubuque, Iowa, Apr. 14, 1954; d. Richard and Myrene (Larson) B.; m. Gary Stephen Dulin, June 2, 1990. BA magna cum laude, St. Olaf Coll., 1976; MA, U. Chgo., 1979, PhD, 1986. Asst. prof. Luther Sem., St. Paul, 1985-90; asst. prof., religion and philosophy dept. Luther Coll., Decorah, Iowa, 1990-95; assoc. prof. religion Gustavus Adolphus Coll., St. Peter, Minn., 1995—; vis. asst. prof. Knox Coll., Galesburg, Ill., 1985, Theologisches Seminar, Leipzig, German Democratic Republic, 1989. Mem. exec. bd. Word and World, 1987-88, 89-90; mem. editorial bd. Dialog, 1992—; translated, edited, introduced selection of writings by Johann Gottfried Herder Against Pure Reason, 1992; contbr. articles to profl. jours. World Coun. of Chs. fellow, 1979-81, U. Chgo. fellow, 1984, Charlotte Newcombe Found. fellow, 1984-85, Assn. Theol. Schs. fellow, 1986, Evang. Luth. Ch. in Am. fellow, 1989, Joyce Found. award, 1993. Mem. Internat. Herder Soc. (exec. bd. 1985-90), Am. Acad. Religion, Soc. for Values in Higher Edn., Am. Soc. for 18th Century Studies, Phi Beta Kappa. Office: Gustavus Adolphus Coll Religion Dept Saint Peter MN 56082

BUNKERS, DOUGLAS FREDERICK, city administrator; b. Cherokee, Iowa, Sept. 29, 1958; s. Darrell Mathew and Gloria Jeanette (Thompson) B.; m. Rebecca Ethel Coleman, Apr. 6, 1986; children: Samuel, Leah. BA, U. Iowa, 1981, MA in Pub. Affairs, 1985. Teaching asst. U. Iowa, Iowa City, 1984-85; asst. to city mgr. City of Alma, Mich., 1985-88, acting city mgr., 1988; city adminstr. City of Madison, Minn., 1988-93, City of Luverne, Minn., 1993-95; city mgr. City of Windsor Heights, Iowa, 1995—; mem. Gov.'s Commn. on Intergovtl. Rels., St. Paul, 1991-95, Gov.'s Commn. on Govt. Innovation, St. Paul, 1993-95. Mem. adv. bd. Southwest Minn. Initiative Fund, Granite Falls, 1989-93; community liaison Minn. Nat. Guard Employer Support, St. Paul, 1990-93. Mem. ASPA, Iowa City/County Mgmt. Assn., Internat. City/County Mgmt. Assn., Internat. Pers. Mgmt. Assn., Govt. and Fin. Officers Assn., Kiwanis (sec. Madison chpt. 1988-93, mem. Urbandale-Merle Hay chpt. 1996—). Home: 3000 University Ave #75 West Des Moines IA 50266 Office: City of Windsor Heights 1133 66th St Windsor Heights IA 50311

BUNKERS, MATTHEW JOHN, meteorologist; b. Dell Rapids, S.D., Sept. 29, 1969; s. James Andrew and Lorraine Gertrude (Schreurs) B.; m. Heather Rae Wallace, Sept. 18, 1993; 1 child, Madalyn Lorraine. BS in Interdisciplinary Scis., S.D. Sch. of Mines and Tech., Rapid City, 1992, MS in Meteorology, 1993. Meteorologist technician Nat. Weather Svc., Rapid City, 1991-93, meteorologist intern, 1993-95, meteorologist, 1995—; rsch. asst. S.D. Sch. of Mines and Technology, 1993-95. Contbr. articles to profl. jours. Mem. Am. Meteorol. Soc., Nat. Weather Assn. Roman Catholic. Home: 109 Centennial St Rapid City SD 57701 Office: Nat Weather Svc 300 E Signal Dr Rapid City SD 57701

BUNNELL, SANDRA JEAN, jewelry designer; b. Detroit, Mar. 1, 1945; d. James and Renee (Choate) Xenakis; m. Richard Bunnell, Oct. 5, 1968 (div. Aug. 1972). Diploma, Centros Europeos de Lenguas y Cultura, Barcelona, Spain, 1966; BA, Wayne State U., 1967. Columnist Detroit Free Press, 1973-77; writer Anthony M. Franco, Detroit, 1976-77, copy dir., account exec., 1978-80; v.p. consumer accounts PR Assocs., Detroit, 1980-83; v.p. pub. relations Berline Group, Birmingham, Mich., 1983-84; pres. Bunnell & Co., Farmington Hills, Mich., 1984-87; pvt. practice communications cons. and writer Detroit/Ann Arbor/Chelsea, Mich., 1987—; designer, jeweler Ann Arbor, 1987—; pres. IronMark, 1991-92; fashion cons. Ann Arbor, 1992—. Assoc. editor Contemporary Authors, 1972-73. Active Leadership Detroit, 1982-83; trustee Franklin Wright Settlements, Detroit, 1983-89, 2d v.p., 1988-89; mem. small bus. adv. coun. to Congressman Sander Levin, 1986; mem. Ypsilanti Women's coun. Recipient commendation Community Relations Report, 1980. Mem. Women in Comm. (pres. Detroit chpt. 1985-86, chmn. nat. pay equity com. 1986-87), Women in the Bus. of Art, Fashion Group, Nat. Assn. Women Bus. Owners.

BUNT, MARION ADAMS, retired administrative secretary/coordinator; b. Port Huron, Mich., Oct. 21, 1916; d. Lewis Richard and Gladys (Wakeham) Adams; m. Floyd Walter Gordon Bunt, Aug. 16, 1941; children: Floyd Walter Gordon Jr., Mary Elizabeth Bunt-Harlan, Theodore James, Terrence Lewis. BA, Oakland U., 1982. Adminstr., sec. Oakland U., Rochester, Mich., 1962-80, coord., 1980-89; ret. Oakland U., 1989. Pres. Women of Oakland U., 1987-89; founding mem., bd. dirs. Oakland Sail; active numerous coms. and offices Cranbrook House and Gardens Aux., including bd. dirs., sec. 1992—, joint exec. bd.; active Cranbrook Ednl. Community; founder Cranbrook Ice Skating Club, Cranbrook Tennis Club; mem. founding com. Cranbrook Music Guild. Recipient Thistle award for meritorious svc., Cranbrook House and Gardens Aux. Mem. LWV, Oakland U. Alumni Assn. (sec. bd. dirs. 1991-93, v.p. 1993-94, various other coms.), Altrusa Club (various coms., ofcl. positions). Home: 4536 Middleton Ct West Bloomfield MI 48323

BUNTING, ROGER KENT, chemistry educator, business owner; b. Creston, Ill., Nov. 27, 1935; s. Robert Williams and Gladys Margaret (Skinner) B.; m. Sheila Louise McGuire, June 7, 1958; children: Bryan, Rachel, Laura, Stephen. BS, U. Ill., 1958, MS, 1961; PhD, Pa. State U., 1965. Rsch. assoc. Ohio State U., Columbus, 1965-66; mem. chemistry faculty Ill. State U., Normal, 1966—; hon. rsch. fellow U. London, 1974-75; rsch. assoc. U. Florence, Italy, 1982, Universidad del Pais Vasco, San Sebastian, Spain, 1993; vis. prof. Ohio State U., 1983; disting. vis. prof. USAF Acad., Colorado Springs, 1987-88; resident rsch. assoc. Jet Propulsion Lab., Pasadena, Calif., 1992; tech. cons. The Eureka Co., Bloomington, Ill., 1976-81. Author: The Chemistry of Photography, 1987; contbr. articles to profl. jours. Recipient numerous rsch. grants. Mem. Am. Chem. Soc., Royal Photographic Soc. (London), Royal Soc. Chemistry (London), Sigma Xi. Home: 1203 Searle Dr Normal IL 61761 Office: Ill State U Dept Chemistry Normal IL 61790-4160

BUNTROCK, ROBERT E., information consultant, organic chemist; b. Mpls., Nov. 19, 1940; s. Eric Frank and Louise Ada (Intorf) B.; m. Gloria Carolyn Kral, June 24, 1961; children: Stephen Robert, Christine Louise. BS in Chemistry, U. Minn., 1962; MA, Princeton U., 1964, PhD, 1967. Rsch. chemist Air Products & Chem., Allentown, Pa., 1967-70, Amoco Oil Co., Whiting, Ind., 1970-71; rsch. info. scientist Amoco Corp., Naperville, Ill., 1971-80, sr. rsch. info. scientist, 1980-85, rsch. assoc., 1985-95; pres. Buntrock Assocs., Inc., Naperville, 1995—; mem. adv. bd. Derwent Ltd., London, 1980-86, Chem. Abstracts Svc., Columbus, Ohio, 1985—, Questel Orbit, McLean, Va., 1989—. Contbr. articles to Database, Online, Jour. Chem. Info. and Computer Sci., 1975-95; patentee in field. Bd. dirs. Naperville Area Transcribing for the Blind, 1973-80. Mem. Am. Chem. Soc. (chmn. divsn. chem. info. 1981, bd. dirs. Chgo. sect. 1985—), Am. Soc. Info. Sci., Assn. Ind. Info. Profls., Sigma Xi. Lutheran. Office: Buntrock Assocs Inc 670 N Eagle St Naperville IL 60563-3024

BURBANK, JOHN THORN, contract cleaning executive; b. St. Paul, Sept. 18, 1939; s. Richard Hart and Rae (Parkins) B.; divorced; children: Jennifer, Leslie, Betsy. Student, U. Minn., 1957-62. V.p. Burbank Burns, Mpls., 1963-65, Twin City Index, Mpls., 1965-68, Pentagon Corp., Mpls., 1968-72, AS Industries, Mpls., 1972-78; pres. Minn. Graphics, Mpls., 1978-84; v.p. Graphics Unltd., Mpls., 1984-87, Perfection Graphics, Mpls., 1987-90; pres. Burbank Svcs., Inc., Edina, Minn., 1990-93; mem. adv. bd. Dakota County Votech, Rosemount, Minn., 1982-91. Nation officer YMCA Indian Princess, Bloomington, Minn., 1975; pres. PTA, Bloomington, 1970; coach Traveling Youth Hockey, Bloomington, 1970-84. With USNR, 1961-63. Mem. Internat. Typesetting Assn. (regional pres. 1976-77, program chmn. 1975, 76). Episcopalian. Home and Office: 44 5th Ave N Hopkins MN 55343-1658

BURCH, DAVID B., financial consultant; b. Monroe, Mich., Feb. 23, 1961. Fin. cons. Smith Barney Inc., Grand Rapids, Mich., 1989—. Bd. advisor Little League Club. With U.S. Army, 1980-83. Mem. Kiwanis (bd. advisor). Republican. Roman Catholic. Office: Smith Barney Inc 99 Monroe Ave NW Ste 200 Grand Rapids MI 49503-2639

BURCH, ROBERT L., state senator, lawyer. BA magna cum laude, Kent State U., 1971; JD, Georgetown U., 1975. Bar: Ohio. Atty. NLRB, Washington and Cleve.; asst. atty. gen. State of Ohio, Columbus, 1981-84; pvt. practice, New Philadelphia, Ohio, 1980—; mem. Ohio Senate, Columbus, 1985—; mem. agr., commerce and labor com., bd. on unreclaimed strip mined lands, coal tech. adv. com., energy, natural resoruces and environ. and health coms., human svcs. and aging coms., mem. joint com. on agy. rule revision. Dep. campaign mgr. Senator John Glenn, 1980. Recipient Conservation Legislator award League Ohio Sportsmen, 1988, Pub. Policy Leadership award Ohio Victims of Crime Program, 1989, Excellence in Govt. award Jefferson C. of C., 1992. Mem. NAACP, Farm Bur., Farmers Union, Moose, Eagles, Elks. Democrat. also: State Senate State Capitol Columbus OH 43215*

BURCH, STEPHEN KENNETH, financial services company executive, real estate investor; b. Fairmont, W.Va., Feb. 1, 1945; s. Kenneth Edward and Gloria Lorraine (Wilson) B.; m. Juliana Yuan Yuan, June 17, 1972 (div. Feb. 1985); children: Emily, Adrien. AB in Econs., Washington U., St. Louis, 1969. V.p. TSI Mgmt., Los Angeles, 1970-71; pres. Investors Choice Cattle Co., Los Angeles, 1972-76; v.p. Clayton Brokerage Co., St. Louis, 1976-84; pres. Yuan Med. Lab., St. Louis, 1976-78; v.p. Restaurant Assocs., St. Louis, 1982-83, Am. Capital Equities, St. Louis, 1984-89; pres., owner Burch Properties, Inc., St. Louis, 1984—; owner Clayton-Hanley, Inc., St. Louis, 1987-88; pres., owner Clayton Securities Services, Inc., St. Louis, 1988—; mng. ptnr. 600 S. Ptnrs., St. Louis, 1976-87, Midvale Ptnrs., St. Louis, 1979—. Bd. dirs. AMC Cancer Rsch. Ctr., 1989-91. Mem. Sigma Phi Epsilon (pres. alumni bd. 1981-87). Office: Clayton Securities Svcs Inc 112 S Hanley Rd Ste 102 Saint Louis MO 63105-3418

BURCH, WILLIAM R., business executive; b. Evansville, Ind., Dec. 19, 1946. BSEE, Evansville Coll., 1968. Pres. Aztech, Inc., Newburgh, Ind., 1990—; cons. Turbo Air, Mayfield, Ky., 1992-93. Democrat. Office: Aztech Inc 309 W 1st St Newburgh IN 47630-1208

BURCHAM, EVA HELEN (PAT BURCHAM), electronics technician; b. Bloomfield, Ind., Apr. 11, 1941; d. Paul Harold and Hazel Helen (Buzan) B. Grad., Blackstone Sch. of Law, 1988, Paralegal Inst., Phoenix, 1991; grad. paralegal, So. Career Inst., Boca Raton, Fla., 1991. With Naval Weapons Support Ctr./Crane Div. Naval Surface Warfare, Crane, Ind., 1967-76, 78-80; electronics technician Naval Weapons Support Ctr., Crane, Ind., 1980—. With U.S. Army, 1976-77, with Res. 1977-81. Named to Am. Women's Hall of Fame. Mem. NAFE (exec. bd. chair), NOW, Am. Soc. Naval Engrs., Soc. Logistics Engrs., Am. Legion, Federally Employed Women, Fed. Women's Program, Profl. Women's Network (pres. 1993, bd. dirs.), Blacks in Govt., Nat. Paralegal Assn. (registered paralegal), Nat. Fedn. Paralegal Assn., Inc., Toastmasters (gov.). Roman Catholic. Home: 200 W Washington St Loogootee IN 47553-2324

BURCHARD, MAX NORMAN, sociology educator; b. Seward County, Kans., May 27, 1925; s. Charlie and Jenny Grace (Swink) B.; m. June Larsen, Sept. 11, 1948 (dec. 1980); children: Denise, Clyde W., Marti, Norman D., Melissa, Brett L., Tracey. AB in Psychology, San Jose State Coll., 1949; MA in Sociology, U. Nebr., 1951, PhD, 1955. Instr. sociology and social work U. Omaha, 1952-54; asst. prof., chair Marietta (Ohio) Coll., 1955-60; assoc. prof., chair U. N.D., Grand Forks, 1960-64; assoc. prof., chair sociology Moorhead (Minn.) State Coll., 1964-68; prof., chair Iowa Wesleyan Coll., Mt. Pleasant, 1968-90, prof. emeritus, 1990—; sociology tchr. U. Md., Okinawa, Japan, Korea, 1990-92; pvt. practice as hypnotherapist, Mt. Pleasant, 1972-90. Author: Sociology, 1967. Sec., pres. S.E. Iowa Planned Parenthood, Mt. Pleasant, 1975-82; mem. county bd. Dem. Ctrl. Com., Henry County, Iowa, 1985-90. 2d lt. USAFR, 1948-53. Mem. Midwest Sociol. Soc. (life, bd. dirs. 1962-64, 80-82), Fraternal Order Eagles, Am. Legion. Home: 624 N McArthur Macomb IL 61455

BURD, FRANCIS JOHN, packaging executive; b. Dubuque, Iowa, Dec. 27, 1940; s. Francis LaVern and Mary F. (Whalen) B.; m. Sharon Ann Dalsing, Aug. 6, 1966; children: David F., Christine A., Catherine A. BA, Loras Coll., 1964. Tchr. St. Mary's Sch., Kieler, Wis., 1965-68; sales exec. St. Regis Paper Co., Dubuque, 1968-84, Georgia-Pacific Corp., Dubuque, 1984-87; mgr. sales and mfg. John Halper Box Co., Mpls., 1987-88; v.p. sales & mktg. Am. Carton & Polybag, Inc., Mpls., 1988—. V.p. Bd. Edn. Nativity Parish, Dubuque, 1977; vol. Loras Coll. Appeal, 1971, Wahlert High Sch.

Appeal, Dubuque, 1984. Recipient Economic Edn. Award Jr. Achievement, Dubuque, 1983, Recognition award Boy Scouts Am., Dubuque, 1984. Mem. Assn. Ind. Corrugated Converters, TAPPI, Presidents Club, Regent's, Kiwanis (dir. 1983-87). Republican. Roman Catholic. Home: 3011 Meyer Ct Saint Paul MN 55109-1547

BURD, WILLIAM A., numismatist; b. Ithaca, N.Y., May 11, 1944; s. Kenneth and Grace Mary (Jones) B.; m. Irene Lantor Burd, Dec. 1972 (div. Mar. 1988); children: Kimberly A., Denise R., Katherine G.; m. Geraldine Ann Schallaci, Apr. 24, 1988; children: Donald R., John M. Tisch. Office mgr. Penn Truck Lines, Syracuse and Boston, 1963-65; asst. to regional mgr. Penn Truck Lines, Buffalo, 1966; acct. Penn Truck Lines, Cleve., 1966-68; asst. to pres. Penn Truck Lines, Phila., 1969-70; terminal mgr. Penn Truck Lines, Cleve., 1971; regional mgr. Penn Truck Lines, Chgo., 1971-76; mgr. rail divsn. Bekins Van Lines, Chgo., 1976-78; gen. mgr. Gold Dust Coin, Inc., Chgo., 1979-95; pres. Darv Coin and Stamp, Inc., Chgo., 1995—. With U.S. Army, 1961-63. Mem. Am. Numismatic Assn. (life mem.), Am. Numismatic Soc., Chgo. Coin Club (editor 1994—). Republican. Roman Catholic. Office: Darv Coin and Stamp Inc 6455 W Archer Ave Chicago IL 60638

BURDETT, BARBRA ELAINE, biology educator; b. Lincoln, Ill., Mar. 18, 1947; d. Robert Marlin and Klaaska Johanna Baker; m. Gary Albert Burdett, Sept. 27, 1968; children: Bryan Robert, Heather Lea, Amanda Rose. AA, Lincoln Coll., 1981; postgrad., Ill. State U. Edn. Core, 1982-83; BS, Millikin U., 1985; postgrad., Western U., 1994—. Cert. tchr., Ill. Tchr. advanced placement biology, botany and human physiology Brown County H.S., Mt. Sterling, Ill., 1985-95; tchr. biology and algebra Pleasant Plains (Ill.) H.S., 1995—; dir. Drama Club, Brown County H.S., 1988-90, dir. sci. fairs; ednl. advisor Nat. Young Leaders Conf. Author: Misty White, 1991, Possums Sing, 1994. Sponsor Children, Inc., Richmond, Va., 1985—, Internat. Wildlife Coalition, North Falmouth, Mass., 1991—; vol. Vets. Hosp., St. Louis, 1988—. Mem. ASCD, Nat. Assn. Biology Tchrs. (Biology Tchr. of Yr. in Ill. 1994), Ill. Sci. Tchrs. Assn., Phi Delta Kappa (newsletter editor 1990), Phi Theta Kappa. Episcopalian.

BURDETT, GEORGE CRAIG, plastics industry executive; b. Scranton, Pa., Mar. 9, 1943; s. George William and Doris Carolyn (Davies) B.; m. Mary Alice Comly, May 25, 1963; children: Stephen Craig, Jonathan Mark, Andrew James. Student, Kennedy-Western U., 1990. Lab. technician E.I. duPont de Nemours, Wilmington, Del., 1962-65; sales rep. Carpenter Motor Freight, Wilmington, 1965-66; cost acct. Stauffer-Hoechst Polymer, Delaware City, Del., 1966-69; contr. Covenant Coll., Lookout Mountain, Tenn., 1969-74; v.p., contr. Armin Industries, South Elgin, Ill., 1974—; cons. in field, Lookout Mountain, 1969-74. Bd. dirs. Pop Warner Football, Elgin, Ill., 1977-79, Elgin Classic Little League, pres., 1980-81; bd. dirs. Westminster Christian Sch., 1977-85, Wheaton Christian H.S., West Chicago, 1990-94. Mem. Am. Prodn. and Inventory Control Soc., Am. Payroll Assn., Inst. Mgmt. Accts., Am. Mgmt. Assn., Beta Gamma Sigma. Home: 9 Bloomsbury Ct Algonquin IL 60102 Office: Armin Industries 1500 N La Fox St South Elgin IL 60177-1249

BURDETT, JAMES RICHARD, golf products innovator; b. Oak Park, Ill., Jan. 4, 1934; s. Paul Eswald and Ruth (Woodward) B.; m. Marilyn Carole Stoker, Aug. 29, 1959; children: Deborah Lyn Dodd, Daniel James, Donna Carole Humphress. Student, Grinnell Coll., 1953-54; BS in Econs., U. Ill., 1956. Owner James R. Burdett, Lombard, 1983-92; pres. Burdett's Inc., 1993—, Master of the Links, Lombard, 1988—; speaker conf. Golf Course Superintendent Assn., Anaheim, Calif., 1993. Mem. Golf Course Supts. Assn. Am., Midwest Assn. Golf Course Supts., Ill. Turfgrass Found. (pres. 1965-66). Mem. Christian Sci. Ch. Office: PO Box 1865 Lombardt IL 60148-1865

BURGDOERFER, JERRY, lawyer; b. Jeffersonville, Ind., May 3, 1958; s. Jerry Jack and Barbara Jean (Hofherr) B. BS, Ind. U., 1980, MBA, 1983, JD cum laude, 1983. Bar: Ill. 1984, U.S. Dist. Ct. (no. dist.) Ill. 1984, U.S. Tax Ct. 1984. Assoc. Adams, Fox, Adelstein, Rosen & Bell, Chgo., 1983-88, ptnr., 1988-89; assoc. Jenner & Block, Chgo., 1989-90, ptnr., 1991—; with Mori Sogo Law Offices, Tokyo, 1991-93. Author articles. Vol. teen living programs Homeless Youth Shelter, 1988—. Named 2d Benton Nat. Moot Ct. Competition, 1982. Mem. ABA, Internat. Bar Assn., Inter Pacific Bar Assn., Ill. Bar Assn., Chgo. Bar Assn., Japan Am. Soc. Chgo., Ind. U. Alumni Club Chgo. (vol. 1988-89), Monroe Club, Econ. Club Chgo., Execs. Club Chgo., Japanese C. of C. and Industry Chgo., Chgo. Coun. on Fgn. Rels., Phi Eta Sigma, Phi Delta Phi, Phi Delta Theta (sec. chpt. 1977-78, co-founder, steering com. Chgo. alumni club 1988-89). Office: Jenner & Block 1 E IBM Plz Ste 3700 Chicago IL 60611-3586

BURGER, GEORGE VANDERKARR, wildlife ecologist, researcher; b. Woodstock, Ill., Jan. 22, 1927; s. Irwin Louis and Nettie Ann (Vanderkarr) B.; m. Jeannine Ingram Willis, June 23, 1949; children: Suzanne Linda Burger Campbell, Christine Melissa Burger Rice, Nancy Willis Burger Smith. BS, Beloit Coll., 1948; MS, U. Calif., Berkeley, 1950; PhD, U. Wis., 1958. Cert. wildlife biologist. Instr. Contra Costa (Calif.) Jr. Coll., 1952-54; field rep. Sportsmen's Svc. Bur., La Crosse, Wis., 1958-62; mgr. wildlife mgmt. Remington Arms Co., Chestertown, Md., 1962-66; gen. mgr. Max McGraw Wildlife Found., Dundee, Ill., 1966-92; commr. Ill. Nature Preserves Commn., 1985-89; mem. Ill. Surface Mining Adv. Coun., 1990-94, Kane County Solid Waste Mgmt. Adv. Com., Geneva, Ill. Author: Practical Wildlife Management, 1975; editor: Pheasants: Symptoms of Wildlife Problems, 1988, (proc.) N.Am. Wood Duck Symposium, 1988. Mem. Kane County Regional Planning Commn., Ill., 1980—, Elgin (Ill.) Parks and Reclamation Commn., 1986—. Sgt. U.S. Army, 1945-46. Wis. Alumni Rsch. Found. fellow, 1954-56; Green Trees Club grantee, 1958; recipient nat. award Nature Conservancy, 1954. Mem. Am. Fisheries Soc., Izaak Walton League of Am., Outdoor Writers Assn. Am., Wildlife Soc. (hon., editor bull. 1972-75). Office: Max McGraw Wildlife Found PO Box 9 Dundee IL 60118-0009

BURGER, HENRY G., anthropologist, vocabulary scientist, publisher; b. N.Y.C., June 27, 1923; s. B. William and Terese R. (Felleman) B.; m. Barbara G. Smith, Nov. 29, 1991. B.A. with honors (Pulitzer scholar), Columbia Coll., 1947; M.A., Columbia U., 1965, Ph.D. in Cultural Anthropology (State Doctoral fellow), 1967. Indsl. engr. various orgns., 1947-51, Midwest mfrs. rep., 1952-55; social sci. cons. Chgo. and N.Y.C., 1956-67; anthropologist Southwestern Coop. Ednl. Lab., Albuquerque, 1967-69; assoc. prof. anthropology and edn. U. Mo., Kansas City, 1969-73, prof., 1973-93, prof. emeritus, 1994—, founding mem. univ. wide doctoral faculty, 1974-93; founder, pub. The Wordtree, Overland Park, Kans., 1984—; lectr. CUNY, 1957-65; adj. prof. ednl. anthropology U. N.Mex., 1969; anthrop. cons. U.S. VA Hosp., Kansas City, 1971-72; speaker at numerous confs. Author: Ethno-Pedagogy, 1968, 2d edit., 1968; editor, compiler: The Wordtree, a Transitive Cladistic for Solving Physical and Social Problems, 1984; selected for exhibit at 3 insts.; selected as a type in Cambridge Ency. of the English Lang., 1995—; mem. editl. bd. Coun. Anthropology and Edn., 1975-80; author linguistic periodical column New Times, New Verbs, 1988—; contbr. to anthologies; author articles. Capt. AUS, 1943-46. NSF Instl. grantee, 1970. Fellow World Acad. Art and Sci., Am. Anthrop. Assn. (life), Royal Anthrop. Inst. Gt. Britain (life); mem. European Assn. for Lexicography, Internat. Soc. for Systems Scis., Internat. Soc. for Knowledge Orgn., English-Speaking Union (v.p. Kansas City chpt. 1995-96), Dictionary Soc. N.Am. (life, terminology com.), Assn. Internationale de Terminologie, Academie Europeenne des Scis., Arts et Lettres (corr.), Soc. Conceptual and Content Analysis by Computer, Columbia U. Club, Phi Beta Kappa. Office: The Wordtree 10876 Bradshaw St Overland Park KS 66210-1148

BURGER, JANETTE MARIE, librarian; b. Union City, Ind., July 9, 1958; d. William Bronson and Janet Sue (Boyle) B.; m. Dan Michael Mraz, Nov. 14, 1980 (div. May 1985). BA, Hanover Coll., 1980; M in Liberal Sci., Northern Ill. U., 1985; MBA, North Ctrl. Coll., 1996. Subs. tchr. Dist. 300 Sch. Corp., Dundee, Ill., 1980-82; libr. Gail Borden Pub. Library, Elgin, Ill., 1982-83, Follett Software Co., 1984—. Democrat. Roman Catholic. Home: 1850 W Highland Ave # 203F Elgin IL 60123-5079 Office: Follett Software 1391 Corporate Dr Mc Henry IL 60050-7041

BURGER, STEPHEN E., religious organization executive; b. St. Paul, Aug. 23, 1940; s. Paul J. and Hope K. (Nelson) B.; m. Delores T. Prohofsky, Dec. 16, 1961; children: Eric L., Linda B. Student, Hamline U., Bethel Coll. Dir. boys clubs Union Gospel Mission, St. Paul, 1959-64; youth dir. City Rescue Mission, New Castle, Pa., 1964-69; supt. York (Pa.) Rescue Mission, 1969-74; exec. dir. Union Gospel Mission, Seattle, 1974-89, Internat. Union Gospel Missions, Kansas City, Mo., 1989—; nat. spokesman for rescue missions; vice chair City Mission World Assn., Sydney, Australia. Office: Internat Union Gospel Missions 1045 Swift North Kansas City KS 64116

BURGESS, JAMES EDWARD, newspaper publisher, executive; b. LaCrosse, Wis., Apr. 5, 1936; s. William Thomas and Margaret (Forseth) B.; m. Catherine Eleanor, Dec. 20, 1958; children: Karen E. Burgess Hardy, J. Peter, Sydney Ann, R. Curtis. Student, Wayland Acad.; BS, U. Wis., Madison. Pub. Ind. Record, Helena, Mont., 1969-71; pub. Tribune, LaCrosse, Wisc., 1971-74; v.p. newspapers Lee Enterprises, Davenport, Iowa, 1974-81; exec. v.p. Lee Enterprises, 1981-84, dir., 1974-85; dir. Madison (Wis.) Newspapers, Inc., 1975-93; pres. Madison Newspapers, Inc., 1984-93; pub. Wis. State Jour., Madison, 1984-94; Past pres. WNA, Meriter Health Svcs. Bd. dirs., v.p. Madison Art Ctr.; chmn. Edgewood Coll., Madison, 1984—; founder Future Madison, Inc.; chmn. SAVE Commn. Mem. Inland Daily Press Assn. (pres., chmn. 1982-84). Home: 6102 S Highlands Ave Madison WI 53705-1113 Office: PO Box 55060 Madison WI 53705-8860

BURGESS, JOHN NORMAN, veterans service officer; b. St. Joseph, Mo., July 17, 1949; s. Keith Lavern and Beatrice Jane (Brooke) B.; m. Joan Marie Farley, Nov. 26, 1972; 1 child, Kimberly Michelle. BSBA in Mgmt., Mo. Western State Coll., 1971; AS in Ednl. and Instrnl. Tech., Cmty. Coll. of the Air Force, 1990, AS in Transp., 1990. Cert. instr. health and human svcs. On the job monitor 139 MAPF Mo AN6, St. Joseph, Mo., 1980-84; drawing monitor, mgr. 139 MSS Mo AN6, St. Joseph, Mo., 1986-87, edn. supr., counselor, 1987—; benefit authorizer, instrnl. tech. asst. Social Security Adminstrn., Kansas City, Mo., 1978-88, claims authorizer, 1989; vets. svc. dir. Mo. Vets. Commn., Maryville, Mo., 1990—. Mem. Maryville Citizen for Cmty. Action, 1990—, v.p., 1992-93; bd. dirs. Maryville R-II Sch. Bd., 1994—. Sgt. USAF, 1971-75. Named 44th Security Police Group Employee of the Month, Mo. Dept. Pub. Safety, 1993.

BURGESS, ROBERT K., construction company executive; b. 1944. BS, Mich. State U., 1966. With Pulte Corp., Bloomfield Hills, Mich., 1983—, v.p. corp. devel., 1983-84, sr. v.p., 1984-85, chief operating officer, exec. v.p., 1985-86, pres., chief operating officer, 1987-93, ceo, pres., 1994—, also bd. dirs. Office: Pulte Corp 33 Bloomfield Hills Pky Ste 200 Bloomfield Hills MI 48304-2946

BURGHER, NORM, electronic engineer; b. Creston, Iowa, July 4, 1953. AAS, S.W. Cmty. Coll., Creston, Iowa, 1989. Electronic engr. technician Shivvers Inc., Corydon, Iowa, 1989—. Office: Shivvers Inc 614 W English Corydon IA 50060

BURHOE, RALPH WENDELL, religion and science educator; b. Somerville, Mass., June 21, 1911; s. Winslow Page and Mary Trenaman (Stumbles) B.; m. Frances Bickford, Aug. 4, 1931 (dec. Aug. 1967); children: Winslow Newton, Laura Jean Burhoe Maier, Thomas Allen, Diana May Burhoe Chase; m. Calla Crawford Butler, Apr. 6, 1969. Student, Harvard, 1928-32, Andover Newton Theol. Sch., 1934-36; Sc.D., Meadville Lombard Theol. Sch., Chgo., 1975; L.H.D., Rollins Coll., 1979. Observer, research asst., librarian, asst. to dir. Blue Hill Meteorol. Obs., Harvard U., 1936-47; asst. sec. Am. Meteorol. Soc., Milton, Mass., 1936-47; treas. Am. Meteorol. Soc., 1942-47; exec. officer Am. Acad. Arts and Sciences, Boston, 1947-64; prof. theology and scis. Meadville Theol. Sch., Chgo., 1964-74, dir. Ctr. for Advanced Studies in Theology and the Scis., 1965-74, prof. emeritus, 1974—; founder Ctr. for Advanced Studies in Religion and Sci., 1973, treas., bd. dirs., 1974-89; co-founder, active in Chgo. Ctr. for Religion and Sci., 1988—. Author: Toward a Scientific Theology, 1981; editor: (with Hudson Hoagland) Evolution and Man's Progress, 1962; author, editor: Science and Human Values in the Twenty-first Century, 1971; editor Zygon: Jour. Religion and Sci., 1966-79, founding editor, 1979—; contbr. to profl. jours. and books. 1st Am. recipient Templeton prize for progress in religion, London, 1980. Fellow AAAS, World Acad. Art and Sci., Am. Acad. Arts and Scis., Inst. on Religion in an Age of Sci. (founder 1954, hon. pres. 1959—), Soc. Sci. Study of Religion (treas. 1965-70, Disting. Career Achievement award 1984); mem. Am. Acad. Religion, Am. Theol. Assn., Inst. Theol. Encounter with Sci. and Tech. Home and Office: Montgomery Place 5550 South Shore Dr Apt 715 Chicago IL 60637-5032

BURHOP, KENNETH EUGENE, physiologist, researcher; b. Grafton, Wis., May 7, 1953; s. Dietrich William and Lorraine (Schutta) B.; m. Christine Vivian Krueger, Aug. 13, 1977; children: James Randall, Kelly Lorraine, Ryan Phillip. MS, U. Wis., 1979, PhD, 1984. Rsch. asst. dept. vet. sci. U. Wis., Madison, 1976-79, 80-84, rsch. specialist dept. preventive medicine, 1979-80; postdoctoral fellow dept. physiology Albany (N.Y.) Med. Coll., 1984-86; postdoctoral fellow Baxter Healthcare Corp., Round Lake, Ill., 1986-87, mgr. dept. physiology, applied scis., 1987-90, dir. biol. scis., 1990—. Contbr. 27 articles and 54 abstracts to profl. jours. Mem. Am. Physiol. Soc., N.Y. Acad. Scis., Am. Soc. for Artificial Organs, Shock Soc., Am. Assn. Blood Banks, Nat. Stroke Assn., Soc. Critical Care Medicine, Internat. Soc. for Artificial Organs, Am. Fedn. Clin. Rsch., Phi Eta Sigma. Democrat. Lutheran. Office: Baxter Healthcare Corp Blood Substitutes Rt 120 and Wilson Rd Round Lake IL 60073

BURK, NORMAN, oral surgeon; b. Dallas, Sept. 28, 1937; s. Rubin and Lena (Shodnisky) B.; m. Beverly Rae Hyken, Aug. 27, 1961; children: Ronald S., Steven J. BS, U. Okla., 1959; DDS, U. Mo., Kansas City, 1962. Diplomate Am. Bd. Oral and Maxillofacial Surgery. Resident in oral surgery Kansas City (Mo.) Gen. Hosp., 1965; practice dentistry specializing in oral surgery Kansas City, Mo., 1965—; mem. staff Truman Med. Ctr., Independence Sanitarium and Hosp.; chief staff Bapt. Meml. Hosp., 1976-77, Menorah Med. Ctr., 1975-85; sec. med. staff St. Joseph Health Ctr., Kansas City, Mo., 1992-93; clin. assoc. prof. U. Mo., Kansas City, 1965085; appointed to Blue Cross/Blue Shield peer review com. for Greater Kansas City Oral Surgeons. Contbr. articles to profl. jours. Bd. dirs. Kehilath Israel Synagogue. Fellow Am. Coll. Oral and Maxillofacial Surgeons, Am. Assn. Oral and Maxillofacial Surgeons, Internat. Congress of Oral Implantologists, Acad. Osseointegration, Am. Coll. Oral and Maxillofacial Surgeons (founder); mem. Kansas City Soc. Oral Surgeons (pres. 1974), Mo. Soc. Oral Surgeons (pres. 1979), ADA, Midwestern Mo. and Kansas City Soc. Oral and Maxillofacial Surgeons, Delta Sigma Delta (advisor 1966-74), Univ. Study Club (pres. 1970), B'nai Brith Lodge. Home: 8400 Delmar Ln Shawnee Mission KS 66207-1824 Office: Burk Ennis & Allen 1010 Carondelet Dr Kansas City MO 64114-4859

BURK, RONALD LEE, traffic safety professional; b. Peoria, Ill., Mar. 19, 1936; s. Kenneth Marion and Phyllis Lee (Eaton) B.; m. Lila Jean Benham, Aug. 9, 1975; children: Robin Lee, Douglas Joseph, Steven Mathew, Dana Lynn. BA, Butler U., 1958. Cert. pers. cons. Cons. Gen. Emp. Enterprises, Indpls., 1962-70; co-owner, pers. cons. HBS & Assoc., Columbus, Ohio, 1971-83; project mgr., traffic safety Ohio Dept. of Pub. Safety, Columbus, 1984—. Recipient Recognition for Minority Ch. program Ohio State Sentate, 1992, Proclamation for Minority Ch. Program City of Toledo, 1992, Cert. of Appreciation U.S. Dept. Transp., 1992, Outstanding Pub. Rels. award Ohio Dept. of Hwy. Safety, 1990, State Occupant Protection award Gov.'s Traffic Safety Com., 1989, Spel. Recognition award, Ohio Dept. of Hwy. Safety, 1990, Nat. award Am. Coalition for Traffic Safety, 1991; honored by Ronald Burk Day in the City, City of Cleve., 1992. Home: 755 Lauraland Dr S Columbus OH 43214

BURKE, BRIAN B., state senator, lawyer; b. Milw., Apr. 19, 1958; s. Thomas Joseph and Mary White (Higgins) B.; m. Patricia J. Coorough, Aug. 7, 1982; children: Colleen Marie, Kathleen Clare, Erin Elizabeth. BA magna cum laude, Marquette U., 1978; JD, Georgetown U., 1981. Bar: Wis. 1981, U.S. Dist. Ct. (ea. and we. dists.) Wis. 1981, U.S. Ct. Appeals (7th cir.) 1983, U.S. Supreme Ct. 1984. Asst. dist. atty. Milwaukee County, Milw., 1981-84; alderman Milw. Common Coun., 1984-88; mem. Wis. Senate, Madison, 1988—. Mem. editl. bd. Georgetown Internat Law Jour.; contbr.: Wisconsin Lawyer, 1992, 94. Trustee Milw. Pub. Libr., 1984-88, Pabst Theatre Bd., Milw., 1984-88; commr. Milw. Met. Sewerage Dist., 1990—, Milw. Redevel. Authority, 1985-88, Hist. Preservation Commn., Milw., 1987-88; exec. bd. Wis. Pub. Utility Inst., 1993—; pub. policy com. of Wis. Trust for Hist. Preservation, 1992—; mem. Dem. Leadership Coun., Nat. Conf. State Legis. Environ. Com. Recipient Wis.'s Environ. Decade Clean 16 award, 1989-94, Bridge Builder's award Nature Conservancy, 1994, Cesar Chavez Humanitarian award Hispanic Leadership Coun., 1994, Friend of Wis. Jewish Cmty. award Wis. Jewish Conf., 1994. Mem. St. Thomas More Lawyers Soc., Hispanic C. of C., Greater Mitchell Street Assn., Phi Beta Kappa. Democrat. Roman Catholic. Office: Wis Senate PO Box 7882 Madison WI 53707-7882

BURKE, DANIEL J., state legislator; b. Chgo., Dec. 17, 1951. Student, Loyola U., Berlitz Sch. Lang., DePaul U. Dep. city clk. Chgo, 1979—; Ill. state rep. Dist. 23, 1991—; mem Edn. Appropriations, Election Law, Elem. & Secondary Edn., Labor and Commerce, Transp. & Vehicles Coms., Ill. Ho. of Reps. Mem. Internat. Mcpl. Clks. Assn. (legis. co-chmn.), Gov. Fin. Officers Assn. Address: 206S-L Stratton Bldg Springfield IL 62706*

BURKE, DERMOT, artistic director; m. Karen Russo; children: Daniel, Kevin, Margaret Kathleen. Ballet master, resident choreographer, artistic dir. Am. Repertory Ballet Co., 1979-92; exec. dir. Dayton (Ohio) Ballet, 1992—. Choreographer Pacific Northwest Ballet, Am. Repertory Ballet, Dayton Ballet. Office: Dayton Ballet 140 N Main Street Dayton OH 45402*

BURKE, JAMES DONALD, museum administrator; b. Salem, Oreg., Feb. 22, 1939; s. Donald J. and Ellin (Adams) B.; m. Diane E. Davies, May 17, 1980. B.A., Brown U., 1961; M.A., U. Pa., 1966; Ph.D., Harvard U., 1972. Curator Yale U. Art Gallery, New Haven, 1972-78; asst. dir. St. Louis Art Mus., 1978-80, dir., chief exec. officer, 1980—; cons., panel mem. IRS, Washington, 1980—. Author: Jan Both, 1974, Charles Meyron, 1974; contbr. articles to profl. jours. Pres. St. Louis Art Mus. Found., 1985—, Gateway Found., 1986—. Fulbright fellow, 1968-69. Mem. Coll. Art Assn., Print Council Am., Am. Assn. Mus., Assn. Art Mus. Dirs. Office: St Louis Art Mus One Fine Arts Dr Forest Park Saint Louis MO 63110

BURKE, JOHN FRANCIS, JR., economist; b. Bath, Maine, Mar. 25, 1937; s. Ruth; m. Lynda Scheer, Sept. 15, 1962 (div.); children: Colleen, George, Maureen, John; m. Nancy A. Fuerst, Aug. 16, 1986; children: Ruth, Patrick. BS, Boston Coll., 1961; MA, U. Notre Dame, 1963, PhD, 1967. Teaching asst. U. Notre Dame, South Bend, Ind., 1963-65; instr. Ind. U., South Bend, 1963-65; asst. prof. Ea. Ill. U., 1965-67; asst. prof. Cleve. State U., 1967-69, assoc. prof. econs., 1970-93, assoc. prof. emeritus, 1994; ptnr. Burke, Rosen & Assocs., Cleve., 1973—; invited lectr. U. Ljubljiana, Yugoslavia, 1989, Brazil, 1979, 86, Mex., 1995, Jamaica, 1995, Grand Cayman, 1995, Bahamas, 1983, French Guiana, 1986; host Cleve. State U. Forum, 1989—; econ. advisor to atty. gen. State of Ohio, 1983-85; staff economist WKYC-TV and NBC, Cleve., 1981-84; host radio talk show WERE Radio, 1983-84; mem. Coll. Entrance Exam. Bd., 1978-81; ad hoc TV commentator Sta. WJW (CBS), Cleve.; expert forensic econ. witness in over 1500 cases; econ. advisor in field. Contbr. numerous articles to profl. jours.; reviewer Rev. of Social Economy, 1971-81. Mem. AAUP, Am. Econ. Assn., Am. Statis. Assn., Assn. for Social Econs., Nat. Assn. Bus. Economists, Atlantic Econ. Assn., Ea. Econ. Assn., Midwest Econ. Assn., Nat. Tax Assn., nat. Acad. Econ. Arbitrators. Office: Burke Rosen & Assocs 2800 Euclid Ave Ste 300 Cleveland OH 44115-2418

BURKE, PAMELA DE WINDT, securities executive; b. Detroit, Oct. 15, 1942; d. Edward Mandell and Betsy (Bope) DeWindt; m. Daniel Burke II, Mar. 11, 1981; children: Heather Steck, Megan S. Berg, Elizabeth Steck. BA in Psychology, Bennington Coll., 1964. Fin. advisor E.F. Hutton & Co., Cleve., 1981-84; v.p. Prudential Securities, Cleve., 1984-94; 1st v.p. McDonald & Co. Securities, Pepper Pike, Ohio, 1994—. Trustee Berkshire Sch., Sheffield, Mass., 1987—; pres. Hathaway Brown Alumnae Coun., Cleve., 1976-80. Republican. Office: McDonald & Co Securities 30050 Chagrin Blvd Ste 150 Pepper Pike OH 44124-5704

BURKE, PAUL E., JR., state senator, investment banker; b. Kansas City, Mo., Jan. 4, 1934; s. Paul E. and Virginia (Moling) B.; m. Debbie Weihe; children: Anne Elizabeth, Kelly Patricia, A. Catherine, Jennifer Marie. B.S. in Bus. Adminstrn., U. Kans., 1956. Mem. Kans. Ho. of Reps., 1972-74; mem. Kans. State Senate, 1975—, pres., 1989—, majority leader, 1985-89; bd. dirs. Kansas, Inc., 1986—; chmn. Legislative Coordinating Coun., 1995; pres.-elect Nat. Conf. State Legislatures, 1990-91, pres., 1992; pres. Nat. Conf. State Legislatures Found., 1994; mem. Fed. Adv. Commn. Intergovtl. Rels., 1993—. Councilman, City of Prairie Village (Kans.), 1959-63; mem. Kans. Turnpike Authority, 1965-69, chmn., 1969; mem. adv. bd. Sec. of Corrections, 1973-78. Capt. USAF, 1956-59; capt. USNR, 1963-88. Mem. Kans. Assn. Commerce and Industry. Republican. Episcopalian. Lodges: Masons, Shriners, Rotary. Address: 26391 Cedar Niles Cir Olathe KS 66061

BURKE, PAUL NORMAN, publishing executive, toy manufacturing executive; b. Detroit, Apr. 22, 1955; s. Carl Andrew and Elaine Rita (Giguere) B.; m. Gretchen Maureen Schneider, Oct. 14, 1982; children: Janelle, Jason. Pres. Stabur East Music, Redford, Mich., 1981—, Stabur Graphics, Inc., Redford, 1982—; pres., chief exec. officer Stabur Holdings, 1983—; pres. Stabur Press, Inc., Detroit, 1986—, Stabur Corp., Livonia, Mich., 1987—, Whiffart Co., Prescott, Ariz., 1989—, Creative Boxers, Inc., Malibu, Calif., 1990—, Stabur/RHPS, Inc., Livonia, 1982—, Can-Am. Music Corp., Toronto, Can., 1990—, Stadium Svcs., Inc., Livonia, 1993—, TMP Internat., Inc. (McFarlane Toys), Livonia, 1994—, TMP-Irwin Licensing Corp., Carson City, Nev., 1994—, TMP Asia, Ltd., Hong Kong, 1995—, McFarlane Design Group, Inc., Cedar Grove, N.J., 1995—. Mem. ASCAP, Soc. Can. Music Pubs., Broadcast Music, Inc. Home: 48269 Hill Top Dr East Plymouth MI 48170 Office: Stabur Corp 11904 Farmington Rd Livonia MI 48150-1724

BURKE, ROBERT HARRY, surgeon, educator; b. Cambridge, Mass., Dec. 22, 1945; s. Harry Clearfield and Joan Rosalyn (Spire) B.; m. Margaret Cauldwell Fisher, May 4, 1968; children: Christopher David, Catherine Cauldwell. Student, U. Mich. Coll. Pharmacy, 1964-67; DDS, U. Mich., 1971, MS, 1976; MD, Mich. State U., 1980. Diplomate Am. Bd. Oral and Maxillofacial Surgery, Am. Bd. Cosmetic Surgery. Pvt. practice cosmetic and reconstructive surgery Ann Arbor, Mich., 1976—; house officer oral and maxillofacial surgery U. Mich. Sch. Dentistry, U. Mich. Hosp., Ann Arbor, 1973-76; clin. asst. prof. dept. oral surgery U. Detroit Sch. Dentistry, 1976-77; adj. asst. rsch. scientist Ctr. Human Growth and Devel. U. Mich., 1976-77, adj. rsch. investigator, 1982-85; clin. asst. prof. Mich. State U., East Lansing, 1978-80, 1987—; house officer surg. emphasis St. Joseph Mercy Hosp., Ann Arbor, 1980-81; adj. rsch. investigator dept. anatomy U. Mich. Med. Sch., 1982-85; clin. asst. prof. oral and maxillofacial surgery U. Mich., 1984-86; lectr. U. Detroit Sch. Dentistry, 1986, assoc. clin. prof. oral and maxillofacial surgery, 1987-90; cons., lectr. dept. occlusion U. Mich. Sch. Dentistry, 1986; head sect. dentistry and oral surgery dept. gen. surgery St. Joseph Mercy Hosp., 1982-87, mem. exec. com. dept. gen. surgery, 1984-87; chmn. com. emergency care rev. Beyer Meml. Hosp., Ypsilanti, Mich., 1986, also active, 1987, 1990—; active staff St. Joseph Meml. Hosp.; courtesy staff Saline (Mich.) Community Hosp., 1978-88; Chelsea (Mich.) Med. Ctr., 1978-88, 90-92, McPherson Community Hosp., Howell, Mich., 1984-87. Mem. editl. bd. Topics in Pain Mgmt., 1985—; contbg. editor Am. Jours. Cosmetic surgery, 1990-91; sect. editor Internat. Jour. Aesthetic and Restorative Surgery, 1992-95, 96—. Campaign chmn. med. and dental sects. United Way Washtenaw County, Ann Arbor, 1982, dental sect. 1983; profl. adv. com. March of Dimes Genesee County Valley Chpt., Flint, 1979; pres. Huron Pkwy. Pla. Condominium, 1984—. Fellow ACS, Internat. Coll. Surgeons (bd. dirs. Mich. chpt., vice regent), Am. Coll. Oral and Maxillofacial Surgeons (v.p. 1987-88, pres.-elect 1989-90, pres. 1991-93), Am. Acad. Aesthetic and Restorative Surgery; mem. AMA, Am. Assn. Craniomaxillofacial Surgeons (pres. 1992—), Internat. Soc. Cosmetic Laser Surgeons (trustee 1992-93, sec. 1992), British Soc. for Oral and Maxillofacial Surgeons (assoc.), European Soc. Aesthetic Surgery and Liposuction, Chalmers Lyons Acad. Oral Surgery, European Assn. for Cranio-Maxillofacial Surgery (assoc.), Washtenaw County Med. Soc. (exec.com. sec. 1987-88, pres. 1990), Inst. Study Profl. Risk (bd. dirs. 1985-90), Victor's Club, Pres.'s Club, Omicron Kappa Upsilon. Congregationalist. Home: 4702

Mulderry Woods Cr Ann Arbor MI 48105 Office: 2260 S Huron Pky Ann Arbor MI 48104-5151

BURKE, ROBERT R., electrical engineer; b. Green Bay, Wis., Sept. 1, 1933. BME, Marquett U., 1955, BEE, 1963. Registered profl. engr., Fla., Ohio, Wis. Mgr. mfg. Siemens Energy & Automation, Cin., 1972-84, mgr. mech. engring., 1984-89, mgr. devel. engring., 1989—. Patentee in field. Lt. U.S. Army, 1956-58. Mem. IEEE. Office: Siemens Energy & Automation 4620 Forest Ave Cincinnati OH 45212-3306

BURKE, SHEILA JANE, financial advisor; b. Columbus, Ohio, Oct. 1, 1949; children: Troy Gussler, Brian Gussler; m. Stanley M. Burke, June 17, 1989; stepchildren: Jocelyn Morris Burke Dustin, Sabrina. CLU; ChFC. Fin. advisor B.C. Christopher Securities (formerly Dome Fin. Svcs.), Westerville, Ohio, 1976—. Contbr. articles to mags. Mem. Internat. Assn. Fin. Planners, Columbus Life Underwriters Soc. Republican. Methodist. Office: BC Christopher Securities 68 Westerview Dr Westerville OH 43081-2682

BURKE, THOMAS JOHN, communications executive; b. Appleton, Wis., Jan. 23, 1947; s. John George and Rosella Sally (Vanderlois) B.; m. Barbara Jean Koth, June 13, 1970; children: Bradley John, Michael James. BSME, Purdue U., 1970; MBA, Fairleigh Dickinson U., 1979. Registered profl. engr., N.J. Salesman Am. Air Filter, Louisville, 1970-72; product mgr. Polycon, Ramsey, N.J., 1972-74; sales engr. Joy Mfg., N.Y.C., 1974-75; sr. sales engr. Joy Mfg., Chgo., 1975-88; pres. Burke Ventures Ltd./Burke Communication Systems, Oak Park, Ill., 1988—; publ. Node News, 1996—; Jaycee trainer Life Dynamics, Chgo., 1983-86; lectr. Leadership Tng., Chgo., 1983-87; cons. Time Mgmt., Chgo., 1983-87; co-owner Minou Cafe & Bakery, Oak Park, Ill., 1986-92. Author: Dream Genesis, 1986, History of Imperial Hotel and Frank Lloyd Wright, 1987; co-pub. Chic Menu Guide. Pres. Oak Park Austin Coun. for Community Rels., 1983-87; mem. edn. com., pub. speaker Frank Lloyd Wright Home and Studio, 1986—; officer Oak Park Mall Merchants Assn., 1988-92; cub master Boy Scouts Am., Oak Park, 1985-89. Mem. Oak Park C. of C. (Athena judge Best Bus. Women of Yr. 1988—), Friends of Small Bus., Entrepreneurial Coun., Jaycees (v.p. 1983-86, Oak Park Jaycee of Yr. 1983), TLC Book Club (co-counder). Home: 742 N Taylor Ave Oak Park IL 60302-1750 Office: Burke Communications Systems PO Box 4152 Oak Park IL 60303-4152

BURKE, THOMAS JOSEPH, civil engineer; b. Grosse Pointe Park, Mich., Sept. 1, 1927; s. Cyril Joseph and Marie Estelle (Sullivan) B.; BCE, Villanova U., 1949; m. Elaine Kiefer, Nov. 10, 1951; children: Judy Lee Burke Brooks, Kathleen Marie Harness, Maureen Elaine Beck, Thomas P. Chmn., Burke Rental Service, Sterling Heights, Mich., 1949—, Cyril J. Burke, Inc., Sterling Heights, Mich., 1949—. Trustee Villanova U., 1980—. Served to lt. USAF, Korea. Mem. ASCE, Detroit Builders Exchange (v.p. 1976-78, dir. 1975-78), Associated Equipment Distbrs. (dir. 1955-58, 75-78), Associated Underground Contractors (dir. 1965-68), Mich. Ready Mix Concrete Assn. (dir. 1960-65), Villanova U. Alumni Assn. (nat. v.p. 1978-79, nat. pres. 1980), Detroit Engring. Soc. Roman Catholic. Clubs: Grosse Pointe Yacht, Otsego Ski, Ocean Reef, Detroit Athletic, Villanova U. of Detroit (pres. 1955-65). Home: 578 Shelden Rd Grosse Pointe MI 48236-2640 also: 688 N Lakeshore Rd Port Sanilac MI 48469-9713 Office: 36000 Mound Rd Sterling Heights MI 48310-4733

BURKE, THOMAS JOSEPH, software engineer; b. Cleve., Oct. 31, 1957; s. Thomas Melvin and Rita Jane (Plicka) B.; m. Amalia Kelly, Aug. 9, 1980; 1 child, Robert Anthony. BS in Math., John Carroll U., 1979; MS in Computer Sci., U. Dayton, 1988. Programmer Soc. Nat., Cleve., 1978-79, NCQ, Dayton, Ohio, 1979-84; sr. software engr., supr. Allen Bradley, Cleve., 1984-92, prin. software engr., 1992-94; prin. engr. Rockwell Software, Cleve., 1994—; dir. software devel. Mirror Images, Beachwood, Ohio, 1984-86; cons. Mannix Enterprises, Cleve., 1986-90; software developer Cloud Nine, Dayton, 1980-84. Patentee in field. Dir. devel. Habitat for Humanity, Chagrin Falls, Ohio, 1994—. Home: 18038 Harvest Chagrin Falls OH 44023 Office: Rockwell Software 747 Alpha Park Highland Heights OH 44143

BURKEN, RUTH MARIE, retail company executive; b. Kenosha, Wis., Sept. 25, 1956; d. Richard Stanley and Anne Theresa (Steplyk) Wojtak; m. James H. Burken, Oct. 15, 1988. AAS, Gateway Tech. Inst., 1976; BA, U. Wis.-Parkside, 1980; AAS, Coll. of DuPage, 1995. Transp. aide Kenosha Achievement Ctr. (Wis.), 1977; lifeguard U. Wis.-Parkside, Kenosha, 1980, library clk., 1978-80; asst. mgr. K Mart Corp., Troy, Mich., 1980-88, regional office supr., 1988, internal auditor, 1989-92, sr. field auditor, 1992—. Mem. NAFE, Distributive Edn. Clubs Am. (parliamentarian 1976), U. Wis.-Parkside Alumni Assn. Roman Catholic. Office: K Mart Internat Hdqs 3100 W Big Beaver Rd Troy MI 48084-3004

BURKET, GAIL BROOK, author; b. Stronghurst, Ill., Nov. 1, 1905; d. John Cecil and Maud (Simonson) Brook; AB, U. Ill., 1926; MA in English Lit., Northwestern U., 1929; m. Walter Cleveland Burket, June 22, 1929; children: Elaine (Mrs. William L. Harwood), Anne, Margaret (Mrs. James Boyce). Pres. woman's aux. Internat. Coll. Surgeons, 1950-54, now bd. dirs. Mus.; nat. vice chmn. Am. Heritage of DAR, 1992-95; pres. Northwestern U. Guild, 1976-78; sec. Evanston women's bd. Northwestern U. Settlement, 1979-81, pres., 1984-86; mem. cen. com., 1986—. Mem. Nat. Trust Hist. Preservation, 1995—. Recipient Robert Ferguson Meml. award Friends of Lit., 1973. Mem. Nat. League Am. Pen Women (Ill. state pres. 1952-54, nat. v.p. 1958-60), Soc. Midland Authors, Poetry Soc. Am., Women in Communications Inc., AAUW (pres. N. Shore br. 1961-63), Ill. Opera Guild (bd. dirs. 1982—, 1st v.p. 1986-91, pres. 1991-93), Daus. Am. Colonists (state v.p. 1973-76), Colonial Dames Am. (chpt. regent 1974-80), Phi Beta Kappa, Delta Zeta. Author: Courage Beloved, 1949; Manners Please, 1949; Blueprint for Peace, 1951; Let's Be Popular, 1951; You Can Write a Poem, 1954; Far Meadows, 1955; This is My Country, 1960; From the Prairies, 1968. Contbr. articles, poems to lit. publs. Address: 1020 Lake Shore Blvd Evanston IL 60202-1433

BURKETT, GORDON R., manufacturing executive; b. Muncie, Ind., June 13, 1937. Pres. 5 Star Machine & Tool, Anderson, Ind., 1983-88, Drives by Design, Anderson, Ind., 1980-87, Gen A Flex Corp., Chesterfield, Ind., 1987—; mem. adv. bd. Drives by Design, 1980—, Ind. State Prision, Pendleton, 1992—. Inventor in field. With USN, 1954-63. Office: Gen A Flex Corp 67 Skyview Dr Chesterfield IN 46017-1056

BURKEY, LEE MELVILLE, lawyer; b. Beach, N.D., Mar. 21, 1914; s. Levi Melville and Mina Lou (Horner) B.; m. Lorraine Lillian Burghardt, June 11, 1938; 1 child, Lee Melville, III. B.A., U. Ill., 1936, M.A., 1938; J.D. with honor, John Marshall Law Sch., 1943. Bar: Ill., 1944, U.S. Dist. Ct., 1947, U.S. Ct. Appeals, 1954, U.S. Supreme Ct.; 1983; cert. secondary tchr., Ill. Tchr. Princeton Twp. High Sch., Princeton, Ill., 1937-38, Thornton Twp. High Sch., Harvey, Ill., 1938-43; atty. Office of Solicitor, U.S. Dept. Labor, Chgo., 1944-51; ptnr. Asher, Gubbins & Segall and successor firms, Chgo., 1951-94; of counsel, 1995—; lectr. bus. law Roosevelt Coll., 1949-52; bd. dirs. First of America Bank. Contbr. numerous articles on lie detector evidence. Trustee, Village of La Grange, Ill., 1962-68, mayor, 1968-73, village atty., 1973-87; commr., pres. Northeastern Ill. Planning Commn., Chgo., 1969-73; mem. bd. dirs. United Ch. Christ, Bd. of Homeland Ministries, 1981-87; mem. exec. com. Cook County Coun. Govts., 1968-70; life mem. Assoc. Bd. La Grange Meml. Hosp., La Grange Area Hist. Soc.; bd. dirs. Better Bus. Bur. Met. Chgo., Inc., 1975-82, Plymouth Place, Inc., 1973-82; mem. exec. bd. S.W. Suburban Ctr. on Aging, 1993—. Brevet 2nd Lt. Ill. Nat. Guard, 1932. Recipient Disting. Alumnus award John Marshall Law Sch., 1973, Good Citizenship medal S.A.R., 1973, Patriot medal S.A.R., 1977, meritorious Service award Am. Legion Post 1941, 1974, Honor award LaGrange Area Hist. Soc., 1987; col. Ky., 1989. Mem. ABA (coun., sect. labor and employment law 1982-87, governance officer 1987—), Ill. Bar Assn., Chgo. Bar Assn., SAR (state pres. 1977), S.R., La Grange Country Club, Order of John Marshall, Theta Delta Chi. Democrat. Mem. United Ch. of Christ. Office: 125 S Wacker Dr Chicago IL 60606-4402

BURKHART, JOHN A, physiatrist, educator; b. Canton, Ohio, Jan. 22, 1942; s. John Arnold and Kathleen Evelyn (Smith) B.; m. Maureen Ann Martin, June 18, 1966; children: Ann Elizabeth, Matthew John, Timothy Martin, Laura Ruth. BSc, Ohio State U., 1963, MD, 1968. Diplomate Am. Phys. Medicine and Rehab., Am. Bd. Electrodiagnostic Medicine. Rotating intern Akron (Ohio) City Hosp., 1968-69; resident in phys. medicine Ohio State U. Coll. Medicine, Columbus, 1969-72, chief resident, 1972, clin. instr., 1971-72, clin. asst. prof., 1974—; pvt. practice, Columbus, 1974—; med. dir. skilled nursing facility Riverside Meth. Hosp., Columbus, 1978—, assoc. med. dir. phys. medicine, 1978—; physician mem. phys. therapy sect. Ohio Phys. Therapy-Occupl. Therapy Bd., Columbus, 1977-83, sec., 1977-80, pres., 1980-83; mem. med. staff Grant Hosp., Children's Hosp., Columbus Cmty. Hosp.; mem. tech. rev. com. cancer control program Nat. Cancer Inst., NIH, 1973-74; chmn. utilization rev. com. Rev. Plus, 1987-90, physician advisor, 1990-91; mem.-at-large med. coun. Health Coalition Ctrl. Ohio, 1993; presenter in field. Author: A Manual of Orthopedic Terminology, 1977; contbr. articles to med. jours. Deacon Upper Arlington Luth. Ch., Columbus, 1971, chmn. youth bd., 1971-72, 74-76, mem. stewardship com., 1975, chmn. bd. stewardship, 1977-78, v.p. congregation, 1979-80, pres., 1980-81, Sunday sch. tchr., 1975-76, mem. bd. lay ministry, 1981-92, mem. bd. social concern, 1982-83, chmn. com. on Christian counseling, 1983-84, mem. nominating com., 1984-85, mem. bd. worship and music, 1984-87; del. Ohio dist. Am. Luth. Ch. Conv., 1980, 81, 86, Columbus Conf., 1986, Am. Luth. Ch., Nat. Conv., 1987; del. Evang. Luth. Ch. Am. Nat. Conv., 1987; bd. dirs. Happy Canine Helpers, 1984—, vice chmn. bd. trustees, 1986-90, chmn., 1990—; team physician Wellington Sch., Columbus, 1983-87; trustee New Directions Evangelistic Assn., Burlington, N.C., 1975-77, Westminster-Thurber Cmty. Retirement Ctr., 1993; bd. dirs. Chapel Ministries, New Smyrna Beach, Fla., 1976-80; dean leader pack 295 Cub Scouts Am., Columbus, 1986-87; asst. baseball, football, soccer and softball coach Little League, 1980-85, 90; mem. exec. com. Wellington Sch. Parents Assn., 1986-88, mem. nominating com., 1986-87, chmn. scholarship com., 1987-88; mem. budget and allocation com. United Way, Columbus, 1975-77. Lt. comdr. M.C., USN, 1972-74. Fellow Am. Acad. Phys. Medicine; mem. AMA, Ohio Med. Assn. (legis. com. 1984-89, del. to ann. conv. 1987-93, chmn. com. on Bur. Workers Compensation 1987-92, spl. honor citation 1984), Ohio Soc. Phys. Medicine (program chmn. 1976-79, 81-85, exec. com. at-large 1985-89, pres.-elect 1986-89, pres. 1989-92), Acad. Medicine Columbus and Franklin County (exec. com. 1990-94, sec.-treas. 1992-94), Christian Med. Soc. (affiliate), Ohio State U. Alumni Marching Band (life), Ohio State U. Coll. Medicine Alumni Assn. (life), Soc. Hipprocrates, Ohio State U. Alumni Assn. (life), President's Club, Buckeye Club, Script Ohio Club, Kappa Kappa Psi, Nu Sigma Nu, Beta Theta Pi. Republican. Home: 4035 Fenwick Rd Columbus OH 43220 Office: Riverside Meth Hosp 3535 Olentangy River Rd Columbus OH 43214

BURKHOLDER, GARY STEPHEN, mental health nursing educator; b. Traverse City, Mich., Mar. 25, 1941; s. Clarence James and Evelyn (Nelson) Boyd; m. Sharon Kay Weigand, June 25, 1966; children: Sharry, Eric. ADN, Northwestern Mich. C.C., Traverse City, 1965; BSN, Wayne State U., 1968, MSN, 1970. Staff nurse Regional Psychiat. Hosp., Traverse City, 1965-66, Kingswood Hosp., Ferndale, Mich., 1966-67; inservice dir. Kingswood Hosp., Ferndale, 1967-69; instr. Northwestern Mich. C.C., Traverse City, 1970-72; instr. Ferris U., Traverse City, 1972-77, off campus program dir., 1977-83; assoc. prof. Ferris U., Big Rapids, Mich., 1983—; founder, adv. bd. dirs. Alcohol Treatment Svcs., Traverse City, 1974; grad. faculty Wayne State Univ., Grand Rapids, 1977-79 mem. adv. bd. Mich. Substance Abuse Adv. Bd. Dist. 3, 1977; founder ADN Mental Health Nurse Educators of Mich. Network, 1991. Mem. Boy Scouts Am., Big Rapids, 1984-88, Rotary Internat., Big Rapids, 1985-89. With USN, 1959-63. Recipient Nat. Excellence in Teaching award Nat. Co-Alliance for Teaching Excellence, Shawnee, Mission, Kans., 1992. Mem. Mich. Nursing Assn. (liaison with mental health div. 1977-80, vice chair edn. 1977-79, bd. dirs. 1978-80). Lutheran. Home: 7462 E Nine Mile Rd Big Rapids MI 49307 Office: Ferris Univ Dept Nursing Big Rapids MI 49307

BURKHOLDER, JAMES PETER, music educator; b. Chapel Hill, N.C., June 17, 1954; s. Donald L. and Jean A. (Fox) B.; m. P. Douglas McKinney, May 29, 1993. AB, Earlham Coll., 1975; MA, U. Chgo., 1980, PhD, 1983. Lectr. U. Chgo., 1979, 81; instr. U. Wis., Madison, 1982-83, asst. prof., 1983-88; assoc. prof. music Ind. U., Bloomington, 1988-96, prof., 1996—, assoc. dean of faculties, 1995—. Author: Charles Ives: The Ideas Behind the Music, 1985 (Irving Lowens award 1987), Basic Concepts of Music, 1991, All Made of Tunes: Charles Ives and the Uses of Musical Borrowing, 1995; editor: Charles Ives and His World, 1996; co-editor: Charles Ives and the Classical Tradition, 1996; contbr. articles to music jours. Co-clk. Friends for Lesbian and Gay Concerns, 1990-94; recording clk. Bloomington Friends Meeting, 1989-93. Fellow Am. Coun. Learned Socs., 1985. Mem. Am. Musicological Soc. (coun. mem. 1986-89, bd. dirs. 1992-94, Alfred Einstein award 1986), Charles Ives Soc. 9bd. dirs. 1984—, pres. 1992—), Coll. Music soc. (bd. dirs. 1996—), Soc. Music Theory, Sonneck Soc. Am. Music. Democrat. Office: Ind Univ School of Music Bloomington IN 47405

BURKMAN, ALLAN MAURICE, pharmacology educator; b. Waterbury, Conn., Apr. 23, 1932; s. Leon Oscar and Anna (Deitcher) B.; m. Katherine Horween, Aug. 8, 1965; children: David Eric, Deborah Rae. BSc, U. Conn., 1954; MSc, Ohio State U., 1955, PhD, 1958. Registered pharmacist, Conn. Asst. prof. pharmacology U. Ill., Chgo., 1958-63; assoc. prof. Butler U., Indpls., 1963-66; assoc. prof. Ohio State U., Columbus, 1966-71, prof., 1971-95, prof. emeritus, 1995—, chmn. div., 1978-87, 94-95; vis. prof. U. Utah, Salt Lake City, 1981-82, Universidad Ctrl. de Venezuela, Caracas, 1994. Co-author: Introduction to Ocular Pharmacology and Toxicology, 1991; mem. editorial rev. bds., referee various profl. and sci. jours.; contbr. articles to profl. and sci. jours., chpts. to books. Recipient R.B. Allen Instructorship award U. Ill., 1963, award for rsch. direction Mead Johnson Co., 1965; grantee Am. Found. Pharm. Edn., 1957-58, NIH, Office Naval Rsch., industry, 1959-95. Mem. Am. Soc. Pharmacology and Exptl. Therapeutics, Soc. Exptl. Biology and Medicine, Am. Pharm. Assn. Home: 2990 Shadywood Rd Columbus OH 43221-2325 Office: Ohio State U Div Pharmacology 500 W 12th Ave Columbus OH 43210-1214

BURLEIGH, ANNE HUSTED, freelance writer; b. Indpls., Sept. 12, 1941; d. Ralph W. and Margaret (Walden) Husted; m. William Robert Burleigh, Nov. 28, 1964; children: David William, Catherine Anne, Margaret Walden. BA, DePauw U., 1963; MA, Ind. U., 1980. Reporter Indpls. Star, 1960-63; now freelance writer Cin.; contbg. editor Crisis Mag.; editorial adv. bd. Modern Age mag. Author: John Adams, 1969, Journey Up the River: A Midwesterner's Spiritual Pilgrimage, 1994; contbr.: The Unbought Grace of Life: Essays in Honor of Russell Kirk, 1994; editor: Education in a Free Society, 1972. Mem. regional bd. dirs. Couple to Couple League, Cin., 1986-90; bd. visitors DePauw U., Greencastle, Inc., 1987-90; bd. dirs. Pregnancy Problem Ctr. E., Cin., 1993—; bd. trustees U. Dallas, 1993—. Mem. Fellowship of Cath. Scholars, Delta Gamma. Republican. Roman Catholic. Home: Turkey Ridge Farm 11213 E Bend Rd Burlington KY 41005

BURMAN, DIANE BERGER, organization development consultant; b. Pitts., Dec. 7, 1936; d. Morris Milton and Dorothy June (Barkin) Berger; m. Sheldon Oscar Burman, Dec. 15, 1926; children: Allison Beth, Jocelyn Holly, Harrison Emory Guy. BA, Vassar Coll., 1958; MA, Middlebury Coll., 1961. Tchr. of French Allderdice High Sch., Pitts., 1960-61, Mamaroneck (N.Y.) High Sch., 1961-64; personnel specialist G.D. Searle & Co., Skokie, Ill., 1972-77, orgn. devel. tng. cons., 1977-78; personnel and orgn. devel. cons. Abbott Labs., North Chgo., 1978-82; orgn. devel. cons., v.p., mgr. career devel. Harris Bank, Chgo., 1982—. Mem. edit. bd. Orgn. Devel. Jour., 1987. Bd. advisors Grad. Sch. Bus. No. Ill. U. Mem. ASTD (bd. dirs. Chgo. career devel. profl. practice area 1987—), Orgn. Devel. Network (exec. dir. Chgo. chpt. 1986-89), Assn. Psychol. Type-Nat. Conf., Orgn. Devel. Inst. (adv. bd. 1987—, chmn. nat. conf. 1990), Nat. Assn. Bank Women, Internat. Assn. Career Mgmt. Profls., Vassar Club (bd. dirs. 1975-80, 95—). Jewish. Home: 247 Prospect Ave Highland Park IL 60035-3357 Office: Harris Bank 111 W Monroe St Chicago IL 60603-4003

BURMEISTER, PAUL FREDERICK, farmer; b. Great Bend, Kans., June 11, 1938; s. Ferdinand Frederick Adam and Gertrude Nellie (Hanson) B. BA in Chemistry and Agr., Ft. Hays State U., 1960; postgrad., U. Kans., 1961. Farmer Claflin, Kans., 1952-61, 64—; with USANG, 1963-69; farmer coop. Kans. Agrl. Experiment Sta., Ft. Hays Br. Sta., Hays, Kans., 1970, Kans. Rural Ctr., Whiting, 1991, 92; panel mem. Kans. Sustainable Agr. Conf., Great Bend and Salina, 1991, 92; mem. Kans. Natural Resource Coun., Topeka, 1975—, Nat. Resources Def. Coun., N.Y.C., 1975—; participant,U. Akron Nat. Energy Forum, 1976, Nat. Low-Level Radioactive Waste Mgmt. Strategy Rev. Workshop, Washington, 1981; participant pub. forum on radioactive wastes Office Radiation Programs, EPA, Denver, 1978; guest speaker, Rapid City, S.D., 1993. Contbr. articles to environ. and agrl. jours. Vol. Am. Peace Corps, Ludhiana, India, 1961-63; local organizer campaign Union of Concerned Scientists, Cambridge, Mass.; lobbyists on environ. protection and conservation issues, Topeka, 1976-80; mem. Renew Am., Washington, 1980—; mem. The Menninger Found., Topeka, 1989—, Environ. Action, 1982—; lay mem. ad hoc task force on ecology Christian lifestyle United Ch. of Christ, 1977-78, commn. on outreach Kans.-Okla. conf., 1988—, network environ. and econ. responsibility; participant Kans. Citizens Forum Com. for Humanities, Topeka, 1987; mem. farmer adv. com. Sunshine Farm Project, Land Inst., Salina, Kans., 1995—. With Kans. Army NG, 1963-69. Recipient Bankers award Banks of Barton County, Kans. and U.S. Soil Conservation Svc., 1990. Mem. Nat. Wildlife Fedn. (life), Nat. Coun. Returned Peace Corps Vols., Nat. Arbor Day Found., World Wildlife Fund (charter), Am. Wind Energy Assn., Am. Solar Energy Soc., Kans. Assn. Wheat Growers, Kans. Farmers Union, Kans. Organic Prodrs., Inc., Friends of the Earth, Cousteau Soc. (founding yr. mem.), Kans. State Hist. Soc. (life), Kans. Wildlife Fedn., Sierra Club (life), Native Forest Coun., Ducks Unlimited Inc., Friends of India, Tau Kappa Epsilon (sec. 1958-59, scholar 1959), Phi Eta Sigma (historian 1958-59), Phi Kappa Phi, Delta Epsilon. Home: RR 1 Box 168 Claflin KS 67525-9802

BURNETT, EUGENE ALLEN, secondary education educator; b. Sycamore, Ill., Apr. 22, 1951; s. Lowell Allen and Virginia Mae (Jackson) B.; m. Yvonne Dee Cartwright, Aug. 6, 1983. BA, Western Ill. U., 1973, MA, 1978. Tchr. Macomb (Ill.) Sr. High Sch., 1974-76; tchr., dept. chair social studies Pontiac (Ill.) Twp. High Sch., 1976—; adv. com. mem. East Ctrl. Ill. Edn. Svc. Ctr., Rantoul, 1991—; evaluator Ill. State Bd. Edn., 1990—. Author: (with others) Understanding the Illinois Constitution, 1986, The History of Livingston County, 1991. Market master Main St. Am. Program, Pontiac, 1990—. Recipient Master Tchr. award State of Ill., 1984; named Outstanding Tchr. Am. History, Ill. Orgn. Daughters of Am. Revolution, 1992, Voice of Democracy Program Tchr. of Yr., VFW, 1990, one of Outstanding Young Men of Am., U.S. Jaycees, 1984; Freedom Found. scholar, 1982; Fulbright-Hays fellow, U.S. Govt., 1977. Mem. Assn. for Advancement of Am. History, Ill. Speech and Theatre Assn., Ill. Coun. for Soc. Studies, Phi Delta Kappa. Home: 702 Mohave Dr Pontiac IL 61764-1538 Office: Pontiac Twp High Sch 1100 E Indiana Ave Pontiac IL 61764-1204

BURNETT, JUDITH JANE, foundation administrator, consultant; b. Muncie, Ind., Aug. 21, 1947; d. Albert Ward and Jane M. (Collins) Burnett; student public schs. Saleswoman, Collins Mobile Home Sales, Muncie, 1970-73; sales mgr. HiWay, Inc., Anderson, Ind., 1973-75; service dir., then ops. mgr. Indiana Homemakers, Inc., Indpls., 1975-80, exec. v.p., 1980-83, also dir.; corp. sec. Mgmt. Alternatives, Inc., Indpls., 1984-85; exec. v.p., dir. Three—I Homemakers, Inc., Illini Homemakers, Inc., 1980-83; dir. Home Care Med. Products Co., 1980-82; adminstr. ECF Med. Billing, 1987-88; adminstrv. Extended Med. Svcs., 1988-92; owner Projects and Promotions, 1988—; exec. dir. Ryan White Found., 1994—; mem. council Central Ind. Health Systems Agy., 1980-83; mgr. Eynon for Congress Campaign, 1985-86; mem. Homemaker, Handyman, Home Health Aide Task Force, 1980-83, sec., 1980-81, Marion County Council Rep. Women, Marion County GOP Strategy Team; vol. access control mgr. Tenth Pan An. Games, 1987. Mem. WINS, U.S. Tennis Writer's Assn., Nat. Fedn. Rep. Women. Baptist. Home: 9459 Timber View Dr Indianapolis IN 46250-1390

BURNETT, RITA MARLINE, dentist; b. Oswego, Kans., Apr. 29, 1954; d. Elizabeth Ann (Bassett) B.; m. Brett LaMarr Ferguson, Dec. 31, 1984; children: Brittny, Helene-Cole, Brett LaMarr Jr. Student, Blackburn Coll., 1972-73; BS, U. Kans., 1976; DDS, U. Mo., Kansas City, 1983. Diplomate Am. Bd. Dentistry. Jr. biologist Midwest Rsch. Inst., Kansas City, Mo., 1976-77; rsch. toxicologist Mobay Chem. Corp., Stillwell, Kans., 1977-79; assoc. in gen. dentistry Anne Johnson DDS, Kansas City, Mo., 1983-84; pvt. practice family dentistry Kansas City, Kans., 1984—. Vol. Wyandotte County chpt. ARC, 1984—, bd. dirs., 1986—; bd. dirs. Humane Soc. of Greater Kansas City, 1995—; mentor Digital Electronics for all area high schs., 1991—; mem. PTA bd. Shawnee Mission Sch. Dsit., 1994—. Named one of Kansas City Globe's 100 Most Influential African-Americans, 1995. Mem. ADA, Assn. Am. Women Dentists, Am. Soc. Dentistry for Children, Kans. Dental Soc., Mo. Dental Soc., Heart of Am. Dental Soc., Greater Kans. City (Mo.) Dental Soc., Wyandotte County Dental Soc., Am. Bus. Women's Assn. (pres. Women in Action chpt., Kans. City, Mo. 1986-87). Baptist. Home: 10195 Farley St Overland Park KS 66212-5433 Office: Ste 219 4631 Orville Ave Kansas City KS 66102-3647

BURNEY, JOAN ROSSITER, columnist, counselor, public speaker; b. Walthill, Nebr., Oct. 23, 1928; d. Emmett William and June Elizabeth (Hitchcock) Rossiter; m. Howard Keith Burney, Sept. 13, 1947; children: Robert, William, John, Juli, Tom, Charles. BA in Comm. and Music cum laude, Mount Mary Coll., 1973; MS in Edn., Wayne (Nebr.) State Coll., 1986; diploma Leadership in Family Ministry, Creighton U., 1984; student comty. caretaking, hospice vol., N.E. Comty. Coll., 1980, 83, 85. Cert. instr. active parenting 1987, setting the limits 1989 Nebr. Alcohol and Drug Abuse Coun. Columnist various newspapers and mags. in Nebr., Iowa, Mo., Colo.; speaker at seminars, workshops, retreats, nationally and internationally, 1972—. Author: (anthologies) The Keepers Vol 1, The Keepers Vol 2, Comes the Dawn; co-author: Sharing the Faith with Your Child (birth to six) (seven to 14); contbr. articles to mags. and newspapers. Founder, pres. Grandparents Outraged by the Abuse of Drugs; bd. dirs. Hartington (Nebr.) Drug and Alcohol Task Force; mem. pub. rels. com. Hartington Found., bd. dirs. Cedar Cath. H.S. Found.; past pres guild Holy Trinity Ch., sch. bd. mem., choir mem. and dir.; mem. liturgy com., family ministry, cantor; bd. mem. Valley Hope Rehab. Ctr., Alcoholism and Drug Abuse Coun. of Nebr. Mem. Soc. Profl. Journalists, Nat. Fedn. Press Women, Nebr. Press Women (past pres., bd. dirs. 1972—), Nebr. Mothers Assn. (pres.), Am. Mothers Inc (nat. bd. 1991—), Am. Assn. Counseling and Devel., Nebr. Counselors Assn., Fellowship of Merry Christians, Nebr. Writers Guild. Republican. Roman Catholic. Home and Office: RR2 Box 118 Hartington NE 68739

BURNHAM, DUANE LEE, pharmaceutical company executive; b. Excelsior, Minn., Jan. 22, 1942; s. Harold Lee and Hazel Evelyn (Johnson) B.; m. Susan Elizabeth Klinner, June 22, 1963; children—David Lee, Matthew Beckwith. BS, U. Minn., 1963, MBA, 1972. CPA, Wis. Sr. v.p. fin., chief financial officer Abbott Labs., North Chgo., 1982-84, exec. v.p., chief financial officer, dir., 1985-87, vice chmn., chief fin. officer, 1987-89, chmn., chief exec. officer, 1990—; bd. dirs. Sara Lee Corp., Evanston Hosp. Corp. Bd. dirs. Mus. Sci. and Industry, Chgo., Lyric Opera, Healthcare Leadership Coun.; trustee Northwestern U.; mem. adv. bd. J.L. Kellogg Grad. Sch. Mgmt.; chmn. Emergency Com. for Am. Trade. Office: Abbott Labs 100 Abbott Park Rd Abbott Park IL 60064-3500

BURNS, AVON LORRAINE, law educator; b. Flint, Mich., Feb. 24, 1952; d. Henry and LouVera (Robinson) Burns. AAS, Ferris State U., 1972, BS, 1974; MS, Mich. State U., 1979; postgrad., Wayne State U., Detroit, 1987—. Govt. intern City of Flint, Mich., 1975-77; ombudsman investigator City of Flint, 1977-78; part-time instr. Mott Community Coll., Flint, 1976-85; plant security supr. and safety engr. Gen. Motors/Chevrolet div., Flint, 1979-85; assoc. prof./coord. criminal justice program Mott Community Coll., 1985—; dir. criminal justice adv. com. Mott Community Coll. Mem. adv. com. Genesee County Sheriff, Nu Paths; bd. dirs. Bruin Club, Youth Svcs. Bur., Crimestoppers, editor newsletter. Recipient Nat. Instrnl. Staff Orgn. Devel. Tchg. Excellence award U. Tex., 1993, Mich. Trends in Occupl. Studies Educator award, 1994, Faculty Recognition Honor cert. Mich. C.C. Consortium. Mem. Acad. Criminal Justice Sci. (exec. counselor, C.C. sect.), Am. Soc. Indsl. Security. Office: Mott Community Coll 1401 E Court St Flint MI 48503-6208

BURNS, DAVE, business executive; b. Indpls., Nov. 24, 1955. BSEE, Purdue U., 1982. Customer engr. Hewlett-Packard, Bloomington, Ind., 1980-86; pres. Med.-Link, Bloomington, 1987—. Com. mem. Community Learning Network, Bloomington, 1994—. Sgt. USMC, 1974-78. Office: Med Link Inc 315 W 17th St Bloomington IN 47404-3453

BURNS, ELIZABETH MURPHY, media executive; b. Superior, Wis., Dec. 4, 1945; d. Morgan and Elizabeth (Beck) Murphy; m. Richard Ramsey Burns, June 24, 1984. Student U. Ariz., 1963-67. Promotion and programming sec. Sta. KGUN-TV, Tucson, 1967-68; programming and traffic sec. Sta. KFMB-TV, San Diego, 1968-69; owner, operator Sta. KKAR, Pomona, Calif., 1970-73; co-owner Evening Telegram Co. (parent co. Murphy Stas.); pres. Morgan Murphy Stas., Madison, Wis., 1976—; dir. Nat. Guardian Life Ins. Co., various media stas. and corps. Trustee Coll. St. Scholastica; bd. dirs. Republic Bank. Mem. Nat. Assn. Broadcasters, Wis. Broadcasters Assn. Republican. Roman Catholic. Clubs: Madison, Nakoma Country; Northland Country (Duluth), Boulders Country (Carefree, Ariz.). Avocations: golf, tennis, travel. Home: 180 Paine Farm Rd Duluth MN 55804-2609 Office: Sta WISC-TV 7025 Raymond Rd Madison WI 53719-5053

BURNS, GARY CURTIS, communications educator; b. Elgin, Ill., June 10, 1952; s. William Eugene and Beatrice Ona (Nagel) B.; m. Deborah Sue Utz, Aug. 11, 1973 (div. 1981); 1 child, Rachel Michelle. BS, U. Ill., 1973; MA, No. Ill. U., 1976; PhD, Northwestern U., 1981. Grad. tchg. asst. speech comm. No. Ill. U., DeKalb, 1975-76; instr. speech U. Mo., St. Louis, 1976-78; grad. tchg. asst. radio, TV and film Northwestern U., Evanston, Ill., 1978-79, grad. rsch. asst., instr. radio, TV and film, 1979; instr. speech U. Mo., St. Louis, 1979-81, asst. prof. speech, 1981-82; asst. prof. radio, TV and film Northwestern U., 1982-84; asst. prof. comm. U. Mo., 1984-88; asst. prof. comm. studies No. Ill. U., 1988-90; assoc. prof. comm. U. Mo., 1988-91; assoc. prof. comm. studies No. Ill. U., 1990—, asst. chair, 1996—; local faculty adv. com. Mus. of Broadcast Comm., Chgo., 1992—; mem. North Area Cmty. Access Bd., St. Louis County, 1984-88, vice chair, 1987-88. Co-editor: Television Studies: Textual Analysis, 1989, Making Television: Authorship and The Production Process, 1990; editor Popular Music and Soc. jour., 1994—; reviewer in field; contbr. articles to profl. jours. Recipient Rsch. grant Assn. for Recorded Sound Collections, 1990. Mem. NARAS, Am. Culture Assn. (governing bd. 1983-86, 91-95, v.p., pres.-elect 1995—), Broadcast Edn. Assn., Internat. Assn. for Study of Popular Music, Soc. for Cinema Studies, Speech Comm. Assn., Univ. Film and Video Assn., and others. Home: 621 W Highland Ave Elgin IL 60123 Office: No Ill Univ Dept Comm Studies De Kalb IL 60115

BURNS, GLENN RICHARD, dentist; b. Marietta, Ohio, Mar. 23, 1951; s. Alphas Gale Burns and Elma June (Sayres) George; m. Linda Edith Bailey, June 10, 1978; children: Geoffrey William, Katharine May. BS in Zoology, Ohio U., 1973; DDS, Ohio State U., 1980. Gen. practice dentistry Lancaster, Ohio, 1980—. Bd. dirs. Lancaster YMCA, Fairfield County, 1985-91; Presbyn. elder. Served to sgt. U.S. Army, 1973-77. Fellow Acad. Gen. Dentistry, 1991. Fellow Pierre Fauchard Acad.; mem. ADA, Ohio Dental Assn., Hocking Valley Dental Soc. (chmn. children's dental health month 1983-86, v.p. 1991, pres. 1993), Acad. Gen. Dentistry, Doctors With a Heart, Christian Dental Soc., Aircraft Owners and Pilots Assn. (Flying Dentist award), Kiwanis (v.p. 1988, 1st v.p. 1989, pres. 1990), Xi Psi Phi (v.p. 1984-88, pres. 1988-92). Republican. Home: 3931 Mudhouse Rd NE Lancaster OH 43130-8716 Office: 208 N Columbus St Lancaster OH 43130-3005

BURNS, JAMES F., communications engineer; b. Rockport, N.Y., July 16, 1925. BS in Television Engring., Am. TV Inst., 1948; postgrad., Cuyahoga C.C., 1974. Registered profl. engr., Ohio. Project engr. Bunker Rano, Cleve., 1968-71, Allen Bradley Co., Cleve., 1971—. Patent in Swing Arm Connection to Rack Module. Tchr. boating safety U.S. Power Squadron, Cleve. Sgt. U.S. Army, 1944-46. Mem. Jeauga County Airport Authority. Home: 1649 Bell Rd Chagrin Falls OH 44022 Office: Allen Bradley Co 747 Alpha Dr Cleveland OH 44143

BURNS, JAMES TIMOTHY, communications company executive; b. Wausau, Wis., May 26, 1946. BS in Mktg., U. Wis., Oshkosh, 1973. Sr. acct. exec. Bus. Incentives, Mpls., 1983-94; v.p. bus. devel. Becker Comm., Inc., Schofield, Wis., 1994—. Mem. sch. bd. Waukasha (Wis.) Cath. Sch. System, 1982-86. Home: 1220 Ayrshire Ln Waukesha WI 53186-6764 Office: Becker Comm Inc PO Box 500 Schofield WI 54476-0500

BURNS, JEFFREY PHILLIPS, music theorist, composer; b. St. Louis, Nov. 6, 1955; s. Herbert J. and Barbara Alice (Gardner) B. AA, Rock Valley Coll., 1978; BA, No. Ill. U., 1983; advanced computer programming cert., Rock Valley Coll., 1987; MusM, U. Wis., Madison, 1995. Keyboardist, composer Tazz R.K.K., DeKalb, Ill., 1979-80; piano accompanist theater arts dept. No. Ill. U., DeKalb, 1979-84; keyboardist, composer Burns Rickert Set, DeKalb, 1980-86; keyboardist, arranger J.P. and the Cats, DeKalb, 1981-83; pianist, arranger The Moonlight Jazz Orch., Rockford, Ill., 1987-89; piano accompanist dance dept. U. Wis., Madison, 1989-93; piano accompanist The Madison Sch. of Ballet, 1989-91; piano instr. Forbes-Meagher Music, Madison, 1993-94, Ward-Brodt Music, Madison, 1995—; accompanist, vocal coach The New Coll. Singers, Madison, 1988-89; pianist, arranger The Winged Steer, DeKalb, 1984. Author: Messiaen's Modes of Limited Transposition Reconsidered, 1995, The Pentatonic Compendium, 1995; composer: Complexications, 1990, The History of the Mystery, 1992. Mem. Wis. Alliance of Composers.

BURNS, JON PERRY, healthcare administrator; b. Sunbury, Pa., Oct. 26, 1957; s. James Harvey and Thelma (Abrogast) B.; m. Druanne R. Patterson, Oct. 16, 1982; 1 child, James Robert. BS in Bus., Bloomsburg U., 1987; cert. in healthcare mgmt., U. N.C., Chapel Hill, 1989. Coord. Geisinger Med. Ctr., Danville, Pa., 1975-79; supr. TRW, Inc., Harrisburg, Pa., 1979-82; mgr. Geisinger Med. Ctr., Danville, Pa., 1982-85, assoc. bus. dir., 1985-88; fin. adminstr. U. N.C. Hosps., Chapel Hill, 1988-92; corp. dir. adminstrv. svcs. Western Res. Care System, Youngstown, Ohio, 1992-95, v.p., chief info. officer, 1995—; v.p. Keysteon Patient Mgmt., Harrisburg, 1985-86, com. chmn., 1984-85. Contbr. articles to profl. jours. Bd. dirs. Chapel Hill (N.C.) Day Care, 1990—. Mem. Am. Guild of Patient Mgmt. (Editors award 1986), Health Care Fin. Mgmt. Assn., Carolina Patient Mgmt. Home: 566 Daffodil Ln Hubbard OH 44425-2737 Office: Western Res Care System 345 Oak Hill Ave Youngstown OH 44502-1429

BURNS, RICHARD RAMSEY, lawyer; b. Duluth, Minn., May 3, 1946; s. Herbert Morgan and Janet (Strobel) B.; divorced; children: Jennifer, Brian; m. Elizabeth Murphy, June 15, 1984. BA with distinction, U. Mich., 1968, JD magna cum laude, 1971. Bar: Calif. 1972, U.S. Dist. Ct. (no. dist.) Calif. 1972, U.S. Ct. Appeals (9th cir.) 1972, Minn. 1976, U.S. Dist. Ct. Minn. 1976, Wis. 1983, U.S. Tax. Ct. 1983. Assoc. Orrick, Herrington, Rowley & Sutcliffe, San Francisco, 1971-76; ptnr. Hanft, Fride, O'Brien, Harries, Swelbar & Burns P.A., Duluth, 1976—; gen. counsel Evening Telegram Co., Superior, Wis., 1982—, Murphy TV Stas., Madison, Wis., 1982—. Chmn. Duluth-Superior Area Cmty. Found., 1988-90; chmn. Quetico Lifecare Corp., Duluth, 1987—; bd. dirs. Minn. Coun. on Founds, United Way of Greater Duluth, Inc., Duluth Airport Authority, Miller Dwan Med. Ctr. Found. Fellow Am. Coll. Trust and Estate Counsel; mem. Calif. Bar Assn., Wis. Bar Assn., Minn. Bar Assn. (chmn. probate and trust coun.), 11th Dist. Bar Assn. (past pres., past chmn. ethics com.), Arrowhead Estate Planning Coun. (pres. 1980), Duluth Area C. of C. (bd. dirs.), Northland Country Club (pres. 1982), Boulders Club, Kitchi Gammi Club, Mpls. Athletic Club. Republican. Home: 180 Paine Farm Rd Duluth MN 55804-2609 Office: Hanft Fride O'Brien Harries Swelbar & Burns PA 1000 First Bank Pl 130 W Superior St Duluth MN 55802-2056

BURNS, ROBERT EDWARD, editor, publisher; b. Chgo., May 14, 1919; s. William Joseph and Sara (Foy) B.; m. Brenda Coleman, May 15, 1948; children: Maddy F., Martin J. Student, De Paul U., 1937-39; Ph.B., Loyola U., Chgo., 1941; PhD (hon.), Rosary Coll., 1983. Pub. relations dir. Cath. Youth Orgn., Chgo., 1943-45, 47-49; exec. dir. No. Ind. region Nat. Conf. Christians and Jews, 1946; exec. editor U.S. Cath. mag.; gen. mgr. Claretian Publs., Chgo., 1949-84. Author: The Examined Life, 1980, Catholics on the Cutting Edge, 1983. Bd. dirs. Thomas More Assn. Recipient St. Francis de Sales award Cath. Press Assn., 1973, Proecclesia et Pontifice award Pope John Paul II, 1984. Home: N 4590 19th Ave Montello WI 53949-7926

BURNS, VIRGINIA LAW, writer; b. Redford, Mich., May 23, 1925; d. Alvin John and Leola Miriam (Wadley) Law; divorced; children: James Ritchie, Duncan Ritchie, Margaret Ritchie. Student, Cranbrook Acad. Art, Bloomfield Hills, Mich., 1943, U. Mich., 1943-47; BA, Mich. State U., 1956. Cert. tchr., Mich. Tchr. elem. schs. State of Mich., 1969-87; editor, pub. Enterprise Press imprint Little People's Books, Lainsburg, Mich., 1978—. Author: (juvenile biographies) Frontier Doctor, 1978, Frontier Soldier, 1980, First Frontiers, 1985, Tall Annie, 1987, Gentle Hunter: Biography of Alice Evans, Bacteriologist, 1992, Four Winds of the Past, 1993; pub.: The Little Puppy That Lost Its Tail; contbr. articles to newspapers and mags. Mem. honors selection com. Mich. Women's Hall of Fame. Recipient Lit. award of merit Hist. Soc. Mich.; nominated one of Mich.'s First Ladies for promoting state history in lit. Mem. Soc. Children's Book Writers & Illustrators (regional advisor), Detroit Women Writers Assn. (chair membership selection com.). Home: 8600 Fenner Rd Laingsburg MI 48848-8702 Office: Enterprise Press 8600 Fenner Rd Laingsburg MI 48848-8702

BURNSIDE, WANDA JACQUELINE, elementary school educator; b. Highland Park, Mich., Mar. 9, 1950; d. Minor and Willie Lee (McCann) Palm; m. Simmie Lee Burnside, Jr., Nov. 4, 1972. BA in Humanities and Social Scis., U. Detroit. Clk. pers. dept. Blue Cross Blue Shield, Detroit, Mich., 1968-69; student asst. dir. libr. U. Detroit Edn. Libr., 1969-72; head clk NARO Fed. Project U.S. Atty.'s Office, Detroit, 1970; editor, office mgr. Detroit Ch. World, 1974-78; SDIP and IIE, ASIP Marygrove Coll., Detroit, 1979-81; elem. tchr. Martin L. King Jr. Ednl. Ctr., Detroit, 1981-88; sales rep. Five Stars Heating, Detroit, 1990-91; exec. sec. Second Ecclesiastical Ch. of God in Christ, Detroit, 1990—, office mgr., 1991—; tchr. Head Start, Detroit, 1967; drama coach Martin L. King Jr. Ednl. Ctr., Detroit, 1980-88; monitor State of Mich. Nurse Lic. Dept., Detroit, 1980-81; tutor private home, Detroit, 1983-87. Author: (poetry) In My Neighborhood, 1972. Mem. Joy of Jesus Ministries, 1975-76, SCLC Detroit chpt., 1993. Recipe contest winner, Fayco Beverage Co., 1979, 2d, Thornapple Valley, 1988, 2d, Progresso Soups, 1989, 1st; cited for laity leadership Congress of Nat. Black Chs., Washington, 1990. Mem. Black Writers Guild, Christian Edn. for Handicapped, Christian Writers Inst., Am. Family Jour. Democrat. Home: 8245 Mendota Detroit MI 48204 Office: Ch of God in Christ Hdqtrs SW Michigan 7045 Curtis Ave Detroit MI 48221

BUROKER, DANIEL JACK, engineer. Welder Kenton (Ohio) Structural, 1985-93; engr. The Mold Makers, Kenton, Ohio, 1994—. Roman Catholic. Home: 417 E Columbus St Kenton OH 43326 Office: The Mold Makers, Inc. 13608 State Rte 68 Kenton OH 43326

BURR, BROOKS MILO, zoology educator; b. Toledo, Aug. 15, 1949; s. Lawrence E. and Beverly Joy (Herald) B.; m. Patti Ann Grubb, Mar. 5, 1977 (div. July 1987); 1 child, Jordan Brooks. BA, Greenville Coll., 1971; MS, U. Ill., 1974, PhD, 1977. Cert. scuba diver, Nat. Assn. Underwater Instrs. Lab. instr. dept. biology Greenville (Ill.) Coll., 1971-72; rsch. asst. Ill. Natural History Survey, Champaign, 1972-77; affiliate scientist Ctr. for Biodiversity Ill. Natural History Survey, Urbana, 1989—; from asst. prof. to prof. dept. zoology So. Ill. U., Carbondale, 1977—; mem. adv. panel U.S. Fish and Wildlife Svc., 1990—; adj. prof. dept. biology U. N.Mex., Albuquerque, 1991—; adj. prof. dept. ecology, ethology and evolution U. Ill., 1993—. Co-author: A Distributional Atlas of Kentucky Fishes, 1986, A Field Guide to Fishes, North America North of Mexico, 1991 (selected as one of Outstanding Acad. Books of 1992 by Choice Mag.); contbr. more than 90 articles to profl. jours. Recipient Paper of Yr. award Ohio Jour. Sci., 1986. Mem. AAAS, Am. Soc. Ichthyologists and Herpetologists (sec., mem. exec. com. 1990-94), Soc. Systematic Zoology, Biol. Soc. Washington, Assn. Systematic Collections, Sigma Xi (Leo M. Kaplan award 1990). Home: 203 W Wedgewood Ln Carbondale IL 62901 Office: So Ill Univ Dept Zoology Carbondale IL 62901-6501

BURR, JACKIE ANN, nursing educator; b. Neosho, Mo., July 20, 1955; d. Howard Calvin and Doris Ann (Brown) Garlow; m. James David Platner, Aug. 5, 1995. LPN, Crowder Coll., 1974, ADN, 1988; BSN, Mo. So. State Coll., 1992. Cert. nurse oper. rm., ACLS provider. Med. express mobile nurse Boulder, Colo., 1992; staff nurse Oak Hill Hosp., Joplin, Mo., 1974-92, Regional Surgery Ctr., Joplin, 1992-94; nursing instr. ADN program sch. nursing Crowder Coll., 1994—; mem. health edn. adv. coun. Crowder Coll., Neosho, 1978-88, 90-94, past sec., past v.p., past pres. Mem. ANA (bd. dirs.), Assn. Oper. Rm. Nurses, Mo. League for Nursing, Mo. So. State Coll. Alumni Assn., Crowder Coll. Alumni Assn. Home: 1220 E 34th St Joplin MO 64804-4023

BURRELL, JOEL BRION, neuroimmunologist, researcher, clinician; b. Orange, N.J., Nov. 27, 1959; s. Robert and Barbara (Miller) B. BS in Biology, Rutgers U., 1982, grad. student, 1983; MD, Temple U., 1987. Diplomate Am. Bd. Med. Examiners. Intern Abington (Pa.) Meml. Hosp., 1987-88; neurology resident The Mt. Sinai Med. Ctr., N.Y.C., 1988-91; neuroimmunology fellow Cleve. Clin. Found., 1991-93; attending physician with pvt. clin. practice, 1993—; asst. clin. prof. Med. Coll. Ohio, 1993—. Presenter in field. Fellow Am. Stroke Coun. of Am. Heart Assn. Recipient Pinnacle award Being Single Mag., 1995. Fellow Stroke Coun. of Am. Heart Assn.; mem. AMA (Physician's Recognition award 1992—), Am. Acad. Clin. Neurophysiology, Internat. Cerebral Hemodynamics Soc., Am. Acad. Neurology, Nat. Med. Assn., Acad. Medicine Cleve., Cleve. Med. Assn., Ohio Acad. Sci., Ohio State Med. Assn., Med. Alumni Assn. Temple U., Temple U. Gen. Alumni Assn., Assoc. Alumni of Mt. Sinai Med. Ctr. of N.Y.C.; Huron County Medical Soc. (Treasurer/Secretary 1995—), New York Academy of Science. Office: Summit Profl Bldg 85 Benedict Ave Ste 103 Norwalk OH 44857-2112

BURRELL, THOMAS J., marketing communication executive; m. Joli Burrell. Founder, chmn. Burrell Communications Group (Burrell Advt. Inc., Burrell Consumer Promotions, Burrell Pub. Rels. Inc.), Chgo., 1971—. Office: Burrell Comm Group Inc 20 N Michigan Ave Chicago IL 60602-4811

BURRIER, GAIL WARREN, physician; b. Newark, Ohio, Apr. 6, 1927; s. Harold I. and Esther M. (Simpson) B.; m. Mary Lou Miller, June 12, 1948 (dec. 1982); children: Dale, Marie. BS, Ohio State U., 1950, MS, 1952, MD, 1956. Diplomate Am. Bd. Family Practice; cert. geriatrist. Intern Grant Hosp., Columbus, Ohio, 1956-57; pvt. practice Canal Winchester, Ohio, 1957-73; dir. family practice Grant Med. Ctr., Columbus, 1973-88; med. dir. Alum Crest Nursing Home, Columbus, 1988—; clin. instr. Ohio State U., Columbus, 1969-74, clin. asst. prof., 1974-81, clin. assoc. prof., 1981—; med. dir. Winchester Place Nursing Home, Canal Winchester, 1983—; med. tech. asst. State of Ohio, Columbus, 1988—. Trustee Columbus Area Mental Health, 1974-81; bd. dirs. Meth. Ch., Canal Winchester, 1959-63; team physician high sch. tournaments, Columbus, 1957—. Fellow Am. Acad. Family Physicians (local pres. 1973); mem. Am. Coll. Physician Execs., AMA, Am. Geriatric Soc., Am. Soc. on Aging, Ohio State U. Alumni Club (pres. Columbus chpt. 1985-86). Republican. Home and Office: 45 Trine St Canal Winchester OH 43110

BURRIS, MERLE HERSHAL, JR., home inspector; b. Sioux City, Iowa, Sept. 20, 1928; s. Merle Hershal and Clara Alice (Olson) B. Sr.; m. Verna Mae Herbold, Sept. 6, 1951; children: Bradley, Sherrie, Jeffrey. Student, Wayne State Coll. Cert. home inspector. Lighting engr., cons. Utility Co. Gas & Electric, Sioux City, Iowa; cert. home inspector Sioux City, Iowa; owner, pres. Home Owners Aware, Ltd., 1985—; cons. Home Buyers, Sioux City, Relocation Co., Home Inspector Network, Iowa. Mem. Masons, Shriners. Republican. Methodist. Home and Office: 2016 S Palmetto St Sioux City IA 51106-3014

BURRIS, ROBERT HARZA, biochemist, educator; b. Brookings, S.D., Apr. 13, 1914; s. Edward T. and Mable C. (Harza) B.; m. Katherine Irene Brusse, Sept. 12, 1945; children: Jean Carol, John Edward, Ellen Louise. B.S., S.D. State Coll., 1936, D.Sc., 1966; M.S., U. Wis., 1938, Ph.D., 1940. NRC fellow Columbia U., 1940-41; faculty U. Wis., Madison, 1941—; prof. U. Wis., 1951-84; chmn. biochemistry Coll. Agr., 1958-70, W.H. Peterson prof. biochemistry, 1976-84, prof. emeritus, 1984—. Recipient Charles Thom award Soc. Indsl. Microbiology, 1977; Nat. Medal of Sci., 1980; Carty award Nat. Acad. Scis., 1984; Wolf award in Agr., 1985; Guggenheim fellow Cambridge U., 1954. Mem. Am. Chem. Soc. (Spencer award 1990), Am. Soc. Biochemistry and Molecular Biology, Am. Philos. Soc., Am. Soc. Plant Physiologists (Stephen Hales award 1968, Charles Reid Barnes award 1977, pres. 1960), Biochem. Soc., AAAS, Am. Soc. Microbiology, NAS, Indian Nat. Sci. Acad. (fgn. assoc.). Home: 1015 University Bay Dr Madison WI 53705-2250

BURROUGHS, PAMELA GAYLE, critical care nurse; b. Dayton, Ohio, July 31, 1957; d. Dale Davis and Anita Madge (Allen) Hallsted; m. Donald W. Burroughs, Oct. 7, 1978; children: Kristin Rene, Kevin Wayne. Diploma, Jewish Hosp. Sch. Nursing, 1977. RN, Ohio. Staff nurse Epp Meml. Hosp., Cin., 1977-78; relief charge nurse ICU, Clermont Mercy Hosp., Batavia, Ohio, 1978-90, supr. patient care, 1990-95, coord. nursing edn., 1991-92, staff nurse ICU, 1993-94, edn. instr., 1992-94, info. svcs. nursing coord., 1994-96, mgr. clin. info. svcs., 1996—; BLS instr. trainer. Mem. AACN.

BURROW, JOHN RANDOLPH, secondary education educator, writer, editor; b. Victorville, Calif., Nov. 13, 1953; s. George Irving and Elizabeth Zane (Miller) B.; m. Janet Kay Norton, May 22, 1982. BA in English and Theatre, Iowa Wesleyan Coll., Mt. Pleasant, 1975; postgrad., St. Ambrose Coll., Davenport, Iowa, 1984, U. Iowa, 1981, 84, 88. Cert. in secondary edn., English/speech, Iowa. Tchr. Ft. Madison (Iowa) Cmty. Sch., 1975-77; tchr., head dept. Andrew (Iowa) Cmty. Sch., 1977—; permanent dir. Peace Pipe Players, Maquoketa, Iowa, 1978—; cons. dir. Mt. Pleasant Cmty. Theatre, 1975—; speaker/cons. Big Bend Writers Conf., 1994-95, Iowa Thespian Soc., Cedar Rapids, 1984. Author: (tech. handbook) Andrew Writing Guide, 1985, 94; contbr. poetry, lit. essays, criticism to Design mag., Critical Thinking/Critical Writing, Iowa Jour. Social Work, others. Mem. MLA, Nat. Coun. Tchrs. English, Soc. for Tech. Comm., Ednl. Theatre Assn., Archaeol. Inst. Am., The Planetary Soc. (charter mem.). Home: 1018 Wesley Dr Maquoketa IA 52060 Office: Andrew Cmty Sch 13 S Marion Andrew IA 52030

BURROWS, CECIL J., judge, lawyer; b. Schuyler County, Ill., Mar. 21, 1922; s. Amos R. and Florence M. (Krohe) B.; m. Virginia Pearson, June 27, 1949; children: Sandra, Carol, Deborah. BS, Western Mich. U., 1944; JD, Northwestern U., 1952. Bar: Ill. 1952. City atty. Pittsfield, Ill., 1957-64; state's atty. Pike County, Ill., 1964-70; sole practice, Pittsfield, to 1970; cir. judge 8th cir. Ill., 1970-90. Served as officer USMC, 1943-46. Mem. Ill. Judges Assn., Pike County Bar Assn., Federalist Soc., Masons, Shriners, Jesters. Home: 437 W Washington St Pittsfield IL 62363-1345 Office: One Professional Pla Pittsfield IL 62363

BURROWS, ROBERT NELSON, American and English literature educator; b. North Reading, Mass., Dec. 21, 1923; s. Frederick Nelson and Mary McIntosh; m. Marion Elsie Jauch, Feb. 24, 1951; children: David, Mark, John. BA, Colo. Coll., 1947; MA, U. Edinburgh (Scotland), 1949, U. Pa., 1956; PhD, U. Pa., 1959. Asst. prof. English Hardin-Simmons U., Abilene, Tex., 1951-54, Ea. Bapt. Coll., St. Davids, Pa., 1954-59; prof. English Ouachita U., Arkadelphia, Ark., 1959-61, East Cen. State Coll., Ada, Okla., 1961-65, U. Wis., Whitewater, 1965—; prof. English Universität Klagenfurt, Austria, 1992; Fulbright prof. Am. studies Keimyung U., Taegu, Korea, 1993. Contbr. articles to profl. jours. Capt. USMC, 1942-46, PTO. Mem. MLA, Nat. Coun. Tchrs. English. Home: 129 N Esterly Ave Whitewater WI 53190-1312

BURT, ROBERT EUGENE, civic organization administrator; b. Bussey, Iowa, June 5, 1926; s. Francis Earl and Grace (Hauenstein) B.; m. Mary Emma Bates, May 5, 1946; children: Kenneth, Roberta, Carl, Rodney, Lori. BA in Human Relations, Mo. Valley Coll., 1953. Exec. dir. USDA, Madera, Calif., 1946-51; dist. exec. Boy Scouts Am., Jefferson City, Mo., 1953-57; dist. exec. Boy Scouts Am., Mpls., 1957-61, dir. camping, 1961-68; scout exec. Boy Scouts Am., Duluth, Minn., 1968-71; dep. regional exec. New Eng. Boy Scouts Am., 1971-72; dir. of program North Cen. Region Boy Scouts Am., Overland Park, Kans., 1972-86; chmn. Eagle Scout scholarship program SAR, Louisville, 1980-87. Author, editor: Camping in Minnesota, 1970, Bruer a Huguenot, 1987, Some Hauenstein/Howenstine/Howenstein Families in America, 1992, Sloggett Families in America, 1992, Our Bates Genealogy, 1993, The Richard Burt Genealogy, 1993. President Weatherby Lake Park Bd.; alderman Weatherby Lake City Coun., 1988. With USAF, 1944-46. Recipient Disting. Service award Nat. Order of Arrow, Duluth, 1986, Medal of Honor, DAR, 1985. Fellow Am. Coll. Genealogists; mem. AARP, SAR (pres. Kans. soc. 1984, registrar and membership sec. 1992—, genealogist gen. 1988-89, Minuteman award 1987), Kans. Huguenot Soc. (pres. 1984-85, registrar 1993), Soc. Descendants Washington's Army at Valley Forge (Mo. Brigade comdr. 1985-89, paymaster gen. 1988-90), Nat. Genealogy Soc., New Eng. Hist. and Genealogy Soc., Welcome Soc. Pa., McConnaughay Soc. Am. (pres. 1992-95), First Families of Ohio, Ind. Pioneers, Iowa Pioneers, Greater Kansas City Dahlia Soc. (pres. 1994-96). Democrat. Methodist. Home: 9708 NW 75th St Kansas City MO 64152-1763

BURTCH, SUSAN MARIE, physical therapist, administrator; b. Waukesha, Wis., Nov. 11, 1958; d. James Harold and Betty Ann (Hertzberg) Otter; m. Michael Anthony Burtch, July 24, 1982; children: Christopher Michael, Matthew James. B degree, U. Wis., La Crosse, 1981. Lic. phys. therapist, Wis. Staff phys. therapist Waukesha Meml. Hosp., 1981-85; staff phys. therapist Wausau (Wis.) Hosp., 1985-89, coord. phys. therapy, 1989-94, mgr. phys. therapy-occupl. therapy, 1994—. Mem. Am. Phys. Therapy Assn., Wis. Phys. Therapy Assn. Roman Catholic. Office: Wausau Hosp 333 Pine Ridge Blvd Wausau WI 54401

BURTLE, DEBRA ANN, needlework and gift shop owner; b. Decatur, Ill., Oct. 24, 1953; d. Albert Eugene and Barbara Ann (Watson) Naab; m. Paul Walter Burtle, July 22, 1978; 1 child, Laura Rose. AA, Lincoln Land C.C., 1973; BS, Ea. Ill. U., 1975; cert., Martha Pullen Sch. Fashion, 1986, Margaret Boyle Sch. Needlework, 1989. Cert. tchr., Ill. Tchr. home econs. Athens (Ill.) Cmty. Unit Sch. Dist., 1977-78, Waverly (Ill.) Cmty. Unit Sch. Dist., 1978-80; instr. adult edn. Sew with Flo, Springfield, Ill., 1980-83, The Quilting Bee, Rochester, Ill., 1980-83, Springfield Crafts and Ceramics Club, 1987—; owner, mgr. Ruffles, Flourishes, and Satin Bows, Auburn, Ill., 1985—; textile judge Christian County Fair, Taylorville, Ill., 194—, Ill. State Fair Springfield, 1992, 93, 94, 95; demonstrator wool spinning Clayville Rural Life Ctr., Pleasant Plains, Ill., 1967-74, Ill. State Fair, Springfield, 1974-75; instr. wool spinning Lincoln's New Salem State Park, Petersburg, Ill., 1969; needlework demonstrator Winter Folk Fest, Blackburn Coll., Carlinville, Ill., 1992. Artisan exhibitor Springfield Art Assn. Fine Art Fair, 1989, others. Winner textile and garment awards Sangamon County Fair, New Berlin, Ill., 1971, Ill. State Fair, 1988, 89, 91, 92, 93, 94, 95; recipient Outstanding Farm Family award Ill. Farmers Union, 1993. Mem. Auburn Jr. Women's Club (sec. 1985), Elegant Stitchers Needlework Guild (v.p. 1986, pres. 1987-89). Home: 5435 Snell Rd Auburn IL 62615-9749 Office: Ruffles Flourishes and Satin Bows 115 N 4th St Auburn IL 62615-1451

BURTLE, PAUL WALTER, farmer; b. Springfield, Ill., May 31, 1950; Walter Jerome and Esther (Bodnar) B.; m. Debra Ann Naab, July 22, 1978; 1 child, Laura Rose. BS in Agriculture, U. Ill., 1972. Farm mgr., operator Burtle Farm, Auburn, Ill., 1972—; chmn. Sangamon County Exec. Extension Coun., Springfield, 1975-76, Sangamon County Agrl. Coun., Springfield, 1983-84, dir. Farm Credit Svcs. of West Cen. Ill., Springfield, 1990, vice chmn. Fed. Land Bank Assn. of West Cen. Ill., Champaign, 1988-90, chm. bd. Farm Credit Svcs. of Cen. Ill. 1995—, Fed. Land Credit Assn., Champaign, 1991; pres. Sangamon County Farmers Union, 1993; dir. exec. bd. Ill. Farmers Union, 1994. Squadman Champaign County Rescue Squad, Urbana, Ill., 1970-72. Recipient Svc. award Champaign County Civil Def., 1972, 4-H Alumni award Sangamon County 4-H Leaders, 1975, Ill. Farmers Union Outstanding Farm Family award, 1993; named Nat. Corn Yield Contest winner Seedtec, Internat., 1985. Mem. Ill. Farm Bur. Fedn., Ill. Farmers Union (exec. bd. 1994), Sangamon County Farmers Union (pres. 1993), Acad. Family Mediators, Mediation Coun. Ill. Democrat. Roman Catholic. Home: 5435 Snell Rd Auburn IL 62615-9749

BURTNESS, DAVID JEFFREY, electrical engineer; b. Janesville, Wis., Apr. 2, 1949. BS in Elec. Engring., U. Wis., 1982; MS in Elec. Engring., U. Mo., Rolla, 1987. Sr. project engr. McDonnell Douglas Corp., St. Louis, 1983—. Lutheran. Home: 1186 English Saddle Rd Florissant MO 63034-3439

BURTON, BETTY JUNE, minister, pastor; b. Muskegon, Mich., June 11, 1923; d. Bernard J. and Louise Ella (Weaver) Mulder; mem. Harold Ver Berkmoes, June 4, 1943 (div. 1966); children: Suzanne, James, Michael, William, Judith, David (dec.); m. Eldon Franklin Burton, June 27,

1971. Student of music, psychology and religion, Hope Coll., 1941-45; student, Garrett Evang. Theol. Sem., 1984-85. Ordained to ministry United Meth. Ch., 1986. Librarian Vassar Hosp. Sch. Nursing, Poughkeepsie, N.Y., 1958-60, Hackley Pub. Library, Muskegon, 1960-64, Boyne City (Mich.) Pub. Library, 1972-74; reporter Ludington (Mich.) Daily News, 1975-81; caseworker Aid to Dependent Children Mich. Dept. Social Services, Hart, 1974-78; pastor various Meth. Chs., Norwood, Barnard and Charlevoix, Mich., 1981-83, Mears (Mich.) United Meth. Ch., 1985, 86; assoc. pastor United Meth. Centenary, Pentwater, Mich., 1986-90; pastor First Congl. Ch. of Central Lake, Mich., 1990-92, Thompsonville (Mich.) Congl. Church, 1992-93; assoc. realtor Shaw Real Estate, Pentwater, 1975-81, Real Estate One, Traverse City, Mich., 1981-82, Century 21 Williams Real Estate, Pentwater, 1986-89. Sec. Pentwater Planning Commn., 1985. Mem. NAFE, Internat. Platform Assn., Am. Platform Assn., Am. Assn. Christian Counselors, Nat. Christian Counselors Assn., Nat. Trust Hist. Preservation, Am. Mus. Natural History, Nat. Audubon Soc., Am. Acad. Ministry, Hist. Soc. Mich., Oceana County Hist. Soc., Kappa Beta Phi (pres. 1943), Xi Gamma Beta (sec. 1970). Republican. Clubs: Women's of Pentwater (v.p. 1986—), Garden of Pentwater (pres. 1986—), Sierra. Home and Office: 4407 Daisy Ln Traverse City MI 49684-8761

BURTON, DANNY LEE, congressman; b. Indpls., June 21, 1938; m. Barbara Jean Logan, 1959; children: Kelly, Danielle Lee, Danny Lee II. Mem. Ind. Ho. Reps., Indpls., 1967-68, 77-80, Ind. State Senate, 1969-70, 81-82; owner ins. and real estate firm, 1968—; mem. 98th-104th Congresses from 6th Ind. dist., 1983—; mem. internat. rels. com. and govt. reform and oversight com.; chmn. western hemisphere subcommittee. Pres. Vols. of Am.; pres. Ind. Christian Benevolent Assn., Com. for Constl. Govt., Family Support Ctr. Served with U.S. Army, 1957-58. Republican. Office: US Ho of Reps 2411 Rayburn Ofc Bldg Washington DC 20515

BURTON, DARRELL IRVIN, engineering executive; b. Ashtabula, Ohio, Sept. 21, 1926; s. George Irvin and Barbara Elizabeth (Streyle) B.; BS in Radio Engring., Chgo. Tech. Coll., 1954; m. Lois Carol Warkentien, Apr. 14, 1951; children: Linda Jean Burton Clinton, Lisa Ann Burton Watts, Lori Elizabeth. R & D engr. Motorola, Inc., Chgo., 1951-60; devel. engr. Hallicrafters, Chgo., 1960-62; chief engr. TRW, Inc., Des Plaines, Ill., 1962-65; devel. engr. Warwick, Niles, Ill., 1965-68; systems mgr. Admiral Corp., Chgo., 1968-76; elec.-electronics lab. mgr. Montgomery Ward & Co., Chgo., 1976-82; staff engr. Wells-Gardner Electronics Corp., Chgo., 1982-85; sr. engr., Zenith Electronics Corp., 1985-91; ret., 1991; pres. Burton Electronics Co., 1992—; tchr. electronics and math. Pres. Addison Homeowners Assn., 1958-60, v.p., 1960-62; mem. Addison Plan Commn., 1960-63; mem. Bd. Edn. Immanuel Luth. Sch., 1985-87, dir. sound/tape min., 1973—. With USNR, 1944. Mem. IEEE, ASTM, Am. Radio Relay League, York Amateur Radio Club (pres. 1984-86, bd. dirs. 1986-90). Republican. Patentee in field. Home: 112 Lawndale Ave Elmhurst IL 60126-3522

BURTON, DRENNA LEE O'REILLY, kindergarten educator; b. Advance, Mo., Apr. 22, 1948; d. Willard and Frances (Moore) Lee; m. Donald Gene Burton, May 25, 1987; children: Jennifer Anne, Heather Lee. BA in Edn., Lambuth U., 1970; MA in Edn., Southeast Mo. State U., 1984. Cert. tchr., Mo. Tchr. med.-dental assts. St. Louis Bus. Coll., 1970; tchr. Bell City (Mo.) R-2 Schs., 1971-74; tchr. 1st grade Delta (Mo.) R-5 Schs., 1974-81, tchr. kindergarten, 1981—; adv. bd. Parents as Tchrs.; adj. faculty Coll. Edn., Southeast Mo. State U., Cape Girardeau. Mem. Mo. State Tchrs. Assn., Community Tchrs. Assn. (sec., treas., v.p.), Mo. Assn. Rural Educators. Office: Delta R-5 Elem Sch PO Box 219 Delta MO 63744-0219

BURTON, GARY L., state legislator; b. Knoxville, Iowa, Aug. 26, 1945; m. Jennifer Grant; children: Dianne, Todd, Lance, Melinda, Tye, Nathan. BS, Ea. N.Mex. U., 1968. Former mem. Joplin (Mo.) City Coun.; Mo. State rep. Dist. 128, 1988—; ins. agt.; mem. energy and environ. com., budget com., appropriations/edn. and transp. coms., ins. com., mines and mining com., state parks com., recreation and natural resources com. Mo. Ho. Reps.; former mem. Joplin Exec. Call Program, econ. devel. market, area solid waste, chamber govt. affairs and Joplin mote tax coms. Mem. Elks, Joplin C. of C., Mo. Life Underwriters, Mo. Spl. Olympics (state treas.). Home: 1829 E 20th St Joplin MO 64804-0932*

BURTON, GLENDEAN MAE, maternal child health consultant, educator; b. Ottawa, Ill., Dec. 13, 1951; d. Glen McDonald and Doris Nadine (Osborne) Morello; m. Edward F. Bouley (div. Dec. 1982); children: Matthew, Lisa. AAS in Nursing, Ill. Valley C.C., Oglesby, 1975; BSN, No. Ill. U., 1981; postgrad., Loma Linda U., 1993. Cert. alcohol and drug counselor. Staff nurse Morris (Ill.) Hosp., 1976-82, Ottawa (Ill.) Community Hosp., 1982-85; intake coord. Alaska Youth Found., Anchorage, 1985-86; adolescent chem. dependency coord. Charter North Hosp., Anchorage, 1986-89; program mgr. chem. dependency svcs. Elmhurst (Ill.) Meml. Hosp., 1989-94; regional maternal child health cons. Ill. Dept. Pub. Health, West Chicago, 1994—; adolescent counselor, med. cons. LaSalle County Coun. on Alcohol and Drug Abuse, Ottawa, 1982-84; instr. nursing Ill. Valley C.C., Oglesby, 1982-84. Author: (tng. manual) A Guide for LaSalle County Youth Workers: Helping Youth Make Positive Choices, 1984. Bd. dirs. Nat. Assn. Alcohol and Drug Abuse Counselors (Anchorage chpt.), 1988; adv. bd. Ptnrs. for Drug Free Youth, Anchorage, 1988. Mem. Ill. Assn. Alcohol and Other Drug Dependency Counselors, Nat. Consortium Reciprocity of Counselors, Nat. Assn. Perinatal Adduction Rsch. and Edn., Ill. Pub. Health Assn. Democrat. Home: 10s680 Lilac Ln Apt 101 Hinsdale IL 60521-6745

BURTON, LAUREL ARTHUR, educator, minister; b. Indpls., Oct. 29, 1943; s. William Newton and Mary Elizabeth (Horn) B.; m. Mary Kay Gisolo, July 28, 1968; children: Annamary Catherine, Anthony William. BS, Ind. U., 1965; ThM, Boston U., 1970, ThD, 1983. Ordained minister United Meth. Ch. 1970. Assoc. dean of chapel Boston U., 1970-71, asst. dean, 1980-82; assoc. pastor Brentwood United Meth. Ch., Denver, 1971-73; pastor 1st United Meth. Ch., Yuma, Colo., 1973-76; chaplain, asst. prof. Millikin U., Decatur, Ill., 1976-78; dean of chapel W.Va. Wesleyan Coll., Buckhannon, W.Va., 1979-80; dir. pastoral care Univ. Hosp./Boston U. Med. Ctr., 1982-89; dir. ministerial studies Harvard U., Cambridge, Mass., 1989-90; Anderson prof. Rush U., Chgo., 1990—; vis. lectr. Harvard U., 1986-89. Author: From Hiding to Healing, 1986, Pastoral Paradigms, 1986; editor Jour. of Health Care Chaplaincy, 1986-90, CareGiver Jour., 1990-95. Bd. dirs. S.W. Denver Cmty. Health, 1971-73, S.W. Boston Cmty. Health, 1982-86, Maracy-Newberry Assn., Chgo., 1994—; pres. bd. dirs. Metro Boston Alliance, 1983-86. Fellow Coll. of Chaplains (Svc. award 1993); mem. Am. Assn. Marriage Family Therapists (clin. mem., approved supr.), Soc. for Bus. Ethics, Assn. for Practical/Profl. Ethics. Office: Rush U 1653 N Congress Pkwy Chicago IL 60612

BURTON, MICHAEL THOMAS, earth science educator; b. New Rockford, N.D., Oct. 28, 1946; s. Myron Andrew and Ovedia Marie (Haakenson) B. BS, N.D. State U., 1971. Cert. tchr., N.D. Tchr. Fargo (N.D.) Pub. Schs., 1971—; owner EdCon, Fargo; ptnr. Operation Physics of N.D., Fargo. Recipient Sci. Tchr. award Pres. U.S., 1987, Achievement in Edn. award Fargo Optimists, 1988. Mem. Am. Meteorol. Assn. (local chpt. v.p. 1988), Nat. Earth Sci. Tchrs. Assn. (pres. 1988-90), Nat. Sci. Tchrs. Assn. (bd. dirs. 1988-90), N.D. Sci. Tchrs. Assn. (pres. 1986-87, N.D. Earth Sci. Tchr. of Yr. 1976), N.D. Edn. Assn. (bd. dirs. 1984-90). Home: 340 Prairiewood Cir Fargo ND 58103 Office: Discovery Jr HS 1717 40th Ave S Fargo ND 58103

BURTON, ROBERT A., transmission manufacturing company executive; b. Chicago Heights, Ill., July 28, 1944. Pres. All Power Transmission Mfg. Co., Green Bay, Wis., 1986—; marine cons. Patentee in field universal joint driveshafts. Office: All Power Transmission Mfg Co 3146 Market St Green Bay WI 54304-5612

BURTON, WOODY, state legislator; b. Indpls., June 11, 1945; m. Volly Burton; children: Woody Lee, Jeff, April Stirling. Student, Ind. U. Real estate broker, mgr., carpenter Better Homes & Gardens; mem. Ind. State Ho. of Reps. Dist. 58, 1988—, mem. elections and apportionment com., mem. ins., corp. and small bus., roads and transp. coms., mem. ways and means com., chmn. fin. com. Mem. Johnson County Coun., 1980-84, County Planning Commn., 1983, County Coun. on Aging, 1983-85. Mem. Nat. Assn. Realtors, Ind. Assn. Realtors, Met. Indpls. Bd. Realtors, Ind. Auctioneers Assn., Greenwood Masonic Lodge, Scottish Rite, Murat Shrine.

BURWELL, ROBERT LEMMON, JR., chemist, educator; b. Balt., May 6, 1912; s. Robert Lemmon and Anne Hume (Lewis) B.; m. Elise Frank, Dec. 23, 1939; children: Mary Elise, Augusta Somervell. A.B., St. John's Coll., Annapolis, Md., 1932; Ph.D. (Procter fellow), Princeton U., 1936. Instr. chemistry Trinity Coll., 1936-39; instr. Northwestern U., 1939-45, asst. prof., 1946, asso. prof., 1946-52, prof., 1952—, Ipatieff prof. chemistry, 1970-80, Ipatieff prof. emeritus, 1980—, chmn. dept. chemistry, 1952-57; Humboldt sr. scientist Tech. U. Munich, 1981; vis. prof. U. Pierre et Marie Curie, Paris, 1982; dir. Internat. Congress Catalysis, 1956-65; chmn. Gordon Research Conf. Catalysis, 1957; sec. Council Internat. Congress Catalysis, 1968-72, v.p., 1972-76, pres., 1980-84; cons. Amoco Corp., 1949-92. Served as lt. USNR, 1942-45. Mem. Am. Chem. Soc. (chmn. div. phys. chemistry 1958-59, mem. council policy com. 1969-72, Kendall award in colloid and surface chemistry 1973, Lubrizol award in petroleum chemistry 1983, Langmuir award 1985), Catalysis Soc. (dir. 1977-81, pres. 1973-77, First Burwell lectr. 1983), Internat. Union Pure and Applied Chemistry (titular mem. colloid and surface chemistry commn. 1969-77). Home: 5700 Williamsburg Landing Dr Williamsburg VA 23185-3775 Office: Dept of Chemistry Northwestern Univ Evanston IL 60208

BURZYNSKI, JAMES BRADLEY, state legislator; b. Christopher, Ill., July 13, 1955; m. Judy Burzynski; 2 children. Ill. state sen. Dist. 35, 1990; mem. exec. appts. com.; chair higher edn. com., ins., pensions and lic. activities coms. Address: 1205 DeKalb Ave Sycamore IL 60178*

BURZYNSKI, THOMAS F., hospice administrator; b. South Bend, Ind., Jan. 1, 1936; s. Frank Theodore and Stephany Josephine (Zaljeski) B.; m. Barbara Chrapek, Aug. 12, 1967 (dec. Apr. 1983); children: John David, Margaret Rose, Susan Marie, Mary Frances. BA, U. Notre Dame, 1954-58. Tchr., football coach St. Adalbert Sch., South Bend, 1959-66; tchr., asst. prin. Marian High Sch., Mishawaka, Ind., 1966-73; exec. dir., field rep. March of Dimes Birth Defects Found., South Bend, 1973-83; exec. dir., pres. Hospice of St. Joseph County, Inc., South Bend, 1983—. Contbr. articles to Jour. Hospice Care. Sec. Inter-city Cath. League, South Bend, 1959-66; chmn. Deaneny Home and Schs. Assn., 1984; bd. dirs. Dismas Ho. of Michiana, 1987-91. Recipient Fr. Jack Hickey award Dismas Ho. of Michiana, 1990, Nora J. McFarland award Indiana Assn. of Health Care, 1993. Mem. Nat. Hospice Orgn., Ind. Assn. Hospices (publicity chair 1984-91, bd. dirs. 1984-91, pres. 1991-92), Michiana Continuity of Care (treas. 1989), Notre Dame Club of St. Joseph Valley. Roman Catholic. Office: Hospice of St Joseph County Inc 108 N Main St Ste 111 South Bend IN 46635

BUSACK, GARY LEE, managed care adminstrator; b. Redwood Falls, Minn., May 15, 1952; s. Arden Helmuth and Pernell Jeanette (Dresow) B.; m. Diana Thelma Humes, Sept. 29, 1973; children: Travis Cameron, Shannon Nicole, Trenton Kyle. BA, U. Minn., 1975; MPH, Yale U., 1980. Diplomate Am. Coll. Health Care Execs.; lic. long-term care adminstr., Minn. Asst. adminstr. Kern Med. Ctr., Bakersfield, Calif., 1981-86; dir. Bakersfield Family Med. Group, 1986; adminstr. Franklin Gen. Hosp., Hampton, Iowa, 1986-92; dir. Sisters of Mercy Health Corp., Des Moines, 1992-94, Unity Health Plans, Sauk City, Wis., 1994—. Bd. dirs. Franklin County Devel. Assn., Hampton, Iowa, 1988-92. Mem. APHA, Iowa Hosp. Assn. (bd. dirs. 1990-92), Hampton Area C. of C. (bd. dirs. 1988-89). Office: Unity Health Plans 840 Carolina St Sauk City WI 53583

BUSCH, AUGUST ADOLPHUS, III, brewery executive; b. St. Louis, June 16, 1937; s. August Anheuser and Elizabeth (Overton) B.; m. Susan Marie Hornibrook, Aug. 17, 1963 (div. 1969); children: August Adolphus IV, Susan Marie II; m. Virginia L. Wiley, Dec. 28, 1974; children: Steven August, Virginia Marie. Student, U. Ariz., 1957-58, Siebel Inst. Tech., 1960-61. With Anheuser-Busch, Inc., St. Louis, 1957—, sales mgr., 1962-64, v.p. mktg. ops., 1964-65, v.p., gen. mgr., 1965-71, exec. v.p., gen. mgr., 1971-74, pres., 1974-75, pres., CEO, 1975-77; chmn. bd., pres. Anheuser Busch Cos., Inc., St. Louis, 1979-87, chmn. bd., pres., CEO, 1987—, also bd. dirs., chmn. bd., pres.; bd. dirs. St. Louis Nat. Baseball Club, Mfrs. Rly. Co., Southwestern Bell Corp., Gen. Am. Life Ins. Co., Emerson Electric Co.; trustee St. Louis Refrigerator Car Co. Exec. bd. St. Louis Boy Scouts Am.; chmn. adv. bd. St. John's Mercy Med. Ctr.; bd. dirs. United Way Greater St. Louis; bd. overseers Wharton Sch., U. Pa. Clubs: St. Louis, Frontenac Racquet, St. Louis Country, Racquet (St. Louis); Noonday, Log Cabin, Stadium. Office: Anheuser-Busch Cos Inc 1 Busch Pl Saint Louis MO 63118-1849*

BUSCH, LAWRENCE MICHAEL, sociologist, researcher; b. N.Y.C., Mar. 27, 1945; s. Raymond and Carol Cecilia (Lewis) B.; Karen V. Hagberg, Dec. 30, 1966; children: Lisa Marion, Rachel Valaria. BA, Hofstra U., 1965; MS, Cornell U., 1972, PhD, 1974. Asst. prof. sociology U. Ky., Lexington, 1974-79, assoc. prof., 1979-85, prof., 1985-90; prof. Mich. State U., 1990—; cons. U.S. AID, Washington, 1978—; mem. sci. adv. bd. CIRAD (French Fgn. Aid Agy.). Co-author: Science, Agriculture Politics of Research, 1983, Food Security in the U.S., 1984, The Agricultural Scientific Enterprise, 1986, Plants, Power, and Profit, 1991, Making Nature, Shaping Culture: Plant, Biodiversity in Global Context, 1995; editor: Science and Agricultural Development, 1981. Grantee NEH, 1981, NSF, 1982, 86, 92, 96, USDA, 1985, 87, 94. Fellow AAAS; mem. Rural Sociol. Soc., Am. Sociol. Assn., Soc. for Agr., Food and Human Values (pres. 1989-90). Office: Mich State U Dept Sociology East Lansing MI 48824

BUSCH, WILLIAM H., engineer; b. Iowa, Nov. 1, 1935; s. Max. F. and Ruby L. (Ruhser) B.; m. Patsy A. Bull; children: Cynthia, Diane, Jill. BS in Civil Engring., U. Iowa, 1959; MS, So. Ill. U., 1979. Prof. Engr., Iowa, Ill.; diplomate Am. Acad. Environ. Engrs. Field engr. Ill. Dept. Pub. Health, Rock Island, 1959-63, engr., 1963-70; field ops. engr. Ill. Environ. Protection Agy., Springfield, 1970-71, sect. mgr., 1971-72, permits sect. mgr., 1972-77, field ops. sect. mgr., 1977--. Mem. Water Pollution Control Fedn. (dir. 1989-92, Bedell award 1989), Am. Acad. Environ. Engrs. (trustee 1987-90, pres. 1993-94), Ill. Assn. Water Pollution Control (pres. 1985-86, dir. 1989-92), Am. Assn. of Engring. Socs. (bd. dirs. 1992—, bd. water environ. rsch. found. 1995—). Lutheran. Office: Busch Environ Engring 2200 Churchill Rd Springfield IL 62702-3406

BUSELT, CLARA IRENE, religious organization administrator; b. Detroit, Jan. 30, 1921; d. Andrew and Bernice (Marcian) Kochanowski; m. Michael Leo Buselt, Apr. 18, 1940; children: Edwin, Nancy, Robert, John, Jane. Student, MacGregor Beauty Coll., Kansas City, 1939. Cosmetician various beauty shops, Leavenworth, 1940-45; surp. dir. Sch. Lunch Program Sacred Heart Cafeteria, Immaculata High, Leavenworth, 1957-68; dietetic worker VA Med. Ctr., Leavenworth, 1968-81; office clk. Storage Box Inc., Leavenworth, 1987—; sr. Times corr., photographer Leavenworth Times, 1990—. Photographer (contest) Congress Americas, 1986. Mem. Sr. Coun. Park and Recreation, Leavenworth, 1988, Sr. Citizen Inc. Kitchen Band, 1993—. Recipient Gov. and First Lady Vol. award Gov. of Kans., 1990, Sr. Citizen of Yr. award Leavenworth County Coun. on Aging, 1994, Sr. Citizen award Am. Assn. Ret. Persons, 1995; named Silver Haired Legislator Leavenworth County, 1993. Mem. Am. Assn. Ret. Persons (recording sec. 1995-96), Women's Div. C. of C., Parish Council Sacred Heart Ch., Sacred Heart Alter Soc. (pres. 1977-87), Am. War Mothers (state pres. 1983-85, nat. color bearer 1985-87, nat. chaplain 1987-89), Cath. Literary Club (pres. 1983-85), Sch. Food Svc. Assn. (charter pres. 1958), St. John Hosp. Guild (pres. 1975-76), Loyal Christian Benefit Assn. (br. pres. 1977-88, nat. trustee 1981—), Daughters Isabella, Arch Diocese Coun. (pres. 1981-83), Nat. Assn. Ret. Fed. Employees, Loyal Christian Benefit Assn. (br. pres. 1977—), Leavenworth County Coun. Aging (chair adv. coun. aging), Ret. Eagles Activity Club (v.p. 1991-93, pres. 1993—). Home: 1413 S 16th St Leavenworth KS 66048-2914

BUSEMAN, KATHLEEN ANNE, ophthalmology nurse; b. Milbank, S.D., Nov. 4, 1954; m. Donald Ray Buseman, Aug. 21, 1976; children: Nicole, Sarah. RN, Sioux Valley Sch. of Nursing, Sioux Falls, S.D., 1976. RN, S.D.; cert. in ophthalmology. Staff RN Sioux Valley Hosp., Sioux Falls, S.D., 1976-78, asst. head nurse, 1978-81; surg. asst. Dr. Byron Hohm, Ophthalmology, Ltd., Sioux Falls, 1981-85; office nurse and insvc. coord. Ophthalmology, Ltd., Sioux Falls, 1985-92, nursing supr., 1993—; organizer, presenter insvcs. for area nursing homes and profl. mtgs. Mem. Am. Soc. Ophthalmic RNs. Home: 3909 S Fairhall Ave Sioux Falls SD 57106-1738 Office: Ophthalmology Ltd 1200 S Euclid Ave Sioux Falls SD 57105-0429

BUSH, BARBARA PIERCE, volunteer, wife of former President of the United States; b. Rye, N.Y., June 8, 1925; d. Marvin and Pauline (Robinson) Pierce; m. George Herbert Walker Bush, Jan. 6, 1945; children: George Walker, John Ellis, Neil Mallon, Marvin Pierce, Dorothy Walker. Student, Smith Coll., 1943-44; hon. degrees, Stritch Coll., Milw., 1981, Mt. Vernon Coll., Washington, 1981, Hood Coll., Frederick, Md., 1983, Howard U., Washington, 1987, Judson Coll., Marion, Ala., 1988, Bennett Coll., Greensboro, N.C., 1989, Smith Coll., 1989, Morehouse Sch. Medicine, 1989. Author: C. Fred Story; Millie's Book; Barbara Bush: A Memoir, 1994. Hon. chair adv. bd. Reading is Fundamental; hon. mem. Bus. Coun. for Effective Literacy; mem. adv. coun. Soc. of Meml. Sloan-Kettering Cancer Ctr.; hon. mem. bd. dirs. Children's Oncology Svcs. of Met. Washington, The Washington Home, The Kingsbury Ctr.; hon. chmn. nat. adv. coun. Literacy Vols. of Am., Nat. Sch. Vols. Program; sponsor Laubach Literacy Internat.; nat. hon. chmn. Leukemia Soc. of Am.; hon. mem. bd. trustees Morehouse Sch. of Medicine; hon. nat. chmn. Nat. Organ Donor Awareness Week, 1982-86; pres. Ladies of the Senate, 1981-88; mem. women's com. Smithsonian Assocs., Tex. Fedn. of Rep. Women, life mem., hon. mem.; hon. chairperson for the Nat. Com. on Literacy and Edn. United Way, Barbara Bush Found. for Family Literacy, Washington Parent Group Fund, Girls Clubs of Am., 10th anniversay Harvest Nat. Food Bank Network; hon. chmn. Nat. Com. for the Prevention of Child Abuse and Childhelp U.S.A.; hon. pres. Girl Scouts U.S; hon. chair Nat. Com. for Adoption; mem. bd. trustees Mayo Clinic Found.; hon. chair Read Am., Boarder Baby Project; mem. bd. visitors M. D. Anderson Cancer Ctr.; hon. chair Leukemia Soc. Am., Children's Literacy Initiative; hon. mem. Reading is Fundamental; ambassador at large Americares; honorary mem. Barbara Bush Found. for Family Literacy. Recipient Nat. Outstanding Mother of Yr. award, 1984, Woman of Yr. award USO, 1986, Disting. Leadership award United Negro Coll. Fund 1986, Disting. Am. Woman award Coll. Mt. St. Joseph, 1987. Mem. Tex. Fedn. Rep. Women (life), Internat. II Club (Washington), Magic Circle Rep. Women's Club (Houston), YWCA. Episcopalian. Office: 10000 Memorial Dr Houston TX 77024-3422

BUSH, CRYSTAL REED, financial planner; b. Chgo., Dec. 14, 1957; d. Alonzo and Elmethra (Luster) Reed; m. Tony Bush, Aug. 12, 1989. BA in History, Roosevelt U., 1979; JD, DePaul U., 1995. Tchr. Chgo. Bd. Edn., 1979-90; pres. Buree Assocs., Chgo., 1990—. Fin. editor The Leguenet, 1991; contbr. articles to jours. Treas., chair program com. Women's Entrepreneur Network, Chgo., 1990-91; treas. League of Black Women, Chgo., 1991-92. Recipient Exceptional Contbn. award to Afro-Am. Cmty. AT&T, 1991, 92, 93. Mem. Nat. Assn. Women Bus. Owners (mem. Chgo. chpt.), Chgo. Bar Assn., Ill. Bar Assn. Home: 8644 S Kenwood Ave Chicago IL 60619-6416 Office: Buree Assocs 14 N Peoria St Ste 100 Chicago IL 60607

BUSH, ERIC THOMAS, state legislator; b. Long Island, N.Y., May 11, 1946; s. Frederic Bush and Claralee (Wiltshire) Whetsell; children from previous marriage: Michael Todd, Sarah Elizabeth; m. Penny L. Bush, Feb. 11, 1984; 1 child, Brett Thomas. AA, Kellogg C.C., 1968; BA, Western Mich. U., 1973, MPA, 1987. Police officer Battle Creek (Mich.) Police Dept., 1970-94; state rep. Mich. Ho. of Reps., Lansing, 1995—; vice chmn. Sr. Citizens com. and veterans affairs com., mem. judiciary and civil, also mem. nat. conf. of state legislators, law enforcement caucus, new bus. and entrepreneurial task force, state emergency med. svcs. coord. com. Chmn. Cmty. Anti-Drug Coalition, 1993—, Metro Auto Theft Task Force; pres. Substance Abuse Coun. of the Greater Battle Creek, 1993; bd. mem. Coalition of the Homeless, 1989; vol. United Way, 1982-90; mem. Domestic Abuse Task Force, 1993—, Sch. Improvement Task Force, 1994—; bd. mem. Silent Observer Program, 1990—, Transitional Living Program, 1989, Safe Place, 1993—. With U.S. Army, 1966-68, Vietnam. Mem. Mich. Assn. Chiefs of Police, Internat. Narcotics Officers Assn., Internat. Homicide Investigator Assn. Methodist. Home: 131 Francis Dr Battle Creek MI 49015-3973

BUSH, EUGENE NYLE, pharmacologist, research scientist; b. McKeesport, Pa., Apr. 14, 1952; s. Nyle E. and Rosalia M. (Merlino) B.; m. Janet Rosemary Ruscitto, May 7, 1977; children: Stephen Michael, Rebecca Renee, Timothy George. BS in Pharmacy, U. Pitts., 1977, PhD in Pharmacology, 1981. Registered pharmacist. Tchg. asst. U. Pitts., 1978-81; staff pharmacist Western Pa. Hosp., Pitts., 1977-81; pharmacologist II Abbott Labs., 1981-84, pharmacologist I, 1984-87; sr. rsch. sci. Abbott Labs., Abbott Park, Ill., 1986-88, rsch. investigator, 1988-89, group leader, endocrine pharmacol., 1989-91; sr. group leader endocrine pharmacol. Abbott Labs., 1991—, assoc. Volwiler rsch. fellow, 1996—. Co-author numerous publs.; contbr. articles to profl. jours. Asst. scoutmaster St. Joseph Ch. troop 60, Boy Scouts Am., Libertyville, Ill., 1994—. Assoc. Volwiler Rsch. fellow, 1996—. Mem. Endocrine Soc., Nat. Eagle Scout Assn., Sigma Xi, Am. Pharm. Assn. Republican, Roman Catholic. Home: 816 Bedford Ct Libertyville IL 60048-3002 Office: Abbott Labs 100 Abbott Park Rd Ap 10 Dept 46R Abbott Park IL 60064-3500

BUSH, GEORGE HERBERT WALKER, former President of the United States; b. Milton, Mass., June 12, 1924; s. Prescott Sheldon and Dorothy (Walker) B.; m. Barbara Pierce, Jan. 6, 1945; children: George W., John E., Neil M., Marvin P., Dorothy W. Koch. BA in Econs., Yale U., 1948; numerous other hon. degrees. Co-founder Bush-OVerbey Oil Devel. Co., 1951; Co-founder, dir. Zapata Petroleum Corp., Midland, 1953-59; pres. Zapata Off Shore Co., Houston, 1956-64; chmn. bd. Zapata Off Shore Co., 1964-66; mem. 90th-91st Congresses from 7th Dist. Tex., 1967-71, Ways and Means com.; U.S. amb. to UN, 1971-73; chmn. Rep. Nat. Com., 1973-74; chief U.S. Liaison Office Peking, People's Republic China, 1974-75; dir. CIA, 1976-77; adj. prof. adminstrv. sci. Rice U., Houston, 1978; V.P. of U.S., 1981-89, Pres. of U.S., 1989-93. Del. Rep. Nat. Conv., 1964, 69; Rep. candidate U.S. senator from Tex., 1964, 70. Lt. (j.g.), pilot USN, WWII. Decorated D.F.C., Air medals (3). Office: 10000 Memorial Dr Houston TX 77024-3422

BUSH, GORDON KENNER, JR., newspaper publisher; b. Athens, Ohio, July 30, 1934; s. Gordon Kenner and Izotta (Ackerman) B.; m. Margene Gilson, Aug. 2, 1958; children: Frederick Gordon, David Gilson. AB, Colgate U., 1956; MBA, Harvard U., 1960. Nat. advt. salesperson Gannetti Co., Rochester, N.Y., 1960-62; asst. pub. Athens Messenger, 1962-65, pub., editor, 1966—; pres. Messenger Pub. Co., Athens, 1972—, sec., treas., 1962-72, pres., treas., 1972-93; mem. com. on state investment Ohio Bd. Regents, 1994—; mem. adv. bd. EW Scripps Sch. Journalism, 1987—. Trustee Ohio U. Found., Athens, 1976-92, Ohio Coalition for Open Govt., 1992-96, Ohio U., Athens, 1975-84, chmn. bd., 1982-83. With U.S. Army, 1956-58. Recipient Ohio Gov.'s award State of Ohio, 1994; hon. alumnus Ohio U., 1984. Mem. Ohio Newspaper Assn. (trustee 1981—, Pres.'s award 1984), Southeastern Ohio Regional Coun. (dir. 1989—, chmn. hwy. users com. 1975—, Comty. Svc. award 1987), Ohio C. of C. (dir. 1972-89, chmn. 1991-92, life dir. 1993). Republican. Office: The Messenger Pub Co Rte 33 N Athens OH 45701

BUSH, SARGENT, JR., English language educator; b. Flemington, N.J., Sept. 22, 1937; s. Sargent and Marion Louise (Roberts) B.; m. Cynthia Bird Greig, June 18, 1960; children: Charles Sargent, James Jonathan. AB, Princeton U., 1959; MA, U. Iowa, 1964, PhD, 1967. Asst. prof. English Washington and Lee U., Lexington, Va., 1967-71; asst. prof. English U. Wis., Madison, 1971-73, assoc. prof., 1973-79, prof., 1979—, chmn. dept. English, 1980-83, assoc. dean for humanities, Coll. Letters and Sci., 1989-94; vis. prof. U. Warwick, Coventry, Eng., 1983-84. Author: (wth George H. Williams, Norman Pettit and Winfried Herget) Thomas Hooker: Writings in England and Holland, 1626-1633, 1975, The Writings of Thomas Hooker: Spiritual Adventure in Two Worlds, 1980, (with Carl J. Rasmussen) The Library of Emmanuel College, Cambridge, 1584-1637, 1986; editor Jour. of Sarah Kemble Knight in Journeys in New Worlds: Early American Women's Narratives, 1990; contbr. articles to profl. jours. With U.S. Army, 1959-60, 61-62. Fellow Coop. Program in Humanities, 1969-70, Am. Coun. Learned Socs., 1974, Inst. for Rsch. in Humanities, 1978, Mass. Hist. Soc. rsch. fellow, 1990; grantee NEH, 1969, 86, Am. Philos. Soc., 1979. Mem. MLA, Am. Lit. Assn., Nathaniel Hawthorne Soc., Cambridge Bibliog. Soc., Assn.

Documentary Editing, Melville Soc., Thoreau Soc. Presbyterian. Home: 4146 Manitou Way Madison WI 53711-3014 Office: U Wis Helen C White Hall Madison WI 53706

BUSHNELL, WILLIAM RODGERS, agricultural research scientist; b. Wooster, Ohio, Aug. 19, 1931; s. John and Dyllone (Hempstead) B.; m. Ann Holcomb, Sep. 20, 1952; children: Thomas H., John A., Mary D. AB, U. Chgo., 1951; BS, Ohio State U., 1953, MS, 1955; PhD, U. Wis., 1960. Plant physiologist agrl. rsch. svc. U.S. Dept. Agr., St. Paul, 1960—; adj. prof. U. Minn., St. Paul, 1973—. Contbr. numerous rsch. articles in plant sci. jours.; editor books in field. Named U.S. Sr. Scientist Alexander Von Humboldt Found., Germany, 1984. Fellow Am. Phytopathological Soc. Office: U Minn Cereal Rust Lab Saint Paul MN 55108

BUSHO, ELIZABETH MARY, nurse, consultant, educator; b. Ellendale, Minn., Feb. 26, 1927; d. Ruben Oscar and Lillian Katherine (Gahagan) B. RN, Kahler Hosps. Sch. of Nursing, 1948. RN, Minn. Oper. rm. staff nurse, Minn., Calif., Colo., 1948-53; oper. rm. head nurse, Mt. Sinai Hosp., Mpls., 1953-61; asst. supr. oper. rm. St. Barnabas Hosp., Mpls., 1961-71; asst. dir. surg. svcs. St. Mary's Hosp., Rochester, Minn., 1971-80, dir., 1980-90; sr. cons. oper. rms. Mayo Med. Ctr., Rochester, 1990-92; ind. cons. surg. svcs., 1992—; instr. Rochester Community Coll. Developer course in oper. rm. nursing. Mem. adv. bd. Rochester Area Vocat. Tech. Inst., Rochester Community Coll., Sigma Theta Tau. Republican. Methodist. Office: 2100 Valkyrie Dr NW Apt 415 Rochester MN 55901-2449

BUSHY, KAREN MARIE, municipal official; b. Chgo., Nov. 28, 1940; d. Joseph E. and Marie K. (Steinmetz) Sherman; m. Gabor A. Bushy, July 17, 1965; children: James, Nancy. Grad. high sch., Chgo. mem. Du Page County Stormwater Mgmt. Com.; mem. small bus. task force Ill. Environ. Protection Agy. Elected pres. Village of Oak Brook, Ill., 1991—, mem. plan commn., 1978-85, trustee, 1985-91. Mem. Oak Brook Assn. Commerce and Industry (bd. dirs.), Du Page Mayors and Mgrs. (v.p., legis. com., inter-govt. rels. com., exec. com.), Du Page County Conv. and Visitors Bur. (bd. dirs.). Republican. Office: Village of Oak Brook 1200 Oak Brook Rd Oak Brook IL 60521-2203

BUSICK, DENZEL REX, lawyer; b. Council Bluffs, Iowa, Oct. 16, 1945; s. Guy Henry and Selma Ardith (Woods) B.; m. Cheryl Ann Callahan, June 17, 1967; children: Elizabeth Colleen, Guy William. BS in Bus. Adminstrn., U. Nebr.-Omaha, 1969; JD, Creighton U., 1971. Bar: Nebr. 1971, U.S. Dist. Ct. Nebr. 1971, U.S. Ct. Apls. (8th cir.) 1975, U.S. Sup. Ct. 1974; Law clk., U.S. Dist. Ct. Nebr., 1970-72; mem. Fraser, Stryker, Veach, Vaughn, Meusey, Olsen & Boyer, Omaha, 1972-78; assoc. Kay & Satterfield, North Platte, Nebr., 1979-80; ptnr. Luebs, Leininger, Smith, Busick & Johnson, Grand Island, Nebr., 1980—. Fellow Nebr. State Bar Found. (bd. dirs.), Am. Coll. Legal Medicine (law); mem. ABA, ATLA, Am. Bd. Trial Advocates (civil diplomate), Nat. Bd. Trial Advocacy (civil diplomate), Am. Bd. Profl Liability Attys. (diplomate), Am. Judicature Soc., Nebr. State Bar Assn. (past mem. ho. of dels., exec. coun., past chmn. ins. com.), Nebr. Assn. Trial Attys. (bd. dirs., 1991-95), Nebr. Lawyers Trust Account Found. (past pres., bd. dirs.), Nebr. State Bar Commn., Kiwanis (past pres. Grand Island chpt.), Phi Alpha Delta. Republican. Contbr. to publs. in field. Home: 3027 Brentwood Pl Grand Island NE 68801-7222 Office: PO Box 790 Wheeler at 1st St Grand Island NE 68802-0790

BUSKIRK, PHYLLIS RICHARDSON, retired economist; b. Queens, N.Y., July 19, 1930; d. William Edward and Amy A. Richardson; m. Allen V. Buskirk, Sept. 13, 1950; children: Leslie, William, Carol, Janet. AB cum laude, William Smith Coll., 1951. Rsch. asst. W.E. Upjohn Inst. for Employment Rsch., Kalamazoo, 1970-75, rsch. assoc., 1976-83, sr. staff economist, 1983-37. Co-editor Bus. Conditions in the Kalamazoo Area, Quar. Rev., 1979-84, asst. editor Bus. Outlook for West Mich., 1984-87. Mem. Civil Svc. Bd. City of Kalamazoo, 1977-91, chmn., 1981-91; trustee First Presbyn. Ch., Kalamazoo, 1984-87, chmn., 1985, 86, mgr. adminstrn. and fin., 1987-92; trustee Sr. Citizens Fund, Kalamazoo, 1984-88, corp. restructuring com. 1985-86. exec. bd. 1986-88; bd. dirs. Heritage Cmty. Kalamazoo, 1988—, chmn. 1995-96; chmn. Kalamazoo County Futures Coms., 1985-86, bd. dirs., 1987-89. Fellow Presbyn. Ch. Bus. Adminstrn. Assn.; mem. Nat. Assn. Ch. Bus. Adminstrn., P.E.O., Kalamazoo Network, YWCA. Home: 3324 Saint Antoine Ave Kalamazoo MI 49006-5522

BUSLER, MICHAEL BRITT, financial manager; b. Phila., June 7, 1950. Owner Honda Yamaha, York, Pa., 1976-83; br. mgr. Merrill Lynch, York, 1983-93, Paine Webber, Muskegon, Mich., 1993—. Chmn. YMCA, York, 1984-93, United Way, York, 1984-93; scoutmaster Boy Scouts. Mem. Rotary. Republican. Lutheran. Office: Paine Webber PO Box 959 945 W Norton Ave Muskegon MI 49443

BUSSE, EILEEN E., special education educator; b. Green Bay, Wis., Oct. 16, 1957; d. Ervin F. and Elaine I. (Behnke) Dohl; m. John F. Busse, July 5, 1980; children: Jessica Lynn, Jeremy John. BS in Elem. and Spl. Edn., U. Wis., Eau Claire, 1979; MS in Spl. Edn., U. Wis., Whitewater, 1985. Cert. tchr. elem. and spl. edn. Tchr. spl. edn./mentally retarded Ithaca (Wis.) Pub. Schs., 1979-80; spl. edn. tchr. Walworth County HCEB Walworth County HCEB, Whitewater, Wis., 1980—; spl. edn. tchr. Lakeview Elem. Sch., 1991—; mem. Walworth County Handicapped Children's edn. Bd.; coop. tchr. U. Wis., Whitewater, 1988—. Author: Student Owned Spelling, 1991, II, 1992, III, 1994. Mem. Gifted and Talented Parent Support Group, Whitewater, 1993—; sch. liaision, founder Caring Parents Support Group, Whitewater, Lakeview, 1988-94, student coun. advisor, Whitewater, 1995—; mem. First English Luth. Ch. edn. com., Whitewater, 1990—, chmn. edn. com., 1993-95, mem. ch. coun., 1993-95; active Girl Scouts U.S.A., 1992—, Boy Scouts Am., 1995—. Recipient Excellence in Edn. award U.S. Dept. Edn., 1984-85. Mem. Coun. for Exceptional Children. Home: 455 Ventura Ln Whitewater WI 53190-1548 Office: Lakeview Elem Sch PO Box 646 Whitewater WI 53190-0646

BUSSE, WILBUR EDWARD, retired engineer; b. Mount Prospect, Ill., June 14, 1919; s. Arthur W. and Ella (Engelking) B.; m. Joyce Ruth Will, May 30, 1953; children: Barbara Ann, Richard Allan, Beverly Ellen, Carolyn Jane. BSCE, U. Ill., 1941; postgrad., U.S. Naval Acad., 1942. Registered profl. engr., Ill., Tex. Commodity industry analyst NPA, Washington, 1951-52; devel. engr. Chgo. Bridge and Iron Co., 1945-52; contracting engr. Chgo. Bridge and Iron Co., Detroit, 1960-65, Houston, 1965-66; dist. sales mgr. Chgo. Bridge and Iron Co., Detroit, 1960-66; divsn. sales mgr. Horton Process divsn. Chgo. Bridge and Iron Co., Oak Brook, Ill., 1966-68; dist. sales mgr. Chgo. Bridge and Iron Co., Detroit, 1969-70; contracting engr. Chgo. Bridge and Iron Co., Cleve., 1971-79, ret., 1979. Inventor floating roof seal hanger, self inflating costume. Served to lt. comdr. USN, 1941-45. Chmn. Alcona County Rep. Com., 1987-94. Mem. Lost Lake Woods Assn. (pres., CEO 1994—, b. dirs. 1992-94). Home: 4116 Black Bear Trail Lincoln MI 48742

BUSSMAN, DONALD HERBERT, lawyer; b. Lakewood, Ohio, July 15, 1925; s. Herbert L. and Hilda L. (Henrichs) B. PhB, U. of Chgo., 1947, JD, 1951. Bar: Ill. 1951. Atty. Swift & Co., Chgo., 1950-84; pvt. practice Chgo., 1985—. With U.S. Army, 1944-46. Mem. ABA, Chgo. Bar Assn., Am. Assn. of Individual Investors, Club Internat. (Chgo.). Office: Ste 702 860 N Dewitt Pl Chicago IL 60611-1721

BUSSONE, FRANK JOSEPH, health association administrator, television broadcaster; b. Pontiac, Ill.; s. Joseph Dominick and Olma Francis (DesCarpentrie) B.; m. Karen Marie Watson, May 27, 1972; 1 child, R.J. BS, Bradley U., 1964, MA, 1966; PhD, U. So. Calif., 1968. Adminstr. Bradley U., Peoria, Ill., 1969-77; v.p., COO Dirksen Congl. Ctr., Pekin and Washington, 1977-80; pres., CEO Sta. WEEK-TV, Peoria, 1980-86; exec. v.p. Eagle Broadcasting Co., N.Y.C., 1985-86; pres., CEO The Proctor Found., Peoria, 1986—; TV broadcaster ESPN SportsChannel, Chgo., 1972—; anchor TV broadcaster Ill. State Basketball Tournament, 1980-91; bd. dirs. BankPlus (Ill.), St. Jude, Memphis; motivational speaker, 1970—. Author: The Tag Line, 1975; editor: Surprising Peoria, 1990; columnist for various newspapers, 1982—. Bd. dirs. Am. Heart Assn., Springfield, Ill., 1991—; TV host St. Jude Telethons, Ill., 1980-86; mem. Presdl. Task Force, Washington, 1988; speaker Bush for Pred. Campaign, Ill., 1988, Edgar for Gov. Campaign, Ill., 1990; mem. Bradley U. Community Bd., 1982—. Recipient Love a Child award Neighborhood House, Peoria, 1987, Citation of Hon. City of L.A., 1968; named to Bradley U. Hall of Fame, 1989, Ill. Basketball Hall of Fame Ill. Coaches Assn., 1983. Mem. Ill. Hosp. Assn., The Dirksen Soc., Creve Coeur Club, Mt. Hawley Country Club, Downtown Rotary Club. Roman Catholic. Home: 53 Hyde Park Dr Morton IL 61550-9534 Office: The Proctor Found 5409 N Knoxville Ave Peoria IL 61614-5016

BUTLER, ALICE CLAIRE, rehabilitation nurse; b. Lander, Wyo., Sept. 9, 1925; d. Donald A. and Violet C. (Carney) Sherlock; m. Harry Wallace Butler, July 25, 1958 (wid. Feb. 1994); children: Gladys Norene, Linda Marie, Janet Christine, Mary Alice, David Paul, Anna Louise, Rebecca Ruth, Philip Clyde, John Glenn, James Sheldon. ADN, Penn Valley Community Coll., 1976; AA, Kansas City (Mo.) Jr. Coll., 1949; BA in Elem. Edn., U. Mo., Kansas City, 1986. RN, Mo.; cert. rehab. nurse. Charge nurse Rehab. Inst., Kansas City; asst. dir. nursing Children's Mercy Hosp., Kansas City, 1977-81; staff relief nurse Clara Manor Nursing Home, Kansas City; part-time nursing coord. Park Lane Med. Ctr., Kansas City. Mem. Assn. Rehab. Nurses, Mo. League for Nursing, Nat. League for Nursing. Home: 4311 Campbell St Kansas City MO 64110-1621

BUTLER, DEBRA SUE, physical therapist; b. Napoleon, Ohio, Jan. 19, 1957; d. Elmer Bernell and Rosalyn Ann (Baker) Junge; m. Robert Lee Phillips, Aug. 1, 1981 (div. Sept. 1985); 1 child, Nathan; m. Joseph Lee Butler, June 4, 1994; children: Jessica, Derek. BS in Elem. Adapted Phys. Edn., Bowling Green (Ohio) State U., 1980; BS in Phys. Therapy, Bowling Green State U., Toledo, Ohio, 1983; M in Spl. Edn., U. of Toledo, 1989. Lic. phys. therapist. Pediatric phys. therapist Henry County Schs., Napoleon, Ohio, 1983-96; cons., SERRC, Bowling Green, Ohio, 1985-95. Sec. Parent Tchr. League, St. Paul's Lutheran, 1990-91, band boosters, 1994-95. Federal grant U. Toledo, 1988-89. Lutheran. Home: V-405 SR108 Rt 1 Napoleon OH 43545

BUTLER, GERALDINE HEISKELL (GERRI BUTLER), designer, artist; b. Detroit, Sept. 6, 1930; d. Artist Kavassel and Geraldine Gentle (Heiskell) B.; student Wright Jr. Coll., 1946; B.E., Chgo. U., 1948; B.A. in Edn. (Delta Sigma Theta Scholar), Chgo. Art Inst., 1949, M.A. in Edn., 1950; postgrad. Harvard U., 1962-64. Tchr. pub. elementary schs., Chgo., 1949-52; tchr. art Chgo. pub. high schs., 1953-61; supr. art Chgo. Bd. Edn., 1962-75; graphic art and media coordinator, dept. instrn. Chgo. Bd. Edn., 1976-77; founder, prin. Gehebu-AK, design cons. services, Chgo., 1976—; founder, prin. Butler Studios, creative designer, Chgo., Wis., 1977—; one-man shows include: Saxon Gallery, Chgo., Roosevelt Hotel, N.Y.C., Henri IV Restaurant, Cambridge, Mass., Hilton Trinidad, B.W.I., Goldstein Gallery, Chgo.; group shows include: Triangle Gallery, Chgo., McCormick Pl., Chgo., Hyde Park Art Center, Chgo., Ill. State Fair, Peninsula Exhbts., Door County, Wis.; represented in permanent collections: rental gallery Art Inst. Chgo., Huntington Hartford Collection, N.Y.C.; judge numerous exhbts. and competitions; art cons. and designer. Mem. Ill. wing CAP, 1963—. Huntington Hartford fellow, 1956-58. Mem. Alumni Chgo. Art Inst., Artists Guild Chgo., Chgo. Soc. Artists, USAF Art Corps, Triangle-Lincoln Park Art Center, Am. Youth Hostels, Delta Kappa Gamma, Delta Sigma Theta. Office: PO Box 220 Fish Creek WI 54212-0220 also: Butler Studios-South 1724 N Cleveland Ave Chicago IL 60614-5603

BUTLER, JAMES MARTIN, science educator; b. Freeport, Ill., Apr. 20, 1948; s. Martin Harvey and Elizabeth Ann (Hillebrecht) B.; B.S., U. Ill., 1970, M.S., Northeastern Ill. U., 1978; M.A., Chgo. State U., 1982; m. Ruth Ann Dratwa, Dec. 17, 1972; children—Dawn Marie, Christine Ann, Kimberly Ann, James Martin, Jennifer Lynn. Tchr. sci., chmn. dept. Thornton Fractional North High Sch., Calumet City, Ill., 1979—. Vice pres. Holy Name Soc., St. Andrew Ch., 1979-81, pres., 1982-83. Mem. Nat. Assn. Biology Tchrs., Am. Assn. Physics Tchrs., Assn. Supervision and Curriculum Devel., Ill. Assn. Biology Tchrs., Ill. Chess Assn., U.S. Chess Fedn., U. Ill. Alumni Assn. (life), Northeastern Ill. U. Alumni Assn., Chgo. State U. Alumni Assn. Club: KC (4 deg.). Home: 426 155th St Calumet City IL 60409-4510 Office: 755 Pulaski Rd Calumet City IL 60409-4030

BUTLER, MARGARET KAMPSCHAEFER, retired computer scientist; b. Evansville, Ind., Mar. 7, 1924; d. Otto Louis and Lou Etta (Rehsteiner) Kampschaefer; m. James W. Butler, Sept. 30, 1951; 1 child, Jay. AB, Ind. U., 1944; postgrad., U.S. Dept. Agr. Grad. Sch., 1945, U. Chgo., 1949, U. Minn., 1950. Statistician U.S. Bur. Labor Statistics, Washington, 1945-46, U.S. Air Forces in Europe, Erlangen and Wiesbaden, Germany, 1946-48; statistician U.S. Bur. Labor Statistics, St. Paul, 1949-51; mathematician Argonne (Ill.) Nat. Lab., 1948-49, 51-80, sr. computer scientist, 1980-92; dir. Argonne Code Ctr. and Nat. Energy Software Ctr. Dept. Energy Computer Program Exch., 1960-91; spl. term appointee Indsl. Tech. Devel. Ctr. Argonne Nat. Lab., 1993—; cons. AMF Corp., 1956-57, OECD, 1964, Poole Bros., 1967. Author: Careers for Women in Nuclear Science and Technology, 1992; editor Computer Physics Communications, 1969-80; contbr. (chpt.) The Application of Digital Computers to Problems in Reactor Physics, 1968, Advances in Nuclear Sci. and Technology, 1976; contbr. articles to profl. publs. Treas. Timberlake Civic Assn., 1958; rep. mem. nomination com. Hinsdale (Ill.) Caucus, 1961-62; coord. 6th dist. ERA, 1973-80; del. Rep. Nat. Conv., 1980; bd. mgr. DuPage dist. YWCA Met. Chgo., 1987-90; mem. computer and info. sys. adv. bd. Coll. DuPage, 1987—; mem. industry adv. bd. computer sci. dept. Bradley U., 1988-91; vice-chair Ill. Women's Polit. Caucus, 1987-90; chair voter's svc. LWV, Burr-Ridge-Willowbrook, 1991-93. Recipient Cert. Leadership, Met. YWCA, Chgo., 1985, Merit award Chgo. Assn. Technol. Socs., 1988; named to Fed. 100, 1991; named Outstanding Woman Leader of DuPage County Sci., Tech. and Health Care, 1992; recipient spl. award Am. Nuclear Soc. Math and Comp. divsn., 1992. Fellow Am. Nuclear Soc. (mem. publs. com. 1965-71, bd. dirs. 1976-79, exec. com. 1977-78, chmn. bylaws and rules com., 1979-82, profl. women in ANS com. 1991-93, reviewer for publs.); mem. Assn. Computing Machinery (exec. com., sec. Chgo. chpt. 1963-65, publs. chmn. nat. conf. 1968, reviewer for publs.), Assn. Women in Sci. (pres. Chgo. area chpt. 1982, exec. bd. 1985-87), Nat. Computer Conf. (chmn. Pioneer Day com. 1985, tech. program chmn. 1987). Republican. Home: 17 W 139 Hillside Ln Hinsdale IL 60521-6062

BUTLER, PATRICIA, protective services official; b. Salem, Mass., Aug. 13, 1958; d. Frank Arthur and Ruth Elizabeth (Bartlett) B. Paramedic degree, Davenport Coll., 1984, AA in Mgmt. of Emergency Med. Svcs., 1987; Mich. Law Enforcement Officers Tng. Coun. cert., Grand Valley State U., 1988; BA in MHR, Spring Arbor Coll., 1994. CEO Whispering Winds, Inc., L'Anse, Mich., 1985—; firefighter Grand Rapids (Mich.) Fire Dept., 1985; security, data entry clerk Lacks Industries, Grand Rapids, 1985-88; loss prevention officer Woodland Mall Security, Kentwood, Mich., 1988-89, Butterworth Hosp., Grand Rapids, 1989; police officer Lakeview Police Dept., 1989, Edmore (Mich.)-Home Mcpl. Police Dept., 1989-90, Coopersville (Mich.) Police Dept., 1989-90; chief police Lakeview Village Police Dept., 1990-94, MSP L'anse Post, 1994—; mem. Mich. Paramedic, 1986—, Mich. Police Chaplains, 1992-94. Mem. NAFE, Nat. Assn. Chiefs, Mich. Chief's Assn. (v.p. 1991-94), Internat. Assn. Women Police, Mich. Assn. Chief of Police, Women Police Mich., Lions. Office: MSP-L'Anse PO Box 100 L'Anse MI 49946-0100

BUTLER, ROBERT ANDREWS, clinical psychologist; b. Lancaster, Calif., June 19, 1955; s. Robert Andrews and Ines Gertrude (Ottaviano) B.; m. Nadine Suzanne Pastor, Dec. 27, 1975; 1 child, Alex Robert. BA, Long Beach (Calif.) State U., 1977; MA, Dominguez Hills State U., 1979; PhD, Washington State U., 1983. Cert. Am Bd. Med. Psychotherapy; lic. psychologist, Wis. Dir. psychology Brown County Mental Health, Green Bay, Wis., 1983-89; pvt. practice psychology Green Bay, 1984-90; clin. dir. anxiety and affective disorders Fox Valley Hosp., Green Bay, 1989-90; dir. divsn. psychology Bellin Psychiat. Ctr., Green Bay, 1991-93; adj. prof. psychology U. Wis., Green Bay, 1983-86; cons. Family Violence Ctr., Green Bay, 1984, Whitman County (Wash.) Mental Health, 1981, St. Vincent Hosp. Sleep Disorders Ctr., 1989—. Contbr. articles to profl. jours. Fulbright fellow. Mem. Am. Psychol. Assn., Wis. Psychol. Assn., Syndicate Nat. Des Psychologues Francais (hon.). Home: 3740 Libal St Green Bay WI 54301-1253 Address: 2020 Riverside Dr Green Bay WI 54301-2300

BUTLER, ROBIN C., financial consultant; b. Balt., Sept. 13, 1959. BA, Miami U., 1981. Fin. cons. Merrill Lynch, Chgo., 1982—. Active various ch. orgns. Office: Merrill Lynch 141 W Jackson Blvd Ste 290 Chicago IL 60604-2905

BUTLER, STEVEN KING, pastor; b. Carter, Miss., Apr. 25, 1930; s. Charlie and Louetta (Wells) B.; m. Jimmie Will Nalls, June 29, 1952; children: Sammie, Salandra, Stephen Sr., Sylvia, Sherman, Shelia, Sandra, Sychem. Cert., Moody Bible Inst., 1954; Master's degree, Nazarene Theol. Sch., 1960. Ordained deacon, 1956, ordained to ministry, 1961, ordained pastor Nazarene All Nations Ch., 1970, ordained to Chgo. dist. ministry Alliance for Youth, 1994. Pres. Chgo. Dist. Min. Alliance for Youth. Bd. dirs. 308 union CTA, Chgo., 1961-82, Appeal for Charity, Chgo., 1984-95; dir. Nazarene Home for Elderly, Chgo., 1979-94. Home: 6500 S Ashland Ave Chicago IL 60636 Office: PO Box 368195 6508 S Ashland Ave Chicago IL 60636

BUTLER, WILLIAM JOSEPH, JR., insurance broker, lawyer; b. Chgo., Feb. 24, 1942; s. William Joseph Sr. and Emily Jane (Mockenhaupt) B.; BS, Coll. of the Holy Cross, Worcester, Mass., 1964; MBA, St. Louis U., 1969; JD, John Marshall Law Sch., 1988; m. Helen Katherine O'Malley, Aug. 28, 1965 (div. 1976); children: Charlotte Anne, Emily Jane. CLU. Mgmt. trainee Clinton E. Frank Inc., Chgo., 1969-70; dist. agt. Prudential Ins. Co., Evanston, Ill., 1970-74, spl. agt., Skokie, Ill., 1974-92; atty. pvt. practice, 1993—. Mem. fin. com. St. Mary's Ch., Lake Forest, Ill., 1980-81, Parish Coun., 1992-95, Edn. Commn., 1993-95, Strategic Planning Com., 1994-95; vol. Lake County Pub. Defender's Office, 1993—; fundraiser Donald Rumsfeld's CAVPAC (Citizens for Am. Values), 1986-87; mem. Vol. Lawyers Program Lake County Bar Assn., 1993—; arbitrator 19th Jud. Cir. Arbitration Ctr., Waukegan, Ill., 1995—. Capt. USAF, 1964-68. Mem. ABA, Ill. State Bar Assn., Chgo. Bar Assn. Republican. Roman Catholic. Office: 1301 N Western Ave # 306 Lake Forest IL 60045-1220

BUTORAC, THOMAS F., electrical engineer; b. May 28, 1957. A in Elec. Engring., Stark Tech. Coll., 1990; A in Electronics & Applied Sci., U. Akron, 1993. Staff engr. Akron Extrudes Inc., Canal Fulton, Ohio, 1989—. Home: 414 Misty Ln Copley OH 44321 Office: Akron Extrudes Inc 1119 N Milan St Canal Fulton OH 44614-9737

BUTTA, DEENA CELESTE, librarian; b. Chgo., June 1, 1950; d. Joseph James and Michaline Ann (Pabisinski) Weglarz; m. William C. Hartray, Apr. 21, 1974 (div. 1983); m. Raymond Peter Butta, June 2, 1984; children: Alexander Michael, Maris Michael, Philip Adrian. BA, Northwestern U., 1972; MLS, Rosary Coll., River Forest, Ill., 1978. Mem. staff Evanston (Ill.) Pub. Libr., 1969-79; libr. Triton C.C., River Grove, Ill., 1981, Libr. of Health Scis., U. Ill., Chgo., 1982-85; family day care provider Starchild Daycare, Chgo., 1985—, also bd. dirs.; staff mem. Des Plaines (Ill.) Pub. Libr., 1995—; counselor Bach Flower Soc., Lynbrook, N.Y., 1987—; mem. Day Care Action Coun., Chgo., 1985—; treas. Echo 33, Chgo., 1988—; Reiki II practitioner; co-founder CARETAKERS, 1996. Panelist TV series Man's Ultimate Destiny, 1992. Presenter Day of Prayer, Monastic Interreligious Dialogue; dancer Old Town Renaissance Consort, 1983—. Mem. Fellowship of Isis (priestess, del. representing fellowship to Parliament of the World's Religions), Eleusis of Chgo. (planning and facilitating com. FOI ann. convs.), Bach Flower Remedy Soc., Sacred Dance Guild, Chgo. Calligraphy Collective. Home: 3334 W Eastwood Ave Chicago IL 60625-5304

BUTTERFIELD, JAMES T., small business owner; b. Galion, Ohio, July 9, 1951; s. Carlos and Ethel Louise (Miller) B.; m. Mary Anne Shaffo, May 17, 1986; children: Jacob Alan, Emily Lauren. Cert. plumbing insp., backflow insp., cert. pipe welder, EPA cert. refrigerant handling technician, lic. low pressure steam operator, cert. automatic sprinkler installer, cert. plumbing contractor, Ohio. Apprentice Don Barnett Plumbing, Galion, Ohio, 1968-69, Rinehart Plumbing and Heating, Galion, 1969-71; owner Butterfield Plumbing and Heating, Galion, 1972—, Galion Sheet Metal, 1982—. Mem. Am. Soc. Sanitary Engrs., Ohio Assn. Plumbing Insps. Home: 375 W Atwood St Galion OH 44833 Office: Butterfield Plumbing and Heating PO Box 33 Galion OH 44833

BUTTERFIELD, JIM, political science educator; b. Lafayette, Ind., Sept. 11, 1955; s. John M. and Dorothy Butterfield; 1 child, Sarah. BA, Ind. U., 1982; MA, U. Notre Dame, 1984, PhD, 1989. Asst. prof. dept. polit. sci. Western Mich. U., Kalamazoo, 1988-93, assoc. prof., 1993—; cons. Detroit Pub. Sch., 1990, City of Kalamazoo, 1991-92; cons. USAID in Russia, 1994-95. Editor: Perestroika from Below, 1991; contbr. scholarly articles to profl. jours. Mem. Am. Polit. Sci. Assn., Am. Assn. for the Advancement Slavic Studies. Home: 220 W Park Vicksburg MI 49097 Office: Dept Polit Sci Western Mich U Kalamazoo MI 49008

BUTTERFIELD, KIMBERLE RAE, account executive; b. Newark, Mar. 29, 1960; d. Raymond P. Luther and Sue (Taylor) Voris; m. David M. Butterfield. BA, Otterbein Coll, Westerville, Ohio, 1982. Loan officer First Fin. Savs., Cin., 1983-93; account exec. Ohio Co., Newark, 1994—. Mem. NAFE (bd. mem. 1994—), Zonta Internat. (bd. mem. 1994—). Democrat. Methodist. Office: The Ohio Co 30 N Park Pl Newark OH 43055-5517

BUTTERFIELD, TODD WENDALL, financial consultant; b. La Harpe, Ill., June 19, 1962. B of Fin., Western Ill. U., 1984. Trader Realcor Shatkin, Chgo., 1984-88; trading advisor Butterfield Trading, Macomb, Ill., 1988-90; fin. cons. Smith Barney Inc., Quincy, Ill., 1990—. Republican. Office: Smith Barney Inc 418 Maine St Quincy IL 62301-3930

BUTTERWORTH, JANE ROGERS FITCH, physician; b. Louisville, Aug. 3, 1937; d. Howard Mercer and Jane Rogers (McCaw) Fitch; m. William Butterworth, Sept. 5, 1958 (div. Feb. 1968); children: Jane Rogers, William Stoddard, Robert Mercer, Benjamin Richard Mallory, Anne Lewis. BS, U. Louisville, 1971, MD, 1974. Rotating intern Humana Hosp. Audubon (formerly St. Joseph's Hosp.), Louisville, 1974-75, resident in radiology, 1975-76; resident in phys. medicine and rehab. Frasier Rehab. (formerly Inst. of Phys. Medicine and Rehab.), Louisville, 1976-80; staff physiatrist Rockford (Ill.) Meml. Hosp., 1980-83; clin. instr. Rockford Sch. Medicine, 1980-83; med. dir. phys. medicine and rehab. Western Res. Care System, Youngstown, Ohio, 1983-86, mem. teaching staff residency program, 1983—; clin. instr. Northeastern Ohio U. Coll. of Medicine, Rootstown, 1983—, chairperson phys. medicine subcoun., mem. acad. rev. and promotions com., 1985-95; adj. faculty Youngstown State U., 1984—; regional med. advisor Rehab. div. Ohio Indsl. Commn., Youngstown, 1985—; mem. admissions com. Northeastern Ohio U. Coll. Medicine, 1988; cons. Vista Ctr., Lisbon, Ohio. Mem. choir St. John's Episcopal Ch., Youngstown, vestrywoman, 1989-91; bd. dirs. Goodwill Industries, Youngstown, 1985-92, advisor rehab. divsn., 1986—, bd. advisors, 1993—; mem. med. rev. staff Hospice, Youngstown, 1984—; dir. med. svcs. Easter Seals Soc., Youngstown, 1987—; mem. med. bd. pub. TV, Youngstown, 1986—; violinist Youngstown State U. Cmty. Orch., 1985; mem. Youngstown Musica Sacra, 1989—; regional med. advisor Rehab. Divsn. Ohio Indsl. Commn., 1984-94. Recipient Community Svc. award St. John's Episcopal Ch., 1988. Mem. AMA, Ohio Med. Assn., Mahoning County Med. Soc. (coun. 1989, alt. del to Ohio Med. Assn. 1990, pres. 1992), Ky. Med. Assn., Jefferson County Med. Soc., Am. Congress Rehab. Medicine, Colonial Dames Soc. Am., Phi Beta, Chi Delta Phi, Kappa Alpha Theta. Republican. Home: 186 Rockland Dr Boardman OH 44512-5921 Office: Western Res Care System Southside Hosp 345 Oak Ave Youngstown OH 44512-6124

BUTTLER, JEWELL ANN, public relations executive; b. Detroit, July 10, 1937; d. John Martin and Grace Katherine (Gibes) Moranda; m. Francis Anthony Buttler, July 28, 1973. BA in Journalism, BS in Econs., Oakland U., 1983. Asst. mgr. communications dept. Greater Detroit C. of C., 1966-73; dir. pub. relations and devel. Ctr. for Creative Studies Coll. of Art and Design, Detroit, 1974-79; dir. pub. relations Detroit Inst. for Children, 1983-96, ret., 1996. Mem. Nat. Assn. Female Execs., Mensa. Home: 5048 Buckingham Pl Troy MI 48098-2602

BUTTRAM, JAMES ALAN, commercial real estate agent; b. Ponca City, Okla., Nov. 12, 1953; s. James Walter and Ardyth Ann (Grover) B.; m. Pamela Ann Colling, May 19, 1989; children: Allison Leigh, Patrick Aaron,

Alex Reed. BSBA, Okla. State U., 1976. Property mgr. Buttram-Bowker Devel. Co., Ponca City, 1976-92; corp. dir. North Park Devel. Co., Ponca City, 1976-92, Ponca Plaza, Ltd., Ponca City, 1976-92; real estate broker Coldwell Banker/Brady Stevens, Joplin, Mo., 1992—. Graduate Leadership Ponca City, 1989. Mem. Am. Bus. Club, Rotary (pres. Pioneer Club 1989, Outstanding Rotarian award 1988, 91, 92, Dist. 5750 Outstanding Rotarian award 1991-92, Disting. Club Citation 1990, dist. chmn. youth leadership awards conf. 1988-90, dir. Pioneer Club 1990, mem. dist. rep. 1990, dist. chmn. membership devel. com. 1991-92). Republican. Home: 507 Eagle Circle Carl Junction MO 64834 Office: Coldwell Banker Brady Stevens Co 2531 E 32nd St Joplin MO 64804-3129

BUTTRAM, JAMES DAVID, publishing company executive; b. Springfield, Mo., May 7, 1941; s. Lester Leo and Ethel Berniece (Thiemer) B. BS, Cen. Mo. State U., Warrensburg, 1971. Contr. Gospel Tract Soc. Inc., Independence, 1965-70, sec./treas., 1970-90, pres., 1991—; pres. Bethel Bible Sch., Port au Prince, Haiti, 1976—; supt. Ebenezer Christian Schs., Haiti, 1983—. Author numerous religious tracts. Editor: Gospel Tract Harvester, 1978—. Active Rep. Nat. Com., 1976—; bd. dirs. Teen Challenge Kansas City, Mo., 1980-82, Bethesda Missionary Fellowship, Bungoma, Kenya, 1988—. Staff sgt. USAFR, 1964-70. Named hon. fellow, Harry S. Truman Libr. Inst., 1978. Mem. Independence C. of C. Mem. Assembly of God Ch. Club: Kiwanis (pres. Independence chpt. 1982-83). Office: Gospel Tract Soc Inc 1105 S Fuller St Independence MO 64050-4221

BUXMAN, KARYN LYNN, nurse; b. St. Louis, July 30, 1956; d. Earl LaMoine and Shirley Lou (Bradley) Rapp; m. Stanley Louis Buxman, June 24, 1978; children: David Louis, Adam Louis. Diploma, Blessing Hosp. Sch. Nursing, 1979; BSN, SUNY, Albany, 1988; MSN, U. Mo., 1990. RN, Mo. Staff nurse Hannibal (Mo.) Clinic, 1979, Levering Hosp., Hannibal, 1979-83, Marion County Dept. Health, Hannibal, 1983; clin. instr. Sch. Practical Nursing, Hannibal, 1983-86; sch. nurse Hannibal Sch. Dist. 60, 1986-88; nurse educator Hannibal LaGrange Coll., 1988-91; psychiat. nurse Mark Twain Area Counseling Ctr., Hannibal, 1990-92; spkr., cons. U.S. and abroad, 1990—; presenter at profl. confs. Co-editor: Nursing Perspectives on Humor, 1995; contbg. editor Jour. Nursing Jocularity, Mesa, Ariz., 1990—, Am. Assn. Therapeutic Humor, 1991—; editor newsletter; mem. editorial bd. Mo. Nurse; contbr. articles to profl. publs.; producer: (4 audios and booklet) Healthcare FUN-damentals, (2 videos) Wit Happens! Managing Conflict with Humor, Humor: The Good, The Bad and the Ugly. Vol. Avenues Abused Women's Shelter, Hannibal, 1989—; mem. sch. bd. Hannibal Pub. Schs. Dist. 60, 1991-94; vestry mem. Trinity Episc. Ch., Hannibal, 1991-94. Mem. ANA, Mo. Nurses Assn. (dist. pres. 1991-93, Nurse of Yr. 1991), Am. Assn. Therapeutic Humor, Internat. Soc. Humor Studies, Nat. Spkrs. Assn., Bus. and Profl. Women Hannibal (Young Bus. Woman 1991), Sigma Theta Tau. Home and Office: HUMORX PO Box 1273 Hannibal MO 63401-1273

BUYER, STEVE E., congressman, lawyer; b. 1959; m. Joni Buyer; children: Colleen, Ryan. BS in Bus. Adminstrn., The Citadel, 1980; JD, Valparaiso U., 1984. Officer Med. Svc. Corps U.S. Army, 1980; spl. att to U.S. Atty. U.S. Army, Va., 1984-87; atty., 1988—; dep. atty. gen. Ind., 1987-88; legal counsel 22nd Theater Army, Saudi Arabia, 1990-91; legal advisor U.S Armed Forces/Western Enemy Prisoner of War Camps/War Crimes Interrogations, Saudi Arabia, 1991; mem. 103d Congress from 5th Ind. Dist., 1993—; com. mem. mil. forces and personnel, vets. affairs, judiciary. Decorated Bronze Star. Republican. Office: US Ho Reps 326 Cannon Washington DC 20515-1405*

BUZZELLI, LAURENCE FRANCIS, lawyer; b. Cleve., Jan. 24, 1943; s. Frank Vincent and Viola J. (Piccolino) B.; m. Judith Louise Shope, July 16, 1966; children: Christopher Laurence, Lauren Marie. BS in Edn., Ohio U., 1965; JD, Cleve. State U., 1973. Bar: Ohio, 1973; cert. secondary tchr., Ohio; lic. comml. pilot. Claims supr., regional analyst Allstate Ins. Co., Cleve. and Hudson, Ohio, 1969-74; atty., mng. atty. Continental Ins. Co./Buckeye Union Ins. Co., Cleve. and Cin., 1977-94; ptnr. Quandt, Giffels & Buck Co., L.P.A., Cleve., 1994—; arbitrator Cuyahoga County Common Pleas Ct., Cleve., 1974, Hamilton and Clermont County Pleas Ct., Cin. and Batavia, Ohio, 1978-83. Served to capt. U.S. Army, 1965-68, Vietnam. Mem. Def. Research Inst., Ohio Bar Assn., Bar Assn. Greater Cleve., Ohio Assn. Civil Trial Attys., Am. Arbitration Assn. (arbitrator), DAV (life). Office: Quandt Giffels & Buck Co LPA 800 Leader Bldg 526 Superior Ave NE Cleveland OH 44114-1460

BYCZKOWSKI, JANUSZ ZBIGNIEW, toxicologist; b. Gdansk, Poland, May 29, 1947; came to U.S., 1979; s. Stanislaw and Halina (Osterczy) B.; m. Janina K. Slosarska, Aug. 6, 1977; children: Ian S., L. Peter. MSc in Toxicology, Acad. Medicine, Gdansk, 1970, PhD in Pharmacology, 1975, DSc in Biochem. Pharmacology, 1979. Cancer rsch. scientist dept. exptl. therapeutics Roswell Park Meml. Inst., Buffalo, 1979-80, 1985-87; adj. ast. prof. pharmacology Acad. Medicine Gdansk, 1980-83; pharmacologist and dir. of pharmacy Internat. Red Cross and Red Crescent, Tobruk, Libya, 1983-84; asst. prof. and rsch. scientist Coll. Pub. Health U. South Fla., Tampa, 1987-91; project scientist and study dir. ManTech. Environ. Tech., Inc., Dayton, Ohio, 1991—; editorial reviewer Bull. Environ. Contamination and Toxicology, Reno, Nev., 1989—, Free Radical Biology and Medicine, Baton Rouge, 1989—, Placenta, Manchester, Eng., 1991—. Contbr. articles to profl. publs., chpts. to books. Active mem. Solidarity, Poland, 1980-83. Recipient Rsch. award 1st degree Sci. Soc. Gdansk, 1975, Polish Pharmacol. Soc. 1977, Ministry Health and Social Welfare of Poland, 1977. Mem. AAAS, Soc. for Rsch. on Polyunsaturated Fatty Acids (pres. 6th sci. meeting 1992—, travel grantee 1992), N.Y. Acad. Scis., Oxygen Soc., Soc. Toxicology, Soc. for Risk Analysis (councilor Ohio chpt. 1994—). Home: 212 N Central Ave Fairborn OH 45324-5006 Office: ManTech Environ Tech Inc PO Box 31009 Dayton OH 45437-0009

BYE, LYNN ELLEN, social work educator; b. Jersey City, Nov. 23, 1950; d. Harry and Phyllis (Paxton) Horgen; m. Douglas Bye. BA, U. Minn., 1972, MSW, 1975; PhD, Rutgers U., 1994. Lic. ind. social worker, Minn. Sch. social worker Dist. 742, St. Cloud, Minn., 1975-95; asst. prof. social work Coll. St. Benedict, St. Joseph, Minn., 1995—. Author publs. in field. Clk. Dist. 912 Sch. Bd., Milaca, Minn., 1978-84; bd. dirs. Cmty. Edn. Adv., Milaca, 1978-81; chair Milaca Vocat. Bd., 1979-80. Recipient Sch. Bd. award Milaca Sch. Bd., 1984. Mem. Minn. Sch. Social Workers Assn. (pres. 1985, Sch. Social Worker of Yr. 1986), Coun. on Social Work Edn. Office: Coll St Benedict 37 College Ave Saint Joseph MN 56374

BYERLY, REX R., state legislator; m. Linda Byerly; 1 child. BS, Nat. Coll., Rapid City, Mich. Computer cons., state rep. dist. 1, 1991—; mem. appropriations com.; chmn. human resources com. N.D. Ho. Reps. Mem. CAP. Mem. Exptl. Aviation Assn., Williston Basin Racing Assn., Moose. Republican. Home: PO Box 968 Williston ND 58802-0968*

BYERS, GEORGE WILLIAM, retired entomology educator; b. Washington, May 16, 1923; s. George and Helen (Kessler) B.; m. Martha Esther Sparks, Feb. 25, 1945 (div. 1953); children: George William, Carolyn Sylvia; m. Gloria B. Wong, Dec. 16, 1955; children: Bruce Alan, Brian William, Douglas Eric. BS, Purdue U., 1947; MS, U. Mich., 1948, PhD, 1952. Asst. prof. dept. entomology U. Kans., Lawrence, 1956-60, curator Snow Entomol. Mus., 1956-83, dir., sr. curator, 1983-88, assoc. prof., 1960-65, prof. entomology, 1965-88, ret., prof. dept. systematics and ecology, 1969-88, chmn. dept. entomology, 1969-72, 84-87, ret., 1988; vis. prof. Mountain Lake Biol. Sta. U. Va., alt. summers, 1961-92, U. Minn., 1970. Author: several book chpts.; contbr. articles to profl. jours. With U.S. Army, 1942-46, 53-56, WWII and Korea; lt. col. M.S.C., USAR, ret. Rackham fellow U. Mich., 1952-53; NSF grantee, 1958-87. Mem. Entomol. Soc. Am. (editl. bd. Annals 1967-72, chmn. 1971-72), Entomol. Soc. Can., Ctrl. States Entomol. Soc. (pres. 1958-59), Entomol. Soc. Washington, Soc. Systematic Biology (editor Syst. Zool. jour. 1963-66), Phi Beta Kappa, Phi Kappa Phi, Sigma Xi. Home: 909 Holiday Dr Lawrence KS 66049-3006 Office: U Kans Dept Entomology Lawrence KS 66045

BYERS, JO ANN, pharmacist; b. Osceola, Iowa; d. Robert Nelson and Carmen June (Waller) B. BS in Pharmacy, Drake U., 1970; MBA, Roosevelt U., 1982. Registered lic. pharmacist, Ill., Tex. Asst. mgr. pharmacy Holy Family Hosp., Des Plaines, Ill., 1977-79; assoc. dir. pharmacy Alexian Bros. Med. Ctr., Elk Grove Village, Ill., 1979-83; ops. mgr. Best Western Regal Inn, Osceola, Iowa, 1983-84; mgr. pharmacy svcs. St. Therese Med. Ctr., Waukegan, Ill., 1984-89; supr. cen. pharmacy Luth. Gen. Hosp., Park Ridge, Ill., 1989-93, asst. dir. pharmacy, 1993—. Dir. N.W. suburban unit Am. Cancer Soc., Chgo., 1980-83; active Order of Rainbow for Girls, worthy advisor; deacon Christian Ch. of Arlington Heights, Ill., 1979-81. Mem. Am. Pharm. Assn., Am. Soc. Health Sys. Pharmacists, Ill. Coun. Health Sys. Pharmacists (editor Keep Posted 1982-83), Order Ea. Star, Lambda Kappa Sigma.

BYERS, SUSANNAH ANTOINETTE, nurse practitioner; b. Michigan City, Ind., Oct. 11, 1932; d. Edward and Henrietta Caroline (Schmidt) Pizarek; m. Jimmy D. Byers, Aug. 1, 1970; children—Patrick John, Jean Marie, Thomas Edward Smeltzer. Diploma, Holy Cross Sch Nursing, South Bend, Ind., 1953; B.S.N., St. Mary's Coll., Notre Dame, Ind., 1954; cert. family nurse practitioner Ind. U.-N.W., 1978. Head nurse Beatty Meml. Hosp., Westville, Ind., 1954-55, adminstrv. supr., 1955-62, psychiat. nursing instr., 1962-71; news editor Westville Indicator, Ind., 1972-77; nurse practitioner Planned Parenthood N.W. Ind., Merrillville, Ind., 1979—. Pres., Town Bd. Trustees Westville, 1979; mem., 1977-80; mem. No. Ind. Regional Planning Comn., 1978-79. Mem. Nurses Assn. Am. Coll. Ob-Gyn (cert.), Nat. Assn. Nurse Practitioners in Reproductive Health Assn., Ind. Assn. Nurse Practitioners in Family Planning (sec. 1985-86, co-chairperson 1986-89), N.W. Ind. Council on the Adolescent. Avocations: sewing; quilting; leaded stained glass. Home: 156 Main St Westville IN 46391 Office: Planned Parenthood 8645 Connecticut St Merrillville IN 46410-6222

BYKERK, G. PATRICK, stockbroker; b. Grand Rapids, Mich., Nov. 26, 1965; s. Gerald M. and Margaret E. (Stahl) B.; m. Becki R. Buit, Apr. 30, 1994. BA in Bus. Adminstrn., Grand Valley U., Allendale, Mich., 1992. V.p. ops. Biker Landscape Maintenance, Caledonia, Mich., 1982-94; stockbroker 1st of Mich. Corp., Grand Rapids, 1994—. Republican. Mem. Christian Reformed Ch. Home: 148 Garland St SE Kentwood MI 49548-4427 Office: 1st of Mich Corp 300 Ottawa Ave NW Ste 150 Grand Rapids MI 49503-2305

BYL, WILLIAM, state legislator; b. May 11, 1946. BS, Calvin Coll. County commr. Kent, Mich.; rep. Mich. State Dist. 75, 1995—; transp. com. Mich. Ho. Reps., conservation com., environ. & Great Lakes com., vice chmn. urban policy com. Address: 1241 Benjamin SE Grand Rapids MI 49506

BYLSMA, SCOTT A., financial consultant; b. Grand Rapids, Mich., June 25, 1963; s. Jay M. and Nancy A. (Ooley) B.; m. Patricia A. Konwinski, Sept. 16, 1989; 1 child, Kasey. BA, Bowling Green (Ohio) State U., 1985. Acct. Coopers & Libran, Grand Rapids, 1985-88; v.p. fixed income Anderson & Co., Grand Rapids, 1988-93; fin. cons. Merrill Lynch, Grand Rapids, 1993—. Named to Hall of Fame Hockey, 1993; mem. Hockey Nat. Team, 1994. Mem. West Walker Sportsman Club. Republican. Mem. Reformed Ch. Home: 0-655 Bylsma Dr NW Grand Rapids MI 49504 Office: Merrill Lynch Frey Bldg 300 Ottawa Ave NW Grand Rapids MI 49503-2304

BYLUND, DAVID BRUCE, pharmacologist, educator; b. Spanish Fork, Utah, Apr. 16, 1946; s. H. Bruce and Rhea (Bowen) B.; m. Elaine C. Thurman, May 27, 1970; children: Carma, Eric, Michelle, Kevin, Jennie, Kristen, Emily. BS, Brigham Young U., 1970; PhD, U. Calif., Davis, 1974. Postdoctoral rsch. fellow Johns Hopkins Med. Sch., Balt., 1975-77; prof. med. sch. U. Mo., Columbia, 1977-89; prof., chmn. U. Nebr., 1989—. Series editor: The Receptors, 1988—. Mem. LDS Ch. Office: U Nebr Med Ctr Pharmacology 600 S 42nd St Omaha NE 68198-6260

BYNER, EARNEST ALEXANDER, professional football player; b. Milledgeville, Ga., Sept. 15, 1962. Student, East Carolina. With Cleve. Browns, 1984-88, 94—; running back Washington Redskins, 1989-94. Office: Cleve Browns 80 1st Ave Berea OH 44017-1238

BYRD, ELLIS CHARLES, automotive executive; b. Youngstown, Ohio, Apr. 8, 1952; s. Ellis and Naomi (Thomas) B.; m. Juanita Marie, Aug. 8, 1981; children: Fatima Marie, Michael Charles, Jason Anthony. BS in Criminal Justice, Youngstown State U., 1980. Planner GM, Lordstown, Ohio, 1991—. Pres. Minority Concerns Commn., Diocese of Youngstown, 1976—; mem. 50/50 Role Model Club, Youngstown, 1993—; grand knight Knights of St. Peter Clauer, 1994—. Roman Catholic. Home: 2806 Rogers Rd Youngstown OH 44511

BYRD, LORENDA SUE, nursing administrator; b. Eureka, Ill., Jan. 31, 1941; d. Denver C. and Sadie M. (Van Sickle) Aucutt; m. Larry L. Byrd, Jan. 2, 1984; children: Scott, Ellen, Leslie, Brian. Diploma, Meth. Hosp. Cen. Ill. Sch., Peoria, 1962; BSN, McKendree Coll., 1981; MSN, So. Ill. U., Edwardsville, 1990. RN, Ill., Mo.; cert. nursing adminstr. ANCC. Staff nurse Charleston Community Hosp., 1962-65; mem. faculty Mennonite Hosp. Sch. Nursing, Bloomington, Ill., 1965-76; head nurse emergency rm. Belleville (Ill.) Meml. Hosp., 1976-80; nurse mgr. med.-surg. oncology dept. St. Elizabeth Med. Ctr., Granite City, Ill., 1980-87; assoc. dir. patient svcs. Alexian Bros. Hosp., St. Louis, 1988-91; dir. nursing St. Joseph Hosp.-West, Lake St. Louis, Mo., 1991—. Mem. "We Can 2000" Cmty. Orgn., Wentzville, Mo., 1992-95, Bus. and Profl. Women, Wentzville, 1993-94. Mem. Am. Orgn. Nurse Execs., Mo. Orgn. Nurse Execs., St. Louis Coun. Nurse Execs. (pres.-elect 1993, pres. 1994), O'Fallen (Mo.) Rotary (sec. 1995, pres.-elect 1996), C. of C. Lake St. Louis (sec. 1994—, bd. dirs. 1994, 96), Sigma Theta Tau.

BYRD, MARK ALAN, institutional researcher, educator; b. Little Rock, Dec. 3, 1957; s. Isaac Durham Jr. and Joellen Rae (Horne) B.; m. Martha Lee Bowling, July 1, 1978; children: Jonathon, Andrew. BA, Ouachita Bapt. U., Arkadelphia, Ark., 1982; postgrad., Henderson State U., Arkadelphia, 1982; MA, U. Ark., 1984; postgrad., U. Mich., 1993. Grad. asst. U. Ark., Fayetteville, 1982-84; rsch. analyst Ark. Dept. Higher Edn., Little Rock, 1984-86; rsch. assoc., computer system adminstr. U. Ark. Cen. Adminstrn., Little Rock, 1986-87; dir. institutional rsch. U. Scranton, Pa., 1987-93, adj. faculty, 1989-93; telecommunication cons. U. Ark. Cen. Adminstrn., 1987; cons. Greater Scranton C. of C. Mem. Assn. for Instutional Rsch., Higher Edn. Data Sharing Consortium (instutional rep.), Am. Assn. Higher Edn., Am. Amateur Racquetball Assn., Exec. Info. Systems Spl. Interest Group, Alpha Kappa Delta. Republican. Home: 2294 Stone Rd Ann Arbor MI 48105-2537

BYRD, RANDALL DUANE, sales engineer, project manager, actor; b. Clinton, Iowa, June 8, 1966; s. John L. and Bonny Jane (Daugherty) B. BS in Indsl. Edn. and Tech., Iowa State U., 1992; postgrad. in Bus. Adminstrn., North Ctrl. Coll., Naperville, Ill., 1994—. Field engr. Terracon Cons. NE, Inc., Des Moines, 1988-90; agy. dir. The Rahmani Agy., Ames, Iowa, 1991-93; profl. actor film and TV, 1989—; sales engr./project mgr. Trans Tech Am., Inc., Carol Stream, Ill., 1993—; comm. cons. Byrd Enterprises, Carol Stream, 1991—. Appeared in Hard Knox, Revenge of the Nerds II and numerous commls.; actor 7 indsl. films; promotional spokesperson. Active Eagle Scout project Savanna Riverfront Beautification, Miss., 1984. Recipient Male Talent of Yr. hon. mention Internat. Modeling and Talent Assn., 1991, winner TV Soap Opera Competition, 1991, winner Theatrical Headshots Competition, 1991, Comdey Monologue Competition 3d runner up, 1991, TV Real People Commls. 3d runner up, 1991, Singing-Male Category 3d runner up, 1991, TV Beauty Commls. hon. mention, 1991; Impromptu and After Dinner Speaking finalist Nat. Forensic Assn., 1992. Mem. Am. Soc. for Quality Control (cert. quality engr.-in-tng.), Soc. Mfg. Engrs. (cert. mfg. technologist), Soc. Plastics Engrs., The Planetary Soc., Nat. Space Soc., The Challenger Ctr. (charter mem.), Sierra Club, Nat. Eagle Scout Assn. (life), Olympic Games Pin Soc. (charter mem.), Iowa State U. Alumni Assn. Office: Trans Tech Am Inc 475 N Gary Ave Carol Stream IL 60188

BYRD, ROBERT RAY, computer science educator; b. Lafayette, Ind., Nov. 23, 1959; s. Ralph Ray and Una Alice (Winchell) B.; m. Kelli Marie Dees, Dec. 17, 1981; children: Michelle, Natasha, Robin. AS in Gen. Sci., York Coll., 1979; BS in Math., Harding U., 1981; MS in Math., Ceighton U., 1992. Cons. Bryd Brain Cons. and Svc., Lake Orion, Mich., 1992—; computer lab. mgr. Mich. Christian Coll., Rochester Hills, Mich., 1992-94, math/computer sci. tchr., 1992-94; project mgr. ARROW EDI Svcs., Elkhorn, Wis., 1994—; computer sci. tchr. Gateway Tech. Coll., Elkhorn, 1994—. Capt. USAF, 1982-92. Mem. IEEE, Air Force Assn. (life). Republican. Mem. Ch. of Christ.

BYRNE, MICHAEL JOSEPH, business executive; b. Chgo., Apr. 3, 1928; s. Michael Joseph and Edith (Lueken) B.; B.Sc. in Mktg., Loyola U., Chgo., 1952; m. Eileen Kelly, June 27, 1953; children—Michael Joseph, Nancy, James, Thomas, Patrick, Terrence. Sales engr. Emery Industries, Inc., Cin., 1952-59; with Pennsalt Chem. Corp., Phila., 1959-60; with Oakton Cleaners, Inc., Skokie, Ill., 1960-70, pres., 1960-70; pres. Datatax Inc., Skokie, 1970-74, Midwest Synthetic Lubrication Products, 1978—, Pure Water Systems, 1984—, Superior Tax Service, 1984—. Served with ordnance U.S. Army, 1946-48. Mem. A.I.M., VFW, Alpha Kappa Psi. Club: Toastmasters Internat. Home: PO Box 916 600 Grego Ct Prospect Heights IL 60070-1636

BYRNE, THOMAS H., investment broker; b. St. Louis, Sept. 16, 1959; s. Patrick H. and Mary L. (Graham) B.; m. Melissa R. Gales, Sept. 24, 1994. BA, St. Louis Christian Ch., 1986; BA magna cum laude, St. Louis U., 1991. Fin. analyst City Corp., St. Louis, 1986-92; investment broker Edward D. Jones & Co., St. Louis, 1992—. Mem. C. of C., Lions. Republican. Home: 27 Fawn Meadow Dr Eureka MO 63025-1207 Office: Edward D Jones & Co 6926 Chippewa St Saint Louis MO 63109-3038

BYRNES, R. JOHN, food packaging company executive; b. Detroit, Nov. 6, 1948; s. Robert J. Byrnes and Gay A. Ahrens; m. Ellen I. Wells, July 17, 1971; children: Nathan J., Alana M. BBA, Western Mich. U., 1970; MBA, U. Detroit, 1974. With GM Co., Detroit, 1972-76, Rockwell Internat., Troy, Mich., 1976-82; mgr. fin. and planning NWL Controls - I.C. Ind., Kalamazoo, 1982, mgr. cost/inventory, 1983, dir. fin., 1983-86; v.p. fin. Columbus (Ohio) Auto Parts Co., 1986-89; v.p. fin. Nestle Dairy Sys., Bad Homburg, Germany, 1989-91, v.p. ops., 1991-92, v.p., gen. mgr., 1992-94; CFO, v.p. Norse Dairy Sys., Columbus, 1994—; bd. dirs. J.W. Blair Inc. Mem. allocation com. United Way, Kalamazoo, 1983-86. With U.S. Army, 1970-72. Mem. German-Am. C. of C., Nat. Assn. MBA Execs., Nat. Assn. Accts. (chpt. treas.). Office: Norse Dairy Sys PO Box 1869 Columbus OH 43216-1819

BYRON, RITA ELLEN COONEY, travel executive, publisher, real estate agent, photojournalist, writer; b. Cleve.; d. Harry James and Marie (Hakey) Cooney; m. Carl James Byron Jr., Nov. 27, 1954 (dec.); children: Carey Lewis, Carl James, Bradford William. Student Cleve. Coll., 1954, Western Res. U., 1955, John Carroll U., 1956; PhD (hon.), Colo. State Christian Coll., 1972. Mgr. European Immigration dept. U.S. Steamship Lines, Cleve., 1956; real estate agt. W.I. White Realtor Inc., Shaker Heights, Ohio, 1965-67, J.P. Malone Realtors Inc., Shaker Heights, 1967-70, Thomas Murray & Assocs., 1971-76, Mary Anderson Realty, Shaker Heights, 1978-79, Barth Brad & Andrews Realtors Inc., Shaker Heights, 1979—, Heights Realty, 1986—; v.p., co-owner Your Connection To Travel, Kent, Ohio, 1980—; v.p., gen. mgr. World Class Travel Agy., 1985—; dir. Travel One div. Quaker Sq., Akron, Travel Trends for Singles, 1985, Playhouse Sq. Travel, 1986, World Class Internat., 1986. Mem. U.S. Figure Skating Assn., 1960—, Wightman Cup Women's Com., 1965—; mem. women's com. Cleve. Mus. of Art, 1969—, Friendship Force Ohio, 1986 ; co-chmn. Cleve. Invitational Figure Skating Competition, 1972—; chmn. Gold Rush Rush, U.S. Ski Team, 1982, Cleve. benefit U.S. Olympic Teams, Midas Touch, 1983, Gran Apres-Ski Prix, 1981, blue ribbon ball Hunt Club for Handicapped; patron Cleve. 500, 1983; originator Benefits Unltd., Exceptional Single Person's, Connections Unltd., 1983; founder, coordinator Singled Out Club, 1983; co-ptnr., adv. bd. The Service Service, 1984; benefit chmn., patroness various balls and fund-raising events; vol. Foster Parents Inc., 1983; vol. Council on World Affairs, 1983, Bellefaire Home for Spl. Children, 1983, Big Sisters Greater Cleve., 1983, Camp Cheerful, 1983, Chisholm Ctr., 1983, Children's Diabetic Camp Ho Mita Koda, 1984, Young Audiences, 1985; adv. trustee Friends of Fairmount Theatre of the Deaf, 1983; mem. Greater Cleve. Growth Assn., 1983. Mem. Western Res. Hist. Soc., Garden Ctr. Greater Cleve., Friends Cleve. Pub. Library, UN Assn. of U.S., Cleve. Council World Affairs, U.S. Ski Ednl. Fund (chmn. benefits), English Speaking Union (jr. bd.), Travel Age Exchange, Globetrotters Internat. Fedn. Women's Travel Orgns., North Coast Exec. Women's Network, Growth Assn., Council on Small Enterprises. Cleve. Real Estate Bd., Cleve. Photographic Soc. (bd. dirs. 1989—), Camera Guild (exec. bd. trustees 1989), Associated Photographers, Photographic Soc. Am. Clubs: Cleve. Skating, Broadmoor World Arena Figure Skating, Colony Beach and Racquet, Suburban Ski, Cleve. Advertising, Communicator's, Towne Hall, Women's City, Gilmour Acad. Women's, Mid-Day, Cleve. Wellesley, Arctic Circle, Intrepid Traveler, Tibet, Mongolia and China Explorers', Himalaya Yeti (1987 Nepal Expdn.), Internat. Chagrin Valley Camera, Nat. Hist. Mus. Photo Soc., Kodochromse Adventure Soc., Nature Artists Soc., Cleve. Astronomical Soc., Archeol. Soc., Holden Aborteum Soc., East Berlin Photo Club, Chagrin Valley Photo Club, Shaker Lakes Nature Club, Met. Parks, Photography Club, Photocrafters, Sanctuary Marsh Photo, Cuyahoga Valley Nat. Pk. Photo Club (assoc. photographer, various photography awards). Co-pub., exec. editor The Single Register (pub. documentary book The Fall of the Wall 1989), other publs.; featured in numerous publs. Home: 18126 Lomond Blvd Cleveland OH 44122-5012 Office: World Class Travel 3520 Ingleside Rd Cleveland OH 44122-5002 also: Es Turo Edificio, Kontiki, Majorica Balearic Islands Spain

BYRUM, DIANNE, state legislator; b. Mar. 18, 1954; d. Cecil Dershem and Mary D.; m. James E. Byrum; children: Barbara Anne, James Richard. AA, Lansing Cmty. Coll.; BS cum laude, Mich. State U. Rep. dist. 68 State of Mich., 1991-94; owner Blackhawk Hardware, Leslie, Mich., 1983—; senator 25th dist. State of Mich., 1995—; minority vice chair agr. and forestry, health policy and sr. citizens; mem. tech. and energy com., capitol com.; chair dem. caucus. Recipient Disting. Citizen award Ingham County Soil Conservation Dist., 1991, Disting. Alumnus award Lansing Cmty. Coll., 1993. Mem. Am. Cancer Soc. (Ingham-Delta br. mem. bd. dirs.), Mich. Retail Hardware Assn., Lansing Regional C. of C., Greater Lansing Safety Coun., S. Lansing Bus. Assn., S. Lansing-Everett Kiwanis, Women Bus. Owners. Democrat. Office: Mich State House 125 W Allegan PO Box 30036 Lansing MI 48909

BYRUM, JUDITH MIRIAM, accountant; b. Bismarck, N.D., Sept. 24, 1943; d. Adolph Mathew and Gertrude Cecelia (Lechner) H.; m. Richard W. Byrum, July 30, 1965 (div. Oct. 1984); children: Thomasin Jane, Toby Oliver; m. Danny D. Jansen, Oct. 21, 1989 (dec. Nov. 1989); m. Jack N. Sutton, June 26, 1993. BS in Acctg., Ariz. State U., 1967. CPA, Ariz., Kans. Underwriter Gt. SW Fire Ins. Co., Mesa, Ariz., 1963-65; staff auditor Touche Ross & Co., London, 1967-69, Arthur Andersen & Co., Kansas City, Mo., 1970-71; treas. John J. Peterson Real Estate, Overland Park, Kans., 1971-75; internal auditor Bus. Men's Assurance Co., Kansas City, 1975-78; chief exec. officer, owner Judith H. Byrum, CPA, Overland Park, 1978—. Contbr. articles to newsletter. Mem. adv. bd. Rockhurst Coll. Women's Ctr., Kansas City, 1977; mem. Congressman Larry Winn II Small Bus. Com., Washington, 1977-80; treas. Trinity Luth. Ch., Mission, Kans., 1990-94. Mem. AICPA (legis. liaison), Am. Woman's Soc. CPAs (treas., v.p. Chgo. 1977-83), Am. Soc. Women Accts. (pres. Kansas City 1980-81), Kans. Soc. CPAs (com. mem. 1977—, pres., v.p., treas. Metro chpt. 1989—, bd. dirs. 1994—), Kansas City Women's C. of C. (v.p. 1980), Beta Alpha Psi. Office: 10550 Marty St Ste 202 Shawnee Mission KS 66212-2557

CACCHIONE, PATRICK JOSEPH, health association executive; b. Syracuse, N.Y., Mar. 19, 1959; s. Nicholas Phillip and Ruth Helen (Liadka) C.; m. Pamela Carol Zurkowski, Oct. 8, 1988. BA, Hobart Coll., 1981; MPA, Am. U., 1983. Rsch. asst. Brookings Instn., Washington, 1982-83; field organizer Mondale for Pres. Campaign, Washington, 1983-84; legis. asst. Office of Congressman Tom Luken, Washington, 1985-86; cons. Am. Express Co., Washington, 1986, Francis, McGinnis and Rees Assocs., Washington, 1986; legis. asst. Law Office of Raymond D. Cotton, Washington, 1987-88; dir. legis. affairs Nat. Assn. Med. Equipment Suppliers, Alexandria, Va., 1988-90; v.p. govt. affairs Daus. of Charity Nat. Health System, St. Louis, 1991—; cons. Cardondelet Health System, St. Louis, 1992—; candidate U.S. House Rep., First Dist. Mo., 1993—. Contbr. articles to profl. publs. Vol. Harriet Woods for Senate, St. Louis, 1986,

Guardian Angels Settlement, St. Louis, 1991-92, Jack Garvey for Cir. Atty., St. Louis, 1992; campaign mgr. Dianne Smith for County Coun., Silver Spring, Md., 1990; bd. dirs. Compton Heights Civic Assn., St. Louis, 1992. Mem. St. Louis Ambassadors, Women in Govt. Rels., Democratic Club, Healthcare Fin. Mgrs. Assn., Network. Democrat. Roman Catholic. Home: 2922 Accomac St Saint Louis MO 63104-1602 Office: Daus of Charity Nat Health System 4600 Edmundson Rd Saint Louis MO 63134-3806*

CACCIOLFI, WILLIAM PETER, JR., small business owner, expolorer; b. Tachi Kawa, Japan, Apr. 9, 1960; s. William Peter and Sara Veronica (Stafford) C.; divorced; children: Koryne Taylor, Nikolas Peter; m. Arati Joshi, Oct. 17, 1989; children: Ava, Anthony Joshi. Grad. high sch., Chicopee, Mass.; student, Wright State U., Fairborn, Ohio. Mental health tech. USAF, Wright Patterson AFB, Ohio, 1978-85; prin. River Athlete Raft Co., Beaver Creek, Ohio, 1984—, New World Expdns., Yellow Springs, Ohio; expdn. leader Nepal, Arab Republic of Egypt, Burma, Thailand, Congo and Nigeria, Venezuela, S.Am. Internationally pub. photographer. Mem. World Wildlife Fund; ofcl. tour operator Whitewater Olympic Games, Spain, 1992. Mem. Internat. Soc. Cryptozoology, Am. Canoe Assn., Nat. Assn. Adventure Tour Operators, Nat. Geographic Soc., Nigerian Conservation Found., New World Explorers Soc.

CADWALLADER, CARL EUGENE, automotive manufacturing engineer; b. Pontiac, Mich., Apr. 22, 1967; s. Carl and Patricia A. (Emrick) C.; m. Kathleen Moore, June 1, 1990. B in Elec. Engring., Mich. Tech. U., 1990, M in Elec. Engring., 1991. Emc engr. GM Corp., Milford, Mich., 1991-93; lead emc engr. GM Lansing (Mich.) Automotive Divsn., 1993-94; mfg. engr. GM Lansing (Mich.) Car Assembly, 1994—. Mem. IEEE. Office: Lansing Automotive Divsn GM M5 15 0Z 920 Townsend Lansing MI

CADY, ELWYN LOOMIS, JR., medicolegal consultant, educator; b. Ames, Iowa, Feb. 21, 1926; s. Elwyn Loomis Sr. and Annabel (Lacey) C.; m. Jane Carolyn Elliott, Jan. 27, 1964 (dec. Dec. 1989); children: James Anson, Kathryn Anne; stepchildren: Martin Norman Jensen III, Paul Elliott Jensen. JD, Tulane U., 1951; BS in Medicine, U. Mo., 1955. Bar: Mo. 1951, U.S. Supreme Ct., 1965. Sci. comml. tchr., athletic dir. and coach Vermillion (Kans.) Rural High Sch., 1948-49; pvt. practice Kansas City, St. Louis, Independence, Mo., 1951—; dir. law-medicine program U. Kansas City, 1951-56; asst. dir. Law-Sci. Inst. U. Tex., Austin, 1956-57, sec. Law-Sci. Acad. Am., 1956-57; of counsel Koenig & Dietz, St. Louis, 1959-74; gen. counsel Elliott Oil, Inc., Independence, 1966—; mem. com. on mgmt. Ea. Jackson County Planned Parenthood Clinics, Independence, 1970-75. Author: (book) Law and Contemporary Nursing, 1961, 1st. rev. edit., 1963; Author: (with others) Immediate Care of the Acutely Ill and Injured, 1974, Cardiac Arrest and Resuscitation, 1958, 3rd rev. edit., 1974, West's Federal Practice Manual, 1960, 3rd rev. edit., 1989, Gradwohl's Legal Medicine, 1954; book reviewer: sci. books and films. Legal Counsel Friends of the Truman Campus, U. Mo.-Kansas City, Independence, 1987—, Comty. Assn. for the Arts, Independence, 1991—; charter mem. Friends of Nat. Frontier Trails Ctr., Independence, 1990—, Independence Hist. Trails City Com., 1991—. With U.S. Army, 1944-45, ETO. Fellow Harry S. Truman Libr. Inst. for Nat. and Internat. Affairs (hon.), Am. Acad. Forensic Sci. (ret.); mem. AAAS (life), Nat. Geog. Soc. (life), Am. Legion (past comdr., judge adv., chaplain, chmn. state blood donor program, chmn. dist. oratorical contest), Phi Alpha Delta (life), Phi Beta Pi, Tau Kappa Epsilon. Home and Office: 1919 Drumm Ave Independence MO 64055-1836

CADY, LOUIS BYRON, psychiatrist; b. Little Rock, June 11, 1955; s. James William and Claire Elizabeth (Benson) C.; m. Janet Lynn Shoemate, May 13, 1984; children: Richard Louis, Marcus James. B.Mus., U. Mo., Kansas City, 1977; M.Mus., U. Mo., 1979; MD, U. Tex., Galveston, 1989. Grad. teaching asst. U. Mo., Kansas City, 1977-79; artist-in-residence in piano and asst. prof. music Howard Payne U., Brownwood, Tex., 1980-83; resident physician The Mayo Clinic, Rochester, Minn., 1989-93; pvt. practice child, adolescent and adult psychiatry Evansville, Ind., 1993—; med. dir. Sleep Diagnostic Ctr. of Ind., 1994-95, Mulberry Ctr. Disordered Eating Program, 1994—; resident in in-patient psychiatry St. Mary's Hosp., Rochester, 1989-93; concert tours as pianist, 1981-83. Chmn. adv. bd. Brown County Citizens Coun. on Drugs, Brownwood, 1981-83. U. Mo. scholar, 1976-77; NIH grantee, 1985, others. Mem. AMA, Am. Psychiatric Assn., Nat. Rifle Assn., Mensa, Rotary. Republican. Baptist. Office: Oak Park Profl Bldg 501 SE 6th St Ste 202 Evansville IN 47713-1219

CADY, PATRICIA ANN, physical therapist assistant; b. Tucson, Nov. 30, 1951; d. James Edward and Faith Alba (Iverson) Gregory; m. Steven Robert Cody Sr., May 31, 1975; 1 child, Steven Robert Jr. AS, Kellogg C.C., Battle Creek, Mich., 1975. Phys. therapist asst. Infant Stimulation Program Doris Klaussen Ctr., Battle Creek, Mich., 1977-78; phys. therapist asst. Oaklawn Hosp., Marshall, Mich., 1978, Leila Hosp., Battle Creek, 1978—, Gary Nederveld & Assocs., Battle Creek, 1978—. Pres. Emmett Twp. Dept. Pub. Safety Aux., Battle Creek, 1985-95. Recipient Recognition award Emmett Twp. Bd., 1989. Mem. Am. Phys. Therapy Assn. (cons. dept. minority internal affairs 1993—, cons. mentor to students 1993—, Spotlight award 1994), Mich. Phys. Therapy Assn., Order Eastern Star. Home: 941 N Wattles Rd Battle Creek MI 49017 Office: G Nederveld & Assocs BCHS Rehab Svcs 300 North Ave Battle Creek MI 49017

CAFFERY, JOHN PATRICK, lumber company salesman, retired, city alderman; b. Davenport, Iowa, July 7, 1932; s. William Thomas and Frances Rella (Dooley) C.; m. Genevieve Ann Hart, Oct. 7, 1957; children: Lisa, William, Cathy. Grad., St. Ambrose Acad., 1951. Policeman Davenport Police Dept., 1954-67; lumber salesman Mueller Lumber Co., Davenport, 1967-93; ret., 1993. Dem. Alderman, City of Davenport, 1985-95. Served with USNR, 1951-77, ret. 1992. Mem. Fleet Res. Assn., Naval Res. Assn. (life), Moose. Roman Catholic. Home: 1507 Florence Ln Davenport IA 52804

CAHAY, MARC MICHEL, electrical engineer, educator; b. Liege, Belgium, Oct. 11, 1959; came to U.S., 1983; s. Oscar and Mary (Bony) C. BS in Physics, U. Liege, 1981; MS in Physics, Purdue U., 1986, PhD in Elec. Engring., 1987. Rsch. scientist dept. nuclear physics U. Liege, 1981-82; substitute tchr. physics various high schs., Belgium, Germany, 1983; teaching asst. physics Purdue U., West Lafayette, Ind., 1983-84, rsch. asst. dept. elec. engring., 1984-87; rsch. scientist Sci. Rsch. Assocs., Glastonbury, Conn., 1987-89; asst. prof. elec. and computer engring. U. Cin., 1989-95, assoc. prof., 1995—; presenter at profl. confs.; co-organizer Superlattices and Microstructures Conf., Cin., 1995. Contbr. articles to profl. publs. Grantee NSF, 1991—. Mem. IEEE, Internat. Soc. Optical Engring., Am. Phys. Soc. (session chmn. 1991), Electro Chem. Soc. (membership chmn. 1992—), Sigma Xi (Young Investigator award 1995), Eta Kappa Nu. Office: Univ Cin 832 Rhodes Hall ECECS Dept Cincinnati OH 45221

CAHILL, ARTHUR RIPLEY, financial executive; b. Springfield, Mo., July 7, 1907; s. Frederick A. and Louise (Ripley) C.; m. Jeannette S. Cahill, Sept. 15, 1934 (dec. July 1987); children: Douglas R., Steven M., Susan S. PhB in Econs., U. Chgo., 1931. Loan discount dept. Harris Trust & Savs. Bank, Chgo., 1931-34; asst. to gen. auditor Fed. Res. Bank, Chgo., 1934-41; asst. treas. Montgomery Ward, Chgo., 1941-48, treas., 1948-49, v.p., treas., 1949-52; asst. treas. Internat. Minerals Corp., Chgo., 1953-54, v.p., treas., 1954-56, v.p., fin., 1956-60; v.p. fin. Brunswick Corp., Skokie, Ill., 1960-72, cons., 1972—. Bd. trustees Coll. of Ozarks, Point Lookout, Mo., 1974—. Mem. Commonwealth Club, Oak Park Country Club, Hickory Hills Country Club, The Tower Club (Springfield, Mo.), Univ. Club Chgo. Republican. Home: 107 Woodleigh Dr S Branson MO 65616-3724

CAHILL, PATRICIA DEAL, radio station executive; b. St. Louis, Oct. 9, 1947; d. Richard Joseph and Dorothy (Deal) C.; children: Lindsay Cahill, Jessica Cahill Crump. BA, U. Kans., 1969, MA, 1971. Continuity dir. Sta. KANU-FM, Lawrence, Kans., 1970, audio reader dir., 1970-73; reporter Sta. KCUR-FM, Kansas City, Mo., 1973-75; news dir. Sta. KMUW-FM, Wichita, Kans., 1975, gen. mgr., 1976-87; gen. mgr. Sta. KCUR-FM, Kansas City, Mo., 1987—; asst. prof. communications studies U. Mo. Kansas City, 1987—; dir. Nat. Pub. Radio, 1982-88, exec. com., 1983-88, chair tech. and distbn., 1985-88. Chmn. Wichita Free U., 1979-81; v.p. Planned Parenthood Kans., 1986-87; bd. dirs. Kansas City Cultural Alliance. Recipient Matrix award Wichita chpt. Women in Communications, 1986, Alumni Honor Citation U. Kans., 1993. Mem. Pub. Radio in Mid Am. (pres. 1979-80, 89-93), Radio Rsch. Consortium (bd. dirs. 1981—), Kans. Pub. Radio Assn. (bd. dirs. 1980-87). Home: 621 W 87th St Kansas City MO 64114-2843 Office: Sta KCUR 5100 Rockhill Rd Kansas City MO 64110-2446*

CAIN, MADELINE ANN, mayor; b. Cleve., Nov. 21, 1949; d. Edward Vincent and Mary Rita (Quinn) C. BA, Ursuline Coll., 1973; MPA, Cleve. State U., 1985. Tchr. St. Augustine Acad., Lakewood, Ohio, 1973-75; clk. coun. legis. aide Lakewood City Coun., 1981-85; legis. liaison Cuyahoga County Bd. Commrs., Cleve., 1985-88; mem. Ohio Ho. of Reps., Columbus, 1989-95; mayor City of Lakewood, Lakewood, Ohio, 1995—. Mem. Cudell Neighborhood Improvement Corp., West Blvd. Neighborhood Assn.; trustee Malachi House. Mem. Lakewood Bus. and Profl. Women, Lakewood C. of C., City Club. Democrat. Roman Catholic. Home: 2169 Glenbury Ave Cleveland OH 44107-5413 Office: Ohio Ho of Reps Lakewood City Hall 12650 Detroit Ave Lakewood OH 44107

CAIN, RICHARD DUANE, small business owner; b. Sullivan, Ill., Mar. 18, 1941; s. Bert and Wilma Ellen (Rhodes) C.; m. Sue Ann Price, May 20, 1967; children: J. Douglas, Ryan M., Bradley P. BS, Ea. Ill. U., 1964; postgrad., U. Ill., Champaign, 1964-66. Mktg. rep. IBM Corp., Springfield, Ill., 1966-75; owner Tom's Grill, Decatur, Ill., 1975—; co-owner Lock, Stock & Barrel, Decatur, 1977-78; tchr. Richland C.C., Decatur, 1984-88. Pres. Decatur Area Convention and Vis. Bur., 1981-83. Sgt. USAR, 1960-66. Recipient Glen Hesler award Ea. Ill. U., 1989. Mem. Ea. Ill. U. Panther Club (pres. 1987), Southside Country Club (pres. 1989-90), Elks, Jaycees (pres. Decatur club 1973), Rotary (pres. Decatur club 1990). Republican. Home: 4 Montgomery Pl Decatur IL 62522-2654 Office: Toms Grill 1856 N Main St Decatur IL 62526-4332

CAIRNEY, KATHRYN JANE, economic development specialist; b. Milw., Sept. 13, 1965; d. Thomas John and Jane Elizabeth (Richards) C. BA in Journalism and Pub. Rels., U. Wis., 1988. Mgr. resource devel. Wis. Humane Soc., Milw., 1988-92; mgr. cmty. rels. Milw. Enterprise Ctr., 1992-94; v.p. Women's Bus. Initiative, Milw., 1994—; freelance cons., Milw., 1992—. Vol. Schlitz-Audubon Ctr., River Hills, Wis., 1990-91, Friends of Wis. Humane Soc., Milw., 1990-93, Nat. Conf. on Bus. Incubation, Buffalo, N.Y., 1994, Milw., 1993. Mem. Nat. Bus. Incubator Assn. (com. mem., Jefferson award 1992), Wis. Bus. Incubator Assn. (bd. dirs., v.p., Pres.'s award 1993), Nat. Soc. Fund Raising Execs. (com. mem. 1989), Wis. Econ. Devel. Assn. (com. mem. 1993—). Office: Womens Bus Initiative Corp 1915 N Martin Luther King Milwaukee WI 53212

CAIRNS, LINDSEY ELIZABETH, health and human services administrator, planner; b. Montreal, Apr. 10, 1966; d. Ian Edward and Margaret Ellen Wheatley. BA (hon.), Queen's U., Kingston, Ontario, 1988; M of Health Sci., U. Toronto, 1992. Post grad. fellow Rush-Presbyn. St. Luke's Med. Ctr., Chgo., 1992-93; govt. and external affairs specialist Chgo. Osteopathic Health Sys., Chgo., 1993-95; dir. network and bus. devel. Southside Health Consortium, Chgo., 1995—; com. mem. Il. Hosp. Assn., Naperville, 1993-94; com. chair Southside Health Consortium, Chgo., 1993-95. COntbr. articles to profl. jours. Vol., tutor Programmed Activities in Correctional Edn., Chgo., 1992—. Office: Southside Health Consortium 10 W 35th St 9th Fl Chicago IL 60616

CALABRESE, LEONARD M., social services administrator; b. Cleve., Nov. 22, 1946; s. Anthony O. and Mary M. (Buzzelli) C. BA magna cum laude, John Carroll U., 1968; MA summa cum laude, Northwestern U., Evanston, Ill., 1974; postgrad., Northwestern U., 1974-78. Cons. in neighborhood devel. Cuyahoga C.C., 1977; assoc. prof. U. Akron (Ohio), 1977-88; cons. in human resources City of Cleve., 1978; exec. dir. Commn. on Cath. Community Action, Cleve., 1987—; ofcl. election observer Nicaragua Elections, 1990; Segundo Montes lectr. John Carroll U., 1993; presenter Internat. Thomas Merton Soc. Conf., 1995. Co-author: Multicultural Diversity Training Manual, 1989; prodr. TV videos, 1985, 88. Active Witness for Peace, 1984, 86; chmn. Consumer Adv. Panel, Cleve., 1989—; commr. Cleve. Poverty Commn., 1990-93; mem. Nat. Urban Ministry Bd., 1993—; bd. dirs. Greater Cleve. Interreligious Task Force on Ctrl. Am., 1991-95, Wings of Hope, Cleve., 1991-95; bd. trustees Collinwood Art Coun., 1990-95, Greater Cleve. Substance Abuse Initiative, 1995—, Cleve. City Club Program Com., 1996; chmn. Clergy and Laity Concerned, Cleve., 1984-85; exec. com. mem. Cuyahoga County Dem. Orgn., 1978-83; nat. bd. Roundtable Soc. Action Dirs., 1995—; mem. Cleve. Workers Rights Bd., 1994—. Named Consumer of Year, Ohio Consumers Coun., Columbus, 1990; recipient William Evans New Frontier award, Am. for Dem. Action, 1991. Mem. Cleve. City Club (program com.). Office: Commn Cath Community Action 1027 Superior Ave E Cleveland OH 44114-2503

CALARCO, N. JOSEPH, theater educator; b. N.Y.C., Mar. 19, 1938; s. Charles and Vincenza (Marrara) C.; m. Margot Demarais, Mar. 1964 (div. 1981); children: Deidre L., Joseph V. AB, Columbia U., 1959, MA, 1962; PhD, U. Minn., 1966. Instr. U. Minn., Mpls., 1964-66; asst. prof. U. Calif., Berkeley, 1966-68; from asst. prof. to prof. theatre Wayne State U., Detroit, 1968—; artistic dir. Wayne State Playwrights' Workshop, 1992-94; pres. TransArt Prodns., N.Y.C., 1982-86; cons. in field. Author: Tragic Being: Apollo and Dionysus in Western Drama, 1968; (play) Telephone: A Play in Three Calls, 1990, Ajax, 1992; prin. theorist of tragedy: Tragedy and Tragic Theory: An Analytical Guide, 1992; contbr. articles to profl. jours.; dir. 50 theatrical prodns. (Best Play of Decade award 1970-80). Bd. dirs. City of Troy (Mich.) Bicentennial Ethnic Festival, 1976. Mem. Dramatists Guild, AAUP, Soc. Stage Dirs. and Choreographers, Assn. Theatre in Higher Edn. Home: 1826 Eastport Dr Troy MI 48083-1719 Office: Wayne State U Dept Theatre Detroit MI 48202

CALCAMUGGIO, LARRY GLENN, lawyer; b. Toledo, Feb. 9, 1951; s. Glenn L. and Darlene M. (Brown) C.; m. Diane L. Seagert, June 30, 1973; children: Jeffrey, Todd, Scott. BBA, U. Toledo, 1973, JD, 1977. Bar: Ohio 1977, U.S. Dist. Ct. Ohio 1979, U.S. Tax Ct. 1984. Auditor Blue Cross N.W. Ohio, Toledo, 1973-75; trust officer Ohio Citizens Bank, Toledo, 1975-78; assoc. Brown, Baker, Schlageter & Craig, Toledo, 1979-80; ptnr. Rohrs, Rimelspach & Calcamuggio, Toledo, 1980-82; trust officer new bus. BancOhio Nat. Bank, Toledo, 1982-84; pvt. practice Toledo, 1984-94; ptnr. Sprenger, Douglas and Calcamuggio Attys., Toledo, 1994-95; pvt. practice Toledo, 1996—; mem. adv. com. legal assisting tech. U. Toledo, 1980-92, instr., 1987-89. Coach Little League Baseball, 1986-92; trustee Luth. Social Svcs., Toledo, 1989-92, sec. 1992. Mem. NRA, Ohio Bar Assn., Toledo Bar Assn., Toledo Estate Planning Coun., Nat. Fedn. Ind. Bus., Toledo Planned Giving Coun. Lutheran. Office: Ste 2 4149 Holland-Sylvania Rd Toledo OH 43623-2590

CALDWELL, CARL HOWARD, dean; b. Charleston, W.Va., May 3, 1944; s. David Louis C. and Doris Kathrine (Cooper) Young; m. Carolyn Ruth Falls, Feb. 20, 1965; children: Christopher Lane, Craig Breton. BA, Anderson Coll., 1966; MA, Ohio U., 1968; PhD, Ind. U., 1975. Prof., history Manchester Coll., North Manchester, Ind., 1971-89, assoc. dean acad. affairs, 1981-84; dean acad. affairs Bridgewater (Va.) Coll., 1989-92; v.p. acad. affairs and dean Franklin (Ind.) Coll., 1992-95, v.p. adminstrn., 1995-96; v.p. acad. affairs Anderson (Ind.) U., 1996—; dir. Ind. Com. U.S.-Arab Rels., 1987-89. NEH Summer fellow, NEH, 1978. Mem. Mid-East Studies Assn., Mid-East Inst. Mem. Ch. of God.

CALDWELL, JESSIE J., quality assurance specialist; b. Ashland, Ky., Nov. 15, 1959. Gen. mgr. DMT Industries, Berea, Ohio, 1980-90; quality assurance mgr. Toolbold Corp., Berea, 1990—. Baptist. Office: Toolbold Corp PO Box 940 Berea OH 44017-0940

CALDWELL, JOHN RANKIN, internist; b. Middletown, Conn., Oct. 11, 1918; s. Rankin Sutton and Jane Brandt (Ulsh) C.; m. Julia Elinor Matthews, Oct. 4, 1947; children: John M., Ann B., Sally B., Beth A., Mark S. BA, Lafayette Coll., 1940; MD, Temple U., 1943. Diplomate Am. Bd. Internal Medicine. Resident Kent Gen. Hosp., Dover, Del., 1946-47; gen. med. practice Dover, Del., 1947-50; grad. student U. Pa., Phila., 1950-51; resident internal medicine Cleve. Clinic, 1951-52; staff physician Henry Ford Hosp., Detroit, 1952-89, head physician divsn. hypertension, 1954-67, staff physician div. metabolic disease, 1967-79, staff physician div. nephrology and hypertension, 1980-89; cons. Blue Cross-Blue Shield of Mich., Detroit, 1989-94; mem. bioethics com. Mich. State Med. Soc., East Lansing, 1989-96. Contbr. over 40 articles to profl. med. jours. Chmn. Physicians for Social Responsibility, Detroit, 1963-68; v.p. Am. Assn. for U.N., Oakland County, Mich., 1963-64, 91-93, pres., 1993-94; chmn. Hypertension Coordinating and Planning Coun. Southwestern Mich., 1973-74. Recipient Laureate award Am. Coll. Physicians, 1989, Disting. Career award Henry Ford Hosp., 1990. Fellow Coun. on High Blood Pressure Rsch., Coun. on Arterio Sclerosis, Am. Coll. Physicians; mem. AMA, Am. Soc. Internal Medicine, Sr. Men's Club of Birmingham. Home: 2259 Avon Ln Birmingham MI 48009-1510

CALDWELL, KENNETH CARSON, manufacturing engineering executive; b. Dayton, Ohio, Sept. 28, 1949; s. Monroe Emert and Myrtle Augusta (Dale) C.; m. Brenda Sue Brown, Dec. 27, 1975; children: Leah Nicole, Adam Kenneth. BSME, GM Engring. and Mgmt. Inst., Flint, Mich., 1972, MS in Mfg. Mgmt., 1988. Registered profl. egnr., Ohio. Project engr. Maremont Brake Products, Nashville, 1976-78; jr. prodn. engr. Delco Moraine div. GM, Dayton, 1972-74, prodn. engr., 1974-76, sr. mfg. engr., 1978-80, gen. supr. mfg., 1980-81, gen. supr. maintenance, 1981-86; gen. supr. mfg. engring. Delco Chassis div. GM, Dayton, 1986-94; mgr. tech. and engring. Allied Systems Automotive, Greenville, Ohio, 1994—. Author: Stack Bonding Clutch Plateswith Induction Heating, 1972. Mem., v.p., pres. Vandalia (Ohio)-Butler City Schs. Bd. Edn., 1988-95; coach Vandalia Pee Wee Football Assn., 1990-94; mem. Montgomery County Joint Vocat. Bd. Edn., Englewood, Ohio, 1991-95; active Vandalia Bapt. Temple. Mem. Ohio Sch. Bds. Assn., Gideons Internat., Lions, Lambda Chi Alpha. Republican. Baptist. Home: 8363 Frederick Pike Dayton OH 45414-1249 Office: Allied-Signal 851 Jackson St Greenville OH 45331

CALDWELL, LYNDALL S., financial advisor; b. Fairfield, Ill., Oct. 20, 1959. BS, So. Ill. U., 1982. Brokerage advisor Chgo., 1989-91; fin. advisor Edward D. Jones, Morton Grove, Ill., 1991-94, Robert Thomas Securities, Northbrook, Ill., 1995—. Reporter articles. Mem. Morton Grove C. of C., Lions (bd. dirs. 1992—). Home: 1008 N Wheeling Rd Mount Prospect IL 60056-1218 Office: Robert Thomas Securities 1353 Shermer Rd Northbrook IL 60062-4546

CALDWELL, MARY ELLEN, English language educator; b. El Paso, Ark., Aug. 6, 1908; d. Clay and Mabel Grace (Coe) Fulks; m. Robert Atchison Caldwell, Feb. 22, 1936; 1 child, Elizabeth. PhB, U. Chgo., 1931, MA, 1933. Instr. English U. Ark., Fayetteville, 1940-42, U. Toledo, 1946-48; from instr. to asst. prof. to assoc. prof. U. N.D., Grand Forks, 1966-79, assoc. prof. emeritus, 1979—, prof. ext. divsn., 1979—. Author: North Dakota Division of the American Association of University Women, 1930-63, A History, 1964; co-author: The North Dakota Division of the American Association of University Women, 1964-84, 2d vol., 1984; contbr. revs. and articles to scholarly jours. Sec. citizen's com. Grand Forks Symphony Assn., 1960-66. Mem. AAUW (life, N.D. state pres. 1968-70), P.E.O., MLA (life), Soc. for Study of Midwestern Lit. (bibliography staff 1973—), Linguistic Cir. of Man. and N.D. (pres. 1981), Melville Soc. Democrat. Episcopalian. Home: 514 Oxford St Grand Forks ND 58203-2847

CALDWELL, SARAH, opera producer, conductor, stage director and administrator; b. Maryville, Mo., Mar. 6, 1924. Student, U. Ark., Hendrix Coll., New Eng. Conservatory, Berkshire Music Ctr., Tanglewood, Mass.; D. Mus. (hon.), Harvard U., Simmons Coll., Bates Coll., Bowdoin Coll. Mem. faculty Berkshire Music Ctr.; dir. Boston U. Opera Workshop, 1953-57; created dept. music theater Boston U.; founded Boston Opera Group (later became Opera Co. of Boston), 1957, sinced served as artistic dir. and condr. Asst. to Boris Goldovsky in direction of New Eng. Opera Co.; operatic directorial debut with Rake's Progress, Opera Workshop, 1953; operatic debut as condr. with Opera Group of Boston, 1957, Carnegie Hall debut with Am. Symphony Orch., 1974; condr. and/or dir. maj. opera cos. in U.S., including N.Y. Met. Opera, Dallas Civic Opera, Houston Grand Opera, N.Y.C. Opera; condr. with maj. orchs. including: Indpls. Symphony, Milw. Symphony, Am. Symphony, N.Y. Philharmonic; condr. at Ravinia Festival, 1976. Recipient Rogers and Hammerstein award.

CALE, JOHN WESLEY, software engineer; b. Springfield, Mo., May 21, 1918; s. John Wesley and Tillie Louise (Parmenter) C.; m. Beryl Opal Burke, June 22, 1941 (div. 1951); children: Vivienne Sheila, Alan Nelson; m. Mary Catherine Brixey, Apr. 2, 1978. B of Religious Edn., New Orleans Bapt. Theol. Sem., 1950; DPs, Loyola U., 1968. Coun. chief N.C. Cherokee Nation, 1944—; quality control engr. electrician Boeing Airplane Co., Wichita, Kans., 1951-56; chief electronics engr. Electronics Labs., Norwood, Mo., 1956-94, software engr., 1993—; Native Am. chief Black Bear Clan, Springfield, 1994—; bd. dirs. S.W. Mo. Indian Ctr.; cons. SeMaNo Elec. Co., Mansfield, Mo., 1956-75. Author computer software. Sgt. USAF, 1938-45. Decorated ETO medal with 2 bronze stars, Victory medal and Am. Def. medal. Native American. Home: 1154 S Pickwick Ave Springfield MO 65804

CALEY, DIANE LEE, library administrator; b. Minot, N.D., Sept. 7, 1935; d. Cyrus and Annette Karine (Lee) Ronnie; m. Carroll Dean Caley, Nov. 25, 1955; 1 child, Christopher Dean. BS, Minot State U., 1972. Libr. asst. Minot Pub. Libr., 1951-67; libr. adminstr. Ward County Pub. Libr., Minot, 1967—. Contbr. articles to profl. jours. Fed. rels. coord. for N.D., Washington, 1990-91; del. White House conf. on Libr. and Info. Svcs., Washington, 1991. Mem. ALA, N.D. Libr. Assn. (chair pub. libr. sect. 1971-82, chair membership com. 1983-85, pres. 1988-90, Presdl. award 1985), Mountain Plains Libr. Assn., Souris Valley Libr. Assn., Thor Lodge/Sons of Norway. Lutheran. Home: 1932 Anderson Dr Minot ND 58703 Office: Ward County Pub Libr 405 3d Ave SE Minot ND 58701

CALHOUN, LARRY DARRYL, art educator; b. Revere, Mo., Oct. 9, 1937; s. Adren Kieth and Neva Isabel (Parker) C.; m. Marilyn Gail Walker, June 9, 1959; children: Eric, Rachael, Robin. BA in Art, Iowa Wesleyan, 1959; MA in Art, U. Iowa, 1961. Art instr. Westmar Coll., LeMars, Iowa, 1961-63; assoc. prof. art Millikin U., Decatur, Ill., 1963-70; assoc. prof. ceramics U. Akron, 1970-76; artist in residence Ill. Arts Coun., Decatur, Ill., 1977; chair, dept. art MacMurray Coll., Jacksonville, 1978—; owner Village Arts, Jacksonville, 1978—; painter, 1989—; ceramist pottery and sculpture, 1961-89. Woodrow Wilson fellowship U. Iowa, 1960-61. Mem. NAACP, AAUP (pres. 1992—). Office: MacMurray Coll 400 E College Ave Jacksonville IL 62650

CALHOUN, LYLA LEA, clinical social worker, consultant; b. Holdrege, Nebr., July 3, 1934; d. Lyle Curtis and Bula Beatrice (Kent) Spongberg; m. Donald Ray Calhoun, Mar. 6, 1954; children: Dennis Blake, Sheryl Ann Calhoun Montford, Shaun Patrick, Scott Alan. Student, Friends U., Wichita, Kans., 1952-53; BA, Wichita State U., 1974; MS in Social Adminstrn., Case Western Res. U., 1986. Diplomate in Clin. Social Work, lic. ind. social worker, Ohio. Social worker ARC, Wichita, 1973-75, Mo. Dept. Human Svcs., Union, 1977-78; clin. social worker Cath. Social Svc. Bur., Medina, Ohio, 1981—, Cornerstone Psychol. Svcs., Medina, 1993—; cons. Hospice Medina County, Medina, 1986-91, Tri County Home Health, 1993-95, Medina County Health Dept., 1989—. Mem. adv. bd. Medina County Ext. Agy., 1985—, Adult Edn. Joint Vocat. Sch., Medina, 1989—, Dept. Human Svcs., Medina, 1989-91; bd. dirs. ARC, Medina, 1980-90. Mem. NASW, Ohio Assn. Social Workers, Mental Health Profls. of Medina County (program chmn. 1990-93, pres. 1994-95). Republican. Mem. Christian Ch. (Disciples of Christ). Home: 3558 Country Club Dr Medina OH 44256 Office: Cath Social Svc Bur 246 Northland Dr Medina OH 44256-1533

CALHOUN, WILLIAM, research pharmacologist; b. Abington, Pa., Nov. 21, 1948; s. John and Olga (Belevich) C.; m. Deborah Jean Kupec, Apr. 18, 1978; 1 child, Jeffrey. BS, Ashland (Ohio) U., 1970; MS, Duquesne Univ., 1972. Med. writer Franklin Inst., Phila., 1975-76; rsch. asst. Temple U., Phila., 1976-78, Osteopathic Med. Ctr. of Phila., 1978-84; sr. scientist Wyeth-Ayerst Rsch., Princeton, N.J., 1984-89; rsch. pharmacologist Abbott Labs., Abbott Park, Ill., 1989-91, clin. rsch. assoc., 1991-95; cons., clin. rsch. assoc. Trilogy Cons. Corp., Waukegan, Ill., 1995—. Contbr. articles to profl. jours. Pres. Jaycees, Hatboro, Pa., 1983-84; advisor ARC, Mundelein, Ill., 1990-93; vice chmn., bd. dirs. Warminster Vol. Ambulance Corp., 1980-84.

Recipient Excellence award ARC, 1991, Outstanding Young Citizen U.S. Jaycees, 1979. Mem. Am. Soc. for Pharmacology and Exptl. Therapeutics, Toastmasters Internat. (area gov., club treas., club pres.), Sigma Xi. Democrat. Presbyterian.

CALLAHAN, DOROTHY MOTT, educational program director; b. Jersey City, N.J., May 4, 1942; d. Raymond F. and Helene A. (Tierney) Mott; children: Christine, Robert, Thomas, Timothy. BS in Home Econs., U. Nebr., Omaha, 1964; MS, U. Nebr., Lincoln, 1977. Counselor, field rep. Alpha Xi Delta Sorority, Evanston, Ill., 1964-65; instr. YWCA, Omaha, 1969-71; ext. agt. home econs. Nebr. Coop. Ext., Omaha, 1974-85; ext. agt., chair U. Nebr. Lincoln Coop. Ext., Omaha, 1985—. Mem. Nat. Assn. Ext. Home Econs. (Disting. Svc. award 1987), Nat. Assn. Ext. 4-H Agts. (Nat. Comms. award 1986, Disting. Svc. 1985), Nebr. Coop. Ext. Assn. (Disting. Ext. Agt. 1991, pres. 1992-93), Nebr. Home Econs. Asn. (conf. chair 1989-90), Omaha Agri-Bus. Assn. (pres. 1988-89), Omicron Nu, Epsilon Sigma Phi. Office: Cooperative Ext 8015 W Center Rd Omaha NE 68124-3106

CALLAHAN, JEAN LESLIE, educator, artist; b. Chgo., Oct. 25, 1937; d. Aaron S. Jr. and Joyce A. (Potter) Gourfain; m. Thomas F. Callahan, Oct. 19, 1963 (dec. July 1977); 1 child, Max G. Ethan. BFA, Art Inst. Chgo., 1959; cert. tchg., U. Chgo., 1960, MA in Social Scis., 1986; cert. tchg., Inst. for Psychoanalysis, Chgo., 1981; cert. hatha yoga, Temple Kriya Yoga, Chgo., 1994. Cert. tchr., Ill., cert. tchr. Hatha Yoga. Presch. art tchr. Y.M.J.C. Youth Ctr., Chgo., 1961-64; kindergarten Bret Harte Sch., Chgo., 1964-67, Kozminski Sch., Chgo., 1967-68, Einstein/Judd Schs., Chgo., 1968-69; kindergarten and primary grades tchr. Judd Sch., Chgo., 1969-71; primary grade tchr. Woodson South Elem. Sch., Chgo., 1981-87; primary grade tchr. Wm. H. Ray Elem. Sch., Chgo., 1987—, grade level chmn., 1994-95; tchr. yoga Temple of Kriya Yoga and Quaker House, Chgo., 1994-95. Artist numerous paintings; author poetry. Recipient scholarships Art Inst. Ch., 1955-59; grantee Chgo. Found. for Edn., 1994-95.

CALLANAN, KATHLEEN JOAN, retired electrical engineer; b. Detroit, Feb. 10, 1940; d. John Michael and Grace Marie (Kleehammer) C. BSE in Physics, U. Mich., 1963; postgrad. in physics Northeastern U., 1963-65; MSEE, U. Hawaii, 1971; diploma in Japanese lang. St. Joseph Inst. Japanese Studies, Tokyo, 1973; cert. in mgmt. Boeing Mil. Airplane Co. Employee Devel., 1985. Vis. scholar Sophia U., Tokyo, 1976-79; elec.-electronic components engr. Boeing Mil. Airplane Co. (named changed to Boeing Def. and Space Group-Product Support Div.), Wichita, Kans., 1979-83, instrumentation design engr., 1983-85, strategic planner for tech., 1985-86, research and engring. tech. supr., 1986-87, electromagnetic effects avionics mgr., 1987-89, elec. and electronics mgr., 1989, design tech. support mgr., 1990-92, engring. leader, 1992-95, ret. 1995. Contbr. articles to profl. jours. Mem. Rose Hill Planning Commn., Kans., 1982-85; coord. Boeing Employees Amateur Radio Soc., Wichita, 1982-83, sec., 1991. Fellow Soc. Women Engrs. (sr. mem., sect. rep. 1981-83, sec. treas. 1985-86, regional bd. dirs. 1983-85, sect. pres. 1987-88); mem. Bus. and Profl. Women, Quarter Century Wireless Assn. (communications com. 1985-86), Assn. of Old Crows (bd. dirs. 1988-91, chpt. pres. 1991). Lodge: Toastmasters (local pre pres. 1985-86, competent toastmaster 1985). Avocations: amateur radio, singing, bowling. Home: 456 Emden St Fort Myers FL 33903-2194

CALLANDER, KAY EILEEN PAISLEY, business owner, retired gifted talented education educator, writer; b. Coshocton, Ohio, Oct. 15, 1938; d. Dalton Olas and Dorothy Pauline (Davis) Paisley; m. Don Larry Callander, Nov. 18, 1977. BSE, Muskingum Coll., 1960; MA in Speech Edn., Ohio State U., 1964, postgrad., 1964-84. Cert. elem., gifted, drama, theater tchr., Ohio. Tchr. Columbus (Ohio) Pub. Schs., 1960-70, 80-88, drama specialist, 1970-80, classroom, gifted/talented tchr., 1986-90, ret., 1990; sole prop. The Ali Group, Kay Kards, 1992—; coord. Artists-in-the Schs., 1977-88; cons., presenter numerous ednl. confs. and sems., 1971—; mem., ednl. cons. Innovation Alliance Youth Adv. Coun., 1992—. producer-dir., Shady Lane Music Festival, 1980-88; dir. tchr. (nat. distbr. video) The Trial of Gold E. Locks, 1983-88; rep., media pub. relations liason Sch. News., 1983-88; author, creator Trivia Game About Black Americans (TGABA), exhibitor of TGABA game at L.A. County Office Edn. Conf., 1990; presenter for workshop by Human Svc. Group and Creative Edn. Coop., Columbus, Ohio, 1989. Benefactor, Columbus Jazz Arts Group; v.p., bd. dirs. Neoteric Dance and Theater Co., Columbus, 1985-87; tchr., participant Future Stars sculpture exhibit, Ft. Hayes Ctr., Columbus Pub. Schs., 1988; tchr. advisor Columbus Coun. PTAs, 1983-86, co-chmn. reflections com., 1984-87; mem. Columbus Mus. Art, Citizens for Humane Action, Inc.; mem. supt.'s adv. coun. Columbus Pub. Schs., 1967-68; presenter Young Author Seminar, Ohio Dept. Edn., 1988, Illustrating Methods for Young Authors' Books, 1986-87; cons. and workshop leader seminar/workshop Tchg. About the Constitution in Elem. Schs., Franklin County Ednl. Coun., 1988; sponsor Minority Youth Recognition Awards, 1994. Named Educator of Yr., Shady Lane PTA, 1982, Columbus Coun. PTAs, 1989, winner Colour Columbus Landscape Design Competition, 1990; Sch. Excellence grantee Columbus Pub. Schs.; Commendation Columbus Bd. Edn. and Ohio Ho. of Reps. for Child Assault Prevention project, 1986-87; first place winner statewide photo contest Ohio Vet. Assn., 1991; recipient Muskingum Coll. Alumni Disting. Svc. award, 1995. Mem. ASCD, AAUW, Assn. for Childhood Edn. Internat., Ohio Coun. for Social Studies, Franklin County Ret. Tchrs. Assn., Nat. Mus. Women in the Arts, Ohio State U. Alumni Assn., U.S. Army Officers Club, Navy League, Liturgical Art Guild Ohio, Columbus Jazz Arts Group, Columbus Mus. Art, Nat. Coun. for Social Studies, Columbus Art League, Columbus Maennerchor (Damen sect.). Republican. Home: 2323 Colts Neck Rd Blacklick OH 43004-9648 Office: The Ali Group Kay Kards PO Box 13093 Columbus OH 43213-0093

CALLAWAY, KAREN A(LICE), journalist; b. Daytona Beach, Fla., Sept. 5, 1946; d. Robert Clayton III and Alice Johnston (Webb) C. BS in Journalism, Northwestern U., 1968. Copy editor Detroit Free Press, 1968-69; asst. woman's editor, features copy editor, news copy editor, asst. makeup editor Chgo. Am. and Chgo. Today, 1969-74; asst. makeup editor Chgo. Tribune, 1974-76, asst. news editor, 1976-81, assoc. news editor spl. sect., 1981—, assoc. news editor vertical publs., 1993—; adviser Jr. Achievement Tribune sponsored co., Chgo., 1976-77; editor Infant Mortality sect., 1989; vis. prof. student chpt. Soc. Profl. Journalists, Northwestern U., 1989. Chmn. class of 1968 20th reunion Northwestern U., 1989, mem. seminar day com., 1989-90, chmn., 1991, mem. alumni bd. dirs. Medill Sch. Journalism, 1991-95, ex-officio mem., 1995—; vol. Northwestern U. Settlement House. Mem. Soc. of Profl. Journalists, Sigma Delta Chi, Kappa Delta. Methodist. Office: Chicago Tribune 435 N Michigan Ave Ste 573 Chicago IL 60611-4001

CALLAWAY, RICHARD EARL, dentist; b. Des Moines, Aug. 9, 1951; s. Grover Earl and Geraldine Anna (Dageforde) C.; m. Nancy Jean Clark, May 2, 1981; children: Scott, Jessica, Lindsey, Rachel. BA, Mo. Western State Coll., 1974; DDS, U. Mo., Kansas City, 1978. Gen. practice dentistry Fremont, Nebr., 1978—. Bd. dirs. Fremont Big Bros./Big Sisters, 1981-87. Named one of Outstanding Young Men of Am., Fremont Jaycees, 1985. Mem. ADA, Nebr. Dental Assn., Omaha Dist. Dental Assn., Tri Valley Dental Soc. (treas. 1980, v.p. 1981), Fremont Jaycees (bd. dirs. 1979-85, v.p. 1985-86, pres. 1986-87), Fremont Tennis Assn. Republican. Lutheran. Lodge: Optimists. Home: 545 N Platte Ave Fremont NE 68025-5273 Office: 1835 E Military Ave Fremont NE 68025-5465

CALLECOD, JOAN D., stockbroker, accountant, auditor; b. Chgo., July 20, 1940; m. Robert Callecod; children: Kimberly Callecod Weinrich, Jennifer, Melissa Callecod Myerholtz. BA in Polit. Sci., Knox Coll., 1962. CPA, Ohio. Auditor IRS, Chgo., 1962-65, MidAm Inc., Bowling Green, Ohio, 1988-91; tax preparer, 1963-75; acct. Karl Somekawa, Wayzata, Minn., 1975-80, Buckingham & Assocs., Findley, Ohio, 1985-88; pvt. practice acctg., Maple Plain, Minn., 1980-85; stockbroker Robert Thomas Securities, Bowling Green, Ohio, 1991—; mem. adv. bd. Cmty. Employment Svc., Bowling Green, 1992—. Trustee First Step, Fremont, Ohio, 1993—, 1st Presbyn. Ch., Bowling Green, 1991-93. Mem. AICPA, Ohio Soc. CPA's, Bowling Green C. of C. (exec. bd. 1993—), Kiwanis (trustee Bowling Green 1993—), B.G.B.N.I. Office: Robert Thomas Securities 745 Haskins Rd Bowling Green OH 43402-1600

CALLEN, RONALD CORLETTE, commissioner, state; b. Port Allegany, Pa., Sept. 25, 1932; s. Harold Napier and Alice Leona (Keagle) C.; m. Carolyn Mae Kamans, Aug. 2, 1957; children: Bruce, Paul, Philip. BA, Wabash Coll., 1954; MA in Physics, Wesleyan U., 1957. Sr. physicist Pratt-Whitney Aircraft, Middletown, Conn., 1957-63; asst. project engr. Atomic Power Devel. Assocs., Detroit, 1963-73; asst. dir. of planning Mich. Pub. Svc. Commn., Lansing, 1973—; exec. dir. nuclear waste program, evaluation office Nat. Assn. of Regulatory Utility Commrs., Washington, 1990-92; cons. U.S. Nuclear Regulatory Commn.; adj. assoc. prof. Mich. State U., East Lansing. Chmn. State Intergovtl. Environ. Rev. Com.; task force chmn. Gov.'s Spl. Commn. on Energy; liaison to Mich. Air Pollution Control Commn., Mich. Environ. Rev. Bd.; co-founder, rep. State Working Group on High Level Nuclear Waste, exec. com. mem.; mem. gov.'s adv. com. on High Level Nuclear Waste Disposal; mem. gov.'s task force on Nuclear Waste. Mem. Nuclear Waste Strategy Coalition (founder, contbr.). Home: 501 McPherson Ave Lansing MI 48915 Office: Mich Pub Svc Commn PO Box 30221 Lansing MI 48909

CALLENDER, JAMES SUTTON, JR., lawyer; b. Mayfield, Ky., Jan. 9, 1965; s. James Sutton Sr. and Patricia Rhea (Dycus) C.; m. Andrea Lynn Schembre, June 11, 1990; 1 child, Ashley Rhea. BA in History, Cleve. State U., 1989; JD, Cleve. Marshall Law Sch., 1992. Bar: Ohio 1992. Assoc. Robert H. Myers, Jr. & Assocs., Painesville, Ohio, 1992-94; ptnr. James S. Callender Jr., Painesville, 1994—. Chmn., pres. Retinitis Pigmentosa Found., Cleve., 1990-93; chmn. Willowick (Ohio) Recreation Bd., 1992-94; vice chmn. bd. trustees Lake County (Ohio) Hist. Soc., 1994—; mem. exec. com. and ctrl. com. Lake County Republican Party. Mem. ABA, Ohio State Bar Assn., Lake County Bar Assn. (grievance com.), Masons. Methodist. Home: 29227 Oakdale Willowick OH 44095 Office: 56 Liberty St Ste 302 Painesville OH 44077

CALLESEN-GYORGAK, JAN ELAINE, special education educator; b. Manistee, Mich., Sept. 21, 1959; d. Carl Wayne and Patsy Arlene (Haglund) Callesen; m. Gregg Gyorgak, Oct. 27, 1990; children: Danielle Marie, Nathaniel Charles, Kristen Lynn, Wayne Anthony. BS in Edn., Bowling Green State U., 1981; M in Curriculum and Instrn., Cleve. State U., 1988. Lic. elem. edn., spl. edn., libr. and media scis. Montessori tchr. Children's Home of Parma (Ohio), 1981-82; kindergarten tchr., coord. Murton's Child Devel. Ctr., Fairview Park, Ohio, 1983-85; spl. edn. tchr.-learning disabilities Cleve. Pub. Schs., 1985—; advisor Safety Patrol, Cleve., 1986—. Mem. ASCD, Cleve. Tchrs. Union, Coun. for Exceptional Children (divsn. learning disabilities). Home: 6283 Surrey Dr North Olmsted OH 44070-4813 Office: Walton Elem Sch 3409 Walton Ave Cleveland OH 44113-4942

CALLIS, PEGGY, library director; b. Princeton, Ind., Apr. 1, 1935; d. Harry Dorsey and Mary Duncan (Fitzsimmons) Keneipp; m. Darwin E. Callis, Feb. 9, 1957; children: Jean Ann Callis Edwards, Eric A. Callis. Student, Ind. U., 1963-55. Acting librarian Owensville (Ind.) Carnegie Pub. Libr., 1978—; chair small libr. divsn. ILF, 1995. Named Citizen of Yr. Watermelon Festival, Owensville, 1991. Mem. Owensville Alumni Assn. (bd. dirs. 1993—). United Methodist. Home: RR 3 Box 130 Owensville IN 47665 Office: Owensville Carnegie Pub Libr 110 S Main St Owensville IN 47665

CALLOW, WILLIAM GRANT, retired state supreme court justice; b. Waukesha, Wis., Apr. 9, 1921; s. Curtis Grant and Mildred G. C.; m. Jean A. Zilavy, Apr. 15, 1950; children: William G., Christine S., Katherine H. PhB in Econs, U. Wis., 1943, JD, 1948. Bar: Wis. Asst. city atty. Waukesha, 1948-52; city atty., 1952-60; county judge Waukesha, 1961-77; justice Supreme Ct. Wis., Madison, 1978-92; asst. prof. U. Minn., 1951-52; mem. faculty Wis. Jud. Coll., 1968-75; Wis. commr. Nat. Conf. Commrs. on Uniform State Laws, 1967—; arbitrator Wis. Employment Rel. Commn.; arbitrator-mediator bus. disputes; arbitration and mediation nat. and internat. res. judge, 1992—. With USMC, 1943-45, with USAF, 1951-52, Korea. With USMC, 1943-45; with USAF, 1951-52, Korea. Recipient Outstanding Alumnus award U. Wis., 1973. Fellow Am. Bar Found.; mem. ABA, Dane County Bar Assn., Waukesha County Bar Assn. Episcopalian.

CALO-ILORETA, MARIA DELIA, nursing educator; b. Butuan City, Agusan, The Philippines, Sept. 28, 1948; d. Salvador Leyson Calo and Dominica Montilla (Sanchez) Calo; m. Alfredo Tabutol Iloreta, May 30, 1980; children: Jaymarc, Sal Francis, Joseph. BSN, U. St. Tomas, The Philippines, 1969; MA in Nursing, NYU, 1977. RN, N.J., N.Y., Kans. Faculty U. St. Tomas, 1969-72; nurse Clara Maass Meml. Hosp., Belleville, N.J., 1973-75, Lenox Hill Hosp., N.Y.C., 1975-79; nursing educator Quality Seminars, Topeka, Kans., 1987—. Sec. Shawnee County Med. Alliance, Topeka, 1993-94; bd. dirs. Internat. Ctr. Topeka, 1993-94. Growth Thru Investment Club (founder, pres. 1994), Filipino-Am. Assn. (founder, sec. 1986-87, pres. 1993-94), U. St. Tomas Alumni Assn. (chmn. scholarship com. 1989-95, sec. 1989-94, lectr.), Sigma Theta Tau. Republican. Roman Catholic. Home: 6715 SW Sherwood Ct Topeka KS 66614

CALVIN, ROCHELLE ANN, development association adminstrator; b. St. Paul, Feb. 28, 1936; d. Peter Herbert and Leah (Noun) Schaffer; m. Arnold Orloff, 1957 (div. 1984); children: Robin, Nadine, Steven; m. Stafford R. Calvin, Nov. 25, 1988. BA, U. Minn., 1958. Dir. woman's divsn. United Jewish Fund, St. Paul, 1979-91, devel. dir., 1991—. Pres. Hadassah, St. Paul, 1977. Jewish. Office: United Jewish Fund 790 Cleveland Ave S Saint Paul MN 55116-1958

CALVIN, STAFFORD RICHARD, academic administrator; b. St. Paul Apr. 6, 1931; s. Carl and Zelda Ida (Engelson) C.; m. Nancy Goldberg (div. 1984); m. Rochelle Ann Schaffer, Nov. 26, 1988; children: Lawrence, Carlton, Loran. BA, U. Minn. 1952, MFA, U. Mexico City, 1954. Pres. Sibley Co., St. Paul, 1953-58, Dealers Distbrs., St. Paul, 1958-65; v.p. Internat. Systems Assn., N.Y.C., 1965-70, Carlson Cos., Mpls., 1970-74; chief exec. officer Calstar, Mpls., 1974-85; v.p. Acad. Learning Ctrs., Inc., St. Paul, 1988-90, pres. Calvin Acad., 1991—; Founder Inst. Essential Edn. Author: Save Your Child, 1989. Democrat. Jewish. Avocations: performing arts, biking, rafting. Office: Calvin Acad 2500 Cleveland Ave N Saint Paul MN 55113-2728

CAMACCI, MICHAEL A., commercial real estate broker, development consultant; b. Youngstown, Ohio, Feb. 6, 1951; s. Martin B. and Viola F. (Conti) C.; m. Susan Hawkins, Oct. 18, 1985; 1 child, Michael Philip. BBA, Youngstown Coll., 1974. Cert. bus. analyst. Acct. U.S. Steel Corp., Youngstown, 1969-80; mgr. sales Soc. Realty, Boardman, Ohio, 1980-81; dir. sales Pop-ins Maid Services, Columbiana, Ohio, 1981-82; bus. broker Eranco Assocs., Girard, Ohio, 1982-86; pres. JMC Realty, Inc., Youngstown, 1986—; pres., broker Camacci Real Estate, 1986—; pres. Hillview Nursing Home, 1988—, Valley View Nursing Home, 1990—, Pyramid Printing, Inc., 1991—; v.p. Wedgewood Property Mgmt., Inc. Mem. Youngstown-Warren Regional Growth Alliance; v.p. Austintown Growth Found. Served with U.S. Army, 1971-77. Mem. Am. Health Care Assn., Ohio Health Care Assn., Nat. Assn. Printers and Lithographers, Internat. Coun. Shopping Ctrs., Youngstown-Warren Area C. of C., Columbiana Area C. of C. Democrat. Roman Catholic. Office: Camacci Real Estate Inc 5533 Mahoning Ave Youngstown OH 44515

CAMARGO, MARTIN JOSEPH, English literature educator; b. Flushing, N.Y., July 23, 1950; s. Mario and Veronica (Burg) C.; m. Sandra Stein, June 6, 1987. AB, Princeton U., 1972; PhD, U. Ill., 1978. Asst. prof. U. Ala., Tuscaloosa, 1979-80; vis. asst. prof. U. Mo., Columbia, 1978-79, asst. prof. English, 1980-85, assoc. prof., 1985-92, prof., 1992—, dir. grad. studies dept. English, 1990-93; essays editor The Mo. Rev., Columbia, 1981-87, 89-90. Author: The Middle English Verse Love Epistle, 1991, Medieval Rhetorics of Prose Composition, 1995; author monograph. Fulbright fellow, Paris, 1974-75; ACLS rsch. fellow, 1984, 96—; Humboldt Rsch. fellow, Tuebingen, West Germany, 1987-88. Mem. MLA (assembly del. 1988-91), Internat. Soc. for History of Rhetoric, Medieval Acad. Am., New Chaucer Soc. Home: 1811 Highridge Dr Columbia MO 65203-1935 Office: U Mo Dept English 107 Tate Hall Columbia MO 65211

CAMBERS, PHILIP WILLIAM, music minister, music educator, pastor; b. Kansas City, Mo., May 5, 1957; s. William Hammond Cambers and Mary Elisabeth (Sharp) Kehrer; m. Sharon Kay thompson, Apr. 28, 1984; children: Ashley Carmen, Jeffrey Philip, Scott William. B of Music Edn., Cen. Mo. State U., 1979, BA of Sci. Edn., 1979. Lic. to preach Assemblies of God, 1987; cert. tchr. music and French. Youth min. First Assembly of God, St. Joseph, Mo., 1982; min. of music Calvary Assembly of God, Toledo, 1982-85, First Assembly of God, Mobile, Ala., 1985, N. Highland Assembly of God, Columbus, Ga., 1985-86, Southside Assembly of God, Jackson, Miss., 1986-92; with First Assembly of God, Honolulu, 1992-94, 1st Assembly of God Ch., East Lansing, Mich., 1994-95; min. of music 1st Assembly of God Ch., Toledo, 1994—; sr. pastor New Life Assembly of God Ch., Ann Arbor, 1995—; tchr. music Calvary Christian Sch., Toledo, 1982-85, Briarcrest Christian Sch., Columbus, Ga., 1985-86, Southside Christian Sch., Jackson, Miss., 1986-92; sr. pastor New Life Assembly of God, Ann Arbor, Mich., 1993—; dist. music dir. Miss. Dist. Coun., Assembly of God, Jackson, 1986-92; host Miss. Dist. Coun. Choral Workshop, Jackson, 1987; adjudicator Nat. Fine Arts Festival Assembly of God, Springfield, Mo., 1988; choral clinician Evangel Assembly of God, Columbus, Miss., 1988-90. Contbr. articles to profl. jours. Choir dir. Children's Choir & Handbell Choir (for nursing homes), Jackson, 1989-90; handbell choir dir. TV comml. Sta. WAPT-TV, Jackson, 1990. Recipient First Place Nat. Assn. Tchrs. Singing, 1979. Mem. Am. Guild English Handbell, Am. Choral Dir.'s Assn. Home: 2112 Ann Arbor Saline Rd Ann Arbor MI 48103 Office: New Life Assembly of God Ch 2118 Ann Arbor Saline Rd Ann Arbor MI 48103

CAMBONI, SILVANA MARIA, resources sociologist; b. Columbus, Ohio; d. Louis and Margherita (DeFeo) C. BA, Ohio State U., 1970, MA, 1971, PhD, 1984. Rsch. assoc. II Ohio State U., Columbus, 1982-84; asst. dir. The Ohio State U. Rsch. Found., Columbus, 1985-88; assoc. dir. rsch. devel. Ohio State U. Rsch. Found., Columbus, 1988—; adj. asst. prof. Ohio State U., 1987—; faculty assoc. The Mershon Ctr., Columbus, 1990-92; dir., founder Human and Natural Resources Preservation Ctr., Columbus, 1988—. Co-editor book; contbr. articles to profl. jours., chpts. to books. Founding com. Hunger & Devel. Coalition of Ohio, Columbus, 1984; dir. pub. rels. UNICEF, Franklin County, 1972. USDA rsch. grantee, 1991, Mershon Ctr. rsch. grantee, 1990. Mem. AAAS, Gamma Sigma Delta. Office: The Ohio State Univ Rsch Found 1960 Kenny Rd Columbus OH 43210-1016

CAMBRIDGE, WILLIAM G., federal judge; b. 1931. BS, U. Nebr., 1953, JD, 1955. With Madgett, Hunter and Cambridge, 1957-63; pvt. practice law Hastings, Nebr., 1964-81; judge 10th Jud. Dist. Nebr., 1981-88; judge U.S. Dist. Ct. Nebr., Omaha, 1988-94, chief judge, 1994—. Hon. trustee Hastings (Nebr.) Coll. 1st lt. U.S. Army, 1955-57, USAR, 1957-65. Mem. ABA, Nebr. Bar Assn., Omaha Bar Assn., 10th Jud. Dist. Bar Assn., Adams County Bar Assn. Office: US Dist Ct PO Box 1076-dts Omaha NE 68101-1076

CAMDEN, DAVID GEORGE, sales executive; b. Hinsdale, Ill., Jan. 21, 1951; s. Kenneth George and Jeanne Audrey (Finnegan) C.; m. Marilyn Lee Childress, July 10, 1976; 1 child, Christopher. BS, Western Ill. U., 1974. Field rep. GMAC, Westchester, Ill., 1974-76; various field and staff positions Chrysler Corp., Elk Grove, Ill., 1976-82; merchandising mgr. Toyota Motor Distbrs., Inc., Englewood, Colo., 1982-84; field ops. mgr. Toyota Motor Distbrs., Inc., Carol Stream, Ill., 1984-86, sr. field ops. mgr., 1986-87; asst. gen. mgr. Toyota Motor Distbrs., Inc., Englewood, 1987-88; sr. asst. gen. mgr. Toyota Motor Distbrs., Inc., West Caldwell, N.J., 1988-93; gen. mgr. Toyota Motor Sales USA, Kansas City, Mo., 64153. Home: 6162 N Mattox Rd Kansas City MO 64151-2500 Office: Toyota Motor Sales USA Kans City Region 11111 NW Airworld Dr Kansas City MO 64153

CAMENGA, DAVID LEROY, neurologist, educator; b. New Berlin, N.Y., Aug. 26, 1938; s. Kenneth Arnold and Evalyn Rosanna (Skaggs) C.; m. Mary Ruth Tilton, June 14, 1959 (div. Mar. 1986); children: Craig Steven, David Lloyd, James Kenneth; m. Joanna Lubicz Woyciechowska, Dec. 31, 1986 (div. Mar. 1993). BS in Quantitative Biology, MIT, 1960; MS in Neurophysiology, U. Wis., 1964, MD, 1965. Diplomate Am. Bd. Psychiatry and Neurology. Intern in internal medicine New England Ctr. Hosp., Boston, 1965-66; resident in neurology Barnes Hosp., Washington U., St. Louis, 1966-69; NINCDS fellow Johns Hopkins U. Sch. Hygiene and Pub. Health, Balt., 1971-73; asst. prof. neurology Emory U. Sch. Medicine, Atlanta, 1973-77; asst. prof. then assoc. prof. neurology U. Md. Sch. Medicine, Balt., 1977-87; neurologist The Duluth (Minn.) Clinic, Ltd., 1987—, chief sect. neurology, 1994—; clin. assoc. prof. U. Minn. Sch. Medicine, Duluth, 1988—; exch. scientist Fogarty Internat. Ctr., Polish Ministry of Health, Warsaw, 1986; assoc. med. dir. Duluth Comprehensive Multiple Sclerosis Ctr., 1988-93, med. dir., 1996; lectr. in field. Author: (with others) Neurologic Emergencies, 2d edit., 1990; contbr. articles to profl. jours. Surgeon USPHS, 1969-71. Recipient Borden Undergrad. Rsrch. award Borden Corp., 1965. Fellow Am. Acad. Neurology; mem. AMA, Minn. Med. Soc. Office: Duluth Clinic Ltd 400 E 3rd St Duluth MN 55805-1951

CAMERA, CHARLES VINCENT, city administrator; b. Lorain, Ohio, Dec. 28, 1954; s. Carmello Leonardo and Carmella Maria (Iemma) C.; m. Kimberly Jean Camera, June 5, 1993; children: Paul, Vincenzo, Mario. Student, LCCC, Elyria, Ohio, 1973, 81—. Laborer City of Lorain, 1976-79, utilityman, 1979-80, operator, 1980-84, heavy equipment operator, 1984-85, foreman, 1985-86, asst.supt., 1986-91, supr. of streets, 1991—; mem. Lorain Beautification Com., 1994—; chair Cmty. Gardens, Lorain, 1993—; mem. Issue II Com., Lorain, 1988—. Bldg. and grounds dir., v.p. Lorain Youth Baseball, 1991—; mem. bldg. fund St. Anthony's Ch., Lorain, 1994—. Mem. City of Lorain Mmgt. Group. Democrat. Roman Catholic.

CAMERIUS, JAMES WALTER, marketing educator, corporate researcher; b. Chgo., June 14, 1939; s. Wilbert Albert and Violet Elna (Johnson) C. BS, No. Mich. U., 1961; MS, U. N.D., 1963; postgrad., U. Okla., 1974-77. Instr. No. Mich. U., Marquette, 1963-67, asst. prof., 1967-81, assoc. prof., 1981-90, prof. mktg., 1990—; lectr. corp. case histories. Author corp. case studies; editor univ. publs. Cir. lay rep. Luth. Ch.-Mo. Synod, 1987-89; pres. Redeemer Luth. Ch., Marquette, 1989-90, sec. to ch. coun., 1990-92, bd. elders, 1993—. Recipient MAGB Disting. Prof. award, 1995; Rsch. grantee Direct Selling Edn. Found., 1987—, Walker L. Cisler Sch. No. Mich. U., 1990, Filene Rsch. Inst., 1994. Fellow Acad. Mktg. Sci.; mem. Am. Mktg. Assn., Soc. Case Rsch. (v.p. 1990-91), N.Am. Case Rsch. Assn., World Assn. for Case Method Rsch. and Application, Econ. Club, Alpha Kappa Psi (alumni award). Democrat. Home: 171 Lakewood Ln Marquette MI 49855-9543 Office: No Michigan Univ Mktg Dept Marquette MI 49855

CAMERON, JAMES GREGORY, utility executive, government official; b. Evansville, Ind., Nov. 16, 1957; s. Thomas Alphonsus and Mary Lucille (Titzer) C.; m. Justine Lee Southard, July 12, 1980; 1 child, Jeanine Elyse. BS in Bus. Adminstrn. accounting, Ind. U., 1979. CPA, Ind. Field examiner, auditor Ind. State Bd. of Accts., Indpls., 1979-84; asst. dir. utility adminstrn. Evansville (Ind.) Water and Sewer Utility, 1984-87, dir. utility adminstrn. and fin., 1988—. Mem. AICPA, Ind. CPA Soc., Govt. Fin. Officers Assn., Am. Water Works Assn., Water Environment Fedn. Office: Evnsville Watr & Sewer Utly Rm 104 1 NW Martin L King Jr Blvd Evansville IN 47708

CAMERON, JEAN ELIZABETH, academic dean; b. Boston; d. Robert H. and Ethel (Cartmell) Cameron; m. Robert O. Linde, June 30, 1983; children: Kent Hiel, Cindy Cameron-Crabbe, Alix Hiel, Elizabeth Hiel, Thomas Hiel; 1 stepchild, Anne Linde. ALA, Golden Valley Luth. Coll., 1974; BA in Religious Studies, U. Minn., 1975, MA in Am. Studies, 1977, PhD in Am. Studies, 1991. Asst. to assoc. dean for humanities and fine arts Coll. Liberal Arts, U. Minn., 1979-81, curriculum coord., computer coord., asst. to dean, 1981-87, dir. Office of Tech. and Space Mgmt., asst. to dean, 1988-90; exec. dir. Assoc. Colls. of the Twin Cities, St. Paul, 1990-94; assoc. acad. dean Coll. of St. Catherine, St. Paul, 1994—. Author: Ann Hutchinson: Guilty or Not?: A Closer Look at Her Trials, 1994; broadcaster Radio Talking Book Network for Blind, St. Paul, 1981-90. Bd. dirs. United Arts, St. Paul, 1990-92. Mem. AAUW, Nat. Coalition Ind. Scholars, Phi Beta Kappa, Phi Kappa Phi (pres. Minn. chpt. 1978-79). Office: Coll St Catherine 2004 Randolph Ave Saint Paul MN 55105

CAMERON, PAUL SCOTT, architect; b. Mansfield, Ohio, June 6, 1940; s. Cecil Paul and Marianne (Flaitz) C.; m. Louise Chapman Foster, Aug. 24, 1968; children: Eleanor Gott, Morgan Scott. Student, Antioch Coll., 1958-61; BA, State U. Iowa, 1966; MA, U. Iowa, 1968; MArch, Washington U., St. Louis, 1976. Registered architect, Mo., Iowa, Ala., Calif., Ga., Ill., Ind., La., Mass., Miss., S.C., Tenn., Tex. Va. Design cons. Form & Environ. Design Group, various locations, 1963-72; teaching fellow U. Iowa, Iowa City, 1966-68; instr. U. No. Iowa, Cedar Falls, 1968-69; designer, architect Henmi & Assocs., St. Louis, 1973-77; planner, architect City of St. Louis, 1977-78; sr. architect Fruco Engrs., St. Louis, 1978-80; project architect HBE Corp., St. Louis, 1980-83; sr. architect, prin. architect Fru-Con Corp., St. Louis, 1983-90; prin. Cameron/Architect, St. Louis, 1990—, Cmty. Design Group, 1995—. Prin. works include corp. office Fru-Con Corp., St. Louis, Shelter Ins. Co., St. Louis, Sherwood Med. Co., St. Louis, Oxychem Corp., Sauget, Ill., Cornerstone Partnership, Wellston, Mo. Mem. AIA, Ethical Soc. St. Louis (trustee 1987—), Carlyle Yacht Club (sec. 1976-77). Home and Office: Cameron Architect 2031 Rutger St Saint Louis MO 63104-2430

CAMERON, RON D., law enforcement retired, security head; b. Rushville, Ind., Aug. 28, 1945; s. Floyd and Mildred (Aldridge) C.; children: Ronnie D. II, Jennifer E. Cameron Mathews. Grad. h.s., Rushville, Ind. Cert. police officer Ind. Law Enforcement Acad., 1969. Patrolman Rushville (Ind.) Police Dept., 1969-72, capt., 1972-73, detective capt., 1973-75, asst. chief, 1975-78, chief, 1978-90; chief investigation internal affairs Ind. Dept. Corrections, 1990-93; dir. security Ind. Soldiers & Sailors Home, Knightstown, Ind., 1993—; bd. dirs. Ind. Chiefs of Police, 1980-85; dir. tng. Police League Ind., 1982-83. Elected mem. Rush County Coun. at Large, 1993-96. Named Police Officer of Yr. Ind. Am. Legion, 1984. Mem. Ind. Assn. Chiefs of Police (life, pres. 1982-83, dir. tng. 1981-87), Ind. Fraternal Order of Police (life). Republican. Home: 1581 US Hwy 52 W Rushville IN 46173 Office: Ind Soliders & Sailors Children's Home Security Dept Knightstown IN 46148

CAMERON, WILLIAM JOHNSON, broadcasting executive; b. St. Louis, Sept. 24, 1946; s. Fred E. and Juliehe E. (Johnson) C.; m. Joan M. Schneider, Oct. 17, 1970; children:L Elizabeth Ann, Matthew William. BS, Ind. U., 1968; postgrad., U. Ill., 1968-68. With Sta. WMAQ-AM Radio, Chgo., polit. editor. Recipient Edward R. Murrow award Radio & TV News Dirs. Assn. Mem. Soc. Profl. Journalists. Office: WMAQ-AM Radio 455 N Cityfront Chicago IL 60611

CAMILLI, PRISCILLA CONSTANCE, art history educator, curator; b. Plymouth, Wis., July 31, 1942; d. George Nicholas and Ione Clemana (Grade) Burkart; m. Charles Lee Camilli, Nov. 30, 1963; children: Michael C., Christopher D., Laura. BA in History, U. Wis., Milw., 1979, MA in Art History, 1983. Lectr. art history Milw. Ctr. for Photography, 1982-84, U. Wis.-Parkside, Racine, 1983-84, Milw. Inst. Art and design, 1983-90; assoc. lectr. art history U. Wis., Milw., 1990—, curator visual resources, 1984—; assoc. lectr. art U. Wis., Waukesha, 1995—; co-curator exhibit on Milw. architect Henry C. Koch, Firestation Gallery, Milw., 1988; guest lectr. Rahr-West Art Mus., Manitowoc, Wis., 1991, Vogel Art Mus., U. Wis., Milw., 1992, U. Wis.-Parkside, 1992. Bd. dirs. Assn. for Retarded Citizens, Milw., 1975-79; mentor YMCA One on One Program, Milw., 1994-95. Mem. Art Librs. Soc. N.Am., Art Libraries Soc. Midwest, Phi Kappa Phi. Office: Univ of Wis Milw Mitchell 151 Dept Art Hist PO Box 413 Milwaukee WI 53201

CAMMA, PHILIP, accountant; b. Phila., May 22, 1923; s. Anthony and Rose (LaSpada) C.; m. Anna Ruth Karg, July 21, 1956 (dec. Aug. 1960); 1 child, Anthony Philip. BS, U. Pa., 1952. CPA, Ohio, Ky. Acct., Main and Co., CPA's, Phila., 1952-53; in-charge acct. Haskins & Sells, CPA's, Phila., St. Louis, Cin. and Columbus, Ohio, 1953-60; controller Marvin Warner Co., Cin., 1960-61, Leshner Corp., 1961-63; mng. ptnr. Camma & Patrick, CPA's, 1963-66; founder Philip Camma Co., CPA's, Cin., 1966—. Served with USAAF, 1942-45, ETO. Mem. AICPA's, Ohio Soc. CPA's, Ky. Soc. CPA's, Nat. Assn. Accts. Republican. Home: 1711D Lakeknoll Dr Cincinnati OH 45231 Office: 700 Walnut St Apt 603 Cincinnati OH 45202-2015

CAMMACK, WILLIAM ROGER, JR., chemical company executive; b. St. Paul, Feb. 17, 1950; s. William Roger and Martha Cammack; m. Susan Kay Balfany, Apr. 29, 1978; children: Christopher Roger, Carmel Ann, William Roger III. BBA, U. Minn., 1974. Sales/noise control specialist Wheel Svc. Inc., St. Paul, 1973-75; v.p., co-owner Martin Wood Specialists, St. Paul, 1976-81; pres., owner C&H Chem. Co., St. Paul, 1980—; bd. dirs. Minn. Chem. Tech. Alliance, St. Paul, 1993-96. Chmn. Cammack Marshall Fund for Children, St. Paul, 1991-94. Mem. Pig's Eye Gyro Club (pres. 1993-95), Rotary (pres. St. Paul chpt. 1995-96).

CAMP, DAVE, congressman; b. Midland, Mich., July 9, 1953; m. Nancy Keil, Sept. 10, 1994; 1 child, Andrew David. BA, Albion (Mich.) Coll., 1975; JD, U. San Diego, 1978. Bar: Mich., Calif., D.C., U.S. Supreme Ct., U.S. Dist. Ct. (ea. dist.) Mich., U.S. Dist. Ct. (so. dist.) Calif. With Riecker, Van Dam, Looby & Barker, 1978-90; spl. asst. atty. gen., 1980-84, adminstrv. asst. to Congressman Bill Schuette, 1985-87; state rep. 102nd Dist. Mich., 1989-91; mem. 102d-104th Congresses from 10th (now 4th) Mich. dist. 102nd-103rd Congresses from 10th (now 4th) Mich. dist., 1991—; mem. ways and means com. Mem. ABA, Midland County Bar Assn. Republican. Office: US Ho of Reps 137 Cannon Washington DC 20515-0003

CAMP, LOREN CLINTON, county engineer; b. Radcliff, Ohio, Mar. 26, 1934; s. Clinton Elmer Camp and Ethyl Frances (Saunders) Byers; m. Esther Marie Nethersole, Sept. 5, 1956 (div. June 1978); children: Nick, Chad, Chase; m. Evelyn Marie Osborne; children: Harold, Denise, Lorena, Eric. Degree in Civil Engring., Ohio State U. Project engr. Rackoff & Assocs., Columbus, Ohio, 1961-66, Tweed & Eriksson, Columbus, 1966-70; city engr. City of Cambridge, Ohio, 1970-72; county engr. Muskingum County, Ohio, 1972—; cons. Loren C. Camp & Assoc., Zanesville, Ohio, 1956-66. Mem. ASCE. Home: 155 Rehl Rd Zanesville OH 43701

CAMP, PAUL ALLEN, publisher, consultant, writer; b. Alton, Ill., Mar. 19, 1949; s. Charles Albert and Dorothy Jean (Whitmer) C.; m. Mary E. Connors, June 24, 1989; 1 child, Conor. BA in Polit. Sci., Washington U., St. Louis, 1971. Editor Friends of the Environment, St. Louis, 1970-72; editor, gen. mgr. St. Louisan Mag., St. Louis, 1972-74; account exec. George Johnson Advt., St. Louis, 1975; editor, pub. St. Louis Today, 1975-76; editor, asoc. pub. The Counselor, Phila., 1977-78, Fairchild Publs., N.Y.C., 1979-82; editor, writer Chgo. Tribune, 1983-90; owner, pub. Checagau Comms., Chgo., 1990-92; pub. Thomson Newspapers, Chgo., 1992—; speaker, cons. Nat. Assn. Splty. Food Trade, N.Y.C., 1986—; cons. Badonsky Restaurant Assocs., Chgo., 1989—. Author: Grand Pioneers of Promotion, 1978, Paul Camp's Chicago Tribune Guide, 1988; author, editor: Zagat Chicago Restaurants, 1992; editor: (textbook) Specialty Advertising, 1984. Organizer, fund raiser Coalition for the Environment, St. Louis, 1972-76; mem. pub. rels. com. Boys and Girls Club Chgo., 1992-93, Conv. and Tourism Bur., Chgo., 1993-94. Mem. Inland Press Assn., Assn. Alternative Postal Sys., Chog. Conv. and Tourism Bur., Mus. Contemporary Art. Office: Thomson Target Media Ste 706 730 N Franklin St Chicago IL 60610

CAMPAGNA, TIMOTHY NICHOLAS, institute executive; b. Chgo., June 8, 1957; s. Nicholas and Dorothy (Hoffmeister) C.; m. Diana Lynn Czarny, Aug. 1, 1981; children: Maria, Joseph. BA, Lewis U., Romeoville, Ill., 1980, MA, 1985. Basketball referee NCAA and Ill. High Sch. Assn., 1976-88; asst. dir. housing Lewis U., 1978-80; tchr. Fairmont Jr. High Sch., Lockport, Ill., 1979-80; tchr., therapist Guardian Angel Home, Joliet, Ill., 1980-82; assoc. dean students DeVry Inst. Tech., Lombard, Ill., 1982-84, dean students, 1984-87; dean adminstrv. svcs. DeVry Inst. Tech., Irving, Tex., 1987-93, dean evening coll., dir. Ctr. Bus. and Industry Ednl. Svcs., 1993-95, dean enrollment mgmt. and mktg., 1994-95; v.p. Am. Inst. Commerce, Davenport, Iowa, 1995—; mem. sch. bd. Holy Family Nazareth. Named Tchr. of Yr., Fairmont Jr. High Sch., 1980, Adminstr. of Yr., DeVry Inst. Tech., 1984. Mem. Nat. Assn. Student Pers. Adminstrs., Am. Assn. Coll. Registrars and Admissions Officers, Nat. Assn. Fgn. Student Advisors, Nat. Assn. Coll. and Univ. Bus. Officers. Roman Catholic. Office: Am Inst Commerce 1801 E Kimberly Rd Davenport IA 52807

CAMPBELL, ALICE SHAW, retired accountant, poet; b. Crawfordsville, Ind., Aug. 29, 1918; d. Chester Monroe and Amy Susan (Peck) Shaw; m. George A. Campbell, Aug. 29, 1936. Student, Ind. U., 1958-74. With State and USDA Soil Conservation Svc., 1952-57, Dept. HEW-Social Security Adminstrn., Lafayette Motor Parts Co., Inc., West Lafayette, Ind., 1979-88. Author: (poetry) Kaleidoscope, 1989; contbr. poetry to publs. including Best Poems of 1995, Treasured Poems of Am., The Desert Sun, In the West of Ireland. Named Golden Poet, World of Poetry, 1989; recipient L.A. Poetry Acad. award presented by Milton Berle, 1993.

CAMPBELL, ANITA JOYCE, computer company executive; b. Jefferson City, Mo., Sept. 24, 1953; d. George Rigsby and Betty Jean (Heade) Sanders; m. Michael Joseph Campbell (div. 1986); children: Kim Erik Seaver, Daniel Joseph Campbell. AAS, Lincoln U., Jefferson City, 1985. Student lab. mgr. Lincoln U., 1985; integrated systems analyst Xerox Corp., St. Louis, 1988-89, ins. industry project mgr., western region ops. mgmt. staff, 1990-91, advanced product specialist, western regions ops. mgmt., 1991, advanced solutions tech. mgr., western region ops. mgmt., 1992-93, tech. market project mgr., rsch. & engring, integrated systems orgn., 1993-94, tech. mktg. mgr. integrated solutions, systems sales and support, 1994-95; tech. con., integrated document solutions Integrated Document Solutions, 1995—; project mgr. state and local govt. Xerox Profl. Doc. Svcs. Bridgeton, Mo., 1996—. Co-developer Delta Plan, 1988. Office staff campaign mgr. for Carter-Mondale Reelection Com., Washington, 1989-90; waterfront dir. Spl. Olympics, Lake of the Ozarks, Mo., 1987; bd. dirs. ARC, Jefferson City, 1986. Home: 912 Leawood Dr Saint Louis MO 63126-1114 Office: Xerox Corp 3221 McKelvey Rd Bridgeton MO 63044

CAMPBELL, BONNIE JO, mathematics educator; b. Kalamazoo, Mich., Sept. 14, 1962; d. Frederick Loesser and Susanna (Herlihy) C.; m. Christopher John Magson. BA in Philosophy, U. Chgo., 1984; BA in Math., Western Mich. U., 1992, MA in Math., 1995, postgrad., 1995—. Cert. tchr., Mich. Pres. Goulash Tours, Inc., Kalamazoo, 1988—. Editor newsletter: The Letter Parade, 1985—; essayist The Letter Parade, 1992. Home and Office: Goulash Tours Inc 1707 Olmstead Rd Kalamazoo MI 49001

CAMPBELL, CAROL NORTON, college official; b. Mpls., July 28, 1944; d. Dale Edward and Betty Lorraine (Huntley) Norton; m. George Carl Anderson, May 5, 1963 (div. Aug. 1973); children: Todd Elove, Robb Norton, Mark Edward; m. John Thomas Campbell, June 5, 1976. BSB in Acctg., U. Minn., 1975. CPA, Minn. Mem. audit staff Coopers & Lybrand, Mpls., 1977-79, audit supr., 1979-81, mgr., 1981-84; dir. acctg. U. Minn., Mpls., 1984-86, controller, treas., 1986-90, assoc. v.p., 1990; v.p., treas. Carleton Coll., Northfield, Minn., 1990—; chmn. adv. coun. Tchrs. Ins. and Annuity Assn.-Coll. Retirement Equity Fund, 1995-96; bd. dirs. United Educators Ins. Risk Retention Group, Inc., 1996—. Bd. dirs. Northfield Hosp., 1991—, chair, 1994-95; bd. dirs. Cannon Valley coun. Girl Scouts U.S., 1991—, treas., 1992—; bd. dirs. WCAL Radio 89.3 FM. Mem. Ctrl. Assn. Coll. and Univ. Bus. Officers (exec. com. 1986-91, pres. 1990), Nat. Assn. Coll. and Univ. Bus. Officers (treas. 1991, vice chmn. 1992, chmn. 1993, bd. dirs. 1990-95), Fin. Execs. Inst., Rotary. Home: 700 Baneberry Ct Northfield MN 55057-3412 Office: Carleton Coll 1 N College St Northfield MN 55057-4001

CAMPBELL, CATHERINE MARY, school system administrator; b. Battle Creek, Mich., May 20, 1941; d. Frederick George and Jennie Lucille (Rowland) Clements; children: Cameron, Michael; m. Raymond Lee Campbell, July 24, 1964. BS, Western Mich. U., 1963, MA, 1966, Ed.S., 1977. Cert. elem. tchr., Mich., ctrl. office administr. Elem. tchr. Portage Pub. Schs., Kalamazoo, Mich., 1963-64, Albion (Mich.) Pub. Schs., 1964-66; tchr. jr. high sch. Albion (Mich.) Pub. Sch.s, 1967-76, dir. community edn., 1976-93; elem. prin. Albion (Mich.) Pub. Schs., 1993—; adj. prof. Western Mich. U., 1991—; lectr. in field. Co-author: History of Albion Public Schools, 1991. Chmn. Leadership Albion; co-chair United Way Fund Drive, Albion, 1992; active Hospital Svc. League, Friends of Libr.; chmn. Albion Coll. Community Campaign, 1994. Recipient Albion Minute Man award Mich. State Legis., 1983. Mem. Nat. Cmty. Edn. Assn., Mich. Elem. Prins. Assn., Mich. Assn. Cmty. Edn. (State of Mich. Outstanding Cmty. Educator 1987), South Ctrl. Adult and Cmty. Edn. Assn. (pres. 1984-85), Albion Area C. of C. (amb.), Rotary, ELT Club, Delta Kappa Gamma (v.p. 1976). Republican. Methodist. Home: 712 Irwin Ave Albion MI 49224-2053 Office: Albion Pub Schs 401 E Michigan Ave Albion MI 49224-1844

CAMPBELL, CHERYL NICHOLS, telecommunications company executive; b. Ocala, Fla., Oct. 25, 1948; d. Ralph Charles and Virginia (Lloyd) Nichols; m. David William, Aug. 21, 1971; children: Andrew, Stephen. Student, U. Hawaii, 1969; BA, Purdue U., 1970; postgrad., U. Pa., Dartmouth Coll. Lic. secondary edn. tchr. Adminstrv. asst. Ind. Bell, Indpls., 1970-71; group mgr. Cin. Bell, 1971-73, staff assoc., 1973-74, staff asst., 1974-78, staff specialist, 1978-81, staff mgr., 1981-87, adminstrv. mgr., 1987-88, dist. mgr., 1988-90; dir. operator and directory svcs., Cin. Bell, 1990-91; dir. govt. affairs Cin. Bell, 1991-93, dir. docket mgmt./issue analysis, 1993-94, regulatory planning v.p., 1995—; operator svcs. adv. group Bell Communications Rsch., Morristown, N.J., 1988—. Mem. steering com. U.S. Figure Skating Championships, Cin., 1978-79; mem. adv. bd. Downtown Montessori Day Care Ctr., Cin., 1981-83, Children's Psychiat. Ctr., Cin., 1984-86; divsn. leader Greater Cin. United Way, 1989-90; chmn. Mayor's Commn. on Children, Cin., 1992—; bd. trustees Children Protective Svcs. Greater Cin. Named one of Outstanding Young Women of Am., 1971, for Best Mktg. Story, Greater Cin. Editors' Assn., 1974, Oustanding Active Mem., Kilgour chpt. Telephone Pioneers of Am., Cin., 1989. Mem. Jr. League Cin. (bd. dirs., evening rep. 1979-80, future planning 1981-82, pub. rels. 1984-85), Telephone Pioneers Am. (Kilgour chpt., bd. dirs., fund raising 1989-90), Jr. Achievement Cin. (corp. vol. coord. 1988-90). Republican. Episcopalian. Office: Cin Bell 201 E 4th St Rm 102-310 Cincinnati OH 45202-4122

CAMPBELL, DANE H., applications engineer; b. Euclid, Ohio, Nov. 3, 1969. BSME, Miami U., Oxford, Ohio, 1993; BAFA, Sinclair U., Dayton, Ohio, 1995. Applications engr. Advanced Assembly Automation, Dayton, 1993—; engr., ptnr. Speedy C, Columbus, Ohio, 1991—. Wrestling/soccer coach, various high schs., Dayton, 1995; active Big Bros./Big Sisters, Dayton, 1995. Roman Catholic. Home: 520 Redwood Ave Dayton OH 45405-5140 Office: Advanced Assembly Auto 313 Mound St Dayton OH 45407-3370

CAMPBELL, DAVID GEORGE, ecologist, researcher; b. Decatur, Ill., Jan. 28, 1949; s. George Robert and Jean Blossom (Weilepp) C.; m. Karen S. Lowell; 1 child, Tatiana Claire. BA, Kalamazoo Coll., 1971; MS, U. Mich., 1973; PhD, Johns Hopkins U., 1984. Exec. dir. Bahamas Nat. Trust, Nassau, 1974-77; ecologist N.Y. Bot. Garden, Bronx, 1984-88, leader Amazon Expdns., 1974-92, research fellow, 1989—; Henry R. Luce prof. in Nations and the Global Environment Grinnell (Iowa) Coll., 1991—; adj. prof. U. Nanjing, People's Republic of China; cons. Internat. Union for Conservation of Nature, 1978-79; biologist and lectr. M.V. World Discoverer in Amazon and Antarctic, 1981-87; biologist Brazilian Antarctic Expdn., 1987-88. Author: The Ephemeral Islands, 1978, The Crystal Desert, 1992; editor: Floristic Inventory of Tropical Countries, 1989; contbr. articles to profl. jours. Fellow John Simon Guggenheim Found., 1989; recipient Fulling award Soc. Econ. Botany, 1987, Houghton Mifflin Lit. fellow, 1992, Pen/Martha Albrand award for nonfiction, 1993, John Burroughs medal, 1994. Fellow Linnean Soc. London. Office: Grinnell Coll Dept Biology Grinnell IA 50112

CAMPBELL, DENNIS G., investment advisor; b. Wichita, Kans., Aug. 15, 1930; m. Betty J. West, May 4, 1954; children: Corby Shields, Lori Dickson. BA, Kans. State U., 1953. Investment advisor Paine Webber, Topeka, 1970-82; co-owner Bee Croft Cole, Topeka, 1982-92; investment advisor Piper Jaffray Inc., Topeka, 1992—. Mem. adv. bd. Jr. Achievement, Topeka, 1985—, Family Trusts, Topeka. Lt. USAF, 1954-56, Korea. Mem. Moose, Elks, Shawnee Country Club, Rotary Club (pres. 1960—). Republican. Office: Piper Jaffray Inc 2445 SW Wanamaker Rd # 100 Topeka KS 66614-4261

CAMPBELL, EDWARD ADOLPH, judge, electrical engineer; b. Boonville, Ind., Jan. 16, 1936; s. Revis Allen and Sarah Gertrude (Hunsaker) C.; m. Nancy Colleen Keys, July 26, 1957; children: Susan Elizabeth Campbell Frisse, Stephen Edward, Sara Lynne. BEE, U. Evansville, 1959; JD, Ind. U., 1965; grad. Nat. Coll. Dist. Attys., U. Houston, 1972, Nat. Jud. Coll. U. Nev., 1978, Am. Acad. Jud. Edn., U. Va., 1979. Bar: Ind. 1965, U.S. Dist. Ct. (so. dist.) Ind. 1965, U.S. Ct. Customs and Patent Appeals 1967, U.S. Supreme Ct. 1973, U.S. Ct. Appeals (fed. cir.) 1982. Patent examiner U.S. Patent Office, Washington, 1959-60; patent adv. U.S. Naval Avionics, Indpls., 1960-65; patent atty. Gen. Elec. Co., Fort Wayne, Ind., 1965-66; ptnr. Weyerbacher & Campbell, attys., Boonville, Ind., 1966-71; pros. atty. 2nd Jud. Cir., Warrick County, Ind., 1971-77; judge Warrick Superior Ct. No. 1, 1977—. Fellow Ind. Bar Found.; mem. IEEE, Ind. State Bar Assn., Ind. Judges Assn., Nat. Coun. Juvenile and Family Ct. Judges, Ind. Coun. of Juvenile and Family Ct. Judges, Warrick County C. of C. (bd. dirs. 1978-84), Sigma Pi Sigma, Phi Delta Phi. Democrat. Methodist. Club: Rolling Hills Country (Newburgh, Ind.). Lodges: Lions, Kiwanis. Home: 911 Julian Dr Boonville IN 47601-9556 Office: Warrick Superior Ct No 1 PO Box 666 Boonville IN 47601-0666

CAMPBELL, F(ENTON) GREGORY, college administrator, historian; b. Columbia, Tenn., Dec. 16, 1939; s. Fenton G. and Ruth (Hayes) C.; m. Barbara D. Kuhn, Aug. 29, 1970; children: Fenton H., Matthew W., Charles H. AB, Baylor U., 1960; postgrad., Philipps U., Marburg/Lahn, Fed. Republic of Germany, 1960-61; MA, Emory U., 1962; postgrad., Charles U., Prague, Czechoslovakia, 1965-66; PhD, Yale U., 1967; postgrad. in ednl. mgmt., Harvard U., 1981. Rsch. staff historian Yale U., New Haven, 1966-68, spl. asst. to acting pres., 1977-78; asst. prof. history U. Wis., Milw., 1968-69; asst. prof. European history U. Chgo., 1969-76, spl. asst. to pres., 1978-87, sec. bd. trustees, 1979-87, sr. lectr., 1985-87; pres., prof. history Carthage Coll., 1987—; fellow Woodrow Wilson Internat. Ctr. for Scholars, Smithsonian Instn., Washington, 1976-77; participant Japan Study Program for Internat. Execs., 1987. Author: Confrontation in Central Europe, 1975; joint editor: Akten zur deutschen auswartigen Politik, 1918-1945, 1966-95; contbr. articles and revs. to profl. jours. Bd. dirs. AAL Mutual Funds, Heritage Bank and Trust, Prairie Sch., Racine, Wis., Kenosha (Wis.) Hosp. and Med. Ctr. Fulbright grantee, 1960-61, 1973-74; Woodrow Wilson fellow, 1961-62, U.S.A.-Czechoslovakia exchange fellow, 1965-66, 73-74, 85. Mem. Am. Assn. for Advancement Slavic Studies, Wis. Assn. Ind. Colls. and Univs. (chmn.), Mid-Day Club (Chgo.), Kenosha (Wis.) Country Club, Rotary (Kenosha), Phi Beta Kappa, Omicron Delta Kappa. Home: 623 17th Pl Kenosha WI 53140-1360 Office: Carthage Coll History Dept Kenosha WI 53140

CAMPBELL, GAVIN ELLIOTT, real estate investor and developer; b. Alton, Ill., Feb. 29, 1960; s. Colin Chandler and Mariana Nicholas (Hardwick) C. BA in Polit. Philosophy magna cum laude, Yale U., 1982; MBA in Fin., U. Chgo., 1989. Analyst internat. trade Ill. Dept. Agr., Springfield, 1982-83; asst. to gov. for planning State of Ill., Springfield, 1983-85; dep. dir. Civic Com., Chgo., 1985-90; assoc. acquisitions LaSalle Advisors Ltd., Chgo., 1990-92, v.p. acquisitions, 1992-93, exec. v.p. acquisitions, 1994-95, prin. acquisitions, 1996—; pres. Chgo. Restoration Group, 1986—. Pres. Latino Chgo. Theater Co., Chgo., 1990-96, Leadership Fellows Assn., Chgo., 1996—; dir. Yale Coll. Alumni Schs. Com., Chgo., 1991-94; com. rep. A.N. Pritzker Local Sch. Coun., 1993—; co-founder, mem. exec. com. Young Leader's Fund, 1994-96. Recipient Gov.'s fellowship, Springfield, 1982; fellow Leadership Greater Chgo., 1987. Republican. Home: 1417 N Hoyne Ave Chicago IL 60622-1802 Office: LaSalle Advisors Ltd 200 E Randolph Chicago IL 60601-1203

CAMPBELL, JAMES E., financial consultant; b. Boone, Iowa, Sept. 13, 1953. BA in Edn., U. No. Iowa, 1975. Tchr. Riverdale H.S., Port Byron, Ill., 1975-79; salesman Wholesale Distbg. Co., Moline, Ill., 1979-85; fin. cons. E.F. Hutton, Rock Island, Ill., 1985-94, Merrill Lynch, Moline, 1994—. Lutheran. Office: Merrill Lynch PO Box 160 4575 16th St Moline IL 61265

CAMPBELL, JOHN W., financial consultant; b. Kirksville, Mo., Aug. 25, 1955. BA, U. Mo., St. Louis, 1978. Br. mgr. Glidden Co., St. Louis, 1973-90; fin. cons. Merrill Lynch, Chesterfield, Mo., 1991—. Office: Merrill Lynch 16100 N Outer 40 Chesterfield MO 63017-1784

CAMPBELL, JOYCE MARIE, elementary education educator; b. Joplin, Mo., Oct. 7, 1936; d. Harold Leroy and Leora Lucille (Whitworth) Cartright; m. Donald Lee Campbell, July 28, 1934; children: Gail Robbyn, Stephen Lee. Grad., Dickerson Bus. Coll., Kansas City, Mo., 1988, Montessori Sch., Kansas City, Mo., 1990. Cert. Montessori tchr. Tchr. Children's Montessori Ctr., Liberty, Mo., 1989—. Author: Shadow of Life, 1991, (poetry) Shadow of a Man, 1989, 91. Choir mem. Pleasant Valley Ch., Liberty, 1989—. Mem. Montessori Tchrs. Assn. Home: 511 Blythe St Liberty MO 64068 Office: Childrens Montessori Ctr 291 Middlebrooke St Liberty MO 64068

CAMPBELL, JUDITH LOWE, child psychiatrist; b. Indpls., Jan. 21, 1946; d. Albert St. Clair and Adele V. (Lobraico) Lowe; m. Robert Frank Campbell, Nov. 30, 1968; children: Christiaan Robert, Kevin Lowe, Geoffrey Ford. BS in Zoology, Butler U., 1967; MD, Ind. U., 1971. Resident in psychiatry Ind. U. Sch. Medicine, 1971-73, fellow in child psychiatry 1973-75; asst. dir. Riley Child Guidance Clinic, Indpls., 1975-79, dir. child psychiatry consultation, liaison svc. to pediatrics, 1975-79; dir. child psychiatry svcs. Riley Hosp. for Children, 1979-85; pvt. practice child psychiatry, Indpls., 1985—; child psychiatry cons. Ctr. for Mental Health of Madison County, Anderson, Ind., 1975-77, Lutheran Child Welfare Assn., Indpls., 1974—, Lutherwood Children's Home, Indpls., 1974—, Jewish Family and Children's Svcs., 1983-84, child and adolescent div. Midtown Cmty. Mental Health Ctr., 1983-85; assoc. med. dir. child and adolescent psychiat. svcs. Cmty. Hosps. of Indpls., Inc., 1989-90; med. dir. outreach svcs. Arbor Hosp. of Greater Indpls., 1990, med. dir. children's unit, 1990-92, pres. med. staff, 1990-92; med. dir. Arbor Hosp., 1992-94. instr. Ind. U. Sch. Medicine, Indpls., 1974-75, asst. prof. dept psychiatry, 1975-89, clin. assoc. prof., 1989—. Vice-precinct committeeman Rep. Party, 1990-94; mem. parent's adv. coun. Butler U., 1989-93, pres., 1990-93. Recipient Physician's Recognition award in Continuing Edn. AMA, 1974, 77; Helen McQuiston award in sci., 1967. Fellow Am. Psychiat. Assn., Ind. Psychiat. Soc. (councilor 1978-80, 90-91, sec. 1981-83, editor newsletter 1981-83, chmn. com. women 1983-92, mem. ethics com. 1992—), Am. Acad. Pediatrics (Ind. br.), Am. Acad. Child and Adolescent Psychiatry, Ind. Coun. Child and Adolescent Psychiatry (sec. 1986-87, pres.-elect 1987-88, pres. 1988-89, Smithsonian Assocs., Indpls. Mus. Art, Indpls. Zool. Soc., Pi Beta Phi. Clubs: Eastern Star, Woodland Country. Contbr. articles on child psychiatry to profl. jours. Research on emotional aspects of burns in children, craniofacial anomalies in children, also sex differences in child and adolescent population groups. Office: 11075 N Pennsylvania St Indianapolis IN 46280-1091

CAMPBELL, KATHLEEN CHARLOTTE MURPHEY, audiology educator and researcher; b. Sioux Falls, S.D., Mar. 20, 1952; d. Chester Humphrey and Ruth Maxine (Thompson) Murphey; m. Craig Anthony Campbell, Nov. 15, 1975. BA, S.D. State U., 1973; MA, U. S.D., 1977; PhD, U. Iowa, 1989. Cert. audiologist. Clin. grad. asst. dept. communication U. S.D., Vermillion, 1976-77; regional audiologist II British Columbia Ministry Health, Cranbrook, 1977-82; audiologist II dept. otolaryngology head and neck U. Iowa, Iowa City, 1983-88, rsch. asst. dept. speech, pathology and audiology, 1985; doctoral fellow Health Svcs. R&D, VA, Iowa City, 1987-88; assoc. prof. div. otolaryngology dept. surgery So. Ill. U. Sch. Medicine, 1989—; cons. Packer Engring., Naperville, Ill., 1992—. Editorial cons. Am. Jour. Audiology, 1992; reviewer Annals of Otolaryngology, 1992; contbr. articles to profl. jours. Mem. Midamerica Playwrights Theatre, Springfield, Ill., 1989—, Sierra Club, Springfield, 1989—. Recipient Clin. Investigator Devel. Award grant NIH, 1990, Small Bus. Innovative Rsch. grant NIH, 1990, Ctrl. Rsch. Coun. grant So. Ill. U., 1991, Children's Miracle Network award So. Ill. U., 1991, 92, Alzheimer Disease Ctr. grant So. Ill. U. Sch. Medicine, 1992. Mem. Am. Speech-Lang.-Hearing Assn., Am. Acad. Audiology, Assn. Rsch. in Otolaryngology, Am. Acad. Otolaryngology-Head/Neck Surgery (assoc.), Mensa. Office: SIU Sch Medicine 301 N 8th St # 5B Springfield IL 62701-1041

CAMPBELL, KENNETH RAY, mechanical engineer; b. Kansas City, Kans., Jan. 4, 1937. BS in Mech. Engring., U. Kans., 1960, M in Mech. Engring., 1967. Registered profl. engr., Kans. Sr. plant engr. AT&T Technologies Inc., Lee's Summit, Mo., 1970-95. Roman Catholic. Home: 6423 W 79th Terr Overland Park KS 66204

CAMPBELL, LESLEY ANN, environmental coordinator; b. Des Moines, Iowa, July 30, 1959; d. Robert Frederick and Sherrill Ann (Cox) Kryselmire. AA, Iowa Western Community Coll., 1979; BS, U. of South Dakota, 1981. County inspector Polk County Phys. Planning, Des Moines, Iowa, 1988; environ. specialist Iowa Dept. Natural Resources, Des Moines, 1988-92; sr. assoc. ESSI, Des Moines, 1992-94; dist. environ. compliance coord. U.S. Postal Svc., Des Moines, 1994—. Mem. NAFE, Environ. Profls. of Iowa, Iowa Groundwater Assn., Beta Sigma Phi (v.p., treas., rec. sec.). Presbyterian. Office: US Postal Svc PO Box 189991 Hawkeye Dist Des Moines IA 50318-9991

CAMPBELL, MALCOLM BYRON, educator; b. Flint, Mich., May 25, 1938; s. Malcolm and Marian Marguerite (Smith) C.; m. Lynn Mildred Ufholz, June 29, 1968 (div. 1977); children: Alycia Lynn, Courtney Jessica; m. Rosie Lanette Mapes, May 31. 1986. AB, U. Mich., 1960, AM, 1961, PhD, 1966. Tchr., English elem. schs., Bloomfield Hills (Mich.) Dist. Schs., 1965-66; asst. prof. edn. Bowling Green State U. (Ohio), 1966-70, assoc. prof., 1970-75, prof., 1975—; cons. Tiffin Devel. Ctr. (Ohio). Lyndon Baines Johnson Found. grantee, 1974; Gerald R. Ford Found. grantee, 1990. Mem. Comparative and Internat. Edn. Soc., Ednl. Excellence Network, Am. Ednl. Studies Assn., Am. Ednl. Research Assn., Spl. Interest Group on Internat. Studies, History of Edn. Soc. Democrat. Author: Non-Specialist Study in the New Universities and Colleges of Advanced Technology in England, 1966; co-editor: Jour. of Abstracts in Internat. Edn., 1971-90, editl. bd. 1990-94, Ednl. Impressions: Readings, 1977; contbr. articles to profl. jours. Home: 729 Ordway Ave Bowling Green OH 43402-2769 Office: Bowling Green State U 556 Ednl Bowling Green OH 43403-0251

CAMPBELL, MARILYN F., association executive, author; b. Terre Haute, Ind., Mar. 4, 1941; d. Carl Wesley and Elsie Fern (Watson) C. BS, Ind. State U., 1962, MA, 1965. Instr., sci. chmn. Danville (Ill.) Area C. C., 1965-69; dep. dir. edn. Vermilion County Conservation Dist., Danville, Ill., 1969-94; exec. dir. Ill. Audubon Soc., Wayne, 1994—; cons. Ill. Nature Preserves Commn., Springfield, 1984-94; mem. adv. comm. Ill. Wildlife Preservation Fund, 1984-94. Columnist Conservation Corner; contbr. Ill. Audubon, Ind. Audubon Quar., Prairie in Vermilion County, At Home in Forest Glen, and Wings and Things. Named Woman of Achievement, AAUW, 1989. Mem. The Nature Conservancy, Cornell Lab. Ornithology. Office: Ill Audubon Soc PO Box 2418 Danville IL 61834

CAMPBELL, MARK ALAN, federal agency administrator; b. Pt. Huron, Mich., Nov. 16, 1950; s. Donald J. and Mary Margaret (Bills) C.; m. Leila Elizabeth Simons, June 24, 1972. Fin. officer Mpls. Housing & Redevel. Authority, 1976-79; single family loan specialist U.S. HUD, Mpls., 1979-83, mgr. (sect. chief), 1983-85, multifamily loan specialist, 1985-92, mgr. (br. chief), 1992—. V.p. Minn. Masonic Found., St. Paul, 1993-96, pres., 1996—; dir. Minn. Masonic Home Cluster Homes, Bloomington, Minn., 1994—, Minn. Masonic Homes Sr. Housing, Bloomington, 1995—, trustee, 1996—; mem. exec. coun. Bloomington Neighborhood Crime Watch Adv. Coun., 1993—. Mem. Mason (Mason of Yr. Richfield lodge # 334 1993, past master Richfield lodge # 334 1993, mem., treas. Cass lodge # 243 1994—, dist. rep. Grand Lodge of Minn. 1990—), Intertel, Mensa, Hennepin Area Masters and Wardens Assn. (sec./treas. 1994—). Home: 8657 22d Ave S Bloomington MN 55425-2107

CAMPBELL, MICHELLE DAWN CLARA, journalist; b. Breckenridge, Minn., May 9, 1970; d. Zachary Taylor and Colleen Kay (Carlson) Roberts; m. Anthony Howard Campbell, July 11, 1992. AA, Bismarck State Coll., 1990; BA in Journalism, Ariz. State U., 1992; MS in Journalism, Northwestern U., 1993. Sports writer The Hazen (N.D.) Star, 1987-88; editor The State Press, Tempe, Ariz., 1990-92; reporter The Mesa (Ariz.) Tribune, 1991; news asst., corr. The Ariz. Republic, Phoenix, 1992-93; Westlake editor The Times, Munster, Ind., 1993-95; reporter The Chgo. Sun-Times, 1995—. Named Coll. Journalist of Yr., Univ. Mag., Chgo., 1992; recipient 1st Place award Ind. SPJ, Indpls., 1994, Kent Cooper award Ind. Assoc. Press Mgmt. Edn. Assn., Indpls., 1995, 1st Place award Nat. Assn. Black Journalists, Phila., 1995. Fellow Poynter Inst. Media Studies, Knight Ctr. Specialized Journalism; mem. Investigative Reporters and Editors, Soc. Profl. Journalists, Kappa Tau Alpha. Home: 17327 S 65th Ave Tinley Park IL 60477 Office: The Chgo Sun-Times 401 N Wabash Ave Chicago IL 60611

CAMPBELL, PATRICIA ELAINE, elementary education educator; b. Cin., Dec. 3, 1943; d. Jake T. and Margaret O. (Hunter) C.; 1 child, Andre. BA in Elem. Edn., Andrews U., 1968; MA in Edn., U. Cin., 1978. Cert. elem tchr., prin. and supr., Ohio. Tchr. elem. Cin. Pub. Schs., 1968—, consulting tchr. Math. Assessment Devel., 1988—; curriculum writer gifted and talented, career edn., programs in math. and sci.; mentor; youth program leader. Chmn. bd. Pvt. Parochial Sch., Cin., 1991-95. Mem. Ohio Maths. Groupg., Cin. Maths. Group, Nat. Coun. Tchrs. Maths. Adventist. Office: Cin Pub Schs 230 E 9th St Cincinnati OH 45202-2138

CAMPBELL, PATTI SUSAN, public relations professional; b. Franklin, Ind., Feb. 29, 1964; d. William Norman and Kathryn Edith (Myers) Campbell; m. Samuel B. Hicks, Dec. 22, 1987. Student, Butler U., Indpls., 1982-86, Franklin Coll., 1988-95. Circulation mgr. The Franklin Newspaper, 1991-93, metro editor, 1993-94; pub. rels. coord. Matinee Musicale of Franklin, 1993—; office adminstr. Ctr. United Meth. Ch., Indpls., 1994—. Editor brochures. Mem. Pi Sigma Alpha, Phi Alpha Theta. Methodist. Home: 2766 Del Prado Dr Indianapolis IN 46221

CAMPBELL, RAYMOND W., surgical nurse; b. Orlando, Fla., Sept. 3, 1956; s. Frank Richard Sr. and Edythe Bertha (Voyles) C.; m. Brenda L. Campbell, May 8, 1978; children: Rachael D., Raymond W. II. AD, Kellogg Coll., Battle Creek, Mich., 1989. Cert. ACLS, emergency med. tech. Indsl. emergency med. technician Ingalls Shipbldg., Pascagoula, Miss., 1976-79; chief urodynamics technician Lucerne Gen. Hosp., Orlando, 1978-79; psychiat. nursing asst. U.S. VA Med. Ctr., Battle Creek, 1980-87; scrub and circulating nurse Battle Creek Health Sys., 1989-94, oper. rm. charge nurse, 1994; scrub and circulating nurse, neurosurg. svcs. coord. Borgess Med. Ctr., 1994—, clin. preceptor, 1994—; mem. oper. rm. safety and infection control policy and procedure com. Battle Creek Health Systems, chmn. oper. rm. product edn. com. Trustee Village of Augusta, Mich., fire marshall and police commr.; ward mission leader Ch. Jesus Christ of LDS, Kalamazoo, 1994-95. With USN, 1974-76. Office: Borgess Med Ctr Surgery Svc 1521 Gull Rd Kalamazoo MI 49001

CAMPBELL, REX, sociology educator; b. Jasper, Mo., Jan. 8, 1931; s. Philip Edward and Lucy Fern (Strecker) C.; m. Mary Higgins, June 12, 1955. PhD, U. Mo., 1965. Prof. sociology U. Mo., Columbia, 1961—; cons., owner Campbell & Assocs., Columbia, 1970-80. Author: Society and Environment, Black Migration; editor jour. The Rural Sociologist, 1988-92; contbr. more than 100 articles to profl. jours. Mem. Columbia City Coun., 1989—; mem. Planning and Zone Commn., City of Columbia, 1982-88. Served with U.S. Army, 1952-54, Korea. Recipient Provost's award for creative extension U. Mo., 1988. Mem. AAAS, Rural Sociol. Soc., Mus. Assocs. (pres. 1992-94), Columbia N.W. Rotary. Office: U Mo 730 Clark Hall Columbia MO 65211

CAMPBELL, RONALD BRUCE, clothing company executive; b. Linton, Ind., Aug. 20, 1946; s. Bruce Everett and Mary Francis (Buckles) C. Student, Vincennes (Ind.) U., 1964-66; BS in Bus., Ind. U., 1973. Cert. residential specialist. Gen. agt. Old Heritage Life Ins., Lincoln, Ill., 1973-74; buyer, mgr. Root's Dept. Store, Terre Haute, Ind., 1974-79; assoc. Pfister Better Homes & Gardens, Terre Haute, 1979-96; with Brooks Brothers, Northbrook, Ill., 1996—. Adv. Ind. State U. Ctr. Econ. Edn.; past v.p. Dance Action Terre Haute; mem. Leadership Terre Haute, 1990-91; bd. dirs. United Ministries. Mem. Terre Haute Bd. Realtors, Nat. and State Bd. Realtors, Vigo County Hist. Soc., Exchange Club, Am. Mktg. Assn., Multiple Listing Assn., Vigo County Ind. U. Alumni Club (past pres. Terre Haute chpt.), Terre Haute C. of C., Delta Sigma Pi (life), Sigma Pi (life). Republican. Baptist. Home: 1202 N Streamwood Vernon Hills IL 60061 Office: Pfister Better Homes Brooks Brothers Northbrook IL

CAMPBELL, ROYCE MICHAEL, agricultural engineer; b. McCook, Nebr., Oct. 6, 1952; s. Frank Lewis and Eula Kathryn (Cordell) C.; m. Joan Marie Hinze, Dec. 29, 1973; children: Jeremy Scott, Erin Nicole, Michelle Rae. BS in Agrl. Engring., U. Nebr., 1974. Registered profl. engr. Nebr. Field engr. Halliburton Services, Liberal, Kans., 1975; design engr. Lenox (Iowa) div. Hoover Universal, 1975-78; product design engr. Henke Machine, Inc., Columbus, Nebr., 1978-84, v.p. engring., 1984—. Pres. Sch. Bd. Dist. 9, Platte County, Columbus, Nebr., 1985—. Mem. Am. Soc. Agrl. Engrs. Roman Catholic. Home: 2990 29th Ave E Columbus NE 68601-7285 Office: Henke Machine Inc PO Box 1006 Columbus NE 68602-1006

CAMPBELL, RYAN D., account executive; b. Marion, Ohio, Aug. 4, 1967. BS in Bus., Ohio State U., 1990. Salesman Plastic Corp., Columbus, Ohio, 1990-94; account exec. The Ohio Co., Columbus, 1994—.

CAMPBELL, S. JACK, investment banker; b. Lafayette, Ind., Apr. 22, 1945; s. J. D. and Betty J. Campbell; m. Pamela A. Campbell; children: Braun C., Drew C. BS, Ball State U., 1967; JD, Ind. U., 1973. Staff asst. Ernst & Ernst, Indpls., 1967-68; staff auditor Ind. Dept. Revenue, Indpls., 1971; staff asst. to mgr. Ernst & Whinney, Indpls., 1971-78; mgr. Ernst & Whinney, South Bend, Ind., 1978-82; ptnr. Ernst & Whinney, Chgo., 1982-84; prin., pres. Merger & Acquisition Strategies Inc., Chgo., 1984—, MASI, Ltd., Deerfield, Ill., 1989—; bd. dirs. Mergers and Acquisition Strategies, Inc., MASI Ltd.; chmn. M&A Internat., Delaware, Md., 1987. Team capt. United Way, South Bend, 1977. With U.S. Army, 1968-70. Mem. ABA, AICPA, Ill. Bar Assn., Ind. Soc. Chgo. (sec. 1992-94, v.p. 1994—), Ill. CPA Soc., Beta Theta Pi (funding coord. Delta Iota chpt. 1994). Office: MASI Ltd 1419 Lake Cook Rd Ste 220 Deerfield IL 60015-5230

CAMPBELL, WILLIAM EDWARD, state hospital school administrator; b. Kansas City, Kans., June 30, 1927; s. William Warren and Mary (Bickerman) C.; m. Joan Josselyn Larimer, July 26, 1952; children: William Gregory, Stephen James, Douglas Edward. Student, U. Nebr., 1944-45, M.S., 1975; student, U. Mich., 1945, Drake U., 1948; B.A., U. Iowa, 1949, M.A., 1950; Ph.D. in Psychology, U. Nebr., Lincoln, 1980. Psychologist Dept. Pub. Instrn., State of Iowa, 1951-52; hosp. adminstr. Mental Health Inst., Cherokee, Iowa, 1952-68; dir. planning and rsch. Dept. Social Svcs., State of Iowa, 1968-69; supt. Glenwood State Hosp. Sch., Iowa, 1969—, Clarinda Mental Health Inst., Iowa, 1979—; assoc. prof. mental health adminstrn. Northwestern U., Chgo., 1982—; pres., bd. dirs. River Bluffs Community Mental Health Ctr.; dir. Shared Mental Health Svcs., Clarinda/Glenwood; founder, chmn. Regional Drug Abuse Adv. Council; adj. prof. Sch. Pub. Health U. Minn., also preceptor grad. students in mental health adminstrn.; vis. faculty Avepane U., Caracas, Venezuela; adj. prof. Coll. Medicine and Health Adminstrn. Tulane U. Author works in field. UN spl. cons. to Venzuela for UNESCO; bd. dirs. Polk County Mental Health; v.p., bd. dirs. Mercy Hosp., Coun. Bluffs, Iowa; state pres. United Cerebral Palsy; charter mem., bd. dirs. Pub. Broadcasting Sta. KIWR, Council Bluffs, Iowa, Glenwood-Mills County Econ. Devel. Found., Inc., 1985—; chartered mem., bd. dirs. Mills County Econ. Devel., 1987, Glenwood Resource Ctr., 1993—. Served with AUS, 1944-46; col. Res. Decorated Army Commendation medal; recipient Meritorious Service medal U.S. Army, 1982. Fellow Assn. Mental Health Adminstrs. (nat. com. chmn. 1970); mem. Assn. Med. Adminstrs., Am. Hosp. Assn. (nat. governing bd. psychiat. services sect., charter panelist nat. adv. panel on mental health services, mem. governing body psychiat. services sect.), Iowa Hosp. Assn., Health Planning Council of Midlands, Assn. Univ. Programs in Health Adminstrn. (mem. nat. task force on edn. of mental health adminstrs.), Am. Assn. on Mental Deficiency (chmn. adminstrn. sect. Region 8), Nat. Rehab. Assn., Assn. for Retarded Children, Mental Health Assn., Phi Beta Kappa. Office: Office of Supt Glenwood State Hosp Glenwood IA 51534

CAMPER, JOHN JACOB, writer, university administrator; b. Toledo, Sept. 8, 1943; m. Cleraine Uguccioni, Mar. 27, 1971 (div. May 1981); 1 child, Sarah; m. Mary C. Galligan, Jan. 9, 1988; 1 child, Joseph. B.A., Kenyon Coll., 1964. Reporter Detroit News, 1965-68; reporter, critic Chgo. Daily News, 1968-78; editorial writer Chgo. Sun-Times, 1979-84; dept. head external relations Regional Transp. Authority, Chgo., 1984-85; media coord. Chgo. World's Fair Authority, 1985; reporter Chgo. Tribune, 1985-90; assoc. chancellor for pub. affairs U. Ill., Chgo., 1990—; bd. dirs. Family Svc. Mental Health Ctr. of Oak Park and River Forest, 1991-95; v.p. Chgo. Pub. Rels. Forum, 1995—. Recipient Peter Lisagor award Chgo. Headline Club, 1983, UPI award, Chgo., 1983, Stick-O-Type, Chgo. Newspaper Guild, 1983, Nat. Assn. Black Journalists award, 1987. Home: 505 River Oaks Dr River Forest IL 60305-1621 Office: U Ill Chgo 1331 University Hall 601 S Morgan St Chicago IL 60607-7100

CAMRAS, CARL BRUCE, ophthalmologist, educator; b. Chgo., Nov. 23, 1953; s. Marvin and Isabelle Lillian (Pollack) C.; m. Nancy Louise Ross, June 3, 1979; children: Melanie, Lucinda. BA, Yale U., 1975; MD, Columbia U., 1979. Diplomate Am. Bd. Ophthalmology. Med. intern Los Angeles County Harbor-UCLA Med. Ctr., Torrance, Calif.; resident in ophthalmology Jules Stein Eye Inst., UCLA Med. Ctr.; asst. prof. ophthalmology Mt. Sinai Med. Ctr., N.Y.C., 1983-87, assoc. prof., 1988-91; prof., vice chmn. dept. ophthalmology U. Nebr. Med. Ctr., Omaha, 1991—. Contbr. articles to Investigative Ophthalmology and Visual Sci., Exptl. Eye Rsch., Current Eye Rsch., Ophthalmology, Am. Jour. Ophthalmology, Archives of Ophthalmology, Ophthalmic Surgery. NIH grantee, 1988—; Heed Ophthalmic Found. fellow, 1983; recipient Travel Fellowship award Assn. for Rsch. in Vision, 1977, Sandoz award, 1979, Alvin Behrens Meml. Fund award, 1979. Fellow ACS, Am. Glaucoma Soc., Am. Acad. Ophthalmology, N.Y. Acad. Medicine, Assn. for Rsch. in Vision and Ophthalmology. Office: Univ Nebr Med Ctr Dept Ophthalmology 600 S 42nd St Omaha NE 68198-5540

CANAAN, DON, journalist; b. N.Y.C., Aug. 14, 1938; s. Louis and Sally Swerdlow; m. Mazal Canaan, Feb. 27, 1975 (div. Feb. 1992); children: Richard, Kenneth, Tamar, Golan. BA in Film Tech., CUNY, 1961; MA in Journalism, Ohio State U., 1984. Cert. audio-visual specialist NASA. Film editor NBC News, N.Y.C., 1961-74; freelance film editor ABC News, Washington, 1977-83; TV prodr. and dir. Ben Gurion U., Beersheva, Israel, 1975-76; supr. audio-video comm. NASA Goddard Space Flight Ctr., Greenbelt, Md., 1979-81; copy editor Downtowner, Cin., 1986-87; staff writer Am. Israelite, Cin., 1987-91; freelance writer, Balt. and Washington, 1977—; Cin. corr. UPI, 1994—; adj. instr. film Rockland C.C., Suffern, N.Y., 1970, Montgomery Coll., Rockville, Md., 1978; system operator Tri-State Online, Cin., 1989—. Author: Horror in Hocking County, 1989; editor: (video) Reasonable Doubt, 1984 (Cin. Blue Chip Cable Commn. award 1989). Vice pres. Howard Community Access Corp., Columbia, Md., 1979-83, Guilford Gardens, Columbia, 1979-83; media cons. Virginia Rhodes Congl. Campaign, Cin., 1992. With U.S. Army, 1956. Recipient award for best film on a shoestring for Welfare Island: Blight of a City, 1969, Freedom: A Long Hard Road, 1971, Peabody citation for American White Paper: Organized Crime in the United States, 1967. Jewish. Home: 8916 Reading Rd Cincinnati OH 45215-3256

CANDEE, BENJAMIN LEROY, JR., retired psychologist, educator; b. Syracuse, N.Y., May 24, 1921; s. Benjamin L. Sr. and Maude G. (Merrill) C.; m. Alice Kemeny Kohn, Jan. 8, 1951 (div. July 1958); m. Jean A. Carey, Dec. 24, 1960; children: William, Amy, Philip. BA, Cornell U., 1941; MS in Edn., Syracuse U., 1945; PhD, U. Nebr., 1955. Cert. sch. psychologist, Ohio; diplomate Am. Bd. Profl. Psychology. Ship's cattleman Brethren Svc. Com., 1946-47; ships purser U.S. Lines, Inc., 1947-48; relief worker Am. Friends Svc. Com., 1949; area officer UN Relief and Works Agy. for Palestine Refugees, Acre, Israel, 1949-50; sch. psychologist Cleve. (Ohio) City Sch. Dist., 1954-77, supr. psychol. svcs., 1977-87; psychology instr. Cuyahoga C.C., Cleve., 1969-71, Cleve. (Ohio) State U., 1973-76; mem. testing com. Ohio Bd. Psychology, Columbus, 1975. Mem. War Register's League, 1940—; activist, organizer Com. on Racial Equality, Syracuse, N.Y., 1941-42; conscientious objector fed. prison, Danbury, Conn., 1946; mem., clinic protector Nat. Abortion Rights League, Cleve., 1992-95. Mem. ACLU, APA, NAACP, Cleve. Psychol. Assn., Cleve. Assn. Sch. Psychologists, Psychologists for Social Responsibility, Planned Parenthood, Sierra Club. Home: 3123 Ludlow Rd Shaker Heights OH 44120

CANJAR, PATRICIA MCWADE, psychologist; b. Pitts., Mar. 14, 1932; d. Robert Malachai McWade and Lillian Kathryn (Seidenstricker) Robb; m. Lawrence N. Canjar, Aug. 4, 1951 (dec. Nov. 1972); 1 son, R. Michael; m. James M. McDonald, Sept. 24, 1977. A.A., Carlow Coll., 1951; B.A., U. Detroit, 1973, M.A., 1975. Lic. psychologist, Mich. Psychologist, Robinwood Clinic, Detroit, 1973-77, Psychol. Resources, Birmingham, Mich., 1977-80, Realistic Living Ctr., Warren, Mich., 1983-85, Behavior Ctr., Birmingham, 1980-84; with Eastwood Cmty. Clinic, Big Beaver, Mich., 1984-94; ret. 1994. Mem. Nat. YWCA Spl. Commn., Boston, N.Y.C. and Washington, 1967; bd. dirs. YWCA, Pitts., 1961-65, Detroit, 1965-67; asst. coordinator United We Sing, Pitts. Music Festival, 1955-65; pres. Carnegie Mellon Women's Club, Pitts., 1963-65, U. Detroit Faculty Wives' Club, 1968-70; mem. State of Mich. Fair Campaign Practices Commn., 1968-70; treas. Grandview Beach Assn., 1982-84, pres., 1984-87. Fellow Am. Psychol. Assn.; mem. Mich. Assn. Profl. Psychologist, Mich. Assn. Alcohol and Drug Abuse Counselors. Democrat. Roman Catholic.

CANNON, BENNIE MARVIN, physical education educator; b. Goshen Pike, Ala., Aug. 20, 1942; s. L.D. and Gussie Lee (Canty) C.; m. Vercilla Brown, Aug. 27, 1966; children: Steven Marvin, Jonathan Benjamin, Noah Christopher. AA, Chgo. City Coll., 1964; BS, Upper Iowa U., 1968; postgrad., U. Ill., 1971-76. Cert. phys. edn., safety and driver edn. tchr., Ill. Tchr. elem. phys. edn. Chgo. Pub. Schs., 1968-69, tchr. gen. sci., 1969-71, tchr. secondary phys. edn., driver's edn., 1971-78, 79—. Fitness specialist del. Dwight David Eisenhower Found., Spokane, Wash., 1992, Driver Edn. Profl. del. Dwight David Eisenhower Found., Spokane, 1996. Mem. AAPHERD, Ill. Assn. Health, Phys. Edn., Recreation and Dance (Quarter Century award Chgo. dist. 1993, Quarter Century Club award state dist. 1994), Nat. Sci. Tchrs. Assn., Ill. H.S. and Coll. Driver Edn. Assn., Nat. Fedn. News, Am. Fedn. Tchrs., Phi Zeta Tau. Democrat. African Methodist Episcopal. Home: 8419 S Indiana Ave Chicago IL 60619-5606

CANNON, VALERIE LYNN, medical laboratory professional; b. Gary, Ind., Jan. 11, 1957; d. Lawrence Wendell and Ruth (Augustus) C. BS, St. Mary's Coll., 1979; cert. med. technologist, Evanston Hosp. Sch. Med. Tech., Ill., 1980; MPA, Ind. U., Gary, 1990. Med. technologist St. Catherine's Hosp., East Chicago, Ind., 1980-82; lab. supr. Meth. Hosp., Merrillville, Ind., 1982-86, phlebotomy supr., 1986-90; lab. mgr. Loyola U. Med. Ctr., Maywood, Ill., 1990-95; cons. Health Care Development Svcs., Northbrook, Ill., 1995—. Named one of Outstanding Young Women Am., 1991. Mem. Am. Soc. Clin. Pathologists, Am. Coll. Healthcare Execs., Soc. Ambulatory Care Profls., Clin. Lab Mgmt. Assn. Methodist. Office: Loyola U Med Ctr 2160 S 1st Ave Maywood IL 60153-3304

CANON, DAVID THEODORE, political science educator; b. Mpls., Apr. 26, 1959; s. Cornelius Baird and Marvis Jean Canon; m. Sarah Fetherston, July 16, 1987; children: Neal Emmerson, Katherine Betts, Sophia Frances. BA in Polit. Sci. with honors, Ind. U., 1981; MA, U. Minn., 1984, PhD in Polit. Sci., 1987. Rsch. fellow Brookings Instn., Washington, 1985-86; asst. prof. Duke U., Durham, N.C., 1986-91, U. Wis., Madison, 1991-94; assoc. prof. U. Wis., 1994—. Reveiwer, book editor: Congress and the Presidency: A Journal of Capital Studies; contbr. articles to profl. jours. Recipient Ind. County scholarship, 1980-81, I.U. Honors Program Rsch. grant, 1980, Hossier Merit scholarship, 1977-78, Ford P. Hall award Ind. U., 1981. Mem. Am. Polit. Sci. Assn. (legis. studies sect.), Midwest Polit. Sci. Assn., So. Polit. Sci. Assn., Phi Beta Kappa. Home: 2521 Kendall Ave Madison WI 53705 Office: Univ Wis Dept Polit Sci 110 N Hall 1050 Bascom Mall Madison WI 53706

CANTONI, LOUIS JOSEPH, psychologist, poet, sculptor; b. Detroit, May 22, 1919; s. Pietro and Stella (Puricelli) C.; m. Lucile Eudora Moses, Aug. 7, 1948; children: Christopher Louis, Sylvia Therese. AB, U. Calif., Berkeley, 1946; MSW, U. Mich., 1949, Ph.D., 1953. Personnel mgr. Johns-Manville Corp., Pittsburg, Calif., 1944-46; social caseworker Detroit Dept. Pub. Welfare, 1946-49; counselor Mich. Div. Vocat. Rehab., Detroit, 1949-50; conf. leader, tchr. psychology, coordinator family and community relations program Gen. Motors Inst., Flint, Mich., 1951-56; from assoc. prof. to prof., dir. rehab. counseling Wayne State U., Detroit, 1956-89. Author books and monographs including: The 1939-1943 Flint Michigan Guidance Demonstration, 1953, Marriage and Community Relations, 1954; (with Mrs. Cantoni) Counseling Your Friends, 1961, Supervised Practice in Rehabilitation Counseling, 1978, Writings of Louis J. Cantoni, 1981, Essays, Theses and Projects in Rehabilitation Counseling, 1989; (with Mrs. Cantoni) Theoretical Underpinnings of Practice in Family Service Agencies, 1990; (poetry) With Joy I Called to You, 1969, Gradually The Dreams Change, 1979, A Festival of Lanternes, 1994; editor: Placement of the Handicapped in Competitive Employment, 1957; co-editor: Preparation of Vocational Rehabilitation Counselors Through Field Instruction, 1985; prin. editor: (poetry) Golden Song Anthology, 1985; editor jours. Mich. Rehab. Assn. Digest, 1961-63, Cathedral Digest, 1973-75; contbr. articles, revs., poems and illustrations. to jours. Judge Mich. regional and nat. essay and poetry contests, 1965-77; bd. dirs. Mich. Rehab. Assn., 1962-64, 78-79, Mich. Rehab. Conseling Assn., 1985-87. Served to 2d lt. AUS, 1942-44. Recipient award for leadership and service Mich. Rehab. Assn., 1964, Mich. Rehab. Counseling Assn., 1985, 87, 88, Outstanding Service award Mich. State Bd. Edn., 1989; South and West ann. poetry award, 1970; Award for Meritorious Service Wayne State U., 1971, 81, 86, 87, 89; Outstanding Service award Poetry Soc. Mich., 1984. Fellow AAAS; mem. AAUP, APA, Coun. of Rehab. Counselor Educators (sec. 1957-58, chmn. 1965-66), Nat. Rehab. Assn., Nat. Congress of Orgns. of the Physically Handicapped, Nat. Assn. of the Physically Handicapped, Nat. Alliance for the Mentally Ill, Am. Inst. Econ. Rsch., Poetry Soc. Am., Mich. Rehab. Assn (pres. 1963-64), Detroit Rehab. Assn. (pres. 1958), Mich. Counseling Assn., Mich. Career Devel. Assn., Internat. Inst. Met. Detroit, World Poetry Soc. (Edwin A. Falkowski Meml. award 1990), Acad. Am. Poets, Detroit Inst. Arts, Friends of Detroit Pub. Libr., Friends of Marshall M. Fredericks Sculpture Gallery, Soc. for Study of Midwestern Lit., U.S. Hist. Soc., Italic Studies Inst., USN Meml., Internat. Sculpture Ctr., Nat. Sculpture Soc., Sculptors Guild Mich., Lladro Collectors Soc., Birmingham-Bloomfield Art Assn., Psychology and the Arts, Poetry Soc. Mich., Detroit Film Soc., Poetry Resource Ctr. Mich., Univ. Club, Scarab Club (Detroit), Phi Kappa Phi, Phi Delta Kappa. Democrat. Episcopalian. Home: 2591 Woodstock Dr Detroit MI 48203-1062

CANTRALL, IRVING J(AMES), entomologist, educator; b. Springfield, Ill., Oct. 6, 1909; s. Ula J. and Elsie M. (LaRue) C.; m. Dorothy Louise Ransom, Dec. 24, 1932; children: Marion Louise, James Bruce. AB, U. Mich., 1935, PhD, 1940. Asst. Mus. Zoology U. Mich., Ann Arbor, 1935-37, tech. asst. Mus. Zoology, 1937-42, from asst. to prof. Zoology, 1949-77; curator Edwin S. George Res., Ann Arbor, 1949-59; curator insects Mus. Zoology U. Mich., Ann Arbor, 1959-77, curator insects emeritus, 1978—, prof. emeritus, 1978—; jr. aquatic biologist TVA, 1942, asst. aquatic biologist, 1942-43; asst. prof. biology U. Fla., Gainesville, 1946-49. Editor Great Lakes Entomologist, 1971-76; contbr. numerous articles on zoology to profl. jours. 1st lt. USAAF, 1943-46. Fellow AAAS; mem. Am. Entomol. Soc., Mich. Entomol. Soc. (pres. 1957-58, editor 1971-76), Soc. for Study of Evolution, Ecol. Soc. Am., Soc. Systematic Zoology, The Orthopterists Soc., Mich. Acad. Sci., Arts and Letters (sec. 1963-65), N.Y. Acad. Sci., Ind. Acad. Sci., Fla. Acad. Sci., Sigma Xi, Phi Kappa Phi, Phi Sigma, Gamma Alpha. Home: 1531 Las Vegas Dr Ann Arbor MI 48103-5765

CANTRELL, JOHN L., secondary education educator; b. Aug. 24, 1945; s. Mance and Maglene (Conley) C. BA, Morehead State U., 1967; MA, la Universidad de Coahuila, Saltillo, Mex., 1971; postgrad., Miami U. Spanish tchr., dir., performing arts instr. Piqua (Ohio) City Schs., 1967-72, Hamilton (Ohio) City Schs., 1972-86, Springfield (Ohio) City Schs., 1987—. V.p. Civic Theatre, Springfield, 1987-89; bd. dirs. Ohio Lyric Theatre, Springfield, 1989-90. Recipient Ohio Gov.'s award for excellence in arts, 1992, Outstanding Citizen award Moose Lodge, 1970, Outstanding Educator award Jaycees, 1981. Mem. NEA, S.W. Ohio Edn. Assn. (chmn. fgn. langs. 1980-82), Ohio Edn. Assn., Ohio Tchrs. Assn. (bd. dirs., theatre dir. 1992), Ohio Theatre Alliance, Ednl. Theatre Assn., Phi Kappa Delta, Theta Kappa Epsilon (v.p. 1966-67). Home: 1853 Winding Trl Springfield OH 45503-2816

CANTRELL, LINDA MAXINE, counselor; b. Ann Arbor, Mich., June 20, 1938; d. Donald LaVerne and Lila Maxine (Crull) Katz; m. Douglas D. Cantrell, Dec. 28, 1963; children: Douglas David Jr., Warren Vincent, Bryan LaVerne. BA, U. Mich., 1960, MA, 1963, postgrad., 1963-65. Cert. secondary tchr., Mich. Caseworker Cook County Dept. Pub. Aid, Chgo., 1960; psychometrist Evanston (Ill.) Schs., 1960-61; rsch. assoc. U. Mich., Ann Arbor, 1961-64; guidance counselor Radcliff Mid. Sch., Garden City, Mich., 1964-66; dir. guidance and counseling St. Mary Acad., Monroe, Mich., 1985-87; counselor, head counselor, instr. Ypsilanti (Mich.) Adult Edn., 1987—; tchr. young adult program Ypsilanti Pub. Schs., 1995—. Rep. precinct leader Ann Arbor, 1971; clk., marker, rec. sec. Thrift Shop of Ann Arbor, 1981—; bd. dirs. Ypsilanti Adult/Cmty. Edn. Adv. Com., 1990—; treas. Burns Park Sch., Ann Arbor, 1978-79; rec. sec. Chapel of Love Ch., 1989—; co-chmn. benefits Ann Arbor Chamber Orch., 1981-82; chmn. ann. benefit Rudolf Steiner Sch. Ann Arbor, 1984-85; treas. Burns Park PTO, 1978-79; vol. Greenhills Schs., 1978-81, St. Paul's Luth. Sch., 1972-73, among others. Recipient Gil Bursley award Rep. Party, 1972, scholarship Chi Omega, 1957. Mem. AAUW (fellowship chmn. 1971-73), Mich. Assn. for Counseling and Devel. (membership chmn. Monroe County chpt. 1986-87), Ypsilanti Fedn. Tchrs. (rec. sec. 1989-91), Mich. Assn. for Acad. Advisors Community Edn., Washtenaw Counselors Assn., Monroe County Counselors Assn. (membership chmn. 1985-87), Ann Arbor Women's City Club (membership com. 1985-87), Ea. Mich. U. Coll. Bus. Wives (program chmn. 1974, pres. 1975), Phi Kappa Phi, Pi Lambda Theta. Office: Ypsilanti Adult Edn Ypsilanti Pub Schs Perry Sch Ypsilanti MI 48197

CANTU, DINO ANTONIO, secondary education history educator; b. Savanna, Ill., Sept. 25, 1961; s. Alfonso A. and Bonnie L. (Wills) C.; m. Sandra Lou Smith, May 12, 1984; childen: Derek Anthony, Dylan Alex. AS in Social Sci., Highland C.C., Freeport, Ill., 1981; BSE in Social Sci. Edn., Ark. State U., 1983, MA in History, 1984, specialist in C.C. Edn., 1989. Tchrs. Cert. Social Studies 7-12, Mo. Tutor PASS Program Ark. State U., Jonesboro, 1982-83, grad. asst. History Dept., 1983-84; military intelligence officer U.S. Army, Ft. Knox, Ky., 1984-88; history instr. Ark. State U., Jonesboro, 1988-89; tchr. Am. history, chair dept. social studies Ste. Genevieve (Mo.) High Sch., 1989—; adj. faculty 1-8-1-8 program St. Louis U., Ste. Genevieve, Mo., 1991—; chairperson Social Sci. Curriculum Com., Ste. Genevieve, Mo., 1991; evaluator North Ctrl. Vis. Com., Ste. Genevieve, Mo., 1992; cooperating tchr. S.E. Mo. State U., Ste. Genevieve, Mo., 1992; rep. NCSS Textbook Com., Washington, 1992—; rep. Governor's Task Force Environ. Edn., 1993-94; rep. ad hoc com. performace standards Mo. Dept. Elem. and Secondary Edn., 1994. Presenter: Civil War Prison Camp, 1984, Rural Traditions, 1991. Commr. Ste. Genevieve (Mo.) Landmarks Commn., 1992—; bd. dirs. Found. for Restoration of Ste. Genevieve, 1993-94; rep. steering com. Ste. Genevieve Hist. Preservation and Tourism, 1993-94. Capt. U.S. Army, 1984-88. Recipient Social Sci. award Highland C.C., Freeport, Ill., 1981, George C. Marshall ROTC award U.S. Army, Ark. State U., 1984, Military Intelligence Acad. award U.S. Army, Ft. Huachuca, Ariz., 1985, Army Commendation medal U.S. Army, Ft. Knox, Ky., 1988; named Outstanding Young Educator, Jaycees, Ste, Genevieve, Mo., 1992, Mo. Social Studies Tchr. of Yr., Mo. Coun. Social Studies, 1994. Mem. Nat. Coun. History Edn. (Mo. com. corr.), Am. Sociol. Assn., Nat. Coun. Social Studies (chair sociology spl. interest group 1993-95), Mo. Coun. Social Studies (v.p.), Mo. Hist. Soc., Orgn. Am. Historians, Pi Gamma Mu, Sigma Phi epsilon, Kappa Delta Pi, Phi Kappa Phi, Phi Alpha Theta. Home: 748 Claymont Dr Sainte Genevieve MO 63670-1815 Office: St Genevieve H S 715 Washington St Sainte Genevieve MO 63670-1237

CANUP, LARRY DALE, data systems specialist; b. Cairo, Ill., Apr. 28, 1955; s. Micah C. and Alberta (Crockett) C.; m. Cheryl Darlene Mace, July 23, 1973; 1 child, Larry Dale Jr. Cert. programmer, Automation Machine Tng. Ctr., Kansas City, Mo., 1973. Cert. Novell engr., advanced AIX adminstr. Computer operator Phoenix Hecht, Geneva, Ill., 1973-74; lead computer operator Cessna Fluid Power, Hutchinson, Kans., 1974-75; systems programmer Tymshare, Wichita, Kans., 1975-77, Vickers Petroleum, Wichita, Kans., 1977-79, Beech Aircraft, Wichita, Kans., 1979-82; mgr. computer tech. BHP Petroleum, Wichita, Kans., 1982-87; supr. online systems Cessna Aircraft, Wichita, Kans., 1987-88; systems support mgr. St. Joseph Med. Ctr., Wichita, Kans., 1988-89; network svcs. mgr. Health Care Data Systems, Wichita, Kans., 1989—. Therapeutic foster parent Caring Connection, Wichita, 1989-90. Recipient Cert. of Merit Ill. State Scholarship Commn., 1973-74. Mem. Data Processing Mgmt. Assn. (publicity dir. 1984-85). Republican. Baptist. Home: 406 Peach Tree Ln Haysville KS 67060-1028

CANUTESON, GREG, state legislator. Mo. State rep., Dist. 34. Address: 623 W Kansas Ave Liberty MO 64068-2126*

CAO, JOHN, investment executive; b. Shanghai; came to U.S., 1990; BBA, U. Mo., Kansas City, 1993. Stockbroker Piper Jaffray Inc., Kansas City, Mo., 1993—; bd. dirs. Chinese-Am. Bus. Svc. Ctr., Inc., Kansas City, Chinese Monthly; v.p. Chinese NEtwork of Kansas City, 1992—. Mem. Kansas City Security Assn. Office: Piper Jaffray Inc 2100 City Ctr Sq 4600 Madison Ave # 1200 Kansas City MO 64112

CAO, XIANG-DONG, mechanical engineer; b. Huangshi, Hubei, China, Dec. 30, 1962; came to U.S., 1989; s. Jiabin and Yun-Nan (Pan) C. BS, Huazhong U. Sci. and Tech., Wuhan, Hubei, 1984; M Space Physics, Grad. Sch. Sci. Acad., Beijing, 1987; MS in Mech. Engring., U. Rochester, 1991, PhD, 1995. Rsch. instr. Chinese Acad. Scis., Beijing, 1987-89; rsch. fellow dept. elect. engring. and computer sci. U. Mich., Ann Arbor, 1995—; conf. presenter in field, including Internat. Sympoium Space Physics, Beijing, 1986, Internat. Quantum-electronics Conf., Vienna, Austria, 1992, 6th Internat. Conf. on Multiphoton Processes, Quebec City, Que., Can., 1993. Contbr. articles to profl. jours.; patentee in field. Recipient natural sci. award 3d class Nat. Found. Sci., 1991. Mem. Optical Soc. Am., Internat. Soc. Optical Engring. Home: 2286 Stone Rd Ann Arbor MI 48105-2537 Office: U Rochester Lab for Laser Energetics 2286 Stone Rd Ann Arbor MI 48105-2537

CAPALDO, GUY, obstetrician, gynecologist; b. Bisaccia, Italy, Jan. 1, 1950; came to U.S., 1958; s. Arturo Nunziante and Maria Carmela (Ciani) C.; m. Kathy Nicita, Apr. 20, 1985. BSEE magna cum laude, U. Dayton, 1972; MS, Ohio State U., Columbus, 1973; MD, Med. Coll. Ohio, 1978. Diplomate Am. Bd. Ob-Gyn. Research asst. Ohio State U., 1973-75; resident in ob-gyn Med. Coll. Ohio, Toledo, 1978-82; practice medicine specializing in ob-gyn Mansfield, Ohio, 1982—; chief ob-gyn. dept. Mansfield Gen. Hosp., 1985—; lab. dir. Mansfield (Ohio) Ob-Gyn Assocs. Contbr. articles to profl. jours. Clinic physician Plan Parenthood, Mansfield, 1982—. Pres. scholar U. Dayton, 1968-72, Univ. fellow Ohio State U., 1972-75. Fellow Am. Coll. Ob-Gyn; mem. AMA, Ohio State Med. Assn., Richland County Med. Soc. Office: Mansfield Ob-Gyn Assocs 500 S Trimble Rd Mansfield OH 44906-3452

CAPERTON, ALBERT FRANKLIN, newspaper editor; b. Hemphill, W.Va., Dec. 31, 1936; s. Albert Harrison and Viola (Hicks) C.; m. Elizabeth Moreland, Jan. 29, 1960; children—Catherine Elizabeth, Robert Harrell. B., Northwestern State U., 1962; M.Jour., Columbia U., 1965; cert. Advanced Mgmt. Program, Harvard U., 1982. Reporter Richmond News Leader, Va., 1962-64; reporter St Petersburg Times, Fla., 1965-67, Tampa Tribune, Fla., 1967-69; asst. city editor Miami Herald, Fla., 1969-72; Broward County editor Miami Herald, Fort Lauderdale, Fla., 1972-75; exec. editor Macon Telegraph & News, Ga., 1975-78, Virginian-Pilot & Ledger Star, Norfolk, 1978-84; mng. editor Indpls. News, 1984-90, Indpls. Star, 1990-95; exec. editor Indpls. (Ind.) Star and News, 1995—. Pres. Crossroads of Am. Coun. Boy Scouts of Am., Indpls., 1991-92; trustee Christian Theol. Sem. With USAF, 1954-57. Mem. Am. Soc. Newspaper Editors, Rotary. Mem. Diciples of Christ. Home: 6432 Landborough North Dr Indianapolis IN 46220-4351 Office: Indianapolis Star 307 N Pennsylvania St Indianapolis IN 46204-1811

CAPLE, SHARON, chemistry educator; b. El Centro, Calif., Jan. 19, 1939; d. Charles Rickter and Mabel Dorothy (Miller) Clough; m. Gerald Caple, Aug. 9, 1964; children: Shelly, Kay, Kris. BS, Chapman U., 1957; secondary credential, No. Ariz. U., 1978, MA in Phys. Sci., 1993. Tchr. chemistry Tuba City (Ariz.) H.S., 1979-83, tchr. chemistry and sci., ESL, 1984-93; tchr. chemistry and math. Camino H.S., Flagstaff, Ariz., 1984-93; instr. chemistry Coconino C.C., Flagstaff, 1994, Ft. Scott (Kans.) C.C., 1994—; chemistry coach for Challenge contest Tuba City H.S. team, 1988-91. Mem. NSTA, Am. Chem. Soc. (speaker edn. div. 1991), Soc. for Advancement Chicanos and Native Ams. (Disting. Svc. award 1992), Phi Kappa Phi. Home: 1401 Bitner Ter Pittsburg KS 66762 Office: Ft Scott CC 2108 S Horton Fort Scott KS 66701

CAPLINGER, PATRICIA E., family nurse practitioner; b. St. Louis, Oct. 6, 1956; d. Julius G. and Wanda L. (Guthrie) Kissel; child from previous marriage, Jeremy Michael Frederiksen; m. Ray E. Caplinger, Dec. 26, 1995. ADN, St. Louis C.C., 1977; BSN, U. State N.Y., 1982; FNP, U. Colo., Denver, 1985. RN, Colo.; CNOR, CNRN; cert. family nurse practitioner. Med. case mgmt. supr. Intracorp., Denver; clin. mgr. Rehab. Svcs. Corp., Eureka, Calif.; family nurse practitioner Burre Clinic, Eureka; pvt. practice Eureka; dir. PM&R Marian Health Ctr., Sioux City, Iowa; family nurse practitioner Lebanon (Mo.) Med. Ctr. Mem. ANA (nursing scholar), ARN, AANP. Home: 23241 Red Oak Dr Lebanon MO 65536

CAPOBIANCO, ERNEST R., advertising executive; b. Providence, Mar. 28, 1960; s. Ernest R. and Florence Capobianco; m. Elske Cordero, Sept. 19, 1992. BSBA, Boston U., 1978; MS in CIS, Bentley Coll., 1988. Fin. profl. Digital Equipment Co., Boston, 1980-86; CFO Rossin Greenberg, Boston, 1986-89, Chiat Day Advt., N.Y.C., 1989-92; exec. v.p., CFO Valentine Radford, Kansas City, Mo., 1992-95; CEO Capobianco Assocs., Kansas City, 1995—; mem. fin. com. AAAA, N.Y.C., 1994—; bd. dirs. Zydekoln, New Orleans. Inventor: (bd. game) Imponderables, 1996. Bd. dirs. Ozanam Sch. for Boys, N.Y.C., 1993—; mem. mktg. com. Mo. Symphony Orch., Kansas City, 1995—.

CAPORALE, D. NICK, state supreme court justice; b. Omaha, Sept. 13, 1928; s. Michele and Lucia Caporale; m. Margaret Nilson, Aug. 5, 1950; children: Laura Diane Stevenson, Leland Alan. B.A., U. Nebr.-Omaha, 1949, M.Sc., 1954; J.D. with distinction, U. Nebr.-Lincoln, 1957. Bar: Nebr. 1957, U.S. Dist. Ct. Nebr. 1957, U.S. Ct. Appeals 8th cir. 1958, U.S. Supreme Ct. 1970. Mem. firm Stoehr, Rickerson, Sodoro & Caporale, Omaha, 1957-66; ptnr. Schmid, Ford, Mooney, Frederick & Caporale, Omaha, 1966-79; judge Nebr. Dist. Ct., Omaha, 1979-81, Nebr. Supreme Ct., Lincoln, 1982—; lectr. U. Nebr., Lincoln, 1982-84. Pres. Omaha Community Playhouse, 1976. Served to 1st lt. U.S. Army, 1952-54, Korea. Decorated Bronze Star; recipient Alumni Achievement U. Nebr.-Omaha, 1972. Fellow Am. Coll. Trial Lawyers, Internat. Soc. Barristers; mem. Order of Coif. Office: Nebr Supreme Ct 2413 St Capitol Bldg Lincoln NE 68509

CAPOUCH, EDWARD ARTHUR, electrical engineer; b. Oak Park, Ill., Jan. 30, 1942; s. Edward James and Laura Ann (Christian) C.; m. Judith Rae Schroeder, Dec. 30, 1967; children: Brett, Christen, Heather. BSEE, Purdue U., 1965. Registered profl. engr., Ill., Calif., Conn., Ky., Mass., Tex. Dir. elec. engring. & design Fluor Daniel, Inc., Chgo., 1965-92; sr. elec. project engr. Sargent & Lundy, Chgo., 1992—. Trustee St. Peter Lutheran Ch., Arlington Heights, Ill., 1985-91. Mem. IEEE (sr., chmn. power engring. soc. Chgo. chpt. 1978-79, sec. Chgo. sect. 1991-92, treas. Chgo. sect. 1992-93, vice chmn. 1993-94, chmn. 1994-95, chpt. rep. power engring. soc. region 4C 1992—, governing bd. power engring. soc. 1992—), Ill. Engring. Coun. (del. 1991-95), Chgo. Assn. Tech. socs. (v.p. 1989-90). Republican. Home: 224 E Kerry Brook Ln Arlington Heights IL 60004-2199 Office: Sargent & Lundy 55 E Monroe St Chicago IL 60603-5702

CAPPARELLI, RALPH C., state legislator; b. Chgo., Apr. 12, 1924; s. Ralph and Mary (Drammis) C.; m. Cordelia Capparelli; children: Ralph, Valerie. BS, No. Ill. U. 1st v.p. 41st Ward Dem. Orgn., Chgo., 1965—; Ill. state rep. Dist. 13, 1971—; asst. majority whip, ex officio mem. Com. Intergovt. Coop. Com., exec. mem. Fin. Inst. Com. and Transp. and Motor Vehicles Com., Ill. Ho. of Reps.; supr. recreation Chgo. Pk. Dist., 1953-67; advisor Columbia Bank, Chgo., 1967—; sec.-treas. Jefferson Travel, 1968—; former tchr. Decorated Battle Star. Mem. Nat. Recreation Soc., Ill. Recreation Soc., Lions, K.C. (4th degree), Eagles, Am. Legion, Sigma Nu. Office: State Capitol Springfield IL 62706

CAPPO, JOSEPH C., publisher; b. Chgo., Feb. 24, 1936; s. Joseph V. and Frances (Maggio) Cacioppo; m. Mary Anne Cappo, May 7, 1967; children: Elizabeth, John. BA, DePaul U., 1957. Reporter, Hollister Publs., Wilmette, Ill., 1961-62; reporter Chgo. Daily News, 1962-68, bus. columnist, 1968-78; columnist Crain's Chgo. Bus., 1978—, pub., 1979-89; v.p. Crain Communications, Inc., 1981-89, sr. v.p. group. pub., 1989-95, sr. v.p. internat., 1996—; pub. Advt. Age, 1989-92, publishing dir, 1992—; dir. Assn. Area Bus. Publs., 1982-88. Bd. dirs.: Off the Street Club, Chgo., 1981—, Chicago Advt. Fedn., 1987-93, Mus. of Broadcast Communications, 1984-1990, Ill. Coun. on Econ. Edn., 1990-95. With U.S. Army, 1959-61. Recipient award Ill. Press Assn., 1962, (with other Daily News staffers) Nat. Headliner award, 1966, Disting. Alumni award DePaul U., 1975, Page One award Chgo. Newspaper Guild, 1978, Peter Lisagor award Sigma Delta Chi, 1978, Outstanding Achievement award in Communication, Justinian Soc. Lawyers, 1979. Author: Future Scope: Success Strategies for the 1990's and Beyond, 1990. Mem. Internat. Advt. Assn. (world bd. 1994—, sr. v.p. 1996—), Econ. Club (Chgo.), Bus. and Econ. Writers (bd. govs. 1984-89), Ill. Small Business Advisory Commn., 1986-90, Internat. Advtsg. Assn., Delta Mu Delta (hon.). Roman Catholic. Office: Crain Communications Inc 740 N Rush St Chicago IL 60611-2525

CAPPS, DENNIS WILLIAM, secondary school educator; b. Phila., Mar. 14, 1944; s. William Hoyle and Alice Gertrude Capps; children: Andrea Diane, Adrienne Kathleen. BSBA, Fairmont State Coll., 1968; MEd, Miami U., 1975, postgrad., 1991-92; postgrad., U. Cin., 1991-92, Wright State U., 1992. Cert. secondary tchr. math., visual arts, Ohio. Secondary schs. tchr. math. Mason (Ohio) City Schs., 1968-89, secondary schs. tchr. visual arts, 1989—; chmn. Youth Arts Exhbn., Summerfair, Cin., 1991—; mem., ofcl. photographer Multi-cultural On-site Curriculum Writing Project, Mex., summer 1993; mem. regional evaluating team North Ctrl. Accrediting Assn. Recipient Jennings Scholarship award Martha Holden Jennings Found., Dayton, Ohio, 1974-75, Golden Apple Tchr. award, Mason City Sch. System, 1988. Mem. NEA, Ohio Edn. Assn., Mason Edn. Assn. (treas. 1975-76, v.p. 1979-80), Nat. Art Edn. Assn., Ohio Art Edn. Assn. (state bd. dirs. 1993-95, presenter conv. 1993, 94, local conv. coord., 1995), S.W. Ohio Art Edn. Assn. (regional dir. 1993-95), Am. Mensa Soc., Intertel, Cin. Art Mus., Contemporary Arts Ctr. Democrat. Home: 8325 Summerbridge Way West Chester OH 45069-1817

CAPSHAW, CHARLES W., investment company executive; b. Oklahoma City, Apr. 10, 1960. BS in Bus., Murray (Ky.) State U., 1983. Corp. intern Merrill Lynch, Evansville, Ind., 1983-84; investment broker, v.p. J.J.B. Hilliard W.L. Lyons Inc., Evansville, 1984—. Bd. dirs. Mesker Park Zoo Found., Evansville, 1994—. Mem. Lions. Office: JJB Hilliard WL Lyons Inc PO Box 98 329 Main St Evansville IN 47701

CAPSHAW, TOMMIE DEAN, judge; b. Oklahoma City, Sept. 20, 1936; m. Dian Shipp; 1 child, Charles W. BS in Bus., Oklahoma City U., 1958; student U. Ark. Coll. Law, Fayetteville, 1958-59; JD, U. Okla., Norman, 1961. Bar: Okla. 1961, Wyo. 1971, Ind. 1975. Assoc. Looney, Watts, Looney, Nichols and Johnson, Oklahoma City, 1961-63, Pierce, Duncan, Couch and Hendrickson, Oklahoma City, 1963-70; trial atty., v.p. Capshaw Well Service Co., Liberty Pipe and Supply Co., Casper, Wyo., SSA, adminstrv. law judge, Evansville, Ind., 1973-75, hearing office chief adminstrv. law judge, 1975—; acting regional chief adminstrv. law judge, Chgo., 1977-78; acting appeals council mem., Arlington, Va., 1980, acting chief adminstrv. law judge, 1984; mem. faculty U. Evansville, 1977, Sch. Law So. Ill. U., 1988—, So. Ind. U., 1990; lectr. in field. Author: A Manual for Continuing Judicial Education, 1981, Practical Aspects of Handling Social Security Disability Claims, 1982, Judicial Practice Handbook, 1990, A Quest for Quality, Speedy Justice, 1991; contbr. numerous articles to profl. jours., chpt. to textbook. Mem. adv. council Boy Scouts Am., scoutmaster, den leader, 1969—, Nat. Jud. Coll. U. Nev.; bd. dirs. Casper Symphony, 1972-73, Casper United Fund, 1972-73, Midget Football Assn., Casper, 1972-73, German Twp. Water Dist., 1984-85; pres. Evansville Unitarian Universalist Ch., 1984-86; performer Evansville Philharm. Orch., 1986—. Recipient Kappa Alpha Order Ct. of Honor award, 1962, Silver Beaver award Boy Scouts Am., 1980, presentation for vol. svc. contbg. betterment of community Office Hearings and Appeals, 1992, presentation outstanding jud. mentor tng. Supreme Ct. Iowa, 1992, presentation disting. mentor tng. Fla. Jud. Coll., 1992. Mem. Okla. Bar Assn., Okla. County Bar Assn. (v.p. 1967), Wyo. Bar Assn., Evansville Bar Assn. (jud. rep. 1986-87, James Bethel Gresham Freedom award, 1988), Young Lawyers Conf. of Okla. County (pres. 1966), Okla. Assn. Def. Council, Okla. City Trial Lawyers Assn., Assn. Adminstrv. Law Judges HHS (bd. dirs. 1979-82, presentation dedicated svc. advancing jud. edn. 1992), Fed. Adminstrv. Law Judges Assn., Oklahoma City U. Alumni Assn. (bd. dirs. 1965). Home: 6105 School Rd # 6 Evansville IN 47720

CARACCIOLO, ENRIQUE ERNESTO, foreign language educator; b. Aug. 15, 1930; came to the U.S., 1981; married; one son. Prof. de Inglés, U. Cordoba, Argentina, 1956; PhD, U. Essex, Eng., 1966. Assoc. prof. U. Cordoba, Argentina, 1960; lectr. in Spanish U. Bristol, Eng., 1962-64; lectr. in lit. U. Essex, Eng., 1966-74, sr. lectr. in lit., 1974-77, reader in lit., 1977-80; prof. Spanish Purdue U., West Lafayette, Ind., 1981—; vis. prof. U. BC.C., Can., 1976-77, Ind. U., fall 1978. Editor: Penguin Book of Latin American Poetry, 1971, Baroque Poetry, 1974; author: Vicente Huidobro y la Vanguardia, 1974, Travesias, 1984; translator: William Blake: Poemas, 1986, W.B. Yeats: Poemas, 1988, John Donne: Poemas, 1987, 88, 90; contbr. articles to profl. jours. Home: 193 Old Bridge Rd Danville KY 40422 Office: Dept Fgn Langs Purdue Univ West Lafayette IN 47907

CARAHER, MICHAEL EDWARD, systems analyst; b. Indpls., Dec. 22, 1953; s. Gregory Thomas and Mary Margaret (Shevlin) C.; m. Jan. 6, 1979 (div. 1986); children: Joseph Michael, Erin Michelle. BA, Butler U., Indpls., 1976. Systems mgr. Alexander Typesetting, Indpls., 1984-88; systems specialist for Weimer Graphics divsn. Shepard Poorman Comm. Corp., Indpls., 1988-94; systems mgr. Shepard Poorman Comm. Corp., 1994—. Vice precinct committeeman Ind. Dem. Party, Indpls., 1972-78, precinct committeeman, 1994. Mem. Ancient Order of Hibernians, Saenger Chor. Democrat. Roman Catholic. Home: 5205 E Washington St Indianapolis IN 46219-6325

CARDEN, ROBERT A., stockbroker; b. St. Louis, Sept. 6, 1963. BS, U. Mo., Rolla, 1985; MBA, S.E. Mo. State U., 1987. Banking officer Merchantile Bank, St. Louis, 1988-93; account exec. MGI Bank, St. Louis, 1993-94; stockbroker Huntleigh Securities Corp., Belleville, Ill., 1994—. Mem. Riverbend Growth Assn., 1992—. Mem. N. Alton Godfrey C. of C. Republican. Roman Catholic. Home: 7017 W Main St Collinsville IL 62234-6635 Office: Huntleigh Securities Corp 11 S High St Belleville IL 62220-2102

CARDER, CHARLES E., retired machine operator, writer; b. Avoca, N.Y., Apr. 11, 1931; s. Wilbur S. and Margaret E. (Wilkerson) C.; m. W. Jean Cheney, Dec. 8, 1950; 1 child, Deborah A. Grad., Ctrl. H.S., Lima, Ohio, 1950; student in indsl. mgmt., Ford Motor Co. Machine operator Baldwin-Lima (Ohio)-Hamilton Corp., 1950-57, Ford Motor Co., Lima, 1957-86; ret., 1986. Freelance columnist and contbg. editor Ohio Out-of-Doors and The Single Shot Exchange mags. City councilman City of Delphos, Ohio, 1992-93, 96—, pres. city coun., 1996—. Mem. Outdoor Writers of Ohio, Assn. Great Lakes Outdoor Writers, Mason, Eagles, Tri-State Gun Collectors (v.p., dir.). Democrat. Methodist. Home: 1309 Pamela Cir Delphos OH 45833

CARDINAL, SHIRLEY MAE, education educator; b. Morann, Pa., May 6, 1944; d. Thomas Joseph and Mary Louise (Nemish) Giza; m. Charles Edward Cardinal, June 11, 1966; children: Julie Ann, Karen Lee. BS, Lock Haven U., 1966; MEd, Pa. State U., 1970. Tchr. Bald Eagle Nittany Corp., Mill Hall, Pa., 1966-68; tchr., supr. Pa. State U., University Park, 1968-76; tchr., chairperson State Coll. (Pa.) Area Schs., 1968-76; primetime educator Oregon-Davis Corp., Hamlet, Ind., 1984—; instr., cons. Dept. Edn., Indpls., 1979—, cons. energy edn., 1980-85, educator linker, 1981—, rep. prime time, 1987—; instr. Ancilla Coll., Donaldson, Inc., 1976—; chair for evaluation North Ctrl. Accreditation Assn., 1988-89, leadership team, 1996; mem. leadership team North Ctrl. Regional Lab., 1991-92, 93-94, 94—, Fermi Nat. Accelerator Lab., 1994—, North Ctrl. Regional Ednl. Lab. Author: Energy Activities with Learning Skills, 1980. Chmn. publicity com. Rep. Orgn. Plymouth, Ind., 1983—; mem. Teacher Talk, Ind. Gov's. Com., 1988-89. Recipient Mankind and Edn. award U.S. Jaycees and Ind. Jaycees, 1981. Mem. Ind. State Tchr. Assn., Marshall County Reading Assn., Pa. State U. Club, Proficiency Bd. Accreditation (chairperson 1996), Phi Delta Kappa (v.p. programs South Bend chpt. 1992-93, v.p. membership 1994-95), Pi Lambda Theta, Sigma Kappa (chmn. Parent Club), Tri Kappa. Roman Catholic. Home: 10101 Turf Ct Plymouth IN 46563-9494

CARDOZO, LUIS EDUARDO, physiologist; b. Montevideo, Uruguay, June 14, 1964; came to U.S., 1988; s. Luis Alberto and Alba (Albarracin) C. BA in Law, U. Uruguay, Montevideo, 1986, BS in Phys. Edn., 1987; MSEd, U. Kans., 1992. Grad. fitness coord. U. Kans., Lawrence, 1989-91; wellness and fitness dir. Kansas City, Kans. C.C., 1991—; fitness cons. and specialist Prairie Life Ctr., Overland Park, Kans., 1991—. Co-chmn. City of Hope, Kansas City, 1995-96; fitness cons. March of Dimes, Kansas City, Mo., 1992—. Mem. Am. Coll. Sports Medicine, Idea Internat. Fitness Profl. Assocs., Nat. Wellness Assn., The Cooper's Clinic (instr.), Aerobics and Fitness Assn. of Am. Office: KCKCC Wellness & Fitness Ct 7250 State Ave Kansas City KS 66112

CARDUCCI, JACK A., investment banker; b. Detroit, June 6, 1963. BS in Mktg. and Mgmt., U. Detroit, 1987. Lic. Nat. Assn. Securities Dealers. Sales/dept. mgmt./merchandise Highland Super Stores, Detroit, 1977-87; investment banker Dean Witter, Troy, Mich., 1988-91, Bentley Lawrence Securities, Birmingham, Mich., 1991—; broker Warren Pension Plan, 1990—. Mem. mayor's steering com. City of Warren, Mich., 1990—. Mem. Italian-Am. C. of C., Cepranese Italian Club. Republican. Roman Catholic. Home: 30036 Moulin Ave Warren MI 48093-3108 Office: Bentley Lawrence Securities 344 N Woodward Ave Ste 301 Birmingham MI 48009-5351

CAREY, CHRISTOPHER JOHN, outdoor education specialist, consultant; b. New Haven, Conn., July 9, 1966; s. Charles Branch and Mary Ann (Bonoff) C. AAS in Environ. Sci., Paul Smiths Coll., 1986; BS in Environ. Edn., Slippery Rock U., 1988. Naturalist Greenkill Environ. Edn. Ctr., Huguenot, N.Y., 1988-89; resource tchr. Joy Outdoor Edn. Ctr., Clarksville, Ohio, 1989-94. Mem. Sierra Club, Cin., 1990-95, Healing Racism Dialogue, Lebanon, 1995. Recipient Chester L. Buxton award Paul Smiths Coll., 1986. Home: PO Box 61 Morrow OH 45152

CAREY, DAVID ARTHUR, physical therapist; b. Pittsfield, Mass., Apr. 17, 1957; s. Robert B. and Aline (Desautels) C.; m. Catherine A. Cameron, Aug. 14, 1993; 1 child, Melody C. Carey. BA magna cum laude, St. Anselm Coll., Manchester, N.H., 1979; MA, Boston U., 1984. Phys. therapist Lake Forest (Ill.) Hosp., 1984-86; phys. therapist, supr. Evanston (Ill.) Hosp.-Northbrook, 1986-93; sr. phys. therapist Lake Forest Health and Fitness Inst., 1993—. Mem. Am. Phys. Therapy Assn. Home: 405 Seafarer Grayslake IL 60030

CAREY, EDWARD MARSHEL, JR., accounting company executive; b. Washington, Pa., June 12, 1942; s. Edward Marshel and Mildred Elizabeth (Bradley) C.; B.S. in Bus. Adminstrn., Greenville (Ill.) Coll., 1964; m. Naomi Ruth Davis, June 1, 1964; children—Martha Ann, Mary Louise. Acct., Gen. Motors Corp., Anderson, Ind., 1964-68, supr. acctg., 1968-70; staff acct. Carter, Kirlin & Merrill, CPAs, Indpls., 1970-74, ptnr., 1974-87, mng. ptnr., 1988—; pres. CKM Mgmt., Inc., Indpls., 1985—. Mem. AICPA (mgmt. of acctg. practice com. 1976-80, chmn. com. 1978-80, mgmt. adv. svcs. com. 1980-83, chmn. com. 1982-83, dir. Indpls. chpt. 1977-83, treas. 1978-79, pres. 1979-80), Nat. Assn. Accountants, Am. Mgmt. Assn., Inst. Internal Auditors (dir.), Greenville Coll. Alumni Assn. (dir., treas. Ind. chpt. 1980-82), Indpls. Athletic Club. Republican. Methodist. Home: 215 Royal Oak Ct Zionsville IN 46077-1039 Office: Carter Kirlin & Merrill CPA's 9102 N Meridian St Ste 555 Indianapolis IN 46260-1809

CAREY, JERALD RAYMOND, investment advisor; b. Kansas City, Mo., Jan. 18, 1939. BSBA, Rockhurst Coll., Kansas City, 1960; postgrad., U. Mo., Tokyo, 1965-66. CFP; cert. flight instr.; cert. scuba diver. Stockbrokeer Stifel Nicolaus, Kansas City, 1968-78; sr. v.p. Weinrich Zitzman, Whitehead, Kansas City, 1978-83; CEO, Carey Co., Kansas City, 1983-89, Carey Fin. Cons., Overland Park, Kans., 1989—. Vol. investment advisor to area retirements homes, 1992—. Named One of Top 20 Brokers in U.S., Registered Rep. mag., 1983. Office: Carey Fin Cons 9604 Nieman Pl Overland Park KS 66214-2260

CAREY, JOSEPH RICHARD, mathematics educator; b. Carroll, Iowa, July 7, 1964; s. Richard Joseph and Catherine Ann (Fitzsimmons) C.; m. Mary Jacqueline Wente, Dec. 30, 1989; 1 child, Benjamin Thomas. BS in Math., Briar Cliff Coll., Sioux City, Iowa, 1987; M of Sch. Math., Iowa State U., 1992. Tchr. math. Shenandoah (Iowa) High Sch., 1987-89; math. tchr. Winterset (Iowa) High Sch., 1991—. Recipient Math. award, Briar Cliff Coll., 1987. Mem. Nat. Coun. Tchrs. Math. Roman Catholic.

CARFORA, JOHN MICHAEL, economics and political science educator; b. New Haven, Conn., July 24, 1950; s. John Michael and Rose Mary (Mitro) C.; m. Linda Louise Palmer, July 22, 1972; 1 child, Rachel Ellen. BS, U. New Haven (Conn.), 1973, M in Pub. Adminstrn., 1975; MS in Econs. and Polit. Sci., London Sch. Econs. and Polit. Sci., 1978; AM, Dartmouth Coll., 1985, EdM Harvard U., 1993. Vis. asst. prof. dept. def., 1979-80; vis. sr. lectr. Poly. of Central London, 1980; research asst. London Sch. Econs. and Polit. Sci., 1980-81; vis. asst. prof. internat. relations So. Conn. State U., New Haven, 1982; lectr. dept. polit. sci. Albertus Magnus Coll., New Haven, 1982-83; lectr. dept. econs. and quantitative analysis U. New Haven, 1982-83; program cons. Dartmouth Coll., 1984-85; asst. prof. internat. econ. Sch. Internat. Tng., 1985-90; v.p. rsch. and acad. affairs, dir. Soviet-Am. projects Global-Genesis, Internat. Cons. (formerly Global Consultancy Group), 1989-91, dir. east and west projects, 1992-94; asst. dean for rsch. and sponsored programs Ind. State U., Terre Haute, 1994-95; dir. grants and sponsored programs Simmons Coll., Boston, 1995—; ednl. cons. USSR Acad. Mgmt., Moscow, 1991-92; cons. Commonwealth Acad. Mgmt., Moscow, 1992-94; lectr. in field. Author book reviews; contbr. articles to profl. jours. Served with USAR, 1970-76. Recipient Roy E. Jenkins award, 1972; fellow Radio Free Europe-Radio Liberty, 1979, Internat. Research and Exchanges Bd., 1981-84. Mem. Am. Assn. Advancement Slavic Studies, Nat. Assn Fgn. Student Advisors (internat. educators), Am. Acad. Polit. Sci., Am. Econ. Assn., Am. Polit. Sci. Assn., Acad. Polit. Sci., N.E. Slavic Assn., Royal Acad. Pub. Adminstrn. (Eng.), Atlantic Econ. Soc., Am. Friends of the London Sch. Econs. (Conn. program chmn. 1981-85, N.H.-Vt. program chmn. 1985-87, alumni bd. dirs. 1983-92). Office: Simmons Coll 300 The Fenway Boston MA 02115-5898

CARGILE, MICHAEL EDWARD, advertising agency executive; b. New Orleans, Jan. 8, 1942; s. Duncan Edward Cargile and Marguerite (Choppin) McCormick; m. Susan Elizabeth Walter, Nov. 26, 1966; children: Christopher, Heather. BA, U. Miss., 1963. Sales mgr. Cleve. Ad. Club, 1966-68; account exec. Watts, Lee and Kenyon, Cleve., 1968-71; account supr. Marschalk Interpublic, Cleve., 1971-75; pres. The Jayme Orgn., Cleve., 1982-89; gen. mgr. Fahlgren Martin, Interpub., Cleve., 1990-92; pres. Communiquik, Cleve., 1992—. Trustee Cleve. Health Mus., 1976-80, Cuyahoga Valley Line Bath, Ohio, 1988—; pres. Hiram Ho. Bd. Trustees, Chagrin Falls, 1975—; trustee Hist. Warehouse Dist., 1990—; mem. Mayor's Pub. Rels. Com., Cleve., 1991—. Named Exec. of Yr. Exec. Women Internat., Cleve., 1987. Mem. Cleve. Art Assn. (trustee 1992), Hillbrook Country Club, The Country Club (Pepper Pike, Ohio). Home: 20725 Shaker Blvd Cleveland OH 44122-2621 Office: Communiquik The Rockefeller Bldg 614 W Superior Ave Ste 774 Cleveland OH 44113-1306

CARGO, REBECCA R., office manager, dairy farmer; b. Rugby, N.D., Aug. 22, 1948. Head bookkeeper Pioneer State Bank, Towner, N.D., 1966-69; income tax preparer Beneficial Fin., Minot, N.D., 1975; asst. to trust dept. v.p. 1st Am. Bank & Trust, Minot, 1979-87; with Soil Conservation Svc., Towner, 1987-88; clk. Rugby Pamida Store, Towner, 1988-89; office mgr. Duchscher & Shinemoen Ins., Rugby, 1989—; with Berthel Fisher & Co., Rugby; dairy farmer, Towner. Roman Catholic.

CARL, ALOYSIUS JEROME, business executive; b. Fort Thomas, Ky., Oct. 3, 1960. BS in Mktg., No. Ky. U., 1983. Divsn. sales mgr. Dunn & Bradstreet, Columbus, Ohio, 1987-88; v.p., sec. Kreller Group, Cin., 1989—; pres. Kreller Bus. Info. Group, Inc., Cin., 1994—; v.p., sec. Kreller Rsch. Solutions, Inc., Cin., 1995—. Roman Catholic. Office: Kreller Bus Info Group Inc 817 Main St Fl 3 Cincinnati OH 45202-2183

CARL, ANGELA REEVES, strategic planning consultant, trainer; b. Maysville, Ky., May 12, 1949; d. William Frank Reeves and Marjorie Jean (King) Miller; m. Edward John Carl, Oct. 2, 1971; children: Cassandra Joy, Anya Suzanne, Lucinda Adrienne. BS in Edn., U. Cin., 1971. Editor Standard Pub. Co., Cin., 1971-72; tchr. Northwest Sch. Dist., Cin., 1972-76; exec. dir. Child Abuse Task Force, Kingston, N.Y., 1984-85; comms. trainer, leadership devel. owner Tng. for Success, Cin., 1989—; child abuse prevention cons., 1984—; chair N.Y. State Fedn. Child Abuse, Albany, 1984-85. Author: Child Abuse: What You Can Do About It, 1985, 3dedit., 1993, Good Hugs, Bad Hugs: How Can You Tell?, 1985, 3d edit., 1993, A Matter of Choice, 1984; contbr. articles to profl. jours. Vol. trainer Clean Up Cin. Conf., 1990; chmn. Fine Arts Fund, Mason, Ohio, 1989, 93, Bloom Where You're Planted Orientation Program, Paris, 1980-81; trainer United Way Cin., 1989-95; children's edn. dir. Mason Ch. of Christ, 1991-92. Mem. ASTD, Jr. League Cin. (chair parent seminar 1988—, chair donor recognition, mentor trainer and advisor Leadership Forum, Star Mem. award 1989, bd. dirs. mem.-at-large 1992, chair tng. and devel. 1993). Home and Office: 1129 Black Horse Run Loveland OH 45140-9021

CARL, DOUG, state legislator; b. Almont, Mich., Aug. 12, 1951; m. Maria; 1 child, Colleen. BA with honors, Mich. State U. Commr. Macomb (Mich.) County, 1980-82; state rep. Mich. Ho. Reps., 1985-87; state senator Mich. State Senate, Dist. 12, 1987—; chmn. transp. & tourism com., chmn. econ. devel. com., vice chmn. fin. com. & sel. com. on bonding, mem. family law, criminal law & corrections com., vice chmn. edn. com., Mich. State Senate. Mem. Mich. Coun. Alcohol Problems. Address: 8533 Nancy Ave Utica MI 48317-5337*

CARLETON, CARLA LOU, theriogenologist, educator; b. Ames, Iowa, May 4, 1949; d. Walter Monroe and Lillie May (Martin) C. BS, Kans. State U., Manhattan, 1977, DVM, 1977; MS, Ohio State U., 1984. Diplomate Am. Coll. Theriogenologists. Veterinarian Hitch Enterprises Master Vet. Svc., Inc., Guymon, Okla., 1977-81; resident Ohio State U. Coll. Vet. Medicine, Columbus, 1981-84; asst. prof. Mich. State U. Coll. Vet. Medicine, East Lansing, 1984-89, assoc. prof., 1989—; cons. to privately owned stud farms, Pune and Gujarat, India, 1992-96; presenter in field. Contbr. chpts. to books. Fellow Queensland and N.S.W., 1990. Mem. AVMA (del. 1993—), Am. Coll. Theriogenologists (nat. cert. exem. com. 1990-95, exam. chair 1993-95, liaison to Am. Bd. Vet. Splties. 1995—), numerous others. Office: Mich State U Coll Vet Med A-117 VMC Dept Large Animal Clin Scis East Lansing MI 48824-1314

CARLIN, CLAIR MYRON, lawyer; b. Sharon, Pa., Apr. 20, 1947; s. Charles William and Carolyn L. (Vukasich) C.; m. Cecilia Julia Reis, Sept. 21, 1971 (div. Mar. 1982); children: Elizabeth Marie, Alexander Myron. BS in Econs., Ohio State U., 1969, JD, 1972. Bar: Ohio 1973, Pa. 1973, U.S. Dist. Ct. (so. dist.) Ohio 1973, U.S. Dist. Ct. (no. dist.) Ohio 1975, U.S. Supreme Ct. 1976, U.S. Ct. Claims 1983, U.S. Ct. Appeals (6th cir.) 1983, U.S. Tax Ct. 1985. Staff atty. Ohio Dept. Taxation, Columbus, 1972-73; asst. city atty. City of Warren, Ohio, 1973-75; assoc. McLaughlin, DiBlasio & Harshman, Youngstown, Ohio, 1975-80; ptnr. McLaughlin, McNally & Carlin, Youngstown, 1980—. Mem. editorial bd. Ohio Trial mag. Mem. Trumbull County Bicentennial Commn., Ohio, 1976; v.p. Svcs. for the Aging, Trumbull County, 1976-77; mem. Pres.' Club Ohio State U. Served to maj. Ohio NG, 1972-82. Mem. ABA, Ohio State Bar Assn. (mem. Negligence Law Com. 1991), Ohio State Bar Coll., Mahoning County Bar Assn. (chmn. legal edn. com. 1985-86, counsel 1986-87), ATLA (bd. govs. 1995—), Ohio Acad. Trial Lawyers (trustee 1988-92, polit. action com. chmn. 1991, exec. com. 1991—, treas. 1992-93, sec. 1993-94, pres.-elect 1994-95, pres. 1995-96), Mahoning-Trumbull Acad. Trial Lawyers (pres. 1991), Ohio State U. Alumni Assn. (pres. Trumbull County chpt. 1985—), Cath. War Vets. (Ohio state commdr., Vet. of Yr. 1988). Democrat. Roman Catholic. Club: Tippecanoe Country (Canfield, Ohio). Lodge: Rotary. Home: 5510 West Blvd Youngstown OH 44512-2527 Office: McLaughlin McNally & Carlin 500 City Centre One Youngstown OH 44503

CARLINER, SAUL A., communications executive; b. Balt., June 18, 1958; s. Louis Elliot and Jodean (Askin) C. BA, Carnegie-Mellon U., 1980; MA, U. Minn., 1987; PhD, Ga. State U., 1995. Info. developer IBM Corp., Rochester, Minn., 1980-86; edn. devel. adminstr. IBM Corp., Atlanta, 1986-88, mktg. programs adminstr., 1988-92; info. architect and founding ptnr. Carliner & Co., Inc., Atlanta, 1992-95; exec. v.p. Fredrickson Comm., Inc., Mpls., 1995—; asst. prof. So. Coll. Tech., Marietta, Ga., 1995-96. Co-editor: Techniques for Technical Communicators, 1993; contbr. articles to profl. jours. Bd. dirs. Minn. Common Cause, St. Paul, 1984-86; chmn. bd. Rochester Citizen's Adv. on Transit, 1985, Friends of Fernbank Mus. and Sci. Ctr., Atlanta, 1990-91; mem. adv. bd. Inst. Jewish Ethics, Phila., 1995—. Recipient Award of Disting. Tech. Comm., Internat. Tech. Pubs., 1987, Carolyn Haskell award Village Writer's Group, 1989, Award of Merit, Internat. Tech. Pubs., 1993. Mem. IEEE Prof. Comms. Soc., Am. Assn. Mus., Soc. Tech. Comm. (internat. pres. 1995-96), Internat. Soc. Performance Improvement (nat. conf. com. 1991-94), The Loft. Jewish. Office: Fredrickson Comms Inc 119 N 4th St Ste 513 Minneapolis MN 55401

CARLISLE, RONALD DWIGHT, nursery owner; b. Bismarck, N.D., Oct. 28, 1940; m. Neva Carlisle, May 18, 1968. BS, Black Hills State Coll., 1966. Policy issue mgr. Provident Life Ins. Co., Bismarck, N.D., 1966-83; workers compensation commr. Bismarck, 1983-85; delivery driver Premium Beverage, Bismarck, 1985-86; owner trees N M Ore, Bismarck, 1986—; mem. N.D. Legislature. Chair Dist. 52-Dist. 30, Bismarck; del. Rep. State Conv., 1976, 78, 80, 82, 84, 86, 88, 90, 92, 94, 96. Served with USN, 1958-62. Recipient Guardian of Small Bus. award NFIB, 1991. Mem. Am. Vets. (life), N.D. Nursery Assn., Elks, NRA. Address: PO Box 222 Bismarck ND 58502-0222

CARLMAN, SUSAN FRICK, reporter; b. Royal Oak, Mich., June 17, 1957; d. Robert Carter Frick and Nancy Gail (Sanders) Chickering; m. Daniel Alton Carlman, Sept. 11, 1982; children: Erin Gail, Samuel Alton, Molly Louise, Cody Rose. BS in Devel. Psychology, Mont. State U., 1981; postgrad., U. Ariz., 1981. Reporter, columnist The Doings Newspaper, Hinsdale, Ill., 1983—; lectr. various community groups, Hinsdale, 1989—. Author: Farmers Market Cookbook, 1988, Gifts From Your Kitchen, 1993. Mem. Ill. Press Assn., No. Ill. Newspaper Assn., Suburban Press Club. Home: 305 W Chicago St Plainfield IL 60544-2017 Office: The Doings Newspapers 118 W 1st St Hinsdale IL 60521-4013

CARLOCK, MAHLON WALDO, financial consultant, former high school administrator; b. Plymouth, Ind., Sept. 17, 1926; s. Thorstine Clifford and Katheryn G. (Gephart) C.; m. Betty L. Dobbs, Aug. 27, 1954; children: Mahlon W. II, Rhena M., Shawn R. BS, Ind. U., 1951, MS, 1956. Tchr. jr. high Martinsville Schs. Corp., Brooklyn, Ind., 1952-53; tchr. high sch. Indpls. Pub. Schs., 1953-63, asst. to dean of boys, 1963-73, asst. dean of boys, 1973-75, bus. mgr., 1976-87; fin. cons. Indpls., 1987—; property builder, owner Ind. and Fla.; lectr. on fin. and real estate; condr. seminars on estate planning and trust. Sgt. U.S. Army, 1945-47. Mem. NEA (life), Indpls. Adminstrs., Ind. Bus. Edn. Assn., Indpls. Edn. Assn. (rep. 1958-63). Republican. Baptist. Lodge: Masons. Home and Office: 9705 E Michigan St Indianapolis IN 46229-2564

CARLOMAGNO, STEPHEN GUIDO, insurance company executive; b. Youngstown, Ohio, Sept. 2, 1948; s. Guido Pepino and Margaret Mary (Strunak) C.; m. Diane Dimichaelangelo, Aug. 14, 1992; children: Rachael Lynn, Stephan Michael; stepchildren: Michael Van Valien, Jacquilyn Van Valien. AA, Kent State U., 1968; cert. in fin. planning, Am. Coll., 1976. Gen. supt. Gen. Motors Corp., Lordstown, Ohio, 1972-73; agt. Nat. Life and Accident Ins. Co., Sharon, Pa., 1973-77; sales staff mgr. Nat. Life and Accident Ins. Co., Youngstown, Ohio, 1977-85; pres., owner S.G.C. Investment Co., Youngstown, 1978—; dist. mgr. Am. Gen. Life and Accident Ins. Co., Youngstown, 1985—; owner Carlomagno and Sons Construction, Inc., Youngstown, 1992—. Fund raising chmn. United Way, Youngstown, 1987, 88. Staff sgt. Green Beret U.S. Army, 1968-72. Decorated Bronze Star. Mem. Pa. Assn. Life Underwriters (bd. dirs. 1981-84, dir. edn. 1982-84, Leaders Roundtable), Youngstown Assn. Life Underwriters (bd. dirs. 1984-85), Nat. Assn. Life Underwriters (Sales Achievement award 1974-76, Nat. Quality award 1974-76), VFW, Gen. Agents and Mgmt. Assn. (Nat. Mgmt. award 1995). Republican. Roman Catholic. Home: 436 Arbor Cir Youngstown OH 44505-1916 Office: Am Gen Life & Accident Ins PO Box 2746 Youngstown OH 44507-0746

CARLOTTI, RONALD JOHN, food scientist; b. Martins Ferry, Ohio, Sept. 20, 1942; s. John Peter and Mary Rose (Pilla) C.; m. Eileen Theresa Dorsey, May 17, 1969; children: Lori Ann, Christina Maria, Jennifer Ann, Theresa Maria. Student, Wheeling (W.Va.) Jesuit Coll., 1960-63; BS, Ohio State U., 1964; MS, W.Va. U., 1966, PhD, 1970. Postdoctoral fellow Dept. Biochemistry, U. Iowa, Iowa City, 1971-72; asst. rsch. scientist Pediatrics Dept., U. Iowa, Iowa City, 1973-74; corp. nutritionist Kellogg Co., Battle Creek, Mich., 1974-77; mgr. nutrition/basic rsch. Frito Lay div. Pepsico, Dallas, 1977-82, prin. scientist new products, 1982-85; sr. rsch. scientist Amway Corp., Ada, Mich., 1985-89; dir. food sci. and tech. Country Home Bakers, Grand Rapids, Mich., 1990-93; pres. Carlotti and Assocs., Grand Rapids, 1994; pres., CEO Natura Inc., Lansing, Mich., 1995—; tech. rep. Snack Food Assn., Crystal City, Va., 1978-82, Grocery Mfrs. of Am., Washington, 1975-77; nutritionist Am. Frozen Food Assn., Washington, 1990-93. Contbr. articles to profl. jours. Pres. Mary Immaculate Sch. Bd., Dallas, 1981-83. Recipient Lovable Spud award, Nat. Potato Promotion Bd., Denver, 1981. Mem. Am. Chem. Soc., Am. Assn. Cereal Chemists, Inst. Food Tech. Roman Catholic. Home: 6921 Maplecrest Dr SE Grand Rapids MI 49546-9208 Office: Natura Inc Ste 1007 3900 Collins Rd Lansing MI 48910

CARLSON, ALAN H., state legislator; b. Nov. 21, 1948; m. Sharon Carlson; 3 children. Student, N.D. Sch. Sci., N.D. State U. Gen. contractor Fargo; state rep. dist. 41, 1993—; Rep. caucus leader; mem. industry, bus. and labor com., natural resources com. N.D. Ho. Reps. Named Fargo Moorhead Builder of Yr., 1988. Mem. N.D. Assn. Builders (pres.), Fargo-Moorhead Home Builders Assn. (past pres.). Republican. *

CARLSON, ALLAN CONSTANTINE, historian; b. Des Moines, May 7, 1949; s. Harry Bernard and Constance Ann Carlson; m. Elizabeth Cecelia Belin, July 1, 1972; children: Anders, Sarah-Eva, Anna, Miriam. AB, Augustana Coll., 1971; PhD in European History, Ohio U., 1978. Asst. dir. office for govtl. affairs Luth. Coun. in the U.S.A., Washington, 1975-78; asst. to pres., history lectr. Gettysburg (Pa.) Coll., 1979-81; exec. v.p. The Rockford (Ill.) Inst., 1981-86, pres., 1986—; mem. Coun. on Families in Am., N.Y.C., 1991—; cons. Family Rsch. Inst., Moscow, 1995, U.S. Dept. Justice, Washington, 1986-87, U.S. Dept. Edn., Washington, 1986-88. Author: From Cottage to Work Station, 1993, The Swedish Experiment in Family Politics, 1990, Family Questions, 1988; co-author: The Family: Is it Just Another Lifestyle Choice?; contbr. articles to profl. jours. Active The Nat. Commn. on Children, Washington, 1988-93; adv. bd. project SHARE U.S. Dept. Health Human Svcs., Washington, 1983-85; leader Boy Scouts of Am., dist. chmn., 1995-96. NEH fellow Am. Enterprise Inst., 1979; recipient George Washington Honor medal Freedoms Found. Valley Forge, 1985, 87. Mem. Phila. Soc. (1st v.p. 1986-87), Rotary (pres. 1994-95), John Randolph Club (bd. dirs., sec. 1993-95), Lutherans for Life (bd. dirs. 1987-92), Phi Beta Kappa. Lutheran. Home: 1324 Camp Ave Rockford IL 61103 Office: The Rockford Inst 934 N Main St Rockford IL 61103

CARLSON, ANDREW RAYMOND, archivist; b. Ludington, Mich., Aug. 19, 1934; s. Louis Peter and Mable Pearl (Genter) C.; m. Linda Inara Volfarts, Sept. 5, 1959; children: Sharon Lee, Andrew Arthur. BA, Western Mich. U., 1960, MA, 1961; PhD, Mich. State U., 1970. Tchr. Galesburg (Mich.)-Augusta Schs., 1961-62, Kalamazoo (Mich) Pub. Schs., 1962-65, Portage (Mich.) Pub. Schs., 1962-65; asst. prof. Ea. Ky. U., Richmond, Ky., 1967-70, Ferris State U., Big Rapids, Mich., 1970-73, Western Mich. U., Kalamazoo, 1973-75; archivist Kalamazoo County, 1976—; adj. prof. Western Mich. U., Kalamazoo, 1989—. Author: Anarchism in Germany, 1972, Germany Foreign Policy, 1970; (with others) Social Protest, Violence & Terror, 1982, Sozialprotest, Gewalt, Terror, 1982; contbr. articles to profl. jours. Adj. treas. Diabled Am. Vets., Allegan, Mich., 1976—; active Fontana Concert Soc. Sgt. U.S. Army, 1952-57. Mem. Am. Hist. Assn. (European sect.), So. Hist. Assn., Internat. Wissenschaftliche Korrespondenz, Internat. Labor & Workers History, German History Soc., German Studies Assn., Am. Philatelic Soc., German Philatelic Soc., Phi Gamma Mu, Phi Alpha Theta. Office: Western Mich U Dept History Kalamazoo MI 49008-5020

CARLSON, ANN MARIE, poet; b. Lansing, Mich., Sept. 3, 1934; d. Cecil Louis and Anna Mae (Kazanowsky) Lamanna; m. Lester D. Carlson, Aug. 28, 1954; children: Michael D., Patrick L., Stephen L. Attended, Lansing C.C., 1977-95, Mich. State U., 1979. Sec. General Motors, Lansing, Mich. Author: (book of poems) Murhooing Sands, 1990, Nuggets in Champagne, 1991, (poem) Virgin in the Street (Arts award HM Gwendolyn Brooks Contest 1987), 1987; editor: (anthology) The Lansing Poetry Club, 1988. Active Waverly Jaycees, 1966. Named Woman of the Yr. Waverly Jaycees, 1966. Mem. Soc. for the Study of Mid-Western Literature, Poetry Soc. Mich. (treas. 1990-95), Lansing Poetry Club (pres. 1985, 92), St. Gerard Church (carnival chmn. 1972). Roman Catholic. Home: 1422 Maycroft Lansing MI 48917

CARLSON, ARNE HELGE, governor; b. N.Y.C., Sept. 24, 1934; s. Helge William and Kerstin (Magnusson) C.; children by previous marriage: Arne H. Jr., Anne Davis; m. Susan Shepard, July 12, 1985; 1 child, Jessica Shepard. BA, Williams Coll., 1957; postgrad., U. Minn., 1957-58. Mem. advt. staff Control Data, Bloomington, Minn., 1962-64; councilman Mpls. City Council, 1965-67; ind. businessman Mpls., 1968-69; legislator Minn. Ho. Reps., St. Paul, 1970-78; state auditor State of Minn., St. Paul, 1978-90, gov., 1991—; bd. dirs. Minn. Land Exch. Bd., St. Paul; trustee Minn. State Bd. Investment, St. Paul, 1979—. Bd. dirs. Exec. Coun., St. Paul; sec. Minn. Housing Fin. Agy., St. Paul, 1979-91; past pres. Pub. Employees Retirement Assn., St. Paul, 1985-88; mem. Nat. Gov.'s Assn., Midwest Gov.'s Assn., Great Lakes Govs.; mem. Nat. Ednl. Goals Panel of Nat. Gov.'s Assn. Bush Found. Leadership fellow, 1971; recipient Children's Champion award Minn. Children's Def. Fund, Nat. Audubon Soc. award, Small Bus. Guardian award Nat. Fedn. Ind. Businesses, 1994, Great Blue Heron award N.Am. Waterfront Mgmt. Plan/U.S. Fish & Wildlife Svc., 1995; named Rep. of Yr. Nat. Ripon Soc., 1993. Bd. dirs. Exec. Coun. St. Paul, sec. Minn. Housing Fin. Agy., St. Paul, 1979-91; past pres. Pub. Employees Retirement Assn., St. Paul, 1985-88; mem. Nat. Gov.'s Assn. (chmn. com. on human resources, mem. Nat. Ednl. Goals Panel), Rep. Gov.'s Assn., Midwest Gov.'s Assn., Great Lakes Govs. Republican. Home: 1006 Summit Ave Saint Paul MN 55105-3033 Office: Office Gov 130 State Capitol Saint Paul MN 55155

CARLSON, BRENT JAMES, engineering designer; b. Ames, Iowa, May 15, 1959. Student, Chippewa Valley Tech. Coll., 1977-80; AAS in Electronics Tech., Waukesha Tech. Coll., 1993. Sr. layout draftsperson Hein-Werner, Waukesha, Wis., 1982-88; engr. Blanton Co., Ashippun, Wis., 1988-90; engring. designer Broan Mfg. Co., Hartford, Wis., 1990-96; design engr. G/S Hydraulics Sales, New Berlin, Wis., 1996—; cons. future bus. analysis design process and devel. Coopers & Lybrand, Re-engring. Orgn., Chgo., 1993-94. Office: Broan Mfg Co 926 W State St Hartford WI 53027-1066

CARLSON, BRIAN JAY, health facility executive; b. Mpls., Mar. 21, 1956; s. John Russell and Shirley Mae Joan (Warholm) C.; m. Ann Margaret Grabau, May 26, 1979; children: Daniel Jordan, Katja Mari, Anja Matia, Peder Christian. BA in Bus. and Hosp. Adminstrn., Concordia Coll., 1978; MSA in Instl. Adminstrn., U. Notre Dame, 1986. Dir. ops. St. Joseph's Med. Ctr., Brainerd, Minn., 1978-80, dir. research and devel., 1980-84, v.p. ops., 1984-95; adminstr. Lake View Meml. Hosp., Two Harbors, Minn., 1995—; engring. cons. St. Joseph's Med. Ctr., Brainerd, 1984-95. Mem. Am. Coll. Healthcare Execs., Am. Mgmt. Assn., Am. Hosp. Assn., Soc. for Hosp. Planning and Mktg., Brainerd C. of C. (mktg. expansion com. 1984-94). Democrat. Office: Lake View Meml Hosp 325 11th Ave Two Harbors MN 55616

CARLSON, CHARLES EVANS, university official; b. Savanna, Ill., Aug. 25, 1941; s. Gustave Bert and Agnes Loretta (Johnson) C.; m. Nancy Jane Wahl, Aug. 10, 1963; children: Courtney E., Darrin C. BA, Carthage Coll., 1963; MA, U. Ill., 1965. Tchr. Polo (Ill.) Community High Sch., 1963-65; instr. history Cen. Mich. U., Mt. Pleasant, 1966-72, regional assoc. dir. Detroit campus, 1973-87, assoc. dir. extended degree programs, 1987—; dir. grants, contracts & spl. projects Detroit Campus, Mt. Pleasant, 1994—; coord. Ams. with Disabilities Act Compliance Detroit Campus, 1994—. Contbr. articles to profl. publs. Mem. Optimist Club. Office: Cen Mich U 131 Rowe Hall Mount Pleasant MI 48859

CARLSON, CURTIS LEROY, corporate executive; b. Mpls., July 9, 1914; s. Charles A. and Letha (Peterson) C.; m. Arleen Martin, June 30, 1938; children: Marilyn Carlson Nelson, Barbara Carlson Gage. BA in Econs., U. Minn., 1937. Salesman, Procter & Gamble Co., Mpls., 1937-39; founder, pres. Gold Bond Stamp Co., Mpls., 1938-84, pres., chmn. bd. dirs., 1938—; chmn. bd. dirs., ceo Carlson Cos., Inc. (formerly Premium Service Corp.); pres. MIP Agy., Inc.; chmn. bd. Radisson Hotel Corp., Radisson Group Inc., Carlson Real Estate Co., Inc., Carlson Holdings, Inc., Carlson Leasing, Inc., TGI Friday's Inc., Dallas, Nordic-Am. Travel, Inc., K-Promotions, Inc., Carlson Mktg. Group, Carlson Travel Group; bd. dirs. Premiums Internat. Ltd.; chmn. Carlson Hospitality Group. Sr. v.p. U. Minn. Found.; chmn. emeritus Swedish Coun. Am.; bd. dirs., founder Boys Club Mpls.; bd. dirs. Minn. Meetings; mem. adv. bd. U. Minn. Curtis L. Carlson Sch. of Mgmt., U. Minn.; adv. coun. U.S. Swedish Found.; mem. Hennepin Ave. Meth. Ch. Mem. Trading Stamp Inst. Am. (dir., founder, pres. 1959-60), Swedish-Am. C. of C. (dir.), U. Minn. Alumni Assn. (honors com.), Sigma Phi Epsilon (vice chmn. bd. trustees), Mpls. Club, Northland Country (Duluth), Minikahda Club, Ocean Reef Yacht (Key Largo), Palm Bay (Miami), Masons, Shriners, Jesters. Office: Carlson Cos Inc PO Box 59159 Carlson Pky Minneapolis MN 55459

CARLSON, DANIEL ERIK, market research executive; b. Mpls., Aug. 21, 1954; s. Donald C. and Marie Aurelia (Moris) C.; m. Karen Ann Noreen, Oct. 31, 1954; children: Kaitlin Marie, Michael Daniel. Student, Concordia Coll., 1972-74, Augsburg Coll., 1974-76, Brown Inst., 1977. Staff announcer WONW Radio, Defiance, Ohio, 1977; studio mgr. Linder Radio Network, Montevideo, Minn., 1977-82; v.p., ops. mgr. Linder Radio Network, Willmar, Minn., 1982-89; gen. sales mgr. Linder Rd. Network, Willmar, Minn., 1980-82; mktg. mgr. The Gallup Orgn., Mpls., 1989-91; v.p., div. mgr. Gallup Poll Media Group, Mpls., 1991—. Mem. Broadcast Promotion and Mktg. Execs., Nat. Assn. Broadcasters, Radio and TV News Dirs. Assn., Nat. Assn. TV Producers and Execs., Minn. Assn. Broadcasters, Kiwanis Club, Lions Club. Lutheran. Home: 10128 Utah Cir S Bloomington MN 55438-2014 Office: The Gallup Orgn 965 Interchange Tower Minneapolis MN 55426

CARLSON, DAVID WAYNE, software company executive; b. Brainerd, Minn., Nov. 9, 1953; s. Harold James and Katherine Allen (Norton) C.; m. Donna Jean Lindahal, July 14, 1974; children: Andrew James, Amethyst Joy (dec.). BS in Math., Pillsbury Coll., 1976, BS in Edn., 1977; BAS in Supervision, U. Minn., 1984; grad., US Army Command & General Staff Coll., 1989; MA in Computer Mgmt., Webster U., 1990. Cert. systems profl., logistician, locksmith, research and devel. mgmt. Inspector County Hwy. Dept., Little Falls, Minn., 1970-71; computer operator Joston's Inc., Owatonna, Minn., 1971-73; engr.'s asst. County Hwy. Dept., Owatonna, Minn., 1973-75; maintenance supr. Pillsbury Coll., Owatonna, Minn., 1975-76; tchr. North Star Acad., Little Falls, 1976-78; army engr. officer U.S. Army, 1978-90, commd. 2d lt., 1979, advanced through grades to maj., 1990; now maj. USAR Army Corps of Engrs., 1990—; system mgr. Cable Am. Corp., St. Robert, Mo., 1990-92; owner, cons. Carlson Home Industries, Waynesville, Mo., 1992—; locksmith, owner Dave's Safe & Lock, 1976-78; adviser Electronics Club, Little Falls, Minn., 1976-78; cons. Cable Am. Corp., Phoenix, 1990—, U.S. Army, Seoul, 1992, U.S. Army Task Force Honduras, 1993, Bus. Network Comm., Inc., Waynesville, 1993—; adj. faculty Webster U., 1995—. Author: (manual) Bridge Anchorage System, 1984, (booklet) Cable TV Instructions, 1991, (computer programs) Dino Trilogy, 1994, Boxes, 1995, Virus: The Game, 1995, Words, 1996, Dino Cards, 1996, Dino Tiles, 1996. Recipient Tech. Knowledge award Locksmith Ledger, 1978. Mem. Math. Assn. Am., Waynesville C. of C., Mensa,

Internat. Thespian Soc., Kiwanis (sec. 1990). Home: 1105 Home Ave Waynesville MO 65583-2231 Office: DynoTech Software 1105 Home Ave Waynesville MO 65583-2231

CARLSON, DONALD A., retired protective services official; b. Muskegon, Mich., Aug. 3, 1926; s. Carl Edwin and Ida Eugenia (Lundeen) C.; m. Jo Ann Katherine Owen; children: Michael Edwin, John Arthur, Kenneth Anton. Student, Kalamazoo (Mich.) Valley C.C. Carpenter various locations, 1946-53; sgt. Kalamazoo (Mich.) Fire Dept., Kalamazoo Pub. Svc. Dept., 1953-84; real estate salesperson Crossroad Real Estate, Portage, Mich., 1984-95; ret., 1995. With U.S. Army, 1944-46, ETO. Methodist. Home: 1943 Lakeshore Dr Allegan MI 49010-9545

CARLSON, E. DEAN, state official. Sec. Dept. Transp., Topeka. Office: Transp Dept Docking State Office Bldg Fl 7 Topeka KS 66612-1568*

CARLSON, ERIC DUNGAN, astronomer; b. Kansas City, Mo., Jan. 19, 1929; s. Harry Gustavus and Avis (Dungan) C.; m. Sandra Maria Ellzey, Oct. 11, 1970; children: Rebecca, Mark. AB, Washington U., 1950; MS, Northwestern U., 1965, PhD, 1968. Sr. astronomer, edn. supr. Alder Planetarium & Astronomy Mus., Chgo., 1968-96, emeritus astronomer, 1996—. Contbr. articles to Astrophys. Jour., Vistas In Astronomy, Publ. Astron. Soc. Pacific. Cpl. U.S. Army, 1954-56, West Germany. Mem. Am. Astron. Soc. Office: Adler Planetarium Astronomy Mus 1300 S Lake Shore Dr Chicago IL 60605-2403

CARLSON, GARY ALBERT, earth science educator; b. York, Nebr., Mar. 11, 1946; s. Clarence Martin and Alverda (Goesch) C.; m. Sharon Laurine Toelle, Dec. 22, 1979. BS in Edn., Midland Luth. Coll., 1968; MEd, Sul Ross State U., 1974; EdD, U. Nebr., 1985. Planetarium dir. Big Spring (Tex.) Ind. Sch. Dist., 1968-75; dir. Lueninghoener Planetarium and Behlen Obs. Midland Luth. Coll., Fremont, Nebr., 1975—, assoc. prof. earth sci., 1975-92, prof., 1992—; curator Midland Lutheran Coll. Arboretum, 1995—. Merit badge counselor Boy Scouts Am., Fremont, 1975—; project dir. Nebr. Com. for Humanities, Lincoln, 1988, vis. scholar, 1989-93; agt. Project Earth Sci. Tchrs. Exploring Exemplary Materials Ctr. for Astrophysics, Smithsonian Astrophys. Obs., Harvard Coll. Obs., 1991; mem. Keep Fremont Beautiful, 1994—. Named Tchr. of Yr., Midland Luth. Coll., 1985, 90. Fellow Internat. Planetarium Soc.; mem. Assn. Astronomy Educators, S.W. Assn. Planetarium Assn. (pres. 1970-71), Gt. Plains Planetarium Assn. (printing editor 1982-93, Disting. Svc. award 1988, Sears-Roebuck Found., Tchg. Excellence and Campus Leadership award 1990), Nebr. Acad. Sci. (Zimmerman Disting. Professor 1995). Democrat. Lutheran. Office: Midland Luth Coll 900 N Clarkson St Fremont NE 68025-4254

CARLSON, GARY L., stockbroker; b. Mpls., Oct. 30, 1942. BA, U. Minn., 1964. V.p. Engler & Budd, Mpls., 1967-91; stockbroker Summit Investment Corp., Bloomington, Minn., 1991—. With U.S. Army, 1964-70. Office: Summit Investment Corp 3800 W 80th St Ste 200 Bloomington MN 55431-4420

CARLSON, GERHARD FREDERICK, school psychologist; b. Manistee, Mich., June 24, 1937; s. Gerhard Enoch and Amethyst Elnora (Bullinger) C.; m. Judith Lynne Kurek, Aug. 1, 1960; children: Pamela Lynne, Elise Nicole. BA, Western Mich. U., 1959, MA, 1963; PhD, Wayne State U., 1969. Cert. sch. psychologist; lic. psychologist, Mich. Tchr. Coldwater (Mich.) Pub. Schs., 1959-60, Harper Creek Pub. Schs., Battle Creek, Mich., 1960-61; sch. psychologist Berrien County Intermediate Sch. Dist., Berrien Springs, Mich., 1961-64, asst. dir. spl. edn., 1966-74; doctoral fellow Wayne State U., Detroit, 1964-66; dir. ednl. program Impact Program, 1970-74; dir. pupil pers. Saudi Aramco Schs., Dhahran, Saudi Arabia, 1974-90; sch. psychologist Everett (Wash.) Pub. Schs., 1990-91; dir. Midwest Admissions, Leysin (Switzerland) Am. Sch., 1992-94. Mem. WNIT Cmty. Adv. Bd., Elkhart, Ind., 1991-94. Served with USNR, USCGR, USCG Aux. Mem. Nat. Assn. Sch. Psychologists, Mich. Assn. Learning Disability Edn. Office: Berrien County Intermediate Sch Dist 711 Saint Joseph Ave Berrien Springs MI 49103-1602

CARLSON, GUY RAYMOND, retired minister, religious organization administrator; b. Crosby, N.D., Feb. 17, 1918; s. George and Ragna Louise (Russum) C.; m. Mae Adeline Steffler, Oct. 7, 1938; children: Gary Allen, Sharon Carlson Bontrager, Paul Raymond. Student, Western Bible Coll., Winnipeg, Man., Can., 1934-35; D. of Div. (hon.), N. Cen. Bible Coll., Mpls., 1968. Ordained to ministry Assemblies of God Ch., 1941. Pastor Assembly of God Tabernacle, Thief River Falls, Minn., 1940-48; Minn. dist. Sunday sch. dir. Assemblies of God Council, Mpls., 1944-48, Minn. dist. supr., 1948-61; pres. N. Cen. Bible Coll., Mpls., 1961-69; asst. gen. supt. Assemblies of God Council, Springfield, Mo., 1970-85, gen. supt., 1986-94; pres. Assemblies of God Theol. Sem., Springfield, 1986-87. Author: Romans, 1962, Salvation, 1963, How to Study the Bible, 1964, The Inspired Scriptures, 1968, The Assemblies of God in Mission, 1970, The Life Worth Living, 1975, Preparing to Teach God's Word, 1975, Spiritual Dynamics, 1976, Our Faith and Fellowship, 1977, The Acts Story, 1978, And He Gave Pastors, 1979, Prayer and the Christian's Devotional Life, 1980; contbr. Commentary on Romans to The Complete Biblical Library, 1989; contbr. articles to profl. jours. Bd. dirs. Cen. Bible Coll., Evangel Coll., Berean Coll., Assemblies of God Theol. Sem., Springfield. Named to Order of Golden Shield, Evangel Coll., 1977. Mem. Nat. Assn. Evangelicals (exec. com., 1983—), Pentecostal Fellowship N.Am. (exec. com., mem. Pentecostal World Conf.).

CARLSON, JON GORDON, lawyer; b. Wakefield, Mich., June 25, 1943; s. John Edwin and Irene Anne (Erickson) C.; m. Jane McCann, June 17, 1965; children: Christine, Eric, Susan. BA, U. Ill., 1965, JD, 1967. Bar: Ill. 1967, Mo. 1990. Assoc. Edward F. O'Malley, East St. Louis, Ill., 1967-68, Kassly, Weihl & Bone, Belleville, Ill., 1968-70; ptnr. Kassly, Weihl, Bone, Becker & Carlson, Belleville, 1970-78, Chapman & Carlson, Ill., 1978-84, Talbert, Carlson & Mallon, Ill., 1985-86, Carlson & Alfeld, Edwardsville, Ill., 1986-87; prin. Jon G. Carlson & Assocs., P.C., Edwardsville, Ill., 1987-94, Carlson, Wendler & Sanderson, Edwardsville, Ill., 1994—, Abelle, Carlson & Sanderson, St. Louis, 1994—. Mem. Ill. Trial Lawyers Assn. (pres. 1987-88). Democrat. Office: 90 Edwardsville Profl Park PO Box 527 Edwardsville IL 62025

CARLSON, KEN H., engineer; b. Detroit, Apr. 1, 1934. Plant engr. Crystlers, Detroit, 1965; room leader La Duke Design Svc., Inc., Warren, Mich., 1966-81; chief engr. Savair, Inc., St. Clair Shores, Mich., 1981—. With U.S. Army, 1950-52. Mem. Am. Legion. Roman Catholic. Office: Savair Inc 33200 Freeway Dr Saint Clair Shores MI 48082-1071

CARLSON, KENNETH GEORGE, data processing executive; b. Duluth, Minn., Dec. 14, 1949; s. George Bernard and Laura Anna (Larson) C.; m. Stephanie Venn Petersen, Sept. 20, 1969; children: Laura, Anna. BSEE, U. Minn., 1972. Cert. in data processing; cert. systems profl. Systems programmer U. Minn. Computer Ctr., Mpls., 1969-74; dept. mgr. United Computing System, Kansas City, Mo., 1974-80; computer scientist Computer Scis. Corp., Falls Church, Va., 1980-82; pres., chmn. bd. LSS Data Systems, Mpls., 1982-86, 87—; v.p. Minn. Supercomputer Ctr., Mpls., 1986-87, asst. to exec. v.p., 1987-90; data processing advisor Johnson Community Coll., Overland Park, Kans., 1975-78; bd. dirs., chief fin. officer Superior Resources, Duluth, 1985—. Mem. Minn. Regional Network (corp. sec. 1987-88). Republican. Mem. United Ch. of Christ. Office: LSS Data Systems 6600 City West Pky Ste 200 Eden Prairie MN 55344-7707

CARLSON, LARRY VERNON, insurance company executive; b. Geneseo, Ill., Apr. 15, 1943; s. Vernon L. and Marjorie I. (Daniels) C.; m. Janet E. Dingwell; children: Kathleen J. Carlson Smith, Laurel E. Carlson Lewis. BS, Iowa Wesleyan Coll., 1965. CLU. Salesman Northwestern Mut. Life, Mt. Pleasant, Iowa, 1965-68; tng. asst. Northwestern Mut. Life, Milw., 1968-71; dir. devel. Northwestern Mut. Life, South Bend, Ind., 1971-81; gen. agt. Northwestern Mut. Life, Columbus, Ohio, 1981—. Chmn. bd. dirs. Goodwill Rehab. Ctr., Columbus, 1991-93; pres. Worthington Hills Civic Assn., Columbus, 1983-84. Mem. CLU Assn. (pres. Columbus chpt. 1993-94), Northwestern Mut. Gen. Agts. Assn. (pres. 1993-94), Gen. Agts. and Mgrs. Assn. (pres. 1982-83, Nat. Mgmt. award 1991), Rotary (Group Study Exch. 1977). Republican. Methodist. Home: 7626 Oakhurst Ln Columbus OH 43235-1642 Office: Northwestern Mut Life 580 S High St Columbus OH 43215-5644

CARLSON, LINDA MARIE, language arts educator, consultant; b. St. Paul, Dec. 24, 1951; d. Kenneth Leroy Carlson and Margaret (Herbison) Berget. BS in English and Polit. Sci., U. Minn., Duluth, 1973, MEd in Rhetorical Theory, 1979; MBA, U. St. Thomas, 1987; postgrad., Rensselaer Poly. Inst., 1992—. Cert. Myers-Briggs Type Indicator adminstrn., cert. tchr., Minn. Tchr. English, curriculum leader Ind. Sch. Dist. 13, Columbia Heights, Minn., 1973-76, publs. advisor, coach, 1974-76; exec. asst. to provost Univ. Minn., Duluth, 1977-80; tech. editor EG and G (U.S. Dept. Energy), Idaho Falls, Idaho, 1980; tchr. English, gifted and talented Ind. Sch. Dist. 11, Coon Rapids, Minn., 1980—, lang. arts curriculum developer, 1981—, publs. advisor, 1982-84, learning styles cons., 1986—, assessment cons., 1989—; performance assessment cons. Minn. State Dept. Edn., St. Paul, 1990—; writing assessment cons. Minn. State Graduation Rulie Pilot Site, St. Paul, 1994—; lang. arts cons. pvt. and pub. schs. Minn. Mem. Minn. Arthritis Found., St. Paul, 1981-90, Commn. on Health and Healing, Mpls., 1984-86, Anoka (Minn.) Handicapped Assn., 1992—. Recipient Golden Apple Teaching award Ashland Oil Co., 1994; All-Univ. scholar Rensselaer Poly. Inst., 1992. Mem. NEA, ASCD, Nat. Coun. for Tchrs. of English, Anoka-Hennepin Edn. Assn. (pub. rels. com. 1980—), Coll. Compositional Comm. Home: 1117 Cottonwood St NW Coon Rapids MN 55448

CARLSON, LYNDON RICHARD SELVIG, state legislator, educator; b. Mpls., Apr. 18, 1940; s. Lyndon C. and Shirley (Gittens) C.; m. Carole Moss, Dec. 7, 1968; children: Tonya, Lyndon Jr., Philip. BS, Mankato State U., 1964. Soc. studies tchr. Mpls. Pub. Schs., 1964—; mem. Minn. Ho. of Reps., St. Paul, 1972—; chmn. edn. com., mem. higher edn. fin. divsn., U. Minn. fin. divsn., K-12 edn. fin. divns.; mem. fin. instns. and ins. com., ways and means com., rules and legis. adminstrn. com., capital investment com. Recipient Pub. Svc. award Met. State U., 1983, Carroll award Minn. Vocat. Assn., 1990, Disting. Svc. award U. Minn. Extension Svc., 1990. Mem. Nat. Conf. State Legislatures (edn. com. 1987) Washington, Minn. Fedn. Tchrs. Office: Minn Ho of Reps 365 State St Saint Paul MN 55155

CARLSON, MARY ISABEL (MARIBEL CARLSON), county treasurer; b. Kinsley, Kans., July 26, 1931; d. Paul Doak and Minnie (Huser) Owen; m. Merle Dean Carlson, Aug. 16, 1952 (dec. 1984); children: James Dean, Gary Lee, Tommy Owen. Grad., Am. Bus. Coll., 1950; postgrad., Hays State U., 1992. Pvt. sec. Equitable of Iowa, Wichita, Kans., 1950-51; exec. sec. Wichita Jr. C. of C., 1951-52; sec. Etling & Beezley, Attys. at Law, Kinsley, 1952-55; dep. Edwards County Register of Deeds, Kinsley, 1967; ins. clk. Taylor & Sons, Ins., Kinsley, 1969-84; treas. County of Edwards, Kinsley, 1984—. Clk. election bd. Logan Twp., Edwards County, 1960-70, judge, 1960-70. Mem. Kans. County Treas. Assn., South Cen. Dist. Kans. County Treas. Assn. (pres. 1990-91, v.p. 1989-90, sec.-treas. 1988-89, hostess spring mtg. 1990). Republican. Methodist. Office: Edwards County Treas PO Box 246 Kinsley KS 67547-0246

CARLSON, MICHAEL PAUL, analytical chemist, toxicologist; b. Scottsbluff, Nebr., Apr. 7, 1952; s. Roy Leonard and Helen Mary (Rudloff) C.; m. Susan Jean Cummings, May 16, 1976; children: Lisa Nicole, Lynn Renee, Beth Christine. BS, U. Nebr., 1974; PhD, 1996; MS, Purdue U., 1976. Analytical chemist Dept. Vet. Sci. U. Nebr., Lincoln, 1980—. Contbr. articles to profl. jours. Maj. USAR, 1988—; with ARNG. Mem. Am. Chem. Soc., Am. Inst. Chemists, Assn. Ofcl. Analytical Chemists Internat. (assoc. referee, bd. dirs. Midwest region, treas. 1986, Assoc. Referee of Yr. 1985, Collaborative Study of Yr. award 1985, Midwest region pres. 1996), U. Nebr. Assn. for Administrv. Devel. (com. 1985—). Roman Catholic. Office: U Nebr Dept Vet and Biomed Sci Rm 145 Vet Diag Ctr Lincoln NE 68583-0907

CARLSON, RANDY EUGENE, insurance executive; b. Central City, Nebr., Jan. 5, 1948; s. Ned Conrad and Bonnie Lee (Norgard) C.; m. Lorraine Marie Cordsen, Sept. 16, 1967; children: Lance, Brent. BA in Edn., Wayne State Coll., 1970. Tchr., coach Elgin (Nebr.) Pub. Schs., 1970-72, Lewiston (Nebr.) Consol. Schs., 1972-74, North Platte (Nebr.) Pub. Schs., 1974-78; sales assoc. Franklin Life Ins. Co., North Platte, 1977-79; mng. gen. agt. Life Investors Ins. Co., North Platte, 1979—; trustee Fortunaires Found., Davenport, Iowa, 1980—; bd. dirs. Life Investors Ownership Trust, Cedar Rapids, Iowa, Life Investors Gen. Agt. Coun., 1993—; mem. Communicating for Agr. Scholarship and Edn. Found., 1985—. Contbr. articles to profl. jours. Mem. North Platte Booster Club, 1983—; designed plan for Nebr. High Sch. Football Playoff Sys., 1973. Mem. Nat. Assn. Life Underwriters (local pres. 1985-86, state membership chmn. 1986-87, local chmn. life underwriter polit. action com. 1993—), Nebr. State Life Underwriters Assn. (regional v.p. 1988-89), Gen. Agts. and Mgrs. Assn., North Platte C. of C. (bd. dirs. 1986—, vice chmn. 1988-89, hmn. 1989-90, chmn. bus. and edn. com. 1991—), North Platte Am. Legion, North Platte Country Club. Republican. Lutheran. Home: 3301 W F St North Platte NE 69101-5866 Office: Carlson and Assocs Inc 717 S Willow St PO Box 969 North Platte NE 69103-0969

CARLSON, RICHARD GREGORY, accountant; b. Chgo., Aug. 24, 1949; s. Richard George and S. Diane (Russell) C.; m. Annette Claire Bonneville, Aug. 30, 1969 (div. May 1982); children: Scott Richard, Amy Kristin; m. Pamela Catherine Punzelt, Sept. 25, 1982. BBA, Western Mich. U., 1971. CPA, Ill. With Deloitte & Touche, Chgo., 1971—, ptnr., 1980—, dir. real estate svc. ctr., 1980-91, mem. nat. real estate com., 1982-91, dirs. client svcs. and devel., 1985-88, mem. Chgo. exec. com., 1985-88, mng. ptnrs. adv. council, 1986-88, mng. dir. nat. real estate svcs., 1991—; Author: Real Estate Accounting and Reporting Handbook, 1995; editor Real Estate Accounting and Taxation Journal, 1991-93, Real Estate Strategies, 1991—. Mem. MIT Real Estate Ctr., 1995—; mem. bd. advisors Real Estate Fin. Jour., 1993—. Contbr. articles to profl. jours. Treas. Grace Luth. Ch., Glen Ellyn, Ill., 1977-78, Luth. Ch. of Ascension, Northfield, Ill., 1979-80; bd. dirs. Western Mich. U. Found., 1986—, mem. investment com., 1986-88, 91—, mem. exec. com., 1988—, vice-chmn., 1992-93, chmn., 1994—; bd. dirs. Pin Oak Homeowners Assn., treas. 1982-86. With USAR, 1971-77. Recipient Disting. Acctg. Alumni award Western Mich. U., 1987, Disting. Alumni award, 1993. Mem. AICPA, Am. Acctg. Assn. (Midwest regional steering com. 1983-87), Ill. Soc. CPAs, Internat. Coun. Shopping Ctrs., Western Mich. U. Alumni Assn. (bd. dirs. 1984-91, treas. 1984-86, pres. 1986-88), Nat. Assn. Real Estate Cos., Nat. Realty Com. (bd. dirs. 1992—), Real Estate Securities and Syndication Inst., Nat. Coun. Real Estate Investment Fiduciaries (acctg. com. 1985—, membership com. 1992—, bd. dirs. 1993—), Plaza Club (Chgo.), Westmoreland Country Club (bd. dirs. 1988-92, treas. 1988-92). Republican. Office: Deloitte & Touche 2 Prudential Plz Chicago IL 60601

CARLSON, RICHARD L., financial consultant; b. Peoria, Ill., June 4, 1955. Fin. cons. Wardel & Reed, Indpls., 1985-87, ABG & Assocs., Indpls., 1987-91, Fin. Network, Indpls., 1991—. Office: Fin Network Inv Corp 6325 Southeast St #A Indianapolis IN 46227

CARLSON, ROGER ALLAN, manufacturing company executive, accountant; b. Mpls., Dec. 12, 1932; s. Carl Albert and Borghild Amanda (Anderson) C.; m. Lois Roberta Lehman, Aug. 20, 1955; children: Gene, Bradley. BBA, U. Minn., 1954. CPA, Minn. Investment mgr. Mayo Found., Rochester, Minn., 1963-83; controller Luth. Hosp. and Homes Soc., Fargo, N.D., 1983-84; v.p., treas. Crenlo Inc., Rochester, 1984-94, also bd. dirs., part owner; instr. seminars, 1971, 82. Pres. Ability Bldg. Ctr., Rochester, 1974-75, United Way, Olmsted County, Minn., 1980; trustee Minn. Charities Rev. Coun., Mpls., 1981-83; bd. dirs. Dr. Samaritan Bethany, Inc., Rochester, Minn., 1991-95. Capt. U.S. Army, 1955-57. Mem. Am. Inst. CPA's, Minn. Soc. CPA's, Nat. Assn. Accts. (pres. So. Minn. chpt. 1969). Home: 4915 Sussex Pl Shorewood MN 55331-9217 Office: Crenlo Inc 1600 4th Ave NW Rochester MN 55901-2573

CARLSON, RUSSELL BUSBY, media specialist; b. Ft. Dodge, Iowa, Sept. 28, 1947; s. Russell Edward and Margaret E. (Busby) C.; m. Marilyn Joyce King, July 1, 1983. BA, U. No. Iowa, 1969, MA, 1975. Media specialist high sch. Nevada (Iowa) Cmty. Schs., 1969—; mem. Ctrl. Iowa Regional Libr. Com., Des Moines, 1990—. Mem. NEA, Iowa State Edn. Assn., Iowa Ednl. Media Assn., Nevada Cmty. Edn. Assn. Home: 701 NW Applewood St Ankeny IA 50021 Office: Nevada High Sch IMC 1001 15th St Nevada IA 50201

CARLSON, THOMAS JOSEPH, lawyer, real estate developer, former mayor; b. St. Paul, Jan. 12, 1953; s. Delbert George and Shirley Lorraine (Willardson) C.; m. Chandler Elizabeth Campbell, July 15, 1973; 1 child, Thomas Chandler. BA, George Washington U., 1975; JD, U. Mo., Kansas City, 1979. Reporter Springfield (Mo.) News-Leader, 1975-76; editor Buffalo (Mo.) Reflex, 1976-77; assoc. Woolsey Fisher, Springfield, 1980-83; pvt. practice law Springfield, 1983-86; ptnr. Carlson & Clark, 1986-93, Carmichael, Carlson, Gardner & Clark, Springfield, 1993-94; mayor City of Springfield, 1982-93; U.S. Bankruptcy trustee Springfield, 1982—; pvt. practice, 1994—; CEO, Resorts Mgmt., Inc., 1995—; lectr. in field. Contbr. articles to profl. jours. Mem. Springfield City Coun., 1983-85, Airport Bd. Springfield, 1994—; chmn. Springfield-Branson Leadership Com., 1993—. Mem. Mo. Bar Assn. (Disting. Young Lawyer award 1989). Presbyterian. Office: PO Box 50280 Springfield MO 65805-0280

CARLSON ARONSON, MARILYN A., English language educator; b. Gothenburg, Nebr., July 24, 1938; d. Harold N. and Verma Elnora (Granlund) C.; m. Paul E. Carlson, July 31, 1959 (dec. Sept. 1988); 1 child, Andrea Joy; m. David L. Aronson, July 8, 1995. BS in Edn., English and Psychology, Sioux Falls Coll., 1960; MA in History, U. S.D., 1973, MA in English, 1992; postgrad., U. S.D. English and social scis. instr., curriculum coord. Beresford (S.D.) Pub. Sch., 1960-78; English and social scis. instr. Sioux Empire Coll., Hawarden, Iowa, 1979-85; instr. of English and ESL Midwest Inst. for Internat. Studies, Sioux Falls, 1985-89; asst. prof. English Augustana Coll., Sioux Falls, 1989—; part time instr. psychology Northwestern Coll., 1985; part time instr. English and lit. Nat. Coll., 1985-88; part time instr. English and history Augustana Coll., 1986-89; presenter in field. Author: Visions of Light: Flannery O'Connor's Themes and Narrative Method, also rev.; published Heroines in Willa Cather's Prairie Novels-Heritage of the Great Plains, 1995 author critiques. Named Tchr. of Yr., 1976; S.D. Humanities scholar, 1993; Bush mini-grantee, 1993; Internat. Studies grantee, 1994. Mem. AAUP, Nat. Coun. Tchrs. English, Nat. Fedn. Music Clubs, Am. Assn. Univ. Profs. Home: 29615 469th Ave Beresford SD 57004-9205 Office: Augustana Coll Dept English 29th St and Summit Ave Sioux Falls SD 57197

CARLTON, ROBERT L., clinical psychologist; b. Murray, Ky., June 1, 1918; s. Albert B. and Ophelia (Hughes) C.; m. Frances Suiter, July 10, 1946; children: Glenn R., Keith H. BS, Murray State U., 1948; MA, Ohio State U., 1950, PhD, 1953. Lic. psychologist, Ohio. Staff psychologist Children's Mental Health Ctr., Columbus, Ohio, 1952-55, chief psychologist, 1955-63, assoc. dir., 1963-82; pvt. practice Columbus, 1982—; clin. asst. prof. dept. psychiatry Ohio State U., Columbus, 1966-77, adj. assoc. prof. dept. psychology, 1972-81. 1st lt. USAF, 1942-46, PTO. Mem. Am. Psychol. Assn., Ohio Psychol. Assn. (spl. recognition award 1972), Cen. Ohio Psychol. Assn. Home: 27 Willow Brook Way Delaware OH 43015-3815

CARLTON, TERRY SCOTT, chemist, educator; b. Peoria, Ill., Jan. 29, 1939; s. Daniel Cushman and Mabel (Smith) C.; m. Claudine Fields, June 11, 1960; children: Brian, David. B.S., Duke U., 1960; Ph.D. (NSF grad. fellow 1960-63), U. Calif., Berkeley, 1963. Mem. faculty Oberlin (Ohio) Coll., 1963—, prof. chemistry, 1976—, chmn. dept., 1980-83; vis. prof. chemistry U. N.C., Chapel Hill, 1976. Co-author: Composition, Reaction and Equilibrium, 1970. Mem. Am. Chem. Soc. Home: 165 Fairway Dr Oberlin OH 44074-1420 Office: Oberlin Coll Dept Chemistry Oberlin OH 44074

CARLUCCI, MARIAN ELAINE, investment company executive; b. Peoria, Ill., Mar. 19, 1964. BA, Ill. U., 1986. Stockbroker Merrill Lynch, Chgo., 1988-89; v.p. investments A G Edwards & Sons Inc., Lake Forrest, Ill., 1989—. Active Humane Soc., Chgo., 1994—, Anti-cruelty Soc., 1994—. Home: 3005 Roslyn Ln E Buffalo Grove IL 60089-4622 Office: A G Edwards & Sons Inc 225 E Deerpath Rd Ste 100 Lake Forest IL 60045-1970

CARMEAN, JERRY RICHARD, broadcast engineer; b. Greenfield, Ohio, Apr. 2, 1938; s. Cloyde B. and Mary F. (Hedges) C.; m. Patricia H. Carmean; 1 child, Steven. BS in Edn., Ohio U., 1965, BS in Elec. Enging., 1984. Registered profl. engr., Ohio; lic. FCC gen. class radiotelephone operator. Tchr. New Philadelphia (Ohio) High Sch., 1965-66; broadcast engr. Ohio U. Telecommunications Ctr., Athens, 1966-81, dir. enging., 1981-92; pvt. broadcast enging. cons., 1992—; cons. Sta. WLGN, Logan, Ohio, 1964—; tech. cons. Sta. 4VEH, Cap hatien, Haiti. Served with U.S. Army, 1961-64. Mem. NSPE, Ohio Soc. Profl. Engrs., Antique Wireless Assn., Soc. Broadcast Engrs., Men for Missions Internat., Athens County (Ohio) Amateur Repeater Assn., The Planetary Soc., Rotary. Home: 16341 Calico Ridge Rd Logan OH 43138-9416 Office: Sta WLGN Logan Broadcasting Co 1 Radio Ln Logan OH 43138-8762

CARMEN, IRA HARRIS, political scientist, educator; b. Boston, Dec. 3, 1934; s. Jacob and Lida (Rosenman) C.; m. Sandra Vineberg, Sept. 6, 1958; children: Gail Deborah, Amy Rebecca. BA, U. N.H., 1957; MA, U. Mich., 1959, PhD, 1964. Asst. prof. Ball State U., 1963-66; assoc. prof. Coe Coll., 1966-68; prof. polit. sci. U. Ill., 1968—; mem. recombinant DNA adv. com. NIH, 1990-94; participant meetings on China-U.S. genetic enging. rsch. andpolicy rels., Beijing, 1991, European-U.S. human genetic experimentation and policy rels., London, Paris, Rome, 1995; program organizer Human Genome Orgn. internat. meeting, Heidelberg, 1996; vis. scholar Yale Law Sch., 1981; vis. lectr. Tamkang U., Taiwan, 1991. Author: Movies, Censorship, and the Law, 1966, Power and Balance, 1978, Cloning and the Constitution, 1985; contbr. articles to profl. jours. Sr. advisor Bush-Quayle Nat. Jewish Campaign Com., 1988; mem. Pres. George Bush's Inaugural Educators Adv. Com., 1989; guest del. Rep. Nat. Conv., 1992; mem. Nat. Rep. Senatorial Com., 1996; mem. Rep. Nat. Com., Nat. Jewish Coalition, Empower Am. Recipient Clarence Berdahl award U. Ill., 1980, 87, 90, All-Campus award for excellence in undergrad. teaching, 1980, William F. Prokasy award, 1995, Harriet and Charles Luckman award, 1995. Mem. AAAS, Am. Polit. Sci. Assn., Phi Beta Kappa. Office: U Ill Dept Polit Sci Urbana IL 61801

CARMICHAEL, R. MARC, gas company executive; b. Muncie, Ind., Feb. 21, 1950; divorced; 2 children. BA, U. Notre Dame, 1972. Mem. Ind. House, 1986-91; Dem. candidate U.S. House, 2nd Dist., Ind., 1996. *

CARMICHAEL, VIRGIL WESLY, mining, civil and geological engineer, former coal company executive; b. Pickering, Mo., Apr. 26, 1919; s. Ava Abraham and Rosevelt (Murphy) C.; m. Emma Margaret Freeman, Apr. 1, 1939 (dec.); m. Colleen Fern Wadsworth, Oct. 29, 1951; children: Bonnie Rae, Peggy Ellen, Jacki Ann. BS, U. Idaho, 1951, MS, 1956; PhD, Columbia Pacific U., San Rafael, Calif., 1980. Registered profl. geol., mining and civil engr., geologist, land surveyor. Asst. geologist Day Mines, Wallace, Idaho, 1950; mining engr. De Anza Enging. Co., Troy, Idaho, Santa Fe, 1950-52; hwy. enging. asst. N.Mex. Hwy. Dept., Santa Fe, 1952-53; asst. engr. U. Idaho, 1953-56; minerals analyst Idaho Bur. Mines, 1953-56; mining engr. No. Pacific Ry. Co., St. Paul, 1956-67; geologist N.Am. Coal Corp., Cleve., 1967-69, asst. v.p. enging., 1969-74, v.p., head exploration dept., 1974-84; travel host Satrom Travel and Tour, Bismarck, N.D., 1988-92; mem., advisor (photogeology) for People to People "Hard Rock" Minerals Del. to China, 1981; mem., leader People to People Coal Mechanization Del. to China, 1982; advisor (photogeology) to Carbocol, Colombia, S.A., 1984-85; mem. Bismarck Scottish Rite Children's Hearing Impairment Bd., 1991—. Asst. chief distbr. DC Emergency Mgmt. Fuel Resources of N.D., 1968-92; bd. dirs., chmn. fund dr. Bismarck-Mandan Orch. Assn., 1979-83; 1st v.p., bd. dirs., chmn. fund dr. Bismarck Arts and Galleries Assn.,1 982-86; mem. and spl. advisor (Minerals) Nat. Def. Exec. Res., 1983—; mem. Fed. Emergency Mgmt. Agy., 1983—; mem. adv. bd. Bismarck Salvation Army, 1988—, chmn., 1993-95; sci. rsch. bd. N.D. Acad. Sci. Found., 1986-91. Recipient A award for sci. writing Sigma Gamma Epsilon; J.C. Penney Golden Rule award finalist, 1996. Mem. Am. Inst. Profl. Geologists (past pres. local chpt.), Breezy Shores Resort and Beach Club (bd. dirs.), Kiwanis (past pres., dist. lt. gov., dist. chmn. internat. found. 1991û), Masons (past master, trustee 1987-92, N.D. Masonic Found. 1987-92, 94—, chmn. 1990-92, Mason of Yr. Bismarck lodge 1992, Gen. Grand Masters award Cryptic Mason Med. Rsch. Found., Knight Comdr. Scottish Rite), Elks, York Rite

(Knight Templar Cross of Honor, Knight of York Cross of Honor). Republican. Home: 1013 N Anderson St Bismarck ND 58501-3446

CARNAHAN, MEL, governor, lawyer; b. Birch Tree, Mo., Feb. 11, 1934; s. A.S.J. and Mary Kathel (Schupp) C.; m. Jean Anne Carpenter, June 12, 1954; children: Roger, John Russell, Robin, Thomas. BA, George Washington U., 1954; JD, U. Mo.-Columbia, 1959. Lt. gov. State of Mo., 1988-93, gov., 1993—; majority fl. leader Mo. Ho. of Reps., Jefferson City, 1965-66; state treas. State of Mo., 1980-84. 1st lt. USAF, 1954-56. Named Outstanding Democrat Mo. Ho. of Reps., 1965, St. Louis Globe, 1965. Mem. Mo. Bar Assn., Order of Coif, Kiwanis (pres. Rolla chpt.), Masons, Shriners. Baptist. Home: PO Box 698 Rolla MO 65401-0698 Office: Office of the Governor PO Box 720 Jefferson City MO 65102-0720

CARNAL, CHRIS D., stockbroker; b. Ann Arbor, Mich., Aug. 29, 1967. BS in Mktg., Miami U., 1985-89. Lic. securities trader series 7, 63. Sales rep. Lenier Worldwide, Troy, Mich., 1989-93; stockbroker First of Mich., Grosse Pointe, 1993—. Instr. adult edn. Grosse Pointe War Meml.; mem. Habitat for Humanity. Mem. Country Club Detroit. Republican. Roman Catholic. Office: First of Mich 16980 Kercheval Ave 2nd Fl Grosse Pointe MI 48230

CARNES, JAMES EDWARD, state legislator; b. Wheeling, W.Va., Feb. 19, 1942; s. Edward A. and Avis E. (Hoop) C.; m. Nancy Ann Taylor, 1962; children: Jeffrey, Karen. Student, Bethany Coll., Coll. of Commerce, Wheeling, W. Va. Book keeper C. V. & W. Coal Co., 1962-69; office mgr. Cravat Coal Co., Holloway, Ohio, 1969—; owner, mgr. Carnes Mobile Home and Appliances, Barnesville, Ohio; sec.-treas. McCants Ins. Agy., Newcomerstown, Ohio; senator State of Ohio, Columbus; former chmn. legis. com. Ohio State Senate, Columbus; mem. Bd. Electors, State of Ohio, 1970-82, Ohio Commn. on Aging; regional chmn. Ohio State Manpower Coun. Pres. Rep. Club, 1970; mem., chmn. Belmont County Ctrl. and Exec. Coms., 1970-82. Finalist in 1959, 60, Prince of Peace Contests, Ohio; named hon. Lt. Gov. State of Ohio. Mem. Belmont County Hist. Soc., Flushing (Ohio) Rotary Club. Office: Senate Bldg Columbus OH 43215

CARNEY, JEAN KATHRYN, psychologist; b. Ft. Dodge, Iowa, Nov. 10, 1948; d. Eugene James and Lucy (Devlin) C.; m. Mark Krupnick, Jan. 1, 1977; 1 child, Joseph Carney Krupnick. BA, Marquette U., Milw., 1970; MA, U. Chgo., Chgo., 1984; PhD, U. Chgo., 1986. Registered Clin. Psychologist, Ill. Reporter Milw. Jour., 1971-76, editorial writer, 1976-79; asst. prof. psychology St. Xavier Coll., Chgo., 1985-86; dir. Lincoln Park Clinic, Chgo., 1986-87; pvt. practice psychotherapist Chgo., 1987—; mem. sci. staff Michael Reese Hosp. Med. Ctr., Chgo., 1987—; instr. Northwestern U. Med. Sch., 1991—; lectr. U. Ill. Coll. Medicine, 1993—. Recipient Best Series Articles, 1975, Best Editorial, 1978, Milw. Press Club, William Allen White Nat. Award for Editorial Writing, 1978, Robert Kahn Meml. Award for Research on Aging, Univ. Chgo., 1985. Mem. APA, Ill. Psychol. Assn., Chgo. Assn. Psychoanalytic Psychology. Home: 915 Burns Ave Flossmoor IL 60422-1107 Office: 55 E Washington St Ste 1219 Chicago IL 60602-2108

CARNEY, LARRY BRADY, telecommunications manager, accountant; b. Poplar Bluff, Mo., Mar. 15, 1948; s. Brady Elvis and Wanda Pauline (Francis) C.; m. Barbara Sue Foster, June 6, 1968; children: Lisa Anne, Steven Wayne, Karen Brooke. BSBA, S.E. Mo. State U., 1970; MBA, So. Ill. U., 1993. CPA, Mo. Auditor, Ernst & Young, St. Louis, 1970-73; internal auditor, acctg. mgr., v.p. contr. Maritz Inc., St. Louis, 1973-80; area mgr. Southwestern Bell Tel., St. Louis, 1980—, cost analyst, 1984-88, mktg. communications analyst, 1988-89, fin. analyst, 1980-81, product mgr., 1990—; staff mgr., industry mgr. AT&T Info. Systems, St. Louis, 1982-84; acctg. instr. Mo. Bapt. Coll., St. Louis, 1981-82, St. Louis Community Coll., 1982-85, Fontbonne Coll., 1992—. With Army N.G., 1970-76. Mem. AICPA, Mo. Soc. CPAs, Alpha Kappa Psi, Beta Gamma Sigma. Republican. Baptist.

CARNEY, RONALD EUGENE, chemist; b. Waukegan, Ill., Mar. 15, 1943; s. Eugene George and Letty Jean (Church) C.; m. Mary Lenore Healy, Nov. 15, 1969; 1 child, Lori Jean. BS in Chemistry, Northeastern Ill. U., 1976. Lab. tech. Abbott Labs., North Chicago, Ill., 1962-77; rsch. chemist Abbott Labs., North Chicago, 1978-82, rsch. chemist I, 1983-87, sr. scientist, 1987-95; assoc. rsch. fellow Abbott Labs., 5, 1995—; speaker in field. patentee in field. Assoc. rsch. fellow Abbott Labs., 1995—. Mem. Am. Chem. Soc., AAAS. Office: Bldg R2B D-451 14th & Sheridan North Chicago IL 60064

CARNEY, SUSAN MARGARET, marketing professional; b. Detroit, Apr. 14, 1960; d. Patrick Grover and Margaret Mary (Flynn) C. BA in History, U. Mich., Dearborn, 1986. Paralegal Bodman, Longley & Dahling, Detroit, 1982-85; pub. relations coordinator AM Gen. Divsn. LTV Aerospace and Def. Co., Livonia, Mich., 1985, pub. relations rep., 1986; pub. relations and advt. rep. AM Gen. Divsn. LTV Aerospace and Def. Co., South Bend, Ind., 1986-88; communications cons., Dearborn, Mich., 1988-89; dir. comm. Mueller Brass Co., Purt Huron, Mich., 1989-91; mgr. corp. comm. AM Gen. Corp., South Bend, Ind., 1991-93; dir. corp. comm. AM Gen. Corp., South Bend, 1993—. Mem. NAFE, Women in Comm. Roman Catholic. Office: 100 E Wayne St Ste 300 South Bend IN 46601

CARO, MELANIE DARLEEN, lawyer; b. Fairborn, Ohio, Dec. 12, 1956; d. Eugene Campbell and Bonnie Jean (Beall) Parkerson; m. Frank Anthony Caro, Jr., May 12, 1984; children: Tracy Hedberg, Alexandra Caro. BA summa cum laude, Washburn U., 1981, JD with honors, 1985. Legal intern Kans. Dept. Revenue, Topeka, 1983-85, atty., 1985-90; asst. U.S. atty. Dept. of Justice/U.S. Atty.'s Office, Topeka, 1990—. Leader Daisy/Girl Scouts U.S., Topeka, 1993; bd. dirs. Washburn Rural Mid. Sch. Parents Orgn., Topeka, 1992, 93, Topeka Gifted Orgn./501 Sch. Dist., 1987-89. Mem. Topeka Women Attys. (bd. dirs. 1989—), Am. Inns. of Ct., Topeka Inns of Ct., Topeka Bar Assn. (bd. dirs. 1986-90), Phi Kappa Phi. Republican. Office: US Attys Office 444 SE Quincy St Topeka KS 66683

CARON, ELISABETH, humanities educator, translator; b. Dombasle, France, Mar. 30, 1946; came to U.S. 1975; d. Jean and Yvonne Antoinette (Fieux) C.; m. Richard Jon Toumi, June 11, 1971; children: Jean U., Richard J. BA, U. Minn., Duluth, 1971; MA, U. Minn., 1978, PhD, 1984. Vis. asst. prof. U. Minn., Mpls., 1984-86, U. Kans., Lawrence, 1986-92; lectr. Loyola U., Chgo., 1992-95; vis. asst. prof. Roosevelt U., Chgo., 1992-95, Ind. U. N.W., Gary, 1995—; guest lectr. U. Chgo., 1993. Author: Les Essais de Montaigne ou les échos satiriques de l'humanisme, 1993; contbr. articles to profl. jours. Mem. MLA (reg. del. 1980-95), Midwest MLA, Assn. Tchrs. of French, Renaissance Soc. Am., Scholars of Early Modern Studies. Home: 1462 W Argyle St #2S Chicago IL 60640

CARON, RONALD JACQUES, professional sports team executive. Scout Montreal Canadiens NHL, 1957-68; gen. mgr. Voyagers Am. Hockey League, 1968-71; asst. to gen. mgr. Montreal Canadiens NHL, 1971-83; gen. mgr. St. Louis Blues, 1983—, v.p. and past gen. mgr., now exec. v.p. Office: St Louis Blues Kiel Ctr 1401 Clark Saint Louis MO 63103*

CARP, RICHARD MERCHANT, educational administrator; b. Madison, Wis., June 10, 1949; s. Abraham and Frances (Merchant) C.; m. Jana Elizabeth Carp, Nov. 6, 1985; children: James, Dylan. BA, Stanford U., 1971; MA, Pacific Sch. Religion, 1977; PhD, Grad. Theol. Union, 1981. Youth dir. St. Mark Episcopal Ch., Berkeley, Calif., 1981-84; program dir. United Meth. Jr. High Ch. Camp, No. Calif., 1985-87; dir., editor Image Bank for Teaching World Religions, Harvard U., 1988—; v.p. acad. affairs Kansas City Art Inst., 1989-91; chair Sch. of Art No. Ill. U., DeKalb, 1991—; bd. advisors TV course WGBH, Boston, 1989-92; co-dir. summer inst. NEH, 1993. Author: (play) Maiden, Mother, Crone: Women and Spirituality in the West, 1987; contbr. chpts. to books. Bd. dirs. Coun. for Arts in Palo Alto (Calif.) and Mid-Peninsula Area, 1976-77, Theatre Community Ctr. of Bay Area, San Francisco, 1979-84; artistic dir. Bur. Western Mythology, San Francisco Bay area, 1977-88; pres., art dir. Arts in Process, Berkeley, 1986-88. NEH grantee, 1987, 89; named to Outstanding Young Men Am., Jaycees, 1984. Mem. Am. Acad. Religion, Assn. for Integrative Studies (bd. dirs. 1992—), Coll. Art Assn., Semiotic Soc. Am., Phi Beta Kappa. Office: No Ill U Sch of Art 215A Arends Bldg De Kalb IL 60115-9984

CARPANZANO, CHRISTINA STEITZ, college administrator; b. Chgo., Dec. 3, 1952; d. Ronald Arthur and Anne Elizabeth (Wolk) Steitz; m. Jay Boundy, May 19, 1979 (div. Jan. 1986); m. Sergio Carpanzano, Dec. 31, 1992; children: Alexander, Anastasia. BA, Lake Forest Coll., 1974; MPA, DePaul U., 1983. Cert. travel cons. Reservation mgr. Internat. Travel Svc., Chgo., 1975-79; sales mgr. Transamerica Air, Chgo., 1979-83; sales profl. United Airlines, Elk Grove Village, Ill., 1983-90; sales mgr. Paging Network, Westchester, Ill., 1990-93; assoc. dean Robert Morris Coll., Chgo., 1992-95; adminstr. Joliet (Ill.) Jr. Coll., 1995—; cons. and advisor Bus. Network, Chgo. Presenter Chgo. Area Bus. Educators, mem. 1993—; mem. Community Svcs., Will County, 1994—. Recipient Outstanding Student award Am. Soc. Pub. Adminstrs., 1983. Mem. AAUW. Democrat. Roman Catholic. Office: Inst Econ Technology Joliet Jr Coll 214 N Ottawa Joliet IL 60432

CARPENTER, DAVID ERWIN, county planner; b. Appleton, Wis., Oct. 20, 1939; s. Erwin Carl and Othilia Mary (Killian) C.; m. Linda Louise Simkins, June 22, 1961 (div. Apr. 15 1983); children: Bradley John, Robert Anthony, Paige Elizabeth; m. Mary Starr (Davis) Griffin, May 18, 1991. BS, U. Wis., 1962, MS, 1979. Planner Wis. Dept. Devel., Madison, 1963-66, Fond du Lac County, Wis., 1966-68; supr. county planning Wis. Dept. Devel., Madison, 1968-69; assoc. dir. Southeastern Wis. Health Systems Agy., Milw., 1969-77; dir. planning St. Mary's Hosp. Med. Ctr., Madison, 1977-84; dir. mktg. St. Mary's Svcs., Madison, 1984-86; pres. David Carpenter Assocs., Madison, 1986-89; dir. planning Dodge County, Juneau, Wis., 1989-95; exec. dir. Dodge County Planning and Devel., Juneau, Wis., 1995—; mgr. Dodge County Heritage Preservation, Beaver Dam, 1991—; vol. Columbus (Wis.) Main Street Program, 1992-95. Author: Solid Waste Recycling Plan, 1991, Outdoor Recreation Plan, 1995. Pres. Wis. Soc. for Health Care Planning, 1982; sec-treas. Ice Age Park & Trail Found., Madison, 1990; pres. Charles E. Brown Archaeol. Soc., Madison, 1992-95; vol. Columbus Downtown Devel. Corp., 1992; trustee Columbus United Meth. Ch., 1992—; mem. exec. com. Flyway Area Labor-Mgmt. Coun., Horicon, 1993—; pres. Rock River Coalition, Watertown, 1995—; mem. Columbus Ad Hoc Econ. Devel. Com., 1994, Friends of Horicon Marsh Internat. Edn. Ctr., 1995—; vice chmn. Greater Columbus Recreation Commn., 1994—. Recipient award Wis. Dept. Devel., Madison, 1992, Forward Wis. award, 1994, Elmer Kohlbeck Friend of Tourism award, 1995. Mem. Am. Planning Assn., Am. Soc. Landscape Architects (affiliate), Meth. Planning and Rsch. (bd.dirs.), Wis. Archaeol. Soc., Phi Sigma Kappa. Office: Dodge County Planning & Devel 127 E Oak St Juneau WI 53039-1329

CARPENTER, DOROTHY FULTON, former state legislator; b. Ismay, Mont., Mar. 13, 1933; d. Daniel A. and Mary Ann (George) Fulton; m. Thomas W. Carpenter, June 12, 1955; children: Mary Ione, James Thomas. BA, Grinnell Coll., 1955. Tchr. elem. schs., Houston, and Iowa City, 1955-58; mem. Iowa Ho. Reps., 1980-94, asst. minority floor leader, 1982-88, chair ethics and state govt. coms., 1992-94; ret., 1994. Pres. Planned Parenthood of Iowa, 1970; bd. dirs. Planned Parenthood Fedn. Am., 1977-80; fin. chmn. Episcopal Diocese of Iowa, 1979-80. Recipient Grinnell Coll. Alumni award, 1980. Republican.

CARPENTER, JOHN EDWARD, marketing professional; b. Lancaster, Ohio, June 17, 1941; s. Leo Walter and Helen M. (Feeman) C.; m. Jennifer Rose Hill; children: Kevin A., Jeanine M., Anthony E. Student, Ohio U., Lancaster, 1974-76. Clk. reports Anchor Hocking Glass, Lancaster, Ohio, 1963-64; agt. life ins. Western & Southern Ins., Lancaster, 1964-65; letter carrier U.S. Post Office, Lancaster, 1965-70; supt. City Cemeteries, Lancaster, 1970-80, Sandusky, Ohio, 1980-87; diocesan dir. Cath. Cemeteries, Toledo, 1987—. With U.S. Army, 1960-63. Mem. Am. Cemetery Assn. (cert., bd. dirs.), Am. Mgmt. Assn., Nat. Cath. Cemetery Conf. (legis. com., trustee), Ohio Cath. Cemetery Conf. (past v.p., sec./treas.), Ohio Assn. Cemetery Supts. and Ofcls. (past pres., legis. and ethics com., exec. com., Allied Meml. Coun.), Am. Legion, Eagles, Toledo Area C. of C., Toledo Better Bus. Bur. Home: 2837 Jodore Ave Toledo OH 43606 Office: Catholic Cemeteries 5725 Hill Ave Toledo OH 43615

CARPENTER, KENNETH RUSSELL, international trading executive; b. Chgo., May 22, 1955; s. Kenneth and Margaret (Lucas) C.; 1 child, Matthew. AS in Aviation, Prairie State Coll., Chicago Heights, Ill., 1979. Respiratory therapist Harvey, Ill., 1980-83; dir., owner, ptnr. Pulmonary Therapy Inc., Harvey, 1983-91; v.p. Home Air Joliet Ltd., Harvey, 1984—; dir., owner Air Systems Internat. Export/Import Med. Equipment, Chicago Heights, 1981—, Air Systems, Ft. Lauderdale, 1991—, Home Ortho Ltd., Harvey, 1985—; pres., CEO Profl. Yacht Svcs., Inc., Chicago Heights, 1987-94; owner CL2 Exporting Inc., Chicago Heights, 1993-95; dir. pub. rels. Lansing (Ill.) Med. Group, 1990; dir. pulmonary rehab. Cardio-Pulmonary Assocs., Munster, Ind., 1990—, CLZ Exporting, 1992—; maj. importer/exporter of durable med. oxygen equipment worldwide. Pilot CAP, 1979-86. With USN, 1973-77. Mem. Am. Assn. Respiratory Therapy (cert.), Nat. Assn. Med. Equipment Suppliers, Ill. Assn. of Med. Equipment Suppliers. Home and Office: 23030 Miller Rd Chicago Heights IL 60411-5932

CARPENTER, MARY LAURE, hospital administrator; b. South Bend, Ind., Oct. 17, 1953; d. Daniel Pierre and Elizabeth Ann (Arigan) Laure; m. Gregory John Ingrassia, Oct. 26, 1974 (div. 1981); m. David James Carpenter, Dec. 30, 1983. Exch. student, France, 1970; student, U. Mo., St. Louis, 1972-74; BA, DePaul U., Chgo., 1988. With Christian Hosp. N.E., St. Louis, 1974-78; patient account mgr. Faith Hosp., Creve Coeur, Mo., 1978-81; telephone collector Tri-County Accounts Bur., Wheaton, Ill., 1981; Medicaid supr. Ingalls Meml. Hosp., Harvey, Ill., 1981-82; owner Medicare Claims Svc., Berkeley, Ill., 1982-84; ops. mgr. Superior Med. Supply, Elmhurst, Ill., 1984-85; bus. mgr. Forest Health Sys.-Forest Hosp., Des Plaines, Ill., 1985-86; asst. adminstr. Vencor/Sycamore (Ill.) Hosp., 1986-89; patient accounts mgr. Linden Oaks Hosp., Naperville, Ill., 1989-91; bus. office mgr. Vencor Hosp. Chgo., Northlake, Ill., 1991-95; pres. Vision Health, Inc., St. Charles, Ill., 1995—; lectr. in field. Mem. Am. Guild Patient Acctg. Mgrs. (v.p. 1979-80, Pres.'s award, 1980, Journalism award 1979), Health Care Fin. Mgmt. Assn., Midwest Hosp. Credit Mgr. Assn. (bd. dirs. 1976-79). Office: Vision Health Inc Box 828 Saint Charles IL 60174

CARPENTER, TIMOTHY W., state legislator; b. Milw., Feb. 24, 1960. BA, U. Wis., Milw., 1982. Former delivery svc. courier; state assemblyman dist. 20 State of Wis., 1984-92, speaker pro tem dist. 9; chmn. health com. Wis. State Assembly; mem. 4th Congl. Dist. Dem. Com., former chmn. Mem. Wilson Park Advancement Assn. Democrat. Home: 2957 S 38th St Milwaukee WI 53215-3519*

CARR, ARTHUR GARNSEY, III, lawyer; b. Newport, R.I., June 15, 1953; s. Arthur Garnsey II and Hilda (Brown) C.; m. Nancy Rita Ahan, Dec. 30, 1989. BA, Oberlin Coll., 1975; JD, New Eng. Sch. Law, 1983. Bar: N.Y., 1984. Banker Ulster Savs. Bank, Kingston, N.Y., 1977-80; atty. Eric K. Copeland, Esquire, Albany, N.Y., 1987-89, Carp, Sexauer & Carr, St. Louis, 1989-94; pvt. practice Kingston, 1984-85, St. Louis, 1994—; immigration law counsel Robert A. Perkins and Assocs., Chgo., 1994—. Author: (legal compliance documents) Labor Condition, 1994. Mem. adv. bd. Salvation Army Harbor Light Ctr., St. Louis, 1994—. Mem. Am. Immigration Lawyers (vice-chair Mo./Kans. chpt. 1991-94), Bar Assn. Met. St. Louis. Office: Ste 1132 225 S Meramec Saint Louis MO 63105

CARR, BONNIE JEAN, professional ice skater; b. Chgo., Sept. 29, 1947; d. Nicholas and Agnes Marie (Moran) Musashe; m. James Bradley Carr, Dec. 8, 1984; children: Brittany Jean, James Bradley II, Brooke Anderson. BS, Northwestern U., 1969; JD (hon.), Loyola U., Chgo., 1978. Skater Adventures on Ice, Mpls., 1961; prin. skater Jamboree on Ice, Chgo., 1961-68; society editor The Free Press, Colorado Springs, Colo., 1969; prin. skater, publicist on tour, asst. lighting dir., tour ednl. tutor Holiday on Ice Internat., 1970-74; skating dir. William McFetridge Sports Ctr., Chgo., 1975-86; choreographer, prin. skater Ice Time, USA, Mundelein, Ill., 1975—; skating coach St. Bronislava Athletic Club, Chgo., 1967-69; publicity dir. Amateur Skating Assn. Ill., Chgo., 1968; founder, dir. skating programs for blind, hearing impaired and mentally handicapped, Chgo., 1975-85; physical fitness advisor Exec. Health Seminars, Chgo., 1979; founder, dir. skating programs Fred Hutchinson Cancer Rsch. Ctr., Seattle, 1985-86; guest speaker Am. Cancer Soc., Columbia, S.C., 1973; conditioning coach Riverside Wellness and Fitness Ctr., Richmond, Va., 1989-91, Southampton Rec. Assn., Richmond, 1991-94; figure & speed skating coach Va. Spl. Olympics, 1991—. Recipient Key to City, Mobile, Ala., 1973, Service Recognition award Special Olympics, Chgo., 1984. Mem. Am. Guild Variety Artists, Am. Coun. on Exercise (cert. 1990-96). Roman Catholic. Home: 1931 Albion Rd Midlothian VA 23113-4148 Office: Ice Time USA 28800 N Gilmer Rd Mundelein IL 60060-9538

CARR, CAROLYN KEHLOR, realtor, fund raiser; b. St. Louis, July 23, 1948; d. James Kehlor Jr. and Jean Wheatly (Costen) C. BA in Art History, U. Mo., 1970, MEd in Learning Disabilities, 1971; Cert. in Spl. Edn. Adminstrn. and Supervision, U. Toledo, 1978—; postgrad. in Edn. Specialist, Cen. Mo. State U., 1988; completed Program on Negotiation, Harvard U., 1991. Learning lab. tchr. Jefferson County Pub. Schs., Lakewood, Colo., 1971-72; resource tchr. Littleton (Colo.) Pub. Schs., 1972-75; learning disabilities/behavior disorder spur. Lucas County Sch. Bd., Toledo, 1975-78; spl. edn. cons. Mo. Dept. Elem. and Secondary Edn., Jefferson City, 1978-80, interagy. supr., 1980-90; due process hearing officer, 1990—; pres. Carr and Assocs. of St. Louis, 1990—; mem. steering com. Mo. Gov.'s Conf. on Health Edn. for Children, 1986; presider working session for decision making profls., div. spl. edn. Mo. Dept. Elem. and Secondary Edn. contact for sch. aged head injury, 1988. Mem. Mo. Interagency Task Force for Persons with Deaf/Blindness, 1989-90; mem. Mediation and Conflict Mgmt. Svcs. Tng., Clayton, Mo.; bd. dirs. Jefferson City Community concert Assn., Very Spl. Arts., Mo., St. Louis Aquires and Ladies Charitabel Found. Recipient Profl. Contbn. award Div. Youth Services, St. Louis region, 1988. Mem. Nat. Assn. State Dirs. Spl. Edn. (life), Coun. Adminstrs. Spl. Edn., Nat. Soc. Arts and Letters (mentor 1994), Capital Kappans (chairperson steering com. 1980-81), Phi Delta Kappa (pres. 1981-92). Episcopalian. Home and Office: 93 Pebblebrook Ln West County MO 63146-5615

CARR, CHARLES WILLIAM, biochemist, emeritus educator; b. Mpls., July 20, 1917; s. Eugene Dickinson and Emma Joanna (Fogelmark) C.; m. Betty Jane Westman, June 16, 1945; children—Ralph William, George Eugene. B.Chemistry, U. Minn., 1938, M.S., 1939, Ph.D., 1943. Research assoc. U. Minn., 1943-46, mem. faculty, 1946-84, prof. biochemistry, 1964-84, prof. emeritus, 1984—, assoc. dept. head, 1976-84. Author: Physiological Chemistry/Biochemistry 1888-1988, 1994; co-author: Physiological Chemistry: Laboratory Directions, 1951. Lalor summer fellow, 1956; grantee NIH, 1952-74. Mem. Am. Soc. Biol. Chemists, Am. Chem. Soc., Minn. Med. Found. Conglist. Home: 6633 Lynwood Blvd Minneapolis MN 55423-2224

CARR, CLAY BRYAN, JR., federal civil service manager; b. Winchester, Va., Sept. 14, 1934; s. Clay Bryan and Elizabeth Caldwell (Hume) C.; m. Dorothy Anita Groves (div. Aug. 1963; 1 child, Clay Bryan III.; m. Helen Muriel McNeil (div. Oct. 1975); m. Gayle Florence Wonders, July 2, 1976. BA, Washington & Lee U., 1956; MDiv, Va. Theological Sem., 1959. Trainee USIA Foreign Svc., Washington, 1964, VA, Portland, Oreg., 1964-65; personnel specialist VA, Fresno, Calif., 1965-66, Def. Depot, Ogden, Utah, 1966-68, Holloman AFB, Alamagordo, N.Mex., 1968-71; civilian personnel officer Kingsley Field, Klamath Falls, Oreg., 1971, Def. Contract Adminstrn. Region, Dallas, 1971-80, Def. Depot, Memphis, 1980-83, Def. Construction Supple Ctr., Columbus, Ohio, 1983-87; chief Def. Logistics Agy. Civilian Personnel Svcs. Support Office, Columbus, 1987—; presenter, moderator, panelist numerous confs., 1975-91. Author: The New Manager's Survival Guide, 1988, Front-Line Customer Service, 1990, The Managers Troubleshooter, 1990, Teampower, 1992, Smart Training, 1993, The Competitive Power of Constant Creativity, 1994; contbr. articles to jours. Bd. dirs. Internat. Soc. for Performance Improvement; pres. Wyo. Assn. for Mental Health, 1961-62, Fed. Bus. Assn., Dallas, 1977-78, Fed. Pers. Mgmt. Assn., Memphis, 1980-83; co-founder, pres. NE Wyo. Assn. for Mental Health, 1962-63; chmn. Otero County Cmty. Action Agy., Alamogordo, 1969-70. Home: 342 E Schrock Rd Westerville OH 43081-3453 Office: DCPSO 3990 E Broad St Columbus OH 43213-1152

CARR, CYNDA ANNETTE, elementary education educator; b. Harper, Kans., June 6, 1948; d. Don Edward and Raquel Ann (Daniels) C. BA, Wichita (Kans.) State U., 1974, MEd, 1980. Tchr. Unified Sch. Dist. 361, Anthony, Kans., 1974—; steering com. Kans. Tchr. of Yr., 1995—; tchr. cons. Kans. Geographic Alliance, 1992—. Trainer Wheatbelt area coun. Girl Scouts U.S., Hutchinson, Kans., 1980-83, 85-92, bd. dirs., 1987-91, active various coms. and task forces; neighborhood chmn. Anthony coun. Girl Scouts U.S., 1985-91, troop leader, 1976-84, 88-89; bd. dirs. Harper County chpt. Am. Cancer Soc., Anthony, 1986—, Anthony United Way, 1987-89; mem. Leadership Harper County, 1994-95; activities counselor Camp Hope/Am. Cancer Soc., 1987; Sunday sch. tchr., mem. choir 1st Congl. Ch., 1990—; sponsor Kids for Saving Earth, 1991—; mem. Soil Conservation Earth Team, 1992—. Named Tchr. of Yr. Harper County Conservation Dist., 1992; recipient Silver Pen award Kans. Edn. Assn., 1987, Thanks Badge award Girl Scouts U.S., 1988, Contbn. to Conservation award Anthony Republican, 1992, Nat. Educator award Milken Family Found., 1994. Home: 401 S Kansas Ave Anthony KS 67003-2624 Office: Anthony Elem Sch 215 S Springfield Ave Anthony KS 67003-2550

CARR, DOLEEN, computer and environmental specialist, consultant; b. Alameda, Calif., Sept. 23, 1950; d. Charles Joseph Ziegler and Dola Faye (Cushing) Peterson; m. Glen Allwin Pellett, June 26, 1971 (div. 1986); children: mark D., Michael J.; m. Danny Lynn Carr, Dec. 29, 1986 (div. 1996). BA, U. Wis., Madison, 1973. Notary Pub., Mich. Budget analyst Ednl. Testing Svc., Princeton, N.J., 1979-80; tech. recruiter Uniforce Svcs., Inc., Rock Hill, S.C., 1983-84; mgr. tng. and documentation Electronic Data Systems Corp., Troy, Mich., 1985-87; tech. writer, trainer, analyst cons. CES, Inc., Troy, 1989-92; pres. D'Carr Co., Inc., Roseville, Mich., 1988-93; tech. writer, trainer, cons. Eaton Corp., Southfield, Mich., 1988-93; pres., CEO Carr-Ben Tech Ltd., Roseville, Mich., 1996—; installer Gt. Plains Acctg., Fargo, N.D., 1990—; cons. Hazardous Materials Info. Exch., Washington, 1989—; cons., tech. writer Saturn Corp., 1991-92, Blue Cross Blue Shield, Southfield, Mich., 1992-93, 95—; tech. wrtier FANUC Robotics, N.A., Inc., Auburn Hills, Mich., 1993-95. Co-author: CIW-Weld Monitor, 1990, 93. Mem. AAUP, ASTD, NAFE, Internat. Platform Assn., Greater Trenton Musicians Union, Profl. Bus. Women's Assn., Macom County Dems., Mich. Dems., Roseville Kiwanis (pres., clown 1994—). Democrat. Roman Catholic. Office: 133 Belmont Ln Whitmore Lake MI 48189

CARR, JACQUELYN, university administrator; b. Morristown, N.J., Oct. 26, 1970; d. James Matthew and Loretta (Russo) C. BS, Fla. State U., Tallahassee, 1992; MEd, Clemson U., 1994. Resident asst. Fla. State U., Tallahassee, 1990-92; resident dir. Clemson (S.C.) U., 1992-94; resident dir. Ohio U., Athens, 1994—, instr., 1994—. Mem. Am. Coll. Pers. Assn. (standing com. for women 1995—), Nat. Assn. Student Pers. Adminstrs., Assn. for Student Jud. Affairs, Ohio Coll. Pers. Assn., Chi Sigma Iota. Roman Catholic. Home: PO Box 5595 Athens OH 45701 Office: Ohio U South Green Office O'Bleness House Athens OH 45701

CARR, MARCELLA IRENE, medical surgical nurse; b. McCook, Nebr., Oct. 9, 1938; d. Carl Oscar and Ruby Marcella (Miller) Peterson; m. Robert Connell Carr, Aug. 20, 1957; children: Brenda Irene Bell, Robert Carl Carr, David Alan Carr. LPN diploma, Mid Plains C.C., 1977; ADN, Dakota Wesleyan U., 1985; BS, U. Nebr., 1987. RN, Kans., Nebr., Fla.; cert. BLS, Am. Heart Assn. Stenographer, clk. Frontier County Welfare Office, Curtis, Nebr., 1954-66; office asst. Charles E. Hranac, M.D., Cozad, Nebr., 1967-75; staff nurse Cozad (Nebr.) Community Hosp., 1977-87; staff nurse part-time Richard Young Hosp., Kearney, Nebr., 1989-93; pool nurse Great Plains Health Alliance, Phillipsburg, Kans., 1987-93; home health nurse Cozad (Nebr.) Cmty. Hosp., 1993-94; house supr. Southview Manor Care Ctr., Cozad, 1994-96; supr. Hilltop Estates, Gothenburg, Nebr., 1996—. Mem. ANA, Nat. League Nursing, Kans. Nurses Assn., Nebr. Nurses Assn., Am. Assn. Ret. Persons, Royal Neighbors Am. (oracle 1964-66), Maccabees, Psi Chi. Republican. Mem. Ch. of Christ. Home: 512 W 11th St Cozad NE 69130-1306 Office: Hilltop Estates 2520 Ave M St Gothenburg NE 69138

CARR, ROBERT WILSON, JR., chemistry educator; b. Montpelier, Vt., Sept. 7, 1934; s. Robert Wilson and Marie (Soucy) C.; m. Betty Lee Elmer, June 21, 1958; children: Kevin, Terrell, Kathryn. B.S., Norwich U., 1956; M.S., U. Vt., 1958; Ph.D., U. Rochester, 1962. NIH fellow Harvard U., 1963-65; asst. prof. U. Minn., 1965-69, asso. prof., 1969-75, prof. dept. chem.

engring. and materials sci., 1975—; vis. prof. U. Cambridge, 1971-72, MIT, 1995; guest prof. U. Göttingen, Fed. Republic Germany, 1982. Asst. editor: Jour. Phys. Chemistry, 1970-80. Served to 1st lt. U.S. Army, 1963. NSF fellow, 1971-72; Fulbright fellow, 1982. Mem. Am. Chem. Soc., Am. Aviation Hist. Soc., Interam. Photochem. Soc., Am. Inst. Chem. Engrs., Sigma Xi. Mem. United Ch. of Christ. Home: 5722 Harriet Ave Minneapolis MN 55419-1807 Office: U Minn Dept Chem Engring and Materials Scis Minneapolis MN 55455

CARR, WILEY NELSON, hospital administrator; b. Dayton, Ohio, Dec. 29, 1940; s. Russell Earl and Anna Lee (Stroud) C.; m. Grace Elizabeth Brown, June 4, 1960 (div.); children: Wiley Nelson, Alison Mary Ann, G. Elizabeth, Joshua William, Joy Kathleen. Student, Miami U., Oxford, Ohio, 1959-62; BSJ, Ohio U., 1963, MS, 1964; MBA, Xavier U., Cin., 1974. Lic. nursing home adminstr., Ky. Dir. pub. rels. Western Coll. for Women, Oxford, 1964-67, dir. devel., 1967-70; dir. devel. and community rels. St. Elizabeth Med. Ctr., Covington, Ky., 1970-74, asst. adminstr., 1974-83; v.p., chief operating officer St. Elizabeth Med. Ctr., Edgewood, Ky., 1983-90; pres., CEO, Porter Meml. Hosp., Valparaiso, Ind., 1990—; bd. dirs. BetterCare, Inc., Cin.; sec. Tri-State Healthcare Laundry, Edgewood, 1989-90. Pres. Tri-State Community Cancer Orgn., Cin., 1988—; bd. dirs. United Way Porter County, Community Devel. Corp., Valparaiso, N.W. Ind. Forum, YMCA Valparaiso. Fellow Am. Coll. Healthcare Execs.; mem. Ind. Hosp. Assn. Republican. Methodist. Home: 601 Stratford Ter Valparaiso IN 46383-2024 Office: Porter Memorial Hospital 814 Laporte Ave Valparaiso IN 46383-5860

CARR, WILLIAM H(ENRY) A., public relations executive, author; b. Albany, N.Y., Nov. 25, 1924; s. John Joseph and Ruby (Sokol) C.; m. Brooks Boeke, Nov. 18, 1984; children: Stephen, Christine, Jennifer, John, Brooks, Beth. Student, U. Chgo., 1944-46. Reporter City News Bur., Chgo., 1943-44, Chgo. Sun, 1944-45, Chgo. Times, 1945-46; news editor ABC, Chgo., 1946-47; pub. relations specialist John Price Jones Co., N.Y.C., 1949-52; assoc. dir. pub. rels. United Community Def. Svcs., N.Y.C., 1952-55; reporter, editor N.Y. Post, N.Y.C., 1955-64; cons. INA Corp., Phila., 1967-71; dir. pub. info. Commonwealth of Pa., Harrisburg, 1971; pres., CEO Jack Raymond & Assocs., Inc., N.Y.C. and Indpls., 1977—. Author: Beauty in the White House, 1961, Those Fabulous Kennedy Women, 1961, What Is Jack Paar Really Like?, 1962, The Basic Book of the Cat, 1962, Medical Examiner, 1963, J.F.K., A Complete Biography, 1963, Diplomatic Immunity (as Eleanor Sydell), 1966, The Age of the Wife Swappers (as John T. Warren), 1966, Savage Scalpel (as Alain Rothstein), 1968, Black Gold, 1969, Perils: Named and Unnamed, 1967, The Emergence of Red China, 1966, The DuPonts of Delaware, 1964 (Best Book of Yr., Friends of Am. Writers), From Three Cents a Week..., 1975, The New Basic Book of the Cat, 1978, Up Another Notch: Institution Building at Mead, 1989. Mem. Gov.'s Task Force on Crime Prevention and Cmty. Involvement, Md., 1968-69; mem. exec. com. Pa. Pub. Com. for Humanities, 1971-76; bd. dirs. 500 Festival Assocs., 1988-93, Ind. Internat. Coun., 1988—; pres. Hemlock Soc. Ind., 1994—, Ind. Advocates for Arts, 1994—; pres. Ind. Citizens for Arts, 1994—. Recipient Albert Schweitzer medal for humanitarianism, Animal Welfare Inst., 1961. Mem. Authors Guild Am., Aircraft Owners and Pilots Assn., Pub. Rels. Soc. Am., Internat. Assn. Bus. Communicators, Confrerie Chevaliers du Tastevin de Bourgogne, Columbia Club Indpls., Overseas Press Club, Nat. Press Club, N.Y. Press Club, Indpls. Press Club. Office: Jack Raymond & Assocs Inc 5235 Roland Dr Indianapolis IN 46228

CARRAHER, CHARLES JACOB, JR., professional speaker; b. Cin., Sept. 22, 1922; s. Charles Jacob and Marcella Marie (Hager) C.; grad. pub. schs., Norwood, O.; m. Joyce Ann Root, June 13, 1947; children—Cynthia A., Craig J. With Cin. Enquirer, 1937-72, office mgr., circulation mgr., adminstrv. asst. to exec. v.p., 1947-66, dir. employee community relations, 1966-72, corp. sec., 1969-72; exec. v.p., partner Cin. Suburban Newspapers Inc., 1973-77; asst. dir. devel. WCET-TV, 1977-79; v.p. Garrett Computer Inc., 1979-81; participant numerous symposia. Mem. bd., v.p. Cin. Conv. and Visitors Bur., 1966-72; mem. Cin. Manpower Planning Council, 1972. Bd. dirs. Central Psychiatric Clinic, 1970-80, Mental Health Assn., 1970-72, Great Rivers council Girl Scouts U.S.A., 1969-74; v.p. bd. dirs. Neediest Kids of All, 1969-72; bd. dirs. Greater Cin. Urban League, 1971-74, 75-78. Served to lt., USAAF, World War II, ETO. Decorated Air medal with cluster. Mem. Greater Cin. C. of C. (chmn. human resources devel. com. 1972), Beta Gamma Sigma. Republican. Methodist. Home and Office: 10848 Lake Thames Dr Cincinnati OH 45242-3105

CARRIER, MARK ANTHONY, professional football player; b. Lake Charles, La., Apr. 28, 1968. BA in Communications, U. So. Calif. Safety Chicago Bears, 1990—. Voted to Pro Bowl, 1990-93; named defensive back The Sporting News All-America team, 1989, free safety The Sporting News NFL All-Pro team, 1991; recipient Jim Thorpe award, 1989. *

CARRIGAN, JOANN, history educator; b. Washington, Ark., Sept. 10, 1933; d. Gray Eugene and Lucile (Monroe) C. BA, Henderson State U., 1953; MA, La. State U., 1956, PhD, 1961. Tchr. Sheridan (Ark.) High Sch., 1953-54; instr. Henderson State Coll., 1959, Nicholls State Coll., Thibodaux, La., summer 1962; asst. prof. La. State U., Baton Rouge, 1962-67, assoc. prof., 1967-69; assoc. prof. history U. Nebr., Omaha, 1970-71, prof. history, 1971—; vis. prof. U. Ala., Tuscaloosa, summer 1967; adj. prof. med. history U. Nebr. Med. Ctr., Omaha, 1973—; program coord. Mo. Valley Hist. Conf., Omaha, 1973-74, 84. Author: The Saffron Scourge: A History of Yellow Fever in Louisiana, 1994; (with others) Disease and Distinctiveness in the American South, 1988; editor: Fortier's History of Louisiana, 1966-72; mng. editor La. History, 1963-69; contbr. articles to profl. jours. Gottlieb scholar La. State U., 1960-61; Andrew Mellon fellow U. Pitts., 1961-62. Mem. Am. Assn. for the History of Medicine, Am. Hist. Assn., La. Hist. Assn., So. Hist. Assn., Orgn. Am. Historians, Phi Alpha Theta. Home: 1633 Country Club Ave Omaha NE 68104-5019 Office: Dept History Univ Nebr at Omaha Omaha NE 68182

CARRIGAN, PAMELA SUE, new resident administrator; b. Des Moines, May 26, 1970; d. Burle Ralph and Alice Louise (Corey) Carrigan. BA in Social Sci. cum laude, U. No. Iowa, Cedar Falls, 1992. Cert. tchr., Iowa. Tchr. social studies and English, 7th, 8th, and 9th grades Twin Wells Indian Sch., Sun Valley, Ariz., 1992-93; tchr. history 9th-11th grades Des Moines Christian Sch., 1993-94; eligibility specialist Systemed Pharmacy, Inc., Des Moines, 1994-96; new resident mgr. Good Samaritan Urban Ministries, Des Moines, 1996—. Vol., Campus Crusade for Christ, L.A., 1992. Mem. Nat. Coun. for the Social Studies (awards com.), Kappa Delta Pi, Phi Alpha Theta, Psi Chi. Republican. Methodist. Office: Good Samaritan Urban Ministries Des Moines IA 50314

CARRILLO, CARMEL J., journalist; b. Chgo., Jan. 11, 1969; d. Joseph S. and Marcia A. (Keller) C.; m. Steven B. Hartline. BA in English and Sociology, U. Ill., 1991. Copy editor Newsday, L.I., N.Y., 1996—. Editor (newsletter) Headlines and Deadlines, 1995-96. Fellow So. Ill. U. Law Sch., 1991; scholar League of United Latin Am. Citizens, 1987, Presdl. scholar U. Ill., 1995. Mem. League of Women Voters, Soc. Profl. Journalists, Nat. Assn. Hispanic Journalists, Soc. of Environ. Journalists (minority fellow, 1995).

CARRINGTON, MICHAEL DAVIS, criminal justice administrator, educator; b. South Bend, Ind., Mar. 9, 1938; s. Herman Lakin and Margaret (Davis) C.; m. Lynn Ogden, Feb. 8, 1958; children: Michael O., Jill A., Elizabeth A., Gretchen L. BA, Ind. U., 1970; MALS, Valparaiso U., 1971. Parole officer State of Ind., South Bend, 1970-71; chief probation officer St. Joseph County, South Bend, 1971-74; dir. pub. safety City of South Bend, 1974-76, mayor's asst., 1976-80; adj. assoc. prof., dir. safety, security, police Ind. U., South Bend, 1979-94; presdl. appointment as U.S. Marshal Northern Dist. of Ind., South Bend, Ind., 1994—; cons. in pvt. security Pan Am. Games, Indpls., 1987; auditor videotape Gavin DeBecker Inc., Studio City, Calif., 1988; security advance agt. Olympic Torch Relay, Ind., 1984, Hands Across Am., Ind., 1986. Author, editor handbook, studies in field. Pres. South Bend Bd. Pub. Safety, 1975; mem. Spl. Crimes Unit adv. bd. St. Joseph County, 1992; mem. St. Joseph-Indiana County Jail Project adv. bd., 1993—; bd.dirs. South Bend Housing Devel. Corp. Recipient Sagamore of Wabash award, 1984; named Ky. Col., 1984, Hon. Big. Brother of Yr., 1974, Outstanding Residential Faculty Mem. awrd Ind. U. South Bend Sch. Pub. and Environ. Affairs, 1992. Mem. Acad. Criminal Justice Soc., Am. Soc. Ind. Security. Methodist. Office: U.S. Marshals Room 233 204 S Main South Bend IN 46601

CARROLL, CHRISTOPHER STEVEN, lawyer; b. L.A., Oct. 2, 1952; s. Charles Lawrence and Avis Rae (Varnadore) C. BA magna cum laude, U. Ill., Chgo., 1974; JD, IIT, Chgo., 1978. Bar: Ill. 1979, U.S. Dist. Ct. (no. dist.) Ill. 1979, U.S. Dist. Ct. (so. dist.) Ill. 1980. Staff atty. State Appellate Prosecutor, Mt. Vernon, Ill., 1979-81; assoc. Benjamin & Shapiro, Chgo., 1981-84, Meloche & Assocs., Chgo., 1985-88; claims atty. Nat. Continental Ins., Cleve., 1988-91; div. litigation mgr. Progressive Ins., Seattle, 1991-93; assoc. Goldberg & Goldberg, Chgo., 1993—. Northside polit. action chmn. Ind. Voters Ill., Chgo., 1971; legis. counsel Mothers Against Drunken Driving, DuPage County, Ill., 1986. Mem. Ill. Trial Lawyers Assn. Democrat. Methodist. Home: 510 W Briar Pl Chicago IL 60657-4625 Office: Goldberg & Goldberg 33 N Dearborn St Chicago IL 60602-3102

CARROLL, ELLEN THERESE, small business owner; b. Chgo., May 23, 1961; d. Carter Donald and Phyllis Estelle (Przybylski) C. AA, Coll. of DuPage, 1982; BA, U. Md., 1990; MA, U. London, 1992. Tour operator, writer Travel Plans Internat., Oak Brook, Ill., 1985-86; editor Capitol Publs., Alexandria, Va., 1986-87; with sales dept. Kennedy Ctr., Washington, 1990; conf. coord. Anderson's Books, Naperville, Ill., 1992-94; owner, operator Carroll Literary Events, Naperville, 1994—; freelance copywriter U.S. News & World Report, Washington, 1987, Congl. Quar., Washington, 1987; creator, organizer Hole in the Wall Gang Camp, Ashford, Conn., 1993—. Mem. Internat. Reading Assn. (bd. dirs. suburban coun., publicity chair 1994—). Office: Carroll Literary Events 511 E North Ave Naperville IL 60540

CARROLL, HOWARD WILLIAM, state senator, lawyer; b. July 28, 1942; s. Barney M. and Lyla (Price) C.; m. Eda Stagman, Dec. 1, 1973; children: Jacqueline, Barbara. BBA, Roosevelt U., 1964; postgrad., Loyola U., 1964-65; JD, DePaul U., 1967. Bar: Ill. 1967. Staff atty. Chgo. Transit Authority, 1967-71; pvt. practice, 1971-74; ptnr. Carroll & Sain, Chgo., 1974—; mem. Ill. Senate, Springfield, 1973—, asst. minority leader, 1993—, chmn. appropriations com., 1977-93; mem. Legis. Info. System Commn., Ill. Comprehensive Health Ins. Bd.; vice chmn. State Employees Suggestion Award Bd.; mem. fed. budget and taxation com. State-Fed. Assembly; mem. Assembly Com. on State's Legis. Fiscal Affairs and Oversight; prof. complemental faculty Rush U. Coll. Health Scis., Chgo.; lectr. in field. Mem. Ill. Ho. of Reps., 1971-72; chmn. fin. com. Chgo. and Cook County Dem. Crtl. Com., 1982-84, treas., 1984—; committeeman 50th Ward Dem. Orgn., 1980—; mem. platform com. Ill. Dem. Com., 1974—; former mem. youth adv. bd. Dem. Nat. Com.; del. nat. and Ill. Dem. convs.; v.p. Young Dem. Clubs Am., 1971-73, also former gen. counsel; mem. exec. bd. Atlantic Alliance Young Polit. Leaders, 1970-73; active numerous civic orgns.; mem. exec. com. Jewish Nat. Fund, 1977—; founder Howard W. Carroll Found. Recipient numerous awards, 1971, including cert. of appreciation Decalogue Soc. Lawyers, 1972, Hemophilia Found. Ill., 1988, City Colls. Chgo., 1992, Disting. Svc. award State of Israel Bonds, 1974, Self-Help Assn., 1986, citation for meritorious svc. DAV, 1986, Legislator of Yr. award Child Care Assn. Ill., 1988, Ill. Coun. on Long Term Care, 1988, Outstanding Legislator award Am. Acad. Ophthalmology, 1989, Legis. Advocacy award Ill. Coun. for Gifted, 1991, Founders medal Montay Coll., 1992; named Ill. Health Care Outstanding Legislator of Yr., 1995. Mem. Chgo. Bar Assn. (Disting. Lawyer and Legislator award 1974), Zionist Orgn. Chgo., Masons (32d degree), B'nai B'rith (bd. dirs. West Rogers Park, chmn. Anti-Defamation League 1978-80, mem. exec. com. and chmn. spl. events Greater Chgo. coun., bd. dirs. Budlong Woods chpt.). Home: 2929 W Albion Ave Chicago IL 60645-4203 Office: Office of Senate Members State Capitol Springfield IL 62706 also: 47 W Polk St Lobby 3 Chicago IL 60605-2000

CARROLL, JEAN GAYTON, healthcare industry consultant; b. Chgo.; d. Loran Delancey and Margaret Gertrude (Hassett) Gayton; m. Walter W. Carroll (dec.); children: Michael Gayton Carroll, Christopher James Carroll. MA, U. Chgo., 1952, PhD, 1967. Dir. rsch. Joint Commn. Accreditation, Chgo., 1967-75; v.p. Delta Sys. Inc., Chgo., 1975-79; mgr. health care Laventhol & Horwath, Chgo., 1980-85; v.p. Neomedica, Inc., Chgo., 1985-87; co-dir. stds. devel. Joint Commn. Accreditation, Chgo., 1987-91, dir. internat. program, 1992-94; mem. policy adv. coun. on healthcare edn. stds. U.S. Dept. Edn., Washington, 1991-96; pres. Lawler Trust, Chgo., 1993-96. Author: Monitoring With Indicators, 1975, annual supplements, 1975—, Restructuring Hospital Quality Assurance, 1985, Monitoring and Measuring Ambulatory Care, 1996. Various positions, vol., chairperson, annual fund drive, others Am. Cancer Soc., Chgo., 1960—. Mem. Internat. Soc. Quality Assurance in Health Care, Hungarian Soc. Quality Assurance in Health Care (adv. coun. 1992-96). Roman Catholic.

CARROLL, JOSEPH CLELBURN, English educator; b. Clay, Ala., Sept. 5, 1949; s. Joseph Edward and Betty sue (Sanders) C.; m. Paula Eleanor Sweet, Dec. 1, 1977; children: Gwendolyn, Michael. BA, U. Calif., Berkeley, 1974, PhD, 1981. Prof. English U. Denver, 1981-85, U. Mo., St. Louis, 1985—. Author: The Cultural Theory of Matthew Arnold, 1982, Wallace Stevens' Supreme Fiction, 1987, Evolution and Literary Theory, 1995. Home: 9038 Old Bonhomme Rd Saint Louis MO 63132 Office: U Mo Saint Louis English Dept 8001 Natural Bridge Rd Saint Louis MO 63121

CARROLL, MARSHA GAIL, critical care emergency nurse; b. Springfield, Mo., Oct. 1, 1952; d. Harley Junior and Barbara Jean (Anderson) Cozad; m. Charles Wilburn Huffman Jr., Aug. 11, 1977 (div. June 1985); m. Richard Edward Carroll, Oct. 29, 1992; 1 stepchild, Alyssa Fawn. ADN, U. Ark., 1975; postgrad., Drury Coll., 1991-95. Cert. ACLS, BCLS, neonatal advanced life support instr., pediat. advanced life support instr., trauma nurse core course instr., prehosp. trauma life support provider and instr., basic trauma life support, emergency nurse provider course instr., advanced trauma nursing course instr.; CEN cert. emergency nursing. Staff nurse, relief charge nurse St. John's Regional Health Ctr., Springfield, Mo., 1976-77, 80-84; staff nurse, relief nurse St. Joseph's Hosp., St. Charles, Mo., 1977-80; staff nurse St. John's Regional Health Ctr., Hammons Life Line, 1984-89, chief flight nurse, 1989-96; staff nurse emergency trauma ctr. St. John's Regional Health Ctr., 1996—. Active Sexual Assault Forensic Exam (SAFE) for Kids Task Force for Greene County. Mem. Nat. Flight Nurses Assn., Nat. Flight Paramedics Assn., Emergency Nurses Assn. (treas. 1988-90, pres.-elect 1996, cert. emergency nurse, Outstanding Emergency Rm. Nurse 1990). Baptist. Office: St. John's Regional Health 1235 E Cherokee St Springfield MO 65804-2203

CARROLL, MELODY J., educator, writer; b. Keokuk, Iowa, Nov. 29, 1960; d. Stanley C. and Hope W. (Johnson) Small; m. Jerry D. Carroll, July 30, 1954; children: Lala Spring, Lanna Jane, Letty May. A, Iowa Wesleyan Coll. Preschool tchr. aide Jaycee Preschool, Ft. Madison, Iowa, 1986-87; assoc. Christian edn. First United Meth. Ch., Ft. Madison, 1990-91; freelance writer United Meth. Publ., Nashville, 1991—; abstract writer Am. Abstract, Ft. Madison, 1995—; cons. First United Meth. Ch., Ft. Madison, 1994-95. Author numerous poems. Recipient 2nd place KC essay contest, Kahoka, Mo., 1976, 77. Mem. Federated Women of Am., P.E.O. (local recording sec.), Christian Edn. Found., Soc. of Poets, Beta Sigma Phi (pres. 1989-90, Chapter Woman of the Year 1991). Home: 2223 Mokena Terrace Fort Madison IA 52627 Office: Freelance Wrtg & Prtg Etc 2223 Mokena Terrace Fort Madison IA 52627

CARROLL, RICHARD, novelist, researcher; b. Kenosha, Wis., Oct. 20, 1961; s. Conrad James and Mary Ann (Gorelik) C. AAS with high honors, Wilbur Wright Coll., Chgo., 1994. Rsch. asst. Consultancy in Action, Milw., 1991—. Home: 10015 28th Ave Kenosha WI 53143

CARROTT, GREGORY T., management consultant; b. Wauseon, Ohio, Apr. 12, 1950; s. John T. and Norma Lee (Boyle) C.; m. Kathleen Ann Biracree Veenker, Sept. 12, 1970 (div. 1978); children: James H., Elizabeth A.; m. Marina Goesswein, June 20, 1981. BA, Lawrence U., Appleton, Wis., 1972; MSJ, Northwestern U., Evanston, Ill., 1973; MBA, U. Chgo., 1981. With Continental Bank, Chgo., 1973-76; dir. Northwest Industries, Chgo., 1976-80; v.p. HDM, Chgo., 1980-85; dir. Borg-Warner Corp., Chgo., 1985-87; ptnr. Egon Zehnder Internat., Chgo., 1987—. Mem. Racquet Club of Chgo. Democrat. Episcopalian. Home: 1415 N Dearborn Pky Chicago IL 60610

CARRUTHERS, CLAUDELLE ANN, occupational and physical therapist; b. Chgo., Nov. 23; d. Veronica Josephine Walker. AA, Golden Valley Luth. Coll., Minn., 1981; BS in Occupational Therapy, U. Minn., 1984; M in Phys. Therapy, U. Iowa, 1991; PhD, U. Minn., 1995. Lic. occupational therapist, Iowa, phys. therapist, Iowa, Minn.; cert. occupational therapist, Minn. Dir., supr., occupational therapist Rehab. Specialists, Inc., Minnetonka, Minn., 1984-86; supr., occupational therapist St. Therese Home, Inc., Mpls., 1986-88; dir., supr., occupational therapist Allied Health Alternatives, Inc., Mpls., 1988-89; occupational therapist St. Luke's Hosp., Cedar Rapids, Iowa, 1989-91; occupational therapist, phys. therapist Fairview Riverside Med. Ctr., Mpls., 1991—; instr., rschr. U. Minn., 1992-95; prof. occupational and phys. therapy Coll. of St. Catherine, 1995—; research in field of virtual reality, neurology/kinesiology; mem. adv. bd. occupational therapy program Anoka Tech. Coll., 1992—; mentor for occupational and phys. therapy students Coll. of St. Catherine's, St. Paul, 1992; mentor for occupational and phys. therapy and women athlete's of color U. Minn. Author publs. in field. Human rights commr. City of Plymouth, 1994—; mem. allocation panel United Way Mpls., 1992; mem. Minn. Zoo, 1986—. Recipienmt Vol. Basketball award Courage Ctr., Golden Valley, Minn., 1987, 89. Mem. Am. Phys. Therapy Assn. (student rep. 1981-83), Iowa Occupational Therapy Assn., Minn. Occupational Therapy Assn., Am. Occupational Therapy Assn., Occupational Therapy Minn.-Dak Assn. (panel presentor 1992), Glende Ski Club (2d v.p. 1987), Martin Luther King Tennis Club, Alpha Kappa Alpha. Office: College of St Catherine Saint Paul MN 55105

CARRUTHERS, PHILIP CHARLES, lawyer, public official; b. London, Dec. 8, 1953; came to U.S., 1962, naturalized, 1971; s. J. Alex and Marie (Calarco) C. BA, U. Minn., 1975, JD, 1979. Bar: Minn. 1979, U.S. Dist. Ct. Minn., 1979, U.S. Ct. Appeals (8th cir.) 1979. Assoc., Nichols & Kruger, and predecessor firm, 1979-81; ptnr. Nichols, Kruger, Starks and Carruthers, Mpls., 1982-84; ptnr. Luther, Ballenthin & Carruthers, Mpls., 1985-93, pvt. practice, 1994—; pros. atty. City of Deephaven, Minn., 1979—, City of Woodland, Minn., 1980—; mem. Minn. Ho. Reps., 1987—. Co-author: The Drinking Driver in Minnesota: Criminal and Civil Issues, 1982. Note and comment editor Minn. Law Rev., 1978-79. Mem. Met. Council of Twin Cities Area, St. Paul, 1983-87; mem. Minn. Ho. of Reps., 1987—, Ho. majority leader, 1993—. Mem. Minn. Trial Lawyers Assn. (bd. govs. 1982-86), Minn. State Bar Assn., Hennepin County Bar Assn. Mem. Democratic Farmer-Labor Party. Roman Catholic. Home: 861-70th Ave N Brooklyn Center MN 55430 Office: 459 State Office Bldg Saint Paul MN 55155

CARSON, GAIL MARIA, fashion designer, marketing consultant; b. Detroit, Nov. 27, 1954; d. Samuel Salvador and Dorothy Marie (Mallard) Dasher; m. Calvin Jerome Carson, Feb. 15, 1975; 1 child, Meredith Jojuan. Student, U. Detroit, 1972-74, Siena Heights Coll., 1982-83; cert. in merchandising, Fashion Inst. Am., 1986. Hostess coffee shop J.C. Penney Co., Southfield, Mich., 1975-78; exec. dir. office ethnic minority higher edn. Wayne State U., Detroit, 1982-86; fashion show coord. Prodns. Plus, Inc., Birmingham, Mich., 1986-91; internat. mktg. cons. Internat. Mktg. Assn., Southfield, 1976—; designer knitwear Needle Classics, Detroit, 1986—, Rio Boutique, Detroit, 1993—. Mem. Winship Cmty. Coun., Detroit, 1976-80; fundraiser, campaigner Judge Bruce Morrow, Detroit, 1992; co-chairperson Mumford High Sch. Alumni, Detroit, 1992—; co-chairperson coun. Scott Meml. United Methodist Ch., Detroit, 1989-91. Recipient Outstanding Leadership award E.B.O.N. Assocs., 1980, Outstanding Achievement award Amway Corp., 1981, Outstanding Young Woman of Am. award, 1983. Mem. Knitter's Guild Am., Mumford H.S. Alumni Assn. and Endowment (co-chairperson 1992—, Outstanding Leadership award 1992), Mom and Dad Club Gesu Sch.

CARSON, JULIA M., state legislator; b. Louisville, July 8, 1938; 2 children. Ed. Ind. U., 1960-62, St. Mary of the Woods, 1976-78. Mem. In. Ho. of Reps., Indpls., 1972-76; mem. Ind. Senate, 1976—. Vice pres. Greater Indpls. Prog. Com.; nat. Democratic committeewoman; trustee YMCA; bd. dirs. Pub. Service Acad. Recipient Woman of Yr. Ind. award, 1974; Outstanding Leadership award AKA; Humanitarian award Christian Theol. Sem. Mem. NAACP, Urban League, Nat. Council Negro Women. Baptist. Office: State Senate State Capital Indianapolis IN 46205 Other: 2530 N Park Ave Indianapolis IN 46205-4261

CARSON, RICHARD MCKEE, chemical engineer; b. Dayton, Ohio, June 6, 1912; s. George E. and Gertrude (Barthelemy) C.; children: Joan Roderer, Linda McCartan. BS in Chem. Engring., U. Dayton (Ohio), 1934. Registered profl. engr., Ohio. Rsch. chemist Dayton Mall Iron Co., 1934-45; pres. Carson-Saeks, Inc., Dayton, 1945-80, Carson & Saeks Cons. Assocs. Inc., Dayton, 1980—; sec.-treas. Cecile Baird, Inc., Hillsboro, Ohio. Mem. AAAS, Am. Chem. Soc. Home: 2310 Kershner Rd Dayton OH 45414-1214

CARSWELL, ROGER L., library director; b. Ottawa, Kans., June 1, 1957; s. Richard Hugh and Mary Jo (Lewis) C.; m. Kristin K. Wolfersperger, Dec. 26, 1983; children: Dwight, Riley, Kyle. BA, McPherson Coll., 1979; MLS, Emporia State U., 1983. Sch. libr. Peabody (Kans.)-Burns Unified Sch. Dist., 1981-83, Wellington (Kans.) H.S., 1983-85; head adult svcs. Emporia (Kans.) Pub. Libr., 1985-91; dir. Pittsburg (Kans.) Pub. Libr., 1991-92, S.E. Kans. Libr. Sys., Iola, 1993—. Author: The Early Years of Osage County, 1982; pub. book: Kansas Periodical Index, 1984—. Bd. dirs. Iola Area United Funds, 1993—, sec., 1995. Mem. Kans. Libr. Assn. (mem. coun. 1986-90, 95—, chmn. state steering com. for humanities programs in librs. 1986-90, 2d v.p. 1995-96), Strategic Tech. Through Area Resources, Kiwanis Club of Iola (sec. 1994—). Office: SE Kansas Library System 218 E Madison Iola KS 66749

CARTER, ARLENE MAE, psychiatric nurse; b. Alliance, Nebr., Oct. 8, 1947; d. Louis and Alice Abigail (Davis) Zahradnicek; m. William Frank Carter, Oct. 11, 1983 (div. 1988); m. Charles Ray Cravens, Aug. 18, 1989. BS, Union Coll., 1970; MS, Loma Linda U., 1974. RN, Colo. Staff nurse ICU, CCU Porter Meml. Hosp., Denver, 1970; staff nurse St. Anthony's Hosp., O'Neill, Nebr., 1970-72; staff nurse ICU, CCU St. Bernadine's Hosp., San Bernardino, Calif., 1972-74; staff nurse West Holt Meml. Hosp., Atkinson, Nebr., 1973-75, N.T. Enloe Meml. Hosp., Chico, Calif., 1977-78; commd. capt. U.S. Army, 1978, advanced through grades to lt. col., 1986; staff nurse, clin. nurse specialist in psychiatry Fitzsimmons Army Med. Ctr., Aurora, Colo., 1978-82; psychiat. clin. nurse specialist U.S. Army MEDDAC, Ft. Campbell, Ky., 1982-87; clin. nurse mgr. residential treatment facility 2d Gen. Hosp., Landstuhl, Germany, 1987-90; clin. nurse specialist psychiatry U.S. Army MEDDAC, Ft. Polk, La., 1990-92; psychiat. case mgr. Gateway to Care, Ft. Polk, 1992-93; psychiat. case mgr. U.S. Army MEDDAC, Ft. Leavenworth, Kans., 1993-96, Ft. Hood, Tex., 1996—; instr. Morningside Coll., Sioux City, Iowa, 1975-76, asst. prof. nursing, 1976-77; mental health cons. Cherry County Hosp., Valentine, Nebr., 1974-75; presenter in field. Contbr. to profl. publs. Recipient Fed. Nursing Svc. award, 1995. Mem. Nat. League Nursing (cert. addictions nurse), Nurses Soc. on Addictions, Assn. of Mil. Surgeons of the U.S. Office: USA MEDDAC Cmty Mental Health Fort Hood TX 76544

CARTER, HAROLD LLOYD, secondary education educator; s. Gustavus and Vennie (Carroll) C. BS, Columbia U., 1960; MA, Ohio State U., 1976. Cert. tchr., Ohio. Legal stenographer, law dept. The Port of N.Y. Authority, N.Y.C., 1954-59; legal stenographer Calif. State Atty. Gens. Office, San Francisco, 1963; history tchr. Buckeye Youth Ctr. Sch., Columbus, Ohio, 1969—, chmn. history dept., 1972-76; history tchr. Circleville (Ohio) Youth Ctr. Sch., 1993-94, Scioto Juvenile Correctional Ctr. Sch., Delaware, Ohio, 1994—; tutor Columbus Pub. Sch., 1976. Author: The African Heritage in Human Biological and Cultural History: From Pre-Historic Times and Early Civilizations, 1995. Vol. ACLU, L.A., 1965; So. Episc. Diocese of Ohio del. Nat. Conf. on Race, Atlanta, 1981; trustee, mem. community rels. com., pers. com. Neighborhood House, Columbus, 1982-88 (Commemoration plaque 1988). Sgt. U.S. Army, 1950-53; ct. reporter Ft. Benjamin Harrison, Ind./Lenggries, Germany; judge advocate sect. V Corps Frankfort, Germany. Mem. NEA, Ohio Edn. Assn., Nat. Coun. Social Studies, World History Assn., Ohio Valley World History Assn., Ohio Acad. History, Ohio State U. Alumni Assn., Alpha Phi Alpha (asst. v.p. 1958-59). Democrat. Episcopalian. Home: 5454 Woodvale Ct Westerville OH 43081-4350

CARTER, JAMES H., state supreme court justice; b. Waverly, Iowa, Jan. 18, 1935; s. Harvey J. and Althea (Dominick) C.; m. Jeanne E. Carter, Mar. 1959; children: Carol, James. B.A., U. Iowa, 1956, J.D., 1960. Law clk. to judge U.S. Dist. Ct, 1960-62; assoc. Shuttleworth & Ingersoll, Cedar Rapids, Iowa, 1962-73; judge 6th Jud. Dist., 1973-76, Iowa Ct. Appeals, 1976-82; justice Iowa Supreme Ct., Des Moines, 1982—. Mem. Disciples of Christ Ch. Office: Iowa Supreme Ct PO Box 5488 Cedar Rapids IA 52406-5488

CARTER, JOHN DALE, organizational development executive; b. Tuskegee, Ala., Apr. 9, 1944; s. Arthur L. and Ann (Bargyh) C.; m. Veronica Louise Helen Hopper, Oct., 12, 1986; children: Annelise Grace, Hopper Carter; AB, Ind. U., 1965, MS, 1967; PhD (NDEA fellow), Case Western Res. U., 1974. Dir. student affairs Dental Sch., Case Western Res. U., Cleve., 1974-75, asst. prof. applied behavioral sci., 1974-90, asst. dean orgn. devel. and student affairs, 1975-78; pres. John D. Carter and Assocs., Inc., Cleve., 1969—; ptnr. Portsmouth Cons. Group, 1984—; chmn. bd. Gestalt Inst. Cleve., 1974-80, chmn. orgn. and systems devel. program, 1980—, program dir., fin. dir. 1981-86, dir. corp. svcs., 1989-95, dean of faculty, 1992-96; mem. exec. bd. Nat. Tng. Labs., 1975-78; faculty Am. U., 1980-90, 94—; mem. Nat. Tng. Labs., 1976—; bd. dirs. Behavioral Sci. Found., Cleve.; exec. bd. Fielding Inst., 1987-89; preceptor Shri Ram Chandra Yoga & Meditation Mission, Sahag Marg, 1993—. Mem. Internat. Assn. Applied Social Scientists, (cert. cons. Internat.), Kappa Alpha Psi (pres. Alpha chpt. 1964-65), Alpha Phi Omega. Author: Counselling the Helping Relationship, 1975, Managing the Merger Integration Process, 1986. Home and Office: 2232 Harcourt Dr Cleveland OH 44106-4622

CARTER, KEVIN ANTHONY, securities company executive; b. Cleve., May 23, 1960. BA, Vanderbilt U., 1982; MBA, Weatherhead Sch. Mgmt., Cleve., 1987. Lic. investment cons. Sr. cons. Ernst & Young, Cleve. and Chgo., 1986-89; sr. analyst LTV Corp., Cleve., 1989-93; v.p., dir. diversity and bus. devel. McDonald & Co. Securities Co., Cleve., 1993—; columnist Kaleidoscope mag., also chmn. adv. bd.; columnist Call and Post newspaper. Chmn. telethon United Negro Coll. Fund; mem. Cleve. Mayor's Neighborhood Lending and Investment Oversight Com., Cleve Mayor's Cmty. Rels. Bd.; chmn. African Am. Bus. Consortium, 1991—; mem. Leadership Class of Greater Cleve. Growth Assn., 1993-94. Recipient H. Naylor Fitzhugh award of excellence, 1993; named One of Top 10 To Watch, Greater Cleve. Success Guide, 1991. Mem. Black Profls. Assn. (past bd. dirs.), Nat. Black MBA Assn. (past bd. dirs.), NAACP (past bd. dirs. Cleve. br.), University Sch. Alumni Assn. (past bd. dirs.), Weatherhead U. Alumni Assn. (past bd. dirs.). Office: McDonald & Co Investment McDonald Investment Ctr 800 Superior Ave Cleveland OH 44114

CARTER, MARILYN PETERSON, securities trader/dealer; b. Columbus, Ohio, Dec. 22, 1963; d. Earle C. Jr. and Marilyn (Miller) Peterson; m. David K. Carter, June 16, 1990. BA, Capital U., Columbus, 1986. Registered sales assoc. Everen Securities, Inc. (formerly Kemper Securities), Dublin, Ohio, 1986—. Active charity work. Home: 1620 E Broad St Apt 707 Columbus OH 43203-2023 Office: Kemper Securities Inc 485 Metro Pl S Ste 150 Dublin OH 43017-5300

CARTER, MARY NASH (MARY CARTER EDGINGTON), advertising executive; b. Cleve., June 23, 1947; d. Arthur Haseltine and Mary-Jessie (Nash) Carter; m. Larry Edgington, Sept. 21, 1984 (div. Aug. 1994). AS, Endicott Coll., Beverly, Mass., 1968. Asst. buyer Mercantile Stores Co., Inc., N.Y.C., 1968-70, buyer, 1970-72; account exec. J J Lane Advt., N.Y.C., 1972-75; v.p., account mgr. Michel-Cather, Advt., N.Y.C., 1975-79; owner Carter Comm., Green Lake, Wis., 1980-84; mgr. advt. and pub. rels. Oshkosh (Wis.) B'Gosh Inc., 1984-88, dir. advt. and pub. rels., 1988-92; dir. client svc. Retail Target Mktg. Sys., Waukesha, Wisc., 1994-95; guest lectr. U. Wis., Oshkosh, 1990-91. Bd. dirs. Evergreen Retirement Cmty., Oshkosh, 1988-94, exec. com., 1989-94; bd. stewards Federated Ch. of Green Lake, 1988-91; vol. Am. Cancer Soc. Mem. Oshkosh Rotary (bd. dirs. 1992-94, pres. elect), Brookfield Sunrise Rotary (pres. elect 1995-96, pres. 1996—), C. of C. (mktg. com. 1990, 95-96). Episcopalian.

CARTER, PAMELA LEE, school system administrator; b. Indpls., Sept. 29, 1949; d. Bernard Marsh and Virginia Lee (Rigsby) Fisher; m. Michael Carter, Aug. 19, 1975. BS in Elem. Edn., Ball State U., 1971, MA, 1973; postgrad., various univs. Cert. tchr., Mich. Kindergarten tchr. Lynn (Ind.) Elem. Sch., 1971-74, Padgett Elem. Sch., Lakeland, Fla., 1974; substitute tchr. Farmington (Mich.) and Clarenceville (Mich.) Pub. Schs., 1975-76; kindergarten tchr. Waverly Community Schs., Lansing, Mich., 1976-86, K-12 curriculum coord., 1985—; nat. lecture staff Gesell Inst. Human Devel., New Haven, Conn., 1986—; resource counselor Willoway Summer Day Camp, Wixom, Mich., 1976; assoc. dir. Meadowbrook Woods Learning Ctr., Novi, Mich., 1975; child devel. cons. Northland Pioneer Coll., Holbrook, Ariz., 1975. Contbr. articles to profl. jours. Named Outstanding Early Childhood Specialist Cen. Mich. Assn. for Edn. Young Children, 1985, Outstanding Young Educator Waverly Jaycees, 1980. Mem. ASCD, Nat. Staff Devel. Coun., Nat. Assn. Edn. Young Children, Assn. for Childhood Edn. Internat., Sierra Club. Office: Waverly Community Schs 620 Snow Rd Lansing MI 48917-4503

CARTER, PAMELA LYNN, state attorney general; b. South Haven, Mich., Aug. 20, 1949; d. Roscoe Hollis and Dorothy Elizabeth (Hadley) Fanning; m. Michael Anthony Carter, Aug. 26, 1971; children: Michael Anthony Jr., Marcya Alicia. BA cum laude, U. Detroit, 1971; MSW, U. Mich., 1973; JD, Ind. U., 1984. Bar: Ind. 1984, U.S. Dist. Ct. (no. dist.) Ind. 1984, U.S. Dist. Ct. (so. dist.) Ind. 1984. Rsch. analyst, treatment dir. U. Mich. Sch. Pub. Health and UAW, Detroit, 1973-75; exec. dir. Mental Health Ctr. for Women and Children, Detroit, 1975-77; consumer litigation atty. UAW-Gen. Motors Legal Svcs., Indpls., 1983-87; securities atty. Sec. of State, Indpls., 1987-89; Gov.'s exec. asst. for health and human svcs. Gov.'s Office, Indpls., 1989-91, dep. chief of staff to Gov., 1991-92; with firm Baker & Daniels, 1992-93; atty. gen. State of Ind., Indpls., 1993—. Author poems. mem. Cath. Social Svcs., Indpls., Jr. League, Indpls., Dem. Precinct, Indpls. Recipient Outstanding Svc. award Indiana Perinatal Assn., 1991, Community Svc. Coun. Ctrl. Ind., 1991, non-profl. healthcare award Family Health Conf. Bd. Dirs., 1991, award for excellence Women of the Rainbow, 1991; named Outstanding Young Woman of America, 1977, Breakthrough Woman of the Year, 1989. Mem. Nat. Bar Assn., Ind. Bar Assn., Coalition of 100 Black Women. Democrat. Office: 402 W Washington St Rm C553 Indianapolis IN 46204-2739*

CARTER, PAULA J., state legislator. Mo. State rep. Dist. 61. Home: 5936 Summit Pl Saint Louis MO 63147-1119 Office: Mo Ho of Reps State Capitol Building Jefferson City MO 65101-1556*

CARTER, RICHARD GLEN, engineering development manager; b. Sharpsville, Ind., Mar. 29, 1936. B, Purdue U., 1958, postgrad. Mgr. engring. devel. Delco Elecs., Kokomo, Ind., 1958—. Patentee in field.

CARTER, ROBERT LEE, automotive company program manager; b. Chgo., Oct. 13, 1954; s. Naggie Lee and Katie Mae (Minter) C.; m. Min Ok Kim, Jan. 18, 1982; children: Kimberly, Jonathan. BS in Engring, U.S. Military Acad., 1978; MS in Adminstrn., Cen. Mich. U., 1989. Commd. 2d lt. U.S. Army, 1978, advanced through grades to capt., 1982; ret., 1983; product engr. Gen. Dynamics Land Systems, Warren, Mich., 1983-84; sr. engr. Gen. Dynamics Land Systems, Sterling Heights, Mich., 1984-87, engring. supr., 1987-90; program analyst Ford Motor Co., Dearborn, Mich., 1990-96; program mgr. Chivas Products, Ltd., Sterling Heights, Mich., 1996—; bd. dirs. Holovision Sys., Inc., Findlay, Ohio. Capt. U.S. Army, 1978-83. Mem. Inst. Cert. Profl. Mgrs. (cert. mgr.), Masons, Phi Beta Gamma, Photographic Gild Detroit. Presbyterian. Home: 23735 Edinburgh Pl Southfield MI 48034-4889 Office: Ford Motor Co 21500 Oakwood Blvd Dearborn MI 48124-4080

CARTER, SALLY PACKLETT, elementary education educator; b. Clovis, N.Mex., May 15, 1948; d. Charles Everett and Marion Jamie (Pippin) Gee; m. Leonard Gene Carter, Mar. 7, 1969; 1 child, Dale Lee. BS in Edn., Ctrl. Mo. State U., 1969, MS in Edn., 1981. Cert. vocat. home econs. grades 7-12, elem. edn. grades K-6, Mo., K-8 elem. edn., home econs. grades 7-12, Ariz. Home econ. tchr. Deepwater (Mo.) High Sch., 1969-71; tchr. grade 7 Deepwater (Mo.) Sch., 1971-73; tchr. grades 1 and 2 Davis R-12, Clinton, Mo., 1974-80; tchr. grade 5 Southeast Elem., Clinton, 1980—. Mem. Nat. Coun. Tchrs. Math., Mo. State Tchrs. (pres. ctrl. dist. 1989-90), Clinton Tchrs. Assn. (pres. 1985, 90, 92), Clinton C. of C., VFW Ladies Aux. Post 1894, Delta Kappa Gamma (1st v.p. Mu. chpt. 1992-94, pres. Mu. chpt. 1994—), Phi Kappa Phi. Home: 248 NE 251st Rd Clinton MO 64735-9329

CARTIER, CHARLES ERNEST, alcohol and drug abuse services professional; b. Chgo., Aug. 4, 1931; s. Charles E. and Kathryn (Hanlon) C.; m. JoAnne Murphy, July 12, 1958; children: Kevin, Julia, Theresa, Carol. BS in Commerce, DePaul U., 1953. Nat. cert. alcohol, drug and addictions counselor. Program asst. Alcoholism Svcs. of Cleve. (Ohio), Inc., 1983-84; community liaison coord. Merrick Hall Adolescent Chem. Dependency Program, Cleve., 1984-86; instr. D.W.I. Counter Attack Project Cleve. (Ohio) State Univ., 1984-92; clin. supr. Fresh Start, Inc., Cleve., 1986-91; rehab. therapist alcohol treatment program VA Med. Ctr., Brecksville, Ohio, 1991—; lectr. Cuya Hoga Community Coll., Sch. of Mental Health Tech., Cleve., 1987—; bd. mem., v.p. Exodus, Inc. Treatment Program, 1986-90. Sgt. U.S. Army, 1953-55. Mem. Nat. Assn. Alcoholism and Drug Abuse Counselors, Ohio Assn. Alcoholism and Drug Abuse Counselors (sec. 1986-91, Hinkle Meml. award for Outstanding Work in the Field of Alcoholism Counseling 1990). Roman Catholic. Home: 9049 Roosevelt Dr Northfield OH 44067-1222 Office: VA Med Ctr 10000 Brecksville Rd Cleveland OH 44141-3204

CARTWRIGHT, CAROL ANN, university president; b. Sioux City, Iowa, June 19, 1941; d. Carl Anton and Kathryn Marie (Weishapple) Becker; m. G. Phillip Cartwright, June 11, 1966; children: Catherine E., Stephen R., Susan D. BS in Early Childhood Edn., U. Wis., Whitewater, 1962; MEd in Spl. Edn., U. Pitts., 1965, PhD in Spl. Edn., Ednl. Rsch., 1968. From instr. to assoc. prof. Coll. Edn. Pa. State U., University Park, 1968-72, from assoc. prof. to prof., 1972-79, dean acad. affairs, 1981-84, dean undergrad. program, vice provost, 1984-88; vice chancellor acad. affairs U. Calif., Davis, 1988-91, prof. human devel., 1988-91; pres. Kent (Ohio) State U., 1991—; founder, co-chair Alliance for Undergrad. Edn., 1986-88; trustee Akron Reg. Devel. Bd., 1991—, Akron Gen. Med. Ctr., 1991—; bd. dirs. Soc. Nat. Bank, Cleve., 1991—, Ohio Edison Co., Akron, 1992—, Republic Engineered Steels, Inc., Massillon, Ohio, 1992—, M.A. Hanna Co., Cleve., 1994—. Editorial bd. Topics in Early Childhood Special Education, 1982-88, Exceptional Education Quarterly, 1982-88. Pres., bd. dirs. Child Devel. Coun. of Center County, Title XX Day Care Contractor, 1977-80; bd. dirs. Center County United Way, State College, Pa., 1984-88; bd. mem. Davis (Calif.) Art Ctr., 1988-91, Davis Sci. Ctr., 1989-91; bd. dirs. Ohio divsn. Am. Cancer Soc., 1993—, nat. bd. dirs., 1993—. Mem. AAUW, Am. Coun. Edn., Am. Ednl. Rsch. Assn., Am. Assn. for Higher Edn., Nat. Assn. State Univs. and Land-Grant Colls., Coun. for Exceptional Children. Roman Catholic. Home: 1703 Woodway Rd Kent OH 44240-5917 Office: Kent State U Office of the President PO Box 5190 Kent OH 44242-0001

CARTWRIGHT, KEROS, hydrogeologist, researcher; b. L.A., July 25, 1934; s. Eugene Ewing and Charlotte Lucy (Searle) C.; m. Sharon Miller, July 5, 1955 (dec.); children: Sylvia, Jennifer; m. Jennifer Elizabeth Moberley, Mar. 9, 1962 (div. Sept. 1988); children: David, Bridget; m. Madalene Rose Tierney, Feb. 16, 1990. AB in Geology, U. Calif., 1959; MS in Geology, U. Nev., 1961; PhD in Geology, U. Ill., 1973. Cert. profl. geologist, profl. hydrologist. Hydrogeologist Humboldt River Rsch. Project, Winnemucca, Nev., 1959-61; hydrogeologist Ill. State Geol. Survey, Champaign, 1961—, head hydrogeology and geophysics section, 1975-84, prin. scientist and head gen. and environ. geology group, 1984-88, prin. rsch. scientist, 1988—; adj. prof. geology No. Ill. U., DeKalb, 1979—, U. Ill., Urbana, 1985—; cons. pvt. practice in hydrogeology, N.Am. and Europe, 1968—, U.S. Environ. Protection Agy. Sci. Adv. Bd., Washington, 1983—, Savannah River Site Environ. Adv., Aiken, S.C., 1988—. Mem. editorial bd. Elsevier Sci. Publ. Jour. of Hydrology, 1982-85; contbr. articles to profl. jours. Named Disting. Lectr. Assn. Groundwater-Water Scientists and Engrs., 1987; recipient Cert. Appreciation U.S. Environ. Protection Agy., 1988. Fellow Geol. Soc. Am. (officer hydrogeology sect. 1975-78, chmn. 1978-79, editorial bd. Jour. Water Resources Rsch. 1975-81, Bull. 1981-83, Birdsall disting. lectr. 1987-88, governing coun. 1993—, chmn. publs. com., George B. Maxey Disting. Svc. award 1991), Explorers Club; mem. ASTM (vice chmn. subcom. D-14 1984-88), Am. Inst. Hydrology (editorial bd. Jour. Hydrological Sci. and Tech. 1985—), Am. Geophys. Union (assoc. editor 1975-81), Am. Water Resources Assn., Internat. Assn. Hydrogeologists (U.S. com. 1985-89). Office: Ill Geol Survey 615 E Peabody Dr Champaign IL 61820-6918

CARTY, JOHN WESLEY, lawyer; b. Lansing, N.C., Oct. 29, 1923; s. John Arthur and Bertha (Eller) C.; m. Doris Frances Barnes, June 27, 1948; children: Dixie Lynne, John Jeffrey. BA, Buena Vista Coll., 1950; JD, Drake U., 1952. Bar: Iowa 1952, U.S. Dist. Ct. (so. dist.) Iowa 1952, U.S. Ct. Appeals (8th cir.) 1965. Assoc. Pryor, Hale, Plock, Riley & Jones, Burlington, Iowa, 1952-54; ptnr. Carty & Jones, Des Moines, 1960-75; pvt. practice Winfield, Iowa, 1955—; Bd. dirs. Farmers Nat. Bank, Winfield, Iowa, pres., chmn. 1985—; pres. Oxidex, Inc., Winfield, 1971—; broker, dir. Winfield Realty Co., 1956—; pres., chmn. Winfield Health Care & Retirement Ctr., 1972-77; dir., sec., treas. Satellite Mill, Inc., 1961-63. Co-author: Business Law & The Cooperative, 1962; assoc. editor Drake U. Law Rev., 1951-52. City atty. City of Winfield, Iowa, 1954-89, City of Wayland, Iowa, 1962-70; mem. Henry County Conservation Bd., Mt. Pleasant, Iowa, 1972-74; chmn. Henry County Compensation Commn., 1987-92; sec. S.E. Iowa Planning Coun., 1973-74; dir. S.E. Iowa Health Care Coun., Ft. Madison, 1974-76; mem. Iowa Archaeol. Soc., 1991—; mem. commn. eminent domain Henry County, 1993—. With combat infantry U.S. Army, 1944-46, ETO. Decorated Combat Infantryman's badge, Bronze star; recipient Spl. award Bur. Nat. Affairs, 1952, Annual award Greene County Conservation Bd., 1987. Mem. Henry County Bar Assn. (pres. 1961-62), S.E. Iowa Bar Assn. (pres. 1962), Iowa State Bar Assn., Iowa Archeol. Soc., Hawkeye Archeol. Soc., Am. Legion, VFW, Masons, Phi Alpha Delta. Baptist. Home: 1586 Oasis Ave Mount Union IA 52644-9506 Office: Carty Law Office Farmers Nat Bank Bldg Winfield IA 52659

CARTY, RAYMOND WESLEY, academic administrator; b. Carlinville, Ill., Jan. 26, 1956; m. Elaine Smith, Apr. 21, 1979; children: Brooke Angelyn, Devan Alicia. AA, Hannibal-LaGrange (Mo.) Coll., 1977; BS, S.W. Bapt. U., 1979; MA, Liberty U., 1990. Registered social worker, Ill. Youth therapist Macoupin County Mental Health Ctr., Ill., 1979-84; minister music and youth Charity Bapt. Ch., Carlinville, 1979-84; assoc. dir. admissions Hannibal-LaGrange Coll., 1984—, assoc. dean of admissions, 1987-95; dean of enrollment mgmt., 1995—. Named one of Outstanding Young Men of Am., 1988. Mem. Mo. Assn. Coll. Admissions Counselors, Ill. Assn. Coll. Admission Counselors. Baptist. Home: 15 Fairway Dr Hannibal MO 63401-3615 Office: Hannibal-LaGrange Coll 2300 Palmyra Rd Hannibal MO 63401-1919

CARY, ARLENE D., retired hotel company sales executive; b. Chgo., Dec. 19, 1930; d. Seymour S. and Shirley L. (Land) C.; student U. Wis., 1949-52; BA, U. Miami, 1953; m. Elliot D. Hagle, Dec. 30, 1972 (div.). Public relations account exec. Robert Howe & Co., 1953-55; sales mgr. Martin B. Iger & Co., 1955-57; sales mgr., gen. mgr. Sorrento Hotel, Miami Beach, Fla., 1957-59; gen. mgr. Mayflower Hotel, Manomet, Mass., 1959-60; various positions Aristocrat Inns of Am., 1960-72; v.p. mktg., McCormick Center Hotel, Chgo., 1972-93; ret. 1993. Active Nat. Women's Polit. Caucus, Internat. Orgn. Women Execs., membership promotion chmn., 1979-80, bd. dirs., 1980-81. Recipient disting. salesman award Sales and Mktg. Execs. Internat., 1977. Mem. Profl. Conv. Mgmt. Assn., Internat. Assn. Exposition Magmt., Hospitality Sales and Mktg. Assn. Internat., Meeting Planners Internat., Am. Soc. Assn. Execs., N.Y. Soc. Assn. Execs., Chgo. Soc. Assn. Execs., Ind. Hotel Alliance (sec. 1986—). Jewish. Home: 6007 N Sheridan Apt 18H Chicago IL 60660

CASADONTE, MICHAEL JOHN, computer technician; b. Flint, Mich., June 8, 1953; s. John and Pauline E. (Powell) C.; m. Charlotte I. Loveland, Jan. 1, 1985; children: Crystal N., CloAnn. AS in Robotics, Charles Stewart Mott Sch., Flint, Mich., 1984; AS in Fluid Power, Charles Stewart Mott Sch., 1984, AS in Electronics, 1985. Computer technician GM-CLCD, Flint, Mich., 1990—; consulting Specialize Ins. Svcs. Grand Blanc, Mich., 1985—, Quantum USA, Clio, Mich., 1989—. Home: 3336 W Wilson Clio MI 48420 Office: GM-CLCD 4100 S Saginaw St Flint MI 48557-2121

CASASANTA, JOSEPH JOHN, III, association director; b. South Bend, Ind., Aug. 30, 1963; s. Joseph John Jr. and Naomi Elizabeth (Rafferty) CasaS.; m. Janelle Lynn Garrett, July 22, 1988; 1 child, Claire Elizabeth. BSEd, Ind. State U., 1987. Phys. dir. YMCA of Greater Indpls., 1988-90; youth and family dir. YMCA of Greater St. Louis, 1990-95; CEO Tri-county YMCA of the Ozarks, Osage Beach, Mo., 1995—; dir. YMCA Cen. Leaders Sch., Jacksonville, Ill., 1993—. Chmn. jail and bail com., Am. Cancer Soc., Osage Beach, 1995. Mem. Rotary, KC, Assn. Profl. Dirs. Roman Catholic. Office: Tri-County YMCA of Ozarks PO Box 541 Osage Beach MO 65065-0541

CASCINO, ANTHONY ELMO, JR., lawyer, insurance executive; b. South Bend, Ind., Aug. 21, 1948; s. Anthony E. and Lorayne (Allegretti) C.; m. Mary Anne Dory, July 28, 1973; children: Anthony Elmo, III, Christine Anne, Caroline Stephanie. B.A., Loyola U., Chgo., 1970; J.D., Ill. Inst. Tech., 1974; MMgt. Northwestern U., 1987. Bar: Ill. 1974, U.S. Dist. Ct. (no. dist.) Ill. 1974, U.S. Supreme Ct. 1986. Div. counsel CF Industries Inc., Long Grove, Ill., 1974-79; sec., gen. counsel Energy Coop., Inc., Rosemont, Ill., 1979-83; v.p., gen. counsel GHR Energy Corp., Good Hope, La., 1983; dep. gen. counsel AM Internat., Inc., Chgo., 1983-86; v.p. bus. devel. Multigraphics div. AM Internat., Mt. Prospect, Ill., 1986-88; exec. v.p., sec., gen. counsel, bd. dirs. United Fin. Group Inc. of Ill., Oak Brook, 1988—; bd. dirs. Oak Brook Property and Casualty Ins. Co., First Oak Brook Corp. Syndicate, United Comml. Affiliated, Inc., Combined Adjustment Co., Inc., Ctrl. States Ins. Cons., Inc.; mem. inquiry bd. Atty. Registration and Disciplinary Commn., 1992; alt. trustee Ill. Ins. Exchange; lectr. Ill. Inst. Continuing Edn., 1986; mem. adv. com. on postgrad. programs, Ill. Inst. Tech., 1987-88. Contbg. author: Commercial Damage, 1984. Mem. ABA, Fed. Energy Bar Assn., Ill. State Bar Assn., Chgo. Bar Assn., DuPage County Bar Assn., Art Inst. Chgo., Lyric Opera of Chgo. (Glencoe chpt.), Bar and Gavel Soc., DuPage Club, Union League Club (Chgo.), Club Internat. (Chgo.). Democrat. Roman Catholic. Home: 385 Lincoln Ave Glencoe IL 60022-1521

CASCINO, DONNA KAY, religious organization administrator; b. Evanston, Ill., Nov. 2, 1949; d. James R. Meinhardt and Dorothea A. (Brey) Lexau; m. Joseph Peter Cascino, Jr., May 25, 1974; children: Kirsten, Elizabeth. BS, St. Cloud (Minn.) State U., 1971; M Pastoral Studies, Loyola U., Chgo., 1983; D Ministry, Grad. Theol. Found., Donaldson, Ind., 1997. Youth/family min. Chaplain's Office Dept. Army, Ft. Sheridan, Ill., 1982-85; dir. religious edn. St. Mary Ch., Buffalo Grove, Ill., 1986-89; campus min. Resurrection H.S., Chgo., 1990-93; dir. Young Christian Formation St. Isaac Jogues Ch., Hinsdale, Ill., 1993-96; religious edn. dir. St. Thomas of Villanova, Palatine, Ill., 1996—; religious edn. dir. Archdiocese Chgo.; family min. Ctr. for Youth Ministry Devel.; alumni bd. mem. Inst. Pastoral Studies, Loyola U., Chgo., 1993-94; deanery I youth ministry coord. Archdiocese of Chgo., 1988-92. Mem. Profl. Assn. Christian Educators, Loyola U. Alumni Assn., Sigma Sigma Sigma (treas. Gamma Nuchpt. 1969-70). Roman Catholic.

CASE, DOUGLAS MANNING, lawyer; b. Cleve., Jan. 3, 1947; s. Manning Eugene and Ernestine (Bryan) C.; m. Marilyn Cooper, Aug. 23, 1969. BA, U. Pa., 1969; JD, MBA, Columbia U., 1973. Bar: N.Y. 1974, N.J. 1975, Calif. 1980, Ohio 1991. Assoc. Brown & Wood, N.Y.C., 1973-77; corp. counsel PepsiCo Inc., Purchase, N.Y. and Irvine, Calif., 1977-83, Nabisco Brands Inc., N.Y.C., East Hanover, N.J. and London, 1983-89; asst. gen. counsel Chiquita Brands Internat., Inc., Cin., 1989-92; pvt. practice Cin., 1993—. Chmn. Olde Colonial Dist.; active Morris-Susssex Area Coun. Boy Scouts Am., 1986-88; sec., trustee Marble Scholarship Com., N.Y.C., 1983-88; bd. dirs. Cin. Opera Guild, 1994—. Mem. ABA, Internat. Bar Assn., Ohio State Bar Assn. (mem. internat. com. 1993—), Cin. Bar Assn. (chair solo and small firm practitioners com. 1995—, continuing legal edn. chair internat. com. 1994—), Quality in Law (chmn.), Munich Sister City Assn. of Grater Cin. (chmn. econ. devel. com. 1995-96), The Lawyers Club of Cin. (exec. com. 1995—, treas. 1996), Morris County Golf Club, Columbia Bus. Sch. Club (N.Y.C., pres., bd. dirs. 1974-79), Kenwood Country Club. Office: 8700 Old Indian Hill Rd Cincinnati OH 45243-3724

CASE, HANK, retired art educator, photographer, wine importer; b. Danville, Ky., Jan. 12, 1938; s. Will Franklin and Margaret (Whitaker) C.; divorced; 1 child, J. Erin. BS, Ball State U., 1964, MA, 1966. Cert. master tchr., Ind. State Tchrs. Assn. Supr. of fine arts Anderson (Ind.) Cmty. Schs., 1964-96; instr. photography Anderson U., 1969-89; free-lance photographer Anderson, 1956—, cons. wine, 1981—; owner Hank Case Wine Imports, 1989—. Bd. dirs. Alliance of Indpls. Mus. of Art, 1992—. Mem. Art Educators Assn. Ind. (life), Confrerie des Chevaliers du Tastevin (chevalier, redacteur 1984—), Confrerie de la Chaine des Rotisseurs (chevalier 1995—), Commanderie du Bontemps de Medoc et des Graves (comdr. 1982—), L'Ordre Mondial des Gourmets Degustateurs, Internat. Wine and Food Soc., Indpls. Wine Soc. (pres. 1981-83), Alpha Phi Gamma, Theta Chi. Home: 823 W 7th St Anderson IN 46016-1056 Office: 823 W 7th St Anderson IN 46016-1056

CASE, RUSSELL P., company executive; b. Sept. 24, 1923. V.p. United Svc. Co., Columbus, Ohio, 1975—. Office: United Svc Co 1345 W Mound St Columbus OH 43223-2205

CASEY, MARTHA LINK, chemist; b. Gaffney, S.C., June 15, 1942; d. Eugene P. and Beulah (Meyer) L.; m. Charles P. Casey, July 20, 1968; 1 child, Jennifer. AB, Bryn Mawr Coll., 1964; PhD, MIT, 1968. Asst. dir. budget planning and analysis U. Wis., Madison, 1978-95, asst. vice chancellor, 1996—; rsch. assoc. U. Wis., Madison, 1974-78, program coord., 1968-74. Bd. dirs. Wis. Alumni Assn., Madison, 1995-97, Madison Opera Guild, 1990—. Mem. Rotary, University Club (pres. 1993-95), Am. Chem. Soc. (nat. councilor 1990—, chmn. Wis. sect. 1980), Assn. Instnl. Rsch. (nat. nominating com. 1995). Office: Univ Wis Office Budget Planning/Anal 500 Lincoln Dr Madison WI 53706

CASEY, MURRAY JOSEPH, physician, educator; b. Armour, S.D., May 1, 1936; s. Meryl Joseph and Gladice (Murray) C.; m. Virginia Anne Fletcher; children: Murray Joseph Jr., Theresa Marie, Anne Franklin, Francis Xavier, Peter Colum, Matthew Padraic. Student, Chanute Jr. Coll., 1954-55, Rockhurst Coll., 1955-56; AB, U. Kans., 1958; MD, Georgetown U., 1962; postgrad., Suffolk U. Law Sch., 1963-64, Howard U., 1965, U. Conn., 1977; MS in Mgmt., Cardinal Stritch Coll., 1984; MBA, Marquette U., 1988. Diplomate Nat. Bd. Med. Examiners, Am. Bd. Ob-Gyn. Intern USPHS Hosp.-Univ. Hosp., Balt., 1962-63; staff physician USPHS Hosp., Boston, 1963-64; rsch. staff Lab Infectious Diseases, Nat. Inst. Allergy and Infectious Diseases, NIH, Bethesda, Md., 1964-66; virologist, resident physician Columbia-Presbyn. Med. Ctr. also Francis Delafield Hosp., N.Y.C., 1966-69, USPHS sr. clin. trainee, 1969-70; fellow gynecol. oncology, resident dept. surgery Meml. Hosp. Cancer and Allied Diseases, Meml. Sloan-Kettering Cancer Ctr., N.Y.C., 1969-71; Am. Cancer Soc. fellow, 1969-71; ofcl. observer in radiotherapy U. Tex. M.D. Anderson Hosp. and Tumor Inst., Houston, 1971; vis. scientist Radiumhemmet Karolinska Sjukhuset and Inst., Stockholm, 1971; asst. prof. ob-gyn U. Conn. Sch. Medicine, 1971-75, asso. prof., 1975-80, dir. gynecologic oncology, 1971-80, also mem. med. bd.; prof., assoc. chmn. dept. ob-gyn U. Wis. Med. Sch., 1980-89; prof., chmn. dept. ob-gyn. Creighton U., Omaha, 1989-94; chief ob-gyn. and dir. gynecologic oncology St. Joseph Hosp., Creighton U. Med. Ctr., Omaha, 1989-94; chief ob-gyn Mt. Sinai Med. Ctr., Milw., 1980-82, dir. gynecologic oncology, 1980-89, also mem. med. exec. com.; chmn. research adv. com., mem. council Conn. Cancer Epidemiology Unit. Editor, contbr. articles in sports medicine to profl. jours., chpts. to books; rsch. in oncogenesis and tumor immunology. Bd. dirs., mem. exec. com., chmn. profl. edn. com. Hartford unit Am. Cancer Soc., dir. Milw. divsn., exec. com. 1985-87, v.p., 1985-86, pres.-elect, 1986-87, 1st v.p. exec. com. Wis. divsn. 1987-89, bd. dirs., chmn. profl. edn. com., 1987-89, bd. dirs., 1989—, exec. com. Nebr. divsn., 1989-93, pub. edn. and communications com., profl. edn. com. vice chair, 2nd v.p., 1990-91, 1st v.p., pres.-elect, 1991-92, pres., 1992-93, bd. dirs. Douglas County unit, 1993—; mem. med. svcs. 1980 Winter Olympic Games, Lake Placid, N.Y.; mem. med. supervisory team U.S. Nordic Ski Team. Lt. (j.g.) USPHS, 1962-64, lt. comdr., 1964-66; col.

USAR, 1988-93. Fellow ACS, Am. Coll. Ob-Gyn; mem. AAAS, Soc. of Gynecol. Surgeons, Cen. Assn. Ob-Gyns., Am. Coll. Sports Medicine, N.Y. Acad. Scis., Am. Soc. Colposcopy, Am. Assn. Gynecologic Laparoscopists, Am. Fertility Soc., Soc. Gynecol. Oncologists, European Soc. Gynecol. Oncologists, New Eng. Assn. Gynecol. Oncologists (pres. 1980-81), Internat. Gynecol. Cancer Soc., Am. Radium Soc., Am. Soc. Clin. Oncology, Internat. Menopause Soc., N.Am. Menopause Soc., Internat. Assn. foir Advancement of Humanistic Studies in Medicine, Soc. Meml. Gynecol. Oncologists (exec. bd. 1979-84; pres. 1982-83), Lake Placid Sports Medicine Soc. (v.p. 1981-84, pres. 1984-86), Am. Urogynecol. Soc., Assn. Mil. Surgeon, Soc. of Gynecol. Surgeons, Cedarburg C. of C. (Ambassadors com. 1983—, dir. 1983-85, chmn. bus. indsl. program com. 1985, 87-88), St. George Soc. Office: Creighton U Sch Medicine Dept Ob-Gyn 601 N 30th St # 4810 Omaha NE 68131-2137

CASH, ALAN SHERWIN, electronics assembly specialist; b. Chgo., Oct. 28, 1938; s. Edward A. and Mildred M. (Miller) C.; m. Carole M. Hoffman, July 31, 1966; children: Susan, Jody. BS in Indsl. Engring., U. Ill., 1961; MBA, Northwestern U., 1969. Registered profl. engr., Calif.; cert. ESD engr. Sr. process engr. Cook Electric Co., Morton Grove, Ill., 1973-75; sr. indsl. engr. Motorola, Carol Stream, Ill., 1975-77; supr. indsl. engring. def. sys. divsn. Northrop Grumman, Rolling Meadows, Ill., 1977-80, mgr. tech. svcs. def. sys. divsn., 1980-84, mgr. advance mfg. tech. def. sys. divsn., 1984-86, mgr. tng. ctr. def. sys. divsn., 1986-95; tech. advisor/tng. specialist, 1995—, DOD category C instr., examiner; engr. Nat. Soldering Std. Working Coms., 1990-93, mem. IPC J-stds. coms.-001, 002, 003, 004, 005, 006, 1990—, mem. IPC ESD task group. Mem. Inst. Indsl. Engring. (pres. North Suburban Ill. chpt. 1982-83, program chmn. Dist. 8, 1984—, spouses program chmn. 1992 internat. conv., Midwest chpt. ESD assoc. libr. chmn.), Inst. Indsl. Engrs., Assn. Old Crows, U. Ill. Alumni Assn., Northwestern U. Alumni Assn., Northwestern Club Chgo., ESD Assn. (Midwest chpt.). Office: Northrop Grumman ESID 600 Hicks Rd Rolling Meadows IL 60008-1098

CASKEY, BETHANY ANNE, artist; b. San Diego, Dec. 29, 1950; d. Bruce and Phyllis Margarite (Forst) C.; m. Russell Austin Kness, Apr. 1, 1988; 1 child, Echo Caskey Kness. BA in Art, Graceland Coll., 1974. Studio artist Albia, Iowa, 1977—; v.p., co-founder and performer Vintage Show Co., Albia, 1985—. Artist: (painting) Cottontail/Iowa Habitat Print, 1985; illustrator for Equine mags., 1990—; designer USET Endurance team logo; contbr. articles to profl. jours. Mem. Am. Acad. Equine Art, Soc. Animal Artists. Office: Vintage Show Co Caskey Gallery PO Box 263 Albia IA 52531-0263

CASKEY, HAROLD LEROY, state senator; b. Bates County, Mo., Jan. 3, 1938; s. James Alfred and Edith Irene (Anderson) C.; AB, Central Mo. State U., 1960; JD, U. Mo., Columbia, 1963; m. Kay Head, 1974; children: Kyle James. Pros. atty., Bates County, 1967-72; city atty., Butler, Mo., 1973-76; individual practice law, Butler, Mo.; asst. prof. NE Mo. State U., 1975-76; mem. Mo. Senate, 1977—. Mem. Mo. Bar Assn., Am. Judicature Soc., Fellowship Christian Politicians, Am. Criminal Justice Educators, Order Coif, Acacia, Phi Alpha Delta, Kappa Mu Epsilon, Alpha Phi Sigma. Baptist. Office: State Capitol Jefferson City MO 65101 also: PO Box 45 Butler MO 64730-0045

CASPERSON, PAUL G., mechanical designer; b. Woodstock, Ill., June 5, 1951. BS, U. Ill., Chgo., 1975; MS, Loyola U., Chgo., 1985. Product developer Kester Solder, Chgo., 1976-78; engr. Zenith Electronics, Chgo., 1978-85; mgr. mech. design Cummins Electronics, Columbus, Ind., 1985—. Contbr. articles on electronic packaging and prodn. to tech. publs.; patentee in heat sinking field.

CASSELL, FRANK HYDE, business educator; b. Chgo., Oct. 12, 1916; s. Frank V. Seymour and Mary Alicia (Robinson) C.; m. Marguerite Ellen Fletcher, Mar. 24, 1940; children: Frank Allan, Thomas W. (dec.), Christopher B. AB, Wabash Coll., 1939; postgrad., U. Chgo., 1946-47. Exec. Inland Steel Co., Chgo., 1948-68; U.S. rep. OECD, Amsterdam, 1966, Paris, 1967; on leave as dir. U.S. Employment Svc., Washington, 1966-68; prof. indsl. rels. Kellogg Grad. Sch. Mgmt., Northwestern U., 1968-85, prof. emeritus orgn. behavior and indsl. rels., 1985—; chmn. bd. employment rsch. and devel. inst. Northwestern U., 1987—; vis. prof. Inst. Am. Studies, Salzburg, Austria, 1957, Inst. Mgmt., Northwestern U., Burgenstock (Luzerne), Switzerland, 1975—; v.p. bd. dirs. Rehab. Inst. Chgo., 1960-66; cons. to govt. and industry in fields manpower, econ. and technol. devel., indsl. rels. and mgmt. Author: The Employment Service: An Organization in Change, 1968, (with Weber and Ginsberg) National Manpower Policies, 1969, (with Jean Baron) Collective Bargaining in the Public Sector, 1976; contbr.: Handbook of Business Strategy, 1985, Handbook of Airline Economics, Emergence of Policy Bargaining, 1996; contbr. articles to profl. jours. Trustee Wabash Coll., 1967-71; chmn. Gov. Ill. Com. Unemployment, 1961-63; chmn. Winnetka (Ill.) Planning Commn., 1973-75; bd. dirs. Chgo. Urban League, 1953-92; bd. dirs., mem. exec. com. Means Services, Inc., 1974-82; co-chmn. Chgo. Mayoral Transition Com., 1983, Chgo. Mayor's Task Force on Steel and S.E. Chgo., 1984-86; adv. Northwestern U.-Am. Iron and Steel Inst. Steel Research Project, 1987-90; advisor set-aside contracts legis. for women and minorities Mayor's Blue Ribbon Panel, Chgo., 1990.; hon. mem. White Mountain Apache Tribe, White River, Ariz., 1967; pres. Op. Able, Chgo., 1991-92. Recipient Disting. Svc. awards U.S. Dept. Labor, 1968, 73. Mem. Indsl. Rels. Assn. Chgo. (pres. 1957-58), Indsl. Rels. Rsch. Assn. (bd. dirs. 1966-69), Am. Econ. Assn., Nat. Planning Assn., Beta Gamma Sigma. Home: 128 Church Rd Winnetka IL 60093-3904 Office: Northwestern U McCormick Sch Engring 2145 Sheridan Rd Evanston IL 60201-2926 Office: Employment R&D Inst 809 Ridge Rd Wilmette IL 60091

CASSELMAN, BARRY, political correspondent, nonprofit administrator, author; b. Erie, Pa., May 24, 1942; s. Hyman Lawrence and Pauline (Masiroff) C. BA with honors, U. Pa., 1964; postgrad., U. Madrid, 1966-67; MFA, U. Iowa, 1969. Tchr. Erie (Pa.) Sch. Dist., 1970-71; editor, pub. Appleseeds newspaper, Chaska, Minn., 1972-73, Many Corners newspaper, Mpls., 1973-86; pres. Preludium News Svc., Mpls., 1986—; polit. corr. The Polit. Report, Washington, 1990—; lectr. Cunard Lines, 1988—; radio commentator Sta. WCCO-AM, Mpls., 1986-91; TV commentator CONUS All News Channel, 1992—. Author: Language, A Magical Enterprise, The Body, 1978, Among Dreams, 1985, (poetry) The Rippling Water Sleeve, 1969, Equilibrium Fingers, 1977. Exec. dir. Internat. Conf. Found., Mpls., 1990—. Office: Internat Conf Found 7600 France Ave S Ste 108 Minneapolis MN 55435

CASSENS, ROBERT GENE, food scientist; b. Morrison, Ill., June 10, 1937; s. Ludwig P. and Ethel (Hinrichs) C.; m. Dessa Cassens, June 11, 1961; children: Martha, Martin. BS, U. Ill., 1959; MS, U. Wis., 1961, PhD, 1963. Asst. prof. food sci. U. Wis., Madison, 1964-67, assoc. prof., 1967-71, prof., 1971—. Author: Nitrite-cured Meat: A FoodSafety Issue in Perspective, 1990, Meat Preservation: Preventing Losses and Assuring Safety, 1994; editor: The Physiology and Biochemistry of Muscle as a Food, 1966, 2d edit., 1970; contbr. over 300 articles to profl. jours. Inst. Food Technologists Rsch. grantee, 1967, Am. Soc. Animal Sci. grantee, 1969, Am. Meat Sci. Assn. grantee, 1971; recipient R.C. Pollock award, 1996. Fellow AAAS. Office: Muscle Biol Lab 1805 Linden Dr W Madison WI 53706-1110

CASSIDAY, DONALD MARION, banker; b. Clinton, Iowa, Jan. 15, 1935; s. Donald Marion and Ruth Abbey (Beil) C.; m. Rosalie J. Yeoman, Jan. 17, 1959; children: Karen Lynn, Terry Jane, Julie. BA in History, Grinnell Coll., 1956; MS in Mgmt., Colo. U., 1968. Commd. 2d lt. USAF, 1956, advanced through grades to col., 1971, ret., 1977; dean Sch. Bus. Aurora (Ill.) U., 1977-85; v.p. corp. devel. Mchts. Bancorp. Inc., Aurora, 1985—; mem. Aurora Airport Adv. Bd., 1989—, Joseph Corp. Adv. Bd., 1994. Co-author: Study of MBA Business Communication Course Needs, 1985; contbr. articles to profl. jours. Pres., bd. dirs. Aurora United Way, 1979-87; bd. dirs. Mercy Ctr. for Health Care Svcs., Aurora, Aurora YMCA, 1995—, Aurora Conv. and Tourism Coun., Aurora Downtown Redevel., 1994—; chmn. Mercy Svcs. Found. Bd., 1996—; bd. dirs., treas. Foxfest Aurora, 1990-95, Freedom Flight Aurora; v.p., bd. dirs. Mental Health Bd., Aurora, 1983-86; dir. Two Rivers coun. Boy Scouts Am., St. Charles, Ill., 1988-95. Recipient Grinnell Coll. Outstanding Alumni award, 1996, Humanitarian award St. John's AME Ch., Aurora, 1988, Community Builders award Masons, Aurora, 1987. Mem. Bank Mktg. Assn., Air Force Assn., Ret. Officers Assn., Aurora U. Alumni Assn. (bd. dirs.), Am. Assn. Higher Edn., Am. Mgmt. Assn., Kiwanis (Aurora chpt. pres. 1986, lt. gov. 1987, Disting. Pres. award 1986, Kiwanian of Yr. 1987), Assn. Individual Devel. (bd. dirs. 1989-95). Republican. Methodist. Office: Mchts Bancorp Inc 34 S Broadway Aurora IL 60505-3335

CASSIDAY, KAREN LYNN, psychologist; b. Salina, Kans., Mar. 18, 1960; d. Donald Marion and Rosalie Jean (Yeoman) Cassiday; m. John Edward Calamari, May 26, 1989. BA, Wheaton Coll., 1982; PhD, Chgo. Med. Sch., 1990. Staff psychotherapist The Anxiety Clinic, Chgo., 1990-91; instr. dept. clin. psychology Chgo. Med. Sch., North Chicago, Ill., 1991—; program dir. Behavior Med, Inc., Lake Bluff, Ill., 1991-92; co-dir. Cognitive Behavioral Treatment Ctr., Arlington Heights, Ill., 1992-95; dir. Anxiety and Agoraphobia Treatment Ctr., Kenosha, Wis., 1995—; cons. Deborah's Place, Chgo., 1987-88. Contbr. articles to profl. jours.; author various manuals. Mem. Psi Chi. Episcopalian. Home: 141 Oak Knoll Dr Lake Villa IL 60046-8997 Office: Anxiety & Agoraphobia Treatment Ctr 10400 75th St #311 Kenosha WI 53142

CASSIDY, EUGENE PATRICK, pathologist; b. N.Y.C., July 21, 1940; s. Eugene Zachary and Anita Hilda (Corsi) C.; m. Hollis Elizabeth Ward, Sept. 25, 1965; 1 child, Meredith. BA, Williams Coll., 1962; MD, Yale U., 1966. Diplomate Am. Bd. Pathology. Intern Yale-New Haven Hosp., Conn., 1966-67; resident then fellow in pathology and lab. medicine Yale U. Med. Ctr., 1967-70; dir. pathology Appalachian Lab. for Occupational Respitory Disease, Morgantown, Wis., 1970-72; pathologist Clarkson Hosp., Omaha, 1972-78, Scripps Hosp., Encinitas, Calif., 1978-84; dir. pathology Marshalltown (Iowa) Med. and Surgical Ctr., 1984—; asst. prof. W.Va. U. Sch. Medicine, Morgantown, 1970-72, U. Nebr. Sch. Medicine, Omaha, 1974-78. Contbr. articles to profl. jours. Served with USPHS, 1970-72. Fellow Internat. Acad. Pathology, Coll. Am. Pathologists, Am. Soc. Clin. Pathologists; mem. AMA, Am. Assn. Blood Banks. Republican. Home: Woodfield Rd Marshalltown IA 50158-3851 Office: Marshalltown Med & Surg Ctr 3 S 4th Ave Marshalltown IA 50158-2924

CASSIDY, FREDERIC GOMES, humanities educator; b. Oct. 10, 1907; s. Walter C. and Camilla (Gomes-Casseres) C.; m. Hélène Lucile Monod, Dec. 26, 1931; children: Frederic Monod, Victor Monod, Claire Monod, Michael Monod. BA, Oberlin Coll., 1930, MA, 1932, HHD (hon.), 1983; PhD, U. Mich., 1938; D.Litt. (hon.), Meml. U. Nfld., 1982, Ind. State U., 1983, U. W.I., 1984, U. Mich., 1986. Faculty Oberlin Coll., 1930-31, U. Strasbourg, France, 1935-36, U. Mich., 1936-39; faculty U. Wis., Madison, 1939—; prof. English U. Wis., 1949-78, prof. emeritus, 1978—; Vis. prof. Columbia, summer 1956, Stanford, 1963-64; editorial cons. Funk & Wagnalls Co., 1964-72. Author: Place Names of Dane County, Wisconsin, rev. edit., 1947, A Method for Collecting Dialect, 1953, Jamaica Talk, 1961, 2d edit., 1971, Dictionary of Jamaican English, 1967, 2d edit., 1980; chief editor: Dictionary of American Regional English, 1965—, vol. 1, 1985, vol. 2, 1991. Recipient Silver Musgrave medal Inst. Jamaica, 1962, Gold Musgrave medal, 1984, Centenary medal, 1980; Fulbright rsch. fellow, 1951-52, 58-59; grantee U.S. Office Edn., 1965-70; grantee Nat. Endowment for Humanities, 1970—; NSF, 1975—. Fellow Am. Acad. Arts and Scis.; mem. Am. Dialect Soc. (past pres.), Soc. for Caribbean Linguistics (pres. 1972-76), Wis. Geog. Names Council, Am. Name Soc. (pres. 1980). Home: 207 N Spooner St Madison WI 53705-4034

CASSIDY, JAMES MARK, construction company executive; b. Evanston, Ill., June 22, 1942; s. James Michael and Mary Ellen (Munroe) C.; B.A., St. Mary's Coll., 1963; m. Bonnie Marie Bercker, Aug. 1, 1964 (d. Dec. 1981); children: Micaela Marie, Elizabeth Ann, Daniel James; m. Patricia Margaret Mary Murphy, Sept. 15, 1984. Estimator, Cassidy Bros., Inc., Rosemont, Ill., 1963-65, project mgr., 1965-67, v.p., 1967-71, exec. v.p., 1971-77, pres., 1978—; trustee Plasterer's Health & Welfare Trust, 1971-92. Area fund leader constrn. industry salute to Boy Scouts Am., 1975; mem. pres.'s council St. Mary's Coll.; chmn. labor liaison com. Laborers Internat. Union N.Am. and Assn. Wall and Ceiling Industries, 1982-85, chmn. labor-mgmt. group, 1985-88; chmn. Chicagoland Assn. Wall and Ceiling Contractors' Carpenters Union Negotiating Team, 1983—. Served with U.S. Army, 1963-64, N.G., 1964-69. Mem. Chgo. Plastering Inst., Builder Uppers Club (pres. 1973-74), Chicagoland Assn. Wall and Ceiling Contractors (pres. 1976-79), Great Lakes Council, Internat. Assn. Wall and Ceiling Contractors (chmn. 1977), Constrn. Employers Assn. Chgo. (dir. 1976—, pres.-elect 1989-90, pres. 1991-93), chmn. com. labor-mgmt. relations 1983—), Chicagoland Safety Council (dir. 1988-92, chmn. joint conf. bd. Cook County 1995—), Assn. Wall and Ceiling Industries Internat. (dir. 1978-81, 88-89, fin. v.p. 1990, 2d vp 1991, pres.-elect 1992, pres. 1993), Park Ridge (Ill.) Country Club (dir. 1994—), Eagle Creek Country Club (Naples, Fla.). Office: Cassidy Bros Inc PO Box 570 Des Plaines IL 60018-0570

CASSIDY, JOHN LEMONT, engineering executive; b. Springfield, Mass., Jan. 2, 1934; s. Elbridge Floyd and Marion (Arent) C.; m. Katherine Helen Carollo, Feb. 9, 1954 (div. Apr. 1970); children: Debbie M. Cassidy Batliner, Sheryl A. Cassidy Batliner, Dennis M.; m. Jane Frances Wahlmeier, Nov. 21, 1974; children: Armon J., Carla A., Monica L. Scheetz. BS in Physics, U. Mo., Kansas City, 1969. V.p. mfg. Hisonic, Inc., Olathe, Kans., 1969-83; v.p. Unimark, Inc., Overland Park, Kans., 1988—; pres. Unimark Svc. Co., 1988-93; sr. judge Am. Water Ski Assn., 1985-91. Coach Kans. Spl. Olympics, chmn. winter games, 1990-95. Sgt. USMC, 1953-56. Recipient Disting. Svc. award Kans. Spl. Olympics, 1990. Mem. U.S. Recreational Ski Assn. (chmn. bd. dirs. 1985-88, Slim Davis award 1988), Kansas City Ski Club (pres. 1983-84), MENSA. Republican. Home: 16000 W 149th Ter Olathe KS 66062-2647 Office: Unimark Inc 9400 Reeds Rd Shawnee Mission KS 66207-2519

CASSIDY, MARY JOAN, historian, consultant; b. Spring Valley, Ohio, Mar. 16, 1939; d. Charles Scott and Mabel Helen (Dakin) Stiles; m. Thomas G. Cassidy, Aug. 21, 1960; children: Patrick Alan, Michael Thomas, Timothy Aaron. BA, Wilmington Coll., 1960; postgrad., Wright State U., 1972—. Cert. tchr. English and history. Tchr. English Franklin (Ohio) City Schs., 1960-62; tchr. English and history Wayne Local Schs., Waynesville, Ohio, 1964-80; antique dealer Past-Is-Prologue Shop, Waynesville, 1987-94; genealogist Waynesville, 1985—; owner Mill Creek Books, Waynesville, 1985—. Cons. Middle Run Cemetery Preservation Assn., Bellbrook, Ohio, 1995—.

CASSIDY, SAMUEL M., banker; b. Lexington, Ky., Aug. 8, 1932; s. Samuel M. Cassidy and Frances Carroll Stevenson; m. Rebecca Jane Hoult, June 9, 1956; children: Francis Cassidy Sabad, James W., Michael, Mary. A.B. in Econs., Duke U., 1958; M.B.A., U. Cin., 1962. Mgmt. trainee 1st Nat. Bank Cin., 1958-62, asst. cashier, 1962-64, asst. v.p., 1964-68, v.p. dept. banks, 1968-74, sr. v.p., 1974-80, exec. v.p., dir., 1980-84, pres., 1984-94, ret., 1994; dir. Leyman Corp., Cin. Group vice chmn. United Appeal, Cin., 1979—; chmn. devel. com. Santa Maria Community Service, Cin., 1981-83; trustee Greater Cin. Better Bus. Bur., 1983—; corp. chmn. Fine Arts Fund, Cin., 1984. Served as sgt. USMC, 1953-56. Mem. Ohio Bankers Assn. (chmn. BancPac program 1985-86), Cin. C. of C. (leadership com. 1980, vice chmn. steering com. 1982-83, ballot issues com. 1984—). Clubs: Commonwealth, Cin. Country, Bankers, Queen City. Home: 7790 Ivygate Ln Cincinnati OH 45242-5120*

CASSIN, JAMES RICHARD, broadcast educator; b. Port Huron, Mich., Oct. 7, 1933; s. Lloyd Gerald Cassin and Gladys Carolyn (Smith) McCarron; m. Winnie Christine Carr, May 2, 1952; children: James R. II, Carolyn Marie Cassin Krecklow. BS in Journalism, Ball State U., 1982; MS in Radio-TV, Butler U., 1984. Enlisted USAF, 1951; served as pub. info. specialist USAF, Japan, Korea, Nev., Tex., Colo., Wis., 1951-71; ret. USAF, 1971; editor internal publs. Am. Fletcher Corp., Indpls., 1972-74; publicity dir. Amateur Athletic Union of U.S., Indpls., 1974-76; prof. broadcasting Def. Info. Sch., Ft. Benjamin Harrison, Ind., 1976-95; adj. prof. Marian Coll., Indpls., 1988-91. Editor industry newspaper Dimensions (Best newspaper award Ind. Bus. Communicators, 1972); editor newletter Kaleidoscope (Award of Merit, Ind. Bus. Communicators, June 1972, Mar. 1973); editor Am. Fletcherline (Best newspaper award Ind. Bus. Communicators, 1974); editor AAU News Mag. (award of month Ind. Bus. Communicators, Feb., Apr., Dec. 1975, Mar. 1976). Mem. Armed Forces Broadcasters Assn., Am. Legion, USAF Thunderbird Alumni Assn., Kappa Tau Alpha, Phi Delta Kappa. Lutheran.

CASSINELLI, JOSEPH PATRICK, astronomy educator; b. Cin., Aug. 23, 1940; s. Herbert John and Louise (Schlottman) C.; m. Mary LeFever; children: Joseph Michael, Carolyn Marie, Mary Kathleen. BS in Physics, Xavier U., 1962; MS in Physics, U. Ariz., 1965; PhD in Astronomy, U. Wash., 1970. Research asst. Kitt Peak Nat. Obs., Tucson, 1963-65; research engr. Boeing Co., Seattle, 1965-66; postdoctoral research assoc. Joint Inst. for Lab. Astrophysics, Boulder, Colo., 1970-72; postdoctoral fellow U. Wis., Madison, 1972-73, asst. prof., 1973-77, assoc. prof., 1977-81, prof., 1981—, chmn. astronomy dept., 1986-89; vis. scientist Space Astronomy Lab., Utrecht, the Netherlands, 1975-76, Space Telescope Sci. Inst., 1991; Donders chair U. Utrecht, 1985. Co-author: Introduction to Stellar Winds, 1996. Langley Abbot research fellow Harvard Smithsonian Ctr. for Astrophysics, 1981; Fulbright research fellow Sonnenborgh Obs., 1986. Mem. Am. Astron. Soc., Internat. Astron. Union. Roman Catholic. Home: 1520 Chandler St Madison WI 53711-2210 Office: U Wis Astronomy Dept 475 N Charter St Madison WI 53706-1507

CASSITY, ANNE ELIZABETH, ; b. Bridgeport, Conn., Jan. 30, 1968; d. Michael Ralph Esposito and Maryanne Volosin Flummer; m. Christopher Cassity, Oct. 7, 1988; 1 child, Jessica Marie. Purchasing agt. Alro Metals, Inc., St. Petersburg, Fla., 1988-91; mother, 1991-93; asst. Medi-Flex Hosp. Products, Overland Park, Kans., 1993-94. Author: We Met By Murder, 1993; Actress (Musical) Kiss Me Kate, 1989. Catechist St. Therese Byzantine Ch., St. Petersburg, Fla., 1987. Named Superior Group Musical, 1985, Superior Improvisation, 1985, Duet Improvisation, 1985, Internat. Thespian Soc. Mem. Internat. Thespian Soc. Byzantine Catholic.

CASSON, CHARLES R., engineer; b. Vicksburg, Miss., Jan. 16, 1947. AS, U. Cin., 1976. Mgr. mfg. svcs. Constellation Steel Mill Equipment Co., Cin., 1965-82; mfg. mgr., chief engr. Rosemont Industries, Inc., Cin., 1982—. Mem. Am. Kennel Club (judge dog shows), K-9 Tng. Assn. Office: Rosemont Industries Inc 1700 West St Cincinnati OH 45215-3438

CASSTEVENS, DAVID PAUL, city administrator; b. Kansas City, Mo., Nov. 8, 1950; s. Emery Reber and Paula Rebecca (Dexheimer) C.; m. Jennifer Jean Shank, Apr. 15, 1977; children: Jessica Blue, Amanda Jean, James Daniel. BA, Washington U., St. Louis, 1973; MPA, Iowa State U., 1987. Intern asst. to city mgr. City of Ames, Iowa, 1983-84; dir. adminstrv. svcs. City of Newton, Iowa, 1984-90; fin. dir. City of Muscatine, Iowa, 1990—. Home: 205 W 11th St Muscatine IA 52761 Office: City of Muscatine 215 Sycamore Muscatine IA 52761

CASSTEVENS, THOMAS WILLIAM, political science educator; b. Fayette, Mo., Feb. 3, 1937; s. Harold T. and Willa G. (Hargis) C.; m. Jeanne Isabel Savery, June 3, 1958; children: Willa Jeanne, Margot Lee. BA in Polit. Sci., Reed Coll., 1959; PhD in Polit. Sci., Mich. State U., 1966. Asst. instr. Mich. State U., 1960-61, instr., 1961-63; asst. rsch. polit. scientist Inst. Govtl. Studies U. Calif., Berkeley, 1963-66, lectr., 1963-64; asst. prof. Oakland (Mich.) U., 1966-69, assoc. prof., 1969-72, prof. polit. sci., 1972—, acting dept. chmn., spring 1973, chmn. dept., 1979-82; vis. fellow dept. math. Dartmouth Coll., Hanover, N.H., 1968-69; vis. scholar Darwin Coll. U. Kent, Canterbury, Eng., fall 1973; vis. prof. U. Delhi (India), winter 1977; Fulbright vis. prof. Jawaharlal Nehru U., New Delhi, 1976-77; vis. prof. Sch. Bus. Adminstrn. Pacific Luth. U., Tacoma, Wash., Oct. 1984; spl. advisor to adminstr. Agy. Internat. Devel., Washington (D.C.), 1982-85; trustee Lillie A. Schwarck Charitable Scholarship Trust, 1988—; lectr. USIA, 1976-77; external examiner Centre for Am. and West European Studies, Sch. Internat. Studies, Jawaharlal Nehru U., 1977—; cons. The White House, 1975-76; lectr., cons. mathematical polit. sci. Nat. Sci. Found. Coll. Sci. Improvement Program Heidelberg Coll., Tiffin, Ohio, 1973; hon. rsch. fellow U. New England, Australia, 1991. Author: (monographs) Politics, Housing and Race Relations: The Defeat of Berkeley's Fair Housing Ordinance, 1965, Politics, Housing and Race Relations: California's Rumford Act and Proposition 14, 1967; editor (with B.K. Shrivastava) American Government and Politics, 1980 (with Lynn W. Eley) The Politics of Fair Housing Legislation, 1968; mem. internat. adv. bd. jour. Asian Affairs, 1982—; contbr. articles and revs. to profl. jours. Science faculty fellow NSF, 1968-69. Office: Oakland U Dept Dept Polit Sci Rochester MI 48309

CASSY, CATHERINE MARY, elementary school educator; b. Granite City, Ill., Aug. 12, 1949; d. George Joseph and Margaret Mary (Pieper) Crawshaw; m. Gene Herschel Cassy, June 5, 1971. BS in Edn., So. Ill. U., 1971; MS, Lindenwood Coll., 1987. Cert. lifetime elem., instrumental music, vocal music tchr., reading specialist, Mo., elem. tchr., Ill. Tchr. music Fowler Elem. Sch., Phoenix, 1972-73; tchr. 5th grade Parkview Elem. Sch., Granite City, 1973-82; tchr. of gifted Maryville Sch., Granite City, 1982-83; tchr. 6th grade and vocal music Henderson Jr. High Sch., St. Charles, 1984-86; tchr. 6th grade, tchr. vocal music Barnwell Jr. High Sch., St. Charles, Mo., 1986-87; tchr. 6th grade M.G. Henderson Elem. Sch., St. Charles, 1987—; cycle chairperson Henderson Sch., 1991—. Mus. dir., performer Showtime Express, Inc., Granite City, 1989—; chair Great Rivers Environ. Edn. Network, 1994-96. Named Tchr. of Yr. Barnwell Jr. High Sch., 1987; recipient Travis Hack Meml. award, 1993, Excellence in Teaching award Emerson Electric, 1993; Nat. Elem. Sci. Leadership grantee Nat. Sci. Resource Ctr., 1993. Fellow Tchr.'s Acad.; mem. NSTA, NEA, Nat. Coun. Tchrs. Math., Mo. Coun. Tchrs. Math., Mo. Sci. Tchrs. Assn., Acad. Sci. St. Louis, Nature Conservancy, Phi Delta Kappa. Home: 2191 Shirlene Dr Granite City IL 62040-2564 Office: Henderson Elem Sch 2501 Hackmann Rd Saint Charles MO 63303-5452

CAST, ANITA HURSH, small business owner; b. Columbus, Ohio, July 11, 1939; d. Charles Walter and Hulda Marie (Ramsey) Hursh; m. William R. Cast, Apr. 1, 1961; children: Jennifer, Carter, Meghan. BA, DePauw U., 1961. Ptnr. Cast Hursh and Assocs., Ft. Wayne, Ind., 1982—; pianist Words and Music, Ft. Wayne, 1983—; owner Anita Cast's Wearable Art, Ft. Wayne, 1986—; cons. for bd. tng. Bd. dirs., pres. Am. Symphony Orch. League, vol., v.p., 1985-86; bd. dirs. WBNI Nat. Pub. Radio, Ft. Wayne; commr. Ind. Gov.'s Mansion Commn., 1987, Ind. Arts Commn., 1979-87; chmn., bd. dirs. Fine Arts Found., Ft. Wayne, 1988; pres. Ft. Wayne Philharmonic, 1977-79; pres., bd. dirs. Friends of Music, Ind. U.; v.p. Leadership Ft. Wayne Adv. Bd., Ind. Endowment of the Arts; chmn. bd. Arts United of Greater Ft. Wayne, 1988-90; pres. Met. YMCA, Ft. Wayne, 1986—; mem. Mayor's Bicentennial Exec. Bd., 1989-94; mem. Ind. Cultural Congress Hon. Com. Lily Endowment Leadership fellow. Republican. Episcopalian. Home and Office: Anita Cast Wearable Art 4401 Taylor Rd Fort Wayne IN 46804-1913

CASTELE, THEODORE JOHN, radiologist; b. New Castle, Pa., Feb. 1, 1928; s. Theodore Robert and Anne Mercedes (McNavish) C.; m. Jean Marie Willse, Oct. 20, 1951; children: Robert, Ann Marie, Richard, Mary Kathryn, Thomas, Daniel, John. BS, Case Western Res. U., 1951, MD, 1957. Diplomate Am. Bd. Radiology, 1962. Intern then resident U. Hosps. Cleve., 1957-61, fellow, 1961-62; dir. of radiology Luth. Med. Ctr., Cleve., 1968-75, 77-89; chief of staff Luth. Med. Ctr., 1975-81; pres. Med. Ctr. Radiologists, Inc., Cleve., 1978-95; v.p. med. and copr. devel. Health Cleve. Inc., 1989-91; chmn. Lakeshore Radiology Inc., Cleve., 1991—; med. editor sta. WEWS-TV-ABC, Cleve., 1975—; chmn. bd. Med. Cons. Imaging Co., Cleve., 1981—; asst. clin. prof. radiology Case Western Res. U. Chmn. Southwestern dist. Greater Cleve. coun. Boy Scouts Am., 1969, 73; mem. bd. med. cons. Cleve. Police Dept., pres., 1988-90; trustee Comty. Dialysis Ctr., Luth. Med. Ctr. Found., chmn. bd. trustees, 1969-75, pres., 1988-90; trustee Case Western Res. U., Blue Cross/Blue Shield Ohio, Greater Cleve. Hosp. Assn., Fairview Health, Luth. Med. Ctr., 1975-80, Fairview Hosp. Found., No. Ohio Lung Assn.; chmn. Health Mus. Cleve., 1996—, Humility of Mary Healthcare Sys., 1995—. With USN, 1946-47. Recipient Order of Merit award Boy Scouts Am., 1971, Silver Beaver award, 1972, Nat. Disting. Eagle Scout award, 1984, Frances Payne Bolton Sch. of Nursing Disting. Svc. award, 1990, Outstanding Philanthropist award Nat. Soc. of Fundraising Execs., 1991; named Knight of the Equestrian, Order of the Holy Sepulchre of Jerusalem, 1993—. Fellow Am. Coll. Radiology; mem. AMA (Physician Spkr. Gold award 1978, 90, Silver 1979, Bronze 1978, Benjamin Rush award 1989, Golden Achievement award 1996, chmn. Ohio del. 1988—), Ohio State Med. Assn. (5th dist. councilor 1977-79, Spl. award 1979), Cleve. Radiol.

Soc. (pres. 1969-70), Cleve. Med. Libr. Assn. (pres. 1996), Case Western Res. U. Med. Alumni Assn. (pres. 1971-72, 91-92, Disting. Svc. award 1987), Cleve. Acad. Medicine (pres. 1974-75, Disting. Mem. award 1990, Disting. Svc. award 1984), Ohio State Radiol. Soc. (Silver award 1990). Home: 18869 Canyon Rd Cleveland OH 44126-1703 Office: 20325 Center Ridge Rd Rocky River OH 44116-3554

CASTENSON, ROGER R., agricultural engineer, association executive; b. Galveston, Tex., Aug. 6, 1943. BSAE, Tex. A&M U., 1972; MBA, Mich. State U., 1977. Rsch. assoc. Blackland Rsch. Ctr., Temple, Tex., 1972-73; mgr. pub. rels., mem. activities Am. Soc. Agrl. Engrs., St. Joseph, Mich., 1973-80, exec. v.p., CEO, 1987—; ops. mgr. Soc. Petroleum Engrs., 1980-81, bus. mgr., 1981-86. Mem. AIChE, Am. Soc. Agrl. Engrs., Soc. Petroleum Engrs., Instn. Engrs. Australia, Coun. Engring. and Sci. Soc. Execs., Sigma Xi, Tau Beta Pi. Office: Am Soc Agrl Engrs 2950 Niles Rd Saint Joseph MI 49085-9601

CASTIGLIONI, DEBRA MARIE, stockbroker; b. St. Louis, Aug. 9, 1965. Owner ins. agy., Clayton, Mo., 1983-88; COO Cutter & Co., Chesterfield, Mo., 1988—. Mem. Securities Industry Assn. Republican. Roman Catholic. Home: 1010 Tara Ridge Ct Ballwin MO 63021 Office: Cutter and Co. 15510 Olive Blvd Chesterfield MO 63017-0710

CASTILLO, ALLAN PAUL, metallurgist; b. N.Y.C., Oct. 6, 1939; s. Baltazar Cruz and Louise Hyacinth (Carruthers) C.; m. Isabella Maria Saum, July 3, 1964; children: Michael Allan, Monique Maria, Eric John. BS in Chemistry, U. New Haven, 1973; MS in Metallurgy, U. Conn., 1980. Technician Union Carbide Corp., Tarrytown, N.Y., 1967-69; sr. engr. Olin Corp., New Haven, 1969-80; sr. group leader Sandusky (Ohio) Internat. Inc., 1981-94; dir. R&D. CC Tech. Inc., Columbus, Ohio, 1994—; mem. faculty, mem. tech. adv. bd. Bowling Green (Ohio) State U., 1985—. With USAF, 1960-65. Mem. TAPPI (liaison 1983—, various coms.), Am. Soc. Materials Internat., Nat. Assn. Corrosion Engrs. (liaison 1988—). Republican. Lutheran. Home: 7320 Parker Rd Castalia OH 44824-9747 Office: CC Tech Svcs Inc 6141 Avery Rd Dublin OH 43016-8761

CASTILLO, MARIO ENRIQUE, artist, educator; b. Rio Bravo, Mexico, Sept. 19, 1945; came to U.S., 1955, naturalized, 1965; s. Manuel Castillo and Maria Enriquez de Allen. cert. Ill. Inst. Design, 1964; BFA, Sch. of Art Inst. Chgo., 1969; MFA, Calif. Inst. of Arts, 1972; postgrad. U. So. Calif., 1969-70, Pasadena City Coll., 1977, Calif. State U. at L.A., 1980-81, Calif. State U., Dominguez Hills, 1986-88, East L.A. City Coll., 1982, Nat. U., Inglewood, Calif., 1989. Designer J.M. Pateros Studios, Inc., Chgo., 1965, Lukas & Assocs., Chgo., 1966; instr. Pilsen Settlement House, Chgo., 1967; comml. artist Chgo. Bd. Edn., 1968; instr. United Christian Cmty. Svc., Chgo., 1968-69; mural dir. Halsted Urban Progress Ctr., 1968, Dept. Human Resources, Chgo., 1969, McHenry Coll., Crystal Lake, Ill., 1992, No. Ill. U., DeKalb, 1993, Joliet Jr. Coll., Ill., 1994, Coll. of Lake County, Grayslake, Ill., 1994, U. Guadalajara, Ocotlan, Mex., 1995, SAIC & Lincoln Park Cultural Ctr., Chgo., 1996; tchg. asst. Calif. Inst. Arts, Valencia, 1970-72, instr., 1972-73; instr. Santa Monica (Calif.) City Coll., 1973; mem. faculty dept. art U. Ill., Champaign, 1973-76; comml. artist, L.A., 1977; instr. art Immaculate Heart Coll., Hollywood, Calif., 1979-80, Pacific Asian Consortium in Edn., 1980-81, E.C.F. Art Ctr., L.A., 1986-90, L.A. Unified Sch. Dist., 1986-90, Instituto Comercial Artistico, Maywood, Calif., 1987, Lexicon Sch. Languages, 1987-88, Plaza de la Raza, 1989-90; mem. faculty art dept. Columbia Coll., Chgo., 1990—; panelist at Northeastern Ill. U., Chgo., 1974, Coll. Art Assn., Chgo., 1975, Columbia Coll., Chgo., 1992, 94, 96, Chgo. Artist Coalition, 1993, Nat. Assn. Chicano Studies, Chgo., 1994, 96, Suburban Fine Arts Ctr., Highland Park, Ill., 1995, U. Guadalajara, Jalisco, 1995; presenter workshop Human Rights Portfolio, Chgo., 1994, Internat. Prints, Chgo., 1994, Humboldt Park, Chgo., 1995; guest lectr. Galeria J.M. Velazeo, Mexico City, 1975, Centro de la Causa, Chgo., 1975, Latino Cultural House, Champaign, 1975, U. Ill., Champaign, 1975, 76, Corpus Christi (Tex.) State U., 1978;, McHenry County Coll., 1991, 92, Northwestern U., 1991, Columbia Coll., Montebello Sch. Dist., 1990, No. Ill. U. DeKalb, 1993, Triton Coll., River Grove, Ill., 1993, 94, Prospectus Gallery, Chgo., 1993, Joliet (Ill.) Jr. Coll., 1994, St. Cloud (Minn.) State U., 1994, Mac Murry Coll., Jacksonville, Ill., 1994, Coll. of Lake County, 1994, Nat.- Louis U., Chgo., 1995, Melrose Park (Ill.) Pub. Libr., 1995, Mobil Art Gallery, Jacksonville, Ill., 1994, Northeastern U., Chgo., 1995, Harold Washington Libr., Chgo., 1995, Munster Ind. Cultural Ctr., 1995, U. Guadalajara, Ocotlan, Jalisco, 1995, 96, CCC Art Gallery, Chgo., 1995, Winnetka (Ill.) Cultural House, 1995, No. Ill. U., De Kalb, 1995, U. Guadalajara, La Barranca Campus, 1996, Lincoln Park Cultural Ctr., Chgo., 1996; art juror Weisman Scholarship CCC, Chgo., 1993, Old Town Art Fair, Chgo., 1993, Hokin Gallery CCC, Chgo., 1995, Weisman Best of Show, Chgo., 1996; curator of art exhibitions U. Ill., Champaign, 1975, Columbia Coll., Chgo., 1994, 95, Triton Coll., 1995, No. Ind. Arts Assn., Munster, 1995, 11th Street Art Gallery CCC, 1995; interior designer El Mercado Co., L.A., 1981-83; regular performer musical program Noches Rancheras, East L.A., Calif., 1981-83; cons. in field. One-man shows include Scholarship and Guidance Assn., Chgo., 1968, Calif. Inst. of the Arts, Burbank, 1971, Valencia, Calif., 1972, Latino Cultural House, U. Ill., Champaign, 1976, Inst. For Hispanic Cultural Studies, Santa Monica, Calif., 1989, Orlando Gallery, Sherman Oaks, Calif., 1989, Sangre De Cristo Arts and Conf. Ctr., Pueblo, Colo., 1991, Prospectus Gallery, Chgo., 1991, 93, McHenry County Art Gallery, 1991, No. Ill. U. Art Gallery, DeKalb, 1993, Atwood Art Ctr., St. Cloud U., 1994, Mac Murry Coll, Jacksonville, Ill., 1994; numerous group shows including: Coll. Lake County, 1987, 94, Northeastern Ill. U., Chgo., 1974, Mus. of Sci. and Industry, Chgo., 195, 90, Krannert Art Mus., Champaign, 1975, Truman Coll., Chgo., 1977, Chgo. Pub. Libr. Cultural Ctr., 1978, Immaculate Heart Coll., 1979, The Mexican Fine Arts Ctr. Mus., Chgo., 1987, 90, 93, 96, Riverside (Calif.) Art Mus., 1989, ARC Gallery, Chgo., 1990, Coll. Of The Canyons, Valencia, Calif, 1990, McHenry County Coll., 1991, Fresno Art Mus., Calif., 1991, San Francisco Art Mus., 1991, San Francisco Mus. of Modern Art, 1991, Albuquerque Mus., 1991, Denver Art Mus., 1991, 93, Prospectus Gallery, 1992, 94, 369 Gallery, Edinburgh, Scotland, 1992, Ill. Governor's Office, Chgo., 1992, Northern Ill. U. Art Gallery, 1993, 95, Chgo. Internat. Art Expo, 1993, San Antonio Mus. of Art, 1993, Nat. Mus. of Am. Art, 1993, Tucson Mus. of Art, 1993, Triton Coll., 1993, 95, St. Augustine Coll., Chgo., 1993, Columbia Faculty Art Exhibit, Lake Geneva, Wis., 1993, Field Mus., Chgo., 1993, 94, U. Chgo., 1993, 94, Chgo. Latino Film Festival, 1994, Las Artes Galeria, Omaha, 1994, Open Windows Gallery, Chgo., 1994, S. Suburban Coll., South Holland, Ill., 1994, Columbia Coll., Chgo., 1994, 95, J.R. Shapiro Gallery, Oak Park, 1994, Cath. Theological Union, Chgo., 1995, John Linsey Gallery, Oak Park, 1995, Hokin Gallery CCC, Chgo., 1995, Oak Park Art League, 1995, Suburban Fine Art Ctr., Highland Park, 1995, Ill. State Art Gallery, Chgo., 1995, Peace Gallery, Chgo., 1995, Reimer Gallery SAIC, Chgo., 1995, Ill. State Mus., Springfield, 1996, Pilsen Artist to Artist, Chgo., 1996, CCC Faculty Exhbn., Chgo., 1996; also film screenings U.S., Europe and Mexico; commd. muralist in public locations and pvt. residences; represented in permanent collections: Sara Lee Corp., Chgo., Mexican Mus. of Fine Arts, Chgo., San Francisco Mus. of Art, San Francisco Mus. of Contemporary Art, Tucson Mus. of Art, San Diego Mus. of Contemporary Art, Latino Inst., Chgo., Columbia Coll., Chgo., Bell Telephone Co., Chgo., Lake Meadows Assn., Chgo., Scholarship and Guidance Assn., Chgo., City of Chgo., San Antonio Art Mus., Guadalupe Cultural Arts Ctr., Denver, Evergreen State Coll., Olympia, Wash., Chicano Humanities and Art Coun., Denver, Ariztlan Inc., Phoenix, Mira, Chgo., Centro Cultural de La Raza, San Diego, San Diego Mus. Art, Albuquerque Mus., San Francisco Mus. Art, San Diego Mus. Contemporary Art, Denver Art Mus., Mex. Mus., San Francisco, Portland Art Mus., Nat. Mus. Am. Art, Washington, also numerous pvt. collections. Recipient numerous awards including: nat. gold medal, gold keys and certs. Scholastic Mag., 1963-65, cert. of merit N.Y. Times, 1965, 1st Prize award, Chgo. Police Dept., 1964, 1st Prize award Chgo. Assn. Commerce & Indus., 1965, 1st pl. U. Ill. Chicago LASP design competition, 1st prize Maldef Art Competition, 1989, 1st pl. ESDC's Archtl. Relief Design Competition for New Homes in Chgo., 1992; artist to represent midwest in nat. workshop, UCLA, 1988, artist to represent Latino culture in Spanish TV comml., 1989, 1st prize Homewood (Ill.) C. of C., 1967, 1st prize Fiesta del Quinto Sol, Chgo., 1974, 1st prize Mus. Sci. and Industry, Chgo., 1975, 1st prize for 18th St. banner design, Chgo., 1994; Am. Film Inst. grantee, 1972; Oakley fellow U. So. Calif., 1969-70; Scholarship and Guidance Assn. grantee, 1965-68, Ford Found. grantee, 1975; named Artst of Yr., Latino Inst., 1991. Composer numerous songs. Home and Studio: 10101 S Avenue M Chicago IL 60617-5925 Office: Columbia Coll Art Dept 600 S Michigan Ave Chicago IL 60605-1901

CASTLE, DIANA CHRISTINE, poet; b. St. Louis, Nov. 14, 1954; d. Gordon Wray Tipton and Doris Marie (Purcell) Sterling; m. Dennis L. Castle, Jan. 11, 1975; children: Sara, Elizabeth, Joanna, Gabriel. AA, Florissant Valley Coll., 1975. Author: (poetry) Muddle Puddle, 1994, Prize of Life, 1995, Squeaky See-Saw, 1995, The See-Saw, 1995, Maiden's Plea, 1995, The Dream Box, 1995, Winter's Dawn, 1995, Who Are You, 1995, Sail Me High, 1995, The Final Voyage, 1995, Twilight, 1995, many others. Lincoln County homeschool coord. Mo. Homeschoolers, 1990-92, 94-95. Home: 3796 Ethington Rd Moscow Mills MO 63362

CASTLE, HOWARD BLAINE, religious organization administrator; b. Toledo, July 15, 1935; s. Russell Wesley and Letha Belle (Hobbs) C.; m. Patricia Ann Haverty, Aug. 12, 1957; 1 child Kevin Blaine. AB, Marion Coll., 1958; postgrad., Valparaiso U., 1960. Pastor The Wesleyan Ch., Valparaiso, Ind., 1958-60, Toronto, Ohio, 1963-69; assoc. pastor Northridge Wesleyan Ch., Dayton, Ohio, 1960-63; exec. dir. gen. dept. youth Wesleyan Ch. Hdqrs., Marion, Ind., 1968-72, dir. field ministries gen. dept. Sunday schs., 1972-74, exec. dir. curriculum, 1980-81; mng. editor WIN Mag., Marion, Ind., 1969-72; asst. gen. sec. Gen. Dept. of Local Ch. Edn., Marion, Ind., 1974-80; gen. dir. estate planning Wesleyan Ch. Internat Ctr., Indpls., 1982—; Editor Ohio dist. The Wesleyan Ch., Columbus, 1961-69; gen. conf. del. The Wesleyan Ch., Anderson, Ind., 1968. Writer: Curriculum-Religious Adult Student/Teacher, 1982—, Light from the Word, 1982—. Mem. Christian Holiness Assn., Christian Stewardship Assn., Christian Mgmt. Assn. Office: The Wesleyan Ch Internat PO Box 50434 Indianapolis IN 46250-0434

CASTLE, JANICE MORRIS, healthcare management consultant; b. Rocky Mount, Va., July 21, 1956; d. Brady Lee and Lena Love (Maxie) Morris. AAS, Va. Western Community Coll., 1976; BSN, Radford U., 1990. RN, Va.; cert. med.-surg. nursing. Asst. head nurse ICU Community Hosp. Roanoke (Va.) Valley, acting head nurse ICU, head nurse chronic respiratory unit, nursing resource coord.; dir. clin. computer svcs. Carilion Health Systems, Roanoke, Va., 1990-95; healthcare mgmt. cons. Superior Cons., Co., Inc., 1995—. Mem. Va. Lung Assn. (bd. dirs. Roanoke Region, pres. 1991-93), Sigma Theta Tau.

CASTLEBURY, GUY A., engineering executive; b. Chgo., Ill., Jan. 11, 1951. BSME, Milw. Sch. Engring., 1973; M in Engring., Gannon U., 1976. Registered profl. engr., Ohio. Design engr. Bucyrus Erie (Pa.), 1973-75; sr. engr. Marion (Ohio) Power Shovel divsn. Dresser Industries, 1975-77; v.p. engring. Conco-Tellus divsn. fo Interlake Corp., Brookfield, Ill., 1977-86; exec. v.p. ACRO Automation Syss., Milw., 1986—. Author: The AGV Handbook, 1990, The AGV Implementation Guide, 1991; contbr. articles to mag. Mem. Milw. Athletic Club. Home: 3613 E Norport Dr Port Washington WI 53074 Office: ACRO Automation Syss Inc 2900 W Greentree Rd Milwaukee WI 53207

CASTOR, CHRISTINA PELAYO, critical care nurse; b. St. Louis, June 3; d. Jacobo E. and Abundia L. (Pelayo) C. AS in nursing, Ind. U., Gary, 1980; BSN, Purdue U., Hammond, Ind., 1983, MS in nursing, 1984; MD, U. Santo Tomas, Manila, The Philippines, 1989. RN, Calif., Ill., Ind., Mich.; CEN; cert. ACLS, PALS, mobile intensive care; cert. trauma nurse. Staff nurse/charge nurse Our Lady of Mercy Hosp., Dyer, Ind., 1980-85, 86, 87; office nurse Conrado P. Castor MD, Munster, Ind., 1984-90; staff nurse Humana Hosp., Hoffman Estates, Ill., 1990; staff nurse/charge nurse emergency rm. St. Margaret Hosp., Hammond, Ind., 1990—. Mem. Emergency Nurse's Assn.

CASTORINO, SUE, communications executive; b. Columbus, Ohio, May 5, 1953; m. Randy Minkoff, Oct. 29, 1983. BS in Speech, Northwestern U., Evanston, Ill., 1975. Grad. fellow Ohio Gov.'s Sch., Columbus, 1975; producer, community affairs WBBM-TV (CBS all-news)), Chgo., 1975; news anchor, reporter Sta. WBBM, Chgo., 1981-86; news reporter WHTH-AM/FM, Newark, Ohio, 1975; news anchor, reporter WERE-AM (NBC all-news), Cleve., 1975-78, WWWE-AM (ABC), Cleve., 1978-81; founder, pres. Sue Castorino: The Speaking Specialist, Chgo., 1986—; guest lectr. various groups in bus., medicine, govt., law, sports, fin., worldwide, 1986—; leader media and presentation skills seminars; pvt. voice coach, 1986—; internat. exec. comm. tng. in media, crisis and issue mgmt. Author: North Shore Mag., 1987—; voice-over and on-camera talent, 1986—. Recipient Golden Gavel award Chgo. Soc. Assn. Execs., 1991, various news reporting awards AP, UPI, Chgo., 1981-86. Mem. Sigma Delta Chi. Office: The Speaking Specialist 435 N Michigan Ave Ste 2700 Chicago IL 60611-4001

CASTRO, DANIEL R., telecommunications administrator; b. Trenton, Mich., Sept. 21, 1955; s. Alden Ray and Wilma Lou (Smith) C.; m. Robin Rena Gillam, June 25, 1977. B in Electronics Enging. Tech., Devry, 1977; MBA, Xavier U., 1982; cert., AT&T Comm. Tng. Program, 1989-90. Tech. writing assoc. Western Electric, Winston-Salem, N.C., 1977-79; tech. writing specialist Western Electric, Columbus, Ohio, 1979-83; engring. instr. AT&T, Cin., 1983-86, network engring. supr., 1986-89, network provisioning mgr., 1990—; sys. engr. AT&T Bell Labs, Red Hill, N.J., 1990; network provisioning mgr. AT&T, Cin., 1990—; Part-time coll. recruiter, Western Electric, Columbus, Ohio, 1978-80. Mem. IEEE (assoc.), Am. Mgmt. Assn., Project Mgmt. Inst. Home: 8004 Thistlewood Dr West Chester OH 45069 Office: AT&T 221 E Fourth St Cincinnati OH 45202

CASTRONOVA, FRANK VINCENT, editor; b. Southfield, Mich., Apr. 15, 1971; s. Frank Charles and Carol Anne (Chmura) C.; m. Gaye Tischler, Sept. 29, 1995. BA in English, Wayne State U., 1993. Sales clk., book buyer Book Ctr. of East Detroit, Mich., 1987-93; sales clk. Borders Book Shop, Beverly Hills, Mich., 1993; rsch. assoc. Gale Rsch. Inc., Detroit, 1993-95, assoc. editor, 1995—. Mem. MLA, Friends of Detroit Pub. Libr. Roman Catholic. Office: Gale Rsch Inc 835 Penobscot Bldg Detroit MI 48226

CASTRONOVO, THOMAS PAUL, architect, consultant; b. Chgo., Apr. 7, 1932; s. Paul Thomas and Nancy (Racina) C. Student, U. Akron, 1949-51; BArch, Ohio State U., 1955. Registered architect, Ohio, Calif., Colo., Fla. Intern architect E.J. Guran, Architect, Akron, Ohio, 1957-58, A.W. Petersen, Architect, Akron, 1958-60; pres., owner Thomas P. Castronovo, Architect, Akron, 1960—. Chmn. Akron Urban Design and Fine Arts Commn.; mem. Akron Civic Design Awards Com., 1972, Akron Regional Devel. Bd., 1983-87. 1st lt. USAF, 1955-57. Mem. AIA (bd. dirs. Akron chpt. 1987-90), Architects Soc. Ohio, Pi Kappa Epsilon (Akron U. chpt., pres. alumni 1982-84, mem. Hall of Fame 1982). Office: 1175 N Main St Akron OH 44310-1047

CATACOSINOS, PAUL ANTHONY, geologist, educator, researcher; b. N.Y.C., Sept. 29, 1933; s. Anthony Adonis and Alice Elpiniki (Cocotos) C.; m. Joan Diane Cook, Jan. 16, 1958; children: Alice E., Andrew C., Diana N. BA, U. N. Mex., 1957, MS, 1962; PhD, Mich. State U., 1972. Exploration geologist Mt. Fuel Supply Co., Salt Lake City, Utah, 1962-66, Consumer's Power Co., Jackson, Mich., 1967-69; prof. geology Delta Coll., Univ. Ctr., Univ. Ctr., Mich., 1969-95; emeritus prof. geology Delta Coll., Univ. Ctr., Mich., 1995—; cons. geologist, pvt. practice, Albuquerque, 1969—. Co-editor: Early Sedimentary Evolution of the Michigan Basin, 1991, Basement and Basins of Eastern North America, 1996; contbr. articles to profl. jours. Recipient Bergstein award for teaching excellence Delta Coll., 1972, 88, Scholarly Achievement award Delta Coll., 1992. Fellow AAAS, Geol. Soc. Am.; mem. Am. Astron. Soc., Mich. Basin Geol. Soc. (pres. 1978-79), Albuquerque Geol. Soc., N.Mex. Geol. Soc., Am. Assn. Petroleum Geologists (cert.; pres. ea. sect. 1988-89, mem. adv. coun. 1989-92, Disting. Svc. award 1989, hon. mem., Nat. Cert. of Merit 1992, Disting. Svc. award 1993), Sigma Xi (pres. Midland chpt. 1994-95).

CATALANO, GERALD, accountant, oil company executive; b. Chgo., Jan. 17, 1949; s. Frank and Virginia (Kreiman) C.; m. Mary L. Billings, July 4, 1970; children: James, Maria, Gina. BSBA, Roosevelt U., 1971. CPA, Ill. Jr. acct. Drebin, Lindquist and Gervasio, Chgo., 1971; jr. acct. Leaf, Dahl and Co., Ltd., 1971-77, prin., 1978-80, ptnr. 1980-82; prin. Gerald Catalano, CPA, Chgo., 1982-83; ptnr. Barbakoff, Catalano & Assocs., 1983-87; pres. Barbakoff, Catalano & Caboor, Ltd., 1988-93, pres., Catalano, Caboor & Co., Ltd., 1993—; v.p. Tri-City Oil, Inc., Addison, Ill., 1983—; treas. Uncle Andy's, Inc., 1991-94; corp. officer Bionic Auto Parts, Inc.; bd. dirs. EDT, Inc., treas., 1993—. Pres. Young Dems., Roosevelt U., 1967-71; trustee U. Ill. Russo Scholarship Fund, 1989—; dir. Elmhurst Jaycees, 1976. Mem. AICPA, ASCAP (assoc.), NARAS (assoc.), Ill. CPA Soc., Theosophical Soc. Roman Catholic. Office: 1000 S York Rd Ste 301 Elmhurst IL 60126-5122

CATEFORIS, DAVID CHRISTOS, art history educator; b. Balt., Apr. 16, 1964; s. Vasily Christos and Mary-Ann Augusta (Baugh) C.; m. Elizabeth Ritchie Seale, Sept. 16, 1989. BA with distinction, Swarthmore Coll., 1986; MA in art history, Stanford U., 1988, PhD in art history, 1992. Rsch. asst. Fine Arts Mus., San Francisco, 1987-88; curatorial asst. Anderson Collection, Menlo Park, Calif., 1988-91; instr. Georgetown U., Washington, 1992, U. Va., Falls Church, Va., 1992; asst. prof. art history U. Kans., Lawrence, Kans., 1992—. Author: Willem De Kooning, 1994; contbr. articles to profl. jours. Recipient Centennial Teaching Asst. award Stanford U., 1989-90. Mem. Coll. Art Assn., Midwest Art History Soc., Am. Studies Assn., Phi Beta Kappa. Office: U Kans Art History Dept 209 Spencer Mus Art Lawrence KS 66045

CATERER, CLAIRE MILDRED, editor, writer; b. Southfield, Mich., Dec. 7, 1965; d. Kenneth Wyburn and Sally Ruth (Scovel) C.; m. Christopher D. Bohling, July 20, 1991; 1 child, Melanie Sarah. BA, U. Kans., 1988. Editl. asst. Woman's Day mag., N.Y.C., 1988-90; project editor HarperCollins Pubs., N.Y.C., 1990-93; editl. dir., founding ptnr. The Editl. Edge, Overland Park, Kans., 1993—; guest lectr. Butler County C.C. Creative Writing Conf., El Dorado, Kans., 1995. Mem. Phi Beta Kappa. Office: The Editl Edge 9109 W 88 Ter Overland Park KS 66212

CATLETT, CHARLES E., computer center administrator, network researcher; b. Kansas City, Kans., Mar. 29, 1960; s. David Leroy and Janice Lavern (Marth) C.; m. Joan Lorene Sandberg, Mar. 10, 1984; children: Amy Elizabeth, Charles Richard, Jonathan Earl David. BS in Computer Engring., U. Ill., 1983. Systems programmer U.S. Army Corps Engrs., Champaign, Ill., 1983-85; rsch. programmer Nat. Ctr. for Supercomputing Applications, Urbana, Ill., 1985-87; mgr. networking Nat. Ctr. for Supercomputing Applications, Urbana, 1985-89, assoc. dir., 1992—. Contbr. chpt. to book Internet System Handbook, 1992. Rsch. grantee NSF, 1988, 90, 93, 94, 95, AT&T, 1988, Advanced Rsch. Projects Agy., 1990, 94, 95. Mem. IEEE (Fred W. Ellersick award 1992), Assn. Computing Machinery, Internet Soc. Office: Nat Ctr for Supercomputing 605 E Springfield Ave Champaign IL 61820-5518

CATLIN, SUSAN LYNN, alcohol and drug abuse psychotherapist; b. Chgo., Dec. 15, 1954; d. Charles Sexton and Dorothy Mary (Good) C. BA, U. Ill., 1977; postgrad., George Williams Coll., 1983; MA, Roosevelt U., 1995. Cert. alcohol and drug counselor. Psychiat. tech. Forest Hosp., Des Plaines, Ill., 1979-85; alcohol counselor Ptnrs. in Psychiatry, Des Plaines, 1985-90; dir., pres. S.L. Catlin and Assocs., Des Plaines, Schaumburg, Ill., 1990—; cons. Advanced Psychiat. Svcs., 1990-94. Fellow Div. of Ill. Addictions, Nat. Assn. Alcoholism and Drug Abuse Counselors. Republican. Methodist. Home: 258 Sierra Pass Dr Schaumburg IL 60194

CATLIN, WILLIAM ARTHUR, police chief; b. Youngstown, Ohio, Dec. 28, 1941; s. Clyde Macky and Margaret (Loftus) C.; m. Mary Rose Corso, Nov. 9, 1963; children: Janet Marie, Judy Marie, Linda Marie. AAS, Kent (Ohio) State U., 1977, BS, 1979; MS, Youngstown (Ohio) State U., 1983; grad., Police Exec. Leadership Coll., 1995. Capt. Niles (Ohio) Police Dept., 1970-86; chief of police Lordstown (Ohio) Police Dept., 1986—; pres. Cavalier Fed. Credit Union. Contbg. author: The Police Personnel System, 1983. With U.S. Army, 1959-62, Korea. Mem. Internat. Assn. Chiefs of Police (pres.), Ohio Assn. Chiefs of Police (past chmn.), Mahoning Valley Chiefs of Police, Lordstown C. of C. Democrat. Byzantine Catholic. Home: 6160 Tod Ave SW Warren OH 44481-9769 Office: Lordstown Police Dept 1583 Salt Springs Rd Warren OH 44481-8625

CATOLINE, PAULINE DESSIE, small business owner; b. Ft. Worth, Dec. 17, 1937; d. Byron Hillis and Dessie Elizabeth (Plumlee) Doggett; children: Sherry Lou, Brenda Lynn; m. Donald Ralph Ackerman, Feb. 19, 1993. BA in Bus. Mgmt. (labor rels. specialty), Hiram Coll., 1989. Notary public, Ohio. Sec. Gen. Am. Life Ins. Co., Ft. Worth, 1956-57, Kelly Girl Svcs., Youngstown, Ohio, 1965-69; legal sec. Burgstaller, Schwartz & Moore, Youngstown, 1962-65, Green, Schiavoni, Murphy & Haines, Youngstown, 1969-71, Flask & Policy, Youngstown, 1971-83; sec. Western Res. Care System, Youngstown, 1983-87, exec. sec., 1987-90; owner, mgr. Pauline's Place, Youngstown, 1993—; legal sec. Henderson, Covington, Stein, Donchess & Messenger Law Firm, 1993-94; exec. adminstrv. asst. to pres. CEO, sr. v.p. Internat. Renaissance Developers, 1994-96; owner Paulne's Place, 1996—. Pres. PTA, Cottage Hills, Ill., 1968-69, brownie and scout leader, 1968-69. Mem. Mahoning County Legal Secs. Assn. (v.p. 1973-74, editor monthly booklet 1974-75), Exec. Link, Missionary Group Club. Democrat. Methodist. Home: 3961 Cannon Rd Youngstown OH 44515-4604

CATTANEO, MICHAEL S., heating and cooling company executive; b. Detroit, May 30, 1948; s. Alex and Bernadine (Krause) C.; m. Nancy Lucille Horsch, Sept. 6, 1969; children: Michael Alex, Jason Ryan. Cert., Lawrence Inst. Tech., 1970, Macomb Coll., 1977. Service tech. Reliable Heating and Cooling, Detroit, 1965-69; service supr. Artic Air Inc., Detroit, 1969-77; supt. Kropf Service Inc., Detroit, 1977-78; v.p., owner Greater Detroit Heating and Cooling, Inc., 1978—; owner J.B. Air Conditioning Inc., 1978—; mech., tech. educator, Career Prep. Ctr., Warren, Mich., 1982-83; tech advisor Macomb Prosecutor's Office div. consumer fraud, Mt. Clemens, Mich., 1985—. Mem. Italian Cultural Ctr. (Warren), Ams. Italian Origin. Republican. Roman Catholic. Office: Greater Detroit Heating and Cooling Inc 18334 E 9 Mile Rd East Detroit MI 48021-1961

CATTELINO, RONALD E., art education administrator; b. Pittsburg, Kans., Oct. 24, 1948; s. Eugene A. and Mary (Mazzloni) C.; m. Toni L. Thiebaud, Mar. 13, 1976; children: Jill L., Rachel J. BSBA, Pittsburg State U., 1970. Chief acct. Kansas City Art Inst., Kansas City, Mo., 1971-75; dir. fin. Kansas City Art Inst., 1975-76, v.p., 1976-89, sr. v.p., 1989—. Bd. dirs. Women's Christian Assn., chmn. 1989-91; bd. dirs. Gillis Ctr., vice chmn., 1985-87. Mem. Alpha Kappa Psi. Office: Kansas City Art Inst 4415 Warwick Blvd Kansas City MO 64111-1820

CAUDILL, CHARLOTTE, publishing executive; b. Mousie, Ky., Sept. 13, 1953; d. J.R. and Susie (Click) Hicks; m. Ted Caudill, Aug. 29, 1977; children: Patrick Theodore, Douglas Wayne. BA, teaching cert., Morehead State U., 1976. Cert. tchr., Ill. Fin. aid advisor Alice Lloyd Coll., Pippa Passes, Ky., 1976-77; libr. asst. Dundee High Sch., Carpentersville, Ill., 1979-80; internat. liaison Cahners Pub. divsn. Reed Elsevier, Des Plaines, Ill., 1980—; participant Chgo. Area Direct Mktg. Basic Course. Author several poems. Mem. Humane Soc., Knott County History Club. Recipient Golden Poet award, 1988, Silver Poet award, 1989. Mem. Direct Mktg. Assn., Sierra Club, Audubon Soc. Home: 1122 Riverwood Dr Algonquin IL 60102-3817 Office: Cahners Pub Co 1350 E Touhy Ave Des Plaines IL 60018-3303

CAUDILL, DORENE JACKSON, editor; b. Indpls., Mar. 17, 1964; d. Wayne Keith Jackson and Linda Sue (Cunningham) Jackson Crow; m. Michael E. Caudill, Feb. 28, 1992. B in Journalism and Spanish, Franklin (Ind.) Coll., 1986; M in Journalism, Ind. U., 1995. Editor newspaper Jefferson County Jour., Arnold, Mo., 1986-87, Belleville (Ill.) News-Democrat, 1987-89; editor mag. City Indpls. Woman, 1989, The Hoosier Farmer, indpls., 1989-93, Saturday Evening Post, Indpls., 1993; editor newspaper The Indpls. Star/News, 1993—; free-lance writer, Indpls., 1989—. Vol. Spanish translator Mex. Fedn. Agr. World Gymnastics Championships, 1992. Mem. Soc. Profl. Journalists (v.p. 1994-95, pres. 1995—), Soc. Collegiate Journalists (vol. judge 1990—), Order Ea. Star, Mensa. Republican. Office: The Indpls Star/News 307 N Pennsylvania St Indianapolis IN 46204

CAUDILL, TOM HOLDEN, logistics director; b. St. Augustine, Fla., June 21, 1945; s. Julian Terrill and Alta Jane (Holden) C.; m. Virginia Mary Kauss, June 26, 1971; 1 child, Mara Julia. BA in History, East Tenn. State

U., 1967, MA in Internat. Rels., 1977; MA in Mgmt. Sci., Webster U., 1980. Instr. English as second lang., polit. sci., mgmt. sci. U.S. Peace Corps, Loei, Thailand, 1970-73; instr. English as second lang., polit. sci., mgmt. sci. Steed Coll., Johnson City, Tenn., 1973-76; instr. Internat. Ctr. U. Tex., Austin, 1976-77; tng. specialist Air Tng. Command USAF, Lackland AFB, Tex., 1977-80; tng. specialist Logistics Command USAF, Wright-Patterson AFB, Ohio, 1980-81, logistics mgmt. specialist, 1981-85, chief, policy and procedures Internat. Logistics Ctr., 1985-88, chief policy and analysis, 1986—, chief plans and devel., 1988; dir. Arabian programs Internat. Logistics Ctr., 1991-95; exec. fellow Woodrow Wilson Sch. Govt. Princeton U., 1995-96; dep. dir. internat. programs Air Force Security Assistance Ctr., 1996—; vis. instr. English as a second lang., polit. sci., mgmt. sci. Antioch Coll., Yellow Springs, Ohio, 1986—; asst. dep. plans policy mgmt. systems, 1988, dir. plans and policy, 1988, tech. lead integrated logistics support, acquisition logistics div., 1988—, instr. mgmt. sci. Author: Textbook in Logistics 1988, Policy Regulations/Procedural Instructions 1986—; contbr. articles to profl. jours., 1987—. Adminstr. Refugee Assistance Program, Greene County, Ohio, 1981-84, AFS chpt. v.p.; Scoutmaster Buckeye Trails coun. Girl Scout U.S., Yellow Springs, 1982-86; active Dayton (Ohio) Coun. on World Affairs, 1984—; pres. local chpt. Am. Field Svc., Greene County, 1988—. Mem LWV (fin. chm. Greene county chpt. 1987—). Democratic. Methodist. Home: 445 W South College St Yellow Springs OH 45387-1422 Office: Air Force Security Assist Ctr AFSAC/IP Wright Patterson AFB OH 45433

CAUFIELD, THOMAS J., financial planner; b. Indpls., Mar. 24, 1959. BA, Coe Coll., Cedar Rapids, Iowa, 1982. Stockbroker Prudential Securities, Indpls., 1983-84; br. mgr. A.G. Edwards & Sons, Quincy, Ill., 1984—. Republican. Episcopalian. Home: 19 Lancaster Dr Quincy IL 62301-8613 Office: AG Edwards & Sons Inc 3325 Maine St Quincy IL 62301-4438

CAULFIELD, JOAN, academic relations coordinator, educator; b. St. Joseph, Mo., July 17, 1943; d. Joseph A. and Jane (Lisenby) Caulfield; BS in Edn. cum laude, U. Mo., 1963, MA in Spanish, 1965, PhD, 1978; postgrad. (Mexican Govt. scholar) Nat. U. Mexico, 1962-63. TV tchr. Spanish, Kansas City (Mo.) pub. schs., 1963-68; tchr. Spanish, French Bingham Jr. High Schs., Kansas City, 1968-78; asst. prin. S.E. High Sch., Kansas City, 1984; prin. Nowlin Jr. High Sch., Independence, Mo., 1984-86, Lincoln Coll. Preparatory Acad., Kansas City, Mo., 1986-88, asst. supt., Kansas City, 1988-89; part-time instr. U. Mo.-Kansas City; dir. English Inst., Rockhurst Coll., summers, 1972-75, coord. sch. coll. rels., 1989—; mem. nat. steering com. Brain-Based Learning Network; assessor dept. elem. and secondary edn. State Mo. Mem. Sister City Commn., Kansas City, 1980—, Kans.' Quality Performance Assessment Team; ofcl. translator to mayor on trip to Seville, Spain, 1969; bd. dirs. Kansas City chpt. NCCJ, Expo '92 World's Fair, Seville, Spain (translator 1992), St. Theresa's Acad., 1991-94, Kansas City Acad. of Learning; selected leadership training Greater Mo.; trainer Harmony in a World of Difference, 1989-93; mem. task force C. of C.bd. dirs. Girls to Women. Named Outstanding Secondary Educator, 1973. Mem. ASCD, Romance Lang. Assn., Nat. Assn. Secondary Sch. Prins., MLA (contbr. jour.), Am. Assn. Tchrs. Spanish & Portuguese, Friends of Seville, Friends of Art, Magnet Schs. Am. (contbr. jour.), Mo. Mid. Sch. Assn. (contbr. jour.), Phi Sigma Iota, Phi Delta Kappa, Delta Kappa Gamma (state scholar 1977-78, contbr. jour. Bulletin), Phi Kappa Phi, Sigma Delta Pi. Presbyterian. Home: 431 W 70th St Kansas City MO 64113-2022 Office: 1100 Rockhurst Rd Kansas City MO 64110-2545

CAUSEY, EARL WAYNE, insurance company executive; b. St. Louis, Feb. 12, 1945; s. Doyle Edward and Virginia Lorene (Book) C.; m. Stella Ann Holtgrieve, Aug. 12, 1966 (dec. Jan. 1995); children: Amanda Book, John Doyle. Student, U. Mo., 1964-67. Svc. rep. Monumental Life Ins. Co., Balt., 1967-74, MFA Ins. Cos., Columbia, Mo., 1974-75, Sentry Ins. Cos., Stevens Point, Wis., 1975-76, Nat. Life and Accident, Nashville, 1976-79; dist. mgr. Farmland Ins. Cos., Des Moines, 1979-84; co-owner, mgr. Causey-Bauer and Assocs., St. Charles, Mo., 1984—. Mem. Ind. Ins. Agts. Am., Profl. Ind. Ins. Agts. Mo. Office: Causey-Bauer & Assocs 119 S Main St Saint Charles MO 63301-2863

CAVANAGH, MICHAEL FRANCIS, state supreme court justice; b. Detroit, Oct. 21, 1940; s. Sylvester J. and Mary Irene (Timmins) C.; m. Patricia E. Ferriss, Apr. 30, 1966; children: Jane Elizabeth, Michael F., Megan Kathleen. BA, U. Detroit, 1962, JD, 1966. Bar: Mich. 1966. Law clk. to presiding justice Ct. Appeals, Detroit, 1966-67; atty. City of Lansing, Mich., 1967-69; ptnr. Farhat, Story, et al., Lansing, Mich., 1969-73; judge 54-A Dist. Ct., Lansing, 1973-75, Mich. Ct. Appeals, Lansing, 1975-82; justice Supreme Ct., Lansing, 1983—, chief justice, 1991-94; supervising justice Sentencing Guidelines Com., Lansing, 1983-94, Mich. Jud. Inst., Lansing, 1986-94; bd. dirs. Thomas M. Cooley Law Sch., 1979-88; with Mich. Justice Project, 1994-95, Nat. Interbranch Conf., 1994-95; chair Mich. Justice project, Lansing, 1994-95; chair Nat. Interbrance Conf., Mpls. Bd. dirs. Am. Heart Assn. Mich., 1982—, chmn. bd. Am. Heart Assn. Mich., Lathrup Village, 1985; bd. dirs. YMCA, Lansing, 1978, chair Mich. Justice Project, Lansing, Mich., chair Nat. Interbranch, Mpls. Mem. ABA, Ingham County Bar Assn., Inst. Jud. Adminstrn. (hon.), Inc. Soc. of Irish/Am. Lawyers (pres. 1987-88). Democrat. Roman Catholic. Home: 234 Kensington Rd East Lansing MI 48823-4006 Office: Mich Supreme Ct PO Box 30052 Lansing MI 48909-7552

CAVANAUGH, JEAN, medical secretary; b. Lake City, Iowa, June 27, 1924; d. Orrin Ellsworth and Golda Mae (Howard) VanHorn; m. Clair Joseph Cavanaugh, 1947; children: Thomas Paul, Kathleen Ann Bowman, Michael John, Terrence Joseph, James Clair. BS in Bus. Edn., Ft. Hays State U., Hays, Kans., 1970, MS in Guidance and Counseling, 1971, Edn. Specialist, 1975. Cert. tchr. Clk., fingerprint classifier FBI, Washington, 1942-44; pollster Gallup Polls, Great Bend, Kans., 1974-82; substitute tchr. Great Bend Sch. Dist., 1971-84; med. sec. Cen. Kans. Med. Ctr., Great Bend, 1974—; bd. dirs. First Bank & Trust Co., Glidden, Iowa. Bd. mem. Unified Sch. Dist. 428, Great Bend, 1979—; exec. sec. Golden Belt Cmty. Concerts, 1979—; sec. Barton County Health Fair Bd., 1983-90, Ret. Sr. Vol. Program, 1985—; bd. dirs. Smoky Hills Pub. TV, 1991—, vp. bd.; active Sr. Ctr. Adv. Bd.; cmty. mem. Wellness Com., 1995-96. Named Woman of Yr., Bus. and Profl. Women, Great Bend, 1976. Mem. AAUW, Am. Med. Assn. Aux. (regional v. p. Midwestern regional 1985-87), So. Med. Assn. Aux. (councilor 1986-89, 92-96, by-laws com. 1992), Northwest Family Cmty. Edn. Unit (sec.), C. of C. (edn. com. 1989—), Pilot Internat. of Great Bend (dir., pres.-elect 1989-90, pres. 1991-92, gov.-elect Kans.-Mo. dist. 1993, pilot gov. Kans.-Mo. dist. 1994-95), Kans. Assn. Middle Level Edn., Nat. Middle Sch. Assn., Kans. Assn. Sch. Bd. Region 8 Legis. (chmn. 1996-97), Athenian and Cosmopolitan Study Clubs, Phi Delta Kappa. Roman Catholic. Home: 5103 Telstar Great Bend KS 67530

CAVANAUGH, PAUL FRANCIS, JR., biochemical pharmacologist; b. Rochester, N.Y., Oct. 23, 1955; s. Paul Francis and Ann Marie Cavanaugh; m. Kathleen Anne Vastola, Apr. 9, 1983; children: Anthony, Samuel. BS in Chemistry, Boston Coll., 1977; PhD in Biochem. Pharmacology, SUNY, Buffalo, 1983. Cancer rsch. scientist Roswell Park Meml. Inst., Buffalo, 1982-86; sr. rsch. investigator Eastman Kodak Co./Sterling Winthrop Inc., Malvern, Pa., 1986-92, Health Care Divsn., Procter and Gamble Co., Cin., 1992-96; vol. assoc. prof. dept. otolaryngology head and neck surgery U. Cin. Coll. of Medicine, 1993—; sr. rsch. investigator Procter & Gamble Pharms., Cin., 1996—. Mem. Am. Assn. Cancer Rsch., Am. Chem. Soc., N.Y. Acad. Sci., Rho Chi. Office: Procert & Gamble Pharms Health Care Divsn 11450 Grooms Rd Cincinnati OH 45242

CAVENDER, JEANNE MCLAREN, artist; b. Monesson, Pa.; d. Hugh Ross and Mary Eleanor (Park) McLaren; m. Carl Franklyn Cavender, June 7, 1947; children: Sandra Moore, Carla, Charles Brauchler, Elizabeth Queen. BA, Denison U., 1945; student classical arranging, Ikenobo Sch., Kyoto, Japan, 1960-70, student modern Japanese flower arranging, 1969-70. Pres. Canton (Ohio) Garden Ctr., 1976, 3rd v.p., 1972, 2d v.p., 1973, 1st v.p., 1974-75; pres. Arboretum Garden Club, Canton, 1958. Editor: (newspaper) Canton Garden Ctr., 1962-63; writer Canton Newspapers, local periodicals, 1964-74; author children's books, short stories and poetry. Mem. Nat. League of Am. Pen Women (Arts and Letters award 1981), Am. Watercolor Soc. (assoc.), Coll. Club of Canton, Ikebana Internat., Sans Souci Garden Club, Hudson Soc. of Arts, Ohio Coun. of Nat. Accredited Flower Show Judges, Nat. Coun. of State Flower Show Judges (master judge). Republican. Lutheran. Home: 3605 Darlington Ave NW Canton OH 44708

CAWELTI, G. SCOTT, English language educator; b. Cedar Falls, Iowa, July 19, 1943; s. Elmer Carlyle and Laverne Inabel (Edwards) C.; m. Martha Jane Waterman, Dec. 1, 1977 (div. Dec. 1995); children: Christa, Jason. BA in Music, U. No. Iowa, Cedar Falls, 1965, MA in English, 1968; PhD in English, State U. Iowa, Iowa City, 1978. Tchr. music Holstein (Iowa) Pub. Schs., 1965-66; instr. English U. No. Iowa, 1968-71, asst. prof., 1971-86, assoc. prof., 1986-95, prof., 1995—, univ. writing advisor, 1988-90; cons. on software Burroughs Corp., Detroit, 1984-85; cons. editor Jour. Creative Behavior, Buffalo, 1992-95. Co-author: (textooks) Introduction to College Writing, 1991, The Inventive Writer, 1993; radio commentator KUNI, Cedar Falls, 1980-95; columnist Waterloo (Iowa) Courier, 1980-95. Recipient award of merit for columns Women in Comms., 1995. Mem. Nat. Coun. Tchrs. English, Iowa Coun. Tchrs. English (pres. coll. sect. 1985-87). Home: 3743 Beaver Ridge Cir Cedar Falls IA 50613 Office: U No Iowa Baker Hall Cedar Falls IA 50614

CAWOOD, ALBERT MCLAURIN (HAP CAWOOD), newspaper editor; b. Harlan, Ky., Nov. 10, 1939; s. Frank Finley and C. Eugene (Barwick) C.; m. Sonia Barreiro, July 3, 1965; children: Romy Lanier, Shuly Xochitl. BA in English, Union Coll., 1962; MA in Journalism, Ohio State U., 1966. Asst. city editor Dayton (Ohio) Daily News, 1966, editorial writer, 1966-82, editorial page editor, 1982—. Vol. Peace Corps, Sierra Leone, 1962-64; chmn. Ohio Com. on Crime and Delinquency, 1969-70. Recipient Disting. Svc. award for Editorial Writing, Nat. Soc. Profl. Journalists, 1968, Walker Stone award for Editorial Writing, Scripps-Howard Found., 1984. Mem. Am. Soc. Newspaper Editors, Nat. Conf. Editorial Writers, Union Coll. Alumni Assn. (pres. 1985-87). Democrat. Home: 211 S Winter St Yellow Springs OH 45387-1730 Office: Dayton Daily News PO Box 1287 Dayton OH 45401-1287

CAYTON, JOHN CHARLES, criminalist, forensic consultant; b. Kansas City, Mo., Sept. 15, 1943; s. Charles Leo Abraham and Georgina Marie (Edson) C.; m. Kathleen Ann DiSanto, Sept. 10, 1962 (div. Dec. 1964); m. Mary Kathleen Fields, May 7, 1965; children: Dianna Marie, Shelley Roxann, Bryant Alan, Kerry Christina. Student, Kansas City (Mo.) Jr. Coll., 1964-67, U. Mo., Kansas City; BS, Ctrl. Mo. State U., Warrensburg, 1974, MS, 1985. With acctg. dept. Bus. Men's Assurance Co., Kansas city, 1958-61; with maintenance dept. Kansas City Terminal R.R., 1966-68; forensic examiner Police Crime Lab. Kansas City (Mo.) Police Dept., 1969-72, firearm and evidence examiner Regional Criminalistic Lab., 1972-74, supr. firearm and evidencesect., 1975-77, chief forensic firearm and tool mark examiner, 1977—; chief warrant officer U.S. Army CId Crime Lab., Frankfurt Germany and Ft. Gullen, Ga., 1980—; keynote speaker 10th Australian-Internat. Forensic Sci. Symposium,Brisbane, 1988. Asst. scout leader Boy Scouts Am., Grandview, Mo., 1966. Served with USAR, 1961—. Recipient award for valor Met. Police Chief and Sheriff Assn., 1976, MeritoriousSvc. award Kansas City Police, 1979, others. Mem. Assn. Firearm and Tool Mark Examiners (disting. life; past 1st v.p. and pres., Disting. Mem. award 1976), Midwestern Assn. Forensic Sci. (charter; firearm com.), Internat. Wound Ballistics Assn., Internat. Assn. for Identification (pres. Mo. div. 1980). Republican. Mem. Ch. of God. Home: 1325 SW Wamsley Rd Osborn MO 64474 Office: Regional Crime Lab 1525 Holmes Kansas City MO 64108

CAYTON, MARY KUPIEC, historian, educator; b. Washington, Mar. 21, 1954; d. Henry Frank and Claire Helen (Carroll) Kupiec; m. Andrew Robert Lee Cayton, Aug. 23, 1975; children: Elizabeth Renanne, Hannah Kupiec. BA in Psychology and English, U. Va., 1976; AM in Am. Civilization, Brown U., 1978, PhD in Am. Civilization, 1981. Postdoctoral fellow Boston (Mass.) U., 1981-82; vis. asst. prof. Sch. Interdisciplinary Studies Miami U., Oxford, Ohio, 1982-88; asst. prof. Am. studies Miami U., Oxford, 1988-91, assoc. dir. univ. honors program, 1987-91, assoc. prof. Am. studies, 1991-92, assoc. prof. history and Am. studies, 1992—; cons. rsch. historian Conner Prairie Pioneer Settlement, Noblesville, Ind., 1983-84. Author: Emerson's Emergence: Self and Society in the Transformation of New England, 1989; co-editor: Encyclopedia of American Social History, 1993 (Dartmouth Honor cert. 1993). Summer Rsch. grantee NEH, 1991. Mem. Am. Studies Assn. (chairwomen's com. 1993-94), Orgn. Am. Historians, Soc. for Historians of the Early Am. Republic (chair book prize com. 1995). Office: Dept History Miami Univ Oxford OH 45056

CAYWOOD, CLARKE LAWRENCE, marketing educator, public relations executive; b. Madison, Wis., Mar. 13, 1947; s. Fred Lawrence and Marjorie Caroline (Clarke) C.; m. Mary Margaret Westing, Dec. 15, 1973; children: Matthew Shields, Emily Margaret, Graham Clarke. BBA, U. Wis., 1969, PhD, 1985; MPA, U. Tex., 1972. Asst. to gov. Exec. Office, Madison, 1969-70; research assoc. Lyndon Baines Johnson Sch. Pub. Affairs, U. Tex., Austin, 1971-72; legis. officer Office of Atty. Gen., Madison, 1972-74; exec. dir. Friends of Channel 21, Sta. WHA-TV, Madison, 1975-76; lectr. U. Wis., Whitewater, 1976-78; asst. prof. Marquette U., Milw., 1978-87; vis. asst. prof. U. Wis., Madison, 1987-89; assoc. prof. Medill Sch. Journalism Northwestern U., Evanston, 1989—; bd. dirs. Direct Selling Edn. Found., Washington, Nat. Telemedia Coun., Madison; cons. IBM-Midwest, Scania, Kreab, Applied Power, Budgetel Corp., Wis., IBM-Europe, State of Wis. Contbr. articles to profl. jours. Adv. council Office of Lt. Gov., Madison, 1988; del. Wis. Rep. Party Conv., 1974-88; campaign dir. Friends of Scott McCallum, Wis., 1986. Mem. Am. Acad. Advt., Am. Mktg. Assn., Assn. Edn. on Jour. and Mass Comm., Arthur W. Page Soc. (trustee), PRSA (nat. hon. chpt.), Beta Gamma Sigma. Republican. Presbyterian. Home: 936 Sheridan Rd Wilmette IL 60091-1938 Office: Northwestern U Medill Sch Evanston IL 60208-1290

CAZABON, GILLES, bishop; b. Verner, Ont., Can., Apr. 5, 1933. Ordained priest, 1960, bishop, 1992. Bishop Diocese of Timmins, Ont., 1992—. Office: Diocese of Timmins, 65 avenue Jubilee est, Timmins, ON Canada P4N 5W4

CECCOLI, ANTHONY J., mechanical design engineer; b. Lakewood, Ohio, July 11, 1965; s. John W. and Mary Lou (Wagner) C.; m. Dianne L. Budd, June 13, 1992. BSME, U. Akron, 1989, BS in Applied Math., 1989. Registered engr.-in-tng., Ohio. Customer engr. CAD EDS, Dayton, Ohio, 1989-90; mech. project engr. Lorain (Ohio) Products, 1990-92; mech. design engr. Allen Bradley, Cleve., 1992—. Patent in Shock and Vibration Mounting at Indsl. Work Station. Mem. Holy Trinity Luth. Ch., Brunswick, Ohio, 1992. Named to Dean's list U. Akron, 1987-88, 88-89. Lutheran. Home: 10495 Westwood Rd Columbia Twp OH 44028 Office: Allen Bradley 747 Alpha Dr Cleveland OH 44143

CECH, DONALD, project manager; b. Chgo., Mar. 15, 1935. B, U. Denver, 1956. Designer Internat. Harvestor, Hinsdale, Ill., 1960-82; project mgr. Case Corp., Hinsdale, Ill., 1988—. Patentee in field. Sgt. U.S. Army, 1988-61.

CECH, JOSEPH HAROLD, chemical engineer; b. Flint, Mich., Oct. 8, 1951; s. Joseph, Jr. and Margaret Luella (Taphouse) C. BS in Chem. Engring., Mich. Tech. U., 1978. Trainee, Menasha Corp., North Bend, Oreg., 1978-79, project engr. molded products div., Watertown, Wis., 1979-84, plastic devel. engr., 1984-86, composite engr., coordinator, 1986-90, sr. process engr., 1990-92, process material supr., 1992-96, material/process mgr., 1996—. Served with USN, 1971-75. Mem. Mensa, Soc. Plastic Engrs., Am. Inst. Chem. Engrs., Nat. Geog. Soc., Watertown Conservation Club. Methodist. Office: 426 S Montgomery St Watertown WI 53094-6132

CECIL, DORCAS ANN, property management executive; b. Greensboro, N.C., Mar. 31, 1945; d. George Joseph and Marianne Elizabeth (Zimmerman) Ernst; m. Richard Lee Cecil, June 8, 1968; children: Sarah, Matthew. BA, U. Ark., 1967. Pres. B & C Enterprises Property Mgmt., Ltd., O'Fallon, Ill., 1977-93, Cecil Mgmt. Group, Inc., O'Fallon and St. Louis, 1993—. Bd. dirs. O'Fallon Pub. Libr., 1983—, v.p., 1986-87, pres., 1987—; sec. St. Vincent de Paul Soc., 1987—; bd. dirs. Leadership Coun. Southwestern Ill., 1994—. Named Realtor of Yr., Belleville Area Assn. Realtors, 1994. Mem. Inst. Real Estate Mgmt. (cert., v.p. 1987, pres. St. Louis chpt. 1990, vice chmn. Nat. IREM std. coms. 1991—, regional v.p. 1992-93, governing councillor 1994—, nat. ethics and discipline hearing bd. 1994—), St. Louis Multi-Housing Coun., Profl. Housing Mgmt. Assn., Cmty. Assns. Inst., Nat. Assn. Realtors, Ill. Assn. Realtors (housing com. 1994—), Belleville Assn. Realtors (bd. dirs. 1991-94, Realtor of Yr. 1994), Mo. Assn. Realtors, Belleville Bd. Realtors C. of C. (bd. dirs. 1987-96, v.p. 1988—, pres. 1992-93), O'Fallon C. of C. Office: Cecil Mgmt Group Inc PO Box 459 O'Fallon IL 62269

CECIL, FRANCES (FRANCES VANDER MYDE), nursing administrator, medical surgical nurse, hotel executive; b. Chgo., Nov. 18, 1945; d. Walter John and Rosemary Christine (Albietz) Vander Myde; m. William Robert Cecil, Feb. 13, 1981; children: Laura Beth Gartner, Jennifer Susan Gartner. Diploma in nursing, Presbyn.-St. Luke's Hosp., Chgo., 1966; BA in Health Svcs. Adminstrn., Governor's State U., 1980, MS in Mgmt., 1980-81; MS, Cardinal Stritch Coll., 1983. RN, Ill., Wis.; cert. BLS, ACLS, cardiac/critical care. ICU/CCU nurse mgr. St. Francis Hosp., Milw.; clin. svcs. adminstr. Midwest Homecare Specialists, Milw.; supr. emergency rm. Door County Meml. Hosp., Sturgeon Bay, Wis.; dir. cardiac telemetry St. Vincent Hosp., Green Bay, Wis.; co-owner The Scofield House Bed & Breakfast, Sturgeon Bay, Wis.; part-time house supr. St. Vincent Hosp., 1990—. Recipient #10 in top 25 Inns U.S.A., 1994. Mem. Am. Orgn. Nursing Execs., Door County C. of C., Wis. Bed and Breakfast Hist. Inns Assn. Home: The Scofield House B&B 908 Michigan St Sturgeon Bay WI 54235-1849

CEDAR, PAUL ARNOLD, church executive, minister; b. Mpls., Nov. 4, 1938; s. Carl Benjamin and Bernice M. (Peterson) C.; m. Jean Helen Lier, Aug. 25, 1959; children: Daniel Paul, Mark John, Deborah Jean. BS, No. State Coll., Aberdeen, S.D., 1960; MDiv, No. Bap. Theol. Sem., 1968; Calif. State U., Fullerton, 1971; DMin, Am. Baptist Sem. of the West, 1973. Ordained to ministry Evang. Free Ch., 1966. Youth for Christ, crusade dir. Billy Graham Evang. Assn., Leighton Ford Team, 1960-65; pastor Evang. Free Ch., Naperville, Ill., 1965-67, Yorba Linda, Calif., 1969-73; exec. pastor 1st Presbyn. Ch. Hollywood, Calif., 1975-81; sr. pastor Lake Ave. Congl. Ch., Pasadena, Calif., 1981-90; pres. Evang. Free Ch. Am., Mpls., 1990-96; chmn., CEO Mission Am., 1995—; guest dean Billy Graham Sch. Evangelism, Mpls., 1983—; vis. prof. Fuller Theol. Sem., Pasadena, Talbot Theol. Sem., La Habra, Calif., Trinity Div. Sch., Deerfield, Ill. Author: How to Make Love Your Motive, 1977, Becoming a Lover, 1978, Seven Keys to Maximum Communication, 1980, Sharing the Good Life, 1980, Communicators Commentary, 1983, Strength in Servant Leadership, 1987, Mastering the Pastoral Role, 1991, Where Is Hope?, 1992. Mem. Internat. Lausanne Com.; chmn. U.S. Lausanne Com. for World Evangelization, 1992—, Internat. Coalition, AD 2000 and Beyond Movement; mem. adv. bd. African Enterprise. Mem. Christian TV and Film Commn. (adv. bd.), Internat. Students, Ron Hutchcraf Ministries, Worldwide Leadership Coun., Caleb Ministries, Leadership Renewal Ctr., John M. Perkins Found., Nat. Prayer Com., Revival Prayer Fellowship, Barnabas Internat., Pioneer Clubs. Office: Evang Free Ch Am 901 E 78th St Minneapolis MN 55420-1334

CEILLEY, ROGER I., dermatologist, oncologist, educator; b. Cedar Falls, Iowa, May 18, 1945; married; children: Elizabeth, John, Michael. BA, U. No. Iowa, 1967; MD, U. Iowa, 1971. Diplomate Am. Bd. Dermatology, Am. Bd. Dermatopathology. Intern U. Colo., 1971-72; resident in dermatology U. Iowa, 1974-77; preceptorship in chemosurgery U. Wis., 1976; instr. dept. dermatology U. Iowa, Iowa City, 1976-77, asst. prof. dept. dermatology, 1977-79, asst. clin. prof. dept. dermatology, 1979—; fellowship dir. Mohs' Micrographic Surgery and Cutaneous Oncology, Des Moines, 1990—; pvt. practice Des Moines, 1979—; mem. adv. and med. couns. of Skin Cancer Found., 1989; mem. credentials com. Univ Hosps., Iowa City, 1977-79, cancer com., 1978-79; mem. tumor bd. Iowa Meth. Med. Ctr., Des Moines, 1980-81, admission com., 1980-81, cancer com., 1983—; advisor on Task Force on Biomed. Comm., 1983-88. Served to comdr. USPHS, 1969-74. Recipient Biering Cup award Med. Libr. Club Des Moines, 1986, Bruner-Biering Cup award Med. Libr. Club Des Moines, 1987-88. Fellow Am. Acad. Dermatology (bd. dirs. 1990, bd. dirs. liaison to bylaws com. 1994-95, pres-elect 1996), Am. Coll. Chemosurgery, Am. Acad. Facial and Plastic Reconstructive Surgery; mem. AMA, Am. Coll. Physicians (assoc.), Am. Thoracic Soc. (assoc.), Student Am. Med. Assn., Okla. Med. Soc., Phoenix Med. Soc., Ariz. Med. Soc., Soc. for Investigative Dermatology, Iowa Dermatol. Soc. (sec.-treas. 1977-79), Am. Soc. for Dermatol. Surgery (pres.-elect 1987), Am. Coll. Chemosurgery, Iowa Med. Soc. (del.), Soc. for Pediat. Dermatology, Am. Acad. Facial and Reconstructive Surgery, Internat. Soc. for Pediat. Dermatology, Polk County Med. Soc. (del. to Iowa Med. Soc. 1984-87), Iowa Dermatol. Soc. (sec.-treas. 1979-80, pres. 1980-81), Am. Soc. for Dermatol. Surgery (bd. dirs. 1981-84, pres. 1988-89), Noah Worcester Soc. (bd. dirs. 1986), Am. Soc. for Dermatol. Surgery (sec. 1983-85, v.p. 1986), Am. Soc. Dermatopathology, Am. Dermatol. Assn., Pacific Dermatology Assn. (hon.), Tau Kappa Epsilon, Beta Beta Beta, Phi Beta Pi, Alpha Omega Alpha. Home: 804 38th St West Des Moines IA 50265 Office: Dermatology Assocs 6000 University Ste 450 West Des Moines IA 50266

CELEBREZZE, ANTHONY J., JR., lawyer; b. Cleve., Sept. 8, 1941; s. Anthony J. and Anne M. C.; m. Louisa Godwin, June 19, 1965; children: Anthony J. III, Catherine, Charles, David, Maria. BS, U.S. Naval Acad., 1963; MS, George Washington U., 1966; JD, Cleve. State U., 1973. Bar: Ohio 1973. Ptnr. Celebrezze and Marco, Cleve., 1975-79; mem. Ohio State Senate, 1975-79; sec. of state State of Ohio, Columbus, 1979-83, atty. gen., 1983-91; ptnr. Porter Wright Morris and Arthur, Columbus, 1991-96, Dinsmore & Shohl, Columbus, 1996—; bd. dirs. Environ. Law Inst., 1989-94. Pres. Joint Vets. Commn. of Cyahoga County, Ohio, 1977; v.p. Lake Erie Regional Transp. Authority, 1972-74; mem. Gt. Lakes Commn., 1975-78, vice chmn., 1977-78, Nat. Environ. Enforcement Coun., 1988-91. With USN, 1963-68, capt. USNR, ret. Decorated Navy Commendation medal, Meritorious Svc. medal; recipient Jeffersonian Lodge award, 1977, Man of Yr. award Delta Theta Phi, Freedoms Found. Honor medal, 1980, 86, Disting. Service award Buckeye Assn. Sch. Adminstrs., 1987. Mem. Nat. Assn. of Atty. Gen. (chmn environ. com. 1985-86, vice-chmn. antitrust com., 1987-88). Democrat. Roman Catholic. Office: Dinsmore & Shohl 175 S 3d St 10th Fl Columbus OH 43215-5134

CELIC, LILLIAN CHRISTINA, consciousness and growth techniques educator; b. Blue Island, Ill., Aug. 20, 1947; d. Urban J. and Antje C. Schellhase; m. Alan J. Iliff, June 11, 1983. BS in Biology, Ill. Inst. Tech., 1969. Med. rschr. U. Chgo. Hosps., 1969-70, Northwestern Meml. Hosp., Chgo., 1971-73, VA Lakeside Hosp., Chgo., 1973-88; rsch. assoc. Northwestern U. Med. Sch., Chgo., 1988-94; cons. in consciousness phenomenology Chgo., 1970—, tchr. charisma and stage presence, 1989—; lectr. corps mem. Lyric Opera of Chgo., 1992—; cons. astrologer, Chgo., 1975—; pub. spkr. in field, 1969—. Contbr. articles to profl. publs. Mem. Nat. Coun. for Geocosmic Rsch. (cert., pres. Chgo. chpt. 1996—), Ill. Soc. for Psychic Rsch. (pres. 1986-87), Rosicrucian Order (regional monitor 1994—), Nefertiti Lodge (master 1984-85), Am. Fedn. Astrologers. Home and Office: 1049 N Leavitt St Chicago IL 60622

CELLA, A. F., chief engineer; b. Detroit, Dec. 11, 1946. BS, GM Inst., 1969. Registered profl. engr., Mich. Test engr. Chrysler, Detroit, 1972-74; project engr. Mech. Tech. Inc., Latham, N.Y., 1974-79; chief engr. Parker Hannifin Corp., Metamora, Ohio, 1979—. Patentee in field; contbr. articles to profl. jours. Office: Parker Hannifin Corp 16810 County Road 2 Metamora OH 43540-9714

CENTA, WILLIAM JAMES, manufacturing executive; b. Cleve., July 17, 1952; s. Andrew Edward and Phyllis Elizabeth (Cleary) C.; m. Renee Maria Halik, Aug. 9, 1975; children: Lauren M., Jennifer M. BBA, Bowling Green (Ohio) State U., 1974; MBA, Cleve. State U., 1977; postgrad., Cleve.-Marshal Law Sch., 1983-84. CPA, Ohio. Dep. dir. acctg. United Way Svcs., Cleve., 1974-76; sr. mgr. Arthur Andersen & Co., Cleve., 1977-84; v.p. fin. Invacare Internat., London, 1984-86; contr. Invacare Corp., Elyria, Ohio, 1986-88; chief fin. officer, chief oper. officer Leemar Steel Co., Inc., Cleve., 1988-90; chmn., chief exec. officer Bentbrook Enterprises Inc., Cleve., 1989-90; v.p. fin. W.S. Tyler, Inc., Gastonia, N.C., 1990-92, v.p. and gen. mgr. media ops., 1992-94; pres. Kal Equip Co., Cleve., 1994-96, Actron Internat., Cleve., 1996—; cons. Hallmark Fin. Group, Inc., Cleve., 1986-92. Mem.

Am. Inst. CPA's, Ohio Soc. CPA's, Beta Gamma Sigma, Alpha Tau Omega. Republican. Roman Catholic. Home: 12466 Bentbrook Ln Chesterland OH 44026-2459 Office: Actron Mfg Co 9999 Walford Ave Cleveland OH 44102-9999

CENTNER, CHARLES WILLIAM, law educator; b. Battle Creek, Mich., July 4, 1915; s. Charles William and Lucy Irene (Patterson); m. Evi Rohr, Dec. 22, 1956; children: Charles Patterson, David William, Geoffrey Christopher. AB, U. Chgo., 1936, AM, 1936, AM, 1939, PhD, 1941; JD, Detroit Coll. Law, 1970; LLB, LaSalle Extension U., 1965. Bar: Mich. 1970. Asst. prof. U. N.D., 1940-41, Tulane U., New Orleans, 1941-42; liaison officer for Latin Am., Lend-Lease Adminstrn., 1942; assoc. dir. Western Hemisphere div. Nat. Fgn Trade Coun., N.Y., 1946-52; exec. Ford Motor Co., Detroit, 1952-57, Chrysler Corp. and Chrysler Internat. S.A., Detroit and Geneva, Switzerland, 1957-70; adj. prof. Wayne State U., U. Detroit, Wayne County Community Coll., 1970—. Author: Great Britain and Chile, 1810-1914, 1941. Lt. comdr. USNR, 1942-45. Mem. ABA, State Bar Mich., Oakland County Bar Assn., Masons. Republican. Episcopalian. Home: 936 Harcourt Rd Grosse Pointe MI 48230-1874

CENTO, WILLIAM FRANCIS, retired newspaper editor; b. St. Louis, Mar. 20, 1932; s. Frank and Augusta (Albietz) C.; m. Vera Ann Shaide, May 16, 1964. BS, St. Louis U., 1954. Gen. assignment reporter East St. Louis (Ill.) Jour., 1954-56; suburban editor Globe-Democrat, St. Louis, 1956-61; copy-editor Post-Dispatch, St. Louis, 1961-62; make-up editor Pioneer Press, St. Paul, 1962-65, wire editor, 1965-67, Sunday editor, 1967-73; graphics editor Pioneer Press & Dispatch, St. Paul, 1974-77; mng. editor St. Paul Dispatch, 1977-84; assoc. editor Pioneer Press, St. Paul, 1984-90; owner Give Me Rewrite, West St. Paul, 1990—; editor, pub. Letter from Minn., West St. Paul, 1995—. Editor: Fifty and Feisty APME: 1933 to 1983, 1983. Recipient numerous awards including Twin Cities Newspaper Guild Page 1 award Makeup 1st pl. award, 1969, 71, 74, 2d pl., 1971, 72, Award of Appreciation, AP Mng. Editors Assn., 1983. Mem. Soc. Profl. Journalists. Roman Catholic. Home: # 103 111 Imperial Dr W West Saint Paul MN 55118-2226

CERA, JACK, state legislator; m. Becky Cera; children: Jaclyn, Bethany Anne. BA, Brown U., 1978. Mem. Ohio Ho. of Reps., Columbus, 1983—; vice chmn. pub. safety and hwys. com., mem. agr. and natural resources com., pub. utilities, fin. and appropriations com., energy and environ. com., coal tech. adv. com. and bd. unreclaimed strip mined lands, mem. radioactive waste adv. com.; mem. Nat. Conf. State Legislators. Recipient Alumni Achievement award Bellaire H.S., 1985. Mem. Bellaire Jaycees, Belmont County Vets. Vietnam War, Sons of Italy, Bellaire Touchdown Club, Italian Am. Club, Eagles. Democrat. Home: 63899 Violet Ln Bellaire OH 43906-9502*

CERE, RONALD CARL, languages educator, consultant, researcher; b. N.Y.C., Oct. 22, 1947; s. Mindie Anthony and Edvige Clelia (Ruggero) C. BA, CUNY, 1968; MA, Queens Coll., 1969; PhD, NYU, 1974. Asst. prof. SUNY, Old Westbury, 1974-77, U. Ill., Urbana, 1977-80, U. Nebr., Lincoln, 1980-83, Gettysburg (Pa.) Coll., 1983-85; prof. Ea. Mich. U., Ypsilanti, 1985-90, 1990—; cons. Trinity Dynamics, N.J., Harcourt Brace Jovanovich, Harper & Collins, D.C. Heath, Prentice-Hall, Random House, Scott Foresman Pub. Cos., 1985—; speaker, presenter in field. Author: Los Fabulistas, 1969, Exito Comercial, 1990; contbr. articles to profl. jours. Recipient James C. Healy award NYU, 1974. Mem. MLA, ASTD, Am. Assn. Tchrs. Spanish and Portuguese (dir. career svcs.), Am.Coun. Teaching Fgn. Langs., Soc. for Intercultural Edn., Tng. and Rsch., Southern Conf. Lang. Teaching (bd. advisors). Home: 2245 Glencoe Hills Dr Apt 7 Ann Arbor MI 48108-3017 Office: Ea Mich U Dept Fgn Langs 219 Alexander Hall Ypsilanti MI 48197-2255

CERNY, JOSEPH CHARLES, urologist, educator; b. Oak Park, Ill., Apr. 20, 1930; s. Joseph James and Mary (Turek) C.; m. Patti Bobette Pickens, Nov. 10, 1962; children: Joseph Charles, Rebecca Anne. BA, Knox Coll., 1952; MD, Yale U., 1956. Diplomate Am. Bd. Urology. Intern U. Mich. Hosp., Ann Arbor, 1956-57, resident, 1957-62; practice medicine specializing in urology, Ann Arbor, and Detroit since 1962—; inst. surgery (urology) U. Mich., Ann Arbor, 1962-64, asst. prof., 1964-66, assoc. prof., 1966-71, clin. prof., 1971—; chmn. dept. urology Henry Ford Hosp., Detroit, 1971—; pres. Resistors, Inc., Chgo., 1960—; cons. St. Joseph Hosp., Ann Arbor, 1973—. Mem. editorial bd. Am. Jour. Kidney Diseases, 1988—; contbr. articles to profl. jours., chpts. in books. Bd. dirs., trustee Nat. Kidney Found. Mich., Ann Arbor, 1988—, chmn. urology council 1987—, exec. com. 1987—, pres. 1988—, disting. svc. award, 1993; bd. dirs. Ann Arbor Amateur Hockey Assn., 1980-83; pres. PTO, Ann Arbor Pub. Schs., 1980. Served to lt. USNR, 1956-76. Recipient Disting. Service award Transplantation Soc. Mich., 1982. Fellow ACS (pres.-elect Mich. br. 1984-85, pres. 1985—); mem. Am. Acad. Med. Dirs., Am. Coll. Physician Execs., Internat. Soc. Urology, Am. Urol. Assn. (pres. Mich. br. 1980-81, pres. North Cen. sec. 1985-86, Manpower com. 1987-88, Jud. Rev. com. 1987-91, tech. exhibits 1987-88, fiscal affairs rev. commn. 1985-89, manpower commn. 1990-92, audit commn. 1992-96, chmn. 1995, exec. commn. 1993—, bd. dirs. 1994—, work force com., publ. com., 1995—, Best Sci. Exhibit award 1978, Best Sci. Films award 1980, 82, audio-visual com., 1994—, program review com. 1994—, urology work force com. 1995—, publs. com. 1995—), Transplantation Soc. Mich. (pres. 1983-84), ACS (pres. Mich. chpt. 1985-86), Am. Assn. Transplant Surgeons, Endocrine Surgeons, Soc. Univ. Urologists, Am. Assn. Urologic Oncology, Am. Fertility Soc, Am. Coll. Physician Execs., Am. Acad. Med. Dirs., S.W. Oncology Group. Republican. Methodist. Clubs: Barton Hills Country; Ann Arbor Raquet . Avocations: tennis, fishing, Civil War. Home: 2800 Fairlane St Ann Arbor MI 48104-4110 Office: Henry Ford Hosp Dept Urology 2799 W Grand Blvd Detroit MI 48202-2608

CERNY, WILLIAM F., state legislator; m. Patricia Cerny. Rep. S.D. State Ho. of Reps. Dist. 29; rep. S.D. State Ho. of Reps. Dist. 25, 1993—, minority whip, mem. appropriations com.; farmer. Home: RR 1 Box 2 Burke SD 57523-9501*

CEROKE, CLARENCE JOHN, engineer, consultant; b. Chgo., Dec. 1, 1921; s. Paul Anthony and Anne (Krieger) C.; m. Violet Marie Lobonc, Sept. 21, 1947; children: Paul, Donald, Robert, Marie, Louise, Karen. BS in mech. Engring., Ill. Inst. Tech., 1943. Reg. profl. engr., Ill. Supr. product devel. U.S.I. Clearing, Chgo., 1969-74; engr. Panduit Corp., Tinley Park, Ill., 1974-75; design engr. Interlake Steel, Chgo., 1975-76; mgr. engring. AFL Industries, West Chicago, 1976-77; design engr. Castle Engring., Chgo., 1977-80; supr. Dreis and Krump, Chgo., 1980-81; project engr. Epstein Process Engring., Chgo., 1981-83; cons. engr. Beacon Engring., Homewood, Ill., 1983-84; engr. Espo Engring., Canton, Ohio, 1984—; owner Beacon Engring., Homewood, 1978—. Patentee in field. Pres. St. Kilians Holy Name Soc., Chgo., 1960; coach Little League Baseball, Chgo., 1959. With USN, 1943-44. Mem. Mt. Carmel Alumni Assn., Pi Tau Sigma, Hall-Fame Racquet Club. Roman Catholic. Home: 4716 Magnolia Dr NE Canton OH 44705-2949 Office: Beacon 4716 Magnolia Canton OH 44705

CERVELLI, THOMAS R., business executive. Mktg. mgr. Ill. Bell, Chgo., 1966-82; v.p. Control Corp., Lisle, Ill., 1982-94; pres. Thomas R. Cervelli, Assocs., Woodridge, Ill., 1994—. With U.S. Army, 1964.

CERVENKA, BARBARA, art educator, artist; b. Cleve., Sept. 28, 1939; d. James J. and Florence (Balzer) C. BA, Siena Heights Coll., 1963; MFA, U. Mich., 1971. Mem. art faculty Siena Heights Coll., Adrian, Mich., 1971-78; mem. adminstrn. Adrian Dominican Sister, Mich., 1978-82; mem. art faculty, asst. dean Sch. Art U. Mich., Ann Arbor, 1982—. Curator (exhbns.) Cuadros of Pamplona, Alta., 1989-95; exhbns. include Dennos Mus., Traverse City, 1992, Ctrl. Mich. U., 1993, Field Mus., Chgo. Bd. dirs. Siena Heights Coll., Adrian, 1985-95. Home: 307 Maple Ridge Ann Arbor MI 48103

CERVENY, KATHRYN M., educational administrator; b. Chgo., May 26, 1939; d. Roland John and Florence Anna (Cooke) Heidenfelder; children: Erick Joseph, Charles George. Student, Milw. Downer Coll., Lawrence U. Distbr., county mgr. Vanda Beauty Counselors, Orlando, Fla., 1965-80; sales assoc., adminstrv. asst. Resource Data Systems, Northbrook, Ill., 1981-87; dept. asst. Northwestern U., Evanston, Ill., 1987—; internat. conf. editl. asst. IEEE, 1994—; pvt. piano tchr. Leadership trainer, dist. commr. Boy Scouts Am.; mem. exec. coun. bd. N.W. Suburban Coun., Mt. Prospect, Ill., 1993—. Recipient Silver Beaver award Boy Scouts Am. Mem. NAFE. Home: 8021 Kilpatrick Ave Skokie IL 60076-3073

CERVILLA, CONSTANCE MARLENE, marketing consultant; b. Lafayette, Ind., Dec. 28, 1951; d. Norman Cimmino and Marilyn Jane (Stonebraker) C. AB, Harvard U., 1974, postgrad., 1974-75. Mktg. asst. Gen. Mills, Inc., Mpls., 1975-76; product dir. Pillsbury Co., Mpls., 1976-78; asst. v.p. Citicorp, N.A., Rochester, N.Y., 1978-80; cons. Bain & Co., Boston, 1980-81; owner, pres. Core Group Mktg., Inc., Mpls., 1981—; co-founder, v.p. Mil. Communications Ctr., Inc., Mpls., 1983-89; co-founder Gift Certificate Ctrs., Inc., 1990—; speaker to bank mktg. orgns. Patentee in field. Mem. Bank Mktg. Assn., Harvard/Radcliffe Club Minn., Mpls. Inst. Arts, Woman's Club Mpls., Wilderness Soc., Nat. Rowing Assn., Harvard Club (N.Y.C.). Office: Core Group Mktg Inc 6436 City West Pky Eden Prairie MN 55344-7712

CESARIO, ROBERT CHARLES, franchise executive, consultant; b. Chgo., Apr. 6, 1941; s. Valentino A. and Mary Ethel (Kenny) C.; m. Susan Kay DePoutee; children: Jeffrey, Bradley. B.S. in Gen. Edn., Northwestern U., 1975; postgrad. in bus. adminstrn. DePaul U., 1975. Mgr. fin. ops. Midas Internat. Corp., Chgo., 1968-73; chief opt. ops. Am. Hosp. Supply Corp., McGaw Park, Ill., 1973-76; v.p. Car X Svc. Systems Inc., Chgo., 1976-78, v.p. oil svcs., 1983-84; v.p. Chicken Unltd. Enterprises Inc., Chgo., 1978-83; pres. Growth Strategies, Inc., 1984-87; pres. CEO Lube Pro's Internat., Inc., 1987—. Served with USMC, 1960-62. Office: Lube Pros Internat Inc 1630 W Colonial Pky Palatine IL 60067-4725

CHACKO, SAMUEL, association official; b. Mezhuveli, Kerala, India, Aug. 1, 1942; came to U.S., 1970; s. Chanda Pillai and Sosamma (Cheriyan) C.; m. Omana Chellimalayil George, May 21, 1979; children: Roshen Samuel, Renee Susan. BA in Econs., U. Kerala, 1963, MA in History, 1966, MA in Polit. Sci., 1968; BA in Social Sci., Olivet Nazarene U., Kankakee, Ill., 1971; MA in Comm., Govs. State U., 1974; postgrad., U. Ill., Chgo., 1981-86. Cert. in gerontology, cmty. nutrition. Dir. dept. aging Kankakee Land Community Action Agy., 1972-76; head sr. citizens dept. Oakland-Livingston Human Svcs. Agy., Pontiac, Mich., 1976-78; dir. Benton Harbor (Mich.) Area Parks and Recreation Bd., 1978-79; program analyst Ill. Migrant Coun., Chgo., 1980-84; dir. energy svcs. Community and Econ. Devel. Assn. Cook County, Inc., Chgo., 1985—; mem. Ill. State Commerce Commn. Task Force on Rewriting Utility Svc. Rules, 1995—, Ill. State Energy Assistance Program Working Group, 1991-93. Vice chmn. State Assn. Dirs. Foster Grandparent Program, 1974-76; chmn. com. on bylaws Nat. Dirs. Assn. Foster Grandparent Programs; bd. dirs. Kankakee-Will County Citizens Coun., 1975-76. Office: Cmty and Econ Devel Assn Cook Cty Inc 224 N Des Plaines Chicago IL 60661-1195

CHADWICK, JOHN EDWIN, financial counselor and planner; b. Mpls., Feb. 6, 1957; s. Edwin Bazley and Roberta Mae (Brown) C.; 2 children. BA, Gustavus Adolphus Coll., St. Peter, Minn., 1979; cert., Am. Coll., Bryn Mawr, Pa., 1989. CFP. Feed ingredient merchandiser Pillsbury Co., Mpls., 1979-81; pres. Chadwick Co., Bloomington, Minn., 1982-84; v.p. sales Red Wing (Minn.) Bus. Systems, 1984-85; fin. counselor CIGNA, Mpls., 1985-88; prin. The Chadwick Group, Inc., Bloomington, Minn., 1989—. Founding chmn. Oak Grove Endowment Com., Bloomington, 1987—. Mem. Nat. Assn. Life Underwriters, Mpls. Assn. Life Underwriters. Presbyterian. Office: The Chadwick Group Ste 2420 Xerxes Ave S Bloomington MN 55431-1136

CHAFFEE, PAUL CHARLES, newspaper editor; b. Racine, Wis., Aug. 10, 1947; s. Raymond Russell and Ellen Mary (Tiles) C.; m. Bonnie Louise Burmeister, Aug. 9, 1969. BA in Journalism, U. Minn., 1969. Reporter Grand Rapids (Mich.) Press, 1969-79, asst. met. editor, 1979-81; met. editor Saginaw (Mich.) News, 1981-88, editor, 1988—; founding mem. adv. bd. dept. journalism Ctrl. Mich. U., Mt. Pleasant, 1987—; pres. bd. dirs. Mich. Assoc. Press Editl. Assn.; bd. dirs. Mid Am. Press Inst. Bd. dirs. Salvation Army, Saginaw, 1986—, St. Charles (Mich.) Cmty. Found., 1994—, Westlund Child Guidance Clinic, 1995—; mem. Leadership Saginaw Steering Bd. Mem. Am. Soc. Newspaper Editors, Mich. State U. Journalism Dept. Hispanic Adv. Assn., Saginaw Country Club. Office: Saginaw News 203 S Washington Ave Saginaw MI 48607-1244

CHAFFEE, RICHARD J., JR., financial planner; b. Worcester, Mass., Mar. 19, 1948; s. Richard J., Sr. and Martha Ann (Kerr) Freeman; m. Jane Hamilton, Sept. 5, 1981; children: Laura Mitchell, Jessica Ann. BA, Franklin & Marshall, 1970; Mgmt./Ins., U. Penn, 1978. Cert. CLU. Life ins. salesman Penn Mutual, Phila., 1970-77; mgmt. MONY, N.Y.C., 1977-82, Phoenix Home, Hartford, Conn., 1982-95; pres., CEO Bus. & Estate Resource, Edina, Minn., 1993-95; pres., CEO Chaffee & Assocs., Edina, 1982-95, Fin. Ptnrs., Edina, 1994-95. Mem. adv. bd. Gutherie Theater, Mpls., 1994-95, St. Katherines, St. Paul, 1995; mem. leadership bd. Lake Harriet Meth. Ch., Mpls., 1994-95. Mem. CLUs, Assn. Adv. Life Underwriters, Gen. Agents and Mgrs. Assn., Nat. Assn. Life Underwriters. Republican. Home: 2409 W 52nd St Minneapolis MN 55410 Office: Bus and Estate Resources Ste 195 7301 OHMS Lane Edina MN 55439

CHAFFIN, LESLIE RENÉE, corporate communications administrator, writer; b. Wichita, Kans., Feb. 20, 1959; d. Gladwin Wilkie and Margrit Hildi (Luthi) C.; m. Jon L. Smith, Aug. 20, 1983; 1 child, Colt W. BA in Journalism-Advt./Pub. Rels., Wichita State U., 1982. Ad coord./copywriter Sheplers, Inc., Wichita, 1980-83; writer/prodr. Stephan Advt. Inc., Wichita, 1983-86; mgr. mktg. and pub. rels. Old Cowtown Mus., Wichita, 1986; sole propr. Idea Hatching Unltd., Wichita and Mulvane, 1987-92; pub./editor/et. al. Saddle Up Newspaper, Mulvane, 1987-90; pub. rels. coord. Starkey Inc., Wichita, 1990-92; adj. instr. Cowley County C.C., Mulvane, 1988-90; dir. comm. Hospice Inc., Wichita, 1992—; freelance writer Thorn Ams., Kans. Coliseum, Wichita, 1985—. Contbr. articles to nat. horse publs. Com. Chair Pack 894, Mulvane, 1994, 95-96; vol. guardian/conservator Kans. Advocacy and Protective Svc., Wichita, 1990—; horse trails vol. Red Brush Fram/Meadowlark Pony Club, Wichita, 1985-93; mem. Munson Primary Staff Devel. Com., Mulvane, 1994-95, mem. Munson Primary Curriculum com., 1993-94. Recipient Pres.'s award Nat. Hospice Orgn., 1992, 93, Addy award for excellence Advt. Fedn. Wichita, 1982, 85, Emerald award KAHC, 1994. Mem. Mulvane Bus. and Profl. Women (Woman of Yr. 1988), Internat. Assn. Bus. Communicators (v.p. comm. 1990-91, v.p. programs 1991-92, v.p. membership 1992-93, pres. 1993-94, sr. del. 1994-95, Bronze Quill, 1992, 93, Gold Quill 1995, Silver Quill, 1995). Office: Hospice Inc 313 S Market Wichita KS 67202

CHAIYABHAT, WIN, risk control professional; b. Bangkok, Jan. 9, 1950; came to U.S., 1967; s. Thavorn and Boonchia (Khomsiri) C.; m. Nancy Benzie, June 1, 1975; children: Whit, Shaun. BS in Engring. Physics, U. Maine, 1973, MEd, 1974; EdD, Boston U., 1981. Teaching asst. physics dept. U. Maine, Orono, 1972-73; teaching fellow Boston U., 1975-76; sect. head data compilation EDP, Petroleum Authority Thailand, Bangkok, 1980-82, asst. dir. corp. planning, adminstrv. mgr. pipeline project, 1982-83; dep. mgr. Delta Engring. & Constrn. Co., Bangkok, 1983-84; tech. rep. highly protected risk dept. Kemper Group, North Quincy, Mass., 1976-79, tech. rep., 1984-86; edn. coord. highly protected risk dept. Kemper Group, Long Grove, Ill., 1986-88; engring. mgr. internat. dept. Kemper Internat. Corp., Chgo., 1988-95; regional dir. risk control Alexander & Alexander, Inc., Chgo., 1995—. Violinist, concert master Boston Light Opera, 1977-79; founder, chmn. bd. Bangkok Symphony Orch., 1982-84; violinist Woodstock (Ill.) Opera Theatre, 1986-88, Fox Valley Symphony Orch., Aurora, Ill., 1986-88. Recipient Cultural award Govt. of Australia, Bangkok, 1983; scholar U. Maine Coll. Engring., 1967-72. Mem. Soc. Fire Protection Engrs., Nat. Fire Protection Assn. (tech. coms. 72, 75 and 16 1988—), Inst. Indsl. Engrs. (sr. mem.). Home: 589 Parkside Ct Crystal Lake IL 60012-3366 Office: Alexander & Alexander Inc Two Prudential Plaza 180 N Stetson Ave Chicago IL 60601-6714

CHALBERG-PLUNKETT, SHERRI LINELL, construction executive; b. Leavenworth, Kans., Mar. 10, 1960; d. Larry Allen and Esther Louise (Martin) C.; m. James Davidson Plunkett, Oct. 25, 1986. BSBA, William Jewell Coll., 1984; MBA, Rockhurst Coll., 1988. Personnel dir. Belger Cartage Service, Kansas City, Mo., 1984-86; v.p. Jim Plunkett, Inc., Kansas City, Kans., 1986—; chief exec. officer Wall Systems Corp., Kansas City, Kans., 1986—. Mem. Home Builders Assn., Assoc. Builders and Contractors, Nat. Assn. Women in Constrn. (dir., recording sec. 1990-91). Republican. Mem. Unity Ch. Home: 7511 NW Tomahawk Ln Kansas City MO 64151-1427 Office: Jim Plunkett Inc 1304 Argentine Blvd Kansas City KS 66105-1537

CHALOUPKA, FRANK JOSEPH, economics educator; b. Cleve., Sept. 10, 1962; s. Frank Joseph and Carol Ann (Jenisek) C. BA, John Carroll U, University Heights, Ohio, 1984; PhD, CUNY, N.Y.C., 1988. Asst. prof. econs. U. Ill., Chgo., 1988-94, assoc. prof., 1994—; rsch. assoc. Nat. Bur. Econ. Rsch., N.Y.C., 1994—. Rsch. grantee Nat. Cancer Inst., 1988-90, 95—, Nat. Inst. Alcohol Abuse and Alcoholism, 1988—, Nat. Inst. Drug Abuse, 1991-96, Robert Wood Johnson Found., 1993—, Ctrs. Disease Control and Prevention, 1994—. Mem. Am. Econ. Assn., Western Econ. Assn., So. Econ. Assn., Eastern Econ. Assn., Midwest Econ. Assn., Am. Pub. Health Assn. Home: 361 Wildwood Dr North Aurora IL 60542-3018 Office: U Ill 601 S Morgan St Chicago IL 60607-7121

CHAMBERLAIN, JOSEPH MILES, retired astronomer, educator; b. Peoria, Ill., July 26, 1923; s. Maurice Silloway and Roberta (Miles) C.; m. Paula Bruninga, Dec. 12, 1945; children: Janet Ann, Susan Louise, Barbara Jean. BS, U.S. Mcht. Marine Acad., 1944; BA, Bradley U., 1947; AM, Tchrs. Coll. Columbia, 1950, EdD, 1962. Instr. Columbia Jr. High Sch., Peoria, 1943; instr. nav. War Shipping Adminstrn., 1944-45; boys sec. YMCA, Peoria, 1946-47; instr. U.S. Mcht. Marine Acad., Kings Point, N.Y., 1947-50; asst. prof. U.S. Mcht. Marine Acad., 1950-52; asst. curator Am. Museum-Hayden Planetarium, N.Y.C., 1952-53; gen. mgr., chief astronomer Am. Museum-Hayden Planetarium, 1953-56, chmn., 1956-64; asst. dir. Am. Mus. Natural History, 1964-68; dir. Adler Planetarium, Chgo., 1968-91, pres., 1977-91, ret., 1991; prof. astronomy Northwestern U., 1968-78; professorial lectr. U. Chgo., 1968-71; led eclipse expdns. to Can., 1954, 79, Ceylon, 1955, Pacific Ocean, 1977, 91, astro-geodetic expdns. to Can., 1956, 57, Greenland, 1958; dean coun. of sci. staff Am. Mus. Nat. History, 1960-62. Co-author: Planets, Stars and Space, 1957; author: Time and the Stars, 1964; also articles on popular astronomy. Active Boy Scouts Am., Met. Chgo. YMCA. Served to lt. USNR, 1945-46; staff Naval Res. Officers Sch. 1953-54, N.Y.C. Mem. Am. Astron. Soc., Internat. Astron. Union, Internat. Planetarium Dirs. Conf. (vice chmn. 1968-77, chmn. 1977-87), Am. Polar Soc., Am. Assn. Museums (mem. council 1965-77, v.p. 1971-74, pres. 1974-75), Phi Delta Kappa, Phi Kappa Phi, Kappa Delta Pi. Republican. Presbyn. (elder). Clubs: University (Chgo.), Tavern (Chgo.), Dutch Treat. Home: 510 W Thousand Oaks Dr Peoria IL 61615-1395

CHAMBERS, DONALD EVERARD, social worker, educator; b. Denver, Oct. 30, 1929; s. Jack Adair and Ruth Wilhelmina (Swenson) C.; m. widowed; children: Kristin, Jane, Timothy. BA, Stanford U., 1950; MSW, U. Nebr., 1952; DSW, Washington U., St. Louis, 1967. Social worker Cath. Charities, Archdiocese of Omaha, 1952-59; dir. mental health svcs. Idaho Dept. Health, Pocatello, 1959-62; social worker Mental Health Inst., Clarinda, Iowa, 1962-64; prof. Sch. Social Welfare U. Kans., Lawrence, 1967—. Author: Social Problems and Social Policy, 1986, 2d edit., 1993 (translated for Chinese edit., Singapore 1993), Evaluating Social Programs, 1992; contbr. numerous articles and rsch. reports to profl. and scholarly jours. Bd. dirs. Shanti Vanuum Rtreat House, Easton, Kans., 1975—. Fulbright rsch. fellow, Costa Rica and Guatemala, 1990-91; British rsch. awardee, 1978-79. Democrat. Roman Catholic. Home: 787 E 1300 Rd Lawrence KS 66046 Office: U Kans Sch Social Welfare 315 Twente Hall Lawrence KS 66044-7509

CHAMBERS, DONALD H., industrial designer; b. Detroit, June 26, 1957; s. Howard Charles and Mary Elizabeth (Johnson) C.; m. Kathleen Marie Abraham, June 28, 1987; children: Donna, Edward. Student, Wayne State U., 1984—. Drafting staff Glad Industries, Detroit, 1979; designer AA Gage Inc., Ferndale, Mich., 1980—. Mem. Tau Alpha Pi. Home: 29594 Westfield St Livonia MI 48150-4042 Office: AA Gage Inc 350 Fair St Ferndale MI 48220-2647

CHAMBERS, ERNEST, state legislator. Mem. from dist. 11 Nebr. State Senate, Lincoln, 1970—, mem. agr., bus. and labor coms., vice chmn. judiciary com., exec. bd. Address: Nebr State Senate State Capitol Rm 1107 Lincoln NE 68509*

CHAMBERS, JAMES S., financial consultant; b. Peoria, Ill., June 23, 1952. BS in Agrl. Econs., U. Mo., 1974. Salesman, then sales mgr. O'Brien Steel Svc., Peoria, 1974-84; fin. cons. Smith Barney Inc., Peoria, 1984—. Republican.

CHAMBERS, JERRY RAY, school system administrator; b. St. Joseph, Mo., Oct. 1, 1947; s. Ray Linden and Betty Allene (Roach) C.; m. Jacqueline Kaye Thomas, Feb. 11, 1967; children: Sandra Kaye, Jennifer Lynn. AS, Mo. Western State Coll., 1967; BA, U. Mo., Kansas City, 1969, MA in Edn. Adminstrn. and History, 1971; postgrad., U. Madras, India, 1974; PhD in Edn. Adminstrn., U. Mo., Kansas City, 1986. Tchr. Lillis High Sch., Kansas City, Mo., 1969; from high sch. tchr. to dir. media svc. Sch. Dist. St. Joseph, 1969-80; supt. schs. Sch. Dist. Washington, Mo., 1990—; coun. pres. ITV Kansas City Pub. TV, 1981-90; assessor Mo. Prin. Assess Ctr., DESE, Jefferson City, Mo., 1987-90; bd. dirs. 353 Econ. Devel. Corp. Washington, 1991—, Network Ednl. Devel., St. Louis, 1993-96; exec. com. Coop. Sch. Dists. St. Louis. Author: Missouri Students Tune IN, 1987, History of Missouri Instructional Television, 1986, Beyond the Bullet Hole, 1988. Bd. dirs. Regional Bluffs Libr., St. Joseph, 1989, United Fund, Washington, 1992-95; campaign co-chmn. Earnings Tax Com., St. Joseph, 1988; chmn. edn. divsn. United Way, St. Joseph, 1986-89, bd. dirs. 1992. Fulbright scholar U.S. Dept. Edn., 1974; recipient Alumni Achievement award U. Mo., Kansas City, 1988, Disting. Alumni award Mo. Western State Coll., 1990, Disting. Leadership award Nat. Assn. Com. Leadership, 1988, Key to City award City of St. Joseph Mayor, 1990. Mem. Am. Assn. Sch. Adminstrs., Lions Club (Washington chpt., St. Joseph Host Club pres. 1989-90, exec. coun. Cooperating Sch. Dists. Greater St Louis). Home: 2 Winchester Ct Washington MO 63090-5314 Office: School Dist Washington PO Box 357 220 Locust St Washington MO 63090-2829

CHAMBERS, LAROYCE FRANCIS, obstetrician, gynecologist; b. Detroit, Dec. 5, 1944; s. Hobart Madra and Alma Bernice (Green) C.; m. Minnie Pearl Smith, July 3, 1971; children: Anthony LaRoyce, Reginald Alan. BS, Wayne State U., 1966; MD, U. Mich., 1970. Diplomate Am. Bd. Ob-Gyn. Intern Chgo. Wesley Meml. Hosp., 1970-71; resident Northwestern U., 1973-76; practice medicine specializing in ob-gyn Ob-Gyn Med. Services, Milw., 1976—; chief dept. ob-gyn Sinai Samaritan Med. Ctr., Milw., 1986—; asst. clin. prof. Med. Coll. Wis., Milw., 1981—, U. Wis. Mem. ethics bd. City of Mequon, Wis., 1986; bd. govs. Wis. affiliate Am. Heart Assn., Milw., 1986; bd. dirs. Univ. Sch. Milw., River Hills, Wis., 1986, Family Services, Milw., 1986. Served to capt., U.S. Army, 1971-73. Baptist. Home: 2720 W Range Line Ct Mequon WI 53092-5325 Office: Newtowne Med Group 8675 N Port Washington Rd Milwaukee WI 53217-2209

CHAMBERS, MARJORIE BELL, historian; b. N.Y.C., Mar. 11, 1923; d. Kenneth Carter and Katherine (Totman) Bell; m. William Hyland Chambers, Aug. 8, 1945; children: Lee Chambers-Schiller, William Bell, Leslie Chambers Trujillo, Kenneth Carter. AB cum laude, Mt. Holyoke Coll., South Hadley, Mass., 1943; MA, Cornell U., 1948; PhD, U. N.Mex., 1974; LLD honoris causa, Ctrl. Mich. U., 1977; LHD (hon.), Wilson Coll., 1980, Northern Michigan U., 1982. Staff asst. Am. Assn. UN, League of Nations Assn., N.Y.C., 1944-45; program specialist dept. rural sociology Cornell U., Ithaca, N.Y., 1945-46, rsch. asst. dept. speech and drama, 1946-48; substitute tchr. Los Alamos (N.Mex.) Pub. Schs., 1962-65; project historian U.S. AEC, Los Alamos, 1965-69; adj. prof. U. N.Mex., Los Alamos, 1970-76, 84-85; pres. Colo. Women's Coll., Denver, 1976-78; dean Grad. Sch. Union Inst., Cin., 1979-82, mem. core faculty Grad. Sch., 1979—; interim pres. Colby-Sawyer Coll., New London, N.H., 1985-86; vis. prof. Cameron U., Lawton, Okla., 1974; commr., vice-chair N.Mex. Commn. on Higher Edn., Santa Fe, 1987-91; chair citizen adv. bd. U.S. Army Command and Gen. Staff Coll., Ft. Leavenworth, Kans., 1990—; mem. bd. dirs. Coun. Ind. Colls. and

Univs., Santa Fe, 1991—; rep. Los Alamos County Labor Mgmt. Bd. Contbr. articles to profl. jours. Chair Los Alamos County Coun., 1976, councilor, 1975-76, 79; candidate N.Mex. 3d Congl. Dist., 1982, lt. gov. N.Mex., 1986; chair Sec. of Navy's Advisor Bd. on Edn. and Tng., Washington and Pensacola, Fla., 1987-89; chair Citizen Bd. of U.S. Army Command and Gen. Staff Coll., Fort Leavenworth, Kans.; acting chair, vice-chair adminstrn. Pres. Carter's Com. for Women, Washington, 1977-80; chair Pres. Ford's Nat. Adv. Bd. on Women's Ednl. Programs, Washington, Los Alamos County Pers. Bd., 1983-90; mem. nat. adv. coun. U.S. SBA, 1990—; mem., editor Los Alamos and N.Mex. Rep. Ctrl. com., 1982—; trustee Colby-Sawyer Coll., New London, N.H., 1980-89; pub. mem. U.S. Dept. State Fgn. Svc. selection bd., 1978; mem. U.S. del. UN Conf. Women, Copenhagen, 1980. Recipient Teresa d'Avila award Coll. St. Teresa, Winona, Minn., 1978, Disting. Woman award U. N.Mex. Alumni Assn., Albuquerque, 1990, N.Mex. Disting. Pub. Svc. award Gov. and Awards Coun., Albuquerque, 1991; named Outstanding N.Mex. Woman Gov. and Com. on Status of Women, Albuquerque, 1988, 89. Mem. AAUW (life), U.S. rep. coun. 1973-75, nat. pres. 1975-79, pres. Edn. Found.), DAR, Bus. and Profl. Women (Los Alamos parliamentarian and dist. parliamentarian 1991-93), Women's Polit. Caucus (gov. bd. conv., keynoter, vice-chair Rep. caucus 1971—), Internat. Women's Forum, N.Mex. Hist. Soc., Los Alamos Hist. Soc. (pres., Sangre de Cristo Girl Scouts "Woman of Distinction" 1996). Presbyterian.

CHAMPION, MARTIN R., health facility administrator, consultant; b. Cin., June 24, 1969; s. Vernon and Libby C.; m. Tonya Champion; children: Ashley, Breanna, Martin. Student, U. Ill., 1987-91. Constrn. mgmt. cons. Davis Environ. Svcs., Elmhurst, Ill., 1988-90; ops. mgr. CCC Info. Svcs., Chgo., 1989-92; IOI UCC Southside Health Project, Chgo., 1992—; pres., CEO M.R. Champion & Assocs., Chgo. Cmty. voters registration 1989—. Named Ill. State Scholar Ill. State Scholarship Commn., Ill., 1987-88. Mem. Alpha Phi Alpha. Democrat. Office: UCC South Side Health Project 1818 E 71st St Chicago IL 60649

CHAMPION, NORMA JEAN, communications educator, state legislator; b. Oklahoma City, Jan. 21, 1933; d. Aubra Dell and Beuleah Beatrice (Flanagan) Black; m. Richard Gordon Champion, Oct. 3, 1953 (dec.); children: Jeffrey Bruce, Ashley Brooke. BA in Religious Edn., Cen. Bible Coll., Springfield, Mo., 1971; MA in Comm., S.W. Mo. State U., 1978; PhD in Tech., U. Okla., 1986. Producer, hostess The Children's Hour, Sta. KYTV-TV, NBC, Springfield, 1957-86; asst. prof. Cen. Bible Coll., 1968-84; prof. broadcasting Evangel Coll., Springfield, 1978—; mem. Springfield City Coun., 1987-92, Mo. Ho. of Reps., Jefferson City, 1992—; adj. faculty Assemblies of God Theol. Sem. Springfield, 1987—, pres. coun.; chmn. bd. Berean U.; frequent lectr. to svc. clubs, ednl. seminars; seminar speaker Internat. Pentecostal Press. Assn. World Conf., Singapore, 1989; announcer various TV commls. Contbr. numerous articles to religious publs. Mem. bd Mo. Access to Higher Edn. Trust, 1990—; regional rep. Muscular Dystrophy Assn.; mem. adv. bd. Chameleon Puppet Theater, 1987; mem. exec. bd. Univ. Child Care Ctr., 1987; hon. chmn. fund raising Salvation Army, 1986; also numerous other bds., hon. chairmanships.; judge Springfield City Schs. Recipient commendation resolution Mo. Ho. of Reps., 1988; numerous award for The Children's Hour; Aunt Norma Day named in her honor City of Springfield, 1976. Mem. Nat. Broadcast Edn. Assn., Mo. Broadcast Edn. Assn., Nat. League Cities, Mo. Mcpl. League (human resource com. 1989, intergovtl. rels. com. 1990), Nat. Assn. Telecom. Officers and Advisors, Internat. Pentesostal Press Assn., Josephson Inst. for Advancement Ethics, Springfield C. of C., Mo. PTA (life). Republican. Mem. Assemblies of God Ch. Home: 3609 S Broadway Ave Springfield MO 65807-4505 Office: Evangel Coll 1111 N Glenstone Ave Springfield MO 65802-2125

CHAMPLIN, MIKE, rancher, former county commissioner; b. Cedar Vale, Kans., June 21, 1958; s. Merl and Virginia (Ponder) C.; m. Kitty M. Stuever, Oct. 16, 1983; children: Marc, Jon, Erin. AA, Hutchinson (Kans.) Jr. Coll., 1978. Rancher, Cedar Vale, 1978-90; co-owner Chautauqua Hills Cattle Co., Cedar Vale, 1990—. Chmn. Chautauqua County Commn., 1984-92, Chautauqua County Soil Conservation Svc., Sedan, Kans., 1978-80, Chautauqua County Solid Waste Commn., 1993—. Mem. Masons (master Chautauqua 1989-91),Lions.

CHAN, CARLYLE HUNG-LUN, psychiatrist, educator; b. Clarksdale, Miss., July 4, 1949; s. Henry Howe and Jennie (Wong) C.; m. Patricia Meyer, June 18, 1977; children: Christopher, Diana. BS, U. Wis., 1971; MD, Med. Coll. Wis., 1975. Diplomate Am. Bd. Psychiatry and Neurology. Resident in psychiatry U. Chgo., 1975-78; asst. prof. Med. Coll. Wis., Milw., 1980-86, assoc. prof., 1986—, dir. residency edn., 1987—; dir. catchment area Milw. County Mental Health Complex, 1981-82; dir. continuing med. edn., 1990; chief psychiatrist Psychiatrist Ctr., Columbia Hosp., Milw., 1982-87; dir. continuing med. edn. Med. Coll. Wis., Milw., 1990—, Soc. Tchg. Scholars, 1994; dir. course annual psychiat. conf., 1982—; dir. Door County (Wis.) Summer Inst., 1987—. Asst. editor Asian-Am. Psychiatry Newsletter, Washington, 1983-84; assoc. editor Acad. Psychiatry Newsletter, 1991-94; contbr. articles to profl. jours. Bd. dirs. Planning Council for Mental Health and Social Service, 1983—. Robert Wood Johnson clin. scholar Yale U., 1978-80; jr. Faculty Devel. award NIMH, 1983-85; Community Devel. award Apple Computer Co., Milw., 1984. Fellow Am. Psychiat. Assn.; mem. Wis. Psychiat. Assn. (pres. Milw. chpt. 1990-91), Assn. Acad. Psychiatry (regional coord. 1987—, regional coord. dir. 1993-96, treas. 1996—), Am. Assn. Dirs. Psychiat. Residency Tng. (sec. 1994-95, pres.-elect 1995, pres. 1996, treas. 1990-92, program com. chair 1993-94), Wis. State Med. Soc., Milw. County Med. Soc. Med. Coll. of Wis., Soc. Teaching Scholars. Office: Med Coll Wis Dept Psychiatry 8701 W Watertown Plank Rd Milwaukee WI 53226-3548

CHAN, HENG-BENG, restaurant manager, wholesale business owner; b. Butterworth, Penang, Malaysia, Apr. 9, 1970; came to the U.S., 1988; s. Khai-Hock and Kim-Eng (Ooi) C. BBA in Entrepreneurship, Wichita State U., 1992, MBA in Mktg., 1994. Line server Morrison Custom Svc., Wichita, 1990; lab asst. Wichita (Kans.) State U., 1990-92; cons. Qualinit, Penang, 1992; grad. tchg. asst. Wichita (Kans.) State U., 1992-94; pres., founder Intrenasionale, Inc., Wichita, 1992—; mgr. Little Caesar's, Wichita, 1994—; dean's student adv. coun. Wichita (Kans.) State U., 1991-94; mem. World Trade Coun., Wichita, 1992-94; cons. Internat. Directory of Young Entrepreneur, Boston, 1994—. Author: Entrepreneur's Resource Book, 1993, student edit., 1994. Vol. Big Bros. and Big Sisters, Wichita, 1991-94; founder Children's Favorite Things, Wichita, 1992; vol. coord. Project Hope, Wichita, 1992—. Mem. Assn. Collegiate Entrepreneurs (membership dir. 1991-92, pres. 1992-94, Spl. Recognition award 1994), Wichita State U. Alumni Assn. (coun. mem. 1994—), Student in Free Enterprise (founding mem.). Home: 2517 N Parkwood Ct Wichita KS 67220 Office: Intrenasionale Inc 2517 N Parkwood Ct Wichita KS 67220

CHAN, HENRY YUN SHING, history educator; b. Hong Kong, Apr. 28, 1947; came to U.S., 1973.; s. Ki (Yu) C.; m. Janet Chau, Nov. 23, 1994. BA, U. Hong Kong, 1968; MA, Ind. U., 1975; PhD, Ind. U, 1987. Asst. master Raimondi Coll., Hong Kong, 1968-70; asst. social welfare officer Social Welfare Dept., Hong Kong, 1970-71; asst. libr. Urban Coun. Pub. Librs., Hong Kong, 1971-72; instr. Ind. U., Bloomington, 1978-87; asst. prof. history Lewis-Clark State Coll., Lewiston, Idaho, 1987-89, Moorhead (Minn.) State U., Moorehead, MN, 1989-94; assoc. prof. history Moorhead (Minn.) State U., 1994—. Bush Profl. Devel. grantee, Moorhead State U., 1993-94. Fellow Internat. Ctr. Asian Studies; mem. Am. Hist. Assn., Assn. Asian Studies, Ind. U. Alumni Assn., Moorhead Cen. Lions Club (pres. 1994-95). Office: Moorhead State U Dept of History Moorhead MN 56560

CHANDLER, DANIEL ROSS, religious studies educator, minister, writer; b. Wellston, Okla., July 22, 1937; s. Ross Crawford and Vernie Imo (Davis) C. BS, U. Okla., 1959; postgrad., Duke U., 1959-62; MA, Purdue U., 1965; postgrad., U. Chgo., 1964-65, U. So. Calif., 1966-67; BD, Garrett Theol. Sem., 1968; PhD, Ohio U., 1969. Ordained deacon United Methodist Church, 1960, elder, 1968. Asst. debate coach Duke U., 1959-62; instr. speech, assoc. debate coach Augustana Coll., Ill., 1965-66; asst. pastor Peoples Ch. Chgo., 1965-66; asst. prof. Ctrl. Mich. U., Mt. Pleasant, 1969-70, SUNY, New Paltz, 1970-71, CUNY, 1971-75; asst. prof. Rutgers U., New Brunswick, N.J., 1976-83, coord. basic speech program Douglass campus, 1976-81; from adj. asst. prof. to adj. assoc. prof. CUNY, 1983-90; adj. prof. Hofstra U., Hempstead, N.Y., 1985-90, N.Y. Inst. Tech., Old Westbury, 1985-89, Loyola U., Chgo., 1991-93, Northeastern Ill. U., Chgo., 1994-95; assoc. dean The Humanist Inst., N.Y.C., 1983-86; mem. planning bd. and creator/coord. internat. interdisciplinary conf. 1993 Parliament of World's Religions, Chgo; grad. asst. Purdue U., 1962-64, U. So. Calif., 1966-67, Ohio U., 1968-69. Author: The Reverend Dr. Preston Bradley, 1971, The Rhetorical Tradition, 1978, Toward Universal Religion, 1996, The 1993 Parliament of the World's Religions; book rev. editor Religious Humanism; contbr. chpts. to books and articles to profl. jours. Recipient Highest Civilian Commendation for Heroism, N.Y.C. Police Dept., 1981, Outstanding Tchr. of Yr. award Golden Key Honor Soc. CCNY, 1988; rsch. grantee W. Clement and Jessie V. Stone Found., 1965-66, Kern Found., 1967, Plandome Veatch Fund, 1983-84, others; Mastand fellow Union Theol. Sem., 1975-76, rsch. fellow Yale Divinity Sch., 1974, 75, 77, 78, vis. fellow Princeton Theol. Sem., 1974, 75, 77, 79, 80, 83, 84; vis. scholar Harvard Divinity Sch., 1972, Sch. Theology Boston U., summer 1975, New Sch. Social Rsch., N.Y.C., 1976-77, Garrett Theol. Sem., summer 1977, postdoctoral rsch. scholar Divinity Sch., U. Chgo., 1992-93. Mem. Theosophical Soc. Am., Am. Acad. Religion, Aurobindo Assn., Vedanta Soc., Fulbright Assn. (fellow summer 1986), Unitarian Universalist Mins. Fellowship (affiliate), Pi Kappa Delta, Tau Kappa Alpha-Delta Sigma Rho. Republican. Hindu. Home and Office: PO Box 953 Evanston IL 60204-0953

CHANDLER, EDWARD WILLIAM, communications systems engineer; b. Milw., Oct. 10, 1953; s. Donald Harold and Helen Aliedia (Wonders) C.; m. Christine Anne Wohl, June 13, 1987; children: Rebecca Marie, Marcella Anne, Mary Elizabeth, Andrew Donald. BS, U. Wis., Milw., 1975; MSEE, Ill. Inst. Tech., 1978; PhD, Purdue U., 1985. Registered profl. engr., Wis. Electronics engr. Communications and Electronics div. Motorola Inc., Schaumburg, Ill., 1976-77; instr. elec. engring. Milw. Sch. Engring., 1977-79, asst. prof., 1979-80, assoc. prof., 1982-84, prof., 1992—, acting head electronic communications engring. tech. program, 1978-79, head, 1979-80, dir. elec. engring. program, 1982-84, dir. MS in Engring. program, 1992—; asst. prof. elec. engring. Marquette U., Milw., 1984-86; sr. engr. Titan Linkabit Corp. (formerly Govt. Systems Div. M/A-COM, Inc.), San Diego, 1986-88, mem. tech. staff, 1988-92; cons. Milw., 1992—; lectr. U. Wis., Milw., part-time 1979-83; grad. instr. rsch. Purdue U., West Lafayette, Ind., 1980-82; rsch. cons. Naval Ocean Systems Ctr., San Diego, 1986. Contbr. articles to profl. jours. David Ross summer grantee, 1981; faculty rsch. grantee Milw. Sch. Engring., 1983; recipient Titan Most Valuable Performer award, 1990, Noel Amherd Tech. Performer award, 1991. Mem. IEEE (sr., newsletter editor Milw. sect. 1985-86), Am. Soc. Engring. Edn., Armed Forces Communications Electronics Assn., Air Force Assn., Triangle, Sigma Xi, Tau Beta Pi, Eta Kappa Nu.

CHANDLER, JAMES BARTON, international education consultant; b. Conway Springs, Kans., May 27, 1922; s. James Perry and Bessie May (Stone) C.; m. Madeleine Racoux, July 27, 1946; children: Paul A., Peter R., Michele A. Chandler Dore. AB, U. Kans., 1947, MA, 1949; postgrad., U. Mich., 1950-54. Asst. prof., fgn. student advisor Ea. Mich. U., 1953-55, 57-58; lang. edn. advisor Okla. A&M/Ethiopia, 1955-57, U. Mich./Laos, 1958-60; tchr. edn., advisor U.S. AID-Laos, Vientiane, Laos, 1960-61, edn. div. chief, 1961-63, asst. dir. manpower, industry, pub. administrn., 1965-69, deputy mission dir., 1969-73; higher edn. advisor U.S. AID-Tunisia, Tunis, Tunisia, 1963-65; dir. Office of Edn. AID, Washington, 1973-76, assoc. asst. adminstr., 1976-77; dir. Internat. Bur. Edn. UNESCO, Geneva, 1977-83; cons. Ann Arbor, 1983-88; St. Louis, 1989—; sec. Rotary, Vientiane, Laos, 1968-69. Arbitrator, mediator BBB. Capt. U.S. Army, 1943-47, ETO. Decorated Bronze Star, 1945; recipient Meritorious Honor award AID, 1973, Disting. Career Svc. award, 1977, Cert. Appreciation Pres. Gerald Ford, 1975, Letter Appreciation Dir. Gen. UNESCO, Geneva, 1983; S.L. Whitcomb fellow U. Kansas, 1948-49; fellow Ford Found., 1951-52. Mem. Am. Numismatic Assn., Am. Contract Bridge League, Am. Acad. Social and Polit. Sci., Am. Fgn. Svc. Assn., Ind. Rights Found., Comparative and Internat. Edn. Soc., Diplomatic and Consular Officers Ret. (regional corr.), Nat. Assn. Ret. Fed. Employees (pres. Ann Arbor chpt. 1986-89, v.p. St. Louis chpt. 1989-90, pres. 1991-93, bd. dirs. 1992-93), Mo. Hist. Soc., Smithsonian Assocs., World Affairs Coun., Fgn. Policy Assn., Acad. Sci. St. Louis, Wilson Ctr. Assn., Heritage Found., Nature Conservancy, Assn. Former Internat. Civil Servants, VFW, Am. Legion, 4th Cavalry Assn., Soc. Fratellanza Italiana, Soc. Francaise St. Louis (bd. dirs., v.p., pres.), Alliance Francaise, St. Louis-Lyon Sister Cities Com., Rotary (bd. dirs.), Phi Beta Kappa, Phi Delta Phi, Phi Kappa Phi. Roman Catholic. Home and Office: 7449 Rupert Ave Richmond Heights MO 63117

CHANDLER, KENSAL R., executive; b. Oregon, Wis., Apr. 22, 1925. BSCE, U. Wis., 1945. Pres., gen. mgr. Koehring divsn. Koehring Co., Milw., 1964-72, group v.p., 1972-77; v.p. Heath Corp., Brookfield, Wis., 1979—. Ensign USN, 1943-46. Republican. Methodist. Home: 15245 Cascade Dr Elm Grove WI 53122

CHANDLER, KEVIN, state legislator; b. Mar. 31, 9160; m. Kathleen Chandler; 1 child. BA, U. Minn.; JD, Cath. U. Am. State senator Dist. 55 Minn. State Senate, 1993—; atty., 1996—. Home: 4567 Lake Ave White Bear Lake MN 55110-3423*

CHANDLER, PAUL MICHAEL, ethnoecologist; b. Erwin, N.C., June 8, 1951; s. James Dixon and Getrude Saylor (Wayne) C.; m. Lillian Xinlian Show, May 17, 1991 (div. Apr. 7, 1992). BA, U. N.C., Chapel Hill, 1973; MS, N.C. State U., Raleigh, 1975; PhD, U. Washington, Seattle, 1990. Vol. vis. prof. Peace Corps Fed. U. Vicosa, Brazil, 1976-78; rsch. asst. Kans. State U., Manhattan, 1978-79; forester Bur. Indian Affairs U.S.D.I., Hoquiam, Wash., 1979-80; forester-in-charge Makah Reservation, Wash., 1980-81; timberlands appraiser Spokane, Wash., 1981-84; freelance writer/photographer White Knight Freelance, Seattle, 1984-86; instr. English Nanjing Forestry U., China, 1987-88; post doctoral researcher U. Wash., Seattle, 1990-91; asst. prof. Natural Resources Ball State U., Muncie, Ind., 1991—; resource mgmt. cons. White Knight Consulting, Seattle, 1985-86. Author: (chpt.) Watershed Management, 1992; author, editor: Agroforestry, 1995; contbr. articles to profl. jours. Campaign mgr. United Way Delaware County, Muncie, Ind., 1992—. Recipient Weyerhaeuser Co. scholarship, Federal Way, Washington, 1987, social sci. fellowship U. Washington, Seattle, 1990. Mem. Soc. Am. Foresters, Ind. Acad. Sci., Ind. consortium for Internat., Ind. Ptnrs, of Am. Office: Dept Natural Resources Ball State University Muncie IN 47306

CHANDLER, THERESA LYNE, sociology educator; b. Naperville, Ill., Feb. 20, 1965; d. Norman Eugene and Aurelia Mary (Mudra) Mariani; m. Michael Douglas Chandler, Aug. 10, 1985; children: Jennifer Elizabeth, Michael Douglas II. BS in Sociology, Ill. State U., 1989, MS in Sociology, 1991; postgrad. studies, U. Iowa, 1993—. Grad. tchg. asst. Ill. State U., Normal, 1989-91, adj. sociology instr., 1991; sociology instr. Spoon River Coll., Canton, Ill., 1991—; adj. sociology instr. Eureka (Ill.) Coll., 1991, U. Iowa, Iowa City, 1995; chmn. Instructional Resources Com., Spoon River Coll., 1994-95, mem. Human Rels. Com., 1993—. Contbr. revs. to Teaching Sociology, Jour. of Social and Personal Rels. Basketball coach 3rd grade girls YMCA, Canton, Ill., 1994-95. Mem. Internat. Network on Personal Relationships, Ill. Sociol. Assn. (presenter at confs.), Midwest Sociol. Soc. (presenter 1993-94), Am. Sociol. Soc., Sociologists Against Sexual Harassment, Soc. for Sci. Study of Social Problems. Office: Spoon River Coll 23235 N Co 22 Canton IL 61520

CHANEY, NORMAN RICHARD, English studies educator; b. Brazil, Ind., Feb. 19, 1935; s. Hareld Ebon and Mildred Calista (Love) C.; children: Elizabeth, Paul, Heather; stepchildren: Adrian, Jacqueline, Vicki. BA in English, U. Indpls., 1960; MA in Comparative Lit., Ind. U., 1961; MDiv in Religion and Lit., Yale U., 1964; MA in Religion and Lit., U. Chgo., 1969, PhD in Religion and Lit., 1975. Tchr. Quinnipiac Coll., Hamden, Conn., 1961-63, Otterbein Coll., Westerville, Ohio, 1964-66, 70—, Elgin (Ill.) C.C., 1966-67; assoc. pastor Grace Meth. Ch., Naperville, Ill., 1967-68; tutor U. Chgo., 1969. Author: Theodore Roethke: The Poetics of Wonder, 1981, Six Images of Human Nature, 1990; contbr. articles to profl. jours. Elder United Meth. Ch., 1964—; pastor Hillsdale (Ind.) Meth. Ch.; singer Columbus (Ohio) Symphony Chorus, 1980-90. With Army Med. Corps, 1954-56. Grantee NEH, 1978, 87, 90, Otterbein Coll., 1961-64. Mem. Am. Philos. Assn., MLA, Am. Acad. Religion. Home: 265 Pawnee Dr Westerville OH 43081 Office: Otterbein Coll Dept English Westerville OH 43081

CHANEY, WILLIAM ALBERT, historian, educator; b. Arcadia, Calif., Dec. 23, 1922; s. Horace Pierce and Esther (Bowen) C. AB, U. Calif., Berkeley, 1943, PhD, 1961. Mem. faculty Lawrence U., Appleton, Wis., 1952—, George McKendree Steele prof. Western culture, 1966—, chmn. dept. history, 1968-71, 95-96; vis. prof. Mich. State U., summer 1958. Author: The Cult of Kingship in Anglo-Saxon England: The Transition from Paganism to Christianity, 1970; Contbr. profl. jours., encys. Jr. fellow Harvard Soc. Fellows, 1949-52; grantee Am. Council Learned Socs., 1966-67. Fellow Royal Soc. Arts; mem. MLA, AAUP, Am. Hist. Assn., Mediaeval Acad. Am., Am. Soc. Ch. History, Conf. Brit. Studies, Archeol. Inst. Am. Episcopalian. Home: 215 E Kimball St Appleton WI 54911-5720

CHANEY, WILLIAM REYNOLDS, forestry and natural resources educator; b. McAllen, Tex., Dec. 2, 1941; s. Harold Glen and Mary (Reynolds) C.; m. Joann Judith Simon, Aug. 24, 1968; children: Brandon, Carey. BS, Tex. A&M U., 1964; PhD, U. Wis., 1969. Rsch. assoc. U. Wis., Madison, 1969-70; prof. dept. forestry and natural resources Purdue U., West Lafayette, Ind., 1970—; vis. prof. Univ. Coll. Wales, Aberystwyth, 1977, N.C. State U., 1987. Contbr. articles to profl. jours., chpts. to books. Scoutmaster Sagamore coun. Boy Scouts Am., 1984-86. Plant Growth Regulation Soc. Am., Internat. Soc. Tropical Forestry, Internat. Soc. Arboriculture. Roman Catholic. Avocation: stamp collecting. Home: 1536 Summit Dr West Lafayette IN 47906-2228 Office: Dept Forestry and Natural Resources Purdue Univ West Lafayette IN 47907

CHANG, THEODORE CHIEN-HSIN, psychologist; b. Shanghai, Kiangsu, Peoples Republic of China, June 21, 1926; came to U.S., 1949; s. Yu-Tung and Yin-Fen (Wen) C.; m. Juana Fay Lee, Dec. 31, 1960. MD, St. John's U., Shanghai, 1947; PhD, NYU, 1957. Cert. tchr., Iowa; cert. psychologist. Psychologist NYU/Bellevue Med. Ctr., N.Y.C., 1954-56, Springfield (Md.) State Hosp., 1957-58, Kans. Neurol. Inst., Topeka, 1958-61, Larned (Kans.) State Hosp., 1961-62, Camarillo (Calif.) State Hosp., 1962-65, Cumberland Comprehensive Care Ctr., Somerset, Ky., 1965-69, VA Med. Ctr., Knoxville, Iowa, 1969-71; sales Lincoln Benefit Life Ins., 1975-93, Life USA , 1993-95. Recipient fellowship Econ. Corp. Adminstrn., 1950-56. Mem. Am. Psychol. Assn., Iowa Psychol. Assn. Home: 105 N Park Lane Dr Knoxville IA 50138-3333

CHANG, YI-CHENG, insurance agent; b. Guang Dong, China, June 24, 1943; came to U.S., 1974; s. Jin-Xin and Man-Hua (Ling) C.; m. Rufina Hoi Tong Chung, Sept. 6, 1975; 1 child, Wen Zhong. BS, Hong Kong Bapt. Coll., 1968; MS, Mich. State U., 1976. Owner Self-Strength Air Conditioning, Hong Kong, 1962-68; asst. lab. mgr. Micro Electronics, Hong Kong, 1968-70; purchasing mgr. Gen. Electronics, Hong Kong, 1970-73; material controller Coltronics Ltd., Hong Kong, 1973-74; purchasing agt. Reese Finer Foods, Elk Grove Village, Ill., 1976-79; import clk. Charlotte Charles, Inc., Chgo., 1979-80; purchasing agt. Commodity Communication Corp., Lombard, Ill., 1980-82; agt., speaker N.Y. Life, Chgo., Ill., 1982—; spkr. minority workshop N.Y. Life, 1987-90, chmns. coun., 1984-94, nat. Chinese market conf., 1993-95; spkr. Chgo. Life Underwriters Assn., South Br., 1989, 91, Inst. for Internat. Rsch., Washington, 1996, others; commentator Chinese radio and TV, Chgo. Author: Easy & Practical Ways of Learning Swimming, 1971; columnist Chinese newspapers; contbr. articles to profl. jours. Mem. Orgn. of Chinese-Ams., Chgo., 1983—; founder, bd. dirs. Chgo. Chinese TV, 1990—; bd. dir. Light-a-Lamp Edn. Found., 1988, 89. Mem. Nat. Assn. Life Underwriters (strategic planning com. 1995), Life Underwriters Assn., Chgo. Life Underwriters Assn. (bd. dirs. 1992-94), Million Dollar Round Table, Chinese Alliance No. Ill., Chgo.-Chinese C. of C. (bd. dirs. 1992), Chinese Am. C. of C. and Professions. Office: 211 W 22nd Pl # 3 F Chicago IL 60616-1901

CHAPMAN, ALBERT LEE, anatomy educator, university dean; b. Anderson, Mo., Nov. 5, 1933; s. Coleman V. and Lorena (Farley) C.; m. Patsy Joan Pickett, Aug. 31, 1958; children: Gregory Paul, Robin Annette, Janette Lee, Jeffrey Coleman. AA, Joplin Jr. Coll., 1954; BA, U. Mo., 1956, U. Mo., 1959; PhD, U. Nebr., Omaha, 1962. Instr. U. Kans., Kansas City, 1962-64, asst. prof. med. ctr., 1964-69, assoc. prof. dept. anatomy, 1969-74, dir. Electron Microscopy Rsch. Ctr., 1973-91, prof., 1974—, acting dean grad. studies med. ctr., 1983-85, dean. grad. studies and research med. ctr., 1985-93, assoc. vice chancellor for rsch. adminstrn., dean, 1993-96; acting exec. vice chancellor U. Kans., 1995, vice chancellor acad. affairs, dean grad. studies & rsch., 1996—; pres. U. Kans. Med. Ctr. Rsch. Inst., Inc., 1992—. Mem. Am. Assn. Anatomists, Am. Soc. Cell Biology, Cen. States Electron Microscopy Soc. (pres. 1979-80, 85-86), Electron Microscopy Soc. Am., Sigma Xi (pres. 1978-79). Office: U Kans Med Ctr Office Grad Studies and Rsch 3901 Rainbow Blvd Kansas City KS 66160-0001

CHAPMAN, ALGER BALDWIN, finance executive, lawyer; b. Portland, Maine, Sept. 28, 1931; s. Alger Baldwin Sr. and Elizabeth (Ives) C.; m. Beatrice Bishop, Oct. 30, 1983; children: Alger III, Samuel P., Andrew I., Henry H. BA, Williams Coll., 1953; JD, Columbia U., 1956. Bar: N.Y. 1957. Pres. Shearson, Hammill & Co., 1970-74; co-chmn. Shearson & Co., 1974-81; vice chmn. Am. Express Bank, 1982-85; chmn., chief exec. officer Chgo. Bd. Options Exchange, 1986—; bd. dirs. Johnson Internat., Smith Barney, Worldwide Funds, HDO. Clubs: Chgo., Racquet Club Chgo.; Metropolitan (N.Y.C.); Attic, Glenview. Home: 1500 N Lake Shore Dr Chicago IL 60610-1624 Office: Chgo Bd Options Exch 400 S La Salle St Chicago IL 60605-1023

CHAPMAN, CONRAD DANIEL, lawyer; b. Detroit, July 31, 1933; s. Conrad F. and Alexandrine C. (Baranski) C.; m. Carol Lynn DeBash, Sept. 1, 1956; children: Stephen Daniel, Richard Thomas, Suzanne Marie. BA, U. Detroit, 1954, JD summa cum laude, 1957; LLM in Taxation, Wayne State U., 1964. Bar: Mich. 1957, U.S. Dist. Ct. (so. dist.) Mich. 1957. Pres., chmn. bd. dirs. Powers, Chapman, DeAgostino, Meyers & Milia and predecessor firms, Troy, Mich., 1964—. Mem. ABA, Detroit Bar Assn., Oakland Bar Assn., Am. Arbitration Assn., Detroit Estate Planning Coun., Oakland Estate Planning Coun., Nat. Assn. Estate Planning Counc., Detroit Athletic Club, Detroit Golf Club, Elks. Office: Powers Chapman DeAgostino 3001 W Big Beaver Rd Troy MI 48084-3101

CHAPMAN, FERN SCHUMER, freelance writer; b. Chgo., Nov. 29, 1954; d. William and Edith (Westerfeld) Schumer; m. Stephen James Chapman, Sept. 10, 1983; children: Ross James, Keith Westerfeld, Isabelle Sarah. Student, Trinity Coll., Oxford, Eng., summer 1974; BA, U. Wis., 1976; MA, Northwestern U., 1977. Washington corr. Berns Bur., 1977-78; staff writer Forbes mag., Washington, 1978-80; reporter Chgo. Tribune, 1980-83; freelance writer Evanston, Ill., 1983—; instr. writing Loyola U., Chgo., 1983-85, Northwestern U., 1990—. Contbr. articles to Fortune, U.S. News and World Report, Wall St. Jour., Washington Post, USA Today, Money, Reason, Washingtonian, Iowa Woman. Boesky fellow Harvard U. Sch. Pub. Health, 1985. Address: 1810 Shore Acres Dr Lake Bluff IL 60044-1339

CHAPMAN, GERALD D., school superintendent; b. Aurora, Ill., Nov. 21, 1943; s. Kenneth William and Helen Faye (Fossler) C.; m. Linda J. Poindexter, July 22, 1966; children: Bradley G., Alison J. BS, No. Ill. U., 1965; MA, Northwestern U., 1968; EdD, Ind. U., 1972. Lic. adminstr., supervision supt., Ind.; cert. adminstrv. supt. K-12, adminstrv. gen. adminstr. K-12, high sch. tchr., Ill. Math. tchr. William Fremd H.S., Palatine, Ill., 1965-71, activities dir., 1970-71, asst. prin., 1972-73; assoc. prin. Hoffman Estates (Ill.) H.S., 1973-74; asst. supt. H.S. Dist. 211, Palatine, 1974-85, assoc. supt., 1985-90, supt. of schs., 1990—; math. lectr. William Rainey Harper Coll., Palatine, 1969-71, 76-82; grad. asst. Ind. U., Bloomington, 1971-72; adv. bd. Cook County Regional Office of Edn. Church elder, treas. St. Paul United Ch., Palatine, 1974-78; coach, ofcl. Palatine Park Dist., 1974-80; mem. Lions Club, Palatine, 1978-82; bd. dirs. C. of C., Palatine, 1990—. Recipient scholarships No. Ill. U., 1961-65, NSF, Northwestern U., 1966-69, Sch. of Edn. Ind. U., 1971-72. Mem. Am. Assn. Sch. Adminstrs., Ill. Assn. Sch. Adminstrs., Northwest 2001 (bd. dirs. 1994—), Northwest Suburbs Supts. Assn. (chmn. 1995—). Office: High Sch Dist 211 1750 S Roselle Rd Palatine IL 60067

CHAPMAN, GILBERT BRYANT, physicist; b. Uniontown, Ala., July 8, 1935; s. Gilbert Bryant and Annie Lillie (Stallworth) C.; m. Loretta Woodward, June 5, 1960 (dec. Sept. 1994); children: Annie L., Bernice M., Cedric N., David O., Ernest P., Frances Q.H., Gilbert Bryant III. BS in Math. and Chemistry, Baldwin Wallace Coll., Berea, Ohio, 1968; MS in Physics, Cleve. State U., 1973; MBA, Mich. State U., 1990; postgrad, Kent State U., Ohio, 1974-76. Phys. sci. technician NASA-Lewis Rsch. Ctr., Cleve., 1953-68, emission spectroscopist, 1968-75, materials engr., 1975-77; sr. rsch. engr. Ford Motor Co., Redford Twp., Mich., 1977-83, project engr., 1983-86; adv. materials testing specialist Chrysler Corp., Highland Park, Mich., 1986-89; adv. materials specialist Chrysler Corp., Madison Heights, Mich., 1989-91, advanced materials and product exec., 1991-95; advanced materials cons., 1995—; chmn. auto. com. '87 Soc. Mfg. Engrs. Composites Group, Dearborn, 1987; chmn. ind. adv. bd. NDE/Ctr., Iowa State U., Ames, 1989, 90; mem. indsl. adv. bd. Inst. for Mfg. Rsch., Wayne State U., Ctrl. State U., U. Tex.-Pan Am.; chair Internat. Symposium on Automotive Tech. and Automation Materials Conf., 1996. Contbr. articles to profl. jours., chpts. to books. Lay leader, elder SDA Ch. of Southfield, Mich., 1983-95; bd. trustees Mt. Vernon Acad., Ohio, 1972-76; lay adv. coun. Ohio Conf. SDA, 1974-77. With USAF, 1959-61. Recipient Group Achievement award, NASA Lewis Rsch. Ctr., 1970, Apollo Achievement award, 1968, Mayor Archer's Proclamation, Motor City Youth Fedn., 1994, Spirit of Detroit award Detroit City Coun., 1994; named one of Best and Brightest Profls., Dollars and Sense Mag., 1993. Fellow Am. Soc. Nondestructive Testing (cert. level III 6 NDT methods); mem. AAAS, ASM (polymer composites program com. paper 1986), ASTM, IEEE, SAE (award for excellence in oral presentation), Am. Chem. Soc., Am. Phys. Soc., Am. Soc. for Composites, Engring. Soc. Detroit (sci. com., ASM/ESD Best Paper award 1993), Fedn. of Analytical Chemists, Nat. Tech. Assn. (Cleve. program com.), Soc. for Applied Spectroscopy (Cleve. vice chair, sec.), Soc. Mfg. Engrs. (chaired CMA adv. bd.), Soc. Physics Students (pres.), Internat. Symposium on Automative Tech. and Automation (chair materials conf. 1996). Home: 17860 Bonstelle Ave Southfield MI 48075-3452 Office: Chrysler Corp 30900 Stephenson Hwy Madison Heights MI 48071-1617

CHAPMAN, JOHN WILLIAM, JR., marketing executive; b. Greensboro, N.C., Mar. 4, 1955; s. John William and Mary Elizabeth (Arndt) C.; m. Judith Arlene Vos, Mar. 28, 1992. BS in Computer Info. Systems, Ohio State U., 1978. Project engr. AccuRay Corp., Columbus, Ohio, 1978-82, mktg. mgr., 1982-84; mgr. demonstrations and exhbns. Combustion Engring., Columbus, 1984-90; project mgr. ABB Indsl. Sys. (formerly ABB Process Automation, Columbus, 1990-92, mgr. solutions ctrs., 1992—. Comm. chmn. disaster svcs. ARC, Columbus, 1988—; mem. Columbus Zoo Docent Assn., 1982—; pres. Cen. Ohio Amateur Radio Emergency Svc., 1988—. Mem. Tech. Assn. Pulp and Paper Industry. Home: 743 Fleetrun Ave Gahanna OH 43230-3267 Office: ABB Indsl Sys 650 Ackerman Rd Columbus OH 43202-4500

CHAPMAN, KATHLEEN HALLORAN, state legislator, lawyer; b. Estherville, Iowa, Jan. 19, 1937; d. Edward E. and Meryl (McConoughey) Halloran; m. Allen Ray Chapman, Apr. 29, 1961; children: Christopher, Stuart. BA, U. Iowa, 1959, JD, 1974. Bar: Iowa 1974, U.S. Ct. Appeals (8th cir.) 1974. Prin. Booth & Chapman, Cedar Rapids, Iowa, 1974—; mem. Iowa Ho. of Reps., Des Moines, 1983-92, vice chmn. judiciary com., 1983-86, vice chmn. ethics com., 1985-88, vice chmn. ways and means com., 1987-88, chmn. rules and adminstrn. com., 1987-88, asst. majority leader, 1989-90, chmn. edn. appropriations, 1991-92; Legis. Coun. Iowa Gen. Assembly, 1987-92; participant Atlantic Exch., 1989. Trustee East Cen. Regional Libr., Cedar Rapids, 1974-80, Tanager Place, Cedar Rapids, 1978—. Toll fellow Coun. State Govts., 1988; named Woman of Yr. Linn County, 1995. Mem. Iowa Bar Assn. (chair adminstrv. law sect. 1995-96). Democrat. Roman Catholic. Office: 425 2d St SE 1010 The Ctr 425 2nd St SE Cedar Rapids IA 52401

CHAPMAN, PAULA ANNE, cultural organization administrator; b. Tiffin, Ohio, Sept. 15, 1960; d. Paul Everett and Mary Virginia (Brosious) Young; m. James Nelson Cook, Sept. 16, 1977 (div. Dec. 1981); children: Nichole Adele, Jessica Theresa, Samantha Rebekah; m. Harry N. Chapman, Dec. 10, 1988. BS in Psychology, Heidelberg Coll., 1982; MA in Polit. Sci., Bowling Green (Ohio) State U., 1987; postgrad., Ball State U., 1994—. Child therapist Sandusky (Ohio) Youth Referral Svc., 1982-83; parole officer State of Ohio, Columbus, 1983-86; dep. dir. Seneca, Sandusky and Wyandot Commn. Mental Health Bd., Tiffin, 1986-87; program dir. WSOS Cmty. Action Commn., Fremont, Ohio, 1987-88; dir. community devel. Seneca Indsl. and Econ. Devel. Corp., Tiffin, 1988-90; exec. dir. Tiffin Area C. of C./Seneca Indsl. & Econ. Devel. Corp., Tiffin, 1988-90; pres. Chapman Cmty. Devel. Cons., Tiffin, 1990-93; dir. devel. St. Francis Health Care Ctr., Green Springs, Ohio, 1993-94, St. Francis Coll., Ft. Wayne, Ind., 1994—; adj. prof. econs. Tiffin U., 1987-94; mem. ednl. adv. bd. Vanguard/Sentinel Vocat. Sch., Fremont, 1989-90; chmn. Tiffin Fair Housing Bd., 1985-90; bd. dirs. Ohio Indsl. Tng. Program, Sandusky, 1988-90, Pvt. Industry Coun., Fremont, Seneca County Revolving Loan Fund, Tiffin; chairperson adv. bd. WSOS. Candidate Seneca County Commr., 1992; docent Ft. Wayne Children's Zoo; active Ft. Wayne Women's Bur.; vol. Legal Svcs. Maumee Valley, Ft. Wayne; mem. fin./devel. com. Ft. Wayne YWCA; mem. mktg. com. Sci. Ctrl., Ft. Wayne; mem. Grad. Ft. Wayne Leadership Works, 1994; vol. house mgr. Ft. Wayne Civic Theatre. Mem. NAFE, Nat. Soc. Fundraising Execs. (mem. N.W. Ind. cluster steering com.), Bus. and Profl. Women's Assn. (Young Career Woman of Yr. 1987, 89), Ft. Wayne C. of C. (mem. VIP com. Ambs. Club), Kiwanis Internat. (mem. Ind. dist. steering com., Iodine Deficiency Disease project, bd. dirs. Ft. Wayne Downtown chpt.). Home: 1721 Woodland Crossing Fort Wayne IN 46825-7228

CHAPMAN, RANDELL BARKLEY, family and emergency physician, medical educator; b. Altus, Okla., July 20, 1955; s. Dale Barkley and Doris Quay (Saunders) C.; m. Sydney Lee Ellison, Mar. 11, 1978; children: Chase Creighton, Cory Lee, Sherry Jordan Barkley. BS in Microbiology, U. Okla., Norman, 1978; MD, U. Okla., Oklahoma City, 1983. Diplomate Am. Bd. Family Practice; lic. in healing arts, Kans. Intern in family medicine Okla. Meml. Hosp., Norman, 1983-84, resident in family medicine, 1984-86; emergency physician Norman Regional Hosp., 1986-87; pvt. practice, Bapt. Care Ctr., Yukon, Okla., 1987-89, Altus, Okla., 1989-91; clin. lab. dir. Family Health Ctr., Derby, 1991-95; prin. physician Rose Hill (Kans.) Med. Ctr., 1995—; mem. med. staff Via Christi Med. Ctr., St. Joseph Campus, Wichita, Kans., 1991—, St. Francis Campus, 1995—, Wesley Med. Ctr., Wichita, 1991—; clin. instr. Butler County C.C., 1991-95. Fellow Am. Acad. Family Practice, Assn. Emergency Physicians; mem. AMA (Physician's Recognition award with spl. commendation for self-directed learning 1995), Am. Coll. Sports Medicine, Assn. Emergency Physicians (charter), Kans. Acad. Family Practice, Sedgewick County Med. Soc. (alternate del. Kans. Med. Polit. Action Com. 1992-94), Sigma Phi Epsilon. Democrat. Methodist. Office: Box 247 1305 Rose Hill Rd Rose Hill KS 67133

CHAPMAN, ROBIN SMITH, psycholinguist, educator; b. Washington, July 1, 1942; d. Nicholas Monroe Smith Jr. and Elizabeth Hightower (Kimbrough) McNees; m. Thomas Woodring Chapman, Nov. 26, 1968 (div.); children: John Kimbrough, Joshua Woodring. BA with high honors, Swarthmore (Pa.) Coll., 1964; PhD, U. Calif., Berkeley, 1967. Rsch. assoc. Wis. R & D Ctr. for Cognitive Learning, Madison, 1967-91; asst. prof. U. Wis., Madison, 1971-75, assoc. prof. communicative disorders, 1975-79, prof. communicative disorders, 1979—; vis. lectr. Airlangga U., Sura Baya, Indonesia, 1977; mem. adv. bd. Silver-Burdette; mem. human devel. and aging study sect. 3 NIH, 1989-92, chair, 1992-94. Editor: Processes in Language Acquisition and Disorders, 1992; contbg. author 25 books on child lang.; contbr. 25 articles to profl. jours.; author 2 books on poetry, 1989, 91. Credentials chair Wis. Fellowship of Poets, 1989-92. NSF fellow, 1964; NIH grantee, 1965-67. Fellow Am. Speech-Lang. Hearing Assn. (mem. publ. bd. 1981-88, editor ASHA monographs 1984-88); mem. Am. Acad. Mental Retardation, Linguistic Soc. Am., Soc. Rsch. in Child Devel., Sigma Xi, Phi Beta Kappa. Democrat. Unitarian. Office: U Wis Comms Disorders 1975 Willow Dr Madison WI 53706

CHAPMAN, STEVEN G., portfolio manager; b. Flint, Mich., July 8, 1947. Sr. portfolio mgr. Smith Barney Inc., Grand Rapids, Mich., 1982—. Sgt. U.S. Army, 1965-68.

CHAPPARS, TIMOTHY STEPHEN, lawyer; b. Cin., July 23, 1952; s. Gregory S. and Helen (Maragos) C.; m. Laurie A. Kress, Dec. 24, 1986 (div. Sept. 1987); m. Laurie A. Kress, Apr. 18, 1990; children: Alexander T., Jake A. BS, Duke U., 1974; JD, U. Cin., 1978. Assoc. Cox & Chappars, Xenia, Ohio, 1978-94, Bryant Law Office, Wilmington, Ohio, 1981—; trial atty. Pub. Defender's Office, Clinton County, Wilmington, 1978-88; lectr. So. State Jr. Coll., Wilmington, 1982. Mem. Ohio Bar Assn., Am. Trial Lawyers Acad., Ohio Acad. Trial Lawyers. Methodist. Home: 2025 Winding Brook Way Xenia OH 45385-9382 Office: Chappars Law Office Box 280 Xenia OH 45385

CHARA, PAUL JOHN, psychology educator; b. Middletown, N.Y., June 13, 1953; s. Paul J. and Linnie I. (Miller) C.; m. Kathleen Ann Leibert, July 21, 1990; children: Christian Paul, Karston John, Kristof Caleb. BA, U. Rochester, 1975; MS, Mont. State U., 1977; PhD, U. Tenn., 1982. Counselor Shadow Mountain Inst., Tulsa, 1984-86, City of Faith Chem. Dependency Ctr., Tulsa, 1986, St. John Med. Ctr., Tulsa, 1986-87; asst. prof. Oral Roberts U., Tulsa, 1982-87; assoc. prof. psychology Loras Coll., Dubuque, Iowa, 1987—; adj. prof. Tulsa Jr. Coll., 1984-86, Langston U., Tulsa, 1982-87; cons. reader Perceptual and Motor Skills jour., Psychol. Reports Jour., 1988-95; reviewer Harper Collins, 1990, Harcourt Brace Jovanovich, 1992—; conv. presenter, Mont., Tenn., Okla., Iowa, Fla., Wis., N.Y., 1976—. Author: Handbook in Scientific Psychology, 1988, Biological/Cognitive Psychology, 1990, 93, The Art of Virtue, 1996; also articles in psychology, sociology and philosophy. Judge, team leader Okla. Sci. Fair, Tulsa, 1986-87; coll. rep. ROTC Selection Com., Dubuque, 1989; coord. adult edn. St. John Episcopal Ch., Dubuque, 1991-92; adult edn. tchr. Galena Ill. Bible Ch. Mem. Coun. Tchrs. Undergrad. Psychology, Am. Psychol. Soc., Nat. Honor Soc. Office: Loras Coll Psychology Dept Dubuque IA 52004

CHARBAUSKI, COLLEEN ANNE, accountant; b. Geneva, Ill., Apr. 11, 1959; d. Joseph Raymond and Marlene Josephine (Schramer) Murphy; m. David Michael Charbauski, Sept. 16, 1989; 1 child, Kevin Michael. AA, Coll. DuPage, 1979; BA, Aurora U., 1993. Acct. Caterpillar, Inc., Aurora, Ill., 1979—; officer Murphy Laundries, Inc., Oswego, Ill., 1989-94; bd. dirs. Giving Employees Meaningful Svc. (GEMS), Aurora. Mem. com. girls and boys basketball coach, Sugar Grove, Ill., 1991-96; bd. dirs. Sugar Grove Athletic Assn., 1993-94; den leader Boy Scouts Am., Sugar Grove, 1993—; mem. St. Anne's Women's Club, Oswego, 1977—; pres. Bus. Resources Social Club, aurora, 1983-85, 88-89, 93-95. Mem. Inst. Mgmt. Accts., Omicron Delta Kappa, Phi Theta Kappa. Republican. Roman Catholic. Office: Caterpillar Inc PO Box 348 Aurora IL 60507-0348

CHARD, LESLIE FRANK, II, English language educator; b. Dunkirk, N.Y., Sept. 2, 1934; s. Leslie Frank and Sarah Helen (Higham) C.; m. Anne Smith, Apr. 6, 1961 (div. Oct. 1975); children: Leslie III, Kathleen M., Sarah E.; m. Diane Engber, Dec. 20, 1980; 1 child, Joseph Samuels. BA, Trinity Coll., Hartford, Conn., 1956, MA, 1958; PhD, Duke U., 1962. Instr. in English Emory U., Atlanta, 1961-64, asst. prof. English, 1964-66; assoc. prof. English U. Cin., 1966-75, prof. English, 1975—, dir. undergrad. studies English, 1991-93. Author: Dissenting Republican, 1972; editor: Urban Resources, 1983-89. Democrat. Office: U Cin Dept English Cincinnati OH 45221-0069

CHAREWICZ, DAVID MICHAEL, photographer; b. Chgo., Feb. 17, 1932; s. Michael and Stella (Pietrzak) C.; student DePaul U., 1957, Northwestern U., 1952; MA in Photography, Profl. Photographers Am. Inc., 1986; m. Catherine Uccello, Nov. 8, 1952; children: Michael, Karen, Daniel. Trainee, Merill Chase, Chgo., 1950-51; dark room technician Maurice Seymour, Chgo., 1951-52; photographer Oscar & Assos., Chgo., 1955-63; owner Dave Chare Photography, Park Ridge, Ill., 1963—; pres., owner C&C Duplicating, Inc., 1978-93. Pres. Oakton Parent Tchr. Club, 1968-69, del. dist. 64 caucus, 1970, 73; mem. centennial photo com., Park Ridge, Ill., 1973; mem. sponsoring com. Park Ridge Men's Prayer Breakfast 1982—. Served with AUS, 1952-54. Mem. Am. Soc. Photographers, Profl. Photographers Assn., Midstate Indsl. Photographers Assn. (treas. 1981, pres. 1984-85). Home: 739 N Northwest Hwy Park Ridge IL 60068-2541 Office: 1045 N Northwest Hwy Park Ridge IL 60068-1805

CHARLA, LEONARD FRANCIS, lawyer; b. New Rochelle, N.Y., May 4, 1940; s. Leonard A. and Mary L. Charla; m. Kathleen Gerace, Feb. 3, 1968 (div. Dec. 1988); children: Larisa, Christopher; m. Elizabeth A. Du Mouchelle, Aug. 27, 1993. BA, Iona Coll., 1962; JD, Cath. U., 1965; LLM, George Washington U., 1971. Bar: D.C. 1967, N.J. 1970, Mich. 1971. Tech. writer IRS, Washington, 1966-67; atty. adv. ICC, Washington, 1967, atty., 1968-69; mgmt. intern HEW, Washington, 1967-68; atty. Bowes & Millner, Transp. Cons., Newark, N.J., 1969-71; atty. legal staff GM, Detroit, 1971-85, sr. counsel, 1985-87, asst. gen. counsel, 1987-89; sr. v.p. Clean Sites Inc., Alexandria, Va., 1989-90; shareholder, Butzel Long, Detroit and Birmingham, Mich., 1990—; mem. faculty Ctr. for Creative Studies, Coll. Art and Design, Detroit, 1978-89, adj. assoc. prof., 1982-89; faculty art U. Mich., 1980, 84-89, adj. asst. prof. 1988-89. Bd. dirs. Gt. Lakes Performing Artists Assocs., 1983-85; bd. dirs. Mich. Assn. Community Arts Agys., 1983-89, 92-93, vice-chair 1986-88, chair, 1988-89; bd. govs. Cath. U. Am. Alumni, 1982, v.p., 1993—; active Info. Network Superfund Settlements, 1988—; bd. regents, Cath. U. Am., 1992—, Birmingham Bloomfield Art Assn., 1987-88, 94-95. Fellow N.Y. State Regents, 1962; scholar Cath. U. Law Sch., 1962-65. Mem. ABA, Mich. State Bar Assn. (chmn. arts sect. 1980-81, Arts Comm. Entertainment and Sports sect. coun. 1979-88, 92—). Office: Butzel Long 150 W Jefferson Ave Ste 900 Detroit MI 48226-4415

CHARLES, ANN KENNETT, editor, publisher; b. Mound City, Kans., Apr. 24, 1951; d. Henry Issac and Alice Christeen (Jackson) McNabb; 1 child, Tyler Kennett; m. Hugh Keeney Charles, July 20, 1991. Program devel. and claims examiner State of Kans. Dept. Human Resources, Parsons, 1975-81; advt. sales rep. Parsons Sun, 1981-82, advt. dir., 1982-85, mktg. dir., 1985-89, asst. to publisher, 1989-90, editor, publisher, pres., 1990—. Founding pres. Mainstreet Pride, Parsons, 1986-93; mem. Kans. Main Street Adv. Bd., Topeka, 1988-91; v.p. Parsons Industries, 1990-92, pres., 1992-95, bd. dirs., 1996—; trustee Mid-Am. Inc., Parsons, 1990-92. Mem. Kans. Press Assn. (bd. dirs. 1986-88, 93—, v.p. 1995—), Kans. Newspaper Advt. Assn. (pres. 1986-88), Parsons C. of C. (bd. dirs. 1988-91). Office: Parsons Pub Co 220 S 18th St PO Box 836 Parsons KS 67357

CHARLESWORTH, PAUL, research chemist, educator; b. Nottingham, Eng., Nov. 22, 1967; arrived in U.S., 1993; s. Kenneth and Margaret (Eason) C. BS in Chemistry and Geology with honors, Keele U., 1990, PhD in Chemistry, 1993. Rsch. chemist Bowling Green (Ohio) State U., 1993-94; rsch. chemist, educator Iowa State U., Ames, 1995—. Contbr. papers to profl. jours. Mem. Am. Chem. Soc., Royal Soc. Chemistry. Home: 12 Walkmill Dr, Hucknall NG158BX, England Office: Iowa State U 3807 Gilman Hall Ames IA 50011

CHARLIER, PATRICIA ANN, lawyer; b. Marshalltown, Iowa, Dec. 24, 1957; d. Tom Carroll Charlier and Phyllis Yvonne (Gallentine) Miller; m. Kelvin Frank Chvojka, May 16, 1981 (div. Apr. 1989); m. Steven Dale Nederhoff, Jan. 18, 1992; children: Jenny Nederhoff, Julie Nederhoff, Jon Nederhoff. BA summa cum laude, Drake U., Marshalltown, 1980; JD, Drake U., Des Moines, 1992. Bar: Ill., U.S. Patent and Trademark Office. Atty. assoc. Jenner & Block, Chgo., 1992-94; intellectual property atty. Nalco Chem. Co., Naperville, Ill., 1995—. Precinct committeeman Republican Party, Troy Twp., Ill., 1995—. Mem. Ill. State Bar Assn., Will County Bar Assn., Will County Woman's Bar Assn., Intellectual Property Law Assn. Chgo., Order of Coif, Phi Beta kappa. Christian. Home: 3413 Christine Ave Shorewood IL 60431

CHARLSON, DAVID HARVEY, executive search company professional; b. Pitts., May 26, 1947; s. Raymond Milton and Helen Joan (Wesley) C.; m. Michal Brooke Riley, Aug. 22, 1969; 1 child, Adam David. BS, U. Ariz., 1969. Personnel dir. internat. div. Bank of Am., San Francisco, 1969-73; mgr. employment Gen. Foods Corp., White Plains, N.Y., 1973-74; staff v.p. Staub-Warmbold Assocs., San Francisco, 1974-76; mng. dir., sr. ptnr. Korn-Ferry Internat., Chgo., 1976-84; exec. v.p., mng. dir. Richards Cons., Chgo., 1984-89; pres., CEO Chestnut Hill Internat. LLC, Chgo., 1989—; cons. Noreast Banks, Mpls., 1978-84, Blue Cross-Blue Shield Ill., Chgo., 1978—, Wards Corp., Chgo., 1993, Sherring-Plough Corp., 1989—, Marrin-Merrill Daw, 1986—; bd. dirs. Universal Casualty Co., Dental Network Am., Kemper Ins. Co., I.V.T. Corp. Contbr. articles to profl. publs. Mem. Oak Park (Ill.) Sch. Dist. Bd. Edn., 1978-80; bd. dirs. U. Chgo. Grad. Sch. Bus., 1982-84, mem. bd. advisors; bd. dirs. Better Boys Found., Chgo., 1982-84; treas. Chgo. Dist. Tennis Assn., 1984-86; chmn. Ill. Citizens for Perot, 1992; sr. advisor Clinton-Gore Presdl. Campaign, 1992, Ill. Dem. Com., 1992—; mem. bd. cons. Little City Found.; mem. bd. advisors Highland Park Hosp. Recipient NFL Players Assn. award Better Boys Found., 1984; named One of Am.'s Top 100 Exec. Recruiters, Harper & Row Publs., One of 150 Top Exec. Recruiters in Am., 1992, One of 200 Top Exec. Recruiters in N.Am., 1994. Mem. Internat. Motor Sports Assn., Pharm. Mfrs. Assn., Assn. Exec. Recruitment Cos., Univ. Club Chgo., Pres.' Club U. Ariz., Sports Car Club Am., Hillcrest Country Club. Home: 1927 Half Day Rd Highland Park IL 60035-1509 Office: Chestnut Hill Internat LLC 12526 High Bluff Dr S S-300 San Diego CA 92130

CHARLTON, BETTY JO, retired state legislator; b. Reno County, Kans., June 15, 1923; d. Joseph and Elma (Johnson) Canning; BA, U. Kans., 1970, MA, 1976; m. Robert Sansom Charlton, Feb. 24, 1946 (dec. 1984); children: John Robert, Richard Bruce. Asst. instr. polit. sci. and western civilization U. Kans., Lawrence, 1970-73; legis. adminstrv. svcs. employee State of Kans., Topeka, 1977-78, legis. aide gov's. office, 1979; mem. Kans. Ho. of Reps., 1980-95, ret., 1995.

CHARMOLI, MARGARET CHARITY, psychologist; b. Virginia, Minn., Dec. 8, 1951; d. Arnold Amadeo and Orvokki Katri (Harju) C. BA, Macalester Coll., St. Paul, 1974; MA, U. Minn., 1979, PhD, 1986. Lic. psychologist, Minn.; lic. marriage and family therapist, Minn. Adminstrv. intern Ramsey County Adminstr., St. Paul, 1974-76; adminstrv. asst. Ramsey County Comty. Human Svcs., St. Paul, 1976-82; grad. asst. Pers. Decisions, Inc., Mpls., 1980-85; counselor Office for Students with Disabilities U. Minn., Mpls., 1982-85, counselor Vocat. Assessment Clinic, 1984-86; psychologist employee assistance program Met. Clinic of Counseling, Mpls., 1985-86; psychologist Met. Clinic of Counseling, Edina, 1986-88, Maplewood (Minn.) Psychol. Assocs., 1988—; mem. annual mtg. com. Minn. Psychol. Assn., St. Paul, 1983-84, 93-96, chair 1994, mem. exec. coun. 1994—, pres.-elect 1995, pres. 1996; APA rep. to Task Force on Psychology and the Handicapped Minn. Psychol. Assn., St. Paul, 1983-86; mem. Steering Com. Minn. Women Psychologists, Mpls., 1986-88, 93-96, 1st Annual Rsch. award 1984. Author: (book rev.) Contemporary Psychology, 1994; contbr. article to profl. jour. Vol. Pooneil Corner, St. Paul, 1970-71, Inn Place, St. Paul, 1970-71, Family Tree Health Clinic, 1973-75, pres., 1977-78; intern Ctr. for Urban Encounter, 1974, Orgn. for a Better St. Paul, 1974; bd. dirs. Neighborhood Health Clinics, St. Paul, 1974-78, Ramsey Action Programs, St. Paul, 1975-76; mem. adv. com. Exodus, Inc., St. Paul, 1977-78; appointments chair Ramsey County Women's Polit. Caucus, St. Paul, 1978-80, co-chair, 1980-81; mem. St. Paul Human Rights Commn., 1980-89, St. Paul Mayor's Blue Ribbon Task Force on Affirmative Action, St. Paul, 1981; vice-chair Equal Opportunities Coalition, St. Paul, 1981-83; founder, chair Rainbow Forum, St. Paul, 1994-95. Recipient Recognition of Svcs. award Ramsey Action Programs, 1975, Recognition of Svcs. award City of St. Paul, 1983, 85, Sen. Nicholas Coleman Meml. Svc. award St. Paul Gay and Lesbian Comtys., 1985, Vol. Cert. of Recognition, State of Minn., 1986, Svc. award St. Paul Human Rights Commn., 1989; spl. doctoral dissertation grantee U. Minn., 1982. Mem. APA, Minn. Psychol. Assn. (pres.-elect 1995, pres. 1996, APA rep. to task force 1983-86, mem. ann. meeting com. 1983-84, exec. coun. 1994-97), Minn. Women Psychologists (mem. steering com. 1986-88, 93-96, treas. 1993-95, 1st Ann. Rsch. award 1984), Minn. Soc. for Clin. Hypnosis, Minn. Coun. Sexual Addiction and Compulsivity (bd. dirs. 1996), Phi Kappa Phi. Democrat. Ecumenical. Home: 1870 Roblyn Ave Saint Paul MN 55104 Office: Maplewood Psychol Assocs 2480 White Bear Ave Maplewood MN 55109

CHARNITSKY, GARY A., engineer; b. Ypsilanti, Mich., Nov. 25, 1949. A, Washtenaw C.C., 1979; student, Oakland C.C. Engr. Republic Dye & Tool, Bellville, Mich., 1973-87; process engr. Graph-Tech, Troy, Mich., 1987-92; product engr. Superior Cam, Madison Heights, Mich., 1992—. Office: Superior Cam 31240 Stephenson Hwy Madison Heights MI 48071-1620

CHARTERS, MICHAEL G., securities company executive; b. Cornwall, Ont., Can., Apr. 8, 1961. BS in Bus., Miami U., Oxford, Ohio, 1983. Investment broker E.F. Hutton, Columbus, Ohio, 1984-89; sr. v.p. Prudential Securities Inc., Columbus, 1989—, mem. president's coun., 1991—. Mem. Springfield Country Club (Ohio), Columbus Shamrock Club, KC. Roman Catholic. Office: Prudential Securities Inc 8101 N High St Ste 150 Columbus OH 43235-1406

CHARTIER, CHARLES ADRIAN, sales executive; b. Tiffin, Ohio, Feb. 4, 1955; s. Victor Howard and Lois Eileen (Dunn) C.; m. Josie Ann Manahan, Dec. 29, 1979; children: Holly Nicole, Heather Ann, Gabrielle Irene. BS in Edn., Ohio State U., 1977; MEd, Bowling Green State U., 1978. Asst. athletic trainer Bowling Green (Ohio) State U., 1978-79; sales rep. McNeil Pharm., Toledo, 1979-87; regional sales mgr. LifeScan, Inc., Monclova, Ohio, 1987—. Mem. Am. Mgmt. Assn., Am. Assn. Diabetes Educators, Am. Diabetes Assn. Home and Office: 7759 Monclova Rd Monclova OH 43542-9701

CHASE, MARIA ELAINE GAROUFALIS, publishing company executive; b. Chgo., Jan. 9, 1957; d. Byron L. and Irene (Mathews) Garoufalis. BS, Manchester Coll., 1979. CPA, Ill. Sr. mgr. Ernst & Young, Chgo., 1979-92; contr., v.p. fin. Fox Valley Press, Inc., Plainfield, Ill., 1993—. Bd. trustees rep., Alumni Assn. bd. dirs. Manchester Coll.; bd. dirs. St. Nectarios Greek Orthodox Ch. Ladies' Soc., Palatine, Ill., 1985-92, pres., 1989-90. Mem. AICPA, AMA, NAFE, Internat. Newspaper Fin. Execs., Ill. CPA Soc., Manchester Coll. Acctg. Alumni Assn., Greek Women's Univ. Club. Office: Fox Valley Press Inc 3101 N Us Highway 30 Plainfield IL 60544-9604

CHASE, REX B., stockbroker; b. Midland, Mich., Apr. 10, 1937. BS, Ctrl. Mich. U., 1959. MBA, 1960. MEd. mgr. Sears Roebuck & Co., Canton, Ohio, 1959-84; registered rep. Dean Witter, Ohio, 1984-90, Butler Wick & Co., Canton, 1990-92; investment mgr. AAA Discount Stock Brokers, Barberton, Ohio, 1992—. Mem. Rotary, Elks. Methodist. Office: AAA Discount Stock Brokers 248 Norton Ave Barberton OH 44203-1932

CHASE, ROBERT WILLIAM, petroleum engineering educator, consultant; b. Scranton, Pa., Oct. 24, 1950; s. Elmer Frank and Doris Lynette (Shafer) C.; m. Carol Ann Leh, Oct. 11, 1975; children: Christopher Robert, Thomas William. BS in Petroleum Engring., Pa. State U., 1972, MS in Petroleum Engring., 1974, PhD in Petroleum Engring., 1980. Engr.-in-tng. Halliburton Svcs., Elkview, W.Va., 1972; rsch. engr. Gulf R & D Corp., Harmarville, Pa., 1974; asst. prof. W.Va. U., Morgantown, 1976-78; prof., dir. petroleum engring. program Marietta (Ohio) Coll., 1978—; cons. Gulf Sci. & Devel. Corp., Harmarville, 1978, Sci. Applications Inc., Morgantown, 1978-79, Columbia Gas, Charleston, W.Va., 1984—. Mem. contemporary Christian musical group Faithful Friends. Mem. contemporary Christian musical group Faithful Friends. Rsch. grantee U.S. Dept. Energy, Morgantown, 1977-78. Mem. Soc. Petroleum Engrs. (bd. dirs. 1991-94), Assn. Petroleum Engring. Dept. Heads (pres. 1990-91), S.E. Ohio Oil & Gas Assn. (adv. com. 1989-91). Republican. Methodist. Office: Marietta Coll 215 Fifth St Marietta OH 45750-3029

CHASE, THEODORE TAYLOR, securities trader; b. Quincy, Ill., May 29, 1932; m. Jean S. Stout, Aug. 23, 1953; children: James, Robert, Steven. B of Edn., Ill. Wesleyan U., 1954, MEd, 1957. Band dir. Glenwood H.S., Chatham, Ill., 1957-75; registered rep. Waddell & Reed, Springfield, Ill., 1975-91, Fin. Network Investment Corp., Rochester, 1991—; profl. musician. Mem. Ill. Symphony Chorus; dir. Ill. Heartland Brass Band. With U.S. Army, 1954-56. Mem. Blue Key. Home: RR 1 Box 174 Chatham IL 62629 Office: Fin Network Investment Corp PO Box 528 203 S Walnut St Rochester IL 62563

CHATFIELD, RUTH CHRISTINA, nurse, researcher; b. Atlanta, July 9, 1956; d. Gene Hall and Norma Jean (Bryant) C. Diploma in nursing, Ga. Bapt. Med. Ctr., Atlanta, 1979; BS in Nursing, Emory U., 1983. RN, Ga.

Staff nurse Windy Hill Hosp., Marietta, Ga., 1979-80; charge nurse Ga. Bapt. Med. Ctr., 1980-83, oncology clinician, 1983-85; clin. educator Humana Women's Hosp., Tampa, Fla., 1985-86; team nurse, coord. nutrition support and pain team H. Lee Moffit Cancer Ctr. and Rsch. Inst., Tampa, 1986-88; mktg. rep. Am. Home Patient Ctrs., Inc., Franklin, Tenn., 1988-89; mgr. Sims Deltec, Inc., St. Paul, 1989—; presenter in field. Contbr. articles to profl. jours. Vol. Am. Cancer Soc., 1982-84; instr. basic cardiac life support Am. Heart Assn., 1985-86. Mem. Internat. Assn. for Study Pain, Am. Soc. for Parenteral and Enteral Nurtition (Fla. bd. dirs. 1988-90), Oncology Nurses Soc., Fla. Assn. Nutrition Support (nurse counselor 1988, 89, newsletter editor 1989, 90, bd. dirs. 1988-90). Republican. Home: 607 SE 12th St Fort Lauderdale FL 33316-2003 Office: Sims Deltec Inc 1265 Grey Fox Rd Saint Paul MN 55112-6967

CHATTERTON, ROBERT TREAT, JR., reproductive endocrinology educator; b. Catskill, N.Y., Aug. 9, 1935; s. Robert Treat and Irene (Spoor) C.; m. Patricia A. Holland, June 24, 1956 (div. 1965); children: Ruth Ellen, William Matthew, James Daniel; m. Astrida J. Vanags, June 4, 1966 (div. 1977); 1 child, Derek Scott; m. Carol J. Lewis, May 24, 1985. BS, Cornell U., 1958, PhD, 1963; MS, U. Conn., 1959. Postdoctoral fellow Med. Sch. Harvard U., 1963-65; rsch. assoc. div. oncology Inst. Steroid Rsch. Montefiore Hosp. and Med. Ctr., N.Y.C., 1965-70; asst. prof. Coll. Medicine U. Ill., 1970-72, assoc. prof. Coll. Medicine, 1972-79; prof. Med. Sch. Northwestern U., Chgo., 1979—; mem. sci. adv. com. AID; chairperson Instl. Review Bd. Northwestern U., 1982-83, Intellectual Properties Com., Northwestern U., 1987-95. Contbr. numerous articles to sci. jours.; patents: method of totally suppressing ovarian follicular devel. and method of ovulation detection. Grantee NIH, 1972-90, 95—, NSF, 1975, 95—, AID, 1971-86, Army Office Rsch., 1987-94. Mem. AAAS, N.Y. Acad. Scis., Am. Chem. Soc., Endocrine Soc., Soc. Gynecologic Investigation, Soc. Study Reprodn., Chgo. Assn. Reproductive Endocrinologists (pres. 1987-88), Sigma Xi, Phi Kappa Phi. Presbyterian (deacon). Home: 6001 N Knox Ave Chicago IL 60646-5821 Office: Northwestern U Prentice 1516 333 E Superio Chicago IL 60611

CHATTIN, DUANE HERBERT, director of media relations; b. Vincennes, Ind., May 11, 1953; s. Herbert O. and Edna M. (McCallister) C.; m. Brenda Kay Braun, May 3, 1980; children: Katie, Lisa. Student, Vincennes U., 1971-72; BA in Journalism/Polit. Sci., Ind. U., 1975. Writer, editor Greater Vincennes (Ind.) Pub. Co., 1977-79; assoc. broker Century 21 Heritage Realty, Vincennes, 1980-82; asst. dir. pub. rels. Vincennes (Ind.) U., 1983-89, dir. media rels., 1989—. Precinct committeeman Knox County Dem. Ctrl. Com., Vincennes, 1982-94; del. Dem. State Conv., Indpls., 1978-94, Dem. Nat. Conv., San Francisco, 1984; mem. Vincennes City Coun., 1984-95. Recipient Above & Beyond the Call of Duty award Vincennes U., 1985, Cmty. award of Merity, Knox County Humane Soc., 1995, 96; named Citizen of Yr. Vincennes Civitan Club, 1995, Outstanding Young Hoosier, Ind. Jaycees, 1984, 91. Mem. United Way of Knox County (pres. 1984-85, 93-94), Knox County Chpt. Red Cross (chmn. 1985-88), Good Samaritan Hosp./LT Hospice (pres. 1991-92), Knox County Humane Soc. (pres. 1982-83, 90-91), Vincennes U. Alumni Assn. (pres. 1983-84, 91-92), Knox County Emergency Food & Shelter (comm. chair 1984-87). Democrat. Roman Catholic. Home: 1120 E Sycamore St Vincennes IN 47591 Office: Vincennes U 1002 N First St Vincennes IN 47591

CHATTIN, JAMES WILLIAM, library director; b. San Mateo, Calif., Aug. 9, 1949; s. Earl William and Jane Ann (Schulz) C.; m. Marian Ruth Judge, Apr. 21, 1990; children: James Michael, Mary Janeann. BA in history, Miami U , Oxford, 1971; MS Info. Media, St. Cloud State U., St. Cloud, 1994. Commd. officer USN, 1971-91; ref. libr. Forest Lake Pub. Libr., Forest Lake, Minn., 1994-95; libr. dir. Carnagie Pub. Libr., Devils Lake, N.D., 1995—. Democrat. Presbyterian. Office: Carnagie Pub Library 623 4th Ave Devils Lake ND 58301

CHAVIANO, HUGO, lawyer; b. Havana, Cuba. Grad., Rutgers U., 1975; JD, Northwestern U., 1978. Assoc. Pretzel & Stouffer, Chgo., 1978-85; ptnr. Broderick & Chaviano, Chgo., 1985-91; prin. Chaviano & Assocs., Chgo., 1991—. Bd. dirs. Dearborn Park Cmty. Corp.; trustee Episcopal Charities; pres., bd. dirs. Hispanic Alliance for Career Enhancement. Mem. Chgo. Bar Assn. (bd. mgrs.), L.Am. Bar Assn. (trustee), Legal Assistance Found. (bd. dirs.), Hispanic Fedn. Ill. C. of C. (trustee), L.Am. C. of C. (trustee), Cuban Am. C. of C. (trustee). Office: Chaviano & Assocs 10 S La Salle St Fl 371 Chicago IL 60603-1002

CHEATHAM, MARY ANN, auditory physiologist, educator, researcher; b. Rockford, Ill., June 1, 1944; d. George Marvin and Edna (Givens) C. BA, U. Kans., 1966; MA, Northwestern U., 1967, PhD, 1983. Rsch. assoc. Northwestern U., Evanston, Ill., 1967-73, instr., 1973-77, rsch. assoc., 1978-81, 84-87, sr. rsch. assoc., 1987-89, rsch. assoc. prof., 1990—. Editl. bd. Audiology and Neuro-Otology, 1995—; contbr. articles to profl. jours. Grantee Deafness Rsch. Found., 1985-87, 90-92; Hugh Knowles Ctr. fellow, 1989—. Fellow Acoustical Soc. Am. (psychol. and physiol. acoutics tech com. 1995—); mem. AAAS, Assn. for Rsch. in Otolaryngology (long-range planning com. 1996—), Sigma Xi. Office: Northwestern U 2-240 Frances Searle Bldg 2299 N Campus Dr Evanston IL 60208-3550

CHEESMAN, JOHN MICHAEL, aeronautics company administrator, civic leader; b. Wichita, Kans., Feb. 4, 1943; s. Norman Carlyle and Anne Lucille (Norris) C.; m. Sharon Lindsey, Feb. 8, 1964; children: Mary Kathleen, Deborah Kristine. AA in Math., Social Scis., Wichita (Kans.) State U., BBA, 1986, MA in Social Scis., 1987; postgrad., Calif. State U., Carson; grad., Inst. Children's Lit., West Redding, Conn., 1993. Cert. quality engr., Kans. Mgr. Guardian Industries, Wichita, 1966-72; supr. Cessna Aircraft Corp., Wichita, 1972-78; stats. analyst Boeing Airplane Co., Wichita, 1978-85; lead engr. Boeing Mil. Airplanes, Wichita, 1985-89; coord. prodn. conformance Boeing Comml. A/P Group, Wichita, 1994. Contbr. articles to religious jours. Vol. United Meth. Urban Ministries Wichita, 1984—; numerous positions local and regional chpts. Boy Scouts Am., including commr. of scouting Quivira coun., Wichita; leader United Meth. Men and Boys Retreat Youth Ministries, 1984—; chmn. United Meth. Neighborhood Outreach, 1988—; chmn. communication com. Grace United Meth. Ch., Wichita, 1988—; vice chmn. endowment com., United Meth. Ch., Wichita; institutional rep. United Meth. Coun. on Ministries, Wichita; active Wichita-Sedgwick County Hist. Mus. Assn., 1985—, Rep. Nat. Com., 1981—, Nat. Rep. Congl. Com., 1986—, Wichita Children's Home, 1989—, Big Bros./Big Sisters, Wichita/Sedgwick County, 1989—; charter mem. Ronald Reagan Trust, 1990; vol. leader Wichita Spl. Olympics, 1985—, chmn.; chmn. adv. bd. Rep. Nat. Com., 1994—, hon. consul-gen. Brit. Honduras, 1994; bd. dirs. Dept. Human Svcs., City of Wichita, 1991—. Recipient Campaign Victory cert., 1983, Presdl. Achievement award Rep. Nat. Com., 1986, cert. of merit, 1990, Congl. cert. of appreciation, 1991; Presdl. cert. of recognition, 1991; Presdl. cert. of appreciation, 1992; Vice presdl. cert. of commendation, 1992; Congl. cert. of merit, 1992; George Meany award Nat. Fedn. Unions, 1986, God and Svc. award United Meth. Ch., 1986, Torch award Kans. West conf. United Meth. Ch., 1986, 88, Community Vol. of Yr. awards Boeing Co., 1987-89, Cross and Flame award United Meth. Ch., 1988, 91, Award of Merit Boy Scouts Am., 1988, Arrowhead Honor award Boy Scouts Am., 1988, God and Svc. award Presbyn. Ch. U.S.A., 1991, William M. Allen award Boeing Corp., 1989, Cert. of Appreciation Nat. Rep. congl. Com., 1990, 91, Whitney M. Young award Salvation Army, 1991, Gold Medal of Honor, World Acad. Poetry, 1992, Poetry award Homer Honor Soc. Internat. Poets, 1992, Wichita's First Citizen award First Nat. Bank, 1992, Disting. Commr. award Boy Scouts Am., 1993, James E. West fellow, 1994, Silver Beaver award, 1994, Albert Einstein medal Acad. Sci. and Engring. Mem. Am. Mgmt. Assn., Adminstrv. Mgmt. Soc., Am. Soc. for Quality Control, Am. Assn. Family Counselors (cert. profl. counselor, nat. adv. bd. 1995—), Wichita State U. Alumni Assn. (life), Wichita State U. Soc. of 1895 (life), Wichita State U. Endowment Assn. (life), The Am. Air Mus. in Britain, Wichita Aero. Hist. Assn./Kans. Aviation Mus., U.S. Hist. Soc., United Meth. Men (past pres.), Nat. Assn. United Meth. Scouters (charter life, coord./chartered organizational rep.), Nat. Assn. Presbyn. Scouters (life), Nat. United Ch. of Christ Assn. Scouters (charter life Nat. Adv. Coun. 1984—), Internat. Soc. Poets, Orders and Medals Soc. Am., Medal of Honor Hist. Soc., Token and Medal Soc. Am., New Life Club (charter), Mensa Soc. (charter), The Augustan Soc. (charter), Mensa Soc. (charter), The Augustan Soc. (charter), Internat. Polo Soc. (charter), Masons (32 degree), Scottish Rite, York Rite, Shriners, Order of the Arrow. Home: 1470 Hornecker St Wichita KS 67235-1050

CHEEVER, RAYMOND CRAIG, publisher, editor; b. Bozeman, Mont., Dec. 25, 1926; s. Hurlbert Craig and Myrtle (Hollier) C.; m. Grace Caroline Wiprud, Dec. 28, 1947; children: Sheryl Lynn, Richard Craig, Julie Caroline. BS in Sales Mgmt., Northwestern U., 1950. Supr. advt. and sales promotion State Farm Ins Cos., Bloomington, Ill., 1950-68; pres., pub. Accent on Living mag., spl. publs. Cheever Pub., Inc., Bloomington, 1956—. Mem. Pres.'s Com. on Employment of Handicapped, 1962-93; participant workshops on disabled, 1976—; founder, bd. dirs. Occupational Devel. Ctr., 1965-79; bd. dirs. Living Independence for Everyone/Ctr. for Ind. Living, Normal, Ill., 1985-89; mem. steering com. establishing consumer divsn. Nat. Rehab. Assn.; mem. adv. group AIA Nat. Barrier Free Environ. Conf., resulting in Nat. Ctr. for Barrier Free Environ. With USNR, 1944-46. Recipient Disting. Svc. award Ill. Coun. for Exceptional Children, 1970, Humanitarian award Pilot Internat., 1977, One-of-a-Kind award People-to-People Com. for Handicapped, 1981, citations for meritorious svc. Pres.'s Com. on Employment of Handicapped. Fellow Assn. for Advancement Rehab. Tech.; mem. Nat. Spinal Injury Assn., Polio Network Ill., Ill. Coalition Citizens with Disabilities. Republican. Presbyterian. Home and Office: PO Box 700 Bloomington IL 61702-0700

CHELETTE, TAMARA LYNNE, biomedical engineer; b. Morgantown, W.Va., July 11, 1962; d. Charles Caruthers and Nancy Ruth (Williams) Cook; m. Murry René Chelette, June 1, 1985; children: Murry René Jr., Andrew John. BS in Engring., Boston U., 1984; PhD of Biomed. Scis., Wright State U., 1994. Registered profl. engr., Ohio. Intern clin. engring. Mass. Eye and Ear Infirmary, Boston, 1983-84; biomed. engr. VA, Little Rock, 1984-86, Dayton, Ohio, 1986-87; biomed. sys. engr. Krug Internat., Dayton, 1987-89; biomed. engr. Armstrong Lab., Wright-Patterson AFB, Ohio, 1989—; adj. prof. Wright State U., Dayton, 1994—. Patentee in field; contbr. articles to profl. jours. Treas. Wright-Patt Young Heroes Assn., Dayton, 1992—. Recipient Outstanding Achievement award Soc. Women Engrs., 1982, Arthur Flemming award, 1995. Mem. IEEE, Aerospace Med. Assn. (assoc. fellow, Innovative Rsch. award 1994, pres. life scis. br. 1996), Engring. in Medicine and Biology Soc., SAFE Assn. (v.p. Wright Bros. chpt. 1994-95), Miami Valley Consortium for Rehab. Tech. Home: 2062 Griffon Pl Centerville OH 45459-6966 Office: Armstrong Lab 2245 Monahan Way Wright Patterson AFB OH 45433-7008

CHEN, DANNY ZIYI, computer scientist, educator; b. Taishan, China, Oct. 15, 1960; came to U.S., 1981; s. Ting-Fang and Rui-Lian (Li) C.; m. Xiaobo Hu, May 27, 1990; children: Florence Yunhang, Francis Xinghang. BS in Computer Sci., U. San Francisco, 1985, BS in Math., 1985; MS in Computer Sci., Purdue U., 1988, PhD in Computer Sci., 1992. Grad. tchg. asst., rsch. asst. Purdue U., West Lafayette, Ind., 1986-92; asst. prof. computer sci. U. Notre Dame, Ind., 1992—; Clark Equipment asst. prof. U. Notre Dame, 1994-95; program com. mem. Internat. Symposium, Honolulu, 1996, Internat. Conf. Xian, China, 1995. Contbr. articles to profl. jours. including Algorithmica, Jour. of the ACM, also others. Recipient Career award NSF, 1996. Mem. IEEE, Assn, for Computer Machinery. Office: U Notre Dame Dept Computer Sci & Engring Notre Dame IN 46556

CHEN, EDEN HSIEN-CHANG, engineering consultant; b. Koachsiung, China, Mar. 1, 1954; came to U.S., 1976; s. Wen-Wu and Wen-Chian (Tien) C.; m. Marilyn L. Haugan, Jan. 18, 1982; children: Jessica, Joshua, Justin, Jerilyn. BS in Indsl. Engring., Chung Yuan U., 1976; MS in Indsl. Engring., N.D. State U., 1980. Sr. engr. Gen. Instruments, Kaohsiung, Taiwan, 1976-78, Litton Industries, Sioux Falls, S.D., 1980-86; engring. mgr. DICKEY-John Corp., Auburn, Ill., 1986-88, TRW, Marshall, Ill., 1988-90; prin. cons. CTI, Springfield, Ill., 1990—; adj. instr. George Washington U., Washington, 1989—, U. Wis., Madison, 1989—; instr. Soc. Automotive Engrs., Warrendale, Pa., 1986—, Soc. Mfg. Engrs., Dearborn, Mich., 1989—. Chmn. Springfield Commn. Internat. Visitors, 1995—, commr., 1992—; advisor Ill. Staet Treas. Pat Quinn, Chgo., 1992-94, Overseas Chinese Affairs Commn., Taipei, Taiwan, 1995—. Office: CTI PO Box 9302 Springfield IL 62791-9302

CHEN, GUI-QIANG, mathematician, educator, researcher; b. Ningbao, Zhejiang, People's Republic of China, May 25, 1963; came to U.S., 1987; parents Zhi-Biao and Jin-Er (Hu) C. BS, Fudan U., Shanghai, People's Republic China, 1982; PhD, Acad. Sinica, Beijing, 1987. Asst. prof. Inst. Systems Sci., Acad. Sinica, 1987; vis. scientist Courant Inst. Math. Scis., N.Y.C., 1987; asst. prof. math. U. Chgo., 1989-94; assoc. prof. math. Northwestern U., 1994-96, prof., 1996—; cons. Argonne Nat. Lab., Chgo., 1989—. Recipient Young Investigator award NSF, Beijing, China, 1987, Nat. Medal of Sci., People's Republic of China, 1989; Alfred P. Sloan Rsch. fellow, 1991; named Excellent Young Scientist, Beijing Soc. for Sci. and Tech., 1988. Mem. Am. Math. Soc., Soc. for Indsl. and Applied Math. Office: Northwestern Univ Dept Math Evanston IL 60208-2730

CHEN, HOLLIS CHING, electrical engineering and computer science educator; b. Chekiang, China, Nov. 17, 1935; came to U.S., 1960; naturalized, 1971; s. Yu-Chao and Shui-Tan C.; m. Donna H. Liu, Sept. 3, 1961 (dec. Apr. 1988); children: Deiree, Hollis. BS, Nat. Taiwan U., 1957; MS Ohio U., 1961; PhD, Syracuse U., 1965. Instr., asst. prof. Syracuse U., N.Y., 1961-67; asst., assoc. prof. Ohio U., Athens, 1967-75, prof., 1975—, acting chmn. dept. elec. and computer engring., 1984-86. Author: Theory of EM Waves, 1983; (with others) Research Topics in EM Wave Theory, 1981; contbr. articles to profl. jours. Mem. AAAS, IEEE (sr.), Internat. Union Radio Sci., Am. Soc. for Engring. Edn., Soc. Indsl. and Applied Math., Math. Assn. Am., Am. Geophys. Union, Optical Soc. Am. Home: 1 Ball Dr Athens OH 45701-3621 Office: Ohio U Sch Elec Engring & Computer Sci Athens OH 45701

CHEN, LEA D., engineering educator, researcher; b. Yuan-Lin, Taiwan, June 1, 1952; came to U.S. 1977; s. Der Hwa and Chun Inn (Wu) C.; m. Yuan Yu Yang, Jun. 16, 1977; one child: Jennifer Anne. BS, Nat. Taiwan U., 1974; MS, Pa. State U., 1979, PhD, 1981. Rsch. asst./assoc. Pa. State U., University Park, 1981, asst. prof., 1981-82; asst. prof. U. Iowa, Iowa City, 1982-86, assoc. prof., 1986-91, prof., 1991—, interim chair mech. engring., 1992-93, chair mech. engring., 1993—; vis. scientist, faculty Air Force Wright Lab., Ohio, 1985-93. Co-editor Turbulence Measurements and Flow Modeling, 1987; co-author Compustion and Flame, Compustion Science and Tech., AIAA Jour. Propulsion and Power, ASME Jour. Heat Transfer. Recipient Aerospace Sci. Meeting Poster Merit award, 1987, Ann. Gallery on Fluid Motion, Am. Phys. Soc., 1986, 87, 92; Old Gold Faculty fellow U. Iowa, 1983; grantee NSF, NASA, Office of Naval Rsch., Air Force Wright Lab., Air Force Office Sci. Rsch. Mem. ASME, AIAA, Combustion Inst., Am. Soc. Engring. Edn., Am. Phys. Soc., AAAS, Sigma Xi. Home: 2010 Rochester Ct Iowa City IA 52245-3246 Office: U Iowa Dept Mech Engring 2204 EB Iowa City IA 52242

CHEN, WAI-KAI, electrical engineering and computer science educator, consultant; b. Nanking, China, Dec. 23, 1936; came to U.S., 1959; s. You-Chao and Shui-Tan (Shen) C.; m. Shirley Shiao-Ling, Jan. 13, 1939; children—Jerome, Melissa. BS in Elec. Engring., Ohio U., 1960, MS in Elec. Engring., 1961; PhD in Elec. Engring., U. Ill., Urbana, 1964. Asst. prof. Ohio U., 1964-67, assoc. prof., 1967-71, prof., 1971-78, disting. prof., 1978-81; prof., head dept. elec. engring. and computer sci. U. Ill., Chgo., 1981—; vis. assoc. prof. Purdue U., 1970-71; hon. prof. Tianjing U., Peoples Republic of China, 1990, Beijin U. of Posts and Telecomms., Beijing U. of Aeronautics and Astronautics, 1992. Author: Applied Graph Theory, 1970, Theory and Design of Broadband Matching Networks, 1976, Applied Graph Theory: Graphs and Electrical Networks, 1976, Active Network and Feedback Amplifier Theory, 1980, Linear Networks and Systems, 1983, Passive and Active Filters: Theory and Implementations, 1986, The Collected Papers of Professor Wai-Kai Chen, 1987, Broadband Matching: Theory and Implementations, 1988, Theory of Nets, 1990, Linear Networks and Systems: Computer-Aided Solutions and Implementations, 1990, Active Network Analysis, 1991, Modern Network Analysis, 1992; editor: Brooks/Cole Series in Electrical Engineering, 1982-84, Advanced Series in Electrical and Computer Engineering, 1984-86; editor in chief Advanced Series in Elec. and Computer Engring., World Sci. Pub. Co., Singapore, 1986—, Jour. Circuits, Systems and Computers, 1989—, The Circuits and Filters Handbook, 1995; assoc. editor: Jour. Circuits, Systems and Signal Processing, 1981—; editor in charge Advanced Series in Circuits and Systems, World Scientific Publ. Co., 1991—. Recipient Lester R. Ford award Math. Assn. Am., 1967, Baker Fund award Ohio U., 1974, 78, Disting. Accomplishment award Chinese Acad. & Profl. Assn. in Mid-Am. , 1985, disting. Guest Prof. award Chuo U., Tokyo, 1987, Outstanding Service award Chinese Acad. & Profl. assn. in Mid-Am., 1988, Outstanding Achievement award Mid-Am. Chinese Sci. & Tech. Assn, 1988, disting. alumnus award Electrical and Computer Engring. Dept. Alumni Assn. U. Ill. Urbana-Champaign, 1988, Alexander von Humboldt award Alexander von Humboldt Stiftung, Fed. Republic of Germany, 1985, hon. prof. award Nanjing Inst. of Technology and Zhejing U., Peoples Republic of China, 1985, The Northeast U. Tech., East. China Inst. Tech., Nanjing Inst. of Posts & Telecommunications, AnHui U., Chengdu Inst. Radio Engring., Wuhan Univ.; Research Inst. fellow Ohio U., 1972, Japan Soc. for Promotion of Sci., 1986, Sr. U. Scholar award U. Ill., 1986, Ohio U. Alumni Medal Merit for Disting. Achievement in Engring. Edn., 1987, hon. prof. award Hangzhan U. of Electronic Tech., Peoples Republic of China, 1990. Fellow IEEE, AAAS; mem. NSPE, IEEE Cirs. and Sys. Soc. (adminstrv. com. 1985-87, exec. v.p. 1987, assoc. editor Trans. on Cirs. and Sys. 1977-79, editor 1991-93, pres.-elect 1993, pres. 1994), Md.-Am. Chinese Sci. and Tech. Assn. (bd. dirs. 1984-86, 89-93, pres. 1991-92), Chinese Acad. and Profl. Assn. Mid-Am. (advisor to bd. dirs. 1984-89, pres. 1986-87), Soc. Indsl. and Applied Math., Assn. Computing Machinery, Tensor Soc. Gt. Britain, Sigma Xi (sec.-treas. Ohio U. chpt. 1981), Phi Kappa Phi, Eta Kappa Nu. Office: U Ill Dept Elec Engring & Computer Sci 851 S Morgan St Rm 1120 Seo Chicago IL 60607-7042

CHEN, ZHENGXIN, computer scientist; b. Nanjing, Jiangsu, China, Oct. 2, 1947; came to U.S. 1983; s. Donald Zhichu and Grace Fang (Chen) C.; m. Mei Zheng, Dec. 19, 1980. BS, East China Normal U., 1982; MS, La. State U., 1985, PhD, 1988. Instr. math. Shanghai Pharm. U., China, 1982-83; asst. prof. computer sci. U. Nebr., Omaha, 1988-94, assoc. prof., 1994—. Referee/reviewer profl. jours.; contbr. numerous articles to profl. jours. UCR grantee U. Nebr., 1990, Travel grantee Office of Naval Rsch., 1987. Mem. IEEE, Assn. Computing Machinery, Am. Assn. Artificial Intelligence. Office: U Nebr at Omaha Durham Sci Ctr # 237 Omaha NE 68182

CHENEY, DAVID WILLI, engineering company executive; b. Wausau, Wis., Mar. 6, 1950; s. Donald Eugene and Patricia Ann (Frederick) C.; m. Maria Aurora Lamadrid Pequeño, Mar. 14, 1981 (dec. 1986). BS in Biology, U. Utah, 1972, BSEE, 1976; MBA, Interamerican U., Bayamon, P.R., 1982. Registered profl. engr., Wis. Engr. Finley Engring. Co., Eau Claire, Wis., 1968-85, ptnr., 1985-89, v.p., 1989—. Mem. IEEE, NSPE, Wis. Soc. Profl. Engrs. Libertarian. Office: Finley Engring Co Inc Box 147 Eau Claire WI 54702

CHENG, BETTY HSIAO-CHIH, computer science educator, researcher; b. Chgo., Apr. 18, 1964; d. John Kwang-Ming and Marjorie S.H. (Chen) Cheng; m. Philip Keith McKinley, July 21, 1990. BS in Elec. Engring. and Computer Sci., Northwestern U., 1985; MS, U. Ill., 1987, PhD, 1990. Program analyst IBM, Research Triangle Park, N.C., 1985; program analyst, developer Data Gen., Research Triangle Park, 1986; software analyst Digital Equipment Corp., Maynard, Mass., 1987; rsch. asst. dept. computer sci. U. Ill., Urbana, 1986-90; faculty fellow NASA JPL/Calif. Inst. Tech., Pasadena, 1993; assoc. prof. computer sci. Mich. State U., East Lansing, 1990—. Contbr. articles to profl. jours. NASA faculty fellow, 1993; grantee NSF, 1992, 94, U.S. Dept. Agr., 1992, 93, 94, EPA, 1994. Mem. IEEE (reviewer Trans. on SE, KE 1990—), Assn. for Computing Machinery. Office: Mich State U Dept Computer Sci A714 Wells Hall East Lansing MI 48824

CHENG, STEPHEN ZHENG DI, chemistry educator, polymeric material researcher; b. Shanghai, Aug. 3, 1949; came to U.S., 1981, naturalization, 1992; s. Luzhong and Jingzhi (Zhang) C.; m. Susan Lian Zhi Xue, June 28, 1978; 1 child, Wendy D.W. BS in Math., East China Normal U., 1977; MS in Polymer Engring., China Textile U., 1981; PhD in Polymer Chemistry, Rensselaer Poly. Inst., 1985. Postdoctoral and rsch. assoc. Rensselaer Poly. Inst., Troy, N.Y., 1985-87; asst. prof. polymer sci. U. Akron, Ohio, 1987-91, assoc. prof. polymer sci., 1991-95, prof. polymer sci., 1995—; faculty rsch. assoc. Maurice Morton Inst. of Polymer Sci., U. Akron, 1987—, faculty rsch. assoc. Inst. Polymer Engring., 1988; vis. prof. sci, U. of Tokyo, 1994; vis. prof. polymer sci. and engring. Sichun Union U., China, 1994—; fgn. mem. acad. steering com. Nat. Polymer Physics Open Lab., Chinese Acad. Sci., 1994—, guest prof. polymer sci. Guangzhou Inst. Chemistry, 1994—, guest prof. polymer sci. Changchun Inst. Applied Chemistry, 1995—; guest prof. polymer materials and engring. Zhengshou U., China, 1994—; mem. orgn. com. The First Conf. Worldwide Young Chinese Chemists, Beijing, 1995; adv. prof. polymer sci. Chinese Textile U., 1995—, Fudan U., 1996—; cons., spkr. in field. Editor: Jour. Macromolecular Sci. Part B, Physics, 1995—; contbr. chpts. to books and articles to profl. jours. Grantee in field; recipient Presdl. Young Investigator award NSF and White House, 1991, Appreciation cert. U. Akron Bd. Trustees, 1992, 94, John H. Dillon Medal, Am. Physical Soc., 1995. Fellow Am. Phys. Soc., N.Am. Thermal Analysis Soc.; mem. Am. Chem. Soc. (Akron Sect. award 1994), Soc. Plastics Engrs., Materials Rsch. Soc., Soc. Advancement Material and Process Engring. Office: U Akron Morton Inst Polymer Sci Akron OH 44325-3909

CHERENZIA, BRADLEY JAMES, radiologist; b. Niagara Falls, N.Y., Aug. 22, 1931; s. Peter and Myrna (Bradley) C.; m. Paula Joyce, Mar. 9, 1978; children: Kevin, Lori, David, Robert, Lisa. BS in Pharmacy cum laude, U. Buffalo, 1953; MD, SUNY Upstate Med. Ctr., Syracuse, 1957. Cert. Am. Bd. Radiology, Am. Bd. Nuclear Medicine. Intern SUNY Upstate Med. Ctr. Hosps., Syracuse, 1957-58; resident in radiology Wayne State U. Sch. Medicine Hosps., Detroit, 1960-63; practice medicine specializing in radiology Diagnostic Radiology Cons., P.C., Warren, Mich., 1965—, also chmn. bd. dirs.; sr. attending radiologist Detroit-Macomb Hosp. Corp., chmn. divsn. diagnostic radiol. quality improvement com., med. care and evaluation com., chmn. radiation safety com.; med. dir. dept. diagnostic radiology Macomb Hosp. Ctr., mem. med. exec. com. Served to capt. M.C., U.S. Army, 1958-60. Mem. AMA, Am. Soc. Nuc. Cardiology, Wayne County Med. Soc., Mich. State Med. Soc., Radiol. Soc. N.Am., Mich. Radiol. Soc., Am. Coll. Radiology, Soc. Nuclear Medicine, Am. Coll. Nuclear Medicine, Am. Coll. Physician Execs., Soc. Radiologists in Ultrasound, Am. Heart Assn., Am. Med. Tennis Assn. Republican. Roman Catholic.

CHERNISH, LELIA MARGARET, developer, fundraiser; b. Collins, Mo., Mar. 19, 1921; d. Aubra F. and Velta Lelia (Nance) Higgins; m. Stanley M. Chernish, June 19, 1949; 1 child, Dwight Landers. Student, Md. U., Ind. U. Tchr. kindergarten Silver Springs, Bethesda, Md., 1945-51; appointed del. White House Conf. on Aging, 1971, Ind. Health Careers, 1974-84; mem. Ind. Impaired Physicians Com., 1976-79; appointee Ind. Mus. Art, 1976-84; appointed bd. trustees Ind. Med. Distbn. Loan Fund, 1977-92, Ind. Med. & Nursing Distbn. Loan Fund, 1981-85; mem. Marion County Impaired Physicians Com., 1983-84; liaison to med. student wives, rec. sec., program, publicity and fin. chmn., historian and by-laws chmn. Ind. State Med. Aux.; pres. Marion County Med. Aux., 1965-66, med. student liaison, historian, United Fund chmn., by-laws com., parliamentarian, chmn. cookbook prodn.; mem., fin. chmn., parliamentarian Boys Club Aux. Mem. Winona Meml. Hosp. Aux.; founder Vol. Observer Program, Ind., 1970-71; mem., yearbook chmn. Alliance of Indpls. Mus. of Art; participant Women United Against Rape, 1975, Sch. Drop Out Program, Diabetes Detection Dr., drug and internat. health activities; regular ct. watcher Indpls. Anti-Crime Crusade; vol. Ronald McDonald House, 1982-94, bd. trustees, chmn. needle art project, facilities com., chmn. 10th anniversary calendar fund raising project, 1992. Recipient Theta Sigma Phi award, 1969, Sagamores of the Wabash award for disting. pub. svc. Gov. Otis R. Bowen, 1977, by Gov. Robert D. Orr, 1981, Ind. Jefferson award, 1982, Lori Kleiman award for svcs. over and above call of duty Ronald McDonald House, 1992; named Ind. Mother of Yr., 1981. Mem. Faculty Women's Club of Ind. U. Sch. Medicine, Hillcrest Garden Club (treas., chmn. flower show), Women in Neighborhood Svc. (WINS), Indpls. chpt. Embroiders Guild of Am. (charter, chmn. nat. embroiders guild exhibit 1989, dean of faculty seminar 1990, co-chmn. nat. seminar, 1992), Mag. Club (pres. 1963-65).

CHERNISH, STANLEY MICHAEL, physician; b. N.Y.C., Jan. 27, 1924; s. Michael B. and Veronica (Hodon) C.; m. Lelia M. Higgins, June 19, 1949;

1 child, Dwight. BA, U. N.C., 1945; MD, Georgetown U., 1949. Diplomate Nat. Bd. Med. Examiners, Am. Bd. Internal Medicine. Intern Washington Gen. Hosp., 1949-51; resident Marion County Gen. Hosp., Indpls., 1953-55; with clin. rsch. div. Eli Lilly & Co., Indpls., 1954-85; from asst. to assoc. in medicine Sch. Medicine, Ind. U., 1957-66, asst. prof., 1967-76, clin. assoc. prof., 1977-80, assoc. prof., 1981-94; rsch. cons. Meth. Hosp., Indpls., 1986—; mem. vis. staff Marion County Gen. Hosp., 1965-94. Contbr. more than 115 articles to profl. jours., chpts. to books. Served with USNR, 1943-45, 50-53, ret. comdr. 1984. Fellow ACP, Am. Coll. Gastroenterology; mem. Am. Coll. Clin. Pharmacology and Therapeutics, AMA (Physicians Recognition award in continuing med. edn. 1972—), Ind. State Med. Soc. (mem. subcommn. on accreditation), Marion County Med. Soc., Assn. Am. Physicians and Surgeons, Am. Fedn. Clin. Rsch., Am. Gastroent. Assn., Sci. Rsch. Soc., Sigma Xi. Office: Meth Hosp Ind Dept Med Rsch PO Box 1367 1701 Senate Blvd Indianapolis IN 46202-1239

CHERRY, C. CONRAD, religious studies educator, author; b. Kerens, Tex., Mar. 31, 1937; s. Charles Curry and Laura (Vaughn) C.; m. Mary Ella Bigony, Aug. 22, 1959; children: Kevin, Cynthia. BA, McMurry U., 1958; MDiv, Drew U., 1961, PhD, 1965. Prof. Pa. State U., University Park, 1964-81; dir. Scholars Press, Atlanta, 1981-88; rsch. prof. Emory U., Atlanta, 1985-88; Disting. prof. Ind. U., Indpls., 1988—; dir. Ctr. for Study of Religion and Am. Culture, Indpls., 1989—; vis. prof. Bryn Mawr (Pa.) Coll., 1976. Author: Theology of Jonathan Edwards, 1966, Nature and Religious Imagination, 1980, God's New Israel, 1972, Hurrying Toward Zion, 1995. Recipient fellowship Soc. Religion and Higher Edn., 1970, fellowship Pa. State U., 1978. Mem. Am. Acad. Religion (Spl. Citation award 1987), Am. Soc. Ch. History, Am. Studies Assn. Office: Ind Univ University Blvd Indianapolis IN 46202

CHERRY, JOHN D., JR., state legislator; b. Sulphur Springs, Tex., May 5, 1951; s. John D. Sr. and Margaret L. (Roark) C.; m. Pamela M. Faris, 1979; children: Meghan M., John D. BA, U. Mich., 1973, MA, 1984. Chmn. 7th Cong. Dist. Dem. Com., Mich., 1973-75; adminstrv. asst. Mich. State Sen. Gary Corbin, 1975-81; Mich. polit. dir. Am. Fedn. State, County & Munic Employees AFL-CIO, 1981-82; state rep. Mich. Ho. Reps., Dist. 79, 1983-86; state senator Mich. State Senate, Dist. 29, 1987-94, Mich. State Senate, Dist. 28, 1995—; minority floor leader, mem. legis. coun., vice chmn. labor com., Mich. State Senate. Mem. Soc. Pub. Adminstrs., Polit. Sci. Assn., Acad. Polit. Sci. Address: 4116 Orme Cir Clio MI 48420-8527 also: State Senate State Capitol Lansing MI 48909*

CHERRY, LINDA LEA, deputy United States marshal; b. Davenport, Iowa, Apr. 6, 1956; d. Francis Eugene and Joan Grace (Rottman) Johnson; m. Bradley Scott Cherry, Mar. 1, 1980; children: Jacob Carl, Lucas Andrew. AA, Des Moines Area Community Coll, 1981; BS, Upper Iowa U., 1992. Cert. peace officer; cert. sex crimes investigator. Cashier Frontier Grocery Store, Polk City, Iowa, 1976; clk. typist Deere Employees Credit Union, Ankeny, Iowa, 1974-76; gas sta. attendant Go-Tane, Ankeny, 1977; radio operator Ankeny Police Dept., 1976-78, detective, 1980-85, 89-90, patrol officer, 1978-80, 85-89; guard U.S. Marshals Svc., Des Moines, 1983-90, dep. U.S. marshal, 1990—, recruiter, pub. info. officer, spl. emphasis program mgr., 1990-95, student intern coord., 1992-95, seized asset specialist, 1994-96; motor vehicle officer Des Moines, 1995—; WITSEC contact U.S. Marshals Svc., Des Moines, 1995—; instr. Ankeny Police Dept., 1980-90; apptd. mem. coun. Iowa Law Enforcement Acad., 1988-90; apptd. mem. E-911 Commn., 1986-88. Named Officer of Yr., Optimist Club, Ankeny, 1981. Mem. NRA (life), Iowa Assn. Police Women (life, pres. 1982-88, Officer of Yr. 1989, fundraising/publicity officer 1992-95), Iowa State Policemen's Assn. (del. 1989), Iowa Assn. Chiefs and Police Officers (legis. com. 1989-90), Internat. Assn. Women Police (life, regional coord. 1986-88, chmn. membership com. 1991-94, rec. sec. 1992-94, pres. 1994-96, immediate past pres. 1996—, life trustee 1996—). Republican. Lutheran. Home: RR 2 Box 30 Elkhart IA 50073-9802 Office: US Marshals Svc 208 US Courthouse Des Moines IA 50309

CHERRY, PETER BALLARD, electrical products corporation executive; b. Evanston, Ill., May 25, 1947; s. Walter Lorain and Virginia Ames (Ballard) C.; m. Crissy Hazard, Sept. 6, 1969; children: Serena Ames, Spencer Ballard. B.A., Yale U., 1969; M.B.A., Stanford U., 1972. Analyst Cherry Elec. Products Corp., Waukegan, Ill., 1972-74, data processing and systems mgr., 1974, treas., 1974-77; v.p. fin. and bus. devel. Cherry Elec. Products Corps., Waukegan, Ill., 1977-80; exec. v.p. Cherry Elec. Products Corp., Waukegan, Ill., 1980-82, pres., chief oper. officer, 1982-86; pres., chief exec. officer Cherry Corp., Waukegan, 1986-92, chmn., pres., 1992—. Trustee Lake Forest Coll., Ill., 1982-90; trustee Lake Forest Hosp., 1982—, chmn., 1989-92. Mem. IEEE, Computer Soc., Chgo. Coun. Fgn. Rels., Econ. Club, Comml. Club, Chgo. Club, Commonwealth Club, Onwentsia Club. Office: Cherry Corp 3600 Sunset Ave Waukegan IL 60087-3214

CHERRY, ROBERT STEVEN, III, municipal agency administrator; b. Chgo., Aug. 13, 1951; s. Robert Lee and Jean Louise (Curry) C. BA, Kensington U., 1988. With Chgo. Pk. Dist., 1968—, aquatic supr., 1983—. Asst. capt. 37th precinct, 7th ward, City of Chgo., 1979-80, precinct capt., 1980-83, asst. precinct capt. 2d precinct, 42d ward, 1984-92, capt., 1992—. Mem. Am. Legion (Post 1976), Young Dems. Am. (Ill. del. 1985), Young Dems. Ill., Young Dems. Cook County, U.S. Water Polo, U.S. Lifesaving Assn., Res. Officers Assn. U.S., Pub. Svc. Employees Union, Lambda Alpha Epsilon. Roman Catholic. Office: Chgo Park Dist 425 E Mcfetridge Dr Chicago IL 60605-2801

CHESEBRO, JAMES WILLIAM, communications educator; b. Mpls., June 24, 1944; s. Floyd Jerome and Jeanette Mary (Campbell) C. BA, U. Minn., 1966, PhD, 1972; MS, Ill. State U., 1967. Instr. Concordia Coll., Moorhead, Minn., 1967-69; tchg. assoc. U. Minn., Mpls., 1969-72; assoc. prof. Temple U., Phila., 1972-81; prof. Queens Coll. CUNY, Flushing, 1981-89; dir. ednl. svcs. Speech Comm. Assn., Annandale, Va., 1989-92; prof. Ind. State U., Terre Haute, 1992—; vis. prof. U. Puerto Rico, San Juan, 1980; adj. prof. George Mason U., Fairfax, Va., 1989-92. Author: Computer-Mediated Communication, 1989; contbr. more than 75 articles on comm. to profl. jours. Recipient Disting. Svc. award Nat. Kenneth Burke Soc., 1993. Mem. Speech commn. Assn. (pres. 1995-96, Golden Ann. Monograph award 1985), Ea. Comm. Assn. (pres. 1982-83, Disting. Svc. award 1989, Hunt Scholarship award 1989). Office: Ind State U Dept Comm Terre Haute IN 47809

CHESLEY, STANLEY MORRIS, lawyer; b. Cin., Mar. 26, 1936; s. Frank and Rachel (Kinsburg) C.; children: Richard A., Lauren B. BA, U. Cin., 1958, LLB, 1960. Bar: Ohio 1960, Ky. 1978, W.Va., Tex., Nev. 1981. Ptnr. Waite, Schneider, Bayless & Chesley Co., Cin., 1960; Contbr. articles to profl. jours. Bd. dirs. Friends of the Plum Street Temple; past chmn. bd. Trustees U. Cin.; past chmn. bd. commrs. on grievances and discipline Supreme Ct. Ohio, active Jewish Welfare Fund Bd., Bonds for Israel Bd.; past pres. Camp Livingston; past chmn. Isaac Wise Temple Religious Sch. Com.; past pres. Jewish Fedn. Cin.; exec. com. U.S. Holocaust Meml. Mus. Mem. ABA, ATLA, Am. Judicature Soc., Fed. Bar Assn., Melvin M. Belli Soc., Ohio Bar Assn., Ky. Bar Assn., W.Va. Bar Assn., Tex. Bar Assn., Nev. Bar Assn., Cin. Bar Assn. Office: Waite Schneider Bayless & Chesley 1513 Central Trust Towers Cincinnati OH 45202

CHESNIN, LEON, waste management and utilization consultant; b. N.Y.C., Mar. 28, 1919; s. Samuel and Anna (Melcher) C.; m. Esther Rae Katz, Sept. 27, 1940; children: Sidney, Harold, Nancy, Gary. BS in Agr., U. Ky., 1940; MS, Ohio State U., 1941; PhD, Rutgers U., 1948. Prof. agr. U. Nebr., Lincoln, 1947-85, prof. emeritus, 1985—; pres. Chesnin Waste Mgmt., Lincoln, 1985—; cons. FDA, U.S. Congress, U.S. Office Tech. Assessment, Fertilizer Inst., Nat. Fertilizer Solutions Assn., Nebr. Livestock Task Force, Rural Affairs Ctr., for U. Nebr.; mcpl. county gov.'s environ. attys., fertilizer industries, livestock and poultry industries, slaughterhouse, galvanizing industries, composting industries. Recipient Environ. Quality awards EPA, 1979, 80, Internat. Man of Yr. award Internat. Biog. Centre, Gt. Britain, 1993. Mem. Agronomy Soc., Soil Sci. Soc. Am., Internat. Soil Sci. Soc., Soil and Water Conservation Soc., Nat. Fertilizer Solution Assn. (hon. mem. award 1970). Home and Office: 3520 S 37th St Lincoln NE 68506-5711

CHESSICK, RICHARD D., psychiatrist; b. Chgo., June 2, 1931; m. Marcia Chessick, Sept. 3, 1953; three children. BS, U. Chgo., 1950, MD, 1954; PhD, Calif. Coast U., L.A., 1977. Diplomate in psychiatry Am. Bd. Psychiatry and Neurology; diplomate in psychoanalysis Am. Acad. Psychoanalysis. Intern Cook County Hosp., Chgo., 1954-55; resident in psychiatry U. Ill. Rsch. and Ednl. Hosp., Chgo., 1955-58; prof. psychiatry Northwestern U., Chgo., 1960—; adj. prof. philosophy Loyola U., Chgo., 1980-87; sr. attending psychiatrist Evanston (Ill.) Hosp., 1972—; examiner Am. Bd. Psychiatry and Neurology, 1974, 76, 79, 82, 88. Author 13 books on psychoanalysis, intensive psychotherapy and philosophy; mem. editl. bd. Am. Jour. Psychotherapy, 1980—, Jour. Am. Acad. Psychoanalysis, 1992—; editor Bull. Am. Soc. Psychoanalytic Physicians, 1993—; contbr. some 200 articles to profl. jours. Surgeon USPHS, 1958-60. Fellow Am. Acad. Psychoanalysis, Am. Psychiat. Assn., Acad. Psychosomatic Medicine, Am. Orthopsychiat. Assn., Am. Soc. for Adolescent Psychiatry; mem. Am. Soc. Psychoanalytic Physicians (sec. 1993-95, pres. 1996-97), German Psychoanalytical Soc. (corr.). Office: 9400 Drake Ave Evanston IL 60203-1106

CHESTER, RUSSELL GILBERT, JR., accountant, auditor; b. Lorain, Ohio, Aug. 6, 1947; s. Russell Gilbert and Elizabeth Jane (Eucker) C.; m. Martha Ann Mamula, Jan. 24, 1970 (div.); children: Sally Ann, Russell Theodore; m. Pamela Jean Huggins, Sept. 26, 1992. BS in Indsl. Mgmt., Purdue U., 1970; grad. with honors, USAF Comm. Analyst Sch., 1971; M Accountancy, Bowling Green State U., 1975. CPA, Ohio; cert. systems profl. Staff and sr. acct. Arthur Andersen & Co., Cleve., 1975-77; chief internal auditor lighting fixture div. ITT, Vermilion, Ohio, 1977-78; comptr., dir. pers. lighting fixture div. Lithonia Lighting, Vermilion, Ohio, 1978-80; supr. internal audit indsl. tech. group ITT, Chgo., 1980-81, mgr. internal audit indsl. tech. group, 1981-83; dir. internal audit natural resources group ITT, Stamford, Conn., 1983-84; dir. audit svcs. Parker Hannifin Corp., Cleve., 1984—; cons. Component Repair Tech. Mentor, Ohio, 1984-86, bd. dirs., 1986—; cons. Chester Tax Svcs., Wakeman, Ohio, 1965—, Echo Valley Golf, Wellington, Ohio, 1975-78, Hereform Farm, New London, Ohio, 1974-80, Avon Lake (Ohio) Florist, 1975-78, Star Supply, Wadsworth, Ohio, 1984-86; mem. acctg. student adv. bd. Cleve. State U., 1990—, Case Western Res. U., 1994-95. Asst. scoutleader Boy Scouts Am., Cleve., 1985; instr. Jr. Achievement, Cleve., 1986. Sgt. USAF, 1970-73. Mem. AICPA, Inst. Mgmt. Accts., Ohio Soc. CPAs, Inst. Internal Auditors (bd. dirs. Cleve.-Akron chpt. 1991—, internat. conf. com. 1994—, chmn. acad. rels. 1991-94, 1st v.p. 1994-95, pres. 1995-96), Assn. for Sys. Mgmt., Mfrs. Alliance for Productivity and Innovation (gen. auditors coun.), Beta Alpha Psi. Republican. Office: Parker Hannifin Corp 17325 Euclid Ave Cleveland OH 44112

CHESTER, STEPHANIE ANN, lawyer, banker; b. Mpls., Oct. 8, 1951; d. Alden Runge and Nina Lavina (Hanson) C.; divorced. B.A. magna cum laude, Augustana Coll., 1973; J.D., U. S.D., 1977; postgrad. C.F.S.C., ABA Nat. Grad. Trust Sch., Evanston, Ill., 1984. Bar: S.D. 1977, Minn. 1979. Asst. counselor Minnehaha County Juvenile Ct. Ctr., Sioux Falls, S.D., 1972-73; child care worker Project Threshold, Sioux Falls, 1973-74; legal intern Davenport, Evans, Hurwitz & Smith, Sioux Falls, 1976; law clk. S.D. Supreme Ct., Pierre, 1977-78; originations dept. buyer Dain Bosworth, Inc., Mpls., 1978-79; v.p., trust officer 1st Bank of S.D., N.A., Sioux Falls, 1979-86; v.p. First Trust Co., Inc., St. Paul, 1986-93; cons. Chester & Stoffels, Inc., St. Paul, 1993-94; lawyer Westby, Chester & Lees, P.A., 1994—; pres. Sioux Falls Estate Planning Coun., 1983-85. Projects and research editor S.D. Law Rev., 1977; author law rev. comment. Mem. fund raising coms. S.D. Symphony, Sioux Falls Community Playhouse, Augustana Coll., 1982-83; mem. S.D. div. Nat. Women's Polit. Caucus; mem. events com. Augustana Coll. Fellows, Sioux Falls, 1984; bd. dirs. YWCA, Sioux Falls, 1984, Sioux Falls Arena/Coliseum, 1985; mem. Sioux Falls Jr. Service League, 1984. Augustana Coll. scholar, 1969-73; Augustana Coll. Bd. Regents scholar, 1973. Mem. S.D. Bar Assn., Minn. Bar Assn., ABA, 2d S.D. Jud. Circuit Bar Assn., Nat. Assn. Bank Women (state conv. com. 1983-85), Phi Delta Phi, Chi Epsilon. Democrat. Lutheran. Clubs: Network, Portia (Sioux Falls). Office: 79 Western Ave N Ste C Saint Paul MN 55102-4616

CHESTER, TIMOTHY J., museum director. Assoc. dir. for collections La. State Mus., 1985-86; asst. dir. Pub. Mus. of Grand Rapids, Mich., 1986-88, dir., 1988—; pres. Mich. Mus. Assn., Grand Rapids, 1995—. Office: Van Andel Mus Ctr 272 Pearl St NW Grand Rapids MI 49504-5371

CHESTNUT, KATHI LYNNE, lawyer; b. Springfield, Mo., Nov. 7, 1959; d. Stanley Carl and Onita Faye (Weir) C. BA in Polit. Sci. summa cum laude, William Woods Coll., 1980; JD, Washington U., St. Louis, 1983. Bar: Mo. 1983, U.S. Dist. Ct. (ea. dist.) Mo. 1983, Ill. 1984, (so. dist.) Ill. 1991, U.S. Ct. Appeals (8th cir.) 1984, U.S. Supreme Ct., 1991. Assoc. Evans and Dixon, St. Louis, 1983-89, ptnr., 1990—; reviewer Mo. Jud. Edn. Com., Jud. Desk Book, Civil Procedure. Mem. Mo. Bar Assn. (contbg. author Mo. Civil Procedure publ. 1988, 90, 95), Ill. Bar Assn., Met. Bar Assn. St. Louis, Order of Coif, Alpha Chi Omega (Sigma Sigma Psi chpt. sec. 1985-86). Republican. Presbyterian. Home: 5318 N Kenrick Parke Dr Saint Louis MO 63119-5047 Office: Evans & Dixon 1200 Saint Louis Pl 200 N Broadway Saint Louis MO 63102-2730

CHEVELDAE, TIM, professional hockey player; b. Melville, Sask., Can., Feb. 15, 1968. Goalie Detroit Red Wings, 1986-94, Winnipeg Jets, 1994—; now with Philadelphia Phantoms (farm team); player NHL All-Star game, 1992. Named to WHL All-Star 1st Team, 1987-88. Office: Philadelphia Phantoms care Core State Spectrum 3601 South Broad St Philadelphia PA 19148*

CHEW, WENG CHO, engineering educator; b. Kuantan, Pahang, Malaysia, June 9, 1953; came to U.S., 1973; s. F.S. Chew and T.L. Goh; m. Chew-Chin Phua, 1977; 2 children. BSEE, MIT, 1976, MSEE, 1978, PhD in Elec. Engring, 1980. Postdoctoral assoc., inst. MIT, Cambridge, 1980-81; mem. profl. staff Schlumberger-Doll Rsch., Ridgefield, Conn., 1981-83; program leader Schlumberger-Doll Research, Ridgefield, Conn., 1983-84, dept. mgr., 1984-85; assoc prof. U. Ill., Urbana, 1985-90, prof., 1990—; presdl. young investigator, 1986; cons. Schlumberger, Ridgefield, 1985—; dir. Ctr. Computational Electromagnetics & Electromagnetics Lab., 1995—. Contbr. more than 140 articles to sci. jours. Fellow IEEE (sr., assoc. editor 1984—); mem. Union Radio Sci. Internat. (guest editor 1985).

CHEYNE, VALORIE E., psychologist; b. Bloomfield Hills, Mich., Apr. 28, 1944; d. Cyril Gordon Browne and Dorothy Ellenor (Neel) Van Kempen; m. Kenneth McLean, July 22, 1967; 1 child, Casey. BA, Mich. State U., 1966; MEd, Wayne State U., 1978; Psy. S., Ctr. for Humanistic Studies, 1983; PhD, Union Inst., 1988. Lic. psychologist, Mich.; cert. tchr., Mich.; cert. social worker, Mich. Tchr. multiply physically hadicapped and learning disabled Farmington (Mich.) Pub. Schs., 1966-72; counselor, psychotherapist, coordinator attention deficit ctr. Human Potential Counseling Ctr., Southfield, Mich., 1968-92; dir. clin. svcs. Human Potential Counseling Ctr., Southfield, 1988—; mem. adj. faculty Ctrl. Mich. U., Mt. Pleasant, Oakland C.C., Union Inst. Pres. bd. Women's Survival Ctr., Pontiac, Mich., 1985—; bd. dirs. Jr. League, Birmingham, Mich., Jr. Women's Assn. for Detroit Symphony Orch. Mem. APA, Mich. Psychol. Assn. (women's issues com.), Mich. Women Psychologists (pres.), Am. Orthopsychiat. Assn., Assn. Humanistic Psychology, Mich. Inter-Profl. Assn., Internat. Coun. Psychologists, Profl. Acad. Custody Evaluators. Congregationalist. Club: Hill and Dale Garden (Farmington) (Pres. 1977-78). Office: 31000 Telegraph Rd Ste 130 Bingham Farms MI 48025-4361

CHIANG, HUAI CHANG, entomologist, educator; b. Sunkiang, China, Feb. 15, 1915; came to U.S., 1945, naturalized, 1953; s. Wentse Chiang and Hsiu Hsiu C.; m. Zoh Ing Shen, Sept. 8, 1946; children: Jeanne, Katherine, Robert. B.S., Tsing Hua U., Peking, China, 1938; M.S., U. Minn., 1946, Ph.D., 1948; D.Sc. (hon.), Bowling Green State U., 1979. Asst. instr. entomology Tsing Hua U., Peking, 1938-40, instr., 1940-44; asst. prof. U. Minn., St. Paul and Duluth, 1954-57; assoc. prof. U. Minn., St. Paul, 1957-60, prof., 1960-83, prof. emeritus, 1984—; cons. UNDP FAO, 1970, 72, 75, 76, 80, 82, 85-88, USDA, 1975-83; mem. sci. del. Am. Entomol. Soc., 1974, NAS, 1975, USDA/EPA, 1978, 81, USDA, 1979, 81, FAO, 1980, 82; sci. panel Coun. Environ. Quality, 1977, U.S. Internat. Comm. Agy., 1979, Internat. Centre Insect Physiology and Ecology, Nairobi, Kenya, 1980, Taiwan Coun. Agr., 1979, 84, Chinese Ministry Agr., 1982. Editor 3 publs.; contbr. over 230 rsch. papers to profl. jours. Recipient cert. USDA, 1975, Disting. Svc. award Am. Inst. Biol. Scis., 1979, Regents Cert. Merit U. Minn., 1984, Disting. Svc. award Ministry Agr. and Coops., Thailand, 1988; named Tchr. of yr. Student Assn., U. Minn-Duluth Campus, 1961; Guggenheim fellow, 1955; Phi Kappa Phi nat. scholar, 1983. Mem. Can. Royal London Entomol. Socs., Am. Entomol. Soc. (hon. mem., sect. chmn., chpt. pres., C.V. Riley award, Master Entomologist award), Hungarian Entomol. Soc. (hon. mem.), Japanese Soc. Population Rsch., Internat. Assn. Ecologists, Internat. Orgn. Biol. Control (pres. Western hemisphere, pres., hon. pres. working group), AAAS, Minn. Acad. Scis., Sigma Xi, Gamma Sigma Delta (Merit award 1983), Phi Kappa Phi (scholar of Yr. award 1982, Minn. chpt.). Home: 1896 Carl St Saint Paul MN 55113-5102 Office: U Minn Dept of Entymology Saint Paul MN 55108-1385

CHICOINE, ROLAND ALVIN, farmer, state official; b. Rural Elk Point, S.D., Dec. 10, 1922; s. Elmire Joseph and Louise Marie (Ryan) C.; m. Evelyn Marie Lyle, June 18, 1945; children: Jeffrey R., David L., Marcia M. Quinn, Daniel B., Timothy K., Brian Elmire, Ellen Little, Nicole Louise Klein. Owner, farmer Elk Point, 1942-90; state rep. S.D. State Legislature, 1980-86, state Sen., 1987-92, state rep., 1993—. Mem. Elk Point Local Dist. Sch. Bd., 1971-80; bd. dirs. Union County Farmers Home Adminstrn.; 4-H leader (40 yrs.) Sioux Livestock 4-H Club, state past pres.. Named 1987 SDS Family of the Yr. Mem. County Crop Improvement Assn. (past chmn. bd. dirs.), County Livestock Improvement Assn. (past chmn. bd. dirs.), S.D. State Irrigators Assn. (past state chmn. and organizer), S.D. Water Congress (past bd. dirs.), Union County Livestock Assn. (resolutions com. 1980—), Fed. Land Bank Assn. (Sioux Falls area chmn., bd. dirs. 1970-84, Omaha 4 state adv. bd. 1976-80), S.C. State 4-H Leaders Assn. (state chmn.), Lions. Democrat. Roman Catholic. Address: RR 2 Box 212 Elk Point SD 57025-9734

CHIKI, FRANK T., small business owner; b. Athens, Ohio, Sept. 9, 1965; s. Shirley A. Chiki; life ptnr. R. Solon Jr., Aug. 22, 1993. Adminstrv. asst. Tri-County Cmty. Action Agy., Athens, 1981-83; prodn. supr. Wells Fargo Investment Advisors, San Francisco, 1987-90; owner MacPower, L.A., 1991-93; typesetter/graphics staff Nationwide Ins. Co., Columbus, Ohio, 1993-94; owner FTC Publs./Visual Impact Comms., Columbus and Indpls., 1994—. Children's activities co-coord. Columbus Arts Festival, 1993; vol. Big Bros./Big Sisters, Columbus Marathon, Oktoberfest, others, 1993-94; vol. mem. Ambassadors, Indpls., 1995. Democrat. Jehovah's Witness. Office: Visual Impact Communication Indianapolis IN 46204

CHILA, ANTHONY GEORGE, osteopathic educator; b. Youngstown, Ohio, Dec. 14, 1937; s. Paul and Anne (Jurenko) C.; m. Helen Paulick, Oct. 9, 1965; 1 child, Anne Elizabeth. BA, Youngstown State U., 1960; DO, Kansas City Coll. Osteopathy and Surgery, 1965. Assoc. prof. family medicine Mich. State U. Coll. Medicine, East Lansing, 1977-78; assoc. prof. family medicine Ohio U. Coll. Medicine, Athens, 1978-83, prof. family medicine, 1983, chief clin. research, 1982; chmn. instl. rev. bd. Ohio U., Athens, 1986-88; George C. Kozma Meml. lectr. Cleve. Acad. Osteo Medicine, 1979, Andrew Taylor Still Meml. lectr., Chgo., 1990, Sutherland Meml. Lectr., San Francisco, 1992. Contbr. numerous articles to profl. jours. Trustee Saint Vladimir's Orthodox Theol. Sem., Tuckahoe, N.Y., 1975-89; active Kootaga Area coun. Boy Scouts Am. Mem. AAAS, Am. Osteo. Assn. (Louisa M. Burns lectr. Clearwater, Fla. 1987), Am. Coll. Gen. Practitioners, Am. Acad. OSteopathy (pres. 1983-84, 85-86, Scott Meml. lectr. Kirksville, Mo. 1984, Thomas L. Northup lectr. Las Vegas 1986, Gutensohn-Denslow award 1995), Cranial Acad., N.Y. Acad. Scis., Am. Assn. Orthopaedic Medicine, Gen. Charles Grosvenor Civil War Round Table. Republican. Office: Ohio U Coll Osteo Medicine Grosvenor Hall Athens OH 45701

CHILDERS, JOHN HENRY, talent company executive, personality representative; b. Hoopston, Ill., July 26, 1930; s. Leroy Kendal and Marie Ann (Sova) C.; m. JoAnn Uhlar, July 27, 1956; children: Michael John, Mark Joseph. Sales rep. Universal Match Corp., Chgo., 1956-59; v.p. sales to pres. Sales Merchandising, Inc., Chgo., 1959-63; chmn. bd., chief exec. officer Talent Enterprise, Inc. and Talent Network, Inc., Skokie, Ill., 1963—. Served as pilot USAF, 1950-56. Mem. Assn. Reps. of Profl. Athletes (v.p.); Internat. Wine and Food Soc., Chaine des Rotisseurs, Les Amis du Vin, Wine finders, Classic Car Club Am., Auburn-Cord-Dusenberg Club. Republican. Roman Catholic. Clubs: Knollwood Country, Lake Geneva Country, PGA Country. Home: 1299 Knollwood Cir PO Box 150 Lake Forest IL 60045-0150 also: 219 Club Cottages Palm Beach Gardens FL 33410 also: 105 S Lake Shore Dr Lake Geneva WI 53147-2038 Office: Talent Enterprise Inc 5200 Main St Skokie IL 60077-2158

CHILDERS, L. DOYLE, state legislator; b. Ironton, Mo., Nov. 25, 1944; s. Lawrence Arlin and Jewel Nicks C. AS, Sch. Ozarks, 1964, BS, 1972; postgrad., Southwestern Mo. State U. Active U.S. Peace Corps., Cen. Am., 1965-69; sci. chmn. Reeds Spring RIV Sch. System, 1972-82; Mo. State rep. Dist. 141, 1983—. Active Reeds Spring Comm. Betterment Assn. Mem. Lions, Delta Kappa Phi. Home: PO Box 127 Reeds Spring MO 65737-0127*

CHILDERS, LAWRENCE JEFFREY, superintendent of schools; b. Newport News, Va., Oct. 24, 1947; m. Susan Lynn Bohn; 1 child, Jeffrey Scott. BS in Edn., Ohio U., 1972; MEd, Xavier U., Cinn., 1978. Cert. profl. secondary tchr., elem. prin., secondary tchr., local supt. and supt. Tchr. elem., jr. high sch., high sch. Tri-Valley LSD, Dresden, Ohio, 1967-80; head coach boys basketball Ohio U., Zanesville, 1977-80; prin., dir. in-sch. suspension, coach varsity boys basketball Maysville Local Sch. Dist., Zanesville, 1980-82; prin. South Zanesville (Ohio) Sch., 1982-85, Newton Elem. Sch., 1985-89; prin. Millersburg (Ohio) Elem. Sch., West Holmes Local Sch. Dist., 1989-91, dir. spl. edn., prin., 1992-93; county supt. Holmes County Office of Edn., Millersburg, 1993-94; supt. Holmes County Ednl. Svc. Ctr., Millersburg, Ohio, 1995—; coach Ohio Regional Campus State Basketball Champions, 1978; developer Parent Vol. Network, 1990, in-sch. post office, 1990—; mem. strategic planning com. for bldg. and grounds improvement West Holmes Local Sch. Dist., 1992—; spkr. Sch. Study Coun. Ohio, 1992; mem. tchr. Expectation and Student Achievement; mem. sch. supt.'s adv. coun. Ashland U., 1993, adj. prof., 1995—; supt.'s rep. Ohio East Regional Tchr. Devel. Ctr., 1994—. Mem. adv. bd. Holmes County 4-H, 1990-92; vol. Buckeye Book Fair, 1991, 92, 93; chair Holmes County Interagy, Cluster, 1994-95. Named Ohio Dist. 12 Coach of Yr., 1983, Muskingum Valley League Coach of Yr., 1983. Mem. ASCD, Ohio Assn. Elem. Sch. Adminstr., Ohio Sch. Bds. Assn., Buckeye Assn. Sch. Adminstrs., North Ctrl. Buckeye Assn. Sch. Adminstrs., Wayne-Holmes County Prins. Assn., Coun. for Exceptional Children, Sch. Study Coun. Ohio, Holmes County C. of C., Phi Delta Kappa. Home: PO Box 192 Millersburg OH 44654-0192

CHILDERS, SUSAN LYNN BOHN, special education educator, administrator, human resources and transition specialist; b. Zanesville, Ohio, Mar. 1, 1948; m. Lawrence J. Childers; 1 child, Jeffrey Scott. AA, Ohio U., 1978, BS in Edn. cum laude, 1982; MEd in Supervision, Ashland U., 1991. Profl. cert. 1-8 elem. tchr., K-12 edn. handicapped and supervision; spl. edn. tchr., Ohio. Educator learning disabilities, developmentally handicapped Maysville Local Sch. Dist., South Zanesville, Ohio, 1982-89; work-study coord. Holmes County Office Edn., Millersburg, Ohio, 1990, editor spl. edn. newsletter, 1990-93, cons., supervisor work-study programming, 1991-93; spl. edn. supr. Wayne County Bd. Edn., Wooster, Ohio, 1993-94; adminstr. severe behavior handicapped program, supr. special edn. Ashland-Wayne County Bd. Edn., Wooster, 1994—; mem. Holmes County Spl. Edn. Adv. Coun., 1990-93, E. Holmes Local Sch. Dist. Strategic Planning Action Team Job/Life Skills, 1993, Regional Adv. Coun. for Ohio's Employability Skills Project, Holmes County Job Placement Adv. Bd., 1991-93; spkr. in field; rep. Ohio Devel. Handicapped Issues Forum; mem. steering com. Ohio Speaks, 1991-94; mem. strategic planning com. Ashland-Wayne County Bd. Edn., 1994-95; mem. Chippewa Local Sch. Dist. Child Care Bd., 1995—; chmn. Direct Student Svcs. Strategic Planning Com., 1995-96; mem. safety com. Ashland-Wayne Ednl. Svc. Ctr., 1994—; mem. svc. coordination com. Wayne County Children and Family First Initiative, 1995, 96. Editor Spl. Edn. Newsletter Holmes County Office Edn., 1990-93. Mem. adv. bd. Holmes County Job Placement, Holmes County Litter Prevention Cmty. Action Plan com., 1993; vol. Ohio Buckeye Book Fair, 1991-93, Holmes County Spl. Olympics, 1990-93, chairperson vols., 1993; mem. jr. assembly Bethesda Hosp., 1970-78; mem. Beaux Arts Zanesville Art Ctr., 1972-78; mem. spl. needs adv. bd.

Ashland-West Holmes Career Ctr., 1990-93; mem. Transition and Comm. Consortium on Learning Disabilities, Ohio U. Alumni Career Resource Network, Holmes County Abuse Prevention Cmty. Action Plan com., 1993, Ohio Staff Devel. Coun., Wayne County Family and Children First Coun. (Clin. Cluster), 1994-96; co-chairperson fundraising com. Creating Connections Symposium, Akron, Ohio, 1994; strategic planning com. Ashland-Wayne County Bd. Edn., 1994-95; bd. dirs. Chippewa Local Sch. Dist. Child Care, 1995—; mem. safety com. Ashland-Wayne Ednl. Svc. Ctr., Wooster, 1994-96, svc. coordination com. Wayne County Children and Family First Initiative, 1995-96; mem. Ashland-Wayne-Holmes Counties Adv. Com. for Tech. and Tng. subcom., Ohio, 1996—; adv. com. for tech. 3-county rep., Ashland, Wynd, Holmes, Ohio, 1996—, mem. A-site tech. tng. com., 1996—, regional rep. for School/Net Communities of Practice, 1996—. Recipient award Muskingum County Office Litter Prevention, 1988, Kids Care Project, 1989, Maysville Bd. Edn. commendation, 1989, Merit award Keep Ohio Beautiful program, 1991, Ohio Future Forum's Exemplary Transition from Sch.-to-Work Model award, 1993, Model Program designation Ohio's Employability Skills Project, 1987, Franklin B. Walter Outstanding Educator award, 1996. Mem. ASCD, Career Edn. Assn., Coun. Exceptional Children, Ohio Rural Edn. Assn., Ohio Sch. Suprs. Assn., Ohio Assn. Vocat. Edn. Spl. Needs Pers., Ohio Assn. Suprs. and Work-Study coords. (award of Excellence 1992, reg. pres. 1993-94), Am. Assn. Univ. Women, Wayne-Holmes Elem. Adminstrs. Assn., Phi Delta Kappa. Home: PO Box 192 Millersburg OH 44654-0192 Office: Kinney Meml Bldg 2534 Burbank Rd Wooster OH 44691-1675

CHILDERS, TERRY LEE, marketing educator, consultant; b. Galesburg, Ill., Dec. 31, 1948; s. Harry K. and Charlotte I. (Shriber) C.; m. Colleen Childers-Fogarty, Apr. 28, 1989; 1 child, Jennifer. BS, Ill. State U., 1971, MS, 1973; MBA, PhD, U. Wis., 1982. Rsch. analyst FS Svcs., Bloomington, Ill., 1975-76; assoc. rsch. adminstr. State Farm Ins., Bloomington, 1976-79; asst. prof. U. Minn., Mpls., 1982-87, assoc. prof., 1987-93, prof., 1993—; mktg. cons. U. Rsch. Consortium, Mpls., 1987—; mem. adv. bd. Minn. Ctr. for Survey Rsch., Mpls., 1988—. Mem. editorial bd. Jour. Bus. Rsch., 1987—, Jour. Consumer Rsch., 1988-90; contbr. articles to profl. jours. McKnight rsch. grantee U. Minn., 1988, U. Minn. grantee, 1988, IBM Corp. grantee, 1987. Mem. APA, Am. Mktg. Assn. (chpt. bd. dirs. 1978-79), Assn. for Comsumer Rsch., Am. Psychol. Soc. Home: 6209 Crescent Dr Minneapolis MN 55436-2530 Office: U Minn Dept Mktg 271 19th Ave S Minneapolis MN 55455-0430

CHILSTROM, HERBERT WALFRED, bishop; b. Litchfield, Minn., Oct. 18, 1931; s. Walfred Emanuel and Ruth (Lindell) C.; m. Ella Corinne Hansen, June 12, 1954; children: Mary, Christopher, Andrew. BA, Augsburg Coll., Mpls., 1954; ThM, Augustana Theol. Sem., Rock Island, Ill., 1958, Princeton Theol. Sem., 1966; EdD, NYU, 1976; DD (hon.), Northwestern Luth. Theol. Sem., Mpls., 1979, Gustavus Adolphus Coll., 1987, Capital U., Columbus, Ohio, 1988, Wittenberg U., 1988, Gettysburg (Pa.) Coll., 1988, Midland (Nebr.) Coll., 1988, Newberry (S.C.) Coll., 1989; LHD (hon.), Capitol U., 1988; DD, Gen. Sem., N.Y., 1990, Susquehanna (Pa.) U., 1991, Gurukul Theol. Inst., Madras, India, 1992, Bethany Coll., Lindsborg, Kans., 1993, Muhlenberg Coll., Allentown, Pa., 1994, Thiel Coll., Greenville, Pa., 1995. Ordained to ministry Luth. Ch., 1958. Pastor Faith Luth. Ch., Pelican Rapids, Minn., 1958-62; prof., acad. dean Luther Coll., Teaneck, N.J., 1962-70; sr. pastor First Luth. Ch., St. Peter, Minn, 1970-76; bishop Minn. Synod, Luth. Ch. Am., Mpls., 1976-87, mem. exec. council, 1978-82; pres., bishop Evang. Luth. Ch. in Am., Chgo., 1987-95; mem. Faith and Order Commn. Nat. Council Chs., N.Y.C., 1982; mem. Commn. for a New Lutheran Ch., 1982-86; v.p. Luth. World Fedn., 1990—. Author: Hebrews, A New and Better Way, 1984, When We Reach for the Sun, 1986, Foundations for the Future, 1987. Mem. Faith and Values (VISN) Cable TV Bd.; trustees Bethphage Mission, Inc., Omaha, 1995—. Decorated Royal Order of North Star (Sweden); recipient Pub. Svc. award Suomi Coll., Hancock, Mich., 1979; Disting. Alumnus citation Augsburg Coll., Mpls., 1979, Augsburg medal, 1995; Pope John XXIII award Viterbo Coll., LaCrosse, Wis., Luth. Sch. Theology, Chgo., 1995, Servus Dei award ELCA, 1995, Fine Arts award Gustavus Adolphys Coll., 1995. Mem. Religious Alliance Against Pornography.

CHILTON, BRADLEY STEWART, criminal justice educator; b. Rockford, Ill., Oct. 28, 1955; s. Ermal Rural and Maybelle Rose (McNair) C.; m. Lisa Marie Hartmann, May 21, 1977. BA, Milton Coll., 1977; JD, U. Toledo, 1980, MA, 1981; MA, U. Wis., 1982; PhD, U. Ga., 1988; MLS, U. So. Miss., 1989. Instr. S.E. Mo. State U., Cape Girardeau, 1985-86; asst. prof. U. So. Miss., Hattiesburg, 1986-89, Wash. State U., Pullman, 1989-93; assoc. prof., dir. criminal justice program U. Toledo, 1993—; pre-law advisor U. Toledo, 1993—. Author: Prisons Under the Gavel, 1991. Mem. Acad. Criminal Justice Scis., Am. Judicature Soc., Am. Polit. Sci. Assn. Congregationalist. Office: U Toledo Dept Polit Sci Pub Adminstr Toledo OH 43606-3390

CHILTON, JEFFREY ETHAN, physicist, researcher; b. Visalia, Calif., Apr. 9, 1971; s. Jerry Ben and Mary Eileen (Guse) C. BS in Physics, U. Iowa, 1993. Rsch. asst. U. Iowa, Iowa City, 1990-93, U. Wis., Madison, 1993—; rsch. asst. Fermi Nat. Accelerator Lab., Batavia, Ill., 1991-92, European Ctr. for Nuclear Rsch., Geneva, 1994. U. Iowa Presdl. scholar, 1989-93, Barry Goldwater scholar, 1992; Nat. Def. Sci. and Engring. fellow, 1993-96, U. Wis. Alumni fellow, 1996. Mem. Am. Phys. Soc. Democrat. Home: 2130 University Ave 40 Madison WI 53705 Office: U Wis Dept Physics 1150 University Ave Madison WI 53706

CHILTON, KENNETH WAYNE, business research director, writer; b. St. Louis, Aug. 22, 1944; s. Thomas L. and Sadie I. (Smith) C.; m. Linda K. Bevirt, Aug. 23, 1965; children: Jennifer L., Thomas K. BS, Northwestern U., 1967, MS, 1968; MSBA, Washington U., 1992; PhD, 1994. Mgmt. sci. cons. McDonnell Douglas Corp., St. Louis, 1968-74; treas., dir. bus. planning Permaneer Corp., Maryland Heights, Mo., 1974-77; owner Auto Sell, Creve Coeur, Mo., 1977; asst. dir. Ctr. for the Study of Am. Bus., Wash. Univ., St. Louis, 1977-80, assoc. dir., 1980-91, dep. dir., 1991-95; dir., 1995—; instr. Fontbonne Coll., Clayton, Mo., 1983-88, Washington U., 1988-91, 95. Co-editor: The Dynamic American Firm, Public Policy Toward Corporate Takeovers, American Manufacturing in a Global Market, Environmental Protection, Regulating for Results; contbr. articles to profl. jours. Mem. Pres. Reagan's Small Bus. Issues Task Force, 1980, Small Bus. Adv. Coun. Rep. Nat. Com., 1984. Recipient Spirit of Freedom award Discussion Club, St. Louis, 1988. Mem. AAAS, Nat. Assn. Bus. Econs., Acad. Mgmt., Assn. for Pvt. Enterprise Edn. Office: Washington U Ctr for Study Am Bus Saint Louis MO 63130-4899

CHILTON, WILLIAM DAVID, architect; b. Tulsa, Jan. 4, 1954; s. Horace Thomas Jr. and Betty Jane (Gray) C.; m. Laura Ann Johnson, Aug. 22, 1981. BA in Architecture, Iowa State U., 1976; MArch, U. Minn., 1980. Registered architect, Minn. Designer CDG, Tulsa, 1976; assoc. architect Olson & Coffey Architects, Tulsa, 1977-78, Leonard Parker Assocs., Mpls., 1980-81; sr. architect Conoco, Inc., Ponca City, Okla., 1981-89; v.p., project mgr. Ellerbe Becket, Inc., Mpls., 1989, sr. project mgr., 1990, v.p., project dir., 1991-93, sr. v.p., project dir., 1994—, dir., 1994-95; dir. The Ellerbe Becket Co., Mpls., 1995—. Prin. works include Milne Point (Alaska) Ops. Complex (award Best of Engring. News Record 1986, Excellence in Architecture award North Ctrl. Okla. chpt. AIA 1987, Honorable Mention Builder mag. 1985), Conoco Corp. Offices, Wilmington, Del. (Excellence in Architecture award North Ctrl. Okla. chpt. AIA 1987), Conoco Office/Housing Facilities, Luanda, Angola, 1985-88, Dow Chem. Corp. Hdqrs. Master Plan, Midland, Mich., 1992, Dow Chem. Global Data Ctr., 1992, Sci. Mus. Minn., St. Paul, 1991—. Recipient Design Achievement award Iowa State U., 1995. Mem. Minn. Soc. AIA (sec. North Ctrl. Okla. chpt. 1986, v.p. 1987, pres. 1988, bd. dirs. 1986-88, bd. dirs. Okla. Coun. 1987-88), Minn. Internat. Ctr., Leadership Mpls., Interlachen Country Club (Edina, Minn.). Lutheran. Home: 101 Maple Hill Rd Hopkins MN 55343-8544 Office: Ellerbe Becket Inc 800 Lasalle Ave Minneapolis MN 55402-2014

CHIN, NEEOO WONG, reproductive endocrinologist; b. Hong Kong, Nov. 27, 1955; came to U.S., 1958; s. Bing Leong and Din Sui (Gee) C.; m. Shelly Loraine Crumrine, June 25, 1977; children: Jason Lei, Taryn Mae. BA, U. Cin., 1977; MD, Ohio State U., 1981. Diplomate Am. Bd. Ob-Gyn. Resident Duke U. Med. Ctr., Durham, N.C., 1981-84; chief resident Duke U. Med. Ctr., Durham, 1984-85; fellow Ohio State U. Coll. Medicine, Columbus, Ohio, 1985-87; teaching staff Good Samaritan Hosp., Cin., 1987—; clin. asst. prof. U. Cin. Med. Ctr., 1987—; dir. assisted reproductive techs. The Christ Hosp., Cin., 1992—; mem. High Sch. for the Health Profl. subcom., Cin., 1989—. Author: (with others) Current Therapy in Obstetrics, 1988; contbr. articles to profl. jours. Named to Honorable Order of Ky. Cols., Gov. Martha Collins of Ky., 1987. Fellow Am. Coll. Ob-Gyn.; mem. AAAS, Am. Fertility Soc., Soc. Assisted Reproductive Tech., Soc. for Immunology Repro., Cin. Ob-Gyn. Soc. (med. malpractice com. 1989—), Acad. Medicine Cin. Office: The Christ Hosp 2123 Auburn Ave Ste 044 Cincinnati OH 45219

CHINEA-SERRANO, JORGE LUIS, ethnic studies educator; b. Toa Alta, P.R., Mar. 13, 1954; s. Jorge and Otilia (Serrano) Chinea-Andreu; m. Terri Veronica Williams, Oct. 15, 1983; children: Marcus Antonio, Mateo Luis, Monica Ashley. BA, Binghamton U., 1980, MA, 1983; PhD, U. Minn., 1994. Vis. lectr. Macalester Coll., St. Paul, 1988-90; asst. prof. Metro. State U., St. Paul, 1989-91, Mankato (Minn.) State U., 1991—; adj. instr. John Jay Coll., N.Y.C., 1983; mem. hispanic learner task force Minn. Dept. Edn., Mankato, 1991-92; cons. The Ford Found., 1989-90; history chair Columbus Quincentennial Com., St. Paul, 1990-92. Bd. dirs. Puerto Rican Family Inst., N.Y.C., 1969-70; Latin music program dir. WHRW-FM Radio, Binghamton, 1979-83; vol. Centro Cultural Chicano, 1985-86. Mem. Am. Soc. Ethnohistory, Am. Hist. Assn., Assn. Caribbean Historians, Nat. Assn. Ethnic Studies, Puerto Rican Studies Assn. Office: Mankato State U Ethnic Studies Dept Box 62 Mankato MN 56002

CHING, WAI YIM, physics educator, researcher; b. Shaoshing, China, Oct. 18, 1945; came to U.S., 1969; s. Di-Son and Hung-Wong (Sung) C.; m. Mon Yin Lung, Dec. 27, 1975; children: Tianyu, Kunyu. BSc, U. Hong Kong, 1969; MS, La. State U., 1971, PhD, 1974. Rsch. assoc., lectr. U. Wis., Madison, 1974-78; asst. prof. U. Mo., Kansas City, 1978-81, assoc. prof., 1981-84, prof. physics, 1984-88, curators' prof., 1988—, chmn. physics dept., 1990—; cons. Argonne (Ill.) Nat. Lab., 1978-82, vis. scientist, 1985-86; vis. prof. U. Sci. and Tech., Hefei, China, 1983. Contbr. articles to profl. jours. Recipient N.T. Veatch award for disting. rsch., 1985; Trustee fellow U. Mo., 1984, 90. Mem. AAAS, Am. Phys. Soc., Am. Ceramic Soc., Am. Vacuum Soc., Materials Rsch. Soc., Sigma Xi. Home: 2809 W 119th St Leawood KS 66209-1104 Office: U Mo Dept Physics 1110 E 48th St Kansas City MO 64110-1718

CHINN, REX ARLYN, chemist; b. Bosworth, Mo., Apr. 5, 1935; s. Loren Herbert and Lima (Stanton) C.; m. Wanda June Williams, May 31, 1959 (dec.); children: Timothy Michael, Sharon Rose Chinn-Heritch, Jonathan Daniel; m. Victoria Loraine Hunter. BS in Chemistry, S.W. Mo. State Coll., 1961; grad., Cleve. Inst. Electronics. Lic. Bapt. minister. Rsch. asst. U. Mo. Med. Ctr., Columbia, 1961-65, William S. Merrell Co., Cin., 1965-67; lab. supr. U.S. Indsl. Chem. Co., Rsch. div., Cin., 1967-72; mgr. quality assurance Cloudsley Co., Cin., 1972-74; dir. tech. affairs Woodson Tenent Labs., Memphis, 1974-77; quality engr. Nat. Ind. for the Blind, Earth City, Mo., 1977-96; owner/mgr. The Master's Image, Maryland Hts., Mo., 1987—; freelance field prodns. KNLC, Channel 24, St. Louis, 1987—; freelance audo rec. for ACTS Inc., 1996—; video cons.; environ. control sys. cons. Contbr. articles to profl. jours; producer/dir.: More Than a Fighting Chance, 1989. With U.S. Army, 1954-56. Mem. Internat. Platform Assn. Republican. Home and Office: The Masters Image 12079 Ameling Rd Maryland Heights MO 63043-4148

CHINTELLA, GEORGE M., manufacturing company executive; b. Sharon, Pa., Dec. 31, 1955. Sr. designer Cleve. Machine Controls, 1979—. Office: Cleve Machine Controls Drafting Dept 7550 Hub Pky Cleveland OH 44125-5705

CHIOU, WEN-AN, science educator, researcher; b. Nan-Chou, Ping-Tung, Taiwan, June 24, 1948; came to U.S., 1973; s. Ter-Tsai and Jane-May (Liaow) C.; m. Nae-Shiang Pan; children: George W., Kathy S. BS in Oceanography, Chinese Culture U., Hwa-Kang, Taiwan, 1970; postgrad. study in geology, Nat. Taiwan U., Taipei, 1971-73; MS in Marine Sci., U. South Fla., 1976; PhD in Oceanography, Tex. A&M U., 1981. Lab. asst. Taiwan Petroleum Exploration Div. Chinese Petroleum Corp., Miao-Li, Taiwan, 1971-72; grad. rsch. tchg. asst. U. South Fla., Tampa, 1973-76, Tex. A&M U., College Station, 1976-80; staff geologist Reservoirs, Inc., Houston, 1981-83, sr. staff geologist, 1983-86; electron microscopist, mgr. Northwestern U., Evanston, Ill., 1986-90, assoc. rsch. prof., 1991—; adj. lectr. U. Houston, Clear Lake, Tex., 1983-86; adj. assoc. prof. Marquette U., Milw., 1990—; cons. rsch. scientist Naval Rsch. Lab., Stennis Space Ctr., Miss., 1988—; v.p. tech. svc. Accumin Analysis Inc., Houston, 1986—. Assoc. editor: Microstructure of Fine-Grained Sediments, 1991; contbr. more than 40 articles to profl. and scholarly jours. 2nd lt. Chinese Army, 1970-71. Recipient Michael Tenenbaum award Iron and Steel Soc., 1994, Sun Yet0Sun scholar Republic of China Govt., 1972, 73; rsch. scholar Chines Ministry Edn., 1972-73. Fellow Royal Microscopial Soc., mem. Am. Geophys. Union, Mineralogical Soc. Am. Mineralogical Soc., Electron Microscopy Soc. Am. (presdl. scholar 1980, Travel Exhibit Poster award 1993, 95), Clay Minerals Soc., Minerals Metals Materials Soc., Microbeam Analysis Soc. Home: 419 Vine St Wilmette IL 60091-3131 Office: Northwestern Univ Dept Material Sci/Engring 2225 N Campus Dr Evanston IL 60208-3108

CHIPMAN, JOHN SOMERSET, economist, educator; b. Montreal, Que., Can., June 28, 1926; s. Warwick Fielding and Mary Somerset (Aikins) C.; m. Margaret Ann Ellefson, June 24, 1960; children: Thomas Noel, Timothy Warwick. Student, Universidad de Chile, Santiago, 1943-44; BA, McGill U., Montreal, 1947, MA, 1948; PhD, Johns Hopkins U., 1951; postdoctoral, U. Chgo., 1950-51; Doctor rerum politicarum honoris causa, U. Konstanz, Germany, 1991. Asst. prof. econs. Harvard U., Cambridge, Mass., 1951-55; assoc. prof. econs. U. Minn., Mpls., 1955-60; prof. U. Minn., 1961-81, Regents' prof., 1981—; fellow Ctr. for Advanced Study in Behavioral Scis., Stanford, Calif., 1972-73; Gubbenheim fellow, 1980-81; vis. prof. econs. various univs.; permanent guest prof. U. Konstanz, 1985-91; bd. dirs. Leuthold Funds, Inc. Author: The Theory of Intersectoral Money Flows and Income Formation, 1951; editor: (with others) Preferences, Utility, and Demand, 1971, Preferences, Uncertainty and Optimality, 1990, (with C.P. Kindleberger) Flexible Exchange Rates and the Balance of Payments, 1980; co-editor Jour. Internat. Econs., 1971-76, editor, 1977-87; assoc. editor Econometrica, 1956-60, Can. Jour. Stats., 1980-82; mem. adv. bd. Jour. Multivariate Analysis, 1988-92. Recipient James Murray Luck award Nat. Acad. Scis., 1981, Humboldt Rsch. award for Sr. U.S. Scientists, 1992. Fellow AAAS, Econometric Soc. (coun. 1971-76, 81-83), Am. Statis. Assn., Am. Acad. Arts and Scis.; mem. NAS, Internat. Statis. Inst., Inst. Math. Stats., Can Econ. Assn., Royal Econ. Soc., Soc. for Advancement of Econ. Theory, History of Econs. Soc. Home: 2121 W 49th St Minneapolis MN 55409-2229 Office: U Minn Dept Econs 1122 Mgmt and Econs Bldg 217 19th Ave S Minneapolis MN 55455-0400

CHIPMAN, MARION WALTER, judge; b. Penokee, Kans., May 5, 1920; s. James Edwin and May Maude (Hatcher) C.; m. Thelma Nadine Clark, Nov. 1, 1941 (div. 1965); m. Nancy Jo Payne, May 28, 1983; children: Clark D., Jill Ellen. AB in Social Sci., Ft. Hays (Kans.) State U., 1942; JD, Washburn U., 1948. Bar: Kans. 1948, U.S. Dist. Ct. Kans. 1948, U.S. Ct. Appeals 1970, U.S. Supreme Ct. 1970. Supt. Prairieview (Kans.) Sch., 1942; atty. County of Graham, Hill City, Kans., 1949-53; counselor County of Johnson, Olathe, Kans., 1967-68; judge 10th Jud. Dist. Kans. Dist. Ct., Olathe, 1980-91. Sgt. USAAF, 1942-46. Mem. ABA (life), Johnson County Bar Assn. (life), Kans. Bar Assn., Am. Judicature, Am. Judge's Assn., Am. Arbitration Assn., Am. Legion, Masons, Shriners, Elks. Methodist. Home: 1012 S Stratford Rd Olathe KS 66062-2117 Office: Kans Dist Ct 10 Jud Dist Johnson County Courthouse Olathe KS 66061

CHISHOLM, GEORGE NICKOLAUS, dentist; b. Pullman, Wash., Sept, 21, 1936; s. Leslie L. and Lila Rene (Cates) C.; D.D.S., U. Nebr., 1960; 1 son, Andrew M. Practice dentistry, Lincoln, Nebr., 1963-83; clin. instr. Coll. Dentistry, U. Nebr., 1976-83. Mem. S.E. Nebr. Health Planning Agy., 1976-82. Served to capt. Dental Corps, USAF, 1960-63. Mem. ADA (del. 1980), Nebr. Dental Assn. (del. 1974-80, trustee 1980-83), Lincoln Dist. Dental Assn. (pres. 1979-80), Sigma Alpha Epsilon, Xi Psi Phi. Mason (32 deg., Shriner). Asst. editor Nebr. State Dental Jour., 1967-69. Home: 1735 S 38th St Lincoln NE 68506-5253

CHISHOLM, MALCOLM HAROLD, chemistry educator; b. Bombay, India, Oct. 15, 1945; came to U.S., 1972; s. Angus MacPhail and Gweneth (Robey) C.; m. Cynthia Ann Truax, May 1, 1982; children: Calum R.I., Selby Scott, Derek Adrian. BS in Chemistry, Queen Mary Coll., London, 1966, PhD in Chemistry, 1969; DSc (hon.), London U., 1981. Postdoctoral fellow U. Western Ont., London, 1969-72; asst. prof. Princeton (N.J.) U., 1972-78; assoc. prof. chemistry Ind. U., Bloomington, 1978-80, prof., 1980-85, Disting. prof. chemistry, 1985—; cons. in field. Editor: Polyhedron, Chem. Comm.; mem. editl. bd. Inorganic Chemistry, Organometallics, Inorganic Chimica Acta; contbr. over 400 rsch. articles to profl. jours. Fellow AAAS, Ind. Acad. Scis., Royal Soc. (London), Royal Soc. for Chemistry (Corday Morgan medal 1981, award for Transition Metal Chemistry, Centenary Lectr. and medal), Am. Chem. Soc. (Akron sect. award 1982, Buck Whitney award 1987, Inorganic Chemistry award). Home: 515 S Hawthorne Dr Bloomington IN 47401-5023 also: 38 Norwich St, Cambridge CB2 1NE, England Office: Ind Univ Dept Chemistry Bloomington IN 47405

CHISM, JAMES ARTHUR, information systems executive, business consultant; b. Oak Park, Ill., Mar. 6, 1933; s. William Benjamin Thompson and Arema Eloise (Chadwick) C. AB, DePauw U., 1957; MBA, Ind. U., 1959; postgrad. advanced mgmt. program U. Pa., 1984; postgrad. sr. exec. devel. program U. Notre Dame, 1988. Mgmt. engr. consumer and indsl. products div. Uniroyal, Inc., Mishawaka, Ind. and N.Y.C., 1959-61, sr. mgmt. engr., office mgr., 1961-63; systems analyst Miles, Inc., Elkhart, Ind., 1963-64, sr. systems analyst, 1965-69, project mgr. distbn./logistics systems, 1969-71, mgr. systems and programming for corp. fin. and adminstrv. depts., 1971-73, mgr. adminstrv. systems and corp. staff svcs., 1973-75, group mgr. consumer products group systems and programming, 1975-79; dir. corp. orgnl. analysis, adminstrn. and staff svcs. Berkeley, Calif., Elkhart, Ind., London, Toronto, Can., Cutter/Miles, 1979-81, dir. advanced office systems and corp. adminstrn. 1982-84; dir. advanced office systems Internat. MIS and Adminstrn., 1984-85, dir. advanced office systems, tng. and adminstrn., 1985-87; exec. dir. Office Info Systems Tng., Fin. and Adminstrn., 1987-90, exec. dir. fin. and adminstrv. svcs. for N.Am. Information Systems and Logistics, 1991-92. CFO, N.Am. Information Systems, 1992-95; ptnr. Heartland Consulting Group, 1995—. Bd. dirs. United Way Elkhart County, 1974-78, 91-94, Arts Indiana Inc. State Coun. Mem., 1995—; bd. dirs. Sorin Soc., Ind. Colls. of Ind. Found., 1986-95, devel. comm., 1992-95; bd. dirs. Snite Mus. Art, 1990—, vice-chmn., 1993-94, chmn. 1994—; sustaining fellows Art Inst. Chgo., 1970— (Ind. Govs. Arts award, 1994); patron Indpls. Mus. Art, 1995—; mem. Coun. of Sagamores of Wabash, 1993—; sponsoring mem. Mich. Arts and Scis. Coun., 1983—. With AUS, 1954-56. Mem. Indpls. Hist. Soc. (life), Common Dataprocessing Assn., Assn. Systems Mgmt. (chpt. pres. 1969-70, div. dir. 1972-77, internat. dir., 1978-80, Merit award 1975, Achievement award 1977, cert. systems profl. 1984, Disting. Svc. award 1986, 25 Yrs. Leadership award 1988, 30 Yr. Commendation award 1994), Disting. Dean's Assocs. of Ind. U. Sch. Bus. Bloomington (computer info. sys. adv. coun. 1980—), Ind. U. Alumni Assn. (life mem.), Well House Soc., Assn. Internal Mgmt. Cons. (exec. com., bd. dirs., v.p.), Fin. Execs. Inst., Econ. Club Chgo., Office Automation Soc. Internat., Nat. Assn. Bus. Economists, DePauw U. Alumni Assn. (Pres.'s Cir., regents program 1989, nat. ann. fund exec. com. 1990—, bd. visitors, 1990-93, alumni assn. bd. dirs. 1994—), Washington C. DePauw Soc. 1993— (exec. com.), DePauw Deke Realty Assn., Delta Kappa Epsilon, Deke Club of N.Y.C. (past pres. bd. dirs. Deke Realty 1986-94), Sigma Delta Chi, Sigma Iota Epsilon, Beta Gamma Sigma, Omicron Delta Epsilon, Alpha Iota Delta. Republican. Episcopalian. Clubs: Morris Park Country (South Bend, Ind.), Univ. Club (Notre Dame, Ind.), Yale Club of N.Y.C.; Skyline Club (Indpls.), Ind. Soc. of Chgo., Deke Club of N.Y.C. Home: 504 Cedar Crest Ln Mishawaka IN 46545-5772 Office: Bayer Corp PO Box 40 1884 Miles Ave Elkhart IN 46515-0040

CHITWOOD, LERA CATHERINE, marketing information professional; b. Columbiana, Ala., Sept. 14, 1942; d. Roy P. and Lizzie Hearn (Erwin) C.; m. John N. Mathys, Mar. 17, 1984 (div. 1992); 1 child, Jonathan Roy Chitwood Mathys. BA in English, Carson-Newman Coll., 1964; MLS, Emory U., 1967; MBA, DePaul U., 1985. Asst. head dept. bus. and sci. Atlanta Pub. Libr., 1964, 66-69; tchr. English, Sequoyah High Sch., Doraville, Ga., 1965; libr. Ill. Inst. Tech. Stuart Sch. Mgmt. and Fin., Chgo., 1970-79; sr. reference libr., asst. prof. bibliography U. Ala., Huntsville, 1979-82; mgr. bus. rsch. Motorola Inc., Schaumburg, Ill., 1985-95; mgr. mktg. John Crane Internat., Morton Grove, Ill., 1995—. Libr. sch. scholar Atlanta Pub. Libr., 1966. Mem. Soc. Competitive Intelligence (CI Rev. columnist, 1991-95), Assn. Global Strategic Info. Home: 208 E Crescent Ave Elmhurst IL 60126-4054

CHIU, ING-MING, biochemistry educator; b. Taipei, Taiwan, July 19, 1952; came to U.S., 1976; naturalized, 1988; s. Shin and Chung Tse (Shih) C.; m. Mei-Ching Liu Chiu, Sept. 4, 1977; children: Cindy Nicole, Katherine Grace. BS, Nat. Taiwan U., 1974; PhD, Fla. State U., 1981. Postdoctoral fellow NIH, Bethesda, Md., 1981-85; sr. investigator Revlon Health Care, Springfield, Va., 1985-86; asst. prof. Ohio State U., Columbus, 1986-91, mem. cancer rsch. ctr., 1986—, assoc. prof., 1991-95; prof., 1995—. Contbr. articles to profl. jours. Lt. missile corps Taiwanese Army, 1974-76. Recipient Fogarty Internat. fellowship NIH, 1981-85, Ohio Cancer Rsch. award, 1988-90, Rsch. Career Devel. award, 1990-95. Mem. AAAS, Am. Soc. Biochemistry and Molecular Biology, Am. Assn. Cancer Rsch. Presbyterian. Home: 8664 Finlarig Dr Dublin OH 43017-9636 Office: Ohio State U 480 W 9th Ave Rm 2052S Columbus OH 43210-1245

CHLEBOWSKI, JOHN FRANCIS, JR., financial executive; b. Wilmington, Del., Aug. 19, 1945; s. John Francis and Helen Ann (Cholewa) C.; divorced; children: J. Christopher, Lauren R. B.S., U. Del., Newark, 1967; M.B.A., Pa. State U., State College, 1971. Fin. analyst Jones & Laughlin Steel, Pitts., 1971-74; mgr., fin. analyst W.R. Grace & Co., N.Y.C., 1974-75; mgr., fin. planner W.R. Grace & Co., Dallas, 1975-77; mgr., asst. treas. W.R. Grace & Co., N.Y.C., 1978-83; v.p. planning Polumbus Co., Denver, 1977-78; v.p. fin. planning GATX Corp., Chgo., 1983-84, v.p. fin., 1984—, v.p. fin., chief fin. officer, 1986-94; pres. GATX Terminals Corp., Chgo., 1994, pres., CEO, 1995. Bd. dirs. Travelers & Immigrants Aid Assn., 1987—, pres. bd. dirs., 1992-93; chief crusader United Way Crusade Mercy, Chgo. Leadership Greater Chgo. fellow, 1984-85. Mem. Econ. Club, McGraw Wildlife Club, Chgo. Club, Beta Gamma Sigma. Roman Catholic. Office: GATX Corp 500 W Monroe St Chicago IL 60661-3630

CHLUBNA, DAVID JOHN, psychotherapist; b. Detroit, Mar. 18, 1953; s. John and Vonda Cleone (DeGeer) C.; m. Sandra Lynne Jacobs, Aug. 14, 1982 (dec. June 1996). BA, Oakland U., Rochester, Mich., 1975; MS, Ea. Mich. U., 1982. Resident mgr. Renaissance House, Inc., Ypsilanti, Mich., 1979-80; resource coord. psychology dept. Ea. Mich. U., Ypsilanti, 1980-82; psychologist intern Huron Valley Child Guidance Ctr., Ypsilanti, 1981-82; career counselor JTPA Kankakee (Ill.) C.C., 1983-84; staff psychotherapist Mental Health Ctr. Kankakee County, Kankakee, 1984-87; mental health coord. Kewaunee County Cmty. Programs, Algoma, Wis., 1987-89; psychotherapist Door County Counseling Svc., Sturgeon Bay, Wis., 1987-93; staff psychotherapist Cath. Social Svc., Green Bay, Wis., 1992-96. Editor Single Child Rev., 1991; editorial bd. Jour. of Mental Health Counseling, 1993; contbr. articles to profl. jours. Mem. ACA, APA (assoc.), Am. Psychol. Soc., Am. Mental Health Counselors, Assn. for Behavior Analysis, Am. Assn. Applied and Preventive Psychology, Am. Ortho-Psychiat. Assn. Home: 1522 Memorial Dr Sturgeon Bay WI 54235-1502 Office: Cath Social Svcs 1825 Riverside Dr Green Bay WI 54305-5825

CHMELL, SAMUEL JAY, orthopedic surgeon; b. Chgo., Aug. 21, 1952; s. Samuel and Elsie (Wauterlek) C.; m. Nancy Jean Aumiller, June 22, 1974; children: Jessica, Carson, Alexis, Lesley, Samuel Jayson. BS, U. Notre Dame, 1974; MD, Loyola U., 1977. Diplomate Am. Bd. Orthop. Surgery. Intern Loyola U. Med. Ctr., Maywood, Ill., 1977-78, resident in orthop. surgery, 1980-84; emergency rm. physician USPHS Indian Health Svc., Chinle, Ariz., 1978-80; attending orthop. surgeon Hines (Ill.) VA Hosp., 1984-88, Shriners Hosp. for Crippled Children, Chgo., 1985-89, Gallup (N.Mex.) Indian Hosp., 1988-89, Humana-Michael Reese Hosp. and Health Plan, Chgo., 1989—; chmn. sect. orthopaedic surgery Humana-Michael Reese HMO, Chgo., 1991—; asst. prof. dept. orthopaedic surgery U. Ill., Chgo., 1991—; clin. instr. in orthop. surgery Loyola U. Med. Ctr., Maywood, 1985-88; asst. prof. dept. orthop. surgery U. Ill., Chgo. Contbr. articles in field to profl. jours. Active Olmsted Hist. Soc. Riverside, Ill.

Sofield travelling fellow Orthop. Rsch. Soc. Gt. Britain, 1985. Fellow ACS, Am. Acad. Orthop. Surgeons; mem. AMA, Ill. State Med. Soc., Ill. Orthop. Soc., Chgo. Med. Soc., Notre Dame Orthop. Soc., Founders' Cir. of Sorin Soc. U. Notre Dame, Alpha Omega Alpha. Office: Humana-Michael Reese Health Plan 2545 S King Dr Chicago IL 60616-2419

CHMIELEWSKI, FLORIAN, state legislator; b. Feb. 10, 1927; m. Patricia Chmielewski; four children. Minn. Agrl. Extension, LaSalle Law Extension U. State senator Dist. 8 Minn. State Senate, 1971-78, 81—; pres. TV Network, 1996—; farmer, 1996—; chmn. Employment Com.; pres. pro tem Transp. & Pub. Transit; mem. rules and Adminsstrn., taxes & tax laws; ex-oficio mem. Intertribal Bd. Coms.; mem. Energy & Cmty. Devel., Fin. Divsn., Vet. & Gen. Taxes Coms. Minn. State Senate. Office: Sturgeon Lake MN 55783 also: State Senate State Capitol Building Saint Paul MN 55155-1606*

CHODZINSKY, DANIEL, design engineer; b. South Bend, Ind., May 12, 1951. Degree in Dye Design, Acme Tech. Sch., South Bend, Ind., 1970. Designer Tool and Die Huckins Tool and Die, South Bend, Ind., 1968-70; machine design Weldun Internat., Bridgeman, Mich., 1979-84; project engr. machine design Able Engring., Inc., South Bend, Ind., 1984—. Roman Catholic. Office: Able Engineering Inc 3605 Gagnon St South Bend IN 46628-4366

CHOINOSKI, RICHARD DENIS, financial executive; b. Washington, Dec. 7, 1941; s. Denis Walter and Alice Victoria (Imanski) C.; divorced; children: Regina Dolores, Richard Christopher. BBA in Acctg., Loyola U., Chgo., 1965, MBA in Acctg., 1972. Chief acct. Loyola U., Chgo., 1965-71; comptroller Village of Rosemont, Ill., 1971-76, Village of Bellwood, Ill., 1976-80; dir. fin. Village of Maywood, Ill., 1980-86; mgr. for bus. affairs Soc. Profl. Journalists, Chgo., 1987-88; budget analyst, purchasing agt. City of Waukegan, Ill., 1988—. Served with U.S. Army, 1965-67. Roman Catholic. Home: 1109 N Sheridan Rd Waukegan IL 60085-2055 Office: City of Waukegan 410 Robert V Sabonjian Pl Waukegan IL 60085-4328

CHOJNA, WOJTEK, philosophy educator; b. Lublin, Poland, Dec. 29, 1957; came to U.S., 1985; s. Henryk and Celina (Pruszkowska) C.; 1 child, Kasia. MA, U. Maria Curie-Sklopowska, Lublin, 1980; PhD, Temple U., 1992. Lectr. U. Maria Curie-Sklopowska, Lublin, 1980-85; teaching asst. Temple U., Phila., 1985-89; adj. prof. St. Joseph's U., Phila., 1988-93; asst. prof. Ohio U., Athens, 1993—. Contbr. articles to profl. jours. Mem. Solidarnosc, Lublin, 1980. Mem. Am. Philosophy Assn., Am. Soc. for Aesthetics, Soc. for Phenomenology and Existential Philosophy, Soc. for Utopian Studies. Office: Ohio U 104 Lindley Athens OH 45701

CHOJNACKI, PAUL ERVIN, pharmacist, pharmaceutical company official; b. Chgo., Dec. 29, 1950; s. Ervin Edward and Monica (Jablonski) C.; m. Doris Warenberg, May 26, 1979; children: Brittany, James. BS in Bus., Chgo. State U., 1975; BS in Pharmacy, St. Louis Coll., 1977; MA in Mktg., Webster U., 1982. RPh, Mo., N.C., Ind. Clk. Filmanowicz Drug, Chgo., 1968-70; stock clk. Sears, Roebuck & Co., Chgo., 1974-75; sales rep. Chgo. Motor Club, 1975-76; pharmacist Family Pharmacy, St. Louis, 1977; sales assoc. Eli Lilly & Co., St. Louis, 1977-84; regional mgr. Hosp. Pharmacies Inc., St. Louis, 1984-85; hosp. rep. Glaxo Inc., St. Louis, 1985-91; State of Ind. dist. mgr. Allen & Hanburys/Glaxo Pharms., Fishers, 1991—; assoc. product mgr. Oral Cephaloporins Glaxo, Inc., 1989. Local campaign worker, St. Louis, 1985. Mem. Am. Pharm. Assn., St. Louis Pharmacists Assn., St. Louis Hosp. Pharmacists Assn., Ind. Pharm. Assn., Ind. Pharmacists Assn., St. Joseph County Pharmacist Assn. (officer 1995, continuing edn. coord.), Alpha Zeta Omega (treas. St. Louis 1977-78, pres. 1978-79). Home and Office: 10110 Bent Tree Ln Fishers IN 46038

CHOLDIN, MARIANNA TAX, librarian, educator; b. Chgo., Feb. 26, 1942; d. Sol and Gertrude (Katz) Tax; m. Harvey Myron Choldin, Aug. 28, 1962; children: Kate and Mary (twins). BA, U. Chgo., 1962, MA, 1967, PhD, 1979. Slavic bibliographer Mich. State U., East Lansing, 1967-69; Slavic bibliographer, instr. U. Ill., Urbana, 1969-73, Slavic bibliographer, asst. prof., 1973-76, Slavic bibliographer, assoc. prof., 1976-84, head Slavic and East European Libr., 1982-89, head, prof., 1984—, dir. Russian and East European Ctr., 1987-89, C. Walter and Gerda B. Mortenson Disting. prof., 1989—, dir. Mortenson Ctr. for Internat. Libr. Programs, 1991—; dir. Mortenson Ctr. for Internat. Libr. Programs., U. Ill., 1991—. Author: Fence Around the Empire: Russian Censorship, 1985; editor: Red Pencil: Artists, Scholars and Censors in the USSR, 1989, Books, Libraries and Information in Slavic and East European Studies, 1986. Mem. ALA, Am. Assn. for Advancement of Slavic Studies (pres. 1995), Internat. Fedn. Libr. Assns. and Instns., Phi Beta Kappa. Jewish. Home: 1111 S Pine St Champaign IL 61820-6334 Office: U Ill Libr 1408 W Gregory Dr Urbana IL 61801-3607

CHORENGEL, BERND, international hotel corporation executive. Pres. Hyatt Internat. Corp., Chgo. Office: Hyatt Internat Hotels Corp Madison Plz 200 W Madison St Chicago IL 60606-3414*

CHOU, CHING-CHUNG, physiology and medical educator; b. Taipei, Taiwan, June 25, 1932; came to U.S., 1960; m. Lucy Ai-shu Tzen Chou, Nov. 15, 1962; children: Jane, Belinda, Michael. MD, Nat. Taiwan U., Taipei, 1958; PhD, U. Okla., Oklahoma City, 1966. Instr. physiology U. Okla., Oklahoma City, 1965-66; asst. prof. physiology and medicine Mich. State U., East Lansing, 1966-69, assoc. prof. physiology and medicine, 1969-73, prof. physiology and medicine, 1973—, assoc. chairperson physiology, 1992—; pres. Splanchnic Circulation Group, 1978-83, exec. sec., 1983—. Author: (book) Physiology of Gastrointestinal Tract, 1968, (book chpt.) Intestinal Motility and Blood Flow, 1989; contbr. numerous articles to profl. jours. Fulbright scholar, Brazil, 1987; recipient Disting. Faculty awards Coll. Medicine Mich. State U., 1988, 89. Fellow Am. Heart Assn.; mem. Am. Physiol. Soc., Am. Gastroent. Assn., Cen. Soc. Clin. Rsch., N.Am. Tiawanese Med. Assn. (bd. dirs. 1990-92), N.Am. Taiwanese Prof. Assn. (bd. dirs. 1993—). Home: 4845 Mohican Ln Okemos MI 48864-1406

CHOU, KUO-CHEN, biophysical chemist; b. Guangdong, China, Aug. 14, 1938; came to U.S., 1980; s. Hsiu-Chi Chou and Bi-Kun Luo; m. Wei-Zhu Zhong, Apr. 12, 1968; 1 child, James Jeiwen Chou. BS, Nanking (Peoples Republic China) U., 1960, MS, 1962; PhD equivalent, Shanghai (Peoples Republic China) Inst. Biochemistry, 1976; DSc, Kyoto (Japan) U., 1983. Jr. scientist Shanghai Inst. Biochemistry, Chinese Acad. Sci., 1976-78, assoc. prof., 1978-79; prof. Chem. Ctr. Lund (Sweden) U., 1979-80; vis. assoc. prof. Max-Planck Inst. Biophys. Chemistry, Göttingen, Fed. Republic Germany, 1979-80; vis. prof. chemistry Cornell U., Ithaca, N.Y., 1980-83, sr. scientist Baker Lab., 1984-85; vis. prof. biophysics U. Rochester, N.Y., 1985-86; sr. scientist Eastman Kodak Co., Rochester, 1986-87, Upjohn Labs., Kalamazoo, Mich., 1987—. Editor Jour. Molecular Sci., 1983-86, Progress in Physics, 1981-85; contbr. more than 130 rsch. articles and rev. papers to profl. jours. Recipient Sci. and Tech. award Shanghai Com. of Sci. and Tech., 1977, Nat. medal of Sci., Nat. Acad. of Sci., China, 1978, Disting. Leadership award Am. Biog. Inst., N.C., 1989, Commemorative medal of Honor, Am. Biog. Inst., 1991; named for Leadership and Achievement, Internat. Biog. Ctr., Cambridge, U.K., 1990. Fellow Am. Inst. Chemistry; mem. AAAS, N.Y. Acad. Scis., Biophysical Soc., Am. Chem. Soc., Sigma Xi. Home: 4416 Woodhaven Dr Kalamazoo MI 49008-3443 Office: Pharmacia & Upjohn Labs Computer-Aided Drug Discov 301 Henrietta St Kalamazoo MI 49007-4940

CHOU, SHELLEY NIEN-CHUN, neurosurgeon, university official, educator; b. Chekiang, China, Feb. 6, 1924; s. Shelley P. and Tse-tsun (Chao) C.; m. Jolene Johnson, Nov. 24, 1956 (div. 1977); children: Shelley T., Dana, Kerry; remarried, 1979. B.S., St. John's U., Shanghai, China, 1946; M.D., U. Utah, 1949; M.S., U. Minn., 1954, Ph.D., 1964. Diplomate: Am. Bd. Neurol. Surgery (mem. bd.). Resident U. Minn. Hosps., 1950-55; practice medicine, specializing in neurosurgery Salt Lake City, 1955-58, Bethesda, Md., 1959, Mpls., 1960—; clin. asst. Coll. Medicine U. Utah, 1956-58; vis. scientist Nat. Insts. Neurol. Diseases and Blindness NIH, 1959; mem. faculty U. Minn., 1960—, assoc. prof. neurosurgery, 1965-68, prof. neurosurgery, 1968-92, head dept. neurosurgery, 1974-89, prof. emeritus, 1992, interim dean med. sch., dep. v.p. med. affairs, 1993-95; mem. Am. Bd. Neurol Surg., 1974-79; mem. residency rev. com. ACGME, 1984-90, chmn., 1987-89. Contbr. numerous articles to profl. jours.; Publs. on studies of intracranial lesions using radioactive angiography techniques; malformations of cerebral vasculature; neurol. dysfunctions of urinary bladder. Mem. AMA, A.C.S. (mem. adv. council neurosurgery 1981-87, mem. grad. Med. edn. com. 1984—), Congress Neurol. Surgery, Soc. Neurol. Surgeons (pres. 1978-79), Am. Acad. Neurol. Surgery (pres. elect 1985-86, pres. 1986-87), Soc. Nuclear Medicine, Am. Assn. Neurol. Surgeons (bd. dirs. 1980-83, v.p. 1984-85), Neurosurg. Soc. N.Am. (pres. 1977-78), N.Y. Acad. Medicine, Forum Univ. Neurosurgeons (pres. 1968-69), AAAS, Phi Rho Sigma. Home: 183 Galtier Pl Shoreview MN 55126-2113 Office: Box 96 UMHC 420 Delaware St SE Minneapolis MN 54455-0392

CHOVAN, JOHN DAVID, biomedical engineer; b. Canton, Ohio, Sept. 14, 1958; s. John Jr. and Esther Lee (Baker) C. BS, Ohio State U., 1980, BS in Audio Recording, 1980, BSEE, 1982, MS, 1984, PhD, 1990. Registered profl. engr., Ohio. Evaluation programs assoc. Nat. Bd. Med. Examiners, Phila., 1985-87; rsch. scientist Battelle Meml. Inst., Columbus, 1991-95; grad. rsch. assoc. Ohio State U., Columbus, 1982-84, lead programmer-analyst, 1984-85, grad. rsch. assoc., 1987-90, postdoctoral researcher, 1990-91, sr. tech. specialist, 1995—. Author: Educom Selected Academic Software, 1990; editor: Preprints of the 1991 IFIP Working Group on Intelligent CAD, 1991; author conf. papers, tech. reports. Mem. Columbus AIDS Task Force, 1985; mem. Ohio State U. AIDS Edn. and Rsch. Com., Columbus, 1987-90, Am. Rose Soc. Recipient numerous baking and cooking state level competitions. Mem. Engring. in Medicine and Biology Soc. of IEEE, Biomed. Engring. Soc., Internat. Neural Networks Soc., Mensa, Knitting Guild Am., Sigma Xi. Home: 135 Arden Rd Columbus OH 43214-3719 Office: Ohio State U JL Camera Ctr 2050 Kenny Rd Columbus OH 43221

CHOW, CHI-MING, retired mathematics educator; b. Tai-Yuan, Shansi, Republic of China, Nov. 15, 1931; came to U.S., 1959; s. Wei-Han Chow and Lu-Tsen Hsu. Cert. tech. officer, Chinese Air Force Tech. Inst., Republic of China, 1954; BS in Math., Ch. Coll. Hawaii, 1962; MS in Math., Oreg. State U., 1965. Tech. officer Chinese Air Force, Republic of China, 1954-59; prof. math. Oakland Community Coll., Farmington Hills, Mich., 1965-92; ret., 1992; student advisor Oakland Community Coll., Union Lake, Mich., 1968; mem. scholar com. Oakland Community Coll., Farmington Hills, 1985—. Contbr. articles to prof. jours. Donor United Fund, Mich., and others. Served to 1st lt. Air Force of Republic of China, 1954-59. Mem. NEA, Mich. Edn. Assn., Oakland Community Coll. Faculty Assn., Pi Mu Epsilon. Home: PO Box 903 Novi MI 48376-0903

CHOWDHURY, ABDUR RAHIM, economics educator; b. Dhaka, Bangladesh, Feb. 12, 1953; came to U.S., 1979; s. Abdul Halim and Rahima Chowdhury; m. Shaheen Ahmed, Jan. 22, 1978; children: Rajib, Raffi. BA in Econs. with honors, Dhaka U., 1976, MA in Econs., 1977; MA in Econs., U. Ky., 1981, PhD in Econs., 1983. Rsch. officer World Bank Resident Mission, Dhaka, 1977-78; rsch. officer planning commn. Bangladesh Ministry of Planning and Fin., Dhaka, 1978-79; teaching fellow dept. econs. U. Ky., Lexington, 1981-82; asst. prof. econs. Bentley Coll., Waltham, Mass., 1983-89; assoc. prof. Marquette U., Milw., 1989—; dir. grad. econ. program, 1991-95; cons. Bangladesh Inst. for Devel. Studies, Dhaka, 1977-78, U.S. Agy. for Internat. Aid, Dhaka, 1987; vis. prof. Johns Hopkins U., 1996. Contbr. over 25 articles to profl. jours. Organizer Civil Liberties Union, Dhaka, 1974, Internat. Students Assn., Waltham, 1984-88. Fulbright scholar in Thailand, 1995-96. Mem. Am. Econ. Assn., So. Econ. Assn., Midwestern Econ. Assn., Ea. Econ. Assn., Atlantic Econ. Assn., Decision Sci. Inst. Office: Marquette U Dept Econ Milwaukee WI 53233

CHOWHAN, NAVEED MAHFOOZ, oncologist; b. Pakistan, Oct. 19, 1960; came to U.S., 1979; Student, Mao and Forman Christian Coll., Pakistan, 1979; MD cum laude, U Cetec, Dominican Republic, 1982. Bd. cert. internal medicine, 1986, hematology, 1992, oncology, 1993. Resident internal medicine Georgetown U. Svc., D.C. Gen. Hosp., Washington, 1983-86; fellowship oncology-hematology SUNY, Stony Brook, 1988-91, clin. asst. prof. dept. medicine divsn. oncology, 1992-94; pvt. practice New Albany, Ind., 1994—; pvt. practice, South Bend, Ind., 1986-88; attending physician Meml. Hosp. and St. Joseph Med. Ctr., South Bend, 1987-88, Floyd Meml. Hosp., New Albany, 1994—, Clark Meml. Hosp., Jeffersonville, Ind., 1994—; mem. Com. on Rsch. Involving Human Subjects, 1993-94; physician pioneer bone marrow transplant program SUNY, Stony Brook, 1994; chair cancer conf., mem. cancer com. and cont. med. edn. com. Floyd Meml. Hosp., 1995—; mem. cancer com. and blood transfusion com. Clark Meml. Hosp., 1995—; investigator, rschrs. and presenter in field. Contbr. articles to profl. jours. Fellow ACP; mem. Am. Soc. Clin. Oncology, Am. Soc. Hematology. Office: Ste 440 1919 State St New Albany IN 47150

CHOYKE, PHYLLIS MAY FORD (MRS. ARTHUR DAVIS CHOYKE, JR.), management executive, editor, poet; b. Buffalo, Oct. 25, 1921; d. Thomas Cecil and Vera (Buchanan) Ford; m. Arthur Davis Choyke Jr., Aug. 18, 1945; children: Christopher Ford, Tyler Van. BS summa cum laude, Northwestern U., 1942. Reporter City News Bur., Chgo., 1942-43, Met. sect. Chgo. Tribune, Chgo., 1943-44; feature writer OWI, N.Y.C., 1944-45; sec. corp. Artcrest Products Co., Inc., Chgo., 1958-88, v.p., 1964-88; pres. The Partford Corp., Chgo., 1988-90; founder, dir. Harper Sq. Press div., 1966—. Author: (under name Phyllis Ford) (with others) (poetry) Apertures to Anywhere, 1979; editor: Gallery Series One, Poets, 1967, Gallery Series Two, Poets—Poems of the Inner World, 1968, Gallery Series Three Poets: Levitations and Observations, 1970, Gallery Series Four, Poets, I am Talking About Revolution, 1973, Gallery Series Five/Poets—To An Aging Nation (with occult overtones), 1977; (manuscripts and papers in Brown U. Library). Bonbright scholar, 1942. Mem. DAR (corr. sec. Gen. Henry Dearborn chpt. 1991-92, treas. 1992-96), Soc. Midland Authors (bd. dirs. 1987-96, treas. 1988-93, pres. 1993-95), Mystery Writers Am. (assoc.), Chgo. Press Vets. Assn., Arts Club Chgo., John Evans Club (Northwestern U.), Poetry Soc. Am. (N.Y.C.), Friends of Lit., Acad. Am. Poets (N.Y.C.). Home: 29 E Division St Chicago IL 60610-2316

CHRISENBERRY, CAROL ANN, music educator; b. Blackwell, Okla., July 26, 1937; d. John Edgar and Sylvia Irene (Kirk) C.; m. Maurice Leland Meade (div.); 1 child, Wiley Maurice Meade. MusB in Voice, U. Okla., 1960, MusM in Voice, 1963; MusB in Edn., Ctrl. State U., 1974. Cert. music educator, Kans.; Orff level I certification. Singer, dancer Kans. City (Mo.) Starlight Theater, 1958-59, Meadow Brok Papermill Playhouse, Millburn, N.J., 1965, Music Fair Enterprises, N.Y.C., 1964-65, Mcpl. Theater, Milw., 1965-66; pvt. voice tchr. Norman and Blackwell, N.Y.C., 1958—; singer, dancer Music Theatre Lincoln Ctr., N.Y.C., 1967-68, Broadway Theatre, N.Y.C., 1967-68; vocal instr. Unified Sch. Dist. 360, Caldwell, Kans., 1974-86; jr. high, sr. high vocal instr. Unified Sch. Dist. 493, Columbus, Kans., 1987-89; music specialist Unified Sch. Dist. 257, Iola, Kans., 1989—; singer Wichita Symphony Chorus, 1986; performer Iola Community Theatre, 1989—. Program chmn. Iola Music Club, 1992. Recipient Am. Guild of Musical Artists award, 1959. Mem. Orgn. Am. Kodaly Educators, Am Orff-Schulwerk Assn., Kans. Music Educators Assn., Kans. Nat. Educators Assn., Actors Equity Assn., Am. Guild Mus. Artists, Music Educators Nat. Conf., Midwest Kodaly Music Educators Am., Iola Music Club, Delta Kappa Gamma. Home: 514 E Neosho St Iola KS 66749-3429 Office: Lincoln Elem Sch 700 N Jefferson St Iola KS 66749-2219

CHRISMER, RICH, state legislator; b. Apr. 9, 1946; m. Mary Margaret Parson, 1972; children: Richard, Anna, Laura, Mark. AA, St. Louis C.C., Florissant Valley. Mo. State rep. Dist. 16; svc. technician. Bd. dirs. Pro-Life Citizen Mo. Mem. K.C. (4th degree). Home: 25 Barkwood Tris Saint Peters MO 63376*

CHRIST, SANDRA LOUISE, customer service representative; b. LaCrosse, Wis., Sept. 23, 1950. Sec. real estate divsn. U.S. Post Office, St. Paul, 1975-76; with computer plating Unisys, Roseville, Minn., 1977-88; customer svc. rep. Stuart-Hooper Co., St. Paul, 1989—. Home: 1351 Minnehaha Ave E Saint Paul MN 55106-4819 Office: Stuart-Hooper Co 162 Wabasha St S Saint Paul MN 55107-1819

CHRIST, VINCENT B., retired sales executive; b. Buffalo, Apr. 1, 1931; s. Arthur Michael and Mary Henrietta (Hattinger) C.; m. Alice Ann Klee, Oct. 13, 1956 (dec. 1986); children: Mary Christ Browne, Daniel, Beth Christ Berman, Karen Christ Krepps, Nancy Christ Drewitt, Andrew; m. Jeanne Andree Macy, Feb. 11, 1989. BS in Pharmacy, U. Buffalo, 1953; MS in Pharmacy, U. Tex., 1956. Lic. pharmacist, N.Y. Med. sales rep. Eli Lilly & Co., Indpls., 1959-65, clin. info. adminstr., 1965-68; med. sales rep. Eli Lilly & Co., Cleve., 1968-90; ret. Lt. (j.g.) USN, 1956-59; lt. comdr. USNR, 1959-67. U. Tex. scholar, teaching fellow, 1953-56. Mem. Kappa Psi, Gamma Iota Ch, Gamma Gamma (pres.). Home: 160 Nantucket Cir Painesville OH 44077-1550

CHRISTENSEN, DAVID ALLEN, manufacturing company executive; b. 1935. BS, S.D. State U., 1957. With John Morrell & Co., 1960-62; with Raven Industries Inc., Sioux Falls, S.D., 1962—, product mgr., 1964-71, pres., chief exec. officer, 1971—. Served with AUS, 1957-60. Office: Raven Industries Inc PO Box 5107 Sioux Falls SD 57117-5107

CHRISTENSEN, ERIK REGNAR, engineering educator, researcher; b. Copenhagen, Denmark, Apr. 17, 1943; came to U.S., 1974; s. Regnar and Margrethe Cathrine (Lou) C.; m. Lone Normann Jensen, Aug. 10, 1968; children: Irene Normann, Eva Normann, Finn Normann. MSEE, Tech. U., Denmark, 1967; Phd in Environ. Engring., U. Calif., Irvine, 1977. Registered profl. engr., Wis. Asst. prof. engring. Tech. Univ. Denmark, Lyngby, 1969-73, assoc. prof., 1973-74; rsch. asst., teaching assoc. U. Calif., Irvine, 1974-77; asst. prof. U. Wis., Milw., 1977-82, assoc. prof., 1982—; cons. Dept. of Justice, Madison, 1986-87, Milw. Met. Sewer Dist., 1989-90; coun. mem. Wis. Coastal Mgmt. Coun., Madison, 1987—; organizer/convener First Internat. Specialized Conf. (IAWQ) on contaminated aquatic sediments, 1993. Author: (with others) Hazard Assessment of Chemicals, 1989. NSF grantee, Washington, 1981-85, 87-89, 90—. Mem. ASCE, Am. Geophys. Union, Internat. Assn. Water Quality, Assn. Environ. Engring. Profs., Soc. Environ. Toxicology and Chems. Office: U Wis Dept Civil Engring and Mechanics 3200 N Cramer St Milwaukee WI 53211-3029

CHRISTENSEN, MARI ALICE, nursing auditor, medicolegal analyst, consultant; b. Omaha, June 13, 1934; d. Benjamin Marion and Alice Minnie (Thompson) Voelte; m. Gerald H. Christensen, Mar. 17, 1956; 1 child, Amy Michaela. Diploma, Nebr. Meth. Coll. Nursing, Omaha, 1955; BSN, U. Nebr., Omaha, 1961; postgrad., Pitts. State U., Ins. Inst. Am., 1992. RN, Nebr.; rehab. nurse certificate, Ga. Nurses Assn. Charge nurse Nebr. Meth. Hosp., Omaha, 1955-56; office nurse Geo. Robertson, M.D., Omaha, 1956-57; surgeon's asst., office nurse Physicians Clinic, Omaha, 1957-74; medicolegal analyst Turner & Boisseau, Chartered, Great Bend, Kans., 1975-82, Schmid, Mooney & Frederick, P.C., Omaha, 1984-89; cons. Mutual of Omaha Ins. Co., 1989-91; nurse auditor, workers compensation case mgr., analyst Mid-Am. Med. Mgmt., Omaha, 1991-92; pvt. nurse auditor, case mgr., medicolegal analyst Omaha, 1992; ret., 1992; rehab. cons. Crawford Rehab., Omaha, 1982. Mem. ANA (exec. com.), Nat. Assn. Legal Assts. (continuing edn. com. 1988), Nebr. Nurses Assn. (sec., bd. dirs. com. mem.), Assn. Oper. Rm. Nurses (sec.), Nat. Disting. Svc. Registry Nursing, Sigma Theta Tau, Gamma Pi Sigma. Home: 11315 Castelar Cir Omaha NE 68144-3085

CHRISTENSEN, MARVIN NELSON, venture capitalist; b. W. Branch, Iowa, July 15, 1927; s. Peter Ancher and Martha Henrietta (Neilsen) C.; m. Mary Lou Miller, Dec. 17, 1949; children: Stephen R., Barbara. BS, U. Iowa, 1950. Pvt. practice ins. and real estate Iowa City, 1955-69; asst. to pres. Gen. Growth Cos., Des Moines, 1970-72; acquisitions dir. Life Investors of Iowa, Cedar Rapids, 1972-80; chmn. and chief exec. officer Bus. Comml. Realty, Denver, 1980—; chmn., CEO Colo. Internat. Devel., Colorado Springs, 1984—; chmn. Byers (Colo.) State Bank, 1987-89, Farmer's State Bank, Waubun, Minn., 1988-96; founder, adminstr. Waubun Area Devel. Enterprises, 1988—. Contbr. many articles to nat. pubs. Lt. (j.g.) USNR, 1944-46. Mem. Am. Bankers Assn., Minn. Bankers Assn., Masons, Elks, Eagles, VFW. Home: RR 2 Waubun MN 56589-9802 Office: Farmers State Bank Main St Waubun MN 56589

CHRISTENSEN, PAMELA KAREN, pediatric nurse; b. Mason City, Iowa, Aug. 5, 1957; d. Buford LeRoy and Violet Mae (Shepherd) C. AS, North Iowa Area Community Coll, Mason City, 1982. Cert. med. asst. Lakeland Med. Acad., Mpls., 1977. Staff nurse pediatrics and med.-surg. unit Boone County Hosp., Boone, Iowa; traveling nurse, pediatrics and adult TravCorps, Malden, Mass.; charge nurse in pediatrics City of Faith, Tulsa; traveling nurse in pediatrics Cross Country Nurses, Boca Raton, Fla.; staff nurse in pediatrics ICU Mayo Med. Ctr./St. Marys Hosp., Rochester, Minn.; speaker Pediatric ICU conf. Contbr. chpt. to pediatric textbook. Mem. Am. Assn. Med. Assts. (past local pres. and state sec.). Home: 329 Chestnut St Osage IA 50461

CHRISTENSEN, RAYMOND GORDON, physician; b. Valley City, N.D., Apr. 3, 1944; s. Irvin Arthur and Phyllis Ione (Myers) C.; separated; children: Kari Rae, Anna Marie. BS in Agr., Wis. State U., River Falls, 1966; MD, U. Wis., 1971. Diplomate Am. Acad. Family Physicians. Intern St. Mary's Hosp., Duluth, Minn., 1971-72; physician Gateway Family Health, Moose Lake, Minn., 1972—; med. advisor Minn. Dept. Health, Mpls., 1991—; rural cons. med. outreach dept. U. Minn., Mpls., 1992; preceptor Rural Physician Program, Mpls., U. Duluth (Minn.) Med. Sch., 1972—; airman med. examiner FAA, Moose Lake. Pres. No. Lakes Health Care Consortium, Duluth, 1984—, Arrowhead Emergency Med. Svcs., Duluth, 1984-91; chair Found. Health Care Evaluation, 1992; founder Rural Access Clinic, Cromwell, Minn., 1992; trustee Minn. Hosp. Assn., Mpls., 1989—, dir. Lake Superior chpt., Duluth, 1989-91. Recipient Louis Goren award Nat. Rural Health Assn., 1989; various awards No. Lakes Health, No. Lakes Consortiuim, Arrowhead EMS Assn., Lake Superior Med. Soc. Mem. AMA, Am. Hosp. Assn., Minn. Med. Assn. (v.p. 1993-95, pres.-elect. 1995-96, cmty. svc. award 1992), Am. Acad. Family Physicians, Minn. Acad. Family Physicians (chmn. bd. dirs. 1990-91, pres.-elect 1992, pres. 1993-94, merit award), Lake Superior Med. Soc. (pres. 1991), Am. Geriatrics Soc., Civil Aviation Med. Assn., Masons (past master Solomon's lodge 1987, 5th dist. rep. Grand Lodge 1991), Scottish Rite, Shriners. Lutheran. Home: 278 County Line Rd E Moose Lake MN 55767-9322 Office: Clinic Ltd Gateway Family Health Moose Lake MN 55767

CHRISTENSEN, RICHARD L., school system administrator; b. Sioux Falls, S.D., July 27, 1937; s. George A. and Janette (Teabrinke) C.; m. Joyce D. Erpenbauch, May 4, 1964; children: Dixie Lynn, Richard Allan. BS, Huron U., 1979; M in Secondary Adminstrn., No. State U., 1983; EdS, U. S.D., 1990. Cert. specialist in edn. adminstr., S.D. Pvt. practice Canova, S.D., 1964-79; tchr. secondary, prin. Forbes (N.D.) Sch. Dist., 1979-84; prin. secondary Marty (S.D.) Indian Sch., 1984-86, Spencer (S.D.) Sch. Dist., 1986-88; supt. schs. Artesian (S.D.) Schs., 1988-91, Herreid (S.D.) Schs., 1991-93, Midland (S.D.) Schs., 1993—. Sec. Midland Comml. Club. With U.S. Army, 1960-63. Mem. KC, Assn. Supts., Supts. of S.D., Phi Delta Kappa. Democrat. Roman Catholic. Office: Midland Sch Dist PO Box 226 Midland SD 57552

CHRISTENSON, CHARLES DUANE, sales executive; b. Austin, Minn., Aug. 26, 1957; s. Vernon Sherman and Beverly Jean (Stauffer) C.; m. Jennifer Lynn Chose, May 3, 1980; children: Jacob Dane, Molly Beth. BS, Concordia Coll., Moorhead, Minn., 1979. Dir. youth ministry Como Park Luth., St. Paul, 1979-81; area sales rep. RJ Reynolds Tobbaco, Mankato, Minn., 1981-84; advt. cons. KTOE/NDOG Radio, Mankato, 1984-86; tech. sales exec. Oakite Products Inc., Mankato, Minn. & Omaha, Nebr., 1986—. Mem. worship com. St. Thomas Luth., Omaha, 1995, chmn. worship com., 1995—. Mem. Soc. of Mfg. Engrs. (sr. mem., Linoln, Nebr. chpt.). Republican. Home: 16817 N Circle Omaha NE 68135 Office: Oakite Products Inc 50 Valley Rd Berkeley Heights NJ 07922

CHRISTENSON, EILEEN ELAINE, geriatrics nurse; b. Fosston, Minn., July 26, 1950; d. Arthur L. and Gertrude E. (Jaworsky) Maruska; m. Leonard Dale Christenson, Mar. 16, 1968; children: Kristy, Dale, Melissa, Alicia. Grad., Thief River Fall Tech. Inst., Minn., 1996. LPN, Ill., N.Mex., Minn. Staff nurse Beltram (Minn.) Nursing Home, 1990—, Clearwater County Meml. Hosp., Bagley, Minn. Troop leader Land O'Lakes coun. Girl Scouts U.S., 1974-89. 1st lt. USAF, 1968-76, Vietnam. Decorated Purple Heart, Silver Cross, Bronze Star (2). Mem. VFW, Am. Legion, Eagles 351. Home: RR 5 Box 330A Bemidji MN 56601-8531

CHRISTENSON, JOHN DONALD, library director, consultant; b. Amherst, Wis., Sept. 2, 1936; s. John Carl and Jane (Smith) C.; m. Ann Fellows Christenson, Sept. 13, 1969; children: Nathaniel, Katharine. BS, U. Wis., Oshkosh, 1962; MS in Libr. Sci., U. Wis., Madison, 1963. Audio visual libr. Madison (Wis.) Pub. Libr., 1963-67; adult svcs. coord. Lake County Pub. Libr., Independence Hill, Ind., 1967-69; cmty. rels. libr. Ferguson Libr., Stamford, Conn., 1969-71; libr. dir. Brevard County Libr., Cocoa, Fla., 1971-75; exec. dir. Traverse des Sioux Libr. Sys., Mankato, Minn., 1975—; cons. Christenson Libr. Cons., Mankato, Minn., 1990—; coun. mem. ALA, Chgo., 1987-91; exec. bd. Pub. Libr. Assn., Chgo., 1995—, Minn. Libr. Assn., Mpls., 1987-91, Assn. Specialized and Coop. Libr. Assn., Chgo., 1983-84. Contbr. articles to profl. jours. Mayor City of Good Thunder, Minn., 1977-91; del. Minn. Dem. Conv., St. Paul, 1984; bd. mem. League of Minn. Cities, St. Paul, 1987-90; chair Blue Earth County Mayor and Clks. Assn., Mankato, Minn., 1988-91. Named Minn. Libr. of Yr., 1985; recipient Exemplanary Svc. award Soutncentral Minn. Libr. Exchange, Mankato, 1995. Mem. Kiwanis Club of Mankato, Mankato Area C. of C., Blue Earth Hist. Soc. Bd., Nicollet County Hist. Soc. Democrat. Episcopalian. Home: 2011 Freeman Dr Saint Peter MN 56082 Office: Traverse des Sioux Libr Sys PO Box 608 110 S Broad St Mankato MN 56002-0608

CHRISTENSON, LINDA, state legislator; m. Duane Christenson; 4 children. BA, Minot State U., MS. English tchr.; mem. from dist. 18 N.D. State Ho. of Reps., Bismarck, mem. judicary, govt. and vet. affairs coms. Bd. dirs. Firehall Cmty. Theater, United Health Svc. Named Martin Luther King Educator of Yr., N.D., 1991. Mem. Grand Forks Edn. Assn. Address: 812 Belmont Rd Grand Forks ND 58201

CHRISTIAN, KENNETH EDWARD, security administration educator; b. Mpls., May 13, 1935; s. Edward Howard and Ruth Leone (Carney) C.; m. Ellen Nora Hallinan, Aug. 24, 1957; children: Lisa M., Jonathan Nicholas. BS, Mich. State U., 1959, MS, 1970, PhD, 1976. Cert. protection profl. Police officer City of Bloomington, Minn., 1959-65; agt. Minn. Crime Bur., St. Paul, 1965-68; fellow U.S. Dept. Justice, Washington, 1968-71; rsch. assoc. Am. Justice Inst., Sacramento, 1971-73; prof. Mich. State U., East Lansing, 1973—; cons. Ariz. State U., 1993, Med. Coll. Va. Hosp., 1992, Uited Arab Emirates, Dubai, 1989, Herman Miller Corp., Zeeland, Mich., 1988, K-Mart Corp., Troy, Mich., 1986, GM Inst., Flint, Mich., 1983. Author: Introduction to Private Security, 1991; mem. editl. bd. Security Jour., 1989—; contbr. articles to profl. jours. Mem. burglary protection coun. Underwriters Labs., 1987—. With U.S. Army. Recipient Pres.' Award Internat. Assn. for Healthcare Security and Safety, 1988. Mem. Am. Soc. Indsl. Security, Internat. Healthcare Security and Safety Found. (bd. dirs. 1986—, Philip A. Gaffney faculty chair), Internat. Found. for Protection Officers (bd. dirs. 1988—, pres. 1991-95). Office: Mich State U Sch Criminal Justice 560 Baker Hall East Lansing MI 48824-1118

CHRISTIANO, MARY HELEN, systems analyst; b. Geneva, N.Y., Sept. 14, 1956; d. Anthony Joseph Christiano and Lucy Ann (Benge) Christiano Farris; 1 child, Andrew Joseph. Cert., Syracuse Sch. Automation, 1975; student, Augsburg Coll., 1990—. Cert. computer programmer, sys. analyst. Asst. head cashier Neisner's Dept. Store, Waterloo, N.Y., 1973-74; lead computer operator Geneva Gen. Hosp., 1976-78; sys. analyst 3M Co., St. Paul, 1979—; v.p. Westbridge Inc., St. Paul, 1992-94. Author, editor: (newsletter) Qualifier, 1985-87. Tutorial adviser St. Paul schs., 1987-92; chpt. leader Riverview Crime Watch, St. Paul, 1989-90; vol. United Negro Coll. Fund, St. Paul, 1993—, Spl. Olympics, Bloomington, Minn., 1992, Toys for Tots, St. Paul, 1991—; mem. Sci. Mus. of Minn., 1991. Mem. Women in Tech. Home: 1572 McAfee St Saint Paul MN 55106 Office: 3M Info Tech 3M Ctr Bldg 224-4S-19 Saint Paul MN 55133-3224

CHRISTIANSEN, RAYMOND STEPHAN, librarian, educator; b. Oak Park, Ill., Feb. 15, 1950; s. Raymond Julius and Anne Mary (Fusek) C.; m. Phyllis Anne Dombkowski, Nov. 25, 1972; 1 child, Mark David. BA, Elmhurst Coll., 1971; MEd, No. Ill. U., 1974. Dept. dir. Elmhurst Coll., Ill., 1971-73; asst. law librarian media services Lewis U., Glen Ellyn, Ill., 1974-77; asst. prof. edn. Aurora U., Ill., 1977-90, assoc. prof., 1990—, media librarian, 1977-82, instructional developer, 1982-89, dir. univ. media svcs., 1985—; media cons., 1977—. Author video series: Rothblatt on Criminal Advocacy, 1975; book: Index to SCOPE the UN Magazine, 1977. Lic. lay min. Episcopal Ch., 1990—. Mem. Assn. Ednl. Communications and Tech., Assn. Tchr. Educators, Assn. Supervision and Curriculum Devel. Home: 424 S Gladstone Ave Aurora IL 60506-5370 Office: Aurora U Libr 347 S Gladstone Ave Aurora IL 60506-4877

CHRISTIANSON, ELIN BALLANTYNE, librarian, civic worker; b. Gary, Ind., Nov. 11, 1936; d. Donald B. and Dorothy May (Dunning) Ballantyne; m. Stanley David Christianson, July 26, 1959; children: Erica, David. BA, U. Chgo., 1958, MA, 1961, Cert. advanced studies, 1974. Asst. librarian, then librarian J. Walter Thompson Co., Chgo., 1959-68; libr. cons., 1968—; asst. prof. Grad. Libr. Sch., U. Chgo., 1981-90, Sch. Libr. and Info. Sci., Ind. U., 1982—, libr., info. svcs. cons., 1968—; editor The Libr. Quarterly Grad. Library Sch. U. Chgo., 1988-90. Chmn. Hobart Am. Revolution Bicentennial Commn., 1974-76; bd. dirs. Hobart Hist. Soc., 1973—, pres., 1980-85, 89—; pres. LWV, Hobart, 1977-79. Recipient Laura Bracken award Hobart Jaycees, 1976, Cert. Achievement Ind. Am. Revolution Bicentennial Commn., 1975; Woman of Yr. award Hobart Bus. and Profl. Women, 1985, Resident Recognition award Northwest Ind. Forum, 1988. Mem. AAUW (pres. Hobart br. 1975-77), ALA, Ind. Libr. Assn., Spl. Librs. Assn. (chmn. advt. and mktg. div. 1967-68), Assn. Library and Info. Sci. Edn., U. Chgo. Grad. Libr. Sch. Alumni Assn. (v.p. 1971-74, 76-77, pres. 1977-79). Unitarian. Author: Non-Professional and Paraprofessional Staff in Special Libraries, 1973; Directory of Library Resources in Northwest Indiana, 1976; Old Settlers Cemetery, 1976; New Special Libraries: A Summary of Research, 1980; Daniel Nash Handy and the Special Library Movement, 1980; co-author: Subject Headings in Advertising, Marketing and Communications Media, 1964; Special Libraries: A Guide for Management, 1981, rev. 3d edit., 1991; mem. editorial adv. bd. New Standard Encyclopedia, 1986—. Home: 141 Beverly Blvd Hobart IN 46342-4346

CHRISTIANSON, FLOYD KENNETH, retired oil company executive; b. Larimore, N.D., Mar. 13, 1917; s. Carl Edwin and Dagmar Asora (Linge) C.; m. Marian Elinor Bakken, June 22, 1941; children: Milo, Sharon Ell. Grad. high sch., Larimore, N.D., 1935. Asst. mgr. S & L Store, Grand Forks, N.D., 1937-43; territory mgr. Amoco Oil Co., Grand Forks, 1944-77; chmn. Oil Ind. Info. Com., 1969. Past pres. Brotherhood United Luth. Ch.; organizer Dollars for Scholars; pres. Lake Agassiz coun. Boy Scouts Am., 1962-63; sec.-treas. emeritus Kiwanis Ednl. Found. Recipient Silver Beaver award Boy Scouts Am., 1959, Lamb award United Luth. Ch., 1960, Circle of Svc. award Circle K. of Kiwanis Internat.; named the Outstanding Young Man of Yr., Jr. C. of C., Grand Forks, 1949. Mem. Kiwanis (pres. 1987-88, sec.-treas. Grand Forks chpt. 1946-77, Minn.-Dakotas dist. 1977-91, sec.-treas. emeritus Minn.-Dakotas dist., sec.-treas. emeritus found., Hixon award 1990, Messer award 1987, Circle Svc. award). Lutheran. Home: 1811 Chestnut St Grand Forks ND 58201-7353

CHRISTIANSON, JAMES DUANE, real estate developer; b. Bismarck, N.D., Aug. 18, 1952; s. Adolph M. and Elizabeth M. (Barnes) C.; m. Deborah Jaeger, Oct. 10, 1987. Student, Bismarck Jr. Coll., 1970, 1971-72, U. N.D., 1971. Lic. pvt. pilot; lic. realtor. Gen. mgr. and supr. Nutrition Search, Bismarck, 1974-76; gen. mgr. Home Still, Inc., Bismarck, 1976-78; v.p. Good Heart Assocs., Bismarck, 1978-82; pres. N. W. Devel. Group, Bismarck, 1982—, First Realty Bismark Inc., 1990-93, N.W. Realty Group, Bismarck, 1994—; chmn. bd. Basin State Bank, Stanford, Mont., 1986-94; mem., vice chair Ctr. City Partnership, 1994—. Supr. editor: Nutrition Almanac, 1975. Mem. Bismarck Centennial Com., 1986-89. Recipient Outstanding Citizen award Mayor and City Commn., Bismarck, 1982. Mem. Downtown Bus. and Profl. Assn. (bd. dirs. 1989—, pres. 1991). Office: N W Devel Group Inc 414 E Main Ave PO Box 1097 Bismarck ND 58502

CHRISTIE, FRED ATHERTON, aerospace engineer; b. Amherst, N.S., Can., July 25, 1936; s. Harold Bent and Edith Alice (Atherton) C.; m. Grace Helen Hogg, Aug. 27, 1960 (div. June 1993); children: Gillian Flemming, Iain Atherton. BS, Dalhousie U., Halifax, N.S., Can., 1958; BE with honors, N.S. Tech. Coll., Halifax, 1960; MSc, U. London, 1964; DSc, Laval U., Quebec City, Can., 1971. Registered profl. engr., Alta. Def. sci. officer Def. Rsch. Bd. Can., Quebec City, PQ, 1964-71; head explosives group Def. Rsch. Establishment Valcartier, Quebec City, PQ, 1971-72, head rocket tech. group, 1972-77, head rockets sect., 1977-78; dir. def. tech. div. Def. Rsch. Establishment Suffield, Medicine Hat, Alta., Can., 1978-88; dir. strategic devel. space sta. project Nat. Rsch. Coun., Ottawa, Ont., Can., 1988-90; v.p. rockets and space Bristol Aerospace Ltd., Winnipeg, Man., Can., 1991-95; sr. indsl. policy advisor Can. Space Agy., 1995-96; v.p. engring. and quality Bristol Aerospace Ltd., Winnipeg, 1996—; councillor, exec., v.p., pres. Can. Aeros. and Space Inst., Que., 1991—, Que. Medicine Hat, Ottawa, Winnipeg and Montreal brs., 1960—; Can. nat. leader (rockets; targets) Tech Coop. Program, 1977-79, 78-88. Contbr. over 60 tech. papers and articles to tech. publs. Pres. Province of Que. Sch. Curling Assn., Quebec City, 1973-77; v.p. Medicine Hat World Jr. Curling Championship, 1981-83. Recipient scholars, 1954-60; Athlone fellow U.K. Bd. of Trade, 1960-63. Fellow Can. Aeros. and Space Inst.; mem. Alta Assn. Profl. Engrs., Geologists and Geophysicists (sr. mem.), AIAA. Office: Bristol Aerospace Ltd, 660 Berry St, Winnipeg, MB Canada R3H 0S5

CHRISTIE, WALTER SCOTT, retired state official; b. Indpls., 1922; s. Walter Scott and Nina Lilian (Warfel) C; m. Betty W. Phelps, Dec. 14, 1991; stepchildren: Thomas G. Phelps, Judith Phelps Cummings. BS in Bus. Adminstrn., Butler U., 1948. CPA, Ind.; cert. fin. examiner. With Roy J. Pile & Co., CPAs, Indpls., 1948-56, Howard E. Nyhart Co., Inc., actuarial consultants, Indpls., 1956-62; with Ind. Dept. Ins., Indpls., 1962-92, dep. commr., 1966-74, adminstrv. officer, 1974-79, sr. examiner, 1979-81, adminstrv. asst., 1981-82, chief auditor, 1982-91, ret., 1991; bd. dirs., sec., treas. Sr. Enterprises. Treas. Delta Tau/Delta House Corp., 1967—, Butler U. With AUS, 1942-45. Named to Hon. Order Ky. Cols. Mem. Ind. Assn. CPA's, Soc. Fin. Examiners (state chmn.), Indpls. Acturarial Club, Nat. Assn. Ins. Commrs. (chmn. zone IV life and health com. 1970-75), Internat. Platform Assn. Episcopalian (assoc. vestryman 1948-60), Optimist Club Downtown Indpls. (bd. dirs., Outstanding Svc. award 1985-87, Optimist of Yr. 1990). Home: 7195 Koldyke Dr Fishers IN 46038-2739

CHRISTISON, JUDY ANN, graphic arts trainer; b. Rochester, Ind., Apr. 23, 1950; d. William Burton and Regina Catherine (Boudreau) Yates; m. Raymond Laurence Bennett, Jr., Dec. 7, 1974 (div. Nov. 1990); children: Rachel Jo, Kyle Michael; m. Dan E. Christison, Oct. 26, 1995. BA, Augustana Coll., 1988; MA, U. Iowa, 1991. Rsch./teaching asst. U. Iowa, Iowa City, 1988-91; evaluator, extended employment case mgr. Handicapped Devel. Ctr., Davenport, Iowa, 1991-93; training coord. Bawden Printing, Eldridge, Iowa, 1993—; adj. faculty Scott Cmty. Coll., Davenport, 1993—, St. Ambrose U., Davenport, 1995—. Mem. ASTD, Assn. Graphic Arts Trainers, Phi Beta Kappa. Jewish. Office: Bawden Printing 400 S 14th Ave Eldridge IA 52748

CHRISTMANN, RANDEL DARVIN, state legislator; b. Hazen, N.D., June 16, 1960. B in Bus. Adminstrn., N.D. State U., 1982. Truck driver, rancher N.D.; state senator dist. 33 State of N.D., Hazen; mem. fin. and taxation com. N.D. State Senate, vice-chmn. natural resources com., vice chmn. interim N.D./S.D. Comm. Mem. NRA, Farm Bur. N.D., Stockmen's Assn. Office: RR 1 Box 120 A Hazen ND 58545

CHRISTNER, DAVID LEE, utilities executive; b. Millersburg, Ohio, Apr. 9, 1949; s. George and Nettie (Swartzentruber) C.; m. Carol Kay Gerber, May 2, 1970. Student, United Electronics Inst., 1970. Cert. elec. safety inspector, Ohio. Electrician Kauffman Supply Co., Millersburg, 1971-73, Charm (Ohio) Plumbing, 1973-75, Dave's Elec. and Plumbing, Berlin, Ohio, 1975-80; quality control officer Skyline Corp., Holmesville, Ohio, 1980-81; elec. safety inspector State of Ohio, Columbus, 1981-94; fin. adviser, stockbroker Life/Health Ins. Sales, 1994—; class instr. Berlin, Ohio, 1984—. Mem. Internat. Traders, Aircraft Owners and Pilots Assn. Republican. Home: PO Box 116 Berlin OH 44610-0116 Office: DL Christner Fin Svcs Inc 5124 SR 39 PO Box 299 Berlin OH 44610

CHRISTOFFEL, KURT MATTHEW, chemistry educator; b. Chgo., Sept. 4, 1953; s. Bertram Francis and Mary Ann (Garstkiewicz) C. BA, Ill. Inst. Tech., 1976, MS in Chemistry, 1979, PhD in Chemistry, 1982. Postdoctoral rsch. fellow dept. chemistry U. Toronto, Ont., Can., 1982-85; asst. prof. chemistry Augustana Coll., Rock Island, Ill., 1985-93, assoc. prof., 1993—; vis. assoc. prof. chemistry W.Va. U., Morgantown, 1991-92; rsch. cons. chemistry dept. Duke U., Durham, N.C., 1991. Contbr. articles to profl. jours. Mem. Am. Chem. Soc., Coun. Undergrad. Rsch., Sigma Xi, Sigma Pi Sigma. Roman Catholic. Office: Augustana Coll Dept Chemistry Rock Island IL 61201-2296

CHRISTOPHER, ALEXANDER GEORGE, transportation company executive; b. Melrose Park, Ill., Apr. 17, 1941; s. George Alexander and Ann (Gianoulis) C.; m. Susan Bernice Breitweiser, May 12, 1979; children: Anna Bernice, Jason Woodrow. BA in Econs., Elmhurst (Ill.) Coll., 1963; postgrad., DePaul U., 1963-64. Mgr. Dunn & Bradstreet, Chgo., 1965-67, various Chgo.-area currency exchs., 1967-71; v.p. Ill. Armored Car Corp., River Grove, 1971-82, dir.-in-exile, 1982-83; pres. Ill. Armored Car Corp., Broadview, 1983-95; chmn., CEO Ill. Armored Car Corp., Broadview, Ill., 1995—; CEO, United Armored Svcs., 1995—; mem. adv. bd. fin. instns. sec. state Ill. With USMCR, 1964-70. Mem. Ind. Armored Car Operators Assn. (pres. 1979-80, chmn. bd. 1980-81, chmn. legis. com. 1988—, bd. dirs. 1989-95), The Exec. Com. Greek Orthodox. Office: Ill Armored Car Corp 2001 W Cermak Rd Maywood IL 60153-4600

CHRISTOPHER, GREGORY ALAN, professional society executive; b. Lafayette, Ind., Jan. 18, 1966; s. John Alton and Joyce (Sayers) C.; m. Tina Smith, June 20, 1992; 1 child, Zachary. BS in Mass Comm., Miami U., Oxford, Ohio, 1988, MBA in Mktg., 1991. Sports rsch. analyst NBC, N.Y.C., 1988; account exec. WWWV-FM, Charlottesvilee, Va., 1988-90; sports mktg. mgr. Purdue U., West Lafayette, Ind., 1990; dir. mktg. and devel. Soc. Profl. Jours., Greencastle, Ind., 1991-94, exec. dir., 1994—; bd. dirs. Ind. Journalism Hall of Fame. V.p. Friends of Plainfield (Ind.) Pub. Libr., 1995. Mem. Am. Soc. of Assn. Execs., Ind. Soc. of Assn. Execs. (Ind. First com.), Greencastle C. of C. (bd. dirs.). Home: 519 Southmore St Plainfield IN 46168

CHRISTOPHER, SHARON A. BROWN, bishop; b. Corpus Christi, Tex., July 24, 1944; d. Fred L. and Mavis Lorraine (Krueger) Brown; m. Charles Edmond Logsdon Christopher, June 17, 1973. BA, Southwestern U., Georgetown, Tex., 1966; MDiv, Perkins Sch. Theology, 1969; DD, Southwestern U., 1990. Ordained to ministry United Meth. Ch., 1970; elected bishop 1988. Dir. Christian Edn. First United Meth. Ch., Appleton, Wis., 1969-70, assoc. pastor, 1970-72; pastor Butler United Meth. Ch., Butler, Wis., 1972-76, Calvary United Meth. Ch., Germantown, Wis., 1972-76, Aldersgate United Meth. Ch., Milw., 1976-80; dist. supt. Ea. Dist. Wis. Conf. United Meth. Ch., 1980-85; asst. to bishop Wis. Conf. Wis. Confs. United Meth. Ch., Sun Prairie, Wis., 1986-88; bishop North Cen. jurisdiction United Meth. Ch., Minn., 1988—. Contbr. articles and papers to religious publs. Bd. dirs. Nat. Coun. Chs. of Christ, 1988—, United Meth. Ch. Bd. of Ch. & Soc., 1988-92, bd. discipleship, 1992—; bd. dirs. Walker Meth. Health Ctr., Mpls., 1988—, Meth. Hosp., Mpls., 1988—, Nat. United Meth. Clergywomen, 1992—; trustee Hamline U., St. Paul, 1988—; gen. and jurisdictional conf. del., 1976, 80, 84, 88; mem. N. Cen. Jurisdiction Com. on Episcopacy, 1984-88, Com. on Investigation, 1980-88, Gen. Bd. Global Ministries, 1980-88, chmn. Mission Pers. Resources Program Dept., 1984-88. Named one of Eighty for the Eighties, Milw. Jour., 1980.

CHRISTOPHERSEN, EDWARD REA, child psychologist; b. Oak Park, Ill., July 15, 1940; children: Hunter, Catherine. MA in Psychology, Mich. State U., 1965; PhD in Psychology, U. Kans., 1970. Chief behavioral pediatrics Children's Mercy Hosp., Kansas City, Mo., 1986—; prof. pediatrics U. Mo. Sch. Medicine, Kansas City, 1988—; lectr. over 300 nat. convs. Aauthor 8 books; contbr. over 150 articles to profl. jours.; over 150 print interviews, 1977—, 300 TV and radio appearances, 1978—; features editor Jour. Devel. and Behavioral Pediat., 1991-96. Bd. gov. Am. Royal Horse Show and Livestock Exhbn., Kansas City. Fellow APA, Acad. Behavioral Medicine; mem. Ambulatory Pediatrics Assn., Soc. Pediatric Rsch., Soc. Behavioral Pediatrics (exec. com.). Office: Childrens Mercy Hosp 2401 Gillham Rd Kansas City MO 64108-4619

CHRISTOPHERSON, CHRISTINE YOUNG, state legislator; b. Jamestown, N.D., Oct. 17, 1950; d. Eugene J. and Esther (Sorensen) Young; m. Thomas D. Christopherson, 1978. Student, N.D. State U., 1968-70, Interstate Bus. Coll., 1970-71. V.p. The Party Store, Rent All, Fargo/Moorhead, N.D., 1978—; state rep. dist. 11, 1993—; mem. human svcs., govt. and vet. affairs coms. N.D. Ho. Reps. Chmn. dist. 51 Rep. Com., 1982—; bd. dirs. Fargo/Moorhead Cmty. Theater. Mem. Fargo/Moorhead Human Soc. (exec. com.), Quota Club, Am. Rental Assn. (N.D. rep. polit. action com. 1982—). Republican. Home: 705 14th St S Fargo ND 58103-2537*

CHRISTOPHERSON, MYRVIN FREDERICK, college president; b. Milltown, Wis., July 21, 1939; s. Fred J. and Inger J. (Haug) C.; m. Anne Christine Marking, June 10, 1967; children: Kirsten, Berit, Bjorn, Nisse. BA, Dana Coll., 1961; MS, Purdue U., 1963, PhD, 1965. Teaching asst., instr. Purdue U., West Lafayette, Ind., 1961-65; asst. prof. speech U. Wis., Madison, 1965-69; assoc. prof. communication U. Wis., Stevens Point, 1969-76, prof. communication, 1976-86, assoc. dean. fine arts and communication, 1970-86; pres. Dana Coll., Blair, Nebr., 1986—; cons. Wis. Telephone, Milw., 1968-78, AT&T, N.Y.C., 1969-71, 1st Fin. Corp., Stevens Point, 1980-86; commr. Nebr. Coordinating Commn. for Post Sec. Edn., 1989-91. Author: Speaker's Trainer's Guide, 1970, The Company Speaker, 1979; editor Jour. of the Wis. Communication Assn., 1978-80. Mem. Nebr. Ednl. Fin. Authority, 1991—, chmn., 1992—; mem. adv. bd. The Lutheran, 1987-94, chmn., 1992-94; bd. dirs. Planned Giving Svcs., Nebr., 1987—, chmn., 1992-94; mem. fund appeal chmn. Meml. Cmty. Hosp., 1994; mem. pastoral call com. First Luth. Ch., 1995. Inducted into Wall of Honor, Unity High Sch., Polk County, Wis.; fellow Palmer Coll. Chiropractic, Palmer Coll. Chiropractic-West. Mem. Assn. Ind. Colls. Nebr. (chmn. 1992-93), Nebr. Ind. Coll. Found. (exec. com. 1990-92, vice chmn. 1992-93, chmn. 1994-95), Luth. Edn. Conf. N.Am. (vice chmn. 1994-95, chmn. 1995-96), Nebr. Ednl. TV Coun. for Higher Edn. (chmn. 1990-91). Office: Dana Coll Office of Pres Blair NE 68008

CHRISTOPOULOS, GEORGE T., investment representative; b. Chgo., Sept. 8, 1957. Lic. series 7 Nat. Assn. Securities Dealers. Owner Starbright Enterprises, Skokie, Ill., 1972-92; investment rep. Edward D. Jones & Co., Skokie, 1992—. Mem. Skokie C. of C. Republican. Greek Orthodox. Office: Edward D Jones & Co 7925 Lincoln Ave Skokie IL 60077-3632

CHRISTOWSKI, HENRY FRANKLIN, school system administrator; b. Spickard, Mo., Apr. 24, 1938; s. Henry and Mabel Lorraine (Crawford) C.; m. Sondra Lou Kemp, June 1962 (div.); children: Jeannine, Joseph, Jeffrey; m. Patricia Luella Taylor, May 23, 1987. BS in Edn., Northeastern Mo. State, 1960; MS in Ednl. Adminstrn., Drake U., 1968. Tchr. Spickard (Mo.) Reorganized Dist., 1960-65; tchr., prin. Norwalk (Iowa) Cmty. Schs., 1965-80, adminstrv. asst. to supt., 1980—; softball coach Dowling H.S., West Des Moines, Iowa, 1989—, Simpson Coll., Indianola, Iowa, 1995—. Author: (videos) Slap Attack, 1993, Hit Doctor, 1994, Catching - the Inner Game, 1995. Home: 412 Center St Norwalk IA 50211

CHROMIZKY, WILLIAM RUDOLPH, accountant; b. Chgo., Jan. 21, 1955; s. Rudolph Joseph and Helen M. (Gniewek) C.; m. Laura Lee Lamoureux, Oct. 24, 1992. BS, No. Ill. U., 1977; M of Mgmt., Northwestern U., 1987. CPA, Ill. Sr. auditor Arthur Andersen & Co., Chgo., 1977-83; supr. internal audit AM Internat., Chgo., 1983-84, mgr. fin. reporting, 1984-85, dir. acctg., 1985; mgr. bus. analysis Premark Internat., Inc., Deerfield, Ill., 1985-87; dir. fin. reporting Premark Internat., Inc., Deerfield, 1987—. Vol. CPAs for the Pub Interest, Chgo., 1990-92; mem. fin. com. Brother Rice H.S., 1995—. Mem. AICPA, Ill. CPA Soc. Home: 9008 Tara Hill Rd Darien IL 60561-8435 Office: Premark Internat 1717 Deerfield Rd Deerfield IL 60015-3977

CHRONISTER, ROCHELLE BEACH, state legislator; b. Neodesha, Kans., Aug. 27, 1939; m. Bert Chronister, 1961; children: Pam, Phillip. AB, U. Kans. State rep. dist. 13 Kans. Ho. of Reps.; former asst. majority leader; sec. for social and rehab. svcs. Kans. Cabinet, 1995—; chmn. Kans. Rep. Party, 1989—. Named Woman of Yr., Neodesha C. of C. Mem. AMA (aux.), Bus. and Profl. Women. Methodist. Home: RR 2 Box 321 A Neodesha KS 66757-9562

CHU, ALEXANDER HANG-TORNG, chemical engineer; b. Taiwan, Republic of China, Oct. 30, 1955; came to the U.S., 1979; s. Wu-Lung and Su-Chin (Cheng) C.; m. Wei Jeng-Chu, June 22, 1981; children: Albert P., Jocelyn C. BS, Nat. Taiwan U., 1977; PhD, U. Wis., 1984. Cert. chem. engr. Rsch. asst. U. Wis., Madison, 1979-84, teaching asst., 1980-84; rsch. engr. Internat. Minerals & Chem., Terre Haute, Ind., 1984-87, project leader, 1987-88; sect. mgr. Abbott Labs., North Chicago, Ill., 1988-95; assoc. rsch. fellow, sect. mgr. Volwiler Soc., 1995—. Contbr. articles to Jour. Chromatography, Analytical Chemistry, Jour. Chem. Rsch., British Chem. Engring. Jour., Internat. Conf. on Separation Tech. Recipient Internat. Edison prize Thomas A. Edison Found., 1973, Book Coupon award, Nat. Taiwan U., 1977, Meritorious Svc. award China Youth Corps, 1975-76, Engr. award Chinese-Am. Inst., 1977. Mem. Am. Inst. Chem. Engrs. (vice chmn. 1986-88), Chinese Inst. Engrs. (pres. 1975-77), Sigma Xi. Office: Abbott Labs 1401 Sheridan North Chicago IL 60064

CHU, DANIEL TIM WO, pharmaceutical researcher; b. Hong Kong, Aug. 5, 1941; came to U.S., 1978; s. K.Y. and S. (Tsui) C.; m. Amy K.T. Kwan, Dec. 5, 1970; children: Dixie, Ernest. BSc, U. Alta., Edmonton, Can., 1967; PhD, U. New Brunswick, Fredericton, Can., 1971. Sr. chemist Abbott Labs., Abbott Park, Ill., 1979-84, group leader, 1985, group leader, assoc. rsch. fellow, 1985-86, project leader, assoc. rsch. fellow, 1986-87, project leader, rsch. fellow, 1987-88, sr. project leader, rsch. fellow, 1988-90, sr. project leader, sr. rsch. fellow, 1990-93; sr. project leader, disting. rsch. fellow, 1993—, dir. antibacterial rsch. disting. rsch. fellow, 1996—; presenter in field. Contbr. articles to profl. jours. Recipient Hamao Umezawa Internat. prize for chemotherapy, 1992, Orgn. Chinese Am. Inc., Asian-Am. Corp. Achievement award, 1993; named Inventor of Yr. Intellectual Property Land Assn. Chgo., 1990. Fellow Am. Inst. Chemists; mem. Am. Chem. Soc., Am. Soc. Microbiology, Sigma Xi. Lutheran. Office: Abbott Labs D-47N AP9A One Hundred Abbott Park Rd Abbott Park IL 60064-3500

CHU, JOHNSON CHIN SHENG, physician; b. Peiping, China, Sept. 25, 1918; came to U.S., 1948, naturalized, 1957; s. Harry S.P. and Florence (Young) C.; m. Sylvia Cheng, June 11, 1949; children—Stephen, Timothy. M.D., St. John's U., 1945. Intern Univ. Hosp., Shanghai, 1944-45; resident, research fellow NYU Hosp., 1948-50; resident physician in charge State Hosp. and Med. Ctr., Weston, W.Va., 1951-56; chief services, clin. dir. State Hosp., Logansport, Ind., 1957-84; active mem. Meml. Hosp., Logansport, Ind., 1968—. Research in cardiology and pharmacology; contbr. articles to profl. jours. Fellow Am. Psychiat. Assn., Am. Coll. Chest Physicians; mem. AMA, Ind. Med. Assn., Cass County Med. Soc., AAAS. Home: 36 E Lake Shafer Monticello IN 47960 Office: Southeastern Med Ctr Walton IN 46994

CHUCK, LEON, materials scientist; b. Balt., Mar. 7, 1955; s. Billy and Yuk Yin C. BSME, U. Md., 1978, MSME, 1984. Ceramic engr. Naval Rsch. Lab., Washington, 1976-79; rsch. engr. Nat. Bur. Stds., Gaithersburg, Md., 1979-86; sr. rsch. engr. Norton Co. High Performance Ceramics Div., Northboro, Mass., 1986-88; owner Advanced Structural Materials Consulting, Auburn, Mass., 1988-89; assoc. materials scientist U. Dayton (Ohio) Rsch. Inst., 1989—; part-time prof. dept. mech. and aerospace engring. U. Dayton, 1990—. Faculty advisor, coach U. Dayton Men's Volleyball, 1991—; chmn. St. Paul's Spares and Pairs Group, Oakwood, Ohio, 1991. Mem. ASME, Am. Ceramic Soc., Am. Soc. Testing and Materials (task group leader 1991—), Am. Soc. Materials, Soc. Automotive Engrs., Soc. Exptl. Mechanics, Soc. Application and Materials Processing Engrs., Nat. Inst. Ceramic Engrs. Home: 560 Oaknoll Dr Springboro OH 45066-9676 Office: U Dayton Rsch Inst 300 College Park Ave Dayton OH 45469-0172

CHUDZINSKI, MARK ADAM, lawyer; b. Chgo., Oct. 13, 1956; s. Brunon and Maria (Chmielinski) C.; m. Barbara Podkul, July 31, 1993; 1 child, Anna. BA, Northwestern U., 1977, MBA, 1981, JD, 1981; Diplome d'Etudes Approfondies, U. Paris, 1982. Bar: N.Y. 1982, Ill. 1990, U.S. Supreme Ct. 1994. Assoc. Coudert Bros., N.Y.C., 1982-85, London, 1985-88, Sydney,

Australia, 1988-89; sr. assoc. Winston & Strawn, Chgo., 1990-95, ptnr., 1995—; acting gen. counsel Ameritech Internat., 1996—; acting gen. counsel Ameritech Internat., 1996—. Articles editor Northwestern Jour. Internat. Law and Bus., 1981. Trustee CETA Inc. (Stas. WTTW-TV and WFMT-FM), Chgo.; mem. adv. bd. Sta. WBEZ-FM, Chgo.; bd. dirs. Chgo. Legal Clinic, Inc., Polish Mus. Am., Polish Am. Congress. Austin scholar 1978; fellow Leadership Greater Chgo., 1990; U.S. Champ Jessup Moot Ct., 1979. Mem. ABA, N.Y. State Bar Assn., Am. Soc. Internat. Law, French-Am. C. of C., German-Am. C. of C., U.S.-Poland C. of C. (founder, chmn. 1991-95). Roman Catholic. Home: 6005 N Oconto Ave Chicago IL 60631-3620 Office: Winston & Strawn 35 W Wacker Dr Chicago IL 60601-1614

CHUKMAN, L(OUIS) D., artist, illustrator; b. Chgo., Aug. 27, 1955; s. Louis (Alojczak) and Mary B. Chukman. BFA, Sch. of the Art Inst. Chgo., 1978. Courtroom illustrator WLS TV, Chgo., 1975—; courtroom illustrator various news agencies, including MacNeal/Lehrer News Hr., ABC TV, Fox Broadcasting, local news agencies in Ill., Wis., Mich., 1975—; storyboard artist Marshall Field & Co., Burson-Marstellar, others, 1981—. Group shows include ARC Gallery, Chgo., West Hubbard Gallery, Chgo., Artemesia Gallery, Chgo., others, 1978—; illustrator: Home and Office Visi-calc Companion, 1982. Mem. Chgo. Artists Coalition, Midwest Aikido Center (pres. bd. dirs. 1987-89). Office: c/o K&K Ltd PO Box 7045 Westchester IL 60154-7045

CHUMMERS, PAUL, performing company executive. Pres., CEO Utah Symphony, Salt Lake City.

CHUN, SHINAE, state official. Dir. Labor Dept., Chgo. Office: 160 N LaSalle Ste C1300 Chicago IL 60601

CHUNG, ALISON LI, information systems specialist; b. Hong Kong, Jan. 2; d. Henry Fook-Kuen and Vivian Po-King (Woo) Li; m. Dean Ilkwon Chung, Feb. 18, 1984; 1 child, Jennifer. BA, Wellesley Coll.; MA, Stanford U.; MBA, U. Chgo., 1986. Programmer Commonwealth Edison, Chgo., 1979-81; systems engr. IBM, Chgo., 1981-84; sr. cons. Price Waterhouse, Chgo., 1984-85, mgr., 1985-86; dir. info. systems Jenner & Block, Chgo., 1986-89, dir. tech., 1989—. Mem. blue ribbon automation com. Recorder of Deed's Office, 1992—; mem. Chgo. Bot. Garden, 1992-96. Mem. IEEE, Data Processing Mgmt. Assn., Am. Soc. Info. Sci., Chgo. Wellesley Club (bd. dirs. 1986-93, admissions chair 1988-89, sec. 1989-92, treas. 1992-93, pres. 1996—), Ravinia Assocs. (bd. dirs. 1989—), Chgo. GSB Club, U. Chgo. Women's Bus. Group. Anglican. Home and Office: PO Box 468 Glencoe IL 60022-0468

CHUNG, DEAN I., business executive, marketing professional; b. Salinas, Calif., May 26, 1958; s. Hai C. and Sue J. (Cho) C.; m. Alison Li, Feb. 18, 1984; 1 child, Jennifer. BA with honors, Williams Coll., 1981; MBA, U. Chgo., 1986. Systems engr. IBM Corp., Northfield, Ill., 1981-84, mktg. rep., 1985-87; account exec. GMD, Westchester, Ill., 1988-89; mgr. The Foster Group, Chgo., 1989-90, prin., 1990-91; dir. Aldon Trading Co., Glencoe, Ill., 1992—. Precinct capt. New Trier Rep. Orgn., Kenilworth, Ill., 1988-96; mem. Recorder of Deeds Blue Ribbon Com., Chgo., 1990; mem. Bus. Vols. for the Arts, Chgo., 1986, 90, Shedd Aquarium Assocs. bd. 1994-96. Mem. Univ. Club of Chgo. (devel. com. 1990-91, admissions com. 1991-94, reciprocal privilege com. 1994-96, billiards and games com. 1994-96), Ill. Squash Rackets Assn., Williams Alumni Club Chgo. (admissions rep. 1985, class agt. 1990—, v.p. 1995—), Chgo. Grad. Shc. Bus. Club. Office: Aldon Trading Co Inc 30 W Monroe St Ste 1400 Chicago IL 60603-2401

CHUNG, PAUL MYUNGHA, mechanical engineer, educator; b. Seoul, Dec. 1, 1929; came to U.S., 1947, naturalized, 1956; s. Robert N. and Kyungsook (Kim) C.; m. E. Jean Judy, Mar. 8, 1952; children: Maurice W., Tamara P. BSME, U. Ky., 1952, MS, 1954; Ph.D., U. Minn., 1957. Asst. prof. mech. engring. U. Minn., 1957-58; aero. research scientist Ames Research Center, NASA, Calif., 1958-61; head fluid physics dept. Aerospace Corp., San Bernardino, Calif., 1961-66; prof. mech. engring. U. Ill., Chgo., 1966-95, head dept. energy engring., 1974-79, dean engring., 1979-94, prof., dean emeritus, 1995—; mem. tech. adv. com. Ill. Inst. Environ. Quality, 1975-77; corp. mem. Underwriters Lab., 1983-95; cons. to industry, 1966—. Author numerous papers in field; author: Electric Probes in Stationary and Flowing Plasmas, 1975, Russian edit., 1978; contbr. chpt. to Advances in Heat Transfer, 1965, to Dynamics of Ionized Gases, 1973. Bd. govs. Redlands (Calif.) YMCA, 1965-67. Fellow AIAA (nat. tech. com. on plasmadynamics 1972-74, com. on propellants and combustion 1976-80); mem. AIChE (nat. com. on internat. activities 1992-94), Am. Soc. Engring. Edn. (exec. bd. engring. dean's coun. 1983-84), Sigma Xi, Tau Beta Pi, Pi Tau Sigma, Phi Kappa Phi. Home: 2003 E Lillian Ln Arlington Heights IL 60004-4215 Office: Univ Ill Off of Dean Chicago IL 60680

CHUPP, DIANA LYNN, textiles and needlework educator; b. Balt., Sept. 6, 1945; d. Grant Lenhardt and Ann Eva (Stellmacher) Boland; m. Larry Dean Chupp, Mar. 1, 1969. AA, Stephens Coll., 1965, BFA, 1967. Display coord. J.C. Penney Co., Dallas, 1966; fashion coord. J.C. Penney Co., Columbia, Mo., 1966-67; mgmt. trainee J.C. Penney Co., Chgo., 1967-68; mdse. mgr. J.C. Penney Co., Gary, Ind., 1968-70, sr. mdse. mgr., 1977-83; employment counselor Roland Employment, Chgo., 1970-71; mgr. Fabricenters Am., Gary, 1971-75; substitute tchr. various schs., Porter County, Ind., 1986—; pvt. tchr., textile, fibers and needlework Valparaiso, Ind., 1989—; owner, importer Diana Lynn Chupp Textile, Fiber, Needle Arts, Valparaiso, 1992—; cons. Victorian home restoration & furnishing, Valparaiso, 1989—. Mem. Ctrl. Neighborhood Assn., Valparaiso, 1990—, porter County Hist. Soc., Valparaiso, 1988; mem. adv. bd. Valparaiso Canine Crusade Against Cancer affiliate Am. Cancer Soc.; active Greyhound Companions. Recipient numerous 1st Place prizes for designing and making clothes, beads and baskets. Mem. Duneland Weavers (sec. 1989-92, chair Interwoven Expressions 1992-93, hospitality 1988-89), Embroidery Guild Am., Ind. Lure Coursing Club. Home and Office: 103 Weston St Valparaiso IN 46383-4669

CHURCH, HARRISON LEON, publishing executive, newspaper; b. St. Louis, June 16, 1941; s. Leon Harry and Helen Caroline Dorothy (Saegesser) C.; m. Harriet Lois Feddersen, Oct. 27, 1988. BS, U. Ill., 1963, MS, 1965, JD, 1971. Bar: N.D. Assoc. prof. Dickinson (N.D.) State Coll., 1971-73; owner, operator Lebanon (Ill.) Advertiser, 1974—. Contbr. articles to mags. Pres., v.p., treas., spokesman Lebanon Hist. Soc., 1964—; bd. dirs. St. Clair County Hist. Soc., Belleville, Ill., 1987-92. Named Cmty. Builder Masons, 1991, prose laureate Am. Amateur Press Assn., 1976; James scholar U. Ill., 1959-60. Home: 10940 State Rt 4 Lebanon IL 62254 Office: Lebanon Advertiser 309 W Saint Louis St Lebanon IL 62254-0126

CHURCH, IRENE ZABOLY, personnel services company executive; b. Cleve., Feb. 18, 1947; d. Bela Paul and Irene Elizabeth (Chandas) Zaboly; children: Irene Elizabeth, Elizabeth Anne, Lauren Alexandria Gadd, John Dale Gadd II. Grad. high sch. Pers. cons., recruiter, Cleve., 1965-70; chief exec. officer, pres. Oxford Pers., Pepper Pike, Ohio, 1973-89, Oxford Temporaries, Pepper Pike, 1979—, Oxford Group Ltd., Inc., 1989—; guest lectr. in field, 1974—; expert witness for ct. testimony, 1982—. Troop leader Lake Erie coun. Girl Scouts U.S., 1980-81; mem. Christian action com. Federated Ch., United Ch. Christ, 1981-85, sub-com. to study violence in rels. to women, 1983, creator, presenter programs How Work Affects Family Life and Re-entering the Job Market, 1981, mem. Women's Fellowship Martha-Mary Circle, 1980—, program dir., 1982-84, 87—; chpt. leader Nat. Coalition on TV Violence, 1983—; mem. The Federated Ch., United Ch. of Christ, Chagrin Falls, Ohio, program dir Mary-Martha Circle, 1982—, christian action com. 1981-85, mem. Mary-Martha Circle, Women's fellowship, 1980—; mem Better Bus. Bur., 1973-82. Mem. Nat. Assn. Pers. Cons. (cert., mem. ethics com. 1976-77, co-chairperson ethics com. 1977-78, mem. bus. practices and ethics com. 1980-82, mem. cert. pers. cons. soc. 1980-82, regional leader for membership 1987—, Pres.'s award 1988), Ohio Assn. Pers. Cons. (trustee 1975-80, 85—, sec. 1976-77, 85-87, chairperson bus. practices and ethics com. 1976-77, 81-82, 1st v.p., chairperson resolutions com. 1981-82, chairperson membership com. 1985-89, 2d v.p. 1987—, Outstanding Svc. award 1987, pres. 1988-89), Greater Cleve. Assn. Pers. Cons. (2nd then 1st v.p., 1974-76, state trustee 1975-80, pres. 1976-77, bd. advisor 1977-78, chairperson bus. practices and ethics com. 1974-76, chmn. nominating com., 1983-88, membership com. 1987-87, arbitration com., 1980, 85-87, fundraising, 1980-89, bd. dirs. 1980-89, trustee 1985-89, program chair 1987-89, Vi Pender Outstanding Svc. award 1977), Euclid C. of C. (small bus. com. 1981, chairperson task force com. evaluating funding in social security and vet.'s benefits 1981), Internat. Platform Assn., Am. Bus. Women's Assn., Nat. Assn. Temp. Svcs., Chagrin Valley C. of C. (leader Chagrin Blvd./East chpt. 1987—, Pres.'s award for Outstanding Contbns. 1988, pres. bd. dirs 1990—), Greater Cleve. Growth Assn. Coun. Small Enterprises, Rotary (vocat. svc. chairperson, program com. 1987—, membership chairperson 1988-89). Home: 8 Ridgecrest Dr Chagrin Falls OH 44022-4218

CHURCH, JAY KAY, psychologist, educator; b. Wichita, Kans., Jan. 18, 1927; s. Kay Iverson and Gertrude (Parrish) C.; BA, David Lipscomb Coll., 1948; MA, Ball State U., 1961; PhD, Purdue U., 1963; m. Dorothy Agnes Fellerhoff, May 21, 1976; children: Karen Patrice Turnbull, Caryn Annice Church Casey, Rex Warren, Max Roger. Chemist, Auburn Rubber Corp., 1948-49; salesman Midwestern United Life Ins. Co., 1949-52; owner, operator Tour-Rest Motel, Waterloo, Ind., 1952-66; tchr., guidance dir., public schs., Hamilton, Ind., 1955-61; counselor Washington Twp. (Ind.) Schs., Indpls., 1961-62; asst. prof. psychology Ball State U., 1963-67, assoc. prof., 1967-71, prof., 1971-88, prof. emeritus, 1988—, chmn. dept. ednl. psychology, 1970-74, dir. advanced grad. programs in ednl. psychology, 1978-81; pvt. practice psychology, 1963—. Mem. Am. Psychol. Assn., Nat. Assn. Sch. Psychologists. Home: 8501 N Ravenwood Dr Muncie IN 47303-9313

CHURCHILL, ROBERT WILSON, state legislator, lawyer; b. Waukegan, Ill., Apr. 10, 1947; s. George Oliver and Helga C. (Carlson) C.; m. Sandra Lee Bartlett, Aug. 5, 1985; children: Abigail Lee, Julia Aubrey, Christine Lizbeth. BA, Northwestern U., Evanston, Ill., 1969; JD, U. Iowa, 1972. Elected del. Rep. Nat. Conv., 1980, 92, 96, alt. del., 1984; trustee Lake Villa (Ill.) Township, 1981-83; rep. Ill. Ho. Reps., 1983—; minority whip Ill. Gen. Assembly, 1987-89, asst. minority leader, 1989-91, dep. minority leader, 1991-94; majority leader, 1995—; chmn. Rep. Ctrl. Com. for Lake County, Ill., 1990-94; co-chmn. Ill. Econ. and Fiscal Commn., Springfield, 1991-95. Mem. ABA, Lake County, Ill. Bar Assn., Ducks Unlimited, Lake Villa Lions, Exchange Club, Moose. Republican.

CHURCHILL, STEVEN WAYNE, state legislator, fund-raising consultant; b. Akron, Ohio, May 8, 1963; s. Wayne Stevenson and Susan (Gurney) C. BA, Iowa State U., 1985. Fin. asst. The Governor Branstad Com., Des Moines, 1986, fin. dir., 1988-90; mktg. mgr. Iowa Dept. Econ. Devel., Des Moines, 1987; devel. officer Simpson Coll., Indianola, Iowa, 1990-93; fundraising cons. The Churchill Group, Johnston, Iowa, 1993—; mem. Iowa Ho. of Reps., Johnston, Iowa, 1992—. Elected State Rep., Ctrl. Iowa, 1992; commr. Iowa Civil Rights Commn., Des Moines, 1991-92; deacon Plymouth Congl. Ch., 1988-91; alumni amb. Iowa State U., 1990-92. Recipient Comdr.'s Award for Pub. Svc., Dept. of the Army, 1991; named one of 10 Outstanding Young Iowans, Iowa Jaycees, 1995. Mem. Johnston C. of C., Urbandale C. of C., Bull Moose Club (pres. 1990-91), Rotary of Des Moines (pres. 1991-92), Sigma Alpha Epsilon (pres. 1989-90, Order of the Lion 1990). Home: 6140 Nottingham Johnston IA 50131-8713 Office: The Churchill Group 6140 Nottingham Johnston IA 50131-8713

CHVALA, CHARLES JOSEPH, state legislator; b. Merrill, Wis., Dec. 5, 1954; s. John Patrick and Mary Ann (Severt) C.; children: Ted, Jessica. BA, U. Wis., 1978, JD, 1978. Atty. DeWitt, Sundby, Huggett & Schumacher, 1979-81, Smith, Chvala & Merg, 1981-83, Boushea, Newton & Seagall, 1983—; lobbyist Citizen's Utility Bd., 1981-82; mem. Wis. State Senate, 1985—, mem. Joint Fin. com., Projects com., radioactive review bd., chmn. state coun. Alcohol & Other Drug Abuse. Nat. Merit scholar. Mem. State Bar Wis., Dane County Bar Assn. also: 304 Parkwood Ln Apt 4 Madison WI 53714-1979 also: State Senate State Capitol Madison WI 53702*

CIANI, ALFRED JOSEPH, language professional, dean; b. N.Y.C., June 29, 1946; s. Joseph Alfred and Aurora Smiles (VanOver) C.; m. Sharon Skolkey, Aug. 16, 1968 (div. 1979); children: Mieke Jo, Gabriel Wolf; m. Lesley Lockwood, Aug. 9, 1980; children: Joseph Alfred, Clinton Lockwood. BA, U. Albany, 1969; MA, Coll. of St. Rose, 1972; EdD, Ind. U., 1974. Tchr. Greater Amsterdam (N.Y.) Schs., 1969-72; rsch. asst. Ind. U., Bloomington, 1972-73; assoc. instr. Ind. U., 1973-74; asst. prof. U. Cin., 1974-79, assoc. prof., 1979—; vis. prof. U. Wis., Milw., 1980; assoc. dean, info. officer U. Cin., 1988-92; pres. Ohio Internat. Reading Assn., Columbus, 1981-82; outside cons., State of Miss., Jackson, 1982-84; cons., U. Oreg. Profl. Devel., Eugene, 1979-80, cons., Nashville Schs., 1982-83; mem. Dean's Cabinet. Author: Motivating Reluctant Readers, 1981; editor: (book series) Reading in Content Areas, 1979-81; rev. editor: Rsch. in Mid. Level Edn., 1995—. Grantee Ford Found., 1990, IBM, 1990. Mem. AAUP, Internat. Reading Assn., Am. Ednl. Rsch. Assn. Assn. Tchr. Educators (nat. com.), Nat. Coun. Tchrs. English, Nat. Mid. Sch. Assn., Nat. Reading Coun., YMCA, Phi Delta Kappa, Kappa Delta Pi. Democrat. Roman Catholic. Office: U Cin Mail Location 02 Cincinnati OH 45221

CIARAMITARO, NICK, state legislator; b. Detroit, Dec. 17, 1951; s. Sam and Catherine (Sooentino) C.; m. Peggy Houlihan. BA cum laude, U. Detroit, 1974; JD, Wayne State U., 1979. City clk. City of Roseville (Mich.), 1977-78; law clk. Mich. Atty. Gen. Frank Kelley & Atty. Michael P. Long, 1977; state rep. Mich. Ho. Reps., Dist. 37, 1979—; mem. appropriations com., Mich. Ho. Reps. Chmn. Macomb County Young Dem., Mich., 1972, vice chmn., 1972-73, officer-at-large, 1972-74; dir. registration Macomb Voters Registrar Com., 1972; alt. del. Dem. State Ctrl. Com., 1971-72; vice chmn. Mich. Young Dem., 1973-75; exec. bd. 12th Congl. Dist. Dem. Com., 1972; assoc. field staff reporter Mich. State Dem. Party, 1973-76; staff mem. U.S. Rep. James O'Hara, 1973-77; del. Dem. Nat. Mid-Term Conf., 1974; mem. exec. bd. Macomb County Dem. Comm., 1974—; mem. Friends Roseville Libr., Roseville Bicentennial Com., treas., 1976—. Mem. Lions, Jaycees, Alpha Sigma Nu. Home: 29127 E Brittany Ct Roseville MI 48066-2049*

CIARLILLO, MARJORIE ANN, musician, educator; b. Cleve., Nov. 1, 1940; d. Nicolo and Madelaine (DaMico) C. AB in Fine Arts, Lake Erie Coll., 1962; cert., U. London, 1962; MA in Musicology, Western Res. U., 1971; postgrad., Ind. U., 1965, 82, 83; cert. Chinese music, Shanghai Conservatory Music, 1983. Dir. lower sch. music dept. Univ. Sch., Shaker Heights, Ohio, 1963-70; br. cood. Cleve. Inst. Music/Beaumont Sch. for Girls, Cleveland Heights, 1971-75; mem. piano faculty Cleve. Inst. Music, 1971—; dir. China Music Project, Cleve., 1980—; musicologist Glen Oak Sch., Gates Mills, Ohio, 1978-82; instr. piano Lake Erie Coll., Painesville, Ohio, 1975-82, other ednl. instns. and pvt. students, 1961—; dir. China Music Project, 1980—; spl. asst. to dean of coll. Case Western Res. U., Cleve., 1987-94; asst. headmaster The Andrews Sch., Willoughby, Ohio, 1994—. Performer Chinese Cultural Arts Symposium, 1988, Cleve. Mus. Art., Cleve. Inst. Music, 1981, 82, 86; performer radio programs on Chinese music WCLV-FM, Cleve., 1981—, WRUW-FM, Cleve., 1987; pianist Cleve. Women's Orch., 1972-75; contbr. articles to arts and scholastic publs. Trustee Andrews Sch., Willoughby, Ohio, 1991-94, Lake Erie Coll, 1975-78. Fellow Ednl. Rsch. Coun., 1968; recipient Disting. Alumna award Andrews Sch., 1978. Mem. AAUW, Adult Edn. Assn. U.S., Am. Musicol. Soc., Assn. Chinese Music Rsch. (founding), Coun. Advancement and Support Edn., Soc. Asian Music, Soc. Ethnomusicology, Mu Phi Epsilon. Office: The China Music Project Inc 334 Claymore Blvd Cleveland OH 44143-1730

CIARLO, FLORA L., state legislator; widowed; 3 children. BS, Nat. Coll. Edn. Ill. state rep. Dist. 80, 1995—; mem. Aging, Cities and Villages, Elem. and Secondary Edn. and Commerce, Indsl. and Labor Coms., 1995—, Ill. Ho. of Reps.; elem. sch. tchr., 1961-67; former educator, program mgr. Bloom Twp. H.S. Dist. Trustee Prairie State Coll.; mem. citizens adv. bd. St. James Hosp. and Health Ctr.; mem. United Way; life mem. PTA. Office: 3331 Chicago Rd Steger IL 60475

CIAVARELLI, MATT D., engineering executive; b. Pittstown, Pa., Aug. 11, 1942. BS, LeTourneau Coll., 1971. Project engr. Phillips Industries, Cleve., 1973-75; product/test engr. Midland Steel, Cleve., 1975-84; quality control mgr. Modern Tool & Dye Co., Cleve., 1984—. With USN, 1964-66. Mem. ASQC. Office: Modern Tool & Die Co 5389 W 130th St Cleveland OH 44130-1034

CICCONE, RICHARD, newspaper editor; b. Sewickley, Pa., Feb. 23, 1940; s. Samuel C. and Mary (Thomas) C.; m. Joan M. Garrity, Nov. 18, 1967; children: Cristin, Richard. Reporter Chgo. Bur. AP, 1962-63, 66-74, news editor, 1974-76; reporter Chgo. Tribune, 1976-77, polit. editor, from 1976, mng. editor, assoc. editor, 1995—. Co-author: Who's Running Chicago, 1979. With USMC, 1963-66, Vietnam. Decorated Bronze star. Office: Chgo Tribune Co 435 N Michigan Ave Ste 356 Chicago IL 60611-4001*

CIERPIOT, CONNIE, state legislator. Mem. Mo. Ho. of Reps., Jefferson City. Republican.

CIESIELSKI, THOMAS GREGORY, bank executive; b. Chgo., Dec. 25, 1949; s. Dennis C. and Helene T. (Bojak) C.; children: Christopher A., Mark R. BA, DePaul U., 1971; M in Mgmt., Northwestern U., Evanston, Ill., 1988. Sr. tng. specialist Fed. Res. Bank Chgo., 1972-74, systems cons., 1974-76, mgr., 1976-81, asst. v.p., 1981-85, v.p., 1985—; mem. coun. bus. assocs. Elmhurst (Ill.) Coll., 1987—; mem. bus. adv. group CAEL, 1996—. Mem. human resources com. Met. YMCA, Chgo., 1988—. Office: Fed Res Bank Chgo 230 S La Salle St Chicago IL 60604-1496

CILZ, DOUGLAS ARTHUR, lawyer; b. Rugby, N.D., Feb. 22, 1949; s. Fred W. and Arliene (Nelson) C.; m. Kathy Ann Walker, June 10, 1972; children: Jennifer, Nicholas. BS, Dickinson State U., 1976; JD, U. N.D., Grand Forks, 1980. Bar: N.D. 1980, U.S. Dist. Ct. N.D. 1980, Minn. 1981, U.S. Tax Ct. 1981, U.S. Claims Ct. 1981. Atty. Qualley Larson & Jones, Fargo, N.D., 1980-81, Pearson & Christensen, Grand Forks, N.D., 1981-87; ptnr. Hamilton, Juntunen, Cilz & Hagen, Grand Forks, 1987—; instr. East Grand Forks (Minn.) Tech. Coll., 1989-92; apptd. spl. asst. atty. gen. Bank N.D., 1993—; apptd. temporary adminstrv. law judge N.D. Office Adminstrv. Hearings, 1995—. Sgt. USAF, 1968-71. Mem. ABA, Minn. Bar Assn., N.D. Bar Assn., Am. Trial Lawyers Assn., Grand Forks C. of C. Lutheran. Office: Hamilton Juntunen & Cilz 218 S 3rd St Grand Forks ND 58201-4732

CIOCHON, RUSSELL LYNN, paleoanthropologist; b. Altadena, Calif., Mar. 11, 1948; s. Val Martin and Glenda Bernice (Timbrook) C.; m. Noriko Ikeda, Nov. 2, 1986. MA, U. Calif., Berkeley, 1974, PhD, 1986. Lectr. U. N.C., Charlotte, 1978-81; rsch. paleontologist U. Calif., Berkeley, 1982-83; rsch. assoc. Inst. Human Origins, Berkeley, 1983-85, SUNY, Stony Brook, 1985-86; asst. prof. U. Iowa, Iowa City, 1987-90, assoc. prof., 1990-96, prof., 1996—; vis. lectr. U. Ariz., Tucson, 1987. Rev. bd. Jour. Human Evolution, 1980-85; mem. editl. bd. Internat. Jour. Primatology, 1990, Am. Jour. Phys. Anthropology, 1996—; series editor: Advances in Human Evolution, 1991-93; co-editor: Oxford Series in Human Evolution, 1995—; editor: Evolutionary Biology of New World Monkeys, 1980, New Interpretations of Ape and Human Ancestry, 1983; author, editor: Primate Evolution and Human Origins, 1987, The Human Evolution Source Book, 1993, Integrative Paths to the Past, 1994; author: Other Origins: The Search for the Giant Ape, 1990, Evolution of the Cercopithecoid Forelimb, 1993. Rsch. grantee Smithsonian Fgn. Currency Program, Washington, 1978, The L.S.B. Leakey Found., Oakland, Calif., 1987, The Nat. Geographic Soc., Washington, 1988, The Wenner-Green Found., N.Y., 1991. Mem. AAAS, Am. Anthropol. Assn., Am. Assn. Phys. Anthropologists, Soc. Systematic Biologists, Phi Beta Kappa. Democrat. Home: 1025 Keokuk St Iowa City IA 52240-3303 Office: Univ of Iowa Dept Anthropology 114 Macbride Hall Iowa City IA 52242-1322

CIOSEK, NANCY CAROL, dietitian, educator; b. Chgo., May 4, 1942; d. Bruno George and Ann Barbara (Krawiec) C. BA in Home Econs., Rosary Coll., 1964; MS in Foods and Nutrition, No. Ill. U., 1972; postgrad., Depaul U. Law Sch., 1975-76. Registered and lic. dietitian; cert. nutrition specialist. Dietitian Chgo. State Hosp., 1965-66; dietary mgr. Read-Chgo. State Mental Health Ctr., Chgo., 1966-69; instr. Wesley-Passavant Sch. Nursing, Chgo., 1969-79; dir. health and nutrition svcs. Community and Econ. Devel. Assn. Cook County, Inc., Chgo., 1980-84; dir. dietetic programs Chgo. State U., 1985-91, assoc. prof., 1985—; mem. adv. com. Ill. Dept. Pub. Health Nutrition Svc., Springfield, 1982-95; mem. Chgo. Area Dietetic Edn. Programs Coun., 1986-90; mem. interdisciplinary faculty Gt. Lakes Geriatric Ctr., Chgo., 1987-90. Author: (with others) Manual of Clinical Dietetics, 3d edit., 1988, The Hunger Handbook, 5th edit., 1988, 7th edit., 1993. Co-founder, mem. Healthy Mothers and Babies Coalition, Chgo., 1982-88; mem. Ill. Caucus on Teenage Pregnancy, Chgo., 1981-88, Ill. Hunger Action Coalition, Chgo., 1985, 88, Ill. Citizens for Better Care, Chgo., 1987-88, Chgo. Hospitality/Food Svc. Careers for Youth Speakers Forum, 1989—; bd. dirs. Suburban Cook County-DuPage County Health Systems Agy., 1983-87, exec. bd., 1985-87; bd. dirs. Health and Medicine Policy Rsch. Group, 1983-90, Suburban Health Planning Assn., 1987-88; mem. dietetic tech. adv. bd. Malcolm X Coll., 1985-92, Wm. Rainey Harper Coll., 1988-93. Named honoree Spl. Supplemental Food Program for Women, Infants and Children 10th Anniversary awards Ceremony Ill. Dept. Pub. Health Region VIII, 1984. Mem. Am. Dietetic Assn. (renal dietetics practice group), Ill. Dietetic Assn. (chair dietetic educators of practitioners 1988-91, co-chair 1992-93), Chgo. Dietetic Assn., Chgo. Nutrition Assn., Ill. Pub. Health Assn., Ill. Assn. Allied Health Profls. (bd. dirs. 1992—). Roman Catholic. Office: Chgo State U 95th and King Dr Chicago IL 60628

CIRCLE, LILIAS WAGNER, honor society administrator; b. Ann Arbor, Mich., Apr. 26, 1928; d. Herbert Phillip and Julia Julia (Kendall) Wagner; m. Robert L. Jones, Dec. 29, 1951 (div. Jan. 1967); children: Lilias, Robert G., Eric D.; m. T. Robert Circle, Dec. 14, 1968; 1 child, Phillip T.; stepchildren: Jane Circle Asmuth, Thomas Rhys. BA in Speech, U. Mich., 1950. Student Interlochen (Mich.) Music Camp, 1944-47, staff, 1950; tchr. English, history Ann Arbor Pub. Schs., 1950-51; tchr. speech Eastern Mont. Coll., Billings, 1957; writer pub. rels. Chgo. Symphony Orch., 1967-68; adminstrv. asst. Leadership Greater Chgo., 1984; nat. sec. and treas. Pi Kappa Lambda, Evanston, Ill., 1984—; essayist, spkr. Lyric Opera Chgo., other orgns., 1986—; violist Evanston Symphony, 1960—; prodr. Savoy-aires, Evanston, 1964-89, soloist choral groups, 1974—. Author program notes Evanston Symphony, 1963—, Symphony II, 1992—, Allied Arts, Chgo. Symphony Chorus, Stagebill, Mostly Music Chamber Music Series, 1993—. Active St. Augustine's Ch., Wilmette, 1973—; class officer U. Mich., 1949—; mem. alumni bd. Interlochen Music Camp, 1979-81. Republican. Episcopalian. Club: Mich. Shores. Office: Pi Kappa Lambda Northwestern U Sch Music Evanston IL 60208-1200

CIROLIA, DONNA MARY, government relations executive; b. Nyack, N.Y., Aug. 19, 1958; d. Philip John and Catherine (Lombardo) C. BA, Lafayette Coll., 1980; MPA, George Washington U., 1982. Environ. protection specialist U.S. EPA, Washington, 1980-84; dir. govt. affairs Water Quality Assn., Washington, 1984-89; mgr. industry and govt. rels. Culligan Internat., Northbrook, Ill., 1989—; lectr. various orgns. Contbr. articles to profl. jours. Mem. Water Quality Assn. (mem. govt. affairs adv. group 1989—), Internat. Bottled Water Assn. (mem. bd. dirs., govt. rels. com. 1992—), Am. Water Works Assn., Nat. Environ. Health Assn., Nat. Rural Water Assn., Pi Alpha Alpha. Office: Culligan Internat One Culligan Pkwy Northbrook IL 60062

CISKY, JON AYRES, state senator; b. Port Huron, Mich., Sept. 6, 1941; m. Lynn M. Williams; children: Jon, Pam. BS, Madonna Coll., Detroit, 1975; MA, U. Detroit, 1976. Sgt. St. Clair (Mich.) County Sheriff Dept., 1970-76; asst. to dir., asst. prof. Abraham Baldwin Agrl. Coll., Tifton, Ga., 1976-78; prof. Saginaw (Mich.) Valley State U., 1978-90; senator Mich. State Senate, Lansing, 1991—; mem. appropriations com. Mich. State Senate, 1991, chmn. corrections, state police, and mil. affairs coms., 1991. Founder, spokesperson Crime Stoppers Mich., 1984-90; bd. dirs. Crime Stoppers Internat., 1986, Saginaw Valley Cime Commn., 1979-82. With Sea Bees, USN. Mem. Am. Soc. Indsl. Security, Mich. Chiefs of Police Assn., Saginaw Valley State U. Faculty Assn., Mich. Criminal Justice Educators Assn., Ea. Mich. Police Chiefs Assn. Republican. Office: Michigan Senate State Capitol Lansing MI 48909

CITRO, JAMES COLLINS, investment executive; b. Chgo., Dec. 10, 1950; m. Kathleen Citro, 1973; children: Melissa, Joseph, Daniel, John, Katherine. BA, Quincy U., 1973. Tchr. St. Peters Sch., Quincy, 1973-75, Quincy Notre Dame Sch., 1975-79; real estate salesman Davis & Assocs., Quincy, Ill., 1979-84; investment broker Kemper Securities Inc., Quincy, 1984—. Bd.

dirs. Quincy Notre Dame Sch., Madonna House, Quincy, United Way, Quincy, Men's Club, St. Peters Ch., Quincy, Muddy River Opera, Quincy, mem. Quincy Sch. Bd., 1996—. Mem. Quincy Country Club. Republican. Roman Catholic. Home: 417 S 24th St Quincy IL 62301-4428 Office: AG Edwards & Sons 3325 Maine Quincy IL 62301

CIULLA, WILLIAM JAMES, import export company executive; b. Chgo., Aug. 1, 1929; s. Charles C. and Helen Bogin; m. Elsie Marie Endler, May 3, 1967. BS, Northwestern U., 1959; MBA, U. Chgo., 1960. Consumer loan officer 1st Nat. Banl Evergreen Park (Ill.), 1950-56; asst. treas. 1st Fed. Savings & Loan Assn., Chgo., 1956-61; treas., bd. dirs. Cantop, Inc., Bola-Cynooyd, Pa., 1961-65; divsn. mgr. Res, Ins. Co., Chgo., 1965-69; mgr. internal audit Chgo. Fed. Savings & Loan Assn., 1969-76; asst. v.p., mgr. bus. devel. 1st Fed. Savings & Loan, 1976-84; exec. v.p. H. Wittur & co., Evanston, Ill., 1984-86; adminstr. C.P.A. Svcs., Inc., Chgo., 1986-88; various positions corp. hqrs. Video Trend, Inc., Des Plaines, Ill., 1988-93; pres., CEO, founder Baron of Florence Enterprises, Inc., Park Ridge, Ill., 1993—; loaned exec. Nat. Alliance Bus., 1980. Sponsor, fundraiser Chgo. Sympnohy Orch., 1995; patron, fundraiser Lyric Opera Chgo., 1995, The of Art Inst., Chgo., 1995, Art Inst. Chgo., 1995; sustaining mem. Judaeo-Christian Inst. Seaton Hall U., South Orange, N.J., 1995, Health Rsch. Inst., Naperville, Ill., 1995' fundraiser United Way, Northbrook, Ill., 1980-84. Mem. German Am. C. of C., Chgo. Coun. Fgn. Rels. Independent. Roman Catholic. Home and Office: 918 N Florence Dr Park Ridge IL 60068-2108

CIZEK, DAVID JOHN, sales engineer, small business owner; b. Chgo., Sept. 29, 1959; s. John Jacob and Cecelia Ursula (Shway) C.; m. Kimberly Ann Kral, May 12, 1984. BSEE, U. Ill., 1981. Asst. sales engr. control div. Westinghouse Electric Co., Chgo., 1981-83; product line engr. control div. Westinghouse Electric Co., Fayetteville, N.C., 1983-85; sales engr. field sales div. Westinghouse Electric Co., Chgo., 1985-86, aerospace and def. automation specialist, 1987-88, engr. distbn. support sales, 1988-94; field sales divsn. sales engr. Cutler-Hammer, 1994-95; pres., owner Lakeridge Electric Supply Co., Inc., Crest Hill, Ill., 1995—. Mem. U. Ill. Alumni Assn., Girl Scouts of Am., Kappa Sigma Alumni Assn. Republican. Presbyterian. Home: 8409 Willow West Dr Willow Springs IL 60480-1139 Office: Lakeridge Electric Supply 1491 Caton Farm Rd Crest Hill IL 60435

CIZMADIA, DAVID PAUL, financial consultant; b. Cleveland Heights, Ohio, May 21, 1968; s. David Sr. and Randy (Shandle) C. BA, Ohio State U., 1991. Intern Res. Capital, Cleve., 1993; fin. cons. Merrill Lynch, Cleve., 1993—. Republican. Roman Catholic. Office: Merrill Lynch 1375 E 9th St Ste 10 Cleveland OH 44114-1724

CLAASSEN, SHERIDA DILL, newspaper executive; b. Columbia, Mo., Nov. 27, 1948; d. Wilben Hubert and Dorothy Louise (Richardson) Dill; m. Arthur Norman Claassen, June 22, 1985; children: April Dill, Christopher Wilben. BJ, U. Mo., 1970; MBA, Pepperdine U., 1981. Editor Graphic Herald, Downers Grove, Ill., 1970-73; area editor Suburban Trib/Chgo. Tribune, 1973-78; copy editor San Jose (Calif.) Mercury, 1978-79, asst. metro. editor, 1979-81; city editor Wichita (Kans.) Eagle, 1981-82, asst. mng. editor, news, 1982-85, dir., R & D, 1985-91, exec. editor, 1991-94, v.p., assoc. pub., 1995—. Bd. dirs. Boys and Girls Club of Wichita, 1995—, Kids Voting Kans., 1995—, Roots & Wings, Wichita, 1989-91, Leaderhip Kans. Class 1989, Leadership 2000 Class 1991, Wichita; bd. advisors Salvation Army of Wichita, 1995—; v.p., bd. dirs. Wichita Festivals, Inc., 1988-91. Recipient Excellence in Entrepreneurship award Knight-Ridder, Inc., 1990. Office: Wichita Eagle PO Box 820 Wichita KS 67201-0820

CLAASSEN, W(ALTER) MARSHALL, employment company executive; b. St. Paul, Jan. 16, 1943; s. Walter Marshall and Marie Christine (Petersen) C.; m. Nancy Rector Alcock, Mar. 2, 1974; children: Katherine, Walter. BA, U. Mo., 1966, BJ, 1966. Sr. adminstr. Honeywell, Inc., Chgo., 1968-74; pers. dir. Lyon-Healy, div. of CBS, Inc., Chgo., 1974-78; mgr., corp. placement CF Industries, Long Grove, Ill., 1978-82; mgr. of recruiting Newark Electronics, Chgo., 1983-84; dir. human resources Swift, div. of Reichold Chem., Downers Grove, Ill., 1984-86, ECM, Inc., Schaumburg, Ill., 1986-87; pres. GBX, Inc., dba Express Personnel Svcs. of Vernon Hills, Ill. and Express Pers. Svcs. of Palatine,, Ill., 1988—. Bd. dirs. Elk Grove-Schaumburg Mental Health Ctr., 1975-77, Pvt. Industry Coun. of Lake County, Waukegan, Ill., 1990—, chmn., 1994—; bd. dirs. Pvt. Industry Coun. Found., 1992—. Lt.(j.g.) USNR, 1966-68. Mem. No. Ill. Bus. Assn., Libertyville-Vernon Hills C. of C., Lake County C. of C., Lincolnshire C. of C., Arlington Heights C. of C., Univ. Mo. Alumni Assn., Phi Delta Theta. Republican. Quaker. Home: 25030 N Pawnee Rd Barrington IL 60010-1380 Office: Express Personnel Svcs 1530 E Dundee Rd Ste # 140 Palatine IL 60067

CLACK, FLOYD, state legislator; b. Houston, Dec. 21, 1940; m. Brenda J. Jones; children: Michael, Mia. BS, Tex. So. U., 1965; MA, Ea. Mich. U., 1972. State rep. Mich. Ho. Reps., Dist. 80, 1983-94, Mich. Ho. Reps., Dist. 48, 1995—; vice chmn. Dem. black caucus, majority whip, mem. standing com. labor, standing con. coll. & univs., standing com. constrn. rev. & women's rights, chmn. standing com. corrections, ad hoc spl. com. alternatives fo rhigh risk students, 2d vice chmn. majority caucus, mahority vice chmn., standing com. civic rights, mem. standing com. mental health, standing com. corp. & fin., standing com. ins., criminal justice com., ad hoc spl. com. studying Mich. fin. inst., Mich. Ho. Reps. Mem. exec. bd. Genesee County Dem. Com., Mich.; co-chmn. Mayor's Hail Task Force; del. Dem. Nat. Conv.; chmn. Genesee County Jackson for Pres. Caucus, Jesse Jackson for Pres. com., Flint, 1988; founder Floyd Clack Cmty Project; chmn. Mott Found. Tribute Com. & Floyd J. McCree Tribute Com.; mem. New Paths, Inc. Adv. Coun.; bd. dirs. Eastside Teen Ctr.; bd. trustees Don Haley Scholar; founder, bd. dirs. Youth Leadership Ins., Flint. Recipient Svc. award Concerned Pastors Assn., 1982, Greater Flint Afro-Am. Hall of Fame, Toll Fel., 1987, David McMahon award Mech. Edn. Assn., 150% Achiever Lansing Stae Jour. Mem. NEA, Am. Corrections Assn., Mich. Corrections Assn., United Tchrs. Flint (chmn. human rels. com.), John W. Stevenson Lodge No. 56, Lions (charter, past v.p., Man of Yr. 1982), Met. C. of C., Urban League, Kappa Alpha Psi. Home: 3120 Helber St Flint MI 48504-2921*

CLAMME, ROSALIE ANN, library director; b. Anderson, Ind., Oct. 31, 1947; d. Allen James and Lena Mae (VanNess) Grose; m. Robert Allen Clamme, June 27, 1969; children: Lisa Rene, Anne Kathryn, Robert David. BS in Journalism, Ball State U., 1969, MLS, 1981. Cert. librarian, Ind. Asst. editor Trap & Field Mag., Indpls., 1970-71; legal sec. Yarling, Funnell, Robinson & Lamb, Indpls., 1971-73; office mgr. Jay County Prosecutor, Portland, Ill., 1974-80; library dir. Jay County Pub. Library, Portland, 1981—; pres. East Ind. Area Library Svc. Authority, 1984-86, Ind. Library Fedn. Endowment, Indpls., 1994—. Dir. United Way of Jay County, 1977-85; treas., co-chair prom parents Jay County H.S., 1987, 92; mem. task force Portland Strategic Plan, 1982-91. Mem. ALA, Ind. Library Fedn., Cinn. League (pres., v.p., founder 1987—), Kappa Kappa, Kappa Sorority (treas. 1981—). Democrat. Lutheran. Home: Route 3 Box 101 Portland IN 47371 Office: Jay County Public Library 131 E Walnut Portland IN 47371

CLANCY, TERRENCE PATRICK, food service executive; b. Milw., May 10, 1955; s. William Francis and Lois Ann (Helmes) C.; m. Mary Regina Freund, May 19, 1979; children: Evan Patrick, Shannon Eileen. BS, U. Wis. Stout, 1979. Asst. dir. food svc. St. Joseph's Hosp., Ft. Wayne, Ind., 1979-81; food svc. dir. Szabo Food Svc. Co., Ft. Wayne, 1981-87; gen. mgr. ARA Svc., Ft. Wayne, 1987-90; pres., CEO Classic Cafe, Inc., Ft. Wayne, 1990—; sec. Am. Soc. Hosp. Food Svc. Adminstrs., Ft. Wayne, 1980--81; chmn. delinquency com. Ins. Employees Fed. Credit Union, Ft. Wayne, 1985-92. Bd. dirs. Anthis Career Ctr., Ft. Wayne, 1990—. Roman Catholic. Home: 6226 Tolbert Ct Fort Wayne IN 46804-4280 Office: Classic Cafe Inc 1300 S Clinton St Fort Wayne IN 46802-3506

CLAPP, BETTY S., journalism educator; b. Garrettsville, Ohio, June 20, 1950; d. Paul C. and Margaret (Newcomb) C. BA, Hiram (Ohio) Coll., 1972; MA, Kent State U., 1982. Editor, mng. editor Western Reserve Mag., Garrettsville, Ohio, 1973-80; editor, assoc. instr. Cleve. State U., 1986-88, lectr., 1990—, adj. faculty, 1993—; part time faculty Lakeland C.C., Kirtland, Ohio, 1991—. coord. regional pub. workshop series for coll. journalists, Cleve., 1994—. Mem. Soc. Profl. Journalists, Coll. Media Advisors, Inc. Office: Cleve State U Dept Comm 2001 Euclid Ave Cleveland OH 44115

CLAPP, C(HARLES) EDWARD, research chemist, soil biochemistry educator; b. Holden, Mass., Aug. 29, 1930; s. Charles Edward and Natalie (Shepard) C.; m. Betty Joyce Huff, June 13, 1953; children: David L., Duane E., Jonathan C., Jay J. BS, U. Mass., 1952; MS, Cornell U., 1954, PhD, 1957. Asst. soil chemist Cornell U., Ithaca, N.Y., 1952-56; organic chemist Agrl. Rsch. Svc., USDA, Beltsville, Md., 1956-61; rsch. chemist Agrl. Rsch. Svc., St. Paul, 1961—; from asst. prof. to prof. U. Minn., St. Paul, 1961—. Author: (with others) Utilization of Municipal Wastewater and Sludge on Land, 1983, Role of Organic Matter in Moder Agriculture, 1986, Humic Substances II: In Search of Structure, 1989, Rhizosphere Dynamics, 1990, Interactions at the Soil Colloid-Soil Solution Interface, 1991, Organic Substances in Soil and Water: Natural Constituents and Their Influences on Contaminant Behaviour, 1991, Humic Substances in the Global Environment and Implications on Human Health, 1994, Advances in Soil Science: Soil Management and Greenhouse Effect, 1995; editor, author (with others): Humic Substances in Soil and Crop Sciences: Selected Readings, 1990, Sewage Sludge: Land Utilization and the Environment, 1994, Humic Substances and Organic Matter in Soil and Water Environment: Characterization, Transformation and Interaction, 1996. Y's men officer YMCA, Roseville, Minn., 1965-70; boy and cub scout leader Boy Scouts Am., Roseville, 1965-75. Hon. Sr. Rsch. fellow U. Birmingham, Edgbaston, Eng., 1988-89, Hebrew U. Jerusalem, Rehovot, Israel, 1989. Fellow Soil Sci. Soc. Am. (rep. to Internat. Humic Substance Soc. 1990—), Am. Soc. Agronomy, Am. Inst. Chemists; mem. Internat. Soil Sci. Soc., Internat. Humic Substances Soc. (chair nominating com. 1986-90, treas. 1993-96), Soil Water conservation Soc., Sigma Xi, Gamma Sigma Delta. Mem. United Ch. of Christ. Office: USDA Agrl Rsch Svc/U Minn 1991 Upper Buford Cir Saint Paul MN 55108-6024

CLARDY, MARY JOANNE, gifted education educator; b. Kansas City, Mo., Sept. 11, 1955; d. Norris Alger and Mary Jane (Brewster) Smith. AA, Miss. County Coll., 1985; BA, Gov.'s State U., University Park, Ill., 1988, MA in English, 1992. Cert. tchr, Ill., Mo.; cert. gifted students tchr., Ill. Tchr. Sch. Dist. #160, Country Club Hills, 1989-94; tchr., coord. gifted program Sch. Dist. #159, Mokena, Ill., 1994—; instr. Mississippi County C.C., summers 1993—; instr. Joliet Jr. Coll. Active NOW. Mem. NEA, Internat. Platform Assn. Home: 206 N East St Wilmington IL 60481

CLARK, C. PHILLIP, III, investment broker; b. St. Louis, Mar. 11, 1958. BS in Bus., Webster Coll., St. Louis, 1981. Fin. planner Cigna Corp., St. Louis, 1981-87; regional mktg. mgr. Montsanto Co., St. Louis, 1988-91; investment broker A.G. Edwards & Sons Inc., St. Louis, 1992—. Bd. dirs. Devel. Disabilities Mo., St. Louis, 1980-83, W.W. Johnson Life, St. Louis, 1988-90, Justice Coun. Ret. Citizens, St. Louis, 1980-83, United Way, St. Louis, 1994—, North Side Cmty. Ctr., St. Louis, 1995—, Citizens of Mo. Children, St. Louis, 1995—. Mem. Nat. Assn. Securities Dealers, Nat. Assn. Securities Profls., Sales and Mktg. Execs., Kappa Alpha. Democrat. Home: 4148 Enright Ave Saint Louis MO 63108-3022 Office: AG Edwards & Sons Inc 1 City Ctr Ste 1300 Saint Louis MO 63101-1893

CLARK, CARL ARTHUR, retired psychology educator, researcher; b. Oak Park, Ill., Sept. 20, 1911; s. Alfred Houghton and Mary (Geist) C.; m. Janet Picquet; 1 child, Peter Picquet. BA cum laude, Colo. Coll., 1948, MA, 1951; PhD, State U. Iowa, 1954. Mem. faculty Colorado Springs High Sch., 1948-50; rsch. asst. State U. Iowa, Iowa City, 1951-53; rsch. assoc. U. Chgo., 1953-54; prof. psychology Chgo. State U., 1954-76, chmn. psycol. dept., prof. emeritus, 1976—; adj. prof. U. Mo.-Rolla, 1976-77; rsch. evaluator Ford Found. projects, Chgo., 1963-66. Mem. editorial bd. Ill. Schs. Jour., 1966-76. Contbr. articles and revs. to profl. jours. Served with U.S. Army, 1942-45. Recipient Outstanding Achievement award Black Students Psychology Assn., 1973. Mem. AAAS, APA, N.Y. Acad. Scis., Sigma Xi. Home: 616 W Washington Ave Kirkwood MO 63122-3835

CLARK, CLIFFORD EDWARD, JR., history educator; b. BayShore, N.Y., July 13, 1941; s. Clifford Edward and Helen (LaPan) C.; m. Grace Williams, Aug. 20, 1966; children: Cynthia Williams, Christopher Allen, Susan McGrath. BA, Yale U., 1963; MA, Harvard U., 1964, PhD in Am. Civilization, 1968. History tutor Harvard U., Cambridge, Mass., 1966-67; instr. Amherst (Mass.) Coll., 1968-69, asst. prof., 1969-70; from asst. to assoc. prof. Carleton Coll., Northfield, Minn., 1970-80, prof. history, 1980—, M.A. & A.D. Hulings Prof. of Am. Studies, 1982—, dir. summer acad. programs, 1984—, chmn. history dept., 1986-89; cons. Minn. Humanities Commn., Mpls., 1976—, Minn. Hist. Soc., Mpls., 1982—; Northfield Sch. Bd., 1978-87; editl. cons. Winterthur Portfolio, Del., 1983-92. Author: Henry Ward Beecher, Spokesman for a Middle-Class America, 1978, The American Family Home, 1800-1960, 1986, (with others) The Enduring Tradition, 1996; editor: Minnesota in a Century of Change: The State and Its People Since 1900, 1989. Mem. Northfield Hist. Preservation Commn., 1986. Fellow Woodrow Wilson Found., 1964, 67; Demonstration grantee NEH, 1978, sr. fellow NEH, 1980; recipient Younger Humanist Summer Stipend, NEH, 1973. Mem. Am. Studies Assn., Am. Hist. Assn., Orgn. Am. Historians, Northfield Hist. Soc. Episcopalian. Home: 718 4th St E Northfield MN 55057-2316 Office: Carleton Coll Dept History One N College St Northfield MN 55057

CLARK, DAVID KEITH, lawyer, real estate developer; b. Lakewood, Ohio, July 28, 1952; s. Don Roger and Patricia Ann (Hunt) C.; m. Beth Moore Malone, June 14, 1980; children: Blaire Megan, Shannon Elizabeth. BArch, U. Ariz., 1977, BSBA, 1977; JD, U. Houston, 1980. Bar: Tex. 1980, U.S. Dist. Ct. (no., so. and ea. dists.) Tex. 1980, U.S. Ct. Appeals (5th cir.) 1980. Law librarian, clk. Baker, Botts, Vinson & Elkins, Houston, 1977-78; assoc. Baker, Brown, Sharman et al, Houston, 1980-82; asst. gen. counsel, devel. officer Cadillac Fairview, Dallas, 1982-87; devel. officer Prentiss Properties Urban Devel., Dallas, 1987-90; v.p. The Equity Group, Chgo., 1990-92; sr. v.p. LaSalle Ptnrs., Chgo., 1992—; bd. dirs. Don R. Clark M.D., P.C., Roswell, N.Mex., 1972—. Chmn. Dallas Urban Design Task Force, Mich. Ave. dist. task force, 1995. Mem. ABA (real estate, probate and trust sects.), Tex. Bar Assn. (real estate, probate and trust sects.), Urban Land Inst., Univ. Club Chgo., Leadership Dallas, Phi Delta Phi. Republican. Methodist. Home: 1184 Cedar Ln Northbrook IL 60062-3544 Office: LaSalle Ptnrs 200 E Randolph Chicago IL 60601

CLARK, GARY DANIEL, nurse anesthetist, educator; b. Granite City, Ill., Nov. 12, 1948; s. William A. and Winifred M. (Young) C.; m. Elizabeth Ann Alben, Aug. 20, 1970; children: Nicole Leigh, Jason Andrew. Diploma, St. Joseph's Sch. Nursing, Alton, Ill., 1969; diploma in grad. studies in nurse anesthesia, Truman Med. Ctr., 1973; cert. advanced clin. hypnosis, Acad. Clin. Hypnosis, 1976; BA in Health Care and Adminstrn., Ottawa (Kans.) U., 1981; cert. in gerontology, So. Ill. U., Edwardsville, 1984, MS in Adminstrn., 1985; EdD, Nova Southeastern U., 1995. RN, Kans., Ill., Mo.; CRNA. Chief nurse anesthetist Jackson County Hosp., Kansas City, Mo., 1973-76; didactic and clin. instr. anesthesia Truman Med. Ctr., Kansas City, 1973-76; pres., chief adminstr. Anestat, Inc., Albany, Mo., 1976-77; staff anesthetist St. Joseph's Hosp., Alton, 1977-80; chief anesthetist St. Anthony's Hosp., Alton, 1980-82; nurse anesthetist, clin. and didactic instr. anesthesia Sch. of Nurse Anesthesia, Washington U. Sch. Medicine, St. Louis, 1986—; adj. faculty So. Ill. U., Edwardsville; project dir. Ctr. for Addictions Rsch. & Edn.; lectr. in field. Med. editor, columnist, contbr. Sr. Citizen newspaper, 1986-90; contbr. lectr. articles to profl. publs. Former bd. dirs., chmn. program com. YMCA; founder, past pres. Alton Swim Team and Parents Club. 1st lt. Med. Svc. Corps, USAF, 1969-71. Mem. Am. Assn. Nurse Anesthetists, Ill. Assn. Nurse Anesthetists, Mo. Assn. Nurse Anesthetists. Roman Catholic. Home: 908 Hampton Ct Godfrey IL 62035 Office: Washington U Sch Nurse Anesthesia 660 S Euclid Ave Saint Louis MO 63110-1010

CLARK, GARY R., newspaper editor; b. Cleve., June 27, 1946; s. Dale Francis and Mary Louise (Rozeski) C.; m. Caryn Elaine Helm, Dec. 18, 1976; children: Jessica Lynn, Brian Michael. BA, Ohio State U., 1973, MA, 1978. Reporter Chronicle-Telegram, Elyria, Ohio, 1973-77; reporter The Plain Dealer, Cleve., 1978-88, state editor, 1988-89, nat. editor, 1989, city editor, 1989-90, mng. editor, 1990—; teaching assoc. Ohio State U., Columbus, 1977-78. Sgt. USMC, 1966-69, Vietnam. Mem. AP Mng. Editors, Am. Soc. Newspaper Editors, Investigative Reporters and Editors, Cleve. City Club. Office: The Plain Dealer 1801 Superior Ave E Cleveland OH 44114-2107*

CLARK, HENRY OGDEN, architect; b. Berwyn, Ill., Dec. 29, 1944; s. Charles Dhority and Agnes Theresa (Ogden) C.; m. Susan Jean Longini, Aug. 1967 (div. Aug. 1970); m. Fran Louise Hodges, Aug. 1991; 1 child, Colette Maria. Student, Reed Coll., 1962-64; BArch, U. Mich., 1969; MS in Creative Intelligence, Maharishi European Research U., Weggis, Switzerland, 1980. Registered architect, Ga., Iowa, Wash., Ca. Intern Anderson, Notter, Boston, 1970-71, Enteleki, Salt Lake City, 1971-73; ctr. chmn. Internat. Meditation Soc., Traverse City, Mich., 1973-75; architect Sizemore Assocs., Atlanta, 1975-79; assoc. prof. art Maharishi Internat. U., Fairfield, Iowa, 1979—; prin. Henry Ogden Clark, Architect, Fairfield, 1987—; v.p., bd. dirs. Merlin's Enterprises Internat., Fairfield, 1985-88; pres. Traverse Bay Group, Fairfield, 1982—, Traverse City, 1988—; bd. dirs. Fairfield Architects and Planners, 1989—; v.p. Maharishi Heaven on Earth Devel. Corp., Malibu, Calif., 1990—; pres., chmn. bd. Maharishi Heaven on Earth Design Corp., Fairfield, 1991—; head architect 7000 Devel. Corp., Fairfield, 1991—. Co-author: Energy Planning for Buildings, 1978. Dir. Maharishi Sthapatya-Ved Inst. N.Am., 1992—; Natural Law Party candidate for Mich. 11th dist. U.S. Ho. of Reps. Recipient State Energy award State of Iowa, 1986. Mem. AIA. Home and Office: PO Box 1231 Fairfield IA 52556-1231

CLARK, JAMES MURRAY, state legislator; b. Indpls., Nov. 3, 1957; m. Janet Campbell. BA, Kenyon Coll., 1979; JD, Ind. U., 1982. Assoc. Clark, Clark, Pappas & Quinn, Attys. at Law, 1982; mem. from dist. 29 Ind. State Senate, Indpls., mem. govt. and regulatory affairs, mem. health and environ. affairs com., mem. ins. and fin. inst. and judiciary coms. Address: 1 Indiana Sq Ste 2200 Indianapolis IN 46204

CLARK, JAMES ROBERT, architect; b. Detroit, Dec. 5, 1950; s. Robert Emerson and Isabel Lucinda (Smith) C.; divorced; children: Shannon Marie, Brian James. BS in Arch., Lawrence Tech. U., 1975, BArch, 1976. Registered architect, Mich. Assessor West Bloomfield (Mich.) Twp., 1976-78; sales engr. Unistrut/GTE, Wayne, Mich., 1978-81, divsn. mgr., 1981-83; br. mgr. Unistrut/GTE, San Antonio, 1983-85; v.p., gen. mgr. Unistrut Corp., Salt Lake City, 1985-87; divsn. mgr. Busch Industries, Grand Rapids, Mich., 1987-93; real estate cons. Century 21 Property Ctr., Caledonia, Mich., 1993—; cons. Jr. Achievement, Salt Lake City, 1985-86. Cubmaster Boy Scouts Am., Grand Rapids, 1988-92; coach Lamar Park Youth, Wyoming, Mich., 1990-93. Home: 432 Pine Vista SE Kentwood MI 49548

CLARK, JEANENNE FRANCES, community health nurse specialist; b. St. Louis, Oct. 1, 1954; d. Pete Jr. and Marie (Risch) Stoplos; m. Richard Edward Clark, June 9, 1974; childen: Richard Paul, Jason Nicholas. Diploma, Jewish Hosp. Sch. Nursing, St. Louis, 1975; BSN cum laude, U. Mo., St. Louis, 1992; MPH, MSN, St. Louis U., 1996. Cert. critical care nurse. Staff nurse, acute medicine Jewish Hosp., St. Louis, 1975-77; critical care nurse, med.-coronary ICU St. Anthony's Med. Ctr., St. Louis, 1977-88; staff nurse level III burn/trauma, respiratory ICU Barnes Hosp., St. Louis, 1988-91; staff nurse trauma ICU St. Louis U. Hosp., 1991-94; pub. health nurse Family Care Health Ctrs., 1994, community health supr., 1994—, acting health svcs. dir., 1995; amb., mem. Critical Care Nursing Delegation, Russia, Hungary, 1992; program coord. Immunization Info. Sys., St. Louis U., 1996. Contbr. articles to profl. jours. Recipient St. Anthony's Star of Excellence award, 1986, Recognition award Barnes Hosp. Nursing Svc., 1990, Dean's Disting. Nurse award U. Mo., St. Louis, 1992; AACN scholar. Mem. ANA (inst. constituent mems. on nursing practice 1991-94), APHA, AACN (clin. practice spl. interest cons. region 14 1990-92, pres. St. Louis chpt. 1991-92, chmn. pub. rels. 1988-90, health care policy and legis. editor St. Louis chpt. 1989-95; cert. corp., exam. writer 1990-92), Mo. Nurses Assn. (2 v.p. 3d dist. 1994-96, coun. nursing practice 1987-91, med.-surg. chmn. 1989-91), Mo. Pub. Health Assn. (2d v.p. St. Louis chpt. 1995-96), LWV, Sigma Theta Tau. Home: 9939 Affton Pl Saint Louis MO 63123-4305

CLARK, JEFFERY D., stockbroker; b. Rochester, N.Y., May 5, 1960. BA, Ohio State U., 1988. Stockbroker Venture Capital, Columbus, Ohio, 1988-92, Prudential Securities, Cin., 1992—. Mem. Cin. Opera. With U.S. Army, 1980-83. Republican. Office: Prudential Securities Inc # 1900 525 Vine St # 1900 Cincinnati OH 45202-3105

CLARK, JOHN W., architect; b. Chgo., July 16, 1954; s. Arthur Dewitt and Jane (Dickson) C.; m. Patricia Nealon, Oct. 1, 1985; children: Adrienne, Anna. Student, Ecole des Beaux Arts, Versailles, France, 1976; BArch, U. Ill., 1977, postgrad., 1978-79; postgrad., Art Inst. Chgo., 1984-86, Northwestern U., 1993-94. Instr. English Formosa Plastic Corp., Taipei, Taiwan, 1973-74; architect Hammond, Beeby & Babka, Chgo., 1977-82; mem. faculty Art Inst. Chgo., 1983-87; ptnr. Cordogan, Clark & Assocs., Chgo., 1984—; cons. Gt. Lakes Solar Engring., 1977-79, Chgo. Park Dist., 1993, Chinese Am. Devel. Corp., 1993; vis. juror Art Inst. Chgo., 1982—, U. Ill., 1982—. Prin. works include Heritage Performing Arts Ctr., Alma, Mich., Hollywood Casino, Aurora, Ill., Citibank, Chgo. and suburban Ilinois, Allen Residence, Oakbrook, Ill., Ford Music, Chgo., Dunham Hall, Aurora U.; represented in permanent collections Chgo. Art Inst., Chgo. Hist. Soc. Recipient Community Beautification award City of Aurora, 1991; Indep. Study grantee Nat. Soc. Arts and Letters, Evanston, Ill. Mem. AIA (Disting. Bldg. award 1989, Divine Detail award 1992, N.E. Ill. and Chgo. chpts.), Arch. Club of Chgo., Arts Club of Chgo. Office: Cordogan Clark & Assocs 716 N Wells St Chicago IL 60610-3510

CLARK, KAREN, state legislator. BS, Coll. St. Teresa, Winona, Minn. Mem. Minn. Ho. of Reps., 1981—, chmn. housing com., mem. various coms. Recipient Martin Luther King, Jr. award, 1987, Minn. Alliance Progressive Leadership award, 1991, Leadership award Nat. Gay & Lesbian Task Force. Office: Minn State Senate State Capital Bldg 503 State Office Bldg Saint Paul MN 55155

CLARK, KENNETH WILLIAM, mechanical engineer; b. Royal Oak, Mich., July 6, 1960; s. Ralph Waldo and Shirley Anne (Cutright) C. BS in Mech. Engring., Mich. Tech. U., 1983. Engr.-in-tng. status, Mich. Design engr. Troy (Mich.) Design Svcs., 1983-84; application engr. NOK, Inc., Bloomfield Hills, Mich., 1984-86, supr. application engring., 1986-88; asst. mgr. application engring. Freudenberg-NOK, Plymouth, Mich., 1988-92, mgr. application engring., 1992-94; mgr. air/fuel systems Auttocom, Plymouth, Mich., 1995-96; mgr. engine sealing Freudenberg-NOK, Plymouth, Mich., 1996—. Mem. Soc. Automotive Engrs. Office: Freudenberg-NOK 47690 E Anchor Ct Plymouth MI 48170-2400

CLARK, KEVIN H., stockbroker; b. Grand Rapids, Mich., Aug. 7, 1956. BA, Hope Coll., 1978. Ltd. ptnr. Edward D. Jones, St. Louis, 1982-89; regional mgr. Raffens Burger Hughes, Indpls., 1989-92; broker JJB Hilliard W L Lyons, Holland, Mich., 1992—; Mem. Holland Sch. Bd., 1994—, Holland Econ. Devel. Corp., 1987—; past pres. Great Holland United Way, 1984-90. Mem. C. of C., Rotary. Republican. Mem. Dutch Reformed Church. Home: 1354 Heather Dr Holland MI 49423-4498 Office: JJB Hilliard W L Lyons Inc 38 W 8th St Holland MI 49423-3104

CLARK, LANCE DAVID, communications educator; b. Huntington, Ind., Aug. 5, 1989; s. Doyle Paule and Janet K. (Geroge) C.; m. Mary Lynn Pfister, Aug. 5, 1989; children: Tianna, Larissa. BA, Huntington Coll., 1989; MA, Regent U., Virginia Beach, Va., 1991. Announcer WKSV Radio Sta., Virginia Beach, 1989-90; prodn. dir. WXRI Radio Sta., Virginia Beach, 1990-91; resident dir. of life Anderson (Ind.) U., 1991-93; instr. comms. Huntington (Ind.) Coll., 1993-95; video producer Brethren Prodns., Huntington, 1993-95. Mem. Expo Com., C. of C., Huntington, 1995. Mem. Nat. Assn. Religious Broadcasters, Soc. Profl. Journalists, Nat. Assn. TV Profls. Republican. United Brethren. Office: Huntington Coll 2300 College Ave Huntington IN 46750

CLARK, LARRY DALE, insurance company executive; b. Muncie, Ind., Oct. 20, 1951; s. Francis Marion and Estil Louise (Dean) C.; m. Sarah Ann Copley, Sept. 19, 1970; children: Michael, Michelle. Student, Am. Coll. CLU. Asst. mgr. Welles Dept. Store, Mincie, Ind., 1967-73, Masons Dept. Store, Mincie, Ind., 1973-74; ins. salesman Nat. Life & Accident, Mincie,

Ind., 1974-82; agy. mgr. Western So. Ins., Cin., 1983—; tchr. new agt. tng. sch. Western & So. Life, Chgo., 1991-94. Coach Youth Basketball, Chatham, Ill., 1988-94; book-keeper Girls High Sch. Basketball Team, Chatham. Mem. Nat. Assn. Life Underwriters, Gen. Agts. and Mgrs. Assn. Home: 743 Hackeberry Dr Chatham IL 62629

CLARK, LAUREL JAN, adult education educator, author, editor, minister; b. Denver, Jan. 29, 1957; d. Clyde C. Dale and Ethelyn (Goldberg) Fuller; m. John Gordon Clark, May 29, 1994. BA with honors, U. Mich., 1978; PsD, Sch. Metaphysics, 1987; DD, Coll. Metaphysics, 1992, DM, 1994. Cert. tchr., Mo.; ordained min. Interfaith Ch. Metaphysics. Tchr. adult edn. Sch. Metaphysics, 1979—; dir., teaching supr. Sch. Metaphysics, St. Louis, Ann Arbor, Mich., 1979-82; field dir. Sch. Metaphysics, 1984-94; cert. counselor Interfaith Ch. Metaphysics, Windyville, Mo., 1987—; author SOM Pub., Windyville, Mo., 1981—; mng. editor Thresholds Quarterly, Windyville, Mo., 1990—; sec. Sch. Metaphysics, Windyville, Mo., 1990—, v.p., 1988—; internat. adv. bd. Unity and Diversity World Coun., L.A., 1995—; bd. dirs. Sch. Metaphysics; spkr. U. Mo., St. Louis, U. Mo., Columbia, Am. Bus. Women's Assn., Boulder (Colo.) Sheriff's Dept., Pa. State Univ., others. Author: Shaping Your Life, 1994, Concentration, 1995; co-author: Power of Structure, 1987, Total Recall, 1993; contbr. articles to profl. jours. Mem. Am. Holistic Health Assn., Interfaith Alliance, Inst. Noetic Scis., Phi Beta Kappa. Home and Office: Sch Metaphysics HCR 1 Box 15 Windyville MO 65783

CLARK, MARK A., stockbroker; b. Grinnell, Iowa, Feb. 5, 1957. Bachelor's, Cornell Coll., 1979. Coll. football coach Western Ky. U., Bowling Green, Ky., 1979-84; asst. football coach Lee High U., Bethlehem, Pa., 1984-89; stockbroker Edward D. Jones & Co., Cedar Rapids, Iowa, 1989—. Republican. Office: Edward D Jones & Co 4015 Mount Vernon Rd SE Cedar Rapids IA 52403-3801

CLARK, MICHEL DESERE, clergyman; b. Kewanee, Ill., Aug. 1, 1951; s. Walter Everett and Betty Elizabeth (Bjornson) C.; m. Karen Lynn Carhart, June 5, 1976; children: Erin Marie, Megan Elizabeth. AB, Augustana Coll., Rock Island, Ill., 1973; MDiv, Luth. Sch. Theology, Chgo., 1977. Ordained to ministry Luth. Ch., 1977. Asst. pastor First Luth. Ch., Decatur, Ill., 1977-79; pastor First Luth. Ch., Sherrard, Ill., 1979-85, Grace Luth. Ch., Knoxville, Ill., 1985—; cons. Evang. Luth. Ch. in Am., Chgo., 1992-95, dean S.W. conf. No. Ill. Synod, rockford, 1988-94, chair pastoral and profl. support com., 1994—. Author: Augsburg Home Bible Study, 1992. Chair Knox Twp. Youth Coun., 1989—. NEH grantee, 1972. Mem. Rotary Internat. Home: 104 Bayard Ave Knoxville IL 61448 Office: Grace Luth Ch South and Timber Knoxville IL 61448

CLARK, NATHAN STEWART, JR., rail transportation company executive; b. Sharon, Pa., Sept. 21, 1959; s. Nathan Stewart and Ruth Mae (Tevendale) C.; m. Mary Kathleen Haessly, Oct. 29, 1988 (div. June 1992); 1 child, Jonathan Andrew; m. Christine Ann Wisniewski, Oct. 16, 1994. BS in Bus. Logistics, Pa. State U., 1984. Cert. in transp. and logistics. Machinery operator Bessemer & Lake Erie R.R. Co., Greenville, Pa., 1978; rail planner Ohio Rail Transp. Authority, Columbus, 1980-81; R.R. expeditor L-E-P Expediting Svc., Pitts., 1981-85; sales trainee Conrail, St. Louis, 1985-86; sales rep. Conrail, Toledo, Ohio, 1986-87; account exec. Conrail, Dearborn, Mich., 1987-90, area mgr., 1990-95, mgr. customer devel., 1995—. Co-author: Bessemer and Lake Erie Railroad - In Color, 1994; co-editor art/poetry mag. Polyphon, 1979. Mem. Am. Soc. Transp. and Logistics (cert. mem., pres. Mich. chpt. 1990, Rsch. Paper of Yr. 1992), Am. Rwy. Engring. Assn. Office: Conrail 17301 Michigan Ave Ste 350 Dearborn MI 48126-2734

CLARK, NOREEN MORRISON, behavioral science educator, researcher; b. Glasgow, Scotland, Jan. 12, 1943; came to U.S., 1948; d. Angus Watt and Anne (Murphy) Morrison; m. George Robert Pitt, Dec. 3, 1982; 1 child, Alexander Robert. BS, U. Utah, 1965; MA, Columbia U., 1972, M.Phil., 1975, PhD, 1976. Rsch. coord. World Edn. Inc., N.Y.C., 1972-73; asst. prof. Sch. Pub. Health Columbia U., N.Y.C., 1973-80, assoc. prof., 1980-81; assoc. prof. Sch. Pub. Health U. Mich., Ann Arbor, 1981-85, prof., chmn. dept. health behavior and health edn., 1985-95, Marshall H. Becker prof. of pub. health, 1995—, dean, 1995—; adj. prof. health adminstrn. Sch. Pub. Health Columbia U., 1988—; prin. investigator NIH, 1977—; mem. adv. com. pulmonary diseases Nat. Heart, Lung & Blood Inst., Rockville, Md., 1983-87, mem. adv. com. for prevention, edn. and control, 1987-91, coordinating com. Nat. Asthma Edn. Program, 1991—; assoc. Synergos Inst., N.Y.C., 1987—. Author: (monograph) Education for Development, 1980; co-author: Evaluation of Health Promotion, 1984; contbr. articles on disease self-management to profl. jours.; editor Health Edn. Quarterly, 1985—; mem. editorial bd. Women in Health, Advances in Health Edn. and Promotion, Home Health Care Services Quarterly. Hon. dir. Freedom from Hunger Found., Davis, Calif., 1980—; bd. dirs. Aaron Diamond Found., 1990—, Family Care Internat., N.Y.C., 1987—, Am. Lung Assn., N.Y.C., 1988—, chair govt. rels., 1994—. Fellow Soc. Pub. Health Edn. (pres. 1985-86, Disting. Fellow award 1987); mem. APHA (chair health edn. sect. 1982-83, Derryberry award in behavioral sci. 1985, Disting. Career award 1994), Am. Thoracic Soc. (Health Edn. Rsch. award Nat. Asthma Edn. Program 1992), Internat. Union Health Edn., Soc. Behavioral Medicine, Coun. Fgn. Rels., Overseas Devel. Coun., Pi Sigma Alpha. Office: U Mich Sch Pub Health 109 S Observatory St Ann Arbor MI 48109-2029

CLARK, PAMELA KAY, school counselor; b. Plymouth, Ind., Apr. 25, 1946; d. Orville Trowbridge and Bea Marie (Hester) Phelps; m. Robert Love Wilkinson Clark, Aug. 30, 1970; children: Allison Jennings, Amber Phelps. BS, Ball State U., 1968, MA in Edn., 1983. Nat. cert. counselor; nat. cert. sch. counselor. Counselor Culver (Ind.) Girls Acad., 1970; tchr. Manual High Sch., Denver, 1968-71, Hamilton Southeastern High Sch., Noblesville, Ind., 1981-83; sch. counselor Noblesville High Sch., 1983-95; counselor North Ctrl. H.S., Indpls., 1995—. Pres., bd. dirs. Zionsville (Ind.) Awareness: Alcohol and Drug Abuse, 1990. Mem. AACD, Am. Sch. Counselor Assn. (chmn. pub. rels. com. 1988-89, Outstanding Leadership citation 1986, 87, 88), Ind. Sch. Counselor Assn. (pres. 1988, author brochure 1985, Past Pres. award 1988), Ind. Assn. for Counseling and Devel. (pres. 1990-91). Episcopalian. Home: 1080 Williamsburg Ln Zionsville IN 46077-1158 Office: North Ctrl HS 1801 E 8th St Indianapolis IN 46240

CLARK, RAYMOND JOHN, Academic Administrator; b. Highland Park, Mich., May 10, 1951; s. John Harold and Mima Jean (Baker) C.; m. Sally Ann Narhi, June 14, 1975; 1 child, Arvid John. AA, Oakland Community Coll., 1971; BS in Animal Husbandry, Mich. State U., 1973, BS Agribus. and Natural Resources Edn., 1974, MA in Agrl. Edn., 1976, PhD in Agrl. and Ext. Edn., 1991. Tchr. Grand Ledge (Mich.) High Sch., 1974-76; instr. Mich. State U., East Lansing, 1976-80; dir. coop. edn. Soumi Coll., Hancock, 1980-81; county extension dir. Mich. State U., Hancock, 1981-84; dist. farm mgmt. agt. Mich. State U., Marquette, 1984-88, acting regional extension supr., 1988-90; county extension dir. Mich. State U., Ontonagon, 1990—; extension advisor Armenian/Am. Extension Project, Stepanavan Region Republic of Armenia, 1993, Stepanavan and Tumanian Regions, 1994; presenter in field. Chmn. agrl. bus. com. Houghton (Mich.) C. of C., 1972-74; bd. dirs. Copper Country Farm Bur., Houghton, 1978-80; bd. dirs., mem. exec. com. Vol. Action Ctr. of the Keeweensaw, 1992—; chair Cmty. Cares Coalition, 1995. Mem. Nat. Assn. Agrl. Extension Agts., Mich. Assn. Agrl. Extension Agts., Mich. 4-H Internat. Assn., Ontonagon County C. of C. (bd. dirs. 1992—), Phi Delta Kappa, Epsilon Sigma Phi (v.p., pres., chair chpt. internat. com. and nat. internat com.). Lutheran. Home: RR 1 Box 54 Pelkie MI 49958-9714 Office: Mich State U 725 Greenland Rd Ontonagon MI 49953-1492

CLARK, RUSSELL GENTRY, federal judge; b. Myrtle, Mo., July 27, 1925; s. William B. and Grace Frances (Jenkins) C.; m. Jerry Elaine Burrows, Apr. 30, 1959; children: Vincent A., Viki F. LLB, U. Mo., 1952. Bar: Mo. 1952. Mem. firm Woolsey, Fisher, Clark, Whiteaker & Stenger, Springfield, Mo., 1952-77; judge U.S. Dist. Ct. (we. dist.) Mo., Kansas City, 1977-91, sr. judge, 1991—. 2d lt. U.S. Army, 1944-46. Fellow Am. Bar Found.; mem. ABA, Internat. Platform Soc., Mo. Bar Assn. (continuing legal edn. com. 1969), Greene County Bar Assn. (dir. 1968-71), Kiwanis (past pres. Springfield chpt.). Democrat. Methodist. Club: Kiwanis (past pres. Springfield chpt.). Office: US Dist Ct 3100 US Courthouse 222 N John Q Hammons Pky Springfield MO 65806-2530

CLARK, STANLEY RALPH, agricultural engineer; b. Abilene, Kans., Oct. 29, 1945; s. Ralph I. and Mary E. (Taylor) C.; m. LeAnn Diehl, Feb. 4, 1964; children: Julia, Brad. BS in Agrl. Engring., Kans. State U., 1967, MS in Agrl. Engring., 1970. Design engr. Allis-Chalmers, Independence, Mo., 1967-68, Hesston (Kans.) Corp., 1974-77; instr. Kans. State U., Manhattan, 1969-73; project engr. Charles Machine, Perry, Okla., 1977-78; advanced devel. engr. Hay & Forage Industries, Hesston, 1979-92; engring. mgr. Gt. Plains Mfg., Assaria, Kans., 1992—. Patentee double sickle mechanism, forage harvesting device, wide windrow pickup , bale shape indicator, seed packing wheel, planter trash wheel, material injection sys. Mem. Hesston Planning Commn., 1984—, Unified Sch. Dist. 460 Bd. Edn., Hesston, 1986-95. Mem. Am. Soc. Agrl. Engrs. (bd. dirs. 1986-88, 95—). Methodist. Office: Gt Plains Mfg Inc PO Box 245 Assaria KS 67416-0218

CLARK, SUSAN MATTHEWS, psychologist; b. Newton, Kans., Aug. 5, 1950; d. Glenn Wesley Matthews and Jane Buckles; m. S. Bruce Clark, Aug. 14, 1971; children: Casandra Jane, Ryan Matthews. BME, Wichita State U., 1971, MME, 1975, MA, 1982; PhD, North Tex. State U., 1985. Elem. tchr. Derby (Kans.) Pub. Schs., 1972-74; profl. musician Amarillo (Tex.) Symphony, 1974-77; psychol. cons. Achenbach Ctr., Hardtner, Kans., 1983-85; psychologist VA Med. Ctr., Wichita, Kans., 1984-85, St. Francis Acad., Inc., Salina, Kans., 1986-89, Psychiat. Clinic Wichita, 1989-93; gen. mgr. Affiliated Psychiat. Svcs., Wichita, 1993-95; psychologist Charter Clinic, Wichita, Kans., 1995—; bd. dirs. Salina Coalition for the Prevention of Child Abuse, 1986-87. Author: Grant, 1987. Bd. deacons Plymouth Congl. Ch., Wichita, 1989-92, mem. bd. Christian Edn., 1993. Recipient: Phi Kappa Phi, Mu Phi Epsilon, Psi Chi. Mem. APA, Nat. Acad. Neuropsychology, Southwestern Psychol. Assn., Kans. Psychol. Assn., Wichita Area Psychol. Assn., Kans. Assn. Profl. Psychologists. Republican. Congregationalist. Office: Charter Clinic 8911 E Orme Ste C Wichita KS 67207

CLARK, THOMAS B., SR., real estate broker; b. Ann Arbor, Mich., Jan. 21, 1943; s. Thomas W. and Helen (Sheldon) C.; m. Dianne Stribley, Dec. 4, 1970; children: Thomas B. Jr., Andrea Lynn. BA, U. Mich., 1964. Dir. rec. U. Mich., Ann Arbor, 1965-70; sr. auditor Touche Ross (now Deloitte and Touche), Detroit, 1970-72; acctg. mgr. E.R.I.M., Ann Arbor, 1972-75; owner/developer Clark Apts., Ann Arbor, 1975—; bd. dirs. Kenitis Corp. Mem. Ann Arbor Apt. Assn. (bd. dirs.). Address: PO Box 7822 Ann Arbor MI 48107-7822 Office: 621 S Forest Ave Ann Arbor MI 48104-3114

CLARK, TONY, state legislator. Student, Mich. State U., 1990-91; BS in Polit. Sci., N.D. State U., 1994, BS in History Edn., 1996. Mem. Dist. 44 N.D. Ho. of Reps., 1994—, mem. edn., govt. and vet. affairs coms.; mem. interim budget on human svcs. com. N.D./S.D. Commn.; sec. Dist. 44 Rep. Com., 1994—. Sec. Dist. 44 Rep. Com.; adult leader Boy Scouts Am. Mem. Phi Kappa Phi. Office: 600 East Blvd Bismarck ND 58505

CLARKE, INGRID GADWAY, academic ombudsman, consultant; b. Bad Homburg, Hesse, Fed. Republic Germany, Sept. 21, 1942; came to U.S., 1964, naturalized, 1982; d. Johann Kajetan and Irmgard (Schneider) Rebholz; m. David Scott Clarke, Dec. 24, 1984. B.A. equivalent, Johann Wolfgang Goethe Universität, Frankfurt, Fed. Republic Germany, 1964; M.A., Memphis State U., 1965; postgrad. Tulane U., 1965-69; Ph.D., So. Ill. U., 1984. Instr. So. Ill. U., Carbondale, 1969-74, univ. ombudsman, 1974—, also chairperson bd. dirs. students' legal assistance program, 1980-86 . Mem. Carbondale Human Relations Com., 1974-76; chairperson Carbondale Fair Housing Bd., 1978-82. Fulbright scholar, 1964-67. Mem. Fulbright Alumni Assn., Univ. and Coll. Ombudsman Assn. (founder and first pres. 1985-86), Soc. Profls. in Dispute Resolution Delta Phi Alpha. Avocations: opera; tennis; skiing. Office: So Ill U Office Univ Ombudsman Carbondale IL 62901

CLARKE, LEWIS DOUGLAS, lawyer; b. Waukegan, Ill., July 4, 1936; s. Lewis D. Sr. and Jean (Sager) C.; m. Deborah A. Wuellner, June 21, 1991; 1 child, Douglas. BA, Denison U., 1958; JD, Am. U., 1965. Asst. corp. counsel D.C., Washington, 1966-70; ptnr. Snyder, Clarke, Fouts & Assocs., Waukegan, Ill., 1970—; commr. State Bar Com. on Character and Fitness, 1993—; lectr. Am. U., Washington, 1968-69; charter mem. Jefferson Inn, Am. Inns of Ct., Ill., 1989—. Contbr. articles to profl. jours. Bd. chmn. Music Ctr. Lake County, Waukegan, 1970-72. Mem. Appellate Lawyers Assn., Ill. State Bar Assn., D.C. Bar Assn., Lake County Bar Assn. (chmn. appellate com. 1987—), Waukegan Yacht Club (judge advocate 1979-89), Waukegan City Club. Home: 1105 W Keith Ave Waukegan IL 60085-1741 Office: Snyder Clarke Fouts & Assoc 700 S Lewis Ave Waukegan IL 60085-6173

CLARKE, MICHAEL ROBERT, lawyer, educator; b. Golden, Colo., Oct. 18, 1966; s. Michael Ellsworth Clarke and Karen Rebecca (Hopper) Clarke-Kraut; m. Christine Marie Hyde, Sept. 14, 1991. BA in Psychology, Quincy (Ill.) Coll., 1988; JD, St. Louis U., 1991. Bar: Mo., Ark. Legal assistance atty. U.S. Army, West Point, N.Y., 1991-92, chief claims atty., 1992-94; criminal def. atty. U.S. Army, Ft. Riley, Kans., 1994—; adj. faculty Upper Iowa U., Ft. Riley, 1995—. Supr. Big Bros./Big Sisters, U.S. Mil. Acad., 1993-94. Capt. U.S. Army, 1991—. Mem. ABA, ATLA, Nat. Assn. Criminal Def. Attys. Democrat. Roman Catholic. Home: 1509 Yorktowne Cir Manhattan KS 66503 Office: US Army Trial Def Svc Patton Hall Fort Riley KS 66442

CLARKE, OSCAR WITHERS, physician; b. Petersburg, Va., Jan. 29, 1919; s. Oscar Withers and Mary (Reese) C.; m. Susan Frances King, June 18, 1949; children—Susan Frances, Mary Elizabeth, Jennifer Ann. B.S., Randolph Macon Coll., 1941; MD, Med. Coll. Va., 1944. Intern Boston City Hosp., 1944-45; resident internal medicine Med. Coll. Va., 1945-46, 48-49, fellow in cardiology, 1949-50; pvt. practice specializing in internal medicine and cardiology Gallipolis Holzer Med. Ctr., Ohio, 1950—; pres., bd. dirs. Holzer Clinic Inc., 1981-89; bd. dirs. Ohio Valley Devel. Co., Gallipolis, Cmty. Improvement Corp.; pres. Ohio State Med. Bd.; chmn. Ohio Med. Edn. and Rsch. Found., Commn. Heart Attack Alert Program NIH, 1995-96; pres. Gallipolis Cty Bd. Helath, 1955—, Gallia County Heart Coun., 1955—. Contbr. articles to med. jours. V.p. Tri-State Regional coun. Boy Scouts Am., 1957; pres. Tri-State Community Concert Assn., 1957-59; trustee Med. Meml. Found., Holzer Hosp. Found. Capt. M.C., AUS, 1946-48, ETO. Recipient John Stewart Bryant pathology award Med. Coll. Va., 1943. Fellow ACP, Royal Soc. Medicine; mem. AMA (chmn. coun. on ethics and jud. affairs 1991—), Am. Heart Assn., Gallia County Med. Soc. (pres. 1953), Cen. Ohio Heart Assn. (Merit medal 1960, trustee), Ohio Med. Assn. (pres. 1973-74, Disting. Svc. citation 1988, Physician of Century 1996), Am. Soc. Internal Medicine (Disting. Internist award 1992), Alpha Omega Alpha, Sigma Zeta, Chi Beta Phi. Presbyterian. Club: Rotary (pres. 1953-54). Home: 108 Spruce Knls Gallipolis OH 45631-1066 Office: Holzer Med Clinic PO Box 344 Gallipolis OH 45631-0344

CLARKE, RICHARD STEWART, security company executive; b. Louisville, Aug. 23, 1934; s. Jesse Edward and Sarah Elizabeth (Pilkerton) C.; m. Constance Jean Koga, Sept. 29, 1956; children: Stewart Michael, Stephen James, Susan Michelle (dec.). BS in Biology/Sociology, Ill. State U., 1958; postgrad., Ill. Benedictine Coll., 1955-56, DePaul U., 1956-57, 80-81, N.E. Mo. State Coll., 1959, U. Chgo., 1960-61. With Autoquip Corp., Chgo., 1952-54, asst. gen. mgr., 1956-57, indsl. engr., 1958-62, prodn. mgr., v.p. mfg., 1962-73; with Ky. Trailer, Louisville, 1953, Shafer Bearing, Downers Grove, Ill., 1955-56; salesman Ency. Britannica, Chgo., 1956; sci. tchr., writer Wilmette (Ill.) Bd. Edn. and Children's Press, 1958-62; pres. Darci Assocs., 1973-82, Alert Security Cons., Inc., Chgo., 1982—; cons. in field; sci. fair dir. Chgo. Area Tchrs. Sci. Assn. and Wilmette Bd. Edn., 1960-62; sci. lectr./writer; trainer indsl. mgmt.; dir. Parassistance Corp., Chgo., 1976-80. Co-designer 3-dimensional board game: Skew, 1958; developer various ednl./sci. rsch. methods; author poetry: The Chicago Spirit, 1988-91; editor: St. Margaret Mary Today, 1992. Com. chmn. South Hinsdale (Ill.) Improvement Assn., 1952-53; mem. Rodgers Park Community Coun., Chgo., 1967—; pres. Northtown Fair Housing Com., Chgo., 1966-67; campaign aide Ill. Constl. Conv., Chgo., 1970-71; leader, sect. pres. Christian Family Movement, Chgo., 1957-70; ch. leader, tchr. St. Margaret Mary Parish Orgn., Chgo., 1966—, coun. pres., 1986-88; bldg. fund chmn. St. Margaret Mary Gym & Social Ctr., Chgo., 1987-89, auxiliary minister, 1982—. Mem. Security Assocs., Nat. Fire & Burglary Alarm Assn., No. Ill. Indsl. Mgmt. Soc. (exec. officer), Kappa Delta Pi (hon. life), Pi Gamma Mu (hon. life). Republican. Roman Catholic. Office: Alert Security Cons Inc 2453 W Morse Ave Chicago IL 60645-4611

CLARKSON, WILLIAM MORRIS, children's pastor; b. Newport, R.I., Feb. 23, 1954; s. George and Lois Ruth (Terwilligar) C.; m. Janice Aiko Enoki, June 16, 1978; children: Kyle Hideo, Keith Hiroshi. BA, Muhlenberg Coll., Allentown, Pa., 1976; MPA, Ball State U., Muncie, Ind., 1977. Advanced cert. in Employee Relations Law, Mich., Ind. Research asst. Ball State U. Bur. Govtl. Research, Muncie, Ind., 1977; field staff cons. Ind. U., Div. Pub. Service, Indpls., 1977-78; adminstrv. asst. City of Midland, Mich., 1978-81, pers. dir., 1981-91; asst. city mgr. for pers. and risk mgmt., 1991-96; adj. instr. pub. adminstrn. Ctrl. Mich. U., Mt. Pleasant, 1982-91, mem. MPA program adv. bd., 1988-91; mem. planning and evaluation com. Mich. Inst. for Pub. Adminstrn., 1989-91; dir. apptd. com. on act 312/PERA Det., Mich. Employment Rels. Commn., 1987-91; chmn. edn. and tng. com. Mich. Mcpl. League, 1991-95; mem., govtl. sector chmn. Midland Area Chamber Quality Coun., 1992-96; mem. Dow Chem. Cmty. Adv. Panel, 1994—. Co-author: Manual Indiana Counties Model Personnel Policies, 1978. Bd. dirs. Salvation Army Adv. Bd., Midland Mich., 1978-81, trustee Meml. Presbyn. Ch., Midland Mich., 1984-87, Loaned Exec. United Way Midland Mich., 1985; vice-chair Midland County Drug Abuse Resistance Edn. Project, 1989-95. Recipient Mcpl. Achievement award Mich. Mcpl. League 1984; named one of Outstanding Young Men of Am., 1981. Mem. Midland Area Soccer League Club Mich. Mem. Assembly of God. Home: 3806 Westbrier Ter Midland MI 48642-6658 Office: City of Midland 333 W Ellsworth St Midland MI 48640-5134

CLARSON, STEPHEN JOHN, chemistry educator, university dean; b. Rawmarsh, Eng., Apr. 20, 1959; came to the U.S., 1985; s. Samuel and Eileen Mary (Hadfield) C.; m. Marie Elizabeth Frantz, Aug. 26, 1989; children: Julia Marie, Heather Marie. BA with honors, U. York, 1980, DPhil, 1985. Chartered chemist. Rsch. fellow U. Cin., 1985-88, asst. prof., 1988-94, assoc. prof., 1994—, asst. dean, 1995—; dir. Polymer Rsch. Ctr., 1995—. Co-author: Siloxane Polymers, 1993; mem. editl. bd. trends in Polymer Sci., 1993—; contbr. articles to sci. jours.; patentee in field in U.S. Mem. Royal Soc. Chemistry, Am. Chem. Soc., Polymer Networks Group (Rubber Divsn.). Office: U Cin Materials Sci Engring Cincinnati OH 45221

CLARY, BRADLEY GRAYSON, lawyer, educator; b. Richmond, Va., Sept. 7, 1950; s. Sidney Grayson and Olive Jean (Beazley) C.; m. Mary-Louise Hunt, July 31, 1982; children: Benjamin, Samuel. BA magna cum laude, Carleton Coll., 1972; JD cum laude, U. Minn., 1975. Bar: Minn. 1975, U.S. Dist. Ct. Minn. 1975, U.S. Ct. Appeals (10th cir.) 1977, U.S. Ct. Appeals (8th cir.) 1979, U.S. Ct. Appeals (6th cir.) 1980, U.S. Ct. Appeals (7th cir.) 1981, U.S. Supreme Ct. 1986, U.S. Ct. Appeals (4th cir.) 1989, U.S. Ct. Appeals (9th cir.) 1991. Assoc. Oppenheimer Wolff & Donnelly, St. Paul, 1975-81, ptnr., 1982—; adj. prof. Law Sch. U. Minn., Mpls., 1985—; adj. instr. William Mitchell Coll. Law, St. Paul, 1995—. Author: Primer on the Analysis and Presentation of Legal Argument, 1992. Vestryman St. John Evangelist Ch., St. Paul, 1978-81, pledge drive co-chmn. 1989-90; mem. alumni bd. Breck Sch., Mpls., 1981-85, 89—, exec. com., 1991—; mem. adv. bd. Glass Theatre Co., West St. Paul, Minn., 1982-87; mem. antitrust adv. panel dept. health State of Minn., 1992-93. Mem. ABA (adv. group antitrust sect. 1987-89, corp. counseling com.), Minn. Bar Assn. (program chmn. antitrust sect. 1986-87, treas. 1987-88, vice-chmn. 1989-90, co-chmn. 1990-92), Phi Beta Kappa. Office: Oppenheimer Wolff & Donnelly 3400 Plaza VII Bldg 45 S 7th St Minneapolis MN 55402

CLARY, ROSALIE BRANDON STANTON, timber farm executive, civic worker; b. Evanston, Ill., Aug. 3, 1928; d. Frederick Charles Hite-Smith and Rose Cecile (Liebich) Stanton; BS, Northwestern U., 1950, MA, 1954; m. Virgil Vincent Clary, Oct. 17, 1959; children: Rosalie Marian Hawley, Frederick Stanton, Virgil Vincent, Kathleen Elizabeth. Tchr., Chgo. Public Schs., 1951-55, adjustment tchr., 1956-61; faculty Loyola U., Chgo., 1963; v.p. Stanton Enterprises, Inc., Adams County, Miss., 1971-89; author Family History Record, genealogy record book, Kenilworth, Ill., 1977—. also lectr. Leader Girl Scouts U.S., Winnetka, Ill., 1969-71, 78-86, Cub Scouts, 1972-77; badge counselor Boy Scouts Am., 1978-87; election judge Rep. Com., 1977—; vol. Winnetka Libr. Genealogy Projects Com., 1995—. Mem. Nat. Soc. DAR (Ill. rec. sec. 1979-81, nat. vice chmn. program com. 1980-83, state vice regent 1986-88, state regent 1989-91, rec. sec. gen., 1992-95), Am. Forestry Assn., Forest Farmers Assn., North Suburban Geneal. Soc. (governing bd. 1979-86), Winnetka Hist. Soc. (governing bd. 1978-90, 95—), Internat. Platform Assn., Delta Gamma (mem. nat. cabinet 1985-89). Roman Catholic. Home: 509 Elder Ln Winnetka IL 60093-4122 Office: PO Box 401 Kenilworth IL 60043-0401

CLASPILL, JAMES LOUIS, finance company executive; b. St. Louis, Dec. 31, 1946; s. Rufus Ira and Alma Elizabeth (Holzum) C.; m. Bonnie Lee Roth, Feb. 13, 1971; 1 child, Jennifer Yvonne. BA in Polit. Sci., S.W. Mo. State U., Springfield, 1968; MBA in Fin., St. Louis U., 1974. Dept. mgr. Venture Stores, St. Louis, 1970-74, J.C. Penny Co., St. Louis, 1974-77; ins. broker, agy. mgr. Aetna Life and Casualty, St. Louis, 1977-82; pres., CEO Claspill Fin. Group, St. Charles, Mo., 1982—; CEO Winterhawk Corp., Channel Islands, 1990—; exec. v.p. Bi-Golden Mfg. Co., 1991—; cons. Bank of Eng., London, 1986—, Garwick Mortgage Bankers, Sydney, Australia, 1986—, Internat. C. of C., 1986-88. Candidate Mo. State Senate, 1978, Dem. candidate 2d dist. Mo. U.S. House of Reps., 1996; campaign organizer Litton for U.S. Senator, 1974. Sgt. U.S. Army, 1968-70, Vietnam. Recipient Million Dollar Round Table award Nat. Assn. of Life Underwriters, 1979, 80, 81. Mem. VFW, Regional Commerce Growth Assn., Better Bus. Bur., St. Charles C. of C., Nat. Hist. Soc., Internat. Assn. Financiers (v.p. 1985-86), Am. Legion, Lions Club. Roman Catholic. *

CLAUSEN, ERIC N., earth science educator, university program director; b. Ithaca, N.Y., July 2, 1943; s. Robert T. and Edna (Rublee) C. BA, Columbia U., 1965; PhD, U. Wyo., 1969. Asst. prof. earth sci. Minot (N.D.) State U., 1968-72, assoc. prof. earth sci., 1972-79, prof. earth sci., 1979—; dir. Midcontinent Inst., Minot State U., 1990—; dir. N.D. Geographic Alliance, 1995—. Home: 1120 11th St NW Minot ND 58703-2114 Office: Minot State Univ Division of Science Minot ND 58707

CLAUSER, ANGELA FRANCES, medical surgical, pediatrics and geriatrics nurse; b. Leavenworth, Kans., June 25, 1955; d. Donald F. Sr. and Agnes Angela (Forge) C. AA, Kansas City (Kans.) Jr. Coll., 1984; BSN, Pitts. State U., 1986. RN, Kans.; cert. provider CPR, Am. Heart Assn. Sec. U.S. Army, Ft. Leavenworth, Kans., 1978, 79-80, USAF Acad., Colorado Springs, Colo., 1981-82, VA, Leavenworth, 1982-84; staff nurse St. John's Hosp., Leavenworth, 1989—, unit edn. coord., 1995—. Mem. Nurses Svc. Orgn., Pitts. State U. Alumni Assn., Kans. City Jr. Coll. Alumni Assn.

CLAUSING, ALICE, state legislator; b. June 7, 1944. BA, U. Wis., Oshkosh. Property mgr.; mem. from dist. 10 Wis. State Senate, Madison, 1992—, mem. child abuse and neglect prevention bd., mem. Minn.-Wis. boundary area com., mem. Miss. River Pkwy. com. Mem. Wis. Assn. of Lakes, John Muir Sierra Club. Office: 1314 Wilson Ave Menomonie WI 54751-2927*

CLAY, FRANKLIN DELANO, advertising executive; b. Ashland, Ky., Apr. 8, 1947; s. Edward and Herma (Holbrook) C.; 1 chld, Jessica C. Student, Columbus Coll. Art and Design, 1965-70. Graphic designer Howard Swink Advt., Marion, Ohio, 1970-73; art dir. George Banta Co., Columbus, 1973-75, Hammeroff Advt., Columbus, 1975-76; owner/pres. Clay Assocs., Columbus, 1976—; lectr. in field. Program chmn. Greater Marion (Ohio) Arts Coun., 1971-73. Recipient Addy award, 1975. Mem. Columbus Soc. Communicating Arts (program dir. 1974-75). Home: 2724 Big Sur Lewis Center OH 43035 Office: 1550 Lewis Center Rd Lewis Center OH 43035

CLAY, MARGARET LEONE, community psychologist, consultant; b. St. Joseph, Mo., Oct. 23, 1923. BS with distinction, U. Mich., 1956, MS, 1958, PhD, 1962. Teaching fellow psychology dept. U. Mich., Ann Arbor, 1958-59, lectr., 1963-71, rsch. asst., 1956-60, asst. rsch. psychologist, 1960-62, assoc. rsch. psychologist Mental Health Rsch. Inst., 1962-82, asst. dir., 1965-68, asst. prof. psychiatry dept. Med. Sch., 1975-82, asst. prof. emeritus, 1982—; pvt. practice human svcs. cons. Hillman, Mich., 1982—; mem.

faculty extension svc. U. Mich. Sch. Pub. Health, Ann Arbor, 1969-72; mem. vis. faculty Rutgers U. Summer Sch. Alcohol Studies, New Brunswick, N.J., 1972-76; mem. bd. rsch. advisors Walden U., Naples, Fla., 1979—; bd. dirs. Thunder Bay Cmty. Health Svcs., 1983—, chmn. bd., 1993-95. Contbr. articles to profl. jours. Mem. Gov.'s Sect. 20 Rev. Com., Lansing, Mich., 1976; mem. Gov.'s Task Force on Drinking Drive Problem, Lansing, 1970-74; bd. mem. Gov.'s Adv. Commn. on Substance Abuse, Lansing, 1976-83; coun. mem. Statewide Health Coord. Coun., Lansing, 1977-83; mem. Mich. Coun. on Crime and Delinquency, Lansing, 1979—, pres., 1981-83; bd. mem. Mich. Coalition on Substance Abuse, 1986—, Shelter, Inc., 1989-92, N.E. Mich. Cmty. Partnership for Prevention, 1991—, No. Regional Acad./Cmty. Health System, 1993—; bd. dirs. Northeast Mich. Comm. Mental Health Bd., 1993—, chmn., 1996—. Recipient Disting. Svc. award Mich. Alcohol and Addiction Assn., 1977, Outstanding Svc. award Mich. Prevention Assn., 1993, Award for Outstanding Svc. in Prevention, 1993; named Vol. of Yr. Nat. Coun. on Alcoholism, Mich., 1985. Mem. APHA, APA (vis. psychologist 1976-78), Am. Assn. Correctional Psychologists (sec.-treas. 1975-77), N.Am. Assn. Alcohol Problems (program chmn. 1970-72), Alcohol and Drug Problems Assn. N.Am. (chmn. rsch. com. 1973-75, program chmn. 1976-78, bd. dirs. 1980-82, Outstanding Svc. award 1978), Mich. Pub. Health Assn. (hon. life, chmn. mental health div. 1969-70). Office: PO Box 251 Hillman MI 49746-0251

CLAY, WILLIAM LACY, congressman; b. St. Louis, Mo., Apr. 30, 1931; s. Irving C. and Luella (Hyatt) C.; m. Carol A. Johnson, Oct. 10, 1953; children: Vicki, Lacy, Michelle. B.S. in Polit. Sci, St. Louis U., 1953. Real estate broker, from 1964; mgr. life ins. co., 1959-61; alderman 26th Ward St. Louis, 1959-64; bus. rep. state, county and municipal employees union, 1961-64; edn. coordinator Steamfitters local 562, 1966-67; mem. 91st-104th Congresses from 1st Mo. dist., 1969—; ranking minority mem. econ. & ednl. opportunity com. Served with AUS, 1953-55. Mem. NAACP (past exec. bd. mem. St. Louis), CORE, St. Louis Jr. C. of C. Democrat. Office: US Ho of Reps 2306 Rayburn Bldg Washington DC 20515-0005*

CLAY, WILLIAM LACY, JR., state legislator; b. St. Louis, July 27, 1956; s. William L. and Carol Ann (Johnson) C.; m. Ivie Lewellen, Jan. 24, 1992. BS in Polit. Sci., U. Md., Coll. Park, 1983. Cert. paralegal; lic. real estate salesman, Mo. State senator Mo. Gen. Assembly, Jefferson City, 1983—. Chmn. Mo. Jesse Jackson 1988 Presdl. Campaign; Jackson del. to 1988 Dem. Nat. Conv.; committeeman to Dem. Nat. Com.; bd. dirs. William L. Clay Scholarship and Rsch. Fund. Mem. Ams. Dem. Action (Outstanding Legis. Mo. chpt. 1985, 86). Roman Catholic. Office: Mo State Senate Capitol Building Jefferson City MO 65101-1556

CLAYBORN, CHRISTIN LYNN, engineer; b. Battle Creek, Mich., May 8, 1968; d. Bill and Gloria (Zink) Clayborn. BS, Western Mich. U., 1990; MBA, Oakland U., 1994. Programmer/analyst Volkswagen Am., Auburn Hills, Mich., 1990-91; cons. Aida Info. Techs., Southfield, Mich., 1992-95; analyst Chrysler Corp., Centaline, Mich., 1993-95; sr. engr. Gen. Dynamics, Sterling Heights, Mich., 1995—; cons., programmer Ford Motor Co., Dearborn, Mich., 1992-93. Computer Sci. Faculty scholar Western Mich. U., Kalamazoo, 1985. Mem. IEEE (chair 1995—), Assn. for Computer Machinery, Upsilon Pi Epsilon (readong sec. 1989-90).

CLAYBORNE, JAMES F., state legislator. Ill. state sen., 1995—. Office: First Ill Bank Bldg 1327 Missouri Ave No 422 East Saint Louis MO 62201

CLAYBOURNE, FRANK, lawyer; b. Albert Lea, Minn., July 7, 1916; s. Morton F. and Nellie (Hill) C.; m. Ingrid Larsen, Sept. 25, 1940; children: Stephen, Philip, Marcia. BA, U. Minn., 1937, LLB, 1943. Bar: Minn. 1943, U.S. Dist. Ct. Minn. 1944, U.S. Ct. Appeals (8th cir.) 1945, U.S. Supreme Ct. 1945. Grain buyer Cargill, Inc., Mpls., 1937-40; naval officer USN, 1943-44; atty. Doherty, Rumble & Butler, St. Paul, 1944—; chmn. Minn. Supreme Ct. Adv. Com. on rules of Criminal Procedure, St. Paul, 1971-91. Gen. counsel Minn. Rep. Party, St. Paul, 1950-74; chmn. St. Paul Rent Control Bd., 1946-48. Fellow Am. Coll. Trial Lawyers; mem. Minn. State Bar Assn. (pres. 1979-80), Midland Hills Country Club, St. Paul Athletic Club, Order of Coif. Home: 2436 Beverly Rd Saint Paul MN 55104-4902 Office: Doherty Rumble & Butler 30 E 7th St 2800 Minn World Trade Ctr Saint Paul MN 55101-4901

CLAYBURGH, RICHARD SCOTT, state legislator; m. Jane Clayburgh; 2 children. BA, Concordia Coll., Moorhead, Minn., 1982; MBA, U. N.D., 1990, JD, 1994. Bar: N.D. 1994, Minn. 1994. Atty., state rep. dist. 17, 1989—; atty. Warcup & Clayburgh, Grand Forks; mem. state and fed. govt., human svcs., vet. affairs, appropriations and govt. ops. divsn. coms. N.D. Ho. Reps. Bd. dirs. N.D. Spl. Olympics, chmn. State Summer Games, 1990, 91; bd. dirs. Grand Forks Sr. Citizen Assn. Mem. ABA, Minn. Bar Assn., N.D. Bar Assn., Nat. Fedn. Ind. Bus., Grand Forks C. of C. Republican. Home: 1109 S 12th St Grand Forks ND 58201-5410*

CLAYPOOLE, ROBERT EDWIN, distribution service company executive; b. Elizabeth, N.J., July 6, 1936; s. Nelson A. and Mary J. (Fox) C.; m. Nancy P. Tetzlaff, May 12, 1962; children: Patricia, N. Catherine, Kimberly, Christine, Robert, Michael. B.C.E., Cornell U., 1959, M.B.A., 1961. Plant mgr. GATX Terminals, Carteret, N.J., 1964-66; mgr. European Ops. GATX Terminals, Barcelona, Spain, 1966-68, GATX European Ops., Antwerp, Belgium, 1968-70; asst. mgr. ops. GATX Terminals, Chgo., 1970-78, v.p. ops., 1978-80, CEO, pres., 1980-94, CEO, chmn., 1994-96; treas., dir. Chgo. Dist. Waterways Assn., 1974-77; dir., treas. Ind. Liquid Terminals Assn., Washington, 1981-83, vice chmn., 1983-84, chmn., 1984-85. Chmn. GATXGood Govt. Program, Chgo., 1981—; pres. Fairhaven Civic Assn., Barrington, Ill., 1976. Recipient Profl. Mgmt. award Cornell Sch. Bus. and Pub. Adminstrn., Ithaca, N.J., 1981. Mem. Cornell Univ. Coun., Beefeater club, Biltmore Country Club, Barrington Tennis Club, The Tower, Stone Harbor Country Club, Sawgrass Country Club, KC. Republican. Roman Catholic. Office: GATX Terminals Corp 500 W Monroe St Fl 43rd Chicago IL 60661-3630

CLAYSON, SUSAN HOLLIS, art historian, educator; b. Chgo.. BA, Wellesley Coll., 1968; MA, UCLA, 1975, PhD, 1984. Asst. prof. art history Wichita State U., 1978-82, U. Ill., Chgo., 1984-85; vis. asst. prof. Northwestern U., Evanston, Ill., 1982-84; asst. prof. Northwestern U., Evanston, 1985-90, assoc. prof. art history, 1991—; McCormick prof. teaching excellence Northwestern U., Evanston, Ill., 1993—, assoc. dean grad. sch., 1995—. Author: Painted Love: Prostitution of French Art of the Impressionist Era, 1991; contbr. articles to profl. jours. ACLS fellow, 1989. Office: Northwestern U Dept Art History 1859 Sheridan Rd Evanston IL 60208

CLAYTON, BRUCE DAVID, pharmacology educator; b. Grand Island, Nebr., Mar. 9, 1947; s. John David and Eloise Regnier (Camp) C.; m. Francine Evelyn Purdy, June 19, 1971; children: Sarah Elizabeth, Beth Anne. Student Hastings Coll., 1965-67; BS, U. Nebr., 1970; D of Pharmacy, U. Mich., 1973. Resident U. Mich., 1972-74; asst. prof. clin. pharmacy Creighton U., Omaha, 1974-77; assoc. prof. Coll. Pharmacy, U. Nebr. Med. Center, Omaha, 1978-85, vice chmn. dept. pharmacy practice, 1978-84, interim chmn., 1984-85; prof., chmn. dept. pharmacy practice, U. Ark. Med. Scis., Little Rock, 1985-87, prof. dept. pharmacy practice, 1985-89; prof., assoc. dean Coll. Pharmacy Butler U., Indpls., 1989—; unit coord. perinatal pharmacy svcs. Univ. Hosps., Omaha, 1978-80; clin. pharmacist pediatrics Ark. Children's Hosp., Little Rock, 1986-89; Ciba-Geigy vis. prof., Australia and N.Z., 1979; S.E. Wright traveling fellow Pharm. Soc. Australia, 1983; lectr. in field. Author: (with S.A. Ryan) Handbook of Practical Pharmacology, 1977, 2d edit., 1980; (with J.E. Squire) Basic Pharmacology for Nurses, 7th edit., 1981, Handbook of Pharmacology in Nursing, 1984, Handbook of Pharmacology, 1987, (with Yvonne Stock) Basic Pharmacology for Nurses, 11th edit., 1996; contbr. articles to profl. jours. Recipient Bristol award for professionalism, 1970; named Nebr. Hosp. Pharmacist of Yr., 1978. Mem. Nebr. Soc. Hosp. Pharmacists (pres. 1978-79, dir. 1979-80), Ind. Soc. Hosp. Pharmacists, Am. Soc. Hosp. Pharmacists (coun. on organizational affairs 1979-82, com. on nominations 1980-85, chmn. 1985, ho. of dels. 1980-88, coun. on ednl. affairs 1987-89, chmn. 1989), Am. Pharm. Assn. (APHA-PAC bd. govs., 1995—), Ind. Pharm. Assn. (bd. dirs. 1991—, v.p. 1995-96), Am. Assn. Colls. of Pharmacy, Rho Chi.

CLAYTON, ROBERT MORRISON, III, state legislator; b. Hannibal, Mo., Aug. 20, 1969; s. Robert M. II and Frances (Price) C. BA, So. Meth. U., 1991; JD, U. Mo., Kansas City, 1994. Ptnr. Clayton, Curl & Rhodes, Hannibal, 1994—; mem. Mo. Ho. of Reps. from 10th dist., 1995—. Sr. articles editor: The Urban Lawyer, 1993. Mem. Historic Bethel German Colony, Hannibal Arts Coun. Recipient Pres.'s award Kansas City Met. Bar Assn. 1994. Mem. Mo. Bar Assn., Hannibal C. of C., Jaycees, Delta Theta Phi, Kappa Alpha. Democrat. Office: Mo Ho of Reps PO Box 1032 Hannibal MO 63401*

CLAYTON, VERNA LEWIS, state legislator; b. Hamden, Ohio, Feb. 28, 1937; d. Matthews L. and Yail (Miller) Lewis; m. Frank R. Clayton, Feb. 4, 1956; children: Valerie Clayton Euneman, Barry L. Office mgr., Village of Buffalo Grove, Ill., 1972-78, village clk., 1971-79, village pres., 1979-91; mem. Ill. Ho. of Reps., Springfield, 1993—. Mem. Lake County Solid Waste Planning Agy. (chmn. tech. com., chmn. agy.), Nat. League of Cities (chmn. transp. and communications steering com.). Recipient Disting. Service award Amvets, 1981. Mem. Northwest Mcpl. Conf. (pres. 1983-84), Chgo. Area Transp. Study Council Mayors (vice chmn. 1981-83, chmn. 1985-91), Mcpl. Clks. Ill. (treas. 1978-79), Mcpl. Clks. Lake County (pres. 1977-78), Ill. Mcpl. League (bd. dirs., v.p. 1985-90, pres. 1989-90), Buffalo Grove Rotary Club (hon. mem.), Buffalo Grove C. of C. (bd. dirs.). Republican. Methodist. Home: 2831 Acacia Ter Buffalo Grove IL 60089-6634 Office: 314 McHenry Rd Ste D-1 Buffalo Grove IL 60089-6749 also: 2119 N Stratton Bldg Springfield IL 62706

CLEARY, MARK W., business executive; b. Detroit, Apr. 22, 1949. BS in Acctg., Xavier U., 1971. CPA, Mich. Sr. v.p. Staubach Co. Midwest Inc., Franklin, Mich., 1988-92; pres. Timmis Cleary Assocs., Bloomfield Hills, Mich., 1992-94; COO Plante & Moran, Cresa, L.L.C., Southfield, Mich., 1994—. Roman Catholic. Office: Plant Moran Cresa LLC 27400 NW Hwy PO Box 307 Southfield MI 48037

CLEARY, ROBERT EMMET, gynecologist, infertility specialist; b. Evanston, Ill., July 17, 1937; s. John J. and Brigid (O'Grady) C.; M.D., U. Ill., 1962; m. June 10, 1961; children—William Joseph, Theresa Marie, John Thomas. Intern, St. Francis Hosp., Evanston, 1962-63, resident, 1963-66; practice medicine specializing in gynecology and infertility, Indpls., 1970—; head Sect. of Reproductive Endocrinology and Infertility, Chgo. Lying-In Hosp., U. Chgo., 1968-70; head Sect. of Reproductive Endocrinology and Infertility, Ind. U. Med. Center, Indpls., 1970-80; prof. ob-gyn Ind. U., Indpls., 1976-80, clin. prof. ob-gyn, 1980—. Recipient Meml. award Pacific Coast Obstetrical and Gynecol. Soc., 1968; diplomate Am. Bd. Ob-Gyn, Am. Bd. Reproductive Endocrinology and Infertility. Fellow Am. Coll. Ob-Gyn, Am. Fertility Soc.; mem. Endocrine Soc.,Soc. Gynecol. Investigation, Pacific Coast Fertility Soc., Soc. Reproductive Endocrinologists, Soc. Reproductive Surgeons, N.Y. Acad. Scis., Sigma Xi. Roman Catholic. Contbr. articles in field to med. jours. Home: 7036 Dubonnet Ct Indianapolis IN 46278-1541 Office: 8091 Township Line Rd Indianapolis IN 46260-2495

CLEARY, SUE ALLENE SHORNEY, communication executive; b. Belding, Mich., Aug. 13, 1935; d. Robert Henry and Agnes Lorraine (Marvin) Shorney; m. Thomas Edward Cleary, June 8, 1956 (div. 1983); children: Margaret Beth, Michael Robert. BA, Denison U., 1957. Tchr. English Newark (Ohio) High Sch., 1957-58; tchr., dept. chair Milw. Downer Sem., 1958-64; tchr. U. Wis., Milw., 1964-68; editor-in-chief Presbyn. Synod of Wis., Madison, 1971-73; exec. sec. Wis. League Women Voters, Madison, 1974-84; adminstrv. asst. Wis. Strategic Devel. Com., Madison, 1984-85; exec. dir. Wis. Pub. Radio Assn., Madison, 1985—. Bd. dirs., pres. Dane County Adminstrs. of Vol. Svcs., Madison, 1986-91; bd. dirs., chair Cen. Wis. Ctr. Vol. Project, Madison, 1974-86; bd. dirs., sec. United Ministries in Higher Edn., 1965-74; bd. dirs., sec., treas. YMCA, Madison, 1982-84, 87-89; pres., bd. dirs. PICADA, 1989-95. Mem. Kappa Delta Pi, Kappa Kappa Gamma (pres. Milw. alumnae 1965-68, Madison, 1970-73). Office: Wis Pub Radio 821 University Ave Madison WI 53706-1412

CLEAVER, EMANUEL, II, mayor, minister; b. Waxahachie, Tex., Oct. 26, 1944; s. Lucky and Marie (McKnight) Cl; m. Dianne Donaldson, June 1970; children: Evan Donaldson, Emanuel III and Emiel Davenport (twins), Marissa Dianne. BA, Prairie View (Tex.) A&M Coll.; ThM, St. Paul Sch. Theology, Kansas City, Mo.; DD (hon.), Baker U., 1988. Ordained to ministry United Meth. Ch. Pastor St. James-Paseo United Meth. Ch.; mayor pro-tem City of Kansas City, 1987-91, mayor, 1991—; Lectr. to chs., schs., civic and social orgns. nationwide. Councilman Fifth Dist. City, 1979-91; chmn. City Coun. Plans and Zoning Com., 1984-87, Policy and Rules Com., 1987-91; mid-cen. regional v.p. So. Christian Leadership Conf., Drum Major for Justice award, 1991; founder, co-chair Kansas City Harmony In A World of Difference. Recipient Centurions Leadership award Greater Kansas City C. of C., 1987, William Yates Disting. Svc. Medallion William Jewel Coll., 1987, Pub. Svc. award Am.-Jewish Com., 1991, Junteenth Man of Yr. award Black Archives of Mid-Am. Inc., 1991, Disting. Citizen award Greater Kansas City Urban Affairs Coun., 1991, Community Svc./Leadership award Webster U., 1991, Disting. Svc. award Park Coll., 1991, Drum Major of Justice award Nat. SCLC, 1991, Friend of Youth award Boys & Girls Clubs, 1991, Outstanding Contbns. to Black Cmty. award Concerned Citizens Black Clergy of Atlanta, 1991, Rainbow award, 1992, 100 Most Influential Kansas Citians award Kansas City Globe, 1991, 92, 93, Bridge Builders award Kansas City Globem 1992, Harold L. Holiday Sr. Civil Rights award NAACP, 1992, Disting. Grad. award St. Paul Sch. Theology, 1993, Kansas City Anti-Apartheid award, 1993, James C. Kirkpatrick Excellence for Govt. award, 1993, Disting. Citizen of Midwest award NCCJ, 1993, Gov. award for local elected ofcl. of yr. State of Mo., 1994. Mem. NAACP, Greater Kansas City C. of C. (Centurions Leadership award 1987), Alpha Phi Alpha. Founder and co-chmn., Harmony In A World of Difference program. Office: Office of Mayor City Hall Fl 29 414 E 12th St Kansas City MO 64106-2705

CLEM, ALAN LELAND, political scientist; b. Lincoln, Nebr., Mar. 4, 1929; s. Remey Leland and Bernice (Thompson) C.; m. Mary Louise Burke, Oct. 24, 1953; children: Andrew, Christopher, Constance, John, Daniel. B.A., U. Nebr., 1950; M.A., Am. U., 1957, Ph.D., 1960. Copywriter, research dir. Ayres Advt. Agy., Lincoln, 1950-52; press sec. to Congressman Carl Curtis of Nebr., 1953-54, Congressman R. D. Harrison of Nebr., 1955-58; info. specialist Fgn. Agrl. Service, Dept. Agr., 1959-60; asst. prof. polit. sci. U. S.D., Vermillion, 1960-62; assoc. prof. U. S.D., 1962-64, prof., 1965—; assoc. dir. Govtl. Research Bur., 1962-76, chmn. dept. polit. sci., 1976-78; ptnr. Opinion Survey Assocs., 1964-88; state analyst Comparative State Elections Project, U. N.C., 1968-73; dir. Mt. Rushmore Presdl. Inst., 1970-71; mem. U.S. Census Bur. Adv. Com. on State and Local Govt. Stats., 1970-74. Author: several books, including Prairie State Politics: Popular Democracy in South Dakota, 1967, The Making of Congressmen: Seven Campaigns of 1974, 1976, American Electoral Politics: Strategies for Renewal, 1981, Law Enforcement: The South Dakota Experience, 1982, The Government We Deserve, 1985, 5th edit., 1995, Congress: Powers, Processes and Politics, 1989; contbr. articles to profl. jours.; editor: Contemporary Approaches to State Constitutional Revision, 1969. Mem. Vermillion City Coun., 1965-69; sr. warden St. Paul's Episcopal Ch., Vermillion, 1971-73, treas., 1996—. Nat. Conv. faculty fellow, 1964. Mem. Mensa, Midwest Polit. Sci. Assn. (exec. council 1970-72, editorial bd. Am. Jour. Polit. Sci. 1971-72), Am. Polit. Sci. Assn., Phi Beta Kappa, Phi Alpha Theta, Pi Sigma Alpha (nat. coun. 1986-89), Sigma Delta Chi. Republican. Club: Vermillion Golf Assn. (pres. 1986-87). Home: 902 Valley View Dr Vermillion SD 57069-3547 Office: Dept Polit Sci U SD Dept Polit Sci Vermillion SD 57069

CLEMENS, DEB FISCHER, state legislator, nursing administrator. DON; mem. S.D. Ho. of Reps., Pierre, 1995—, mem. health and human svcs., local govt. coms., 1995—. Democrat.

CLEMENS, RICHARD PAUL, JR., electrical engineer; b. Omaha, Sept. 30, 1956; s. Richard Paul, Sr. and Mary Ann (Greco) Clemens; m. Diane Bertha Snyder, May 30, 1981; children: Heather L. Brady, Beth A. Clemens. BSEE, U. Nebr., Lincoln, 1981. Registered profl. engr., Nebr. Design engr. Omaha Pub. Power Dist., Omaha, 1981-83, sr. design engr., 1983-85, lead elec. design engr., 1985-87, supr. simulator svcs., 1987-90, supr. elec./I & C engring., 1990-91, outage dir., 1991-95. Recipient Hon. Admiral-Navy of Nebr. award State of Nebr., 1972; ednl. scholar. Lincoln Engrs. Club, 1980. Mem. Am. Nuclear Soc. (interim chmn. 1987), NSPE (Young Engr. of Year 1985, program chmn. chpt. dir. 1990-92), IEEE, Profl. Operators' Soc. Republican. Office: Omaha Pub Power Dist PO Box 399 Fort Calhoun NE 68023

CLEMENS, T. PAT, manufacturing company executive; b. Hibbing, Minn., July 26, 1944; s. Jack LeRoy and Mildred (Cross) C.; div. 1992; children: Patrick Michael, Heather Kristen. BS in Econs. and Mgmt., St. Cloud State U., 1968; student of theology, Coll. St. Thomas, 1985-87. Sales adminstr. Transistor Electronics Co., Eden Prarie, Minn., 1969; head instnl. sales Chiquita Brands, Edina, Minn., 1970; dist. sales mgr. Menley & James Labs., Phila., 1971-75; owner, pres. T.P. Clemens Labs., Eagan, Minn., 1975—; instr community edn. Rosemount, Minn., 1977-78; bd. dirs. Rosemount Hockey, 1977-78, Relocation Assistance Assn. Am., 1984-85; v.p. Sch. Dist. #196 Booster Club, 1984-85; lectr. econs. to corps., high schs. and colls. in U.S., Scotland, Ireland, and Jamaica, 1979—. Author, editor: How Prejudice and Narcissism Control Economics of the United States and the World, 1979. Mem. Rosemount Cmty. Edn. Bd., 1985, chmn., 1986-87; chmn. speakers bur. Citizens Steering Com., 1984-85; coach Little League, 1970-82, 88-91; coach high sch. weight lifting team, 1975—; vol. worker with comatose children Kids 'n' Kinship program, 1988-92. Recipient letter of recognition for stopping armed robbery Dakota County Atty.'sDept., 1993. Mem. Internat. Platform Assn., Kids-N-Kinship Program. Home and Office: 1276 Vildmark Dr Eagan MN 55123-2801

CLEMENT, DANIEL ROY, III, accountant, assistant nurse, small business owner; b. Kirtland, Ohio, Apr. 2, 1943; s. Roy A. Jr. and Evelyn Violet (Hale Chase) C.; m. Jennifer Ilean Handley, July 10, 1965 (div. 1975); children: Elizabeth Ann Clement Baitt, Catherine Lynn Clement Holder; m. Barbara Jane Griffiths, Dec. 10, 1985. Student, Fenn Coll., 1961-63, Alexander Hamilton Inst., 1963-67, Am. Inst. of Banking, 1963-65, Lakeland Coll., 1965-70, Case Western Res. U., 1970-73, Lake Erie Coll., 1973-85. Shipping and cost acctg. Mentor (Ohio) Products, 1961; acctg. asst. N.Y. Cen. Transport, Cleve., 1963-65; acct. mgr. Am. Soc. of Metals, Novelty, Ohio, 1965-67; corp. fleet mgr. Addressograph Multigraph, Euclid, Ohio, 1967-72; treas. Debevec Salo & Assocs., Painesville, Ohio, 1972-74; with sales Pontiac Cadillac-Record Shack, Mentor, 1974-78; shipping coord. Ajax Mfg., Euclid, 1978-82; notary pub. Active Jr. C. of C., Mentor, Willoughby, Brunswick, Novelty, Lake County, 1962-78; mem. Congl. Task Force Pres. Bush, 1981-94. Republican. Methodist. Home and Office: 344 N Saint Clair St Painesville OH 44077-4039

CLEMENTS, MARY MARGARET, retired educator; b. Glasgow, Scotland, Dec. 23, 1925; came to U.S., 1928; d. Peter MacIntyre and Margaret Service (Mackay) Somerville; m. Carl Emery Clements, Aug. 28, 1954; children: Robert Peter, Margaret Ann Clements Fleming. BA in Edn., U. Akron, 1946; MA in History, U. Mich., 1950. Permanent cert. tchr., Ohio. Tchr. English, history and Spanish, Brunswick (Ohio) H.S., 1946-47, Covington (Ohio) H.S., 1947-51, Xenia (Ohio) Ctrl. H.S., 1951-58, Notre Dame Acad., Chardon, Ohio, 1970-74; tchr. Spanish, Villa Angela Acad., Cleve., 1968-70; tutor for pupil pers. Euclid (Ohio) Sch. System, 1963-67, 91-94, chmn. English dept. summer sch., 1980-91; ret., 1994; tchr. Spanish, English, and History Euclid (Ohio) Sch. System, 1995-96. Sec., coord. united thank offering Diocesan Episcopal Ch. Women, 1981-94; editor Episcopal Ch. Women's News Notes, 1984-94; mem., host family Am. Field Svc., Euclid, 1961-94; pres. PTA Coun., Euclid, 1974-76; provost Deanery Episcopal Ch., Cleve., 1993-95; trustee Ctr. for Human Svcs., Cleve., 1976-86; mem., past pres. Meridia Euclid Hosp., 1976-94; mem. Women's Caucus, Euclid, 1978-82; circulation mgr. Church Life Episcopal newspaper Diocese of Ohio, 1995. Recipient award for civic leadership Du Pont, 1980. Mem. AAUW (pres. 1978-80, Faculty Wives Assn. (pres. 1963-65). Home: 55 E 213th St Euclid OH 44123-1064

CLEMENTS, MICHAEL CRAIG, health services consulting executive, retired renal dialysis technician; b. Cin., Sept. 17, 1945; s. Marvin Hubert and Mildred Helen (Rabe) C.; m. Minnie Faye Pospisil, Dec. 1, 1972; children: Melissa Ayn, Michael Aaron. Student, U. Cin., 1968-70; EMT/paramedic, Good Samaritan Health Ctr., 1980. Cert. renal dialysis technician. Hemodialysis technician Christ Hosp., Cin., 1968-79; tech. svcs. dir. Dialysis Clinic, Inc., Cin., 1980-91; pres. Critical Care Svcs., Inc., Mason, Ohio, 1987—; firefighter/paramedic Mason Vol. Fire Co., 1978-85, EMS tng. officer, 1984, EMS capt., 1985. Contbr. articles to profl. jours. Mem. Mason Environ. Adv. Commn., 1990—, vice chmn., 1992-93, bus. and parent curriculum review com. Mason City Schs., 1992; employer advisor coop. program Cin. Tech. Coll. Biomed. Engring. Tech., 1986-91. With USN, 1964-70. Mem. AAMS, Assn. for Advancement of Med. Instrumentation, Ohio Acad. Sci. Mem. Ch. of Christ. Office: Critical Care Svcs Inc PO Box 252 1083A Reading Rd Mason OH 45040

CLEMENTS-SARBER, MARY KATHY, rehabilitation nurse; b. St. Louis, July 24, 1949; d. Horace G. and Naomi (Quigley) Mead; birthmother: Eileen Howard; m. Alan L. Clements, Apr. 20, 1968 (div. Feb. 1990); children: Troy Alan, Trevor, Kelli; m. Richard Earl Sarber, Aug. 10, 1991; children: Lauren, Dana. Diploma, South Chicago Sch. Nursing, 1983. RN, Ill.; cert. CRRN; cert. case mgr. Staff nurse St. James Hosp., Chicago Heights, Ill., 1983-84, U. Chgo., 1984-87; dir. mktg. Cares, Inc., Lansing, Ill., 1987-88; exec. dir. Rehab. Achievement Ctr., Hazel Crest, Wheeling, Ill., 1987—, Lisle, Ill., 1987—. Bd. dirs. Am. Heart Assn., Chgo., 1992—, ABBY Found., Flossmoor, Ill., 1988—, Exec. Exch., Flossmoor, 1992; pub. spkr. MADD, Chgo., 1989-91; apptd. govs. adv. coun. for brain and spinal cord injuries, State of Ill.; sec. coun. chair Nat. Head Injury Assn., 1994. Recipient Blue Chip award U.S. C. of C. for Healthcare, 1995; inducted into Entrepreneur Hall of Fame by Arthur Andersen, U. Ill., 1993. Mem. No. Ill. Assn. Rehab. Nurses (bd. dirs. 1990), Ill. Head Injury Assn. (mem. adv. bd. 1988-92, chair state conf. 1990), Nat. Spinal Cord Injury Assn. (chair nat. conf. 1992), Nat. Assn. Women Bus. Owners, Chgo. Southland C. of C. (bd. dirs. 1994—, vice chair commn. 1995, 96, Bus. Person of Yr. award 1993). Roman Catholic. Office: Rehab Achievement Ctr 17512 E Carriageway Dr Hazel Crest IL 60429-2006

CLEMMONS, JAMES H., engineering executive; b. Winter Haven, Fla., May 5, 1930. B, Ill. Inst. Tech., 1964. Engr. Sun Stran Corp., Rockford, Ill., 1980-88; pres. Specsystems, Inc., Freeport, Ill., 1988—. Contbr. articles to profl. jours. With USAF, 1951-55. Lutheran. Office: Specsystems Inc 1205 S Chicago Ave Freeport IL 61032-5744

CLEMONS, RONALD DALE, journalism educator; b. Marshall, Mo., Jan. 5, 1939; s. W.L. and Elsie Faye (Nelson) C.; m. Bonnie Lou Lazenby, May 29, 1960 (dec. 1969); m. Molly Jean Kuhlemeyer Wiseman, Apr. 27, 1982. BS in Edn., Ctrl. Mo. State U., 1961; MA in Journalism, U. Mo., 1965; postgrad., U. Minn., 1966. Tchr. Windsor (Mo.) High Sch., 1961-64, Truman High Sch., Independence, Mo., 1964—; dept. chair Independence Schs., 1978—; dir. Blair Summer Sch. for Journalism, Blairstown, N.J., 1978-91, Nat. Journalism Scholars Acad., Hightstown, N.J., 1994—, summer media workshop U. Mo., Columbia, 1980—. Asst. editor C:Jet, 1969-74; contbr. articles to profl. jours. Design editor jour. Jackson County Hist. Soc., Independence, 1990—; creative writing chair Cmty. Assn. for Arts, Independence, 1993—. Named Nat. Journalism Tchr. Yr. Dow Jones, 1977. Mem. Journalism Edn. Assn. (pres. 1978-83, Carl Towley award 1984), Mo. Journalism Edn. Assn. (pres. 1966-68), Journalism Educators Met. Kans. City (pres. 1966-68), Soc. Profl. Journalists, Columbia Scholastic Press Assn. (Gold Key award 1981), Phi Delta Kappa. Republican. Baptist. Home: 309 E Partridge Independence MO 64055

CLERY, ROGER G., communications educator, telecommunications consultant; b. Oak Pk., Ill., Feb. 27, 1945; s. Roger and Doris (Direck) C.; m. Carolsue H. Clery, Dec. 19, 1988. BS, No. Ill. U., 1967, MBA, 1968; PhD, Greenwich U., Hilo, Hawaii, 1995. Cert. data processing Inst. Certification Computer Profls. Instr., program coord. Coll. of DuPage, Glen Ellyn, Ill., 1981-82; assoc. prof. Roosevelt U., Chgo., 1983—. Mem. Lombard Jaycees (pres. 1978-79), Telephone Collectors Internat.

CLEVELAND, ROBERT HAROLD, artist, designer; b. Washington, Ind., Oct. 14, 1922; s. Harold and Mary (McNamara) C.; m. Roma Madge McDaniel, Aug. 11, 1948; children: Jane Cleveland, Karen Cleveland Register. Pilot cadet, USAF, 1942; AA, Vincennes U., 1946; BS, Centre Coll., 1950. Chief engring. designer Howard Foundary, Indpls., 1952-54; artist, designer Herf Jones, Inc., Indpls., 1955; artist Rhoads, Humphreys & Adams, Indpls., 1956-58; artist, owner Cleveland Art Studio, Indpls., 1958-65; prodn. supr. Repro Art, Cin., 1965-77; v.p. Artco, Inc., Cin., 1977-92; ret., 1992. Mem. Rep. Nat. Com., Cin. 2d lt. USAF, 1949-51. Decorated D.F.C., Air medal with four oak leaf clusters; recipient 3 Presdl. Citations, 1963. Mem. 91st Bombardment Group Meml. Assn., Art Dirs. Club, VFW. Roman Catholic. Home: 6740 High Meadows Dr Cincinnati OH 45230-3805

CLICK, MARIANNE JANE, credit manager; b. Marion, Ohio, Aug. 2, 1949; d. Raymond E. and Martha C. (Robinson) C. BS in Edn., Ohio State U., 1971. Cert. consumer credit exec. Various positions Western Auto Supply, Delaware, Ohio, 1973-87; dept. mgr. Western Auto Supply, Kansas City, Mo., 1988-89, dir. revolving ops., 1989—. Bd. dirs. Consumer Credit Counseling Svcs., Kansas City, 1992—, sec., 1995-96. Mem. Internat. Credit Assn., Credit Assn. Greater Kansas City (bd. dirs. 1991—, 2nd v.p. 1995-96, 1st v.p. 1996-97), Internat. Assn. Credit Card Investigators, Mchts. Rsch. Coun., Alpha Lambda Delta. Office: Western Auto Supply Co 5777 Deramus Ave Kansas City MO 64120-1261

CLIFF, JOHNNIE MARIE, mathematics and chemistry educator; b. Lamkin, Miss., May 10, 1935; d. John and Modest Alma (Lewis) Walton; m. William Henry Cliff, Apr. 1, 1961 (dec. 1983); 1 child, Karen Marie. BA in Chemistry, Math., U. Indpls., 1956; postgrad., NSF Inst., Butler U., 1960; MA in Chemistry, Ind. U., 1964; MS in Math., U. Notre Dame, 1980. Cert. tchr., Ind. Rsch. chemist Ind. U. Med. Ctr., Indpls., 1956-59; tchr. sci. and math. Indpls. Pub. Schs., 1960-88; tchr. chemistry, math. Martin U., Indpls., 1989—, chmn. math. dept., 1990—, divsn. chmn. depts. sci. and math., 1993—; adj. instr. math. U. Indpls., 1991. Contbr. rsch. papers to sci. jours. Grantee NSF, 1961-64, 73-76, 78-79, Woodrow Wilson Found., 1987-88; scholarship U. Indpls., 1952-56, NSF Inst. Reed Coll., 1961, C. of C., 1963. Mem. AAUW, NAACP, NEA, Assn. Women in Sci., Urban League, N.Y. Acad. Scis., Am. Chem. Soc., Nat. Coun. Math. Tchrs., Am. Assn. Physics Tchrs., Nat. Sci. Tchrs. Assn., Am. Statis. Assn., Am. Assn. Ret. Persons, Neal-Marshall-Ind. U. Alumni Assn., U. Indpls. Alumni Assn., U. Notre Dame Alumni Assn., Ind. U. Chemist Assn., Notre Dame Club Indpls., Kappa Delta Pi, Delta Sigma Theta. Democrat. Baptist. Home: 405 Golf Ln Indianapolis IN 46260-4108 Office: Martin U 2171 Avondale Pl Indianapolis IN 46218-3867

CLIFFORD, MICHAEL, electrical engineer; b. Cin., Sept. 5, 1956. BSEE, Ohio U., 1978. Elec. engr. Cin. (Ohio) Milacron, 1978-90, Goldcrown Machinery, Cin., 1990—.

CLIFFORD, NAOMI, librarian; b. Glenwood, Minn., June 26, 1940; d. Clifford and Ruth Lydia (Meilicke) Flom; m. John Edward Clifford, July 20, 1963 (div. Apr. 10, 1973); m. Mark M. Gormley, Aug. 23, 1975. BA, UCLA, 1963; MLS, Case Western Reserve U., 1979. Libr. asst. UCLA, 1963-67; asst. libr. U. Mo., St. Louis, 1967-74; collection devel. libr. Case Western Reserve U., Cleve., 1975-77; nat. office libr. Ernst & Young, Cleve., 1977-95; asst. dir. Ctr. for Bus. Knowledge Earnst & Young, Cleve., 1995—. Mem. Spl. Librs. Assn. (officer, mem. networking com. 1979-85). Office: Ernst & Young 1660 W 2d St Cleveland OH 44113

CLIFFORD, RITA KAY, nursing school administrator; b. Ashland, Kans., Oct. 1, 1940; d. Ernest Leslie and E. Regina (Carleton) Harris; m. Jack Carter, Dec. 23, 1968; 1 child, Christina Lee. BSN, U. Kans., 1962, PhD, 1981; MS in Psychiat. Nursing, Boston U., 1964. Staff nurse Peter Bent Brigham Hosp., Boston, 1962-64; instr. U. Kans. Sch. Nursing, Kansas City, 1964-67, asst. prof., 1967-71, assoc. prof., 1971—, asst. dean, 1974-92, assoc. dean, 1992-95, acting dean, 1995—; mem. adv. bd. Nursing and Health Careers Resource Ctr., Kansas City, 1989—. Contbr. articles to profl. jours. and chpts. to books. Planning com. Women's Concern Conf. II, Kansas City, 1982, Women's Agenda II Nat. Conf., Kansas City, 1988; phone capt. Johnson County (Kans.) Humane Soc., 1990. Named Disting. Alumnus U. Kans. Nurses Alumni Assn., 1992. Mem. ANA, Nat. League of Nursing, Midwest Nursing Rsch. Soc., Midwest Alliance in Nursing (bd. dirs. 1995-97), Kans. State Nurses Assn. (pres. dist. II 1988-90), steering com. 1989-91), Sigma Theta Tau (internat. del. 1991, pres. Delta chpt. 1992-94, internat. heritage commn. 1996-98). Office: U Kans Sch Nursing 3901 Rainbow Blvd Kansas City KS 66160-0001

CLIFTON, AUDRIENNE KAY, education educator, sociologist; b. Mt. Pleasant, Iowa, June 1, 1938; d. Rene and Naomi (Cottrell) C. BS in Sociology and Biology, Iowa Wesleyan Coll., 1960; MA in Recreation Outdoor Edn., U. Iowa, 1964, PhD in Sociology, 1973; MSW, U. Ill., 1984. Asst., assoc. prof. Ill. State U., Normal, 1968-78; co-owner Women's Woodworks, Champaign, Ill., 1978-81; adj. faculty Ill. Wesleyan U., Bloomington, Ill., 1980-83, Parkland Coll., Champaign, Ill., 1978-83, Ill. State U., Normal, 1982-83; drug counselor, evaluation specialist Project Oz, Bloomington, 1980-83; grad. asst. McKinley Health Ctr. U. Ill., Urbana, 1983-84; adj. faculty U. Cin., 1986-88; prof. sociology and social work Coll. of Mount St. Joseph, Cin., 1984—. Co-author of books and chpts. in books; contbr. articles to profl. jours. Vol. Girl Scouts, 1968-84, Coun. on Aging, Cin., 1984-94; pres. Women Faculty Assn., Ill. State U., Normal, 1968-78; chair faculty devel., v.p., pres. Faculty Coun., chair dept. behavioral scis. Coll. of Mount St. Joseph, Cin., 1989—; mem. City of Cin. Human Svcs. Adv. Com., 1990-94; bd. dirs. Price Hill Civic Club, Cin., 1995—; mem. eco-neighborhood com. Imago, Cin., 1993—; pres. Women's Rsch. and Devel. Ctr. Named Tchr. of Yr., Coll. of Mount St. Joseph, 1986; grantee State of Ohio Women's Health Month, Fed. Health and Human Svcs.. Mem. Coun. on Social Work Edn., Soc. for Applied Anthropologists, Assn. for Cmty. Orgn. and Social Adminstrn., Women's R&D Ctr. (pres. 1987—), Earth Connection (bd. dirs. 1994—). Democrat. Methodist. Office: Coll of Mount St Joseph 5701 Delhi Cincinnati OH 45233

CLIFTON, KELLY HARDENBROOK, biology educator; b. Spokane, Wash., July 22, 1927; s. John Minton and Nora Marie (Toole) C.; m. Mayre-Lee Harris, Aug. 27, 1949; children: Kelly H. Jr., William H., Brice M. BA honors, U. Mont., 1950; MS, U. Wis., 1951, PhD, 1955. Postdoctoral fellow Children's Cancer Rsch. Found., Boston, 1955-56, rsch. assoc., 1956-59; from asst. prof. to prof. radiology U. Wis., Madison, 1959-67, prof. human oncology and radiology, 1975-95, prof. emeritus human oncology, 1995—; spl. rsch. fellow Nat. Cancer Inst. at Karolinska Inst., Stockholm, 1970-71; chief of rsch., bd. dirs. Radiation Effects Rsch. Found., Hiroshima and Nagasaki, Japan, 1980-82. Contbr. over 100 articles to profl. jours. Bd. dirs. Madison Gen. Hosp. Med. Surg. Found., 1984-91. With USCG, 1945-46. Grantee Am. Cancer Soc., U. Wis., 1960-83, U.S. Nat. Cancer Inst., U. Wis., 1972—, Dept. of Energy, U. Wis., 1984-95; named Disting. Alumnus U. Mont., 1995. Mem. Am. Assn. for Cancer Rsch., Soc. for Exptl. Biology and Medicine (chmn. Wis. sect. 1963-64), Radiation Rsch. Soc., Sigma Xi (nat. lectr. 1990-92). Home: 1218 University Bay Dr Madison WI 53705-2253 Office: K4/330 U Wis Comprehensive Cancer Ctr 600 Highland Ave Madison WI 53792-0001

CLIMER, BETH JANE, health information technology coodinator, educator; b. St. Louis, July 16, 1954; d. Warren Eugene and Bruce May (Coppedge) Kozozenski; m. Jack C. Climer, Nov. 26, 1977; children: Ty, Lance. Student, S.W. Mo. State U., 1974; BS, Coll. St. Mary, 1977. Registered record adminstr. Med. record adminstr. Mo. State Chest Hosp., Mt. Vernon, 1977-83; asst. dir. med. records Cox South, Springfield, Mo., 1985-86, inpatient coder, 1991-92; med. record cons. Allied Health Cons. Corp., Liberty, Mo., 1989-91, Springfield, 1985—; coord., instr. Ozarks Tech. C.C., Springfield, 1992—; adj. faculty mem., mem. adv. com. for health info. mgmt. program Stephens Coll., Columbia, 1985—. Mem. Am. Health Info. Mgmt. Assn., Mo. Health Info. Mgmt. Assn. (elected nominating com. 1995-96), Ozark Area Health Info. Mgmt. Assn. (elected del. 1994-95). Home: 825 Lloyd Dr Rogersville MO 65742-9135 Office: Ozarks Tech C C NTM-1923 E Kearney Springfield MO 65803

CLINE, CHARLES WILLIAM, poet, pianist, rhetoric and literature educator; b. Waleska, Ga., Mar. 1, 1937; s. Paul Ardell and Mary Montarie (Pittman) C.; m. Sandra Lee Williamson, June 11, 1966; 1 son, Jeffrey Charles. Student, U. Cin. Conservatory of Music, 1957-58; AA, Reinhardt Coll., 1957; BA, George Peabody Coll. for Tchrs., 1960; MA, Vanderbilt U., 1963; LittD, World U., 1981; DFA (hon.), Australian Inst. Coordinated, 1996; diploma (hon.), Inst. des Affaires Internat., 1996. Asst. prof. English Shorter Coll., Rome, Ga., 1963-64; instr. English West Ga. Coll., Carrollton, 1964-68; manuscript procurement editor Fideler Co., Grand Rapids, Mich, 1968; assoc. prof. English Kellogg Community Coll., Battle Creek, Mich., 1969-75, prof. English and resident poet, 1975—; chmn. creative writing sect. Midwest Conf. on English, 1976; condr. poetry readings and workshops. Piano recitals at Internat. Congress on Arts and Comm., 1992, 93, 94, 95; author: Crossing the Ohio, 1976, Questions for the Snow, 1979, Ultima Thule, 1984, (with Amal Ghose and others) Wholeness of Dream, 1989; editor: Forty Salutes to Mich. Poets, 1975; contbr. Gifts of Music, 1994; contbr. poems to jours. and anthologies. Decorated knight comdr. Lofsensischen Unsiniusordens, 1991, knight Order of Knights Templars of Jerusalem, 1991, knight Order of Circulo Nobilario de los Caballeros Universales, 1993, knight Order of Holy Grail, 1996, baron Royal Order of the Bohemian Crown, 1996, count Order of San Ciriaco, 1996; recipient Order of Pegasus poetic achievement Olympoetry Movement, 1966, Poetry awards Modus Operandi, 1975, Internat. Belles-Lettres Soc., 1975, Poetry Soc. Mich., 1975, N. Am. Mentor, 1977, 78, Lit. Prize World Inst. Achievement, 1986, 88, Star of Distinction, 19th Internat. Congress on Art and Comm., St. John's Coll., U. Cambridge, 1992, Disting. Participation medallion 20th Congress, Cambridge, Mass., 1993, diplôme d'Honneur á Littèrature et Musique, Inst. des Affaires Internats., 1996; resolutions recognition Kalamazoo City Commn., Mich. Ho. of Reps. and Senate, 1981, others. Fellow World Literary Acad. (founding, prize 1983), Internat. Soc. Lit. (life), Am. Biog. Inst. (life, World Fellowship award 1987, Internat. Hall of Leaders 1988, hon. advisor rsch. bd. advisors nat. divsn. 1994); mem. Tagore Inst. Creative Writing Internat. (life), World Poetry Soc. Intercontinental, Centro Studi e Scambi Internazionali (Poet Laureate award, Diploma di Benemerenza, Diploma d'Onore), Accademia Leonardo da Vinci, Poetry Soc. Am., Poets and Writers Inc., Acad. Am. Poets, Am. Biog. Inst. Rsch. Assn. (dep. gov.), Internat. Biog. Assn. (life patron), World U. Roundtable, Internat. Biog. Ctr. (dep. dir. gen. 1991, 20th Century award for achievement 1992, World Intellectual 1993), Accademia Internationale di Pontzen (distintivo palmato 1991, lauro d'oro for literary merit 1991), Maison Internat. des Intellectuels, Acad. M.I.D.I., Wordsworth-Coleridge Assn., Assn. Lit. Scholars and Critics. Presbyterian. Office: Kellogg Community Coll 450 North Ave Battle Creek MI 49017-3306

CLINE, DONALD ALAN, management consultant; b. Ft. Belvoir, Va., Aug. 7, 1954; s. Robert Bird and Janet Louise (Krahn) C.; m. Terri Lynn Stroehmer, Dec. 27, 1975; children: Stephanie, Heather, Aaron. BS in Nuclear Engring., U. Mo., Rolla, 1975, MS in Engring. Mgmt., 1976. Nuclear fuels engr. Tennessee Valley Authority, Chattanooga, 1977-80, power planning specialist, 1980-82; corp. planning engr. Union Electric Co., St. Louis, 1982-86, quality improvement sr. engr., 1986-94, internal audit supervising engr., 1994—; examiner Mo. Quality Award, Jefferson City, Mo., 1993. Pres. Hillsboro (Mo.) R-3 Bd. of Edn., 1995, Redeemer Luth. Ch., 1985; treas. Hillsboro Fire Protection Dist., 1992—, vol. firefighter/EMT, 1989-94; mgr., coach Hillsboro Little League, 1988-92. Mem. The Planning Forum, Hillsboro Comty. Civic Club. Home: 27 Ridgewood Dr Hillsboro MO 63050

CLINE, DOROTHY MAY STAMMERJOHN (MRS. EDWARD WILBURN CLINE), educator; b. Boonville, Mo., Oct. 19, 1915; d. Benjamin Franklin and Lottie (Walther) Stammerjohn; grad. nurse U. Mo., 1937; BS in Edn., 1939, postgrad., 1966-67; MS, Ark. State U., 1964; m. Edward Wilburn Cline, Aug. 16, 1938 (dec. May 1962); children: Margaret Ann (Mrs. Rodger Orville Bell), Susan Elizabeth (Mrs. Gary Lee Burns), Dorothy Jean. Dir. Christian Coll. Infirmary, Columbia, Mo., 1936-37; asst. chief nursing svc. VA Hosp., Poplar Bluff, Mo., 1950-58; tchr.-in-charge staff State Tng. Ctr. No. 4, Poplar Bluff, 1959-66, Dorothy S. Cline State Sch. #53, Boonville, 1967-85; instr. U. Mo., Columbia, 1973-74; cons. for workshops for new tchrs., curriculum revision Mo. Dept. Edn. Mem. Butler County Council Retarded Children, 1959-66; v.p. Boonslick Assn. Retarded Children, 1969-72; sec.-treas. Mo. chpt. Am. Assn. on Mental Deficiency, 1973-75. Mem. NEA, Mo. Tchrs. Assn., Am. Assn. on Mental Deficiency, Council for Exceptional Children, AAUW (v.p. Boonville br. 1968-70, 75-77), Mo. Writers Guild, Creative Writer's Group (pres. 1974—), Columbia Creative Writers Group, Eastern Center Poetry Soc., Laura Speed Elliott High Sch. Alumni Assn., Bus. and Profl. Women's Club, Smithsonian Assn., U. Mo. Alumni Assn., Ark. State U. Alumni Assn., Internat. Platform Assn., Mo. Hist. Soc., Boonslick Hist. Soc., Friends Historic Boonville, Delta Kappa Gamma, PEO. Mem. Christian Ch. Home: 603 High St Boonville MO 65233-1212

CLINE, LINDA BLAIR, accountant; b. Nashville, Nov. 1, 1950; d. Frank Williamson and Mary Elizabeth (Hayes) Blair; m. William Chambers Cline, July 3, 1971; children: Polly, Sarah, William, Blair. AB, Duke U., 1971; MA, George Peabody Coll., 1972; M of Mgmt., Northwestern U., 1978. CPA, Ill. Sr. acct. Touche Ross & Co., Chgo., 1978-80; prin. Linda B. Cline, CPA, Glencoe, Ill., 1981-89; chief operating officer APTE, Inc., Evanston, Ill., 1990—. Treas., bd. dirs. Nat. Lekotek Ctr., Evanston, 1981-88, bd. advisors, Innotek, Ill., 1989—; active Duke U. Alumni Adv. Com., Durham, N.C., 1979—, Jr. League of Chgo., 1972—. Mem. AICPA, Ill. CPA Soc., Nat. Orgn. on Disability. Episcopalian.

CLINE, LINDA JEAN, reading educator; b. Salem, Ohio, July 18, 1948; d. Henry Richard and Elsie Louise (Boor) C. BS, Ind. State U., 1970; MEd, Ashland U., 1984. Cert. elem. tchr., secondary tchr., supr. Tchr. English, journalism, newspaper advisor Galion (Ohio) High Sch., 1970-72; tchr. 4th and 5th grade Colonel Crawford Schs., Bucyrus/North Robinson, Ohio, 1973-74; tchr. chpt. 1 reading Plymouth Local Schs., Plymouth/Shiloh, Ohio, 1975—, coord. right-to-read program, 1983—, coord. chpt. 1, 1989-90, mem. supt.'s master planning com., 1990-92, mem. prin.'s adv. com., 1992-93. Pres. United Meth. Women 1st United Meth. Ch., Shelby, Ohio, 1985-87, 94, lay speaker, 1988—. Scholar State of Ind., 1966. Mem. NEA, Ohio Edn. Assn., Plymouth Edn. Assn. (pres. 1979-81), Order Ea. Star (Worthy Matron 1977, 81, 95, Grand Rep. N.H. 1979), Alpha Sigma Alpha (corr. sec. 1966—), Sigma Tau Delta. Republican.

CLINE, PAUL ANDERSON, health facilities adminstrator; b. Tampa, Fla., Jan. 1, 1963; s. Bennie Anderson and Heidi Yvonne (Harvey) C.; m. Teresa Lyn Koudelka, Oct. 8, 1988; 1 child, Alexandria Elizabeth. BS in Med. Tech., Ohio State U., 1986; MS in Health Svcs. Adminstrn., Ctrl. Mich. U., 1993. Med. technologist Ohio Dept. Mental Health, Columbus, 1986-89, St. Ann's Hosp., Westerville, Ohio, 1987-91; tech. supr. Futuremed Lab., Columbus, 1991-92, lab. mgr., 1992-93; lab. cons. Tek Lab. Cons., Lewis Center, Ohio, 1993—; lab. mgr. Morrow County Hosp., Mt. Gilead, Ohio, 1993—; mem. adv. bd. Marion (Ohio) Tech. Coll., 1993—. Mem. Saddlebrook Civic Assn. (pres., v.p. 1991-92), Ohio State U. Allied Med. Alumni Assn. (pres. 1990-93). Home: 2868 Brookhaven Dr Lewis Center OH 43035 Office: Morrow County Hosp 651 W Marion Rd Mount Gilead OH 43338

CLINE, SANDRA WILLIAMSON, elementary education educator; b. San Francisco, Dec. 10, 1944; d. Wilburn Woodrow and Hazel Stewart (Cochrane) Williamson; m. Charles William Cline, June 11, 1966; 1 child, Jeffrey Charles. BA, Western Mich. U., 1970, MA, 1973; MA, Western Mich. U., 1986. Cert. tchr., Mich. 1st-3rd grade tchr. Portage Mich. Pub. Schs., 1971—, mem. sch. effectiveness team and report card rev. com., 1988-92, mem. sci. writing team, 1989—; mentor coach Western Mich. U.; mus. co-dir. Lake Ctr. Elem. Sch., Portage, 1982-83, student tchr., mentor, safety patrol advisor, 1st grade chairperson, state com. for social studies, writing chairperson, 1988-94. Vol. Portage Police, 1992—; assoc. coord. city emergency sys., 1995—. Recipient Congress medallion for disting. participation, 1992-93. Mem. NEA, ASCD, NSTA, Am. Fedn. Police (Nat. Patriotism award 1994), Nat. Coun. Tchrs. English, Assn. for Study of Coop. in Edn., Mich. Edn. Assn., Portage Edn. Assn. (exec. bd., membership chairperson, elem. grievance chair, negotiating team), Mich. ASCD (conf. com.), Phi Delta Kappa. Home: 2170 Sanibel Is # A-3 Kalamazoo MI 49024-8616 Office: Lake Ctr Elem Sch 10011 Portage Rd Kalamazoo MI 49002-7249

CLINEFELTER, RUTH ELIZABETH WRIGHT, historian, educator; b. Akron, Ohio, Nov. 2, 1930; d. Cyril and Ruth Elizabeth (Dresher) Wright. BA, U. Akron, 1952, MA, 1953; MLS, Kent State U., 1956. Serials libr. U. Akron, 1953-61, social scis. rsch. libr., 1961-76, humanities rsch. libr., 1977-83, social scis. humanities bibliographer, 1983—; lectr. in gen. studies U. Akron, 1960, instr. bibliography, 1956-59, asst. prof. bibliography, 1959-77, assoc. prof. bibliography, 1977-84, prof. bibliography 1984—; resource person NEH, Ohio; mem. joint study com. Am. History Rsch. in Ohio Ohio Hist. Soc., 1969-70; mem. acad. affairs com. Ohio Faculty Senate, 1971-72; mem. hist. abstracts bibliographic svc. ABC Clio Users Bd., 1978-79. Contbr. articles to profl. jours. Trustee Akron Area Women's History Project; active Citizens AGainst Sys. Abuse, Humane Soc. Greater Akron, Nat. Trust for Hist. Preservation, Progress Through Preservation, Summit County Hist. Soc., Cascade Locks Park Assn., Pet Guards Shelter. Mem. Acad. Libr. Assn. Ohio, AAUP, Am. Hist. Assn., Assn. for Bibliography of History, North Am. Conf. British Studies, North Cen. Women's Studies Assn., Ohio Acad. History, Ohio Classical Assn. Democrat. Episcopalian. Home: 1377 Hadden Cir Akron OH 44313-6505 Office: U Akron Bierce Libr Akron OH 44325

CLINGAN, DONALD FRANK, retired clergyman; b. Atchison, Kans., Feb. 25, 1926; s. Frank E. and Hazel Ellen (Hall) C.; m. Jacqueline Stephenson, Aug. 26, 1952; children: Stephen Frank, Jane Ellen Clingan Reynolds. BA, Phillips U., 1950; BDiv, Tex. Christian U., 1952, MDiv, 1955; DMin, Christian Theol. Sem., Indpls., 1978; Grad. Cert. in Gerontology, U. Oreg., 1976-79. Ordained clergyman, Disciples of Christ. Minister First Christian Ch., Lyons, Kans., 1955-60; sr. minister First Christian Ch., Manhattan, Kans., 1960-65; dir. of program planning, dept. World Outreach Edn. Disciples of Christ (Divsn. Homeland Ministries), Indpls., 1965-70; exec. dir. dept. svcs. to congregations Nat. Benevolent Assn./Disciples of Christ Ch., Indpls., 1970-80; exec. dir. Nat. Ctr. on Ministry with the Aging, Indpls., 1980-84; sr. minister First Christian Ch., Springfield, Ill., 1984-92; founding pres. Nat. Interfaith Coalition on Aging, Athens, Ga., 1972-74, exec. dir., 1974-75, bd. dirs.; pres. Inst. on Religion and Aging, Indpls., 1972-84. Author: (camp curriculum) Sincerely Yours, 1964, (curriculum) Christian Living Encounters, 1969, (book) Aging Persons in the Community of Faith, 1975; co-author: Aging: God's Challenge to Church and Synagogue, 1996. Del. White House Conf. on Aging, Washington, 1971, 1995, ofcl. observer, 1981. Sgt. U.S. Army Corps, 1944-46. Recipient George E. David award for Noteworthy Ministry with the Aging, Inst. on Religion and Aging, Indpls., 1984, Nat. Spiritual Well-Being award Nat. Interfaith Coalition on Aging, 1984. Mem. Ill./Wis. Region of the Christian Ch., Kiwanis, Phi Mu Alpha, Blue Key. Democrat. Home: 41 Westwood Terrace Springfield IL 62702

CLOHESY, WILLIAM WARREN, philosophy educator; b. Chgo., July 31, 1946; s. John Cecil and Mary Evelyn (Ahern) C.; m. Stephanie June Jagucki, June 19, 1971. BS in Humanities, Loyola U., Chgo., 1964-68; MA, So. Ill. U., 1968-71; PhD, New Sch. for Social Rsch., N.Y.C., 1981. Instr. Loyola U., Chgo., 1967, asst. prof., 1982-83; teaching asst. So. Ill. U., Carbondale, 1969; adj. prof. Montclair State Coll., Upper Montclair, N.J., 1981-82; asst. prof. Rochester (N.Y.) Inst. Tech., 1983-86, rsch. assoc., 1986-87; lectr. U. Belgrano, Buenos Aires, 1987; asst. prof. U. No. Iowa, Cedar Falls, 1987-93, assoc. prof., 1993—; mem. BSN adv. com. Allen Coll., Waterloo, Iowa, 1991—. Editor: Ethics at Work, 1992; contbr. articles to profl. jours. Rsch. and faculty devel. grant W.K. Kellogg Found., 1995, Symposium grant Iowa Humanities Bd., 1991-92, Symposium grant NEH, 1991-92, Fulbright fellowship to Argentina, 1987, Kurt Riezler Meml. awar New Sch. for Social Rsch., 1982. Mem. Am. Philos. Assn., Hegel Soc. Am., Hume Soc., N.Am. Soc. for Social Philosophy, N.Am. Kant Soc., Soc. for the Advancement of Am. Philosophy. Democrat. Roman Catholic. Office: U No Iowa Dept Philosophy Cedar Falls IA 50614-0501

CLONTZ, NITA M. BARNES, stockbroker; b. Burns, Oreg., Jan. 26, 1957. AD, Bauder Coll., 1977. Heavy equipment operator Internat. Union Oper. Engrs., Wash., Oreg. and Idaho, Oreg. and Idaho, 1976—; stockbroker Firm 1 Securities, Dodge City, Kans., 1988-89; v.p. Perkins Smart & Co. Inc., Pratt, Kans., 1989—. Trustee Pratt C.C., 1994—; bd. dirs. Leadership 2000, Pratt, 1993—, Pratt County Integrated Cmty. Health Devel. Bd., 1994—, Spirit 2000 Retail/Svc. Commn.; vol. Spl. Olympics, Miss. Kans. Pageant. Mem. Pratt C. of C., Rotary, Kiwanis (past pres., Kiwanian of Yr. 1993). Office: Perkins Smart & Co Inc PO Box 8543 307 S Main Pratt KS 67124

CLOR, HARRY M., political scientist, educator; b. Springfield, Ill., July 20, 1929; s. Joseph J. and Sophie Lois (Goldstein) C.; m. Margaret Bessey Hyink, June 26, 1966; children: Kate, Laura. BA, Lawrence U., 1951; PhD, U. Chgo., 1967. Instr. Basic Program Liberal Edn. U. Chgo., 1960-64; prof. Kenyon Coll., Gambier, Ohio, 1965—. Author: Obscentity and Public Morality, 1968, Public Morality and Liberal Society, 1996; contbr. articles to profl. jours. With U.S. Army, 1952-54. Grantee Bradley Found., 1993. Mem. Nat. Assn. Scholars, Ohio Assn. Scholars, Univ. Ctrs. for Rational Alternatives. Home: PO Box 597 Gambier OH 43022 Office: Kenyon Coll Political Sci Dept Gambier OH 43022

CLOSSON, BONNIE LEIGH, rehabilitation clinical nurse; b. Chgo.. BSN, U. Md., Balt., 1961; M of Rehabilitation Counseling, Bowling Green State U., 1981; MS in Nursing, U. Wis., Eau Claire, 1991. RN, Minn.; cert. gerontol. clin. nurse specialist, cert. rehab. nurse. Head nurse emergency rm. Univ. Hosp., Balt.; instr. Akron (Ohio) City Hosp. Sch. Nursing; pub. health nurse Guam Pub. Health Dept., Agana; instr. Buckeye Sch. Nursing, Napoleon, Ohio, 1972-81; head nurse rehab. St. Mary's Hosp., Rochester, Minn., 1981-83, asst. dir. nursing edn., 1983-89, dir. ednl. svcs., 1989-90; rehab. clin. nurse specialist Mayo Clinic, Rochester, Minn., 1990—. Chpt. reviewer Nursing People Experiencing Neurol. Disorders, 1990. Elder First Presbyn. Ch., Rochester, 1991-94, deacon, 1986-89. Recipient Excellence in Nursing award U. Wis., 1990, grant St. Mary's Hosp., 1989. Mem. ANA (cert. gerontol. clin. nurse specialist, cert. rehab. RN), Assn. Rehab. Nurses (continuing edn. reviewer 1991-95, rehab. nurses cert. bd. 1995—), Minn. Nurses Assn. (chmn. continuing edn. approval program 1987-89), Am. Assn. Spinal Cord Injury Nurses, Sigma Theta Tau, Phi Kappa Phi. Office: Mayo Clinic St Marys Hosp 1216 2nd St SW Rochester MN 55902-1906

CLOUD, GARY LEE, engineering educator; b. Muskegon, Mich., Sept. 8, 1937; s. Kenneth Melvin and Eliene Pearl (Ruggles) C.; m. Elizabeth Anne Fee, July 30, 1972; children: Sarah, Abigail. BSME, Mich. Tech. U., 1959, MS in Engring. Mech., 1961, PhD in Applied Mechanics, 1966. Registered profl. engr., Mich. Asst. prof. Mich. State U., East Lansing, 1966-70, assoc. prof., 1970-79, prof., 1979—; lectr. U. Zambia, Lusaka, 1969; sr. rsch. assoc. Air Force Materials Lab., Dayton, Ohio, 1975-76; NSF fellow Imperial Coll., London, 1976-77; cons. numerous firms in field, 1970—. Contbr. 100 articles to profl. publs. Musician Opera Co., Steiner Chorale, Lansing, Mich., 1961—. Grantee NSF, 1980, NIH, 1980, others; recipient Withrow Teaching Excellence award, 1992, Outstanding Engring. Educator award Mich. Soc. Profl. Engrs., 1992; named Mich. State U. Disting. Faculty award 1994, Withrow Disting. Scholar award, 1995. Mem. Soc. Exptl. Mechanics (pres. 1993-94, Best Paper award 1989), Soc. Photo-Optical Instrumentation Engrs., Brit. Soc. Strain Measurement. Methodist. Office: Mich State U Materials Sci & Mechanics A332 Engring Bldg East Lansing MI 48824

CLOUS, JAMES M., electrical equipment company executive, engineer; b. Traverse City, Mich., July 22, 1959; s. August J. and Beverly J. (Kroetsch) C.; m. Mimi M. O'Connell, June 28, 1979 (div. July 1983). AS, Northwestern Mich. Coll., 1979; BSME, Mich. Tech. U., 1981. Sales engr. Louis Allis-Litton, Houston, 1981-83; dist. mgr. Louis Allis-Magnetek, Baton Rouge, 1984-85, GEC Automation Projects, Houston, 1986-88; regional mgr. Ross Hill Controls, Houston, 1989-91; nat. sales mgr. ABB Indsl. Systems, New Berlin, Wis., 1991-94; v.p. sales and mktg. Ideal Electric, Mansfield, Ohio, 1994—; pvt. practice mktg. cons., Houston, 1987-91. Mem. Nat. Rep. Com., Washington, 1988. Mem. IEEE. Republican. Roman Catholic. Office: 330 E 1st St Mansfield OH 44902-7756

CLOUSE, JOHN DANIEL, lawyer; b. Evansville, Ind., Sept. 4, 1925; s. Frank Paul and Anna Lucille (Frank) C.; m. Georgia L. Ross, Dec. 7, 1978; 1 child, George Chauncey. AB, U. Evansville, 1950; JD, Ind. U., 1952. Bar: Ind. 1952, U.S. Supreme Ct. 1962, U.S. Ct. Appeals (7th cir.) 1965. Assoc. firm James D. Lopp, Evansville, 1952-56; pvt. practice law, Evansville, 1956—; guest editorialist Viewpoint, Evansville Courier, 1978-86, Evansville Press, 1986—, Focus, Radio Sta. WGBF, 1978-84; 2d asst. city atty. Evansville, 1954-55; mem. appellate rules sub-com. Ind. Supreme Ct. Com. on Rules of Practice and Procedure, 1980. Pres. Civil Svc. Commn. Evansville Police Dept., 1961-62, v.p. 1988; pres. Ind. War Memls. Com., 1963-69; mem. jud. nominating com. Vanderburgh County, Ind., 1976-80; dir. Ind. Fed. Cmty. Defender Project, Inc., 1993—. With inf. U.S. Army, 1943-46. Decorated Bronze Star; named one of World's Most Travelled Man Guinness Book of Records, 1993, Most Travelled Man, 95-96. Fellow Ind. Bar Found.; mem. Evansville Bar Assn. (v.p. 1972), Ind. Bar Assn. (chmn. com. on civil rights 1991-92), Selden Soc., Pi Gamma Mu. Republican. Methodist. Club: Travelers Century (L.A.). (L.A.). Home: 1369 E Chandler Ave Evansville IN 47714-1951 Office: 1010 Hulman Bldg Evansville IN 47708

CLOUTIER, MARTIN, agricultural economist, researcher; b. Montreal, Quebec, Canada, Apr. 29, 1966; Came to the U.S., 1992; s. Robert Cloutier and Monique Montpetit. BSc, McGill U., Montreal, 1989, MSc, 1993. Rsch. asst. McGill U., Montreal, 1989-92; asst. program coord. Internat. Inst. for Agrifood Mgmt., Paris, 1995; rsch. asst. U. Ill., Urbana, 1992—. Contbr. articles to profl. jours. Mem. Am. Agrl. Econs. Assn., Canadian Agrl. Econs. and Farm Mgmt. Soc. (Outstanding Master's Thesis award 1993), Internat. Agribusiness Mgmt. Assn. Office: U Ill Dept Agrl Econs 1301 W Gregory Dr Urbana IL 61801

CLOWE, CURTIS JAMES, environmental chemist; b. Hastings, Nebr., Jan. 29, 1959; s. Derrel Dean and Gloria Ann (Nanninga) C.; divorced; children: Anthony James, Kelsey Danae. BA in Chemistry, Hastings (Nebr.) Coll., 1984. Cert. profl. closer, Nebr. Analytical chemist Midwest Labs., Omaha, 1984-85; quality control chemist SmithKline Beckman, Omaha, 1985-87; quality control mgr. Platte Chem. Co., Fremont, Nebr., 1987-89; environ. specialist Farmland Industries, Omaha, 1989-91; environ. chemist Woodward-Clyde Cons., Omaha, 1991-93; mgr. environ. chemistry Woodward-Clyde Fed. Svcs., Omaha, 1993-95, mgr. in-plant svcs., 1996—; industry rep. Nebr. State Emergency Response Commn., Lincoln, 1990-94; mem. environ. and safety task force ConAgra, Omaha, 1990. Contbr. articles to profl. jours. Mem. Am. Chem. Soc., Am. Indsl. Hygiene Assn., Nebr. Indsl. Coun. on Environment. Republican. Methodist. Avocations: swimming, golf, raquetball, fishing, hunting. Office: Woodward-Clyde Fed Svcs 101 S 108th Ave Omaha NE 68154-2621

CLUCAS, JOHN M., company executive; b. Kewanee, Ill., Feb. 1, 1950. BS in Edn., Ill. State U., 1978. Registered prin., NASD. Br. office mgr. Edward D. Jones, Stevens Point, Wis., 1981-86; pres. Linsco Pvt. Ledger, Inc., Stevens Point, Wis., 1986—. Treas., bd. dirs. Big Bros./Big Sisters, Portage County, Wis., 1990-93; bd. dirs. United Way, Portage County, 1987—; instr. adult edn. U. Wis., Stevens Point, 1985-88. Recipient Athletic scholarship Ill. State U., 1974-78. Mem. Wis. MANX Soc. (v.p. 1992—), Kiwanis (bd. dirs. 1984—). Office: Linsco Pvt Ledge Inc 1265 Main St Stevens Point WI 54481-2864

CLUSKEY, GERALD ROBERT, accounting educator; b. Peoria, Ill., Jan. 17, 1947; m. Eve J. Killebrew, Aug. 30, 1954. BS in Acctg., Bradley U., Peoria, 1971; MS in Human Resource Mgmt., U. Utah, 1978; DBA in Acctg., So. Ill. U., 1994. CPA, Ill. Cons. Fails Mgmt. Svc., Raleigh, N.C., 1980-82; tng. officer Ill. Air N.G., Peoria, 1982-94; acctg. faculty Bradley U., Peoria, 1985—. Lt. col. USAF, 1971-80, Ill. Air N.G., 1982-94. AF-ROTC scholar, 1970. Mem. AICPAs, Inst. Mgmt. Asscts. (v.p. edn. 1984—), Am. Acctg. Assn. Republican. Roman Catholic. Home: 2919 W Rohmann Ave West Peoria IL 61604-4839 Office: Bradley Univ 1501 W Bradley Ave Peoria IL 61625

CLYBURN, LUTHER LINN, real estate broker, appraiser; b. Evansville, Ind., May 17, 1942; s. Luther and Robbie (Cobb) C.; children: Lisa Michelle, Luther Brent. Grad., Am. Savs. and Loan Inst., 1970; ABA, Pontiac (Mich.) Bus. Inst., 1972; BS, Detroit Coll. Bus., 1972; M of Bus. Mgmt., Cen. Mich. U., 1983. Chief loan officer First Fed. Savs. and Loan Assn. Oakland, Pontiac, 1964-74; assoc. broker Bateman Real Estate Corp., Pontiac, 1975-77; regional rep. United Guaranty Residential Ins., Troy, Mich., 1977-83; sr. account mgr. Investors Mortgage Ins. Co., Boston, 1983-87; real estate broker, appraiser White Lake, Mich., 1977—, Clyburn Appraisal Svcs., White Lake, 1987—. Project dir., capt.: (documentary film) Angels of the Sea, 1982 (N.Y. Film Festival award 1983). Capt., comdr. "Noble Odyssey" Tng. Ship, Mt. Clemens, Mich., 1977-89; dir., comdr. U.S. Naval Sea Cadet Corps Great Lakes div., Mt. Clemens, Mich., 1973—; nat. bd. dirs. U.S. Naval Sea Cadet Corps, 1988; project dir. Interseas Inc., Pontiac, 1982; ship capt. Great Lakes Botanical Island research project for Cranbrook Inst. Sci. (Thunder Bay Islands, Lake Huron, 1987, Islands of Green Bay, 1989, 90); dir. of Underwater Cinitofu; capt. Pride of Mich., 1989—. Recipient Cert. Appreciation award Southfield Bicentennial Commn., 1976, Letter of Commendation award Sec. of Navy, 1983, Quality People award Meritorious Cmty. Svc., 1993, Oakland County Q2 award, 1993, Unsung Hero award Mich. Ho. of Reps., 1994. Mem. Internat. Ship Masters Assn., Navy League of U.S., Am. Soc. Appraisers, Mich. Assn. Real Estate Appraisers. Home and Office: 9000 Gale Rd White Lake MI 48386-1411

CLYMER, DAVID HOISINGTON, real estate broker; b. Wichita, Kans., Aug. 31, 1924; s. Rolla Anderson and Elizabeth Clymer; m. Betty Cruse, Aug. 30, 1946 (div. Dec. 1968); children: Sara Lee, Richard Andrew; m. Sherry Louise Clymer, Dec. 18, 1969. BJ, Kans. U., 1948. Mng. ptnr. weekly newspapers LaCrosse, Medicine Lodge, Oakley, 1948-58; with El Dorado (Kans.) Times, 1958-88; real estate broker and developer, 1960—; now with Re/Max Preferred, El Dorado; developer Oz Cable. With U.S. Army, 1943-46. Mem. Am. Legon, VFW, Elks, Moose, El Dorado C. of C., El Dorado Country Club, Masons (33 deg.), Shriners. Republican. Presbyterian. Office: Re/Max Preferred 114 W Central El Dorado KS 67042

CLYNE, MICHAEL ANDREW, political consultant; b. Evergreen Park, Ill., Nov. 30, 1954; s. Eugene J. and Dolores M. (Higgins) C. Student, U. Notre Dame, 1972-76. Staff GM Acceptance Corp., Chgo., 1978-80; assoc. Cook County States Atty.'s Office, Chgo., 1981-86, Palos Venture, Palos Heights, Ill., 1986-96; polit. cons. Citizens for Devine, Chgo., Ill., 1996—. Mem. South Cook County Environ. Action Coalition. Named Ill. State Scholar, 1972. Mem. Chgo. Acad. Scis., Chgo. Hist. Soc., East Beverly Assn., Irish-Am. Alliance (treas. 1995-96), Irish Am. Cultural Inst., Gaelic Park, Irish Am. Heritage Ctr., Irish Am. Partnership, Celtic League, Mensa, Irish Fellowship Club Chgo.. Roman Catholic. Home: 1831 W 104th St Chicago IL 60643-2848 Office: Citizens for Devine 54 W Illinois St Chicago IL 60610

COADY, MICHAEL GARY, engineering supervisor; b. Kokomo, Ind., July 16, 1952; s. Robert Emmett and Allwyn Corrine (Samuels) C.; m. Deborah Lynn Staggs, Oct. 28, 1972; children: Jaime Lyn, Abbe Nicole. BSME/EE, Gen. Motors Inst., 1975; MS in Mfg. Mgmt., GMI Engring. Mgmt. Inst., 1993. Printed circuit bd. mfg. engr. Delco Electronics, Kokomo, 1976-80, printed circuit bd. and hybrid engring. group leader, 1981-87, hybrid engring. supr., 1988-93, strategic planning and tech. supr., 1994—; traffic engring. software cons. A & F Engring., Indpls., 1982-88. Patentee in field; contbr. articles to profl. jours. Adminstrv. bd. St. Luke's United Meth. Ch., Kokomo, 1985-88, staff/parish rels. com. chmn., 1989-91, nominating com., 1992-94; pres. bd. trustees Kokomo Ctr. Township Schs., 1993-94, v.p. bd. trustees, 1992-93, apptd. bd. trustees, 1992-94, elected trustee, 1994—; mem. curriculum com. Darrough Chapel Elem. Schs., Kokomo, 1991-92, tech. team, 1989-91; mem. Howard County Coalition for Decency, Kokomo, 1988-89, Kokomo H.S. Booster Club, 1991—; book buddy Elwood Hayes Elem. Sch., Kokomo, 1994; leader Elks Cancer Drive, 1989-92. Mem. Soc. Mfg. Engrs. (pres. 1985-86), Internat. Soc. Hybrid Microelectronics, Nat. Sch. Bds. Assn., Ind. Sch. Bds. Assn. (master bd. mem.). Republican. Home: 1211 W Cadillac Dr Kokomo IN 46902-2551 Office: Delco Electronics 700 E Firmin St Kokomo IN 46904-9005

COASE, RONALD HARRY, economics educator; b. Willesden, Eng., Dec. 29, 1910; came to U.S., 1951; s. Henry Joseph and Rosalie (Giles) C.; m. Marian Ruth Hartung, Aug. 7, 1937. B of Commerce, London Sch. Econs., 1932, DSc, 1951; Dr. Rer. Pol. honoris causa, Cologne U., Fed. Republic Germany, 1988; D of Social Sci. (hon.), Yale U., 1989; LLD (hon.), Washington U., St. Louis, 1991, U. Dundee, Scotland, 1992; DSc (hon.), U. Buckingham, Eng., 1995. Sir Ernest Cassel Travelling scholar, 1931-32; asst. lectr. Dundee Sch. Econs., 1932-34, U. Liverpool, Eng., 1934-35; from asst. lectr. to lectr. to reader London Sch. Econs., 1935-51; prof. U. Buffalo, 1951-58, U. Va., Charlottsville, 1958-64; prof. U. Chgo., 1964—, now Clifton R. Musser prof. emeritus, sr. fellow in law and econs. Law Sch.; statistician, then chief statistician Central Statis. Office, Offices War Cabinet, Eng., 1941-46. Author: British Broadcasting, A Study in Monopoly, 1950, The Firm, the Market and the Law, 1988, Essays on Economics and Economists, 1994; editor Jour. Law and Econs., 1964-92. Rockefeller fellow, 1948; fellow Center for Advanced Study Behavioral Scis., 1958-59; sr. research fellow Hoover Instn., Stanford U., 1977; recipient Nobel Prize in econ., 1991. Fellow Am. Acad. Arts and Scis., Am. Econ. Assn. (disting.), The Brit. Acad. (corr.), European Acad.; mem. Royal Econ. Soc., Mont Pelerin Soc. Home: 1515 N Astor St Chicago IL 60610-1655 Office: U Chgo Laird Bell Law Quadrangle 1111 E 60th St Chicago IL 60637-2702

COATES, CAROLINE M., marketing administrator; b. Detroit, Sept. 1, 1965; d. Joseph Hudy and Virginia R. Fisher; m. Richard A. Coates, Oct. 10, 1987. BA, Ctrl. Mich. U., 1987. Intern reporter Morning Sun, Mt. Pleasant, Mich., 1986; mktg. coord. Athletic Tng. Svcs., Inc., Mt. Pleasant, Mich., 1986-87; comms. coord. Traverse City (Mich.) Conv. Bur., 1987-90; spl. sects. editor Noverr Pub., Inc., Traverse City, 1989-90; mktg. dir. Coldwell Banker Schmidt Realtors, Traverse City, 1990—. Asst. press sec. Dem. Congl. Candidate, Mt. Pleasant, 1986. Mem. Soc. Profl. Journalists, Traverse Ad Club, Sigma Iota Epsilon. Office: Coldwell Banker Schmidt 402 W Front St Traverse City MI 49686-2664

COATS, DANIEL RAY, senator; b. Jackson, Mich., May 16, 1943; s. Edward R. and Vera E. C.; m. Marcia Crawford, Sept. 4, 1965; children: Laura, Lisa, Andrew. B.A., Wheaton (Ill.) Coll., 1965; J.D. cum laude, Ind. U., 1971. Bar: Ind. 1972. Mem. 97th-100th Congresses from 4th Dist. Ind., Washington, 1981-89; Dist. rep. U.S. Congressman Dan Quayle, 1976-80; U.S. senator from Ind., 1989—. Pres., Big Bros./Big Sisters, Ft. Wayne, Ind. Served with U.S. Army, 1966-68. Office: US Senate 404 Russell Senate Bldg Washington DC 20510-1403

COATS, JAMES O., state legislator; m. Alice Coats. BS, N.D. State U. Tchr., ret., state rep. dist. 34, 1991—; mem. industry, bus. and labor, polit. subdvsns. coms. N.D. Ho. Reps. Recipient Golden Rule award, 1991. Mem. VFW, Am. Legion (dept. comdr.), Mandan Golden Age Club (pres.), Elks, Eagles, Amvets. Democrat. Home: 1704 Sunset Dr Mandan ND 58554-1628*

COBANE, JOSEPH L., retired manufactures agent; b. Detroit, June 24, 1928. BS, U. Mich., 1950, MBA, 1951. Pres. Metamora Products, Meta Mora, Mich., 1966-75; chmn. bd. Cobane Corp., Grosse Point Woods, Mich., 1966-93, ret., 1993. Co-inventor returnable plastic container for textile fabric. 1st lt. USAF, 1951-54. Mem. Otsego Ski Club. Republican. Presbyterian.

COBB, CECELIA ANNETTE, counselor; b. Dayton, Ohio, June 22, 1944; d. Fred E. and Margaret Laverne (Ogle) C.; m. Robert A. Fackler, June 25, 1966 (div. Mar. 1981); m. James A. McCluskey, June 18, 1983; 1 child, James Christian. BS, Ohio U., 1967; MA in Teaching, Saginaw Valley State Coll., 1978; MA in Counseling, Oakland U., 1993. Lic. profl. counselor, Mich.; cert. tchr., Mich. Tchr. L'Anse Creuse Pub. Schs., Mt. Clemens, Mich., 1966-91, counselor, 1993—; cons. Establishment Crisis Ctr., Mt. Clemens, 1968-70; supr. tchr. Mich. State U., Lansing, 1970-72; leader pilot project Quest Inc., Findlay, Ohio, 1982-83. Provider shelter for homeless, Mt. Clements, 1983-93. Mem. NEA, Am. Sch. Counseling Assn., Mich. Edn. Assn., Mich. Sch. Counseling Assn., Macomb County Assn. Counseling and Devel., Chi Sigma Iota. Democrat. Home: 38098 Lakeshore Dr Harrison Township MI 48045-2855 Office: L'Anse Creuse Pub Schs 36727 Jefferson Ave Harrison Township MI 48045-2917

COBB, CLAYTON LEIGH, academic advisor; b. Racine, Wis., Jan. 15, 1970; s. Dorothy Ann Cobb. BA in English, Vitebro Coll., 1993; MS in cultural founds. edn., U. Wis., Milw., 1995. Admission counselor Vitebro Coll., La Crosse, Wis., 1993-94; acad. advisor student support svcs. U. Wis.-Parkside, Kenosha, 1995—; presenter in field. Home: 2000 E Newberry Blvd Milwaukee WI 53211 Office: U Wis Parkside 9000 Wood Rd Box 2000 Kenosha WI 53141

COBLE, PAUL ISHLER, advertising agency executive; b. Indpls., Mar. 17, 1926; s. Earl and Agnes Elizabeth (Roberts) C.; A.B., Wittenberg U., 1950; postgrad. Case-Western Res. U., 1950-53; m. Marjorie M. Trentanelli, Jan. 27, 1951; children—Jeffery Mansfield, Sarah Anne Davis, Douglass Paul Coble. Reporter, Springfield (Ohio) Daily News, 1944; reporter, feature writer Rockford (Ill.) Register-Republic, 1947-48; account exec. Fuller & Smith & Ross, Inc., Cleve., 1949-57; dir. sales promotion McCann Erickson, 1957-63; dir. sales devel. Marschalk Co., 1963-65, v.p., 1965-70, sr. v.p., 1970-73; pres. Coble Group, 1973—; chmn. bd., sec.-treas. Hahn & Coble. Inc., advt., mktg. and pub. relations, 1977—; pub. Islander mag., Hilton Head Island, S.C., 1973-83; asst. prof. advt. W.Va. U., 1982-83. Chief instr. Cleve. Advt. Club Sch., 1961-73. Active fund raising drives for various charitable and youth orgns. Served with AUS, 1944-46. Mem. Sales and Marketing Internat., Assn. Indsl. Advertisers, Cleve. Advt. Club, Newcomen Soc., River Oaks Racquet Club, Sea Pines Country Club, Cleve. Rotary. Contbr. articles to profl. pubs. Home: 37 Club Course Dr Hilton Head Island SC 29928-3137

COBLITZ, DAVID BARRY, chief technical specialist; b. Ashtabula, Ohio, Oct. 1, 1949; s. Sandford E. and Leah Pearl (Shapiro) C.; m. Sandra Gay Tischler, Dec. 26, 1976; children: Brian, Evan, Aaron. BS in Physics, Case Inst. Tech., 1971; MS in Optical Engring., U. Rochester, 1973. Computer programmer Wheeler Mfg. Corp., Ashtabula, 1967-71; engr. Xerox Webster Rsch. Ctr., Webster, N.Y., 1972; staff engr. McDonnell Douglas Electronics, St. Charles, Mo., 1973-83; br. mgr. DCS Corp., Alexandria, Va., 1983-89; tech. devel. and integration specialist McDonnell Douglas, St. Louis, 1989—. Contbr. articles to profl. jours.; patentee multipurpose adaptive filter, reflection elimination method. Home: 15306 Schoettler Estates Dr Chesterfield MO 63017-5461 Office: McDonnell Douglas MC0642233 PO Box 516 Saint Louis MO 63166-0516

COBURN, DWIGHT D., mechnical designer; b. Charlois, Pa., Jan. 26, 1953. AD in Mech. Design, Hawkeye C.C., Waterloo, Iowa, 1977. Mech. designer Deere & Co., Waterloo, 1977—. Mem. Waterloo Cmty. Schs. PTA, pres., 1990-95; coord. mentor ptnrs. Ptnrs. in Edn./John Deere, Waterloo, 1992-95. Office: Deere & Co PO Box 8000 Waterloo IA 50704-8000

COBURN, RONALD MURRAY, ophthalmic surgeon, researcher; b. Detroit, Aug. 25, 1943; s. Sidney and Jean (Goldberg) C.; m. Barbara Joan Levy, Feb. 21, 1969; children: Nicholas Scott, Lauren Joy. BS, Wayne State U., 1965, MD, 1969. Diplomate Am. Bd. Ophthalmology, Am. Bd. Eye Surgery (surg. examiner). Dir. The Coburn Clinic, Dearborn, Mich., 1976—; chief ophthalmology Straith Hosp. for Spl. Surgery, Southfield, Mich., 1985—; cons. CooperVision, Inc., Bellevue, Wash., 1985-88, Alcon Surg., Inc., Ft. Worth, 1988—. Co-author: Lens-Stat Intraocular Lens Modeling System; editorial advisor Phaco and Foldables, 1990. Trustee Straith Hosp. for Spl. Surgery, 1986—. Capt. Mich. N.G., 1969-76. Fellow ACS, Internat. Coll. Surgeons, Soc. Eye Surgeons, Royal Soc. Medicine (London), Leadership Soc. ACS; mem. AAAS, Am. Soc. Cataract and Refractive Surgery, Am. Diabetes Assn., Mich. Ophthal. Soc., Wayne County Med. Soc., Rsch. To Prevent Blindness, N.Y. Acad. Scis., Internat. Assn. Ocular Surgeons, Internat. Eye Found., Soc. Geriatric Ophthalmology, Soc. for Excellence in Eye Cre, Internat. Glaucoma Congress, Phi Beta Kappa. Home: 1490 W Long Lake Rd Bloomfield Hills MI 48302-1340 Office: The Coburn Clinic 19855 Outer Dr Dearborn MI 48124-2037

COCHRAN, DALE M., state legislator; b. Ft. Dodge, Iowa, Nov. 20, 1928; s. Melvin and Gladys C.; m. Jeannene Hirsch, 1952; children: Deborah, Cynthia, Tamara. BS, Iowa State U., 1950. Rep. Iowa State Rep. Dist. 14, 1965-86; spkr. of house Iowa Ho. of Reps., 1975-78, exec. com. mem. nat. conf. state legis. and coun. state govt., chmn. agrl. and food policy com. nat. conf. state legis.; sec. agrl. Iowa, 1987—; owner of farm; dir. Iowa Rural Devel. Policy Coun.; pres. Midwestern Assn. State Depts. Agrl. and Mid-Am. Int. Agrl. Trade Coun. Farm editor: Ft. Dodge Messenger. Recipient Altig award Nat. Fedn. Blind, Sweepstakes award Friends of Agrl. Mem. Iowa Assn. Soil (hon. life), Iowa Soybean Assn. (bd. dirs. 1969-75), Lions, Elks, Pi Kappa Phi, Gamma Sigma Delta. Office: Agr & Land Stewardship Dept Wallace Bldg 9th and Grand Des Moines IA 50319*

COCHRAN, LESLIE HERSCHEL, university administrator; b. Valparaiso, Ind., Apr. 24, 1939; s. Robert H. and Dellcena (Marquart) C.; m. Linda Stockman, May 20, 1978; children: Troy, Kirt, Leslee. B.S., Western Mich. U., 1961, M.A., 1962; Ed.D., Wayne State U., 1968. Mem. faculty Central Mich. U., Mt. Pleasant, 1968-80, assoc. dean, 1970-75, dean fine and applied arts, 1975-76, vice provost, 1976-80; provost S.E. Mo. State U., Cape Girardeau, 1980-92; pres. Youngstown (Ohio) State U., 1992—; mem. accreditation team North Ctrl. Assn., Chgo., 1982—. Author: Advisory Committee in Action, 1980, Innovative Program in Industrial Education, 1970, Administrative Commitment to Teaching, 1989, Publish or Perish: The Wrong Issue, 1992. Trustee Butler Inst. Am. Art, Western Res. Health Care System, N.E. Ohio Med. Coll. Japan Soc. Promotion of Sci. fellow Tokyo, 1976. Mem. Nat. Assn. Indsl. and Tech. Tchr. Edn. (pres. 1976), Rotary. Office: Youngstown State U Office of Pres Youngstown OH 44555

COCHRAN, MARY ANN, nurse educator; b. Chgo., Dec. 12, 1951; d. Lawrence Donovan and Mary Gracz (Capizzi) Lee; m. Thomas Lee Cochran, Mar. 12, 1971; 1 child, Nathan Edgar. Diploma in nursing, St. Joseph's Hosp., Joliet, Ill., 1973. RN, Ill.; cert. post anesthesia nurse. Staff nurse Silver Cross Hosp., Joliet, 1973—, stafff nurse ICU, 1979—, in-svc. educator post anesthesia care unit, 1987-92, BLS instr., 1987—. Mem. AACN, Am. Soc. Post Anesthesia Nurses, Ill. Soc. Post Anesthesia Nurses (membership chair 1990-92, ways & means chair 1992-95, Ill. dist. 1 dir. 1995—). Office: Silver Cross Hosp 1200 Maple Rd Joliet IL 60432-1439

COCHRAN, WILLIAM C., state legislator; b. New Albany, Ind., Aug. 25, 1934; m. Judith Ann Bocard; children: Sherry Lee, Rex Charles, Richard Paul. Student, Ind. U. Realtor Brooks Realtors; rep. Dist. 72 Ind. Ho. of Reps., 1974—, vice chmn. interstate coop. com., mem. judiciary com., ways and means com. Clk. Cir. Ct., Floyd County, 1967-74; vol. March of Dimes. Recipient Outstanding Cmty. Svc. award, 1970. Mem. VFW, FOB, Manzanita Tribe Redmen, Elks, Masons. Home: 4330 Green Valley Rd New Albany IN 47150-4258*

COCKBURN, EVE GILLIAN, newsletter editor; b. Astley, Eng., Mar. 3, 1924; came to U.S., 1948; d. Thomas and Alice (Speakman) Fairhurst; m. Aidan Cockburn, June 26, 1945 (dec. 1981); children: Gillian Margaret, Erika June, Vivien Jo, Alistair Aidan, Alison Francesca. BA with honours, Oxford U., 1945, MA, 1958. Sci. and health columnist Berkshire Evening Eagle, 1954-55; syndicated sci. and health columnist Pakistani newspapers, including Civil and Mil. Gazette, 1958-60; founder, editor Dance Newsletter, Detroit, 1969-74; co-founder, editor newsletter Paleopathology Assn., Detroit, 1973—, dir., 1981—; Mem. Antiquaries Bd., Detroit Inst. of Arts, 1971—. Editor Woman and Health, 1959-60, Mummies, Disease, and Ancient Cultures, 1980 (Med. Writers Am. award 1981); mem. editl. bd. Jour. Paleopathology, 1988—, contbg. editor, 1991; mem. sci. com. Cronos, 1990-92. Mem. World Coun. on Mummy Studies, 1992—, hon. com. The Origin of Syphilis in Europe, Toulon, France, 1993. Fellow Zool. Soc. London; mem. Am. Assn. Phys. Anthropologists. Office: Paleopathology Assn 18655 Parkside Detroit MI 48221-2208

COCOZZOLI, GARY RICHARD, library director; b. Detroit, Oct. 27, 1951; s. Berto and Yolanda Virginia (Ronchetto) C. BA in Geography, Wayne State U., Detroit, 1973, MLS, 1974. With serials and interloan dept. Lawrence Inst. Tech., Southfield, Mich., 1975-81; dir. libr. Lawrence Tech. U., Southfield, 1981—; mem. exec. bd. Mich. Libr. Consortium, 1994—. Author: (with others) German-American History and Life, 1980, Japan's Economic Challenge, 1988; reviewer: Am. Reference Books Annual, 1985—. Bd. dirs. Mich. Libr. Consortium, 1994—; pres. Cambridge Village Assn., Southfield, 1987—. Recipient Disting. Alumnus award Wayne State U. Lib. Sci. Program, 1990. Mem. ALA, Mich. Libr. Assn. (acad. div. bd. 1986-88, continuing edn. com. 1992-94), Spl. Librs. Assn. (career devel. com. 1987-88), S.E. Mich. League Librs. (chair 1988-90), Coun. on Resource Devel. (chair Oakland County, Mich. 1990-91), Toastmasters Internat. Office: Lawrence Tech U 21000 W 10 Mile Rd Southfield MI 48075-1051

CODUTI, PHILIP JAMES, legal association admininstration; b. Chgo., Aug. 14, 1968; s. Philip James and Mary Cathirine C. AAS, South Suburban Coll., South Holland, Ill., 1990; BA, Gov.'s State U., University Park, Ill., 1992; MA, 1994. Military police investigator U.S. Army, U.S. Army Reserve, Rosemont, Ill., 1987—; police officer Thornton Police Dept., 1990-92; rsch. asst. Gov.'s State U., University Park, Ill., 1990-94; prof., 1994—; asst. to the Undersheriff Cook County Sheriff's Office, Chgo., 1994—; adminstr. of Grants and Planning, 1994—; liberal arts adv. bd. Gov.'s State U., University Park, Ill., 1993—; anti-violence trainer Ill. TASC, Chgo., 1993—; criminal justice adv. bd. Gov.'s State U., University Park, Ill., 1994—, S. Suburban Coll., S. Holland, Ill., 1994—. Trustee Ill. Bd. Gov.'s, Springfield, Ill., 1993-94. Recipient Army Achievement medal U.S., Army, Chgo., 1992; named Grad. Studnet of Yr. Gov.'s State U., University Park, Ill., 1994, Nat. Dean's List, Nat. Dean's List., University Park, Ill., 1994. Democrat. Roman Catholic. Office: Cook County Sheriff Richard J Daley Ctr Rm 704 Chicago IL 60602

CODUTTI, JERRY LUIS, steel manufacturing executive; b. Rosario, Santa Fe, Argentina, Apr. 6, 1953; came to U.S. 1965; s. Enzo Radil and Olga Naomi (DiPado) C.; m. Lydia Ann Watson, Feb. 14, 1981; 1 child, Nicholas Alan. Student, Va. Mil. Inst., 1972-76. Supr. RECO Industries, Co., Richmond, Va., 1977-84, prodn. supt., 1984-86; supr. Paul Mueller Co., Springfield, Mo., 1986-88, supt. of supports, 1988-90, supt. of mfg., 1991—; plant mgr. Alhstrom, Princeton, N.J., 1990-91; dir. mfg. Paul Mueller Co., Springfield, Mo., 1991-96, mfg. engring. and quality assurance mgr., 1995—. Office: Paul Mueller Co Phelps Ave Springfield MO 65802

CODY, AELRED JOSEPH, editor, priest; b. Oklahoma City, Feb. 3, 1932; s. Joseph Francis Cody and Frances Margaret Tucker. BA, St. Meinrad Coll., 1956; Sacrae Theologia Licentiatus, U. Ottawa, Ont., Can., 1958, Sacrae Theologiae Doctor summa cum laude, 1960; Sacrae Theologia Licentiatus, Pontifical Bibl. Inst./Commn., Rome, 1962, Sacrae Scipturae Doctor summa cum laude, 1968; diploma, French Bib. and Archaeol. Sch., Jerusalem. Ordained priest, 1957; professed Benedictine, 1952. Prof. Old Testament and ancient Near East studies S. Anselmo, Pontifical Bible Inst., Rome, 1968-78; organist Abbazia di S. Anselmo, Rome, 1968-76; procurator gen. in Roman Curia Am.-Cassinese & Swiss-Am. Benedictine Congregations, Rome, 1975-78; master of novices and juniors St. Meinrad (Ind.) Archabbey, 1978-92; mem. pres.'s coun. Swiss-Am. Benedictine Cong., 1981-96, mem. legal com., 1984—, chmn. legal com., 1990—; assoc. editor Cath. Bib. Quar., St. Meinrad, 1987-92, gen. editor, 1993—; mem. ofcl. Oriental Orthodox-Roman Catholic Consultation in U.S., Nat. Conf. of Cath. Bishops and Standing Conf. of Oriental Orthodox Bishops, 1981—; consultor for Holy See, Mixed Commn. Roman Cath. Ch. and World Alliance Ref. Chs., 1970. Author: Heavenly Sanctuary and Liturgy in the Epistle to the Hebrews, 1960 (prize of Christian Rsch. Found. Harvard U. 1960), A History of Old Testament Priesthood, 1969, Ezekiel, 1984; contbr. to profl. jours. and encycs.; mem. editl. bd. Biblica, Rome, 1968-73; mem. editl. com., consultative com. Concilium, Nijmegen, 1969-91. Mem. Royal Coll. Music (assoc., London), Royal Coll. Organists (assoc., London), Internat. Orgn. for Study of Old Testament, Internat. Assn. for Coptic Studies, Am. Oriental Soc., Soc. Bib. Lit., Cath. Bib. Assn. Am. (life, trustee 1984-87, exec. bd. 1993—). Home: St Meinrad Archabbey Saint Meinrad IN 47577 Office: The Cath Bib Quar St Meinrad Archabbey Saint Meinrad IN 47577

COE, FREDRIC L., physician, educator, researcher; b. Chgo., Dec. 25, 1936; s. Lester J. and Lillian (Chaitlen) C.; m. Eleanor Joyce Brodny, May 5, 1965; children: Brian, Laura. A.B., U. Chgo., 1955; M.S., U. Chgo., 1957; M.D., U. Chgo., 1961. Diplomate Am. Bd. Internal Medicine. Intern Michael Reese Hosp., Chgo., 1961-62, resident, 1962-65; resident U. Tex. S.W. Med. Sch., 1967-69; chmn. nephrology Michael Reese Hosp., 1972-82; prof. medicine U. Chgo., 1977—, prof. physiology, 1979—; chmn. nephrology A.M. Billings Hosp., Chgo., 1982—; founder, pres. Litholink Corp. Author: Nephrolithiasis, 1978, 2d edit. (with J. Parks), 1987, (with B. Brenner and F.C. Rector) Renal Physiology, 1986, Clinical Nephrology;

editor: Renal Therapeutics, 1978, Nephrolithiasis, 1980, Hypercalciuric States, 1983, (with M. Favus) Disorders of Bone and Mineral Metabolism, 1993; editor-in-chief Yearbook of Nephrology; editor: (with others) Kidney Stones: Medical and Surgical Management, 1996. Served to capt. USAF, 1961-67. Grantee NIH, 1977—. Fellow ACP; mem. Am. Soc. Clin. Investigation, Am. Physiol. Soc., Assn. Am. Physicians. Jewish. Home: 5490 S South Shore Dr Chicago IL 60615-5920 Office: U Chgo Med Ctr 5841 S Maryland Ave Chicago IL 60637-1463

COE, JOHN WILLIAM, management consultant; b. Highland Park, Mich., Oct. 2, 1924; s. C. Leroy and Grace Lamont C.; m. Sally Childs, Oct. 24, 1953; children: John Childs, Daniel William. BS in Indsl.-Mech. Engring., U. Mich., 1949. Acct. Charles L. Coe and Assocs., 1949; buyer J.L. Hudson Co., Detroit, 1950-58, div. mdse. mgr., 1959-81, v.p., gen. mgr. stores, 1981-83; Champion Enterprises Inc. v.p. mktng. 1982-84, dir. 1970-91; pres. Coe and Assocs., 1984—. Dist. chmn. United Found.; bd. dirs. Planned Parenthood League, Inc. Lt. (j.g.) USNR, 1943-46. Mem Northland-Eastland Mchts. Assn. (dir., past pres.), Mensa, Country Club Detroit, Econ. Club Detroit, Rotary (past pres.), Trout Unltd., Am. Mus. Fly Fishing, Psi Upsilon Alumni Assn. (bd. dirs.), U. Mich. Alumni Club. Republican. Episcopal. Home: 295 Lothrop Rd Grosse Pointe MI 48236-3405

COE, LINDA MARLENE WOLFE, marketing development, photographer; b. Logan, Ohio, Apr. 5, 1941; d. Kenneth William and Mary Martha (Eddy) Wolfe; m. Frederic Morrow Coe, Sept. 15, 1962; children: Christopher, Jennifer, Peter, Michael. BFA, Columbus Coll. of Art and Design, 1978. Freelance photographer Columbus, 1978—; sec., receptionist Plaza Dental, Columbus, 1983; sec. Worthington (Ohio) Dental Group, 1983-85; mktg. and devel. adminstr. Custom Corp. Gift Svc., Worthington, 1985-92, Grandparents Living Theatre, 1993, Premiums & Promotions, Inc., 1995—; trustees Met. Women's Ctr., Columbus, 1986-87. Docent trainee Columbus Mus. Art, 1982-83; mem. Worthington Arts Coun., 1982, 83, 85, 87, 89-93, 94. Mem. Zephrus League, Phoenix Soc., Nat. Soc. Fund Raising Execs., Women's Bus. Bd., Columbus Bus. and Profl. Women, Columbus C. of C., Cols. C. of C., Pres'. Roundtable (com. 1985—), Columbus Coll. Art and Design Alumni Assn. Republican. Roman Catholic. Home: 320 E South St Worthington OH 43085-3771 Office: 684 New York Ave Columbus OH 43201-2945

COE, MICHUAL WILLIAM, physical therapist; b. Emporia, Kans., Aug. 31, 1950. EdD; JCB, EdD, Cath. U., 1983; BS in Phys. Therapy, Ind. U., Indpls., 1985. Lic. phys. therapist, Ill., Ind. Rehab. supr. Healthmark, Indpls., 1985-88, v.p., 1987-89; dir. phys. therapy Vermillion County Hosp., Clinton, Ind., 1988-91, Valley Rehab., Terre Haute, Ind., 1991—; pres., sec., treas. Rehab. Svcs., Inc., Terre Haute, 1991. Mem. Am. Phys. Therapy Assn. (Mary McMillan scholar 1985, pvt. practice sect., Ind. chpt.), Nat. Assn. Rehab. Agys. Home: 3484 John Hinkle Pl Bloomington IN 47408 Office: Valley Rehab 788 S 3rd St Terre Haute IN 47807-4653

COEN, LARRY PAUL, geologist, environmental manager; b. St. Louis, Nov. 7, 1949; s. Willard Clark and Verona Evelyn (Pirkl) C.; m. Laura Ann Rebori, June 5, 1971; children: Rebekah, Joshua, Rachael. BS in Geology, U. Mo., Rolla, 1971, MS in Geology, 1973. Cert. profl. geologist Am. Inst. Profl. Geologists; cert. hazardous materials mgr., Inst. Hazardous Materials Mgrs. 2d lt. Army Air Def. Artillery, Anchorage, Alaska, 1973-75, 1st lt., 1975-77; field geologist Standard Oil Ohio, Pitts., 1977-87; land reclamation specialist Mo. Dept. Natural Resources, Jefferson City, 1987-89, environ. specialist, 1989-90, environ. unit chief, 19990-939, environ. sect. chief, 1993—. Mem. Gov.'s Lead Poisoning Commn., Jefferson City, 1994—. Recipient Gov.'s Productivity award Gov. Mo., Jefferson City, 1991, 95, U.S. EPA Streamlining award Region VII, Kansas City, Mo., 1992. Mem. Am. Inst. Profl. Geologists, Assn. Mo. Geologists. Democrat. Mem. Assembly of God. Home: 1017 Moreau Dr Jefferson City MO 65101 Office: Mo Dept Natural Resources PO Box 176 205 Jefferson St Jefferson City MO 65102

COERVER, ELIZABETH ANN, data base consultant; b. St. Louis, Sept. 4, 1941; d. Harrison Fredrick and Virginia (Marks) C. BA, Fontbonne Coll., St. Louis, 1963. Supr. McDonnell Douglas, St. Louis, 1969-71, cons., 1971-74; sr. cons. McDonnell Douglas, Washington, 1974-75, Phoenix, 1975-77; sr. cons. Mcauto Internat., London, 1977-79; prin. cons. Mcauto Internat., Bonn, Germany, 1979-80; prin. cons. Mcauto Benelux, Hilversum, The Netherlands, 1980-82, Dublin, Ireland, 1982-84; sr. cons. McDonnell Douglas, St. Louis, 1984-93, prin. specialist IS tech., 1993—. Author: (class) IMS Application Programming, 1971, Data Base Design, 1972, Master Terminal Operations, 1972. Mem. AAUW. Office: McDonnell Douglas PO Box 516 Saint Louis MO 63166-0516

COFFEE, VIRGINIA CLAIRE, civic worker, former mayor; b. Alliance, Nebr., Dec. 8, 1920; d. James Maddigan and Adelaide Mary (Forde) Kennedy; BS, Chadron State Coll., 1942; m. Bill Brown Coffee, June 21, 1942; children: Claire, Sara, Virginia Anne, Sue. High sch. prin., Whitman, Nebr., 1942; bookkeeper Coffee & Son, Inc., Harrison, Nebr., 1965—, officer, 1967—, pres., 1987—; dir. Friends of Agate Fossil BEOS, Inc., 1988, v.p. 1988—; mayor City of Harrison, 1978-80. Leader, Girl Scouts U.S.A., 1953-63; mem. Harrison Elem. Sch. bd., 1958-64; mem. liaison com. Chadron State Coll., 1975; pub. rels. chmn. Nebr. Cowbelles, 1968; sec. NW Stock Growers, 1971-73; corp. officer Ft. Robinson Centennial, 1973-88; officer Gov.'s Ft. Robinson Centennial Commn., 1973-75; hon. gov. Nebr. Centennial, 1967; chmn. Sioux County Bicentennial, 1973-77; trustee Nebr. State Hist. Soc. Found., 1975—, Village of Harrison, 1973-80, Chadron State Coll. Found., 1995—; bd. dirs. Harrison Cmty. Club, Inc., 1983-86, officer, 1984-86; apptd. Sioux County Vis. com. 1989—; apptd. adm. Nebr. Navy, 1992. Recipient Disting. Svc. award Chadron State Coll., 1994. Mem. Nebr. State Hist. Soc. (life, dir. 1979-85, 2d v.p. 1982-84, 1st v.p. 1984-85, com. for marker to honor Harrison centennial 1985-86), Wyo. State Hist. Soc., Cardinal Key Honor Frat., Sioux County Hist. Soc. (bd. dirs. 1975-81, 83-84, 87-90, pres. 1988-90, co-pres., sec., v.p.) Sioux county history book com. 1985-86, contbr. articles. Roman Catholic. Clubs: Nebr. Cattle Women, Ladies Community, Westerners Corral Internat., Harrison Cmty. Inc. Chmn. compilation com. book Sioux County Memoirs of Its Pioneers, 1967; coordinator Harrison sect. book Nebraska Our Towns, 1988. Address: PO Box 336 Harrison NE 69346-0336

COFFEY, DENNIS JAMES, technology consultant; b. Detroit, Nov. 11, 1940; s. James Patrick Coffey and Gertrude Viola Rinne Coffey Schultz; m. Joyce Crim (div. 1967); children: Jordan Collard, Denise Van Patten, Dennis Michael; m. Kathryn Osborne (div. 1988); children: James Donald, Andrew Joseph. BA, Wayne State U., 1990, MEd, 1992. Artist, writer, producer Maverick/MGM Records, Detroit, 1964-68, Sussex/Buddah Records, L.A., 1970-74, West Bound/Atlantic Records, Detroit, 1974-78; studio guitarist Motown Records, Detroit, 1968-76; v.p., co-owner Theocoff Prodns., Detroit, 1978-80, Glen Ridge, N.J., 1980-82; free-lance guitarist Farmington Hills, Mich., 1982-85; instrnl. technologist GM, Warren, Mich., 1985-89, Detroit Art Svcs., Troy, Mich., 1989-92; tng. cons. Farmington Hills, Mich., 1993-94; tng. mgr. ISI Robotics Inc., Warren, 1994-95. Artist, writer and producer record albums including Hair and Thangs, 1969, Evolution, 1971, Going For Myself, 1972, Electric Coffey, 1973, Instant Coffey, 1974, Finger Lickin Good, 1975, Back Home, 1976, A Sweet Taste of Sin, 1978, Motor City Magic, 1988, Under the Moonlight, 1990. With U.S. Army, 1959-61. Recipient 3 cert. gold singles Rec. Industry Assn. Am., cert. gold album, Australia, award for best instrumental record NATRA, 1972, Alumni Acad. Achievement award Wayne State U. Coll. Lifelong Learning, 1995; named top instrumentalist and outstanding prodr. Record World, 1978; featured on cover Cashbox mag., 1972. Mem. ASTD, Nat. Soc. Performance and Instrn., Am. Fedn. Musicians, Mich. Soc. Instructional Tech. (hon. Achievement award 1991, Recognition award 1992), Broadcast Music Inc. (Citation Achievement award), Soc. for Tech. Communication (award 1991). Lutheran.

COFFEY, DOUGLAS WAYNE, mental health nurse; b. Columbus, Nebr., June 9, 1958; s. Wayne L. and Helen B. (Guenther) C.; m. Claudia G. Black, June 16, 1979; 1 child, Jeremiah Jason. BA in Edn., Wayne (Nebr.) State Coll., 1980; ASN, U. Nebr. Med. Ctr., Omaha, 1983, BSN, 1984, MSN, 1994. RN, Nebr., Tenn. Charge nurse Nebr. Psychiat. Inst., Omaha; dept. coord. psychiatry Hendersonville (Tenn.) Hosp.; unit mgr. med.-surg. unit Bergan Mercy Med. Ctr., Omaha; house supr. St. Joseph Ctr. for Mental Health, Omaha, dir. support svcs.; dir. hosp. quality improvement and support svcs. St. Joseh Ctr. for Mental Health, Omaha. With U.S. Army Res., 1980—. Home: 7383 Madison St Ralston NE 68127-4350

COFFEY, JAMES LEO, semi-retired pediatrician, family practitioner; b. Wellman, Iowa, July 5, 1919; s. Elmer Ivan and Lola Edna (Oldaker) C.; m. Eleanore Irene Smith, May 17, 1944; children: Steve James, Margaret Irene, John Cecil. BS, U. Iowa, 1943, MD, 1945. Fellow in pediatrics St. Louis Children's Hosp., 1947-49; pediatrician pvt. practice Phoenix, 1949-51; family practice Fairfax, Mo., 1951-55, Emmetsburg, Iowa, 1955-85; adj. emergency room physician Ft. Dodge, Mason City, Emmetsburg, 1985—. Bd. dirs. Iowa Lakes Cmty. Coll., Estherville/Emmetsburg, Iowa, 1966-70; bd. dirs., funding chmn. Five Island Lake Bd., Palo Alto County, Iowa, 1989—. Capt. U.S. Army, 1947. Named Man of Yr., Emmetsburg C. of C., 1968, 94. Mem. Am. Coll. Cardiology, Am. Bd. Family Practice (charter), Iowa Acad. Family Practice (life), Iowa State Med. Soc. (life). Democrat. Episcopalian. Home: 13 N Madison Emmetsburg IA 50536

COFFEY, PAUL, professional hockey player; b. Weston, Ont., Can., June 1, 1961. Hockey player Edmonton (Can.) Oilers, 1980-87, Pitts. Penguins, 1987-92; with L.A. Kings, 1992, Detroit Red Wings, 1993—; mem. OMJHL All-Star second team, 1979-80, NHL All-Star second team, 1980-81, 83-84, 89-90, first team, 1984-86, 88-89, Stanley Cup championship teams, 1984, 85, 87, 91; player NHL All-Star Game, 1982-86, 88-94. Recipient James Norris Meml. trophy, 1984-86; named All-Star second team, 1981-82, 83-84, 87-87, 89-90, first team, 1984-85, 85-86, 88-89. Office: Detroit Red Wings 600 Civic Center Dr Detroit MI 48226-4408*

COFFIELD, CURTIS STEVEN, music director; b. Madison, Ohio, Nov. 20, 1969; s. Eugene Ray and Dinah J. (Evans) C.; m. Jennifer Lynne Gasterland, Dec. 19, 1991. Student, Lee Coll., 1987-88, Kilgore Coll., 1988-89, Christ for the Nations Inst., 1990-91, Normandale Coll., 1992. Ordained minister Ch. on the Rock World Outreach Center. Program dir., disc jockey KBCL Radio Sta., Shreveport, La., 1989-90; youth min. Life Tabernacle, Shreveport, 1989-90; dir. youth and music Christian Outreach Internat., Minnetonka, Minn., 1991-93; min. music Ch. on the Rock, St. Peters, Mo., 1993-95, Resurrection Life Ch., Grandville, Mich., 1995—. Vocalist Lee Coll. Campus Choir, Cleveland, Tenn., 1987-88; dir. Young Life Club, Shreveport, 1990; vocalist Living Praise, Dallas, 1990-91; featured musical performer Youth for the Nations Conf., Dallas, 1994. Presdl. scholar Lee Coll., Cleveland, 1988. Republican. Home: 4660 Orchard Ct Grandville MI 49418 Office: 5600 Ivanrest SW Grandville MI 49418

COFFIN, BERTHA LOUISE, telephone company executive; b. Atlanta, Aug. 19, 1919; d. William Wesley and Bertha Louise (Marsh) Mendenhall; m. J. Donald Coffin, Feb. 14, 1943 (dec. Sept. 1978). BA, U. Kans., 1940. Med. technologist Midwest Research Lab., Emporia, Kans., 1940-43; ins. agt. Coffin Ins. Agy., Council Grove, Kans., 1943—, sole owner, mgr., 1978-82; treas. Council Grove Telephone Co., 1947-50, sec.-treas., 1950-78, pres., gen. mgr., chmn. bd., 1978—; del. legis. confs. Nat. Tel. Coop. Assn., 1986, 88, 91, 92, 94, comem. comml. co. com., 1987-91, mem. govt. affairs com., 1996—; founder, pres., chmn. bd. Kans. Personal Comm. Svcs. Ltd., 1995—. Copy preparation for book The Story of the Santa Fe Trail, 1982; author: History of Council Grove Telephone Company, 1991; ann. civic sects. tel. directory. Pres. various lit. clubs, Council Grove, 1945-72; speaker various civic, polit. and religious groups, 1962—; mem. adv. coun. Manhattan Christian Coll., 1983-86, trustee, 1986-92, 93—, chmn., 1991-92. Mem. Kans. Telecomm. Assn. (bd. dirs. 1992-95), Ind. Tel. Pioneers (dir. 1984-92). Democrat. Office: PO Box 272 Council Grove KS 66846-0272

COFFIN, ROBERT PARKER, architect, engineer; b. Chgo., Aug. 6, 1917; s. Charles Howells and Irene (Parker) C.; m. Emily Elizabeth Magie, Jan. 7, 1944; children: Betsy, Robert Jr., Barbara, John. BEngring., Yale U., 1939. Registered profl. engr., Ill., architect, Ill., Wis., Minn., Mo., Ind., Mich., Ky. Field engr. Commonwealth Edison, Chgo., 1939-50; architect Shaw Metz and Dolio, Chgo., 1950-56; ptnr. Coffin and Scherschel, Barrington, Ill., 1956—. Pres., sec. Long Grove (Ill.) Sch. Bd. Dist. 96, 1950-56; trustee Long Grove Village, 1956-59, pres., 1959-81, chmn. plan commn., 1981—. Lt. (j.g.) USN Air Corps, 1942-46. Recipient 5 Gold Key awards Nat. Home Builders Assn. Mem. AIA (emeritus), ASCE (life), Am. Soc. Archtl. Historians, Interfaith Forum on Ch. Architecture. Office: Coffin and Scherschel Ltd 119 North Ave Barrington IL 60010-3220

COFFING, JANET S., principal, special education educator; b. Oak Hill, Ohio, Dec. 28, 1951; d. William T. and Marion L. Coffing. BS in Edn. magna cum laude, Cen. Mich. U., 1974; MEd, Mich. State U., 1978. Cert. spl. edn. tchr., Mich. Tchr. spl. edn. Fowler (Mich.) Pub. Schs., 1974-93, mem. sch. improvement team, 1989-90, 91-92; tchr. spl. edn. Sault Ste. Marie (Mich.) Pub. Schs., 1993-95, elem. prin., 1994—; mem. local planning team Nat. Assistance Project of Spl. Edn. Tech., 1985-88. Vol. Clinton Meml. Hosp., St. Johns, Mich., 1986-93. Vol. of the Yr., 1992. Mem. NEA, ASCD, Mich. Edn. Assn., Mich. Assn. for Learning Disabilities Educators, Coun. for Exceptional Children, Mich. Elem. and Mid. Sch. Prins. Assn. Office: Washington Elem Sch 1200 Ryan Ave Sault Sainte Marie MI 49783-2626

COFFMAN, CURTIS M., securities company official; b. Columbus, Ohio, Nov. 18, 1966. BS in Computer Sci., Heidelburg Coll., 1989. Lic. series 62 and 63 Nat. Assn. Securities Dealers. Account exec. Corna Securities Inc., Columbus, 1990-94, sr. account exec., 1994—. Vol. Columbus Park and Recreation Bd. Home: 594 Tansy Ln Westerville OH 43081-5672 Office: Corna Securities Inc 5302 Mckitrick Blvd Columbus OH 43235-7366

COGAN, DOLORIS COULTER, public relations executive; b. Potter, Nebr., July 28, 1924; d. George Albert and Margaret Ann (Jensen) C.; children: Thomas James, Richard Brian, Douglas George. BA, Wesleyan U., 1945; MS, Columbia U., 1946. Editor Inst. Ethnic Affairs, Washington, 1946-49; dir. rsch. Inter-Am. Indian Affairs, Washington, 1949-50; adminstrv. asst. Office Territories, Washington, 1950-55; account rep. Leo Miller Assocs., Westport, Conn., 1964-65; mgr. pub. rels. Pepperidge Farm, Norwalk, Conn., 1965-72; dir. pub. rels. Miles Labs., Inc., Elkhart, Ind., 1972-87; pres. Cogan Communications, Elkhart, 1988—. Producer: (indsl. film) Miles in Perspective, 1984 (3d place award 1985). Trustee Wesleyan U., Lincoln, Nebr., 1973-79. Mem. Am. Mktg. Assn., Am. Women Radio and TV (pres. 1976-77), Pub. Rels. Soc. Am., Altrusa Club. Democrat. Unitarian. Home and Office: 1616 N Bay Dr Elkhart IN 46514-4270

COGER, RICK, health science facility administrator, educator; b. Pineland, S.C., June 30, 1940; s. Martin and Mary (Brantley) C.; m. Lillian Annette Beasley, July 28, 1964; children: Brenton Raval, Tiffany Ashelia. BS, Savannah State U., 1962; MA, Ball State U., 1965; PhD, Ohio State U., 1972. Cert. secondary tchr., S.C. Asst. prof. Miss. Valley State U., Itta Bena, Miss., 1965-67, Cen. State U., Wilberforce, Ohio, 1967-70; adminstrv. assoc. Ohio State U., Columbus, 1970-72; prof. Wilberforce U., 1972-75; asst. dir. instructional design South Cen. Regional Med. Edn. Ctr. VA Med. Ctr., St. Louis, 1975-91; program dir. Continuing Edn. Ctr. Dept. Vets. Affairs, St. Louis, 1991—; adj. prof. Concordia U. Wis., St. Louis, Mo., 1993—; arbitrator BBB, St. Louis, 1984—; ednl. evaluator Nat. Accrediting Commn. of Cosmetology Arts and Scis., Washington, 1983—; instrnl. designer Am. Med. Record Assn., Chgo., 1978-81. Author: (book) Developing Effective IS, 1975; editor Jour. Allied Health, 1977, Jour. Bio-Communications, 1982; designer various video programs (Gold award 1985). Vol. Peace Corps, Belize City, Belize, 1962-64; bd. dirs. PTO Oakville Elem. Sch., St. Louis, 1980-84; pres. Cross of Christ Luth. Ch., 1984-86; mem. sch. improvement leadership team, mem. tech. task force for Mehlville Sch. System,; mem. parents adv. com. Oakville Sr. High Sch. Named Disting. Leader, Am. Leadership Coun., 1984-85; recipient various awards VA, 1979, 82, 84, 85, Tng. Officers award U.S. Govt., 1979, Disting. Leadership award, 1989, Internat. Leaders in Achievement award, 1990. Mem. Am. Tech. Assn., Health Edn. Media Assn., Am. Counc. Comparative Edn., Health Scis. Communication Assn. (program mem. 1987), Phi Delta Kappa. Home: 2781 Brandenberg Ln Saint Louis MO 63129-4009 Office: Continuing Edn Ctr Dept Vets Affairs Jefferson Barracks Saint Louis MO 63129

COGGS, G. SPENCER, state legislator; b. Milw., Aug. 6, 1949; s. Calvin Jr. and Erma (Bryant) C.; m. Gershia Christina Brown, 1971; children: Mariama, Kijana. AA, Milw. Area Tech. Coll., 1975; BS, U. Wis., Milw., 1976. Former health officer, postal worker, printer City of Milw.; mem. from dist. 16 Wis. State Assembly, Madison, 1982-92, 93—, chmn. spkr.'s task force on gang violence, mem. com. on urban and local affairs, com. on rules, mem. com. on children and human svcs., com. on colls./univs., mem. coms. on employment and tng.; mem. com. on criminal justice and pub. safety, vice chmn. majority caucus; mem. Wis. State Job Tng. Coord. Coun., Job Tng. Partnership Act, 1983—. Mem. Milw. Truancy Com.; mem. N.W. Corridor Rapid Transit Adv. Com., Sherman Park Rapid Transit Adv. Com.; bd. dirs. Isaac Coggs Cmty. Health Ctr. Mem. NAAPC, Urban League (bd. dirs., health and social svc. com.), Wis. Pub. Health Assn., Nat. Conf. State Legislators (mem. transp. and comms. com.). Home: 3732 N 40th St Milwaukee WI 53216-3027*

COHASSEY, JOHN FREDRICK, writer; b. Pontiac, Mich., Nov. 2, 1961; s. Theodore F. C. and Nancy (Aldrich) Chubb; m. Gretta Ann Abu-Isa, May 22, 1993. A of Psychology, Oakland C.C., 1985; B of History, Oakland U., 1990; MA in History, Wayne State U., 1993. Freelance writer Detroit, 1993—. Author: Toast of the Town: The Life and Times of Sunnie Wilson, 1996; contbr. articles to jours. Home: 2410 Woodrow Wilson West Bloomfield MI 48324

COHEN, ALAN DAVID, packaging company executive; b. Madison, Wis., Aug. 15, 1946; s. Israel S. and Belle (Cohen) C.; m. Gail B. Baird, Aug. 22, 1971. Student, U. ARiz., Guadalajara, Mex., 1965; BA, U. Wis., 1968; MBA, Loyola U., Chgo., 1971. Cert. fin. planner. Credit mgr. CB&K Supply, Janesville, Wis., 1972-74; fin. analyst Allis Chalmers, Matteson, Ill., 1974-75; credit mgr. W. Braun Co., Chgo., 1975-78, dir. fin., 1978-82, v.p. mktg., 1982-84, v.p., CFO, 1984—; instr. De Paul U., Chgo., 1984—, advisor, 1986—. Author book revs. Mem. Internat. Assn. Fin. Planners. Office: W Braun Co Chicago IL 60606

COHEN, ALAN R., neurosurgeon; b. N.Y.C., Feb. 15, 1952; m. Joann Coons, May 28, 1978; children: Nathan, Jeremy. BA summa cum laude, Harvard U., 1974; MD, Cornell U., 1978. Resident in internal medicine Dartmouth Hosps., Hanover, N.H., 1978-79; resident gen. surgery NYU Med. Ctr., N.Y.C., 1979-80; fellow in neurology The Nat. Hosp. Queen Square, London, 1982; resident and chief resident, neurosurgery NYU Med. Ctr., N.Y.C., 1980-87; chief of pediatric neurosurgery Floating Hosp./New Eng. Med. Ctr., Boston, 1988-94, Rainbow Babies and Children's Hosp., Cleve., 1994—; assoc. prof. neurosurgery Case Western Res. U., Cleve., 1994—. Editl. bd.: Internat. Jour. of Minimally Invasive Neurosurgery. Fellow Am. Coll. Surgeons; mem. AMA, Am. Assn. Neurol. Surgeons (sect. pediatric neurol. surgeons, young neurosurgeons com.), Congress of Neurol. Surgeons, Phi Beta Kappa. Office: Case Western Res Univ Hosp Dept Neurosurgery 2074 Abington Rd Cleveland OH 44106

COHEN, ALBERTO, cardiologist; b. Rio de Janeiro, Aug. 12, 1932; came to U.S., 1959; s. Nessim and Anneta (Rabischoffsky) C.; m. Bertha Kalichztein, Dec. 27, 1958; children: Deborah Cohen Stein, Annabel, Miriam Cohen Disner. BS, Edn. Rui Barboza, Rio de Janero, 1952; MD, Brazil U., Rio de Janero, 1958. Diplomate Am. Bd. Internal Medicine, Am. Bd. Cardiovascular Disease; cert. bd. med. examiners, Ariz., Fla., Tex., Calif. Intern Robert Wood Johnson Med. Ctr., New Brunswick, N.J., 1959-60; resident Detroit-Macomb Hosp., 1960-61; fellow cardiology medicine Harper Hosp., Detroit, 1961, Detroit Gen. Hosp., 1963-65; practice medicine specializing in cardiology and internal medicine Mt. Clements and Clinton Twp., Mt. Clements, Mich., 1966—; attending staff St. Joseph's Mercy Hosp.; mem. attending cardiology staff Sinai Hosp., Detroit, 1995—, cardiologist, 1995—; instr. medicine Wayne State U., Detroit, 1964-65, asst. prof. medicine, 1965-67, clin. asst. prof. medicine, 1967-87. Contbr. numerous articles to profl. jours. Pres. Macomb County Heart Unit, 1974-77. Fellow ACP, Am. Coll. Chest Physicians, Am. Coll. Angiology, Am. Coll. Internat. Physicians, Am. Coll. Cardiology, Internat. Coll. Angiology; mem. AMA, Brazilian Soc. Medicine, Brazilian Soc. Cardiology, Am. Soc. Internal Medicine, Mich. Soc. Internal Medicine (trustee 1974-77), Mich. State Med. Soc., Wayne County Med. Soc., Macomb County Med. Soc., Am. Heart Assn. (fellow sci. coun. clin. cardiology), Detroit Heart Club (pres. 1989-90). Jewish. Home: 1477 Lochridge Rd Bloomfield Hills MI 48302-0734

COHEN, ALLAN RICHARD, broadcasting executive; b. Bklyn., Dec. 27, 1947; s. Ike and Fae C.; m. Roberta Segal, July 12, 1970; children: Evan, Stacie. BS, Hofstra U., 1970; MM, Poly. Inst. Bklyn., 1976. Electronics engr. Sperry Systems Mgmt. Div., Great Neck, N.Y., 1970-74; with CBS/Viacom, 1974—; dir. planning and adminstrn. WCBS-TV, 1977-79; v.p. personnel CBS Broadcast Group, 1979-80; v.p., gen. mgr. Sta. KMOX-TV, St. Louis, 1980-86, Sta. KMOV-TV, St. Louis, 1986—; lectr. in comm. and journalism Washington U., St. Louis; mem. affiliates adv. bd. CBS. Restaurant critic, travel editor St. Louis Bus. Jour. Vice chmn. bd. dirs. St. Louis Symphony; bd. dirs. Paraquad, Jewish Hosp., United Way, Variety Club; mem. adv. bd. Nat. Coun. Jewish Women, St. Louis. Recipient Flair awards, Emmy awards. Mem. NATAS (v.p. St. Louis chpt. 1987-88, pres. 1989-91), Mo. Broadcasters Assn. (bd. dirs.), Ill. Broadcasters Assn., Nat. Assn. Broadcasters, St. Louis Jr. League (adv. bd.), Westwood Club, St. Louis Variety Club (bd. dirs.).

COHEN, BRUCE ROBERT, finance company executive; b. Chgo., June 4, 1961; s. Benjamin B. and Bernice Lorraine (Grinker) C.; m. Lisa Ann Cohn, July 16, 1989. BA, Tufts U., 1983; MBA, U. Chgo., 1989. Mgr. real estate Pell, Rudman & Co., Boston, 1985-86; sr. v.p. Enterprise Savings Bank, Chgo., 1986-89; pres. Cohen Realty Svcs., Chgo., 1989-93; mng. dir. mcht. banking Cohen Fin., Chgo., 1993—; vis. lectr. Tufts U., 1984-86. Bd. dirs. Coun. Jewish Elderly, Chgo., 1988—, Thresholds, Chgo., 1994—, Young Leaders United, Chgo., 1993—, Std. Club, Chgo., 1994—. Recipient Hill award Tufts U., Boston, 1982, Lewis F. Manley award, 1983. Mem. Nat. Assn. Indsl. & Office Profls., Nat. Realty Com., Urban Land Inst. Office: Cohen Fin 2 N LaSalle Ste 800 Chicago IL 60602

COHEN, CHERYL DIANE DURDA, communications executive; b. Mpls., Jan. 26, 1947; d. Joseph and Dolores Catherine (Monahan) Durda; m. Miles Jon Cohen, June 24, 1967; children: Christopher, Michael, Brian, Katherine Kelly. BA, U. Minn., 1978; grad. Owner/Pres. Mgmt. program, Harvard U., 1992. Writer Aeration Industries Internat. Inc., Chaska, Minn., 1982-85, communications asst., 1985-86, communications mgr., 1986-88, v.p. pub. rels., 1988-93, v.p. mktg. and pub. rels., 1993—; also bd. dirs. Aeration Industries Internat. Inc., Chaska. Editor AIRE-02 News, 1985—, AQUA-02 News, 1988—; contbr. articles on water restoration and aquaculture to U.S. and internat. profl. jours., also conf. proc.; film editor, producer, 1986—. Bd. dirs. Minn. Assn. Retarded Citizens, Mpls., 1984-85, The Joseph Durda Found., 1990—; St. David's Sch. for Exceptional Children, Minnetonka, 1980-85; mem. adv. bd. Minnetonka Schs. CARE, Minn., 1982-92; dir. communications Minnetonka Football Assn., 1986-92, founding mem., 1986; mem. adv. coun. U. Minn. Women's Intercollegiate Athletics; founding mem. Minnetonka Basketball Club, 1984; active legis. testimony, lobbying, pub. speaking Adv. for Severely Disabled, 1981—; mem. U. Minn. Gopher Football Team's Parent Club, 1988-92; mem. USAF Acad. Parents Club, 1992-93, Harvard-Radcliffe Club Minn., 1992—; co-facilitator Devel. Capable Young People series for Minnetonka community, 1983-84. Mem. Water Pollution Control Fedn., World Aquaculture Soc., Asian Fisheries Soc., Chesapeake Bay Found., Clean Water Found., U. Minn. Alumni Assn., U. Minn. Presidents Club (chartered), Minn. Press Club, Booster Club (producer cable TV sports show 1988—, co-chair publicity 1988-92), Harvard Bus. Sch. Club Minn. (alumni mem.), Hazeltine Nat. Golf Club. Roman Catholic. Office: Aeration Industries Internat Inc 4100 Peavey Rd Chaska MN 55318-2344

COHEN, EDWARD, state official. Commr. Dept. Correction, Indpls. Office: IGCS Rm E334 302 W Washington St Indianapolis IN 46204*

COHEN, EDWARD LAWRENCE, state agency administrator; b. Mobile, Ala., Sept. 17, 1950; s. Samuel A. and Rose (Feldman) C.; m. Karen Sue Graber. BA, Ind. U., 1975. Co-owner Silver Maple Prodns. Co., Indpls., 1977-78; energy edn. specialist Cmty. Action Against Poverty, Indpls., 1978-80; energy cons. Rsch. & Planning Assocs., Inc., Indpls., 1980-81; mgr.

Energy Conservation, Indpls., 1981-82; energy auditor Energy Conservation Analysis, Inc., Indpls., 1982-83; program dir. Divsn. of Energy Policy Ind. Dept. of Commerce, Indpls., 1983-90; program dir. Ind. Dept. Environ. Mgmt., Indpls., 1990-93, chief source reduction and recycling br., 1993-94, chief ops. branch, 1994—; bd. dirs. Eastside Cmty. Investments, Indpls., 1979-81; sec. bd. Alternative Tech. Assn., Indpls., 1978-80; bd. dirs. Ind. Recycling Coalition, Indpls., 1990-91; bd. pres., co-founder, pres. Ecology House of Indpls., 1992-95. Producer, dir.: What Energy Crisis?, 1975; developer, trainer: (tng. course) Residential Energy Auditing, 1980; author: (tng. manuals) Commercial Energy Auditing, 1981. Coord. Indpls. Sun Day Com., 1978; co-founder Indpls. Citizens for Recycling, 1990. Recipient Svc. to the Environ. award Ind. Dept. Environ. Mgmt., 1991, Environ. Impact award, 1992, Open Window award Positive Change Network, 1992. Home: 5605 Kingsley Dr Indianapolis IN 46220-3433 Office: PO Box 6015 Indianapolis IN 46206-6015

COHEN, GABRIEL MURREL, editor, publisher; b. Louisville, Aug. 31, 1908; s. Isaac and Jenny (Rosenbaum) C.; m. Helen Aronovitz, Sept. 22, 1938; children: Lawrence, Theodore, Miriam, Debbie, Ben-Zion, Jennie, Hermine, Rena. A.B., U. N.C., 1930. Reporter Louisville Herald-Post, 1927-28, 30-31; founder, editor, pub. Ky. Jewish Chronicle (now Ky. Jewish Post and Opinion), Louisville, 1931—, Ind. Jewish Post, Indpls., 1935—, Mo. Jewish Post and Opinion, St. Louis, 1948-92, Nat. Jewish Post (now Nat. Jewish Post and Opinion), Indpls., 1948—. Founding chmn. Am. Jewish Press Assn., 1944—. Home: 7984 Lieber Rd Indianapolis IN 46260-2835 Office: Nat Jewish Post & Opinion 2120 N Meridian St Indianapolis IN 46202-1308

COHEN, MARVIN RICHARD, real estate management executive; b. N.Y.C., Nov. 1, 1947; s. Hyman Elias and Goldie (Schwartz) C.; m. Jane E. Richman, Dec. 23, 1973; children: Jennifer Richman, Rebecca Richman. BA, U. Calif., Berkeley, 1969, PhD in Polit. Sci., 1975; MA in Polit. Sci., Columbia U., 1970; MA in Social Svcs. Adminstrn., U. Chgo., 1979. Sr. planner Mass. Dept. Planning, Brockton, 1973; asst. prof. U. Tex., Dallas, 1975-77; sr. staff assoc. Chgo. Cmty. Trust, 1979-86; dir. Children, Youth and Families Initiative Chgo. Cmty Trust, 1991-96; program dir. Local Initiative Support Corp., Chgo., 1987-89; rsch. fellow Chapin Hall for Children U. Chgo., 1989-90, lectr. Sch. Social Svc. Adminstrn., 1984-92; sr. v.p. Investors Realty and Mgmt. Corp., Chgo., 1996—; dir. Leadership Greater Chgo., 1983-86; chmn. fin. rev. bd. Investors Realty and Mgmt. Corp., Chgo. Co-chair Coalition of Comty. Founds. for Youth, Kansas City, Mo., 1992-96; chmn. Grantmakers for Children, Youth and Families, Washington, 1993-96; treas. Nat. Assn. Child Advocates, 1992-96. Columbia U. fellow, 1969, Florence G. Heller fellow U. Chgo., 1978. Home: 460 Lincoln Ave W Highland Park IL 60035 Office: IRMCO 2300 Lincoln Park West Chicago IL 60614

COHEN, MAX MARK, surgeon; b. Glasgow, Scotland, Feb. 11, 1939; came to U.S., 1987; s. Harry and Rachel (Goldstein) C.; children: Simon, Talya; m. Marilyn Silverstein. MB ChB, U. Glasgow, 1963. Intern U. Glasgow Hosps., 1963-64, resident surgery, 1964-69; surgical rsch. fellow U. B.C., 1969-70, Harvard U., Cambridge, Mass., 1970-71; chief resident surgery Vancouver Gen. Hosp., 1971-72; asst. prof. surgery, then assoc. prof. surgery U. B.C., Vancouver, Can., 1972-80; assoc. prof. surgery, then prof. surgery U. Toronto, Ont., Can., 1980-87; prof. surgery U. Pa., Phila., 1987-94, U. Colo., Denver, 1989-94; chmn. surgery Grad. Hosp., Phila., 1987-89; prof. surgery Wayne State U., Detroit, 1994—; chmn. surgery Rose Med. Ctr., Denver, 1989-94; dir. Rose Videoscopic Surgery Ctr., Denver, 1991-94; chief surgery Grace Hosp., 1994—. Editor: Biological Protection with Prostaglandins (2d vols.), 1985; editorial bd. Can. Jour. Surgery, 1983-87, Jour. Laparoendoscopic Surgery, 1992—; assoc. editor Clin. and Investigative Medicine, 1985-89; contbr. articles to profl. jours. Grantee Med. Rsch. Coun. Can., 1974-86. Fellow ACS, Royal Coll. Surgeons Edinburgh, Royal Coll. Surgeons Can.; mem. Soc. Am. Gastrointestinal Endoscopic Surgeons, Soc. Univ. Surgeons, Undersea Med. Soc., Am. Gastroenterology Assn., Am. Coll. Physician Execs., Can. Assn. Gen. Surgeons (chmn. rsch. com. 1984-87), Anti Def. League (bd. dirs. 1992). Office: Grace Hosp 6071 W Outer Dr Detroit MI 48235

COHEN, MILLARD STUART, diversified manufacturing company executive; b. Chgo., Jan. 17, 1939; s. Lawrence Irmas and Myra Paula (Littmann) C.; BS in Elec. Engring., Purdue U., 1960; m. Judith E. Michel, Aug. 2, 1970 (dec. Dec. 1995); children: Amy Rose, Michele Lauren. Design engr. GTE Automatic Electric Labs., Northlake, Ill., 1960-66; chief elec. engr. Nixdorff Krein Industries, St. Louis, 1966-68, dir. data processing, 1968-72, treas., 1970—, v.p., 1980-85, pres., 1985—, exec. v.p. Nixdorff Chain, 1972-76, pres. Grape Expectations, 1976—, also dir. Dist. commr. Boy Scouts Am., 1968-72; judge Mo. State Fair; mem. Mo. State Wine Adv. Bd., 1980—, vice-chmn., 1983, 93; mem. St. Louis County Restaurant Commn., 1979—, Augusta (Mo.) Wine Bd., 1981—. Recipient award of merit French Wine Commn., 1972. Mem. ACM, IEEE, Mensa, Les Amis du Vin, Chaine des Rotisseurs, Commanderie de Bordeaux. Jewish (trustee temple), Internat. Wine and Food Soc. (gov. Ams. 1985—). Club: St. Louis. Home: 11233 Ladue Rd Saint Louis MO 63141-8318 Office: PO Box 419050 Saint Louis MO 63141-9050

COHEN, PHYLLIS JOANNE, nurse; b. Freeport, Ill., May 18, 1935; d. Leonard Lawrence and Elsie Hedwig (Schmoldt) Dickman; m. Ralph Cohen, May 17, 1953 (div. 1967); children: Jeffry Alan, Douglas Neil. AS with honors, Highland Community Coll., Freeport, Ill., 1980. LPN, Ill.; RN, Ill., Fla., Ga. Nurse Freeport Meml., Ill., 1977-81; traveling nurse Holy Cross Hosp., Ft. Lauderdale, Fla., 1981-82, Palms of Pasadena, St. Petersburg, Fla., 1982-83, West Paces Ferry, Atlanta, 1983-86, Md. Gen. Hosp., Balt., 1986-87, Chandler Gen. Hosp., Atlanta, 1987—; nurse Eggleston Hosp., Atlanta, 1987, St. Francis Med. Ctr., Honolulu, 1990-91; staff nurse Swedish Am. Hosp., Rockford, Ill., 1988-90; staff nurse Rockford Meml. Hosp., 1992-94, nurse psychiat. unit, 1994—; bd. dirs. Freeport Meml. Hosp., Ill. Artist: Oil Painting Empty Rooms (Blue Ribbon award 1968); Poet: Poetry, Contemplation (Golden Poets award 1986, 88); Before It's Gone (Golden Poets award 1987), Change of Seasons (Golden Poets award 1988), A Letter From Dad (Golden Poets award) 1989. Vol. St. Anthony Aux., Rockford, 1960-61, Contact, 1974-75; mem. YWCA. Mem. Nat. Assoc. Smithsonian Inst., Alumni Assn. of Nurses, Phi Theta Kappa. Republican. Home: 1393 US Highway 20 E Freeport IL 61032-9699 Office: Rockford Meml Hosp 2400 N Rockton Ave Rockford IL 61103-3623

COHEN, RANDALL B., stockbroker; b. Charleston, S.C., May 25, 1971; s. David L. and Linda G. (Golding) C. BAS, Ind. U., 1993. Stockbroker Olde Discount Corp., Glenview, Ill., 1993—. Office: Olde Discount Corp Ste #100 1701 E Lake Ave Glenview IL 60025-2085

COHEN, RICHARD J., state senator; b. Oct. 5, 1949. BA, Northwestern U.; JD, William Mitchell Coll. Law. State rep. Dist. 64B Minn. Ho. of Reps.; senator Dist. 64 Minn. State Senate, 1986—; atty., 1996—; chmn. State Govt. Divsn. Fin. Com.; mem. Crime Prevention com., Ethics & Campaign Reform & Judiciary coms. Office: 591 Cretin Ave S Saint Paul MN 55116-1127 also: State Senate State Capital Building Saint Paul MN 55155-1606*

COHEN, RICHARD LAWRENCE, writer; b. Bronx, N.Y., Mar. 22, 1952; s. Nathan G. and Jean Roslyn (Fiddle) C.; m. Ann Adair Althouse, May 19, 1973 (div. Sept. 1987); children: John, Christopher; m. Susan Baker Empson, July 10, 1994; 1 child, Eric Cohen Empson. BA, U Mich., 1973. Editl. asst. Scott Meredith Lit. Agy., N.Y.C., 1973-79; lectr. creative writing U. Wis., 1988. Author: (books) Domestic Tranquility, 1981, Don't Mention the Moon, 1983, Say You Want Me, 1988, Writer's Mind: Crafting Fiction, 1994. Recipient Hopwood Short Fiction award U. Mich., 1973; fellow Cultural Affairs Commn., 1995. Jewish.

COHEN, ROBERT ALAN, agricultural administrator, educator; b. Akron, Ohio, May 7, 1953; s. Ralph and June Laverne (Peck) C.; m. Margaret Elaine Murphy, Dec. 7, 1973 (div. Oct. 1992); children: Benjamin, Daniel, Michael, Karen, Tamara; m. Paula Moyen Bardige, Mar. 19, 1993; children: Marissa, Leigh. BA, U. Akron, 1973; MA, Ohio State U., 1975. Cert. secondary tchr., Ohio. Program dir. Sta. WWWJ, Johnstown, Ohio, 1976-80; sales mgr. Sta. WZZT, Johnstown, 1980-83; tchr. Licking Heights Sch. Dist., Summit Station, Ohio, 1983-84; acad. dir. Park Coll., Columbus, Ohio, 1983-91; grad. teaching assoc. Ohio State U., Columbus, 1974-77; instr. dept. comm. Ohio State U., Mansfield, 1986—; gen. mgr. Sta. WAPQ, Mansfield, 1990-93; instr. North Ctrl. Tech. Coll., Mansfield, Ohio, 1989-93; regional mgr. Vol. in Overseas Coop. Assistance, Columbus, 1993—; instr. Agrl. Tech. Inst., Wooster, Ohio, 1990—. Author: Introduction to Cooperatives, 1993; co-author (screenplays) Lost But Not Forgotten, 1990, Dangerous Cartel, 1991. Recipient Thomas J. Evans Teaching Excellence award Ohio State U., Newark, 1988, Coop. Educator of Yr. award Ohio Coun. Coops., 1994. Mem. NRA (life), Nat. Coop. Bus. Assn., Nat. Press Club, Coop. Communicators Assn., Assn. Coop. Educators, Ohio Ag Coun., Country Music Assn. Office: 6161 Busch Blvd Ste 209 Columbus OH 43229

COHEN, VALERIE M., physical therapist; b. N.Y.C., Dec. 16, 1965; d. Stanely I. and Yvonne S. (Sayagh) C. BS in Phys. Therapy, Northeastern U., 1988; MS in Athletic Tng., Ind. State U., 1991, MS in Exercise Sci., 1992. Registered phys. therapist, Kans. Supr. phys. therapy Quest I Phys. Therapy, Ramsey, N.J., Union Hosp., Terre Haute, Ind., 1991-92; dir. rehab. svcs. Terre Haute (Ind.) Regional Hosp., 1992-93; phys. therapist Lawrence (Kans.) Meml. Hosp., 1994, Mt. Oread Rehab., Lawrence, 1994—. spkr. in field. Massage therapist Elite Med. Unit Care, Boston Marathon, 1988-90; guest participant North Vermillion (Ind.) H.S., 1991; coord. of county activities Steroid Awareness Week, Terre Haute, 1992; vol. asst. Terre Haute (Ind.) Triathalon, 1992; vol. athletic trainer Hoop-It-Up, Indpls., 1992, Rose Hulman Basketball, Terre Haute, 1993; vol. massage therapist Greater Kans. City (Mo.) Marathon, 1994. Invited To be ATC for USOCTC, Lake Placid, N.Y., 1994, invited to be PT/ATC for USA Track and Field Nat. Pole Vault Summit, Reno, 1995. Mem. AAHPERD, Am. Phys. Therapy Assn. (orthopedic, sports and aquatic sect mem. Kans. com. mem.), Nat. Athletic Trainers Assn., Olympic Sports Medicine Assn., Mo. Sports Massage Team, Nat. Rehab. Network. Home: 3806 Elizabeth Ct Lawrence KS 66049-4156 Office: Mt Oread Rehab 3510 Clinton Pky Pl Lawrence KS 66047

COHN, ANNE HARRIS, health planner, health science association administrator; b. Evanston, Ill., Jan. 16, 1945; d. Nathan and Marjorie (Kurtzon) C.; m. Michael Teitz, Mar. 25, 1973 (div. Dec. 1978). BA in Sociology, U. Mich., 1967; MA in Med. Sociology, Tufts U., 1970; MPH in Health Adminstrn., U. Calif., Berkeley, 1972, DrPH in Health Adminstrn., 1975. Lectr. sch. pub. health U. Calif., Berkeley, 1975-78; legis. aide Senator Albert Gore, Jr., Washington, 1978-79; spl. asst. to sec. HHH, Washington, 1979-80; exec. dir. Nat. Com. Prevention Child Abuse, Chgo., 1980—; adv. bd. Nat. Resource Ctr. Child Abuse, Denver, 1986—, Nat. Assn. Children of Alcoholics, South Laguna, Calif., 1987—. Contbr. articles to profl. jours., newspapers, encys. Assoc., bd. dirs. Berkeley Planning Assocs., 1973-78; bd. dirs. Nat. Congress Parents and Tchrs., Chgo., 1985-87. White House fellow, 1979-80. Fellow AAAS (Congl. sci. fellow 1978-79); mem. Internat. Soc. Prevention Child Abuse and Neglect (sec. 1986—), Am. Pub. Health Assn., Soc. Research in Child Devel. Office: Nat Com Prevention Child Abuse 332 S Michigan Ave Ste 950 Chicago IL 60604-4304

COHN, BARRY L., financial executive; b. Cleve., Apr. 1, 1960. BBA, Ohio U., 1982. Account exec. Cowen & Co., Cleve., 1983-92; v.p. Dean Witter, Cleve., 1992-93; sr. v.p., br. mgr. Rodman & Renshaw Inc., Pepper Pike, Ohio, 1993—. Jewish. Office: Rodman & Renshaw 5288 Ridgebury Blvd Pepper Pike OH 44124-1209

COHN, LUCILE, psychotherapist, nurse; b. Kokomo, Ind., Apr. 17, 1924; d. Jacob and Anna (Kaplan) Kohn; m. Norman Cohn; children: Richard Alan, Robert Irving. PhD, Marquette U. Cert., registered med. clin. hypnotherapist. Cons. psychotherapist Cardinal Stritch Coll., Milw., 1982—; pvt. practice psychotherapy Milw., 1980—; prof. nursing Columbia Coll. Nursing, Milw., 1976—, Carroll Coll. Nursing, Waukesha, Wis., 1976—; profl. vol. dying patients and grieving families, nursing homes and hosps. Contbr. chpt. to textbook. 1st lt. U.S. Army Nurse Corps. Mem. Am. Med. Psychotherapists Assn. (diplomate and fellow), Women's Assn. Orgn. Rehab. Through Tng., Am. Assn. Grief Counselors, Hadassah, U. Wis. Union. Democrat. Jewish. Home: 929 N Astor St Unit 2406 Milwaukee WI 53202-3438

COHN, SCOTT HOWARD, television and radio news correspondent; b. Chgo., Feb. 8, 1960; s. Daniel Harris and Lillian Liselotte (Klopstock) C.; m. Jessica Elizabeth Simonson, Nov. 23, 1985; children: Nathan George, Justin Reid. BA in Journalism, U. Wis., 1981. Reporter Sta. WYEN, Des Plains, Ill., 1978; reporter, anchor Wis. Pub. Radio, Madison, 1978-81; announcer Sta. WHA-TV, Madison, 1980-81; desk asst. Sta. WEAU-TV, Madison, 1981; reporter, anchor Stas. WEAU-TV, WAXX-FM and WAYY, Eau Claire, Wis., 1981-82; anchor, corr. Sta. WZZM-TV, Grand Rapids, Mich., 1982-89; corr. CNBC, N.Y.C., 1989-90; chief midwest corr. CNBC, Chgo., 1990-95; nat. corr., 1995—; commentator Sta. WGVU-TV, Grand Rapids, 1988-89. Video prodr. Temple Emanuel, Grand Rapids, 1988-89. Recipient 1st place award radio feature N.W. Broadcast News Assn., 1982; outstanding achievement award AP, Mich., 1983, 1st place award for individual reporting, 1986; outstanding achievement award UPI, Mich., 1983, 1st place award for spot news coverage, 1986, for investigative reporting, 1987, for feature reporting, 1988; nominee Cable Ace awards, 1992, 93, Citation of Merit, Deadline Club NYC, 1994. Mem. Soc. Profl. Journalists (bd. dirs. Madison campus chpt. 1980-81, award for best spot news coverage Grand Rapids 1984), U. Wis. Alumni Assn., Radio and TV News Dirs. Assn. Office: CNBC 141 W Jackson Blvd Ste 1771 Chicago IL 60604-2908

COHN, STANLEY ALAN, cell biology educator; b. Denver, Nov. 12, 1957; s. Louie and Evelyn Lynn (Shames) C.; m. Sara Hurwitz Cohn, Aug. 11, 1985; children: Rachel Beth, Jacob Samuel. BS in Chemisty with honors, Calif. Inst. of Tech., 1979; PhD in Biology, U. Colo., 1986. Postdoctoral rschr. Nat. Jewish Ctr. for Immunology and Respiratory Medicine, Denver, 1986-89; asst. prof. DePaul U., Chgo., 1989-96, assoc. prof., 1996—. Bd. dirs. Niles Twp. Jewish Congregation, Skokie, Ill., 1982—. Postdoctoral fellowship Am. Cancer Soc., 1987-89; rsch. grant NSF, 1994—. Fellow Royal Soc. of Arts (Silver medal 1979); mem. AAAS, Am. Soc. for Cell Biology, Internat Soc. for Diatom Rsch., Coun. for Undergrad. Rsch. Democrat. Home: 8033 Tripp Skokie IL 60076 Office: DePaul Univ Biology Dept of Biology 1036 W Belden Ave Chicago IL 60614

COKINOS, CHRISTOPHER ANDREW, writer, educator, environmental activist; b. Indpls., Jan. 13, 1963; s. George Clinton and Marjorie (Klotz) C.; m. Elizabeth Caroline Dodd, May 14, 1988. BA in English, Ind. U., 1986; MFA, Washington U., 1991. Editor Ind. U., Bloomington, 1988-89; editor, adminstr. Kans. Regents Network, Manhattan, 1989-90; adj. faculty, instr. Kans. State U., Manhattan, 1991—, asst. dir. NEH regional tchrs. inst., 1994-96. Author: Killing Seasons, 1993; editor poetry Am. Nature Writing newsletter, 1994-96; contbg. editor Orgn. and Environ.; contbr. articles and poems to profl. jours. Co-chair Riley County for Clinton/Gore, Kans., 1992. Recipient Robert Gross award in poetry Woodley Press, 1993. Mem. Assn. Study of Lit. and Environ., Robinson Jeffers Assn., No. Flint Hills Audubon (bd. dirs. 1991—), Kans. Audubon Coun. (pres. 1995—). Democrat. Office: Kans State U English Dept Denison Hall 122 Manhattan KS 66506

COLAIZZI, JOSEPH JOHN, homeless services professional, clergyman; b. Pitts., Oct. 27, 1944; s. Joseph and Edith (Marino) C.; m. Marilyn Frances Davis, Nov. 14, 1982; children: Joseph John, Janna Marisa. BFA, U. Cin., 1966; MDiv, Nazarene Theol. Sem., Kansas City, Mo., 1987. Ordained elder, Ch. of the Nazarene, 1987. Floor dir., asst. lighting dir. WQED-TV, Pitts., 1966-67, prodn. coord., dir., 1968-71; studio supr. WHAS-TV, Louisville, 1967-68; dir. instrnl. TV Carnegie Mellon U., Pitts., 1971-73; self employed, 1974-75; dir. Crisis Care, assoc. Pastor Lamb's Manhattan Ch. of the Nazarene, N.Y.C., 1976-82, dir. ops., 1982-83; student Nazarene Theol. Sem., Kansas City, Mo., 1983-87; exec. dir. Kansas City Rescue Mission, 1985—; mem. adv. bd. Adult Basic Edn. fr Homeless, Kansas City Sch. Dist., 1988-90; mem. adv. bd. Health Care for the Homeless, Kansas City, 1990—; mem. steering com. Urban project Ch. of the Nazarene, Kansas City, 1994-95; mem. ptnrs. steering com. ACCESS Exploring Solutions for Homeless Mentally Ill, Kansas City, 1994—; co-chmn. Homeless Svcs. Coalition, Kansas City, 1995—. Bd. dirs., pres. Meadowridge Housing Coop., Blue Springs, Mo., 1991-93, 96—, v.p., 1993-95. Recipient Eagle award-Outstanding Leadership, Kansas City Dist. Ch. of the Nazarene, 1991, Disting. Svc. award Kansas City Rescue Mission, 1994, Kansas City First Ch. of the Nazarene, 1995. Office: Kansas City Rescue Mission 1520 Cherry Kansas City MO 64108

COLBERT, THOMAS BURNELL, history and literature educator; b. Carroll, Iowa, Sept. 23, 1947; s. Walter Delmar and Marie Anne (Schnuettgen) C.; m. Pamela Jeanette Moffatt, Dec. 28, 1978; 1 child, Matthew. Student, Buena Vista Coll., Storm Lake, Iowa, 1967; BA in History, U. Iowa, 1969, MA in History, 1975; PhD in History, Okla. State U., 1982. Grad. teaching asst. Okla. State U., Stillwater, 1975-79, 80-81; vis. instr. history Huron (S.D.) Coll., 1979-80; prof. history and lit., chmn. social scis./phys. edn. div. Marshalltown (Iowa) Community Coll., 1981—. Contbr. articles and book revs. to hist. jours. and encys., 1976—. Bd. dirs. Rena Van Orman Youth Group Home, Inc., Marshalltown, 1983-91; mem. ctrl. com. Dem. Party of Marshall County, Marshalltown, 1984-88. With USN, 1970-74. NEH fellow Iowa State U., 1990, 94, U. Ariz., 1993. Mem. Am. Hist. Assn., Orgn. Am. Historians, Agrl. History Soc., Western History Assn., So. Hist. Assn., Okla. Hist. Soc., State Hist. Soc. Iowa (trustee 1991—), Hist. Soc. Marshall County (bd. dirs. 1982-85), Des Moines Civil War Roundtable, Phi Alpha Theta, Phi Kappa Phi. Democrat. Episcopalian. Home: 1707 Olson Way Marshalltown IA 50158-4078 Office: Marshalltown CC 3700 S Center St Marshalltown IA 50158-4760

COLE, ELSA KIRCHER, lawyer; b. Dec. 5, 1949; d. Paul and Hester Marie (Pellegrom) Kircher; m. Roland J. Cole, Aug. 16, 1975; children: Isabel Ashley, Madeline Aldis. AB in History with distinction, Stanford U., 1971; JD, Boston U., 1974. Bar: Wash. 1974, U.S. Supreme Ct. 1980, Mich. 1989. Asst. atty gen., rep. dept. motor vehicles State of Wash., Seattle, 1974-75, asst. atty. gen., rep. dept. social and health svcs., 1975-76, asst. atty. gen., rep. U. Wash., 1976-89; gen. counsel U. Mich., Ann Arbor, 1989—; presenter ednl. issues various confs. and workshops. Contbr. articles to profl. jours. Mem. Nat. Assn. Coll. and Univ. Attys. (chair profl. devel. com. 1990-91, mem. nominations and site selection coms. 1987-88, program 1988-89, 89-90, 91-92, 92-93, fin., articles and by-laws coms. 1988-89, co-chair student affairs sect. 1987-88, 88-89, honors and awards ethics com. 1991-92, bd. dirs. 1988-91), Wash. State Bar Assn. (chair law sch. liaison com. 1988-89), Wash. Women Lawyers (pres. Seattle-King County chpt. 1986, v.p. membership, state bd. 1987, 88, state chair candidate endorsement com. 1987, 88), Seattle-King County Bar Assn. Congregationalist. Office: U Mich Office of the Gen Counsel 4020 Fleming Bldg Ann Arbor MI 48109

COLE, GRETCHEN BORNOR, distribution and service executive; b. Detroit, Nov. 12, 1927; d. Maurice Frank and Dora Levina (Richardson) Bornor; m. Ernest James Cole, Mar. 31, 1951; (div. May, 1981); children: Cynthia, Sara Ann. BA, DePauw U., 1949; MSW, Wayne State U., 1980. Cert. social worker, Mich. Regional sec. Kenyon and Eckhardt, Detroit, 1951-52; office mgr. W.O. Earl Assocs., Detroit, 1952-54; social worker St. Joseph Mercy Hosp., Pontiac, Mich., 1981-82; with Detroit Air Compressor and Pump Co., Ferndale, Mich., 1963-80, sec., 1981, v.p., 1982, chmn., pres., 1990—, also chmn. bd. dirs.; regional dir., v.p. Atlas Copco Distbr. Assn., 1987-90; mem. Atlas Copco Compressors Coun. Bd., 1990-92. Named one of Top 50 Woman Bus. Owners State of Mich., 1986, 94, one of Top 25, 1996. Mem. Women's Econ. Club, Nat. Assn. Women Bus. Owners, Econ. Club Detroit, Founder's Soc., Detroit Inst. Arts, Oakland County C. of C. (exec. bd. 1994—, chair mktg. com., bd. dirs. 1994—), Alpha Chi Omega. Republican. Episcopalian. Office: Detroit Air Compressor & Pump Co 3205 Bermuda St Ferndale MI 48220-1060

COLE, JEFFREY CLARK, college development professional; b. Toledo, Jan. 20, 1966; s. Frank Herbert Jr. and Mary Terese (Clark) C. BA, U. Toledo, 1989, postgrad., 1990—. Admissions counselor U. Toledo, 1989-92, devel. officer, 1992—; instr. comm. U. Toledo, 1992—. Editor-in-chief The Collegian, 1988-89. Pres. student govt. U. Toledo, 1987-88; subcom. mem. City Toledo Sesquicentennial Celebration, 1987; mem. speakers bur. Keep Toledo-Lucas County Beautiful, 1989; alumni bd. dirs. St. Francis deSales High Sch., Toledo, 1989-92; mem. bd. mgrs. Univ. YMCA, 1991—; mem. alumni affiliate steering com. U. Toledo Coll. Arts and Scis., 1992—, mem. profl. staff coun., 1993—, chair, 1995-96. Mem. Blue Key Nat. Honor Soc. (hon.), Toledo Press Club (award 1989, Excellence in Media award 1995), Nat. Soc. Fundraising Execs., Soc. Profl. Journalists, Toledo Club. Republican. Home: 3843 Woodmont Rd Toledo OH 43613-4323 Office: U Toledo 2801 W Bancroft St Toledo OH 43606-3328

COLE, JOHN A., service management electronic publishing; b. Garrett, Ind., Feb. 23, 1954; s. Franklin R. and Kathlyn L. (Redmund) C.; m. Pamela S. Elliott, June 2, 1979; children: Elliott R., Kathlyn E. BS, Ind. U., 1976. CPA. Auditor Arthur Young CPAs, Indpls., 1976-77; fin. specialist Nat. Industries, Louisville, 1977-78; sr. analyst, auditor Mead Corp., Dayton, Ohio, 1978-82; controller Mead Pub. Paper, Escanaba, Mich., 1982-86; dir. bus. mgmt. Mead Data Ctrl., Dayton, 1986-88, market dir., 1988-90, dir. strategy, 1990-93, v.p. mktg. and products, 1993-94; v.p. mktg. and products Lexis-Nexis, Dayton, 1994—. Home: 8795 Toft Trees Springboro OH 45066 Office: Lexis-Nexis PO 933 9443 Springboro Pike Dayton OH 45401

COLE, KATHLEEN ANN, advertising agency executive; retired social worker b. Cin., Nov. 22, 1946; d. James Scott and Kathryn Gertrude (Borisch) Cole; BA, Miami U., 1968; MSW, U. Mich., 1972; MM, Northwestern U., 1978; m. Brian Brandt, Mar. 21, 1970. Social worker Hamilton County Welfare Dept., Cin., 1969-70, Lucas County Children Svcs. Bd., Toledo, 1970-74, East Maine Sch. Dist., Niles, Ill., 1974-77; account supr. Leo Burnett Advt. Agy., Chgo., 1978-93; primary therapist, Lifeline, Chgo., 1994-95; acct. supr. GreenHouse Comm., 1995—; field instr. Loyola U., Chgo., 1976-77. Mem. Acad. Cert. Social Workers (mem. pub. rels. task force), Nat. Assn. Social Workers, Miami U. Alumni Assn. (dir. 1976—), Northwestern U. Prof. Women's Assn., Kellogg Alumni Assn., North Shore United Meth. Congregation. Home: 414 Kelling Ln Glencoe IL 60022-1113

COLE, ROLAND JAY, lawyer; b. Seattle, Dec. 15, 1948; s. Robert J. and Josephine F. (Carrow) C.; m. Elsa Kircher, Aug. 16, 1975; children: Isabel Ashley, Madeline Aldis. AB in Econs. magna cum laude, Harvard U., 1970, M Pub. Policy, 1972, PhD in Pub. Policy, JD, 1975. Bar: Wash. 1975, U.S. Supreme Ct. 1980, U.S. Dist. Ct. (we. dist.) Wash. 1984, Mich. 1989. Rsch. scientist Battelle Human Affairs Rsch. Ctrs., Seattle, 1975-83; assoc. Appel and Glueck, P.C., Seattle, 1984-89; gen. counsel Indsl. Tech. Inst., Ann Arbor, Mich., 1990-94; founder, exec. dir. Software Patent Inst., 1994—; founder, dir. MIS; bd. dirs. Cobro Pub., Inc., Lynnwood, Wash., 1984-90. Co-author: Government Requirements of Small Business, 1980, The Containment of Organized Crime, 1984; co-programmer Quadrant I software program, 1983. HUD fellow, 1970-71. Mem. Assn. Personal Computer User Groups (dir., founding pres. 1986), Wash. Athletic Club. Congregationalist. Office: Software Patent Inst 2901 Hubbard St Ann Arbor MI 48105-2467

COLE, SARAH, law enforcement librarian; b. Ill., Nov. 8, 1963; d. David and Carol (Schrader) C. BA, North Cen. Coll., Naperville, Ill., 1985; MA in Libr. Studies, No. Ill. U., 1988. Law enforcement libr. North East Multi-Regional Tng., North Aurora, Ill., 1988—. Editor Precious Nonsense newsletter, 1984—. Active Midwestern Gilbert and Sullivan Soc., North Aurora. Mem. Spl. Librs. Assn., Ill. Librs. Assn., Nat. Sheriffs Assn. Office: NE Multi-Regional Tng 1 Smoke Tree Plz Ste 111 North Aurora IL 60542

COLE, THEODORE JOHN, osteopathic physician; b. Covington, Ky., May 30, 1953; s. John N. and Florence R. (Bruener) C.; m. Ellen Cole; children: Joren, Emily, Kevin. BA, Centre Coll., Danville, Ky., 1975; MA, Western Ky. U., 1978; DO, Ohio U., 1986. Diplomate Am. Osteo. Bd. Gen. Practice, Nat. Bd. Osteo. Examiners. Psychologist Comprehensive Mental Health Svcs., St. Petersburg, Fla., 1978-82; intern Detroit Osteo. Hosp., 1986-87; resident Doctors Hosp., Columbus, Ohio, 1987-88; pvt. practice, West Chester, Ohio, 1989—; preceptor Ohio U. Coll. Osteo. Medicine, Athens, 1990—, U. Cin. Med. Sch., 1990—; dir. So. Ohio Coll. Nursing. Coach, Soccer Assn. for Youth, West Chester, 1989, 90, Liberty Sports Orgn., West Chester, 1990. Mem. Am. Osteo. Assn., Am. Assn. Osteopathy, Am. Coll. Gen. Practitioners, Ohio Osteo. Assn., Am. Acad. Environ. Medicine, Cranial Acad., Am. Acad. Advancement of Medicine. Office:

West Chester Family Practice 9678 Cincinnati Columbus Rd Cincinnati OH 45241-1071

COLE, THOMAS FERGUSON, architect; b. Camden, N.J., July 5, 1935; s. Floyd Howard and Georgiana (Ferguson) C.; m. June Kleinjohn, Dec. 21, 1959; children: Jennifer Brook, Sarah Ferguson McCartney. BS, U. Cin., 1960. Cert. arch. Ohio, Ky., Tenn., W.Va., Tex., Fla., La., Ala., Miss., Mo., Minn., N.J.; cert. interior designer Fla., Tex.; class II plans examiner, Ohio. From archl. draftsman to intern arch. Cordes-Pressler-Houck and Assocs., Cin., 1960-64; from arch. to sec./treas. F.W. Pressler & Assocs., Cin., 1965-73; prin. Thomas F. Cole, Arch., Batavia, Ohio, 1973-83; prin., sec./treas. Cole & Russell Archs., Cin., 1983—; sec. Batavia Twp. Zoning Commn., 1974-78; pres. Bella Vista Non-Profit Housing Corp., Batavia, 1978. search com. for supt. Rollman Psychiat. Inst., Cin., 1979; trustee Cin. Cmty. Chest & Coun., 1970-77; chmn., vice chmn. Clermont County Bd. Mental Health & Mental Retardation, Batavia, 1974-80; chmn. adv. bd. Ursuline H.S., Brown County, Ohio, 1979-80. Mem. AIA, Ohio Soc. Archs., Batavia Rotary Club (pres. 1983), Beta Theta Pi. Republican. Presbyn. Home: 2419 Bauer Rd Batavia OH 45103 Office: Cole & Russell Archs 2368 Victory Pkwy Cincinnati OH 45206

COLE, WILLIAM R., bank executive; b. 1939. With First Am. Bank Mich. NA, Kalamazoo, 1960—, sr. v.p., 1973-82, pres., CEO, 1982—, chmn. bd. dirs.; v.p. First Am. Bank Corp. Office: 1st Am Bank Mich NA 108 E Michigan Ave Kalamazoo MI 49007-3908*

COLEMAN, CHARLES W., state legislator; b. Milw., Aug. 7, 1932; Children: Steven, Michael, Scott, Kristi, Carson, Casey. BBA, U. Wis., 1954, MS, 1959. Instr. polit. sci., farmer. Mem. Walworth County Farm Bur. Mem. Am. Legion, Elks. Home: N7230 Krahn Dr Whitewater WI 53190-4389*

COLEMAN, GARY WILLIAM, elementary education educator; b. Davenport, Iowa, Dec. 16, 1945; s. Robert Earl and Mildred Margaret (Mast) C.; m. Janice Marie Coleman, Dec. 29, 1973; children: Heidi Marie, Sean Robert. BS in Elem. Edn., U. S.D., 1987; BSBA, Ariz. State U., 1969. Cert. elem. tchr., EMT, S.D. Tchr. Marty (S.D.) Indian Sch., 1987-91, Parkston (S.D.) Elem. Sch., 1991—; acct./bookkeeper Ulland Bros Constrn., Austin, Minn.; realtor assoc. Myre-Sorenson Real Estate, Albert Lea, Minn.; bldg. constrn. contractor, landscaper, Alcester, S.D. Sgt. USAF, 1969-73. Mem. NEA, Parkston Edn. Assn. (v.p. 1995-96, pres. 1996—).

COLEMAN, GEORGE MICHAEL, chemical company executive; b. Cleve., Mar. 5, 1953; s. George M. and Patricia A. (Harrold) C.; m. Deborah M. Zalar, Feb. 19, 1977 (div. 1989); children: Sean, Kate. BS in Biology, John Carroll U., 1975. Prodn. supr. Republic Steel Corp., Cleve., 1975-79; acct. rep. Calgon Corp. div. Merck and Co., Cleve., 1979-81; mktg. mgr. Calgon Corp. div. Merck and Co., Pitts., 1981-82, regional sales mgr., 1982-83, mgr. mktg., comml. devel., 1983-84; mgr. new bus. devel. biotechnology Standard Oil Chem Co Specialties div. (now BP Chems. Internat.), Cleve., 1984-87; gen. mgr. Adhesive Products div. and Electronic Materials Group BP Chems. Am., Cleve., 1987-90; owner, pres. Innobond Adhesive Corp., Cleve., 1990—. Patentee in field. Republican. Roman Catholic. Clubs: Cleve. Yachting, Holden Arboretum. Home: 1235 W 6th St Apt 5D Cleveland OH 44113-1301 Office: Innobond Adhesive Corp 1235 W 6th St Ste 5D Cleveland OH 44113-1301

COLEMAN, GLORIA JEAN, chemical manufacturing company professional; b. Hannibal, Mo., May 9, 1952; d. Gene Hughes and Joan (Wiley) Carroll; m. Larry Dean Coleman, Nov. 25, 1971. BBA, Culver-Stockton Coll., Canton, Mo., 1992. Cert. profl. sec. Sec., bookkeeper, cashier Western-So. Life Ins., Hannibal, Mo., 1970-77; exec. sec. Marion County Mut. Savs. and Loan, Hannibal, 1977; acctg./info. svcs. dept. sec. Am. Cyanamid, Hannibal, 1977-85, users svcs. coordinator, 1985-88, analyst office systems, 1988-90, analyst computer edn. and tng., 1990-94; supr. computer edn. and tng., 1995—; mem. adv. bd. Hannibal area Vocat. Tech. Sch. Bus. Edn. Com., 1985-91; pub. speaker area schs. and svc. orgns., Quincy, Ill., Hannibal, Springfield, Mo., 1986—. Bd. dirs. ARC, Hannibal; mentor Bus. and Profl. Women's Club, Hannibal, 1985-86,also coord. individual devel. program for pub. speaking; fundraiser Convocom Pub. Broadcasting Sta., Quincy, 1986, Hannibal, 1988. Mem. Cert. Profl. Sec. Acad., Profl. Secs. Internat. (sec. Quinsippi chpt. 1984-85, v.p. Heartland chpt. 1988-89, pres. 1989-91, parliamentarian 1991-93, pres. Mo. div. 1993-94, Sec. of Yr. 1985), Kiwanis (Early Bird 1990-94). Mem. Assembly of God Ch. Home: 106 Butternut Dr Hannibal MO 63401 Office: Am Cyanamid PO Box 817 Hannibal MO 63401-0817

COLEMAN, JAMES J., JR., investment company executive; b. St. Louis, Mar. 8, 1946; s. James J. Coleman; m. Terry S. Esterbrook Spazt, Nov. 20, 1993; 3 stepchildren. Investment broker Steifel, Nicolaus, St. Louis, 1968-83, J. Thall & Co., St. Louis, 1983-87; v.p. A.G. Edwards & Sons Inc., St. Louis, 1987—. With USAR, 1964-70. Mem. St. Louis Athletic Club, Boone Valley Golf Club. Republican. Roman Catholic. Home: 429 Cheshire Farm Ln Saint Louis MO 63141-8503 Office: AG Edwards & Sons Inc 1 City Ctr Ste 1300 Saint Louis MO 63101-1893

COLEMAN, ROBERT LEE, retired lawyer; b. Kansas City, Mo., June 14, 1929; s. William Houston and Edna Fay (Smith) C. BMus in Edn., Drake U., 1951, LLB, U. Mo., 1959. Bar: Mo. 1959, Fla. 1973. Law clk. to judge U.S. dist. ct. (we. dist.) Mo., Kansas City, 1959-60; assoc. Watson, Ess, Marshall & Enggas, Kansas City, 1960-66; asst. gen. counsel Gas Service Co., Kansas City, 1966-74; v.p., corp. counsel H & R Block, Inc., Kansas City, 1974-94; ret., 1994. Served with U.S. Army, 1955-57. Mem. ABA, Kansas City Bar Assn., Lawyers Assn. Kansas City.

COLEMAN, ROY EVERETT, secondary education educator, computer programmer; b. Chgo., Oct. 16, 1942; s. William Everett and Evelyn (Johnson) C.; m. Dianna Joy Uchida, Nov. 12, 1988. BS in Physics, Ill. Inst. of Tech., 1964; MS in Physics, DePaul U., 1974; Sci. Edn., Ill. Inst. of Tech., Chgo., 1990; Computer Sci., Chgo. State U., Chgo., 1984. Physics tchr. Morgan Park High Sch., Chgo., 1965—, St. Xavier Coll., Chgo., 1977-80; S.M.I.L.E. staff specialist Ill. Inst. of Tech., Chgo., 1982—, computer edn. staff, 1988—; dir. comp. lit. Chgo. Pub. Sch., 1983-84; treas., pres. Am. Assn. of Physics Tchrs. Chgo. Author: Equipment Evaluation, 1982; co-author: Physics Text Evaluations, 1984. Mem. Pursuit of Excellence Com., Chgo., 1982-88, Scholarship Com., 1985-89. Recipient Phoebe Aperton Hurst award Nat. PTA, Washington, 1985, Tchr. of Yr. award Chgo. PTA, 1978, 80, Presdl. award of Excellence, U.S. Dept. Edn., 1987, Supt. award Chgo. Pub. Schs., 1979, 80, H.S. Tchr. of Astronaut Dr. Mae C. Jemison award, Kohl Internat. Tchg. award, 1994; Tandy Tech. scholar, 1995; finalist Golden Apple awards, 1995. Mem. Am. Assn. Physics Tchrs., Sports Car Club Am. (Ind. N.W. region). Home: 5436 S Kimbark Ave Chicago IL 60615-5284

COLEMAN, STEPHEN ROBERT, psychology educator; b. Malden, Mass., Sept. 6, 1942; s. Gerard Joseph and Alice Irene (Ryan) C.; m. Katherine Ann Brase, Dec. 30, 1967; children: Jason G., David F. BA magna cum laude, U. Mass., 1965; postgrad., Ind. U., 1965-66; MA, U. Iowa, 1970, PhD, 1972. Instr. in psychology Cleve. State U., 1971-72, asst. prof., 1972-78, assoc. prof., 1978-89, prof. psychology, 1989—; manuscript reviewer Brooks/Cole Pub. Co., Pacific Grove, Calif., 1985—. Cons. editor Behavior and Philosophy, 1987—; mem. editl. bd. Behavior Analyst, 1988-90; contbr. articles to profl. jours. Sec. bd. trustees Neighborhood Counseling Svc., Cleve., 1986-88; team mgr. Suburban Hockey League, Cleveland Heights, Ohio, 1988-92. NSF predoctoral fellow, 1965-68, Woodrow Wilson fellow, 1965; named Vol. of Yr., Neighborhood Counseling Svc., 1988. Mem. APA, Forum for History of Sci. in Am., Cheiran Soc., Phi Beta Kappa. Home: 12664 Klatka Dr Chardon OH 44024 Office: Cleve State U 2399 Euclid Ave Cleveland OH 44115

COLEMAN, TROY LEE, computer company executive; b. Lynchburg, Va., June 13, 1961; s. Marvain Arnold and Bessie Rose (Evans) C.; m. Christine Terri Buhrke, Dec. 7, 1985; children: Maegan Christine, Tyler Lee. BA in Computer Sci., Concordia Coll., 1987. Programmer Concordia Coll., River Forest, Ill., 1983-87, Arthur Andersen & Co., Chgo., 1987-88; data base adminstr. Anixter Bros. Inc., Skokie, Ill., 1988-91, Moore Bus. Forms, Lake Forest, Ill., 1991-92; mgr. data base adminstrn. Ameritech., Hoffman Estates, Ill., 1992-94; pres. Coleman Cons. Inc., Lindenhurst, Ill., 1994—; mem. Internat. DB2 Users Group, 1996 N.Am. Planning Com. Elder Bethel Luth. Ch., Gurnee, Ill., 1994—. Mem. Midwest Database Users Group, Internat. DB2 Users Group (spkr. 1994—). Republican. Home: 795 Colony Ave Lindenhurst IL 60046 Office: Coleman Cons 795 Colony Ave #1STF Lindenhurst IL 60046-7831

COLES, GRAHAM, conductor, composer; b. London, May 7, 1948; arrived in Canada, 1951; s. Walter Harold and Phyllis Irene Gwendoline (Conn) C. MusB, U. Toronto, 1972, MusM, 1974, EdB, 1991. Music dir. Kitchener-Waterloo (Ont.) Chamber Orch., 1985—. Composer numerous instrumental and vocal compositions. Mem. Can. League Composers, Can. Music Ctr. (assoc. composer), Assn. Can. Orchs. Home: 76 Cedar Crest St, Kitchener, ON Canada N2N 1Y2 Office: Kitchener Waterloo Chamber Orch, PO Box 34015, Kitchener, ON Canada N2N 3G2

COLES, LORRAINE MCCLELLAN, vehicle maintenance analyst; b. Chgo., Nov. 1, 1929; d. Wiley and Cornelia (Robinson) Packnett; m. Sam Taylor, Feb. 10, 1947 (div. 1962); children: Diana, Arvetta Lorraine, Samuel Joseph, Conella Elizabeth; m. Earskin G. Coles, Jan. 3, 1982. Student, Truman Coll., Chgo., 1980, Loop Coll., 1982-84, U. Okla. Postal Acad., Norman, 1981-83, City-Wide Coll., 1988; cert. in travel and tourism, Nat. Radio Inst., 1991. Asst. forelady Diana Sportswear, Chgo., 1951-52; sr. balancer Spiegel's, Inc., Chgo., 1959-60; intermittent claims examiner Ill. Dept. of Labor, 1963-72; with U.S. Postal Svc., Chgo., 1960-90; acting fleet mgr. U.S. Postal Svc., Gary, Ind., 1981; supt. delivery and vehicle maintenance U.S. Postal Svc., Chgo., 1986-89, acting mgr. delivery and retail programs, 1989, ret., 1990; travel cons. Beautiful Travel Svcs., Ltd., Chgo., 1989—. Mem. Scheme Rev. Com., Chgo., 1986-90. Mem. NAFE, LWV, Nat. Assn. Commd. Travel Agts., Nat. Geog. Soc., Black Bus. and Profl. Women's Assn., Presbyn. Women's Assn. (sec. 1986-90, pres. 1990—), Sr. Friends. Home: 233 E Wacker Dr Apt 1405 Chicago IL 60601-5108

COLGROVE, THOMAS MICHAEL, landscape architect; b. Painesville, Ohio, Dec. 16, 1930; s. Melvin Samuel and Agnus Mary (Oswald) C.; m. Lois Martha Roffman, June 1, 1957; children: Nancy M., Ruth A., Thomas M., Tracy S. BS, Ohio State U., 1954, B.Landscape Arch., 1955. Reg. landscape architect, Kans. Landscape architect Stuart M. Mertz Assocs., Clayton, Mo., 1955-60, Abbey & Dickens, Inc., Rochester, N.Y., 1960-63; v.p. Hare & Hare, Inc., Kansas City, Mo., 1963-74; dir. landscape arch. G. Butler Assocs., Inc., Kansas City, 1974-89; pres. Thomas Colgrove Assoc., Prairie Village, Kans., 1989—; mem. Coun. Landscape Archtl. Registration Bd., 1989—. Chmn. City Bd. Parks and Recreation, Prairie Village, Kans., 1972-82; chmn. Kans. Bd. Tech. Professions, Topeka, 1988—. Recipient Trustee award, Nelson Gallery of Art, 1972, Plant Am. award, Am. Assn. Nurserymen, 1966, 62, 61. Mem. Am. Soc. Landscape Architects (trustee 1965-70), Mo. Parks and Recreation Assn., Nat. Parks and Conservation Assn., Mo. Assn. landscape Architects (pres. 1964-67), Kans. Assn. Landscape Architects (pres. 1967-70), Profl. Grounds Assn. Republican. Episcopalian. Home: 9024 Rosewood Dr Shawnee Mission KS 66207-2229 Office: Thomas Colgrove Assocs 9024 Rosewood Dr Shawnee Mission KS 66207-2229

COLLENS, LEWIS MORTON, university president, legal educator; b. Chgo., Feb. 10, 1938. BS, U. Ill., Urbana, 1960, MA, 1963; JD, U. Chgo., 1966. Bar: Ill. 1966. Assoc. Ross, Hardies, Chgo., 1966-67; spl. asst. to gen. counsel EEOC, Washington, 1967-68; asst. prof. Ill. Inst. Tech., Chgo. Kent Coll. Law, 1970-72, assoc. prof., 1972-74, prof., 1975—; dean Coll. Law, Ill. Inst. Tech., 1974-90, pres., 1990—; bd. dirs. Amsted Industries, Inc., Dean Foods Co., Inc. Bd. dirs. Met. Plan Coun., pres. Coun. of of Pres. of the Tchrs. Acad. for math. and Sci., dir. Ill. Coalition; pres. Leadership Greater Chgo. Mem. ABA, Ill. Bar Assn., Chgo. Bar Assn., Am. Law Inst., Econ. Club of Chgo. (dir.), Order of Coif. Office: Ill Inst Tech 10 W 33rd St Rm 223 Chicago IL 60616-3730

COLLETT, RANDAL RAY, telecommunications administrator; b. Kansas City, Mo., Nov. 21, 1952; s. Howard L. and Marjorie (Flatt) C.; m. Jaclynn S. McLain, July 22, 1973 (dec. Aug. 1982); 1 child, Carrie N.; m. Rachel A. Muenks, May 31, 1986; children: Zachary R., Margaret A. BS, Kans. State U., 1974; M of Pub. Adminstrn., U. Mo., 1988. Income maintenance worker Kans. Dept. of Social and Rehab. Svcs., Cottonwood Falls, Kans., 1974-78; computer operator FAA, Kansas City, Mo., 1978-80; comm. cons. Southwestern Bell, Kansas City, 1980-82; account exec. AT&T, Jefferson City, Mo., 1982-86; maj. accounts rep. United Telephone Co., Jefferson City, Mo., 1986-90; telecomm. mgr. Ctrl. Mo. State U., Warrensburg, 1990—; steering com. No. Telecom DMS-100 Centrex User Group, Raleigh, N.C., 1992—. Mem. Assn. of Coll. and Univ. Telecomm. Adminstrs. (co-producer video 1994, pres. 1994-95, exec. v.p. 1993-94, v.p. 1992-93, region dir. 1991-92, Achievement award 1992, 94). Republican. Methodist. Home: 15729 Woodson Overland Park KS 66223 Office: Ctrl Mo State Univ Humphreys Bldg Rm 200 Warrensburg MO 64093

COLLEY, SUSAN JANE, mathematician, educator; b. N.Y.C., May 20, 1959; d. Edward Malcolm and Jane (Hochstadter) Morris; m. William Clarence Colley III, July 20, 1980; 1 child, Diane Elizabeth. SB in Math., MIT, 1979, PhD in Math., 1983. Asst. prof. math. Oberlin (Ohio) Coll., 1983-88, assoc. prof., 1988-95; dept. chair, 1994—, prof., 1995—. Contbr. articles to profl. publs. including Procs. of Am. Math. Soc., Am. Math. Monthly, Advanced in Math., Comm. in Algebra, Lecture Notes in Math., Contemporary Math. Compositio Math. Danforth Found. grad. fellow, 1979-83, Keck fellow in natural scis. Oberlin Coll., 1986. Mem. Am. Math. Soc., Math. Assn. Am. (cons.), Nat. Coun. Tchrs. of Math., Assn. for Women in Math. Democrat. Jewish. Office: Oberlin Coll Dept Math King Bldg Oberlin OH 44074

COLLIE, JOHN, JR., insurance agent; b. Gary, Ind., Apr. 23, 1934; s. John and Christina Dempster (Wardrop) C.; student Purdue U., 1953; AB in Econs., Ind. U., 1957; assoc. risk mgmt. m. Jessie Fearn Shaw, Aug. 1, 1964; children: Cynthia Elizabeth, Douglas A.H., Jennifer Fearn. Operator, Collie Optical Lab., Gary, 1957-62; owner, operator Collie Ins. Agy., Merrillville, Ind., 1962—; pres. Collie Realty and Investment, Ins. and Fin. Advisory, Lake Mich. Global Industries; lectr. High Frontier; dist. chmn. 1st dist. Ind. for com. to secure High Frontier; mem. employer support Guard & Res., Dept. Def. Lt. col. U.S. Army Res., 1957-86; instr. Command and Gen. Staff Coll., 1973-77. Mem. Ind. Ins. Agts. Assn., Mil. Order World Wars, Res. Officers Assn. (sec., pres. N.W. Ind. chpt., v.p. Ind. chpt.), Leadership Council Am.; Nat. Fedn. Ind. Bus., Guardian, Merrillville C. of C. (legis. com.), Phi Kappa Psi. Republican. Methodist. Clubs: Masons (32 deg.), Shriners. Home: 871 Camelot Mnr Portage IN 46368-6632 Office: PO Box 10148 5600 Broadway Merrillville IN 46411

COLLIER, BEVERLY JOANNE, elementary education educator; b. Grand Haven, Mich., Oct. 28, 1936; d. Joseph Frank and Anne (Mary) Snyder; divorced; children: Ann, Cindy. Student, U. Mich., 1955-57; BA, Western Mich. U., 1965. Cert. elem. tchr., Mich. 1st grade tchr. Fruitport (Mich.) Community Schs., 1965-93; retired, 1993. Contbr. articles to local newspapers. Active Grand Haven (Mich.) Presbyn. Ch., 1955—. Mem. ASCD, NEA, Muskegon Edn. Assn., Mich. Edn. Assn. (past regional rep.), Mich. Assn. Ret. Sch. Personnel (Muskegon County chpt.). Home: 1235 Washington Ave Grand Haven MI 49417-1627 Office: Fruitport Cmty Sch 305 Pontaluna Rd Fruitport MI 49415-9652

COLLIER, DAVID ENGLISH, electrical engineer, consultant; b. Indpls., Nov. 11, 1960; s. Thomas Leslie and Florence Edna (Vasbinder) C.; m. Ginger Lynn Stamps, Mar. 18, 1995. BS in Computer Engring., U. Evansville, 1984; MBA, Butler U. Engr. Benerson Corp., Evansville, Ind., 1984; software engr. Naval Avionics Ctr., Indpls., 1985-90; project engr. Naval Air Warfare Ctr., Indpls., 1990—. Contbr. articles to profl. jours. Mem. IEEE, IEEE Computer Soc. (chmn. Cen. Ind. chpt. 1992-93). Home: 5410 N Sherman Dr Indianapolis IN 46220

COLLIER, NATHAN MORRIS, musician, music educator; b. Clinton, Okla., July 23, 1924; s. Lotan Morris and Annie Carlletta (Willsey) C.; m. Frances Aleta Snell, June 24, 1955; children: Susan Aleta Kowalski, Ray Morris. MusB, U. Okla., 1949; MusM, Eastman Sch. Music, U. Rochester, 1951. String music cons. Lincoln (Nebr.) Pub. Schs., 1951-68; asst. concertmaster Lincoln Symphony Orch., 1953—; assoc. concertmaster Omaha (Nebr.) Symphony, The Nebr. Sinfonia, 1977-78, acting concertmaster, 1978, first violin, 1956-79; first violinist Lincoln String Quartet, 1951—; concertmaster Lincoln Symphony, Lincoln Little Symphony, 1977-78; asst. prof. violin and theory Nebr. Weslyan U., Lincoln, 1968-84; string tchr. St. John Luth. Sch., Seward, Nebr., 1983-89; vis. instr. music Concordia Tchrs. Coll., Seward, 1985, 90; asst. concertmaster Nebr. Chamber Orch., 1973-91, acting concertmaster on occasion; guest prin. violinist Des Moines Symphony, 1979, 87, prin. second violinist, 1979—; concertmaster Omaha Pops Orch., 1988—; guest violinist, violist with The Myron Cohen and the Midlands String Quartets, 1985—; with the Met. String Quartet, Omaha, 1988—; 1st violinist Avanti String Quartet, 1990; asst. prof. music Kans. State U., Manhattan, 1980-81, condr. symphony orch., 1980-81; pvt. tchr. and 1st violinist with the KSU Resident String Quartet, 1980-81; viola instr., chamber music coach summer course U. Nebr., Lincoln, 1991; concertmaster and soloist Nebr. Camerata-Orch. Berlin tour 1992; guest violinist/violist Hastings (Nebr.) Symphony, 1990—; cons., lectr. in field, arranger of numerous compositions for string quartet 1980—; mem. adv. bd. Rocky Ridge Music Ctr., 1972—. Tchr., co-organizer Brownville (Nebr.) Summer Music Festival, 1972-77. With USN, 1943-46. U.S. Govt. grantee 1966-67. Mem. Am. String Tchrs. Assn. (Pvt. Studio Tchr. of Yr. 1994), Music Tchrs. Nat. Assn. (natonally cert., 1994—), Music Educators Nat. Conf., Violin Soc. Am., Lincoln Music Tchrs. Assn., Nat. Sch. Orch. Assn., NEA, Nebr. State Edn. Assn., Lincoln Musicians Assn., Omaha Musicians Assn., Internat. Soc. of Bassists (Helen Haggie Arts award 1995). Democrat. Methodist. Composer various musical pieces. Home: 4544 Mohawk St Lincoln NE 68510-4838

COLLIN, THOMAS JAMES, lawyer; b. Windom, Minn., Jan. 6, 1949; s. Everett Earl and Genevieve May (Wilson) C.; m. Victoria Gatov, Oct. 11, 1985; children: Arielle, Elise, Sarah. BA, U. Minn., 1970; AM, Harvard U., 1972; JD, Georgetown U., 1974. Bar: Ohio 1975, U.S. Dist. Ct. (no. dist.) Ohio 1975, U.S. Ct. Appeals (10th cir.) 1977, U.S. Supreme Ct. 1980, U.S. Ct. Appeals (6th cir.) 1981, U.S. Ct. Appeals (8th cir.) 1982. Law clk. to Judge Myron Bright U.S. Ct. Appeals, 8th Cir., St. Louis, Mo., 1974-75; assoc. Thompson, Hine & Flory, Cleve., 1975-82, ptnr., 1982--. Author: Ohio Business Competition Law, 1994, (with others) Criminal Antitrust Litigation Manual, 1983, Protecting Intellectual Property Under Ohio Law, 1989; contbr. articles to profl. jours. Active Citizens League, Cleve., 1987—, bd. trustees, 1994—, v.p., 1995—. Mem. ABA (chair bus. torts and unfair competition com., antitrust sect. 1995—), Ohio State Bar Assn. (bd. govs. antitrust sect. 1988—). Republican. Home: 7879 Oakhurst Dr Cleveland OH 44141-1123 Office: Thompson Hine & Flory 3900 Society Center 127 Public Square Cleveland OH 44114-1216

COLLINGS, BETTY, artist, curator, writer; b. Wanganui, New Zealand, Jan. 15, 1934; came to U.S., 1962; d. Florence Anne Stent; m. Edward William Collings, Apr. 4,1953; children: Jane, Christopher. BFA, Ohio State U., 1970, MFA, 1974. Dir. Ohio State U. Gallery, Columbus, 1974-80; pres. The Artists' Orgn., Ohio, 1984-87, program dir., 1987—; ind. artist, 1964—, ind. writer and curator, 1981—; mem. New Zealand-U.S. Arts Found., 1981-89; bd. dirs. ISIS Symmetry, 1995—. Exhibited works in solo shows at Ohio State U., 1974, New Gallery, Cleve., 1976, Concourse Gallery, Grad. Ctr. CUNY, 1983, Bertha Urdang Gallery, 1979-90, Gallery Vistavka, Ukraine Union of Artists, Kiev, 1992, others; numerous group exhbns. including Purdue U., Columbus Art Mus., Islip Mus., Ohio U. at Lancaster, Israeli Mus., U. Akron, Urdang Gallery, ISIS Symmetry, Washington, 1995; author and subject of articles. Mem. Internat. Critics Assn. (Am. sect.). Office: 1991 Hillside Dr Columbus OH 43221-4120 Studio: 780 King Ave Columbus OH 43212

COLLINGS, GILBEART HOOPER, JR., physician; b. Anderson, S.C., Aug. 16, 1919; s. Gilbeart H. and Hazel Winifred (Cover) C.; m. Margaret George Pitts, Feb. 28, 1942; children: Margaret Patricia, June Elizabeth, Gilbeart Hooper III, George Frederick. BS, Clemson A&M Coll., 1937; MD, Emory U., 1941; MPH, Johns Hopkins U., 1945. Intern Md. Gen. Hosp., 1942; surgeon Bethlehem Steel Co., Sparrows Point, Md., 1942-46; chief occupational health br. Army Environ. Health Lab., Army chem. Ctr., Md., 1955-57; med. dir. Crane Co., Chgo., 1957-59, Standard Oil Co. (Ind.), Chgo., 1959—. Contbr. articles to sci. publs. Mem. AMA, APHA, Indsl. Med. Assn., Med. Dirs. Forum, Am. Indsl. Hygiene Assn., Am. Acad. Occupational Medicine, Am. Coll. Preventive Medicine, Ill. Med. Soc., Chgo. Med. Soc., Cen. States Soc. Indsl. Medicine and Surgery. Presbyterian. Office: 910 S Michigan Ave Chicago IL

COLLINS, ALLAN MEAKIN, cognitive scientist, psychologist, educator; b. Orange, N.J., Aug. 7, 1937; s. Clinton and Sarah Amy (Meakin) C.; m. Anne Marjorie Linstead, Aug. 24, 1963; children: Antony, Elizabeth. MA in Communication Scis., U. Michigan, 1962, PhD in Psychology, 1970. Sr. scientist Bolt, Beranek & Newman Inc., Cambridge, 1967-82, prin. scientist, 1982—; prof edn. and social policy Northwestern U., Evanston, Ill., 1989—; co-dir. Ctr. for Tech. in Edn., Bank St. Coll. of Edn., N.Y.C., 1991-94; lectr. various colls. and univs. Editor: Representation and Understanding, 1975, Cognitive Science, 1976-80, Readings in Cognitive Science, 1988; author: The Cognitive Structure of Emotions, 1988. Guggenheim fellow, 1974, Sloan fellow, 1980. Mem. AAAS, Nat. Acad. Edn., Cognitive Sci. Soc. (chmn. 1979-80, goving. bd. 1979-87), Am. Assn. for Artificial Intelligence (fellow 1990), Am. Edni. Rsch. Assn. Home: 135 Cedar St Lexington MA 02173-6516 Office: BBN Corp 70 Fawcett St Cambridge MA 02138

COLLINS, BARBARA BALLIN, lawyer; b. Chgo., Jan. 17, 1955; d. Orrin Bernard and Hilda (Kraimen) Ballin; m. Gregory Dean Collins, Apr. 30, 1982; children: Hayley B., Allison B. BA, U. Ill., Champaign, 1976; JD, Chgo.-Kent Coll. Law, 1979. Bar: Ill. 1979. Law clk. to Judge Trapp 4th Dist. Ill. Appellate Ct., Springfield, 1979-81; trial atty. U.S. Dept. of Justice, Washington, 1981-83; asst. atty. gen. Ill. Atty. Gen. Office, Springfield, 1984-86; staff atty. Ill. EPA, Springfield, 1986-87; assoc. Morse, Giganti & Appleton, Springfield, 1987-90; mem. Stratton & Nardulli, Springfield, 1990—. Mem. Ctrl. Ill. Womens Bar Assn. (treas. 1990-91, v.p. 1991-92, pres. 1992-93). Jewish. Home: 1404 S Park Ave Springfield IL 62704-3464 Office: Stratton & Nardulli 725 S 4th St Springfield IL 62703-2244

COLLINS, BARBARA-ROSE, congresswoman; b. Detroit, Apr. 13, 1939; d. Lamar N. Sr. and Versa (Jones) R.; widowed; children: Cynthia Lynn, Christopher Loren. Student, Wayne State U. Commr. Human Rights Commn., Detroit, 1974-75; Mich. state rep., 1975-81; councilwoman City of Detroit, from 1982; mem. 102nd-103rd Congresses from 13th (now 15th) Mich. dist., 1991—, ranking minority mem. govt. reform & oversight subcom. on postal svc., mem. transp. & infrastructure com.; regional coord. Nat. Black Caucus of Local Elected Officials, 1984. Chmn. Detroit City Coun. Task Force on Teenage Violence, 1985. Recipient Disting. Cmty. Svc. award Shrines of Black Madonna Pan African Orthodox Christian Ch., 1981, Devoted Svc. award Metro Boy Scouts Am., 1984, Invaluable Svc. award Pershing H.S., Detroit, 1985. Office: 401 Cannon Washington DC 20515-2215 also: Dist Office One Kennedy Sq 719 Griswold Ste 2006 Detroit MI 48226*

COLLINS, CARDISS, congresswoman; b. St. Louis, Sept. 24, 1931; m. George W. Collins (dec.); 1 child, Kevin. Ed., Northwestern U.; hon. degree, Winston-Salem State U., Spelman Coll. Barber Scotia Coll.; sec. Ill. Dept. Revenue, then acct., revenue auditor; mem. 93d-103d Congresses from 7th Ill. Dist., 1973—; ranking minority mem. govt. reform & oversight com.; former chair. govt. activity and transp. subcom.; former majority whip-at-large; former chair Congl. Black Caucus, sec.; former chair Mems. Congress for Peace through Law. Mem. NAACP, The Chgo. Network, The Links. Mem. Nat. Coun. Negro Women, Chgo. Urban League, Black Women's Agenda, Alpha Gamma Pi, Alpha Kappa Alpha. Democrat. Baptist. Office: US Ho of Reps 2308 Rayburn Bldg Washington DC 20515-0005*

COLLINS, CHARLES PATRICK, emergency physician; b. Evanston, Ill., July 31, 1947; s. James Francis Jr. and Jeanne (Moss) C.; m. Barbara Lukes, June 18, 1977; children: Charles Bernard, Courtney Barbara, Christopher Burgess. BA in Econ., Mich. State U., 1969; MD, Loyola U., Maywood, Ill., 1977; MS in Bioengring., U. Ill., Chgo., 1989. Diplomate Am. Bd.

Emergency Medicine. Pres. Collins Med. Rsch./Svc., Oak Brook, Ill., 1978—. Woodrow Wilson fellow Harvard U., 1969; Returning scholar U. Chgo., 1983. Home: 700 Acorn Hill Ln Hinsdale IL 60521

COLLINS, DANA JON, financial executive; b. Grand Rapids, Mich., July 15, 1956; s. Daniel Hiltz and JoAnne M. (Smee) C. BBA with honors, U. Mich., 1978. CPA, Mich. Staff acct. Ernst & Whinney, Jackson, Mich., 1978-82; mgr. Ernst & Whinney, Jackson, 1982-86; CFO, treas. Fetzer Broadcasting Svc., Inc., Kalamazoo, 1986—, also bd. dirs.; exec. v.p., treas., bd. dirs. W.C.A. Holdings, Inc. Mem. AICPA, Mich. Assn. CPAs, Inst. Mgmt. Accts. (treas. 1984-86, exec. v.p. 1989, pres. 1990-91, bd. dirs. local chpt. 1984-92, nat. bd. dirs. 1992—). Republican. Home: 7094 Jamaica Ln Kalamazoo MI 49001-9402 Office: Fetzer Broadcasting Svc Inc 5168 Sprinkle Rd Kalamazoo MI 49002-2055

COLLINS, JAMES FRANCIS, lawyer, financial consultant; b. Evanston, Ill., July 31, 1943; s. James Francis Jr. and Jeanne (Moss) C.; m. Ann Peake Rogers, Apr. 5, 1983. BSc in Mktg., U. Louisville, 1969, JD, 1977; JD, Xavier U., 1971; MEd in Bus. Adminstrn. Bar: Ky. 1977, Ill. 1977, Fla. 1978, U.S. Dist. Ct. (we. dist.) Ky. 1978, U.S. Mil. Ct. Appeals 1978, U.S. Tax Ct. 1978, U.S. Customs Ct. 1978, U.S. Ct. Appeals (6th cir.) 1980, U.S. Supreme Ct. 1980, U.S. Dist. Ct. (so. dist.) Ind. 1981, U.S. Dist. Ct. (mid. dist.) Fla. 1982, Wis. 1989, Ind. 1989; cert. secondary tchr., Ill., Ky., Ohio. Br. mgr., mcht. rep. Household Fin. Corp., Chgo., 1962-66; tchr. bus. Jefferson County Bd. Edn., Louisville, 1968-77; pvt. practice Louisville, 1977-82; criminal def. trial lawyer Pub. Defender, Sanford, Fla., 1982-83; pvt. practice Schaumburg, Ill., 1984—; arbitrator, chairperson Cir. Ct. Cook. County, Mandatory Ct. Annexed Arbitration, 1990—; part-time instr. in comml. and internat. law Watterson Coll., Louisville, 1974-75. Dist. ct. judge candidate Jefferson County, Ky., 1981; cir. ct. judge candidate Dem. Primary, Chgo., 1986, 88, 92, 96; appellate ct. judge candidate, Chgo., 1990, Dem. Primary, Chgo., 1994; Dem. cir. ct. judge candidate, 1996; mem. S.E. Side Community Orgn.; legal counsel election day Dem. Party of Proviso Twp., 1985-90, 37th Ward of Chgo., 1991-94, 27th Ward of Chgo., 1991-94, election day legal counsel to Sen. Richard Hendon, 1989—; mem. Berkeley (Ill.) Citizens Party, 1987. Recipient ICLE 32 Hour Bankruptcy Course award, 1985, Recognition award Berkeley (Ill.) Citizens party, 1986, Continuing Legal Edn. recognition award Ky. Bar Assn., 1987, 91, 92, 93, 94, 95, Recognition awards Westside Chgo. Black Polit. Leaders Assn., 1990, 92, Recognition award Cook County Dem. Party Fair Coalition, 1992, Continuing Legal Edn. Recognition award Ky. Bar Assn., 1994; named Disting. Citizen of Louisville, Ky. by Mayor Harvey Slone, 1976, Hon. Cpt. Belle Louisville by County Judge Exec. Todd Hollenbach, 1974, Hon. Ky. Col. by Gov. Wendel Ford, Lt. Gov. Thelma Stoval, 1974. Mem. Internat. Platform Assn., Chgo. Bar Assn. (Ill. indsl. commn. worker's compensation com., adminstrv. law com.), U. Louisville Bus. Sch. Alumni Assn., Xavier U. Alumni Assn., Sigma Delta Kappa. Office: 3 Golf Ctr PO Box 68042 Schaumburg IL 60168-0042

COLLINS, JAMES GREGORY, civil engineering company executive; b. LaPorte, Ind., Feb. 11, 1939; s. Donald Leroy and Alice Teresa (Fick) C.; m. Barbra Jeanne, June 10, 1961 (div. Aug. 10, 1990); children: Kathleen, Andrea, Jennifer. BA in Math., Notre Dame U., 1961, BSCE, 1962. Registered profl. engr., Fla. Spl. rep. western sales divsn. domestic sales Caterpiller Tractor Co., 1964-67; v.p. earthmoving and bridge divsn. Canonie Constrn. Co, Ind./Mich., 1967-71; v.p. ops. Capital Dredge & Dock Corp., Pa., Mich., Ohio, 1971-75; v.p. marine divsn. Roger J. Au & Son Inc, Ind., Mich., N.Y., Miss., Ohio, 1976; pvt. practice constrn. Mich., Minn., Ohio, Mo., Miss., 1976-80; prin. stockholder, CEO Trident Marine Inc., South Haven, Mich., 1980-84; owner, pres. Trident Tech. Svcs. Inc., South Haven, 1985—. Patentee in field. Capt. U.S. Army Corps Engrs., 1962-64. Mem. ASCE, Am. Constrn. Arbitration Assn. (constrn. panel), Notre Dame Club of Kalamazoo, Notre Dame Club of Stuart (Fla.), KC. Roman Catholic. Home and Office: 1435 Clarke Pl South Haven MI 49090

COLLINS, JAMES TROY, JR., academic administrator; b. Savannah, Ga., Oct. 31, 1940; s. James Troy and Bertis (Bland) C.; m. Elizabeth Wylly, Sept. 14, 1963; children: James T. III, Wylly Habersham, Susan Lachlan Collins Ivy. BS, U. Ga., 1961, JD, 1964. Pvt. tax practice Ga., Mo., 1964-77; dir. fin. divsn. Miller Brewing Co., Milw., 1977-96; dir. Deloitte and Touche Multistate Tax Ctr., U. Wis., Milw., 1996—; v.p. bd. dirs. U. Wis., Milw., 1992—; pres. bd. dirs. St. Michael Hosp., Milw., 1992-93. Editor: Jour. of State Taxation, 1982—, Jour. of Property Tax Mgmt., 1982—. Treas. Joint Orgn. for Better Sewers, Milw., 1983—; pres. Blue Ridge Fund-S.S.W., Milw., 1994—. Recipient Philip Morris Chmn.'s award, 1981, Philip Morris Silver Ring award, 1988; named Wis. Outstanding Tax Profl., 1994. Republican. Presbyterian. Home: 5817 N Lake Dr Milwaukee WI 53217 Office: U Wis 2200 E Kenwood Blvd Milwaukee WI 53217

COLLINS, JAY MICHAEL, stockbroker; b. Fargo, N.D., Dec. 18, 1947. BA in Econs. and Govt., St. John's U., Collegeville, Minn., 1969. Owner, mgr. Collins Constrn., Fargo, 1969-81; stockbroker Dain Bosworth Inc., Fargo, 1981-83, Piper Jaffray Inc., Fargo, 1993—. Bd. govs. Dakota Heartland Health Sys., Fargo, 1995—. Republican. Roman Catholic. Office: Piper Jaffray Inc 51 Broadway Fargo ND 58102-4970

COLLINS, LINDA LOU POWELL, contract manager; b. Michigan City, Ind., May 6, 1957; d. Ronald Edward Powell and Betty Louise (Gruenberg) Will; m. Aug. 15, 1981 (div. May 18, 1983); m. Edward T. Collins, oct. 14, 1989; 1 child, Elizabeth Louise. BA in English, Purdue U., 1980; MBA, St. Francis Coll., Fort Wayne, Ind., 1988. Cert. purchasing mgr.; cert. profl. contracts mgr. Head expeditor Graham Electronics, Ft. Wayne, Ind., 1981-82; expeditor solid state Magnavox Electronic Systems Co., Ft. Wayne, 1982-83, assoc. buyer, 1983-85, buyer, 1985-87, subcontract adminstr., 1987-88, sr. contract adminstr., 1988-93, contract mgr., 1993—; bus. writing instr. Ind.-Purdue U., Ft. Wayne, 1990-91; seminar instr. Nat. Contract Mgmt. Assn., 1991-92. Mem. Civic Theater Dirs.' Cir., Ft. Wayne, 1989—; property trustee St. Joseph United Meth. Ch., Ft. Wayne, 1992, choir mem., 1993-95. Recipient Woman of Achievement award YWCA, 1996. Fellow Nat. Contract Mgmt. Assn. (program chair 1990-91, v.p. 1991-92, mem. chair 1993-93, v.p. programs/facilities 1993-94, v.p./sec. 1994-95, regional mem. chair 1994-96, nat. functional dir. mem. retention 1994-95, v.p. membership 1995-96, nat. dir. 1996—, James E. Cravens Meml. award 1993, Blanch Witte Hon. Mention award 1996); mem. Purdue U. Alumni Assn., Magna Health Club (v.p. 1990-91, mem. chair 1991-95, sec. 1995-96), Magnavox Mgmt. Club Ind. (facilities chair 1990-91, bd. dirs. 1993-96), Alpha Gamma Delta (altruism chair 1977-78). Republican. Office: Magnavox Electronic Systems Co A Hughes Def Comms Co 1010 Production Rd Fort Wayne IN 46808-1164

COLLINS, MARIE ANN, civil engineer; b. Morganfield, Ky., Nov. 6, 1957; d. R. Eugene and Ann (Hancock) C. BSCE, U. Ky., 1980; MSCE, U. Mo., Rolla, 1989. Registered profl. engr., Mo. Design engr. I Booker Assocs., Inc., St. Louis, 1980-88; with Met. St. Louis Sewer Dist., St. Louis, 1988—, mgr. of plan rev., 1996—. Mem. com. City of Maryland Heights (Mo.) Bd. Code Appeals, 1986—; commr. Mo. Seismic Safety Commn. Mem. ASCE (chpt. rep. zone III Younger Mem. Coun. 1988-89, nominating com. 1990-91, 92, chpt. dir. 1991-95, Young Engr. of Yr. St. Louis chpt. 1988), Mo. Soc. Profl. Engrs. (chpt. dir. 1988-91, chpt. treas. 1991-92, chpt. sect. 1992-93, chpt. v.p. 1993-94, chpt. pres.-elect 1994-95, chpt. pres. 1995-96), Engrs. Club St. Louis (dir. 1988-91, chmn. young engrs. com. 1987-88, Young Engr. of Yr. 1989). Roman Catholic. Office: Met Saint Louis Sewer Dist 2000 Hampton Ave Saint Louis MO 63139-2934

COLLINS, MARY ELLEN, human resources executive; b. Indpls., Jan. 24, 1949; d. Carl William and Hester (Dawson) McConn; m. Thomas N. Wininger, June 19, 1971 (div. 1981); m. Larry Wayne Collins, Dec. 15, 1983; 1 child, Ann Marie. Diploma in nursing, Holy Cross Coll., 1969; BS, Coll. of St. Francis, 1981; MS, Ind. U., 1984; PhD in Orgnl. Behavior, Union Inst., Cin., 1993. Edn. coord. Cmty. Hosp., Indpls., 1969-84; dir. tng. Middletown (Ohio) Regional Hosp., 1984-87; pres. People Power Cons. Svc., Cin., 1987—; adj. prof. Coll. Mt. St. Joseph, Ohio, 1988-93. Editl. bd. Strategic Governance for Non Profit Orgns., (newsletters) Teamwork, Quality One. Adminstrv. chair Deerfield Ch., Maineville, 1987-89. Mem. ASTD (bd. dirs. Cin. chpt. 1988-89), Assn. for Psychol. Type (pres., founder Greater Cin. chpt. 1992—, bd. dirs. Gt. Lakes region, Internat. New Leader award 1993), Assn. Quality Participation (healthcare adv. bd., Disting. Faculty mem.), Internat. Visitors Ctr., Women Entrepreneurs, Inc. Methodist.

COLLINS, MARY ELLEN KENNEDY, librarian, educator; b. Pitts., Feb. 28, 1939; d. Joseph Michael and Stella Marie (Kane) Kennedy; m. Orpha Collins. BA, Villa Maria Coll., 1961; MLS, U. Pitts., 1970, PhD, 1980. Tchr., Pitts. Catholic Schs., 1962-65; tchr., Anne Arundel County Schs., Annapolis, 1965-67; legal sec., firm Joseph M. Kennedy, Pitts., 1967-70; cataloger Newport News (Va.) Libr. System, 1970-71; reference librarian Glenville (W.Va.) State Coll., 1971-80; asst. prof. libr. sci. Ball State U., Muncie, Ind., 1980-83; reference librarian, asst. prof. Purdue U., West Lafayette, Ind., 1983-88, assoc. prof., 1988—. Author: Education Journals and Serials: An Analytical Guide, 1988; contbr. articles to profl. jours. Sec. Presbyn. Ch., 1973-74, pres., 1974-76, bd. deacons, 1979-80; chmn. library com., Muncie, 1981-83; mem. belle com. W.Va. Folk Festival, 1973-80. Recipient Title III advanced study grant, 1977-78, Disting. Edn. and Behavioral Scis. Libr. award Assn. Coll. and Rsch. Librs., ALA, 1994. Mem. ALA (reference books rev. com. 1979-82, profl. devel. com. 1983-87, mem. Ednl. Behavioral Scis. (sect.-problems of access and control of ednl. materials 1984-88, curriculum materials com. 1988—, adult libr. materials com. 1988—), Ind. Library Assn., Spl. Libraries Assn., Assn. Coll. and Rsch. Libraries, Am. Assn. U. Profs., Assn. Ind. Media Educators, Assn. Am. Libr. Schs., AAUW (corr. sec. 1981-82), Delta Kappa Gamma, Sigma Sigma Sigma, Beta Phi Mu. Republican. Office: Purdue U HSSE Libr West Lafayette IN 47907

COLLINS, MICHAEL R., lawyer, business executive; b. Oak Park, Ill., July 3, 1961. BBA, U. Mich., 1983; JD, DePaul U., 1986. Sec., treas. North Shore & Ctrl. Ill. Freight Co., Chgo., 1983—; ptnr. Collins and Collins, Chgo., 1985—; v.p. Dearborn F, Chgo., 1988—; ptnr. Wolverine Leasing Ptrns., Chgo., 1990—; pres. Video Ednl. Prodn. Ltd., Chgo., 1990—, North Shore Interstate, Inc., Chgo., 1993—. Producer (instructional video) How To Play the Guitar Now, 1990. Dir. Community Health Care Plans, Inc., Chgo., 1994-95; mem. Lawyers for the Creative Arts, 1990-95; coach Hinsdale Little League, 1995—. Roman Catholic. Office: 332 S Michigan Ave Ste 1758 Chicago IL 60604-4404

COLLINS, MOIRA ANN, graphics and communications company executive, calligrapher; b. Washington, Dec. 16, 1942; d. Peter William and Louise (Carroll) Collins; m. Andrew Joseph Griffin, Aug. 21, 1965; children: Andrew Fitzgerald, Timothy Collins. BA, U. Toronto (Ont., Can.), 1964; MA in Teaching, Northwestern U., 1965; MEd in Urban Studies, Northeastern U., Chgo., 1968. Tchr., Chgo. Bd. Edn., 1965-68; studied with profl. calligraphers, scribes and illuminators, Haystack Mountain Sch., Deer Isle, Maine, 1973, U. Calif. Santa Cruz, 1973-74; freelance calligrapher, 1974-78; mem. publicity and promotional staff Swallow Press, Chgo., 1978-79; owner Letters, Chgo., 1979—; pres. Astrogram, Chgo. 1986; intern Gestalt Inst. of Toronto & Oasis Ctr, Chgo., 1986-87. HEW fellow Northeastern U., 1967-68. Author, contbr.; Celebration: Anais Nin, 1975; contbr. to Goodfellow Rev. of Crafts, 1979. Calligrapher: Erotica, 1976, Chgo. Rev., 1978. Chmn. fund-raising Van Gorder Walden Sch., Chgo., 1979-80. Mem. Chgo. Calligraphy Collective (co-founder, chmn. 1976-77, pres. 1978-79, hon. mem.), Soc. Scribes N.Y., Soc. Scribes and Illuminators (Eng.), Friends Calligraphy Calif. Democrat. Roman Catholic. Home: 3920 N Lake Shore Dr Apt 9N Chicago IL 60613-3449 Office: 533 Lake Front Dr Beverly Shores IN 46301

COLLINS, RICHARD WARD, labor union administrator, secondary education educator; b. Appleton, Wis., Mar. 7, 1943; s. Russell Ward and Eleanore A. (Marx) C.; m. D. Debra Berndt, Oct. 2, 1976; children: Emily E.B., Benjamin W.B., Anne Lindsay. BS, U. Wis., 1965; MA, U. Wis., LaCrosse, 1972. Tchr. Waupun (Wis.) H.S., 1972-89; v.p. Wis. Edn. Assn. Coun., Madison, 1984-89, pres., 1989—; pres. Wis. Coalition Am. Pub. Employees, Madison, 1985-89. Chmn. Wis. Ed. Assn. Polit. Action Com., Madison, 1989—; exec. v.p. Wis. CitizenAction, Milw., 1995. Capt. U.S. Army, 1967-69, Vietnam. Unitarian. Home: 221 Declark St Beaver Dam WI 53916-1709 Office: Wis Edn Assn Coun PO Box 8003 Madison WI 53708

COLLINS, ROSS FRANCIS, communications educator; b. Fargo, N.D., Dec. 21, 1954; s. Dorothy I. (Castonia) Collins. BS, BA, Moorhead State U., 1978; MA, U. Warwick, Eng., 1980; PhD, U. Cambridge, Eng., 1992. Staff writer Forum of Fargo-Moorhead, Fargo, 1978-79; pvt. practice comm. cons. Moorhead, Minn., 1981-84; instr. mass comm. Moorhead State U., 1984-87, comm. officer, 1988-89, 91; comm. officer U. N.D., Grand Forks, 1991-92, asst. prof., 1993; asst. prof. N.D. State U., 1993—. Author: Images, 1986 (booklet) Backing Up Bluffs, 1985, also monographs and articles in field. Scholar Am. Friends of Cambridge U., 1989-90, French History Soc., 1989-90, Rotary Found., 1989-90; Overseas Rsch. Student, Brit. Govt., 1987-90. Mem. Assn. for Edn. in Journalism and Mass Comm., Am. Journalism Historians Assn. Home: 1017 7th St S Fargo ND 58103-2709 Office: ND State U Dept Sch Comm Fargo ND 58105

COLLINS, SUSAN J., management services company; b. Mpls., Minn., Sept. 29, 1945. Asst. v.p. Norwest Bank, Mpls., 1968-86, Midwest Fed. Saving & Loan, Mpls., 1986-88; v.p. Accounts Receivable Mgmt. Svcs., Mpls., 1988—. Mem. Gen. Fedn. Women's Clubs of Minn. Office: Accounts Receivable Mgmt Svcs P O Box 20154 Minneapolis MN 55420-0154

COLLINS, THOMAS WILLIAM, caterer, consultant; b. Lewiston, Idaho, Nov. 4, 1926; s. William James and Mary (Egan) C.; m. Mary Charlene Tracy, Aug. 1, 1947 (dec. Apr. 1984); children: Kathleen, William, Charles. Grad. high sch., Staples, Minn., 1944. Owner Collins Cafe, Park Rapids, Minn., 1947-63, Tom Collins Restaurant, Walker, Minn., 1963-83, Tom Collins Catering, Walker, 1983—. Author: Collins Cooking Secrets, 1981. Fundraiser DFL, 1976-83; adv. bd. Lake Country Food Bank, Mpls., 1981-86. Served with USN, 1945-46, 51-52. Recipient Recognition award Mont. Gov., 1978, cert. of Spl. Congl. Recognition, 1995; Tom Collins Day proclaimed by Minn. Gov., 1977. Mem. Assn. Great Lakes Outdoor Writers, Am. Legion. Lodge: Masons (sr. warden 1958), Shriners. Home and Office: PO Box 33 Walker MN 56484-0033

COLLINS, VERNON E. (RICK COLLINS), manufacturing company executive; b. Lewiston, Maine, June 9, 1948; s. Elden Ross and Elaine Beverly (Robinson) C.; div.; 1 child, Jordan Vernon. BS in Engring. Mgmt., Norwich U., 1970; MS in Arctic Engring., U. Alaska, 1986, MS in Civil Engring., 1988. Constrn. mgr., supr. S.A. Collins & Son, Inc., Rangeley, Maine, 1964-69; project engr. New Eng. Telephone, 1970-71; CEO 89th Ord Det U.S. Army, Ft. Benning, Ga., 1971-74; logistics chief and CEO 696th Ord Co and HHC 6th Ord Bn., 1974-75; COO 543rd Ord Det, U.S. Army, Ft. Leonard Wood, Mo., 1976-78; chief spl. ops. J-3 8th U.S. Army, Seoul, Korea, 1979; CEO U.S. Army, Fort Richardson, Alaska, 1979-81; sr. project mgr. Alyeska Pipeline Svc. Co., Anchorage, 1981-88, exec. mgr. pipeline stas. 1 and 2, 1988-90; marine terminal exec. mgr. Alyeska Pipeline Svc. Co., Valdez, Alaska, 1990-93; chmn., pres., CEO Bliss-Salem Inc., Salem, Ohio, 1994—. Author: (adventure stories) Hunting in Alaska, 1981; contbr. articles to profl. jours. Pres. and chmn. of bd. Valdez C. of C., 1991-93; bd. dirs. State C. of C., Juneau, Alaska, 1991-93; coll. coun. Valdez C.C., 1992; bd. dirs. Valdez Devel. Inst., 1992. Col. USAR ret. Recipient Meritorious Svc. medal U.S. Army, 1975, 79, 81, Army Commendation medal U.S. Army, 1974, 84. Mem. ARC, Project Mgmt. Inst., Equality Lodge #497 Masonic (lectr. 1975—), Valdez C. of C. (pres. 1991-93, chmn. bd.), State C. of C. (bd. dirs. 1991-93). Democrat. Home: 803 Highland Ave Salem OH 44460-2572 Office: 530 S Ellsworth Ave Salem OH 44460-3067

COLLINS, WALTON ROBERT, writer, educator; b. Phila., Feb. 15, 1930; s. Walton Robert and Margaret (Missett) C.; m. Carolyn Huebner, June 11, 1952; children: W. Robert, Mary Carol (dec.), Jeanne, John, Margaret. AB, U. Notre Dame, 1951; MPA, Ind. U., South Bend, 1976. Asst. editor Indsl. Maintenance Mag., Phila., 1951-53; mng. editor Alexandria (Ind.) Times-Tribune, 1953-57; reporter South Bend Tribune, 1957-61, assoc. editor, 1961-69; asst. to chancellor Ind. U., South Bend, 1969-83; editor Notre Dame Mag., 1983-95; free-lance writer/editor, 1995—; adj. assoc. prof. U. Notre Dame, 1983—, Ind. U., South Bend, 1970-84. Contbr. numerous articles to mags. and newspapers. Recipient numerous awards for Notre Dame Mag., 1983—. Mem. Soc. Profl. Journalists, South Bend Press Club (past pres.), Sibley Soc. Mag. Editors. Home: 2201 Riverside Dr South Bend IN 46616-2151

COLLOTON, JOHN WILLIAM, university health care executive; b. Mason City, Iowa, Feb. 20, 1931; s. Harold and Miriam (Kelly) C.; m. Mary Ann Hagglund, Oct. 8, 1960; children—Steven, Laura, Ann. B.A. with high honors, Loras Coll., 1953; M.A., U. Iowa, 1957. Hosp. relations rep. Hosp. Service Inc. of Iowa, Des Moines, 1957-58; with U. Iowa, Iowa City, 1958—; assoc. dir. U. Iowa Hosps. and Clinics, 1969-71, dir., asst. to univ. pres. for statewide health svcs., 1971-93; v.p. statewide health svcs. U. Iowa, 1993—; bd. dirs. Baxter Internat., Inc., Nat. Med. Waste Inc., Iowa State Bank & Trust Co., MidAm. Energy Co., Premier Anesthesia, Atlanta, 1992, Assn. Health Svcs. Rsch., 1992; cons. HIH; pres. adminstrv. bd. Assn. Am. med. Colls. Coun. of Teaching Hosps., 1979-80; mem. presdl. search com. Assn. Am. Med. Colls., 1984; mem. adv. bd. Duke U. Hosp., 1985; mem. task force on acad. health ctrs. Commonwealth Fund, chmn. selection com. exec. nurse leadership program, 1983; mem. prospective payment commn. Congl. Office Technology Assessment, 1983; chmn. bd. dirs. Iowa-S.D. Health Svcs. Corp. (now Blue Cross and Blue Shield Iowa, Blue Cross S.D.), 1993—. Contbr. articles to profl. pubs. Served with Finance Corps U.S. Army, 1953-55. Fellow Am. Coll. Hosp. Adminstrs.; mem. Inst. Medicine NAS, Am. Hosp. Assn. (con. on financing 1977, med. edn. com. 1984-87), Iowa Hosp. Assn. (chmn. bd. trustees 1977-78, trustee 1978—), Am. Assn. Hosp. Planning, Assn. Am. Med. Colls. (chmn. 1987-88, disting. svc. mem. 1991), Johnson County (Iowa) Med. Soc., U. Iowa Alumni Assn., Rotary. Roman Catholic. Home: 1899 Brown Deer Rd Coralville IA 52241-1160 Office: U Iowa Hosps & Clinics 200 Hawkins Dr Iowa City IA 52242-1009

COLOMBO, FREDERICK J., lawyer; b. Detroit, Dec. 7, 1916; s. Louis J. and Irene Elizabeth (McKinney) C.; m. Frances Elizabeth Fisher, June 12, 1947; children: William, Joan, Richard, John. AB, U. Mich., 1938, JD, 1940. Bar: Mich. 1940, U.S. Dist. Ct. (ea. dist.) Mich. 1940, U.S. Ct. Appeals (6th cir.) 1940, U.S. Supreme Ct. 1940. Ptnr. Colombo and Colombo, P.C., Birmingham, Mich., 1945-86, of counsel, 1987—. Trustee emeritus Harper Grace Hosp., Detroit; chmn. spl. gifts com. United Found.; mem. exec. com. Mich. Republican Party. Mem. ABA, Mich. State Bar Assn., Am. Judicature Soc., Detroit Bar Assn., Oakland County Bar Assn., Cardinal Club (past pres., Detroit), Cardinal Club (past pres., Detroit). Roman Catholic.

COLONNA, ROCCO J., state legislator; m. Shirley J. Colonna; children: Tina Marie Colonna Rini, Lavaine Anne Colonna Cates, Danny V.M. BA, U.S. Armed Forces Inst.; postgrad., Internat. Data Processing Inst., Cuyahoga C.C., Baldwin Wallace Coll. Mem. Ohio Ho. of Reps., Columbus, 1975—; chmn. econ. devel. and small bus. com., labor-mgmt. com., mem. rules com., ways and means com., devel. financing adv. bd., select com. for tech., linked deposit adv. com., rep. to speaker on econ. devel. policy bd., mem. turnpike oversight com., motor vehicle inspection and maintenance program and policy planning com. Former mem. Brook Park (Ohio) Planning Commn., Brook Park Zoning and Bldg. Bd. Appeals; mem. Brook Park City Coun., 1970-74; mem. Ohio Gov.'s Tripartite Labor and Mgmt. Adv. Commn. Recipient Outstanding Leadership award Ohio C. of C., 1986, Legislator of Yr. award food industry com. Ohio Coun. Retail Mchts., 1980, AMVETS, 1990. Mem. Ohio Aerospace Inst., Am. Legion, Holy Name Soc., Eagles. Democrat. Home: 6477 Wolf Rd Cleveland OH 44142-3873*

COLONNA, WILLIAM MARK, accountant; b. Joliet, Ill., Jan. 18, 1956; s. William and Lorraine (Govednik) C. BA in Acctg., Lewis U., 1974-78. Cost acct., asst. acctg. mgr. Insta-Foam Products, Joliet, Ill., 1978-86; cost acct. Durkee Foods, Joliet, 1986-88; chief acct. mgr. Lennon Wallpaper Co., Shorewood, Ill., 1988-90; pres., owner William M. Colonna Acctg. and Tax Svc., Crest Hill, Ill., 1990—; contr. Whiteford Warehouse & Distbn., Joliet, 1992—, Midwest Motor Svc. Co. of Ill., Inc., Joliet, 1992—; sec., Joliet St. Anne Credit Union, Crest Hill, Ill., 1980—, also bd. dirs. Home: 1718 Dearborn St Joliet IL 60435-2550

COLONY, DAVID CARL, civil engineering educator; b. Mt. Holly, N.J., civil engineering educator, Oct. 17, 1924; s. David Carl and Sadie Ella (Bedwell) C.; m. Selma Jane Rowe, Mar. 29, 1946; children: Judith A., Stephen F., James A. BCE, George Washington U., 1948; MSE, U. Mich., 1950, PhD, 1972. Registered profl. engr. and surveyor, Ohio. Jr. engr. Wickersham & Chance, Naval Archs., Washington, 1948-49; divsn. engr. City of Toledo, 1950-51, commr. of bldg. inspection, 1954-57; prin. engr. T.C. Biebesheimer Engrs., Toledo, 1957-63; mem. faculty U. Toledo, 1963—, prof. emeritus, 1994—; engring. cons. City of Toledo, 1965-93, Ohio Dept. Transp., Columbus, 1967-93. Contbr. articles to profl. jours. Lt. USN, 1945-46, 51-54. Named Outstanding Engring. Educator, Ohio Soc. Profl. Engrs.; recipient 1st place award Nat. Asphalt Paving Assn., 1982; faculty fellow NSF, 1966. Fellow ASCE (Toledo sect., Civil Engr. of Yr. 1984). Office: Civil Engineering Dept Univ of Toledo 2801 W Bancroft Toledo OH 43606

COLOSIMO, KAREN ELIZABETH, academic administrator; b. Lincoln, Nebr., Mar. 5, 1936; d. Glenn Paul and Mildred Evelyn (Carper) Bahr; m. Clark A. Springman (div. May 1972); children: Jeffrey Clark, Jennifer Lynn (dec.), Gregory Andrew, David Stuart; m. William Colosimo, June 23, 1973. Student, U. Nebr., 1954-56, George Williams Coll., Downers Grove, Ill., 1970-71. Adminstrv. asst. State of Nebr., Lincoln, 1954-56; adminstrv. asst. to v.p. George Williams Coll., Downers Grove, 1968-80, dir. devel. rsch., 1980-84; rsch. cons. John Pruehs & Assocs., Naperville, Ill., 1985-88; mktg. asst. Mid Am. Fed., Naperville, 1988-90, dir. advancement scis. Aurora (Ill.) U., 1990-93, dir. donor rsch., 1993—. Mem. Compassionate Friends bd., Hinsdale, Ill., 1978-80, Aurora area Fundraisers, 1989—; mem. adv. bd. Fox Valley Arts Coun., Geneva, Ill., 1990—; mem. DuKane Valley coun., Batavia, 1991—. Mem. Aurora C. of C., Midwest Scottish Deerhound Club Am. (pres. 1990-93, 95—, bd. dirs. 1991—), Scottish Deerhound Club Am. (pres. 1995—). Methodist. Home: 2750 Harvey Rd Oswego IL 60543 Office: Aurora Univ 347 S Gladstone Ave Aurora IL 60506

COLOSIMO, MARY LYNN SUKURS, psychology educator; b. Chgo., Aug. 14, 1950; d. Charles Paul and Charlotte Pearl (Bartkus) S.; m. Ronald Alfred Colosimo, Nov. 26, 1977; children: Elizabeth Catherine, Victoria Carmella, Christina Charlotte, Diana Clare. BA, Bradley U., 1972, MA, 1974; PhD, U. Chgo., 1981. Cert. tchr., Ill. Tchr. Lincoln (Ill.) High Sch., 1973-75; counselor Lyle Elem. Sch., Bridgeview, Ill., 1975-78; prof. St. Xavier Coll., Chgo., 1984-86; prof. ednl. psychology, tchg. methods, coord. tchr. interns field placements Trinity Christian Coll., Palos Heights, Ill., 1988—; pvt. practice as counselor, cons., Orland Park, Ill., 1983-90; educator, dir. summer program for gifted elem. students, after-sch. enrichment program women's ministry, retreat work, small group leader Cmty. Life Ch., Lockport, Ill.; researcher in field. Contbr. articles to profl. jours. Mem. ACA, ASCD, AAUW, Am. Ednl Rsch. Assn., Assn. Rsch. Value Issues in Counseling, , Assn. Christian Therapists, Am. Assn. Christian Counselors, Nat. Gifted Edn. Assn., Ill. Gifted Edn. Assn., Nat. Assn. Guidance Counselors, Ill. Assn. Guidance Counselors, Phi Kappa Phi.

COLTEN, HARVEY RADIN, pediatrician, educator; b. Houston, Jan. 11, 1939; s. Oscar Aaron and Zina Mae (Radin) C.; m. Susan J. Kaplowitz, July 29, 1959; children: Jennifer J., Lora, Charles Thomas. B.A., Cornell U., 1959; M.D., Western Res. U., 1963; M.A. (hon.), Harvard U., 1978. Diplomate Am. Bd. Allergy and Clin. Immunology, Am. Bd. Pediatrics. Intern Univ. Hosps., Cleve., 1963-64, resident in pediatrics, 1964-65; resident in pediatrics Children's Hosp. of D.C., Washington, 1968-69; rsch. assoc. Nat. Inst. Child and Human Devel., NIH, Bethesda, Md., 1965-67; asst. prof. pediatrics George Washington U., 1969-70; asst. prof. pediatrics Harvard U., 1970-73, assoc. prof., 1973-79, prof., 1979-86; chief div. cell biology, dir. cystic fibrosis program Children's Hosp. Med. Ctr., Boston, 1976-86; Harriet B. Spoehrer prof. pediats. Washington U. Med. Sch., St. Louis, 1986—, chmn. dept. pediatrics, 1986-95, prof. molecular microbiology, 1986—; pediatrician-in-chief Children's and Barnes Hosps., 1986-95, Jewish Hosp., 1986-90; pediatrician Children's, Barnes and Jewish Hosps., 1995—; past chmn. pediatric allergy Nat. Inst. Allergy and Infectious Disease Task Force on Asthma and Allergy; past mem. Nat. Inst. Child and Human Devel. Task Force on Cystic Fibrosis; past bd. dirs. rsch. rev. com. Nat. Cystic Fibrosis Found.; past mem. pulmonary diseases adv. com. NIH. Assoc. editor Jour. Immunology, 1971-74, Immuno-chemistry, 1972-75, Jour. Allergy and Clin.

Immunology, 1977-80, New Eng. Jour. Medicine, 1978-81, Jour. Clin. Investigation, 1982-85, Am. Jour. Respiratory Cell and Molecular Biology, 1988-91, New Insights into CF, 1993; mem. editorial bd. Molecular and Cellular Biochemistry, 1983-87, Jour. Pediatrics, 1981-88, Jour. Clin. Immunology, 1985-89, Ann. Rev. Immunology, 1986-90, Clin. Immunology and Immunopathology, 1987-91, Blood, 1987-92, New England Journal of Medicine, 1990—, Jour. Biomedical Sci., 1992—, Proc. Assn. Am. Physics, 1995—; contbr. articles to profl. jours. Past vice chmn., bd. dirs. Parents As Tchrs. Nat. Ctr.; past mem. pediatric scientist program selection com. AMSPDC; mem. sci. adv. coun. Mar. Dimes; mem. Nat. Heart, Lung, Blood Adv. Coun., NIH. Recipient Spl. faculty rsch. award Western Res. U., 1963, E. Mead Johnson award, 1979. Fellow AAAS, Am. Acad. Allergy and Immunology, Am. Acad. Pediatrics; mem. Fedn. Am. Socs. for Exptl. Biology (mem. fin. com.), Inst. Medicine of NAS (mem. coun.), E. Mead Johnson Award Program Com. (past chmn.), Am. Assn. Immunologists (sec.-treas.), Am. Soc. Clin. Investigation, Assn. Am. Physicians, Soc. Pediatric Rsch., Am. Pediatric Soc., Am. Thoracic Soc., Cen. Inst. for Deaf (bd. mgrs.), Am. Soc. Biochem. & Molecular Biol., St. Louis Pediatric Soc. Office: Dept Pediatrics Washington U Sch Medicine 1 Children's Pl Saint Louis MO 63110

COLTON, VICTOR ROBERT, real estate developer, investor,; b. Detroit, Apr. 30, 1930; s. McArthur and Lottie S. BA, Wayne State U., 1952; DDS, U. Detroit, 1956. Owner V. Robert Colton, D.D.S. Dental Clinic, Detroit, 1956-84; owner, dir. Lakewood Devel. Co., Inc., Southfield, Mich., 1974-81, Monetary Investment Group Inc., Southfield, Mich., 1975-90, Clean Rooms Internat., Grand Rapids, Mich., 1984-90, Macomb Biotech., Inc., Romeo, Mich., 1984-90, Polymeric Processes Inc., Tecumseh, Mich., 1984—, Toth Aluminium Corp., Vacherie, La., 1986—, Strong Point, Inc., Newport Beach, Calif., 1986—, Airsensors, Inc., Seattle and Cerritos, Calif., 1988—, Accor Tech., Inc., Bellevue, Wash., 1988—, Clifton Engring. Co., Inc., Three Rivers, Mich., 1989-91, Movie Am. Corp., Atlanta, 1989-91, RCM Internat., Inc., Sylvan Lake, Mich., 1991—, Am. Artists Film Corp., Atlanta, 1991—, RCH Investments, Inc., Southfield, Mich., 1994—; trustee Monetary Realty Trust, Southfield, 1978-82; owner, dir. Primus Fin. Svcs., Inc., Grand Rapids, 1983-88; owner cons. Cartrex Corp., Grand Rapids, 1984-88. Home: 7340 Creek View West Bloomfield MI 48322-3515 Office: RCH Investments Inc 25130 Southfield Rd Ste 100 Southfield MI 48075

COLVARD, MICHAEL DAVID, periodontist, oral medicine and laser surgery specialist; b. Salem, Ore., Oct. 11, 1954; s. William Douglas and Othelene (Lee) C.; m. Kathleen Marie Perkowitz, July 14, 1984; children: Christopher Michael, Jonathon David. BA in Edn., Ariz. State U., 1978; DDS, Loyola U., 1985, cert. periodontist, 1985-87; postgrad., U. Ill., 1993—. Diplomate Am. Acad. Pain Mgmt. Surg. asst. Evanston (Ill.) Hosp., 1978-85; pvt. practice Schaumburg, Ill., 1985—; vis. lectr. Dept. Oral and Maxillofacial Surgery Loyola U., Maywood, Ill., 1990-95; clin. asst. prof. Stritch Sch. Medicine Loyola U., 1995—; adj. prof. dental hygiene William R. Harper Coll., Palatine, Ill., 1987—. Speaker Am. Acad. Gen. Dentistry, 1988—. Named One of Outstanding Young Men Am., U.S. Jaycees, 1975, Outstanding Dental Corp. Officer of Air Nat. Guard, 1991; recipient Outstanding Achievement medal, Air Force, 1994, Air Force Meritorious Medal, 1992, Order of the Med. Minuteman N.G. Bur., Washington, 1991. Fellow Am. Acad. Oral Medicine, Am. Soc. Laser Medicine and Surgery; mem. ADA, Am. Acad. Periodontology (speaker 1988—), Assn. of Mil. Surgeons, Air Force Assn., Aerospace Medicine Assn., Nat. Jr. Coll. Athletic Assn. (all-Am. 1st team gymnastics 1975). Republican. Office: Ste 1 South 650 E Higgins Schaumburg IL 60173

COLVIN, ROBERT ALAN, neurobiology educator; b. Buffalo, Apr. 26, 1953; s. John D. and Martha (Jaworska) C. BA, SUNY, Buffalo, 1975; PhD, Rutgers U., 1980. Instr. U. Conn. Health Ctr., Farmington, Conn., 1980-85; asst. prof. pharmacology Oral Roberts U., Tulsa, 1985-90; assoc. prof. biology Ohio U., Athens, 1990—. Office: Coll Osteopathic Medicine Ohio Univ Athens OH 45701

COLWELL, JOHN EDWIN, retired aerospace scientist; b. Bellaire, Kans., Sept. 2, 1930; s. Clyde Theodore and Ida Mae (Swank) C. BS in Chemistry, Kans. State U., 1952; postgrad., Harvard U., 1952-53; PhD in Phys. Chemistry, U. Pa., 1958. Rsch. chemist Shell Oil Co., Wood River, Ill., 1952; staff scientist Rocketdyne divsn. N.Am. Aviation, Canoga Park, Calif., 1958-61; mem. tech. staff The Aerospace Corp., El Segundo, Calif., 1961-72, cons., 1972-73; cons. NASA, 1970-72. Bd. dirs. Ctrl. Kans. Libr. System, Great Bend, 1977-81, 89-93; vice chmn. Smith County Rep. Ctr., 1986-90, chmn., 1990-94; trustee Blaine Twp., Bellaire, 1981—; treas. Smith County Hist. Soc., 1990-93. 1st lt. USAF, 1953-55. Fellowships Harvard fellow Harvard U., 1952-53, NSF fellow U. Pa., 1957-58. Mem. Am. Legion (post comdr. 1991-93), Sigma Xi, Phi Kappa Phi, Theta Xi. Republican. Home: RR 2 Box 54 Lebanon KS 66952-9500

COLYER, RICHARD ALLEN, business executive; b. Cin., July 20, 1946; s. B.F. and Neva E. (Morrow) C. BBA, Stetson U., 1968; MBA, Fla. State U., 1970. Sales cons. Bapt. Village Retirement Ctr., Pompano Beach, Fla., 1972-73; asst. br. mgr. Conn. Gen. Life Ins. Co., Ft. Lauderdale, Fla., 1973-74; v.p. devel. Evangelism Explosion Internat., Ft. Lauderdale, 1974-81; v.p. Serve Internat., Atlanta, 1981-85; sr. devel. cons. McConkey/Johnson, Inc., Atlanta, 1985-90; pres. Mktg. Opportunities Network, Atlanta, 1987-91, Devel./Mgmt. Group, Columbus, Ohio, 1988—; v.p. for devel., bd. dirs. Bible Lit. Internat., Columbus, 1993—. Contbr. to mag. The Word Around Us, 1994—. Mem. bd. deacons Karl Rd. Bapt. Ch., Columbus, 1993-95, mem. long range planning com., 1995—, mem. coalition of missions com., 1995; bd. dirs. Chapel for the Exceptional, Meth. Hour Internat., and Son-Scape Re-creation Ministries, St. Louis, 1988-93. 1st lt. AUS, 1970-72, Vietnam. J.S. Aspley scholar, 1968. Mem. Evang. Devel. Assn., Vineyard Christian Fellowship. Republican. Home: 5128 Sassafras Rd Columbus OH 43229 Office: Bible Lit Internat 625 E North Broadway Columbus OH 43214

COMBS, M. JAY, utilities executive; b. Guymon, Okla., Sept. 3, 1952; s. Clyde George and Leona Margaret (Pafford) C.; m. Patricia Ann Felix, Mar. 5, 1981 (div. May 1995); 1 child, Jay Michael. BS Mech. Engring. Tech., Okla. State U., 1976. Supr. maintenance Pub. Svc. Co. Okla., Lawton, 1976-91; mgr. power sta. UtiliCorp Power Svcs., Great Bend, Kans., 1991—. Mem. IEEE, Soc. Automotive Engrs. (assoc.). Office: UtiliCorp Power Svcs Mullergren Sta PO Box 170 Great Bend KS 67530-0170

COMERFORD, JOSEPH FRANCIS, manufacturing executive; b. Phila., May 29, 1926; s. James J. and Anne Marie (Gillies) C.; m. Mary Margaret Mullen, Feb. 19, 1949; children: Mary-Jo, Sheila Marie, John Joseph, James Patrick. Salesman Gen. Foods, Phila., 1946-50, Whitman Chocolates, Phila., 1951-54, Shaw-Walker, N.Y.C., 1954-56; indsl. salesman Atlas Precision, 1956-59; salesman, regional mgr., advt. mgr. Bendix Corp., 1960-80; exec. v.p. Jacobsen & Daw, Chgo., 1980-85; prin. Comerford Tooling & Accessories, Palatine, Ill., 1985—. With USN, 1945-46, World War II, 51-52, Korea. Mem. Soc. Mfg. Engrs., Carbide Engrs., K.C., Elks, Am. Legion. Home and Office: Comerford Tooling & Access 902 E Paddock Dr Palatine IL 60067

COMIENSKI, JAMES SIGMON, secondary education educator, planetarium director; b. Cleve., Nov. 6, 1948; s. Sigmon James and Martha Helen (Chernus) C.; m. Barbara Ann Lutz, July 1, 1978. B.A. in Geology, Case Western Res. U., 1970; postgrad. Ohio State U., Cleve. State U., U. Akron, 1974—. Traffic checker schedule dept. Regional Transit Authority, Cleve., 1966-68, 69-70, 72; sci. tchr., planetarium dir. Lakewood (Ohio) Schs., 1973—; cons. earth sci. curriculum North Ridgeville, 1977; lectr. bird migration; asst. instr. Ohio Sea Grant Edn., summer, 1981; co-writer sci. project activities for Ohio Sea Grant, Crustal Evolution Edn. Project, National Air Space Mus./NASA activity booklets; photographer for wife's doll articles in National/International Mags. Ruling elder Lakewood Presbyterian Ch., 1981-89; v.p. Bay Village Hist. Soc., 1990-92, trustee, 1992—. Served with U.S. Army, 1970-72. Fellow Great Lakes Planetarium Assn. (edn. com.); mem. Nat. Sci. Tchrs. Assn., Cleve. Astron. Assn. (exec. council), Assn. Astronomy Educators, Internat. Soc. Planetarium Educators, Cleve. Mus. Natural History, Cleve. Regional Council Sci. Tchrs., Cleve. Regional Assn. Planetarians, Lakwood Tchrs. Assn., Ohio Educators Assn., Nat. Earth Sci. Tchrs. Assn., Aerospace Educators Assn., Western Res. Hist. Soc., Nat. Geog. Soc., Planetary Soc., Ctr. Environ. Edn., NEA, Bay Village Hist. Soc., Smithsonian Assoc. Democrat. Co-writer sci. project activities. Home: 420 Bassett Rd Cleveland OH 44140-1803 Office: Lakewood Schs 14100 Franklin Blvd Cleveland OH 44107-4516

COMISAR, CHRIS FARAH-LYNN, advertising executive; b. Cin., Jan. 4, 1952; s. Fred Louis and Ada Marie (Davis) C. BSBA, U. So. Calif., 1976. Profl. Photographer, Certification in Papermaking. Gen. mgr. Berchmann Roofing Co., Cin., 1976-78; advt., photography Art & Film Photography Studios, Cin., 1978-79; papermachine cons. Pulp, Paper Turner & Sheets, Cin., 1979-81; pres. chief exec. officer Camera Ready Graphics, Cin., 1981-88; pres. J.L. Reese & Assocs., Madeira, Ohio, 1988—; cons. engr. Turner & Sheets Inc., Cin., 1985-87. Mem. Big Bros. Am. Recipient Photography award, Cin. Nova Arts Coun., 1978. Mem. Cin. Speech & Hearing Soc. (interpreter). Republican. Office: 7919 Kenwood Rd Cincinnati OH 45236

COMISKEY, NANCY, publishing executive. Mng. editor The Indpls. News. Office: The Indpls News PO Box 145 Indianapolis IN 46206*

COMMEAN, PAUL KEVIN, electrical engineer; b. Du Quoin, Ill., July 13, 1959; s. Paul Dean and Naomi Ruth (Fred) C.; m. Rebecca Anne Meyer, Mar. 10, 1990; children: Angela Hanna Michelle, Hannah Christine Elisabeth, Michelle Kristie Anna. BEE with honors, Ga. Tech., 1982. Sr. engr. McDonnell Douglas Corp., St. Louis, 1982-85, Cencit Inc., St. Louis, 1985-91; sr. rsch. engr. Mallinckrodt Inst. Radiology, St. Louis, 1992—; gen. mgr. Anything Sewn, St. Louis, 1992—. Contbr. articles to profl. jours. Home: 951 Newport Ave Webster Groves MO 63119 Office: Mallinckrodt Inst Radiology 510 S Kingshighway Blvd Saint Louis MO 63110

COMMERS, TIM, state legislator; b. May 1966. BA, Olaf Coll. State rep. Minn. Ho. Reps., Dist. 38A, 1992—; mem. com. & econ. devel., environ. & natural resources, fin., gen. legis., bet. affairs & elections coms., Minn. Ho. Reps. Home: 2370 Lexington Ave S Mendota Heights MN 55120-1261*

COMMITO, RICHARD WILLIAM, podiatrist; b. Chgo., May 2, 1951; s. Mario Fiore and Aileen Margaret Commito. BS, U. Ill., Chgo., 1972; DPM, Ill. Coll. Podiatric Medicine, 1976. Diplomate Nat. Bd. Podiatry Examiners, Am. Bd. Podiatric Surgery, Am. Bd. Profl. Disability Cons., Am. Bd. Forensic Examiners, Am. Coun. Cert. Podiatric Physicians and Surgeons, Am. Acad. Pain Mgmt. Podiatrist Chgo., 1976—; dir. podiatry svcs. Community Hosp., Evanston, Ill., 1978-80; cons. staff podiatry Ridgeway Hosp., Chgo., 1981—; owner Conserv Environ. Products, FootDoc Products, NewFoot Pharmical; dir. podiatry svc. Lawndale Pla. Surgicenter, Chgo.; ind. med. examiner of counsel R. S. Connors Assocs., Chgo. Bd. dirs. Little Village unit Boys Clubs, 1981—, mem. One Hundred Club, 1982, 400 Club, Marshall Square unit, 1981-82; mem. Art Inst. Chgo., 1980-96, Lincoln Park Zool. Soc., Chgo., 1980-96. Fellow Acad. Ambulatory Foot Surgery, Am. Inst. Foot Medicine (cert.); mem. Soaring Soc. Am., Ill. Podiatry Edn. Group, Am. Podiatric Med Assn., Ill. Podiatry Soc., Am. Med. Soc. Vienna (life), Nat. Assn. Professions, Am. Coll. Forensic Examiners, Am. Bd. Profl. Disability Consultants, Am. Soc. Podiatric Legal Medicine, Am. Podiatric Circulatory Soc., Am. Acad. Pain Mgmt., Am. Soc. Podiatric Physicians and Surgeons, Am. Coun. Cert. Podiatric Physicians and Surgeons (cert.), Internat. Inst. Reflexology (cert.), Am. Pain Soc., Nat. Assn. of the Self-Employed, Internat. Inst. Continuing Med. Edn. Roman Catholic.

COMPTON, DAVID BRUCE, international management consultant; b. Dayton, Ohio, Sept. 27, 1952; s. Hall W. and Joan E. (Reinheimer) C.; m. Danielle M. Dufour, Apr. 19, 1986; children: Kyle Hall, Benjamin David, Zachary James. BS, No. Ariz. U., 1976; M in Internat. Mgmt., Am. Grad. Sch. Internat. Mgmt., 1977. Cons. Harris Graham and Ptnrs., London, 1978-81, Wyatt Co., Stamford, Conn., 1981-84; mgr. internat. benefits dept. Motorola, Inc., Chgo., 1984-86; dir. internat. benefits dept. Dart & Kraft, Chgo., 1986; dir. employee benefits dept. Premark Internat. subs. Dart & Kraft, Chgo., 1986-89, dir. internat. compensation and benefits dept., 1989—; pres., dir. HR Solutions, Inc., 1991—. Mem. Internat. Platform Assn., Soc. Human Resource Mgmt., Am. Compensation assn., Assn. Human Resource Systems Profls. Home: 550 Carpenter Dr Palatine IL 60067-3706 Office: HR Solutions PO Box 175 Palatine IL 60078-0175

COMPTON, ROGER PAUL, financial consultant; b. Osaka, Japan, Jan. 30, 1951; came to U.S., 1957; Supr. Exxon Corp., Houston, 1971-91; fin. cons. Merrill Lynch, Chesterfield, Ill., 1991-94, Stifel Nicolaus & Co., Alton, Ill., 1994—. Chmn., vol. St. Louis chpt. ARC, 1971—; v.p. Jaycees, 1975—. Republican. Roman Catholic. Office: Stifel Nicolaus & Co # 100 322 State St Alton IL 62002

COMSTOCK, ROBERT J., mechanical draftsman; b. Topeka, Kans., Feb. 15, 1963. Student, Platte Vo-Tech Coll. Machinist Didde Web Tech., Emporia, Kans., 1981-82; draftsman Didde Web Press, Emporia, 1990—; machinist Machine Instrument, Houston, 1982-84; draftsman Sunflower Metal, Topeka, 1984-85; lab tech., draftsman Aeroquip Corp., Lawrence, Kans., 1985-90. Office: Didde Web Press PO Box 1088 Emporia KS 66801-1088

CONABLE, GORDON M., library director; b. Buffalo, Jan. 5, 1947; s. William Gouinlock and Miriam (Meyer) C.; m. Irene Hackett Shortall, Sept. 13, 1975; 1 child, Edward James. BA, Antioch Coll., Yellow Springs, Ohio, 1969; MSLS, Columbia U., 1976. Assoc. dir. Ft. Vancouver (Wash.) Regional Libr., 1979-88; dir. Monroe (Mich.) County Libr. System, 1988—; lectr., presenter workshops on librs., intellectual freedom and censorship, 1987—. Contbr. papers to profl. publs. Trustee Monroe County Employees Retirement Sys., 1988—, vice-chair, 1995—; trustee Tears of Joy Theatre, Vancouver, 1980-88, chair, 1981-85; chair Vancouver City Charter Commn., 1985; treas. bd. trustees Freedom to Read Found., 1988-89, 96—, v.p., 1990-91, pres., 1992-95. Recipient Best of Show award Western Art Dirs., 1977; named Mich. Pub. Servant of Yr., 1994, Freedom to Read Found. Roll of Honor, 1996. Mem. ALA (life, mem. coun. 1991—), Pub. Libr. Assn., Libr. Adminstrn. and Mgmt. Assn., Mich. Libr. Assn., Detroit Suburban Librs. Roundtable, Mich. Class VI Libr. Dirs. Assn. Office: Monroe County Libr System 3700 S Custer Rd Monroe MI 48161-9774

CONANT, STEVEN GEORGE, psychiatrist; b. Elkhart, Ind., July 8, 1949; s. Hubert Eugene and Ruth (Weaver) C. BA in Zoology with distinction, DePauw U., 1971; MD, Ind. U., 1975. Diplomate Am. Bd. Psychiatry and Neurology. Intern Ind. U. Med. Ctr., Indpls., 1975-76, resident in psychiatry, 1976-78, asst. prof. psychiatry, 1978-80, asst. clin. prof. psychiatry, 1988-93; cons. psychiatry Gallahue Mental Health Ctr., Indpls., 1979-85; staff psychiatrist Metro Health, Indpls., 1983—; staff privileges at Meth. Hosp., Indpls., 1979—; cons. psychiatrist Ind. Prison Sys., 1986, Ctrl. State Hosp., 1992-94, Hamilton Ctr., 1994—. Mem. Conductor's Cir. Indpls. Symphony, 1984—, Indpls. Symphonic Choir Orch., 1976-83; trustee Indpls. Mus. Art, 1988—. Mem. AMA, Am. Acad. Clin. Psychiatrists, Mensa, The Hoosier Group, Wash. DePauw Soc. Republican. Presbyterian. Office: Metro Health 4850 Century Plaza Rd Indianapolis IN 46254-2483

CONATON, MICHAEL JOSEPH, financial service executive; b. Detroit, Aug. 3, 1933; s. John Martin and Margaret Alice (Cleary) C.; m. Margaret Ann Cannon, Sept. 3, 1955; children—Catherine, Macaira, Michael, Margaret, Elizabeth. B.S., Xavier U., 1955. Public accountant Stanley A. Hitter, C.P.A., Cin., 1956-58; controller The Moloney Co., Albia, Iowa, 1958-61; v.p. fin. The Midland Co., Cin., 1961-80, sr. v.p., chief fin. officer, 1980-83, exec. v.p., chief fin. officer, 1983-88; pres., chief operating officer The Midland Co., 1988—; also dir. The Midland Co., Cin.; bd. dirs. Key Corp Bank, BBI Mktg. Svcs., Inc.; interim pres. Xavier U., 1990-91. City councilman, Albia, 1959-61; trustee, chmn. bd. Xavier U., 1983—. Served to lt. USMC, 1955-56. Mem. Fin. Execs. Inst., Cin. Soc. Fin. Analysts, Athenaeum of Ohio (trustee), Met. Club (chmn. bd.). Home: 701 Reisling Knls Cincinnati OH 45226-1735 Office: The Midland Company 537 E Pete Rose Way Cincinnati OH 45202-3599

CONATSER, JOHN EDWARD, health care services executive, accountant; b. Nashville, Ark., Mar. 23, 1952; s. Eunice Edward and Lois Marie (Holton) C.; m. Deborah Goldman, Aug. 10, 1980; children: Nicole, Graham. BA, Hope College, 1974; MBA, U. Mich., 1976. CPA, Ill. CPA Touche, Ross & Co., Chgo., 1976-79, Arthur Young & Co., Chgo., 1979-82, Goldman, Conatser & Co., Chgo., 1983-93; pres. Berkshire Healthcare Group, Lincolnshire, Ill., 1994—. Trustee Village of Lincolnshire,1993—. Mem. Am. Assn. CPAs, Ill. CPAs Soc., Ill. Health Care Assn., Ill. Assn. Health Care Admin., Phi Beta Kappa. Republican. Jewish. Office: Berkshire Healthcare Group PO Box 220 Lincolnshire IL 60069

CONATY-COOLEY, DONNA MARIE, music educator, oboist; b. Elliot Lake, Ont., Can., Oct. 4, 1959; d. Philip and Bernadete (Knowles) Conaty; m. Brigham John Cooley, Dec. 1, 1990. MusB summa cum laude, U. No. Colo., 1981; MusM, Yale U., 1984. Affiliate faculty oboe SUNY, Purchase, 1985; adj. instr. U. Evansville, Ind., 1985-89; assoc. prof. oboe Ohio U., Athens, 1989—; prin. oboe Evansville Philharm., 1985-89, Owensboro Symphony, 1985-89, Promusica Chamber Orch., Columbus, Ohio, 1992—, 2d oboe, 1990-92, Cabrillo Music Festival Orch., Santa Cruz, Calif., 1993—; oboist Spoleto Festival Orch., Charleston, S.C. and Spoleto, Italy, 1985, 86, Bach Aria Festival, Stony Brook, N.Y., 1987, 92. Mem. Internat. Double Reed Soc., Music Educators Nat. Conf., Music Tchrs. Nat. Assn. (cert.), Am. Fedn. Musicians, Pi Kappa Lambda. Democrat. Office: Ohio Univ Sch Music 440 Music Bldg Athens OH 45701

CONAWAY, MARY ANN, dean; b. Pulaski, Ill., Nov. 3, 1940; d. Harry Sr. and Anna Mary (Walsh) Tolar, m. Larry Kay Conaway, June 25, 1960; children: Mary Kay, Larissa Jean, Stephen Patrick. BS, So. Ill. U., 1962; MEd, U. Mo., 1980; PhD, St. Louis U., 1991. Cert. secondary tchr., Mo.; lic. profl. counselor, Mo. Secondary tchr. Equality (Ill.) High Sch., 1962-63; data processor Blue Bell Meat Packing Plant, DuQuoin, Ill., 1963-64; secondary tchr. Dixon (Mo.) High Sch., 1964-66; ednl. cons. St. Louis, 1980-83; marriage, family therapist Christian Psychol. and Family Svcs., St. Louis, 1983-87, Psychologists & Educators, St. Louis, 1987-88; min. single adults and family Fee Fee Bapt. Ch., Bridgeton, Mo., 1988-89; min. edn. Concord Bapt. Ch., St. Louis, 1989-91; asst. prof. psychology Mo. Bapt. Coll, St. Louis, 1992-93, dean of students, 1993—. Mem. ACA, Am. Assn. Marriage and Family Therapists, So. Bapt. Assn., Family Mins., Pi Lambda Theta, Chi Sigma Iota. Democrat. Office: Mo Baptist Coll One College Park Dr Saint Louis MO 63141

CONDELLONE, TRENT PETER, real estate developer; b. Belleville, Ill., Sept. 28, 1969; s. Peter Charles and Carroll Helen (Malano) C.; m. Angela Marie Trader, June 21, 1991 (div. Oct. 1995). Student, Mo. So. State U., 1990, Evangel Coll., Springfield, Mo., 1991. Pres. Edgewater software Corp., Matthews, N.C., 1985-87; owner Sta. KØ8AT-TB, Cabool-Houston, Mo., 1988-89; chief reserve officer City of Willard, Mo., 1991-93; pres. Condellone Properties, Springfield, 1990-93; chief of police City of Battlefield, Mo., 1993-94; pres. Mo. Property Investments, Springfield, 1994—; owner Flying Armadillo Restaurants, Inc., Springfield, Mo., 1996—; sec. bd. advisors Meml. Hosp., Houston, 1988-91. Author: Iron Wondea-Clipless Stand Machine, 1996. State chmn. Teen Age Reps., 1987-90 (Mo. Teen Age Rep. of Yr. 1990); state bd. dirs. Young Reps., 1987-90, Coll. Reps., 1989-90; pres. Evangel Coll. Reps., 1989-90. Mem. Internat. Callulator Collectors, Pacyderms. Republican. Office: Mo Property Investments Inc PO Box 2741 Springfield MO 65801

CONDRON, BARBARA O'GUINN, metaphysics educator, school administrator, publisher; b. New Orleans, May 1, 1953; d. Bill Gene O'Guinn and Marie Gladys (Newbill) Jackson; m. Daniel Ralph Condron, Feb. 29, 1992; 1 child, Hezekiah Daniel. BJ, U. Mo., 1973; MA, Coll. Metaphysics, Springfield, Mo., 1977, DD, D Metaphysics, 1979. Cert. counselor; ordained min. Interfaith Ch. Metaphysics. Field rep. Sch. Metaphysics, New Orleans, 1978-80; dir. Interfaith Ch. Metaphysics, 1884-89; pres. Nat. Hdqs., Sch. Metaphysics, Windyville, Mo., 1980-84, chmn. bd., prof., 1989—; CEO SOM Pub., Windyville, 1989—; guest lectr., instr. Wichita State U., 1977, U. New Orleans, 1979, La. State U., 1981, Am. Bus. Womens Assn., 1982, U. Mo., Kansas City, 1984, Unity Village, 1985, Kans. Dept. Social Svcs. Conf., Topeka, 1986, U. Mo., Columbia and St. Louis, 1986, Mo. Tchrs. Conf., St. Louis, 1991, U. Okla., Norman, 1988-89, Parliament of World's Religions, Chgo., 1993, many others; creator Sch. Metaphysics Assocs., 1992; initiator Universal Hour Peace, 1995; initiator, advisor Nat. Dream Hotline, 1988—; radio and TV guest, 1977—. Author: What Will I Do Tomorrow?, Probing Depression, 1977, Search for a Satisfying Relationship, 1980, Strangers in My Dreams, 1987, Total Recall: An Introduction to Past Life & Health Readings, 1991, Kundalini Rising, 1992, Dreamers Dictionary, 1994, The Work of the Soul: Past Life Recall & Spiritual Enlightenment, 1996, First Opinion, 1996; series editor When All Else Fails; editor-in-chief Thresholds Jour., 1990—; editor Wholistic Health and Healing Guide, 1992—; also numerous poems. Mem. Internat. Platform Assn., Am. Bus. Women's Assn., Interfaith Ministries, Kundalini Rsch. Network, Planetary Soc., Heritage Found., Sigma Delta Chi. Office: Sch Metaphysics Nat Hdqs Windyville MO 65783

CONDRON, DANIEL RALPH, academic administrator, metaphysics educator; b. Chillicothe, Mo., Jan. 30, 1953; s. Ralph Wesley and Rosa Irene (Garber) C.; m. Barbara Gail O'Guinn, Feb. 29, 1992; 1 child, Hezekiah Daniel. BS, U. Mo., 1975, MS, 1978; DDiv, Coll. Metaphysics, Springfield, Mo., 1982, D in Metaphysics, 1985. Cert. counselor; ordained to ministry Interfaith Ch. of Metaphysics. Dir. Sch. Metaphysics, Des Moines, 1980, Kansas City, Mo., 1981; regional dir. Sch. Metaphysics, Colo., 1982-85, Chgo. and Detroit, 1985-90; pres. bd. nat. hdqs. Sch. Metaphysics, Windyville, Mo., 1988—; chancellor, prof. Coll. Metaphysics, Windyville, Mo., 1990—; teaching asst. U. Mo., Columbia, 1977; sales and mgmt. cons. Am. Media, Des Moines, 1980-83; speaker in field including Parliament of the World's Religions, Chgo., 1993. Author: Dreams of the Soul, 1991, Permanent Healing, 1992, Universal Language of Mind, 1994, Understanding Your Dreams, 1994, Seven Secret Keys to Prosperity and Abundance, 1996; pub. jour. Thresholds Quar., 1988—; internat. radio and TV guest including BBC, RAdio Hong Kong, Voice of Am., 1979—. Mem. Sch. Metaphysics Assocs. (pres.), Nat. Space Soc., Planetary Soc., Alpha Gamma Rho, Alpha Zeta. Republican. Home: HCR 1 Box 15 Windyville MO 65783 Office: Sch Metaphysics Nat Headquarters Windyville MO 65783

CONES, VAN BUREN, electronics engineer, consultant; b. Indpls., July 4, 1918; s. Ben and Fanette (Miller) C.; m. Eloise Winifred Knoll, Sept. 8, 1951; children: Diane Lee Cones Serban, Anita Sue Cones Cohee. BSEE, Purdue U., 1940; postgrad., Mass. Inst. Tech., 1942, Harvard U., 1942. Registered profl. engr., Ind. Field engr. Powers Regulator Co., Indpls., 1940-42, 46-52; electronics engr. Naval Avionics Ctr., Indpls., 1952-84; pvt. practice Indpls., 1984—. Post comdr. Am. Legion, Indpls., 1974. Capt. USAF, 1942-46. Mem. IEEE, NSPE. Methodist. Home: 5503 Skyridge Dr Indianapolis IN 46250-1749

CONIDI, DANIEL JOSEPH, private investigation agency executive; b. Chgo., Mar. 11, 1957; s. Joseph Frank and Gloria (Zimmerman) C. BS, SUNY, Albany, 1983; MA, Chgo. State U., 1987. Lic. pvt. detective, Ill., Wis., Ind. Owner, mgr. Conidi Enterprises, Chgo., 1979-81; pres. Daniel J. Conidi-Assocs., Chgo., 1981—; cons. Office Cook County Sheriff, Chgo., 1983-90; freelance lectr., 1983—. Author: Professional Investigative Methods, 1984, Private Investigators Training Manual, 1986. Del. Cook County Rep. Conv., 1987. Recipient cert. of appreciation Boys Town, 1982; named Ky. col. State of Ky., 1987. Mem. World Assn. Detectives, Internat. Police Congress, Coun. Internat. Investigators, Nat. Assn. Investigations and Security, Fraternal Order Police, NRA (life), Navy League (life), Univ. Club, Masons, Shriners. Presbyterian. Home: 500 Ashland Ave River Forest IL 60305-1825 Office: 734 N LaSalle St Ste 1082 Chicago IL 60610

CONKLIN, ROBERT EUGENE, electronics engineer; b. Loveland, Ohio, Apr. 21, 1925; s. Charles and Alberta (Reynolds) C.; m. Virginia E. McCann, June 14, 1952; children—Carl Lynn, Jill Elaine Conklin Bradford. B.S. in Edn., Wilmington Coll., 1949, B.S. in Sci., 1949. Electronic scientist Electronic Technol. Lab., Wright-Patterson AFB, Ohio, 1951-55; electronic engr. AF Avionics Lab., Wright-Patterson AFB, 1956-60 supervisory elec. engr., 1960-72, cons. electronic engr., 1972-78, supervisory electronic engr., 1978-82, electronic engr. (VHSIC), 1982-84; cons. engr. REC Electronics, Fairborn, Ohio, 1984—; mem. Inst. Nav., 1968-72. Mgr. Babe Ruth Boys' Baseball, 1969-74; mgr. and pres. Little League, Fairborn, 1965-68. Served with USAAC, 1943-46. Mem. IEEE. Republican. Quaker. Lodge: Lions (Fairborn) Home: 114 Wayne Dr Fairborn OH 45324-5228 Office: 47 N Broad St Fairborn OH 45324-4863

CONLEY, DIANA MAE, computer sales and service franchise owner; b. Corry, Pa., May 1, 1942; d. William and Mae (Stoltz) Conley; m. William Sadowski, Dec. 31, 1965 (div. Mar. 1984); 1 child, Jeffrey Sadowski. LPN, Miller Hosp., St. Paul, 1964; BS, Governors State U., Park Forest, Ill., 1974. Nurse Miller Hosp., 1964-66; tchr. Dist. 145, Oak Forest, Ill., 1975-78; mgr., owner ComputerLand Downers Grove, Ill., 1978—; mem. mktg. coun. ComputerLand, San Francisco, 1984-89; mem. Novel Dealer Coun., Provo, Utah, 1987-89. Mem. Nat. Assn. Women Bus. Owners (bd. dirs., pres. Chgo. chpt. 1993-94, Woman Bus. Owner of Yr. award Chgo. chpg. 1993, Ill. winner Blue Chip Enterprise award 1993), Downers Grove C. of C. (bd. dirs. 1991—), Ill. Womens Bus. Ownership Coun. (chair 1994—). Office: ComputerLand 148 Ogden Ave Downers Grove IL 60515-2322

CONLEY, MICHELLE DIANE, investment consultant; b. Parkersburg, W.Va., Feb. 7, 1964; d. David O. and Pauline M. (House) C.; m. William M. Hegarty Jr., Oct. 23, 1993. BS, Kent (Ohio) State U., 1986. Salesman Roulston & Co., Cleve., 1987-89; v.p. Hickory Inn Advisor, Cleve., 1989-91; investment cons. McDonald & Co., Cleve., 1991—. Bd. advisors Nat. Black MBA Assn., Cleve., 1992—; bd. dirs., chair fin. com. YWCA, Cleve., 1993—; bd. dirs. Fedn. Cmty. Planning, Cleve., 1994—; bd. dirs. Lake Erie Girl Scouts, 1995—. Mem. Womens City Club. Republican. Methodist. Office: McDonald & Co Securities 800 Superior Ave 19th Fl Cleveland OH 44114

CONLEY, SARAH ANN, health facility administrator; b. Richmond, Ind., Sept. 14, 1942; d. Harry Herbert and Mary Janet Kercheval; m. Philip Howard Conley, Apr. 5, 1963 (dec.); children: Christine L., Philip Douglas. BS, Purdue U., 1964; postgrad., U. Cin., 1965. Elem. tchr. Southwest Local Schs., Harrison, Ohio, 1964-66; svc. office mgr. Renault of Dayton (Ohio), 1970-73; mgr. Office of Charlotte Ames, Xenia, Ohio, 1974-77; bus. mgr. Radiol. Physicians, Inc., Dayton, 1977-79, Nat. Tractor Pullers Assn., Columbus, Ohio, 1979-85; HMO adminstr. Cen. Benefits Mutual Ins. Co., Columbus, 1985-90; adminstr. Orthopedic and Neurol. Cons., Columbus, 1990—. Mem. Am. Coll. Med. Practice Execs. (cert.), Ohio Med. Group Mgmt. Assn. (pres. 1993-94), MidOhio Med. Mgmt. Assn., Med. Group Mgmt. Assn., Licking County Bus. and Profl. Women (pres. 1989-91). Democrat. Methodist. Office: Orthopedic and Neurol Cons 70 S Cleveland Ave Westerville OH 43081-1329

CONLON, JAMES CHARLES, state legislator; m. Janice D. Winters; 7 children. BS, U. Notre Dame; MEd, Pa. State U. Tchr.; rep. Dist. 19 Ind. Ho. of Reps., 1990—, mem. cities and towns, edn. coms., mem. local govt. and natural resources coms., mem. urban affairs com., dep. spkr. pro tem. Mem. Crown Point (Ind.) City Coun., 1980-90; bd. mem. works and Pub. Safety, Crown Point, 1985-90, mem. planning com., 1987-90. Home: 341 Maple Ln Crown Point IN 46307-4544*

CONLON, PATRICK C., health facility administrator, nurse educator; b. Sioux City, Iowa, July 24, 1962; s. James Ambrose and Mary Lee Emily (Donahue) Conlon. Diploma in Nursing, St. Joseph Mercy Hosp., Sioux City, 1986; BSN, Briar Cliff Coll., Sioux City, 1988, BA in Psychology. Cert. in gen. nursing practice; cert. diabetes educator; cert. BCLS; cert. case mgr. Staff nurse, charge nurse Marian Health Ctr., Sioux City, 1979-89; staff nurse Western Med. Svcs., Sioux City, 1987-89; asst. nurse mgr., orthopaedic nurse adminstr. Michael Reese Hosp. and Med. Ctr., Chgo., 1989-91; edn. dir. ADA Iowa Diabetes Childrens Camp, 1989-93; health team coord., nurse educator, teaching faculty Triangle D Childrens Diabetes Camp, No. Ill., 1990-93; dir., clin. coord. diabetes edn. Mt. Sinai Hosp., 1991-96. Manuscript reviewer Jour. of Care Mgmt.; contbr. articles to profl. jours. Mem. ANA (chmn. 1992-94), Am. Nurses Credentialing Ctr., Am. Diabetes Assn. (bd. dirs., camp com. No. Ill. affiliate, peer reviewer of recognition program 1994—), Iowa Nurses Assn. (nursing adminstrn. commn. 1993-97), Am. Psychol. Soc. (charter), Nat. Nurses in Bus. Assn. (charter), St. Joseph Mercy Sch. Nursing Alumni Assn., Am. Assembly for Men in Nursing, Am. Assn. Diabetes Educators (manuscript reviewer jour.), Diabetes Educators Chgo. Area (v.p. 1991-92, pres.-elect 1992-93, pres. 1993-94, past pres./symposium chair 1994-95), Sigma Theta Tau, Alpha Tau Delta. Home: 2059 Roundtable Rd Sergeant Bluff IA 51054-9743 Office: Mt Sinai Hosp and Med Ctr Dept Medicine F-908 15th and California Ave Chicago IL 60608

CONLY, MICHAEL FREDERICK, architect; b. Indpls., May 3, 1945; s. Morris Frederick and Harriet Rosalie (Bishop) C.; m. Elaine Andrea May, Oct. 24, 1948; children: Ryan Bishop, Megan Casey. BS in Architecture, U. Cin., 1969; grad., Harvard Grad. Sch. Arch. Registered arch., Ind., Ky., Ohio, Ill., Minn., Mo., Tenn., Kans., Va., N.C., Okla., Colo., Ariz., Conn., Iowa. Grad. architect James Architects, Indpls., 1970-72; staff architect Cooler, Schubert, Olds, Inc., Indpls., 1972-78; v.p., bd. dirs. CSO/Architects, Inc., Indpls., 1978-80; sec. corp., exec. v.p. CSO/Architects, Inc., 1980-88, treas., exec. v.p., 1988—; pres. CSO Equities, Inc., Indpls., 1986—; v.p., treas. Anthemius Corp., Indpls., 1987—; mgr. ISODORUS, LLC, 1996—; sec., bd. dirs. Indpls. AIA, 1988-91, Damar Children's Homes, Camby, Ind., 1990—. Lead arch. Ind. State Mus. Complex and Ind. Hist. Soc. Hdqrs. Mem. Govs. Club, Indpls., 1988, Ind. Bus. Coun., 1989-95, Ind. Hist. Soc., 1994—, Ind. Dem. Party Gold Circle, 1996—. Recipient Best Adaptive Reuse Design award City of Indpls., 1979, Monumental Achievement award City of Indpls./Power Co., 1986, Corp. Campus Design award Associated Gen. Contractors, 1990, 92. Mem. AIA (bd. dirs. 1986, pub. awareness 1989, sec. Indpls. chpt. 1989, 90), Am. Correctional Assn., Ind. Sheriffs Assn., Ind. Corrections Assn. Home: 3630 Haverhill Dr Indianapolis IN 46240-3646 Office: CSO Architects Inc 9100 Keystone Crossing Indianapolis IN 46240-2154

CONMY, PATRICK A., federal judge; b. 1934. BA, Harvard U., 1955; JD, Georgetown U., 1959. Bar: Va. 1959, N.D. 1959. Ptnr. Lundberg, Conmy et al, Bismarck, N.D., 1959-85; mem. Bismarck City Commn., 1968-76; state rep. N.D. House Reps., Bismarck, 1976-85; judge U.S. Dist. Ct. N.D., Bismarck, 1985—. Office: US Dist Ct Fed Bldg 220 E Rosser Ave Rm 411 PO Box 1578 Bismarck ND 58502-1578

CONN, PHILIP WESLEY, university president; b. Decatur, Ala., Jan. 4, 1942; s. Charles William and Edna Louise (Minor) C.; m. Donna Kay Taylor, Dec. 18, 1971; children: Chadwick Austin, Philip Cason, Cynthia Louise, Christina Anne. BA, Berea (Ky.) Coll., 1963; Diploma in Social Policy, Inst. Social Studies, The Hague, Netherlands, 1966; MA, U. Tenn., 1972; MPA, U. So. Calif., 1982, DPA, 1991. Tchr. West Coast Christian Coll., Fresno, Calif., 1963; field rep. Vols. in Svc. to Am., Washington, 1965; asst. exec. dir. Bradley/Cleveland Community Action Corp., Cleveland, Tenn., 1967; dir. alumni affairs Berea Coll., 1968-70; pub. rels. advance dir. Combs/Carroll Campaign Staff, Louisville, 1971; exec. dir. Legis. Rsch. Commn., Frankfort, Ky., 1972-77; assoc. prof. sociology, v.p. univ. and regional svcs. Morehead (Ky.) State U., 1977-84; assoc. prof. mgmt., v.p. for univ. advancement Cen. Mo. State U., Warrensburg, 1985-94; prof. bus., pres. Dickinson (N.D.) State U., 1994—; mem. exec. com. Gov's. Adv. Commn. on Tourism, Frankfort, 1977-79; bd. chmn. Stas. KMOS-TV and KCMW-FM, Warrensburg, 1985-94. Contbr. articles to profl. publs.; editor The Berea Alumnus, 1968-70. Trustee City of Lakeview Heights, Ky., 1980; chmn. Morehead/Rowan County Indsl. Devel. Authority, 1982; vice chmn. Gateway Area Devel. Dist., Owingsville, Ky., 1984; bd. dirs. Ky. Humanities Coun., Inc., Lexington, 1977-82, Ky. Archives and Records Commn., Frankfort, 1973-77; assoc. dir. Appalachian Vols., Berea., 1964. Named Outstanding Young Man of Ky. Jaycees, 1977, Outstanding Young Man of Yr. Frankfort Jaycees, 1976. Mem. Am. Soc. Pub. Adminstrn., Coun. for Advancement and Support of Edn., Am. Assn. for Higher Edn., Am. Assn. of State Colls. and Univs. (N.D. state rep. 1994—), Nat. Assn. of Intercollegiate Athletics (mem. coun. of pres. 1996—), Warrensburg (Mo.) C. of C. (bd. dirs. 1990-93), Berea Coll. Alumni Assn. (pres. 1976-77, spl. merit 1977), Rotary (fellow The Hague 1965-66), Phi Kappa Phi. Democrat. Methodist. Office: Dickinson State U 104 May Hall Dickinson ND 58601-4711 Office: Dickinson State U Dickinson ND 58601-4896

CONNALLY, SANDRA JANE OPPY, art educator; b. Crawfordsville, Ind., Feb. 10, 1941; d. Thomas Jay and Helen Louise (Lane) Oppy; m. Thomas Maurice Connally, Nov. 9, 1962; children: Leslie Erin Connally Hosier, Tyler Maurice. BS, Ball State U., 1963, MA, 1981. Freelance writer Muncie, Ind., 1971-76, art/freelance, 1964-81; substitute tchr. Muncie (Ind.) Community Schs., 1980-81, art tchr., 1981—. Two women shows include Emens Auditorium, Ball State U., 1983; juried shows include Ball State U. Small Drawing and Sculpture, 1964, Alford House/Anderson (Ind.) Fine Arts Ctr., Winter Show, 1979, 80, 81, Summer Show, 1981, Historic 8th St. Exhbn., 1981, Patrons Watercolor Gala, Oklahoma City, 1983, Whitewater Valley Annual Drawing, Painting and Printmaking Competition, Richmond, Ind., 1983; represented in numerous pvt. collections; contbr. short stories to profl. publs. Grantee Container Corp. Am., 1981, Ball State U. Mus. Art/Margaret Ball Meml. Fund, 1992, Robert B. Bell, 1993, 94, 95; recipient achievement award Ind. Dept. Edn., 1992-93, 94, Nat. Gallery Videodisc Competition, 1993; named disting. UniverCitizen Ball State U., 1992. Mem. NEA, Ind. State Tchr. Assn., Muncie Tchrs. Assn., Internat. Platform Assn., Nat. Art Edn. Assn., Art Edn. Assn. Ind. Republican. Methodist. Home: 2351 W Warwick Rd Muncie IN 47304-3346

CONNELL, JOHN M., mechanical engineer; b. Decauter, Ill., Aug. 22, 1938; s. Frank S. and Emily (Dostelak) C.; m. Nadine Mary Broom, June 15, 1962; 1 child, Kathleen. BS in Mech. Engring., Valpraiso U., 1960. Application engring. mgr. Parker Hannatin Corp., Des Plaines, Ill., 1967-85; chief engr. B & H Machine Inc., Minerva, Ohio, 1985—. Republican. Roman Catholic. Office: B & H Machine Inc PO Box Box 96 Lincoln Way W Minerva OH 44657-0096

CONNELL, KATHRYN MCQUOWN, medical educator; b. N.Y.C., Oct. 19, 1945; d. Norman A. and Dolores (Milleville) McQuown; m. David W. Connell, June 1973; 1 child, Reed M. BA, Brown U., 1967; MPH, U. Calif. Berkeley, 1975. Tchr. English as Fgn. Lang. Inst. Mex.-N.Am. Rels. Culturales, Mexico City, 1967-69; various positions Planned Parenthood Alameda, San Francisco, 1969-81; coord. inpatient quality assurance San Francisco Gen. Hosp., 1983-85; exec. asst. to state health commn. Ind. State Dept. Health, Indpls., 1985-88; project coord. Midwest AIDS Tng. and Edn. Ctr., Indpls., 1988—; exec. dir. Clin. Tng. Assocs., Inc., Indpls., 1995—; adj. asst. prof. Ind. U. Sch. Nursing, Indpls., 1994; HIV Tng. cons., Indpls., 1991—; dir. Planned Parenthood Ctrl. and So. Ind., Indpls., 1995—, Ind. Cmty. AIDS Action Network, Inc., Indpls., 1995—. Contbr. articles to profl. jours. Home: 620 Oakwood Dr Indianapolis IN 46260

CONNELLY, JOHN DOOLEY, social service organization executive; b. Chgo., Sept. 8, 1946; s. John Joseph and Mary (Dooley) C. BS, Xavier U., 1968; MA, Northeastern Ill. U., 1973; PhD, Cornell U., 1976. Spl. edn. tchr. Spl. Edn. Dist., Lake County, Gurnee, Ill., 1969-73; asst. prof. spl. edn. Ea. Ky. U., Richmond, Ky., 1973-76; div. dir., acting exec. dir. City of Chgo. Health Sys., 1977-80; exec. dir. Jobs for Youth Chgo., 1980—; bd. dirs. Emergency Loan Fund, Chgo., 1983-88. Founding mem. Health and Medicine jour., 1984. Chmn. Pegasus Players Theatre, Chgo., 1982-87; bd. dirs. Health and Medicine Policy Rsch. Group, Chgo., 1983-84, 92—, Chgo. Literacy Coordinating Coun., 1988-90; Clarence Darrow Cmty. Ctr., Chgo., 1983-88, Gov.'s Task Force on Youth, 1986-87; mem. steering com. Chgo. Initiative, 1992-95; bd. dirs., AIDS Care, 1992-94; co-chair Chgo. Lab. for Change; active Soc. Svcs. Adv. Coun., Ill. Dept. Pub. Aid, 1989—; mem. Chgo. Com. Urban Opportunity, 1993-94, Mayor's Task Force on Youth, 1994—, adv. com. City Chgo. Cmty. Devel., 1994—. Roman Catholic. Office: Jobs for Youth Chgo 50 E Washington St Chicago IL 60602-2100

CONNELLY, JOHN JAMES, retired oil company technical specialist; b. Lima, Ohio, Aug. 14, 1935; s. Robert Vincent and Helen Josephine (Hay) C.; m. Aug. 22, 1959 (dec. Aug. 1991); children: Thomas, Kathleen, Joseph, Patrick; m. Virginia Connelly, July, 1993. BSChemE, Ohio State U., 1958; MBA with honors, Baldwin Wallace U., 1975. Registered profl. engr., Ohio. Engr. Std. Oil of Ohio, Lima, 1958-63; rsch. assoc. Battelle Meml. Inst., Columbus, Ohio, 1963-65; tech. specialist Owens Corning Fiberglas, Granville, Ohio, 1965-67; sr. engr. Std. Oil of Ohio, Lima, 1967-71; tech. program analyst Std. Oil of Ohio, Cleve., 1971-74, linear program specialist, 1974-78, fed. affairs analyst, 1978-81; project leader Std. of Ohio/Brit. Petroleum Am., Cleve., 1981-92; tech. specialist BP Am., Cleve., 1992-95; retired, 1995; part time technical specialist Paramount Tech. Svcs., 1995—; instr. Ohio State U., Lima, 1961-63. Advisor Jr. Achievement, Lima, 1960-62; treas. Harding Middle Sch. PTA, Lakewood, Ohio, 1975-77, Music Parents Assn., Lakewood, 1978-80, Sch. Bd. Candidate Treas., Lakewood, 1981. Mem. Soc. of Friends. Home: 23749 Wonneta Pky Westlake OH 44145-2733

CONNER, LELAND LAVON, Indian lorist; b. Logan, Ohio, May 9, 1930; s. Foster Everett and Ida May (Cullison) C.; m. Doris Ann Keller, 1953; children: Lavonna Sue, Gregory Lee, Kay Annette, Melinda Lou. Indian lore speaker Conner Indian Show, Logan, 1960—. Author: The Vengeance of Lewis Wetzel, 1980; contbr. articles to profl. publs. Pres. Hocking County Hist. Soc., Logan, 1977-78, v.p., 1975-76; chmn. ARC Blood Program, Logan, 1976-77. With U.S. Army, 1951-53. Recipient Schiele award for Excellence in Indian Lore Schiele Mus., Gastonia, N.C., 1987, Proclamation of Recognition Ohio Ho. Reps., 1988. Mem. Am. Indian Lore Assn. (nat. dir. 1988—, Catlin Peace Pipe award 1979), Continental Confederation of Adopted Indians (Continental chief 1988—), Pipestone Indian Shrine Assn. Home and Office: Am Indian Lore Assn 960 Walhonding Ave Logan OH 43138-1868

CONNOR, DANIEL G., stockbroker; b. Mpls., Dec. 8, 1948. BA, U. Okla., 1972. Precious metals broker, Mpls., 1982-86; stockbroker Dean Witter, Wayzata, Minn., 1986-92, Smith Barney Inc., Bloomington, Minn., 1992—. Mem. Hopkins (Minn.) Bd. Edn., 1993—. Libertarian. Jewish. Office: Smith Barney Inc 3600 W 80th St Ste 110 Bloomington MN 55431-4506

CONNOR, DAVID THOMAS, chemist; b. Batley, Yorkshire, Eng., Nov. 6, 1939; came to U.S., 1965; s. Lawrence and Mary Josephine (Timlin) C. BSc, U. Manchester, Eng., 1962, MSc, 1963, PhD, 1965. Rsch. assoc. U. Chgo., 1966-68; scientist, then sr. scientist Warner-Lambert/Parke-Davis, Morris Plains, N.J., 1969-77; rsch. assoc., sr. rsch. assoc. Warner-Lambert/Parke-Davis, Ann Arbor, Mich., 1977-84, dir. allergy and inflammation chemistry, 1984—. Contbr. chpt. to book and over 100 articles to profl. jours. Mem. Am. Chem. Soc., Inflammation Rsch. Assn., N.Y. Acad. Scis. Home: 2453 Antietam Dr Ann Arbor MI 48105-1470 Office: Warner Lambert Parke-Davis 2800 Plymouth Rd Ann Arbor MI 48105-2430

CONNOR, MARY RODDIS, foundation administrator; b. Marshfield, Wis., May 14, 1909; d. Hamilton and Catherine S. (Prindle) Roddis; m. Gordon R. Connor, July 20, 1929 (dec. 1986); children: Mary I. Pierce, Gordon P., Catherine Dellin, David (dec.), Sara W. Connor. Student, Wellesley Coll., 1927-28; student, U. Wis., 1929. Corp. sec. Connor Lumber and Land Co., Connor Forest Industries, Wausau, Wis., 1954-78; co-founder, exec. dir. Camp Five Mus. Found., Inc., Laona, 1968—; bd. dirs., v.p. Hamilton Roddis Found.; pres. Connor Found., Forest History Assn. Wis., 1975-87; v.p. Gordon R. Connor Charitable Found.; mem. Nat. Women's Adv. Coun., Am. Forest Products Inst., 1960-78; active Mary Roddis Connor U. Wis. Endowment Fund, 1992. Author: A Century with Connor Timber, 1972, Forestry Futures and Conservation Misconcepts, 1946, 2d rev. edition, 1947; contbr. articles to various publs. Legis. chmn. 7th Dist. Wis. Fedn. Rep. Women, 1963-65, bd. dirs., 1955-65, vice chmn. 1955-59; del. Rep. county, state, nat. conventions, 1962; vice chmn. Marathon County; Rep. vice chmn. Recipient Gov.'s Wis. Heritage Tourism award, 1993, State Hist. Soc. Wis. Award of merit, 1970, 90, Outstanding Achievement in Environ. Protection Svcs. award U.S. EPA, 1987, Forest History Assn. Wis. Mus. award, 1978, Nat. Award in Edn. Arbor Day Found., 1975. Mem. Wis. Mayflower Soc., Colonial Dames (Wis. Soc.), The Hugenot Soc. of Wis., Bascom Hill Soc. (U. Wis.), Lake States Resource Alliance, Inc., Lake States Women in Timber, Inc., Forest History Assn. of Wis., State Hist. Soc. of Wis., Nat. Trust for Hist. Preservation, Wausau chpt. DAR (nat. vice chmn. resolutions 1965-68, Wis. state chmn. nat. def., 1962-65, nat. conservation chmn. 1974-77, recipient many awards). Home: 1011 8th St Wausau WI 54403-4956

CONOVER, NANCY ANDERSON, secondary school counselor; b. Manhattan, Kans., July 8, 1943; d. Howard Julius and Wilma June (Katz) Anderson; m. Gary Hites Conover, Aug. 10, 1968; children: Chad Anderson, Cary Hites. BS in Edn., Kans. State U., 1965; MEd, Wichita State U., 1991. Cert. sch. counselor, tchr., Kans. Tchr. Flint (Mich.) Sch. Dist., 1965-66, Unified Sch. Dist. 259, Wichita, Kans., 1967-68, Overland Park (Kans.) Sch. Dist., 1968-70; bus. mgr., sec.-treas. Gary Conover, D.D.S., Wichita, 1985-94; sch. counselor Unified Sch. Dist. 259, Wichita, 1991-94; secondary sch. counselor Unified Sch. Dist. 385, Andover, Kans., 1994—. Mem. Am. Counselors Assn., Kans. Assn. Counselors, Kans. Dental Aux. (sec. 1970-74), Wichita Dist. Dental Aux. (pres. 1970-75), Jr. League Wichita (adminstrv. v.p. 1978-82), Gamma Phi Beta, Phi Kappa Phi Honor Soc. Republican. Lutheran.

CONOVER, PHILLIP GLEN, investment broker; b. Quincy, Ill., Jan. 22, 1944. BA, Ariz. State U., 1966, MA, 1970. History tchr., basketball coach Quincy Notre Dame, 1973-77; investment broker Everen Securities, Quincy, 1978—. Past bd. dirs. John Wood. C.C., 1983-89; chmn. Nat. Arthritis Telethon, 1995—. Mem. Quincy Exch. Club (pres. 1986), Mart Heinen Club (bd. dirs. 1992—), Northside Businessmen (mem. City Loan com.). Home: Sherwood Lake Est. # 6 Quincy IL 62301 Office: Everen Securities Inc 535 Main St Quincy IL 62301-2906

CONRAD, CHARLES PHILLIP, musician, educator; b. Indpls., Mar. 26, 1954; s. Joseph P. and Patricia G. (Keenaugh) C.; m. Ann Marie Calvert, May 19, 1976. BMus, Ind. U., 1976; MMus, Butler U., Indpls., 1983; Dr. of Arts in Music, Ball State U., Muncie, Ind., 1994. Pvt. trumpet instr. Indpls., 1970—; freelance profl. trumpeter, 1976—; prin. trumpet Indpls. Brass Quintet, 1990—; condr. Greencastle (Ind.) Chamber Orch., 1985-90; music dir. John Knox Presbyn. Ch., Indpls., 1990—, Indpls. Athenaeum, 1991-95; condr. Indpls. Symphonic Band, 1989-94, music dir., 1994—. Author: Fred Jewell (biography), 1994; contbr. articles to profl. jours.; composer/arranger numerous works for band, orch., choir. Mem. Carmel (Ind.) Arts Coun., 1993—. Mem. Internat. Trumpet Guild (pub. rels. dir. 1992—), Condrs. Guild, Am. Mus. Instrument Soc., Hist. Brass Soc., Sonneck Soc., Delta Chi. Presbyterian. Home: 410 2d Ave NE Carmel IN 46032

CONRAD, DONALD LEWIS, sociology educator, clergyman; b. Goshen, Ind., Aug. 15, 1927; s. Mirl A. and Eva May (Reiff) C.; m. Margaret Ruth D'Arcy, Aug. 26, 1950; children: Gregory Mahlon, Joel Bryce, Christine Ruth, Loren Paul. BA, Bethel Coll., Mishawaka, Ind., 1950; MA, Mich. State U., 1958; PhD, U. Notre Dame, 1971; postgrad., Ind. U., South Bend, 1965-67. Ordained to ministry Missionary Ch., 1957. Pastor Missionary chs., Ind., Mich., 1951-62; registrar, dir. admissions Bethel Coll., 1962-71, prof. sociology, 1962-96, chmn. div. social scis., 1971-86, dir. adult programs and self-study, 1987-90; adj. and vis. prof. Ind. U., Purdue North Cen. U., Asbury Sem., 1972-84; cons. South Bend Model Cities, 1968-69; cons. United Way, 1968-69; rep., officer No. Ind. Consortium for Edn., 1973-82; rep. Urban Consortium, South Bend, 1973-75; advisor Headstart, St. Joseph County, Ind., 1983-85; NIMH rsch. trainee U. Notre Dame, 1967-70. Author: Mileau and Morale, 1971; also chpts. to book. Bd. dirs. Group Home, South Bend, 1973-75, Cerebral Palsy Assn., 1973-75; rep., mem. exec. com. A.C.C.E.S.S. social svc. network, Mishawaka, 1978-92; bd. dirs., v.p. Hubbard Hill Retirement Estates, Elkhart, Ind., 1987-96; exec. bd. Miss. Ch. Hist. Soc., 1979—; trustee Miss. Sch. Archives & Hist. Coll., 1992—. Named Alumnus of Yr., Bethel Coll. Alumni Assn., 1984. Mem. Am. Sociol. Assn., North Ctrl. Sociol. Assn., Ind. Acad. Social Scis., Nat. Assn. Evangs. (social action com. 1975-92), Nat. Geog. Soc. Republican. Office: Bethel Coll 1001 W Mckinley Ave Mishawaka IN 46545-5509

CONRAD, JOSEPH LAWRENCE, Slavic language educator; b. Kansas City, Mo., June 26, 1933; s. Lawrence Herman and Marguerite (Smith) C.; divorced; children: Belinda, Karla, Allan. BA, U. Kans., 1955; PhD, U. Tex., 1961. From instr. to asst. prof. Fla. State U., Tallahassee, 1959-62; from asst. prof. to assoc. prof. U. Tex., Austin, 1962-66; from assoc. prof. to prof. U. Kans., Lawrence, 1966—. Author book; contbr. numerous articles to profl. jours. Grantee Inst. Internat. Edn., 1955-56, Internat. Rsch. and Exch. Bd., 1964-86. Mem. AAAS (chair various coms.), Am. Assn. Tchrs. Slavic and East European Langs., Soc. Slovene Studies, others. Office: U Kans Dept Slavic Langs 2134 Welscoe Lawrence KS 66045

CONRAD, KENT, senator; b. Bismarck, N.D., Mar. 12, 1948; m. Lucy Calautti, Feb. 1987; 1 child, Jessamyn Abigail. Student, U. Mo., 1967; BA, Stanford U., 1972; MBA, George Washington U., 1975. Asst. to tax commr. State of N.D. Tax Dept., Bismarck, 1974-80, tax commr., 1981-86; U.S. senator from N.D. Washington, 1987—. Democrat. Office: care US Senate 724 Hart Senate Office Bldg Washington DC 20510

CONRAD, SISTER LINDA, elementary school educator; b. Lorain, Ohio, Apr. 26, 1951; d. Chester Clifford and Virginia Ann (Smith) C. BA, Notre Dame Coll., Cleve., 1987; MEd, Notre Dame Coll., South Euclid, Ohio, 1996. Cert. tchr., Ohio; mem. Sisters of Notre Dame. Tchr. Julie Billiart Sch., Lyndhurst, Ohio, 1977-85, St. Francis Sch., Cleve., 1987-92, Gesu Sch., Cleve., 1992-94; dir. ctr. for excellence in edn. Notre Dame Coll. Ohio, South Euclid, 1994—; dir. Project Stars Grant, Cleve., 1991-92, Tchr. Thinking in Art Curriculum Grant, Cleve., 1993-94; moderator Student Coun., Cleve., 1988-92. Roman Catholic. Office: Notre Dame Coll 4545 College Rd South Euclid OH 44121-4228

CONRAD, LORETTA JANE, educational administrator; b. Wooster, Ohio, Aug. 9, 1934; d. Donald William and Celia Irene (Smith) C.; B.Mus. Edn. cum laude, Coll. of Wooster, 1956; M.Mus. Edn., U. Colo., 1969; postgrad. cert. supervision/adminstrn. (Univ. scholar), John Carroll U., 1978. Tchr., Avon Lake (Ohio) public schs., 1956-61, Dept. Def., Europe and Far East, 1961-64, Bay Village (Ohio) Bd. Edn., 1964-73, Elyria (Ohio) public schs., 1973-78; asst. prin. Bay Village Bd. Edn., Bay High Sch., 1978-84, Bay Middle Sch., 1984-89; edn. dir. Riverside Acad.; music clinician, adjudicator; pvt. tchr. piano; accompanist, dir. ch. choir, Luth. Ch., 1966-80, children's choir Lakewood United Meth. Ch., 1989-92. Area rep. for recruitment, mem. music com. Coll. of Wooster. Presser scholar, 1955-56; Annie Webb Blanton scholar, Delta Kappa Gamma, 1968. Mem. Ohio Assn. Secondary Sch. Prins., Nat. Assn. Secondary Sch. Prins., Assn. Secondary Curriculum Devel., Ohio Middle Schs. Assn., Phi Delta Kappa, Delta Kappa Gamma, Alpha Delta (state music rep.), Coll. Club West (bd. dirs., historian), Three Arts Club Lakewood (chmn. scholarship grant fund). Democrat. Lutheran. Club: Quota (pres. 1985-87). Home: 1650 Cedarwood Dr Cleveland OH 44145-1862

CONRAD, MELVIN LOUIS, biology educator; b. Kiowa, Kans., Mar. 10, 1927; s. Marvin Bearl and Elsie Louise (Murphy) C.; m. Eula Montes Vieira, Apr. 3, 1954; children: Albert Vieira Conrad, Celia Conrad Theiler, Daniel Vieira Conrad. BA in Biology, Southwestern Coll., 1950; MA, George Peabody Coll. Tchrs., 1956; PhD, U. Mo., 1980. Edn!. missionary Meth. Ch., Brazil, 1950-54; tchr. biology and gen. sci. McLeansboro (Ill.) Twp. High Sch., 1956-58; asst. prof. biology Oxford (Ga.) Coll. Emory U., 1958-67; from asst. prof. to prof. plant taxonomy N.E. Mo. State U., Kirksville, 1967-91, prof. emeritus, 1991—; vis. instr. botany U. Ga., Athens, 1967; mem. teaching staff Reis Biol. Sta., St. Louis U., nr. Steelville, Mo., 1988—; reviewer Army C.E., 1985. Bd. dirs. ARC, Kirksville, 1984-93, chmn. Adair County chpt. 1985, dir. blood svcs., 1993. Mem. Mo. Native Plant Soc. (pres. 1983-85), Am. Soc. Plant Taxonomists, Lions Internat. (dist. gov. 1983-84, other offices), Beta Beta Beta, Phi Sigma. Republican. Home: 1014 Dickinson Kiowa KS 67070

CONRAD, MICHAEL EARL, computer scientist, researcher; b. N.Y.C., Apr. 30, 1941; s. Earl Phillip and Anna Alyse (Abrams) C.; m. Deborah Antoinette Jones, Sept. 18, 1965; 1 child, Emily. AB, Harvard U., 1963; PhD, Stanford U., Palo Alto, Calif., 1970. Postdoctoral fellow Ctr. for Theoretical Studies U. Miami, Coral Gables, Fla., 1969-71; postdoctoral scholar dept. math. U. Calif., Berkeley, 1970-72; asst. prof. Inst. for Info. Sci. U. Tübingen, Fed. Republic of Germany, 1972-75; assoc. prof. dept. biology CCNY, N.Y.C., 1974-75; assoc. prof. dept. computer and communication scis. U. Mich., Ann Arbor, 1975-79; prof. dept. computer sci. Wayne State U., Detroit, 1979—; adj. prof. dept. biol. scis. Wayne State U., 1979-88, bd. govs. disting. univ. fellow, 1985-87; co-mng. editor BioSystems, 1983—; chmn. Fgn. Applied Sci. Assessment Ctr. panel on molecular electronics, McLean, Va., 1988-89; spl. vis. prof. Japanese Ministry of Edn., Tech. U., Nagaoka, 1987; disting. lectr. Computer Soc. IEEE, 1990-91; exch. scientist NAS, 1980, 83, 87; U.S. India exch. scientist, 1984; vis. prof. S.E. Univ., Nanjing, 1991—; fgn. mem. Russian Acad. Natural Scis., 1993—; vis. scholar Cavendish Lab., Cambridge U., 1979-82; vis. scientist Inst. for Chemistry, U. Mex., 1995. Author: Adaptability, 1983; co-editor: Physics and Mathematics of the Nervous System, 1974, Physical Principles of Neuronal and Organismic Behavior, 1973; assoc. editor: Chaos, Solitous and Fractals, 1991—; contbr. over 200 articles to scientific pubs. Mem. Soc. for Math. Biology (bd. dirs. 1983-86, sec., newsletter editor 1985-92), Internat. Soc. Molecular Electronics and Biocomputing (pres. 1993-94), Assn. for Computing Machinery, Biophys. Soc., IEEE Computing Soc. Office: Wayne State U Dept Computer Sci Detroit MI 48202

CONRAD, ROBERTA, municipal official, tax consultant; b. Milton, Iowa, Feb. 3, 1936; d. Leroy Martin and Lala Kate (Miller) Harward; m. John W. Conrad, June 19, 1953; children: John William, Rosalyn Conrad Nottke, James S. (dec.). Student, Iowa Wesleyan Coll., Mt. Pleasant, 1954; advanced income tax acctg., Block Tax Tng., Kansas City, Mo., 1972-94; IRS Tax Tng., U. Ill., Champaign, 1980. Sec. Green Lumber Co., Milton, Iowa, 1951-53; recording sec. United Meth. Ch., Aroma Park, Ill., 1969-73; treas. United Meth. Ch., Aroma Park, 1975-81; tax practitioner H and R Block, Kankakee, Ill., 1972-75; office mgr. H and R Block, Kankakee, 1975-93; trustee village bd. Village of Aroma Park, 1983-93, pres., 1993-97; vice chmn. planning commn. a divsn. of Ill. Dept. Transport., Kankakee, 1994; sec. Kankakee County Mayors Assn., 1994-95, vice chmn., 1995-96. Founder Young Homemakers, Milton, Iowa, 1960; mem. Kankakee County Home Extension, 1960-63, steering com. Kankakee County Devel. Corp., 1995-96. Mem. Kankakee Area C. of C. Republican. Home: 101 S Perar Aroma Park IL 60910 Office: Village of Aroma Park 107 W Front Aroma Park IL 60910

CONROY, JOE, state legislator; m. Mary Ann Macksood; children: Kevin, Kelly, Tim, Christine. State senator Mich. State Senate, Dist. 28, 1985-94, Mich. State Senate, Dist. 29, 1995—; mem. appropriations com., higher edn. & tech. com., Mich. State Senate; mem. human svc. com. & health com. Nat. Conf. State Legis. Office: 6095 Mapleridge Dr Flint MI 48532-2119 also: State Senate State Capital Lansing MI 48909*

CONROY, THOMAS HYDE, lawyer; b. Beloit, Kans., Feb. 6, 1922; s. Thomas Emmett and Ida Ruth (Hyde) C.; m. Helen Regina Supple, Nov. 27, 1952; children: Thomas William, Sheila Anne, Regina Marie, Joseph Patrick (dec.). AB, U. Kans., 1945, LLB, 1949. Bar: Kans. 1949. Assoc. Ralph H. Noah, Beloit, 1949-52; city atty. City of Beloit, 1953-55, 67-81; county atty. County of Mitchell, Kans., 1957-65; ptnr. Hamilton & Conroy, 1965; pvt. practice law Beloit, 1965—; owner, developer Conroy Place, 1965—. Bd. dirs. Mitchell County Hist. Soc., Inc. 1972—, 1st v.p., 1972-75, pres., 1975-77; trustee Mitchell County Hosp., 1965-87, pres. 1965-73, Marymount Coll. of Kans., 1983-88. Mem. ABA, Kans. Bar Assn., Am. Legion, Lions, KC (state adv. 1958-59), Phi Kappa, Phi Delta Phi. Home: 721 E 3rd St Beloit KS 67420-2830 Office: 209 E Main St Beloit KS 67420-3211

CONSEY, KEVIN EDWARD, museum administrator; b. N.Y.C., Jan. 15, 1952; s. Edward and Dorothy (Kemmann) C.; m. Susan Mary Kirsch, Aug. 26, 1972. BA, Hofstra U., 1974; M in Mus. Practice, MA, U. Mich., 1977. Dir. Emily Lowe Gallery, Hofstra U., Hempstead, N.Y., 1977-80, San Antonio Mus. Art., 1980-83; dir., chief exec. officer Newport Harbor Art Mus., Newport Beach, Calif., 1983-89, Mus. Contemporary Art, Chgo., 1989—; panelist profl. devel. Nat. Endowment for Arts, Washington, 1987-88, panelist challenge grant, 1988, panelist mus. program, 1989-90, panelist F.A.C.I.E., 1991-94. Hofstra U. scholar, 1970-74, Guggenheim Mus. intern, 1976; grantee Nat. Mus. Act, 1976-77. Mem. Assn. Art Mus. Dirs., Coll. Art Assn. Office: Mus Contemporary Art 220 E Chicago Ave Chicago IL 60611-3204

CONSOLA, MARY FRANCES, actuary, consultant; b. Chgo., Aug. 29, 1946; d. Anthony Patsy and Mary Frances (Reilly) C. BA, Mundelein Coll. of Loyola U., Chgo., 1968; MM, Northwestern U., 1987. Actuarial asst. Globe Life Ins., Chgo., 1968-73; asst. v.p. PolySystems, Inc., Chgo., 1973-80; asst. actuary Nat.-Ben Franklin Life, Chgo., 1980-82, Am. Bankers Ins. Group, Miami, Fla., 1982-84; cons. Capsco Software, Rosemont, Ill., 1984-86; mgr. Jerome F. Seaman & Assocs. Inc., Northfield, Ill., 1986—. Mem. Chgo. Actuarial Assn. (pub. rels. com.), Kellogg Alumni Club of Northwestern U. (career devel. com.). Roman Catholic. Office: Jerome F Seaman & Assocs 550 W Frontage Rd Northfield IL 60093-1202

CONSTABLE, JOHN, advertising executive; b. 1943. Pvt. practice London, 1964-76; with Cramer Krasselt Co., Milw., 1976-78; with Laughlin/Constable Inc., Milw., 1978—, now v.p., sec. Office: Laughlin/Constable Inc 207 E Michigan St Milwaukee WI 53202-4905*

CONSTANTINESCU, GHEORGHE M., veterinarian; b. Bucharest, Ilfov, Romania, Jan. 20, 1932; came to U.S., 1984; U.S. citizen 1989; s. Mircea and Elisabeta (Mateescu-Capetineanu) C.; m. Ileana Anghelina, Mar. 1, 1979; children: Alexandru Razvan, Adina Elizabeth. Student, Liceul Gh. Lazar, Bucharest, 1950; DVM, Faculty Vet. Medicine, Bucharest, 1955, PhD, 1964; Dr honoris causa, U. Agrl. Scis. Banat-Timisoara, Romania, 1992, U. Agrl. Scis., Bucharest, 1995. Bd. cert. in vet. diagnostic lab. pathology. Lab. chief Faculty of Vet. Medicine, Bucharest, 1955; scientific researcher Zootech. Rsch. Inst., Bucharest, 1958-59; doctor-medic vet. Zool. Garden, Bucharest, 1959-62; circuit doctor-medic vet. Agrl. Coun., Panciu-Galati, Romania, 1962-63; head breeding sect. Agrl. Coun., Panciu-Galati, Romania, 1963-65; head and assoc. prof. vet. anatomy Faculty of Vet. Medicine, Timisoara, Romania, 1965-82; assoc. prof. vet. anatomy U. Mo. Coll. Vet. Medicine, Columbia, 1984-92, prof., 1992—; v.p. Agrl. Coun., Panciu-Galati, 1963-65; sci. sec. Agronomic Inst. Timisoara, Romania, 1974-76; assoc. dean Faculty of Vet. Medicine, Timisoara, 1976-77; mem. internat. com. on vet. gross anatomical nomenclature, 1988—. Author: Comparative Anatomy, 4 vols., 1971-74, Comparative and Topographic Anatomy of Domestic Animals, 1978, Topographic Anatomy Domestic Mammals, 1982, Clinical Dissection Guide for Large Animals, 1991, Illustrated Veterinary Anatomical Nomenclature, 1992. Mem. European Assn. Vet. Anatomists, Union Soc. Med. Scis. Romania, Soc. Vet. Med. Romania, Am. Assn. Vet. Anatomists, Am. Assn. Anatomists, World Assn. Vet. Anatomists, Fedn. Am. Socs. for Exptl. Biology, Nat. Computer Graphics Assn. Home: 5800 Spiva Crossing Rd Hallsville MO 65255-9717 Office: U Mo Coll Vet Medicine 1600 W Rollins Rd Columbia MO 65203-1756

CONTE, LOU, artistic director, choreographer; b. DuQuoin, Ill., Apr. 17, 1942; s. John and Floy Mae (Saunders) C. Student Ellis DuBoulay Sch. Ballet, Chgo., 1961-68, So. Ill. U., 1960-62, Am. Ballet Theatre Sch., N.Y.C., 1964-66. Choreographer musicals Mame, 1972, Boss, 1973; choreographer Milw. Melody Top, 1966; dir. Lou Conte Dance Studio, Chgo., 1974—; artistic dir. Hubbard St. Dance Co., Chgo., 1977—; lectr. Mem. Actors Equity Assn., AFTRA. Office: Hubbard St Dance Co 218 S Wabash Ave Chicago IL 60604-2306

CONTI, PAUL LOUIS, management consulting company executive; b. Utica, N.Y., Sept. 3, 1945; s. Louis Joseph and Dorothy Mae (Kellogg) C.; m. Lee Ann Scheuerman, Apr. 18, 1970; children: Meghan Elizabeth, Dawn Michelle. BA, So. Ill. U., 1972, MBA, 1974. Sr. cons. Lester B. Knight & Assocs., Chgo., 1974-76; dir. pers. Applied Info. Devel., Oak Brook, Ill., 1976-80; v.p. Comsi, Inc., Oak Brook, 1980-82; chief exec. officer Prestige Mgmt. System, Inc., Glen Ellyn, Ill., 1982-86; v.p. human resources Rand McNally & Co., Skokie, Ill., 1986-87; assoc. dir. Ernst & Young (formerly Ernst & Whinney), Chgo., 1987-93; regional v.p. Alexandria Alexander, Inc., Chgo., 1993—; bd. dirs. So. Ill. U. Coll. Bus. Adminstrn. Lobbyist Invest in the Future, Invest in Edn., State of Ill., 1988; bd. dirs., exec. com. So. Ill. U.-Carbondale Found., 1991—, pres., 1994—. Named to So. Ill. U. COBA Hall of Fame, 1988; named Community Ambassador So. Ill. U., 1980. Mem. Soc. Human Resource Profls., Soc. Human Resources Mgmt., Human Resources Mgmt. Assn. of Chgo., Employment Mgmt. Assn., Pontikes Ctr. for Mgmt. Info. (bd. dirs. 1989—), So. Ill. U. Alumni Assn. (pres. 1986-88, bd. dirs. 1986—, exec. com. 1991—), Ideal Club (pres. 1986-88), McCullom Lake Club. Republican. Roman Catholic. Home: 635 S Park Blvd Glen Ellyn IL 60137-6977

CONTIE, LEROY JOHN, JR., federal judge; b. Canton, Ohio, Apr. 2, 1920; s. Leroy John and Mary M. (DeSantis) C.; m. Janice M. Zollars, Nov. 28, 1953; children: Ann L., Leroy John III. BA, U. Mich., 1941, JD, 1948; JD (hon.), U. Akron, 1993. Bar: Ohio 1948, U.S. Dist. Ct. (no. dist.) Ohio, 1953, U.S Supreme Ct. 1959. Law dir. City of Canton, 1952-60; chmn. Canton City Charter Commn., 1963; mem. Stark County Bd. Elections, Canton, 1964-69; judge Common Pleas Ct., Stark County, 1969-71, U.S. Dist. Ct., No. Dist. Ohio, Cleve., 1971-82, U.S. Ct. Appeals (6th cir.), Cin., 1982—; now senior judge U.S. Ct. Appeals (6th cir.). Trustee Stark County Legal Aid Soc., Canton chpt. ARC; mem. adv. bd. Walsh U., Canton, U. Akron Law Coll. With AUS, 1942-46. Mem. Am., Ohio, Stark County, Summit County, Cuyahoga County, Akron bar assns., Am. Judicature Soc., U.S. Jr. C. of C. (internat. senator), Canton Jr. C. of C. (trustee), Stark County Hist. Soc., Stark County Wilderness Soc., Am. Legion, Sigma Phi Epsilon (Nat. citation award), Phi Alpha Delta., Omicron Delta Kappa, K.C. Club (4 deg.), Elks Club. Roman Catholic. Office: US Ct Appeals 365 US Courthouse 2 S Main St Akron OH 44308-1813

CONTIGUGLIA, JOSEPH JUSTIN, preventive medicine physician, internist; b. N.Y.C., Jan. 8, 1948; s. Joseph and Doris (Justin) C.; m. Sylvie Blaise, Nov. 23, 1982; children: Dorothy Justine, Joseph Henry, Catherine Emily. AB in Sociology, Columbia Coll., N.Y.C., 1969; MD, U. Siena (Italy), 1975; MPH and Tropical Medicine, Tulane U., 1981; MBA, St. Mary's U., San Antonio, 1990. Diplomate Am. Bd. Preventive Medicine, Am. Bd. Med. Mgmt. Resident internal medicine Cabrini Med. Ctr., N.Y.C., 1975-78; commd. USAF, advanced through grades to col.; chief hyperbaric medicine USAF Clinic, Kadena AFB, Okinawa, Japan, 1978-80; resident aerospace medicine USAF Sch. Aerospace Medicine, Brooks AFB, San Antonio, 1980-82; chief aeromed. svcs. USAF Hosp., Seymour Johnson AFB, Goldsboro, N.C., 1982-85; chief occupational medicine and environ. health Royal Australian Air Force, Canberra, Australia, 1985-87; chief aerospace medicine div. Air Tng. Command, Randolph AFB, San Antonio, 1987-90; hosp. comdr. USAF Hosp., Reese AFB, Lubbock, Tex., 1990-92; dep. comdr. 5th med. group comdr. 5th aerospace medicine squadron, Minot AFB, N.D., 1992—; comdr. 5th Air Transportable Hosp.; clin. assoc. prof. preventive medicine and rural health U. N.D. Sch. Medicine, 1992—. Editor: Flight Surgeons Check List, 1982. Fellow Royal Soc. Medicine, Am. Coll. Preventive Medicine, Aerospace Med. Assn. (chmn. mil. aviation safety subcom., chmn. AIDS subcom.); mem. ACP, Am. Col. Physician Execs., Am. Soc. Tropical Medicine and Hygiene, Royal Aero. Soc., Aviation Med. Soc. Australia and New Zealand. Republican. Roman Catholic. Home: 111 Glacier Dr Minot ND 58704-1310 Office: 5AMDS/CC Minot AFB ND 58705

CONVERY, PATRICK GEORGE, orthopedic surgeon; b. Paterson, N.J., July 4, 1953; s. Patrick Hugh and Constance (Donato) C.; m. Marilyn Jean Glaser, Aug. 3, 1975; children: Kristen, Ellen, Matthew, Steven. BA in Chemistry, Montclair State Coll., 1975; MD, Bowman Gray Sch. Medicine, 1979. Diplomate Am. Bd. Orthopedic Surgery. Resident Pa. State U., Hershey, 1979-84; practice medicine specializing in orthopedic surgery Budd Lake, N.J., 1984-85; orthopedic surgeon Univ. Mednet, 1985—, chief dept. surgery, 1994—; active staff Lake County Hosp., Willougby, 1986—, Euclid Gen. Hosp., 1986-94, Univ. Hosps. Cleve., 1994—; chief dept. surgery Univ. Mednet, 1994—; mem. adv. bd. Kerr Brumbaugh Rehab. Ctr., Mentor, Ohio, 1987—; med. dir. Lake Hosps. Rehab. and Wellness Ctr. Fellow Am. Acad. Orthopaedic Surgeons; mem. Ohio State Med. Assn., Lake County Med. Soc. (pres. 1992—), Cleve. Orthopaedic Soc. Democrat. Roman Catholic. Home: 8280 Eagleridge Ln Concord OH 44077-9797 Office: Mednet Euclid Clinic 18599 Lake Shore Blvd Euclid OH 44119-1039

CONVISER, RICHARD JAMES, law educator, lawyer, publications company executive; b. Chgo., Apr. 4, 1938; s. Jack and Florence Conviser; 1 child, Ryan Elizabeth. B.A., U. Calif.-Berkeley, 1959, J.D., 1962; Dr. Jur, U. Cologne, Fed. Republic Germany, 1964. Bar: Calif. 1962, Ill. 1965. Assoc. Baker & McKenzie, Chgo., 1965-67; dep. European dir. European Office of Ill., Brussels, Belgium, 1968-69; prof. law DePaul U., Chgo., 1969-73, Chgo.-Kent Coll. Law, Ill. Inst. Tech., 1973—; sr. v.p. Harcourt Brace Pubs., N.Y.C., from 1980; chmn., chief exec. officer Harcourt Brace Legal & Profl. Publs., Inc., Chgo., 1967—; founder, dir. BAR/BRI Bar Rev., Chgo.; founder, dir. Conviser & Duffy CPA Rev., Chgo.; bd. dirs. Harcourt Profl. Edn., Exchange Nat. Bank, Chgo., Conviser-Duffy CPA Rev. Author: The Modern Philanthrophic Foundation: A Comparative Legal Analysis, 1965, The Law of Agency and Partnership, 1993; mng. editorial dir. Gilbert Law Summaries, L.A., 1978—. Mem. North Dearborn Pk. Assn.; trustee Emory U. Sch. Law, Atlanta, Libr. Internat. Rels., Inst. Internat. Edn. Fellow Col. W. Dinkelspiel Found., 1960-62, Newhouse Found., 1960-62; Ford Found. internat. law fellow, 1962-64. Mem. ABA, Calif. Bar Assn., Ill. Bar Assn., Chgo. Bar Assn. Clubs: Racquet of Chgo., Saddle and Cycle (Chgo.). Home: 1518 N Dearborn Pky Chicago IL 60610-1402 Office: Harcourt Brace Legal & Profl Publs Inc 176 W Adams St Ste 2100 Chicago IL 60603-3603

CONWAY, JOHN PAUL, retired steel executive; b. Summit, N.J., May 20, 1924; s. Thomas Francis and Mary Magdalene (Spencer) C.: m. Helen Elizabeth Hermes, Sept. 4, 1948; children: Agnes, John Paul, Edward, Mary M., Raymond F., Anne, Joseph, Hugh G., Margaret, Frances. BA, Loras Coll., 1949; postgrad., No. Ill. U. Acct. Northwestern Steel & Wire Co., Sterling, Ill., 1950-65, mgr. acctg., 1965-70, asst. contr., 1970-75, contr., 1975-80, v.p. fin., sec., treas., dir., 1980-86; adv. dir. Allendale Midwest Adv. Bd., Chgo., 1982-86; bd. dirs. Dillon Found., Sterling, 1980—, Cath. Found. of the Rockford (Ill.) Diocese, 1991—. Vol. bus. mgr. St. Mary's Ch., Sterling; bd. dirs. United Way, Sterling, 1975-80. Served with USN, 1943-46, ETO, PTO. Home: 1408 1st Ave Sterling IL 61081

CONWAY, MARK ALLYN, lawyer; b. Dayton, Ohio, Dec. 13, 1957; s. Allyn Walter and Doris Jean (Wright) C.; m. Dawn Elizabeth Manning, July 31, 1982; children: Ashley Wright, Alexandra Mills. BA, Denison U., 1980; JD, Calif. Western Sch. of Law, 1983; LLM in Taxation, Georgetown U., 1984. Bar: D.C. 1983, U.S. Tax Ct. 1983, Calif. 1988, Ohio 1991. Ptnr. Thompson, Hine & Flory P.L.L., Dayton, 1990—. Mem. ABA (real property, probate and trust law sect.), D.C. Bar Assn. (taxation sect. Washington chpt.), Calif. Bar Assn. (real property, probate and trust law sect. 1988—), Dayton Racquet Club. Republican. Presbyterain. Home: 5712 Price Hill Pl Dayton OH 45459-1428 Office: Thompson Hine & Flory PLL 2000 Courthouse Plz NE Dayton OH 45402

CONWAY, NEIL JAMES, III, land title company executive, lawyer, writer; b. Cleve., Feb. 15, 1950; s. Neil J. and Jeanne Louise (Gensert) C.; m. Maureen Dolan; children: Seanna, Neil James (V, Declan, Liam. BSBA, John Carroll U., 1972; MBA, Suffolk U., 1974; JD, Antioch Sch. Law (named change to The U. of D.C.), 1983. Bar: Ohio, 1983, U.S. Dist. Ct. (no. dist.) Ohio, 1983, U.S. Supreme Ct., 1987, D.C., 1988. Auditor U.S. Dept. Interior, Arlington, 1974-77; systems acct. Mil. Dist. Washington, 1978-79; legal intern Govt. Accountability Project, Washington, 1980-81; jud. intern presiding judge U.S. Dist. (no. dist.) Ct. Ohio, 1982; legal asst. Spiegel & McDiarmid, Washington, 1982-83; pvt. practice Painesville, Ohio, 1983—; from title examiner to pres. Conway Land Title Co., Painesville, 1983—; adj. prof. legal studies Lake Erie Coll., Painesville, Ohio. Author: American Protestants for Truth About Ireland; editor in chief Antioch Law Jour., 1982-83, Am. Soc. for Internat. Law Human Rights Newsletter, 1995; pub. The Ohio Irish Times, 1993—; contbr. articles to profl. jours. Mem. Lake County Econ. Devel. Coun.; mem. Lawyers Com. for Human Rights, N.Y.C. Capt. USAR, 1972-81. Recipient First Pl. writing competition Gaelic League, Columbus, Ohio, 1992-94. Mem. ABA, Am. Soc. Internat. Law (Dean Rusk award 1980), Ohio Bar Assn. (real property sect., internat. law com.), Lake County Bar Assn. (co-author real estate symposium 1989), Brehon Law Soc. N.Y., Ohio Land Title Assn., Lake County Bd. Realtors (Affiliate of Yr. 1986), Painesville Title Assn. (pres. 1985-86), Women's Coun. Realtors (treas. 1984-86, historian 1991), Irish Am. Cultural Inst. (Editl. citation Ohio Irish Bull. 1990), Lake-Geauga Legal Aid Soc. (adv. bd. 1984-87), Amnesty Internat., MacBride Prin.'s coalition of Ohio (co-founder 1990), Smithsonian Instn. Democrat. Roman Catholic. Home: 10930 Bradley Ct Concord OH 44077-2443

CONWAY, ROBERT G., office manager; b. Cleve., Mar. 13, 1947. AB in Polit. Sci., Kenyon Coll., 1969; MBA, Cornell U., 1972. Office mgr. Centennial Securities, Westlake, Ohio, 1989—. Office: Centennial Securities Ste #250 24601 Center Ridge Rd Westlake OH 44145-5600

CONWAY, THOMAS WILLIAM, biochemist, educator; b. Aberdeen, S.D., June 6, 1931; s. James L. and Agnes (Mullen) C.; m. Mary Patricia Leadon, July 6, 1957; children: Catherine A., James M. BS, Coll. St. Thomas, St. Paul, 1953; MA, U. Tex., 1955, PhD, 1962. Postdoctoral fellow Rockefeller U., N.Y.C., 1962-64; asst. prof. U. Iowa, Iowa City, 1964-68, assoc. prof., 1968-73, prof. biochemistry, 1973—; mem. NIH Physiol. Chem. Study Sect., 1975-79, chmn., 1976-78; Am. Cancer Soc. vis. scholar ICRF Labs., London, 1980-81, vis. prof. U. Chile, 1968. Co-author: Biochemistry: A Case-Oriented Approach, 1974, 6th rev. edit., 1996. 1st Lt. USAF, 1953-58. Named Rosalie B. Hite fellow, U. Tex. Austin, 1958-62, NSF fellow Rockefeller U., N.Y.C., 1962-64, vis. scholar Am. Cancer Soc., London, 1980-81. Mem. Am. Soc. Biol. Chemists, Am. Chem. Soc., Soc. de Biologia de Chile (hon.), Sigma Xi (pres. U. Iowa chpt. 1978-79). Roman Catholic. Home: 1 Wellesley Way Iowa City IA 52245-3830 Office: U Iowa Dept Biochemistry Iowa City IA 52242

CONWAY, TYRRELL, molecular microbiologist; b. Bartlesville, Okla., Nov. 20, 1957; s. Paul S. Conway and Joyce M. (Mayfield) Stephens; m. Sharri Suzanne Kinney, Mar. 9, 1985; children: David Justin, Gracen Elizabeth. BS, Okla. State U., 1979, PhD, 1984. Faculty rsch. asst. U. Fla., Gainesville, 1985-88; assoc. prof. U. Nebr., Lincoln, 1988-92, 92-94, 1989-94; assoc. prof. Ohio State U., 1994—; sci. adv. coun. Nebr. Ctr. for Biotech., Lincoln, 1989—. Contbr. articles to Jour. Bacteriology and Applied Environ. Microbiology, Molecular Microbiology. Recipient Layman award U. Nebr., 1991, Fling summer rsch. fellowship, 1988, Basic Energy Scis. grant U.S. Dept. Energy, 1990, 93, Nebr. Energy Office grant, 1990. Mem. AAAS, Am. Soc. Microbiology, Soc. for Indsl. Microbiology. Office: The Ohio State U Dept Microbiology 376 BioSci Bldg Columbus OH 43210

CONWAY, WILLIAM FREDERICK, SR., business founder; b. Pitts., Dec. 6, 1928; s. Dewitt Huss and Olive Katherine (Frederick) C.; m. Betty Allen, Mar. 19, 1953; children: William Frederick Jr., Allen, Winifred. BA, Duke U., 1950. Traffic mgr. George Koch Sons, Inc., Evansville, Ind., 1954-65; vice chmn. Discount Labels, Inc., New Albany, Ind., 1965—. Author: 9 books on Civil War and related history, 1987—; arranger concert band music, 1954—; prodr. weekly internat. religious radio program, Jeffersonville, Ind., 1985—. Trombonist Corydon (Ind.) Concert Band, 1985—, River City Concert Band, 1990—; curator Conway Fire Mus., 1990—. With USAF, 1950-53. Republican. Office: Discount Labels Inc PO Box 709 New Albany IN 47151-0709

CONYERS, JAMES E., sociology educator; b. Sumter, S.C., Mar. 6, 1932; s. Emmett C. and Crenella C. (Clinkscales) C.; m. Joan L. Farris, June 6, 1956 (div. Nov. 1978); children: Judy Y., James E. Jr., Jennifer J. AB in Sociology, Morehouse Coll., 1954; MA in Sociology, Atlanta U., 1956; PhD in Sociology, Wash. State U., 1962. Instr. LeMoyne Coll., Memphis, 1955-56; tchg. fellow Wash. State U., Pullman, 1958-62; asst. prof. sociology Ind. State U., Terre Haute, 1962-64; assoc. prof. sociology Atlanta (Ga.) U., 1964-68; full prof. sociology Ind. State U., Terre Haute, 1968—; selection com. Nat. Fellowship Fund, Atlanta, 1973-78; mem. advisory panel for sociology NSF, Washington, 1975-77; mem., predoctoral fellow NRC, Washington, 1994-95. Co-author: Black Youth in a Southern Metropolis, 1968, Black Elected Officials, 1976, (pamphlet) A Brief History of Association of Black Sociologists, 1991; co-editor: Sociology for the Seventies, 1972; editl. bd. Phylon, 1966-68, Western Jour. Black Studies, 1987-93. Bd. mem. Terre Haute (Ind.) Symphony Assn., 1979-85; v.p. West Ctrl. Ind. Civil Liberties Union, 1986-87. Mem. Am. Sociol. Assn., North Ctrl. Soc. Assn. (coun. 1991), Assn. Social and Behavioral Scis. (pres. 1970-71, W.E.B. DuBois award 1981), Assn. Black Sociologists (pres. 1973-74, Disting. Scholar award 1994), Young Men Civic Club, NAACP (life mem.). Democrat. Unitarian. Home: 5862 E Cougar Dr Terre Haute IN 47802 Office: Dept Sociology Ind State Univ Terre Haute IN 47802

CONYERS, JOHN, JR., congressman; b. Detroit, May 16, 1929; s. John and Lucille (Simpson) C.; m. Monia Estes; children: John Jr., Carl Edward. B.A., Wayne State U., 1957, J.D., 1958; LL.D., Wilberforce U., 1969. Bar: Mich. 1959. Legis. asst. to Congressman John Dingell, 1959-61; sr. ptnr. firm Conyers, Bell & Townsend, 1959-61; referee Mich. Workmen's Compensation Dept., 1961-64; mem. 89th-103rd Congresses from 1st (now 14th) Mich. dist., 1964—; former chmn. Govt. Ops. Com., former chmn. subcom. on legis. and nat. security; ranking mem. Judiciary Com.; Past dir. edn. Local 900, United Auto Workers; mem. adv. council Mich. Liberties Union; gen. counsel Detroit Trade Union Leadership Council; vice chmn. nat. bd. Ams. for Democratic Action; vice chmn. adv. council ACLU; an organizer Mems. Congress for Peace through Law; bd. dirs. numerous other orgns. including African-Am. Inst., Commn. Racial Justice, Detroit Inst. Arts, Nat. Alliance Against Racist and Polit. Repression, Nat. League Cities. Sponsor, contbg. author: Am. Militarism, 1970, War Crimes and the American Conscience, 1970, Anatomy of an Undeclared War, 1972; contbr. articles to profl. jours. Trustee Martin Luther King Jr. Ctr. for Non-Violent Social Change. Served to 2d lt. AUS, 1950-54, Korea. Recipient Rosa Parks award SCLC. Mem. NAACP (exec. bd. Detroit), Kappa Alpha Psi. Democrat. Baptist. Office: 2426 Rayburn Ofc Bldg B Washington DC 20515-0005

COOGAN, FRANK NEIL, health and social services administrator; b. Watertown, Wis., June 14, 1929; s. Neil Christopher and Lilian (Nelson) C.; m. Mary Louise Block, Apr. 14, 1951; children: Michael, Thomas, Karen. BS, U. Wis., 1951, MSW, 1955. Psychiatric social worker VA, 1955-62; dist. mental health cons. Wis. State Div. Mental Hygiene, 1962-65; dir. Bur. Alcohol and Other Drug Abuse, Wis. Dept. Health, 1965-77; v.p. DePaul Health Corp., 1977-90; behavioral health cons. Corphealth, West Allis, Wis., 1990-94; psychotherapist Family Social and Psychotherapy Svc., 1994—. With U.S. Army, 1951-53. Fellow Am. Coll. Addiction Treatment Adminstrs.; mem. Alcohol and Drug Problems Assn. N. Am. (chmn. membership com.), Wis. Alcohol and Drug Treatment Providers Assn. (bd. dirs.), Wis. Assn. Alcohol and Other Drug Abuse (bd. dirs., Outstanding Profl. award 1990). Lutheran. Home: 2127 S 99th St Milwaukee WI 53227-1452

COOK, ALEXANDER BURNS, museum curator, artist, educator; b. Grand Rapids, Mich., Apr. 16, 1924; s. Gorell Alexander and Harriette Florence (Hinze) C.; m. Marilyn Bierschwal Coffey, Aug. 11, 1992; B.A., Ohio Wesleyan U., 1949; M.S., Case Western Res. U., 1967. Editorial cartoonist, artist Cleve. Plain Dealer, 1949-55; account exec. Edward Howard & Co., Cleve., 1955-61; spl. art tchr. Cleve. Pub. Schs., 1964-88; curator exhibits Inland Seas Maritime Mus. (formerly Gt. Lakes Mus.), Vermilion, Ohio, 1970-78, curator, 1978—, chmn. mus. operating com., 1977—. Trustee, Berkshire Condominium Owners Assn., 1981-83, pres., 1982-83. Served with AUS, 1943-45. Recipient award of honor Ohio Wesleyan U., 1955; Distinguished Achievement award Gt. Lakes Hist. Soc., 1973; 1st pl. award for editorial cartoons Union Tchr. Communications Assn., 1980, 81, 82, 87. Mem. Gt. Lakes Hist. Soc. (exec. v.p. 1959-64, v.p. 1964—, trustee, mem. exec. com. 1959—), Ohioana Library Assn., Akron Art Mus., Cleve. Mus. Art, Am. Soc. Marine Artists, Assn. for Great Lakes Maritime History, Chgo. Maritime Soc., Delta Tau Delta, Pi Delta Epsilon, Pi Sigma Alpha. Republican. Episcopalian. Contbr. editorial cartoons to Reid Cartoon Collection, U. Kans. Jour. Hist. Center, The Critique, 1975—; editorial adviser, numerous articles to Inland Seas, 1957—, The Chadburn, 1976—; cover illustrations for Ohioana Quar., 1979—; book cover illustrations Dodd, Mead & Co., 1984. Paintings represented in pvt. collections, 1960—; executed mural depicting Gt. Lakes shipping Gt. Lakes Mus., 1969. Mem. The English Speaking Union. Avocations: gardening, sailing, model railroading.

COOK, ANDA SUNA, civil rights advocate; b. Riga, Latvia, Mar. 15, 1935; came to U.S., 1952.; d. Janis Suna and Erna Alexandra (Kletnieks) Sirmais; m. William E. Cook, May 27, 1961; children: Lisa Inara Hamilton, Inta Marie Mitterbach, John William. Student, Augustana Coll., Sioux Falls, S.D., 1954-55, Cleve. State U., 1970-85; MS, Case Western Res. U., 1989. Lic. real estate agt. With Cuyahoga Plan of Ohio, Inc., Cleve., 1976-91, dir. resource devel., 1988-91; exec. dir. Living in Cleve. Ctr., 1992—; v.p. regional div. U.S. Orgn. Internat. Trade, Inc., Cleve., 1989—; price analyst U.S. Steel Corp., Cleve., 1955-62; pres. ASC Cons.-Orgn. Devel., Cleve., 1988; presenter World Latvian Sci. Congress, Riga, 1991. Writer 60 Years of Leage of Women Voters, 1980; writer, prodr. Vol. Affirmative Mktg. Agreement in Action, 1989. Bd. dirs. Dept. Human Svcs., Cuyahoga County, 1984-93, Cudell Sr. Adv. Coun., 1980-85; trustee Friends of Cleve. Met. Housing Authority, 1986-92; active Cuyahoga C.C. Adv. Bd., 1980—; bd. trustees Citizens League, Cleve., 1989-95, Housing Advocates, 1996—;

chair Cleve. PTA, 1972-73; pres. Louisa May Alcott Elem. Sch. PTA, Cleve., 1971-72, LWV, Cleve., 1975-77. Recipient Dedicated Svc. award The Cuyahoga Plan, Cleve., 1985, Cleve. Leadership award United Way, 1976, Cleve. Area Bd. Realtors Fair Housing award, 1993. Mem. Am. Soc. Tng. and Devel. Democrat. Lutheran. Home: 9801 Lake Ave Cleveland OH 44102-1230 Office: US Orgn Internat Trade Inc 9801 Lake Ave 4d Cleveland OH 44102

COOK, CHARLES F., food industry consultant executive; b. Bratislava, Slovakia, Sept. 13, 1937; came to U.S., 1953; s. Frank and Gerda (Hecht) C.; m. Jean E. Thurber Cook, Feb. 14, 1992; children: Jeffrey, Kimberley, Kristofer. BS, Oregon State U., Corvallis, 1958; MS, U. Wis., Madison, 1961, Phd, 1963. Dir. Oscar Mayer, Madison, Wis.; managing ptnr. Cook & Thurber, Middleton, Wis. Mem. Recycle Market Devel. Bd., Madison. Office: Cook & Thurbor 4898 Foxfire Trl Middleton WI 53562

COOK, CHARLES TERRENCE, library director, consultant; b. Portsmouth, Ohio, June 20, 1949; s. Leonard C. and Callie L. (Newman) C.; m. Marchetta Piccolo, Sept. 2, 1975 (div. Feb. 1979); 1 child, Ann Elizabeth. Student, Ohio U., Portsmouth, 1967-68; BA, Ohio State U., 1971; MSLS, U. Ky., 1973. Asst. dir. Portsmouth Pub. Libr., 1973-75, libr. dir., 1975—. Ch. trustee Ch. of Christ, Portsmouth. Mem. ALA, Ohio Libr. Assn. (legis. com. 1985-86), Ohio State U. Alumni Assn., Hon. Order of Ky. Cols. Home: 1233 23rd St Portsmouth OH 45662-2955 Office: Portsmouth Pub Libr 1220 Gallia St Portsmouth OH 45662-4217

COOK, GARY L., state legislator; m. Cheryl Cook. Grad., Ind. Law Enforcement Acad. Police officer/patrolman Plymouth (Ind.) Police Dept.; rep. Dist. 17 Ind. Ho. of Reps., 1990—, mem. county and twp. govt. affairs, environ. affairs com., mem. pub. safety, rds. and transp. coms., chmn. internstate coop. com., rds. transp. com., ranking minority mem. Mem. Marshall County Right to Life, Plymouth Arts Commn. Mem. FOB, Lions. Home: 11385 9th Rd Plymouth IN 46563-8324*

COOK, JEANNE G., historian, genealogist; b. Wadsworth, Ohio; d. Ralph D. and Rose M. Garn; m. William A. Cook; children: William Jeffrey, Julie L. Cook Boatwright, James A. BA, Hiram Coll., 1947. Woman's supr. City Recreation Dept., Wadsworth, 1947-51; libr. Cleve. City Schs., 1953-55; physician's office receptionist Cleve., 1978-81; self-employed genealogist, historian Parma Heights, Ohio, 1982—; lectr. in field. Editor Mayflower Newsletter, 1991-95; author: (poetry) The Blue of Autumn, 1990 (Golden Poet award), also numerous genealogies and slide programs. Vol. craft instr. City of Parma Heights, 1968-75. Mem. Western Res. Hist. Soc. (vol. libr. 1980—, mem. geneal. com. 1981—), Parma-Cuyahoga Genealogy Soc. (pres. 1986—), Daus. Am. Colonists (state sec. 1993—, regent local chpt. 1991-95), 1st Families of Ohio (lectr. 1982—), Cleve. Colony Mayflower Descendants (bd. assts., pub. rels. com. 1987—), Hiram Coll. Club of Women. Home: 6428 Nelwood Rd Parma Heights OH 44130

COOK, JEANNINE HARRISS, educational administrator, educator; b. St. Louis, Dec. 3, 1929; d. Lester Raymond and Mabel (Gruner) Harriss; m. Edward Bruce Cook, May 2, 1953; 1 child, Bruce Harriss. BFA, Washington U., St. Louis, 1951. Dir. community edn. and arts Affton (Mo.) Sch. Dist., St. Louis, 1951—; lectr. art edn. Washington U., 1969—, St. Louis U., 1980—. Mem. Mo. Adv. Coun. on Hist. Preservation, 1990—, St. Louis County Hist. Bldg. Commn., 1990-94; pres. Save Grant's White Haven Inc., St. Louis County, 1990—, Affton Hist. Soc., 1982-85; bd. dirs. Jefferson Nat. Expansion Hist. Assn., 1992—, Mo. Alliance for Hist. Preservation, 1992—, pres., 1994—. Mem. Affton C. of C. (bd. dirs. 1986—). Presbyterian. Home: 9533 Trinadad Ln Saint Louis MO 63126-3124

COOK, JUDITH ANN, academic program director; b. Quincy, Ill., Aug. 25, 1948; d. William McQuinn and Irma Dell (Underwood) Cox; m. Neil Allen Cook, June 5, 1971; children: Joshua McQuinn, Sara Aine. BA, Augustana Coll., 1970. Speech clinician Henry-Stark Edn. Dist., Kewannee, Ill., 1970-72, Rock Island (Ill.) Pub. Schs., 1972-75; tchr. ESL Iowa Lakes C.C., Spencer, 1980-82; dir. Reach Out to Single Parents Clay County Citizen Awareness Coun., Spencer, 1983-84; dir. Upward Bound/Talent Search Iowa Lakes C.C., Emmetsburg, 1984-89; exec. dir. Planning and Devel. Iowa Lakes C.C., Estherville, 1989—. Mem. MAEOPP (bd. dirs.), Iowa MAEOPP (pres. 1984), Nat. Coun. Resource (tape libr. coord. 1989, state of Iowa dir. 1995-96), Rotary Internat., Aid Assn. for Luths. Br. (pres. 1978). Office: Iowa Lakes Cmty Coll 19 S 7th St Estherville IA 51334

COOK, LOIS ANNA, chemistry educator; b. Canton, Ohio, June 15, 1924; d. Ransom Harold and Freda Belle (Babcock) Barr; m. Aaron Sylvester Cook, Aug. 9, 1950; children: Barbara Ann Cook Picini, Douglas Allan Cook. BA, Coll. of Wooster (Ohio), 1945; MS, Ohio State U., 1948; PhD, Union Inst., Cin., 1980. With Pillsbury Mills, Mpls., 1948-49; instr. chemistry Middlebury (Vt.) Coll., 1949-50; chemist Univis Lens, Dayton, Ohio, 1950-51, Matls. Lab., Wright Patterson AFB, Ohio, 1951-54; position classifier Wright Patterson AFB, Dayton, 1954-55; instr. chemistry Wright State U., Dayton, 1964-74, asst. prof. chemistry, 1974-87, prof., 1987, dir. coll. counseling, 1970-73, asst. dean Coll. Sci. and Engring., 1973-86, asst. dean Coll. Sci. and Math., 1986-87; ret., 1987; dir. west dist. Ohio Jr. Acad. Sci., Wright State U., 1984—, project dir. Links to Learning Project, 1990-92. Contbr. articles to profl. jours. Trustee Westminster Presbyn. Ch., 1991-94. Centennial honoree, Ohio Acad. Sci., 1991, Award for Outstanding Profl. Achievement, Affiliate Socs. Coun. of Engring. and Sci. Found. of Dayton for Profl. Accomplishments, 1988; inducted into Ohio Women's Hall of Fame, 1985. Fellow Ohio Acad. Sci. (exec. com. 1984-96, Centennial honoree 1991), Am. Inst. Chemists; mem. AAUP, AAUW (br. pres. 1985-87, corp. liaison for Wright State U. 1973-87, state pres. 1983-85, corp. rels. chmn. 1985-87), Am. Chem. Soc., Nat. Fedn. Bus. and Profl. Women's Clubs, DAR, Assn. Women in Sci. (chmn. Engring. amd Math. Consortium Ohio 1986-96). Home: 1020 Hampshire Rd Dayton OH 45419-3713

COOK, MARJORIE ELLEN LIND, nursing administrator; b. Logansport, Ind., Oct. 31, 1942; d. Frank A. and Florence M. (Weiand) Lind; m. Rudolph W. Cook, Oct. 30, 1970 (dec. July 1978); 1 child, Franklin R. BSN, Ind. U., 1964, MSN, 1969. RN, Ind.; lic. nurse, Fla.; cert. nursing adminstrn. advanced ANA. Staff RN VA Med. Ctr., Indpls., 1964-67; staff RN, instr. Cmty. Mental Health Ctr., Indpls., 1968-69; DON St. Mary's Hosp., West Palm Beach, Fla., 1969-70; supr. nursing Arden Hill Hosp., Cmty. Mental Health Ctr., Goshen, N.Y., 1971-72; instr. Mt. St. Mary's Coll., Newburg, N.Y., 1973-76; head nurse VA Med. Ctr., Bay Pine, Fla., 1976-78; asst. chief nurse VA Med. Ctr., Poplar Bluff, Mo., 1978-81, Danville, Ill., 1981-83; chief VA Med. Ctr., Ft. Wayne, Ind., 1983-86, Topeka, 1986—; mem. adv. coun. to coll. RN program, Poplar Bluff, Danville, Ft. Wayne; mentor new students VA Med. Ctr., Topeka, 1989; mem. adv. coun. Sch. Nursing Kans. U., Kans.; mem. adj. faculty Sch. Nursing Baker U. and Sch. Nursing Kans. U., 1991-96. Mem. nursing adv. coun. ARC, Topeka, 1992. YMCA Leadership honoree, 1992; Mayor's Commn. on Status of Women honoree, 1992; NIH scholar, 1968; recipient U.S. Govt. Adminstrv. Svc. award Greater Kans. City Fed. Exec. Bd., 1996. Mem. AAUW (pres. 1980-81), ANA, Am. Orgn. Nurse Execs., Bus. and Profl. Women, Soroptimist Internat. of Topeka, Leadership Va., VA Spkrs. Bus., Sigma Theta Tau (com.), Pi Lambda Theta. Methodist. Home: 3121 SW Staffordshire Rd Topeka KS 66614-4386 Office: VA Med Ctr 2200 SW Gage Blvd Topeka KS 66622-0001

COOK, RUSSELL ELBERT, JR., electrical engineer; b. Hartford, Conn., Nov. 7, 1969; s. Russell E. and Myrna L. (Butz) C. BSEE, We. New Eng. U., 1991. Electronics engr. Naval Undersea Warfare Ctr., Newport, R.I., 1991-94, Alliant Techsys., Mpls., 1994-96; ADC Telecomms., 1996—. Mem. IEEE, Tau Beta Pi. Home: 5437 Maryland Ave N Crystal MN 55428 Office: Alliant Techsystems MN11-2920 600 2nd St NE Hopkins MN 55343

COOK, STANTON R., media company executive; b. Chgo., July 3, 1925; s. Rufus Merrill and Thelma Marie (Borgerson) C.; m. Barbara Wilson, Sept. 23, 1950 (dec. Nov. 1994). BS in Mech. Engring., Northwestern U., 1949. With Shell Oil Co., 1949-51; with Chgo. Tribune Co., 1951-81, v.p., 1967-70, exec. v.p. and gen. mgr., 1970-72, pres., 1972-74, pub., 1973-90, CEO, 1974-76, chmn., 1974-81; dir. Tribune Co., 1972-96, v.p., 1972-96, pres., 1974-88, chmn., 1989-92, CEO, 1974-90; chmn. Chgo. Nat. League Ball Club, Inc., 1990-94; bd. dirs. AP, 1975-84, 2d vice chmn., 1979-84; bd. dirs. Newspaper Adv. Bur., 1987-92, Am. Newspaper Pubs. Assn., 1974-82; dep. chmn., bd. dirs. Fed. Res. Bank Chgo., 1980-83, chmn., 1984-85; bd. dirs. Robert R. McCormick Tribune Found., 1990—. Trustee Robert R. McCormick Trust, 1972-90, Savs. and Profit Sharing Fund of Sears Employees, 1991-94, U. Chgo., 1973-87, Mus. Sci. and Industry, Chgo., 1973—, Field Mus. Natural History, Chgo., 1973—, Gen. Douglas MacArthur Found., 1979—, Northwestern U., 1987—, Shedd Aquarium Soc., 1987—, Am. Newspaper Pubs. Assn. Found., 1973-82. Mem. Newspaper Assn. Am. (bd. govs. 1992), Chgo. Coun. Fgn. Rels. (bd. dirs. 1973-93), Comml. Club (past pres.), Econ. Club (past pres., life mem.).

COOK, WAYNE EVANS, music educator; b. Pearsall, Tex., Dec. 16, 1939; s. George Evans and Loreen Ruth Cook; m. Marlene Bruce Cook, Aug. 28, 1965; children: Julie, Sheri, Leslie. BMus, U. North Tex., 1962; MS in Music Edn., U. Ill., 1964; postgrad., Eastman Sch. Music, 1965. Instr. music Ind. State U., Terre Haute, 1964-66; asst. prof. music U. Wis., Milw., 1966-73; assoc. prof. music U. Wis., 1973-79, prof. music, 1979—; dir. grad. studies in music U. Wis., Milw., 1985—, assoc. dean sch. of fine arts, 1983-84, chmn. dept. of music, 1993—; profl. trumpet performer Freel Artist in City, Milw., 1966—. Dir. music Abiding Savior Luth. Ch., Milw., 1978-89; prin. trumpet Festival City Symphony, Milw., 1968—, utility trumpet Milw. Symphony Orch., 1966-80; prin. trumpet Skylight Opera Orch., Milw., 1970-84. Mem. Internat. Trumpet Guild, Nat. Assn. of Schs. of Music, Nat. Assn. of Coll. Wind and Percussion Instrs. Democrat. Congregationalist. Home: 4133 N Woodburn St Shorewood WI 53211 Office: Dept Music Univ Wis PO Box 413 Milwaukee WI 53201

COOK, WELLS FRANKLIN, education educator; b. Ovid, Mich., May 20, 1928; s. Wayne Baldwin and Beatrice Cecelia (Stuart) C.; m. Lois Arlene Anderson, Apr. 2, 1930; children: Natalie Ruth Cook Hermes, Annette Jean, Wayne Earl. BS, Cen. Mich. U., 1950; MA, U. Mich., 1955; PhD, Mich. State U., 1974. Tchr. Owosso (Mich.) High Sch., 1950-51; instr. Co. Clk.'s Sch., Ft. Jackson, S.C., 1951-53; tchr. Fenton (Mich.) High Sch., 1953-57; tchr., coord. co-op Royal Oak (Mich.) Pub. Schs., 1957-67; prof., vocat. tchr. educator, dept. bus. info. sys. Ctrl. Mich. U., Mt. Pleasant, 1967—; cons., lectr. Mich. Mcpl. League, Ann Arbor, 1979—, Mich. Twps. Assn., Lansing, 1979—; evaluator Career Colls. Assn., Washington, 1979—. Author manuals. Recipient Spl. Recognition award Mich. State Bd. Edn., 1993. Mem. NEA, Mich. Edn. Assn., Nat. Bus. Edn. Assn., Mich. Career Coords. Assn. (pres. 1979-80, Outstanding Svc. awards 1983, 93), Mich. Occupl. Tchr. Educators Assn. (pres. 1988-91), Mich. Vocat. Curriculum Leaders (bd. dirs. 1989-91), Mich. Assn. for Career Edn. (bd. dirs. 1985-90), Nat. Assn. Parliamentarians. Methodist. Office: Ctrl Mich Univ Dept Bus Info Sys 320C Grawn Hall Mount Pleasant MI 48859

COOKE, ANNE E., administrative assistant; b. Columbus, Ohio, Mar. 18, 1966. BA, Stevens Coll., Columbia, Mo., 1988. Sales asst. Smith Barney Inc., St. Louis, 1988-89, Bank One Securities Corp., Columbus, 1989-90, Merrill Lynch, Columbus, 1990-91; adminstrv. asst. McDonald & Co. Securities Inc., Columbus, 1991—. Mem. Columbus Stock and Bond Club. Office: McDonald & Co Securities Inc One Columbus Bldg Ste 1600 Columbus OH 43215

COOKE, BRIAN F., financial advisor; b. Bunkerhill, Ind., May 26, 1967. BS, Ind. U., 1987. Sales rep. E G Brooks, Indpls., 1989-90, Mammars, Indpls., 1990-92; v.p. investments Prudential Securities, Indpls., 1992—. Mem. Pres. Coun., 1994—, Pinnacle Conf. Harvard, 1995—. Mem. Nat. Assn. Sales Profls. (v.p. 1992—), Pinrod Soc. (bd. dirs. 1995—). Home: 7999 Evanston Rd Indianapolis IN 46240-2731 Office: Prudential Securities Inc 8888 Keystone Xing # 200 Indianapolis IN 46240-4609

COOKE, JOHN DAVID, financial advisor; b. Peru, Ind., Sept. 16, 1940. Bus. degree, Butler U., 1962. Fin. advisor Thompson McKinnan, Indpls., 1967-89; sr. v.p. investments Prudential Securities, Indpls., 1989—. Chmn. Cmty. Hosp. North, Indpls., 1992. With USAF, 1962-67. Named Outstanding Broker Register Rep., 1994; inductee Broker Hall of Fame, Rsch. Mag., 1994. Mem. Hawthorn Country Club (bd. dirs.). Office: Prudential Securities # 200 8888 Keystone Xing # 200 Indianapolis IN 46240-4609

COOLER, THECLA BEHRENS, university administrator, international advisor; b. Wellington, New Zealand, Nov. 3, 1938; came to U.S., 1973; d. John Fredrick and Bessie Irene (Gilooly) Behrens; m. Richard Morrall Cooler; children: Aram Sebastian Yaacov, Amycla Sieglinde Yael. BMus with honors, Victoria U., Wellington, 1972; MA in Art History, No. Ill. U., 1981, EdD in Adult Edn., 1996; Licentiate in Piano, Trinity Coll. Music, London, 1971. Cert. med. bacteriologist, New Zealand. Rsch. asst. Addenbrooke's, U. Cambridge, Eng., 1964-65; rsch. assoc. Academisch Ziekenhuis, Utrecht, Netherlands, 1965-68; staff hematologist Alexander's Pathology, Wellington, 1969-71; coord. honors program No. Ill. U., DeKalb, 1984-86, asst. dir. internat. student and faculty office, 1986—; S.E. Asian studies counselor Ctr. , No. Ill. U., 1988—. Cert. instr. AIDS prevention ARC, DeKalb, 1994—. Burmese Fgn. Lang. Study grantee No. Ill. U., 1985. Mem. Assn. Asian Studies, Nat. Assn. Fgn. Student Affairs Ill. (co-founder, pres. 1991-93), Rotary.

COOLEY, JACK LEE, engineering manager; b. Salina, Kans., Feb. 24, 1930; s. Lee S. and Mabel Cooley; m. Freida L., Dec. 10, 1955; children: Anita Jo, Mary Kathryn. Engring. mgr. FMC Corp., Itasca, Ill., 1973-80, Environment One Corp., Schenectady, N.Y., 1980-89, Hycor Corp., Lake Bluff, Ill., 1989—. Methodist. Office: Hycor Corp 29850 N Hwy 41 Lake Bluff IL 60044

COOLEY, JAMES LUMBERT, stockbroker; b. Flint, Mich., Feb. 13, 1942. Student, Albion Coll., 1963; BS in Bus. and Polit. Sci., Mich. State U., 1966. Stockbroker Francis I. Dupont, Detroit and Flint, 1967-74, Dean Witter Reynolds, Detroit, 1974—. Active Jaycees, Flint, Mich., 1970. Mem. Detroit Rotary Club, Nat. Ski Patrol, Bayview Yacht Club. Methodist. Office: Dean Witter Reynolds 333 W Fort St Fl 17 Detroit MI 48226-3134

COOLEY, NANCY JO, university administrator; b. Cadillac, Mich., June 28, 1952; d. Gordon and Frances Perry (Hiller) Berghorst; m. Jeffery Lynn, Aug. 25, 1973. BS in Edn., Ctrl. Mich. U., Mt. Pleasant, 1974; MA in Tchg., Oakland U., Rochester, Mich., 1977; PhD, U. Mich., 1988. Lic. tchr. grades K-8, ages 0-25 spl. edn. Tchr. Lapeer (Mich.) Pub. Schs., 1974-78; tchr. cons. Kearsley Schs., Flint, Mich., 1978-81; dir. Cooley Reading Clinic, Lapeer, Mich., 1981-88; faculty tchr. edn. Ctrl. Mich. U., Mt. Pleasant, 1989-93, dept. chair, 1993-95, spl. asst. to provost, 1995, asst. vice provost, 1995—; mem., past adv. bd. Mich. Coun. Presvc. Edn., Detroit, 1990-96;mem. Tchr. Edn. Admissions Bd., Mt. Pleasant, 1995-96. Vol. Forfar Biol. Field Sta., Andros Island, Bahamas, 1991, Playscape, Mt. Pleasant, 1994. Mem. Internat. Soc. Tech. Edn., Assn. Managing and Using Info. Tech. in Higher Edn., Mich. Assn. Computer Users in Learning, Internat. Reading Assn., Mich. Assn. for Colls. of Tchr. Edn. (treas. 1995-96), Phi Beta Delta. Office: Ctrl Mich U Warriner 382 Mount Pleasant MI 48858

COOLEY, WENDY, judge, lawyer; b. Birmingham, Ala., Jan. 1, 1948. BS, Ea. Mich. U., 1968; MA, U. Mich., 1971; JD, U. Detroit, 1982. cert. spl. edn. tchr., Mich. Spl. edn. cons. Detroit Bd. Edn., 1971-80; assoc. Kirk & McCargo, Detroit, 1982-84; judge Mich. 36th Dist. Ct., Detroit, 1984—; host TV show Winning Ways CBS; instr. Wayne County C.C., Detroit, 1979-84. Contbr. articles to various publs. Bd. dirs. U.Detroit, Wayne County Cmty., Wayne County Econ. Growth; speaker various ch. and cmty. groups, Detroit area; radio hostess Sta. WNIC, Detroit; active Leadership Detroit, Second Ebeneezer Bapt. Ch.; mem. Mich. Martin L. Ling Holiday Commn.; apptd. to Mich. Correction Officer Tng. Coun., 1987. Mem. Mich. Dist. Judges Assn., Mich. State Bar Assn., Eastern Star, Delta Sigma Theta. Office: Mich 36th Dist Ct 421 Madison St Detroit MI 48226-2358

COOLEY, WILLIAM EDWARD, regulatory affairs manager; b. St. Louis, Mar. 7, 1930; s. Charles Frederic and Lillian Marie (Williams) C.; m. Marion Grace Sherman, June 5, 1952; children: Charles, Marilyn, Harold, Noele. AB, Cen. Coll., 1951; PhD, U. Ill., 1954. Rsch. chemist Procter & Gamble Co., Cin., 1954-61, product devel. chemist, 1961-65, product devel. group leader, 1965-75, product devel. regulatory sect. mgr., 1975-90, regulatory affairs sect. mgr., 1990-91; worldwide regulatory coordination sect. mgr., 1991-94; pres. Cooley Cons., Inc., 1994—; bd. dirs. Nonprescription Drug Mfrs. Assn., Washington, 1987-91. Contbr. articles to profl. jours.; inventor, patentee in field. Mem. Am. Assn. Dental Rsch., Internat. Assn. Dental Rsch., Nonprescription Drug Mfrs. Assn., Assn. Food Drug Ofcls., Regulatory Affairs Profl. Soc. (bd. editors 1990), Drug Info. Assn. Republican. Home: 531 Chisholm Trl Cincinnati OH 45215-2517 Office: Cooley Cons Inc 531 Chisholm Trail Wyoming OH 45215

COOLEY, WILLIAM EMORY, JR., radiologist; b. Charlottesville, Va., Jan. 28, 1941; s. William Emory Sr. and Madelle Elizabeth (Fullen) C.; m. Janella Mahoney Haney, Dec. 26, 1966; children: Angela Janette, William Emory, James Haney. BA, Emory U., 1963; MD, U. Va., 1967. Diplomate Am. Bd. Radiology. Rotating intern. U.S. Naval Hosp., Phila., 1967-68; resident radiology U.S. Naval Regional Med. Ctr., Phila., 1972-75; radiologist U.S. Naval Regional Med. Ctr., Portsmouth, Va., 1975-76, asst. chief radiology, 1976-77; radiologist Bloomington (Ill.) Radiology S.C., 1977-79, pres., 1979—; chief radiologist Brokaw Hosp., Normal, Ill., 1979-85, St. Joseph Hosp., Bloomington, Ill., pres. med. staff, 1981; med. dir. radiology Bromen Health Care System, Bloomington, 1985—, pres. med. staff, 1990. Mem. citizens adv. coun. Sch. Dist. 87, Bloomington, 1981-84; v.p. McLean County unit Am. Cancer Soc., 1989-90, pres., 1990-94. Comdr. USN, 1966-77. Fellow Am. Coll. Radiology (alt. councillor 1987-92, councillor 1993—); mem. AMA, Radiol. Soc. N.Am., Am. Roentgen Ray Soc., Am. Inst. Ultrasound Medicine, Ill. Radiol. Soc. (exec. com. 1986—, pres. 1994-95), Ctrl. Ill. Radiol. Soc. (pres. 1990-91), Bloomington Country Club, Masons. Republican. Presbyterian. Office: Bloomington Radiology SC 200 S Towanda Ave Normal IL 61761-2132

COOMBER, JAMES ELWOOD, English language educator; b. Freeport, Ill., Jan. 17, 1942; s. Elwood Lowell and Vi Anna Margaret (Schoonhoven) C.; m. Eleanor Ruth McKinnon, June 11, 1966; children: Sarah Ellen, Matthew James. BS, U. Wis., Platteville, 1964; MA, U. Wis., Madison, 1966, PhD, 1972; postgrad., U. Ariz., 1989. Prof. English Concordia Coll., Moorhead, Minn., 1966—, chair dept. English, 1984-88, 96—; vis. prof. U. Calgary, Alta., Can., 1979, 81; adj. faculty Hamline U., St. Paul, 1982—, N.D. State U., Fargo, 1972—; faculty mem. Prairie Writing Project, Moorhead, 1977-82; dir. Concordia Conf. on Reading and Writing, 1983—; cons. to pub. schs., Minn., N.D. Co-author: The English Book, 1981, Macmillan Spelling, 1983, Vocabulary for College Reading and Writing, 1984, Wordskills, 1990, Words for Success, 1996; contbr. articles to profl. jours. Active Bread for the World, Washington, 1988—. Nat. Teaching fellow U.S. Dept. Edn., 1969. Mem. Conf. Coll. Composition and Communication, Nat. Coun. Tchrs. English, Minn. Coun. Tchrs. English, Sierra Club. Democrat. Episcopalian. Office: Concordia Coll Dept of English Moorhead MN 56562

COON, SAUNDRA KAY, home health nurse, small business owner; b. San Francisco, Oct. 31, 1943; d. Earl and Peggy Leona (Tripple) Raby; m. Robert T. Burns, Dec. 19, 1981 (div. Nov. 1987); 1 child, Gagen A. Coon. Student, U. Kansas City, Mo., 1961-62, Penn Valley C.C., 1963-64, 91-94, Coll. of Redwoods, 1973-87, U. Mo., Kansas City, 1994-95. Exec. sec. Kansas City Coll. Osteopathy and Surgery, 1963-66; office mgr. pvt. practice med. office, Mendocino and Ft. Bragg, Calif., 1973-88; med. office cons. Mendocino, 1977-88; owner Sound Explosion, Jamaica, W.I., 1987-89, Village Imports, Kansas City, 1988—; med. sec. pvt. practice med. office, Kansas City, 1990-92. Contbr. poetry to Nat. Libr. of Poetry: Best Poems of 1994, 95, also to profl. jours.; photographs exhibited in group show Kaw Valley Arts and Humanities, 1991; photography televised on KQED, 1994. Chair membership Congress of Racial Equality, Kansas City, 1963-66; mem. So. Poverty Law Ctr., Montgomery, Ala., 1986, Mendocino Environ. Ctr., Ukiah, Calif., 1990; mem. Nat. Abortion Rights Action League, 1989, Greenpeace, Women in the Arts, Ptnrs. U.S.A./Para Brazil, Rainforest Alliance Network; bd. dirs. Global and Multicultural Edn. Ctr., 1993—, chair, 1994. Mem. Internat. Platform Assn., Planned Parenthood of Greater Kansas City, Amnesty Internat., Habitat for Humanity, Sierra Club, Greater Kansas City Greens Club, Deer Creek Golf Club. Democrat. Humanist. Home: 1017 E 68th St # 1 Kansas City MO 64131

COONEY, PATRICK RONALD, bishop; b. Detroit, Mar. 10, 1934; s. Michael and Elizabeth (Dowdall) C. B.A., Sacred Heart Sem., 1956; S.T.B., Gregorian U., Rome, 1958, S.T.L., 1960; M.A., Notre Dame U., 1973. Ordained priest Roman Cath. Ch., 1959 ordained bishop, 1983. Assoc. pastor St. Catherine Ch., Detroit, 1960-62; asst. chancellor Archdiocese of Detroit, 1962-69, dir. dept. worship, 1969-83; rector Blessed Sacrament Cathedral, 1977-83; regional bishop Roman Cath. Ch., Detroit, 1983-89; apptd. bishop Diocese of Gaylord, Mich., 1989—. Office: Diocese of Gaylord Pastoral Ctr 1665 32 W Gaylord MI 49735

COOPER, BONNIE SUE, state legislator; b. Jan. 13, 1934; m. Daniel L. Cooper, 1956. State rep. dist. 32 Mo. Ho. of Reps., 1982—. Republican. Home: 413 NW 58th St Kansas City MO 64118-4017 Office: Mo Ho of Reps State Capitol Building Jefferson City MO 65101-1556*

COOPER, CAROLYN ANNETTE, proofreader, journalist; b. Cleve., Mar. 29, 1965; d. Joseph and Lavonia (PItts) C. BA in Rhetoric and Mass Comm., Kent State U., 1989; MA in Journalism and Mass Comm., Kent State U., Strongsville, Ohio, 1994; postgrad. studies Counseling Psychology, Vision Christian Bible Coll., 1995—. Tchr.'s aide Stephen E. Howe Sch., Cleve., 1982; tchr. Kiddie Tots Nursery, Cleve., 1983, Collinwood Cmty. Day Care, Cleve., 1984; student libr. Kent (Ohio) State U., 1985-89; proofreader Bus. Stationery, Inc., Cleve., 1995—; participant Kent State's Journalism and Mass Comm. Inst. for Minority Students, 1990; pub. rels. specialist Ausar Ctr. Cleveland Heights, Ohio, 1992—; freelance writer Cleve. Plain Dealer, 1993—. Contbr. articles to profl. jours. Booth offl. Cleve. Bd. of Elections, 1991—; pub. rels. specialist for candidate Cleve. City Coun., 1993-94; mem. focus group Sta. WEWS-TV, Cleve., 1995. Mem. Soc. Prof. Journalists, YMCA, Full Gospel Evanglistic Ctr. (pub. rels. specialsit 1994—), Sigma Gamma Rho. Democrat. Pentacostal. Home: PO Box 6-08114 Cleveland OH 44108

COOPER, DAVID DALE, American studies educator; b. Phoenix, Sept. 2, 1948; s. Dale C. and Marylee Cooper; m. Christina P. Cooepr, June 10, 1977. BA, U. Calif., Santa Barbara, 1970; PhD, Brown U., 1977. Lectr. U. Calif., Santa Barbara, 1978-88; assoc. prof. Am. thought and lang. Mich. State U., East Lansing, 1988—. Author: Thomas Merton's Art of Denial, 1989, Writing in the Public Interest, 1995. Dir. Svc.-Learning Writing Project, East Lansing, 1992—. Office: Mich State U Dept Am Thought Lang 229 Bessey Hall East Lansing MI 48824

COOPER, DONNA RUTH, corporate librarian; b. Cleve., Mar. 8, 1948; d. Gerald Charles and Ruth Estelle (Hunter) Hollis; m. Herman L. Cooper, June 5, 1982. CPS, Detroit Sch. Bus., 1982. Adminstrv. asst. ANR-Pipeline Co., Detroit, 1979-82, corp. libr., 1982—. leader Girl Scouts U.S., Benton Harbor, Mich., 1967-68; sec., bd. dirs. Rackham Symphony Choir, Detroit, 1993-95; active Archdiocesan Chorus, Detroit, adminstrv. asst., 1995-96. Office: ANR Pipeline Co 500 Renaissance Ctr Detroit MI 48243

COOPER, ELAINE JANICE, physical therapist; b. Detroit, Apr. 26, 1937; d. Morris and Sally (Mack) Braverman; divorced; children: Jeffrey, Michael, Jonathan. BS, U. Mich., 1959; cert. in massage therapy. Supr. Rehab. Inst., Detroit, 1959-61; cons. Redford (Mich.) Community Hosp., 1963-73; cons. in field Detroit, 1970-78; asst. dir. William Beaumont Hosp., Royal Oak, Mich., 1979-81; pres., cons. Cooper & Assoc. Physical Therapy P.C., Farmington Hills, Mich., 1981—; cons. Drs. Sobel & Castle, Detroit, 1965-66. Mem. Am. Phys. Therapy Assn. (edn. com. 1969), Mich. Phys. Therapy Assn., Biofeedback Soc. Mich., Am. Massage Therapy Assn., Mich. Dance Assn., Mich. State C. of C. (health care com.), Brookfield Highlands Club (chmn. land devel., restrictions coms. 1979-85). Office: Cooper & Assocs Phys Therapy PC 31800 Northwestern Hwy Ste 110 Farmington MI 48334-1663

COOPER, GEORGE KILE, business educator; b. Bushnell, Ill., Apr. 5, 1920; s. George Kile and Lula Belle (Robison) C.; m. June Anna Cardell, June 12, 1948; children: Kyle, Ernest, Ruth Anne, William, Jeanne, Andrew. BEd, Western Ill. State U., 1942; MBA, Ind. U., 1951; PhD, U.

Mich., 1962. Cert. secondary sch. tchr., Ill. Bus. tchr. Reynolds (Ill.) Community High Sch., 1946-47; student teaching coordinator Western Mich. U., Kalamazoo, 1948-55, head bus. edn. dept., 1955-62; head bus. edn. and adminstrv. office mgmt. dept. Eastern Ill. U., Charleston, 1962-73, prof. bus. edn. and adminstrv. office mgmt., 1962-82, prof. emeritus, 1982—; vis. research and devel. specialist Ctr. for Vocat. and Tech. Edn., Ohio State U., Columbus, 1973-74. Treas. Wesley United Meth. Ch., Charleston, 1983-93, trustee, 1994—; chmn. Ill. Curriculum Coun., 1980-81. With AUS, 1942-46. Recipient Alumni Achievement award Western Il.. U., 1994; Cooper Hall namin in honor, Ea. Ill., U., 1991. Mem. Ill. Bus. Edn. Assn. (pres. 1971-72, disting. svc. award 1975), Ill. Vocat. Asns. (treas. 1965-69), Ill. State U. Annuitants Assn. (pres.-elect 1986-87), Eastern Ill. U. Annuitants Assn. (pres. 1984-86), Pi Omega Pi (nat. pres. 1966-68), Delta Pi Epsilon (pres. chpt. 1960-61), Phi Delta Kappa (pres. chpt. 1980-81, alt. del. 1986-87). Home: 708 Taft Ave Charleston IL 61920-4135

COOPER, J. MICHAEL, advertising executive; b. 1949. Grad., Southwest Mo. State U., 1971. CPA. With Associated Wholesale Grocers, 1971-72, Gen. Grocer Co., 1972-73, McLean Enterprises, 1973-74, Paul Mueller Co., 1974-78; pvt. practice as acct., 1978-81; with Lawrence Photo-Graphic, 1981-84; with Noble & Assocs., Springfield, Mo., 1984—, now sec., CFO. Office: Noble & Assocs 336 S Barnes Ave Springfield MO 65801*

COOPER, JAMES ALBERT, JR., electrical engineering educator; b. Columbus, Miss., Feb. 5, 1946; s. James Albert and Juanita (Perkins) C.; m. Barbara Crowder, Aug. 3, 1968; children: David Alan, Katherine Liann. BSEE, Miss. State U., 1968; MSEE, Stanford U., 1969; PhD, Purdue U., 1973. Mem. tech. staff Sandia Labs., Albuquerque, N.Mex., 1968-69; grad. rsch. asst. Sch. Elec. Engring. Purdue U., West Lafayette, Ind., 1970-72, prof., 1983—, dir. Purdue Optoelectronics Rsch. Ctr., 1986-89; mem. tech. staff Bell Labs., Murray Hill, N.J., 1973-83. Contbr. numerous articles to jours., chpts. to books; patentee in field. Fellow IEEE (assoc. editor Trans. on Electron Devices 1983-86). Republican. Mem. United Methodist Ch. Office: Purdue U Sch Elec & Computer Engring 1285 EE Bldg West Lafayette IN 47907-1285

COOPER, JAMES CLINTON, social services administrator, consultant; b. Brinson, Ga., Feb. 3, 1929; s. James and Hattie Lue (Speights) C.; m. Anne Elizabeth Brown, July 14, 1959. BA, Savannah State U., 1956; MSW, Atlanta U., 1958. Lic. ind. social worker, Ohio. Clin. social worker VA Hosp., Tuskegee, Ala., 1958-61; social work supr. State Hosp., Fulton, Mo., 1961-64; dir. resident ctr. Community Action for Youth, Cleve., 1964-67; exec. dir. Goodrich-Bell Social Settlement, Cleve., 1967-69; dir. social svc. Cleve. State Hosp., 1969-74, Fairhill Mental Health Ctr., Cleve., 1974-84; dir. social svc. Cleve. Psychiat. Inst., 1984-85, cons. on quality assurance, 1985-95; owner Northcoast Vending Co., Cleve., 1992—; pres., chief exec. officer Wayne Morrie, Inc., cons., Cleve., 1983—. Bd. dirs. Hough Area Devel. Corp., Cleve., 1967-77, 1st vice-chmn., 1976-77. Sgt. U.S. Army, 1951-53. Recipient Editors' Choice award Nat. Libr. Poetry, 1993; NASW fellow U. Pitts., 1977-79. Mem. Acad. Cert. Social Workers, Nat. Assn. Quality Assurance Profls. Home: 14420 Onaway Rd Cleveland OH 44120-2841

COOPER, JANELLE LUNETTE, neurologist, educator; b. Ann Arbor, Mich., Dec. 11, 1955; d. Robert Marion and Madelyn (Leonard) C.; children: Lena Christine, Nicholas Dominic. BA in Chemistry, Reed Coll., 1978; MD, Vanderbilt U., 1986. Diplomate Nat. Bd. Med. Examiners; diplomate in neurology Am. Bd. Psychiatry and Neurology; registered med. technologist Am. Soc. Clin. Pathologists. Med. technologist Swedish Hosp. Med. Ctr., Seattle, 1978-80, U. Wash. Clin. Chemistry, Seattle, 1980-82, Vanderbilt U. Hosp., Nashville, 1983-84; intern medicine Vanderbilt U. Med. Ctr., Nashville, 1986-87, resident neurology, 1987-90; instr. neurology Med. Coll. Pa., Phila., 1990-91, asst. prof., clerkship dir., 1991—, mem. curriculum com., 1990-91, vis. asst. prof., 1991-95; neurologist Greater Ann Arbor Neurology Assocs., 1991-93; dir. neurological svcs., med. dir. Industrial Rehab. Program St. Francis Hosp., Escanaba, Mich., 1993—; founder, dir. No. Neuroscis., Escanaba, 1993—; physician MCP Neurology Assocs., Phila., 1990-91; emergency rm. physician Tenn. Christian Med. Ctr., 1989-90. Contbr. articles to Annals of Ophthalmology, Ophthalmic Surgery. Vol. Rape and Sexual Abuse Ctr., Nashville, 1988-90; mem. adminstrv. bd. Edgehill United Meth. Ch., Nashville, 1989-90; mem. editorial bd. Nashville Women's Alliance, 1989-90; bd. dirs. Upper Peninsula Physicians Network; mem. adv. bd. Perspective Adult Daycare Ctr., 1996—. Recipient Svc. award for outstanding contbns. Rape and Sexual Abuse Ctr., 1990; epilepsy minifellow Bowman Gray U., 1995. Mem. AMA (physician's Recognition award 1989-92), NOW, AAAS, NAFE, Am. Med. Women's Assn., Am. Acad. Neurology, Am. Psychol. Soc., Mich. State Med. Soc., N.Y. Acad. Scis., Upper Peninsula Physician Network (bd. dirs. 1995—), Aircraft Owners and Pilots Assn., Women in Aviation Internat. (charter). Democrat (mem. nat. com.). Methodist. Home: 519 S 8th St Escanaba MI 49829-3608 Office: Northern Neurosciences 3415 Ludington St Ste 201 Escanaba MI 49829-1300

COOPER, JOHN ARNOLD, financial analyst; b. Detroit, Oct. 27, 1917; s. Gage Whitman and Helen Dorothy (Danger) C.; m. Sylvia Grace, Sept. 6, 1941 (div. 1977); 1 child, Maud Cooper Granzow; m. Virginia Bailey Svagr, Mar. 11, 1977 (dec. 1981); m. Anny Marion Van Dyke, Apr. 9, 1983. BA, Williams Coll., Williamstown, Mass., 1939; MBA, Mich. State U., 1968. CFA, Inst. Chartered Fin. Analysts. Treas. Cooper Supply Co., Detroit, 1941-44, sec., 1944-56, pres., 1956-67; v.p. Texas Industries, Inc., Dallas, 1963-67; pres. Cooper, Van Dyke Assocs. Inc., Bloomfield Hills, Mich., 1970—; pres. Transit Mixed Concrete Inst. Met. Detroit, 1952-53, 55-77, Builders Exch., Detroit, 1967-68. Class agt. Williams Coll., 1989-94; chmn. preservation fund drive The Cmty. House, Birmingham, Mich., 1995—. Lt. (j.g.) USNR, 1944-46. Fellow Fin. Analysts Fedn.; mem. Mich. Trucking Assn. (mem. bd. govs. 1958-63), Am. Trucking Assn. (bd. dirs. 1961-63), Inst. Chartered Fin. Analysts, Fin. Analysts Soc. Detroit (pres. 1980-81, chmn. profl. conduct/ethics com. 1988—), Assn. Investment Mgmt. and Rsch., Associated Gen. Contractors Detroit, Williams Club N.Y., Beta Gamma Sigma. Republican. Episcopalian. Office: Cooper Van Dyke Assocs Inc 1100 Woodward Ave Ste 238 Bloomfield Hills MI 48304-3971

COOPER, JOHN WESLEY, school system administrator; b. Selma, Ala., Apr. 15, 1953; s. Thurston Othello and Ruth Marcella (White) C.; m. Joan Margaret Schneider, May 3, 1975; children: John Wesley III, Michael Joseph, Megan Joy. BA, Fla. State U., 1975, MA, 1976; PhD, Syracuse U., 1982. Rsch. asst. Am. Enterprise Inst., Washington, 1979-81; asst. prof. of philosophy and religion Bridgewater (Va.) Coll., 1981-82, asst. prof. and dean for acad. affairs, 1982-84, assoc. prof. and dean for acad. affairs, 1984-87; sr. rsch. fellow Ethics and Pub. Policy Ctr., Washington, 1987-89; pres. James Madison Inst. for Pub. Policy Rsch., Tallahassee, Fla., 1989-94; pres., headmaster Wichita (Kans.) Collegiate Sch., 1994—; adj. prof. Wichita State U., 1995—. Author: (book) The Theology of Freedom, 1985; co-editor: The Corporation: A Theological Inquiry, 1981; editor: Private Property, Land Use Policy and Growth Management, 1990. Vice-chmn. Fla. Conservative Union, Gainesville, 1993-94; dir. Montessori Inst. of North Fla., Tallahassee, 1991-94, State Policy Network, Ft. Wayne, Ind., 1991-94; cons. Nat. Endowment for the Humanities, Washington, 1985. Mem. Kans. Assn. of Non-Govt. Schs., Ind. Schs. Assn. of the Southwest (bd. dirs. 1994—), Phila. Soc. (trustee 1993—), Heritage Found. Resource Bank, Kans. Health Ethics (bd. dirs. 1994—), Rotary, Phi Beta Kappa, Phi Delta Kappa, Theta Chi Beta. Republican. Presbyterian. Office: Wichita Collegiate Sch 9115 E 13th St Wichita KS 67206

COOPER, LEE MOLLIN, fire training specialist; b. Chgo., Sept. 17, 1939; s. William and Ione (Robbins) C.; m. Carolyn Jo Allman, Jan. 24, 1960; children: Laura, Douglas, James. BA, U. Minn., 1984, cert. in fire protection, 1987, MEd, 1994. Cert. tchr., Wis., Minn. Foreman Minneapolis Glass Co., St. Louis Park, Minn., 1960-64; police officer City of Hopkins, Minn., 1964-72; driver Smith Ambulance Co., Mpls., 1972-73; supt. traffic svc. City of Hopkins, 1973-85; fire svc. instr./supr. Wis. Indianhead Tech. Coll., New Richmond, 1985—; security officer IDS-Oxford, Mpls., 1975-80, Marriott Corp., Bloomington, Minn., 1984-85; tchr. Minn. Regional Fire Sch., 1982—; instr. Fire Insts. Assn. Minn. Schs., 1992-93. Firefighter Minnetonka (Minn.) Vol. Fire Dept., 1968-89; vol. Hopkins Raspberry Festival, 1974-85; chairperson Environ. Health Group, St. Croix County Cmty Health Assessment, 1995. Mem. Am. Critical Incident Stress Found., Am. Tech. Edn. Assoc., Am. Vocat. Assn., Nat. Fire Protection Assn., Internat. Mcpl. Signal Assn. (past pres.), Internat. Assn. Arson Investigators, Internat. Soc. Fire Svc. Instrs., Internat. Fire Photographer Assn., Internat. Assn. Fire Chiefs, Wis. Soc. Fire Svc. Instrs., Wis. Fire Inspectors Assn., Fire Dept. Safety Officers Assoc., Wis. State Fire Chief's Assn., Fire Instrs. Minn. (bd. dirs., pres.), Wis. Vocat. Assn., Minn. Alumni Assn., Wis. State Firefighter Assn., Minn. Assoc. Emergency Med. Technicians (nationally registered), Aircraft Owners & Pilots Assn. Home: 11618 Friar Ln Minnetonka MN 55305-4338 Office: Wis Indianhead Tech Coll 1019 S Knowles Ave New Richmond WI 54017-1738

COOPER, REGINALD RUDYARD, orthopedic surgeon, educator; b. Elkins, W.Va., Jan. 6, 1932; s. Eston H. and Kathryn (Wyatt) C.; m. Jacqueline Smith, Aug. 22, 1954; children—Pamela Ann, Douglas Mark, Christopher Scott, Jeffrey Michael. B.A. with honors, W.Va. U., 1952, B.S., 1953; M.D., Med. Coll. Va., 1955; M.S., U. Iowa, 1960. Diplomate Am. Bd. Orthopedic Surgeons (examiner 1968-70). Orthopedic surgeon U.S. Naval Hosp., Pensacola, Fla., 1960-62; assoc. in orthopedics U. Iowa Coll. Medicine, Iowa City, 1962-65; asst. prof. orthopaedics U. Iowa Coll. Medicine, 1965-68, assoc. prof. orthopedics, 1968-71, prof. orthopedics, 1971—, chmn. orthopedics, 1973—; research fellow orthopedic surgery Johns Hopkins Hosp., Balt., 1964-65; exchange fellow to Britain for Am. Orthopedic Assn., 1969. Trustee Jour. Bone and Joint Surgeons, 1989—, chmn. 1993—. Trustee Nat. Easter Seals Research Found., 1977-81, chmn., 1979-81. Served to lt. comdr. USNR, 1960-62. Mem. Iowa, Johnson County Med. Socs., Orthopedic Rsch. Soc. (sec.-treas. 1970-73, pres. 1974-75), Am. Acad. Orthopedic Surgeons (Kappa Delta award for outstanding rsch. in orthopedics 1971), Canadian, Am. Orthopedic Assns., N.Y. Acad. Sci., Assn. Bone and Joint Surgeons, AMA, Am. Rheumatism Assn., Am. Acad. Cerebral Palsy, Am. Acad. Orthopedic Surgeons (chmn. exams. com. 1978-82, sec. 1982, 2d v.p. 1985-86, 1st v.p. 1986-87, pres. 1987-88, ortho residency rev. com. 1989-95, chmn. 1993-95). Home: 201 Ridgeview Ave Iowa City IA 52246-1625 Office: U Iowa Hosps & Clinics 450 Newton Rd Iowa City IA 52242

COOPER, ROBERT G., investment executive; b. Syracuse, N.Y., Aug. 18, 1940. Lic. stockbroker. Photographer Syracuse, 1960-61; mgr. Piggly Wiggly, Macon, Ga., 1969-71; lineman REC, Macon, 1971-74; salesperson Greer Carver, Topeka, 1974-86; investment exec. Paine Webber, Topeka, 1986—. Sgt. USAF, 1960-68. Mem. VFW, Am. Legion. Republican. Methodist. Home: 3743 SW Sena Dr Topeka KS 66604-1754 Office: Paine Webber 634 S Kansas Ave Topeka KS 66603-3804

COOPER, ROBERT JAMES, purchasing consultant; b. St. Louis, Dec. 27, 1929; s. William McKinley and Lucille Evelyn (Floyd) C.; m. Joan Kathleen Gray, Nov. 20, 1932; children: Bruce John, Anne Muriel. Student, Ruskin Coll., Oxford, Eng., 1954-55. Asst. purchasing agt. Absorbant Cotton Co., St. Louis, 1960-65; purchasing agt. Christian Hosp., St. Louis, 1965-67; dir. purchasing St. John's Mercy Med. Ctr., St. Louis, 1967-86; purchasing cons. St. Louis, 1986—; lectr. in field; condr. seminars/workshops in field. Contbr. articles to profl. jours. With USAF, 1950-54. Mem. Nat. Assn. Purchasing Mgmt., Nat. Assn. Hosp. Purchasing Mgmt. (pres. 1974-76, fellow), Assn. Hosp. Purchasing Agts. of Greater St. Louis (pres. 1968). Democrat. Episcopalian. Home: 7955 Big Bend Blvd Saint Louis MO 63119-2703

COOPER, ROGER, state legislator; b. Nov. 8, 1944; m. Margie. BA, Rockford Coll.; postgrad., Mankato State U. State rep. Minn. Ho. Reps., Dist. 15B, 1986—; vice chmn. econ. devel. com., mem. govt. oper. com., vice chmn. health & human svc. com., mem. gen. legis., bet affairs & elec. agrl., hyman svcs. fin. divsn. & local govt. & met. affairs com., Minn. Ho. Reps. Home: PO Box 461 260 S 6th St Bird Island MN 55310*

COOPER, SCOTT KENDRICK, professional baseball player; b. St. Louis, Oct. 13, 1967. Baseball player Boston Red Sox, 1986-94; with St. Louis Cardinals, 1994—; mem. Am. League All-Star Team, 1993, 94. Office: St. Louis Cardinals 250 Stadium Plz Saint Louis MO 63102

COOPER, SIGNE SKOTT, retired nurse educator; b. Clinton County, Iowa, Jan. 29, 1921; d. Hans Edward and Clara Belle (Steen) Skott. BS, U. Wis., 1948; MEd, U. Minn., 1955. Head nurse U. Wis. Hosp., Madison, 1946-48; instr. U. Wis. Sch. Nursing, Madison, 1948-51, asst. prof., 1952-57, assoc. prof., 1957-62; prof., assoc. dean U. Wis. Sch. Nursing, 1948-83, prof. emeritus, 1983—; prof. U. Wis. Extension, 1955-83. Contbg. author: American Nursing: A Biographical Dictionary, Vol. 1, 1988, Vol. 2, 1992; contbr. articles to profl. jours. 1st Lt. U.S. Army Nurse Corps, 1943-46. Recipient NLN Linda Richards award, ANA Honorary Recognition award, Adult Edn. Assn. Pioneer award; named Fellow Am. Acad. Nursing. Mem. ANA, Am. Assn. for History Nursing, Wis. Nurses Assn. (pres.).

COOPER, THOMAS DAVID, metallurgical engineer, consultant; b. Dayton, Ohio, Apr. 7, 1932; s. Arnold Leroy and Edna Catherine (Guthrie) C.; m. Katherine Ann Ambrose, Dec. 26, 1953; children: Theresa Deborah, Michael Bruce, Stephen Jeffrey. BS in Metall. Engring., U. Cin., 1955; MS in Metall. Engring., Ohio State U., 1964. Registered profl. engr., Ohio. Jr. engr. Westinghouse Electric Corp., Pitts., 1955-56; project engr., sr. project engr. USAF Materials Lab., Wright-Patterson AFB, Ohio, 1956-61, sect. chief, br. chief, various brs., 1961-76, br. chief materials integrity, 1976-91, divsn. chief systems support, 1991-95, ret., 1995; sr. program mgr. Universal Technology Corp., Dayton, Ohio, 1995—; presenter in field. Co-editor: Prevention of Structural Failure - The Role of Quantitative Nondestructive Evaluation, 1975; Oxide Dispersion Strengthening, 1966; contbr. chpts. to books, articles to profl. jours. Capt. USAFR, 1956-58. Recipient Disting. Alumnus award U. Cin. Coll. Engring., 1972, USAF Meritorious Civilian Svc. award, 1992. Fellow Am. Soc. Metalls. Internat., Am. Soc. Nondestructive Testing; assoc. fellow AIAA; mem. Soc. Automotive Engrs. (Franklin Kolk Air Transport award 1991, Arch T. Colwell Coop. Engring. medal 1992). Home: 542 Rader Dr Vandalia OH 54377 Office: Universal Technology Corp 4031 Colonel Glenn Hwy Dayton OH 45431-1600

COOPER, WAYNE ALLEN, state government administrator; b. Mason City, Iowa, Mar. 9, 1950; s. William H. and Muriel L. (Larsen) C.; m. Jean Martin, July 21, 1971; 1 child, Kimberly Nicole. AA, Waldorf Coll., Forest City, Iowa, 1970; BA, Wartburg Coll., Waverly, Iowa, 1972. Agt., auditor, tng. instr. Iowa Dept. Revenue and Fin., Des Moines, 1974-82; regional mgr. Iowa Dept. Revenue and Fin., Council Bluffs, 1982-92; taxpayer svcs. mgr. Iowa Dept. Revenue and Fin., Des Moines, 1992—. Mem. state ctrl. com. Iowa Dem. Party, Des Moines, 1990-94. Recipient Jim Ludwig Meml. award Iowa Dem. Party, 1994. Mem. Rolm Users Group Iowa, Luth. Brotherhood (v.p. 1990-92), Heartland Collectors Club (co-pres. 1994—). Office: Iowa Dept Revenue and Fin Hoover State Office Bldg Des Moines IA 50319

COOPER-LEWTER, MARCIA JEAN, fine arts educator, administrative assistant; b. Petersburg, Va., Nov. 2, 1959; d. Andrew Ezekiel and Lillian (Bonner) Wyatt; m. Nicholas Charles Cooper-Lewter, Nov. 29, 1986. BS in Elem. Edn., Va. State U., Ettrick, 1984; MEd in Spl. Edn., 1993. Lic. minister, 1987; ordained to clergy, 1990. Tchr. Marion (Ind.) Community Schs., 1985-86, Inglewood (Calif.) Unified Schs., 1986-87; office mgr. C.R.A.V.E. Christ Counseling, Tustin, Calif., 1986—; asst. minister New Garden of Gethsemane B.C., L.A., 1987-90; assoc. minister New Hope Bapt. Ch., St. Paul, 1990—; assoc. pastor New Garden of Gethsemane B.C., L.A., 1990—; assoc. minister New Hope Bapt. Ch., 1990—; pres. C.R.A.V.E. Christ Singers, L.A., 1987-90; adminstr. asst. Eldorado Bank, Orange, Calif., 1988-90; tchr. fine arts Mpls. Sch. Dist., 1990—; with Wyatt, Cooper-Lewter Consulting, Shoreview, Minn., 1986—; founder, dir. "Diversity in Motion" program for A.A. students, 1992—; stage dir. "Babu's Magic" with reknown dancer Chuck Davis, 1994. Mem. C.R.A.V.E. Christ Ministries (Relax in Christ, Affirm with Christ, Visualize Christ, Experience Christ); nominated to Pres.'s Commn., White House Fellowships, 1993. Imagination grant Star Tribune, 1994, 1995-96, Fulbright grant to Namibia Africa Curriculum Waiting, 1996, U. Wis.-Madison African Studies grant, 1995-96. Mem. NAFE, Alpha Kappa Alpha.

COOPER-LEWTER, NICHOLAS CHARLES, psychotherapist, educator, minister; b. Washington, June 25, 1948; s. Ernest Charles and Constance (Hoage) Cooper; m. Marcia Jean Wyatt; children: Michelle, Sonia, Sean, Nicholas. BA, Ashland U., 1970; MSW, U. Minn., 1976; PhD, Calif. Coast U., 1988; LHD, Treamer Sch. Religion, 1976. Lic. marriage family therapist, Minn., marriage family child counselor, Calif. Rsch. specialist Ctr. Youth Devel. and Rsch. U. Minn., St. Paul, 1972-73; group worker Hallie Q Brown MLK Ctr., St. Paul, 1973-74; teaching asst. Sch. Social Work, U. Minn., St. Paul, 1974-75; field investigator, rep. City of St. Paul Human Right Dept., 1974; owner, dir. Cooper-Lewter Cons., Minn., Calif., 1978—, C.R.A.V.E. Christ Counseling Ctrs., Minn., Calif., 1984—; sr. pastor New Garden of Gethsemane B.C., L.A., 1985-90; founder, chief exec. officer C.R.A.V.E. Christ Ministries, St. Paul, 1987—; assoc. minister New Hope Bapt. Ch., St. Paul, 1990-93; assoc. prof. Bethel Coll. and Sem., St. Paul, 1990-95, coord. McKnight Found. cultural diversity grant, 1991-95; founder, CEO Cooper-Lewter Rites of Passage, Inc., St. Paul, 1995—; founder, pastor, CEO Committed by Choice Ministries, Inc., Mpls., 1995—; consulting agt. Met. Protection Bur., St. Paul, 1993—. Co-author: Soul Theology: Heart of American Black Culture, 1986. Mem. NAACP, Nat. Assn. of Social Workers, Acad. Cert. Social Workers, Am. Acad. Med. Hypnoanalysts (cert.), Rotary Internat., Omega Psi Phi (founder Xi Theta chpt.).

COOPERRIDER, TOM SMITH, botanist; b. Newark, Ohio, Apr. 15, 1927; s. Oscar Harold and Ruth Evelyn (Smith) C.; m. Miwako Kunimura, June 13, 1953; children: Julie Ann, John Andrew. BA, Denison U., 1950; MS, U. Iowa, 1955; PhD, 1958. Instr. biol. scis. Kent (Ohio) State U., 1958-61, asst. prof., 1961-65, assoc. prof., 1965-69, prof., 1969-93, emeritus prof., 1993—, curator herbarium, 1968-93, dir. bot. gardens, 1972-93; mem. editorial bd. Univ. Press, 1976-79; on leave as asst. prof. dept. botany U. Hawaii, 1962-63; NSF rschr. Mountain Lake Biol. Sta., U. Va., summer 1958; faculty mem. Iowa Lakeside Lab., U. Iowa, summer 1965; cons. endangered and threatened species U.S. Fish and Wildlife Svc. Dept. Interior, 1976-83; cons. Davey Tree Expert Co., 1979-85, Ohio Natural Areas Coun., 1983; bd. dirs. Bot. Gardens, 1972-93. Author: Ferns and Other Pteridophytes of Iowa, 1959, Vascular Plants of Clinton, Jackson and Jones Counties, Iowa, 1962, The Dicotyledoneae of Ohio, Part 2, 1995; editor: Endangered and Threatened Plants of Ohio, 1983. Active YMCA-YWCA Students in Govt., Washington, 1950; personnel placement U.S. Census Bur., Washington, 1950-51; Quaker Internat. Vol., Fed. Republic Germany, 1951. Served with U.S. Army, 1945-46. Recipient Osborn award Ohio Biol. Survey, 1994; dedicatee Kent Bog State Nature Preserve, Ohio Dept. Natural Resources, 1995; NSF predoctoral fellow, 1957-58. Fellow AAAS, Ohio Acad. Scis. (chair Ohio flora com. 1969—), Explorers Club; mem. Am. Soc. Plant Taxonomists, Internat. Assn. Plant Taxonomists, Bot. Soc. Am., Nature Conservancy, Wilderness Soc., So. Appalachian Bot. Soc., Blue Key, Sigma Xi. Home: 548 Bowman Dr Kent OH 44240-4512

COOPER-SERVAITES, PAMELA SUE, nursing administrator; b. Flint, Mich., July 8, 1941; d. Francis S. Jr. and Pauline A. (Ringle) Pierce; m. Kenneth Cooper, June 22, 1963 (div. Aug. 1968); children: Kenneth Jr., Robert; m. Jerome Servaites, Nov. 16, 1991; stepchildren: Mathew, Mara. RN, Miami Valley Hosp. Sch.Nursing, Dayton, Ohio, 1962; BS, St. Joseph's Coll., North Windham, Maine, 1981. Quality assurance nurse VA Med. Ctr., Dayton, 1981; dir. nursing Med. Pers. Pool, Dayton, 1982, Nurses Calling, Dayton, 1983-84, Nursing Systems, Dayton, 1985-86; dir. utilization rev. and quality assurance All Care, Inc., Dayton, 1987, Wright Choice Health Plan, Dayton, 1987; cons. long term care facilities Dayton, 1985—; dir. nursing Covenant House, Dayton, 1989-90, Stillwater Ctr., Dayton, 1990-93, Kettering (Ohio) Convalescent Ctr., 1993-94; dir. provider rels. IHS at Spring Creek, Huber Heights, Ohio, 1994-95; case mgr. IHS Dayton Post Acute Network, Dayton, Ohio, 1995—; bd. dirs. Joint Vocat. Schs. Practical Nursing, Dayton, 1990—. Mem. Nat. Assn. Dirs. Nursing Adminstrn./Long Term Care, Ohio Assn. Dirs. Nursing Adminstrn./Long Term Care, Miami Valley Continuity of Care Coun. Episcopalian. Home and Office: 7816 Port Cir Centerville OH 45459-4106

COOPERSMITH, BERNARD IRA, obstetrician, gynecologist, educator; b. Chgo., Oct. 19, 1914; s. Morris and Anna (Shulder) C.; m. Beatrice Klass, May 26, 1940; children: Carol, Cathie. BS cum laude, U. Ill., 1936, MD cum laude, 1938. Diplomate Am. Bd. Ob-Gyn. Intern Michael Reese Hosp., Chgo., 1938-39, resident in ob-gyn., 1939-42; pvt. practice medicine specializing in ob-gyn. Chgo., 1942—; mem. staff Prentice Women's Hosp. of Northwestern Meml. Hosp., Michael Reese Hosp., Mt. Sinai Hosp., Chgo. Maternity Ctr.; asst. prof. ob-gyn Northwestern U. Med. Sch., Chgo., 1948—. Contbr. articles to profl. jours. Pres. Barren Found. Chgo., 1971-73. Fellow ACS; mem. AMA, Ill. Med. Soc., Chgo. Med. Soc., Chgo. Gynecol. Soc., Cen. Assn. Ob-Gyn, Am. Coll. Ob-Gyn, Alpha Omega Alpha. Jewish. Clubs: Bryn Mawr Country, Carleton. Home: 1110 N Lake Shore Dr Chicago IL 60611-1054 Office: 680 N Lake Shore Dr Ste 1030 Chicago IL 60611-4402

COORDSEN, GEORGE, state legislator; b. Fairburg, Nebr., Aug. 13, 1935; m. Janice Fegter, 1956; children: Debra (Mrs. David Fangmeier), Kevin, Valerie (Mrs. Brice). Farmer Nebr.; mem. from 32d dist. Nebr. State Senate, Lincoln, 1987—, mem. banking, comml. and com. com., vice chmn. revenue and bldg. maintenance com. Chmn. Nebr. Grail & Sorghum Bd., 1981-86; dir. U.S. Feed Grains Coun., 1981-86. Named to Hall of Fame, Nebr. Agr., 1989. Address: RR 1 Box 122 Hebron NE 68370-9780 also: State Legislature State Capitol Lincoln NE 68509*

COPELAND, CHRISTINE SUSAN, therapist; b. Milw., Jan. 8, 1949; d. Walter Horace and Doris Esther (Becker) C. BA in Psychology, Valparaiso (Ind.) U., 1971; MS in Psychology, U. Wis., 1974. Psychologist Curative Workshop, Green Bay, Wis., 1974-77, No. Wis. Ctr. for Developmentally Disabled, Chippewa Falls, Wis., 1977-86; behavior therapist Midelfort Clinic, Eau Claire, Wis., 1986-93, Systems Counseling and Cons., Inc., Eau Claire, 1994-95; pvt. practice Chippewa Falls, Wis., 1995—. Mem. APA (assoc.), Am. Assn. Mental Retardation, Assn. for Advancement of Behavior Therapy, Wis. Psychol. Assn., C.H.A.D.D., Beta Sigma Phi (officer Wis. chpt. 1977—, Woman of the Yr. 1979). Home and Office: 17962 W Edgewater Dr Chippewa Falls WI 54729-8753

COPELAND, FRED E., state legislator; b. Cooter, Mo., June 12, 1932; m. Patricia Ann Weber, 1952 (div.); m. Ginna Lee Hequembourg, 1980; children: Fred, Lisa Ann, Leslie Ann. Student, Ark. State Coll. State rep. dist. 161 Mo. Ho. of Reps., 1960—; real estate exec. and farmer. Home: 30 Greenbriar Dr New Madrid MO 63869-1225*

COPELAND, HENRY JEFFERSON, JR., former college president; b. Griffin, Ga., June 13, 1936; s. Henry Jefferson and Emory (Drake) C.; m. Laura Harper, Dec. 21, 1958; children—Henry Drake, Eleanor Harper. B.A., Baylor U., 1958; Ph.D, Cornell U., 1966. Instr. Cornell U., Ithaca, N.Y., 1965-66; asst. prof. history Coll. Wooster, Ohio, 1966-69; assoc. dean Coll. Wooster, 1969-74, dean, 1974-77, pres., 1977-95, prof. history, 1995—. Woodrow Wilson fellow, 1960. Democrat. Presbyterian.

COPPOCK, JANET ELAINE, mental health nurse; b. Tipton, Ind., June 2, 1954; d. Jack Donavon and Bonnie Ruth (Luse) Weismiller; divorced; children: Jonathan Andrew, Daniel Jason. Student, Ball State U., 1972-73; ASN, Ind. U., Kokomo, 1977. RN, Ind. RN charge staff and med.-surg. Tipton County Meml. Hosp., Ind., 1977-79; RN psychiatric staff Howard Cmty. Hosp., Kokomo, 1987-89; pvt. nurse Kokomo, 1989-95; RN psychiatric and addiction treatment, instr. Koala Hosp. & Counseling Ctr., Kokomo, 1995—; instr. parenting edn. Kinsey Youth Ctr., Kokomo, 1995—. Author: Poetic Reflections, Expressions and Inspirations, 1986, Faithful Resolutions, 1993. Recipient Golden Poet award World Poetry Orgn., 1987, 88. Mem. Nurses Svc. Orgn., Writers' Ctr. Indpls., Ind. U. Alumni Assn. (life), Kokomo H.S. Band Boosters, PTA Kokomo Ctr. Schs. Republican. Home: 2711 President Ln Kokomo IN 46902 Office: Koala Hosp & Counseling Ctr 2715 S Albright Kokomo IN 46902

CORAM, COLLEEN ANN (O'BRIEN), Spanish language educator; b. Columbia, Mo., Jan. 4, 1949; d. Thomas D. and Madelyn Ruth (Schuering) O'Brien; m. Steven B. Coram,, Feb. 24, 1967; children: Melissa Coram Addison, Amy Coram Harris. BA in Spanish and English Edn., Kearney State Coll., 1985, MA Spanish Edn., mid. sch. endorsement, 1990. Cert.

mid. sch./secondary edn. Spanish and English, Nebr. Paraprofl. Learning Skills Ctr., Kearney, 1983-85; libr. Reference/Interloan Ctr. Kearney State Coll., 1984-86; Spanish educator Kearney Jr. H.S. (now named Horizon Mid. Sch.), 1986—; co-owner Coram-Lind Spanish Lang. Cons., Kearney, 1992—. Co-author: (reference guidebook) Quick Reference Guide-Spanish for Medical Professionals, 1992. Recipient Spl. Recognition Christa McAuliff award, 1993. Mem. NEA, Nebr. Fgn. Lang. Assn., Nebr. Frameworks (fgn. lang. facilitator 1995—), Kearney Edn. Assn. (treas. 1992, 93), Alpha Delta Kappa. Roman Catholic. Home: RR3 Box 15A Kearney NE 68847 Office: Horizon Middle Sch 913 W 35th Kearney NE 68847

CORAN, ARNOLD GERALD, pediatric surgeon, educator; b. Boston, Apr. 16, 1938; s. Charles and Anne (Cohen) C.; m. Susan Williams, Nov. 17, 1960; children: Michael, David, Randi Beth. BA cum laude, Harvard U., 1959, MD cum laude, 1963. Diplomate Am. Bd. Surgery, Am. Bd. Thoracic Surgery, Am. Bd. Pediatric Surgery, Am. Bd. Surg. Critical Care. Intern Peter Bent Brigham Hosp., Boston, 1963-64, resident in surgery, 1964-68, chief surg. resident, 1969; resident in surgery Children's Hosp. Med. Ctr., Boston, 1965-66, sr. surg. resident, 1966, chief surg. resident, 1968; instr. surgery Harvard, Cambridge, Mass., 1967-69; asst. clin. prof. surgery George Washington U., 1970-72; head physician pediatric surgery Los Angeles County-U. So. Calif. Med. Center, 1972-74; asst. prof. surgery U. So. Calif., 1972-73, assoc. prof., 1973-74; prof. surgery U. Mich., Ann Arbor, 1974—; head sect. pediatric surgery U. Mich. Hosp., 1974—; Surgeon-in-chief Mott Children's Hosp. Editor Pediatric Surgery Internat.; contbr. over 300 articles to profl. jours. Served to lt. comdr. MC AUS. Fellow ACS; mem. Am. Acad. Pediatrics, Am. Surg. Assn., Soc. Univ. Surgeons, Am. Pediatric Surg. Assn., Western, Central surg. assns. Home: 505 E Huron St Apt 802 Ann Arbor MI 48104-1541 Office: C S Mott Childrens Hosp Pediatric Surgery Assocs Ann Arbor MI 48109-0245

CORBET, DONALD LEE, audio company executive, technical systems educator; b. Dayton, Ohio, Dec. 1, 1959; s. John Rodger and Barbara Lou (Timmerman) C.; 1 child, Jessica Lea. Student, Wright State U., 1978-80, Capitol U., Columbus, Ohio, 1991—; cert. NCR service, NCR, Columbia, S.C., 1986; cert. communication theory, Codex, Boston, 1987; student, Capital U., 1991—. Computer cons. Radio Shack, Dayton, 1981-82; computer service tech. Reynolds and Reynolds, Peoria, Ill., 1982-84; tech. systems instr. Reynolds and Reynolds, Dayton, 1984-91; sr. instr., 1991-94, team leader tech. tng., 1994—; cert. repair, trainer Compaq Computers, Houston, Calif., 1995—; owner D. L. Cobet Audio, Dayton, 1980—; career developer Success Motivation Inst., Waco, Tex., 1986-88; bd. dirs. Mgmt. Documentation Assn., Dayton; cons. SIGI Wittenburg U., Springfield, Ohio, 1982; speaker various clubs and lodges. Author: Understanding Customer Satisfaction, 1987; co-author: Everybody's Guide to P.C.'s, 1986; composer (recs.) Thunder Road Theme, 1985, Twister film soundtrack, 1986, Chrysler Interactive Training Theme; producer, dir. various ednl. computer videos. Recipient Dayton Music Link award Hands Across Am., 1986. Home: 10317 Black Birch Dr Centerville OH 45458-9473 Office: PO Box 1005 Dayton OH 45401-1005

CORBETT, FRANK JOSEPH, advertising executive; b. N.Y.C., July 5, 1917; s. Daniel and Frances (Manson) C.; m. Dolores Pierce, May 23, 1959; children: Kenneth, Beverly. Ph.G., Columbia U., 1938; postgrad., U. So. Calif., 1947, UCLA, 1947, NYU, 1945-46. Pharmacy mgr. N.Y.C., 1938-41; sales rep. Upjohn, Inc., N.Y.C., 1941-43; dist. sales mgr., mgr. market research dept. William R. Warner Co., N.Y.C., 1944-46; dir. product devel. and market research, advt. mgr., also asst. to dir. sales Harrower Lab., Inc., Glendale, Calif., 1946-51, Jersey City, 1946-51; account exec. Jordan-Sieber Advt. Agy., Chgo., 1951-55; ptnr., v.p. Jordan, Sieber & Corbett (advt.), 1955-60; cons. pharm. field, 1960-61; founder, pres. Frank J. Corbett, Inc. (advt.), 1961-78, chmn. bd., 1978-93, vice chmn., 1993—. Mem. Nat. Wholesalers Drug Assn., Midwest Pharm. Advt. Club, Pharm. Mfrs. Assn. Home: 1320 N State Pky Chicago IL 60610-2118 Office: Frank J Corbett Inc 211 E Chicago Ave Chicago IL 60611-2616*

CORBETT, GAIL ANN, plant ecologist, educator; b. Rapid River, Mich., May 23, 1936; d. Joseph and Charlotte Marie (Ames) Rushford; m. Robert Guy Corbett, Aug. 31, 1959; children: Erica Ann, Jonathan Matthew. BA, U. Mich., 1958, MS, 1960, PhD, 1967. Rsch. asst. U. Mich., Ann Arbor, 1958-59, teaching fellow, 1959-61; instr. West Va. U., Morgantown, 1963, rsch. assoc., 1968-69; lectr. U. Akron, Ohio, 1977; instr. Western Res. Acad., Hudson, Ohio, 1987-88; instr. Ill. State U., Normal, 1990, adj. prof., 1990—, lectr., 1994, 95, 96; cons. Odot Rsch. Geology dept., U. Akron, 1975, Frank Thomas & Assocs., Canton, Ohio, 1980, Seagull Devel. Corp., Canal Fulton, Ohio, 1983-84; vol. Cuyahoga Valley Nat. Recreation Area, Peninsula, Ohio, 1984-89. Contbr. articles to profl. jours. Mem. Svc. League, Morgantown, W.Va., 1967-69; vol. Parklands Found., Bloomington, Ill., 1993—. Recipient Orion Scott award, U. Mich., 1954, Bradley Moore Davis award, 1958, Rackham fellowship, 1961, NSF fellowship, 1961. Mem. AAAS, Am. Forestry Assn., Am. Soc. Plant Taxonomists, Ecological Soc. Am., So. Appalachian Botanical Club, Nature Conservancy, Audubon Soc., Sigma Xi, Phi Sigma. Home: 504 Wellesley Dr Normal IL 61761-2445

CORBETT, JOHN DUDLEY, chemistry educator; b. Yakima, Wash., Mar. 23, 1926; s. Alexander Hazen and Elizabeth (Dudley) C.; m. Irene Lienkaemper, Aug. 7, 1948; children: John Scott, Julia Barton, James Dudley. B.S. cum laude, U. Wash., 1948, Ph.D. (duPont research fellow), 1952. Asst. prof., asso. chemist Iowa State U. dept. chemistry and Ames Lab. AEC (now Dept. of Energy), 1952-58; asso. prof., chemist Iowa State U. and Ames Lab. AEC, 1958-63, prof., sr. chemist, 1963—, disting. prof. scis. and humanities, 1983—, chmn., div. chief, 1968-73, program dir., materials chemistry, 1974-78; chmn. molten salts Gordon Research Confs., 1963, mem. council, 1964-67; cons. E.I. duPont de Nemours & Co., 1956-63, 73-79, Oak Ridge Nat. Lab., 1969-72, Monsanto, 1977-78. Contbr. articles to profl. jours. Served with USNR, 1944-46. Recipient A. von Humboldt Sr. U.S. scientist award, 1985, Outstanding Sci. Accomplishments award U.S. Dept. Energy, 1987, Sustained Outstanding Rsch. in Materials Chemistry award, 1995, J.C. Bailar Jr. medal U. Ill., 1988. Mem. Nat. Acad. Scis., Am. Chem. Soc. (councilor, past chmn. Ames sect., Iowa award 1984, Midwest award 1985, award in inorganic Chemistry 1986), AAUP, Sigma Xi, Phi Lambda Upsilon, Phi Kappa Phi, Pi Mu Epsilon, Delta Tau Delta. Episcopalian. Home: 2337 Woodview Dr Ames IA 50014-8259

CORBETT, SUZANNE ELAINE, food writer, film producer, marketing executive, food historian; b. St. Louis, Jan. 23, 1953; d. George Edward and Opal Laverne (Duncan) Traxel; m. James Joseph Corbett, Jr., July 17, 1970; 1 child, James J. III. BA, Webster U., 1994, MA in Media Comm., 1995. Cert. culinary profl. Tchr. Inst. Continuing Edn. St. Louis C.C., 1976—; tchr. cmty. edn. Lindbergh Sch. Dist. Pub. Schs., St. Louis, 1983-89; confectioner/caterer Suzanne Corbett Seasonal Confections, St. Louis, 1977-84; test baker Fleishman's Yeast, St. Louis, 1983; food stylist St. Louis, 1980—, rsch. cons./food mktg. and rsch. food/product history, 1994; rsch. cons. PanCor Prodns., 1994—; food historian/folklorist St. Louis County Parks and Recreation, Mo. Hist. Soc., St. Louis Art Mus., Colonial Dames Am.; food media trainer Internat. Assn. Culinary Profls., 1990; ALHFAM lectr. in field. Author: Cowpuncher's Provision, 1988, River Fare, 1990, Pharoh's Pheast-Food from the Nile, 1991, Tips from Missouri Win Country, 1993; food writer, cookbook editor St. Louis Bugle food editor, columnist, 1991-96; columnist Sr. Circuit Newspaper. Bd. dirs. St. Louis South sect. Am. Heart Assn., Historyonics Theatre Co.; mem. Mo. Grape and Wine Adv. Bd. Recipient Folklife Greentree grant award Ralston Purina, 1989, grant award Commerce Bank, 1990, grant award Wetterau Foods, 1991. Mem. Women in Communications (pres. St. Louis chpt. 1996—, Communication awards 1989, 90, 91, 92, 93, 94, 95, 96), Mo. Press Women (past pres., Communication award 1989, 96, Communicator of Yr. 1993), Victorian Soc. Am. (past pres. St. Louis chpt.), James Beard Found. (charter), Am. Inst. Wine and Food, Internat. Assn. Culinary Profls. (cert., culinary historian Boston and Ann Arbor, internat. conf. com. 1990), Assn. Ind. Video and Filmmakers, St. Louis Press Club (former co-editor Courier, Pres.' award, Press Club Charitable Fund pres. 1993-94), Nat. Fedn. Press Women (Communication and Writing awards), Nat. Trust for Hist. Preservation, St. Louis Culinary Soc. (sec., bd. dirs.), Order Eastern Star. Roman Catholic. Home and Office: 5850 Pebble Oak Dr Saint Louis MO 63128-1412

CORBETT, WILLIAM ARNOLD, securities broker, writer; b. Chgo., July 5, 1947; s. Thomas Cyril and Dorothy Huttman Corbett; m. Deborah Jane Holden, Aug. 13, 1973; children: Charles, Leah, Stephan, Nora. Student, Marquette U., 1965-66; BA, U. Mich., 1969. Cert. fin. planner; registered investment advisor. Real estate salesman Schmidt Real Estate-Klotzbach Realty, Traverse City, Mich., 1974-79; securities broker Manley Bennett McDonald & Co., Traverse City, 1980-84; asst. branch mgr. First of Mich. Corp., Traverse City, 1984-87, securities broker, 1987—, br. mgr., 1994—; owner, editor Corbett Comms. Co., Traverse City, 1994—. Author: Financial Guide for Catholics, 1989; editor Grand Traverse Rep., 1992—; contbr. articles to religious mags. Mem. fin. coun. Immaculate Conception Cath. Ch., Traverse City, 1985-93; Cath. Diocese of Gaylord, Mich., 1993—; mem. bldg. adv. com. Goodwill Industries, Traverse City, 1989-90; mem., cert. user Traverse Cmty. TV, 1994—; exec. com. Grand Traverse GOP, 1992—. Recipient Golden Elephant award Grand Traverse GOP, 1995. Mem. Grand Traverse Area U. of Mich. Club (pres. 1984-86, alumnus of the year 1987), Ancient Order of Hibernians (sec. 1988-89, Lord Mayor Traverse City 1990), Elks. Home: 1405 Randolph St PO Box 1125 Traverse City MI 49685-1125 Office: First of Michigan Corp 10850 E Traverse Hwy Traverse City MI 49684-1315

CORBIN, BRIAN ROLAND, religious human services administrator; b. Winslow, Maine, July 18, 1962; s. Maurice Donald Joseph and Nancy Carolyn (Violette) C.; m. Donna Marie DeBlasio, July 25, 1992. BA, Cath. U., 1984; ABD, MIT, 1987, postgrad. Rsch. intern Ctr. of Concern, Washington, 1980-84; rsch. asst. Cath. U. of Am., Washington, 1981-84; asst. to pres. Ctr. for Sci. in Pub. Interest, Washington, 1984; rsch. asst., teaching asst. MIT, Cambridge, 1984-87; dir. Cath. Diocese of Youngstown, Ohio, 1987—; pres./CEO Cath. Charities Housing Opportunities Corp., Youngstown, 1995—; cons. DF Econs. Corp., Cambridge, Mass., 1986-88; bd. dirs. Campaign for Human Devel., Youngstown, Cath. Relief Svcs., Youngstown; chairperson Coalition for Community Investment, Youngstown, 1989-92, Cath. Conf. Ohio, Columbus, 1990-92. Contbr. articles to jours. Active Citizens League, Youngstown, 1989-92, AIDS Task Force, Youngstown, 1988-92, City Housing Bd., Youngstown, 1991-92; coord. Leadership Youngstown/Warren, 1991-92; mem. joint com. on religion and politics, MIT-Harvard U., 1985-87,; mem. joint com. on polit. devel., MIT-Harvard, 1986-87. Mem. Am. Polit. Sci. Assn., Roundtable of Social Action Dirs. Office: Cath Diocese of Youngstown 144 W Wood St Youngstown OH 44503-1005

CORBIN, DAVID R., state legislator; b. July 20, 1943; m. Betty Corbin. Mem. Ho. of Reps., Topeka, 1990-92; U.S. senator from Kans. Topeka, 1993—; chmn. agrl. com.; mem. edn., assessment and taxation coms.; farmer and commodity broker; market analyst Kans. Agrl. Network, 1983—. Mem. Farm Bur., Livestock Assn., Nat. Assn. Farmbroadcasters, El Dorado and Augusta C. of C., Lions, Kiwanis. Republican. Home: RR 1 Box 73 Towanda KS 67144-9742*

CORBIN, MARK R., project engineer; b. Redbud, Ill., May 15, 1954. BS in Mech. Engring., Kans. State U., 1987. Project engr. McCracken Concrete Pipe Machine, Sioux City, Iowa, 1987—. Patentee in field. Leader Boy Scouts, Sioux City, 1990—. Republican. Lutheran. Office: McCracken Concrete Pipe Machine PO Box 1708 Sioux City IA 51102-1708

CORBIN, ROBERT L., state legislator; b. Appleton, Wis., Dec. 8, 1922; s. Lyle Dalton and Minnie (Yokers) C.; m. Edith Peters, 1948; children: Carol, Lynn Corbin Costanza. BA, Otterbein Coll. Buyer Rike Kumler, 1940-53; exec. pres. Foodcraft Mgmt. Corp., 1953-64, pres., 1964-79; mem. Oho Ho. of Reps. Columbus, 1977—, asst. majority floor leader, 1996. Named Restaurateur of Yr., Miami Valley Restaurant Assn., 1963. Mem. Ohio Restaurant Assn. (past pres.), Walnut Grove C. of C., Otterbein Coll. Alumni Assn. (past pres.), Dayton Agonis Club (past pres.), Pi Kappa Phi. Methodist. Home: 135 Shadybrook Dr Dayton OH 45459-1930*

CORCORAN, JAMES ALBERT, firefighter; b. Sumpter, S.C., May 8, 1951; s. George I.S. and Wilma Louise (Beckmann) C. BS magna cum laude, Madonna U., 1989. Capt. firefighter City of Southfield, Mich., 1974—. With U.S. Army, 1970-72, Germany. Mem. Internat. Assn. Firefighters, Sierra Club (svc. award 1991), Am. Sailing Inst. (instr.). Home: 2593 Columbia Berkley MI 48072 Office: City of Southfield 26000 Evergreen Southfield MI 48075

CORCORAN, KEVIN MICHAEL, newspaper reporter; b. Indpls., June 2, 1965; s. Michael Joseph and Joan Phyllis (Yauch) C.; m. Trisha Kim Essig, June 26, 1993. BS in Journalism, Ind. U., 1988. Corr. AP, Indpls., 1987-88; Sears congl. intern U.S. Rep. Peter Kostmayer, Washington, 1988; reporter The Jour.-Gazette, Ft. Wayne, Ind., 1988-91; statehouse reporter The News-Sentinel, Indpls., 1991-95, The Times of N.W. Ind., Indpls., 1996—; advisor, co-founder Ind. H.S. Journalism Partnership Project, 1994—. Active Big Bros., Indpls., 1993—; host parent Adventures in Real Comm., 1995. Recipient Fraternal Order of Police award, 1989, 1st Pl. Journalism award Hoosier State Press Assn., 1992, Journalist of Yr. award Ind. Trial Lawyers Assn., 1993, Sch. Bell award Ind. State Tchrs. Assn., 1993, Friend of H.S. Press award Ind. H.S. Press Assn., 1995, Washington Monthly Jour. award 1995. Mem. Soc. Profl. Journalists (3 awards 1993), Nat. Inst. for Computer Assisted Reporting, Investigative Reporters and Editors (2 awards 1990), Indpls. Press Club. Roman Catholic. Home: 805 N Audubon Rd Indianapolis IN 46219 Office: The Times 155 W Washington St Ste 220 Indianapolis IN 46204

CORCORAN, MARY ALICE, medical surgical nurse, educator; b. West Point Twp., Wis., Sept. 19, 1934; d. Roman P. and Agnes M. (Ryan) Boehmer; m. Edward J. Corcoran, Aug. 16, 1958; children: Patrick, Bridget (dec.). Diploma, St. Mary's Sch. Nursing, Milw., 1955; cert. pub. health nurse, Marquette U., 1957. RN, Wis.; cert. diabetes educator. Nurse clinician IV U. Wis. Univ. Health Svc., Madison, 1967—. Mem. hypertension faculty Am. Heart Assn., 1978-94. Mem. Am. Diabetes Assn. (Wis. bd. dirs. 1985-91, Vol. of Yr. award 1988, Program Vol. of Yr. award 1994, Outstanding Svc. award), Am. Assn. Diabetes Educators. Office: U Wis Health Svc 1552 University Ave Madison WI 53705-4084

CORDELL, STEVEN MARK, small business owner; b. Kansas City, Mo., Aug. 18, 1955; s. Arthur Orville and Eva (Miller) C.; m. Sandra Sue Price, Oct. 24, 1981; 1 child, Elizabeth Ann. AA, Penn Valley Coll., 1975; BA, U. Mo., 1977; MBA, Mid Am. Nazarene Coll., 1994. Store mgr. Radio Shack, Kansas City, 1977-78; sales rep. Harris-Hansen Co., Grandview, Mo., 1978-80; jr. ptnr. Palatine Engring., Mission, Kans., 1980-82; sales engr. T. L. Dowell and Assoc., Overland Park, Kans., 1983-85; sales mgr. Independent Electric, Kansas City, 1985-89; gen. mgr. North Supply div. United Telecom, North Kansas City, 1989-91; lead quality facilitator network ops. U.S. Sprint Corp., Overland Park, Kans., 1991-94; owner Money Mailer of South Johnson County, Olathe, Kans., 1994—. Mem. Kansas City Blues Soc., Rotary of Olathe, Olathe C. of C., Phi Theta Kappa. Home: 14405 S Kaw Dr Olathe KS 66062-4864 Office: Money Mailer South Johnson County 14405 S Kaw Dr Olathe KS 66062-4864

CORDERMAN, DOUGLAS GEORGE, retired non-profit organization executive; b. Ft. Sill, Okla., Sept. 3, 1931; s. W. Preston and Virginia (Sandt) C.; m. Joan Jaeckel, Nov. 30, 1974; children: Susan, David, Lisa, John, Jean, Daniel. A.B., Dartmouth Coll., 1952; J.D., Harvard U., 1955; D.S. (hon.), Fla. Inst. Tech., 1976. Contract adminstr. Gen. Dynamics Corp., Rochester, N.Y., 1958-60; mgr. contracts Dresser Industries, Houston, 1960-62; asst. mgr. adminstrn. McDonnell Aircraft Co., St. Louis, 1962-64; mgr. contracts Electronics and Space div. Emerson Electric Co., St. Louis, 1964-69, dir. adminstrn., 1969-71, v.p. adminstrn., 1971-78, sr. v.p., 1978-88; corp. dir. Product Liability, 1988-90; pres. U. S. Nat. Sr. Sports Orgn., 1990-95. Contbr. articles to profl. publs. Mem. vestry Good Shepherd Episcopal Ch., St. Louis, 1995—, St. Timothy's Episcopal Ch., St. Louis, 1975-78, 81-83; mem. alumni council Dartmouth Coll., Hanover, N.H., 1979-81; bd. dirs. U.S. Olympic Com., 1990-95. Fellow Nat. Contract Mgmt. Assn. (nat. pres. 1975-77, Blanche Witte Meml. award 1970, hon. life mem.); mem. Am. Def. Preparedness Assn. (bd. dirs. St. Louis chpt. 1973-88, pres. 1981-82), Nat. Security Indsl. Assn. (hon. life mem., trustee 1980-90, exec. com. 1985-90, chmn. 1987-88), Navy League (hon. life mem.). Republican. Club: Norwood Hills Country (St. Louis). Avocations: family, running, skiing, swimming, triathlons.

CORDES, EUGENE HAROLD, pharmacy and chemistry educator; b. York, Nebr., Apr. 7, 1936; s. Elmer Henry and Ruby Mae (Hofeldt) C.; m. Shirley Ann Morton, Nov. 9, 1957; children: Jennifer Eve, Matthew Henry James. B.S., Calif. Inst. Tech., 1958; Ph.D., Brandeis U., 1962. Instr. chemistry Ind. U., Bloomington, 1962-64, asst. prof., 1964-66, assoc. prof., 1966-68, prof., 1968-79, chmn., 1972-78; exec. dir. biochemistry Merck, Sharp and Dohme Research Labs., Rahway, N.J., 1979-84, v.p. biochemistry, 1984-87; v.p. research and devel. Eastman Pharmaceuticals, Malvern, Pa., 1987-88; pres. Sterling Winthrop Pharms. Rsch. div. Sterling Winthrop Inc., Collegeville, Pa., 1988-94; prof. U. Mich., Ann Arbor, 1995—. Author: (with Henry Mahler) Biological Chemistry, 1966, 2d. edit., 1971, Basic Biological Chemistry, 1969, (with Riley Schaeffer) Chemistry, 1973; also articles. NIH Career Devel. award, 1966; Alfred P. Sloan Found. fellow, 1968. Mem. AAAS, Am. Soc. Biol. Chemists. Home: 220 Barton North Dr Ann Arbor MI 48105-1016

CORDES, SAM MEADE, agricultural economist; b. Sturgis, S.D., Nov. 15, 1943; s. Milton C. and Hallie Alaska (Funk) C.; m. Patricia Ellen Brown, Dec. 21, 1985; children: Kelly, Jill, Carter, Tanya. BS in Agrl. Economics, S.D. State U., 1967; PhD in Agrl. Economics, Wash. State U., 1973. Exec. dir. gov's. task force on rural affairs Gov's. Office, Olympia, Wash., 1971-72; from asst. to assoc. prof. agrl. econs. Pa. State U., State College, 1972-85; head dept. agrl. econs. U. Wyo., Laramie, 1985-89; head dept. agrl. econs. U. Nebr., Lincoln, 1989-94, prof. agrl. econs., 1989—, dir. Ctr. for Rural Revitalization, 1991—; mem. HSS Nat. Adv. Com., Washington, 1988-92, USDA Nat. Adv. Com., Washington, 1992; commr. Nebr. Rural Devel. Commn., Lincoln, 1993—; faculty cons. CSRS, USDA, Washington, 1993—. Author: (with others) Rural Health Services, 1994; contbr. articles to profl. jours.; exec. producer: (film) Condition Critical, 1981 (Ace award 1983). Trustee Ctr. Cmty. Hosp., State College, 1983-85; mem. Nebr. Agrl. Rels. Coun., Lincoln, 1990—, Nebr. Agribusiness Club, Lincoln, 1990—. Named regional finalist White House Fellowship Program, Washington, 1981; recipient Disting. Rschr. award Nat. Rural Health Assn., Kansas City, Mo., 1996. Mem. Internat. Assn. Agrl. Econs., Am. Agrl. Econs. Assn. (bd. dirs. 1994—), Coun. on Food, Agr. and Rsch. Econs. (bd. dirs. 1993—), Coun. on Agr., Sci. and Tech., Rural Sociol. Soc. Office: Univ Nebr 58 Filley Hall Lincoln NE 68583

CORDONI, BARBARA KEENE, special education educator; b. Peoria, Ill., Dec. 21, 1933; d. Edward Leland Keene and Grace (Wolpert) Werner; m. Gregory Walter Kupiec, June 9, 1984; children: Mark, Heather, Lance, Tara. BA, Southwestern U., 1955; MEd, Duke U., 1974, EdD, 1976; D in Ednl. Psychology. Certified Sch. Psychologist Specialization in Learning Disabilities. Tchr. Catskills (N.Y.) Pub. Sch., 1955-56, Oneonta (N.Y.) Pub. Sch., 1956-57; dir. Nursery Sch., Woodstock, N.Y., 1959-62; dir. pvt. sch. Merritt Island, Fla., 1967-72; resource tchr. Brevard County Schs., Merritt Island, 1972-73; clin. instr. Duke U., Durham, N.C., 1973-75; asst. prof. Greensboro (N.C.) Coll., 1975-77, So. Ill. U., Carbondale, Ill., 1977-81; assoc. prof. So. Ill. U., Carbondale, 1981-87, prof., 1987—; coordinator So. Ill. U. Clin. Ctr. Achieve Program, Carbondale, 1977—; cons. in field. Author: Living with a Learning Disability, 1987, rev., 1990; contbr. numerous articles to profl. jours. Mem. Ill. Gov.'s Adv. Council, Springfield, Ill., 1982-90; participant Pres.'s Commn. for Employment of the Handicapped, Washington. Named Outstanding Woman of the Year, 1970, Brevard County Tchr. of the Year, 1972, Fla. Dist. Tchr. of the Year, 1973; recipient Disting. Teaching award, 1977, Wallace Phillips Meml. Award for Outstanding Svc. in the Field of Learning Disabilities, 1977. Mem. Coun. for Exceptional Children, Learning Disabilities Assn. Am., N.C. Assn. for Rsch. in Edn., Am. Ednl. Rsch. Assn., Nat. Orton Soc., Internat. Acad. for Rsch. in Learning Disabilities, Golden Key, Kappa Delta Pi, Phi Delta Kappa. Democrat. Methodist. Home: 2037 W Lake Rd Murphysboro IL 62966-5630 Office: So Ill U Dept Ednl Psych/Spl Edn Carbondale IL 62901

CORDRY, JIM A., investment broker; b. Rosebud, S.D., Mar. 23, 1951. BFA, U. S.D., 1976. Investment broker Dain Bosworth, Inc., Overland Park, Kans., 1990—. Mem. Profls. Offstage. Office: Dain Bosworth Inc # 100 9401 Indian Creek Pky Ste 100 Overland Park KS 66210-2007

CORE, EDWARD K., state legislator, farmer; m. Joyce Core; children: Tony, Elizabeth Core Orts. BSc, Ohio State U.; postgrad. Antioch Coll. Farmer Rushsylvania, Ohio; mem. Ohio Ho. of Reps. Columbus. Former commr. Logan County, Ohio; former supr. Logan Soil and Water Conservation Dist. Grantee NSF. Mem. Ohio Cattlemen's Assn., Farm Bur., Nat. Fedn. Ind. Bus., AMVETS, NRA, Elks, Sigma Phi Epsilon. Republican. Home: 2450 County Road 118 Rushsylvania OH 43347-9756*

COREY, GLENN MICHAEL, artist, educator; b. Detroit, June 28, 1950; s. Fred Mike and Virginia (Elnicki) C. BA, Mich. State U., 1972; BFA, Wayne State U., 1974, MSLS, 1985; MFA, Schiller Internat. U., Strasbourg, France, 1979; MA, U. N.C., 1984. Cert. continuing edn. Instr. art history N.C. Cen. U., Durham, 1983, Ctr. for Creative Studies, Detroit, 1988-91; tchr. Troy (Mich.) Sch. Dist., 1972—, tennis coach, 1975-77, 79-80, 1986—. One-man shows include C.A.D.E. Gallery, Detroit, 1981, Art Sch. Gallery, Carrboro, N.C., 1982, Western Md. Coll., 1991; exhibited in groups shows, 1977—. Mem. Nat. Art Edn. Assn., U.S. Profl. Tennis Assn. (tennis profl. 1990—), U.S. Tennis Assn. Democrat. Home: 1812 Wickham St Royal Oak MI 48073-1162 Office: Troy Sch Dist 4400 Livernois Rd Troy MI 48098-4777

COREY, JUDITH ANN, educator; b. Peoria, Ill., Dec. 1, 1937; d. Lyle William and Eileen A. (Zigrang) Springston; m. Thomas W. Corey, Aug. 12, 1961; children: John William, Jeffrey Michael, Gregory Lyle, Mark Andrew. BA in Bus., English, Marycrest Coll., 1960; MA in Counseling, Bradley U., 1972. Lic. clin. profl. counselor. Tchr. Riverview Sch., Spring Bay, Ill., 1960-61, Lincoln Sch., East Peoria, Ill., 1963-64; counselor Bradley U., Peoria, Ill., 1972-73; clin. psychologist intern Zeller Zone Ctr., Peoria, Ill., 1973; dean students Morton (Ill.) High Sch., 1974-85; tchr. Jefferson Sch., Morton, 1985—. Campaign work Grace Bunn Lievens Ill. Rep., 89th Dist. Ill., Morton, 1994. Mem. NEA, Ill. Edn. Assn., Ill. State Deans Assn. (historian 1982-84, membership chmn. 1984-85), Morton Edn. Assn. (mem. exec. com. 1989-93, v.p. 1993-95, newsletter editor 1987-90), Phi Kappa Phi (life), Kappa Gamma Pi, Pi Lambda Theta. Roman Catholic. Home: 20432 N Tennessee Ave Morton IL 61550 Office: Jefferson Sch 220 E Jefferson Morton IL 61550

CORFMAN, THOMAS A., editor, newspaper; b. Michigan City, Ind., Dec. 10, 1954; s. Rex M. and Loretta C. (Cullen) C.; m. Carol A. Brook, Sept. 7, 1988; children: Samuel Brook, Jack Brook. BA, Northeastern Ill. U., 1978; MA in English, Vanderbilt U., 1980; JD, DePaul U., 1983; MS in Journalism, Northwestern U., 1990. Assoc. Gensen & Steinback, Chgo., 1983—; pvt. practice Chgo., 1986-90; mng. editor Chgo. Reporter, 1991—. Office: The Chicago Reporter 332 S Michigan Ave Ste 500 Chicago IL 60604-4394

CORIDEN, JOHN P., investment broker; b. Hammond, Ind., Mar. 15, 1945; m. Kathleen L. Dalrymple, Aug. 26, 1978; children: John K., Daniel P. BS, John Carroll State U., 1967; MBS, Ind. U., 1976. Mgr. internat. mktg. Bettele Lab., Columbus, Ohio, 1978-88; investment broker Raffensberger Hughes, South Bend, Ind., 1988-90, A. G. Edwards & Sons Inc., South Bend, 1990—. Pres. Christians in Commerce, South Bend, 1993—; past pres. local kidney found., South Bend, 1992-94; past v.p. Parish Coun., South Bend., 1992—. With U.S. Army, 1969-71. Mem. John Carroll Alumni Assn. (pres. 1985-87). Roman Catholic. Home: 17663 Waxwing Ln South Bend IN 46635-1328 Office: A G Edwards & Sons Inc PO Box 1378 205 W Jefferson South Bend IN 46624

CORK, DONALD BURL, electrical engineer; b. Terre Haute, Ind., Aug. 10, 1949; s. Clay Jr. and Margaret M. (Ellis) C.; m. Carolyn R. Lewis, Nov. 18, 1978. BSEE, U. Evansville, Ind., 1971. Owner Ellcor Electric, West Union, Ill., 1971-73; test engr. Zenith Radio, Paris, Ill., 1973-78, mfg. engr., 1978-81; design engr. TRW Electronics, Marshall, Ill., 1981-84, electrical engr. coord., 1984-88, program mgr., 1988—. Mem. West Union (Ill.) Fire Dept.,

1969—, trustee, 1995; elder West Union Christian Ch. Mem. Eta Kappa Nu, Ea. Ill. Hamateurs (pres. 1971-73), West Union Firemans Assn. (v.p. 1977-78, treas. 1989), Old Nat. Trail Firefighters'. Republican. Home: RR 1 Box 5 West Union IL 62477-9701 Office: TRW TED PO Box 279 Marshall IL 62441-0279

CORKILL, DUANE, electrical, mechanical engineer; b. Mar. 30, 1942. Student, Olivetti, Terrytown, N.Y. Designer Bainbridge R&D, Topeka, Kans., 1978; engring. designer Seymoure Inc., Topeka, 1980-90; pres. Midwest BRD Inc., Topeka, 1990—. Patentee (6) in field. Advisor Vo-Tech. Sch., Topeka.

CORLETTE, ELIZABETH ANN, primary education educator; b. Cleve., Dec. 17, 1965; d. Donald Joseph and Shirley Mae (Campbell) Logar; m. Patrick James Corlette, July 22, 1995. BS in Edn., Slippery Rock U., 1988; MS, Syracuse U., 1989; student, Cleve. State U., 1993. Cert. elem. tchr., Ohio. Tchr. preschoolers with spl. needs Euclid (Ohio) City Schs., 1988-95, Westerville (Ohio) City Schs., 1995—. Vol. Rainbow Babies' and Children's Hosp., Cleve., 1992-95, Friendship Connection Deepwood Ctr., Mentor, Ohio, 1991-95. Mem. Nat. Assn. Edn. Young Children, Autism Soc. Am. Office: Presch Office Hanby Elem Sch 56 S State St Westerville OH 43081

CORLEY, JENNY LYND WERTHEIM, elementary education educator; b. Lincoln, Ill., June 18, 1937; d. Robert Glenn and Nancy Lynd (Hoblit) Wertheim; m. William Gene Corley, Aug. 9, 1959; children: Anne Lynd Corley Baum, Robert William, Scott Elson. BS in Music Edn., U. Ill., 1959, MS in Music Edn., 1961; postgrad., U. Ill., Loyola U., 1985—. Tchr. choral music Mahomet (Ill.)/Seymour K-12, 1959-61; supr. music Fairfax County (Va.), 1961-63; Tchr. music Highland Park (Ill.) 107, 1969, dir. gifted edn., 1969-70; tchr. music Glenview (Ill.) 34, 1981—; sec.-treas. Corley Agroleum Properties, 1993—; water safety instr./trainer ARC; lifeguard instr./trainer Cmty. First Aid, 1995. Dir. mid-Am. bd. ARC, Chgo., 1980-86. Recipient Heart of Gold United Way, 1992, Community Svc. award Ill. Park & Recreation Assn./Ill. Assn. Park Dists., 1994, Disting. Svc. award Boys and Girls Swimming Official, Ill. High Sch. Assn., 1994. Mem. Music Edn. Nat. Conf., North Shore Music Tchrs. Assn. (treas. 1987-90), Jr. League Chgo. (treas. 1978-81), Sigma Alpha Iota, Phi Delta Kappa (found. chmn. 1994—), U. Ill. Music Alumnae (pres. bd. dirs. 1995—). Presbyterian. Home: 744 Glenayre Dr Glenview IL 60025-4411 Office: Springman Sch 2701 Central Rd Glenview IL 60025-4134

CORMANICK, ROSA-MARIA MORENO, academic program coordinator; b. Guatemala, Guatemala, Sept. 4, 1946; d. Armando and Lily (Cordon) Moreno; children: Liza Maria, Angie Michele, David William. Diploma, Liceo Bilingue, Guatemala, 1964; BA, Ohio State U., 1982, MA in Higher Edn. Adminstrn., 1995. Fgn. dept. asst. Banco del Agro, Guatemala, 1964-66; regional mgr. asst. gen. food div. Incasa, Guatemala, 1966-68; translator/asst. human rsch. ctr. Ohio State U., Columbus, 1968-69, dirs. asst. internat. program, 1969-71, acad. program coord. dept. Slavic and East European langs., 1971—; v.p./treas. St. Anthony Sch. Bd., Columbus, 1982-86; bd. dirs. St. Francis DeSales Sch., Columbus, 1991-95; liaison on the comms. and edn. team Adminstrv. Resource Mgmt. Sys. Project, 1996—. Mem. Dobro Slovo Slavic Honor Soc., Phi Kappa Phi. Office: Ohio State U Slavic Dept 232 Cunz Hall 1841 Millikin Columbus OH 43210

CORMICAN, TERRY D., electrical engineer; b. Sullivan, Ind., June 11, 1956. BEE, DeVry Inst., Chgo., 1981. Sr. engr. Vorne Industries, Itasca, Ill., 1980—. Mem. PTA Central H.S., Salem, Wis., 1993-94. Office: Vorne Industries 1445 Industrial Dr Itasca IL 60143-1849

CORNEIL, HAMPTON GASKILL, oil company executive; b. St. Joseph, Mo., Feb. 11, 1914; s. Alonzo Nelson and Mary Emma (Gaskill) C.; m. Laura Pauline Anderson, Feb. 1, 1941 (dec. Jan. 1987); children: Paul Hampton, Mary Elizabeth. BSChemE, Okla. U., 1936. Registered profl. engr., Tex. Chem. engr. Exxon Corp., Baytown, Tex., 1936-52; exec. Exxon Corp., Baytown, Houston, 1952-62, N.Y.C., 1962-79; bd. dirs. Stake Tech. Corp., Ltd., Norval, Ont., Can., 1981—. Contbr. numerous articles to profl. jours.; patentee in field. Mem. SAR (Delaware Crossing chpt.), Am. Inst. Chem. Engring. (emeritus), Am. Chem. Soc. (emeritus). Republican. Presbyterian. Home and Office: 32 Le Mans Ct Shawnee Mission KS 66208-5219

CORNELSEN, PAUL FREDERICK, manufacturing and engineering company executive; b. Wellington, Kans., Dec. 23, 1923; s. John S. and Theresa Albertine (von Klatt) C.; m. Floy Lila Brown, Dec. 11, 1943; 1 son, John Floyd. Student, U. Wichita, 1939-41, 45-46; BS in Mech. Engring, U. Denver, 1949. With Boeing Airplane Co., 1940-41, Ralston Purina Co., St. Louis, 1946—; v.p. internat. div. Ralston Purina Co., 1961-63, adminstrv. v.p., gen. mgr. internat. div., 1963-64, v.p., 1964-68, dir., 1966—, exec. v.p., 1968-78, vice-chmn. bd., chief operating officer, 1978-81, pres. internat. group, 1964-77; pres., chief exec. officer Moehlenpah Industries Inc., St. Louis, 1981-82; chmn., chief exec. officer Mitek Inc. (formerly Moehlenpah), St. Louis, 1982-93; cons. Cornelsen Assocs., Chesterfield, Mo., 1993—; chmn. bd. dirs. Purina Mills Inc.; founding mem. L.Am. Agribus. Investment Corp., 1970—; founding mem. industry coop. program UN Agys., Rome. Trustee Ill. Coll., Jacksonville. 1st lt. AUS, World War II, AUS, Korea. Decorated Silver Star. Home: 506 Fox Ridge Rd Saint Louis MO 63131-3402 Office: 400 Chesterfield Ctr Ste 400 Chesterfield MO 63017-4800

CORNETT, PAUL MICHAEL, SR., lawyer; b. Chgo., Jan. 24, 1949; s. Paul Elvon and Phyllis (Pedone) C.; m. Marianne Elizabeth Hofer, Aug. 14, 1971; children: Paul Michael Jr., Matthew Charles, Nicholas Robert. BBA, Western Mich. U., Kalamazoo, 1971; JD, Marquette U., Milw., 1974. Bar: Supreme Ct. Wis., 1974. Officer, capt. legal asst. USAR, Green Bay, Wis., 1974-87; assoc. atty. Mazza Law Offices, New Berlin, Wis., 1974-75; pvt. practice Shawano, Wis., 1975-77; asst. dist. atty. Shawano County, Menominee County, Wis., 1977-78; dist. atty., corp. coun. Shawano and Menominee County, Wis., 1978-82; assoc., corp. counsel Direnzo and Bomier, Neenah, Wis., 1982-84; ptnr., corp. counsel Van Hoof, Van Hoof and Cornett Law Offices, Little Chute, Wis., 1984-93; ptnr., 1993—; pro bono atty. Legal Svcs. N.E. Wis., Appleton, 1990—; atty. Village of Combined Locks (Wis.) 1984—, Darboy (Wis.) Sanitary Dist., 1984—, Town of Buchanan, Wis., 1984—; mentor to juvenile offender Outagamie County Juvenile Offender Program, Appleton, Wis., 1995—; lawyers in the classroom State Bar of Wis., 1974—; judge Mock Trial Competition, Appleton, Wis., 1993—. Bd. dirs., 1989—, chmn. bd., 1995-96, Heart of Valley C. of C., Kaukauna, Wis.; pres. Little Chute (Wis.) Businessman's Assn., 1994-95; pal to 9 yr. old boy Outagamie County PAL Program, Appleton, Wis., 1994—; bd. mem., chmn. bd., big brother Big Bros. and Big Sisters of Shawano County, Wis., 1976-82. 2nd lt. U.S. Army, 1974. Recipient Dedication award Shawano and Menominee Counties, Wis., 1982, Army Commendation medal, 1987, Army Achievement medal, 1985, USAR, Washington. Mem. KC, State Bar of Wis., Outgamie County Bar Assn., Optimist Internat. Republican. Roman Catholic. Home: 532 Vandenbroek St Little Chute WI 54140 Office: Van Hoof Van Hoof & Cornett Law Offices 200 E Main St Little Chute WI 54140

CORNFIELD, DARLENE, state legislator; b. Aug. 3, 1953; m. John A. Cornfield. Mem. Kans. Ho. of Reps., Topeka, 1990—. Republican. Home: 7 Weatherly Ct Valley Center KS 67147-8547 Office: Kans Ho of Reps State Capitol Topeka KS 66612*

CORNING, JOY COLE, state official; b. Bridgewater, Iowa, Sept. 7, 1932; d. Perry Aaron and Ethel Marie (Sullivan) Cole; m. Burton Eugene Corning, June 19, 1955; children: Carol, Claudia, Ann. BA, U. No. Iowa, 1954. Cert. elem. tchr., Iowa. Tchr. elem. sch. Greenfield (Iowa) Sch. Dist., 1951-53, Waterloo (Iowa) Community Sch. Dist., 1954-55; mem. Iowa Senate, Des Moines, 1984-90, asst. Rep. leader, 1989-90; lt. gov. State of Iowa, Des Moines, 1991—; bd. dirs. Iowa Nat. Bankshares Corp. Pres. Cedar Falls (Iowa) Sch. Bd., 1975-83; state pres. Iowa Talented and Gifted, 1975-77; mem. adv. bd. Waterloo Comty. Playhouse, Cedar Arts Forum; bd. dirs. Iowa Housing Fin. Authority, Des Moines, 1981-84, Iowa Assn. Sch. Bds., Des Moines, 1983-84, Iowa Peace Inst., 1987-91; mem. Edn. Commn. of States, 1987-90, The Caring Found., 1989—. Named Citizen of Yr., Cedar Falls C. of C., 1984; recipient ITAG Disting. Svc. to Iowa's Gifted and Talented Students award, 1991, Pub. Svc. award Iowa Home Econs. Assn., 1994, Friend of Math. award Iowa Coun. Tchrs. of Math., 1995, Iowa State Edn. Assn. Human Rels. award 1996; recognized for Extraordinary Advocacy for Children of Iowa chpt. Nat. Com. for Prevention of Child Abuse. Mem. AAUW, LWV, PEO, Nat. Assn. for Gifted Children (mem. adv. bd. 1991—), Delta Kappa Gamma, Alpha Delta Kappa. Republican. Mem. United Ch. of Christ. Office: State Capitol Office Of Lt Gov Des Moines IA 50319

CORNS, MARVIN A., corporate executive. BA in Comml. Advt., Columbus Coll. of Art and Design, 1975. Auditor Marriott Corp., Cleveland, 1970-75; v.p. Dorcy Internat., Inc., Columbus, 1975—. Office: Dorcy Cycle Corp 3985 Groves Rd Columbus OH 43232-4138

CORNWELL, PAUL M., JR., architect; b. Wheeling, W.Va., Nov. 28, 1966; s. Paul M. Sr. and Penny S. (Kain) C. BS, Kent State U., 1988, BArch, 1989. Registered architect, Ohio. Estimator/field rep. Evick Cons., Inc., St. Clairsville, Ohio, summer 1987, summer 1988; intern architect Brubaker/Brandt, Inc., Columbus, Ohio, 1989-92, Maddox-NBD/Brubaker-Brandt, Inc., Dublin, Ohio, 1992-93, NBBJ, Columbus, 1993-95, Fanning/Howey Assocs., Dublin, Ohio, 1995—; ind. contractor Amway Corp., Ada, Mich., 1991—; architect/engr. C.H.K. Degvel., Belmont, Ohio. Scolar Ruritan Internat., Am. Inst. Architects, Honors Coll. Kent State U. Republican. Lutheran. Home: 5818 Scenic Edge Blvd Dublin OH 43017-2525 Office: Fanning/Howey Assocs Inc 4930 Bradenton Ave Dublin OH 43017

CORONATO, JAMES ALLEN, publishing executive, author; b. Dallas, Apr. 24, 1956; s. E.T. and Patricia Ann (Allen) C.; m. Celeste Constance White, Aug. 3, 1989. BS with highest distinction, Pa. State U., 1978; MS, Carnegie Mellon U., 1980, PhD, 1988. Registered profl. engr.-in-tng., Pa. Pres. Coronato Construction Co., Montclair, N.J., 1975-77; staff engr. Langan Engring. Assocs., Clifton, N.J., 1978; teaching asst. Carnegie Mellon U., Pitts., 1978-80, rsch. asst., 1983-88; sr. rsch. engr. Weidlinger Assocs., N.Y.C., 1981-83; pres. Consolidated Ideas, Shevlin, Minn., 1988—; ptnr. Neill & Assocs., Austin, Tex., 1991; adj. prof. math. Austin C.C., 1991; adj. prof. physics Bemidji (Minn.) State U., 1992; cons. Materials Engring. & Testing, Export, Pa., 1984-85, Expert Techs., Inc., Pitts., 1984-86, Rizzo Assocs., Pitts., 1987; speaker The Learning Network, Austin, 1989. Contbr. articles to profl. jours. Harold A. Thomas scholar, 1983, Richard King Mellon scholar, 1983. Home: RR 1 Box 244 Shevlin MN 56676-9628

CORPORON, CHARLES EDWARD, employment agency owner; b. Arcadia, Kans., Oct. 18, 1927; s. George William and Portteus Virginia (Stephens) C.; m. Therese M. Quirk, Dec. 27, 1986; 1 child, Randy. BS in Edn., Pittsburg (Kans.) State U., 1950, MS, 1951. Zone tng. mgr. Allstate Ins., Northbrook, Ill., 1971-77; corp. tng. dir. Western Pub. Co., Racine, Wis., 1977-83; pres. Wis. Novelty Co., Milw., 1983-86, Quirk-Corporon & Assocs., Inc., Milw., 1986—; bd. dirs., former pres. Ins. Nat. Search, Milw. Staff sgt. Counter-Intelligence Corps, 1945-47. Mem. Nat. Ins. Recruiters Assn. Office: Quirk-Corporon & Assocs Inc 1229 N Jackson Ste 205 Milwaukee WI 53202

CORR, ROBERT MARK, computer company executive; b. Macon, Ga., Oct. 17, 1948; s. Edward and Nancy (Green) C.; m. Patricia Ann McKibben, Mar. 14, 1970; children: Kevin Matthew, Amy Elizabeth. Bachelor of Indsl. Engring., Ga. Tech. U., 1971; MBA with honors, Mich. State U., 1985. Sr. engr. assembly div. GM, Atlanta, 1968-75; sr. staff asst. assembly div. GM, Warren, Mich., 1975-78; supt. mfg. assembly div. GM, Framingham, Mass., 1978; planning dir. GM, Mexico City, 1978-80; sr. adminstr. fin. staff Gen. Motors, Detroit, 1980-84; dir. internat. Pacific ops. Electronic Data Systems, Warren, 1984-86; dir. tech. planning Electronic Data Systems, Troy, Mich., 1986-87, regional mgr., 1988-91; divsn. mgr. EDS Capital Svcs., Detroit, Mich., 1992-95, EDS VSSM, Troy, Mich., 1995—; pres. Advancement of Tech. Through Strategic Cooperation, Warren, 1986-87. Contbg. editor Info World, 1985-88. Mem. Founders Soc., Detroit Inst. Arts, 1987—; commr. Boy Scouts Am., Detroit, 1984-86. Mem. Internat. Platform Assn., Strategic Planning Inst., Am. Productivity and Quality Ctr., Phi Kappa Phi, Beta Gamma Sigma. Office: EDS Capital Svcs Ste 727 750 Tower Dr #524 Troy MI 48007-7019

CORRELL, VERNON W., state legislator; m. Laura Correll. Mem. Kans. Ho. of Reps., Topeka, 1993—. Democrat. Home: PO Box 214 Oswego KS 67356-0214*

CORRIGAN, MARK H.N., psychopharmacology director; b. Boston, July 2, 1957; married. BA in English/Psychology with honors, U. Va., 1979, MD, 1984. Intern and resident in psychiatry Maine Med. Ctr., Portland, Maine, 1984-87, chief resident in psychiatry, 1987-88; staff psychiatrist Clin. Rsch. Unit, Dorothea Dix Hosp., 1988, assoc. dir., clin. rsch unit, 1989-93; clin. asst. prof. U. N.C., Chapel Hill, 1989-93, dir. traumatic stress studies program, 1991-93; assoc. dir. psychopharmacology The Upjohn Co., Kalamazoo, Mich., 1993—; libr. com. Dorthea Dix Hosp., 1989-92; quality assurance com. Maine Med. Ctr., 1988, resident edn. steering com., 1987; admissions com. U. Va. Med. Sch., 1984; pvt. practice Triange Psychiat. Assocs., Raleigh, N.C., 1989-92; cons. Rocky Mount Mental Health Clinic, N.C., Bath-Brunswick Mental Health Clinics, 1988, Main Correctional Ctr., Windham, Maine, 1988; lectr., presenter in field. Contbr. articles to profl. jours. Recipients grants. Mem. Am. Psychiat. Assn., So. Assn. for Rsch. in Psychiatry, N.C. Psychiat. Assn. (rsch. com., pub. rels. com. mem), Intenrat. Soc. for Taumatic Stress Study (scientific program com. 1993), NIMH Ctr. for Psychoneuroendocrinology in Adults and Children. Office: The Upjohn Co 7000 Portage Rd Kalamazoo MI 49009

CORSAW, ARDITH, geriatrics nurse, administrator; b. Decatur, Ill., Sept. 10, 1950; d. Everette Eugene and Norma L. (Swarm) Kirkman; m. David Corsaw, Dec. 19, 1971; children: Adam, Tara, Karen. Diploma, Decatur Meml. Hosp., 1971. RN. Pvt. duty nursing, charge nurse med.-surg. unit Graham Hosp., Canton, Ill., 1972-82; nurse Hooper-Holmes Port-A-Medic, Peoria, Ill., 1982-83; office nurse family practice physician's office, Cuba, Ill., 1982-87; factory first-aid sta. relief nurse Caterpillar, Inc., Mapleton, Ill., 1986-88; nursing supr., insvc. dir. Heartland of Canton (Ill.), Health Care and Retirement Corp., 1988-91, DON, 1991-92; quality assurance coord., rehab. coord. Health Care and Retirement Corp., 1992; DON Sprucewood Health Care, 1992-96, Ill. River Correctional Ctr., 1996—; supr. nursing, clin. support br. chief ambulatory svcs. McDill AFB. Ill. Air N.G. Nurse Exec., 1971-95, MOS Comdr. 1995—. Mem. Assn. Air N.G. Nurses, Alliance Air N.G. Flight Surgeons, Assn. Mil. Surgeons U.S., N.G. Assn. U.S., N.G. Assn. Ill. Home: 8442 E Beaver Pass Rd Smithfield IL 61477-9716

CORSER, MAUREEN SLAGG, librarian, media specialist; b. Seattle, July 8, 1942; d. Maynard Owen and Bertha May (Bunnell) Slagg; m. George Albert Corser, Apr. 8, 1962; children: George Patrick, John Kevin, Carin Glendyne. BA in Econs., Wash. State U., Pullman, 1964; AM in LS, U. Mich., 1976. Cert. tchr., Mich. Media specialist Carman-Ainsworth Sch., Flint, Mich., 1972-79; libr., media specialist Flint Cmty. Schs., 1979—; mem. Genesee County Adv. Bds. on Media, Tech., Math./Sci., Microcomputers, 1980—. Editor Media Spectrum, 1995—. Officer, chair voter svc., budget chair LWV of Mich., 1965—. Mem. Mich. Edn. Assn. (rep.), Mich. Assn. for Media in Edn. (sec. 1984-85), Phi Delta Kappa (v.p. 1983), Delta Kappa Gamma, Phi Chi Theta, Phi Beta Mu. Unitarian. Home: 5151 Laramie Ln Bridgeport MI 48722-9525 Office: Flint Cmty Schs 2138 W Carpenter Rd Flint MI 48505-1997

CORSON, JAMES ALLEN, business official; b. Ankara, Turkey, Nov. 2, 1959; came to U.S., 1960; s. Robert Richard and Catherine Maureen (Peterson) C.; m. Allison Jo Brown, June 7, 1986; children: Sean T., Jordyn R. BSBA, U. Nebr., Omaha, 1986; MBA, Creighton U., 1990. Acctg. clk. Airlite Plastics, Omaha, 1979-83; campus rep. Miller Brewing Co., Omaha, 1982-84; bartender, mgr. Big Fred's Pizza, Omaha, 1984-89; sales rep. Pace Membership Warehouse, Omaha, 1989; mem. mgmt. staff Keystone/Medicine Chest, Missouri Valley, Iowa, 1990—. Mem. Creighton Grad. Bus. Assocs., Sigma Tau Gamma Alumni (v.p., sec.).

CORSON, THOMAS HAROLD, manufacturing company executive; b. Elkhart, Ind., Oct. 15, 1927; s. Carl W. and Charlotte (Keyser) C.; m. Dorthy Claire Scheide, July 11, 1948; children: Benjamin Thomas, Claire Elaine. Student, Purdue U., 1945-46, Rennsselaer Poly. Inst., 1946-47, So. Meth. U., 1948-49. Chmn. bd. Coachmen Industries, Inc., Elkhart, Ind., 1965—; also chmn. bd. Coachmen Industries, Inc. (numerous subs. cons.); bd. dirs. First State Bank, Middlebury, R.C.R. Sci. Inc., Goshen, Ind.; chmn., sec. Greenfield Corp., Middlebury. Adv. coun. U. Notre Dame; past trustee Ball State U.; dir., past vice chmn. Interlochen (Mich.) Arts Acad. and Nat. Music Camp. Served with USNR, 1945-47. Mem. Ind. Mfrs. Assn. (past dir.), Elkhart C. of C. (past dir.), Ind. C. of C. (bd. dirs.), Capitol Hill Club, Royal Poinciana Golf Club, Elcona Club (past dir.), Masons, Shriners. Methodist. Home: PO Box 504 Middlebury IN 46540-0504 Office: Coachmen Industries Inc 601 E Beardsley Ave Box 3300 Elkhart IN 46515

CORTRIGHT, HELEN RAE, banker; b. Madison, Ohio, July 27, 1963; d. Raymond Earl and Evelyn Helen (Friedrich) Wolf; m. Ricky Lee Cortright, Oct. 16, 1982; 1 child, Rebecca Chelsea. Grad. high sch., Jefferson, Ohio. Cashier Ben Franklin's Store, Jefferson, 1980-82; mem. factory staff Lake City Plating, Ashtabula, Ohio, 1982; cashier, cook Mr. Hero's, Jefferson, 1982-83; cashier Fashion Bug, Jefferson, 1983-84; asst. mgr. Cinema Ctrs., Ashtabula, 1985-88; branch ops. supr. Peoples Savs. Bank, Ashtabula, 1984—. Mem. Am. Bus. Women's Assn. (treas. 1989-90). Home: 5269 State Route 46 S Jefferson OH 44047-8533 Office: Peoples Savs Bank 4200 Park Ave Ashtabula OH 44004-6857

CORWIN, GREGG MARLOWE, lawyer; b. Mpls., May 4, 1947; s. Gerald Sidney Corwin and Shirley Mae (Nathenson) Nadler; m. Frances Gail Shapiro, mar. 21, 1971; children: Mitchell, David. BA summa cum laude, U. Minn., 1969, JD cum laude, 1972. Bar: Minn. 1972, U.S. Dist. Ct. Minn. 1972, U.S. Ct. Appeals (8th cir.) 1976, U.S. Supreme Ct. 1977. Assoc. Fred Burstein Law Firm, Mpls., 1972-77; ptnr. Cortlen Cloutier, Mpls., 1977-78; pvt. practice, Mpls., 1978—. Capt. USAF. Mem. ABA, Minn. Bar Assn., Hennepin County Bar Assn., Phi Beta Kappa. Democrat. Jewish. Office: 1660 Hwy 100 Ste 508 E Minneapolis MN 55416-1534

COSGROVE, CHARLES HENRY, theology educator; b. Denver, July 8, 1954; s. Charles Henry and Marjorie Martha (Holtorf) C.; m. Debbie Lee Fredericks, June 20, 1975; 1 child, Katherine. BA, Bethel Coll., 1976; MDiv, Bethel Theol. Sem., 1979; PhD, Princeton Theol. Sem., 1985. Asst. prof. New Testament No. Bapt. Theol. Sem., Lombard, Ill., 1985-89, assoc. prof. New Testament, 1989-95, prof. New Testament, 1995-96; prof. New Testament studies, Christian ethics No.Bap. Theol. Sem., Lombard, Ill., 1996—. Author: The Cross and the Spirit, 1988; editor: Faith and History, 1990; contbr. articles to profl. jours. Mem. Soc. Bibl. Lit., Modern Lang. Assn., Chgo. Soc. Bibl. Rsch. Home: 4230 Raymond Ave Brookfield IL 60513 Office: No Bapt Theol Sem 660 E Butterfield Lombard IL 60148

COSGROVE, JIM, plant manager, product liability consultant; b. Manchester, Eng., Oct. 15, 1941; came to U.S., 1979; BS equivalent, U. Manchester, Eng., 1967. Engring. mgr. Joy Mfg., Eng. & U.S., 1977-88; plant mgr. Vanair Mfg., New Buffalo, Mich., 1988—. Co-inventor compression unit, patented. Mem. Inst. Mech. Engring. (Eng.). Home: 3606 Michinda Ct Michigan City IN 46360-1066 Office: Vanair Mfg Inc 19015 US Hwy 12 New Buffalo MI 49117

COSNER, RAYMOND ROBERT, aeronautical engineer; b. Charleston, W.Va., Dec. 18, 1949; s. Robert Ronald and Winona (Hinkley) C.; m. Mary Elizabeth Stuesse, May 23, 1979; children: Linda Maria, Sam Alan. BS, MS in Aero. Engring., Purdue U., 1972; PhD in Aeronautics, Calif. Inst. Tech., 1976. R & D engr. McDonnell Aircraft Co., St. Louis, 1975-88, computational fluid dynamics applications mgr., 1988-96, aerodynamic design tech. mgr., 1996—; adj. prof. Ohio State U., 1993. Contbg. author: Applied Computational Aerodynamics, 1990; contbr. numerous tech. papers to profl. publs. McDonnell Douglas rsch. and engring. fellow, 1991. Assoc. fellow AIAA (adv. coun. 1987-88, Outstanding Young Profl. Engr. 1980, Outstanding Tech. Paper 1983). Home: 12765 Castlebar Dr Saint Louis MO 63146-3732 Office: McDonnell Douglas Corp Mailcode 1067126 PO Box 516 Saint Louis MO 63166

COSNER, THURSTON LAWRENCE, retired psychology educator, psychologist; b. Clairton, Pa., Jan. 10, 1937; s. Thurston and Edna Marie (Morris) C.; m. Sandra Lee Sutton, Dec. 19, 1969 (div. 1980); children: Jennifer A., Timothy T.; m. Janet Ehlert, Dec. 3, 1983; stepchildren: Theodora Martis, James Martis. BS in Psychology, Pa. State U., 1961; MA in Psychology, Bowling Green State U., 1963; PhD in Psychology, Kent State U., 1983. Lic. psychologist, Ohio. Vocat. psychology Cuyahoga County Div. Child Welfare, Cleve., 1963-64; ct. psychologist Cuyahoga County Ct. Common Pleas, Cleve., 1964-66; prof. psychology Cuyahoga C.C., Cleve., 1965-95; pvt. practice Beachwood, Ohio, 1976—; child psychologist Parmadale Children's Village, Parma, Ohio, 1966-69; clin. psychologist We. Res. Habilitatin Ctr., Sagamore Hills, Ohio, 1969-70; cons. psychologist, dir. Evaln. & Devel. Assn., Cleve., 1971—; supr. psychology Vocat. Guidance Svcs., Cleve., 1972-76; adj. faculty mem. Kent (Ohio) State U. grad. sch., 1978-82; mem. schs. faculty Chautaugua (N.Y.) Instn., 1987-90; presenter workshops in field, 1968—. Contbr. articles to profl. jours. With USAF, 1954-58. Recipient Disting. Prof. award Cuyahoga C.C. Student Senate, 1968, Cosse award, 1986; award of honor Cleve. AFL-CIO, 1971. Mem. APA, Ohio Psychol. Assn., Midwestern Psychol. Assn., Cleve. Psychol. Assn. Home: 19401 Beach Cliff Blvd Rocky River OH 44116-1713 Office: Cuyahoga CC 21625 Chagrin Blvd Ste 200 Beachwood OH 44122

COSPER, ANDREA VERBIE, management consultant; b. Brookline, Mass.; d. Andrew Sotir and Verbie Eudell (Brown) Bregou; m. Anthony Joseph Leech, Aug. 21, 1971 (div. May 1985); m. William Madison Cosper III, Nov. 16, 1990. AA in Bus., Wentworth Jr. Coll., 1987; BS in Bus. Mgmt. summa cum laude, Tarkio Coll., 1988. Mgr. adminstrv. svcs. Mgmt. Recruiters, Bridgeton, Mo., 1972-82; br. mgr. Ballwin (Mo.) Bus. Ctrs., 1982-83; v.p., co-owner PSS, St. Charles, Mo., 1983-85; dir. Mgmt. Info. Svcs. Fitronetics, Inc., Kansas City, Mo., 1985-87; cons. A L Consulting, Lexington, Mo., 1983—; habilitation specialist Higginsville (Mo.) Habilitation Ctr., 1988-90, 93—, habilitation specialist II, 1993—; cons. Desco Med. Co., Milw., 1983—. Mem. St. Louis Tng. Club. Home: RR 1 Box 76 Lexington MO 64067-9708

COSS, JOHN EDWARD, archivist; b. Spring Valley, Ill., Apr. 2, 1947; s. Edward Francis and Doris (Leonard) C.; m. Sherry Lee Ushman, June 4, 1973 (div. May 1979); 1 child, Stephen John; m. Brenda Lynn Gibson, May 30, 1981; 1 stepchild, Anthony Robert. AA, Ill. Valley Community Coll., 1967; BA, Northwest Mo. State U., 1970. Archivist Ill. State Archives, Springfield, 1971—. Mem. Ill. Fedn. Archivists, Archival Technicians & Photographers, Springfield Trades & Labor Coun. (del.). Methodist. Home: RR 1 Box 170 Buffalo IL 62515-9753 Office: Dept Archives and Records Ill Sec State Archives Bldg Springfield IL 62756

COSTELLO, JERRY F., JR., congressman, former county official; b. Sept. 25, 1949. County bd. chmn. St. Clair County, Ill.; dir. ct. services and probation 20th Jud. Cir. Campaign; chmn. Heart Assn., Belleville, Ill., 1983; vice chmn. Ill. div. United Way, 1984, chmn., 1985; mem. 100th-103rd Congresses from 21st (now 12th) Ill. Dist., 1988—; mem. budget com., mem. transp. and infrastructure com. Bd. dirs. Ill. Ctr. for Autism; active St. Clair County Big Bros./Big Sisters, Belleville Women's Crisis Ctr., Children's Ctr. for Behavioral Devel.; helped establish St. Clair County chpt. Vets. Outreach Info. Ctr.; mem. East St. Louis Econ. Opportunity Commn., Ill.; vice chmn. Southwestern Ill. Bus. Devel. Fin. Corp., 1985—; bd. dirs. So. Ill. Leadership Council; pres. Urban Counties Council of Ill. Recipient cert. of Appreciation, Bus. and Profl. Women's Assn., 1985; honored Citizens League for Adequate Social Services; 1985 AAHMES Court #84, Daus. ISIS Ann. Humanitarian award, Gene Hughes award Ill. Ct. Services and Probation Assn. Office: US Congress 2454 Rayburn Washington DC 20515-1312*

COSTIN, JAMES D., performing arts company executive. BA in Theater, U. Calif., L.A., 1959; MA in Theater, U. Mo., Kansas City, 1966. Cert. German linguist, 1956. Mgr. Fox West Coast Theatres, L.A., Calif., 1954-56; German linguist Army Security Agency, U.S. Army, 1956-59; editor

Great Lakes News, 1960-61; asst. stage mgr to stage mgr. Am. Ballet Theatre, 1961-62, co. mgr., 1962-63; asst. gen. mgr. Washington D.C. Ballet Guild/Am. Ballet Theatre, 1963-64; co-founder, adminstrv. dir. Mo. Repertory Theatre, U. Mo., Kansas City, 1964-67; playwright in residence U. Mo., Kansas City, 1966-67; adminstrv. dir. of theatre U. Mo., 1968-72, asst. to the provost, dir. office of cultural events, 1972-76, asst provost for performing arts mgmt., 1976-79, vice provost, chief academic fiscal officer, 1979—; exec. dir./playwright in residence Mo. Repertory Theatre, Inc., 1979—; cons. Internat. Theatre Inst., Great Lakes Shakespeare Festival, Kansas City Ballet. Author: (play) Laity, 1964, Lee, 1966, Ageina, 1969, The Curious Adventures of Alice, 1988, Jekyll, 1989; (stage productions) Ageina, The Curious Adventures of Alice, Jekyll; (co-author play with James Lee) The Holy Terror, 1967. Com. mem. Mayor's Com. Save The Starlight Theater, Save the Phiharmonic Orchestra; bd. dirs. State Ballet Mo., Kans. City Arts Coun. Lt. USNR 1968-71. Recipient Best Playwright award UCLA, 1959, Pirouette award, 1987. Office: Mo Repertory Theatre 4949 Cherry St Kansas City MO 64110-2229

COTE, JOHN JOSEPH, medical student; b. Omaha, Nov. 29, 1968; s. Laurence Joseph and LuCinda Kay (Scantlin) C. BS in Biology, Loyola Marymount U., L.A., 1991; postgrad., Creighton Med. Sch., 1995—. Debate instr. Loyola Marymount U., 1991-92; tchr. biology Loyola High Sch., L.A., 1991-92, 92-94, dir. of debate, 1991-94; asst. dir. of debate Creighton U., Omaha, Nebr., 1994—. Nat. Lincoln-Douglas Debate champion, 1989. Mem. AMA, AAAS, Nat. Forensic League, Am. Mus. Natural History, N.Y. Acad. Scis., Sigma Xi, Eta Sigma Phi, Delta Sigma Phi. Roman Catholic. Home: 5618 S 104th St Omaha NE 68127-3020

COTTER, JEFFREY GENE, tool designer; b. Granite, Ill., Feb. 2, 1963; s. Wayne Keith and Karen Lee (Shaver) C.; m. Yvette Denise Perigen, July 28, 1988; 1 child, Jacob. BS in Mech. Engrng., U. Mo., Rolla, 1986. Tool designer Erhardt Tool Machine Co., St. Louis, 1987—. Mem. Soc. Mech. Engr. Home: 2029 Cottage Ave Granite City IL 62040-3941 Office: Erhardt Tool Machine Co 2224 N 10th St Saint Louis MO 63102-1421

COTTER, PATRICIA EWING, human resource specialist; b. Albany, N.Y., Feb. 26, 1956; d. Maurice Duane and Jacqueline (Jenniches) Ewing; m. Thomas Peter Cotter, Sept. 8, 1985. Student, SUNY, Oneonta, 1974-75; MSW, SUNY, Albany, 1980; BS in Social Work summa cum laude, Syracuse U., 1978. Cert. sr. profl. in human resorces. Counselor Summit Med. Ctr., Atlanta, 1981-82; asst. mgr. Concept Mgmt. Inc., Atlanta, 1982-83, gen. mgr., 1983-84, dir. recruiting and tng., 1984-86; mgr. recruiting and placement Rich's, Duluth, Ga., 1986-90; mgr. of employment BANC ONE, 1990-95, v.p. human resources, 1996—. Bd. trustees Ballet Met. Office: 191 W Schrock Rd Columbus OH 43271-1048

COTTON, LARRY, ranching executive. Office: Premier Beef Cattle Inc 305 Amos Rd Howell MI 48843*

COUCH, LEON WHELAND, III, music educator, performer; b. Gainesville, Fla., Sept. 1, 1970; s. Leon Worthington II and Margaret (Wheland) C. BS in Physics, U. Fla., 1992, BA in Math., 1992, MusB with high honors, 1992; MusM in Organ Performance and Music Theory, Cin. Coll. Conservatory Music, 1995; postgrad. in organ perfromance, Cin. Coll. Cons. Music, 1995—. Musician Gainesville and Cin., 1987—; computer programmer Phys. Plant divsn. U. Fla., Gainesville, 1988-89; organist Trinity Episc. Ch., Melrose, Fla., 1991-92, Ascention Luth. Ch., Cin., 1992-93, Disciples Christian Ch., Hamilton, Ohio, 1994-95; music dir. Concordia Luth. Ch., Cin., 1995—; tutor sci., math. and music, U. Cin., 1992—, tchg. asst. music theory, 1993-95, tchg. asst. organ performance, 1995—; cons. Gainesville, 1988—. Composer various music selections, 1988—. Mem. Am. Guild Organists, Soc. Physics Students, Soc. Music Theory, Phi Beta Kappa, Pi Kappa Lambda, Phi Kappa Phi. Methodist. Home: 3204 Bishop St Cincinnati OH 45220 Office: Univ Cin Keyboard Divsn Coll Conserv Music Cincinnati OH 45220 Ch. Office: Concordia Luth Ch 1133 Clifton Hills Ave Cincinnati OH 45220

COUFAL, CHARLES FRANCIS, electrical engineer; b. Omaha, Sept. 7, 1956. Student of elec. engring., U. Nebr., 1984—. Engr. AT&T, Omaha, 1978—. Office: AT&T PO Box 37000 Omaha NE 68137-9000

COUGHLIN, FRED R., securities executive; b. Winchester, Ill., May 24, 1920. BS, U. Ill., 1940, MS, 1941. Pres. Alton State Bank, East Alton, Ill., 1968-77; v.p. Longrow Securities, Alton, Ill., 1992—. Staff sgt. U.S. Army, 1943-45. Mem. VFW. Republican. Presbyterian. Office: Longrow Securities Inc PO Box 160 # 400 200 W 3d St Alton IL 62002

COUGHLIN, MARY LYNN, physical therapist; b. Battle Creek, Mich., Mar. 26, 1959; d. Louis A. and Katherine (Velzing) O'Daniel; m. H. Richard Coughlin, June 18, 1983; children: Melanie, Stephen. BS in Phys. Therapy, U. Evansville, Ind., 1981; M Health Sci., U. Indpls., 1993. Lic. phys. therapist Mich., Fla. Staff phys. therapist Saginaw (Mich.) Gen. Hosp., 1981-86, supr. phys. therapy, 1986-90, asst. dir. phys. medicine, 1990-93, dir. phys. medicine, 1994; phys. therapist HealthTrak Rehab., Bay City, Mich., 1994—. Mem. adv. bd. PTA Program Delta Coll., Univ. Ctr., Mich., 1993, 4-H Horseback Riding for Handicappers, Mich. State U., Lansing. Mem. Am. Phys. Therapy Assn. (Mich. chpt.). Office: HealthTrak 903 N Euclid Ste 3 Bay City MI 48706

COULDWELL, WILLIAM TUPPER, neurosurgeon; b. Vancouver, B.C., Can., Dec. 15, 1955; s. William John and Janet Mary (Tupper) C.; m. Marie Francoise Simard; children: Sandrine, Mitchell, Genevieve. MD, McGill U., 1984, PhD, 1991. Resident in neurosurgery U. So. Calif., L.A., 1984-89; fellow neuroimmunology Montreal Neuri. Inst., 1989-91, fellow epilepsy surgery, 1990; fellow neurosurgery CHUV, Lausanne, Switzerland, 1990-91; asst. prof. dept. neurol. surgery U. So. Calif., L.A., 1991-95, assoc. clin. prof., 1995—; ICU dirs. com. U. So. Calif. Med. Ctr., L.A., 1991-95; assoc. clin. prof. U. N.D., Minot, 1995—. Contbr. articles to profl. jours. Recipient Preuss award Am. Assn. Neurol. Surgeons, 1991, Clinician Investigator award, 1993; Med. Rsch. Coun. Can. Centennial fellow, 1990; McGill U. scholar, 1984, Wood Gold medal. Fellow ACS; mem. Am. Assn. Neurol. Surgeons (joint sect. on tumors 1991—), Congress of Neurol. Surgeons. Office: Trinity Med Ctr 1 Burdick Expressway W Minot ND 58701

COULSON, ELIZABETH ANNE, physical therapy educator; b. Hastings, Nebr., Sept. 8, 1954; d. Alexander and Marilyn (Marvel) Shafernich; m. William Coulson, Feb. 14, 1986. Student, Wellesley Coll., 1972-73; BS in Edn., U. Kans., 1976; cert. in phys. therapy, Northwestern U., Chgo., 1977; MBA, Keller Grad. Sch. Mgmt., 1985; postgrad., U. Ill., 1991. Lic. phys. therapist, Ill. Assoc. prof. dept. phys. therapy Chgo. Med. Sch., North Chicago, Ill., chmn. dept. phys. therapy, 1993-96. Contbr. articles to profl. jours. Trustee Northfield Twp., Ill., 1993—; state rep. candidate 57th dist., 1996. Mem. APHA, Am. Phys. Therapy Assn. (Ill. del. 1986-93, chief del. 1991-93), Ill. Phys. Therapy Assn. (chmn. jud. com. 1989-91). Home: 1701 Sequoia Trl Glenview IL 60025-2022

COULTER, CHRISTOPHER JAY, industrial professional; b. Wyandotte, Mich., Nov. 24, 1963. AS, Henry Ford C.C., Dearborn, Mich., 1986. Structural steel detailer Holmstrom Detailing Svc., Livonia, Mich., 1988-90; project engr. Titus Welding, Farmington Hills, Mich., 1990-93; project mgr. Ferro-Tech Inc., Wyandotte, Mich., 1993—. Republican. Roman Catholic. Office: Ferro Tech Inc 467 Eureka Rd Wyandotte MI 48192-5841

COULTON, MARTHA JEAN GLASSCOE (MRS. MARTIN J. COULTON), library consultant; b. Dayton, Ohio; d. Lafayette Pierre and Gertrude Blanche (Miller) Glasscoe; m. Martin J. Coulton; children: Perry Jean, Martin John. student Dayton Art Inst., 1946-47. Dir., Milton (Ohio) Union Pub. Libr., 1968-89; libr. cons., Centerville, Ohio, 1989—. Named Outstanding Woman Jaycees, 1978-1979; recipient Spl. Recognition award Ohio Ho. Reps., 1989. Mem. ALA, Ohio Library Assn., Miami Valley Library Orgn. (sec. 1981, v.p. 1982, pres. 1983), Internat. Platform Assn., Puppeteers of Am., DAR, Union Internat. Marionnette, Amnesty Internat., Pub. Citizen Health. Home and Office: 6029 Buggywhip Ln Dayton OH 45459-2407

COUNSELL, LEE ALBERT, dentist, educator, Hispanist; b. Neillsville, Wis., July 5, 1923; s. Clarion and Henrietta (Clemens) C. D.D.S., Northwestern U., 1948; B.A., U. Wis.-Madison, 1949; diploma grad. pedodontics Forsyth Dental Center, Boston, 1949; M.P.H., U. Mich., 1967; M.A. Spanish, So. Ill. U., 1984. Commd. lt. Dental Corps, U.S. Navy, 1950, advanced through grades to comdr., ret., 1972; intern staff Naval Hosp., Gt. Lakes, Ill., 1950; asst. dir. dept. pediatric dentistry Marquette U., 1952-54; practice pediatric dentistry, Milw. and Washington, 1954-55; house staff Naval Hosp., Boston, 1959-62; dir. dental dept. Naval Constrn. Bn. Center, Davisville, R.I., 1964-66; head preventive dentistry program Naval Base, Gt. Lakes, Ill., 1968-70; asst. chief clin. investigations div. Naval Dental Research Inst., 1971, chief, 1972; asst. dir. Bur. Dental Health, Div. Health, State of Fla., 1972-73; fellow U. Dundee (Scotland), 1973; research assoc. Am. Dental Assn., Chgo., 1973-74; assoc. prof. So. Ill. U., Carbondale, 1974-77, adj. assoc. prof., 1979-86; apptd. adj. prof. Northwestern U., 1990; cons. dental health edn., 1977-86, dental pub. health, 1977-86. Decorated Navy Commendation medal, 1972. Fellow Am. Assn. Endodontists, Am. Coll. Dentists; mem. ADA (life), G.V. Black Soc. (life), Organ Hist. Soc., Xi Psi Phi (life), Phi Kappa Phi, Omicron Kappa Upsilon (hon. mem.). Episcopalian. Contbr. numerous articles to profl. publs. Home: 140 E Franklin Pl #107 Lake Forest IL 60045

COUNTER, JAMES A., financial planner; b. Wabasha, Minn., Apr. 3, 1941. MS, Am. Sch. Fin., 1988. Lic. life underwriter; ChFC. Fin. planner Counter & Assocs., New Richmond, Wis., 1964—; pres. Econ. Devel. Commn., New Richmond, 1985—; bd. dirs. N.W. Savs. Bank, New Richmond. Mem. United Way of Great St. Croix County, New Richmond, 1992—, St. Croix Devel. Commn., New Richmond, 1995. Office: Counter & Assocs 134 S Knowles Ave New Richmond WI 54017-1727

COUNTRYMAN, ELLEN WITT, hospital administrator; b. Pineville, Ky., Dec. 18, 1951; d. Cecil and Sylvia (Tolliver) Witt; m. Daniel Lee Countryman, Jan. 2, 1972; children: Sarah Ellen, Kathryn Elizabeth. Student, Ball State U., 1986-88; grad., Ind. U., 1993. Sec., dispatcher Franklin (Ohio) Police Dept., 1971; legal sec. De Armond & De Armond Law Office, Anderson, Ind., 1972; exec. sec. J.C. Penney Distbrn. Ctr., Anderson, 1972-74; reading tutor, aide Jay Sch. Corp., Portland, Ind., 1974-79; billing clk. Jay County Hosp., Portland, 1979-80, med. records clk., 1980-86, interim dir. med. records, 1986-87, dir. health info. mgmt. and med. staff svcs., 1988—. Mem. Headwaters Heritage, Portland, 1983-88, pres., 1983-86; deacon Presbyn. Ch., Portland, 1984-86, pres., 1986, trustee; mem. solicitation com. Jay Arts Coun.; mem. cmty. rels. com. Jay County Hosp.; mem. Jay County Friends of the Libr.; mem. Dem. Women's Com., pres., 1994; bd. dirs. Literacy Coalition, 1992—. Mem. Nat. Assn. Med. Staff Svcs., Am. Health Info. Mgmt. Assn., Ind. Health Info. Mgmt. Assn., Altrusa Internat., Cincinnatus League, Phi Theta Kappa. Democrat. Office: Jay County Hosp 500 W Votaw St Portland IN 47371-1322

COUNTS, DONALD R., furniture maker; b. St. Louis, May 26, 1961; m. Elizabeth Ann Counts; 5 children. H.S., Salem H.S., 1979. Rep. nom. for U.S. House of Reps., 1994; Rep. candidate 1st dist. Mo. U.S. House Reps., 1996. Apostolic Pentacostal. Office: PO Box 648 Florissant MO 63033*

COURANT, PAUL NOAH, economist, educator; b. Ithaca, N.Y., Jan. 5, 1948; s. Ernest David and Sara (Paul) C.; m. Katherine Olive Johnson, Sept. 21, 1969 (div. 1984); children: Ernest Mendel, Noah Albert; m. Marta Ann Manildi, Jan. 30, 1988; 1 child, Samuel Robinson Manildi. BA, Swarthmore Coll., 1968; MA, Princeton U., 1972, PhD, 1973. Jr. economist Coun. Econ. Advisers, Washington, 1969-70, sr. economist, 1979-80; asst. prof. econs., pub. policy U. Mich., Ann Arbor, 1973-78, assoc. prof., 1978-84, prof. econs. and pub. policy, 1984—, dir. Inst. Pub. Policy Studies, 1983-87, 89-90, chair econs. dept., 1995—; mem. Task Force on Long-Term Econ. Growth, State of Mich., 1983-84; cons. Mich. Dept. Commerce, Lansing, 1984-85, Congl. Budget Office, Washington, 1988-89; bd. dirs. Mich. Future, Bingham Farms, 1991—. Author: America's Great Consumption Binge, 1986; co-author: Economics, 1973, 11th edit., 1996; contbr. articles to profl. jours. Mem. econs. com. Sierra Club, San Francisco, 1984-90. Grantee NSF, 1976-77, 79-81, 94—, Rockefeller Found., 1985-87, Nat. Cancer Inst., 1992-95. Mem. Am. Econ. Assn., Assn. Pub. Policy Analysis and Mgmt. (mem. policy council 1994—), Nat. Tax Assn. Office: Univ Mich Dept Econs 611 Tappan Ave Ann Arbor MI 48109-1220

COURSON, ROGER LEE, agricultural educator; b. Galesburg, Ill., June 1, 1931; s. Lester Dale and Eva (Dexter) C.; m. Joanne Delores Root, Apr. 14, 1952 (dec. Nov. 1990); children: Jerry L., Michael K., David W.; m. Donna Rose Huffmaster, July 6, 1991. BS, U. Ill., 1952, MS, 1955, PhD in Agr./Agronomy, 1965. Vocat. agr. tchr. Crescent-Iroquois Commun. High Sch., Crescent City, Ill., 1953-58, Henry (Ill.) High Sch., 1958-60; agronomy and horticulture specialist Vocat. Agr. Svc., U. Ill., Urbana, 1960-77, prof., head, 1977—; asst. head agr. communications and edn., media specialist, Urbana, 1988-90; teaching material specialist Egerton U., Kenya, 1986, 88; program and facilities specialist Chgo. High Sch. for Agrl. Sci., 1984-85; computer cons. Am. Dairy Sci. Assn., Champaign, Ill., 1984-87; in planning and devel. U. Algeria, Blida, 1976-77. Author: Soil Fertility and Fertilizers, 1981; editor: Anatomy of Seeds, 1977; contbr. chpts. to book, articles to profl. jours. Trustee Ill. Found. FFA, Springfield, Ill., 1977—; sec.-treas. PTA, Champaign, 1968-72; asst. coach Little League Baseball, Champaign, 1975-85. Recipient Friends of Vocat. and Tech. Edn. award Ill. Vocat. Assn., 1992, Outstanding Svc. to Agr. award Nat. Vocat. Agr. Tchrs. Assn., 1987, 90; named Hon. Am. Farmer, Nat. FFA, 1982. Mem. Weed Sci. Soc. Am., Sigma Xi, Gamma Sigma Delta (sec. 1965-70), Alpha Tau Alpha, Pi Alpha Xi. Home: 2104 Madison Ct Champaign IL 61820-7564 Office: U Ill 1401 S Maryland Dr Urbana IL 61801-4732

COURTNEY, DARREL GENE, investment executive; b. Oskaloosa, Iowa, Jan. 10, 1949. Degree in indsl. rels. and psychology, U. Iowa, 1972. Ins. agt. Am. Family, Iowa City, 1972-75; investment exec. Dain Bosworth Inc., Iowa City, 1979—. Mayor City of Iowa, 1992-93; coun. mem. City Coun. Iowa City, 1985-93. Mem. Rotary, Elks (bd. trustees 1995). Office: Dain Bosworth Inc 112 S Dubuque St Iowa City IA 52240-4009

COURTNEY, EUGENE WHITMAL, computer company executive; b. East St. Louis, Ill., Jan. 3, 1936; s. Eugene and Goldie Genell (Mitchell) C.; m. Barbara Ann Beckwith, Aug. 1, 1959; children: Kevin Eugene, Kyle Patrick. BSEE, Princeton U. with honors, 1957. Exec. v.p., gen. mgr., dir. Digital Sci. Corp., San Diego, 1970-75, pres., chief exec. officer, 1975-79; dir. Digital Sci./Europe, 1975-79; v.p. corp. devel. Topaz, Inc., San Diego, 1979; v.p. corp. devel. Nat. Computer Systems, Mpls., 1980-81, v.p., gen. mgr. scanning div., 1981-83, group v.p., 1983-88; exec. v.p., COO, dir. HEI Inc., Victoria, Minn., 1988-90; pres., CEO, 1990—; prin. and dir. Triangle Tool and affiliates, 1988—; bd. dirs. DRS Data and Rsch. Svcs. plc, Milton Keynes, Eng., SFT Solutions From Tech., Mpls., Datakey, Inc., Mpls.; mem. Minn. Software Tech. Com., 1985-86. Contbr. articles to profl. jours. Trustee, v.p. engring. San Diego Hall of Sci., 1974-79; mem. State of Calif. gov.'s task force on edn. and industry, 1977-78; mem. Rancho Santa Fe (Calif.) Park and Recreation Bd., 1978; mem. tech. adv. bd. Minn. Dept. Corrections, Shakopee, 1985-86. Am. Electronics Assn. (nat. bd. dirs., chmn. San Diego coun. 1976-79, chmn. Minn. coun. 1993—), Princeton Club (N.Y.C.). Republican. Home: 7312 Claredon Dr Minneapolis MN 55439-1722 Office: HEI Inc PO Box 5000 Victoria MN 55386-5000

COURTNEY, JERRY L., social welfare administrator; b. Knoxville, Tenn., Mar. 11, 1955; s. Bertha Darlis (Lowe) C.; m. Sarah Jane Donohue, Nov. 11, 1989; children: McKenzie Lynn, Emmett Lawrence. BS, Berry Coll., 1977. Dir. Camp Kanuga, Hendersonville, N.C., 1982-85; exec. dir. Y Camp Pendalonan, Montague, MIch., 1985-91, YMCA Storer Camps, Jackson, Mich., 1991—. Bd. dirs. Camp Michimac, Southfield, Mich., 1991-95, Spl. Days Camp, Kalamazoo, 191-95. Named one of Outstanding Young Men Am., 1989, 92. Home and Office: 7260 S Stony Lake Rd Jackson MI 49201

COURTNEY, VERNON S., museum administrator; b. Hampton, Va., Nov. 2, 1946; s. Vernon S. and Myrtle C. (Charity) C.; m. Cassandra A. Hill, Sept. 28, 1974; 1 child, Aliya D. AB, Harvard Coll., 1969; MEd, Pa. State U., 1978. Asst. to dir. Robeson Ctr. Pa. State U., University Park, 1978-80; from dir. instnl. adv. to exec. asst. to pres. Wilberforce (Ohio) U., 1980-87; asst. dir. Nat. Afro-Am. Mus., Wilberforce, 1987—. Woodrow Wilson Found. fellow, 1981-84. Mem. Alpha Phi Alpha (v.p. chpt.). Office: Nat Afro-Am Mus PO Box 578 Wilberforce OH 45384

COUSSENS, FRANK J., investment company executive; b. South Bend, Ind., Jan. 13, 1946. Assoc., Davenport U., Grand Rapids, Mich., 1966. Pvt. builder South Bend, 1966-81; v.p. Merrill Lynch, South Bend, 1981—. Office: Merrill Lynch 404 S Columbia St PO Box 4013 South Bend IN 46699

COVAULT, LLOYD R., JR., hospital administrator, psychiatrist; b. Troy, Ohio, Feb. 3, 1928; s. Lloyd R. and Anne Marie (Grisez) C.; m. Janet Eileen Davidson, June 12, 1951; children: Sheryl Ann, Jane Helen, Michael Lee, Roger Ken. BA, Miami U., Oxford, Ohio, 1950; MD, Ohio State U., 1954. Extern Orient (Ohio) State Inst., 1953-54, staff physician, 1954-57, clin. dir., 1957-66, asst. supt., 1968-70; pvt. practice Columbus, 1968-75; psychiat. trainee Cen. Ohio Psychiat. Hosp., Columbus, 1966-68, psychiatrist, 1982-85; supt. Columbus State Inst., 1970-74; med. dir. North Cen. Community Mental Health Ctr., Columbus, 1974-79; assoc. prof. psychiatry Ohio State U. Med. Sch., 1975-76; cons. psychiatrist North Cen. Community Mental Health Ctr., Columbus, 1985-90; dir. S.E. Mental Health Ctr., Columbus, 1979-82, asst. med. dir., 1985-86, cons. psychiatrist, 1986—; med. dir. Charles B. Milles Mental Health Ctr., Marysville, Ohio, 1989-95; med. dir. VA Hosp., Chillicothe, Ohio, 1995—, psychiatrist, 1995—; mem. Franklin County Mental Health and Retardation Bd., 1970-74, Ohio Dept. Mental Health, ret. 1983; cons. psychiatrist Madison County Mental Health Ctr., London, 1984-85, Ohio Correction Complex, Orient, 1988-89, Chillecother VA Hosp., 1995—; 1st med. coord. Netcare Admission Unit Ctrl. Ohio Psychiat. Hosp., 1985-87; founding father Physicians Assn. Ohio Dept. Mental Health, 1956-68, pres. 1957. Fellow Am. Assn. Mental Retardation (life, chmn. adminstrn. state chpt. 1974-75), Am. Psychiat. Assn. (life); mem. Ohio Psychiat. Assn., Neuropsychiat. Soc. Ctrl. Ohio (pres. 1973-74), Mental Health Supts. Assn. (pres. Ohio dept. 1973-74). Home: 11092 Darby Creek Rd Orient OH 43146-9797 Office: SE Mental Health Ctr 16 W Long St Columbus OH 43215 also: Chillicothe VA Hosp 17273 State Rt 104 Chillicothe OH 45601-0999

COVEY, WILLIAM BENNETT, JR., English language and literature educator; b. Chgo., Feb. 3, 1960; s. William B. and Marie F. (DeBeney) C. AS in Bus., Waubonsee C.C., Sugar Grove, Ill., 1980; BA in English, No. Ill. U., 1983, MA in English, 1987; PhD in English, Purdue U., 1996. Cert. secondary teacher, Ill. Teaching asst. No. Ill. U., DeKalb, 1986-87, instr., 1987-88; teaching asst. Purdue U., West Lafayette, Ind., 1988—. Purdue U. faculty grantee, 1994—. Mem. MLA, Nat. Coun. Tchrs. English, Soc. Cinema Studies, Soc. Critical Exch., U. Film and Video Assn., Phi Kappa Phi, Sigma Tau Delta. Office: Purdue U Dept English Heavilon Hall # 443 West Lafayette IN 47907

COVINGTON, EDWARD JAMES, author, retired physicist; b. Flint, Mich., May 18, 1931; s. John Clinton and Violet Emiline (Girard) C.; m. Mary Lou Tobin, July 25, 1953; children: Nancy, David. BS in Physics, Mich. State U., 1955, MS in Physics, 1956. Rsch. physicist Gen. Electric Co., Schenectady, N.Y., 1959-60, Cleve., 1961-92; ret., 1992. Author: A Man From Maquoketa: A Biography of Matthew Luckiesh, 1992, Franklin Silas Terry (1862-1926), Industrialist: Paragon of Organization, Harmony and Generosity, 1994. Home: 669 Gloucester Dr Highland Heights OH 44143

COVINGTON, PATRICIA ANN, university administrator; b. Mt. Vernon, Ill., June 21, 1946; d. Charles J. and Lois Ellen (Combs) C.; m. Burl Vance Beene, Aug. 10, 1968 (div. 1981). BA, U. N.Mex., 1968; MS in Ed., So. Ill. U., 1974, PhD, 1981. Teaching asst. So. Ill. U., Carbondale, 1971-74, prof. art, asst. dir., 1974-88, asst. dir. in admissions and records, 1988—; bd. dirs. Am. Coun. on Edn., Nat. Com. for Army.Am. Coun. on Edn. Registry Transcript; mem. tech. com. Ill. Articulation Initiative, Ill. Bd. Higher Edn.; vis. curator Mitchell Mus., Mt. Vernon, 1977-83, judge dept. conservation; mem. panel Ill. Arts Coun., Chgo., 1982; faculty advisor European Bus. Seminar, London, 1983; edn. cons. Ill. Dept. Aging, Springfield, 1978-81, Apple Computer, Cupertino, Calif., 1982-83; mem. adminstrv. profl. coun. So. Ill. U., 1989-92; presenter in field. Exhibited papercastings in nat. and internat. shows in Chgo., Fla., Calif., Tenn., N.Y. and others, 1974—; author: Diary of a Workshop, 1979, History of the School of Art at Southern Illinois University at Carbondale, 1981; reviewer Mayfield Pub., Random House, (with William C. Brown) Holt, Reinhart & Winston. Bd. dirs. Humanities Couns. John A. Logan Coll., Carterville, Ill., 1982-88; mem. Ill. Higher Edn. Art Assn., chmn. bd. dirs., 1978-88; mem. Post-Doctoral Acad., 1981-95; sec. adminstrv. profl. coun., 1989-90; lifetime mem. Girl Scouts U.S., 1988—, del. 1992, 93. Grantee Kresge Found., 1978, Nat. Endowment for the Arts, 1977, 81, Ill. Bd. Higher Edn. HECA grantee, 1994, 95; named Outstanding Young Woman of Yr. for Ill., 1981, Woman of Distinction Girl Scouts U.S.. Fellow Ill. Ozarks Craft Guild (bd. dirs. 1976-83); mem. Am. Assn. Coll. Registrars and Admissions Officers, Ill. Assn. Coll. Registrars and Admissions Officers (chair so. dist., exec. com. 1992-93, nominating com. 1993-94), Spinx (hon.), Phi Kappa Phi. Presbyterian. Home: 389 Lake Dr Murphysboro IL 62966-5955 Office: So Ill U Admissions and Records Carbondale IL 62901

COWAN, ARNOLD RICHARD, finance educator, researcher; b. Chgo., Sept. 7, 1955; s. William Lemuel and Dorothy Grace (Johnson) C.; m. Christine Anne Corbin, June 14, 1980; children: Andrew, Anna, Jonathan. BA, Augustana Coll., 1977; MA in Econs., U. Iowa, 1980, MS in Stats., 1985, PhD of Fin., 1988. Instr. Augustana Coll., Rock Island, Ill., 1980-83; lectr. Wayne State U., Detroit, 1987-88; asst. prof. Iowa State U., Ames, 1988-94, assoc. prof., 1994—. Author: (software) Eventus 6.2; contbr. articles to profl. jours. Mem. Am. Fin. Assn., Fin. Mgmt. Assn. Internat. (Outstanding Paper 1994), Midwest Fin. Assn., We. Fin. Assn. Lutheran. Office: Iowa State Univ 300 Carver Hall Ames IA 50011

COWAN, DALE HARVEY, internist, lawyer; b. Cleve., Jan. 25, 1938; s. Milton Jerome and Clara (Umans) C.; m. Deborah Wolowitz, Jan. 28, 1967; children: Rachel, Morris Benjamin, William Ezra. AB, Harvard U., 1959, MD, 1963; JD, Case Western Res. U. Diplomate Am. Bd. Internal Medicine. Bar: Ohio 1981. Intern Cleve. Met. Gen. Hosp., 1963-64, resident, 1964-65, 67-70; practice medicine specializing in internal medicine, hematology and oncology; dir. hematology and oncology Marymount Hosp., Cleve., 1982—; asst. prof. medicine Case Western Res. U., Cleve., 1970-75, assoc. prof., 1975-84, clin. prof. environ. health scis.) 1985—, assoc. Health Systems Mgmt. Ctr., 1982-90; of counsel firm Burke, Haber & Berick, 1984-86; spl. cons. President's Commn. on Bioethics, Washington, 1981-82; mem. nat. adv. coun. Nat. Heart Lung and Blood Inst., Bethesda, Md., 1982-85. Author: Preferred Provider Organizations, 1984; co-editor Human Organ Transplantation, 1987; contbr. articles to profl. jours. Bd. dirs. Bur. Jewish Edn., 1977-87, Northeast Ohio affiliate Am. Heart Assn., 1982-86; pres. Ohio/W.Va. Oncology Soc., 1990-94. Served to lt. comdr. USPHS, 1965-67. Fellow ACP, Am. Coll. Legal Medicine; mem. Am. Soc. Hematology, Am. Soc. Clin. Oncology, Am. Assn. for Cancer Research, AMA, Nat. Health Lawyers Assn. (bd. dirs. 1988-94), Am. Acad. Hosp. Attys., Am. Soc. Law and Medicine, ABA. Home: 19600 Shaker Blvd Cleveland OH 44122-1830 Office: 6100 W Creek Rd #15 Cleveland OH 44131-2133

COWAN, DAVID MICHAEL, neuropsychologist; b. Kansas City, Mo., June 20, 1957; s. Lawrence and Patricia (Pennington) C.; m. Victoria Lynn Downes; 1 child, Caitlin Anne. BS, Mich. State U., 1979; MA, U. Detroit, 1982, PhD, 1985. Lic. psychologist, Mich. Staff psychologist St. Joseph Mercy Hosp., Pontiac, Mich., 1986-87, Wyandotte (Mich.) Hosp., 1987-88, Providence Hosp., Southfield, Mich., 1988-92; dir. rehab. neuropsychology St. Joseph Mercy Hosp., Pontiac, 1992—; owner Health Psychology Assocs., Pontiac, 1993—. Editor: Michigan Hospital Practice Handbook, 1994. Mem. APA, Am. Bd. Forensic Examiners, Nat. Acad. Neuropsychology, Mich. Psychol. Assn. (chair hosp. practice com. 1989-92). Office: 1411 Woodward Ave Ste 201 Bloomfield Hills MI 48302

COWAN, JOHN WILLARD, writer, management consultant, priest; b. Mpls., Dec. 24, 1935; s. Charles Willard and Ruth Astroot (Green) C.; m. Edith Ann Meissner, May 20, 1972; children: Benjamin, David. BA, St. Paul Seminary, 1957. Ordained priest Roman Catholic Ch., 1961. Parish priest Archdiocese St. Paul, 1961-69; orgn. specialist Honeywell, Mpls., 1969-71; cons. REB, Inc., Mpls., 1971-78; pvt. practice Mpls., 1974-77; sr.

cons. edn. Control Data Corp., Mpls., 1977-85, prin., quality cons., 1980-85; pvt. practice St. Paul, 1985—; priest Episcopal Diocese Minn., 1981. Author: Self-Reliant Manager, 1977, Small Decencies, 1992, The Common Table, 1993. Recipient Cons. of Yr. award Minn. chpt. Am. Soc. Tng. & Devel., 1989. Home and Office: 1498 Goodrich Ave Saint Paul MN 55105-2318

COWAN-RICKS, CARREL, historical archaeologist; b. Lansing, Mich., Dec. 1, 1945; d. William Joseph and Ella Louvisa (Jones) Cowan; m. Norville Ricks, Nov. 22, 1984 (div. July 1986). BA in Anthropology, Wayne State U., 1984, MA in Anthropology, 1989, cert. in archival adminstrn., 1990, postgrad., 1990—. Teaching asst. Wayne State U., Detroit, 1988-90, anthropology instr., 1988-91; vis. asst. prof. hist. archaeology Clemson U., 1991-93; vis. lectr. U. Toledo, 1989, 91; mem. adv. bd. Nat. Park System, 1992-95; historian Mich. Hist. Ctr., Lansing, 1994—; peer rev. panelist Ctr. for Field Rsch., Watertown, Mass., 1992, Foley Sq. African Burial Ground, N.Y.C., 1993—; reviewer Hist. Archaeology, 1993; Black history sites com. mem. Detroit Hist. Mus., 1983-91; interpreter Henry Ford Mus. and Greenfield Village, Dearborn, Mich., 1989-91, project coord. African Am. family life, history and culture, 1989; contract archaeologist Cowan and Co., Albuquerque, 1985-87; contract compliance officer U.S. Dept. HHS, Chgo., 1985, pub. info. officer, 1976-79; mem. field crew archaeol. survey Oshara Tradition Ea. N.Mex. State U., 1982, Springstead Farm site Wayne State U., 1982-85, field asst., 1988; lab. tech. Anthropology Mus., Detroit, 1982-83, Cowan and Co., 1987; prin. investigator dept. hist. houses Clemson U., S.C., 1991-93; N.Mex./Ariz Hist. cemetery project La Villa Elena project Cowan and Co., 1987; crew chief hist. Fort Wayne Cemetery excavation Wayne State U., 1990; contract archaeologist, archival rschr., oral historian Elmwood Logging Camp Gilbert/Commonwealth Inc., Iron County, Mich., 1986; cons. Hunnicutt Cemetery Restoration and Indexing Project, Keowee Key Garden Club, Salem, S.C., 1991-92, Old Bethel Restoration Project, African Am. Cemetery Rsch., Indexing and Restoration Project, McClellanville, S.C., 1992-92, Keese Barn Project African Am. Hist. Site Restoration Project, Pendleton, S.C., 1991-92; lectr., reviewer, presenter in field. Editor Mich. Archaeologist, 1991; contbr. articles to profl. jours. Mem. adv. bd. Home Instrn. Program for Presch. Youngsters, Detroit, 1990-91; faculty friend vol. Wayne State Friends program, Detroit, 1990-91. Fellow Thomas C. Rumble, 1990-92, S.C. Humanities Coun., 1993. Mem. Conf. Mich. Profl. Archaeologists, Coun. S.C. Profl. Archaeologists, Mich. Archeol. Soc. (exec. bd. dirs. 1988—, pres.-elect 1989-90, pres. 1990-91, past pres. 1991-92, trustee S.E. chpt. 1982, 90-92, sec. 1984-85, pres. 1988-90), Am. Anthropol. Assn., Assn. Black Anthropologists, Archeol. Soc. S.C., Inc., Soc. for Hist. Archaeology, So. Anthropol. Soc. Republican.

COWDERY, ROBERT DOUGLAS, consulting geologist; b. Lyons, Kans., Aug. 20, 1926; s. Herman Rayburn and Blanche (Charles) C.; m. Mary Sue Barlow, Oct. 9, 1954; children:; Craig Douglas, Patricia Lynn. BS in Geology, Kans. State U., 1949; postgrad., U. Denver, 1953-54, Colo. Sch. Mines, 1963-64, U. Colo., 1963-71, Wichita State U., 1979-88. Geologist Cities Svc. Oil Co., Oklahoma City-Gt. Bend, Kans., 1949-51; staff geologist Petroleum Inc., Wichita, Kans., 1951-53; dist. geologist Petroleum Inc., Denver, 1953-56, div. geologist, 1956-57, Rocky Mountain exploration mgr., v.p., 1967-75; exploration mgr., v.p. Petroleum Inc., Wichita, 1975-85, pres., dir. exploration, 1985-88; ret., 1988; cons. geologist Wichita, 1988—. Pres. bd. dirs. Episcopal Social Svcs. S.W. Convocation, Wichita, 1989-90. Sgt. AUS, 1944-46. Recipient Disting. Svc. award Kans. State U. Coll. Arts and Scis., 1991; inducted into Kans. Oilmen's Hall of Fame. Mem. Am. Assn. Petroleum Geologists (cert., hon., v.p. 1983-84, v.p. divsn. profl. affairs 1987-88, pres.-elect 1990-91, pres. divsn. profl. affairs 1991-92, pres., Disting. Svc. award divsn. profl. affairs 1994), Am. Inst. Profl. Geologists (cert.), Rocky Mountain Assn. Geologists (hon., pres. 1973), Kans. Geol. Soc. (hon., pres. 1986, Presdl. citation 1978), Kans. Geol. Found. (pres. 1990—, Disting. Svc. award 1991, Pres.'s award 1993), Soc. Ind. Profl. Earth Scientsts (Kans. Geol. Found. (pres. 1990—, Disting. Svc. award 1991, Pres.'s award 1993), Soc. Ind. Profl. Earth Scientsts (Kans. chpt. chmn., bd. dirs. 1995— national sec. 1996-97), Archaeol. Assn. South Ctrl. Kans. (v.p. 1988-89, pres. 1990-93), So. Am. Archaeologists, Wyo. Geol. Soc., Oklahoma City Geol. Soc., West Tex. Geol. Soc., Panhandle Geol. Soc., Petroleum Club (bd. dirs. 1988-91, sec. 1991), Kiwanis (Downtown bd. dirs. 1993, sec. 1995-96), Phi Kappa Phi, Sigma Gamma Epsilon, Beta Theta Pi. Home: 7520 E 21st St # 10 Wichita KS 67206 2: 107 N Market St Ste 1007 Wichita KS 67202

COWELL, BILL, minister; b. Clay Center, Kans., July 6, 1939; s. Horace Edward and Dorothy Katherine (Jenkins) C.; m. Carole Ann Weber, July 7, 1963; children: Mary Elizabeth, Rebecca Ruth, Grace Ann, Daniel Levi, Sarah Suzanna. BS, Kans. State U., 1961; MDiv, Wheaton Coll., 1965. Ordained minister. Pastor Calvary Bapt. Ch., Hoisington, Kans., 1965-68, Emmanuel Bapt. Ch., Marion, Kans., 1968-72; prin. Victory Christian Acad., Hutchinson, Kans., 1972—; pastor Village Ch., Hutchinson, 1974-90; dir. Heart Ministries, Inc., Hutchinson, 1971—. Republican. Baptist. Home and Office: PO Box 2068-19 S Victory Rd Hutchinson KS 67504

COWIE, NORMAN EDWIN, credit manager; b. Balt., Nov. 24, 1958; s. Graham Norman Cowie and Jane Ardythe (Wertzler) Seekman; m. Sandra Jo Twaddle, Oct. 19, 1985; children: Samantha Lynn, Lauren Alexandra. AA, Kalamazoo Valley (Mich.) C.C., 1978; BBA magna cum laude, Western Mich. U., 1980. Cert. credit exec. Nat. Assn. Credit Mgmt. Mgr. Assocs. Fin. Co., Mich., Ill., 1980-85; region credit supr. Westinghouse Electric Supply, Elmhurst, Ill., 1985-89; v.p. fin., corp. credit mgr. Evergreen Oak Electric Sales and Supply, Crestwood, Ill., 1989—; chmn. Elec. Distbrs. Credit Group, Park Ridge, Ill., 1990-92; bd. dirs. Chgo. Midwest Credit Mgmt. Assn., Park Ridge; spkr. Nat. Elec. Contractors Assn., DuPage, Ill., 1991, Chgo. Plumbing & Heating Wholesalers Credit Group, Oak Brook, Ill., 1994; moderator Roundtable Discussion, Ill. Mechanic's Lien Law, Park Ridge, 1994, Ill. Mechanic's Lien Seminar, Rosemont, Ill., 1995. Author: (comic) Short Circuit, 1992; contbr. articles to profl. jours. Mem. Improved Constn. Practices Com. (chmn. Ill. chpt. 1993—), Chgo. Midwest Credit Mgmt. Legis. Com. (chmn. 1992-95). Home: 2822 Hawkshead New Lenox IL 60451 Office: Evergreen Oak Electric Supply 13400 S Cicero Crestwood IL 60445

COWLER, ROSEMARY ELIZABETH, English educator, college administrator; b. Ft. Wayne, Ind., May 10, 1925; d. John Ambrose and Rosella Elizabeth (Plummer) C. BA, Douglass Coll., New Brunswick, N.J., 1946; MA, Ind. U., 1949; PhD, Yale U., 1956. Instr. Lake Forest (Ill.) Coll., 1955-57, asst. prof., 1957-62, assoc. prof., 1962-68, prof., 1968-95, dir. grad. program, 1990—; trustee Lake Forest Acad., 1987-95. Author: Shadow and Substance: A Discussion of Pope's Correspondence, 1966; editor: Twentieth Century Interpretations of Pamela, 1966, The Prose Works of Alexander Pope, Vol. II: The Major Works 1625-1744, 1986 (Rose Mary Crawshay Prize Brit. Acad. 1987). Pres. lake Forest Libr. Bd., 1972-79; bd. mem. Friends Lake Forest Libr., 1987-93. Recipient Outstanding Tchr. award Inland Steel-Ryerson Found., 1981; grantee Widener Libr. Harvard U., 1959, Am. Coun. Learned Socs., 1961, Ford Found., 1968, Lake Forest Coll., 1974, NEH, 1984, 88, Douglass Soc., 1989; named Hotchkiss Presdl. chair Lake Forest Coll., 1992. Mem. AAUP (chpt. pres. 1963), Am. Soc. 18th Century Studies, MLA (reader, evaluator), Modern Humanities Rsch. Assn. (Am. sec., treas. 1988-92), North Ctrl. Commn. Instns. Higher Edn. (evaluator, commr. 1973-75), Phi Beta Kappa (chpt. sec. 1962-95). Democrat. Home: 700 Green Briar Ln Lake Forest IL 60045-3217 Office: Lake Forest Coll 555 N Sheridan Rd Lake Forest IL 60045-2338

COWLES, ERNEST LEE, academic administrator, educator, consultant, researcher; b. Lead, S.D., Aug. 9, 1949; s. Leon Andrew and Freeda (Kaubisch) C.; m. Ellison Bell Fuller, Sept. 4, 1970. BA, U. So. Fla., 1971; MS, Rollins Coll., 1976; PhD, Fla. State U., 1981. Probation and parole officer I & II Fla. Probation Parole Commn., Central, Fla., 1971-76; psychologist Fla. Dept. Offender Rehab., Clearmont, 1976; asst. prof. Northeast Mo. State U., Kirksville, 1978-1984, assoc. prof., 1984-85; dir. div. classification and treatment Mo. Dept. Corrections and Human Svcs., Jefferson City, 1985-89; assoc. prof., prin. investigator Ctr. Study Crime Delinquency & Corrections So. Ill. U., Carbondale, 1989-94; dir. Ctr. Legal Studies U. Ill., Springfield, 1994—; cons. Kirksville Police Dept., 1984, 10th Jud. Cir. Juvenile Div., Hannibal, Mo., 1983; with Nat. Inst. Justice U.S. Dept. Justice, Washington, 1985—, Fed. Bur. Prisons, 1989, Bur. Justice Assistance, 1990—. Contbr. articles to profl. jours. and chpts. to books. Exec. bd. Lincoln Legal Papers, 1994—. Active Boy Scouts Am.; mem. Gov.'s Task Force on Rape. Law Enforcement Asst. Adminstrn. fellow, 1976-78. Mem. Am. Soc. Criminology, Acad. Criminal Justice Scis., Am. Correctional Assn., Justice Rsch. & Stats. Assn. (exec. bd. 1993), Mensa. Home: 1312 Community Dr Springfield IL 62703

COWLES, JOHN, JR., publisher, women's sports promoter; b. Des Moines, May 27, 1929; s. John and Elizabeth (Bates) C.; m. Jane Sage Fuller, Aug. 23, 1952; children: Tessa Sage Flores, John, Jane Sage, Charles Fuller. Grad., Phillips Exeter Acad., 1947; AB, Harvard U., 1951; LittD (hon.), Simpson Coll., 1965. With Cowles Media Co. (formerly Mpls. Star and Tribune Co.), 1953-83, v.p., 1957-68, editor, 1961-69, pres., 1968-73, 79-83, editorial chmn., 1969-73, chmn., 1973-79, dir., 1956-84; pres. Harper's Mag., Inc., 1965-68, chmn. bd., 1968-72; dir. Harper & Row, Pubs., Inc., N.Y.C., 1965-81; chmn. Harper & Row, Pubs., Inc., 1968-79; dir. Des Moines Register & Tribune Co., 1960-84, Farmers & Mechanics Savs. Bank, Mpls., 1960-65, Cowles Comms., Inc., N.Y.C., 1960-65, Equitable Life Ins. Co. Iowa, Des Moines, 1964-66, 1st Bank Systems, Inc., Mpls., 1964-68, A.P., N.Y.C., 1966-75, Midwest Radio-TV, Inc., Mpls., 1967-76; fitness instr. Sweatshop Fitness Ctr., St. Paul, 1989-93; guest artist Bill T. Jones/Arnie Zane & Co., 1990-92; vice chmn. Women's Profl. Fastpitch, L.L.C., Mpls., 1995—. Mem. adv. bd. on Pulitzer Prizes, Columbia U., 1970-83; campaign chmn. Mpls. United Fund, 1967; bd. dirs. Guthrie Theatre Found., 1960-71, pres., 1960-63, chmn., 1964-65; trustee Phillips Exeter Acad., 1960-65; bd. dirs. Walker Art Ctr., 1960-69, 87-92, Minn. Civil Liberties Union, 1956-61, Urban Coalition Mpls., 1968-70, Mpls. Found., 1970-75, German Marshall Fund U.S., 1975-78; bd. dirs. Am. Newspaper Pubs. Assn., 1975-77, mem. govt. affairs com., 1976-79. Served to 2d lt. AUS, 1951-53. Named one of ten outstanding men of year U.S. Jr. C. of C., 1964. Mem. Greater Mpls. C. of C. (dir. 1978-81, chmn. stadium site task force 1977-82). Clubs: Minneapolis (Mpls.).

COWLES, ROBERT L., state legislator; b. July 31, 1950. BS, U. Wis., Green Bay, 1975. Mem. from dist. 75 Wis. State Assembly, Madison, 1983-87; mem. from dist. 2 Wis. State Senate, Madison, 1987—; mem. Gov.'s Coun. on Recycling and Environ. Edn. Bd.; mem. joint com. on fin. Wis. House Reps. Office: 2424 Ducharme Ln Green Bay WI 54301-1912*

COWLES, ROLLIN JAMES, III, public health administrator; b. Burlington, Iowa, Mar. 30, 1921; s. Rollin James Jr. and Ruth Whitlatch (Smith) C.; m. Betty Irene Miller, Apr. 1, 1945; children: R.J. IV, Catherine, Anne, Christina, David, Molly. Student, Iowa State U., 1939-41, DVM, 1950. Vet. medicine pvt. practice Burlington, Iowa, 1950-76; adminstr. county health unit Des Moines County, 1976-86; chmn. pub. health Health Bd., Des Moines County, 1965-86, other offices, 1950-76. Chmn. Sr. Citizens Ctr., Burlington, Iowa, 1970-96, UN SE Iowa (pres. 1995—); advisor Boy Scouts Am. Explorer Post, Burlington, 1970-95; advisor Boy Scouts Am. Explorer Post, Burlington, 1970-90 (Silver Beaver award 1970); vol. Planned Parenthood, Burlington, 1960-86; vol. trail work in Nat. Forests, Nat. Parks and Monuments, 1986—. Sgt. maj. AUS, 1941-46, 1st lt. vet. corps. U.S. Army Res., with 113th cav. Iowa Nat. Guard. Mem. Responsible Sr. Vol. Program, Habitat for Humanity, Sierra Club (chmn. Leopold Group 1960-95), Am. Hiking Soc., Nature Conservancy. Republican. Home: 5256 Ferres Ln Cynclyf Farm Burlington IA 52601-9030

COWLES, RONALD EUGENE, church administrator; b. Ottumwa, Iowa, Jan. 30, 1941; s. Fred Howard and Bertha Ilelah (Sammons) C.; m. Rowena Rae Miller, Apr. 30, 1959; children: Richard Eric, David Allen, Rebecca Ruth. BA, Ottawa (Kans.) U., 1963; BD, MDiv, Ctrl. Bapt. Theol. Sem., Kansas City, Kans., 1966; D of Ministry, U. Bibl. Studies, 1991. Pastor Dry Ridge Bapt. Ch., Uniontown, Kans., 1961-63, First Bapt. Ch., Easton, Kans., 1963-66, Renwick (Iowa)-Corwith Parish, 1966-72, First Bapt. Ch., Pella, Iowa, 1972-86; assoc. exec. min. S.D. Bapt. Conv., Sioux Falls, 1986-91; exec. min. Am. Bapt. Chs. Dakotas, Sioux Falls, 1991—; bd. trustees Sioux Falls Coll., Ctrl. Bapt. Theol. Sem., Kansas City. Mem. Lions (pres. 1971), Rotary (bd. dirs. 1980-82). Office: Am Bapt Chs 1524 S Summit Ave Sioux Falls SD 57105-1632

COWLEY, BENJAMIN DOLLAR, nephrologist, molecular biologist; b. Louisville, Oct. 18, 1956; s. Benjamin Dollar and Mary Francis (Hammond) C. Student, Rice U., 1974-77; MD, Baylor U., 1981. Diplomate Am. Bd. Internal Medicine/Nephrology. Intern, then resident in internal medicine U. Kans. Med. Ctr., Kansas City, 1981-84, fellow in nephrology, 1984-85, fellow in biochemistry, 1985-87, rsch. instr., 1986-87, asst. prof. medicine, 1989-94; assoc. prof. medicine, 1994—; adj. asst. prof. biochemistry, molecular biology U. Kans. Med. Ctr., Kansas City, 1989—; guest scientist NIH, Bethesda, Md.,1987-89. Contbr. articles to Procs. of NAS, Jour. Biol. Chemistry, Am. Jour. Physiology, Jour. Clin. Investigation. Grantee Kans. Heart Assn., Topeka, 1990, Polycystic Kidney Rsch. Found., Kansas City, 1990. Mem. AAAS, Am. Soc. Cell Biology, Am. Fedn. Clin. Rsch., Am. Soc. Nephrology, Ctrl. Soc. Clin. Rsch., Sigma Xi. Home: 5847 Howe Dr Shawnee Mission KS 66205-3441 Office: Univ Kans Med Ctr 4015 Sudler 39th St at Rainbow Blvd Kansas City KS 66160

COWLING, MICHAEL RAY, communications educator; b. Mt. Carmel, Ill., Jan. 16, 1953; s. Harold Vernon and Helen Louise (Houchin) C.; m. Melanie Therese Grzesiak, Sept. 2, 1972; children: Matthew Ryan, Audrey Ann. BA in Journalism, Ea. Ill. U., 1975; MS in Journalism, U. Ill., 1976. Copy editor Champaign (Ill.) News Gazette, 1975-76; sports copy desk chief Champaign-Urbana (Ill.) Courier, 1976-77; asst. news editor Joliet (Ill.) Herald-News, 1977-82; copy editor Chgo. Sun-Times, 1982-86; nat. news editor L.A. Times, 1986-94; asst. prof. journalism U. Wis. Oshkosh, 1994—; cons. Thomson Newspaper, Appleton, Wis., 1995—; textbook reviewer St. Martin's Press, N.Y.C., 1994—. Fellow Freedom Forum, 1995, William Weld fellow Am. Press Inst., 1995. Mem. Soc. Profl. Journalists, Assn. Edn. in Journalism and Mass Comm., Kappa Tau Alpha. Office: U Wis Journalism Dept 800 Algoma Blvd Oshkosh WI 54901

COWLING, RANDAL KEITH, minister; b. Killeen, Tex., Nov. 13, 1957; s. Marion F. and Ollie L. (Hosey) C.; m. Doris Jean Lorenz, May 28, 1978; children: Jennifer Ann, Emily Megan. BA, SW Bapt. Coll., 1979; MDiv, Midwestern Bapt. Sem., 1989. Ordained to ministry So. Bapt. Conv., 1987. Interim minister edn., ch. extension intern Park Hill Bapt. Ch., Kansas City, Mo., 1986-87; dir. ch. and community ministries Clay-Platte Bapt. Assn., Kansas City, 1987-89, dir. ch. programs, 1988-89; founder, pastor Boardwalk Chapel, Atlantic City, 1989-95; dir. Atlantic City Ministries, 1989-95; founder, co-pastor Iglesia Bautista Hispana, Atlantic City, 1990, Hope Fellowship Ch., Galloway Township, N.J., 1991-95; dir. missions So. Bapts. of Kaw Valley, Topeka, 1995—. Compiler (community ministries manual) Northland Directory, 1987. Co-founder-pres., v.p. Northland Homes Partnership, Kansas City, 1988. Named Outstanding Young Man of Am., Jaycees, Kansas City, 1987, 89. Mem. South Jersey Bapt. Assn. (sec.-treas. ministers fellowship 1989—), So. Bapt. Social Svcs. Assn. (charter, v.p. publs.), Assn. Resort and Leisure Mins. Office: So Bapts of Kaw Valley 2300 SW 29th St Topeka KS 66611

COWLISHAW, MARY LOU, state legislator; b. Rockford, Ill., Feb. 20, 1932; d. Donald George and Mildred Corinne (Hayes) Miller; m. Wayne Arnold Cowlishaw, July 24, 1954; children: Beth Cowlishaw McDaniel, John, Paula Cowlishaw Rader. BS in Journalism, U. Ill., 1954. Mem. editorial staff Naperville (Ill.) Sun newspaper, 1977-83; mem. Ill. Ho. of Reps., Springfield, 1983—, chmn. elem. and secondary edn. com., 1995—, vice-chmn. pub. utilities com., 1995—, mem. joint Ho.-Senate edn. reform oversight com., 1985—; mem. Ill. Task Force on Sch. Fin., 1990—; vice chmn. Ho. Rep. Campaign Com., 1990—; co-chair Ho. Rep. Policy Com., 1991—; chmn. edn. com. Nat. Conf. State Legislatures, 1993—; mem. Joint Com. Adminstrv. Rules, 1992—; commr. Edn. Commn. of the States, 1995—; chair, Ill. Women's Agenda Task Force, 1994—. Author: This Band's Been Here Quite a Spell, 1983. Mem. Naperville Dist. 203 Bd. Edn., 1972-83; co-chmn. Ill. Citizens Coun. on Sch. Problems, Springfield, 1985—. Recipient 1st pl. award Ill. Press Assn., 1981, commendation Naperville Jaycees, 1986, Golden Apple award Ill. Assn. Sch. Bds., 1988, 90, 92, 94, Outstanding Women Leaders of DuPage County award West Suburban YWCA, 1990, Activator award Ill. Farm Bur., 1996; named Best Legislator, Ill. Citizens for Better Care, 1985, Woman of Yr., Naperville AAUW, 1987, Best Legislator, Ill. Assn. Fire Chiefs, 1994, Outstanding Edn. Adv. Indian Prairie Sch. Dist. 204, 1994, Legislator of Yr., Ill. Assn. Pk. Dists., 1995; commr. Edn. Commn. of the States, 1994—. Mem. Am. Legis. Exchange Council, Conf. Women Legislators, Nat. Fedn. Rep. Women, DAR, Naperville Rep. Women's Club (pres. 1994—). Methodist. Home: 924 Merrimac Cir Naperville IL 60540-7107 Office: 552 S Washington St Ste 119 Naperville IL 60540-6669

COX, CLIFFORD ERNEST, deputy superintendent, chief information officer; b. Chgo., Apr. 28, 1942; s. Clifford Ernest and Beulah May (Lynn) C.; m. Scenobia Butler, June 20, 1964; children: Clifford, Fred, Sean. BA, U. Chgo., 1964, MBA, 1966; postgrad., No. Ill. U., 1988—. Cert. in data processing. Sr. systems engr. IBM, Chgo., 1966-69; v.p. MIS Golden Fifty Pharm., Chgo., 1969-71; sr. mgr. Arthur Andersen & Co., Chgo., 1971-79; pres. Cenox Systems, Inc., Chgo., 1979-81; chief info. officer Chgo. Pub. Schs., 1981-92; deputy supt. Detroit (Mich.) Pub. Schs., 1992—; lectr. Keller Grad Sch. Mgmt., 1986-89; del. Ill. Regional White House conf., 1990. Contbr. articles to profl. jours. Bd. dirs. Assn. House, Chgo., 1991; mem. Chgo. Assembly. Home: 1526 Chateaufort Pl Detroit MI 48207-2717 Office: Detroit Pub Schs 5057 Woodward Ave Detroit MI 48202-4000

COX, DAVID CARSON, media company executive; b. Orange City, N.J., July 31, 1937; s. Earl Byron and Ruth Elinor (Carson) C.; m. Vicki Bever, Aug. 29, 1958; children: Brian Bever, Carson Burns. AB magna cum laude with honors in Econs., Stanford U., 1959; MBA, Harvard U., 1961. V.p., gen. mgr. Lawry's Foods, Inc., Los Angeles and Paris, 1962-75, Litton Microwave Co., Mpls., 1975-79, Toro Co., Mpls., 1979-81; exec. v.p., chief operating officer Cowles Media Co., Mpls., 1981-85, pres., chief operating officer, treas., 1984-85, pres., chief exec. officer, 1985—, corp. sec., 1983-84, dir., 1982—; bd. dirs. Nat. Computer Systems, Mpls., Tennant Co., Mpls., NWNL Cos., Inc. Trustee Macalester Coll., Mpls.; bd. dirs. Guthrie Theater, 1977-86, v.p., 1982, pres., 1983-85, chmn., 1985—; bd. dirs. Minn. Bus. Partnership, Inc., 1985—, United Way Mpls., 1991—. Lt. U.S. Army, 1962-64. Mem. Newspaper Assn. Am. (chair postal affairs subcom. 1991—, vice chair com. on govt. and legal pub. policy 1992—, bd. dirs. 1991—), Coun. Fgn. Rels. Mpls., Harvard Bus. Sch. Club, Stanford Alumni Club, Minikahda Club, Mpls. Club. Office: Cowles Media Co 329 Portland Ave Minneapolis MN 55415*

COX, JUSTIN B., editor; b. Seagrove, N.C., Jan. 27, 1934; s. Justin B. and Ruth (Farlow) C.; m. Golda Rae Garner, Dec. 28, 1958. AB, High Point (N.C.) Coll., 1955; postgrad., U. N.C., Greensboro, 1960-62. Cert. secondary tchr., N.C. Tchr. Siler City (N.C.) Pub. Schs., 1955-56, Asheboro (N.C.) Pub. Schs., 1958-69; dir. pub. rels. Wings and Wheels Mus., Santee, S.C., 1969; editor-in-chief Exptl. Aircraft Assn., Oshkosh, Wis., 1970—. Editor, pub., writer, owenr quar. mag. Sportsman Pilot, 1981—; editor-in-chief, writer monthly mag. Sport Aviation, 1970—. Served with USN, 1956-58. Recipient Journalism award Aviation/Space Writers Assn., 1988. Mem. Exptl. Aircraft Assn., Aircraft Owners and Pilots Assn., Antique Airplane Assn. Office: Exptl Aircraft Assn PO Box 3086 Oshkosh WI 54901-3086

COX, MARY E., physics and engineering educator, consultant; b. Detroit, Nov. 11, 1937; d. Willis H. and Dorothy E. (Nicholls) Buckles; 1 child, Kendall M. Cox. AB, Albion Coll., 1959; MA, U. Mich., 1961; PhD, UCLA, 1984. Tutor in physics Sommerville Coll. U. Oxford, Eng., 1977-78, demonstrator Clarendon Lab., 1977-78; instr. physics U. Mich.-Flint, 1966-71; asst. prof. physics U. Mich.-Flint, Flint, 1971-76, assoc. prof. physics, 1976-84, chmn. dept. physics and astronomy, 1976-77, acting dean, 1981-82; rsch. assoc. The Crump Inst. for Med. Engring., 1982-84, rsch. scientist, 1984-87; assoc. prof. physics and engring. U. Mich.-Flint, 1984-88; prof. physics and engring. U. Mich.-Flint, Flint, 1988—, chmn. dept. physics and engring. sci., 1987-89, 92—. Contbr. articles to profl. jours. Recipient Ralph and Marjorie Crump prize for excellence in med. engring., 1984; NSF grantee, 1977-78. Mem. Optical Soc. Am., Am. Assn. Physics Tchrs. (pres. Mich. sect. 1975), Materials Rsch. Soc. Office: U Mich-Flint Dept Physics & Engring Sci 303 E Kearsley St Flint MI 48502-2186

COX, MARY LINDA, maintenance industry executive; b. Alton, Ill., July 3, 1946; d. William M. and Helen (Winters) C. BA, McKendree Coll., 1970; MBA, So. Ill. U., 1977; postgrad. date St. Louis U., 1984—. Exec. dir. Girl Scouts U.S., 1969-76; instr. So. Ill. U., Edwardsville, 1976-80; mgr. Smith-Scharff, St. Louis, 1980-81; account exec. AT&T, Tulsa, 1981-82; pres. Mo. Disposable Products, St. Louis, 1982-91, Am. Comml. Cleaning, pres., CEO, 1987—; v.p. Devel. Family Svcs. and Vis. Nurse Assn., Alton, Ill., 1992-94. Media specialist Tenn. Rep. Party, 1974; bd. dirs., pub. rels. chmn. YWCA, Alton, 1st v.p., pres.; mem. fin. com., 1st v.p. Greater St. Louis coun. Girl Scouts U.S., pres., 1993; mem. youth panel United Way St. Louis; planning chmn., mem. Greene County Hist. Soc., City of Wood River planning commn., White House Com. on Librs.; active United Cerebral Palsy, 1994. Mem. Central Bus. Assn. (v.p. 1985), Am. Comml., Beta Gamma Sigma (chpt. pres. 1978-79). Office: Am Comml Cleaning 4 E Lorena Ave Wood River IL 62095-1710

COX, MICHAEL MATTHEW, biochemist; b. Wilmington, Del., May 19, 1952; s. Louis William and Helen Rita (Keenan) C.; m. Beth Leslie Birnbach, Aug. 8, 1986; children: Thomas Halpern and Benjamin Louis (twins). BA in Biology, U. Del., 1974; PhD in Biochemistry, Brandeis U., 1980. Asst. prof. U. Wis., Madison, 1983-87, assoc. prof., 1987-92, prof., 1992—, asst. chair dept., 1993—; ad hoc study sect. NIH, Washington, 1988, 90, microbial physiology and genetics study sect., 1993-95. Asst. editor Jour. Biol. Chemistry, 1991—; contbr. articles to Critical Rev. of Biochemistry and Molecular Biology, Ann. Rev. Biochemistry, Nucleic Acid Rsch. jour. Recipient Rsch. Career Devel. award NIH, 1984-89, Dreyfus Tchr.-Scholar award Camille and Henry Dreyfus Founds., Inc., 1986-91; Shaw fellow Milw. Found., 1983-88; Basil O'Connor Starter Rsch. grantee March of Dimes, 1984-86. Mem. AAAS, Am. Chem. Soc. (Eli Lilly award 1989), Am. Soc. for Biochemistry and Molecular Biology. Office: U Wis-Madison Dept Biochemistry 420 Henry Mall Madison WI 53706-1502

COX, PAUL NOEL, law educator; b. Salt Lake City, Mar. 17, 1949; s. Herman Wilford and Carole Jeanne (Christmas) C.; m. Margaret Koven, Jan. 6, 1973 (div. Nov. 1979); 1 child, Jennifer Cox; m. Christine Allyson Eland, Aug. 5, 1988. BS, Utah State U., 1971; JD, U. Utah, 1974; LLM, U. Va., 1980. Bar: Utah. Asst. prof. Valparaiso (Ind.) U., 1980-83, assoc. prof., 1983-84, prof., 1984-86; prof. Ind. U., Indpls., 1986—. Author: Employment Discrimination, 1987, 2d edit., 1992, Employment Discrimination, Cases and Commentary, 1991. Capt. USAF, 1974-78. Mem. Order of the Coif, Phi Kappa Phi. Office: Ind U Sch Law 735 W New York St Indianapolis IN 46202

COX, RAY L., state legislator; m. Judy Cox. Mem. Ho. of Reps., Topeka, 1993—; investment broker. Home: 824 S 131st St Bonner Springs KS 66012-9604*

COX, VANDE LEE, critical care nurse; b. Takoma, Md., June 21, 1954; d. Vego Larkin and Lanette Lucille (Cunningham) Gooch; divorced; children: Andrea, Nathenial. Diploma, Deaconess Hosp. Sch. Nursing, 1976; BSN, U. Evansville, Ind., 1980, MSN, 1989. RN, Ind.; CEN, CCRN; cert. PALS, ACLS, TNCC, BTLS, ACLS instr. Nurse emergency rm. Deaconess Hosp., Evansville, 1976-77; clin. instr. Deaconess Hosp. Sch. Nursing, Evansville, 1980-85; clin. instr. ICU and med./surg. unit U. Evansville, 1989; critical care nurse Welborn Hosp., Evansville, 1989-90, emergency rm. nurse, 1990—; charge nurse Thunder on the Ohio, 1991; clin. instr. Ivy Tech., Evansville, 1992. Mem. Emergency Nurses Assn., Critical Care Nurses Assn., Sigma Theta Tau. Home: 3417 Koring Rd Evansville IN 47720-2612 Office: Welborn Hosp 401 SE 6th St Evansville IN 47713

COY, PATRICIA ANN, special education director, consultant; b. Beardstown, Ill., Apr. 2, 1952; d. Ben L. and Dorothy Lee (Hubbell) C. BS in Elem. and Spl. Edn., No. Ill. U., 1974; MS in Spl. Edn., Northeastern Ill. U., 1976, MA in Spl. Edn., 1978; MEd in Spl. Edn., Northeastern U., 1984; postgrad., No. Ill. U., 1988—. Cert. elem. and spl. edn. tchr.; cert. counselor. Mental health supr. Waukegan (Ill.) Devel. Ctr., 1974-77; ednl. therapist Grove Sch. and Residential Program, Lake Forest, Ill., 1977-78; dir. residential svcs. N.W. Suburban Aid for the Retarded, Park Ridge, Ill., 1978-83; exec. dir. The Learning Tree, Des Plaines, Ill., 1983—; dir. residential svcs. Augustanan Ctr. Luth. Social Svcs. of Ill., Chgo., 1984-86, dir. planning and evaluation, 1986-93, dir. community svc., 1993-95; exec. dir. Blare House Inc., Des Plaines, Ill., 1995—; behavior advisor Habilitative Systems, Inc., Chgo., 1985-88; program coord. Human Resource Devel. Inst., Chgo., 1986-89; project dir. Support Svcs. Ill., Inc., Chgo., 1987-91; dir. TranSteps Inc. Steps for Success for Adults with Learning Differences, 1991—. Contbr. articles to profl. jours. Mem. Coun. for Exceptional Children, Am. Assn. Mental Deficiency, Chgo. Assn. Behavioral Analysis, Behavior Analysis Soc. Ill., Assn. for Supervision and Curriculum Devel., Nat. Rehab. Assn., Coun. for Disability Rights, Assn. for Learning Disability, Profls. in Learning Disabilities, Cwens, Echoes, Mortar Bd., Kappa Delta Pi. Democrat. Mem. United Ch. of Christ. Home: 8936 N Parkside Ave Apt 118 Des Plaines IL 60016-5517 Office: TranSteps 7144 N Harlem Ave Ste 344 Chicago IL 60631-1017 also: Blare House 960 Rand Rd Ste 216 Des Plaines IL 60016

COY, WILLIAM RAYMOND, civil engineer; b. Omaha, Nov. 28, 1923; s. Vern Elmer and Edna Mae (Seymour) C.; m. Geraldine Petra Zaback, July 31, 1943; children: Carol Sue, William R. Jr., Russell B., Steven D., Marcus R. Student, Omaha Mcpl. U., 1944, 45. Registered profl. engr., N.D. Lab. technician U.S. Army CE, 1946-57; paving engr. CE, Albuquerque Dist., Roswell, N.Mex., 1958-61; chief materials testing CE Ballistic Missile Constrn., Minot and Grand Forks, N.D., 1961-65; engr.-in-charge CE Green River Dam, Campbellsville, Ky., 1965-68; chief concrete sect. CE Div. Lab., Omaha, 1968-78; chief materials engr. CE Missouri River Div., Omaha, 1978-87; assessor, constrn. technology Nat. Inst. Standards and Tech., Omaha, 1987—. With USN, 1945-46. Mem. Soc. Am. Mil. Engrs., Am. Concrete Inst. Home: 3226 S 44th Ave Omaha NE 68105-3815

COYLE, MARTIN ADOLPHUS, JR., lawyer; b. Hamilton, Ohio, June 3, 1941; s. Martin Adolphus and Lucille (Baird) C.; m. Sharon Sullivan, Mar. 29, 1969 (div. Dec. 1991); children: Cynthia Ann, David Martin, Jennifer Ann; m. Linda J. O'Brien, July 31, 1993. BA, Ohio Wesleyan U., 1963; JD summa cum laude, Ohio State U., 1966. Bar: N.Y. 1967. Assoc. Cravath, Swaine & Moore, N.Y.C., 1966-72; chief counsel securities and fin. TRW Inc., Cleve., 1972-73, sr. counsel, asst. sec., 1973-75, asst. gen. counsel, asst. sec., 1976, asst. gen. counsel, sec., 1976-80, v.p., gen. counsel, sec., 1980-89, exec. v.p., gen. counsel, sec., 1989—; sec. TRW Found., 1975-80, trustee, 1980—. Co-inventor voting machine. Pres. Judson Retirement Cmty., 1986-88, trustee, 1986-90; nat. chmn. Ohio Wesleyan U. Assocs., 1987-89; chmn., sec. Martin A. Coyle Found.; trustee Berea Coll., 1989— Chautauqua Inst., 1990—, Fairhill Inst. for the Elderly, 1990—, Univ. Hosps. Health Systems, Inc., 1990—, Ohio Wesleyan U., 1992—; mem. steering com. Cleve. Aquarium, 1990-92. Mem. ABA, Am. Soc. Corp. Secs. (pres. Ohio regional group 1978-80, nat. dir. 1981-87, nat. chmn. 1985-86), Assn. Gen. Counsel (sec.-treas. 1992-94, 2d v.p. 1994-95, pres. 1996—, exec. com. 1992—), Ohio Bar Assn., Bar Assn. Greater Cleve., Hillbrook Club, Union Club. Home: 29 Shoreby Dr Bratenahl OH 44108-9999 Office: TRW Inc 1900 Richmond Rd Cleveland OH 44124-3719

COYNE, ANN, social work educator; b. Medford, Mass., June 26, 1936; d. Edward James Jr. and Catherine Mary (Stokes) Gaffey; m. Dermot Patrick Coyne, June 15, 1957; children: Patrick J., Brian D., Thomas M., James E., Catherine A., Gerard W. BA, Cornell U., 1958; MSW, U. Nebr., 1975, PhD, 1980. Dir. community services Lancaster Office Mental Retardation, Lincoln, Nebr., 1971-75; assoc. prof. social work U. Nebr., Omaha, 1975-88, prof. social work, 1988—; dep. dir. State Dept. Social Services, Lincoln, 1981-82; pres. Coyne & Assocs., Lincoln, 1978—; project dir. Child Welfare Tng. Inst., Lincoln, 1982-87; bd. dirs. Adoption Links Worldwide. Contbr. articles to profl. jours. Bd. dirs. Child Guidance Ctr., Lincoln, 1975-81, Crime and Community, Lincoln, 1983-85, Nebraskans for Peace, Lincoln, 1985, Nebraskans for Nicaraguan Children, 1987-95, Voices for Children in Nebr., 1987-92, Assn. Pediatricians United Health Children Nicaragua, 1995, v.p.; chmn. Gov.'s Planning Coun. on Devel. Disabilities, 1986-90. Mem. Nat. Assn. Social Workers, Child Welfare League of Am. (cert.), Sigma Xi. Democrat. Catholic. Home: 1130 N 79th St Lincoln NE 68505-2007 Office: Univ Nebr Sch Social Work Annex # 40 Omaha NE 68106

COYNE, MARY JEANNE, state supreme court justice; b. Mpls., Dec. 7, 1926; d. Vincent Mathias and Mae Lucille (Steinmetz) C. BS in Law, U. Minn., 1955, JD, 1957. Bar: Minn. 1957, U.S. Dist. Ct. Minn. 1957, U.S. Ct. Appeals (8th cir.) 1958, U.S. Supreme Ct. 1964. Law clk. Minn. Supreme Ct., St. Paul, 1956-57; assoc. Meagher, Geer, Markham & Anderson, Mpls., 1957-70, ptnr., 1970-82; assoc. justice Minn. Supreme Ct., St. Paul, 1982—; mem. Am. Arbitration Assn., 1967-82; mem. bd. conciliation Archdiocese St. Paul and Mpls., 1981-82; instr. U. Minn. Law Sch., Mpls., 1964-68; mem. Lawyers Profl. Responsibility Bd., St. Paul, 1982; chmn. adv. com. rules of civil appellate procedure Minn. Supreme Ct., St. Paul, 1982—, chair adv. com. rules of civil procedure, 1984—. Editor: Women Lawyers Jour., 1971-72. Mem. ABA, Minn. State Bar Assn., Nat. Assn. Women Lawyers, Nat. Assn. Women Judges, Minn. Women Lawyers Assn., U. Minn. Law Alumni Assn. Office: Minn Supreme Ct 422 Minn Jud Ctr 25 Constitution Ave Saint Paul MN 55155-1500

COZ, MARY KATHLEEN, respiratory therapist; b. Ravenna, Ohio, Aug. 1, 1952; d. John and Kathleen (Bronson) C. A in Secretarial Sci., U. Akron, 1972, A in Respiratory therapy, 1979, BS, 1986, MS in Tech. Edn., 1990. Registered and lic. respiratory therapist. Sec. Kent (Ohio) Bd. Edn., 1970; exec. sec. Ernst & Ernst, Akron, Ohio, 1972-75; respiratory therapist, tech. support assoc. Akron City Hosp. Summa Health Syss., 1977—. Mem. Am. Assn. Respiratory Care, Ohio Soc. Respiratory Care, Nat. Bd. Respiratory Care. Roman Catholic. Home: 1236 Chelton Dr Kent OH 44240-3240 Office: Akron City Hosp 525 E Market St Akron OH 44304-1619

COZORT, AMBER LYNNE, nurse; b. West Plains, Mo., Jan. 4, 1963; d. Norris Bert and Chlora Ivene (Brickey) C. BSN, Rockhurst Coll. and Rsch. Coll. of Nursing, Kans. City, Mo., 1985. Psychiat. staff nurse Cox Med. Ctr. North, Springfield, Mo., 1985; psychiat. technician Park Cen. Hosp., Springfield, 1985-86; orthopedic staff nurse St. John's Regional Health Ctr., Springfield, 1986—. Mem. com. St. John's Med. Explorer Post 339, 1989-90, pres., 1990-91; mem. Greene County Rep. Party-TARGET; mem. Rep. Nat. Com., 1995; mem. com. S.W. Mo. Nurses Recognition Dinner, 1992-94, chair, 1994—. Mem. Mo. Nurse Assn. (corr. sec., past bd. dirs., 4th dist. nominating com., mem. med.-surg. spl. interest group 1993-95, sec. 1996—, region F regional dir. 1994—, mem. MONA-PAC com. 1996—), Nat. Assn. Orthopedic Nurses, Rsch. Nursing Alumni Assn., Rsch. Coll. Nursing Alumni Assn., Rsch. Coll. Nursing Honor Soc.

CRABB, BARBARA BRANDRIFF, federal judge; b. Green Bay, Wis., Mar. 17, 1939; d. Charles Edward and Mary (Forrest) Brandriff; m. Theodore E. Crabb, Jr., Aug. 29, 1959; children: Julia Forrest, Philip Elliott. A.B., U. Wis., 1960, J.D., 1962. Bar: Wis. 1963. Assoc. Roberts, Boardman, Suhr and Curry, Madison, Wis., 1962-64; legal rschr. Sch. Law, U. Wis., 1968-70, Am. Bar Assn., Madison, 1970-71; U.S. magistrate Madison, 1971-79; judge U.S. Dist. Ct. (we. dist.) Wis., Madison, 1979—, chief judge, 1980-96, dist. judge, 1996—; mem. Gov. Wis. Task Force Prison Reform, 1971-73. Membership chmn., v.p. Milw. LWV, 1966-68; mem. Milw. Jr. League, 1967-68. Mem. ABA, Nat. Assn. Women Judges, State Bar Wis., Dane County Bar Assn., U. Wis. Law Alumni Assn.(defender svcs. com. jud. conf.). Home: 741 Seneca Pl Madison WI 53711-2950 Office: US Dist Ct PO Box 591 120 N Henry St Madison WI 53701-0591

CRABB, DELBERT ELMO, state legislator; b. McPherson, Kans., Sept. 27, 1916; s. Paul C. and Louise (Molzen) C.; m. Georgana Oelrich, 1937; 1 child, Gary Conn. Student, McPherson Coll., 1934-36; BS, U. Kans., 1938, MS, 1946. Mayor City of McPherson, 1981-87; mem. Kans. Ho. of Reps., Topeka; chmn. McPherson County Rep. Com., Kans., 1968-74. Mem. McPherson Sch. Bd. Edn., 1949-61 (pres. 3 yrs.). With AUS, Am. Theatre. Mem. Nat. Assn. Music Merchants, Res. Officers Assn., Kans. Music Merchants Assn., Elks, VFW, Am. Legion Res. Officers Assn., Phi Delta Kappa. Home: 1532 N Walnut St Mc Pherson KS 67460-1824*

CRABB, KENNETH WAYNE, obstetrician, gynecologist; b. Glendive, Mont., June 17, 1950; s. Kenneth Willard and Marjorie Jane (Martin) C.; m. Gwen Aldean Wendelschafer, June 8, 1974; children: Kenneth Wendel, Richard David. BS with honors in Biochemistry, U. Iowa, 1971, MD, 1975. Diplomate Am. Bd. Ob-Gyn. Intern, then resident in ob-gyn St. Paul Ramsey Med. Ctr., 1975-79; practice medicine specializing in ob-gyn St. Paul, 1979—; clin. asst. prof. ob.-gyn. U. Minn., Mpls., 1981-82, clin. assoc. prof., 1989—; vice chmn. dept. ob.-gyn. United Hosp., St. Paul, 1984-86, 91-93, pharm. and therapeutics com., 1980-84, cance com., 1995—; preceptor family practice resident St. John's Hosp., St. Paul, 1979—, maternal health com., 1979-88, cancer com., 1984-85; quality assurance com. St. Joseph's Hosp., St. Paul, 1981-83; mem. Med. Affairs Coun. for Health One, 1989-93; chmn. bd. dirs. ParaNatal Svcs., Inc., 1990-94; bd. dirs. Preferred One Physicians Assn., 1987—, pres. 1994-96, Preferred One PPO, Preferred One Mgmt. Co.; physician advisor Medtrac, Health Mark, Found. for Health Care Evaluation. Trustee Actors Theatre of St. Paul, 1980-90, bd. dirs, 2d v.p., 1984-85; mem. council Grace Luth. Ch., 1984-87; bd. dirs. Indianhead Council Boy Scouts Am., 1986—. Recipient Eagle Scout award Boy Scouts Am., 1966, Appreciation award Am. Acad. Family Physicians, 1979-90. Fellow Am. Coll. Ob-Gyn. (jr. fellow dist. chmn. 1978-79, jr. fellow adv. coun. 1978-80, chmn. 1989 Dist. VI meeting, appreciation award 1978-79, chmn. higher edn. loan program com. 1989-91, adv. coun. Minn. sect. 1996—), Am. Fertility Soc.; mem. AMA (Physicians Recognition award 1985, 88, 90, 93, 96), Ctrl. Assn. Obstetricians & Gynecologists, Am. Soc. Coloscopy & Cervical Pathology, Am. Assn. Gynecologic Laparoscopists, Minn. Med. Assn. (nominating com. 1986-87, legis. com. 1988-94, vice chmn. 1989-94, med. practice and planning com. 1995—, vice chmn. 1995—), Minn. Obstetric and Gynecologic Soc. (program com. 1984), Ramsey Med. Soc. (bd. trustees 1993-94, med. practice com. 1982-87, del. 1983, 85-87, fin. com. 1984-89, med. svc. com. 1986-88, nom. com. 1992-93, polit. action com. 1988—, pres.-elect 1995, pres. 1996), Assn. Profs. Ob-gyn., Found. Health Care Evaluation, Rotary (chmn. various coms. 1983-84, 87-88, bd. dirs. 1984-86, 89-91, v.p. 1991-92, pres. 1992-93, sgt. at arms 1986-87), Phi Beta Sigma, Omicron Delta Kappa, Phi Beta Phi (sec. U. Iowa chpt. 1972-73, 2d vice archon 1982-83, supreme sec. treas. 1984-89, supreme archon 1989-92). Office: Advanced Specialty Care for Women 310 Smith Ave N Ste 390 Saint Paul MN 55102-2378

CRAFT, BEVERLY JO, library director; b. Kinsley, Kans., July 30, 1931; d. Joseph Olaf and Rubie Helen (Hatfield) C. BA, Wichita State U., 1964. Exec. sec. Larned (Kans.) State Hosp., 1955-62; kindergarten tchr. Hutchinson (Kans.) Schs., 1964-69, Bur. Indian Affairs, Manderson, S.D., 1971-72; libr. dir. Kinsley Pub. Libr., 1972—; co-chair Kans. State Tchrs. Assn. Ann. meeting, 1968-69; rep., com. mem., treas., mem. search com. Southwest Kans. Libr. Sys., Dodge City, 1972—. Com. mem. Edwards County Centennial Com., Kinsley, 1973; county rep. Iroquois Ctr. Mental Health Hdqs., Greensburg, Kans., 1985-86. Mem. Eastern Star (conductress 1975-77), Delta Kappa Gamma (chmn. various coms. Beta Iota chpt. 1973—). Republican. Methodist. Office: Kinsley Libr 208 E Eighth St Kinsley KS 67547

CRAHAN, JACK BERTSCH, manufacturing company executive; b. Peoria, Ill., Aug. 24, 1923; s. John F. and Ann B. (Bertsch) C.; m. Peggy Furey, Sept. 9, 1944; children—Patrick Michael, Colleen Mary, Kevin Furey. BS, U. Minn., 1948. With Flexsteel Industries, Inc., Dubuque, Iowa, 1948—, plant mgr., 1950-54, gen. mgr., v.p., 1955-70, exec. v.p., 1970-84, pres., 1985-89, vice-chmn., chief ops. officer, 1989-90, chief exec. officer, 1990—, chmn. bd. dirs.; bd. dirs. Dubuque Bank and Trust Co., Dubuque Racing Assn.; trustee United Steel Workers Am. Pension Fund. Bd. regents Loras Coll., 1967-80, 81—; bd. dirs. Xavier Hosp., 1969-78, Boys Club Am., 1981—. Served with USNR, 1942-43; Served with USMC, 1943-46, 51-52. Decorated D.F.C. (2), Air medal (6). Mem. Am. Furniture Assn. (bd. dirs. 1974-80). Republican. Roman Catholic. Home: 1195 Arrowhead Dr Dubuque IA 52003-8594 Office: Flexsteel Industries Inc Brunswick Indsl Block PO Box 847 Dubuque IA 52001

CRAIG, ELIZABETH LOUISE, management consultant; b. Chgo., Feb. 10, 1951; d. Lewis Kurtzman and Betty Jane (O'Neill) Kinne; m. James J. Craig Jr., Mar. 31, 1973. BS with high distinction, U. Minn., 1973; MBA cert., U. St. Thomas, 1983; MBA, Coll. of St. Thomas, 1989. Cert. in family and consumer scis. Educator Edina (Minn.) Pub. Schs., 1973-82, area leader, 1979-82; pres., founder Craig Group Internat., Eden Prairie, Minn., 1982—; invited spkr. Coll. of Advanced Edn., Perth, Western Australia, 1988. Author: Don;t Slurp Your Soup, A Basic Guide to Business Etiquette, 1991 (Book award 1992), 2d rev. edit., 1996; author: (with others) Careers, 1991. Adv. coun. Eden Prairie Community Ednl. Svcs., 1994—. Recipient New Achiever award, 1984. Mem. Eden Prairie Women's Network (founding pres. 1982-91), Mktg. Communicators Assn., Midwest Ind. Publishers Assn. (spl. interest group 1992—), Minn. Women's Consortium (mem. leaders of today and tomorrow 1994—).

CRAIG, HURSHEL EUGENE, agronomist; b. Chrisman, Ill., May 18, 1932; s. Thomas Hurshel and Letha Mae (Short) C.; m. Zada Pauline Honnold, Dec. 29, 1954; children: Toni Jane, Tina Jean. Student, Ea. Ill. U., 1951, Ill. State U., 1956; BS, U. Ill., 1958, MS, 1970, postgrad., 1974. Mgr. Lime Svc. Co., Chrisman, Ill., 1959-61; br. mgr. Remole Soil Svc., Inc., Potomac, Ill., 1961-64, home office mgr., 1966-67; ptnr., agronomist Harris Fertilizer, Inc., Farmer City, Ill., 1967-69; farm cons. Gifford (Ill.) State Bank, 1964-66; instr. agr. Danville (Ill.) Area Community Coll., 1970-80; agronomy cons. and ptnr. C & S Pro-Farm Svcs., Ridge Farm, Ill., 1977-80; agronomy cons. Ag-Vantage, Westerville, Ohio, 1980-85; soils analysis sales CLC Labs Ind., West Lafayette, 1985-90, agronomy cons., 1987—; soil and plant tissue analysis sales Cal-Mar Soil Testing Lab., West Lafayette, 1990—. Co-author: Career Awareness Test for Agriculture Students and Prospective Spouses, 1974. Chmn. adminstrv. coun. Bismarck (Ill.) United Meth. Ch., 1989-91. With U.S. Army, 1952-54. Mem. Ill. Fertilizer and Chem. Assn., Profl. Crop Cons. Ill. (pres. 1992), Ill. Soil Testing Assn. Methodist. Home and Office: 16916 E 2690 North Rd Danville IL 61834-6067

CRAIG, JOHN ROBERT, broadcast and cinematic arts educator, researcher; b. New Kensington, Pa., Dec. 21, 1947; s. Raymond R. and Ann (Facemyer) C.; m. Linda Kay Raybuck, Dec. 26, 1971; children: Shea, Tyson, Daedre. BS inEdn., Clarion U. of Pa., 1969, MS, 1971; PhD, U. Mo., 1981. Sports dir. WWCH Radio, Clarion, 1966-69; mem. faculty N.W. Mo. State U., Maryville, 1971-80; mem. faculty Ctrl. Mich. U., Mt. Pleasant, 1980—, chair dept. broadcast and cinematic arts, 1993-96; text reviewer Focal Press. Contbr. articles to Lit./Film Quar., Jour. Evolutionary Psychology, Other Dimensions, Edn., Feedback, Journalism Educator. Baseball coach Mt. Pleasant Farm League, 1988-90; mem. percussion crew Mt. Pleasant High Marching Band, 1995. Mem. NEA, Broadcast Edn. Assn., Internat. Assn. on the Fantastic in the Arts, Assn. for Evolutionary Psychology, Speech Comm. Assn. Home: 6033 E Broadway Mount Pleasant MI 48858 Office: Ctrl Mich U 340 Moore Hall Mount Pleasant MI 48859

CRAIG, JUDITH, bishop; b. Lexington, Mo., June 5, 1937; d. Raymond Luther and Edna Amelia (Forsha) C. BA, William Jewell Coll., 1959; MA in Christian Edn., Eden Theol. Sem., 1961; MDiv, Union Theol. Sem., 1968; DD, Baldwin Wallace Coll., 1981; DHL, Adrian Coll., 1985, Otterbein Coll., 1993. Youth dir. Bellefontaine United Meth. Ch., St. Louis, 1959-61; intern children's work Nat. Coun. of Chs. of Christ, N.Y.C., 1961-62; dir. Christian edn. 1st United Meth. Ch., Stamford, Ct., 1962-66; inst. adult basic edn. N.Y.C. Schs., 1967; dir. Christian edn. Epworth Euclid United Meth. Ch., Cleve., 1969-72, assoc. pastor, 1972-76; pastor Pleasant Hills United Meth. Ch., Middleburg Heights, Ohio, 1976-80; conf. council dir. East Ohio Conf. United Meth. Ch., Canton, 1980-84; bishop United Meth. Ch., Mich. area, 1984-92, West Ohio area, 1992—; mem. Nat. Task Force on Itineracy, 1977-80; responder to World Coun. of Chs. (document on Baptism, Eucharist and Ministry 1975); gen. conf. del., 1980, 84; mem. United Meth. Publ. House Bd., 1992—; bd. dirs. U.S. Health Corp.; frequent lectr. and preacher; bd. trustees 27 institutions in West Ohio. Contbr. articles to ministry mags. Bd. dirs. YWCA, Middleburg Heights, 1976-80. Recipient Citation of Achievement William Jewell Coll., 1985, Woman of Achievement award YWCA, 1995. Office: 32 Wesley Blvd Worthington OH 43085

CRAIGHEAD, WENDEL LEE, film and video producer, director; b. Burr Oak, Kans., May 30, 1936; s. Alfred and Eva May (Burton) C. Student, Kans. State U., 1954-55; BA, Bethany (Okla.) Nazarene Coll., 1959; postgrad., U. Mo., Kansas City, 1962-63. Film editor Calvin Prodns., Kansas City, 1959-63, film dir., 1963-68; v.p., mgr. producer services Calvin Communications, Kansas City, 1968-75, producer, 1975-80, producer, v.p. sales, 1980-82; owner Craighead Film & Video, Prairie Village, Kans., 1982—. Dir. A Place in History, 1969 (Cine Golden Eagle award 1970); producer, dir. We Proceeded On: The Expedition of Lewis and Clark 1804-1806 (blue ribbon Am. Film Festival 1992); producer, dir. 60 motion pictures. Mem. Assn. N.Am. Radio Clubs (nat. exec. sec. 1970-72), Nat. Rwy. Hist. Soc., Smoky Hill. Rwy. Hist. Soc., Friends of Nat Frontier Trail Ctr. Republican. Nazarene. Home and Office: 2110 W 74th Ter Shawnee Mission KS 66208-3437

CRAIGO, GORDON EARL, engineer; b. Glasgow, W.Va., June 17, 1951. BS in Nuclear Engring., U. Fla., Gainesville, 1977; MS in Edn., Nat.-Louis U., 1995. Field engr. General Electric, Oak Brook, Ill., 1978-84; pres., owner Craigo Tech. Svc., Inc., Woodridge, Ill., 1984—. Office: Craigo Tech Svcs Inc 6s235 Steeple Run Dr Ste 12G Naperville IL 60540-3769

CRAIN, JOHN KIP, school system administrator; b. Urbana, Ohio, June 14, 1956; s. William Frederick and Patricia Ann (Bumgardner) C.; m. Rebecca Ann Ireland, July 11, 1980; children: Amanda Ann, Tiffany Kay, Kelly Jo. BS in Edn. summa cum laude, Ohio State U., 1985, MA, 1987; predoctoral, Bowling Green State U., 1992—. Cert. tchr., supr. dir., prin., asst. supt., supt., Ohio. Drafter, office mgr. Crain Bldgs., Mechanicsburg, Ohio, 1974-82; tchr. drafting Springfield (Ohio)-Clark County Joint Vocat. Sch., 1982-86; supr. Eastland Vocat. Schs., Groveport, Ohio, 1986-91; dir. Oregon (Ohio) City Schs., 1991—; bd. dirs. Ohio Indsl. Tng. Program, Toledo; co-chair skill olympics Ohio Vocat./Indsl. Clubs Am., Columbus, 1987-89; presenter workshops. Author and editor catalog Eastland Vocat. Schs., 1987. Vol. St. Charles Hosp. Emergency Rm., 1991—; bd. dirs. Ea. Comty. YMCA,Toledo, 1992-94. Pres.'s sr. scholar Ohio State U., 1984. Mem. Am. Vocat. Assn. (life), Ohio Vocat. Assn. (life), Ohio Vocat. Dirs. Assn., Ohio Assn. Secondary Sch. Adminstrs., Bay Area Jr. C. of C. (state dir. 1991-94), Oregon Area C. of C., Kiwanis (bd. dirs. 1991-95, pres. 1995-96 East Toledo chpt.), Ohio Vocat. Indsl. Club Am. (regional advisor 1984-86, asst. dir. summer leadership camp 1985-86, chairperson state skill olympics 1986, 87, author and editor program guidelines 1985, local advisor notebook 1986), Phi Delta Kappa, Pi Lambda Theta, Omicron Tau Theta. United Methodist. Home: 2036 Coe Ct Perrysburg OH 43551-5600 Office: Oregon City Schs 5721 Seaman Rd Oregon OH 43616-2600

CRAMER, DAVID WARREN, investment banker; b. Campbell, Ohio, Sept. 16, 1966. BA, Kent State U., 1990. Lic. series 7 Nat. Assn. Securities Dealers; lic. real estate and life ins. broker, Mich. Investment banker The Ohio Co., Muskegon, Mich., 1991—. With Army N.G., 1988—. Mem. Ducks Unltd., Optimists. Republican. Roman Catholic. Office: The Ohio Co 427 Seminole Rd Muskegon MI 49444-3747

CRAMER, JANIS R., educational art specialist, artist; b. Tiffin, Ohio, Oct. 26, 1963; d. Walter Cletus and Regina Marie (Hartzell) Beat; m. Thomas A. Cramer, Oct. 30, 1987; children: Nicholas David. BS in Art Edn., Bowling Green State U., 1986. Cert. tchr., Mich., Ohio. Freelance artist Battle Creek, Mich., 1986—; gallery mgr. Decor Corp., Kalamazoo, 1987-90; art specialist Crestline (Ohio) Exempted Village Schs., 1986-87, Art Ctr. Battle Creek, 1988—, Battle Creek Pub. Schs., 1990—; seminar coord. E.K. Kellogg Corp., Battle Creek, 1991; mem. sch. improvement core team Battle Creek Pub. Schs., 1991—, dist. sch. improvement team, 1994—; participant Koyo Corp. Japanese Tchr. Exch., 1995. One-woman shows include Sam & Diane's (photography, hon. mention), 1990, B.C. Focus Photography, 1990, Pen Dragon's Calligraphy Show, Kalamazoo, 1991, Mich. Artists Competition, Battle Creek Art Ctr., 1993; student artwork published in book, Peace Ribbon, 1985. Active Battle Creek Hist. Soc., 1992; mem. City of Battle Creek Historic Commn., 1996—; vol. Food Bank S. Ctrl. Mich., 1990—; founding, fundraiser mem. Empty Bowls. Recipient Gallery Art Video Disc, Nat. Gallery Art, 1993; W.K. Kellogg expert-in-residence program grantee, 1995. Mem. Nat. Art Edn. (Mich. Art Edn. Assn. region 4 liaison), Mich. Art Edn. Assn., Mich. Alliance for Arts, United Arts Coun. Calhoun County (grantee 1991, 92, 94), Leila Arboretum Soc. Roman Catholic. Home: 24 Garrison Ave Battle Creek MI 49017-4730

CRAMER, MICHAEL WILLIAM, insurance executive; b. London, Feb. 14, 1924; came to U.S., 1939; s. William and Belle (Klauber) C.; m. Martha Lorena Deckman, Jan. 20, 1951; 1 child, Bruce Edward. BSBA, Washington U., St. Louis, 1947. CLU. Clk., group claims Gen. Am. Life Ins. Co., St. Louis, 1947-51; inventory control clk. Fred Campbell Auto Supply Co., St. Louis, 1951-55; sales and planning rep. Equitable Life Assurance Soc., St. Louis, 1955—. Active St. Louis Artists Guild, 1990; pres. Permanent Endowment Found., 1991-94, chmn. spl. funds com., 1994—, pres. council 1995—; bd. dirs. City of Univ. City (Mo.) C. of C. Mem. Life Underwriters Assn. St. Louis (bd. dirs. 1972-78, award 1987, nominee Life Underwriter of Yr. 1994), Estate Planning Coun. St. Louis, Assn. CLU and ChFC (bd. dirs. St. Louis chpt., chmn. student sponsorship com. through 1993, Meritorious Svc. award 1993), IW Club Varsity Athletics Alumni Washington U. (mem. exec. com. 1991—). Home: 718 Audubon Dr Saint Louis MO 63105-2906 Office: 8182 Maryland Ave Ste 1000 Saint Louis MO 63105-3786

CRAMER, WILLIAM ANTHONY, biochemistry and biophysics researcher, educator; b. N.Y.C., June 11, 1938; s. Robert and Sylvia (Blumstein) C.; m. Hanni Aebersold, Sept. 11, 1964; children: Rebecca, Jean-Marc, Gabrielle, Nicholas. BS, MIT, 1959; MS, U. Chgo., 1960, PhD, 1965. NSF post doctoral fellow U. Calif., San Diego, 1965-67; research assoc. U. Calif., 1967-68; asst. prof. dept. biol. scis. Purdue U., West Lafayette, Ind., 1968-73; assoc. prof. Purdue U., 1973-78, prof., 1978—, assoc. head dept., 1984-86; Henry Koffler prof. biol. scis. Purdue U., West Lafayette, Ind., 1995—; head panel predoctoral fellowships in biophysics and biochemistry NSF, 1979, mem. molecular biology panel, 1980-82, mem. cellular biochemistry panel, 1989-91; mem. panel competitive grants USDA, 1983-84; chmn. Gordon Conf. on Photosynthesis; mem. phys. biochemistry study sect. NIH, 1991—. Author textbook on bioenergetics; editor: Archives Biochemistry and Biophysics, 1979-91, Biochim. Biophys. Acta, 1983—, Photosynthesis Rsch., 1989—, Jour. Bioenergetics Biomembranes, 1991—; contbr. articles to profl. jours. Recipient Rsch. Career Devel. awrd NIH, 1970-75, H.N.McCoy award for sci. achievement Purdue U., 1988, Kettering award Sm. Soc. Plant Physiologists, 1996; EMBO fellow U. Amsterdam, 1974-75, Alexander von Humboldt fellow Max-Planck Inst., Frankfurt, 1992, John Simon Guggenheim fellow, 1992-93. Mem. Am. Soc. Biol. Chemists, Protein Soc., Biophys. Soc. (chmn. bioenergetics subgroup 1989-92, organizing com. "Biophys. Discussions" 1992, program chair 40th annual meeting 1996). Office: Purdue U Dept Biol Sci Lilly Hall of Life Sciences West Lafayette IN 47907

CRANDALL, LEE ALDEN, medical sociologist, educator; b. Alexandria Bay, N.Y., Aug. 27, 1947; s. Frank D. and Althea (Morse) C.; m. Terry Anne Russell, Aug. 26, 1967 (div. 1988); children: Mark William, Timothy Russell; m. Sherril L. Aversa, Nov. 6, 1993. AA, Jefferson C.C., 1967; BA, SUNY-Potsdam, 1969; MS, Purdue U., 1973, PhD (USPHS fellow), 1976. Asst. research scientist U. Fla. Coll. Medicine, Gainesville, 1976-77, asst. prof. depts. community health and sociology, 1977-81, assoc. prof., 1981-91, prof., 1991-94; prof., head dept. cmty. health, U. Ill., Urbana Champaign, 1994—; tchr.; research adminstr. Bd. dirs. Fla. affiliate Am. Heart Assn., 1991-94, Ill. affiliate, 1994—. Mem. Alpha Kappa Delta, Phi Kappa Phi. Episcopalian. Contbr. numerous articles in field to profl. jours. Home: 2904 Timbergate Rd Champaign IL 61821 Office: U Ill Dept Community Health MC588 1206 S 4th St Champaign IL 61820

CRANDALL, NEAL H., substance abuse counselor; b. Springfield, Ohio, Apr. 4, 1952; s. Vaughn Jack and Virginia Carol (Fotheringham) C.; m. Ellen Holster, Dec. 27, 1977 (div. 1981); 1 child, Benjamin Jack; m. Pamela Kay Davis, Sept. 4, 1993. BA in Polit. Sci. and Econs., Earlham Coll., 1974; MEd in Counseling and Chem. Dependency, Wright State U., 1995. Pub. New Soc. Pub., Phila., 1978-79; peace edn. sec. Am. Friends Svc. Com., Dayton, Ohio, 1980-81; substance abuse counselor McKinley Hall, Springfield, 1994—. Bd. dirs. House of the People, Dayton, 1989—; spl. events coord. African-Am. Cultural Week, Inc., Yellow Springs, Ohio, 1991—; co-founder, co-chair Miami Valley Unemployed Coalition, Greater Dayton, 1982-87; co-chair Rainbow Coalition, Greene County, Ohio, 1988; founder Coalition for Survival, Yellow Springs, 1980-82; co-founder Greene Environ. Coalition, Greene County, 1989-91. Recipient Meritorious Svc. award African Am. Cultural Week, Inc., 1993. Mem. Am. Counselors Assn., Ohio Counselors Assn. Quaker. Home: 360 W North College # 115

Yellow Springs OH 45387 Office: McKinley Hall 1101 E High St Springfield OH 45505

CRANDELL, DWIGHT SAMUEL, museum executive; b. Parke County, Ind., Nov. 30, 1943; s. Terence Wesley and Alice Ruth (Cox) C.; m. Rachel Louise Wentworth, June 14, 1965; children: Jeremy, Abigail, Joanna, Joshua. B.A., Principia Coll., 1965; M.A., SUNY-Oneonta, 1974. Asst. in research and adminstrn. Mt. Vernon (Va.) Ladies Assn. of the Union, 1965-66; exhibits coordinator, ednl. docent Children's Mus., Indpls., 1972-73, curator exhibits research and planning, 1973-77, collections dir., 1977-81; dir. devel., asst. dir. St. Louis Sci. Ctr., 1981-82, exec. dir., 1982-94, v.p. programs and ops., 1992-95, v.p. ops., 1996—; bd. dirs. Wild Canid Rsch. and Survival Ctr., 1983-88, 91-95. Served to capt. USAF, 1966-71. Nat. Mus. Act travel grantee, 1973. Mem. Am. Assn. Museums, Midwest Museums Conf., Mo. Museums Assocs. (v.p. 1983-85, pres. 1986-87, 94-95), Assn. Sci-Tech. Ctrs. (bd. dirs. 1983-85), St. Louis Area Mus. Collaborative, Rotary. Christian Scientist. Office: Saint Louis Sci Ctr 5050 Oakland Ave Saint Louis MO 63110-1404

CRANDELL, JODIE LEIGH, environmental specialist; b. Evansville, Ind., Nov. 4, 1959; d. William Lawrence and Wilma Izetta (Coffman) Woolley; m. Mark Theodore Brown, Nov. 30, 1985 (div. Dec. 1990); m. G.R. Crandell, Mar. 26, 1992. BA, Ind. U., 1983, postgrad., 1983-85. Intern Ind. Infrastructure Inc., Indpls., summer 1985; enforcement specialist Indpls. Air Pollution Control Div., 1985-89; environ. engr. Chrysler-Indpls. Foundry, 1989-90; plant environ. control adminstr. Chrysler Corp.-Indpls. Foundry, 1990-91; corp. environ. engr. Copeland Corp., Sidney, Ohio, 1991-92; rsch. assoc. Ind. Environ. Inst., Indpls., 1992-94; environ. cons. Keramida Environ. Inc., 1994—. Mem. Am. Foundrymen Soc. (environ. com. Chgo. chgp. 1989-91), Piqua Area Environ. Coun., Copeland Mgmt. Assn., Ind. Cast Metals Assn. (bd. dirs. Indpls. chpt. 1990-91), Air and Waste Mgmt. Assn., Phi Beta Kappa, Nat. Wildlife Fedn., World Wildlife Fund, Nature Conservancy. Home and Office: 2220 Fisher Ave Speedway IN 46224-5033

CRANE, FAYE, small business owner; b. Amery, Wis., Dec. 2, 1947; d. Vaemond Hall and Irene C. (L'Allier) C.; 1 child, Camille Mills Seifert. Grad. high sch., Milltown, Wis. Premiums statis. clk. State Farm Ins., St. Paul, 1968-73; pension adminstrn. asst. Mut. Svc. Ins., St. Paul, 1973-78; dist. dir. Avon Products, Inc., Morton Grove, Ill., 1978-79; sales rep. Midwest Bus. Sys., Duluth, Minn., 1979-84, REM's Inc., Grand Rapids, Minn., 1984; pres. prodn. Presto Print, Grand Rapids, 1984—. Mem. No. Minn. Citizen's League, Grand Rapids, 1984—, Nat. Mus. Women in the Arts, 1988—; commr. City of Grand Rapids Planning Commn., 1990-94; bd. dirs. Grand Rapids Econ. Devel. Authority, 1994—. Mem. NAFE, Nat. Fedn. Bus. and Profl. Women (treas. nat. conv. 1992), Minn. Fedn. Bus. and Profl. Women (mem. promotion com. 1982-92, emblem chmn. 1982-83, found. chmn. 1983-84, exec. dir., chmn. 1984-85, editor 1987-90, v.p. 1992-93, pres. 1994-95), Grand Rapids Bus. and Profl. Women (pres. 1985-86). Home: PO Box 404 Grand Rapids MN 55744-0404 Office: Presto Print 516B S Pokegama Ave Grand Rapids MN 55744-3525

CRANE, FREDERICK LORING, biochemistry educator; b. Montague, Mass., Dec. 12, 1925; s. Frederick Turner and Gertrude Irene (Stange) C.; m. Helen Marguerite Eggerth, Apr. 8, 1950 (dec. Mar. 1980); children: Richard, Katherine, Eleanor, Thomas; m. Marilyn Ann Marquardt, Mar. 13, 1982. BS, U. Mich., 1950, MS, 1951, PhD, 1953; MD (hon.), Karolinska Inst., Stockholm, 1989. Fellow Enzyme Inst., U. Wis., Madison, 1953-59; asst. prof. chemistry U. Tex., Austin, 1959-60; assoc. prof. biology Purdue U., West Lafayette, Ind., 1960-62, prof., 1962-94, prof. emeritus, 1994; vis. prof. Wenner Gren Inst., U. Stockholm, 1963-64; vis. fellow in biochemistry Australian Nat. U., Canberra, 1970-71, 79-80; vis. prof. cell biology U. Cordoba, Spain, 1994-95; mem. molecular biology rev. panel NSF, Washington, 1969-71; dir. advanced rsch. workshop NATO, Cordoba, 1988. Editor: Plasma Membrane Oxidoreductases in Control of Animal and Plant Growth, 1989, Oxidoreduction at the Plasma Membrane Relation to Growth and Transport, Vol. 1, 1990, Vol. 2, 1991; mem. editorial bd. Biochimica et Biophysica Acta, 1968-91; rev. editor Jour. Bioenergetics and Biomembranes, 1980-91. With U.S. Army, 1944-46, World War II. Recipient Eli Lilly award Am. Chem. Soc., 1961, silver medal U. Bologna, Italy, 1989, award for rsch. on coenzyme Q, Folkers Found, 1996. Mem. Am. Soc. Biol. Chemistry, Am. Soc. Plant Physiologists, Plant Growth Soc. Am., Am. Soc. for Cell Biology. Office: Purdue U Dept Biology West Lafayette IN 47907

CRANE, JEROME CALVIN, JR., college, university administrator; b. Chgo., Oct. 18, 1967; s. Jerry Calvin and Ruby Jewel (Jenkins) C. BA, Drake U., 1989. Cert. claims adjuster, Ill. Profl. athlete L.A. Raiders, Dallas Cowboys, L.A., Dallas, 1989; claims adjuster Economy Fire& Casualty, Freeport, Ill., 1989-91; coll. admissions specialist Triton Comty. Coll., River Grove, Ill., 1991-95; asst. dir. admissions Midwestern U., Downers Grove, Ill., 1995—; staff facilitator Scout Camp (Pro football), Chgo., 1995-96; sr. program specialist U.S. Dept. Edn., Maywood, Ill., 1996—; bd. advisors Triton C.C., River Grove, 1993-95; mentor student support svcs., 193-95. Participant in food drive and transport Fellowship of Christian Athletes, Des Moines, 1988; Big Brother, City of Freeport, 1992; supr. Punt, Pass & Kick, Athletes in Edn., Chgo., 1994; mem. faculty for basic life skills, Mighty God Tabernacle Ch., Chgo., 1995. Recipient Umpire Appreciation award Southeast Baseball League, Chgo., 1983, Rookie Appreciation award L.A. Raiders, 1989, Comty. Leadership award, Comtys. with God, Inc., Chgo., 1992; recognized as Guide to Experts, Fellowship of Christian Athletes, Des Moines, 1988. Mem. Nat. Assn. Coll. Admission Counselors, Ill. Assn. Coll. Admission Counselors, Ill. Coun. for Coll. Attendance, Nat. Assn. Minority Med. Educators. Democrat. Roman Catholic. Office: CEDA Talent Search 515 St Charles Rd Maywood IL 60513

CRANE, PATRICIA SUE, probation services administrator, social worker; b. Rockway, N.Y., Jan. 17, 1948; d. Herbert Milton and Miriam (Rosenblum) Brager; m. Marvin J. Crane, May 2, 1971; 1 child, Elizabeth A. BA, U. Wis., 1969; MS in Criminal Justice with honors, Wayne State U., 1984. Cert. social worker. Dir. probation svcs. 52d dist. ct. 1st div. State of Mich., Novi, 1979—. Jewish. Home: 5042 Meadowbrook Dr West Bloomfield MI 48322-1570 Office: 52nd Dist Ct 1st Divsn 48150 Grand River Ave Novi MI 48374-1222

CRANE, PHILIP MILLER, congressman; b. Chicago, Ill., Nov. 3, 1930; s. George Washington III and Cora (Miller) C.; m. Arlene Catherine Johnson, Feb. 14, 1959; children: Catherine Anne, Susanna Marie, Jennifer Elizabeth, Rebekah Caroline, George Washington V, Rachel Ellen, Sarah Emma, Carrie Esther. Student, DePauw U., 1948-50; B.A., Hillsdale Coll., 1952; postgrad., U. Mich., 1952-54, U. Vienna, Austria, 1953, 56; M.A., Ind. U., 1961; Ph.D., 1963; LL.D., Grove City Coll., 1973, Nat. Coll. Edn., 1987; Doctor en Ciencias Politicas, Francisco Marroquin U., 1979. Advt. mgr. Hopkins Syndicate, Inc., Chgo., 1956-58; teaching asst. Ind. U., Bloomington, 1959-62; asst. prof. history Bradley U., Peoria, Ill., 1963-67; dir. schs. Westminster Acad., Northbrook, Ill., 1967-68; mem. 91st-104th Congresses, 12th (now 8th) Ill. Dist., 1969—, Ways and Means Com. Author: Democrat's Dilemma, 1964, The Sum of Good Government, 1976, Surrender In Panama: The Case Against the Treaty, 1978; contbr.: Continuity in Crisis, 1974, Crisis in Confidence, 1974, Case Against the Reckless Congress, 1976, Can You Afford This House?, 1978, View from the Capitol Dome (Looking Right), 1980, Liberal Cliches and Conservative Solutions, 1984. Dir. rsch. Ill. Goldwater Orgn., 1964; mem. nat. adv. bd. Young Ams. for Freedom, 1965—; bd. dirs. Am. Conservative Union, 1965-82, chmn., 1976; bd. dirs., chmn. Intercollegiate Studies Inst.; bd. advisors Ashbrook Ctr., Ashland U., 1983—, univ. trustee, 1988-93; founder Rep. Study Com., 1972—, chmn., 1984; commr. Commn. on Bicentennial U.S. Constn., 1986-91; trustee Hillsdale Coll. Recipient Distinguished Alumnus award Hillsdale Coll., 1968, Independence award, 1974, William McGovern award Chgo. Soc., 1969, Freedoms Found. award, 1973; named Ill. Statesman's Father Yr., 1979. Mem. ASCAP, VFW (award 1978), Am. Hist. Assn., Orgn. Am. Historians, Acad. Polit. Sci., Am. Acad. Polit. and Social Scis., Am. Legion, Phila. Soc., B'nai B'rith (award 1978), Phi Alpha Theta, Pi Gamma Mu. Office: 233 Cannon House Bldg Washington DC 20515

CRANEY, TERRANCE LEE, physics educator; b. Eau Claire, Wis., June 6, 1950; s. Sidney Harold and Loretta (Oatman) C.; m. Diane E. Otto, June 10, 1988; children: Michael S., Taylor L. BS, U. Wis., Eau Claire, 1974; MS, U. Wis., Superior, 1977. Physics, math. instr. N.E. Wis. Tech. Coll., Green Bay, 1974-95. Campaign mgr. State Rep. Sharon Metz, Green Bay, 1980-86, State Rep. Mary Lou VanDreel, Green Bay, 1986-92; del. to Dem. Nat. Conv., Atlanta, 1988, N.Y.C., 1992. Mem. Wis. Vocat. Assn. (Tchr. of Yr. 1984, 88), Wis. Edn. Assn. Coun. (v.p. 1991-95, pres. 1995—). Democrat. Home: 1218 Tramore Tr Madison WI 53717 Office: WEAC PO Box 8003 Madison WI 53708

CRANT, JAMES MICHAEL, business educator; b. Ft. Myers, Fla., May 9, 1961; s. Jesse James and Carol (Presson) C.; m. Teresa Ann Meisel, July 23, 1983; children: Julia, Brian. BSBA, U. Fla., 1983, MBA, 1985; PhD, U. N.C., 1990. Asst. prof. mgmt. U. Notre Dame, Ind., 1990-96, assoc. prof. mgmt., 1996—. Mem. editl. bd. Jour. of Mgmt., 1995—; contbr. articles to profl. jours. Mem. Acad. Mgmt. Office: U Notre Dame PO Box 399 Notre Dame IN 46556

CRARY, SELDEN BRONSON, physicist; b. Schenectady, N.Y., May 10, 1949; s. Selden Bronson and Marjorie Darlene (Simpson) C.; m. Susan Florence Engert, Sept. 19, 1975; 1 child, Kathryn Simpson. ScB, Brown U., 1971; MS, U. Wash., 1973, PhD, 1978. Asst. prof. physics dept. Amherst (Mass.) Coll., 1978-82; sr. rsch. scientist GM Rsch. Labs., Warren, Mich., 1983-87, staff rsch. scientist, 1987-88; pres. Mich. Microsensor, Inc., Ann Arbor, 1988—; asst. rsch. scientist dept. elec. engring. and computer sci. U. Mich., Ann Arbor, 1988—; vis. asst. prof. dept. physics and astronomy U. Mass., Amherst, 1981-83. Designer (computer software) I-OPT, CAEMEMS; contbr. articles to profl. jours. Office: 1301 Beal Ave Ann Arbor MI 48109-2122

CRARY, SHARON ANNE, needlework designer; b. Morristown, N.J., Jan. 17, 1953; d. Randolph and Virginia Bette (Joostema) Smith; m. John Gerald, July 8, 1972; children: Laura, Megan, Benjamin. Grad. high sch., Saranac Lake, N.Y. Sec. U. of the Ozarks, Clarksville, Ark., 1972-76, 2d Bn. 42d FA, Crailsheim, Germany, 1978-80, Swisher & Ackerson Attys., St. Petersburg, Fla., 1982-83; sec., asst. Cardinal Industries, College Park, Ga., 1984-85; designer, owner The Crary Collection, Wahiawa, Hawaii, 1985-87, Sharon Anne Designs, Ft. Leavenworth, Kans., 1989-90; designer, owner, needlework tchr. Sharon Anne Designs, Evans Mills, N.Y., 1990-92; nnedlework adviser Ft. Drum (N.Y.) Officers Wives Club, 1990-92. Designer original needlework designs The Stitchery, 1990, 91, 92. 2d grade asst. Evans Mills Primary Sch., 1990-91; ways and means chairperson Ft. Drum Officers Wives Club, 1991-92. Mem. Heartland Stitch Counters Soc. (sec. 19889-95), Heartland Stitch Counters Soc. (bd. dirs. 1992—). Republican. Home and Office: Sharon Anne Designs 4504 Parkway Dr Leavenworth KS 66048

CRATER, TIMOTHY ANDREWS, medical student; b. Winston-Salem, N.C., Aug. 27, 1966; s. John Lee Crater and Nancy Denton Hafner; m. Debra Marie Schuh, Feb. 14, 1992. BA in History, Wake Forest U., 1989; student field arty. officers basic course, Ft. Sill Arty. Sch., Okla., 1990; officers tng., U.S. Army Airborne Sch., Ft. Benning, Ga., 1990, 1st Infantry Divsn. Nuclear, Biol. & Chem. Sch., Ft. Riley, Kans., 1991; premed., Kans. State U., 1994; student, U. Kans. Sch. Medicine, 1994—. Commd. 2d lt. U.S. Army, 1989, advanced through grades to 1st lt., 1992; fire support officer hdqs. battery 1/5 field arty. Ft. Riley, Desert Storm, 1990-91; fire direction officer bravo battery 1/5 field arty. Ft. Riley, 1991-92, targeting officer hdqs. battery 1/5 field arty., 1992—; honorably discharged, 1993; history of medicine fellow U. Kans., summer 1995. Decorated Bronze Star for Valor, Dept. Def., 1991, Army Achievement medal with oak leaf cluster Dept. Army, 1991, Army Commendation medal, 1992, S.W. Asia Svc. medal Dept. Def., 1991, Kuwait Liberation medal Govt. Saudi Arabia, 1992, Parachutist Badge. Mem. 5th Arty. Regtl. Assn., Am. Mensa, Soc. of Big Red One, Phi Beta Kappa. Republican. Home: 10851 Hauser Ct Lenexa KS 66210-3747

CRAWFORD, ALVIN HOWELL, pediatrician, orthopedist; b. Memphis, Tenn., Aug. 28, 1939; s. Robert S. and Irma (Myers) C.; m. Alva Jean Jamison, Feb. 23, 1962; children: Carol, Alvin Jr. BS, Tenn. A&I U., 1960; MD, U. Tenn., 1964. Intern Boston Naval Hosp., 1964-65; resident U.S. Naval Hosp., Boston, 1966-68, staff orthopaedic surgeon, 1971; fellow Mass. Gen. Hosp., Boston, 1968-69, New England Bapt. Hosp., Boston, 1969, Children's Hosp. Boston, 1970-71, Alfred I. DuPont Hosp., Del., 1974; staff orthopaedic surgeon Naval Regional Med. Ctr., San Diego, 1971-75; cons. Children's Health Ctr., San Diego, 1971-75; courtesy staff Paradise Valley Hosp., National City, Calif., 1973-75; team physician San Diego Coll., 1975; assoc. surgeon pediatric orthopaedics Henry Ford Hosp., Detroit, 1975-77; dir. orthopaedic surgery and pediatrics Children's Hosp., Cin., 1977—, U. Cin. Hosp., 1981—; cons. Surgeon Gen. of USN, 1977—; vis. prof. King Hussein Med. Ctr., Amman, Jordan, 1979, 81. Editor Jour. Nat. Med. Assn.; cons. editor Clin. Orthopaedics and Related Rsch.; editl. bd. Jour. Pediatric Orthopaedics, 1980—; contbr. chpts. to numerous books; contbr. articles to profl. jours. Mem. N. Avondale Neighborhood Assn., NAACP; bd. dirs. Ohio Nat. Life Ins., Pa. Life Ins. Capt. USNR, 1962—. Decorated Navy Commendation medal; Recipient Outstanding Residents award Boston Orthopaedic Club, 1970; Carl Berg Traveling fellow, 1972; grantee Nat. Med. Sloan Found., 1962-64. Fellow Am. Acad. Cerebral Palsy, Am. Acad. Orthopaedic Surgeons, Am. Acad. Pediatrics, Am. Coll. Surgeons; mem. AMA, Am. Orthopaedic Assn., Assn. Tissue Bank Surgeons, Nat. Med. Assn., Pediatric Orthopaedic Soc. N.Am., Scoliosis Rsch. Soc., Soc. Mil. Orthopaedic Surgeons, Midwest Found. for Med. Care, Inc., Ohio Orthopaedic Soc., Ohio State Med. Assn., Cin. Acad. Medicine, Cin. Med. Assn., Cin. Orthopaedic Club, Cin. Pediatric Soc., C.L. Mitchell Soc., Greater Cin. Scoliosis Soc., Queen City Orthopaedic Club, Children's Hosp. Alumni Assn., Alpha Omega Alpha. Home: 3963 Winding Way Cincinnati OH 45229 Office: Childrens Hosp Med Ctr 3333 Burnet Ave Cincinnati OH 45229

CRAWFORD, ANDREA STEEN, village official; b. Chgo., July 20, 1963; d. John G. and Susan M. Crawford; m. Stephen L. Steen. BA, Kalamazoo Coll., 1985; MPA, U. Wis., 1987. Budget analyst State of Wis., Madison, 1986; adminstrv. intern City of Madison, 1986-87; adminstrv. asst. Village of Wilmette, Ill., 1987-89, asst. fin. dir., 1989-90; village adminstr. Village of Maple Bluff, Madison, 1990—. Mem. Internat. City Mgmt. Assn., Wis. City Mgmt. Assn. (exec. bd. 1993—, v.p. 1995-96), La Follette Inst. Alumni Assn. of U. Wis. (pres. 1991-94).

CRAWFORD, CARL WALLACE, corporate communications executive; b. Kennett, Mo., Nov. 26, 1939; s. Carl F. and Marie Katherine (Houston) C.; m. Fleda B. Anderson, Aug. 15, 1964; 1 child, Kimberly Fleda. BS in Journalism, U. Memphis, 1962; postgrad. fellow, Northwestern U., 1967. Bur. chief, Little Rock The Comml. Appeal, Memphis, 1963-66, urban affairs editor, 1966-69; dir. pub. rels., then customer rels. mgr. Memphis Light, Gas & Water, 1969-76; exec. v.p. Valley Products Co., Memphis, 1977; mgr. environ. info. TVA, Chattanooga, 1978-79, mgr. power info., 1979-85, mgr. nuclear info., 1985-88; dir. communications Am. Electric Power, Columbus, Ohio, 1988-90; pres. The Strategy Group Inc., Dublin, Ohio, 1990—; adj. prof. pub. rels., U. Tenn., Chattanooga, 1982-88; mem. pub. affairs com., sec. U.S. Com. Energy Awareness, Washington, 1984—, Edison Electric Inst., Washington, 1988—. Bd. dirs., Memphis-Shelby County Bd. Mental Health, 1974-79. Sgt. USAF, 1962-66, Southeast Asia. Recipient Pub. Affairs Reporting award, Am. Polit. Sci. Assn., 1967. Mem. Pub. Rels. Soc. Am., Soc. Profl. Journalists, Am. Pub. Power Assn. (chmn. pub. info. com. 1976), Tenn. Mcpl. Electric Power Assn. (founding chmn. 1978), C. of C., Privateer Yacht Club. Republican. Episcopalian. Office: The Strategy Group Inc 290 Beckley Ln Dublin OH 43017-1346

CRAWFORD, DAVID MARK, public relations executive; b. Circleville, Ohio, May 25, 1958; s. David and Delores Jane (Akers) C.; m. Mary N. Houston, July 14, 1984; 1 child, Christine. BA in Journalism, Ohio State U., 1980. Reporter Circleville Herald, 1980-84, editor, 1984-86; media rels.-program mgr. Ohio State U. Hosps., Columbus, 1986—. Coun. mem. Circleville City Coun., 1988-95, pres., 1996. Mem. KC (officer). Office: Ohio State U Med Ctr 450 W 10th Ave Columbus OH 43210

CRAWFORD, GEORGE DAVID, credit, collections executive; b. Milw., Apr. 2, 1930; s. Gabriel Desmond and Rose Vivian (Daniels) C.; m. Lois Ann Foote, June 30, 1951; children: Paul, Guy, Virginia, Georgeanne, Adam. Grad. high sch., Milw. Mgr. Milw. Accts. Svc., 1958-70; from dist. supr. to v.p. ops. Nat. Accts. Systems Inc., Chgo., 1970; exec. v.p., chmn. bd. N.W. Collectors, Inc., Rolling Meadows, Ill., 1970—. Commr. Zoning Bd. Appeals, Elk Grove Village, Ill., 1981—; trustee Elk Grove Village Libr., 1981. With USN, 1946-50. Mem. VFS (life), KC (Columbian award 1976). Republican. Home: 3613 E Lake Shore Dr Wonder Lake IL 60097-8502 Office: Northwest Collectors Inc 3601 W Algonquin Rd Rolling Meadows IL 60008-3126

CRAWFORD, JEAN ANDRE, clinical therapist; b. Chgo., Apr. 12, 1941; d. William Moses and Geneva Mae (Lacy) Jones; student Shimer Coll., 1959-60; BA, Carthage Coll., 1966; MEd, Loyola U., Chgo., 1971; postgrad. Nat. Coll. Edn., Evanston, Ill., 1971-77, Northwestern U., 1976-83; m. John N. Crawford, Jr., June 28, 1969; lic. profl. counselor; cert. sch. counselor Nat. Bd. Cert. Counselors, elem. edn., spl. edn. and pupil personnel services, Ill. Med. technologist, Chgo., 1960-62; primary and spl. edn. tchr. Chgo. Pub. Schs., 1966-71, counselor maladjusted children and their families, 1971-88; counselor juvenile first-offenders, 1968-88, post-secondary vocat. counselor, 1988-93; tchr., transition coord. Cook County Dept. Corrections Alternative High Sch., Chgo., 1993-94; clin. therapist St. Mary of Nazareth Hosp. Ctr., Chgo., 1994—. Vol. Sta. WTTW-TV; vol. counselor deaf children and their families; counselor post-secondary students; vol., mem. community devel. bd. New City YMCA, 1987-92. Mem. scholarship com. Chgo. Urban League. Mem. AACD, Ill. Assn. Counseling and Devel., Am. Sch. Counselors Assn., Ill. Sch. Counselors Assn., Ill. Vocat. Counselors Assn., Am. Mental Health Counselor Assn., Ill. Mental Health Counselor Assn., IIll. Assn. Advancement Black Ams. in Vocat. Edn., Coun. Exceptional Children, Coordinating Coun. Handicapped Children, Shimer Coll. Alumni Assn. (sec. 1982-84), Phi Delta Kappa. Home: # 1200 601 E 32nd St Chicago IL 60616-4054 Office: 2233 W Division St Chicago IL 60622-3043

CRAWFORD, LINDA D., data company executive; b. Trenton, Mo., Dec. 6, 1954; d. Harold E. and Polly A. (Craig) Johnson; m. Randall D. Crawford, July 1, 1978; children: Rebecca, Beth, Olivia. BS in Acctg., North Western U., Maryville, Mo., 1976. Owner Linda Crawford, Kansas City, 1988-90; contr. Mintur Mktg., Shawnee Mission, Kans., 1989—; v.p. HP/Data divsn. Hickerson Phelps, Assocs., Inc., Kansas City, 1990—, Henderson HP, Kansas City, 1992—. Mem. PTA, Girl Scouts Am. Mem. Kansas City Fin. Adv. Club (past pres. 1991). Presbyterian. Office: Hickerson Phelps, Assoc Inc 2300 Main St Ste 140 Kansas City MO 64108-2415

CRAWFORD, WILLIAM A., state legislator; b. Indpls., Jan. 28, 1936; 4 children. Student, Ind. Vo-Tech. Coll. Exec. dir. Ind. Christian Leadership Conf.; rep. Dist. 51 Ind. Ho. of Reps., 1972-91, rep. Dist. 98, 1991—, ranking mem. constn. law com., vice chmn. pub. health com., mem. ways and means com., mem. cts. and crime com., environ. affairs com.; cons. outreach Ind. Vo-Tech. Coll., Region 8. Active Urban Union, Indpls. Black Caucus, Ind. Black Caucus, Indpls. Neighborhood Housing Partnership. Mem. NAACP, Ind. Black Expo, NBCSL. Home: 3731 Station St Apt C4 Indianapolis IN 46218-1481*

CRAWLEY, RICHARD ALAN, arbitrator, mediator; b. Pontiac, Mich., Jan. 16, 1947; s. Rochard L. and Charlene (Prall) C.; children: Derek A., Devonie A. BSBA, Ferris State U., 1974. Pers. supr. Consumers Power, Jackson, Mich., 1974-78; mgr. human resources Quinex Corp., Houston, 1978-85; pres. HR Cons., Inc., Jackson, 1985—; instr. Jackson C.C., 1994—. Author: Mediation and Arbitration, 1993. Bd. dirs. Goodwill Industries, Jackson, 1982-84, Soc. Jackson Bus., 1985-89; mem. Econ. Understanding Com., Jackson, 1982-84. Capt. U.S. Army, 1966-72, Vietnam. Decorated Bronze Star, Army Commendation medal with V device oak leaf cluster, Disting. Flying Cross, 37 air medals and V device, Vietnamese Cross of Gallantry. Mem. Am. Arbitration Assn., Vietnam Helicopter Pilots Assn., Disabled Am. Vets. Republican. Methodist. Home and Office: 5030 Ann Arbor Rd Jackson MI 49201-8801

CRAYCRAFT, ALLIE V., JR., state legislator; m. Juanita Craycraft. Material mgr. Detroit Diesel Allison; with Hydra-Matic, Muncie, Ind.; rep. Dist. 26 Ind. State Senate, 1978—, ranking minority mem., ethics com., mem. govt. and regulatory affairs com., mem. transp. and interstate coop. com., mem. legis. appointment and elec. com., ranking minority mem. pensions/labor com., pub. policy com. Precinct committeeman, 1968—; trustee Liberty Twp., 1970-74; mem. Delaware County Welfare Bd., 1970-78; chmn. Delaware County chpt. Am. Heart Assn.; mem. Liberty-Perry Athletic Booster Club. Mem. Amvets (chmn. Delaware County chpt.), Muncie Lions. Office: 9501 E Jackson St Selma IN 47383-9508 also: State Senate State Capital Indianapolis IN 46204*

CRAYTON, BILLY GENE, physician; b. Holden, Mo., May 15, 1931; s. John Reuben and Carrie Zona (Head) C.; student Central Mo. State Coll., 1948-49; BS, Stetson U., 1958; postgrad. U. Kansas City, summer 1955; MD, U. Mo., 1962. Intern, Mound Park Hosp., St. Petersburg, Fla., 1962-63; practice gen. medicine Latham Hosp., California, Mo., 1963-64, Kelling Clinic and Hosp., Waverly, Mo., 1964-88, vice chief of staff, 1980-88; preceptor in community health and med. practice U. Mo. Sch. Medicine, Waverly, 1968-88; sec., dir. Kelling Hosp., Inc., 1969-80; pres. Kelling Clinic, 1971-88; med. dir. Waverly Ambulance Co., 1985-86; pres. Riverview Heights, 1972-88. Adviser, Mo. chpt. Am. Assn. Med. Assts., 1973-79. Adviser, Explorer Post Boy Scouts Am., 1968-70. Served with AUS, 1952-54. Fellow Am. Acad. Family Physicians. Baptist. Home: 1231 W 69th Ter Kansas City MO 64113-2054

CREAGER, GARY S., transportation engineer; b. Ashville, Ohio, Nov. 23, 1941; s. Kirby A. and Emily Adelade (Kurtz) C.; m. Patricia L., July 8, 1972; children: Tina M. Creager Perdue, Robert W., Matthew W. BSCE, Fenn Coll., 1965; postgrad., Yale U., 1965-66. Registered profl. engr., Ohio. Asst. traffic studies engr. Ohio Dept. Transp., Columbus, 1966-69, asst. traffic rev. engr., 1969-81, traffic control engr., 1981-90, design svcs. engr., 1990—; chairperson subcom. advanced traffic info. systems Intelligent Vehaicle Hwy. Systems, Columbus, 1994-95. Co-author: (booklet) Park & Ride Guidelines, 1978. Fellow Inst. Transp. Engrs. (Young Engr. of Yr. award 1975, Ohio sect. treas. 1994, sec. 1995). Home: 10455 Hayden Run Rd Amlin OH 43002 Office: Ohio Dept Transp 25 S Front St Columbus OH 43215

CREAMER, BRUCE CUNNINGHAM, retired safety educator, property manager; b. Champaign, Ill., Oct. 27, 1941; s. Carl Moore and Eunice (Cunningham) C.; m. Judith Ann Pride, June, 1968 (div. Apr. 1972). BS in Indsl. Edn., U. Ill., Urbana, 1964, MS in Libr. Sci., 1972, CAS in Libr. Sci., 1975. Auditorium mgmt. U. Ill. Assembly Hall, Urbana, Ill., 1968-70; documents libr. U. Ill. Library, Urbana, Ill., 1972-74; property mgr. Creamer Interests, Champaign, Ill., 1975—; instr. motorcycle rider program U. Ill., Urbana, Ill., 1977-81, project coord. motorcycle rider program, 1982-93; chmn. Curriculum Com., Ill. Cycle Rider Training Program, Springfield, Ill., 1982-86. Co-author: Motorcycle Rider Program, 1982. Bd. dirs. Preservation and Conservation Assn. 1st lt. USAF, 1964-67. Mem. Presidents Coun. U. Ill., U. Ill. Alumni Assn., Air Force Assn., Am. Motorcyclist Assn., Civil Air Patrol, Loyal Order of Moose. Home: 1015 W Daniel St Champaign IL 61821-4517

CREASMAN, VIRENA WELBORN (RENE CREASMAN), retired elementary and secondary school educator, genealogist, researcher; b. Lebanon, Nebr., Feb. 10, 1909; d. Lawrence Morgan and Auretta Iva (Daffer) Welborn; m. Sam Doran Creasman, May 8, 1929 (dec. Jan. 1982); children: Gary W., Lee-Ellen Creasman Matzke. AA, McCook Jr. Coll., 1928; B in Edn., U. Nebr., 1962; postgrad., Kearney State Coll., 1967, Creighton U., 1968. Cert. elem., secondary tchr. Tchr. Rural Sch. grades 1-8, Red Willow County, Nebr., 1928-29; elem. tchr. McCook (Nebr.) City Schs., 1949-67, tchr. jr. high reading, English, 1968-76; tchr. genealogy, rschr. McCook Coll. and Southwest Nebr. Genealogy Soc., 1976—; rschr. state and local genealogy confs., 1976—. Vol., mem. Nebr. Hist. Soc. and Mus., High Plains Hist. Soc. and Mus., 1980—. Recipient Plaque of Appreciation from High Plains Hist. Soc. and Mus., 1990, Cert. of Appreciation from Nebr. State Hist. Soc. and Mus., 1989, Genealogist of Yr. cert. Southwest Nebr. Genealogy Soc., 1984, Appreciation of Svc. award as thrift shop coord. Congl. Ch., 1984-90. Mem. AAUW (chpt. leader 1962—), DAR (chpt. regent and registrar 1976—), NOW, LWV, UN Assn. U.S.A., Sierra Club,

Arbor Day Found., Humane Soc., Assn. Retired Tchrs. (local pres. 1976—, nat., state), Delta Kappa Gamma (publicity com.), Eastern Star, Daus. of the Nile, Shriners Auxilliary, Genealogy Socs. (nat., local, state, libr. local chpt.). Democrat. Home: 8 Parkview Dr Mc Cook NE 69001-2248

CREBS, P(AUL) TERENCE, lawyer; b. St. Louis, Apr. 14, 1938; s. Edward Rudd and Edith Ruth (Beppler) C.; m. Carol Ann Kring, June 17, 1961 (div. 1987); children: Paul T. Jr., Susan J.; m. Karen Charlotte Hensel, July 25, 1987. AB, Washington U., St. Louis, 1960, JD, 1962. Bar: Mo. 1962, U.S. Dist. Ct. (ea. dist.) Mo. 1962, U.S. Ct. Appeals (8th cir.) 1962, U.S. Ct. Appeals (7th cir.) 1977, U.S. Ct. Appeals (10th cir.) 1988, U.S. Dist. Ct. (so. dist.) Ill. 1989, U.S. Supreme Ct. 1990. Ptnr. Fordyce & Mayne, St. Louis, 1962-76, Gallop, Johnson, Crebs & Neuman, St. Louis, 1976-81, Peper, Martin, Jensen, Maichel & Hetlage, St. Louis, 1981-87, Herzog, Crebs & McGhee, LLP, St. Louis, 1987—. Assoc. editor Washington U. Law Quar., 1961-62. Bd. dirs. North Ctrl. and South Ctrl. Regional Ctrs. for Deaf-Blind, Mpls. and Dallas, 1972-78; mem. Met. St. Louis Devel. Disability Coun., 1974-80, Presbyn. Children's Svcs., 1989-92. Mem. ABA (fin. officer coun. mem. tort and ins. practice sect. 1983-89), Internat. Assn. Def. Counsel (chair accident life and health com. 1979-80), Fedn. Ins. and Corp. Counsel (vice-chair bus. torts sect. 1990-94, vice chair life health and disability sect. 1993-94, chmn. employment litigation and civil rights sect. 1994—), Mo. Bar Assn., Mo. Orgn. Def. Lawyers, Bar Assn. Met. St. Louis, St. Louis County Bar Assn., Trial Attys. Am. (v.p., dir. 1994—). Presbyterian. Office: Herzog Crebs & McGhee LLP 1 City Ctr 24th Fl 515 N 6th St Saint Louis MO 63101-1842

CREIGHTON, DEAN F., manufacturing company executive; b. Dart, Ohio, Aug. 15, 1925. Grad., high sch., 1943. Ptnr. Creighton Machine Co., New Matamoras, Ohio, 1946—. Chmn. Bd. Pub. Affairs, New Matamoras, 1955-85. With U.S. Army, 1944-46. Mem. Odd Fellows. Office: Creighton Machine PO Box 277 New Matamoras OH 45767-0277

CREIGHTON, W. EDWARD, food products executive; b. 1931. Ptnr. Creighton Bros. LP, Warsaw, Ind., 1952—, Crystal Lake LP, Warsaw, Ind. Office: Creighton Bros LP 4217 E Old Rd 30 Warsaw IN 46580*

CRESSEY, BRYAN CHARLES, lawyer; b. Seattle, Sept. 28, 1949; s. Charles Ovington and Alice Lorraine (Serry) C.; m. Christina Irene Petersen, Aug. 19, 1972; children: Monique Joy, Charlotte Lorraine, Alicia Lin. BA, U. Wash., 1972; MBA, Harvard U., 1976, JD, 1976. Bar: Wash. 1976, Ill. 1977. Sr. investment mgr. First Chgo. Investment Corp., Chgo., 1976-80; prin. Golder, Thoma, Cressey, Rauner, Inc., Chgo., 1980—; chmn., bd. dirs. Cable Design Techs., Inc., Golf Enterprises, Dallas; bd. dirs. Paging Network, Inc., Am. Habilitation, Houston, Am. MedServe, Chgo., Ullo Internat., Boston. Bd. dirs. Planning Infant Welfare Soc., Chgo., 1984—, Jr. Achievement, Chgo. Home: 500 W County Line Rd Barrington IL 60010-9629 Office: Golder Thoma Cressey Rauner Inc 6100 Sears Tower Chicago IL 60606

CRESSMAN, KARL, mechanical engineer; b. Lansing, Mich., Oct. 12, 1959; s. H. Keith and Katherine Mary C. BSME cum laude, U. Ill., 1984. Registered profl. engr. 1992. Mech. engr. Cummins Electronics, Columbus, Ind., 1984-88, Cummins Engring. Co., Columbus, 1988; sr. CAD design engr. Harman Motive, Martinsville, Ind., 1989—. Vol. Housing Partnerships, Columbus, 1990; mem. Columbus Ind. Philharmonic, 1988—. Mem. Soc. Automotive Engrs., Soc. Mfg. Engrs.

CREW, J. BURNER, stockbroker; b. Cleve., June 11, 1956. BA in Econs., Columbia U., 1978. Sales rep. Republic Steel, Greenwich, Conn., 1978-81; regional mgr. Alcoa, Canaan, Conn., 1981-85; owner Crewcon, Schaumburg, Ill., 1985-87; stockbroker E.F. Hutton, Cleve., 1987-88, Prescott Ball & Turbin, Cleve., 1988-90, Kemper Incorp., Cleve., 1990-91, McDonald & Co. Securities Inc., Pepper Pike, Ohio, 1991—. Youth vol. Bethel A.M.E. Zian, Cleve., 1993—. Republican. Methodist. Office: McDonald & Co Securities 30050 Chagrin Blvd Ste 150 Pepper Pike OH 44124-5704

CREWS, DAVID TERENCE, federal employee; b. Wichita, Kans., Oct. 16, 1942; s. David Franklin and Helen Jane (Macredie) C.; m. Myo Yon O, Jan. 29, 1989; children: David Alexander, Christopher Robert. BA in Sociology, Kans. State U., 1966; Graduate, Squadron Officers Sch., 1976, Air Command Staff Coll., 1979, Nat. Def. U., 1982; Cert. Supervision/Computer Applications, Wichita State U., 1989. Cert. emergency mgr. Commd. USAF, 1968, advanced through grades to maj., 1980, ret., 1988; owner Crews Corp., Inc., Clearwater, Kans., 1989-93; dir. emergency mgmt. Reno County, Hutchinson, 1993-95; dep. sect. chief for info. and planning sect. FEMA Region VII, 1995—; avionics officer Geodetic and Cartographic Svc., Topeka, Kans., 1969-70; avionics officer Norton AFB, Calif., 1972-74, Keflavic, Iceland, 1974-76; inspector gen. NORAD/Air Def. Command, Colorado Springs, 1976-80; chief logistics plans Air Def. Command, Langley AFB, Va., 1980-82; chief maintenance ops. Pacific Air Forces, Osan, Korea, 1984-87. Editor Ninety-Three newsletter, 1990. Mayor City of Clearwater, 1991—. Maj. CAP. Decorated Meritorious Svc. medal with oak leaf cluster, Joint Svc. Commendation medal, USAF Commendation medal with 2 oak leaf clusters, Vietnameses Cross of Gallantry with a bronze palm. Mem. Am. Soc. Profl. Emergency Planners, Rural Mayors Assn. Sedgwick County (chair 1993), Radio Amateur Civil Emergency Svcs., Air Force Sgts. Assn., Kans. Emergency Preparedness Assn., Nat. Coordinating Coun. on Emergency Mgmt., Internat. Assn. Fire Chiefs, Am. Radio Relay League, Assn. Pub. Safety Communications Ofcls., Nat. Assn. for Search and Rescue, VFW, Am. Legion (comdr. 1989-91), Nat. Eagle Scout Assn. (life), Air Force Assn. (life), Ret. Officers Assn., Lions. Methodist. Home: 150 S Grain Clearwater KS 67026-0296

CRIDER, ROBERT AGUSTINE, international financier, law enforcement official; b. Washington, Jan. 3, 1935; s. Rana Albert and Terasa Helen (Dampf) C.; student law enforcement U. Md., 1959-63; m. Debbie Ann Lee, Feb. 1960. Police officer Met. Police Dept., Washington, 1957-67; substitute tchr., bldg. trades instr. Maries R-1 Sch., Vienna, Mo., 1968-70; vets. constrn. tng. officer VA Dept. Edn., Mo., 1968-70; constrn. mgr. Tectonics Ltd., Vienna, 1970-79; owner, dir. R-A Crider & Assocs., St. Louis, 1979—; bd. dirs. TI-CO Investment Corp., Langcaster Corp. Served with USAF, 1952-56. Mem. Assn. Ret. Policemen, Internat. Conf. Police, Internat. Assn. Chiefs of Police, Nat. Police Assn., World Future Soc., Internat. Platform Assn., Mo. Police Chiefs Assn., Mo. Sheriff's Assn., Am. Correctional Assn., Law Enforcement Intelligence Assn., Internat. Drug Enforcement Assn., Nat. Assn. Fin. Cons., Internat. Soc. Financiers, Am. Legion, St. Louis Honor Guard. Roman Catholic. Clubs: Lions, K.C. (4th deg.). Home: PO Box 109 Vienna MO 65582-0109 Office: R-A Crider & Assocs PO Box 3459 2644 Roseland Ter Saint Louis MO 63143-2304

CRIDER, RUTH LEE, community health nurse, nursing administrator; b. St. Genevieve County, Mo., Aug. 23, 1936; d. Glen Allen and Ruby Ethel (Holmes) McDowell; m. Joseph E. Crider, June 28, 1957; children: Joseph Allen, Cheryl Lynette, Michael Ervin. ADN, So. Mo. State U., 1987, BSN, 1991. RN, Mo.; CHN III. Nurse, adminstr. Oreg. County Health Dept., until 1983, adminstr., 1994—; RN, registrar Oreg. & Howell Counties, 1983-94; registrar Oregon County, 1994—. Mem. Mo. League for Nursing (assoc.), Mo. Pub. Health Assn.

CRISP, CHERYL LEE, pediatric rehabilitation nurse; b. Shelbyville, Ind., Feb. 25, 1959; d. Raymond Lee and Lillian Orpha (McClain) C. ADN, Ind. Ctrl. U., 1980. Cert. rehab. nurse, cert. devel. disabilities nurse. Staff nurse Heritage House Children's Ctr., Shelbyville, 1980-84, asst. DON, 1984-85, supr., 1986-87; staff nurse James Whitcomb Riley Hosp., Indpls., 1985-86; staff nurse Lifelines Children's Rehab. Hosp., Indpls., 1987-89, nurse mgr., 1989-91, house mgr., 1991-95; clin. care coord. pediatric and rehab. Vis. Nurse Svc., Inc., Indpls., 1995—. Mem. Assn. Rehab. Nurses, Ind. Assn. Rehab. Nurses, Assn. for the Care Children's Health, Devel. Disabilities Nursing Assn. Baptist. Office: Vis Nurse Svc 4701 N Keystone Ave Indianapolis IN 46205-1563

CRISS, DARLENE JUNE, English language educator; b. Potwin, Kans., Feb. 4, 1931; d. Leroy Eckard and Sarah Caroline (Weber) Edwards; m. James Harold Criss, July 18, 1948; children: Melissa Colleen, Melinda Collette, James Anthony, Michael Jordan, Troy Mitchell, Shayne Lee. BA, Wichita State U., 1976, MEd., 1979. Cert. tchr., Kans. Tchr. English Unit Sch. Dist. 265, Goddard (Kans.) High Sch., 1976—, chmn. dept. lang. arts, 1979—; lectr. on creativity, 1977—; adviser yearbook, 1976-91, Prism, 1976—. Editor (newsletter) Sunflower Seeds, 1974-84; contbr. poetry to English Jour. Leader Camp Fire Girls, Wichita, dist. program leader, Wichita 1960-65; area chair Am. Heart Assn., Wichita 1958-73; pres. South High PTA, Wichita, 1969-71. Recipient Wakan award Camp Fire Girls, Wichita, 1968; named one of 5 state finalists Tchrs. in Space Program, 1985, Outstanding Young Tchr., Goddard Sch. Dist., 1985. Mem. NEA, Kans. Edn. Assn., Goddard Edn. Assn. (chief negotiator 1981-84), Nat. Assn. Tchrs. English, Kans. Assn. Tchrs. English, Mensa (life, nat. rep. internat. bd. dirs. 1987-95, nat. sec. 1988-91, nat. 1st vice chmn. 1991-95, chmn. 1995—, bd. dirs. 1995—, editor nat. bull. 1982-84, editor Isolated M newsletter 1984-95, pub. agt. Internat. Mensa Jour. 1985-91, Disting. Svc. award 1986). Democrat. Presbyterian. Home: 2311 S Santa Fe St Wichita KS 67211-4942 Office: Goddard High Sch 501 S Main Goddard KS 67052

CRISSMAN, PENNY M., state legislator; b. Nov. 20, 1943; m. Charles; children: Mitzi, Mark. Student, Ea. Mich. U., Oakland U. Mayor Rochester, Mich., 1989-92; rep. Mich. Dist. 45, 1993—; mem. Rochester City Coun., 1985-92; asst. Rep. whip Mich. Ho. Reps., 1993—, co-chair com. on civil rights & women's issues, edn. com., higher edn. com., local govt. coms., pub. health coms. Recipient disting. citizenship award Rochester Elks, 1992. Mem. Rochester C. of C., Optimists, Oakland U. Press Club. Office: Mich Ho of Reps PO Box 30014 Lansing MI 48909-7514*

CRIST, LEWIS ROGER, insurance company executive; b. Takoma Park, Md., Oct. 9, 1935; s. Howard Roger and Dorothy Ada (Massey) C.; m. Connie M. Combs, Mar. 29, 1980. Student, U. Md., 1953-54, 58-60. Br. mgr. CNA Ins. Cos., St. Louis, 1961-85; dir. Mo. Div. Ins., Jefferson City, Mo., 1986-88; pres. The Bar Plan Ins. Co., St. Louis, 1988-93, Vallifacts, Inc., St. Louis, 1995—; chmn. Inter-Co. Arbitration Com., Omaha, 1971, Spl. Arbitration Com., New Orleans, 1975; mem. Nat. Panel Consumer Arbitrators, New Orleans, 1975-76, Nat. Supplemental Health Ins. Panel, Washington, 1987-88; bd. dirs. Gateway Ins. Co., Cameron Mutual Ins. Co. Mem. Alzheimers Task Force, Jefferson City, 1986-88. With U.S. Army, 1954-57. Mem. Omaha Claim Mgrs. Coun. (pres. 1973), Ins. Inst. New Orleans (bd. dirs. 1976-78), La. Property Assn. (bd. dirs. 1974-77, Ins. Co. Execs. Assn. (pres. 1983), Ins. Regulatory Examiners Soc., Mo. Ins. Edn. Found. (pres. 1994 bd. dirs.), IRES Found. (bd. dirs. 1989—). Republican. Episcopalian. Home: 175 Cherry Hills Meadows Dr Grover MO 63040-1649 Office: Crist & Assocs 175 Cherry Hills Meadows Dr Grover MO 63040-1649

CRISWELL, CHARLES HARRISON, analytical chemist, environmental and forensic consultant, executive; b. Springfield, Mo., Jan. 9, 1943; s. John Philip and Elba Anne (Denton) C.; m. Joyce LaVonne Louth, Apr. 26, 1968; 1 child, Christina Rachel. AB in Chemistry and Biology, Drury Coll., 1967; postgrad., U. Mo., 1967-68. Cert. hazardous materials and waste specialist, cert. profl. environ. health specialist, cert. profl. chemist, qualified environ. profl., hazardous materials emergency responder-ops./tech./specialist levels; registered hazardous substances profl. Dir. Water Pollution Control Labs City of Springfield, 1968-72, chief Water Pollution Sect., 1972-80; pres., chmn. bd. dirs. Cons. Analytical Svcs. Internat., Springfield, 1979—; assoc. Environ. Planning Assocs., Inc., 1985—; adj. faculty, spl. instr. in environ. law Drury Coll.; apptd. by gov. mem. Mo. Hazardous Waste Mgmt. Commn., 1978; mem. Mo. Joint Commn. on Hazardous Waste Mgmt. Legis., statewide ad-hoc Com. on Regulations; mem. curriculum adv. com. Environ. Resource Ctr., Crowder Coll.; tech. advisor S.W. Mo. Household Hazardous Waste Project; spkr. in field, nationwide. Contbr. more than 70 papers, presentations, articles to profl. jours. Active Springfield Employees Activities Club, Thirteen Gallon Club of ARC, Friends of Zoo; judge Southwest Mo. Regional Sci. Fair; vice chmn., 1990-93, chair 1993—, mem. numerous subcoms. Greene County Local Emergency Planning Com.; ruling elder 1st and Calvary Presbyn. Ch., elected for life, 1974, elected clk. of session, 1996—, deacon, sr. high sch. youth advisor, active numerous coms.; mem. permanent jud. commn. John Calvin Presbytery, 1977-85, 93—, treas., 1975—; mem. spl. adminstrv. commns. Presbytery Synod Gen. Assembly Inter-judicatory Consultation on Long Range Ch. Fin., also assoc. stated clk. and other offices; alumni bd. dirs. Greenwood Lab. Sch., 1992—, pres., 1993—, chmn. bd., 1993—. Recipient Gift of Time award for cmty. svc. Springfield Area Coun. Chs., C. of C., others; named Pheresis Donor of Yr., ARC, 1988. Fellow Am. Inst. Chemists; mem. ASTM (mem. subcom. on environ. assessment of real estate), Am. Inst. Biol. Scis., Am. Chem. Soc. (charter, mem. com. on environ. analytical methodology Ozarks sect.), Nat. Assn. Safety Health Profls., nat. Assn. Environ. Profls., Nat. Environ. Health Assn., Internat. Union Pure and Applied Chemistry (affiliate), Assoc. Industries Mo. (mem. environ. com., mem. hazardous waste task group), Mo. Acad. Sci., Mo. Waste Control Coalition, Mo. Rural Water Assn., Mo. Water and Sewerage Conf. (sect. pres. 1975), Mo. Water Enrivon. Assn. (pres., mem. exec. com. 1977-83, chmn. 1979-80, newsletter assoc. editor, chmn. numerous coms. and confs., award of merit 1991, 92, 93), Nat. Environ. Tng. Assn., Hazardous Materials Control Resources Inst., Inst. Profl. Environ. Practice, Assn. Ofcl. Analytical Chemists, Analytical Lab. Mgrs. Assn., N.Am. Hazardous Materials Mgmt. Assn. (internat. bd. dirs.), Water Environ. Fedn. (chmn./asst. chmn. nat. confs., Arthur Sidney Bedell award), Mensa (life), Springfield Area C. of C. (mem. environ. com., chairperson emergency preparedness and cmty. right to know subcom.), Beta Beta Beta, Phi Mu Alpha, Gamma Alpha. Republican. Office: Cons Analytical Svcs Internat 1437 S Summerplace Springfield MO 65809-2247

CRISWELL, JOHN, business executive; b. Canton, Ohio, Sept. 5, 1929. Ptnr. Pro-Machine, Canton, Ohio, 1976-85; pres. Gewell Machine & Comco Inc., Canton, Ohio, 1985—. Mem. Canton C. of C., Elks. Office: Gewell Machine & Comco Inc PO Box 7369 Canton OH 44705-0369

CRISWELL, SCOTT LEE, JR., computer automation consultant; b. Lansing, Ill., May 22, 1967; s. Scott and Susan (Bowie) C. AS, Thornton C.C., 1988; BSBA, Governor State U., 1990, MBA, 1991. Lic. real estate broker, Ill. & Ind. Dog groomer The Pet Set, Lansing, Ill., 1981—; video engr. TPS Video, Lansing, 1985—; real estate sales rep. C.J. Frank & Son, Lansing, 1988—, tax preparer, 1991—; registered rep. Fortis Investors, Inc., St. Paul, 1989—; owner, mgr. C2 Bus. MicroComputer Cons., Lansing, 1991—, Big Boring Criswell's Firearms, Lansing, 1993—, Scott's Computer Stuff, Lansing, 1993—; CEO InMedia Inc., Lansing, 1994-95; owner Criswell and Assocs., Lansing, 1995—. Home: 2155 Indiana Ave Lansing IL 60438-2104 Office: C2 Cons 3448 Ridge Rd Lansing IL 60438-3102

CRITELLI, PAUL JOSEPH, psychologist; b. Rochester, N.Y., Mar. 11, 1949; s. Joseph and Mary (Campanozzi) C. BA, Iona Coll., 1970; MA, Fordham U., 1972, PhD, 1978. Lic. clin. psychologist, Mich. Chief psychologist Care Unit, Grand Rapids, Mich., 1978-81; pvt. practice psychology Grand Rapids, 1979—, Greenville, Mich., 1987—; asst. dir. Terrap of Mich., Grand Rapids, 1986—, dir., 1989-93; dir. Psychol. Mgmt. Assocs., Grand Rapids, 1989—; co-dir. student personal advising ctr Davenport Coll., Grand Rapids, 1990—; adj. lectr. Holy Family Coll., Phila., 1976-78; humor cons. Producer: (tv series) Psychology in Focus, 1986 (1st place Philo T. Farnsworth Competition 1986), Magic with Paul, 1986 (1st place Philo T. Farnsworth Competition 1986), (twice weekly tv segment-NBC affiliate) Focus with Dr. Critelli, 1993—. Speaker on anxiety disorders, use of humor in stress mgmt., fraudulent faith healing, occult frauds; lectr. seimnars on stress mgmt. to industry. Recipient Marky award Magic Mktg. Seminar, Albuquerque, 1990. Mem. APA, Mich. Psychol. Assn., Soc. Am. Magicians (chairperson contest of magic 1989—), Psychic Entertainers Assn. Home: 858 Iroquois Dr SE Grand Rapids MI 49506-3373 Office: 4829 E Beltline Ave NE Grand Rapids MI 49505-9747

CRITTENDEN, MARY LYNNE, science educator; b. Detroit, Oct. 27, 1951; d. William and Marie (Ryall) C. BS, Wayne State U., 1974; MS, U. Detroit, 1984; postgrad., Wayne State U., 1991—. Tchr. sci. Detroit Bd. Edn., 1974-77, Highland Park (Mich.) C.C., 1980—; faculty rschr. Air Force program Wright Patterson AFB, Dayton, Ohio, 1991; speaker Mich. Ednl. Occupational Assn., 1989, Liberal Arts Network Devel., Lansing, Mich., 1990, 95; presider QEM, Math., Sci. Engring. Conf., Detroit, 1996. Author ednl. materials; contbr. to profl. publs. Mem. AAAS, Am. Chem. Soc. (outreach program 1992—), Civic Ctr. Optimist Club (bd. dirs. 1991-94, coord. scis. 1990-94), Mich. C.C. Biologists, Human Anatomy and Physiology Soc. Home: 15386 Alden St Detroit MI 48238-2104 Office: Highland Park C C Glendale at 3rd Highland Park MI 48203

CROAK, FRANCIS R., lawyer; b. Janesville, Wis., Feb. 19, 1929; s. Francis Joseph and Virginia (Blakey) C.; m. Susan Nolte, Aug. 15, 1953 (dec.); m. 2d, Judith Torbenson, Apr. 30, 1976; children: Carolyn, Martha, Daniel, David, Joseph. BS, U. Wis., 1950, JD, 1953. Bar: Wis. 1953, U.S. Ct. Appeals (7th cir.) 1960, U.S. Supreme Ct. 1980. First asst. dist. atty. Milwaukee County, Wis., 1956-60; ptnr. Cook & Franke S.C., Milw., 1960—; lectr. in law Marquette U., 1972-74, U. Wis., 1973-78. Mem. Wis. Jud. Coun., 1971-82. Pres. Greater Milw. Open, 1995—. Served to 1st lt. U.S. Army, 1953-56; to col. USAR, 1956-80. Fellow Am. Coll. Trial Lawyers; mem. Am. Law Inst. Democrat. Clubs: Milwaukee Athletic, Westmoor Country. Home: 12555 W Grove Ter Elm Grove WI 53122-1974 Office: 660 E Mason St Milwaukee WI 53202-3830

CROAK, JOHN H., investment representative; b. St. Louis, June 14, 1952; s. William T. and Jewell S. (Schmitz) C.; m Cindy M. Marcum, July 10, 1982; 1 child, Justin. BS in Bus. Mgmt./Mktg., S.W. Mo. State U., Springfield, 1976. Self-employed St. Louis, 1988-92; investment rep. Edward D. Jones & Co., Florissant, Mo., 1992—. Mem. Florissant C. of C. Mem. United Ch. of Christ. Home: 12904 Walnutway Ter Saint Louis MO 63146-6044 Office: Edward D Jones & Co 1152 Shackelford Rd Florissant MO 63031-4369

CROAT, THOMAS BERNARD, botanical curator; b. St. Marys, Iowa, May 23, 1938; s. Oliver Theodore and Irene Mary (Wilgenbush) C.; m. Patricia Swope, Sept. 4, 1965; children: Anne Irene, Thomas Kevin. BA, Simpson Coll., 1962; MA, U. Kans., 1966, PhD, 1967. Tchr. sci. pub. schs., Virgin Islands and Iowa, 1962-64; research botanist Mo. Botanical Garden, St. Louis, 1967-71, P.A. Schulze curator of botany, 1977—; vis. fellow Smithsonian Tropical Research Inst., Ancon, Canal Zone, 1968-71; adv. com. NSF Resources in Systematic Botany, 1972-74; faculty assoc. biology Washington U., St. Louis, 1970—; adj. faculty U. Mo., St. Louis, 1974—; adj. assoc. prof. St. Louis U., 1982—. Author: Flora of Barro Colorado Island, 1978. Contbr. articles to profl. jours. Served as pfc U.S. Army, 1956-58, Fed. Republic Germany. Recipient Rsch. award Soc. Sigma Xi, 1975. Grantee NSF, 1972—, Nat. Geog. Soc., 1973, 83, 86, 89, 95, NEA, 1975, 79. Mem. Am. Soc. Plant Taxonomists, Assn. Tropical Biology, Internat. Soc. Plant Taxonomists, Internat. Aroid Soc. (hon. bd. 1978-84), Botanical Soc. Am. Republican. Roman Catholic. Avocations: Welding, electronics, auto repair, construction. Home: 5600 Hill View Dr Pacific MO 63069-3523 Office: Mo Bot Garden PO Box 299 Saint Louis MO 63166-0299

CROCKETT, GEORGE EPHRIAM, secondary education educator; b. Chgo., July 5, 1940; s. Edmund and Ethel Teva (Cowan) C.; m. Ethelene Standifer, Nov. 25, 1968; children: Patricia Johnson, Ronald O'Neal, Michael O'Neal. BS, Ill. State U., 1964; MA in History, Northeastern Ill. U., 1981; postgrad., U. Ill., Champaign. Cert. tchr., Ill. History tchr. John Marshall Metro High Sch., Chgo., 1964—, chmn. social studies dept., 1992—; tng. specialist John Marshall Metro Evening High Sch., 1966-69, counselor, 1980-83; cons. curriculum guide Chgo. Bd. Edn., 1970. Active Cen. Meml. Bapt. Ch., Chgo., 1957—; mem. com. explorer scouts Boy Scouts Am., 1977-79; mem. Citi-Educators Team Project, DePaul U., 1989. Recipient Tchr. of Yr. award Chgo. Bd. Edn., 1974, Black Educator award Push Found., 1977, Blum-Kovler Ednl. Found. award, 1984, merit award N. Eastern Ill. Alumni, 1985, Midwest Community award, 1990—. Mem. Ill. Coun. Social Studies, Chgo. Social Studies, Chgo. Afro-Am. Tchrs. Assn., Chgo. Area Alliance Black Sch. Educators, NAACP, Nat. Urban League, Midwest Community Coun., Operation Push, So. Christian Leadership Conf. Home: 3130 W Fulton St Chicago IL 60612-1728 Office: John Marshall Met High Sch 3250 W Adams St Chicago IL 60624-2901

CROCKETT, JAMES EDWIN, physician, educator; b. Kansas City, Kans., Oct. 20, 1924; s. John Edward and Orva Rose (Ramsey) C.; m. Martha Adam, June 8, 1949; children: Kevin, Brian, Cara. BA, Park Coll., 1945; MD, U. Kans., 1949. Diplomate Am. Bd. Internal Medicine and Cardiovascular Diseases. Intern U.S. Naval Hosp., Long Beach, Calif., 1949-50; resident U. Kans. Med. Ctr., Kansas City 1950-56; asst. prof. medicine U. Kans. Sch. Medicine, Kansas City, 1956-58, assoc. prof., 1958-63, dir. cardiology, 1960-63; clin. prof. medicine U. Mo.-Kansas City Sch. Medicine, 1972—; mem. adv. bd. Chinese Inst. Cardiology, Beijing, 1984—; co-founder, cons. cardiologist Mid-Am. Heart Inst., Kansas City, mem. adv. bd., 1980—. Author: Your Heart, 1983, 2d edit., 1990; contbr. articles to profl. jours. Bd. dirs. St. Lukes Hosp. Research Found., 1973-75. Served to lt. USN, 1949-57. Fellow ACP, Am. Coll. Cardiology (bd. trustees 1965-67, 71-73, treas. 1966-67, sec., bd. govs. 1972-74, assoc. editor Accel. 1969-81, Cummings Internat. Teaching award, 1967). Republican. Episcopalian. Clubs: River, Carriage. Avocations: music, reading, tennis. Home: 5049 Wornall Rd Kansas City MO 64112-2423 Office: Cardiovascular Cons Office Pres 4320 Wornall Rd Kansas City MO 64111-3201

CROIS, JOHN HENRY, local government official; b. Chgo., Jan. 13, 1946; s. Henry F. and Dorothy M. (Priebe) C. BA, Elmhurst Coll., 1969; MA, U. Notre Dame, 1972. Asst. village mgr. Village of Oak Lawn, Ill., 1975-85; village mgr. Village of Westchester, Ill., 1985; dir. West Cook County Solid Waste Agy., 1990—; coord. Oak Lawn Swine Flu Immunization Program, 1976. Mem. ASPA, West Cen. Mcpl. Conf. (chmn. intergovtl. com. 1991), Chgo. Area Transp. Study Coun. Mayors (no. cen. region), Internat. City Mgmt. Assn., Ill. City Mgmt. Assn., Metro-Mgrs. Assn., St. Germaine's Men's Club. Home: 10233 Karlov Ave Oak Lawn IL 60453-4235 Office: 10300 W Roosevelt Rd Westchester IL 60154-2568

CROLL, ROBERT FREDERICK, educator, economist; b. Evanston, Ill., Feb. 3, 1934; s. Frederick Warville and Florence (Campbell) C.; m. Sandra Elizabeth Bell, June 15, 1968; 1 child, Robert Frederick. BSBA, Northwestern U., 1954; MBA (Burton A. French scholar) with high distinction, U. Mich., 1956; DBA, Ind. U., 1969; DLitt, John F. Kennedy Coll., 1970. Instr. Ind. U. Sch. Bus., Bloomington, 1956, researcher in bus. econs., 1960-62; mng. dir. Motor Vehicle Industry Research Assocs., Evanston, 1962-63; personal asst. to speaker Ill. Ho. of Reps., 1963-65; asst. prof. bus. adminstrn. Kans. State U., 1965-66; asst. prof. Inst. Indsl. Relations, Loyola U. Chgo., 1966-70; assoc. prof. Sch. Bus. Adminstrn., Central Mich. U., 1970-76, prof., 1976—. Mem. platform committee Ind. Republican Com., 1958; Ind. del. Young Rep. Nat. Conv., 1959; nat. chmn. Youth for Goldwater Orgn., 1960-61; chmn. coll. clubs Young Rep. Orgn. Ill., 1960-62; treas. Young Rep. Orgn. Ill., 1963-65; asst. chief page Rep. Nat. Conv., 1964; mem. Mt. Pleasant City Charter Commn., 1973-76. Trustee estate of F.W. Croll, Chgo., 1959—; bd. govs. Clarke Hist. Library, 1986—. Recipient Grand prize Gov. of Ind., 1958. Accredited personnel diplomate Am. Soc. Personnel Adminstrn. Accreditation Inst. Mem. Soc. Automotive Engrs., Am. Inst. Mgmt., Soc. Advancement Mgmt., Am. Econ. Assn., Mt. Pleasant C. of C., Young Ams. for Freedom (founder 1960, vice chmn. 1962-63), Phila. Soc. (founder 1964), Beta Gamma Sigma, Delta Sigma Pi Key, Phi Delta Kappa, Phi Kappa Phi, Pi Sigma Alpha, Delta Mu Delta, Sigma Pi, Alpha Kappa Psi, Sigma Iota Epsilon, Phi Chi Theta, Pi Omega Pi., Phi Beta Delta. Episcopalian. Clubs: Little Harbor (Harbor Springs, Mich.); Mount Pleasant Country. Author: Fall of an Automotive Empire: A Business History of the Packard Motor Car Company, 1945-1958, others. Contbr. articles to profl. jours. Home: 1224 Glenwood Dr Mount Pleasant MI 48858-4328 Office: Ctrl Mich U Dept Mgmt Mount Pleasant MI 48859

CROMER, EARLE GEORGE HAYWARD, JR., editor, electrical and chemical engineer, consultant; b. Chgo., May 4, 1924; s. Earle George Hayward Sr. and Myrtle Alma (Erdmann) C.; m. Carol Milyko Kimball, July 30, 1952 (div. Feb. 1962); 4 stepchildren; m. Evelyn Eileen Draege, June 22, 1963; children: Susan Leslie, Earle George Hayward III. BSEE, Northwestern U., 1949, BSChemE, 1949. Design engr. Sperry Gyroscope Co., Great Neck, N.Y., 1949-52; rsch. engr. Internat. Minerals & Chem. Corp., Bartow, Fla., 1952-54; design engr. Victor Adding Machine Co., Chgo., 1954-59; sr. project engr. Radiation Counter Labs., Morton Grove, Ill., 1959-60, Streeter-Amet Co., Grayslake, Ill., 1960-66; mng. editor Milton S. Kiver Publs., Inc., Chgo., 1966-72, assoc. editor, 1972-75; editorial/engring. cons. Mt. Propect, Ill., 1975-79; mng. editor Lake Pub. Corp., Libertyville, Ill., 1979-89; tech. editor Lake Pub./An IHS Group Co., Libertyville, 1989-92; contbg. editor PennWell Pub. Co. Advanced Tech. Group, Westford, Mass., 1992-93; ret., 1994. Contbr. articles to profl. jours. including Electronic Instrument Digest, Electronic Packaging and Prodn., Microelectronic Mfg. and Testing, Microelectronics Mfg. Tech., Hybrid Circuit Tech., Solid State Tech., Microlithography World; French horn player with orchs. including Staten Island Symphony, Pt. Washington Symphony, Tampa Philharm., St. Petersburg Symphony, Clearwater Symphony, N.W. Symphony Orch., 1950-89. With U.S. Army, 1944-46. Mem. AAAS, IEEE (life). Republican. Episcopalian. Home: 622 N Main St Mount Prospect IL 60056-2113

CROMLEY, JON LOWELL, lawyer; b. Riverton, Ill., May 23, 1934; s. John Donald and Naomi M. (Mathews) C. BS, U. Ill., 1958; JD, John Marshall Law Sch., 1966. Bar: Ill. 1966. Real estate title examiner Chgo. Title & Trust Co., 1966-70; pvt. practice, Genoa, Ill., 1970—; mem. firm O'Grady & Cromley, Genoa, 1970—; bd. dirs. Citizen's First Nat. Bank, 1984-92, Kingston Mut. Ins. Co., Genoa Day Care Center, Inc. Mem. ABA, Am. Judicature Soc., Am., Ill. State Bar Assn., Chgo. Bar Assn., DeKalb County Bar Assn. Home: 130 Homewood Dr Genoa IL 60135-1260 Office: O'Grady & Cromley 213 W Main St Genoa IL 60135-1145

CRONE, ANNA LISA, Russian literature educator; b. Bklyn., June 9, 1946; d. James Clarence Jr. and Ethel Margaret (Donnelly) C.; m. Vladimir Donchik, July 12, 1982; 1 child, Liliana Donchik. BA in Russian Lit., Goucher Coll., 1967; MA in Russian Lang. and Lit., Harvard U., 1969, PhD in Russian Lang. and Lit., 1975; LHD (hon.), Goucher Coll., 1988, D Honoris Causae, 1988. From instr. to asst. prof. Russian and Russian lit. Johns Hopkins U., Goucher Coll., Balt., 1971-74; tchr., translator Associated Jewish Charities, Balt., 1974-75; researcher Radcliffe Inst., Harvard U., Cambridge, Mass., 1975-76; from asst. prof. to assoc. prof. Slavic langs. and lits. U. Chgo., 1977—. Author: (scholarly study) Rozanov and the End of Literature, 1978; editor, contbr.: New Studies in Russian Language and Literature, 1986; mem. editl. bd. Russian Lang. Jour., Ency. of Russian Literature, Ency. of the Essay; contbr. articles to profl. jours. Mem. Univ. Senate U. Chgo., 1992-95. Nat. Def. Fgn. Lang. fellow, 1967-71, Woodrow Wilson fellow, 1967. Mem. Am. Assn. Tchrs. of Slavic and East European Langs., Am. Assn. Advancement of Slavic Studies, Stochastic Soc. (pres. 1991-92, 96-97), Phi Beta Kappa. Democrat. Office: U Chgo Slavic Dept 1130 E 59th St Chicago IL 60637-1543

CRONICK-LEONARD, ANNE BERTHA, retired psychiatrist; b. Kalamazoo, May 18, 1910; d. Menno John and Elizabeth (VanderTill) Bosma; m. Charles Herbert Cronick, Feb. 28, 1938 (div. 1948); children: Karen Anne, Charles Herbert; m. Alan Thomas Leonard, Oct. 12, 1957. BA, Calvin Coll., Grand Rapids, Mich., 1932; MD, U. Mich., 1936. Intern Women's Hosp., Cleve., 1936-37; resident City Hosp., Cleve., 1937-38; assoc. psychiatrist Fair Oaks Villa Sanitarium, Cuyahoga Falls, Ohio, 1938-39; resident in psychiatry Inst. of Pa. Hosp., Phila., 1939-40; pvt. practice, Youngstown, Ohio, 1940-46; assoc. psychiatrist Child Guidance Clinic, Grand Rapids, 1946-48, dir., 1948-50, cons., 1950-52; cons. Child Guidance Clinic, Muskegon, Mich., 1952-57; pvt. practice, Muskegon, 1950-93, ret., 1993. Mem. adv. bd. Hackley Adult Mental Health Clinic, Muskegon, 1954-56; mem. Citizens Action Comn. for Edn., North Muskegon, Mich., 1959-60; mem., v.p. Nutritional Svcs. Older Ams., Muskegon, 1974-77. Mem. AMA, Am. Psychiat. Assn., Soc. for Study Multiple Personality and Dissociation, Mich. Med. Assn., Muskegon County Med. Soc. Methodist. Home: 915 Oak Crest Ln Jenison MI 49428

CRONIN, DAN, state legislator; b. Nov. 7, 1959. BA, Northwestern U., 1981; JD, Loyola U., 1985. Campaign coord. Congressman John E. Porter, 1981; law clk. spl. prosecution divsn. Ill. Atty. Gen. Office, 1983; minority leader Ill. Ho. of Reps., 1985-87; with DuPage County State's Atty.'s Office, 1987-89; Ill. State sen. Dist. 39, 1993—; mem. Elem. and Secondary Edn., Gen. Svcs. Appropriations and Health Care Coms.; atty. Kemp & Capanna, Ltd., Oak Brook, Ill. Mem. YMCA. Mem. ABA, ATLA,Ill. Bar Assn., DuPage County Bar Assn., Am. Cancer Soc., Lions, KC. Address: 105 E 1st St Elmhurst IL 60126*

CRONIN, JAMES WATSON, physicist, educator; b. Chicago, Ill., Sept. 29, 1931; s. James Farley and Dorothy (Watson) C.; m. Annette Martin, Sept. 11, 1954; children: Cathryn, Emily, Daniel Watson. A.B., So. Methodist U. (1951); Ph.D., U. Chgo. Asst. physicist Brookhaven Nat. Lab., 1955-58; asst. prof. Princeton, 1958-65, prof. physics, 1965-71; prof. physics and astronomy U. Chgo., 1971—; Loeb lectr. physics Harvard U., 1967; participant early devel. spark chambers; co-discoverer CP-violation, 1964; lectr. Nashima Found., 1993. Recipient Research Corp. Am. award, 1967; John Price Wetherill medal Franklin Inst., 1976; E.O. Lawrence award ERDA, 1977; Nobel prize for physics, 1980; Sloan fellow, 1964-66; Guggenheim fellow, 1970-71, 82-83. Mem. Am. Acad. Arts and Scis., Nat. Acad. Sci. (council mem.), Am. Phys. Soc. Home: 5825 S Dorchester Ave Chicago IL 60637-1764 Office: U Chgo Enrico Fermi Inst 5630 S Ellis Ave Chicago IL 60637-1433*

CROOK, EMIL ALBERT, construction company executive; b. Edwardsville, Ill., Mar. 3, 1935; s. Raymond Joseph and Laverne Ann (Kraft) C.; children: Sally Jo Wilkinson, Pamela Rae Wallace. Grad. high sch., Edwardsville. Owner Crook Constrn. Co., Edwardsville, 1961-74; owner, pres. Mark IV Builders, Edwardsville, 1974-85; owner Landmarke Supply Co., Edwardsville, 1970-85; pres. Vail Elec. Co., Edwardsville, 1974-84, Leenco Investments, Edwardsville, 1970-85; owner Sun Constrn. Co., Alton, Ill., 1985-91, Sun Enterprises, Alton, 1991—; pres., owner Suncon Inc., Alton, 1991—; mem. bd. Holiday Shores Inc., Edwardsville, 1969-77. With U.S. Army, 1967-69. Mem. Associated Builders and Contractors, So. Ill. Builders Assn. (bd. mem. 1971-88, v.p. 1981, pres. 1982). Home: 116 Windward Pl Alton IL 62002 Office: Suncon Inc PO Box 435 Alton IL 62002

CROOK, STEPHEN RICHARD, sales and marketing management consultant; b. Madison, Wis., Apr. 20, 1963; s. Richard John and Marcia Jane (Monroe) C.; m. Laura Ann Nabhan, Sept. 10, 1988. AS in Computer Sci. with highest honors, Purdue U., 1985, BS in Indsl. Engring., 1985; MS in Ops. Rsch., Stanford U., 1986; MBA, Northwestern U., 1992. Systems engr. AT&T Bell Labs. Inc., Naperville, Ill., 1985-88; design engr. Smart House Venture, Upper Marlboro, Md., 1986-88; product mgr. new product devel. planning AT&T Network Systems Inc., Lisle, Ill., 1989-90; product mgr. intelligent network bus. planning AT&T Network Systems Inc., Naperville, Ill., 1990-92; assoc. strategy discipline Gemini Consulting, Chgo., 1992-93; mgr. ZS Assocs., Evanston, Ill., 1993—. Inventor Smart House telephone gateway. Mem. Alpha Sigma Phi, Tau Beta Pi, Alpha Pi Mu. Office: ZS Assocs 1800 Sherman Ave Evanston IL 60201-3777

CROPPER, REBECCA LYNN, radiological engineer, radioactive waste engineer; b. LaGrange, Ky., Nov. 8, 1957; d. Clyde Carter and Dorothy Jean (Neblett) C. BA in Physics, Hanover Coll., 1979; MS in Health Physics, Ga. Inst. Tech., 1982. Radiol. control and safety technician U.S. Ecology, Inc., Louisville, 1979-81; rsch. asst. Ga. Inst. Tech., Atlanta, 1981-82; radiol. engr. Bechtel Nat., Inc., Oak Ridge, 1982-85; supervising engr. Impell Corp., Lincolnshire, Ill., 1985-90; licensing dir. Chem-Nuclear Systems, Inc., Springfield, Ill., 1990-92; prin. mem. tech. staff Ralph M. Parsons Co., Cin., Ohio, 1992-93; program health and safety mgr. Parsons Engring. Sci., Inc., Denver, 1993—. Mem. ASTM, Health Physics Soc., Am. Nuclear Soc.

CROPSEY, ALAN LEE, state legislator, lawyer; b. Paw Paw, Mich., June 13, 1952; s. Harmon George and Ruth Marian (Lindsay) C.; m. Erika Lynn Rumminger, Nov. 24, 1979; children: Joel Daniel, Gabriel Michael, Nathaniel Samuel, Evamarie Barbara. B of Math. Edn., Bob Jones U., 1975; JD, Cooley Law Sch., 1978. Bar: Mich., 1978. State senator 30th dist. Mich. Senate, 1983-86; state rep. 88th dist. Mich. Ho. of Reps., 1981-82, state rep. 86th dist., 1993—. Office: Kallman & Cropsey 205 W Saginaw St Lansing MI 48933-1239

CROSBIE, ROWENA GLADYS, management consultant; b. Winnipeg, Manitoba, Canada, Dec. 30, 1963; came to the U.S., 1991; d. Ronald Albert and Eileen Ethel (Trembath) Wilson; m. Daniel Wallace Berrie, Oct. 14, 1989 (div. 1992); m. Theodore Marlowe Crosbie, Nov. 24, 1992; 1 child, Jonathan Marlowe. CIM, U. Manitoba, 1991. Adminstr. Credit Union Stab Fund, Winnipeg, 1987-88; controller Garst Seed Co., Winnipeg, 1988-90; tng. specialist ICI Seeds, Des Moines, 1990-93; pres. Tero Internat., Inc., Earlham, Iowa, 1993—; trainer, cons., keynote speaker numerous orgns. including Buick Motor Divsn., Flint, Mich., 1993—, Drake U., Des Moines, 1994—, Allied Ins., Des Moines, 1994—, Zeneca/ICI, Wilmington, Del., 1991—. Author: (tng. manual) Impact: How to Speak Your Way to Success, 1993. Mem. Am. Soc. for Tng. and Devel., Canadian Inst. for Mgmt. Office: Tero Internat Inc 3524 Filmore Ct Earlham IA 50072

CROSBY, DONALD P., mechanical engineer; b. Jacksonville, Fla., Oct. 5, 1962. BSME, U. Mo., Rolla, 1984. Project engr. Billy Goat Industries, Lee's Summit, Mo., 1985-87, Dixon Industries Inc., Coffeyville, Kans., 1987—. Patentee in field. Mem. Soc. Mfg. Engrs. (v.p. 1995). Republican. Office: Dixon Industries Inc PO Box 1569 Coffeyville KS 67337-0945

CROSBY, GILBERT M., business analyst; b. Lodi, Ohio, June 15, 1939; s. Carleton Henry and Marian Lucille (Moutoux) C.; m. Patricia Diane Kaetzel Crosby, July 27, 1968; children: Gilbert Alexander, Karen Diane. BS in Edn., Ashland (Ohio) U., 1964. Vol. U.S. Peace Corps., Musoma, Tanzania, 1964-66; surveyor Great Lakes Constrn. Co., Cleve., 1966-67; mktg. rep. Caterpillar Inc., Peoria, Ill., 1967-69; engine dist. mgr. N.Y., Pa., 1969-75; Oh., W.Va., 1969-75; engine regional mgr. Caterpillar Australasia Ltd., Manila, Philippines, 1976-79; OEM sales mgr. Caterpillar Inc., Peoria, Ill., 1980-82; mktg. program cons., 1983-90, sr. industry analyst, 1990—; adv. bd. Truck Blue Book, Chgo., 1989-92. Bd. trustees Cat Trail Pub. Water Dist., Germantown Hills, Ill., 1991—; asst. scoutmaster Boy Scout Troop 162, Germantown Hills, Ill., 1983-90. Mem. Orpheus Club, Ch. of Brethren. Mem. Ch. of Brethren. Home: 1174 N Elm Ct East Peoria IL 61611-5404 Office: Caterpillar Inc 100 NE Adams Peoria IL 61629

CROSBY, LAVON KEHOE STUART, civic leader; b. Hastings, Nebr., Apr. 25, 1924; d. Charles William and Kathryn Marie (Farrell) Kehoe; m. Lester Stuart, Oct. 9, 1948 (dec. 1970); children—Mary Stuart Bolin, Michael, Timothy, Frederick Stuart; m. Robert B. Crosby, May 22, 1971. BA, U. Nebr., 1987. Asst. to pres. Hastings Tribune Corp., Nebr., 1941-68; mem. staff U.S. Senator Roman Hruska, Washington, 1968-71; mem. Nebr. State Legislature, 1988—; mem. Appropriations Com., 1988—, mem. Nebr. Retirement Systems com., 1992—, chmn. com. on coms., 1994—. Chmn. music com. Cathedral of Risen Christ Choir, Lincoln, Nebr.; pres. Lincoln Community Playhouse Guild; bd. dirs., chmn. membership com. Lincoln Community Playhouse; v.p., bd. dirs. Lincoln Symphony Guild; bd. dirs. Lincoln Symphony Orch. Assn., 1972-82; founder Nebr. Found. for Humanities; mem. Lincoln Symphony Found. Bd., 1984—; bd. dirs. Friends of Ctr. for Great Plains Studies, 1984—; vice chmn. Nebr. Arts Council, 1981-82, chmn., 1982-85; past mem. and sec. Pershing Auditorium Bd.; pres. Nebr. Legis. Ladies League, 1977-78; adv. bd. Cath. social Services Bur.; budget chmn. Nebr. Mother's Assn.; chmn. legis. affairs Diocesan Council Cath. Women; v.p. Heritage League, Lincoln, 1985—; pres. Cornhusker Republican Women, 1974-75. Recipient Mayor's Arts award, Lincoln, 1985, Gov.'s Arts award, Nebr., 1986, YWCA Tribute to Women award, 1993. Mem. Nebr. Club (Lincoln). Home: 3440 Hillside St Lincoln NE 68506-5737 Office: State Legislature State Capital Lincoln NE 68516

CROSS, BONHAM E(LWOOD), retired newspaper account executive; m. Marie Swanberg; children: Randi Lawrence, David. News photographer Star Tribune, Mpls., then with advt. dept.; ret. Chmn. Minn. Coun. for Hearing Impaired, interim exec. dir., 1991; mem. adv. com. Metro Regional Svc. Ctr. for Hearing Impaired; mem. Legis. Coalition for Hearing Impaired. Named Man of Yr., Minn. Assn. Deaf Citizens, 1987; recipient various awards for news photography. Home: 3662 Shady Oak Rd Minnetonka MN 55305-4223

CROSS, DELBERT RAY, electronic systems engineer; b. McAlistar, Okla., June 15, 1954. BSEE, U. Akron, 1990. Electronic sys. engr. Interbold, North Canton, Ohio, 1991—. Mem. Highmill Ch. of the Resurrection, North Canton, 1992—, Music Ministry, 1994—, Promise Keepers, 1994—. Seaman USN, 1972-74. Republican. Office: Interbold PO Box 3091 5995 Mayfair Rd Canton OH 44720-1550

CROSS, DOLORES EVELYN, university administrator, educator; b. Newark, Aug. 29, 1938; d. Charles and Ozie (Johnson) Tucker; children: Thomas E., Jane E. BA in Elem. Edn., Seton Hall U., 1963; MS, Hofstra U. 1968; PhD in Higher Edn. Adminstrn., U. Mich. 1971; hon. doctorates Marymount Coll., Skidmore Coll., Hofstra U., Elmhurst Coll. Asst. prof. edn. Northwestern U., Evanston, Ill. 1971-74; assoc. prof. Claremont Grad. Sch., Calif., 1974-78; vice chancellor CUNY, 1978-81; prof. Brooklyn Coll., 1978-81; pres. N.Y. State Higher Edn. Service Corp., Albany, 1981-88; assoc. provost, assoc. v.p. academic affairs U. Minn., Mpls., 1988-90; pres. Chgo. State U., 1990—; bd. dirs. Coll. Bd., Campus Compact, Assn. Black Women in Higher Edn., No. Trust Co.; sr. cons. South Africa's Historically Black Colls. Editor: Teaching in a Multicultural Society, 1978; bd. dirs. Field Mus., Chgo. Urban League, Leadership for Quality Edn., Chgo. Area Fulbright Scholars Program; Tosney award, Amer. Assn. of Univ. Admin., 1995. Mem. NAACP (life), Am. Edn. Research Assn., Am. Council on Edn. (bd. dirs.), Women Execs. in State Govt. (adv. bd.), Commercial Club (Chgo.). Avocations: running, hiking, bicycling, theater, writing. Office: Chgo State U Office of the President 95th St King Dr Chicago IL 60628

CROSS, HAROLD ZANE, agronomist, educator; b. Portales, N.Mex., Dec. 25, 1941; s. Guy Edner and Hagabelle (Lawson) C.; m. Glenda Faye Wilhoit, Nov. 24, 1961; children: Carter Dale, Carson Lee, Curtis Don, Cathryn Faye. BS with honors, N.Mex. State U., 1965, MS, 1967; PhD, U. Mo., 1971. Rancher Elida, N.Mex., 1965-67; grad. rsch. asst. N.Mex. State U., Las Cruces, 1965-67; NDEA fellow U. Mo., Columbia, 1967-71; asst. prof. N.D. State U., Fargo, 1971-77, assoc. prof., 1977-82, prof., 1982—; cons. Agrl. Inst. Osijek, Yugoslavia, 1984, CIMMYT, Mexico City, 1984, Eli Lilly Co., Indpls., 1987. Contbr. numerous articles to profl. jours. Crops judge N.D. Winter show, Valley City, 1973-94. Santa Fe Rwy. scholar, 1961-62; NDEA fellow, 1967-71; recipient Outstanding Sr. Rsch. award N.D. State U. Coll. Agr., 1992. Mem. Crop Sci. Soc. Am. (editor for maize germplasm 1989-92), Am. Soc. Agronomy, Sigma Xi, Phi Kappa Phi, Gamma Sigma Delta, Alpha Zeta. Office: ND State U Dept Plant Sci Fargo ND 58105

CROSS, JOAN ELAINE, nurse, insurance company representative; b. Cin., June 22, 1945. Diploma in Nursing, Bethesda Hosp. Sch. Nursing, Cin., 1966. Cert. assoc. in risk mgmt. Ins. Inst. of Am. Staff nurse emergency dept. Jewish Hosp., Cin., 1966-70; nurse, team leader ICU, critical care unit Bethesda Hosp., Cin., 1970-73, critical care instr., 1978-82; staff nurse ICU Christ Hosp., Cin., 1973-78; sr. risk mgmt. rep., med. svcs. St. Paul Fire and Marine Ins. Co., Cin., 1982—. Mem. NAFE, ARC, Am. Soc. Healthcare Risk Mgrs., Ohio Soc. Healthcare Risk Mgrs., Ky. Soc. Healthcare Risk Mgrs. Office: St Paul Fire and Marine Ins Co 250 W Court St Cincinnati OH 45202-1054

CROSS, THOMAS H., state legislator; b. Nashville, July 31, 1958; m. Eugenia Hovater; 1 child, Eloise Reynolds. BA, Ill. Wesleyan U., 1980; JD, Samford U., 1983. Asst. state's atty. Kendall County, Ill., 1983-92; Ill. state rep. Dist. 84; mem. Judiciary I and II, Transp., Fin. Insts. and Elections-State Govt. Coms., 1993—, Ill. Ho. of Reps.; atty. Law Offices of Ingemunson, Yorkville, Ill., 1986—. Recipient Humanitarian award Sr. Servants, 1990, 91. Mem. Yorkville C. of C. (bd. dirs. 1988—), Kendall County Found. (chmn. 1986-92), Oswego Lions (bd. dirs. 1990—), Navy League (judge adv. 1990—), Theta Chi. Office: 541 Countryside Ctr Yorkville IL 60560

CROSSAN, JOHN ROBERT, lawyer; b. Buchannon, W.Va., May 31, 1947; s. Thomas Benjamin Jr. and Margaret Windsor (Hicks) C.; m. Monique Margaretha Scheen, Dec. 22, 1973; children: Ashley Margaret, Aubry Kelly. BS with honors, U. Va., 1969; JD, U. Chgo., 1974. Bar: Ill. 1974, U.S. Dist. Ct. (no. dist.) Ill. 1974, U.S. Ct. Appeals (4th and 10th cirs.) 1978, U.S. Ct. Appeals (7th cir.) 1979, U.S. Ct. Appeals (fed. cir.) 1983, U.S. Ct. Appeals (6th cir.) 1989, U.S. Supreme Ct. 1985. Staff atty. Ill. Task Force N.E. Ill. Pub. Transp., Chgo., 1972-73; assoc. Hill, Van Santen, Steadman, Chiara, Chgo., 1973-77; assoc., then ptnr. Cook, Wetzel and Egan, Ltd., Chgo., 1978-88; counsel Willian, Brinks, Hofer, Gilson and Lione, Chgo., 1989-90; ptnr. Brinks, Hofer, Gilson & Lione, Chgo., 1991—; dir. Va. Engring. Found., 1996—. Author: Quick Guide to the Patent Law, 1994; contbr. articles to profl publs. Pres. aux. bd. Chgo. Architecture Found., 1983-85. Mem. Chgo. Yacht Club, Lakeshore Athletic Club. Home: 2825 N Cambridge Ave Chicago IL 60657-6018 Office: Brinks Hofer Gilson & Lione NBC Tower Ste 3600 Chicago IL 60611

CROSSLAND, ANN ELIZABETH, psychotherapist; b. Cambridge, Ohio, Apr. 24, 1940; d. H. Stewart and Laura Geraldine (Geese) Hastings; m. Eugene Joseph Szmuc, Nov. 30, 1963 (dec. Oct. 1976); m. Richard Ray Crossland, July 16, 1988; children: Rae Ann, Nancy, Carol. BS in Edn., Kent State U., 1965; MSEd in Counseling, U. Akron, 1981. Third grade tchr. Bertha Bradshaw Elem. Sch., Rootstown, Ohio, 1963-64; substitute tchr. Kent (Ohio) City Schs., 1967-84, Portage County Schs., Ravenna, Ohio, 1979-84; assoc. tchr. severely handicapped Portage County Schs., Ravenna, 1984-88, H.S. tchr. severe behavior handicap, 1988-92; therapist Child & Adolescent Svc. Ctr., Canton, Ohio, 1992—. Bd. dirs., facilitator Oncology Support Group, Akron, 1977-81; bd. dirs., vol. trainer, counselor WomanShelter, Ravenna, 1980-87; organizer, group facilitator Portage County Cancer Group, Ravenna, 1982-83; mem. steering com. Portage County Adolescent Network, Ravenna, 1987-92. Mem. ACA, Am. Mental Health Counselors Assn., Delta Kappa Gamma (Theta chpt.). Democrat. Unitarian Universalist. Office: Child & Adolescent Svc Ctr 1226 Market Ave N Canton OH 44714-2604

CROSSLIN, ANNA ERIKO, association executive; b. Tokyo, Aug. 24, 1950; d. Harry Edward and Mary Mieko (Negishi) Peterson; m. Wayne E. Crosslin, Nov. 14, 1987; 1 child, Clare Eriko. BA, Washington U., 1972; DHL, Webster U., 1992. Pres., CEO Internat. Inst., St. Louis, 1978—; mem. Mo. adv. coun. U.S. Commn. on Civil Rights, 1992-95; participant Leadership St. Louis, 1985-86. Pres. 39th St. Redevel. Corp., St. Louis, 1991-93, Shaw Neighborhood Improvement Assn., 1993-94; bd. dirs. Tech. Assistance Corp., St. Louis, 1991—. Mem. Japanese Am. Citizens League, Kappa Kappa Gamma. Home: 3651 Shenandoah Ave Saint Louis MO 63110-4011 Office: Internat Inst 3800 Park Ave Saint Louis MO 63110-2514

CROTTS, CAROLYN PEARL, school librarian; b. Dodge City, Kans., Nov. 3, 1935; d. Ed LaVerne and M. Pearl (Suiter) DeVore; m. Johnny LaVelle Hager, Mar. 27, 1955 (dec. Sept. 1958); children: Diane, Johnny, Jeffrey; m. Robert Gene Crotts, Aug. 25, 1960; children: Roseanne, Sandra, Sharon, David. BA, Ft. Hays Kans. State Coll., 1961; MLS, Emporia (Kans.) State U., 1995. Cert. tchr. English, elem. edn., libr., Kans. Elem. libr. Unified Sch. Dist. 351, Macksville, Kans., 1967-69; high sch. librarian, tchr. 8th grade lang. arts Unified Sch. Dist. 371, Montezuma, Kans., 1965-66, tchr. 6th grade, 1969-72, high sch. and elem. libr., 1972-87; high sch. libr. Unified Sch. Dist. 102, Cimarron, Kans., 1987—. Mem. ALA, NEA, Kans. Nat. Edn. Assn.-Cimarron-Ensign (treas. 1992—), Kans. Libr. Assn., Kans. Assn. Sch. Librs. (v.p. Dist. V 1995-96), Kans. Assn. for Ednl. Comms. and Tech., Lambda Iota Tau. Mem. Christian Ch.-Disciples of Christ. Office: Cimarron HS Libr 400 N 5th St PO Box 489 Cimarron KS 67835-0489

CROUCH, HARLAN EVERETT, business executive; b. Freeport, Ill., Aug. 16, 1937. Adminstr. Coleman Clinic Ltd., Canton, Ill., 1973-86; v.p. Williams and Co. Cons., Sioux City, Iowa, 1986—; adj. asst. prof. Sch. of Medicine, So. Ill. U., Springfield, 1976-81. Contbr. articles to profl. jours. Mayor City of Canton, Ill., 1977-81. Mem. Associated Acctg. Firms Internat. (chmn. cons. com. 1992-93). With USMC, 1955-58. Republican. Home: 2947 Sunset Cir Sioux City IA 51104-4021 Office: Williams and Co Cons 814 Pierce St Sioux City IA 51101-1004

CROUSE, JAMES LYLE, physician; b. Cairo, Ill., Apr. 29, 1926; s. George Homer and Sue Avis (Sale) C.; m. Maureen Terona Tremaiu Crouse, Sept. 20, 1958; children: James C., Michelle R., Kathryn A., Matthew T. BA, So. Ill. U., Carbondale, 1947-54; BS, U. Ill., Chgo., 1954-56; MD, 1954-58. Rotating internship Ill. Ctrl. Hosp., Chgo., 1958-59; surgical resident, 1959-60; chief of staff St. Mary's Hosp., Cairo, Ill., 1960-63; active staff Meml. Hosp., Carbondale, Ill., 1971-90; staff, 1990—; clinic staff Primary Care Medicine, Cardondale, Ill., 1975—. Staff sgt. Arny Air Corps, 1943-46. Recipient Disting. Flying Cross 1945, Air Med. with oak cluster 1945, Army Air Corps.; named Physician of Yr. Carbondale (Ill.) Clinic, 1976. Fellow Royal Soc. Medicine, 1980—. Republican. Roman Catholic. Home: 2711 Sunset Dr Carbondale IL 62902-2347

CROUT, CHARLES JOHN, engineering company executive; b. Chambersburg, Pa., May 6, 1947; s. Shirley John and Anna Geraldine (Gunder) C.; m. Brenda J. Stepler, Aug. 10, 1969; children: Charles John, Brian, Johanna. AA, Pa. State U., 1967, BS, 1971; postgrad. U. Wis., Pa. State U., George Washington U. Draftsman, Pangborn div. Carborundum Corp., Hagerstown, Md., 1967-69; design engr. Chambersburg Engring. Co., 1971-78, sr. engr., 1978-87, engring. mgr., 1988-94, v.p. Forging Devel., Inc., 1995—; cons. machine design and control; tchr. Chambersburg Vo-Tech. Sch., evenings 1978. Sunday sch. supt. Second Luth. Ch., 1978-82, ch. council sec., 1972-74, v.p., 1976-78, pres., 1979-81, 85—; pres. Thaddeus Stevens Elem. Sch. PTO, 1981-83, treas., 1984-85; vol. adult leader Boy Scouts Am. Co-author, co-instr.: Institute of Forging Die Design, Basic Principles, 1989 . Registered profl. engr., Pa. Mem. ASME, NSPE, Pa. Soc. Profl. Engrs., SME, Forging Industry Edn. and Research Found., Forging Industry Assn. (mem. tech. com.). Co-author: Impact Die Design, 1984, 90, Concepts of FOrging, 1995, Forge Engr. & Die Design, 1995; contbr. articles to profl. jours.; patentee in field. Office: Forging Devel (Internat) Inc 29102 Detroit Rd Cleveland OH 44145

CROW, MARY JO ANN, elementary education educator; b. Blytheville, Ark., July 13, 1935; d. Clarence and Myrtle Evelyn (Johnson) Williamson; m. Ernest W. Crow, June 4, 1960; children: Jennifer Evelyn, Steven Ernest. BA, Ctrl. Coll., 1957; postgrad. U. Nebr., 1957-60; tchr. cert., Eureka Coll., 1978-81; MS in Edn., Ill. State U., 1993. Cert. tchr. grades K-9, Ill. Lab. tech. U. Nebr. Coll. Medicine, Omaha, 1960-61, VA Hosp., Omaha, 1962-65; chem. tech. USDA Lab., Peoria, Ill., 1965-68; tchr. jr. high sci. Metamora (Ill.) Grade Sch., 1981—; presenter in field. Contbg. author: Celebrating Science, 1991; contbr. articles to profl. jours. Active Groundwater Protection Com., Lakeview Mus., Sun Found. Named one of Ill. Outstanding Sci. Tchrs., Ill. State U./NSF, 1988-91, Tchr. of Yr., Peoria area Sigma Chi. Mem. NEA, Nat. Sci. Tchrs. Assn., Ill. Sci. Tchrs. Assn., Ctrl. Mo. Amateur Astronomer. Office: Metamora Grade School 815 E Chatham Metamora IL 61548

CROW, SAM ALFRED, federal judge; b. Topeka, May 5, 1926; s. Samuel Wheadon and Phyllis K. (Brown) C.; m. Ruth M. Rush, Jan. 30, 1948; children: Sam A., Dan W. BA, U. Kans., 1949; JD, Washburn U., 1952. Ptnr. Rooney, Dickinson, Prager & Crow, Topeka, 1953-63, Dickinson, Crow, Skoog & Honeyman, Topeka, 1963-70; sr. ptnr. Crow & Skoog, Topeka, 1971-75; part-time U.S. magistrate, 1973-75, U.S. magistrate, 1975-81; judge U.S. Dist. Ct. Kans., Wichita, 1981-92, Topeka, 1992—; lectr. Washburn U. Sch. Law; participant adv. com. on criminal rules Jud. Conf., 1990—; mem. 10th Cir. Jud. Coun., 1987-88; founder Topeka Inn of Ct., pres., 1992-94; criminal rules adv. com.'s liaison Ct. Adminstrn. and Case Mgmt. Com.'s Subcom. on Criminal Case Mgmt., 1994—; bd. dirs. Riverside Hosp., Wichita, 1986-92; lectr. in field. Bd. rev. Boy Scouts Am., 1960-70, cubmaster, 1957-60; mem. vestry Grace Episcopal Ch., Topeka, 1960-65; chmn. Kans. March of Dimes, 1959, bd. dirs. 1960-65; bd. dirs. Topeka Council Chs., 1960-70; mem. Kans. Hist. Soc., 1960—; pres., v.p. PTA.; bd. govs. Washburn Law Sch. Alumni Assn., 1993—. Col. JAGC, USAR, ret. Fellow Kans. Bar Found.; mem. ABA (del. Nat. Conf. Spl. Ct. Judges 1978, 19), Kans. Bar Assn. (trustee 1970-76, chmn. mil. law sect. 1965, 67, 70, 72, 74, 75), Kans. Trial Lawyers Assn. (sec. 1959-60, pres. 1960-61), Nat. Assn. U.S. Magistrates (com. discovery abuse), Topeka Bar Assn. (chmn. jud. reform com., chmn. bench and bar com., chmn. criminal law com.), Wichita Bar Assn., Wichita Lawyers Club, Topeka Lawyers Club (sec. 1964-65, pres. 1965-66), Am. Legion, Shawnee Country Club, Delta Theta Phi, Sigma Alpha Epsilon. Office: US Dist Ct 444 SE Quincy St Topeka KS 66683

CROWDER, BARBARA LYNN, lawyer; b. Mattoon, Ill., Feb. 3, 1956; d. Robert Dale and Martha Elizabeth (Harrison) C.; m. Lawrence Owen

Taliana, Apr. 17, 1982; children: Paul Joseph, Robert Lawrence, Benjamin Owen. BA, U. Ill., 1978, JD, 1981. Bar: Ill. 1981. Assoc. Louis E. Olivero, Peru, Ill., 1981-82; asst. state's atty. Madison County, Edwardsville, Ill., 1982-84; ptnr. Robbins & Crowder, Edwardsville, 1985-87, Robbins, Crowder & Bader, Edwardsville, 1987-88, Crowder & Taliana, 1988—. Co-editor ISBA Family Law Newsletter, 1993; co-author chpts. in ISBA Family Law Handbook, 1995; contbr. articles to profl. jours. Chmn. City of Edwardsville Zoning Bd. Appeals, 1986-87; committee woman Edwardsville De, Precinct 15, 1986—; mem. City of Edwardsville Planning Commn., 1985-87; bd. dirs. Madison-Bond County Workforce Devel. Bd., 1995-96. Named Best Oral Advocate, Moot Ct. Bd., 1979, Outstanding Young Career Woman, Dist. XIV, Ill. Bus. and Profl. Women, 1986; recipient Alice Paul award Alton-Edwardsville NOW, 1987, Outstanding Working Woman of Ill. Ill. Fed. of Bus. and Profl. Women, 1988-89, Woman of Achievement YWCA, 1996; recipient Athena award Edwardsville/Glen Carbon C. of C., 1991. Fellow Am. Acad. Matrimonial Lawyers; mem. ABA, Ill. Bar Assn. (assoc. mem. family law sect. coun. 1990-93, mem. 1994—, co-editor family law newsletter 1993, vice chair 1996—), Ill. Fedn. Bus. and Profl. Women (parliamentaria dist. XIV 1991-92), Women Lawyers Assn. Met. East (pres. 1986), Edwardsville Bus. and Profl Women's Club (pres. 1988-89, 95-96, treas. 1989-90, Woman of Achievement award 1985, Jr. Svc. award 1987), UI Ill. Alumni Assn. (v.p. met.-east club 1994-95, bd. dirs. 1995—). Democrat. Home: 1409 Lantz Ct Edwardsville IL 62025 Office: Crowder & Taliana 216 N Main St Edwardsville IL 62025-1604

CROWE, SHELBY, educational specialist, consultant; b. Irvine, Ky., July 5, 1935; s. Claude and Lena (Clem) C.; m. Ina House, May 22, 1961 (div. 1977); children: Craig, Cara; m. Bonnie Wohlslagel, Aug. 6, 1977; children: Tyler, Trisha, Matthew. BA in Edn., Ea. Ky. U., 1958; MEd, Miami U., Oxford, Ohio, 1961; PhD in Ednl. Founds., Ohio State U., 1980. Cert. permanent spl. K-12 art edn. tchr., Ohio. Tchr. Cin. Pub. Schs., 1958-66; tchr. McGuffey Lab. Sch. Miami U., Oxford, Ohio, 1966-70; prof. edn. Wright State U., Dayton, Ohio, 1970-88, U. Dayton, 1988-90; ednl. specialist Dorothy Lane Markets, Dayton, 1990—; cooperating tchr. U. Cin., 1960-66; instr. Ohio U., 1966; instr. Morehead (Ky.) State U., summers 1964-65; adj. prof. Union for Experimenting Colls. and Univs., Cin., 1982; condr. insvc. workshops, presenter in field local, regional, state and nat. level. Contbr. book revs. to various publs. Recipient Teaching Excellence award Wright State U. Coll. Edn., 1981, 82, Wright State U. Alumni Assn., 1982, Faculty Mem. of Yr. award Wright State U. Student Govt., 1985,. Mem. NEA, ASCD, AAUP, Nat. Coun. for Scoial Studies Edn., Ohio Confedn. Tchr. Edn. Orgns., Ohio Edn. Assn., Nat. Art Edn. Assn. (Students Best Educator award 1973), Ohio Art Edn. Assn., Phi Delta Kappa. Home: 412 Corona Ave Dayton OH 45419-2605

CROWLEY, ANN M., nutrition educator; b. Elkton, S.D., Mar. 20, 1923; d. Walter Joseph and Matilda Marie (Harms) Cassidy; widowed; children: Kate, Tom, Colleen, Mike, Kevin, William, John. BS, U. Minn., 1944, MS, 1957; PhD, U. Iowa, 1977. Registered dietitian. Dir. dietary Abbott Hosp., Mpls., 1960-65; dir. nutrition U. Iowa, Iowa City, 1965-77; pres. Health Care Svcs., Iowa City, 1977—. Author: (book) Menu Plan With Ann, 1980. Mem. aux. Mercy Hosp., Iowa City, 1993—; vol. Birthright, Iowa City, 1993—. Mem. Soc. for Advancement of Food Svc. Rsch., Internat. Food Mktg. (Dir. of Yr. 1980). Office: Health Care Svcs 125 S Mt Vernon Dr Iowa City IA 52245

CROWLEY, ELIZABETH MARLENE, management consultant; b. LeCenter, Minn., Dec. 30, 1940; d. Roman Aloysius and Elizabeth Winifred (Cummings) Malinski; m. John Patrick Crowley, Aug. 3, 1963; children: Elizabeth J., John S., Ann B. BS in English, History, Mankato State U., 1960; MS in Orgn. Devel., U. Wis., Green Bay, 1985. English instr. various schs., Minn., Calif., Wis., 1960-69; communications instr. Northeast Wis. Tech. Coll., Green Bay, 1973-74, human resources devel. cons., coordinator, 1974-83; pres. Human Resources Devel. Cons., Green Bay, 1979-83; exec. dir. Fin. Mgmt. Concepts, Green Bay, 1983-85; asst. to pres. Univ. Bank, Green Bay, 1983-85; pres. Crowley, Lautenbach & Assocs., Green Bay, 1985—; chmn. The Exec. Com., 1993—. Contbr. articles to profl. jours. Bd. dirs. Brown County Hist. Soc., Green Bay, 1978-85, YMCA, 1986—, Family Svc. Assn., 1994—, Green Bay Symphony, 1995—. Recipient Wis. YMCA Key Leader award. Mem. Assn. Mgmt. Cons. (v.p. 1987—), Am. Assn. Univ. Women (v.p. 1969-83), Am. Soc. Tng. and Devel., Ind. Bus. Assn. Wis. Roman Catholic. Office: Crowley Lautenbach & Assocs PO Box 112 Green Bay WI 54305-0112

CROYLE, BARBARA ANN, health care management executive; b. Knoxville, Tenn., Oct. 22, 1949; d. Charles Evans and Myrtle Elizabeth (Kellam) C. BA cum laude in Sociology, Coll. William and Mary, 1971; cert. corp. tax and securities law Inst. Paralegal Tng., 1971; JD, U. Colo., 1975; cert. program mgmt. devel. Colo. Women's Coll., 1980; MBA, U. Denver, 1983. Bar: Colo. 1976. Paralegal Holland & Hart, Denver, 1972-73; law clk. Colo. Ct. Appeals, Denver, summer 1976; assoc. firm Shaw Spangler & Roth, Denver, 1976-77; mgr. acquisitions/lands Petro-Lewis Corp., Denver, 1977-85; mgr. strategic planning Westinghouse, Transp. Div., 1985-87; mng. dir. Benefit Resource Mgmt. Group (subs. Blue Cross We. Pa.), 1987-92; COO and v.p. D.T. Watson Rehab. Hosp., 1992-93; adminstr. dir. Franciscan Med. Ctr., Dayton, Ohio, 1994—; tchr. oil and gas law Colo. Paralegal Inst., 1978, 79; arbitrator Am. Arbitration Assn.; mediator Dayton Mediation Ctr. Mem. NAFE, ABA, Pa. Bar Assn., Inst. Noetic Scis., Am. Coll. Healthcare Execs. (ethics com., assoc.). Home: 330 Jones St Dayton OH 45410-1104 Office: Franciscan Med Ctr 601 S Edwin C Moses Blvd Dayton OH 45408-1424

CRUM, JAMES FRANCIS, waste recycling company executive; b. Pitts., July 23, 1934; s. Frank J. and Martha (Huffman) C.; m. Madeleine Jones, July 3, 1957; children: Cynthia Anne, James Joseph. BMechE, U. Rochester, 1956. Trainee to supt. transp. U.S. Steel Corp., Braddock, Pa., 1959-74; supt. transp. U.S. Steel Corp., South Chgo., Ill., 1974-75; supt. operating maintenance U.S. Steel Corp., South Chgo., 1975-76; asst. div. supt. iron U.S. Steel Corp., Gary, Ind., 1976-83; div. mgr. iron. U.S. Steel div. USX, Gary, 1983-88; exec. v.p., chief oper. officer McGraw Construction Co., Middletown, Ohio, 1988-92; dir. bus. devel. Nat. Recovery Systems, East Chicago, Ind., 1992-95, dir. ops., 1995—; adv. coun. South Suburban Hosp., 1993—; bd. dirs. South Suburban Hosp. Found. Vol. U. Rochester Admissions Network, N.Y., 1987—; cons. Clean City Coalition, Gary, 1988—. Mem. AIME, Eastern States Blast Furnace Assn., Western States Blast Furnace Assn. (bd. dirs. 1985-88), Assn. Iron & Steel Engrs. Republican. Roman Catholic. Home: 736 Central Park Ave Flossmoor IL 60422-2220 Office: Nat Recovery Systems 5222 Indianapolis Blvd East Chicago IN 46312-3838

CRUM, JOE CLAY, state legislator. Mem. Mo. Ho. of Reps., Jefferson City. Democrat.

CRUMP, CONSTANCE LOUISE, journalist; b. Detroit, Aug. 20, 1948; d. William B. and Marion A. (Wass) C. BA, U. Mich., 1969. Pers. asst. Detroit Free Press, 1970; gen. mgr. Kitchen Port Inc., Ann Arbor, Mich., 1970; acct. Carty's Music Co., Ypsilanti, Mich., 1971, U. Cellar Inc., Ann Arbor, 1972-80; freelance writer Ypsilanti, 1980-82; sr. feature writer Ann Arbor News, 1982-89; retailing, arts and entertainment reporter Crain's Detroit Bus., 1989-93; mgr. mktg. comm. Jon Greenberg & Assocs., Southfield, Mich., 1993—. Contbr. articles to local newspapers and nat. mags. including Billboard, Weightwatchers, Art and Antiques Weekly, Ohio Antiques Rev., Detroit Free Press, Detroit Mo.; contbg. editor Detroit Monthly, 1990-92; restaurant reviewer Detroit Mo. Mag. Mem. Culinary Historians of Am., Preservation Wayne, Mich. Theater Found., The Ark Coffeehouse, Ann Arbor Art Assn. (former dir.), Ypsilanti Heritage Found., Nat. Trust for Hist. Preservation, Cityscape Detroit. Office: Jon Greenberg & Assocs 29355 Northwestern Hwy Southfield MI 48034-1053

CRUMP, GWYN NORMAN, engineer; b. Granite Falls, N.C., Dec. 14, 1932; m. Frederick Andrew Sr. and Annie Mae (Bowman) C.; m. Amy Brown, June 11, 1960; children: Gwyn Norman Jr., James R., Melanie L. BSEE, N.C. State U., Raleigh, 1959; postgrad., U. Pitts., 1960-61. Sr. engr., engring. mgr. Miller Electric Mfg. Co., Appleton, Wis., 1969-73; chief elec. engr. Tektran Div. Air Products & Chem., Allentown, Pa., 1973-76; sr. elec. engr. R & D Hobart Bros. Co., Troy, Ohio, 1976-83, mgr. govt. bus., 1983-87; pres. Crump Enterprises, Troy, 1987-88, Spencer, Ohio, 1993—; ops. mgr. govt. bus. Controlled Systems Inc., Fairmont, W.Va., 1988; sr. rsch. project engr. Rohr Industries MP&T Dept., Chula Vista, Calif., 1989-92; cons. Hobart Bros., Seoul, 1980. Inventor SCR arc weld power supply, arc weld robots, space shuttle automatic plasma arc weld sys., power transformer insulation and sound level reduction sys., titanium med. implant tooling. Chmn. com. Boy Scouts Am., Newark and Troy, 1972-79; town councilman Sykesville (Md.) City Coun., 1967-69. With USAF, 1951-55. Mem. IEEE (life sr.), Am. Welding Soc. (silver mem., nat. safety com.), Nat. Elec. Mfrs. Assn. (com. on label and safe practices), Nat. Contract Mgrs. Assn., ANSI (nat. safety com.), Air Force Assn., Am. Def. Preparedness Assn., Nat. Mgmt. Assn. (bd. dirs., charter). Republican. Lutheran. Office: Crump Enterprises 6800 Spencer Rd Spencer OH 44275-9779

CRUMP, WAYNE F., state legislator; b. Belleville, Ill., June 26, 1950; m. Nancy C. Allen, 1974. Student, Belleville Area Coll. Former dep. sheriff Washington County, Mo., 1975-82; state rep. dist. 152 Mo. Ho. of Reps., 1983—; cattle farmer. Democrat. Home: 606 Pine St Potosi MO 63664-1644*

CRUMPINE, JOHN C., mechanical engineer; b. Beloit, Kans., Oct. 1, 1949. BS in Mech. Engring., Kans. State U., 1971. Sr. product engr. Richardson Mfg. Co., Cawker City, Kans., 1971-87, Exmark Mfg. Inc., Beatrice, Nebr., 1987—. Patentee in field. Chmn. fin. Cencentary United Meth., Beatrice, 1992; bd. trustees Cencentary United Meth. Ch., Beatrice, 1995. Republican. Office: Exmark Mfg Inc 2101 Ashland Ave Beatrice NE 68310-1252

CRUTE, BEVERLY JEAN, minister; b. Kansas City, Mo.; d. Robert Scott and Rossie Nell (Locke) C. BA, Baker U., Baldwin City, Kans., 1961; MA, U. Mo., Kansas City, 1969; PhD, Boston Coll., 1981; MDiv, Princeton Theol. Sem., 1984. Ordained to ministry Presbyn. Ch. (USA), 1985. Summer intern Berkeley (Mo.) Presbyn. Ch., 1981-83; sem. asst. Faith Presbyn. Ch., Medford, N.J., 1981-82, First Presbyn. Ch., Morrisville, Pa., 1982-83; asst. pastor First Presbyn. Ch., Willmar, Minn., 1984-85, assoc. pastor, 1986-92; dir. pastoral care, chaplain, hospice chaplain Rice Meml. Hosp., Willmar, 1992—; vis. lectr. Washington U., St. Louis, 1980; lectr. Boston Coll., Chestnut Hill, Mass., 1974-79; instr. North Shore Cmty. Coll., Beverly, Mass., 1972-79; dean women Baker U., Baldwin City, Kans., 1967-71, instr. sociology, 1967-71; tchr. Shawnee Mission H.S. Dist., Kans., 1961-67; chmn. Presbytery Social Justice Com., Willmar, 1985-90, 94—, chair, 1994—; mem. Synod Work Group in Social Justice, 1989-94, moderator, 1991-92. Author: (instr.'s guide) Introduction to Sociology, 1979; contbr. numerous book revs. in Theology Today, 1982-85. Mem. City of Willmar Heartland Express Bd., 1990-92, Kandiyohi County Probation Coun. Adv. Bd., 1991-94, Kandiyohi County Children's Trust Fund Coun., 1990-94, Willmar Ministerial Assn., 1985—, pres., 1989-90, bd. dirs. 1996—. Recipient Disting. Svc. award, Kiwanis, 1990, Spiritual Aims award, Minn.-Dakotas Dist., 1989-90. Mem. AAUW (bd. dirs. 1992—), Am. Sociol. Assn., Kiwanis (bd. dirs. 1991-94), Zeta Tau Alpha. Home: 1128 Par Ln Willmar MN 56201-4891 Office: Rice Meml Hosp 301 Becker Ave SW Willmar MN 56201-3395

CRYER, PHILIP EUGENE, medical educator, scientist, endocrinologist; b. El Paso, Ill., Jan. 5, 1940; s. Clifford Eugene and Carol Ruth (Cherry) C.; m. Susan Odette Shipman, Dec. 23, 1963 (div. May 1990); children: Philip Clifford, Justine Laurel; m. Carolyn Elizabeth Havlin, Sept. 16, 1994. BA, Northwestern U., 1962, MD, 1965. Diplomate Am. Bd. Internal Medicine, diplomate Am. Bd. Endocrinology and Metabolism. Intern Barnes Hosp., St. Louis, 1965-67; fellow in endocrinology Barnes Hosp./Washington U., 1967-68, resident in medicine, 1968-69, 71-72; investigator Naval Med. Rsch. Inst., Bethesda, Md., 1969-71; from instr. to assoc. prof. Washington U. Sch. Medicine, St. Louis, 1971-80, prof., 1981—, Irene E. and Michael M. Karl prof. endocrinology/metabolism, 1995—, dir. gen. clin. rsch. ctr., 1978—, dir. div. endocrinology, diabetes and metabolism, 1985—; Connaught-Novo lectr. Can. Diabetes Assn., 1987; Pimstone lectr. Soc. Endocrinology, Metabolism and Diabetes, South Africa, 1989; Kellion lectr. Australian Diabetes Soc., 1992; Plenary lectr. Japan Diabetes Soc., 1994. Author: Diagnostic Endocrinology, 1976, 2d edit., 1979, 61 book chpts.; editor: Diabetes; mem. editl. bd. Jour. Clin. Investigation, Am. Jour. Physiology, Jour. Clin. Endocrinology and Metabolism; contbr. over 260 articles to profl. jours. Recipient Rorer Clin. Investigator award Endocrine Soc., 1988, Rumbough Sci. award Juvenile Diabetes Found., 1989, Banting medal Am. Diabetes Assn., 1994, Excellence in Clin. Rsch. award NIH, 1994. Fellow ACP; mem. Am. Fedn. Clin. Rsch. (councilor 1979-80), Am. Soc. Clin. Investigation (v.p. 1985-86), Assn. Am. Physicians, Am. Diabetes Assn. (pres. 1996—), Phi Beta Kappa, Alpha Omega Alpha. Office: Washington U Sch Medicine 660 South Euclid Ave Box 8127 Saint Louis MO 63110

CUBA, ROBERT GREGORY, customer technical support administrator; b. St. Louis, Apr. 11, 1959; s. Raymond Joseph and Evelyn Cecelia (Stein) C.; m. Margaret Mary Haines, Sept. 3, 1983. AAS in Quality Control, St. Louis C.C., 1989; BA in Mgmt., Nat.-Louis U., 1991, MS in Mgmt., 1993. R & D technician Carter Automotive, St. Louis, 1981-83, statis. mfg. analyst, 1983-84; R & D technician Sherwood Med. Co., St. Louis, 1984-86; packaging quality supr. Chevron Chem. Co., Maryland Heights, Mo., 1986-89; quality improvement specialist Chevron Chem. Co., San Ramon, Calif., 1989-93; dir. customer tech. support, quality mgr. Continental Sprayers, Inc., St. Peters, Mo., 1994—; speaker in field. Mem. Am. Soc. Quality Control (cert. quality engr.), Engrs. Club of St. Louis. Home: 206 Oakwood Terrace Ct Ballwin MO 63021-8358

CUBBAGE, DIANA, school system administrator; b. Mar. 24, 1941; d. Jacob Henry and Lucy Laura (McClure) Dick; m. Norman Cubbage, Aug. 10, 1963; children: Wendy Cubbage Post, Erik. BA in History and Polit. Sci., Friends U., Wichita, 1963, BS in Phys. Edn., 1963; MA in Polit. Sci., Wichita State U., 1974; EdD in Ednl. Adminstrn., U. Kans., 1986. Tchr. Wichita Pub. Schs., 1963-75; asst. prin. Wichita H.S. North, 1975-78; 1st assoc. prin. Wichita H.S. N.W., 1978-80; prin. Hamilton Traditional Alt. Sch., Wichita, 1980-83, Wichita East H.S., 1983-84, Mayberry Jr. H.S., Wichita, 1985-87; div. dir. Jr. High Schs.-Wichita, 1987-88; area supt. Wichita Pub. Schs., 1988-93, asst. supt. equity and support svcs., 1993-94; supt. Moline/Cola Valley Sch. Dist. 40, Moline, Ill., 1994—. Bd. dirs. Boys and Girls Club, Moline, 1994—, Jr. Achievement, Moline, 1994—, United Way, 1995, Arrowhead Boys Ranch, Moline, 1994—; pres. Violence Prevention Inst., Wichita, 1993; trustee Trinity Sch. Nursing, 1996. Recipient Jr. Achievement Bronze Leadership award 1996; named Outstanding Alumna Friends U., 1988, Outstanding Educator Wichita Jaycees, 1975. Mem. ASCD, Am. Assn. Sch. Adminstrs., Ill. Assn. Sch. Adminstrs., Ill. Women's Assn., Urban Supts. Assn. Am., Rotary, Phi Delta Kappa, Delta Kappa Gamma. Office: Moline Sch Dist 40 1619 11th Ave Moline IL 61265

CUCKLER, TAD, consultant; b. Athens, Ohio, Feb. 11, 1958; s. William Raymond and Phyllis Eileen (Goldsberry) C. BA in Polit. Sci. and Anthropology, Ohio U., 1990, MA in Internat. Affairs, 1991. Owner, pres. Cuckler Cons. Inc., Shade, Ohio, 1990—; instr. cultural diversity and internal rels. Ohio U., Athens, 1991—. Author: Prospectives from the Farm, 1996. Bd. dirs. Athens Friends Internat. Students. With M.I., U.S. Army, 1977-81. Mem. Rotary, Masons, Kiwanis. Republican. Mem. United Brethren Ch. Home and Office: 1050 Carter Rd Shade OH 45776

CUDABACK, JIM D., state legislator; b. Riverdale, Nebr., Apr. 12, 1938. Student, Kearney State Coll. Rental property mgr. Nebr.; mem. from dist. 36 Nebr. State Senate, Lincoln, 1990—, vice chmn. agr. com., mem. gen. affairs com., gov., mil. and vet. affairs com., mem. health and human svc. com., intergovt. coop. com., past mem. bldg. maintenance com. Mem. Buffalo County Bd. Commrs.; mem. Ctrl. C.C. Adv. Bd.; past pres. Cmty. Concert Assn.; active Gibbon Good Samaritan Village; pres., mem. adv. bd. Buffalo County Hist. Soc. Office: Nebr State Senate State Capitol Rm 1124 Lincoln NE 68509*

CUDDIHY, JUNE TUCK, pediatrics nurse; b. Buffalo, June 15, 1936; d. John R. Sr. and Monica A. (Donahue) Tuck; m. Robert V. Cuddihy, Aug. 24, 1957; children: Robert V., Timothy, Kathleen. BSN, D'Youville Coll., Buffalo, 1957; MA, Seton Hall U., 1972, MSN, 1979. Cert. primary care nurse practitioner. Pub. health nurse Monroe County, Rochester, N.Y.; health coord. Early Childhood Learning Ctrs. N.J., Morristown; asst. prof. Seton Hall U., South Orange, N.J., 1977-81, William Paterson Coll., Wayne, N.J., 1981-94; clin. assoc. Coll. Nursing Ohio State U., 1994—; cons. Berkeley BioMedical Group, Inc., 1991—. Contbr. articles to profl. jours. Named Outstanding Grad. Student, Seton Hall U., 1979. Mem. ANA (vice chmn. bd. examiners for cmty. health nursing practice, chmn. sch. nurse practice subcom.), N.J. State Nurses Assn., Nat. Child Abuse Assn., Nat. Burn Victim Found., Pub. Health Assn., Sigma Theta Tau. Home: 8798 Killie Ct Dublin OH 43017-8333 Office: Ohio State U Coll Nursing Dept Cmty Parent Child Psyc 1585 Neil Ave Columbus OH 43210-1289

CUFFE, STAFFORD SIGESMUND, automotive engineer, consultant; b. Kingston, Jamaica, Dec. 4, 1949; came to U.S., 1970; s. Edwin Syndey and Leida C. (Sasso) C.; m. Dorothy Cummings, Sept. 15, 1973; children: Keisha, Kendra. AAS, N.Y.C. Community Coll., 1975; BS in Engring. Tech., CCNY, 1977; MS in Adminstrn., Ctrl. Mich. U., 1993; PhD in Adminstrn./Mgmt., Walden U., 1995. Project engr. PPG Inds. Inc., Wichita Falls, Tex., 1977-79; mfg. engr. Ford Motor Co., Tulsa, 1979-85; sr. mfg. engr. Ford Motor Co., Lincoln Park, Mich., 1985-90; sr. mgr. engr. Rsch. & Engring. Ctr. Ford Motor Co., Dearborn, 1992-95; sr. mfg. engr. Glass Tech. Ctr. Ford Motor Co., 1992—; mem. Dearborn (Mich.) plant modernization team (Japanese venture), 1990-92; cons. in field. Bd. dirs. Tulsa Jaycees, 1981; tech. advisor Boy Scouts Am., Tulsa, 1982; exec advisor Jr. Achievement of S.W. Mich., 1986; fund raiser United Way Found. of Mich., 1988. Mem. IEEE (nat. chmn. glass industry com. 1990—), Soc. Mfg. Engrs., Rotary (Southfield Mich. chpt.). Democrat. Roman Catholic.

CUHAJ, GEORGE, publishing executive; b. Astoria, N.Y., Jan. 8, 1960. AAS, N.Y.C. C.C., 1978; BBA, CUNY, 1985. Computer systemmgr. Am. Numismatic Soc., N.Y.C., 1981-88; chief usher St. Patrick's Cathedral, N.Y.C., 1988-89; catalogue prodn. mgr. Stack's Rare Coins, N.Y.C., 1990-94; mng. editor Numismatic Catalog Divsn. Krause Publs., Iola, Wis., 1995—. Bd. dirs. Bklyn. Tech. Rsch. Found., 1987—. Recipient Silver Beaver award Boy Scouts Am., N.Y.C., 1993. Mem. Am. Medallic Sculpture Assn. (pres. 1994). Home: PO Box 433 Iola WI 54945-0433

CULLEN, CHAD C., business executive; b. Williamsburg, Va.. MBA, Ea. Mich. U., 1973. Mfg. engr. GM, Detroit, 1970-85; v.p. Internat. Quality Inst., Canton, Mich., 1985—. Mem. Am. Soc. for Quality Control (cert. quality engr.), Soc. for Mfg. Engrs. (sr. mem.). Republican. Office: 363 Country Club Ct Canton MI 48188-3026

CULLEN, DAVID A., state legislator; b. Milw., Feb. 1, 1960; married; 1 child. BA, U. Wis., 1981; JD, Marquette U., 1984. Mem. from dist. 13 Wis. State Assembly, Madison, 1990—. Mem. Milw. Sch. Bd., 1983-90, pres., 1987-90; bd. dirs. Friends of Sch. Edn., U. wis.; mem. Statewide Presch.-Grade 5 Adv. Coun. Mem. Wis. Bar Assn. Home: 2845 N 68th St Milwaukee WI 53210-1206*

CULLEN-BENSON, SCOTT PAUL, employee assistance professional; b. Honolulu, June 19, 1952; s. Paul Fredrick and Beverly Davis Benson; m. Cathrine Ann Cullen, June 3, 1978; children: Justin, Brendan, Michael. BA, Ohio State U., 1974; MA, Ill. State U., 1987. Cert. employee assistance profl.; cert. supr. alcohol and other drug abuse counseling. Psychiat. technician Upham Hall, Ohio State U. Hosps., Columbus, 1974-75; child care worker Dept. Children and Family Svcs., State of Ill., Bloomington, 1976-77; addiction clinician St. Mary Hosp., Quincy, Ill., 1977-83; regional employee assistance coord. Reynolds Metals Co., McCook, Ill., 1983—. Mem. Employee Assistance Profl. Assn. (pres. Chgo. chpt. 1992-94), Internat. Employee Assistance Profl. Assn. (North Ctrl. regional rep. 1995—). Office: Reynolds Metals Co 1st Ave and 47th St Mc Cook IL 60525-3294

CULLERTON, JOHN JAMES, state senator, lawyer; b. Chgo., Oct. 28, 1948; s. John James and Mary Patricia (Tyrrell) C.; m. Pamela J. Wilson, Sept. 8, 1979; children: Maggie, John, Garritt, Kyle, Josephine. BS, Loyola U., 1970, JD, 1974. Bar: Ill. 1974. Asst. pub. defender Cook County, Chgo., 1974-79; state rep. State of Ill., Springfield, 1979-91, state senator, 1991—; from assoc. to ptnr. Fagel & Haber, Chgo., 1987—. With U.S. Nat. Guard, 1970-76. Democrat. Roman Catholic. Office: Fagel & Haber 140 S Dearborn St Chicago IL 60603-5202*

CULTER, JOHN DOUGHERTY, chemical engineer; b. Tulsa, May 1, 1937; s. Gail Curtis and Virginia Belle (Dougherty) C.; m. Patricia Ann Woodall, June 20, 1957 (div. 1968); children: Karen Gail, Shawna Lynn; m. Shirley Arlene Seiler, Nov. 27, 1968; children: Judith Ann Leavesley, Kirk Harris Leavesley. BS in Petroleum Engring., U. Tulsa, 1959, MS in Petroleum Engring., 1961; PhD in Chem. Engring., U. Mo., Rolla, 1976. Rsch. engr. Continental Oil Co., Ponca City, Okla., 1960-69; sr. rsch. engr. Am. Enka Co., Ashville, N.C., 1973-76; mgr. polymer and converting tech. St. Regis Corp., West Nyack, N.Y., 1976-84; sr. prin. scientist Gen. Mills Inc., Mpls., 1984—; pres. Advanced Material Engring. Inc., Edina, Minn., 1988—; cons. on packaging materials and polymer processing. Contbr. articles to profl. jours.; patentee in field. Sgt. USAF, 1960-61. Mem. TAPPI, Soc. Rheology, Am. Chem. Soc., Soc. Plastics Engrs. Office: Gen Mills Inc 9000 Plymouth Ave N Minneapolis MN 55427-3870

CULVER, DAVID ALAN, aquatic ecology educator; b. Oak Ridge, Tenn., Feb. 14, 1945; s. Joseph Simpson and Ella Elizabeth (Smart) C.; m. Virginia Ruth Nagel, Sept. 7, 1967; children: Timothy David, Cynthia Diane. BA, Cornell U., 1967; MS, U. Wash., 1969, PhD, 1973. Asst. prof. biology dept. Queen's U., Kingston, Ont., Can., 1973-75; asst. prof. zoology dept. Ohio State U., Columbus, 1975-81, assoc. prof., 1981-95, prof., 1995—; co-dir. young scholars minority program in biology Ohio State U., Columbus, 1988-94; vis. scientist U. Adelaide, Australia, 1984-85; exec. com. Ohio Sea Grant Coll. Program, Columbus, 1983—; dir. tchrs. tng. program Howard Hughes Med. Inst., Columbus, 1989-94; mem. Rsch. Group on Zebra Mussels in Gt. Lakes Basin, Columbus, 1989—; cons. Va. Electric Power Co., Mt. Storm, W.Va., 1991—. Contbr. articles to sci. jours. With U.S. Army, 1969-71. Fellow Coop. Inst. for Limnological and Ecosys. Rsch., NOAA; numerous rsch. grants including U.S. Dept. Interior, 1976-82, EPA, 1977-78, Dept. Commerce, 1980-83, 92—, Ohio Dept. Natural Resources and Ohio Biol. Survey, 1982-83, U.S. Fish and Wildlife Svc., 1983-84, 87-92, 93—, Ohio Sea Grant Program, 1983-92, 90—, North Ctrl. Regional Aquaculture Ctr., USDA, 1990-91; also tng. grants. Mem. Ecol. Soc. Am., Am. Soc. Limnology and Oceanography, Am. Fisheries Soc., Internat. Assn. for Gt. Lakes Rsch., Internat. Assn. for Theoretical and Applied Limnology, Australian Soc. for Fish Biology, Sigma Xi. Democrat. Office: Ohio State U Dept Zoology 1735 Neil Ave Columbus OH 43210-1220

CULVER, ROBERT DUNCAN, religious educator; b. Yakima County, Wash., July 19, 1916; s. Sinyeard Carpenter and Emma Eugenie (Mondor) C.; m. Arlene Leola Hoyt, Jan. 29, 1937 (dec. 1974); children: Douglas, Keith, Lorraine; m. Celest Fay Knipmeyer, Nov. 20, 1975. AB, Heidelberg Coll., 1945; BD, Grace Theol. Sem., 1945, MTh, 1947, ThD, 1952. Ordained min., Brethren Ch. Prof. Old Testament Hebrew Grace Theol. Sem., Winona Lake, Ind., 1945-51; prof. Old Testament and Hebrew Trinity Sem., Chgo., 1951-54; prof. Bible and philosophy Wheaton (Ill.) Coll., 1953-62; prof. Bible Northwestern Coll., Mpls., 1962-64; chmn. theology Trinity Evang. Divinity Sch., Deerfield, Ill., 1964-75; spl. lectr. in theology, 1976—. Author: Daniel and Later Days, 1967, Life of Christ, 1976, A Biblical View of Civil Government, 1975. Mem. Evang. Theol. Soc., Soc. Bibl. Lit. Home: Rt # 1 Box 166 Houston MN 55943

CULVER, ROBERT ELROY, osteopathic physician; b. Toledo, Oct. 1, 1926; s. Elroy and Helen Mary C.; m. Sallie Jane Corder, June 10, 1972; children: Diana L., Galen R., Ronald A., Richard A., Patricia A., Robert B. B.S., U. Toledo, 1951; D.O., Chgo. Osteo. Medicine, 1959. Cert. med. boxing profl. Intern Sandusky Meml. Hosp., Ohio, 1960; practice medicine specializing in family practice and sports medicine Oregon, Ohio, 1960—; health commr. Village of Harbor View, 1990—; dir. osteo. svcs. Riverside Hosp., 1996—; mem. City of Oregon Bd. Health, staff Parkview, Riverside, Toledo, Mercy Hosps.; physician Oregon Sch. Sys.; police surgeon City of Oregon; chief dep. coroner, 1978-80; chmn. wrestling divsn. physicians Nat. AAU; U.S. med. rep. Fedn. Internat. Lute Amateur; physician U.S. Wrestling Team; med. dir. World Cup of Wrestling; pres. Northwestern Ohio

AAU; 3rd v.p. Ohio AAU; med. cons. Ohio Profl. Boxing Commn. Mem. Air Force Mus., Toledo Mus. Art; dir. Toledo Zoo; mem. Smithsonian Instn.; apptd. to sr. coun. of Ohio Acad. of Sci., 1993. With C.E., U.S. Army, 1944-46; col. Ohio Def. Svc. Recipient commendation Ohio Ho. of Reps., 1983, 93, honor award Oreg. Sch. Sys., 1983; named Outstanding Team Physician State of Ohio, 1984, World Sports Medicine Hall of Fame, 1993. Mem. Am. Osteo. Assn., Ohio Osteo. Assn., 1st Dist. Acad. Osteo. Medicine (state trustee, past pres.), Am. Coll. Gen. Practitioners in Osteo. Medicine and Surgery, Ohio Osteo. Assn. Physicians and Surgeons, Chgo. Coll. Osteo. Med. Alumni Assn., Ohio Acad. Sci. (mem. sr. coun.), NRA (life), U. Toledo Alumni Assn. (life), Air Force Assn., Aircraft Owners and Pilots Assn., Nat. Hist. Soc., Ohio Hist. Soc., Am. Legion, Atlas Club, Masons, Elks, Shriners. Methodist. Office: 5517 Corduroy Rd Oregon OH 43616-1511

CULVERWELL, ROSEMARY JEAN, principal, elementary education educator; b. Chgo., Jan. 15, 1934; d. August John and Marie Josephine (Westermeyer) Flashing; m. Paul Jerome Culverwell, Apr. 26, 1958; children: Joanne, Mary Frances, Janet, Nancy, Amy. BEd, Chgo. State U., 1955, MEd in Libr. Sci., 1958; postgrad., DePaul U., 1973. Cert. supr., tchr. Tchr. Otis Sch., Chgo., 1955-59; tchr., libr. Yates Sch., Chgo., 1960-61, Nash Sch., Chgo., 1962-63, Boys Chgo. Parental, 1969-72, Edgebrook and Reilly Schs., Chgo., 1965-67; counselor, libr. Reilly Sch., Chgo., 1968, tchr., libr., asst. prin., 1973, prin., 1974—. Pres. Infant Jesus Guild, Park Ridge, Ill., 1969-70; troop leader Girl Scouts U.S., Park Ridge, 1967-69; sec. Home Sch. Assn., Park Ridge, 1969, v.p. spl. projects, 1970; mem. Ill. Svc. Ctr. Six Governing Bd., 1994. Recipient Outstanding Prin. award Citizens Schs. Com., Chgo., 1987, For Character award, 1984-85, Whitman award for Excellence in Edn. Mgmt., 1990, Local Sch. Coun. award Ill. Bell Ameritech, 1991, Ill. Disting. Educator award Milken Family Found. Nat. Educators, 1991, Ill. Edn./Bus. Partnership award, 1994, 96. Mem. AAUW, LWV (chmn. speakers bur. 1969), Delta Kappa Gamma, Phi Delta Kappa. Home: 1929 S Ashland Ave Park Ridge IL 60068-5460 Office: FW Reilly Sch 3650 W School St Chicago IL 60618-5358

CUMMIN, ALFRED S(AMUEL), retired chemist; b. London, Sept. 5, 1924; came to U.S., 1940, naturalized, 1948; s. Jack and Lottie (Hainesdorff) C.; m. Sylvia E. Smolok, Mar. 24, 1945; 1 child, Cynthia Katherine. BS, Poly. Inst. Bklyn., 1943, PhD in Chemistry, 1946; MBA, U. Buffalo, 1959. Rsch. chemist S.A.M. labs., Manhattan Project, Columbia U., 1943-44; plant supr. Metal & Plastic Processing Co., Bklyn., 1946-51; rsch. chemist Gen. Chem. div. Allied Chem. & Dye Corp., N.Y.C., 1951-53; sr. chemist Congoleum Nairn, Kearny, N.J., 1953-54; supr. dielecs-advance devel. Gen. Elec. Co., Hudson Falls, N.Y., 1954-56; mgr. indsl. products rsch. dept. Spencer Kellogg & Sons, Inc. (Textron), Buffalo, 1956-59; mgr. plastics div. Trancoa Chem. Corp., Reading, Mass., 1959-62; assoc. dir. product devel. service labs. chem. div. Merck & Co., Inc., Rahway, N.J., 1962-69; dir. product devel. Borden Chem. div. Borden Inc., N.Y.C., 1969-72; tech. dir. Borden Chem. div. Borden Inc., 1972-73; tech. dir. Borden Inc., 1973-78, v.p. product safety and quality, 1978-81, v.p. sci. and tech., 1981-89, sr. v.p. sci. and tech., 1989-91; assoc. dir. Ctr. for Packaging Sci. and Engring./Rutgers U., 1991—; advisor to the dir. Ctr. for Advanced Food Technology/Rutgers U., 1994—; rschr. in polymers, electrochemistry, and food packaging; mem. exec. com. Food Safety Coun., 1976-81, trustee, chmn. mem. com., 1976-81; bd. dirs. Formaldehyde Inst., 1977-86, vice chmn., 1982-86, mem. exec. com., 1981-86, mem. med. com., 1977-86, steering com., 1977-86; bd. dirs. Internat. Life Scis. Inst., 1986—, Nutrition Found., 1986—, Risk Assessment Inst., 1986—, Rsch. Inst., 1986—; bd. dirs., treas. Health and Environ. Sci. Inst., 1990—; instr. Poly Inst. Bklyn., 1946-47; asst. prof. Adelphi Coll., 1952-54; prof. math. sci. U.S. Merchant Marine Acad., 1954; seminar leader Am. Mgmt. Assn.; prof. mgmt. NYU Sch. Mgmt., 1968—; mem. Inst. Food Technologists, 1945—, mem. fin. com., 1993—, mem. Found. Fund Drive com., 1993-95, mem. bd. dirs. Packaging Divsn., 1995—. Contbr. articles to profl. jours. Recipient cert. award Fedn. Socs. Paint Tech., 1965. Mem. ASTM, Am. Chem. Soc. Fedn. Coatings Tech., Inst. Food Tech., Synthetic Organic Chems. Mfg. Assn. (dir. 1977-84), Paint Rsch. Inst., Inst. Food Technologists (fin. com. 1992—).

CUMMING, MARION F., forensic consultant; b. Heidelberg, Germany, Apr. 21, 1949; came to U.S., 1955; d. Raymond and Anneliese (Ridinger) Malenfant; m. Michael T. Cumming, Aug. 1, 1970; children: David, Becky. RN, Grace Hosp. Sch. Nursing, Detroit, 1970; student, U. Wis., Oshkosh, 1980, U. Wis., Manitowoc, 1980-82, Graceland Coll., 1992—. RN, Wis. RN Holy Family Hosp., Manitowoc, Wis., 1970-77; cert. cardiopulmonary resuscitation instr. Manitowoc, Wis., 1971-77, life. ins. phys. examiner, 1977-78, chief dep. coroner, 1975-79, county coroner, 1979-93; emergency dept. RN Holy Family Meml. Med. Ctr., Manitowoc, Wis., 1993—; owner, cons. Coroner/Med. Examiner Resources, Manitowoc, Wis., 1993—; developer and participant tng. and seminars Wis. Dept. Justice, Bur. Tng. and Stds., 1979, 81, 83, Wis. Coroners and Med. Examiners Assn., 1975—, U. Wis., Green Bay, 1987, Fin. Analysis Tng., Manitowoc, 1989, Disaster Mgmt. Tng., Madison, 1989, Clin. Forensic Nursing Tng., Green Bay, 1992, Doug Miller Symposium, Madison, 1993, Nat. Assn. Med. Examiners, Ft. Worth, 1993, Charleston, S.C., 1994, Internat. Assn. Forensic Nurses, Sacramento, Calif., 1993, Tyson Corner, Va., 1994, numerous seminars and workshops, 1970—; spkr. Wis. Sudden Infant Death Rsch. and Counseling Ctr., expert on Oprah Winfrey Show, Chgo., 1991; presenter 12th Dist. Nurses Assn., 1980, 91, Wis. Coroners and Med. Examiners Assn., 1980, 93, Manitowoc County Coun. on Aging, 1981, Manitowoc County Chpt. of Compassionate Friends, 1982, Manitowoc Chpt. Alcoholics Anonymous, 1982, Nursing Home Adminstrs. of Wis., Green Bay, 1984, Wis. Coun. of Cath. Women, 1986, Wis. Assn. Pub. Sch. Adminstrs. conf., Mishicot, 1986, Wis. State Assembly Com. on Health Testimony, Madison, 1987, Annual Wis. Sudden Infant Death Rsch. and Counseling Ctr. Profl. Seminars, Milw., 1987, 88, Green Bay, 1991, Bus. and Profl. Women. conf., Manitowoc, 1988, Wis. Women's Legis. conf., Milw., 1988, Wis. Emergency Mgmt. Assn., 1988, Wis. Funeral Dirs. Assn. regional conf., Mineral Springs and Port Washington, 1990, Annual Nat. Conf. of the Musculoskeletal Transplant Found., Atlantic City, 1990, Fox Valley Nurses Assn., Manitowoc, 1991, Manitowoc Sr. Citizen Peer Counselor Tng., 1992, N.E. Wis. Emergency Nurses Assn, Appleton, 1992, 94, Manitowoc Police Dept. cont. edn. sessions, 1992, ARC Nat. Field Leadership meeting, Anaheim, Calif., 1993, Internat. Assn. Forensic Nurses sci. assemblies, Sacramento, Calif., 1993, Tyson Corner, Va., 1994, others; advisor Wis. Dept. Health Info. Publs., 1986, Nat. Transp. Safety Bd., 1987-88, 89-90;. Contbr. articles to profl. jours. Mem. Dem. Party, 1978—, mem. scholarshp com., 1983; mem. Manitowoc County Emergency Med. Svcs. Coun., 1980-93, pres., 1986, 87; mem. adv. bd. Manitowoc County Chpt. Compassionate Friends, 1980—; leader Cub Scouts, Boy Scouts Am., 1980-85; mem. Lakeshore Women's Network, 1981-88, James Monroe Parent-Tchr. Com., 1983-89, pres., 1985-86, 86-87; mem. Yorktown House Cmty. Based Residential Facility Cmty. Coun., 1987—, Whitetails Unltd., 1987-89; mem. police and fire commn. City of Manitowoc, 1993—; mem. steering com. to bring hospice to Manitowoc, 1985; mem. State Registrar's Task Force, 1985-88, Reedsville H.S. Suicide Prevention Task Force, 1986-93, AMA Task Force on Teen Suicide Prevention, 1986, catalyst for a Nat. Geriat. Suicide Prevention Study, 1989; chairperson of the post-mortem com. Manitowoc County AIDS Task Force, 1987-83; mem. alcohol and other drug abuse task force Two Rivers/Mishicot Area United Way, 1989-90; mem. com. to determine location and type of safety bldg. City of Manitowoc, 1989; mem. coroner/med. examiner use of lab task force Wis. State Lab. Hygiene, 1989-90; mem. reassessment of toxicology sect. state crime lab Wis. Atty. Gen.'s Office, 1991—; founder Manitowoc County Chpt. Survivors of Suicide, 1983, Manitowoc County Critical Incident Stress Debriefing Team, 1992. Recipient Recognition award Manitowoc Lions Club, Wis. Atty. Gen.le, 1992, Manitowoc County Sheriff's Office, 1993, Manitowoc City Police, 1993, Newton First Response award, 1993, Wis. State Registrar's award, 1993, Gov. Tommy Thompson's Commendation, 1993. Mem. Wis. Coroners and Med. Examiner Assn. (chairperson ethics com. 1981—, exec. bd. dirs. 1982-83, 90-91, mem. past pres. group 1990—, mem. legis. com. 1979—, adminstrv. v.p. 1984-85, ednl. v.p. 1986-87, pres. 1988-89, mem. quality assurance stds. practice com. 1990—, Recognition award 1990), Internat. Assn. Coroners and Med. Examiners, Wis. County Constnl. Officers Assn. (2d v.p. 1989, 1st v.p. 1990-93, Recognition award 1989), Wis. Sudden Infant Death Rsch. and Counseling Ctr. (cmty. coun. 1989-93), Internat. Assn. Forensic Nurses (charter, exec. bd. dirs. 1993-96, asst. chairperson medicolegal death investigation coun. 1993—), Am. Bd. Forensic Examiners. Democrat. Roman Catholic. Home: 2124 S 13th St Manitowoc WI 54220

CUMMINGS, ERWIN KARL, data processing executive; b. Toledo, June 19, 1954; s. Idell and Mae Sue (Jones) C. AS in Electronic Engring., U. Toledo, 1976, BS in Bus. Svcs., 1981; postgrad., Bowling Green State U., 1990—. Computer operations analyst Owens-Ill. Inc., Toledo, 1972-73; telecommunications analyst Owens-Ill. Inc., Toledo, 1975-78, ops. and planning analyst, 1978-81, software systems analyst, 1981-83, sr. data communications analyst, 1983-86, lead data communicatons analyst, 1986-89, mgr. voice and data communications, 1989—. Pres. Christian Youth Fellowship, Phillips Temple, 1971-72, young adult tchr., 1971-79, supt. Sunday sch., 1979-81, asst. supt., 1983-87, sec. steward bd., 1983-93, head basketball coach, 1986-87, chmn. budget com., 1988-89; bd. dirs. Rosa Morgan Enrichment Ctr., 1988-92, chmn. fin. com., 1989-92, treas., 1990-92; mem. Christian Appalachian Project, 1989—. Mem. NAACP (life), DAV (Comdrs. Club 1985—), YMCA Century Club, Nat. Assn. Systems Programmers, Black Data Processing Assocs., Sacred Heart Automobile League, TV30/FM91, United Way Comdrs. Club. Democrat. Methodist. Home: 1180 Bernath Pky Toledo OH 43615-6742 Office: Owens-Ill Inc 1 Seagate Toledo OH 43666-1000

CUMMINGS, JERRE D., transportation manager; b. Wisconsin Rapids, Wis., Dec. 18, 1936; s. Harry A. and Harriet A. (Turner) C.; m. Virginia L. Ramsdell, Aug. 25, 1956; children: Deborah, Diane, Daniel, David, Dean. Traffic Mgmt. Degree, Humboldt Inst., Mpls., 1957. Rate clk. Gross Common Carriers, Wisconsin Rapids, Milw., Wis., 1956-59; routing and rate clk. Inland Steel Products, Milw., 1959-63; traffic mgr. Wis. Bridge & Iron, Milw., 1963-64, Phenix Mfg. Co., Milw., Shawano, 1964-80; distbn. and warehouse mgr. Phenix Mfg. Co., Shawano, 1980-88, garage door works mgr., 1988-90; transp., warehouse mgr. A. Sturm & Sons, Manawa, Wis., 1990—. Hunter safety instr. Wis. Dept. Natural Resources, Shawano, 1974-76; dir. Shawano Econ. Devel. Corp.; pres. Parent Tchr. League, St. James Luth. Sch., bd. Christian edn.; ; chmn. Shawano Area United Fund; del. Hwy. 29/Fox Cities Connection Coalition; pres. N.E. Wis. Delta Nu Alpha, Green Bay, 1985, v.p. 1996—; elder St. Paul Luth. Ch., 1993-95; steering com. St. Paul Luth. Sch., 1992—. Mem. Wis. Motor Carrier Assn., Fox Valley Traffic Club (dir. 1995-96), Shawano County Recreation Assn. (bd. dirs., chmn. newspaper recycling program, chmn. Shawano County Fair booth), Shawano Rotary Club (chmn. Shawano centenial com.), Red River Sportsman Club (treas. 1986-89), Manawa Lions Club (sec. 1992-96), Toastmasters Internat., Shawano C. of C. (mem. indsl. devel. com., ex officio bd. mem.). Republican. Lutheran. Home: E 6728 Butternut Rd Manawa WI 54949

CUMMINGS, JOAN E., health facility administrator, educator. BA, Trinity Coll., 1964; MD, Loyola U., 1968. Diplomate Am. Bd. Internal Medicine, Geriatric Medicine. Med. internship St. Vincent Hosp., Worcester, Mass., 1968-69; med. residency Hines VA Hosp., Hines, Ill., 1969-71; sr. residency Nephrology Hines VA Hosp., 1971-72, ambulatory care svc. chief gen. med. section, 1971-84, med. dir., hosp. based home care, 1972-87, chief, intermediate care svc., 1984-87, assoc. chief of staff, extended care and geriatrics, 1987-90, med. dir., extended care center, 1987-90, dir., 1990—; asst. prof. Clinical Medicine U. Ill., 1976-82; asst. prof. Clinical Medicine Loyola U., 1983-91, assoc. prof. Clinical Medicine, 1991—; mem. ad hoc com. on primary care U. Ill., 1980-82, coll. edn. policy com. U. Ill., 1980-82, State Ill. Emergency Med. Svc. Coun., 1981-83, Comprehensive Health Ins. Plan Bd. State Ill., 1990—, Med. Licensing Bd. State Ill., 1992—, exec. com. Chgo. Fed. Exec. Bd. State Ill., 1992—; program dir. Loyola/Hines Geriatric Fellowship Program, 1987-90. Contbr. to profl. mags. and jour. Recipient Disting. Svc. award Abraham Lincoln Sch. Med. Univ. Ill., 1979, 81, Leadership award VA, 1980, Certificate of Appreciation award VA, 1980, Laureate award Am. Coll. Physicians, 1990. Fellow Am. Coll. Physicians; mem. AMA (Ill. delegation 1985—, vice speaker ho. delegates 1987-89), Chgo. Med. Soc. (pres. Hines-Loyola Branch 1982-83), Ill. State Med. Soc. (trustee 1984—, chmn. com. on Ill. med., 1988—, speaker ho delegates 1989-91, exec. com., 1989-91, policy com., 1989—), Am. Coll. Physicians (councilor Ill. chpt. 1984—), Chgo. Geriatric Soc., Am. Geriatric Soc. Office: PO Box 5000 5th Ave & Roosevelt Rd Hines IL 60141-5000

CUMMINGS, MAXINE GIBSON, elementary school educator; b. Tupelo, Miss., Oct. 7, 1940; d. T. Ruben and Maggie (Ruff) Gibson; m. Willie B. Cummings, Aug. 15, 1964; 1 child, Stanley. BS, Barber-Scotia Coll., Concord, N.C., 1962; MA, Northeastern Ill. U., Chgo., 1974. Cert. tchr., N.C., Ill. Tchr. Walter Reed Elem. Sch., Chgo., 1963-75, reading tchr., 1975-82, social studies tchr., 1982-85; reading resource tchr. Arna Bontemps Sch., Chgo., 1985-91, ESEA lab. tchr., 1991—; counselor Westside YWCA, Chgo., 1963-68; chmn. reading com. Bontemps Sch., 1986-92, chmn. activity com., 1992-93. Contbr. articles to profl. jours. Mem. Vol. Edna White Century Garden; sec. S.W. Morgan Parkk Civic Assn., Chgo., 1990-92; block rep. Neighborhood Watch Program, Chgo., 1989-90; trustee Morgan Park Presbyn. Ch., peace and justice com. Grantee Chgo.-Incentive, 1987, NEH, 1984, Northeastern Ill. U., 1980. Mem. Minority Students of Chgo. Area (recruiter), Barber-Scotia Alumni Club (sec. 1989-92), Pi Lambda Theta. Home: 11116 S Longwood Dr Chicago IL 60643-4043 Office: Bontemps Elem Sch 1241 W 58th St Chicago IL 60636-1931

CUMMINGS, RICHARD J., otologist; b. Topeka, Nov. 18, 1932; s. John Edward and Mary J. (Harrington) C.; m. Laura Roberta Herring, Dec. 21, 1956; children: Thomas, Anne, William, John. BA, U. Kans., 1954, MD, 1957. Intern St. Benedict Hosp., Ogden, Utah, 1957-58; resident U. Okla. Med. Ctr., Oklahoma City, 1959-62; practice medicine specializing in ear, nose, throat Colorado Springs Med. Clinic, Colo., 1961-62; practice medicine specializing in otology Wichita (Kans.) Ear Clinic, 1962—; clin. asst. prof. U. Kans. Sch. Medicine; pres. med. staff St. Francis Hosp., Wichita, 1974-75; mem. med. staff St. Joseph Hosp., Wichita, pres., 1990-91; host M.D. Radio program, Wichita, 1978-79. Contbr. articles to med. jours. Bd. dirs. Kans. State Bd. of Healing Arts, 1981-83, Kans. Commn. for Deaf and Hearing Impaired, 1988-91; mem. Kans. tissue transplantation com. ARC, 1990-94; chmn. St. Joseph Charity Classic Tournament, 1981; physician's group chmn. United Way Campaign, 1968, 69, 77, 84; mem. U. Kans. Athletic Bd., 1991-95. With USPHS, 1958-59. Fellow ACP, ACS, Am. Acad. Otolaryngology; mem. AMA, Am. Audiol. Soc., Kans. Med. Soc., Kans. Ear Nose Throat Soc. (pres. 1975), Wichita Surg. Soc. (pres. 1989), Sedgwick County Med. Soc. (pres. 1978), Otosclerosis Study Group, Hearing Conservation Assn., Pan Am. Soc. Otolaryngology, Wichita Cochlear Implant Program (bd. dirs.), Rotary (bd. dirs. Wichita chpt. 1978-79), U. Kans. Nat. Alumni Assn. (bd. dirs. 1979-84, vice chmn. 1994-95, chmn. 1995-96). Home: 1258 Burning Tree Dr Wichita KS 67230-1410 Office: 427 N Hillside St Wichita KS 67214-4917

CUMMINGS, WILLIAM ROBERT, JR., business executive; b. Detroit, July 13, 1937; s. William Robert Sr. and Geraldine Alberta (Leffel) C.; m. Jo Ann Sauser; children: William, Michael, Steve, David, Kim. B of Gen. Studies in Math., U. Nebr., 1970. Commd. 2nd lt. USAF, 1959, advanced through grades to lt. col., 1975, ret., 1978; owner Bill's Shell Svc., Ft. Wayne, Ind., 1980—, Cummings Shell Svc., Ft. Wayne, 1980—, Cummings Shell Svc. II, Ft. Wayne, 1993—; bd. dirs., vice chmn. Northeastern Rural Electric Mgmt. Coop., Columbia City, 1986; bd. dirs. Wabash Valley Power Assn. Arbitrator Better Bus. Bur., Ft. Wayne; ward chmn. Rep. Party. Decorated Air medal with thirteen oak leaf clusters, Meritorious Svc. medal with oak leaf clusters, Cross of Gallantry with Palm. Mem. Air Force Assn. (life, state pres. Ind.), Order of Daedalians (life). Republican. Home: 12031 Mahogany Dr Fort Wayne IN 46804-4513 Office: 8903 Lima Rd Fort Wayne IN 46818-1854

CUMMINS, GREGORY EDWARD, sales and marketing specialist; b. Indpls., Oct. 10, 1963; s. Jerry Edward and Jean Margaret (Kirschner) C. BS, Ball State U., 1986. Pub. rels. mgr. Better Bus. Bur., Muncie, Ind., 1985-86; residential sales rep. PSI Energy, Plainfield, Ind., 1987-89, sr. sales rep., 1989-91, comml. DSM program coord., 1991-92; sales specialist Monsma Mktg. Corp., Indpls., 1993—. Active Jr. Achievement, Jaycees, C. of C., United Way. Mem. Home Builders Assn., Realtors Assn., Knights of Columbus. Democrat. Roman Catholic. Home: 3804 Cranberry Dr Greenfield IN 46140 Office: Monsma Mktg Corp 7800-A Records St Indianapolis IN 46226

CUNIBERTI, BETTY ALENA, journalist; b. San Francisco, June 13, 1951; d. Henry Leopold and Vivian Bernice (Rymerson) C.; m. Francis Michael Canavan, Oct. 20, 1984; children: Angela Teresa, Oscar Cuniberti. BA, U. So. Calif., 1973. Sports writer San Bernardino Sun, 1973-76, San Francisco Chronicle, 1976-77, Washington Post, 1977-79, Washington Star, 1979-81; writer politics, gen. L.A. Times, Washington, 1981-90; free-lance journalist Clemson, S.C., 1990-92, Lake Quivira, Kans., 1992-93; metro columnist Kansas City Star, 1994—. Vol. counselor Am. Cancer Soc. "Reach to Recovery" Group, Washington, 1988. Moses Creative Writing scholar, U. So. Calif., 1973; recipient Nat. Headliner award, N.J. Press Club, 1981. Democrat. Address: 262 Arapaho Cir E Lake Quivira KS 66106-9717

CUNNINGHAM, BILLIE M., accounting educator; b. Joliet, Ill., Apr. 2, 1946; d. William Morgan and Mildred Jane (Watson) Klett; m. Robert T. Cunningham, Feb. 27, 1971; 1 child, Dana Marie. BBA, North Tex. State U., 1968, MBA, 1975, PhD, 1980. Applications programmer Burroughs Corp., Dallas, 1969-71; software programmer USAA, San Antonio, 1971-72; asst. prof. Tex. Christian U., Ft. Worth, 1980-85; prof. Collin County C.C., Plano, Tex., 1986-93; Disting. lectr. U. North Tex., Denton, 1993-94; adj. asst. prof. U. Mo., Columbia, 1994—; mem. reaffirmation com. So. Assn. Colls. and Schs., West Palm Beach, Fla., 1991, DeKalb Coll., Decatur, Ga., 1992, Brevard C.C., Cocoa, Fla., 1993; mem. acctg. edn. workshop planning com. Tex. Tech U., Lubbock, 1992; mem. acctg. adv. bd. Brookhaven Coll., Dallas, 1993; ad hoc reviewer Issues in Acctg. Edn., Sarasota, Fla., 1993; review bd. accounting ed. A Journal of Theory, Practice and Rsch, Greenwich, Conn. 1995—; breakout leader student lyceum Fedn. Schs. Accountancy/Ernst & Young, Vero Beach, Fla., 1993; grant reviewer KPMG Peat Marwick, Montvale, N.J., 1994. Author: (textbooks) Accounting: Principles and Applications, 5th edit., 1986, Financial Accounting, Principles and Applications, 5th edit., 1986, Accounting: Basic Principles, 5th edit., 1986; mem. editl. rev. bd. Acctg. Edn.: A Jour. of Theory Practice and Rsch., 1995—; contbr. articles to profl. jours.; speaker at numerous confs. Chair pedagogical resources subcom. on critical thinking Fedn. Schs. Accountancy, St. Louis, 1994, chair pedagogical resources com., 1995-96; com. mem. Second Century Breakfast Com., U. North Tex., 1991-92, mentor Cmty. Mentors Program, 1991-93. Recipient Nat. Teaching Excellence award Nat. Inst. for Staff and Orgnl. Devel., 1989, Exemplary Acctg. Educator award Mo. Assn. Acctg. Educators, 1995; Tex. Christian U. summer rsch. grantee, 1981, 82. Mem. Am. Acctg. Assn. (program adv. com. 1990-91, coun. 1991-92, acctg. edn. adv. com. 1992-94, v.p. 1994-96, sec.-editor 2-yr. coll. sect. 1989-90, vice-chair 2-yr. coll. sect. 1990-91, chair 2-yr. coll. sect. 1991-92, coord. regional reps./officer at large 2-yr. coll. sect. 1991-92, curriculum revision com. 2-yr. coll. sect. 1993-94, vice-chair tchg. and curriculum sect. 1996-97), Acad. Acctg. Historians (edn. com. 1990-94), Gamma Phi Beta, Phi Delta Kappa, Alpha Kappa Psi. Office: U Mo Columbia Sch Accountancy 328 Middlebush Hall Columbia MO 65211

CUNNINGHAM, CHARLES ERNEST, physics educator; b. Long Beach, Calif., May 26, 1964; s. Charles Owen and Mary Catherine (Just) C.; m. Paula Lynn Shanklin, Sept. 6, 1986. BS in Physics, Harvey Mudd Coll., Claremont, Calif., 1986; MS in Physics, Stanford U., 1987, PhD in Physics, 1992. Teaching asst. Stanford (Calif.) U., 1987-88, rsch. asst., 1986-92; postdoctoral rschr. Lawrence Livermore (Calif.) Nat. Lab., 1992-93, guest rschr., 1993-94; asst. prof. Grinnell (Iowa) Coll., 1993—. Contbr. articles to profl. jours. Recipient Cottrell Coll. Sci. award Rsch. Corp., 1994-96; NSF fellow, 1986-89, Harris fellow, 1996-97. Mem. AAUP, Am. Phys. Soc., Am. Assn. Physics Tchrs., Soc. Photo-Optical Instrumentation Engrs., Coun. Undergrad. Rsch., Sigma Xi. Office: Grinnell Coll Physics Dept Grinnell IA 50112

CUNNINGHAM, CHERYL M., business executive; b. Feb. 15, 1948. M in Counseling Psychology, Ill. State U., 1972. Mgr. Catherine McAuley Health Systems, Ann Arbor, Mich., 1985-89; v.p. Mulvihill Cunningham Inc., Ann Arbor, 1989—. Mem. Ann Arbor Pers. Assn. (bd. dirs.). Office: Mulvihill Cunningham Inc 900 Victors Way Ste 350 Ann Arbor MI 48108-2735

CUNNINGHAM, DONALD OTTO, business owner; b. Madison, Wis., Aug. 30, 1930; s. William Otto Cunningham and Goldie Murriel Dary; m. Rose Mary Gasser, May 20, 1951; children: Debra Kay, Theresa Lorraine, Jeffory Allan. Commd. 2d lt. U.S. Air Force, 1946, advanced through grades to sr. master sgt., 1962, ret., 1963; owner Cunningham Svc. Ctr., Madison, Wis., 1965-72, ret., 1972. Mem. VFW (state comdr. 1958-59), Elks, Am. Legion, Purple Hearts, DAV. Home: 5217 Knightsbridge Rd Madison WI 53714-3419

CUNNINGHAM, KAREN LEE, marketing professional; b. St. Louis, Sept. 23, 1949; d. Everett R. and Madelyn Marie (Restivo) Saddler; m. David G. Cunningham, May 4, 1970 (div. 1974). Attended, Ind. State U., 1967-69, Butler U., 1975. Cmty. affairs rep. Am. Fletcher Nat. Bank, Indpls., 1969-80; owner Corporate Art Cons., Indpls., 1980-83; dir. pub. rels. and spl. events L.S. Ayres & Co., Indpls., 1983-85; dir. pub. rels. and promotions Drum Corps Internat., Lombard, Ill., 1986; dir. bus. devel. Schmidt Assocs. Archs. Inc., Indpls., 1987-90; dir. mktg., bus. devel. and pub. rels. Eden Design Assocs., Inc., Carmel, Ind., 1990—. V.p. bd. dirs. Cathedral Arts, Inc., Indpls., 1978-86; mem. adv. coun. Humana Hosp., Indpls., 1983-85; mem. steering com. Eiteljorg Mus., Indpls., 1988-89; city govt. liaison Arts Coun. Indpls., 1989; mem. numerous coms. Meth. Hosp. Task Core, Indpls., 1987—, 500 Festival Assocs., Indpls., 1989—; bd. dirs. Ind. State Mus., Indpls., 1990—; mem. adv. bd. Ind. State U., Terre Haute, 1994—;. Mem. Pub. Rels. Soc. Am., Ind. Soc. Pub. Rels. Profls., Internat. Facility Mgmt. Assn. (bd. dirs., Affiliate Member of Yr. 1993), Soc. Mktg. Profl. Svcs. (bd. dirs.), Network Women in Bus. (bd. dirs. 1978-82, Networker of Yr. 1984). Home: 8516 Hague Rd Indianapolis IN 46256-3441 Office: Eden Design Assocs Inc 111 Congressional Blvd Ste 120 Carmel IN 46032-5652

CUNNINGHAM, MILAMARI ANTOINELLA, anesthesiologist; b. Cody, Wyo., Oct. 4, 1949; d. Milo Leo and Mary Madeline (Haley) Olds; m. Michael Otis Webb, June 4, 1970 (div. Feb. 1971); m. James Kenneth Cunningham, June 14, 1975. BA with honors, U. Mo., 1971, MD, 1975. Diplomate Am. Bd. Anesthesiologists. Intern and resident U. Mo., Columbia, 1975-78; jr. ptnr. Anesthesiologist, Inc., 1979-82, ptnr., 1982-86; owner Cunningham Anesthesia, 1986—; dir. anesthesia dept. Ellis Fischel Cancer Ctr., 1991-92; acting chief anesthesia Harry S. Truman Meml. Vets. Hosp., 1994-95; mem. med. staff Columbia Regional Hosp., Boone Hosp. Ctr., Columbia U. Mo. Hosp. and Clinics, Columbia; cons. staff Audrain Med. Ctr., Mexico, Mo., Harry S Truman Meml. Vets. Hosp., Columbia. Active Mo. Med. Polit. Action Com., 1991—, Friends of Music, Friends of Libr., Boone County Fair, 1978-94, with ham breakfast divsn., 1978-85, with draft horse and mule show, 1986-88; bd. dirs. A Call to Serve Mo., 1996—. Fellowship Am. Coll. Anesthesiologists, 1977. Mem. AMA (physicians recognition award 1978, 85, 87, 91, 95), Am. Soc. Regional Anesthesia, Am. Med. Women's Assn., Internat. Anesthesia Rsch. Soc., Mo. Soc. Anesthesiologists (v.p. 1986-87, pres. elect 1987-88, pres. 1988-89, Am. Soc. Anesthesiologists del. 1989—), Boone County Med. Soc. (alt. del. 1986, del. 1987-89, membership chair 1982-84, sec.-treas. 1996—), Mo. State Med. Assn. (commn. econs. third party payors 1986—, chair 1989), Vis. Nurses Assn. (bd. dirs. 1982-89, chair 1984-86, adv. bd. 1989-93), Phi Beta Kappa. Home: 8202 S Bennett Dr Columbia MO 65201-9804 Office: PO Box 1301 Columbia MO 65205-1301

CUNNINGHAM, NOBLE E., JR., history educator, writer; b. Evans Landing, Ind., July 25, 1926; s. Noble E. and Mary Mae (Cunningham) C.; m. Dana Gulley, Aug. 20, 1954. BA, U. Louisville, 1948; MA, Duke U., 1949, PhD, 1952. Instr. history Wake Forest (N.C.) Coll., 1952-53; asst. prof. U. Richmond, Va., 1953-58, assoc. prof., 1958-64; assoc. prof. U. Mo., Columbia, 1964-66, prof. history, 1966—, Byler Disting. prof., 1980-81, Middlebush prof., 1986-88, Curators' prof., 1988—; vis. prof. Columbia U., N.Y.C., summer 1965; mem. coun. Inst. Early Am. History and Culture, Williamsburg, Va., 1982-85. Author: The Jeffersonian Republicans, 1957, The Jeffersonians Republicans in Power, 1963, The Process of Government Under Jefferson, 1978, The Image of Thomas Jefferson in the Public Eye, 1981, In Pursuit of Reason: The Life of Thomas Jefferson, 1987, Popular Images of the Presidency From Washington to Lincoln, 1991, The Presidency of James Monroe, 1996; mem. editl. bd. Jour. So. History, 1974-78, Jour. of Early Republic, 1985-89. With U.S. Army, 1944-46. Recipient Guggenheim fellowship, John S. Guggenheim Found., 1959-60, fellowship

NEH, 1970-71, 91-92. Fellow Soc. Am. Historians; mem. Am. Antiquarian Soc., Am. Hist. Assn., So. Hist. Assn., Orgn. Am. Historians (exec. bd. 1971-74), Phi Beta Kappa. Office: Univ Mo Columbia Dept History Columbia MO 65211

CUNNINGHAM, PATRICIA ANNE, costume and textiles educator; b. Houston, Sept. 5, 1937; d. Guy Clement and Clara (Talley) C. AA, Stephens Coll., Columbia, Mo., 1957; BS, U. Ill., 1959, MS, 1961; PhD, Fla. State U., Tallahassee, 1980. Asst. prof. U. Conn., Storrs, 1985-86; asst. prof. Bowling Green (Ohio) State U., 1979-85, from assoc. prof. to prof., 1985-95; prof. dept. textiles and consumer scis. Ohio State U., Columbus, 1996—. Editor/author: (essays) Dress and Popular Culture, 1991, Dress in American Culture, 1993; contbr. essays to Making the American Home, 1987; contbr. articles to Dress Jour. Mem. Costume Soc. Am. (bd. dirs. 1986-95, pres. Region III 1986-88, editor 1993—), Internat. Textile and Apparel Assn., Popular Culture Assn. (area chair), Phi Kappa Phi, Phi Upsilon Omicron, Omicron Nu. Office: Ohio State U Textiles & Consumer Scis Heil Ave Campbell Hall Columbus OH 43210

CUNNINGHAM, PATRICK JAY, laboratory engineer; b. Terre Haute, Ind., Jan. 9, 1962. BSME, So. Ill. U., 1984. Rsch. technician Twin Disc Inc., Rockford, Ill., 1985-88; lab. engr. Barber Colman Co., Loves Park, Ill., 1988-90; mgr. engring. lab. John S. Barnes Corp., Rockford, Ill., 1990—. Mem. Soc. Automotive Engrs. (Rockford-South Beloit sect.), Fluid Power Soc. Office: John S Barnes Corp 2222 15th St Rockford IL 61104-7313 Address: 2011 E State St Rockford IL 61104

CUNNINGHAM, PATRICK JOSEPH, III, therapist; b. Chgo., Nov. 29, 1950; s. Patrick Joseph and Sally Mary (Kmiotek) C.; m. Mary Ellen Davis, Sept. 18, 1993. BS, Western Ill. U., 1975; MA, Governors State U., 1979. Cert. tchr., Ill.; cert. addictions counselor; clin. cert. substance abuse counselor. Acad. advisor Triton Coll., 1975-80, biofeedback trainer, 1976-80, acting records evaluator, 1978-79, mem. faculty, 1980; alcoholism counselor The Abbey, Winfield, Ill., 1981, St. Joseph Hosp., Joliet, Ill., 1981-84; addictions counselor Pape and Assocs., Wheaton, Ill., 1984-87; instr. addiction counselor tng. Coll. of DuPage, Glen Ellyn, Ill., 1985-87; dir. addictions counselor tng. program Coll. of DuPage, Glen Ellyn, 1986-87; pvt. practice addictions counselor Naperville, Ill., 1987; staff mem. REACH Found., Westmont, Ill., 1988-91, co-leader, 1989, group leader, 1991; adj. faculty addictions program Nat.-Louis U., Lombard, Ill., 1990-92. Mem. staff REACH Found., Westmont, Ill., 1988; resource person Warrenville Cenacle, 1992; corr. sec. Libertarian Party of Ill., 1993-94. Mem. Nat. Assn. Alcoholism and Drug Abuse Counselors, Nat. Assn. for Children of Alcoholics (exec. svc. bd. Ill. chpt. 1988, v.p. 1989), Alpha Delta Omega (faculty). Office: 800 W 5th Ave Apt 101D Naperville IL 60563-8966

CUNNINGHAM, PAULA DIANE, community college administrator; b. Akron, Ohio; d. David Samuel and Mattie Pauline (Mason) Marsh; m. Darius Lee Cunningham, Aug. 29, 1970; children: Darius Lee II, Dana Leigh. BA in Journalism, Mich. State U., 1981, M in Labor and Indsl. Rels., 1991. Legis. asst. Mich. State Capitol, Lansing, 1975; exec. dir. Profl. Devel. Ctr., Lansing, 1985-86; assoc. prof. bus. Lansing C.C., 1985-92, dir. profl. devel., 1992-94, dir. pub. info., 1994—; cons. to Kellogg Found., Battle Creek, Mich., 1991—, Lansing Bd. Water and Light, 1993—. Bd. dirs. Capitol Area United Way, Lansing, 1995—, Impression and Sci. Mus., Lansing, 1994—, Martin Luther King Holiday Commn., 1995—; mem. com. ARC, 1995—. Recipient Master Tchr. award U. Tex., 1992. Mem. Nat. Mktg. and Pub. Rels. Assn., Nat. Inst. for Staff and Orgnl. Devel., Pub. Rels. Soc. Am., Am. Soc. Staff and Orgnl. Devel. Office: Lansing CC PO Box 40010 Lansing MI 48901-7210

CUNNINGHAM, RAYMOND LEO, research chemist; b. Easton, Ill., Jan. 5, 1934; s. Raymond J. and Minnie G. (Vaughn) C. BA, St. Ambrose U., Davenport, Iowa, 1955. Phys. sci. aid in chemistry Nat. Ctr. Agrl. Utilization Rsch USDA Agrl. Rsch. Svc., Peoria, Ill., 1957-61, chemist Nat. Ctr. Agrl. Utilization Rsch., 1961-78, rsch. chemist Nat. Ctr. Agrl. Utilization Rsch., 1978—. Contbr. articles to profl. jours. With U.S. Army, 1958. Co-recipient R&D 100 award R&D mag., 1988. Fellow Am. Inst. Chemists; mem. AAAS, Am. Assn. Cereal Chemists, Am. Chem. Soc. Home: 1108 W MacQueen Ave Peoria IL 61604-3310 Office: Nat Ctr Agrl Utilization Rsch USDA 1815 N University St Peoria IL 61604-3902

CUNNINGHAM, SARAH MARGARET, orthopedics nurse; b. Weston, W.Va., Nov. 27, 1936; d. William Golf and Kathryn Irene (Holbert) Henry; m. Edward Charles Cunningham, Aug. 2, 1958; children: Timothy M., Edward W., Charles H., Jeanne M., Patrick J. BSN, Coll. Mt. St. Joseph on Ohio, 1958. RN, Ohio; CNOR. Oper. rm. staff nurse Good Samaritan Hosp., Cin., 1958-59; surg. staff nurse Holmes Hosp., Cin., 1960; staff nurse labor and delivery Kettering (Ohio) Meml. Hosp., 1966-75, staff nurse oper. rm., 1975-83; staff nurse, surgery nurse clinician Children's Med. Ctr., Dayton, Ohio, 1983-85, surg. staff nurse, 1985-90, resource nurse in orthopedics, 1990—. Author: (film) The Neonate: Perioperative Consideration, 1990. Mem. Assn. Oper. Rm. Nurses (v.p. Dayton chpt. 1990-92, pres. elect 1995—, mem. nat. nominating com. 1992-94), Nat. Assn. Orthopedic Nurses. Republican. Roman Catholic. Home: 4798 Marshall Rd Kettering OH 45429-5721 Office: Childrens Med Ctr 1 Childrens Plaza Dayton OH 45404

CUPP, ROBERT RICHARD, state senator, attorney; b. Bluffton, Ohio, Nov. 9, 1950; s. William Henry and Pearl Margaret (Keifer) C.; m. Lisbeth Ann Cochran, July 29, 1978; children: Matthew R., Ryan W. BA, Ohio Northern U., 1973, JD, 1976. Bar: Ohio. Prosecutor, asst. city law dir. City of Lima, Ohio, 1976-80; county commr. Allen County, Lima, 1981-84; ptnr. Cupp and Smith, Attys., Lima, 1983-86; mem. Ohio Senate, 1985—; ptnr. Cupp and Jenson, Attys., Lima, 1986-93; pres. Bd. County Commrs., Allen County, Ohio, 1981, 82, 84; chmn. Gilmor Commn. Sch. Funding, 1987-88; commerce and labor com. chmn. Ohio Senate 1989-94; com. chmn. Fin. Instns. Ins. and Commerce, 1995—; majority whip Ohio Senate, 1995—. Co-author: Ethics and Discipline in Ohio, 1977. Co-chmn. Midwest Fedn. Coll. Reps., 1974; exec. bd. Black Swamp coun. Boy Scouts Am.; chmn. League of Coll. Republican Clubs, 1972-73. Mem. Allen County and Ohio State Bar Assn. Methodist. Office: 2021 Allentown Rd # 3 Lima OH 45805-1850

CURBY, VICKI MORGAN, academic program director; b. High Point, N.C., May 18, 1948; d. Lester Cletus and Luna Ellen (Cates) Morgan; m. Jon Kent Curby, Mar. 27, 1971; children: Ann Morgan, Peter Graham. BA, Wake Forest U., 1968; MS, Fla. State U., 1969; PhD, U. Mo., 1978. Coord. women students So. Meth. U., Dallas, 1969-70; assoc. dean students Guilford Coll., Greensboro, N.C., 1970-73; coord. student svcs. U. Mo., Columbia, 1973-78, 79-80; dean student devel. Western Carolina U., Cullowhee, N.C., 1978-79; postdoctoral intern U. Mo., Columbia, 1980-81, rsch. assoc., 1981-82, asst. dir. learning ctr., 1982-93, dir. McNair program, 1989—, dir. spl. programs, 1994—, adj. prof., 1995—; reviewer U.S. Dept. of Edn., Washington, 1993, 95; cons. in field. Editor jour. McNair, 1993-95. Precinct chairperson Dem. Com., Guilford County, N.C., 1972. Recipient Ruth Strang Rsch. award Nat. Assn. Women Deans, Adminstrs. and Counselors, 1979; named Outstanding Young Women Am., 1972, 80. Mem. Nat. Coun. Equal Ednl. Opportunity Assns., Nat. Assn. Grad. Admission Pers., Coun. Grad Schs., Show-Me Basenji Club (sec.-treas. 1991-92, 94-95, pres. 1992-93), Columbia Mo. Kennel Club (show chmn. 1980), Kappa Delta Pi, Phi Delta Kappa. Home: 8761 N Reams Rd Centralia MO 65240-9783 Office: U Mo Grad Sch McNair Scholars Program 431 Lewis Hall Columbia MO 65211

CURFMAN, FLOYD EDWIN, engineering educator; b. Gorin, Mo., Nov. 16, 1929; s. Charles Robert and Cleo Lucille (Sweeney) C.; m. Eleanor Elaine Fehl, Aug. 5, 1950; children: Gary Floyd, Karen Elaine. BSCE, U. Mo., 1958; BA in Math. Edn., Mt. Mary Coll., 1988. Registered profl. engr., Wis., Mo.; cert. tchr., Wis. Forest engr. U.S. Forest Svc., Rolla and Harrisburg, Mo., Ill., 1958-70; engring. dir. U.S. Forest Svc., Milw., 1970-84; chief tech. engr. U.S. Forest Svc., Washington, 1984-86; teacher Wauwatosa (Wis.) High Sch., 1987-89; tchr. Our Lady of Rosary, Milw., 1989-96; retired, 1996. Author: (booklet) Forest Roads-R-9, 1973; co-author: (tng. manual) Transportation Roads, 1966. Co-leader Boy Scouts Am., Harrisburg, 1958-62; activities coord. Community Action Com., Brookfield, 1970-76; bike and hiking trails com. City of Brookfield (Wis.), 1982-83; program chair Math Counts, 1982. With U.S. Army, 1952-54. Mem. ASCE (program chair, Letter Nat. award 1970), NSPE (coms. 1970-86), Nat. Coun. Tchrs. Math., Wis. Soc. Profl. Engrs. (pres. Milw. chpt. 1982-83, State Recognition award 1983). Home: 1755 N 166th St Brookfield WI 53005-5114

CURIELLI, JOHN PETER, lawyer; b. Elkhorn, Wis., Sept. 6, 1946; s. Peter John and Leona (Biagi) C.; m. Catherine Mary Colletti, Jan. 18, 1969; 1 child, Peter J. BS, DePaul U., 1969, JD, 1972. Bar: Ill., 1972, U.S. Dist. Ct. (no. dist.) Ill., 1973, U.S. Ct. Appeals, U.S. Ct. Customs and Patent Appeals, U.S. Ct. Military Appeals, U.S. Supreme Ct. Pvt. practice Chgo. and Barrington, Ill., 1972—; legis. asst. Sen. Loukas, Sen. Laurino. Author: Starting A Law Practice and Surviving, 1973. Chmn., sec. bd., life mem. Italian Cultural Ctr.; pres. joint civic com. Italian Ams. Youth Divsn., asst. com. chmn.; adv. bd. Reed Mental Hosp.; mem. DePaul U. Endowment Bd., exec. com. Coll. Law; chmn. bd. dirs. Crimestoppers of Lake County; pres., trustee, legal adv. Italian-Am. C. of C.; bd. dirs. Barrington Area C. of C., Barrington Area Hist. Soc.; asst. chmn. Youth Com. for Annunzio; mem. Law Student Workers for Judge Berg Campaign; founding mem. Chgo. Police Mus.; active Day Commerce Coun. Mem. ABA (mem. real estate com., law sch. divsn. rep.), FBA, Am. Judicature Soc., Chgo. Bar Assn. (mem. law related edn. com.), Ill Bar Assn., Lake County Bar Assn., Day Commerce Coun., Chgo. Patrolman's Assn., Chgo. Police Mus., Giovanni Pasquali Benevolent Soc., Finance Soc., Columbian Club of Chgo., Crimestopper Bd. of Lake County, Mazzini-Verdi Club, DePaul Soc. of Fellows, Italian Am. Sports Hall of Fame (life), Kiwanis (pres., bd. dirs. Ridgewood-Chgo. chot., treas. bd. dirs. Barrington chpt., lt. gov. Divsn VIII), Masons, Phi Alpha Delta Frat. Office: Law Offices 557 N Hough St Ste A Barrington IL 60010

CURL, EILEEN DEGES, nursing educator; b. Oakley, Kans., Sept. 28, 1954; d. Leonard and Dorothea Anna (Engel) Deges; m. Donald Dewane Curl, Aug. 7, 1982. BS in Nursing summa cum laude, Marymount Coll. Kans., 1976; MS, U. Colo. Health Sci. Ctr., 1977; PhD, The Univ. Tex. at Austin, 1992. Staff nurse Hadley Regional Med. Ctr., Hays, Kans., 1976; dist. nurse cons. Kans. Dept. Health & Environment, Hays, 1979-81; assoc. prof. nursing Fort Hays State U., Hays, 1981—; apptd. mem. Kans. State Bd. Nursing, 1994—. Apptd. Kans. State Bd. Nursing. Grantee Nurse Traineeship, Wagner Fellowship. Mem. Kans. Nurses Assn. (editorial bd., state bd. dirs., second v.p.), Sigma Theta Tau (Region 2 Dissertation award 1995). Office: Fort Hays State U Dept Nursing 600 Park St Hays KS 67601-4009

CURL, THOMAS LEONARD, magazine editor; b. McAllen, Tex., Feb. 18, 1948; s. Robert L. and Mary Alice (Parker) C.; m. Lynda Kay Bowers, Nov. 27, 1971; 1 child, Robert Bowers. BS in Agrl. Journalism, Tex. A&M U., 1970. Info. specialist Tex. Agrl. Extension Svc., 1970-72; assoc. editor Progressive Farmer Mag., Dallas, 1972-76; regional editor Progressive Farmer Mag., Memphis, 1976-81; mng. editor Progressive Farmer Mag., Birmingham, Ala., 1981-82, So. Living Mag., Birmingham, 1982-87; editorial dir. Progressive Farmer Mag., Birmingham, 1987-91; editor-in-chief So. Progress Corp., Birmingham, 1991-93; editor Country Mag., pres. Reiman Publs., Greendale, Wis., 1995—. Author: Beef Cattle, 1980. Elder 1st Christian Ch. (Disciples of Christ), Birmingham, 1984-94. Mem. Am. Agrl. Editors Assn. Avocations: gardening, tennis, woodworking, reading. Office: Reiman Publs 5400 S 60th St Greendale WI 53129-1404

CURL, WILLIAM DONALD, securities dealer; b. Charles City, Iowa, Jan. 16, 1952; s. Donald Morris and Lola Winifred (Bucknell) C. BA, UCLA, 1990. V.p. sales Wedbush Noble Cooke, Claremont, Calif., 1980-83, Rauscher Pierce Refsnes, Beverly Hills, Calif., 1983-84, Bateman, Eichler, Hill Richards, Woodland Hills, Calif., 1984-90; pvt. investor Dubuque, Iowa, 1990—. Cen. com. Clark County Rep. Party, Las Vegas, 1976-80, del. Rep. State Conv., 1976-80. Fellow Cato Inst.; mem. Am. Hist. Assn., SAR., Heritage Found., Woodrow Wilson Internat. Ctr. for Scholars. Libertarian. Roman Catholic. Office: PO Box 1597 Dubuque IA 52004-1597

CURLEY, JAMES R., stockbroker. Pres., CEO Geldermann Inc., Chgo. Office: Geldermann Inc 440 S La Salle St Fl 20 Chicago IL 60605-1028*

CURLISS, JAMES ANDREW, journalist; b. Wilmington, Ohio, May 11, 1973; s. James Robert and Debora June (Young) C. Student, U. Toledo. Sports editor The Collegian, Toledo, 1992-93, mng. editor, 1993-94, editor-in-chief, 1994-95, projects editor, 1995—; news reporter The News & Observer, Raleigh, N.C., 1995, The Dispatch, Columbus, Ohio, 1994, Dallas Morning News, 1996; news asst. The Blade, Toledo, 1994—. Recipient first place awards Columbia Scholastic Press Assn., 1994, 95; named Best in Nation Am. Scholastic Press Assn., 1994. Mem. Investigative Reporters and Editors, Soc. Profl. Journalists (v.p. 1993, Best in Region award 1994, 95), Newspaper Guild. Methodist. Home: 720 Wards Corner Rd Loveland OH 45140

CURLS, PHILLIP B., state legislator; b. Kansas City, Mo., Apr. 2, 1942; s. Fred A. and Velma E. (Wagner) C.; m. Melba Jean Dudley, 1964; children: Phillip B. II, Michael Jay, Monica Joy Bianca, Louis Brandon Audley III. BS, Rockhurst Coll., 1965. State senator dist. 9 Mo., 1982—; del. Dem. Nat. Conv., 1980; contractor, broker and appraiser. Office: 3832 Myrtle Ave Kansas City MO 64128-2749 also: State Senate State Capitol Building Jefferson City MO 65101-1556*

CURRAN, BRAD D., electrical technician; b. Dover, Ohio, Dec. 26, 1949. Student, Kent State U., Tuscarawas County, Ohio, 1968-69, 85-88. Elec. and electronic technician Barmet Aluminum, Urichsville, Ohio, 1988-90; elec. technician Joy Techs. Inc., New Philadelpia, Ohio, 1990—; advisor tech. prep. program consortium Kent State U., Tuscarawas County, 1995. Sgt. U.S. Army, 1969-78, Germany. Methodist.

CURRAN, JAMES FRANCIS, dentist; b. Cleve., Mar. 26, 1932; s. Paul Stanley and Genevieve Agnes (Morgan) C.; children: Deborah Ann, Sean Francis, Therese Marie, Patricia Holly; m. Eleanor Tribble, Nov. 30, 1991. BS, John Carroll U., 1950; DDS, Marquette U., 1959. Gen. practice dentistry, Cleveland Heights, Ohio, 1961-80; gen. dental cons. Gen. Electric Co., Ohio, 1965-80; gen. dentist Euclid Clinic Found. (Ohio), 1980—. Served with U.S. Army, 1959-61. Mem. ADA, Ohio Dental Assn. Office: 18599 Lake Shore Blvd Euclid OH 44119-1039

CURRAN, MICHAEL D., computer consultant; b. Quincy, Ill., Sept. 23, 1945; m. Cathy Curran; 3 children. BA, U. Ill., 1969. Mem. Ill. House, 1983-95; Dem. candidate U.S. House, 19th Dist., Ill., 1996. Home: 441 Jackson Pky Springfield IL 62704-1923*

CURRAN, MICHAEL WALTER, management scientist; b. St. Louis, Dec. 6, 1935; s. Clarence Maurice and Helen Gertrude (Parsons) C.; m. Jeanette Lucille Rawizza, Sept. 24, 1955 (div. 1977); children: Kevin Michael, Karen Ann, Kathleen Marie (dec.), Kimberly Elizabeth; m. Mary Jane Lemanek, Aug. 18, 1981. B.S., Washington U., St. Louis, 1964. With Monsanto Co., St. Louis, 1953-65; supervisory positions dept. adminstrv. services Monsanto Co., 1956-64, research technician inorganic chems. div., 1964-65; sr. ops. research analyst Pet Inc., St. Louis, 1965-68; pres. Decision Scis. Corp., St. Louis, 1968—; also dir. Decision Scis. Corp.; Co-author: Handbook of Budgeting, 1981, 3d edit., 1993, Applied Cost Engineering, 2d edit., 1996; contbr. articles to profl. jours; developer theories of bracket budgeting and range estimating. Co-author: Handbook of Budgeting, 1981, 3d editl., 1993, Applied Cost Engineering, 2d edit., 1996; contbr. articles to profl. jours.; developer theories of bracket budgeting and range estimating. Adviser Jr. Achievement, St. Louis, 1958-59; active United Way, 1958-62. Mem. Inst. Mgmt. Scis. (chmn. St. Louis chpt. 1971-72), Ops. Research Soc. Am., Am. Assn. Cost Engrs. (chmn. risk mgmt. com. 1991—), Project Mgmt. Inst., Soc. Cost Estimating and Analysis, Internat. Platform Assn., Mensa, Intertel, Sigma Xi, Alpha Sigma Lambda. Office: Decision Scis Corp PO Box 28848 Saint Louis MO 63123-0048

CURRIE, BARBARA FLYNN, state legislator; b. LaCrosse, Wis., May 3, 1940; d. Frank T. and Elsie R. (Gobel) Flynn; AB cum laude, U. Chgo., 1968, AM, 1973; m. David P. Currie, Dec. 29, 1959; children: Stephen Francis, Margaret Rose. Asst. study dir. Nat. Opinion Rsch. Ctr., Chgo., 1973-77; part time instr. polit. sci. DePaul U., Chgo., 1973-74; mem. Ill. Ho. of Reps., 1979—, chmn. House Dem. Study Group, 1981-83, asst. majority leader, 1993, asst. minority leader, 1995. Mem. adv. bd. Harriet Harris YWCA; v.p. Chgo. LWV, 1965-69; mem. ACLU, Hyde Park-Kenwood Cmty. Conf., Ind. Voters of Ill.-Ind. Precinct Orgn., Hyde Park Coop. Soc., Ams. for Dem. Action. Named Best Legislator, Ind. Voters of Ill., 1980, 82, 84, 86, 88, 90, 92, 94, Best Legislator, Ill. Credit Union League, Outstanding Legislator, Ill. Hosp. Assn., 1987; recipient Ethel Parker award 1982, 86, 88, 90, 94, Leon Despres award, 1991, Ill. Environ. Coun. award, Ill. Cmty.Action Agys. award, Ill. Women's Polit. Caucus Lottie Holman O'Neill award, Susan B. Anthony award, honor award Nat. Trust Historic Preservation; awards Welfare Rights Coalition of Orgns., Ill. Pub. Action Coun., Chgo. Heart Assn.; named Legislator of Yr., Ill. Nurses Assn., 1984, Nat. Assn. Social Workers, 1984, Ill. Women's Substance Abuse Coalition, 1984; recipient BEST BETS award Nat. Ctr. Policy Alternatives, 1988, Svc. award Nat. Ctr. For Freedom of Info. Studies, 1989, Beautiful Person award Chgo. Urban League, 1989, Friend of Labor award Ill. AFL-CIO, 1990, Ill. Maternal and Child Health Coalition award, 1990, Ill. Hunger Coalition award, 1991, Cert. of Appreciation SEIU Local 880, 1989, March of Dimes, 1988, Chgo. Tchrs. Union, Ill. Hosp. Assn., Ptnr. Vision award Families' and Children's AIDS Network. Mem. ACLU (bd. dirs. Ill.), Ill. Conf. Women Legislators, Nat. Order Women Legislators. Contbr. article to publ. Office: Ill Gen Assembly 300 State House Springfield IL 62704-1757

CURRY, BILL PERRY, physicist, consultant; b. Hopkinsville, Ky., Mar. 14, 1937; s. John Kiser and Lena (Calvert) C.; m. Uta Wundmueller, Dec. 2, 1961 (dec. Jan. 1971); children: Regina Ellen, William Alfred; m. Gretchen Fleming, Mar. 14, 1992. AB in Physics, Vanderbilt U., 1959; MS in Physics, U. Tenn., 1965; PhD in Elec. Engring., Kennedy-Western U., Agoura Hills, Calif., 1990. Rsch. engr. ARO Inc., Arnold Air Force Station, Tenn., 1960-66; physicist Physics Internat. Co., San Leandro, Calif., 1966-68; sr. physicist Lawrence Livermore (Calif.) Lab., 1968-73; rsch. scientist, program mgr. STD Rsch. Corp., Arcadia, Calif., 1973-76; sr. rsch. engr. Sverdrup/ARO, Inc., Arnold Air Force Station, 1976-81; sr. physicist, engr. CALSPAN Corp., Arnold Air Force Station, 1981-87; cons. Argonne (Ill.) Nat. Lab., 1986, physicist, 1987-94; cons. EMSciTek Consulting Co., 1994—; part-time lectr. Calif. State Coll., Hayward, 1968-70; lectr., cons. N.Am. Rockwell Corp., Rocketdyne Corp., Canoga Park, Calif., spring 1972; cons. experience includes chem. lasers, 1972, smoke detectors, 1994, x-ray tube design, 1995. Contbr. articles to profl. jours. Mem. task force on world hunger So. Calif. Synod of Presbyn. Ch., Arcadia, 1975; session mem. 1st Presbyn Ch., Downers Grove, Ill., 1987-90. Founders scholar Vanderbilt U., 1955-59. Mem. IEEE, Am. Phys. Soc., Am. Assn. Aerosol. Rsch., Sigma Xi. Home and Office: 22W101 McCarron Rd Glen Ellyn IL 60137-7053

CURRY, DAVID LEE, writer; b. Springfield, Ill., Jan. 10, 1942; s. George Bruce Sr. and Jessie Lee (Ebel) C. Student, Trinity Coll., 1960-63. Advt. dir. OGR Svc. Corp., Springfield, 1965-76; press aide Ill. Capital Devel. Bd., Springfield, 1977-81; speechwriter, press aide Office of Ill. Atty. Gen., Chgo., 1982-89; speechwriter ADA, Chgo., 1989—. Editor, pub. (lit. mag.) Apple, 1967-76; author: (poems) Here, 1970, Theatre, 1973, Contending to be the Dream, 1979 (Spl. Dist. Elliston Book awards 1979). Writing fellow Nat. Endowment for the Arts, 1976, Residency fellow YADDO, 1977. Home: 2045 N Dayton St Chicago IL 60614-4309 Office: ADA 211 E Chicago Ave Chicago IL 60611-2616

CURRY, JANE ANNE, writer, educator, performer; b. Indpls., Mar. 23, 1945; d. James Alton and Norma (Werden) C.; m. David Lee Lund, Mar. 25, 1978. BA in English, Hanover Coll., 1967; MA in Am. Studies, U. Mich., 1970, PhD, 1975. English tchr. Waterford (Conn.) High Sch., 1967-69; asst. prof. English and Am. Studies Lafayette Coll., Easton, Pa., 1974-78; free lance writer, performer Mpls., 1978—; ind. scholar-performer Minn. Chautauqua, 1981-84, 88-92. Author: The River's in My Blood, 1983, Marietta Holley, 1996; editor, performer Samantha Rastles the Woman Question, 1983; performer Just Say Know, Nice Girls Don't Sweat, Miz Wizard's Science Secrets; contbr. essays, articles and book revs. to various publs. Vol. Big Sisters, Big Brothers, Mpls., 1985-87; coach girl's basketball Seward Community Ctr., Mpls. 1988, '89. Grantee NEH summer stipend, 1977, Am. Coun. Learned Socs., 1977, Minn. Hist. Soc., St. Paul, 1991. Mem. AAUW, Nat. Women's Studies Assn., Women's Sports Found., Minn. Ind. Scholars Forum (bd. dirs. 1980-83), Women Historians of Midwest (bd. dirs. 1980-86, coord. nat. conf. 1982). Home and Office: 5048 37th Ave S Minneapolis MN 55417-1525

CURRY, JOHN PATRICK, insurance company executive, management consultant; b. Logan, W.Va., May 3, 1934; s. Albert Bruce and Mary Naomi (Shugert) C.; m. Patricia Jean Blessington, Oct. 26, 1956; children: Joseph Patrick, Mary Patricia. Kathleen Anne, Carmen Frances, John Gregory. Student St. Charles Coll., Catonsville, Md., 1949-52; B.A., U. Notre Dame, 1956; M.S. in Ops. Research, Western Mich. U., 1976. Lic. profl. cons., Mich. Agt., Conn. Mut. Life Ins. Co., 1959-65; gen. agt. Occidental Life Ins. Co., Los Angeles, 1965-66; pres. Investment Assocs. Inc., 1966-69; gen. agt. Fed. Life Ins. Co., Peoples Home Life Ins. Co. and Home Assurance Cos., 1969-71; actuarial cons. Am.-Brit. Ins. & Annuity Co., Ltd. (Bermuda), Battle Creek, Mich., 1979-87; mgmt. cons., 1971-88; owner, mgr. Nat. Search Cons., exec. search firm, Kalamazoo; owner, operator Curry Supply Co., Portage, Mich., 1978-83; pres. The Consulting Group, Inc. (Del.), Kalamazoo, 1985—; pres. The Pilot Co., Turks and Caicos Islands, 1985-90; dir. Anglo-Am. Ins. Co., Ltd. (Bermuda), 1979-87. Served with U.S. Army, 1957-59. U. Notre Dame scholar, 1952-55; Pat O'Brien scholar, 1956. Republican. Roman Catholic. Clubs: Sertoma (charter dir. 1961-64) (Kalamazoo). Home: 7226 Rockford St Kalamazoo MI 49002-4122

CURRY, JULIE A., state legislator. Ill. state rep. Dist. 101, 1995—. Office: 101 A Ashland Ave Mount Zion IL 62549

CURRY, RAYMOND HOWARD, physician; b. Lexington, Ky., June 5, 1956; s. Howard Jr. and Venita (Dawson) C. AB, U. Ky., 1977; MD, Washington U., St. Louis, 1982. Diplomate Am. Bd. Internal Medicine, spl. cert. in geriatric medicine. Resident in internal medicine McGaw Med. Ctr. Northwestern U., Chgo., 1982-85; internist Northwestern Med. Faculty Found., Chgo., 1985—; mem. staff Northwestern Meml. Hosp., Chgo., 1985—; dir. undergrad. edn. dept. medicine Northwestern U. Med. Sch., Chgo., 1992—; mem. staff VA Lakewide Med. Ctr., Chgo., 1988—; instr. Northwestern U. Med. Sch., Chgo., 1985-89, asst. prof., 1989—. Mem. ACP, Soc. Gen. Internal Medicine, Am. Acad. Physician and Patient, Phi Beta Kappa. Office: Northwestern U Med Sch Dept Medicine 250 E Superior St Ste 296 Chicago IL 60611-2914

CURRY, WILBUR, mechanical engineer; b. Selina, Ohio, Feb. 28, 1948. BS in Indsl. Arts, Miami U., Oxford, Ohio, 1975. Project engr. Cincinnati Milacron Inc., Cin., 1977—. Contbr. articles to profl. jours. Pres. Softball League, Milford, 1995—. With USN, 1968-72. Republican. Roman Catholic. Office: Cincinnati Milacron Inc 4701 Marburg Ave Cincinnati OH 45209-1025

CURTIS, CANDACE A., state legislator; m. Michael Curtis; 1 child, Jameson. BA, Mich. State U., 1982. Environ. health Genesee County Health Dept. Mich.; dep. ct. clk. 67th Dist. Ct., Mich.; chair Genesee County Commrs.; rep. Mich. Dist. 51, 1993—. Mem. Genesee County Dem. Com. Mem. Farm Bur., South End Dem. Club. Office: Mich Ho of Reps PO Box 30014 Lansing MI 78909-7514*

CURTIS, CAROL EDITH, library director; b. West Point, N.Y., Aug. 6, 1952; d. Wesley James and Irene Helen (Kinnaird) C.; m. Charles Sylvester Allen, June 27, 1989 (div. May 23, 1994). AB, Smith Coll., 1974; MS, Columbia U., 1978; MA, Coll. William and Mary, Williamsburg, Va., 1981. Curator manuscripts New Eng. Hist. Geneal. Soc., Boston, 1975-77; asst. dir. devel. Smith Coll., Northampton, Mass., 1977-81; devel. officer for founds. N.Y. Pub. Libr., N.Y.C., 1981-82; reference libr. Springfield (Mo.)-Greene County Libr., 1984-85; asst. prof. libr. sci., reference libr. Drury Coll., Springfield, 1985-91; libr., dir. libr. svcs., asst. dean learning resources ctr. Ozarks Tech. C.C., Springfield, 1991—. Bd. dirs. Alliance for the Mentally Ill, Springfield, 1995—, Mo. Coalition of Alliances for the Mentally Ill, 1995—. Mem. Mo. Libr. Assn., League of Women Voters, Smith Coll.

Alumnae Assn. (life). Office: Ozarks Tech CC 815 N Sherman Springfield MO 65802

CURTIS, ELAINE ROSE, environmental writer, consultant; b. Chgo., Feb. 1, 1925; d. Fredrick William and Elsie Rose (Fitzli) Litzkow; m. Raymond Roddy Curtis, Aug. 1, 1923; children: Christine, Scott Raymond. Grad. h.s., Chgo. Designer, illustrator: (poetry) Earth Song, 1976; contbg. environ. writer South Bend (Ind.) Tribune, 1979-82, Niles (Mich.) Daily Star, 1982-95. Mem. Citizens for Environ. Protection (sr. advisor 1984-95), Four Flags Garden club, The Prairie club. Home: 620 N 16th St Niles MI 49120

CURTIS, GEORGE MARTIN, III, history educator; b. Washington, Apr. 11, 1935; s. George Martin and Louise (Scully) C.; m. Julie Anne Vogel; children: Rebecca Lyn, Louise Page, Anne McClary, Sarah Wilcox, Jessica Ruth. BA, U. Iowa, 1958; MA, U. Kans., 1963; PhD, U. Wis., 1970. Asst.-assoc. prof. Mont. State U., Bozeman, 1968-73; rsch. assoc. Colonial Williamsburg Found., Va., 1973-75, Papers of John Marshall, Williamsburg, 1975-80; adj. prof. Coll. William and Mary, Williamsburg, Va., 1973-80; assoc. prof. Hanover (Ind.) Coll., 1980-84, prof., 1984—, chmn. dept. history, 1987—. Editor: Lincoln Legal Papers, Springfield, Ill., 1986-87, Southern Essays of Richard Weaver, 1987. Recipient Bayhnam award for tchg. Hanover Coll., 1984, 89, 94; grantee Colonial Williamsburg Found., 1967, Lilly Endowment, 1988; fellow NEH, 1971-72. Mem. Am. Soc. Legal History, Am. Hist. Assn., Ind. Hist. Soc., Ky. Hist. Soc., Orgn. Am. Historians. Home: 1251 S Riverview Dr Hanover IN 47243-9026 Office: Dept History Hanover College Hanover IN 47243

CURTIS, JAMES MALCOLM, Russian language educator; b. Florence, Ala., Apr. 16, 1940; s. Malcolm C. and Earsel (Smith) C.; m. Victoria Oswald, Sept. 3, 1962 (div. June 1973); 1 child, Elizabeth Helen; m. Donna M. Elvey, Apr. 2, 1983. BA, Vanderbilt U., 1962; MA, Columbia U., 1964, PhD, 1968. Vis. asst. prof. U. Calif., Berkeley, 1966-68; asst. prof. Russian U. Mo., Columbia, 1968-72, assoc. prof., 1972-79, prof., 1979—. Author: Culture as Polyphony, 1978, Solzhenitsyn's Traditional Imagination, 1984, Rock Eras, 1987. Democrat. Mem. Unity Ch. Office: U Mo Dept GRAS 451 GCB Columbia MO 65211

CURTIS, JEAN TRAWICK, library director; b. Washington; d. Ivory Wilson and Dannie May Trawick; divorced; children: Karen Elizabeth Phoenix, Jeffrey Lynn Phoenix. BA in Library Scis., Howard U., 1958; MLS, U. Md., 1971. Children's librarian D.C. Pub. Library, Washington, 1958-69, reader's adviser, 1965-69; field worker young adults Enoch Pratt Free Library, Balt., 1971-75, regional librarian, 1975-78, chief of extension, 1978-85; deputy dir. Detroit Pub. Library, 1986-87, dir., 1987—; Dir. New Detroit, Inc., 1987—; adv. bd. library services and constrn. act Library of Mich., 1987; bd. dirs. Southeastern Mich. League of Libraries. Treas. Mich. Coun. for Humanities. Mem. ALA (visionary leaders 20/20 com., libr. of Mich.-interdependancy and funding task force), Pub. Libr. Assn. (met. librs. sect.), Mich. Libr. Assn., U. Ctr. Cultural Assn. (dir. 1987—), Zonta Internat. (v.p., pres.-elect Detroit sect. 1993-94). Office: Detroit Pub Libr 5201 Woodward Ave Detroit MI 48202-4007*

CURTIS, SARAH E. C., securities sales associate; b. Peoria, Ill., Nov. 9, 1959. Degree in radio and TV, So. Ill. U., 1980. CFP. Sales assoc. Kemper Securities Inc., Bloomington, Ill., 1987—. Mem. McClain County C. of C. (women's divsn.).

CURTLER, HUGH MERCER, JR., educator; b. Charlottesville, Va., Dec. 31, 1937; s. Hugh Mercer and Nancy Dangerfield (Elsroad) C.; m. Linda Edith Lockwood, June 15, 1962; children: Hugh Mercer III, Rudolph Hirsch. BA, St. John's Coll., 1959; MA, Northwestern U., 1962, PhD, 1964. Instr., asst. prof. U. R.I., Kingston, 1964-66; asst. prof. Midwestern Coll., Denison, Iowa, 1966-68; from asst. prof. to prof. S.W. State U., Marshall, Minn., 1968—. Author: A Theory of Art, 1981, Vivas as Critic, 1982, What is Art?, 1984, Ethical Argument, 1993. Md. State scholar, State of Md., 1955-59; Northwestern U. fellow, Evanston, Ill., 1961-64, Younger Humanist fellow, NEH, 1971-72. Am. Philos. Assn. Home: Box 102 Cottonwood MN 56229 Office: Southwest State U Marshall MN 56258

CURTRIGHT, ROBERT EUGENE, newspaper critic and columnist; b. Kansas City, Mo., Aug. 27, 1944; s. Leslie Odean and Wilma Jean (Kraus) C. BA in Journalism, U. Kans., 1966, MA in Journalism, 1968. Reporter Coffeyville (Kans.) Jour., 1969-74; reporter Wichita (Kans.) Eagle-Beacon (name changed to The Wichita Eagle 1990), 1974-76, spl. bicentennial editor, 1976, movie critic, 1976—, TV columnist, 1981—. Mem. TV Critics Assn. (sec. 1993-95, newsletter editor 1993—, v.p. 1995—). Office: Wichita Eagle 825 E Douglas Ave Wichita KS 67202-3512

CUSHING, RALPH HARVEY, chemical company executive; b. Buffalo, Nov. 3, 1922; s. Benjamin Ralph and Ella Mabel (Lukens) C.; m. Edith Elizabeth Smith, Nov. 27, 1947; children: Sharonrose, Paul Ralph. BS ChemE, Drexel U., 1952. Chem. engr. Bristol Labs., Syracuse, N.Y., 1952-60; project engr. Mobay Chem. Co., Pitts., 1960-63; sr. project engr. Gulf Research Co., Harmarville, Pa., 1963-65; sr. researcher, mgr. engring., dir. coordinated computer services, sr. cons. Enron Corp. (formerly No. Nat. Gas Co.), Omaha, 1965-86; pres. CISSCO, Inc., Omaha, 1968—. Patentee corrosion protection of pipelines; contbr. articles to profl. jours. Lay minister Meth. Ch., Pitts., 1960-63. Served to cpl. U.S. Army, 1944-46, CBI. Mem. Am. Inst. Chem. Engrs., Am. Assn. Cost Engrs., Nat. Assn. Corrosion Engrs. (corrosion specialist 1978—). Republican.

CUSHMAN, KENNETH DEAN, business owner; b. Gary, Ind., June 2, 1945; s. Lon Albert and Marie Claire (Moore) C. Bus. diploma, Wright Coll., Chgo., 1967; student, Northwestern U., 1968-70, Elmhurst Coll., 1972, U. Wis., 1977—. Dir. mktg. Miller & Melby Firms, Chgo., 1972-73; mktg. coord. Daverman Assocs., Inc., Grand Rapids, Mich., 1974-75; dir. mktg. Dow Assocs., Inc., Midland, Mich., 1976-80; owner K.D. Cushman Interests, Ltd., Carmel, Ind., 1980—; mng. ptnr. Signature Group, Inc., Carmel, 1985—. Assoc. mem. Am. Inst. Planners (cert. bldg. ofcl. and code adminstr.); mem. Am. Planning Assn. (charter), Met. Assn. Urban Designers and Environ. Planners, Mich. Non-Profit Homes Assn. Home and Office: KD Cushman Interests Ltd/ The Signature Group Inc 1107 Golfview Dr Carmel IN 46032-2766

CUSTINE, CHRISTOPHER G., computer programmer; b. Wichita, Kans., Jan. 3, 1971. Lic., pilot, Kans. Computer programmer Q Corp. Engring., Denby, Kans., 1989—; cons. in field. Office: Q Corp Engring 301 River St Derby KS 67037-1528

CUTHBERT, ROBERT LOWELL, product specialist; b. Bay City, Mich., June 28, 1939; s. Lowell Robert and Katherine Ann (Popp) C.; m. Carol Ann Barcia, Apr. 23, 1960; children: Steven Robert, Douglas Brian, Kristi Ann. Student, Bay City Jr. Coll., 1957-59, Delta Coll., 1966-67. Lab. tech. coatings Dow Corning Corp., Midland, Mich., 1964-70, silicone acrylic rsch., 1970-72, electronic tech., 1972-78, solar cell rsch., 1978-81, electrical prodn. tech. rep., 1981-88, masonry products tech. rep., 1988-90, product specialist, 1990—. Contbr. articles to profl. jours. With USAF, 1959-63. Mem. Am. Soc. Testing and MAterials, Am. Radio Relay League, Elks. Democrat. Methodist. Office: Dow Corning Mail C02230 Midland MI 48686

CUTLER, (ROBERT) BRUCE, author; b. Evanston, Ill., Oct. 8, 1930; s. Richard Schuyler and Dorothea Leslie (Wales) C.; m. Tina Cirelli, July 3, 1954 (Apr. 1993); children: David, John, Ann; m. Emily Grizzard, Sept. 9, 1995. Student, Northwestern U., Evanston, Ill., 1949; BA with highest distinction, U. Iowa, 1951; MS, Kans. State U., 1957; postgrad., Universita degli Studi, Naples, Italy, 1957-58. Mem. staff Am. Friends Svc. Com., Phila., 1951-55; grad. asst. Kans. State U., Manhattan, 1955-57, instr., 1958-60; instr., asst. prof., assoc. prof., prof., disting. prof. Wichita (Kans.) State U., 1960-87, Adele M. Davis disting. prof. humanities, 1987; vis. prof. English seminar U. Bern, Switzerland, 1975-76. Playwright: A Brave Man's Part, 1987, The Keats of Comedy, 1989, East Lynne, 1991; author: The Massacre at Sand Creek, 1995, others. Fulbright grantee, Italy, 1957-58, Paraguay, 1965, Spain, 1968-69; Nat. Endowment for Arts creative writing fellow, 1989, Bush artist fellow Bush Found., 1990-91. Mem. Dramatists Guild. Home and Office: 1759 Grand Ave # 301 Saint Paul MN 55105

CUTLER, BRUCE, electron microscopist; b. Chgo., Apr. 19, 1943; s. Chaim and Edith (Daum) C.; m. Lucy Janet Ehrlich, Sept. 4, 1964; children: Matt, Melissa. BS, CCNY, 1964; PhD, U. Minn., 1970. Rsch. fellow entomology U. Minn., St. Paul, 1969-71, jr. scientist vet. obstetrics, 1971-73, rsch. assoc. genetics and cell biology, 1974-78; rsch. assoc. pathology St. Paul Ramsey Med. Ctr., 1978-80; asst. scientist Sch. Dentistry U. Minn., Mpls., 1981-85; rsch. svc. VA Med. Ctr., Mpls., 1986-89; dir. electron microscopy lab. U. Kans., Lawrence, 1989—; cons. Tel Tech. Co. Reviewer Jour. Arachnology, Entomological News, New Zealand Jour. Zoology; contbr. chpt. to book and numerous articles to profl. jours. Chair subcom. on invertebrates Minn. Adv. Com. on Endangered Species Act, 1984-87. Mem. Am. Arachnological Soc., Microscopy Soc. Am., Brit. Arachnological Soc., Sigma Xi. Office: U Kans Electron Microscopy Lab Haworth Hall Lawrence KS 66045-2106

CUTLER, NORMAN BARRY, funeral service executive; b. Chgo., Mar. 5, 1942; s. Jerome and Hannah (Feinberg) C.; m. Gail Weinstein, June 30, 1965; children: Brett, Rebecca. BSBA, Northwestern U., 1964, MBA, Kellogg Sch. Mgmt., Northwestern U., 1965. Mgmt. trainee First Nat. Bank of Chgo., 1965-66; pres. Weinstein Family Svcs., Inc. (formerly Weinstein Bros. Inc.), Wilmette, Ill., 1966—, pres., 1972—; pres. Levitt-Weinstein, Inc., North Miami Beach, Fla., 1979—; exec. v.p. Beth David Meml. Gardens, Hollywood, Fla., 1985—, Mt. Nebo Meml. Gardens, Miami, Fla.; gen. ptnr. Wilmette Computer Assocs., Dixie Ptnrs., N.M.B. Assocs.; faculty Worsham Coll., Skokie, Ill., 1981-82. Gen. co-chmn. Channel 11 Pub. TV auction, 1974-75; bd. govs. Congregation Am Shalom, Glencoe, Ill., v.p., pres., 1986-88; bd. dirs. North Suburban Jewish Community Ctr., 1975—, also past pres.; bd. dirs. Ctrl. Bd. Jewish Community Ctrs. Chgo, 1993—; pres. Bernard Horwich Jewish Community Ctr., 1993—; bd. govs. Nat. Found. Funeral Svc., Des Plaines, Ill., 1991—. Mem. Jewish Funeral Dirs. Am. (pres. 1985-86, bd. govs.), Acad. Profl. Funeral Svc. Practice (pres. 1988-89), B'nai B'rith (v.p.). Office: 111 Skokie Blvd Wilmette IL 60091-3055

CUTLER, STEVE KEITH, state legislator; b. Britton, S.D., June 2, 1948; s. Keith and Kathryn (Olson) C.; m. Penny Louise Jones, 1969; children: Jennifer, Shanda. BS, S.D. State U., 1970, MS, 1971. Asst. material engr. S.D. Dept. Transp., 1971-74; rep. S.D. State Ho. of Reps. Dist. 2, 1984—, vice chmn. Taxation Com., mem. legis. procedure, state affairs and taxation coms. Named Outstanding Freshman Civil Engr., ASCE, 1967, Outstanding Sr. Civil Engr., ASCE, 1972. Mem. Am. Legion (legis. officer 1985), Claremont Cmty. Club, Claremont Sportsman Club, Sigma Tau, Chi Epsilon. Office: RR 1 Box 4 Claremont SD 57432-9707*

CUTRONE, THOMAS A., investment broker; b. Seattle, Oct. 5, 1960. BA, U. Ariz., 1983; MA, Quincy U., 1988. Mgr. Quincy (Ill.) Music Ctr., 1983-88; investment broker Searson Leaman, Quincy, 1988-89, A G Edwards, Quincy, 1989—. Bd. dirs. Civic Music Assn., Quincy, 1994—; mem. Quincy Band, 1990—. Mem. Quincy Yacht Club (bd. dirs. 1993—), Quincy Boat Club, Island Club, Springlake Country Club, Elks. Roman Catholic. Home: 4 Peaceful Vly Quincy IL 62301-8895 Office: A G Edwards & Sons Inc 3325 Maine St Quincy IL 62301-4438

CUTSHALL, REX RALPH, management and accounting educator, administrator; b. Washington, Ind., June 3, 1962; s. Ralph L. and Virginia M. (O'Dell) C.; m. Michelle A. Driver, May 16, 1992. AS in Bus., Vincennes (Ind.) U., 1982; BS in Bus., Ind. State U., 1984; MBA, U. Evansville (Ind.), 1988. Cert. consumer arbitrator, cert. purchasing mgr. Purchasing agt. Aristokraft, Inc., Jasper, Ind., 1984-86; sr. buyer Johnson Controls, Inc., Vincennes, 1986-87; asst. prof. bus. Vincennes U., 1987-92, chmn. dept. mgmt. and acctg., 1992—. Author: Business Statistics: Microcomputer Experiences Using Minitab, 1989. Mem. Am. Soc. for Quality Control, Nat. Assn. Instrnl. Adminstrns., Phi Delta Kappa. Office: Vincennes U Business Divsn Vincennes IN 47591

CUTTER, GARY LEE, corn breeder, researcher; b. Milan, Ind., May 21, 1948; s. Marvin Henry and Helen L. Cutter; m. Karen Sue Cutter, Apr. 8, 1972; children: Richard, Rebeka, Micah, Timothy, Sara. BS, Purdue U., 1970, MS, 1972; PhD, U. Wis., 1975. Corn breeder Cargill, Inc., Monticello, Ill., 1975-77; rsch. sta. mgr. Cargill, Inc., Seward, Nebr., 1977-80; regional rsch. mgr. Cargill, Inc., Covington, Ohio, 1981-88; agronomy svcs. mgr. Cargill, Inc., Waco, Tex., 1988-89; prodn. rsch. mgr. Cargill Hybrid Seeds, Aurora, Ill., 1989-94; parent seed mgr. Cargill Hybrid Seeds, Pontiac, Ill., 1994—. Mem. Am. Soc. Agronomy, Sigma Xi, Phi Kappa Phi, Beta Sigma Psi (chpt. v.p. 1969-70). Office: Cargill Hybrid Seeds PO Box 557 Pontiac IL 61763

CUTTER, JEFFREY S., secondary education educator, music educator; b. Royal Oak, Mich., July 20, 1956; s. George E. and Joy G. (Dolby) C. MusB with distinction, Wayne State U., 1978, MEd, M in Ednl. Leadership/Administrn., 1994. Cert. tchr., Mich. Performing arts facilitator Warren (Mich.) Consol. Community Edn., 1980—; student activities dir. Warren High Sch., 1987-92, auditorium mgr., 1987-92, dir. bands, 1985-92; dir. bands Fuhrmann Middle Sch., 1982—. Vice chmn. Warren Cultural Commn. Mem. Mich. Sch. Band and Orch. Assn. (pres. dist. XVI). Home: 32774 McConnell Ct Warren MI 48092-3111 Office: Fuhrmann Mid Sch 5155 E 14 Mile Rd Sterling Heights MI 48310-6534

CUTTER, JOHN MICHAEL, dentist; b. Columbus, Ohio, May 28, 1952; s. John Raymond and Betty Mae (Paripovich) C.; m. Alice May Mcquitty, Aug. 6, 1977 (div. May 1984); 1 child, John David Benjamin; m. Linda Ann Hovis-Smith, Oct. 20, 1990. BA, Ohio State U., 1974, DDS, 1976. Pvt. practice family dentistry and laser-assisted care Fairfield, Ohio, 1976—, Loveland, Ohio, 1993—; assoc. staff dental outpatient dept. Jewish Hosp. Cin., 1977-80, courtesy staff mem. 1980-84; also dental outpatient rep. to med. records and ambulatory care com.; instr. radiology div. dental hygiene U. Cin., 1977, supervising dentist clin. affairs; clin. dentist Rockdale Elem. & Condon Schs. for Handicapped, 1977-79; founding mem., trustee DenCare, 1986-89. Contbr. articles to profl. jour. Sr. clin. dentist Cin. Bd. Edn.; mem. programming com. Southwestern Ohio chpt. Am. Heart Assn., 1983; co-chmn. fin. com., ch. bd. Lindenwald United Meth. Ch., 1982;. Mem. ADA, Ohio Dental Assn., Acad. Gen. Dentistry (nat. spokesdentist in laser-assisted dentistry), Am. Endodontic Soc., Internat. Acad. Laser Dentistry, Cin. Dental Soc. (assoc.), Keely Dental Soc. (co-chmn. programming com. 1980, chmn. continuing edn. 1979-82, editor Keely Bull. 1982-85, mem.-at-large coun. 1982), Psi Omega. Republican. Office: 1251 Nilles Rd Fairfield OH 45014-7205

CUTTILL, RAYMOND FRANCIS, JR., psychologist; b. Evergreen Park, Ill., Oct. 16, 1958; s. Raymond Francis Cuttill and Grayce Claire (Sigler) Brown; m. Mary Louise Stur; children from previous marriage: Kristen Leigh-Ann, Timothy Raymond, Heather Marie, David Aaron. BA in Clin. Psychology, Purdue U., 1992; MA Applied Behavioral Scis. Coursework, Valparaiso U., 1993; MA in Applied Psychology, U. Chgo., 1994; MA in Applied Theology, Liberty Payne Coll., 1995. Admissions clk. Purdue U., Hammond, Ind., 1986-90, rsch. psychology tech., 1990-92; lectr., psychologist pvt. practice, 1995—; realtor Coldwell Banker, 1st Am., Chesterton, Ind., 1995—; facilitator Nat. Alliance Businessmen, Valparaiso, Ind., 1994; speaker, guest lectr., philospher, motivational seminar conductor. Author: The Divine Station, 1986, The End-Times Survival Guide, 1993, The Dead Among Us, 1996., Comes As a King, 1996. Mem. Nat. Assn. Realtors, Adminstrv. Mgmt. Soc., Proter (Ind.) C. of C., Phi Kappa Theta. Republican. Home: 2827 Bryant St Portage IN 46368 Office: Coldwell Banker 1st Am Porter Ave Chesterton IN 46368

CVENGROS, JOSEPH MICHAEL, manufacturing company executive; b. Pana, Ill., Oct. 8, 1931; s. Joseph John and Mary Berniece (Sturgeon) C.; m. Mary Elizabeth Ainsworth, Feb. 11, 1956; children: Joseph J., Mary E., Andrew T., Katherin A., J. Michael, Roert A., David L., Susan M. BABS, Washington U., St. Louis, 1955; MBA, Northwestern U., 1960. Pers. mgr. Continental Baking Co., Chgo., 1956-57; asst. to chmn. bd. dirs. Automatic Canteen Co. divsn. ITT, Chgo., 1957-65; cons. Spencer Stuart and Assoc., Chgo., 1965-68; investor High Tech., Inc., Chgo., 1968—; chmn. bd. dirs., CEO Anaconda Metal Hose divsn. Anamet, Inc., Glen Ellyn, Ill., 1984—. Fellow Econ. Club Chgo. Office: Anamet Inc 739 Roosevelt Rd Glen Ellyn IL 60137-5877

CYR, ARTHUR, professional society administrator; b. L.A., Mar. 1, 1945; s. Irving Arthur and Frances Mary Cyr; children: David Arthur, Thomas Harold, James Price. BA, UCLA, 1966, MA, 1967; AM, Harvard U., 1969, PhD, 1971. Teaching fellow Harvard U., 1970-71; program officer internat. and edn.-research divs. Ford Found., 1971-74; asst. prof. polit. sci., adminstr. UCLA, 1974-76; program dir. Chgo. Council Fgn. Relations, 1976-81, v.p., 1981-96; pres., CEO chgo. World Trade Ctr., 1996—; lectr. U. Chgo., Northwestern U.; mem. adv. coun. Ctr. for Internat. Bus. Edn., U. Ill. Author: Liberal Politics in Britain, 1977, rev. edit., 1988, British Foreign Policy and the Atlantic Area, 1979, U.S. Foreign Policy and European Security, 1987, After the Cold War--American Foreign Policy, Europea and Asia, 1996; contbr. articles to profl. jours. Mem. Internat. Inst. Strategic Studies, Am. Polit. Sci. Assn., N.Y. Coun. Fgn. Rels., Century Assn., Harvard Club (N.Y.C.), Econ. Club, Univ. Club (Chgo.), Phi Beta Kappa. Home: 929 Merchandise Mart Chicago IL 60654

CZACH, MARIE, art historian; b. Chgo.; d. Joseph Thomas and Esther Edna (Ciesielski) C. BFA, Sch. Art Inst. Chgo., 1967; MA in Ednl. Psychology, Columbia U., 1968; PhD in Art History, U. Ill., 1985. Rsch. assoc. George Eastman House, Rochester, N.Y., 1968-70; asst. curator photography Art Inst. Chgo., 1970-72; dir. history of photographic studies Columbia Coll., Chgo., 1972-74; dir. art mus. Western Ill. U., Macomb, 1974-78; grant writer, mgr. South Suburban Coll., South Holland, Ill., 1994—; guest curator St. Louis Art Mus., 1974-78.

CZARNECKI, CARY JOHN, librarian; b. Chgo., Nov. 21, 1946; s. John Anthony and Irene Therese (Slezak) C.; m. Donna Mae Czarnecki, Aug. 5, 1972. AB in English, John Carroll U., 1968; MA, DePaul U., 1974; MALS, Rosary Coll., 1983. Tchr. English, Loyola Acad., Wilmette, Ill., 1969-78; account exec. Burroughs Corp., Chgo., 1978-79; employee benefits cons. Martin E. Segal Co., Chgo., 1980-81; adult services libr. Oak Park Pub. Library, Ill., 1982-83; reference librarian Oak Lawn Pub. Libr., Ill., 1983-85; head reference dept. Hinsdale (Ill.) Pub. Libr., 1985-88; asst. dir. Oak Park Pub. Libr., 1988-93; dir. Niles Pub. Libr. Dist., 1993—. Book reviewer Internat. Jour. Revs. in Library and Info. Sci. John Carroll U. Pres.'s scholar, 1964. Mem. ALA, Ill. Library Assn. Roman Catholic. Club: John Carroll U. Glee (pres. 1967-68). Home: 412 51st St Western Springs IL 60558-1907 Office: 6960 Oakton St Niles IL 60714

CZARNEZKI, MARY ANN, women's studies educator; b. Milw., Dec. 31, 1953; d. Herald Joseph and Shirley (Glisch) Schroeder; m. Joseph John Czarnezki, Dec. 20, 1975; children: Jason, Jamie Marie. BSN, U. Wis., Milw., 1976, MSN, 1982, PhD in Urban Studies, 1995. RN, Wis.; cert. clin. specialist in child and adolescent psychiat. and mental health nursing. Psychiat. nurse Child/Adolescent Treatment Ctr., Milw., 1976-78, supr. nursing svcs., 1979-84, asst. adminstr., 1984-87; instr. Milw. County Sch. Nursing, 1978-79; lectr. U. Wis.-Parkside, Kenosha, 1988; advocacy specialist Legal Aid Soc. Milw., 1988-92; lectr. U. Wis., Milw., 1991—; mem. Wis. Legis. Study Com. on Child Care Regulation, 1987-89. Active administrv. appeals bd. City of Milw., 1989—. Named one of Outstanding Young Women Am., 1987; recipient Leadership awrd YWCA of Greater Milw., 1985. Mem. U Wis.-Milw. Alumni Assn., U. Wis.-Milw. Nursing Alumni Assn., ANA. Democrat. Roman Catholic. Home: 7004 W Van Beck Ave Milwaukee WI 53220 Office: U Wis Milw Dept Sociology PO Box 413 Milwaukee WI 53201

CZARNIECKI, MYRON JAMES, III, art museum director, cultural planner; b. San Francisco, 1948; s. Myron James Jr. and Laura Maxine (Atwood) C.; m. Anne Frances Dixon, 1976; children: Mark James, Laura Anne, Katherine Elizabeth, John Dixon. Student, Xaverius Coll., Antwerp, Belgium, 1966-67; B.A., Wabash Coll., 1971; postgrad., Sch. Art Inst. Chgo., 1971-72. Instr. photography Wabash Coll., 1970-71; with dept. mus. edn. Art Inst. Chgo., 1971-74; dir. edn. and state services The Ringling Museums, 1974-76; dir. Miss. Mus. Art, Jackson, 1976-83, Minn. Mus. Am. Art, St. Paul, 1983-93; pres., CEO S/RI Cultural Planners, St. Paul, 1993—; curator-in-residence USIA, Sofia, Bulgaria, 1982; cons. Nat. Endowment for the Arts, NEH, Inst. Mus. Svcs., Minn. State Arts Bd.; lectr. Art Inst. Chgo., 1972-74, SUNY-Binghamton, 1985-94; founding dir. Miss. Inst. Arts and Letters, 1978-83; sec. Minn.-Cuba Cultural Exch., Havanna, 1985, 87, 91; mem. Minn. Designer Selection Bd., 1990—, chmn., 1992-94, vice-chmn., 1995—; mem. Minn. Cultural Diversity Task Force, 1991-94; pres. bd. dirs. Inst. Photographic Studies, 1994—; del. White House Conf. on Travel and Tourism, 1995. Author or editor numerous exhbn. catalogs; mem. editl. bd. Art in Religious and Theol. Studies, 1991—. Bd. dirs. Intermedia Arts Minn., 1986-91, Pub. Art St. Paul, 1987-95, exec. com. 1994—; bd. dirs. Art Ctr. St. John's U., 1991-95, Chautaqua on the River, 1993—; founding mem. Am. Mus. Asmat Art, 1995. Mcknight Found. fellow, 1989, Salzburg Seminars fellow, 1989; Raymond Fund grantee, 1972-73; Am. Field Svc. scholar, 1966-67. Mem. Am. Assn. Mus. (membership chmn. 1988-91), Internat. Coun. Mus. Office: S/RI Cultural Planners 123 Farrington Saint Paul MN 55102-2101

CZERAK, GERALD STEPHEN, marketing professional; b. Chgo., Sept. 3, 1943; s. Stephen F. and Dorothy (Plywack) C.; m. Judith Mary Karolewicz, Sept. 10, 1966; children: Kevin James, Victoria Lynn, Brian Thomas. BA, DePaul U., 1966; MS in Journalism, Northwestern U., 1967; MBA in Mktg., Ill. Benedictine Coll., 1991. Reporter City New Bur., Chgo., 1966; mng. editor Ragan & Assocs., Chgo., 1967-69; dir. pub. info. Ill. Benedictine Coll., Lisle, 1969-78, dir. mktg. communication, 1978-92; mktg. and media coord. Hawthorne Credit Union, Naperville, Ill., 1994-95; asst. mgr. Chgo. office Thomas Howell Group, Downers Grove, Ill., 1995—. Editor Ill. Benedictine mag., 1972-90. Mem. Pub. Rels. Soc. Am., Am. Mgmt. Assn., Mgmt. Assn. Ill.

CZESWIK, FREDERICK RANDALL, human resources executive, consultant; b. Rapid City, S.D., Nov. 14, 1946; s. Florian Rudolph and Muriel Mercedes (Anderson) C.; m. Joanne Lynn Ventura, Jan. 2, 1987. BA, Augustana Coll., Sioux Falls, S.D., 1969. Pers. adminstr. Control Data Corp., Mpls., 1969-71; v.p. human resources and adminstrn. Farm Credit Svcs., St. Paul, 1971-77; v.p. human resources Mich. Nat. Corp., Lansing, 1977-79; v.p. employee rels. Norwest Corp., Mpls., 1979-81; dir. human resource devel. Ecolob, Inc., St. Paul, 1982-87; pres., mng. ptnr. Soll Czeswik Assocs., Inc., Mpls., 1987-92; sr. v.p. Lee Hecht Harrison (merger), 1992-94; co-owner Carlson & Czeswik, Inc., Mpls., 1995—. Pres. bd. dirs. Compas, St. Paul, 1986-91, Theatre in the Round., Mpls., 1974; deacon Ho. of Hope Presbyn. Ch., St. Paul, 1988-91. Mem. ASTD, Twin Cities Pers. Assn., Am. Soc. Pers. Adminstrn., Human Resource Planning Soc., Rotary (bd. dirs. 1993—), St. Paul Athletic Club (bd. dirs. 1989). Office: Carlson & Czeswik Northland Plaza #995 3800 W 80th St Minneapolis MN 55431

CZOSNYKA, HELENA JULIA, humanities educator; b. East St. Louis, Ill., Jan. 2, 1957; d. John Leo and Anne Felicia (Pikul) C. BA, St. Louis U., 1978, MA, 1984, PhD, 1991. Cert. K-12 tchr., Mo. Acad. advisor St. Louis U., 1987-92, adj. instr., 1987-91, adj. asst. prof., 1991-92; asst. prof. St. Louis Coll. Pharmacy, 1992—; adj. asst. prof. Maryville U., St. Louis, 1991—. Asst. editor Auslegung, 1982—. Vol. St. Mary's Hosp., East St. Louis, 1993-94. Fulbright scholar Warsaw U., Poland, 1989-90. Mem. Am. Acad. Religion, Am. Assn. Colls. Pharmacy, Am. Cath. Hist. Assn., Polish Nat. Alliance, Kosciuszko Found., Polish-Am. Cultural Soc., Pi Delta Phi. Office: St Louis Coll Pharmacy 4588 Parkview Pl Saint Louis MO 63110

CZYSZ, DAVID EUGENE, law enforcement professional; b. Milw., Apr. 20, 1948; s. Eugene A. Winiarski and Marcella (Spychala) Czysz; m. Sandra Ann Br, Sept. 24, 1966; children: Carla, Michele, David Jr.; m. Beth Lynn Formella, July 1987. Sheet metal worker apprentice grad., Milw. Area Tech. Coll., 1972. Lab. worker Allen-Bradley Co., Milw., 1966-67; sheet metal apprentice Wis. Heating Co., Milw., 1967; sheet metal apprentice and journeyman Downey Co., Milw., 1967-72; sheet metal journeyman Butter-Fetting Co., Milw., 1972-73; dep. sheriff sgt. Milw. County Sheriff's Dept., Milw., 1973—; swat team mem.-leader Milw. County Sheriff's Dept., 1975-84, swat team sniper and intelligence officer, 1984—, narcotics undercover officer, 1980-90. tng. officer swat, narcotics/surveillance ops., 1975—; command post officer Tactical Narcotics Team, 1991—; unit sgt. Milw. Metro. Drug Enforcement, 1993—; swat team sniper, 1994—. Mem. Wis. Intelligence Officers, Milw., 1980-87, Midwest Cycle Intelligence Orgn., Milw., 1980-88, Nat. Wildlife Fedn., 1988-89. Recipient award U.S. Atty.'s Office,

Milw., 1988, letter of commendation FBI-Milw., 1984, Forrest County Sheriff's Dept., 1985, Jefferson County Sheriff's Dept., 1987, Milw. Police Dept., 1989, Hometown Hero award Eagles Club, 1984. Mem. Assn. swat Pers. Wis. (bd. dirs. 1986-87), Wis. Narcotics Enforcement Officers Assn. (bd. dirs. 1990—), Internat. Narcotics Enforcement Officer's Assn., Nat. Geog. Soc., NRA. Republican. Roman Catholic. Office: Milw County Sheriffs Dept 821 W State St Milwaukee WI 53233-1427

DABAREINER, THOMAS JOHN, transportation planner; b. Jefferson, Wis., Feb. 9, 1956; s. Jack and Lois (Rindfleisch) D.; m. Audrey Stewart, Oct. 9, 1993. BS in Environ. Sci., U. Wis., Green Bay, 1978; MA in City Planning, U. Iowa, 1982. Asst. dir. Brown County Energy Conservation Ctr., Green Bay, 1978-79; transp. planner N.W. Mcpl. Conf., Mt. Prospect, Ill., 1983-86, Village of Schaumburg, Ill., 1986—; speaker in field. Contbr. articles to profl. jours. Active Ice Age Park and Trail Found., Pewaukee, Wis., 1991—, Nature Conservancy Corp., 1992—; bd. dirs. Schaumburg Twp. Dem. Party; contbg. Dem. Nat. Com., 1983—. Recipient Personal Merit award Helicopter Assn. Internat., 1992. Mem. Am. Planning Assn., Transp. Rsch. Bd. Roman Catholic. Home: 718 Sturnbridge Ln Schaumburg IL 60173-5930 Office: Village of Schaumburg 101 Schaumburg Ct Schaumburg IL 60193-1881

DABBAGH, MAHMOUD, electrical engineer; b. Quwait, Aug. 13, 1962; came to the U.S., 1980; BSEE, So. Ill. U., 1986, M in Elec. Engring., 1988. Engr. Coin Acceptorsinc, St. Louis, 1987-92, sr. elec. engr., 1993—; sr. software engr. Critic Care Sys. Inc., Milw., 1992-93. Office: Coin Acceptorsinc 300 Hunter Ave Saint Louis MO 63124-2081

DABERKO, DAVID A., banker; b. Hudson, Ohio, 1945. BA, Denison U., 1967; MBA, Case Western Res. U., 1970. Mgmt. trainee Nat. City Bank, Cleve., 1968-72, asst. v.p., 1972-73, v.p. bank investment divsn., dept. head met. lending divsn., 1973-80, sr. v.p. corp. banking, 1980-82, pres., 1987-93; exec. v.p. corp. banking Nat. City Corp., Nat. City Bank, Cleve., 1982-85; pres., bd. dirs. Nat. City Bank (formerly BancOhio Nat. Bank), Columbus, 1985-87; dep. chmn. Nat. City Corp., Cleve., 1987-93, pres., CEO, 1993-95, CEO, 1995—; dir. Fed. Res. Bank, Cleve., Student Loan Mktg. Assn., Washington. Trustee Am. Contemporary Music Ctr. Devel. Corp., Cleve. Tomorrow, Greater Cleve. Growth Assn., Greater Cleve. Coun. Boy Scouts of Am., Case Western Res. U., Hawken Sch., Neighborhood Progress, Ohio Found. Ind. Colls., Univ. Cir. Inc., Univ. Hosp. Health Sys.; co-chair Harvest for Hunger Campaign, 1992, 93. Mem. Bankers Roundtable, Greater Cleve. Roundtable (trustee). Office: Nat City Corp 1900 E 9th St Cleveland OH 44114-3484

DABROWSKI, EDWARD JOHN, television technical director; b. Chgo., Nov. 16, 1957; s. Edward J. and Justina J. (Grilc) D. BS in Elec. Engring., Ill. Inst. Tech., Chgo., 1979. Engr. Sta. WMAQ-TV, Chgo., 1976-83, tech. dir., 1983—; enrg.-in-charge The Jenny Jones Show, 1995. Tech. dir. (NBC afternoon spl.) The Sixth Street Kids, 1984, (WMAQ-TV docu-drama) Fast Break to Glory: Dusable Panthers, 1988, Chgo. Sisslin (Chgo. Emmy award 1989), Chgo. Bears Pre-Season football, 1993. Mem. IEEE, Soc. Broadcast Engrs., NATAS (Emmy nominations Chgo. chpt. 1986), Nat. Assn. Broadcast Employees and Technicians (steward Chgo. chpt. 1981-87, Am. Radio RElay Lague (life), Chgo.-Suburban Radio Assn., Mus. Broadcast Comm. (charter), Am. Fraternal Union, Slovens Nat. Benefit Soc. (rec. sec. lodge 449). Democrat. Roman Catholic. Office: Sta WMAQ-TV NBC Tower 454 N Columbus Dr Chicago IL 60611-5501

DABROWSKI, ELIZABETH MARIE, chemistry educator; b. Cleve., May 19, 1950; d. Thaddeus Victor and Elizabeth Agnes (Krawczynski) D. BS cum laude, John Carroll U., 1972; MS in Chemistry, Case Western Res. U., 1974. Sci. tchr. Hebrew Acad. Cleve., Cleveland Heights, Ohio, 1973-74, St. Ignatius H.S., Cleve., 1974-76; chemistry tchr. Magnificat H.S., Rocky River, Ohio, 1979—, co-chair sci. dept., 1995—; mem. energy edn. adv. bd. Centerior Energy, Cleve., 1983—; chemistry instr. Cuyahoga C.C., Parma, Ohio, 1991—, chemistry lectr. John Carroll U., U. Heights, Ohio, 1995—. Author: Reteaching Worksheets and Teacher's Guide to Overheads, Chemistry, 1995; editor (lab. manual) Chemistry. Head usher Playhouse Square Found., Cleve., 1984—. Mem. AIAA, MENSA, Am. Chem. Soc. (local sect. H.S. affiars co-chair 1994—), Iota Sigma Pi. Roman Catholic. Office: Magnificat High Sch 20770 Hilliard Rd Rocky River OH 44116

DAFOE, CHRISTOPHER RANDY, marketing, healthcare education professional; b. Wilkesboro, N.C., Oct. 26, 1962; s. Alfred Walter Brett and Verna Irene Dafoe. LLB, Somerset, Ilminster,, 1985-89; BEd, York U., North York, Ont., Can., 1991; MEd, Greenwich U., 1992, PhD, 1994; DD (hon.), United Luth. Ch. Sem., Modesto, Calif., 1989. Ordained to ministry Luth. Ch., 1990; incardinated as monsignor Ecumenical Jacobite Orthodox Cath. Ch. of Antioch, 1994; lic. primary/jr. level tchr., psychotherapist, Ark., Ont., Mo., W.Va., Brazil; cert. LCSW, CCSW; registered play therapist. Dir. mktg. Info. Interchange Co. Ltd., Freehold, N.J., 1983-93; regional v.p. Sundance Rehab. Corp., Indpls., 1993—; chair. Profl. Paralegal Assn., Ont., Can., 1985-93; cons. Internat. Mktg. Inst., London, 1989—. Named Prince of Medina by Patriarch of Antioch, Baron of San Nicandro by Coun. of Westphalia. Mem. Internat. Lawyers Assn., Internat. Bar Assn., World Jurist Assn., Soc. Psychotherapy and Psychodrama, Notary Assn., Knights Templar (adjutor gen., adjutor 1987-91, Duke of Tyre, 1989), Coun. Seven Sages (H.S.H. sovereign prince, grand master of the order). Home: RR 3 Box 275 Cloverdale IN 46120-9202 Office: Sundance Rehab Corp 101 W Ohio St Fl 20 Indianapolis IN 46204-1906

DAFT, WILLIAM STANLEY, physician; b. Colfax, Iowa, Sept. 24, 1957; s. Stanley Price and Patricia Ann (Tomlonovic) D.; m. Jan Renee Irven, July 20, 1991; children: Stephani, Christi, Cameron. BS in Pharmacy, U. Iowa, 1980; DO, U. Osteo. Medicine & Health Scis., Des Moines, 1987. Diplomate Am. Bd. Family Practice. Asst. dir. pharmacy Skiff Meml. Hosp., Newton, 1980-83; physician Burlington (Iowa) Area Family Practice, 1991—; chief of medicine and family practice Burlington Med. Ctr., 1996—. Mem. AMA, Am. Acad. Family Physicians, Am. Coll. Osteo. Gen. Practitioners, Iowa Osteo. Med. Assn., Iowa Med. Soc., Iowa Acad. Family Physicians, Des Moines County Med. Soc. Office: Burlington Area Family Practice Ctr 1201 W Agency Rd West Burlington IA 52655-1645

D'AGATI, JOHN R., mechanical engineer; b. Sharon, Pa., July 6, 1938. BS in Mech. Engring., Ohio U., 1961. Project engr. Preformed Line Products, Cleve., 1961—. Patentee in field. Mem. IEEE, Soc. Plastics Engrs. Office: Preformed Line Products R & E 660 Beta Dr Cleveland OH 44143-2319

DAGGETT, HORACE CLINTON, retired state legislator; b. Prescott, Iowa, May 15, 1931; s. Donald Earl and Mildred Ann Daggett; m. Ruth Arlene Daggett, Sept. 28, 1952; childrne: Dennis Gene, Debra Denise, Douglas Dee. Grad. high sch., Prescott. Farmer Adams County, Iowa, 1949-91; mem. Iowa Ho. of Reps., 1972-96; ret., 1996. Mem. Lenox Sch. Bd., 1968-71. Sgt. major Iowa ANG, 1950-89. Republican. Baptist. Home: 400 N Bureau St Creston IA 50801-1945 Office: Iowa Ho. of Reps Des Moines IA 50319

DAGGETT, ROXANN, state legislator; b. Mar. 10, 1947; m. Dave Daggett, Aug. 20, 1967; 2 children. Student, Concordia Coll., 1965-67; BS, U. N.D., 1968. Motivational spkr.; rep. Dist. 11A Minn. Ho. of Reps., 1994—.

DAGLI, CIHAN HAYREDDIN, engineering educator; b. Ankara, Turkey, Oct. 18, 1949; came to U.S., 1985; s. Kenan and Zuhre (Kavlakoglu) D.; m. Refia Oner, Nov. 3, 1975; children: Cagri, Ediz. BS in Indsl. Engring., Middle East Tech. U., Ankara, 1971, MS in Indsl. Engring., 1972; PhD in Engring. Prodn., U. Birmingham, Eng., 1979. Cert. engr., Turkey. From teaching asst. to instr. Middle East Tech. U., Ankara, 1972-76, from asst. to assoc. prof., 1979-85; british coun. rsch. fellow U. Birmingham, 1976-79; assoc. prof. U. Mo., Rolla, 1988-95, prof., 1995—; vis. assoc. prof. Wichita (Kans.) State U., 1985-88; indsl. and engring. dept. chmn. Middle East Tech. U., Ankara, 1979-82; cons. U.N. Indsl. Devel., Ankara, 1980, AT&T Bell Laboratories, N.J., 1989. Editor: Artificial Neural Networks for Intelligent Manufacturing; co-editor: Intelligent Engineering Systems Through Artificial Neural Networks, Vol. 1, 1991, Vol. 2, 1992, Vol. 3, 1993, Vol. 4, 1994, Vol. 5, 1995, Intelligent Systems in Design and Manufacturing, 1994; contbr. articles to profl. jours. Aspirant lt. Turkish Army, 1975. British Coun. Rsch. fellow, 1976-79; Ed Smith Rsch. grant U. Mo., Rolla, 1989, 90. Mem. Internat. Neural Network Soc. Spl. Interest Group-Midwest (chmn. 1990—), Internat. Found. for Prodn. Rsch. (bd. dirs. 1987—), Inst. Indsl. Engring. (chmn. Wichita chpt. 1987-88). Home: 401 Greenbriar Dr Rolla MO 65401-3694 Office: Univ Missouri 205 Engineering Management Rolla MO 65401

DAHIYA, RAJBIR SINGH, mathematics educator, researcher; b. Rattangarh, Haryana, India, Dec. 3, 1940; came to U.S., 1968; s. Ram S. and Kesar (Devi) D.; m. Krishna Tavathia, Dec. 11, 1966; children: Madhu, Ranjan. PhD, Birla Inst. Sci. and Tech., Pilani, India, 1967. Lectr. Birla Inst. Sci. and Tech., 1967-68; asst. prof. math. Iowa State U., Ames, 1968-72, assoc. prof., 1972-78, prof., 1978—; reviewer math. revs. Zentrallblat; referee applied math. jours. Contbr. over 100 articles on delay and advanced differential equations, transform theory and spl. functions to U.S., European and Australian profl. jours. Mem. Am. Math. Soc. Democrat. Hindu. Home: 3144 Sycamore Rd Ames IA 50014 Office: Iowa State U Dept Math Ames IA 50011

DAHL, GERALD LUVERN, psychotherapist, educator, consultant, writer; b. Osage, Iowa, Nov. 10, 1938; s. Lloyd F. and Leola J. (Painter) D.; m. Judith Lee Brown, June 24, 1960; children: Peter, Stephen, Leah. BA, Wheaton Coll., 1960; MSW, U. Nebr., 1962; PhD in psychotherapy (Hon.), Internat. U. Found., 1987. Juvenile probation officer Hennepin County Ct. Svcs., 1962-65; cons. Citizens Coun. on Delinquency and Crime, Mpls., 1965-67; dir. patient svcs. Mt. Sinai Hosp., Mpls., 1967-69; clin. social worker Mpls. Clinic of Psychiatry, 1969-82, G.L. Dahl & Assocs., Inc., Mpls., 1983—; assoc. prof. social work Bethel Coll., St. Paul, 1964-83; spl. instr. sociology Golden Valley Luth. Coll., 1974-83; pres. Strategic Team-Makers, Inc., 1985—; adj. prof. U. Wis., River Falls, 1988-90. Founder Family Counseling Svc., Minn. Baptist Conf., bd. stewards, 1994—; bd. dirs. Edgewater Baptist Ch., 1972-75, chmn., 1974-75; vice-chmn. bd. stewards Minnetonka Bapt. Ch., 1995. Mem. AAUP, Am. Assn. Behavioral Therapists, Pi Gamma Mu. Author: Why Christian Marriages Are Breaking Up, 1979; Everybody Needs Somebody Sometime, 1980, How Can We Keep Christian Marriages from Falling Apart, 1988, The Sandwich Family, 1995; contbr. articles to profl. jours. Office: 4825 Highway 55 Ste 140 Minneapolis MN 55422-5155

DAHL, HARRY WALDEMAR, lawyer; b. Des Moines, Aug. 7, 1927; s. Harry Waldemar and Helen Gerda (Anderson) D.; m. Bonnie Sorensen, June 14, 1952; children: Harry Waldemar, Lisabeth (dec.), Christina. BA, U. Iowa, 1950; JD, Drake U., 1955. Bar: Iowa 1950, U.S. Supreme Ct. 1965, Fla. 1970, Nebr. 1983, Minn. 1984. Assoc. Steward & Crouch, Des Moines, 1955-59; Iowa dep. indsl. commr. Des Moines, 1959-62, commr., 1962-71; pres., prin. Law Offices of Harry W. Dahl, P.C., 1972—; of counsel Underwood, Gillis and Karcher, Miami, 1972-77; adj. prof. law Drake U., Des Moines, 1972—; exec. dir. Internat. Assn. Indsl. Accident Bds. and Commns., 1972-77; pres. Workers' Compensation Studies, Inc., 1974-92, Workers' Compensation Svcs., Inc., 1978-92, Hewitt, Coleman & Assocs. Iowa, Inc., 1975-79; mem. adv. com. Second Injury Fund, Fla. Indsl. Rels. Commn. Author: Iowa Law on Workmen's Compensation, 1975; editor: ABC Newsletter, 1964-77. Bd. counselors Drake U. Law Sch., 1990-93. With USRN, 1945-46. Recipient Adminstrs. award Internat. Assn. Indsl. Accident Bds. and Commns., 1967. Mem. Am. Trial Lawyers Assn. (chmn. workers' compensation sect. 1973), ABA (chmn. workers' compensation com. 1974-76), Iowa Bar Assn. (chmn. workers' compensation com. 1984-89), Fla. Bar (bd. govs. 1988-90), Nebr. Bar Assn., Minn. Bar Assn., Internat. Bar Assn., Am. Soc. Law and Medicine (coun. 1975-82), Iowa Assn. Workers' Compensation Lawyers (co-founder, past pres.), Coll. of Workers Compensation Inc. (co-founder, regent), Swedish Pioneer Hist. Soc., Am. Swedish Inst., Sco. of the Goths (founder, pres.), Des Moines Pioneer Club, East High Alumni Assn. (pres. 1975-76), Grand View Coll. Alumni Assn. (bd. dirs. 1993—), Order of Coif, Masons, Shriners, Sertoma (chmn. bd. dirs. 1974-75). Lutheran. Home: 3005 Sylvania Dr West Des Moines IA 50266-2150 Office: 974 73rd St Ste 16 Des Moines IA 50312-1026

DAHL, LAUREL JEAN, human services administrator; b. Chgo.; d. James Edward and Gladys Uarda (Boquist) Findlay; m. Philip Nels Dahl, Aug. 29, 1970; children: Eric Nels, John Philip. BA, Trinity Coll., 1970; MS in Human Svcs., Nat. Louis U., 1992. Cert. sr. alcohol and other drug preventionist. Tchr. Grove Sch., Lake Forest, Ill., 1971, Little Bear Child Care Ctr., Waukegan, Ill., 1975-77; sec. to dir. Strang Funeral Home, Antioch, Ill., 1981-87; comptroller, office mgr. Village of Antioch, 1987-92; prevention specialist Lake County Dept. of Health: Mental Health Div., 1992; community coord. Fighting Back Project of Lake County, Round Lake, Ill., 1992-94; prevention adminstr. No. Ill.Coun. on Alcoholism and Substance Abuse, Lake, 1994—; adj. faculty Nat. Louis U., 1994—. Mem. Antioch Comty. H.S. Bd. Edn., 1987-95, pres., 1991-95, sec., 1989-91; mem. Antioch Comty. H.S. Drug Task Force, MADD; past pres. PTO; mem. adv. bd. WAY; bd. dirs. COURAGE; vice chair Human Svc. Coun., 1994-96, chmn., 1996—; mem. peer rev. com. Ill. Alcohol and Other Drug Abuse Profl. Cert. Assn., 1996—; mem. women's bd. No. Ill. Coun. on Alcoholism and Substance Abuse, 1996—; pres. Human Svc. Coun., 1996—. Recipient commendation for Gt. Lakes Naval Tng. Ctr. for Drug Edn. for Youth, 1994-95, Disting. Svc. award Ill. chpt. Nat. Sch. Pub. Rels. Assn., Enrique Camarena "One Person Can" award, 1995. Mem. Alliance Against Intoxicated Motorists, Ill. Student Assistance Profls., Ill. Assn. for Prevention. Home: PO Box 613 Antioch IL 60002-0613

DAHL, LAWRENCE FREDERICK, chemistry educator; b. Evanston, Ill., June 2, 1929; s. Lawrence Gustave and Anne (Stuessy) D.; m. June Lomnes, Sept. 1, 1956; children: Larry, Eric, Christopher. BS in Chemistry, U. Louisville, 1951; PhD, Iowa State U., 1956; DSc (hon.), U. Louisville, 1991. Postdoctoral fellow Ames (Iowa) Lab. AEC, 1957; from instr. to assoc. prof. chemistry U. Wis., Madison, 1957-64, prof., 1964-78, R. E. Rundle chair, 1978—, Hilldale chair and prof., 1991—; Brotherton rsch. prof. U. Leeds, 1983. Recipient inorganic chemistry award Am. Chem. Soc., 1974, Disting. Alumnus award U. Louisville Coll. Letters and Sci., 1983, sr. U.S. scientist Humboldt award Alexander von Humboldt Stiftung, 1985, R.S. Nyholm medal Royal Soc. Chemistry, 1985, P. Chini medal Italian Soc. Chemistry, 1989, J.C. Bailar Jr. medal U. Ill., 1990, Hilldale award in phys. scis. U. Wis., 1994; named to Hon. Order Ky. Cols., 1982; Alfred P. Sloan fellow, 1963-65, Guggenheim fellow, 1969-70, 1st Alumnus fellow U. Louisville Coll. Letters and Sci., 1990. Fellow AAAS, N.Y. Acad. Sci., Am. Acad. Arts and Scis.; mem. NAS. Home: 4817 Woodburn Dr Madison WI 53711-1345 Office: Univ of Wis Dept of Chemistry 1101 University Ave Madison WI 53706-1322

DAHL, MARILYN GAIL, psychotherapist, nurse; b. Louisville, Dec. 6, 1946; d. James Blair and Dorothy Emma (McDermott) Swartzwelder; m. Charles Dalton Weaver, Dec. 30, 1967 (div. Apr. 1969); m. Donald Allan Dahl, Sept. 18, 1985. BSN, U. Ky., 1968; MEd in Clin. Counseling, The Citadel, 1987. Lic. profl. counselor, Ill. Instr. med.-surgical nursing Sch. Nursing Ky. Bapt. Hosp., Louisville, 1973-79; child psychiat. nurse Norton's Children's Hosp., Louisville, 1980-81; asst. prof., psychiat. nurse Sch. Nursing, U. Louisville, 1981-82; primary therapist/child psychiat. nurse Children's Treatment Service, Louisville, 1982-83; instr. psychiat. nursing Sch. Nursing Bellarmine Coll., Louisville, 1983-84; adult and geritric therapist Seven Counties Services, Louisville, 1984; psychiat. nurse So. Pines Hosp., Charleston, S.C., 1985-86; rev. specialist S.C. Peer Rev. Orgn., Charleston, 1986-87; psychotherapist Ctr. for Change, Charleston, 1987-88; pvt. practice North Charleston, 1988-94; hospice nurse Condell Home Health Agy., Libertyville, Ill., 1994-95; home health nurse Manpower Temporary Agy., Waukegan, Ill., 1996—; hospice nurse Hospice of Charleston, Inc., 1991-92; pub. health nurse Trident Home Halth Svcs., 1992; mental health profl. Charleston/Dorchester Mental Health Ctr., 1993. Vol. Hospice of Louisville, Inc., 1978-85; mem. steering com. Highlands Adult Day Ctr., Louisville, 1984-85; bd. dirs. Ashley River Fire Dept., Charleston, 1986-90, chair, 1989-90; mem. ladies aux. Ashley River Fire Dept., 1985-94; mem. test rose panel Jackson & Perkins, 1989-91. Named to Honorable Order Ky. Cols., Commonwealth of Ky., 1977. Mem. ACA, Am. Assn. for Mental Health Counselors. Home: 2117 Edgewood Rd Waukegan IL 60087-1442

DAHLE, JOHANNES UPTON, academic administrator; b. Ada, Minn., Nov. 28, 1933; s. Upton Emmanuel and Marte (Goli) D.; m. Arlene Isabel Powell, Dec. 27, 1956; children—Randall Douglas, Lisa Johanna. B.S., U. Minn., 1956, M.A., 1966. Choral dir. U. Minn., Mpls., 1960-62, 63-66; dir. choirs Macalester Coll., St. Paul, 1962-63; dir. student activities and univ. programs U. Wis.-Eau Claire, 1966-71, dir. univ. ctrs., 1971-84, dir. devel., 1984-95, ret., 1995. Pres., dir. Eau Claire Conv. Tourism Bur., 1979-84; v.p., dir. Eau Claire Regional Arts Council, 1982-84; bd. dirs. United Way of Eau Claire. Served to capt. USAF, 1956-60. Mem. Internat. Assn. Coll. Unions, Council for Advancement and Support Edn., Phi Kappa Phi (sec. 1982-84), Omicron Delta Kappa (sec. 1981-84), Phi Mu Alpha Sinfonia. Mem. United Ch. of Christ. Lodge: Kiwanis (pres. Eau Claire chpt. 1975-76). Home: 1725 Coolidge Ct Eau Claire WI 54701-4033

DAHLQUIST, JOEL POWELL, university administrator; b. Wichita, Kans., May 6, 2955; s. Jackson Oliver and Jane (Orr) P.; m. Rochelle Dawn Dahlquist, Nov. 25, 1992; children: Julian, Erin, Dennis. BA, Wichita (Kans.) State U., 1980; PhD, U. Iowa, 1989. Dir. criminal justice Moorehead (Minn.) State U., 1987—. Contbr. articles to profl. jours. Office: Moorhead State U Criminal Justice Dept Moorhead MN 56563

DAHMS, WILLIAM LAURITZ, broadcasting executive; b. Oconomowoc, Wis., Mar. 13, 1959; s. Hilbert William and Ruth Olive (Moore) D. Cert. mktg. and human behavior, Carroll Coll., 1984, BS, 1985; student classical voice, Wis. Conservatory Music, 1989-92. Broadcasting sales and copywriter WTKM AM and FM Radio, Hartford, Wis., 1988-93; a founder Sta. WTKM, Oconomowoc, 1992; vol. tchr. Oconomowoc Mid. Sch., 1992-96; pres., treas. Lauritz and Co., Ltd.; creator Bicycle DJ radio character, Interstate Radio Network, Chgo., 1995. Author: The Art of Gourmet Dining, 1977 (1st place award Wis. Distributive Edn. Clubs Am., 3d place award Nat. Distributive Edn. Clubs Am.); commd. to paint epiphany banners St. John the Evangelist Cathedral, Milw., 1994. Soloist, cantor Dr. Martin Luther Ch., Oconomowoc, Reformation Ch., Brookfield, Wis.; fundraiser bicycle tour St. Augustine to San Diego for Kiwanis Internat., 1995, St. Paul to New Orleans, 1994; fundraiser bicycle tour Seattle to Atlantic City for Am. Lung Assn., 1988, Keep Calm Bicycle tour around Lake Michigan, 1993. Mem. Am. Lung Assn. (Nat. honors 1988, 90), Milw. Symphony Chorus, Milw. Singers, United Performing Arts Fund Milw., Kiwanis (sec. 1992-95, Outstanding Achievement award Wis.-Upper Mich. chpt. 1994), Greater Oconomowoc Area C. of C. (amb. 1989-93). Lutheran. Home and Office: 317 N Lake Rd Oconomowoc WI 53066-2821 also: Lauritz & Co Ltd 317 N Lake Rd Oconomowoc WI 53066-2821

DAHN, CARL JAMES, aerospace engineer; b. Chgo., June 22, 1936; s. Carl E. and Genevieve (Bardon) D.; BS in Aero. Engring., U. Minn., 1959; m. Rose E. Kucenski, May 25, 1974. Cert. chem. engr.; registered profl. engr. Rocket propulsion devel. engr. Aerojet Gen. Corp., Azusa, Calif., 1959-61, propulsion and explosives devel. engr., 1962-63; chief engr. Omega Ordanace Co., Azusa, 1961-62; propulsion and explosives specialist Honeywell, Inc., Mpls., 1963-68; system safety rsch. engr. IIT Rsch. Inst. Systems Hazard Analysis, Chgo., 1968-74; hazards engring. specialist Polytechnic, Inc., Chgo., 1974-77; pres. Safety Cons. Engrs., Inc., Rosemont, Ill., 1977—; instr. explosives, guns and ballistics, engring. hazards analysis, electrostatics hazard; cons. in same field; researcher dust explosions. Patentee in explosives field. Asst. scout master Mpls. St. Paul coun. Boy Scouts Am., 1962; area dir. Parents Without Partners, 1973; ward chmn. Rep. Com., 1964; ward chmn. Dem. Com., 1973. Mem. Am. Soc. Safety Engrs., ASTM (com. sec.), System Safety Soc., Soc. Explosives Engrs., Nat. Soc. Profl. Engrs. Democrat. Roman Catholic. Rschr. dust explosion potentials. Home: 400 N Wheeling Rd Prospect Heights IL 60070-1329 Office: 2131 Hammond Dr Schaumburg IL 60173-3811

DAIE, JALEH, researcher, science educator, academic administrator; b. Iran, 1948; came to U.S., 1973; d. M.A. and D.Z. Daie; m. Roger E. Wyse. BS, U. of Ahwaz, Iran, 1970; MS, U. Calif., Davis, 1975; PhD, Utah State U., 1981. Postdoctoral fellow Agrl. Rsch. Svc. U.S. Dept. Agr., Logan, Utah, 1980-82; rsch. asst. prof. Utah State U., Logan, 1983-85; assoc. prof. Rutgers U., New Brunswick, N.J., 1985-89, prof., 1989-93, dir. interdisciplinary plant biology grad. program, 1989-92, dept. chmn., 1989-92; dir. Ctr. for Interdisciplinary Studies in Turfgrass Scis. Rutgers U., New Brunswick, 1991-93; also chmn. George H. Cook Honors Rutgers U., New Brunswick, N.J., 1987-91; sr. sci. advisor to v.p. for acad. affairs U. Wis. System, Madison, 1993-96; prof. U. Wis., Madison, 1993—; vis. scholar, Australia, 1988; keynoter, cons. in field. Featured Leaders of Sci., The Scientist, 1994; Henry Rutgers Rsch. fellow, 1985, Tchg. Acad. fellow U. Wis., 1994; inducted into Hall of Fame Women in Tech. Internat., 1996. Fellow AAAS; mem. Assn. for Women in Sci. (pres. 1996-98), Coun. of Sci. Soc. Presidents (bd. dirs. 1996), N.Y. Acad. Scis., Sigma Xi (pres. 1989-90), Phi Kappa Phi. F. Office: U Wis Birge Hall 430 Lincoln Dr Madison WI 53703

DAILEY, MARY, counselor, educator; b. Rockford, Ill.; d. Frank W. and Anne F. (Faley) D.; m. John E. Clay, Oct. 20, 1973. BS, Rosary Coll.; MS, Ill. Inst. Tech., 1979; postgrad., Northwestern U., 1989-90. Cert. addiction counselor, Ill. Caseworker Cath. Charities, Chgo., 1973-76; family therapist Lambs, Libertyville, Ill., 1979-81; counselor, trainer Parkside Med. Svcs., Chgo., 1981-85; coord. student assistance New Trier Twp. High Sch., Winnetka, Ill., 1985—; cons. Gerald T. Rogers Prodns., Skokie, Ill., 1990—. Author: Group Counseling for Children of Alcoholics, 1989; contbr. articles to profl. jours. Mem. com. Mayor Daley's Com. on Child Care, Chgo., 1976, White House Conf. on Drugs, 1988; mem. Regional Prevention Group, North Suburban Cook County, 1986-89; mem. Village of Wilmette (Ill.) Youth Commn., 1988-92; founding mem., co-chair New Trier Youth Consortium; mem. New Trier Twp. Health and Human Svcs. Com. Mem. Employee Assistance Profls. Assn., Ill. Assn. Student Assistance Profls. (pres. 1991-92), Welfare Pub. Rels. Forum (bd. dirs. 1976-77), Ill. Addiction Counselor Cert. Bd., Ill. Alcohol and Drug Dependency Assn. Home: 229 6th St Wilmette IL 60091-3437 Office: New Trier Twp High Sch 385 Winnetka Ave Winnetka IL 60093-4238

DAILY, WILLIAM ALLEN, retired microbiologist; b. Indpls., Nov. 10, 1912; s. Thomas Alvin Daily and Mary Bernice Swengel; m. Eva Fay Kenoyer, June 24, 1937. BS, Butler U., 1936; MS, Northwestern U., 1938. Asst. sr. microbiologist Eli Lilly Co., Indpls., 1941-77. Co-author: Coccoid Myxophceae, 1956, History of Indiana Academy of Science 1885-1984, 1984. Curator cryptogamic bot. herbarium biology dept. Butler U., Indpls. 1941—. Mem. Ind. Acad. Sci. (pres. 1958), Phycological Soc. Am. (pres. 1958), Bot. Soc. Am., Sigma Xi. Republican. Home: 5884 Compton St Indianapolis IN 46220-2653

DAJANI, ESAM ZAPHER, pharmacologist; b. Jaffa, Palestine, May 30, 1940; came to U.S., 1958; s. Zapher Rageb and Mamdouha (Dajani) D.; m. Najwa Said Beidas, July 16, 1964; children: Mona, Zapher, Nora. BS in Pharmacy, U. Mo., 1963; MS in Pharmacology and Med. Chemistry, Auburn U., 1966; PhD in Pharmacology, Purdue U., 1969. Sr. pharmacologist Rohm and Hass Co., 1968-72; sr. rsch. investigator G.D. Searle and Co., Chgo., 1972-74, group leader, 1974-80, chmn. G.I. diseases, 1974-80, sect. head, 1980, asst. dir., 1980-82, dir., 1982-85, dir. Cytotec sci. and med. affairs, 1985-87, dir. clin. rsch., 1987-93; pres. Internat. Drug Devel. Cons., Long Grove, Ill., 1993—; mem. editl. adv. bd. Drug Devel. Rsch., Dallas, 1983-93, Jour. Assn. Acad. Minority Physicians, Bklyn., 1992—, Jour. Physiology and Pharmacology, Krakow, Poland, 1993—; adj. prof. medicine UCLA, 1984-95; adj. prof. medicine Loyola U., Chgo., 1995—. Editor: Gastrointestinal Cytoprotection, 1987; author: (with others) Prostaglandins and GI Mucosa, 1987, Pharmacology of Misoprostol, 1989, Prostaglandins and Esophagus, 1991, Pharmaceutical Industry Perspective, 1991, Prevention and Treatment of Ulcers induced by NSAIDS, 1995; contbr. numerous rsch. papers, book chpts., and presentations in field; patentee in field. Mem. Arab-Am. Anti-discrimination Com., Washington, 1972, Arab-Am. U. Grads., Washington, 1991. Recipient Edward M. Queeny award, Monsanto Corp., 1991; named Disting. Alumnus Purdue U., 1991. Fellow Am. Coll. Gastroenterology; mem. Am. Soc. Pharmacology and Exptl. Therapeutics, Am. Gastroent. Assn., Am. Pharm. Assn., European Soc. Gastroenterology and Endoscopy, Assn. Acad. Minority Physicians, N.Y. Acad. Sci., Rho Chi, Phi Kappa Phi. Office: Inter Drug Devel Cons Corp Divsn Mid Gulf USA Inc 1549 RFD Long Grove IL 60047-9532

DALAMBAKIS, CHRISTOPHER A., sales executive, systems market manager; b. Dayton, Ohio, Mar. 11, 1960; s. Angelo George Dalambakis and Irene Chacos; m. Judy Ann Schneider, July 28, 1984. BS in Biology, U. Cin., 1983. Asst. mgr. Brendamour's, Dayton, 1978-79; asst. to dir. U. Cin. Alumni Assn., 1982-83; service rep. United Technologies Otis, Chgo., Cin., 1983-84; new equipment rep. United Technologies Otis, Cin., 1984-86; dist. mgr. Steelcase, Inc., Cin., 1986—. Mem. exec. com. U. Cin. McMicken Coll. Bd. Govs., 1987-93; pres. student body, trustee U. Cin., 1981-82; bd. dirs., chmn. com. Cin. Art Mus. Friends Assn., 1989-94; bd. trustees Cin. Fire Mus., 1994—; trustee Nat. Hemophilia Found., 1995—; active Nat. Trust for Hist. Preservations, 1990-94. Named Outstanding Young Man of Am., Jaycees, 1982. Mem. Metro Men's Spirit (hon. 1980—), Am. Student Assn. (nat.dir. 1981-83), Cincinnatus (hon. 1980-83), U.S. Senatorial Club, Sigma Sigma (pres. 1982-83, social chmn. 1990—). Republican. Greek Orthodox. Home and Office: 3759 Old Heritage Ct Loveland OH 45140-5506

DALE, KENNETH RAY, computer executive; b. Garnett, Kans., Aug. 22, 1948; s. Earnest Kenneth and Dorothy Mae (Root) D.; m. Sheila Rae Talbott, June 23, 1979; children: Anne Marie Camp, Carolee Talbott. BA, Washburn U., 1978. Programmer trainee Kans. Power and Light Co., Topeka, 1978-79, programmer, 1979-80, sr. programmer, 1980-81, programmer, analyst, 1981-82, sr. programmer, analyst, 1982-83, systems analyst, 1983-85; programmer, analyst Vol. Shoe Corp., Topeka, 1985-86, sr. programmer, analyst, 1986-87, computer ops. shift mgr., 1987-88, lead programmer, analyst, 1988-91; pvt. practice cons. Overbrook, Kans., 1991-92; staff analyst Profl. Resources Inc., Shawnee Mission, Kans., 1992; tech. svcs. cons. CAP Gemini Am, Overland Park, Kans., 1992—. With USN, 1967-70. Mem. Am. Mgmt. Assn., Data Processing Mgmt. Assn., Masons. Democrat. Home: PO Box 444 605 Walnut Overbrook KS 66524-0444

DALE, STEPHEN GLENN, political science educator; b. St. Joseph, Mo., July 24, 1955; s. Stanley Irvin and Glenda (Gerard) D. BS, Mo. Western State Coll., 1978; MA, Sul Ross State U., Alpine, Tex., 1980; PhD, U. Mo., Columbia, 1992. Instr. Tex. A&I U., Kingsville, 1987-93; panelist on presdl. election Corpus Christi (Tex.) Caller Times, 1988. Mem. Am. Polit. Sci. Assn., Am. Soc. Pub. Adminstrn.

DALESSIO, STEWART, criminology educator; b. Butler, Pa., Apr. 16, 1961. BA, Stetson U., 1984; MS in Criminology, Fla. State U., 1987, PhD, 1993. Grad. asst. Fla. State U., 1985-86, rsch. asst., 1986-88; rsch. assoc. Fla. Dept. Corrections, 1988-89; cons. Justice Rsch. and Stats. Assn., 1992-93; vis. asst. prof. Ind. U.-Purdue U., Ft. Wayne, 1994—, adj. prof. 1993. Contbr. articles to profl. jours. Capt. mil. police, U.S. Army, 1989-91, Panama, Saudi Arabia. Mem. Alpha Phi Sigma.

DALEY, ROBERT EMMETT, foundation executive, retired; b. Cleve., Mar. 13, 1933; s. Emmett Wilfred and Anne Gertrude (O'Donnell) D.; m. Mary Berneta Fredericks, June 7, 1958; children: Marianne Fredericks, John Gerard. BA in English, U. Dayton, 1955; MA in Polit. Sci., Ohio State U., 1968, MA in Pub. Adminstrn., 1976. Local govt. reporter, Washington corr., fin. editor Jour. Herald, Dayton, Ohio, 1957-65, pub. affairs reporter, 1967; staff writer Congressional Quarterly, Inc., Washington, 1966; pub. affairs reporter Dayton Daily News, Dayton, 1969; dir. pub. affairs & communications Charles F. Kettering Found., Dayton, 1977-94, ret., now assoc., 1994—; part-time copy boy, sports reporter Jour. Herald, Dayton, 1953-55. Past pres., bd. trustees St. Joseph Home for Children; former mem. adv. bd. Ctr. for Religious Telecomms., U. Dayton; traveling press sec. sen. candidate John J. Gilligan, 1968, for gubernatorial candidate, 1970-71, asst. to Gov. Gilligan, 1971-75; media rels. dir. Nat. League of Cities, Washington, 1976-77; mem. Montgomery County Hist. Soc.; past mem. Ind. Sector Pub. Info. & Edn. Com. With U.S. Army, 1955-57. Mem. Pub. Rels. Soc. Am., Communications Network in Philanthropy, Soc. Profl. Journalists, Nat. Press Club, KC, Ancient Order Hibernians. Roman Catholic. Home: 888 Cranbrook Ct Dayton OH 45459-1525 Office: Charles F Kettering Found 200 Commons Rd Dayton OH 45459-2788

DALEY, RONALD EUGENE, playwright, poet, director, producer; b. Washington, Sept. 24, 1945; s. Russell Eugene and Dorothy Sybil (Krouse) D.; m. Amelia Lenhart Smith, Aug. 26, 1967 (div. Sept. 1983); m. Virginia Ann Bean, Nov. 7, 1986; children: Jackson Phillip Wesley, Bryan Augustin, Geoffrey Eugene. BA in Philosophy, North Park Coll., 1967; MA in English with honors, Roosevelt U., 1968; MA in Drama, Syracuse U., 1975. Instr. English/Philosophy Malcolm X C.C., Chgo., 1968-70, Orange County C.C., Middletown, N.Y., 1970-73; instr. English N.Y.C. C.C., Bklyn., 1975-78; dir./designer many theatre cos., 1978-80; producer Jerron Prodns., N.Y.C., 1980-81; assoc. artistic dir. New World Theatre, N.Y.C., 1981-82; artistic dir. Nat. Shakespeare Co., N.Y.C., 1982-85; resident dir./producer Riverside Shakespeare Co., N.Y.C., 1986; exec. dir. RED Prodns., Argyle, Wis., 1985—; guest dir. Broom St. Theatre, Madison, 1987-94, Classic Theatre, N.Y.C., 1979-84, AMDA Studio One, N.Y.C., 1977-78, Camden (Maine) Shakespeare Festival, 1979. Author plays off Broadway including Beyond the Veil, Damphools and Wowsers, Argyle Wisconsin 53504, In the Matter of John David Hutchins, It's Gotta Be the Shoes, Nobody Dies, 5:45, Badger Orpheus, The Third Blackhawk War, Journeys with Nanabozo, The Abrazo, The Knight of the Burning Pestle, The Red Palace; editor Amphibious Maneuvers. Cons., dir. Argyle Sesquicentennial Com., Argyle, 1994; prodr. Free Shakespeare in the Parks, N.Y.C., 1986. Mem Soc. of Stage Dirs. and Choreographers, Dramatists Guild, Chgo. Area Playwrights, Theatre Comm. Group, U.S. Holocaust Meml. Mus., ACLU. Home: 17740 River Rd Argyle WI 53504

DALEY, VINCENT RAYMOND, JR., real estate executive, consultant; b. Evanston, Ill., June 21, 1940; s. Vincent R. and Carole V. (Johnson) D.; m. Viola Elizabeth Bursiek, May 6, 1967; children: Kathleen Marie, Colleen Patricia. AA, Lincoln Coll., 1961; BS, Loyola U., Chgo., 1963; student in real estate, Roosevelt U., 1964. From salesman to store mgr. Sears Roebuck & Co., Chgo., 1962-73; v.p., cons. Kencoe Corp., Des Plaines, Ill., 1973-74; pres. Daley & Assocs., Chgo., 1974—. Mem. Econ. Devel. Com., State of Ill., Springfield, 1985-88; legis. asst. 8th Legis. Dist., Chgo., 1985-93. Men. Chgo. Bd. Realtors (life) (bd. dirs.), Nat. Assn. Realtors (bd. regents), Ill. Assn. Realtors (bd. dirs.), Realtors Land Inst. (bd. govs.), Realtors Nat. Mktg. Inst. (CCIM), Internat. Real Estate Fed. (sr. cert. valuerer, registered internat. mem., cert. investment financier). Democrat. Roman Catholic. Home: 1807 N Orleans Chicago IL 60614 Office: Daley & Assocs 77 W Washington Ste 920 Chicago IL 60602-2801

DALGLISH, LUCY ANN, lawyer; b. Mpls., Mar. 24, 1959; d. James Mark and Joanne Elizabeth (Speikers) D. BA, U. N.D., 1980; MSL, Yale U., 1988; JD, Vanderbilt U., 1995. Bar: Minn. 1995. Reporter Grand Forks (N.D.) Herald, 1978-80, St. Paul Dispatch, 1979, 80-81, St. Paul Pioneer Press., 1981-89; night city editor ST. Paul Pioneer Press, 1989-90, nat./fgn. editor, 1991-93; rsch. asst. Freedom Forum, Nashville, 1993-95; assoc. Dorsey & Whitney, Mpls., 1995—; instr. Hamline U., St. Paul, 1989, 90. Nat. chair Project Watchdog, Greencastle, Ind., 1990-92. Yale Law Sch. fellow, 1987-88. Mem. Soc. Profl. Journalists (bd. dirs. 1987-91, nat. chairwoman, freedom of info. com. 1991-95; recipient Wells Meml. Key 1995), First Amendment Congress (nat. bd. mem. 1991—), Minn. AP Assn. (v.p. 1991-93), Investigative Reporters and Editors, Sigma Delta Chi Found. (bd. dirs. 1990-91), Minn. Bar Assn. (bar/media com. 1992-93, 95). Roman Catholic. Office: Dorsey & Whitney 220 S 6th St Minneapolis MN 55402

DALIN, JEFFREY BRIAN, dentist; b. St. Louis, Sept. 16, 1956; s. Harry A. and Lillian (Fiman) D.; m. Debbie Goldberg; children: Jamie, Zachary, Andrew. BA in Chemistry, Emory U., 1976; DDS, Ind. U., Indpls., 1980. Dentist Dalin Dental Assocs. Ltd., St. Louis, 1980—. Author: Oral Manifestations of Eating Disorders, 1982. Fellow Am. Coll. Dentists, Acad. Gen. Dentistry; mem. ADA, Mo. Dental Assn., Greater St. Louis Dental Soc. (editor bull., spokesperson, award of merit 1988, Gold medal 1996). Office: 522 N New Ballas Rd # 382 Saint Louis MO 63141

DALLAS, DANIEL GEORGE, social worker; b. Chgo., June 8, 1932; s. George C. and Azimena P. (Marines) D.; B.A., Anderson (Ind.) Coll., 1955; B.D., No. Bapt. Theol. Sem., 1958; M.S.W., Mich. State U., 1963; M.Div., No. Bapt. Theol. Sem., 1972, D.Min., 1981; m. G. Aleta Leppien, May 26, 1956; children—Paul, Rhonda. Mem. faculty Mich. Dept. Corrections, Mich. State U., 1963-66; med. social adminstr. Med. Services div. Mich. Dept. Social Services, 1966-68; cons. Outreach Center of DuPage County, 1976—, also dir. social service Meml. Hosp. of DuPage County, Elmhurst, Ill., 1968—; therapist, lectr. Traffic Sch., Elmhurst Coll.; pvt. practice; indsl. cons. Mem. Elmhurst Sr. Citizen Commn., 1976—. Recipient Outstanding Service award Mental Health Assn. Ill., 1978. Mem. Nat. Assn. Social Workers, Soc. Hosp. Social Work Dirs., Am. Hosp. Assn., Nat. Registry of Health Care Providers, Mental Health Assn. Chgo. Club: Rotary. Contbr. articles to profl. jours. Office: 242 N York St Ste 203 Elmhurst IL 60126-2747

DALLURA, SAL ANTHONY, physician; b. Flushing, N.Y., Nov. 7, 1960; s. Russ and Mayann (Taranto) D.; m. Donna Ann Baldassare, Aug. 6, 1983 (div. Mar. 1993); children: Christopher Anthony, Corinne Elizabeth; m. Stacy Elizabeth Carberry, July 1, 1995; 1 child, Matthew Anthony. BS, U. Notre Dame, 1982; DO, N.Y. Coll. Osteo. Medicine, 1986. Diplomate Am. Acad. Family Physicians. Mng. ptnr. Flashner Med. Ptnrship., Babylon, N.Y., 1989-91; assoc. physician Moriches Med. Care, Center Moriches, N.Y., 1989-91, Digiovanna, Massepequa Park, N.Y., 1991-92; physician Tippecanoe Family Physicians, Tipp City, Ohio, 1992—; physician mng. ptnr. After Hours Family Care, Tipp City, 1994—. Mem. Am. Osteo. Assn., Am. Coll. Family Practice, Am. Coll. Legal Medicine. Republican. Roman Catholic. Office: 450 N Hyatt St Tipp City OH 45371-1433

DALMAN, JESSIE FIESSELMANN, state legislator; b. Detroit, May 17, 1933; d. Friedrich and Isabella (Stevenson) Fiesselmann; m. Ronald A. Dalman, 1957; children: Ronald L. II, Friedrich Charles, Kristina Marie. BA, Mich. State U., 1955; MA, U. Mich., 1958. Researcher Survey Rsch. Ctr. U. Mich., 1957-59; tchr. Holland (Mich.) Pub. Schs., 1959-60; commr. Ottawa County, Mich., 1979-91; rep. Mich. Dist. 90, 1991—; chmn. bd. Ottawa County Commn., 1989, 90; exec. com. Ottawa County Rep. Com., 1980—; dist. rep. Rep. Fred Upton, 1988-903. Recipient leadership award Western Mich. Health Sys. Agy., 1984, svc. award LWV, 1986. Mem. LWV (charter mem. Holland chpt., treas. 1971—), Holland Hist. Trust (past pres.), Mich. Right to Life, Holland Coun. Arts, Ctr. for Women in Transition, Kappa Alpha Theta. Address: PO Box 2398 Holland MI 49422-2398*

DALRYMPLE, JACK, state legislator; m. Betsy Dalrymple; 4 children. BA, Yale U. Farmer, state rep. dist. 22, 1985—; chmn. appropriations com. N.D. Ho. Reps.; bd. dirs. Prairie Pub. TV, N.D. State u. Devel. Found., Golden Growers Coop.; mem. Edn. Broadcasting Coun.; co-founder Share House Inc. Recipient Outstanding Young Farmer award, 1983. Mem. Cass Coounty Rural Water Users Assn. (past bd. dirs.), Casselton Econ. Devel. Found., Univ. Pres. Agr. Club (pres.), Durum Growers Assn. (bd. dirs.), Jaycees. Republican. Address: PO Box 220 Casselton ND 58012-0220*

DALTON, PATRICIA JOYCE, medical technologist; b. Belleville, Ill., Feb. 16, 1950; d. Murlin H. and Joyce Eileen (Shuemaker) Bannister; m. Samuel James Dalton, Sept. 9, 1972; children: Christopher, Jeffrey, Todd, Rebecca. Med. Technologist, St. Elizabeth Hosp., Belleville, 1972; BS, Stetson U., Deland, Fla., 1973. Lic. med. technologist, Ill. Med. technologist Mo. Bapt. Hosp., Town and Country, Mo., 1972-75, Meml. Hosp., Belleville, 1975-77; med. technologist Anderson Hosp., Maryville, Ill., 1988-89, blood bank supr., 1989—. Mem. Sch. Bd., Collinsville, Ill., 1983—, treas., 1990—; pres. PTA Coun., Collinsville, 1987-88; pres. Am. Cancer Soc., Collinsville, 1992-93. Mem. Am. Assn. Blood Banks, Ill. Assn. Sch. Bds. (Master Sch. Bd. Mem. 1992), Ill. Assn. Blood Banks, Mid-Am. Assn. Blood Banks. Home: 128 Westridge Collinsville IL 62234 Office: Anderson Hospital PO Box 1000 Maryville IL 62062

DALTON, RUTH MARGARET, retired pathologist; b. Chgo., Apr. 30, 1926; d. Maurice Jewett and Madeline Irene (Murphy) D. Student, DePaul U., 1946-48; BS, U. Ill., Chgo., 1950, MD, 1953. Diplomate Am. Bd. Pathology. Intern Madison (Wis.) Gen. Hosp., 1953-54, resident in pathology, 1954-57; resident in pathology Phila. (Pa.) Gen. Hosp., 1957-58; pathologist St. Francis Med. Ctr. Assocs. in Lab. Medicine, La Crosse, Wis., 1958-86; instr. St. Francis Hosp. Sch. Med. Tech., La Crosse, 1958-86; ret., 1986; instr. Madison (Wis.) Gen. Hosp. Sch. Med. Tech., 1954-57; lectr. in field; past inspector Am. Assn. Blood Banks; pres. bd. advisors Viterbo Coll., La Crosse, 1978-81; past med. adv. com. Badger Regional Red Cross Blood Ctr., Madison; past adv. bd. Community-Med. Dietetics Program Viterbo Coll.; bd. dirs. Viterbo Coll. Mem. Girl Scout Am. (life, pers. com., bd. dirs. Riverland chpt.); past bd. mem.La Crosse (Wis.) Symphony Orch.; bd. dirs. La Crosse (Wis.) Community Found., Riverfront Found. Fellow Am. Soc. Clin. Pathologists; mem. Am. Assn. Blood Banks, Internat. Soc. Pathologists, AAAS, Univ. Ill. Alumni Assn. (life), Nat. Wildlife Fedn. (life), Rotary. Roman Catholic. Home: N1946 Forest Ridge Dr La Crosse WI 54601-2467

DALTON, TOM K., financial advisor; b. Toledo, Nov. 21, 1970. BBA, U. Toledo, 1994. Registered rep. N.Y. Stock Exch. Fin. planner IDS, Toledo, 1992-93; fin. cons. Smith Barney, Toledo, 1993-94; fin. advisor Prudential Securities, Columbus, Ohio, 1994—; lectr. fin. seminars. Mem. Young Reps., Columbus, 1992—. Mem. Network Profls. Inc. Office: Prudential Securities Inc 8101 N High St # 150 Columbus OH 43235-1406

DALY, JOSEPH LEO, law educator; b. Phila., July 31, 1942; s. Leo Vincent and Genevieve Delores (McGinnis) D.; m. Kathleen Ann Dolan, July 24, 1965; children: Michael, Colleen. BA, U. Minn., 1964; JD, William Mitchell Coll. Law, 1969. Bar: Minn. 1969, U.S. Dist. Ct. Minn. 1970, U.S. Supreme Ct. 1972, U.S. Ct. Appeals (8th cir.) 1973, U.S. Ct. Appeals (D.C. cir.) 1974; cert. mediator and arbitrator alternative dispute rev. bd. Minn. Supreme Ct. Ptnr. Franke & Daly, Mpls., 1969-74; prof. law Hamline U. Sch. Law, St. Paul, 1974—; arbitrator Pub. Employment Rels. Bd., St. Paul, 1974—, Am. Arbitration Assn., N.Y.C., 1980—, U.S. Fed. Mediation and Conciliation Svc., Washington, 1988—, for the states of Minn., Hawaii, Idaho, Ind., Mass., Mich., N.D., Pa., Oreg., Wisc., V.I and City of L.A.; arbitrator Bur. Mediation Svcs., St. Paul, 1978—; vis. scholar Ctr. for Dispute Resolution, Willamette U., Salem, Oreg., 1985; facilitator Minn. Internat. Health Vols., Kenya, 1985; observer Philippine Constl. Conv., Manila, 1986; participant European Arab Arbitration Congress, Bahrain, 1987; human rights investigator in the Philippines, 1989; vis. scholar U. Oslo, 1990, 91, 92; lectr. on trial skills for human rights lawyers, The Philippines, 1989; lectr. to leaders at Site 2 Cambodian Refugee Camp, Thai/Cambodian border, 1989; lectr. U. Cluj-NAPACA, Romania, 1991; vis. lectr. for developing countries Internat. Bar Assn., 1991-92; lectr. U. Tirana, Albania, 1992, London, 1993, Nat. Econs. U., Hanoi, Vietnam, 1993, 94, Danang (Vietnam) Poly. U., 1993, Ho Chi Minh Econs. U., Saigon, Vietnam, 1993, U. Hanoi Law Sch., 1994, U. Modena, Italy, 1994, Hanoi, Danang and Saigon, 1995, Phnom Penh, Cambodia, 1995. Co-author: The Law, the Student and the Catholic School, 1981; co-author, editor: The Student Lawyer: A High School Handbook of Minnesota Law, 1981, rev. edit., 1986, Strategies and Exercises in Law Related Education, 1981, International Law, 1993, The American Trial System, 1994; contbr. more than 50 articles to profl. jours. Mem. Minn. Legislature Task Force on Sexual Exploitation by Counselors and Therapists, St. Paul, 1984-85, Nat. Adv. Com. on Citizen Edn. in Law, 1982-85; bd. dirs. Scenic Am., Washington, 1989-92. Recipient Spurgeon award Mayor and Citizens of St. Paul and Indianhead Scouting, 1983; fellow U. Miss. Law Sch. Mem. ABA (contbg. editor Preview of U.S. Supreme Ct. Cases mag. 1984—), Internat. Bar Assn. (London, vis. lectr. for devel. countries 1991—), Minn. State Bar Assn., Minn. Lawyers Internat. (human rights com., rep. to Philippine Constl. Conv. 1986), St. Paul Athletic Club, Phi Alpha Delta. Office: Hamline U Sch Law 1536 Hewitt Ave Saint Paul MN 55104-1205

DALY, PATRICK F., real estate executive, architect; b. Chgo., Jan. 25, 1949; s. John F. and Margaret M. (Gleason) D.; m. Shirley J. Kimus, June 25, 1971; children: Sean P., James P. BArch with honors and distinction, U. Ill., Chgo., 1972, BA in Archtl. History with honors and distinction, 1972. Cert. arch., Ill. Prin. Patrick F. Daly Archs. & Engrs., Chgo., 1975-77; chmn. bd. Armanco, Inc., Chgo., 1977—, PFDA, Inc., Chgo., 1975—, DEI, Inc., Chgo., 1980—, Dalan Devel. Corp., Chgo., 1986—; pres. Dalan/Jupiter, Inc., Chgo., 1987—; mng. ptnr. Rising Sun Riverboat Casino and Resort, LLC, Chgo., 1995—; bd. dirs. Internat. Marine & Gaming, Inc., Empire Cruise Lines, Inc. Contbr. articles to profl. jours. chmn. Ill. Ambs., Chgo., 1990—; vice chmn. Met. Pier & Expn. Authority, Chgo., 1985—; commr. Nat. Adv. Commn. U.S. Dept. Labor, Washington, 1991-93; trustee Fund Am. Studies, 1993—, Univ. Ill. Found., 1993—, Inst. Cmty. Empowerment, 1991—; chmn. Chancellor's Corp. adv. com. U. Ill., Chgo., 1995—; adv. bd. mem. Ind. Univ. Ctr. Real Estate Studies, 1994—; exec. com. bd. dirs. UNICEF, Chgo., 1994—. Recipient Spectemur Agendo Scholarship and Leadership award, 1967, Jr. Citizen of Yr. award Chgo. Jr. C. of C., 1967, Alumni Achievement award U. Ill., 1993; I.M.B.A.C. scholar, 1967, SERRA scholar, 1967, Cardinal Stritch scholar, 1967, James scholar, 1967. Fellow Internat. Biog. Assn. (life); mem. Ind. Univ. Ctr. Real Estate Studies (adv. bd.), Arts Club, Univ. Ill. Alumni Assn. (pres.-elect 1995—), Chgo. Club, Tavern Club. Office: Daly Group 615 N Wabash Ave Chicago IL 60611

DALY, WALTER JOSEPH, physician, educator; b. Michigan City, Ind., Jan. 12, 1930; s. Walter Hayes and Nellie Martha (Stipp) D.; m. Joan Brown, June 12, 1953; children: Lois Kay, Alice Louise. AB, Ind. U., 1951, MD, 1955. Diplomate Am. Bd. Internal Medicine. Intern Ind. U., 1955-56, resident, 1956-57, 59-62, instr. medicine, 1962-63, asst. prof., 1963-65, assoc. prof., 1965-68, prof., 1968-77, John B. Hickam prof., 1977-80, J.O. Ritchey prof., 1980-95, J.O. Ritchey prof. emeritus, 1995—; chmn. dept. medicine, 1970-83, dean Sch. Medicine, 1983-95; dean emeritus Ind. U., 1995—; dir. Regenstrief Inst. Health Rsch., 1976-83. Capt. M.C., U.S. Army, 1957-59. Mem. ACP (master, gov. 1980-84), Am. Physiol. Soc., Cen. Soc. Clin. Rsch. (pres. 1980-81), Am. Soc. Clin. Investigation, Am. Clin. and Climatol. Assn., Assn. Am. Physicians. Home: 2048 Oldfields Indianapolis IN 46228 Office: Ind U Sch Medicine 1120 South Dr Indianapolis IN 46202-5135

DAMATO, RALPH JAMES, systems engineer; b. Endicott, N.Y., Mar. 6, 1958. BS in Oceanographic Engring., Fla. Inst. Tech., 1982. Mech. engr. Sparton Electronics, Jackson, Mich., 1982-85, sr. mech. engr., 1988-93; sr. mech. engr. HRB Singer, State College, Pa., 1985-86; sr. design engr. Nat. Waterlift & Controls, Kalamazoo, Mich., 1986-88; sr. sys. engr. Xycom, Inc., Saline, Mich., 1993—. With USCG Aux., Flotilla 17-05, Jackson, Mich., 1989—. Recipient 3d place award for design of free fall piston Corer Lincoln Arc Welding, 1982. Office: Xycom Inc 750 N Maple Rd Saline MI 48176-1641

DAMER, LINDA K., music educator; b. Springfield, Ill., Dec. 5, 1938; d. J. Fred and Mary Jane (Thurmond) Welsh; children: Diana, Cynthia, John. BA, William Jewell Coll., 1959; MA, Boston U., 1967; EdD, U. N.C., Greensboro, 1979. Tchr., Kearney (Mo.) Public Schs., 1959-60, Consolidated Sch. Dist. 1, Kansas City, Mo., 1960-63, Wellesley (Mass.) Pub. Schs., 1963-64, Newton (Mass.) Pub. Schs., 1966-67, Smyth County (Va.) Pub. Schs., 1969-72, Washington County (Va.) Pub. Schs., 1973-76, Burlington (N.C.) Pub. Schs., 1978-79; grad. teaching asst. U. N.C., Greensboro, 1977-78; assoc. prof. music Ind. State U., Terre Haute, Ind., 1979-88, prof. music, 1988—. U. N.C., Greensboro fellow, 1976-77. Mem. Music Educators Nat. Conf. (editorial bd. Music Educators Jour., chair editl. com. Music Educators Jour.), Ind. Music Educators Assn., Am. Orff Schulwerk Assn., University Club, Pi Kappa Lambda, Phi Delta Kappa, Sigma Alpha Iota. Home: 8370 Chapel Pines Dr Indianapolis IN 46234-2137 Office: Ind State U Dept Music Terre Haute IN 47809

DAMERY, D. RODNEY, commodities and stockbroker, farmer; b. Decatur, Ill., July 8, 1950. BA, U. Ill., 1972. Farmer, Blue Mound, Ill., 1972—; commodities and stockbroker Blunt Ellis & Lowe, Decatur, 1980-92, A.G. Edwards & Sons Inc., Decatur, 1992—. Republican. Methodist. Office: AG Edwards & Sons Inc PO Box 3580 2884 N Monroe Decatur IL 62525

DAMIN, DAVID E., technology integration company executive; b. Tell City, Ind., Jan. 29, 1947; s. Earl Louis and Emma Louise (Gilliland) D; m. Mary James Greenfield, Nov. 28, 1970. BS in Elec. Engring., Auburn U., 1973; MA in Mgmt., Webster U., 1980. Electronics technician U.S. Navy, various locations, 1965-73, advanced through grades to lt. comdr., 1973-85; founder/v.p. Ind. ops., gen. mgr. Sci. Applications Internat. Corp., San Diego, 1985—; founder, coord. Winter Harbor Ctr., N.H. Coll., 1974; mem. mfg. com. Ind. BMT Corp., Skip Barber race driver. Mem. Gov.'s task force Mfg. Excellence Modernization; bd. advisors Ind. State U. Sch. of Tech.; mem. St. Lawrence Ch., Salvation Army Assn., Habitat for Humanity. Decorated Naval Commendation medal, Meritorious Svc. medal, Joint Svc. Commendation medal; recipient U.S. Naval Inst. award, 1973; named one of Outstanding Young Men of Am., 1975. Mem. Naval Cryptologic Vets. Assn., Auburn Alumni Assn. (pres. Indy Club), St. Meinrad Sem. Alumni Assn., Am. Soc. Naval Engrs., Ind. Chamber Com., Hudson Inst. Agenda for Am. Mfg. Competitivesness Task Force, Indpls. Rotary, Sports Car Club Am. (driver), Mid-Am. Electric Vehicle Consortium, Nat. Electronics Mfg. Productivity Ctr., Hoosier Auto Racing Fans, U. S. Auto Club, 500/400 Festival Assn., Soc. Old Crows, Ind. Electrical Mfgs. Assn. (bd. dirs.), Ind. Software Assn. Democrat. Home: 10635 Cheapeake Dr N Lawrence IN 46236 Office: SAIC 6330 Castleplace Dr Indianapolis IN 46250-1902

DAMON, BILL L., manufacturing engineer; b. Knox City, Mo., May 18, 1938. A in Fluid Power Specialty, Air Force Tech. Sch., Amarillo, Tex., 1962. Project leader, sr. mfg. engr. Emerson Elec. Co., St. Louis, 1973—. Patent for Motor Component Package, Motor Mfg. Process. With USAF, 1961-65. Office: Emerson Elec Co 8011 W Florissant Ave Saint Louis MO 63136

DAMON, CHRISTOPHER ANDREW, health association executive, lawyer; b. Milw., Nov. 9, 1951; s. Andrew Christ and Katherine John (Vangalis) D.; m. Connie Henderson, July 23, 1983; 1 child, Laura Katherine. BA, Beloit Coll., 1973; MA, U. Wis., 1974, JD, 1977. Bar: Wis. 1977. Assoc. dir. for legal affairs Wis. Bankers Assn., Madison, 1977-80; legis. atty. AMA, Chgo., 1980-86, dir. dept. health care rev., 1986-90; exec. dir. Accreditation Assn. for Ambulatory Health Care, Skokie, Ill., 1990—. Trustee Oak Park (Ill.) Pub. Libr., 1993—. Mem. Chgo. Assn. Healthcare Execs. (pres.-elect 1995-96, pres. 1996—). Office: Accreditation Assn Ambulatory Health Care 9933 Lawler Ave Skokie IL 60077-3703

DAMON, CINDY IRENE, nurse; b. Rochester, Minn., Sept. 1, 1958; d. Raymond Louis and Corrine Ida (Clark) Hinze; m. Darrel James Damon, July 5, 1986; children: Deanna, Jared, Deidre. Grad., St. Mary's Sch., Rochester, 1978; BS, U. Wis., Milw., 1992. LPN, Ill.; RN, Ill. Nursing asst. Ostrander (Minn.) Care Ctr., 1975-76, Madonna Towers, Rochester, 1976-77; nurse St. Marys Hosp., Rochester, 1981-86; asst. to dispatcher Elk River Concrete Co., Shakopee, Minn., 1980-81; nurse Rochester Meth. Hosp., 1981-86, Victory Meml. Hosp., Waukegan, Ill., 1986—. Mem. Wis. State Nurses Assn. (bd. dirs. 1995—), Kenosha/Racine Nurses Assn. (bd. dirs. 1994—), Golden Key Honor Soc., Sigma Theta Tau. Methodist.

DAMSCHRODER, REX, state legislator; m. Rhonda Damschroder; children: Alex, Anthony. BA, Bowling Green State U., 1974; MBA, Tiffin U., 1994. Mem. Ho. of Reps. State of Ohio, Columbus, 1994—. Mem. Sandusky County Rep. Ctrl. Com.; mem. bd. Terra C.C. Mem. Farm Bur., Twp. Trustees Assn., Fremont (Ohio) C. of C., Kiwanis. Republican.

DANBOM, DAVID BYERS, history educator; b. Denver, Mar. 29, 1947; s. Raymond Carl and Rowene Caroline (Byers) D.; m. Karen Renee Poor, June 19, 1971; children: Elizabeth Poor, Mark Raymond. BA, Colo. State U., 1969; MA, Stanford U., 1970, PhD, 1974. Prof. history N.D. State U., Fargo, 1974—; editor N.D. Inst. for Regional Studies, Fargo, 1981-92. Author: The Resisted Revolution, 1979, The World of Hope, 1987, Our Purpose is to Serve, 1990, Born in the Country, 1995; editor: Publicly Sponsored Agricultural Research, 1988. Sec. bd. dirs. Red River Valley Heritage Soc., Moorhead, Minn., 1987-92; mem. Fargo Hist. Preservation Commn., 1990—. Named N.D. Prof. of Yr., Coun. Advancement and Support of Edn., 1990, Disting. Prof., Fargo C. of C., 1990; recipient Faculty Achievement award Burlington No., 1990. Mem. Agrl. History Soc. (bd. dirs. 1990-94, pres. 1990-91), Orgn. Am. Historians (membership com. 1990-95), Soc. Historians of the Gilded Age and Progressive Period. Office: ND State U Dept History Fargo ND 58105

D'ANCA, JOHN ARTHUR, psychotherapist, educator; b. Chgo., Apr. 19, 1950; s. John Joseph and Josephine Rose (Bartolotta) D.; m. Carol Amendola; 1 son, Matthew John. BA, DePaul U., 1972; MA, Governors

State U., 1975; C.A.S., No. Ill. U., 1978, EdD, 1982, PsyD Chgo. Sch. Profl. Psychology, 1996. Mem. counseling faculty Fenwick High Sch., Oak Park, Ill., 1973-75; instr. psychology, counselor Triton Coll., River Grove, Ill., 1975-78; assoc. dir. Ball Found., Glen Ellyn, Ill., 1978-79; prof. student devel. Oakton Coll., Des Plaines, Ill., 1979—; intern in psychology svc. Edward Hines Jr. VA Hosp., Hines, Ill., 1990—; cons. Molex Internat., 1986; lectr. in field; cons. Ill. Dept. Edn., Am. Med. Technologists, Goodwill Industries Internat. Bd. dirs. Chgo. Bd. of Mental Health, Northwest, 1974-75; mem. Oakton Coll. Crusade of Mercy Appeal, 1982. Sears grantee, 1986—. Mem. NEA, APA, Internat. Soc. Traumatic Stress Studies, Ill. Edn. Assn., Am. Soc. Clin. Hypnosis, Soc. Clin. and Experimental Hypnosis, Joint Civic Commn. Italian Americans, Midwest Psychol. Assn., N.Am. Assn. Adlerian Psychology, Ill. Guidance and Personnel Assn., Ill. Coll. Personnel Assn., Phi Delta Kappa. Contbr. articles to profl. jours. Home: 520 E Butterfield Rd Elmhurst IL 60126-4638 Office: 1600 E Golf Rd Des Plaines IL 60016-1234

DANDO, WILLIAM ARTHUR, geography and geology educator; b. Newell, Pa., June 13, 1934; s. Carl Frederick and Myrtle Jane (Foster) D.; m. Caroline Zaporowski, July 19, 1958; children: Christina Elizabeth, Lara Margaret, William Arthur II. BS, Calif. U. Pa., 1959; MA, U. Minn., 1962, PhD, 1969. Vis. instr. U. Manitoba, Winnepeg, Can., 1961; instr. U. Md., College Park, 1965-66, lectr., 1967-69, asst. prof., 1970-75; assoc. prof. U. N.D., Grand Forks, 1975-80; prof. U. N.D., 1980-89, chair geography, 1977-82; prof. Ind. State U., Terre Haute, 1989—, chair geography, geology and anthropology, 1989—; acting chair anthropology Ind. State U., 1993-95; prin. investigator NIH Multiple Sclerosis Project, 1988-91, NSF Phys. Geography Inst., 1992—, Dept. Edn. Project GEO, 1992—, Geo-Technology-GIS Project, 1995—. Author: Introduction to Maryland, 1970, The Geography of Famine, 1980, A Reference Guide to World Hunger, 1991, Russia and the Independent Nations of the Former USSR: Geofacts and Maps, 1995; editor: Innovations in Land Use Management, 1977, World Hunger and Famine, 1995. Pres. Univ. Luth. Ch., Grand Forks, 1979, Christus Rex Luth. Campus Ministry, 1979-87, N.D. Luth. Campus Ministry Com. 1986-88; chairperson fin. com. Trinity Luth. Ch., Terre Haute, 1992—, v.p., 1996-97. Recipient Disting. Tchg. Achievement award Nat. Coun. for Geographic Edn., 1986, Burlington Northern Found. Faculty Achievement award, 1988, Illustrious Alumni Calif. State U. award, 1976. Mem. Assn. Am. Geography (chair Mid. Atlantic divsn. 1973-74, chair Great Plains-Rocky Mt. divsn. 1978-80, chair West Lakes divsn. 1994-95), Assn. N.D. Geographers (pres. 1976-80), Geography Educators Network Ind. (dir. devel. 1991—), Sigma Xi (U. N.D. chpt. pres. 1986-87, Ind. State U. chpt. v.p. 1991-92, pres. 1992-93, Individual Excellence in Scientific Rsch. award 1983). Lutheran. Home: 7785 S Carlisle Rd Terre Haute IN 47802-9343 Office: Ind State U Dept Geography Geology Anthropology Terre Haute IN 47809

D'ANDREA, DEBORAH DAWN, nursing consultant, critical care nurse; b. Chgo.. ADN, Prairie State Coll., Chgo. Heights, Ill., 1970; BA in psychology, Lewis U., 1980, BSN, 1984. RN, Ill., Fla. Staff nurse post anesthesia recovery-surg. ICU Cook County Hosp., Chgo., 1970-72; staff nurse surg. ICU U. Chgo. Hosp. and Clinic, 1972-75, dir. utilization review dept., 1975-79; cons. profl. review orgn. utilization review Chgo. Found. Med. Care, 1979-81; staff nurse psychiat. adolescent Chgo. Lake Shore Hosp., 1981-82; staff nurse psychiat. adolescent and adult Charter Barclay Hosp., 1982-84; utilization review quality assurance nurse Grant Hosp., Chgo., 1982-84, educator staff devel., 1983-84; staff nurse trauma ctr. Cook County Hosp., 1984-86; staff nurse emergency trauma Louis A. Weiss Hosp., Chgo., 1986-88; utilization review coord. Charter Barclay Hosp., 1986-90; prin. Deborah D. D'Andrea & Assoc., 1989—; legal nurse cons. Jeffrey M. Goldberg & Assoc., Chgo., 1991; owner Med. Legal Cons. Assoc., Chgo., 1992—. Recipient Internat. Woman of Yr., 1992-93. Mem. AALNC, ATLA, Am. Assn. Legal Nurse Cons. (bd. dirs. 1994), Nat. Nurses Bus. Assn., Emergency Nurses Assn. Home and Office: Med Legal Consulting Assoc 716 W Briar Pl Ste 3 Chicago IL 60657-4515

DANE, WILMER RAY, fire chief; b. Jackson, Mich., Jan. 5, 1953; s. Russell H. and Cecile M. (Cox) D. A of Applied Arts and Scis., Jackson C.C., 1978; BS, U. New Haven, West Haven, Conn., 1985; grad., Nat. Fire Acad., Emmitsburg, Md., 1988; MPA, Eastern Mich. U., 1994. Firefighter, emergency med. technician Summit Twp. Fire Dept., Jackson, 1972-80; coord. La. State U. Fire Fighter Tng. Program, Baton Rouge, 1980-81; chief adminstrv. fire marshal, enforvement div. La. State Fire Marshal's Office, Baton Rouge, 1981-86; fire chief Three Rivers (Mich.) Fire Dept. and Ambulance Co., 1986-88, Scio Twp. Fire Dept., Ann Arbor, Mich., 1988—; mem. subcom. Gov.'s Fire Safety Task Force, Lansing, Mich., 1991; voting mem. Joint Coun. Fire Svc. Orgns., Lansing, 1990-91. Mich. rep. Congl. Fire Svc. Caucus and Inst., Washington, 1989—. Named Citizen of Yr., Denham Springs (La.) Kiwanis Club, 1985. Mem. Nat. Fire Protection Assn., Internat. Fire Chiefs Assn., Washtenaw Area Mut. Aid Soc. (sec.-treas. 1989-94), Mich. Fire Svc. Instrs. Assn., Soc. Nat. Fire Acad. Instrs., Soc. Exec. Fire Officers (charter mem., at-large dir. 1988-91), Mich. Fire Chiefs Assn. Office: Scio Twp Fire Dept 1055 N Zeeb Rd Ann Arbor MI 48103-1472

DANFORTH, JOHN CLAGGETT, senator, lawyer, clergyman; b. St. Louis, Sept. 5, 1936; s. Donald and Dorothy (Claggett) D.; m. Sally B. Dobson, Sept. 7, 1957; children: Eleanor, Mary, Dorothy, Johanna, Thomas. BA with honors, Princeton U., 1958; BD, Yale U., 1963, LLB, 1963, MA (hon.); LHD (hon.), Lindenwood Coll., 1970, Ind. Central U.; LLD (hon.), Drury Coll., 1970, Maryville Coll., Rockhurst Coll., Westminster Coll., Culver-Stockton Coll., St. Louis U.; DD (hon.), Lewis and Clark Coll.; HHD (hon.), William Jewell Coll.; STD (hon.), Southwest Bapt. Coll.; hon. deg., Va. Theol. Sem., 1990, Holy Cross Coll., 1992, Harris Stowe Coll., 1992, Wash. U., 1995. Bar: N.Y. 1964, Mo. 1966, D.C. 1994. With firm Davis Polk Wardwell Sunderland & Kiendl, N.Y.C., 1964-66; ptnr. Bryan, Cave, McPheeters and McRoberts (now Bryan Cave), St. Louis, 1966-68, 95—; atty. gen. State of Mo., 1969-76; U.S. senator from Mo., 1976-94; ordained deacon Episc. Ch., 1963, priest, 1964; asst. rector N.Y.C., 1963-66; assoc. rector Clayton, Mo., 1966-68, Grace Ch., Jefferson City, 1969; hon. assoc. St. Alban's Ch., Washington, 1977-94; chmn. Mo. Law Enforcement Assistance Council, 1973-74; asst. chaplain Meml. Sloan-Kettering Cancer Ctr. of N.Y.C.; asst. rector Ch. of Epiphany in N.Y.C., Ch. of St. Michael and St. George, Clayton, Mo.; hon. canon Christ Ch. Cathedral, St. Louis. Republican nominee U.S. Senate, 1970; assoc. rector Ch. of the Holy Communion, Univ. City, Mo., 1995—. Recipient Disting. Svc. award St. Louis Jr. C. of C., 1969, Disting. Missourian and Brotherhood awards NCCJ, Presdl. World Without Hunger award, 1985, Disting. Lectr. award Avila Coll., Chancellors medal UMKC, 1995; named Outstanding Young Man Mo. Jr. C. of C., 1968, St. Louis Man of Yr., 1994; Alumni fellow Yale U., 1973-79. Mem. Mo. Acad. Squires, Alpha Sigma Nu (hon.). Republican. Office: Bryan Cave LLP Ste 3600 1 Met Sq 211 N Broadway Saint Louis MO 63102

DANFORTH, WILLIAM HENRY, retired academic administrator, physician; b. St. Louis, Apr. 10, 1926; s. Donald and Dorothy (Claggett) D.; m. Elizabeth Anne Gray, Sept. 1, 1950; children: Cynthia Danforth Prather, David Gray, Maebelle Danforth Reed. A.B., Princeton U., 1947; M.D., Harvard U., 1951. Intern Barnes Hosp., St. Louis, 1951-52; resident Barnes Hosp., 1954-57; now mem. staff; asst. prof. medicine Washington U., St. Louis, 1960-65, asso. prof., 1965-67, prof., 1967-95; vice chancellor for med. affairs Washington U., 1965-71, chancellor, 1971-95; chmn., bd. trustees Washington U., St. Louis, 1995—; pres. Washington U., St. Louis, 1995—; pres. Washington U. Med. Sch. and Assoc. Hosps., 1965-71; co-chair Barnes-Jewish Hosp., 1995—; program coord. Bi-State Regional Med. Program, 1967-68; dir. Ralston Purina Co., McDonnell Douglas Corp., Ralcorp Holdings, BJC Health Svcs. Trustee, chmn. bd. Danforth Found.; trustee Am. Youth Found., 1963—, Princeton U., 1970-74; pres. St. Louis Christmas Carols Assn., 1958-74, chmn., 1975—; co-chair Barnes/Jewish Hosp., 1996—; bd. dirs. BJC Health Systems, 1996—. Named Man of Yr. St. Louis Globe-Democrat, 1978. Fellow AAAS, Am. Acad. Arts and Scis.; mem. Inst. Medicine. Home: 10 Glenview Rd Saint Louis MO 63124-1308 Office: Washington U West Campus Campus Box 1044 7425 Forsyth Blvd Ste 262 Saint Louis MO 63105-2198

DANGEL, STEVEN R., financial executive; b. L.A., July 31, 1946. BS, Ferris State U., 1968; MSB, Cen. Mich. U., 1972. Asst. v.p. Paine Webber, Muskegon, Mich., 1973-88, Merrill Lynch, Muskegon, 1988—. Pres. Muskegon Civic Theater, 1990—; pres.-elect Youth Soccer Leagues, 1994—. Mem. Muskegon Rotary Club (pres. 1986—), Country Club.

D'ANGELO, RICHARD ARTHUR, medical systems company executive; b. Steubenville, Ohio, Mar. 4, 1959; s. Edward and Esther D'Angelo; m. Barbara E. Miller, Sept. 13, 1986; children: Eric, Melanie. BA in Chemistry, Wittenberg U., Springfield, Ohio, 1981; MS in Organic Chemistry, Ohio U., 1986. Mgr. tech./mkt. GE Electromaterials, Coshocton, Ohio, 1985-90; product mgr. GE Super Abrasives, Columbus, Ohio, 1990-92; pres. Genasystems, Columbus, 1993-95; mgr. mktg. and bus. devel. GE Med. Systems, Milw., 1995—. Office: GE Med Systems PO Box 414 NB 911 Milwaukee WI 53201

DANIEL, ALAN, internist, cardiologist; b. N.Y.C., July 7, 1942. BA cum laude, Amherst Coll., 1963; MD, Harvard U., 1967. Diplomate Am. Bd. Internal Medicine, Diplomate Am. Bd. Med. Examiners. Internship Phila. Gen. Hosp., 1967-69, residency, 1971-72; instr. U. Rochester (N.Y.) Med. Sch., 1972-75, asst. prof. medicine, 1975-77; clin. asst. prof. medicine U. Wis. Med. Ctr., Milw., 1977-86, clin. assoc. prof. medicine, 1986—; clin. asst. prof. medicine Med. Coll. Wis., Milw., 1979—; chief div. cardiology St. Michael's Hosp., Milw., 1988-92; chmn. cardiology edn. com. Columbia Hosp., Milw., 1988-92. Mem. bd. govs. Wis. Heart Assn., 1985—. Grantee Genessee Valley Heart Assn., 1974-75; NIH fellow, 1974-76. Fellow ACP, Am. Coll. Cardiology (councilor Wis. chpt. 1993-95), Am. Heart Assn., Coun. Clin. Cardiology; mem. Phi Beta Kappa. Home: 1443 E Goodrich Ln Fox Point WI 53217-2950 Office: 1575 N River Center Dr Milwaukee WI 53212

DANIEL, LLOYD, state legislator. Mem. Mo. Ho. of Reps., Jefferson City. Democrat.

DANIEL, MICHAEL EDWIN, insurance agency executive; b. Indpls., Sept. 8, 1948; s. Richard E. and Margret A. (Phillips) D.; m. Jeanne L. Nobbe, Sept. 29, 1979; children: Whitney Marie, Lindsay Michelle, Tyler Edwin. BA, Principia Coll., Elsah, Ill., 1970; German lang. degree, Dept. Def., Monterey, Calif., 1971. Sales mgr. Mr. Ins. of Ind., Indpls., 1973-77; pres. Ind. Ins. Svcs., Inc., Greenwood, 1977—, Ins. Svc., Inc., 5, 1990—; v.p. Brown County Water Utility, Helmsburg, Ind., 1982-85. Leader Johnson County 4-H, 1993—. With U.S. Army, 1970-73. Mem. Ind. Ins. Agts. Assn., Profl. Ins. Agt. Assn. (treas. Indpls. region 1990), Ind. Trail Riders Assn., BMW Motorcycle Owners Am. Christian Scientist. Office: Ind Ins Svcs Ste P 3115 Meridian Parke Dr Greenwood IN 46142-9414

DANIELEWICZ, CLAUDIA ANNE, quality assurance engineer; b. Niagara Falls, N.Y., Aug. 8, 1964; d. Chester Albert and Florence Carolyn (Pasek) D. AS in Engring., Erie C.C., 1984; BS in Engring., Rochester Inst. Tech., 1987, MS in Engring., 1993. Cert. quality assurance/mech./process engr. Farm equipment oper. Danielewicz Dairy Farms, Sanborn, N.Y., 1984-93; intern mech. engring. Sohio Electro Mineral, Niagara Falls, N.Y., 1984-85, Vets. Hosp., Batavia, N.Y., 1985-86; sales assoc. Gold Circle, Niagara Falls, 1987-88; asst. planner Cambridge Instruments, Buffalo, N.Y., 1988; engr. mfr., quality Par Foam Products, Buffalo, N.Y., 1988-92; engr. quality assurance Avm (Arvin/Gabirel), Marion, S.C., 1992; quality assurance engr. GenCorp Automotive, Batesville, Ark., 1993-94; process/quality assurance engr. Courtaulds Thatcher Tubes, Woodstock, Ill., 1994-95; quality assurance engr. Statis. Resource Quality Network GM Corp., Pontiac, Mich., 1995—. Mem. ASME, Am. Soc. Quality, Nat. Soc. Profl. Engrs. Home: 4286 Saunders Settlement Rd Sanborn NY 14132-9411 Office: General Motors Corp Truck Grp Code 483-510-3F5 2000 Centerpoint Pkwy Pontiac MI 48341-3147

DANIELS, DAN LEE, aeronautical engineer; b. Mpls., Apr. 18, 1957. Supr. engring. Watkins Aircraft Supply, Glenwood, Minn., 1987—. Office: Watkins Aircraft Supply PO Box 100 Glenwood MN 56334-0100

DANIELS, DAVID WILDER, conductor, music educator; b. Penn Yan, N.Y., Dec. 20, 1933; s. Carroll Cronk and Ursula (Wilder) D.; m. Jimmie Sue Evans, Aug. 11, 1956; children: Michael, Abigail, Andrew. AB, Oberlin Coll., 1955; MA, Boston U., 1956; MFA, U. Iowa, 1963, PhD, 1963. Instr. music Culver-Stockton Coll., Canton, Mo., 1956-58; music librarian Berkshire Athenaeum, Pittsfield, Mass., 1958-61; asst. prof. U. Redlands, Calif., 1963-64, Knox Coll., Galesburg, Ill., 1964-69; asst. prof. Oakland U., Rochester, Mich., 1969-71, assoc. prof., 1971-85, prof., 1985—, chmn. dept., 1982-88; music dir. Warren Symphony, Mich., 1974—, Pontiac-Oakland Symphony, Pontiac, Mich., 1977—; pres. Mich. Orchestra Assn., 1981-83. Author: Orchestral Music, 1972, rev. edit., 1982; editor: Avanti newsletter, 1982-86. Mem. Am. Symphony Orchestra League, AAUP, Coll. Music Soc., Conductors Guild (bd. dirs. 1986-94, sec. 1989-91, v.p. 1991-94). Home: 1215 Gettysburg Ct Rochester Hls MI 48306-3819 Office: Oakland U Dept Music Theatre & Dance Rochester MI 48309-4401 also: Warren Symphony Orch 4504 E 9 Mile Rd Warren MI 48091-2548

DANIELS, DORAL LEE, education educator; b. Clinton, Ind., Nov. 2, 1925; s. Oather and Orva Rosetta (Stinson) D.; m. Frances Elizabeth Hyslop, Nov. 8, 1945; children: Mark, Kirk, Brett. BS, Ind. State, 1949; MA, Ball State U., 1954. Tchr. Parksley (Va.) High Sch., Accomack County Sch. Corp., 1946-47; 6th grade tchr. Cicero (Ind.) Twp. Sch. Corp., 1950-51, Tipton (Ind.) Sch. Corp., 1951-55; mid. sch. tchr. Kokomo (Ind.)-Center Twp. Sch. Corp., 1955-92; assoc. instr. Ind.'s Tech. Coll., Kokomo, 1992—. Sec. Assn. for Childhood Edn., 1955-78, Kokomo Tchr.'s Assn., 1950-88, Nat. Edn. Assn., 1950-88; pres. Schoolmasters, Kokomo, 1955-90, Ind. State Tchrs. Assn., 1950-88; commr. Boy Scouts Am., 1955-87. With USN, 1943-46, ETO, PTO. Fellow Kokomo Wood Carvers Assn. (sec.-treas. 1980); mem. Ea. Woodland Woodcarvers Convers Ind., VFW, Nat. L.S.J.T. Assn., Landing Ship Tank Assn. Ind. (plank owner 1994), Ind. Dist. Past Lt. Govs. Assn., Elks, Kiwanis (pres. 1971, lt. gov. 1993-94, Col. J.L. McCulloch award 1994). Methodist. Home: 1800 Executive Dr Kokomo IN 46902-3015 Office: Kokomo Center Twp Sch Corp PO Box 2188 Kokomo IN 46904-2188

DANIELS, DORIA LYNN, manufacturing executive; b. Kent, Ohio, Apr. 22, 1951; d. Eli and Henrietta (Johnson) D. BBA, Kent State U., 1973; postgrad., Old Dominion U., 1975-76, Akron U., 1984-86. Cert. S.A.P. Ptnr. Acad. Mgmt. trainee Cardinal Fed. Savs., Cleve., 1973-74; acctg. mgr. People Savs. and Loan, Hampton, Va., 1974-77; ins. agt. John Hancock Mut. Life Ins., Hampton, 1977-79; prodn. planner Little Tikes Mfg., Hudson, Ohio, 1979—;, 1979-95; project mgr. Transaction Info. Sys., N.Y.C., 1995—; co-founder, pres. Thomas Anderson Devel. Corp., 1986; bus. cons. Lyondell Petrochem. Houston, 1994; SAP/R3 cons. mgr. Union Carbide Co., Danbury, Cann., 1995. Mem. Kent (Ohio) Bd. Edn., 1987, Shade Tree Commn. Kent City Coun., 1987; Rep. candidate ward 3 coun. seat, Kent, 1969; co-founder, chmn. Thomas Anderson Devel. Corp., Kent, 1986—; bd. advisers Portage County ARC, 1991—, chair fin. com., treas.; del. to Russia, Citizen Ambassador Program, 1993. City of Kent scholar, 1969; recipient Gov.'s Recognition award Gov. of Ohio, 1986, commendation from Ohio Ho. of Reps., 1987, Ohio House of Reps. State Commendation for record service to the Kent community, 1987, Kent Edn. Assn. awards, 1988. Mem. NAACP (life, polit. advisor), Am. Prodn. Inventory Control Soc. (publicity dir. 1993), NAFE, Internat. Platform Assn., Nat. Coun. Negro Women. Baptist. Office: Transaction Info Sys 111 Boradway 10th Fl New York NY 10006

DANIELS, FLETCHER, state legislator; b. Muskogee, Okla., Sept. 8, 1919; m. Sybil Daniels, 1946. Former postal employee; state rep. dist. 41 Mo. Ho. of Reps. Democrat. Home: 3537 Askew Ave Kansas City MO 64128-2650*

DANIELS, KURT R., speech and language pathologist; b. Chgo., Oct. 22, 1954; s. Donald R. and Phyllis D. (Lenz) D.; m. Renee Perry, July 5, 1980. BS, Ea. Ill. U., 1976, MS, 1977. Cert. clin. competence speech/lang. pathology; lic. speech/lang. pathologist, nursing home adminstr; tchr's. cert. spl. K-12th grades. Hearing and speech specialist Shapiro Devel. Ctr., Kankakee, Ill.; dysphagia specialist W.A. Howe Devel. Ctr., Tinley Pk., Ill.; cons. in field; presenter in field of dyspharia and developmental disabilities. Recipient Editor's Choice award Nat. Libr. Poetry, 1994, 95. Mem. Am. Speech, Lang. and Hearing Assn., Ill. Network for Augmentative and Alternative Comm., Internat. Soc. Poets.

DANIELS, LEE ALBERT, state legislator; b. Lansing, Mich., Apr. 15, 1942; s. Albert Lee and Evelyn (Bousfield) D.; m. Pamela Mesha; children: Laurie Lynn, Rachael Lee, Julie, Thomas, Christina. BA, U. Iowa, 1965; JD, John Marshall Law Sch., 1967. Rep. precinct committeeman, 1965-74; mem. bd. auditors York Twp., Ill., 1966-73; vice chmn. York Twp. Rep. Comty. Orgn., 1973-74; former minority spokesman judiciary com. Ill. Ho. of Reps.; spl. asst. atty. gen., 1973-75; Ill. state rep. 46th Dist., 1975—, majority whip, 1981-82, minority leader, 1983-94; speaker of the House, 1995—; full ptnr. Katten, Muchin & Zavis, 1984-91; ptnr. Bell, Boyd & Lloyd, Chgo., 1992—. Trustee Elmhurst Hosp. Recipient Everett McKinley Dirksen award, 1995; named one of Outstanding Legislators in Country, Nat. Rep. Legis. Assn., 1991, Legislator of Yr., Ill. Hosp. Assn., 1986, DuPage Mayors and Mgrs. Conf., 1995. Mem. ABA, Ill. Bar Assn., DuPage County Bar Assn., Shriners, Masons, Moose. Home: 611 N York Rd Elmhurst IL 60126 Office: State House Rm 316 Springfield IL 62706*

DANIELS, MARK LEE, secondary education educator; b. Terre Haute, Ind., Nov. 13, 1948; s. Doral Lee and Frances Elizabeth (Hyslop) D.; m. Ofelia Cisneros, June 14, 1986; children: Christopher James, Tyler Lee. BS, Purdue U., 1971, M, 1986. Automotive tchr. Twin Lakes High Sch., Monticello, Ind., 1971; tchr. of indsl. arts Kekionga Jr. High Sch., Fort Wayne, Ind., 1974-78; tchr. of power South Side High Sch., Fort Wayne, 1978-79; tchr. of electricity, graphic arts, and reading Northrop High Sch., Fort Wayne, 1979-89; tchr. of indsl. arts, video coms., and social studies Blackhawk Mid. Sch., Fort Wayne, 1989-93, tech. coord., gifted and talented coord., 1993—; dir. Fort Wayne Pk. Dept., 1974-78. With U.S. Army, 1971-74. Mem. NEA, Ind. Indsl. Tech. Edn. Assn. (Outstanding State Chmn. 1993), Tech. Educator Ind. (Meritorious Tchr. 1993), Fort Wayne Edn. Assn., Masons, Shriners, Disabled Am. Vets. Methodist. Home: 2934 Wilderness Rd Fort Wayne IN 46845-1699 Office: Blackhawk Mid Sch 7200 E State Blvd Fort Wayne IN 46815-6478

DANIELS, MICHAEL RAYMOND, accountant; b. Chgo., Jan. 20, 1952; s. Raymond F. and Betty L. (Smiley) D.; m. Linda Carol Merrell, Aug. 2, 1975; 1 child, Donna Carol. BBA, Loyola U., Chgo., 1972. Cost supr. Smoler Bros., Inc., Chgo., 1973-78; labor acct. Ekco Housewares, Chgo., 1978-81; plant acct. Intercraft Ind., Chgo., 1981-83; cost supr. Wilson Jones Co., Chgo., 1983-85; sr. cost acct. Everco Ind., Skokie, Ill., 1985-89, Switchcraft Inc., Chgo., 1989—. Editor-in-chief Wicker Pack Times, 1965. Sec. Ch. of Christ, Chgo., 1972-75, bible instr., 1973—, dir., 1987—, min., 1975—, elder, 1995; bronze leader DAV, Chgo., 1995. Mem. Am. Legion award, 1965. Mem. Lane Tech. Alumni Assn. Republican.

DANNER, PATSY ANN (MRS. C. M. MEYER), congresswoman; b. Louisville, Ky., Jan. 13, 1934; d. Henry J. and Catherine M. (Shaheen) Berrer; m. Lavon Danner, Feb. 12, 1951 (div.); children: Stephen, Stephanie, Shane, Shavonne.; m. C.M. Meyer, Dec. 30, 1982. Student, Hannibal-LaGrange Coll., 1952; B.A. in Polit. Sci. cum laude, N.E. Mo. State U., 1972. Dist. asst. to Congressman Jerry Litton, Kansas City, Mo., 1973-76; fed. co-chmn. Ozarks Regional Commn., Washington, 1977-81; mem. Mo. State Senate, 1983-1992, 103rd Congress from 6th Mo. dist., 1993—; mem. internat. rels. com., transp. and infrastructure com. Roman Catholic. Home: 6 Nantucket Ct Smithville MO 64089-9605 Office: US House of Representatives Office of House Members 1323 Longworth Washington DC 20515*

DANNESSA, KAREN LYNN, musician, professor; b. Youngstown, Ohio, Mar. 5, 1962; d. Samuel Thomas and Loretta Ellen (Clouser) D.; m. Henry H. Grabb, May 30, 1992. MusB, Youngstown State U., 1985; MusM, Mich. State U., E. Lansing, 1987; Mus D, Fla. State U., Tallahassee, 1994. Tchg. asst. Fla. State U., Tallahassee, Fla., 1987-89; assoc. prof. music Pitts. State U., Pitts., Kans., 1989—; invited performer U. Okla. Clarinet Symposium, 1993, Internat. Clarinet Assn. Conv., 1995, Mont.-Idaho Clarinet Festival, 1995. Author: Annotated Bibliography of Contemporary Trios, 1994; contbr. articles to profl. jours. Mem. Nat. Fed. of Music Clubs, Coll. Music Soc., Midwest Clarinet Soc., Internat. Clarinet Assn., Pi Kappa Lambda (v.p. 1994—). Democrat. Office: Pittsburg St Univ 1701 S Broadway Pittsburg KS 66762

DANNLEY, RALPH LAWRENCE, retired chemistry educator; b. Chgo., June 25, 1914; s. William Harry and Marie Caroline (Soderstrom) D.; m. Hannah Margaret Dannley, Dec. 1950; children: Lynn Marie, William Franklin, Melinda Lee. BS in Chem. Engring., U. Denver, 1936; PhD, U. Chgo., 1943. Instr. U. Chgo., Ill., 1942-43; dir. drying oil rsch. Devoe & Raynolds Co., Inc., Louisville, 1943-45; from instr. to prof. Case Western Res. U., Cleve., 1945-81, prof. emeritus, 1981; cons. in field. Contbr. articles to profl. jours.; patentee in field. Rsch. grantee. Mem. Am. Chem. Soc., Phi Lambda Upsilon. Home: 3691 Runnymede Blvd Cleveland Heights OH 44121

D'ANNUNZIO, JOHN ANTHONY, construction executive, technology consultant; b. Detroit, Nov. 13, 1964; s. August Benny and Catherine Rose (Cicillini) D'A.; m. Gina D'Annunzio, Oct. 21, 1989; children: Nikolis Giavonni, Alec Michael. BBA, Detroit Coll. Bus., 1987; postgrad., Lawrence Tech. U., 1991. Ops. mgr. Mich. Roofing Co., Detroit, 1987-90; cons. Detroit Roofing Inspection Svc., Warren, Mich., 1990-91; pres. Paragon Roofing Tech., Troy, Mich., 1991—; tech. assessor, counsel U.S.-China roofing tech. transfer Ministry Bldg. Materials, People's Republic China. Contbr. articles to profl. publs. Mem. ASTM (mem. various coms. and subcoms.), ASCE, AIA, Constrn. Specifications Inst., Roof Cons. Inst. Republican. Roman Catholic. Office: Paragon Roofing Tech 1700 W Big Beaver Rd Ste 360 Troy MI 48084-3530

DANOFF, I. MICHAEL, art center director, writer, educator; b. Chgo., Oct. 22, 1940; s. Maurice and Matilda (Price) D.; children: Sharon, Brian. B.A., U. Mich., 1962; M.A., U. N.C., 1964; Ph.D., Syracuse U., 1970. Asst. prof. Dickinson Coll., Carlisle, Pa., 1970-73; curator U. Tex., Austin, 1973-74; chief curator Milw. Art Mus., 1974-80, assoc. dir., 1977-80; dir. Akron Art Mus., Ohio, 1980-84, Mus. Contemporary Art, Chgo., 1984-88, San Jose Mus. Art, 1988-91, Des Moines Art Ctr., 1991—; acquisitions dir. HHK Found., Milw., 1977-82; panelist Nat. Endowment for Arts, Washington, Wis. Arts Bd., Madison, Ohio Mus. Assn., Columbus, 1980, Calif. Arts Coun., 1989; lectr. San Jose (Calif.) State U., 1989. Curator art exhbns. including Peter Halley: Paintings 1989-92, Andy Warhol: Print Portfolios, Jeff Koons, 1988, Robert Mangold, 1984, Emergence and Progression, 1979; co-organizer art exhbns. including Image in American Painting and Sculpture, 1981, Gerhard Richter, 1988, Compassion and Protest: Recent Social and Political Art From the Eli Broad Family Found. Collection; art juror Milw. Conf. Ctr., 1979, Akron State Office Bldg., 1983. Active Milw. Forum, 1976-80. Syracuse U. fellow, 1968-70; NEA Mus. Prof. fellow, 1973. Mem. Intermus. Conservation (trustee 1982-84), Assn. Art Mus. Dirs., Coll. Art Assn.

DANTZMAN, GREGORY PETER, design engineer; b. Cudahay, Wis., Jan. 27, 1965; s. Thomas George and Charlotte Ruth (Ropicky) D.; m. Deanna Rose Nitkowski, Apr. 9, 1988; children: Rebecca, Zachary. BSEE, Milw. Sch. Engring., 1987, MSEM, 1993. Lic. engr.-in-tng., Wis. Product svc. engr. drives divsn. GE, Erie, Pa., 1987-89; control design engr., systems design engr. drives systems divsn. Allen-Bradley, Mequon, Wis., 1989-93; elec. engr. CH2M Hill, Milw., 1993-94; project engr. Bucyrus-Erie Co. South, Milw., 1995—. Mem. IEEE, Engring. Mgmt. Soc. Roman Catholic. Home: N60w23874 Butternut Ln Sussex WI 53089-3746

DARANY, GEORGE THOMAS, advertising and transportation company executive; b. Detroit, Mar. 12, 1956; s. Theodore George and Ethel Elizabeth (Joseph) D. BA in Econs., U. Mich., 1978. Real Estate lic., 1994. Cons. Dearborn (Mich.) C. of C., 1978-80, City of Dearborn, 1979-82; mgr. The Musicland Group, Dearborn, 1982-86; pres., owner Classic Trolley Co., Dearborn, 1986—. Bd. dirs. Karmanos Cancer Inst., Dearborn, 1990—, Dearborn City Beautiful Commn., 1990—; elected precinct del., 1994. Mem. Dearborn C. of C. (bd. dirs. 1993—), Met. Detroit Conv. Bur. Roman Catholic.

DARBY, L.E. JACK, public services and properties administrator; b. Stickney, W.Va., Nov. 29, 1945; s. William Thomas and Erma Ethel (Adkins) D.; m. Bertha Mae, Mar. 31, 1972; children: Jacqueline Susanne, James Thomas. BBA, Baldwin Wallace Coll., 1983; MPA, Cleve. State U., 1994. Pipefitter L.T.V. Steel Corp., Cleve., 1969-88; dir. pub. svcs. and properties City of North Royalton, Ohio, 1988—; bd. dirs. No. Ohio Svc. Dirs. Assn., 1992-94. Coun. rep. City of North Royalton, 1985-88. Served with USN, 1963-66. Mem. Am. Pub. Works Assn. (No. Ohio chpt. Exec. Pub. Adminstr. of Yr. 1994). Home: 12500 Pinebrook Dr North Royalton OH 44133 Office: City of North Royalton 11545 Royalton Rd North Royalton OH 44133

DARIN, FRANK VICTOR JOHN, management consultant; b. Detroit, Feb. 16, 1930; s. Frank Peter and Marie D.; m. Barbara Nelson Lynn, July 13, 1957; children: Lynn A., Pamela L. BA in econs., Yale U., 1952; JD, U. Va., 1957. Bar: Mich. 1958. Labor rels. mgr. Ford Motor Co., Dearborn, Mich., 1957-64; dir. indsl. rels. office Ford Motor Co., Valencia, Venezuela, 1965-68; corp. pers. rels. mgr. Ford Motor Co., Dearborn, 1969-82, bus. ops. dir., 1983-87, v.p. Ford Fund, dir. corp. affairs staff, 1988-95; cons. sr. exec. mgmt. Darin Corp. Cons., Inc., Dearborn, Mich., 1995—. Bd. dirs. Henry Ford Health Sys., Dearborn, 1991—, New Detroit, Inc., 1991-95, Detroit Econ. Growth, 1993—, Spoleto Festival U.S.A., Charleston, S.C., 1990-93, Van Patrick Found., Detroit, 1990—; CEO rep. bd. Detroit Renaissance, Inc., 1991-95; bus. advisor Coun. Interlochen (Mich.) Acad. Arts, 1989-95. 1st lt. U.S. Army, 1952-54, Korea. Mem. Greater Detroit C. of C. (bd. dirs. 1991-95, vice chmn. 1994-95), Dearborn Country Club, Renaissance Club (Detroit). Episcopalian. Office: Darin Corp Cons Inc Ste 200 429 N Beech Daly Rd Dearborn Heights MI 48127

DARLING, ALBERTA STATKUS, state legislator, marketing executive, former art museum executive; b. Hammond, Ind., Apr. 28, 1944; d. Albert William and Helen Anne (Vaicunas) Statkus; m. William Anthony Darling, Aug. 12, 1967; children—Elizabeth Suzanne, William Anthony. BS, U. Wis., 1967. English tchr. Nathan Hale High Sch., West Allis, Wis., 1967-69, Castle Rock High Sch., West Allis, Colo., 1969-71; community vol. worker Castle Rock High Sch., West Allis, Milw., 1971—; mem. Wis. State Assembly, 1990-92, Wis. State Senate, 1992—; cons. orgn. devel., Milw., 1982—; dir. mktg. and communications Milw. Art Mus., 1981-88; exec. dir. mktg. architectural firm, 1988-90; State Rep. Wis., 1990—, mem. urban edn. com., children and human svcs. com., tourism com., homelessness com., teeenage pregnancy com., vice chmn. gov.'s housing policy commn., assembly coms. Pres. Community Action Seminar for Women, 1979-80; a founder Goals for Greater Milw. 2000, 1980-84; co-chair Action 2000, 1984-86; co-chmn. Icebreaker Am. Winterfestival; chmn. Community Action Seminar for Women, 1988; bd. dirs., exec. com. United Way, Milw., 1982—, chair project 1985, 1984-85, chmn. policy com. 1988; founder Today's Girls/Tomorrow's Women, Milw., 1982—; pres. Jr. League Milw., 1980-82, Planned Parenthood Milw., 1982-84, Future Milw., 1983-85; vice chmn. State of Wis. Strategic Planning Council, 1988—, chmn. small bus./entrepreneur com.; mem. Greater Milw. Com.'s Mktg. Task Force, 1987-88; chmn. United Way Policy Com., 1987-88; participant Bus. Ptnrs. White House Conf., 1987; mem. summerfest adv. com. on Winter Festivals, 1989; founder Women's Fund of Milw. Found; actuve Juvenile Justice Leadership Com. Recipient Vol. Action award Milw. Civic Alliance, 1984, Community Service award United Way, 1984, Leader of Future award Milw. Mag., 1988, Nat. Assn. Community Leadership Orgn. award, 1986, Today's Girls/Tomorrow's Women Leadership award, 1987, Future Milw. Community Leadership award, 1988, Friend of Edn. Leadership award Head Start, 1994, William Steiger Humanitarian award, 1994. Mem. Greater Milw. Com., TEMPO Profl. Women, Am. Mktg. Assn. (Marketer of Yr. 1984), Pub. Relations Soc. Am., Ctr. for Pub. Representation (state bd. 1988), ARC (bd. dirs., exec. fin. coms. 1987—), Women's Fund (steering com. 1988), Internat. Assn. Bus. Communicators, Greater Milw. Com. Republican. Home: 1325 W Dean Rd Milwaukee WI 53217-2537 Office: State Capitol PO Box 7882 Madison WI 53707-7882

DARLING, LAWRENCE DEAN, engineering computing executive; b. Springfield, Ill., Dec. 20, 1936; s. John Darling and Virginia (Siltman) Vice; divorced; 1 child, Tena Louise. BSME, Northwestern U., 1960. Registered profl. engr., Ill. With Allis-Chalmers, Springfield, 1956-74; product engr. Fiat-Allis, Springfield, 1974-83; engring. computing mgr. automotive appliance controls ops. Eaton Corp., Carol Stream, Ill., 1984-89, mgr. engring. computing., 1989—. Named Outstanding Dir., Springfield Jaycees, 1964; recipient Student Achievement award Wall St. Jour., 1960. Mem. Am. Soc. Mech. Engrs. Baptist. Office: Eaton Corp AACO 191 E North Ave Carol Stream IL 60188-2019

DARLING, SHARON SANDLING, museum director; b. Mitchell, S.D., Feb. 28, 1943; d. Joseph Davis and Barbara M. (Fixmer) Sandling; m. Mikell C. Darling, Apr. 15, 1972. BA, N.C. State U., 1965; MAT, Duke U., 1967. Curator Chgo. Hist. Soc., 1972-86; dir. Motorola Mus., Motorola, Inc., Schaumburg, Ill., 1986—. Author: Chicago Metalsmiths, 1977, Chicago Ceramics and Glass, 1981, Chicago Furniture, 1984 (C.F. Montgomery award 1985), Teco: Art Pottery of the Prairie School, 1989. Mem. ASID (hon.). Home: 4n227 Burr Rd Saint Charles IL 60175-6104 Office: Motorola Inc 1297 E Algonquin Rd Schaumburg IL 60196-4041

DARLINGTON, JUDITH MABEL, clinical social worker, Christian counselor; b. Deckerville, Mich., Nov. 29, 1942; d. Wallace and Mabel Lillian (Rich) Cole; m. Clare Robert Darlington, Dec. 15, 1962; children: Debra Lynn, Dawn Elizabeth. BA, Mich. State U., 1962; MSW, U. Mich., 1983. Tchr. Limestone (Maine) Presque Isle Schs., 1963-64; substitute tchr. Crestwood Sch. Dist., Dearborn Heights, Mich., 1971-74; monitor, tchr. Renewing Life Ministries, Annandale, Va., 1976-82; clin. social worker Westland (Mich.) Counseling Svc., 1983-84; family therapist, counselor Family Svc. of Detroit and Wayne County, Wyandotte, Mich., 1984-86; specialist substance abuse Plymouth (Mich.) Family Svc., 1986-87; exec. dir. Christian Conciliation Svc. of S.E. Mich., Detroit, 1987-90; pvt. practice clin. social worker/family therapist Brighton, Mich., 1990—; speaker in field. Mem. NASW (cert.), Am. Assn. Christian Counselors (charter), Christian Women's Club (chmn. Livonia chpt. 1981—), Inst. for Christian Conciliation, Kappa Delta Pi. Presbyterian. Home: 7911 Debora Dr Brighton MI 48116-9462 Office: 8137 W Grand River Ave Ste C Brighton MI 48116

DARLINGTON, OSCAR GILPIN, historian, educator; b. Downingtown, Pa., Feb. 21, 1909; s. Oscar Gilpin and Emily Jane (Bareford) D.; m. Miriam Howe Wilson, Dec. 31, 1938; children: Helen Spear, Dawn, Mahlon Spear, Phoebe, Lynette, Gerbert, Eunice, Emily-Jane, Bernice. BA, Pa. State Coll., 1932, MA, 1933; PhD, U. Pa., 1938; student, Harvard U., summer 1931, Temple U., summer 1932. Asst. in ancient and mediaeval history U. Pa., 1934-38; instr. history Hofstra Coll., N.Y.U., 1938, asst. prof., 1939, assoc. prof., 1940, prof., 1941-50, chmn. dept. history, 1942-50, dir. summer session, 1949; prof. history, polit. sci., head dept., dir. area social scis. Champlain Coll., SUNY, 1950-53; acad. dean InterAm. U. P.R., 1953-55; dean Coll. Liberal Arts, Ohio No. U., Ada, 1955-66, European-Am. Study Center, Basel, Switzerland, 1967-68; prof. European history Ohio No. U., 1968—, dir. summer session, 1956-59; faculty adviser Student Christian Assn., Champlain Coll.; bd. dirs. Regional Council for Internat. Edn., 1964-72. Author: The Travels of Odo Rigaud, Archbishop of Rouen (1248-1275), 1940, (with others) Contemporary Europe: A Symposium, 1941, Causes and Consequences of World War II, 1948, Glimpses of Nassau County History, 1949, (newspaper column) History Back of the News, 1942-45, articles revs. hist. jours.; editor, trustee: Nassau County Hist. Jour, 1944-50. Nat. trustee Children's Internat. Summer Villages; mem. Ada Sch. Bd., 1976-83, Ohio State Cabinet; pres. Trumbull County Ohio Gideon Camp, 1989-92, zone leader, 1991-94, coord. Area C, 1995—. Mem. NEA, L.I. Hist. Soc., Mediaeval Acad. Am., Am. Hist. Assn., Am. Soc. Ch. History, Am. Acad. Social and Polit. Sci., Soc. Preservation and Encouragement Barbershop Quartet Singing in Am. (Lima Beane chpt.), U.S. Power Squadron, Gideon Internat., Torch Club (Lima, pres. 1961), Youngstown Torch Club, Phi Alpha Theta, Pi Gamma Mu, Phi Kappa Psi, Sigma Delta Pi. Republican. Presbyterian (elder). Home: 503 Robbins Ave Niles OH 44446-2411

DARNELL, GERALD THOMAS, automotive industry executive; b. Detroit, Apr. 21, 1942; s. William C. and Nadine L. (Evans) D.; m. Janet M. Harns, Feb. 14, 1981; 1 child, Rebecca F. AB, Wayne State U., 1971; BA, Faith Coll., Morgantown, Ky., 1973; MA, Pacific Western U., 1987; Grad. Exec. Program, Northwestern U., 1991. Various supr. and adminstrv. positions Chevrolet Motor Div., Detroit, 1968-84; mgr. quality inst. GM, Troy, Mich., 1984-88; mgr. corp. quality and reliability GM, Detroit, 1988, dir. corp. quality and reliability, 1989-92; v.p. Automotive Industries divsn. Lear Corp., Rochester Hills, Mich., 1993—; instr. Wayne State U., Detroit, 1976-84; cons. Darnell Assocs., Clarkston, Mich., 1979-84; mem. exec. adv. bd. continuing edn. Engring. and Mgmt. Inst. of GMI Inst., 1989-90; mem. bd. examiners Malcoln Baldrige Nat. Quality Award, 1991-93; chmn. bd. examiners Mich. Quality Leadership Award, 1994; trustee Mich. Quality Coun., 1994-95. Bd. dirs. YMCA Camping Svcs. Detroit Area. Mem. Assn. for Quality and Participation, Inst. Cert. Profl. Mgrs. (cert.), Am. Soc. for Quality Control (sr. mem.), Orgn. Devel. Inst. (cert.), Nat. Mgmt. Assn. (edit. advisor Quality Observer mag.). Home: 8753 Sharon Dr White Lake MI 48386-3475 Office: Lear Corp Automotive Industries Divsn 2998 Waterview Dr Rochester Hills MI 48309-3484

DAROFF, WILLIAM C., political consultant, public policy analyst; b. Miami Beach, Fla., Nov. 30, 1968; s. Robert Barry and Jane Linda (Abrahams) D. BA summa cum laude, Case Western Reserve U., 1995, postgrad., 1995—. Lead advanceman Kemp for Pres., Washington, 1986-88, Bush-Quayle '88, Washington, 1988; spl. asst. U.S. Dept. Energy, Washington, 1989-90; campaign mgr. Brachman for State Treas., Columbus, Ohio, 1990; spl. asst. to gov. State of Ohio, Columbus, 1990-92; dep. dir. Ohio Dept. Liquor Control, Columbus, 1992-93; pres. W. Daroff Consultants, Shaker Heights, Ohio, 1994—. Sports editor East Side News, 1984-86; mem. editl. bd. Pub. Pers. Mgmt., 1991-92. Rep. nominee for Ohio State Rep., 11th Dist., 1994; mem. exec. com. Cuyahoga County Rep. Orgn., Cleve., 1987-88, 91—, mem. ctrl. com., 1987-88, 94—; alt. del. Rep. Nat. Conv., 1996. Named to Honorable Order of Ky. Cols., 1992; recipient Meritorious Svc. award 4th Ward Rep. Club, 1989, 91, 93. Fellow Soc. for Am. Baseball Rsch., mem. Cleve. Ripon Club, Columbus Athletic Club, Capital Club, Monday Thing Club (membership director 1989--). Republican. Jewish. Office: W Daroff Consultants 14260 Larchmere Blvd Shaker Heights OH 44120

DART, STEPHEN HOWARD, lawyer, insurance company executive; b. Lansing, Mich., Jan. 17, 1953; s. John Harvey and Margaret Lorraine (Welch) D.; m. Abby Baker, 1986; children: Jackson Carroll, Joseph Baker, Will Stephen, Lily Meredith. BA, Harvard U., 1975; MA, Oxford U., 1977; JD, Harvard U., 1980. Asst. prosecuting atty. Ingham County Prosecutor's Office, Lansing, Mich., 1980-81; dir. devel. Calif. Trial Lawyer's Assn., L.A., 1986-87; ptnr. MacLean, Seaman, Laing & Guilford, East Lansing, Mich., 1987-89; chief oper. officer Mich. Physicians Mutual Liability Co., East Lansing, Mich., 1989—; pres., CEO Superior Employers Plan, 1993.

DART, THOMAS J., state legislator; b. May 22, 1962. BA, Providence Coll., 1984; JD, Loyola U., 1987. Former asst. state atty. Ill.; Ill. state rep. Dist. 28; fl. leader, minority spokesman Rev. Com.; mem. Judiciary I Com. and Legis. Com. on Juvenile Justice; lectr. St. Xavier Coll. Recipient Disting. Svc. award Com. for Honest Govts., Disting. Lectr. award DeBoer Com. for Children's Rights, Exceptional Legis. award Office of Pub. Guardians. Address: 2032-J Stratton Bldg Springfield IL 62706*

DASCHLE, THOMAS ANDREW, senator; b. Aberdeen, S.D., Dec. 9, 1947; m. Linda Hall Daschle; children: Kelly, Nathan, Lindsay. B.A., S.D. State U., 1969. Fin. investment rep.; chief legis. aide, field coordinator Sen. James Abourzek, 1973-77; mem. 96th-97th Congresses from 1st S.D. Dist., 98th-99th Congresses at large, 1983-87; U.S. senator from S.D., 1987—, senate minority leader 104th Congress, 1995; Mem. Agrl. Nutrition & Forestry Com., Sen. Dem. Sterring & Coor. Com., Sen. Dem. Tech & Comm. Com., Chmn. Sen. Dem. Conf. Com., Chmn, Sen. Dem. Policy Com. Served to 1st lt. USAF, 1969-72. Recipient Nat. Commdr.'s award Disabled Am. Vets., 1980; named Outstanding Young Man of Yr., U.S. Jaycees, 1981. Democrat. Roman Catholic. Office: US Senate 509 Hart Senate Bldg Washington DC 20510*

DASTYCH, DIANE SUE, critical care nurse; b. Aurora, Ill., Oct. 2, 1948; d. Leo William and Virginia Mae (Knudson) Johnson; m. Theodore E. Dastych. Diploma in nursing, Silver Cross Hosp., Joliet, Ill., 1968; BSN, Lewis U., 1981; MS in Health Svc. Adminstrn., Coll. St. Francis, 1994. Staff nurse Silver Cross Hosp., Joliet, 1968-69; staff nurse, supr. Morris (Ill.) Hosp., 1969-72; staff nurse critical care St. Joseph Med. Ctr., Joliet, 1973-77, charge nurse 3-11 Med. ICU, 1977-82, asst. nurse mgr. med. intensive care unit/coronary intensive care unit, 1982-91, nurse mgr. Cardiovascular-ICU/cardiovascular-stepdown unit, 1991-94; patient care mgr. med.-surg. unit, 1994—; substitute clin. nursing instr. Joliet Jr. Coll.; chairperson Ill. Nat. Nurses Week St. Joseph Med. Ctr., 1990, 91; CPR instr. Mem. AMSN (Greater Joliet chpt. treas.-elect 1992-93). Office: St Joseph Med Ctr 333 Madison St Joliet IL 60435-8200

DATCHER, JEWELL ANTOINETTE, health insurance company consultant; b. Detroit, Aug. 21, 1948; d. Mack A. Jr. and Julia Maria (Oliver) McCartha; m. William Jerome Datcher, Sept. 7, 1968; 1 child, Antonia Latrece. BRE cum laude, William Tyndale Coll., Farmington Hills, Mich., 1984; BA in Bus. Adminstrn., Marygrove Coll., Detroit, 1992; MEd in Instnl. Tech., Wayne State U., 1995; postgrad., Word of Faith Internat. Christian Ctr., 1995—. Dir. Christian edn. Detroit Inst. for Bibl. Studies, 1988-89; customer svc. rep. II Blue Cross-Blue Shield Mich., Detroit, 1966-85, sr. trainer, 1985-87, supr. tng. and quality, 1987-89, tech. writer, 1989-90, lead performance analyst, 1990-91, interim supr., team leader, 1992-93, team leader, instnl. developer, 1991-94; project coord. benefit delivery svcs., 1994—; cons., del. Afro-Am. Mennonite Assn., Detroit, 1979; rep. missions tour to Ecuador, S.Am., William Tyndale Coll., 1980. Mem. TMBC Pastor's Chorus. Grosse Pointe Women's Aux. scholar, William Tyndale Coll., 1983, Marygrove scholar Marygrove Coll., 1985-92. Mem. ASTD, NAACP, Nat. Mgmt. Assn., Marygrove Coll. Alumni Assn., William Tyndale Coll. Alumni Assn.

DATTA, RATHIN, chemical engineer; b. Calcutta, India, Nov. 11, 1948; came to U.S., 1970; s. Amulya N. and Karuna Datta; m. Alicia Reyes, Sept. 14, 1974. BTech, Indian Inst. Tech., Kanpur, 1970; PhD, Princeton U., 1974. Engring. assoc. Merck & Co., Rahway, N.J., 1974-78; sr. engr. Exxon Rsch. & Engring. Co., Linden, N.J., 1978-82; rsch. scientist, sect. leader Corn Products/CPC Internat., Summit, Ill., 1982-87; v.p. rsch. Mich. Biotech. Inst., Lansing, Mich., 1987-92; tech. cons. Chgo., 1992—; advisor waste mgmt. and bioengring. Argonne Nat. Lab., 1992—; chief tech. officer NTEC EdSep Inc., Mt. Prospect, Ill., 1995—; mem. rsch. com. Nat. Corn Growners Assn., St. Louis, 1991-93. Mem. editl. bd. Jour. Indsl. Microbiology, Linden, N.J., 1985-90; contbr. articles to profl. jours., chpts. to books; patentee in field. Grantee U.S. Dept. Energy, USDA, others. Mem. AAAS, AIChE (Ernest E. Thiele award 1996), Am. Chem. Soc., Soc. Indsl. Microbiology, Water Pollution Control Fedn., Inst. Food Technologists, Sierra Club. Home and Office: 442 W Melrose St # 3 Chicago IL 60657-3834

DATTA, SYAMAL KUMAR, medical educator, researcher; b. Cuttack, Orissa, India, Sept. 21, 1943; came to U.S., 1967; s. Jitendra Nath and Kalyani (Hazra) D.; m. Tapati Chaudhury, 1976; 1 child, Ronjon. BS, U. Calcutta, India, 1960, MB, BS, 1966. Diplomate Am. Bd. Internal Medicine. Resident in medicine Cook County Hosp., Chgo., 1969-71, fellow in hematology, 1971-72; rsch. assoc. Tufts U./New Eng. Med. Ctr., Boston, 1972-74, instr. in medicine, 1974-76, asst. prof. medicine, 1976-79, assoc. prof. medicine, 1979-85, prof. medicine, 1985-93; Solovy Arthritis-Rsch. Soc. prof., prof. medicine Northwestern U. Med. Sch., Chgo., 1993—; sr. faculty mem. grad. program immunology Sackler Sch., Boston, 1975-93; mem. study sects. NIH, Bethesda, 1987—. Assoc. editor Jour. Immunology, 1984—. Leukemia Soc. Am. fellow, 1972-74; Am. Cancer Soc. scholar, 1975-78. Mem. AAAS, Am. Assn. Immunologists, N.Y. Acad. Scis., Am. Coll. Rheumatology. Office: Northwestern Univ Med Sch Arthritis Div Ward 3-315 303 E Chicago Ave Chicago IL 60611-3008

DAUME, DAPHNE MARIE, editor; b. Grand Rapids, Mich., June 17, 1924; d. Selden Bennett and Elizabeth Marie (Hixson) D. BS, Northwestern U., 1945; MA, Columbia U., 1948. Copy editor Ency. Britannica, Chgo., 1948-59, asst. editor, 1959-64, assoc. editor, 1964-73, editor, Book of Yr., 1973-93; ret., 1993. Bd. dirs. LWV, Chgo., 1970; co-pres. Chgo. LWV, 1992-93, pres., 1993-96. Mem. Women in Communications, Inc., Coun. on Fgn. Rels. (Chgo.). Democrat. Episcopalian. Home: 1545 W Chase Ave Apt 208 Chicago IL 60626-2110 Office: LWV 332 S Michigan Ave Ste 1142 Chicago IL 60604-4305

DAUNER, MARVIN K., state legislator; b. Dec. 4, 1927; m. Shirley Ann; 5 children. County commr., 1974-86; state rep. Minn. Ho. Reps., Dist. 9B, 1986—; vice chmn. health & human svc., mem. agrl. housing, taxes & transp. & transit coms., Minn. Ho. Reps. Named Outstanding Young Farmer, 1960. Mem. Farm Bur. Fedn. Home: RR 2 Box 21 Hawley MN 56549-9506*

D'AURORA, JAMES JOSEPH, psychologist, consultant; b. Canton, Ohio, Feb. 10, 1949; s. James Joseph Sr. and Arsilia (Lombardi) D'A.; m. Denise Marie Linkenhoker, Dec. 28, 1974; children: Andrew David, Elizabeth Clare. BA, U. Notre Dame, 1971; MEd, Kent State U., 1974; PhD, U. Minn., 1984. Lic. psychologist, Minn., marriage and family therapist, Minn. Pre-major adv. Coll. of Liberal Arts U. Minn., Mpls., 1974-75; intern Bach Inst., Mpls., 1975-77, staff psychologist, 1977-79; psychologist Loring Family Clinic, Mpls., 1979-81; pvt. practice Mpls., 1981-86; cons. psychologist Solstice: A Ctr. for Psychotherapy and Learning, St. Paul, 1986-89; pvt. practice St. Paul, 1989—; cons. in field, 1975—; researcher Family Renewal Ctr., Mpls., 1982-85, Golden Valley Health Ctr. Psychology Subsect., 1988-92. Lectr., lay homilist preacher Christ the King Ch., mem. parish pastoral coun., 1991-96; interim sch. bd. Christ the King-St. Thomas the Apostle Sch., 1992, bd. rs., 1992—, mem. governance com., 1992. Mem. APA, Minn. Psychol. Assn. (chairperson ins. com. 1988-94), Notre Dame Club Minn. (bd. dirs. 1986-91, sec. 1987-88, v.p. 1988-89, pres. 1989-90). Mem. Democratic Farm Labor Party. Roman Catholic. Home: 5536 Merritt Cir Edina MN 55436-2026 Office: 91 Snelling Ave N Ste 200 Saint Paul MN 55104-6753

DAVANZO, JOHN CHARLES, emergency medical services educator; b. Dearborn, Mich., Mar. 8, 1968; s. Antenore Charles and Mary Ann C. (Slowinski) D.; m. Kimberly Mitchell, Oct. 21, 1995. BSc in Emergency Med. Svcs. Mgmt., Madonna U., 1992; AAS in Nursing, Regents Coll., Albany, N.Y., 1995. Cert. paramedic, N.Y., Mich. EMT, paramedic Taylor Ambulance Svc., Detroit, 1986-90; emergency med. svcs. instr.-contingent Madonna U., Livonia, Mich., 1987-91; corps tng. officer St. John Ambulance Brigade, Windsor, Ont., 1988-90; parmamedic Richmond (Mich.) Lenox Emergency Med. Svc., 1989-94; ALS dir. United Ambulance Svc., Taylor, Mich., 1990-93; CEO Life Star Assocs. Inc., Detroit, 1990—; emergency med. svcs. instr. trainer Kellogg C.C., Battle Creek, Mich., 1993—; adj. faculty Henry Ford C.C., Dearborn, 1987-93; cons. Premier Ambulance, Oak Park, Mich., 1992-94, Southeastern Mich. EMS Acad., Troy, 1994—; cons., dive master Blue Water Dive Rescue, Southfield, Mich., 1994—; photographer Am. Image Press, Lewisville, N.C., 1994—. Author: Emergency Protocols, 1994; editor: KCC Medical First Responder Instructor Manual, 1993. High adventure cluster chmn. Detroit (Mich.) Area Coun., 1984-86; asst. scout master Troop 1130, Dearborn, 1986-92. Mem. Nat. Assn. EMT's, Mich. Assn. EMT's, Soc. Mich. EMT Instr. Coords., Profl. Assn. Dive Instrs., Internat. Freelance Photographers Orgn., Nat. Eagle Scouts Assn. Roman Catholic. Home: 125 Pine Knoll Dr Battle Creek MI 49017 Office: Kellogg CC 450 North Ave Battle Creek MI 49017

DAVENPORT, CARL A., marketing professional; b. Greenville, Ky., Mar. 18, 1954; s. William S. and Edna Marie (Cardwell) D.; m. Susan C. Ayres, Mar. 17, 1993; children: Mark Anthony, Brian James, Eric John, Abigail Susan, Scott Thomas. BBA, So. Calif. U. V.p. mktg. Universal Products, Chgo., 1974-78; mktg. mgr. Gas City Ltd., Frankfurt, Ill., 1978-86; pres. Davenport Fin. Svcs., Willow Springs, Ill., 1992—; cons., bd. trustees Oil, Chem. and Atomic Workers, Argo, Ill., 1992-93; mktg. cons. Cupid's Corner Book Sales, Chgo., 1992-94. Contbr. articles to newspapers. Active Willow Springs Residential Club, 1992—. Mem. Argo-Summit Masons, Shriners, Star Craft Club of Ill. (1st v.p. 1990-91), Medinal Shrine Temple, Medinah World Famous Clowns (clown), Lions Club of Summit, United Computer Specialists of Am., Ill. Newspaper Assn. of Writers. Home: 109 N Nolton Willow Springs IL 60480

DAVENPORT, JOHN B(RIAN), librarian, archivist. BA magna cum laude, Macalester Coll., 1973; MA in Librarianship, U. Denver, 1974; MA in History, U. Minn., 1986; PhD in History, U. Minn, 1994. Asst. curator spl. collections U. N.D., Grand Forks, 1974-76; head of spl. collections U. St. Thomas, St. Paul, 1977—, acting dir. librs., 1989-91. Mem. editl. bd. Eire Ireland, 1989-96, LOGOS: A Jour. Cath. Thought and Culture, 1995—, New Hibernia Rev., 1996—; contbr. articles to profl. jours. Mem. Archdiocesan Commn. on Alcoholism, St. Paul, 1986-87. Mem. Am. Conf. Irish Studies, Manuscript Soc., Midwest Archives Conf., Twin Cities Archives Roundtable (sec. 1992-94), Luxembourg Heritage Soc. Am. (bd. dirs. 1994—). Office: Univ Saint Thomas 2115 Summit Ave Saint Paul MN 55105-1048

DAVENPORT, MARY ERICKSON, physical therapist, swim coach; b. Mason City, Iowa, Feb. 29, 1960; d. John Arthur Jr. and Marguerite Francis (Enbusk) E.; m. Rustin Thomas Davenport, Aug. 8, 1987; children: Kathleen Hope, Rex Rustin. BS in Phys. Edn., Iowa State U., 1982; cert. in phys. therapy, U. Iowa, 1984, MA in Phys. Therapy, 1990. Lic. phys. therapist, Iowa. Staff phys. therapist St. Joseph Mercy Hosp., Mason City, 1984-86, work ctr. clin. mgr., 1988-90; staff phys. therapist St. Luke's Hosp., Cedar Rapids, Iowa, 1986-87; rsch. asst. U. Iowa, Iowa City, 1987-88; asst. H.S. swim coach Mason City Sch. Dist., 1993-94; part-time phys. therapist North Iowa Mercy Health Ctr., 1990-94; phys. therapist asst. program leader North Iowa Area C.C., Mason City, 1994—. Sec. Am. Heart Assn., Mason City, 1989-93; pres., mem. St. Maria's Cir.-St. Joseph's Parish, Mason City, 1992—. Mem. Am. Phys. Therapy Assn., Iowa Phys. Therapy Assn. (bd. dirs. 1982—). Roman Catholic. Office: North Iowa Area CC 500 College Dr Mason City IA 50401

DAVENPORT, NYRA J., social work administrator; b. Dayton, Ohio, Dec. 6, 1951; d. Robert Lee Sr. and Virginia Ruth (Middleton) Cartwright; m. Edgar Davenport, Jr.; children: Jarrod, Justin. AA, Sinclair Coll., 1973; BA, Wright State U., 1975, MS, 1991. Lic. social worker, Ohio. Clk. Wright Patterson AFB, Dayton, 1969; sec. Luth. Ch. Am., Dayton, 1971-74; rehab. specialist City of Dayton, 1976-78; employment specialist Ohio Bur. Employment, Dayton, 1978-79; social worker Dept. Human Svcs., Dayton, 1979-82, Sr. Ctr. of Greater Dayton, 1982; case mgmt. specialist State of Ohio, Columbus, 1982-85; asst. dir., case mgmt. svcs. Montgomery County Bd., Dayton, 1985—; owner, cons. NJO Cons., Dayton, 1988—. Evangelist Christ Temple Apostolic Ch., Dayton, 1987-93; mem. Gov. of Ohio Task Force, 1990; vol. Housing Now!, Dayton and Columbus, 1986, 89, 90, Issue One-Housing, Dayton, 1990, Dayton Mohawks Basketball Program, 1988—; pres. Bethesda Temple, 1993—; founder Davenport Ministries, 1993. Recipient Doer award Dayton Spl. Edn. Ctr., 1986, 90. Mem. AACD, Assn. Adult Devel./Aging, Minority Health and Social Welfare Coalition, Black Family Coalition of Dayton, Ministerial Alliance. Democrat. Home: PO Box 26066 Trotwood OH 45426-0066 Office: 8114 N Main St Dayton OH 45415-1702

DAVENPORT, THOMAS HERBERT, small business owner; b. Sandusky Ohio, Mar. 15, 1933; s. Orme and Elva Mae (Bragg) D.; m. Annetta Henman, June 22, 1963; children: Deborah Ann, Mark Thomas, Brenda Kay. Grad., Coyne Electronic Sch., 1954-55. Lic. FCC gen. radio telephone. Clk. Nickel Plate R.R., Bellevue, Ohio, 1951-52, 53-54; electronic technician various firms, Sandusky, 1955-56; prin. Bellevue Radio and TV, 1955—. Numerous inventions in field. Cpl. U.S. Army, 1952-53, 2d. lt USAF Aux., 1980-84. Mem. Am. Legion. Republican. Home: 111 Seneca Dr Bellevue OH 44811-1635 Office: Bellevue Radio & TV 109 W Center St Bellevue OH 44811-1351

DAVID, BARBARA MARIE, medical, surgical nurse; b. Wisconsin Rapids, Wis., Mar. 3, 1935; d. Stanley Spencer and Olga Agatha (Bissig) Stark; m. Russell Paul David, Jan. 19, 1957; children: Dennis James, John Paul. Diploma, St. Joseph's Hosp. Sch. Nursing, Marshfield, Wis., 1956. Cert. med./surg. nurse, clin. nurse 3. Asst. to dir. nursing rsch. St. Joseph's Hosp., head nurse, ICU, staff nurse. Mem. ANA, Wis. Nurses Assn. (treas. dist. 18), Acad. Med.-Surg. Nurses, Nat. League Nurses. Home: 2007 S Maple Ave Marshfield WI 54449-4957

DAVID, HERBERT ARON, statistics educator; b. Berlin, Dec. 19, 1925; came to U.S., 1957, naturalized, 1964; s. Max and Betty (Goldmann) D.; m. Vera Reiss, May 13, 1950 (dec.); 1 child, Alexander John; m. Ruth Finch, Dec. 1, 1992. B.Sc., Sydney U.(Australia), 1947; Ph.D., Univ. Coll. London U., 1953. Rsch. officer Commonwealth Sci. and Indsl. Rsch. Orgn., Sydney, 1953-55; sr. lectr. dept. stats. U. Melbourne, Australia, 1955-57; prof. stats. Va. Poly. Inst., 1957-64; prof. U. N.C., Chapel Hill, 1964-72; dir. stat. lab., head dept. stats. Iowa State U., Ames, 1972-84, prof. stats., 1972-96, Disting. prof. liberal arts and scis., 1980-96, prof. emeritus, 1996—. Author: The Method of Paired Comparisons, 1963, 2d edit., 1988, Order Statistics, 1970, 2d edit., 1981; co-editor: Advances in Biometry, 1996. Recipient J. Shelton Horsley award Va. Acad. Scis., 1963, Wilks award in Army Rsch., 1983. Fellow AAAS, Am. Statis. Assn., Inst. Math. Stats.; mem. Biometric Soc. (editor Biometrics 1967-72, pres. 1982-83), Internat. Statis. Inst. Jewish. Home: 460 Westwood Dr Ames IA 50014-3570

DAVID, MURPHY SAMUEL, physician; b. Tiruchirapalli, Madras, India, Dec. 31, 1931; came to U.S., 1962; naturalized, 1981; s. M.D. and Kamalam (Tucker) D.; m. Indra Mary Thomas, May 30, 1960; 1 child, Rena Marie Vantine. BS, Madras Christian Coll., 1955; MB and Surgery, U. Madras at Vellore, 1960; MPA, Syracuse U., 1974. Diplomate Am. Bd. Family Practice, Am. Bd. Surgery. Resident in surgery St. Joseph's Hosp., Syracuse, N.Y., 1963-67, physician, coord. surg. edn., 1970-75; resident, research fellow Queen's U., Kingston, Ontario, Canada, 1968-69; physician on staff Detroit Indsl. Clinic, Southfield, Mich., 1975—. Mem. Tamil Sangam of Mich. Republican. Episcopalian. Home: 1330 Fieldway Dr Bloomfield Hills MI 48302-0830

DAVID, RONALD E., mechanical engineer, consultant; b. Detroit, Aug. 3, 1940. AS, Electronics Inst., 1964, Wayne State U., 1967. Design room leader Engring. Svcs., Southfield, Mich., 1964-72; chief mech. engr. Sesco Inc., Detroit, 1972—. Vol. local church; coach Little League Baseball. Mem. SME. Home: 6310 Meyer Ave Brighton MI 48116-2024

DAVIDS, CARY NATHAN, physicist, researcher; b. Edmonton, Alberta, Can., Sept. 28, 1940; came to U.S., 1962; s. David Edward and Ruth (Shragge) D.; m. Judith Weller, June 12, 1967; children: Barry S., Martin D. BSc in Physics with honors, U. Alberta, Edmonton, 1961; MSc, U. Alberta, 1962; PhD in Nuclear Physics, Calif. Inst. Tech., 1967. Postdoctoral Calif. Inst. Tech., Pasadena, 1967; rsch. assoc. Mich. State U., East Lansing, 1967-69; asst. prof. U. Tex., Austin, 1969-74; physicist Argonne (Ill.) Nat. Lab., 1974-95, sr. physicist, 1996—; sec., steering com. Nat. Radioactive Beam Facility, 1990—; guest assoc. physicist Brookhaven Nat. Lab., 1973; vis. scholar Enrico Fermi Inst., U. Chgo., 1974-76, sr. rsch. assoc., 1976-79; sr. vis. fellow dept. physics U. Manchester, 1977; prof. physics U. Jyvaskyla, Finland, 1986; adj. prof. physics Vanderbilt U., 1994—. Contbr. over 50 articles to profl. jours. Alfred P. Sloan Found. fellow U. Tex., 1973-76. Fellow Am. Phys. Soc. Office: Argonne Nat Lab 9700 Cass Ave Lemont IL 60439-4803

DAVIDS, GREGORY M., state legislator; b. Aug. 28, 1958; m. Bonnie; 3 children. BS, Winona State U., 1979; postgrad., Mankato State U. Mayor City of Preston (Minn.), 1987-91; state rep. Minn. Ho. Reps., Dist. 31B, 1991—; mem. fin. instr. & ins., health & human svc., human svc. fin. divsn. & housing coms., Minn. Ho. Reps. Mem. Lions. Home: PO Box 32 Preston MN 55965-0032*

DAVIDSON, BONNIE JEAN, gymnastics educator, sports management consultant; b. Rockford, Ill., Nov. 19, 1941; d. Edward V. and Pauline Mae (Dubbs) Welliver; m. Glenn Duane Davidson, June 4, 1960 (dec. Oct. 1993); children: Lori Davidson Aamodt, Wendy Davidson Seerup. Student, Rockford Coll., 1965, Rock Valley Coll., Rockford, 1969-77. Founder, owner, dir. Gymnastic Acad. Rockford, 1977-95; pres., dir., owner Springbrook, Ltd., swim and tennis club, Rockford, 1986-95; rep. trampoline and tumbling com. AAU, 1989—; coach nat. and world champion athletes; mgr., judge, head del. U.S.A. gynmastics teams, 1980—; speaker, lectr., clinician in field.; mem. organizing coms. world championships, also others, 1982—. Contbr. World Book Ency. Bd. dirs. U.S. Olympic Com., 1995—, U.S.A. Gymnastics, 1991—; instr. ARC. Named one of Most Interesting People, Rockford mag., 1987; recipient YWCA Janet Lynn Sports award, 1996. Mem. Internat. Fedn. Trampoline and Tumbling (internat. judge, mem. tech. com. 1986—, del. to congress 1976-86), Internat. Fedn. Sports Acrobats (internat. judge), U.S.A. Trampoline and Tumbling Assn. (nat. tumbling chairperson 1980-88, advisor 1988—, Coach of Yr. award 1980, Outstanding Contbn. to the Sport award 1987, 96, Master of Sport award 1989), U.S. Sports Acrobatics Fedn. (v.p. 1984—), Nat. Judges Assn. (exec. dir.). Republican.

DAVIDSON, CLIFFORD OSCAR, humanities educator; b. Fairbault, Minn., Oct. 29, 1932; s. Ole Frederick and Maude (Simons) D.; m. Audrey Ekdahl, July 4, 1954. BS, St. Cloud State U., 1954; MA, Wayne State U., 1961, PhD, 1966. H.S. tchr. Howard Lake (Minn.) Pub. Schs., 1955-56, Atwater (Minn.) Pub. Schs., 1958-59; grad. asst. Wayne State U., Detroit, 1959-61, instr., 1961-65; asst. prof. English Western Mich. U., Kalamazoo, 1965-72, assoc. prof., 1972-79, prof., 1979-89, prof. English and Medieval Studies, 1989—, exec. editor Early Drama, Art and Music, 1976—. Author: From Creation To Doom, 1984, On Tradition, 1992, also others; editor: Illustrations of the Stage, 1991, Tretise of Miraclis Pleying, 1993, also others; co-editor Comparative Drama, 1967—. With Corp. of Engrs., U.S. Army, 1956-58. Recipient Disting. Scholar award Western Mich. U., 1985. Mem. Medieval Acad. of Am., Renaissance Soc. of Am., Internat. Soc. for the Study of Medieval Drama. Episcopal. Home: 2006 Argyle Ave Kalamazoo MI 49008 Office: Medieval Inst. Western Mich U Kalamazoo MI 49008

DAVIDSON, DONALD W., education educator; b. Prairie Grove, June 8, 1936; s. Emmett and Eugenia (Dorman) D.; m.Ruthanna Davidson, Aug. 9, 1969; children: Charlotte, Ruth Ellen. BA, U. Minn., 1959; PhD, Rutgers U., 1963. Past prof. U. Ala., Tuscaloosa, 1963-65; asst. prof. biology U. Wis., Superior, 1965—. Office: U of Wisconsin Dept Biology/Med Technology Superior WI 54880

DAVIDSON, FRED, education educator; b. Chgo., Dec. 10, 1954; s. Harry Vincent and Thalia (Heim) D. BA, U. Ill., 1976, MA, 1981; PhD, UCLA, 1988. Cert. secondary tchr., speech and English, Ill. Vol. Peace Corps, Liberia, West Africa, 1976-78; rsch., teaching asst. U. Ill., Urbana-Champaign, Ill., 1979-81; intern, lectr. ESL Ohio U., Athens, 1981-83; rsch., teaching asst. UCLA, 1983-88; rsch. advisor U. Cambridge Local Examinations Syndicate, Cambridge, U.K., 1988-89; program evaluator Ill. State Bd. Edn., Springfield, Des Plaines, Ill., 1989-90; asst. prof. English as internat. lang. U. Ill., Urbana-Champaign, 1990-96, assoc. prof., 1996—. Author: Principles of Statistical Data Handling, 1996; contbr. articles to profl. jours. Recipient Cert. of Appreciation, Ministry of Edn., Republic of Liberia, 1978, Teaching Excellence awards UCLA, 1983-88, U. Ill., 1979-81, 90—. Mem. TESOL, Nat. Peace Corps Assn., Am. Ednl. Rsch. Assn., Nat. Coun. Tchrs. English, Lang. Testing Rsch. Colloquim (archivist), Phi Kappa Phi (chair internat. lang. testing assn. task force on testing stds.). Home: 208 Dodson Dr E Urbana IL 61801 Office: U Ill Urbana Champaign Divsn English as Internat Lang 707 S Mathews Ave Urbana IL 61801-3625

DAVIDSON, JAMES WILSON, clinical psychologist; b. Muncie, Ind., Apr. 22, 1950; s. James Wayne and Mary Marguerite (Sanford) D.; m. Nancy Lee Hendershott, Aug. 30, 1969; children: Melissa Ann, Amanda Corynne, Kevin Patrick. BS, Mich. State U., 1972; PhD, Kent State U., 1975; postgrad., Ashland (Ohio) Theol. Sem., 1980-82. Ordained to ministry Assemblies of God, 1988. Coord. Ctr. on Rsch. and Evaluation, Ashtabula, Ohio, 1974-77; pres. The Children's Ctr., Ashtabula, 1978-80, Computech Data Systems, Ashtabula, 1978-82; v.p. Davidson Assocs., Ashtabula, 1977-86; assoc. pastor First Assembly of God, Ashtabula, 1986-88; sr. pastor Metro Ch., Cleve., 1988-94; CEO Heart and Hand Found., Cleve., 1988—, LifeLine Counseling Ctr., 1994—; dir. Ohio Dist. Coun. Urban Missions Ministries, Columbus, 1990—. Recipient 414th Point of Light award White House, 1991, Health award UNICEF, 1992, 93, Ptnr. Agy. Excellence award CMHA, 1992, 93; Kent State U. fellow, 1973-74. Mem. APA, Am. Assn. Christian Counselors. Republican. Home: 2627 Courtland Blvd Cleveland OH 44118 Office: Heart and Hand Found PO Box 93813 2570 Woodhill Rd Cleveland OH 44104-5813

DAVIDSON, JO ANN, state legislator; children: Julie, Jenifer. Mem. Ohio Ho. of Reps., Columbus, 1981—, now minority whip; mem. fin., ethics and stds. and rules coms., house speaker, minority leader, mem. joint com. on mental retardation and devel. disabilities. Mem. Reynoldsburg (Ohio) City Coun., 1968-77; former vice chmn. Ohio Turnpike Commn.; trustee Franklin U., U. Findlay, Ohio; mem. Columbus Area Women's Polit. Caucus. Named Legislator of Yr., Nat. Rep. Legislators Assn., 1991; named to Ohio Women's Hall of Fame, 1991. Mem. Oho C. of C. (v.p. spl. programs), Rotary. Home: 6870 E Livingston Ave Apt B Reynoldsburg OH 43068-3058 Office: OH Ho of Reps State House Columbus OH 43215*

DAVIDSON, JOHN HUNTER, agriculturist; b. Wilmette, Ill., May 16, 1914; s. Joseph and Ruth Louise (Moody) D.; m. Elizabeth Marie Boynton, June 16, 1943; children—Joanne Davidson Hildebrand, Kathryn Davidson Bouwens, Patricia. B.S. in Horticulture, Mich. State U., 1937, M.S. in Plant Biochemistry, 1940. Field researcher agrl. chems. Dow Chem. Co., Midland, Mich., 1936-42, with research and devel. dept. agrl. products, 1946-72, tech. adviser research and devel. agrl. products, 1972-80, tech. adviser govt. relations, 1980-84, cons., 1984—. Served to lt. USNR, 1945. Mem. Am. Chem. Soc., Am. Soc. Hort. Sci., Weed Sci. Soc., Am. Pathol. Soc., Phi Kappa Phi, Alpha Zeta. Republican. Presbyterian. Club: Exchange of Midland. Contbr. articles on plant pathology and weed control to profl. jours. Home: 4319 Andre St Midland MI 48642-3779

DAVIDSON, JOHN KENNETH, SR., sociologist, educator, researcher, author, consultant; b. Augusta, Ga., Oct. 25, 1939; s. Larcie Charles and Betty (Corley) D.; m. Josephine Frazier, Apr. 11, 1964; children: John Kenneth Jr., Stephen Wood. Student, Augusta Coll., 1956-58; BS in Edn., U. Ga., 1961, MA, 1963; PhD, U. Fla., 1974. Asst. prof. dept. psychology and sociology Armstrong State Coll., Savannah, Ga., 1963-67; asst. prof. sociology Augusta Coll., 1967-74; acting chmn., asst. prof. dept. sociology Ind. U., South Bend, 1974-76; assoc. prof. sociology U. Wis., Eau Claire, 1976-78, prof., 1978—, chmn. dept. sociology, 1976-80, asst. spl. projects to dean grad. studies and univ. rsch., 1987-91, coord. family studies, 1990—; cons. family life edn.; rsch. cons. dept. ob-gyn. Med. Coll. Ga., Augusta, 1969-74, pediatrics, 1972-73, also assoc. dir. health care project, 1971-73, rsch. instr., summer 1971, rsch. assoc., summer 1972-73, rsch. cons. dept. community dentistry, 1974-79; program coord. Community Devel. in Process Phase II and III, Title I Higher Edn. Act of, 1965, 1970; mem. sociology and anthropology com. Univ. System Ga., 1970-74, chmn. curriculum sub-com., 1970-72; dir. Sex Edn., The Pub. Schs. and You project Ind. Com. on Humanities, 1975. Author: (textbooks) Marriage and Family, 1992, Marriage and Family: Change and Continuity, 1996; assoc. editor Jour. Marriage and the Family, 1975-85, Sociol. Inquiry, 1986-92; reviewer Jour. Deviant Behavior, 1979-90, Sociol. Spectrum, 1985—; cons. editor Jour. Sex. Rsch., 1991-95; contbr. articles to profl. jours. Past state chmn. pub. affairs Ind. Assn. Planned Parenthood Affiliates, 1975-76; past mem. Eau Claire Coordinating Council; Former bd. dirs. Planned Parenthood North Cen. Ind., also past chmn. pub. affairs com., 1975-76; former mem. bd. dirs., 1st v.p. and mem. resources allocation com. Wis. Family Planning Coordinating Council; former mem. bd. dirs. and mem. exec., info., internat. and edn. coms., chmn. social sci. rsch. com. Assn. for Vol. Sterilization; past pres. citizens adv. bd. Eau Claire and Chippewa Falls Planned Parenthood Clinics; past mem. dirs. Planned Parenthood of Wis., Inc.; former mem. Eau Claire County Adv. Health Forum, Eau Claire County Task Force on Family Planning; past mem. Eau Claire Task Force on Teen Pregnancy. Mem. Am. Sociol. Assn., Am. Assn. Family and Consumer Scis., Wis. Assn. Family and Consumer Scis., Wis. Assn. Family and consumer Scis., Wis. Sociol. Assn., so. Sociol. Soc., Mid-South Sociol. Assn., Midwest Sociol. Soc., Groves Conf., Nat. Coun. Family Rels. (past chmn. com. stds. and criteria for cert., former mem. devel. com. and cert. com.), Wis. Coun. Family Rels. (bd. dirs., exec. com., past pres.), Soc. Sci. Study Sex., Tex. Coun. Family Rels., Augusta Coll. Alumni Soc., U. Fla. Alumni Soc., U. Ga. Alumni soc., Pres. Club. U. Wis.-Eau Claire, Kappa Delta Pi, Phi Kappa Phi (chpt. pres. 1991-92, mem. Nat. Forum editl. com. 1992—), Phi Theta Kappa, Alpha Kappa Delta (editor nat. newsletter 1979-83, nat. v,p. 1992-94, nat. pres.-elect 1994-96, pres. 1996—, mem. exec. coun. 1992—). Episcopalian. Home: 1305 Nixon Ave Eau Claire WI 54701-6574 Office: U Wis Dept Sociology Eau Claire WI 54702

DAVIDSON, MARSHA EILEEN, communications executive; b. Cleve., Dec. 6, 1950. BA, Baldwin-Wallace Coll., 1983. Dir. profl. devel. Am. Soc. for Pers. Adminstrn., Berea, Ohio, 1977-83; ops. mgr. New Cleve. Women Mag., Berea, 1984-87; dir. membership Assn. for Systems Mgmt., Berea, 1987-93; pres. Eagle Communications, Berea, 1993—. Mem. Nat. Assn. Self Employed. Office: Eagle Communications 667 Shakespeare Dr Berea OH 44017-1132

DAVIDSON, MARY THERESA, educational administrator; b. Dodge City, Kans., Mar. 18, 1952; d. Alfred Peter and Marcella Mae (Hattrup) Heeke; m. Thomas Darwin Davidson, June 3, 1972; children: Matthew Braxton, Amanda Christine. AB in French, Ft. Hays State U., 1972, MS in Counseling, 1973, postgrad., 1984-85, 91—. Tchr. French and German Douglass (Kans.) H.S., 1973-74; counselor, elem. sch. Unified Sch. Dist., Ulysses, Kans., 1983-85, prin., 1985-92; prin. Felten Mid. Sch., Hays, Kans., 1992-93; counselor Hays H.S., 1974-76, prin., 1993—; speaker and presenter in field; mem. external adv. bd. Ft. Hays State U. Dept. Edn., 1991—, instr., 1986, 90, 91; mem. North Cen evaluation team Tribune (Kans.) Sch. Dist., 1988. Pres. Grant County Fair Bd., Ulysses, 1991 (Outstanding Svc. to Cmty. 1991); councilwoman Ulysses City Coun., 1985-88; parliamentarian Gen. Fedn. Women's Clubs, Kans., 1984 (State Vol. of Yr.); bd. dirs. Grant County Recreation Swim Team, Ulysses, 1982-87; chair NCA Sch. Improvement Vis. Team at Great Bend H.S. and Garden City H.S.; mem. Kans. State Curriculum Adv. Coun., Kans. State Licensure Assessment Com. Am. Products Inc. scholar, 1969; named Outstanding Adminstr. of Yr., Ulysses C. of C., 1987. Mem. AAUW (pres. 1983-85), Kans. Assn. Secondary Sch. Prins. (pres. 1992-93, pres. S.W. area VI 1988-90, chmn.-elect 1986-88, state coord. 1995—, Prin. of Yr. award 1989), Kans. Assn. Mid. Sch. Adminstrs. (dist. II rep. 1986—), Kans. State H.S. Activities Assn. (Hall of Fame selection com. 1995—). Republican. Roman Catholic. Home: 3004 Cherry Hill Dr Hays KS 67601-1431 Office: Hays High Sch 2300 E 13th St Hays KS 67601-2646

DAVIDSON, OSHA GRAY, writer; b. Passaic, N.J., May 22, 1954; s. Sol M. and Penny (Goldfinger) D.; m. Mary Gray, May 21, 1989; children: Sienna, Sarah, Liam. BA in English, U. Iowa, 1982. Chief writer "The County" Iowa State Assn. of Counties, Des Moines, 1972; editor/pubr. The Grapevine, Iowa City, 1982-85; assoc. editor U. Iowa Alumni Rev., Iowa City, 1985-87; asst. editor Recruitment & Retention in Higher Education, 1987—; cons. "Troublesome Creek" documentary for the Am. Experience, 1991-96. Author: Broken Heartland, 1990, Under Fire, 1993, The Best of Enemies, 1996; contbr. numerous articles to profl. jours. Coord. Iowa Divestment Coalition, Des Moines, 1983-84. Ford Found. grantee, 1988, Fund for Investigative Journalism grantee, 1988; Ctr. Internat. and Comparative Studies U. Iowa scholar, 1995-96, Dept. Am. Studies scholar, 1995-96; Pulitzer nomination for "Best of Enemies", 1996. Mem. nat. Writers Union. Home and Office: 14 S Governor St Iowa City IA 52240-5208

DAVIDSON, RICHARD ALAN, data communications company executive; b. Chgo., June 25, 1946; s. Jacob Aaron and Belle Rina (Feldman) D.; m. Sharyn Gail Ellman, Aug. 19, 1973; children: Kevin Scott, Caryl Elise. BSEE, U. Mich., 1970; MBA, Northwestern U., 1975. Project engr. Motorola, Inc., Schaumburg, Ill., 1967-74; ptnr. Feature Film Svcs., Skokie, Ill., 1974-77; mgr. planning Motorola, Inc., Schaumburg, Ill., 1977-78, mgr. mktg., 1978-79; tech. dir. Voice & Data Systems, Chgo., 1979-82; engring. mgr. Infolink Corp., Northbrook, Ill., 1982-84; pres. Davidson Data Communications, Lake Forest, Ill., 1984—; v.p. engring. Feature Film Svcs., Skokie, 1976—. Inventor pay TV system; contbr. articles to profl. jours. Unit commr. Boy Scouts Am., Lake County, Ill., 1989—; comms. officer USAF Aux. CAP, 1991—. Recipient Cert. of Appreciation Boy Scouts Am., 1990. MEm. IEEE, Assn. for Computing Machinery, Assn. for MBA Execs., North Shore Radio Club (tech. dir.), Tau Delta Phi. Republican. Jewish. Home and Office: 1900 S Millburne Rd Lake Forest IL 60045-4112

DAVIDSON, SOL M., author, management consultant; b. Newark, Dec. 13, 1924; s. Isidore and Helen (Black) D.; m. Penny Davidson, June 19, 1949; children: Cliff, Ron, Osha. BA in Journalism, La. State U., 1945; MA, NYU, 1950, PhD in Am. Civilization, 1960. Ednl. dir. Beneficial Fin. Sys., Morristown, N.J., 1947-60; dir. ops. Dial Fin. Co., Des Moines, 1960-71; asst. to pres. Northwestern Bell Telephone Co., Des Moines, 1971-74; pres. Davidson, Wyatt & Assocs., Des Moines, 1975—; pres. adv. bd. Broadlawns Hosp., Des Moines, 1964-65. Author: Culture and the Comic Strips, 1959, The Cultivation of Imperfection, 1965, The Power of Fiction, 1967, Wild Jake Hiccup, 1992. Pres. Bds. Internat. Edn., Iowa, 1968-69, Ptners. of the Ams., Des Moines, 1969-70; pres. adult edn. adv. coun. Des Moines Schs., 1962-63; bd. dirs. Jewish Fedn., Des Moines, 1969-70; chmn. human rights commn. City of Des Moines, 1968-69. Served with USN, 1945-47. Recipient Nat. Action in Edn. award Better Homes and Gardens, 1962. Jewish. Home: PO Box 5115 Des Moines IA 50306 Office: Davidson Wyatt & Assocs PO Box 5115 Des Moines IA 50306-5115

DAVIES, GEORGE JAMES, physical therapist, educator; b. La Crosse, Wis., June 9, 1947; m. Carol J. Riley, June 7, 1969; children—Scott, Steven. B.A. in Health and Phys. Edn., Trenton (N.J.) State Coll., 1969, M.Ed. with high honors, 1972; postgrad. Rutgers U., 1973, Columbia U., 1973-75, Fairleigh-Dickinson U., 1974, U. Wis., 1977, U. Wis.-La Crosse, 1978. Cert. phys. therapist Columbia U., 1975; lic. phys. therapist Wis.; cert. athletic trainer Nat. Athletic Trainers Assn.; cert. exercise technician Am. Coll. Sports Medicine; cert. emergency med. technician Nat. Registry of Emergency Med. Technicians, Wis.; cert. cardiopulmonary resuscitation instr., trainer Am. Heart Assn.; cert. cardiopulmonary resuscitation instr., standard first aid and personal safety instr., advanced first aid and emergency care instr., ARC. Student athletic trainer Trenton (N.J.) State Coll., 1967-79, grad. asst. in health and phys. edn., 1971-72; instr. health and phys. edn. Bergen Community Coll., Paramus, N.J., 1972-74, athletic training cons., 1974-75; mem. faculty, asst. prof. phys. therapy U. Wis.-La Crosse, 1975-80, assoc. prof., 1980—, dept. chmn., 1978-79, clin. supr., 1979—, vis. asst. prof. grad. program Inst. Grad. Health Scis., 1980—, prof. phys. therapy; nat. faculty mem. U.S. Sports Acad., Mobile, Ala., 1977—; mem. staff La Crosse (Wis.) Exercise Program, 1976—; assoc. dir., bus. mgr. sole practice Orthopaedic and Sports Phys. Therapy, La Crosse, 1979—; cons. in field; exec. dir. Western Wis. Sports Med. Served with USMC, 1969-70. Recipient Cramer Products Athletic Tng. award, 1981; grantee numerous profl. orgns. and govt. agys. Mem. Am. Phys. Therapy Assn. (pres. sports phys. therapy sect. 1992, editor jour., chmn. publs. com.), Am. Coll. Sports Medicine, Nat. Athletic Trainers Assn., Great Lakes Athletic Trainers Assn., Wis. Athletic Trainers Assn., Nat. Registry Emergency Med. Technicians, Wis. Registry Emergency Med. Technicians, Nat. Jogger's Assn., Phi Epsilon Kappa (nat. merit scholar, key award 1972), Sigma Xi. Am. Baptist. Author: (with J. Tesch, et al) Laboratory and Field Tests for Cross Country Skiers, 1980; co-editor: Textbook of Physical Therapy: Orthopaedics and Sports, 1984; contbr. chpts. to books, over 50 articles to profl. jours.; editor Sports Medicine column Cardio-Gram, La Crosse, 1976—, Isokinetics and Exercise Science; co-editor Jour. Orthopaedic and Sports Phys. Therapy, 1979—. Home: 1707 Jennifer Ct Onalaska WI 54650-3135 Office: U Wis 2036 Cowley Hall La Crosse WI 54601-3791

DAVIES, SARA BETH, educator, writer; b. Springfield, Ill., May 14, 1938; d. Thompson Holt and Mary Elizabeth (Burge) Burckhartt; m. John William Organ,May 3, 1958 (dec. July 1966); children: Beth Huff, Paul, Lynn Miller; m. Albert Dean Seegert, May 10, 1968 (div. Aug. 1974); 1 child, Kristin Holt Burckhartt; m. Robert Arden Davies, July 23, 1975. BS, U. Evansville, 1975; MA in Libr. Sci., U. So. Ind., 1994. Exec. dir. Leadership Evansville, Ind., 1979—; founding sec., treas. NACLO, 1979-81; sec., bd. dirs. Leadership Evansville, 1985—. Pres. Cmty. Found. Alliance, 1992—; 1st v.p. IN Donors Alliance, 1992—; Exec. Cmty. Am. Judicature Soc, Chgo., 1994—; Chair. Citizen Cmty. for Future of IN Co. Mem. Leadership Am., See Jane Run, Vanderbergh Cmty. Found., Anew A Network of Evansville Women (v.p), Rotary (Evansville bd. dirs.). Office: Leadership Evansville 310 Main St Ste 2-B Evansville IN 47708

DAVILA, EDWIN, lawyer; b. Cleve., June 21, 1954; s. Emilio and Maltilda Davila. BA, Coll. of Wooster, Ohio, 1976; JD, Cleve. U., 1983. Bar: Ohio 1984, U.S. Dist. Ct. (so. and no. dists.) Ohio 1984, U.S. Ct. Appeals (6th cir.) 1984, U.S. Dist. Ct. (no. dist.) Tex. 1988, U.S. Ct. Appeals (5th cir.) 1988. With Prosecutor's Office City of Cleve., 1982-83; asst. atty. gen. Atty. Gen.'s Office State of Ohio, Columbus, 1983-84; law clk. Ohio Ct. Appeals, Cleve., 1984-85; assoc. Smith & Schnacke, L.P.A., Dayton, Ohio, 1985-87, Arter & Hadden, Canton, Ohio, 1987-89, Ross & Robertson, Canton, 1989-91; pvt. practice Canton, Ohio, 1991—. Mem. Am. Trial Lawyers Assn., Ohio Bar Assn., Ohio Acad. Trial Lawyers, Canton Bar Assn. Office: 836 Savannah Ave NE Canton OH 44704-1260

DAVIO, JOHN JOSEPH, publishing executive; b. Southfield, Mich., July 28, 1944; s. Charles and Helen D.; m. Nancy Anne Beulow, July 10, 1965; children: Cheryl, Stephen. Mgr. Tedrick Photos, Southfield, 1965-75; owner, photographer, framer Photoworld, Rochester, Mich., 1975-86; v.p., treas., publisher, asst. editor A.D. Images, Rochester, 1985—; v.p., publisher, editor Arrathoon-Davio Publ. Co., Rochester, 1995—. Editor: S.S. Duke: Make It With Steel, 1995, Woody Discovers a New Kind of Tree,, 1996, Men Who Changed the World, Vol. I The Henry Ford Story, 1996, Vol. II The First Birdmen: Wilbur and Orville Wright, 1996; contbr. (photos) to Metal Construction News, 1996, and Metal Home Digest, 1996. Office: The Arrathoon-Davio Publ Co PO Box 80547 Rochester MI 48308-0001

DAVIS, AIMEE J., financial consultant; b. Ft. Wayne, Ind., Aug. 5, 1955; m. Doug Davis; children: Kelly, Kristine. Student, U. Purdue, 1975-76. Lic. series 65, 63, 7. Asst. to contr. Ft. Wayne Nat. Bank, 1976—; fin. cons. Merrill Lynch, Ft. Wayne, 1979—. Bd. dirs. Ludwig Park Assn., Ft. Wayne, 1994—. Mem. Optimist Club (bd. dirs. 1993—). Republican. Roman Catholic.

DAVIS, ALICE BERNICE STORLIE, physical therapist; b. Whalen, Minn., Jan. 21, 1921; d. Arthur Edwin Storlie and Ingeborg Bellah Hanson Zehren; m. Ronald Chester Davis, July 15, 1944 (div. Dec. 1981); children: Kent Loren and Scot Colin (twins), Daniel Bruce, Ronald Clark. Student, Winona (Minn.) State Coll., 1940; Cert. in Phys. Therapy, Mayo Clinic, Rochester, Minn., 1943. Registered phys. therapist, Minn.; lic. cosmetologist. Phys. therapist St. Vincent's Hosp., Billings, Mont., 1944-45, Mpls. Curative Workshop, 1946-51, St. Joseph's Hosp., St. Paul, 1968-73, Regency Manor, St. Paul, 1974-89, Midway Manor, St. Paul, 1974-89; dir. and supr. phys. therapy M.J. Hellman Nursing Home, Richfield, Minn., 1973-88; ret. Sec. WELCA, Highview Christian Luth. Ch., Farmington, Minn., 1993-95; rep. Northfield Retirement Aux., 1990. Named Miss Winona (Minn.), 1939. Mem. Am. Phys. Therapy Assn. (life), Afternoon Cir. (leader Bible study 1992-95), Sons of Norway (refreshment coord. 1992-95), Order Ea. Star. Republican. Lutheran. Home: 25399 Cedar Ave W Rt 2 Farmington MN 55024-9670

DAVIS, CHARLES F., financial consultant; b. Effington, Ill., Nov. 3, 1938; m. Judith A. Sliefer, Dec. 23, 1961; children: Michael Foster, Stephen Shannon. BA, U. Ill., 1961; MA, Fla. Inst. Tech., 1968. V.p. Piping & Design, Indpls., 1979-82; owner, mgr. 1st Affiliate, Effingham, 1982-88; mgr. Robert Thomas Securities, Effingham, 1988—. Contbr. articles to profl. publs.;

prodr. videos. Bd. dirs. Sr. Citizens Orgn., Effingham, 1990—. 1st lt. U.S. Army, 1961-63. Named Engr. of Yr., NASA, 1978. Republican. Methodist. Office: Robert Thomas Securities 605 W Jefferson Ave Effingham IL 62401-2362

DAVIS, CHRISTINE EURICH, elementary education educator; b. Lansdale, Pa., Apr. 6, 1937; d. Christian John Eurich and Geraldine (Butz) Snyder; m. Stanley Lewis Davis Jr., July 2, 1960; children: Heidi Christine Marshall, John Stanley Davis. BS in Elem. Edn., Millersville (Pa.) U., 1958; MA, Nat. Louis U., 1985. Elem. tchr. York Ave. Sch., Lansdale, Pa., 1958-60, Lindop Sch., Broadview, Ill., 1960-62; elem. tchr. Sch. Dist. 97, Oak Park, Ill., 1972-93, mem. curriculum devel. staff, 1980-93, review rsch. grants, 1989-93, whole lang. staff developer, 1989—, mem. strategic plan com., 1989-90; tchr. staff developer Ill. Writing Project, Oak Park, 1983—; mem. Consortium Ednl. Change, Oak Park, 1987-93. Mem. Oak Park Ednl. Found., 1990-93; mem. bd. pastoral svc. United Ch. of Christ, Oak Park, 1993-96, vice chair, 1994-95, chair, 1995-96, mem. ch. coun., 1995—, vice chmn., 1996—. Mem. NEA, ASCD, AAUW, Ill. Edn. Assn., Oak Park Tchrs. Assn. (mem.-at-large 1986-87, treas. 1987-88, pres. 1988-90), Chgo. Ministerial Assn., Delta Kappa Gamma (chair profl. growth 1987-89, v.p. program com. 1994-96), Phi Delta Kappa (rsch. chair 1992-93, pres. 1994—). Democrat. United Ch. of Christ. Home and Office: Davis Ednl Media 600 N Lombard Ave Oak Park IL 60302-1720

DAVIS, CHRISTOPHER KEVIN, equipment company executive; b. Ogden, Utah, Apr. 8, 1959; s. James LaVerne and Margaret Mary (Brewer) D.; m. Christine Marie Davis, Oct. 27, 1984; children: Jennifer Lee, Christopher Kevin, Kelly Anne. A in Liberal Arts, Meremac Coll., St. Louis, 1979; B of Gen. Studies, U. Mo., St. Louis, 1988. Lic. in real estate sales. Prodn. supr. Survival Tech., St. Louis, 1982-84; salesman Cardinal Properties Real Estate Co., St. Louis, 1981-84; packaging supr. Sigma Aldrich Chem., St. Louis, 1984-85; sales mgr. Gen. Turf and Grounds Equipment Co., St. Louis, 1985-86; sales mgr. TNT Golf Car & Equipment Co., St. Peters, Mo., 1986-91, gen. mgr., 1991-93; pres., gen. mgr. Gateway Power Equipment, St. Louis, 1993—. Mem. Missouri Valley Turfgrass Assn., Missouri Valley Golf Course Supts., Profl. Grounds Maintenance Assn., So. Ill. Golf Course Supts., Ozark Golf Course Supts. Roman Catholic. Office: Gateway Power Equipment Co 1600 Fairview Saint Louis MO 63132

DAVIS, C(LAUD) NEAL, academic administrator, educator, service club executive, fund development specialist; b. Moko, Ark., Nov. 3, 1936; s. Claud Delbert and Freda Margaret (Gilliam) D.; m. Frances Patricia Duncan, June 16, 1977; children: Cathy Sue, Claud Michael, Cary Mark, Carol Kim, Connie Beth, Cory Mitchel. BA, William Jewell Coll., 1958; MA, N.E. Mo. State U., 1963; PhD, U. Mo.-Kansas City, 1970. Advanced cert. fund raising exec. Asst. mgr. Western Auto Supply Co., Mpls., Kansas City, 1958-59; owner, mgr. Davis Family Shoe Store, Edina, Mo., 1960-64; tchr., coach Hurdland (Mo.) H.S., 1960-61; dean of men and related roles William Jewell Coll., Liberty, Mo., 1961-67; dean students Elmhurst Coll., Ill., 1967-73; pres., prof. Judson Coll., Portland and The Dalles, Oreg., 1973-82; gov. Rotary Dist. 5100, Oreg./Wash., 1981-82; v.p., dean devel. and pub. relations Hannibal-LaGrange Coll., Mo., 1982-85; dir. devel. S.E. Mo. State U., Cape Girardeau, 1985-86; assoc. sec. programs and devel. Rotary Internat., Evanston, Ill., 1986-89; dir. Holt Internat. Childrens Svcs., Eugene, Oreg., 1976-90; v.p. devel. Saint Paul's Coll., Lawrenceville, Va., 1990-93; exec. v.p. Nat. Exch. Club, Toledo, 1993-95; v.p. devel. & pub. affairs Heidelberg Coll, Tiffin, Ohio, 1995—; lectr. in field. Author (with others) Better People, 1981, The World and They that Dwell Within, 1990, Quotes for the Bathroom Wall, 1996; contbr. articles to profl. jours. Vice chmn. Council Related Agys., Hannibal, 1984-85. Lay speaker various chs., Mo., Oreg., 1958—. Mem. Nat. Soc. Fund Raising Execs. (officer Greater Toledo chpt.), Am. Assn. Higher Edn. (life). Am. Assn. for Counseling and Devel., Am. Coll. Personnel Assn., Phi Delta Kappa, Rotary (past dist. gov., various offices, Paul Harris fellow, Tiffin club), Four-Way Test Assn. (bd. dirs., sec.), Exch. Club Toledo. Democrat. Avocations: public speaking, photography, writing, international adoption, church related service. Home: 5047 Brenden Way Sylvania OH 43560-2222 Office: Heidelberg Coll 310 E Market Tiffin OH 44883

DAVIS, CORNELIA HAVEN CASEY, civic leader; b. Greenville, Ill., Sept. 17, 1909; d. George Farnum and Cornelia (Ravold) Casey; m. Frank V. Davis, May 9, 1936; children: James Casey, Thomas Wait (dec.), Andrew Waggoner. AB, Millikin U., 1931. Statistician Bond County (Ill.) Emergency Relief Commn., 1934-36; sec.-treas. E.H. Paul Co., Hookdale, Ill., 1957-67, Davis & Royer, Inc., Greenville, 1967-73. Pres. Greenville PTA, 1944-45; mem. Utlaut Meml. Hosp. Found., 1957, Aux. historian, 1958-59, pres. 1966-67, rec. sec., 1969-70; chmn. Bond County ARC, 1962-64, vice chmn. Ill. fund, 1966, chmn. territorial fund, 1967-68, 69, mem. resolutions com.; bd. dirs. Bond County Tb Assn., 2d v.p., 1965-67, pres. 1969-70; 1st v.p., chmn. Christmas Seals fund drive Heritage Trail Tb and Respiratory Disease Assn., 1970-71; chmn. Greenville and Bond County Bicentennial Commn.; bd. dirs. Greenville Sesquicentennial, 1965. Recipient Good Citizenship medal SAR, 1962, Disting. Service award Greenville Jaycees, 1981. Mem. Ill Hist. Soc. (life), Bond County Hist. Soc. (charter, life, pres., bd. dirs.), Bond County Fair Assn. (life), DAR (various coms. and offices 1935—, including dir. 6th div. 1955-56, state corr. sec. 1956-58, state chmn. 50-Yr. Club nat. chpt. 1983-90, nat. chaplain 1990-91, Benjamin Mills chpt. registrar 1992-94, 94—), Children Am. Revolution (various offices 1955—, hon. sr. state pres.), U.S Daus. War of 1812 (various offices 1963—, hon. state pres.), Ill. Ct. Women Descs. Ancient and Hon. Arty. Co. (various coms.), Daus. Am. Colonists (chmn. Ill. colonial com.), Col. Daus. 17th Century (various com. and offices 1961—, hon. pres. gen.), Colonial Dames of Am. (rec. sec. local chpt. XII 1969-71, 77-81, pres. 1981-83), Nat. Soc. Magna Charta Dames, Soc. Descs. Colonial Clergy, Ill. Geneal. Soc., Bond County Art and Cultural Assn. (bd. dirs., sec.), Sons and Daus. Pilgrims (Okla. chpt., chmn. constn. and bylaws com. 1977), Nat. Gavel Soc., Nat. Soc. Daus. Colonial Wars, Order of Crown in Am., South Cen. Ill. Women's Golf Assn. (chmn. 1953, 66, 71) Nat. Trust Hist. Preservation, Cousteau Soc., Sovereign Colonial Soc., Americans of Royal Descent, Family of Bruce Soc. Am., Order of Washington, Bond Co. Geneological Soc. (life), Greenville Garden Club (pres., rec. sec. 1954-56), Contemporary Club (past pres., rec. sec.), Delta Delta Delta. Republican. Episcopalian. Home and Office: Luther Villas 707 Hoffmeister Dr Altamont IL 62411

DAVIS, DANIEL JOSEPH, SR., religious organization executive, pastor; b. St. Paul, Dec. 18, 1946; s. Joseph A. and Gloria Y. (Roberts) D.; m. Janet L. Poppy, Feb. 12, 1944; children: Daniel J. Jr., Carole L. AB magna cum laude, Morningside Coll., 1968; ThM, U. Chgo., 1970, AM, 1972. Ordained to ministry Christian Ch., 1976. Asst. prof., instr. Pa. State U., State College, 1976-80; pastor 1st Christian Ch., Vinton, Iowa, 1980-84; sr. min. Cen. Christian Ch. (Disciples of Christ), Waterloo, Iowa, 1984-88; assoc. regional min. Christian Ch. in Nebr., Lincoln, 1988-93; adminstr. Cotner Coll. Commn. on Continuing Edn., Lincoln, 1988-93; exec. sec. Interch. Ministries of Nebr., Lincoln, 1993—; mem. coun. for alt. dispute resolution Supreme Ct., Nebr., 1992—; mem. adv. coun. Coll. Human Resources and Family Scis., U. Nebr., Lincoln, 1994—; cons. ch. conflict for 7 denominations in 5 states, 1987—; cons. orgnl. devel. and sys. edn. throughout Midwest, 1985—. Author: Acts: God Shows No Partiality, 1995, (curriculum) 500th Anniversary of Columbus, 1992, (chpt.) Young Adult Ministry Manual, 1984. mem. rural unemployment task force Job Tng. Partnership Act, Cedar Rapids, Iowa, 1982; mem. Rural Response Partnership coalition of pub. and pvt. agys., Lincoln, 1993—. Recipient Outstanding Comty. Ministry/Human Svc. Agy. award Gov. of Iowa, 1986; Ralph E. Cecill scholar U. Chgo., 1970. Mem. Nat. Assn. Ecumenical Staff. Office: Interch Ministries of Nebr # 411 215 Centennial Mall S Lincoln NE 68508-1888

DAVIS, DANNY K., healthcare consultant, educator; b. Parkdale, Ark., Sept. 6, 1941; m. Vera Davis; 2 children. BA, Ark. A. M. & N. Coll., 1961; MA, Chgo. State U., 1968; PhD, Union Inst., 1977. Chgo. alderman, 1979-90; commr. Cook. County, 1990—; candidate Chgo. mayor, 1991; dem. candidate 7th dist. Ill. U.S. House of Reps., 1996. Office: 5730 W Division Chicago IL 60651*

DAVIS, DARRELL L., automotive executive; b. Sharon, Pa., Aug. 8, 1939; s. Paul Darrell and Dorothy Jane (Snyder) D.; m. Jacqueline Donna Pain, July 18, 1986; children: Paul Darrell II, Robert Tod. BS, Youngstown State U., 1963; cert. Stanford Exec. Program, Stanford U., 1987; cert. Global Leadership Program, U. Mich., 1993. Svc. rep., warranty mgr., dist. mgr., asst. zone mgr. Chrysler Motors Corp., Orlando, Fla., 1966-77; zone mgr. Chrysler Motors Corp., Omaha, 1977-78, Troy, Mich., 1978-79; nat. distbn. mgr., regional mgr., gen. mgr. import export ops., gen. sales mgr. Chrysler Motors Corp., Detroit, 1979-88; pres., chief exec. officer Alfa Romeo Distbrs. N. Am., Orlando, 1988-91; gen. sales mgr. Chrysler Corp., Orange, Calif., 1991-93; v.p. Chrysler Internat. Corp., Detroit, 1993-95; gen. mgr. Europe Chrysler Corp., Detroit, 1993-95; pres., COO Chrysler Fin. Corp., Southfield, Mich., 1995—. Lt. U.S. Army, 1963-65. Republican.

DAVIS, DEBORAH CECILIA, auditor; b. Mt. Pleasant, Mich., Aug. 7, 1952; d. Arthur Francis Schaefer and Ninamae Ellen (Confer) Reber. BBA summa cum laude, Western Mich. U., 1974. CPA. Acct. Phoenix Optical, Bay City, Mich., 1968-70; analyst 2nd Nat. Bank, Saginaw, Mich., 1970-72; CPA Deloitte & Touche, Saginaw, Mich., 1975-77; cost acct. AC Sparkplug div. GM, Flint, Mich., 1977-78; corp. auditor GMC, Detroit, 1980; sr. statistician Detroit Diesel Allison div. GM, 1980-83; sr. budget, forecast analyst Cen. Foundry divsn. GM, Saginaw, 1983-91; fin. dir. City of Bay City, Mich., 1991-94; corp. contract supplier auditor GM, 1994—.

DAVIS, DEBORAH LEAH, quality systems engineer; b. Elizabeth, N.J., Dec. 8, 1963. BS in Indsl. Engring., GM Inst. Engring. & Mgmt., Flint, Mich., 1986; MS in Applied Stats., Oakland U., Auburn Hills, Mich., 1988. Cert. quality engr. Am. Soc. Quality Control. Reliability engr. Gen. Motors, Linden, N.J., 1981-87; quality and mfg. engr. Ford Motor Co., Dearborn, Mich., 1987-95; sr. quality engr. Johnson & Johnson, Cin., 1995—. Named Mgmt. Honor Soc. GM Inst., 1984. Office: Ethicon Endo-Surgery 4545 Creek Rd Cincinnati OH 45242

DAVIS, DIANE E., securities company official; b. Detroit, Sept. 10, 1946; m. Dennis Davis, Apr. 12, 1973; 1 child, Todd. Lic. series 7 and 63 Nat. Assn. Securities Dealers. Sales assoc. CF Capital, Cin., 1980-85, Hilliard Lyons, Carmel, Ind., 1985-88, Prudential Securities Inc. (formerly Thomas McKinnen), Indpls., 1988—. Mem. Carmel Women's Bus. Assn. Office: Prudential Securities Inc 8888 Keystone Xing Ste 200 Indianapolis IN 46240-4609

DAVIS, DONALD L., electrical engineer; b. Pasadena, Calif., Oct. 28, 1946. B, U. Wis., 1969. Registered profl. engr., Ill. Project engr. Warner Electric, South Beloit, Ill., 1974-77; chief engr. R & D Systems, Roscoe, Ill., 1977-79; pres. Electro Cam Corp., Roscoe, Ill., 1979—. Patentee in field. Mem. SAE. Office: Electro Cam Corp 13647 Metric Rd Roscoe IL 61073-7637

DAVIS, DONALD W., government official; b. Youngstown, Ohio, May 28, 1943; s. Donald M. and Mary A. (Hoovler) D.; m. Carol A. Baker, Jan. 27, 1968; children: Andrew, Eric. BBA, Ohio U., 1966. Claims rep. Social Security Adminstrn., Highland Park, Mich., 1966, Columbus, Ohio, 1968-70; field rep. Social Security Adminstrn., Bay City, Mich., 1970-71; ops. supr. Social Security Adminstrn., Ann Arbor, Mich., 1971-73; asst. dist. mgr. Social Security Adminstrn., Marietta, Ohio, 1973-78; dist. mgr. Social Security Adminstrn., Portsmouth, Ohio, 1978—. Adv. com. Area Agy. on Aging, Dist. 7, Rio Grande, Ohio, 1982-95, bd. dirs., 1996—, sec.-treas., 1995—; pres. Ret. Sr. Vol. Program, Portsmouth, 1989-95; mem. adv. com. Coalition for Elderly Supportive Svcs., Portsmouth, 1991—; asst. coach Wheelersburg (Ohio) H.S. Soccer Program, 1985-91; pres. St. Peters Ch. Parish Coun., 1991-92. With U.S. Army, 1966-68. Recipient William A. Jenkins award Svcs. to Aging Area Agy. Aging, 1995. Mem. Fed. Exec. Assn. Southeastern Ohio (treas. 1989—, Mem. of Yr. 1991), Wheelersburg Kiwanis (pres. 1992-93, Disting. Pres. award 1993, dist. membership chmn. 1994-95, treas. 1996—), Marietta Civitan Club (v.p. 1977-78, Svc. award 1977). Office: Social Security Adminstrn 923 Findlay St PO Box 1259 Portsmouth OH 45662

DAVIS, DORATHEA, state legislator. State rep. dist. 63 Mo. Ho. of Reps. Democrat. Office: Mo Ho of Reps State Capitol Building Jefferson City MO 65101-1556*

DAVIS, EVELYN MARGUERITE BAILEY, artist, organist, pianist; b. Springfield, Mo.; d. Philip Edward and Della Jane (Morris) Bailey; student pub. schs., Springfield; student art Drury Coll.; piano , organ student of Charles Cordeal; m. James Harvey Davis, Sept. 22, 1946. Sec., Shea and Morris Monument Co., before 1946; past mem. sextet, soloist Sta. KGBX; past pianist, Sunday sch. tchr., mem. choir East Ave. Bapt. Ch.; tchr. Bible, organist, pianist, vocal soloist and dir. youth choir Bible Bapt. Ch., Maplewood, Mo., 1956-69, also executed 12 by 6 foot mural of Jordan River; pvt. instr. piano and organ, voice, Croma Harp, Affton, Mo., 1960-71, St. Charles, Mo., 1971-83; Bible instr. 3d Bapt. Ch., St. Louis, 1948-54; pianist, soloist, tchr. Bible, Temple Bapt. Ch., Kirkwood, Mo., 1969-71; asst. organist-pianist, vocal soloist, tchr. Bible, Bible Ch., Arnold, Mo., 1969; faculty St. Charles Bible Bapt. Christian Sch., 1976-77; organist for Dr. Jack Van Impe Crusades and Dr. Oliver B. Green Crusades; organist, pianist, soloist, bible tchr., dir. youth orch., music arranger, floral arranger Bible Bapt. Ch., St. Charles, 1971-78; organist, vocal soloist, floral arranger Bible tchr. Faith Missionary Bapt. Ch., St. Charles, 1978-82; organist, floral arranger, vocal soloist Bellview Bapt. Ch., Springfield, Mo., 1984-90; tchr. piano, organ, voice, organist, Springfield, Mo., 1983—; pianist Golden Agers Pk. Crest Bapt. Ch., Springfield, Mo., 1991; interior decorator and floral arranger, also organist and vocal soloist for weddings and funerals. Fellow Internat. Biog. Assn. (life), Am. Biog. Inst. Rsch. Assn. (life); mem. Nat. Guild Organists, Nat. Guild Piano Tchr. Auditions, Internat. Platform Assn. Composer: I Will Sing Hallelujah, (cantata) I Am Alpha and Omega, Prelude to Prayer, My Shepherd, O Sing unto The Lord A New Song, O Come Let Us Sing unto The Lord, The King of Glory, The Lord Is My Light and My Salvation, O Worship the Lord in the Beauty of Holiness, The Greatest of These is Love, Prayer to the Lord Our God, We Will Sing Praises, His Name is Jesus, From Bethlehem's Manger to the Cross, also numerous hymn arrangements for organ and piano. Home: 5135 East Farm Rd 174 Rogersville MO 65742-9434

DAVIS, FOSTER, editor. Mng. editor St. Louis Dispatch. Office: St Louis Post Dispatch 900 N Tucker Blvd Saint Louis MO 63101*

DAVIS, F(RANCIS) KEITH, civil engineer; b. Bloomington, Wis., Oct. 23, 1928; s. Martin Morris and Anna (Weber) D.; BSCE, S.D. State U., 1950; m. Roberta Dean Anderson, May 25, 1957; 1 child, Mark Francis. With firm Howard, Needles, Tammen & Bergendoff, Kansas City, Mo., 1950—, asst. chief structural designer, 1960-65, project mgr., sect. chief, 1965-76, dep. chief structural engr., 1976-79, chief engr., 1979—. Bd. advisers N.W. Kans. Area Vocat. Tech. Sch., 1977-80, chmn., 1979-80. Served with AUS, 1951-53. Registered profl. engr., Mo., Ind., Nebr., Mich., Colo., Ariz., Oreg. Fellow ASCE; mem. NSPE, Mo. Soc. Profl. Engrs., Am. Ry. Engring. Assn. (tech. com. 1981—). Club: Homestead Country. Home: 5024 Howe Dr Shawnee Mission KS 66205-1465 Office: PO Box 419299 1201 Walnut Kansas City MO 64141

DAVIS, FREDERICK ATHIE, management executive; b. Detroit, Apr. 9, 1938; s. Leonard Athie Davis and Edna Irene Smith Smalley; m. Patricia Ann O'Keefe, Oct. 12, 1957; children: Laurel A. Smith, Lynnette A., Harner, Leah A. Davis-Bellucci, Lucynda A. Thrushman. Student, St. Clair Community Coll., 1973, U.S. Power Squadron, 1974-75, U.S.C.G. Auxiliary, 1981-85. Lic. internat. radio operator; lic. capt. USCG Master; comml. towing endorsement. Owner, operator Lake Appliance Sales and Svc., Belleville, Mich., 1959-62; svc. technician RCA Svc. Co., Ferndale, Mich., 1962-66; owner, operator Home Appliance Svc. Co., Port Austin, Mich., 1966-83; police officer Village Port Austin, 1968-78; owner, operator TMS Mfrs. Rep., Mich., 1985-88; sales rep., test boat operator Henry H. Smith and Co., various locations, Mich. and Fla., 1985-88; pres. Thumb Marine Inc., Charter and Salvage, Port Austin, 1970—; owner, capt. Miss Port Austin Perch Charter Boat, Port Austin, 1983—; owner, operator Assistance Towing Svc., 1991—; marine cons. Club Marine Boat/U.S. (Lloyds of London), Fla., 1989—; marine surveyor, 1982—; state Mich. instr. Boating and Snowmobile H.S., 1972-78; instr. U.S. Power Squadron, Bad Axe, 1975-80, USCG Aux. B S & S Classes, Port Austin, 1981-85, flotilla 15-09 Comdr., 1981-83, div. 15 vice capt., 1985. Author boating safety co. Fla. Keys Angler, Mich. Mariner and Mich. Out-of-Doors, Huron Daily Tribune, Woods N Water News, Powerboat, Sea Mag., Boating Mag., Heartland Boating, Bay City Times, Boating World, Trailer Boats. Mem. Port Austin Village Coun., 1975-77; vol. fireman Village of Port Austin, 1970—, ambulance attendant, 1970-75; mem. ad hoc com., bd. dirs. Thumb Area Gt. Lakes State Bottomland Preserve Huron County, 1984-88. Recipient Life Saving awards Port Austin Village Coun., Huron County Sheriff's Dept., Pub. Svc. commendation USCG, 1991. Mem. Thumb Area Charter Capts. Assn., Port Austin C. of C. (v.p. 1972, 83-84, pres. 1991), Nat. Charterboat Assn., Mich. Charterboat Assn., Port Austin Boat Club. Home and Office: Thumb Marine Inc 28 Railroad Port Austin MI 48467 also: PO Box 1866 Key Largo FL 33037-2641

DAVIS, FREEMAN MILTON, II, university adminstrator, educator, consultant, per; b. Nashville, Mar. 8, 1950; s. Freeman Milton and Lila (Padgett) D.; m. Olga Idriss Sneed, Jan. 22, 1978; children: Erika Iman, Julian Gershom. BA in Performance, Juilliard Sch., 1977. Bd. dirs./jr. exec. Benasa Found. Orgn., L.A., 1978-79; acct. exec. Diversified Fin. Planners, Beverly Hills, Calif., 1979-81; sales mgr. Allprint Printing Co., Santa Ana, Calif., 1980-84; quality control trainer Wats Telemarketing, Lincoln, Nebr., 1984-85; spl. edn. asst. Everett Jr. H.S., Lincoln, Nebr., 1984-85; ops./data engry mgr. United Phone Book Advertisers, Inc., Lincoln, Nebr., 1985-88; dir./coord./program specialist econ. div. Lincoln City Govt., 1988-91; cons./contr./broker/agt. Davis Consulting, Lincoln and Manhattan, 1991—; adminstr./instr. Kans. State U., Manhattan, 1994—; mem. adv. bd. Nebr. Pub. Radio, Lincoln, 1990-93. Bd. dirs. Leadership Lincoln, 1990-93; pres., bd. dirs. Cmty. Bus. Assn. Nebr., Lincoln, 1990-93; bd. dirs. Lincoln YMCA, 1990-93, Lincoln Bus. Innovation Ctr., 1991-92, Manhattan Arts Coun., 1994—; commr. Nebr. 125th Statehood Anniversary Commn., Lincoln, 1990-93; team mem. Mayoral Transition Team, Lincoln, 1991; advisor, participant Strategic Planning Retreat, Lincoln, 1989. Named Minority Adv. of Yr., U.S. Small Bus. Adminstrn., 1990. Home: PO Box 1984 Manhattan KS 66505-1984 Office: Kans State Univ Multicultural Affairs Manhattan KS 66506

DAVIS, GARDINER B., lawyer; b. Des Moines, Iowa, Apr. 29, 1953; s. Blaine A. and Marie R. (McGeorge) D.; m. Laura A. Ziegler, Nov. 14, 1992; children: Julia, Eleanor. AB, Princeton (N.J.) U., 1975; JD, U. Iowa, 1978. Bar: Mo., Kans., Iowa. Atty. Spencer, Fane, Britt & Browne, Kansas City, Mo., 1978—; chair civil law and procedure com. Kansas City Metro. Bar Assn., 1990; mng. editor Iowa Law Review, 1977-78; pres. Gillis Ozanam Spofford Consortium, Kansas City, 1995—. Chair Gillis Ctr., Kansas City, 1996—. Mem. Iowa State Bar Assn. Office: Spencer Fane Britt & Browne Ste 1400 1000 Walnut St Kansas City MO 64106

DAVIS, GORDON BITTER, business educator; b. Idaho Falls, Idaho, Aug. 9, 1930; s. Orson P. and Olive (Bitter) D.; m. LaNay Marie Flint, Aug. 19, 1954; children: Alison, Jennifer, Clark, Flint. BA in Polit. Sci., Idaho State U., 1955; MBA, Stanford U., 1957, PhD in Bus., 1959; hon. doctorate, U. Lyon, France, 1990, U. Zurich, Switzerland, 1995. CPA. Cons. Touche Ross & Co., N.Y.C., 1959-61; prof. European Inst. for Advanced Studies in Mgmt., Brussels, 1972-73; Shaw prof. info. sys. Nat. U. Singapore, 1986-87; prof. U. Minn., Mpls., 1961—, Honeywell prof. MIS, 1977—; U.S. rep. tech. com. 8, Internat. Fedn. for Info. Processing, Geneva, 1983—, chmn., 1989-95. Author: Introduction to Electronic Computers, 1965, 2d rev. edit., 1977, Computer Data Processing, 1969, rev. edit., 1973, Management Information Systems, 1974,rev. edit., 1985, Managing Information, 1992, others. Bishop LDS Ch., St. Paul, 1972-75, 89-92. Mem. AICPA (cons. 1966-67), Info. Sys. Audit and Control Assn., Am. Acctg. Assn., Assn. for Computing Machinery, Informs, Data Processing Mgmt. Assn., Computer Soc., Assn. for Info. Sys. Office: U Minn Carlson Sch Mgmt 271 19th Ave S Minneapolis MN 55455-0430

DAVIS, GRANT M., investment consultant; b. Shaker Heights, Ohio, Feb. 25, 1964. BA, Ohio State U., 1987. Spl. events coord. Proserve, Washington, 1987-88; regional mgr. Stuffin' Turkey, Balt., 1988-90; mgr. Bakers Furniture, Cleve., 1990-93; investment cons. McDonald & Co. Securities, Pepper Pike, Ohio, 1993—. Participant Big Bros., 1991-95; solicitor Macabi Games, 1995. Mem. Beachwood C. of C., Beechmont Country Club (trustee 1994-95). Republican. Jewish.

DAVIS, GREGORY THOMAS, marine surveyor; b. Evergreen Park, Ill., Jan. 19, 1952; s. Bernard Thomas and Helen Therese (Keehan) D.; m. Christine Ellen Luka, Aug. 25, 1975; children: Brian Thomas, Bonnie Jean. BA, Coll. of Santa Fe, 1973. Cert. marine surveyor, fire and explosion investigator, bd. cert. forensic examiner. Adjuster Gen. Adjustment Bur., Chgo., 1973-74; marine surveyor Graham Miller Ltd., London, 1974-76; marine surveyor, pres. Davis and Co. Ltd., Lisle, Ill., 1977—; guest lect. Tec Core, Wheeling, Ill., 1990—; mem. ad hoc com. on marine fuel U.L. Marine, Northbrook, Ill., 1986—; mem. Am. Bd. Forensic Examiners. Contbr. articles to profl. jours. Mem. Nat. Assn. Marine Surveyors (chmn. ins. com. 1982-95), Am. Boat and Yacht Coun., Nat. Fire Protection Assn., Am. Soc. for Non-destructive Testing, Nat. Assn. Fire Investigators, Internat. Assn. Arson Investigators, Nat. Assn. Marine Investigators, Soc. of Naval Architects and Marine Engrs. Office: Davis and Co Ltd 1989 University Ste I Lisle IL 60532

DAVIS, HARLAN R., design engineer; b. Manchester, Iowa, May 15, 1954. AD in Mech. Design, North Ctrl. Tech. Coll., Wausau, Wis., 1987. Project engr. IMI Cornelius, Mason City, Iowa, 1988—. Patentee in field. Office: IMI Cornelius PO Box 1527 Mason City IA 50402-1527

DAVIS, HENRY BARNARD, JR., lawyer; b. East Grand Rapids, Mich., June 3, 1923; s. Henry Barnard and Ethel Margaret (Turnbull) D.; m. Margaret Lees Wilson, Aug. 27, 1946; children: Caroline Dellenbusch, Laura Davis, George B. BA, Yale U., 1945; JD, U. Mich., 1950; LLD, Olivet Coll., 1983. Bar: Mich. 1951; U.S. Dist. Ct. (we. dist.) Mich. 1956, U.S. Ct. Apls. (6th cir.) 1971, U.S. Supreme Ct. 1978. Assoc. Allaben, Wiarda, Hayes & Hewitt, 1951-52; ptnr. Hayes, Davis & Dellenbusch, Grand Rapids, 1952—. Mem. Kent County Bd. Commrs., 1968-72, Community Mental Health Bd., 1970-94, past chmn.; trustee, sec. bd. Olivet Coll., 1965-91, chmn. law com., 1975-91, trustee emeritus 1991—; chair Grand Rapids Historic Preservation Com., 1977-79. Republican. Trustee, East Congregational Ch., 1979-81. Served with USAAF, 1943-46; Philippines. ABA, Mich. Bar Assn., Grand Rapids Round Table (pres. 1969). Lodge: Masons. Home: 30 Mayfair Dr NE Grand Rapids MI 49503-3831 Office: 535 Fountain St NE Grand Rapids MI 49503-3421

DAVIS, H(UMPHREY) DENNY, publisher; b. Fayette, Mo., May 8, 1927; s. Lionel Winchester and Sarah Elizabeth (Denny) D.; m. Barbara Ellen Hartsgrove, June 6, 1954; 1 child, Thomas Shackelford. Student, Central Meth. Coll., Fayette, 1944-45, 46-47; BJ, U. Mo., 1949. Reporter, wire editor S.E. Missourian, Cape Girardeau, 1949-54; corr. UPI, Oklahoma City, Tulsa, Denver, 1954-55; exec. UPI, Albuquerque, 1955-56; bur. mgr. UPI, Lima, Peru, 1955-58; mgr. for Brazil UPI, Rio de Janeiro, 1958-68; mgr. no. div. Latin Am. Mexico City, 1968-75; regional exec. Charlotte, N.C., 1975-78; founder, owner pub. Wood Creek Corp., Fayette, 1978—; editor Fayette Advertiser and Democrat-Leader, Fayette, 1984—. Author profl. manual; contbr. articles to mags. and newspapers. Chmn. Fayette Planning and Zoning Commn., 1980-87; chmn. Howard County Rep. Cen. Com., Fayette, 1982—; pres. Franklin or Bust, Inc., Fayette, 1988—; mem. Santa Fe Trail Nat. Historic Trail Nat. Adv. Coun., 1991—. With USN, 1945-46, 50-51. Mem. NRA, Santa Fe Trail Assn., Fayette Round Table Club (pres. 1989-90), Fayette Area C. of C. (pres. 1979), Fayette Area Heritage Assn. (v.p. 1989-91), Am. Legion. Republican. Episcopalian. Home: 400 N Church St Fayette MO 65248-1125 Office: Wood Creek Corp 202 E Morrison St Fayette MO 65248-1306

DAVIS, JAMES EDWARD, historian, educator; b. Detroit, Sept. 27, 1940; s. William Franklin and Mable Fern (Corley) D.; m. Joanna Katherine Young, Dec. 22, 1966; children: Mary Suzanne, Kathleen Corley. AB, Wayne State U., 1962, MA, 1966; PhD, U. Mich., 1971. Cert. secondary tchr., Mich. Tchr. Dearborn (Mich.) Pub. Schs., 1963-71; prof. history Ill. Coll., Jacksonville, 1971—; adv. bd. We. Ill. Regional Studies Assn.,

Macomb, 1981—; cons. Elliott State Bank, Jacksonville, 1982, 89-91, Farmers State Bank, Jacksonville, 1986. Author: Frontier America, 1977; editor: Dreams to Dust, 1989, The People of Jacksonville, 1991; contbr. articles to profl. jours. Mem. Orgn. Am. Historians, Soc. Historians for Early Am. Republic, Midwest Sociol. Assn., Ill. State Hist. Soc. (dir. 1988-91, Disting. Svc. award 1977), The Club (pres., sec.). Office: Ill Coll Dept History 1101 W College Ave Jacksonville IL 62650-2212

DAVIS, JAMES HAROLD, banker; b. Kansas City, Mo., July 14, 1943; s. Hunter P. and Pearle (Haas) D.; m. Penelope Wheeler, Aug. 17, 1968; children: J. Hunter, Melissa Beth, Renee Wheeler. BSBA, Northwestern U., Evanston, Ill., 1965, MBA, 1968. Sr. v.p. Continental Ill. Nat. Bank, Chgo., 1965-83; pres. The Oreg. Bank, Portland, 1983-85; exec. v.p. corp. banking, sr. lending officer The Boatmen's Nat. Bank, St. Louis, 1986—. Adv. coun. assoc. Northwestern Grad. Sch. Mgmt.; social chmn. Winnetka Platform Tennis Assn.; mem. Winnetka (Ill.) Presbyn. Ch., Oreg. chpt. Young Pres.'s Orgn.; assoc. gen. chmn. United Way of Columbia, willamette; bd. dirs. Goodwill Industries, Mo. Colls. Fund; bd. trustees St. Louis Children's Hosp.; bd. dirs., exec. coun. and fin. adv. coun. U.S. Olympic Festival, 1994. Mem. Northwestern U. Alumni Assn., Northwestern Club of St. Louis, Oswego Lake Country Club, Mo. Athletic Club, Bellerive Country Club, Creve Coeur Racquet and Paddle Club, Chgo. Yacht Club, Delta Upsilon. Methodist. Office: Boatmens Nat Bank 1 Boatmens Plz 800 Market St Saint Louis MO 63101-2500*

DAVIS, JAMES LLOYD, state legislator; b. Frankfort, Ind., July 28, 1928; s. Lloyd E. and Florence M. (Norris) D.; m. Barbara Ann Scott, 1953; children: Megan Davis Sheets, Beth, Thomas J., William S. BS, Purdue U., 1953. Real estate broker Goar Assocs., 1953—; rep. dist. 28 Ind. Ho. of Reps., 1982—, ranking mem. agr. com., chmn. agr. and rural devel. com., mem. pub. policy com., labor and employment, ethics com., mem. elec. com., vet. affars com., asst. chmn. Rep. Caucus; farmer. Chmn. Clinton County Rep. Com., Ind., 1985-85. Mem. Am. Legion, Elks, Moose, Masons, Shriners, Sigma Chi. Home: 1351 Forest Dr Frankfort IN 46041-3255*

DAVIS, JAMES LEE, business executive; b. Indpls., May 28, 1953; s. Robert Fanton and Mary Elizabeth (Barth) D.; m. Michelle Diane Rutkowski, Oct. 11, 1975; children: Bradley J., Jennifer N., Adam B. AA, West Shore Coll., 1976. Dir. materials West Shore Hosp., Manistee, Mich., 1976-79; exec. sales rep. Surgikos, Inc., Grand Rapids, Mich., 1979-83; midwest div. mgr. Surgikos, Inc., St. Louis, 1983-89; area bus. mgr. Johnson & Johnson, St. Louis, 1989-90; corp. bus. mgr. Johnson & Johnson, Mpls., 1991-96; bus. cons., 1996—. Pres. Vets. Outreach, Scottville, Mich. 1976, Homeowners Assn., Ballwin, Mo., 1985; mem. Citizens Adv. Com.-Congress., St. Louis, 1989-90; bd. dirs. Kirkwood (Mo.) Youth Hockey, 1990—. Sgt. U.S. Army, 1972-74. Mem. Internat. Platform Assn., Am. Soc. Hosp. Materials Mgrs., Mich. Soc. Ctrl. Supply (sterilization specialist 1983). Republican. Home: 18546 Pheasant Ridge Rd Prior Lake MN 55372-9323

DAVIS, JANE STRAUSS, business owner; b. Chgo., July 3, 1944; d. Joseph Loeb and Leanore (Purvin) Strauss; m. Muller Davis, Dec. 28, 1963; children: Melissa Davis Smith, Muller Jr., Joseph. BA with honors in Am. Culture, Northwestern U., 1980, postgrad. studies in Am. History, 1980-81. With residential sales Kenneth Friend Realty, Winnetka, Ill., 1971-74, J.H. Kahn Realty, Glencoe, Ill., 1974-77; v.p. personal trust dept. Harris Trust & Savs. Bank, Chgo., 1983-89; v.p. Bankers Trust Co. Pvt. Bank, Chgo., 1989-90; founder Jane Davis Connections, Chgo., 1991—, Connections Next Step, 1993—, Young Chgo. Authors, 1992-95, Charlotte.Com, Inc., Chgo., 1996—; founder Charlotte Com, Inc.; dir. Met. Family Svcs. Mem. woman's bd. Rush-Presbyn.-St. Luke's Med. Ctr., Chgo., 1978—; co-chmn. med. rsch. campaign Michael Reese Med. Ctr., Chgo., 1982-96; mem. costume com. Chgo. Hist. Soc., 1980-90; mem. campaign for gt. tchrs. Northwestern U., Evanston, Ill., 1988-90, mem. vis. com., 1989—, mem. coun. of 100; mem. Chgo. Symphony Orch. Woman's Assn., 1990—; mem. coun. Children's Meml. Hosp. Med. Rsch. Inst., 1991—; mem. Coun. of 100, The Chgo. Bd.; chmn. 50th anniversary day celebration Roosevelt U., Chgo., 1995, co-chmn. Itzhak Pearlman concert, 1996.

DAVIS, JEFFERSON BATES, microbiologist, consultant; b. Grosse Pointe Farms, Mich., Aug. 1, 1955; s. Ronald Wilfred and Virginia Dorothy (Bates) D. BS in microbiology, U. Mich., Ann Arbor, 1977; postgrad., Columbia U., 1978-79. Cons. sci. and govt. select fortune co., 1986—; cons. fiscal crisis Fed. Govt., Washington, 1989-90, cons. gene analysis for biotechnology, 1994—. Mem. Am. Fed. of Police, Am. Rifle Assn., Elks (exalted ruler 1988-91), Lions (zone chmn. 1989-90). Republican. Home: 325 Bedford St Alpena MI 49707

DAVIS, JOSEPH LLOYD, educational administrator, consultant; b. Crawfordsville, Iowa, May 4, 1927; s. Whitfield and Jane (Lloyd) D.; m. Margaret Florence Cooper, Dec. 28, 1949; children: Stephen Joseph, Thomas Whitfield, Jane Ellen. BSc, Ohio State U., 1949, MA, 1955, PhD, 1967. Reporter Ohio State Jour., 1943-49, 52-53; tchr. Morey Jr. High Sch., Denver, 1949-52, Central High Sch., Columbus, Ohio, 1953-54; asst. dir. adminstrv. research Columbus Public Schs., 1954-56, dir. publs. and public info., 1956-60, exec. asst. to supt., 1960-64, asst. supt. spl. services, 1964-77, supt. of schs., 1977-82; exec. dir. Ohio Coun. Vocat. Edn., 1985-96; trustee Ctr. of Sci. and Industry; past pres. Columbus Rotary; adj. prof. Ohio State U., 1983—, mem. provost's external adv. bd. on tchg., 1995—. Mem. Ohio Gov.'s Human Resource Investment Coun., 1995—. With USN, 1945-46, 50-51. Recipient award for civic leadership Columbus Area C. of C., 1980, Liberty Bell award Columbus Bar Assn., 1980; named to Pub. Schs. Hall of Fame, Columbus, Ohio, 1993. Mem. Am. Assn. Sch. Adminstrs. (disting. svc. award 1989). Nat. Sch. Pub. Rels. Assn. (pres.'s award 1980), Am. Vocat. Assn., Ohio State U. Acad. Supts. (founder, dir. emeritus), Ohio Vocat. Assn., Buckeye Assn. Sch. Adminstrs., Nat. Soc. Study Edn., Horace Mann League, Rotary (Rotarian of Yr. award 1994), Phi Delta Kappa, Epsilon Pi Tau (laureate), Kappa Delta Pi. Presbyterian. Office: 750 Brooksedge Blvd Westerville OH 43081-2881

DAVIS, JOY LEE, English language educator; b. N.Y.C., Apr. 3, 1931; d. William Henry and Genevieve (Rhein) Belknap; m. Peter John King, Aug. 26, 1955 (div. Feb. 1985); children: William Belknap King, Russell Stuart King; m. John Bradford Davis, Jr., July 5, 1986. AB, Wellesley Coll., 1952, AM, 1953; PhD, Rutgers U., 1968; postgrad., Oxford (Eng.) U., 1978. Tchr. English Dana Hall Sch. for Girls, Wellesley, Mass., 1953-54; instr. English U. Mo., Columbia, 1954-55, Boston U., 1955-56; tchr. English Brookline (Mass.) High Sch., Spartanburg (S.C.) High Sch., 1956-60; prof. English Ohio Wesleyan U., Delaware, 1966-71, Hamline U., St. Paul, 1972-74, U. Minn., Mpls., 1974-77, Coll. St. Thomas, St. Paul, 1977-88; lectr., dir. Joy Davis Seminars, St. Paul, 1988—; prof. MA in Liberal Studies Program, Hamline U., 1993—. Pub. poetry in New World Writing and Crisp Pine Anthology; lit. criticism in Midwest Quar., 1993, Jour. Grad. Liberal Studies, 1996. Bd. trustees Ramsey County Arts and Sci. Coun., St. Paul, 1974-80. Wellesley Coll. scholar, 1952. Mem. AAUW (dd. dirs., chair ednl. equity com. 1991, Svc. awrd St. Paul br. 1983), Midwest MLA, Mpls. Inst. Fine Arts, Minn. Club (bd. dirs. 1982-88), New Century Club (bd. dirs., spl. subjects chmn.) Schubert Club (bd. dirs., chmn. mus. com.), Wellesley Coll. Club (regional campaign com.), Delta Kappa Gamma. Republican. Presbyterian. Home and Office: 4312 Pond View Dr Saint Paul MN 55110-4155

DAVIS, KATHRYN WARD, fundraising executive; b. Florence, S.C., Oct. 11, 1949; d. Richard Dixon Ward and Kathryn (McFarland) Duncan; m. Michael R. Bumgardner, Feb. 16, 1974 (div. Nov. 1982); children: Carolyn E., Christopher G.; m. David Addison Davis, May 28, 1983. BA in English, U. N.C., 1971. Dir. devel. WFAE Radio, U. N.C., Charlotte, 1980-82, WUNC Radio, U. N.C., Chapel Hill, 1982-84, U. N.C. Hosps. Med. Found., Chapel Hill, 1984-87, St. Joseph Med. Found., Balt., 1987-88; exec. dir. MCG Found., Mt. Clemens, Mich., 1989-95; dir. devel. Leader Dogs for the Blind, Rochester, Mich., 1995—; fundraising coun. Macomb County Lit. Coun., Mt. Clemens, 1991. Tutor Macomb County Reading Ptnrs., 1992; cons. Jr. Achievement, Detroit, 1991. Named Disting Svc. Toastmasters, Chapel Hill, 1986. Mem. Nat. Soc. Fundraising Execs., Mich. Assn. Hosp. Devel. (pres. 1990-92), Assn. Healthcare Philanthropy (cert., region VI dir. 1994-96), Kiwanis of Sterling Heights (bd. dirs. 1994—, pres. 1996-97), Women's Econ. Club. Republican. Epsicopalian. Office: Leader Dogs for the Blind 1039 S Rochester Rd Rochester MI 48307

DAVIS, KAY, state legislator. Mem. S.D. Ho. of Reps., Pierre; mem. edn. and retirement laws coms. Democrat.

DAVIS, KENNETH MORTON, artist, art historian, educator; b. Cleve., Apr. 18, 1939; s. Max and Frieda (Gevelber) D.; m. Carol Ann Gold, Jan. 30, 1964; children: Aaron Richard Harley, Bradley Marlen. BS, Western Reserve U., Cleve., 1962, MA, 1964; MFA, U. Cin., 1966; MA, Ohio State U., 1968, PhD, 1993. Teaching asst. U. Cin., 1964-66; teaching asst. Ohio State U., Columbus, 1966-68, instr. II, div. recreation, 1966-68; from asst. to assoc. prof. Ball State U., Muncie, Ind., 1968-77, prof. art, 1977—. Works exhibited in shows at Cleve. Mus., Dayton Art Inst., Evansville Mus., Swope Gallery, Terre Haute, Ind., also several univ. museums; contbg. author: Gardner's Art Through the Ages, 9th edit., 1990. Trustee Temple Beth-El Congregation, Muncie, 1980—. Mem. Am. Philatelic Soc., Assn. Historians Am. Art, Mailer's Postmark Permit Club. Home: 2731 S Parkway Dr Muncie IN 47304-5128 Office: Ball State U Dept Art Muncie IN 47306

DAVIS, KENNETH WAYNE, English language educator, business communication consultant; b. Chariton, Iowa, June 22, 1945; s. Wayne Pitman and Jeanne Frances (West) D.; m. Bette Hargrove, Nov. 28, 1970; Cassandra Alice, Evan Thomas. BA, Drake U., 1967; MA, Columbia U., 1968; PhD, U. Mich., 1975. From asst. prof. English to assoc. prof. U. Ky., Lexington, 1975-88; assoc. prof. to prof. Ind. U.-Purdue U., Indpls., 1988—; bus. cons., Lexington, 1977-88; pres. Komei, Inc., 1994—. Author: Better Business Writing, 1983, (with others) Business Communication for the Information Age, 1988, Rehearsing the Audience, 1988, (with others) Writing: Process, Product, and Power, 1993; prodr.: 2001: Lessons in Leadership videoconf., 1991; numerous other books and articles. bd. dirs. Shepherd's House, Inc., Lexington, 1986-88. Sgt. U.S. Army, 1968-71. Woodrow Wilson fellow, 1967; recipient Faculty Service award Nat. Univ. Continuing Edn. Assn., 1987. Mem. ASTD, Nat. Coun. Tchrs. English, Conf. Coll. Compsoition Comm., Assn. Bus. Comm., Assn. Profl. Comm. Cons., World Bus. Acad., Amnesty Internat. Episcopalian. Home: 7856 Clarendon Rd Indianapolis IN 46260-3513 Office: Ind U-Purdue U Dept English 425 University Blvd Indianapolis IN 46202-5148

DAVIS, LARRY ALLEN, lawyer; b. Chgo., June 9, 1950; s. Lee J. and Lynn (Koralchick) D.; m. Caryn Jacobs, Sept. 23, 1978; children: Shanna, Brandon, Merrill. BA, Northwestern U., 1973; JD, DePaul U., 1976. Bar: Ill. 1976, U.S. Dist. Ct. (no. dist.) Ill. 1976. Atty. Sec. of State, State of Ill., Chgo., 1976-80; pvt. practice Chgo., 1980-82; ptnr. Davis & Riebman, Des Plaines, Ill., 1982—; lectr. Ill. Inst. Continuing Legal Edn., Chgo., 1984-96. Author: (with others) Defense of DUI, 1984-96; contbr. articles to profl. jours. Cert. of Recognition NW Suburban Bar Assn., Palatine, Ill., 1985-90. Mem. Ill. State Bar Assn. (chair traffic laws and cts. sect. coun. 1992-93, Cert. of Recognition 1995), Chgo. Bar Assn. (chmn. traffic laws com. 1987-88, lectr. 1984-90, Cert. of Recognition 1995). Office: Davis & Riebman Ltd 960 Rand Rd Ste 210 Des Plaines IL 60016-2355

DAVIS, LARRY MICHAEL, military officer, health-care consultant; b. Lodi, Ark., Mar. 30, 1947; s. Harmon Odell and Jeanice (White) D.; m. Linda Ruth Blanchard, Mar. 22, 1969; children: Elizabeth Blanchard, Brooke Alison. BS, U. Ark., 1969; MA, Pepperdine U., 1978; postgrad., USAF Air U., 1975, 83-84. Commd. 2nd lt. USAF, 1969, advanced through grades to col., 1985; navigator, instr. navigator 596th Bombardment Squadron; radar navigator 62d Bombardment Squadron, 1971-75; instr. navigator, asst. curriculum mgr. 450th Flying Tng. Squadron, Mather AFB, Calif., 1975-76; asst. navigator sect. chief Standardization and Evaluation divsn. 323rd Flying Tng. Wing, Mather AFB, Calif., 1976-78; air ops. staff officer Tng. Analysis div. HQ Air Tng. Command, Randolph AFB, Tex., 1978-79; chief navigation tng. HQ Air Tng. Command, Randolph AFB, Tex., 1979-81; air ops. officer 99th Strategic Reconnaissance Squadron Beale AFB, Calif., 1982-83, wing chief of inspection 9th Strategic Reconnaissance Wing, 1983-84; reconnaissance ops. staff officer, reconnaissance emergency war order plans officer, chief reconnaissance plans divsn. HQ Strategic Air Command, Offutt AFB, Nebr., 1984-87; comdr. 3550th USAF Recruiting Squadron, Indpls., 1987-89; comdr. 3555th USAF Recruiting Squadron Milw., 1988; dep. comdr. 3501st USAF Recruiting Group, Hanscom AFB, Mass., 1989-91; health-care cons., customer svc. mgr. Electronic Data Systems, Indpls., 1991—. Decorated D.F.C., Air medal with three oak leaf clusters. Mem. Internat. Platform Assn., Ret. Officers Assn., Air Force Assn., Rotary (mem. health sharing com. 1989-90), Blue Key, Alpha Zeta, Alpha Gamma Rho. Methodist. Home: 11503 Chloe Ct Indianapolis IN 46236-8708 Office: Electronic Data Systems 950 N Meridian St Indianapolis IN 46204

DAVIS, LAURIE LEE, special education educator; b. Evanston, Ill., Oct. 16, 1965; d. Richard Aubrey and Sue Ann (Wheelock) Hunt; m. John Glen Davis, July 29, 1989; 1 child, Julia Marie. BS, Iowa State U., 1987; student, Nat. Louis U., 1988-90. Cert. tchr., Ill. Spl. edn. asst. Lake Forest (Ill.) Sch. Dist. 67, 1987-88; tchr. spl. edn. Palatine Community Consolidated Dist. 15, Palatine, Ill., 1988-89, Arlington Heights (Ill.) Sch. Dist. 25, 1989-93; team leader spl. edn. Arlington Heights (Ill.) Sch. Dist. 25, 1992—, 1992-93; ret. Home: 4406 Meadowlark Ln La Crosse WI 54601

DAVIS, LINDA WILES, biology educator; b. Cedar Rapids, Iowa, Feb. 20, 1945; d. Leslie E. and Eleanor (Deadman) Wiles; m. Lawrence C. Davis, July 22, 1967; children: Colin C., Steven L. BA, Swarthmore Coll., 1967; MS, Kans. State U., 1988. Instr. biology Kans. State U., Mahattan, 1989—. Author: Weed Seeds of the Great Plains, 1993. Office: Kansas State Univ Divsn Biology 213 Ackert Hall Manhattan KS 66506

DAVIS, MARVIN RALPH, business executive; b. Lebanon, Ohio, Nov. 30, 1922; s. Marvin Flegal and Aurelia (Turner) D.; m. Doris Helen Summer, Oct. 15, 1949; children: Kerry M., Robert A., Lisa S. Davis Drake. BSME, U. Cin., 1949, ME, 1955; MSc, Ohio State U., 1961; PhD, Columbia Pacific U., San Rafael, Calif., 1981. Sr. mech. engr. Nat. Cash Register Co., Dayton, Ohio, 1941-51; v.p. Quality Elec. Co., Dayton, 1953-54; prodn. test pilot USAF, Inglewood, Calif., 1951-53; cicilian dir. sys. procurement office USAF, Wright-Patterson AFB, Ohio, 1954-86; mgmt. cons. Beavercreek, Ohio, 1986—; chmn. bd., pres., CEO Rahcon Corp., Beavercreek, 1992—. Chmn. Valleywood Incorp. Com., Beavercreek, 1970. Sheffield Found. scholar, 1942, 48. Mem. VFW, 467th Bomb Group Assn. (pres. 1995-96), Am. Legion, 2d Air Divsn., 8th Air Force Heritage Mus., 8th Air Force Hist. Soc., Inc. Republican. Lutheran. Home: 1143 Kenora Cir Beavercreek OH 45430

DAVIS, MARY ELIZABETH, speech pathologist, educator, counselor; b. Larned, Kans., July 1, 1930; d. LeRoy D. and Katheryn (Herndon) Harris; m. W.G. Davis, Apr. 3, 1969; children: Pam Koch, Michelle Dalton; 1 stepchild, Wendy Garton. BA, Calif. State U., Fresno, 1959, MA, 1982. Cert. resource specialist, speech pathologist tchr., deaf tchr., counselor, Calif. Dir. recreation and occupl. therapy Wyo. State Hosp., Evanston, 1956-58; tchr. Fresno Unified Sch. Dist., 1960-80, Barton County C.C., Great Bend, Kans., 1990—. Mem. Am. Counseling Assn. Home: 534 W 4th St Larned KS 67550

DAVIS, MICHAEL WARREN REES, journalist, public relations executive; b. Buffalo, May 10, 1931; s. John Erle and Laura Gertrude (Huckleberry) D.; m. Mary Katherine Mattison, Jan. 5, 1957 (dec. Jan. 1986); children: Penelope, Elizabeth, John; m. Karen Lynn Schwarz, Apr. 21, 1990; 1 stepchild, Laura Ann Crandall. BA, Yale U., 1953; MS, Ea. Mich. U., 1983. Reporter The Miami News, 1955-57; asst. bur. mgr. Bus. Week McGraw-Hill Publ. Co., Detroit, 1957-60; from reporter pub. rels. staff to mktg. projects mgr. Ford Motor Co., Detroit, 1960-85; dir. corp. comms. Evening News Assn., Detroit, 1985; corp. comms. dir. The Detroit News, 1986; exec. dir. Detroit Hist. Soc., 1987-92; trustee Nat. Automotive History Collection, Detroit, 1994—; v.p. Univ. Culture Ctr. Assn., Detroit, 1987-92; cons. Engrng. Soc. Detroit, 1994—. Co-author: America's Favorite Homes, 1990, The Ford Fleet, 1994; editor: The Technology Century, 1995. Mem. Pub. Rels. Soc. Am., Nat. Soc. Fund Raising Execs., Soc. Automotive Engrs., Automotive Press Assn., Soc. Archtl. Historians. Episcopalian. Home: 1919 Cedar Hill Dr Royal Oak MI 48067

DAVIS, MONIQUE D. (DEON DAVIS), state legislator; b. Chgo., Aug. 19, 1936; d. James and Constance (Dutton) McKay; divorced; children: Robert Jr., Monique C. Conway. BS in Edn., Chgo. State U., 1967, MS in Guidance and Counseling, 1976. Tchr. Chgo. Bd. Edn., 1967-86, coordinator, 1986—; mem. Ill. Ho. of Reps. from 27th dist., 1987—, vice chmn. elem. and secondary edn. com. Mem. legis. com. Chgo. Area Alliance Black Sch. Edn., 1982-84, Independent Voters of Ill.-Independent Precinct Orgns., Chgo., 1982-83; coordinator 21st ward, Citizens for Mayor Washington, 1985, 87. Recipient GRIT award Roseland Womens Orgn., 1987; named a Tchr. Who Makes a Difference PTA, 1978, 85. Mem. Chgo. Area Tchrs. Alliance (chmn.), Christian Bd. Edn. (bd. dirs. 1978-82), Phi Delta Kappa. Mem. United Ch. of Christ. Office: Ill Ho of Reps State Capitol Springfield IL 62706*

DAVIS, MULLER, lawyer; b. Chgo., Apr. 23, 1935; s. Benjamin B. and Janice (Muller) D.; m. Jane Lynn Strauss, Dec. 28, 1963; children: Melissa Davis Smith, Muller, Joseph Jeffrey. Grad. with honors, Phillips Exeter (N.H.) Acad., 1953; B.A. magna cum laude, Yale U., 1957; J.D., Harvard U., 1960. Bar: Ill. 1960, U.S. Dist. Ct. (no. dist.) Ill. 1961. Practice law Chgo., 1960—; assoc. Jenner & Block, 1960-67; ptnr. Davis, Friedman, Zavett, Kane & MacRae, 1967—; lectr. continuing legal edn., matrimonial law and litigation; legal adviser Michael Reese Med. Research Inst. Council, 1967-82. Author: (with Sherman C. Feinstein) The Parental Couple in a Successful Divorce, Illinois Practice of Family Law, 1995; mem. editorial bd. Equitable Distbn. Jour., 1984—; contbr. articles to law jours. Bd. dirs. Infant Welfare Soc., 1975-96, hon. bd. dirs., 1996—, pres., 1978-82; co-chmn. gen. gifts 40th reunion Phillips Exeter Acad., chair class capital giving, 1994—. Capt. U.S. Army, Ill. N.G., 1960-67. Fellow Am. Acad. Matrimonial Lawyers, Am. Bar Found.; mem. ABA, Fed. Bar Assn., Ill. Bar Assn., Chgo. Bar Assn. (matrimonial com. 1968-83, sec. civil practice com. 1979-80, vice chmn. 1980-81, chmn. 1981-820, Chgo. Estate Planning Coun., Legal Aid Soc. (vice chmn. 1991—), Law Club Chgo., Tavern Club, Lake Shore Country Club, Chgo. Club. Republican. Jewish. Home: 1020 E Westleigh Rd Lake Forest IL 60045-3330 Office: 140 S Dearborn St Chicago IL 60603-5202

DAVIS, PAMELA J., nursing educator; b. Dayton, Ohio, Aug. 17, 1959; d. F. Thomas Jr. and Peggy Jean (Leugers) P. BSN, Wright State U., 1984, MS, 1994. Staff RN newborn ICU Michael Reese Hosp., Chgo., 1984-86, Miami Valley Hosp., Dayton, 1986-87; staff RN newborn ICU Children's Med. Ctr., Dayton, 1987-88, staff nurse pediatric surgery, 1988-89; staff devel. coord. Catalpa Manor, N.H., 1993-94; instr. Miami Jacobs Coll., 1996—. Home: 578 Thoma Pl Vandalia OH 45377-1464

DAVIS, ROBERT EDWARD, judge; b. Topeka, Aug. 28, 1939; s. Thomas Homer and Emma Claire (Hund) D.; div.; children: Edward, Rachel, Patrick, Carolyn. BA in Polit. Sci., Creighton U., 1961; JD, Georgetown U., 1964. Bar: Kans. 1964, U.S. Dist. Ct. Kans. 1964, U.S. Tax Ct. 1974, U.S. Ct. Mil. Appeals 1965, U.S. Ct. Mil. Review, 1970, U.S. Ct. Appeals (10th cir.) 1974, U.S. Supreme Ct. 1982. Pvt. practice Leavenworth, Kans., 1967-84; magistrate judge Leavenworth County, 1969-76, county atty., 1980-84, judge dist. ct., 1984-86; judge Kans. Ct. Appeals Jud. Br. Govt., Topeka, 1986-93; justice Kans. Supreme Ct., Topeka, 1993—; lectr. U. Kans. Law Sch., Lawrence, 1986-95. Capt. JAGC, U.S. Army, 1964-67, Korea. Mem. Am. Judges Assn., Kans. Bar Assn., Leavenworth County Bar Assn. (pres. 1977), Judge Hugh Means Am. Inn of Ct. Charter Orgn. Lawrence. Roman Catholic. Home: 317 Woodlawn Dr Lawrence KS 66049-1839 Office: Justice Robert E Davis 301 W 10th Ave Topeka KS 66612

DAVIS, ROGER PAUL, history educator; b. Warren, Ohio, May 5, 1950; s. Paul William Davis and Lavina Elizabeth (Rooks) Davis Barbour; m. Cecelia Mary Clark, July 10, 1971; 1 child, Daniel Paul. BA in History, English, Youngstown State U., 1972; MA in History, U. Ariz., 1973, PhD in Latin Am. History, 1983. Cert. community coll. tchr., Ariz. Contract researcher Terramar Internat. Svcs., Tucson, 1984; assoc. faculty Pima C.C., Tucson, 1985; asst. prof. U. Nev., Las Vegas, 1985-86; asst. prof. Kearney (Nebr.) State Coll., 1986-89, assoc. prof., 1989-91; assoc. prof. U. Nebr., Kearney, 1991—; vis. lectr. Am. Grad. Sch. Internat. Mgmt., Glendale, Ariz., 1984; reader Ednl. Testing Svc. AP Exams, 1987—. Contbr. articles to profl. publs. Chair Buffalo County Dem. Party, Kearney, 1992-94, 94-96, publicity officer, 1990-92, 96—; chair Kearney/Tomorrow Ctr. Task Force, 1989-90, U. Nebr. Kearney United Way Campaign, 1991, 92, 94; chair editl. bd. The Platte Valley Rev., 1990—; pres. U. Nebr. Kearney Faculty Senate, 1992-93; v.p. U. Nebr. Kearney Edn. Assn., 1993—; mem. adv. bd. Nebr. State Hist. Records, 1996—. Mem. North Ctrl. Conf. Latin Americanists (sec. 1991, membership/comms. chair 1992, program chair 1993, pres.-elect 1994, pres. 1995), Am. Hist. Assn., Conf. on Latin Am. History, Comparative and Internat. Edn. Soc., Phi Alpha Theta. Office: Univ Nebraska History Dept Kearney NE 68849

DAVIS, SHERIE KAY, special education educator; b. Cin., Dec. 2, 1956; d. Earl Myron and and Irene (Alexander) Huffman; m. Dana Allen, June 18, 1985; 1 child, Lauren Nicole. BS in Edn. and Home Econs., U. Cin., 1979, MEd in Spl. Edn., 1980. Tchr. mid. sch. developmentally handicapped Ross Local Sch. Dist., Hamilton, Ohio, 1980-85, substitute tchr., 1985-87; substitute tchr. Three Rivers Local Sch. Dist., Cleve., 1985-87; tchr. high sch. developmentally handicapped New Miami Local Schs., Hamilton, 1987-92; tchr. to developementally handicapped Talawanda City Schs., 1992—; facilitator leadership conf. New Miami Care Team, Hamilton, 1989—; presenter Coun. for Exceptional Children-State Conv., Dayton, Ohio, 1990; coach varsity volleyball, jr. varsity basketball. Coach Three Rivers Knothole Baseball Assn., Cleve., 1991—. Recipient Quality Initiatives award Southwestern Ohio Spl. Edn. Regional Resource Ctr., Ohio, 1988. Mem. Coun. for Exceptional Children. Home: 608 N Miami Ave Cleves OH 45002-1029 Office: Talawanda High Sch 101 W Chestnut St Oxford OH 45056-2619

DAVIS, STEPHEN S., stockbroker; b. Huntsville, Ala., Mar. 24, 1965. BA, So. Ill. U., Carbondale, 1987. Securities broker Robert Thomas Securities, Effingham, Ill., 1988—. Mem. Effingham Jaycees, Masons. Libertarian. Office: Robert Thomas Securities PO Box 430 605 W Jefferson Effingham IL 62401

DAVIS, STEVE, state legislator; b. Sept. 22, 1949; m. Carol Keck; children: Shane, Shelly. Student, Lewis and Clark C.C., So. Ill. U. Hwy. commr. Wood River Twp., Ill., 1981-94; former mem., treas. Madison County Dem. Cen. Com.; Ill. state rep. Dist. 111, 1995—; mem. Aging, Appropriations-Edn., Environ. and Energy and Transp. Coms., 1995—, Ill. Ho. of Reps.; draftsman R. W. Booker and Assocs., 1970; sr. civil engr. Sterling Engrng. Co., 1970-73, Volz Engrng. and Survey, 1973-75, PHO Inc., 1975-78; operator Amoco Oil Co., 1978-80; pres. Steve Davis and Assocs., 1980-82. Bd. dirs. Family Svc. and Vis. Nurse Assn. Mem. Moose, Am. Legion (post 214), Ill. Legis. Sportsmans Caucus. Office: 29 N Wood River Rd Wood River IL 62095

DAVIS, WAYNE JOSEPH, engineering educator; b. Tell City, Ind., Sept. 2, 1948; s. Oliver Lloyd and Margaret Elizabeth (Harpenau) D.; m. Frances Anne Migielicz, Feb. 30, 1989. BS in Engring. Sci., Purdue U., 1970, MS in Engring. Sci., 1971, PhD, 1975. Rsch. asst. Purdue U., West Lafayette, 1973-75; from asst. prof. gen. engring. to assoc. prof. U. Ill., Urbana, 1975-87, prof. gen. engring., 1988—, prof. mech. and indsl. engring., 1992—; cons. Ill. Emergency Svcs., Springfield, Ill., 1979-80, U.S. Dept. Energy-Purdue U., West Lafayette, 1982-84, U.S. Army Rock Island (Ill.) Arsenal, 1988-89, 91; cons., collaborator Nat. Inst. Stds. and Tech., Gathersburg, Md., 1986-93. Author 4 book chpts.; contbr. numerous articles to profl. jours. Mem. various coms. St. Patrick Ch., Urbana, 1975—. NSF fellow Purdue U., 1971-74, Norcus Rsch. fellow U. Wash., Richland, 1976; numerous rsch. grants. Mem. ASME, Inst. Ops. Rsch. and Mgmt. Sci. Roman Catholic. Home: 9 Azalea Ct Savoy IL 61874 Office: U Ill Dept Gen Engring 104 S Mathews Ave Urbana IL 61801

DAVIS, WAYNE PITMAN, public relations specialist; b. Phillipsburg, Mo., Sept. 9, 1920; s. William Riley and Alice (Pitman) D.; m. Jeanne Frances West, May 28, 1944 (dec. June 1975); children: Kenneth Wayne, Polly Jeanne Davis Montgomery (dec.); m. Ferne Gater Bonomi, Apr. 20, 1991. BA, The Principia Coll., 1939; B of Journalism, U. Mo., 1941; MS, Iowa State U., 1988. Publisher The Moravia (Iowa) Union, 1942-45; mgr. The Mille Lacs Messenger, Isle, Minn., 1946-47; publisher The Seymour (Iowa) Herald, 1947-77; dir. mktg., pub. rels. & sales Iowa State Ctr., Ames, 1977-87; instr. Iowa State U., Ames, 1988—. Mem., chmn. Bd. Mcpl., Seymour, 1969-75; pres. Genoa & Seymour Farmers Mutual Telephone Co., 1954-61; dir., v.p. Ctrl. Iowa Symphony Bd., Ames, 1989—. 2d lt. U.S. Army, 1945-46. Decorated Meritorious Svc. medal. Mem. Pub. Rels Soc. Am. (accredited, sec. ctrl. Iowa chpt. 1980-8, bd. dirs. 1982-85), Iowa Newspaper Found. (bd. dirs. 1989—, pres. 1992), Reserve Officers Assn., Soc. Profl. Journalists, Am. Legion, Lions (pres. Ames chpt. 1954-77). Republican.

DAVIS, WILLIAM C., JR., lawyer; b. Knoxville, Tenn., Jan. 27, 1948; s. William C. and Burla A. (Monger) D.; m. Elaine Elizabeth Quinn, Sept. 18, 1971; children: Jeff, Tim, Ruth, Mike. BS in Chemistry, U. Ill., 1970, JD, 1974. Atty. pvt. practice, Lewistown, Ill., 1975—. Dir., Lewistown High Sch. Acad. Found., 1990—. Mem. Toastmasters. Office: Davis Law Office 257 W Lincoln Ave Lewistown IL 61542-1406

DAVIS, WILLIAM R., financial planner, stockbroker; b. Dixon, Ill., Oct. 27, 1949. BA, Ill. State U., 1975, MA, 1985. CFP. Counselor Youth Farm, Peoria, Ill., 1972-75, St. Joseph Home for Children, Mpls., 1975-76; therapist John M. Scott Ctr., Bloomington, Ill., 1986-89; fin. planner IDS Fin. Svcs., Champaign, Ill., 1989-92, Edward D. Jones & Co., Champaign, 1992—. Sgt. USAF, 1968-72, Vietnam. Mem. Internat. Assn. Fin. Planners.

DAVIS-CARTEY, CATHERINE BERNICE, bank executive; b. N.Y.C., Jan. 14, 1954; d. Edward James Doyle Davis and Adele Helen (Dixon) Cartey. BA, Simmons Coll., 1975; EdM, Harvard U., 1978. Program cons. United Community Svcs. Met., Detroit; comml. credit analyst Nat. Bank Detroit Comml. Lending Div., 1980-82; dir. comml. devel. Detroit Econ. Growth Corp., 1982-93; v.p. Mich. Nat. Bank, Bloomfield Hills, 1993—; pres. CDC Consulting, Southfield, Mich., 1985—. Author: Neighborhood Economic Development Strategies, 1989. Mem. exec. com. L.S. of Jesus; mem. fin. planning United Way Southeastern Mich., mem. allocations com.; dir. pers. com. Women's Econ. Club, Detroit; chmn., life mem. Comml. Real Estate Women, Troy, Mich., 1990—, Bus. Role Model/Detroit Pub. Schs., 1987-93; mem. exec. com. Ctrl. Bus. Dist. Assn. Mem. Harvard Club Eastern Mich. Office: Mich Nat Bank 1533 N Woodward Ave Bloomfield Hills MI 48304-2861

DAVISON, DEAN, public relations executive; b. Mercer, Mo., Jan. 8, 1960; s. George F. and Jean (Johnson) D.; m. Patricia Ellen Braymer, Oct. 26, 1985; children: Laura Patricia, Maria Ellen. BJ, U. Mo., Columbia, 1982, BA in Econs., 1982. Reporter, anchor WBAY-TV, Green Bay, Wis., 1982-85; assignment editor-producer KCTV, Kansas City, Mo., 1985-88; account exec. West Assocs. Advt., Leawood, Kans., 1988-89; v.p. Barkley & Evergreen, Fairway, Kans., 1989—. Team leader pub. rels. campaign Legacy of Leadership, Harry S Truman Libr., 1994—; bd. dirs. Project Neighborhood, 1994—; mem. comms. adv. bd. Kans. divsn. Am. Cancer Soc., 1994-95; mem. fin. coun. St. Joseph Ch., 1993—. Mem. Pub. Rels. Soc. Am. (15 Prism awards, APR accreditation), Mo. Mil. Acad. Alumni Assn. (bd. dirs. 1988—). Roman Catholic. Office: Barkley & Evergreen 423 W 8th St Kansas City MO 64105

DAVISON, LUELLA MAY, organization executive, retired writer; b. Woonsocket, S.D., Apr. 26, 1922; d. Milton Israel and Blanche Lyda (Dilley) Brady; m. Kenneth Earl Davison, Oct. 10, 1940; children: Suzanne, Pamela. Grad. high sch., Pontiac, Mich. Freelance writer Inter-Lake News, Mich., 1965-72. Vol., mem. youth, recruiting and escort coms. Pontiac Gen. Hosp., 1984-89; founder Grandparents Anonymous, Sylvan Lake, Mich., 1976, Mich. Grandparents and Grandchildrenns Day, Mich., 1985. Recipient Nat. Grandparent of Yr. award The Nat. Coun. for Observance of Grandparents' Day, 1982, Michiganian of Yr. award Mich. mag. Detroit News, 1982, award Waterford Village Sch., 1984. Home: 1924 Beverly St Sylvan Lake MI 48320-1506

DAVISON, SID I., JR. See **DIAMOND, DAVID**

DAVISON, WALTER SEARS, JR., civil engineer; b. Gibbs, Mo., Oct. 3, 1931; s. Walter Sears and Mary Christina (Umbarger) D.; m. Ellen Margaret Kirkpatrick Korbitz, May 26, 1962; children: John Walter, Jane Ellen. BS in Agr., U. Mo., 1957, BS in Agr. Engring., 1959. Registered profl. engr., Mo., land surveyor, Mo. Agr. engr., project civil engr. Soil Conservation Svc. USDA, Bethany, Higginsville, Mo., 1959-64; civil engr. Mo. River Basin Planning Staff USDA, Columbia, Mo., 1965-67; city engr. City of Kirksville, Mo., 1967-73; city engr., dir. pub. works City of Clinton, Mo., 1973-78; dir. pub. works, city engr., head dept. engring. City of Kirksville, 1978—. Author: Thomas Caldwell Davison, A Book On Genealogy, 1970. Active First Meth. Ch., Kirksville. Sgt. U.S. Army, 1959-61. Mem. NSPE, SAR (Braxton C. Pollard chpt.), Am. Pub. Works Assn. (pres. Mo. Chpt. 1981, Highest award 1994), Mo. SAR, Mo. Soc. Profl. Engrs. (pres. Northeast chpt.), Mo. Assn. Registered Land Surveyors, Am. Legion Post #20, Moose Lodge #1751. Home: 868 College Park Dr Kirksville MO 63501-1869

DAVISON, WARREN GATES, civil engineer; b. Eldora, Iowa, Nov. 8, 1926; s. Paul Thompson and Ruby Winefred (Gates) D.; m. Marilyn June March, Nov. 3, 1946; children: Patricia Kay, Sherry Lynn, Linda Jean, Diana Rae. BSCE, Iowa State U., 1953. Asst. to county engr. Hamilton County, Webster City, Iowa, 1953-56; engr. Emmett County, Estherville, Iowa, 1956-60, Cerro Gordo County, Mason City, Iowa, 1960-89; pvt. practice pub. rels. Mason City, Iowa, 1989-92; res. insp. Fed. Emergency Mgmt. Assn., Kansas City, Mo., 1993—. Pres. Jefferson PTA, Mason City, IA, 1967. Recipient Engring. Mgmt. Achievement award Nat. Assn. County Engrs., 1965, award of Merit Iowa Good Rds. Assn., 1967; named Engr. of Yr., Iowa County Engrs. Assn., 1966. Home: 407 S Louisiana Ave Mason City IA 50401-4443

DAWLEY, DONALD LEE, information systems educator; b. Amanda, Ohio, Feb. 21, 1936; Mem. Data Processing Mgmt. Assn. (internat. com., sec.-treas. 1987, bd. dirs. 1988-92, exec. v.p. 1990, pres. 1991-92; v.p. for adminstrn. Greater Cin. chpt. 1995, treas. 1996), Internat. Bus. Schs. Computer Users Assn. (pres. 1988-92, bd. dirs. 1984—, chmn. bd. dirs. 1989—), Assn. for Sys. Mgmt., Assn. for Ednl. Data Sys., Soc. Data Educators, Assn. Computing Machinery, Ohio Mgmt. Info. Sys. Dirs. Assn. (founder, past pres.), Beta Gamma Sigma, Omicron Delta Kappa. BS in Edn., Kent State U., 1959; AA in Bus., U. Calif., Victor Valley, 1966; MBA in Bus., U. Hawaii, Far East div., 1968; MS in Logistics Engring., Air Force Inst. Tech., Dayton, Ohio, 1970; D in Bus. Adminstrn., George Washington U., 1980-81. Cert. systems profl., data processor. Enlisted USAF, 1959, advanced through grades to lt. col.; with data processing and logistics inspection Hdqrs. USAF, Washington, 1973-75; with data processing plans Def. Logistics Agy., Washington, 1973-75, Air Force Logistics, Dayton, 1978; resigned USAF, 1979; from instr. to assoc. prof. mgmt. info. sys. Miami U., Oxford, Ohio, 1979—, asst. chair Mgmt. Info. Systems, 1985-93; cons. J.M. Smucker Co., Orrville, Ohio, 1982, McCullough-Hyde Hosp., Oxford, 1986-93; speaker in field. Author: Auditor Data Processing Knowledge Requirements, 1984; also articles. Mem. Edn. Spl. Interest Group. Decorated Medal of Honor (foreign), Bronze Star. Mem. Data Processing Mgmt. Assn. (internat. com., sec.-treas. 1987, bd. dirs. 1988-92, exec. v.p. 1990, pres. 1991-92, v.p. adminstrn. Cin. chpt. 1995, treas. 1996), Internat. Bus. Schs. Computer Users Assn. (pres. 1988-92, bd. dirs. 1984—, chmn. bd. dirs. 1989—), Assn. for Sys. Mgmt., Assn. for Ednl. Data Sys., Soc. Data Educators, Assn. Computing Machinery, Ohio Mgmt. Info. Sys. Dirs. Assn. (founder, past pres.), Beta Gamma Sigma, Omicron Delta Kappa. Baptist. Home: 323 Sandra Dr Oxford OH 45056-2540 Office: Miami U Decision Scis-MIS Dept 301 Upham Oxford OH 45056

DAW-SCHMIDT, KENNETH GLENN, law professor; b. Des Moines, Oct. 12, 1956; s. Glenn Erwin and Daw-Schmidt and Barbara Jane Bloom; m. Elizabeth Ross Birch, Aug. 16, 1980; children: Nicholas, Nathaniel, Eleanor Birch. BA, U. Wis., 1978, MA, 1981, JD, 1981, PhD, 1984. Bar: Wis. 1982, Minn. 1984, Ohio 1987. Clk. legal dept. UAW, Detroit, 1980; counsel labor com. Minn. House of Reps., 1982-84; assoc. Previant, Goldberg, and Uelman, Milw., 1984-86; prof. law U. Cin., 1986-91, U. Wis., 1994—, Ind. U., 1991—. Recipient Parker award, U. Mich., 1984, Scholarly Paper award, Assn. Am. Law Schs., 1990; Niezer Faculty fellow, Indiana U., 1993, Whistler Faculty fellow, 1995. Mem. Law and Soc. Assn., Am. Econ. Assn., Indsl. Rels. Rsch. Assn. (bd. dirs.), Am. Assn. Univ. Profs. (exec. com. 1994—, rep. nat. coun. 1993—). Democrat. Episcopalian. Office: Ind U Sch of Law Third St and Indiana Ave Bloomington IN 47405

DAWSON, CAROL, state legislator; b. July 28, 1945; m. Donald. Grad., Ft. Hayes State U., 1967. Mem. dist. 110 Kans. State Ho. of Reps., 1990—; now tchr. Home: 458 E 3rd St Russell KS 67665-2118 Office: Kans Ho of Reps State Capitol Topeka KS 66612*

DAWSON, CRAIG WILLIAM, city official; b. Pontiac, Mich., Sept. 24, 1956; s. Lloyd J. and Frances G. (Mansfield) D. BA with distinction, U. Kans., 1978, MPA, 1981. Planning intern City of Overland Park, Kans., 1977; intern. Office of Spl. Asst. to Gov. of Kans., Topeka, 1978; adminstrv. asst. pub. works divsn. City of St. Louis Park, Minn., 1979-80, adminstrv. asst., office of city mgr., 1981-84; asst. to city mgr. City of Eden Prairie, Minn., 1984-95; asst. city mgr. City of Maplewood, Minn., 1995—. Contbr. articles to profl. jours. Mem. Citizens League, Mpls., 1980—. Edwin O. Stene scholar U. Kans., 1978-79, Summerfield scholar, 1975-78. Mem. Assn. Met. Municipalities, Minn. Assn. Urban Mgmt. Assts. (chair profl. devel. 1992-93, bd. mem. 1996—), Internat. City/County Mgmt. Assn. (assoc.), Phi Beta Kappa. Office: City of Maplewood 1830 County Rd B Maplewood MN 55109-2797

DAWSON, JAMES BUCHANAN, computer consulting firm executive; b. Cin., Aug. 26, 1956; s. Frederick Stewart and Norma Juanita (Brooks) D.; m. Mae LaVerne Tunney, July 7, 1975 (div. Dec. 1988); children: Sherry LaVerne, James Gregory; m. Kathleen Maria Hanson, Feb. 1, 1992; 1 child, Kathleen Jaimiann. BS, Ohio State U., 1983; MS in Elec. Engring., U. Cin., 1989. Electronic warfare signlas intelligence cryptanalyst U.S. Army Security Agy., 1974-83, U.S. Marine Corps, 1983-92; adj. faculty Ind. U./Purdue U., Indpls., 1992-95; pres., founder, sr. cons. Ctrl. Ind. Computer Cons., Inc., Elwood, 1995—; adj. faculty Ivy Tech. State Coll., Indpls., 1994—; mem. tech. adv. bd. Elwood Cmty. Schs., 1994—. Founder Elwood Volks March Club, 1995. Sgt. USMC, 1974-92. Decorated Army Commendation medal (2). Mem. IEEE, Ind. Software Assn., Ctrl. Ind. Assn. for Computing Machinery, Madison County Amateur Radio Club (instr. 1992—), Elwood C. of C. Home: 10207 North State Rd 37 Elwood IN 46036 Office: Ctrl Ind Computer Cons Inc PO Box 402 Elwood IN 46036

DAWSON, JAMES RICHARD, fire and safety engineer; b. Fond du Lac, Wis., July 1, 1936; s. Cecil V. and Helen (Greider) D.; m. Martha Bromley, June 10, 1959; cildren: Heather Joy Dawson Cudworth, Jamie Dawson Strebing. Cert. safety profl., master fire fighter. With Mut. Fire Inspection Bur. New Eng., Salem, Mass., 1959-61, Home Ins. Co., Milw., 1961-65; safety dir. Amron Corp. div. Gulf and Western Co., Waukesha, Wis., 1965-69; fire and safety engr. Ind. U., Bloomington, 1969—. Pres. Waukesha Safety Council, 1969. Mem. Am. Soc. Safety Engrs., Nat. Fire Protection Assn., Vets. of Safety, Ind. Twp. Trustees Assn. (Twp. Trustee of Yr. 1985), Ind. Vol. Fireman's Assn., Fraternal Order Police. Republican. Presbyterian. Home: 3899 E Bethel Ln Bloomington IN 47408-9509 Office: Ind U Poplars Rm 705 400 E 7th St Bloomington IN 47405-3085

DAWSON, LARRY ROSS, transportation marketing professional; b. St. Louis, Dec. 30, 1946; s. Ross Hinton and Viola Ruth (Seitz) D.; m. Karen Gail Wilson, June 7, 1969; children: Kurt Patrick, Joshua John. BS, Southwest Mo. State U., 1968. Cert. tchr., Mo. Rsch. analyst United Van Lines, Inc., Fenton, Mo., 1972-74, substitute svc. coord., 1974-76, mgr. air freight, 1976-79, mgr. rates and tariffs, 1984-86, mgr. brokerage and forwarding, 1986-90, mgr. spl. commodities, 1990-91, mgr. mktg., 1991—; mgr. internat. household goods pricing United Internat., Fenton, Mo., 1979-81, mgr. internat. commodities, 1981-84; Midwest dir. Suddath Transp. Svcs., 1994—; cert. chmn. Transp. Brokers Conf. Am., 1989-91, Midwest v.p., 1989-91, bd. dirs., 1990-91. Author manuals. Mem. adv. bd. Washington (Mo.) Sch. Dist. Bd. Edn., 1977; ward chmn. Mo. Rep. party, Franklin County, 1983. 1st lt. U.S. Army, 1969-72. Mem. Nat. Def. Transp. Assn., Nat. Indsl. Transp. League, Coun. Logistics Mgmt., Elks, Jaycees (pres., v.p. Washington unit,1 973-84), Franklin County Country Club. Home: 1207 Caroline Dr Washington MO 63090-4905

DAWSON, THOMAS THIEL, insurance company executive; b. West Lafayette, Ohio, Mar. 7, 1935; s. Marcus Thiel and Esther Tilla (Cochran) D.; m. Evelyn Ann Iacobellis, Aug. 25, 1956; children: Thomas Scott, Steven Michael, Gregory James, Douglas Joseph. Student, Ohio State U., 1957-59; BBA with honors, Northwood Inst., 1989. CPCU. Stock clk. Arcade Drug Store, Newark, Ohio, 1949-53; laborer Pure Oil Co., Newark, 1953-59; rate clk. State Farm Ins. Co., Newark, 1959-60, svc. supr., 1960-68, asst. supt., 1968-71, ops. supt., 1971—; cons. ins. program City of Newark, 1984-85. Mem. Heath (Ohio) Bd. Zoning Appeals, 1961; councilman City of Heath, 1969. Recipient Outstanding Alumni award Northwood Inst., 1990. Mem. Soc. CPCU (continuing profl. devel. award 1987), Columbus Neighborhood Housing (bd. trustees), Am. Soc. CLU (assoc.), Oldsmobile Club Am., Newark Maennerchor, K.C. Republican. Roman Catholic. Home: 1140 Surrey Dr Newark OH 43055 Office: State Farm Ins Co 1440 Granville Rd Newark OH 43093-0001

DAY, ANNE WHITE, retired registered nurse; b. Cin., July 9, 1926; d. Pinkney McGill and Anna Pearl (Glendenning) White; m. Raymond Eric Parker, Mar. 6, 1948 (div. 1969); children: Douglas McGill, Stephanie Morse. Diploma, Christ Hosp. Sch. Nursing, Cin., 1947. RN, Ohio; cert. chem. dependency nurse Consol. Assn. Nurses in Substance Abuse. Staff nurse to asst. head nurse Holmes div. U. Cin., 1948-84; nursing supr. Villa Hope Extended Care Facility, Cin., 1970-72; staff nurse Hillenbrand Nursing Home, Cin., 1980-82, Emerson A. North Hosp., Cin., 1982-94. Vol. Group Against Smoke Pollution, Cin., 1989—; donor Zoo, Cin., 1989—, Voters for Choice, Ohio, 1989—, Ams. for Non-Smokers Rights, Calif., 1989—, Action on Smoking or Health, 1989—, Stop Teenage Addiction to Tobacco; tutor for adult literacy. Mem. DAR (life). Episcopalian.

DAY, CELESTA, nursing educator, religion educator; b. Jefferson, Iowa, Aug. 5, 1935; d. Earl William and Anabel Marie (Cuddy) D. BS in Biology/Nursing, Viterbo Coll., 1964; MBA in Health Adminstrn., George Washington U., 1966; MA in Spirituality, Mundeline Coll./Loyola, 1979; postgrad., U. St. Thomas, St. Paul, 1993—. RN, Iowa; lice. home nursing adminstr. Staff nurse St. Anthony Hosp., Carroll, Iowa, 1956; dir. nursing St. Joseph's Meml. Hosp., Hillsboro, Wis., 1959-61, adminstr., 1966-70; supr. emergency St. Francis Hosp., La Crosse, Wis., 1961-63, planner, 1979-83, adminstr., 1983-88; resident hosp. adminstrn. St. Vincent's Med. Ctr., N.Y.C., 1965-66; v.p. Franciscan Sisters of Perpetual Adoration, La Crosse, 1970-78, mission effectiveness dir., 1989—; officer numerous hosps., chs., nursing homes; Mem. U.S. Catholic Mission Coun., 1976-80; fin. coun. Diocese La Crosse, 1979—; speaker Emerging Wisdom Assembly; co-coord. Clarefest '93; mem. think tank Catholic Health Facility Mission Dirs., 1993-94. Mem. State Coun. Health Care Coverage for Uninsured, 1985-87, State Health Policy Coun., 1986-88, Legis. Coun. Rsch. Surrogacy, 1988-89. Mem. Catholic Health Assn. (chmn. bd. dirs., pub. policy com.). Office: Franciscan Sisters Perpetual Adoration 912 Market St La Crosse WI 54601

DAY, CHARLES ROGER, public relations manager, journalist; b. Middletown, Ohio, Aug. 15, 1921; s. Joseph Scrivener and Pearl Violet (Farmer) D.; m. Dorothy Jane Hauselman, Aug. 14, 1943; children: Charles R., Martha Ann, Mary Jane, Robert H. AB in History, Fenn Coll. (now Cleve. State U.), 1945. News editor, writer Sta. WGAR, Cleve., 1943-46, news dir., 1946-71; news dir. Sta. WEWS-TV, Cleve., 1963-65; dist. mgr. pub. rels. Ohio Bell Telephone Co., Cleve., 1971-88; ret., 1988. Mem., pres. Bd. Edn., South Euclid-Lyndhurst, Ohio, 1962-83; pub. mem., bd. trustees Cleve. Bar Assn., 1983-86, jud. rev. com., 1983-94; mem. comm. commn. Inter-Ch. Coun. Greater Cleve., 1973—. Recipient Disting. Svc. award Fenn Coll. Alumni Assn., 1954, 1st Place Radio News Reporting award AFTRA, Cleve., 1951, 57-60; named to Journalism Hall of Fame Cleve. Press Club, 1988. Mem. Radio-TV News Dirs. Assn. (bd. dirs., v.p. 1956), Soc. Profl. Journalists (Cleve. chpt., pres. 1966, Disting. Svc. award 1982). Home: 1416 Ford Rd Cleveland OH 44124

DAY, JOSEPH WILLIAM, educator; b. Spokane, Wash., July 28, 1948; s. James Watson and Winnifred Mary-Jane (Putt) D.; m. Leslie Elizabeth Preston, June 19, 1976. AB, Gonzaga U., 1970; MA, Stanford U., 1974, PhD, 1978. Vis. instr. U. Southern Calif., L.A., 1974-75, 78, Ind. U., Bloomington, Ind., 1975-77; asst. prof. The Coll. Wooster, Wooster, Ohio, 1978-83; asst. prof. Wabash Coll., Crawfordsville, Ind., 1983-89, assoc. prof., 1990—; scholarship com., Classical Assn. MidWest & South, 1988-90; gennadeion com., Am. Sch. Classical Studies, 1991-93. Author: The Glory of Athens, 1980; contbr. articles to profl. jours. Recipient Woodrow Wilson fellowship Woodrow Wilson Found., 1970, followship NEH, 1984, ACLS, 1990-91, NEH, 1980. Mem. Am. Philological Assn., Classical Assn. MidWest & South, Alumni Assn. Am. Sch. Classical Studies, Ind. Classical Conf. Home: 608 Sugar Tree Rd Crawfordsville IN 47933 Office: Wabash Coll Crawfordsville IN 47933

DAY, LYN TIBBITS, fundraising consultant; b. Rockford, Ill., Aug. 5, 1935; d. Laurence H. and Evelyn (Kellogg) Tibbits; m. Richard A. Day, Aug. 19, 1956; children: Eric Richard, Sylvia Elise. BA, Boston U., 1957; MEd, U. Cin., 1968. Dir. Three Rivers Coop Nursery Sch., Cleves, Ohio, 1968-74; educator Babies Milk Fund, Cin., 1974-79; dir. rsch. U. Cin. Found., 1980-84; sr. cons., ptnr. Staley/Robeson/Ryan/St. Lawrence, Inc., Cin., 1984-95; ret., 1995. Trustee, vice chair Wilmington (Ohio) Coll., 1986—; bd. dirs. Friends of Women's Studies, U. Cin., 1988-91. Mem. Am. Prospect Rsch. Assn. (pres. 1991, treas. 1992), Nat. Soc. Fundraising Execs. (cert.). Mem. Soc. of Friends. Office: Staley Robeson Ryan et al 635 W 7th St Cincinnati OH 45203-1513

DAY, MICHAEL JOSEPH, English educator; b. Syracuse, N.Y., June 6, 1956; s. Robert Grinnell and Rosemary Little (Trelease) D.; m. Takako Nishiyoshi, Mar. 10, 1984; 1 child, Emelia Maiko. BA in English, Dartmouth Coll., Hanover, N.H., 1978; MA in English, U. Wyo., 1982; PhD in Rhetoric, U. Calif., Berkeley, 1992. Grad. student instr. English U. Wyo., Laramie, 1980-82; vis. instr. dept. lang. and culture Osaka U., Toyonaka, Japan, 1982-83; vis. instr. English Mukogawa Women's U., Nishinomiya, Japan, 1983-85; vis. instr. liberal arts Kobe (Japan) U., 1985-86; grad. student instr. rhetoric dept. U. Calif., Berkeley, 1986-90, rsch. asst., 1990-92; asst. prof. English S.D. Sch. Mines & Tech., Rapid City, 1992—. Author: (with others) Computer Mediated Communication in the Online Classroom, 1995; creator (software) Stylex. Mem. MLA, Nat. Coun. Tchrs. English (assoc. chair assembly on computers and English), Great Plains Alliance for Computers and Writing (regional co-dir. 1993—), S.D. Coun. Tchrs. English. Office: SD Sch of Mines & Tech 501 E Saint Joseph St Rapid City SD 57701

DAY, PHYLLIS ARLENE, marketing professional; b. Cleve., July 29, 1961; d. Sheldon Lee and Lynda Kay (Gerowin) Berkman; m. Daniel James Day, June 20, 1981 (div. Nov. 1988); children: Lauren, Stephen. BA in Fashion Mdse. Bus. Adminstrn., Ursuline Coll., 1984. Asst. buyer Lollipop Shop, Cleve., 1983-87; buyer Munchins Closet, Cleve., 1987-88; asst. dept. mgr. Saks Fifth Ave, Cleve., 1988; asst. coord. Summerfare, Cleve., 1989; exec. asst. New Cleveland Campaign, Cleve., 1989-91, program dir., 1991-92; community rels. coord. Rainbow Babies and Childrens Hosp., Cleve., 1992-94; mgr. comms. and events Ernst & Young LLP, 1995—; exec. producer C-TV Cablevision Prodn., Cleve., 1991-92. Mem. mayor's pub. rels. adv. com., Cleve., 1991—, ProCleveland, 1991. Jewish. Home: 32407A Hamilton Ct # 104 Solon OH 44139-5790 Office: Ernst & Young 1300 Huntington Bldg 925 Euclid Ave Cleveland OH 44115

DAY, RICHARD H., state legislator; b. Mar. 9, 1937; m. Janet; 4 children. BA, Winona State U., 1968. State senator Minn. State Senate, Dist. 28, 1991—; mem. agrl. & rural com., con. com. & health & human svc. com., Minn. State Senate. Mem. Eagles, Elks, KC. Home: PO Box 736 Owatonna MN 55060-0736*

DAYS, RITA DENISE, state legislator; b. Minden, La., Oct. 16, 1950; d. Marion and Juliette (Mitchell) Heard; m. Frank S. Days, June 17, 1972; children: Elliott Charles, Natalie Rechelle, Evelyn Jeanine. BMus, Lincoln U., 1972. Tchr. Webster Parish Sch. Bd., Minden, La., 1972; clk. typist Urban League of St. Louis, 1973-74, asst. dir. pub. info., 1974, placement interviewer, 1974-76; office supr. Burroughs Corp., St. Louis, 1976-80; sec., admissions counselor Jewish Coll. of Nursing, St. Louis, 1989-93; mem. Mo. Ho. of Reps., St. Louis, 1993—; chair elections com. Mo. Ho. of Reps., St. Louis, treas. Mo. Legis. Black Caucus, mem. Supreme Ct. Task Force on Children and Families; mem. Interagy. Coordinating Coun. part H. Active Ptnrs. for Kids, 1993—, New Sunny Mount Bapt. Ch.; sec. Women Legislators Mo.; bd. mem. Project Respond.; past bd. dirs. Normandy Sch. Dist. Mem. Alpha Kappa Alpha. Democrat. Office: Mo Ho of Reps State Capitol Building Jefferson City MO 65101-1556

D'AZZO, JOHN JOACHIM, electrical engineer, educator; b. N.Y.C., Nov. 30, 1919; s. Domenick and Jacqueline (Cappello) D'A.; m. Betty G. McBride, June 13, 1953; 1 child, Dennis. BEE, CCNY, 1941; MSEE, Ohio State U., 1950; PhD, Salford U., Eng., 1978. Registered profl. engr., Ohio. Quality control engr. Western Electric Co., Kearney, N.J., 1941-42; devel. engr. Air Materiel Command, Wright Patterson AFB, Ohio, 1942-46; prof. elec. engring., dept. head Air Force Inst. Tech., Wright Patterson AFB, Ohio, 1947—. Author: Feedback Control System Analysis and Synthesis, 1960, 2d edit., 1966, Linear Control System Analysis and Design, 1975, 4th edit., 1995. Served to 2d lt. U.S. Army, 1945-46. Named Outstanding Engr. Affiliate Socs. Ohio, 1962, 86. Fellow IEEE, AIAA (assoc.); mem. Am. Soc. for Engring. Edn., Sigma Xi, Tau Beta Pi, Eta Kappa Nu. Roman Catholic. Home: 3923 Winthrop Dr Beavercreek OH 45431-3148 Office: Air Force Inst Tech 2950 P St Wright Patterson AFB OH 45433-7765

DEAHL, F. RICHARD, stockbroker; b. Deadwood, S.D., July 18, 1945. BA, DePauw U., Greencastle, Ind., 1967; MA, Ball State U., Muncie, Ind., 1970. Mktg. rschr. Wheelerbrater Frey, Mishawaka, Ind., 1970-76; broker Prudential Securities, South Bend, Ind., 1976—. Mem. adv. bd. trustees Salvation Army, South Bend, 1994—; pres. Izaak Walton League, St. Joseph, Mo., 1987—. Mem. C. of C, Kiwanis. Republican. Congregationalist. Home: 50822 Mercury Dr Granger IN 46530-9795 Office: Prudential Securities Inc 431 E Colfax Ave Ste 100 South Bend IN 46617-2790

DEAHL, WARREN ANTHONY, lawyer; b. South Bend, Ind., Sept. 18, 1918; s. Floyd Anthony and Sarah Talitha (Rosenbury) D.; m. Marjorie Katherine Sears, Nov. 29, 1941; children: Floyd R., John O. Student, U. Mich., 1937-38, U. Notre Dame, 1938-41; BA in Econs., U. Notre Dame, Ind., 1941; JD, U. Notre Dame, 1944. Bar: Ind. 1944, U.S. Dist. Ct. (no. dist.) Ind. 1946, U.S. Ct. Appeals (7th cir.) 1947, U.S. Supreme Ct. 1971. From assoc. to ptnr. Oare, Thornburg, McGill & Deahl (and predecessor firms), South Bend, 1946-64, Thornburg, McGill, Deahl, Harman, Carey & Murray, South Bend, 1964-82; ptnr. Barnes & Thornburg, South Bend, 1982-85, of counsel, 1985—; pres. Bus. Devel. Corp., South Bend, 1982, mem. exec. com. and bd. dirs.; instr. law U. Notre Dame, Ind., 1948, 69; instr. bus. law Ind. U., South Bend, 1947-50; past v.p. New Bus. Facilities, Inc., South Bend. Vestryman St. Michael's Episcopal Ch., South Bend, 1984-85; solicitor Kiwanis Crippled Children's Fund, Snite Mus., Notre Dame, 1990, South Bend Symphony, 1988-93; trustee YMCA, South Bend, 1964-65; bd. dirs. Project Future, South Bend, 1985. Sgt. U.S. Army, 1943-46, ETO. Decorated Bronze Star. Fellow Am. Bar Found., Ind. Bar Found.; mem. ABA, Ind. Bar Assn., St. Joseph County Bar Assn. (bd. govs., pres. 1972-73), Am. Arbitration Assn. (cert.), St. Joseph County C. of C., Inc. (bd. dirs., pres. emeritus 1964, disting. bus. leader award 1988). Office: Barnes & Thornburg 100 N Michigan St South Bend IN 46601-1630

DEAK, CHARLES KAROL, chemist; b. Budapest, Hungary, Sept. 26, 1928; s. Karoly and Ida (Benes) D.; came to U.S., 1955, naturalized, 1961; BS, Eotvos Coll., Budapest, 1948; student Sorbonne, Paris, 1949; postgrad. Wayne State U., 1957-61; bd. cert. forensic examiner; m. Jenny Bocinski,

Apr. 9, 1958; children: James, Christine. With Frankel Co., Inc., Detroit, 1957-73, quality control mgr., 1968-71, mgr. tech. svcs., 1971-73; pres. Analytical Assocs., Inc., Detroit, 1973-92; pres. C.K. Deak Tech. Svcs., Inc., 1992—. Cert. profl. chemist. Fellow Am. Inst. Chemists; mem. Am. Chem. Soc., ASTM, Am. Soc. Metals, Assn. Analytical Chemists, Photog. Soc. Am. Roman Catholic. Patentee in chem. firefighting agts. and dense metal separation. Club: Internat. Brotherhood Magicians. Home: 29844 Wagner Dr Warren MI 48093-8635

DEAL, DANIEL E., stockbroker; b. Holland, Mich., Jan. 31, 1967. BF, Western Mich. U., Kalamazoo, 1989; LLB, U. Detroit, 1992. Stockbroker Smith Barney Inc., Grand Rapids, Mich., 1992—. Republican. Methodist. Office: Smith Barney Inc 99 Monroe Ave NW Ste 200 Grand Rapids MI 49503-2639

DEAL, WILLIAM THOMAS, school psychologist; b. Canton, Ohio, Dec. 18, 1949; s. Richard Lee and Rheta Lucille (Gerber) D.; m. Paula Nespeca, Aug. 5, 1972. BS, Bowling Green State U., 1972; MA, John Carroll U., 1977; postgrad. Kent State U., 1979—. Sci. tchr. Westlake Schs., 1972-76, head bldg. sci. dept., 1974-76; intern sch. psychologist Garfield Heights Schs., 1976-77, sch. psychologist, 1977—; pvt. practice psychology, Parma Heights, Ohio, 1982-84. Alternate mem. adv. council Cuyahoga County Spl. Edn. Service Ctr., 1977—. Recipient Cert. of Recognition, Garfield Heights Bd. Edn., 1980; Outstanding Achievement award Cleve. Assn. for Children with Learning Disabilities, Inc., 1980; named Psychologist of Yr. Cleveland Sch., 1990. Mem. Nat. Assn. Sch. Psychologists, United Teaching Profession, Ohio Sch. Psychology Assn., Cleve. Assn. Sch. Psychologists, Phi Delta Kappa. Republican. Mem. Reformed Ch. Home: 5290 Kings Hwy Cleveland OH 44126-3059 Office: 4900 Turney Rd Cleveland OH 44125-2501

DEALOIA, MICHAEL CHRISTIAN, financial analyst, researcher; b. Dayton, Ohio, Mar. 9, 1969; s. Dominic Antonio and Leah (Watson) D. BSBA, Xavier U., 1991; MBA in Fin. and Mktg., Case Western Res. U., 1996. Writer, rechr. Patterson Pub., Cin.; mutual fund rep. Fidelity Investments, Cin.; software application specialist Reynolds Reynolds, Ft. Lauderdale, Fla.; mktg. cons. Formtec Inc., Cleve.; assoc. corp. banking Nat. Citibank, 1996—; fin. cons. Conservadox Films, LTD, Ft. Lauderdale, Fla., 1993-94. Author of poems. V.p. Sawgrass Young Republicans, Ft. Lauderdale, Fla., 1993-94; assoc. Broward County Young Republicans, Ft. Lauderdale, Fla., 1993-94. Roman Catholic. Home: 2087 East Fourth #207 Cleveland OH 44115

DEAN, GEORGE R., state legislator; b. Kansas City, Kans., Sept. 12, 1933; m. Ethel J. Haley, 1957. BSEE, U. Kans., 1959; MSEE, Wichita State U., 1969. Former aerospace engr.; mem. Kans. Ho. of Reps. Topeka; bd. dirs. Kans. Tech. Enterprise Corp. Bd. dirs. Spl. Olympics, Very Spl. Arts Kans.; adv. bd. University Kans. EECS. Mem. Inst. Elec. and Electronic Engrs. (Region 5 Profl. award 1983, Centenial award 1984, Profl. Acheivement award 1988), Am. Legion, Aircraft Owners and Pilots Assn. Democrat. Home: 2646 Exchange St Wichita KS 67217-2928*

DEAN, MICHAEL L., business administration educator; b. Stamford, Conn., Feb. 9, 1942; s. Stanley R. and Belle (Katzman) D.; m. Carol L. Hoffman, Mar. 21, 1965; children: Jeff, Julie. BA, U. Mich., 1963; MBA, Ohio State U., 1965, PhD, 1971. Asst. brand mgr. Procter & Gamble, Cin., 1965-68; pres. ADI Rsch., Cin., 1976-89; pres. rsch. divsn. MATRIXX Mktg., Inc., Cin., 1990-93, corp. rsch. dir., 1993-95; asst. prof. mktg. U. Cin., 1971-75, assoc. prof., 1975-84, prof. bus. adminstrn., 1985—; mem. adv. bd. Scarlet Oaks Vocat. Ctr., Cin., 1979-80; expert witness Trademark Litigation Res., 1993. Contbr. articles to profl. jours. Endower EXCEL (Excellence in Classrm. Edn. and Learning) award, 1991—. Recipient Excellence in Pvt. Enterprise Edn. award Freedoms Found., Valley Forge, Pa., 1979. Mem. Am. Mktg. Assn., Mktg. Rsch. Assn.

DEAN, THOMAS KEITH, English and American studies educator; b. Rockford, Ill., Mar. 14, 1959; s. Donald N. and Margit K. (Finney) D.; m. Susan M. Prepejchal, July 27, 1985; children: Nathaniel Prepejchal, Sylvia Prepejchal. MusB in Music History and Lit., No. Ill. U., 1982, BA in English, 1982, MA in English, 1984; PhD in English, U. Iowa, 1991. Grad. teaching asst. No. Ill. U., DeKalb, 1982-84, U. Wis., Madison, 1984-86; tchg. fellow U. Iowa, Iowa City, 1986-91; asst. prof. English Cardinal Stritch Coll., Milw., 1991-95, coord. freshman seminar, 1993-95; lectr. Am. thought and lang. Mich. State U., East Lansing, 1995—; test item writer Am. Coll. Testing, Iowa City, 1988—; textbook reviewer Prentice Hall, Englewood Cliffs, N.J., 1993—; bibliographer Frank Norris Studies, Midamerica, ASLE Bibliography, 1988—; founder, dir. Place and Comty. Studies Inst.; presenter papers in field. Contbr. articles to profl. jours. Vol. Cmty. Vols. for Internat. Programs, Mich. State U., East Lansing, 1995—; textbook reader Office of Programs for Handicapped Students, Mich. State U., East Lansing, 1995—; mem. Audubon Nature Ctr., Milw., 1994-95, Riverside Nature Ctr., Newburg, Wis., 1992-94. Study grantee NEH, 1995. Mem. AAUP, MLA, Am. Soc. Environ. History, Am. Lit. Assn., Midwest Modern Lang. Assn., Western. Lit. Assn., Whitman Studies Assn., Popular Culture Assn., Assn. for the Study of Lit. and Environment (v.p. 1993-94, devel. officer 1994—), Nature in Legend and Story (bd. dirs., v.p. 1996—, editor newsletter), Soc. for Study of Am. Indian Lits., Frank Norris Soc. (pres.), Orion Soc. Office: Mich State U Dept Am Thought and Lang Ernst Bessey Hall East Lansing MI 48824

DEANGELIS, ALDO A., state senator; b. Chgo. Hts., Ill., Mar. 25, 1931; grad. Knox Coll., Galesburg, Ill., 1954; postgrad. U. Chgo., Govs. State U.; m. Meredith Roberts; 4 children. Founder, pres. Dial Tube, 1961-65; co-founder, past pres. Vulcan Tube and Metals Co., 1969-78; mem. Ill. State Senate, 1978—, now asst. majority leader; bd. dirs. Bank of Homewood. Bd. dirs. United Way of Chgo. Hts. Served with U.S. Army, 1954-56. Mem. C. of C., Mfrs. Assn. Chgo. (dir.). Republican. Office: State Senate State Capital Springfield IL 62706*

DEANGELO, ANTHONY JAMES, architect; b. Des Moines, Oct. 24, 1956; s. Jimmie Robert and Mary Rose (Carpino) DeA.; m. Amy Katherine Petted, June 26, 1991; children: Nicholas. BArch, U. Ark., 1980; postgrad., NYU, 1985-86, Inst. Design & Constrn., Bklyn., 1982, Poly. of Cen. London, 1980. Registered architect N.Y., Mass., Ill., Iowa; registered contractor, Iowa. Designer Robert Rodin, Architect, N.Y.C., 1981; project engr. Richard Balser Assocs., Engrs., N.Y.C., 1982; design assoc. Stephen Lepp, P.C., Architect and Planner, N.Y.C., 1983; asst. project mgr. Rafael Vinoly Architects, P.C., N.Y.C., 1984; owner Architectura N.Y., N.Y.C., 1985-88; project mgr. David Leibowitz, Architects/Planners, N.Y.C., 1989-90; owner de Angelo Architecture & Devel., LC, N.Y.C., L.A., Des Moines, 1990—; tchr. archtl. photography U. Ark., 1979. Designer assoc. wks. pub. in Archtl. Record, Progressive Arch., Interiors, N.Y. Times. Mem. AIA (com. for long range planning 1990, pub. affairs com. for internat. rels. 1990, scholastic award in field of arch. 1979), N.Y. Assn. Architects, Nat. Coun. Archtl. Registration Bds. (cert.), Tau Sigma Delta, Omicron Delta Kappa. Home and Office: 5813 Waterbury Cir Des Moines IA 50312-1321

DEARDORFF, JOHN MILTON, JR., camera manufacturing executive; b. Villa Park, Ill., Sept. 17, 1935; s. John Milton and Dorothy Izella Anna (Witt) D.; m. Clare Lillian Greenwood, June 10, 1961 (div. Dec. 1989); children: Stephen John, Therese Marie. Student, Elmhurst Coll., 1963-64, Coll. of DuPage, 1977-85. From machinist to pres. L. F. Deardorff & Sons Inc., Chgo., 1948-88; pres. D.P.P.I., Valparaiso, Ind., 1989—. Engr., designer specialized photog. equipment for Chgo. Police Dept., NASA, Met. Mus. Art, USDA, also aerial mapping projectors for Sidwell Studios, Army Map Svc. Active Boy Scouts Am., 1972-85. With U.S. Army, 1958-60. Recipient numerous certs. from camera clubs and assns. Mem. Midstates Indsl. Photographers Assn. (membership chmn. 1954—, citation 1984). Republican. Methodist. Home and Office: 58 Lincolnway Valparaiso IN 46383-5522

DEATZ, GEORGE B., automotive industry executive; b. Sept. 11, 1944. BA in Forestry, U. Mo., 1964. Bus. mgr. Chezik Buick, Kansas City, Mo., 1977-83, Don Wessel Oldsmobile, Springfield, Mo., 1983-89; v.p. Automotive Resources Devel, Springfield, 1989—. Author automotive-related tng. books. With U.S. ANG, 1963-69. Office: Automotive Resources Devel 3754 S Glenstone Ave Ste 103 Springfield MO 65804-4486

DEBARTOLO, EDWARD JOHN, JR., professional football team owner, real estate developer; b. Youngstown, Ohio, Nov. 6, 1946; s. Edward J. and Marie Patricia (Montani) DeB.; m. Cynthia Ruth Papalia, Nov. 27, 1968; children: Lisa Marie, Tiffanie Lynne, Nicole Anne. Student, U. Notre Dame, 1964-68. With Edward J. DeBartolo Corp., Youngstown, Ohio, 1960—, v.p., 1971-76, exec. v.p., 1976-79, chief adminstrv. officer, 1979-94; pres., CEO, 1995—; owner San Francisco 49ers, 1977—; chmn. bd. DeBartolo Realty Corp., 1994—; chmn., CEO DeBartolo Entertainment, Inc. Trustee Youngstown State U., 1974-77; nat. adv. coun. St. Jude Children's Rsch. Hosp., 1978—, local chmn., 1979-80; chmn. local fund drive Am. Cancer Soc., 1975—; mem. Nat. Cambodia Crisis Com., 1980—; chmn. 19th Ann. Victor Warner award, 1985, City of Hope's Spirit of Life Banquet, 1986; apptd. adv. coun. Coll. Bus. Adminstrn. U. Notre Dame, 1988; adv. coun. Nat. Assn. People with AIDS, 1992; bd. dirs. Cleve. Clinic Found., 1991; lifetime mem. Italian Scholarship League. With U.S. Army, 1969. Recipient Man of Yr. award St. Jude Children's Hosp., 1979, Boy's Town of Italy in San Francisco, 1985, Sportsman of Yr. award Nat. Italian Am. Sports Hall of Fame, 1991, Cert. of Merit, Salvation Army, 1982, Warner award, 1986, Silver Cable Car award San Francisco Conv. and Visitors Bur., 1988, Nat. Football League Man of Yr. award Football News, 1989, Svc. to Youth award Cath. Youth Orgn., 1990, Hall of Fame award Cardinal Mooney High Sch., 1993. Mem. Internat. Coun. Shopping Ctrs., Italian Scholarship League (life), Tippecanoe Country Club, Fonderlac Country Club, Dapper Dan Club (dir. 1980—). Office: Edward J DeBartolo Corp PO Box 3287 Youngstown OH 44513-3287 also: care San Francisco 49ers 4949 Centennial Blvd Santa Clara CA 95054-1229

DEBEAR, RICHARD STEPHEN, library planning consultant; b. N.Y.C., Jan. 18, 1933; s. Arthur A. and Sarah (Morrison) deB.; m. Estelle Carmel Grandon, Apr. 27, 1951; children: Richard, Jr., Diana deBear Fortson, Patricia deBear Talkington, Robert, Christopher, Nancy deBear Naski. BS, Queens Coll. CUNY, 1953. Sales rep. Sperry Rand Corp., Blue Bell, Pa., 1954-76; pres. Libr. Design Assocs., Plymouth, Mich., 1976—, Am. Libr. Ctr., Plymouth, 1981—; bldg. cons. to numerous librs., 1965—. Mem. ALA, Mich. Libr. Assn. (oversight com. Leadership Acad. 1990—). Office: Libr Design Assocs Inc 1149 S Main St Plymouth MI 48170-2213

DEBERUSSAERT, KENNETH JOSEPH, state legislator; b. Mt. Clemens, Mich., Apr. 10, 1954. Aide U.S. Rep. David Bonior; rep. Mich. State Dist. 75; senator Mich. State Dist. 11, 1995—; chmn. consumers com. Mich. Ho. Reps., agriculture, conservation, recreation & environ. com., liquor control com., transp. com. Mem. New Baltimore Hist. Soc., Macomb County Farm Bur., Oakland U. Alumni Assn., Friends of Catholic Social Svc. Address: 50241 Bellaire St New Baltimore MI 48047

DE BLASIS, JAMES MICHAEL, artistic director, producer, stage director; b. N.Y.C., Apr. 12, 1931; s. James and Sarah (de Felice) de B.; m. Ruth Hofreuter, Aug. 25, 1957; 1 child, Blythe. BFA, Carnegie Mellon U., 1959, MFA, 1960. Mem. drama faculty Carnegie Mellon U., 1960-62; head drama dept. Onondaga C.C., Syracuse, N.Y., 1963-72; head Opera Workshop, Syracuse, 1969-70; adv. of opera Corbett Found., Cin., 1971-76; gen. dir. Cin. Opera Assn., 1973-87, artistic dir., 1988-96; internat. ind. stage dir. of opera, 1962—. Artistic advisor, Pitts. Opera, Inc., 1979-83. With U.S. Army, 1951-53. Recipient award Omicron Delta Kappa, 1959, Alumni award Bellaire High Sch., 1974, award in arts adminstrn. Gov. Ohio, 1989, Post/Corbett award for performing artist Corbett Found./Cin. Post, 1989. Mem. Actors Equity, Am. Guild Mus. Artists, Drama Alumni Carnegie Mellon U., Beta Theta Pi. Republican. Episcopalian.

DE BOER, DARRELL WAYNE, agricultural engineer; b. Hull, Iowa, Oct. 4, 1940; s. James C. and Grace (Sneller) De B.; m. Ruth Bleeker, Aug. 4, 1960; children: Michael, Pamela. MS, Iowa State U., 1964, PhD, 1969. Staff engr. Iowa Natural Resources Coun., Des Moines, 1964-65; rsch. assoc. Iowa State U., Ames, 1965-69; assoc. prof. S.D. State U., Brookings, 1969-78, prof., 1978—. Contbr. articles to profl. jours. Elder Faith Reformed Ch., Brookings, 1978, deacon, 1971. Named Educator of Yr., C. of C., Brookings, 1990. Mem. Am. Soc. Agrl. Engrs. (chmn. irrigation group 1988-90, Nat. Rsch. Paper award), Soil and Water Conservation Soc. Office: PO Box 2120 Brookings SD 57007

DE BOOR, CARL, mathematician; b. Stolp, Germany, Dec. 3, 1937; m. Matilda C. Friedrich, Feb. 6, 1960 (div. Sept. 12, 1984); children—C. Thomas, Elisabeth, Peter, Adam; m. Helen L. Bee, Jan. 2, 1991. Student, Universitaet Hamburg, 1956-59, Harvard U., 1959-60; Ph.D., U. Mich., 1966. Rsch. mathematician Gen. Motors Research Labs., 1960-64; asst. prof. math., computer sci. Purdue U., 1966-68, assoc. prof., 1968-72; prof. math., computer sci. U. Wis.-Madison, 1972—; vis. staff mem. Los Alamos Sci. Labs., 1970—. Author: (with S. Conte) Elementary Numerical Analysis, 1972, 80, A Practical Guide to Splines, 1978, (with J.B. Rosser) Pocket Calculator Supplement for Calculus, 1979, (with K. Höllig and S. Riemenschneider) Box Splines, 1993. Fellow Am. Acad. Arts and Scis.; mem. NAE, Soc. Indsl. and Applied Math., Phi Beta Kappa. Office: U Wis Depts Computer Scis Math Madison WI 53706

DE BRANGES DE BOURCIA, LOUIS, mathematics educator; b. Paris, Aug. 21, 1932; s. Louis and Diane (McDonald) deB.; m. Tatiana Jakimow, Dec. 17, 1980; 1 child, Konstantin. BS, MIT, 1953; PhD, Cornell U., 1957. Prof. Purdue U., Lafayette, Ind., 1962-88, disting. prof. of math., 1989—. Fellow Sloan Found., 1963-66, Guggenheim Found., 1967-68; recipient Humboldt prize Alexander Humboldt Found., 1986-88, Ostrowski prize Alexander Ostrowski Found., 1989. Home: Hameau de l'Yvette, Batiment D Chemin des Graviers, F-91190 Gif Sur Yvette France Office: Purdue U Dept Math Lafayette IN 47907-1395

DEBRINCAT, SUSAN JEANNE, nutritionist; b. Detroit, Oct. 7, 1943; d. Lloyd Brode and Florence Claire (Majewski) Greenleaf; m. Raymond Frank DeBrincat, June 19, 1965; children: David Lloyd, Mark Joseph. BS magna cum laude, Mich. State U., 1965. Cert. med. technologist, Am. Soc. Clin. Pathologists. Med. technologist Harper Hosp., Detroit, 1965-66, South Macomb Hosp., Warren, Mich., 1966; art teacher YWCA, Berkley, Mich., 1969-80; master coord. Shaklee Corp., West Bloomfield, Mich., 1977—; lifetime master Shaklee Corp., West Bloomfield, 1990—; nutritional counselor, fashion, color, image, makeup counselor, mgmt. and leadership trainer, motivational speaker, pres. club & found. club for Shaklee Corp.; interior designer. Painter oil, acrylic, watercolors. Mem. Rep. Nat. Com. Pres.'s Club, Found. Club, Phi Kappa Phi, Delta Zeta. Roman Catholic. Office: DeBrincat Assocs 30475 Birchway Dr Franklin MI 48025-1503

DEBRULER, ROGER O., state supreme court justice; b. 1934. AB, LLB, Ind. U. Bar: Ind. 1960. Dep. city prosecutor City of Indpls., 1960-63; judge Ind. Cir. Ct., Steuben County, 1963-68; justice, also chief justice Supreme Ct. of Ind., 1968—. Office: Ind Supreme Ct 200 W Washington St Rm 321 Indianapolis IN 46204-2732*

DE BUHR, LARRY EUGENE, director of education botanical gardens; b. Rock Rapids, Iowa, Nov. 21, 1948; s. Herman Henry and Ethel Marie (Christensen) De Buhr; m. Astrid Mary Olsson, Aug. 13, 1977; children Martha Astride, Jackson Eugene. BS, Iowa State U., 1971; MA, Claremont Grad. Sch., 1973, PhD, 1976. Faculty mem. Cotley Coll., Nevada, Mo., 1977-80; asst. dir. and asst. prof. biology U. Mo., Kansas City, 1980-90; dir. edn. Mo. Botanical Gardens, St. Louis, 1990—; mem. review panel NSF, Washington, 1990, 93; adv. bd., environ. sci. Webster U., St. Louis, 1992; cons. Frederik Meijer Gardens, Grand Rapids, Mich., 1993-94; master site planning panel Chgo. Botanic Garden, 1994. Contbr. articles to profl. jours. Bd. dirs. Open Space Coun., St. Louis, 1991-95; pres. St. Louis Magnet Sch. Commn., 1993-95. Mem. Sigma Xi, Phi Kappa Phi. Office: Mo Botanical Garden PO Box 299 Saint Louis MO 63166

DECASTELL, WILLIAM E., mechanical engineer, consultant; b. Bogota, Colombia, Feb. 5, 1930; came to U.S., 1952.; BS, U. So. Calif., 1959. Mech. engr. March Mfg. Co., Glenview, Ill., 1965—. Mem. social clubs. Home: 435 W Miner St Arlington Heights IL 60005-1308 Office: March Mfg Co 1819 Pickwick Ln Glenview IL 60025-1306

DECHART, DANIEL W., financial consultant; b. Kansas City, Mo., Mar. 4, 1969. BS in Bus., Emporia (Kans.) State U., 1993. Fin. planner IDS, Topeka, 1993-94; fin. cons. Merrill Lynch, Kansas City, 1995—. Office: Merrill Lynch 801 W 47th St Ste 501 Kansas City MO 64112-1252

DECIO, ARTHUR JULIUS, manufacturing company executive; b. Elkhart, Ind., Oct. 19, 1930; s. Julius A. and Lena (Alesia) D.; m. Patricia George, Jan. 6, 1951; children: Terrence, Jamee, Linda, Jay, Leigh Allison. Student, DePaul U., 1949-50; DBA (hon.), Salem Coll., W.Va., 1973; LLD, U. Notre Dame, 1975, Ind. State U., Terre Haute, 1978; LLD (hon.), St. Mary's Coll., Notre Dame, Ind., 1996; D. Bus. (hon.), Vincennes U., 1991; D Humanitarian Svc. (hon.), Hillsdale Coll., 1993. Pres. Skyline Corp., Elkhart, 1956-72; chmn. bd., chief exec. officer Skyline Corp., 1959—; bd. dirs. Schwarz Paper Co., Morton Grove, Ill., NIPSCO Industries, Inc., Hammond, Ind., Quality Dining, Inc., Mishawaka, Ind.; past bd. dirs. Banc One Ind. Corp., Indpls., Rodman & Renshaw Capital Group Inc., Chgo., Greencroft Found., Elkhart, Ind., Bank One, Indpls., Michiana Pub. Broadcasting Corp., Elkhart, founding dir., charter bd. dirs.; past bd. dirs. Foremost Corp. Am., Grand Rapids, Mich., Midwest Commerce Banking Co., Elkhart, Fed. Res. Bank Chgo.; past mem. adv. council Coll. Commerce DePaul U.; past bd. govs. NFL Alumni; founding dir. Elkhart (Ind.) Community Found. Dir. Spl. Olympics Internat., Washington; fellow, trustee U. Notre Dame; past mem. adv. bd. Goshen (Ind.) Coll., Ind. U., South Bend; coun. advisors Ctr. for the Homeless, South Bend; past mem., pres. coun. Ind. U.; past mem. Logan Cmty. Adv. Coun., South Bend; past chmn. Elkhart Urban League Membership Drive, Elkhart Gen. Hosp. Major Expansion Drive, Bicentennial Commn. Elkhart County, Salvation Army New Hdqrs. Bldg. Drive; hon. chmn. Salvation Army Christmas Fund Drive, 1972-95; past mem. Commn. on Presdl. Scholars, Presdl. appointment, 1978; pres. Elkhart Gen. Hosp. Found.; past dir. Nat. Italian-Am. Found., Washington; past chmn. adv. coun. United Way, Elkhart, past dir., campaign chmn., 1966; past dir. Cath. Diocese of Ft. Wayne-South Bend, bd. dirs. diocesan fin. coun.; trustee Aux Chandelles Trust for Mentally Retarded, Elkhart; past chmn., trustee Holy Cross Coll., Notre Dame, Ind.; trustee Hillsdale (Mich.) Coll.; life mem., past chmn., chmn. exec. com. nat. adv. bd. Salvation Army, Washington; conf. chmn. Salvation Army Adv. Orgns. Conf., London, 1989; life mem. NAACP, exec. bd. Elkhart County chpt., 1980-82; chmn. Salvation Army capital campaign, 1990; co-chmn. capital campaign Sta. WNIT-TV Pub. TV, 1991; life mem., trustee Marmion Mil. Acad., Aurora, Ill.; bd. advisors Mundelein (Ill.) Sem. of U. St. Mary of the Lake; past dir. Elkhart Urban League, Elkhart Gen. Hosp., No. Ctrl. Ind. Med. Edn. Found., South Bend, Nat. Jr. Achievement; past dir. Jr. Achievement Elkhart, pres. 1965-66; past trustee Stanley Clark Sch., South Bend, LaLumiere Sch., Laporte, Ind.; mem. Coun. on Devel. Choices for the 80's, Urban Land Inst.; Presdl. appointment Low Income Housing task force, 1970; past Presdl. appointee as commr. Christopher Columbus Quincentenary Jubilee Commn., Washington; mem. Internat. Summer Spl. Olympics Com., Inc., 1987; co-chmn. capital campaign Assn. for Disabled of Elkhart County, 1985; hon. chmn. capital campaign for Elkhart Cmty. Day Care Ctr., 1987; bd. govs. Ind. Colls. of Ind.; chmn. annual bishop's appeal fund drive Diocese of Ft. Wayne-South Bend, 1987; bd. dirs., past chmn. Regional Approach for Progress, South Bend; past pres. Elkhart Park Found. Inc. Recipient U. Portland (Oreg.) medal, 1972, Golden Plate award Acad. Achievement Dallas, 1967, Others award Salvation Army, 1972, William Booth award Salvation Army, 1987, Alexis de Tocqueville Soc. award United Way Am., 1987, Sagamore of the Wabash award State of Ind., 1977, 85, Community Service award Elkhart County br. NAACP, 1980, Marmion Centurion award Marmion Mil. Acad., 1979, Achievement award Jr. Achievement, 1974, Humanitarian award Elkhart Urban League, 1981, Community Service award Elkhart Urban League, 1977 Disting. Am. award Moose Krause chpt. NFL Found. and Hall of Fame, 1984, Book of Golden Deeds award Elkhart Noon Exchane Club, 1984, E. M. Morris award Div. Bus. and Econs., Ind. U.-South Bend, 1985, Alumni Leadership award Marmion Mil. Acad., 1964, Wall of Fame award Assn. for the Disabled, 1985; Salvation Army Hon. Adv. Bd. Mem. award, 1971, Columbus Day award for outstanding Italian-Am., 1973, Elkhart Bar Assn. Liberty Bell award, 1976, Aux Chandelles Village Found. OK award, 1976, Life Hon. Membership award Elkhart Urban League, 1980, Outstanding Contbn. award Elkhart Urban League, 1982, Nat. Italian-Am. Found. Career Achievement award, Washington, 1984, Disting. Citizen of Yr. award No. Ind. council Boy Scouts Am., 1988, Ind. Individual Philanthropist of Yr. award, 1984, Mobile Home Hall of Fame, 1975, Industry Man of Yr. award Iowa Manufactured Housing Assn., 1976, Calif. Manufactured Housing Assn., 1977, N.J. Manufactured Housing Assn., 1977. Arthur J. Decio Vol. of Yr. award established by Elkhart United Way, 1984, Journi Industrialist of Yr. award The Exec. Jour. Bd. Dirs., 1989, Howard J. Kenna, C.S.C. award Congregation of Holy Cross, Ind. Province U. Notre Dame, 1989, John J. Cavanaugh award U. Notre Dame Alumni Assn., 1989, James R. Price/Automated Builder Achievement in Housing award Automated Builder mag., 1990, Man of Yr. award Notre Dame Club of St. Joseph Valley, 1990, Ind. Spl. Cause award Ind. Assn. Rehab. Facilities, 1991, Helping Hands award Hospice St. Joseph County, Inc., 1991, Labor Humanitarian award United Labor Agy., Elkhart, Ind., 1991, Alumni of Yr. award St. Vincent's Parish, Elkhart, 1993, John W. Meaney Founders award Michiana Pub. Broadcasting Corp., 1993, Disting. Aux. Svc. Cross Salvation Army Internat. Hdqrs., London, 1995, Cross of Hope award Bros. of Holy Cross and Holy Cross Coll., Notre Dame, 1996. Mem. Manufactured Housing Inst., Mobile Home Mfrs. Assn. (past bd. dirs., pres. and chmn. Washington affairs com.), Ind. Acad. (apptd. 1978), Chgo. Pres. Assn., Chief Execs. Orgn., World Bus. Coun., Marmion Benedictine Abbey (life affiliate, Aurora, Ill.), Knights of Malta; hon. mem. Elkhart Rotary Club. Roman Catholic. Clubs: Chicago, Tavern (Chgo.); Country of Fla. (Village of Golf); Delray Beach Yacht (Fla.); Ocean of Fla. (Ocean Ridge); Signal Point Country (Niles, Mich.). Home: 3215 Greenleaf Blvd Elkhart IN 46514-4357 Office: Skyline Corp 2520 Bypass Rd Elkhart IN 46514-1518

DECKER, JOHN WILLIAM, steel company executive; b. Cleve., July 15, 1948; s. James William and Betty Erdmann (Smith) D.; m. Elaine Marie Metz, Aug. 30, 1971; children: Amanda Elaine, Gregory John. BS, Lincoln Meml. U., 1966-70; MEd, Kent (Ohio) State U., 1970-72. Cert. tchr., adminstr., Ohio. Elem. tchr. Parma (Ohio) City Schs., 1970-78; corp. sec., treas. Decker Steel & Supply, Inc. (formerly Decker Reichert Steel & Supply, Inc.), Cleve., 1978-83, v.p., 1983-85, pres., chmn., chief exec. officer, 1985—. Ruling elder Parma South Presbyn. Ch., Parma Heights, Ohio, 1979-81, 83-92, clk. of session, 1983-94; mem. Am. Theater Orgn. Soc., Playhouse Square Vol. Group; co-chmn. cmty. fin. com. Parma City Schs., 1994—. Mem. Greater Cleve. Growth Assn. Republican. Lodge: Masons. Home: 9634 Greenbriar Dr Cleveland OH 44130-4756 Office: 4500 Train Ave Cleveland OH 44102-4515

DECKER, PETER WILLIAM, academic administrator; b. Grand Rapids, Mich., Mar. 20, 1919; s. Charles B. and Ruth E. (Thorndill) D.; m. Margaret I. Stainthorpe, June 10, 1944; children: Peter, Marilyn, Christine, Charles. BS, Wheaton Coll., 1941; postgrad. Northwestern U., 1942-43, U. Mich., 1958-60; DSc, London Inst. Applied Rsch., 1973, LLD, 1975, DSTh, Midwestern Baptist Bible Sem., 1995. With advt. dept. Hotels Windermere, Chgo., 1942, Princess Pat Cosmetics, Chgo., 1943; market rsch. investigator A.C. Nielson Co., Chgo., 1944-48; pres. Peter Decker Constrn. Co., Detroit, 1948-60; sales mgr. Century Chem. Products Co., Detroit, 1961-62, v.p., 1962-63, pres., 1963-75; sr. ptnr. G & D Advt. Assocs., 1967-78; v.p., treas., exec. dir. Christian Edn. Advancement, Inc., 1975-95; registrar, instr. N.T. Greek, Missions and Theology Birmingham (Mich.) Bible Inst., 1973-86; prof. Midwestern Baptist Coll., 1984—, dir. student fin. aid, 1984—, trustee, 1985—, mem. exec. com., 1986—, asst. to pres., 1985-90, treas., 1991-95; bd. dirs., prof., trustee Midwestern Bapt. Bible Seminary, 1995—. Author: Getting to Know New Testament Greek, Christology, The Pauline Epistles. Scout master, Boy Scouts of Am., 1956-61, neighborhood commr., 1961-66, scout master, 1956-61, merit badge counselor, emeritus, 1979—; mem. Bd. Rev., Beverly Hills, Mich., 1957-63; chmn. Bd. Rev. Southfield Twp., Mich., 1964-67; past pres., Beverly Hills Civic Assn., 1956, bd. dirs. 1953-57; trustee, deacon, Baptist ch., instr. Bible Inst.; bd. dirs. Mich. Epilepsy Ctr. and Assn., 1957-71, exec. com., 1962-67. Recipient Arrowhead Honor award Boy Scouts Am., 1965. Mem. AAAS, ASTM, Mich. Edn. Assocs., Inc. (exec. com. 1994—, treas. 1994-95), Detroit Soc. Model Engrs. (pres.

1958, 62, bd. dir. 1955-71), Chem. Splty. Mfg. Assn., Nat. Geog. Soc., Internat. Platform Assn., Smithsonian Instn. Assocs., Archaeol. Inst. Am., Bibl. Archaeol. Soc., Bible-Sci. Assn., Creation Rsch. Soc., Mich. Student Fin. Aid Assn., Midwest Assn. Student Fin. Aid Adminstrs. Republican. Avocations: biographies, writings of great Christians. Home: 32210 Rosevear St Beverly Hills MI 48025-3921 Office: Midwestern Baptist Coll 825 Golf Dr Pontiac MI 48341-2354

DECKER, RANDY J., machine company executive; b. Dubuque, Iowa, May 17, 1962; s. Vincent Elmer and Evelyn Lavina (Hansen) D.; m. Joni Sue McDermott, May 2, 1992; 1 child, Sydney. Gen. machining degree, NITI, Peosta, Iowa, 1982. Foreman Webber Metals, Cascade, Iowa, 1983-89; pres. Decker Precision Machining, Peosta, 1989—. Roman Catholic. Office: Decker Precision Machining PO Box 9 Peosta IA 52068-0009

DECKER, RUSSELL S., state legislator; b. May 25, 1953. Mem. from dist. 29 Wis. State Senate, Madison, 1990—, mem. rural econ. devel. bd. Active Habitat for Humanity; mem. apprentice com. United Way; rep. for bricklayers union. Home: 5106 Apache Ln Schofield WI 54476-2003*

DECKROSH, HAZEN DOUGLAS, retired state agency educator and administrator; b. Defiance, Ohio, Apr. 13, 1936; s. Lawrence L. and Martha L. Deckrosh; m. Carol Ann Everett, Nov. 25, 1970; children: Stephanie, Todd, Douglas, Nadia Nicole. BS, Ohio No. U., 1959; MEd, U. Toledo, 1980. Cert. tchr., Ohio. Phys. edn. and history tchr., coach Waynesfield (Ohio)-Goshen Jr. High Sch., 1959-61; coach, history, phys. edn. tchr. Coshocton (Ohio) Sacred Heart High Sch., 1961-63; health-phys. edn. tchr., coach West Holmes Jr. High Sch., Millersburg, Ohio, 1965-70; tchr. history and govt., coach Elida High Sch., 1973-77; occupational work experience tchr.-coord., coach Spencerville (Ohio) High Sch., 1973-77; occupational work edn. tchr., coord. Four County Vocat. Sch., Archbold, Ohio, 1977-82; vocat. supr. Jefferson County Vocat. Sch., Steubenville, Ohio, 1986-87; occupational work experience tchr., coord. Ohio Dept. of Youth Svcs., Columbus, 1987-94; ret., 1994; pres. DYS Coordinators, Columbus, 1990-94; ski instr. Swiss Valley, Mich., 1995—; GED instr. Correction Ctr. Northwest Ohio. Editor: Threaded Fasteners, 1987; contbr. articles to profl. publs. Mem. Am. Youth Hostels, Lima, 1972—. Mem. NEA, Ohio Edn. Assn., Am. Vocat. Assn., Ohio Vocat. Assn., Occupl. Work Experience Coords. Assn. (state adv. coun., Lima rep. 1977-80, Columbus rep. 1991-94), Full Gospel Bus. Men's Fellowship Internat., Gideons Internat. (treas.), 5th Dist. Ofcls. Assn. (v.p., rules interpreter), Capitol West Umpires Assn. (rules interpreter 1991-93), Lima Umpires Assn. (sec.-treas. 1973-77), Ret. Tchrs. Assn. (pres.), Alpha Sigma Phi. Republican. Home: 12265 County Rd I 50 Montpelier OH 43543

DE COURTEN-MYERS, GABRIELLE MARGUERITE, education educator, researcher; b. Fribourg, Switzerland, Aug. 8, 1947; came to U.S., 1979; d. Maurice Edmond and Margrit (Wettstein) De Courten; m. Ronald Elwood Myers, Apr. 18, 1981; 1 child, Maximilian. BSBA, Akademikergemeinschaft, Zurich, Switzerland, 1967; MD, U. Zurich, 1974. Resident in psychiatry Hopital Psycho-Geriatrique, Gimel, Switzerland, 1974-75; resident in pediatrics U. Hosp. Zurich, 1977; resident in neuropathology U. Hosp. of Lausanne, Switzerland, 1976-78; rsch. assoc. NIH, Bethesda, Md., 1979-80; fellow in neuropathology Coll. of Medicine U. Cin., 1980-83, asst. prof. neuropathology Coll. of Medicine, 1983-88, assoc. prof. neuropathology Coll. of Medicine, 1988-89, tenured assoc. prof. Coll. of Medicine, 1989—; cons. Vets. Affairs Med. Ctr., Cin., 1983—, Children's Hosp. Med. Ctr., Cin., 1984—, Good Samaritan Hosp., Cin., 1990—. Grantee VA, 1985—, NIH, 1986-90, 93—, Am. Heart Assn., 1991-94, Am. Diabetes Assn., 1995. Mem. AAAS, Am. Assn. Neuropathologists, Am. Acad. Neurology, AAUP, Soc. Acad. Emergency Medicine, Soc. Exptl. Neuropathology. Office: U Cin Coll of Medicine 231 Bethesda Ave Cincinnati OH 45229-2827

DEDERT, STEVEN RAY, marketing professional, consultant; b. Franklin, Ind., Feb. 17, 1953; s. Ralph Edward and Martha Elizabeth (Weisman) D.; children: Eric Allen, Tammi Michelle. AA, St. John's Coll., Winfield, Kans., 1973; BSBA, U. Denver, 1975. CPA, Ind. Audit sr. Coopers & Lybrand, Indpls., 1975-78; controller Am. Med. Mgmt., Inc., Indpls., 1978-82, Moorfeed Corp., Indpls., 1982-84; chief fin. officer, controller Midwest Energy Mgmt., Indpls., 1984-86; pres. Cleaning Solution, Inc., Indpls., 1986-89; chief fin. officer, dir. ops. Corinthian Pharm. Systems, Inc., Indpls., 1990-93; ptnr. Hometown Living Ctrs., Inc., Indpls., 1991—; cons. acct., 1980—. Treas. bd. dirs. Greater Indpls. Assn. for Luth. Secondary Edn., 1978-82; mgr. Franklin Twp. Little League, 1985-87. Mem. Ind. CPA Soc., AICPA. Home: PO Box 39251 Indianapolis IN 46239-0251 Office: 115 N Pennsylvania Ste 856 Indianapolis IN 46204

DEDO, DOROTHY JUNELL TURNER, real estate company executive, civic worker; b. Norway, Mich., Oct. 17, 1920; d. Raymond and Esther Elvira (Junell) Turner; m. Lewis Joseph Dedo, Dec. 24, 1945; children: Craig Turner, Drew Jonathan. Student, U. So. Calif., 1939-40; AB with honors, U. Mich., 1942; postgrad., U. N.D., 1942, Marquette U., 1942-43. Cert. tchr., Wis. Safety person Kearney & Trecker Corp., Milw., 1942-43; supr. Town of Shelby, La Crosse, Wis., 1973-77, clk., 1977-81, chmn., 1981-85; pres. Turner Lands, Inc., Milw., 1985—; supr. County of LaCrosse, 1990-94. Contbr. numerous articles to La Crosse Tribune. Prodr., dir., actor La Crosse Children's Theater, 1959-65; sales mgr., actor La Crosse Cmty. Theatre, 1965-69; sec. Western Wis. Health Planning Orgn., 1964-68; chmn. Christian edn., mem. coun. English Luth. Ch., 1969-72; nominations chmn. bd. advisors Viterbo Coll., 1971-92; bd. dirs. Luth. Hosp. Found., 1978-90; bd. dirs. Winding Rivers Libr. Sys., 1990-95, v.p., 1994-95; sec. Wis. Towns Assn., 1973-85; v.p. La Crosse Area Devel. Corp., 1981-85; mem. La Crosse Area Planning Com., 1981-85; pres. La Crosse County Rep. Women, 1976-78. Lt. comdr. USNR, 1943-55. Recipient Dionysos award in bus. La Crosse Community Theatre, 1965, Women of Yr. award La Crosse Bus. and Profl. Women, 1982, Tribute to Outstanding Woman award YWCA, La Crosse, 1983. Mem. AAUW (pres. LaCrosse 1974-76, Wis., 1981-83, named grant honoree 1977), AARP, Viterbo Coll. Pres.'s Club, Heritage Club, LaCrosse Country Club, Pearl Investment Club (pres. 1988-91), Earthwatch, Alpha Kappa Delta, Alpha Lambda Delta, Alpha Chi Omega. Home: 5870 W Cedar Rd La Crosse WI 54601

DEDONATO, DONALD MICHAEL, obstetrician/gynecologist; b. Bridgeport, Conn., Apr. 25, 1952; s. Michael Anthony and Mary Jane (Zawadski) DeD.; m. Susan Mary Naulty, June 15, 1974; children: Mark Dominic, David Nicholas. BA in Chemistry cum laude, Coll. Holy Cross, 1974; MD, Loyola U., Maywood, Ill., 1977. Intern Loyola Foster McGaw Hosp., Maywood, Ill., 1977-78; resident Ohio State U. Hosp., Columbus, Ohio, 1978-81; ob-gyn. Ob-Gyn. Assocs., Arlington Heights, Ill., 1981-87, DeDonato, Goodnough and Geittmann, Ob-Gyn, Arlington Heights, 1987-92; pres. N.W. Women's Cons., Arlington Heights, 1993—; Clin. instr. Northwestern U. Med. Ctr., Chgo., 1981—. Recipient CIBA award. Mem. AMA, Am. Assn. Med. Colls. (Loyola rep.), Chgo. Med. Soc., Ill. State Med. Soc., Am. Bd. Ob-Gyn., Am. Assn. Gyn. Laparoscopists, Garden Camera (pres. 1985-86, 92-93), Phi Beta Kappa, Alpha Sigma Nu. Office: NW Womens Cons 1614 W Central Rd Arlington Heights IL 60005-2490

DEE, IVAN RICHARD, book publisher; b. Chgo., Mar. 11, 1935; s. Jack Arthur and Jeanette Rose (Melcher) D.; m. Sandra Cohen, June 21, 1959 (div. 1973); m. Phyllis Kirz, Aug. 3, 1977 (div. 1981); m. Barbara Burgess, Apr. 15, 1989; children: Alexander, Sara, Jacob, Gabriel. BJ, U. Mo., 1956, MA, 1957. Pres. Ardivan Press, Macon, Ga., 1960-61; v.p., editor-in-chief Quadrangle Books, Chgo., 1961-72; assoc. editor Chgo. Tribune Book World, Chgo., 1972-73; exec. editor Pubs.-Hall Syndicate, Chgo., 1973-74; editor-in-chief Chicagoan Mag., Chgo., 1974-75; dir. pub. affairs Michael Reese Hosp. and Med. Ctr., Chgo., 1975-89; pres. Ivan R. Dee, Inc., Chgo., 1989—. V.p. South Side Planning Bd., Chgo., 1975-89; commr. Chgo. Baseball League, 1978—. Lt. (j.g.) USN, 1957-60. Office: Ivan R Dee Inc 1332 N Halsted St Chicago IL 60622-2637

DEE, SCOTT ALLEN, veterinarian; b. Rochester, Minn., Sept. 27, 1958; s. Richard Walter and Pauline Kay (Anderson) D.; m. Lisa Ann Bell, Oct. 9, 1993. BA in Biology, Gustavus Adolphus Coll., 1981; MS in Veterinary Microbiology, U. Minn., 1985, DVM, 1987, PhD in Vet. Medicine, 1996. Diplomate Am. Coll. Vet. Microbiologists. Vet., ptnr. Swine Health Ctr., Morris, Minn., 1987—; mem. adv. bd. Swine Health and Prodn., St. Paul, 1991—, NOBL Labs., Sioux Ctr., Iowa, 1992—, Pfizer Animal Health, Lee Summit, Mo., 1994—; spkr. Internat. Porcine Reproductive and Respiratory System Conf., Copenhagen, 1995, St. Paul, 1992; del. Conf. Rsch. Workers in Animal Disease, 1995. Author: Veterinary Clinics of North America: Swine Reproduction, 1992, Current Veterinary Therapy III, 1993,; splty. editor Compendium Continuing Edn., 1995; contbr. articles to profl. jours. Recipient First Decade award Gustavus Adolphus Coll., 1991. Mem. AVMA, Am. Assn. Swine Practitioners (Swine Practitioner of Yr. 1996), Minn. Vet. Med. Assn., Minn. Acad. Vet. Practice. Office: Swine Health Ctr 621 Pacific Ave Morris MN 56267

DEERING, TERRY WILLIAM, state legislator; b. Du Quoin, Ill., Nov. 7, 1958; s. Ernest and Virdell Nell (Heck) D.; m. Reita Jean Peradotta, Sept. 3, 1983; children: Greyson Tyler, Clayton Burke, Allyssa Morgen. Grad. high sch., Nashville, Ill. Delivery person Lorenz Distbg. Co., Nashville, 1976-77; equipment oper. Pitts Quarry, Radom, Ill., 1977-78; machine oper. Gen. Tire & Rubber Co., Mt. Vernon, Ill., 1978-79; equipment oper. Kinkaid Stone Co., Campbell Hill, Ill., 1979; coal miner Arch of Ill., Percy, 1979-90; elected mem. Ill. Gen. Assembly, Springfield, 1990—. Village trustee Village of DuBois, Ill., 1978, village pres., 1979-90; officer Ill. Jaycees, DuBois, 1977-81. Mem. KC, Troopers Lodge. Democrat. Roman Catholic. Office: Dist Office PO Box 268 121 E Adams St Nashville IL 62263*

DEERING, THOMAS EDWIN, academic administrator; b. St. Louis, Nov. 20, 1948; s. Edwin Joseph and Virginia Maria (Thomas) D.; m. Carol Ann Greenwood, June 8, 1984; children: Ian Christopher. BS in Social Studies Edn., U. Mo., 1973, MEd in History and Philosophy of Edn., 1974, EdS in Ednl. Adminstrn., 1979, EdS in Curriculum and Instrn., 1988, PhD in Social and Phil. Founds. of Edn., 1985; MA in History, S.E. Mo. State U., 1981; MA in Philosophy, U. Ill., 1993. Tchr. Pub. Schs., Mo., 1974-80; instr. U. Mo., Columbia, 1980-81, staff liaison, 1987-88; dir. U. Mo., Rolla, 1995—; prin. Mo. State Dept. Elem. and Secondary Edn., Hannibal, 1983-84; staff cons. Mo. State Tchrs. Assn., Columbia, 1984-85; asst. prof. Lambuth U., Jackson, Tenn., 1985-86, Mo. Valley Coll., Marshall, 1986-87; assoc. prof. North Ctrl. Coll., Naperville, Ill., 1988-95; cons. Mo. State Tchrs. Assn., Columbia, Mo., 1983-94. Contbr. articles to profl. jours. Mem. Am. Ednl. Studies Assn., Assn. Tchr. Educators, History of Edn. Soc., State Hist. Soc. Mo. Home: 723 Republic Rolla MO 65401

DEES, DAVID P., retired minister; b. Princeville, Ill., Jan. 4, 1926; s. Jesse W. and Frances (Sherwood) D.; m. Elizabeth O. Dees, May 26, 1956; children: Mary E., Rebekah F., Paul D. BPh, Ill. Wesleyan U., 1949; MDiv, Garrett Evang. Theol. Sem., Evanston, Ill., 1953. Ordained to ministry, Meth. Ch. Minister United Meth. Ch./Ctrl. Ill. Conf., 1951-91; ret.; adj. prof. Ill. State U., Normal, 1991—. Trustee Ill. Wesleyan U., Bloomington, 1976—, Evenglow Lodge, Pontiac, Ill., 1991—. Mem. Ill. State U. Sr. Profls., Ill. Wesleyan U. Alumni Assn., Kiwanis. Republican. Home: 908 Hastings Dr Bloomington IL 61701

DEETS, CAROL ANNE, health science educator; b. Princeton, Ill., Mar. 27, 1938; d. Laurence Edwin and June (McDermott) D. Diploma in Nursing, Presbyn. Hosp., Charlotte, N.C., 1960; BS, Queens Coll., 1961; MN, Ind. U., 1966, D in Edn., 1971. Instr. Jackson Hosp. Sch. of Nursing, Miami, 1961-65, U. S.C., Columbia, 1966-68; asst. prof. U. Tex., Austin, 1971-72, dir. Ctr. for Health Care Rsch., 1972-77; prof. Ind. U., Indpls., 1980-92, acting assoc. dean for grad. program, 1989-91; assoc. dean for rsch., dir. Inst. for Nursing Rsch. U. Cin., 1992—; rsch. cons. VA Hosp. Nursing Dept., Mason, Ind., 1991-94, Indpls., 1978-86, San Antonio, Tex., 1974-75; presenter in field. Mem. Am. Ednl. Rsch. Assn., NLN, AAUP, Sigma Theta Tau, Pi Lambda Theta. Methodist. Home: 4225 Easton Ln Burlington KY 41005 Office: Univ Cin Coll Nursing/Health 3110 Vine St ML 0038 Cincinnati OH 42551-0038

DEFFENBAUGH, DAVID PAUL, SR., writer, artist; b. Peoria, Ill., July 29, 1948; s. Oliver Dewey and Agnes June (Walker) D.; m. Pamela Louise Martin, May 1, 1970 (div. 1989); children: Victoria Marie, David Paul Jr., Emma Florence; m. Sharon Mindy Brender, Oct. 29, 1989; 1 stepchild, Jeremiah; 1 child, Isaiah. Newspaper printer Lowell (Ind.) Tribune, 1965-68, 70-72; security officer Raco Security, Bradly, Ill., 1972-74; security chief Drost Resorts Inc., Roselawn, Ind., 1974-82; corrections officer Ill. Dept. Corrections, Joliet, 1982-84; writer, artist David Deffenbaugh Enterprises, Sparland, Ill., 1984—. Contbr. short stories to periodicals. With U.S. Army, 1968-70. Mem. Am. Legion, N.Am. Fishing Club, Peoria Casting Club, Ministries of Sparland (Ill. pres.). Mem. Pentecostal Ch. Home and Office: David Deffenbaugh Enterprises RR2 Box 15 Sparland IL 61565-9507

DEFRANCO, ANTHONY, sales representative; b. New Haven, Jan. 3, 1957. BA, Temple U., 1978. Candidate for Boston Sch. Bd., 1984; Dem. candidate for U.S. House, 1992, 96. Roman Catholic. Office: Rte 3 Box 403 De Soto MO 63020*

DEGELBECK, GRETCHEN MAY, library director; b. Vassar, Mich., Apr. 2, 1934; d. Clair Adolph and LaRue Carolyn (Long) Gugel; m. Gerald L. Degelbeck, Mar. 11, 1953; children: Richard Louis, Steven Michael. Student, Ctrl. Mich. U., Mt. Pleasant, 1952-53. Asst. libr. Marlette (Mich.) Twp. Libr., 1968-83; dir. libr. Marlette Dist. Libr., 1984—; mem. Sanilac County Libr. Bd., Sandusky, Mich., 1974—; mem. White Pine Libr. Bd., Saginaw, Mich., 1990-92. Mem. Marlette City Coun., 1976-88; mem. Zoning Bd. of Appeals, City of Marlette, 1984—, mem. Planning Commn., 1991—; mem. bd. of session First Presbyn. Ch., treas., 1965-68. Named Citizen of Yr., Marlette C. of C., 1992; recipient Cert. of Excellence, Loleta Fyan Rural Libr. Conf., 1993. Mem. Philomathean Club (former pres.). Home: 6273 Oakes St Marlette MI 48453

DEGERSTROM, JAMES MARVIN, engineering manager; b. Owosso, Mich., Aug. 9, 1933; s. John Marcellus and Emma Judith (Folkadahl) D.; m. Ann Blandford, July 3, 1964. BSME, Mich. State U., 1955; MBA, DePaul U., 1966. Cert. plant engr., 1991. Adminstrv. asst. Sunbeam Corp., Chgo., 1955-61; mfg. supt. Internat. Register Co., Inc., Chgo., 1961-65; sr. engr. Kitchens of Sara Lee, Inc., Deerfield, Ill., 1965-71; pres. Edmanson Bock Caterers, Chgo., 1972; mgr. bldg. ops. Jewel Cos., Inc., Barrington, Ill., 1972-81; dir. plant ops. Copley Meml. Hosp., Aurora, Ill., 1981-86; dir. plant ops. Little Co. Mary Hosp., Evergreen Park, Ill., 1986-88; dir. facilities Oak Park Hosp., 1988-89; mgr. plant engring. Honeywell, Inc., Joliet, Ill., 1989-90; dir. facilities mgmt. S. Suburban Hosp., Hazel Crest, Ill., 1990—; bd. dirs., treas. Credit Union, Kitchens of Sara Lee, 1966-70. With USAF, 1957-65. Recipient cert. of recognition, Am. Inst. Plant Engrs. Nat. Conf., 1977. Mem. Am. Inst. Indsl. Engrs., Am. Inst. Plant Engrs. (sec. 1977-79, pres. chpt. 5 1991), Toastmasters (dist. officer 1982-86, pres. 1981, area gov. 1982, lt. gov. 1983-84, dist. gov. 1984-85). Home: 102 Knollwood Ct Oak Brook IL 60521-1518

DEGEUS, WENDELL RAY, photographer; b. Des Moines, Feb. 1, 1948; s. Raymond G. and Thelma Z. (Hollingsworth) DeG. A. in Photography, Hawkeye Inst. Tech., 1973. Cert. EMT, basic trauma life support. Lab mgr., head tech. Midwest Photo Svc., Galesburg, Ill., 1975-80; sr. prodn. specialist TGS Tech. Inc./EROS Data Ctr., Sioux Falls, S.D., 1980-92, Hughes STX Corp/EROS Data Ctr., Sioux Falls, S.D., 1992—. Vol. Hot Line 58, Crisis Intervention, Galesburg, 1977-78; mem. Minnehaha County Rescue Squad, Sioux Falls, 1988—. Mem. Am. Soc. Photogrammetry and Remote Sensing, Internat. Platform Assn., S.D. EMT Assn. (state tng. officer dist. 2 1993—), Nat. Assn. EMS Physicians. Democrat. Mem. Wesleyan Ch. Home: 300 N Kiwanis Ave Apt 105 Sioux Falls SD 57104-2551

DEGNITZ, DOROTHY ELSIE, nurse; b. Wis., Aug. 13, 1936; d. Fredrick William and Elsie Emily (Lawrenz) D. BSN, Northwestern U., 1959; cert., Frontier Sch. of Nursing, 1968; diploma in nursing edn., Armidale (Australia) Coll., 1981; MA in Social Sci., Azusa (Calif.) Pacific U., 1986. Instr. in psychiat. nursing Sch. of Nursing Evanston (Ill.) Hosp., 1960-66; missionary nurse tchr. Bd. for Mission Svcs., St. Louis, 1966-67, 68-70, Papua New Guinea, 1971-87; nursing supr. infirmary and nights Bethesda Luth. Home and Svcs., Watertown, Wis., 1987-94, part-time staff nurse, 1994—. Mem. Nat. League for Nursing, Wis. Nurse's Assn. (membership com.), APHA. Home: 1202 S 9th St Watertown WI 53094-6604

DE GRAFFENRIED, MICHEAL, public service educator; b. Buffalo; s. John Willie and Viola (Whitmore); m. Delonda K. Gant; 1 child, Rebecca Lee Anne. BA in History and Communications, Canisius Coll., 1981; MS in Pub. Affairs, SUNY, Buffalo, 1987. Supr. YMCA Light House Program, Buffalo, 1980-81; counselor Upward Bound, Ohio, 1982; legal asst. Coll. Law U. Toledo, 1982; pub. adminstr. human rights div. State of N.Y., Buffalo, 1984-85, Erie County Indsl. Devel., Buffalo, 1984-85; bus. counselor Small Bus. Devel. Ctr. SUNY at Buffalo (N.Y.) Coll., 1986; mgmt. intern City of Ft. Worth, 1986-87; adminstrv. asst. to mgr. City of Kalamazoo, Mich., 1987-89; legis. rsch. analyst Mich. Ho. of Reps., Lansing, 1989-91; tchr. Kalamazoo Pub. Schs., 1991-93, behavior specialist, 1993-96; coord. gang prevention through targeted outreach program Prevention Works, 1996—; treas. Minority Bus. Opportunity Com., Buffalo, 1984-86, sec. steering com., 1985-86. Author: Mental Health, 1980, Human Rights, 1980, Job Safety, 1980. Asst. youth counselor Nazareth Ch., Toledo, 1981-82; tutor Adopt-A-Sch., Ft. Worth, 1986-87; vol. summer youth tennis asst., Kalamazoo, 1988; dir. pub. rels. Eternal Life Community Choir, Kalamazoo, 1988; asst. coord. Double Dutch Competition, Kalamazoo, 1988; spl. events coord. ch. Conquering Faith Family Ch., 1991-93, Good News Deliverance Ctr. Ch., 1993—; vol. Big Bros. Big Sisters, Kalamzoo, 1988--. Legal edn. grantee U. Toledo, 1981-82; Dr. Martin Luther King scholar, 1977-81, Home Growth scholar, 1995; HUD fellow, 1984. Home: 429 Reed Ave Kalamazoo MI 49001-2833 Office: Prevention Works Gang Prev Thru Outreach 505 W Vine St Kalamazoo MI 49008

DEGROW, DAN L., state legislator; b. Ann Arbor, Mich., Jan. 28, 1953; m. Cheryl L. Simpson, 1981; children: Allison, Kelsie Sue, Stephen. Grad., Mich. State U., 1975; JD, Wayne State U., 1978. Rep. Mich. State, 1980-82; senator Mich. Dist. 28, 1982-94, Mich. Dist. 27, 1995—; vice chair appropriations com. Mich. State Senate, chmn. K-12 & edn. subcom., cmty. coll. com., capital outlay, budget and oversight com., jud. com., legis coun; ptnr. Nicholson, Fletcher, West & DeGrow, 1979—. Active St. Clair County Rep. Com. Mem. NAACP, Assn. Retarded Citizens, Mich. Bar Assn., St. Clair County Bar Assn., Phi Beta Kappa. Office: State Senate Office State Capitol Lansing MI 48909-7536*

DEHART, EILEEN, state legislator; b. Sept. 15, 1948. Grad., Mich. State U. Staff Rep. Justine Barns; rep. Mich. State Dist. 18, 1995—; conservation, environ. and Great Lakes com. Mich. Ho. Reps., sr. citizens com., vet. affairs com. Address: PO Box 30014 Lansing MI 48909-7514

DEHLER, STEVE, state legislator; b. 1950; m. Jean; 2 children. BA, St. John's U. State rep. Minn. Ho. Reps., Dist. 14A, 1993—. Home: PO Box 337 Saint Joseph MN 56374-0337*

DEHNER, JOSEPH JULNES, lawyer; b. Cin., Nov. 28, 1948; s. Walter Joseph and Bess (Humphries) D.; m. Noel Julnes, Nov. 19, 1983; children: Holly Julnes, Sara Julnes. AB, Princeton U., 1970; JD, Harvard Law Sch., Cambridge, Mass., 1973. Bar: Ohio 1973, U.S. Dist. Ct. (no. and so. dists.) Ohio 1975, Fla. 1986, U.S. Dist. Ct. (ea. dist.) Ky. 1988, U.S. Ct. Internat. Trade 1992. Law clk. to judge U.S. Court Appeals, Cleve., 1973-75; assoc. Kyte, Conlan, Wulsin & Vogeler, Cin., 1975-79, Frost & Jacobs, Cin., 1979—; chmn. Universal Transactions Inc., 1991-95; co-mgr. Ukraine Investments ltd. Author: Structured Settlements and Periodic Payment Judgments, 1986, A Guide to Soviet Businesspeople on American Business Law, 1991, Doing Business in Russia, 1992, Dispute Resolution and China, 1994, A Foreign Investors Guide to Ukraine, 1995; contbr. articles to profl. publs. Sec., v.p. Cin. Preservation Assn., 1978-86; mem. Cin. Planning Commn., 1984-85; pres. Charter Com. Greater Cin., 1982-86; chmn. Cin.-Kharkov Sister City Project, 1988-91; trustee Princeton U., 1970-74, Ohio Hist. Soc., 1974-78. Mem. ABA, Internat. Bar Assn., Ohio State Bar Assn. (chmn. internat. law com. 1989-91), Cin. Bar Assn., Sixth Cir. Jud. Conf. Episcopal. Home: 822 Yale Ave Terrace Park OH 45174-1258 Office: Frost & Jacobs 2500 PNC Ctr 201 E 5th St Cincinnati OH 45202-4117

DEHNER, PHIL MICHAEL, financial consultant; b. Lincoln, Ill., Feb. 2, 1943; s. Fredrick Vincent and Mona Dels (Lutz) D.; m. Connie Louise Hudspeth, July 18, 1964; children: Fredrick Vincent, Carlton Edward, Michelle Louise. BA in Mgmt., Sagamen State U., Springfield, Ill., 1982. Engr. Eaton Corp., Lincoln, Ill., 1979-84; fin. cons. Smith Barney Inc., Decatur, Ill., 1984—. With USN, 1961-73. Mem. Elks. Republican. Roman Catholic. Home: 829 N Kickapoo St Lincoln IL 62656-1864 Office: Smith Barney Inc 3090 N Main St Decatur IL 62526-2301

DEHOOGH, NOREEN BETH, secondary education educator, school system administrator; b. Orange City, Iowa, Aug. 26, 1943; d. Harold Edwin and Ella Harmina (Giesen) DeJager; m. Theodore M. DeHoogh, Feb. 10, 1967; children: Nathan Mark, Derek Michael. BS, Northwestern Coll., 1961. Cert. secondary edn. tchr., Iowa. Tchr. West Sioux Community Sch., Hawarden, Iowa, 1965-66; tchr. Sioux Center (Iowa) Community Sch., 1966-71, sec., 1980-81, bus. mgr., 1981—; tchr. Dordt Coll., Sioux Center, 1975-80. Mem. com. Troop 211 Boy Scouts Am., Sioux Center, 1990—; treas. Pack 211 Cub Scouts, Sioux Center, 1986-90; dir. First Reformed Ch. Children's Choir, 1964—. Mem. First Reformed Ch. Women (cabinet 1990), Am. Legion Aux. (sec. 1996). Office: Sioux Center Community Sch 550 9th St NE Sioux Center IA 51250-2004

DEININGER, DAVID GEORGE, judge; b. Monroe, Wis., July 9, 1947; s. Wilbur Emerson and Anna Emilie (Karlen) D.; m. Mary Carol Nussbaum, June 4, 1969; children: Jonathan David, Christopher Jacob, Emilie Joanne. BS, U.S. Naval Acad., 1969; JD, U. Wis., 1978. Bar: Wis. 1978, Ill. 1978, U.S. Dist. Ct. (we. dist.) Wis. 1978. Ptnr. Benkert, Spielman, Asmus & Deininger, Monroe, 1978-87; legislator Wis. State Assembly, Madison, 1987-94; of counsel Brennan, Steil, Basting & MacDougall, S.C., Monroe, 1988-94; cir. ct. judge Green County, 1994-96. Active Monroe Sch. Bd., 1986-89, Monroe Theatre Guild, 1980—; chmn. Green County Rep. Cen. Com., Monroe, 1982-84. Lt. USN, 1969-75. Mem. Green County Bar Assn. (pres. 1982-83), Wis. State Bar Assn., Am. Legion, VFW, Optimists (pres. Monroe chpt. 1984-85). Home: 1803 11th St Monroe WI 53566-1842 Office: Ct Appeals Dist IV Madison WI 53703-3330

DEINZER, GEORGE WILLIAM, public welfare organization administrator; b. Tiffin, Ohio, Nov. 1, 1934; s. Harvey Charles and Edna Louise (Harpley) D.;. A.B., Heidelberg Coll., 1956; postgrad., Washington U., 1956-57. Asst. to dir. phys. plant Heidelberg Coll., 1957-58, admissions counselor, 1958-60, dir. admissions, 1960-71, dir. fin. aids, assoc. dir. admissions, 1971-80; exec. dir. Tiffin-Seneca United Way, 1980-85; adminstr. Seneca County (Ohio) Dept. Human Services and Children's Services, 1985—; voting rep. Coll. Entrance Examination Bd., 1963-80; fin. aid cons. Nat. Collegiate Athletic Assn.; cons. Ohio Scholarship Funds, 1960-61. Contbr. articles to profl. jours. Pres., chmn. allocations com., bd. dirs. United Way; pres. lay bd. Mercy Hosp.; treas., bd. dirs. N.W. Ohio Health Planning Assn., co-chmn. steering com., 1984; mem. legis com. Ohio Citizens Coun., 1981-88, human svcs. task force, 1984—; pres. Seneca County Mus. Found.; treas. Tiffin Theatre, Inc.; mem. Seneca Indsl. and Econ. Devel. Corp. Bd., 1983-88; chmn. Tiffin Area Devel. and Pub. Rels. Dirs., 1984—, Charter Rev. Commn., Tiffin, 1990-91; mem. W.S.O.S. Community Action Coun. bd., 19906. Mem. Organ Hist. Soc., Am. Theatre Organ Soc., Nat., Ohio (regional coordinator, treas., state trainer, chmn. needs analysis com.) assns. student fin. aid adminstrs., Ohio Athletic Conf. Fin. Dirs. (past chmn.), Am. Personnel and Guidance Assn., Am. Coll. Personnel Assn., Council Ohio United Way Execs., Farm Bur., Ohio Hist. Soc., U.S. Naval Inst., Buckeye Sheriffs Assn., N.W. Ohio and Ohio Human Service Dirs., Rotary (dir., pres. 1982-83, gen. sec.-elect 1990—), Elks, Beta Beta Beta. Republican. *Died Apr., 1993.*

DEITRICH, LAWRENCE WALTER, mechanical engineer, nuclear engineer; b. Pitts., Oct. 17, 1938; s. Leon Lawrence and Margaret (Stillman) D.; m. Patsy Ann Smith, Sept. 5, 1964; 1 child, David Steven. BME, Cornell U., 1961; MSME, Rensselaer Poly. Inst., Troy, N.Y., 1963; PhD, Stanford U., 1969. Group leader Argonne (Ill.) Nat. Lab., 1972-74, sect. mgr., 1974-79, spl. asst. to assoc. lab. dir., 1979-80, assoc. div. dir., 1980-93, div. dir. reactor engring., 1994—, dir. Internat. Nuclear Safety Ctr., 1995—. Contbr. articles to profl. jours. Fellow Am. Nuclear Soc.; mem. ASME, Am. Nuclear Soc. (chmn. nuclear reactor safety div. 1987-88, bd. dirs. 1992-

95), Sigma Xi. Office: Argonne Nat Lab RE/208 9700 Cass Ave RE/208 Argonne IL 60439-4803

DEJULIO, ELLEN LOUISE, special education administrator; b. Jersey City, June 7, 1946; d. Fred J. and Mary F. (Burns) DeJ. AB in English and Edn., Immaculata (Pa.) Coll., 1968; MEd in Ednl. Therapy, Nat.-Louis U., Evanston, Ill., 1973, CAS in Adminstrn./Supervision, 1982; EdD, Vanderbilt U., 1993. Cert. in ednl. adminstrn., learning disabilities, elem./secondary edn., social-emotional disorders, educable and trainable mentally handicapped. Dir. summer program St. Mary of Providence Ctr., Elverson, Pa., 1967-82; tchr. 2d grade Hillcrest Sch., Downers Grove, Ill., 1968-72; spl. edn. tchr. Longfellow Sch., Downers Grove, 1972-73, Fairmount Sch., Downers Grove, 1973-80; asst. dir. S.E. region Sch. Assn. for Spl. Edn., DuPage County, Ill., 1983-85; dir. spl. svcs. Downers Grove Grad. Sch. Dist. 58, 1980—; cons. St. Mary of Providence Ctr., 1983-86. Recipient Community Svc. award Ill. Assn. Parks and Recreation/Downers Grove Park Dist. Mem. ASCD, Coun. for Exceptional Children, Assn. for Severely Handicapped, Art Inst. Chgo., Morton Arboretum, Ill. Women Adminstrs., Ill. Adminstrs. of Spl. Edn., Delta Kappa Gamma. Home: 2235 Durand Dr Downers Grove IL 60515-4267 Office: Downers Grove Grade Sch Dist 58 1860 63rd St Downers Grove IL 60516-2471

DEKORSI, ANN ELIZABETH, public relations professional; b. Austria, Oct. 26, 1947; came to U.S., 1953; d. Paul and Elizabeth (Wenzel) D.; children: Heidi Marie, Kristina Ann, Sarah Elizabeth; m. Peter Rohde, 1995. AA, U. Wis., Waukesha, 1984; BA in Mass Communication, Journalism, U. Wis., Milw., 1986. Lic real estate broker, Wis. Community rels. coord. Milw. Jewish Home, 1987; pub. and promotion coord. Park and Recreation Dept. City of Waukesha, 1988; asst. dir. pub. rels. Milw. Sch. Engring., 1988-89, assoc. dir. pub. rels., 1990-91, dir media rels., 1992—; cons. IGM Robotics, Milw., 1990-91. Contbr. articles to profl. jours. and mags. Pub. rels. cons. Ind. Senate Campaign, Milw., 1988. Faculty scholar U. Wis., Waukesha, 1983, scholar AAUW, 1983-84, Harry J. Grant scholar Milw. Jour., 1985. Mem. Soc. Profl. Journalists, Pub. Rels. Soc. Am. (Dorothy Thomas Black award Wis. chpt. 1986), Women in Communications (co-chair regional conf. 1990).

DEKREY, DUANE LEE, farmer, rancher; b. Jamestown, N.D., June 20, 1956; s. John Edward and Alpha Ann (Whitman) DeK.; m. Jan M. DeKrey, June 18, 1983; children: Tyler John, Peder Robert. BS in Agr., N.D. State U., 1978. Tchr. agrl. edn. Devils Lake (N.D.) Sch., 1979; farmer, rancher JD Acres, Tappen, N.D., 1979—; mem. N.D. Senate, Bismarck, 1990-92. Capt. U.S. Army, 1978—. Mem. Nat. Cattlemen's Assn., N.D. Stockmen Assn., Farm Bur. (pres.), Res. Officers Assn., LAND (state dir.), Masons. Republican. Congregationalist. Home: RR 1 Box 94 Tappen ND 58487-9514

DE KRUIF, WILLIAM RAYMOND, electronics executive, electrical engineer; b. Oak Park, Ill., Apr. 22, 1960; s. Willard Rice and Joan (Singley) D.; m. Vivian Everosk, July 12, 1986; children: Paul, Karena, Erik. BS, Colo. State U., 1983; BSEE, U. Colo., 1989; MBA in Mgmt., Northwestern U., 1994. Bus. dir. Motorola Inc., Chgo., 1989—. Mem. IEEE. Republican. Home: 9 Nathan Rd 18-01, Regency Park 248730, Singapore Office: Motorola Innovation Ctr, Ang Mo Kio Industrial Park, Singapore 569088, Singapore

DELABBIO, DARYL JOSEPH, county administrator; b. Detroit, July 20, 1953; s. Quinto Joseph and Clara Theresa (Gubienski) D.; m. Constance Rose Schoonover, July 23, 1977; children: Juliette Rose, Gianina Rae, Laurel Joy. BA, Aquinas Coll., 1974; MPA, Wayne State U., 1977; M of Mgmt., Aquinas Coll., 1994. Adminstrv. coord. City of Rockwood, Mich., 1977-78; adminstrv. asst. City of Garden City, Mich., 1978-80, dir. adminstrv. svcs., 1980-84; city mgr. City of Rockford, Mich., 1984-95; asst. county adminstr. Kent County, Grand Rapids, Mich., 1995—; coun. mem. Grand Valley Met. Coun., Grand Rapids, 1991-95; bd. dirs. Citizens League of Greater Grand Rapids, 1993-94. Recipient Bus. Assn. of Yr. award Rockford Bus. & Profl. Women's Assn., 1991, Hruby scholarship for Leadership & Svc., Aquinas Coll., 1990-94. Mem. Am. Soc. for Pub. Adminstrn., Mich. Mcpl. League (sec. region 5, 1991-92, trustee 1994-95), Mich. City Mgmt. Assn. (bd. dirs. 1981-83), Rockford Jaycees (sec. 1987-89, Jaycee of Yr. award 1990), Kiwanis (pres. Garden City 1983-84, Kiwanian of Yr. award 1983). Republican. Office: Kent County PO Box 561 300 Monroe Ave NW Grand Rapids MI 49503

DELANEY, CORNELIUS FRANCIS, philosophy educator; b. Waterbury, Conn., June 30, 1938; s. Patrick Francis and Margaret (Gavigan) D.; 1 child, Cornelius Francis Jr. MA, Boston Coll., 1961; PhD, St. Louis U., 1967. Prof. philosophy U. Notre Dame, Notre Dame, Ind., 1967—, chmn. philosophy dept., 1972-82, dir. honors program, 1989—. Author: Mind and Nature, 1969m The Synoptic Vision, 1977, Science, Knowledge and Mind, 1993, The Liberalism-Communitarianism Debate, 1994, New Essays on the Philosophy of C.S. Pierce, 1996. Recipient Madden award U. Notre Dame, 1974, Bicentennial award Boston Coll., 1976, Pres.'s award U. Notre Dame, 1984, Sheedy award U. Notre Dame,1987. Mem. Am. Cath. Philos. Assn. (pres. 1985), C.S. Peirce Soc. (pres. 1986), Am. Philos. Assn. (exec. com. 1983-85). Office: U Notre Dame Dept Philosophy Notre Dame IN 46556

DELANEY, JEAN MARIE, art educator; b. Jersey City, Nov. 14, 1931; d. John Francis and Genevieve Mary (Boulton) Reilly; m. Donald Kendall Delaney, Dec. 29, 1956; 1 child, Laura Marie. BA in Art Edn., Fairmont (W.Va.) State U., 1954; MA in Clin. Psychology, Loyola Coll., Balt., 1979; PhD in Art Edn., U. Wis., Milw., 1992. Cert. art tchr., prin., supr., Md. Tchr. English and social studies Reedurban Sch., Stark County, Ohio, 1954-56; art tchr. Perry Hall High Sch., Stark County, 1956-57, Margaret Brent High Sch., St. Mary's County, Md., 1957-59, Middle River Mid. Sch., Baltimore County, Md., 1959-62; home and hosp. tchr. Harford County (Md.) Bd. Edn., 1968-78; lectr. art appreciation U. Md. Extension, Harford County, 1971-76; art educator Baltimore County Bd. Edn., 1979-93; assoc. prof. art edn. S.W. Mo. State U., Springfield, 1993—; cons. Salisbury (Md.) State Coll., 1987; adj. prof. art edn. Md. Inst. Coll. Art, Balt., 1988-89; cons. bd. examiners and art edn. Nat. Tchr.'s Exam. test devel. com. ETS, Princeton, N.J., 1988-92. Author: Art Image, 6th Grade Units, 1988; editor: Art Scholarships, 1988; editor videotape Ernest Goldstein: Art Criticism, 1987; author, editor curriculum guide. Recipient Youth Art Month award of excellence Art and Craft Materials Inst., 1989, grant to coordinate Crayola Dreammakers program for Ctrl. Region U.S. and Can., 1994-96. Mem. Nat. Art Edn. Assn. (Eastern Region Art Educator award of yr, 1989, Nat. Secondary Art Educator award of yr. 1990), Md. Art Edn. Assn. (state coun. 1985—, v.p. arts advocacy 1988-89, pres.-elect 1992—, Md. Art Educator of Yr. 1988), Internat. Soc. for Edn. Through Art. Home: 634 S National Ave Apt 402 Springfield MO 65804-0065 Office: Southwest Missouri State U 901 S National Ave Springfield MO 65804-0027

DELANGE, WALTER L., state legislator; b. Grand Rapids, Mich., Nov. 9, 1931; s. Walter and Harriet DeL.; m. Lois A. Lindhout, 1951; three children. Mem. Kentwood City (Mich.) Bd. Rev., 1981; commr. Kent County, Mich., 1982; rep. Mich. Dist. 72, 1983—; majority caucus chmn. Mich. Ho. Reps., chmn. Rep. policy com., chmn. human resources & labor com., transp. com., regulatory com. Dir. Grand Rapids Home Builders Assn.; v.p. Mich. Assn. Home Builders, 1979-82, bd. dirs.; bd. dirs. Millbrook Christian Sch.; Sunday sch. tchr. Millbrook Christian Reformed Ch., former deacon, elder, tchr. catechism, clk. Home: 1075 Amberwood West Dr SW Grand Rapids MI 49509-9784*

DELAPA, JUDITH ANNE, business owner; b. Bad Axe, Mich., Feb. 1, 1938; d. John Vincent and Ellen Agatha (Peters) McCormick; m. James Patrick DeLapa, Jan. 10, 1959; children: Joseph Anthony, James P. II, John M., Gina M. BS, Mich. State U., 1959, MA, 1985. Tchr. various schs., Mich., 1959-64; co-founder Saluto Foods Corp., Benton Harbor, Mich., 1963-76; founder Earthtone Interiors, St. Joseph, Mich., 1977-82, High Impact Mktg. Svcs., Grand Rapids, Mich., 1987—; mktg. cons., writer various clients, nationwide. Author: High-Impact Business Strategies, 1993. Bd. dirs. Econ. Club Grand Rapids, Grand Rapids Symphony Orch. Judith A. DeLapa Perennial Garden named in her honor Michigan State U. Office: High Impact Mktg Svcs 2505 E Paris Ave SE Grand Rapids MI 49546-6100

DELAROSA, DENISE MARIA, legal administrator; b. Oakland, Calif., Dec. 30, 1954; d. David and Doris Elizabeth (Cantrell) Eirich; m. Robert Joseph Turocy, Dec. 30, 1972 (div. 1976); children: Robert Justin, Shannon James; m. Oscar Quiroga DeLaRosa, May 1, 1983 (div. 1992). AAS, Truman Coll., 1983; BABA, DePaul U., 1987. Legal adminstr. Taylor, Miller, Sprowl, Hoffnagle & Merletti, Chgo., 1985-91, Leonard M. Ring & Assocs., Chgo., 1991-93, Boehm, Pearlstein & Bright, Ltd., Chgo., 1994-95, Purcell & Wardope Chartered, Chgo., 1995—; ESL tutor Literacy Vols., Chgo, 1985-86. Mem. ABA (assoc.), Ill. Bar Assn. (assoc.), Assn. Legal Adminstrs. Democrat. Roman Catholic. Office: Purcell & Wardope Chartered 300 S Wacker Dr Ste 800 Chicago IL 60606

DELAURENTI, JOHN LEWIS, judge; b. Shelbyville, Ill., May 10, 1933; s. John Charles and Grace Agnes (Broom) D.; m. Leanne Dorothy DeLine, Apr. 9, 1960 (dec. 1991); children: Suzanne L., John R., James L., Elena M.; m. Betty Faye Klenke, Oct. 1, 1992. BA, U. Ill., 1955; JD, Valparaiso U., 1961. Bar: Ill. 1961, Mo. 1968, U.S. Dist. Ct. (so. dist.) Ill. Pvt. practice Jacoby Patton Manns, Alton, Ill., 1961-63; v.p., staff legal counsel Germania S/L, Alton, 1963-67; pvt. practice Roy McGee Firm, Piedmont, Mo., 1967-68, Greenville, Ill., 1968-72; state's atty. Bond County, Greenville, 1968-72; judge State of Ill., Bond County Cir. Ct., 3d Cir., Greenville, Edwardsville, Ill., 1972—; bd. dirs. Southwestern Ill. Law Enforcement Commn., 1970-77; mem. mng. bd. Ill. State's Atty., 1968-72. Contbr. articles to profl. jours. Active 1st Ill. Conservation Congress, Springfield, 1993, Ill. Wetlands Survey Commn. Ill. Dept. Natural Resource, 1995. Lt. col. USAFR, 1956-82. Recipient Law Enforcement award Ill. Dept. Conservation, 1988. Mem. Ill. Judges Assn. (disciplinary com. 1989-95), Ill. State Bar Assn. (Supreme Ct. rules com. 1992-95, pub. rels. com. 1986-92, environ. law com. 1970-72), Bond County Bar Assn. (pres. 1969-74, 81-85), Madison County Bar Assn., Southwestern Ill. Ret. Officers Assn., Am. Legion, Masons, Rotary. Methodist. Home: Rt 2 Box 91 Pocahontas IL 62275 Office: Bond County Circuit Ct 200 W College Greenville IL 62246

DELAY, WILLIAM RAYMOND, communications executive; b. Texarkana, Tex., June 16, 1929; s. Raymond Wallace and Flora Thomas (Greenwood) DeL.; m. Mary Elinor Dolson, Oct. 2, 1954; children—Martha, Nancy. B.S. in Journalism, U. Kans., William Allen White Sch. Journalism, 1951; postgrad. Mead Johnson Inst., 1958-59, Counter Intelligence Corps. Sch., 1951. Reporter Kansas City Kansan, 1951; reporter, copy editor Kansas City Times, 1953-56; pub. relations mgr. Mead Johnson & Co., 1956-60; dir. pub. relations Am. Acad. Family Physicians, 1960-71, dir. communications div., 1971—, founder Am. Acad. Family Physicians Reporter, 1974; advt. promotion mgr. Am. Family Physician mag., 1962-69; instr. pub. relations U. Mo.-Kansas City, 1979; lectr. pub. relations NYU, U. Kans. U. Nev.; mem. profl. adv. coun. dept. communication Cen. Mo. State U., Warrensburg. With U.S. Army, 1951-53. Recipient U.S. C. of C. Disting. Achievement award, 1962; Gold medal N.Y. Film Festival, 1967. Fellow Pub. Relations Soc. Am. (Silver Anvil award 1980; Prism award Kansas City chpt. 1980, 85; Profl. of Year award 1982, President's award 1985); mem. Kansas City Press Club, Nat. Assn. Sci. Writers, Am. Assn. Med. Soc. Execs., Soc. Tchrs. Family Medicine, Acad. Health Services Mktg., Southwest High Sch. Found. (pres.), Midwest Ear Inst. (bd. dirs.), Sigma Delta Chi. Roman Catholic. Contbr. to book: Kansas City Out Loud. Office: 8880 Ward Pky Kansas City MO 64114-2706

DELEO, JAMES A., state legislator; b. Chgo., Aug. 10, 1951; m. Ann Filishio, 1991. Ed., Loop Jr. Coll., DePaul U. Real estate salesman; mem. from 16th dist. Ill. Ho. of Reps., 1985-92; mem. Ill. State Senate, 1993—. Mem. Joint Civic Com. Italian-Ams. *

DE LEONARDIS, NICHOLAS JOHN, banker; b. Chgo., Nov. 13, 1929; s. John and Marie (Janik) De L.; m. Mary Ellen Kloss, Aug. 17, 1957; children: Deborah Marie, Valerie Ann, Nicolette Mary, Regina Ellen, John Paul. BS, De Paul U., 1951, MA, 1968. Salesman Asher J. Goldfine & Co., Chgo., 1953-55. Mem. trust dept. staff First Nat. Bank Chgo., 1955-63, with mcpl. sales dept., 1963-65, v.p. money mkt. ctr., 1965-80, v.p., chmn. money mgmt. com., 1980-85; sr. v.p., treas. La Salle Nat. Bank, subs. Algemene Bank Nederland, N.V., 1985-90; sr. v.p., chmn. asset and liability com. La Salle Nat. Corp.; exec. in residence dept. fin. De Paul U., Chgo., 1990—, lectr., 1968-78, dir. DePaul-People's Republic China Project, 1990-95; grad. sch. banking U. Wis., Madison, 1980-87; mem. Dixon Assn. for Retarded Citizens, 1984, Gov.'s task force on Future of Mental Health in Ill., 1986-87; commn. review the state's mental health code, 1988, adv. com. Devel. at disabilities Dept. of Mental Health and Developmental Disabilities, Ill., 1993—. Contbr. articles to profl. publs. Bd. trustees, past chmn. Found. Hearing and Speech Rehab., Chgo., 1968-92; pres. Dixon (Ill.) Assn. Retarded Citizens, 1984. Mem. Union League Chgo., Delta Mu Delta, Beta Gamma Sigma. Office: De Paul U Dept Fin 1 E Jackson Blvd Ste 6126 Chicago IL 60604-2201

DE LERNO, MANUEL JOSEPH, electrical engineer; b. New Orleans, Jan. 8, 1922; s. Joseph Salvador and Elizabeth Mabry (Jordan) De L.; BE in Elec. Engring., Tulane U., 1941; MEE, Rensselaer Poly. Inst., 1943. Registered profl. engr., Ill., Mass; m. Margery Ellen Eaton, Nov. 30, 1946 (div. Oct. 1978); children—Diane, Douglas. Devel. engr. indsl. control dept. Gen. Electric Co., Schenectady, 1941-44; design engr. Lexington Electric Products Co., Newark, 1946-47; asst. prof. elec. engring. Newark Coll. Engring., 1948-49; test engr. Maschinenfabrik Oerlikon, Zurich, Switzerland, 1947-48; application engr. Henry J. Kaufman Co., Chgo., 1949-55; pres. Del Equipment Co., Chgo., 1955-60; v.p. Del-Ray Co., Chgo., 1960-67; pres. S-P-D Svcs. Inc., Forest Park, Ill., 1967-81, S-P-D Industries, Inc., Berwyn, Ill., 1981—; mem. standards making coms. Nat. Fire Protection Assn. Internat. Lt. (j.g.) USNR, 1944-45, to lt. comdr., 1950-52. Fellow Soc. Fire Protection Engrs.; mem. IEEE (sr., life), Ill. Soc. Profl. Engrs., Am. Water Works Assn. Home: 36w760 Stonebridge Ln Saint Charles IL 60175-4931 Office: 3105 Ridgeland Ave Berwyn IL 60402-3568

DELGADO, CLARA SUE, university administrator; b. Dayton, Ohio, Sept. 26, 1952; d. Paul D. and Jo Ellen (Wilson) Liesenhoff; m. Raúl Escalón, Sept. 1, 1977 (div. Sept. 1987); 1 child, Tania; m. Maximo Delgado, Feb. 23, 1990. BA, Murray (Ky.) State U., 1974; MA, Wright State U., 1984. Instr. idioms Global Inst. Langs., Valencia, Spain, 1972-74; instr. idioms, culture Miami U., Oxford, Ohio, 1974-77; instr. idioms, counselor Pan Am Lang. Inst., Reynosa, Mex., 1977-79; instr. idioms, culture The English Lang. Inst., Dayton, 1980-86, dir., cons., 1986—; advising dir. internat. students U. Dayton, 1994—; accrediting specialist ACICS, Washington, 1988—; cons., cross-cultural spkr. AFIT, SOCHE, Fairborn, Ohio. Author: Speaking American English, 1985, Hispanics in the U.S., 1993. Steering com. Dayton Ednl. Levy, 1995; founding bd. dirs. Project READ, Dayton, 1987—; adv. bd. Kettering (Ohio) Even Start, 1992—. Mem. Japan-Ohio Network, Am. Assn. Intensive English, Nat. Orgn. Fgn. Students, Tchrs. English to Spkrs. Other Langs. Office: Eng Lang/Multicult Inst Univ of Dayton 300 College Park Dr Dayton OH 45469-0319

DELL, THOMAS CHARLES, nurse anesthetist; b. Port Huron, Mich., May 28, 1959; s. John W. and Lois M. (Bell) D.; m. Peggy L. Reynolds, July 2, 1983; children: Adam, Aubree, Andrea. AS, St. Clair County Community Coll., Port Huron, Mich., 1979; BSN, No. Mich. U., 1981; BS, Mercy Coll. Detroit, 1985. RN, Mich.; cert. nurse anesthetist. Nurse Marquette (Mich.) Gen., 1981-83; nurse Mercy Hosp., Port Huron, 1983-85, nurse anesthetist, insvc. coord., 1985-88; nurse anesthetist Saber Salisbury and Assoc., Southfield, Mich., 1988-89; chief nurse anesthetist McKenzie Meml. Hosp., Sandusky, Mich., 1989—. Mem. Am. Assn. Nurse Anesthetists, Mich. Assn. Nurse Anesthetists.

DELLAS, MARIE C., retired psychology educator and consultant; b. Buffalo; d. Theodore Andrew and Katherine (Callos) D. BS cum laude, State U. Coll., Buffalo, 1945; MEd, U. Buffalo, 1967; PhD, SUNY, Buffalo, 1970. Asst. editor Urban Edn. Jour., Buffalo, 1966-67; rsch. asst. SUNY, Buffalo, 1967-69; asst. prof. psychology Ea. Mich. U., Ypsilanti, 1969-73, assoc. prof., 1973-79, prof., 1979-93; mem. adv. bd. Inst. Study Children and Families, 1983-93. Author: Dellas Identity Status Inventory, 1979, 81, Creative Thinking Applied to Problem Solving Manual, 1993; contbr. articles to profl. jours.; mem. bd. editors Midwestern Ednl. Researcher, 1980-87, Urban Edn. Jour., 1977-94. Recipient Josephine N. Keal award Women's Commn., 1980, 85, 86; Grad. Rsch. grantee Ea. Mich. U., 1980-84. Mem. APA, Am. Ednl. Rsch. Assn., Nat. Assn. Gifted Children, Midwestern Ednl. Rsch. Assn., Midwestern Psychol. Assn., Mich. Acad. Gifted, Pi Lambda Theta. Home and Office: 2201 Acacia Park Dr # 312 Lyndhurst OH 44124

DELMONT, MIKE, state legislator; b. May 19, 1940; m. Virginia Delmont; 5 children. Former radio comm. coord. Minn. state rep. Dist. 51A, 1993—. Home: 9561 Griggs Ave Circle Pines MN 55014-3413*

DELMORE, LOIS M., state legislator; m. Michael Delmore; 2 child. Student, U. N.D. Tchr. English Red River H.S.; senator Dist. 43 N.D. State Senate, mem. judiciary and polit subdivsn. coms. Mem. N.D. State Tchrs. Assn. Home: 714 S 22d St Grand Forks ND 58201

DE LONG, DALE RAY, chemicals executive; b. Oelwein, Iowa, Dec. 11, 1959; s. Jack Rollis and Shirley (Follett) De L.; m. Joyce Lynn Bazan, Aug. 15, 1981; children: Nicolas, Kymberly, Sabrina. Office mgr. 3D Inc., St. Joseph, Mich., 1978-82; v.p. 3D Inc., Benton Harbor, Mich., 1982-94; financing exec., broker, cons., 1994—; pres. Darci Corp., Benton Harbor, 1987-94. Mem. Exch. Club. Republican. Office: Profl Loan Funding 800 Port St Saint Joseph MI 59085

DELONG, DONALD REED, accountant; b. Muskegon, Mich., Sept. 3, 1946; m. Susan K. Jourden; children: Kristy, Andrew. BS in Acctg., Ferris State U., Big Rapids, Mich., 1968. CPA, Mich. Staff acct. Alexander Grant & Co., Muskegon, 1970-75; co-founder Brickley Delong, P.C., Muskegon, 1975—, mng. ptnr., pres., 1985—; co-owner, officer Raydon Lumber Co., Inc., Shoreline Group, Inc., Shoreline Land Co.; ptnr. KIMA Properties, Van Mill Square; mem. adv. bd. dirs. No. Boiler and Mech. Contractors, Inc., 1978—, Croton Devel. Co., 1978—, J. Mollema & Sons, Inc., 1980; mem. acctg. com. Mich. Dept. Edn., 1986—. Co-author: State of Michigan School Accounting Manual, 1989. Bd. dirs., pres. YMCA, Muskegon, 1991, bd. dirs. Camp Pendaleuan, 1993—; chmn. bd. trustees McGraft Ch., Muskegon, 1988-90. Mem. Mich. Assn. CPAs (state acctg. com. 1982—). Office: Brickley Delong PC PO Box 999 500 Terrace Plz Muskegon MI 49443

DELONG, LEA ROSSON, art historian; b. Ferriday, La., June 13, 1947; d. Aaron Kenneth and Patsy Ruth (Smith) Rosson; m. Harris Coggeshall DeLong, Sept. 1, 1979; children: Timothy Rosson DeLong, Catherine Rosson DeLong. AA, Cottey Coll., Nevada, Mo., 1967; BA, U. Okla., 1971; MA, U. Kans., 1973, PhD, 1983. Assoc. prof. Drake U., Des Moines, 1976-90; adj. curator Des Moines Art Ctr., 1989-91; adj. assoc. prof. dept. art Drake U., Des Moines, 1990—. Author: The Art of Alexandre Hogue: Nature's Forms/Nature's Forces, 1994, (exhbn. catalogue) New Deal Art of the Upper Midwest, 1989; co-author: New Deal Mural Projects in Iowa, 1983, (essay) Chemistry Imagined: Reflections on Science, 1994. Mem. Coll. Art Assn. Democrat. Roman Catholic.

DELONG, MARK RANDALL, English language educator, director; b. Duluth, Minn., Oct. 23, 1954; s. Wallace Eugene and Delores Romelle (Erickson) DeL.; m. Arlene Ann Alden, Aug. 11, 1979; children: Derek Randall, Aaron Michael, Sarah Elizabeth. Student, U. Göttingen, Federal Republic of Germany, 1974-75; BA magna cum laude, Oklahoma City U., 1977; postgrad., U. Tübingen, Federal Republic of Germany, 1978-79; AM, Duke U., 1981, PhD, 1987. Asst. for devel. and rsch. talent identification program Duke U., Durham, N.C., 1984-85, staff writer talent identification program, 1987-88, acting dir. talent identification program, 1988-89, dir. ops. talent identification program, 1989-94; dir. Ctr. for Talent Devel., Northwestern U., 1994—; asst. prof. dept. English Northwestern U., 1994—; asst. dir. The Humanist as Reformer seminar NEH, Durham, 1984-85; seminar leader White House Commn. on Presdl. Scholars, Washington, 1989; adv. bd. Richard Whitted Inst., Durham, 1989; moderator acad. talent conf. NSF, Durham, 1989; policy implementation com. Duke U., Durham, 1988, adj. asst. prof., 1989-94. Editor: Reflective Writing, 1990; editor: (newsletter) Insights, 1989-90; contbr. articles to profl. jours. Pres. Am. Assn. Gifted Children, 1993-95; bd. dirs. Presdl. Scholar Found., 1994—; mem. ad hoc com. N.C. Govs. Lang. Inst., Winston-Salem, 1986-87; testifier com. appropriations U.S. Senate, Washington, 1989. Trustee Leadership scholar Oklahoma City U., 1973-74, German Exchange scholar Pädagogische Hochscule Niedersachsen, Göttingen, 1974-75; Rotary Internat. fellow, Tübingen, Federal Republic of Germany, 1978-79. Mem. MLA, South Atlantic MLA, Southeastern Renaissance Conf. Home: 2204 Forestview Rd Evanston IL 60201-2010 Office: CTD Northwestern Univ 617 Dartmouth Pl Evanston IL 60201-2811

DE LORENZO, ORINDO ARTURO (DINO), director of engineering; b. Detroit, July 30, 1960. AS, I.T.T. Tech., Fort Wayne, Ind., 1980. Design/detailer Babcox & Wilcox, Akron, Ohio, 1980-82; dir. engring. Randell Mfg., Weidman, Mich., 1982—. Republican. Roman Catholic. Office: Randell Mfg Co 0520 S Coldwater Rd Weidman MI 48893-9609

DE LOS ANGELES, REYNALDO ADRILLANA, psychiatrist, consultant; b. Manila, July 2, 1945; came to U.S., 1976.; s. Amancio Nicdao and Consolacion (Adrillana) D.; m. Olivia Paula Olmedo, Jan. 25, 1947 (dec.); children: Karlo, Reynaldo Amancio II, Olivia Renee, Oliver Rinaldi. BS, U. of the East, Quezon City, Philippines, 1964, MD, 1969. Diplomate Am. Bd. Addiction Medicine, Am. Bd. Forensic Medicine, Am. Bd. Forensic Examiners. Med. dir. New Horizons Community Mental Health, Clinton, Okla., 1982-83; clinical dir. Western State Hosp., Ft. Supply, Okla., 1983-86, Muskogee Regional Med. Ctr., Psychiatric Intervention Ctr., Muskogee, Okla., 1986-88; med. dir. Muskogee Psychiatric Clinic, Muskogee, Okla., 1986-89; active staff Shawnee Mission Med. Ctr., Overland Park, Kans., 1989-91; med. dir. Chem. Dependency Unit Richard H. Young Hosp., Kearney, Nebr., 1991—, chief med. officer, 1993-95; chmn. dept. psych. Good Samaritan Hosp., Kearney, Nebr., 1993—; bd. dirs. Good Samaritan Health Sys., Kearney, 1993-95. Recipient physician's recognition award AMA., 1982—. Mem. Am. Psychiat. Assn., Acad. Clin. Psychiatrists, Acad. Psychomatic Medicine. Home: 2014 W 36th St Kearney NE 68847-2211

DELTON, MARK, investment company executive; b. Mt. Vernon, N.Y., May 2, 1960; s. David and Freida (Eckhaus) D.; m. Jennifer Adams, Sept. 22, 1990; children: Adam, Madeline. BS in Fin., U. Del., 1982. Co-owner tennis bus., Ft. Wayne, Ind., 1982-87; 1st v.p., br. mgr. Smith Barney, Ft. Wayne, 1987—. Co-author: Business Manual for Tennis Pros, 1985. Active Heart Assn. Selbalsy, Ala. Office: Smith Barney Inc 1 Summit Sq 8th Fl Fort Wayne IN 46802

DELUCA, PETER R., financial planner; b. St. Louis, Mar. 21, 1948; s. Philip and Vita (Crimi) DeL.; m. Tana M. Nasco, Dec. 21, 1970; children: Peter R. Jr., Anthony M. Musician St. Louis, 1969-72; mailer Nardmann, St. Louis, 1972-87; fin. planner FFP Sec./1st Fin. Planners, Chesterfield, Mo., 1987—. Roman Catholic. Office: FFP Sec/1st Fin Planners 400 Chesterfield Ctr Chesterfield MO 63017-4800

DELUCCA, LEOPOLDO ELOY, otolaryngologist, head and neck surgeon; b. Santurce, P.R., Nov. 1, 1952; s. Leopoldo Claudio and Laura Iris (Juncos) DeL.; m. Judith Lynn McClellan, June 11, 1977; children: Lauren Denise, Gina Fay. Pre-med. degree, U. P.R., 1973; MD, Jefferson Med. Coll., Phila., 1977. Diplomate Am. Bd. Otolaryngology. Otolaryngologist Ft. Dodge (Iowa) Med. Ctr., 1981-86; practice medicine specializing in otolaryngology Ft. Dodge, 1986—; active med. staff Trinity Regional Hosp., Ft. Dodge, 1981—, chief of surgery, 1985—, pres. med. staff, 1991—; vol. faculty Coll. Osteo. Medicine and Surgery, Des Moines, 1981-82. Bd. dirs. Trinity Regional Hosp., 1993—. Fellow ACS, Am. Acad. Otolaryngology-Head and Neck Surgery, Am. Acad. Facial Plastic and Reconstructive Surgery. Republican. Roman Catholic. Home: 2626 Woodland Dr Fort Dodge IA 50501-7130 Office: Physicians Office Bldg 200 Kenyon Rd Ste 200 Fort Dodge IA 50501-5762

DELUHERY, PATRICK JOHN, state senator; b. Birmingham, Ala., Jan. 31, 1942; s. Frank B. and Lucille (Donovan) D.; B.A. with honors, U. Notre Dame, 1964; B.Sc. (Econ.) with honors, London Sch. Econs., 1967; m. Margaret Morris, 1973; children: Allison, Norah, Rose. Legis. asst. U.S. Senator Harold Hughes, Washington, 1969-74; legis. asst. U.S. Senator John Culver, Washington, 1975; asst. prof. econs. and bus. adminstrn. St. Ambrose U., Davenport, Iowa, 1975—; mem. Iowa State Senate, 1979—; ins. agt.,

1989—. Democrat. Roman Catholic. Home: 11839 100th Ave Davenport IA 52804-9110 Office: Iowa Senate Statehouse Des Moines IA 50319

DE LURGIO, STEPHEN ANTHONY, management educator; b. St. Louis, June 27, 1945; s. Louis J. and Amelia Barbara (Machler) De L.; m. Ina C. Kimmel, Nov. 10, 1969; children: Stephen A. II, Patrick M. BSME, U. Mo., 1967; MBA, St. Louis U., 1971, PhD, 1976. Design engr. Emerson Electric, St. Louis, 1967-70; project engr. Coinco Inc., St. Louis, 1970-74; asst. prof. mgmt. Sangamon State U., Springfield, Ill., 1974-76; prof. U. Mo., Kansas City, 1976—. Co-author: (books) Quantitative Models for Business Decisions, 1980, Forecasting Systems for Operations Management, 1991, Forecasting Theory, 1997; contbr. articles to profl. jours. Bd. dirs. Animal Health Inst., St. Louis, 1985—. U. Kansas City Faculty fellow U. Kansas City Trustees, 1986. Fellow Am. Prodn. and Inventory Control Soc. (chmn. 1984-89, mem. Cert. Com. 1984-89); mem. The Inst. of Man Sci., Inst. of Indsl. Engrs., Internat. Inst. of Forecasters, Decision Scis. Inst. Office: U Mo Bloch Sch Bus Kansas City MO 64110

DEL VALLE, MIGUEL, state legislator; b. P.R., July 24, 1951; m. Lupe; 4 children. BA, Northeastern Ill. U., MA. Mem. dist. 2 Ill. State Senate, 1987—; chmn. consumer affairs, vice chmn. com. and econ. devel., mem. appropriations II, higher edn., revenue and elections and reapportionment coms. Office: 2218 N Lamon Ave Chicago IL 60639-3236 also: Ill State Senate Capitol Bldg Springfield IL 62706*

DELZER, JEFF W., state legislator. Student, Dawson C.C. Farmer/rancher; rep. Dist. 8 N.D. Ho. of Reps., 1991-92, 95—, mem. indsl., bus. and labor and transp. coms. Home: HCR 1 Box 12 Douglas ND 58735-9611

DEMAAGD, GERALD ROBERT, data security consultant; b. East Grand Rapids, Mich., Oct. 20, 1936; s. Gerald and Gordelia Gertrude (Kleinheksel) DeM.; m. Joan Klingaman, Aug. 13, 1960; children: Karen Sue, Shawn Marie, Ursula Joy and Thomas Alan (twins). BS in Econs., Mich. State U., 1962; MBA in Mgmt., Western Mich. U., 1970. Cert. info. sys. security profl., Internat. Info. Sys. Cert. Consortium, Inc.; cert. data processing, Data Processing Mgmt. Assn.; cert. sys. profl. Assn. for Sys. Mgmt. Unit computer operator, computer operator, programmer Fisher Body Divsn., GM, 1962-67; programmer analyst, sys. analyst, sr. sys. analyst Lear Siegler Inc. (Smith Industries), 1967-73; sr. sys. analyst fin. sys. Steelcase Inc., Grand Rapids, Mich., 1982-95, data security cons., 1995—. Columnist Mgmt. Acctg., 1983-84; contbr. articles to profl. jours. Docent Meyer May House. Lance cpl. USMC, 1958-61. Recipient award Grand Rapids chpt. Nat. Assn. Accts., 1982. Mem. Computer Security Inst., Info. Sys. Security Assn. Office: Steelcase Inc CH-3W-18 PO Box 1967 901 44th St Grand Rapids MI 49501

DEMAREE, DAVID HARRY, utilities executive; b. Chgo., Oct. 17, 1939; s. Harry Stambough and Alve (Barnes) D.; m. Brenda Faye Locke, Mar. 2, 1962; children: David Christopher, Dawn Claire. BS in Math., Ga. State U., 1965; grad., U. Wis., 1972; diploma, Grad. Sch. Banking. Audit officer Continental Ill. Bank & Trust Co., Chgo., 1966-73; v.p. Utilities, Inc., Northbrook, Ill., 1973-85; v.p. ops., sec. Utilities, Inc., Northbrook, 1985-94; sr. v.p., sec. Utilities, Inc., 1994—; cons. USAF, Chgo., 1984; expert witness 11 state utility commns. water and sewer utilities. Speaker on disaster planning Nat. Assn. of Regulatory Utility Commrs. Mem. Am. Water Works Assn., Nat. Assn. Water Cos., Lake Barrington Shores Country Club, Mission Hills Country Club, N. Suburban YMCA, Navy League, Ducks Unltd., Phi Kappa Tau Alumni Assn. (Chgo. chpt. pres. 1968-73), Phi Kappa Tau (bd. govs. 1963-64). Republican. Episcopalian (vestry). Office: Utilities Inc 2335 Sanders Rd Northbrook IL 60062-6108

DEMARS, KAREN, marketing professional; b. Pontiac, Mich., July 22, 1941. Student Med. Tech., Mich. State U., 1962; AS, Lawrence Tech. U., Southfield, Mich., 1981. Various positions in med. field William Beaumont Hosp., Royal Oak, Mich., 1962-82; sales agt. Real Estate ONE, Milford, Mich., 1985—; v.p. mktg. Smith Ross, Inc, Fenton, Mich., 1987—; pres. Milford Highland. Contbr. articles to jours. in field of med. tech. Mem. Am. Assn. Bloodbanks, Am. Assn. Clin. Pathologists, Zont Internat. Office: Smith Ross Inc 1440 Torrey Rd Fenton MI 48430-1340

DEMARS, ROBERT A., state legislator; b. Chgo., Apr. 30, 1930; s. Alphonse I. DeMars and Annabel J. Erickson; m. Doris Faye Lockard, 1963. AA, Flint Jr. Coll.; BA, Eastern Mich. U., MA. Tchr. Lincoln Park, Mich., 1956-82; rep. Mich. Dist. 25, 1982—; mem. city coun. Lincoln Park, Mich., 1965-67, mayor, 1967-71, city treas. 197-82. Editor The Mich. Tchr., 1959-61. Col. Mich. Emergency Vols. State Defense Force. With U.S. Submarine Svc. Named veteran of yr. 1985, Lincoln Park. Mem. Kiwanis, Jaycees, VFW, Amvets, Am. Legion, Eagles, Odd Fellows, Moose, Optimists, Shriners, Masons, Scottish Rite, Mich. Fedn. Tchrs. (v.p. 1957-61). Home: 833 Mayflower Ave Lincoln Park MI 48146-2942 Address: PO Box 30014 Lansing MI 48909-7514*

DEMERS, JUDY LEE, state legislator, university dean; b. Grand Forks, N.D., June 27, 1944; d. Robert L. and V. Margaret (Harming) Prosser; m. Donald E. DeMers, Oct. 3, 1964 (div. Oct. 1971); 1 child, Robert M.; m. Joseph M. Murphy, Mar. 5, 1977 (div. Oct. 1983). BS in Nursing, U. N.D., 1966; MEd, U. Wash., 1973, postgrad., 1973-76. Pub. health nurse Govt. D.C., 1966-68, Combined Nursing Service, Mpls., 1968-69; instr. pub. health nursing U. N.D., Grand Forks, 1969-71, assoc. dir. Medex program, 1970-72, dir., family nurse practitioner program, 1977-82, assoc. dir. rural health, 1982-85, dir. undergrad. med. edn., 1982-83, assoc. dean, 1983—; rsch. assoc. U. Wash., Seattle, 1973-76; mem. N.D. Ho. of Reps., 1982-92; mem. N.D. Senate, 1992—; cons. Health Manpower Devel. Staff, Honolulu, 1975-81, Assn. Physician Asst. Programs, Washington, 1979-82; site visitor, cons. AMA-Com. Allied Health Edn. Accreditation, Chgo., 1979-81. Author: Educating New Health Practitioners, 1976; mem. editorial bd.: P.A. Jour., 1976-78; contbr. articles to profl. jours. Sec., bd. dirs. Valley Family Planning and Edn. Ctr., Grand Forks, N.D., 1982—; exec. com., bd. dirs. Agassiz Health Systems Agy., Grand Forks, 1982-86; mem. N.D. State Daycare Adv. Com., 1983-93, Mayor's Adv. Com. on Police Policy, Grand Forks, 1983-85, N.D. State Foster Care Adv. Com., 1985-87, N.D. State Hypertension Adv. Com., 1983-85, Gov.'s Com. on DUI and Traffic Safety, 1985-91, Statewide Adv. Com. on AIDS, 1985-90; bd. dirs. Casey Found. Families First Initiative, 1988—, Comprehensive Health Assn. N.D., 1993—, United Health Found, 1990—, Northern Valley Mental Health Assn., 1994—; mem. adv. bd. Mountainbrooke (formerly Friendship Place), 1992—; adv. com. Ruth Meiers Adolescent Ctr., Grand Forks, 1988—; mem. Commn. on Future Structure of VA Health Care, 1990-91; bd. dirs. Quad County Community Action Agy, 1991—; mem. Resource and Referral Bd. Dirs., 1990—; mem. caring coun. N.D. Blue Cross and Blue Shields Caring Program for Children; coun. mem. N.D. Health Task Force, 1992-94. Recipient Alpha Lambda Delta award, 1963, Pub. Citizen of Yr. award N.D. chpt. Nat. Assn. Social Workers, 1986, Golden Grain award N.D. Dietitics Assn., 1988, Person of Yr. award U. N.D. Law Women Caucus, 1990, Legislator of Yr. award Northern Valley Labor Coun., 1990, N.D. Martin Luther King Jr. award, 1990, Legislator of Yr. award N.D. Mental Health Assn., 1993, Dick Shea award for contbn. to high edn. AAUP, 1995, Voices award N.D. Children's Caucus, 1995; U. Wash. regional med. program service fellow, 1972-73; Toll fellow, 1989, U. Wash. Kellogg Allied Health fellow, 1972. Mem. AAUW, NOW, ACLU, LWV, Am. Nurses Assn., N.D. Nurses Assn. (mem. cabinet on edn. and practice 1982-86, Nurse of Yr. 1983), Am. Pub. Health Assn., Am. Ednl. Research Assn., N.D. Pub. Health Assn., N.D. Mental Health Assn., The ARC (Assn. for Retarded Citizens), Pi Lambda Theta, Sigma Theta Tau. Democrat. Home: 1826 Lewis Blvd Grand Forks ND 58203-1642 Office: U ND Sch Medicine 501 N Columbia Rd Grand Forks ND 58203-2817

DEMERSSEMAN, MICHAEL, state legislator, lawyer. Bar: S.D. Mem. S.D. Ho. of Reps., Pierre. Republican.

DEMETER, NANCY FORD, cultural resources management specialist; b. Royal Oak, Mich., Dec. 19, 1967; d. Merle Lee and Doreen (Shea) Ford; m. R. Paul Eisenstein Jr., Sept. 22, 1979 (div. Sept. 1988); m. C. Stephan Demeter, Mar. 8, 1990; 1 child, Sarah Colleen. BA summa cum laude, Wayne State U., 1986, MA in Anthropology, 1990. Cert. Master Gardener Jackson County Coop. Ext. and Mich. State U. Mus. mgr. Wayne State U., Detroit, 1989-90, instr. anthropology, 1990; editor-in-chief, mktg. specialist Commonwealth Cultural Resources Group, Jackson, Mich., 1990-92, dir. adminstrv. and tech. svcs., 1992—; instr. comm. and tech. writing Jackson C.C., 1992—; editorial chmn. The Michigan Archaeologist, Lansing, Mich., 1989-92, editor Datum Points (Mich. Archeol. Soc. newsletter), 1991—. Tutor Literacy Vols. of Am., Detroit, 1987-90, Jackson Literacy Coun., 1990-91; bd. dirs. Cascades Humane Soc., Jackson, 1991-92. Recipient Assistantship, Wayne State U., 1989-90. Mem. Mich. Archeol. Soc. (1st v.p. 1989-90, pres. elect 1990-91, pres. 1991-92), Soc. for Am. Archaeology, Govtl. Affairs Network (state rep.), Am. Anthrop. Assn., Nat. Trust for Hist. Preservation, Soc. for Hist. Archaeology, Soc. for Indsl. Archaeology, Assn. Profl. Comm. Cons., Coun. on Mich. Archaeology, Soc. for Tech. Comm., Golden Key, Phi Beta Kappa. Republican. Office: Commonwealth Cultural Resources Group Inc 2530 Spring Arbor Rd Jackson MI 49203-3602

DE METZ, DELLA CHRISTINE, executive, writer, social consultant; b. Elkhart, Ind., Jan. 14, 1959; 1 child, Nathan Allen Flores. Student, Purdue U., 1977-78, Ivy Tech. Vocat. Coll., 1994—. Retail sales Pepsico Franchise, Elkhart, Ind., 1980; bus. mgmt. McGrory Corp., Elkhart, Ind., 1990-91, bus. fin., 1990-91; entrepreneur DC & Co., Elkhart, Ind., 1990—. Author of poems. Vol. Homeless Shelter, Elkhert, 1993, Greenpeace, The Wilderness Soc., Washington, 1993, World Wildlife Fund, Sierra Club, Washington, 1993. Recipient Silver Poet award, The World of Poetry, Calif., 1990. Mem. Am. Mgmt. Assn. (mgmt. assoc. 1993), Nat. Wildlife Fedn., Internat. Soc. Poets, Nat. Linb. Poetry.

DEMEULENAERE, CHRISTOPHER JOHN, physical therapist; b. Waverly, Iowa, Aug. 24, 1963; s. Edward Paul and Rose Marie (O'Donnell) D.; m. Ann Marie Meisner, Aug. 25, 1990; 1 child, Rachael Ann. BS in Phys. Therapy, Marquette U., 1985; MBA, Cardinal Stritch Coll., 1994. Lic. phys. therapist, Wis. Staff phys. therapist St. Mary's Med. Ctr., Racine, Wis., 1985; phys. therapy dir. Northview Home, Waukesha, Wis., 1986-87; phys. therapist, cons. Wilkonson Sportsmedicine Ctr., Oconomowoc, Wis., 1988; dir. outpatient svcs. Parkway Therapy Clinic, Milw., 1989-91; case mgr., phys. therapist All Saints VNA, Racine, 1991—; adj. faculty, kinesiology instr. Milw. Area Tech. Coll., 1989—; back care and injury prevention cons. Shared Therapeutic Svcs., Milw., 1989-91. Capt. USAR, 1985—. Decorated Army Achievement medal, Res. Component Achievement medal. Mem. Am. Phys. Therapy Assn. (key contact 1993-94), Wis. Phys. Therapy Assn. (chair legis. action com. 1990-91, pub. rels. com. 1995—), K.C. (3d degree). Roman Catholic. Home: 6828 Juliana Dr Franklin WI 53132

DEMOREST, ALLAN FREDERICK, retired psychologist; b. Omaha, Dec. 20, 1931; s. Byron Peter and Minerva Gladys (Heine) D.; 1 child, Steven M. BA, U. Omaha, 1957; MA, U. Mich., 1959, postgrad., 1960. Lic. psychologist, Iowa, Nat. Register Health Svc. Providers. Counselor Mayor's Com. on Skid Row Problems, Detroit, 1959-61; psychologist Macomb County Schs., Mt. Clemens, Mich., 1961-64; chief psychologist Jasper County Mental Health Ctr., Newton, Iowa, 1964-68; exec. dir. North Cen. Iowa Mental Health Ctr., Ft. Dodge, 1968-75; pvt. practice Ft. Dodge, 1968-85; psychologist Iowa Luth. Hosp., Des Moines, 1985-87; clin. dir. United Behavioral Systems, Des Moines, 1987-94, sr. psychologist, 1994-96; cons., pvt. practice, Des Moines, 1996—; cons. psychologist Des Moines, 1996—; adj. prof. psychology Buena Vista Coll., Ft. Dodge, 1974-85. Contbr. articles on rational therapy to profl. jours. Founding bd. dirs. Rape and Sexual Assault Victim Program, Ft. Dodge, 1976-85, Family Violence Ctr., Ft. Dodge, 1976-85, Youth Shelter Svcs., Ft. Dodge, 1979. With U.S. Army, 1952-54, Korea. Recipient appreciation award Community Mental Health Ctrs. Assn., 1968, community svc. award Iowa Dept. Human Svcs., 1985. Fellow Inst. Rational Psychotherapy; mem. Am. Psychol. Assn., Midwestern Psychol. Assn., Iowa Psychol. Assn., Adminstrv. Mgmt. Soc. (pres. Ft. Dodge 1979-80, 84-85), Iowa Assn. for Advancement Psychology (pres. 1984, Appreciation award 1988), Elks (Exalted Ruler 1979). Home and Office: 4225 Hickman Rd Des Moines IA 50310-3334

DE MOTT, JOHN EDWARD, journalist; b. Topeka, Kans., Aug. 15, 1923; s. Howard Chauncey and Willa Nancy (Fitzpatrick) De M.; m. Vera Belle Martin, Sept. 9, 1925. BS in Edn., U. Kans., 1946; MA in History/Govt., Kansas City U., 1960; MA in English/History, U. Mo., Kansas City, 1960; PhD, Northwestern U., 1971. News reporter/editor Kansas City Star, Mo., 1946-62; asst. prof. U. Kans., Lawrence, 1962-67; instr. Northwestern U., Evanston, Ill., 1967-71; assoc. prof. No. Ill. U., DeKalb, 1971-76, Temple U., Phila., 1976-80; prof. journalism Memphis State U., 1980-93; news/editorial cons. Terre Haute (Ind) newspapers, 1976-77; chmn. dept. journalism Memphis State U., 1984-87. Co-author: The Journalist's Prayerbook, The University City News Service; contbr. articles to profl. jours. Vice pres. World Affairs Council of Memphis, 1988-89; mem. News and Info. com., Nat. Council Chs., 1988—. Recipient Pell Mell "Big Story" award, NBC, 1952; Golden Dozen award, Internat. Soc. Weekly Newspaper Editors, 1988; Community Svc. award, Nat. Conf. Christians and Jews, 1988. Mem. Soc. Profl. Journalists, Religion Newswriters Assn., Internat. Soc. Weekly Newspaper Editors, Assn. for Edn. in Journalism and Mass Comm. Baptist. Home: 221 W 48th #308 Kansas City MO 64112-2427

DEMPSEY, GARY LEE, electrical and computer engineering educator; b. Greensboro, N.C., Nov. 12, 1955; s. Garland Lee and Ruby Aileen (Chandler) D.; m. Dana Lynn Barrington, Sept, 8, 1979. BSEE, U. N.C., 1982; MSEE, U. Va., 1986, PhDEE, 1991. Registered profl. engr., Ill., Va. Elec. engr. GE, Waynesboro, Va., 1982-83; elec. engr. Comdial Corp., Charlottesville, Va., 1983-88, cons. elec. engr., 1988-92; vis. prof. engring. U. Va., Charlottesville, 1991; asst. prof. elec. and computer engring. Bradley U., Peoria, Ill., 1992—; cons. elec. engring. Caterpillar Corp., Peoria, 1994—. Contbr. articles to profl. jours. Equipment grantee Tektronix Corp., U. Va., 1991. Mem. IEEE, NSPE, AAUP, Tau Beta Pi, Pi Mu Epsilon, Eta Kappa Nu. Office: Bradley Univ 1501 W Bradley Ave Peoria IL 61625

DEMPSEY, JAMES RANDALL, academic administrator; b. Mobile, Ala., Sept. 28, 1954; s. James Everett Dempsey and Jacqueline Elizabeth (Crick) Atkinson; m. Barbara Ann Belisle, July 24, 1981; children: Justine Marie, Isabeau Jacqueline. BA, U. Chgo., 1984; MPA, U. Tex., 1986. Fiscal asst. U. Chgo. Grad. Sch. Bus., 1980-82, mgr. info. svcs., 1982-84; budget analyst City of Ft. Worth, 1986-88; adminstrv. asst. U. Chgo. Irving B. Harris Grad. Sch. Pub. Policy Studies, Chgo., 1988-89, dir. budget, 1989-91, assoc. dean, 1991—; bd. dirs. Credit Union U. Chgo., 1995—, chmn. 1996—. Author: (with others) Taxonomy of Regulation, 1986; editor: Regulation in Texas, 1986. Staff sgt. USAF, 1974-78. Title VI Lang. fellow U.S. Dept. Edn., 1985-86. Office: U Chgo Irving B Harris Grad Sch Pub Policy Studies 1155 E 60th St Chicago IL 60637-2745

DEMPSEY, JERRY, state legislator; m. Joanne; 4 children. BA, U. St. Thomas; MA, U. Wis., River Falls. State rep. Minn. Ho. Reps., Dist. 29A, 1993—; mem. capital investment, econ. devel., infrastructure & regulation fin. govt. ops., gaming, regulated indsl. & energy coms., Minn. Ho. Reps., 1993—. Address: 1017 14th St W Hastings MN 55033-2560*

DENBO, JERRY L., state legislator; b. Bradford, Ind., Apr. 24, 1950; m. Donna Denbo; children: Robbie, Marey. BS, Ind. U., 1972, MS, 1975. Owner Denbo & Assocs.; rep. Dist. 62 Ind. Ho. of Reps., 1990—, mem. aging com., mem. environ. affairs, edn., ins. coms., corps. and small bus., rds. and transp. com. Mem. bd. Spring's Valley Sch.; active Dist. Club Scout Coun. Mem. NRA, Sons of Am. Legion, Ind. U. Alumni Assn., Masons, Gideons. Home: RR 1 Box 329 French Lick IN 47432-9801*

DENBOW, CARL JÓN, university official; b. Mpls., Nov. 24, 1944; s. Carl Herbert and Stefania Adalborg (Björnson) D.; m. Hannah Jane Halley, June 22, 1968; children: Carl William, Heather Michelle, Jennifer Marie. BSJ, Ohio U., 1968, PhD in Mass Communication, 1973; MA in Journalism, Ohio State U., 1969. Occupational info. writer Ohio Bur. Employment Svcs., Columbus, summer 1968; instr., asst. prof. journalism Marshall U., Huntington, W.Va., 1970-74; asst. prof., assoc. prof. journalism and radio-TV Murray (Ky.) State U., 1974-77, grad. coord., 1974-77, acting chmn. dept., summer 1976, founding mem. faculty senate, 1974-75; dir. pub. rels. Kirksville (Mo.) Coll. Osteo. Medicine, 1977-78; dir. communication Coll. Osteo. Medicine, Ohio U., Athens, 1978—, founding editor Ohio D.O. mag., 1978—; mem. adv. bd. Still Nat. Osteo. Mus.; mem. editorial adv. bd. Am. Osteo. Assn. Contbr. articles to profl. jours. With USN, 1964-66. Recipient 1st place journalism award Am. Osteopathic Assn., 1977, 2d pl. Radio Journalism award Am. Acad. Family Physicians, 1987, Exceptional Achievement award Coun. for Advancement and Support Edn., 1984; NDEA fellow, 1969-70. Mem. Assn. Edn. Journalism & Mass Communication, Soc. Profl. Journalists, Kappa Tau Alpha. Home: 63 Morris Ave Athens OH 45701-1939 Office: Ohio U Coll Osteo Medicine Athens OH 45701

DENDRINOS, DIMITRIOS SPYROS, urban planning educator; b. Argostoli, Kefalonia, Greece, Sept. 2, 1944; came to U.S., 1969; s. Spyros H. and Iris Anninou (Kavalieratou) D. Diploma archtl. engring., U. Thessaloniki (Greece), 1968; M Urban Design, Washington U., St. Louis, 1971; PhD in City and Regional Planning, U. Pa., 1975. Prin. planner Middlesex County Planning Bd., New Brunswick, N.J., 1975; asst. prof. U. Kans., Lawrence, 1975-79, assoc. prof., 1980-83, prof. urban planning, 1983—, dir. urban and transp. dynamics lab., 1989—; vis. rsch. fellow U.S. Dept. Transp., Washington, 1979-80; sr. tech. advisor UN, People's Republic of China, 1988. Author: Urban Evolution, 1985, The Dynamicsof Cities, 1992; editor-in-chief Social-Spatial Dynamics, 1989-94; hon. editor, founder Jour. Discrete Dynamics in Nature and Society, 1996—; mem. editl. bd. Geog. Analysis, 1990-95, Sistemi Urbani, 1989—, Annals Regional Sci., 1993—; reviewer Math. Revs., 1989—; contbr. over 100 articles to sci. jours. Grantee U.S. Dept. Transp., Washington, 1980, NSF, Washington, 1981, 84, 85, IBM, 1990. Mem. Internat. Geographic Union. Nonlinear Sociospatial Dynamics Soc.

DENDURENT, SHARON DRWALL, university administrator; b. St. Paul, Mar. 18, 1945; d. David Frank and Henrietta Grace (Janikowski)Drwall; m. Harold Oscar Dendurent, June 12, 1970; children: Catherine, Christine. BS, Winona State U., 1967; MA, Northwestern U., 1970; MPh, Roosevelt U., 1971; MEd, U. Maine, Orono, 1976. Vol. Peace Corps, Senegal, 1967-69; instr. social sci. De Lourdes Coll., Des Plaines, Ill., 1971-72; field dir. upward bound program U. Maine, Orono, 1972-75, asst. dean students, 1976-81, assoc. dean students, 1981-85; dean of students Cornell Coll., Mt. Vernon, Iowa, 1985-94; MBA advisor Sch. Mgmt., U. Iowa. Mem. U. Maine Profl. Staff Assn. (treas. 1982-83, pres. 1983-84), Iowa Student Pers. Assn. (treas. 1989-90, pres. 1992-93), Iowa State Edn. Assn. (UniServ dir. 1994-95). Home: 718 8th Ave N Mount Vernon IA 52314-1135

DENES, MICHEL JANET, physical therapist, consultant in rehabilitation; b. Detroit, Apr. 29, 1950; d. Seymore Bernard and Clarine (Stierer) Swartz; m. George Denes, Jan. 22, 1984; 1 child, Zachary Todd. BS in Phys. Therapy, U. Mich., 1972. cert. in phys. therapy; cert. in neuro-devel. treatment in adult hemiplegia. Staff phys. therapist Sinai Hosp. of Detroit, 1972-77, supr., phys. therapist, 1977-78, chief phys. therapy supr., 1979-88; phys. therapist Rehab. Physicians, P.C., Birmingham, Mich., 1989; phys. therapy cons. closed head injury program Spl. Tree Rehab. Sys., Birmingham, 1989—; adj. instr. Wayne State U. Coll. Allied Health Professions, Detroit, 1982-90; lectr. in field. Mem. Neurodevel. Treatment Assn., Am. Acad. Oral Medicine. Office: Spl Tree Rehab Sys Ste 300 2100 E Maple Rd Birmingham MI 48009-6516

DE NEVERS, ROY OLAF, retired aerospace company executive; b. Strasburg, Sask., Can., Dec. 30, 1922; s. Edouard Albrecht V.V. and Christy Helen (Hunt) de N.; divorced; children Gregory Frank (dec.), Sara Dianne. BS in Econs., U. London, 1963; BA in Econ. History, U. Winnipeg (Can.), 1971. Served to lt. comdr. Royal Can. Navy, 1946-67; chief contract adminstr., aircraft repair and overhaul Bristol Aerospace Ltd., Winnipeg, MB, Can., 1968-83; originator co. operating procedure Bristol Aerospace Ltd., Winnipeg, Man., Can., 1983-86. Editor aero. mag., 1956-60. Founder, mem. Commonwealth Air Tng. Plan Mus.; mem. We. Can. Aviation Mus. Served to flight lt. Royal Can. Air Force, 1941-45. Decorated DFC, 1945, Aircrew Europe Star, 1945, France and Germany Clasp, 1945, Def. medal CD, 1945. Mem. Naval Officers Assn. Can. (pres. Winnipeg br.), Canadian Naval Air Group Assn., Three Score Plus Circle, Can. Aeros. and Space Inst. (assoc. fellow), Masons. Mem. Adventist Ch. Clubs: Royal Air Force (London), Fleet Air Arm Officers (London). Address: Group 2 Box 9 Rte 1, Anola, MB Canada R0E 0A0

DENGLER, ROBERT ANTHONY, professional association executive; b. Upper Darby, Pa., Aug. 23, 1947; s. Anthony William and Harriet Josephine (Schneider) D.; m. Renee Faith Aird, Oct. 26, 1985. BS, Drexel U., 1970, MBA, 1972. Cert. assn. exec., mtg. profl. Cons. Orgn. Devel., Phila., 1972-73; dir. tng. & edn. Parkview Meml. Hosp., Ft. Wayne, Ind., 1973-76; dir. human resource mgmt. Americana Healthcare Corp., Chgo., 1976-82; corp. mgr. Human Resource Tng. and Devel. Means Svc. Inc., Chgo., 1982-83; dir. physician services West Suburban Hosp. Med. Ctr., Oak Park, Ill., 1983-85; assoc. dir. Assoc. Equipment Distributors, Oak Brook, Ill., 1985-88; exec. v.p. Internat. Reprographic Assn., Oak Brook, 1988-92; exec. dir. Data Processing Mgmt. Assn., Park Ridge, Ill., 1993-94; pres. Riverside (Ill.) Assn. Svcs., Inc., 1994—. Bd. dirs. Riverside C. of C., 1996, Chgo. Mercedes-Benz Club, 1986; mem. Riverside Village Fin. Com., 1996; recording sec. Riverside Econ. Devel. Commn., 1996. Capt. USAR, 1972-80. Mem. Inst. of Mgmt. Consultants, Am. Soc. Assn. Execs., Chgo. Soc. Assn. Execs., Profl. Convention Mgmt. Assn., Riverside C. of C. (bd. dirs. 1996—), Chgo. Mercedes-Benz Club (bd. dirs. 1996—), Mensa. Home: 294 Lionel Rd Riverside IL 60546-2204

DENHAM, BRADLEY C., financial counselor; b. Logansport, Ind., Nov. 19, 1950; children: Sarah, Audrey. BS, Ind. U., 1973. Br. mgr., CFO, fin. cons., compliance officer E.Y. Denham & Co., Logansport, 1974-83; fin. counselor Raffensperger Hughes, Logansport, 1983—. Mem. adv. bd., mediator Bapt. Temple, Logansport, 1994—; mem. Logansport Planning Commn., 1994—; mem. Cass County Family YMCA Endowment, Logansport, 1994—. Mem. Rotary (pres. Logansport). Republican. Home: 1310 Peter St Logansport IN 46947-1932 Office: Raffensperger Hughes PO Box 718 Logansport IN 46947-0718

DENHAM, JANET, investment broker; b. Logansport, Ind., Jan. 10, 1953; d. Max and Anna Pashion Brandt. BA, Purdue U., 1975, MA, 1977. Investment broker E Y Denham Co., Logansport, 1979-82, Raffensperger Hughes, Logansport, 1983—. Past pres., mem. United Way of Cass County, Logansport, Big Bros./Big Sisters, Cass County; chair edn. Bapt. Temple, Logansport. Mem. Logansport C. of C., Tri Kappa (past chair), Indpls. Stock and Bond Club. Republican. Presbyterian. Home: 817 Ridgeview Est Logansport IN 46947-8803

DENHAM, PATRICIA EILEEN KELLER, law librarian; b. Columbus, Ohio, Mar. 1, 1952; d. William Waite and Eileen Catherine (Miller) Keller; m. Richard Whitley Denham, Oct. 10, 1981 (div. Mar. 1986); 1 child, Michael Richard. BS, Findlay Coll., 1974; MSLS, U. Ky., 1978. Acquisitions libr. Supreme Ct. Ohio Law Libr., Columbus, 1974-76; acquisitions libr. Robert S. Marx Law Libr., U. Cin., 1978-88, head preservation and archives, 1988—; libr. Rendigs, Fry, Kiely & Dennis, Cin., 1979-85. Editor Tech. Svcs. Law Libr., 1990-94. Mem. AAUW, NOW, AAUP, Assn. Women Faculty, Am. Assn. Law Librs. (travel grantee 1984), Ohio Regional Assn. Law Librs. Episcopalian. Office: U Cin Robert S Marx Law Libr PO Box 210142 Cincinnati OH 45221-0142

DENHART, CHARLES FORD, physician; b. Zanesville, Ohio; s. Paul Raymond and Ruth Ann (Ford) D. BA, Hope Coll., 1972; MD, Ohio State U., 1975. Diplomate Am. Bd. Phys. Medicine and Rehab., Am. Bd. Electrodiagnosis. Asst. prof. Ohio State U., Columbus, 1978-79; pvt. practice Des Moines, 1980—; med. dir. Younker Rehab. Ctr., Des Moines, 1992—. Bd. dirs. On With Life, Ankeny, Iowa, 1989-95. Mem. AMA, Am. Acad. Electrodiagnosis, Am. Acad. PM&R. Episcopalian. Office: Younker Rehab Ctr 1200 Pleasant St Des Moines IA 50409

DENKEWALTER, KIM RICHARD, lawyer; b. Chgo., May 7, 1948; s. Walter J. and Doris A. (Gast) D. BA, Loyola U., Chgo., 1971; JD, U. Ill., Chgo., 1974. Bar: Ill. 1974, U.S. Dist. Ct. (no. dist.) Ill. 1974, U.S. Ct. Appeals (7th cir.) 1977, U.S. Supreme Ct. 1979. Ptnr., Abramovic, Denkewalter & Ryan, Northfield, Ill., 1974-79; pres. Denkewalter & Assocs.,

Northfield, 1979-85; pres. Denkenwalter, Angelo & Minkow, 1986—; real estate broker, Chgo., 1978—; guest lectr. Am. Coll. Emergency Physicians, Rosemont, Ill., 1979-84. Pres. 539 Stratford Condo Assn., Chgo., 1985-86, sec. 1985-86, bd. dirs. 1985-86, treas. 1985-86; mem. Hoopis Fin. Group, Northfield, Ill. Served with USAR, 1970-76. Named EMT-A (hon.) Ill. Dept. Pub. Health, 1983. Mem. Ill. State Bar Assn., Chgo. Bar Assn., Assn. Trial Lawyers Am., ABA, Mission Hills Country Club. Home: 14 Darlington Dr Lake Zurich IL 60047-8055 Office: Denkewalter Angelo & Minkow 790 W Frontage Rd Winnetka IL 60093-1204

DENKO, JOANNE D., psychiatrist, writer; b. Kalamazoo, Mich., Mar. 29, 1927; d. John S. and Marian Mildred (Boers) Decker; m. Charles Wasil Denko, June 17, 1950; children: Christopher Charles, Nicholas Charles, Timothey Charles. BA summa cum laude, Hope Coll., 1947; MD, Johns Hopkins U., 1951; MS in Psychiatry, U. Mich., 1963. Lic. psychiatrist Md., Ill, Mich., Ohio. Pvt. practice Columbus, Ohio, 1961-68; staff psychiatrist Fairview Gen. Hosp., Cleve., 1968—; pvt. practice Rocky River, Ohio, 1968—; cons. Juvenile Diagnostic Ctr., Columbus, 1967-68, VA Hosp., Cleve., 1968-72, Cmty. Mental Health Ctrs., Greater Cleve., 1974-80; clin. instr. Case Western Res. U., Cleve., 1981-83. Author: Through the Keyhole at Gifted Men and Women, 1977, (monograph) The Psychiatric Aspects of Hypoparathyroidism, 1962; contbr. articles to profl. jours.; author poetry, 1960—. Mem. AAAS (reviewer children's books), Cleve. Astron. Soc. (bd. dirs. 1984-86), Mensa (Cleve. area br. pres. 1986-87), Great Books Discussion Group (Rocky River, chmn. 1985-92, 94—), Kiwanis Internat. Russian Orthodox. Home and Office: 21160 Avalon Dr Cleveland OH 44116-1120

DENMAN, MARK A., mortgage protection insurance company official; b. Columbus, Ohio, Jan. 13, 1963. Student, Ohio State U., 1981. Lic. series 7 Nat. Assn. Securities Dealers. Cook fried chicken franchise, Columbus, 1980-82; with Lombard Securities Inc., Columbus, 1982—. Office: Lombard Securities Inc PO Box 361162 947 E Johnstown Columbus OH 43236

DENN, CYRIL JOSEPH, insurance career agent; b. Mankato, Minn., Jan. 23, 1948; s. Bertram Henry and Hildegard M. (Drummer) D.; m. Sandra Lee Jones, Oct. 22, 1966 (div. 1970); m. Darlene Kay Wittrock, Apr. 19, 1974; children: Darcy Ann, Amanda Kay, Cassandra Jo. BS, Mankato State U., 1977, 5-yr. cert., 1982. CLU, ChFC. Factory laborer Kato Engring. Co., Mankato, 1971-74; sales rep. Met. Life, Mankato, 1974-76, sales mgr., 1976-79, sales rep., 1979-82; mktg. specialist Met. Life, Aurora, Ill., 1982-83; br. mgr. Met. Life, Sioux Falls, S.D., 1983-84, sales rep., 1984-86; regional mgr. Cath. Aid Assn., St. Paul, 1986-89; mgr. Prudential Ins. Co., Sioux Falls, 1989-91, Aberdeen, S.D., 1992-94; asst. mgr. Farm Bur. Fin. Svcs., Aberdeen, 1995-96; career agt. Farm Bur. Fin. Svcs., Mankato, Minn., 1996—. Mem. sch. bd. St. Clair (Minn.) Pub. Sch., 1981-83. With U.S. Army, 1968-71, Thailand. Fellow Life Underwriters Tng. Coun.; mem. Nat. Assn. Life Underwriters (nat. quality award 1975-89, nat. sales achievmeent award 1975-89), Sioux Falls Life Underwriters Assn. (bd. dirs. 1991-92, edn. chmn., co-chmn. life underwriting tng. coun.), Gen. Agy. Mgrs. Assn. (career devel. award 1994), Aberdeen Life Underwriters Assn. (bd. dirs. 1992-96, sec.-treas. 1994-95, pres. elect 1995-96), S.D. Life Underwriters Assn. (co-chmn. life underwriters tng. coun. 1993-96, fellow 1993), Am. Soc. CLU's and ChFC's (pres. Ea. S.D. chpt. 1992-93, midwest liaison team 1992—, mem. devel. com. 1994—, coord. video teleconf. 1992-96), S.D. Planned Giving Coun. (steering com. 1994-95, v.p. programs/newsletter chair 1995—), S.D. Pony of Americas Club (bd. dirs. 1986—, pres. 1987-89), Midwest Pony of Americas Club (pres. 1988-91, horse show chmn. 1989), Am. Legion. Republican. Roman Catholic.

DENN, JAMES N., commissioner. Commr. Minn. Dept. Transp., St. Paul; mem. exec. com. Transp. Rsch. Bd. Office: Transportation Dept 395 John Ireland Blvd Saint Paul MN 55155

DENNERT, H. PAUL, state legislator. Rep. S.D. State Ho. of Reps. Dist. 2, mem. Transp., Agr. and Natural Resources Com.; farmer, cattleman. Home: RR 1 Box 45 Columbia SD 57433-9742*

DENNEY, LUCINDA ANN, relocation services executive; b. Akron, Aug. 7, 1938; d. Charles Andrew and Madora Heinretta (Frederick) Shetter; m. Jon E. Denney; children: Mary, Jon, Andrew. BA cum laude, Ohio Wesleyan U., 1960. Cons. Cleve., 1978—; dir. corp. relocation Hackett & Arnold, Inc., Cleve., 1991—. Mem. adv. coun. to pub. rels. com. Mus. Arts Assn.; exec. com. Cleve. Orch., jr. com. 1968-84; mem. adv. com. Rock'n Roll Hall of Fame, Cleve., 1986-94, Shaker Heights (Ohio) Citizens League, Cleve. Opera Coun., Shaker Heights Youth Ctr., 1982—, also v.p.; trustee Boy Scouts Am., 1984—, Jr. League Cleve., 1968-95, Big Bros./Big Sisters of Greater Cleve., 1968-84, St. Luke's Hosp. Jr. Bd., 1968-84, St. Luke's Hosp. Assn., 1988—; mem. Leadership Cleve., 1981-93, pres. 1993-94. Named one of 1977 Most Interesting Persons, Cleve. Mag.; recipient Outstanding Pace Setter award Directory of Greater Cleve.'s Enterprising Women, 1985, Disting. Alumni award Cuyahoga Falls H.S., 1988. Mem. 20th Century Club, Mortar Bd., Alpha Theta Pi, Kappa Alpha Theta. Republican. Methodist.

DENNEY, ROGER W., small business owner; b. Buffalo Center, Iowa, Feb. 7, 1947. Foreman Winnibago Industries, various locations, Iowa, 1968; owner Westside R&B Tool, Garner, Iowa, 1972—. Patentee in field. Office: Westside Mgr Co PO Box 162 Garner IA 50438-0162

DENNING, MELINDA SUE, nurse; b. Hillsboro, Ill., Aug. 26, 1962; d. Richard Lee and Lila Marie (Crigler) Chaplin; m. David Lewis Denning, Aug. 1, 1981. BSN, Kaskaskia Coll., 1985. RN. Staff nurse, RN Sunnydale Acres Care Ctr., Vandalia, Ill., 1985-87, care plan nurse, RN, 1987-88; ADON Cherrywood Health Care Ctr., Vandalia, Ill., 1988-89; staff nurse, RN Van Dyke Convalescent Ctr., Effingham, Ill., 1989-91; dir. of nursing Cherrywood Health Care Ctr., Vandalia, 1992-93, psychiat. rehab. svcs. coord., 1993—; nurse Don Olivewood Health Care Ctr., Shelbyville, Ill., 1993-95; CNA instr., DON Cherrywood Health Care Ctr., Vandalia, Ill., 1995—, dir. nursing, 1995—; CNA instr. Kaskaskia Coll., Centralia, Ill., 1990-91, rehab. nursing instr., 1990-91; CPR instr. Am. Heart Assn., Vandalia, 1991—. Methodist. Home: RR 1 Box 308 Vandalia IL 62471-9771 Office: Cherrywood Health Care Ctr 1500 W St Louis Ave Vandalia IL 62471

DENNIS, MARCIA LYNN, speech and language pathologist; b. Danville, Ill., Apr. 7, 1949; d. Arnold Leroy and Florena Grace (Starr) Raaum; m. William Michael Dennis, June 3, 1973; children: Justin M., Heather Erin. BS in Edn., Ea. Ill. U., 1971; postgrad., U. Ill., 1980-84, Ill. State U., 1973; MS, Ill. State U., 1991. Cert. elem. tchr., Ill.; lic. speech-lang. pathologist, Ill. Speech-lang. therapist Streator (Ill.) Schs., 1971-72, Fithian (Ill.) Elem. Sch., 1972-73; tchr. 1st grade Dwight (Ill.) Elem. Sch., 1973-74; tchr. speech therapy and reading Cornell (Ill.) Grade Sch., 1975-77; speech-lang. pathologist Decatur (Ill.) Pub. Schs., 1978-87, Metcalf Lab. Sch., Ill. State U., Normal, 1987-93; clin. supr., instr. speech audiology dept. Ill. State U., 1993—. Sec. Parents Anonymous, 1980-87; dir. vacation bible sch. St. Paul's Luth. Ch., Decatur, 1984-85, supt. Sunday sch., 1986. Mem. Am. Speech and Hearing Assn., Nat. Students Speech and Lang. Assn., Ill. Speech and Hearing Assn., Lincolnland Speech and Hearing Assn. (past officer), Ctrl. Ill. Speech & Hearing Assoc., Kappa Delta Pi, Alpha Gamma Delta.

DENNIS, PETER RAY, environmental corporate executive; b. Milw., Nov. 21, 1938; s. Raymond Wilbur and Elizabeth Susan (Oliver) D.; m. Mary Joan Dennis, July 22, 1977; children: Matthew Lee, Rebecca Ann. BS, U. Wis., 1962, LLB, 1964. Bar: Wis. 1964, U.S. Dist. Ct. (we. dist.) Wis. 1964. Pres. Peter R. Dennis & Assocs., Madison, Wis., 1961-66, Neoflex Rubber, Co., Madison, Wis., 1966-68; Poly-R Corp., 1966-68; cons. Chas. R. Feldstein Co., Chgo., 1968-73; exec. v.p. Idrex, Inc., Chgo., 1973-86; pres. Hazardnet, Inc., Chgo., 1986—, Geomar, Inc., 1994—. Dir. Frankfort (Ill.) Devel. Corp., 1988-91, St. Peters United Ch. of Christ, Frankfort, 1989-92. Mem. ABA (corp. sec. 1964—), Wis. Bar Assn., Air Waste Mgmt. Assn. (Lake Mich. sec. 1990—), Ill. Mfrs. Assn. (environ. com. 1973-85), Masonic Lodge, Medinah Temple, Joliet Shrine Club. Home: 150 Walnut St Frankfort IL 60423-1464 Office: Hazardnet Inc PO Box 404 Frankfort IL 60423-0404

DENNIS, (MARY) RUTH, retired librarian; b. Bloomfield, Iowa, July 16, 1907; d. Claude Charles and Nora Jane (Townsend) Atwood; m. Donald A. Dennis, Sept. 11, 1932 (div. Dec. 1955); children: Larry, Mary Jo Bousek. Student, Ottumwa Heights Jr. Coll., Ottumwa, Iowa, 1927-28; cert. in libr. sci., USDA Grad. Sch., 1964. Libr. asst. Ottumwa Pub. Libr., 1929-31; agt. Met. Life Ins. Co., Marshalltown, Iowa, 1943-45; continuity writer Sta. KFJB, Marshalltown, 1953-56; housemother Signa Alpha Epsilon, Iowa City, 1956-57; libr. asst. U. Iowa, Iowa City, 1957-59; cataloging asst. U.S. Bur. Census, Andrews AFB, Md.; reference libr. U.S. Weather Bur. Libr., Washington, 1959-64; asst. libr. USDA, Peoria, Ill., 1964-66; libr. Herbert Hoover Presdl. Libr., Branch, Iowa, 1966-72; ret., 1972. Author: Homes of the Hoovers, 1986, The Wit and Wisdom of Herbert Hoover, 1995. Bd. dirs. Cedar County chpt. Am. Cancer Soc., Tipton, Iowa, 1987—; past pres. West Branch Heritage; v.p. Friends Eniow Pub. Libr., West Branch. Mem. Herbert Hoover Presdl. Libr. Assn., Questers (historian Red Cedar chpt., past pres.), Order Ea. Star (worthy matron, 1971, 81). Republican. Mem. Christian Ch. (Disciples of Christ). Home: 204 Cookson Dr West Branch IA 52358

DENNIS, WILLIAM CULLEN, foundation officer; b. Richmond, Ind., Nov. 19, 1941; s. David Worth and Tresa (Justice) D. AB, Earlham Coll., 1963; MA, Yale U., 1964, PhD, 1971. Asst. prof. history Denison U., Granville, Ohio, 1968-75, assoc. prof. history, 1975-84, prof. history, 1984; dir. publs. Liberty Fund, Inc., Indpls., 1985-87, program officer, 1987-90, sr. program officer, 1990—. Contbr. articles to profl. jours. Woodrow Wilson fellow, 1963-64, Richard M. Weaver fellow Intercollegiate Studies Inst., 1964-65. Mem. Phila. Soc. (pres. 1987-88), Beta Theta Pi. Republican. Mem. Soc. of Friends. Office: Liberty Fund Inc Ste 300 Ste 228 8335 Allison Pointe Trl Indianapolis IN 46250-1687

DENOYER, GEORGIA ANN, consultant, educator; b. Trenton, Mich., July 17, 1948; d. Lloyd George and Vera Eunice (Lawrence) Robertson; m. Thomas James DeNoyer, Sept. 7, 1968; 1 child, Matthew. AA, Oakland Community Coll., 1981, AAS, 1982; BS in Liberal Arts, USNY, Albany, 1986; AAS in Nursing, Schoolcraft Coll., 1989. RN; cert. EKG tech.; cert. phlebotomy tech.; cert. med. asst. with clin. specialty; cert. hypnotherapist, stress mgmt. counselor, CPR/first aid instr., ARC; cert. ch. nurse instr., ARC. Med. asst. Davis-Smith Med.-Dental Employment Svc., Southfield, Mich., 1982-84; phlebotomist Nat. Health Labs., Oak Park, Mich., 1984-86; pres., owner Affirmative Mgmt. Group, Inc., Canton, Mich., 1986-90; phlebotomist Oakwood Hosp., Dearborn, Mich., 1988, emergency rm. nurse Canton Ctr., 1990-91; nurse emergency rm. Sinai Hosp., Detroit, 1989-90; instr. Ross Tech. Inst., Ann Arbor, Mich., 1991-92; instr. med. asst. program South Lyon Pub. Schs., 1990-91, Ross Career Schs., 1990—, Schoolcraft Coll., 1991—; faculty Baker Coll. Allied Health, 1994-95; owner Holistic Alternatives, 1995—. Vol., Oakwood Hosp., 1984-88, Catherine McAuley Health Ctr., Ann Arbor, Mich., 1984-89. Mem. NAFE, Am. Assn. Med. Assts. (chpt. treas. 1987-88), Intertel, NLN, Am. Assn. Women in Cmty. Colls., Mensa, Am. Holistic Nurses Assn., Internat. Assn. Counselors and Therapists. Roman Catholic. Home: 12853 10 Mile Rd South Lyon MI 48178-9187

DENT, CATHERINE GALE, secondary education educator; b. Salem, Mo., Apr. 20, 1953; d. James Ferguson and Virgina Gale (Martin) Dent; m. Robert David Wells, Aug. 30, 1980 (div. Aug. 1990); m. Michael E. Schafer, Apr. 8, 1992; stepchildren: Heather Schafer, Cole Schafer. Student, U. Mo., 1971-74, 91—, Longview Commun. Coll., Lee's Summit, Mo., 1975, S.W. Bapt. U., Bolivar, Mo., 1985. Lic. funeral dir.; cert. secondary tchr., Mo. Feature writer, reporter Dent County Headliner, 1972-74; acctg. clk. Assn. of Unity Chs., Unity Village, Mo., 1974-77; graphic artist The Salem News, 1979; adminstrv. asst. Ozark Lead Co.-Kennecott Corp., Sweetwater, Mo., 1979-82; ch. organist United Meth. Ch., Salem, 1977—; music tchr. Salem, 1983—; substitute tchr. Salem R-80 Sch. Dist., 1991—. Bd. dirs. Salem Arts Coun., 1984—; mgr. Salem Community Jazz Band, 1985—; accompanist Salem Community Choir, 1984—, Salem R-80 Sch. Sys. Music Dept., 1990—; dir. Temple Carillons Handbell Choir, Salem, 1985-94. Recipient Children's award Cosmopolitan Club; named to Outstanding Young Women in Am., 1985. Mem. Salem Computer Club, Dent County Hist. Soc., Order Ea. Star, Salem Rebekah Lodge, Fraternal Order of Eagles Ladies Aux., Internat. Order Rainbow for Girls (Grand Cross of Color 1968), Sorosis Club (pres. 1992-93), Cosmopolitan Club (sec. 1994—). Democrat. Methodist. Home: 1200 W Center St Salem MO 65560-2736

DENT, RICHARD LAMAR, professional football player; b. Atlanta, Dec. 13, 1960. Student, Tenn. State U. Defensive end Chicago Bears, 1983-94, San Francisco 49ers, 1994—; part-owner men's clothing store, Chgo. Mem. Pro-Bowl Team, 1984-85, 90, 93, recipient Jack Griffin Award, 1995. *

DENT, ROGER EUGENE, psychometrist; b. Canton, Ohio, Aug. 15, 1937; s. Earl LeRoy and Thelma Genevieve (Adrian) D. BS in Commerce, Ohio U., 1959. Psychometrist Psychometrical Svc. Co., Canton, 1963—; sec.-treas. Nat. Fedn. Flemish Giant Rabbit Breeders, 1979—, newsletter editor. Lt. col. USAR, 1960-88. Mem. Am. Rabbit Breeder's Assn. (life mem.), Sigma Nu. Presbyterian. Home and Office: 233 Aultman Ave NW Canton OH 44708-5524

DENTON, JOAN CAMERON, reading educator; b. Chgo.; d. Wallace William and Ruth Elizabeth (Nothof) Cameron; m. Robert Eastman Denton, Aug. 16, 1958; children: Marianne, Lynn, Robert. BS in Edn., Northwestern U., Evanston, Ill., 1954; MS in Spl. Edn. and Reading, U. Nebr., 1982. Tchr. English and social studies Berwyn (Ill.) Pub. Schs.; tchr. devel. and advanced secondary reading Omaha Pub. Schs., reading diagnostician; lead tchr. Reading Svcs.; mem. external visitation team/reading Boys Town Schs.; supr. summer literacy ctr., instr. U. Nebr., Omaha; mem. instrl. dist. coms.; former mem. rev. bd. Reading Tchr.; co-chair Metro Reading Coun. Lit. Project Listening Libr.; mem. reading leadership team Omaha Pub. Schs.; coord. OPS/AT&T Reading Pioneers Assisting Literacy in Schs. Program. Mem. NEA, Nebr. Edn. Assn., Omaha Edn. Assn., Internat. Reading Assn., Nebr. State Reading Assn., Met. Reading Coun., Assistance League Omaha, Phi Delta Kappa, Alpha Xi Delta (alumnae chpt.). Office: Omaha Pub Schs 3215 Cuming St Omaha NE 68131-2000

DENTON, RAY DOUGLAS, insurance company executive; b. Lake City, Ark., May 16, 1937; s. Ray Dudney and Edna Lorraine (Roe) D.; BA, U. Mich., 1964, postgrad., 1969-70; JD, Wayne State U., 1969, postgrad., 1964-65; m. Cheryl Emma Borchardt, Mar. 9, 1964; children: Ray D., Derek St. Clair, Carter Lee (dec.). Claims rep. Hartford Ins. Co., Crum & Forster, Detroit, and Am. Claims, Chgo., 1962-73; partner Chgo. Metro Claims, Oak Park, Ill., 1974-75; founder, pres. Ray D. Denton & Assocs., Inc., Hinsdale, Ill., 1975—. Mem. Pi Kappa Alpha, Phi Alpha Delta. Office: 930 N York Rd Ste 14 Hinsdale IL 60521-2991

DEORIO, ANTHONY JOSEPH, surgeon; b. Chgo., June 27, 1945; s. Joseph John and Catherine Marie Deorio; m. Janet Ann Balskus, Jan. 10, 1970; children: Joseph, Catherine. BS, Loyola U., Chgo., 1967; MD, Loyola U., Maywood, Ill., 1971. Diplomate Am. Bd. Surgery. Intern St. Joseph Hosp., Chgo., 1971-72; resident in surgery Loyola Med. Ctr., Maywood, 1972-76, clin. instr. surgery, 1976-77, asst. prof. surgery, 1977—; pvt. practice Resurrection Hosp., Chgo., 1977—, dir. surg. edn., 1977—, chmn. dept. surgery, 1984-88, sec. med. staff, 1986-88; assoc. examiner Am. Bd. Surgery, 1993, 96. Contbr. articles to profl. jours. Fellow ACS; mem. AMA, Ill. Med. Soc., Chgo. Med. Soc., Chgo. Surg. Soc., Ill. Surg. Soc., Alumni Assn. Stritch Sch. Medicine (bd. govs.), Columbian Club, KC, Blue Key, Alpha Omega Alpha. Roman Catholic. Office: 7447 W Talcott Ave Chicago IL 60631-3745

DEPASCO, RONNIE NICK, state legislator; b. Kansas City, Mo., Mar. 19, 1943; s. Nick and Mildred Anderson DePasco; m. Martha McAdam; children: Carrie E., Kelly L., Kacie A. Grad., Maple Wood Jr. Coll., 1966. State rep. dist. 37 Mo. Ho. of Reps., 1976-80, 82-92; state senator dist. 11 Mo. State Senate, 1993—; chmn. accounts com., budget and local govt. com. Mo. Ho. of Reps., co-chmn. redistricting and appropriations coms.; vice chmn. consumer protection and environ. com. Mo. State Senate, mem. fin. and govt. inst., ins. and housing, labor and indsl. rels., transp. and tourism coms. Recipient Appreciation award Mo. C. of C., 1984, Fraternal Order of Police, 1985, Sch. Dist. Greater Kansas City, 1986, Recognition award Mo. U., 1987. Mem. KC, Mo. Liquor Assn., Entrepreneur and Small Bus. Com., Nat. Com. State Legislators, Moose, Allied Dem. Assn. (chmn.). Home: 925 Cleveland Ave Kansas City MO 64127-1535*

DEPAUL, JOHN PHIL, construction company executive, firefighter; b. Chgo., Apr. 25, 1963; s. Sam and Margaret (DiNardo) DeP. Student, Joliet Coll., 1984—, Kankakee Coll. Lic EMT, emergency rescue technician and paramedic; state cert. firefighter II, Ill., Haz. Mat. Tech. B, Ill., FAE, ACLS, PALS, PHTLS. Capt. Romeoville (Ill.) Emergency Svcs., 1981-91, 93-94; computer operator Spiegel, Westmont, Ill., 1984-92; owner TCB Constrn., Romeoville, 1981—; firefighter, emergency med. technician Romeoville Fire Dept., 1991—; mgr. Med-Care Ambulance, Morios, Ill., 1994-95; owner BLS Instructional, Roeoville, Ill., 1995—; with field response unit DuPage County Office Emergency Mgmt., Wheaton, Ill., 1991-93; CPR instr., Romeoville Fire Dept., 1991—; first aid instr. N.E. Emergency Mgmt. Coun., Wheaton, 1987-94; firefighter Elwood Fire Dept., 1994-95. Stage mgr. Miss Romeoville Pageant, 1981—; mem. Community Edn. Coun., Romeoville, 1981-86; mem. Community Access League, Romeoville, 1982-85. Recipient awards for vol. work. Mem. Prehosp. Care Providers Ill. (charter), Team 911 (charter), Nat. Fire Protection Agy., Will County Pub. Safety Answering Positions, To The Rescue (charter mem.). Republican. Roman Catholic. Home and Office: 507 Amherst Ave Romeoville IL 60446-1301

DEPIANTE, EDUARDO VICTOR, nuclear engineer; b. Córdoba, Argentina, Feb. 20, 1959; s. Marco Osvaldo Antonio and Corina (Berón) D. BS in Nuclear Engring., Nat. U. Cuyo, Argentina, 1981; PhD, MIT, 1988. Rsch. and devel. engr. Nat. AEC, S.C. de Bariloche, Argentina, 1981-84; teaching asst. Nat. U Cuyo, S.C. de Bariloche, Argentina, 1981-84; rsch. asst. MIT, Cambridge, Mass., 1985-88; researcher Oak Ridge (Tenn.) Nat. Lab., 1988; postdoctoral assoc. MIT, 1988-89; researcher Argonne (Ill.) Nat. Lab., 1990—. Contbr. articles to profl. jours. Mem. Am. Nuclear Soc., Soc. for Computer Simulation, Sigma Xi, Alpha Nu Sigma.

DEPKE, NANCY GALLAGHER, marketing professional; b. Sandusky, Ohio, Oct. 5, 1932; d. Paul A. Gallagher and Elizabeth (Senn) Shambaugh; widowed; children: Deidre, Marianne, Meighan, John Jr. BSJ, Ohio U., 1954. Reporter Cleve. Press, 1954-61; pub. rels. dir. Cleve. Music Sch. Settlement, 1972-77, Sta. WVIZ-TV, Cleve., 1977-79; mktg. dir. Cleve. Ballet, 1979-85, Pa. Ballet, Phila., 1985-87, Cleve. Play House, 1987-89; pres. Depke & Assocs., Cleve., 1989—; cons. Pitts. Ballet Theater, Ballet Met., Columbus, Ohio. Mem. Press Club Cleve. (past pres.), Ad Club, Women in Communications.

DEPPE, ANDREW DENYSE, health care systems planner; b. Chgo., Sept. 12, 1962; s. Martin Louis and Margaret Ruth (Atwater) D. BA in English lit., Oberlin Coll., 1985; MPH, U. Ill., Chgo., 1993. Pub. rels. asst. Margie Korshak Assoc., Chgo., 1985-87; freelance editor Chgo., 1987-89; dir. pub. affairs AIDS Found. Chgo., 1989-91; rsch. specialist Dept. Med. Edn., Chgo., 1991-93; health care systems planner Chgo. Dept. Health, 1993—; advocacy com. mem. AIDS Found. Chgo., 1993—. Vol. Horizons Anti-Violence Project, Chgo., 1988-91; bd. dirs. Lesbians/Gay Voter Impact, Chgo., 1988-92; mem. Wellington Ave. Ch. Christ, Chgo., 1987—. Mem. APHA, Oberlin Lesbian, Gay and Bisexual Alumni (founding mem., nat. steering com.). Home: 4004 N Clarendon # 1 Chicago IL 60613 Office: Chgo Dept Health 333 S State St Chicago IL 60604

DE PUMA, RICHARD DANIEL, classical archaeology educator; b. Brockway, Pa., May 15, 1942; s. Daniel Di Paolis and Mary Concetta (De Santis) De P.; m. Rea Ann Scovill, Dec. 28, 1965 (div. Mar. 1972); 1 child, Julian Daniel. BA in Art History, Swarthmore Coll., 1964; MA in Archaeology, Bryn Mawr Coll., 1967, PhD in Archaeology, 1969. Instr. classical archaeology U. Iowa, Iowa City, 1968-69, asst. prof., 1969-74, assoc. prof., 1974-86, prof., 1986—; rsch. assoc. Field Mus. Natural History, Chgo., 1984—; mem. adv. bd. Am. Jour. Archaeology, 1985—, Etruscan Studies, 1991—. Author: Etruscan Tomb Groups, 1986, Corpus Speculorum Etruscorum, 1987, 93, Roman Portraits, 1988; co-editor: Rome and India, 1991, Murlo and the Etruscans, 1993, Corpus Vasorum Antiquorum, 1996. Mem. Archaeol. Inst. Am., Coll. Art Assn., Nat. Inst. Etruscan Studies (fgn.). Office: U Iowa Art History Dept Iowa City IA 52242

DE RAN, SUSAN LOUISE, financial consultant; b. Dayton, Ohio, Feb. 20, 1952; d. Robert G. and D. Louise (Johnson) Deis. BBA, U. Toledo, 1982, MBA, 1989. Sec. Hayes Albion Corp., Tiffin, Ohio, 1973-76, Owens-Ill. Inc., Toledo, Ohio, 1976-79; cashier Owens-Ill. Inc., Toledo, 1979-80, act. control asst., acct., 1983-84; cost and budget supr. Owens-Ill. Inc., 1984-88; sr. fin. bus. analyst Owens-Ill. Inc., Toledo, 1988-89; sr. fin. analyst Libbey-Owens-Ford Co., Toledo, 1989-91; sr. bus. analyst Zimmer Inc., Warsaw, Ind., 1991-92; prin., mgmt. cons. Hackett Group, Hudson, Ohio, 1992-95; fin. cons. Ernst & Young, LLP, Cin., 1995—. Mem. Natl. Assn. Female Exec. Office: Ernst & Young LLP 1300 Chiquita Ctr 250 E Fifth St Cincinnati OH 45202

DERANGO, MARY LAURA KEUL, service occupation careers counselor; b. Racine, Wis., Nov. 13; d. Kelly DeRango and Filomena Covelli; m. Richard C. Keul, Sept. 12, 1953; 1 child, Susan Keul. BE, U. Wis., Parkside, 1972; MEd in Counseling and Pers., Marquette U., 1977; student, U. London, 1979. Elem. tchr. Kenosha Unified Sch. Dist., 1972-81; health careers counselor Gateway Tech. Coll., Kenosha, 1981-90; gen. counselor Gateway Tech. Coll., Racine, Wis., 1990—; cons. CHAMP/pre-coll. program U. Wis.-Parkside, Kenosha, 1982-84; moderator, mem. planning com. Woman to Woman Conf., Milw., 1985; mem. Wis. Gov.'s State Coun. on Affirmative Action, 1987. Active Racine Teen-Age Parent Self-Sufficiency Program, Kenosha Alcohol and Drug Abuse Coun.; mem. accreditation com. Am. Assn. Med. Assts.; sec. Cath. Jr. League; vol. counselor Planned Parenthood; vol. Kenosha Hospice Alliance, Am. Cancer Soc.; vol. reader for the blind Edn. and Reading Svc. Mem. ACCD, Am. Assn. Women in Community and Jr. Colls., Nat. Mgmt. Assn., Wis. Assn. for Counseling and Devel., S.E. Wis. Assn. for Counseling and Devel., Wis. Student Pers. Assn., Wis. Assn. for Vocat. and Adult Edn. Roman Catholic. Home: 23 Globe Heights Dr Racine WI 53406 Office: Gateway Tech Coll 1001 S Main St Racine WI 53403-1501

DERAPS, LARRY, customer service representative; b. Dallas, Feb. 21, 1951; m. Toni Deraps; 4 children. AA, Florissant Valley Jr. Coll., 1972. Rep. candidate for U.S. House, 9th Dist., Mo., 1996. Office: Larry Deraps for US Congress 148 Hastings Way Saint Charles MO 63301*

DE REGNIER, KEVIN VINCENT, osteopath; b. Spencer, Iowa, July 28, 1957; s. Richard Vincent and Beverly Kathryn (Sloan) de R.; m. Raenelle Leone Starr, Aug. 1, 1981; children: Andrea Nicole, Christopher Vincent. BA, U. No. Iowa, 1981; DO, U. Osteo. Medicine and Health, Scis., 1985. Diplomate Nat. Bd. Examiners for Osteo. Physicians and Surgeons; cert. in gen. practice Am. Coll. Osteo. Gen. Practitioners. Chief intern Des Moines Gen. Hosp., 1985-86, chief resident, gen. practice, 1986-87; owner, physician Madison County Med. Assocs., P.C., Winterset, Iowa, 1987—; adj. asst. prof. U. Osteo. Medicine and Health Scis., Des Moines, 1991—; med. examiner Madison County, Winterset, 1987—; bd. dirs. Earlham Care Program, Winterset, Union State Bank, Winterset; chief med. staff Madison County Meml Hosp., Winterset, 1990-91, 92-93. Mem. Madison County Assn. for Spl. People, Winterset, 1991—; elder First United Presbyn. Ch., Winterset, 1995—. Mem. Am. Coll. Osteo. Gen. Practitioners (pres. elect Iowa chpt. 1996), Am. Osteo. Assn., Am. Coll. Osteo. Family Physicians (pres. elect Iowa chpt. 1996), Iowa Osteo. Med. Assn. (bd. dirs. 1991-93, v.p. 1993-94, pres.-elect 1994-95, pres. 1995-96, immediate past pres. 1996—). Republican. Presbyterian. Office: Madison County Med Assocs 60 Court St PO Box 192 Winterset IA 50273

DERGE, DAVID RICHARD, political science educator; b. Kansas City, Mo., Oct. 10, 1928; s. David Richard and Blanche (Butterfield) D.; m. Elizabeth Anne Greene, Sept. 4, 1951 (dec. Mar. 1971); children—David Richard III, Dorothy Anne; m. Patricia Jean Williams, Sept. 2, 1972; children—William David, Mary Jennifer. A.B., U. Mo., 1950; A.M., Northwestern U., 1951, Ph.D., 1955; LL.D., Hanyang U., Korea, 1973. Instr. U. Mo., 1954-56, Northwestern U., summer 1955; mem. faculty Ind.

U., 1956-72, prof. polit. sci., 1965-72, dean adminstrn., exec. v.p., 1968-72; pres. So. Ill. U., Carbondale, 1972-74, prof. polit. sci., 1974—; pres. Behavioral Research Assocs., 1968—; mem. U.S. Adv. Commn. Internat. Ednl. and Cultural Affairs, 1969-76; White House cons. Exec. Office of President, 1970-72; cons. higher and internat. edn. Dept. Health, Edn. and Welfare, 1971-72; sec., dir. Midwest Univs. Consortium for Internat. Activities, 1967-72; pres. Ill. Joint Council Higher Edn., 1972; bd. dirs. Ill. Ednl. Consortium for Computer Services, 1972; sec. Acad. Assn Midwest Univs. Author: Public Leadership in Indiana, 1969, Institution Building and Rural Development, 1968, The World of American Politics, 1968; also articles. Mem. City Council, Bloomington, Ind., 1963-67. Served with AUS, 1946-48; Served with USNR, 1952-88; comdr. Res. ret., lt. col. CAP., 1987—. Grantee Social Sci. Research Council, 1957; grantee Eagleton Inst. Practical Politics, 1959; grantee Citizenship Clearing House, 1961; recipient Sigma Delta Chi Teaching award, 1963, Weatherly Distinguished Teaching award Ind. U., 1964, Outstanding Teaching award So. Ill. U., 1987; named Outstanding Young Man Ind. Ind. Jr. C. of C., 1963. Mem. Am. Polit. Sci. Assn., U.S. Naval Inst., Phi Beta Kappa, Pi Sigma Alpha, Alpha Pi Zeta, Alpha Kappa Psi, Phi Delta Kappa, Kappa Sigma. Presbyn. Clubs: Bloomington Squash Racquets, La Table Six. Home: Spring Arbor Lake 53 Briar Ridge Rd Carbondale IL 62901

DERKS, IRVIN L., engineering executive; b. Zeeland, Mich., Oct. 2, 1944. AD, Ferris State U., 1967. Engr. product project Addison Products Co., Addison, Mich., 1967-72; chief engr. McGraw Edison, Albion, Mich., 1972-76; v.p. engring. Bard Mfg., Bryan, Ohio, 1976—; bd. dirs. A.R.I., Washington. Patentee in field. Mem. adv. com. N.W. State Tech. Coll., Archibold, Ohio, 1984—. With U.S. Army, 1962-65. Mem. Moose. Methodist. Home: 13419 County Road H Bryan OH 43506-9406

DEROO, SALLY A., biology and geology educator. BS, Eastern Mich. U., 1958; MS, U. Mich., 1961, postgrad., 1967-89; postgrad., Wayne State U., 1964-68, Ohio State U., 1995—. Cert. elem. tchr., middle level, all subjects K-8; cert. high sch. level environ. scis., social studies, English, econs. 9-12; cert. tchr. mentally handicapped and emotionally impaired K-12. Asst. prof. sci. Ea. Mich. U., Ypsilanti, 1958-63, asst. prof. biology and geology, 1968—, cons., 1958-89, tchr. spl. edn., cons., 1989—; tchr. sci. and geology Plymouth-Canton Cmty. Schs., 1963-95; curriculum specialist Ctrl. Mich. U., 1989-90; instr. dept. tchr. edn. Mich. State U., 1994—; mem. staff student tchr. edn. Dept. Edn. Madonna U.; advisor Salem H.S., 1990—, Wayne State U., Detroit, 1995—, Pitts. State U., Kans. at Greenbush, 1996; mem. satellite conf. Tchrs. Making a Difference, 1990; mem. support team Sci. Teaching Edn. STEP adv. bd. Madonna U., Livonia, Mich.; mem. math. and sci. challenge grant design com. Wayne County, 1991; adv. bd. SEMSplus Mich. Envirothon; mem. adv. com., issues author sci. curriculum support guides Mich. Dept. Edn., 1989-90; mem. adv. coun. Mich. Dept. Edn.; mem. Mich. curriculum frameworks joint steering com., 1992—, mem. writing com. h.s. proficiency exam., 1993, 94, 95—, mem. adv. com. h.s. sci. proficiency test, 1993, 94, 95-96; dist. commr. Wayne County Sail Dist. U.S. Dept. Agriculture; project chairperson Project Cattail, Tchrs. and Students Making an Environ. Difference, 1992—; project dir. Gt. Lakes-Thunderbay Gt. Lakes Basin Work Shop, Alpena, Mich., 1993; facilitator numerous workshops; presenter in field. Author: (newsletter) Fledgeling, 1990—, (teaching manuals) Exploring Our Environment; contbg. writer Detroit Free Press sci. page; contbr. articles to sci. mags.; writer, dir. 26-week sci. TV series Explore with Me; sci. editor Ann Arbor Pubs., 1968-86; elem. publ. editor Mich. Sci. Tchrs.; adv. (tv waste mgmt. series) Neuton's Apple. Active Rouge River Restoration, 1988—, Friends of Mattaei Bot. Gardens Ann. Flower Show; established Model Adopt-a-Stream Project "River Watch" for Rough River Water Shed, 1994. Recipient Outstanding Educator award Mich. Jaycees, 1963, Best of West Edn. award, 1984, Outstanding Svc. Recognition award Mich. Assn. Mid. Sch. Educators, 1989, 90, gov.'s citation State of Mich., 1990, 91, Tchr. of Yr. Program award IBM, 1990, Can Doers award Mich. Tech. Coun., 1993; named Outstanding Sci. Educator, Metro Detroit Sci. Tchrs. Assn., 1994. Mem. NEA, Nat. Sci. Tchrs. Assn. (presenter, local leader), Mich. Sci. Tchrs. Assn. (dir.-at-large, outreach conf. chairperson), Nat. Mid. Level Sci. Tchrs. Assn., Nat. Resource Def. Coun., Mich. Sci. Leaders Assn. (bd. dirs.), Mich. Edn. Assn., Sci. Curriculum Devel. Assn. (mid. sch. goal-based curriculum), Wayne County Task Force (intermediate sch. dist. writing team 1989), Mich. Alliance for Outdoor Edn., Detroit Zool. Inst., Internat. Joint Commn. (Gt. Lakes), Mich. Reading Assn. (sci. conf. chairperson 1992-93), Phi Delta Kappa (editor newsletter U. Mich. chpt.).

DERR, LEE E., chemical company executive; b. St. Joseph, Mo., June 12, 1948; s. LeRoyce Eugene and Helen Marie (Smith) D.; m. Mary Jo Saldi, Nov. 5, 1986; children: Lindsay, Marie. BS in Bus. Adminstrn., U. Mo., 1970. CPA, Kans., Mo. V.p., fin. and treas. Wulfsberg Electronics, Inc., Overland Park, Mo., 1976-84; group v.p. B.C. Christopher Securities, Kansas City, Mo., 1984-85; pres. Pyrotech Corp., Leawood, Kans., 1985—; pres. Interchem (N.A.) Industries, Inc., Overland Park, 1985—. Mem. AICPA. Home: 8690 Woodland Ave Shawnee Mission KS 66220-3106 Office: Interchem Industries Inc 9135 Barton St Overland Park KS 66214-1720

DERRICK, DEBORAH BALL, communications specialist; b. Syracuse, N.Y., Aug. 20, 1952; d. Thomas Martin and Joyce Virginia (DeLine) Ball; m. Thomas Charles Derrick, Sept. 29, 1978; children: Kristina, Jonathan. BA, Drake U., 1981; grad. student, U. Nebr., Omaha, 1994—. Program specialist City of Syracuse, N.Y., 1975-77; planner Ctrl. Iowa Regional Assn., Des Moines, 1977-82; MIS supr., contract mgmt. coord. Ctrl. Iowa Employment and Tng. Consortium, Des Moines, 1982-84; adminstrv. asst. Francis & Assocs., Des Moines, 1984-85; mktg. coord. Wells Engrs., inc., Omaha, 1985-90; adminstrv. asst. to dean U. Nebr. Med. Ctr., Omaha, 1990-92; comms. specialist U. Nebr.-Lincoln, Omaha, 1992—. Editor (with others) PCI Bridge Manual, 1995—; contbr. feature articles and stories to profl. jours. Chair bd. Christian edn. First Ctrl. Congl. United Ch. of Christ, Omaha, 1988-90, mem. bd. music, 1993—. Recipient Jim Raglin Media award Am. Cancer Soc., 1995, Beat Feature Story award UNo Gateway Newspaper, 1995. Mem. Nat. Fedn. Press Women, Soc. Profl. Journalists. Home: 5411 Western Ave Omaha NE 68132 Office: U Nebr Lincoln Engring Bldg Rm 118 60th and Dodge Omaha NE 68182-0461

DERTIEN, JAMES LEROY, librarian; b. Kearney, Nebr., Dec. 14, 1942; s. John Ludwig and Muriel May (Cooley) D.; m. Elaine Paulette Mohror, Dec. 26, 1966; children—David Dalton, Channing Lee. A.B., U. S.D., 1965; M.L.S., U. Pitts., 1966; MPA, U. S.D., 1995. Head librarian Mitchell Pub. Library, S.D., 1966-67; head librarian Sioux Falls Coll., S.D., 1967-69; acting dir. libraries U. S.D., Vermillion, 1969-70; head librarian Vets. Meml. Pub. Library, Bismarck, N.D., 1970-75, Bellevue Pub. Library, Nebr., 1975-81; libr. dir. Siouxland Librs., S.D., 1981—. Pres., bd. dirs. Vol. and Info. Ctr., Sioux Falls, 1991-93. Mem. ALA, Mountain Plains Library Assn. (pres. 1978-79, editor newsletter 1982—), S.D. Library Assn. (pres. 1986-87). Unitarian. Lodge: Rotary. Home: 1602 Carter Pl Sioux Falls SD 57105-2019 Office: Siouxland Librs 201 N Main Ave Sioux Falls SD 57102-0303

DERWINSKI, DENNIS ANTHONY, dentist; b. Chgo., Oct. 18, 1941; s. Anthony Joseph and Julie Donata (Pochron) D.; m. Mary Pamela Butler, Feb. 11, 1964 (div. Dec. 1975); children: Julie, Nancy, John, Amy, Mollie, Camy; m. Gayle Marie Sondelski, Oct. 8, 1977; 1 child, Anthony. DDS, Marquette U., 1965. Resident Cook County Hosp., Chgo., 1967-68; dentist Riverview Dental Assocs., Wausau, Wis., 1968-81; also pres. Riverview Dental Assocs., Wausau, 1971-81; dentist, pres. Hosp. Dental Assocs., Wausau, 1981-92; with Westhill Profl. Ctr., Wausau, 1989—; vice chmn. Wausau Hosp. Dental Staff, Wasau, 1983-87, chmn., 1987-90. Contbr. articles to profl. jours. Dental chmn. United Way, Wausau, 1983; pres. Montessori Sch. Wausau, 1984; bd. dirs. St. Francis Cabrini Sch., 1978-85. Served to capt. USAF, 1965-67. Fellow Acad. Gen. Dentistry (cert.); mem. Soc. Occlusal Studies, ADA, Wis. Dental Assn. (Continuing Edn. award), Am. Equilibration Soc. Republican. Roman Catholic. Club: Wausau. Home: 1209 E Crocker St Wausau WI 54403-2378 Office: Westhill Profl Ctr 2800 Westhill Dr Ste 104 Wausau WI 54401-3769

DERZON, GORDON M., hospital administrator; b. Milw., Dec. 28, 1934; married. B.A., Dartmouth Coll., 1957; M.H.A., U. Mich., 1961. Adminstrv. resident Bklyn. Hosp., 1960-61, adminstrv. asst., 1961-63, asst. exec. dir., 1963-65, exec. dir., 1966-67; exec. dir. State U. Hosp., Bklyn., 1967-68, Kings County Hosp. Center, Bklyn., 1968-74; supt. U. Wis. Hosps. and Clinics, Madison, 1974—; assoc. prof. SUNY, 1967-74; clin. prof. U. Wis.; dir. Marshall Erdman & Assocs., Pace Med. Systems; mem. bd. Univ. Hosp. Consortium. Contbr. articles to profl. jours. Mem. Am. Hosp. Assn. (past chmn. pub. gen. hosp. sect.). Home: 3440 Topping Rd Madison WI 53705-1439 Office: U Wis Hosp & Clinics 600 Highland Ave Madison WI 53792-0001

DESIDERIO-BUCCI, JOHN, designer and developer of custom exhibits; b. Gorizia, Italy, May 23, 1934; came to U.S., 1959.; EE, U. Ljubljana, Yugoslavia. Owner Bucci Internat., Chgo. Designer, producer shows, including the exhibit for the Italian Cultural Ctr. ofChgo., Mus. Sci. and Industry, Chgo., Blue Island Hist. Soc., Chgo.; builder custom trade show exhibits; designer, builder Le Sabre automobile, 1963, The Trieste automobile, 1967; developed prototypes of two electric cars; designer of furniture, art objects, archtl. residences. Recipient Gold medal Italian Cultural Ctr., 1976. Mem. Italian Cultural Ctr., Italian C. of C. Home: 5869 N Lansing Chicago IL 60646

DESLAURIERS, MARIE ROXANNE LORRAINE, research scientist; b. Montreal, Que., Can., Oct. 2, 1947; m. Rajmund Lewis Somorjai. BSc in Exptl. Biology, U. Laval, Que., 1968; PhD in Biochemistry, U. Ottawa, Ont., 1972. Asst. rsch. officer NRC of Can., Ottawa, 1972-79, assoc. rsch. officer, 1979-86, sr. rsch. officer, 1986-88, group leader, 1988-90, sect. head, 1990-92; group leader NRC of Can., Winnipeg, Man., 1992—; adj. prof. U. Ottawa, 1988—, U. Man., 1992—, U. Winnipeg, 1993—. Author of manuscripts. Grantee Natural Scis. and Engring. Coun. Can., 1994—, Heart and Stroke Found., 1995-97. Fellow Internat. Soc. for Heart Rsch., Soc. Magnetic Resonance (mem. subcom. on student stipends 1995—); mem. Natural Scis. and Engring. Rsch. Coun. (mem. cell biology grant selection com. 1992—), Am. Heart Assn., Internat. Soc. for Heart Rsch., Can. Biophys. Soc. (sec. 1993-96).

DESLEY, JOHN WHITNEY, medical illustrator; b. Old Mystic, Conn., May 17, 1925; s. Clifford James and Hester (Walbridge) D.; m. Janice Reed, Dec. 22, 1951 (dec. Sept. 23, 1993); children: Christopher, Rebecca, Timothy, Rachel, Leah, Louisa; m. Margaret Wakeman Abell, Aug. 31, 1996. BFA, Vesper George, Boston, 1950; M in Med. Illustration, Mass. Gen. Hosp., 1952; student, U. Conn., 1950. Asst. med. artist Mass. Gen. Hosp., Boston, 1951-52; chief med. artist VA Hosp., Birmingham, Ala., 1952-58; med. illustrator U. Minn., Mpls., 1958-63, Mayo Clinic, Rochester, Minn., 1963-90; freelance med. illustrator Rochester, 1990—. Illustrator for med. books, 1985—, (textbook) Cardiac Surgery, 1985; designer bicentennial medallion City of Rochester, 1976, bicentennial print design, 1977. chmn. sch. bd. Bamber Valley Sch., Rochester, Minn., 1973-75. With USN, 1943-46. Home: 609 Sumac Rd Lewisville NC 27023-9555

DE SMET, IMOGENE LORRAINNE MARIE, classicist, educator; b. Colome, S.D., Aug. 24, 1928; d. Charles Ferdinand and Ida Louise (Van Overschelde) De S. BA in English, St. Mary of the Wasatch, 1953; MA in English, Creighton U., 1960; PhD of English, U. Toronto, 1970. Tchr. English Armour (S.D.) H.S., 1953-57, Centerville (Iowa) C.C., 1959-60, Hot Springs (S.D.) H.S., 1960-61; prof. English Coll. St. Catherine, St. Paul, 1961-63, U. Wis. Stevens Point, 1968—; bd. dirs. Bishop's Ednl. Endowment Fund, La Crosse, Wis. Contbr. chpt. in book and articles to profl. jours. Dir. lector ministry St. Stanislaus Parish, Stevens Point, 1988—. Fulbright grant to teach English in The Netherlands, 1957-58; grantee Wis. Arts Coun. Mem. Chaucer Soc., Medieval Soc. Am., Midwest Modern Lang. Assn., Stevens Point Doll Club (pres. 1990-92), Delta Kappa Gamma (pres. 1992-94, publ. grant 1990), Sigma Tau Delta (faculty advisor). Home: 1417 Illinois Ave Stevens Point WI 54481

DESMOND, JANE C., fine arts educator. BA, Brown U., 1973; MFA, Sarah Lawrence Coll., 1975; postgrad., U. N.C., 1984-85; MA, Yale U., 1991, PhD in Am. Studies, 1993. Freelance dancer, choreographer various concert performances, N.Y., N.C., 1975-86; movement designer The Handmaid's Tale (Screenplay), 1990; asst. prof. theatre Cornell U., Ithaca, N.Y., 1975-80; artist-in-residence, faculty, dir. Duke in N.Y. Arts Prog. Duke U., 1982-93; assoc. prof. Am. studies, women's studies U. Iowa, Iowa City, 1993—; co-dir. Internat. Forum for U.S. Studies; cons. The Nat. Faculty of the Arts and Scis., 1989-90, N.Y. State Coun. on the Arts, 1979-81, others. Contbr. articles to profl. jours. and publs.; co-producer (film) Chuck Davis: Dancing through West Africa, 1987 (Nat. CINE Golden Eagle 1987); participant various broadcasts and screenings including nat. PBS broadcasts, 1988, 89, Monterey Film Festival, 1989, others; curated exhibits: Phys. Evidence: New Explorations of the Video Body, 1992, Video, Politics, and Performance, 1990, Eighties Artists: New Performances on Video, 1989, others. Rose Herrick Jackson fellow in Am. Art, Yale U. Art Mus., 1987-88; recipient Univ. Dissertation fellowship, Yale U., 1991-92; fellow NEH, 1980, 93, others; grantee N.C. Arts Coun., Mary Duke Biddle Found., N.C. Ctr. for Pub. TV, N.Y. State Coun. on Arts, Helene Wurlitzer Found., Z.B.S. Found. for Exptl. Audio, others. Office: Univ of Iowa Am Studies Program 202 Jefferson Bldg Iowa City IA 52242

DE SNYDER, SOAMI SANTIAGO, audiologist; b. Phila., Feb. 4, 1963; d. Angel Luis and Julia Maria (Santiago) Santiago; m. Victor Abram Snyder, July 2, 1988. BS, U. P.R., Mayaguez, 1983; MS, Med. Sci. Sch., San Juan, P.R., 1985; postgrad., Ohio State U., 1989—. Audiology intern VA Hosp., Pitts., 1987-88; audiologist Menonnite Gen. Hosp., Aibonito, P.R., 1986-87; with Coll. Health Related Professions U. P.R. Med. Sci. Campus, San Juan, 1989; tchr. assoc. Ohio State U., Columbus, 1989. Contbr. articles to El Nuero Dia Newspaper. Mem. Pro-Life Orgn., San Juan, 1983, Orgn. Speech Pathology and Audiology P.R. student corps, San Juan, 1983. Recipient Student Clin. Excellence award OPPHLA-P.R., 1985. Mem. Am. Auditory Soc., ASHA, OPPHLA of P.R., Am. Acad. Audiology, Alexander Graham Bell Assn. for the Deaf, Ohio Coun. Audiology, Acoustic Soc. Am., P.R. Acad. Audiology (founder), Mich. Acad. Audiology, Tri-Beta. Home: Calle 5 N 18 Reina de Los Angeles Gurabo PR 00778 Office: Coll Health Related Professions Med Scis Campus Audiology Program PO Box 365067 San Juan PR 00936

DESOUZA, JOAN MELANIE, psychologist; b. Bombay, Sept. 17, 1956; came to U.S., 1987; d. Anthony Julius and Natalia Marie (Alvares) deS.; m. John Alec Krzewinski, Sept. 7, 1990. BA in Psychology with honors, U. Bombay, 1976; BS in Guidance and Counseling, Wayne State U., 1984, MA in Psychology, 1986, PhD in Ednl. Psychology, 1991. Lic. psychologist, Mich.; cert. sch. psychologist. Grad. asst. Wayne State U., Detroit, 1984-85; editor, mem. part-time faculty Inst. Gerontology, Detroit, 1985-87; extern St. Joseph Mercy Hosp., Pontiac, Mich., 1986; psychologist Huron Valley Mens' Facility, Ypsilanti, Mich., 1987-96, Huron Valley Ctr., 1996—; cons. Arab-Am. cmty., Detroit, 1988, Ctr. Behavior and Medicine, 1994—. Co-author: (handbook) Medicare Survey Project: Effectiveness of DRG's, 1987; editor (newsletter) Info. on Aging, 1985-87. Intern Parents and Children Together, Detroit, 1984; activist for Laotian community and immigrants Internat. Inst., Detroit, 1983; asst. soup kitchen Mother Theresa's order, Detroit. Grad. profl. scholar Wayne State U., 1985, Rumble fellow, 1986-87, 87-88; parenting skills grantee for low-functioning child abusers Mich. Dept. Edn., Lansing, 1989-90, Spl. Edn. grantee, 1995; recipient Bob Richardson Meml. award for excellence in correctional edn. and rsch., 1995. Mem. APA, Mich. Psychol. Assn., Mich. Assn. Sch. Psychologists, Pi Lambda Theta (Detroit chpt.). Roman Catholic. Home: 203 Russell St Saline MI 48176-1133 Office: Huron Valley Ctr 3511 Bemis Rd Ypsilanti MI 48197

DESROSIERS, ANNE BOOKE, performing arts administrator; b. Bradford, Pa., Sept. 30, 1938; d. Benjamin and Twila Mae (Schwab) Booke; m. Roger Isadore DesRosiers, Dec. 27, 1960; children Marc, Diana, Berinthia. BA in English, U. Fla., 1960. Tchr. Rantoul (Ill.) Elem. Sch., 1961-63, Oogontz Jr. H.S., Phila., 1969-73; dir. adult edn. Guadaloupe Ctr., Salt Lake City, 1974-77; dir. devel. Repertory Theater of St. Louis, 1977-85, St. Louis Zoo, 1985-88; pres. DesRosiers & Assocs., St. Louis, 1988—; mng. dir. Great Lakes Theater Festival, Cleve., 1993—. Mem. Nat. Soc. Fund Raising Execs. (cert., Exec. Leadership Inst. 1990, Outstanding Fund Raising St. Louis chpt. 1988), Cleve. Cultural Coalition (vice chair 1995—). Republican. Jewish. Home: 1 Bratenahl Pl # 1102 Bratenahl OH 44108 Office: Gt Lakes Theater Festival 1501 Euclid Ave Ste 423 Cleveland OH 44115-2108

DESTAFFANY, SANDRA RUSSELL, childbirth educator, author; b. Billings, Mont., Mar. 15, 1957; d. Alexander Emmett and Cleora Jean (Saunders) Russell; m. Joe Lee DeStaffany, Oct. 13, 1979; children: Naomi Jo, Andrea Renee, James Russell. BS, Mont. State U., 1979. cert. childbirth educator. Childbirth educator Conrad (Mont.) Childbirth Edn. Assn., 1983—; U.S. we. dir. Inter Childbirth Edn. Assn., Mpls., 1990-92, pres. elect 1992-94, pres. 1994-95. Contbr. numerous articles to profl. jours.

DETERDING, DIANA MARGARET, advertising agency executive; b. Akron, Nov. 9, 1949; d. Frank Charles and Margaret Audrey (Penzenik) LaSalle; m. William Joseph Sanders, Mar. 25, 1972 (div. 1979); children: Aaron Michael, Phillip Andrew; m. Richard Lee Deterding, Apr. 4, 1981. AA, U. Akron, 1972. Sec. U. Akron, 1969-72; office mgr. Buckeye Fence Co., Akron, 1979-84; designer/writer Dymar Agy., Akron, 1980-83; pres. Dymar Agy., Inc., Gurnee, Ill., 1984—; cons. Smithsonian Nat. Mus. Natural History, Washington, 1989-91. Contbr. articles to profl. jours. Bd. dirs. No. Ill. Coun. for Alcoholism and Substance Abuse, 1994—, adminstrv. v.p. women's bd., 1994. Recipient Design award HOW Mag., 1990; named Woman of the Yr. Wadsworth Jaycee Women, 1979, 83; named to Ohio Jaycee Women Hall of Fame, 1981. Mem. U.S. Equine Mktg. Assn. (pres. chmn. bd. 1989-90), Women's Bus. Exch. (pres. 1988-89), Horse Coun. of Ill. (bd. dirs. 1991-94), Am. Horse Pubs., Am. Horse Coun. Republican. Lutheran. Office: Dymar Agy Inc 1300 N Skokie Hwy Ste 101 Gurnee IL 60031-2144

DETHOMASIS, BROTHER LOUIS, college president; b. Bklyn., Oct. 6, 1940; s. Costantino and Anna (Maggio) DeT. B.S. in Fgn. Service,, Georgetown U., 1963; Ph.D., Union Grad. Sch., 1982. Tchr. LaSalle Acad., Providence, 1969-71; assoc. headmaster LaSalle Mil. Acad., Oakdale, N.Y., 1971-73, pres., 1976-84; v.p. for fin. The Christian Brothers, Narragansett, R.I., 1973-76; pres. St. Mary's Coll., Winona, Minn., 1984—. Author: The Finance of Education, 1978; Investing With Options, 1981; Social Justice, 1982; My Father's Business, 1984. Recipient Pres.'s medal for Christian edn., St. John's Coll. High Sch., 1985, Christian Edn. award Franz W. Sichel Found., 1974. Roman Catholic. Home and Office: PO Box 30 700 Terrace Heights Winona MN 55987-0030*

DETORE, ARTHUR WILLIAM, insurance company executive; b. Boston, May 30, 1953. BA in Greek Classics, Harvard U., 1975; MD, Tufts U., 1980; student, U. Tenn. Diplomate Am. Bd. Internal Medicine. Med. dir. Lincoln Nat. Life Ins. Co., Ft. Wayne, Ind., 1986-91; med. dir., chief knowledge engr. Lincoln Nat. Risk Mgmt., Ft. Wayne, Ind., 1991-94; v.p. strategic planning Lincoln Nat. Reins. Cos., Ft. Wayne, Ind., 1994—. Author: (with others) Life Underwriting With Knowledge-Based Systems, 1992; patentee in field. Mem. AMA, ACP, Am. Acad. Ins. Medicine, Am. Med. Informatics Assn. Office: Lincoln Nat Reins Co 1700 Magnavox Way Fort Wayne IN 46804

DETSCH, DONALD D., business executive; b. Allentown, Pa., Apr. 25, 1947; s. Dewey William Detsch and Jacquline (Mullin) Pfingstl. BSBA, U. Dayton, 1969; MBA, U. Miami, 1985; PhD, St. Louis U., 1993. Chief fiscal officer Lehigh Valley Drug & Alcohol Abuse Services, Allentown, 1969-76; treas. Whitehall (Pa.) Twp., 1976-79; dir. fin. Village of North Palm Beach, Fla., 1979-80; treas. City of Ft. Lauderdale, Fla., 1980-81; v.p. Fla. F.A.A. Fed. Credit Union, Miami, 1981-83; pub. funds officer Citicorp Savs. of Fla., Miami, 1983-87; sr. fin. analyst Citicorp Mortgage, Inc., St. Louis, 1987-89, Pioneer Railroad Co., Inc., Chillicothe, Mo., 1987-91; ptnr. Bus. Cons. Assocs., St. Louis, 1991—; treas. Pioneer R.R. Co., Inc., Chillicothe, Mo., also bd. dirs., 1987; instr. U. Miami, Fla., 1986-87, chief fin. officer, bd. dirs. West Jersey R.R. Co., 1989, Wabash & Grand River Ry., 1990, Ala. R.R. Co., 1991; pres. CompuTrain, LLC. Democrat. Office: CompuTrain LLC PO Box 49 Belleville IL 62222-0049

DETTELBACH, JOHN A., investment company executive; b. Cleve., Sept. 4, 1936; m. Cynthia Gollub, July 11, 1959. BA, Cornell U., 1959; LLB, Cleve. State U., 1964, MBA, 1987. Fin. advisor Horm Blow & Week, Cleve., 1960-69; self-employed fin. advisor Cleve., 1969-86; v.p. Kemper Securities Inc., Cleve., 1986—; advisor TEC Corp. Execs., Cleve., 1991—. Cpl. U.S. Army, 1960-65. Jewish. Office: Kemper Securities Inc 1300 N Point Tower 1001 Lakeside Ave E Cleveland OH 44114-1151

DETTMER, HELENA R., classics educator; d. Terry Stone; children: Dan, Heather, Mike, Anne. BA in Classics, Ind. U., 1972; MA/PhD, U. Mich., 1976. Asst. prof. U. Iowa, Iowa City, 1976-83, assoc. prof., 1983—, chair, 1993—; co-editor Syllecta Classica, 1989—. Author: Horace: A Study in Structure, 1983, Love By the Numbers: Form and Meaning in the Poetry of Catullus, 1996; contbr. articles to profl. jours. Mellow fellowship Duke U., 1977-78; faculty scholarship, 1986-89. Mem. Classical Assn. of Middle West and South (pres.-elect 1995-96, pres. 1996-97). Am. Philolog. Assn. Office: Univ Iowa 112 Schaeffer Iowa City IA 52242

DETWILER, DONALD SCAIFE, historian, educator; b. Jacksonville, Fla., Aug. 19, 1933; s. Donald Jacob and Hazel (Scaife) D.; m. Ilse Elisabeth Kellner, Mar. 28, 1956; children: Stephan Donald (dec.), Henry Donald. BA in History, George Washington U., 1954; Dr.phil. cum laude, Göttingen U., Germany, 1961. From instr. to asst. prof. Montgomery Coll., Md., 1962-65; asst. prof. W.Va. U., Morgantown, 1965-67; asst. prof. history So. Ill. U., Carbondale, 1967, now prof.; vis. res. prof. Nat. Taiwan U., 1987. Author: Hitler, Franco und Gibraltar, 1962; Germany: A Short History, 1976, 2d edit., 1989; (with Ilse E. Detwiler) West Germany, World Bibliographical Series vol. 72, 1987; translator, editor: Hitler: The Man and the Military Leader, 1972, reprinted 1986; editor: World War II German Military Studies (24 vols.), 1979; supplement to Official War Diary of the OKW, 1979; War in Asia and the Pacific (15 vols.), 1980; contbr. articles to encys. and profl. jours. Dir. So. Ill. Univ. Carbondale-U.S. Inter. Communication Agy. German-Am. Hist. Textbook Project, 1979-82; records in Detwiler Collection Hoover Inst. Archives, Stanford, Calif. Lt. USAFR, 1954-57. Rsch. fellow Inst. for European History, Mainz, Fed. Republic Germany, 1960-61; Am. Philos. Soc. grantee, 1969, 74; Am. Council Learned Socs. and German Acad. Exchange Service grantee, 1978. Mem. WWII Studies Assn. (chmn., vice chmn. Internat. Com. History of WWII), Com. on History in Classroom (co-chmn.), Assn. Bibliography History (coun. mem., past pres.), Am. Hist. Assn., Conf. Group on Cen. European History, Soc. for Mil. History, U.S. Commn. on Mil. History, German Studies Assn., Rotary, Phi Beta Kappa. Episcopalian. Home: 201 S Travelstead Ln Carbondale IL 62901-2223 Office: So Ill U Dept History Carbondale IL 62901-4519

DETWILER, SUSAN MARGARET, information brokerage executive; b. Bklyn., Dec. 8, 1953; d. Marshall and Anna (Dembrofsky) Pallas; m. Mark Fredrick Detwiler, Mar. 13, 1977; children: John Marshall, Elizabeth Ann. BS, SUNY, Albany, 1974; MBA, U. Mich., 1976. Market analyst Am. V. Mueller, Niles, Ill., 1976-80; mgr. market rsch. Zimmer Inc., Warsaw, Ind., 1980-85; pres. S.M. Detwiler & Assocs., Inc., Ft. Wayne, Ind., 1985—; pub. Database of Med. Market Sources. Editor: The Detwiler Directory of Medical Market Sources. Mem. Med. Surg. Market Rsch. Group (past pres.), Assn. Ind. Info. Profls. (past v.p.), Regulatory Affairs Profl. Soc. Assn., Am. Hosp. Assn. Democrat. Office: PO Box 15308 Fort Wayne IN 46885-5308

DEUCHLER, SUZANNE LOUISE, state legislator; b. Chgo., July 21, 1929; m. Walter E. Deuchler Jr.; children: Mark, Maryll. BA, U. Ill. Mem. Ill. Ho. of Reps., Springfield, 1980—. Mem. Aurora reg. adv. com., Ill. Dept. Children and Family Svcs., 1976, citizens adv. bd., Aurora U., 1981; bd. dirs. Copley Meml. Hosp., 1982. Mem. AAUW, Altrusa, Bus. and Profl. Women. Republican. Office: Ill Ho of Reps State Capitol Springfield IL 62706*

DEUTSCH, HAROLD FRANCIS, biochemist, researcher, educator; b. Sturgeon Bay, Wis., Sept. 2, 1918; s. Frank Joseph and Anna Catherine (Spahn) D.; m. Patricia Josephine Slidell, Aug. 8, 1942 (div. Nov. 1964); 1 child, Carolyn Frances; m. Regine Erika Merz, Dec. 15, 1965. PhB, U. Wis., 1940, PhD, 1944. Asst. prof. U. Wis., Madison, 1945-47, assoc. prof., 1947-54, prof., 1954-88, prof. emeritus, 1989—; vis. prof. U. Brazil, Rio de Janeiro, 1950, U. Sao Paulo, Brazil, 1954, Hokkado U., Japan, 1972, 81, U. Pretoria, 1988, Osako U., 1990. Rockefeller fellow Nobel Med. Inst.,

Stockholm, 1950-51; Alexander von Humboldt prof. Fed. Republic of Germany, 1987. Mem. AAAS, Am. Soc. Biochemistry and Molecular Biology, Am. Chem. Soc., Am. Soc. Immunology. Office: Univ Wis 1300 University Ave Madison WI 53706-1510

DEUTSCH, WILLIAM REAUGH, trade association executive; b. Jacksonville, Ill., May 18, 1924; s. William W. and Helen (Reaugh) D.; m. Mary Therese Kaler, Jan. 24, 1950; children: William Michael, Denise Deutsch Hall, Mary Michelle Deutsch Trost. Student, Ill. Coll., Jacksonville, 1942-46. Pres. Wm. R. Deutsch Advt., Jacksonville, Ill., 1948-68; exec. v.p. Ill. Petroleum Marketers Assn./Ill. Assn. Convenience Stores, Springfield, Ill., 1968-94; ret., 1994; exec. dir. Ill. Innkeepers Assn., Jacksonville, 1954-67, Ill. Assn. Life Cos., Jacksonville, 1963-67; bd. dirs. Ill. Hwy. Users Conf., Springfield, 1959-94; part-time exposition coord. Western Petroleum Marketers Assn., 1994—. Mem. Am. Assn. of Assn. Execs., Petroleum Mktg. Edn. Found., Petroleum Marketers Assn. Am. (sec., v.p., pres., exec. com., exec. rep. on legis. com.), Ill. Assn. of Assn. Execs. Home: 2015 Mound Rd Jacksonville IL 62650-2201 Office: 15209-B Ivory Dr Fountain Hills AZ 85268

DEVANEY, CYNTHIA ANN, real estate broker, educator; b. Gary, Ind., Feb. 6, 1947; d. Charles Barnard and Irene Mae (Nelson) Burner; m. Harold Verne DeVaney, Nov. 23, 1974 (dec. 1981). BS, Ball State U., 1970, MS, 1972; postgrad., Ind. U. and Purdue U., 1974-76. Cert. real estate broker, Ind. Real estate broker Century 21 McColly Realtors, Merrillville, Ind., 1979-86; real estate broker Better Homes and Gardens McColly Realtors, Merrillville, 1986—, with Pres.' Coun.; tchr. Merkley Elem. Sch., Highland, Ind., 1969—. Active Schubert Theater Guild, Chgo. Mem. N.W. Ind. Bd. Realtors (Million Dollar Club), Nat. Bd. Realtors, Jr. Ind Hist. Soc., Innsbrook Country Club, Match Point Tennis Club. Democrat. Methodist. Home: 607 E 78th Pl Merrillville IN 46410-5624 Office: McColly Better Homes & Gardens 9143 Indianapolis Blvd Hammond IN 46322-2504

DEVASSIE, TERRY LEE, publishing executive; b. Columbus, Ohio, Oct. 27, 1939; s. Robert William and Laura Belle (VanOrsdel) DeV.; m. Lola Faye Sandifer, June 21, 1964; children: Trevor Lane, Thad Lamont. BA in Indsl. Design, Columbus Coll. Art & Design, 1964. Clk., sta. mgr. Columbus Dispatch, 1957-70, div. mgr., 1970-71, asst. to circulation dir., 1971-77, state circulation mgr., 1977-79, circulation mgr., 1979-81, asst. circulation dir., 1981—; ptnr. Preston-Strat Investments, 1993—; pres., CEO Creative Inserts Co., 1992—; owner, designer TLD Design, Columbus, 1964-69; architect-designer Eagle Real Estate/Builders, Columbus, 1968-70; extrusion designer Plaskolite, Inc., Columbus, 1968-69. Pub. speaker on newspapers and hosps.; designer of drive-up newspaper rack; patentee on graphic inserts for newspaper racks. Bd. dirs. St. Anthony Mercy Hosp., Columbus, 1987-91, St. Anthony Mercy Hosp., Columbus, 1987-91, St. Anthony Mercy Hosp., Columbus, 1987-91; bd. govs., mem. exec. com. Shriners Hosp. Burn Ctr., Cin., 1986—; bd. govs. Lexington Unit of Shriners Hosp., 1991. Mem. Ohio Circulation Mgrs. (pres. 1982, founder Pres.'s award 1982, Pres.'s award 1986), Ohio Newspaper Assn. (chmn. conv. 1983, Pres.'s award 1984), Internat. Circulation Mgrs. Assn. (chmn. Internat. Newspaper Carrier Day 1982-84, Pres.'s award 1992), Newspaper Assn. Am. (newspaper coun.), Press Club Ohio (pres. 1983-84), Charity Newsies, Masons (33 degree), Shriners (Illustrious Potentate Aladdin Temple 1995, imperial pub. rels. com. 1995). Republican. Methodist. Home: 5808 Lapaz Ct Westerville OH 43081-4112 Office: Columbus Dispatch 5300 Crosswind Dr Columbus OH 43228-3600

DEVENDORF, LOUISE MARIE, promoter, writer; b. LeRoy, Mich., Apr. 5, 1939; d. Louis George and Lucille Mariam (Dean) Hinkley; m. Richard George Devendorf, Aug. 10, 1974; 1 child, Laurie Anne Hinkley Walker. Grad. high sch., 1957. Underwriter asst. Mich. Mut. Liability, Grand Rapids, 1957-63; dance instr. Arthur Murray Studio, Grand Rapids, 1959-61; insp. Wolverine Worldwide, Big Rapids, Mich., 1965-85; office mgr. Advt. Assocs., Grand Rapids, 1985-89; free-lance writer and promoter Reed City, Mich., 1989—. Author: Some Nostalgia Pertaining to Pearls, 1995, (poetry) War in Haiti, 1996. Mem. City Coun., Reed City, 1988—; mem. ex officio Libr. Bd., Reed City, 1992—; bd. dirs. Osceola Cares, Osceola County, 1993—; active Phone Tree, Reed City, 1995—; musician Furniture City Orch., 1957-59. Recipient award Internat. Soc. Poets, 1996. Home: PO Box 91 Reed City MI 49677

DEVINE, (JOSEPH) LAWRENCE, drama critic; b. N.Y.C., Sept. 21, 1935; s. John Justin and Hazel (Tippit) DeV.; m. Genevieve Christian, Aug. 29, 1959 (div. 1968); children: John Justin II, Ellen Morse; m. Lucy Memory Williamson, July 26, 1968 (dec. Oct. 1985); m. Lois Waterman, July 23, 1988. Student, Georgetown U., 1953-54, U. Mich., 1954; BS in Journalism, Northwestern U., 1957. Drama critic Miami (Fla.) Herald, 1962-67; entertainment editor, drama and film critic L.A. Herald-Examiner, 1967-68; entertainment editor, drama critic Detroit Free Press, 1968—; assoc. dir. Critics Inst., Eugene O'Neill Meml. Theater Ctr., Waterford, Conn., 1973—; mem. faculty drama critics U. Detroit, 1974; NEH profl. fellow U. Mich., Ann Arbor, 1975-76; fellow NEH seminar for critics of arts, Washington, 1977; William Randolph Hearst vis. fellow U. Tex., Austin, 1995; mem. nat. new playwrights jury Am. Coll. Theatre Festival, critic-in-residence festivals, 1978-94; mem. Pulitzer prize nominating jury in drama, 1981-82, 91-92, 93-94; panelist Forums on Theater of the Absurd, London, 1986, Stanislavsky Anniversary, Moscow, 1988. Contbr. articles to profl. jours., revs. to newspapers, mags. Served with AUS, 1958-62. Recipient Amoco gold medal of excellence Am. Coll. Theatre Festivals, 1982, Gov.'s Art award, 1993. Mem. Am. Theater Critics ASsn. (chmn. exec. com. 1979-81), Internat. Assn. Theater Critics (U.S. del. biennial congresses Tel Aviv 1981, Mexico City 1983, E. Berlin 1987, Warsaw 1992), Beta Theta Pi, Sigma Delta Chi. Home: 657 Lincoln Rd Grosse Pointe MI 48230 Office: Detroit Free Press 321 W Lafayette Blvd Detroit MI 48226-2705

DEVINE, MARY VIRGINIA, author, researcher; b. Racine, Wis., Apr. 20, 1945; d. Joseph Thomas and Virginia Arlene (Musil) D. BA, Dominican Coll., Racine, 1966; MA, U. Wis., 1967; PhD, Wayne State U., 1972. Author: (books) Brujería, 1981, Magic from Mexico, 1992.

DEVINE, MAUREEN ELIZABETH, curator; b. Detroit, Dec. 9, 1958; d. Herbert William and Helen Gertrude (Durber) D.; m. Lawrence Anthony Baranski, Feb. 10, 1990. BFA, Western Mich. U., 1982; postgrad., Wayne State U., 1990—. Gallery asst. Detroit Gallery of Contemporary Art, 1979-86; gallery mgr. Gryphon Gallery, Grosse Pointe, Mich., 1986-88; head curator Edsel & Eleanor Ford House, Grosse Pointe, 1988—. Mem. Am. Assn. Mus. Office: Edsel & Eleanor Ford House 1100 Lake Shore Rd Grosse Pointe Shores MI 48236

DEVINE, TERRY MICHAEL, newspaper editor; b. Watertown, S.D., Dec. 13, 1945; s. Russell LeRoy and Margaret Evelyn (Adams) DeV.; m. Patricia Rae Engler, July 25, 1969; children: Taylor Alan, Nathan Lee, Erin Renae. BS, S.D. State U., 1972. Reporter Watertown Pub. Opinion, 1963-65, Sioux Falls (S.D.) Argus Leader, 1969-70; newsman AP, Sioux Falls, 1970-72, Pierre, S.D., 1972-73; newsman-supr. AP, Mpls., 1973-74; corr. AP, Sioux Falls, 1974-75; broadcast exec. AP, Mpls., 1975-78, news editor, 1978-81; news editor Forum Fargo (N.D.)-Moorhead, 1981-85; mng. editor Forum Fargo (N.D.)-Moorehead, 1985—. Sgt. USMC, 1965-69, Vietnam. Mem. AP Mng. Editors Assn. (nat. edn. com. 1986--), Am. Legion (post baseball com. 1986--), Shanley Quarterback Club (pres. 1987--). Republican. Roman Catholic. Home: 1116 17th St N Fargo ND 58102-3329 Office: Forum Pub Co 101 N 5th St Box 2020 Fargo ND 58102*

DEVITT, JOHN WILLIAM, physicist; b. Bayshore, N.Y., Oct. 25, 1959; s. John Gerald and Faith Mary (Fitzgerald) D. BS in Physics, SUNY, Stonybrook, 1981; MS in Physics, Ohio State U., 1984. Lab. asst. Physics Dept., SUNY, Stonybrook, 1980-81; grad. rsch. asst. Physics Dept. Ohio State U., Columbus, 1981-84; infrared evaluation specialist GE Aircraft Engines, Cin., 1984-86, infrared inspection specialist, 1986-88, lead scientist infrared measurements, 1988—. Contbr. articles to profl. jours.; numerous patents in field. Recipient Sanford Moss Meml. Engring. award, 1993. Mem. Soc. Photo Optical Engrs., ASTM. Home: 220 Cannonade Dr Loveland OH 45140-7104 Office: GE Aircraft Engines 1 Neumann Way Mail Drop G104 Cincinnati OH 45215-1915

DEVLIN, JOHN PAUL, performing arts educator; b. Deerfield, Mass., Aug. 24, 1964; s. James Arthur and Mary Regina (Praetz) D.; m. Carol Anne Buttry, Apr. 9, 1961; 1 child, Patrick John. BA in Theatre and History, Allegheny Coll., 1986; MA in Am. History, Syracuse U., 1988, MFA in Drama, 1991. Various positions Black Hills Playhouse, Custer, S.D., 1985-91; proprs. grad. asst. Syracuse (N.Y.) Stage, 1988-91; proprs. carpenter Milw. Repertory Theatre, 1991-94; proprs. artisan Proprs. Prodn., Milw., 1991-94; carpenter No. Stage Co., Milw., 1994; shop asst. U. Wis., Milw., 1994-95; supr., tech. dir., instr. Marquette U., Milw., 1994—. Mem. Theatre Comms. Group, Nat. Soc. Hist. Preservation. Office: Marquette U Helfaer Theatre 525 N 13th St Milwaukee WI 53233

DEVOE, ROBERT DONALD, visual physiologist; b. White Plains, N.Y., Oct. 7, 1934; s. Frank Kenneth and Martha (Josselyn) DeV.; m. Joanne Mattson, July 9, 1960 (div. 1986); children: Catherine Ellen, Edward Edgar; m. Gwendolyn Latta Berghorn, May 20, 1989 (div. 1992). AB, Oberlin Coll., 1956; PhD, The Rockefeller U. From asst. to assoc. prof. Med. Sch. Johns Hopkins U., Balt., 1961-83; prof. Sch. of Optometry Ind. U., Bloomington, 1983—; grantee referee NIH, Washington, 1968—, NSF, Med. Rsch. Coun., Eng., 1973—, B.C. Health Rsch. Found., 1993—, Australian Rsch. Coun., 1993—; manuscript referee to numerous jours., 1960—; rsch. sabbatical Max-Planck Inst. für Biol. Kybernetic, Tübingen, Germany, 1973-74, Sch. Optometry, U. New South Wales, Australia, 1993. Mem. adv. bd. Jour. Comparative Physiology, Berlin, 1983-86; contbr. articles to profl. jours. Recipient Sr. Sci. award Alexander von Humboldt Found., Bonn, Germany, 1973-74; grantee NIH, 1962-91. Mem. AAAS, Assn. for Rsch. in Vision and Ophthalmology, Soc. for Neurosci., Serious Macintosh User's Group (treas.), Alpine Ski Club, Sigma Xi, Phi Beta Kappa. Democrat. Office: Ind U Sch Optometry 800 E Atwater Ave Bloomington IN 47405-3680

DEVOLPI, ALEXANDER, physicist; b. N.Y.C., Feb. 28, 1931; s. Paul Bonaventura and Bertha (Gaber) DeV.; m. Helen Genopolis, 1955 (div. 1977); children: Paul, Dean, Marina, Gregory; m. Judith Carol Klaye, Jan. 14, 1978 (div. 1993). BA in Journalism, Washington and Lee U., 1953; MS in Nuclear Engring. Physics, Va. Poly. Inst., 1957, PhD in Physics, 1967. Physicist, tech. mgr. nuclear diagnostics Argonne (Ill.) Nat. Lab., 1958-90, mgr. treaty verification technology, 1990—; cons., bd. dirs. Fuel Ctrs. Corp. Am., South Bend, Ind., 1970s, U.S.-USSR Disarmament Project, 1985-92. Author: Proliferation, Plutonium, and Policy, 1979; co-author: Born Secret, 1981; contbr. rev. articles on nuclear weapons proliferation, cineradiography, nuclear instrumentation and treaty verification technology to tech. jours. Exec. com. Alliance to End Repression, Chgo., 1969-92. Lt. comdr. USNR, 1953-56. Fellow Am. Phys. Soc.; mem. AAAS, Am. Nuclear Soc., Fedn. Am. Scientists (nat. coun. 1987-92). Office: Argonne Nat Lab Bldg 207 Argonne IL 60439

DEVRIENDT, DAVID MARK, crop adviser, agronomist; b. Fridley, Minn., Apr. 28, 1962; s. Ronald Edward and Jeanette (Petersen) DeV.; m. Mary Bethania Welch, July 11, 1987; children: Mitchell James, Andrea Jean. BS in Agr., U. Wis., 1989. Agronomist Cenex Land-O-Lakes, Kewaunee, Wis., 1990-91, Mt. Horeb (Wis.) Farmers Coop Cenex Land-O-Lakes, 1992-96; agronomy mgr. Middleton (Wis.) Farmers Coop-Cenex Land-O-Lakes, 1996—. Mem. Am. Soc. Agronomy.

DEVRIES, BEVERLY MAE, research recruitment specialist; b. Chgo., Aug. 28, 1935; d. William Fredrick and Wanda Theresa (Kobielusz) Richter; divorced; children: Tracy Lynn DeVries Tucker, April Ann DeVries Alexopaulos. BS, Western Mich. U., 1986, MA, 1994. RN, Mich.; lic. profl. counselor. Staff nurse Mary Free Bed, Grand Rapids, Mich., 1956-57, Butterworth Hosp., Grand Rapids, 1957-63; market researcher Kalamazoo (Mich.) Rsch., Inc., 1965-67; patient educator Bronson Meth. Hosp., Kalamazoo, 1967-78; recruitment supr. Upjohn Rsch. Clinics, Kalamazoo, 1978-95; document reviewer for AIDS rsch. Trilogy Cons. Corp., Kalamazoo, 1995—. Mem. Vol. Action Program. Mem. NAFE, ACA, Ethics Soc., Psi Iota Xi. Democrat. Lutheran. Office: Pharmacia & Upjohn 7000 Portage Rd Kalamazoo MI 49001

DE VRIES, DAVID JOHN, reference assistant; b. Kalamazoo, Nov. 1, 1952; s. Marvin Eugene and Rena (Vander Veen) De V. BA in History, Western Mich. U., 1975, MS in Libr., 1981, MA in History, 1987, MA in Polit. Sci., 1994. Numerous positions Kalamazoo Pub. Libr., 1969-90, local history, reference asst., 1990—. Organist St. Martin of Tours Episcopal Ch., Kalamazoo, 1991—; vol. Kalamazoo Found., 1993, 94, 95. Mem. Am. Guild Organists, Hist. Soc. Mich., Phi Alpha Theta. Republican. Home: 809 Turwill Ln Kalamazoo MI 49006 Office: Kalamazoo Pub Libr 315 S Rose St Kalamazoo MI 49007

DEVRIES, RICHARD BOYD, entrepreneur; b. Muskegon, Mich., Aug. 20, 1953; s. Richard Boyd and Lou Ann (Hobby) DeV. BA in Sci. Biol. Medicine with honors, Wayne State U., 1974; postgrad., Western Mich. U., 1974-75, U. Miami, 1975-77. EKG supr. Trauma Ctr. Bapt. Hosp., 1975-77; prof. rels. rep. Blue Cross & Blue Shield, 1977-80; retail mgr. Jordan Marsh, 1980-83; tng. mgr. Am. Express, 1983-84; mktg.-promotions dir. mktg. adminstrn. Allnet Comms., Inc., 1984-87; founder, owner, exec. dir. De Vries & Assocs., Inc., 1986—. Mem. adv. police dept. City of Chgo., 1991-95; trustee Design Industries Found. for AIDS, Chgo.; bd. dirs. Ill. AIDS Found., vice chmn.; bd. dirs. I.G.L.T.F., Names Project Ill., White Crane Wellness Ctr.; chmn., assoc. bd. dirs. Weiss Meml. Hosp.; advisor com. to Paul Simon 9th Congl. Dist., U.S. Senate, mem. citizens com. to re-elect Ellis B. Levin state rep. 5th Dist., State of Ill.; mem. citizens to re-elect Mayor Richard Daley, City of Chgo., dep. voter registrar, elections judge; mem. Ill. States Attys. Adv. Coun., State of Ill.; seniority adv. com. U. Chgo.; mem. adopt-a-child program Uhlich Children's Home. Recipient U.S. Pillar award Philanthropy Assn. U.S., 1995. Mem. ACLU, Pub. Rels. Soc. Am., Nat. Assn. Self-Employed, Chgo. Area Tech. Assistance Providers, Chgo. Profl. Networking Assn., Donors Forum of Chgo., Nat. Soc. Fundraising Execs., Assn. Vol. Adminstrs., Ill. Assn. Nonprofit Orgns., Publicity Club (Chgo), Univ. Club (Chgo.), Variety Club (Ill.). Democrat. Unitarian.

DE VRIES, ROBERT JOHN, investment banker; b. Pella, Iowa, Aug. 18, 1932; s. John G. and Anna (Kool) m. Patricia Lynn Jackson, Dec. 22, 1962; children: Robert John Jr., Garrett Andrew. BBA, U. Tex., Austin, 1958; MBA, Harvard Grad. Sch. of Bus., Boston, 1960. Registered principal. Security analyst Cyrus J. Lawrence & Sons, N.Y.C., 1960-64, Jas. H. Oliphant and Co., N.Y.C., 1964-66; investment banker William D. Witter Inc., N.Y., 1966-68; v.p. Mgmt. Planning Inc., Princeton, N.J., 1968-73; pres. Cryomed Devices, Inc., Princeton, 1973-80; v.p. Smith Barney, Harris Upham, 1981-84; pres., dir., founder Robert J. De Vries and Co., Inc., Kansas City, 1984—; dir. Aesculapian Concepts, Ltd. Served with USAF, 1952-56. Inst. of Chartered Fin. Analyst, Harvard Club of N.Y., Beta Gamma Sigma. Republican. Presbyterian. Home: 6309 W 102nd St Shawnee Mission KS 66207-1719 Office: De Vries and Co 800 W 47th St Kansas City MO 64112-1251

DE WAART, EDO, conductor; b. Amsterdam, Netherlands, June 1, 1941. Grad. with honors for oboe, Amsterdam Conservatoire, 1962. Oboist, Concertgebouw Orch., Amsterdam, 1963-64, asst. condr., 1966-67; asst. to Leonard Bernstein, N.Y. Philharm., 1965-66; condr. Rotterdam (Netherlands) Philharm., 1967-79, also prin. condr., music dir.; condr. Netherlands Wind Ensemble, 1967-71; condr., music dir., San Francisco Symphony Orch., 1977-85; music dir. Minn. Orch., 1986-95; artistic dir. Netherlands Radio Philharm. Orch., 1989—; chief condr., artistic dir. Sydney (Australia) Symphony Orch., 1993—; guest condr., Amsterdam Concertgebouw, Berlin Philharm., Boston Symphony, Chgo. Symphony, San Francisco Symphony, London Symphony, Cleve. Orch., N.Y. Philharm., Phila. Orch., Sydney (Australia) Symphony Orch., Mostly Mozart Festival, N.Y.C.; condr.: new prodn. Lohengrin, Beyreuth Festival, summer 1979; new prodn. Wagner's Ring, San Francisco Opera, 1985; rec. artist, Philips Records, Virgin Classics, rec. with major European orchs. including New Philharmonia, English Chamber Orch., Royal Philharmonic Orch., Dresden State Orch., Minn. Orch. Recipient 1st prize Metropoulos Competition, N.Y.C., 1964. Office: RFO NOB-Muziekcentrum van, de Omroep Postbus 10, 1200 JB Hilversum The Netherlands also: 52 Williams St Level 5, Sydney NSW 2011, Australia

DEWEESE, JUNE LAFOLLETTE, librarian; b. Trenton, Mo., Aug. 25, 1951; d. Robert D. and Kathryn (Snyder) LaFollette; m. Gary W. DeWeese, June 3, 1972. BA, U. Mo., 1972, MA, 1973. Info. libr. Ellis Libr./U. Mo., Columbia, 1974; head geology libr. U. Mo., Columbia, 1975; libr. social sci./bus. Ellis Libr/.U. Mo., 1975-90, head access svcs., 1990—, interim head tech. svcs., 1994-96. Contbr. articles to profl. jours. Mem. ALA, Mo. Libr. Assn., Columbia Bus. and Profl. Women's Orgn. (pres. 1992-93), Delta Kappa Gamma, Beta Phi Mu. Methodist. Home: 1321 Weaver Columbia MO 65203 Office: U Mo 102A Ellis Libr Columbia MO 65201

DEWEESE, KEITH PATRICK, cinematology researcher; b. Detroit, Aug. 21, 1962; s. Harry Atley and Kathleen Ann (Bennett) DeW. BA, U. Cen. Fla., 1987; MS, Fla. State U., 1989; MA, Columbia Coll., 1994. Libr. Chgo. Pub. Libr., 1990-92, Columbia Coll., Chgo., 1992-94; researcher Columbia Coll., 1994—; adv. bd. Internat. Cinema Mus., Chgo., 1994—. Contbr.: Reel Women, 1992; contbr. to profl. publs. Mem. ALA, Assn. Coll. & Rsch. Librs. Democrat. Roman Catholic. Office: Columbia Coll 600 S Michigan Ave Chicago IL 60626

DEWEY, CRAIG DOUGLAS, operations executive; b. Milw., Apr. 8, 1950; s. RalphEarl and Suzanne Dewey; m. Madeline A. Reedy, Sept. 28, 1989. BSME, U. Wis., 1974. Registered profl. engr., Wis. Mgr. engring. Harnischfeger Corp., Milw., 1974-83, dir. engring., 1986-90; chief engr. Fairmont Railway Motors, Fairmont, Minn., 1983-86; v.p. engring. Pemco, Inc., Sheboygan, Wis., 1990-91; dir. engring. Quad/Tech, Sussex, Wis., 1991-92, dir. ops., 1992—. Patentee in field. Mem. Mensa. Home: 7155 N Green Tree Ct River Hills WI 53217-3708 Office: Quad/Tech N64w23110 Main St Sussex WI 53089-3230

DEWINE, R. MICHAEL, U.S. Senator, lawyer; b. Springfield, Ohio, Jan. 5, 1947; s. Richard and Jean DeWine; m. Frances Struewing, June 3, 1967; children: Patrick, Jill, Rebecca, John, Brian, Alice, Mark, Anna. BS in Edn., Miami U., Oxford, Ohio, 1969; JD, Ohio No. U., 1972. Bar: Ohio 1972, U.S. Supreme Ct. 1977. Asst. pros. atty. Greene County, Xenia, Ohio, 1973-75, pros. atty., 1977-81; mem. Ohio Senate, 1981-82, 98th, 99th, 100th, 101st Congress from 7th Ohio dist., Washington, 1983-90; lt. gov. State of Ohio, Columbus, Ohio, 1991-94; mem. U.S. Senate, 1995—. Republican. Roman Catholic. Home: 2587 Conley Rd Cedarville OH 45314-9525

DEWING, DENIS EUGENE, school counselor; b. Oshkosh, Wis., July 8, 1940; s. Robert Clarence and Loretta Marie (Karst) D.; m. Cheryl Lee White, Aug. 5, 1967; children: Jesse Jonathan, Jamie Paul. BA, Cath. U. of Am., 1963; MS, U. Wis., Milw., 1970. Profl. sch. counselor (pre-k-12); cert. traffic sch. instr. French and Latin tchr. Francis Jordan H.S., Milw., 1963-64; French, Am. History and World Geography tchr. Lourdes Acad., Oshkosh, 1966-67; tchr., counselor Dominican H.S., Whitefish Bay, Wis., 1967-70; guidance dir. St. Mary's H.S., Menasha, Wis., 1970-75; counselor grade 6-9 Maplewood Jr. H.S., Menasha, 1975-78; counselor grade 9-12 Menasha Sr. H.S., 1978-88; elem. sch. counselor Jefferson, Nicolet, Clovis Grove, Menasha, 1988-93; counselor grade 9-12 Menasha Sr. H.S., 1993—; numerous coms. Menasha Sch. Dist., 1975—. Author: (booklet) Scholarship and Financial Aid Information, 1994. Screener Best Friends of Neenah-Menasha, Inc., 1990—; lectr., small group leader, bd. religious edn. mem., St. Bernard Cath. Ch., Appleton, Wis., 1980—; pres., bd. dirs. Youth-Go Inc., Neenah, 1983-89. Achievements include Appreciation Plaque and Gavel Youth-Go, Inc., 1983-89. Mem. Wis. Sch. Counselor Assn., Am. Fedn. Tchrs., Wis. Fedn. Tchrs., Menasha Tchrs. Union. Roman Catholic. Home: 1112 Visgro St Menasha WI 54952 Office: Menasha HS 420 7th St Menasha WI 54952

DEWITT, MICHELLE LYNN, media company administrator; b. Grand Haven, Mich., Nov. 13, 1962; d. Glen William DeWitt and Mary Elizabeth (Boyd) Vivian. AA in Bus., Muskegon Community Coll., 1983; BBA, Western Mich. U., 1985. Office mgr. Tony Betten Ford, Grand Rapids, Mich., 1985-89; acct. exec. Structural Concepts/Olsten Temporary Svc., Spring Lake, Mich., 1989-90; media dir. The VertiMark Group Inc., Grand Rapids, 1990-96; mgr. devel. and promotions Gnu Media, Grand Rapids, Mich., 1996—. Mktg. cons. ARC, Grand Rapids, 1992-93; social events com. Am. Cancer Soc., 1994-95. Mem. Am. Mktg. Assn., Bus. and Profl. Advt. Assn. (treas. Western Mich. chpt. 1992-93), Bus. Mktg. Assn. Western Mich. (pres. 1993-94, membership com. 1994-95). Home: 460 Hampton Ln NW Apt 2A Walker MI 49544 Office: Gnu Media 1324 Lake Dr SE Ste 2 Grand Rapids MI 49506

DEWITT, SHEILA HOBBS, research director; b. Medina, N.Y., May 23, 1960; d. Arnold James and Marcia June (Cady) Hobbs; m. Joseph Arthur DeWitt, Sept. 5, 1992; 1 child, Leah Therese. BA in Chemistry, Cornell U., 1981; PhD in Chemistry, Duke U., 1986. Lab. rsch. asst. FMC Agrl. Chem. Divsn., Middleport, N.Y., 1979-81; rsch. chemist FMC Agrl. Chem. Divsn., Princeton, N.J., 1982, process chemist, 1986-88; prep lab. supr. Duke U., Durham, N.C., 1983, teaching asst., 1982-86, rsch. asst., 1983-86; scientist Parke-Davis Pharm. Rsch., Ann Arbor, Mich., 1988-89, sr. scientist, 1989-91, rsch. assoc., 1991-93, sr. rsch. assoc., 1993-95, chmn. molecular diversity project team, 1993-95; tchr. nat. workshops and short courses; chmn. nat. symposia. Mem. editl. bd. Pharm. News, Molecular Diversity and Drug Discovery Today jours.; contbr. articles to sci. jours.; pioneer in lab. robotics, 1995. Recipient SCITEL-TNO award, 1994. Mem. AAAS, N.Y. Acad. Sci., Am. Chem. Soc., Ann Arbor Art Assn., Ann Arbor Womens Painters, Phi Lambda Upsilon (v.p. 1985-86), Sigma Xi. Office: Parke-Davis 2800 Plymouth Rd Ann Arbor MI 48105-2430

DEWITZ, LOREN, state legislator; m. Judith DeWitz; 2 children. BS, N.D. State U. Farmer, state rep. dist. 14, 1991—; mem. appropriations, human resources divsn. coms. N.D. Ho. Reps.; bd. dirs. Kidder Co. Water Resource. Recipient Great Am. Family award, 1980. Mem. VFW, 4-H (leader), Farm Bur., Am. Legion. Republican. Home: RR 1 Box 82 Tappen ND 58487-9619 Office: ND Ho of Reps State Capitol Bismarck ND 58505*

DEWOODY, GEARY MICHAEL, marketing professional; b. Sherman, Tex., Dec. 15, 1947; s. Henry L. and Ima Jean (Jones) DeW.; m. Johnnie Dee Russell, May 29, 1971 (div. June 3, 1975); m. Susan Kay Atkinson, June 12, 1976. EdB, U. Okla., 1970; AA in Computer Sci., Tulsa Jr. Coll., 1983; MBA in Mktg., U. Rochester, 1992. Tchr. various, Okla., 1970-78; sales mgr. Saied Music Co., Tulsa, 1978-83; systems analyst Occidental Petroleum, Tulsa, 1983-87, Eastman Kodak, Rochester, N.Y., 1987-88; mgr. exec. support systems Eastman Kodak, Rochester, 1989-92; mgr. field tech. support Eastman Kodak, Chgo., 1993-94, dir. tech. mkt. devel., 1995—. Pres. DuPage South Camp, Gideons Internat., Lisle, Ill., 1993-95; pres. Toastmasters, Tulsa, 1983-85. Republican. Home: 2547 Sun Valley Rd Lisle IL 60532 Office: Eastman Kodak Co 343 State St Rochester NY 14650

DEWOSKIN, ALAN ELLIS, lawyer; b. St. Louis, Sept. 10, 1940; s. Samuel S. and Lillian (Sachs) DeW.; m. Iris Lynn Shapiro, Aug. 15, 1942; children: Joseph, Henry, Franklin. BA, Washington U., St. Louis, 1962, JD, 1965; postgrad. U.S. Army Command and Gen. Staff Coll., 1978, U.S. Army War Coll., 1985. Bar: Mo. 1968, U.S. Dist. Ct. (ea. dist.) Mo. 1968, U.S. Ct. Appeals (8th cir.) 1969, U.S. Ct. Mil. Appeals 1976, U.S. Supreme Ct. 1990. Pvt. practice law, St. Louis, 1968-82, prin. Alan E. DeWoskin, P.C., St. Louis, 1982—. Active Boy Scouts Am. Col. JAGC, USAR Ret., 1962-92. Fellow Am. Bar Found.; mem. ABA (chmn. gen. practice sect. 1985-86, mem. Ho. of Dels., 1986-87, assembly del. 1988-91, standing com. mil. law, 1988-91, standing com. assembly resolutions 1988-91, vice chmn. task force solo and small firm practitioners), Assn. Trial Lawyers Am., Mo. Bar Assn. (chmn. gen. practice com. 1987-90, chmn. computer interest groups 1988-90), Bar Assn. Met. St. Louis (mem. exec. com. 1993-94, bd. govs. 1994-95, chmn. solo and small firm sect., 1993-95), Mo. Assn. Trial Attys. (exec. com. 1993-94, bd. govs. 1994-95, chair sect. solo and small firms practitioners 1993-95), Masons (past master, dir. 1972—). Home: 14030 Deltona Dr Chesterfield MO 63017-3311 Office: 225 S Meramec Ave Ste 426 Saint Louis MO 63105-3511

DEXHEIMER, KATHRYN ELAINE, adult day care and health promotion executive; b. Independence, Mo., July 30, 1948; d. Elner Earl and Mary Louise (Pratt) Fye; m. Gregory R. Dexheimer, Mar. 2, 1970; 1 child, Deborah Diane. Diploma, Independence Sanitarium and, Hosp. Sch. Nursing, 1970; BSN, Graceland Coll., 1987; MSN, U. Mo., Kansas City, 1989. RN, Mo., Kans.; cert. BLS. Staff nurse VA Med. Ctr., Kansas City,

Mo., 1970-72, St. Luke's Hosp., Kansas City, 1975-77; instr. Kansas City (Mo.) Bd. Edn., 1977-78, Independence (Mo.) Bd. Edn., 1978-82; nurse coord. adult day care Independence (Mo.) Sanitarium and Hosp., 1982-84; rsch. cons. ANA, Kansas City, 1989; adj. faculty Webster Univ., Kansas City, 1990; nursing instr. Avila Coll., Kansas City, 1990-94; health promotion mgr. Clinicare, Kansas City, 1994—; adj. faculty Avila Coll., 1994. Mem. Mo. Nurses Assn. (bd. dirs. 1994), Midwest Nursing Rsch. Soc., Reorganized Ch. of Jesus Christ of Latter Day Saints Profl. Nurses Assn., Sigma Theta Tau (sec. chpt. 1992), Phi Kappa Phi. Office: Vis Nurse Assn Svcs of Health Midwest 527 W 39th St Kansas City MO 64111-2925

DEYNEKA, PETER, JR., religious organization executive; b. Chgo., Sept. 13, 1931; s. Peter and Vera (Demidovich) D.; m. Anita Marson, June 15, 1968. BA in Bibl. Lit., Wheaton Coll., 1953; MDiv, No. Bapt. Sem., 1957; Doctorate (hon.), No. Bapt. Seminary, 1996. Missionary Slavic Gospel Assn., Ecuador, Argentina, 1961-63; asst. dir. Slavic Gospel Assn., Chgo., 1966-74; pres. Slavic Gospel Assn., Wheaton, Ill., 1975-91; dir. Russian Bible Inst., Buenos Aires, 1962-63; missionary, chaplain U.S. Army Seoul, Republic of Korea, 1963-65; elder Coll. Ch., Wheaton, 1983-85; guest lectr. Fuller Theol. Sem., 1984, Grad. Sch., Wheaton Coll., 1984; pres. Russian Ministries, Wheaton, 1991—; guest spkr. TV and radio programs; cons. on religion in USSR and Eastern Europe, Billy Graham Assn., Trans World Radio, others. Co-author: Christians in the Shadow of the Kremlin, 1974, Peter Dynamite, 1975, A Song in Siberia, 1977. Mem. Interdenominational Fgn. Mission Assn. (bd. dirs.), S.Am. Crusades (bd. dirs.), Soc. for Study Religion and Communism (bd. dirs. 1979-81), Romanian Missionary Soc. (bd. dirs.), Soc. for Ctrl. Asian Nationalities (coun. advisors), The Commission (1992—). Office: Russian Ministries PO Box 496 1415 Hill St Wheaton IL 60189

DEYO, RICHARD ARTHUR, insurance agent, investment officer; b. Detroit, June 4, 1952; s. Leroy and Marian Evelyn (Powers) D.; m. Sara Marie Wood, May 22, 1976; 1 child, Brian Richard. Attended, Ea. Mich. U., Ypsilanti, 1970-72; cert., Bob Jones U., Greenville, S.C., 1975; BS in Pre Seminary, Baptist Bible Coll. of Pa., Clarks Summit, 1982; attended, Ball State U., Muncie, Ind., 1986-87. Polit. action com. coord. Butcher For Congress, Kokomo, Ind., 1986; asst. mgr. vol. svcs. PAX, Indpls., 1987; investment rep. First Affiliated Securities, Kokomo, 1987-89; ins. agent Northwestern Mutual Life, Kokomo, 1989-94, 95—; investment officer Robert W. Baird & Co., Inc., Kokomo, 1989-94, 95—; cons. fundraising Moody Broadcasting Network Moody Bible Inst., Kokomo, 1993-94; dir. pub. relations Ind. Family Inst., Indpls., 1994; cons. fundraising The Catalyst Group, Kokomo, 1995—. Columnist local newspaper. Del. Republican State Conv., Indpls., 1988, 92; precinct committeeman Republican Party, Kokomo, 1988, 90, 92, 94, 96; pres. Habitat For Humanity, 1990-91; pres., chmn. bd. dirs., project mgr. Ctrl. Ind. Christian Broadcasting Inc., Kokomo, 1991-93; pres., chmn. bd. Ctrl. Ind. Christian Ministries, 1994—. Mem. Kokomo Assn. of Life Underwriters (v.p. 1996—), Kokomo/Howard County C. of C. (mem. Legis. Affairs Com., 1992—). Baptist. Home and Office: Northwestern Mutual Life 2626 S 200 E Kokomo IN 46902

DHALIWAL, AMRIK SINGH, biology educator; b. Punjab, India, Nov. 17, 1934; came to U.S. 1957; s. Kapur Singh and Kishan Kaur (Bajwa) D.; m. Gurmeet Gill, Nov. 18, 1962; children: Roopinder Kaur, Deepinder Kaur. MA, Utah State U., 1959, PhD, 1962. Postdoctoral fellow Utah State U., Logan, 1962-64, rsch. assoc., 1965-66; asst. prof. biology Loyola U., Chgo., 1966-71, assoc. prof. biology, 1971-75, prof. biology, 1975—. Home: 1415 Woodhill Dr Northbrook IL 60062-4660 Office: Loyola U 6525 N Sheridan Rd Chicago IL 60626-5311

DHAMEE, M(OHAMMED) SAEED, anesthesiology educator; b. Simla, India, July 8, 1936; came to U.S., 1971; s. M. Ibrahim and Talat (Khatoon) D.; m. Margaret Angela Egan; children: Yousuf I., Saleem. MB, BS, Dow Med. Coll., Karachi, Pakistan, 1960. Diplomate Am. Bd. Anesthesiology. Resident physician Jinnah Postgrad. Med. Ctr., Karachi, 1961-62, United Oxford (Eng.) Hosps. (Cowley and Osler), 1962-64; resident physician, registrar Hallam Hosp., West Bromwich, Eng., 1965-68, post registration resident ob-gyn., 1971; registrar Dudley Rd. Hosp., Birmingham, Eng., 1968-71; asst. physician, cons. West Bromwich Group Hosps., 1971; resident in anesthesiology Med. Coll. Wis., Milw., 1971-74, asst. prof. anesthesiology, 1974-81, assoc. prof., 1981-85, prof., 1985—, dir. cardiac anesthesia, 1979-81, vice chmn. dept. anesthesiology, 1989—; clin. dir. anesthesia Milwaukee County Med. Complex, Milw., 1980-92. Contbr. articles to profl. jours., chpts. to books. Fellow Am. Coll. Anesthesiology, Royal Soc. Medicine, Milw. Acad. Medicine; mem. Assn. Univ. Anesthesiologists, Am. Soc. Anesthesiologists, Soc. Cardiovascular Anesthesiologists, Am. Soc. Critical Care Medicine, Internat. Anesthesia Rsch. Soc., History of Anesthesia Soc., Am. Assn. for History of Medicine, Assn. Pakistani Physicians N.Am. (pres. Wis. chpt. 1996—), Milw. Soc. Anesthesiologists (treas. 1982-83), Westmoor Country Club. Home: 20795 Bradford Ln Brookfield WI 53045-1706 Office: Med Coll Wis Dept Anesthesiology 8700 W Wisconsin Ave Milwaukee WI 53226-3512

DHILLON, ROBIN K. J. S., cardiac, thoracic and vascular surgeon; b. Singapore City, Singapore, Sept. 11, 1958; came to U.S., 1970; s. Karam Singh and Gurbachan Kaur Dhillon; m. Sharon Marie Dhillon, Mar. 31, 1989; children: Kathryn Murro, Aleksander Karam. BS in Biology, Wash. State U., 1980; MD, Hahnemann U., 1986. Diplomate Am. Bd. Surgery. Intern in gen. surgery Univ. Hosps. Cleve., 1986-88; resident in gen. surgery U. Miss. Med. Ctr., Jackson, 1988-91, fellow in cardiothoracic surgery, 1991-93; fellow in transplantation Tex. Heart Inst., Houston, 1993; pvt. practice, Denver, 1993-94, Rapid City, S.D., 1994—. Fellow ACS (assoc.), Soc. Thoracic Surgeons (assoc.); mem. Am. Coll. Chest Physicians. Office: Cardiac Vascular & Thoracic Surgery PC 350 N Elk St Ste B Rapid City SD 57701

DHUSSA, RAMESH CHANDRA, geography educator; b. Dumka, Bihar, India, Jan. 21, 1938; came to U.S., 1974; s. Sardari Lal and Lajwanti Dhussa; m. Aruna Kapoor, Mar. 23, 1977; children: Ruchika, Ankita. BA with honors, Patna (India) U., 1959, MA, 1961; MA, Akron U., 1976; PhD, Kent State U., 1986. Lectr. Magadh U., Bodhgaya, India, 1962-74; teaching fellow Kent (Ohio) State U., 1978-79; lectr. U. Akron (Ohio), 1980-88; vis. asst. prof. SW Mo. State U., Springfield, 1988-89; vis. asst. prof. Drake U., Des Moines, Iowa, 1989-92, asst. prof., 1992—. Author short stories. Mem. Assn. Am. Geographers, Nat. Assn. Geographers India (life), Geography Alliance Iowa (steering com. 1991—). Hindu. Office: Drake U Dept Geography Des Moines IA 50311

DIAL, DAVID EMORY, library director; b. Cleve., Apr. 17, 1955; s. Robert Joel and Donna Louise (Hudson) D.; m. Sharon Ann Takacs, May 18, 1985; children: Andrew J., Amy Elizabeth, Melissa Marie. BA, Baldwin-Wallace Coll., 1977; M of Libr. and Info. Sci., Clarion State U., 1978. Dir. New Madison (Ohio) Pub. Libr., 1978-82, Grafton-Midview Pub. Libr., Grafton, Ohio, 1982—. Co-author Lorain County Funding Formula, 1991. Mem. Grafton Devel. Com., 1992. Mem. ALA, Ohio Libr. Coun., Miami Valley Librs. Consortium (sec. 1981), Lorain County Libr.'s Coun. (pres. 1994), Grafton Bus. Assn. (sec. 1995), Kiwanis Club Grafton-Midview. Republican. Home: 382 Chapel Cir Berea OH 44017

DIAL, DENISE LORRAINE, historian; b. Ottumwa, Iowa, Apr. 16, 1957; d. Charles Francis and Barbara Jean (Knox) D.; m. Claude Ross Harryman, Jan. 19, 1980. AA, Indian Hills Coll., 1988; BA, William Penn Coll., 1990; MA, N.E. Mo. State U., 1992; postgrad., Iowa State U., 1992—. Instr./grad. asst. Iowa State U., Ames, 1992—. Master sgt. USAR, 1979—. Mem. Am. Hist. Assn., Midwest Polit. Sci. Assn., Phi Alpha Theta. Home: RR 1 Box 84 Moulton IA 52572-9732 Office: Iowa State U Ross Hall Ames IA 50011

DIAL, ELEANORE MAXWELL, foreign language educator; b. Norwich, Conn., Feb. 21, 1929; d. Joseph Walter and Irene (Beetham) Maxwell; BA, U. Bridgeport (Conn.), 1951; MA in Spanish, Mexico City Coll., 1955; PhD, U. Mo., 1968; m. John E. Dial, Aug. 27, 1959. Mem. faculty U. Wisc.-Milw., 1968-75, Ind. State U., Terre Haute, 1975-78, Bowling Green (Ohio) State U., 1978-79; asst. prof. dept. fgn. langs. and lits. Iowa State U., Ames, 1979-85, assoc. prof. 1985—; cons. pub. co.; participant workshops; del. 1st World Congress Women Journalists and Writers, Mex., 1975, also mem. edn. commn. NDEA grantee, 1967; Center Latin Am. grantee, 1972; Nat. Endowment Humanities summer seminar UCLA, 1981, U. Calif.-Santa Barbara, 1984; active Gov's. Commn. on Fgn. Langs. and Internat. Studies, 1988-95. Mem. Am. Assn. Tchrs. Spanish and Portuguese, Midwest MLA, MLA, N. Central Council Latin Americanists, Midwest Assn. Latin Am. Studies, Clermont County Geneal. Soc., Ohio Geneal. Soc., Caribbean Studies Assn., Phi Beta Delta, Phi Sigma Iota, Sigma Delta Pi. Contbr. articles and revs. to scholarly jours. Home: 190 North St Batavia OH 45103-2911 Office: Iowa State U Ames IA 50011

DIAMANT, ALFRED, political science educator; b. Vienna, Austria, Sept. 25, 1917; came to U.S., 1940, naturalized, 1942; s. Ignatz and Julia (Herzog) D.; m. Mary Ann Redmon, Mar. 18, 1943; children—Steven R., Alice L. Student, Textilschule Vienna, 1935-36; A.B. with highest honors, Ind. U., 1947; M.A., Yale, 1950, Ph.D., 1957. Textile engr. Austria, Yugoslavia, U.S., 1936-38, 40-42; from instr. to assoc. prof. polit. sci. U. Fla., 1950-60; assoc. prof. to prof. polit. sci. Haverford Coll., 1960-67, chmn. dept., 1963-67; prof. polit. sci. and west European studies Ind. U., Bloomington, 1967—; chmn. dept. Ind. U., 1977-80, dir. grad. studies, 1969-71, dir. West European studies program, 1971-77; Vis. assoc. prof. polit. sci. Yale U., 1958-59, Columbia, summer 1961; vis. prof. Ruhr U. Bochum, 1966-67; vis. scholar Fund for the Future, U. Alta., 1983; co-chmn. Coun. for European Studies, 1976-79; cons. U.S. Office Edn., 1965-66, Temple U., 1977, 84, Dickinson Coll., 1980, Am. Scandinavian Found., 1977—, U. Kerala, India, 1977, 79; sr. rsch. assoc. European adminstrn. rsch. project, 1966-70; guest scholar Brookings Instn., 1980-81. Author: Austrian Catholics and the First Republic: Democracy, Capitalism and the Social Order, 1918-34, 1960 (trans. into German, Italian 1964), Modellbetrachtung der Entwicklungsverwaltung, 1967; contbr. Approaches to Development: Politics, Administration and Change, 1966 ,Temporal Dimensions of Development Administration, 1970, Frontiers of Developmental Administration, 1971, Sozialstruktur und Politik in Frankreich, 1976, Worker's Self-Management: The West European Experience, 1977, The Cost of Federalism, 1984, Politikwissenschaftliche Entwicklungslaenderforschung, 1986; assoc. mng. editor Jour. Politics, 1950-55; editorial bd. Adminstrn. and Society, 1968-84; contbr. chpts. to 7 books, numerous articles to profl. jours.; work reprinted in 7 readers. Vestryman Trinity Episcopal Ch., Bloomington, 1970-73, 77-80, 84-87, 94-95. Decorated Purple Heart, Bronze Star.; Tchr. study grantee Danforth Found., 1955; Fulbright travel grantee, 1966; Guggenheim fellow, 1973-74; Fulbright sr. research grantee, 1973-74; AMOCO Teaching award, 1975; recipient Alumni Teaching award Ind. U., 1985. Mem. Am. Polit. Sci. Assn., Internat. Polit. Sci. Assn., Midwest Polit. Sci. Assn. (v.p. 1971-72), AAUP (chmn. Haverford Coll. chpt. 1962-64), De Tocqueville Soc., Phi Beta Kappa, Pi Sigma Alpha. Democrat. Home: 938 Juniper Pl Bloomington IN 47408

DIAMOND, DAVID (SID I., JR. DAVISON), communications educator; b. Howard, S.D., 1936; s. Imogene (Reeve) Davison. BS in Journalism, U. So. Miss., 1958; MA in Profl. Writing, U. So. Calif., 1982; MA in English, N.W. Mo. State U., 1986; PhD in English, Columbia Pacific U., 1992. With programming dept. RKO-Gen. Broadcasting, L.A., 1965-66, Westinghouse Broadcasting, L.A., 1967-68, RKO-Gen. Broadcasting KFRC, San Francisco, 1968-71, CBS, San Francisco, 1972-76, KIIS Radio, L.A., 1971-75, Cox Communications, San Francisco, 1976-82. Author: (as Link Pennington) Slade Western series; author two works of poetry. With U. S. Army, 1958-59. Home: Box 966 Spearfish SD 57783 Office: Comm Dept Black Hills State U Spearfish SD 57799

DIAMOND, DEBORAH BEROSET, writer; b. Flint, Mich., Feb. 1, 1960; d. John Edward and Martha Jean (Hastings) Beroset; m. Michael Alan Diamond, May 29, 1988 (div. 1996); children: Tova Beroset, Simone Beroset. B Journalism, U. Mo., 1987. Staff writer Gulf News, Dubai, United Arab Emirates, 1980-81; freelance writer Dubai, 1981-83; intern Ladies' Home Jour., N.Y.C., 1986; freelance writer Columbia, Mo., 1986—; instr. journalism Westminster Coll., Fulton, Mo., 1988, U. Mo., Columbia, 1993, 95. Editor, Vet. Med. Rev. mag., Columbia, 1987-90; contbg. editor Ladies' Home Jour., N.Y.C., 1994—; contbr. articles to various publs. Mem. Am. Soc. Journalists and Authors, Nat. Book Critics Circle, Investigative Reporters and Editors, Soc. Profl. Journalists. Democrat. Jewish. Home and Office: 1740 W River Bluff Ct Columbia MO 65201-9374

DIAMOND, EUGENE CHRISTOPHER, lawyer, hospital administrator; b. Oceanside, Calif., Oct. 19, 1952; s. Eugene Francis and Rosemary (Wright) D.; m. Mary Theresa O'Donnell, Jan. 20, 1984; children: Eugene John, Kevin Seamus, Hannah Rosemary, Seamus Michael. BA, U. Notre Dame, 1974; MHA, St. Louis U., 1978, JD, 1979. Bar: Ill. 1979. Staff atty. AUL Legal Def. Fund, Chgo., 1979-80; adminstrv. asst. Holy Cross Hosp., Chgo., 1980-81, asst. adminstr., 1981-82, v.p., 1982-83, counsel to adminstr., 1980—, exec. v.p., 1983-91; exec. v.p., COO St. Margaret Mercy Healthcare Ctrs., Hammond, Ind., 1991-93, pres. CEO, 1993; cons. Birthright of Chgo., 1979—, mem. benefit com., 1981—; bd. dirs. Hammond C. of C., 1993, North West Ind. Forum. Mem. Ill. State Bar Assn., Chgo. Bar Assn. Mgmt. Roman Catholic. Office: St Margaret Mercy HealthcareCtrs 5454 Hohman Ave Hammond IN 46320-1931

DIAMOND, SUSAN ZEE, management consultant; b. Okla., Aug. 20, 1949; d. Louis Edward and Henrietta (Wood) D.; m. Allan T. Devitt, July 27, 1974. AB (Nat. Merit scholar, GRTS scholar), U. Chgo., 1970; MBA, DePaul U., 1979; Cert. office automation profl. Dir. study guide prodn. Am. Sch. Co., Chgo., 1972-75; publs. supr. Allied Van Lines, Broadview, Ill., 1975-78, sr. account svcs. rep., 1978-79; pres. Diamond Assocs. Ltd., Melrose Park, Ill., 1978—; condr. seminars Am. Mgmt. Assn. Author: How to Talk More Effectively, 1972, Preparing Administrative Manuals, 1981, How to Manage Administrative Operations, 1981, How to be an Effective Secretary in the Modern Office, 1982, Records Management: A Practical Guide, 1983, 3d edit., 1995; co-author: Finance Without Fear, 1983; editor Mobility Trends, 1975-78; contbr. numerous articles to profl. jours. Mem. Inst. Mgmt. Accts., Assn. Records Mgrs. and Adminstrs., Am. Mgmt. Assn., Assn. Info. and Image Mgmt., Adventuresses of Sherlock Holmes, Delta Mu Delta. Office: 2851 Pearl Ave Melrose Park IL 60164-1421

DIAS, JERRY RAY, chemistry educator; b. Oakland, Calif., Oct. 26, 1940; s. Francis Frederick and Margurette Ruth (Bass) D.; m. Barbara Jean Turner, July 13, 1959; children: Harvey William, Jennifer Jean. BS with honors in Chemistry, San Jose State U., 1965; PhD, Ariz. State U., 1970. Chem. technologist Filters Inc., Milpitas, Calif., 1959-61; chem. technologist, supr. trainee Amelco, Mt. View, Calif., 1962; chem. technologist, plating supr. Huggins Lab., Sunnyvale, Calif., 1963-64; rsch. asst. San Jose (Calif.) State Coll., 1964-65; grad. teaching asst. Ariz. State U., Tempe, 1965-66; night instr. Chabot Coll., Hayward, Calif., 1970-72; asst. prof. chemistry U. Mo., Kansas City, 1972-78, assoc. prof., 1978-84, prof., 1984—; cons. chemist region VII, EPA, Kansas City, summers 1979-80, Johnson County (Kans.) Emergency Preparedness, 1988—; Chinese lectr. to Yan Tai, 1990; Fulbright lectr., 1980. Author: Polycyclic Hydrocarbons, Parts A and B, 1987, 1988, Molecular Orbital Calculations Using Chemical Graph Theory, 1993; contbr. over 100 articles to profl. jours. Predoctoral fellow NIH, 1967-70, postdoctoral fellow Stanford U., 1970-72, faculty fellow U. Kansas City, 1995-96. Fellow Am. Inst. Chemists; mem. ASTM, NSPE, AICE, Am. Chem. Soc., Am. Electroplater's Soc. Republican. Roman Catholic. Office: U Mo Dept Chemistry Kansas City MO 64110-2499

DIASIO, RICHARD LEONARD, power transmission executive, sports facility executive; b. Bridgeport, Conn., Nov. 25, 1937; s. Daniel Joseph and Rose Sarah (Agasi) D.; m. Julia Ann Krhla, Oct. 14, 1961; children: Richard J., Laura L., Christopher S. AS in Mech. Engring., Bridgeport Engring. Inst., 1965. Engr. U.S. Elec. Motors, Milford, Conn., 1962-64; sales profl. Reliance Electric, Hamden, Conn., 1964-66; sales mgr. Dynamatic div. Eaton Corp., Fairfield, N.J., 1966-72; mgr. regional sales Harnischfeger Corp., Woodbridge, N.J., 1972-74; mgr. nat. sales Kanematsu-Gosho, South Plainfield, N.J., 1974-77; dir. mktg. Ind. Gear Works, Indpls., 1977-78, gen. mgr., 1978-80; pres. Ind. Power Transmission Systems, Inc., Indpls, 1980—; pres. Putnam Park Corp., Putnam County, Ind., 1990—. With USAF, 1955-59. Mem. Soc. Mfg. Engrs. (sr.), Dramatists Guild, Authors League Am. Republican. Roman Catholic. Office: Ind Power Transmission Sys 470 E Northfield Dr Brownsburg IN 46112

DIAZ, KEVIN BRUCE, journalist; b. Genoa, Italy, Oct. 25, 1957; s. Henry George and Muriel Mae (Matthews) D.; m. Jean Ann Baker, May 30, 1980 (div. Oct. 1984); m. Judy Anne Glunz, Aug. 20, 1994. BA in Philosophy with honors, George Washington U., 1980; MA in Journalism/Mass Comm., U. Minn., 1984. Mng. editor Minnesota Daily, Mpls., 1983-84; reporter Star Tribune, Mpls., 1984—. Reporter: newspaper series on gangs (Minn. AP award 1991). Mem., steward Newspaper Guild of the Twin Cities, Mpls., 1984—. Mem. Soc. Profl. Journalists. Office: Star Tribune 425 Portland Ave Minneapolis MN 55488

DIAZ-FRANCO, CARLOS, surgeon, anatomist, anesthesiologist; b. Valparaiso, Chile, Nov. 9, 1956; came to U.S., 1985; s. Ismael Segundo and Aida Rosa (Franco-Huerta) Diaz-Labarca; m. Jennifer Ann Leepard, Mar. 31, 1989 (div. May 1993). MD, U. Valparaiso, Chile, 1981. Instr. anatomy Sch. of Medicine Univ. Valparaiso, Chile, 1982; surgery resident U. Valparaiso, Chile, 1982-85; asst. prof. anatomy, surgery Univ. Valparaiso, Chile, 1983-89; vis. prof. anatomy Med. Coll. of Ohio, Toledo, 1985-86, 88-89; surgeon, pvt. practice Valparaiso U. Hosp., Chile, 1986-89; surgery resident Sinai Hosp., Detroit, 1990-91, anesthesiology resident, 1991-94; with dept. anesthesia Cook County Hosp., Chgo., 1994—. Contbr. articles to profl. jours. Grantee WHO, 1985-86, Ednl. Commn. for Foreign Med. Grads., 1988-89. Fellow AMA, Am. Soc. Anesthesiologists, Latin Am. Soc. Regional Anesthesia. Roman Catholic.

DICARLO, DAVID LAWRENCE, facilities maintenance professional; b. Natick, Mass., Apr. 2, 1957; s. Victor Joseph and Delia (Russo) DiC.; m. Mary Louise Farnsworth, Jan. 2, 1982; children: Matthew, Timothy, Thomas. BS in Bus. Adminstrn., Duquesne U. cert. architectural drafter. Draftsman Salvucci Engrs., Pitts., 1975-77; store mgr. Picway Shoes The Kobacker Co., Columbus, Ohio, 1981-83, area supr. Picway Shoes, 1983-85, asst. mgr. store ops., 1985-91, property mgr., 1991-94; mgr. facilities svc. and maintenance Discovery Zone, Inc., Chgo., 1994—; Mem. bd. dirs., founder Profl. Retail Store Maintenance Assn., 1995—; mem. bd. dirs. Maintenance Adv. Bd. Store Planning, Equipment and Construction Svcs. (SPECS), 1995—. Democrat. Roman Catholic. Home: 22 W 416 Tamarack Dr Glen Ellyn IL 60137 Office: Discovery Zone Inc 110 E Broward Blvd Fort Lauderdale FL 33301

DICE, JEFFREY NILES, health care administrator; b. Indpls., Aug. 22, 1948; s. Niles L. and Suzanne (Murdock) D.; m. Mary Virginia Merrell, Oct. 30, 1993. BA, U. Evansville, 1970; MSW, Ind. U., 1975. ACSW. Caseworker Vanderburgh County Dept. Pub. Works, Evansville, Ill., 1970-72; social worker Welborn Bapt. Hosp., Evansville, 1973; regional social worker cons. United Mine Workers Health and Retirement Funds, Evansville, 1975-76; dir. partial hospitalization Green River Comp. Care Ctr., Henderson, Ky., 1976-77; v.p. Welborn Bapt. Hosp., Evansville, 1977—. Bd. dirs. Vand. County United Way, Evansville, 1995, Neighborhood Ecom. Coun., Evansville, 1985—, ARC, 1987-94. Child abuse prevention grant Am. Legion Child Welfare Assn., 1980. Mem. Rotary. Office: Welborn Bapt Hosp 401 SE 6th St Evansville IN 47713

DI CHIERA, DAVID, performing arts impresario; b. McKeesport, Pa., Apr. 8, 1937; s. Cosimo and Maria (Pezzaniti) DiC.; m. Karen VanderKloot, July 20, 1965 (div. 1992); children: Lisa Marie, Cristina Maria. B.A. summa cum laude in Music, UCLA, 1956, M.A. in Composition (scholar), 1958, Ph.D. in Musicology, 1962; certificate in composition and piano (Fulbright Research grantee), Naples Conservatory of Music, 1959. Instr. music U. Calif., Los Angeles, 1960-61; asst. prof. music Oakland U., Rochester, Mich., 1962-65; chmn. music dept. Oakland U., 1966-73; founder, gen. dir. Mich. Opera Theatre, Detroit, 1971—; founding dir. Music Hall Center for the Performing Arts, Detroit, 1973—; artistic dir. Dayton Opera Assn., 1981-92; gen. dir. Opera Pacific, Costa Mesa, Calif., 1985—; trustee Nat. Opera Inst.; adj. prof. Oakland U., Wayne State U. Producer, dir.: Overture to Opera series for, Detroit Grand Opera series, 1963-71; Composer various works for piano, violin, orch., voice; author articles on Italian opera for various encyclopedias; contbr. revs. and articles to music jours. Mem. Arts Com. New Detroit, Inc.; trustee, mem. exec. com. Music Center for Performing Arts; mem. Arts Task Force City of Detroit. Recipient Atwater Kent award U. Calif., Los Angeles, 1961; Certificate of Appreciation City of Detroit, 1970; citation Mich. Legislature, 1976; Michaelangelo award Boys' Town of Italy, 1980; award Arts Found. of Mich., 1981; President's Cabinet award U. Detroit, 1982; George Gershwin fellow, 1958; named A Michiganian of Yr., 1980; cavaliere della Repubblica Italiana. Mem. Am. Arts Alliance (exec. com.), Nat. Opera Assn., Internat. Assn. Lyric Theatre (v.p.), Am. Symphony League, Am. Musicol. Soc., OPERA Am. (pres. 1979-83), AAUP, Phi Beta Kappa, Phi Mu Alpha Sinfonia. Club: Detroit Athletic. Office: Mich Opera Theatre 104 Lothrop Rd Detroit MI 48202-2703 also: Opera Pacific 9 Executive Cir Ste 190 Irvine CA 92714-6734

DICK, PATRICIA A., counselor; b. Indpls., Mar. 31, 1929; d. Harold D. and Mary R. (Crockett) Barton; m. Richard D. Dick, Sr., June 21, 1947; children: G. Daniel, Richard D. Jr., Lynda S., Kevin D., Deborah D. AA, Wm. Rainey Harper Coll., Palatine, Ill., 1976; BA, Mundelein Coll., Chgo., 1978; MA, Northeastern Ill. U., Chgo., 1984; postgrad., Alfred Adler Inst., Chgo. Cert. sr. addiction counselor, clin. hypnotherapist; nat. cert. counselor. Counselor in pvt. practice Barrington, Ill., 1979—. Contbr. articles on alcoholism to local papers. Mem. Am. Mental Health Counselor Assn., Nat. Assn. Alcoholism and Drug Counseling, Nat. Assn. for Adult Children of Alcoholics, Am. Assn. for Counseling and Devel., Nat. Guild of Hypnotists, Internat. Assn. Marriage and Family Counseling. Roman Catholic. Office: 28662 W Northwest Hwy Barrington IL 60010-5928

DICK, ROBERT MICHAEL, financial planner; b. Harvey, N.D., Dec. 16, 1963; s. Walter Charles and Agnes Caroline (Braaten) D.; m. Mary Joann Marchus, June 27, 1987; children: Jeffrey David, Brendan Robert. BBA, U. N.D., 1987. CFP. Partsman Dick's Auto Supply, Harvey, N.D., 1978-87; fin. planner Fin. Planning Svcs., Minot, N.D., 1987-95, mng. fin. planner, 1991—; fin. planner Fin. Advantage Brokerage Svcs., Inc., Minot, 1995—. Contbr. articles to newspapers. treas. Bread of Life Luth. Ch., Minot, 1989, vice-chmn., 1992. Mem. Inst. CFP, Minot Assn. Life Underwriters, Minot Country Club. Republican. Office: Fin Advantage Brokerage Svc 17 S Main Minot ND 58701

DICKEL, CHARLES TIMOTHY, education educator; b. Portland, Nov. 4, 1946; s. Herman Anderson and Elnora Elizabeth (Dillow) D.; m. Gail Janet Maurer, Aug. 4, 1973; children: Sara, Timothy, Andrew. BA, Whitman Coll., 1968; MS in Edn., Ind. U., 1971, EdD, 1973. Assoc. instr. edn. Ind. U., Bloomington, 1970-73; child devel. specialist Umatilla Intermed Edn. Dist., Pendelton, Oreg., 1973-76; asst. prof. edn. Creighton U., Omaha, 1976-82, asst. to dean coll. arts & scis., 1981-83, assoc. prof. edn., 1982-89, assoc. dean coll. arts & scis., 1988-90, prof. edn., 1989—, chair edn. dept., 1995—. Bd. dirs. Omaha Cath. Archdiocese Sch. Bd., 1993—, Madonna Sch., Omaha, 1995—, St. Pius/St. Leo's Sch., Omaha, 1995—, Nebr. Network for Ednl. Renewal, 1995—. Mem. Am. Counseling Assn. Independent. Roman Catholic. Office: Criehton U Edn Dept 2500 California Plz Omaha NE 68178-0106

DICKENS, JACQUELINE B., management systems executive; b. Winston-Salem, N.C., Mar. 3, 1941; d. Garland Bryant and Elizabeth (Realles) Bass; m. Floyd Dickens Jr., Oct. 31, 1964; children: Daphne, Floyd III, Karen. BS, Hampton (Va.) Inst., 1963; MSW, Ohio State U., 1978. Cons. Forest Pk., Ill., 1972-86; v.p. 21st Century Mgmt. Svcs., Inc., West Chester, Ohio, 1986—. Co-author: The Black Manager Making It In The Corporate World, 1982. Bd. dirs. YMCA, Cin., 1994; vol. Family Svcs. Cin., 1970-73; cons., vol. chs. racial issues, Cin., 1973-76. Mem. Bankers Club. Roman Catholic. Home: 8752 Eagle Ridge Rd West Chester OH 45069

DICKENS, ROBERT ALLEN, psychiatrist; b. Manitowoc, Wis., July 31, 1941. BA, Lawrence Coll., 1963; MD, Tufts U., 1967. Diplomate Am. Bd. Psychiatry and Neurology. Intern U. Wis. Hosps., Madison, 1967-68; resident Boston VA Hosp., 1970-72; pvt. practice Worcester, Mass., 1975-88, Manitowoc, Wis., 1989—. Trustee Rahr-West Art Mus. Capt. M.C., USAF, 1968-70. Mem. AMA, Am. Psychiat. Assn., Am. Acad. Clin. Psychiatrists. Home: PO Box 215 Manitowoc WI 54221-0215 Office: 1117 S 8th St PO Box 215 Manitowoc WI 54221-0215

DICKENSON, H. H., professional society administrator. Field rep. Am. Hereford Assn., Kansas City, Mo., 1960-68, dir. mktg., 1968-74, exec. v.p., 1974—; mem. U.S. Com. Internat. Livestock Trade; bd. dirs. Am. Royal. Mem. Nat. Western Assn., U.S. Beef Breeds Coun. (past pres.), Nat. Pedigree Livestock Coun. (past pres.). Office: Am Hereford Assn 1501 Wyandotte Kansas City MO 64108

DICKERSON, ALLEN BRUCE, interior designer, consultant; b. St. Joseph, Mich., June 8, 1938; s. Harold Clyde and Lucille Anne (Thornton) D.; m. Arlene Virginia Bator, Mar. 26, 1965; children—Scott Denek, Maribeth Anne. B.S. in Indsl. Engring., U. Mich., 1961, M.B.A., 1962; cert. N.Y. Sch. Interior Design, 1967. Sr. indsl. engr. Bohn Aluminum & Brass Co., Detroit, 1962-65, engring. ctr. adminstr., 1965-68, prodn. mgr., 1968-70, asst. plant mgr., 1970-72; plant mgr. DuWel Products Co., Bangor, Mich., 1972-74, corp. chief indsl. engr., 1974-75; contract and residential interior designer Klingman's, Grand Rapids, Mich., 1975—; tchr. South Haven Community Edn. Program, 1977, Western Mich. U., 1975, Am. Soc. Interior Designers, 1980-81. Author: Rental Condominiums-Interior Design for Fun and Profit, 1978, Vacation Home Furnishings, 1984, Decorating with Collectibles, 1990, Showcase of Interior Design- Midwest Edition, 1993. Trustee First United Meth. Ch., South Haven, Mich.; bd. dirs. Van Buren County (Mich.) ARC, 1965-68, Grand Rapids Symphony Designer Showhouse, 1993; coord. Concord Coalition 6th Dist. Mem. Am. Inst. Indsl. Engrs., Am. Soc. Interior Designers, Nat. Council Interior Design Qualification, South Haven C. of C. (com. chmn.), Internat. Lightning Class Assn. Republican. Methodist. Clubs: South Haven Yacht; Shrine (Grand Rapids); Rotary. Home: 30 N Shore Dr N South Haven MI 49090-9169 Office: Eastbrook Mall 3525 28th St SE Grand Rapids MI 49512-1652

DICKERSON, GORDON EDWIN, animal geneticist, biologist; b. La Grande, Oreg., Jan. 30, 1912; s. Malcolm Gordon and Olive (Merrifield) D.; m. Myra Elizabeth Warren, Sept. 11, 1933; children: Alfred Gordon, Malcolm John, Davis Warren, Dean Ames. BS, Mich. State U., 1933; MS, U. Wis., 1934, PhD, 1937. Instr. U. Wis., Madison, 1935-41; geneticist Bur. Animal Industries USDA, Ames, Iowa, 1941-47; prof. animal sci. U. Mo., Columbia, 1947-52; geneticist, dir. rsch. Kimber Farms, Inc., Fremont, Calif., 1952-65; geneticist rsch. br. Can. Agriculture, Ottowa, Ont., Can., 1965-67; prof. animal sci. U. Nebr., Lincoln, 1967-87; rsch. geneticist U.S. Meat Animal Rsch. Ctr., Agrl. Rsch. Svc., USDA, Lincoln, 1967-87, collaborator, 1987—. Editor: Proceedings 3rd World Congress on Genetic Applied Livestock Production, 1987; contbr. articles to profl. jours. V.p. Mayor's Com. on Internat. Friendship, Lincoln, 1968—; pres. UN Assn., Lincoln, 1989-92. Fellow AAAS, Am. Soc. Animal Sci. (breeding and genetics award 1970, Morrison award 1978); mem. Am. Dairy Sci. Assn., Genetics Soc. Am., Am. Genetics Assn., World Poultry Assn., Brit. Soc. Animal Production, U. Nebr. Emeritus Assn. (pres. 1988-89), Poultry Sci. Assn., Sigma Xi (pres. U. Nebr. chpt. 1987-88), Gamma Sigma Delta (Internat. Disting. Svc. Agr. award 1990). Republican. Presbyterian. Office: U Nebr A218 Ans Lincoln NE 68583

DICKERSON, MARTHA ANN, health facility administrator; b. Iowa City, Feb. 2, 1953; d. Wilbur R., Jr. and Phyllis (Schroeder) D. Diploma, Mass. Gen. Hosp. Sch. Nursing, Boston, 1975; BS, Iowa State U., 1978; MS, Rush U., 1983, postgrad. Head nurse, adminstrv. ednl. svcs. coord. Michael Reese Hosp. Med. Ctr., Chgo., 1978-87; clin. health edn. supr., corp. mgr., staff devel. Michael Reese Health Plan, Chgo., 1987-90; clin. svcs. mgr., nat. dir. nursing Buddy Systems, Inc., Chgo., 1990-92; corp. dir. clin. rsch. and spl. projects Cardiac Alliance, Inc., Chgo., 1992-95; mgr. cardiac care unit CareMed Chgo. (formerly Vis. Nurse Assn. Chgo.), 1995—; rsch. in field. Contbr. articles to profl. jours. Mem. AACN, Am. Soc. Health Edn. and Tng., Intravenous Nurses Soc., Am. Soc. Parenteral and Enteral Nutrition, Am. Heart Assn. (Chgo. divsn., chair CPR targeted activity group 1992-95, nat. CPR faculty 1992-95), Ill. Nurses Assn., Ill. League Nursing (pres. 1988-89), Sigma Theta Tau (eligibility com., by-laws com., rec. sec.). Home: 1522 W Thorndale Ave Chicago IL 60660-3326

DICKESON, LUDMILA WEIR, organization administrator; b. Maryville, Mo., June 16, 1941; d. Benjamin Franklin and Ludmila Martha (Vavra) Weir; m. Robert Celmer Dickeson, June 22, 1963; children: Elizabeth Ann, Cynthia Marie. BSE, U. Mo., 1963, MEd, 1966. Cert. tchr., Colo., Ariz., Mo. Tchr. Columbia (Mo.) Pub. Schs., 1963-69; tchr., tutor Madison Sch. Dist., Phoenix, 1979-81; first lady U. No. Colo., 1981-91; dir. Right to Read of Weld County, Inc., 1989-91; mgr. Noel/Levitz Ctrs. for Instnl. Effectiveness, Iowa City, 1991-95; mgr. tng. programs USA Group Noel-Levitz, Indpls., 1995—; com. mem. Ariz. Bd. of Edn. Statewide Textbook Adoption Com., Phoenix, 1979-80. Campaign chmn. United Way Weld County, 1988; pres.-elect Greeley (Colo.) Philharm. Orch. Assn., 1989, pres., 1990; pres. No. Colo. coun. Camp Fire, Inc., 1985-87; trustee Flagstaff (Ariz.) Community Hosp., 1979. Mem. AAUW (rec. sec. 1968-69), PEO (pres. 1974, 84), Rotary, Delta Kappa Gamma, Pi Lambda Theta, Kappa Alpha Theta. Congregational. Home: 11650 Woods Bay Ln Indianapolis IN 46236 Office: USA Group Noel-Levitz 8350 Craig St Indianapolis IN 46250

DICKEY, JULIA EDWARDS, aviation consultant; b. Sioux Falls, S.D., Mar. 6, 1940; d. John Keith and Henrietta Barbara (Zerell) Edwards; m. Joseph E. Dickey, June 18, 1959; children: Joseph E., John Edwards. student DePauw U., 1958-59; AB, Ind. U., 1962, MLS, 1967, postgrad., 1967. Asst. acquisitions libr. Ind. U. Regional Campus Librs., 1965-67; head tech. svcs. Bartholomew County Libr., Columbus, Ind., 1967-74; dir. reference svcs. Southeastern Ind. Area Library Svc. Authority, Columbus, 1974-78, exec. dir., 1978-80; pres. Jedco Enterprises, 1981—; legis. strategy chmn. Ind. Library Coop. Devel., 1975; dir. Ind. Libr. Trustees Assn. Governance Project, 1982. Mem. Columbus exec. bd. Mayor's Task Force on Status of Women, 1973-76; del. Ind. Sch. Nominating Assembly, 1973-75, 75-77; bd. dirs. Human Svcs. Inc. (Bartholomew, Brown and Jackson Counties community action program), 1975-79, sec., 1975, v.p., 1979, pres., 1976-78; elder First Presbyterian Ch. of Aurora, Ind. (session mem. 1996—); mem. adv. coun. Ind./Nat. Network Study, 1977-78; adv. coun. Salvation Army Local, 1984-88; bd. dirs. Columbus Women's Ctr.; precinct coord. Vols. For Bayh, 1974; sheriff Columbus 1st precinct, 1975, clk., 1976-77, insp., 1978, judge, 1980-83; treas. Hayes for State Rep. Com., 1978, 82—. Named Outstanding Young Woman Am., 1973. Mem. ALA, Ind. Library Assn. (dist. chmn. 1972-73, chmn. library edn. div. 1980-81, ad hoc com. on legis. effectiveness, 1982, various coms.), Library Assts. and Technicians Round Table (chmn. 1968-69), Tech. Services Round Table (chmn. 1971-72, sec. library planning com. 1969-72), AAUW (pres. 1973-75), Bartholomew County Library Staff Assn. (pres. 1975-76), Exptl. Aircraft Assn. (charter pres. chpt. 729, Inc. 1981, advisor 1982, sec. 1984-85, treas., 1990—; Ind. EAA Council (pres. 1982-88, advisor 1988—, internat. EAA conv. antique/classic mgmt. team 1988—), Internat. Expt. Aircraft Assn. (Major Achievement award 1983, Antique Airplane Assn., First Tuesday, Psi Iota Xi (thrift shop steering 1985-94, v.p. thrift shop chmn. 1986-87, Mem. of Yr. 1988-89, pres. elect 1991-92, pres. 1992-93, advisor 1993-94, mem. state assn. project com. 1992-93, constn./by-laws com. 1993-94), Review Club of Lawrenceburg, Ind. (corr. sec. 1996—), Zonta Club (newsletter editor Tel-Zon 1981-89, recording sec. 1984-85, treas. 1990-93, v.p. 1993-94). Home and Office: 55 Oakey Ave Lawrenceburg IN 47025-1538

DICKEY, R. KEVIN, financial planner, consultant; b. Quantico, Va., Feb. 15, 1957. BS, S.W. Mo. State U., 1979. Pricing forecast analyst W. Bayerry, St. Louis, 1980-81; marine pers. mgr. Clipper Lines, Clayton, Mo., 1983-87; fin. planner/cons. Equity Fin. Inc., St. Louis, 1987—. Mem. fin. com. Gethsemane Luth. Ch., St. Louis, 1960. Home: 4801 Sunnyview Dr Saint Louis MO 63128-1934 Office: Equity Fin Inc 11648 Gravois Rd Ste 130 Saint Louis MO 63126-3034

DICKEY, WILLIAM A., stockbroker; b. Mpls., Oct. 14, 1954. Mgr. Crystal (Minn.) Marine, 1985-94; stockbroker Dain Bosworth Inc., Edina, Minn., 1994—; bd. dirs. Muskee Inc., Alexandria, Minn. Office: Dain Bosworth Inc 6600 France Ave S Ste 250 Edina MN 55435-1800

DICKINSON, DANIEL OLIVER, aviation executive; b. Waukegan, Ill., June 7, 1950; s. Oliver L. and Ann (Spink) (dec.) D.; m. Nancy Reeves, Apr. 9, 1973; children: Ann Elizabeth, Laura Jane. B of Mech. Engring., Western Ill. U., 1972. Sales mgr. Aircraft Sales Corp., Waukegan, 1973-77; pres., owner Gen. Aviation Svcs., Inc., Lake Zurich, Ill., 1977—, Gen. Aviation Techs., GAS/Wilson, Inc. Pres. Acorn Assn., Hawthorn Woods, Ill., 1989. Mem. EAA, Nat. Aircraft Resale Assn. (bd. dirs. Washington chpt. 1990—, v.p. 1991-92, pres., CEO 1992-94, vice chmn. 1994-96), Aircraft Owners and Pilots Assn. Republican. Mem. United Ch. of Christ. Home: 9 Lydia Ct Lake Zurich IL 60047-9065 Office: Gen Aviation Svcs Inc 430 Telser Rd Lake Zurich IL 60047

DICKINSON, MAE, state legislator; b. Feb. 8, 1933. Student, Ind. U., Martin Coll., Ivy Tech. Coll. Quality inspector GM; rep. Dist. 95 Ind. Ho. of Reps., 1992—, mem. elections and apportionment, cities and towns com., mem. families, children and human affairs, pub. safety coms., vice chmn. labor and employment com. Precinct committeewoman; del. Dem. Nat. Conv.; ward chmn. Named Breakthrough woman in Area of Polit. Coalition of 100 Black Women. Mem. NAACP, Urban League, Uniated Auto Workers, A. Philip Randolph Inst. (Pres.'s award 1990), Flamingo Social and Charity Club, Coalition of Black Trade Unionists. Home: 5455 N Arlington Ave Indianapolis IN 46226-1607 Office: Ind Ho of Reps State Capitol Indianapolis IN 46204*

DICKINSON, WILFRED ARTHUR, construction executive; b. Riceville, Iowa, Dec. 16, 1956. V.p. Schwab Constrn. Svc., Winona, Minn., 1978—. Asst. scoutmaster Boy Scouts, Winona, 1994. Mem. Eagles, Jaycees (pres. 1989-90). Roman Catholic. Office: Schwab Constrn Svc PO Box 528 Winona MN 55987-0528

DICKMAN, CRAIG STEVEN, retail, distribution-consulting company executive; b. Oshkosh, Wis., July 23, 1960; s. Llewellyn Herman and Betty Jane (Klemp) D.; m. Karen Jean Thomson, June 4, 1983; children: Megan, Brenden. BS, U. Wis., Green Bay, 1982; MBA, U. Wis., Oshkosh, 1987. Ops. supr. Schneider Nat., Inc., Green Bay, 1983-86, regional mgr., 1986-87; mgr. ops. Catenation, Inc. a SHADE Co., Green Bay, 1987-88; mgr. logistics svcs. SHADE Info. Systems, Inc., Green Bay, 1988-92, dir. strategic planning, 1992-94; pres. The MD2 Group, Inc., Green Bay, 1994—; mem. adv. bd. N.E. Wis. Tech. Coll., Green Bay, 1989—, instr., 1992—. Mem. Green Bay Housing Authority, 1990-94, Brown County (Wis.) Solid Waste Bd., 1992-94, Green Bay City Coun., 1990-92, Brown County Criminal Justice Bd., 1992-94, Brown County Bd. Suprs., 1990-92; 1st vice chmn. Rep. Com. Green Bay, 1994—. Mem. Coun. Logistics Mgmt., World Future Soc., Am. Assn. Polit. Cons. Home: 1210 Western Meadows Dr Green Bay WI 54313-1324 Office: The MD2 Group Inc 2190 S Ashland Ave Green Bay WI 54304

DICKOW, JAMES FRED, management consultant; b. Chgo., Mar. 27, 1943; s. Fred H. and Margaret I. (Arnold) D.; m. Yvonne A. Zabilka, Aug. 20, 1966; children: Michael J., Christine Y. BSME, Purdue U., 1965, MSME, 1967. Cert. mgmt. cons. Mech. engr. CPC Internat., Argo, Ill., 1965-66; engr. dynamics McDonnell-Douglas Corp., St. Louis, 1967-70; cons. Drake Sheahan/Steward Dougal, Chgo., 1970-71; dir. distbn. planning Will Ross Div. G.D. Searle, Milw., 1971-80; dir. distbn. Gentec Healthcare, Milw., 1980-82, R&J Med. Supply, Milw., 1982-83; exec. v.p., ptnr. Kowaski-Dickow Assoc. Inc., Mequon, Wis., 1983—. Mem. Coun. Logistics Mgmt. (pres. Milw. roundtable 1978-79), Phi Kappa Theta (bd. dirs., nat. pres., pres. Ind. alumni 1980—). Home: 10011 N Miller Ct Thiensville WI 53092-6180

DICKSON, BRENT E., state supreme court justice; b. July 18, 1941. BA, Purdue U., 1964; JD, Ind. U., Indpls., 1968. Bar: Ind. 1968, U.S. Ct. Appeals (7th cir.) 1972, U.S. Supreme Ct. 1975; cert. civil trial advocate NBTA. Pvt. practice Lafayette, Ind., 1968-85; sr. ptnr. Dickson, Reiling, Teder & Withered, 1977-85; justice Ind. Supreme Ct., Indpls., 1986—; adj. prof. Sch. of Law Ind. U., 1992—. Past pres. Tippecanoe County Hist. Assn.; mem. dean's adv. coun. Sch. Liberal Arts Purdue U., 1990-94; mem. adv. bd. Heartland Film Festival, 1995—. Mem. ABA, Ind. State Bar Assn., Indpls. Bar Assn., 7th Cir. Bar Assn., Ind. Judges Assn., Am. Judicature Soc., Inst. Jud. Adminstrn. Office: Ind Supreme Ct 306 Statehouse Indianapolis IN 46204-2213

DICKSON, RICHARD EUGENE, plant physiologist; b. Carbondale, Ill., Sept. 13, 1932; s. J. M. and Elizabeth (Krysher) D.; m. Carol Overlease, Sept. 15, 1956; children: Carol Elizabeth, Diane Lynn, Nancy Lee. MS, So. Ill. U., 1962; PhD, U. Calif., Berkeley, 1968. Rsch. plant physiologist USDA-Forest Svc., Ames, Iowa, 1968-70, Rhinelander, Wis., 1970—. Assoc. editor Forest Sci. Jour., 1986-92; mem. editl. rev. bd. Tree Physiology, 1993-95; contbr. chpt. to Forest Tree Ecophysiology, 1991, Physiology of Trees, 1991, Response of Plants to Stress, 1991. With USMC, 1951-54. Recipient Outstanding Alumni award Sch. of Agrl., So. Ill. U., 1968, Alumni Achievement award Coll. of Agrl., So. Ill. U., 1990, Svc.-wide Disting. Sci. award USDA Forest Svc., 1991, Disting. Svc. award 1993. Home: 1608 Thornapple Dr Rhinelander WI 54501-2130 Office: Forestry Scis Lab PO Box 898 Rhinelander WI 54501-0898

DICKSON, ROBERT FRANK, nursing home executive; b. Carbondale, Ill., Oct. 23, 1933; s. Jason Milburn and Elizabeth (Krysher) D.; m. Roberta Joan Mellican, May 16, 1964; children: Kevin, Craig, Angela, Rebecca. BS, So. Ill. U., 1960. With Farm Credit System, Ill., 1960-67; credit. rep. Fed. Intermediate Credit Bank, St. Louis, 1967-70; adminstr. Union County Hosp., Anna, Ill., 1970-72; v.p. Heritage Enterprises, Inc., Bloomington, Ill., 1972-85, exec. v.p., 1985—. Contbr. articles to mag. Served with USN, 1952-56. Mem. Ill. Health Care Assn. (bd. dirs. 1975-82, 85-86, pres. 1979, 85), Am. Health Care Assn. (bd. dirs. 1979-82, 86). Republican. Presbyterian. Lodge: Kiwanis. Home: 705 Bradley Dr Bloomington IL 61701-2203 Office: Heritage Enterprises Inc 115 W Jefferson St Bloomington IL 61702-3188

DICOLA, VINCENT C., industrial engineer; b. Pitts., Apr. 21, 1946. BS in Indsl. Design, U. Cin., 1969. Cert. in indsl. design, Ky. Staff designer FESCO, Pitts., 1969-71; design mgr. Thomas Industries, Fort Atkinson, Wis., 1971-89, LSI Lighting, Cin., 1990—. Patentee in field. With USAR, 1969-79. Mem. Clifton Track Club. Roman Catholic. Office: L S I Lighting Systems PO Box 42728 10000 Alliance Rd Cincinnati OH 45242-4706

DIDICH, JAN, hospice consultant; b. Lorain, Ohio, Nov. 20, 1952; d. Harry and Helen (Zaborniak) Murawski; m. Aaron N. Didich, May 12, 1979; 1 child, Aaron M. BSN, St. John Coll. of Cleve., 1975; MA in Community Psychology, N.E. Mo. State U., 1982. Asst. head nurse/charge nurse Cleve. Clinic Hosp., 1975-79; charge nurse neonatal ICU Kirksville (Mo.) Osteopathic Hosp., 1979-80; charge nurse ICU Grim-Smith Hosp., Kirksville, 1981-83; asst. instr. N.E. Mo. State U., Kirksville, 1980-83; hospice nurse Hospice of Cen. Iowa, Des Moines, 1984; community nurse Community Nursing Svcs., Mt. Holly, N.J., 1984; dir. patient svcs. Samaritan Hospice, N.J., 1985-86; advanced clin. nurse palliative care, 1986-87; dir. Tricare Hospice, Bellefontaine, Ohio; cons. Cleve. Clinic Found., 1988-90. Contbr. articles to profl. jours. Mem. ANA, Ohio Nurses' Assn., Nat. Hospice Orgn., Ohio Hospice Orgn., AAUW.

DIEDERICH, ANNE MARIE, college president; b. Cleve., Apr. 8, 1943. BA in English, Ursuline Coll. for Women, 1966; MA in Ednl. Adminstrn., John Carroll U., 1975; PhD in Edn. Policy and Leadership, Ohio State U., 1988. Joined Order St. Ursula, Roman Cath. Ch., 1961. Tchr. Villa Angela Acad., Cleve., 1966-70, asst. prin., 1971-76, prin., 1976-82; tchr. Beaumont Sch. for Girls, 1982-84; pres. Ursuline Coll., Pepper Pike, Ohio, 1986—. Mem. Leadership Cleve. '89. Dan H. Eikenberry scholar Ohio State U., 1985; William R. and Marie A. Flesher fellow Ohio State U., 1986. Mem. Phi Kappa Phi. Office: Ursuline Coll Office of Pres 2550 Lander Rd Pepper Pike OH 44124-4398

DIEHL, CAROL LOU, library director, retired, library consultant; b. Milw., Aug. 10, 1929; d. Gilbert Fred and Erna Lou (Braeger) Doepke; m. Russell Phillip Diehl, Aug. 8, 1953; children: Holly Lou Diehl Nelson, Jeffrey Phillip. BS, U. Wis., Madison, 1951; MA, U. Wis., Oshkosh, 1971. Tchr. English, libr. Port Washington (Wis.) High Sch., 1951-54, Minoqua (Wis.) High Sch., 1954-55; libr. Ozaukee High Sch., Fredonia, Wis., 1964-65, Vernon County Tchrs. Coll., Viroqua, Wis., 1965-67; libr. media coord. Manawa (Wis.) Sch. Dist., 1973-77; dir. libr. media svcs. Sch. Dist. of New London, Wis., 1977-95; ret., 1995; lectr. U. Wis., Oshkosh, 1993, 95—; v.p. Coun. on Libr. and Network Devel., Madison, 1979; pres. Lake Forest Bd. Dirs., Eagle River, Wis., 1987-89; libr. cons. Thern Design Ctrs. Inc., 1994—; lectr. U. Wis.-Oshkosh, 1995—. Author: (with others) School Library Media Annual, 1985-87; news corr. Appleton (Wis.) Post Crescent, 1971-81; contbr. articles to profl. jours. Mem. Fox Valley Symphony League; mem. exec. com. Waupaca County Grand Ole Party, chair, 1994—, vice chmn., 1991-94; del.-at-large White House Conf. Libr. and Info. Svcs., 1991. Named Wis. Sch. Libr. Media Specialist of Yr. Assn. Ednl. Comm. and Tech., 1992. Mem. ALA (mem. legis. com. 1986-91, chairperson ALA White House Conf. Libr. and Info. Svcs. 1992-95, mem., 1995—, legis. assembly chairperson 1989-90, mem. membership com. 1995-97), AASL (legis. chmn. 1987—, mem. planning and implementation task force White House Conf. 1990-92), Wis. Libr. Assn. (fed. rels. coord. 1990-91), Assn. Wis. Sch. Adminstr. (mem. edn. svcs. commn. 1986-96), Wis. Ednl. Media Assn. (mem. legis. com. 1986-93, Excellence award 1992), Futurae Club of Manawa, Phi Delta Kappa. Republican. Lutheran.

DIEHL, NANCY ELIZABETH, physical therapist; b. Cleve., Feb. 25, 1955; d. Richard Earl and Elizabeth Josephine (Platten) D. BS, Ft. Hays State U., 1977; MS, U. Ariz., 1978; BS, U. Kans., 1989. Lic. phys. therapist, Kans., Mo. Athletic trainer U. N.Mex., Albuquerque, 1978-79; instr., athletic trainer U. Ariz., Tucson, 1979-80, Emporia (Kans.) State U., 1980-87; phys. therapist Trinity Luth. Hosp., Kansas City, Mo., 1989-90; instr. phys. therapy edn. Kansas City U. Med. Ctr., 1990-91, phys. therapist, athletic trainer Sportsmedicine Inst., 1991-94; phys. therapist, athletic trainer Shawnee Mission (Kans.) Med. Ctr., 1994—. Chpt. sponsor Fellowship of Christian Athletes, Emporia, 1980-87. Mem. Nat. Athletic Trainers Assn., Kans. Athletic Trainers' Soc., Am. Phys. Therapy Assn., Kans. Phys. Therapy Assn. Office: Shawnee Mission Med Ctr 75th & I-35 Shawnee Mission KS 66204

DIEMAND, KIM EUGENE, human resources executive; b. Camden, N.J., Nov. 5, 1953; s. Eugene August and Ruth (Maute) D.; m. Jan Elizabeth Ratcliffe, Oct. 7, 1975; children: Megan, Michael, Andrew. AA, Coll. DuPage, 1977; BS, No. Ill. U., 1978. Office mgr. Diemand Printing Co., Chgo., 1978-79; indsl. engr., estimator Henry Pratt Co., Aurora, Ill., 1979-80; personnel mgr. Marmon/Keystone Corp., Lemont, Ill., 1980-81; plant personnel mgr. Gen. Mills Inc. Package Foods Div., Lodi, Calif., 1981-83; employee rels. mgr. The Gorton Group div. Gen Mills, Gloucester, Mass., 1983-90; dir. human resources McKesson Drug Co., Romeoville, Ill., 1990—. Chief spokesman, mem. personnel bd. Town of Essex (Mass.), 1985-86. Sgt. USMC, 1971-75. Mem. Am. Soc. Human Resource Mgrs., U.S. Parachute Assn., Carillon Golf Club. Office: McKesson Drug Co 1319 Enterprise Dr Romeoville IL 60441-1050 Address: 194 Muirfield Forest Ct Saint Charles MO 63304-0416

DIENER, JEAN BROCK, science educator, author; b. St. Louis, Aug. 8, 1925; d. William Jean Harris and Edith Emma (Tacke) Brock; m. Roy M. Diener, June 26, 1973. BS, U. Ill., 1947; MA in Edn., Washington U., 1959. Analytical chemist Bluline Chem. Co., St. Louis, 1947-50; lab. asst. Prestite Engring. Co., St. Louis, 1950-52; rsch. chemist Olin Industries, East Alton, Ill., 1952-58; tchr. sci. Normandy Jr. H.S., St. Louis, 1959-65, Clayton (Mo.) H.S., 1965-87; tchr. biology Mark Twain Summer Inst. for Gifted Students, Clayton, 1959-66; project coord. biotech. edn. project Math. and Sci. Edn. Ctr., St. Louis, 1987-90; ret., 1990. Author: (textbook) Patterns and Process of Science, 1969, (book) Teaching Tales and Theory, 1991; contbr. articles to profl. jours. Recipient Educator award Sci. Tchrs. of Mo., 1976. Mem. Nat. Sci. Tchrs. Assn. (life, Career Edn. in Sci. award 1979), Nat. Assn. Biology Tchrs., Wilderness Soc. (life), Nature Conservancy, Kappa Delta Pi. Home: 9752 Old Warson Rd Saint Louis MO 63124

DIENHART, CHARLOTTE MARIE, retired anatomy and cell biology educator; b. Sioux Falls, S.D., Aug. 14, 1923; d. Arthur Peter and Mary Agnes (Donahue) D. BS, Coll. St. Catherine, 1945; MS, State U. Iowa, 1947; PhD, Mich. State U., 1960. Registered dietitian. Instr. Coll. St. Catherine, St. Paul, 1948-57; instr. Emory U., Atlanta, 1960-65, asst. prof., 1966-75, assoc. prof., 1975-86, prof. emerita, 1986—. Author: (textbook) Basic Human Anatomy and Physiology, 1967, Spanish edit., 1969, French edit., 1975, 3d edit., 1979. Lt. comdr. USNR, 1952-78. Summer fellow NSF, 1956. Mem. Am. Assn. Clin. Anatomists, Sigma Delta Epsilon, Sigma Xi, Delta Phi Lambda, Omicron Nu, Beta Beta Beta. Democrat. Roman Catholic. Home: 1666 Coffman St # 112 Saint Paul MN 55108

DIERCKS, EILEEN KAY, educational media coordinator, elementary education educator; b. Lima, Ohio, Oct. 31, 1944; d. Robert Wehner and Florence (Huckemeyer) McCarty; m. Dwight Richard Diercks, Dec. 27, 1969; children: Roger, David, Laura. BSEd, Bluffton Coll., 1962-66; MS, U. Ill., 1968. Tchr. elem. grades Kettering City Schs. (Ohio), 1966-67; children's libr. St. Charles County, St. Charles, Mo., 1968-69; libr. Rantoul (Ill.) High Sch., 1970-71; elem. tchr. Elmhurst (Ill.) Sch. Dist., 1971-72; media coordinator Plainfield (Ill.) Sch. Dist., 1980—; evaluator Rebecca Caudill Young Readers' Book Award, 1990—. Founder, treas. FISH orgn., Plainfield, 1975-78; pres. Ch. Women United, 1974; sec. Plainfield Community TV Access League, 1987-89; treas. Plainfield Congl. Ch., 1983-88; bd. dirs. Cub Scouts, 1983-86; leader Girl Scouts U.S., Plainfield, 1985—; mem. Bolingbrook (Ill.) Community Chorus, 1986-90. Mo. State Libr. scholar, 1967, Naperville chpt. Valparaiso Univ. Guild, treas., 1993-95. Mem. ALA, NEA, Ill. Edn. Assn., Plainfield Assn. Tchrs., Ill. Sch. Libr. Media Assn. (membership chmn. 1992-93, mem. awards com. 1994—), Plainfield Athletic Club (sec. 1984-86), Rotary (Plainfield chpt., treas. 1994-95, v.p. 1995-96), Delta Kappa Gamma (Beta Rho, treas. 1993—), Pi Delta, Beta Phi Mu. Home: 13440 S Rivercrest Dr Plainfield IL 60544-8979 Office: Plainfield Sch Dist # 202 611 Fort Beggs Dr Plainfield IL 60544-1877

DIERKS, MERTON LYLE, veterinarian; b. Ewing, Nebr., July 2, 1932; s. Lyle P. and Alys G. (Sanders) D.; m. Gloria Lee Zoeller, Dec. 27, 1958; children: Jon Martin, Thomas Lyle, Christopher Joseph, M. Stephanie. BS in Agriculture, U. Nebr., 1954; DVM, Kans. State U., 1961. Pvt. practice Ewing, 1961-73; ptnr. practice O'Neill, Nebr., 1973-92; mem. 40th dist. Nebr. Legislature, Lincoln, 1986—; chmn. com. on agr. Nebr. Legislature, Lincoln, 1993-96; bd. dirs. St. Anthony's Hosp. Pres. Bd. Edn., Ewing, 1970-84. Lt. USAF, 1954-56. Recipient Outstanding Grassland Conservation award Nebr. Assn. Resource Dists., 1987, 96. Mem. Nebr. Vet. Med. Assn. (Nebr. Veterinarian of Yr 1986, pres. 1983), AVMA, U.S. Animal Health Assn., Comml. Club (pres. 1962-63). Democrat. Roman Catholic. Home: PO Box 38 Ewing NE 68735-0038 Office: State Legislature State Capital Lincoln NE 68516

DIETERICH, RUSSELL BURKS, obstetrician/gynecologist; b. Springfield, Ill., May 9, 1943; s. Charles Russell and Irma Rebecca (Burks) D.; m. Lynn Ellen Heidinger (div. July 1976); 1 child, Kristen; m. Barbara Ann Browning (div. May 1990); children: Paula, Pamela, Patrick; m. Irene Lorraine Carroll, June 27, 1992; children: Kathleen Carroll, Jonathon Carroll. BA, Knox Coll., 1965; MD, U. Ill., 1970. Diplomate Am. Bd. Ob-Gyn., Nat. Bd. Med. Examiners. Intern Blodgett Meml. Hosp., Grand Rapids, Mich., 1970-71, resident, 1971-74; chief of staff ob-gyn. USAF Hosp., Whiteman AFB, 1975-76; chief ob-gyn. Barnes St. Peters (Mo.) Hosp., 1986-87; chief ob-gyn. St. Joseph Hosp., St. Charles, Mo., 1987-89, chief of staff, 1989-90; pres. Dieterich Ob/Gyn Assn., Inc., St. Charles, 1981-95; clin. instr. Sch. Medicine Mich. State U., 1973-74, Sch. Medicine Wash. U., St. Louis, 1988—; speakers bur. Syntex Labs.; adv. bd. Life Seekers, St. Charles. Prodr., condr. (mus. rec.) Sentimental Journey by Request, 1985. Bd. mgrs. St. Charles County YMCA, 1985—; internat. mem. Community YMCA, St. Charles, 1985—; bd. dirs. United Svcs. for the Handicapped, Inc., St. Charles, 1994—. Maj. USAF, 1974-76. Recipient Harvard Book prize Associated Harvard Clubs, 1960, Disting. Alumni award Sigma Nu. Fellow Am. Coll. Ob-Gyn. (presenter, Ephraim McDowell award 1974); mem. AMA, Internat. Soc. for Advancement of Humanistic Studies of Gynecology, Am. Assn. Gynecol. Laproscopists, Am. Fertility Soc., St. Louis Gynecol. Soc. Republican. Free Evangelical. Home: 6 Vicksburg Sta Saint Charles MO 63303-6143 Office: Heritage Ob-Gyn Assocs 2730 S Highway 94 Ste 202 Saint Charles MO 63303-5677

DIETERLE, BRIAN DAVE, internist; b. Minot, N.D., Apr. 4, 1941; s. Dave and Bertha (Hoffer) D.; divorced; children: Karen, Gale, Andrea. BS in Pharmacy, N.D. State U., 1963, MS, 1964; PhD, U. Ariz., 1970; MD,

Am. U. Caribbean, Brit, West Indies, 1988. Resident Good Samaritan Hosp., Cin., 1989-92; pharmacist various retail stores, 1963-84; pvt. practice Branson, Mo., 1992—; rsch. assoc. Duke U., Durham, N.C., 1970-71; sales rep., broker Dean Witter Reynolds, Reno, Nev., 1971-78; assoc. prof. environ. studies Bemidji (Mo.) State U., 1981-82. Contbr. articles to profl. jours. Named Athlete of Yr., N.D. State U., 1963; Am. Foundn. Pharmacy Edn. fellow, 1964-69. Mem. ACP, Mo. Med. Soc., Tri Lakes Med. Soc. (pres. 1993-95), Rho Chi. Republican. Office: 221 Skaggs Rd Ste 201 Branson MO 65616

DIETERLEN, PAUL LEROY, veterinarian; b. Clark County, Ind., May 16, 1932; s. Altus and Nellie Beatrice (Mahan) D.; m. Janet Helen White, June 16, 1957; children: Jeffrey, Laurie, Susan. D in vet. medicine, Ohio State U., 1957. Lic. vet. Ind., Mich. Pvt. practice Nappanee, Ind., 1957-89; vet. area supr. Ind. State Dept. Health, Indpls., 1990—; mem., pres., Bd. Vet. Examiners, Indpls. Bd. trustees Wa-Nee Cmty. Pub. Sch., Nappanee, 1992—. Recipient Sagamore Wabash award Gov. Ind., 1985. Mem. Ind. Vet. Med. Assn. (pres., dir., Vet. Svc. award 1995), Am. Vet. Med. Assn., Am. Assn. Bovine Practitioners, Michiana Dist. Vet. Med. Assn. (pres., dir.). United Methodist. Home: 1004 Northwood Dr Nappanee IN 46550 Office: ISDH-Meat & Poultry Div 1300 Michigan St Indianapolis IN 46206

DIETMEYER, DONALD LEO, electrical engineer; b. Wausau, Wis., Nov. 20, 1932; s. Henry Joseph and Erna M. (Zastrow) D.; m. Carol White, Jan. 26, 1957; children—Karl Peter, Elizabeth Mary, Anne Katherine, Diana Lee. B.S. in Elec. Engring, U. Wis., Madison, 1954, M.S., 1955, Ph.D., 1959. Mem. faculty U. Wis., Madison, 1958-63, 64—; prof. elec. and computer engring. U. Wis., 1967—, assoc. dean Coll. Engring., 1983-95; sr. engr. IBM Corp., Poughkeepsie, N.Y., 1964. Author: Logic Design of Digital Systems, 1978, 3d rev. edit., 1988, Conlan Report, 1983. Served with AUS, 1957. Recipient Western Electric Fund award, 1972. Fellow IEEE; mem. Computer Soc., Assn. Computing Machinery, Sigma Xi. Home: 2211 Waunona Way Madison WI 53713-1619 Office: 1415 Engineering Dr Madison WI 53706-1691

DIETRICH, JAMES J., JR., freight company executive, consultant; b. Chgo., Jan. 21, 1943; s. James J. and Ruth M. (Hubert) D.; m. Mary Ann Obrut Dietrich, Jan 16, 1965, Mchelle R., James A. BA in Acctg., Walton Sch. of Commerce, Chgo., 1963. Auditor Bore-Warner Corp., Chgo., 1963-64, IIT Rsch. Inst., Chgo., 1964-65; controller Graphic Sys., Rockwell Internat., Chgo., 1965-76, Engine Divsn. Allis Chalmers Corp., Harvey, Ill., 1976-78; CFO Daubont Chem. Co., Oakbrook, Ill., 1979; v.p., gen. mgr. Engine and Indsl. Truck Divsn. Allis-Chalmers Corp., Milw., AC Reorganization, Milw., 1987—, Houston Dynamic Svc., Howton, Tex., 1991-92, Pro Set Inc, Dallas, 1993-94; regional v.p. SkyKing Freight Sys., Chgo., 1994—; bd. dirs. Engine Mfr. Chgo., 1984-87, Indecon, Inc., Cutler, Wis., 1987-92, Indsl. Truck Assn., Chgo., 1985-87; pres. J.J. Dietrich, Jr. & Assocs., Tinley Park, Ill., 1987—. Republican. Roman Catholic. Home: 5656 W 171st Pl Tinley Park IL 60477

DIETRICH, LINNEA SANDBERG STONESIFER, art educator; b. Lebanon, Pa., July 26, 1944; d. Frederick A. and Elsie Leona (Sandberg) Stonesifer; 1 child, Rick. BA, Am. U., Washington, 1966; MA, U. Del., 1967; PhD, 1973. Asst. prof. U. S.Fla., Tampa, Fla., 1968-85; prof., 1985-89; chair, full prof. Miami U., Oxford, Ohio, 1989-94; prof., 1994—; scholarship com. Gibson Found., Cin., 1989—; cons. Cin. Art Mus., 1989—, lectr. 1989—. Contbr. articles to profl. jours. Mem. Common Cause, Tampa, 1968-88, AUdubon Soc., Tampa, Oxford, 1968—. Named Excellence in Teaching U. S.Fla., Tampa, 1989; recipient Women's Inst. for Freedom of the Press, Washington, 1983. Mem. Coll. Art Assn., 19th Century Studies, Phi Kappa Phi. Office: Art Dept Miami University NAB 16 Oxford OH 45056

DIETRICH, RONALD G., electrical engineer; b. East Lansing, Mich., May 31, 1941. BSEE, Mich. State U., 1963. Prin. engr. Magnavox Corp., Ft. Wayne, Ind., 1963-77; owner Fremont (Ind.) Hardware, 1977-87; staff engr. Philips Techs., Auburn, Ind., 1991—. With U.S. Army/USNG, 1958-63. Mem. Masonic Lodge. Republican. Baptist. Home: 136 Clear Lake Dr Fremont IN 46737 Office: Philips Techs 813 S Grandstaff Dr Auburn IN 46706-2944

DIETRICH, SUZANNE CLAIRE, instructional designer; b. Granite City, Ill.; d. Charles Daniel and Evelyn Blanche (Waters) D.; BS in Speech, Northwestern U.; MS in Pub. Communication, Boston U., 1967; postgrad. So. Ill. U., 1973-83. Intern, prodn. staff Sta. WGBH-TV, Boston, 1958-59, asst. dir., 1962-64, asst. dir. program Invitation to Art, 1958; cons. producer dir. dept. instructional TV radio Ill. Office Supt. Pub. Instruction, Springfield, 1969-70; dir. program prodn. and distbn., 1970-72; instr. faculty call staff, speech dept. Sch. Fine Arts So. Ill. U., Edwardsville, 1972-73, grad. asst. for doctoral program office of dean Sch. Edn., 1975-78; rsch. asst. Ill. public telecommunications study for Ill. Public Broadcasting Coun., 1979-80; cons. and rsch. in communications, 1980—; exec. producer, dir. TV programs Con-Con Countdown, 1970, The Flag Speaks, 1971. Mem. sch. bd. St. Mary's Cath. Sch., Edwardsville, 1991-92; mem. cable TV adv. com. City of Edwardsville, 1994—, co-chair, 1996-97; bd. dirs. Goshen Preservation Alliance, Edwardsville, 1992-94, pres., 1995-97. Roman Catholic. Home: 1011 Minnesota St Edwardsville IL 62025-1424

DIETZ, MARGARET JANE, retired public information official, tutor; b. Omaha, Apr. 15, 1924; d. Lawrence Louis and Jeanette Amalia (Meile) Neumann; m. Richard Henry Dietz, May 30, 1949 (dec. July 1971); children: Henry Louis, Frederick Richard, Susan Margaret, John Lawrence (dec.). BA, U. Nebr., 1946; MS, Columbia U., 1949. Wire editor Kearney (Nebr.) Daily Hub, 1946-47; state society editor Omaha World-Herald, 1947-48; library aide Akron (Ohio) Pub. Libr., 1963-66, publicity and display dir., 1966-74, editor Owlet, 1966-74; pub. info. officer Northeastern Ohio Univs. Coll. Medicine, Rootstown, 1974-85, dir. Office of Comm., 1985-87, ret. 1987; writer Ravenna (Ohio) Record-Courier, 1988-92; cons. Kent (Ohio) State U. Sch. Music, 1988-91. Mem. culture and entertainment com. Goals for Greater Akron, 1976; pres. bd. Weathervane Cmty. Playhouse, Akron, 1982-85, sec. to the bd., 1988-93, trustee, 1991-93, historian, 1993—, chair 60th anniversary season, 1994-95; trustee Family Svcs. Summit County, Ohio, 1980-94, dist. trustee, 1994—, Am. Heart Assn., Akron dist., 1986-91, Mobile Meals Found., Akron, 1988-91; v.p. Friends of Akron-Summit County Pub. Libr., 1988-94, pres., 1994-95; student tutor LEARN Literacy Coun., 1988-94, trustee 1988-95. Author: Akron's Library: Commemorating Twenty Five Years on Main Street. Recipient Trustee award Weathervane Community Playhouse, 1985, Family Svcs. Bernard W. Frazier award, 1994, John S. Knight award Soc. Profl. Journalists, 1995, Mary Kerrigal O'Neil award Women in Comm., 1995. Mem. Women in Comm., LWV (edn. found. 1989-92, newsletter editor Akron 1957-60), College Club, Press Club, Akron Women's City Club. Home: 887 Canyon Trl Akron OH 44303-2401

DIETZ, RICHARD ALAN, engineer; b. Almont, Mich., Apr. 26, 1950; s. William T. and Velma C. D.; m Barbara Ann Dietz, Apr. 3, 1971; children: Sandra Ann, Dana Lyn. AD, Wayne State U., 1970. Designer Pioneer Engring., Warren, Mich., 1968-71; chief engr. Hydra Lock Corp., Warren, Mich., 1979—; mem. adv. bd. S.W. Tech. Macomb, Warren, 1993—. Patentee in field. Home: 7272 22 Mile Rd Utica MI 48317-2302

DIETZ, ROWLAND ERNEST, real estate manager; b. Cin., Oct. 26, 1920; s. William C.F. and Bertha (Stephens) D.; divorced; children: Christopher P., Brian Luther. BA, Swarthmore Coll.; MA, Columbia U., 1946, PhD, 1962. Instr. polit. sci. CCNY, N.Y.C., 1945-47, U. Cin., 1948-49; asst. prof. govt. Western Coll., Oxford, Ohio, 1963-68; pres. RE Dietz & Co. REal Estate Mgmt., Cin., 1952—; sec., trustee Ft. Washington Trust, Cin., 1970-88; trustee Better Housing League, Cin., 1953-64; dir., pres. Inst. Real Estate Mgmt., Cin., 1955-57. V.p. Cin. Coun. World Affairs, 1957; trustee, dir. City Charter Com., Cin., 1952-65; trustee Human Rels. Com., Cin., 1955-57; v.p., trustee Friends of CCM, Cin., 1995-96; mem. Cincinnatus Assn., Cin., 1975-95. Mem. Univ. Club., Master Gardner Assn. Gr. Cin. (dir. exec. com. 1994-96). Home: 2596 Perkins Ln Cincinnati OH 45208 Office: RE Dietz & Co Inc 225 E 6th St Cincinnati OH 45202

DIFILIPPO, JUDITH MURAIDA, rehabilitation nurse; b. Chgo., Apr. 5, 1947; d. Joseph S. and Mary Jane (Lippert) Muraida; m. Donald N. DiFilippo, Jan. 15, 1972; children: Anthony, Victoria. BS, St. Xavier U., Chgo., 1969; MS, St. Xavier Coll., Chgo., 1978. RN, Ill.; cert. rehab. RN. Staff nurse Mercy Hosp. and Med. Ctr., Chgo., 1969-71, asst. dir. nursing svc., 1980-84, rehab. clin. nurse specialist, 1984-88; instr. Evang. Sch. Nursing, Oak Lawn, Ill., 1971-74, St. Xavier Coll., 1978-83; unit mgr. Rush-Presbyn.-St. Luke's Med. Ctr., Chgo., 1988-94; rehab. advanced practice nurse specialist Advocate Home Health Svc., Oak Brook, Ill., 1994—; mem. commn. on accreditation ANCC, Washington, 1990-94. Pres. Queen of Martyrs Sch. Bd., Evergreen Park, Ill., 1984-86, boys' basketball coord., 1987-88, co-chair parish coun., 1996; troop leader Evergreen Park area Girl Scouts U.S., 1982-85. Mem. ANA, Ill. Nurses Assn. (dist. pres. 1986-88), Assn. Rehab. Nurses (treas. No. Ill. chpt. 1989-90, nat. chmn. film festival 1990, nat. conf. chmn. 1992, pres.-elect No. Ill. chpt. 1993, pres. 1994, region 4 dir. 1995—), St. Xavier Alumni Assn. (past officer, bd. dirs.), Sigma Theta Tau (Excellence in Nursing Practice award Alpha Omicron chpt. 1987). Home: 3608 W 117th St Chicago IL 60655-4201 Office: Advocate Home Health Care Rush Presbyn St Lukes Med Ctr 1441 Branding Ln Downers Grove IL 60515

DIGIACOMO, ROBERT JAMES, purchasing and merchandising professional; b. Chgo., Oct. 18, 1950; s. Rene Alphonse and Rosella Marie (MastAndrea) DiG.; m. Julianne Salmi, Feb. 9, 1973 (div. 1989); 1 child, Matthew James. BS in Commerce, DePaul U., 1973. Asst. buyer Carson Pirie Scott & Co., Chgo., 1973-74, div. sales mgr., 1975-76, buyer, 1976-77; buyer Target Stores, Mpls., 1977-79; sr. buyer Lechmere, Inc., Woburn, Mass., 1979-83, div. mdse. mgr., 1984-87; v.p. merchandising Rent-A-Ctr., Wichita, Kans., 1987-95; v.p., dir. merchandising Thorn Europe, London, 1996—; com. mem. NATM Buying Group, N.Y.C., 1979-85, Thorn Procurement Group, London, 1988-90. Named Buyer of Yr. Telecommunications mag., 1983. Home: 1450 S Webb Rd Apt 422 Wichita KS 67207-4257 Office: Rent A Ctr 8200 Rent A Center Dr Wichita KS 67226-2706

DIGIOVANNA, JOSEPH W., JR., physical therapist; b. St. Louis, Mar. 16, 1961; s. Joseph W. Sr. and Adele Mary (Allain) DiG.; m. Mary Ann Dallas, May 28, 1994. BS in Phys. Therapy, St. Louis U., 1984. Cert. specialist in orthopedic phys. therapy; manual therapist. Staff therapist Tulane Med. Ctr., New Orleans, 1984-86; staff therapist, v.p. Wayzata (Minn.) Phys. Therapy, 1986-92; gen. mgr. NovaCare Outpatient Rehab., Wayzata, 1992—; clin. instr., Coll. of St. Catherine, Mpls., 1992—; lectr. Clin. Specialty Educators, 1993—. Mem. Am. Phys. Therapy Assn. (program com. chair 1989-93), Am. Acad. Manipulative Phys. Therapy (assoc. fellow). Office: Novacare Outpatient Rehab Divsn 1 Carlson Pky #235 Plymouth MN 55416

DIGIOVANNI, LARRY JOSEPH, human resources executive; b. Phila., Sept. 23, 1948; s. Salvatore and Viola (Lafen) DiG.; m. Susan Marie Pacelli, June 27, 1975. BBA, LaSalle U., Phila., 1970. Adminstrv. systems analyst Reliance Ins. Cos., Phila., 1971-74; salary analyst ICI Ams., Wilmington, Del., 1974-75; compensation and benefits specialist Mobil Chem. Co., Macedon, N.Y., 1975-77; compensation cons. NL Industries, Hightstown, N.J., 1977-79; mgr. compensation Hercules, Inc., Wilmington, 1979-82, dir. human resources, 1985-88; v.p. human resources aerospace div. Hercules, Inc., Salt Lake City, 1982-85; v.p. human resources Hercules Aerospace Co., Wilmington, Del., 1988-95, Aerospace Sys. Group Alliant Techsystems, Inc., Hopkins, Minn., 1995—; mem. adv. com. Del. Gov.'s Compensation Com., Wilmington, 1980-82. Mem. adv. group Nat. Alliance of Bus., Salt Lake City, 1984-85; bd. dirs. Utah Health Cost Mgmt. Found., Salt Lake City, 1983-85. Served with USN, 1971-73. Mem. Am. Compensation Assn., Aerospace Industries Assn. (human resources coun. 1987—). Republican. Roman Catholic. Office: Alliant Techsystems Inc MN11-1015 600 Second St NE Hopkins MN 55343

DIGMAN, LESTER ALOYSIUS, management educator; b. Kieler, Wis., Nov. 22, 1938; s. Arthur Louis and Hilda Dorothy (Jansen) D.; m. Ellen Rhomberg Pfohl, Jan. 15, 1966; children: Stephanie, Sarah, Mark. BSME, U. Iowa, 1961, MSIE, 1962, PhD, 1970. Registered profl. engr., Mass. Mgmt. cons. U.S. Ameta, Rock Island, Ill., 1962-67; mgmt. instr. U. Iowa, Iowa City, 1967-69; head applied math. dept. U.S. Ameta, Rock Island, Ill., 1969-74, head managerial tng. dept., 1974-77; assoc. prof. mgt. U. Nebr., Lincoln, 1977-84, dir. grad. studies in mgmt., 1982—, prof. mgmt., 1984-87, Leonard E Whittaker Am. Charter disting. prof. mgmt., 1987-93, Met. Fed. Bank disting. prof. mgmt., 1993-95; First Bank disting. prof. mgmt. U. Nebr., 1995—; dir. Ctr. for Tech. Mgmt. and Decision Scis., 1992-94; interim dir. Gallup Rsch. Ctr., 1994-95; mem. adv. bd. Ctr. for Albanian Studies, 1992—; cons. various orgns., 1963-72; sec. treas. Mgmt. Svcs. Assocs. Ltd., Davenport, Iowa, 1972-77; owner L.A. Digman and Assocs., Lincoln, 1977—; gen. ptnr. Letna Properties, Madison, Wis., 1978—. Author: Strategic Management, 1986, 3d edit., 1995, Network Analysis for Management Decisions, 1982; contbr. articles to profl. jours. Recipient Dist. award SBA, 1980, Certs. of Appreciation Dept. of Def., 1972. Fellow Decision Scis. Inst. (charter, program chmn. 1986, pres. 1987-88, coord. doctoral consortium 1989, strategy/policy track chmn. 1991, v.p. 1992-94, strategic mgmt. track chmn. internat. meeting 1993, chair long-range planning com. 1995-96); mem. IEEE, Strategic Mgmt. Soc. (founding), Acad. of Mgmt., Strategic Leadership Forum, Pan Pacific Bus. Assn., Inst. for Ops. Rsch. and Mgmt. Scis. (founding), MBA Roundtable (charter, steering com.), Firethorn Country Club, Confrerie de la Chaine Rotisseurs. Roman Catholic. Home: 7520 Lincolnshire Rd Lincoln NE 68506-1635 Office: U Nebr 277 CBA Lincoln NE 68588

DI LIELLO, SALVATORE, data processing executive, educator; b. Naples, Campania, Italy, Dec. 29, 1958; came to U.S., 1974; s. Antonio and Concetta (Strazzullo) Di L. BS, Youngstown State U., 1984, postgrad. Cert. systems profl. Microfilm supr. City of Warren, Ohio, 1980-81, data processing operator, 1981-82, data processing coordinator, 1982-83, data processing supr., 1983-85, data processing mgr., 1985—; instr. Bd. Edn., Warren, 1983—. Writer computer software Final Billing Utility System, 1981. Mem. Data Processing Mgmt. Assn. (pres. 1985-86, Plague 1986), U.S. Jaycee's Warren Chpt. (fellow). Roman Catholic. Home: 926 Terra Alta St NE Warren OH 44483-3929 Office: City of Warren 391 Mahoning Ave NW Warren OH 44483-4634

DILL, DOUGLAS ARTHUR, investment counselor; b. Columbus, Ohio, Apr. 3, 1968. BA, Bowling Green U., 1991. Lic. securities dealer. Investment counselor Sweeney Cartwright, Columbus, 1991-93, McDonald & Co. Securities, Cleve., 1993—. Contbr. articles to profl. jours. Bd. dean's coun. Bowling Green State U., 1993; assoc. cabinet United Way, Cleve., 1994—; fundraiser Alzheimer's orgn., Cleve., 1995—; mem. Young Reps. Office: McDonald & Co Securities 2100 Society Bldg 800 Superior Ave E Cleveland OH 44114-2601

DILL, ELLEN RENÉE, minister; b. Detroit, Jan. 2, 1949; d. Clarence Lorenzo and Melvin Elizabeth (Knowles) D.; divorced; children: Christopher Edward Brown, Crystal Elizabeth Brown. BA, Nazareth Coll. Mich., 1972; MDiv, Garrett Evang. Sem., Evanston, Ill., 1979; postgrad., Northwestern U., Evanston, Ill., 1979-82; DMin, Chgo. Theol. Sem., 1995. Lic. to ministry United Meth. Ch., 1974, ordained 1985. Teaching asst. Head Start St. Agnes Ch., Detroit, 1966-68; tchr. Eastside Vicariate Sch., Detroit, 1972-77; pastor St. Luke United Meth. Ch., Chgo., 1980-82; assoc. pastor First United Meth. Ch., Chgo., 1982-84; pastor Clair-Christian United Meth. Ch., Chgo., 1984-88, Community United Meth. Ch., Markham, Ill., 1988-90, Woodlawn United Meth. Ch., Chgo., 1990-93; Oakland Ave. United Meth. Ch., 1993; pastor Homer-Immanuel United Meth. Ch., 1995; condr. seminar on women in ministry Garrett Evang. Sem., 1981, condr. seminar on ch. and soc., 1980, instr. continuing edn. seminar for clergy in adminstrn., 1987; bd. dirs. So. Dist. Bd. Ordained Ministry, Bd. Ch. Bldg. Location; mem. So. Dist. Coun. on Ministries, So. Dist. Strategy Com.; former chmn. No. Ill. Conf. Bd. Edn., So. Dist. Bd. Edn.; former asst. chmn. bd. edn. United Meth. Ch.; mem. Detroit Conf. Elders Orders, 1985; asst. spiritual dir. Walk to Emmaus, 1988-90, 92, spiritual dir. men's walk, 1991; mem. No. Ill. Conf. Commn. on Status and Role of Women, 1991-93, United Meth. Found., U. Chgo., 1990-93; mem. monitoring com. Ill. Conf. Configuration; mem. planning com. Western Dist. Lab. Sch.; invocation Chgo. City Coun. meetings, 1990, 91, 93; chairperson Minn. Conf. Commn. on Religion and Race, 1995—; mem. Minn. Conf. Coun. on Ministries, 1995—; mem. Ethics Minority Concerns Commn., Minn. Conf., 1993—. Co-author: Teachers Guide: Two Hundred Years of American Methodism, 1981; editorial advisor The Christian Ministry jour., 1987—; contbr. articles to profl. jours. Bd. dirs. Carroll M. Felton Jr. Housing Found., 1992-93; asst. dean Pembroke Inst., 1992; bd. dirs. Austin Christian Law Ctr., 1983-93, Child Serve Cmty. Coun., Chgo., 1984-88, Garrett-Evang. Sem., 1978; area chair Mayor's Com. to Keep Detroit Beautiful, 1965. Recipient citation Mayor's Com. To Keep Detroit Beautiful, 1966, citation for excellence in journalism Mich. Press Assn., 1978; Hartman scholar, 1979; Dempster Grad. fellow, 1980, Hartman fellow, 1981. Mem. NAFE, Nat. Assn. Bus. and Profl. Women, Internat. Platform Assn., Black United Meths. for Ch. Renewal (citation for svc. 1982, planning com. jurisdictional meeting, bd. dirs.), Clergy Cluster, Ecumenical Ministerial Assn., Women of the 90s (exec. com. 1992-93), Minn. Coun. of Chs. (bd. dirs. 1994—), Mpls. Initiative AgainstRacism, Mpls. Coun. Ch. (ministries divsn.). Home and Office: 457 S Baker St Winona MN 55987

DILL, WILLIAM JOSEPH, newspaper editor; b. Carmi, Ill., May 8, 1935; s. Hurshell Lloyd and Alma Lucille (Newby) D.; m. Marie Emilie Hubert, Aug. 14, 1965; children: Kevin Joseph, Kathleen Marie, Lisa Marie, Christopher Hubert. BS in Journalism, So. Ill. U., 1961. Reporter, editor AP, Chgo., 1961-65, asst. bur. chief, 1965-69; bur. chief AP, Balt., 1969-71, Nashville, 1971-73, Charlotte, N.C., 1973-76, Mpls., 1976-81; editor The Forum, Fargo, N.D., 1981—; juror Pulitzer Prize, 1985-86, 86-87. Served with USN, 1953-57. Named Journalism Alumnus of Yr., So. Ill. U., 1970. Fellow Am. Soc. Newspaper Editors; mem. Soc. Profl. Journalists (pres. local chpt. 1970-71). Roman Catholic. Home: 105 19th Ave N Fargo ND 58102-2351 Office: The Forum PO Box 2020 Fargo ND 58107-2020

DILLARD, DEAN INNES, English language educator; b. Melvern, Kans., Aug. 13, 1947; s. Alva Everett and Dorothy Marie (Whitney) D. BS in Edn., Emporia (Kans.) State U., 1969, MA, 1975, postgrad., 1977; postgrad., Ft. Hays State U., Hays, Kans., 1980. Tchr. English Unified Sch. Dist. 379, Clay Center, Kans., 1969-70; tchr. English and social studies Unified Sch. Dist. 208, WaKeeney, Kans., 1972-84; instr. English Neosho County C.C., Chanute, Kans., 1984—, chair divsn. liberal arts, 1996—; mem. fine arts task force Neosho County Community Coll., Chanute, 1990-91. With U.S. Army, 1970-71. Mem. MLA, Nat. Coun. Tchrs. English, Assembly on Lit. for Adolescents (life), Midwest Modern Lang. Assn., Kans. Assn. Tchrs. English (exec. bd. 1981-84), Neosho County Community Coll. Educators Assn., Am. Legion, VFW, Chanute Lions Club (zone chmn. 1988-90), Kappa Delta Pi. Republican. Home: 732 S Washington Ave Chanute KS 66720-2713 Office: Neosho County C C 1000 S Allen Ave Chanute KS 66720-2639

DILLARD, KIRK WHITFIELD, lawyer, state senator; b. Chgo., June 1, 1955; s. Edward Floyd and Martina Raye (Whitfield) D.; m. Carol E. Crumbaugh, Mar. 16, 1985. BA, Western Ill. U., 1977; JD, DePaul U., 1982. Bar: Ill. 1983, U.S. Dist Ct. (no. dist.) Ill. 1983, U.S. Dist Ct. (cen. dist.) Ill. 1984, U.S. Dist. Ct. (ea. dist.) Mich. 1988. Staff cons. Ill. State Senate, Springfield, 1977-81; atty., dir. legis. affairs Ill. Office Gov., civ-ingfield, 1982-87; chief of staff Ill. Office Gov., Springfield, 1991-93; judge State of Ill. Ct. of Claims, Springfield, 1987-90; ptnr. Lord, Bissell & Brook, Chgo., 1987—; mem. Ill. Senate, 1993—; legal writing and moot ct. tutor DePaul U. Coll. Laws, 1981-82; guest lectr. Loyola and DePaul U. Coll. Law, Chgo. Rep. precinct committeeman DuPage County, Wheaton, Ill., 1988; mem. Union League Chgo., Bi-State 3rd Airport for Chgo. Study Commn., Ill. Coalition. Named Legislator of the Yr. for Civil Justice, Am. Legis. Exch. Coun., 1995. mem. ABA (Best performance in land use and local govt. law courses award Urban, State and Local Govt. sect. 1982), Ill. Assn. Def. Trial Counsel, Ill. State Bar Assn., Western Ill. U. Alumni Coun. (pres. 1989-92), Blue Key, Phi Alpha Delta. Methodist. Home: 120 Rosalie Ct Hinsdale IL 60521-3165 Office: Lord Bissell & Brook 115 S La Salle St Chicago IL 60603-3801

DILLAVOU, JOHN G., stockbroker, former educator; b. Champaign, Ill., Jan. 12, 1925. BS, Regis Coll., Denver, 1948. Stockbroker Hayden Stone, Champaign, 1965-69, Walston & Co., Champaign, 1969-73, A.G. Edwards & Sons Inc., Champaign, 1973—. Staff sgt. USAAF, 1943-45. Mem. Champaign Country Club (bd. dirs.). Republican. Roman Catholic. Home: 3509 Lakeshore Dr Champaign IL 61821-5201 Office: AG Edwards & Sons Inc 100 Trade Centre Dr Champaign IL 61820-7237

DILLE, ROLAND PAUL, college president; b. Dassel, Minn., Sept. 16, 1924; s. Oliver Valentine and Eleanor (Johnson) D.; m. Beth Hopeman, Sept. 4, 1948; children—Deborah, Martha, Sarah, Benjamin. B.A. summa cum laude, U. Minn., 1949, Ph.D., 1962, LHD (hon.), 1995. Instr. English U. Minn., 1953-56; asst. prof. St. Olaf Coll., Northfield, Minn., 1956-61; asst. prof. English Calif. Lutheran Coll., Thousand Oaks, Calif., 1961-63; mem. faculty Moorhead (Minn.) State U., 1964-94, pres., 1968-94; ret., 1994; chmn. Commn. on Instns. Higher Edn. of N. Cen. Assn. of Colls. and Schs., 1991. Author: Four Romantic Poets, 1969; contbr. numerous articles and revs. to profl. jours. Treas. Am. Assn. State Colls. and Univs., 1977-78, bd. dirs., 1978-80, chmn., 1980-81; mem. Nat. Coun. for Humanities, 1980-86; vice-chair Commn. on Higher Edn., North Cen. Assn., 1989-91, chair, 1991-93. With inf. AUS, 1944-46. Disting. Svc. to Humanities award given by Minn. Humanities Commn. named in his honor; named one of 100 most effective Am. coll. pres., 1987. Mem. Phi Beta Kappa. Home: 516 9th St S Moorhead MN 56560-3519 Office: Moorhead State U 11th St S Moorhead MN 56560-9980

DILLE, STEPHEN EVERETT, farmer, state legislator, veterinarian; b. Mpls., Mar. 16, 1945; s. Donald Everett and Bonnie Marie (Anderson) D.; m. Pamela Jane Johnson, July 5, 1975; children: Nicholas, Kaisa, Spencer, Mitchell. BS, U. Minn., 1967, DVM, 1969. Vet. advisor USAID, South Vietnam, 1969-73; mem. faculty Coll. Vet. Medicine U. Minn., St. Paul, 1973-75; pvt. vet. practice Litchfield, Minn., 1975—; crop livestock farmer Dassel, Minn., 1975—, twp. supr., 1977-84; county commr. Meeker County, Minn., 1985-86; rep. Dist. 21A Minn. Ho. of Reps., St. Paul, 1987-92; state senator Dist. 20 Minn. State Senate, St. Paul, 1993—. Republican. Home: 69800 305th St Dassel MN 55325-2912 Office: Minn State Senate 103 SOB Saint Paul MN 55155

DILLIN, S. HUGH, federal judge; b. Petersburg, Ind., June 9, 1914; s. Samuel E. and Maude (Harrell) D.; m. Mary Eloise Humphreys, Nov. 24, 1940; 1 child, Patricia Wright. A.B. in Govt, Ind. U., 1936, LLB, 1938, LLD, 1992; D of Civil Law (hon.), Ind. State U., 1990. Bar: Ind. 1938. Ptnr. Dillin & Dillin, Petersburg, 1938-61; U.S. dist. judge So. Dist. Ind., 1961—, chief judge, 1982-84; mem. Jud. Conf. U.S., 1979-82, mem. exec. com., 1980-82, mem. Jud. Conf. Com. on Ct. Adminstrn., 1983-89, chmn. subcom. on fed.-state rels., 1983-89; mem. Jud. Panel on Multidist. Litigation, 1983-92; sec. Pub. Svc. Commn. Ind., 1942; mem. Interstate Oil Compact Commn., 1949-52, 61. Mem. Ind. Ho. of Reps. from Pike and Knox Counties, 1937, 39, 41, 51, floor leader, 1951; mem. Ind. Senate from Pike and Gibson Counties, 1959-61, pres. pro tem, 1961. Capt. AUS, 1943-46. Recipient Disting. Alumnus award Ind. U. Coll. Arts and Scis., 1985, Ind. U. Sch. Law, 1987. Mem. Am. Bar Assn., Ind. State Bar Assn., Fed. Bar Assn., 7th Cir. Judges Assn. (pres. 1977-79), Am. Judicature Soc., Delta Tau Delta, Phi Delta Phi. Democrat. Presbyn. Club: Indianapolis Athletic. Office: US Dist Ct 255 US Courthouse 46 E Ohio St Indianapolis IN 46204-1903

DILLING, KIRKPATRICK WALLWICK, lawyer; b. Evanston, Ill., Apr. 11, 1920; s. Albert W. and Elizabeth (Kirkpatrick) D.; m. Betty Ellen Bronson, June 18, 1942 (div. July 1944); m. Elizabeth Ely Tilden, Dec. 11, 1948; children: Diana Jean, Eloise Tilden, Victoria Walgreen, Albert Kirkpatrick. Student, Cornell U., 1939-40; BS in Law, Northwestern U., 1942; postgrad., DePaul U., 1946-47, L'Ecole Vaubier, Montreux, Switzerland; Degré Normal, Sorbonne U., Paris. Bar: Ill. 1947, U.S. Dist. Ct. (no. dist.) Ill., Ind., Mich., Md., La., Tex., Okla., Wis., Idaho, U.S. Ct. Appeals (2nd, 3rd, 5th, 7th, 8th, 9th, 10th, 11th, fed. and D.C. cirs.), U.S. Supreme Ct. Ptnr. Dilling and Dilling, Chgo., 1948—; counsel Cancer Control Soc., Nat. Coun. for Improved Health; bd. dirs. Eagle Sci. Co., Klaire Labs., V.E. Irons, Inc.; v.p. Midwest Medic-Aide, Inc.; spl. counsel Herbalife (U.K.) Ltd., Herbalife Australisia Pty., Ltd.; lectr. on pub. health law. Contbr. articles to pub. health publs. Bd. dirs. Adelle Davis Found. 1st lt. AUS,

1943-46. Recipient Humanitarian award Nat. Health Fedn. Mem. ABA, Ill. Bar Assn., Chgo. Bar Assn., Assn. Trial Lawyers Am., Cornell Soc. Engrs., Am. Legion, Air Force Assn., Pharm. Advt. Club, Rolls Royce Owners' Club, Tower Club, Cornell U., Chicago Club, Delta Upsilon. Republican. Episcopalian. Home: 1120 Lee Rd Northbrook IL 60062-3816 Office: 150 N Wacker Dr Chicago IL 60606-1611 Also: 75560 Calle dur Sur Indian Wells CA 92210

DILLINGHAM, JOHN ALLEN, marketing professional; b. Kansas City, Mo., Jan. 9, 1939; s. Jay B. and Frances (Thompson) D.; m. Nancy Jane Abbott, Sept. 4, 1965; children: Allen Edwards, William Kemp. AS, Wentworth Mil. Acad., 1958; AB in Polit. Sci., U. Mo., 1961, MS in Pub. Adminstrn., 1962. Br. mgr. W.R. Grace Co., Mt. Vernon, Ill., 1964-68; pres. Sho-Hawk Industries, Kansas City, Mo., 1968-72; v.p. comml. loans Traders Nat. Bank, Kansas City, 1972-79; sr. v.p. sales and mktg. Garney Constrn. Co., Kansas City, 1979-95; bd. dirs. Kansas City Conv. and Vis. Bur., 1976-80, Boatmen's Bank, Northland, Kansas City; chmn. Clay County Indsl. Devel. Authority, 1980—, Clay County EDC, 1972-74; mem. pres. adv. bd. for extension U. Mo., 1972-80. Trustee Wentworth Mil. Acad., Lexington, 1978-80, 93—; state chmn. Mo. 4H Found., Columbia, 1985-90; mem. ctrl. governing bd. Children's Mercy Hosp., Kansas City, 1987-92; bd. dirs. Northland Cmty. Fund, Kansas City, 1988—, Kansas City Sports Commn., 1990-93; treas. Harry S. Truman Scholarship Nat. Alumni Assn., 1979-90; mem., v.p. Kansas City Bd. Police Commrs., 1990-95; chmn. Kansas City Mcpl. Asst. Corp., 1984—; mem. Nat. 4H Resource Devel. Com., 1990-92; exec. bd. Heart of Am. coun. Boy Scouts Am., 1993—; 1st bd. dirs. alumni assn. U.S. Command and Gen. Staff Coll., Ft. Leavenworth, Kans., 1993—; dir. DARE of Greater Kansas City, 1995—, CMSU Found. Warrensburg, 1995. Recipient Faculty Alumni award U. Mo., Columbia, 1981, Silver Beaver award Boy Scouts Am. Heart Am. coun., 1992, Harry S. Truman Scholarship Appreciation plaque, 1993, Cmty. Svc. award Park Coll., 1993, Pub. Svc. award Mo. State Univ., 1994; named one of 100 Most Influential Kans. Citizens, Ingrams Mag., 1993. Mem. Northland C. of C. (Quality of Life award), KC Kings, Gold Coaters (pres. 1979-89), Native Sons Kansas City (bd. dirs. 1991-92), Sigma Alpha Epsilon (KC Alumni Assn. pres. 1976, Honor Man 1988, trustee Nat. Found. 1987-93, Nat. Disting. Svc. award 1993). Democrat. Mem. Disciples of Christ Ch. Home: 4040 NW Claymont Dr Kansas City MO 64116-1751 Office: Garney Constrn Co 924 Livestock Exch Bldg Kansas City MO 64102

DILLMAN, LOWELL THOMAS, physics educator; b. Huntington, Ind., Aug. 26, 1931; s. Lloyd Everett and Nancy Marie (Walther) D.; m. Mary Alice Bagwell, Apr. 18, 1954; children: John Mark, Anne Elizabeth, Mary Susan, Bradford Louis. BA, Manchester Coll., 1953; MS, U. Ill., 1955, PhD, 1958. Asst. prof. Ohio Wesleyan U., Delaware, 1958-63, assoc. prof., 1963-69, prof. physics, 1969—; cons. Health & Safety Rsch. Div., Oak Ridge (Tenn.) Nat. Lab., 1967-90. Co-author: MIRD: Radionuclide Data and Decay Schemes, 1989, Radionuclide Transformations, 1983; contbr. over 30 articles to sci. jours. Recipient Herbert Welch Meritorious Teaching award Ohio Wesleyan U., 1980. Mem. Am. Phys. Soc., Am. Assn. Physics Tchrs., Ohio Sect. Am. Phys. Soc. (treas. 1970-80), Sigma Xi. Democrat. Unitarian. Office: Ohio Wesleyan U Science Hall Delaware OH 43015

DILLMAN, NORMAN GREGG, electronics engineering educator; b. Carlisle, Iowa, Sept. 5, 1938; s. Franklin Gregg and Avis Mae (Mumford) D.; m. Phyllis Ann Clark, Aug. 10, 1957; children: David Scott, Linda Sue, Mark Alan. BS, Iowa State U., 1960, MS, 1962, PhD, 1965. Instr. Iowa State U., Ames, 1963-65; assoc. prof. U. Mo., Rolla, 1965-74; engr., engring. mgr. Hewlett Packard Co., Ft. Collins, Colo., 1974-90; prof. Kans. State U., Manhattan, 1990—; engr. Autonetics, Downey, Calif., summer 1962-64, Hughes Aircraft, Fullerton, Calif., summer 1966; adj. prof. U. P.R., Mayaguez, 1982-84; vis. prof. U. Tex., El Paso, 1988-90. Contbr. articles to profl. jours.; patentee in field. Recipient Edn. medal Govt. of South Vietnam, 1974. Mem. IEEE (sr., engring. accreditation evaluator 1983—). Unitarian. Office: Kans State U 261 Durland Hall Manhattan KS 66506-5100

DILLON, HERMAN G., state legislator; b. Junction City, Kans., Nov. 22, 1926; s. Henry James and Nellie C. (Stillwell) D.; m. Betty Jane Childs, 1947; 1 child, Diana J. Dillon Allen. Kans. state rep. Dist. 32, 1977—. Mem. Armourdale Bus. and Home Owners Assn., Teamsters Union Local 41, Southside and Armourdale Dem. Club. Mem. Optimists. Home: 611 S Coy St Kansas City KS 66105-2011*

DILLON, HOWARD BURTON, civil engineer; b. Hardyville, Ky., Aug. 12, 1935; s. Charlie Edison and Mary Opal (Bell) D.; m. Bonny Jean Garard, May 19, 1962; 1 child, Robert Edward. BCE, U. Louisville, 1958, MCE, 1960; postgrad., Okla. State U., 1962, Mich. State U., 1962-65. Registered profl. engr., Ind. Instr. U. Louisville, Ky., 1958-60; from assoc. prof. to prof. Ind. Inst. Tech., Ft. Wayne, 1960-62; NSF fellow Okla. State U., Stillwater, 1962; NSF grantee, instr. Mich. State U., East Lansing, 1962-67; head civil engring. dept. MW Inc. Cons. Engrs., Indpls., 1967-83; project mgr. civil div. SEG Engrs. & Cons., Indpls., 1983-91; pvt. civil engring. cons. Howard B. Dillon, Cons. Engr., Indpls., 1991—; asst. dir. to local pub. road needs study for Ind., 1970; mem. design com. for dams in Ind., 1974—; spl. cons. to Ind. Dept. Nat. Resources on dams, 1980—; mem. infrastructure com. for State of Ind., 1984—. Contbr. articles to profl. jours. Committeeman Wayne 52 precinct, Indpls., 1972-86; vice-ward chmn. Wayne South Twp., Indpls., 1986-87. Hazelett and Erdal scholar, 1957-58, W.B. Wendt scholar U. Louisville; recipient Order of Engr. award Purdue U., 1993. Mem. ASCE (Outstanding Civil Engring. Grad. award 1958), NSPE, Am. Soc. Engring. Edn., ASTM, Internat. Soc. Found. Engrs., Mil. Engrs., Internat. Acad. Sci. Ind. Water Resources Assn., Nat. Audubon Soc., Optimists (pres. Suburban West chpt. 1972-74, bd. dirs. 1974-78, sec. 1992-94, lt. gov. ind. dist. 1972-74, Optimist of Yr., 1995); Chi Epsilon. Democrat. Baptist. Home and Office: 6548 Westdrum Rd Indianapolis IN 46241-1843

DILLON, HUGH J., stockbroker; b. Mpls., Nov. 13, 1962. BS, U. Minn., 1985. Stockbroker Summit Investment Corp., Bloomington, Minn., 1980—. Mem. KC. Republican. Roman Catholic.

DILLON, MICHAEL C., stockbroker; b. Davenport, Iowa, Aug. 3, 1966. BA, U. Ill., 1988. Investment cons. Comerica Bank, Skokie, Ill., 1988-93; sr. investment cons. Bank One, Evanston, Ill., 1993-94; investment advisor David A. Noyes & Co., Skokie, 1994—. Mem. Evanston Gold Club. Republican. Office: David A Noyes & Co 8707 Skokie Blvd Ste 100 Skokie IL 60077-2200

DILLON, PHILLIP MICHAEL, construction company executive; b. Ypsilanti, Mich., July 15, 1944; s. Robert Timothy and Maxine Helen (Elliott) D.; student Mich. State U., 1962-66; m. Phyllis Louise Brooks, Jan. 21, 1978; children: Richard, Debora, Michael, Robert, Karen. Store mgr. Morse Shoe, Inc., Detroit, 1964-68, asst. dir. store planning and constrn., Canton, Mass., 1968-72; dir. store planning and constrn. Stride Rite Corp., Boston, 1972-74; sr. v.p. Capitol Cos., Inc., Arlington Heights, Ill., 1974-81; chmn. bd., chief exec. officer Standard Cos., Inc., Palatine, Ill., 1982-83; co-owner, sr. v.p. Eagle Constrn. Corp., 1983-88; chief exec. officer Dillon Enterprises Ltd., Lemont, Ill., 1988—; bd. dirs. Dillon Enterprises, Ltd.; co-owner, bd. dirs., chmn. Ominitech, Inc.; co-owner, bd. dirs., sr. ptnr. Internat. Developers Partnership, Dillon Farm Partnership Mich., Dillon Yo Ranch Partnership Tex. Mem. Inst. Store Planners, Assn. Gen. Contractors Am., Builders Assn. Chgo., Land Owners Assn. (archtl. rev. com.), Green Acres Sportsman Club, Tex. Longhorn Breeders Assoc. Roman Catholic. Office: 50 E New Ave Lemont IL 60439-3666

DILLON, THOMAS RAY, financial planner; b. Alton, Ill., Dec. 16, 1948; s. Elmer Charles Dillon and Doris Jean (Autery) Drewes; m. Eileen Frances Fudala, June 1, 1974; 1 child, Brett. BS in Indsl. Mgmt., Purdue U., 1971. Cert. fin. planner. Account exec. Merrill Lynch, St. Louis, 1975-77, Dean Witter, St. Louis, 1977-82; dir. fin. services div. Bruno, Stolze & Co., St. Louis, 1982—. Contbr. articles to fin. jours.; author, editor radio show Tip of the Week, 1980-82. Speaker various civic orgns., St. Louis, 1980-86; bd. dirs. Optimists Club of West Port, St. Louis, 1978-82. Mem. Internat. Assn. Fin. Planning (v.p. St. Louis chpt. 1982-84, pres. 1984-86, bd. dirs. Atlanta hdqrs. 1986-88), Inst. Cert. Fin. Planners (bd. dirs. St. Louis chpt. 1984-86), Registry Fin. Planning Practitioners. Office: Bruno Stolze & Co Inc 12444 Powerscourt Dr Ste 230 Saint Louis MO 63131-3619

DI MENZA, SALVATORE, psychologist; b. Chgo., May 2, 1938; s. Salvatore and Bartalomea (Gallina) diM. A.B., DePaul U., 1960, M.A., 1964; postgrad. Loyola U., 1961-64, Ill. Inst. Tech., 1964, 68-72. Dir. research Ill. Drug Abuse Program, Chgo., 1972-73; dir. mgmt. systems Ill. Drug Abuse Program, 1973; dir. drug abuse div. Joint Commn. Accreditation of Hosps., Chgo., 1973-76, assoc. program dir. for planning and devel., 1976-78; mng. partner Health Resources Mgmt. Systems, Chgo., 1978-80; pres. AGI, Rolling Meadows, Ill., 1981-84; v.p. J.W. Crawford Assos., Inc., Chgo., 1979-80; research and eval. cons. Cook County Research and Eval. Project, Inc., Chgo., 1985-86; spl. asst. to dir., Nat. Inst. on Drug Abuse, Rockville, Md., 1986-89; acting dep. dir. Office of Treatment Improvement, Rockville, 1990-91; dir. spl. projects group Substance Abuse and Mental Health Svcs. Adminstrn., 1991-92; policy analyst Office of Nat. Drug Control, 1992-93; pres. Rehabilitation Systems, Inc., 1993-95; instrnl. asst. Wayne State U., Detroit, 1995—; cons. bus. formation and mgmt.; developer nat. standards for providing drug abuse treatment svcs., also large scale employee assistance programs and mental health svcs. for industry, drug abuse policies, clin. mgmt. systems. Recipient Superior Achievement award State of Ill., 1972, Spl. Recognition award Office Asst. Sec. Health, 1992, Recognition award Dept. Alcoholism and Substance Abuse, 1995. Contbr. articles to profl. jours. Home: 2837 S Princeton Ave Chicago IL 60616-2609

DIMERCURIO, PETER N., financial consultant; b. Saginaw, Mich., Mar. 6, 1946. BA, Saginaw Valley State U., 1974; MA, Salve Regina U., 1989, U.S. Naval Coll., 1990. Fin. cons. Merrill Lynch, Traverse City, Mich., 1994—. Contbr. articles to profl. jours. Col. U.S. Army, 1969-94. Mem. KC, VFW, Traverse City C. of C., Kiwanis, Elks. Roman Catholic. Office: Merrill Lynch 12935 S West Bay Shore Dr # 400 Traverse City MI 49684-5453

DINARDO, RUSSELL ANTHONY, architect; b. Monongehala, Pa., Jan. 27, 1967; s. Ronald and Ruth Anne (Magera) DiN. BArch cum laude, U. Cin., 1995. Machine technician Teledyne Republic, Cleve., 1984-85, 89; intern architect Glick/Boehm and Assocs., Charleston, S.C., 1991-92, Michael Schuster Assocs., Cin., 1992-93; teaching asst. U. Cin., 1992-94; intern architect Michael Graves Architects, Princeton, N.J., 1993—; designer DiNardo Designs, Ohio and N.J., 1992—; illustrator/cons. Avondale Redevel., Cin., 1994-95; planning cons. City of Covington, Ky., 1994-95. Adv. com. U. Cin. Sch. Arch., 1990, 94; vol. Spl. Olympics, Tex., Ohio, S.C., 1985-95; cert. coach Pop Warner Football, Charleston, 1987-89. Sgt. USAF, 1985-89. Hixon, Inc. scholar, 1994, City Blue scholar Cleve. Women's League, 1993-94, NWIC scholar, 1994; recipient medal Alpha Rho Chi, 1995; inductee N. Ridgeville H.S. Hall of Fame, 1996. Mem. Am. Inst. Arch. Students (v.p. 1990-92), Air Force Assn., Nat. Trust Historic Preservation, Golden Key.

DINDA, MICHAEL W., business executive; b. Mars Hill, Maine, Oct. 5, 1945. Franchise owner Tuff Kote Din, Ft. Huron, Mich., 1979-80; nat. acct. mgr. Control Data Corp. Edn. Divsn., Southfield, Mich., 1981-87; gen. mgr. United Tng. Svcs. Corp., Southfield, 1988—. With U.S. Army, 1967-69. Republican. Roman Catholic. Home: 1277 Elliott Madison Heights MI 48071

DINGELL, CHRISTOPHER DENNIS, state legislator; b. Washington, DC, Feb. 23, 1957; s. John David and Helen (Henebry) D.; 1 child, Gabrielle. BSc, U. Mich., 1978; JD, Detroit Coll. Law., 1986. Engr. Ford Motor Co., Detroit, 1979-80, Rouge Steel Co., 1980-86; senator Mich. Dist. 7, 1987—; family law com. Mich. State Senate, criminal law & corrections com., mental health com., human resources com., sr. citizens com., natural resources & environ. affairs com.; atty. Sommers, Schwartz, Silver & Schwartz, 1989—. Vol. Dem. Nat. Conv. Mem. Engring. Soc. Detroit, Econ. Club Detroit, Mich. Jaycees, Polish Roman Catholic Union, Mich. United Conservation Club, K. of C. Office: State Senate State Capital Lansing MI 48909*

DINGELL, JOHN DAVID, JR., congressman; b. Colorado Springs, Colo., July 8, 1926; s. John D. and Grace (Bigler) D. BS in Chemistry, Georgetown U., 1949, JD, 1952. Bar: D.C. bar 1952, Mich. bar 1953. Park ranger U.S. Dept. Interior, 1948-52; asst. pros. atty. Wayne County, Mich., 1953-55; mem. 84th-88th Congresses from 15th dist., Mich., 1955-65, 89th-104th Congresses from 16th dist., Mich., 1965—; mem. migratory bird conservation commn.; ranking mem. commerce com. Served as 2d lt. inf. AUS, 1945-46. Office: US Ho of Reps 2328 Rayburn Ho Bldg Washington DC 20515

DINKINS, THOMAS ALLEN, III, construction equipment company executive; b. St. Louis, Dec. 29, 1946; s. Thomas Allen and Catherine (Fabick) D.; m. Donna Marie Berra, Apr, 29, 1967 (div.); 1 child, Thomas Allen IV; m. Patricia Anne Sundling, Nov. 29, 1986; 1 child, Catherine Anne. Student, Christian Brothers Coll., St. Louis, 1964, St. Louis U., 1964-66. Parts clk. John Fabrick Tractor Co., Fenton, Mo., 1962-66; field engr. Honeywell Info. Systems, St. Louis, 1970-74; systems analyst John Fabick Tractor Co., Fenton, Mo., 1974-78, asst. service mgr., 1981-84, service ops. mgr., 1984-85; v.p. product support John Fabick Tractor Co., Mo., 1985-86; exec. v.p. John Fabick Tractor Co., Fenton, Mo., 1988—; v.p. branch mgr. Fabrick Bros. Equipment Co., Sikeston, Mo., 1986-88; systems cons. AED R&S Corp., Oak Brook, Ill. 1981-82. Mem. bd. regents Linn State Tech. Coll., 1995—. With USAF, 1966-70. Named Airman of the Quarter, USAF Communications Service, Forbes AFB Kans. 1968. Mem. Eastside Rivermen's Indsl. Assn., Nat. Model R.R. Assn. (life), Constrn. Equipment Dealers Assn. (past pres. 1993), Propeller Club Port of St. Louis, Sunset Country Club. Republican. Roman Catholic. Home: 12808 Pointe Dr Saint Louis MO 63127-1742 Office: John Fabick Tractor 1 Fabick Dr Fenton MO 63026-2928

DINOLFO, PAUL CARMEN, religious organization administrator; b. Evergreen Park, Ill., July 23, 1952; s. Paul Anthony and Nella (Sabatini) D.; m. Marcia Lynn Kinney, Sept. 2, 1973; children: Michelle, Lisa, Daniel. BA in Chemistry, Mich. State U., 1974. Dir. Work of Christ Cmty., Lansing, Mich., 1975—, v.p., 1983-94, pres., 1994—; pres., owner Christian Specialty Shop, Lansing, 1979-89; trustee Work of Christ Sharing Fund, Lansing, 1985—; pastor Cornerstone Ch., Lansing, 1989—; dir. Christian Childcare Ctr., East Lansing, Mich., 1989—, Servant Ministries, Ann Arbor, Mich., 1990-92; pres. UCO Missions, Lansing, 1992—. Editor newsletter Cmty. & Mission News, 1994—. Republican. Evangelical. Office: Work of Christ Cmty 1516 Jerome St Lansing MI 48912

DINUCCI, JOSEPH V., stockbroker; b. Lowell, Mass., July 10, 1938. BS, Norwich U., Northfield, Mass., 1960. Stockbroker A.G. Edwards & Sons Inc., Cedar Rapids, Iowa, 1965—, mem. chmn.'s coun., 1989—. Capt. U.S. Army, 1960-65. Mem. Masons, Shriners. Republican. Lutheran. Office: AG Edwards & Sons Inc PO Box 75010 425 2d St SE Cedar Rapids IA 52407

DIPPLE, ELIZABETH DOROTHEA, language professional, English educator; b. Perth County, Ontario, Can., May 8, 1937; d. Frederick and Sybilla Katherine (Schmidt) D. BA with honors, U. Western Ontario, London, Ontario, Can., 1959; MA, Johns Hopkins U., 1961, PhD, 1963. Asst., assoc. prof. English U. Wash., Seattle, 1963-71; prof. English Northwestern U., Evanston, Ill., 1971—. Author: (book) Plot, 1970, Iris Murdoch: Work for the Spirit, 1982, The Unresolvable Plot: Contemporary Fiction, 1988; contbr. many articles to profl. jours. Office: Northwestern U Dept of English Evanston IL 60208-2240

DIPPOLITO, DANIEL F., electrical engineer; b. Warren, Ohio, Dec. 31, 1962; s. Siore C. and Marie J. (Fricano) D. BS in Elec. Engring., Youngstown (Ohio) State U., 1991. Engr. Konwal Engring. Svcs., Warren, 1986-91; project engr. Gen. Motors Packard Electric, Warren, 1991—. Mem. U.S. Power Squadron, Raleigh, S.C., 1990—. Office: Gen Motors Packard Electric PO Box 431 Warren OH 44486-0001

DI PRIMA, STEPHANIE MARIE, educational administrator; b. Chgo., Aug. 29, 1952; d. Joseph and Ann Marie (Albate) Di P. BA in English, Rosary Coll., 1974; MEd in Adminstrn. and Supervision, Loyola U., Chgo., 1979. Tchr. St. Vincent Ferrer Sch., River Forest, Ill., 1974-78; prin. Our Lady of Hope Sch., Rosemont, Ill., 1978-81, Sacred Heart Sch., Winnetka, Ill., 1981-84, St. Monica Sch., Chgo., 1984-91, St. Martha Sch., Morton Grove, Ill., 1991—; instr. Rosary Coll., River Forest, Ill. Mem. NAESP, ASCD, Nat. Cath. Ednl. Assn., Ill. Prins. Assn., Ill. Assn. Supervision and Curriculum Devel., Women in Mgmt., Archdiocesan Prins. Coalition for Arts. Office: St Martha Sch 8535 Georgiana Ave Morton Grove IL 60053-2909

DIRE, JEFFREY MICHAEL, mariage and family therapist, pastoral counselor; b. Niles, Ill., Apr. 29, 1953. BEd, DePaul U., 1975; MEd, Northwestern U., 1976; MDiv, Luth. Sch. Theology, Chgo., 1981; D Min, Fuller Theol. Sem., Pasadena, Calif., 1985. Ordained to ministry Luth. Ch., 1981. Clin. dir. Assocs. in Pastoral Psychotherapy, Downers Grove, Ill. Mem. Am. Assn. Pastoral Counselors (cert.), Am. Assn. Marriage and Family Therapists (clin.). Office: Assocs in Pastoral Psychotherapy 6900 Main St Downers Grove IL 60516-3454

DIROLL, DAVID JOHN, lawyer; b. Youngstown, Ohio, June 2, 1951; s. Robert Joseph and Catherine Lucia (Petergal) D.; m. Deborah Ann Tavenner, July 28, 1984; children: Benjamin, Caroline. BA, Youngstown State U., 1974; JD, Ohio State U., 1977. Bar: Ohio 1977. Staff atty. Ohio Legis. Svc. Commn., Columbus, 1977-85; policy chief Gov.'s Office Criminal Justice Svcs., Columbus, 1985-91; dir. Ohio Criminal Sentencing Commn., 1991—; dir. Gov.'s Com. on Prison and Jail Crowding, Columbus, 1985-90; faculty Ohio Jud. Coll., 1992, 95, 96, Nat. Conf. State Legislators, 1992, Ohio State U. Learning Guild, 1990, Ohio CLE Inst., 1995, 96; mem. Lt. Gov.'s Work Group on Prison Crowding, 1992, Lt. Gov.'s Task Force on Parole, 1992-94, Gov.'s/Chief Justice's Task Force on Pre-Sentence Investigations, 1995; mem. steering com. Ohio Ctr. Law-Related Edn., Columbus, 1990, Ohio Risk Think Tank, 1992-95; judge Ohio Mock Trial, 1990, 91, 92, 93; chmn. legis. work group Dept. Alcohol and Drugs, Columbus, 1990. Author, editor: Victorian Village Handbook, 1988; contbr. articles to publs. Mem. City Coun. Appeals Task Force, Columbus, 1988, Downtown Housing Task Force, Columbus, 1988, Victorian Village Traffic Com., 1994-95; chmn. Victorian Village Commn., Columbus, 1987-96; com. chair Victorian Village Tour of Homes, Columbus, 1986-94; youth soccer coach, 1994-96, youth soccer coach, 1996. Recipient Cert. of Appreciation, Columbus City Coun., 1987, 88, Recognition award Crime Victims Assistance Program, Akron, 1989, Pub. Policy Leadership award Ohio Ct. of Claims Victims Program, 1996; named one of Outstanding Young Men Am., 1987. Mem. Victorian Village Soc. (trustee 1987-89, tour com. 1986-90, program chair 1984-85), Columbus Landmarks Assn., Douglas Cmty. Assn. Home: 804 Neil Ave Columbus OH 43215-1330 Office: Ohio Criminal Sentencing Co 513 E Rich St Ste 100 Columbus OH 43215-5376

DISBROW, LYNN MARIE, communication educator; b. Chgo., Sept. 2, 1961; d. Ervin John and Patricia Ann (Grabarek) Lodyga; m. Michael Ray Disbrow, July 14, 1984; children: Matthew Ray, Nicole Marie. BA, Ind. U., South Bend, 1982; MA with distinction, Emerson Coll., Boston, 1986; PhD, Wayne State U., Detroit, 1989. High sch. program mgr. Jr. Achievement of Michiana, Inc., South Bend, 1982-84; account exec. AM The WNDU Stas., South Bend, 1984; instr. Emerson Coll., Boston, 1985-86; instr. Wayne State U., Detroit, 1986-87, grad. teaching asst., 1987; lectr. Ind. U., South Bend, 1988; lectr. I Sinclair C.C., Dayton, Ohio, 1989-90, asst. prof., 1993—; asst. prof. comm. U. Dayton, 1990-92. Author conv. papers Mass. Comm. Assn., 1985, Speech Comm. Assn., 1986-91, 94, 96, Ctrl. State Comm. Assn., 1989, 91-92, 94-96, others; mem. editl. bd. Ohio Speech Jour., 1993, N.D. Jour. Speech and Theatre, 1992. Rumble fellow, 1986-87. Mem. Speech Comm. Assn., Ctrl. States Comm. Assn., Speech Comm. Assn. Ohio (exec. bd. 1995-96). Republican. Roman Catholic.

DISBROW, MICHAEL RAY, aerospace supplier company executive; b. Highland Park, Mich., June 12, 1959; s. Arthur Ray and Vivian (Childress) D.; m. Lynn Marie Lodyga, July 14, 1984. BSME, Purdue U., 1981; MBA, Harvard U., 1986. Co-op. assoc. BFGoodrich Co., Akron, Ohio, 1978-81; axle engr. Bendix Automotive Brake Sys. divsn. Allied Signal, Inc., South Bend, Ind., 1982-83, R & D engr., 1983-84, disc brake engr., 1984, mgr. strategic planning, 1986-87, mgr. Far East bus. planning, 1987-88, mgr. N.Am. joint venture programs, 1988; internal cons. Fram divsn. Allied Signal, Inc., East Providence, R.I., 1985; dir. svc. ctr. Hartzell Propeller, Inc., Piqua, Ohio, 1988-94, v.p. Dornier 328 program, 1994-95, v.p. product support, 1995—. Prodn. advisor Jr. Achievment of Michiana, South Bend, 1982-83, exec. advisor, 1983-84. Named Prodn. Advisor of Yr., Jr. Achievment of Michiana, 1983; fellow The Little Family Found., 1984, 85, Allied Signal Inc., 1984-86. Mem. Tau Beta Pi. Republican. Methodist. Home: 820 Shafor Blvd Oakwood OH 45419-3450 Office: Hartzell Propeller Inc One Propeller Pl Piqua OH 45356

DITCH, KEVIN JESSE, design engineer; b. St. Louis, July 13, 1957; s. Jesse Smith and Virginia Ruth Ditch. A.Bus. Mgmt., St. Louis C.C., 1986; BA in Bus. Adminstrn., Fontbonne Coll., St. Louis, 1996. Sr. mfg. engr. Emerson Electric, St. Louis, 1978-90; design engr. Atlas Soundolier, Fenton, Mo., 1990—. Patentee on stand for articles. With U.S. Army, 1975-78. Republican. Roman Catholic. Home: 4238 Bordeaux Dr Saint Louis MO 63129-3810 Office: Atlas Soundolier 1859 Intertech Dr Fenton MO 63026-1926

DITMAR, RONALD L., JR., financial company executive; b. Grand Rapids, Mich., Dec. 12, 1954. Investment rep. Edward D. Jones, St. Louis, 1985-90; v.p. br. mgr. Raffenberger Hughes, Indpls., 1990-92, Robert W. Baird & Co. Inc., Big Rapids, Mich., 1992—. Mem. Arts Coun., Grand Rapids, 1988—. Mem. Big Rapids C. of C., Rotary. Office: Robert W Baird & Co Inc 110 Sanborn Ave Big Rapids MI 49307-1736

DITMARS, DONALD MELICK, JR., plastic surgeon; b. Trenton, N.J., Nov. 5, 1934; s. Donald Melick Ditmars; m. Anne Theresa Marr, June 4, 1960; children: Donald, Kristin, Kathryn. AB, Princeton U., 1956; MD, Cornell U., 1960. Diplomate Am. Bd. Surgery, Am. Bd. Plastic Surgery. Plastic surgeon Henry Ford Hosp., Detroit, 1970—, divsn. head plastic surgeon, 1981—. Author: (with others) Tendon Repairs, 1991, Finger Tip Injuries, 1990, Hand Local Anesthesia, 1990. Capt. U.S. Army, 1965-67. Fellow ACS; mem. Am. Soc. Plastic and Reconstructive Surgeons, Am. Soc. for Surgery of the Hand, Am. Assn. for Hand Surgery (v.p. 1979), Midwest Assn. of Plastic Surgeons (v.p. 1992), Mich. Assn. Plastic Surgeons (pres. 1975), Mich. State Med. Soc. Office: Henry Ford Hosp 2799 W Grand Blvd Detroit MI 48202-2608

DITTHARDT, ALFRED ROBERT, electronics engineer; b. Wausau, Wis., Aug. 28, 1935; s. Alfred and Agnes Clara (Lucht) D.; m. Mary Isabel McIver, Aug. 29, 1959; children: Mark, Laurie Ditthardt Norton. BSEE, Northwestern U., Evanston, Ill., 1957; postgrad., Ill. Inst. Tech., Chgo., 1963. Sr. devel. engr. Motorola Inc., Chgo., 1954-61; project engr. Zenith Radio, Chgo., 1961-71, rsch. engr., 1972-79; project engr. Northrop Corp., Rolling Meadows, Ill., 1971-72; mgr. product planning Knowles Electronics, Itasca, Ill., 1979-90; pres. ARD Cons., Wheeling, Ill., 1990—; cons. Hearing Industries Assocs., Washington, 1981-90. Pres. Northfield Woods Homeowners, Glenview, Ill., 1975-76, 90-94. With U.S. Army, 1959-67. Mem. IEEE (sessions chmn. Chgo. conf. 1978), Acoustical Soc. Am. Office: ARD Cons 1333 Oakmeadow Ct Wheeling IL 60090-6939

DITTMAN, MARK ALLEN, environmental safety officer; b. Green Bay, Wis., Aug. 18, 1950; s. Paul William and Norma Jean Dittman; m. Theresa Petri, Aug. 19, 1978; 1 child, Adam F. BS in Biology, U. Wis., Stevens Point, 1972; BS in Biomed. Engring., Milw. Sch. Engring., 1978. Cert. healthcare exec.; cert. healthcare safety profl. Clin. engr. Lakeland Hosp., Elkhorn, Wis., 1978-80; clin. engr. Henry Ford Hosp., Detroit, 1980-86, safety officer, 1986—. Mem. Am. Soc. Hosp. Engrs., Assn. Advancement Medicine Inst., Am. Coll. Healthcare Execs. (diplomate). Republican. Roman Catholic. Office: Henry Ford Hosp 2799 W Grand Blvd Detroit MI 48202-2608

DITTMAN, RICHARD HENRY, physics educator; b. Sacramento, July 5, 1937; s. Henry Thomas and Mary Consolata D.; m. Maria Mathilde Keszler, Dec. 27, 1962; children: Susanna Maria, Veronica Cecilia. BS in Physics cum laude, Santa Clara U., 1959; PhD in Physics, U. Notre Dame, 1965. Rsch. asst. Fairchild Semiconductor, Mountain View, Calif., summer 1959-62, U. Notre Dame, Ind., 1959-65; guest scientist Fritz-Haber-Institut, Berlin, 1965-66; asst. prof. U. Wis., Milw., 1966-71, assoc. prof., 1971-90, chair physics dept., 1972-75, assoc. dean letters and sci., 1975-77, prof. physics, 1990—; vis. prof. Physikalisches Institut, Fribourg, Switzerland, fall 1985, summer 1989. Author: (with Glenn Schmieg) Physics in Everyday Life, 1979; (with Mark Zemansky) Heat and Thermodynamics, 1981, 96. Chmn. Bookfellows of Milw., 1978, Mariner Neighborhood Assn., Milw., 1991; mem. Cath. Commn. on Intellectual and Cultural Affairs. Recipient Catherine Sexton Scholarship, Santa Clara U., 1955-59, Uhrig Teaching award, 1971, Undergrad. Teaching award U. Wis.-Milw., 1989. Mem. Am. Assn. Physics Tchrs., Wis. Soc. Sci. Tchrs., Alpha Sigma Nu, Nat. Assn. Scholars. Roman Catholic. Home: 3454 N Murray Ave Milwaukee WI 53211-2817 Office: UWM Physics Dept PO Box 413 Milwaukee WI 53201-0413

DITTMER, SHARON JUANITA, prison nurse; b. Litchfield, Ill., Sept. 16, 1941; d. Norman William and Vera Christine (Jackson) Sumpter; m. James Jerry Dittmer, Mar. 22, 1963; children: James William, Jerry Alan. Diploma, Meml. Hosp. Sch. of Nursing, Springfield, Ill., 1962. RN, Ill, Ky., Ind. Psychiat. staff Madison (Ind.) State Hosp., 1963-64, Norton's Infirmary, Louisville, 1964-68; clinic supr. Louisville Meml. Hosp., 1968-70; obstetrics staff Harrison County Hosp., Corydon, Ind., 1973-75; house supr. Frazier Rehab. Ctr., Louisville, 1979-85; prison nurse Ind. Dept. Corrections, Tell City, 1991—; mem. state quality assurance com. Ind. Dept. Corrections, Indpls., 1991-92. Chairperson community svcs. com. Am. Heart Assn., Crawford County, Ind., 1977-79. Recipient Key to City of Louisville, Mayor, 1969, State Disting. Program award, Am. Heart Assn., Ind. 1973. Mem. Ind. Correctional Nurses Assn. (state rep. 1991-92). Home: RR 1 Box 282 Marengo IN 47140-9745

DITTOE, ROBERT BRADLEY, account executive; b. Cleve., Sept. 2, 1956; s. Joseph Moran and Florence (Phillips) D.; m. Carol Anette Areen, Sept. 26, 1992; children: Erin Phillips, Nicholas Frank. BA, Kent State U., 1986. Ops. dir., news anchor Chillicothe (Ohio) Cablevision, Channel 2, 1986-88; salesman Sta. WCHO, Washington Court House, Ohio, 1987-88; disc jockey Sta. WCOL, Columbus, Ohio, 1991; ops. dir., morning personality WBEX Stas. WKKJ and WBEX, Chillicothe, 1988-93; evening announcer Sta. WYMJ, Dayton, Ohio, 1993-94; midday announcer WDOL, Dayton, 1994-95; acct. exec. Cellular One, Dayton, 1995—. Vice pres. Chillicothe Civic Theatre, 1992-93. Named Most Popular Disc Jockey in Ross County, 1989-92. Mem. AmBucs, Kiwanis. Republican. Roman Catholic. Home: 1627 Mayo Ave Kettering OH 45409-2022 Office: Cellularone 937 S Patterson Dayton OH 45402

DITZLER, JEFFREY L., plastics engineer; b. David City, Nebr., Oct. 29, 1948. A, Milford S.E. C.C., 1969. Mold maker Molex Inc., Lincoln, Nebr., 1980-84; owner, CEO Nebr. Mold & Enging., Lincoln, 1984-92; mgr. tooling Garner Industries, Lincoln, 1992—; seat adv. bd. machine tool dept. Milford C.C., 1993—; adv. bd. Gateway Electronics, 1993—; bd. dirs. Nebr. Plastics Engrs. Coach City Recreational Softball; vol. Salvation Army. Mem. Soc. Plastics Engrs. (sr.).

DIUGUID, LINCOLN ISAIAH, chemist; b. Lynchburg, Va., Feb. 6, 1917; m. Nancy Ruth Greenlee, July 8, 1955 (dec.); children: David, Lewis, Renee, Vincent. BS magna cum laude, W. Va. State U., 1938; MS, Cornell U., 1939, PhD, 1945, post doctorate, 1945-47. Head chemistry dept. Ark. State Coll., Pine Bluff, 1939-43; analytical chemist Pine Bluff Arsenal, 1942-43; pres., founder Du-Good Chem. Lab. and Mfrs., St. Louis, 1947—; chmn. phys. sci. dept. Harris Stowe State Coll., St. Louis, 1949-82, prof. emeritus, 1982—; vis. prof. chemistry Washington U., St. Louis, 1966-68; cons. chemist VA Hosp., Jefferson Barricks (Mo.) Hosp., 1968-78, Intertherm Co., St. Louis, 1964—. Contbr. numerous articles to profl. jours.; chpts. to books; patentee in field. V.p. Leukemia Guild Mo. and Ill., St. Louis, 1963; trustee Leukemia Guild Am., St. Louis, 1968-82. Recipient Disting. Educators award Harris Stowe Alumnae, 1985, Carver award Sigma Gamma, 1979. Fellow Am. Inst. Chemists; mem. AAUP, Am. Chem. Soc., Assn. Cons. Chemists and Chem. Engrs., Ethical Soc., Sigma Xi, Phi Kappa Phi, Omega Psi Phi (v.p. 1950-51, Man of Yr. award 1960). Home: 3645 Lafayette Ave Saint Louis MO 63110-2613 Office: Du-Good Chem Lab and Mfrs 1215 S Jefferson Ave Saint Louis MO 63104-1903

DIULIO, ALBERT JOSEPH, university president, priest; b. Laona, Wis., Feb. 14, 1943; s. Albert Joseph and Louise Frances (Bradle) D. BS, Marquette U., 1965, AM, 1969; MDiv, Weston Sch. Theology, Cambridge, Mass., 1974; MA, Stanford U., 1976, PhD, 1979, MBA, 1983. Joined S.J., Roman Cath. Ch., ordained priest, 1974. Mem. faculty Campion H.S., Prairie Du Chien, Wis., 1969-70, 73-74, headmaster, 1970-71, 74-75; asst. dean Coll. Arts and Scis. Marquette U., Milw., 1978-80, mem. bus. faculty, 1983-84, assoc. dean Sch. of Bus., 1984-86, pres., 1990—; asst. to pres. Loyola Marymount U., L.A., 1980-81; pres. Xavier U., Cin., 1986-90, Marquette U., Milw., 1990—; bd. dirs. Baird Mutual Funds, Allen-Edmonds Shoe Corp. Mem. Task Force to rev. governance Milw. County Med. Complex, Mayor's Com. Police and Cmty. Rels.; Midwest Express Airlines Conf. USA: active Milw. Ethnic Coun., Greater Milw. Com. Recipient Equestrian Order of the Holy Sepulchre of Jerusalem, Outstanding Bus. Leadership award Marquette U., World of Difference award AndiDefamation League, 1995, Person of the Yr. award Justinian Soc. of Lawyers, 1995; Lockheed fellow Stanford U. Bus. Sch. Mem. NCAA (pres.'s commn.), Assn. Jesuit Colls. and Univs. (exec. com., bd. dirs. 1986—), Wis. Found. Ind. Coll., Milw. Country Club, Milw. Club, Univ. Club (Milw.), Milw. Athletic Club, Phi Delta Kappa, Alpha Sigma Nu, Beta Gamma Sigma, Beta Alpha Psi. Home and Office: Marquette U PO Box 1881 Milwaukee WI 53201-1881

DIVINE, THOMAS L., stockbroker; b. Beloit, Wis., Dec. 25, 1935. BA, U. Wis., 1958. Rep. Williams Dickey, Ft. Worth, 1969-83; stockbroker Piper Jaffray Inc., Ames, Iowa, 1983—. With U.S. Army, 1958-60. Mem. Ames C. of C., KC, Rotary, Jaycees, Elks. Office: Piper Jaffrey Inc PO Box 72 402 Main St Ames IA 50010

DIX, NANCY, state senator; m. Robert C. Dix. BS, Drake U. With Ohio Dept. Commerce, Columbus; pres. W.E. Shrider Co., Newark, Ohio; tchr., coach Heath H.S.; mem. Ohio Senate, Columbus, 1994—; vice chmn. energy, natural resources ane environ. com., mem. fin. instns. and ins., hwy. and transp. and agr. coms. Former bd. dirs. United Way; mem. Ctrl. Ohio Health Coalition; mem. devel. com. Am. Heart Assn. Named Freshman Legislator of Yr., Nat. Rep. Legislators Assn., cert. of distinction United Conservatives. Mem. Newark Area C. of C., Rotary. Office: OH Ho of Reps State Capitol Columbus OH 43215*

DIX, ROLLIN C(UMMING), mechanical engineering educator, consultant; b. N.Y.C., Feb. 8, 1936; s. Omer Houston and Ona Mae (Cumming) D.; m. Elaine B. VanNest, June 18, 1960; children: Gregory, Elisabeth, Karen. B.S.M.E., Purdue U., 1957, M.S.M.E., 1958, Ph.D., 1963. Registered profl. engr., Ind., Ill. Asst. prof. mech. enging. Ill. Inst. Tech., Chgo., 1964-69, assoc. prof., 1969-80, prof., 1980—, assoc. dean for computing, 1980—; cons. mech. design Bronson & Bratton, Inc., Chgo., 1965—; dir. Bimet Corp., Morris, Ill. Patentee road repair vehicle, method for vestibular test. Served to 1st lt. U.S. Army, 1960-61. Fellow ASME; mem. Am. Soc. Engring. Edn., Soc. Mfg. Engrs. Home: 10154 S Seeley Ave Chicago IL 60643-2037 Office: Ill Inst Tech 10 W 31st St Chicago IL 60616-3729

DIXON, GEORGE DAVID, radiologist; b. Valley City, N.D., Mar. 27, 1936; s. George Sherman and Isabel Ruth (Eaton) D.; m. Carol Marie Vennerstrom, Feb. 28, 1958; children: Barbara Sarah, George David Jr. Student, Willamette U., 1954-55; BA, U. N.D., 1959; MD, Tulane U., 1961. Diplomate Am. Bd. Radiology. Intern St. Luke's Hosp., Duluth, Minn., 1961-62; gen. practice Lenont-Peterson Clinic, Cook, Minn., 1962-64; resident in radiology Mayo Clinic, Rochester, Minn., 1964-66, 68-70; radiologist St. Luke's Hosp. Radiol. Group, Inc., Kansas City, Mo., 1970—, sec., 1971—; clin. prof. radiology U. Mo. Sch. Medicine, Kansas City, 1985—; sec.-treas. med. staff St. Lukes Hosp., 1992, v.p. med. staff, 1993, pres. med. staff, 1995. Mem. edit. adv. bd. Miller-Freeman Pubs., Inc., 1979—; contbr. articles to med. jours. Pres. Interdenominational Christian Youth Council, Fargo, N.D., 1953-54; lay leader Indian Heights United Meth. Ch., Overland Park, Kans., 1977-79. Served to capt. U.S. Army, 1966-68, Vietnam. Fellow Am. Coll. Radiiology (alt. councilor Mo.), Am. Heart Assn., Soc. Cardiovasc. and Interventional Radiology; mem. AMA, Mo. State Med. Soc., Mo. Radiol. Soc. (bd. dirs.), Met. Med. Soc., Greater Kansas City Radiol. Soc. (sec. 1978-79, treas. 1977-78, pres.), Radiol. Soc. N.Am. (counselor Western Mo. dist. 1988-92), Am. Roentgen Ray Soc., New Eng. Hist. Geneal. Soc., Wally Byan Caravan Club (Kansas City), Masons, Phi Beta Kappa, Beta Theta Pi, Phi Beta Pi. Republican. Home: 10416 Mohawk Ln Shawnee Mission KS 66206-2551 Office: St Lukes Hosp Dept Radiology P O Box 119000 Kansas City MO 64171-9000

DIXON, JAMES WALLACE, financial marketing consultant; b. St. Cloud, Minn., Apr. 4, 1938. BA, Coll. of St. Thomas, 1960. CPA, Minn., Wis. CFO St. Clare Hosp., Monroe, Wis., 1967-72; pres. Dixon/MRD & Co., West Bend, Wis., 1991—, Dixon & Assoc. Ltd., West Bend, 1974—. Inventor snow shovel with auger. Republican. Roman Catholic. Office: Dixon & Assocs Ltd 825 N River Rd West Bend WI 53095-2669

DIXON, JOHN FULTON, village manager; b. Bellingham, Wash., Dec. 17, 1946; s. Fulton Albert and Patricia (Broderick) D.; m. Karen Elizabeth Creagh, May 19, 1973; children: Neil, Craig. BS, Bradley U., 1971; M in Mgmt., Vanderbilt U., 1973. Asst. village mgr. Village of Hoffman Estates, Ill., 1974-76, village mgr., 1980-86; dir. village svcs. Village of Roselle, Ill., 1976-79; asst. village mgr. Village of Schaumburg, Ill., 1979-80; village adminstr. Village of Lake Zurich, Ill., 1986-87; village mgr. Village of Mt. Prospect, Ill., 1987-92; village adminstr. Village of Lake Zurich, 1992—; mgr. exec. bd. dirs. N.W. Suburban Mcpl. Joint Action Water Agy., Hoffman Estates, 1980-92; mem. exec. bd. dirs. N.W. Cen. Dispatch, Arlington Heights, Ill., 1987-92. Troop com. chmn. Boy Scouts Am., 1989-93. Recipient Chief Scout's award Gov. Gen. of Jamaica, Kingston, 1970; Adminstrv. fellow Woodrow Wilson Found., 1973-74, Houston fellow Vanderbilt U., 1972-73; Baker scholar Vanderbilt U., 1971-73. Mem. Met. Chgo. City Mgrs. Assn. (bd. dirs., pres. 1986-87), Ill. City Mgmt. Assn. (bd. dirs., pres. 1990-91), Rotary (bd. dirs. 1989—). Roman Catholic. Home: 248 Sebby Ln Lake Zurich IL 60047-1358 Office: Village of Lake Zurich 70 E Main St Lake Zurich IL 60047-3204

DIXON, MARGUERITE ANDERSON, retired nursing educator; b. Pitts., May 18, 1930; d. William Orlando and Ida Mary (Taylor) Anderson; m. Relyea M. Dixon, June 15, 1952 (dec.); children: Marguerite Elise Dixon-Roper, Relyea Paul. BSN, U. Ill., Chgo., 1959; BA, Andrews U., Berrien Springs, Mich., 1952; MSN, U. Ill., Chgo., 1971, PhD, 1982. Rsch. asst. Coll. Dentistry U. Ill.; adminstrv. nurse I, II & III U. Ill. Hosp., asst. dir. nursing; asst. prof., coord. grad. program psychiat. nursing U. Ill., Chgo., 1985-90; acting dean Chgo. State U., 1990-93. Contbr. articles to profl. jours. Mem. Mayor's Task Force on Women's Health, Chgo., 1993—; pres. local host. bd., 1994. Mem. ANA, Ill. Nurses Assn., Sigma Theta Tau Internat.

DIXON, SALLY FOY, arts administrator; b. Seattle, Feb. 25, 1932; d. Fred Calvert and Elizabeth Jane (Hamilton) Foy; children: John Iversen Dixon,Jr., Steven Hamilton Dixon, Alexander Foy Dixon. Curator film dept. Carnegie Mus. Art, Pitts., 1970-76; ind. cons., 1976-78; acting exec. dir. Film in the Cities, St. Paul, 1978-79; program dir. Bush Artist Fellowships, The Bush Found., St. Paul, 1980—; sr. cons. Alpert Calif. Arts Awards, L.A., 1994—; cons. Pew Artist fellowships, Phila., 1991-92; bd. dirs. Graywolf Press, St. Paul, Friends Sch. of Minn., Mpls.; lectr., mem. numerous panels, bds., others. Actress Dream Sphinx Opera, 1972, L'Amico Frieds Glamourous Friends, 1973, Aged in Wood, by Roger Jacoby, 1974. Home: 438 Laurel Ave Saint Paul MN 55102

DIXON, TERRY PHILLIP, academic administrator, educational consultant; b. Cin., May 8, 1946; s. Henry Phillip and Annabel (Kincaid) D.; m. Evelyn Bowman, Dec. 23, 1969. BS in Chemistry, Biology, Cumberland Coll., 1968; MS in Elem. Edn., Ill. State U., 1978; EdD., U. Nebr., 1988. Cert. elem. tchr., Mo., Ill.; cert. secondary sci. tchr. Tchr. biology, coach Cissna Park (Ill.) High Sch., 1968-69; tchr. Gilman (Ill.) Elem. Sch., 1969-78; chmn. div. Tarkio (Mo.) Coll., 1978-89; cons. higher edn. Williams Dixon Assocs., Tarkio, 1979-86; cons. Dixon & Assocs., Killeen, Tex., 1989—; v.p. acad. affairs U. Cen. Tex., Killeen, 1989-93, Clarkson Coll., Omaha, Nebr., 1993—; instnl. evaluator Am. Coun. of Edn. and Sch. Coun. of Small Bus.; v.p. bd. dirs. Lewis, Dixon and Assocs., 1992—. Mem. Community Revitilization Com., Tarkio, 1985-89; vice chmn. bd. dirs. N.W. Mo. Learning Ctr., Tarkio, 1986-89; mem. fin. com. Ctrl. Tex. Alcoholic Rehab. Ctr., Temple, 1990-93. Mem. Assn. Tchr. Educators, Rotary, Nebr. Educators Assn., Mo. Unit Assn. Tchr. Edn., Greater Killeen C. of C. (mem. small bus. coun.), Phi Delta Kappa. Baptist. Home: 101 S 42nd St Omaha NE 68131-2715 Office: Clarkson Coll 101 S 42nd St Omaha NE 68131-2715

DIXON, WESLEY MOON, JR., venture capital executive; b. Evanston, Ill., Oct. 18, 1927; s. Wesley Moon and Katherine (Strawn) D.; m. Suzanne Searle, May 23, 1953; children: Katherine Dixon Thomson, Carolynn Frances, John Wesley. B.A., Yale U., 1950. Salesman, Owens-Ill. Co., 1950-54; with G.D. Searle & Co., Skokie, Ill., 1954-84, pres., 1972-77, vice chmn., 1977-84; v.p. Earl-Kinship Capital Corp., Northbrook, Ill., 1984—. Trustee Lake Forest (Ill.) Coll., Art Inst. Chgo.; bd. dirs. Lake Forest Hosp., Up With People, Rehab. Inst. Chgo. Mem. Chgo. Council Fgn. Relations (dir.). Republican. Episcopalian. Clubs: Onwentsia (Lake Forest); Chgo. (Chgo.), Mid-Am. (Chgo.), Comml. (Chgo.), Econ. (Chgo.), Commonwealth (Chgo.). Office: Earl-Kinship Capital Corp 400 Skokie Blvd Suite 675 Northbrook IL 60062

DIXON, WILLIAM GORDON, JR., geologist; b. Sedalia, Mo., Nov. 28, 1931; s. William Gordon and Nellie Caroline (Wade) D.; m. Phyllis M. Thomas, June 13, 1954; children: William T., Rebecca S., Sally E., Thomas G., Timothy T. BS, Ind. U., 1958, AM, 1966. Lic. profl. geologist, Wis.; cert. profl. geologist, Ind. Geologist Soil Testing Svcs., Inc., Chgo., 1958-59, Harza Engring. Co., Chgo., 1961-63, Layne-Western Co., Aurora, Ill., 1963-64; engring. geologist Testing Svc. Corp., Wheaton, Ill., 1964-73; sr. field engr. Dames & Moore, Park Ridge, Ill., 1974-75; staff geologist Ill. State Geol. Survey, Champaign, Ill., 1975-91; sr. environ. geologist ASI Environ. Technologies, Arlington Heights, Ill., 1992-93, Environ. S/E, Inc., Glen Ellyn, Ill., 1994-95; cons. Practical Environ. Cons., Inc., 1996—. Contbr. tech. reports to profl. publs.; contbr. numerous articles to profl. jours. Pvt. first class U.S. Army, 1954-56. Mem. Am. Inst. Profl. Geologists, Assn. Engring. Geologists (dir. 1981-82), Ill. Assn. Environ. Profls. (dir. 1988-89, sec. 1989), Ill. Groundwater Assn., Masons (master Euclid lodge # 65 1978, excellent High Priest Euclid chpt. # 13 Royal Arch 1987-89). Methodist. Home: 210 N Wright St Naperville IL 60540-4750

DIZNEY, ROBERT EDWARD, retired secondary education educator; b. Harlan, Ky., May 22, 1937; s. Robert Edward and E. Beatrice (Rowland) D. BA, Berea (Ky.) Coll., 1961; MEd, Miami U., Oxford, Ohio, 1987, postgrad., 1992—. Cert. tchr., Ohio. Tchr. Lockland (Ohio) City Schs., 1961-62, Deerfield Local Schs., Kings Mills, Ohio, 1962-70; tchr., chmn. dept. English Fairfield (Ohio) City Schs., 1971-94; adj. instr. Miami U., Oxford, Ohio, 1992—; cons. writing Miami U. Ohio Writing Project, 1984—; co-dir. Miami U. Tchr.-Rsch. Network, 1992—; adj. instr. Miami U., 1992—. Contbr. articles to profl. jours. Recipient Ashland Oil Tchr. Achievement award 1993, Hugh Morrison Scholarship Miami U., 1995. Mem. Nat. Coun. Tchrs. English, Internat. Soc. for Philos. Enquiry, Intertel, Mensa, Phi Delta Kappa. Democrat. Roman Catholic. Home: 5340 Dellbrook Dr Fairfield OH 45014-3308 Office: Miami U 363 McGuffey Hall Oxford OH 45056

DOAN, JOE COAPSTICK, insurance agency executive; b. Havre de Grace, Md., Aug. 5, 1944; s. Joe Taylor Doan and Mary Jean (Coapstick) Bache; m. Linda Kay Huckleberry, Aug. 3, 1974; children: Angela Michelle, Julia Grace. BSME, Purdue U., 1966; MBA, Cornell U., 1968. CPCU; cert. ins. counselor. Mech. foreman Inland Steel Co., East Chicago, Ind., 1968-71; ins. agt. Coapstick Ins. Agy., Inc., Frankfort, Ind., 1971—, pres., 1979—; bd. dirs. The Farmers Bank, Frankfort; bd. dirs., treas. Frankfort Devel. Corp., 1983—. Trustee Clinton County Hosp., Frankfort, 1983—; bd. dirs. Frankfort Main St., Inc., 1990-93; bd. dirs., treas. Ptnrs. in Progress, Clinton County, Ind., 1990—; fundraising profl. Clinton County Family YMCA, Inc., Frankfort, 1995. Mem. Ind. Hosp. Assn. (bd. dirs. 1991-94), Ind. Ins. Agts. Ind., Frankfort Rotary Club (past pres.), Elks, Moose, Masons, Scottish Rite, Frankfort Country Club (pres. 1979-80). Republican. Presbyterian. Home: 801 Eastwood Dr Frankfort IN 46041 Office: Coapstick Ins Agy Inc 259 E Walnut St Frankfort IN 46041

DOANE, WILLIAM MCKEE, chemist, researcher; b. Covington, Ind., Sept. 26, 1930; s. Earl Edward and Mildred Rowena (McKee) D.; m. Joan Marie Polk, June 6, 1952; children: Diane Elizabeth, Steven William, Robert Alan, Karen Marie. BS, Purdue U., 1948-52, PhD, 1955-62. Prin., tchr. Ind. Schs., Attica, 1954-55; rsch. asst. Purdue U., West Lafayette, Ind., 1955-62; rsch. chemist Nat. Ctr. Agrl. Utilization Rsch., USDA/ARS, Peoria, Ill., 1962-1971; rsch. leader Nat. Ctr. Agrl. Resources, Peoria, Ill., 1971-95; sr. rsch. assoc. prof. Bradley U., Peoria, 1995—; chemistry lectr. Bradley U., Peoria, 1965—. Editor: 2 sci. books; contbr. over 200 articles to sci. publs. Active planning commn. City of Morton, Ill., 1981-86. Recipient Disting. Svc. award USDA, Washington, 1976, 87, Superior Svc. awards, 1979, 88, Inventor of Yr. award Assn. Advancement of Inventions, Washington, 1977, Corn Industry award Nat. Corn Growers Assn., St. Louis, 1989, Tech. Transfer award Agrl. Rsch. Svcs., 1988, 93, Alsberg-Schoch Meml. award Corn Refiners Assn./Am. Assn. Cereal Chemists, 1993; inducted into ARS Sci. Hall of Fame, 1995. Mem. Am. Chem. Soc., Am. Assn. Cereal Chemists, Contr. Release Soc., Soc. Plastic Engrs.

DOBBINS, FREDA J., librarian; b. Hutchinson, Kans., June 1, 1940; d. Mahlon F. and Verna (Detter) Stauffer; m. James R. Dobbins, Aug. 3, 1968; children: Jared S., Janelle K. BA, Southwestern Coll., 1962; MA, U. Denver, 1963. Head adult svcs. Hutchinson Pub. Libr., 1964-67; sys. cons. S. Ctrl. Kans. Libr. Sys., Hutchinson, 1967-68; reference libr. Main Post Libr., Fort Knox, Ky., 1968-69; from dir. ext. to legis. reference libr. Kans. State Libr., Topeka, 1970-78; dir. Pottawatomie Wabaunsee Regional Libr., St. Marys, Kans., 1985—. Bd. dirs. Friendly Acres Retirement Ctr., Newton, Kans. Mem. ALA, Kans. Libr. Assn. (legis. com. 1993—). Methodist. Home: RR 2 Box 105 Goff KS 66428 Office: Pottawatomie Wabaunsee Regional Libr 306 N 5th Saint Marys KS 66536

DOBIS, CHESTER F., state legislator; b. Gary, Ind., Aug. 15, 1942; s. Jack F. and Veronica (Kordys) D.; m. Darlene Zimmerman, 1971. Student, Ind. U. N.W., 1961. Sales rep. Standard Liquors; v.p. govt. svc. Gainer Bank, 1972—; banker, v.p. govt. svc. NBD Bank; rep. Dist. 13 Ind. Ho. of Reps., 1970—, vice chmn. fin. inst., mem. house adminstrn. com., mem. pub. policy, vet. affairs, ethics com., mem. interstate coop. com., rules and legis. procedure com., spkr. pro tem, asst. minority floor leader. Mem. exec. bd. N.w. Ind. Regional Planning Commn.; vice pres. Ross Twp. Dem. Club, Merrillville, Ind., 1968—; bd. dirs. Lake County Young Dems., 1969-70; pres. Ross Twp. Young Dems., 1970—; vol. Lake Area United Way, Lake County Assn. Retarded, Polish Am. Dem. Club. With Ind. N.G. Named One of Top Freshman Legislators, Ind. Gen. Assembly, 1971. Mem. Nat. Coun. State Legislators, Gary Sportsmen Club, PNA Silver Bell. Home: 6565 Marshall Ct Merrillville IN 46410-2859*

DOBMEYER, DOUGLAS CHARLES, media and social issues executive; b. Kendallville, Ind., May 12, 1949; s. Cornelius Paul and Mabel Frances Dobmeyer; m. Candace Huber, Oct. 15, 1977; children: Amelia, Paul. BA, Ind. U., 1971. Housing coord. Community/Econ. Devel. Assn. Cook County, Inc., Chgo., 1980-81; exec. dir. Residents for Emergency Shelter, Chgo., 1982-85, Ctr. for Street People, Chgo., 1983-85, Pub. Welfare Coalition, Chgo., 1986-94; bd. dirs. Lakeview Towers Preservation Corp., Chgo. Bd. dirs., founding pres. Lakefront SRO Corp., Chgo., 1985-91; bd. dirs. Chgo. Coalition for Homeless, 1983-88, pres., 1985-87; bd. dirs. Voice of the People in Uptown, Chgo., 1979-88, pres., 1979-81, 84-86; commr., sec. Chgo. Low Income Housing Trust Fund, 1989—; mem. Mayor's Task Force on the Homeless, Chgo., 1983-89; mem. Social Svcs. Adv. Coun., Chgo., 1987-94; mem. Jobs Opportunity Adv. Coun., Chgo., 1993; legis. chair Religious Task Force to Oppose Legalized Gambling, 1993—. Co-recipient Civic Contbn. award LWV Chgo., 1988, Cmty. Svc. fellowship, Chgo. Cmty. Trust, 1994-95.

DOBRAUC, ANTONE JOHN, JR., securities company official; b. Joplin, Mo., Dec. 6, 1935; s. Antone J. Dobrauc. BS, U. Mo., 1962; postgrad., N.Y. Inst. Fin., 1970. Registered rep., ltd. ptnr. Edward D. Jones & Co., St. Louis, 1970—; br. mgr. Kemper Securities Inc., Pittsburg, Kans., 1985—. Contbr. articles to newspaper. Mem. bd. Colgan H.S., Pittsburg, 1992—. Mem. Rotary, Masons, Shriners. Republican. Roman Catholic. Home: 3006 Woodgate Pittsburg KS 66762 Office: Everen Securities Inc 2521 N Broadway St Pittsburg KS 66762-2620

DOBRIN, SHELDON L., architect; b. Chgo., June 2, 1945; s. Max and Sophie (Schuman) D.; m. Marlene K. Smith, Jan. 26, 1969; children: Stefanie, Jonathan. BArch, Ill. Inst. Tech., 1969, BS, 1970. Registered architect, Ill., Ind., Wis. Architect Form Assocs., Chgo., 1969; tchr. Chgo. Bd. Edn., 1969-72; architect Robert L. Friedman, Chgo., 1972-78, v.p., 1978-90; prin. Friedman, Dobrin and Assocs., Northbrook, Ill., 1984-90; pres. Dobrin Assocs., Ltd., Northbrook, 1991—. Contbr. articles to profl. jours. Docent Chgo. Archtl. Found., 1971-78; mem. caucus bd. Highland Park Sch. Dist., 1988; mem. Highland Park Historic Preservation Commn., 1988—. Recipient Spl. Recognition for Archtl. Design awards, 1985, 88, 89. Mem. AIA (Chgo. chpt. voting del. convs. 1985, 88, 89, com. chair 1993 conv.), Nat. Coun. Archtl. Registration Bds. (cert.), Nat. Trust Hist. Preservation, Art Inst. Chgo., Alpha Epsilon Pi. Office: Dobrin Assocs Ltd Ste 1C 401 Huehl Rd Northbrook IL 60062-2300

DOBRINSKI, EVERETT, state legislator; m. Peggy Dobrinski; 2 children. Farmer, chmn. Velendrye Elec. Coop., state rep. dist. 4, 1993—. Mem. Threshers Assn. Democrat. Home: RR 1 Box 62A Makoti ND 58756-9519*

DOBRONSKI, AGNES MARIE, state legislator; b. Detroit, Apr. 21, 1925; d. Clarence Robert and Agnes Frieda (Franz) Dobronski; m. James Z. Cichocki, June 27, 1987; stepchildren: Thomas, Jerry. BS, Detroit Coll. Bus., 1970; MA, Eastern Mich. U., 1975. Bus. mgr. Dearborn (Mich.) Pub. Schs., 1943-80; exec. dir. Retirement Coord. Coun., Lansing, Mich., 1980-85; mem. Mich. Ho. of Reps., 1987-88, 91—. Trustee Dearborn Bd. Edn., Henry Ford Community Coll., 1980-86. Recipient Disting. Alumna award Detroit Coll. Bus., 1974, Disting. Citizen award Henry Ford Cmty. Coll., 1987, Disting. Alumni award Henry Ford Cmty. Coll., 1989; named Sch. Adminstr. of Yr. Dearborn PTA Council, 1978. Democrat. Lutheran. Home: PO Box 1948 Dearborn MI 48121-1948 Office: House of Reps State Capitol Lansing MI 48909-7514

DOBSON, TRACY ANNE, law educator; b. Ann Arbor, Mich., Oct. 8, 1945; d. John Steuer Dobson and Mary Eliza (Gordy) Rae; children: Noah Cooper, Cheyney Cooper. BA, U. Mich., 1967, JD, 1978. Legal dir. Pub. Interest Rsch., Lansing, Mich., 1978-80; advocacy dir. Mich. Consumer's Coun., Lansing, 1980-81; from. asst. prof. to prof. bus. law Mich. State U., 1981-93, prof. fisheries & wildlife, 1993—; asst. dean internat. studies & programs, 1991-95, assoc. dean, 1995—. Chair East Lansing Commn. on the Environ., 1990-93. Fulbright scholar, 1996. Mem. NOW, Am. Fisheries Soc., Soc. Conservation Biology, The Wildlife Soc., Phi Kappa Phi. Home: 1244 Cedarhill Dr East Lansing MI 48823 Office: Mich State U Internat Studies & Programs 207 International Ctr East Lansing MI 48824-4035

DOBYNS, JOHN, state legislator; b. Mar. 8, 1944. BA, U. Wis. Law enforcement officer; mem. from dist. 52 Wis. State Assembly, Madison, 1992—. Former councilman Fund du Lac, Wis. Office: 33 S Berger Pky Fond Du Lac WI 54935-3003*

DOCHERTY, JOHN JOSEPH, microbiologist; b. Youngstown, Ohio, Dec. 5, 1941; s. John Henry and Viola Jean (Sovak) D.; m. Pamela Ann Kaminsky, Aug. 21, 1965; children: Patricia, Susan. BA, Youngstown U., 1964; MS, Miami U., Oxford, Ohio, 1966; PhD, U. Ariz., 1970; postgrad., Pa. State U. Coll. Medicine, 1972. Asst. prof. microbiology Pa. State U.,

University Park, 1972-76, assoc. prof., 1976-86; prof. microbiology, immunology Coll. Medicine Northeastern Ohio U., Rootstown, Ohio, 1987—, chair dept., 1987—; cons. in field. Grantee NIH, Dept. Agriculture. Mem. Am. Soc. Microbiology, Am. Soc. Virology, Assn. Med. Sch. Microbiology & Immunology Chairs, Phi Sigma, Alpha Omega Alpha. Home: 7531 Diagonal Rd Kent OH 44240-5954 Office: Northeastern Ohio U Dept Microbiology/Immunology Coll Medicine Rtc 44 Rootstown OH 44272

DOCHNAHL, MARK EDWARD, municipal government official; b. Madison, Wis., Aug. 7, 1951; s. William J. and Joan E. (Fisher) D.; m. Faye Ann Dochnahl, Dec. 30, 1978. AA, MATC, 1974. Supt. pub. works City of Ft. Atkinson, Wis., 1974—. Mem. Wis. Urban Forestry Coun., Am. Pub. Works Assn., Wis. Arborist Assn., Internat. Soc. Arboriculture, So. Wis. Assn. Pub. Works Supts. (past pres. 1989), Kiwanis (past pres. 1984). Home: 613 East St Fort Atkinson WI 53538

DOCKHORN, ROBERT JOHN, physician, educator; b. Goodland, Kans., Oct. 9, 1934; s. Charles George and Dorotha Mae (Horton) D.; m. Beverly Ann Wilke, June 15, 1957; children: David, Douglas, Deborah. AB, U. Kans., 1956, MD, 1960. Diplomate Am. Bd. Pediat. Intern Naval Hosp., San Diego, 1960-61; resident in pediat. Naval Hosp., Oakland, Calif., 1963-65; resident in pediat. allergy and immunology U. Kans. Med. Ctr., 1967-69, adj. asst. prof. pediat., 1969—; resident in pediat. allergy and immunology Children's Mercy Hosp., Kansas City, Mo., 1967-69, chief divsn., 1969-83; practice medicine specializing in allergy and immunology Children's Mercy Hosp., Prairie Village, Kans., 1969-94, U. Mo. Med. Sch., Prairie Village, Kans., 1969-94; pres. Internat. Med. Tech. Cons., Inc., Kansas City, 1979—; pres. I.M.T.C.I. (Internat. Med. Tech. Cons., Inc.), Kansas City, 1979—; founder, CEO Internat. Med. Tech. Cons., Inc., Prairie Village, Kans., subs. Immuno-Allergy Tech. Cons., Inc., Clin. Rsch. Cons., Inc. Contbr. articles to med. jours.; co-editor: Allergy and Immunology in Children, 1973. Fellow Am. Acad. Pediatrics, Am. Coll. Allergists (bd. regents 1976—, v.p. 1978-79, pres. 1981-82), Am. Assn. Cert. Allegists (pres. 1991—), Am. Acad. Allergy; mem. AMA, Kans. Med. Soc., Johnson County Med. Soc., Kans. Allergy Soc. (pres. 1976-77), Mo. Allergy Soc. (sec. 1975-76), Joint Coun. Socio-Econs. of Allergy (bd. dirs. 1976—, pres. 1978-79). Home: 8510 Delmar Ln Shawnee Mission KS 66207-1926

DOCKTERMAN, MICHAEL, lawyer; b. Davenport, Iowa, Dec. 14, 1954; s. Jerome and Elaine (Epstein) D.; m. Laura Di Giantonio, Sept. 25, 1983; 1 child, Eliana. BA, Yale U., 1975; JD, Duke U., 1978. Bar: Ill. 1978, U.S. Dist. Ct. (no. dist.) Ill. 1978, U.S. Dist. Ct. (ea. dist.) Mich. 1986, U.S. Dist. Ct. (ctrl. dist.) Ill. 1988, U.S. Dist. Ct. (so. dist.) Ill. 1991, U.S. Dist Ct. (we. dist.) Mich. 1994, U.S. Ct. Appeals (7th cir.) 1978, U.S. Ct. Appeals (4th, 6th and fed. cirs.) 1990, U.S. Ct. Appeals (2d cir.) 1993, U.S. Supreme Ct. 1992. Ptnr. Wildman, Harrold, Allen and Dixon, Chgo., 1978—. Co-author: IICLE Class Actions, 1986, 92; contbg. author: ABA Criminal Antitrust Litigation Manual, 1996; contbr. articles to profl. jours. Active Chgo. Vol. Legal Svcs., 1983—; adult bd. dirs. Greater Midwest region B'nai B'rith Youth Orgn., 1985—; bd. dirs. KAM Isaiah Israel Congregation, 1993—, Duke Law Alumni Assn., 1995—; trustee Max and Gretel Janowski Fund, Chgo., 1992—; mem. The Chgo. Com., Chgo. Coun. on Fgn. Rels. Recipient Award for Advocacy Internat. Acad. Trial Lawyers, Leadership Devel. award B'nai B'rith Youth Orgn. Fellow Pvt. Adjudication Found.; mem. ABA, Chgo. Bar Assn., Legal Club Chgo., B'nai B'rith Justice Lodge. Office: Wildman Harrold Allen Dixon 225 W Wacker Dr Chicago IL 60606-1224

DOCKTOR-SMITH, MARY ANN, employee benefits consultant; b. Indpls., Jan. 26, 1957; d. Leo Edward and Geraldine Marie (Staudt) Docktor; m. Randolph Davis Smith, July 11, 1981. Student, Loyola U., Chgo., 1988—. Cert. Qualified Pension Adminstr. Asst. dir. pension adminstrn. Indpls. Life, 1976-78; pres. Pen-Ad, Inc., Chgo., 1978-82; mgr. Aetna Life Ins. Co., Chgo., 1982-83; pres. Creative Pensions, Inc., Chgo., 1982-84, EBI Employee Benefits, Inc., Chgo., 1984—, The Flag Docktor Inc., Chgo., 1993—; treas. Adv. Flag Co., Inc., Chgo., 1983—. Co-author: The Only Tax-shelter You'll Ever Need, 1991; column author: Gene Balliett Report, 1984—; contbr. articles to profl. jour. Vol. adult reading tutor Literacy Chgo.; donor Ayn Rand Inst., Marina Del Rey, Calif., 1990—; mem. chmn.'s coun. Rep. Nat. Com. Acad. scholar Otto Lehman Found., Chgo., 1991-94. Mem. Am. Soc. Pension Actuaries, N.Am. Vexillogical Assn. (chmn. pub. rels. com., corr. sec. 1993—), Chgo. Coun. Fgn. Rels., Golden Key, Alpha Sigma Nu, Alpha Sigma Lamda, Pi Sigma Alpha. Republican. Office: EBI Employee Benefits Inc 4949 W Diversey Ave Chicago IL 60639-1705

DOCTOR, KENNETH JAY, editor; b. L.A., Jan. 5, 1950; s. Joseph and Ruth (Kazdoy) D.; m. Katherine Conant Francis, June 14, 1971; children: Jenika, Joseph, Katy. BA in Sociology, U. Calif., Santa Cruz, 1971; MS in Journalism, U. Oreg., 1979. Editor, pub. Willamette Valley Observer, Eugene, Oreg., 1975-82; mng. editor Oreg. Mag., Portland, 1982-84; mng. editor, features Boulder (Colo.) Daily Camera, 1984-86; assoc. editor, features St. Paul Pioneer Press, 1986-90, mng. editor, features, 1990-94, mng. editor, 1994—; chair Knight-Ridder Task Force on Family Readers, Miami, Fla., 1991. Recipient Achievement award Oreg. Civil Liberties Union, Eugene, 1982. Mem. Soc. Newspaper Design, AP Mng. Editors, Am. Soc. Newspaper Editors. Office: St Paul Pioneer Press 345 Cedar St Saint Paul MN 55101-1014

DODD, JAMES MICHAEL, secondary education educator; b. Indpls., June 30, 1947; s. Samuel James and Marie Margaret (Rector) D. BA, Ind. State U., 1973; MA, No. Ill. U., 1978, MS in Edn. Cert. sec. edn. tchr., Ill. Tchr. social studies H.S. Dist. 99, Downers Grove, Ill., 1969—. mem. Medinah Temple. Recipient award of merit Those Who Exel-Ill. Bd. Edn., 1995. Mem. Downers Grove Edn. Assn. (pres. 1989-95), Chgo. Coun. on Fgn. Rels., Scottish Rite, Hon. Order of Ky. Cols., Internat. Soc. Tech. Edn. Office: Cmty HS South 1436 Norfolk Downers Grove IL 60516

DODD, LEON POWELL, JR., aerospace executive; b. Nashville, Dec. 18, 1956; s. Leon P. Sr. and Ann D. (Whitehead) D.; m. Ellen Marie Shannon, Sept. 17, 1983; 1 child, Benjamin David. BS in Bus. Industry, East Tex. State U., 1983, MS in Tech., 1989. From tech. publs. to total quality mgr. Lockheed Martin, Ft. Worth, 1980-92, quality assurance program mgr., 1992-93; dir. advanced quality Aeronca Inc., Middletown, Ohio, 1993—. Contbr. articles to profl. jours. With USAF, 1975-80. Named Outstanding Young Man of Am., 1987. Republican. Roman Catholic. Office: Aeronca Inc 1712 Germantown Rd Middletown OH 45042

DODD, STEPHEN COWL, chemical engineer; b. Aurora, Ill., Jan. 21, 1952; s. John Cowl and Marion Ida (McDonald) D.; B.S. in Chem. Engring., Purdue U., 1974; S.M. in Chem. Engring., M.I.T., 1976; m. Margaret Ann Raskopf, Dec. 17, 1978; children—Christopher John, Catherine Adele, Jeffrey Cowl. Chem. engr. Aurora Paperboard Co. div. Davey Co., 1977-78, corporate chem. engr., Jersey City, 1978-80, asst. mill mgr., 1980, Downington, Pa., 1980-83, asst. v.p. research and devel., 1983-85, v.p. research and devel., dir., 1985-95, v.p. mfg., 1995—. Patentee in field. Mem. TAPPI, Am. Inst. Chem. Engrs., Am. Chem. Soc., Instrument Soc. Am., Sigma Xi. Republican. Home: 2571 Whiteway Ct Aurora IL 60504-5275 Office: Davey Co 705 N Farnsworth Ave Aurora IL 60505-2433

DODDS, BRENDA KAY, nurse; b. Wheeling, W.Va., July 14, 1961; d. Ray Charles and Kathryn June (Ries) D. BS, Graceland Coll., 1983; A in Child Devel., 1990. RN. Staff nurse Resthaven Retirement Home, Independence, Mo., 1983-84; staff nurse telemetry unit Columbia Independence Regional Health Ctr., 1983—; camp nurse Mo-Kan Salvation Army Camp, Kansas City, Mo., 1984; dental asst. Ronald E. Jennings, DDS P.C., Independence, 1985-87; sch. nurse Noland Child Devel. Ctr., Independence Pub. Sch. Dist., 1988—, head tchr., 1990—, morning supr., 1993—. Vol. ARC, Independence, 1983—, Voluntary Action Ctr., 1987—; vocalist Independence Messiah/Festival Choir, 1983—; musician Independence Symphony Band, 1988—. Mem. Nat. Assn. for Edn. Young Children, Mo. Nurses Assn., Profl. Nurses Assn., Mensa.

DODDS, CLAUDETTE LA VONN, radio executive and consultant; b. Lenapah, Okla., Sept. 2, 1947; d. Willie Lee and Dora (Harrell) Davis; m. Donald Howard Dodds, Jan. 14, 1965 (div. June 1982); children: Clarence Adam, Donyielle Alana, Erin Michelle. AAS with honors, Kennedy-King Coll., 1984; BA, U. Ill., Chgo., 1989. Newscaster, newswriter Sta. WKKC-FM, Chgo., 1983-84, news dir., 1984-85, program and music dir., 1985, sta. mgr., 1985-87; research asst. Vernon Jarrett Chgo. Sun Times, 1988-89; exec. asst. to pres. Sta. WVON, Chgo., 1989; asst. sta. mgr. Sta. WYCA-FM, Crawford Broadcasting Co., Chgo., Hammond, Ind., 1989-90; mem. adv. com. Coll. Broadcasting, 1985-87; cons. Chgo. Nite Life, 1985-87, Hayes & Co., 1986—, Morning Show/Danny Jack Sta. KWEZ, Monroe, La., 1986—, Sta. WKKC-FM, Future Records, 1988—; music rschr. Let's Dance, Chgo., 1986-88; broadcast asst. Sta. WVON, Chgo., 1989, exec. bd. Young People's Network Sta. WKKC-FM, 1988—, Youth on the Move, 1994, facilitator YPN workshops, 1994. Producer: (TV special) Messiah, 1985, Youth on the Move, 1994; producer, writer (radio and TV specials) Dr. Martin Luther King, 1985-86; producer, hostess (radio specials) Englewood Parade, 1986, Bud Billiken Parade, 1986; mag. music reporter, 1987; editor current affairs newsletter, 1992. Mem. Dem. Student task force, Chgo., 1984, Student Disciplinary Bd., Chgo., 1986; coord. Concerned Studies for Broadcasting Equipment, 1984; mem. task force for AIDS Prevention, 1993—, cons. AIDS task force, mem. program evaluation com., 1994—; vol. Darrell Stingley Youth Found., 1994; bd. dirs. Midwest Ctr. for Comprehensive Svc.; active caring for patients with HIV/AIDS, providing med. svcs., housing and counseling. Recipient Alumni Recognition award Kennedy-King Coll., 1993. Mem. Coalition Labor Union Women, Families Advocating Injury Reduction, Ams. for Legal Reform, Order of Eastern Star (Cable chpt. # 108 Prince Hall), Sorority and Heroines of Jericho (Rahab Ct. # 61), Sigma Gamma Rho (Delta Sigma chpt.). Home and Office: 305 W 69th St Chicago IL 60621-3720

DODENHOFF, HELEN JEAN, curator, archivist; b. Detroit, Apr. 30, 1938; d. Charles Frederick Dodenhoff and Martha Jean (Miller) Merry. BA, Smith Coll., 1960; MA, Wayne State U., 1974, cert. in archival adminstrn., 1988. Jr. curator Detroit Inst. Arts, 1961-62, asst. curator, 1962-73; curator Grosse Pointe (Mich.) Hist. Soc., 1980—; archivist Grosse Pointe Woods (Mich.) Hist. Commn., 1987-89, 95—, U. Liggett Sch., Grosse Pointe, 1988-93, 94—. Vol. allocations com. United Way S.E. Mich., Detroit, 1978-92, spl. grants & agency admissions com. United Way S.E. Mich., 1992-96, capital fund evaluation and allocation com. United Way S.E. Mich., 1995-96; bd. dirs. St. Mary's Cmty. Ctr., Detroit, 1979-94; rschr. Nat. Soc. Colonial Dames in Mich., Detroit, 1981-92; mem. adv. com. Sr. Citizen Info., Grosse Pointe, 1980—. Mem. AAUW, Soc. Am. Archivists, French-Can. Heritage Soc., Mich. Archival Assn., Detroit Hist. Soc., Jr. League Detroit (sustainer, bd. dirs. 1976-77). Episcopalian.

DODERER, MINNETTE FRERICHS, state legislator; b. Holland, Iowa, May 16, 1923; d. John A. and Sophie S. Frerichs; BA, U. Iowa, 1948; m. Fred H. Doderer, Aug. 5, 1944 (dec. 1991); children: Dennis, Kay Lynn. Mem. Iowa Ho. of Reps. 1964-69, 80—, minority whip, 1967-68, chairperson ways and means com., 1983-88, chair commerce com., 1989-90, chair small bus., econ. devel. and trade com., 1991-92; mem. Iowa Senate, 1970-79, pres. pro tem, 1975-76; vis. prof. Stephens Coll., Iowa State Univ. (both 1979); vice-chairwoman Iowa Interstate Cooperation Commn., 1965-66; Vice-chairwoman Democratic Party Johnson County, 1957-60; vice chairperson com. on budget and taxation Nat. Conf. State Legislator's; mem. Dem. Nat. Com., 1968-70, Dem. Nat. Policy Council Elected Ofcls., 1973-76; chairwoman Iowa del. Internat. Women's Yr. Del. Bd. fellows Iowa Sch. Religion. Recipient Disting. Service award Iowa Edn. Assn., 1969, Wilson award Commn. on Status of Women, 1989, Gold Seal award Iowa Coalition Against Domestic Violence, 1995; named to Iowa Women's Hall of Fame, 1978; named Woman of Yr. Iowa City Sr. Ctr., 1995. Mem. LWV, Pioneer Lawmakers (pres. 1993-95), Delta Kappa Gamma (hon.). Democrat. Methodist.

DODGE, MICHAEL LEE, small business owner; b. Ludington, Mich., May 5, 1968; s. Ross Donald and MaryAnn (Boening) D. A in Mgmt. and Mktg., Lansing (Mich.) C.C., 1989. Ind. rep. Equinox Intenat., Novi, Mich., 1992—; owner Am. Comm. Network Distbr., Lansing, 1992—, One Step Ahead Computer Preventive Maintenance, Lansing, 1993—, Chem-Dry of Grand Ledge, Lansing, 1994—. Office: One Step Ahead 8518 Eaton Hwy Grand Ledge MI 48837-9237

DODGEN, JOHN N., manufacturing executive; b. Sapulpa, Okla., June 22, 1926; s. Claude W. and Pearl M. (Glass) D.; m. Wanda Lou Edwards; children: James, Mary Lou, John C.T., Lori. BA, Ottawa U., 1956; PMD, Harvard U., 1961. V.p. distbn. farm equipment Dodgen & Co., Fort Dodge, Iowa, 1947-56; v.p. mfg. and distbn. farm equipment Dodgen Assembly Mfrs., Sioux City, Iowa, 1956-58; pres. mfg. and distbn. farm equipment Silbaugh Mfg., Humboldt, Iowa, 1958-61; pres. mfg. farm and indsl. equipment Dodgen Industries, Inc., Humboldt, 1961—; pres. Dodgen Leasing Corp., Humboldt, 1954—, Born Free, Inc., Humboldt, 1969—, Fiberglass Fabricators, Inc., Humboldt, 1984—, Dodgen Mobile Technologies, Humboldt, 1990—; bd. trustees Ottawa (Kans.) U., 1964—; bd. dirs. Iowa Assn. Bus. and Industry. Office: Dodgen Industries Inc Hwy 169 N Humboldt IA 50548

DODOHARA, JEAN NOTON, music educator; b. Monroe, Wis., Feb. 21, 1934; d. Albert Henry and Eunice Elizabeth (Edgerton) Noton; BA, Monmouth (Ill.) Coll., 1955; MS, U. Ill., 1975, adminstrv. cert., 1980, EdD, 1985; m. Laurence G. Landers, June 7, 1955 (div.); children: Theodore Scott, Thomas Warren, Philip John; m. Edward R. Harris, Nov. 27, 1981 (dec.); stepchildren: Adrianne, Erica; m. Takashi Dodohara, Aug. 7, 1988; 1 stepchild, Eve D. Dodohara. Tchr. music schs. in Ill. and Fla., 1955-76; tchr. ch. music for children, 1957-72; tchr. music Dist. 54, Schaumburg, Ill., 1976-93; teaching asst. U. Ill., 1979. Named Outstanding Young Woman of Yr., Jaycee Wives, St. Charles, Mo., 1968; charter mem. Nat. Mus. Women in Arts. Mem. NEA (life), AAUW, Music Educators Nat. Conf. (life), Ill. Educators Assn. (life), Elgin Area Ret. Tchrs. Assn., U. Ill. Alumni Assn. (life), Mortar Bd., Mensa, Delta Kappa Pi. Mem. United Ch. of Christ. Home: 1068 Hampshire Ln Elgin IL 60120-4905

DODSON, BRUCE J., funeral director; b. Alma, Mich., Oct. 9, 1937; s. Floyd S. and Bertha M. (Van Vynck) D.; m. Carolyn K. McCracken, Jan. 24, 1970; children: Eric, Joshua. AA, Northwood Inst., Midland, Mich., 1961; cert. Mortuary Scis., Wis. Inst. Mortuary Scis., Milw., 1962. Automobile sales Edmore, Mich., 1955-58; mgr. Stebbins Funeral Home, Stanton, Mich., 1962-69; owner Dodson Funeral Home, St. Ignace, Mich., 1969—; pres. Dist. Funeral Dirs. 9, 1974-78. Mem. Stanton City Coun., 1963-68, St. Ignace City Coun., 1981-83; mem. Gov.'s Task Force for Mackinac Bridge Fin., 1986-87; mayor City of St. Ignace, 1983—; chmn. Mackinac Straits Hosp. Bd., 1989-91, vice chmn., 1991-92; co-founder St. Ignace Antique Auto Show, 1976—; mem. Mackinac County Bldg. Authority, 1993—, chair, 1995-96. Named St. Ignace Citizen of the Yr. C. of C., 1992. Mem. Nat. Funeral Dirs. Assn., Mich. Funeral Dirs. Assn. (bd. govs. 1978-81), Mich. Assn. Mayors, Automobile Club Am. (life, nat. judge), Classic Car Club Am., Motor City Packard Club (charter), Family Motor Coach Assn. (life). Methodist. Home and Office: 240 Mccann St Saint Ignace MI 49781-1651

DODSON, CARL EDWARD, nuclear engineer, real estate agent, executive, minister; b. Chgo., July 8, 1956; s. John Eddie and Birdie (Dodson) Allen; m. Peggy E. Dodson; children: LaTressa, LaTisha, LaTonya, Carl Jr., Barry. A in Engring., State Tech. Inst. at Memphis, 1980. Lic. FCC 3d class, lic. Tenn. Bd. Realtors, lic. minister. Engring. aide Spl. Design, Knoxville, Tenn., 1980-82, Sequoyah Nuclear Plant, Knoxville, Tenn., 1982-84; design engr. Sequoyah Nuclear Plant, Soddy, Tenn., 1985-88; real estate agt. Holmes Real Estate Co., Knoxville, Tenn., 1989-91; pres., chief exec. officer Ezra Inc., Knoxville, 1990-91; sr. technician, analyst Weston Gulf Coast, University Park, Ill., 1992-94; pharm. technician Centeon, Kankakee, Ill., 1994—; assoc. pastor Shiloh Full Gospel Bapt. Ch., Kankakee. Author (software): New Student, 1980. Mem. Nat. Inst. Certification in Engring. Technologies, Jaycees (Chattanooga). Home: 278 S Nelson Ave Kankakee IL 60901-4303

DOEGE, THEODORE CHARLES, retired physician; b. Lincoln, Nebr., Dec. 11, 1928; s. Arthur John August and Erna Marie (Lohrmann) D.; m. Ann Elizabeth Edmondson, June 23, 1957; children: Rebecca Ann, Andrew Theodore. AB, Oberlin Coll., 1950; MD, U. Rochester, 1958; MS, U. Wash., 1965. Diplomate Am. Bd. Preventive Medicine. Intern U. Utah Sch. of Medicine, Salt Lake City, 1958-59; sr. asst. surgeon USPHS, Atlanta, 1959-61; asst. resident U. Wash., Seattle, 1961-63; chief resident, pediatrics King County Hosp., Seattle, 1963; asst. prof. dept. preventive medicine U. Wash., Seattle, 1965-67; assoc. prof. U. Ill., Chgo., 1967-95; dir. dept. environ. pub. and occupational health AMA, Chgo., 1977-86, sr. scientist, 1984—; assoc. prof. epidemiology U. Ill., Chgo., 1972-95, dir. dept. environ. pub. occupl. health, 1977-86; dir. dept. risk assessment AMA, Chgo., 1988-90, mem. dept. preventive medicine and pub. health, 1990—; sr. mem. U. Ill. Grad. Coll., 1974-95; vis. assoc. prof. Chiangmai U., Thailand, 1967-70; cons. APHA, Washington, 1973, Carter Ctr. Project, Emory U., Atlanta, 1984, Nat. Safety Coun., Chgo., 1989; cons. on grant applications USPHS, Am. Cancer Soc., 1988; reviewer for med. jours., 1975—. Contbr. articles to profl. jours; editor or co-editor books in field. Mem. CAC Underwriters Labs., Inc., Northbook, Ill., 1980-95, corp. mem., 1984-95. Parachutist Med. Svc. Corps, U.S. Army, 1950-52. Recipient Howard Frank Jr. scholarship Oberlin (Ohio) Coll., 1946-50, Heumann and Rekers scholarships U. Rochester Sch. Med. Dentistry, 1957. Fellow APHA, Am. Coll. Epidemiology; mem. AAAS, AMA, Sigma Xi. Lutheran. Home: 5518 S Garfield Ave Hinsdale IL 60521-5013

DOEHR-BLANCK, DENISE LOUISE, special education educator; b. Milw., Feb. 10, 1963; d. Dennis DeWayne and Mary Lou (Viola) Doehr; m. Timothy James Blanck, June 24, 1989. BA in Early Childhood Edn., Mt. Mary Coll., 1985; MA in Spl. Edn., Cardinal Stritch Coll., 1989. Tchr. grade 1 St. Jude the Apostle, Wauwatosa, Wis., 1985-89; pvt. practice edn. therapist Wauwatosa, 1986-90; edn. specialist Northbrooke Psychiat. Hosp., Brown Deer, Wis., 1989-91; instr. Waukesha County Tech. Coll., Pewaukee, Wis., 1990-91; edn. therapist Comprehensive Mental Health Svcs., Milw., 1990-92; pvt. practice ednl. therapist West Allis, Wis., 1991—; spkr., spl. ednl. therapist Northbrooke Hosp., Brown Deer, Wis., 1989-91; spl. edn. jr. h.s. tchr. St. Francis, Milw., 1993—; acad. coord. St. Francis Children's Ctr., 1994—. Columnist: Ask the Teacher, Chadd Tiddings, 1994—. Mem. Friends of the Milw. Symphony Orch., Zoo Pride. Theresa Ross scholar Mt. Mary Coll., 1983, 84. Mem. Coun. for Exceptional Children, Internat. Reading Assn., Wis. Reading Assn., Orton Dyslexia Soc. (sec. Wis. br. 1987-88), Learning Disabilities Assn. Wis., Children with Learning Disabilities, Nat. Assn. for Child and Adults with Learning Disabilities, Ch.A.D.D. of S.E. Wis. (sec. 1988-95). Republican. Roman Catholic. Home: 1109 S 90th St Milwaukee WI 53214-2838 Office: St Francis 6700 N Port Washington Rd Milwaukee WI 53217-3919

DOELL, JAMES F., electrical engineer; b. Hammond, Ind., Aug. 11, 1966; s. Leonard Arnold and Judith Ray (Abney) D.; m. Cecilia Ann Feldkamp May 7, 1988. BSEE, Purdue U., 1988. Engr. Ill. Power Co., Bloomington, 1988-89; engr. I Pub. Svc. Co., Terre Haute, Ind., 1989-90; engr. II PSI Energy, Columbus, Ind., 1990-91, planning engr., 1991—. Mem. IEEE. Home: 3730 Indianwood Dr Columbus IN 47203-2511 Office: PSI Energy 2727 Central Ave Columbus IN 47201-3124

DOELLMAN, ANTHONY T., state official; b. Quincy, Ill., Oct. 8, 1946; s. Ralph George and Esther Juanita (Mueller) D.; m. Paulette Louise Molitor, Aug. 17, 1974; children: Charles, Ralph, John, Elizabeth, Lauretta, Joseph, Marian, Theodore. BA, Quincy U., 1972; grad., Ill. State Police Command Coll, Springfield, 1994. Vocational assessment specialist Ill. Dept. of Rehab. Svcs., Springfield, 1972-78; cliams mgr. Horace Mann Ins., Springfield, 1978-80; budget analyst Ill. Dept. of Pub. Aid, Springfield, 1980-82; tng. NCO U.S. Army, Springfield, 1982-86; pub. svc. adminstr. Ill. State Police, Springfield, 1986—; Pres. County Vittles and Things, Athens, Ill., 1995—. Bd. dirs. Athens Unified Sch. Dist. 213, 1988-92, 94—; chmn. food com. Athens Rodeo Com., 1993-95; scoutmaster troop 52 Boy Scouts Am., 1993. With U.S. Army, 1968-69, Vietnam. Recipient Svc. plaque Athens Sch. Bd., 1992. Mem. Am. Legion (life), Setoma (bd. dirs. 1994-95), VFW (life). Republican. Roman Catholic. Home: RR 2 Box 285A Athens IL 62613

DOELLMAN, MICHAEL ANTHONY, librarian; b. Quincy, Ill., Feb. 11, 1945; s. Ralph George and Esther Juanita (Mueller) D.; m. Patricia Louise Lyons, Oct. 6, 1973. BA in English, Quincy Coll., 1970; MSLS, Case Western Res. U., 1977; postgrad., No. Ill. U., 1971, U. Akron, 1979-81. Ref. libr. Burton (Ohio) Pub. Libr., 1971-82, cataloger, 1982-84; assoc. dir. adult svcs. Elkhart (Ind.) Pub. Libr., 1984-90, assoc. dir. tech. svcs., 1990—, system adminstr., 1990—; v.p. Customers of Dynix, Inc., 1996—. With U.S. Army, 1963-71. Mem. ALA (notable books com. 1990-91), Ind. Libr. Fedn., Cath. Libr. Assn. Home: PO Box 97 Notre Dame IN 46556-0097 Office: Elkhart Pub Libr 300 S 2nd St Elkhart IN 46516-3183

DOEPKER, J(OHN) FREDERICK, JR., plastic surgeon; b. Lima, Ohio, Mar. 22, 1949; s. John Frederick and Elizabeth (Merritt) D.; children: John, Justin, Ashley, Derek. BA in Math., Ind. U., 1971; MD, Ind. U., Indpls., 1976. Diplomate Am. Bd. Plastic Surgery. Resident in gen. and plastic surgery Butterworth Hosp., Grand Rapids, Mich., 1976-81; fellow in plastic surgery Vanderbilt U., Nashville, 1981-82; practice medicine specializing in plastic surgery Evansville, Ind., 1982—. Past v.p. Vanderburgh County Am. Cancer Soc., Evansville, 1984-88; bd. dirs. Leadership Evansville, 1989—. Fellow ACS; mem. Am. Soc. Plastic and Reconstructive Surgeons, Vanderburgh County Med. Soc., Am. Med. Assn., John B. Lynch Soc., Lipolysis Soc. N.Am., Ferris Smith Soc., So. Med. Assn., Phi Rho Sigma Med. Soc. Office: 2701 Lincoln Ave Evansville IN 47714-1627

DOERINGER, FRANKLIN M., historian, educator; b. Cleve., Oct. 2, 1940; s. Frank J. and Bertha Ann (Warek) D.; m. Frederica Cagan, Dec. 28, 1975; children: Adam Henry, Andrea Cagan. BA, Columbia Coll., 1962; PhD, Columbia U., 1971. Asst. prof. Chinese Columbia U., N.Y.C., 1970-71; Nathan M. Pusey prof. history and East Asian studies Lawrence U., Appleton, Wis., 1972—; chair East Asian langs. and cultures, 1989-96. Author: Discovering the Global Past, 1995; contbr. articles to profl. jours. Curriculum rev. com. mem. Appleton Bd. Edn., 1991—. Grantee 3M Found., 1990, Chiang Ching Kuo Found., 1993. Mem. Internat. Soc. Chinese Philosophy, Am. Hist. Assn. Office: Lawrence Univ Dept History Appleton WI 54915

DOERMANN, HUMPHREY, foundation administrator; b. Toledo, Nov. 13, 1930; s. Henry John and Alice (Robbins Humphrey) D.; m. Elisabeth Adams Wakefield, Jan. 7, 1956; children: Elisabeth M., Eleanor H., Julia L. AB, Harvard U., 1952, MBA, 1958, PhD, 1967; LLD (hon.), Xavier U., La., 1990; LHD (hon.), Coll. St. Scholastica, 1993, U. St. Thomas, 1996. Asst. to com. on admissions and scholarships Harvard, 1955-56; reporter Mpls. Star, 1958-60; asst. to bus. mgr. Mpls. Star & Tribune Co., 1960-61; dir. admissions Harvard, 1961-66; asst. to dean Harvard (Faculty of Arts and Scis.), 1966-69, asst. dean for financial affairs, 1970-71; lectr. on edn. Harvard (Grad. Sch. Edn.), 1967-71; exec. dir. Bush Found., St. Paul, 1971-78; pres. Bush Found., 1978—; cons. Coun. Higher Edn. Va., 1969, W. Va. Bd. Regents, 1970; bd. overseers Harvard Coll., Harvard U., 1973-79; bd. dirs. Coun. on Founds., Washington, 1985-92, chmn. bd. 1990-92; trustee Found. Ctr., N.Y.C., 1975-83, chmn. bd. 1982-83; chmn. Minn. Coun. on Founds., 1981-85, Coll. Bd., N.Y.C., 1994—; mem. selection com. Nat. Merit scholarships, 1965-67; chmn. Minn. Legis. Task Force on Student Aid, 1993; mem. regents candidate adv. coun. U. Minn. Author: Crosscurrents in College Admissions, rev. edit, 1970, Toward Equal Access, 1978; cons. editor Change mag., 1991—; contbr. articles to Found. News, other jours. Mem. Belmont (Mass.) Town Meeting, 1969-70. Served to lt. (j.g.) USN, 1952-55. Mem. Belmont (Mass.) Town Meeting, 1969-70; dist. chmn. Rhodes Scholarship Selection Com. Lt. (j.g.) USN, 1952-55. Home: 736 Goodrich Ave Saint Paul MN 55105-3524 Office: Bush Found E-900 E First Nat Bank Bldg Saint Paul MN 55101

DOERRING, FREDRICK LORENZ, retired engine service company executive; b. Luana, Iowa, Jan. 3, 1928; s. Lorenz August and Beatrice Caroline (Palas) D.; m. Lillian Marie Takach, June 1953; children: Joseph F., Linda Mae, Richard L., Thomas Alan. BA, Upper Iowa U., 1953. various positions, Iowa, 1949-69; Svc. mechanic, asst. shop mgr. Allen Supply Co., Svc. Saw Co., Inc., Cedar Rapids, Iowa, Des Moines, 1955-69; instr., advisor NABS DMACC Labor Dept. Consortium, Des Moines, 1970-71; v.p., gen. mgr. Svc. Saw Co. Inc., Des Moines, 1972-81; owner, CEO Accel Small Engines, Des Moines and Ankeny, Iowa, 1982-84; pres., CEO Fred/Rick

Svcs. Inc., West Des Moines, Iowa, 1985-94; cons. Nat. Gypsum Co., Ft. Dodge, Iowa, 1979. Active Iowa Children's Home Soc., Des Moines 1960-69, Des Moines Police Dept., Des Moines, 1994—. With U.S. Army Air Corps, 1946-49. Republican. Mem. Evangelical Free Ch. Home: 324 E Hughes Des Moines IA 50315

DOGGETT, JOHN NELSON, JR., clergyman; b. Phila., Apr. 3, 1918; s. John Nelson and Winola (Ballard) D.; BA, Lincoln U., 1942; MDiv, Union Theol. Sem., N.Y.C., 1945; MEd, St. Louis U., 1969, PhD, 1971; m. Juanita Toley, Aug. 2, 1973; children by previous marriage: Lorraine, John, William, Kenneth Riddick. Ordained to ministry United Methodist Ch., 1943; civilian chaplain South Gate Community Ch., San Francisco, 1945-47; organizing pastor Downs Meml. Meth. Ch., Oakland, Calif., 1947-49; pastor Scott Meml. Meth. Ch., Pasadena, Calif., 1950-53, Hamilton Meml. Meth. Ch., L.A., 1953-64, Union Meml. United Meth. Ch., St. Louis, 1964-76; dist. supt. United Meth. Ch., St. Louis, 1976-82; sr. pastor Grace United Meth. Ch., St. Louis, 1982-85; ret. pastor Cabanne United Meth. Ch., 1986-89; staff Pastoral Counseling Inst., St. Louis, 1968-89; pres. Midwest Cons., 1989—. instr. founds. edn. Harris Tchrs. Coll., St. Louis, 1971-75; assoc. prof. practical theology Met. Coll., St. Louis, 1976-77; commr. Nat. Coun. Chs. of Christ, 1981-84. Pres. bd. dirs. St. Louis C.M.C. Retirement Village Ctr., Cen. Med. Ctr. Hosps., St. Louis, 1973-86 ; pres. St. Louis NAACP, 1971-81, Limelight Mag., assoc. publ. staff, Clergy Coalition Ch. Health Commn., Ea. Mo. AIDS Summit, 1990; bd. dirs. United Way St. Louis, 1974-81; mem. Commn. on Alternatives to Prison, 1981, Citizens Com. Mo. Dept. Corrections, 1974-80, Mayor's Task Force on Crime, Mo. Minority Health Task Force; trustee Mo. Hist. Soc., 1986—, John N. Doggett St. Louis Internist program, 1996; adv. com. St. Louis U. Sch. Social Work; advisor John and Juanita Doggett Scholarships at St. Paul Sch. Theology, Kansas City, Mo., Lincoln U., Pa.; mem. Interfaith Clergy Coun., 1980-85, World Meth. Coun., St. Louis U. Pres. Coun.; mem. mayor's ambs., 1980-90, World Affairs Coun., ACLU, 1986-93,; project friend St. Louis Drug Free Schs., 1992-95. Named Minister of Year, St. Louis Argus Newspaper, 1971, J.N. Doggett Day proclaimed by Mayor of St. Louis, 1996; recipient Outstanding Alumni award St. Louis U., 1981, Human Rights award E.P. Lovejoy Soc., Martin Luther King Alpha/Anheuser-Busch Spl. Plaque, M.L. King Day Plaque award Job Corp., 1990, Hon. Citizen Martin Luther King award Huntsville, Ala., 1993, Drum Major award NCCJ, 1994, Alpha Kappa Alpha Sorority Life Time Excellence Plaque, Award of Merit Urban League Metro. St. Louis, 1994, Charter BMCR Caucus award, 1994, Outstanding Alumni award Lincoln U., 1996, Founder's Day award Lincoln U., 1996. Mem. Am. Assn. Pastoral Counselors (emeritus), Metro Ministers Coalition, 1981-91, UN Assn. (clergy-pub. edn. com.), Shriner Masons, Phi Delta Kappa, Alpha Phi Alpha (nat. chaplain emeritus, D. Bowles/R. Anderson Svc. award, regional hall fame 1987, midwest region R. Cannon, gen. pres. Alpha Phi Alpha Fraternity Plaque, 1995, nat. presdl. proclamation, 1994, Renaissance IV Excellence Svc. plaque Epsilon Lambda chpt. 1994). Home: 4466 W Pine Blvd Apt 2C Saint Louis MO 63108-2327

DOHMEN, FREDERICK HOEGER, retired wholesale drug company executive; b. Milw., May 12, 1917; s. Fred William and Viola (Gutsch) D.; BA in Commerce, U. Wis., 1939; m. Gladys Elizabeth Dite, Dec. 23, 1939 (dec. 1963); children: William Francis, Robert Charles; m. Mary Alexander Holgate, June 27, 1964. With F. Dohmen Co., Milw., 1939-82, successively warehouse employee, sec., v.p., 1944-52, pres., 1952-82, dir., 1947—, chmn. bd., 1952-82. Bd. dirs. St. Luke's Hosp. Ednl. Found., Milw., 1965-83, pres., 1969-72, chmn. bd., 1972-73; bd. dirs. U. Wis., Milw. Found., 1976-79, bd. visitors, 1978-88, emeritus mem. 1988—; assoc. chmn. Nat. Bible Week, Laymen's Nat. Bible Com., N.Y.C., 1968-82, council of adv., 1983—; elder Presbyn. Ch.; bd. dirs. Riveredge Nature Ctr., Newburg, Wis., 1993-94. Mem. Nat. Wholesale Druggists Assn. (chmn. mfr. relations com. 1962, resolutions com. 1963, mem. of bd. control 1963-66), Nat. Assn. Wholesalers (trustee 1966-75), Druggists Service Council (dir. 1967-71), Wis. Pharm. Assn., Miss. Valley Drug Club, Beta Gamma Sigma, Phi Eta Sigma, Delta Kappa Epsilon, University Club, Town Club (Milw.). Home: 3903 W Mequon Rd Mequon WI 53092-2727

DOHMEN, MARY HOLGATE, retired primary school educator; b. Gary, Ind., July 28, 1918; d. Clarence Gibson and Margaret Alexander (Kinnear) Holgate; m. Frederick Hoeger Dohmen, June 27, 1964; children: William Francis, Robert Charles. BS, Milw. State Tchrs. Coll., 1940; M of Philosophy, U. Wis., 1945. Cert. tchr., Wis. Tchr. primary grades Baraboo (Wis.) Pub. Schs., 1940-43, Whitefish Bay (Wis.) Pub. Schs., 1943-64. Contbr. articles, story, poems to various pubs. Bd. dirs. Homestead H.S. chpt. Am. Field Svc., Mequon, Wis., 1970-80; mem. Milw. Aux. VNA, 1975—, 2d v.p., 1983-85, Milw. Pub. Mus. Enrichment Club, 1975—, Boys and Girls Club of Greater Milw., 1986—; vol. Reading is Fun program, 1987—, Milw. Symphony Orch. League, 1960—, Ptnrs. in Conservation, World Wildlife Fund, Washington, 1991—, Milw. Art Mus. Garden Club, 1979—, com. chmn., 1981-86; mem. Chancellor's Soc. U. Wis.-Milw., 1991—; travel lectr. various orgns., 1980—. Mem. AAUW, Milw. Coll. Endowment Assn. (v.p. 1987-90, pres. 1991-93), Bascom Hill Soc. (U. Wis.), Woman's Club Wis., Alpha Phi (pres. Milw. alumnae 1962-64), Pi Lambda Theta (pres. Milw. alumnae 1962-64), Delta Kappa Gamma. Republican. Presbyterian. Home: 3903 W Mequon Rd Mequon WI 53092-2727

DOHNALEK, DONALD WENCESLAUS, radiologist; b. Chelsea, Iowa, Sept. 11, 1925; s. Charles and Theresa Katharine (Kaufman) D.; m. Katharine T. Tepesch, Dec. 27, 1947 (dec.); children: Donna, Patrice, Jonathan, James, Marianne. Student, Loras Coll., Dubuque, Iowa, 1943-44, Notre Dame (Ind.) U., 1944-45; MD, U. Iowa, 1949. Diplomate Am. Bd. Radiology. Pvt. practice Waukon, Iowa, 1952-56; radiology resident U. Colo., Denver, 1956-59; radiologist various hosps. Iowa, 1959-62; radiologist River Falls (Wis.) Hosp., 1962—, Minn. Dept. Corrections, Stillwater, 1969—; chief of staff River Falls Area Hosp., 1972-73, Myrtue Meml. Hosp., Harlan, Iowa, 1961-62. Mem., clk. River Falls Sch. Bd., 1970—. Lt. comdr. USN, 1949-52. Mem. KC (Grand Knight 1953—). Republican. Roman Catholic. Home and Office: W10361 879th Ave River Falls WI 54022

DOHNÂNYI, CHRISTOPH VON, musician, conductor; b. Berlin, Sept. 8, 1929; s. Hans and Christina (Bonhoeffer) von D.; m. Anja Silja, Apr. 21, 1979; children: Julia, Benedikt, Olga. Student, U. Munich, Hochschule fuer Musik, Munich, Fla. State U., Berkshire Music Ctr.; doctorate (hon.), Oberlin Coll., Cleve. Inst. Music, Case Western Res. U. Coach, condr. Frankfurt (Germany) Opera, 1952-57, gen. music dir., artistic dir., 1968-77; gen. music dir. Lubeck, Germany, 1957-63, Kassel, Germany, 1963-66; dir. West German Radio Symphony, Cologne, 1964-70; artistic dir., prin. condr. Hamburg (Germany) State Opera, 1977-84; music dir. designate Cleve. Orch., 1982-84, music dir., 1984—; guest condr. in U.S. and Europe; prin. guest condr. Philharmonia Orch., London, 1994—. Numerous recordings including 5 symphonies of Mendelssohn, opera Lulu, Petrouchka Suite, opera Wozzeck with Vienna Philharmonic, symphonies of Beethoven, Brahms, Schumann, Dvorak, Mahler, Mozart, Schubert and Bruckner with Cleve. Orch. Decorated l'Ordre des arts et des lettres (France), cross Order of Merit (Germany), comdr. cross Republic of Austria; recipient Richard Strauss prize, Munich, 1951, Bartok prize, Hungary, 1982, Goethe medal City of Frankfurt, 1979, Comdr. of Yr. award Mus. Am., 1992. Office: Cleve Orch 11001 Euclid Ave Cleveland OH 44106-1796

DOLAN, JAN CLARK, state legislator; b. Akron, Ohio, Jan. 15, 1927; d. Herbert Spencer and Jean Risk (Morton) Clark; m. Walter John Dolan, Apr. 22, 1950 (dec. July 1986); children: Mark Raymond, Scott Spencer, Gary Clark, Todd Alvin. BA, U. Akron, 1949. Home svc. rep. East Ohio Gas Co., Akron, 1949-50; dietitian Akron City Hosp., 1950-51; tchr. Brecksville (Ohio) Sch. Dist., 1962-66; adminstr. Orchard Hills Adult Day Ctr., West Bloomfield, Mich., 1978-83; mem. Farmington Hills (Mich.) City Coun., 1975-88, Mich. Ho. of Reps., Lansing, 1989—. Mayor City of Farmington Hills, 1978, 85; elder Presbyn. Ch. Republican. Home: 22587 Gill Rd Farmington Hl MI 48335-4037 Office: Mich Ho of Reps State Capitol Bldg Lansing MI 48909

DOLAN, JAY PATRICK, history educator; b. Bridgeport, Conn., Mar. 17, 1936; s. Joseph T. and Margaret (Reardon) D.; m. Patricia McNeal, May 26, 1973; children: Patrick, Mark. STL, Gregorian U., 1962; PhD, U. Chgo., 1970. Asst. prof. dept. theology U. San Francisco, 1970-71; dir. Charles and Margaret Hall Cushwa Ctr. Study Am. Catholicism, Notre Dame, Ind., 1977-93; asst. prof. U. Notre Dame, Ind., 1971-77, assoc. prof., 1977-86, prof. history, 1986—; vis. prof. Boston Coll., 1991; Fulbright prof. U. Coll., Cork, Ireland, 1986; cons. numerous orgns. including Lilly Endowment Program on Cath. Colls. for Women, 1994, Lilly Fellows Program in Humanities and Arts, 1991-95, N.Y. Irish History Project, 1990-95, De Smet Project Washington State U., 1988-92, Congregational History Project U. Chgo., 1987-81, many others. Author: The American Catholic Experience: A History from Colonial Times to the Present, 1985, Catholic Revivalism: The American Experience 1830-1900, 1978, The Immigrant Church: New York's Irish and German Catholics, 1815-1865, 1975; co-author: Transforming Parish Ministry: The Changing Roles of Catholic Clergy, Laity and Women Relgious in the United States, 1930-80, 1989; editor: Mexican Americans and the Catholic Church 1900-1965, 1994, Puerto Rican and Cuban Catholics in the U.S. 1900-65, 1994, others; mem. numerous editl. bds.; referee numerous jours. and pubs. Vol. Hospice, South Bend, Ind., 1979-81, Ctr. for Homeless, South Bend, 1990—. Rsch. grantee Lilly Endowment, 1991-92, Word of God Inst., 1976; fellow Am. Coun. Learned Socs., 1978-79, Rockefeller fellow U. Chgo., 1969-70, Shelby Cullom Davis Ctr. Princeton U., 1973-74; named Alumnus of Yr. U. Chgo. Divinity Sch., 1987. Mem. Am. Cath. Hist. Assn. (chair joint spring meeting 1992, pres. 1995), Am. Soc. Ch. History (mem. exec. coun. 1977-80, Centennial com. 1982-88, chair program com. 1983, 87, 90, pres. 1987, chair nominating com. 1988), Immigration History Soc. (mem. exec. coun. 1988-91), Statue of Liberty-Ellis Island Found., Inc. (mem. history com. 1983-90), Am. Acad. Religion, U. Chgo. Divinity Sch. Alumni Coun. Home: 51411 Harrington Dr Granger IN 46530 Office: U Notre Dame Dept History Notre Dame IN 46556

DOLAN, THOMAS PATRICK, insurance company executive; b. LaSalle, Ill., Mar. 13, 1936; s. Francis Henry and Josephine (Quigley) D.; 1 child, Elizabeth. BSBA, U. Ill., 1960. Asst. dept. mgr. Transamerica Life Cos., L.A., 1960-69, systems coord., 1969-72, dept. mgr., 1972-78, asst. v.p., sub div. mgr., 1978-86, 2d v.p., div. mgr., 1985—. Fellow Life Mgmt. Inst. Home: 2929 Grand Ave Kansas City MO 64108-3221 Office: Transamerica Occidental 1100 Walnut St Kansas City MO 64106-2109

DOLASINSKI, STEVEN GEORGE, manufacturing engineer; b. Chgo., Mar. 14, 1957. B, Ill. Inst. Tech., 1979. Process engr. John Deer, Moline, Ill., 1979-84; program mgr. United Techs., Syracuse, N.Y., 1984-87; dir. mfg. tech. Comml. Intertech, Youngstown, Ohio, 1987—; vocat. adv. bd. Youngstowns State U., 1988—. Mem. ASME, MADD, SAE, AGMA. Office: Comml Intertech 1775 Logan Ave Youngstown OH 44505-2622

DOLD, ROBERT BRUCE, journalist; b. Newark, Mar. 9, 1955; s. Robert Bruce and Margaret (Noll) D.; m. Eileen Claire Norris, July 10, 1982; children: Megan, Kristen. BS in Journalism, Northwestern U., 1977, MS in Journalism, 1978. Reporter Suburban Trib, Hinsdale, Ill., 1975-83; reporter Chgo. Tribune, 1983-90, mem. editl. bd., 1990-95, dep. editl. page editor, columnist, 1995—. Columnist Chgo. Enterprise, 1991-95; critic: Downbeat Mag., 1980-84; commentator: Chgo. Week in Rev., 1987—. Bd. dirs. Jazz Inst. Chgo., 1980-83. Recipient Peter Lisagor award Sigma Delta Chi, 1988, Pulitzer prize for editorial writing, 1994. Mem. Am. Soc. Newspaper Editors. Roman Catholic. Home: 501 N Park Rd LaGrange Park IL 60526 Office: Chgo Tribune 435 N Michigan Ave Chicago IL 60611-4001

DOLDER, ANGELA MARIE, physical therapist, educator; b. Union City, Ind., Nov. 23, 1964; d. Carl Otis and Sarah Anne (Brandewie) Sharp; m. Timothy Edward Dolder, Oct. 14, 1989; 1 child, Catherine Anne. BS in Phys. Therapy, Ohio U., 1988. Staff phys. therapist St. Ann's Hosp., Westerville, Ohio, 1988-89, Dublin (Ohio) Phys. Therapy, 1989-91, Grady Meml. Hosp., Delaware, Ohio, 1991-94; acad. coord. clin. edn. Ohio State U., Columbus, 1994—. Mem. Am. Phys. Therapy Assn. (cert., assembly rep. Ohio chpt. 1994-96), Ohio Phys. Therapy Assn. Roman Catholic. Office: Ohio State U 1583 Perry St Rm 306 Columbus OH 43210

DOLE, ROBERT J., senator; b. Russell, Kans., July 22, 1923; s. Doran R. and Bina D.; m. Elizabeth Hanford, Dec. 1975. Student, U. Kans., 1941-43, U. Ariz.; A.B., Washburn Mcpl. U., Topeka, 1952, LL.B., 1952; LL.D. (hon.), Washburn U., Topeka, 1969. Bar: Kans. 1952. Mem. Kans. Ho. of Reps., 1951-53; sole practice Russell, Kans., 1953-61; Russell County atty., 1953-61; mem. 87th Congress from 6th Dist., Kans., 88th-90th congresses from 1st Dist., Kans., U.S. Senate from Kans., 1969-96; chmn. Rep. Nat. Com., 1971-73; Senate majority leader U.S. Senate from Kans., 1985-86, Senate Rep. leader, 1987-96; Rep. vice-presdl. candidate, 1976; Rep. presdl. candidate, 1996. Chmn. Dole Found. Served with AUS, 1943-48, World War II. Decorated Purple Heart (2), Bronze Star with 2 clusters. Recipient Horatio Alger award Horatio Alger Assn. Disting. Ams., 1988. Mem. Am. Legion, VFW, DAV, 4-H Fair Assn., Kappa Sigma. Methodist. Clubs: Masons, Shriners, Elk, Kiwanis. Office: US Senate 141 Hart Senate Bldg Washington DC 20510 Office: Office of Majority Leader S230 The Capitol Washington DC 20510-1902

DOLEMAN, CHRISTOPHER JOHN, professional football player; b. Indpls., Oct. 16, 1961; m. Toni; 1 child, Taylor Marie. Student, U. Pitts. With Minn. Vikings, 1985-94; defensive end Atlanta Falcons, 1994—. Player NFL Pro Bowl, 1987, 88, 89, 90, 92, 93; defensive end on The Sporting News All-Pro Team, 1989, 92. *

DOLICH, IRA J., marketing educator, business consultant; b. Yorktown, Tex., Dec. 14, 1934; s. H. Jack and Judith (Simon) D.; m. Phyllis Lynn Shay, Jan. 30, 1965; children: Jared, Michael. BSME, U. Tex., 1957, MBA, 1964, PhD in Bus. Adminstrn., 1967. Chief engr. Structural Metals, Inc., Seguin, Tex., 1957-58; maintenance engr. Sherwin Aluminum Plant: Reynolds, Engleside, Tex., 1960-62; from asst. prof. to assoc. prof. Pa. State U., State College, 1967-77; mktg. specialist U.S.A. Postal Rate Commn., Washington, 1973-74; chmn. dept. mktg. U. Nebr., Lincoln, 1977-81, dir. agribus. program, 1981-86; dean Coll. Bus. Drake U., Des Moines, 1986-89, prof. mktg., 1989—; cons. in field; expert witness in mktg. and bus. Author: Analysis and Decision Making, 1971; also articles. V.p. Lincoln Employee Assistance Program, 1983-86; chair mktg. com. Des Moines Symphony Assn., 1987-92; pres. Bd. Jewish Edn. and Culture, Des Moines, 1993-95. Capt. USAF, 1958-60, Greece. AACSB fellow, 1973; NSF fellow, 1971. Mem. Am. Mktg. Assn. (pres. Lincoln chpt. 1984), Assn. for Consumer Rsch., Masons, Rotary Internat. (dir. 1984-86). Jewish. Office: Drake U Coll Bus and Pub Adminstrn Des Moines IA 50311

DOMBECK, WAYNE LESLIE, product designer; b. Milw., Mar. 23, 1947. Student, U. Wis., Green Bay, 1993—. Sr. product designer Briggs & Stratton, Milw., 1965—. Patent for Fuel Filter Cap. St. USAF, 1966-69. Roman Catholic.

DOMBROWSKI, FRANK R., manufacturing engineer; b. Kingston, Ill., Mar. 7, 1937. Specialist mfg. engr. Gen. Electric, DeKalb, Ill., 1966-88; sr. process engr. Marathon Electric, Lebanon, Mo., 1988-90; sr. mfg. engr. Fasco Indistries, Cassville, Mo., 1990—. Patentee in field. Mem. City Coun., Village of Kingstown, Ill., 1979-88; mem. sch. bd. Genoa County Dist. Sch., Genoa, Ill., 1980-88. Roman Catholic.

DOMBROWSKI, MARK ANTHONY, librarian; b. Oshkosh, Wis., Dec. 13, 1940; s. Alexander Joseph and Veronica Ellen (Gaber) D. BS in English cum laude, U. Wis., Oshkosh, 1966; MSLS, U. Wis., 1968, specialist cert., 1973. Asst. libr. acquisitions Forrest R. Polk Libr. U. Wis., Oshkosh, 1968-74, head libr. acquisitions, 1974-75; libr. dir. Siena Heights Coll., Adrian, Mich., 1975—; cons. St. Catherine Coll. Libr., Springfield, Ky., 1985. Contbr. articles to profl. jours. Mem. YMCA. With USN and USNR, 1959-66. Legis. scholar State of Wis., 1963-65, scholar Ziegler Found., 1966; Edns. Professions Devel. Act fellow Wis. Dept. Edn., 1972. Mem. ALA, MLA, Am. Culture Assn., Nat. Librs. Assn., Mich. Libr. Assn. (v.p. 1981-82, 87-88), Mich. Libr. Consortium (chmn. bd. 1981-83), Phi Beta Mu, Phi Kappa Delta, Kappa Delta Pi, Phi Beta Sigma. Roman Catholic. Office: Siena Heights Coll 1247 E Siena Heights Dr Adrian MI 49221-1755

DOMBROWSKI, PAUL MATTHEW, English educator; b. Pitts., Dec. 22, 1948; s. Joseph J. and Mary Delores (Yaksick) D.; m. Judith Dillon, June 10, 1988; children: Diana, Eileen. BA, Ind. U., 1970; MEd, Pa. State U., 1984, MA, 1987; PhD, Rennsselaer Poly. Inst., 1990. Claims rep. U.S. Social Security Adminstrn., Champaign, Ill., 1975-80; asst. prof. Ohio U., Athens, 1990—. Editor: Humanistic Aspects of Technical Communication, 1994; contbr. articles to profl. jours. Sgt. USAF, 1971-75. Mem. MLA, Assn. Tchrs. Tech. Writing, Nat. Coun. Tchrs. English, Rhetoric Soc. Am. Home: 17 Andover Rd Athens OH 45701 Office: Ohio U Dept English Athens OH 45701

DOMJAN, LASZLO KAROLY, newspaper executive; b. Kormend, Hungary, Apr. 19, 1947; came to U.S., 1956; s. Frank and Violet (Pinter) D.; m. Louise Replogle, June 6, 1969; children: Andrew P., Eric S. BJ, U. Mo., 1969. Copy editor St. Louis Globe-Democrat, 1969; reporter, bureau chief UPI, St. Louis, 1969-81; reporter, night city editor St. Louis Post-Dispatch, 1981—, exec. city editor, 1987-96; projects editor, 1996—. Author, editor: Dioxin: Quandary for the 80s, 1983 (numerous awards); author: (reporter series) Hungary: Thirty Years After, 1986; editor: (series) Prosecutorial Corruption (1993 Pulitzer prize finalist). Active Leadership St. Louis. Recipient Herb Trask award Sigma Delta Chi, St. Louis, 1968. Mem. Press Club of Met. St. Louis, Investigative Reporters and Editors. Roman Catholic. Office: St Louis Post-Dispatch 900 N Tucker Blvd Saint Louis MO 63101-1069

DOMKE, GARY EDWARD, securities company executive; b. St. Louis; s. Charles Fred and Eleanor (Webbers) D.; m. Yvonne Anderson; m. Constance Lowe; m. Lee Frieger, May 6, 1995; 1 child, Yvette Lynn. Student, U. Mo., St. Louis, 1971-76, St. Louis U., 1977-80. Registered principal. Registered rep. R. G. Mills and Co., St. Louis, 1969-71, R. Rowland & Co., St. Louis, 1971-80; v.p. tax shelters, mut. funds WZW Cornerstone, St. Louis, 1980-82; v.p. Prudential Securities, St. Louis, 1982-94; v.p., resident mgr. Stifer Nicolaus & Co. Inc., 1994-96; v.p. pvt. and corp. accounts Oppenheimer & Co., Inc., Clayton, Mo., 1996—; cons. various CPA and lawfirm. Served to capt. U.S. Army, 1965-69. Republican. Office: Oppenheimer & Co Inc 7701 Forsyth Clayton MO 63105

DOMMERMUTH, WILLIAM P., marketing consultant, educator; b. Chgo.; s. Peter R. and Gertrude (Schnell) D.; m. H. Joan Hasty, June 6, 1959; children: Karin, Margaret, Jean. BA, U. Iowa; PhD, Northwestern U., 1964. Advt. copywriter Sears, Roebuck & Co., Chgo.; sales promotion mgr. Sears, Roebuck & Co.; asst., then asso. prof. mktg. U. Tex., Austin, 1961-67; asso. prof. U. Iowa, Iowa City, 1967-68; prof. So. Ill. U., Carbondale, 1968-86, U. Mo., St. Louis, 1986—; CEO The Toerner/Tigrun Group; Cons. bus. firms. Author (with Kernan and Sommers): Promotion: An Introductory Analysis, 1970, (with Andersen) Distribution Systems, 1972, (with Marcus and others) Modern Marketing, 1975, Modern Marketing Management, 1980, Promotion: Analysis, Creativity and Strategy, 1984, 2d edit., 1989; contbr. articles to profl. jours. Mem. Am. Mktg. Assn., Am. Psychol. Assn., So. Mktg. Assn., Midwest Mktg. Assn., The Oxford Club, Phi Beta Kappa, Beta Gamma Sigma, Theta Xi, Delta Sigma Pi. Home: 7242 S Roland Blvd Saint Louis MO 63121-2619 Office: The Toernerl Tigrun Group Ste 427 9648 Olive Blvd Saint Louis MO 63132

DOMPKE, NORBERT FRANK, retired photography studio executive; b. Chgo., Oct. 16, 1920; s. Frank and Mary (Manley) D.; m. Marjorie Gies, Dec. 12, 1964; children: Scott, Pamela. Grad. Wright Jr. Coll., 1939-40; student Northwestern U., 1946-49. Cost comptroller, budget dir. Scott Radio Corp., 1947; pres. TV Forecast, Inc., 1948-52, editor Chgo. edit. TV Guide, 1953, mgr. Wis. edit., 1954; pres. Root Photographers, Inc., Chgo., 1955-91, also chmn. bd. dirs; bd. dirs. Root Studio, Inc., 1991-96, ret., 1996. Adv. com. photography & audiovisual tech., So. Ill. U., 1980-81; adv. bd. Gordon Tech. High Sch., 1979-86. Co-founder TV Guide, 1947. With USAAC, 1943-47. CPA, Ill. Mem. NEA, Nat. Sch. Press Assn., Nat. Collegiate Sch. Press Assn., United Photographers Orgn. (pres. 1970-71), Profl. Photographers Am., Profl. Sch. Photographers Am. (v.p. 1966-67, 87-88, sec.-treas. 1967-69, pres. 1969-70, dir. 1971-78, treas. 1985-86, sec. 1986-87, pres. 1988-89), Photo Mktg. Assn. (recipient disting. svc. award 1992), Photographic Art & Sci. Found. (hall of fame elector 1969-96), Ill. Small Bus. Men's Assn. (dir. 1970-73), Chgo. Assn. Commerce and Industry (edn. com. 1966-94), Ill. High Sch. Press Assn., North Cen. Assn. (visitation com. 1986), Chgo. Bible Soc. (bd. advisors), Ill. C. of C., International. Home: 175 N Harbor Dr Apt 2602 Chicago IL 60601-7345

DOMSKY, IRVING ISAAC, chemist; b. Racine, Wis., Feb. 3, 1930; s. William S. and Gertrude (Kramer) D.; m. Barbara Carol White, Mar. 12, 1964 (dec. Aug. 1984); children: Deborah, Zave, Temirah, Oron; m. Marilyn Chubin, July 3, 1990. BS, U. Wis., 1951, PhD, 1959. Postdoctoral fellow Yale U., New Haven, Conn., 1958-60; cancer rsch. scientist Chgo. Med. Sch., 1960-64; rsch. scientist Abbott Labs., North Chgo., 1964-67, Armour & Co., Chgo., 1967-73; group leader Quaker Oats Co., Barrington, Ill., 1973-74, Chemetron Corp., Chgo., 1975-77; lab. dir. Allied Labs., Ltd., Villa Park, Ill., 1977—, pres., 1977-93. Editor: Recent Advances in Chromatography, 1972; contbr. articles to profl. jours. Cpl. U.S. Army, 1951-53. Mem. Chgo. Chromatography Discussion Group (sec. 1971-72, pres. 1972-73). Democrat. Jewish. Home: 6820 N Francisco Ave Chicago IL 60645 Office: Allied Labs Corp 716 N Iowa Ave Villa Park IL 60181

DONADEY, ANNE, comparative literature and women's studies educator. BA, U. Nice, 1984, MA, 1985; PhD, Northwestern U., 1993. Lectr. U. Tex., Austin, 1985-87; tchg. asst. Northwestern U., Evanston, 1988-93; asst. prof. U. Iowa, Iowa City, 1993—. Mem. AAUW, MLA, Am. Assn. Tchrs. of French, Midwest MLA, African Lit. Assn., Women in French. Office: U Iowa Women's Studies 202 Jefferson Bldg Iowa City IA 52242

DONAHEY, BEVERLY ELLINGER, elementary education educator; b. Lancaster, Ohio, Nov. 20, 1948; d. Lloyd Leonard and Nellie Catherine (Konkler) Ellinger; 1 child, Patrick William. BS, Ohio U., 1970, MS, 1972, postgrad., 1988, 89; postgrad., Goddard U., 1992. Cert. tchr., home econs. tchr., Ohio. Instr. home econs. Marion Harding High Sch., 1971-72; instr., then asst. prof. Ohio Coop. Ext. Svc. The Ohio State U., Columbus, 1972-79; instr. Tri-County Joint Vocat. Sch., Nelsonville, Ohio, 1980-81, family life tchr., 1988-89; tutor learning disabled students Logan (Ohio)-Hocking Sch. Dist., 1981-82, substitute tchr., 1987-88; program coord. Fairfield County Bd. Mental Retardation-Devel. Disabilities, Lancaster, Ohio, 1982-86; tchr. home econs. Trimble Mid. Sch., Glouster, Ohio, 1989-92; tchr. Trimble Elem. Sch., Glouster, 1992—; pvt. tutor, 1987—. Mem. Am. Assn. Family and Consumer Scis., Trimble Local Tchrs. Assn., Ohio U. Alumni Assn., Ohio Assn. Family and Consumer Scis., Hocking Hills Arts and Crafts Assn., Kappa Delta Pi, Phi Upsilon Omicron. Democrat. Lutheran. Home: 913 Mohican Ave Logan OH 43138-1847

DONAHOE-FILLMORE, BETSY KAY, physical therapist; b. Urbana, Ohio, Sept. 8, 1966; d. William A. and Doris E. (Robison) D. BS in Allied Health summa cum laude, Ohio State U., 1988; MS in Phys. Therapy, U. Indpls., 1992. Phys. therapist Children's Hosp. Med. Ctr., Cin., 1988—; assoc. prof. phys. therapy Andrews U., Dayton, Ohio, 1994—. Mem. Am. Phys. Therapy Assn. (dist. chair Ohio chpt. S.W. dist. 1992—, pediat. cert. specialist 1993, state rep. 1993—), Cin. Alumnae Panhellenic (corr. sec. 1993—, pres. 1995—), Phi Mu (alumnae pres. 1992-93). Home: 992 Walnut Ct Mason OH 45040-2011 Office: Children's Hosp 3333 Burnet Ave Cincinnati OH 45229-3026

DONAHUE, JOHN EDWARD, lawyer; b. Milw., Aug. 22, 1950; s. Joseph Robert and Helen Ann (Kelly) D.; m. Maureen Dolores Hart, Sept. 20, 1974; children: Timothy Robert Hart, Michael John Hart. BA with honors, Marquette U., 1972; JD, U. Wis., Madison, 1975. Bar: Wis. 1975, U.S. Dist. Ct. (we. and ea. dists.) Wis. 1975. Assoc. Weiss, Steuer, Berzowski and Kriger, Milw., 1975-80; ptnr. Weiss, Berzowski, Brady and Donahue, Milw., 1981—; guest lectr. Marquette U., Milw., 1976-90; presenter programs Wis. Inst. CPAs, 1984—, Minn. Soc. CPAs, 1992—; expert witness. Past chmn. bd. trustees, past chmn. bd. dirs., past chmn. bd. govs. Mt. Mary Coll., Milw., 1984—, past pres., bd. dirs. com. chmn. Met. Milw. Civic Alliance, 1980—, Children's Hosp. Found., Milw., 1984—; mem. steering com. Greater Milw. Initiative, 1989-92; v.p., bd. dirs. Future Milw., 1984-88; scoutmaster, past cubmaster Boy Scouts Am., 1990—. Recipient citation Milwaukee County Bd. Suprs., 1990, spl. svc. award Met. Milw. Civil Alliance, 1990, silver beaver award Boy Scouts Am., 1995; named outstanding instr. AICPA, 1991. Mem. ABA, Wis. Bar Assn., Milw. Bar Assn., Wis. Retirement Plan Profls., Greater Milw. Employee Benefits Coun., Kiwanis

Club (pres. Milw. unit 1989-90, Outstanding Kiwanian 1989-95, Kiwanian of Yr. 1993). Office: Weiss Berzowski Brady and Donahue 700 N Water St Milwaukee WI 53202-4206

DONAHUE, JOHN LAWRENCE, JR., paper company executive; b. Chgo., Nov. 9, 1939; s. John Lawrence Sr. and Margaret (Bollinger) D.; m. Maureen Anne Forbes, June 20, 1964; children: John L. III, Thomas James, Michael Patrick, Margaret Anne. BS in Marine Engring., U.S. Merchant Marine Acad., 1961. Lic. marine engr. Marine engr. Am. Export Lines, N.Y.C., 1961-64; chief engr. Gen. Box Co., Des Plaines, Ill., 1964-74; dir. engring. Mead Container Corp., Cin., 1974-82; pres. Donahue & Assocs. Internat., Inc., Milford, Ohio, 1982—. Trustee, treas. Milford Community Fire Dept. Inc., 1983—. Served to lt. USNR. Mem. Tech. Assn. Pulp and Paper Industry, Assn. Ind. Corrugated Converters. Republican. Roman Catholic. Office: 2002 Ford Cir Ste H Milford OH 45150-2748

DONAHUE, LAURA KENT, state senator; b. Quincy, Ill., Apr. 22, 1949; d. Laurence S. and Mary Lou (McFarland) Kent; m. Michael A. Donahue, July 16, 1983. B.S., Stephens Coll., 1971. Mem. Ill. State Senate, Quincy, 1981—. Mem. Lincoln Club of Adams County, Ill. Fedn. Republican Women. Mem. P.E.O. Lodge: Altrusa. Office: Ill State Senate State Capitol Springfield IL 62706*

DONAHUE, MICHAEL PETER, manufacturing engineer; b. Racine, Wis., July 13, 1967. BS in Indsl. Engring., U. Wis., Milw., 1992. Mfg. engr. Nissan Forklift Corp., Marengo, Ill., 1993—. Mem. AIAA, ASME, Soc. Mfg. Engrs., Soc. Automotive Engrs. Roman Catholic. Office: Nissan Forklift Corp 240 N Prospect St Marengo IL 60152

DONAHUE, SHIRLEY OHNSTAD, elementary education educator; b. Darlington, Wis., Aug. 29, 1937; d. Joseph and Edna L. (Peterson) Ohnstad; m. John V. Donahue, Aug. 20, 1960; children: Roger K., Jeffrey J. BS, U. Wis., Platteville, 1959; MS, No. Ill. U., 1978. Cert. tchr., Ill. Tchr. Freeport (Ill.) Sch. Sys., 1959-62, Belvidere (Ill.) Sch. Sys., 1962-64, Pecatonica (Ill.) Sch. Sys., 1964-66, Orangeville (Ill.) Sch. Sys., 1966-67, Rock Falls (Ill.) Sch. Sys., 1967-93; ret. Rock Falls (Ill.) Sch. System, 1993. Co-author gifted student curriculum materials. Mem. liturgical com. St. Mary's Ch., Sterling, Ill., 1980-84, aux. min., 1980-94; mem. Friends of Sterling Pub. Libr., v.p. 1990-93, 96, pres. 1995; bd. dirs. YWCA, sec. bd. dirs., 1994-95; mem. Cmty. Gen. Hosp. Med. Aux., 1993—, co-chair sr. health ins. program, 1994—; pres. Community Gen. Hosp. Aux., 1995-96. Recipient Western Ill. Master Tchr. award, 1991. Mem. Rock Falls Elem. Edn. Assn. (chmn. polit. action com. for edn. 1985-87), Ill. Edn. Assn., NEA, AAUW, Sterling Democratic Women. Roman Catholic. Home: 303 W 12th St Sterling IL 61081-2201

DONALD, EDWARD MILTON, JR., graphic designer; b. Detroit, Jan. 11, 1947; s. Edward Milton Sr. and Rosa Marie (Stockell) D.; divorced; children: Christopher Jarrod, Emily Hope, Joshua Andrew. Cert. in Advt. Design, Coll. of Art & Design, Detroit, 1975. Freelance graphic designer Ministry of Natural Resources, Toronto, Can., 1969-74; teaching master Cambrian Coll. of Applied Arts & Tech., Sudbury, Can., 1974-76; sr. art dir. Batten Burton Durstine & Osborne, Troy, Mich., 1976-79; art supr. J. Walter Thompson, Detroit, 1979-83; group supr. Leo Burnett, Southfield, Mich., 1983-88; assoc. creative dir. Deleeuw Ferguson & Assocs., Birmingham, Mich., 1988-90; v.p., assoc. creative dir. The Hopkins Group, Farmington Hills, Mich., 1990—; instr. Ctr. for Creative Studies Coll. of Art & Design, Detroit, 1977-93. Recipient 1st Pl. U.S. TV Commls. Festival, 1981, Gold award Creative Advt. Club Detroit, 1981, CLIO cert. CLIO awards adv. bd., 1982. Mem. Am. Inst. Graphic Arts, Founders Soc. Detroit Art Inst., Graphic Artists Guild (N.Y.). Office: The Hopkins Group 33533 W 12 Mile Rd Ste 130 Farmington Hills MI 48331

DONALD, WILLIAM WALDIE, agronomist; b. Lynbrook, N.Y., Feb. 16, 1950; s. Kay and Florence (Waldie) D.; m. Patricia Ann Rincker, July 26, 1974; children: Mark K., Dennis C. BSc, SUNY, Stony Brook, 1972; MSc, U. Minn., 1974; PhD, U. Wis., 1977. Postdoctoral fellow USDA Agrl. Rsch. Svc., Fargo, N.D., 1977-78, rsch. agronomist, 1980-88; asst. prof. agronomy Colo. State U., Ft. Collins, 1978-80; rsch. agronomist USDA Agrl. Rsch. Svc., Columbia, Mo., 1988—. Assoc. editor Weed Tech.; author 50 articles in sci. jours. on Can. thistle, jointed goatgrass and weed control in cereals. Mem. Weed Sci. Soc. Am. (monograph editor 1985-89), Am. Soc. Agronomy, Sigma Xi. Home: 1905 Iris Dr Columbia MO 65202-1238 Office: USDA Agrl Rsch Svc U Mo 244 Agrl Engring Columbia MO 65211

DONALDSON, SANDRA MARIE, English educator; b. Buffalo, N.Y., Aug. 29, 1943; d. Donald Macmillan and Margaret Marie (Nielsen) D.; m. Lonny B. Winrich, June 3, 1989. BA, SUNY, Buffalo, 1968; MA, U. Conn., 1970; PhD, 1977. Part time inst. Eastern Conn. State Coll., Willimantic, 1970-77; asst. prof. U. N.D., Grand Forks, 1977-82, assoc. prof., 1982-94, dir. women's studies program, 1982-85, 1996—, prof. English, 1994—; assoc. editor Victorian Lit. and Culture. Author: Elizabeth Barrett Browning, An Annotated Bibliography, 1993; contbr. articles to profl. jours. Organizer Planned Parenthood of N.D., Grand Forks, 1994. Fellow Armstrong Browning Libr., Newberry Libr., U. Tex. Humanities Rsch. Ctr. Mem. MLA, Browning Inst., Nat. Women's Studies Assn., Virginia Woolf Soc., Margaret Atwood Soc. Home: 606 S 4th St Grand Forks ND 58201 Office: English 7209 University of North Dakota Grand Forks ND 58202

DONALDSON, VIRGINIA LEE, librarian; b. Leavenworth, Kans., Feb. 24, 1950; d. Leo Otto and Lorene Marie (Koebrich) Schrick; m. Wayne Lee Donaldson, Sept. 1, 1979; children: Rebecca Lee, Matthew Lee; stepchildren: Michael Lee, Jennifer Elizabeth. BA, Morningside Coll., 1972; MA in Librarianship, U. Denver, 1977. Cert. tchr., Kans. Clk. Western Hills Area Ednl. Agy., Sioux City, Iowa, 1972; librarian Washington Elem. Sch., Atchison, Kans., 1972-82; instr. Benedictine Coll., Atchison, Kans., 1973-74; librarian Atchison High Sch., 1982—. Leader Girl Scouts U.S.A., Atchison, 1986-90; Kans. Scholars' Bowl coach, 1989—. Mem. NEA, Kans. Assn. Sch. Librarians, Am. Assn. Univ. Women, Beta Phi Mu. Democrat. Roman Catholic. Home: 712 Fletcher Ave Atchison KS 66002-3144 Office: Atchison High Sch 1500 Riley St Atchison KS 66002-1513

DONESA, ANTONIO BRAGANZA, neurosurgeon; b. Manila, July 27, 1935; came to U.S., 1959, naturalized, 1969; s. Alfonso Pinson and Flora (Braganza) D.; m. Barbara Louise Quinn, Nov. 30, 1962; children: Carmen, Christopher. BS, U. Philippines, 1955, MD, 1959. Intern St. Mary's Hosp., Waterbury, Conn., 1959-60; resident Huron Road Hosp., 1960-61, U. Ala. Med. Ctr., Birmingham, 1961-65; pvt. practice neurosurgery Ft. Wayne, Ind., 1966—; pres., dir. Neurosurgery, Inc., Ft. Wayne, 1971—; mem. staff Parkview Hosp., Ft. Wayne, St. Joseph's Hosp., Ft. Wayne, Luth. Hosp., Ft. Wayne; cons. Marion (Ind.) Gen. Hosp.; founder, past pres. Liberty for Am. Minority Physicians, LAMP Legal Fund. Recipient Leadership award March of Dimes, 1972, Cert. of Appreciation, Heart Fund, 1971, others. Mem. AMA, Assn. Philippine Physicians in Am. (Community Svc. award 1983), Ft. Wayne Acad. Medicine and Surgery, Ind. Philippine Med. Assn. (past. pres.), Am. Coll. Internat. Physicians (founder, exec. dir. 1978-90, chmn. 1985, Leadership award 1975, Disting. Fellow award 1982), Ind. State Med. Assn., Allen (Ft. Wayne, pres. 12th dist. 1985-86) County Med. Soc. (pres. 1990-91), Congress Neurol. Surgeons, Soc. Philippine Neurol. Surgeons in Am. (past pres.), Neurosurg. Soc. Ind., Soc. Philippine Surgeons Am., U. Philippines Med. Alumni Soc. in Am. (nat. pres. 1985-87, Disting. Alumnus Overseas 1985), Masons, Shriners, Summit Club. Office: 3030 Lake Ave Fort Wayne IN 46805-5428

DONHISER, WILLIAM JAMES, pediatric dentist; b. California, Md., July 27, 1957; s. James Robert and Louis Bernice (Cowan) D.; m. Kathleen Marcia Rauch, Apr. 25, 1992. BS in Physiology with honors, U. Wyo., 1979; DDS, Med. Coll. Va., 1983; cert. pediatric dentistry, Children's Med. Ctr., Dayton, Ohio, 1985. Diplomate Pierre Fauchard Acad. Pvt. practice Black Hills Pediatric Dentistry, Rapid City, S.D., 1985—; chmn. Surg. Ctr. Black Hills, Rapid City, 1996—; dept. head Rapid City Regional Hosp.; pres. Black Hills Dental Soc. Mem. Am. Soc. Dental Anesthesiology, Am. Soc. Dentistry Children, Am. Acad. Pediatric Dentistry (state pres.), Black Hills Dist. Dental Soc. Office: Black Hills Pediatric Dentistry 700 Sheridan Lake Rd Rapid City SD 57702

DONKIN, JAMES RICHARD, internal auditor; b. Christopher, Ill., Aug. 4, 1949; s. John and Dorothy Ellen (Hogg) D.; m. Mary Fay Hildebrand, Oct. 12, 1984; children: Sean, Mathew. BS in Mgmt., So. Ill. U., 1973. Audit specialist Ill. Dept. Conservation, Springfield, 1974-85, dir. internal audits, 1989; audit mgr. Ill. Dept. Pub. Aid, Springfield, 1985-88, dir. internal audits, 1989—; mem. gov.'s cost control task force Ill. State. Govt., Springfield, 1985. Chairperson budget and fin. Christ Episcopal Ch., Springfield, 1988-92, sr. warden, 1993; chairperson audit com. Episcopal Diocese Springfield, 1992, treas., 1992—. Mem. Inst. Internal Auditors (cert., pres. 1982-84, internat. membership com. 1984-85, chair program commn. Midwest regional conf., Disting. Svc. award 1989, bd. dirs. Springfield chpt. 1994—). Home: 35 Skyview Dr Springfield IL 62702-1532

DONKIN, SCOTT WILLIAM, chiropractor; b. Rapid City, S.D., June 8, 1955; s. Wilmar and Jeanne Elaine (Sherwood) D.; m. Mary Pat Brugh, Oct. 7, 1977; children: Elizabeth, Peter. Student, Midland Luth. Coll., 1973-76; D Chiropractic, Tex. Chiropractic Coll., 1980. Diplomate Am. Chiropractic Bd. Occupational Health. Pvt. practice Donkin Chiropractic Clinic, Lincoln, Nebr., 1980—; lectr. to chiropractic colls.; cons. Sitting on the Job, Lincoln, 1987—. Author: Sitting on the Job, 1988; inventor Sidewalk Shuffleboard, 1988; contbr. articles to profl. jours., mags. Mem. Am. Chiropractic Assn. (pres. coun. on occupl. health), Nebr. Chiropractic Physicians Assn., Am. Chiropractic Bd. Occupl. Health (treas.). Office: Chiropractic Assocs PC 5540 South St Ste 200 Lincoln NE 68506-2117

DONLEY, PAUL E., newspaper publisher; b. Springfield, Mo., May 13, 1951; s. Raymond G. and Lillian B. (Johnson) D.; m. Gayle L. Rebmann, Oct. 23, 1971; children: Alex J., Timothy P. B in Journalism, U. Mo., 1974. Mng. editor Jacksonville (Ark.) Daily News, 1974-77; pub. Spiro (Okla.) Graphics, 1979-85, Aurora (Mo.) Advertiser, 1985—. Mem., rep. Rep. Ctrl. Com., Lawrence County, Mo., 1995. Mem. Aurora C. of C. (bd. dirs. 1985-89), Rotary Internat. (treas. Aurora club 1984—). Methodist. Home: Rontel Box 166-C1 Aurora MO 65605 Office: Aurora Advertiser PO Box 509 32 W Olive Aurora MO 65605

DONLEY, SARAH LYNN, computer programmer/analyst; b. Carthage, Ill., Nov. 17, 1964; d. Gary Dean and Carol Jean (Galloway) Vest; m. Gary Lee Donley, Nov. 14, 1987; children: Jill Suzanne, Thomas Dale. AS in Computer Sci., John Wood Commun. Coll., Quincy, Ill., 1984; BS in Computer Sci., Quincy Coll., 1986. Clk. Quincy Pub. Libr., 1981-87; clk. Gardner-Denver, Quincy, 1986-89, programmer trainee, cons., 1987-89, programmer, 1989-90, programmer/analyst, 1991-94. Named to Outstanding Young Women in Am., 1991. Lutheran. Home: RR 2 Box 185A Mendon IL 62351-9528

DONNELLY, CHARLES FRANCIS, management consultant, lawyer; b. Toronto; came to U.S., 1949; s. Edward A. and Margaret Jane (Doyle) D.; m. JoAnn McCarthy, June 28, 1952; children: Charles Francis, Mary, Kathleen, Mark, David, Joanna. B in Commerce, U. Toronto, 1949; JD, Fordham U., 1953. Bar: N.Y. 1953, Mich. 1964. Assoc. Hughes Hubbard & Reed, N.Y.C., 1953-58; v.p., gen. counsel S.H. Kress & Co., N.Y.C., 1958-64; assoc. counsel Ford Motor Co., Dearborn, Mich., 1964-67; exec. v.p. Bendix Corp., Detroit, 1967-77; vice chmn., chief adminstrv. officer Bendix Corp., 1977-80, dir., 1968-80; counsel Clark, Klein & Beaumont, Detroit, 1980-82; mgmt. cons., 1982—; vis. prof. mgmt. Lake Superior State Coll., Sault Ste. Marie, Mich., 1981-87. with RCAF, 1942-45. Mem. N.Y. Bar Assn., Mich. Bar Assn., Pinnacle Peak Country Club. Office: 6711 E Camelback Rd Scottsdale AZ 85251-2062

DONNELLY-KEMPF, MOIRA ANN, nursing administrator; b. Toledo, June 11, 1963; d. Gerald M. and Ruth Ann (Crawford) Donnelly; m. Ronald W. Kempf, Aug. 31, 1985. Diploma, Mercy Sch. Nursing, Toledo, 1983; student, Eastern Mich. U., St. Joseph's Coll., 1992. RN. Clin. rehab. nurse Meml. Hosp., South Bend, Ind., 1983-84, U. Mich. Med. Ctr., Ann Arbor, 1985-87; med. claims nurse analyst Kapner Wolfberg & Assocs., Van Nuys, Calif., 1988-89; sr. auditing specialist Intracorp, Southfield, Mich., 1989-94; sr. early intervention specialist Intracorp, 1994—. Mem. Mercy Sch. Nursing Alumnae Assn.

DONNEM, SARAH LUND, financial analyst, non-profit and political organization consultant; b. St. Louis, Apr. 10, 1936; d. Joel Y. and Erle Hall (Harsh) Lund; m. Roland W. Donnem, Feb. 18, 1961; children: Elizabeth Prince, Sarah Madison. BA, Vassar Coll., 1958. Tech. aide, computer programmer Bell Labs., Whippany, N.J., 1959-60; chmn. placement vol. opportunities N.Y. Jr. League, 1972-73, asst. treas. 1974-75, chmn. urban problems relating to mental health, 1967-69, mem. project rsch. com., 1967-71, chmn., 1973-74, mem. bd. mgrs. 1973-74; chmn. cmty. rsch. Washington Jr. League, 1970-71, mem. bd. mgrs., 1970-71; mem. Stratford Hall (N.Y.) Com., 1970—; bd. dirs. East Side Settlement House, Bronx, N.Y., 1972—, v.p., 1975-76, chmn. Nat. Horse Show Benefit, 1976, winter antiques show com., 1994—, co-chmn. adv. com., 1991-94, mem. nominating com., 1990—, mem. investment com., 1993—; bd. dirs. Stanley M. Isaacs Neighborhood Ctr., N.Y.C., 1973-76, v.p., 1975-76; bd. dirs. Presbyn. Home for Aged Women, N.Y.C., 1974-76, v.p., 1976; mem. exec. bd. N.Y. Aux. of Blue Ridge Sch., 1971-75, sec., 1965-67, pres., 1973-75; budget and benevolence com. Brick Presbyn. Ch., N.Y.C., 1973-76, mem. social svc. com., 1973-74, chmn. fgn. students com., 1963-64. Bd. dirs. Search and Care, N.Y.C., 1973-76, Project LEARN, Cleve., 1990-96; chmn. Literacy Fund, 1991-95; Friends of Project LEARN, 1986—; mem. Fedn. Cmty. Planning, Cleve., Coun. on Older Persons, 1978-82, mem. Future Planning Task Force, 1980-81, Commn. on Social Concerns, 1982-84; trustee Golden Age Ctrs. Greater Cleve., 1979-92, investment com., 1993, 1st v.p., 1980-81, pres., 1981-85, chmn. Western Res. Antiques Show, 1979, 80, Western Res. Hist. Soc. (womens adv. coun. 1977, coord. sec. 1978); mem. women's com. Cleve. Orch., 1979-85, Vassar Coll. Cleve. sec. 1980-82, v.p. 1983, pres. 1984-86; AAVC Club Liason Com. 1986-89, chmn. regional program com., 1987-89, chmn. Vassar in Chgo. Conf. 1989; bd. dirs. Cleve. Ballet, 1980—, exec. com., 1981, fin. com., 1982-88, 95—, mem. ballet sch. com., 1985-88, nominating com., 1988-90, 95—; co-chmn. Yale Ball, 1983; bd. advisers Ret. Sr. Vol. Program, 1982, trustee, 1983-90, chmn. long range planning comm., 1986, sec. 1987-89; mem. Family Friends Adv. Coun., 1987-89; trustee Fairmount Presbyn. Ch., 1985-88, mem. long range planning com. United Way, Cleve., 1985-87; coord. Friends of Voinovich, 1987-89; womens advisory com. Voinovich for Governor, 1990; chmn. Voinovich Task Force On Aging, 1990-91, Ohio Adv. Coun. on Aging, 1991—, legis. com., 1994—, chmn., 1995—, Plain Dealer adv. counsel for elderly coverage, 1991-93; chmn. Johns Hopkins Parents Fund, 1986-88, Congl. Life Ministry, 1996—, Project LEARN 15th Anniversary celebration (with Barbara Bush, hon. chmn.), 1989-90; coord. Decorative Arts Trust Cleve. Symposium, 1996; mem. Leadership Cleve. Class 1992; mem. Cleve. Presbytry; del White House Conf. on Aging, 1995. Named Vol. of Yr. N.Y. Jr. League, 1975; recipient Sustainer Svc. award Jr. League Cleve., 1990. Mem. Nat. Inst. Social Scis. (mem. memberships com. 1972—, trustee 1984—). Nat. Soc. of Colonial Dames. Republican. Clubs: Colony (N.Y.C.); Chevy Chase (Washington); Intown, Vassar, Jr. League Cleve., Kirtland (Cleve.). Address: 2945 Fontenay Rd Shaker Heights OH 44120

D'ONOFRIO, PETER JOSEPH, protective services official, educator; b. Bronx, N.Y., Sept. 20, 1947; s. Elia Danato and Chella Concetta (Diorio) D'O.; m. Sharon Warner, Oct. 17, 1971 (div. 1976); m. Barbara Ann Jefferson, Dec. 10, 1977; children; Randyll Thomas, Robyn Margaret Smith. AAS, Sinclair C.C., Dayton, Ohio, 1973; BSBA, U. Dayton, 1974, MBA, BS in Edn., 1975; AAS in Fire Sci., Columbus State C.C., 1988; grad. exec. fire officer program, Nat. Fire Acad., Emmitsburg, Md., 1993. Registered paramedic, fire, EMS instr., fire safety inspector, Ohio. Fire tng. officer, emergency med. svcs. tng. coord. Ohio Fire Acad., Reynoldsburg, 1984—; mem. faculty paramedic edn. Grant Med. Ctr., Columbus, 1987—; mem. adj. faculty Nat. Fire Acad., 1989—; firefighter, paramedic, insp., investigator Miami Twp. Fire Divsn., Miamisburg, Ohio, 1980-84; emergency rm. technician Kettering (Ohio) Med. Ctr., 1978-79; firefighter, paramedic Huber Heights (Ohio) Fire Divsn., 1976-78; instr. Sinclair C.C., 1977-84; lectr. Bowling Green (Ohio) Fire Sch., Ohio State Firefighters Conf., Am. Med. Writers Assn., Fire Dept. Instrs. Conf., others. Editor, pub. (newsletter) North South Med. Times, 1984—. Vol. firefighter Kettering Fire Dept., 1974-80; vol. paramedic Minerva park (Ohio) Fire Dept., 1992-95, Truro Twp. (Ohio) Fire Dept., 1995—. Mem. Internat. Rescue and Emergency Care Assn. (conf. lectr.), Internat. Assn. Fire Fighters (charter, hon.), Nat. Registry EMT's, Ohio Soc. Fire Svc. Instrs. (bd. dirs. 1985-87), Ohio EMT Instrs. Assn., Mil. Order Loyal Legion of U.S., Hon. Order Ky. Cols., VFW (Meritorious Svc. award 1977), Soc. Civil War Surgeons (pres., CEO 1988—). Home: 243 Bristol Dr SW Reynoldsburg OH 43068-9653 Office: Ohio Fire Acad 8895 E Main St Reynoldsburg OH 43068-3397

DONOHUE, CARROLL JOHN, lawyer; b. St. Louis, June 24, 1917; s. Thomas M. and Florence (Klefisch) D.; m. Juanita Maire, Jan. 4, 1943 (div. July 1973); children: Patricia Carol, Christine Ann Donohue Smith, Deborah Lee Donohue Wilucki; m. Barbara Lounsbury, Dec., 1978. AB, Washington U., St. Louis, 1939, LLB/JD Magna cum laude, 1939. Bar: Mo. 1939. Ptnr. Husch, Eppenberger, Donohue, Cornfeld & Jenkins, St. Louis, 1949—. Author articles in field. Campaign chmn. ARC, St. Louis County, 1950; mem. ad. com. Child Welfare, St. Louis, 1952-55; mem. exec. com. Slum Clearance, 1949, bond issues coms., 1995; mem. bond issue com. St. Louis County Bond Issue, screening and supervisory coms., 1955-61, county citizen's com. for better law enforcement, 1953-56, chmn. com. on immigration policy, 1954-56; mayor City of Olivette, Mo., 1953-56; chmn. St. Louis County Bd. Election Commrs., 1960-65; chmn. com. Non-Partisan Ct. Plan; vice chmn. bd. Regional Commerce and Growth Assn. (lifetime recognition award 1996); pres. St. Louis C.C. Found.; bd. dirs. Downtown St. Louis, Inc. (leadership award 1996), Civil Entrepreneurs Orgn., Caring Found., Gateway Mayors Emeritus Inc., Anti-Drug Abuse Edn. Fund. Comdr. USN, WWII. Decorated Bronze Star medal, Navy and Marine Corps medal; recipient Disting. Alumni award Washington U., 1991, Good Guys award NOW, 1995. Mem. ABA, Mo. Bar Assn. (past bd. govs., chmn. ann. meeting, editor jour. 1940-41), St. Louis Bar Assn. (past pres., v.p., treas., Disting. Lawyer award 1992), Order of Coif, Mo. Athletic Club, Univ. Club, Omicron Delta Kappa, Sigma Phi Epsilon, Delta Theta Phi. Office: Husch & Eppenberger 100 N Broadway Ste 1300 Saint Louis MO 63102-2706

DONOHUE, JOHN JAMES, management analyst; b. Brighton, Mass., Mar. 22, 1963; s. John Jerome and Patricia Catherine (Kelly) D.; m. Chris Hiley, Aug. 8, 1992. BA, Gettysburg Coll., 1985; MPA, Drake U., 1994. Tech. writer Sigma Data Svcs. Corp., Washington, 1985-87; documentation specialist The Orkand Corp., Washington, 1987-91; programmer/analyst U.S. Bur. Labor Stats., Washington, 1991-92; mgmt. analyst Iowa Dept. Revenue and Fin., Des Moines, 1993—. Coord. phone bank operation Arlington (Va.) Dem. Com., 1988; pres. Arlington Young Dems., 1989, treas., 1990. Named one of Outstanding Young Men of Am., 1992. Mem. ASPA, So. Polit. Sci. Assn., Pi Alpha Alpha. Presbyterian. Home: 3211 30th St Apt F39 Des Moines IA 50310 Office: Iowa Dept Revenue and Fin Hoover State Office Bldg Des Moines IA 50319

DONOVAN, JAMES ROBERT, business equipment company executive; b. Wichita, Kans., Apr. 11, 1932; s. Karl Genevay and Louise (Silcott) D.; A.B., Harvard U., 1954, M.B.A., 1956; m. Ottilie Schreiber, July 2, 1955; children—Amy Louise, Robert Silcott; m. Margaret Jones Esty, Oct. 31, 1981. Mgr. sales adminstrn., market research Hickok, Inc., Rochester, N.Y., 1956-59, regional sales mgr., 1959-62, asst. nat. sales mgr., 1963-65; group program mgr. Xerox Corp., Stamford, Conn., 1965-68, mktg. mgr. spl. products, 1968-70, mgr. copier products, 1970-72, dir. corp. pricing and competitive activity, 1972-78, dir. corp. mktg. strategy and planning, 1978-83; sr. v.p. corp. mktg. McDonnell Douglas Automation Co., St. Louis, 1983-84; v.p. mktg., planning Info. Systems Group, McDonnell Douglas Corp., St. Louis, 1984-87; pres., Bus. Adv. Services, Inc., Naples, Fla., 1987— . Vice pres. Family Service, Rochester, 1971-72; dir. Family and Children's Services, Stamford, 1972-79; dir. Rochester Sales Execs. Club, 1966-71; mem. mktg. adv. bd. Columbia U. Bus. Sch., 1978-86; v.p. United Way of New Canaan, 1982-83; bd. dirs. Family Service Am., 1986-91. Mem. Harvard Alumni Assn. (dir. 1978-83), Harvard Bus. Sch. Alumni Assn. (dir. 1982-85), Pelican Bay (Fla.) Property Owners' Assn. (bd. dirs. 1994—). Clubs: Harvard (pres. Rochester 1971-72, pres. Fairfield County 1976-78, pres. St. Louis 1986-87, pres. Naples, Fla. 1991-93), Harvard Bus. Sch. (pres. Rochester 1972, chmn. Westchester/Fairfield 1973-74); Woodway Country (Darien, Conn.), The Club at Pelican Bay (Naples), Hole-in-the-Wall Country (Naples).

DONOVAN, JOHN VINCENT, consulting company executive; b. Chgo., May 13, 1924; s. Timothy Vincent and Mabel (Hederman) D.; m. Patricia Hasselhorn, Dec. 29, 1950; children: James, Timothy, Walter. AB, DePauw U., 1947, postgrad. in law, 1947-48; postgrad. in bus., Northwestern U., 1949-54. Mem. adminstrv. staff Swift-Brazil, 1947-50; asst. treas. Mid State Corp. Mobil Homes, Union City, Mich., 1951-55; gen. mgr. Bailey Corp., cosmetics, Chgo., 1955-58; sales mgr. Dole Corp., Honolulu, 1958-61; chmn. Intercon Rsch. Assocs. Ltd., Evanston, Ill., 1961—. Past bd. dirs. Ind. Voters Ill., Chgo. Lt. (j.g.) USNR, 1942-45. PTO. Mem. AAAS, Licensing Execs. Soc., Assn. Corp. Growth, World Future Soc., Chgo. Athletic Assn., Mich. Shores Club. Home: 431 Laurel Ave Wilmette IL 60091-2809 Office: Intercon Rsch Assocs Ltd 6865 N Lincoln Ave Chicago IL 60646-2644

DONOVAN, LAURIE B., state legislator; b. Little Falls, N.Y., Dec. 14, 1932; m. William Donovan, 1958; four children. BA, Pratt Inst.; MA, Syracuse U. State rep. dist. 74 Mo. Ho. of Reps., 1983—. Active Coun. Mental Retardation. Home: 7 Ipswich Ct Florissant MO 63033-4816 Office: Miss State Senate State Capitol Building Jefferson City MO 65101-1556*

DONOVAN, LESLIE D., SR., state legislator; m. Mary (Sissy) Donovan. Kans. state rep. Dist. 94, 1993—, auto dealer, investor. Home: 110 S Rainbow Lake Rd Wichita KS 67235-8508*

DONOVAN, ROBERT J., electrical engineer; b. Cleve., Mar. 27, 1955. AS, Lakeland C.C., Mentor, Ohio, 1978; student, Cleve. State U. Asst. mgr. Pick & Pay Supermarkets, Cleve., 1969-78; road electrician Consolidated Rail Corp., Cleve., 1978-80; elec. project engr. Webb TRIAX, Chardon, Ohio, 1980—. Vol. local ch. Roman Catholic. Office: Webb TRTAX 215 5th Ave Chardon OH 44024-1001

DOOLEY, J. GORDON, food scientist; b. Nevada, Mo., Nov. 15, 1935; s. Howard Eugene and Wilma June (Vanderford) D.; B.S. with honors in Biology, Drury Coll., Springfield, Mo., 1958; postgrad. (NSF grantee) U. Mo., Rolla, 1961, (NSF grantee) Kirksville (Mo.) State Coll., 1959; M.S. in Biology (NSF grantee), Brown U., 1966; postgrad. bus. mgmt. Alexander Hamilton Inst., 1973-75, No. Ill. U., 1964. Tchr. sci. Morton West High Sch., Berwyn, Ill., 1963-64; dairy technologist Borden Co., Elgin, Ill., 1964-65; project leader Cheese Products Lab., Kraft Corp., Glenview, Ill., 1965-73; sr. food scientist Wallerstein Co. div. Travenol Labs., Inc., Morton Grove, Ill., 1973-77; mgr. food sci. GB Fermentation Industries, Inc., Des Plaines, Ill., 1977-79, mgr. product devel., 1979-82; group leader Food Ingredients div. Stauffer Chem. Co., Clawson, Mich., 1982-84; sr. research scientist Schreiber Foods, Inc., Green Bay, Wis., 1984-87, DMV Ridgeview, LaCrosse, Wis., 1987-92; mgr. regulatory affairs, info. svcs., DMV USA, LaCrosse, 1992-95; rsch. scientist AMPC, Inc., Ames, Iowa, 1996—; sci. lectr. seminars, Mexico, 1975; assoc. mem. Ad Hoc Enzyme Tech. Com., 1978—; dairy research adv. bd. Utah State U.; del. in field. Recipient Spoke award Nevada (Mo.) Jr. C. of C., 1960. Speaker, reporter People to People Sanitarians del. to China, 1989. Mem. Am. Dairy Sci. Assn., Inst. Food Technologists, Am. Chem. Soc., Cousteau Soc., Am. Inst. Biol. Scis., Nat. Sci. Tchrs. Assn., Whey Products Inst., Beta Beta Beta, Phi Eta Sigma. Republican. Presbyterian. Clubs: Toastmasters Internat. (pres. Baxter Labs. club 1976-77); Brown U. (Chgo.). Patentee in food and enzyme tech. field; contbr. sci. articles to profl. jours. Home: care AMPC Inc PO Box 645 Ames IA 50010 Office: DMV USA 2340 Enterprise Ave La Crosse WI 54603-1713

DOOLEY, JOHN ANTHONY, clinical psychologist, pain center director; b. St. Louis, Oct. 25, 1953; s. John Alvin and Cecelia Marie (Ortiz) D.; m. Cynthia Joanne Parkin, May 1, 1981. BA in Psychology, St. Louis U., 1974; MA in Psychology, Wayne State U., 1980, PhD in Psychology, 1985. Lic. Psychologist, Mich. Psychologist Gertrude Levin Pain Ctr., Detroit, 1980-85, chief psychologist, 1985-88, dir., 1988—; ptnr. Clin. Psychology Cons., Farmington Hills, Mich., 1985—; cons. Total Therapy Mgmt., Detroit, 1992-94; asst. prof. Wayne State U. Sch. Med., 1992—; mem. Pain Advisory Com. Harper Hosp., Detroit, 1990—, Hutzel Hosp., Detroit, 1994—. Contbr. chpts. to books including Crash Injury and Impairment, 1986, Head and Neck Injury, 1994. Bd. dirs. Catholic Youth Orgn., Detroit. Fulbright fellow, Berlin, 1975-76. Mem. APA, Am. Pain Soc., Internat. Assn. for the Study of Pain, Mich. Coun. on Pain, Phi Beta Kappa, Psi Chi. Roman Catholic. Office: Gertrude Levin Pain Ctr 4727 St Antoine Detroit MI 48201

DOOLIN, PAUL F., radiologist; b. Ill., May 17, 1926; s. Francis Patrick and Sadye Catherine (Murphy) D. AB, Ill. Coll.; MS, U. Ill., 1953; PhD, Case Western Res. U., 1958; MD, Loyola U., Broadview, Ill., 1979. Asst. prof. biology W & J Coll., Washington, Pa., 1959-60; assoc. prof. biology Ill. State U., Normal, 1960-64; dir. ultra struct res. lab Hines VA Med. Ctr., Ill., 1964-74; assoc. prof. anat./path. Loyola U. Med. Ctr., Broadview, Ill., 1968-74; fellowct/ult sound Hahneman Med. Ctr., Phila., 1983-84; fellow nuclear medicine St. Barnabas Med. Ctr., Livingston, N.J., 1984-85; clin. instr. radiology U. Ill. Med. Ctr., Chgo., 1990—; staff radiologist WSUA Med. Ctr., Chgo., 1990—. Contbr. articles to profl. jours. With USNR, PTO.

DORE, JAMES FRANCIS, financial services executive; b. Milford, Mass., Apr. 5, 1946; s. James Edwin and Frances Sofia (Crochunas) D.; m. Teresa Lorenzo, June 15, 1968; children: Judith, Jill, James. BS in Fin., Boston Coll., 1968; MBA with high distinction, Babson Coll., 1971. With fin. mgmt. program instrument dept. GE, Lynn, Mass., 1969-71, mgr. customer acctg. instrument dept., 1971-73; mgr. mfg. cost acctg. silicone products div. GE, Waterford, N.Y., 1973-76, mgr. ops. analysis silicone products div., 1976-79; corp. fin. analyst GE, Fairfield, Conn., 1979-83, mgr. internat. fin., 1983-85; exec. v.p., chief fin. officer Capital Mortgage Ins. GE, Raleigh, N.C., 1985-90; chief fin. officer GE Capital Mortgage Corp., Raleigh, 1990-93; sr. v.p. Employers Reins. Corp. (GE Capital), Overland Park, Kans., 1993—; pres. Puritan Excess Surplus Lines, Overland Park, 1995—; v.p. GE Global Ins. Holdings. 1st lt. U.S. Army, 1968-74. Roman Catholic. Home: 4008 W 123rd St Leawood KS 66209-2218 Office: Employers Reins Corp 5200 Metcalf Ave Overland Park KS 66202-1265

DORGAN, BYRON LESLIE, senator; b. Dickinson, N.D., May 14, 1942; s. Emmett P. and Dorothy (Bach) D.; m. Kimberly Olson Dorgan; children: Scott, Shelly (dec.), Brendon, Haley. BBA, U. N.D., 1965; MBA, U. Denver, 1966. Exec. devel. trainee Martin Marietta Corp., Denver, 1966-67; dep. tax commr., then tax commnr. State of N.D., 1967-80; mem. 97th-102nd congresses from N.D., 1981-92; U.S. senator from N.D., 1992—; asst. Dem. floor leader U.S. Senate, 1996—; mem. Commerce, Sci. and Transp. Com., Select Com. on Indian Affairs, Dem. Policy Com., 1992—; mem. Govt. Affairs Com.; vice chmn. Spl. Com. on Ethics; instr. econs. Bismarck (N.D.) Jr. Coll., 1969-71. Contbr. articles to profl. jours. Recipient Nat. Leadership award Office Gov. N.D., 1972. Mem. Nat. Assn. Tax Adminstrs. (exec. com. 1972-75). Office: US Senate 713 Hart Senate Office Bui Washington DC 20510

DORMAN, MARK JOSEPH, financial services agent; b. Cleve., Nov. 19, 1964; s. Joseph Patrick and Bride (McGhee) D.; m. Tanya Dee Yoskovich, Aug. 6, 1988; children: Aidan Joseph, Andrew Edward. BBA in mktg., Cleve. State U., 1989. Sales rep. New Eng. Fin., Cleve., 1987-91; ptnr. Berbe & Dorman, Cleve., 1991—; apptd. to 1995 Dean's Search Com. James J. Nance Coll. Bus. Cleve. State U., 1995. Mem. Nat. Assn. Life Underwriters, Estate Planning Coun. Cleve., Am. Soc. CLU & ChFC, Million Dollar Round Table, Cleve. State U. Alumni Assn. (dir. 1995-96), Cleve. State U. Bus. Assn. (pres. 1993-94). Republican. Roman Catholic. Office: Beebe & Dorman 1120 Chester Ave Apt 310 Cleveland OH 44114

DORMEIER, BUFF P., investment professional; b. Ft. Wayne, Ind., Dec. 1, 1969. BS in Bus. and Urban Regional Planning, Ind. State U., 1992. Planning asst. Johnson County Planning, Franklin, Ind., 1993; investments profl. Paine Webber, Ft. Wayne, 1993—; lectr. investment seminars, 1993—. Author: (newsletter) Financial Matters, 1993—. Founder Praise Luth. Ch., Ft. Wayne; mem. Jr. Achievement, Ft. Wayne, 1993—. Mem. Delta Tau Corp.

DORN, JOHN, state legislator; b. Dec. 28, 1943; m. Kathleen; 3 children. BA, John's U.; MA, U. Wis. State rep. Minn. Ho. Reps., Dist., 24A, 1986—; vice chmn. appropriations com., mem. edn.-higher edn. fin. divsn., environ. & natural resources & local govt. & met. affairs coms., Minn. Ho. Reps. Home: 1021 Orchard Rd Mankato MN 56001-4522*

DORNER, DOUGLAS BLOOM, vascular surgeon, educator; b. Iowa City, Iowa, Aug. 4, 1941; s. Ralph A. and Gene (Bloom) D.; married, 1970; children: Gillian Austin, Hillary Howell. BA magna cum laude, Amherst Coll., 1963; MD cum laude, Harvard U., 1967. Diplomate Am. Bd. Surgery, Am. Bd. Gen. Vascular Surgery, Nat. Bd. Med. Examiners. Physician intern in surgery U. Calif., San Francisco, 1967-68, asst. resident in surgery, 1968-70, sr. resident, 1971-72, chief resident, 1972-73; surg. registrar St. James' Hosp., London, 1970-71; pvt. practice medicine specializing in vascular surgery Des Moines, 1974—; chief surgery Broadlawns-Polk County Hosp., Des Moines, 1977-78; co-dir. peripheral vascular lab. Iowa Meth. Med. Ctr., Des Moines, 1977—, chief surgery, 1980-81, 88-91; co-dir. peripheral vascular lab. Iowa Luth. Hosp., Des Moines, 1980-88; dir. med. edn. Iowa Meth. Med. Ctr., Des Moines, 1994—; instr. surgery u. iowa, Iowa City, 1973, clin. asst. prof., 1981—; vis. prof. Gunderson Clinic, La Crosse, Wis., 1984, St. James' Hosp., London, 1985, Dublin, Ireland, 1987; cons. VA Med. Hosp., Des Moines, 1980—; dir. med. edn. Iowa Meth. Med. ctr., 1994—; sr. v.p. med. edn. & rsch. Cen. Iowa Health System, 1996—. Contbr. numerous articles to profl. and scholarly jours. Capt. USAR, 1967-77. Nat. Merit scholar, 1959. Fellow ACS (Iowa chpt. scholarship award com., credentials com., chmn. Iowa com. on applicants 1976—); mem. AMA, Naffziger Surg. Soc., Polk County Med. Soc. (councillor 1979-81, trustee 1981-83, pres.-elect 1983, pres. 1984), Iowa Med. Soc. (chmn. program com. sci. session 1982), Am. Trauma Soc., Iowa Acad. Surgery (program chmn. 1981, resident paper award com.), Midwest Surg. Assn. (councillor 1983-85, sec. 1985-88, pres. elect 1989-90, pres. 1990-91), Soc. Clin. Vascular Surgery, Internat. Soc. for Cardiovascular Surgery, Midwestern Vascular Surg. Soc. (membership com.), Soc. Non-Invasive Vascular Tech., Western Surg. Assn., Peripheral Vascular Surg. Soc., Phi Beta Kappa, Sigma Xi, Med. Libr. Club Des Moines (sec. 1989-90), Des Moines Club, Wakonda Club. Home: 5220 Waterbury Rd Des Moines IA 50312-1922 Office: Ste 100 1440 Pleasant St Des Moines IA 50314

DORR, JAMES SUHRER, writer; b. Pensacola, Fla., Aug. 12, 1941; s. Frank James and Betty (Suhrer) D.; m. Ruth Michelle Clark, Aug. 16, 1975 (div. Aug 8, 1982). BS, MIT, 1964; MA, Ind. U., 1968. Tech. writer Wrubel Computing Ctr., Bloomington, Ind., 1969-74, chief tech. writer, 1974-79, editor, 1979-81; writer, mktg. cons. The Stackworks, Bloomington, Ind., 1982; freelance writer Bloomington, Ind., 1982—; Assoc. editor: Bloominton (Ind.) Area Mag., 1983-86. Author: (poems) Towers of Darkness, 1990; contbr. more than 300 articles to mags. and newsletters, poems and over 90 short stories to anthologies and mags. Mem. Bloomington (Ind.) Traffic Commn., 1974-86. Mem. Sci. Fiction and Fantasy Writers of Am., Horror Writers Assn., Sci. Fiction Poetry Assn. Home: 1404 E Atwater Bloomington IN 47401

DORR, ORRIN JOSEPH, county drain commissioner, farmer; b. Chgo., Oct. 11, 1940; s. Orrin Joseph and Marcella Erna (Kruse) D.; m. Fay Alexis Yarborough, Nov. 22, 1976; children: Marcella Erna, Orrin Joseph V. H.s. grad., Lawrence, Mich. Twp. supr. Waverly Twp., Lawrence, Mich., 1985-92; twp. assessor Waverly Twp., Lawrence, 1985-92; county drain commr. Van Buren County, Paw Paw, Mich., 1993—. Mem. Van Buren County Planning Commn., Paw Paw, Mich., 1992-93, Dowagiac River Restoration, Paw Paw, 1993—; adminstr. P.A. 347 Mich. Dept. Natural Resources, Plainwell, 1994—. Recipient Graham Woodhouse award for intergovt. effort Southwestern Mich. Commn., 1994. Mem. Mich. Assn. County Drain Commrs., Van Buren County Flywheelers Assn., J.I. Case Historic Soc. Republican. Home: 41793 46th St Lawrence MI 49064 Office: Van Buren County Ct House 212 E Paw Paw St Paw Paw MI 49079

DORR, STEPHANIE TILDEN, psychologist; b. Orlando, Fla., Sept. 21, 1950; d. Luther Willis Tilden II and Lillian Murfee (Grace) Owen; m. Darwin Dorr, May 21, 1986. AA, El Camino Coll., 1975; BA, U. N.C., 1985; MA, Western Carolina U., 1991. Cons. psychologist Sylva (N.C.) Psychol. Assocs., 1991-92; staff psychologist Park Ridge Hosp., Naples, N.C., 1992, Blue Ridge Ctr., Asheville, N.C., 1991-93; pvt. practice psychology Asheville, 1991-93; project mgr. Sedgwick County Dept. Mental Health, Wichita, Kans., 1993-95; pvt. practice psychotherapy and psychol. assessment Counseling and Mediation Ctr., Wichita, Kans., 1995—; adj. faculty Kans. Newman Coll., Wichita, 1995—; presenter in field. Contbr. articles to profl. publs. Mem. APA, Internat. Rorschach and Projective Techniques Soc., Soc. for Personality Assessment, Soc. for Psychologists in Mgmt., Psychoanalytic Study Group (sec. 1989-93, award 1993), Western N.C. Psychol. Assn. (mem.-at-large 1985-93, pres.-elect 1993), Psi Chi, Pi Gamma Mu. Episcopalian. Office: The Counseling and Mediation Ctr Inc 334 N Topeka Wichita KS 67202

DORSEY, GILBERTA A., investment broker, trust specialist; b. Quincy, Ill., Oct. 14, 1952; m. Jeff A. Dorsey, Feb. 5, 1988; children: Roni Sue, Rene Ann. Registered series 7 Nat. Assn. Securities Dealers. Owner, mgr. Gilberta Styling Salon, Quincy, 1976-84; saleswoman Quincy Mcht., 1985-86, Sta. WTAD, Quincy, 1986-90; investment broker A.G. Edwards & Sons Inc., Quincy, 1990—. Mem. Quincy Visitors Bur., 1992—. Mem. LWV, Am. Bus. Women, Spring Lake Country Club. Office: AG Edwards & Sons Inc 3325 Maine St Quincy IL 62301-4438

DORSO, JOHN, state legislator; b. Mpls., June 12, 1943; s. Carmen T. and Jean D. Dorso; m. Susan James, 1987; children: Victor, Louis, Carmen, Danielle, Amy, Todd. BA, Coll. St. Thomas, 1967. V.p. Dorso Trailer Sales, Fargo, pres. semi trailer sales and leasing; mem. N.D. Ho. of Reps. Dist. 46, 1984—; majority leader N.D. Ho. of Reps.; mem. sts. and hwys. com., transp. com.; chmn. industry, bus. and labor com., majority leader N.D. Ho. Reps.; bd. dirs. Behavioral Health Care, Inc.; pres. N.D. Drivers. Chmn. dist. 46 N.D. Rep. Com., 1981-83, United Rep. Com., Fargo, 1983-84. Recipient Legislative Vision award, 1991, 93, Lignite Pub. Svc. award, 1993. Mem. N.D. State U. Teammakers (pres. 1982-83), N.D. Motor Carriers Assn., Fargo C. of C. Home: PO Box 7310 Fargo ND 58109-7310*

DORWEN, FRANZ F., administrator; b. Stughtgart, Germany, July 14, 1942; came to U.S., 1967; B, German State Sch. Cons. Hesser Corp., Vaihlinben, Germany, 1967-78; plant supr. Mimco Corp., Crystal Lake, Ill., 1978—. Office: Nimco Corp 4012 US Hwy 14 PO Box J Crystal Lake IL 60014

DORWICK, KEITH, educator; b. Chgo., Oct. 18, 1957; s. Charles J. and Peg (Flaherty) D. BA in English, DePaul U., 1989; MA in English, U. Ill., Chgo., 1991, postgrad. in English, 1992—. Tchg. asst. U. Ill., Chgo., 1989-96, grad. coord. student computer assisted instrn. lab., 1989-92; asst. dir. Evening Writing Ctr., 1994-95; rsch. asst. U. Ill., Chgo., 1995-96, instrnl. media planner Office of Acad. Affairs, 1996—; spkr. Conf. on Coll. Composition and Comm., Boston, 1991, San Diego, 1993, Washington, 1995, Milw., 1996; com. mem. grad. curriculum com. U. Ill.-Chgo., 1994-95, com. on computers and composition for Conf. on Coll. Composition and Comm., 1995—; spkr. Internat. Congress on Cross-Dressing, Gender and Sex, Northridge, Calif., 1995; workshop leader U. Ill., Chgo., 1995-96; spkr. Allerton C.C./Univ. English Articulation Conf., Monticello, Ill., 1995, Conf. on Christianity and Lit., Santa Clara, Calif., 1995; workshop leader pre-conv. workshops Conf. Coll. Composition and Comm., Milw., 1996; co-investigator for several grants awarded to dept. English, U. Ill., Chgo., 1995, assoc. head E-Works dept. English, 1996—. Editor: Not-So-Silent Voices: Writings by English 152 Students, 1995; guest editor: Works and Days 27-28: Conversations for Jim Berlin: The Future of Cultural Studies, vol. 14, 1-2, 1996; contbr. articles to profl. jours. including Notable Internet Resource Academe Today and Tchg. in the Cmty. Colls. Jour. Deacon, aspirant Episcopal Ch. Mem. MLA, Nat. Coun. Tchrs. English, Alliance for Computers and Writers, Milton Soc. am. Home: 555 W Cornelia Ave Apt 1811 Chicago IL 60657-2737 Office: Univ Ill Chgo Office Acad Affairs M/C 105 601 S Morgan Chicago IL 60607

DOSÉ, FREDERICK PHILIP, JR., art historian, art and antiques appraiser, consultant, liquidator; b. Chgo., Sept. 9, 1946; s. Frederick P. and Alfa Elaine (Bahr) D.; m. Dee Hampton Keehn, June 8, 1985. BA, Northwestern U., 1968, MA, 1981. Faculty, art historian Northeastern Ill. U., Chgo., 1974-75, Colgate U., Hamilton, N.Y., 1976-80, Ray Coll., Chgo., 1984—; fine arts and antiques appraiser for ins., probate, divorce, Evanston, Ill., 1980—; art critic Chgo. Journal, 1982-85; curator, dir. Chgo. br. Daniel B. Grossman Gallery, 1983; agt., broker Charles Lipson Antiquities, Jamaica Plain, Mass., 1985—; ct. apptd. liquidator, 1987—; expert, witness in field. Co-author: Value, Insurance and Loss of Fine Art; author (catalogue) Wilson Irvine, 1984; contbr. articles to profl. jours. Judge Old Town Art Fair, Chgo., 1991. Mem. Coll. Art Assn., Internat. Soc. Appraisers (contbg. editor bull. 1981—), Newberry Libr. Assocs., Friends of Victoria & Albert Mus., Furniture History Soc. London, Soc. for Ancient Numismatics, Am. Numismatics Assn., Archaeol. Inst. Am., Napoleonic Soc. Am.

DOTSON, JOHN LOUIS, JR., newspaper executive; b. Paterson, N.J., Feb. 5, 1937; s. John Louis and Evelyn Elizabeth (Nelson) D.; m. Peggy Elaine Burnett, Apr. 4, 1959; children: John, Damon, Christopher, Brandon, Leslie. B.S., Temple U., 1958, Doctor of Journalism (hon.), 1981. Reporter Newark News, 1959-64; gen. assignment reporter Detroit Free Press, 1965; with Newsweek Mag., 1965-83; corr. Detroit, 1965-69; corr. L.A., 1969-70, bur. chief, 1970-75; news editor N.Y.C., 1976-77, sr. editor, 1977-83; asst. to exec. editor Phila. Inquirer, 1983-84; exec. asst. to pres. Phila. Newspapers, Inc., 1984-85, dir. night ops., 1986-87; pres., pub. Daily Camera, Boulder, Colo., 1987-92; pub. Akron (Ohio) Beacon Jour., 1992—; bd. dirs. Robert C. Maynard Inst. Journalism Edn., 1974—, treas., 1974-78, chmn., 1980-84, 93—; mem. Pulitzer Prize Bd., 1991—; bd. dirs. Inventure Place; mem. nat. adv. bd. Poynter Inst. for Media Studies. Mem. bd. visitors John S. Knight Fellowships, Stanford U., 1983—, Sch. Journalism, U. N.C., Chapel Hill, 1987—; mem. adv. bd. Sch. Journalism and Mass Comms., U. Colo., Boulder; trustee Akron Cmty. Found., 1993—, chmn., 1995—; mem. exec. com. Akron Regional Devel. Bd.; mem. governing bd. Summit Edn. Initiative. Office: Akron Beacon Jour 44 E Exchange St Akron OH 44328-0001

DOTY, DAVID SINGLETON, federal judge; b. Anoka, Minn., June 30, 1929. BA, U. Minn., 1961, LLB, 1961; LLD (hon.), William Mitchell Coll. Law. Bar: Minn. 1961, U.S. Ct. Appeals (8th and 9th cirs.) 1976, U.S. Supreme Ct. 1982. V.p., dir. Popham, Haik, Schnobrich, Kaufman & Doty, Mpls., 1962-87, pres., 1977-79; instr. William Mitchell Coll. Law, Mpls., 1963-64; judge U.S. Dist. Ct. for Minn., Mpls., 1987—. Mem. Adv. Com. on Civil Rules, Adv. Com. on Evidence Rules; trustee Mpls. Libr. Bd., 1969-79, Mpls. Found., 1976-83. Fellow ABA Found.; mem. ABA, Minn. Bar Assn. (gov. 1976-87, sec. 1980-83, pres. 1984-85), Hennepin County Bar Assn. (pres. 1975-76, adv. com. on civil rules 1993—), Am. Judicature Soc., Am. Law Inst. Home: 23 Greenway Gables Minneapolis MN 55403-2145 Office: US Dist Ct 670 US Courthouse 110 S 4th St Minneapolis MN 55401-2221

DOTY, KAREN M., state legislator, lawyer; m. David Levey. BS, Old Dominion U., 1973; MA, U. Akron, 1977, JD, 1981. Bar: Ohio. With Ardmore Inc., Akron, 1980-85, pres., 1983-85; mem. Ohio Ho. of Reps., Columbus. Me. Akron Mayor's Task Force on Juvenile Violence; mem. steering com. Internat. Yr. of Family. Named Legislator of Yr., Nat. Rep. Legislators Assn., 1991; named to Ohio Women's Hall of Fame, 1991. Mem. ABA, Ohio Bar Assn., Akron Bar Assn. Home: 1345 Jefferson Ave Akron OH 44313-7621 Office: OH Ho of Reps State House Columbus OH 43215*

DOTY, ROBERT J., account executive; b. Belleville, Ill., June 19, 1942. BA, Northwestern Okla. U., 1968; MS, So. Ill. U., Edwardsville, 1972. Program mgr. Ill. Dept. Labor, East St. Louis, 1969-82; account exec. Advest Inc., Belleville, 1982—. Mem. fin. adv. bd. Spl. Children Inc., Belleville, 1989—; co-chmn. adv. bd. Sch. Dist. Red Bud, Ill., 1992—. With U.S. Army, 1964-66. Recipient award Friends of Ill. Edn., 1993, svc. award Red Bud Cmty., 1994. Mem. Soc. Mayflower Descs., Musket Athletic Assn., Farm Bur., Lions (past v.p. and pres. Red Bud, svc. award 1995). Baptist. Office: Advest Inc 13 Park Pl Belleville IL 62221-2967

DOUBLEDAY, JAMES FRANK, English language educator; b. Madison, Wis., Oct. 31, 1936; s. Neal F. and Frances H. (Honey) D.; m. K. O'Brien, Mar. 3, 1960 (div. Dec. 1972); 1 child, Mary; m. Sandra Lee Schnell, July 13, 1977. BS in English, Northwestern U., 1958; MS in libr. sci., U. Ill., 1959, PhD in English, 1967. Part-time instr. Cornell U., Ithaca, N.Y., 1964-65; instr. Elmira (N.Y.) Coll., 1965-68, asst. prof., 1968-69; asst. prof. Univ. Notre Dame, Ind., 1969-76, Jandi Shapur U., Ahwaz, Iran, 1976-78, Rio Grande (Ohio) Coll., 1978-87; assoc. prof. U. Rio Grande, 1987-93, prof., 1993—. Editor: Creative Writer's Handbook, 1984; contbr. articles to profl. jours. Scholar Northwestern U., Evanston., Ill., 1954-58; summer fellow U. Ill., Urbana, 1964. Mem. AAUP, Nat. Coun. Tchrs. of English, Tchrs. of English to Spkrs. of Other Langs., Southeastern Med. Assn., U.S. Chess Fedn. Episcopalian. Home: 1318 Patriot Rd Gallipolis OH 45631 Office: Dept English U Rio Grande Rio Grande OH 45674

DOUGHAN, THOMAS BRUCE, banker; b. Dubuque, Iowa, Sept. 26, 1960; s. Roger and Elizabeth (Becker) D. BA in Fin., Loras Coll., 1983. V.p. Farmers State Bank, Northwood, Iowa, 1996—; asst. high sch. golf coach, 1992-95. Vol. Sen. Baker Pres. campaign, Dubuque, 1979. Mem. Moose, Rochester Traver Ski Club (treas. 1993-94, 94-95), Northwood C. of C., Northwood Men's Club. Republican. Roman Catholic.

DOUGHERTY, CHARLOTTE ANNE, financial planner, insurance and securities representative; b. Canton, Ohio, Nov. 9, 1947; d. Myron Martin and Wilma Rose Brown; m. John Edwin Dougherty, Jr., Feb. 14, 1976; 1 child, John Edwin. BA, Miami U., Oxford, Ohio, 1969; postgrad. Kent State U. (Ohio), 1971-73. Cert. fin. planner. Social worker Summit County Welfare, Akron, Ohio, 1971-73; research coordinator Tufts U., Medford, Mass., 1973-74; corp. recruiter Lincoln Nat. Sales Corp., Ft. Wayne, Ind., 1976-79; registered rep. Lincoln Nat. Life, Cin., 1980—, LNC Equity Sales Corp., Cin., 1989—. Contbr. articles to profl. jours. Mem. Inst. Cert. Fin. Planners, Internat. Assn. Fin. Planners (v.p. Cin. chpt. 1990—), Internat. Assn. for Fin. Planning (pres.-elect Cin. chpt. 1991, pres. 1992-93), Nat. Assn. Life Underwriters, Cin. Assn. Life Underwriters. Office: Oxford Fin Group 8044 Montgomery Rd Ste 400W Cincinnati OH 45236-2923

DOUGHERTY, DANIEL ALLAN, insurance claims manager; b. Great Falls, Mont., Feb. 17, 1951; s. John Alexander and Mariluise (Routzahn) D.; m. Rebecca Louise Baldwin, June 24, 1972; children: Kyle Patrick, Bryn Christine, Colleen Rebecca. BA, Mont. State U., 1973; postgrad., U. Mont., 1976, SUNY, 1976. CPCU, 1991. Tchr. Sch. Dist. #1, Great Falls, Mont., 1973-77; sales Northwestern Nat. Life, Great Falls, Mont., 1977-78; claims adjuster Sentry Ins. Group, Mpls., 1978-85, claims unit mgr., 1985-87; property claim specialist Sentry Ins. Group, Stevens Point, Wis., 1987-89, property claims mgr., 1989—; presenter in field. PRes. bd. dirs. Monteverdi Master Chorale, Stevens Point, 1991; dir. Touch of Brass Handbell Choir, Stevens Point. Mem. Chartered Property Casualty Underwriters Soc. Home: 5219 Howard Ave Stevens Point WI 54481-5656 Office: Sentry Ins 1421 Strongs Ave Stevens Point WI 54481-2918

DOUGHERTY, J. PATRICK, state legislator; b. Decatur, Ill., June 30, 1948; s. James Francis and Bernadine Brennan Dougherty; m. Beverly Anne Martin, 1973; children: Erica Maureen, Bridget Colleen, Elizabeth Kathleen. BA, Quincy Coll., 1970; postgrad., Kenrick Theol. Sem., 1970-72. State rep. dist. 98 Mo. Ho. of Reps., 1979-82, dist. 67, 1983—; caseworker divsn. family svc. St. Louis County, Mo., 1974-78; devel. dir. Marianist Apostolic Ctr.; mem. adv. bd. Fanning Cmty. Sch.; mem. adv. com. Crippled Children; mem. legis. com. United Way Greater St. Louis. Named Outstanding Freshman Legislator Mo. Assn. Pub. Employees, 1979—; recipient Citizen Labor Energy award, 1984, Rutherford T. Phillips award Humane Assn., 1984, Svc. award Mo. Humane Soc., 1984. Home: 4031 Parker Ave Saint Louis MO 63116-3719*

DOUGHERTY, JANET KAY, ambulatory surgery and recovery room nurse; b. Belleville, Ill., Dec. 2, 1959; d. James Ralph and Frances (Baer) Mueller; m. David G. Dougherty, Apr. 23, 1988. Diploma, St. Luke's Hosp., 1980; BSN, Elmhurst Coll., 1986; MSN in Nursing Adminstrn., Loyola U., 1991. RN, Ill., Mo. Staff nurse St. Elizabeth's Hosp., Belleville, 1980-81; staff nurse gen. surg. Rush-Presbyn.-St. Luke's Med. Ctr., Chgo., 1981-85, asst. head nurse gen. surgery, 1985-87, staff nurse ambulatory surgery, 1987-89, asst. head nurse ambulatory surgery, 1989-91, asst. unit leader ambulatory/recovery rm., 1991-93; unit dir. ambulatory/recovery rm., 1993—. Mem. Am. Acad. Ambulatory Care Nurses, Nat. Assn. Orthopedic Nursing, Sigma Theta Tau. Home: 104 S Cornell Ave Villa Park IL 60181-2620 Office: Rush Presbyn St Lukes Ctr 1650 W Harrison St Chicago IL 60612

DOUGHERTY, JOHN A., county official; b. Peoria, Ill., Dec. 1, 1958; s. J. Robert and Joyce A. (Stell) D.; m. Ruthanna M. Torbet, Sept. 8, 1987; children: Christina, Amy. AAS, Ill. Ctrl. Coll., 1986; BA, Ea. Ill. U., 1987; postgrad., Ill. State U., 1993. Mgmt. asst. County of Peoria, Peoria, Ill., 1989-91, budget asst., 1991-94, budget officer, 1994—. Prodr., dir. cable TV show Peoria County Today, 1994—. Bd. dirs. Yule Like Peoria, 1992. Mem. ASPA (chpt. pres. 1994-95), Govt. Fin. Officer Assn., Ill. Govt. Fin. Officers Assn., Internat. City/County Mgmt. Assn. (affiliate). Home: 2326 N Atlantic Peoria IL 61603 Office: County of Peoria 324 N Main Rm 401 Peoria IL 61603

DOUGHERTY, PETER P., securities company executive; b. Cleve., Aug. 11, 1954. BA in History, John Carroll U., 1976. Asst. dir. fin. City of Euclid, Ohio, 1980-86; v.p. Dougherty & Assocs., Cleve., 1986-89; regional v.p. Travelers Ins. Co., Cleve., 1989-91; v.p. McDonald & Co. Securities Inc., Pepper Pike, Ohio, 1991—. Bd. dirs. Lakeland Coll. Found., Cleve., 1991—, Villa Angela-St. Joseph H.S. Found., Cleve., 1993—. Mem. Am. Mgmt. Assn., Rotary (past pres. Euclid, dist. gov. Cleve.). Republican. Roman Catholic. Office: McDonald & Co Securities Inc 30050 Chagrin Blvd Ste 150 Pepper Pike OH 44124-5704

DOUGHERTY, THOMAS, information services executive; s. Harry A. and Mary E. Dougherty; m. Lucille A. Tammetta, Aug. 7, 1965; children: Timothy, Erica. BSBA, Rochester Inst. Tech., 1970. Info. systems mgr. IBM Corp., Endicott, N.Y., 1984-85, tech. asst., 1985, plans and controls mgr., 1985-86; lab. ops. mgr. IBM Product Lab., Endicott, 1986-87, site info. systems mgr., 1987-88; I&TSS dir. IBM U.S.-N.E. Region, Endicott, 1988-92; gen. mgr. aerospace and ctrl. delivery ISSC, St. Louis, 1992—; mem. DPMA, 1982-88; dir. Rochester (N.Y.) Inst. Tech., 1984-88. Adv. mem. Broome County C. of C., 1986-89; dir. Boy's Club Endicott, 1987-90; bd. dirs. Youth in Need, St. Charles, 1995—. Office: ISSC 325 J S McDonnell Blvd Hazelwood MO 63042

DOUGHTEN, MARY KATHERINE (MOLLY DOUGHTEN), retired secondary education educator; b. Belvidere, Ill., Apr. 26, 1923; d. Edwin Albert and Theora Teresa (Tefft) Loop; m. Philip Tedford Doughten, Oct. 15, 1947; children: Deborah Doughten Hellriegel, Susan Doughten Myers, Ann Doughten Fichenscher, Philip Tedford Jr., David, Sarah Doughten Wiggins. BA, DePauw U., 1945; MS, Western Res. U., 1947. Social worker Children's Svcs., Cleve., 1947, San Antonio, 1948-49; tchr. English Indian Valley High Schs., Gradenhutten, Ohio, 1962-66; tchr. English and sociology New Philadelphia (Ohio) High Sch., 1966-86. Bd. dirs. Tuscarawas Valley (Ohio) Guidance Ctr., 1950-62, Cmty. Mental Health Care, Inc., formerly Mental Health Svcs. Cmty. Profl. Svcs., 1974-82, 84-92, pres., 1979-81, Alcohol, Drug and Mental Health Svcs. Bd., formerly Cmty. Mental Health Alcohol and Drug Svcs., Tuscarawas-Carroll County, 1992—, v.p. 1996—; bd. dirs. Tuscarawas County Juvenile Judges Rev. Bd., 1984—, Tuscarawas County United Way, 1960-67, ARC, PTA, 1955-58, coun. pres., 1960-62, mental health chmn. state bd., 1963-65, libr. chmn., 1966-68, Mobile Meals, 1986—, Dem. Women, 1986—, Hospice, 1987—, State C.C. Bd., 1965-68; founder, bd. dirs. Ohio Cmty. Mental Health Svcs., Columbus, 1970-80s; founding com. Kent State U. Tuscarawas campus, 1960s; bd. dirs. Tuscarawas County U. Found., 1994—, v.p., 1996—. Recipient Mental Health award Community and Profl. Svcs., 1978; Martha Holden Jennings scholar, 1975-76. Mem. AAUW (sec. 1962, v.p. 1996—), Ohio Ret. Tchrs. (sec. 1987-89), New Philadelphia Edn. Assn., Friends of Libr., Chestnut Soc. (bd. dirs. 1987-91), Tuscarawas County Med. Aux. (pres. 1959-60, state bd. 1960-64), Union Hosp. Aux. (bd. dirs. 1986—, editor 1986—), DAR, Coll. Club (scholarship chair 1989-91), Union County Club, Atwood Yacht Club, Lady Elks, Mortar Bd., Phi Beta Kappa, Alpha Chi Omega, Theta Sigma Phi. Democrat. Presbyterian. Home: 204 Gooding Ave NW New Philadelphia OH 44663

DOUGHTY, ANTHONY RUTGERS, small business owner; b. Evanston, Ill., June 28, 1938; s. William Howard and Elizabeth (Sargent) D.; m. Patricia Lynn Fuller, Sept. 5, 1964; 1 child, Charles F. Doughty. BA, Williams Coll., 1960. Buyer Marshall Field & Co., Chgo., 1964-69, Dayton/Hudson Corp., Mpls., 1969-71; store mgr. Associated Dry Goods Corp., Mpls., 1971-75; sales mgr. Braun's Fashions, Inc., Mpls., 1975-76; pres., CEO Doughty Dry Goods, Inc., Walker, Minn., 1977—. Contbr. articles to mags. and newspapers. Pres. No. Minn. Pub. TV, Bemidji, 1992-93. Mem. Walker C. of C., Antique Automobile Club Am., Veteran Motor Car Club Am., Horseless Carriage Club Am. Office: Doughty Dry Goods Inc P O Box 699 Walker MN 56484

DOUGLAS, DARYL D., mechanical and design engineer; b. Peoria, Ill., Aug. 25, 1937. Student, U. Minn. Project designer Owatonna (Minn.) Machinery Corp., 1982-86; mech. and design engr. Tech. Inc., Red Wing, Minn., 1986—; advisor on drafting Albert Lea (Minn.) Coll., 1973-75. Patentee in field. Mem. choir Grace Bapt. Ch., Owatonna, 1965—. Republican. Home: 1050 11th Ave NE Owatonna MN 55060-1985

DOUGLAS, DAVID WAYNE, mechanical design consultant; b. Athens, Ohio, Nov. 26, 1960. Jr. designer Autopak Systems, Columbus, Ohio, 1977-79; lead mech. designer Liebert Corp., Columbus, Ohio, 1979-94; mech. design cons. Vanner Weldon, Inc., Hilliard, Ohio, 1994—. Advisor, program planner Youth Groups, Mt. Gilend, 1990-95. Mem. Am. Motorcycle Assn. Office: Vanner Weldon Inc 5282 Reynolds Dr Hilliard OH 43026-1260

DOUGLAS, GEORGE HALSEY, writer, educator; b. East Orange, N.J., Jan. 9, 1934; s. Halsey M. and Harriet Elizabeth (Goldbach) D.; A.B. with honors in Philosophy, Lafayette Coll., 1956; M.A., Columbia U., 1966; Ph.D., U. Ill., 1968; m. Rosalind Braun, June 19, 1961; 1 son, Philip. Tech. editor Bell Telephone Labs., Whippany, N.J., 1958-59; editor Agrl. Expt. Sta., U. Ill., Urbana, 1961-66, instr. Dept. English, 1966-68, asst. prof. English, 1968-77, assoc. prof. English, 1977-88; prof. English, 1988— . Mem. Am. Studies Assn., MLA, Am. Bus. Communication Assn. (editor jour. bus. communication 1968—). Author: H.L. Mencken Critic of American Life, 1978, The Teaching of Business Communication, 1978, Rail City: Chicago and Its Railroads, 1981, Edmund Wilson's America, 1983, Women of the Twenties, 1986, The Early Days of Radio Broadcasting, 1987, The Smart Magazines, 1991, All Aboard: The Railroad in American Life, 1992, Education Without Impact: How Our Universities Fail the Young, 1992, Skyscraper: A Social History of the Tall Building in America; editor: History of Bus. Writing; contbr. articles to profl. jours, television documentaries. Home: 2125 Melrose Dr Champaign IL 61820-7547 Office: U Ill Dept English Urbana IL 61801

DOUGLAS, KENNETH JAY, food products executive; b. Harbor Beach, Mich., Sept. 4, 1922; s. Harry Douglas and Xenia (Williamson) D.; m. Elizabeth Ann Schweizer, Aug. 17, 1946; children: Connie Ann, Andrew Jay. Student, U. Ill., 1940-41, 46-47; J.D., Chgo. Kent Coll. Law, 1950; grad., Advanced Mgmt. Program, Harvard, 1962. Bar: Ill. 1950, Ind. 1952. Spl. agt. FBI, 1950-54; dir. indsl. relations Dean Foods Co., Franklin Park, Ill., 1954-64, v.p. fin. and adminstrn., 1964-70, chmn. bd., chief exec. officer, 1970-87, chmn. bd., 1987-89, vice-chmn., 1989-92; bd. dirs. Richardson Electonics, Ltd., Andrew Corp., Loyola Univ. Health System; chmn. West Suburban Med. Ctr. Chmn. bd. trustees West Suburban Hosp. Med. Ctr., Oak Park, Ill.; mem. bd. overseers Ill. Inst. Tech./Chgo.-Kent Coll. Law; mem. Chgo. Com. With USNR, 1944-46. Mem. Chgo. Club, Econ. Club, Execs. Club, Comml. Club (Chgo.), Oak Park Country Club, River Forest Tennis Club, Steamboat Springs (Colo.) Country Club, Old Baldy Country Club (Wyo.). Republican. Office: 1101 Lake St Ste 403 Oak Park IL 60301-1048

DOUGLAS, ROBERT LEE, lawyer; b. Chgo., Nov. 12, 1936; s. Clinton Arnold and Blance Omara (Perkins) D.; m. Ida Marie Chalstrom, Mar. 18, 1960; 1 child, Clinton Arnold II. BA, Eastern Ill. U., 1961; LLB, U. Ill., 1965. Bar: Ill. 1965, U.S. Dist. Ct. (no. dist.) 1966, U.S. Ct. Appeals (7th cir.) 1966, U.S. Dist. Ct. (ea. dist.) 1968, U.S. Dist. Ct. (so. dist.), U.S. Supreme Ct. 1983. Assoc. Peterson, Lawry, Rall, Barber & Ross, Chgo., 1965-67; pvt. practice Robinson, Ill., 1967—; mem. U. Ill. Pres. Coun. Del. Thomas Jefferson Constnl. Conv., Chgo., 1985; profl. chmn. Am. Cancer Soc., Robinson, 1967; del. Crawpac, Robinson, 1985—. With USN, 1954-57, PTO. Mem. ABA, ATLA, Ill. Trial Lawyers Assn. (bd. mgrs. 1985-87), Crawford County Bar Assn. (ad. 1967, pres. 1978), Ill. State Bar Assn., Am. Angus Assn., Am. Legion, Quail Creek Country Club, Elks, Moose. Democrat. Methodist.

DOUGLASS, CAROL SUZANNE, counselor; b. Wichita, Kans., Nov. 27, 1955; d. Harry Marvin and Anne Eileen (Brinkman) D. BS in Psychology, U. Kans., 1977; MEd, North Tex. U., 1991. Adminstrv. asst. Campus Crusade for Christ, San Bernardino, Calif., 1977-78; campus ministry staff Campus Crusade for Christ, Tallahassee, Fla., 1979-82; campus ministry dir. Japan Campus Crusade for Christ, Tokyo, summer 1982, women's coord., 1983, campus ministry staff, summer 1985; researcher, writer editing dept. Campus Crusade for Christ, Dallas, 1984-86, counselor Japanese ministry staff, 1987—; home office coord., coord. Japan People Link, Inc., 1993—. Researcher, writer editing dept. Becoming a Friend and Lover, 1986; researcher: Building A Relationship That Lasts, 1988; editor, advisor: Faith: A 31 Day Experiment, 1985, Standing Strong in a Godless Culture: A 31 Day Experiment, 1986. Student worker Project Concern, Appalachian Mountains, 1972; coord. evangelism and discipleship Internat. Friendship Program, So. Meth U., Dallas, 1984-88; host family Internat. Friendship Program, So. Meth. U., Dallas, 1984-88. Mem. AACD, Internat. Assn. Marriage and Family Counselors, Nat. Right to Life. Home and Office: 4910 McCoy Shawnee KS 66226

DOUMA, HARRY HEIN, social service agency administrator; b. Richmond, N.Y., Mar. 12, 1933; s. Hein and Ida D. (Van Der Veer) D.; m. Carole Marie Piening; June 21, 1958; children:Daniel H., Deborah Joy, Crystal A. BA in Philosophy, Shelton Coll., 1960; MDiv, Faith Theol. Sem., 1965. Ordained to ministry, 1965. Pastor Port Monmouth (N.J.) Ch., 1955-60; chaplain Edward R. Johnstone Tng. and Research Ctr., Bordentown, N.J., 1960-65; pastor Times Beach (Mo.) Bible Ch., 1965-67, Ist Bapt. Ch., Pilot Knob, Mo., 1967-76; founder, pres., pastor Penuel, Inc., Ironton, Mo., 1973—. Author The Book of Revelation for the Layman, 1971. Mem. Rep. Presdl. Task Force. Served with USN, 1953-55. Recipient Dir.'s Cmty. Leadership award FBI of St. Louis, 1995. Home: Rt 1 Box 593 326 Michael Ln Ironton MO 63650 Office: Penuel Inc PO Box 367 Ironton MO 63650-0367

DOUTHWAITE, JULIA VIGLIONE, French literature educator; b. Seattle, Mar. 10, 1958; d. Geoffrey Kingsley Douthwaite and Mary Louise Somerville; m. Richard Raymond Viglione, June 7, 1986; children: Nicolas Charles, Maximilian Raymond. BA, U. Wash., 1981, MA, 1984; PhD, Princeton U., 1990. Asst. prof. French Ariz. State U., Tempe, 1989-91, U. Notre Dame, Ind., 1991—. Author: Exotic Women: Literary Heroines and Cultural Strategies in Ancien Regime France, 1992. Recipient Clifford prize Am. Soc. for Eighteenth-Century Studies, 1995; NEH fellow, 1993, 95—, Lilly Endowment fellow, 1992. Office: Univ Notre Dame Dept Romance Lang and Lit 343 O'Shaughnessy Notre Dame IN 46556

DOUTT, GERALDINE MOFFATT, retired educational administrator; b. Warren, Mich., Apr. 16, 1927; d. Stanford and Wilhelmine (Ewaldt) Moffatt; m. Robert G. Doutt; children: Eric Robert, Gerald George. B.S. in Occupational Therapy, Eastern Mich. U., Ypsilanti, 1952, M.A. in Edn., 1959; E.D.S. in Spl. Edn., Wayne State U., Detroit, 1968. Tchr., Van Dyke Pub. Schs., Warren, 1963-65, tchr. educable mentally impaired, 1965-67, tchr. cons. for emotionally impaired, 1967-69, dir. spl. edn., 1969-90, ret. Chmn. Macomb County Interagy. Council, 1968-69. Mem. Mich. Assn. Dirs. Spl. Edn., Nat. Council Exceptional Children, Delta Kappa Gamma. Home: 22919 Playview St Saint Clair Shores MI 48082-2085 also: Treasure Island Higgins Lake PO Box 412 Higgins Lake MI 48627-0412

DOVRING, FOLKE, land economics educator, consultant; b. Rystad, Sweden, Dec. 6, 1916; came to U.S., 1960, naturalized, 1968; parents Karl Gustav and Naemi (Arnman) Ossiannilsson; m. Karin Dovring, May 30, 1943. PhD, Lund (Sweden) U., 1947. Assoc. prof. Lund U., 1947-53; statistician, economist FAO, UN, Rome, 1953-60; prof. land econs. U. Ill., Urbana, 1960-87, prof. emeritus, 1987—; cons. UN Econ. Commn. for Europe, Geneva, 1953, OECD, Paris, 1963-64, World Bank, AID, USDA, Dept. Energy, Washington, 1967-79; spkr. Yale Law Sch., 1993-94. Author: (15 books including) Riches to Rags, 1984, Productivity and Value, 1987, Farming for Fuel, 1988, Inequality, 1991, Leninism, 1996; contbr. over 200 other publs. to profl. jours. Mem. publicity campaign on fuel farming Voice of Am., Washington and other nationwide mass media, 1990-91. Rockefeller Found. fellow, 1953-54. Mem. Cosmos Club (Washington). Democrat. Home: 613 W Vermont Ave Urbana IL 61801-4824

DOVRING, KARIN ELSA INGEBORG, author, poet, playwright, communication analyst; b. Stenstorp, Sweden, Dec. 5, 1919; came to U.S., 1953, naturalized, 1968; m. Folke Dovring, May 30, 1943. Grad., Coll. Commerce, Gothenburg, Sweden, 1936; MA, Lund (Sweden) U., 1943, PhD, 1951; Phil. Licentiate, Gothenburg U., 1947. Journalist several Swedish daily newspapers and weekly mags., 1940-60; tchr. Swedish colls.; rsch. assoc. of Harold Lasswell Yale U., New Haven, 1953-78; fgn. corr. Swedish newspapers, Italy, Switzerland, France and Germany, 1956-60; freelance writer, journalist, 1960—; represented by Joseph Nicoletti Hollywood, Calif., 1994—; vis. prof. Internat. U., The Vatican, Rome, 1958-60, Gottingen (W.Ger.) U., 1962; lectr. U.S. Army, Peace Corps, numerous univs. including Yale U., U. Wis., McGill U., U. Iowa, U. Warsaw, Poland; rsch. assoc. U. Ill., Urbana, 1968-69; invited contbr. Social Sci. Rsch. Coun., 1988; featured speaker Ann. Conf. Law and Policy, Yale U. Law Sch., 1992, 93; interviewee radio and TV programs; writer Ill. Alliance to Prevent Nuclear War, radio, theater; Hollywood songwriter; plays for TV movies. Author: Songs of Zion, 1951, Land Reform as a Propaganda Theme, 3d edit., 1965, Road of Propaganda, 1959, Optional Society, 1972, Frontiers of Communication, 1975 (short stories) No Parking This Side of Heaven, 1982, Harold D. Lasswell: His Communication with a Future, 1987, 2d edit., 1988, Forked Tongue? Body-Snatched English in Political Communications, 1989, (novel) Heart in Escrow, 1990, (poems) Faces in a Mirror, 1995, Shadows on a Screen, 1996; contbr. numerous articles to mags. Recipient Swedish Nat. award for short stories Bonniers Pub. House Stockholm, 1951. Mem. NOW, Société Jean Jacques Rousseau of Geneva (hon. life), Inst. Freedom of Press (life asso.), Internat. Biog. Centre (Cambridge, England) (hon., adv. coun.). Democrat. Address: 613 W Vermont Ave Urbana IL 61801-4824 Office: care Creative Network Nicoletti Music Co PO Box 2818 Newport Beach CA 92659

DOW, JEAN LOUISE, school system business administrator; b. Mattoon, Ill., Dec. 20, 1955; d. Paul Leroy and Maria (Brandlhofer) Smith; m. Chris Alan Pfeiffer, June 1, 1974 (div. Nov. 1979); 1 child, Lisa Marie; m. Max L. Balch, Jr.; 1 child, Alex Max. BS in Bus., Ea. Ill. U., 1977, MBA, 1980, PhD, 1993. Office mgr. ED Buxton & Assocs., Charleston, Ill., 1974-77; personnel mgr. Unibuilt Structures, Charleston, 1977-80; asst. dir./bus. Eastern Ill Area Spl. Edn., Mattoon, 1980—. Ill. Assn. Sch. Bus. Ofcls. (scholarship 1984, com. mem. 1984—), Assn. Sch. Bus. Ofcls. (exhibitors scholarship 1990), Ill. Adminstrs. Spl. Edn. Republican, Kappa Delta Pi. Baptist. Avocations: sewing; jogging; swimming; racquetball; tennis.

DOW, WILLIAM GOULD, electrical engineer, educator; b. Faribault, Minn., Sept. 30, 1895; s. James Jabez and Myra Amelia (Brown) D.; m. Edna Lois Sontag., Oct. 24, 1924 (dec. Feb. 1963); children—Daniel Gould, David Sontag; m. Katherine Bird Keene, Apr. 2, 1968; stepchildren—John S. Keene, Margaret Keene Hannan, Karen Keene Day. BS, U. Minn., 1916, EE, 1917; MSE, U. Mich., 1929; DSc (hon.), U. Colo., 1980. Registered profl. engr., Mich. Diversified engrng. and bus. experience, 1917-26; faculty, dept. elec. engrng. U. Mich., Ann Arbor, 1926-65; prof. elec. engrng. U. Mich., 1945-65, chmn. dept. elec. engrng., 1958-64, prof. emeritus, 1966—; sr. research geophysicist Space Physics Research Lab., 1966-71; electronics cons. Nat. Bur. Standards, 1945-55; research staff Radio Research Lab., Harvard, 1943-45, assignment, U.K., winter 1944-45; sci. adv. com. Harry Diamond Labs., 1953-64; bus. mgr. Lang. Studies Abroad, Spain, summers, 1965-74; Mem. vacuum tube devel. com. NDRC, World War II; (European vacuum tube research survey), 1953; mem. rocket and satellite research panel, 1946-60; U.S. tech. panel on rocketry IGY, 1956-59; made world tour for space research and engrng. edn. survey, 1969-70; Charter mem. bd. trustees Environmental Research Inst. Mich., 1972-90, trustee emeritus, 1990—. Author: Fundamentals of Engineering Electronics, 1937, rev. 1952, Very High Frequency Techniques (co-author), 2 vols, 1947; Contbr. tech. articles in field; patentee trochoidal nuclear fusion system. Served as lt. C.E. U.S. Army, World War I. Recipient medal, award in elec. engrng. edn. IEEE, 1963. Fellow IEEE (bd. editors 1941-54), Engrng. Soc. Detroit, AAAS; mem. AAUP, Am. Phys. Soc., Am. Inst. Aeros. and Astronautics, Am. Geophys. Union, Nat., Mich. socs. profl. engrs., Am. Astronautical Soc., N.Y. Acad. Scis., Am. Soc. Engrng. Edn., Am. Welding Soc., Nat. Electronics Conf. (dir. 1949-52, chmn. bd. 1951), Sigma Xi, Tau Beta Pi, Eta Kappa Nu. Episcopalian. Clubs: Mason. (Minn.), Cosmos (Washington). Home: 915 Heatherway St Ann Arbor MI 48104-2833

DOWD, JAMES PATRICK, bookseller, writer; b. Chgo., Apr. 26, 1937; s. James Patrick and Mary Margaret (Healy) D.; m. Frances Marie Allevato, Aug. 4, 1962; children—Mary Frances, Daniel James, Matthew Joseph. Student Wright Jr. Coll., 1956-58, Harper Coll., 1984, Elgin Community Coll., 1986, AS, 1988. With Spraying Systems Co., Wheaton, Ill., 1958-78, owner operator Dowd's Book Shoppe, St. Charles, Ill., 1978-80; tech. specialist Fermi Nat. Accelerator Lab., Batavia, Ill., 1980-86, task order adminstr., 1986-88, fabrication specialist, 1986-92; retired 1992. mem. SSC task force, 1984-88, Elgin (Ill.) Community Coll., 1986-88; hist. cons. Potawatomi Indian Statue Com., St. Charles. Editor: Life of Black Hawk, 1974. Author: Built Like A Bear, 1979, Custer Lives, 1983, The Potawatomi-A Native American Legacy, 1988; contbr.: Images of the Mystic Truth, 1981, Some Misconceptions of Custer and the Battle of the Little Big Horn, 1986, On Becoming and Being a Neshnabe, 1988, Alien, 1988, Great Poets of the Western World, 1989, All Same...All Same..., 1989, Footsteps Along the Fox, 1989, Indian Paul Revere, 1990, Wabansi, 1992. Mem. Roman Cath. Ch., Chgo. With U.S. Army, 1961-63. Mem. First Am.'s Coun. of Friends (treas.), Chgo. Corral of Westerners (assoc. editor). Avocations: collector of scarce and rare western Americana, Northern Ill. Field Archaeology. Home: 38w281 Toms Trail Dr Saint Charles IL 60175-6037 Office: Fermi Nat Accelerator Lab PO Box 500 Batavia IL 60510-0500

DOWDEN, CRAIG PHILLIPS, human resources executive; b. Cleve., Dec. 11, 1947; s. Edmund Van Dyke and Margaret (Phillips) D.; m. Jennie Riffe, June 4, 1970; children: Brett, Travis. BS in Indsl. Mgmt., Purdue U., 1970, MS Indsl. Rels., 1972. Adminstr. union rels. GE Silicones, Waterford, N.Y., 1972-73; compensation specialist GE Maj. Appliance, Columbia, Md., 1973-74; union rels. specialist GE Appliance Components, Ft. Wayne, Ind., 1974-75; mgr. rels. GE Mining Products, Houston, 1975-77; mgr. personnel practices GE Carboloy Systems, Warren, Mich., 1977-79, mgr. union rels., 1979-84; dir. employee rels. OMI Internat. Corp., Warren, 1984-87; mgr. employee rels. GE Carboloy Systems, Warren, 1987; dir. human resources Carboloy Inc., Warren, 1987-90; v.p. human resources Thrall Car Mfg. Co., Chicago Heights, Ill., 1990-91, v.p. adminstrn., 1991—. Pres. Calumet coun. Boy Scouts Am. Mem. Soc. for Human Resource Mgmt. Home: 3115 Heather Hill Ct Flossmoor IL 60422-2024 Office: Thrall Car Mfg Co 2521 State St Chicago Heights IL 60411-4357

DOWDEN, RUSSELL H., JR., career officer; b. Bauxite, Ark., Jan. 13, 1943; s. Russell H. Sr. and Donnie Lee (Watts) D.; m. Linda Marilyn Fowler, Aug. 19, 1963; children: Kevin Reed, Leigh Ann Dowden Chester, Stacy Lynn. BS in Acctg., Ark. State U., 1965; MBA in MIS, Mgmt., Ind. U., 1975; diploma, U.S. Army War Coll., 1985. Commd. 2d lt. U.S. Army, 1980, advanced through grades, 1995; comptr. U.S. Ctrl. Command, Tampa, Fla., 1980-83; chief fin. svcs. U.S. Army Europe, Heidelberg, Germany, 1983-84; student U.S. Army War Coll., Carlisle, Pa., 1984-85; dir. long range plans U.S. Army Fin. and Acctg. Ctr., Indpls., 1985-87; dir. resource mgmt. U.S. Army Signal Ctr., Ft. Gordon, Ga., 1987-89; comdr. 7th fin. group U.S. VII Corps, Stuttgart, Germany, 1989-91; dir. combat devels. Soldier Support Ctr., Ft. Benjamin Harrison, Ind., 1991-92; comdt. U.S. Army Fin. Sch., Ft. Benjamin Harrison, Ind., 1992-94; spl. asst. to commdg. gen. Soldier Support Ctr., Ft. Benjamin Harrison, Ind., 1994—. Contbr. articles to profl. jours. Chmn. Combined Fed. Campaign, Ft. Benjamin Harrison, 1991; Eagle awards com. Boy Scouts Am., Indpls., 1994-95. Named Educator or Yr., Asst. Sec. of Army, 1994; named to Hall of Heroes, Ark. State U., 1994. Mem. U.S. Army Fin. Corps Assn. (pres. 1992-94, Disting. Mem. of Regiment 1992, Fin. Corps Hall of Fame 1992), Am. Soc. Mil. Comptrs. (pres. 1986-87), Assn. U.S. Army, (treas., membership chair 1984-94), Fin. Corps Regimental Assn. (pres. 1992-94), Lambda Chi Alpha. Home: 652 Lawton Loop Indianapolis IN 46216 Office: Office of Commdg Gen Soldier Support Center Fort Harrison IN 46216

DOWDY, JOHN, company executive; b. St. Joseph, Mo., July 29, 1947. BS in Computer Sci., U. Mo., 1974. Sr. tech. specialist Encore Computer Corp., Earth City, Mo., 1976-93; pres. Portable Innovations, Inc., St. Charles, Mo., 1994—. With U.S. Army, 1967-71, Vietnam; USAR, 1990-91, Desert Storm. Mem. Nat. Assn. Factoring Profls. Office: Portable Innovations Inc PO Box 52 Cottleville MO 63338-0052

DOWDY, LINDA KATHERINE, psychiatric and geriatric nurse; b. Jonesboro, Ark., Aug. 15, 1943; d. Eugene Joe and N. Katherine (Pierce) Riegler; m. Luther Joe Dowdy, Aug. 15, 1983; children: Wendy E., Kenneth E. and Katherine H. Garrison. Diploma, St. John's Sch. Nursing, Springfield, Mo., 1974; student, So. Meth. U., Drury Coll., S.W. Mo. State U. Cert. gerontol. nurse. Institutional adv. nurse Div. Aging Div. of Health, State of Mo., Springfield, 1979-83; dir. nursing Greene County Nursing and Health Ctr., Springfield, 1983-85; dir. community health svcs. ARC, Springfield, 1985-88; staff sr. adult psychiat. unit. St. John's Regional Health Ctr., Springfield, 1988-92, staff nurse psychiat. ICU, 1988-95; unit coord. Mercy Villa St. Johns Regional Health Ctr., Springfield, 1995—; profl. practice com. St. John's Regional Health Ctr., 1992-94, sys. rev. com., 1994-95. Chmn. staying healthy after 50 com. Sr. Outreach Program, St. John's Regional Health Ctr., Springfield, Mo. Recipient Health Edn. award Am. Cancer Soc., 1987. Mem. Mo. League of Nursing. Home: 4786 S Farm Rd 213 Rogersville MO 65742-9412 Office: St Johns Regional Health C Marion Ctr A Unit 1235 E Cherokee St Springfield MO 65804-2203

DOWEIKO, JEANETTE MARIE, orientation and mobility specialist, educator; b. Milw., June 15, 1955; d. Charles Walter and Jean Ann (Krueger) Snyder; m. Harold E. Doweiko, Aug. 4, 1984. BS, U. Wis., Milw., 1978; MA, U. No. Colo., 1980; MS in Edn., No. Ill. U., 1989. Cert. tchr., Minn., Tex. Tchr. visually impaired Dawson (Minn.)-Boyd Sch. Dist., 1984-88; orientation and mobility specialist Ceder River Ednl. Svcs. Coop., Austin, Minn., 1988-91; V.I./O. & M. specialist La Crosse (Wis.) Sch. Dist., 1991—. Mem. Assn. for Edn. and Rehab. Blind and Visually Impaired (cert.), Ill. Assn. Orientation and Mobility Specialists, Kappa Delta Pi. Home: 1207 Oak Ave N Onalaska WI 54650-2121

DOWNER, ROBERT NELSON, lawyer; b. Newton, Iowa, July 15, 1939; s. Lowell William and Mabel Mary (Hannon) D.; m. Jane Alice Glafka, May 29, 1971; children: Elise Michele, Andrew Nelson. BA, U. Iowa, 1961, JD, 1963. Bar: Iowa 1963, U.S. Dist. Ct. (so. dist.) Iowa 1963, U.S. Dist. Ct. (no. dist.) Iowa 1964. Assoc. Meardon Law Office, Iowa City, 1963-68; ptnr. Meardon, Sueppel & Downer, Iowa City, 1969-71, Meardon, Sueppel, Downer & Hayes, Iowa City, 1972—; dir., sec. KRNA, Inc., Iowa City, 1975—, Iowa City Tennis & Fitness Ctr., 1987-93; trustee The Oaknoll Found., Iowa City, 1990—; dir. Christian Retirement Svcs., Inc., Iowa City, 1967-82, Iowa State Bar Found., 1996—. Pres. Greater Iowa City Area C. of C., 1979; bd. trustees Iowa City Pub. Libr., 1971-75; chair adminstrv. bd. First United Meth. Ch., Iowa City, 1985-87; del. Rep. Nat. Conv., New Orleans, 1988; mem. Iowa Supreme Ct. Commn. on Continuing Legal Edn., 1975-83, Task Force on Domestic Abuse, 1993-94; bd. dirs. Iowa City Area Devel. Group, 1993—. Recipient Excellence in Svc. award Legal Svcs. Corp. Iowa, 1996. Fellow Am. Coll. Trust & Estate Counsel, Am. Bar Found., Iowa State Bar Found.; mem. ABA, Iowa State Bar Assn. (chair probate, property and trust law com. 1988-90, chair probate sect. 1990-93, v.p. 1993-94, pres.-elect 1994-95, pres. 1995-96), Johnson County Bar Assn. (pres. 1976), Rotary Club Iowa City (pres. 1988-89). Republican. Methodist. Home: 2029 Rochester Ct Iowa City IA 52245-3246 Office: Meardon Sueppel Downer & Hayes PLC 122 S Linn St Iowa City IA 52240-1830

DOWNEY, CHRISTINE, state legislator; b. Abilene, Kans., Mar. 26, 1949; children: Amy, Matthew, Erin. Elem. and mid. sch. tchr., 1975-93, Kans. state senator Dist. 31, 1996—; adj. prof. Bethel Coll., 1990-93. Pres., bd. dirs. Newton Cmty. Children's Choir, 1991-92. Mem. Kans. Nat. Edn. Assn. (pres. 1990), Newton Nat. Edn. Assn. (pres. 1989). Home: 1205 Boyd Ave Newton KS 67114-1574*

DOWNEY, DEOBORAH ANN, systems specialist; b. Xenia, Ohio, July 22, 1958; d. Nathan Vernon and Patricia Jaunita (Ward) D. Assoc. in Applied Sci., Sinclair C.C., 1981, student, 1986-91; BA, Capital U., 1994. Jr. programmer, project mgr. Cole-Layer-Trumble Co., Dayton, Ohio, 1981-82; sr. programmer, analyst, project leader Systems Architects Inc., Dayton, 1982-84, Systems and Applied Sci. Corp. (now Computer Sci. Corp.), Dayton, 1984; analyst Unisys, Dayton, 1984-87; systems programmer Computer Sci. Corp., Fairborn, Ohio, 1987—; cons. computer software M&S Garage/Body Shop, Beavercreek, Ohio, 1986-87. Mem. NAFE, Am. Motorcyclist Assn., Sinclair C. C. Alumni Assn., Cherokee Nation Okla., Cherokee Nat. Hist. Soc. Democrat. Mem. United Ch. of Christ.

DOWNEY, JOHN WILHAM, composer, pianist, conductor, educator; b. Chgo., Oct. 5, 1927; s. James Bernard and Augustina (Haas) D.; m. Irusha Czuszakivna; children: Lida, Marc. MusB, DePaul U., 1945; MusM, Chgo. Mus. Coll., 1951; Docteur es Lettres (PhD), U. Paris-Sorbonne, 1957; Prix de Composition (scholar), Paris Conservatory, 1956. Assoc. prof. Chgo. City Coll., 1958-64; prof. music U. Wis., Milw., 1964-86, disting. prof., 1986—; lectr. music theory De Paul U., Chgo., 1960-64, Roosevelt U., Chgo., 1961. Author: La Musique Populaire dans l'Oeuvre de Bela Bartok, 1966; composer Eastlake Terrace (piano solo), 1959, Edges (piano solo, 1960), Pyramids (piano solo, 1961), Portrait No. 1 (piano solo, 1980), Gasparo Records, Jingalodeon for Orchestra, 1968, recorded with Cala Records, 1991, Cello Sonata, CRI label, 1968, Symphonic Modules (orchestral Suite No. 1), 1972, Agort, woodwind quintet, recorded with Orion label, 1973, Gasparo Records, 1989, Adagio Lyrico: 2 pianos, What If? (composition for mixed choir, solo timpany and brass octet), Octet for Winds, 1954, A Dolphin, voice and chamber ensemble, 1974, recorded with Orion Label, 1974, Gasparo Records, 1989, Lydian Suite, 1975, Gasparo Records, String Quartet II, 1975, Gasparo Records, 1976, Crescendo (for large percussion ensemble), 1977, High Clouds and Soft Rain (for mixed flute choir), 1977, The Edge of Space (Fantasy for Bassoon and Orch.), 1977, recorded with Chandos Records, 1978, Silhouette (solo Doublebass), 1980, Qu'en Avez-vous Fait? (for voice and piano), 1984, Prayer for string trio, 1984, Piano Trio, 1984, Declamations for Large Orch., 1985, recorded with Cala Records, 1991, Discourse for Oboe with String Orch. and Harpsichord, 1986, recorded with Cala Records, 1991, Recombinance for Doublebass and Piano, 1987, Concerto for Doublebass and Orch., 1987, recorded with Cala Records, 1991, Suite of Psalms for a cappella mixed choir, 1988, Fanfare For Freedom for symphonic winds, 1990, Call for Freedom for symphonic winds, 1991, Yad Vashem-An Impression (piano solo), 1991, (chamber orch.), 1994, Memories (piano solo) 1991, Ode to Freedom, for symphony orchestra, 1992, Symphony No. 1, 1993, Rough Road (guitar and flute), 1994, Angel Talk (for eight cellos), 1995, Rememberance-The Swing Set, Reminder-Hungry Squirrel, Reaffirmation-Red Rose, 1995, Song Suite (high voice and piano), 1995, Ghosts (for 12 violins), 1995, Soliloquy (for solo English Horn) 1996, also electronic and computer music; resident artist, MacDowell Colony, summers 1971, 75-77, 82-83, 92, 94, falls 1978, 85, Millay Colony, summer 1991; rec. artist (album) John Downey Plays John Downey, 1987; 5 orchestral works recorded by the London Symphony Orch.: Jingalodeon, Declamations, Concerto for Double Bass and Orch., Discourse for Oboe, Harpsichord and String Orch., The Edge of Space. Decorated Chevalier de l'Ordre des Arts et des Lettres, France, 1980; scholar Fulbright France, 1952-54, winter, 1979, 80, Fulbright Australia, summer, 1987, French Govt., 1954-55; teaching fellow, 1955-56; German Govt. teaching fellow, 1956-57; Copley Found. grantee, 1956-57, 57-58; recipient awards U. Wis., 1971, 73, 75, 77, 79, 83, 87, 93, 95, Ford Found., 1976, Ctr. for L.Am. Studies of the U. Wis.-Milw. award, 1988, NEA, 1977, 83, 94, Moebius award, 1985, New Music for Young Ensembles award, 1986, Walter Heinrichsen award Am. Acad. and Inst. Arts and Letters, 1990, Meet the Composer awards, 1988, 90, 92, 93; named Music Citizen of Yr. Civic Music Assn. of Milw., 1980, Musician of the Yr. Milw Sentinel, 1993; Wis. Arts Bd. Composition fellow,

1991. Mem. Am. Soc. Univ. Composers, Am. Music Ctr., ASCAP (awards 1974—), Am. Fedn. Musicians, Wis. Contemporary Music Forum (founder, chmn. 1970—), Soc. of Composers, Ctr. 20th Century Studies, De Paul U. Alumni Assn. (Disting. Alumni award 1969), Phi Kappa Phi, Delta Omicron (nat. patron), Mu Phi Alpha (Disting. Musician award 1987, other awards 1974-86), Sigma Alpha Iota (Extraordinary Mus. Achievet award Milw. Alumnae chpt. 1986). Office: U Wis Sch Fine Arts Music PO Box 413 Milwaukee WI 53201-0413

DOWNEY, JOSEPH FRANCIS, publishing executive; b. Lima, Ohio, Oct. 16, 1916; s. Thomas and Anna Elizabeth (Ley) D. LittB, Xavier U., Cin., 1939; MA in English, Loyola U., Chgo., 1946, MEd, 1951; PhL, West Baden (Ind.) Coll., 1942, STL, 1949. Ordained priest, Soc. of Jesus, Roman Catholic Ch. Asst. dean arts and sci. U. Detroit, 1951-53; registrar and instr. U. St. Mary of Lake, Mundelein, Ill., 1953-58; dean arts and scis. John Carroll U., Cleve., 1958-62; asst. provincial Detroit Jesuit Province, 1962-69; mng. editor America Mag., N.Y.C., 1969-73; dir. Loyola of Lakes Retreat House, Akron, Ohio, 1974-85; editl. dir. Loyola Univ. Press, Chgo., 1989-96. Editor: (anthology/book) Prose and Poetry for Enjoyment, 1948; copy editor: Christ Our Life, 1986, Correct Writing, 1988, Paragraph Writing Plus, 1989. Mem. Butterfield Country Club. Home: 201 Dempster St Evanston IL 60201 Office: Loyola Univ Press 3441 N Ashland Ave Chicago IL 60657

DOWNEY, NORMA JEAN, special education educator; b. St. Louis, Nov. 22, 1935; d. Richard Ott and Wilma Agnes (Gadd) Swope; m. Wilton Holt Downey, Oct. 27, 1961; children: Richard Wilton, Robert William, stepchild, Darlene Downey Jackson. BS in Spl. and Elem. Edn., U. Mo., 1977; postgrad., Maryville Coll.; MA in Edn., Wash. U., 1982. Head teller, clk. Laclede Gas Co., St. Louis, 1954-55; sales, exec. trainer Famous Barr Co., St. Louis, 1955-57; field rep. Minn. Mining and Mfg., St. Paul, 1957-60; regional sales mgr. Continental Am. Stamp Co., Jacksonville, Ill., 1960-61; dept. mgr. Famous Barr Co., St. Louis, 1961-62; with Downey Inc., 1962-77; tchr. Wentzville (Mo.) Sch. Dist., 1977; campaign mgr. D. Beestman for State Rep., St. Louis, 1982; tchr. special edn Spl. Sch. Dist., St. Louis, 1977—; adj. instr. Maryville U., 1991—. Author Keys to Success for Learning Disabled Students, 1982. Mem. Community Leadership Program for Teachers, 1991-92. Mem. NEA (bd. dirs. spl. dist. 1982—, pres. 1982-84), Conf. on Edn., Coun. for Exceptional Children, Assn. for Reterded Children, Mo. NEA (bd. dirs. 1985-91), Women In Arts, World Affairs Coun., St. Louis Leadership for Tchrs., LWV (variousactivities), Women's Polit. Caucus, Phi Delta Kappa (treas. 1995—). Democrat. Methodist. Home: 1820 Chelmsford Ct Saint Louis MO 63146-3734

DOWNING, CYNTHIA HURST, therapist, addiction and abuse specialist; b. Fort Wayne, Ind., Sept. 10, 1942; d. James Dickson Hurst and Bernadette (Dygert) Lawyer; m. James S. Downing, Sept. 9, 1961 (div. 1979); children: David, Elizabeth, Jeffrey. BA in Psychology, Ursuline Coll., 1980; MA in Human Svcs., John Carroll U., 1982; PhD, Saybrook Inst., 1991. Lic. profl. counselor, Ohio; cert. chm. dependency counselor III, Ohio; nat. cert. addiction counselor II, master addiciton counselor. Counselor United Meth. Alcohol and Chem. Counseling, Berea, Ohio, 1980-82; clin. dir. Earthrise Recovery Svcs., Inc., Chagrin Falls, Ohio, 1982—; clin. dir. chem. dependency Brentwood Hosp., Cleve., 1985; coord. case study, instr. Ctr. Applied Scis. Corp. Nat. Relapse Prevention Cert. Sch., Chgo., 1988—. Author: Triad: The Evolution of Treatment for Chemical Dependency, 1989; mem. editorial adv. bd. Behavioral Health Mgmt. mag., 1991—; contbr. articles to profl. jours. Mem. Nat. Assn. Alcoholism and Drug Abuse Counselors, Nat. Assn. Relapse Prevention Specialists (charter), Assn. Humanistic Psychology, Internat. Soc. for the Study of Dissociation. Office: Earthrise Recovery Svcs Inc 25 W Summit St Chagrin Falls OH 44022-2724

DOWNING, MAUREEN K., nurse; b. Atwood, Kans., Apr. 3, 1959; d. Glenn Arnold and Verna Mary (White) Reilley; m. Keith Irvin Downing, Apr. 8, 1978; children: Erin Hannah, Sarah Lynn, Ryan Keith.; Diploma nursing, Colby Cmty. Jr. Coll., 1980. LPN. Shift charge nurse Good Samaritan Soc., Colby, Atwood, Kans., 1980-85, Lantern Park Manor, Colby, 1988-93; owner, operator K&H Farming, Colby, 1978—; disaster coord. Lantern Park Manor, 1992-93, newsletter editor, 1991-92. Vol. PTA. Republican. Roman Catholic. Home: RR3 Box 300 Colby KS 67701

DOYLE, CONSTANCE TALCOTT JOHNSTON, physician, educator; b. Mansfield, Ohio, July 8, 1945; d. Frederick Lyman IV and Nancy Jean Bushnell (Johnston) Talcott; m. Alan Jerome Demsky, June 13, 1976; children: Ian Frederick Demsky, Zachary Adam Demsky. BS, Ohio U., 1967; MD, Ohio State U., 1971. Diplomate Am. Bd. Emergency Medicine. Intern Riverside Hosp., Columbus, Ohio, 1971-72; resident in internal medicine Hurley Hosp., U. Mich., Flint, 1972-74; emergency physician Oakwood Hosp., Dearborn, Mich., 1974-76, Jackson County (Mich.) Emergency Svcs., 1975-95; core faculty St. Joseph Merch Hosp./U. Mich. Emergency Residency, Ann Arbor, 1975-95; attending emergency physician St. Joseph Mercy Hosp., Ann Arbor, 1995—; cons. Region II EMS, 1978-79, disaster cons., co-chmn. emergency med. svcs. disaster com., 1983-95; St. Joseph Mercy Hosp., Ann Arbor, 1995—; survival flight physician helicopter rescue svc. U. Mich., 1983-91; course dir. advanced cardiac life support and chmn. advanced life support com. W.A. Foote Meml. Hosp., Jackson, 1979-85; clin. instr. emergency svcs., dept. surgery U. Mich., 1981—; faculty combined emergency medicine residency St. Joseph Mercy Hosp.-U. Mich., Ann Arbor, 1995—; instr. EMT refresher courses, Jackson County, Jackson C.C. Contbg. author: Clinical Approach to Poisoning and Toxicology, 1983, 89, May's Textbook of Emergency Medicine, 1991, Schwartz Principles and Practice of Emergency Medicine, 1992, Reisdorff Pediatric Emergency Medicine, 1993; contbr. articles to profl. jours. Fellow Am. Coll. Emergency Physicians (pres. Mich. disaster com. 1987-88, bd. dirs. Mich. 1979-88, chmn. Mich. disaster com. 1979-85, mem. nat. disaster med. svcs. com. 1983-85, chmn. 1987-88, cons. disaster mgmt. course Fed. Emergency Mgmt. Agy. 1982, treas. 1984-85, emergency med. svcs. com. 1985, pres. 1986-87, councillor 1986-87, chair steering com. policy sect., 1994—, mem. disaster sect., 1995—), Nat. Assn. Coll. Emergency Physicians (vice chair sect. of disaster med. svcs. 1990-92, nat. disaster subcom. 1989-90, chair subsection psychol. rehab. svcs., disaster med. svcs. 1992-94, chair policy and legis. 1994—, task force on hazardous materials 1993—, steering com. sect. disaster medicine 1994—, exec. com. sect. disaster medicine 1995—, sec. sect. careers in emergency medicine); mem. ACP, Am. Med. Women's Assn., Am. Assn. Women Emergency Physicians, Mich. Assn. Emergency Med. Technicians (bd. dirs. 1979-80), Careers in Emergency Medicine (sec. 1995—), Mich. State Med. Soc., Jackson County Med. Soc., Sierra Club. Jewish. Home: 1665 Lansdowne Rd Ann Arbor MI 48105-1052 Office: St Joseph Mercy Hosp Dept Emergency Medicine Ann Arbor MI 48109

DOYLE, FRANCIS ROBERT, law librarian, law educator; b. Cambridge, Mass., June 2, 1938; s. Francis Patrick and Gertrude Agnes (Shaughnessy) D.; m. Nancy Louise Gegan, Nov. 18, 1967; children: Barry, Christopher, Adam. BA in Polit. Sci., Boston U., 1963; JD, New England Sch. Law, 1972; MLS, U. Calif., Berkeley, 1977. Cert. law librarian. Reference asst. law sch. libr. Harvard U., Cambridge, Mass., 1955-67; dir. Middlesex Law Libr. Assn., Cambridge, 1967-72; reference libr. U. Calif. Law Libr., Berkeley, 1972-78; dir. law libr., prof. law Loyola U., Chgo., 1978—; bd. dirs. Law Libr. Microform Consortium, Honolulu, 1982-88, Loyola U. Employees Credit Union, Chgo., 1979—; mem. adv. bd. Health Law Inst. Loyola U., Chgo., 1984—. Author: Searching the Law--The States, 1988, 2d edit., 1994; co-author: Searching the Law, 1987; asst. editor Index to Multilateral Treaties, 1965; contbr. articles to profl. jours. Active Ill. Spina Bifida Assn., Chgo., 1987-92. Mem. ALA, Am. Assn. Law Librs. Home: 2400 Grant St Evanston IL 60201-2110 Office: Loyola U Law Libr 25 E Pearson St Chicago IL 60611-2055

DOYLE, JAMES E(DWARD), state attorney general; b. Washington, Nov. 23, 1945; s. James E. and Ruth (Bachhuber) D.; m. Jessica Laird, Dec. 21, 1966; children: Augustus, Gabriel. Student, Stanford U., 1963-66; AB in History, U. Wis., 1967; JD cum laude, Harvard U., 1972. Bar: Ariz. 1973, Wis. 1975, U.S. Dist. Ct. N.Mex. 1973, U.S. Dist. Ct. Ariz. 1973, U.S. Dist. Ct. Utah 1973, U.S. Dist. Ct. (we. dist.) Wis. 1975, U.S. Dist. Ct. (ea. dist.) Wis. 1976, U.S. Ct. Appeals (10th cir.) 1974, U.S. Ct. Appeals (7th cir.) 1985, U.S. Supreme Ct. 1989. Vol. Peace Corps, Tunisia, 1967-69; atty. DNA Legal Svcs., Chinle, Ariz., 1972-75; ptnr. Jacobs & Doyle, Madison, Wis., 1975-77; dist. atty. Dane County, Madison, 1977-83; ptnr. Doyle & Ritz, Madison, 1983-90; of counsel Lawton & Cates, Madison, 1990-91; atty. gen. State of Wis., Madison, 1991—. Mem. ABA, Wis. Bar Assn. (bd. dirs. criminal law sect. 1988), 7th Cir. Bar Assn. (chair criminal law sect. 1988-89). Democrat. Roman Catholic. Office: Office Atty Gen PO Box 7857 114 State Capitol Madison WI 53707-7857

DOYLE, JOSEPH ARTHUR, freelance sports writer; b. Shullsburg, Wis., Oct. 1, 1920; s. John Richard and Olive Bridgetta (Comiskey) D.; m. Juanita Pearl Lees, Feb. 5, 1949 (div. Oct. 1985); children: Roberta, John, Kathy, Mary, Gail, Nancy; m. Doris Ann Gapski Linville, Nov. 15, 1985; children: Mark Linville, Cheryl Linville. AB, U. Notre Dame, 1949. Lic. real estate and isn. salesman, Ind. Writer-editor South Bend (Ind.) Tribune, 1949-51, sports editor, 1951-81, emeritus sports editor and columnist, 1981—; sports copy editor Tampa (Fla.) Tribune, 1981-85; ret., 1985, freelance sports writer, 1985—. Author: Fighting Irish--A Century of Notre Dame Football, 1987. Pres. St. Joseph County Coun. for Retarded, 1964-69. With USAAF, 1943-46, ETO, lt. col. USAF Res. ret. Named Man of Yr., St. Joseph Valley Alumni Assn., 1966. Mem. Football Writers Am. (pres. 1979-80), Univ. Club, K.C., Elks. Democrat. Roman Catholic. Home: 5914 Aberdeen Dr South Bend IN 46614-6382

DOYLE, LAURETTA DARICE, secondary educator; b. Lansing, Mich., Feb. 8, 1954; d. Leo Harry and Geraldine (Hoff) D.; m. Barry Martin Frechette, July 11, 1979; children: Jedediah Doyle, Jacquetta Elyse. BS in Edn., U. Wis., 1992; MA in Edn., St. Mary's U. Minn., 1995. Cert. middle and high sch. tchr. in geography, Wis. Natural resource asst. DNR Blue Mound (Wis.) State Park, 1976-79; waiter Goble's, Mount Horeb, Wis., 1983-85; waiter, restaurant mgr. Cajun Cafe, Madison, Wis., 1985-90; waiter Botticelli's, Madison, 1991-92, Nordika, Mount Horeb, 1992-93; substitute tchr. various schs., 1992-93; teen parent coord. Cooperative Edn. Svc. Agy., Fennimore, Wis., 1993-94; learning lab coord. Dodgeville (Wis.) H.S., 1994-96; mem. bldg. cons. team Dodgeville High Sch., 1994-95, student support team, 1995-96, h.s. technology com., 1995-96; bd. dirs., acting sec. Gen. Store Whole Foods Coop, Mount Horeb, 1982-85. Bible sch. tchr. United Ch. Christ, Barneveld, Wis., 1983, Sunday sch. tchr., 1984-86, soloist ch. choir, 1985-86; vol. tchr. aide Pecatonica Elem. Sch., Hollandale, Wis., 1991. Mem. Wis. Coun. Social Studies, Assn. Am. Geographers, ASCD, Wis. Alliance Concerned with Sch.-Age Parents. Home: 1497 Paulson Rd Hollandale WI 53544-9313 Office: Dodgeville HS 912 W Chapel St Dodgeville WI 53533

DOYLE, O'BRIEN JOHN, JR., emergency medical services consultant, lobbyist; b. Detroit, July 31, 1950; s. O'Brien John Doyle Sr.; m. Sue Ann Woulf, Sept. 6, 1980; children: Catherine Ann, Colleen Elizabeth. Student, Mich. State U., 1970-72; paramedic cert., Vo-Tech. Coll., St. Paul, 1980-81; BA in Human Svcs., Metro State U., St. Paul, 1986. Exec. asst. Mich. Legislature, Lansing, 1972-77; com. aide Ill. Gen. Assembly, Chgo., 1977-79; spl. asst. Gov. Minn., St. Paul, 1979-82; ops. dir. Divine Redeemer Ambulance, South St. Paul, Minn., 1982-84; mktg. dir. Health One Transp., St. Paul, 1984-86; pres. Doyle Consulting, Apple Valley, Minn., 1986—; legis. cons. Health One Corp., Mpls., 1986—, Minn. Ambulance Assn., Mpls., 1986, 91-92, Minn. Hosp. Assn., Mpls., 1991, Mayo Med. Ctr., 1995—, Minn. Air Med. Coun., 1995—; candidate for state senate, 1988. Contbg. editor Trade Jours, 1992—; pub. Capitol Update, 1986—, Rule Promulgation in Michigan, 1973; EMS contr. to Fed. Healthcare (Clinton) Reform proposal, 1993-95; columnist Jour. Emergency Med. Svcs. Adv. 916 Vocat. Coll., White Bear Lake, Minn., 1989—. Mem. Citizens League, Osman Shrine, Scottish Rite. Roman Catholic. Home and Office: 12893 Floral Ave Apple Valley MN 55124-7971

DOYLE, RICHARD HENRY, IV, lawyer; b. Elgin, Ill., Aug. 8, 1949; s. Richard Henry and Shirley Marian (Ohms) D.; m. Debbie Kay Cahalan, Aug. 2, 1975; children: John Richard, Kerry Jane. BA, Drake U., 1971, JD, 1976. Bar: Iowa 1976, U.S. Dist. Ct. (no. and so. dists.) Iowa 1977, U.S. Ct. Appeals (8th cir.) 1977, U.S. Supreme Ct. 1986. Asst. atty. gen. Iowa Dept. Justice, Des Moines, 1976-77; assoc. Lawyer, Lawyer & Jackson, Des Moines, 1977-79; assoc. Law Offices of Verne Lawyer & Assocs., Des Moines, 1979-93, Reavely, Shinkle, Bauer, Scism, Reavely & Doyle, Des Moines, 1993, Michael J. Galligan Law Firm, P.C., Des Moines, 1994—. Contbr. articles to profl. jours. With U.S. Army, 1971-73. Fellow Iowa Acad. Trial Lawyers; mem. ABA, ATLA, Blackstone Inn of Ct., Iowa Trial Lawyers Assn., Iowa Bar Assn., Iowa State Bar Assn. (jud. adminstrn. com.), Polk County Bar Assn., SAR (registrar Iowa 1983-94, v.p. 1994—), Order of the Founders and Patriots of Am., Phi Alpha Delta (chpt. pres. 1975). Home: 532 Waterbury Cir Des Moines IA 50312-1316 Office: Michael J. Galligan Law Firm PC The Plaza 300 Walnut St Ste 5 Des Moines IA 50309-2239

DOYLE, WENDELL E., retired band director, educator; b. Higbee, Mo., July 8, 1940; s. Travis E. and Hattie Erma (Webb) D.; m. Julia Ann Vail, June 23, 1963; children: Dora Michelle, Michael E., Melissa Kae. BS in Edn., Northeast Mo. State U., 1962; MEd in Music, U. Mo., 1967. Cert. lifetime tchr., Mo. Band dir. Braymer (Mo.) C-4, 1962-68, Brookfield (Mo.) R-3, 1968-72, Platte County (Mo.) R-III, 1972-92; ret., 1992; exchange tchr. Platte County R-III Schs., Warwickshire, Eng., 1984. Pres. Barry Heights Homes Assn., 1986—; minister of music Park Bapt. Ch., Brookfield, 1968-72, Northgate Bapt. Ch., Kansas City, 1972-85. Mem. Mo. State Tchrs. Assn. (pres. Greater Kans. City dist. 1978), Music Educators Nat. Conf., Mo. Music Educators Assn., Mo. Bandmasters Assn. (sec.), Phi Delta Kappa, Phi Beta Mu (pres. 1990-91, Outstanding Band Dir. award Lambda chpt., 1993), Rotary (sec., treas. Braymer, Mo. 1966-68). Democrat. Lodge: Rotary (sec., treas. Braymer, Mo., 1966-68). Home: 2330 NW Powderhorn Dr Kansas City MO 64154-1311

DOYLE, WILLIAM JAY, II, business consultant; b. Cin., Nov. 7, 1928; s. William Jay and Blanche (Gross) D.; m. Joan Lucas, July 23, 1949; children: David L., William Jay, III, Daniel L. BS, Miami U., Oxford, Ohio, 1949; postgrad., U. Cin., 1950-51, Xavier U., 1953-54, Case Western Res. U., 1959-60. Sales rep. Diebold, Inc., Cin., 1949-52, asst. br. mgr., 1953-57, asst. regional mgr., 1957-62, regional mgr., 1962-74; founder, pres. CEO Ctrl. Bus. Group divsn. Ctrl. Bus. Equipment Co., Cin., 1974-89, chmn., 1989-95; dir. parent co. and divs. Cen. Bus. Group div. Cen. Bus. Equipment Co., Cin., 1974-95; ret., 1995; mem. area contractor's coun. Spacesaver Corp., 1985-89; speaker on bus systems, security concepts. Contbr. articles to co. and trade publs.; developer new concepts in tng., cash and securities handling, mobile and mechanized storage and filing, and other areas of bus. systems. Mem. Armstrong Chapel, Methodist ch., Indian Hill, Ohio, adminstrv. bd, 1987-89. Mem. Bus. Systems and Sales Mgmt. Assn. (nat. bd. dirs. 1977-79, 81-85, pres. 1981-83, 84-85), Inst. of Mgmt. Accts., Ivy Hills Country Club, Masons, Shriners, Republicans. Republican. Home: 7705 Pine Isle Ct Cincinnati OH 45244-2560

DOZE, CARLA SUE LARUE, critical care geriatrics nurse; b. Ardmore, Okla., Nov. 4, 1962; d. Carl C. and Beatrice E. (Knutson) LaRue; m. Devan D. Doze, Jan. 24, 1982; children: Brandon L., Michael D., Carl Ham. LPN, Seward County C.C., 1982, ADN, 1988. RN, Kans. Charge nurse, shift supr. Liberal (Kans.) Good Samaritan Ctr., 1982-88; charge nurse, shift supr. Wheat Ridge Park Care Ctr., Liberal, 1988-90, dir. of nursing, 1990-91; staff nurse Southwest Med. Ctr., Liberal, 1992-95; quality assurance coord. Good Samaritan Ctr., Liberal, Kans., 1995—; allied health program adv. bd. Seward County C.C., Liberal, 1990-91; day camp nurse Santa Fe coun. Boy Scouts Am., Liberal, 1991. Home: 822 S Calhoun Ave Liberal KS 67901-3912 Office: Liberal Good Samaritan Ctr 2160 Zinnia Ln Liberal KS 67901

DRABIK, HARRY FRANCIS, writer; b. Chgo., Sept. 7, 1944; adopted s. Stephen Joseph and Julia Emily (Thomas) D. BS, U. Minn., 1967, postgrad., 1974-75. Cert. lang. arts secondary tchr., Minn. Instr. Boy Scout Coun., Hibbing, Minn., 1962-73; tchr. Ind. Sch. Dist. 166, Grand Marais, Minn., 1968-78; survey archaeologist Ont. Heritage & Ministry Culture & Comm., Thunder Bay, Can., 1979-87; writer, rschr. Hovland, Minn., 1978—. Author: Spirit of Canoe Camping, 1981, Spirit of Winter Camping, Guide to Canoe Camping, 1987, The Real Log Cabin, 1994; contbr. numerous articles to mags., profl. jours. Plaintiff Tower Commn., Cook County, Minn., 1988-90. Grantee Ont. Heritage Found., 1979-84. Mem. Ont. Archaeol. Soc., Friends of Boundary Waters (lobbyist 1978). Liberal. Roman Catholic. Home: PO Box 547 W115 Hovland MN 55606-0547

DRAFKE, MICHAEL WALTER, business educator, consultant; b. Joliet, Ill., Mar. 23, 1954; s. Raymond and Jeanette (Reich) D.; m. Kathleen Elizabeth Little, Nov. 9, 1985; children: Adam Michael, Erik Michael, Alex Michael. AA, Coll. of DuPage, Glen Ellyn, Ill., 1974; BS, U. Nev., Las Vegas, 1976; MS, Nat. Coll. Edn., Evanston, Ill., 1983. Registered radiography technologist. Chief radiologic technologist Ivinson Meml. Hos., Laramie, Wyo., 1976; clin. instr. in radiography Sherman Hosp., Elgin, Ill., 1977-79; instr. radiography Coll. of DuPage, 1979-83, dir. radiography program, 1983-90, prof. bus., mktg. and mgmt., 1990—; continuing edn. lectr. Ill. Hosp. Assn., Naperville, 1986-90; cons. Mosby-Time-Mirror Pubs., St. Louis, 1990—, F.A. Davis Pubs., Phila., 1988—, Irwin Pubs., Homewood, Ill., 1992—, Austin Press, Flossmoor, Ill., 1993—; mktg cons., 1990—. Author: National Radiography Certification Exam 4, 1986, Trauma and Mobile Radiography, 1990—, Working in Healthcare, 1994—; editor Ill. State Soc. Radiol. Technologists Jour., 1989—; contbr. articles to profl. jours. IBM Computer grantee League for Innovation, 1988; recipient Outstanding Tchrs. award Ill. C.C. Trustees Assn., 1989, Teaching/Learning Excellence award Ill. C.C. Bd., 1993, Connections 2000 award Ill. State Bd. of Edn., 1996. Mem. NEA, Am. Mgmt. Assn., Nat. Bus. Educators Assn., Authors Guild, Am. Mktg. Assn., Ill. State Soc. Radiol. Technologists, Phi Kappa Phi. Home: 18 Evergreen Pl Lemont IL 60439-3838 Office: Coll of DuPage 22d and Lambert Glen Ellyn IL 60137-6599

DRAGOVIC, LJUBISA JOVAN, medical examiner, consultant; b. Belgrade, Yugoslavia, June 12, 1950; s. Jovan Krsto and Ikonia D.; m. Jadranka Bogdanovic, Dec. 1, 1974; children: Aleksandra, Jovan, Andrija, Aleksandar-Filip, Ana, Michael-Jakov, Adriana. MD, U. Belgrade, 1975. Diplomate Am. Bd. Pathology, Am. Bd. Anat. Pathology, Am. Bd. Neuropathology, Am. Bd. Forensic Pathology. Resident in pathology Queens U., Kingston, Ont., Can., 1978-80, chief resident, 1980-81, sr. resident, 1981-83; sr. neuropathology resident divsn. neuropathology U. Toronto, 1983-84; forensic pathology fellow Office of Chief Med. Examiner, State of Md., Balt., 1986-87; asst. med. examiner Wayne County Med.-Examiner's Office, Detroit, 1987-90, acting chief med. examiner, 1988; chief med. examiner, chief forensic pathologist Oakland County, Pontiac, Mich., 1991—; neuropathology rsch. cons. Lafayette Clinic, Detroit, 1986-92; cons. neuropathologist Harper Hosp., Detroit, 1987-92, VA Hosp., Allen Park, Mich., 1988—, Detroit Receiving Hosp., 1989-93; forensic pathology cons. Jackson (Mich.) County, 1992—. Contbr. articles to profl. jours. Recipient Russell S. Fisher award Tissue Bank Internat., 1986. Fellow Coll. Am. Pathologists; mem. AMA, U.S.-Can. Acad. Pathology, Am. Assn. Neuropathologists, Am. Acad. Forensic Scis., Internat. Soc. Neuropathology, Nat. Assn. Med. Examiners, Mich. Soc. Pathologists, Mich. Assn. Med. Examiners, Can. Assn. Pathologists. Mem. Ea. Orthodox Ch. Office: Oakland County Med Examiner 1200 N Telegraph Rd Pontiac MI 48341-1032

DRAGUN, JAMES, soil chemist; b. Detroit, July 29, 1949; s. Henry George and Stella (Kubilus) D.; married, June 16, 1973; children: Nathan, Heather. BS, Wayne State U., 1971; MS, Pa. State U., 1975, PhD, 1977. Soil chemist U.S. EPA, Washington, 1978-82, Kennedy/Jenks, San Francisco, 1982-84, E. C. Jordan, Southfield, Mich., 1984-87, Stalwart Environ., Auburn Hills, Mich., 1987-88; soil chemist, pres. Dragun Corp., Farmington Hills, Mich., 1988—; prof. Wayne State U., Detroit, U. Mass., Amherst. Author: The Soil Chemistry of Hazardous Materials, 1988; author 2 scientific handbooks; editor-in-chief Sci. Jour.; contbr. over 70 articles to profl. publs. Recipient Disting. Svc. award U.S. EPA, 1980, Disting. Svc. award Liquid Indsl. Control and Waste Mgmt. Assn., 1990. Mem. Sigma Xi, Phi Kappa Phi. Office: Dragun Corp 30445 Northwestern Hwy Ste 260 Farmington Hills MI 48334

DRAJESKE, MARK HOWARD, aeronautical engineer, software engineer; b. Chgo., Sept. 26, 1962; s. Philip William and Diane Joy (Suemnicht) D.; m. Michelle Annette Jones, Aug. 24, 1991. BS in Aero. Engring., Purdue U., 1985, MS in Aeronautics and Astronautics, 1989. Flight dynamics rsch. engr. McDonnell Aircraft Co., St. Louis, 1988-91; sr. software engr. FAAC Inc., Ann Arbor, Mich., 1991-96; rsch. engr. Cybernet Sys., Ann Arbor, Mich., 1996—. Contbr. articles to profl. jours. Mem. AIAA.

DRAKE, B. MAX, finance executive; b. Center, Ohio, Jan. 5, 1910; s. C.C. and Mirilla (Stireves) D.; m. Marion A. Hodges, June 6, 1934; children: David L., Ellen, James, Steven, Paul. BS in dairy svc., Ohio State U., 1933. Farm mgr. Scudden Dairy Farm, Friendship, Ohio, 1933-34; 4H club agent Ohio State U. at Medina County ext., Medina, Ohio, 1934-39; farm mgr. L. Bromfields Malabar Farm, Lucas, Ohio, 1939-43; gen. mgr. Noba Inc., Tiffin, Ohio, 1943-77; exec. dir. Hills Co. Ind. Dev. Comm., Hillsdale, Mich., 1991-92, Reading Tax Increment Fin. Auth., Reading, Mich., 1992—. Pres. Ohio State Libr., Columbus, 1969, Ohio State U. Agr. Alumni Assn., 1958, nat. Assn. of Animal Breeders (Pioneer award 1991), Tiffin, Ohio, 1946-51; pres. bldg. trustees Hillsdale Meth Ch., 1985. Recipient Marvin Howell award for disting. svc., 1992. Mem. Hillsdale Kiwanis Club (pres. 1984), Hillsdale C. of C. (bd. dirs. 1990). Republican. Methodist. Home: 2285 Cedar Dr Reading MI 49274

DRAKE, MICHAEL W., designer; b. Lorrain, Ohio, Apr. 6, 1952. Student, S.W. Mo. State U., Springfield, 1974. Designer Rupp Industries, Mansfield, Ohio, 1974-75, Galion (Ohio) Iron Works, 1969-70, 74, Hydranamics Inc., Galion, 1976—. Co-founder Heartbeat of Morrow City, Mt. Gilead, Ohio, 1983. Cpl. USMC, 1970-72. Home: 5067 County Road 57 Galion OH 44833-9652

DRAKE, RICHARD FRANCIS, state senator; b. Muscatine, Iowa, Sept. 28, 1927; s. Frank and Gladys (Young) D.; student Iowa State U.; BS, U.S. Naval Acad., 1950; m. Shirley Jean Henke; children: Cheryll Dee, Ricky Lee. Commd. ensign U.S. Navy, advanced through grades to lt. comdr., 1954; capt. minesweeper U.S.S. Crow; farmer, mgr., 1954—; mem. Iowa Senate, 1968—. Chmn. Young Republican Orgn. Iowa, 1954-56; adminstrv. asst. Muscatine County Rep. Com., 1956-57, chmn., 1958-66; 1st dist. chmn. Rep. party, 1966-72; chmn. Nat. Task Force Rail Line Abandonment and Curtailment; chmn. states and rail problems Midwestern Council State Govts., 1978-79. Named One of Ten Outstanding Legislators of Yr. Nat. Rep. Lesislators Assn. Mem. Farm Bur., Masons, Elks, Order Eastern Star. Lutheran. Office: State Senate State Capitol Des Moines IA 50319

DRAKE, ROBERT ALAN, state legislator, animal nutritionist, mayor; b. Canton, S.D., July 6, 1957; s. Theodore Francis and LaRayne Margaret (Hoffman) D.; m. Pamela Sue Wiechmann, 1977; children: R. Ryan, Kimberly Margaret, Kendra Kay. BS, S.D. State U., 1979, MS, 1981. Animal nutritionist McFleeg Feeds, Bowdle, S.D., 1981—; mayor City of Bowdle, 1988—; mem. S.D. Ho. of Reps., Pierre, 1995—. Supr. Edmunds County Conservation Dist., 1984—; chmn. N.E. Coun. Govts., Aberdeen, S.D., 1992—; pres. Bowdle Cmty. Club, 1985-86, Bowdle Devel. Corp., 1992—. Republican.

DRALLE, LAMBERT R., paper merchant owner; b. Milw., Oct. 3, 1929; s. Herbert Louis and Eleanor Louise (Lambert) D.; m. Marye Ann Siegert, June 16, 1951; children: Janet, Lynn, Robert, James. BBA, U. Wis., 1951. Sales rep. Dralle Paper Co., Milw., 1954-74, sales mgr., 1974-84, v.p., CEO, 1984-93, pres., CEO, 1993—; adv. com. Hudson Pulp and Paper Corp., N.Y.C., 1967-70; adv. bd. United Group, Monroe, La., 1985-90, Consolidated Distributors, Monroe, La., 1990-95. With USN, 1951-54. Republican. Lutheran. Home: 18880B Wilderness Ct Brookfield WI 53045 Office: Dralle Paper Co N29W22798 Marjean Ln Waukesha WI 53186

DRAPER, DAVID EUGENE, seminary president; b. Hagerstown, Md., Feb. 6, 1949; s. James Thomas and Irene Virginia (Seylar) D.; m. Linda Marie Mills, June 26, 1971; 1 child, Andrew Thomas. BS, Frostburg (Md.) State Coll., 1971; MDiv, Winebrenner Sem., Findlay, Ohio, 1979; MEd, Bowling Green (Ohio) U., 1985, PhD, 1988. Ordained to ministry Chs. of God, Gen. Conf., 1978. Pastor Mt. Pleasant Ch. of God, Mt. Victory, Ohio, 1976-79; assoc. in ministry Chs. of God, Findlay, 1979-82; dir. devel. Winebrenner Sem., Findlay, 1982-85, v.p., 1985-88, pres., 1988-90; trustee U. Findlay, 1989-91; mem. Fellowship of Evang. Sem. Pres.; bd. dirs. Great

Commn. Ministries, 1992—. Co-author: Bound but Free, 1978. Adv. bd. Trust Corps Bank, Findlay, 1987-89. Lilly grantee, 1987. Republican. Home: 3218 St Andrews Dr Findlay OH 45840-2945 Office: Winebrenner Sem 701 E Melrose Ave Findlay OH 45840-4416

DRAPER, NORMAN RICHARD, statistician, educator; b. Eng., Mar. 20, 1931; came to U.S., 1955; s. Norris and Helen (Draper). BA, Cambridge (Eng.) U., 1954, MA, 1958; PhD, U. N.C., 1958. Tech. officer, statistician plastics div. Imperial Chem. Industries, 1958-60; mem. Math. Research Center, U. Wis.-Madison, 1960-61, mem. faculty, 1961—, prof. statistics, 1966—, chmn., 1967-73; vis. prof. Imperial Coll., London, fall 1967, 68. Author: (with H. Smith) Applied Regression Analysis, 1966, 2d edit., 1981, (with G.E.P. Box) Evolutionary Operation, 1969, (with W. E. Lawrence) Probability: An Introductory Course, 1970, (with G.E.P. Box) Empirical Model Building and Response Surfaces, 1987. Recipient Max-Planck-Forschungs-Preis, Alexander von Humboldt-Stiftung, 1994. Fellow Royal Statis. Soc., Am. Statis. Assn., Inst. Math. Statistics, Am. Soc. Quality Control (lectr. 1963—); mem. Internat. Statis. Inst., Biometric Soc. Address: Univ of Wisconsin 1210 W Dayton St Madison WI 53706-1613

DRASKOVITS, JAMES F., investment broker; b. South Bend, Ind., Nov. 20, 1940. Investment broker Paine Webber, South Bend, 1976-78, Prudential Securities, South Bend, 1978-88, A G Edwards & Sons Inc., South Bend, 1988—. With USN, 1959-61. Office: A G Edwards & Sons Inc PO Box 1378 205 W Jefferson South Bend IN 46624

DRAY, DWIGHT LEROY, retired school system administrator; b. Carrollton, Ohio, Apr. 15, 1918; s. William Andrew and Florence Emma Dray; m. Nellie Pauline Clark, Jan. 29, 1941 (dec. 1981); children: Mark Stanley, Paula Louise Dray Claypool; m. Eva Mae King, July 17, 1982. BA, Mount Union Coll., Alliance, Ohio, 1957; MA, U. Toledo, Ohio, 1964; postgrad., U. Akron, Ohio. Investigator Ohio Dept. Liquor Control, Columbus, 1946-48; carpenter Kintz Constrn. Co., Alliance, Ohio, 1948-50; clerk Penn R.R., Canton, Ohio, 1950-56; tchr. Perkins local schs., Sandusky, Ohio, 1956-63; elem., jr. high prin. Mapleton Local Schs., Ashland, Ohio, 1963-70; dir. schs. Mene Grande Oil Co., Caracus, Venezuela, 1970-71; supt. schs. Madison County local schs., Lore City, Ohio, 1971-75; curriculum coord. Guernsey Co. schs., Cambridge, Ohio, 1975-84. Contbr. articles to profl. jours. Councilman Cambridge City Coun., 1979-80, 91-95; pres. Cambridge Rotary Found., 1988-93; pres. Guernsey County Scholarship Found., 1990-93; chmn. fin. com. Boy Scouts Am., Zanesville, 1989-90. With U.S. Army, 1942. Named Educator of Yr. Phi Delta Kappa, Zanesville, 1983; Ford Found. scholar Western Carolina U., 1971; Paul Harris fellow Rotary Internat., Evansville, Ind., 1989. Mem. Am. Legion (commander 1960-61), Disabled Am. Vets (life), Phi Delta Kappa, Rotary (pres. 1983-84), Masons. Republican. Protestant. Home: 925 Avon Dr Cambridge OH 43725-2123

DRAZNIN, WAYNE MICHAEL, artist, educator; b. Chgo., May 3, 1950; s. Herman J. and Florence L. (Patt) D. BA, Columbia Coll., Chgo., 1987; MFA, U. Ill., Chgo., 1989. Instr. Columbia Coll., Chgo., 1987-89; assoc. prof. Cleve. Inst. Art, 1989—; intern Mus. Contemporary Photography, Chgo., 1985-87; dir. New Works Gallery, U. Ill., Chgo., 1987-89. Artist; installations include Surveillance Series, 1993, Marked as AnOther, 1995; guest curator and curatorial cons.; author articles. Lilly Found. grantee, 1990; Fulbright scholar, Belgrade, 1991 (cancelled by U.S. State Dept. due to civil war). Home: 322 Overlook Park Dr Cleveland OH 44110 Office: Cleve Inst Art 11141 East Blvd Cleveland OH 44106

DREBUS, JOHN RICHARD, systems engineer; b. Madison, Wis., Feb. 11, 1951; s. Richard William and Hazel Mae (Redford) D.; m. Pamela Kay Perfetto, Jan. 5, 1974; children: Bethea Lynn, Scott Bryan, Cynthia Ann. BA in Zoology, Ind. U., 1973; MS in Mgmt., Purdue U., 1983; Honor Grad., Command & Gen. Staff Coll., 1991. Commd. 2d lt. U.S. Army, 1973, advanced through grades to lt. col., 1994; armor officer U.S. Army, Baumholder, Germany, 1973-77; armor officer, capt. U.S. Army, Fort Knox, Ky., 1977-81; mfg. assoc. Am. Can Co., Hammond, Ind., 1983-84; project mgr. The System Works, Marietta, Ga., 1984-87; bus. rels. specialist Electronic Data Systems, Warren, Mich., 1988-91; supr. Electronic Data Systems, Ypsilanti, Mich., 1991-93; systems engr. Electronic Data Systems, Troy, Mich., 1993—; project officer Army Force Modernization Team, Fort Knox, 1979-80. Contbr. articles to profl. jours. Dir. sch. bd. Faith Luth. Sch., Marietta, Ga., 1986-88; mem. bd. evangelism St. John Luth. Ch., Rochester, Mich., 1990-92; treas. ann. fund drive St. John Luth. Sch., Rochester, 1992-95; bd. mem. Boy Scout Troop 188, Rochester Hills, Mich., 1993-95. Lt. col. USAR, 1995—. Recipient Disting. Mil. Grad award U.S. Army, 1973, Army Commendation medal, 1977, Army Parachute Badge, 1973. Mem. IEEE, N.Y. Acad. Sci., U.S. Army Armor Assn., Assn. of U.S. Army, Mensa. Republican. Lutheran. Home: 1631 Ridgecrest Rd Rochester Hills MI 48306-3159 Office: Electronic Data Systems 300 E Big Beaver Troy MI 48738

DREBUS, RICHARD WILLIAM, pharmaceutical company executive; b. Oshkosh, Wis., Mar. 30, 1924; s. William and Frieda (Schmidt) D.; m. Hazel Redford, June 7, 1947; children—William R., John R., Kathryn L. Belin. BS, U. Wis., 1947, MS, 1949, PhD, 1952. Bus. trainee Marathon Paper Corp., Menasha, Wis., 1951-52; tng. mgr. Ansul Corp., Marinette, Wis., 1952-55; asst. to v.p. Ansul Corp., 1955-58, marketing mgr., 1958-60; dir. personnel devel. Mead Johnson & Co., Evansville, Ind., 1960-65; v.p. corporate planning Mead Johnson & Co., 1965-66, internat. pres., 1966-68; v.p. internat. div. Bristol-Myers Co. (merger Mead Johnson & Co. with Bristol-Myers Co.), N.Y.C., 1968-77, sr. v.p., 1977-78, v.p. parent co., 1978-85, sr. v.p. pharm. research and devel. div., 1985-89, ret., 1989. Past bd. dirs. Jr. Achievement S.E. Conn., Meriden Silver Mus.; past bd. dirs. Meriden-Wallngford United Way, chmn. fund raising drive, 1988-89; trustee emeritus Quinnipiac Coll. Served with AUS, 1943-45. Decorated Combat Inf. Badge, Purple Heart, Bronze Star. Mem. APA, N.Y. Acad. Scis., U. Wis. Bascom Hill Soc., Oshkosh Country Club, Oskhosh Power Boat Club, North Shore Country Club, Phi Delta Kappa. Home: 3720 Pau Ko Tuk Ln Oshkosh WI 54901-7332

DRENGLER, WILLIAM ALLAN JOHN, lawyer; b. Shawano, Wis., Nov. 18, 1949; s. William J. and Vera J. (Simmonds) D.; m. Kathleen A. Hintz, June 18, 1983; children: Ryan, Jeffrey, Brittany. BA, Am. U., 1972; JD, Marquette U., 1976. Bar: Wis. 1976, U.S. Dist. Ct. (ea. and we. dists.) Wis. 1976. Assoc. Herrling, Swain & Drengler, Appleton, Wis., 1976-78; dist. atty. Outagamie County, Appleton, 1979-81; corp. counsel Marathon County, Wausau, Wis., 1981—; vice chmn. Wis. Council on Criminal Justice, Madison, 1983-87. Mem. nat. Dem. delegation, 1974-76; mem. adminstrv. com. Wis. Dems., Madison, 1977-81, 86-88; chmn. local Selective Svc. Bd., Wausau, 1982-89; judge adv. CPT, Wis. Army N.G., 1989—; bd. dirs. Wausau Youth/Little League Baseball, 1988—, team mgr., 1994—. Mem. ABA (chair com. on govt. lawyers, sect. state and local govt. 1991-93, bylaws com. govt. and pub. sect. lawyers divsn. 1993—), LWV, KC, Nat. Assn. County Civil Attys. (dir. 1986-88, v.p. 1988-91, pres. 1991-92), Nat. Assn. Counties (bd. dirs. 1991-92, taxation and fin. steering com. 1991-93, deferred compensation adv. com. 1993-95, justice and pub. safety steering com. 1994-95), State Bar Wis. (govt. lawyers divsn., bd. dirs. 1982-86, sec. 1986-87, pres. 1989-91, professionalism com. 1987-91, 92—), Nat. Eagle Scout Assn., Kiwanis (lt. gov. 1985-86, club pres. 1989-90, chair past lt. govs. coun. 1990-91), Elks. Roman Catholic. Office: Marathon County 500 Forest St Wausau WI 54403-5554

DRESBACH, DAVID PHILIP, financial consultant, educator; b. Columbus, Ohio, Feb. 23, 1947; s. Donald Philip and Marilyn Jo (Armstrong) D.; m. Vicki Elaine Smith, Feb. 25, 1966 (div. 1980); children: Chad, Andrew; m. Mary Louise Mathes, Nov. 29, 1980. MA, Ohio U., 1972. Adminstr. Ohio Univ., Athens, 1969-73; regional mgr. State of Ohio, Columbus, 1973-77, adminstr., 1977-79; adminstr. State of Minn., St. Paul, 1979-82; mgr. Evensen Dodge, Inc., Mpls., 1983-84, v.p., 1985-93; v.p. Springsted, Inc., St. Paul, 1993-95, coord. higher edn. group, 1993-95, newsletter editl. bd. mem., 1994; pres. Dresbach & Assocs., Inc., St. Paul, 1995—; lectr., adj. prof. Ohio U., Athens, 1969-74, Franklin U., Columbus, 1975, Columbus Tech. Inst., 1976-79, Met. State U., Mpls., 1980, U. Minn., Mpls., 1980-84. Author poetry anthologies, 1970, 90, 91, 93; contbr. articles to profl. jours. Soccer coach, chmn. Grove City Kids Assn., 1977-79. Named Boss of Yr. Am. Businesswomen's Assn., St. Paul, 1980. Mem. Nat. Coun. Higher Edn. Loan Programs, Inst. CFPs (cert.), Internat. Platform Assn., Am. Assn. Individual Investors, Fin. Profls. Assn., Mpls. Inst. Art, Acad. Am. Poets, Southview Country Club. Office: Dresbach & Assocs Inc 710 Mager Ct Ste 100 Saint Paul MN 55118-4356

DRESBACH, MARY LOUISE, state higher education administrator; b. St. Paul, Feb. 17, 1950; d. Ernest Joseph and Kathryn Marion (Lauer) Mathes; m. David Philip Dresbach, Nov. 29, 1980. BA, Coll. St. Catherine, 1972; postgrad., U. St. Thomas, 1979-80; MA, Coll. of St. Catherine, 1995. Tchr. St. Paul Pub. Schs., 1974-78; mgr. contracts, budget and human resources Minn. Higher Edn. Svcs. Office, St. Paul, 1978—; speaker Minn. Quality Conf., 1994, chair, 1996. Contbg. author Leading Edge Newsletter. Mem. AAUW, Am. Bus. Womens Assn. (sec. 1979-80), Nat. Assn. Exec. Women, Mpls. Inst. Arts, Met. Mus. Art, Dakota County Leadership Initiative, Minn. Ctr. for Women in Govt., Minn. Coun. Mgrs., Phi Beta Kappa, Pi Gamma Mu.

DRESSEL, IRENE EMMA RINGWALD, alcoholism and family therapist; b. Enderlin, N.D., Oct. 26, 1926; d. Albert William and Emma Anna Magdelena (Trapp) Ringwald; m. Clarence Irvin Dressel, Jr., Mar. 13, 1946 (div. Nov. 1972); 1 son, Keith Alan. Student pub. schs., Casselton, N.D. Cert. Master addiction counselor, N.D.; cert. chem. dependency counselor, Minn. Alcoholism counseling trainee Heartview Found., Mandan, N.D., 1974-75, family therapy intern, 1975-76, family counselor, 1976-77, supr. family mems. program, 1978; designer, supr. family program The Meadows, Wickenburg, Ariz., 1978-79; treatment programs cons., dir. consultation dept. Johnson Inst., Mpls., 1979-81; assoc. dir. chem. dependency unit Presbyn. Hosp., Oklahoma City, 1981-83; supr. adolescent counseling staff United Recovery Ctr., Grand Forks, N.D., 1983-85; dir. Irene Dressel Counseling, Grand Forks, 1985-89; program dir. the Dressel Ctr., Fargo, N.D., 1989-90, ret., 1990; FDR/DIR Your Level Best, 1996; cons. S.W. Inst. Alcohol Studies, Norman, Okla., Kans. Alcoholism Counselors Assn., Okla. Assn. Alcoholism and Drug Abuse; lectr. U. N.D., Grand Forks, N.D. Sch. Alcohol Studies. Mem. N.D. Alcoholism Counselors Assn., Nat. Alcoholism and Drug Addiction Counselors Assn., Am. Assn. Counseling and Devel., Democrat. Lutheran.

DREW, RICHARD ALLEN, electrical and instrument engineer; b. Milw., Jan. 10, 1941; s. Frank Emmons and Irene Louise (Wollaeger) D. BSEE, Milw. Sch. Engring., 1970. Registered profl. engr., Wis. Instrument engr. Nekoosa Papers Inc., Port Edwards, Wis., 1970-74; sr. instrument engr. Nekoosa Papers Inc., Port Edwards, 1974-85, Specialty Systems Inc., Mosinee, Wis., 1985-87; chief elec. and instrument engr. Zimpro Environ. Inc., Rothschild, Wis., 1988—. With USAF, 1963-67. Recipient Outstanding Svc. award Pulp and Paper Industry Div., Instrument Soc. Am., 1983, Outstanding Alumnus award Milw. Sch. of Engring., 1985. Mem. Instrument Soc. Am. (sr. mem. chpt. pres. 1974-75), Am. Radio Relay League (life mem.), Milw. Sch. of Engring. Alumni Orgn. (chpt. pres. 1991-95). Office: Zimpro Environ Inc 301 W Military Rd Rothschild WI 54474-1944

DREXLER, MARY SANFORD, financial executive; b. Pontiac, Mich., Apr. 19, 1954; d. Arthur H. and Kathryn S. (Sherda) Sanford; m. Brian Day, 1975 (div. 1978); m. York Drexler, 1980. BS, Ea. Mich. U., Ypsilanti, 1976, MA, 1979; postgrad., Walsh Coll., Troy, Mich., 1983. CPA, Mich. Spl. edn. tchr. Oakland Schs., Pontiac, Mich., 1976-83; staff auditor Coopers & Lybrand, Det., 1983-84; sr. auditor Coopers & Lybrand, Det., Mich., 1984-86; asst. contr. Webasto Sunroofs Inc., Rochester Hills, 1986-88; contr. Inalfa Hollandia, Inc., Farmington Hills, Mich., 1988—, v.p. fin., 1992—; bd. dirs. Coun. for Exceptional Children, Oakland County 1976--83. Bd. Dirs. Neighborhood Civic Assn., Troy, 1986—. Mem. Inst. Mgmt. Accts., Oakland County, Mich. Assn. CPA Mich., Forest Lake Country Club. Office: Inalfa Hollandia Inc 26700 Haggerty Rd Farmington Hills MI 48331-5714

DREXLER, RICHARD ALLAN, manufacturing company executive; b. Chgo., May 14, 1947; s. Lloyd A. and Evelyn Violet (Kovaloff) D.; m. Clare F. Stunkel, Aug. 24, 1990; children by previous marriage: Dan Lloyd, Jason Ian. B.S., Northwestern U., 1969, M.B.A., 1970. Staff v.p. Allied Products Corp., Chgo., 1973-75, sr. v.p. adminstrn., 1975-79, exec. v.p., chief fin. officer, adminstrv. officer, 1979-82, exec. v.p., chief operating officer, 1982, pres., chief operating officer, 1982-86, pres., chief exec. officer, 1986-93, chmn., pres., chief exec. officer, 1993—. Office: Allied Products Corp 10 S Riverside Plz Ste 400 Chicago IL 60606-3709

DREXLER, RUDY MATTHEW, JR., professional law enforcement work dog trainer; b. Elkhart, Ind., Jan. 16, 1941; s. Rudy Matthew Sr. and Elaine Irene (Hardman) D.; m. Patricia Ann Overmyer, Apr. 4, 1981; children: Scott M., Tina S. Thode. Student, Purdue U., 1960-63. V.p. Custom Booth Mfg. Corp., Elkhart, Ind., 1962-80; pres. Orchard Kennels, Elkhart, Ind., 1964-79; pres., treas. Rudy Drexler's Sch. for Dogs, Inc., Elkhart, Ind., 1980—; lectr. civic orgns.; instr. U. Del. Continuing Edn., Wilmington, 1978. Named to Honorable Order of Ky. Colonels, 1989; named hon. dep. Middlesex County Sheriff's Dept., New Brunswick, N.J., 1984, Daviess County Sheriff's Dept., Owensboro, Ky., 1988, Fairfield County Sheriff's Dept., Lancaster, Ohio, 1982. Mem. Midwest Police K-9 Assn. (founder 1984, tng. dir. 1984-87), Am. Soc. Law Enforcement Trainers (charter mem.), Internat. Narcotics Enforcement Officers Assn. (assoc. mem.), Can. Police K-9 Assn. (assoc. mem.), Nat. Police Res. Officers Assn. (hon. mem.), Moose. Office: Rudy Drexler's Sch for Dogs 50947 County Road 7 Elkhart IN 46514-8853

DREYER, ALEC GILBERT, independent power producer; b. Murphysboro, Ill., Mar. 15, 1958; s. Gilbert Dean and Norma Mae (Cluster) D.; m. Sheri L. Snider, July 26, 1980; children: Hillary Christine, Ahren Grant. BA in Polit. Sci. and Acctg., U. Ill., 1980; MBA with honors, Washington U., 1987. CPA, Ill., Mo. Staff acct. Price Waterhouse, St. Louis, 1980-82, sr. acct., 1982-85, mgr., 1985-88, sr. mgr., 1988-92; contr. Ill. Power Co., Decatur, 1992-94, treas., contr., 1994-95; pres. Illinova Generating Co., Decatur, 1995—. Asst. treas. Com. To Expand Cervantes Conv. Ctr., St. Louis, 1987-88; mem. Citizens Adv. Coun., Edwardsville, Ill., 1990-91; chmn. pers. svcs. divsn. United Way Macon County, Ill., 1994, co-chmn. campaign drive, 1995, chmn. campaign drive,1996. Mem. AICPAs, Ill. Soc. CPAs, Phi Beta Kappa, Beta Gamma Sigma. Republican. Baptist. Home: 976 Stevens Creek Cir Forsyth IL 62535 Office: Illinova Generating Co 2828 N Monroe St Decatur IL 62526-3269

DREYFUSS, PATRICIA, chemist, researcher; b. Reading, Pa., Apr. 28, 1932; d. Edmund T. and Anna J. (Oberc) Gajewski; m. M. Peter Dreyfuss, Jan. 30, 1954; children: David Daniel, Simeon Karl. BS Chemistry, U. Rochester, 1954; PhD, U. Akron, 1964. Postdoctoral fellow U. Liverpool (Eng.), 1963-65; rsch. chemist B.F. Goodrich, Brecksville, Ohio, 1965-71; rsch. assoc. Case Western Res. U., Cleve., 1971-73, sr. rsch. assoc., 1973-74; rsch. assoc. Inst. Polymers Sci., U. Akron, Ohio, 1974-84; sr. rsch. scientist, rsch. prof. Mich. Molecular Inst., Midland, 1984-90; vis. rsch. fellow U. Bristol, 1972; cons. in field, 1974—; vis. prof. Polish Acad. Scis., Poland, 1974; adj. prof. Cen. Mich. U., Mt. Pleasant, Mich. Tech U., Houghton, 1986-92, Mich. Molecular Inst., Midland, 1990-92. Author: Poly (Tetrahydrofuran), 1982; contbr. numerous articles to profl. jours.; co-author books. Flutist West Suburban Philharmonic Orch., Lakewood, Ohio, 1969-75, Midland (Mich.) Community Orch., 1990—; Explorer advisor Explorer post 2069 Boy Scouts Am., Akron, 1975-81; sec., bd. dirs. Adhesion Soc., 1976-88; treas. LWV, 1959-60; mem. ensemble Blessed Sacrament Ch., Midland; occasional flute soloist. Centennial scholar U. Rochester, 1950-54; Sohio fellow U. Akron, 1960, NSF Coop. Grad. fellow, 1961-63, Internat. fellow AAUW, 1964-65, NIH Spl. fellow, 1972-73. Mem. Am. Chem. Soc. (cen. region mtg. chmn. 1984-90, loc. sec. chmn., vice chmn., sec. and bd. dirs. Akron chpt. 1974-84, bd. dirs. Midland chpt. 1985-89, Outstanding Leadership Performance award 1981, Disting. Svc. award Akron chpt. 1985), AAUW (bd. dirs. Akron chpt.). Home: 3980 Old Pine Trl Midland MI 48642-8891

DREZDZON, WILLIAM LAWRENCE, mathematics educator; b. Milw., Feb. 19, 1934; s. Edward Kenneth and Mildred Mary (Schneider) D.; BS in Math., St. Mary's U., 1957; MS in Math. (Esso Oil Co. fellow), Ill. Inst. Tech., 1964; m. Frances Anita Sikes; children: Gregory Francis, Andrea Louise. Tchr. math., chemistry St. Michael's High Sch., Chgo., 1957-59, Lane Tech. High Sch., Chgo., 1959-66; software design engr. A.C. Electronics div. Gen. Motors, Oak Creek, Wis., 1966-67; prof. math., chmn. dept. Kennedy-King Coll., Chgo., 1967-71; prof. math. and learning lab. coordinator Oakton C.C., Des Plaines, Ill., 1971—; vis. prof. U. New Orleans, 1982-84; cons. nat. calculus survey, 1975. NSF grantee, 1961-65, 91; Chgo. Bd. Edn. grantee, summer 1964; NSF coop. program, 1971, 72; Chautauqua Course grantee, 1975-80. Mem. Math. Assn. Am. (chmn. jr. coll. com. Ill. sect., 1971-74, membership and pub. rels. com. 1992-93), No. Ill. Math. Assn. C.C.s (founding pres., 1971, 72, mem. nat. math. assessment com.), Am. Math. Assn. Two-Yr. Colls. (chmn., 1975, pres. 1979), Nat. Math. Assn., Ill. councils tchrs. math., Ill. Assn. C.C.s (pres. 1979), Met. Mathematics Club of Gtr. Chgo., Chgo. Astronomical Soc., Adler Planetarium Soc., Ill. Assn. Personalized Learning Programs, Analytic Psychology Club of Chgo., Lyric Opera Guild of Chgo., New Orleans Opera Assn., Delta Epsilon Sigma. Regional editor Math. Assns. of Two-Year Colleges Jour., 1970-82; author: Curriculum Guide of Transfer Courses for the Ill. Community College Board, 1974; Math. Research and Teaching Techniques, 1973, 76, 85; contbr. articles to jours. Home: 1600 Ashland Ave Des Plaines IL 60016-6606 Office: Oakton CC 1600 E Golf Rd Des Plaines IL 60016-1234

DRICHTA, CLARENCE JAMES, music educator, conductor, violinist; b. Milw., Apr. 20, 1937; s. Erwin Anthony and Florence Mary (Kleczka) D.; m. Pamela Gail Hoffman, Aug. 15, 1967 (div. 1991); children: David Stoner, Jeffrey Hoffman. BA in Music Edn., St. Louis Inst. Music, 1960; MA, So. Ill. U., Edwardsville, 1967. Conductor St. Louis Concert Chorale, Ancora Musica, 1957-60; assoc. conductor Midwest Opera Co., St. Louis, 1958-60; asst. prof. music-orch. U. Mo., St. Louis, 1971-74; orch. dir. Kirkwood (Mo.) High Sch., 1976-91; violin instr., conductor St. Louis Conservatory and Sch. for Arts, 1991-93; violin instr. Baldwin-Wallace Coll., Berea, Ohio, 1993—, Cleve. Inst. Music, 1993—; conductor, musical advisor Alton (Ill.) Symphony, 1965-68, 73-90; conductor Parma Ohio Symphony, 1968-71. Bd. dirs. Apollo's Fire-Baroque Orch., Cleve., 1994—; trustee Cleve. Orch., 1969-71. Mem. Am. String Tchrs. Assn., Music Educators Nat. Conf., Nat. Sch. Orch. Assn., Am. Symphony Orch. League, Phi Mu Alpha (Outstanding Alumni 1988), Cleve. Chamber Music Assn. (bd. dirs. 1994—). Republican. Episcopalian. Home: 2 Bratenahl Pl # 2D Bratenahl OH 44108-1167

DRICKAMER, HARRY GEORGE, retired chemistry educator; b. Cleve., Nov. 19, 1918; s. George Henry and Louise (Strempel) D.; m. Mae Elizabeth McFillen, Oct. 28, 1942; children: Lee Charles, Lynn Louise, Lowell Kurt, Margaret Ann, Priscilla. B.S., U. Mich., 1941, M.S., 1942, Ph.D., 1946; Dr. Chem. Scis. (hon.), Russian Acad. Sci., 1994, Dr. Chem. Sci. h.c., 1994. Chem. engr. Pan Am. Refining Corp., 1942-46; asst. prof. U. Ill. at Urbana, 1946-49, assoc. prof., 1949-53, prof. chemistry, chem. engring. and physics, 1953-90, prof. emeritus, 1990—. Recipient Bendix award, 1968, P.W. Bridgman award Internat. Assn. High Pressure Sci. and Tech., 1977; Michelson-Morley award Case Western Res. U., 1978, John Scott award City of Phila., 1984, Alexander von Humboldt award W.Ger., 1986, Robert A. Welch prize Welch Found., 1987, Disting. Profl. Achievement award U. Mich. Alumni Assn., Elliot Cresson medal Franklin Inst., 1988, Nat. Medal of Sci., 1989; Guggenheim fellow, 1952. Fellow Am. Acad. Arts and Scis., Am. Phys. Soc. (Buckley Solid State Physics award 1967), Am. Geophys. Union; mem. NAS, NAE, Am. Chem. Soc. (Ipatieff prize 1956, Langmuir award in chem. physics 1974, Debye award in phys. chemistry 1987), Am. Inst. Chemists (Chem. Pioneers award 1983, Gold medal 1996), Am. Inst. Chem. Engrs. (Colburn award 1947, Alpha Chi Sigma award 1967, Walker award 1972, W.K. Lewis award 1986), Faraday divsn. Royal Soc. Chemistry (London), Am. Philos. Soc., Ctr. for Advanced Studies, Russian Acad. Sci. Home: 304 E Pennsylvania Ave Urbana IL 61801-5129

DRINKO, JOHN DEAVER, lawyer; b. St. Marys, W.Va., June 17, 1921; s. Emery J. and Hazel (White) D.; m. Elizabeth Gibson, May 14, 1946; children: Elizabeth Lee Sullivan, Diana Lynn Martin, John Randall, Jay Deaver. AB, Marshall U., 1942; JD, Ohio State U., 1944; postgrad., U. Tex. Sch. Law, 1944; LLD (hon.), Marshall U., 1980, Ohio State U., 1986, John Carroll U., 1987, Capital U., 1988, Cleve. State U., 1990; DHL (hon.), David N. Myers Coll., 1990, U. N.H., 1992, Baldwin-Wallace Coll., 1993, Ursuline Coll., 1994. Bar: Ohio 1945, D.C 1946, U.S. Dist. Ct. (no. dist.) Ohio 1958. Assoc. Baker & Hostetler, Cleve., 1945-55, ptnr., 1955-69, mng. ptnr., from 1969, sr. adviser to mng. com.; chmn. bd. Cleve. Inst. Electronics Inc., Double D Ranch Inc., Ohio; bd. dirs. Cloyes Gear and Products Inc., McGean-Rohco Worldwide Inc., Orvis Co. Inc., Preformed Line Products Inc., The Standard Products Co. Trustee Elizabeth G. and John D. Drinko Charitable Found., Orvis-Perkins Found., Thomas F. Peterson Found., Mellen Found., Hostetler Found., The Cloyes-Myers Found., Ohio State U. Found., Marshall U. Found.; founder Consortium of Multiple Sclerosis Ctrs., Mellen Conf. on Acute and Critical Care Nursing, Case Western Res. U. Disting. fellow Cleve. Clinc Found., 1991; Ohio State Law Sch. Bldg. named in his honor, 1995; inducted into Bus. Hall of Fame, Marshall Univ., 1996. Mem. ABA, Am. Jud. Assn., Bar Assn. Greater Cleve., Greater Cleve. Growth Assn., Ohio State Bar Assn., Jud. Conf. 8th Jud. Dist. (life), Soc. Benchers, Case Western Res. U. Law Sch. Assn., Cleve. Play House, Cleve. Civil War Round-table, Mayfield Country Club, Union Club, Univ. Club, The Club at Soc. Ctr., O'Donnell Golf Club, Order of Coif, 33o Scottish Rite Mason, Knight Templar, York Rite, Euclid Blue Lodge No. 599 (Jesters, Shrine, Grotto). Republican. Presbyterian. Home: 4891 Middledale Rd Cleveland OH 44124-2522 also: 1245 Otono Dr Palm Springs CA 92264-8445 Office: Baker & Hostetler 3200 Nat City Ctr 1900 E 9th St Cleveland OH 44114-3401

DRISCOLL, CHARLES FRANCIS, financial services company executive, investment adviser; b. Dubuque, Iowa, July 8, 1943; s. Francis Clarence and Grace Ellen (Shanahan) D.; m. Marie Kathleen McGowan, Aug. 19, 1967; children: Sean, Erin. BA in Econs., Loras Coll., 1968. CLU; registered investment advisor; accredited estate planner. Sr. account mgr. NCR Corp., Davenport, Iowa, 1968-74, St. Louis, 1974-76; fin. planner Mass. Mut. Life Ins. Co., St. Louis, 1976—; pres. Driscoll and Assocs., St. Louis, 1989—; equity sales coord. MML Investor Svcs., Inc., St. Louis, 1983-88. Chmn. Edgewood Program Alumni Recovery Fund, St. John's Mercy Hosp., St. Louis, 1988-90. Mem. Nat. Assn. Life Underwriters, Am. Soc. CLU and ChFC, Estate Planning Coun. St. Lo. Republican. Roman Catholic. Home: 2324 Manor Lake Ct Chesterfield MO 63017-7817 Office: # 1810 100 N Broadway Saint Louis MO 63102

DRISCOLL, DIANE DUFFEY, financial consultant; b. Cin., July 1, 1951. BA, Manhattanville Coll., Purchase, N.Y., 1973. V.p. First Nat. Bank, Chgo., 1975-82; fin. cons., asst. v.p. Merryll Lynch, Chgo., 1982-93; fin. cons., v.p. Smith Barney Inc., Northbrook, Ill., 1993—. Mem. North Shore Womens Paddle League, Lake Forest Country Club. Office: Smith Barney Inc 5 Revere Dr Fl 5 Northbrook IL 60062-1566

DRISCOLL, JENNIFER KAY, public relations executive; b. Austin, Minn., Nov. 6, 1965; d. Maurice W. and Kathleen E. (Tax) D.; m. Steven B. Lundeen, Aug. 28, 1993. BA in English, Coll. St. Catherine, 1988; MBA in Fin., U. St. Thomas, 1991. Intern pub. affairs City of Mpls., 1987-88; editor Northwestern Fin. Rev., Mpls., 1988-91; pub. rels. account exec. Shandwick, Mpls., 1991-93; pub. rels. mgr., v.p. Dain Bosworth Inc., Mpls., 1993-96; dir. Inter Regional Fin. Group, Mpls., 1996—; freelance writer Bank Holding Co. Assn., Richfield, Minn., 1989-94. Contbr. articles to newspapers and mags. Bd. dirs. Am. Diabetes Assn., Mpls., 1994—, chair pub. rels. com., 1993—, sec., 1996—. Mem. Pub. Rels. Soc. Am., Securities Industry Assn. Pub. Rels./Advt. Roundtable, Coll. St. Catherine Alumnae Assn. (bd. dirs. 1993-95), Mpls. C. of C. (mem. Leadership Mpls. 1994-95), Phi Beta Kappa, Kappa Gamma Phi, Delta Phi Lambda. Office: Dain Bosworth Inc 60 S 6th St Minneapolis MN 55402

DRISCOLL, MARK, draftsman; b. Beloit, Wis., Mar. 31, 1971. A in Drafting and Design, Dunwoody Inst., Mpls., 1991. Sr. salesperson Shop/Co, Beloit, Wis., 1987-89; draftsman Beloit Corp., Beloit, Wis., 1989—. Recipient Dunwoody scholarship Beloit Corp., 1989. Roman Catholic. Home: 1904 McKinley Beloit WI 53511 Office: Beloit Corp 1 Saint Lawrence Beloit WI 53511-6246

DROEL, WILLIAM LOUIS, educator; b. Rochester, N.Y., July 28, 1948; s. Louis W. and Alice (Melvin) D.; m. Mary Ann Gallagher, Oct. 19, 1985;

children: Elizabeth, Robert. BA, St. John Fisher Coll., 1970; MA, Mundelein Coll., 1982. Assoc. dir. Orgn. for Better St. Paul, 1972-74; dir. Office Urban-Ethnic Affairs, Buffalo, 1975-77; tchr. Notre Dame High Sch., Niles, Ill., 1978-80; campus min., instr. Moraine Valley Community Coll., Palos Hills, Ill., 1981—; cons. Fund for Intercultural Edn., Chgo., 1988—; officer Nat. Ctr. for the Laity, 1980—. Author: Confident and Competent, 1987; editor Initiatives, 1981—; host TV series Conversation on Faith, 1985—. Pres. Zone 32 Pantry, Chgo., 1982—; bd. dirs. S.W. YMCA, Alsip, Ill., 1986-90, S.W. Cath. Cluster Project, Chgo., 1989—. Mem. Cath. Campus Ministry Assn. Democrat. Office: Newman Ctr PO Box 311 Worth IL 60482-0311

DROPKIN, ALLEN HODES, lawyer; b. Chgo., Oct. 26, 1930; s. Nathan I. and Zelda (Hodes) D.; m. Corrine S. Rose, Aug. 22, 1954; children: Ruth, David, Zachary, Noah. AB, U. Chgo., 1948, JD, 1951. Bar: Ill. 1951, D.C. 1956. Assoc. Arvey, Hodes & Mantynband, Chgo., 1951-54, 57-61; asst. states atty. Cook County, Ill., 1954-56; spl. counsel subcom. on housing, banking/currency com. U.S. Ho. of Reps., Washington, 1956; ptnr. Arvey, Hodes, Costello & Burman, Chgo., 1961-91, Fishman & Merrick PC, 1992—. Pres. Bd. Jewish Edn., Chgo., 1975-78, Midwest Region United Synagogue Am., 1981-84; dir. Jewish Cmty. Ctrs., Chgo., 1972-76, Chgo. Jewish Hist. Soc., 1995—. Mem. Ill. State Bar Assn. Home: 1340 N Astor St Chicago IL 60610 Office: Fishman & Merrick PC 30 N La Salle St Chicago IL 60602-2508

DROSTE, JEAN RASMUSEN, educational consultant; b. DeKalb, Ill., May 30, 1941; d. Russel Nelferd Rasmusen and Mary Edna (McAllister) Giles; m. Dieter Hans Droste, Sept. 2, 1967 (div. 1992); children: Stephen, Lora. AA, Monmouth Coll., 1961; BS, U. Wis., 1964, MA, 1966. Ford Found. tchr. intern Janesville (Wis.) High Sch., 1963-64; instr. polit. sci. & history Lea Coll., Albert Lea, Minn., 1966-67; caseworker St. Louis County Welfare Dept., 1967-68; staff dir. Ohio Commn. on Edn. Improvement, Columbus, Ohio, 1989-91; exec. asst. Office Gov., Columbus, Ohio, 1991-93; ednl. cons., 1993—. Author: (with others) University Women - A Series of Essays, 1980. Sch. bd. v.p. Circleville (Ohio) City Schs., 1978-83, pres., 1984-89; sch. bd. mem. Pickaway Ross Joint Vocat. Sch., Chillicothe, Ohio, 1982-89. Recipient Civic Leadership award Ohio Assn. Gifted Children, 1987; nominee AAUW Woman of Yr., 1990. Mem. AAUW (pres. 1973-77), Ohio AAUW, Ohio LWV, Rotary (Circleville Club). Presbyterian. Home: 670 Ridgewood Dr Circleville OH 43113-1134

DROVDAL, DAVID (SKIP), state legislator; m. Kathy Drovdal; 4 children. Student, Minot Col. Bus.; diploma, Western Coll. Auctioneering. Retailer, state rep. dist. 39, 1993—; mem. edn. and natural resources com. N.D. Ho. Reps. Mem. Watford City Interim Edn. Fin. Com. Named Watford City Fireman of Yr. Mem. Watford City C. of C., Lions (Lion of Yr. 1993). Home: HC 1 Box 22 Arnegard ND 58835-9726*

DROZD, PHYLLIS ANN, business owner; b. Allegan, Mich., July 26, 1932; d. Edward and Wilma (Busfield) Moored; m. Thomas Drozd, June 20, 1953; children: Julie, T. Jon, Jay H. Sec. Cresent Machine Co., Allegan, Mich., 1949-55; egg retailer Tom & Phyllis Drozd, Allegan, Mich., 1953-79, farmer, 1953-85; co-owner Drozd Seed, Allegan, Mich., 1953—. Pres. Allegan County Sch. Dist., 1978—; treas., 1965-78; sec.-treas. Allegan County Sch. Bds. Assn., 1991-92; pres. Allengan Bus. & Profl. Women, 1986-87, 91-92, 1st sr. v.p., 1984-85; bd. dirs. Mich. Assn. Sch. Bds., 1993—; mem. various ednl. coms. Home and Office: 537 32nd St # M40 Allegan MI 49010-9763

DROZDA, JOSEPH MICHAEL, author; b. Chgo., Aug. 3, 1943; s. Albert and Bozena J. (Milonski) D.; m. Cynthia Elizabeth Gartin, Aug. 21, 1971; children: Joseph M. Jr., Patricia B. BS, Ind. U., 1969. Sales rep. EBSCO Industries, Columbus, Ohio, 1969-70; pres. The Stewart Howe Alumni Service, West Lafayette, Ind., 1970-79, Drozda Burchell Advt., Lafayette (Ind.) and Indpls., 1974-79; chmn. fin. Dole For Pres. Com., Alexandria, Va., 1979; sales mgr. Gibraltar Mausoleum Corp., Ind., Minn., Pa., 1980-84; v.p. sales Gibraltar Mausoleum Corp., Indpls., 1984-90; pres. N.Am. Cemeteries, Inc., Indpls., 1990—. Author, editor: Chi Omega 50 Years at Indiana, 1972, Hub City History, 1984, Tailgater's Handbook, 1996; contbr. articles to profl. jours. Precinct committeeman Rep. Party, Lafayette, 1979; cons. Haig for Pres. Com., Alexandria, 1979; v.p. Downtown Bus. Ctr. Corp., Lafayette, 1979. Served to maj. U.S. Army, 1966-69, Vietnam. Mem. Pub. Relations Soc. Am., Kappa Sigma (Dist. Grand Master 1972-78). Presbyterian. Lodge: Rotary (pres. Republic, Pa. club 1983-84). Office: NAC Inc PO Box 526 Brownsburg IN 46112-0526

DRUCKER, BARRY JULES, environmental health specialist; b. St. Louis, Dec. 29, 1940; s. Morris Josef and Geraldine Drucker; m. Sandra Leta Lew, June 10, 1968; 1 child, Marlon. BA, So. Ill. U., 1969; MA, Webster U., 1976; MPH, St. Louis U., 1992. Registered sanitarian.; cert. profl. environ. health specialist. Chemist St. Louis City Health Dept., 1970-76; sr. research technician Washington U. Sch. Medicine, St. Louis, 1976-77; sanitarian Mo. Dept. Mental Health, St. Louis, 1977-79; sanitarian, supr. Mo. Dept. Health, St. Louis, 1979-82; program mgr. St. Louis County Health Dept., Clayton, Mo., 1982—; assoc. dir. Mo. Restaurant Assn., St. Louis, 1982—; mem. Mo. Food Adv. coun., Jefferson City, 1982—, St. Louis County Restaurant com., 1982; vice chmn. Mo. Bd. Certification for Sanitarians, Jefferson City, 1987-89, 90-91, mem., 1986-91; adj. faculty St. Louis U., 1992—; mem. Mo. State Milk Bd., Jefferson City, 1995—; mem. adv. bd. Sch. Pub. Health St. Louis U., 1996—. Peer reviewer Jour. of Environ. Health, 1985—; contbr. articles to profl. jours. With USAF, 1960-64. Mem. Mo. Environ. Health Assn. (pres. 1985-86, publ. awards 1986, 87, 88, 93, Sanitarian of Yr. 1987), St. Louis Area Pub. Health Assn. (pres. 1986-87, mem.-at-large 1992—), Mo. Pub. Health Assn. (bd. dirs. 1986-87, pub. award 1988, 93), Nat. Environ. Health Assn. (bd. dirs. 1984-86, Cert. of Merit 1987, Jour. Editor's award 1994). Home: 19250 River Ridge Ln Wildwood MO 63005-3818 Office: St Louis County Health Dept 111 S Meramec Ave Saint Louis MO 63105-1711

DRUCKREY, GERALD RICHARD, ophthalmologist; b. Long Beach, Calif., Jan. 9, 1933; s. Richard Adolph and Evelyn Alvina (Moede) D.; m. Marilyn Mae Sievert, June 11, 1955; children: Dawn Suzanne, Sara Joanne, Scot Richard. MD, Marquette U., 1957. Diplomate Am. Bd. Ophthalmology. Intern Tripler U.S. Hosp., Honolulu, 1957-58; resident ophthalmology Walter Reed Gen. Hosp., Washington, 1959-62; pvt. practice, Beloit, Wis., 1965—; past chmn. dept. surgery, past pres. med. staff, past chmn. instnl. rev. bd. Beloit Meml. Hosp.; past pres. med. staff Beloit Clinic. Maj. M.C. U.S. Army, 1957-65. Fellow Am. Acad. Ophthalmology; mem. Am. Soc. Cataract and Refractive Surgery, Wis. Acad. Ophthalmology. Office: Beloit Clinic 1905 Huebbe Pky Beloit WI 53511-1842

DRUGAN, CORNELIUS BERNARD, school administrator, psychologist, musician; b. Youngstown, Ohio, July 23, 1946; s. Francis Edward and Erminia (Costarella) D.; m. Kathleen Anne Cowhard, Aug. 17, 1968; children: Jonelle Kathryn, Noelle Marie. BS, Heidelberg Coll., 1968; AM, John Carroll U., 1970; PhD, Walden U., 1980. Cert. supt.; lic. psychologist. Tchr. Warrensville City Schs., Warrenville Heights, Ohio, 1968-72; intern psychologist Garfield Heights (Ohio) City Schs., 1972-73; psychologist Belmont (Ohio) County Schs., 1973-80; supr. Union Local Schs., Belmont, 1980-83, pupil personnel dir., 1983-87; adminstr. Streetsboro (Ohio) City Schs., 1987—; tchr. Warrenville Heights Recreation Dept., 1968-72, Southgate Music, Maple Heights, Ohio, 1970-73; instr. Cleve. State U., 1970-72; advisor Belmont County Career Ctr., St. Clairsville, Ohio, 1980-86. First place piano competition Portage Music Tchr. Assn., Ravenna, Ohio, 1964. Mem. Buckeye Assn. Sch. Adminstrs., Jaycees (Jaycee of Month, St. Clairsville, Ohio chpt. 1975), Ohio Assn. Secondary Sch. Adminstrs., K.C. (council 5173), Phi Delta Kappa. Home: 3138 Robin Dr Ravenna OH 44266-9548 Office: Streetsboro High Sch 1900 Annalane Dr Streetsboro OH 44241-1729

DRUKKER, BRUCE H(IGHSTONE), obstetrics and gynecology educator; b. Passaic, N.J., Sept. 8, 1934; s. Henry L. and Sylvia H. Drukker; m. Esther Verna VanManen, June 19, 1956; children: Stephen, Cynthia, Jeffery. BS, Calvin Coll., 1956; MD, Cornell U., 1959. Diplomate Am. Bd. Ob-Gyn, Nat. Bd. Med. Examiners. Resident physician Henry Ford Hosp., Detroit, 1960-64, sr. staff physician, 1966-73, chmn. dept. ob-gyn, 1973-84; prof., chairperson dept. ob-gyn, coll. human medicine Mich. State U., East Lansing, 1984—; Clin. prof. ob-gyn U. Mich., Ann Arbor, 1976-83. Contbr. articles to profl. jours. Served to capt. U.S. Army M.C., 1964-66. Fellow Am. Coll. Ob-Gyn.; mem. Ctrl. Assn. Ob-Gyn. (trustee 1986-88, pres. 1993-94), Assn. Profs. Gynecology and Obstetrics, Am. Soc. Breast Disease, Soc. Gynecol. Oncologists, Soc. Gynecol. Surgeons. Office: Mich State Univ Dept of Ob/Gyn and Reproductive Biology Clin Ctr East Lansing MI 48824-1315

DRUMMOND, DOROTHY WEITZ, geography education consultant, educator, author; b. San Diego, Dec. 19, 1928; d. Frederick W. and Dora (Weidenhofer) Weitz; m. Robert R. Drummond, Sept. 5, 1953 (dec. June 1982); children: Kathleen, Gael, Martha. AB, Valparaiso U., 1949; MA, Northwestern U., 1951. Cert. tchr., Ind. Social studies tchr. Woodrow Wilson Jr. High Sch., Oxnard, Calif., 1949-50; editorial asst. Am. Geog. Soc., N.Y.C., 1951-53; substitute tchr. Vigo County Sch. Corp., Terre Haute, Ind., 1960-67; social studies tchr. Ind. State U. Lab. Sch., Terre Haute, 1963-64; geog. edn. cons., author, workshop presenter, Terre Haute, 1953—; adj. asst. prof. geography Saint Mary-of-the-Woods (Ind.) Coll., 1967—, Ind. State U., Terre Haute, 1990—; dir. project GEO, Ind. State U., 1992-96; cons. McGraw-Hill, Scott-Foresman, Agy. for Instrnl. Tech., Hudson Inst.; bd. dirs. GIS for the Twenty-First Century, Ind. State u., 1996—. Author: The World Today, 3d edit., 1971, People on Earth, 3d edit., 1988, World Geography, 1989; contbr. numerous articles to profl. jours. Bd. dirs. Mental Health Assn. Wabash Valley, Terre Haute, 1984-93, Coun. on Domestic Abuse, Terre Haute, 1987-92, United Ministries Ctr., Terre Haute, 1991-94; organizer, leader ednl. tours to China, 1986, 88, Australia, 1993, 96. Fulbright scholar, Burma, 1957-58; grantee Geography Educators Network Ind., 1988-96, Ind. Commn. Higher Edn., 1990, 92, 94, NSF, 1993, 95, U.S. Dept. Edn., 1992-96. Mem. Ind. Coun. Social Studies, Geography Educators Network Ind. (bd. dirs.), Nat. Coun. Geog. Edn. (pres. 1990), Nat. Coun. Social Studies, Nat. Sci. Tchrs. Assn., Am. Geographers.

DRURY, DAVID MICHAEL, electrical engineer, educator; b. Casco, Wis., Aug. 1, 1951; s. Raymond and Marie Drury. BSEE, Milw. Sch. of Engring., 1972; PhD, Marquette U., 1978. Lic. profl. engr., Wis. Devel. engr. Motorola Communications Div., Schaumburg, Ill., 1972-76; mem. tech. staff Sandia Nat. Labs., Albuquerque, 1978-87; assoc. prof. U. Wis., Platteville, 1987—; cons. Insight Industries, Platteville, 1988-89, Kaul-Tronics, Inc., Richland Center, Wis., 1995. Contbr. articles to IEEE Jour. Quantum Electronics, IEEE Transactions on Microwave Theory and Techniques, IEEE Transactions on Edn., Galliean Electrodynamics. Arthur J. Schmitt fellow Arthur J. Schmitt Found., 1978. Mem. IEEE (Frank Cowan scholarship 1977), Sigma Xi (assoc.). Home: 960 Stonebridge Rd Apt 3 Platteville WI 53818-2036 Office: U Wis-Platteville Dept Elec Engring 1 University Plz Platteville WI 53818-3012

DRYER, SHAWN PETER, secondary education educator; b. Manistee, Mich., Nov. 3, 1946; s. R.E. and Wanda Helen Dryer; m. Juanita Kay McClain, June 14, 1969; children: Kelly Ann, Cory Jacob. BA, Cen. Mich. U., 1968; MA, Western Mich. U., 1973, EdD in Ednl. Leadership, 1980. Cert. sci. tchr., elem. tchr., sch. adminstr. Waterfront dir. Lake City (Mich.) Kiwanus, 1966-68; elem. tchr. Battle Creek (Mich.) Pub. Schs., 1968-86; tchr. of academically talented, 1985; sci. educator Mich. Partnership for New Edn. Dist. Leadership Acad., 1987-96,, 1992; biology researcher U. Mich., Pellston, 1989; grievance chmn. Battle Creek Edn. Assn., 1991-93, chief negotiator, 1993, 96; bd. dirs., NEA rep., 1993-96; intern Upjohn Educators, 1994. Mem. Rep. Inner Cir., Washington, 1986-88, Earthwatch, Watertown, Mass., 1990-91, 95; observer World Hot Air Balloon Championships, Battle Creek, 1987-93, 96; judge Seiko Youth Challenge, 1993-95; panelist Home Testing Panelist, Newspapers in Edn., 1980-96; appropriations bd. United Fund of Battle Creek, 1989, 91, 94, 95, 96, Wednesday Night Golf Assn. Recipient Excellence in Edn. award W.K. Kellogg Found., Battle Creek, 1986, grantee 1993; recipient Classrooms of Tomorriw award State of Mich., Lansing, 1990; grantee NSF, U. Mich., 1989, Battle Creek Pub. Schs. Computer award, 1991. Mem. Libr. Congress (assoc.), Internat. Platform Assn., Mich. Sci. Tchrs. Assn., Nat. Audubon Soc., Rails and Trails Conservancy, Nature Conservancy, Bass Anglers Sportsman Soc., Wilson Ctr. Assocs., Am. Mus. Natural History. Lutheran. Office: Northwestern Jr High 176 Limit St Battle Creek MI 49017-2139

DRZEWIECKI, GARY FRANCIS, state legislator; b. Pulaski, Wis., Oct. 29, 1954; s. Wallace and Marcella Drzewiecki; m. Julie Pakanich, 1982; children: Eric, Matthew, Michelle, Tiffany. Student, U. Wis., Stout, 1972-73. Owner, perator Pulaski Fin. Ctr.; pres. Pulaski Econ. Devel. Corp.; mem. from dist. 30 Wis. State Senate, Madison; chair state govt. ops. and corrections coms. Bd. dirs. Tri County Res. Squad, 1989—; past pres. Village of Pulaski; Bd. dirs. Brown County Planning Commn. Mem. Optimists, Lions. Home: 419 Washington St Pulaski WI 54162*

D'SOUZA, AUSTIN, manufacturing executive; b. Nanthur, Karnataka, India, Aug. 8, 1950; came to U.S., 1981; s. Gaulbert and Rose D'Souza; m. Theresa Lilly Pinto, Oct. 25, 1980; children: Anita, Anil, Atina, Angel. MBA, Pacific We. U., 1982, PhD, 1984. Mfg. coord. Wesley Jessen Corp., Chgo., 1981-95; mfg. mgr. IPI Med. Products, Chgo., 1995-96; with Courtsey Corp., Buffalo Grove, 1996—. Author: Adarsh Yuvajan, 1978, (play) Ankwaar Celly, 1979; actor Kala Sampath, 1980. Mem. spl. com. India Cath. Assn. Am., 1992-93; mem. pastoral coun. St. Bernardine Ch., 1991—, mem. sch. bd., 1991—; chmn. leadership com. Chgo. Archdiocese, 1992—. Mem. Chgo. Damayan Lions (sec. 1990-91, v.p. 1991-92, pres. 1992-93, dist. 1A Lions environ. chmn. 1993—, dist. 1A publicity and pub. rels. chmn. 1994, zone chmn. 1995, region chmn. 1996, Pres. Appreciation award 1991, Lion of Yr. 1992, Melvin Jones fellow 1993, 100% Pres. award 1993, Internat. Found. Honor Roll 1994, Schering Plough Excellence award 1994, Lions Internat. Pres. Appreciation award 1995, dist. Lion of yr. award 1996), Kala Sampath Lions (founder 1996), Filippin Am. Coun. Chgo. (del. 1991—). Home: 906 Dunlop Ave Forest Park IL 60130-2059 Office: Courtsey Corp 800 Corporate Grove Dr Buffalo Grove IL 60089

D'SOUZA, HARRY J., mathematics educator; b. Mangalore, India, Dec. 24, 1955; came to U.S., 1978; s. Joseph and Lily D'S.; m. Marianne P. McGrath, July 8, 1994. BS, St. Xavier's Coll., 1976; MS, U. Bombay, 1978; MS, PhD, U. Notre Dame, 1983. Asst. prof. math. U. Mich., Flint, 1983-89, assoc. prof. math., 1989—; mem. exec. com. U. Mich., 1995—, acad. affairs adv. bd., 1994—, grad. bd., 1994—, svcs. adv. bd., 1994—, math. club advisor, 1992-94. Advisor Amnesty Internat., 1992-94. Math. fellow St. Xavier's Coll., 1976-78. Office: U Mich Dept Math Flint MI 48502-2186

DU, DING-ZHU, mathematician, educator; b. Qigihaer, China, May 21, 1948; s. Jin-Gao and Ai-Hua (Xu) D.;m. Shu-Mei Li, Jan. 20, 1977; 1 child, Hong-Wei. MS, Chinese Acad. Scis., Beijing, 1982; PhD, U. Calif., Santa Barbara, 1985. Asst. prof. Inst. of Applied Math., Beijing, 1981-82; postdoctoral Math. Scis. Rsch. Inst., Berkeley, Calif., 1985-86; asst. prof. MIT, Cambridge, 1986-87; prof. Inst. of Applied Math., Beijing, 1987-90; rsch. assoc. Princeton (N.J.) U., 1990; prof. U. Minn., Mpls., 1991—. Author: Convergence Theory of Feasible Direction Methods; editor: Gradient Projection Methods in Linear and Nonlinear Programming, 1988, Combinatorics, Computing and Complexity, 1989; contbr. over 95 articles to profl. jours. Mem. Am. Math. Soc. Office: U Minn Computer Sci Dept Minneapolis MN 55455

DUBEY, STEPHEN ARTHUR, accountant; b. Chgo., Feb. 14, 1947; s. Donald Morton Dubey and Josephine (Halpern) Scott; m. Diane Ellen Eulenberg, Apr. 17, 1969; children: Karla, Geoffrey, Shoshana. BS, U. Ill., 1969. CPA, Ill. Staff acct. Seidman & Seidman CPAs, Chgo., 1969-73; ptnr. Fisher & Dubey CPAs, Chgo., 1973-76; pres. Stephen A. Dubey Ltd. CPAs, Lincolnwood, Ill., 1976-88; ptnr. Adler & Assocs., Ltd., Skokie, Ill., 1988-92; owner Stephen A. Dubey, CPAs, Chgo., 1992-95; ptnr. Best of Israel Tours, 1995—. Bd. dirs. Skokie Solomon Schechter Day Sch., 1982; fin. sec. Congregation Shaare Tikvah, 1984-86, pres., 1987-89, chmn. bd. dirs., 1990-91; mem. North Suburban Synagogue Coun., Mercaz, N.Y., 1987-90; mem. president's coun. midwest region United Synagogue Am. Mem. AICPA, Ill. Soc. CPA's, Lions. Office: 730 N Franklin #302 Chicago IL 60610

DUBOIS, MARK BENJAMIN, utility executive; b. Peoria, Ill., Sept. 27, 1955; s. Benjamin John and Marjorie Abigail (Black) DuB.; m. Jeri Rene Simmons, May 24, 1975; 1 child, Benjamin Robert. BS with high distinction, U. Ariz., 1977; MA, U. Kans., 1981. Rsch. asst. State Biol. Survey Kans., Lawrence, 1978-81; systems programmer Cen. Ill. Light Co., Peoria, 1982-84, operating software supr., 1984-85, gen. supr. data processing ops. sect., 1985-88, gen. supr. applications systems sect., 1988-90, security adminstr. staff info. systems, 1990-91, gen. supr. data processing ops. sect., 1991-93, staff info. system planning admin., 1993-95, sr. market rsch. adminstr., 1995—; part-time instr. nat. sci. and computer literacy Midstate Coll., 1987—; rsch. affiliate Ill. Nat. Hist. Survey, Urbana, Ill., 1988—; cons. identifier, Ctr. for Insect Identification, Lansing, Mich., 1988—. Bd. dirs. Spl. People Encounter Christ, Peoria, 1982-83; treas. Religious Edn. Activities for Cmty. Handicapped, Lawrence, 1978-81; cons. Jr. Achievement, 1987-88; mem. sch. bd. Father Sweeney Sch. for Academically Gifted, 1989-91; chmn. Utility Info. Systems Exchange, 1991-92; amb. Lakeview Mus. Arts Scis., 1992-95, guest curator, 1993-95. Mem. AAAS, Data Processing Mgmt. Assn., Internat. Union for Study Social Insects, Entomol. Soc. Am., Am. Inst. Biol. Scis., Mid-Am. Paleontol. Soc., Cen. States Entomol. Soc., Kans. Acad. Sci., Animal Behavior Soc., Cambridge Entomological Club, Soc. Systematic Zoology, Sigma Xi, Phi Kappa Phi, Alpha Zeta, Gamma Sigma Delta (agrl. honoraries). Contbr. articles on entomology and personal computer software to profl. jours. Home: 116 Burton St Washington IL 61571-2509 Office: Cen Ill Light Co 300 Liberty St Peoria IL 61602-1400

DUBOWSKY, SONDRA, zoologist; b. Wichita, Kans., July 13, 1965; d. Edward Lee and Juanita Faye (Waddell) D. BS in Biology, BA in Chemistry, Southwestern Coll., 1989; MS, Emporia State U., 1991. Teaching assistantship Emporia (Kans.) State U., 1989-91, rsch. assistantship, 1990-91; teaching and rsch. assistantship N.D. State U., Fargo, 1992-93; adj. faculty Butler County C.C., 1996—. Contbr. articles to profl. jours. Mem. Am. Soc. Zoologists, Soc. for Study Reproduction, AAAS.

DUCHARME, HOWARD MAURICE, philosopher, educator; b. Saginaw, Mich., June 4, 1950; s. Howard Maurice and Kathryn (Grigsby) D.; m. Karen Sue Griffith, May 30, 1975; children: Dustin G., David J. BA, Hope Coll., 1972; postgrad., Western Ill. U., 1977-78; MA, Trinity Divinity Sch., 1980; DPhil, Oxford (Eng.) U., 1984. Instr. philosophy Coll. Lake County, Grayslake, Ill., 1979-80, Chapman Coll. Extension, Gt. Lakes, Ill., 1980; tutor in morals Oriel Coll., Oxford (Eng.) U., 1982; asst. prof. philosophy U. Tenn., Knoxville, 1984-85; asst. prof. philosophy U. Akron, Ohio, 1986-91, assoc. prof. philosophy, 1991—; chair dept. philosophy, 1996—; vis. asst. prof. bioethics Coll. of Medicine, U. Fla., Gainesville, 1986; bioethicist Coll. of Medicine, Northeastern Ohio Univs., Rootstown, 1986—, mem. instl. rev. bd., 1992—; ethics com. Akron Gen. Med. Ctr., 1986—; reviewer for various pubs., 1986—; speaker at ednl. instns. Cons. Jour. of History of Philosophy, St. Louis, 1991—, Jour. Clin. Ethics, 1992; contbr. articles on philosophy, bioethics, theology to scholarly publs. Coach area soccer teams. Grantee Inst. for Advanced Studies in Christianity and Religious Pluralism, U. Wis., 1985. Mem. Am. Philos. Assn., Hastings Ctr., Tyndale Fellowship. Office: Univ Akron 302 Olin Hall Akron OH 44325

DUCHARME, THOMAS ANDREW, fire protection specialist, educator; b. Columbus, Ohio, Aug. 24, 1955; s. Robert Lewis and Eileen Marie (Buchanan) DuC.; m. Denise Ann LeMaster, June 11, 1983; 1 child, Nicole Kathryn. AAS in Fire Sci. with honors, Columbus State Cmty. Coll.; BS in Fire Protection/Safety with honors, U. Cin., 1996. Cert. fire safety inspector, Ohio. Lt. Jackson Twp. Fire Dept., Grove City, Ohio, 1975—; cons., pres. Fire Safety Educators and Assocs., Grove City, 1987—; dir. Safety Town, Grove City, 1987—; rep. Police and Fire Retirement Bd., Columbus, Ohio, 1988—; adj. instr. Ohio Fire Acad., Reynoldsburg, 1990—, Nat. Fire Acad., Emmitsburg, Md., 1990—. Author: (instructional manuals) Counseling Juvenile Firesetters, 1990, Safety Town, 1990. Instr. ARC, Columbus, 1980-85; mem. Press Club Ohio, Columbus, 1989—. Recipient Cross of Honor, Internat. Supreme Coun. Order of DeMolay, 1981, Cmty. Svc. award Columbus Dispatch, 1989. Mem. Internat. Assn. Fire Fighters (charter, pres. local chpt. 1988-92), Masons, Phi Theta Kappa. Republican. Home: 5382 Thornhill Ct Grove City OH 43123 Office: Jackson Twp Fire Dept PO Box 517 Grove City OH 43123

DUCHEK, MICHAEL GERARD, mechanical engineer; b. St. Louis, May 3, 1966; s. Thomas Jefferson and Mary Alberta (Stricker) D. AA in Math., St. Louis Community Coll., 1986, AA in Engring. Sci., 1986; BSME, Purdue U., 1990. Engring. coop. McDonnell Douglas Corp., St. Louis, 1987-90, flight test engr., 1990-91; gen. engr. Def. Mapping Agy. Aerospace Ctr., St. Louis, 1991-93; mech. engr. Def. Mapping Agy. Hydrographic/Topographic Ctr., Washington, 1993-94; resident mech. engr. VA Hosp., Columbia, Mo., 1994-95; grad. teaching asst. U. Mo.-Rolla, 1996—. Recipient Congressional award, U.S. Congress, 1988. Mem. ASME (chpt. treas. 1989), Soc. Am. Mil. Engrs., Engrs. Club St. Louis, KC, Phi Theta Kappa Internat. Honor Soc. (regional alumni officer 1994-96, Stalcup Nat. award 1987, Regional Hall of Honor 1988, regional pres. 1987-88). Roman Catholic. Home: 1104 N Rolla St # 3 Rolla MO 65401 Office: U Mo-Rolla Dept Mech & Aerospace Engri MC Annex Rm 211D Rolla MO 65409-1350

DUCHON, ROSEANN MARIE, business owner, consultant; b. Cleve., Jan. 16, 1950; d. Steve and Mary (Bobak) Gaydos; m. Ronald Joseph Duchon, Oct. 11, 1969 (div. 1994); children: Michelle, Teresa, Megan, Kevin, Jason. Student, Kent (Ohio) State U., 1983-84. Sec. ETC, Inc., Cleve., 1968-69; sec., model Bobbie Brooks, Inc., Cleve., 1969-71; instr. childbirth edn. Childbirth Edn. Assn. Cleve., 1971-83; office mgr. 3690 Corp./Devel. Systems, Beachwood, Ohio, 1984-85, Park Pl. Bus. Services, Hudson, Ohio, 1985-86; owner Hudson Secretarial Services, 1986, Exec. Office Services, Hudson, 1987—, Hudson Telephone Answering Services, Hudson, 1988—; pres. R.M. Duchon, Inc., 1991, Western Reserve Staffing Svcs., 1992—. Chmn. Hudson League for Service, 1980-82; active Better Bus. Bur., 1989-90. Mem. Hudson Bus. and Profl. Women (nominating com. 1985-86, pres. 1986-87, region mem. chmn., Ohio state membership chair 1993-94), Hudson C. of C., Nat. Assn. Secretarial Svcs., Nat. Fedn. Indep. Bus., Women's Network. Roman Catholic. Office: Exec Office Svcs PO Box 541 Hudson OH 44236-0541

DUCK, VAUGHN MICHAEL, software company executive; b. Rockford, Ill., Sept. 13, 1943; s. Vaughn Victor and Virginia Stella (Cielisz) D.; m. Sandra Jean Carlstrom, Jan. 27, 1968; children: Kirsten Lee, Kendra Edith. Assocs., Inst. Automation, Chgo., 1963. Dir. MIS G.C. Electronics, Rockford, 1964-67; gen. mgr., v.p. Computer Svcs. Ctr., Rockford, 1968-79; pres. Integrated Micro Systems, Rockford, 1980-82, pres. Govtl. Data Systems, Rockford, 1983-85; exec. v.p. Bus. Records Corp., Dallas, 1986-87; pres. Interactive Software Products, Rockford, 1988—. Developer: (software) Election Mgmt. System, 1984, Retail Operations System Exec., Rose, 1988, Unix Retail POS System, UX/POS, 1991; Inventor election ballot processor, PEPS, 1980. Republican. Office: Interactive Software Products 2704 Broadway Rockford IL 61108-2127

DUCKETT, BERNADINE JOHNAL, retired elementary principal; b. Flint, Mich., Aug. 7, 1939; d. John and Bernice (Robinson) Edwards: m. Ellis Duckett Jr., Apr. 15, 1963; children: Bruce Devlon, Janeen Jae; 1 stepchild, Ellis III; m. Charles Teaberry (div. June 1960). BS in Edn., Ctrl. Mich. U., 1962; MA in Ednl. Adminstrn., U. Mich., 1966; Reading Specialist, Mich. State U., 1970; postgrad., Flint (Mich.) C.C., 1989-92. Cert. elem. tchr., Mich. Classroom tchr. Dort Elem. Sch., Flint, 1959-65; reading tchr. Dort & Dewey Elem. Sch., Flint, 1965-67; instrnl. specialist Doyle and Dewey Elem. Sch., Flint, 1967-71; asst. prin. Dewey, Merrill & Cook Elem. Sch., Flint, 1971-74; prin. Garfield & Elem. M.L. King, Flint, 1974-96; ret., 1996; presenter, mem. Internat. Ednl. Symposium, Rome, 1988-92, Flint Schs. Employee of Month Program, 1985-92. Author: Diet on the Lighter Side, 1988, My Grandparents Said Go 4 It, 1989; author joint books: Bicentennial Sch. Cookbook, 1976, Tapestry, 1988, URA Winner, 1994; contbr. articles to mags. and newspapers. Fundraiser Walk-a-Thons, United Negro Coll. Fund, Children's Miracle, Flint, 1991, Crim Race for Spl. Children, Flint, 1989-94, Riverbend Striders, Flint, 1993-95; mem., presenter Consortium to Prevent Child Abuse, 1990; vol. St. Joseph Hosp. Aux., Flint, 1990-95; mem. Greater Flint Afro-Am. Sports Hall of Fame, 1992; mem. com. Aiding Hard of Hearing, Quota Club Internat., Flint, 1994. Grantee Flint Cmty. Schs., 1990-93; recipient Outstanding Educator plaque NAACP, Flint Intern Plaque, 1986, Flint OBE Pioneer Plaque, 1993, Ednl. Contbns. as Family award, 1993, Walker medal Leukemia Soc., 1996. Mem. Nat. Assn. Elem. Sch. Prins. (dir. founds. 1992-94, cons., student discipline Focus Group on

Ethnic Minorities 1981, 92, 94, Outstanding Svc. Plaque 1993), Nat. Assn. Media Women (sec. Flint chpt. 1989-92, Media Woman of Yr. 1990), Mich. Assn. Elem. and Mid. Sch. Prins. (chairperson awards, mem. conf. planning and summer camp com., treas., membership chair, del., presenter 1977-92, certs. 1985, 87, 91, plaque 1990), Nat. Alliance Black Sch. Educators (presenter 1993), Internat. Platform Assn., Flint Assn. Elem. Prins. (sec., election chair, social chair 1980-93), Global Network of Schs., U. Mich. Alumni Assn. Home: 3720 Circle Dr Flint MI 48507-1879

DUDA, ZENON MICHAEL, podiatrist; b. Chgo., Apr. 28, 1955; s. Wasyl and Paraskevia (Konoba) D.; children: Katherine Marika, Hania Mary. BS, Loyola U., Chgo., 1977; D Podiatric Medicine, Ill. Coll. Podiatric Medicine, 1981. Diplomate Am. Bd. Podiatric Surgery. Mem. teaching staff Lindell Hosp., St. Louis, 1984-87, Central Med. Ctr., St. Louis, 1988; adj. clin. prof. dept. podiatric medicine Pa. Coll. Podiatric Medicine, Phila, 1986-87; pvt. practice Cape Girardeau, Mo., 1981—; mem. staff Deaconess Hosp., Perry County Meml. Hosp., Twin Rivers Regional Med. Ctr.; mem. staff dept. surgery S.E. Hosp.; mem. Am. Bd. Podiatric Orthopedics. Fellow Am. Coll. Foot and Ankle Surgeons; mem. Am. Podiatric Med. Assn., Am. Assn. Hosp. Podiatrists, Mo. State Podiatric Med. Assn. Mem. Ch. of Scientology. Home: 2520 Tulip Ln Cape Girardeau MO 63701-3635 Office: 1345 Mt Auburn Rd Cape Girardeau MO 63201

DUDE, MARY ANN, women's health nurse, medical paralegal; b. Milw., Mar. 25, 1949; d. Rupert George and Florence Mary (Chuppa) Jonas; m. Robert James Dude, Oct. 4, 1975; children: Ann, Carolynn. BSN, U. Wis., Milw., 1971. RN, Wis. Staff nurse St. Luke's Hosp., Milw., 1971-73; charge nurse St. Francis Hosp., Milw., 1973-74; instr. Sacred Heart LPN Sch., Milw., 1974-81; maternity nurse Family Health Plan, Milw., 1985-88; med. paralegal Gillick, Murphy, Wicht, Milw., 1988-91; educator Planned Parenthood, Milw., 1991-92; sci. aide New Berlin Pub. Schs., Milw., 1989-93. Pres. Cleveland Heights Elem. PTO, New Berlin, 1987-90, New Berlin West Mid. PTO, 1988-91; parent rep. Gifted and Talented Task Force, New Berlin, 1988-96; pres. New Berlin Supporters of Talented and Gifted Edn., 1992—, bd. dirs., 1994-96; tour guide Historic Milw., Inc., 1993-96. Mem. Paralegal Assn. Home: 3145 S Manor Ct New Berlin WI 53151-4382

DUDEK, EDWARD FRANCES, library administrator; b. Chgo., Nov. 17, 1944; s. Edward Francis and Harriette (Gronkowski) D.;m. Irene Gabrielle Dudek, June 15, 1974. BA, DePaul U., Chgo., 1967. MA, 1972; MILS, Rosary Coll., River Forest, Ill., 1987. Tchr. St. Rita H.S., Chgo., 1968-87; libr. adminstr. Summit (Ill.) Pub. Libr. Dist., 1988—. Office: Summit Pub Libr Dist 6209 S Archer Rd Summit IL 60501

DUDEK, FELICIA ANNE, rehabilitation counselor; b. Chgo., Aug. 30, 1947; d. Edmund and Bernice (Rak) Funk; m. John Dudek, Sept. 6, 1969; 1 child: Elizabeth. BS in Psychology, Ill. Inst. Tech., 1972, MS in Rehab. Counseling, 1974. Lic. clin. profl. counselor, Ill.; cert. rehab. counselor, alcohol and drug counselor. Alcoholism therapist Grant Hosp., Chgo., 1974-79, dir. alcoholism counselor tng. program, 1978-79; mem. adj. faculty Cen. YMCA Community Coll., Chgo., 1981-82; coord. substance abuse tng. Nat.-Louis U., Evanston, Ill., 1984—; pvt. practice Chgo., 1979—. Contbr. articles to profl. jours. Bd. dirs. Glenview Youth Svcs., 1984-86, Glenview Citizens for Alcohol and Drug Awareness, Glenview, 1984, Ill. Alcohol and Other Drug Abuse Profl. Cert. Assn., Inc., 1993—, pres., 1995. Mem. ACA (chair Ill. Alcohol/Drug Counselor Tng. Program Dirs.' consortium, 1989-92), Nat. Rehab Assn., Ill. Rehab. Assn., Ill. Alcohol and Drug Dependence Assn. Roman Catholic. Office: 30 N Michigan Ave Ste 1926 Chicago IL 60602-3605

DUDERSTADT, JAMES JOHNSON, university president; b. Ft. Madison, Iowa, Dec. 5, 1942; s. Mack Henry and Katharine Sydney (Johnson) D.; m. Anne Marie, June 24, 1964; children: Susan Kay, Katharine Anne. B in Engring. with highest honors, Yale U., 1964; MS in Engring. Sci, Calif. Inst. Tech., 1965, PhD in Engring. Sci. and Physics, 1967. Asst. prof. nuclear engring. U. Mich., 1969-72, assoc. prof., 1972-76, prof., 1976-81; dean U. Mich. (Coll. Engring.), 1981-86; provost, v.p. acad. affairs U. Mich., 1986-88, pres. univ., 1988—. AEC fellow, 1964-68; recipient E. O. Lawrence award U.S. Dept. Energy, 1986, Nat. medal of Tech., 1991; named Nat. Engr. of Yr., NSPE, 1991. Fellow Am. Nuclear Soc. (Mark Mills award 1968, Arthur Holly Compton award 1985); mem. NAE, Am. Phys. Soc., Nat. Sci. Bd. (chair 1991—), Am. Acad. Arts & Scis., Sigma Xi, Tau Beta Pi, Phi Beta Kappa. Office: U Mich Office of Pres 2074 Fleming Ann Arbor MI 48109

DUDLEY, DURAND STOWELL, librarian; b. Cleve., Feb. 28, 1926; s. George Stowell and Corinne Elizabeth (Durand) D.; m. Dorothy Woolworth, July 3, 1954; children: Jane Elizabeth, Deborah Anne. BA, Oberlin Coll., 1948; MLS, Case Western Res. U., 1950. Librarian, Marietta (O.) Coll. Library, 1953-55, Akron (O.) Pub. Library, 1955-60; librarian Marathon Oil Co., Findlay, O., 1960-74, sr. law librarian, 1974-86; supr. tech. services dept. Findlay-Hancock County Pub. Library, Findlay, 1986-88. Mem. Spl. Libraries Assn. Presbyterian (deacon). Home: 865 Maple Ave Findlay OH 45840-5013

DUDLEY, PAUL V., bishop; b. Northfield, Minn., Nov. 27, 1926; s. Edward Austin and Margaret Ann (Nolan) D. Student, Nazareth Coll., St. Paul Sem. Ordained priest Roman Cath. Ch., 1951. Titular bishop of Ursona, aux. bishop of St. Paul-Mpls, 1977-78; bishop of Sioux Falls S.D., 1978—. Office: Chancery Office PO Box 5033 Sioux Falls SD 57117-5033

DUDLEY, RONN J., engineering manager; b. Marrow, Ohio, Nov. 2, 1958. Assoc. Mech. Engring., Columbus Tech. Inst., 1982, Assoc. Indsl. Engring., 1982; postgrad., Franklin U. Cert. employment mgr. Columbus Ohio Mgmt. Assn. Mgr. engring. labs. EBCO Mfg. Co., Columbus, Ohio, 1981—. Bd. dirs. EBCO Employees Credit Union, Columbus, 1994—. Republican. Presbyterian. Home: 4135 Leather Stocking Trl Gahanna OH 43230-1527 Office: EBCO Mfg Co 265 N Hamilton Rd Columbus OH 43213-1311

DUDYCZ, WALTER W., state legislator; b. Chgo., Mar. 11, 1950; m. Oksana; 2 children. Grad., Chgo. Citywide Coll., Chgo. Police Acad. Police detective City of Chgo., 1971-84; mem. dist. 7 Ill. State Senate, 1985—; mem. appropriations I com., exec. appointment com., vet affairs and admin. com., minority spokesman, elec and reapportionment com., legis. rsch. unit com., Alzheimers task force com., mem. state gov. orgn. ad admin., transp. com., asst. rep. leader. Office: 6143 N Northwest Hwy Chicago IL 60631-4115 also: Office of Senate Members State Capitol Springfield IL 62706*

DUDZIK, TED EDWARD, law enforcement official; b. Whiting, Ind., Sept. 14, 1925; s. John A. and Rose (Gibala) D.; m. Edna Szymanski, May 30, 1949; children: Karen, Rosanne. BS in Criminal Justice, St. Joseph Coll., 1950, AA in Corrections, 1952; BA in Psychology, Calumet Coll., 1955; grad., FBI Acad., 1958, Sch. Narcotics U.S. Dept. Treasury, 1960, Northwestern U. Traffic Inst. Cert. probation officer, Ill. Capt. of detectives Whiting Police Dept., Ind., 1948-71, ret.; dir. law enforcement & police records program Nat. Safety Coun., Chgo., 1971—, staff rep. to traffic records com., traffic law enforcement and adjudication com., awards com., congress planning com., developer, adminstr. ann. forum on traffic records systems; firearms dealer; mem. law enforcement com. Transp. Rsch. Bd., Washington; mem. 4 tech. coms. Internat. Assn. Chiefs of Police, Va. Staff sgt. USMC, 1943-1946. Office: Nat Safety Coun 444 N Michigan Ave Chicago IL 60611-3903

DUECKER, ROBERT SHELDON, bishop; b. Medina County, Ohio, Sept. 4, 1926; s. Howard LaVerne and Sarah Faye (Simpson) D.; m. Marjorie Louise Clouse, June 13, 1948; children: Philip Lee, Christine Cay Duecker Isle. B in Religion, AB, Indiana Wesleyan U., 1948; BD, MS, Christian Theol. Sem., Indpls., 1952, DD (hon.), 1969; DPS (hon.), Kendall Coll., 1996. Ordained to ministry United Meth. Ch., 1952. Pastor Dyer (Ind.) United Meth. Ch., 1952-54; sr. pastor Gethsemane United Meth. Ch., Muncie, Ind., 1954-62, Grace United Meth. Ch., Hartford City, Ind., 1962-65, 1st United Meth. Ch., Warsaw, Ind., 1965-70, Simpson United Meth. Ch., Ft. Wayne, Ind., 1970-72; dir. No. Ind. Conf. Coun. Ministries United Meth. Ch., Marion, 1973-77; dist. supt. No. Ind. Conf. United Meth. Ch., Ft. Wayne, 1977-82; sr. pastor High St. United Meth. Ch., Muncie, 1982-88; bishop Chgo. area United Meth. Ch., 1988—; trustee United Theol. Sem., Dayton, Ohio, 1985-88, Kendall Coll., Evanston, Ill., 1988—, North Ctrl. Coll., Naperville, Ill., 1988—, Garrett Theol. Sem., Evanston, 1988—; mem. gen. bd. publ. United Meth. Ch., 1988-92, gen. bd. higher edn. and ministry, 1992—, univ. senate, 1992—; mem. adv. coun. Ams. United for Separation of Ch. and State. Author: Tensions in the Connection, 1982; also monographs. Mem. Kosciusko County Health Planning Coun., Warsaw, Ind., 1968-70; bd. dirs. Goodwill Industries, Ft. Wayne, Muncie, 1977-88; former pres. Del. County Mental Health Assn., Muncie. Named Sagamore of the Wabash Gov. of Ind., 1988. Mem. Coun. of Religious Leaders of Met. Chgo. (pres. 1996—), Coun. Bishops United Meth. Ch., North Ctrl. Jurisdiction Coll. Bishops, Kiwanis, Rotary, Theta Phi. Office: United Meth Ch 8765 W Higgins Rd Chicago IL 60631-4101

DUEHOLM, ROBERT M., state legislator; b. June 7, 1945. BA, U. Wis. Assemblyman Wis. State Dist. 28; bd. dirs. Inter-County Leaders; acct. mgr. Honeywell Corp.; adv. bd. Indianhead Tech. Coll. Address: 904 Hwy 48 Luck WI 54853

DUEL, WARD CALVIN, health care consultant; b. Fond du Lac, Wis., Mar. 13, 1924; s. Myrton M. and Matie Rose (Tidyman) D.; m. Madelyn Mae Kressin, Oct. 1, 1950; children: Ward Rick, Christine Selma, Roxanne Matie, Beth Dawn. BS, U. Wis., 1950; postgrad., Marquette U., 1955-57; MPH, U. Calif., Berkeley, 1959. Registered sanitarian, Ill., Calif., Nat. Environ. Health Assn. Sanitarian City of Kenosha (Wis.), 1951-59; br. office mgr. Lake County Health Dept., Waukegan, Ill., 1959-65; dir. health Skokie (Ill.) Dept. Health, 1965-68, McHenry County Health Dept., Woodstock, Ill., 1968-70; asst. dir. pub. and environ. health AMA, Chgo., 1971-81; chief environ. health City of Chgo., 1981-82; dir. Mid-Ohio Valley Dept. Health, Parkersburg, W.Va., 1982-83; dir. environ. health, pub. and mental health Choctaw Indians, Phila., 1984-85; cons. on environ. health to prisons, juv. detention ctrs. and mental hosps. in 44 states and D.C., 1985—; active Nat. Com. on Correctional Health Care; capt. U.S. Pub. Health Svc. Commn. Corps Res., 1958—; lectr. in field. Co-editor: Clinical Implications of Air Pollution Research; author monographs: Physicians Guide to Solid Waste, 1975, Physicians Guide to Air Pollution, 1973-80, Flood Area Health Guide, 1961; contbr. articles to profl. jours. Served in U.S. Army, 1945-46. Decorated Bronze Star for Heroism; recipient Theta award Defenders, 1969, Samuel J. Crumbine award Single Svc. Inst., 1963, Walter S. Mangold award nat. Environ. Health Assn., 1978, Outstanding Citizen award Ill. Dept. Edn., 1984, Jour. Environ. Health Editors award, 1979. Mem. ASME, ASHRAE, Nat. Environ. Health Assn. (pres. 1967-68), Wis. Environ. Health Assn. (pres. 1957-58), Ill. Environ. Health Assn. (pres. 1964-65), Am. Pub. Health Assn. (fellow 1967), Am. Correctional Assn., Am. Jail Assn. (nat. stds. com. 1993—). Lutheran. Home and Office: 4907 N West St Mc Henry IL 60050-7968

DUELL, DANIEL PAUL, artistic director, choreographer, lecturer; b. Rochester, N.Y., Aug. 17, 1952; s. Seth Joseph and Ellen Catharine (Newton) D. Diploma, Profl. Children's Sch., N.Y.C., 1970; scholarship student, Sch. Am. Ballet, 1969-72. Mem., N.Y.C. Ballet, 1972-87, soloist, 1977-79, prin. dancer, 1979-87; choreographer in repertoire of Ballet Hispanico, N.Y., Dayton Ballet, Ballet Chgo.; mem. edn. dept., N.Y.C. Ballet; now artistic dir., choreographer Ballet Chgo. Mem. Sch. Am. Ballet Assn., Dance/USA, Chgo. Dance Coalition. Office: Ballet Chgo 185 N Wabash Ave Ste 2300 Chicago IL 60601-3607

DUEWEL, WESLEY LUELF, religious organization executive; b. St. Charles, Mo., June 3, 1916; s. Louis John and Ida L. Duewel; m. Elizabeth Dolly Raisch; children: John, Christine, Darlene. BTh, God's Bible Coll., Cin., 1939; MEd, U. Cin., 1949, EdD, 1952; DD (hon.), Taylor U., Upland, Ind., 1982. Pres. Allahabad (India) Bible Sem., 1946-65; chmn. Evang. Frellowship of India, New Delhi, 1963-65; v.p. OHS Internat., Greenwood, Ind., 1966-68, pres., 1969-83, pres. emeritus, 1995—; chmn. Evang. Fgn. Missions Assn., Washington, 1970-72; mem. bd. adminstrs. Nat. Evang. Assn., Wheaton, Ill., 1970—. Author: Touch the World, 1986, Let God Buide, 1988, Mighty Prevailing Prayer, 1990, Ablaze for God, 1989, Measure Your Life, 1992, Revival Fire, 1995, Open Your Life to God, 1996. Life bd. trustees Asbury Theol. Sem., Wilmore, Ky., 1970-96. Recipient World Evang. fellowship N. Am. Coun., Wheaton, 1975-94; named Disting. Alumnus God's Bible Coll., Cin., 1988, Holliness Exponent of Yr. Christian Holiness Assn., 1988. Fee Methodist. Home: 617 Horton Greenwood IN 46142 Office: OMS Internat Greenwood IN 46142

DUEWER, ELIZABETH ANN, biology educator; b. Champaign, Ill., June 21, 1937; d. Robert Koehn and Ella Faye Hubbard; m. Raymond George Duewer, Aug. 31, 1963; children: John Robert (dec.), Mary Elizabeth, Julia Ann. BS with honors, U. Ill., 1960, MS, 1962; postgrad., Duke U., 1962-63; PhD, U. Ariz., 1971. From lectr. to sr. lectr. U. Wis., Platteville, 1979—. Vol. Sci. Olypiad, Girl Scouts U.S., 4-H. Mem. Am. Bryological and Lichenological Soc., Brit. Lichen Soc., Soc. of Sigma Xi.

DUEWER, RAYMOND, horticulturist; b. Ill., Mar. 28, 1926; s. John William and Mattie Elizabeth (Dippel) D.; m. Elizabeth Ann Hubbard Duewer, Aug. 31, 1963; children: John Robert (dec.), Mary Elizabeth, Julia Ann. BS, U. Ill., Urbana, 1961; MS, 1962; PhD, U. Ariz., Tucson, 1969. Asst. prof. U. Wis., Platteville, 1969-75; assoc. prof., 1975-84, prof., 1984-95; coach U. Wis. Pi Alpha Xi Nat. Collegiate Flower Judging Contest, 1980, 82-95. Merit badge leader Boy Scouts Am., Platteville, Wis., 1977-80; project leader Platteville City Doers 4H Club, Platteville, Wis., 1979—. Recipient Scholarly Activity Improvement Fund award, U. Wis., Great Britain, 1988, Platteville, 1992-93. Mem. Am. Soc. for Horticultural Sci., Am. Horticultural Soc., The Nature Conservancy, Sigma Xi. United Methodist. Home: 1975 Old Lancaster Rd Platteville WI 53818

DUFF, CRAIG, agricultural products executive. Pres. Beef Belt Feeders, Inc., Scott City, Kansas. Office: Beef Belt Feeders Inc PO Box 651 Scott City KS 67871*

DUFF, JANET MARIE, insurance company executive; b. St. Louis, Nov. 25, 1958; d. Joseph John and Wanda Lee (Bice) McHale; m. Steven Lynn Ryan, Jan. 11, 1981 ((div. Oct. 21, 1991); children: Lauren Noel Duff, Thomas Ian Duff; m. Michael Houston Duff. BA in Bus. Adminstrn. cum laude, Lindenwood Coll., St. Charles, Mo., 1994. Internal auditor Auto Club of Mo., St. Louis, 1979-84; cons. Tillinghast/Towers Perrin, St. Louis, 1984-91; mgr. Ins. Control May Dept. Stores Co., St. Louis, 1991-92; ins. analyst NGIC, St. Louis, 1992-93; claim analyst, database coord. Clark Refining & Mktg., St. Louis, 1993—; budget chairperson Soc. Ins. Rsch., Atlanta, 1993, 94; mem. NAFE. Lay reader, chilren's ministry United Meth. Ch., St. Peters, Mo., 1995. Recipient Linden Scroll St. Charles, 1993, 94. Mem. Mo. Assn. Self Insureds, Sigma Tau. Office: Clark Refining & Mktg 8182 Maryland Ave Saint Louis MO 63105

DUFF, JOHN BERNARD, college president, former city official; b. Orange, N.J., July 1, 1931; s. John Bernard and Mary Evelyn (Cunningham) D.; m. Helen Mezzanotti, Oct. 8, 1955 (div.); children: Michael, Maureen, Patricia, John, Robert, Emily Anne; m. Estelle M. Shanley, July, 1991. B.S., Fordham U., 1953; M.A., Seton Hall U., 1958; Ph.D., Columbia U., 1964; DHL (hon.), Seton Hall U., 1976, Northeastern U., 1982, Emerson Coll., 1983, Lincoln Coll., 1993. Sales rep. Remington-Rand Corp., 1955-57, dist. mgr., 1957-60; mem. faculty Seton Hall U., 1960-70, prof. history, 1968-70, acad. v.p., 1970-71, exec. v.p., acad. v.p., 1971-72, provost, acad. v.p., 1972-76; pres. U. Lowell, Mass., 1976-81; chancellor of higher edn. State of Mass., 1981-86; commr. Chgo. Pub. Libr. System, 1986-92; pres. Columbia Coll., Chgo., 1992—; mem. Gov.'s Commn. to Study Capital Punishment, 1972-73; chmn. bd. dirs. Mass. Corp. Ednl. Telecommunications, 1983—; dir. Mass. Tech. Park Corp., Bay State Skills Corp. Author: The Irish in the United States, 1971, also articles.; Editor: (with others) The Structure of American History, 1970, (with P.M. Mitchell) The Nat Turner Rebellion: The Historical Event and the Modern Controversy, 1971, (with L. Greene) Slavery: Its Origin and Legacy, 1975. Dem. candidate to U.S. Congress, 1968; mem. State Bd. Edn., 1981-86; chmn. Livingston Town Dem. Com., 1972-76; bd. dirs. Merrimack Regional Theatre, 1981-84, Mass. Higher Edn. Assistance Corp., 1981-86, Chgo. Metro History Fair ; trustee Essex County Coll., 1966-70, Mass. Community Coll. System., St. John's Prep. Sch., Danvers, Mass.; chmn. Lowell Hist. Preservation Commn., 1979-86; mem. adv. bd. Wang Inst., 1979-81; mem. bd. visitors Emerson Coll., 1986-90; pres. Nat. Coun. of Heads of Public Higher Edn. Systems; mem. nat. adv. com. on accreditation and indsl. eligibility U.S. Dept. Edn., 1981-82; mem. Ill. Lit. Coun., 1986-92, adv. com. Ill. State Libr., 1986-92. With U.S. Army, 1953-55. Mem. Fedn. Ind. Coll. and Univ. Ill. (sec., treas.). Club: K.C.

DUFF, MARC CHARLES, state legislator; b. Port Washington, Wis., July 4, 1961; s. James Wayne and Marlyn (Hoffman) D. BS, U. Wis., Whitewater, 1983; MA, U. Wis., Madison, 1985. Legis. asst. Wis. State Rep. Tom Ourada, Madison, 1985-87; sr. analyst rep. caucus staff Wis. State Assembly, Madison, 1987-88, mem. from dist. 84, 1988-92, 93—. Chmn. New Berlin (Wis.) Roadway Beautification Com., 1987—; supr. Dist. 31, Waukesha County, 1988-89. Mem. Rotary Club. Home: 1811 S Elm Grove Rd Waukesha WI 53151-2605*

DUFFY, JAMES JOSEPH, engineer; b. Pawhuska, Okla., Aug. 28, 1917; s. James Leo and Margretta Marsden (Wittlinger) D.; m. Edna Jean Laramie, Aug. 15, 1953; children: Paul Edward, Donald Lawrence. BSME, Rice U., 1941; MS in Auto Engring., Chrysler Inst., 1948. Registered profl. engr., Mich. Jr. petroleum engr. Humble Oil and Refining Co., Houston, 1941-42; engine devel. engr. Chrysler Corp., Detroit, 1948-52, resident engr., 1952-54; auto transmission engr. Ford Motor Co., Dearborn, Mich., 1954-59, steering design engr., 1962-65, adv. steering design engr., 1965-90, tech. specialist advanced steering, 1990-95 (ret.); valve design engr. AiRsch., Phoenix, 1959-62. Patentee in field. 1st lt. USAF, 1943-45, SW Pacific. Recipient Disting. Inventor award Intellectual Property Owners, 1988. Mem. Soc. Automobile Engrs., Tau Beta Pi, Sigma Xi. Republican. Lutheran. Home: 35594 Orangelawn St Livonia MI 48150-2539

DUFFY, KATHLEEN MAY, retired community health nurse; b. Lima, Ohio, May 7, 1930; d. Leonard Joseph and Florence Elizabeth (Niles) Kagey; m. John Francis Duffy, June 14, 1952; children: Kathie, Karla, Sharon. Student, Ind. U., 1951-81; diploma, Meth. Hosp. Sch. of Nursing, Indpls., 1952; student, Marian Coll., 1981. Orthopedic supr. Meth. Hosp., Indpls., 1952; obstet. charge nurse Sacred Heart Hosp., Garrett, Ind., 1954-56; sch. nurse N.W. Hendricks Schs., Lizton, Ind., 1966-73; pub. health clinic nurse Health and Hosp. Corp. Marion County, Indpls., 1985-90; pub. health nurse Health, Hosp. Corp. Marion County, Indpls., 1961-65, 73-85, 90-92, Marion County Health Dept., 1993—; mem. Silver Striders Adv. Com. Named Woman of the Day, Sta. WIRE. Mem. Ind. Pub. Health Assn., Women's Health Task Force, Ind. Race Walkers, Silver Striders. Home: 5850 Buick Dr Indianapolis IN 46224-5321

DUFFY, NORMAN VINCENT, chemistry educator; b. Washington, Nov. 1, 1938; s. Norman Vincent and Glenn Mae (Drury) D.; m. Marianne Youdell, Oct. 13, 1962; children—Norman Vincent III, Mary Virginia, Joseph Leslie, Anne-Marie, Maureen Glenn. B.S., Georgetown U., 1961, Ph.D., 1966. From asst. prof. to assoc. prof. chemistry Kent State U., Ohio, 1966-1980; from asst. dean arts and scis. to assoc. dean, 1973-1976, prof. chemistry dept. 1980—, chmn. dept., 1981—. Contbr. articles to profl. jours. Contbr. articles to encys. Producer ednl. films in field. Mem. Am. Chem. Soc., The Chem. Soc., Sigma Xi. Roman Catholic. Home: 1317 Denise Dr Kent OH 44240-1606 Office: Kent State U Chemistry Dept Kent OH 44242

DUFFY, NORMAN VINCENT, III, news director; b. Washington, Jan. 28, 1964; s. Norman Vincent Jr. and Marianne (Youdell) D.; m. Amie Lynn Vargo. BA in Telecomm., Kent State U., 1986, BA in Polit. Sci., 1987; MA in Mass Media, Miami U., 1989; postgrad., U. Ill. Host Sta. WKSU-FM, Kent, Ohio, 1984-86; news anchor, reporter Sta. 4ZZZ-FM, Brisbane, Australia, 1986; asst. prodr. Radio 74, Geneva, Switzerland, 1987; news anchor, reporter Sta. WMUB-FM, Oxford, Ohio, 1988-89; reporter Sta. WILL-AM, Urbana, Ill., 1989, host, prodr. of morning edit., 1989-95, news dir., 1995—; vis. lectr. U. Ill., 1994—. Recipient Best Investigative Report Ill. AP, 1992, Best Radio Feature, 1990, Best Radio Enterprise AP, 1990; recipient Cert. of Merit ABA, 1992. Mem. Soc. of Profl. Journalists (v.p. 1995), Ill. News Broadcasters Assn., AEJMC, Phi Kappa Phi. Office: WILL Radio 810 S Wright St Urbana IL 61801

DUFFY, PAMELA ANN, physical therapist; b. Marshalltown, Iowa, July 13, 1954; d. Francis John and Georgia Ann (Fetter) D. BS in Zoology and Phys. Edn., Iowa State U., 1976; BS in Phys. Therapy, U. Pa., 1978. Lic. phys. therapist, Pa., N.J., Iowa. Staff phys. therapist Albert Einstein Med. Ctr., Phila., 1978-80; mgr. phys. therapist Phila. Inst. Pain & Trauma, 1980-81; staff phys. therapist Garden State Cmty. Hosp., Marlton, N.J., 1981-82, Ottumwa, Iowa, 1982, Iowa Meth. Med. Ctr., Des Moines, 1982-83, Iowa Orthopaedic Sports Medicine Ctr., Urbandale, Iowa, 1983-85; owner, phys. therapist Duffy & Assocs. Phys. Therapy, P.C., Windsor Heights, Ankeny, Iowa, 1985—; phys. therapy advisor Traveler's Ins., 1994—; chmn. Ankeny Leadership Inst., 1993—; bd. dirs. Brenton Bank, Ankeny. Bd. dirs. Arthritis Found., Des Moines, 1993-95; active Easter Seals of Iowa, Des Moines, 1988-91. Named Up and Comer Iowa Bus. Leader Des Moines Register, 1992. Mem. Iowa Phys. Therapy Assn. (Olive C. Farr Disting. Svc. award 1992), Am. Phys. Therapy Assn. (chmn. nominating com. 1978—), Ankeny C. of C., Greater Des Moines C. of C. Democrat. Roman Catholic. Home: 2833 J Ave Adel IA 50003-8260 Office: Duffy & Assocs Phys Therapy 925 E 1st St Ste L Ankeny IA 50021

DUFFY, WILLIAM EDWARD, JR., retired education educator; b. Fostoria, Ohio, Aug. 30, 1931; s. William Edward and Margaret Louise (Drew) D.; B.S., Wayne State U., 1958, M.Ed., 1960; Ph.D., Northwestern U., 1967; m. Sally King Wolfe, Nov. 21, 1958 (div. 1978). Tchr. social studies Detroit pub. schs., 1957-61; instr. Northwestern U., Evanston, Ill., 1961-65; asst. prof. edn. U. Iowa, Iowa City, 1965-70, assoc. prof., 1970-94, coordinator Soc. Found. Edn. program, 1978-93, chmn. div. founds., postsecondary edn., 1981-88; ret., 1994; lectr. in field. Served with USAF, 1951-54. Fellow John Dewey Soc., Philosophy of Edn. Soc.; mem. Am. Ednl. Research Assn., History of Edn. Soc., Am. Ednl. Studies Assn. Editorial bd. Ednl. Philosophy Theory, 1969-71; contbr. book revs. and articles to profl. publs. Home: 376 Samoa Pl Iowa City IA 52246-3632

DUGGAN, JERRY C., investment banker; b. Kansas City, Mo., Jan. 25, 1942. BS in Bus., Coll. William and Mary, 1964. Asst. v.p. Stern Bros. & Co., Kansas City, Mo., 1965-74; v.p. br. mgr. Rheinholt & Garchner, Kansas City, Mo., 1974-79, Newhart, Cook & Co., St. Louis, 1979-80; v.p. rsch. Stern Bros. & Co., Kansas City, Mo., 1980-85; investment banker Duggan & Co. Investment Securities, Leawood, Kans., 1985—; cons. Oppenheimer Industries, L.A., 1991-92. Mem. Kansas City Securities Assn., Am. Royal Livestock and Horse Show Assn. (gov. 1970—), Saddle and Sirloin Club (com. chair 1968—). Republican. Home: 2701 W 86th St Leawood KS 66206-1403 Office: Duggan & Co Invest Secur # 210 4701 College Blvd Leawood KS 66211-1658

DUGGAN, LESTER W., lawyer, insurance claims manager; b. St. Louis, Jan. 12, 1922; m. Barbara Jane McCollum; 5 children. Attended, St. Louis U., 1946-47, JD, 1950. Mayor City of Ferguson, 1960-62; judge Mo. Cir. Ct., 1985-90. Office: 523 McDonough St Saint Charles MO 63301*

DUGGAN, PATRICK JAMES, federal judge; b. 1933. BS in Econs., Xavier U., 1955; LLB, U. Detroit, 1958. Pvt. practice law Brashear, Duggan & Tangora, 1959-76; judge Wayne County Cir. Ct., 1977-86, U.S. Dist. Ct. (ea. dist.) Mich., Detroit, 1987—; prof. Madonna U., Livonia, Mich. Chmn. Livonia Family YMCA, 1970-71; mem. bd. trustees Madonna U., 1970-79. Mem. Mich. Jaycees (pres. 1967-68). Office: US Dist Ct 251 Theodore Levin US Courthouse 231 W Lafayette Blvd Detroit MI 48226-2719

DUHME, CAROL MCCARTHY, civic worker; b. St. Louis, Apr. 13, 1917; d. Eugene Ross and Louise (Roblee) McCarthy; m. Sheldon Ware, June 12, 1941 (dec. 1944); 1 child, David; m. H. Richard Duhme, Jr., Apr. 9, 1947; children: Benton (dec.), Ann, Warren (dec.). AB, Vassar Coll., 1939. Tchr. elem. sch., 1939-41, 42-44; moderator St. Louis Assn. Congl. Chs., 1952; dir. Christian edn. First Congl. Ch., St. Louis, 1959-62, trustee, 1964-66, mem. ch. coun., 1974-75, 84-85, 87-89, bd. deaconesses, 1978-81, bd. deacons, 1982-85, 92-95; chmn. bd. Christian Edn., 1987-88; former bd. dirs. Community Music Schs., St. Louis, Community Sch., Ch. Women United, John

Burroughs Sch., St. Louis Bicentennial Women's Com., St. Louis Jr. League; pres. St. Louis Vassar Club; pres. bd. dirs. YWCA, St. Louis, 1973-76, chmn. ann. fund, 1989-90; bd. dirs. North Side Team Ministry, 1968-84, Chautauqua (N.Y.) Instn., 1971-79, mem. adv. coun. to bd., 1987—; adv. coun. Mo. Bapt. Hosp., 1973-89; exec. com. bd. dirs. Eden Theol. Sem., 1981-95, presdl. search com. 1986-87, 92-93, v.p. bd. dirs., 1991, chmn. 150th Anniversary com., 1996—; sec. bd. dirs. UN Assn., St. Louis, 1976-84, coun. of advisors, 1993—; pres. bd. dirs. Family and Children's Svc. Greater St. Louis, 1977-79; mem. chancellor's long-range planning com. Washington U., 1980-81, mem. Nat. Coun., Sch. Social Work, 1987—; chmn. Benton Roblee Duhme Scholarship Fund; trustee Joseph H. and Florence A. Roblee Found., St. Louis, 1984—, pres., 1984-90, bd. dirs.; chmn. Chautaugua Bell Tower Scholarship Fund, 1964—; bd. dirs. Nat. Inland Waterways Libr., St. Louis Merc. Libr. Mem. corp. assembly Blue Cross Hosp. Svc. of Mo., 1978-86. Recipient Mary Alice Messerley award for volunteerism Health and Welfare Coun. St. Louis, 1971; Vol. of Yr. award, YWCA, 1976; Woman of Achievement award St. Louis Globe Democrat, 1980; Outstanding Lay Woman nomination Mo. United Ch. of Christ, 1991; Outstanding Alumna award John Burroughs Sch., 1992. Home: 8 Edgewood Rd Saint Louis MO 63124-1817

DUITSMAN, STEVEN R., financial consultant; b. Champaign, Ill., Apr. 28, 1959; m. Mary Duitsman; children: Patrick, Nicholas. A of Aviation Electronics, U. Ill., 1981. Retail mgr. Case Merchandise, 1978-93; fin. cons. Merrill Lynch, Bloomington, Ill., 1993—. Mem. Toastmasters. Office: Merrill Lynch # 116 2103 N Veterans Pky Bloomington IL 61704-0908

DUKAS, PHILIP ALEXANDER, association executive; b. Tokyo, June 28, 1954; s. Alexander Nicholas and Edith Dukas; m. E. Katherine Coffin, Mar. 25, 1978; children: Alexandra, Briana. BS, Va. Polytech. Inst., 1977; MBA, Ohio State U., 1989. CEO Nat. DHIA, Columbus, Ohio, 1992—; mem. nat. rules com. Dairy Herd Improvement Assn.; U.S. rep. Internat. Com. on Animal Rec. Contbr. articles to profl. jours. Recipient Pacesetter award Ohio State U., 1988. Mem. Dairy Shrine, Am. Soc. Assn. Execs., Am. Mktg. Assn., U.S. Animal Health Assn., Nat. Quality Cert. Com., Nat. Mastitis Coun. (bd. dirs.), Internat. Standards Orgn. (U.S. rep.), Pacesetter Club (bd. dirs.). Home: 9551 Lake Of The Woods Dr Galena OH 43021-9622 Office: DHIA 3021 E Dublin Granville Rd Columbus OH 43231-4031

DUKES, JACK RICHARD, history educator; b. Indpls., Jan. 21, 1941; s. Richard Eugene and Kathleen (Cox) D.; m. Joanne Petty, June 15, 1963; children: Gregory Scott, Richard Aaron. BA, Beloit Coll., 1963; MA, No. Ill. U., 1965; PhD, U. Ill., 1970. Asst. prof. Macalester Coll., St. Paul, 1969-70; asst. prof. Carroll Coll., Waukesha, Wis., 1970-75, assoc. prof., 1975-83, prof. 1983—, chmn. dept. history, 1972—, dir. Russian Area Studies program, 1972-75; vis. assoc. prof. U. Calif., Santa Barbara, 1980-81; Scholar-Diplomat U.S. Dept. State, 1977; mem. exec. comm. Wis. Inst. for the Study of War, Peace and Global Cooperation, 1988-92. NEH fellow SUNY, Albany, 1974; U. Ill. assoc. in Russian history, 1977; NEH fellow in residence, U. Calif., Santa Barbara, 1977-78, St. Petersburg, Russia, 1992; fellow U. Calif. Inst. for Global Conflict and Cooperation, 1989; recipient Benjamin F. Richardson Excellence in Teaching, Rsch. and Ednl. Innovation Faculty award, 1991, Disting. Svc. citation Beloit Coll., 1993; named Hon. Citizen, City of Kokshetau, Kazakhstan, 1995. Mem. Am. Hist. Assn., Am. Assn. for Advancement Slavic Studies, Conf. Group Study Central European History, Soc. History Am. Fgn. Rels., German Studies Assn., Waukesha Sister Assn. (pres. 1989-91, exec. dir. 1991—). Author: (with Joachim Remak) Another Germany: A Reconsideration of the Imperial Era, 1987; contbr. articles to profl. jours. Home: 114 W Laflin Ave Waukesha WI 53186-6230 Office: Carroll Coll Dept History Waukesha WI 53186

DULBERGER, REID EDWARD, economic development executive; b. Jersey City, N.J., Dec. 24, 1956; s. Ira and Betti (Mogil) D.; m. Judith Ann Botch, Oct. 19, 1986; 1 child, Jacob Robert. AA, Miami Dade Cmty. Coll., Miami, Fla., 1973; BA, Fla. Internat. U., 1975; MA, Georgetown U., 1977; MS, Carnegie Mellon U., 1984. Cert. fin. profl. Coal policy analyst U.S. Dept. Energy, Washington, 1984-85; financial analyst U.S. Dept. Housing & Urban Devel., Washington, 1985-86; deputy dir. devel. City of Syracuse, Syracuse, N.Y., 1986-91; sr. v.p. Youngstown Warren Regional Chamber, Youngstown, Ohio, 1991—; sec., YSU Tech. Devel. Corp., Youngstown, 1991—; com. co-chair, bd. dirs., Mahoning-Columbiana Training Assn., Youngstown, 1993—; bd. dirs. CASTLO Cmty. Improvement Corp., Struthers, Ohio, 1994—. Adv. com. Trumbull Correctional Inst., Warren, Ohio, 1994—; planning com. Youngstown/Mahoning Co. United Way., 1993—; bd. dirs., com. co-chair Temple Rodef Sholom, Youngstown, 1993—; pres. Temple Rodef Sholom Brotherhood, 1993—. Recipient Presdl. Mgmt. Internship award U.S. Office Pers. Mgmt., 1984; Monetary award for Superior Svc. U.S. Dept. Energy, 1985. Mem. Ohio Devel. Assn., Am. Planning Assn., Am. Econ. Devel. Coun., Nat. Coun. Urban Econ. Devel. Home: 2240 Selma Ave Youngstown OH 44504 Office: Youngstown Warren Regional Chamber 1200 Stambaugh Bldg Youngstown OH 44503

DULC, JAMES M., application engineer; b. Cleve., Jan. 18, 1953. BS in Engring. Tech., Miami U., Oxford, Ohio, 1976. Applications cons. Mfr. Software and Svcs., Cin., 1978-83; regional tech. mgr. Encode, Nashua, N.H., 1985-87; application engr. SDRC, Milford, Ohio, 1987-88; sys. cons. Comuterland, Cin., 1988-90; application engr. Intergraph, Cleve., 1990—; cons. product knowledge Intergraph. Office: Intergraph 9885 Rockside Rd Ste 100 Cleveland OH 44125-6200

DULL, CLIFFORD JOHN, religious groups analyst; b. Richland Ctr., Wis., Jan. 11, 1946; s. Clifford LaVerne and Olive Clare (McKittrick) D.; m Helen Marie Kirkpatrick, June 12, 1970. BA in History, Milligan Coll., 1968; MA in Classics, U. Wis., 1970, PhD in History, 1975; Cert. in Book Pub., NYU, 1980. Vis. asst. prof. U. Colo., Boulder, 1975-76; faculty mem. Roanoke Bible Coll., Elizabeth City, N.C., 1976-77; lectr. Carthage Coll., Kenosha, Wis., 1977-78; editorial cons. Standard Pub., Cin., 1978-79; lectr. U. Wis.-Washington County, West Bend, 1980; computer specialist Def. Logistics Agy., Columbus, Ohio, 1980—. Contbr. articles and book revs. to profl. jours. and articles to books. Elder Upper Arlington Christian Ch., Columbus, 1983—. Mem. Assn. Ancient Historians, Am. Inst. Archaeology, Disciples of Christ Hist. Soc., Am. Soc. Ch. Soc. Home: 225 Tibet Rd Columbus OH 43202

DULLOCK, SCOTT ANTHONY, manufacturing executive; b. Jackson, Mich., Jan. 18, 1970; s. Anthony Edward and Merrily Louise (Mault) D. Student, Jackson C.C., 1988-93. Cashier, stock, gas attendent Lansing Ave Beer Co., Jackson, Mich., 1983-88; prodn. supr. Jackson Flexible Products, 1988—; residential builder The House Drs., Jackson, 1993—. Mem. Nat. Assn. Self Employed, Jackson Area Landlord Assn. Roman Catholic. Home and office: 531 Barrett Ave Jackson MI 49202

DULLY, FRANK EDWARD, JR., physician, educator; b. Hartford, Conn., Jan. 19, 1932; s. Frank Edward and Monica Theresa (Cooney) D.; m. Rebecca Sue Akers, Apr. 23, 1982; children: Kathleen, Ann, Margaret, David, Nancy, Tammy. BS, Coll. of Holy Cross, 1954; MD, Georgetown U., 1958; MPH, U. Calif., Berkeley, 1970. Diplomate Am. Bd. Preventive Medicine. Rotating intern D.C. Gen. Hosp., Washington, 1958-59; resident in family practice Bridgeport (Conn.) Hosp., 1959-60; resident in aerospace medicine Naval Aerospace Med. Inst., Pensacola, Fla., 1970-72; pvt. practice Shelton, Conn., 1960-64; commd. lt. USN, 1964, advanced through grades to capt., 1972; served with Destroyer Squadron 14, 1964-65; USN student flight surgeon, 1965-66; sr. med. officer USS Hornet, 1966-68, Naval Air Sta., Glynco, Ga., 1968-69; aerospace medicine resident USN, Pensacola, Fla., 1970-72; sr. med. officer USS Enterprise, 1972-74; dir. tng. Naval Aerospace Med. Inst., Pensacola, 1974-77; sr. med. officer First Marine Aircraft Wing, 1977-78, Pacific Fleet Naval Air Force, 1978-82; commanding officer Naval Aerospace Med. Inst., 1982-85; instr. aviation safety Naval Postgrad. Sch., Monterey, Calif., 1985-87; ret., 1987; field assoc. prof. Inst. Safety and Systems Mgmt. U. So. Calif., L.A., 1987-90, cons. aviation med., 1990-94; lectr. aviation safety worldwide, 1978—; tchr. safety N.W. Airlines, Mpls., 1988-90; cons. in aviation medicine U. So. Calif., 1990—. Co-editor: U.S. Navy Flight Surgeon Manual, 1976; contbr. over 40 articles on aviation medicine to med. jours. Decorated Legion of Merit, Air medal with oak leaf cluster, Meritorious Svc. medal. Fellow ACP, Am. Coll. Preventive Medicine, Aerospace Med. Assn.; mem. Internat. Acad. Aviation and Space Medicine, Soc. U.S.-Naval Flight Surgeons (pres. 1980, 81, 83), Internat. Soc. Air Safety Investigators, Am. Helicopter Soc., Am. Model Yachting Assn., St. Louis Admirals R/C Boat Club, Scale Ship Modelers Assn. N.Am., Tailhook Assn., Flight Safety Found., USS Enterprise Assn. Republican. Roman Catholic. Home: 2522 Briarcliff Dr Newburgh IN 47630-8604

DULMES, STEVEN LEE, computer science educator; b. Sheboygan Falls, Wis., Apr. 29, 1957; s. Warren Lynn and LaVerne (Wensink) D.; m. Renee Kay VandeVrede, Dec. 2, 1989. BS in Mech. Tech., Purdue U., 1981; MS in Computer Sci., DePaul U., Chgo., 1995. Design engr. Harnischfeger Corp., Cedar Rapids, Iowa, 1981-84; mfg. specialist Ohmeda div. BOC, Madison, Wis., 1984-85; mfg. engr. EDS div. GM, Oak Creek, Wis., 1985-87; instr. computer aided design Coll. Lake County, Grayslake, Ill., 1987—; cons. Baxter Healthcare Corp., Round Lake, Ill., 1989—. Pres. Cedar Valley Running Assn., cedar Rapids, 1981-83; adviser Jr. Achievements, Cedar Rapids, 1983; active Calvary Meml. Ch., Racine, Wis., 1990. Republican. Home: 3531 Sherwood St Racine WI 53406-5245 Office: Coll Lake County 19351 W Washington St Grayslake IL 60030-1148

DUMAINE, DANIEL JEROME, musician, composer, musical director; b. St. Louis, Oct. 10, 1963; s. William R. and Sallie C. (Mapp) DuM.; m. Jessica Juliana Smoot, June 4, 1988; children: Nicole, Xavier, Maxine. BA, Webster U., 1985. Musical conductor Ruppert's Orch., St. Louis, 1990-92; music dir. Divine Praise Co., St. Louis, 1994—, Black Composers Repertory Chorus, St. Louis, 1995—, St. Alphonsus Rock Ch., St. Louis, 1988—, Marriott West Hotel, St. Louis, 1993—; music dir., adv. bd. McDonald's Gospelfest, St. Louis, 1992-94. Composer: A Difference, 1991 (compact disc, Billboard award, 1991), Soulful Mass of St. Alphonsus, 1993 (compact disc, Billboard award, 1993), It's Time, 1994 (winner St. Louis Song Contest, 1995). Founder, annual fund-raising concert for the needy, MAT Ctr., St. Louis, 1994—. Named Nat. Youth of the Yr. Nat. Assn. Negro Musicians, N.Y.C., 1986, one of "40 People Under 40 Who Are Making a Difference in St. Louis" St. Louis Mag., 1991; recipient McDonald's Gospelfest Heritage award, St. Louis, 1994. Home: 1944 Venita Dr Saint Louis MO 63114

DUMAS, TYRONE PIERRE, architect, construction manager, consultant; b. Milw., July 11, 1952; s. Augustus Elerby and Darlene (Elerby) Ingram; m. Ceciel Harrell Dumas, Aug. 18, 1973; children: Maurice A., Danielle S.; foster children: Latrice Harrell, Stonia Harrell. AArch, Milw. Area Tech. Coll., 1975; BArch, U.Wis., Milw., 1977. Construction bldg. inspection dept. City Milw., 1977-79; corporate engr. Miller Brewing Co., Milw., 1979-86; constrn. mgr. Heike/Design Assn. Inc., Brookfield, Wis., 1986; with Dumas Cons. Specialties, Milw., 1986—. Vol., speaker United Way, Milw., 1984-86; vol. speaker Milw. Pub. Schs., 1984-86; asst. basketball coach Bethlehem Luth. Sch.; trustee Bethlehem Luth. Ch., steward various coms. Recipient Merit award State of Wis., 1973, Role Model of Yr. award Milw. Pub. Sch., 1983-84, Community Service award Miller Brewing Co., 1985. Mem. AIA (assoc.), Wis. Soc. Architects (assoc.), Project Mgmt. Inst., U.S. Brewers Acad., Constrn. Specifications Inst. (assoc.), U.W. Milw. Alumni Assn. Lutheran. Home and Office: 5963 N 78th St Milwaukee WI 53218-1712

DUMKE, MELVIN PHILIP, dentist; b. Sleepy Eye, Minn., Jan. 23, 1920; s. Herman Gustav and Else Ida (Battig) D.; D.D.S., U. Minn., 1943; m. Phyllis Lorraine Steuck, June 25, 1950; children: Pamela, Bruce, Shari. Practice dentistry, Sleepy Eye, 1946-50, Morgan, Minn., 1950-66, Mankato, Minn., 1966—. Lectr. dental assts. Mankato State Coll., 1967-69. Mem. Town Council, Morgan, 1960-65. Bd. control Martin Luther Acad., New Ulm, Minn., 1965-79; bd. dirs. The Luth. Home, Belle Plaine, Minn., 1981—; pres. Luth. Congregation, 1970, 86-87. Served to capt., Dental Corps, AUS, 1943-46. Fellow Royal Soc. Health, Internat. Coll. Dentists, Am. Coll. Dentists, Pierre Fouchard Acad.; mem. ADA (ho. of dels. 1977-87), Minn. Dental Assn. (chmn. peer rev. com. 1973-79, mem. ho. of dels. 1978-89, pres. 1983-84, guest of honor 1993), So. Dist. Dental Soc. (exec. coun., trustee 1988-89), South Cen. Dental Study Club (pres. 1970), Fedn. Dentaire Internationale, U. Minn. Alumni Assn., V.F.W. (recipient Distinguished Service award 1966, comdr. 1965), Am. Legion, Lions (pres. 1965, 74, zone chmn. 1975), Mankato Golf Club, U. Minn. Sch. Dentistry Century Club, Psi Omega. Home: 364 Carol Ct Mankato MN 56003-3300 Office: 430 S Broad St Mankato MN 56001-3703

DUNAGAN, GWENDOLYN ANN, special education educator; b. Youngstown, Ohio, Sept. 27, 1941; d. Charles Jefferson and Emma Juanita (Alexander) Hicks; m. Willie Miles, 1966; 1 child, Byron Keith Miles; m. Kenneth Robert Dunagan, July 1, 1972. BS in Edn., Youngstown U., Ohio, 1963; postgrad., Ashland U., 1986-89. Cert. elem. tchr., Ohio, learning disabilities tchr., Ohio, tchr. to severe behavior disorder, Ohio. Elem. tchr. Youngstown Bd. Edn., 1963-67, 1968-72; adminstr., tchr. Free Kindergarten Assn., Youngstown, 1967-68; liaison home-sch. Alliance (Ohio) Bd. Edn., 1972-86, tchr. disadvantaged pupils, 1986-89, intervention tchr. learning disabilities, 1989-90, tchr. specific learning disabilities, 1990-94, tchr. spl. edn., 1990-96; contestant, winner TV show Price is Right; group leader Youngstown Detention Ctr. Contbr. articles to profl. mags., area newspapers. Pres. Domestic Violence Shelter, Alliance, 1990-92, hon. mem., 1992—; pres. John Slimack Homeless Shelter, Alliance, 1989-93; pres., founder Cmty. Civic Com., Alliance, 1987—; treas. Altrusic Civic Club, Alliance, 1988-91; mem. choir Holy Temple Ch. God in Christ, Alliance, 1972—, mem. usher bd. dirs., fin. sec., sec. Sunday sch., 1989—; chairperson Alliance Area Desert Storm Celebration, 1991; mem. Family Counseling Ctr., YWCA, Dr. King Birthday Celebration Com.; mem. Dr. Martin Luther King Jr. Steering Com., 1995; tchr. Prayer and Bible Band, 1990—; adv. bd. Salvation Army, 1994—. Honored for community svc. Stark County Community Action Agy., 1990. Mem. NAFE, AAUW, Alliance Edn. Assn. (Dowling scholarship com.), NAACP (2d v.p. 1990-93), McKinley Reading Assn., Quota Club, Alpha Kappa Alpha. Home: 1115 S Seneca Ave Alliance OH 44601-4068

DUNASKISS, MAT J., state legislator; b. Pontiac, Mich., Sept. 21, 1951; s. Frank and Aldona (Suvedis) D.; m. Diane L. Tench, 1978; three children. AA, Oakland C.C., 1971; BA, U. Mich., 1973, MA, 1976. Tchr. Lake Orion (Mich.) Cmty. Sch., 1974-78; commr. Oakland County, Mich., 1979-80; rep. Mich. Dist. 61, 1980-90; senator Mich. Dist. 16, 1991—; chmn. tech. & energy com. Mich. State Sen., vice chmn. natural resources & environ. affairs com., local, urban & state affairs com. Recipient cmty. svc. award Lake Orion Area Jaycees, 1981. Mem. Oakland County C. of C., Optimists, K. of C., Lake Orion Lake Assn., St. Joseph Catholic Ch. Usher's Club. Home: 40 Nakomis St Lake Orion MI 48362-1228 Address: 535 Cushing Lake Orion MI 48362*

DUNAWAY, FRANK ROSSER, III, emergency physician; b. Albuquerque, Sept. 2, 1953; s. Frank Rosser and Constance (Durham) D.; m. Marcia Lee Moore, May 24, 1975 (div. 1990); children: Melissa Sommer, Amanda Durham, Vanessa Lee; m. Amy Jane Rutledge, Apr, 7, 1990; children: Kiera Elizabeth Eirwyn, Reagan Kailean Maira. BS, Duke U., 1975; MD, U. Ill., 1988. Diplomate Am. Bd. Emergency Medicine, Nat. Bd. Med. Examiners. Resident inspector nuclear engr. U.S. Nuclear Regulatory Commn., Glen Ellyn, Ill., 1982-84; resident emergency physician St. Francis Med. Ctr., Peoria, Ill., 1988-91; attending emergency physician Qualified Emergency Specialists Inc., Cin., 1991-93; med. dir. emergency svcs., chmn. dept. emergency medicine Proctor Hosp, Peoria, 1993—, cons. hyperbaric physician, 1996—; v.p. Proctor Emergency Physicians, P.C., Peoria, 1995—; consulting physician Hyperbaric Medicine, 1996—. Contbr. articles to profl. jours. Lt. US Navy, 1975-82. Fellow Am. Coll. Emergency Physicians. Republican. Episcopalian.

DUNBAR, MARY ASMUNDSON, communications executive, investor and public relations consultant; b. Sacramento, Calif., Feb. 6, 1942; d. Vigfus Samundur and Aline Mary (McGrath) Asmundson; m. Robert Copeland Dunbar, June 21, 1969; children: Geoffrey Townsend, William Asmundson. BA in English Lit., Smith Coll., 1964; MA in Communications, Stanford, 1967; MBA in Fin., Case Western Res. U., 1985. Cert. pub. rels. profl. Tchr. Peace Corps, Cameroun, Africa, 1964-66; writer, editor Ednl. Devel. Corp., Palo Alto, Calif., 1967-68, Addison-Wesley, Menlo Park, Calif., 1969-70; free lance writer, editor various, Cleve., 1970-85; account exec. Edward Howard & Co., Cleve., 1985-87; account exec. Dix & Eaton, Inc., Cleve., 1987—, v.p., 1992—. Author publs. in field (Arthur Page award 1990, IABC award 1987, Women in Communications award 1987). Trustee Cleve. Scholarship Program, 1993—, Cleve. Coun. World Affiars, 1994—. Recipient scholarship Smith Coll., Northampton, Mass., 1960-64; fellowship Stanford Univ., Palo Alto, Calif., 1967. Mem. Smith Coll. Club Cleve., Pub. Rels. Soc. Am., Nat. Investor Rels. Inst. (membership Cleve.-Akron chpt.), Cleve. Soc. Security Analysts, Cleve. Com. Fgn. Rels. Republican. Episcopalian. Home: 2880 Fairfax Rd Cleveland OH 44118-4014 Office: Dix & Eaton Inc 1801 E 9th St Ste 1300 Cleveland OH 44114-3103

DUNCAN, CLEO, state legislator; m. John Duncan. BS, Ball State U.; MS, Purdue U. Sales rep. Gray & Gray Specialties; mem. Ind. State Ho. of Reps. Dist. 67, mem. edn., pub. policy, ethics and vet. affairs com., mem. roads and transp. com., vice-chmn. environ. affairs com. Councilman Greensburg, Ind.; pres. Decatur County Solid Waste Bd.; mem. Greensburg City Planning Commn., Decatur County Coun. Youth; founder Project HELP. Mem. Greensburg C. of C., Decatur County Found.

DUNCAN, JAMES STACY, accountant, community college administrator; b. Abingdon, Va., June 8, 1962; s. Robert Cleveland and Geneva Anne (Davidson) D.; m. Beverly Brooks, Feb.16, 1990; children: James David, Melissa Danielle, Kaylyn Marie. BS, Berea (Ky.) Coll., 1984; MA, Tusculum Coll., 1990. Cert. netware engr. V.p. ops. Duncans, Saltville, Va., 1987-91; asst. dir. fin. aid Va. Tech., Blackburg, 1991-93; dir. fin. aid U. Ill., Springfield, 1993-94, Columbus (Ohio) State C.C., 1994—; mem. adv. com. VA, Roanoke, Va., 1989-91; bd. dirs. Duncans; pres. Duncan Techs., Hilliard, Ohio, 1994—. Bd. dirs. Salt Theater Corp., Saltville, 1994—; mem. com. Columbus Found., 1995, Ctrl. Benefits, Inc., Columbus, 1994-95. Lt. USMC, 1985-87. Carl Perkins grantee U.S. Dept. Edn., 1995. Mem. Am. Mgmt. Assn. Democrat. Home: 5379 Taylor Lane Ave Hilliard OH 43026 Office: Columbus State CC 550 E Spring St Columbus OH 43215

DUNCAN, LOUIS D., building and safety director; b. Detroit, May 22, 1945; s. Hugh and Gladys Marie (Knas) D.; married, June 5, 1971 (widowed Aug. 1989); children: Aaron, Danielle. Student, Henry Ford C.C., Dearborn, Mich., Ea. Mich. U. Dir. bldg. and safety dept. City Hall City of Dearborn, Dearborn, 1965—. Mem. KC.

DUNCAN, ROYAL ROBERT, publisher; b. Bloomington, Ill., May 6, 1952; s. Robert E. and Audrey L. Gresham (Mossberger) D. AA, Rock Valley Coll., Rockford, Ill., 1972; BS, Bradley U., 1974. Sales mgr. Sports Svcs., Peoria, Ill., 1975-77, 4-B Advt., East Peoria, Ill., 1977-78; pres. Royal Pub., Peoria, 1978—. Home: 7600 N Galena Rd Peoria IL 61615-9751 Office: 7620 Harker Dr Peoria IL 61615-1849

DUNCAN, STEPHEN C., stockbroker; b. Waukegan, Ill., Oct. 19, 1938. BS in Fin., Mich. State U., 1961. Stockbroker Mullaney Wells Co., Chgo., 1962-69, Summers & Co., Ft. Wayne, 1969-72, Roney & Co., Ft. Wayne, 1972-75, Headford & Co., Ft. Wayne, 1975-84, Investment Mgmt. and Resources, Ft. Wayne, 1984—; owner Retirement Plan Mgmt., Ft. Wayne, 1989—. Office: Investment Mgmt & Resources 813 Fulton St Fort Wayne IN 46802-2111

DUNCANSON, DONALD GEORGE, retired encyclopedia editor; b. L.A., Feb. 26, 1928; s. George H. and Addie (Biddison) D. BA, U. So. Calif., L.A., 1953; MA, Harvard U., 1954; postgrad., U. Chgo., 1954-56. Lexicographer Funk & Wagnalls Inc., N.Y.C., 1956-57; assoc. editor Scott, Foresman & Co., Chgo., 1958-64, Sci. Rsch. Assocs., Inc., Chgo., 1964-67; editor Ency. Britannica, Inc., Chgo., 1967-73, 77-93. With USN, 1946-49. Democrat. Home: 3605 Sarah St Franklin Park IL 60131-1632

DUNEA, MARY MILLS, governor's aide; b. Des Moines; d. George Sturginne and Mary Brackett (Sweney) Mills; m. John Robert Barr (div.); children: Mary Louise, John Mills; m. George Dunea; 1 child, Melanie Serena Alexandra. AB, Grinnell Coll. Pub. rels. dir. Cook County Hosp., chgo., 1968-70, Comprehensive State Health Planning Agy., chgo., 1970-73, Chgo. Tchrs. Union, 1975-77; book reviewer WGN Radio-Roy Leonard Show, Chgo., 1980-92; owner Walton Books, Inc., Chgo., 1978-84; asst. to the sec. Staff of Sec. of State Jim Edgar, Chgo., 1984-91; asst. to the gov. Staff of Gov. Jim Edgar, Chgo., 1991—; bd. dirs. Internat. Vis. Ctr., Chgo., English Speaking Union, Chgo.; Chgo. com. mem. Coun. on Fgn. Affairs, 1993—. Mem. campaign staff Dick Ogilve for Gov., Chgo., 1968, Jim Edgar for Gov., Chgo., 1990. Recipient award Ill. Ctr. for the Book, Chgo., 1990, Grand Decoration of Honor, The Republic of Austria, 1994. Fellow The Royal Soc. Arts; mem. Woman's Athletic Club, Cliff Dweller Club, Skyline Club, Carlton Club. Republican. Methodist. Home: 222 E Chestnut St Chicago IL 60611 Office: Office of Gov 100 W Randolph St Chicago IL 60601-3218

DUNHAM, MICHAEL D., design engineer; b. Garden City, Kans., May 26, 1966. BS in Mech. Engring. Tech., Pitts. State U., 1989. Design engr. Rimpull Corp., Olathe, Kans., 1989—. Republican.

DUNHAM, MICHAEL HERMAN, human services agency executive; b. Dayton, Ohio, Mar. 30, 1951; s. Robert Fredrick and Marjory Katherine (Fortune) D.; m. Nancy Lynn Cross, July 2, 1977; children: Lisa Yandow Olson, A. Richard Yandow. Student, Kent State U., 1970-72, U. Vt., 1975-77; BA in sociology, U. Wis., 1980. Rsch. assoc. U. Wis., Madison, 1977-84; dir. managed care Univ. Health Care, Inc., Madison, 1984-86; dir. fiscal affairs Health & Hosps. Corp., N.Y.C., 1986-88; CEO Total Health HMO, Inc., N.Y.C., 1988-89; pres., CEO Practice Mgmt., Inc., Madison, 1989-92, Cmty. Care Mgmt., Inc., Madison, 1992—; faculty mem. CASSP Inst., Georgetown U., Washington, 1992-96. Contbr. chpts. to books, articles to profl. jours. Mental health Interagy. Coun. State Wis., Madison, 1992-94, grad. med. edn. rev. commn., 1986, cert. need adv. com., 1984-86. Mem. N.Y. State HMO Coun. (exec. bd. 1988), Wis. Assn. Family & Children's Agys. Presbyterian. Home: 405 Elmside Blvd Madison WI 53704 Office: Cmty Care Mgmt Inc 16 N Carroll St Ste 640 Madison WI 53703

DUNIGAN, DENNIS WAYNE, real estate executive; b. Cin., Apr. 28, 1952; s. Park George and Hazel Edna (Hines) D. AA, U. Cin., 1974, BBA, 1975. Salesman Comey and Shepherd, Inc., Cin., 1978-79; property mgr. Dunigan Properties, Cin., 1980—; assoc. T.J. Carter Realty, Cin., 1984—. Contbr. articles to profl. jours. Chmn. trans. com. Reagan for Pres. Cin., 1980--; active Cin. Hist. Soc., Mus. of Nat. Hist., 1987--, Cin. Zoo, 1987--, Contemporary Arts Ctr., Cin., 1988--, The Taft Mus., 1988--; contbg. mem. Cin. Art Mus., 1987—. Mem. U. Cin. Alumni Assn., Ohio Assn. Realtors, Cin. Bd. Realtors, Nat. Baseball Hall of Fame and Mus. Republican. Home: 6022 St Regis Dr Cincinnati OH 45236-4218

DUNIPHAN, J. P., state legislator, small business owner. Mem. S.D. Ho. of Reps., Pierre, mem. commerce and local govt. coms. Republican.

DUNIVENT, JOHN THOMAS, artist, educator; b. Moberly, Mo., Apr. 24, 1928; s. Everett B. and Bertha (Goetze) D. Student, St. Louis U., 1946-47; BFA, Washington U., St. Louis, 1951; postgrad., Berkshire Music Ctr., Lenox, Mass., 1951; MA, N.Mex. Highlands U., 1957. Asst. prof. drama dept. Fontbonne Coll., St. Louis, 1967-71; lectr. photography and society U. Mo., St. Louis, 1984, 90; lectr. history of photography Washington U. Sch. Fine Arts, St. Louis, 1987; art instr. Parkway Sch. Dist., St. Louis County, Mo., 1960-67, 71-94; vis. prof. art edn. U. Maine, Portland, summers 1971, 72. Illustrator (ink drawings, book) Amerind: Gestural Communication for the Speechless, 1978, (photographs, book) St. Louis Currents, 1986; painter ann. midyear show Butler Inst. Am. Art, Youngstown, Ohio, 1981; solo exhibit of photographs Ctr. for Met. Studies, U. Mo., St. Louis, 1988. Panel mem. master tchr. symposium U. Kans. Sch. Fine Arts, Lawrence, 1985; bd. dirs. Young Audiences, Inc., St. Louis, 1968-74, 80-83. Spl. agt. Counter Intelligence Corps, U.S. Army, 1952-54. Recipient award for pastel painting Chautauqua (N.Y.) Inst., 1959. Home and Office: 607 Forest Ct Saint Louis MO 63105-2759

DUNKEL, NANCY ANN, banker; b. Manchester, Iowa, Sept. 5, 1955; d. Marvin John and Olga Teresa (Bildstein) Helle; m. Kenneth James Dunkel, June 12,1976; children: Jill Marie, Todd Michael. Student, Loras Coll., 1986. Exec. sec. R.L. Luehrsmann, Dyersville, Iowa, 1975-77; sr. v.p., loan officer Farley (Iowa) State Bank, 1977-90; exec. v.p., cashier State Bank Worthington, Iowa, 1991—, also bd. dirs. Bd. dirs. Dyersville Area Found. for Future, 1989—; eucharistic minister St. Francis Xavier Basilica, Dyersville, 1987—; mem. Worthington Centennial Exec. Com., 1992-93; mem. bd. dirs., sec. Worthington Cmty. Club, 1994—; treas. Farley Mid. Sch. PTA, 1996-98. Recipient Iowa Disting. Woman Banking award Northwestern Fin. Review, 1993. Mem. Fin. Women Internat. (Iowa State pres. 1990-91, Iowa pub. affairs chmn. 1992, v.p. N.E. Iowa group 1993-94, pres. 1994-95), Iowa Bankers Assn. (chmn. consumer svcs. com. 1987-88, mem. mgmt. com. 1994—), Dubuque County Bankers Assn. (pres. 1989-90). Democrat. Roman Catholic. Home: 11822 Hickory Ln Dyersville IA 52040-9500 Office: State Bank Worthington 110 1st Ave W Worthington IA 52078

DUNLAP, CONNIE SUE ZIMMERMAN, real estate professional; b. Defiance, Ohio, Mar. 3, 1952; d. John Eldon and Loisann (May) Zimmerman; m. Joseph Richard Dunlap, Dec. 20, 1972; children: Brad, Todd, Eric. Student, MacMurray Coll., 1970-71, Ohio State U., 1973; BA, Wayne State U., 1989. Grad. Realtor Inst.; cert. residential specialist, 1991. Dental hygienist Dr. A. Lamar Byrd, San Diego, 1973-75; realtor, assoc. broker Champion & Baer, Inc., Grosse Pointe, Mich., 1986-95, Bolton-Johnston Assocs., Grosse Pointe Farms, Mich., 1995—; mem. Grosse Pointe Bd. Realtors, Macomb Bd. Realtors. Mem. Jr. League of Detroit, 1981—. Nat. Merit scholar Mature and Returning Women Wayne State U., Detroit, 1985-89. Mem. Phi Beta Kappa, Kappa Alpha Theta. Republican. Presbyterian. Home: 544 University Pl Grosse Pointe MI 48230-1640 Office: Bolton-Johnston Assocs 18332 Mack Ave Grosse Pointe MI 48236-3219

DUNLAP, DAVID HOUSTON, judge; b. Columbia, Mo., Apr. 24, 1947; s. James Vardeman and Cynthia May (Roby) D.; m. Dana Sue Coburn, Apr. 23, 1982. BA, Southwest Mo. State U., 1969, MA, 1971; JD, U. Mo., 1975. Assoc. Campbell, Morgan & G, Kansas City, Mo., 1975-82; editor Mo. Law Tape, Inc., Kansas City, 1982-86; judge Howell County Cir. Ct. (37th cir.), West Plains, Mo., 1986—; cons. appellate law, Mo., 1982-86; profl. judge USA Nat. Debate team, 1972, 73. Author, editor: (audio tapes) Legal Ednl., 1974-86. Speaker Mo. Right-to-Work Com., Kansas City, 1978; bd. dirs. St. Francis' Farm, West Plains, Mo., 1986-90; mem. Mo. Task Force on Gender and Justice, 1990-93. Am. Forensic Assn. grantee, 1971. Mem. Mo. Bar Assn., Mo. Judicial Conf., Ozark Gastronomic Soc. (bd. dirs. 1983—). Home: 728 Monk St West Plains MO 65775-2908 Office: Howell County Cir Ct Assoc Div Howell County Courthouse West Plains MO 65775

DUNLAP, RICHARD LOWELL, foundation administrator, church organist; b. Passaic, N.J., Aug. 7, 1950; s. Robert Lindzay and Lenora (Willis) D.; m. Dianne Jeter, June 30, 1973; children: Stephen Richard, Ryan Lowell, David Michael. BMus, So. Meth. U., 1972, MFA, 1974. Arts program dir. Okla. Arts and Humanities Coun., Okla. City, 1973-75; assoc. faculty Okla. City U., 1975; dep. dir. Mich. Coun. For the Arts, Detroit, 1975-91, Mich. Coun. for Arts and Cultural Affairs, Detroit, 1991-95; program officer The Kresge Found., Troy, Mich., 1995—; music dir., organist Plumbrook Bapt. Ch., Sterling Heights, Mich., 1977-86, Presbyn. Ch. of Utica, Sterling Heights, 1989—. Bd. dirs. Am. Bapt. Chs. of S.E. Mich., Detroit, 1984-86, Great Lakes Arts Alliance, Cleve., 1985-86, Arts Midwest, Mpls., 1985-87; panelist Nat. Endowment for the Arts, Washington, 1987-93; mem. adv. bds. Ohio Arts Coun., Columbus, 1987-95; elder, clk. of session Presbyn. Ch. of Utica, Sterling Heights, Mich., 1988-93; bd. dirs. Concerned Citizens for the Arts in Mich., Detroit, 1995—; trustee The Art Ctr., Mt. Clemens, Mich., 1995—; mem. Sterling Heights Cultural Commn., 1996—; panelist N.J. State Coun. on the Arts, 1996; mem. citizens adv. coun. Detroit Dept. of Cultural Affairs, 1996—. Home: 39641 Karola Dr Sterling Heights MI 48313 Office: The Kresge Found PO Box 3151 Troy MI 48007-3151

DUNLAP, WILLIAM DEWAYNE, JR., advertising agency executive; b. Austin, Minn., Apr. 8, 1938; s. William D. and Evelyn (Hummel) D.; m. Lois Mary Apple, Sept. 23, 1961; children: Kristin, Leslie, Brenda. B.A., Carleton Coll., 1960. Brand mgr. soap Procter & Gamble, Cin., 1960-69; asst. postmaster gen. U.S. Postal Svc., Washington, 1970-75, chmn. postmaster gen.'s customer coun., 1971-75, chmn. stamp adv. coun., 1972-75; pres. MCA Advt., Westport, Conn., 1976-81; chmn. Campbell-Mithun Esty, Mpls., 1981—. Mem. Minn. Bus. Partnership; bd. dirs. Operation Smile Internat.; chmn. Minn. chpt. United Way. Mem. Am. Assn. Advt. Agys., Greater Mpls. C. of C. Lutheran. Home: 951 Springhill Rd Wayzata MN 55391-9553 Office: Campbell-Mithun-ESTY 222 S 9th St Minneapolis MN 55402-3310*

DUNLAVY, BRUCE MERRITT, environmental engineering executive; b. Yankton, S.D., Feb. 9, 1950; s. John Thomas and Rose (Eisenoff) D.; m. Sandra Joan Scott Farnsworth, Jan. 11, 1983; stepchildren: Stephen Gaylord Farnsworth II, Louis Andrew Farnsworth, Mark Gregory Farnsworth. AB in History with honors, Kenyon Coll., 1971; MA in History, Bowling Green State U., 1976. Registered sanitarian, Ohio; cert. class III wastewater works operator, Ohio. Asst. to chief chemist Divsn. of Sewerage and Drainage, Columbus, Ohio, 1971-72; water microbiologist Ohio Dept. Health, Bowling Green, 1973-74; environ. scientist Ohio EPA, Bowling Green, 1974-83, environ. engr., 1983-89, environ. supr., 1989-90, environ. mgr., 1990—. Co-author: EPA Survival Manual, 1986; mem. editl. bd. Ohio's Health mag., 1973-74; contbr. articles to profl. jours. Mem. Ohio Environ. Health Assn. Office: Ohio EPA 347 N Dunbridge Rd Bowling Green OH 43402-9398

DUNN, DAVID LEWIS, surgeon, researcher; b. Pontiac, Mich., Dec. 4, 1952; s. Lewis Edgar and Mary Elizabeth (Potts) D.; m. Patricia K. Felton. BS, U. Mich., 1973, MD, 1977; PhD, U. Minn., 1985. Intern U. Minn. Hosp., 1977-78, resident gen. surgery, 1978-85, transplant fellow, 1985-86; asst. prof. U. Minn., Mpls., 1985-89, assoc. prof., 1989-92, prof. surgery, 1993-95, Jay Phillips prof. and head of surgery, 1996—. Contbr. over 200 articles to profl. jours. Sandoz fellow, 1985; NIH grantee, 1983, 88, 91, 95. Fellow ACS; mem. Am. Soc. Transplant Surgeons, Soc. Univ. Surgeons, Surg. Infection Soc. (pres.), Assn. Acad. Surgery (pres.-elect), Am. Surg. Assn., Halsted Soc., Alpha Omega Alpha. Office: U Minn Mayo Meml Bldg Meml Bldg PO Box 242 420 Delaware St SE Minneapolis MN 55455-0374

DUNN, FLOYD, biophysicist, bioengineer, educator; b. Kansas City, Mo., Apr. 14, 1924; s. Louis and Ida (Leibtag) D.; m. Elsa Tanya Levine, June 11, 1950; children: Andrea Susan, Louis Brook. Student, Kansas City Jr. Coll., 1941-42, Tex. A&M U., 1943; BS, U. Ill., Urbana, 1949, MS, 1951, PhD, 1956. Research assoc. elec. engring. U. Ill., Urbana, 1954-57; research asst. prof. elec. engring. U. Ill., 1957-61, assoc. prof. elec. engring. and biophysics, 1961-65, prof., 1965—, prof. elec. engring., biophysics and bioengring., 1972-95; faculty mem. Beckman Inst. for Advanced Sci. and Tech.; prof. emeritus, 1995—; dir. bioacoustics research lab. U. Ill., 1976—, chmn. bioengring. faculty, 1978-82; vis. prof. dept. microbiology U.C. Coll., Cardiff, Wales, 1968-69; vis. sr. scientist Inst. Cancer Research, Sutton, Surrey, Eng., 1975-76, 82-83, 90; vis. prof. Inst. Chest Diseases and Cancer, Tohoku U., Sendai, Japan, 1982, 89-90, U. Nanjing, Nanjing, People's Republic of China, 1983; mem. radiation study sect. NIH, 1976-81; steering com. NSF Workshop on Interaction of Ultrasound and Biol. Tissues, 1971-72; chmn. WHO working group on health aspects of exposure to ultrasound radiation, London, 1976; mem. FDA tech.-elec. products radiation stds. com. 1974-76, NIH bioengring., radiation and diagnostic radiology study sects., 1970-81; faculty mem. Beckman Inst. Advanced Sci. and Tech. Editorial bd. Jour. Acoustical Soc. Am., Ultrasound in Medicine and Biology, Ultrasonics, Critical Reviews in Acoustics, Handbook of Acoustics, and Encyclopedia of Applied Physics; contbr. articles on biophys. acoustics to profl. jours. Trustee Hensley Twp., Ill., 1980-81. With AUS, 1943-46. NIH Spl. Rsch. fellow, 1968-69, Am. Cancer Soc.-Eleanor Roosevelt-Internat. Cancer fellow, 1975-76, 82-83, Fulbright fellow, 1982-83, Japan Soc. for Promotion of Sci. fellow, 1982, Fogarty Internat. fellow, 1990; recipient U. Ill. Sr. Scholar award, 1988, medal Spl. Merit Acoustical Soc. Japan, 1988, AIUM/WFUMB History Med. Ultrasound Pioneer award, 1988. Fellow AAAS, IEEE (Engring. Medicine and Biology Soc. Career Achievement award 1995, Edison medal 1996), Am. Inst. Med. and Biol. Engring., Acoustical Soc. Am. (assoc. editor Jour., pres. 1985-86, Silver medal 1989), Am. Inst. Ultrasound in Medicine (William J. Fry Meml. award 1984, Joseph H. Holmes Basic Sci. Pioneer award 1990), Inst. Acoustics (U.K.); mem. NAS, NAE, Am. Inst. Physics, Biophys. Soc., Japan Soc. Ultrasound in Medicine (hon.), Sigma Xi, Sigma Tau, Eta Kappa Nu, Tau Beta Pi, Pi Mu Epsilon, Phi Sigma, Phi Sigma Phi. Home: 2631 E Avenida de Maria Tucson AZ 85718 Office: U Ill Bioacoustics Rsch Lab 1406 W Green St Urbana IL 61801-2918

DUNN, FLOYD EMRYL, psychiatrist, neurologist, consultant; b. Wilkes-Barre, Pa., Apr. 25, 1910; s. Adrian Anson and Frances Amanda (Culver) D.; m. Wilda Kathryn Lauer, Aug. 14, 1943; children: Kathryn Alice (dec.), Deborah Lee. Student, Temple U., 1929-32; DO, Phila. Coll. Osteo. Medicine, 1936. Diplomate Am. Osteo. Bd. Neurology and Psychiatry. Resident in neurology, psychiatry Still-Hildreth Hosp., 1941-45, staff psychiatrist, 1945-49; chmn. div. neurology, psychiatry Kirksville Coll. Osteo. Medicine, 1945-48, Kansas City Coll. Osteo. Medicine, U. Health Scis., Mo., 1949-68; mem. staff VA Hosp., Knoxville, Iowa, 1968-76, chief psychiatry svc., 1970-76; clin. prof. neurology, psychiatry Coll. Osteo. Medicine, Des Moines, 1970-74; mem. Nat. Bd. Examiners for Osteo. Physicans and Surgeons, 1965-74, Excellence award, 1974, cons. neurology, psychiatry, Chgo., 1974—; cons., examiner sect. of disability determinations Mo. Dept. Elem. and Secondary Edn., Jefferson City, 1985—. Author: (monograph) History of the American College of Neuropsychiatrists, 1984. Contbr. articles to profl. jours. Mem. Iowa Adv. Coun. on Mental Health Ctrs., Des Moines, 1972-78, Abou Ben Adhem Temple, Cen. Regional Adv. Coun. for Comprehensive Psychiat. Svcs., Columbia, Mo., 1978-86. Fellow Am. Coll. Neuropsychiatrists (life, sec.-treas. 1948-52, pres. 1954-55, 63-64, Disting. Svc. award 1967, Disting. Fellow award 1984, 1st Fellows' Lecture Honoree 1989), Am. Assn. on Mental Deficiency; mem. Am. Osteo. Assn. (life, editorial cons. publs. 1958-95, del. 1960-69, pres.'s adv. coun. 1973), Mo. Assn. Osteo. Physicians and Surgeons (hon. life, del. 1958-69, v.p. 1969-70), Phi Sigma Gamma (pres. grand coun. 1952-53, coun. sec.-treas. 1953-59, editor Speculum 1959-65, Meritorious Svc. award 1965, 87-91, exec. sec.-treas. grand coun. 1980-95, editor Speculum 1995—), Am. Coll. Neuropsychiatrists and Am. Osteopathic Assn. (cons., examiner of neurology and psychiatry residency tng. programs 1988-91), Lions (pres. Gravois Mills, Mo. chpt. 1984-85, sec. 1985-88, del. to internat. conv. 1985, 86, 87), Masons (32d degree), Elks (life), Alpha Phi Omega. Republican. Methodist. Avocations: photography, travel, journalism. Home: RR 3 Box 504A Gravois Mills MO 65037-9431

DUNN, FRANK (FRANCIS MICHAEL DUNN), banker; b. Sigourney, Iowa, Feb. 27, 1933; s. John Michael and Marie Catherine (Strohman) D.; m. Maryann Lee Peiffer, Aug. 18, 1956; children: Katrina, Theresa, Michael, Nancy, Kelly, Patrick. Student, U. Denver, 1957-66, U. Colo., Denver, 1959-66; grad., So. U. Ill. Grad. Sch. Banking, Carbondale, 1973. Ordained deacon Roman Cath. Ch., 1992. Real estate broker, mortgage banker, ins. broker Denver, 1956-66; exec. v.p., dir. E. Dubuque (Ill.) Savs. Bank, 1967-76; cons. in banking E. Dubuque, 1976-80; v.p., dir. Tri-State Bank, E. Dubuque, 1980-84; pres., dir. First Nat. Bank, Glidden, Iowa, 1984-86; v.p., dir. and br. mgr. Swea City State Bank/Graettinger (Iowa) Bank Office, 1986-93; CEO, dir. Iowa Fin. Cons. Ltd., Estherville, 1993—; mgr., owner, broker Iowa Realty, Estherville, 1994—. Mem. Joint County Sch. Bd., 1973-76; bd. dirs. Horizons Unltd., 1990—; pres. bd. dirs. Estherville Youth Corp., 1993; organizer, developer, pres. Dunlieth Park & Pool, Jo Daviess County, Ill., 1972. organizer, developer, pres. Dunlieth Park & Pool, Jo Daviess County, Ill., 1972; bd. dirs. area handicap agy. Horizons Unltd. Mem. Ill. Bankers Assn. (agr. com. 1968-75), Iowa Bankers Assn. (agr. com. 1985-87), Thunder Hill Country Club (bd. dirs., organizer, treas. 1972-76), Lions (pres., bd. dirs. 1967-76). Roman Catholic. Office: Iowa Financial Cons 103 N 9th St Estherville IA 51334-2212

DUNN, HELEN ELIZABETH, retired secondary school educator; b. Peoria, Ill., July 14, 1930; d. Albert Edward and Corinne Ada (Rudel) Joos; m. Harry Christie Dunn, Feb. 4, 1951; children: Pamela Elizabeth Dunn Baumann, Patricia Louise Dunn Marshall. BS in Edn., Bradley U., 1951, MA in Guidance/Counseling, 1969. Tchr. Pub. Schs. of Hawaii, Lanai City, 1951-54, Ulupalakua, 1954-56; tchr. Pub. Schs. of Peoria, 1956-69; English LaSalle (Ill.)-Peru H.S., 1970-71; counselor, tchr. Peru (Ill.) Pub. Schs., 1971-89; ret., 1989. Contbr. poems to books: The Best Poems of the '90s, 1992, Distinguished Poets of America, 1993, Best Poems of 1995, 1995. Mem. NEA (del. 1951-56, rep. 1957-69, life mem.), LWV (bd. dirs. 1973-89, treas. 1982-89), Ret. Tchrs. Assn. (mem. legis. com. 1991-96), PEO, Peoria Women's Club, Delta Kappa Gamma (pres. 1968-70, 78-80, 92-94), Sigma Kappa (alumni chpt., pres. 1962, 91), Phi Lambda Theta. Methodist.

DUNN, HORTON, JR., organic chemist; b. Coleman, Tex., Sept. 3, 1929; s. Horton and Lora Dean (Bryant) D. BA summa cum laude, Hardin-Simmons U., 1951; MS, Case Western Res. U., 1975, PhD, 1979. Instr. chemistry Hardin-Simmons U., 1951; ONR fellow Ohio State U., Columbus, 1951-52; teaching fellow in chemistry Purdue U., Lafayette, Ind., 1952-53; rsch. chemist Lubrizol Corp., Cleve., 1953-70, dir. tech. info. ctr., 1970-79, supr. rsch. div., 1980—; chmn. bd., bus. mgr. Isotopics, Cleve., 1964-67, editor, 1961-63. Contbr. articles to profl. jours.; patentee in field. Treas. Cleve. Cir. Decorative Arts Trust, 1990-91, 93—, v.p., 1992-93; active Cleve. Art Assn., Cleve. Mus. of Art, Rock and Roll Hall of Fame, Mus. Founders Club. Fellow Am. Inst. Chemists; mem. AAAS, SAR (life), Am. Chem. Soc. (treas. Cleve. chpt. 1968-70, chmn. 1987, bd. dirs. 1990—), Am. Soc. for Info. Sci. (chpt. pres. 1973-74), Royal Soc. Chemistry, Soc. Tribologists and Lubrication Engrs., Nat. Coun. Met. Opera, Royal Oak Soc. (life), Cleve. Tech. Soc. Coun. (treas. 1987), Cleve. Art Assn., Univ. Club, Cleve. Club, Cleve. Play House Club, Rock and Roll Hall of Fam Mus. Founders Club (charter). Home: 530 Sycamore Dr Cleveland OH 44132-2150 Office: 29400 Lakeland Blvd Wickliffe OH 44092-2201

DUNN, J. TERRANCE, financial company executive, consultant; b. Kansas City, Mo., Nov. 10, 1939; s. Robert Emmett and Marian Elizabeth (Robison) D.; m. Kathryn Sue Gaines, Oct. 6, 1962 (div. Dec. 1991); 1 child, Elizabeth Leeann Dunn Steel. Student, Ctrl. Mo. State U., 1958; MS, Am. Coll., Byrn Mawr, Pa., 1992. CLU; ChFC. Mgmt. trainee Manulife Fin., Toronto, Ont., Can.; Kansas City, Mo., 1962-66; agy. trainer L.A., 1966-67; asst. gen. mgr. Santa Ana, Calif., 1967-69; gen. mgr. Spokane, Wash., 1969-71, L.A., 1971-77, Honolulu, 1977-80, Cin., 1980-87, Chgo., 1987-93; chmn., CEO, Jonathan Group, Chgo., 1993—. Bd. dirs., mem. exec. com. Boys Hope, Northridge, Ill., 1987—. Lt. U.S. Army N.G., 1962-68. Recipient Outstanding Leadership award San Fernando Valley Assn. Life Underwriters, 1976, Cin. Gen. Agts. and Mgrs. Assn., 1987. Mem. Am. Soc. CLU's and ChFC's (nat. bd. dirs. 1989-92, nat. dirs. coun. 1992-93, nat. chmn. student membership 1991-93, Outstanding Leadership award Hawaii chpt. 1980, Cin. chpt. 1987). Republican. Office: Jonathan Group 222 S Riverside Pl Ste 1520 Chicago IL 60606

DUNN, JAMES BERNARD, mining company executive, state legislator; b. Lead, S.D, June 27, 1927; s. William Bernard and Lucy Marie (Mullen) D.; m. Elizabeth Ann Lanham, Sept. 5, 1955; children: Susan, Thomas, Mary Elizabeth, Kathleen. BS in Bus. Adminstrn. and Econ., Black Hills State U., 1962. Heavy equipment mechanic Homestake Mining Co., Lead, 1947-62, asst. dir. pub. relations, 1962-78, dir. pub. affairs, 1978; mem. S.D. Ho. Reps., Pierre, 1971-72; mem. S.D. State Senate, Pierre, 1973—, asst. majority leader, 1989-92, asst. minority leader, 1993-94, asst. majority leader, 1995-96; exec. com. Nat. Conf. State Legislatures, 1979-81, 93-94, Coun. State Govt., 1983—; chmn. Midwestern Conf. Coun. of State Govts., 1984; bd. dirs. S.D. Blue Shield, S.D. Automobile Assn. Editor: Homestake Gold Mine 1876-1976, 1976, Bulldog Mountain Silver Mine, 1978. Bd. dirs. S.D. State Hist. Soc., Pierre,. 1971—; chmn. bd. trustees Adams Mus., Deadwood, S.D., 1962—. With U.S. Army, 1945-47. Republican. Roman Catholic. Home: 619 Ridgeroad Lead SD 57754 Office: State Senate State Capitol Pierre SD 57501

DUNN, JEFFREY W., stockbroker; b. Mpls., June 7, 1959. Stockbroker Dean Witter Reynolds, Bloomington, Minn., 1988—. Republican. Office: Dean Witter Reynolds 8300 Norman Center Dr Ste 1150 Bloomington MN 55437-1027

DUNN, JOHN FRANCIS, lawyer, state representative; b. Logansport, Ind., Dec. 24, 1936; s. John Francis and Bertha (Newman) D.; m. Barbara Burke, Feb. 10, 1962; children: John F. III, Robert E., William M., Nancy L. BS in Chem. Engring., U. Notre Dame, 1958, JD, 1961. Bar: Ill. 1961, Ind. 1961, U.S. Dist. Ct. (so. dist.) Ill. 1961, U.S. Ct. Appeals (4th cir.) 1962. Atty. Standard Oil Ind. (now Amoco), Chgo., 1961-64; assoc. Morey and Dunn, Attys., Decatur, Ill., 1964-74; ptnr. Dunn and Fichter, Attys., Decatur, Ill., 1975-85; pvt. practice Decatur, Ill., 1986—. State rep. Ill. Gen. Assembly, Springfield, 1974-94, asst. majority leader; city councilman City of Decatur, 1971-74. Democrat. Roman Catholic. Office: 330 Millikin Ct Decatur IL 62523-1399

DUNN, LEONARD E., financial executive; b. Chgo., May 6, 1942. BS, Ill. Inst. Tech., 1962. Owner Dunn Enterprises, Milw., 1962-90; v.p. fin. cons. Richard Cholfector, Milw., 1990, Smith Barney Inc., Milw., 1990—.

DUNN, PAUL LEVI, city official; b. Lincoln, Nebr., June 24, 1965; s. Robert Arthur and Dolores Ann (Sugden) D. BS, U. Nebr., 1988. Mgr. Sound & Spirit Contemporary Christian Singers, Lincoln, 1984-88; loaned exec. United Way of N.Y.C., 1987-88; prodn. asst. Kimball Recital Hall, Lincoln, 1986-91; rsch. asst. Lincoln Recycling Office, 1989-91; comml. recycling specialist Orange Community Recycling, Chapel Hill, N.C., 1991-94; recycling coord. City of Omaha, 1994—; chmn. Environ. Joint Strategy Action Team, Lincoln, 1990-91; mem. Nat. Waste Prevention Task Force, 1995—. Co-author, editor: (manual) Backyard Composting, 1991; creator, designer Junk Mail Terminator, 1993; news columnist Watching Our WasteLine, 1991-94. Chmn. Campus Ministry Bd., Lincoln, 1988-90. Mem. Am. Planning Assn., Nebr. Recycling Assn. (bd. dirs. 1995—). Republican. United Methodist. Home: 5322 Corby St Apt 12 Omaha NE 68104-4224 Office: City of Omaha 5600 S 10th St Omaha NE 68107-3501

DUNN, RALPH, state legislator; b. Pinckneyville, Ill., Feb. 28, 1914; m. Ellen Dunn; 4 children. Grad., Pinckneyville Cmty. H.S., 1933. Real estate investor; mem. from 115th dist. Ill. Ho. of Reps., 1973-85; mem. Ill. State Senate, 1985—; mem. higher edn. com., appropriations II com., elem. and secondary edn. com., 1985—. Del. 6th Constnl. Conv., 1969-70. Office: RR 3 Box 150 Du Quoin IL 62832-9427 also: State Senate State Capital Springfield IL 62706*

DUNN, REBECCA JO, state legislator; d. Francis G. and Eldred (Wagner) D. BA, U. S.D., 1967; MA, U. Hawaii, 1972. Senator S.D. State Senate Dist. 15, 1993—; mem. legis. exec. bd., corrections com., S.D. State Senate Dist. 15; profl. spkr. in field. Author: The Pearl of Potentiality, Co-A, 1979. Mem. PEO, Downtown Rotary, Hawaii Yacht Club, Kappa Alpha Theta. Home: 320 N Summit Ave Sioux Falls SD 57104-2933*

DUNN, ROBERT SIGLER, engineering executive; b. Cin., Aug. 13, 1926; s. John W. and Mirian S. (Sigler) D.; m. Barbara A. Rigdon, June 26, 1949; children: Anne Dunn Stockman, John R., Mark A. BSME, BSEE, Purdue U., 1949. With Collins Radio Co., Cedar Rapids, Iowa, 1949-72; regional v.p., gen. mgr. Collins Radio Co., Cedar Rapids; v.p. ops. King Radio Corp., Olathe, Kans., 1973-91; also bd. dirs. King Radio Corp., Olathe; pvt. cons., 1991—; Mem. Iowa State Bd. Engring. Examiners, 1969-72. Bd. dirs., v.p. Olathe Comm. Hosp., 1982-90; chmn. bd. trustees Olathe Health Sys.; chmn. bd. trustees Miami County Med. Ctr.; mem. bd. advisors Kans. U. Sch. Engring., 1979—. Mem. IEEE, NSPE, Am Soc. Quality Control, Rotary, Pi Tau Sigma, Eta Kappa Nu, Tau Beta Pi. Home and Office: 15320 Melrose Pl Overland Park KS 66221-9556

DUNN, WILLIAM BRADLEY, lawyer; b. Newark, Dec. 2, 1939; s. Ernest William and Ruth Harriet (Bradley) D.; m. Judy Ann Shepherd, Aug. 2, 1988; children: John, Peter, Brian, Kelly. AB, Muskingum Coll., 1961; JD, U. Mich., 1964. Bar: Mich. 1964. Mem. Clark Hill PLC (formerly Clark, Klein & Beaumont), Detroit, 1964—; lectr. in field. Contbr. articles to legal jours. Mem. ABA (chair sect. real property, probate and trust law 1989-90, ho. of dels. 1990—, standing com. on professionalism 1993—), Am. Coll. Real Estate Lawyers (pres. 1983-84), Anglo-Am. Real Property Inst., Urban Land Inst. Episcopalian. Home: 6398 Catalpa Ct Troy MI 48098-2231 Office: Clark Hill PLC 1001 Woodward Ave Detroit MI 48226-1962

DUNSMORE, ALLISON ROSINA TIPPMAN, marketing executive; b. Kalamazoo, Mich., Aug. 25, 1954; d. Melvin and Rosina (Meier) Tippman; m. David Kent Dunsmore, Mar. 1, 1975; children: Victoria, Christine. Student, Western Mich. U., 1972-75. Mgr. Ft. Polk (La.) Thrift Shop, 1978; art instr. Hanau Mil. Community, Hanau, Germany, 1981-82, Ft. Knox (Ky.) Recreation Dept., 1983; customer svc. rep. Do-It Corp., South Haven, Mich., 1984-85, store system specialist, 1985-87, mktg. exec., 1987—; dir. South Haven Mold & Tool, 1992—; ptnr. Retailers for Maximun Packaging Effectiveness, 1995. Author: Hang Tab Headers (3rd Place 1986), Bottle Neck Tabs (2d Place 1991), Colore Hang Tabs (Hon. Mention 1989). Chmn. Jr. Achievement, 1992, exec. bd. mem., 1991. Recipient Community Svc. award Ft. Polk Mil. Community, 1979, V.I.P award Vinyl Packaging Coun., 1992. Mem. Nat. Office Products Assn., Am. Craft Coun. Industry. Lutheran. Office: Do-It-Corp PO Box 592 73475 8th Ave South Haven MI 49090-9769

DUPUIS, ROBERT, retired principal; b. Detroit, Sept. 25, 1926; s. Luther Henry and Mabel Agnes (Desmond) D.; m. Loretta Jean Gardner, Aug. 20, 1949; children: Denise Jean Dupuis Morey, Diane Lynne. BA, Wayne State U., 1950, MEd, 1955, Edn. Specialist, 1964. Cert. tchr., counselor, adminstr. Tchr. Detroit Pub. Schs., 1950-57, counselor, 1957-63, asst. principal, 1963-66, principal, 1966-84; bd. trustees Orgn. Adminstrs., 1980-84; tchr. training cons. Wayne County Intermediat Sch. Dist., Mich., 1984-87. Author: Bunny Berigan: Elusive Legend of Jazz, 1993; contbr. articles to popular jours. Officer Grosse Pointe Unitarian Ch., Mich., 1960—; mem. citizens adv. com. Grosse Point Schs., 1964; staff congressman John Conyers re-election com., Detroit, 1993. Mem. Internat. Assn. Jazz Record Collectors, Mich. Jazz Record Collectors (pres. 1989-91). Democrat. Home: 725 Lincoln Road Grosse Pointe MI 48230

DUQUETTE, DAVID WILLIAM, engineering consultant; b. St. Paul, May 26, 1958; s. William Frederick and Barbara Ann (Tunell) D.; m. Mary Kay Harris, June 8, 1991; 1 child, Emily Rose. BA, Concordia Coll., 1980; PhD, U. Wis., 1985. Asst. prof. U. Nebr., Lincoln, 1988-95; owner Complete Light Solutions, Mpls., 1995—; mem., pres. Open Harvest Natural Food Corp., Lincoln, 1989-94. Contbr. articles to profl. jours. Postdoctoral fellow Harvard Coll. Observatory, Cambridge, Mass., 1985-88. Mem. IEEE, Optical Soc. Am. Office: Complete Light Solutions 5101 13th Ave S Minneapolis MN 55417

DURAN, F. R. RICK, management consultant; b. Pullman, Wash., June 13, 1952; s. Servet A. and Martha Tucker Duran; m. Sheila Ann Marin, June 5, 1976; children: Danica, Gage, Logan, Brayden. BA in Gen. Interdisciplinary Studies, U. Wash., 1976, BA in Environ. Design, 1977; MArch, U. Ill., 1979, MBA, 1979. Mng. assoc. Lester B. Knight & Assocs., Inc., Chgo., 1981-84; asst. gen. mgr. Met. Fair and Expn. Authority, Chgo., 1984-86; v.p. Balcor Co./Am. Express, Skokie, Ill., 1986-87; pres., sr. mktg. exec. Archinomics Group, Winnetka, Ill., 1986-90, 93—; v.p. internat. rels. ECE Project Mgmt. Internat., Hamburg, Germany, 1990-93. Contbr. articles to profl. jours. Bd. dirs., mktg. chair Chgo. String Ensemble, 1995—; bd. dirs. Sch. Dist. 36 Task Forces, 1995—. Mem. Am. Assn. Cost Engrs., Nat. Assn. Corp. Real Estate Execs., Internat. Real Estate Inst., Internat. Coun. Shopping Ctrs., Urban Land Inst., Profl. Svcs. Mgmt. Assn. Office: Archinomics Group Inc 342 Forest St Ste 300 Winnetka IL 60093

DURBIN, RICHARD JOSEPH, congressman; b. East St. Louis, Ill., Nov. 21, 1944; s. William and Ann D.; m. Loretta Schaefer, June 24, 1967; children: Christine, Paul, Jennifer. B.S. in Econs., Georgetown U., 1966, J.D., 1969. Bar: Ill. 1969. Chief legal counsel Lt. Gov. Paul Simon of Ill., 1969; mem. staff minority leader Ill. Senate, 1972-77, parliamentarian, 1969-77; practice law, 1969—; assoc. prof. med. humanities So. Ill. U., 1978—; mem. 98th-103rd Congresses from 20th Dist. Ill., 1983—; mem. appropriations com.; ranking min. mem. appropriations subcom. on ag. Campaign worker Sen. Paul Douglas of Ill., 1966; staff Office Ill. Dept. Bus. and Econ. Devel., Washington; candidate for Ill. Lt. Gov., 1978; staff alt. Pres.'s State Planning Council, 1980; advisor Am. Council Young Polit. Leaders, 1981; mem. YMCA Ann. Membership Roundup, YMCA Bldg. Drive, Pony World Series; bd. dirs. Cath. Charities, United Way of Springfield, Old Capitol Art Fair, Springfield Youth Soccer; mem. Sch. Dist. 1986 Referendum Com., Springfield NAACP. Democrat. Roman Catholic. Office: US House of Reps 2463 Rayburn Bldg Washington DC 20515-0005*

DURBIN, (MARGARET) ROSAMOND, marketing executive; b. Shelbyville, Ind., Feb. 25, 1952; d. Willard Clyde and Irma Frances (Havens) Sandefur; m. Timothy Mark Durbin, Dec. 27, 1986. BA in English, Xavier U., 1974. Office mgr. Pryde, Inc., Cin., 1975-77; media mgr. Intermedia, Inc., Cin., 1977-80; media dir. Caldwell-Van Riper, Inc., Ft. Wayne, Ind., 1980-82; media supr. Jerrico/Abbott Advt., Lexington, Ky., 1982, Marsteller, Inc., Chgo., 1982-85; mgr. Midwest mktg. Pearle Vision Ctr., Chgo., 1985-86; v.p. Bonsib Inc. Mktg. Svcs., Indpls., 1986-94; pres. Durbin Mktg. Inc., 1994—; guest lectr. Ind. U.-Purdue U., Indpls. Pres. YWCA, Ft. Wayne, 1982; mem. local advt. rev. bd. Ctrl. Ind. BBB. Mem. Am. Mktg. Assn., Advt. Club Indpls., Nat. Wildlife Fedn., Xavier Alumni Assn. Republican. Roman Catholic.

DURDAHL, CAROL LAVAUN, psychiatric nurse; b. Crookston, Minn., Jan. 18, 1933; d. Elmer Oliver and Ovidia (Olson) Durdahl; m. Hans A. Dahl, May 22, 1956 (div. 1983); children: Hana Sorensen, Carla Pederson. RN, St. Lukes Hosp., Duluth, Minn., 1953; BA in Human Svcs., Met. State U., St. Paul, 1982. Staff nurse various hosps., Minn., 1953-59; human svcs. tech. Willmar (Minn.) State Hosp., 1970-74, supplemental tchr., 1974-83; staff nurse Rice Meml. Hosp., Willmar, 1983-86; utilization rev. various nursing homes, Willmar, 1985-86; tchr. Willmar Area Vocat. Tech. Inst., 1986; dir. nurses Glenmore Recovery Ctr., Crookston, Minn., 1986-88; shift supr. Golden Valley (Minn.) Health Ctr., 1988-92; with crisis dept. Hennepin County Med. Ctr., 1988—; managed care of psychiat. and substance abuse MCC Managed Behavioral Care, Mpls., 1992. Contbr. articles to profl. jours. Mem. AAUW, Bus. and Profl. Women, League Women Voters (pres. and state bd.), Federated Women, Does. Republican. Lutheran. Home: 6450 York Ave S Apt 403 Minneapolis MN 55435-2341 Office: Hennepin County Med Ctr 701 Park Ave Minneapolis MN 55415-1623

DURFLINGER, ELIZABETH WARD, retired zoology educator and university dean; b. Ft. Wayne, Ind., July 8, 1912; d. Louis Clinton and Elizabeth Margaret (Fields) Ward. BA, Western Coll., Oxford, Ohio, 1933; MA, U. Cin., 1934, PhD, 1939. Instr. U. Cin., 1939-40; asst. prof. zoology Butler U., Indpls., 1940-44, assoc. prof., 1944-54, prof., 1954-75, dean women, 1940-65; ret., 1975; cons. on human anatomy George F. Cram Co., Indpls., 1975-80. NSF fellow Ohio State U., 1969. Mem. Ind. Acad. Sci., Sigma Xi, Phi Kappa Phi (life mem. sec. Butler U. chpt. 1956-59). Republican. Presbyterian. Home: 1010 Oakwood Trl Indianapolis IN 46260-4021

DURHAM, CHARLES JOSEPH, management consultant; b. Mendota, Ill., Apr. 25, 1928. BA in Chemistry, Knox Coll., 1952. V.p. C.J. Durham Cons. Co. Ltd., Moline, Ill., 1981—. With U.S. Army, 1946-48, Korea. Mem. Am. Chem. Soc. Office: 5202 26th Avenue A Ct Moline IL 61265-5665

DURKEE, TIMOTHY JAMES, physician; b. Chgo., Feb. 14, 1957; s. James and Theresa Dorothy (Markewicz) D.; n. Cheryl L. Johanson, Sept. 2, 1983; children: Megan Ann. BS, Wheaton Coll., 1980; MD, U. Ill., 1993, PhD in Physiology/Molecular Biology, 1993. Secondary sch. tchr. Dists. 108, 59, 214, Arlington Heights, Ill., 1981-85; physician Loyola U. Med. Ctr., Maywood, Ill., 1993—; mem. adv. bd. Ill. Bd. Higher Edn., Springfield, 1983-85. Contbr. articles to profl. jours. Dir. youth ministry, counselor, Mt. Prospect (Ill.) Bible Ch., 1985—, deacon, 1992-94; bd. dirs. Silver Birch Ranch, Inc., 1985-93; vol. physician, Crisis Pregnancy Ctr., Oak Brook, Ill., 1995—. Recipient 2nd Place Young Investigator award Chgo. Assn. Reproductive Endocrinologists, 1992. Fellow: Am. Coll. Ob. Gyn. (jr.), Am. Soc. Reproductive Medicine (jr.); mem. Am. Med. Assn. (Outstanding Scientific Rsch. 1992), Soc. Study Reproduction, Am. Physiol. Soc., Chgo. Assn. Office: Loyola U Med Ctr 2160 S First Ave Elk Grove Village IL 60007

DURKET, MARK J., stockbroker, educator; b. East Liverpool, Ohio, Nov. 6, 1953. BS, Miami U., Oxford, Ohio, 1976; MBA, Xavier U., Cin., 1983. Stockbroker Legge Mason Wood Walker, Cin., 1983-89, Ross Sinclaire & Assocs Inc., Cin., 1989—. Mem. Univ. Club, Stock and Bond Club, Sigma Phi Epsilon. Republican. Lutheran. Office: Ross Sinclaire & Assocs Inc 36 E 7th St Ste 1550 Cincinnati OH 45202-4434

DURKIN, JAMES B., state legislator. BS, Ill. State U.; JD, John Marshall U. Former asst. state atty. Cook County; former asst. atty. gen. Ill.; pres. Proviso Twp. Rep. Orgn.; Ill. state rep. Dist. 44, 1995—; mem. Elec. and State Govt., Higher Edn., Judiciary and Criminal and Pers. and Pensions Coms., 1995—, Ill. Ho. of Reps. Vice-chmn., bd. trustees Triton Coll. Mem. Chgo. Bar Assn., Fenwick Bar Assn. (bd. dirs.). Office: 10544 W Cermak Rd Westchester IL 60154

DURKIN, KEVIN THOMAS, retired marketing professional; b. Evergreen Park, Ill., July 14, 1956; s. Anthony Frances and Margaret Mary (Noon) D. Student, Columbia U., Chgo., 1976, U. Ill., 1977. Wholesale svc. rep. Flying Tigers, Chgo., 1987-89; account exec. Fed. Express, Chgo., 1989-91; mktg. rep. DonTech, Chgo., 1991-93, ret., 1993. Author: Dusting Off Dreams, 1994, Dark Side of the Moon, 1995. Community rep. Oak Park Police Dept., 1994-95. With USN, 1976-78. Mem. Am. Heritage Soc. With USN, 1976-78. Democrat. Roman Catholic. Home: 1234 S Austin # 1N Oak Park IL 60302

DURNELL, EARL, rancher; b. Cabool, Mo., Dec. 4, 1935; m. Emily Gay Spencer; 6 children. Student, Southwest Mo. State U., 1954-56. Rep. candidate for U.S. House, 1992, 96. Baptist. Office: Earl Durnell for Congress Com 102 County Rd 5990 Cabool MO 65689*

DURNIL, GORDON KAY, lawyer, diplomat, arbitrator, political party official; b. Indpls., Feb. 20, 1936; s. J. Ray and E. Merle Durnil; m. Lynda L. Powell, Mar. 1, 1963; children—Guy S., Cynthia L. B.S., Ind. U., 1960, J.D., 1965. Bar: Ind. 1965. Sales rep. Franklin Life Ins. Co., 1956, Moore Bus. Forms, Inc., 1960; sole practice, Indpls., 1965—; profl. arbitrator, mediator, Indpls., 1993—; active Republican Party, 1960—, publicity com. Marion County com. (Ind.), 1966-67, campaign coordinating com., mem. campaign coordinating com. Ind. State Com., 1968-80, mem. congressional coordinating com., 1973-74, campaign dir., 1978, state chmn., 1981-89; campaign mgr. for numerous candidates; mem. Exec. Council Rep. Nat. Com., 1985-89; chmn. Midwestern Rep. State Chmn. Assn., 1988-89, Ind. del. chmn., del. to 1984 and 1988 Rep. Nat. Conv.; nominated by the Pres. and confirmed by U.S. Senate U.S. chmn. Internat. Joint Commn. U.S. and Can., 1989—; head of del. U.N. Conf. on Environment and Devel., Rio de Janeiro, 1992; v.p. Ind. Ornamental Iron Works, Inc., 1960-65; dep. prosecutor Marion County (Ind.), 1965-66; legal counsel Ind. Fedn. Young Republicans, 1965-68; spl. asst. Office of Bus. Service U.S. Dept. Commerce, 1971. Pres. Emmerich Manual High Sch. Alumni Assn., 1968; justice of peace Washington Twp. (Ind.), 1967-70; bd. dirs. Our House, Inc. (Ind. Ronald McDonald House); chmn. Marion County Election Bd., 1978-81. Served with U.S. Army; Korea. Mem. Ind. Bar Assn., Am. Assn. Polit. Cons., Soc. Profls. in Dispute Resolution. Presbyterian. Author: The Making of a Conservative Environmentalist, 1995; editor: The Marion County Republican Reporter, 1966-71. Office: Internat Joint Commn 1250 23rd St NW Ste 100 Washington DC 20037-1164

DURO, MARCIA CULP, temporary employment agency official; b. Joliet, Ill., Mar. 13, 1954; d. Donald Elbert and Doloras Evon (Casper) Culp; m. Franklin James Duro, May 3, 1975; children: Amanda Marie, Jacob Culp. Student, Freeport (Ill.) C.C., 1972-74. Travel agt. Buehler Travel, Monroe, Wis., 1982-85; svc. rep. Manpower Internat. Inc., Monroe, 1985-87; svc. rep. Manpower Internat. Inc., Peru, Ill., 1987-88, mgr., 1988-89, dist. mgr. Chgo. South Western dist., 1991—; mem. adv. bd. 1st State Bank, Peru, 1992—, Illinois Valley C.C., Oglesby, 1991-93. Mem. Mendota (Ill.) Sch. Bd. 287, 1990-95; internat. rep. to Hanover (Germany) Indsl. Fair, Ctrl. Ill. Corridor Coun., 1992, 94, 95. Recipient Jaycette Project of Yr. award Wis. Jaycettes, 1980, Jaycette of Yr., 1981, Leadership Dynamics award 1985. Mem. Ill. Valley Pers. Assn. (pres. 1989-96), Ill. Valley Area C. of C. (pres. bd. 1994—, chmn. ann. auction 1992-93, internat. rep. to Hanover Indsl. Fair 1992, 93, 94, 95, 96). Office: Manpower Internat Inc 3941 Frontage Rd Peru IL 61354-1113

DURR, EDWARD E., insurance agent; b. Chamisal, N.Mex., Jan. 28, 1947; s. Laurence F. and Frances M. (Martinez) D.; m. Lita Prickfit, Apr. 15, 1968 (div. Aug. 1974); children: Crystal, Rachel. BS in Theology, Platte Valley Coll., 1968; MS in Counseling, Ft. Hays (Kans.) State U., 1984. Interviewer I Kans. State Employment Svc., Goodland, 1970-72; interviewer II Kans. State Employment Svc., Garden City, Kans., 1972-74; coll. counselor The Garden City C.C., 1974-87; legalization adjudicator Immigration and Nat. Svc., 1987; sales rep. Mutual of Omaha Ins., 1987-90; vocat. rehab. counselor State of Kans., 1991-92; agt.-at-large, 1992—. Bd. pres. Mexican Am. Ministries, Garden City, 1985-86; bd. dirs. Svc. Employment Redevelopment, Garden City, 1980-85, Okla. Rural Opportunities, Garden city, 1979-82, Harvest Am., Garden City, 1983-85; precinct com. chmn. Rep. Party, Garden City, 1980-84; vol. ARC, 1993-94. Mem. Profl. Hispanic Orgn. (guard 1990). Home: PO Box 39 Garden City KS 67846

DURST, ALAN R., mechanical engineer; b. Warren, Ohio, Jan. 25, 1952; s. Robert Wayne and Donna Jean (Irwin) D. A in Mech. Engring., ATES Tech. Sch., 1974. Draftsman engring. United Telephone Sys., Warren, 1975-80; checker engring. dept. Kennametal Inc., Cleve., 1980—. Presbyterian. Office: Kennametal Inc 6865 Cochran Rd Solon OH 44139-4335

DURST, GARY MICHAEL, management trainer, speaker; b. Mt. Clemens, Mich., May 21, 1945; s. Carl William and Rosaline Rita (Constance) D.; m. Margaret Ellen O'Reilly, Sept. 2, 1966, (div. May 1977); children: Gregory, John, David. BA, Oakland U., 1966; MA, Mich. St. U., E. Lansing, 1968; PhD., Loyola U., 1972. Tchr. Avondale Pub. Sch., Auburn Hieghts, Mich., 1966-68; counselor/adminstr. U. of Ill. Med. Cntr., Chicago, 1968-69; assoc. dean of students Elmhurst Coll, Ill., 1969-72; v.p. Great Western Learning Systems, Denver; pres. Training Systems, Inc., Evanston, Ill., 1974--. Author: Napkin Notes: On the Art of Living 1979, Management By Responsibility, 1982. Named Prominent Training Professional- McMilan Co. 1986. Mem. Assoc. of Humanistic Psychology, Am. Soc. of Training And Devel. Office: Tng Systems Inc PO Box 788 Evanston IL 60204-0788

DURST, MARK P., maintenance administrator; b. Chgo., June 2, 1955. AD, Triton Coll., 1976. Maintenance electrician GE, Chgo., 1977-79; field svc. engr. Burgmaster, L.A., 1979-89; maintenance supr. Viking Pump, Cedar Falls, Iowa, 1989—; mem. curriculum adv. bd. Hawkeye Jr. Coll., Waterloo, Iowa, 1992—. Office: Viking Pump PO Box 8 Cedar Falls IA 50613-0008

DURYEE, HAROLD TAYLOR, insurance executive; b. Willoughby, Ohio, Feb. 11, 1930; s. Gerald Fancher and Margaret Grace (Taylor) D.; m. Phyllis Annette Painter, June 18, 1966. AB, Kenyon Coll., 1951. Field rep. Mahoning Valley Coun., Boy Scouts Am., Youngstown, Ohio, 1951-56; mgr. claims svcs. Nationwide Ins. Cos., Canton, 1956-65; legis. and field dir. Ohio Rep. Party, Columbus, 1965-70, exec. dir., 1970-77, cons., 1980-81; dep. adminstr. Ohio Bur. Workers' Compensation, Columbus, 1977-84; exec. dep. adminstr. Fed. Ins. Adminstrn., Washington, 1984-86; adminstr. fed. ins. Fed. Emergency Mgmt. Agy., Washington, 1986-90; dir. Ohio Dept. Ins., 1991—; Trustee, exec. com. Griffith Found. for Ins. Edn. Vice chmn. North Canton City Planning Commn., 1958-67; precinct committeeman Stark County Cen. Com., 1958-72; organizer North Canton Rep. Com., 1958, chmn., 1960-72; sec. North Canton Area Devel. Com., 1959-64; chmn. North Canton City Charter Commn., 1960; campaign mgr. U.S. Rep. Frank T. Bow, 1962, Oliver P. Bolton for U.S. Congress, 1964, Clarence J. Brown, Jr. for U.S. Congress, 1965; state chmn. Ohio League Young Rep. Clubs, 1962-63; nat. vice chmn. Young Rep. Nat. Fedn., 1963-65. Recipient Disting. Svc. award Jaycees, 1961, Civic Affairs award Rotary, 1964, Meritorious Svc. award Fed. Emergency Mgmt. Agy., 1989, Disting. Civilian Svc. medal, Fed. Emergency Mgmt. Agy., 1990. Mem. Nat. Assn. Ins. Commrs. (mem. exec. com. 1992-95), Acad. Polit. Sci., Univ. Club. Episcopalian. Home: 925 City Park Ave Columbus OH 43206-2511 Office: Ohio Dept Ins 2100 Stella Ct Columbus OH 43215-1067

DURZINSKY, DENNIS STEVEN, cardiothoracic surgeon, educator; b. Anderson, Ind., July 15, 1957; s. Lawrence S. and Harriett J. (Dickey) D.; m. Jill L. Cassidy, May 9, 1982. BA, Northwestern U., 1978; MD, Ind. U., 1982. Intern in gen. surgery U. Wis., Madison, 1982-83, resident in gen. surgery, 1983-86, chief resident in gen. surgery, 1986-87; registrar Gloucestershire Royal Hosp., Gloucester, Eng., 1987-88; fellow in cardiothoracic surgery U. Utah, Salt Lake City, 1988-90; asst. prof. surgery Med. Coll. Ohio, Toledo, 1990—, chief cardiothoracic surgery, 1993—. Contbr. articles to profl. jours. Fellow ACS; mem. AMA, Soc. Thoracic Surgeons, Internat. Soc. Heart and Lung Transplantation, Phi Beta Kappa, Alpha Omega Alpha. Office: Med Coll Ohio Dept Surgery 3000 Arlington Ave, PO Box 10008 Toledo OH 43699

DUSSMAN, JUDITH ANN, publishing executive; b. Chgo., Aug. 23, 1947; d. Thomas Raymond and Dorothy M. (Stalzer) D.; div. 1985; children: John Thomas, Douglas Jude, Luke Price, Katherine Cannon. BA, Northwestern U., 1969; postgrad., Fordham U., 1974; JD, Loyola U., 1975. Bar: Ill. 1993, U.S. Dist. Ct. (no. dist.) Ill. 1993. Advt. sales mgmt. Chgo. Sun Times, Daily News, 1970-77, New York Trib, 1977-78, New York Times, Golf Digest, Tennis, 1979-81; assoc. pub. Ofcl. Airline Guides mag. div. Dun & Bradstreet, Oak Brook, Ill., 1981-83; pub. New Connections mag. Dun & Bradstreet, N.Y.C., 1984; circulation dir. Ofcl. Airlines Guide, Oak Brook, Ill., 1985-87; chief exec. officer, gen. mgr. Wordright Enterprises Inc., Evanston, Ill., 1987-89. Contbg. editor: (book) Where The Fun Is, 1968; footnote editor: (book) Re-issue Of The Impending Crisis Of The South, 1969. Bd. dirs., chmn. legal com. Kemeys Cove Condo., Scarborough, N.Y., 1976-80; mem. Friends Brookfield Zoo; pres. parents' coun. Ill. Math. and Sci. Acad., 1992—; vol. atty Office of Pub. Guardian, Cook County. Mem. MENSA, Am. Electronics Assn., Midwest Chpt. Speakers Com., Chgo. Assn. Direct Mktg., Am. Soc. Travel Agts. Educators Forum, Ill. Bar Assn., DuPage Bar Assn., Chgo. Bar Assn., Direct Mktg. Assn., Women in Mgmt., Advt. Women N.Y., Loyuola Law Alumni, Northwestern U. Alumni Assn., Cross Country Flying Club, DuPage County Bar Assn., Chgo. Coun. Lawyers, DuPage Assn. Women Lawyers, Ill. Bar Assn., Zonta, Chi. Omega. Roman Catholic. Club: Sales and Mktg. Exec. N.Y. Home: 46 S Madison St Hinsdale IL 60521-3236 Office: Dussman and Assocs Hinsdale IL 60521

DUTTA, HIRIAN MOYEE, biologist, educator; b. Patna, Bihar, India; came to the U.S., 1966; s. Trailokha N. and Sarujobala (Dutta) D.; m. Ashok K. Dutt, Jan. 19, 1958; children: Rinku, Jhumu D. Kohts. PhD, Leiden U., 1968. Asst. prof., chmn. dept. sci. N.H. Coll., Manchester, 1966-68; asst. prof., chmn. dept. biology Walsh Coll., North Canton, Ohio, 1968-70; vis. asst. prof. Kent (Ohio) State U., 1970-75, asst. prof., 1975-80, assoc. prof., 1981-89, prof., 1990—; dir. KSU-Leiden Univs., 1978—; vis. prof. Inst. Zoology Jagellonian U., Krakow, Poland, 1978, Polish Acad. Scis. Inst. Zoology, 1989, Paradenia U., Sri Lanka, 1991; invited spkr. India Sci. Congress Assn. ann. conf., 1994, India Inst. Sci., 1995, Internat. Symposium on Water/Air Transitions in Biology, 1996. Author: Functional Morphology of the Head of Anabas Testudineus, 1968; editor: Fish Morphology Horizon of New Research, 1996; contbr. chpts. to books, articles to profl. jours. Faculty advisor Kent State Indian Assn., 1976-82, Kent State U. Bangladesh Student Assn., 1983-89. Fulbright lecturing/rsch. fellow, 1991; Smithsonian Instn. grantee, 1990-93. Mem. AAAS, Indian Assn. Freshwater Biology (mem. editorial bd.), Am. Soc. Ichyologists and Herpetologists, Am. Soc. Zoologists, Ohio Acad. Sci., Indian Assn. Greater Akron (v.p. 1979, pres. 1980). Office: Kent State U Dept Biology 256 Cunningham Stall Kent OH 44242

DUTTERA, BRIAN CLEVE, financial consultant and sales manager; b. York, Pa., Oct. 6, 1963; s. Joel Cleve and Sheridan Patricia (Adams) D.; m. Holly Christine Leible, July 24, 1984; children: Jared Everett, Amber Michele, Emily Daniele. AA, Ambassador U., 1984. Electronic assemblyman York, 1981-82; sr. account rep. Don Barr Inc., Mansfield, Ohio, 1985-87; fin. cons. Merrill Lynch, Mansfield, 1987-93; sr. fin. cons., asst. v.p. Merrill Lynch, Sandusky, Ohio, 1993—, sr. fin. cons., v.p. Coach basketball Youth Opportunities United, Mansfield, Ohio and Ft. Lauderdale, Fla., 1985-93, volleyball and track, Mansfield, 1985-93, basketball and volleyball, Cleve., 1993—. Mem. Better Bus. Bur. (bd. dirs. 1990—), Ambassador Spokesman Club (pres. 1988, 94-95). Home: 304 Wexford Dr Huron OH 44839-1462 Office: Merrill Lynch 1st Fl 4406 Timber Commons Dr Sandusky OH 44870

DUTTLINGER, LINDA M., education educator; b. Michigan City, Ind., Apr. 6, 1948; d. Francis and Virginia C. (Baird) Rooney; m. Richard C. Duttlinger, Jan. 30, 1971; children: Benjamin, David, Fred. BA, Purdue U., 1971, MS, 1973, PhD, 1979. Life tchr. lic., Ind. Tchr. North Judson (Ind.) Schs., 1971-75; grad. instr. Purdue U., West Lafayette, Ind., 1975-79; adj. faculty Purdue North Central, Westville, Ind., 1980-84, mem. staff, 1984-85, asst. prof., 1985-90, assoc. prof., 1990—; v.p. Jasper County Ext. Bd., Rensselaer, Ind., 1991-96; mem. Michigan City ABE/GED Adv. Bd., 1992—. Author: Technical Writing with World Processing, 1987. Club leader 4-H, Wheatfield, Ind., 1990—. Mem. Nat. Assn. Devel. Edn., Ind. Assn. Devel. Edn. (Outstanding Educator 1990), Correctional Edn. Assn., Kappa Delta Pi, Alpha Sigma Lambda. Home: 5376 E State Rd 10 San Pierre IN 46374 Office: Purdue U North Ctrl 1401 S US 421 Westville IN 46391

DUVALL, DARIN LEE, electronic publishing specialist, educator; b. Glendale, Calif., July 31, 1966; s. Frank Lonkert and Sandi Lee (Copenhaver) D.; m. Laura Lynn Steiger, June 21, 1992. BS in Psychology, Calif. State U., Northridge, 1989, MA in Human Factors, 1992. Multimedia designer Philips Interactive Media, L.A., 1992-93; electronic pub. specialist U. Ill., Urbana, 1994—; chair electronic pub. com. Info. Svcs./UIUC, Urbana, 1994—; conflict mgmt. cons. Heartland Coll., Bloomington, Ill., 1994. Coord. world wide weblibr. VISTA, 1995. Mem. Agrl. Communicators in Edn., Assn. for Computing Machinery (scholarship com. 1993—). Democrat. Home: 610 Old Farm Rd Bloomington IL 61704 Office: U Ill 47 Mumford Hall Urbana IL 61801

DUVANENKO, VICTOR J., electronic engineer; b. Leningrad, USSR, Nov. 10, 1962; came to U.S., 1976; s. Valery and Tamara (Serotinsky) D.; m. Elizabeth Ann Alexander, Jan. 15, 1987;children: Natalie, Abbigail, Alexander. BSEE, Purdue U., 1980-84; MSEE, N.C. State U., 1989-90. Design engr. VLSI Intel Corp., Santa Clara, Calif., 1984-88; jr. founder Silicon Engring., Scotts Valley, Calif., 1988; sr. mem. tech. staff Truevision, Inc., Indpls., 1991—. Contbr. articles to profl. jours. Mem. IEEE, Assn. Computing Machinery. Home: 8441 Thornhill Dr Indianapolis IN 46256-1526 Office: Truevision Inc 7340 Shadeland Station Way Indianapolis IN 46256-3919

DUXBURY, ROBERT NEIL, state legislator; b. Mar. 14, 1933; s. Joy Chase and Lois Mae (McNeil) Duxbury; m. Rose Ann Radcliffe, 1953; children: Robert Neil Jr., Kathryn Ann Duxbury Meyer, Dale Lynn, Dean Douglas, Brian Richard. BS, S.D. State U., 1956. Sec. of Agrl. S.D., 1975-79; senator S.D. State Senate, 1979-86; rep. S.D. Ho. of Reps. Dist. 5; former minority leader, former mem. legis. procedure com. Dist. 22; currently mem. appropriations com. S.D. Ho. Reps.; farmer, rancher. Mem. Farmers Union, Hand County Livestock Improvement Assn. Home: RR 2 Box 58 Wessington SD 57381-8905*

DVORAK, CLARENCE ALLEN, microbiologist; b. Cedar Rapids, Iowa, July 6, 1942; s. Clarence Louis and Lily Ann (Duda) D. BS, Iowa State U., 1969. Microbiologist Penford Products Co., Cedar Rapids, 1969—, analytical chemist, 1970-81, sci. photographer. Mem. AAAS, TAPPI, Am. Soc. Microbiology, Soc. Indsl. Microbiology. Home: 1231 Sierra Dr NE Apt 10 Cedar Rapids IA 52402-6541

DVORAK, JANE ANN, property management executive; b. Cin., Dec. 19, 1955; d. Ralph Harold and Mary Elizabeth (Rodenberg) Teke; m. Alan Eugene Dvorak; Mar. 19, 1977. BBA, Ohio U., 1977. Part-time emergency med. tech. Southeast Ohio Emergency Med. Services, Athens, Ohio, 1977-80; patient coordinator O'Bleness Hosp., Athens, 1977; loan officer Athens Credit Union, 1978-79; mgr. Athens Mall JMB Property Mgmt. Corp., 1980-87; v.p. Athens Marine & Tire Inc., 1987-91; gen. mgr. Univ. Mall Beerman Realty, Athens, 1990—; bd. dirs. Athens Pvt. Industry Coun., 1985-87. Pub. rels. coord. Athens County Emergency Mgmt. Svcs., 1985-94; exec. dir. Athens chpt. Big Bros./Big Sisters, 1989-92; mem. USCG Aux., 1990—, staff officer, 1992-93, flotilla comdr., 1994-96; mem. Athens County Crime Solvers Anonymous; mem. Program com. Am. Heart Assn., 1993-96. Mem. Internat. Coun. Shopping Ctrs., Athens C. of C. (bd. dirs. 1983-87), Athens Crime Solvers Anonymous, Phi Mu (house corp. v.p. 1984-87). Home: 14525 Kincade Rd Athens OH 45701-9444 Office: U Mall Mgmt 1002 E State St Athens OH 45701-2149

DVORAK, MICHAEL A., state legislator; b. South Bend, Ind., Oct. 24, 1948; s. William E. and Marilyn J. (Radican) D.; m. Kathleen Braunsdorf, 1970; children: Ryan, Todd, Sean, Brett, Carrie, Brady, Casey, Tyler. BA, Loyola U., Chgo., 1970; JD, Western State U., San Diego, 1975. Ptnr. Hahn, Walz, Knepp, Dvorak & Higgins, South Bend, 1977—; dep. pros. atty. Santislaus County, Modesto, Calif., 1975-77; rep. Dist. 8 Ind. Ho. of Rep., 1986—, chmn. rules and legis. procedure com., rnaking minority mem., mem. cts. and criminal code com., mem. families, children and human affairs com. Mem. Ind. State Bar Assn., St. Joseph County Bar Assn. Home: 51815 Lake Knoll Ct Granger IN 46530-7080*

DVORKIN, LOUIS, neuropsychologist; b. Phila., July 24, 1951; s. Benjamin and Eleanor (Braverman) D.; m. Jori Harriet Potiker, May 30, 1977 (div. July 1980); m. Gail Myra Apple, Oct. 18, 1987; children: Lauren, Adam, Elyse. BA in Psychology, Am. U., 1972; MA in Psychology, Wayne State U., 1978, PhD in Psychology, 1980; postgrad. in aging psychology, U. Mich., 1977. Lic. psychologist, Mich. Staff psychologist Rehab. Inst., Detroit, 1980-83; dir. neuropsychology Wyandotte (Mich.) Hosp. and Med. Ctr., 1983-87; pres. Louis Dvorkin PhD & Assocs., West Bloomfield, Mich., 1988—; cons. in neuropsychology Ctr. for Forensic Psychiatry, Ann Arbor; mem. adj. med. staff Crittenton Hosp., Rochester, Mich., 1992—; mem. med. staff Pontiac (Mich.) Osteopathic Hosp., 1990—, Sinai Hosp., Detroit, 1990—; mem. adj. mem. staff Rehab. Inst., 1980—. Fellow Adminstrn. on Aging, 1979, Wayne State U., 1975-76. Mem. APA, Mich. Psychol. Assn. (ethics com. 1994—), Internat. Neuropsychol. Soc., Nat. Acad. Neuropsychology, Am. Bd. Forensic Examiners, Psi Chi. Jewish. Home: 4948 Lakebluff Ct West Bloomfield MI 48323-2426 Office: Louis Dvorkin PhD & Assocs 6450 Farmington Rd Ste 101 West Bloomfield MI 48322-4456

DWENGER, THOMAS ANDREW, engineer; b. Dayton, June 17, 1945; s. Ferdinand Bernard and Velma Theresa (Woeste) D.; m. Brenda Lee Langsdon, May 28, 1966; children: Kelly, Kevin. BSME, Ind. Inst. Tech., Ft. Wayne, 1969. Staff tire designer The Goodyear Tire and Rubber Co., Akron, Ohio, 1968-72; sr. tire designer The Goodyear Tire and Rubber Co., Luxembourg, 1972-77; sect. head aircraft tires sect. The Goodyear Tire and Rubber Co., Akron, Ohio, 1977-84, chief engr., 1984—. Inventor asymmetric tread aircraft tire, 1988. Mem. Stark County Soil & Water Conservation Dist., Canton, Ohio, 1989—, Evang. Luth. Ch. Am. Strategy for Akron Area, 1987-91; treas. Luth. Coun. Greater Akron, 1988-92; elder, fin. sec., mem. coun. St. John/St. Paul Evang. Luth. Ch., pres. ch. coun., 1991-92. Mem. Soc. Automotive Engrs. (chmn. A-5C subcom. on aircraft tires 1988—), Tire and Rim Assn. (chmn. aircraft tire subcom. 1985-87, 89-90, 92, del. to Internat. Standards Orgn., 1986—), Rubber Mfrs. Assn., Aircraft Tire Engring. Com., Goodyear Antique Auto Club (treas. 1990-93, sec. 1993—), Farm Bur. Home: 3611 Moonglo St NW Uniontown OH 44685-8027 Office: Goodyear Tire & Rubber Co PO Box 3531 # B Akron OH 44309-3531

DWYER, DEBORAH JEAN, management educator; b. Cin., May 22, 1956; d. Charles Edward and Ivy (Devonshire) D. BA, U. Cin., 1984, MA, 1985; PhD, U. Nebr., 1989. Realtor Duff Bros. Realty, Middletown, Ohio, 1975-77, Century 21 Realty, Middletown, 1977-78; pres. Baron Personnel of Springdale, Cin., 1978-81; sales rep. Orkin Exterminating, Cin., 1981-84; assoc. prof. U. Toledo, 1989—. Mem. Acad. Mgmt., Midwest Acad. Mgmt. (membership chair), Soc. Human Resource Mgmt., Toledo Pers. Mgmt. Assn., Area Human Resource Assn. Democrat. Presbyterian. Office: U Toledo Dept Mgmt 2801 W Bancroft Toledo OH 43606-3390

DWYER, DENNIS D., information technology executive; b. Oak Park, Ill., July 19, 1943; s. John J. and Jessie M. Dwyer; m. Carolyn R. Schultz, Apr. 29, 1967; children: David, Julianne. Various positions Harris Bank, Chgo., 1967-83, mgr. info. tech. planning, 1983-86, v.p. tech. facilitation, 1986—; resolutions chmn. Cooperating Users of Burroughs Equipment, Detroit, 1978-82; cons. Unisys mainframe computers. Pres. Hunting Ridge Homeowners Assn., 1983-85; mem. Palatine Plan Commn., 1984—, chmn., 1989—.

Recipient Tom Grier award for Excellence Unisys Users Group, 1988. Home: 1032 Raven Ln Palatine IL 60067-6649 Office: Harris Bank PO Box 755 Chicago IL 60690-0755

DWYER, WILLIAM T., investment broker; b. North Smithfield, R.I., Dec. 21, 1955; m. Debrah Ann Burnette, Jan. 1, 1984; 1 child, Darren L. BS, Bryant Coll., 1977. Prin. profl. cleaning svc. Smithfield, R.I., 1975-82; regional leader Edward D. Jones & Co., Salem, Ill., 1983—. Mem. C. of C., Rotary. Republican. Lutheran. Office: Edward D Jones & Co 521 W Main St Salem IL 62881-1402

DYBEK, STUART, English educator, writer; b. Chgo., Apr. 10, 1942; s. Stanley and Adeline (Sala) S.; m. Caren Bassett, Feb. 7, 1967; children: Anne, Nicholas. BS, Loyola U., Chgo., 1964, MA, 1967; MFA, U. Iowa, 1973. Tchr. U.S. V.I. Sch., St. Thomas, 1968-70, U. Iowa, Iowa City, 1970-73; prof. English Western Mich. U., Kalamazoo, 1973—; vis. prof. creative writing Princeton (N.J.) U., 1991, U. Calif., Irvine, 1995. Author: (poetry) Brass Knuckles, 1979; (fiction) Childhood and Other Neighborhoods, 1980, The Coast of Chicago, 1990. Guggenheim fellow, 1982; recipient Whiting Writers award, 1985, O. Henry first prize, 1985, Acad. award in fiction Am. Acad. Arts and Letters, 1994, PEN/Malamud award, 1995. Mem. PEN. Home: 320 Monroe St Kalamazoo MI 49006-4436 Office: Western Michigan U Dept English Kalamazoo MI 49008 also: care Amanda Urban Intl Creative Mgt 40 W 57th St New York NY 10019-4001

DYER, CYNTHIA MYERS, library director; b. Camp Lejeune, N.C., June 26, 1955; d. Louis B. and Shirley Jean (Shimon) Myers; m. Grant E. Dyer, Nov. 24, 1984; children: Katherine Elizabeth, Sarah Caroline. BA, U. Iowa, 1977, MLS, 1978. Tech. svcs. librarian Simpson Coll., Indianola, Iowa, 1978-83, dir. library svcs., 1983—, assoc. prof., 1994—; program co-chmn. Iowa Gov.'s Pre-White House Conf. on Librs., 1990-91; mem. Blue Ribbon Task Force on Librs., 1988; mem. adv. bd. Cen. Iowa Regional Libr., 1987-88. Contbr. articles to profl. jours. Pres. Simpsin Guild, Indianola, 1995-96; spkr. on AIDS, 1992—; chmn. various libr. adv. coms., 1986—, Women's History Month, 1990-91, 96; tri-chmn. Campus Capital Campaign, 1990. Mem. ALA, Iowa Libr. Assn. (acad. and rsch. librs. conf. planner 1979, 82, 95, exec. bd. dirs. 1984-86, 88-90, pres. 1989, nominating com. 1991-93, strategic planning com. 1993), Iowa Libr. Assn. Found. (v.p. 1990-92, chmn. distbn. 1991-92, pres. 1993-94, chair continuity com. 1995), Iowa Pvt. Acad. Librs. (chmn. 1986, panelist 1993), Indianola Breakfast Club (bd. dirs. 1988-90), Rotary (speaker for various groups), Phi Beta Kappa, Phi Beta Mu, Epsilon Sigma. Democrat. Office: Simpson Coll Dunn Libr # 508 Nc Indianola IA 50125

DYER, ROBERT THEODORE, power producer executive; b. Jacksonville, Fla., Nov. 15, 1945; s. Theodore Mains Dyer and Mildred Inez (Fuqua) Patrick; m. Robin Jean Dizor, Sept. 1, 1973 (div. Aug. 1992); children: Robert Christopher, Robin Nicole, Sabrina Jean, Nicholas Theodore. BSEE, U. Fla., 1971; MBA, U. North Fla., 1979. Engr. in tng. Jacksonville (Fla.) Electric Authority, 1971-73, div. chief, 1974-80; power systems engr. Walt Disney World, Orlando, Fla., 1973-74; v.p. adminstrn. Plains Electric G&T Coop. Inc., Albuquerque, 1980-89; v.p. bulk power and indsl. devel. Midland (Mich.) Cogeneration Venture, 1989-94; gen. mgr. Wholesale Power Svcs., Inc., Indpls., 1994-95; mgr. bulk pwoer mktg. Cinergy Svcs., Indpls., 1995—. Contbr. articles to profl. jours. With USAF, 1963-67, Vietnam. Mem. NSPE (chpt. pres. 1987-88). Baptist. Home: 3359 Heather Ridge Dr Apt 2 Indianapolis IN 46214-1884 Office: Cinergy Power Mktg/Trading 251 N Illinois St Ste 1410 Indianapolis IN 46204-1927

DYER, WILLIAM EARL, JR., retired newspaper editor; b. Kearney, Nebr., May 15, 1927; s. William Earl and Hazel Maud (Hosfelt) D.; m. Betty M. Meisinger, June 26, 1967; children—Lee Michael, Scott William. B.A., U. Nebr., 1949. Reporter, Nebraska City Daily News Press., 1943-44; reporter, copy editor The Lincoln Star (Nebr.), 1948-50, city editor, 1951-60, exec. editor, 1960-92; pres. Nebr. AP Editors, 1964; author: Headline: Starkweather, 1993. Pres., Lincoln Unitarian Ch., 1962-63; state chmn. Nebr. We Shake Hands Indian Project, 1958-60; mem. Nebr. Adv. Com. on Indian Law Enforcement, 1960-62; mem. State Adv. Com. to Welfare Dept., 1970-73, 80-84. Served with AUS, 1945-46. Named Hon. Mem., Omaha Indian Tribe. Mem. AP Mng. Editors Assn., Phi Beta Kappa, Sigma Delta Chi. Democrat. Club: Open Forum. Home: 1115 Fall Creek Rd Lincoln NE 68510-4947 Office: Jour-Star Printing Co PO Box 81609 926 P St Lincoln NE 68501

DYKES, KATHRYN A., community health nurse, educator, administrator; b. Racine, Wis., Sept. 11, 1951; d. Frank R. and Stella Korzilius; m. Herman J. Dykes, Apr. 2, 1977; children: Kathryn, Stephanie, John. BS, Coll. St. Teresa, Winona, Minn., 1973; MSN, U. Wis., Oshkosh, 1996. Cert. in infection control, CPR, BLS, Emergency Response instr. trainer. Critical care staff nurse Milwaukee County Med. Complex, Milw.; case mgr./home health Vis. Nurse Assn., Milw.; staff., case mgmt. home health Vis. Nurses of Family Svc. Assn., Green Bay, Wis., staff devel. coord., dir. nursing. Recipient Presdl. award Community Svc., 1990; named Vol. of Yr. Brown County, Wis., 1990, Outstanding Vol. Wis. Crisis Ctr., 1989. Mem. Assn. for Practitioners in Infection Control, Transcultural Nurses Soc., Nat. Parish Nurses Assn., Health Ministries Assn. Office: Visiting Nurses 300 Crooks St Green Bay WI 54301

DYKSTRA, DAVID ALLEN, corporate executive; b. Kalamazoo, Feb. 5, 1938; s. Alle and Elizabeth (VanderHorst) D. m. Kathryn Ann DeNio, Aug. 4, 1962 (div. Nov. 1985); children: Brian Thayer, Kristen Lee, Holly Beth. BBA, Western Mich. U., 1966. Pres. Dyco Corp., Portage, Mich., 1970—; realtor Crossroads Real Estate, Kalamazoo, Mich, 1994—; cons. Waste Industry, Mich., 1976-82; owner Dairy World Yogurt Shops; with Callander, Woollam & Britigan Comml. Realtors. Bd. dirs. Portage C. of C., 1980-83, mem. econ. devel. com.; alt. del. Rep. Conv., Mich., 1984. Mem. Safari Club Internat. (bd. dirs. Mich. chpt.), Ducks Unltd. (mem. com.), Beacon Club. Republican. Mem. Reformed Ch. Home: 7221 W V W Ave Schoolcraft MI 49087-9447 Office: Crossroads Real Estate 6443 S Westredge Kalamazoo MI 49002

DYKSTRA, ROBERT, retired education educator; b. Vesper, Wis., Feb. 26, 1930; s. John and Anna (Holstein) D.; m. Lou Ann Conselman, Oct. 6, 1956; children: S. Kim, Paul, Randall. BS in Elem. Edn., U. Wis., River Falls, 1957; MA in Ednl. Psychology, U. Minn., 1959, PhD in Ednl. Psychology, 1962. Cert. elem. edn. Elem. tchr. Cedar Grove (Wis.) Pub. Sch., 1954-55; asst. prof. U. Minn., Mpls., 1962-64, assoc. prof., 1965-69, prof., 1970-73, chair dept. curriculum and instrn., 1974-85, prof., 1986-93, ret., 1993. Co-author: Teaching Reading, 1974, Language Arts: Teaching and Learning Effective Use of Language, 1988; contbr. articles to profl. jours. With U.S. Army, 1952-54. Elected to Reading Hall of Fame, 1996; U.S. Office Edn. rsch. grantee, 1963, 65. Mem. Nat. Coun. Tchrs. of English (mem. exec. com. 1969-71), Nat. Conf. on Rsch. in English (pres. 1984-85), Twin City Area Reading Coun. (pres. 1990-91), Internat. Reading Assn. (mem. pub. com. 1975-77), Nat. Reading Conf. (mem. pub. com. 1978-80). Lutheran. Home: 1998 16th St NW Saint Paul MN 55112-5555

DYLAG, HELEN MARIE, healthcare administrator; b. Cleve., Oct. 14, 1950; d. Stanley John and Helen Agnes (Jarkiewicz) D. BSN, St. John Coll., Cleve., 1971; MS, Ohio State U., 1973. RN, Ohio. RN V.A. Adminstrn. Hosp., Brecksville, Ohio, 1971-72; clin. specialist, psychiat.-mental health nursing Marymount Hosp./Mental Health Ctr., Garfield Heights, Ohio, 1973-78, dir. consultation and edn. dept., 1978-84, dir. Ctr. for Health Styles, 1984-88; adminstrv. dir. Women's Healthcare Ctr./St. Luke's Hosp., Cleve., 1988-90; adminstrv. dir. dept. of psychiatry MetroHealth Med. Ctr., Cleve., 1990—. Contbg. author: Nursing of Families in Crisis, 1974, Distributive Nursing Practice: A Systems Approach to Community Health, 1977; producer and host "Health Styles" TV Talk Show, 1987-88; contbr. articles to profl. jours. Trustee The Stroke Assn. of Ohio, Cleve., 1990-91; mem. Women of Achievement com., Women's City Club, Cleve., 1989-91. Recipient award Greater Cleve. Hosp. Assn., 1981, Innovator award Am. Hosp. Assn./Ctr. for Health Promotion, 1985. Mem. Assn. Mental Health Adminstrs., Am. Coll. Healthcare Execs., Healthcare Adminstrs. Assn. of Northeast Ohio, Sigma Theta Tau. Home: 5709 Onaway Oval Cleveland OH 44130-1642 Office: Metro Health Med Ctr 2500 Metrohealth Dr Cleveland OH 44109-1900

DYREGROV, MICHAEL See BAKER, JOHN STEVENSON

DZIADYK, BOHDAN, botany and ecology educator; b. Aschaffenburg, Germany, Mar. 26, 1948; came to U.S., 1950; s. Iwan and Maria (Jaroszuk) D.; m. Marietta Jay Johnston, Mar. 23, 1974; children: Jennifer Maria, Joseph Walter. BA, Southern Ill. U., 1970, MS, 1980; PhD, N.D. State U., 1982. From instr. to assoc. prof. botany and ecology Augustana Coll., Rock Island, Ill., 1980-96, prof., 1996—, co-dir. environ. studies program, 1981—, dir. coll. field sta., 1991—; chmn. biology dept., 1992-95; bd. dirs. Quad Cities Bot. Ctr. Contbr. articles to profl. jours. Sgt. AUS, 1970-73. Pew Sci. Program researcher and grantee, 1988-94. Mem. Ecol. Soc. Am., Ill. Native Plant Soc., Ctr. for Plant Conservation, Ill. State Acad. Sci. (pres. 1993-95), Alpha Phi Omega (adv. and scouting coord. 1981—), Sigma Xi (pres. John Deere chpt. 1987-88). Office: Augustana Coll Dept Biology 639 38th St Rock Island IL 61201-2210

DZIERZYNSKI, HAROLD THOMAS, automotive executive; b. Spring Valley, Ill., June 5, 1963; s. Harold William and Patricia Anne (Hynds) D. BS in Mfg., Bradley U., 1987. Gen. mgr. Valley Ford, Inc., Spring Valley, Ill., 1987—. Pres. Spring Valley Bus. Owners' Assn., 1990, 93; chmn. Spring Valley Coal Mine Devel. Com., 1990—. Mem. Spring Valley Jaycees, Ladd Moose Lodge, Spring Valley Lions Club. Home: 323 E Minnesota Spring Valley IL 61362 Office: Valley Ford Inc 225 E Saint Paul Spring Valley IL 61362

DZIUK, PHILIP JOHN, animal scientist educator; b. Foley, Minn., Mar. 24, 1926; s. Edmund William and Ellen Catherine (Carlin) D.; m. Patricia Rosemary Weber, Sept. 29, 1951; children: Corinne, Constance, Rita, Catherine, Kenneth, Ronald, Carl. BS, U. Minn., 1950, MS, 1952, PhD, 1955. From rsch. asst. to rsch. assoc. U. Minn., Mpls., 1950-55; from asst. prof. to prof. U. Ill., Urbana, 1955-88, prof. emeritus, 1988—; cons. Upjohn, Abbott, Eli Lilly, Am. Cynamid, Schering, Batelle; reviewer of grants NIH, Bethesda, Md., 1982-86, USDA, Beltsville, Md., 1983-89. Contbr. peer reviewed publs. in sci. and profl. jours. With USN, 1945-46. Fellow Lalor Found., 1958, 61, Pig Industry Devel. Authority, Eng., 1961; recipient Achievement in Rsch. award Am. Fertility Soc., 1970, Sr. Scientist award Alexander von Humboldt Found., 1981. Mem. AAAS, KC, Am. Assn. Anatomist, Am. Soc. Animal Scis. (fellow 1987, Rsch. in Physiology award 1971), Soc. Study of Fertility, Soc. Study of Reproduction (dir., pres. 1987-88, Disting. Svc. award 1989), Lions Internat. (pres., sec. 1992-94), Sigma Xi, Gamma Alpha, Phi Kappa Phi, Phi Zeta, Gamma Sigma Delta, Alpha Zeta. Office: U Ill Dept Animal Scis 1207 W Gregory Dr Urbana IL 61801-3838

DZUBACK, MARY ANN, historian, educator; b. Chattanooga, Tenn.; d. Joseph Philip and Juanata Jayne (Childers) D.; m. Peter Alan Best, Dec. 29, 1983; stepchildren: Nicholas Alan Best, Christopher Robert Best. BA, Franconia Coll., 1974; MA, Columbia U., 1981, PhD, 1987. From asst. to assoc. prof. Washington U., St. Louis, 1987—. Author: Robert M. Hutchins, 1991. Rsch. grantee Rockefeller Archive Ctr., 1994, grantee Spencer Found., 1994—. Mem. Am. Hist. Assn., Am. Ednl. Rsch. Assn., Orgn. Am. Historians, History of Edn. Soc.

EACHUS, ALAN CAMPBELL, chemist; b. Champaign, Ill., July 11, 1939; s. Joseph Jackson and Ruth Margaret (Porter) E.; m. Ruth Elaine Briggs June 10, 1961; children: Donald Andrew, Timothy Alan. BS in Chemistry, Syracuse U., 1960; PhD in Organic Chemistry, SUNY, Syracuse, 1964; MBA in Fin. & Mktg., Northwestern U., 1975. Project coord. U.S. Army Missile Command, Redstone Arsenal, Ala., 1964-66; rsch. chemist Dow Chem. Co., Midland, Mich., 1966-70; sr. rsch. chemist Masury-Columbia Co., Melrose Pk., Ill., 1970-72; tech. svc. rep. Comml. Solvents Corp., Hillside, Ill., 1972-76; product mgr. IMC Chem. Group, Des Plaines, Ill., 1976-79; market mgr. IMC Chem. Group, Des Plaines, 1979-82; dir tech. svcs. Angus Chem. Co., Northbrook, Ill., 1982-91, mgr. tech. svc., 1991-95; dir. tech. support, 1995—. Contbr. articles to profl. jours. including Jour. Am. Chem. Soc., Chem. Times & Trends, Paint & Coatings Industry, Internat. Jour. of Cosmetic Scis., Chimica Oggi, Siefen, Ole Fette und Wachse, Pharm. Mfg. Internat., Cosmetics and Toiletries Mfg. Worldwide. Capt. U.S. Army, 1964-66, ret. col. USAR, 1992. Recipient Army Commendation medal, 1966. Mem. Am. Chem. Soc., N.Y. Acad. Scis., Am. Assn. Pharm. Scientists, Soc. Indsl. Microbiology. Home: 644 S Michigan Ave Villa Park IL 60181-2817 Office: Angus Chem Co 1500 E Lake Cook Rd Buffalo Grove IL 60089-6553

EADES, DAVID CLUTHE, real estate developer; b. Evansville, Ind., Feb. 3, 1935; s. Alvin Quiller and Oramay (Cluthe) E.; m. Jane Y. Chen, Feb. 20, 1959; children: Elizabeth Frank, Katherine Grill, Jennifer, Rebecca, Amelia. AB, Wabash Coll., 1955; MBA, U. Mich., 1956, MS, 1959; PhD, Ind. U., 1962. Asst. prof. SUNY, Oneonta, 1962-64; postdoctoral fellow NIH, Urbana, Ill., 1964-65; asst. prof. U. Ill., Urbana, 1965-70, assoc. prof., 1970-71; gen. ptnr. Eades Properties, Champaign, Ill., 1971—; gen. ptnr. Regency Cos., Savoy, Ill., 1973—; mng. gen. ptnr. Regency Assocs., Champaign, 1982—. Contbr. articles to profl. jours. Founder, dir., pres. Alvin Eades Ctr., Jacksonville, Ill., 1984-91; trustee Eades Found., Champaign, 1970—; bd. dirs. Carle Found., Urbana, 1972-81. Mem. Champaign County C. of C. (bd. dirs. 1990-91). Office: Regency Assocs 1701 Broadmoor Dr Ste 200 Champaign IL 61821

EADS, THOMAS MARTIN, food scientist educator; b. Pitts., Dec. 9, 1951; s. David Kirk and Florence Helen (Di Domenicis) E. BS in Biophysics, Penn State U., 1973; PhD in Molecular Biophysics, Fla. State U., 1981. Rsch. biochemist Rohm & Haas Co., Springhouse, Pa., 1973-75; grad. rsch. assoc. Fla. State U., Tallahassee, Pa., 1975-80; postdoctoral fellow U. Minn., Mpls., 1981-83, U. Rochester, N.Y., 1983-84; group leader, sr. scientist Kraft Foods, Glenview, Ill., 1985-89; assoc. prof. food sci. Purdue U., West Lafayette, Ind., 1990—; cons. Hershey Foods and other cos., 1990-95; founder, pres. Molecular Origins, Inc., Indpls., 1995. Author: (book) Molecular Origins of Food Functionality; mem. editorial bd. Jour. Magnetic Resonance Analysis, 1994; author, co-author of various profl. jours. Grantee Showalter Trust, 1993, A.E. Staley Mfg. Co., 1993-94; named Carl Fellers Vis. prof. U. Mass., 1995. Mem. Inst. Food Technologists, Am. Chem. Soc., Am. Oil Chemist's Soc., Sierra Club. Office: Purdue U 1160 Smith Hall W Lafayette IN 47907

EADY, LYDIA DAVIS, publishing executive; b. Kokomo, Ind., May 4, 1958; d. Henderson Sheridan and Ruth Vinita (Patterson) Davis; m. Jacquès Wayne Eady; 1 child, Andrew Jacquès. BA magna cum laude, Howard U., 1980. Reporter trainee Sta. WRTV-TV, Indpls., 1980-81; writer, researcher Johnson Pub. Co., Chgo., 1981-82, asst. dir. pub. relations, 1983, assoc. producer Ebony/Jet Celebrity Showcase, 1983, dir. promotion, 1983-85, v.p. promotion, 1985—. Recipient cert. Merit Circulation Direct Mail awards, 1984, Communications Excellence to Black Audiencies, 1986, 88, 89, Woman of Substance award, 1994. Mem. League Black Women, Nat. Women of Achievement, Chgo. Assn. Black Journalists, Howard U. Alumni Assn., Women's Advt. Club Chgo. Mem. African Methodist Episcopal Ch. Office: Johnson Pub Co 820 S Michigan Ave Chicago IL 60605-2103

EAGLE, CURTIS WILLIAM, civil engineer; b. Ft. Wayne, Ind., Nov. 13, 1957; s. Curtis Dale and Joan Darlene (Brilinski) E.; 1 child, Allison Suzanne Eagle. AS, Alpena (Mich.) C.C., 1977; BS, Mich. Technol. U., 1979. Registered profl. engr., Ohio, Mich. Plant engr., mgr. Insultherm Corp., Alpena, 1979-80; design engr. Eagle Engring. Co. Inc., Alpena, 1980; asst. to city engr. City of Portage (Mich.), 1980-84; city engr., dir. svc. City of Trotwood (Ohio), 1984-91; v.p. Eagle Engring. and Utility, Alpena, 1991-94; city engr. City of Tiffin (Ohio), 1994—; exec. sec. Tiffin Bd. Zone Appeals, Tiffin, 1994—; coord. disaster svc. Tiffin Disaster Svcs., Tiffin, 1995—; bd. dirs. Eagle Co., Alpena. Exec. sec. Tiffin Fair Housing Bd., Tiffin, 1994—. Mem. Tiffin Jaycees. Home: 4974 Township Rd 1173 Tiffin OH 44883 Office: Office of City Engr 51 E Market St Tiffin OH 44883

EAGLEMAN, JOE R., meteorologist, educator; b. Howell County, Mo., Oct. 9, 1936; s. Edward B. and Ella M. (Crawford) E.; m. Doris L. Kugel; children: Gregory T., Kristy L., Kent E. BS, U. Mo., 1959, MS, 1961, PhD, 1963. Asst. prof. U. Kans., Lawrence, 1963-67, assoc. prof., 1967-75, prof. meteorology, 1975—; expert witness U.S. Ho. of Reps., Washington, 1973, Kans. Senate, Topeka, 1991, IRS, Washington, 1980. Author: Visualization of Climate, 1976, Meteorology, 2d edit., 1985, Severe and Unusual Weather, 1990, Air Pollution Meteorology, 2d edit., 1996. Mem. Am. Meteorol. Soc. Republican. Mem. Ch. of Christ. Office: U Kans Dept Physics & Astronomy Lawrence KS 66045

EAGLES, DEREK M., project engineer; b. Mancaton, Can., Apr. 6, 1949; came to the U.S., 1973; BS in Mech. Engring., U. Alberta, Can., 1972. Registered profl. engr., Iowa. Engr. John Deere, Dubuque, Iowa, 1973-77; project engr. John Deere Product Engring., Waterloo, Iowa, 1977—. Patentee in field. Mem. Am. Soc. Engrs., Soc. Automotive Engrs. Office: John Deere Product Engring PO Box 8000 Waterloo IA 50704-8000

EAGLY, ALICE HENDRICKSON, social psychology educator; b. L.A., Dec. 25, 1938; d. Harold Martin and Josara Alberta (Whyers) Hendrickson; m. Robert Victor Eagly, Sept. 8, 1962; children: Ingrid Victoria, Ursula Elizabeth. BA, Radcliffe Coll., 1960; MA, U. Mich., 1963, PhD, 1965. Asst. prof. Mich. State U., East Lansing, 1965-67; asst. to assoc. to full prof. U. Mass., Amherst, 1967-80; vis. asst. prof. U. Ill., Champaign, 1970-71; vis. assoc. prof. Harvard U., Cambridge, Mass., 1974-75; prof. social psychology Purdue U., West Lafayette, Ind., 1980-95, Northwestern U., Evanston, Ill., 1995—; MacEachern Meml. lectr. U. Alta., 1985; vis. prof. U. Tuebingen (Germany), 1991-92. Author: Sex Differences in Social Behavior: A Social Role Interpretation, 1987, (with Shelly Chaiken) The Psychology of Attitudes, 1993; cons. editor Jour. Personality and Social Psychology: Attitudes and Social Cognition, 1979—, mem. editorial bd., 1983—; cons. editor Psychology of Women Quar., 1978-86, also others; contbr. articles to profl. jours. Recipient Disting. Pub. award, Assn. for Women in Psychology, 1978, Gordon Allport Intergroup Rels. prize, Soc. Psychol. Study Social Issues, 1976; Nat. Merit scholar, 1956-60, Fulbright fellow, 1960-61, Woodrow Wilson fellow, 1961-62, NSF fellow, 1962-65; various rsch. grants. Mem. APA (citation as disting. leader for women in psychology com. on women in psychology), Soc. Personality and Social Psychology (pres. 1981), Donald Campbell award for disting. contbn. to social psychology 1994), Soc. for Exptl. Social Psychology (exec. com. 1973-76, 81-83), Midwestern Psychol. Assn., Phi Beta Kappa, Sigma Xi. Office: Northwestern U Dept Psychology Swift Hall 2029 Sheridan Rd Evanston IL 60208

EAKES, LINDA M., telecommunications executive, consultant; b. Borger, Tex., Aug. 2, 1957; d. Earl Dean and Pauline Marie (Overlin) Murphy. BA, N. Tex. State U., Denton, 1978. Mgr. nat. tng. U.S. Telephone Inc., Dallas, 1980-85; dir. mktg. Telesphere Internat., Oakbrook, Ill., 1985-90; v.p. customer svc. Capital Network Inc., Autin, Tex., 1990-92; dir. client svcs. Value-Added Communications, Dallas, 1992-93; v.p. mktg., bd. dirs. Telecom. resources, Inc., Kansas City, 1993—; sec., bd. dirs. Telecom. Resources, Inc., Kansas City, 1993—; cons. Integretel Inc., San Jose, 1994—. Author (Poetry) Farm Journal, 1974; co-author: Competitive Operator Services in the U.S., 1989. Mem. Dem. Party. Mem. NOW, Comptel, Operator Svc. Providers Am., S.W. Telecom. Assn., APCC. Democrat. Office: TRI 8 Victory Ln # 200 Liberty MO 64068-1903

EAMAN, FRANK DWIGHT, lawyer; b. Stamford, Conn., Nov. 21, 1944; s. James Benjamin E. and Elizabeth Marie (Darrow) Willoughby; m. Allyn Carol Biener, May 24, 1974 (div. 1988); 1 child, Elizabeth; m. Julie Ann Kiefer, June 1, 1991. AB, U. Chgo., 1967; JD, U. Mich., 1971. Bar: Mich. Supreme Ct., 1971, U.S. Supreme Ct., 1984. Student atty. Washtenaw County Legal Aid, Ann Arbor, Mich., 1969-70; atty. Gage, Burgess, et al., Detroit, 1971-74; shareholder Eaman & Ravitz, P.C., Detroit, 1974-88, Bellanca, Beattie & DeLisle, Detroit, 1988—; commr. State Appellate Defender Commn., Detroit, 1988—. Recipient Arthur Von Briesen award Nat. Legal Aid & Defender Assn., 1983. Fellow State Bar Found.; mem. Criminal Def. Attys. Mich. (pres. 1986-90), Mich. State Bar Assn. (chairperson task force on assigned counsel standards 1986-91), Legal Aid and Defender Assn. Detroit (bd. dirs., v.p. 1974-86). Office: Bellanca Beattie DeLisle 20480 Vernier Rd Harper Woods MI 48225

EAMES, EARL WARD, JR., management educator, development specialist; b. Morris, Minn., Oct. 22, 1923; s. Earl Ward and Camilla (Hendricks) E.; m. Anyes de Horst, June 26, 1954; children: Elizabeth Anne, Earl Ward III, Erik Michael, Christopher Paul. SB, MIT, 1949. Vice pres., then pres., dir. Consultants Inc., Boston and Amsterdam, Netherlands; prodn. specialist Found. Productivity Research, Helsinki, Finland; pres. Gen. Mgmt. Assos., Boston; Royal Danish consul New Eng.; sr. assoc. Cresap, McCormick & Paget, N.Y.C., 1963-66; exec. v.p. Spl. Metals Inc., 1966; pres., chief exec. officer, dir. Council Internat. Progress in Mgmt., N.Y.C.; vis. prof. and mgmt. consultancy advisor UN Indsl. Devel. Orgn., Nigeria, 1978-80; advisor on small-scale industry UN Indsl. Devel. Orgn. World Bank, various locations, 1980-86; pres. UN Assn. Minn., 1991-92, 94; mem. nat. com., vice chair CCDP UN Assn., 1991—; adj. prof. Augsburg Coll., 1986—, U. St. Thomas, 1988—; mem. Minn. Gov.'s Commn. on Nat. and Cmty. Svc., 1994—; chmn. bd. trustees Nat. Svc. Secretariat, 1966—. Author: Managerial Requirements 1966, Non-Woven Fabrics, 1970; Contbr. Training Managers: The International Guide, 1969, University Involvement in Industrial Development, 1979. Served with USNR, 1942-46. Mem. Acad. Polit. Sci., MIT Alumni Assn., Calhoun Beach Club. Home: 2601 Sunset Blvd Minneapolis MN 55416-4286

EARL, FRANK D., manufacturing company executive; b. Austin, Minn., July 17, 1961. Student, Milw. Sch. Engring., 1980-81; A.Mech. Tech., Parkland Coll., Champaign, Ill., 1984. Engr. technician Superior Ill. Corp., Decatur, Ill., 1984-85; draftsman S&R Engring., Urbana, Ill., 1985-87; detail draftsman IMI Cash Value, Decatur, 1987-94; product designer Hydro-Gear, Sullivan, Ill., 1994—. Mem. Ill. Heartland Auto CAD Users Group (librarian 1994-95), Sports Car Club Am. (regional sec. 1995). Roman Catholic. Office: Hydro Gear 1411 S Hamilton St Sullivan IL 61951-2263

EARLE, JAMES A., educational administrator; b. St. Louis, Aug. 18, 1945; s. William C. Earle Jr. and Dorothy C. (Kersting) Wieck; m. Portia K. Newport, June 13, 1970; children: James A. Jr., John W. BS in Edn., Cen. Mo. State U., 1968; MS, NE Mo. U., 1973; PhD, U. Ill., 1981; adminstrv. cert., So. Ill. U., 1987. Cert. phys. edn. and health tchr., elem. prin., supt., Mo. Elem. sch. prin., dir. state and fed. programs Sch. Dist. Riverview Gardens, St. Louis, 1986—; adj. prof. NE Mo. State U., Kirksville. Recipient Bravo award St. Louis County, 1991. Mem. ASCD, NAESP, AAHPERD, Mo. Assn. Elem. Sch. Prins., Phi Delta Kappa, Phi Epsilon Kappa. Home: 3905 Sunnyvale Ct Florissant MO 63034-3217 Office: Sch Dist Riverview Gardens 1370 Northumberland Dr Saint Louis MO 63137-1413

EARLE, MARY MARGARET, marketing executive; b. Newberry, Mich., June 26, 1947; d. William Loren and Naida Theresa (Ward) E. Student, St. Mary's Coll., Notre Dame, Ind., 1965-67. Cert. employment cons. Receptionist Western Girl World, San Francisco, 1968-69; receptionist, sec. Advanced Memory Systems, Sunnyvale, Calif., 1969-71; career cons. Qualified Personnel, Madison, Wis., 1972-75; VIP asst. Summit Sports Arena Grand Open, Houston, 1975, S. Petroleum Gp/OTC, Houston, 1976, Astrodomain Assn., Houston, 1976-77; bus. mgr. Mobile Colo TV Prodn., Houston, 1977-80; broadcast bus. affairs dir. G.D.L. & W. Adv., Houston, 1980-90; broadcast talent cons. Willis, Tex., 1990-93; mktg. cons., pvt. practice Marquette, Mich., 1993-95; pres. IXL Creative-Mktg. Excellence, Marquette, Mich., 1996—; modeling judge Page Parks Sch. Modeling, Houston, 1988-91; cons. industry/union rels. AFTRA/SAG, Houston, 1985-92. Houston mem. Fashion Group, 1989-90; sec. Bluebell Estates Assn., Willis, 1991, pres. 1992; pub. rels. vol. Women's Ctr. seminars, Houston, 1984-85. Named Disting. Salesman of Yr. Sales and Mktg. Execs., Madison, 1973, 74. Mem. Adminstrv. Mgmt. Soc. (cons. ofcl. panel 1974), Pers. Adminstrs. Soc., Am. Assn. Advt. Agys. (so. broadcast policy com.), Lake Superior Art Assn. (bd. dirs. 1996—). Home and Office: 612 County Road 480 Marquette MI 49855-9411

EARLEY, ANTHONY FRANCIS, JR., utilities company executive, lawyer; b. Jamaica, N.Y., July 29, 1949; s. Anthony Francis and Jean Ann (Draffen) E.; m. Sarah Margaret Belanger, Oct. 14, 1972; children: Michael Patrick, Anthony Matthew, Daniel Cartwright, Matthew Sean. BS in Physics, U. Notre Dame, 1971, MS in Engring., 1979, JD, 1979. Bar: Va. 1980, N.Y. 1985, U.S. Ct. Appeals (6th cir.) 1981. Assoc. Hunton & Williams, Richmond, Va., 1979-85, ptnr., 1985; gen. counsel L.I. Lighting Co., Hicksville, N.Y., 1985-89, exec. v.p., 1988-89, pres., COO, 1989-94, also bd. dirs.;

pres., COO The Detroit Edison Co., 1994—, also bd. dirs.; bd. dirs. Mutual Am. Contbr. articles to profl. jours. Mem. adv. coun. Coll. Engring., U. Notre Dame. Served to lt. USN, 1971-76. Mem. ABA. Roman Catholic. Office: Detroit Edison Co 2000 Second Ave Detroit MI 48226*

EARLY, BERT HYLTON, lawyer, legal search consultant; b. Kimball, W.Va., July 17, 1922; s. Robert Terry and Sue Keister (Hylton) E.; m. Elizabeth Henry, June 24, 1950; children—Bert Hylton, Robert Christian, Mark Randolph, Philip Henry, Peter St. Clair. Student, Marshall U., 1940-42; A.B., Duke U., 1946; J.D., Harvard U., 1949. Bar: W.Va. 1949, Ill. 1963, Fla. 1981. Assoc. Fitzpatrick, Marshall, Huddleston & Bolen, Huntington, W.Va., 1949-57; asst. counsel Island Creek Coal Co., Huntington, W.Va., 1957-60, assoc. gen. counsel, 1960-62; dep. exec. dir. ABA, Chgo., 1962-64, exec. dir., 1964-81; sr. v.p. Wells Internat., Chgo., 1981-83, pres., 1983-85; pres. Bert H. Early Assocs. Inc., Chgo., 1985-94, Early Cochran & Olson, Chgo., 1994—; dir. Am. Bar Found., Chgo., 1993-95; instr. Marshall U., Huntington, W.V.a, 1950-53; cons. and lectr. in field. Bd. dirs. Morris Meml. Hosp. for Crippled Children, 1954-60, Huntington Pub. Libr., 1951-60, W.Va. Tax Inst., 1961-62, Huntington Galleries, 1961-62; mem. W.Va. Jud. Coun., 1960-62, Huntington City Coun., 1961-62; bd. dirs. Cmty. Renewal Soc., Chgo., 1965-76, United Charities Chgo., 1972-80, Hinsdale (Ill.) Hosp. Found., 1987-93, Internat. Bar Assn. Found., 1987-89; bd. dirs. Am. Bar Endowment, 1983—, sec., 1987-89, treas., 1989-91, v.p., 1991-93, pres., 1993-95; mem. vis. com. U. Chgo. Law Sch., 1975-78; trustee Davis and Elkins Coll., 1960-63; mem. Hinsdale Plan Commn., 1982-85. 1st lt. AC, U.S. Army, 1943-45. Fellow Am. Bar Found. (bd. dirs. 1993-95), Ill. Bar Found. (charter); mem. ABA (ho. of dels. 1958-59, chmn. young lawyers divsn. 1957-58, Disting. Svc. award young lawyers divsn. 1983), Am. Law Inst. (life), Internat. Bar Assn. (asst. sec. gen. 1967-82), Nat. Legal Aid and Defender Assn., Legal Aid Soc. Chgo., Am. Judicature Soc. (bd. dirs. 1981-84), Fla. Bar, W.Va. Bar Assn., Chgo. Bar Assn. Presbyterian. Office: Early Cochran & Olson Inc 401 N Michigan Ave Ste 515 Chicago IL 60611

EARLY, JUDITH K., program evaluation director; b. Evansville, Ind., 1954; d. Forrest M. and Dorothea E. Early. BA, Brescia Coll., 1976; MS, So. Ill. U., 1985, RhD, 1991. Cert. vocat. evaluator. Work activity supr. So. Ind. Rehab. Svcs., Inc., Boonville, 1976-78; vocat. evaluator Evansville Assn. for Retarded Citizens, 1978-85; vocat. evaulator Evaluation and Developmental Ctr., Carbondale, Ill., 1985-88; grad. asst., program evaluator So. Ill. U., Carbondale, 1988-90, rsch. and teaching asst., 1990-91; exec. dir. Albion Fellow Bacon Ctr., Evansville, Ind., 1991-93; family svcs. dir. Goodwill Family Ctr., Evansville, 1993-95, program evaluation dir., 1995-96, dir., 1996—. Contbr. articles to profl. publs. Bd. dirs. So. Ill. Ctr. for Ind. Living, Carbondale, 1990-91; bd. dirs., youth worker 1st United Meth. Ch., Carbondale, 1989-91; v.p. Altrusa of Evansville, 1993-94; bd. dirs. Youth as Resources, 1995—; chmn. Transitional Svcs., Inc., Human Rights Com., 1992—. Mem. ACA, AAUW, Nat. Rehab. Assn. (accessibility site surveyor 1990—), Vocat. Evaluation and Work Adjustment Assn. (chmn. student affairs com. 1988-90, Student Lit. award 1987), Ill. Rehab. Assn. (bd. dirs. 1989-91), Ill. Vocat. Evaluation and Work Adjustment Assn. (chmn. mem. 1989-91, pres. 1991—, Disting. Svc. award 1989), Am. Assn. Mental Retardation, Assn. Retarded Citizens, Kiwanis (sec. North Park chpt. 1993-94). Office: Goodwill Family Ctr 1351 W Buena Vista Rd Evansville IN 47710-3338

EARLY, THOMAS MICHAEL, educator; b. Worcester, Mass., June 25, 1942; s. Luke John and Mabel Catherine (Hill) E.; m. Marie Elena Antonioli, Jan. 22, 1966; children: Ptrick Michael, Kathleen Michelle. BS, North Adams State Coll., Mass., 1964; MA, Ctrl. Mich. U., Mt. Pleasant, 1979. Lic. tchr. Mass., Ind. Commd. 2d lt. USMC, 1964, advanced through grades to col., 1987; mem. gen. staff 1st Marine Brigade, Kanohe, Hawaii, 1978-80; mem. admirals staff Comdr. in Chief Pacific Fleet, Honolulu, 1980-82; mem. gen. staff 4th Marine Amphibious Brigade, Norfolk, Va., 1982-85, Fleet Marine Force Atlantic, Norfolk, 1985-92; comdg. officer Comm. Officer Sch., Quantico, Va., 1989-92; prof. Tulane U., New Orleans, 1992-94; head leadership dept. J.W. Riley H.S., South Bend, Ind., 1994—. Contbg. author: Ambush Valley, 1990. Decorated 3 Legions of Merit, Bronze Star with Combat V, Purple Heart, 2 Meritorious Svc. medals. Mem. Armed Forces Comm. Agy. (pres. 1989-92, Legion of Merit 1992). Republican. Roman Catholic. Home and Office: 50695 Ridgemoor Way Granger IN 46530

EARNHART, DON BRADY, retired charitable foundation executive; b. Marion, Ind., Aug. 5, 1925; s. Don A. and Bernice (Brady) E.; m. Suzanne Kersting, Aug. 5, 1950; children: Elizabeth Ann, Susan, Stephen. B.S., Ind. U., 1949, LLD (hon.), 1986; LHD (hon.), U. Indpls., 1994. C.P.A., Ind. With Ernst & Ernst (C.P.A.s), Indpls., 1949-53; with Inland Container Corp., Indpls., 1953-72; asst. treas. Inland Container Corp., 1957-60, sec., asst. treas., 1961-64, sec.-treas., 1965-67, v.p., treas., 1968-72; adminstrv. trustee, sec.-treas. Krannert Charitable Trust, 1973-88, ret., 1988; bd. dirs. Indpls. Life Ins. Co., former chmn. bd. Pendleton Banking Co., Ind. Former mem. adv. bd. Ind. U.-Purdue U. at Indpls.; mem. Cmty. Svc. Coun. Met. Indpls.; chmn. edn. study team Ind. Gov.'s Economy Program, 1969; trustee emeritus U. Indpls.; trustee, past treas. Indpls. Mus. Art; former bd. dirs., treas. Indpls. Met. YMCA; former bd. dirs. Indpls. Symphony Orch.; trustee; former bd. dirs. Indpls. Zoo, Fine Arts Soc. of Indpls., Indpls. Health Inst., Jr. Achievement, Indpls., Greater Indpls. Progress Com.; bd. dirs., past treas. Ind. U. Found. Served with U.S. Mcht. Marine, 1943-46. Designated Sagamore of Wabash by Gov. Ind., 1969, 89; recipient Disting. Alumni Svc. award Ind. U., 1993. Mem. Ind. Assn. C.P.A.s (past dir., sec.), Indpls. C. of C. (past dir.), Ind. U. Sch. Bus. Alumni Assn. (past exec. council). Home: 7275 Lakeside Dr Indianapolis IN 46278-1616

EASON, ALPHONSO LEE, state agency administrator; b. Detroit, Nov. 2, 1967; s. Lorenzo Lee and Sadie Mae (James) E. BS, No. Mich. U., 1989; MPA, Drake U., 1993. Comty. devel. specialist U.S. Senator Carl Levin, Detroit, 1989; dean's asst. No. Mich. U., 1990; residence hall dir. Drake U., Des Moines, 1990-93, intern student fin. planning, 1991, intern office admissions, 1991-92; budget analyst Iowa Dept. Human Svcs., Des Moines, 1993; pub. assistance officer Iowa Emergency Mgmt. divsn., Des Moines, 1993-94; program planner Iowa Dept. Pub. Def., Des Moines, 1994—; intern Office of City Mgr., West Des Moines, 1992. Bd. dirs. KAPSI Found. Inc., Des Moines, 1994—; childcare worker Young Women's Resource Ctr., Des Moines, 1993-94. Named one of Outstanding Young Men Am., 1993. Mem. Internat. City/County Mgrs. Assn., NAACP (exec. com. 1994—), Toastmasters, Kappa Alpha Psi. Home: 2824 Grand Ave Apt 106 Des Moines IA 50312 Office: State of Iowa Hoover Bldg Des Moines IA 50319

EAST, MARK DAVID, physician; b. Baton Rouge, July 22, 1955; s. Charles Ray and Gloria Lee (Fairbanks) E.; m. Cara Elizabeth Sherk; children: Nicole, Sara, Mark, Kyle, Erin. BS in Pharmacy, U. Miss., 1978; DO, U. Health Scis., Kansas City, Mo., 1983. Diplomate Nat. Bd. Examiners. Pharmacist asst. mgr. Sav-On Drugs, Inc., McComb, Miss., 1978-79; intern Normandy Hosps., St. Louis, 1983-84; resident in internal medicine Normandy Osteo. Hosps., St. Louis, 1984-87; fellow in pulmonary, critical care and environ. medicine U. Mo., Columbia, 1987-89; physician pulmonary, critical care, internal medicine Tri-County Pulmonary Medicine, St. Peters, Mo., 1989-90, Lake Internal Med. Specialists, Osage Beach, Mo., 1990—; med. dir. ICU and cardiopulmonary dept. Lake of the Ozarks Gen. Hosp., Osage Beach, 1990—; chmn. dept. medicine Lake Ozarks Gen. Hosp., 1991—, chmn. infection control and pharmacy & therapeutics com., 1991—. Asst. scoutmaster 14th World Scout Jamboree, Boy Scouts Am., Lillehammer, Norway, 1975, patrol leader 13th World Jamboree, Fuminamiya City, Japan, 1971, staff mem. 8th Nat. Scout Jamboree, Moraine State Park, Pa., 1973. Mem. AMA, Am. Osteo. Assn., Am. Thoracic Soc., Mo. Assn. Osteo. Physicians, Sigma Sigma Phi, Phi Delta Chi. Republican. Methodist. Office: Lake Internal Medicine Specialists Med Office Bldg Ste 102 Osage Beach MO 65065

EASTBURN, JEANNETTE ROSE, religious publishing executive; b. Huntington, Ind., Mar. 18, 1916; d. Elmer Fyson and Iva Jerusha (Rose) Connett; widowed. BS, Bethel Coll., Mishawaka, Ind., 1973. ordained World Bible Way Fellowship, 1990. Mgr. Calvary Bookstore, South Bend, Ind., 1952-54; sec. Meml. Hosp., South Bend, 1954-58, Pvt. Day Christian Sch. Calvary Temple, South Bend, 1958-64; tchr. South Bend Pub. Schs., 1964-78; ednl. cons. KDSA Radio, Wichita, Kans., 1978-80; pub. Christian Comm., Inc., Wichita, 1980—. Contbr. articles to profl. jours. Mem. AAUW, Order Eastern Star, Amanranth, White Shrine, Ky. Cols., Epsilon Sigma Alpha, Gamma Sigma, Phi Delta Kappa. Republican. Home: 6434 N Hillside St Wichita KS 67219-1805

EASTBURN, RICHARD A., consulting firm executive; b. West Chester, Pa., Jan. 16, 1934; s. Louis W. and Alma S. (Shellin) E.; BA, Shelton Coll., 1956; MST, N.Y. Theol. Sem., 1959; MEd, Temple U., 1970; MBA, Columbia U., 1979; m. Heidi Fritz, June 15, 1963 (dec. 1991); children: Karin J., R. Marc; m. Carol Mc Devitt, Oct. 24, 1993. Ordained to ministry Am. Baptist Conv., 1959; minister, Laurelton, N.J., 1959-61; dir adult programs Central YMCA, Phila., 1961-65; dir. Opportunities Industrialization Ctr., Phila., 1965-67; mgr. tng. and devel. Missile & Surface Radar div. RCA, Moorestown, N.J., 1967-68, mgr. mgmt. devel. govt. and comml. systems sector, dir. mgmt. devel., 1969-71; group mgr. personnel for internat. field mktg. & svc. Digital Equipment, Maynard, Mass., 1971-75; corp. dir. orgn. and productivity devel. Am. Standard, Inc., N.Y.C., 1975-79; corp. dir. mgmt. devel. edn. and staffing TRW, Inc., Cleve., 1979-85; pres. Retirement Cmty. Concepts, 1981-88, founder Laurel Lake Retirement Cmty., Hudson, Ohio, 1985; sr. v.p. Strategic Mgmt. Group of Phila., 1985-88; exec. dir. mfg. Studies Bd. NAS, 1989-90; pres. Mgmt. Ops. Solutions, Chagrin Falls, Ohio, 1990—; chmn. The Executive Com. of Cleve., 1988—; producer, moderator Ask the Clergy, Sta. WIP, Phila., 1965-67; bd. dirs./advisors Travaco Mgmt. Systems, Wellsboro (Ohio) Foundry, Camet Corp., Johnson Industries, exec. program adv. bd. U. Ind., Burlington County (N.J.) Cmty. Com., 1967-69; pres. Rehab. Am., Inc., 1991-93. Recipient Disting. Cmty. Svc. award Shelton Coll. Alumni, 1956; Dedicated Service award Phila. March of Progress, 1967. Mem. Am. Soc. Tng. and Devel. (dir., 1979-80), Chagrin Valley C. of C., 1986—, Cleve. Advanced Mfg. Program, 1986—, Ops. Mgmt. Assn., Soc. Mfg. Engrs., Am. Prodn. and Inventory Control Soc., Wembley Swim and Tennis Club, A & A Sportsman Club. Mem. United Ch. Christ. Home and Office: 15511 Russell Rd Chagrin Falls OH 44022-2669

EASTMAN, NATHAN LEROY, realtor, appraiser; b. Kimball, Nebr., Mar. 29, 1921; s. Leon Roy and Emma Anna (Dudek) E.; m. Elizabeth G. (Gailey) June 1, 1942; children: George M., Andrew R., William R., James H., John C., Thomas F. BS, U. Wyo., 1952. Owner Eastman Realty & Ins., Kimball, 1947—. Mem., pres. Kimball Sch. Bd. Maj. USAF, 1942-46, 51-53. Mem. Kimball Rotary Club, Rotary Internat. (dist. gov. 1992-93). Methodist. Home: 800 East 6th St Kimball NE 69145 Office: 601 S High School St Kimball NE 69145

EATON, KARL F(RANCIS), insurance executive, consultant; b. Sewal, Iowa, July 16, 1925; s. Stewart E. and Jessie L. (Holmes) E.; m. Martha J. Adams, Mar. 20, 1950; 1 child, Jay A. BA in Math., U. Mo., Kansas City, 1949. Actuarial asst. Bus. Men's Assurance Co., Kansas City, 1948-54, mgr. EDP, 1954-62; contr. Guarantee Mut. Life Co., Omaha, 1962-67; v.p. Employers Reins. Corp., Kansas City, 1967-88; owner, mgr. ins. cons. Eaton Cons. Svcs., Shawnee Mission, Kans., 1988—. Scoutmaster Boy Scouts Am., Prairie Village, Kans., 1966, dist. chmn., Kansas City, Kans., 1982; pres. Truman Med. Ctr. Aux., Kansas City, Mo., 1991-93. Sgt. U.S. Army, 1944-46, ETO. Recipient award of merit Boy Scouts Am., 1979, Silver Beaver award, 1982, Auxilian of Yr. award Truman Med. Ctr. Aux., 1987. Fellow Life Mgmt. Inst.; mem. Life Office Mgmt. Assn. (automation II com. 1963-67), Casualty Actuarial Soc. (assoc.), Am. Acad. Actuaries, Mo. Assn. Hosp. Auxs. (bd. dirs. dist. III 1995-96, 3rd v.p. 1996—), Kansas City Actuaries Club (prs. 1955-56). Republican. Presbyterian. Home: 13740 Pembroke Cir Leawood KS 66224-4203 Office: 9000 W 67th St Shawnee Mission KS 66202-3631

EATON, MICHAEL CHRISTOPHER, accounting technician; b. Columbus, Ohio, Aug. 8, 1959; s. Ronald Andrew and Rosaleen Ann (Murnane) E.; m. Charlene Ann Gutmann, Nov. 6, 1993. AS, Burlington C.C., 1984. Contracting specialist Def. Supply Ctr., Columbus, 1996—. Active Feinstein Found. to Help Hunger. Sgt. USAF, 1980-86. Mem. K.C. (chancellor 1994—, 4th degree 1994, Dep. Grand Knight 1996), DAV (life). Republican. Roman Catholic. Home: 720 E Mithoff St Columbus OH 43206 Office: DSCC Columbus Ctr 3990 E Broad St Columbus OH 43216

EATON, ROBERT JAMES, automotive company executive; b. Buena Vista, Colo., Feb. 13, 1940; s. Eugene Hiram and Mildred Inez (Stokes) E.; m. Cornelia Cae Drake, June 28, 1964; children: Scott C., Matthew D. B.S.M.E., U. Kans., 1963. Exec. engr. engring. staff GM, Warren, Mich., 1974-75, chief engr. small family car project Chevrolet div., 1975-76, chief engr. corp. car programs engring. staff, 1976-79; asst. chief Oldsmobile div. GM, Lansing, Mich., 1979-82, dir. reliability, 1982; v.p. advanced product and mfg. engring. staff GM, Lansing, Detroit, 1982-86; v.p. and group exec. Tech. Staffs Group GM, 1986-88; pres. GM Europe, Zurich, Switzerland, 1988-92; vice-chmn., chief operating officer Chrysler, 1992-93, chmn., CEO, 1993—; chmn. bd. dirs. SAAB Automobile; bd. dirs. Internat. Paper Co. Mem. indsl. adv. coun. Coll. Engring., Stanford U., 1986—, U. Mich.; chmn. indsl. adv. group Stanford Inst. for Mfg. and Automation, 1984-86; bd. chmn. Met. Ctr. for High Tech., 1982-88; dir. Detroit Renaissance, United Way of Southeastern Mich., Econ. Alliance for Mich., Detroit Symphony Orch., Mich. Leaders Health Care Group. Chevalier du Tastevin, 1989—. Fellow Soc. Automotive Engrs. (chmn. tech. bd. 1986-87, fin. com. 1985—, chmn. Engring. Expo), Engring. Soc. Detroit (co-chmn. membership com. 1986-87, bd. dirs.); mem. NAE, Am. Automobile Mfrs. Assn. (chmn., dir.), Indsl. Tech. Inst. (bd. dirs. 1982-85), Electronic Data Systems (bd. dirs. 1984-89), Group Lotus (bd. dirs.), Bus. Coun., Bus. Roundtable, U.S./Japan Bus. Coun., Pres.'s Adv. Com. on Trade Policy & Negotiations. Office: Chrysler Corp 1000 Chrysler Dr Auburn Hills MI 48326*

EATON, THOMAS NEWTON, cartoonist; b. Wichita, Mar. 2, 1940; s. Newton A. and Betty E. (Cooper) E.; m. Shara J. Pinkley, June 24, 1967. BFA, U. Kans., 1962. Writer/artist Hallmark Cards, Inc., Kansas City, Mo., 1962-66; art editor Scholastic Mags., Inc., N.Y.C., 1966-68; freelance cartoonist Kansas City, Mo., 1968—. Author, illustrator numerous books including: Chicken-Fried Fudge, 1970, Flap, 1972, Captain Ecology, Pollution Fighter, 1974, Otis G. Firefly's Phantasmagoric Almanac, 1975, Popnut, Tom Eaton's Book of Marvels, Rufus Crustbuster and the Earth Patrol, 1978, others; author/illustrator Holiday Greeting Cards, Super Valentines to Cut and Color, others; illustrator: The Penguins are Coming!, 1969, Steven and the Green Turtle, 1970, An Animal for Alan, 1971, Leo Lion Looks for Books, 1972, Count On Leo Lion, 1973, The Sleep-Leaping Kangaroo, 1973, Puzzle Panic, 1977, The Beastly Gazette, 1977, Play Ball, Joey Kangaroo!, 1980 and numerous others; contbr. cartoons to Look, Saturday Evening Post, Playboy, othrs: writer and artist Dink and Duff, Webelos Woody, Tiger Cubs, Pedro, Cub Corner (cartoon features for Boys' Life), 1984—. With U.S. Army, 1963-65. Home: 911 West 100 St Kansas City MO 64114

EBBITTS, MARK HOBART, travel service professional; b. Kansas City, Mo., Oct. 29, 1949; s. Robert H. and Catherine Ann (Bodde) E.; m. Babs Faulk Fleming, July 20, 1975 (div. 1986); 1 child, Brian Faulk. BEE, U. Mo., 1971, MEE, 1972. Registered profl. engr., Mo. Automatic controls engr. Procter and Gamble Co., Albany, Ga., 1972-75; plant engring. supr. Dow Chem. Co., Rocky Flats, Colo., 1975-77; pres. Shelton Travel Svc., Kansas City, Mo., 1977—; dir. Fin. Bldg. Assn., Kansas City, 1986-89, pres., 1988—. Patentee in field. Mem. Am. Soc. Travel Agts., Friends of Art, Friends of Kansas City Zoo, Kansas City Club, 1212 Club, C. of C. Republican. Roman Catholic. Home: 1007 Romany Rd Kansas City MO 64113-2014 Office: Shelton Travel Svc Inc 4800 Belleview Ave Kansas City MO 64112-1321

EBBS, GEORGE HEBERLING, JR., management consulting company executive; b. Sewickley, Pa., Sept. 20, 1942; s. George Heberling and Mae Isabelle (Miller) E.; m. Agnes Rak, 1989; children: Stacey Kirsten, Cynthia Lynn, George Heberling III. BS in Engring., Purdue U., 1964; MBA, U. Wash., 1966; PhD in Bus., Columbia U., 1970. Sr. engr. Boeing Co., Seattle, 1966; assoc. Booz Allen & Hamilton, N.Y.C., 1969-72, sr. v.p., 1974-86; v.p. Fry Cons., N.Y.C., 1973; chmn., pres. The Canaan Group, Park City, Utah, 1986—; adj. prof. Columbia U., N.Y.C., 1978-80. Trustee Utah Opera. Bronfman fellow, Columbia U., N.Y.C., 1967; Purdue Old Master. Mem. Met. Opera Club, Wings Club, Iron Key, Omicron Delta Kappa, Beta Gamma Sigma. Presbyterian. Home: 14 Canyon Ct Park City UT 84060 Office: The Canaan Group Ltd PO Box 680580 2052 Prospector Ave Park City UT 84068

EBEL, A. JAMES, broadcasting consultant; b. Waterloo, Iowa, May 13, 1913; s. Louis August and Lillian Stubbs Ebel; m. Elouise Lenore Hanson, May 26, 1935; children: Marilyn, James, Marjorie, Douglas. BA, U. Iowa, 1937, MS, U. Ill., 1943. Registered profl. engr., Ill. Radio engr. Stas. KFJB, KDGE, WMT, WBAA, 1929-37; chief engr. U. Ill. Br. Svc., Urbana, Ill., 1937-46; pres. Sta. KXIC, Iowa City, 1952-53; pres., gen. mgr. Cornhusker TV Corp., Lincoln, Nebr., 1954-85; broadcast cons. A. James Ebel, Lincoln, Nebr., 1955—; pres., dir. Sta. KMEG-TV, Sioux City, Iowa, 1969-85; USA del. World Adminstrv. Radio Conf., Geneva, 1971, 77, 79, 83, 88; mem. Frequency Mgmt. Adv. Commn., Washington, 1971—, New Tech. Com. Communications, 1971—; chmn. ABC, CBS, NBC Affiliates Assn. Satellite Com., Lincoln, 1970-88. Contbr. articles to profl. jours. Bd. dirs. Fed. Res. Bank., Omaha, Nebr., 1969-73, Doane Coll., Crete, Nebr., 1974—; mem. Press, Radio, TV Commn. Luth. Ch. Am., 1967-72. Recipient Abe Lincoln Broadcast Achievement award So. Bapt. Ch., 1976, Image of Excellence award Grand Island C. of C., 1984, Innovator award U. Nebr., 1994; named Engring. Man of Fame Nebr. Broadcasters Assn., 1974, Disting. Journalist Kappa Tau Alpha, 1985. Mem. IEEE (sr.), Maximum Svc. Telecasters (mem. engring. com., Engring. award 1973). Republican. Lutheran. Office: A James Ebel Broadcast Consulting PO Box 81891 Lincoln NE 68501-1891

EBEL, JAMES V., adjusting company executive; b. Creighton, Nebr., Dec. 15, 1943; s. Victor A. and Laura C. (Fuchtman) E.; m. Jane A. Kissack, Dec. 25, 1947; children: James V. II, Jason R. BS in Bus., U. Nebr., 1966. CPCU; assoc. risk mgmt. Claim adjuster Wausau Ins. Co., Kansas City, Mo., 1966-72; home office cons. Wausau Ins. Co., Wausau, Wis., 1972-76; liability mgr. Wausau Ins. Co., Portland, Oreg., 1976-77; regional casualty mgr. Wausau Ins. Co., Syracuse, N.Y., 1977-80; regional claim mgr. Wausau Ins. Co., Chgo., 1980-86; regional mgr. Toplis & Harding, Inc., Chgo., 1986-90, pres., CEO, 1990—. With U.S. Army Nat. Guard, 1961-67. Mem. Nat. Risk Retention Assn. (sec., v.p. 1990-92), Profl. Liability Underwriters Soc., CPCU. Office: Toplis & Harding Inc 222 S Riverside Pl Chicago IL 60606

EBERG, H. RICHARD, investment banker and broker; b. Indpls., Sept. 26, 1932; m. Marilyn F. Thomas, Apr. 1, 1953; children: Vickie, Lynn Eberg Fitzpatrick, Steven Michael (dec.), Barry Keith. BA, Ind. U., 1954, MA in Econs., 1957. Investment broker Ind. Nat. Bank, Indpls., 1961-68; self-employed, Indpls., 1968-75; sr. v.p. Traub Co., Indpls., 1975—; bd. dirs. Kenen-Stalh, Indpls. Bd. dirs. Indpls. Boys Club. Lt. (j.g.) USNR, 1951-57. Recipient award Indpls. Boys Club. Mem. Cmty. Bankers Assn., Sertoma (past pres. Indpls.), Indpls. Yacht Club (commodore, award). Republican. Methodist. Office: Traub Co Inc 320 N Meridian St Indianapolis IN 46204-1719

EBERHARD, WILLIAM THOMAS, architect; b. St. Louis, Apr. 11, 1952; s. George Walter and Bettie Alma (Seilkop) E.; m. Cynthia Ann Hardy, Aug. 20, 1977 (div. 1981); m. Linda W. Bayer, Dec. 5, 1986; children: Elena Lynn, Alysse Marie. BArch, U. Cin., 1976; postgrad. Archtl. Assn., London, 1974. Registered arch. Ohio, Mich., Pa., Fla., D.C., Ill., Mo. V.p. Visnapuu & Assocs. Inc., Cleve., 1972-82; prin.-in-charge Oliver Design Group, Cleve., 1983—; v.p., prin.-in-charge Grubb & Ellis, Cleve., Detroit, Pitts., 1989—, Grubb & Ellis Nat. Accounts Team, 1987-90. Author: Public Interiors, 1986, Professional Office Design, 1988, Docket, 1988, Facility Design & Managment, 1990, 91, Contract Design, 1995; contbr. articles to profl. jours. Profl. team leader Inst. Urban Design, Cleve., 1983; mem. evangelism com. First Bapt. Ch. of Greater Cleve., 1990—. Recipient Best Comml. Interior Design Project award NAIOP, 1991-96, Best Office Interior Design Project award, 1992, Best Renovation Project, 1995, Design award Nat. Inst. Bus., 1992, 93, Best Comml. Space, 1993, NAIOP Design award Best Pub. Space, 1993, Best Renovation Project, 1995, 1st. Pl. award Build Ohio Competition, 1992, AIA, 1993, Cleve. Chpt. Design award AIA, 1993, 94, Ohio Area Design awards AIA, 1994-95, Internat. Int. Design awards, 1992, 94, 95. Mem. AIA (chpt. sec. 1982-84, 2 Design awards, 1993, 1 Design award, 1994), Internat. Facility Mgrs. Assn., Cleve. Art Assn., Nat. Trust for Hist. Preservation, Inst. Urban Design, Am. Soc. Interior Designers (assoc.), Seminotic Soc. Am. (founding), Design Forum of Cleve. (founding 1990—, pres. 1991—), Club Soc. Ctr. (founding), Cleve. Design Task Force (founding), Shaker Heights Country Club (house com., design com.), Union Club of Cleve. Avocations: drawing, photography, tennis, snowmobiling, golf. Home: 2867 Torrington Rd Shaker Heights OH 44122-3408 Office: Oliver Design Group One Park Pla 1111 Chester Ave Cleveland OH 44114-3516

EBERLEY, HELEN-KAY, opera singer, classical record company executive, poet; b. Sterling, Ill., Aug. 3, 1947; d. William Elliott and P. (Conneely) E. MusB, Northwestern U., 1970, MusM, 1971. Chmn., pres. Eberley-Skowronski, Inc., Evanston, Ill., 1973-92; founder H.K.E. Enterprises, 1993—, pres., 1993—; circulation libr. Evanston Pub. Libr., 1995—; artistic coord. Eberley-Skowronski, Inc., 1973-92; founder EB-SKO Prodns., 1976, tchr., coach, 1976—; exec. dir., performance cons. E-S Mgmt., 1985-92; featured artist Honors Concert, Northwestern U., 1970, Master Class and guest lectr. various colls. and univs.; music lectr. rep. Harvard Club, Chgo.; numerous TV and radio talk show appearances and interviews. Operatic debut in Peter Grimes, Lyric Opera, Chgo., 1974; starred in: Cosi Fan Tutte, Le Nozze Di Figaro, Dido and Aeneas, La Boheme, Faust, Tosca, La Traviata, Falstaff, Don Giovanni, Brigadoon, others; jazz appearances with Duke Ellington, Dave Brubeck; performing artist Oglebay Opera Inst., Wheeling, W.Va., 1968, WTTW TV/PBS, Chgo., 1968; solo star in: Continental Bank Concerts, 1981-89, United Airlines-Schubert, Schumann, Brahms, Mendelssohn, Faure, Mozart, Duparc/Wolf, Supersta. WFMT Radio, Chgo., 1982-90; featured artist with North Shore Concert Band, 1989; starring artist South Bend Symphony, 1990, Mo. Symphony Soc., 1990, Milw. Symphony, 1990; spl. guest artist New Studios Gala Sta. WFMT, 1995; prodr.-annotator Gentlemen Gypsy, 1978, Strauss and Szymanowski, 1979, One Sonata Each: Franck and Szymanowski, 1982; starring artist-exec. prodr. Separate But Equal, 1976, All Brahms, 1977, Opera Lady, 1978, Eberley Sings Strauss, 1980, Helen-Kay Eberley: American Girl, 1983, Helen-Kay Eberley: Opera Lady II, 1984; performed Am. and Can. nat. anthems for Chgo. Cubs Baseball Team, 1977-83, Chgo. Bears Football, 1977; also starred in numerous concert recital and symphony appearances, Europe, Can., U.S.; author: Angel's Song, 1994, The Magdaleva Poems, 1995, ChapelHeart, 1996. Docent Art Inst. Chgo.; vol. Chgo. Christian Indsl. League, Evanston Shelter for Battered Women, Rape Victim Adv.; mem. Mayor's founding com. Evanston Arts Coun., 1974-75; judge Ice-Skating Competition, Wilmette (Ill.) Park Dist., 1974-77, bd. dirs., 1973-77; bd. dirs. Ctr. for Voice, 1994—. Recipient Creative and Performing Arts award Ind. Jr. Miss. and South Bend Jr. Miss, 1965, Milton J. Cross award Met. Opera Guild, 1968; prize winner Met. Opera. Nat. Auditions, 1968; F.K. Weyerhauser scholar Met. Opera, 1967. Mem. People for Ethical Treatment of Animals, Am. Soc. for Prevention of Cruelty to Animals, Am. Guild Mus. Artists, Internat. Platform Assn., Whale Adoption Project, Amnesty Internat., Environ. Def. Fund, Doris Day Animal Found., Humane Soc., Greenpeace (physicians com. for responsible medicine). Clubs: St. Mary's Acad. Alumnae Assn., Delta Gamma. Office: HKE Enterprises 1726 Sherman Ave Evanston IL 60201-3713

EBERLEY, KELLY ANN, physical therapist; b. Sterling, Ill., Dec. 14, 1960; d. Richard Joseph and Theresa (Kernan) E. Student, U. Minn., 1979-82; BS, Ithaca Coll., 1984. Lic. phys. therapist, Minn. Phys. therapist Univ. Health Care Ctr., Mpls., 1984-85, Midway Hosp., St. Paul, 1985-90, Univ. Park. Phys. Therapy, St. Paul, 1990-93, Inst. for Athletic Medicine, St. Paul, 1993, Comprehensive Phys. Therapy and Sports Medicine, Coon Rapids, Minn., 1994—; leader Parkinson's Support Group, St. Paul, 1988-90. Bd. dirs. Townhome Assn., Oakdale, Minn., 1994-96. Mem. Am. Phys. Therapy Assn.

EBERT, DOUGLAS EDMUND, banker; b. Washington, Oct. 21, 1945; s. Edmund Francis and Lathelia Marie (Keesey) E.; m. Carol Bernice Hedwall, Apr. 11, 1981; children: Elizabeth Anne, Leslie Anne, Kevin Edward. B.A., Williams Coll., 1968. Asst. sec. Mfrs. Hanover Trust Corp., N.Y.C., 1969-72, asst. v.p., 1972-73, v.p., 1973-76, sr. v.p., dep. gen. mgr., 1976-82, exec. v.p., 1982-85, sr. v.p. investment banking sector, 1985-90; pres., CEO S.E. Bank N.A., Miami, 1990-91, also chmn. bd. dirs., 1990-91; with Lincoln Fin.

Corp., Fort Wayne, Ind., 1992-93; pres., COO Mich. Nat. Bank, Farmington Hills, 1993—; pres., chief exec. officer, S.E. Banking Corp., 1990—, Miami, also bd. dirs. Bd. dirs. Cancer Research Ctr. Mem. Com. Econ. Devel., Bankers Assn. Fgn. Trade, U.S. Bus. Council, Bank Adminstrn. Inst., Assn. Res. City Bankers. Office: Mich Nat Bank 27777 Inkster Rd Farmington Hills MI 48334*

EBERT, ROGER JOSEPH, film critic; b. Urbana, Ill., June 18, 1942; s. Walter H. and Annabel (Stumm) E.; m. Chaz Hammelsmith, July 18, 1992. BS, U. Ill., 1964; postgrad., U. Cape Town, South Africa, 1965, U. Chgo., 1966-67; LHD (hon.), U. Colo., 1993. Editor Daily Illini, 1963-64; pres. U.S. Student Press Assn., 1963-64; staff writer News-Gazette, Champaign-Urbana, Ill., 1958-66; film critic Chgo. Sun-Times, 1967—, US mag., 1978-79, NBC-TV News, Chgo., 1980-83, ABC-TV News, Chgo., 1984—, N.Y. Post, N.Y.C., 1986-88, N.Y. Daily News, 1988-92, Compu Serve, 1991—; pres. Ebert Co., Ltd., 1981—; Microsoft Cinemania, 1994—; instr. English Chgo. City Coll., 1967-68; lectr. film criticism, fine arts program U. Chgo., 1969—; Kluge fellow U. Va., 1995-96; lectr. film Columbia Coll., Chgo., 1973-74, 77-80; cons. Nat. Endowments for Arts and Humanities, 1972-77; juror film festivals. Co-host (TV shows) Sneak Previews, PBS, 1976-82, At the Movies, syndicated, 1982-86, Siskel & Ebert, syndicated, 1986—; broadcaster: Movie News, ABC Radio, 1982-85; author: An Illini Century, 1967, (screenplay) Beyond the Valley of the Dolls, 1970, Beyond Narrative: The Future of the Feature Film, 1978, A Kiss Is Still A Kiss, 1984, Roger Ebert's Movie Home Companion, 1986-93, Roger Ebert's Video Companion, 1994—, (with Daniel Curley) The Perfect London Walk, 1986, Two Weeks in the Midday Sun, 1987, Behind the Phantom's Mask, 1993, Ebert's Little Movie Glossary, 1994, Roger Ebert's Book of the Movies, 1996; co-author: The Future of the Movies. Recipient Overseas Press club, 1963, award Chgo. Headline Club, 1963, award Chgo. Newspaper Guild, 1973, Pulitzer prize, 1975, Emmy award, 1979; Rotary fellow, 1965, Kluge fellow in film studies U. Va., 1995-96. Mem. Newspaper Guild, Writers Guild Am. West, Nat. Soc. Film Critics, Acad. TV Arts and Scis., Studebaker Drivers' Club, Arts Club of Chgo., Cliff Dwellers (Chgo.), Acad. Club (London), Sigma Delta Chi, Phi Delta Theta. Office: Chgo Sun-Times Inc 401 N Wabash Ave Rm 110 Chicago IL 60611-3532

EBNER, FRANK HENRY, chaplain; b. Elk River, Minn., June 14, 1922; s. Eric Emil and Bernadette Rose (Stenglein) E. Student, St. John's U., Collegeville, Minn., 1940-42; grad., St. Paul (Minn.) Seminary, 1947. Ordained Cath. priest. Asst. pastor St. Boniface Ch., Melrose, 1947-51; pastor St. Francis Xavier Ch., Sartell, Minn., 1957-77, St. Mary of Mt. Carmel Ch., Long Prairie, Minn., 1977-81, St. Andrew Ch., Elk River, 1981-93; retired, 1993. Chmn. Sherburne County chpt. ARC. With USAF, 1951-57, PTO; Col. USAFR, 1951-82. Recipient Golden Crusader award Venezuelan Mission, Am. Legion Americanism award, 1993, WCCO Radio Good Neighbor award, 1993. Mem. VFW, Mil. Chaplains Assn. of U.S.A. (nat. pres. 1988-90, Res. Officers Assn. of the U.S., K of C, Nat. Retired Tchrs. Assn., Cath. War Vets. Home: 10339 Parrish Ave NE Elk River MN 55330-7135

EBY, MARTIN KELLER, JR., construction company executive; b. Wichita Falls, Tex., Apr. 19, 1934; s. Martin and A. Pauline (Kimbell) E.; m. Melodee Stanley, Aug. 20, 1955; children: Stanley, Suzanna, David. B.S. in Civil Engring, Kans. State U., 1956. Registered profl. engr., Kan. With Martin K. Eby Constrn. Co., Inc., Wichita, Kan., 1956—; engr., project mgr., v.p. Martin K. Eby Constrn. Co., Inc., 1956-67, pres., 1967-92, chmn., 1979—; bd. dirs. Intrust Bank in Wichita, Intrust Fin. Corp., SBC Comms. Inc.; mem. engring. adv. coun. Kans. State U., Manhattan, 1970—. Bd. dirs. Kans. Pub. Policy Inst., chmn.; mem. Kans. State U. Coll. of Engring. Hall of Fame, 1989—; chmn. Constrn. Industry Polit. Action Com. of Kans., Topeka, 1978. Mem. ASCE, NSPE, Kans. Engring. Soc., Wichita Profl. Engring. Soc., Chief Execs. Orgn., Beavers (bd. dirs.), Moles (hon.). Congregationalist. Home: 624 N Longford Ln Wichita KS 67206-1818 Office: Martin Eby Constrn Co Inc PO Box 1679 610 N Main St Wichita KS 67203-3601

ECCKER, SCOTT S., financial consultant; b. Danville, Ill., Jan. 5, 1957. BBA, U. Mich., 1988. V.p. Merrill Lynch, Grand Rapids, MI, 1980—. Recipient Photographic award Ill. Press Assn., 1979. Office: Merrill Lynch Frey Bldg 300 Ottawa Ave NW Grand Rapids MI 49503-2304

ECK, BERNARD JOHN, engineer; b. Springfield, Ill., May 2, 1928; s. Edward Franz and Pauline (Schafer) E.; m. Janice May Carlson, Apr. 7, 1956; children: William, Robert, John, James, Julie. BS, Mo. Sch. Mines, Rolla, 1950; postgrad., Columbia U., 1967. Technologist U.S. Steel, Chgo., 1950-57; dir., prodn. engr. Griffin Wheel Co., Chgo., 1957-88, sr. tech. advisor, 1988-91; dir. tech. svc. Amsted Industries Internat., Chgo., 1991-94; rlwy. engring. cons. Elmhurst, Ill., 1994—; chmn. Elmer A. Sperry Bd. of Award, N.Y.C., 1989. Contbr. articles to profl. jours. and chpt. to book. Past pres. Country Club Highland Homeowners Assn., Elmhurst, Ill, 1961; pres. St. Charles Borromeo Sch. Bd., Bensenville, Ill., 1975, past v.p. adv. bd. 1965; precinct committeeman Reps., Elmhurst, 1961-69. Sgt. U.S. Army, 1951-53, Korea. Recipient Commendation medal, U.S. Army, 1952, Bronze Star, 1953. Fellow ASME (chmn. Rail Transp. Div. 1984-85, sec.-treas. 1983-84, chmn. adv. com.); mem. ASTM (chmn. subcom.). Roman Catholic. Home and Office: 155 Fairlane Ave Elmhurst IL 60126-3622

ECKDAHL, WENDY ANN, research officer; b. N.Y.C., Aug. 13, 1966; d. Robert Lawrence Gustafson and Nancy Kay Lehman; m. Joseph Carl Eckdahl, Oct. 10, 1987; children: Jessica Ruby, Adam Joseph. AAS in Bus. Mgmt., U. Minn., 1991; student, Met. State U., 1994—. Rsch. asst. Carleton Coll., Northfield, Minn., 1991-94; rsch. officer Carleton Coll., Northfield, 1994—. Mem. Assn. Profl. Rschrs. for Advancement. Democrat. Unitarian Universalist. Home: 21795 Vernon Ave Lakeville MN 55044 Office: Carleton Coll Devel One North College St Northfield MN 55057

ECKEL, HAL, information systems specialist; b. Bowling Green, Ohio, Mar. 25; s. Harold and Elva (Scribner) E.; m. Sylvia Mihalik, Aug. 27, 1960; children: Ted, Erik. BS in Math., Bowling Green State U., 1962, MS in Computer Sci., 1978. Mgr. info. systems Owens Illinois, Toledo, 1968-69; dir. info. systems Bowling Green (Ohio) State U., 1969-73; mgr. info. systems Owens-Corning Fiberglas, Toledo, 1973-79, Arco, Louisville, 1979-85, Computer Corp. Am., Boston, 1985-86, GE, Louisville, 1986-89; dir. info. systems Haworth, Holland, Mich., 1989—; advisor Western Mich. U., Kalamazoo, 1989—, Grand Rapids (Mich.) C.C., 1990—. Contbr. tech. papers to profl. publs. 1st lt. USAF, 1962-65. Mem. Data Processing Mgmt. Assn. (pres. 1992-93). Republican. Roman Catholic. Home: 351 Stoneharbor Rd Holland MI 49424 Office: Haworth 1 Haworth Ctr 3-36 Holland MI 49423

ECKERLINE, PETER EDWARD, financial consultant; b. Framingham, Mass., Oct. 28, 1960; s. Charles A. and Elenor B. (Jones Buckley) E.; m. Martha Ann Otto, Sept. 19, 1992. BA, U. Wis., Eau Claire, 1982, MA, 1983. Sr. fin. cons., v.p. Merrill Lynch, Edina, Minn., 1983—; advisor Chrms. Club, Edina, 1991—. Active Adopt-a-Family, Edina, 1987—, Ch. of St. George, Orono, Minn., Toys for Tots, Edina, 1987—, Twin City Builders Assn., Edina, 1991—. Mem. Pres. Club, Wayzata Country Club. Republican. Roman Catholic. Home: 2555 Fox St Wayzata MN 55391-9338 Office: Merrill Lynch 3400 W 66th St Ste 190 Edina MN 55435-2109

ECKERT, ERNST R. G., mechanical engineering educator; b. Prague, Czech Republic, Sept. 13, 1904; came to U.S., 1945, naturalized, 1955; s. Georg and Margarete (Pfrogner) E.; m. Josefine Binder, Jan. 30, 1931; children: Rosemarie Christa Eckert Kohler, Elke, Karin Eckert Winter, Dieter. Diploma Ing., German Inst. Tech., Prague, 1927, Dr.Ing., 1931; Dr. habil., Inst. Technology, Danzig, 1938; Dozent, Inst. of Technol., Braunschweig, Germany, 1940; hon. doctorates, Inst. Tech., Munich, 1968, Purdue U., 1968, U. Manchester, Eng., 1968, U. Notre Dame, 1970, Poly. Inst. Romania, Jassy, 1973, U. Minn., 1995. Registered profl. engr., Minn. Chief engr., lectr. Inst. Technology, Danzig, 1934-38; sect. chief thermodynamics Aero. Research Inst., Braunschweig, 1938-45; prof., dir. Inst. Technology, Prague, 1943-45; cons. USAF, 1945-49, Lewis Flight Propulsion Lab., NASA, 1949-51; prof. mech. engring. dept. U. Minn., 1951-73, dir. thermodynamics and heat transfer and of heat transfer lab., 1955-73, Regents' prof. emeritus mech. engring., 1973—; former vis. prof. Purdue U.; cons. Gen. Electric Co.; former cons. Trane Co.; U.S. rep. aerodynamics panel Internat. Com. Flame Radiation. author: (with Drake) Introduction to the Transfer of Heat and Mass, 1950, 2d edit., 1959, Heat and Mass Transfer, (translated by J.F. Gross), 1963; others in German, Russian, and Chinese, (with Goldstein) Measurement Techniques in Heat Transfer, 1970, 2d edit., 1976, (with Drake) Analysis of Heat and Mass Transfer, 1972; Chmn. hon. editorial adv. bd. Internat. Jour. Heat and Mass Transfer; former editor: Thermal Scis. series, Wadsworth Pub. Co., Belmont, Cal.; editor: Thermo and Fluid Dynamics; co-chmn. adv. editorial bd.: Heat Transfer-Japanese Research; co-editor: Energy Developments in Japan; chmn. hon. editorial adv. bd.: Letters in Heat and Mass Transfer; editorial adv. bd.: Numerical Heat Transfer; contbr. articles to sci. mags. Mem. Nat. Commn. Fire Prevention and Control, 1970-73. Recipient Max Jacob Meml. award, 1961, Disting. Teaching award U. Minn., 1965, award Western Electric Fund, 1965, gold medal French Inst. Energy and Fuel, 1967, Vincent Bendix award, 1972, Alexander von Humboldt U.S. sr. scientist award, 1980, A.V. Luikov medal, 1979, Aircraft Gas Turbine Tech. award, 1994, gold medal Czech Acad. Sci., 1994, Founders award Nat. Acad. of Engring., 1995; rsch. fellow Japan Soc. Promotion Sci., 1982. Fellow N.Y. Acad. Scis., AIAA; mem. ASME (hon.), NAE (Gold medal and Founders award 1995), Wissenschaftliche Gesellschaft für Luft und Raumfahrt, Sigma Xi, Pi Tau Sigma, Tau Beta Pi. Home: 60 W Wentworth Ave W Saint Paul MN 55118-3881 Office: Mech Engring Dept U Minn Minneapolis MN 55455

ECKERT, WINFIELD SCOTT, health science association administrator; b. Lancaster, Ohio, May 30, 1936; s. George Lewis and Blanche Tyson (Wilson) E.; m. Jo Ann Sheridan, Aug. 11, 1956; children: Cynthia, Michael, Cathy. Student, Ohio State U., 1956-57, Ohio State U., Lancaster, 1960-65. Draftman Anchor Hocking Glass, Lancaster, 1954-56, Alden E. Stilson Engrs., Columbus, Ohio, 1956-59; machine designer Diamond Power Specialty Corp., Lancaster, 1959-65, Varo Engr. Ltd., Columbus, Ohio, 1972-74; adminstr., pres., treas. Crestview Manor Nursing Home, Inc., Lancaster, 1971--; bd. dirs. Heritage Pharmacy, Lancaster, 1979--. Councilman, Lancaster City, 1961-65; deacon First Presbyn. Ch., 1959-64; dir. Crestview Village Ltd., 1986. Mem. Ohio Acad. of Nursing Homes, Am. coll. Health Care Adminstrs. Republican. Home: 4765 Vista Dr Canal Winchester OH 43110-9235 Office: Crestview Manor Nursing Home Inc 925957 Becks Knob Rd Lancaster OH 43130

ECKSTEIN, NORMAN R., management consultant; b. Neptune, N.J., Aug. 24, 1943; s. Arthur and Reba (Pobiner) E.; m. Bridget Cynthia Tuman, Dec. 17, 1970; children: Deborah Lynn, Glenn Alan. BS, MIT, 1965, MS, 1968. Cert. mgmt. cons. Staff project mgr., assoc. buyer Montgomery Ward, Chgo., 1966-71; installation mgr. Alexander Proudfoot Co., Chgo., 1972-75, chief of installations, 1976-77; dir. profit improvement cons. Coopers & Lybrand, Chgo., 1977-81; pres. The Eckstein Co., Chgo., 1981-83; mktg. dir. Sportmart, Inc., Niles, Ill., 1983-84; project mgr. United Rsch. Corp., Morriston, N.J., 1985-86, Stikon Corp., Ft. Lee, N.J., 1987-89; pres. Eckstein Mgmt. Cons., Chgo., 1989—; adv. bd. Entrepreneurship Inst., Chgo., 1990—; exec. com. MIT Enterprise Forum, Chgo., 1990-92. Bd. dirs., treas./v.p. fundraising Young Leadership Jewish United Fund, Chgo., 1978-83; bd. dirs. Bur. on Jewish Employment Problems, Chgo., 1979—, Bd. Jewish Edn., 1979-85. Mem. Inst. Mgmt. Cons. (bd. dirs., v.p. Chgo. chpt. 1993-94, exec. v.p. 1994—). Home: 489 Sunset Rd Winnetka IL 60093-4231 Office: Eckstein Mgmt Cons 645 N Michigan Ave Chicago IL 60611-2814

EDBERG, JEFFREY SCOTT, real estate broker, marketing professional; b. Iowa City, Iowa, Sept. 24, 1951; s. Robert Anderson and Patricia Ruth (Frankenfeld) E.; m. Patricia Tanner (div.); m. Jacqueline Carol Ann Brooks, Mar. 15, 1985; 1 child, Fiona Ann Edberg. Owner, broker Denier, Inc., Tucson, 1980-85; sales mgr. Premier Homes, Tucson, 1985-86; owner Edberg Investment, Phoenix, 1986-89; comml. broker Cornish & Carey, Sacramento, Calif., 1989-92; programmer/analyst Brokerage Info. Svc., Sacramento, 1991-92; mktg. mgr. Aquadrill Inc., Iowa City, Iowa, 1992-95; ptnr. Coldwell Banker Anderson-Bender, Realtors, Iowa City, 1995—; cons. Iowa City Homebuilders, 1994-95. Author: (computer software) Win Fleet, 1994. Mem. Airplane Owners and Pilots Assn., Iowa City Bd. Realtors, Nat. Bd. Realtors, Assn. of Info. Systems Profls. Republican. Home: 572 Linder Rd Iowa City IA 52240 Office: Coldwell Banker Anderson Bender Realtors 44 Sturgis Corner Dr Iowa City IA 52246

EDDIE, RUSSELL JAMES, state legislator, sales executive; b. Wayne, Nebr., June 9, 1938; s. Robert Alex and Myrtle (Kruse) E.; m. Gladys Ann Pederson, Aug. 6, 1960; children: Julie, Thomas, Robert, Steven. BA, Buena Vista Coll., 1960. Tchr. Clayton Pentral Cmty. Sch., Royal, Iowa, 1961-66; farmer Storm Lake, Iowa, 1966-89; mem. Iowa Ho. of Reps., 1989—; sales exec. E-D Assocs., Storm Lake, 1991—. Mem. BU County Hist. Soc., Pork Prodrs. Assn., Farm Bur., Kiwanis Internat. Republican. Lutheran. Home: 1101 Pierce Dr Storm Lake IA 50588-2744

EDDY, CHARLES ALAN, chiropractor; b. Kansas City, Mo., Feb. 20, 1948; s. Sam Albert and Ella Louise (Gani) E.; m. Donna Darlene Perry, Oct. 23, 1971. Student, U. Mo., Kansas City, 1967; D in Chiropractic, Cleveland Chiropractic, Kansas City, 1970. Diplomate Nat. Bd. Chiropractic Examiners. Pvt. practice chiropractic Kansas City, 1970—; mem. peer rev. bd. Blue Cross and Blue Shield, Kansas City, 1972; pres. hon. bd. govs. Bapt. Hosp., Kansas City, 1993-94; cons. Quality Corp., Overland Park, Kans., 1988. Leader, profl. musician Chuck Eddy Band, Kansas City, 1966—; res. officer Kansas City Police Dept., 1970-77, sgt., 1977-82, capt., 1982-94; vice chmn. Citizens Assn., candidate for City Coun., Kansas City. Mem. Am. Chiropractic Assn., Mo. State Chriopractic Assn., Mo. Dist. II Chiropractic Assn. (bd. dirs.), Cleve. Chiropractic Coll. (trustee 1990, vice chmn. 1992, 93, 94, 95), Cleve. Chiropractic Alumni Assn. (v.p., bd. dirs. 1990—, ambassador's soc. 1983—, chmn. 1990-96), Optimist Club of Landing (pres. 1980, lt. gov. Mo. dist. 1982), Am. Lebanon Syrian Men's Club (pres. 1988-91, chmn. bd. 1992), St. Andrews Soc. (drummer in pipe band), DeMolay Legion Hon. (sec. 1988, treas. 1990, vice dean 1991, dean 1992), Pipes and Drums of Ararat (treas. 1977-90, pres. 1985, dir. 1989, 90), Elks, Shriners (divan of Ararat shrine temple, publicity chmn. 1991-92), Royal Order Jesters, Order Quetzalcoatl. Episcopalian. Home: 406 W 109th St Kansas City MO 64114-4910 Office: 8301 State Line Rd # 108 Kansas City MO 64114-2019

EDELMAN, ANN BROOK, small business owner, writer; b. Cleve., Aug. 6, 1949; d. Harvey and Sally (Schwartz) Levine; m. Steve Edelman, Dec. 4, 1983; 1 child, Crystal. BA, Ohio State U., 1972; postgrad., Ashland U., 1990—. Cert. tchr. in specific learning disabilities, severe behavior handicapped and art. Learning disability tchr. Groveport (Ohio) Madison Schs., 1991—; owner, pres. Cherrystone Books, Reynoldsburg, Ohio, 1993—. Author: Cherry Stone Farms Meatless Cooking, 1993, Diet of the Future Cookbook, 1995. Natural Law Party candidate U.S. Congress, 1996. Recipient cooking contest award Eastside Messenger Newspaper, Columbus, Ohio, 1986. Mem. Alumni History Art Dept., Jewish Vegetarian Soc. Office: Cherry Stone Books PO Box 615 Reynoldsburg OH 43068

EDELMAN, DANIEL JOSEPH, public relations executive; b. N.Y.C., July 3, 1920; s. Selig and Selma (Pfeiffer) E.; m. Ruth Rozumoff, Sept. 3, 1953; children: Richard, Renee, John. Grad., Columbia U., 1940; MS, 1941. Reporter Poughkeepsie (N.Y.) newspapers, UPI, 1941-42; news writer CBS, 1946-47; staff mem. Edward Gottlieb & Assocs., 1947; pub. rels. dir. Toni Co., Chgo., 1948-52; owner 32 offices Daniel J. Edelman, Inc., Chgo., 1952—; founder, owner 31 offices Daniel J. Edelman, Inc. (a.k.a. Edelman Pub. Relations Worldwide), 32 other locations in U.S., Can., Mexico, Europe, Asia-Pacific. Mem. Ill. Lottery Control Bd., 1974; mem. comm. com. Boy Scouts Am., Chgo.; chmn. vis. com. U. Chgo. Libr., 1976; bd. dirs. Ill. Children's Home and Aid Soc., Chgo.; chmn. sustaining fellows individual campaign Chgo. Art Inst., 1982; bd. dirs. Lyric Opera Chgo.; mem. Philanthropy Task Force/Chgo. United, 1988; dir. Comm. for Econ. Growth of Israel. With U.S. Army, 1942-46. Recipient Disting. Alumnus award Columbia U., 1988, John Jay award Columbia U., 1990; named Pub. Rels. Profl. of Yr. Pub. Rels. News, 1993, Agy. of Yr. Inside PR Mag., 1993. Fellow Pub. Resl. Soc. Am. (past chmn. counselor sect., 26 Silver Anvil awards), Publicity Club Chgo., Young Pres. Orgn. (chmn. Chgo. chpt. 1963), Chief Execs. Orgn., Arthur Page Soc., Chgo. Club, Std. Club, Harmonie Club, Mid-Am. Club, Casino Club, Phi Beta Kappa. Jewish. Home: 1301 N Astor St Chicago IL 60610-2186 Office: Edelman Pub Rels Amoco Bldg 200 E Randolph St Chicago IL 60601-6436

EDELSON, DAVID, hospital administrator; b. N.Y.C., Jan. 28, 1919; s. Max Etish and Frieda (Epstein) E.; m. Miriam Osnovitz, Apr. 3, 1943; children: Richard, Jeffrey. BA, NYU, 1948; MSW, Columbia U., 1950; MS in Hosp. Adminstrn., Northwestern U., Chgo., 1958. Dir. USA-Travelers Aid, Belleville, Ill., 1952-54; chief social worker Evansville (Ind.) State Hosp., 1954-56, Dixon (Ill.) State Hosp., 1956-57; asst. supt. East Moline (Ill.) State Hosp., 1958-62; supt. Dixon Devel. Ctr., 1962-78; program policy advisor Dept. of Mental Health, Springfield, Ill., 1978-81; bd. commr. Lee County Ill., Dixon, 1982-92; v.p. Northwestern Ill. Area Agy. on Aging, Rockford, 1992-93, pres., 1993-95; presenter in field. Bd. dirs. Access Svcs., 1990—, v.p., 1994—; bd. dirs. Nat. Assn. Supts., 1970-78. 1st lt. USAF, 1942-45. Recipient Leadership award Ill. Assn. for the Mentally Retarded, 1968, Gov.'s award for unique achievement, 1994. Jewish. Home: 1938 Phillip Dr Dixon IL 61021-9232

EDELSTEIN, TERI J., museum administrator, educator; b. Johnstown, Pa., June 23, 1951; d. Robert Morten and HuldaLois (Friedhoff) E. BA, U. Pa., 1972, MA, 1977, PhD, 1979; cert. NYU, 1984. Lectr., U. Guelph, Ont., Can., 1977-79; asst. dir. for acad. programs Yale Ctr. for Brit. Art, New Haven, 1979-83; dir. Mt. Holyoke Coll. Art Mus., South Hadley, Mass., 1983-90, dir. Skinner Mus., 1983-90, mem. faculty dept. art, 1983-90; dir. Smart Mus. Art, U. Chgo., 1990-92, sr. lectr. U. Chgo. dept. of art, 1990—; dep. dir. Art Inst. of Chgo., 1992—; mem. adv. bd. Sculpture Chgo., Mus. Loan Network, Knight and Pew Founds. Yale Ctr. Brit. Art fellow, NEA fellow; Penfield scholar U. Pa., 1975. Mem. Coll. Art Assn., Artable, Am. Assn. Museums, Am. Soc. 18th Century Studies, Chgo. Network, Walpole Soc. Office: Art Inst Chgo 111 S Michigan Ave Chicago IL 60603-6110

EDEN, JAMES GARY, electrical engineering and physics educator, researcher; b. Washington, Oct. 11, 1950; s. Robert Otis and Joyce (West) E.; m. Carolyn Sue Thomas, June 10, 1972; children: Robert Douglas, Laura Ann, Katherine Joy. BS, U. Md., 1972; MS, U. Ill., 1973, PhD, 1975. Teaching asst. elec. engring. dept. U. Ill., Urbana, Jan.-June 1972, rsch. asst., 1972-75, asst. prof. elec. engring. dept., 1979-81, assoc. prof., 1981-83, prof. elec. engring. dept. and rsch. prof. Coordinated Sci. Lab, 1983—, assoc. dean Grad. Coll., 1994—, mem. physics grad. rsch. faculty, asst. dean Coll. Engring., 1992-93; postdoctoral rsch. assoc. NRC, Washington, 1975-76; rsch. physicist Naval Rsch. Lab., Washington, 1976-79; assoc. mem. Ctr. for Advanced Study, U. Ill., 1987-88; mem. program com. Conf. on Lasers and Electro-Optics, 1982, 83, 88, 89, 94-97; chmn. Engring. Found. Conf. Ultraviolet Lasers, 1987, co-chair, 1990, 94; program chair ann. meeting IEEE Lasers and Electro-Optics Soc., 1990, conf. chair, 1992; program vice chmn. Interdisciplinary Laser Sci. Conf. V, 1989; program chair ILS V, 1990, conf. chair ILS VII, 1992; bd. govs. Lasers and Electro-Optics Soc., 1991-93, v.p. for tech. affairs, 1993-95. Author: Photochemical Vapor Deposition, 1992; editor IEEE Jour. Spl. Topics in Quantum Electronics, 1996—; assoc. editor Photonics Tech. Letters, 1988-94; contbr. over 120 articles to profl. jours.; patentee for 12 inventions. Recipient Rsch. Publ. award Naval Rsch. Lab., 1978, Beckman Rsch. award U. Ill., 1988-89, IBM Rsch. award U. Ill., 1984. Fellow IEEE, Optical Soc. Am., Am. Phys. Soc.; mem. Tau Beta Pi, Eta Kappa Nu, Sigma Xi, Phi Kappa Phi. Republican. Home: 513 Taylor Dr Mahomet IL 61853-9246 Office: U Ill Everitt Lab 1406 W Green St Urbana IL 61801-2918

EDEN, NORMAN NACHUM, insurance agent; b. Grodno, Poland, Sept. 27, 1920; came to U.S., 1938; s. Abraham Pinkus and Shytra (Rothenberg) Rajgrodski; m. Shulamit Gootman Eden, Dec. 19, 1943; 1 child, Avi Don. BA, U. Cin., 1947, MA, 1953. Asst. econ. rsch. Office of Prime Min., Israel, 1948-52; pres. NN Eden Agy., Cin., 1956-82, Midwest Exec. Ins. Agy., Cin., 1980-95; lectr. Judaic Studies U. Cin., 1985. With U.S. Army, 1942-46. Democrat. Jewish. Home: 3120 E Galbraith Rd Cincinnati OH 45236 Office: Midwest Exec Ins Agy 3120 E Gailbraith Rd Cincinnati OH 45236

EDENS, RUDI R., manufacturing engineer, administrator; b. Detroit, Oct. 6, 1931. BS, Lawrence Inst. Tech., 1954. Owner, mgr. Falcon Tool Co., Warren, Mich., 1959-93; gen. mgr. Centenniel Mold, Inc., Sterling Heights, Mich., 1993—. Inventor: 4 patents in mfg. field. Sgt. Army Engr. Corps, 1952-53. Mem. Soc. Plastic Engrs., Soc. Mfg. Engrs. (sr.). Lutheran. Office: Centennial Mold Inc 44038 Phoenix Dr Sterling Heights MI 48314-1463

EDGAR, JIM, governor; b. Vinita, Okla., July 22, 1946; m. Brenda Smith; children: Brad, Elizabeth. Grad., Eastern Ill. U., 1968; postgrad., U. Ill., Sangamon State U., 1971-74. Legis. intern pres. pro tem Ill. Senate, 1968; key asst. to speaker ho. Ill. Ho. of Reps., 1972-73; aide to pres. Ill. Senate, 1974, to Ho. minority leader, 1976; mem. Ill. Ho. of Reps., 1977-79; dir. legis. affairs Ill. Gov., 1979-80; sec. state State of Ill., 1981-91; gov. State of Ill., 1991—; co-lead gov. Nat. Gov.'s Assn. Transp. Com., 1995-96; chair Edn. Commn. of States, 1993-94; chair Nat. Gov.'s Assn. Com. on Econ. Devel. and Commerce, 1992-93; pres. Coun. State Govts., 1992-93; chair Gov.'s Ethanol Coalition, 1992-93; chair Nat. Gov.'s Assn. Com. on Econ. Devel. and Tech. Innovation, 1991-92. Precinct committeeman, treas. Coles County Rep. Com., 1974; dir. state svc. Nat. Conf. State Legislatures, 1975, 76; mem. campaign com. Ill. Ho. of Reps.; pres. Nat. Assn. Secs. of State, 1988; exec. com. Coun. State Govts., 1988, v.p. exec. com., 1991, pres., 1992-93; bd. dirs. Nat. Commn. Against Drunk Driving, 1989; chmn. Ill. Literacy Coun., 1989; chmn. Edn. Commn. of the States, 1993-94; chmn. Gov.'s Ethanol Coalition, 1992-93; pres. Bd. Coun. State Govts. Mem. Nat. Govs. Assn. (chmn. econ. devel. and commerce com. 1992-93, strategic planning rev. task force 1991—, past chmn. task force on edn., mem. edn. goals panel, chair com. econ. devel. and technol. innovation 1991-92, edn. commn. of states 1993-94, co-lead gov. transp. com. 1995-96), Coles County Hist. Soc. (pres. 1976-79). Baptist. Office: Office of Gov 207 State House Springfield IL 62706-0001

EDGINGTON, MARY CARTER See CARTER, MARY NASH

EDLAND, ROBERT WILLIAM, radiation oncology educator; b. Madison, Wis., Feb. 14, 1932; s. Alfred O. and Ella W. (Freund) E.; m. Carole F. McGinley, Sept. 17, 1955; children: Christopher, Anne, Christina, David. BS, U. Wis., 1953, MD, 1956. Diplomate Am. Bd. Radiology. Chmn. radiation oncology dept. Gundersen Clinic, La Crosse, Wis.; clin. prof. radiation oncology U. Wis., Madison, 1978—, radiation oncology Med. Coll. Wis., 1983—. Contbr. articles to profl. jour. Served to lt. col. USMC, 1956-67. Fellow Am. Coll. Nuclear Medicine, Am. Coll. Radiology (bd. chancellors 1991—), Royal Soc. Health; mem. Am. Soc. Therapeutic Radiology and Oncology (pres. 1986-87). Home: 2200 Hickory Ln La Crosse WI 54601 Office: 1836 South Ave La Crosse WI 54601-5429

EDLUND, RICHARD J., state legislator; b. Kansas City, Dec. 5, 1924; s. Earl Edwin and Mary (Lia) E.; m. Eileen Edlund, 1971; children: John, Jack, Jim, Mike. Kans. state rep. Dist. 33, 1990—, mem. labor and indsl. appropriations com., ret. businessman; labor cons. for sheltered workshops. Bd. dirs. Nat. Fedn. of the Blind. Mem. Nat. Fedn. for the Blind (treas. 1974-88, pres. 1971-90), Kiwanis, Masons. Home: 6734 Montana Ct Kansas City KS 66111-2351*

EDMISTON, DELORES P., nurse; b. Chattanooga, Oct. 11, 1946; d. Robert Arthur and Geneva Fincher (Miller) Phillips. RN, Ga. Bapt. Sch. Nursing, Atlanta, 1967; BSN, McKendree Coll., Lebanon, Ill.; MA in Speech, So. Ill. U., 1994. RN, Ill. Staff nurse Egleston Children's Hosp., Atlanta, Alton (Ill.) Meml. Hosp., Alton Mental Health and Devel. Disabilities Ctr. Mem. ANA, Ill. Nurses Assn. NAFE, Speech Commn., Phi Kappa Pi. Home: 1261 Brown St Alton IL 62002-6750

EDMONDS, JOHN, state legislator; m. Marta Edmonds. Pub. acct.; mem. Kans. State Ho. of Reps. Dist. 112.

EDMUNDS, NANCY GARLOCK, federal judge; b. Detroit, July 10, 1947; m. William C. Edmunds, 1977. BA cum laude, Cornell U., 1969; MA in Teaching, U. Chgo., 1971; JD summa cum laude, Wayne U., 1976. Bar: Mich. 1976. With Plymouth Canton Public Schools, 1971-73; law clk.

Barris, Sott, Denn & Driker, 1973-75; law clk. to Hon. Ralph Freeman U.S. Dist. Ct. (ea. dist.) Mich., 1976-78; ptnr. litigation sect. Dykema Gossett, 1984-92, resident Oakland County, 1986-92; judge U.S. Dist. Ct. (ea. dist.) Mich., 1992—; trustee Hist. Soc. U.S. Dist Ct. (ea. dist.) Mich. Bd. trustees Temple Beth El; mem. bus. and profl. women's divsn., lawyers' divsn. Jewish Welfare Fedn./Allied Jewish Campaign; mem. Saginaw Valley State U. Bd. Control, 1991-92. Mem. ABA, Fed. Judges Assn., Nat. Assn. Women Judges, Federalist Soc., State Bar Mich. (chair U.S. cts. com. 1990-91). Office: US Dist Ct 211 US Courthouse Detroit MI 48226-2799

EDMUNDS, NIEL ARTHUR, vocational education educator, consultant, researcher; b. Marion, Iowa, Sept. 19, 1931; s. Niel R. and Helen June (Oxley) E.; m. Carol J. Gesiriech, Aug. 9, 1958; children: Jane Elizabeth Edmunds Shook, Ann Louise. BS in Edn., Nebr. State Tchrs. Coll., 1958, MS in Edn., 1960; EdS, U. S.D., 1966; EdD, Utah State U., 1968. Cert. profl. adminstr., Nebr., secondary tchr., Nebr. Tchr., coach Hartington (Nebr.) High Sch., 1958-61; prin. Wausa (Nebr.) H.S., 1961-67; prof., dean, assoc. v.p. Wayne (Nebr.) State Coll., 1969-77; prof. U. Nebr., Lincoln, 1977-86; assoc. prof. U. Mo., Columbia, 1986-89; prof. U. Nebr., Lincoln, 1989—; cons. numerous high schs. and high edn., 1980—. Contbr. articles to profl. jours. With U.S. Army, 1952-54. Recipient Disting. Alumnus award Coll. Engring. Utah State U., 1989; named Indsl. Arts Tchr. of Yr.-State of Nebr., Am. Indsl. Arts Assn., 1965. Mem. Am. Vocat. Assn. (pres. 1988-89, bd. dirs. 1984-90, Leadership award 1989), Internat. Tech. Edn. Assn., Nebr. Vocat. Assn. (bd. dirs. 1984-92, Disting. Svc. award 1987-90, Arch of Fame award 1990), Internat. Vocat. Assn., Am. Tech. Assn., Omicron Tau Theta, Epsilon Pi Tau. Methodist. Home: 6400 Chesterfield Ct Lincoln NE 68510-2361 Office: Univ Nebr 513 Nebraska Hall Lincoln NE 68588-0515

EDMUNDSON, CHARLES WAYNE, mechanical engineer, communications executive; b. Fairhope, Ala., July 23, 1942; s. Charles Vogel and Helen Bell (Winberg) E.; m. Linda Louise Lingren, June 13, 1964 (div. 1984); m. Jane Marie Byerlotzer, Apr. 11, 1986; children: Charles Bryan, Elizabeth Courtney, Joseph Michael. BSME, Texas A & M U., 1965. Registered Profl. Engr. Student Engr. Southwestern Bell Telephone Co., Dallas, 1964, staff asst., 1965, asst. engr., 1965, engr., 1967-68; sr. engr. Southwestern Bell Telephone Co., San Antonio, Tex., 1969-71; supr. engr. Southwestern Bell Telephone Co., San Antonio, 1971-73, equipment engr., 1973-76; div. staff supr. Southwestern Bell Telephone Co., St. Louis, 1976-79, div. mgr., 1979-93, dir. strategic sourcing, 1993-96, dir. regional sourcing, 1996—; dir. Gateway Metro Credit Union, St. Louis, 1983—; pres. St. Louis Area Constrn. Users Coun., 1988-91. Campaign Chmn. United Way Campaign, Southwestern Bell Telephone Co., St. Louis 1985. Capt. U.S. Army Corps of Engrs. 1966-68, Germany. Named Young Engr. of the Yr. Bexar Chpt., Tex. Soc. of Prof. Engr., San Antonio, 1973-74. Mem. ASME (San Antonio Sec., treas. 1972-73, sec. 1973-74, chmn. 1974-75), Tex. Soc. Profl. Engrs. (dir. 1972-73, sec./treas. State PEI 1975-76), Gateway A&M Club (pres. 1988-89), Tex. A&M Former Students Assn. (nat. rep. 1990-95), Foreman Supr. Club (pres. 1988-89, 93). Republican.

EDSON, DANIEL CHARLES, educational administrator; b. Flint, Mich., Oct. 22, 1951. BS, Ctrl. Mich. U., 1972; MS, Mich. State U., 1979. Med. technologist Sparrow Hosp., Lansing, Mich., 1978-79; surveys operation mgr. Coll. Am. Pathologists, Traverse City, Mich., 1980-90; pres. Am. Proficiency Inst., Traverse City, 1991—; mem. adv. bd. Nat. Accreditation for Practice Quality, Ann Arbor, Mich., 1994—. Contbr. articles to profl. jours. Vol., dir. Med. Clin., Traverse City, 1994—. Office: Am Proficiency Inst 419 E 8th St Traverse City MI 49686-2626

EDSON, WAYNE E., dentist, consultant; b. Marinette, Wis., July 4, 1947; s. E.J. Edson and Anita (Pearson) Edson Sebero; m. Linda Mary Hullison, Apr. 3, 1971; children: William Earl, Erin Hullison, Thomas John. BS, U. Wis.-Madison/Milw., 1973; DDS, Northwestern U., 1977. gen. practice dentistry, Winnetka, Ill., 1982—. Pres. Kenilworth United Fund, 1983-84, bd. dirs., 1981—; com. mem. Kenilworth Baseball, 1978-83. Served with USN, 1965-72. Mem. Chgo. Dental Soc., Ill. State Dental Soc., ADA. Roman Catholic. Avocations: hunting; fishing, curling. Clubs: John Evans of Northwestern U., G.V. Black Soc. of Northwestern U., Kenilworth, Chgo. Curling Club. Home: 624 Exmoor Rd Kenilworth IL 60043-1021 Office: 450 Green Bay Rd Kenilworth IL 60043-1074 also: 1 E Delaware Pl Chicago IL 60611

EDWARDS, ALISYN ARDEN, psychologist; b. Winfield, Kans., Nov. 8, 1960; d. Warren Dale and Vera Colleen (Edwards) A. BA, U. Kans., 1982; M Marriage and Family Therapy, Abilene Christian U., 1984. Registered psychologist; registered marriage and family therapist. Psychotherapist Mental Health Ctr. East Cen. Kans., Emporia, 1988-90; psychologist Sedgwick County Dept. Mental Health, Wichita, Kans., 1990-92; psychotherapist MCC Behavioral Care, Wichita, 1992-93, R & L Counseling & Referral Svc., Wichita, 1993-94; psychologist El Dorado Correctional Ctr, Eldorado, 1994—; intra-familial sexual abuse treatment team Mental Health Ctr. East Cen. Kans., Emporia, 1988-90. Violinist Mid-Kans. Symphony Orch., Friends U. Community Symphony, 1991-92; mem. Run Wichita team Leukemia Soc. 1995. Mem. Am. Assn. Marriage and Family Therapy (clin.), Kans. Assn. Marriage and Family Therapy. Office: El Dorado Correctional Facility PO Box 311 El Dorado KS 67042-0311

EDWARDS, CHARLES ARTHUR, fundraising consultant; b. Chgo., May 7, 1940; s. Arthur Lewis and Kathleen (McGinnis) E.; children: Valerie Kathleen, Jennifer Anne. AB, U. Chgo., 1965. Pres. The Edwards Group, Grayslake, Ill., 1984—. Mem. exec. com. Nat. Alumni Fund Bd., U. Chgo., 1975-77, Conn. Gov.'s Com. on Arts and Tourism, 1973-75; mem. Nat. Alumni Cabinet, U. Chgo., 1969-72; chmn. New Eng. Conf. Devel. Group, Am. Assn. Mus., 1977-78; bd. dirs. Pegasus Players, Chgo., 1988-89; bd. trustees Anne S.K. Brown Military Coll., Brown U. Libr., Providence, R.I., 1994—. With U.S. Army, 1958-62. Decorated Officer Order of Polonia Restituta and Cross of Merit 2d Class (London). Mem. Nat. Soc. Fund Raising Execs. (cert., bd. dirs. Chgo. chpt. 1986-89, asst. treas. 1988-89), Art Mus. Devel. Assn. (pres. 1976-77), Ill. St. Andrew Soc. (bd. govs. 1989-95, v.p. 1992-95), Royal Humane Soc. (gov. 1991—), Intelligence Corps Assn. (hon. life), Newport Arty. Co. (hon.), Victory Club (London). Congregationalist. Office: Edwards Group PO Box 622 Grayslake IL 60030-0622

EDWARDS, CHARLES C., JR., newspaper publisher; b. Denver, Jan. 5, 1947; s. Charles C. and Sue Cowles (Kruidenier) E.; m. Harriet Hubbell, June 24, 1979; children: Hayley, Emily. BA in History, U. Colo., 1970; postgrad. Drake U., 1973. Advt. salesman Des Moines Register, 1970-74, news reporter, 1974-79, circulation dir., 1979-82, advt. dir., 1982-84, mktg. dir., 1984, pres., pub., 1984—; bd. dirs. Norwest Bank, Des Moines. V.p. Des Moines Art Ctr., 1985; trustee Gardner Cowles Found., Inc., Des Moines; bd. dirs. Iowa Coll. Found., Des Moines; pres. Iowa Group for Econ. Devel.; mem. bd. govs. Drake U. Republican. Congregationalist. Avocations: running, tennis, golf. Office: Des Moines Register & Tribune Co PO Box 957 715 Locust St Ste 957 Des Moines IA 50309*

EDWARDS, DAVID B., education coordinator; b. Waukegan, Ill., Aug. 16, 1957; s. Norman B. and Rhoda M. (Robinson) E. BS in Biol. Scis., Ill. State U., 1978; MA in Health Scis. Mgmt., Webster U., 1993. Assoc. sanitarian McLean County Health Dept., Normal, Ill., 1979-81, sanitarian, 1981-87, sr. sanitarian, 1987-89; instutional sanitarian cons. Lake County Health Dept., Waukegan, Ill., 1989-95; continuing edn. coord. Victory Meml. Hosp., Waukegan, Ill., 1995—; dir. Le Roy (Ill.) Emergency Ambulance Svc., 1987-89. Vol. paramedic Antioch (Ill.) Rescue Squad, 1990—. Named Eagle Scout. Mem. Nat. Environ. Health Assn., Nat. Assn. EMTs, Ill. Environ. Health Assn., Alpha Phi Omega. Office: Victory Meml Hosp 1324 Sheridan Rd Waukegan IL 60085

EDWARDS, ELIZABETH A., marketing educator; b. Nagoya, Japan, Oct. 1, 1957; came to U.S., 1960; d. John A. and Elizabeth R. (Rice) E.; m. Carsten Jonat, May 6, 1995. BS in Math., U. Mich., 1979, MS in Math., 1981, MBA, 1988, PhD in Bus. Adminstrn., 1992. Systems and ops. rsch. analyst Ford Motor Credit Co., Dearborn, Mich., 1981-83; fin. analyst Ford Motor Co., Dearborn, 1983-86; rsch. and tchg. asst. U. Mich., Ann Arbor, 1986-91; vis. lectr. U. Mich., Dearborn, 1991-92; asst. prof. mktg. Coll. Bus., Eastern Mich. U., Ypsilanti, 1992-96, assoc. prof., 1996—. Mem. APA, Assn. Consumer Rsch., Am. Mktg. Assn., Assn. Fin. Counseling and Planning Edn. Office: Eastern Mich U Coll Bus Mktg Dept 469 Owen Bldg Ypsilanti MI 48197

EDWARDS, ESTHER G., museum administrator, former record, film and entertainment company executive; b. Oconee, Ga.; d. Berry and Bertha Ida (Fuller) Gordy; m. George H. Edwards, Apr. 12, 1951 (dec.); 1 son (by previous marriage), Robert Bullock. Ed., Howard U., Wayne State U. Sr. v.p., sec., dir. Motown Record Corp., Detroit, 1959-1988; sec., dir. Jobete Music Pub. Co., Inc., 1959—; sr. v.p., corporate sec. Motown Industries, Hollywood, Calif., 1973-88; chmn., CEO Motown Hist. Mus., Detroit, 1985; dir. Bank of the Commonwealth, 1972-79. Bd. dirs. Detroit Econ. Growth Corp.; founder, exec. dir. Gordy Found., 1968—; chmn. Wayne County Dem. Women's Com., 1956; Mich. del.-at-large Dem. Nat. Conv., 1960; bd. dirs. Martin Luther King Ctr. for Non-Violent Social Change; trustee Founders Soc. of Detroit Inst. Arts; mem. corp. Lawrence Tech. U., Southfield, Mich.; chmn. Motown Hist. Mus. Inc., Detroit, 1985—; commr. Mich. Hist. Commn., 1989-95. Mem. Greater Detroit C. of C. (treas., exec. bd. 1973-79), Met. Detroit Conv. and Visitor's Bur. (dir.), Econ. Club Detroit (dir.), African Am. Heritage Assn. (founder, chmn.), Alpha Kappa Alpha, Gamma Phi Delta. Office: Motown Hist Mus 2648 W Grand Blvd Detroit MI 48208-1237

EDWARDS, IAN KEITH, obstetrician, gynecologist; b. Spartanburg, S.C., Mar. 2, 1926; s. James Smiley and Georgina (Waters) E.; m. Glenda Melissa Joselyn, Dec. 27, 1968; children—Darien, Jennifer, Carol, Terry. A.B., Duke U., 1949, M.D., 1953. Diplomate Am. Bd. Ob-Gyn. Spl. study pediatrics St. Bartholomew's Hosp., London, 1952; resident in ob-gyn Grady Meml. Hosp., Atlanta, 1955-58; chief ob-gyn Valley Forge (Pa.) Army Hosp., 1958-61; practice medicine specializing in ob-gyn Olney, Ill., 1969—; ptnr. Trover Clinic, Madisonville, Ky., 1961-68, Weber Med. Clinic, Olney, 1969—; dir. dept. ob-gyn Weber Med. Clinic, 1970-74, 78-83, 93-95, Richland Meml. Hosp., 1989-95; chmn. bd. dirs. Weber Med. Clinic, 1983-87, med. dir., 1987-95; ret., 1995; chief staff Hopkins County Hosp., Ky., 1967-68, Richland Meml. Hosp., Olney, 1974-76; clin. instr. ob-gyn. U. Ky. Med. Ctr., Lexington, 1965-68; cons.; vice-chmn. Ill., sec. ACOG, adv. coun. dist. VI, 1990-93. Contbr. articles to med. jours. Citizen amb. Profl. Exchange Program, Moscow and St. Petersberg, Russia, 1992; mem. found. com. Olney Central Coll., long range planning and bldg. com. Served to capt. M.C., U.S. Army, 1954-55; Korea. Fellow ACOG (Ill. sec. dist. VI, vice chmn. 1990-93); mem. AMA, Phila. Obstet. Soc., Ill. Med. Soc., Hopkins County Med. Soc. (pres. 1968), Richland County Med. Soc. (pres. 1974-76), Am. Soc. Colposcopists and Cervical Pathology, Am. Assn. Gynecol. Laparoscopists, So. Ill. Med. Assn., Am. Legion. Democrat. Methodist. Office: Weber Med Clinic 1200 N East St Olney IL 62450-2432

EDWARDS, J. MICHELE, conductor, educator; b. Ottumwa, Iowa, Jan. 2, 1945; d. Frederick Finch and Jean (Coleman) Benedict; m. Robert George Edwards (dec. Apr. 1981). MusB, U. Iowa, 1967, MA, 1970, D of Mus. Arts, 1983. Grad. asst. U. Iowa, Iowa City, 1969-71; condr. Harmonia Mundi, Mpls., 1976—; from instr. to prof. Macalester Coll., St. Paul, 1974—, dir. faculty devel., 1987-88, dir. Women's/Gender Studies, 1988-91, 93-95; vis. assoc. prof. U. Iowa, 1989; dir. music Mayflower Ch., Mpls., 1976-87; mem. music adv. panel Minn. State Arts Bd., St. Paul, 1987. Author: Literature for Voices in Combination, 1977; reviewer for CHOICE, Internat. Alliance for Women in music Jour., Am. Music; contbr. chpts. to books, articles to profl. jours. and encys. Participant Pierre Boulez Conducting Workshop, Carnegie Hall, 1991. Grantee ACLS, 1986, 95, Am. Philos. Soc., 1986, Mellon Found., 1987, 88, Japanese Ministry Edn., 1990, Wallace Found., 1991, 91-92, 92-93, 95. Mem. Am. Musicol. Soc. (program chair Midwest chpt. 1992-93, bd. dirs. gay and lesbian study group), Internat. Schütz Soc., Am. Fedn. Musicians, Am. Choral Dirls. Assn. (Julius Herford Dissertation award 1983), Coll. Music Soc. (edit. rev. bd. symposium 1989-91, 95—, nat. com. on status of women 1988-93), Pi Kappa Lambda. Home: 1844 Rome Ave Saint Paul MN 55116-2029 Office: Macalester Coll Music Dept 1600 Grand Ave Saint Paul MN 55105-1801

EDWARDS, JOHN DAVID, investment executive; b. Gallipolis, Ohio, Apr. 14, 1958; s. Vernard David and Virginia Isabelle (Tate) E. Student, Rio Grande Coll., 1976-78. V.p. VD Edwards Ins. Agy., Inc., Pomeroy, Ohio, 1979-85, pres., 1985-86; pres. CLC Ltd. Gold and Silver, Inc., Athens, Ohio, 1987-88; presiding ptnr. NXS Investment Club, Pomeroy, 1988—. Mem. High Frontier, Va., 1987; chmns. advisor U.S. Congl. Adv. Bd., Washington, 1987; charter mem. Ronald Reagan Trust, Washington, 1988; mem. Rep. Presdl. Task Force, Washington, 1988. Recipient Medal of Honor, High Frontier, 1987. Mem. Am. Def. Preparedness Assn. (life), U.S. Naval Inst. (assoc.), Assn. of U.S. Army, Am. Numismatics Assn., Am. Film Inst., Nat. Geog. Soc., Players Club Internat. (charter mem.). Methodist. Home: 100 Union Ave Pomeroy OH 45769-1000

EDWARDS, JUDITH ELIZABETH, advertising executive; b. St. Louis, May 22, 1933; d. Archie Earl and Ivy Elizabeth (Jones) Hector; m. George N. LaMont Jr., Jan. 9, 1960 (div. Oct. 1965); m. Gary W. Edwards, Nov. 25, 1966; stepchildren: Michael Brent, David Reed Edwards. Grad. high sch., St. Louis, 1951; student, Brown's Bus. Coll., St. Louis. Exec. sec., asst. to chmn. Rep. Nat. Com., Washington, 1958-60; dep. to county clk. Vandervurgh County, Evansville, Ind., 1972-76; sec.-treas. Edwards Outdoor Advtg., Carmi, Ill., 1979—; mem. Evansville Health Planning Coun., 1974-76. Pres. White County Rep. Women's Club, Carmi, 1989—, White County Hosp. Aux. Named Ky. Col. Mem. Carmi Bus. and Profl. Women's Club, Carmi C. of C., Kiwanis, Order Ea. Star, Sigma Alpha. Methodist. Office: PO Box 250 Carmi IL 62821-0250

EDWARDS, KARIN REDEKOPP, piano educator; b. Winkler, Man., Can., Mar. 13, 1948; d. Jacob Peter and Elsa (Sawatzky) Redekopp, Mark Allen Edwards, June 8, 1973. Teaching cert., U. Man., Winnipeg, 1967, BMus., 1970; M. Music, Ind. U., 1972, D. Music, 1983. Accompanist Winnipeg Mennonite Children's Choir, 1963-70; asst. instr. Ind. U., Bloomington, Ind., 1970-71; faculty mem. Wis. Conservatory of Music, Milw., 1974-80; instr. piano Carroll Coll., Waukesha, Wis., 1980-87; pianist Milw. Symphony Chorus, 1980-87; keyboardist Milw. Symphony Orch., 1980-87; asst. prof. Wheaton (Ill.) Coll., 1987-92, assoc. prof., 1992—; lectr. at convs. and univs.; judge contests. Performer with orchs., chamber groups, soloist on radio and TV, including CBC, CBC-TV, NPR affiliates; duo pianist Redekopp and Edwards; performer on compact disc Karin Redekopp Edwards Plays Chopin, Liszt, Eckhardt-Gramatté, 1990. Doctoral fellow Can. Coun., 1972, 73; recipient Assoc. Royal Conservatory Toronto, Gold medal, 1968. Mem. Ill. Music Tchrs. Assn. (workshop chair 1988—), Music Tchrs. Nat. Assn., Coll. Music Soc., Am. Liszt Soc. Mennonite. Office: Wheaton Coll Dept Music Wheaton IL 60187

EDWARDS, MARILYN, state legislator. State rep. dist. 105 Mo. Ho. of Reps. Office: Mo Ho of Reps State Capitol Building Jefferson City MO 65101-1556*

EDWARDS, RICHARD ALAN, banker; b. Minot, N.D., Apr. 26, 1957; s. Duane LaVoy Sr. and Virginia Ione (Lyson) E.; m. Deon Rae Schmidt, June 3, 1989. BBA, Minot State Coll., 1979. Bank teller Norwest Bancorp., Minot, 1977-80; bank examiner N.D. Dept. Banking, Fargo, 1980-85; loan adminstrn. officer Banks of Iowa, Inc., Des Moines, 1985-88, asst. v.p. loan adminstrn., 1988-90, v.p. loan rev., 1990-91; v.p. credit adminstrn. Firstar Corp. of Iowa, Des Moines, 1991-92, 1st v.p. credit adminstrn., 1992-95, sr. v.p. credit adminstrn., 1995—. Mem. Am. Inst. Banking, Robert Morris Assocs., Sigma Tau Gamma. Lutheran. Home: 2820 Eula Dr Des Moines IA 50322-4258

EDWARDS, RONALD GARY, librarian, historical researcher; b. Wausau, Wis., July 19, 1948; s. Chester Paul Valentine and Alma Esther Ida (Mueller) E.; m. Patricia Ann Lankford, Oct. 1, 1982; 1 child, Cassidy Ford. BA, U. Wis., Milw., 1976, MLIS, 1985, MS, 1987; postgrad., Marquette U., 1989—. In mgmt. Volume Shoe Corp., Topeka, 1980-84, Armel, Inc., Ft. Lauderdale, Fla., 1985-86; in ednl. sales B. Dalton/Software Etc., Milw., 1986-87; librarian, instr. Concordia U., Mequon, Wis., 1987-92; head libr., asst. prof. Bowling Green (Ohio) State U., 1993—; liaison Wis. Libr. Assn.-Found. Adv. Bd., Madison, 1992-93; mem. Libr. Coun. Met. Milw., 1987-93, mem. continuing edn. com., 1991-92. Author articles and revs. Mem. Ohioana Children's Lit. Award Com., 1995-96. Marquette scholar, 1990-91. Mem. ALA, Wis. Libr. Assn. (chair libr. careers com. 1992-93), Assn. Coll. and Rsch. Librs./Instrn. Sect. (edn. and behavioral scis. sect., curriculum materials com. 1993—, instrn. for diverse populations com. 1991-92), Acad. Libr. Assn. Ohio, Pi Lambda Theta. Home: 931 Partridge Ln Bowling Green OH 43402-4370

EDWARDS, RUSSELL J., manufacturing executive; b. Chgo., July 8, 1952; s. Russell and Nora (Rochford) E.; m. Kathy Ann Monroe; children: William Russell, Michael Patrick. B in Mgmt., Nat. Louis U., 1991; A in HVAC and Refrigeration, Morton Coll., 1986. Cutter Fabrico, Chgo., 1969-73; br. mgr. Dole Refrigerating, Chgo., 1973-79; pres. Cool Way Refrigeration, Lyons, Ill., 1979—; instr. Morton Coll., Cicero, Ill., 1985—. Pres. sch. bd. Lyons Sch. Dist. 103, 1989—. Republican. Roman Catholic. Home: 8627 Patricia Dr Lyons IL 60534-1042 Office: Cool Way Refrigeration PO Box 268 Lyons IL 60534-1042

EDWARDS, SCOTT BRIAN, health facility administrator; b. Royal Oak, Mich., June 19, 1956; s. Edgar Willard and Betty Jane (Johnson) E.; m. Candace Kay Snyder, Apr. 5, 1986. BA in Chemistry, Kalamazoo Coll., 1978; pharmacology, U. Mich., 1979; MD, Wayne State U., 1983; MPH, Johns Hopkins U., 1989. Diplomate Am. Bd. Internal Medicine, Am. Bd. Preventive Medicine, Specialist in Occupl. Medicine. Vol. rschr. NIH, Bethesda, Md., 1976; intern, resident Internal Medicine, lectr. Ind. U., Indpls., 1983-88; fellow Occupl. Medicine, resident Johns Hopkins U., Balt., 1988-90; med. dir. Occupl. Medicine Network, South Bend, Ind., 1991—; cons. Occupl. Safety and Health Adminstrn., Washington, 1989, Internat. Assn. Fire Fighters Union, Washington, 1989. Bd. dirs. Gospel Ctr. Missionary Ch., 1992-94, stewardship and fin. 1993-94. Mem. ACP, APHA, AMA, Am. Coll. Occupl. and Environ. Medicine, Soc. Occupl. and Environ. Health. Office: St Joseph' Med Ctr Occupl Medicine Network 1010 N Bendix Dr South Bend IN 46628

EDWARDS-KULIKOWSKI, ERNESTINE VIVIAN, writer; b. Bells, Tenn., Dec. 17, 1956; d. Robert Andrew and Simmons Edwards; m. Leon T. Kulikowski, Dec. 17, 1976. PhD in Physiology, U. Chgo., PhD in Polit. Sci.; LLD, U. Ill., Chgo. Sec. Opportunity Pub. Co., Chgo., 1970-79; tchr. South Shore High Sch., Chgo., 1980-87. Mem. Chatonooga (Tenn. sec. 1980). Democrat. Home: 1857 E 81st St Chicago IL 60617

EFTIMOFF, ANITA KENDALL, educational consultant; b. Granite City, Ill., May 3, 1927; d. David Harlow and Ollie Lorena (Galloway) Kendall; m. Vasil Eftimoff, June 14, 1959; 1 child, James Kendall. BA, Washington U., St. Louis, 1949; MA, So. Ill. U., Edwardsville, 1978, EdD, 1983. Cert. in multiple gen. edn., spl. edn., Ill. Spl. edn. instr. Community Unit 9, Granite City, 1968-83; ednl. cons. Efti Enterprises, Granite City, 1982—; program dir. At-Risk Presch. Grant, Granite City, 1986—; del. NDEA Conf. Ea. Mich. U., Ypsilanti, 1968, Gifted Edn. Conf. Ill. Office of Edn., Springfield, 1975-77; adminstrv. intern Ill. State Bd. Edn., Springfield, 1981. Editor: Symphony Youth Orch. Newsletter, 1991—, Symphony Vol. Key Notes Newsletter, 1991-93. Bd. dirs. Ill. Gov.'s Adv. Coun. on Women's Affairs, Springfield, Rape Crisis and Sexual Abuse Ctr., So. Ill. U., 1978-82, Family Resource Ctr.; chmn. adopt-a-friend St. Louis Ambs., 1982-84, co-chmn. Vets. Day, 1984-86; chmn. St. Louis Symphony Youth Orch., 1985—, St. Louis Symphony Young Artists Competitions, 1993—; mem. aux. St. Louis Children's Hosp., 1980; v.p. mus. activities St. Louis Symphony Vol. Assn.; bd. pres. Ill. Ctr. for Autism, 1993. At-risk presch. grantee Ill. Bd. Edn., 1986—. Mem. World Coun. for Gifted and Talented Children, Nat. Assn. for Gifted Children, Assn. for the Gifted, Ill. Council for the Gifted, Women's Assn. (bd. dirs. 1961—, pres. 1989-91), St. Louis Symphony Women's Assn., AAUW, Delta Kappa Gamma, Phi Delta Kappa. Lodges: Daus. of Nile, Rotary-Anns. Home: 2800 Michigan Ave Granite City IL 62040-3536 Office: At-Risk Presch Program 2300 W 25th St Granite City IL 62040-2025

EGAN, PATRICK DENNIS, organizational development consultant; b. Mpls., Nov. 4, 1959; s. Thomas B. Egan and Sharon (Wegscheider) Cruse. BA in Comm., U. Colo., 1983; MBA, U. St. Thomas, 1991. Human resources rep. Cargill, Inc., Mpls., 1983-88; employment mgr. Medtronic, Inc., Mpls., 1988-91, orgnl. devel. cons., 1991—; human resource advisor Possibilities, Inc., Las Vegas, 1991. Columnist Hill and Isles Press, 1995. Pres. East Isles Residents Assn., Mpls., 1990—. Mem. Phi Beta Kappa. Home: 2632 Humboldt Ave S Minneapolis MN 55408 Office: Medtronic 7000 Central Ave NE Minneapolis MN 55432

EGBERT, RANDALL H., dentist, financial consultant; b. Wausau, Mich., Apr. 1, 1947. BS, U. Iowa, 1969, DDS, 1972. Dentist Milford, Ohio, 1975—; pres. Hudson Fin. Cons., Milford, 1990—; bd. dirs. Quest Mgmt., Reno. Editor: Hand Colored Photography, 1995. Leader Boy Scouts Am., 1990-95; founder, organizer Extended Shadowing Programs, Milford, 1992—; active Cooperative of Edn. for Participants, Milford, 1980—. Capt. USAF, 1972-75. Rotary. Lutheran. Office: 1188 State Route 131 Milford OH 45150-2711

EGE, SCOTT CHARLES, physical therapist; b. Hammond, Ind., June 3, 1965; s. Charles Frederick and Donnelle Susan (Potadle) E.; m. Diane Lynn Peterson, June 16, 1990. BA, U. Iowa, 1988; MS in Phys. Therapy, U. Osteo. Medicine/Health Sci., Des Moines, 1990. Lic. phys. therapist. Phys. therapy aide in pvt. home Iowa City, Iowa, 1987-88; staff phys. therapist St. Anthony Med. Ctr., Rockford, Ill., 1990-94, coord. occupl. rehab., 1994—, indsl. cons., 1993—. Youth counselor Broadway Covenant Ch., Rockford, 1990-93, First Covenant Ch., Rockford, 1994—, youth commn. mem., 1994—. Mem. Am. Phys. Therapy Assn. (orthopedic sect.), Ill. Phys. Therapy Assn. (dist. rep. 1992-94). Office: St Anthony Med Ctr 5666 E State St Rockford IL 61108

EGGAN, LAWRENCE CARL, math and computer science educator; b. Fargo, N.D., Jan. 10, 1935; s. Elmer Melford and Esther Emily (Guernsey) E.; m. Janet Francis Windecker, Sept. 1956 (div. Mar. 1969); children: Peter Cornelius, Reneé Annette, Nicole Denise; m. Christine Ann Wright, Dec. 18, 1971; children: Kevin Carl, Emily Elizabeth. BA, Pacific Luth. U., 1956; MS, U. Oreg., 1958, PhD, 1960. Asst. prof. math. U. Mich., Ann Arbor, 1960-65; assoc. prof., chair math. dept. Pacific Luth. U., Tacoma, 1965-68; assoc. prof., then prof. math. Ill. State U., Normal, 1968-73, 73-84, prof. applied computer sci., 1984—, chair applied computer sci., 1984-94; vis. prof. math. U. London, 1963-64, 76-77, U. West England, Bristol, 1994-95; vis. assoc. prof. math. U. Oreg., Eugene, summers 1966, 67, 68; cons. Srinakarinwirot U., Bangkok, Thailand, 1990, Logic of Computers Corp., U. Mich., 1962-66; bd. advisors Info. Resource Mgmt. Assn., Harrisburg, Pa., 1991-96; assoc. editor math. revs. U. Mich., 1979-81. Co-author: Mathematics: Models and Applications, 1979; contbr. articles to profl. publs. Bd. dirs. Heartland Freenet, Peoria and Bloomington, 1991-94; vol. Bloomington chpt. ARC, 1981-85. Recipient James Armstrong award Ill. Math. Assn. C.C., 1987. Mem. Math. Assn. Am. (pres. Ill. sect. 1972-73), London Math. Soc., Assn. for Computing Machinery, Sigma Xi (rsch. award 1960). Lutheran. Office: Ill State U ACS Dept Campus Box 5150 Normal IL 61790-5150

EGGERS, JAMES WESLEY, executive search consultant; b. Des Moines, Feb. 7, 1925; s. Paul William and Opal Imo (Cardiff) E.; m. Marjorie Mardell Freel, Aug. 2, 1947; children: James S., Barbara Bucher, Mark D. Grad., Knoxville High Sch., 1943. Farmer Knoxville, Iowa, 1948-55; sales rep. Iowa Power & Light Co., Des Moines, 1953-60, Cedar Rapids, Iowa, 1960-62; sales exec. Thomas D. Murphy Co., Red Oak, Iowa, 1962-67; pres., owner Eggers Cos., Omaha, 1967—; bd. dirs. Nebr. State Bank, Omaha; owner, mgr. Exec. Realty and Mgmt. Co., Omaha, 1979—. Bd. dirs. local Meth. Ch.; chmn. local dist. George Bush for Pres. campaign, Nebr., 1988; chmn. State of Nebr. Merit Coun., Lincoln, 1979-83; chmn. and mem. various civic bds. Mem. Nebr. Assn. Pers. Cons. (pres. 1974-75), Nat. Assn. Pers. Cons. (mem. nat. com. 1979-83, cert.), Omaha C. of C. (bd. dirs. 1980-83), Rotary (bd. dirs. Omaha chpt. 1983—, sgt.-at-arms 1986-90), Masons, Shriners. Republican. Office: Eggers Cons Co Inc Eggers Plz 11272 Elm St Omaha NE 68144-4731

EGGERT, RUSSELL RAYMOND, lawyer; b. Chgo., July 28, 1948; s. Ralph A. and Alice M. (Nischwitz) E. AB, U. Ill., 1970, JD, 1973; post-grad., Hague Acad. Internat. Law, The Netherlands, 1972. Bar: Ill. 1973, U.S. Supreme Ct. 1979. Assoc. U. Ill., Champaign, 1973-74; asst. atty. gen. State of Ill., Chgo., 1974-79; assoc. O'Conor, Karaganis & Gail, Chgo., 1979-83; legal counsel to Ill. atty. gen., Chgo., 1983-87; ptnr. Mayer, Brown & Platt, Chgo., 1987—. Contbr. various articles to profl. jours. Mem. ABA. Democrat. Office: Mayer Brown & Platt 190 S La Salle St Chicago IL 60603-3410

EGGING, DON A., mechanical engineer; b. Sidney, Nebr., Sept. 16, 1952. BS in Mech. Engring., Mont. State U., 1977. Project engr. Egging Co., Gurley, Nebr., 1977—. Patentee in field. Mem. KC. Roman Catholic. Home: 2382 Maple St Sidney NE 69162-1865 Office: 12145 Road 38 Gurley NE 69141-6511

EGGLESTON, HARRY, optometrist; b. Dec. 31, 1941; m. Julie Kassebaum; 1 child. Student, Benedictine Coll., 1959-61; BA, St. Louis U., 1962; BA, MA, Creighton U., 1966; MD, U. Cin., 1972. Rep. candidate for U.S. House 9th Dist., Mo., 1996. With USAF, 1967-69. Roman Catholic. Address: Eggleston for US Congress PO Box 128 Saint Charles MO 63302*

EGLOFF, FRED ROBERT, manufacturers representative, writer, historian; b. Evanston, Ill., Nov. 30, 1934; s. Edward Gottfried and Pearl Elizabeth (Fischrupp) E.; m. Sharon Lee Geyer, June 30, 1962. BS in Commerce, Loyola U., 1956. Asst. adv. mgr. The Englander Co., Chgo., 1956-57; indsl. film svc. Accurate Cinema Svc., Chgo., 1960-62; indsl. sales The EMF Co., Chgo., 1962-69, Avery Internat., Azusa, Calif., 1969-77, The Stanley Works, Hartford, Conn., 1977-78; mfg. rep. ARTCO, Chgo., 1979—; v.p., bd. dirs. Westerners Internat., Oklahoma City, 1982—; cons. ALA, Chgo., 1982—; tchr. New Trier Extension, Wilmette, Ill., 1985—. Author: El Paso Lawman, 1982; editor Westerners Brand Book, 1986—; contbr. articles to profl. jours. Bd. dirs. Wilmette Hist. Soc., 1973-77; hist. cons. Wilmette Hist. Mus., 1978; com. mem. Save the Depot Preservation, Wilmette, 1974; sec. Wilmette Sailing Assn., 1974. Capt. U.S. Army, 1957-59. Mem. Western History Assn., Western Writers Am., Soc. Midland Authors, Chgo. Corral the Westerners (sheriff 1978-80, sidewinder 1984), Windy City BMW Car Club Am. (pres. 1976, Big Wheel 1972), Vintage Sportscar Club (sec. 1972-80), Nat. Cowboy Hall Fame. Republican. Roman Catholic. Home: 2035 Greenwood Ave Wilmette IL 60091-1439 Office: ARTCO 2035 Greenwood Ave Wilmette IL 60091-1439

EHLERS, VERNON JAMES, congressman; b. Pipestone, Minn., Feb. 6, 1934; m. Johanna Meulink, 1958; children: Heidi, Brian, Marla, Todd. Student, Calvin Coll.; AB, U. Calif., Berkeley, 1956, PhD in Physics, 1960. Tchg. asst. U. Calif., Berkeley, 1956-57, rsch. asst., 1957-60, lectr. in physics, 1960-66; prof. physics Calvin Coll., 1966-83; mem. Mich. State Ho. of Reps., 1983-85, Mich. State Senate, 1986-94, 103d Congress from 3d Mich. Dist., 1994—; active Gov. Milliken's Task Force on Environ. Problems, 1977, Kent County Rep. Com., Kent County Rep. Exec. Com., Kent County Bd. Commrs., 1975-83, chmn., 1979-82, Mich. Toxic Substance Control Commn., 1982; asst. floor leader Mich. State Ho. of Reps., mem. house oversight com., mem. transp. and infrastructure com., mem. sci. com. Contbr. articles to profl. jours. NATO Post-doctoral Rsch. fellow U. Heidelberg, Germany, 1961-62, Sci. Faculty fellow NSF, 1971-72, fellow Calvin Coll. Ctr. for Christian Scholar, 1977-78. Mem. AAAS, Am. Phys. Soc., Am. Assn. Phys. Tchrs., Mich. Assn. Environ. Profls. Mem. Christian Reformed Ch. Home: 1848 Morningside Drive NE Grand Rapids MI 49503 Home: 1848 Morningside Dr SE Grand Rapids MI 49503 Office: Federal Bldg 110 Michigan NW Grand Rapids MI 49503

EHLERT, NANCY LYNNE, elementary education educator; b. Columbus, Ohio, Jan. 25, 1954; d. Ralph E. and Eleanor G. (Seymour) Ater; m. Arthur William Ehlert, Oct. 3, 1987; 1 child, Benjamin Curtis. BA, Bowling Green State U., 1976; MEd, Ohio State U., 1980, postgrad., 1981-92. Tchr. Worthington (Ohio) City Schs., 1976—; cons. tchr. Ohio State U./NIH Grant Project, Columbus, 1992-93; pilot tchr. BSCS Sci. Curriculum Field Test, Worthington, 1992-93, Soc. Automotive Engrs., Worthington, 1992; strategy for success team Worthington City Schs., 1990; testing software com human growth and devel. grant project NIH, 1995-96; venture capitol grant writing com. Staff Devel. in Restructure our Sch. Environ., 1996. Recipient 1992 Excellence Category Innovation award, 1992. Mem. Nat. Sci. Tchrs. Assn., Omega Phi Alpha Nat. Svc. Sorority (nat. alumni adminstrn. 1981-82). Theosphist. Office: Worthington City Schs 1850 Sutter Pky Powell OH 43065-9240

EHLERT, PAUL EDWARD, insurance company representative; b. Waverly, Iowa, Sept. 7, 1932; s. Henry Ehlert and Edith Mae (Hall) Shindley; m. Phyllis Ann Fickess, July 21, 1952; children: Mark, Wesley, Timothy, Brian, Melissa, Jennifer. BA, U. No. Iowa, Cedar Falls, 1967; MA, Cen. Mo. State U., 1979. Risk improvement rep. Employers Mut. Co., Des Moines. Office: Employers Mut Co 717 Mulberry Des Moines IA 50309

EHLMANN, STEVEN E., state legislator; b. St. Charles, Mo., Dec. 6, 1950; m. Jean Poggmeier, 1988. BA, Furman U., 1973; MA, U. Mo., 1975; JD, Washington U., 1985. Former tchr., ptnr. law firm. State rep. dist. 19 Mo. Ho. of Reps., mem. higher edn. and judiciary coms., tourism, recreational and cultural affairs, St. Charles Citizens Participatory Adv. Com.; state senator dist. 23, 1993—. Mem. Salvation Army, Boys Club Am. Home: 2941 Wentworth Saint Charles MO 63301*

EHRE, MILTON, Slavic languages and literature educator; b. N.Y.C., Apr. 15, 1933; s. Isaac and Sylvia (Weissberg) E.; m. Roberta Greene, June 9, 1963; children: Joelle, Julieanne. BA cum laude, CCNY, 1955; MA, Columbia U., 1966, PhD, 1970. Tchr. English N.Y.C. Bd. Edn., 1956-63; asst. prof. U. Chgo., 1967-72, assoc. prof., 1972-81, prof., 1981—. Author: Oblomov and His Creator: The Life and Art of Ivan Gonchârov, 1973, Isaac Babel, 1986; editor and translator The Theater of Nicolay Gogol, 1980; translator Chekhov for the Stage, 1992; mem. edtl. bd. Slavic and E. European Jour. Columbia U. Pres.'s fellow, 1964-66, Guggenheim fellow, 1975-76, Fulbright-Hays fellow, 1984, 90. Mem. Am. Assn. Advancement Slavic Studies, Am. Assn. Tchrs. Slavic and E. European Langs., Joseph Jefferson Awards Com. of Chgo. Jewish. Office: U Chgo Slavic Dept 1130 E 59th St Chicago IL 60637

EHRENHAFT, JOHANN LEO, surgeon; b. Vienna, Austria, Oct. 10, 1915; came to U.S., 1934, naturalized, 1939; s. Felix and Olga (Steindler) E.; m. Jean Lovett, Oct. 17, 1953; 1 son, John Bruce. Student, U. Vienna, 1933-34; M.D., U. Iowa, 1938. Diplomate: Am. Bd. Surgery. Intern Johns Hopkins Hosp., 1938-39, Halsted fellow in surgery, 1939-40; resident surgery U. Iowa, 1940-42, 45-47, instr., 1947-48, asso., 1948-49, asst. prof., 1949-51, asso. prof., 1951-53, prof. surgery, 1953—; fellow in thoracic surgery Barnes Hosp., St. Louis, 1948-49; chmn. div. thoracic surgery U. Iowa Hosps., Iowa City, 1949-86, prof. emeritus, 1986—; Mem. Council on Cardiovascular Surgery, Am. Heart Assn., 1952—, Bd. Thoracic Surgery, Inc., 1966—. Editorial bd.: Annals Thoracic Surgery, 1964—; Contbr. articles on thoracic and cardiovascular surgery to med. jours. Served to maj. AUS, 1942-46. Fellow A.C.S.; mem. AMA, Am. Surg. Assn., Am. Assn. Thoracic Surgery, Am. Heart Assn., Soc. Univ. Surgeons, Am., Central, Pan-Am. surg. assns., Am. Coll. Chest Physicians (past regent), Internat. Cardiovascular Soc., Soc. Thoracic Surgeons, Soc. Vascular Surgery, Société Internationale de Chirugie, Sigma Xi, Alpha Omega Alpha. Home: 325 Beldon Ave Iowa City IA 52246-3503

EHRLICH, GEORGE, retired art history educator, researcher; b. Chgo., Jan. 28, 1925; s. Joseph and Mathilda (Kun) E.; m. Mila J. Smith, May 26, 1956; children: Paul S., Matthew C. BS, U. Ill., 1949, MFA, 1951, PhD, 1960. Instr. art history U. Mo., Kansas City, 1954-56, asst. prof., 1956-62, assoc. prof., 1962-66, prof., 1966-92, prof. emeritus, 1992—; rsch. on archtl. history. Author: Kansas City, Missouri, 1992; co-author: (with David H. Sachs) Guide to Kansas Architecture, 1996; curator exhbn. Art of the Tall Bldg., 1985. Mem. Kansas City Landmarks Commn., 1979-89; bd. dirs. Hist. Kansas City Found., 1978-84. 1st lt. USAAF, 1943-46, USAF, 1951-53, PTO. Mem. Soc. Archtl. Historians (bd. dirs. 1979-82). Home: 5505 Holmes St Kansas City MO 64110-2725

EHRLICH, LARRY G., educator; b. Russell, Kans., Mar. 25, 1939; s. Rolland A. and Mildred I. (Glynn) E. AB, U. Kans., 1961, MA, 1962; PhD, Northwestern U., 1968. Asst. prof. Rockhurst Coll., Kansas City, Mo., 1962-70, U. No. Colo., Greeley, 1970-73; assoc. prof. U. Mo., Kansas City, 1973—. Author: Effective Speaking & Listening, 1995. Pres., bd. dirs. Good Samaritan Project, Kansas City, 1993-95. Mem. Assn. surg. Technologists (pres., bd. dirs.), Speech Comm. Assn. Lutheran. Home: 2216 W 50th St Westwood Hills KS 66205-2028

EICH, PETER M., engineering executive; b. Merrilville, Ind., Mar. 14, 1960. BS, Purdue U., 1982. Mgr. NTN Bearing Corp., Mt. Prospect, Ill., 1982—. Contbr. articles to profl. jours. Coach Little League. Mem. SAE. Office: NTN Bearing Corp PO Box 7604 Mount Prospect IL 60056-7604

EICHHOLZ, MARK JOSEPH, lawyer; b. St. Louis, Nov. 7, 1957; s. Bernard Joseph and Nancy Lee (Wolf) E.; m. Joanne Roberta Ditzler, Nov. 22, 1980 (div. Feb. 1992); children: Neil Andrew, Drew Charles. BA, Benedictine Coll., 1980; MBA, U. Kans., Lawrence, 1985; JD, U. Mo., Columbia, 1988. Bar: Mo. 1988, Kans. 1989. Economist/fin. bank analyst Fed. Reserve Bank of Kans. City, Kansas City, Mo., 1981-85; lawyer Armstrong, Teasdale Law Firm (successor to Dietrich Davis), Kansas City, 1988-91, Witt & Hicklin, P.C., Platte City, Mo., 1991-92, Hacker, Hinkle & Hackler, Olathe, Kans., 1993—. Contbr. articles to profl. jours. Bd. dirs. Olathe Babe Ruth Baseball, Olathe Citizens Police Adv. Bd. Recipient Wall St. Jour. award Benedictine Coll., Atchison, 1980. Mem. Kans. Bar Assn., Mo. Bar Assn., Johnson County Bar Assn., Olathe C. of C., Lawyers Assn. of Kansas City. Republican. Roman Catholic. Home: 13120 S Brougham Olathe KS 66062 Office: Hackler Hinkle & Hackler 201 N Cherry Olathe KS 66061

EICHHORN, ARTHUR DAVID, music director; b. St. Louis, Oct. 13, 1953; s. Arthur Louis and Adele (Stankunas) E. BA, Concordia U., River Forest, Ill., 1975, MA, 1976; MA, Webster U., 1986. Cert. elem. tchr., Ill., Mo. Dir. music St. John Luth. Ch., Mt. Prospect, Ill., 1974-76, Our Savior Luth. Ch., Springfield, Ill., 1976-81, Holy Cross Luth. Ch., St. Louis, 1981-91, Timothy Luth. Ch., St. Louis, 1991—. Mem. Choristers Guild (pres. local chpt. 1990-92), Music Educators Nat. Conf., Mo. Music Educators Assn., Am. Guild Organists, Assn. Luth. Ch. Musicians. Republican. Home: 7116 Mardel Ave Saint Louis MO 63109-1123 Office: Timothy Luth Ch 6704 Fyler Ave Saint Louis MO 63139-2239

EICHHORN, BRADFORD REESE, management consultant; b. Cleve., Jan. 24, 1954; s. Charles Albert Jr. and Jeanne Yvonne (Reese) E.; m. Dawn Lynette Mattern, Feb. 25, 1980; children: Serena Ruth, Reese Aaron, Hannah Dawn. BS in Computer Sci. magna cum laude, Cleve. State U., 1975, MS in Operations Research summa cum laude, 1977. Cert. data processor, systems profl. Mgr. applications devel. Control Data Corp., Lakewood, Ohio, 1976-83; sr. cons. Coopers & Lybrand, Cleve., 1983-84; mgr. bus. systems Ferro Corp., Independence, Ohio, 1984-89; mgr. systems and programming Forest City Enterprises, Cleve., 1989-95; mgr. Claremont Tech. Group, Cleve., 1995—; treas. Blossom Property Devel., Cleve., 1985-87. Contbg. editor Hinckley Record, 1993. Chmn. fin. com. All Saints Luth. Ch., Olmsted Falls, Ohio, 1984-85; chmn. endowment fund Our Saviour Luth. Ch., Hinckley, Ohio, 1989-93, sec. stewardship and fin. com., 1986-87; Christian fin. counselor; chmn. deacons Medina Alliance Fellowship, 1993-94, elder, 1995—; dir. Compassion Inc., Ashland, Ohio, 1995—. Mem. Beta Gamma Sigma. Home: 149 Salem Ct Hinckley OH 44233-9639 Office: Claremont Tech Group 600 Superior Ave Cleveland OH 44114

EIDE, EUGENE GERHARD, tool and die company executive; b. Valley Stream, N.Y., June 20, 1921; s. Gerhard Nicholi and Eleanor (Weiss) E.; m. Betty Jane Johnson, Aug. 19, 1948; children: Karen, Gerald, Richard, Ellen. BS in Marine Engring., Kings Point Merchant Marine, 1944. Chmn. bd. Justrite Machine Works Inc., Kansas City, Mo., 1960-95. Commdr. Merchant Marines, 1940-47, WWII. Presbyterian. Home: 7801 Colonial Dr Prairie Vlg KS 66208-4643 Office: Justrite Machine Works Inc 5335 Brighton Ave Kansas City MO 64130-3219

EIDSNESS, PAT, state legislator. Dir. spl. programs; mem. S.D. Ho. of Reps., Pierre; mem. health, human svcs. and transp. coms. Republican.

EIGEL, CHRISTOPHER JOHN, real estate executive; b. Evanston, Ill.; s. Jack William and Martha Eloise (English) E.; m. Carolyn Koenig, Mar. 23, 1968; children: Jeffrey Christopher, Edward Drummond, Amy Elizabeth. BA, U. Ill., 1967; MBA, U. Chgo., 1969. Mktg. rsch. officer The Northern Trust Co., Chgo., 1969-74; exec. v.p. and gen. sales mgr. Koenig and Strey Inc., Wilmette, Ill., 1974—. Mem. real estate adv. bd. Oakton C.C., Des Plaines, Ill. Mem. Ill. Assn. Realtors (bd. dirs. 1986-88), North Shore Bd. Realtors (bd. dirs. 1980-88, pres. 1987), U. Ill. Alumni Assn. (bd. dirs. 1993—), Glenview Ednl. Found. Home: 630 Windsor Rd Glenview IL 60025-4453 Office: Koenig and Strey Inc 3201 Old Glenview Rd Wilmette IL 60091-2942

EIKENBERRY, KEVIN LEON, training consultant; b. Ludington, Mich., May 26, 1962; s. Phillip L. Eikenberry and Janet M. (Lindamood) Wallis; m. Lori A. West, Aug. 30, 1986; 1 child, Parker. BS in Agriculture, Purdue U., 1984. Sales rep. Chevron Chem. Co., Evansville, Ind., 1986; mktg. coord. Chevron Chem. Co., San Francisco, 1986-88; tng. coord. Chevron Chem. Co., San Ramon, Calif., 1988, telemarketing mgr., 1988-90; tng. cons. Chevron Corp., San Francisco, 1990-93; pres., tng. cons. Performance Ptnrs., Indpls., 1993—. Contbr.: Active Training Designs, 1995, McGraw Hill Training and Development Yearbook, 1995. Mem. N.Am. Simulation and Gaming Assn. (bd. dirs. 1993—), Am. Soc. Tng. and Devel., Internat. Soc. for Permance Improvement, Internat. Alliance for Learning, Purdue Agrl. Alumni Assn. (bd. dirs. 1993—). Office: Performance Ptnrs 7035 Buffridge Way Indianapolis IN 46278

EILERT, BUTCH ALLEN, mechanical engineer; b. Beloit, Kans., Oct. 3, 1958. AD in Mech. Engring., N. Ctrl. Kans. Vocat., 1990; A in Mech. Engring., Kans. Coll. of Tech, 1990. Auto machanic N. Ctrl. Kans. Votech., 1976-78; machinist R&M Auto Parts, Beloit, Kans., 1978-88; mech. engr. Mac Equipment, Sabetha, Kans., 1991, Wenger Mfg., Sabetha, Kans., 1992—; mem. adv. bd. North Ctrl. Kans. Votech., 1980-82. Mem. Tau Omicron Tau (v.p. 1990, sr. rep. mech. engr. dept. 1990). Republican. Office: Wenger Mfg 714 Main Sabetha KS 66534

EILERT, MARK ANTHONY, agricultural engineer; b. Beloit, Kans., Nov. 11, 1960; s. Donald Leo and Dolores Mae (DeLude) E. BS in Agrl. Engring., Kans. State U., 1983. Registered profl. engr. Kans., Nebr., Fla. Design engr. Kent Mfg. Co., Inc., Tipton, Kans., 1991—; cons. in field. Patentee in field. Lt. comdr. civil engr. corps. USNR. Mem. ASCE, NSPE, Am. Soc. Agrl. Engrs., KC. Republican. Roman Catholic. Home: RR 4 Box 11 Beloit KS 67420-9087 Office: Kent Mfg Co Inc PO Box 126 Tipton KS 67485-0126

EINBINDER, SUSAN LESLIE, literature educator, rabbi; b. Ridgewood, N.J., Dec. 9, 1954; d. Seymour K. and Julia M. (Morrison) E. BA in English magna cum laude, Brown U., 1976; MHL, Hebrew Union Coll., 1983; MA in English and Comparative Lit., Columbia U., 1978, MPhil, 1986, PhD in Comparative Lit., 1991. Ordained rabbi, 1983. Vis. lectr., chaplain to Jewish students Colgate U., Hamilton, N.Y., 1987-88; adj. prof. gen. studies NYU, N.Y.C., 1990-92; adj. prof. Manhattan Sch. Music, N.Y.C., 1991-92; vis. lectr. U. Md., College Park, 1992-93; asst. prof. Hebrew lit. Hebrew Union Coll., Cin., 1993-96; assoc. prof. Hebrew Union Coll., 1996—. Translator: (novella) IYA (Shimon Ballas), 1995; contbr. articles to profl. jours. and confs. Bd. dirs. Prospect House, Cin., 1995—; spkr. at cmty. orgns. Fellow Fulbright Found., 1986-87, Nat. Found. for Jewish Culture, 1988-89. Mem. MLA, Cen. Conf. of Am. Rabbis, Nat. Assn. Profs. of Hebrew, Assn. for Jewish Studies. Office: Hebrew Union Coll Jewish Inst Religion 3101 Clifton Ave Cincinnati OH 45220

EINHORN, EDWARD MARTIN (EDDIE EINHORN), professional baseball team executive; b. Paterson, N.J., Jan. 3, 1936; s. Harold Benjamin and Mae (Lippman) E.; m. Ann Magdelene Pelachik, Apr. 24, 1962; children: Jennifer, Jeffrey. AB, U. Pa., 1957; JD, Northwestern U., 1960. Radio sports announcer Sta.-WXPN, Phila., 1954-57; founder, pres. Midwestern Sports Network, Chgo., 1957-61; founder, pres. TV sports Inc. (name changed to TVS 1968, became subs. Corinthian Broadcasting Corp. 1973), N.Y.C., 1961-65, pres., chief exec. officer, 1965-78; exec. producer CBS Sports Spectacular, N.Y.C., 1978—; pres. Chgo. White Sox, 1981-93, vice chmn., 1993—; founder Sports Vision Chgo., 1982; dir. Corinthian Broadcasting Corp., 1973-77; format com. mem. Major League Baseball; co-architect Baseball Network; TV cons. U.S. Olympic Com.; initiator 200 hour Olympic TV package, 1990; TV cons. U.S. Figure Skating Assn., Internat. Skating Union. bd. dirs. Chgo. Bulls. Editor-in-chief Jour. Air Law and Sci., 1959-60, Northwestern Jour. Criminal Law Sci., 1958-60; producer (TV spl.) Gossamer Albatross, Flight of Imagination (Emmy award 1980). Recipient Honor award Naismith Basketball Hall of Fame, 1973, Merit award Nat. Basketball Coaches, 1973, Victor award City of Hope, 1974. Mem. Nat. Acad. Radio, TV Arts and Scis., Internat. Radio, TV Soc., Nat. Assn. TV Program Execs., Nat. Assn. Coll. Dirs., Nat. Assn. Basketball Coaches (TV negotiation com.) Profl. Baseball Assn. (TV com. mem. 1992-95, sr. Am. League rep. on player devel. negotiating com.). Office: Chgo White Sox 333 W 35th St Chicago IL 60616-3621

EINHORN, MARTIN B., physics educator; b. Dayton, Ohio, Aug. 14, 1942; s. Aaron Howard and Rosalind (Rosen) E.; m. Vibeke Gjoe Geleff, Feb. 18, 1967; children: Michael, Linda. BS, Calif. Inst. Tech., 1965; PhD, Princeton U., 1968. Post-doctoral fellow Stanford (Calif.) Linear Accelerator Ctr., 1968-70, Lawrence Berkeley (Calif.) Lab., 1970-72; post-doctoral fellow Fermi Nat. Accelerator Lab., Batavia, Ill., 1972-73, staff physicist, 1973-76; assoc. rsch. scientist U. Mich., Ann Arbor, 1976-79, assoc. prof., 1979-83, prof. physics, 1983—; chair adv. bd. Theoretical Advanced Study Inst., Boulder, Colo., 1984-91, dep. dir. Inst. for Theoretical Physics, U. Calif., 1990—. Contbr. 60 articles to profl. jours. Mem. high energy physics adv. panel Dept. of Energy, Washington, 1983-87. Fellow Am. Phys. Soc.; mem. AAUP, AAAS. Office: Inst Theoretical Physics UC Santa Barbara Santa Barbara CA 93106

EINHORN, STEPHEN EDWARD, mergers and acquisitions executive, consultant, investment banker; b. Bklyn., June 25, 1943; s. Benjamin and Rosalind (Nuss) R.; m. Nancy Lore, May 22, 1965; children: David, Daniel. BA, Cornell U., 1964; postgrad., U. Pa., 1964-65; MSChemE, Bklyn. Polytech. Inst., 1967. With Adelphi Paint Co., Carlstadt, N.J., 1965-75; pres. Einhorn Assocs., Inc., Milw., N.J., 1975—; mergers and acquisitions chem. industry specialist concentrating on paints and adhesives; spkr. Nat. Paint and Coatings Assn., Atlanta, 1993, Powder Coatings Inst., Palm Springs, 1993. Author: If You Try to Please Everybody..., 1983, Employee Stock Option Plans, 1985; contbr. articles to profl. jours.; patentee on handling latex paint, 1978. Mem. Cornell Club of Wis. (pres. 1987-90). Home: 8205 N River Rd Milwaukee WI 53217 Office: 2323 N Mayfair Rd Ste 490 Milwaukee WI 53226

EINODER, CAMILLE ELIZABETH, secondary education educator; b. Chgo., June 15, 1937; d. Isadore and Elizabeth T. (Czerwinski) Popowski; student Fox Bus. Coll., 1954; BEd in Biology, Chgo. Tchrs. Coll., 1964; MA in Analytical Chemistry, Gov.'s State U., 1977; MA in Adminstrn. and Supervision, Roosevelt U., 1986; postgrad 1992—. m. Joseph X. Einoder, Aug. 5, 1978; children: Carl Frank, Mark Frank, Vivian Einoder, Joe Einoder, Tim Einoder, Sheila Einoder, Jude Einoder. Secretarial positions, Chgo., 1955-64; tchr. biology Chgo. Bd. Edn., 1964—, tchr. biology and agr., 1975-81, tchr. biology, agr. and chemistry, 1981—; human rels. coord. Morgan Park High Sch., Chgo., 1980—, tchr. biology Internat. Studies Sch., 1983—, mem. adv. bd., 1989—; career devel. cons. for agr. related curriculum. Bds. dirs., founding mem., author constn. Community Coun., 1970—; bd. dirs., edn. cons. Neighborhood Coun., 1974; rep. Chgo. Tchrs. Union, 1969; exec. bd. dir. The Lira Ensemble, 1996—. Mem. Phi Delta Kappa, Iota Sigma Pi. Home: 10637 S Claremont Ave Chicago IL 60643-3101 Office: 1744 W Pryor Ave Chicago IL 60643-3457

EINSELEN, KENNETH LEE, civil engineer; b. Peru, Ind., Nov. 5, 1954; s. John Harold and Carolyn (Agness) E.; m. Cynthia Lisa Jean Bateman, Dec. 27, 1980; children: John Michael, Mark Andrew, Lisa Marie, Lydia Anne, Matthew David. BSCE, Purdue U., 1976, MSCE, 1977. Registered profl. engr., Ind. Airport engr. A & E Engring., Indpls., 1977-82; transp. engr. Mid-States Engring., Indpls., 1982-83; county hwy. engr. County of Miami, Peru, 1984—. Mem. ASCE, United Meth. Men (pres. McGrawsville chpt. 1990-91). Office: Miami County Rm 101 County Courthouse Peru IN 46970

EISEN, DAVID JOHN, librarian; b. Zeeland, Mich., Dec. 11, 1949; s. Albert J. and Mary Jane (DeGraaf) E.; m. Barbara JoAnn Fredricks, June 10, 1972; 1 child, Deanne Elizabeth. BA, Calvin Coll., Grand Rapids, Mich., 1972; MA, U. Va., 1974; MLS, U. Mich., 1974. Head adult svcs. Mishawaka-Penn Pub. Libr., Mishawaka, Ind., 1975-78, adminstrv. asst. to dir., 1977-78, acting dir., 1978-79, dir., 1980—; libr. sci. lectr. Ind. U., South Bend, 1977—. Author: Biographical Index, 1978, Vital Statistics Index, 1987, Vital Statistics Index to St. Joseph County, Indiana, Newspapers, 1831-1912, 1995; editor: Mishawaka Mosaic, 1983. Adv. bd. pres. Mishawaka Salvation Army, 1991-94; v.p. ACCESS, Mishawaka, 1990-92, pres., 1993—. Named Mishawaka Man of the Yr. Mishawaka Bus. Assn., 1982. Mem. ALA, Ind. Libr. Assn., Mishawaka Bus. Assn. (pres. 1985), Area 2 Libr. Svcs. Authority (pres. 1983, 99, 94-95), Grand Valley Hist. Soc., Lions (sec. 1986-94, pres. 1995—), Beta Phi Mu. Christian Ref. Ch. Home: 1112 E 3rd St Mishawaka IN 46544-2735 Office: Mishawaka-Penn Pub Libr 209 Lincoln Way E Mishawaka IN 46544-2084

EISEN, MARLENE RUTH, psychologist, educator; b. Chgo., Nov. 23, 1931; d. William and Sophia Maria (Brounwine) Friedlander; m. Lee B. Andalman, Aug. 2, 1963 (dec. July 1974); children: Martin Price, Dan Price, Robert; m. Sydney B. Eisen, June 6, 1979. Student, U. Wis., 1948-51; BA, Roosevelt U., Chgo., 1952; MA, U. Chgo., 1967, PhD, 1977. Tchr. Ravinia Nursery Sch., Highland Park, Ill., 1952-56; nursery sch. tchr. Country Schs., North Hollywood, Calif., 1958-61; kindergarten tchr. Sch. Dist. #65, Evanston, Ill., 1962-73; coord. early childhood program U. Chgo., 1974-75; coord. early childhood program, assoc. prof. Harper Coll., Palatine, Ill., 1976-84; pvt. practice cons. ednl. programs Evanston, 1972-86; assoc. faculty Ill. Sch. Profl. Psychology, Chgo., 1982—; pvt. practice psychotherapy Chgo., 1977—; mem. faculty tchr. edn. program Inst. Psychoanalysis, Chgo., 1984-95; cons. Evanston Sch. Dist. #65, 1967; chmn. adv. bd. early edn. program Harper Coll., Palatine, 1976-84; presenter papers and workshops at various confs., univs., community ctrs., parents groups, ednl. groups and profl. orgns. Contbr. articles to profl. jours. Fellow APA; mem. Soc. Clin. and Exptl. Hypnosis, Am. Soc. Clin. Hypnosis. Office: 1603 Orrington Evanston IL 60201-5000

EISENSTEIN, PHYLLIS LEAH, writer, writing educator; b. Chgo., Feb. 26, 1946; d. Irving Walter and Sylvia (Davidson) Kleinstein; m. Alex Beau Eisenstein, Sept. 8, 1966. BA, U. Ill., Chgo., 1981. Tchr. writing Columbia Coll., Chgo., 1989—. Author: Born to Exile, 1978 (Balrog 1978), Shadow of Earth, 1979, Sorcerer's Son, 1979, In the Hands of Glory, 1981, The Crystal Palace, 1988, In the Red Lord's Reach, 1989. Recipient Readers award SF Chronicle mag., N.Y.C., 1981, Balrog award Foolcon Sci. Fiction Conv., Johnson City, Kans., 1978. Mem. Sci. Fiction Writers Am., Authors Guild.

EISERMANN, ECKEHARD HERMANN, corporate executive; b. Munich, Jan. 13, 1943; came to U.S., 1980; s. Gunter Ludwig and Lisa (Klusmann) E.; m. Karin Ursula Pfeiffer, May 8, 1968; children: Philip Okken, Lukas Georg. BS, Tech. U., Clausthal, Fed. Republic of Germany, 1964; MS in Engring., Tech. U., Berlin, 1967, PhD in Engring., 1969. Application mgr. M&P, Cologne, Fed. Republic of Germany, 1975-77, sales mgr., 1977-80; gen. mgr. M&P, Lorain, Ohio, 1980-87; pres. M&P, Inc., North Olmsted, 1987—. Home: 4499 Mapleview Dr Vermilion OH 44089-3431

EISLER, MILLARD MARCUS, financial executive; b. Toledo, Ohio, Mar. 31, 1950; s. Joseph R. and Marilynn (Gross) E. BS, Ind. U., 1972; MBA, Cornell U., 1977. CPA, Ill., Mass., N.H. Auditor Arthur Andersen & Co., Boston, 1977-79; mgr. internat. acctg. Wheelabrator-Frye, Inc., Hampton, N.H., 1979-81; mgr. ops. analysis and audit GCA Corp., Bedford, Mass., 1981-85; mgr. cost acctg. and fin. analysis Precision Sci., Inc., Chgo., 1985-86, contr., chief fin. officer, 1986-89; tax preparer H&R Block, Inc., Chgo., 1989-92; tax preparer H&R Block, Inc., Lincoln, Nebr., 1993, quality control mgr., 1994; dist. mgr. H&R Block, Inc., Madison, Wis., 1994—; bd. dirs. Franklin Software Co., Arvada, Colo.; lectr. Northeastern Ill. U., Chgo., 1986-88. Mem. Ind. U. Alumni Assn., Cornell U. Alumni Assn. of Wis. Democrat. Jewish. Home: 834 S Gammon Rd Madison WI 53719-1381 Office: H&R Block 1240 S Park St Madison WI 53715-2102

EISNER, GAIL ANN, artist, educator; b. Detroit, Oct. 17, 1939; d. Rudolph and Florence (White) Leon; m. Marvin Michael Eisner, June 14, 1959 (dec. Feb. 1993); 1 child, Alan. Rsch. fellow, Art Inst. Chgo., Art Student League of N.Y.; BFA, Wayne State U. One-woman shows include Worthington Art Ctr., Ohio, OK Harris/David Klein Gallery, Birmingham, Mich., Sinclair Coll., LRC Gallery, Dayton, Ohio, U. Mich. Hosps., Ann Arbor; group shows include Islip Art Mus., East Islip, N.Y., Columbia (Mo.) Coll., Tubac (Ariz.) Ctr. of the Arts, Ft. Wayne (Ind.) Mus. of Art, C.W. Post Coll., Brookville, N.Y., NAWA, Jacob K. Kavits Ctr., N.Y.C., Schoharie County Coun. of the Arts, Cobbleskill, N.Y., ARC Gallery, Chgo., McPherson (Kans.) Coll., Med. Coll. Ga., Augusta, Heckscher Mus. Art, Huntington, Nassau County Mus. Art, Roslyn, N.Y., Guild Hall, East Hampton, N.Y., Castle Gould, Sands Point, N.Y., Pastel Soc. Am., N.Y.C., Carrier Found., Belle Meade, N.J., Hill Country Arts Found., Ingram, Tex., Cunningham Meml. Art Gallery, Bakersfield, Calif., Henry Hicks Gallery, Bklyn. Hgts., U. N.D., Grand Forks, Nassau C.C., Garden City, N.Y., Trenton (N.J.) State Coll., Wenatchee Valley (W.Va.) Coll., Del Mar Coll., Corpus Christi, Tex., Minot (N.D.) State U., Ctrl. Mo. State U., McNeese State U., Lake Charles, La., Worthington Art Ctr., Ohio, Art Ctr., Mt. Clemens, Mich., Oakland C.C., Mich., Krasl Art Ctr., St. Joseph, Mich., Fontana Concert Soc., Kalamazoo, Mich., Art Ctr. Battle Creek, Mich., Ctrl. Mich. U., Mt. Pleasant, Birmingham (Mich.) Bloomfield Art Assn., Cmty. House, Birmingham, Sch. of Art Inst., Chgo., Cheekwood Mus. Art, Nashville, Grand Rapids (Mich.) Mus. Art, Flint (Mich.) Inst. Arts, Ariana Gallery, Royal Oak, Mich., Judith Paul Gallery, Medford, Oreg., The Art Collector, San Diego, Gwenda Jay Gallery, Chgo., Columbia Greens Coll., Hudson, N.Y., Worthington (Ohio) Art Ctr.; permanent collections include Rabobank, Chgo., Resurrection Hosp., Kanai (Hawaii) Hotel, Jules Joyner Designs, Royal Oak, Mich., The Lumber Store, Chgo., others, also pvt. collections. Recipient Adriana Zahn award Pastel Soc. Am., Heckscher Mus. award, Our Visions: Women in Art award Oakland C.C., 1995. Mem. Nat. Assn. Women Artists (Sara Winston Meml. award 1992), N.Y. Artist Equity Assn., Art Student League N.Y. (Sidney Dickinson Meml. award), Birmingham Bloomfield Art Assn. Office: Gail Eisner Studio 104 W 4th St Ste 303 Royal Oak MI 48067-3808

EITINGON, DANIEL BENJAMIN, insurance executive; b. N.Y.C., Nov. 20, 1950; s. Mark and Aimee Brigitte (Berline) E. BBA, Hofstra U., 1977; postgrad., LaSalle U., Mandeville, La. CPCU; assoc. in risk mgmt.; assoc. in underwriting; accredited customer svc. rep.; accredited advisor in ins. Dir. mktg. BHK&R Inc., Mpls., 1982-89; v.p., broking exec. Alexander & Alexander, Inc., Mpls., 1990-95; pres., CEO Outsource Ins. Svcs., Ltd., Mpls., 1995—. Mem. Soc. CPCUs (Minn. chpt. media contact com.), Soc. Ins. Trainers and Educators, Twin Cities Ins. Club. Democrat. Jewish. Home: 3782 Kipling Ave S Saint Louis Park MN 55416 Office: Outsource Ins Svcs Ltd 3208 W Lake St #160 Minneapolis MN 55416

EITRHEIM, NORMAN DUANE, bishop; b. Baltic, S.D., Jan. 14, 1929; s. Daniel Tormod and Selma (Thompson) E.; m. Clarice Yvonne Pederson, Aug. 23, 1952; children: Daniel, David, John, Marie. BA, Augustana Coll., 1951; BTh, Luther Sem., St. Paul, 1956; LHD (hon.), Augustana Coll., 1988. Pastor 1st English Luth. Ch., Tyler, Minn., 1956-63, St. Philips Luth. Ch., Fridley, Minn., 1963-76; asst. to pres. Luther Northwestern Sem., St. Paul, 1976-80; bishop S.D. dist. Am. Luth. Ch., Sioux Falls, 1981-87; bishop S.D. Synod Evang. Luth. Ch. in Am., Sioux Falls, 1988-95. Staff sgt. USAF, 1951-52.

ELDER, MARJORIE JEANNE, English language educator; b. Salina, Kans., July 3, 1921; d. Raymond Berl Sr. and Maye (Whitney) E. BS in Edn., Ind. Wesleyan U., 1945, BA, 1947, DLitt (hon.), 1995; MA in Speech, U. Wis., 1950; PhD in English, U. Chgo., 1963. Tchr. county schs. Cloud County, Kans., 1939-41; tchr. Gas City (Ind.) Schs., 1946-49; instr. Ind. Wesleyan U., Marion, 1949-52, asst. prof., 1952-58, assoc. prof., 1958-64, prof., 1964-67, chair div. modern lang. and lit., 1967-87, prof. English, 1964—; historian of Ind. Wesleyan U. history, Marion. Author: Nathaniel Hawthorne: Transcendental Symbolist, 1969, The Lord, The Landmarks, The Life, 1994. Named Disting. Alumnus Ind. Wesleyan U., 1945. Mem. MLA of Am., Nat. Coun. of Tchrs. of English, Hawthorne Soc., Melville Soc. Republican. Office: Ind Wesleyan U 4201 S Washington St Marion IN 46953-4974

ELDON, LAURA P., stockbroker; b. Royal Oak, Mich., Sept. 26, 1965. Lic. series 7 Nat. Assn. Securities Dealers. Med. sec. Dr. Edward R. Heil, Troy, Mich., 1985-88; sales asst. Smith Barney Inc., Southfield, Mich., 1989—. Roman Catholic. Office: Smith Barney Inc 2000 Town Ctr Ste 1800 Southfield MI 48075-1151

ELDRED, HEATHER ANN, librarian; b. Racine, Wis., Sept. 4, 1942; d. Sverre S. and Fern (Fulton) Elsmo; m. John Walter Eldred, Feb. 26, 1966. BA, U. Wis., 1964, MLS, 1965. Cert. libr., Wis. Children's libr. Cudahy (Wis.) Pub. Libr., 1966; cataloger/acting dir. Marquette U. Law Sch. Libr., Milw., 1966-70; cataloger Holy Redeemer Coll., Union Grove, Wis., 1970-72; cons. Wis. Valley Libr. Svc. Wausau, Wis., 1972-75, system administrator, 1975-83, dir., 1983—. Mem. ALA, Wis. Libr. Assn. (v.p. to pres.-elect 1987, pres. 1988, past pres. 1989, Muriel Fuller award 1995). Methodist. Office: Wisconsin Valley Libr Svc 300 N First St Wausau WI 54403

ELDREDGE, CHARLES CHILD, III, art history educator; b. Boston, Apr. 12, 1944; s. Henry and Priscilla Marion (Bateson) E.; m. Jane Allen MacDougal, June 11, 1966; children: Henry Gifford, Janann Bateson. B.A., Amherst Coll., 1966; Ph.D., U. Minn., 1971. Curator asst. Minn. Hist. Soc., St. Paul, 1966-68; mem. edn. dept. Mpls. Inst. Arts, 1967-69; teaching assoc. art history U. Minn., 1968-70; asst. prof. art history, curator collections Spencer Mus. Art, U. Kans., Lawrence, 1970-71; dir. mus. Spencer Mus. Art, U. Kans., 1971-82, assoc. prof., 1974-80, prof., 1980-82; dir. Nat. Mus. Am. Art, Washington, 1982-88; Hall disting. prof. of Am. art U. Kans., Lawrence, 1988—; C.H. Hynson vis. prof. U. Tex., Austin, 1985; trustee Watkins Cmty. Mus., Lawrence, 1972-76, Assn. Art Mus. Dirs., 1982, 87, Reynolda House Mus. Am. Art, 1986-88, Amherst Coll., 1987-93; trustee Georgia O'Keefe Found., 1989-95; rsch. assoc. Smithsonian Instn., 1988—; founder Smithsonian Studies in Am. Art, 1987. Author: Marsden Hartley: Lithographs and Related Works, 1972, Ward Lockwood, 1894-1963, 1974, American Imagination and Symbolist Painting, 1979, Charles Walter Stetson, Color and Fantasy, 1982, Pacific Parallels: Artists and the Landscape in New Zealand, 1991, Georgia O'Keeffe, 1991, Georgia O'Keeffe: American and Modern, 1992, Canyon Suite: Early Watercolors by Georgia O'Keeffe, 1994; co-author: The Arcadian Landscape: 19th Century American Painters in Italy, 1972, Art in New Mexico, 1900-1945, 1986, American Originals: Selections from Reynolda House, Mus. of American Art, 1990; gen. editor The Register of Mus. Art, 1971-82; editl. bd. Am. Studies, 1974-77. Smithsonian Instn. fellow Nat. Collection Fine Arts, 1979; Fulbright scholar N.Z., 1983; Found. Visitor fellow U. Auckland, 1993, Smithsonian fellowship Nat. Mus. of Am. Art, 1995; recipient Outstanding Alumnus award U. Minn., 1986. Mem. Coll. Art Assn. Am., Am. Studies Assn., Am. Assn. Mus., Assn. Art Mus. Dirs., Authors Guild. Office: U Kans Dept Art History 209 Spencer Mus Art Lawrence KS 66045

ELDRIDGE, CARRIE WOODARD, history researcher, teacher, consultant; b. Jenkins, Ky., Mar. 30, 1943; d. Jesse Joe and Edith Alicia (Allison) Woodard; m. Robert Stanley Eldridge, Dec. 17, 1965; children: Alicia Colleen, Robert Michael. AB in Secondary Edn., Marshall U., 1966, MS in Geography, 1982. Tchr. Lawrence County Schs., Rock Hill, Ohio, 1966; band dir. Lawrence County Schs., Symmes Valley, Ohio, 1975; tchr. Kanawha County Schs., Nitro, W. Va., 1967-68, Cabell County Schs., Huntington, W. Va., 1969-72; substitute tchr. Bd. of Edn., Ohio and W. Va., 1976-90, Chesapeake, Ohio, 1990-95; sec. Marshall U. Grad. Students, Huntington, W. Va., 1982; free lance writer, researcher, Huntington, 1985-95. Author: Cabell County Deed Book vols. I-V, 1985, 86, 88, 89, 93, Cabell Marriages, 1809-1850, 1988, Cabell County Will Book I, 1820-1848, Cabell Cemeteries Vol. I, North of US 60, Vol. II, South of U.S. 60, Vol. III, Huntington, 1990-91, Water: Key to County Formation and Highway Location in Virginia, 1992, Cabell County Census Locator 1810-1850, 1992, Looking at the Personal Diaries of William F. Dusenberry, 1992, Mason County, W.Va. Marriages, 1806-1850, 1992, A Gazetteer of Harrison County, W.Va., 1992, Lost Records: 1853 Pay Roster of Washington Aqueduct, 1993, 1860 Cabell County Census, 1994, 1870 Cabell County Census, 1994, Cabell County Minute Book 3, 1826-1835, 1994, Washington County, Ohio, Tax List of 1817 and non-resident taxes of 1801, 1994, Greenbottom Baptist Church 1836-1853, 1995, Cabell County Fee Book, 1826-1839; mapmaker: (maps) Extinct Towns of Cabell County, 1982, Cabell County Cemeteries, 1990, Cabell County Census Locator, 1992, Historic Towns of Harrison County W.Va., 1992; editor Mountain News newsletter for Mining Your History Found., 1996. Advisor 4H Club Lawrence County, Ohio, 1969-94. Mem. KYOWVA, Va. Genealog. Soc., Gamma Theta Upsilon. Home: 3118 CR 31 Big Branch Chesapeake OH 45619-9780

ELDRIDGE, GARY LYNN, personnel director, emergency medical technician; b. Batesville, Ind., Feb. 9, 1956; s. Kenneth and Glenora Faye (Bryant) E.; m. Margaret Jane Tucker, June 29, 1980; children: Amanda Lynn, Whitney Morgan. BA in History, Berea Coll., 1984. Cert. EMT, Ind. Radio announcer, salesperson Sta. WIXI-Radio, Lancaster, Ky., 1978-79, 81, Sta. WKXO-Radio, Berea, Ky., 1979-80, 80-81; with Cin. Enquirer, 1984-85; hist. site asst. mgr. Whitewater Canal State Hist. Site, Metamora, Ind., 1985-89; pub. access coord. Divsn. Fish & Wildlife, Indpls., 1989-93, tng./pers. officer, 1993—. Mem. Dearborn County Rep. Men's Club, Aurora, Ind., 1993—; bd. dirs. Dearborn County 4-H, Aurora, 1993—; pres., sec. Manchester (Ind.) PTO, 1988-91; EMT Sunman (Ind.) Area Life Squad, 1994—. Home: 13960 Burns Rd Milan IN 47031 Office: DNR-Divsn Fish & Wildlife 402 W Washington Rm W 273 Indianapolis IN 46204

ELEY, JOHN DUANE, electrical engineer, consultant; b. Beloit, Wis., May 20, 1951; s. Charles Albert and Thelma Margeret (Wayne) E.; m. Lucinda Lynn Noack, June 16, 1979; children: Maria Ann, Andrew John, Daniel Paul. BSEE, U. Wis., 1974; postgrad., Cardinal Stritch Coll., 1991—. Registered profl. engr., Wis. Elec. engr. McCleary Industries, South Beloit, Ill., 1975-80; elec. design engr. Ipsen Industries, Rockford, Ill., 1980-85; elec. project engr. Ill. Water Treatment Co., Rockford, 1985-88; v.p. R & D, Brocon Inc., Beloit, 1984-88; applications and controls engr. Eclipse-Dungs Controls Co., Rockford, 1988—. Mem. TAPPI (engring. com.), Instrument Soc. Am. Mem. New Apostolic Ch. Home: RR 4 Box 202 Beloit WI 53511-9804 Office: Eclipse-Dungs Controls Co 1665 Elmwood Rd Rockford IL 61103-1211

ELGER, WILLIAM ROBERT, JR., accountant; b. Chgo., Mar. 20, 1950; s. William Robert and Grace G. (LaVaque) E.; m. Kathryn Michele Johnson, July 10, 1971; children: Kimberly, William, Kristin, Joseph. AS in Applied Sci., Coll. of DuPage, Glen Ellyn, Ill., 1970; BS magna cum laude, U. Ill.-Chgo., 1972. CPA, Ill. Staff acct. Ernst & Whinney, Chgo., 1973, in-charge acct., 1973-74, sr. acct., 1974-78, mgr., 1978-82, sr. mgr., 1982-88; chief fin. officer U. Ill. Eye and Ear Infirmary, 1988-89; CFO U. Mich. Med. Sch., Ann Arbor, 1989—; presenter various confs. in field Ernst & Whinney, Chgo., 1980-88. Author, developer: (tng. course) Auditing Third Party Reimbursement, 1986, 87. Active Union League Civic and Arts Found., Chgo., 1982-89, Union League Found. for Boys and Girls Clubs, Chgo., 1982-89; treas. Newport Assn., Carol Stream, Ill., 1982-83; coach Tri-City Soccer Assn., St. Charles, Ill., 1984, 87, Saline Soccer Assn., 1990, 91, 93, 94, 95, Salene H.S. Soccer Club, 1995. Mem. AICPA, Healthcare Fin. Mgmt. Assn. (advanced mem., acctg. and reimbursement com. 1982-87, chpt. task force com. 1986, 87, auditing com. 1986, 87, Spl. Recognition award 1986), Ill. Soc. CPAs (mem. long term healthcare com. 1983, hosps. com. 1988-89), Nat. Coun. Univ. Rsch. Adminstrs., Assn. of Univ. Technology Mgrs., Med. Group Mgmt. Assn. Methodist. Office: U Mich Med Sch M7336 1301 Catherine St Ann Arbor MI 48109-0624

ELGUEZABAL, LUIS EMILIO, food distribution company executive; b. Cienfuegos, Cuba, Nov. 6, 1944; came to U.S., 1960, naturalized, 1969; s. Domingo and Dolores (Hernandez) E.; B. Bus. Sci., Tulane U., 1965; m. Dora Angelica Palma, Aug. 22, 1965; children: Dora Angelica, Luis Emilio. With Chiquita Brands Co., 1966-72, 78—; dir. internat. info. systems support group, Framingham, Mass., 1978—; owner, operator Servicios Electronicos de Datos, S.A., Panama, 1972-78. Mem. Data Processing Mgmt. Assn., Internat. IBM Users Group (past chmn.), Data Processing Mgmt. Assn. Roman Catholic. Home: 3033 Prestwicke Dr Edgewood KY 41017 Office: Chiquita Brands Co 250 E 5th St Cincinnati OH 45202-4103

ELIASON, JON TATE, electrical engineer; b. Menominee, Mich., Mar. 23, 1938; s. Edwin Adolph and Irene Albertyn (Longlais) E.; m. Barbara Ann Love, July 2, 1960 (div. Dec. 1980); children: Ellen Artimese, Eric Alan, Eileen Amber; m. Kathleen Ann Vitell, May 25, 1996. BS in Sci. Engring., U. Mich., 1960; MS in Physics, Oreg. State U., 1966. Registered profl. engr., Ala. Engr. Vallecitos Nuclear Lab. GE, Pleasanton, Calif., 1964-66; sr. staff engr., engring. cons. Sperry Rand Corp., Huntsville, Ala., 1966-76; sr. staff engr. Martin Marietta Corp., Denver, 1976-84; master program engr., group engr. Sundstrand Corp., Rockford, Ill., 1984-92; engr. Insight Industries, Inc., Platteville, Wis., 1993-96, Insight Info. Inc., Platteville, Wis., 1996—. Patentee in field. Recipient New Tech. award NASA, 1973, 75; Regents/Alumni scholar U. Mich., 1956-60. Mem. IEEE, AIAA, Am. Phys. Soc., Sigma Pi Sigma, (chpt. pres. 1963-64). Office: PO Box 7231 Rockford IL 61126-7231

ELIASON, LARRY ELMER, education educator; b. Detroit, Oct. 8, 1936; s. Alfred O. and Evelyn W. (Aldridge) E.; m. Linda J. Macy, Aug. 7, 1971. BA in Edn., Western Wash. Coll., Bellingham, 1961, std. gen. cert., 1965; MA, U. Iowa, 1976. Cert. permanent profl. tchr. Iowa. Tchr. Highline Pub. Schs., Burien, Wash., 1961-69, Oskaloosa (Iowa) Pub. Schs., 1969—; adj. instr. edn. William Penn Coll., Oskaloosa, 1970—, N.E. Mo. U., Kirksville, 1973, Vennard Coll., University Park, Iowa, 1987—, Ctrl. Coll., Pella, Iowa, 1988—; advisor, bd. mem. Jack & Jill Presch., Oskaloosa, 1974-79; chmn. supt adv. bd. pub. schs., Oskaloosa, 1971-75; human rels. adv. bd. William Penn Coll., Oskaloosa, 1974-79. Mem. bd. Oskaloosa Pub. Libr., 1986-89. With Signal Corps U.S. Army, 1955-58. Named Outstanding Tchr. Hoover Presdl. Libr., West Branch, Iowa, 1991. Mem. NEA, Iowa Edn. Assn., Oskaloosa Edn. Assn. Mem. Soc. of Friends. Home: 1709 Lacey Dr Oskaloosa IA 52577 Office: Whittier Sch 604 North B Oskaloosa IA 52577

ELITZIK, PAUL, publishing executive; b. N.Y.C., May 11, 1945; s. Harold and Mary (Bunin) E.; m. Margaret Wiedmann, June 29, 1974; children: Laurie, Nicholas. BA, CUNY, 1966; AM in Classical Philosophy, Harvard U., 1971. Dir. Lake View Press, Chgo., 1981—; faculty advisor student newspaper Sch. of Art Inst. Chgo., 1984-95, dir. student publs. dept., 1995—; cons. Sch. Art Inst. Chgo. Press, 1993—; v.p. Ill. Book Pubs. Assn., 1994—. Woodrow Wilson fellow Woodrow Wilson Found., 1966-67. Office: Lake View Press PO Box 578279 Chicago IL 60657

ELKINS, JAMES PAUL, physician; b. Lincoln, Nebr., Mar. 20, 1924; s. James Hill and Antonia (Wohler) E.; MD, U. Va., 1947; m. May Hollingsworth Reynolds, June 15, 1946; children—Patricia May Elkins Riggs, Paulette Frances Elkins Phillips, James Barrington. Cert. Emergency Med. Svcs. Commn. Intern, DePaul Hosp., Norfolk, Va., 1947-48; resident in ob-gyn Alexandria (Va.) Hosp., 1948-49, Franklin Sq. Hosp., Balt., 1949-50, St. Rita's Hosp., Lima, Ohio, 1950, Tripler Army Hosp., Honolulu, 1953-54; practice medicine specializing in ob-gyn, Indpls., 1954-73; chief ob-gyn St. Francis Hosp., Beech Grove, Ind., 1965-66; mem. teaching staff Gen. Hosp., Indpls., 1954-73; dep. coroner Marion County, 1965-74; ret. med. cons. disability determination div. Ind. Rehab. Svcs.; ringside physician Ind. State Athletic Commn., Ind. Golden Gloves, Indpls. Pal Club, 1976-86; retired med. cons. Served with AUS, 1949-54. Recipient Fred Deborde Award Ind. Golden Gloves, 1985. Mem. Am. Coll. Ob-Gyn, Ind. State Med. Assn., Marion County Med. Soc., Indpls. Press Club (hon. life), Police League Ind., Fraternal Order Police, Nat. Sojourners, Ind. Sports Corp. (charter gold mem.), U.S. Auto Club (life), Phi Chi. Clubs: Ind. Pacers Booster (charter), Thundering Herd Booster Indpls. Colts (charter mem.). Lodges: Masons, Shriners (life). Home: 11603 Boone Dr Indianapolis IN 46229-9610

ELKINS, KEN JOE, broadcasting executive; b. Prenter, W.Va., Oct. 12, 1937; s. Ernest Eugene Elkins and Gay (Avis) Dodrill; married; children: James, Diana. Student, Nebr. U., 1966-69. Engr. Sta. KETV-TV, Omaha, 1960-67, asst. chief engr., 1967-70, ops. mgr., nat. sales, gen. sales mgr., 1972-75, gen. mgr., 1975-80; chief engr. Sta. KOUB-TV, Dubuque, Iowa, 1970-71, gen. mgr., 1971-72; gen. mgr. Sta. KSDK-TV, St. Louis, 1980-81; v.p., CEO Pulitzer Broadcasting Co., St. Louis, 1981-84, pres., CEO, 1984—; bd. dirs. Commerce Bank St. Louis, Maximum Svc. Telecasters, Washington, BMI; pres. Nebr. Broadcasters, Omaha, 1979-80; chmn. NBC Affiliate Bd. Govs. Bd. dirs. BJC Health Sys. With USAF, 1957-61. Inducted into Nebr. Broadcasters Hall of Fame, 1990. Mem. Nat. Assn. Broadcasters (1st amendment com. Washington chpt. 1986-91, 1st amendment com. 19866), Found. Broadcasters Hall of Fame (bd. dirs., trustee 1990), TV Operators Caucus, Algonquin Club. Home: 720 Twin Fawns Dr Saint Louis MO 63131-4722 Office: Pulitzer Broadcasting Co 101 S Hanley Rd Ste 1250 Saint Louis MO 63105-3406

ELKINS, SHARON PATRICIA, nursing educator; b. Monticello, Ky., Jan. 30, 1948; d. James G. and Mary J. (Jones) Ragan; m. Garis Elkins Jr., June 18, 1966; children: Alicia Jael, John Garis, Amy Elizabeth. ASN, Ind. U., 1985, BSN, 1992; MS, Ball State U., 1996. Nursing edn. coord. Henry County Meml. Hosp., New Castle, Ind., 1985—. Mem. Sigma Theta Tau. Home: 7679 E 100th N Hagerstown IN 47346

ELLEFSON, KAREN ANN, physical therapist; b. Milw., Mar. 23, 1945; d. Stanley Vincent and Mary (Dounar) Zbikowski; m. Julian John Ellefson, Nov. 2, 1968; children: Kirsten Ann, Lindsay Ann. BS in Phys. Medicine, U. Wis., 1968. Staff phys. therapist Curative Workshop, Green Bay, Wis., 1969-70, St. Francis Hosp., Milw., 1970-72, Sage Nursing Home, Milw., 1972-75, Wis. Therapy Svcs., Waukesha, 1975-84, Sport Clinic Greater Milw., Wauwatosa, 1984-85; owner, dir. pvt. practice Phys. Therapy Ctr. of Waukesha, 1985—; cons. Waukesha Sports Medicine, 1994—; mem. adv. bd. Sch. Edn., Phys. Therapy Ctr., U. Wis., Madison, 1994—. Mem. Am. Phys. Therapy Assn., Wis. Phys. Therapy Assn., Wis. Ind. Phys. Therapists (treas., bd. dirs. U. Wis. chpt. 1994—), Wis. Alumni Assn., Envisions. Roman Catholic. Home: W 273 N 893 Rabby Ln Waukesha WI 53188

ELLERHOFF, ROGER DALE, securities company executive; b. Ames, Iowa, May 17, 1955. BBA in Fin., U. Iowa, 1978. Salesman Plumbers Supply, Iowa City, 1978-82; agt., registered rep. various ind. ins. cos., Iowa City, 1982-90; sr. v.p. MidAm. Securities Mgmt. Co., Iowa City, 1990—. Lutheran. Office: MidAm Securities Mgmt Co 103 E College St Ste 100 Iowa City IA 52240-4008

ELLFELDT, HOWARD JAMES, orthopedic surgeon; b. Kansas City, Mo., Feb. 11, 1937; s. Howard James and Peggy Maude (Bowen) E.; m. Dee Anne Park, June 18, 1960; children: Kimberly, Jeffrey, Kamela, Kent. AB, U. Kans., 1959, MD, 1963. Cert. Am. Bd. Orthopedic Surgery. Intern U. Kans., 1963-64, intern in orthopedic surgery, 1964-68; pvt. practice specializing in orthopedic surgery Kansas City, Mo., 1970—; team physician Kansas City King's Basketball Club, 1972-84, Kansas City Chief's Football Club, 1973-90; chief of staff Rsch. Med. Ctr., Kansas City, 1984-85, bd. dirs. 1986-92; bd. dirs. Rsch. Health Svcs., Kansas City, 1985-91; pres. Rsch. Comprehensive Health Care, Inc., 1985-91. Bd. dirs. K-Life, Shawnee Mission, Kans., 1983-86. Served to maj. U.S. Army, 1968-70, Vietnam. Fellow Am. Acad. Orthopedic Surgeons; mem. ACS (diplomate), Am. Orthopedic Soc. for Sports Medicine, Am. Coll. Sports Medicine, Alpha Omega Alpha. Republican. Episcopalian. Club: Mission Hills (Kans.) Country. Home: 5701 W 119th St Overland Park KS 66209-3722 Office: Kans City Bone and Joint Clinic 6420 Prospect Ave Ste 207T Kansas City MO 64132-4127

ELLING, LADDIE JOE, agronomist, educator; b. Lawton, Okla., June 18, 1917; s. Otto Henry and Helen Mae (Pool) E.; m. Bethene Secrist, Aug. 15, 1942 (dec. 1974); children: Joe Kerry, Mary Elizabeth, Jean Anne Elling Edin; m. Helen Marie Wierschke, Mar. 27, 1976. BS, Okla. A&M Coll., Stillwater, 1941; MS, U. Minn., St. Paul, 1948, PhD, 1950. Instr. U. Minn., St. Paul, 1950, rsch. assoc., 1950-53, asst. prof. agronomy, 1953-58, assoc. prof., 1958-68, prof., 1968-85, prof. emeritus, 1985—; cons. Barzen Seed Co., Mpls., 1960-61, Peterson Biddick Co., WAdena, Minn., 1985-92. Contbr. articles to profl. jours. Pres. Arden Hills North Homes Assn., 1988-92. Capt. U.S. Army, 1941-46. Recipient Horace T. Morse Teaching award, U. Minn., 1970. Fellow Crop Sci. Soc. Am.; mem. Torch Internat. (pres. 1988-90), Alpha Zeta, Gamma Sigma Delta, Phi Sigma, Phi Theta Kappa. Methodist. Home: 1472 Arden View Dr Saint Paul MN 55112-1942

ELLINGER, JOHN MICHAEL, university administrator; b. Columbus, Ohio, Oct. 19, 1948; s. Harley Andrew and Florence Louise (Karn) E.; m. Clair Elizabeth Wuichet, June 20, 1970; children: Eve Melinda, Daniel Matthew, Justin Marc. BS, Ohio State U., 1970, MS, 1972; postgrad., Kent (Ohio) State U., 1975-76, Ind. U., 1980. Acad. advisor Ohio State U., Columbus, 1970-72; coord. FBPA Tri-County Joint Vocat. Sch., Nelsonville, Ohio, 1972-73; coord. FBPA Wayne County Career Ctr., Smithville, Ohio, 1976-79, supr., 1976-79; assoc. dir. Ohio Unions-Ohio State U., Columbus, 1979-83, dir., 1983-88; asst. v.p. Agrl. Administr.-Ohio State U., Columbus, 1988-94; dir. A.R.M.S. Project Ohio State U., 1994—. Co-author Outdoor Awareness, 1979. Chairperson United Way-Ohio State U., 1991-94, Ameriflora '92, 1989-93; trustee Columbus Assn. for Childbirth Edn., 1980-86. Capt. USAF. Recipient Hon. Degree Ohio FFA Assn., 1992, Disting. Svc. award Ohio Spl. Olympics, 1984. Mem. Ohio Staters, Inc., Upper Arlington Civic Assn., Am. Vocat. Assn. (life), Ohio State U. Alumni Assn. (life, Wayne County 1975-77), Sphinx Hon. (advisor 1986—), Alpha Zeta (trustee, 1981-89, Disting. Svc. 1988), Assn. of Coll. Unions Internat. (Disting. Svc. 1995). Republican. Methodist. Office: Ohio State U R501 2050 Kenny Rd Columbus OH 43221

ELLINGSON, JULIE ANN SCHAFF, public relations professional; b. Bismarck, N.D., July 14, 1974; d. Martin Lawrence and Angie Elizabeth (Leintz) Schaff; m. Chad Jason Ellingson, July 21, 1995. AS, Bismarck State Coll., 1993; BS, N.D. State U., 1995. Reporter Mandan (N.D.) News/Bus. Jour.; comm. dir. N.D. Stockmen's Assn., Bismarck. Mem. Soc. Prof. Journalists, Pub. Rels. Student Soc. Am. Roman Catholic. Home: 2100 County Rd 135 Saint Anthony ND 58566 Office: ND Stockmens Assn 407 S 2nd St Bismarck ND 58504

ELLINGSON, LYNN MARIE, flight attendant; b. Mpls., June 5, 1957; d. Marvin Leslie and Jeanette Amanda (Tollefson) E. Student, Oxford U., Eng., 1977-78; BA in English magna cum laude, St. Olaf Coll., 1979; postgrad., U. Minn., 1988, 94; MALS summa cum laude, Hamline U., 1993. Secondary tchr. Kodaikanal Internat. Sch., Tamil Nadu, India, 1979; freelance writer, photographer, 1979—; flight attendant N.W. Airlines, St. Paul, 1980—; writer, photographer, graphic designer corporate newsletter, 1989; guest speaker various chs. and schs. 1981—. Author, photographer travel articles Inflight Mag. 1985, 86, 87. Vol. pub. and correctional schs., 1976-79, Mother Teresa's Missionaries of Charity, Calcutta, India, Home for the Dying, 1981, 82; orphan escort Ams. for Internat. Aid, 1981, 92. Home: 13791 Heywood Ct Saint Paul MN 55124-6519 Office: NW Airlines MS 575 Mpls St Paul Airport Saint Paul MN 55111

ELLINGTON, HOWARD WESLEY, architect; b. Anthony, Kans., Mar. 2, 1938; s. John Wesley and Cressie May (Wilson) E.; m. Nelda Lee Newlin, Sept. 5, 1959; children: Howard Wesley II, Eric John, Craig Alan, Amy Lee. BArch, U. Kans., 1961. Registered architect, Kans., N.Mex., Mo., Ohio. Prin. Howard W. Ellington, AIA, Architect, Wichita, Kans., 1979—; co-owner Gallery Ellington, Wichita; founding trustee Kans. Cultural Trust, Wichita, 1985—; mem. bldg. and grounds com. Wichita Ctr. for Arts, trustee, 1995; bd. dirs. arts com. Ulrich Mus., Wichita; founding trustee, exec. dir. Allen-Lambe House Found., Wichita, 1990—. Editor: The Prairie Print Makers, 1984. Trustee Wichita Ctr. for the Arts, 1995—; bd. dirs. Wichita-Sedgwick County Arts & Humanities Coun., 1996—. Recipient Kans. Preservation award, 1993, Pedestal award, 1996. Mem. Friends of Wichita Art Mus., Western Penn. Conservation, Nat. Trust Historic Preservation, Chgo. Archtl. Found., Frank Lloyd Wright Home and Studio Found., Birger Sandzen Meml. Gallery. Republican. Episcopalian. Office: 350 N Rock Rd Wichita KS 67206-2257

ELLIOTT, BARBARA JEAN, librarian; b. Bluffton, Ind., Oct. 2, 1927; d. Dale A. and Gwendolyn I. (Long); m. Robert J. Elliott, June 13, 1949; 1 son, Michael Roger. B.S. with honors, Ind. U., 1949, M.L.S., 1979. Dir. tech. info. services uranium div. Mallinckrodt Chems., St. Louis, 1949-59; research librarian Petrolite Corp., Webster Groves, Mo., 1961-63; head tech. services St. Frances Coll., Ft. Wayne, Ind., 1974-76; dir. Bluffton-Wells County Pub. Library, 1976-95, ret. Pres. Wells County Found., 1995. Mem. ALA, Ind. Library Assn. (fed. legis. coordinator), LWV of Ind. (state sec. 1981-83, chmn. health care 1983-89, 3d vice pres. 1985-86), Ind. Bus. and Profl. Women (pres., dist. dir. 1988-93). Club: Bluffton Garden (v.p. 1983-87), Wells Co. Coun. on Aging (sec. 1996—, pres., 1996—). Home: 6831 SE State Rd 116 Bluffton IN 46714-9420

ELLIOTT, BRUCE R., electronics engineer; b. Marquette, Wis., Aug. 20, 1968. BSEE, U. Wis., Platteville, 1992. Electronics design engr. Standish Industries, Lake Mills, Wis., 1992—. Mem. IEEE. Republican. Home: 1199 N 4th St Watertown WI 53098-3235 Office: Standish Industries W 7514 Hwy V Lake Mills WI 53551

ELLIOTT, EDDIE MAYES, academic administrator; b. Grain Valley, Mo., Sept. 12, 1938; s. Franklin E. and Edna Mae (Rowe) E.; m. Sandra Temple, Nov. 23, 1960; children: Glenn, Gregg, Grant. AB, William Jewell Coll., 1960; MA, Columbia U., 1964; EdD, U. No. Colo., 1969. Tchr. Harrisonville (Mo.) High Sch., 1960-61, Excelsior Springs (Mo.) Pub. Schs., 1961-63, The Trinity Sch., N.Y.C., 1963-64; mem. faculty dept. phys. edn. CUNY, 1964-65; chmn. athletics, coach Mo. Valley Coll., Marshall, 1965-71; dir. grad. studies Wayne (Nebr.) State Coll., 1971-73, dean spl. studies, 1973-75, v.p., 1975-82, pres., 1982-85; pres. Cen. Mo. State U., Warrensburg, 1985—; assoc. Ctr. for Planned Change, 1975-82; mem. adv. bd., bd. dirs. Nebr. Coun. on Econ. Edn., 1977-83; bd. incorporators Higher Edn. Strategic Planning Inst., 1981—; mem. Coun. Pub. Higher Edn. Mo.; bd. advisors Apple Restaurants Europe. Mem. land-grant mission adv. com. U. Mo. Named outstanding faculty mem. Wayne State Coll., 1973, to U. No. Colo. Alumni Hall of Fame, 1989; recipient Disting. Svc. award Wayne State Coll., 1986, Cecil R. Martin award William Jewell Coll., 1960, citation for achievement, 1986, Disting. Alumni award, 1986. Mem. AAUP, AAHPERD, Am. Assn. State Colls. and Univs. (task force on emerging issues, bd. dirs.), Assn. Governing Bds. (adv. com. on strengthening governance of pub. univs.), Am. Assn. Higher Edn., Am. Coll. Sports Medicine, North Ctrl. Assn. Evaluation Teams, Nat. Coun. Accreditation of Tchrs., Am. Assn. State Colls. & Univs. (chair pres.'s commn. tchr. edn. 1993-94), Mo. Corp. for Sci. and Tech., Warrensburg C. of C., Phi Kappa Phi. Office: Cen Mo State U Office of Pres Warrensburg MO 64093

ELLIOTT, LORA LOUISE, training executive; b. Indpls., Dec. 21, 1962; d. John Russell and Luella Lee (Greer) E. BS, U. Indpls., 1988. Mgr. Noble Roman's, Indpls., 1990-91, tng. dir., 1991-92, svc. trainer, 1990—. 1st lt. USAR, 1982—. Mem. NAFE, VFW. Republican. Methodist. Home: 5925 Dewey Ave Indianapolis IN 46219-7208 Office: USAR 21st TAACOM (CA) 2625 Kessler Blvd North Dr Nd Indianapolis IN 46222-2216

ELLIOTT, MARK T., state legislator; b. Carthage, Mo., July 18, 1956; m. Denise Ann Severn, 1976; children: Rhett Thomas, Haley Dawn, Hillery Ann. Student, Drake U., Mo. So. State Coll. State rep. dist. 126 Mo. Ho. of Reps., former state rep. dist. 127, asst. minority whip, mem. agrl. bus. com., appropriations natural and econ. resource, ethics com., human rights and resources com. Mem. Farm Bur. Home: 2 S Main St Webb City MO 64870-2326*

ELLIOTT, PEGGY GORDON, university president; b. Matewan, W.Va., May 27, 1937; d. Herbert Hunt and Mary Ann (Renfro) Gordon; children from previous marriage: Scott Vandling III, Anne Gordon. B.A., Transylvania Coll., 1959; M.A., Northwestern U., 1964; Ed.D., Ind. U., 1975. Tchr. Horace Mann High Sch., Gary, Ind., 1959-64; instr. English Ind. U. N.W., Gary, 1965-69, lectr. Edn., 1973-74, asst. prof. edn., 1975-78, assoc. prof., 1978-80, supr. secondary student teaching, 1973-74, dir. student teaching, 1975-77, dir. Office Field Experiences, 1977-78, dir. profl. devel., 1978-80, spl. asst. to chancellor, 1981-83, asst. to chancellor, 1983-84, acting chancellor, 1983-84, chancellor, 1984-92; instr. English Am. Inst. Banking, Gary, 1969-70; pres. U. Akron, Ohio, 1992—; vis. prof. U. Ark., 1979-80, U. Alaska, 1982; bd. dirs. Lubrizol Corp., A. Schulman Corp., Akron Tomorrow, Ohio Aerospace Consortium, Ohio Super Computer Com.; holder VA Harrington disting. chair edn., 1994—. Author: (with C. Smith) Reading Activities for Middle and Secondary Schools: A Handbook for Teachers, 1979, Reading Instruction for Secondary Schools, 1986, How to Improve Your Scores on Reading Competency Tests, 1981, (with C. Smith and G. Ingersoll) Trends in Educational Materials: Traditionals and the New Technologies, 1983, The Urban Campus: Educating a New Majority for a New Century, 1994, also numerous articles. Bd. dirs. Meth. Hosp., N.W. Ind. Forum, N.W. Ind. Symphony, Boys Club N.W. Ind., Akron Symphony, NBD Bank, John S. Knight Conv. Ctr., Inventure Pl., Akron Roundtable, Cleve. Com. Higher Edn. Recipient Disting. Alumni award Northwestern U., VA Disting. Alumni award, 1994, numerous grants; Am. Council on Edn. fellow in acad. adminstrn. Ind. U., Bloomington, 1980-81. Mem. Assn. Tchr. Educators (nat. pres. 1984-85, Disting. Mem. 1990), Nat. Acad. Tchrs. Edn. (bd. dirs. 1983—), Ind. Assn. Tchr. Educators (past pres.), North Ctrl. Assn. (commn. at large), Am. Assn. State Colls. and Univs. (bd. dirs.), Am. Coun. Edn. (bd. dirs.), Leadership Devel. Coun. ACE, Ohio Inter Univ. Coun. (chair), Internat. Reading Assn., Akron Urban League (bd. dirs.), P.E.O., Phi Delta Kappa (Outstanding Young Educator award), Delta Kappa Gamma (Leadership/Mgmt. fellow 1980), Pi Lambda Theta, Chi Omega. Episcopalian. Home: 856 Sunnyside Akron OH 44303 Office: U Akron Office of Pres Akron OH 44325-4702

ELLIOTT, PETER R., athletic organization executive; b. Bloomington, Ill., Sept. 29, 1926; s. Joseph Norman and Alice (Marquis) E.; m. s. Joan Connaught Slater, June 14, 1949; children: Bruce Norman, David Lawrence. B.A., U. Mich., 1949. Asst. football coach Oreg. State U., 1949-50, U. Okla., 1951-55; head football coach Nebr. U., 1956, U. Calif., Berkeley, 1957-59, U. Ill., 1960-66, U. Miami, Fla., 1973-74; dir. athletics U. Miami, 1974-78; asst. football coach St. Louis Cardinals, 1978; exec. dir. Pro Football Hall of Fame, Canton, Ohio, 1979—. Served with USNR, 1944-45. Named to Mich. Sports Hall of Fame, 1983, Coll. Football Hall of Fame, 1994. Mem. Am. Football Coaches Assn. (Region 8 Coach of Yr. 1958, Region 5 Coach of Yr. 1963). Presbyterian. Home: 3003 Dunbarton Ave NW Canton OH 44708-1818 Office: Nat Football Mus Inc 2121 Harrison Ave NW Canton OH 44708-2613

ELLIOTT, ROBERT BETZEL, physician; b. Ada, Ohio, Dec. 8, 1926; s. Floyd Milton and Rose Marguerite (Betzel) E.; m. Margaret Mary Robichaux, Aug. 26, 1954; children: Howard A., Michael D., Robert Bruce, Douglas J., John C., Joan O. BA, Ohio No. U., 1949; MD, U. Cin., 1953. Diplomate Am. Bd. Family Practice. Intern Charity Hosp., New Orleans, 1953-54; resident in pathology Bapt. Meml. Hosp., Memphis, 1958-59; practice medicine specializing in family practice Ada, 1959—; mem. staff Ohio No. U. Health Service, Ada, 1960-70; coroner Hardin County, 1973-93. Mem. Ada Exempted Village Sch. Bd., 1960—, pres., 1966-69, 72—, v.p. 1971—. Named Ohio Family Physician of Yr., 1985. Mem. AMA, Ohio State Med. Assn., Hardin County Med. Soc. (pres. 1964), Am. Acad. Family Physicians, Ohio Acad. Family Physicians, Lima Acad. Family Physicians, Am. Coll. Health Assn. Democrat. Presbyterian. Lodges: Masons, Elks. Home: 4429 State Route 235 Ada OH 45810-9509 Office: 302 N Main St Ada OH 45810-1112

ELLIOTT, SUSAN SPOEHRER, information technology executive; b. St. Louis, May 4, 1937; d. Charles Henry and Jane Elizabeth (Baur) Spoehrer; m. Howard Elliott Jr., Sept. 2, 1961; children: Kathryn Elliott Love, Elizabeth Gray. AB, Smith Coll., 1958. Systems engr. IBM, St. Louis, 1958-66; pres., founder Sys. Svc. Enterprises, Inc., St. Louis, 1966—; systems analyst Mo. State Dept. Edn., Jefferson City, Mo., 1967-70; systems coord. Boatmen's Nat. Bank, St. Louis, 1979-83; bd. dirs., mem. exec. com. Mo. Automobile Club; class C dir., dep. chmn. Fed. Res. Bd., St. Louis, 1996—, St. Louis Zoo; bd. dirs. St. Louis Regional Commerce and Growth Assn., sec. bd. dirs., 1991-94. Trustee, vice chmn. Mary Inst., St. Louis, 1976-89, Webster U., 1987—; commr., vice chmn. St. Louis Civil Svc. Commn., 1985-86, Mo. Lottery Commn., Jefferson City, 1985-87; mem. corp. partnership coun. St. Louis Sci. Ctr.; mem. pres.'s adv. coun. area coun. Girl Scouts U.S.; class C dir., dep. chmn. Fed. Res. Bank St. Louis, 1996—. Mem. Internat. Women's Forum. Republican. Presbyterian. Office: Sys Svc Enterprises Inc 795 Office Pky Ste 101 Saint Louis MO 63141-7166

ELLIOTT-WATSON, DORIS JEAN, psychiatric, mental health and gerontological nurse educator; b. Caney, Kans., Dec. 6, 1932; d. Alva Orr and Mary Amelia (Boyns) Elliott; children Marsha Jean Watson, Sherwood Elliott Watson. BE, U. Miami, Fla., 1952, MEd, 1954; EdD, Pacific Western U., 1982; BSN, U. Kans., 1985; AS in Psychology, Kansas City (Kans.) C.C., 1989; AA in Music, Kansas City C.C., 1994. RN, Kans., Mo.; cert. clin. specialist gerontology nurse, gerontology nurse generalist, psychiat.-mental health nurse, med.-surg. nurse, ANCC; cert. elem. to jr. coll. tchr., Kans., Mo.; lic. adult care home adminstr., Kans. Tchr. learning disabled, gifted, emotionally disturbed Shawnee Mission, Kans., 1961-76; instr. hospitalized psychiat. and med.-surg. children U. Kans. Med. Ctr., Kansas City, 1979-82; pvt. practice, gerontol. nurse educator Bonner Springs, Kans., 1985—; libr. U. Miami, 1952, Kans. U., 1978; nurse ARC, Kansas City, 1985—; nurse educator Am. Heart Assn., Kansas City, 1985—; program designer mainstreaming spl. needs children into regular classrooms, 1969; specialist geriatric sexuality nursing homes, 1986. Editor Park Stylus, Parkville, Mo., 1952; author, speaker Kansas City area, 1950—. Tutor-organizer Tutoring Vol.Orgn. for Inner City Children, 1965-68; sustaining mem. Rep. Nat. Com., Washington, 1978—, rep. Congl. Com., 1978—, Rep. Senatorial Com., 1978—; pres. Young Reps., Kansas City, 1960; mem. Rep. Nat. Conv. Platform Planning Com., 1995; patron, charter mem. Kaw Valley Cmty. Choir, 1990-92; mem. Kansas City Cmty. Choir, 1992—, mem. tour of cathedrals Christ Ch., Oxford and King's Coll., Eng., 1993; mem. Mid. Am. Nazarene Coll. Cmty. Choir, 1993—, Leavenworth Cmty. Carnegie Choir, 1994—. Recipient Coast to Coast 2810 miles award Am. Running and Fitness Assn., 1994; inducted Rep. Nat. Hall of Honor, Rep. Nat. Conv., 1992. Mem. ANA (coun. on gerontol. nurses, coun. for cmty., primary care and long term care nursing practice, coun. for nursing rsch.), NEA (life, del. state conv. 1980, nat. conv. 1973), Kans. Nurses Assn., U. Kans. Alumni Assn., Bus. and Profl. Women, Order Ea. Star (Electra 1982, Martha 1994, Marshal 1995, Assoc. Conductress 1996), Order Rainbow for Girls (worthy advisor 1950), Am. Volkssport Assn. (Tri-Athlete 1993, 94, 95, 4500 Km Walking award 1993, 5500Km 1994, Sunflower State Games Athlete 1993, 94, 95, Sooner State Games Athlete award 1994, 95, Mid-Am. Walking Marathon 1994, 6500 Km Walking award 1995), Tiblow Trailblazers Walking Club (pres. 1993—), Nat. Wildlife Fedn. (cert. backyard wildlife habitat 1994), Kappa Delta Pi, Pi Delta Epsilon, Phi Theta Kappa, Alpha Kappa Delta, Phi Alpha Theta. Home and Office: 231 Sheidley Ave Bonner Springs KS 66012-1410

ELLIOTT-ZAHORIK, BONNIE, nurse, administrator; b. Algona, Iowa. AAS, Coll. Lake County, Grayslake, Ill., 1979; student, U. Iowa; BS, Coll. St. Francis, Joliet, Ill., 1988; MSM, Nat. Louis U., Evanston, Ill., 1989; doctoral fellow, Walden U., Mpls., 1995—. RN, Ill.; CCRN; cert. nurse adminstr.-advanced; cert. critical care preceptor and instr. Evening nurse dir. Victory Meml. Hosp., Waukegan, Ill., 1991—; adminstrn./mgmt. doctoral fellow Walden U., Mpls., 1995—. Contbr. articles to profl. jours. Mem. AACN, Ill. Coun. Nurse Mgrs. (pres. Region 2B).

ELLIS, ARTHUR BARON, chemist, educator; b. Lakewood, Ohio, Apr. 4, 1951; s. Nathan and Carolyn Joan (Agulnick) E.; m. Susan Harriet Trebach, Nov. 9, 1975; children: Joshua, Margot. BS, Calif. Inst. Tech., 1973; PhD, MIT, 1977. Asst. prof. chemistry U. Wis., Madison, 1977-82, assoc. prof., 1982-84, prof., 1984-86, Meloche-Bascom prof., 1986—. Editor: Chemistry and Structure at Interfaces, 1986; patentee in field; contbr. articles to profl. jours. Fellow A.P. Sloan Found., 1981, H.I. Romnes fellow U. Wis., 1985, Guggenheim fellow, 1989; recipient Nat. Catalyst Tchg. award Chem. Mfrs. Assn., 1994. Mem. Am. Chem. Soc. (Exxon fellow 1980), Electrochem. Soc. Jewish. Office: U Wis Dept Chemistry 1101 University Ave Madison WI 53706-1322

ELLIS, BRENDA LEE, mathematician, computer scientist, consultant, educator; b. Norfolk, Va., Jan. 4, 1965; d. Lester and Annie Mae (Leak) E. BS cum laude, Norfolk State U., 1987; postgrad., Old Dominion U., 1988-89, Cleve. State U., 1991, Hampton U., 1994. Computer clk. Naval Electronics Systems Engrng. Ctr., Portsmouth, Va., 1986-88; rsch. asst. Old Dominion U., Norfolk, 1988-89; computer analyst Dept. Def., Ft. Meade, Md., 1989; mathematician NASA Lewis Rsch. Ctr., Cleve., 1989—; lab. dir., instrnl. support Norfolk State U., 1993-95; tutor SAT tutorial Bethel H.S., 1994; panelist Sonia Kovalesky Math. Day, Cleve. State U., 1990-92, workshop facilitator Nat. Soc. Black Engrs., 1996; guest spkr. Math. Counts Workshop, 1991; mentor Hampton U., 1994; tax preparer H&R Block, 1994. Author: Tips for Effective Study: From F to A, 1996. Usher Rock Ch., Virginia Beach, 1983-91, Mt. Calvary Bapt. Ch., Cleve., 1991; vol. Combined Fed. Campaign, Cleve., 1991, Norfolk Community Hosp., 1982; tutor, mentor, sci. fair coord. East Tech. High Sch., Cleve., 1991-92; meet dir. Lake Erie Indoor Track Field Championship, 1992. Recipient 1st pl. North Coast Relays, 1991-92, Group Achivement awards NASA, 1991, 93-94, Svc. award, 1995, Appreciation award Norfolk State U., 1995. Mem. IEEE, NAFE, Am. Bus. Womens Assn., Nat. Tech. Assn. (exec. sec. Cleve. chpt.), Assn. Computing Machinery (acting sec. 1986-87), Norfolk State U. Alumni (co-chair spl. projects com. 1993), Worth Sharing Comm., Black Data Processing Assn., Bus. and Profl. Women Orgn. (Young Careerist of Yr. 1996), Internat. Platform Assn., Over the Hill Track Club (v.p. 1991-92), Beta Kappa Chi. Baptist. Office: NASA Lewis Rsch Ctr 21000 Brookpark Rd Cleveland OH 44135-3127

ELLIS, MICHAEL EUGENE, documentary film producer, writer, director; b. Murphysboro, Ill., Aug. 1, 1946; s. Robert Eugene and Lula May (Williams) E. BS, So. Ill. U., Carbondale, 1971. Asst. to pres. So. Ill. U., 1970; asst. dir. Ill. Info. Svc., Springfield, 1971-72; mgr. press rels. Ill. Ho. of Reps., Springfield, 1973-77; dep. dir. com. Rep. Nat. Com., Washington, 1977; pres. Lincana Corp., Springfield, 1978-80; mgr. mktg. presentations Ill. Dept. Commerce, Springfield, 1980-91; prin. The DV Partnership, Loami, Ill., 1993—; dir. devel. and pub. rels. Sparc Inc., Springfield, 1993—. Coauthor: Work and the College Student, 1975; author: Elements of Political Public Relations, 1977; author film scripts, 1983—. Dir. comm. Pres. Ford Com. in Ill., Chgo., 1976; mem. Ill. Rep. Com., Springfield, Rep. Presdl. Task Force, Washington, Sangamon Rep. Found., Springfield. Recipient Gold Award Advt. Assn., Springfield, Ill., 1987-89. Mem. Internat. Communications Industry Assn., Am. Film Inst., Assn. for Multi Image Internat., World Affairs Coun.. Home: 627 Witherspoon Dr Springfield IL 62704 Office: Sparc Inc 1 Sparc Ctr Plz 232 Bruns Ln Springfield IL 62702

ELLIS, MICHAEL G., state legislator; b. Neenah, Wis., Feb. 21, 1941; married. BS, U. Wis., Oshkosh, 1965. Horse breeder, farmer; mem. Wis. State Assembly, Madison, 1970-82; mem. from dist. 19 Wis. State Senate, Madison, 1982—, former minority leader, now majority leader; Alderman City of Neenah. Office: 1752 County Road Gg Neenah WI 54956-9762 also: State Senate State Capitol Madison WI 53702*

ELLIS, NANETTE C., home-based specialist; b. Georgetown, Tex., Aug. 1, 1943; d. Ernest Nelson and Gladys Beatrice (Anderson) Johnson; m. Howard Norman Ellis, July 18, 1970; children: Jay, Heidi, Kirsten. BS, Tex. Luth. Coll., Sequin, 1965; MEd, Lincoln U., Jefferson City, Mo., 1990. Rsch. technician Shrine Burns Hosp. for Crippled Children, Galveston, Tex., 1966-70, U. Tex. Med. Br., Galveston, 1965-66, 70-71; dir. family planning OEO, Galveston, 1971-72; in-sch. suspension supr. Dubuque (Iowa) Sr. High Sch., 1979-80; substitute tchr. Cheylin High Sch., Bird City, Kans., 1980-84; tchr. sci. Jefferson City High Sch., 1984-90; guidance counselor Russellville (Mo.) High Sch., 1990-95; home-based specialist Luth. Child and Family Svcs., Randolph County, Ill., 1996—. Contbr. articles to profl. jours. Primary election judge Rep. Party, Galveston, 1968-72; county sec., del. to Rep. State Confs., 1966, 70; v.p. Cheyenne County Com. on Alcohol and Drug Abuse, St. Francis, Kans., 1981-84; mem. subcom. Human Rels. Commn. for Prison Reform, Galveston, 1969-70; dir. Trinity Luth. Confirmation Choir, 1984-92; mem. com. on discipline Evang. Luth. Ch. in Am., 1991-97; multicultural change team Cen. States Synod, 1991-95, parish ministry Assoc. Cen. States Synod. Recipient various awards. Mem. Am. Assn. Christian Counselors. Home: Box 280 Campbell Hill IL 62916 Office: Lutheran Child & Family Svcs Ill 2408 Lebanon Ave Belleville IL 62221

ELLIS, PETER, editor. Mng. editor Argus Leader. Office: Argus Leader PO Box 5034 200 S Minnesota Ave Sioux Falls SD 57117-5034*

ELLIS, TRAVIS KYLE, research and development project leader; b. Pocahontas, Iowa, Jan. 4, 1971. Project leader Gomaco Corp., Ida Grove, Iowa, 1991—. With U.S. Army, 1988-92. Recipient Top 100 New Product award Equip. News, 1993. Mem. Pheasants Forever. Office: Gomaco Hwys 59 and 175 Ida Grove IA 51445

ELLIS, WILLIAM RAY, soil scientist, agronomist researcher; b. Hanford, Calif., Aug. 16, 1952; s. Chester Wayne and Laura Janette (Milwee) E.; m. Peggy Elaine Glessner, May 27, 1952; children: Karin Christine, Bethany Jane. AS, Fresno City Coll., 1973; BA, Calif. State U., Fresno, 1975; MS, Wash. State U., 1979; PhD, U. Minn., 1982. Cert. profl. soil scientist, agronomist. Rsch. scientist USDA ARS, St. Paul, 1982-84; dir. Urbana Labs., St. Joseph, Mo., 1985-89, Seedbiotics, St. Joseph, Mo., 1989-95; dir. ops. Urbana Labs., St. Joseph, Mo., 1995—; bd. dirs. Alfalfa Crop Adv. Com. USDA, Beltsville, Md., 1986—; mem. sci.adv. coun. Am. Seed Rsch. Found., 1991—. Author: (book chapter) Plant Proteolytic Enzymes, 1986, Breeding Legumes for Enhanced Symbiotic Nitrogen Fixation, 1984. Bd. dirs. Allied Arts Coun., St. Joseph, 1989-91; solicitor United Way, St. Joseph, 1988-91. Mem. AAAS, Am. Soc. Microbiology, Crop Sci. Soc. Am., Soil Sci. Soc. Am., Am. Soc. Agronomy, St. Joseph Host Lions Club (dir. 1992—). Office: Urbana Labs PO Box 1393 Saint Joseph MO 64502-1393

ELLISON, DAVID WALTER, editor; b. Columbus, Ohio, Aug. 25, 1949; s. Walter Eugene and Laura Irene (Stecher) E.; m. Barbara Jean Robbins, Aug. 23, 1969; children: Mark Douglas, Margaret Anne. Student, Huntington Coll., 1969-74. Dept. worker Kroger Co., Piqua, Ohio, 1970-83; editor IRS, Covington, Ky., 1985—. Coord. scouting Boy Scouts Am., Bright, Ind., 1984—. Home: 1291 Morgan Rd West Harrison IN 47060

ELLMAN, JUNE CHRISTINE, research consultant; b. Vermillion, S.D., June 26, 1950; d. Marvin Milton Scholten and Evely Marie Kuyper; m. Craig Robert Ellman, Aug. 4, 1972 (div.); children: Christina, Alexander, Angela. BS in Edn., Moorhead State Coll., 1972; MA in Edn., Augustana Coll., 1987; DEd, U. S.D., 1991. Asst. prof. Chadron (Nebr.) State Coll., 1992-94; cons., owner Rsch. Consulting Svc., Brookings, S.D., 1995—; vis. asst. prof. SUNY, Oswego, 1991-92. Mem. orgn. com. S.D. Parent to Parent Orgn., Sioux Falls, 1985-88; pres. local orgn. S.D. Edn. Assn., Brandon, 1981. Mem. APA (affiliate), Phi Delta Kappa. Address: 1929 8th St Brookings SD 57006-2528

ELLMANN, SHEILA FRENKEL, investment company executive; b. Detroit, June 8, 1931; d. Joseph and Rose (Neback) Frenkel; BA in English, U. Mich., 1953; m. William M. Ellmann, Nov. 1, 1953; children: Douglas Stanley, Carol Elizabeth, Robert Lawrence. Dir. Advance Glove Mfg. Co., Detroit, 1954-78; v.p. Frome Investment Co., Detroit, 1980—. Mem. U. Mich. Alumni Assn., Nat. Trust Hist. Preservation. Home: 28000 Weymouth Ct Farmington Hills MI 48334

ELLSTROM-CALDER, ANNETTE, marketing manager, clinical medicine educator; b. Duluth, Minn., Dec. 19, 1952; d. Raymond Charles Ellstrom and Ruth Elaine (Bloomquist) Larson; m. Jeffrey Ellstrom-Calder, July 30, 1982; children: Hannah, Ian. BA in Social Work, Psychology, Sociology, Concordia Coll., 1974; MSW, U. Wis., 1978. Group therapist N.D. State Indsl. Sch., 1973; social worker Fergus Falls (Minn.) State Hosp., 1974, Jackson County Dept. Social Services, Black River Falls, Wis., 1975-77; sr. clin. social worker U. Wis. Hosp., Madison, 1979-90, clin. instr. medicine, 1989—; mktg. mgr. Med. Media Assocs., Madison, 1990—; cons. Waupun (Wis.) Meml. Hosp., 1979-84, lectr. grad. sch. social work U. Wis., Madison, 1979-82, prin. investigator in rsch. U. Wis. Hosp., Madison, 1985—. Editor: A Guide to Patients and Families, 1984; mem. editl. bd. Advances in Renal Replacement Therapy; contbr. articles to profl. jours. Del. trustee, bd. dirs. Nat. Kidney Found., N.Y.C., 1983-91, chmn. bd. dirs., Milw., 1985-87, vice chmn., 1983-85, sec., 1982-83, chmn. patient svcs. com., 1981-82, bd. dirs., 1981—, chmn. nat. tng. and edn. com., mem. nat. patient svcs. com., N.Y.C., 1987-91, mem. pers. com., bd. dirs. Madison chpt., 1979-80; bd. dirs. Combined Health Appeal Wis., 1990—, sec., 1992—; mem. nat. rsch. com. Am. Assn. Spinal Cord Injury Psychologists and Social Workers, N.Y.C., 1988—. Recipient Health Advancement award Nat. Kidney Found. Wis., 1985, Vol. Yr. award Nat. Kidney Found. Wis., 1984, Vol. Service award Nat. Kidney Found. Wis., 1983, Nat. Nephrology Social Worker of Yr. Merit award Nat. Kidney Found. and Council of Nephrology Social Workers, 1987; hon. adoptee Winnebago Indian Tribe, 1978; named Outstanding Young Wisconsinite Wisc. Jaycees, 1988. Mem. Council Nephrology Social Workers (nat. v.p. 1984-86, nat. exec. com. 1984-86, Nat. Nephrology Social Worker Yr. award 1987, mem. Nat. Rsch. Rev. com. 1996—), Nat. Assn. Social Workers, Pi Gamma Mu. Democrat. Office: Medical Media Assocs 585 Science Dr Ste B Madison WI 53711

ELLSWORTH, CYNTHIA ANN, counseling administrator; b. Springfield, Ohio, Jan. 19, 1950; d. Donald Harry and Jeanne Marie (Glover) E. BE, Western Conn. State U., 1972; M in Spl. Edn., Ohio U., 1976; Postgrad., Ohio State U., 1985-86; MS in Counseling, U. Dayton, 1988. Tchr. LBD Fed. Hocking Schs., Stewart, Ohio, 1972-76; supr. EMR/LBD Vinton County Schs., McArthur, Ohio, 1976-77; tchr. Southwestern City Schs., Grove City, Ohio, 1977-88, sch. counselor, 1989—. Mem. ACA, Am. Sch. Counselors Assn., Phi Delta Kappa. Office: 194 Winfall Dr Gahanna OH 43230-6204

ELMEN, GARY WARREN, principal; b. Chgo., Feb. 13, 1947; s. Warren N. and Oween C. (Michelson) E.; m. ELizabeth Caldwell, Apr. 4, 1980; children: Kathryn, Lindsay, Brittany. BA, U. Ill., 1968, MEd, 1970, EdD, 1995. Cert. tchr., Ill. Tchr. Downers Grove (Ill.) N. H.S., 1968-83, dean of students, 1983-84; asst. prin. Downers Grove S. H.S., 1984-87; prin. Waubonsie Valley H.S., Aurora, Ill., 1987—; mem. govs. property tax adv. commn. State of Ill., Springfield, 1974; trustee Golden Apple Found. for Excellence in Teaching, Chgo., 1989-96; chmn. Legis. Commn., Ill. H.S. Assn., Bloomington; mem. State Supts. Adv. Com., 1994-96. Elected trustee Ill. Tchrs. Retirement System, Springfield, 1979-91. Recipient Golden Achievement award Nat. Sch. Pub. Rels. Assn., 1986, Ill. Those Who Excel Merit award, 1995. Mem. ASCD, NEA (life), Am. Assn. Sch. Adminstrs., Nat. Assn. Secondary Sch. Prins., Ill. Prins. Assn., Kiwanis Internat., Phi Beta Kappa. Lutheran.

ELMER, W. OWEN, state legislator; b. McCook, Nebr., June 13, 1938; m. Donny J. Hoyt, 1959; children: Crinda K. (Mrs. McConville), Sharma L. (Mrs. Dunder), Lewis E., Jeana R. (Mrs. Kruger). Student, U. Nebr., 1956-58. Former agribusinessman Nebr.; mem. from dist. 44 Nebr. State Senate, Lincoln, 1986—, vice chmn. natural resources com., mem. agr. and gen. affairs coms. City councilman, Indianola, Nebr. Mem. Nebr. Petroleum Marketers, Nebr. Fertilization and Chem. Assn., Masons, Shriners, Rotary, Elks. Office: Nebr State Senate State Capitol Rm 2104 Lincoln NE 68509 also: State Legislature State Capital Lincoln NE 68516*

ELMETS, CRAIG ALLAN, dermatologist; b. Des Moines, Aug. 16, 1949; s. Harry B. and Charlotte Irene (Musin) E.; m. Laurie Beth Melamed, June 30, 1985; children: Joshua Philip, Michael William, David Benjamin. BA, U. Iowa, 1967-71, MD, 1971-75. Intern U. Kans. Med. Ctr., Kansas City, 1975-76, resident internal medicine, 1976-78; resident dermatology U. Iowa Hosps., Iowa City, 1978-80; fellow immunodermatology U. Tex. Health Sci., Dallas, 1980-82; asst. prof. dermatology Case Western Res. U., Cleve., 1982-88, asst. prof. gen. med. scis., oncology, 1987-88, assoc. prof. gen. med. scis. oncology, 1988-94, prof. gen. med. scis. oncology, 1994—, assoc. prof. environ. health scis., 1991—; attending physician U. Hosps. Cleve., 1982—, chief immunodermatology svc., 1987—; attending physician Cleve. VA Med. Ctr., 1990—; chief photodermatology svc., 1994—; dir. Skin Diseases Rsch. Ctr. N.E. Ohio NIH'; mem. rsch. adv. panel Rainbow Babies and Childrens Hosp., Cleve., 1990—. Editor: Photoimmunology, 1995; Mem. editorial bd. Photodermatology, Photoimmunology, Photmedicine, Jour. Investigative Dermatology, 1996—; sect. editor Experimental Dermatology; assoc. editor Photochemistry and Photobiology, 1994—, Jour. Immunology, 1995—; tech. adv. com. Edison Biotechnology Ctr.; rsch. adv. com. Diabetes Assn. Greater Cleve.; ad hoc reviewer gen. medicine study sect. NIH; contbr.

articles to profl. jours. Recipient Frederic E. Mohs award Skin Cancer Found., 1986, New Investigator Rsch. award NIH, 1983-86, Rsch. Career Devel. award 1987-92. Mem. ACP, AAAS, Am. Acad. Dermatology (com. on occupational health, com. sci. and poster exhibits, chmn. com. on scientific and poster exhibits 1995—, EPA/NIEHS liaison com. 1995—), Soc. Investigative Dermatology (midwest chmn. 1986-89, mem. com. 1991-94, com. chmn. 1993-94), Am. Assn. Immunologists, Am. Soc. for Photobiology, Am. Assn. for Cancer Rsch., Ohio Dermatological Soc., Cleve. Dermatological Soc. Home: 3962 White Oak Trl Cleveland OH 44122-4722 Office: U Hosps Cleve 2074 Abington Rd Cleveland OH 44106-2602

ELMORE, JEFFREY MICHAEL, engineering consultant; b. Huber Heights, Ohio, Jan. 29, 1968; s. Donald and Barbara E.; m. Linda S., Apr. 4, 1992; 1 child, Michael. BS Mech. Engring., Purdue U., 1991; postgrad., Capital U. Staff engr. Ajax Superior, Springfield, Ohio, 1991-92; project engr. Cooper Energy Svcs., Mt. Vernon, Ohio, 1992-94, supr. stds. & procedures, 1994—. Patentee in field. Mem. ASME. Office: Cooper Energy Svcs 105 N Sandusky St Mount Vernon OH 43050

ELROD, WILLIAM CORBIN, aerospace engineering educator; b. Walhalla, S.C., Dec. 28, 1928; s. William Crayton and Alice Dewitt (Corbin) E.; m. Emma Carolyn Reid, Aug. 9, 1952; children: Miriam, Mary, Alice, Elizabeth, William. BME, Clemson U., 1949, MME, 1951; PhD, U. Mich., 1965. Registered profl. engr., S.C. Project engr. USAF Equipment Lab., Wright-Patterson AFB, Ohio, 1951-55; project engr., sect. chief USAF Aeromed. Lab., Wright-Patterson AFB, 1957-61; asst. prof. Clemson (S.C.) U., 1961-67; assoc. prof. Air Force Inst. Tech., Wright-Patterson AFB, 1967-87, prof., 1987-93. Contbr. articles to profl. jours. and chpts. to books. Capt. USAF, 1953-61, lt. col. USAFR, 1961-77. Fellow AIAA (assoc., mem. tech. com. 1978-95); mem. ASME (sect. chmn. 1965-95), Affiliate Socs. Coun. Dayton (com. chair 1987-95), Honor Seminars Met. Dayton (chair, vice chair, sec. 1984-95), Am. Def. Preparedness Assn. (life), NRA (life), Mil. Ops. Rsch. Soc., Tau Beta Pi, Sigma Xi, Phi Kappa Phi, Phi Eta Sigma, Sigma Gamma Tau. Home: 4669 Bath Rd Dayton OH 45424

ELSEA, SANDRA JEANNE, community health nurse, clinical specialist; b. Orchard, Nebr., Aug. 28, 1937; d. Gail Roy and Edna Louise (Leach) Brodie; m. Neil Leroy Elsea, June 14, 1969 (dec. Feb. 1989); children: Cathleen Amber, Brenda Kay, Bradley Alan. BSN, U. Nebr., Omaha, 1958; MSN, U. Wash., 1964. RN, Nebr; cert. CPR. Staff nurse obstetrics U. Nebr., 1958-59, head nurse obstetrics, 1959-63; instr. U. Nebr. Coll. Nursing, 1964-66, asst. prof., 1966-69; chief project nurse maternal health and family planning project Omaha Douglas County Health Dept Vis. Nurse Assn., 1969-72; staff nurse York (Nebr.) Gen. Hosp., 1974-75; asst. prof. U. Nebr. Coll. Nursing, 1977-85; also coord. 1st yr. assoc. degree program, 1984-85; nurse coord. low birth weight risk assessment risk reduction program Vis. Nurse Community Health Svcs., 1985-86, dir. client svcs., 1986-87; cons. Maternity Nursing Vis. Nurse Assn., Omaha Douglas County Health Dept., 1969-72, Nebr. State Dept. Health, 1990. Contbr. articles to profl. jours. Co-leader Jr. Girls Scout Troop, 1980-82; instr. prenatal parent edn. classes York, 1974-75; officer, rm. mother Millard Sch. System PTO; parent sponsor, home ch. group leader Chi Rho, Faith Christian Ch. Recipient nurse traineeship USPHS, 1963. Mem. ANA (liaison maternal child health nursing conf. group 1965, planning com. 1983-84), Nebr. Pub. Health Assn., Nebr. Nurses Assn. (dist. II chmn. nominating com. 1961, dist. II bd. dirs. 1990-92), U. Nebr. Sch. Nursing Alumni Assn. (pres., bd. dirs. 1965-67), Sigma Theta Tau. Democrat. Mem. Christian Ch.

ELSTEN, CATE, financial consultant; b. Cin., Apr. 22, 1957; d. Walter and Melba (Callahan) E.; m. Arthur S. Beeman, Oct. 6, 1984. BA, Oberlin Coll., 1979; MBA, U. Wis., 1981. Dir. fin. Playhouse Sq., Cleve., 1981-84; sr. sales analyst Dayton Hudson Corp., Mpls., 1984-87; mgr. fin. planning Aveda, Mpls., 1988; chief oper. officer Sign Cons., Inc., Mpls., 1989-90; mgr. Ernst & Young, Mpls., 1990-92; dir. Coopers & Lybrand, Mpls., 1992—. Bd. dirs. Minn. Advocates for Human Rights, Mpls., Civic Leadership Found.; prs. New Dance Ensemble, Mpls., 1985-95. Mem. Licensing Execs. Soc., Phi Beta Kappa, Beta Gamma Sigma.

ELSTEN, STAN, mechanical engineer. Grad., Wichita (Kans.) Sch. of Bus., 1969. Cert. journeyman machinist, Kans. Machinist Galena (Kans.) Precision, 1969, Vickers Sperry, Joplin, Mo., 1970-73, Ingersol Rand, Baxter Springs, Mo., 1974, B.F. Goodrich Co., Miami, Okla., 1975-85, Sterling/IMM, Riverton, Kans., 1985—. Patentee (5) in field. Office: PO Box 11 Riverton KS 66770-0011

ELSTON, THOMAS LEE, firefighter, emergency medical technician; b. Omaha, Nov. 19, 1949; s. Robert Nicholas and Adeline (Dulacki) E.; m. Judith Ann Sobol, Sept. 17, 1982; 1 child, Elissa Ann. BS, Ill. State U., 1972. Owner Prairie People's Pottery, Peoria, Ill., 1973-75; clk. Allied War Surplus, Peoria, 1974-76; mgr. Kay-Bee Toys Store, Bloomington, Ill., 1976-77; firefighter, medic Normal (Ill.) Fire Dept., 1977—; ptnr. Double T Honey Co., 1978-86; owner Amber Bee Co., Bloomington, 1987—. Mem. Town of Normal Fgn. Fire Tax Bd., 1991-96, pres., 1992-96. Mem. Internat. Fire Fighters Assn. (sec. local 2442 1982—), Am. Philatelic Soc., Heart of Ill. Beekeepers Assn. (trustee 1989-92, sec. 1994-96). Roman Catholic. Home: Box 346-D 9 Brentwood Rd RRD 1 Bloomington IL 61704-9752

ELTZ, ROBERT WALTER, bioprocess technologist; b. Callicoon, N.Y., June 22, 1932; s. Carl George and Adele (Markert) E.; m. Deborah Lee Kinkaid, Nov. 24, 1962; children: Karen, Kurt, Kirsten. BS in Biology/Chemistry, Rensselaer Poly. Inst., 1953; PhD in Microbiology, Cornell U., 1958. Rsch. microbiologist Chas. Pfizer & Co., Bklyn., also Groton, Conn., 1957-61, Sun Oil Co., Marcus Hook, Phila., Pa., 1961-70; biol. process devel. dir. E.R. Squibb & Sons, Inc., New Brunswick, N.J., 1970-80; tech. dir. Krause Milling Co., Milw., 1980-82; bioprocess devel. dir. Monsanto Co., St. Louis, 1982-90, bioprocess tech. dir., 1990-94; indsl. R&D mgmt. cons., 1994—; mem. Hungarian workshop on indsl. econs. Nat. Acad. Sci., 1991. Mem. Am. Chem. Soc. (chmn. div. biochem. tech. 1981-82, James M. Van Lanen Disting. Svc. award 1984), Am. Soc. for Microbiology, Sigma Xi. Home and Office: 727 Cedar Field Ct Chesterfield MO 63017-5727

ELVENDAHL, SUSAN J., stockbroker; b. Mpls., Sept. 26, 1953. BA in Bus. Adminstrn., U. Minn., 1977. Sales asst. Dean Bosworth, Mpls., 1985-88; stockbroker Dean Witter Reynolds, Bloomington, Minn., 1988—. Democrat. Lutheran. Home: 7145 Valley View Rd Edina MN 55439-1656 Office: Dean Witter Reynolds 8300 Norman Center Dr Ste 1150 Bloomington MN 55437-1027

ELVIG, MERRYWAYNE, real estate manager; b. Anoka, Minn., Jan. 16, 1931; d. Wayne Leroy and Erma Lou (Greenwald) Ridge; m. Donald Keith Elvig, June 15, 1955 (div. 1972); children: Amy, David. AA, Cottey Jr. Coll., 1951; BS, U. Minn., 1953. Tchr. Anoka Hennepin Sch. Dist., Anoka, 1953-56; with med. records div. East Main Clinic, Anoka, 1972-78; real estate mgr. Skurdal Properties, Anoka, 1978-79; mgr. Belma Properties, Anoka, 1986—, ABC Travel, Anoka, 1979-93; v.p. Walker Meth. Residence Group, 1990—; chmn. Walker Plaza, 1994—, Walker on the River, 1994—; travel counselor Am. Automobile Assn., 1994—. Commr. Housing Redevel. Authority, Anoka, 1978, chmn., 1984—; bd. dirs. Walker Sr. Housing Corp., Anoka, 1986—, Walker Meth. Sr. Housing, Inc., 1988—; v.p. Walker Meth. Sr. Property Mgmt. Group, 1990—; treas. Anoka Devel. Corp., 1986—; charter and life mem. aux. Mercy Med. Ctr., coon Rapids, Minn., 1965—, bd. dirs., 1965-71; mem. Greenhaven Study Com., Anoka, 1986-90, Anoka County Hist. Soc., 1987—, Anoka North Ctrl. Bus. Dist. Study Commn., 1993—; vol. Anoka coun. Girl Scouts U.S., 1963-65; chmn. Am. Cancer Soc., 1962-65; moderator 1st Congl. Ch., Anoka, 1984-86; vol. coord. City of Anoka, 1995—; deacon 1st Congregational Ch., 1995—. Mem. Am. Soc. Travel Agts. (bd. dirs. 1986—), Minn. Exec. Women in Travel (treas.), Minn. Exec. Women in Tourism, Internat. Fedn. Women's Orgns., Anoka Landowners' Assn., Anoka Area C. of C. (pres. 1985), Kiwanis (bd. dirs.), Philanthropic Ednl. Orgn. Sisterhood (pres. 1966-68), Philolectian Club (pres. 1965-67), Greenhaven Women's Golf Club (pres. 1987-89). Republican. Home: 1933 Cressy Ave Anoka MN 55303-1920 Office: AAA Minnesota 3027 Coon Rapids Blvd Coon Rapids MN 55433

ELWIN, JAMES WILLIAM, JR., dean, lawyer; b. Everett, Wash., June 28, 1950; s. James William Elwin and Jeannette Georgette (Zichy-Litscheff) Sherman; m. Regina K. McCabe, Oct. 25, 1986. BA, U. Denver, 1971, MA, 1972; JD, Northwestern U., 1975. Bar: Ill. 1975, U.S. Dist. Ct. (no. dist.) Ill. 1975, U.S. Ct. Appeals (7th cir.) 1977, U.S. Supreme Ct. 1980. Trial atty. antitrust div. U.S. Dept. Justice, Chgo., 1975-77; asst. dean sch. law Northwestern U., Chgo., 1977-82, assoc. dean, 1982—, exec. dir. Corp. Counsel Ctr., 1984—; planning dir. Corp. Counsel Inst., Garrett Corp. and Securities Law Inst., Chgo., 1983—; dir. Short Course for Pros. Attys., 1981—, Short Course for Def. Lawyers in Criminal Cases, Chgo., 1979—. Bd. dirs. Legal Assistance Found. of Chgo., 1985—; vice chmn. Gov.'s Adv. Coun. on Criminal Justice Legis., 1986-91. Fellow German Acad. Exch. Svc., 1986; Fulbright scholar Germany, 1990. Mem. Chgo. Coun. Fgn. Rels. (mem. Chgo. com.), Chgo. Bar Assn. (bd. mgrs. 1983-85), Chgo. Bar Found. (bd. dirs. 1985-93, pres. 1989-91), Ill. Inst. Continuing Legal Edn. (chmn. 1987-88), Am. Law Inst., Legal Club (pres. 1991-92), Univ. Club, Law Club City of Chgo., Phi Beta Kappa, Pi Gamma Mu. Office: Northwestern U Sch Law 357 E Chicago Ave Chicago IL 60611-3008

ELY, LAWRENCE ORLO, retired surgeon; b. Guthrie Center, Iowa, Dec. 13, 1919; s. John Emerson and Luella Mabel (Knapp) E.; m. Dorothy Maxine Jenkins, Aug. 23, 1942; children: Patricia Anne, Lawrence Orlo, Stephen Craig, Bennett Knapp, Carolyn Elizabeth. BA, State U. Iowa, 1942, MD, 1943, MS, 1948, PhD, 1950. Diplomate Am. Bd. Gen. Surgery. Intern Mt. Carmel Mercy Hosp., Detroit, 1943-44; instr. dept. physiology Med. Sch., State U. Iowa, Iowa City, 1946-48, resident, instr. dept. surgery, 1948-52; pvt. practice gen. surgery Des Moines, 1952-85; mem. staff Iowa Luth. Hosp., Des Moines, 1952-85, Mercy Med. Ctr., Des Moines, 1952-85, Iowa Meth. Med. Ctr., Des Moines, 1952-86; cons. Iowa Blue Cross-Blue Shield, 1985-86, Iowa Found. for Med. Care, 1985-86. Sect. head United Campaign, Des Moines, 1958-60; mem. Des Moines Opera Bd., 1973—, pres., 1973-78; mem. Health Planning Coun. of Iowa Med. Corp., 1970-78; bd. dirs., pres. Ramsey Home, 1988-94; bd. dirs. Civic Music Assn. Des Moines, 1984—; mem. steering com. Friends of the Arts, Drake U., Des Moines. Capt. M.C., U.S. Army, 1944-46. Fellow ACS; mem. AMA, Iowa Med. Soc., Polk County Med. Soc. Republican. Mem. Disciples of Christ Ch. Home: 3500 Fleur Dr Des Moines IA 50321-2650

ELY, WAYNE HARRISON, broadcast engineer; b. Alliance, Ohio, Aug. 31, 1933; s. Dwight Harrison and Mable Evellen (Jones) E.; m. Roslyn Rose Ambrose, June 14, 1964 (div. Nov. 1981): children: Eric (dec.), Kevin, Gayle, Mitchell; m. Linda Kay Grubb, July 22, 1989. Student Mount Union Coll., 1955-56, Ohio U., 1956-62. Transmitter engr. Sta. WOUB-FM-TV, Ohio U., Athens, 1958-62; studio field engr. ABC, N.Y.C., 1962-66, 67-72; studio engr. CBS, N.Y.C., 1966-67; transmitter supr. Sta. WOUC-FM-TV, Ohio U., Quaker City, 1972-91; retired, 1991—; technical adv./vol. Muskingum Perry Career Ctr. Radio-TV Dept., 1991—; tchr. radio tech. Ohio U., Zanesville. Served with C.E., U.S. Army, 1952-54. Mem. Soc. Broadcast Engrs. (profl. broadcast engrs. cert.). Home: 140 Riley Rd Norwich OH 43767-9722

EMANUEL, BRIAN PATRICK, sanitarian; b. Chgo., Nov. 3, 1956; s. Clarence John and Renee A. (Weidman) E.; m. Irene Mary Kreuger, Feb. 28, 1981; children: Bridget M., Celeste K., Brett C., Emily J. BS in biology, bus. mgmt., Northeastern Ill. U., 1977; MPH, U. Ill., Chgo., 1993. Assoc. sanitarian Lake County Health Dep., Waukegan, Ill., 1978-79; environ. health coord. City of Park Ridge, Ill., 1979—; instr. cmty. hygiene and food protection, U. Ill. Chgo., 1993—. Mem. Nat. Environ. Health Assn. (registered sanitarian), Internat. Assn. Milk, Food Environ. Sanitarians, Ill. Environ. Health Assn. (sec. 1988), N.W. Mcpl. Conf. Health Dirs. (chmn. 1985-88). Roman Catholic. Office: City Park Ridge 505 Butler Pl Park Ridge IL 60068

EMARA, MOHAMED AMIN, immunologist; b. Cairo, Feb. 1, 1946; came to U.S., 1976, naturalized, 1981; m. Samia Mahmoud, June 10, 1973. BSc and 2d honor degree in agr. sci., Cairo U., 1967, MSc in Agr. Chemistry, 1977; med. tech. diploma, St. Alexis Hosp., Cleve., 1975; MSc in Bioloby, Cleve. State U., 1981, PhD in Immunology, 1986. Cert. med. tech. Am. Soc. Clin. Pathologists. Rsch. assoc. in soil chemistry Agrl. Rsch. Ctr., Cairo, 1968-75; med. technologist St. Alexis Hosp., Cleve., 1976-78; med. technologist, head chemistry Lakewood (Ohio) Hosp., 1977-82; evening charge med. technologist St. John Hosp., Cleve., 1979-87; postdoctoral fellow in immunology Duke U., Durham, N.C., 1987-89; asst. prof. clin. pathology, assoc. dir. Tissue Typing Lab., East Carolina U. Sch. Medicine, Greenville, N.C., 1989-92; assoc. staff investigator Henry Ford Hosp., Detroit, 1992-93, staff investigator, 1993—, dir. Transplant Immunology Rsch. Lab., 1992—, assoc. dir. Tissue Typing Lab., 1992—. Contbr. articles and abstracts to sci. jours. Recipient award N.C. Bd. Sci. and Tech., 1990; grantee Cleve. State U., 1984-85, starter grantee Ea. Carolina U., 1989-90, also others. Mem. Am. Soc. for Histocompatability and Immunogenetics, Am. Assn. Immunologists, Transplantation Soc., S.E. Organ Procurement Found. (Bernard Amos Sandoz Young Investigator award 1987). Home: 5103 Bayside Dr Troy MI 48098 Office: Immune & Diagnostic Lab Inc Ste 350 32905 West 12 Mile Rd Farmington Hills MI 48334

EMEAGWALI, DALE BROWN, molecular biologist; b. Balt., Dec. 24, 1954; d. Leon Robert and Johnnie Doris (Baird) Brown; m. Philip Emeagwali, Aug. 15, 1981; 1 child, Ijeoma. BA in Biology, Coppin State Coll., 1976; PhD in Microbiology, Georgetown U., 1981. Teaching asst. sch. medicine Georgetown U., Washington, 1977-80; postdoctoral fellow Nat. Inst. Allergy and Infectious Diseases, Bethesda, Md., 1981-84, Uniformed Svc., U. Health Sci., Bethesda, 1985-86; rsch. assoc. U. Wyo., Laramie, 1986-87; sr. rsch. fellow U. Mich., Ann Arbor, 1987-88, asst. rsch. scientist, 1989-92; rsch. assoc. U. Minn., St. Paul, 1992—, lectr., 1992—. Contbr. articles to sci. jours., chpts. to books. Vol. Sci. Mus. Minn., St. Paul. 1993. Grantee NSF, 1990, Am. Cancer Soc., 1990. Mem. AAAS, Sigma Xi. Office: U Minn 250 Biosci Ctr 1445 Gortner Ave Saint Paul MN 55108-1095

EMERSON, RICHARD DONALD, investment broker; b. Creston, Iowa, June 13, 1947. BS, Iowa State U., 1969. News reporter Sta. WMT Radio-TV, Cedar Rapids, Iowa, 1969-73; dir. comty. rels. Kirkwood C.C., Cedar Rapids, 1973-74; asst. dir. alumni assn. Iowa State U., Ames, 1974-77; v.p. alumni adminstrn. Case Western Res. U., Washington, 1977-80; exec. dir. alumni assn. U. Colo., Boulder, 1980-87, U. Iowa, Iowa City, 1987-94; investment exec. Dain Bosworth Inc., Iowa City, 1994—. Mem. U. Athletic Club (pres. 1995), Iowa City C. of C. (pres. 1995), Kappa Sigma (dist. grand master 1994-95), Optimist Club, Rotary. Methodist. Office: Dain Bosworth Inc 112 S Dubuque St Iowa City IA 52240-4009

EMERSON, ROBERT, state legislator; b. Alpena, Mich., Mar. 23, 1948; s. Melvin Frances and Elaine (Larmer) E.; m. Judy Samuelson, 1981; children: Melanie Erica, Phillip James, Erin Samuelson. Student, Wayne State U., 1969-69, U. Mich., 1970-71. Legal aide Mich. Ho. Reps., Lansing, 1978-79; rep. Mich. Dist. 81, 1980-94, Mich. Dist. 49, 1995—. Address: 1025 Kensington Ave Flint MI 48503-5311 Address: PO Box 30014 Lansing MI 48909-7514*

EMERSON, THOMAS EUGENE, anthropology educator; b. Chippewa Falls, Wis., May 31, 1945; s. Bernard Thornton and Pearl Emerson; m. JoAnne Adams, Jan. 13, 1978; children: Nils A., Kjersti E., Hans T.; stepchildren: Samuel I. Adams, Fredrick G. Adams, Andrew J. Adams. BA, U. Wis., Eau Clair, 1968; MA, U. Wis., Madison, 1977, PhD, 1995. Pvt. archaeol. contractor Madison, 1970-77, Caldwell, Wis., 1982-84; field dir. U. S.D., Vermilion, 1978-79; site dir. U. Ill., Urbana, 1979-82; chief archaeologist Ill. Hist. Preservation Agy., Springfield, Ill., 1984-94; dir. Ill. transp. archaeol. rsch. program U. Ill., Urbana, 1994—. Author: Mississippi Stone Images in Illinois, 1982, Florence Street Site, 1983, BBB Motor Site, 1984, Dyroff-Levin Site, 1984; editor: Early Woodland Archaeology, 1986, Cahokia and Mississippi Hinterlands, 1991, Calumet and Fleur-de-lys, 1992, Highway Into the Past, 1993. Bd. dirs. Upper Miss. Valley Archaeol. Rsch. Found., Chgo., 1973-76, Northeastern Archaeol. Found., Madison, Wis., 1974-77. Fellow Ill. Archaeol. Survey (editor 1994); mem. Nat. Assn. State Archaeologists (Ill. rep. 1984-94), Soc. Am. Archaeology (Ill. rep. com. on pub. archaeology 1984-94), Wis. Archaeol. Soc., Soc. Hist. Archaeology, Southwestern Archaeol. Conf., Plains Anthropological Soc. Roman Catholic. Home: 114 8th St Lincoln IL 62656 Office: U Ill Dept Anthropology 109 Davenport Hall Urbana IL 61801

EMERT, TIMOTHY RAY, lawyer; b. Independence, Kans., Jan. 29, 1940; s. Walter Glen and Fern LaVon (Braschler) E.; m. BarbaraA. Meitner, Aug. 22, 1964; children: Kate, Jennifer, Babs. BS in Journalism, U. Kans., JD. Bar: Kans. 1965. Ptnr. Scovel, Emert, Heasty and Chubb, Independence. Senator 15th dist. State of Kans.; bd. dirs. Independence C. C. Found., Class LTD; commr. Uniform Laws Conf.; mem. Kans. Judicial Coun.; former bd. dirs. Independence Bd. Edn., Independence Pub. Libr., Kans. State Bd. Edn., Kans. State H.S. Activities Assn., Kans. Commn. on Pub. Broadcasting, William Inge Festival Found., Kans. Commn. on Edn. Restructuring and Accountability Corp. for Change, Kans.; vol. Kans. Advocacy and Protective Svcs.; mem. adv. bd. Manor Nursing Home, Independence. Mem. S.E. Kans. Bar Assn., Kans. Bar Assn., Independence C. of C., Rotary. Republican. Roman Catholic.

EMERY, FRANK EUGENE, publishing executive; b. Wichita, Kans., May 14, 1934; s. Frank A.C. and Nellie Mae (Bloss) E.; m. Sara Manette Marble, Nov. 3, 1956 (div. 1983); children: Frank Michael, Mark W., Timothy T., Todd A.; m. Sandra Kay Adamson, June 28, 1988. BA, U. Kans., 1955, MD, 1959. Diplomate Am. Bd. Orthopedic Surgery, Nat. Bd. Med. Examiners. Intern U. Kans. Med. Ctr., Kansas City, 1959-60, resident radiology, 1960-61, resident gen. surgery, 1961-62; resident orthopedic surgery U. Tex. Med. Br., Galveston, 1968; fellow Orthopedic Rsch. and Edn. Found. U. Edinburgh, Scotland, 1968; pvt. practice specializing in orthopedic surgery Springfield, Mo., 1969-73; asst. prof. surgery, orthopedics U. Tex. Med. Br., Galveston, 1973-77, assoc. prof. surgery, orthopedics, 1977-78, dir. Arthritis Minimal Care Unit, 1975-76; pub. Ft. Scott (Kans.) Tribune, 1980—; pres. Tribune Monitor Co., Ft. Scott, 1982—; bd. dirs. Tribune Monitor Co., Ft. Scott, Gateway Comm., Wichita; gen. ptnr. Hotel Ptnrs., I, II, III, IV, Wichita. Contbr. articles to med. publs. V.p. Mo. and Ark. River Basins Assn., 1984-86; co-chmn. Gov.'s Task Force Pub. Sector Funding, Kans., Main St. Program, Topeka, 1985-86; chmn. basin adv. com. Kans. Water Authority, Topeka, 1986-90; bd. dirs. Kans. C. of C. and Industry, Topeka, 1990-91. Lt. comdr., surgeon USPHS, 1991-93. Pediatric psychiatry fellow NIH, 1957; fellow United Cerebral Palsy Found., 1967-68. Fellow Am. Acad. Orthopedic Surgeons; mem. Kans. Press Assn., Inland Press Assn., Am. Soc. for Surgery of the Hand, Sigma Xi, Nu Sigma Nu, Delta Upsilon. Home: RR 9 Box 575-a Springfield MO 65809-9137 Office: Fort Scott Tribune 6 E Wall St Fort Scott KS 66701-1423

EMERY, JAMES W., state legislator; m. Elaine Emery; 1 child. Senator S.D. State Senate Dist. 30; chmn. transp. com., vice-chmn. agr. and natural resources com., mem. judiciary, commerce, health and human svc. and local govt. com., S.D. State Senate. Home: 515 Belair Dr Custer SD 57730-1009*

EMERY, JOHN A., electrical engineer; b. Evanston, Ill., Apr. 30, 1959. BSEE, Milw. Sch. Engring., 1983. Registered profl. engr., Wis. Engr. Emerson Electric, St. Louis, 1983-92; co-owner, engr. Emery Machine & Tool Co., Oconomowoc, Wis., 1992—. Mem. Nat. Fedn. Ind. Bus., Mil. Vehicle Preservation Assn.

EMERY, LARRY C., financial executive; b. Poplar Bluff, Mo., June 15, 1939. BA, Washington U., St. Louis, 1961. Investment cons. Merrill Lynch, Kansas City, Mo., 1968-78, Smith Barney, Kansas City, Mo., 1978-90, Kidd Peabody, Kansas City, Mo., 1990-94; account v.p. Paine Webber, Kansas City, Mo., 1995—. Contbr. articles to newspapers. Mem. Optimist Club (Optimist of Yr. 1979-80), Optimist Youth Club. Republican. Lutheran. Office: Paine Webber # 500 700 W 74th St Kansas City MO 64114-1310

EMISON, EWING RABB, JR., lawyer; b. Vincennes, Ind., Feb. 3, 1925. AB, DePauw U., 1947; LLB, Ind. U., 1950. Bar: Ind. 1950. Ptnr. Emison Doolittle Kolb & Roellgen, Vincennes. Mem. Wabash Valley Interstate Commn., 1959-62, Ind. Flood Control and Water Resources Commn., 1961-65; mem. bd. visitors Ind. Univ. Sch. Law, 1984-87. Mem. ABA (sects. on litigation, econs. of law practice), Ind. State Bar Assn. (bd. of mgrs. 1975-77, chmn. ho. of dels. 1979, pres. 1986-87), Internat. Assn. Def. Counsel, Am. Judicature Soc., Phi Delta Phi. Office: Emison Doolittle & Roellgen PO Box 215 8th and Busseron Sts Vincennes IN 47591

EMMETT, RITA, professional speaker; b. Chgo., Apr. 12, 1943; d. Thomas Henry Dorney and Helen Fischer; m. Bruce Karder, May 21, 1994; children: Robb Sean, Kerry Shannon. BA in English, Northeastern Ill. U., 1979; MS in Adult and Cont. Edn, Nat. Louis U., Evanston, Ill., 1985. Coord. edn. programs Leyden Family Svc., Franklin Park, Ill., 1977-95; mem. adj. faculty Triton Coll., River Grove, Ill., 1977—, Wright Coll., Chgo., 1985—; pres. Emmett Enterprises, Inc., Des Plaines, 1994—; presenter seminars in field. Author: Family Communications Handbook, Great Speakers Anthology; contbr. articles to newspapers. Pres. Parent's Club, River Grove, 1987-88; keynote spkr. Gov.'s Mansion, Springfield, Ill. Mem. Bus. and Profl. Women (Achievement award 1986), Assn. Consultation and Edn. (sec.), Ill. Prevention Network, Century Club, Nat. Spkr.'s Assn., Profl. Spkr.'s of Ill. (bd. dirs. 1995, 96). Roman Catholic.

EMMONS, JOANNE, state senator; b. Big Rapids, Mich., Feb. 8, 1934; d. Ray J. and Emma M. (Von Glahn) Gregory; m. John Francis Emmons, June 9, 1956; children: Sarah, Dorothy. BS, Mich. State U., 1956; degree in pub. svc. (hon.), Ferris State U., 1992. Tchr. Mecosta (Mich.) High Sch., 1956-58; treas. Big Rapids Twp., 1976-86; state rep. State of Mich., Lansing, 1987-91, state senator, 1991—. Chair Mecosta County Rep. Com., 1976-80; vice chair 10th dist. Rep. Com., 1984-86; bd. dirs. Luth. Child and Family Svcs., 1990—. Named Nat. Rep. Legislator of Yr., Nat. Assn. State Legislators, 1993, Legislator of Yr., Mich. Twp. Assn., 1993. Mem. Am. Legion Aux., Mich. Farm Bur. (legis. com. 1970—), Omicron Delta Kappa. Home: 13904 Northland Dr Big Rapids MI 49307 Office: Mich State Senate State Capitol Lansing MI 48909

EMMOTT, DAVID FIELDING, physician, urologist; b. Stillwell, Okla., Aug. 31, 1953; s. Ralph Cameron Emmott and Isabel Graeme (Wrifht) Emmott-Haller; m. Helen Malissa Clark, Apr. 1, 1978; children: Cameron, Elizabeth, Margaret. BA in History, U. Okla., Norman, 1975; MD, U. Okla., Oklahoma City, 1979. Urologist Urology Cons., Shawnee Mission, Kans., 1985—; chmn. dept. surgery Bethany Med. Ctr., Kansas City, Kans., 1991-92; chmn. surgery quality com. Shawnee Mission (Kans.) Med. Ctr., 1994, sec. treas. med. staff, 1995—. Mem. Kansas City Urologic Soc. (sec. 1994-95), Johnson County Med. Soc., Phi Beta Kappa. Episcopalian. Office: Urology Cons 8901 W 74th St Ste 308 Shawnee Mission KS 66204

EMPEN, DAN R., electrical engineer; b. Freeport, Ill., July 2, 1966. BS, Ill. Inst. Tech., 1992. Engr. Zenith Electronics, Melrose Park, Ill., 1990-92; electrical engr. Motorola AIEG, Northbrook, Ill., 1992—. Mem. SAE. Roman Catholic. Office: Motorola AIEG 4000 Commercial Ave Northbrook IL 60062-1829

EMRICH, JEFFREY PAULING, food products executive; b. Evanston, Ill., Nov. 4, 1948; s. Charles Lyman and Barbara Mary (Boettcher) E.; m. Nancy Haddaway Jones Emrich, Dec. 27, 1978; children: Charles William Haddaway Emrich, Parker Henry Van Nes Emrich. BA, Brown U., Providence, 1970; M of Urban and Regional Planning, George Washington U., 1980. Analyst Gladstone Assocs., Washington, 1975-78; cons. Tischler, Montasser Assocs., Washington, 1978-81; v.p. fin., corp. treas. Custom Food Products, Inc., 1981-91; prin. Concepts Internat. Ltd., Wilmette, Ill., 1991—. Trustee Evanston (Ill.) Hist. Soc., 1988-92, Evanston (Ill.) Cmty. Found., 1994—; mem. Zoning Amendment Com., Evanston, Ill., 1989-92;. Mem. Inst. Food Technologists, Union League Club of Chgo, Ausable Club. Republican. Episcopalian.

EMRICK, DONALD DAY, chemist, consultant; b. Waynesfield, Ohio, Apr. 3, 1929; s. Ernest Harold and Nellie (Day) E.; B.S. cum laude, Miami U., Oxford, Ohio, 1951; M.S., Purdue U., 1954, Ph.D., 1956 Grad. teaching asst. Purdue U., Lafayette, Ind., 1951-55; with chem. and phys. research div. Standard Oil Co. Ohio, 1955-64, research asso., 1961-64; cons., sr. research chemist research dept. Nat. Cash Register Co., Dayton, Ohio, 1965-72, chem. cons., 1972—. Mem. AAAS, Am. Chem. Soc., Phi Beta Kappa, Sigma Xi. Patentee in Field. Contbr. articles to profl. jours. Home: 4240 Lesher Dr Dayton OH 45429-3042

ENCK, JOHN, computer analyst; b. Lewisburg, Pa., Aug. 14, 1956; s. Herbert and Birdine (Kline) E.; m. Marlene Bennett, July 9, 1982; children: Leanne, Sean. BA, Antioch Coll. Svc. mgr. Systems Rsch., Okemos, Mich., 1978-81, Burroughs Corp., Okemos, Mich., 1985-88; v.p. Dale Computer Corp., Okemos, Mich., 1985-88; analyst Forest Computer, Okemos, Mich., 1988—. Author: A Managers Guide to Multivendor Networks, 1991, Navigating the AS/400, 1993, The Quintessential Guide to PC Support, 1993, LAN to Wan Interconnections, 1995; contbr. articles to profl. jours.

ENDLICH, LEATRICE ANN, therapist; b. Topeka, Aug. 27, 1928; d. Harry and Roselle (Dauer) E.; m. Howard L. Swartzman, June 27, 1950 (div. Aug. 1984); children: Susan Swartzman Freeman, Steven Swartzman, Julie Swartzman Krop. BA, Mills Coll., 1950; MSW, U. Kans., 1963. Social worker Jewish Family and Children's Services, Kansas City, Mo., 1968-73, dir. family life edn., 1973-77; pvt. practice clin. social work Prairie Village, 1977-78; teaching assoc. dept. child psychiatry U. Kans. Med. Ctr., Kansas City, 1978-84; day treatment therapist Gillis Ctr., Kansas City, 1984-86; pvt. practice, 1986-88; dir. client svcs. Good Samaritan Project, Kansas City, 1988-94, ret., 1994; past bd. dirs. Crittenden Ctr., Kansas City; co-chmn. Kansas City Ryan White Planning Coun., 1994—. Mem. adv. com. Kans. Behavioral Scis. Regulatory Bd., 1983; mem. Menorah Med. Ctr. Aux. (life), Kansas City, Friends of Art, Kansas City, Lyric Opera Guild, Kansas City, William Jewell Coll. Fine Arts Guild; trustee Conservatory Music, Kansas City, 1988-92; mem. adv. bd. Johnson County Nursing Ctr., 1988—; bd. dirs. Jewish Family and Children Svcs., 1988-92; mem. nat. com. HIV-AIDS, Union of Am. Hebrew Congregations, 1993—. Named Kans. Social Worker of Yr. Mokan Unit of Nat. Assn. Social Workers, 1992; recipient Administrs. Achievement award Health Care Financing Adminstrn., 1995, Ribbon of Hope award, 1995, AIDS Cmty. Svc. award. Mem. Nat. Assn. Social Workers, Acad. Cert. Social Workers (cert.), Nat. Coun. Jewish Women (life mem. Mo. chpt.). Democrat. Home: 12239 Ash St Shawnee Mission KS 66209-3513

ENDRES, KATHLEEN LILLIAN, journalism educator; b. Toledo, Ohio, May 1, 1949; d. Lawrence John and Bridget (Tierney) Barber; m. Fredric Franklin Endres, June 7, 1969; children: Stephanie, Jon-Fredric. BA, U. Md., 1972, MA, 1975; PhD, Kent State U., Ohio, 1985. Reporter EDP News Svcs., Washington, 1970-72, Datamation Mag., Washington, 1972-73; assoc. editor Babcox Pubs., Akron, Ohio, 1974-75; instr. Kent (Ohio) State U., 1975-77; mng. editor Crain Comms., Akron, 1977-78; asst. prof. Bowling Green (Ohio) State U., 1985-87; assoc. prof. U. Akron, 1987—; judge Neal awards Am. Bus. Press, N.Y.C., 1987-94. Editor: Trade, Industrial, and Professional Periodicals of the United States, Women's Periodicals of the United States, Consumer Magazines, Women's Periodicals of the United States: Social and Political Issues; contbr. articles to profl. jours., chpts. to books. Mem. coord. com. Women's Studies, U. Akron, 1989-94, 95—. Assn. Bus. Pubrs. grantee, 1987, Bowling Green State U. grantee, 1986, Women in Comms. grantee, 1980; recipient Student's Choice award, U. Akron, Phi Eta Sigma, 1990. Mem. Women in Comms. (chpt. advisor 1987-92), Assn. for Edn. in Journalism and Mass Comms., Akron Press Club. Office: Univ of Akron Sch Communications Akron OH 44325-1003

ENDSLEY, JANE RUTH, nursing educator; b. Harrisburg, Ill., Oct. 14, 1942; d. Clifford B. Bond and Haroldene (Malone) Miller; m. William R. Endsley, June 6, 1964. Grad., Deaconess Hosp. Sch. Nursing, Evansville, Ind., 1963; student, So. Ill. U., 1968; BSN cum laude, U. Evansville, 1978. RN, Ind., Ill. Staff nurse Deaconess Hosp., 1963-64; psychiat. nurse med.-surg. emergency room and obstetrics Ferrell Hosp., Eldorado, Ill., 1964-68, DON, 1969-70; DON, Good Shepherd Nursing Home, Eldorado, 1971-72; instr. nursing Southeastern Ill. U., Harrisburg, 1973—; cons. parents too soon Egyptian Pub. Health Dept., Eldorado, 1985. Vice chmn. Pvt. Industry Coun., Harrisburg, 1983-91; precinct committeeperson Harrisburg Dem. Com., 1986-90; donor chmn. ARC, Harrisburg, 1970—; instr. CPR to civic orgns. and students, 1980-87; pres. Peartree Antiques, Inc., 1995. Mem. AAUW, Ill. Nurses Assn. (nominating com. 1975), Southeastern Ill. Coll. Edn. Assn. (pres. 1988-91), Faculty Wives and Women Southeastern Ill. Coll. (sec.-treas. 1974-75), Sigma Theta Tau. Home: PO Box 345 1075 Shawnee Hills Rd Harrisburg IL 62946-4943

ENG, JOSHUA, business executive; b. Hong Kong, Mar. 9, 1955. BFA in Comm., No. Ill. U., 1979. Design dir. Gailen Assoc., Highland Park, Ill., 1982-85; sr. design cons. Hill and Knowlton Pub. Rels., Chgo., 1985-88; pres. Fish Eng Ptnrs. Inc., Chgo., 1988—. Vol. Make-A-Wish Found. of Ill., Chgo., 1987-89. Recipient Gold award Fin. World, 1987, 5 Desi awards Design Guild, 1985-88. Republican. Office: Fish Eng Ptnrs Inc 431 S Dearborn St Chicago IL 60605-1121

ENGEL, ALBERT JOSEPH, federal judge; b. Lake City, Mich., Mar. 21, 1924; s. Albert Joseph and Bertha (Bielby) E.; m. Eloise Ruth Bull, Oct. 18, 1952; children: Albert Joseph III, Katherine Ann, James Robert, Mary Elizabeth. Student, U. Md., 1941-42; A.B., U. Mich., 1948, LL.B., 1950. Bar: Mich. 1951. Ptnr. firm Engle & Engel, Muskegon, Mich., 1952-67; judge Mich. Circuit Ct., 1967-71; judge U.S. Dist. Ct. Western Dist. Mich., 1971-74; circuit judge U.S. Ct. Appeals, 6th Circuit, Grand Rapids, Mich., 1974-88, chief judge, 1988-89, sr. judge, 1989—. Served with AUS, 1943-46, ETO. Fellow Am. Bar Found.; mem. ABA, Fed. Bar Assn., Mich. Bar Assn., Cin. Bar Assn., Grand Rapids Bar Assn., Am. Judicature Soc., Am. Lgion, Phi Sigma Kappa, Phi Delta Phi. Episcopalian. Club: Grand Rapids Torch. Home: 5497 Forest Bend Dr SE Ada MI 49301-9005

ENGEL, BERNARD FRANCIS, humanities educator; b. Spokane, Wash., Nov. 25, 1921; s. Ignatius L. and Katherine (McDonald) E.; m. Adele Say Engel, Dec. 23, 1946. BA, U. Oreg., 1946; MA, U. Chgo., 1949; PhD, U. Calif., Berkeley, 1956. Reporter, city editor Register-Guard, Eugene, Oreg., 1946-48; prof. English U. Idaho, Moscow, 1949-50, Oreg. State U., Corvallis, 1952-53, Sacramento (Calif.) State U., 1953-57; prof. Am. thought and lang. Mich. State U., East Lansing, 1957-90; chmn. dept. Am. thought and lang. Mich. State U., East Lansing, 1967-77; bd. mem. Coll. Conf. Composition. Author: Marianne Moore, 1964, revised edit., 1989, CD-Rom, 1996, 12 other books; contbr. articles to profl. jours. Vol. Hospice, Lansing, Mich., 1990—; bd. mem. ACLU Mich., 1991-93. With U.S. Army, 1942-45, ETO. Fulbright schoalr U. Argentina, 1963; rsch. grantee Nat. Humanities Coun., 1978. Mem. MLA (mem. del. assembly), Soc. Midwestern Lit. (pres. 1970-71), Marianne Moore Soc., Popular Culture Assn. Home: PO Box 4002 East Lansing MI 48826

ENGEL, L. PATRICK, state legislator; b. South Sioux City, Nebr., May 18, 1932; m. Dee Smith, 1952; children: Kathie, Kim, Jeff, Julie, Michael. Student, U. Nebr. Ins. agt. State Farm Ins., South Sioux City, Nebr.; commr. Dakota County, Nebr.; senator State of Nebr., Lincoln, 1994—; mem. appropriations com. Nebr. Senate. Mem. South Sioux City Sch. Bd., fin. com. St. Michael's Ch., South Sioux City Comty. Sch. Cardinal Found. Mem. KC (past grand knight, dist. dep.), Mended Hearts (chpt. 41), Sertoma, Toastmasters. Office: Nebr State Senate State Capitol Rm 1518 Lincoln NE 68509

ENGEL, LESLIE CARROLL, cell and molecular biologist, researcher; b. St. Louis, Nov. 9, 1949; d. William Reeves and Carroll Ann (Becker) E.; m. Robert Fulton Scheef, Dec. 31, 1976. BA, U. Mo., 1976, MA, 1980; PhD, Case Western Res. U., 1984. Muscular Dystrophy Assn. postdoctoral fellow Case Western Res. U., Cleve., 1984-85; NIH postdoctoral fellow U. Calif., San Francisco, 1985-89; rsch. specialist health scis. dept. Monsanto Co., St. Louis, 1989—; cons. vascular cell biology group Washington U., St. Louis, 1991—. Contbr. articles to profl. jours. Vol. sci. literacy program Sch. Dist. Webster Groves/Monsanto Co., 1991—. Recipient Arthur F. Hughes Meml. award for outstanding original rsch. Case Western Res. U., 1985. Mem. Am. Soc. Cell Biology, Tech. Community Monsanto.

ENGEL-ARIELI, SUSAN LEE, physician; b. Chgo., Oct. 7, 1954; d. Thaddeus S. Dziengiel and Marion L. (Carpenter) Kasper; m. Udi Arieli. BA, Northwestern U., 1975; MD, Chgo. Med. Sch., 1982. Med. technician G.D. Searle, Skokie, Ill., 1972, 73, assoc. dir., 1983-84; dir. U.S. Regional Clin. Support G.D. Searle, 1984-86; rsch. editorial asst. U. Chgo., 1974; rsch. assoc. Loyola U., Maywood, Ill., 1977-78; intern Rush Presbyn. St. Lukes Hosp., Chgo., 1982-83; resident U. Chgo., 1983; mgr. hosp. products div. Abbott Labs., Abbott Park, Ill., 1986-87; bd. govs., dep. gov. Am. Biog. Inst. Rsch. Assn., 1988; vis. prof. Rush Presbyn.-St. Luke's Hosp., Chgo., 1985, faculty assoc., 1985; assoc. investigator, asst. prof. medicine King Drew Med. Ctr., UCLA, 1985-90; practical cardiology panel experts, 1988; Med. World News Rev. panel, 1988; bd. dirs. Am. Soc. Handicapped Physicians, acting v.p.; bd. dirs. fundraising, chmn. Vestibular Disorders Assn. Author: How Your Body Works, 1994, C-D Rom version, 1995; contbr. articles to profl. and scholarly jours. Bd. govs. Art Inst. Chgo., 1985—, mem. aux. bd., 1988—, mem. multiple benefit coms., 1984—, vice chmn. Capital Campaign, 1984-85; mem. pres. com. Landmark Preservation Coun., Chgo., 1984-90, chmn. multiple coms. polit. candidates, 1986; bd. dirs. Marshall unit Chgo. Boys Clubs, 1984—; mem. benefit com. Hubbard St. Dance Co. 10th Gala, 1988, Victory Garden's Theatre Ann. Benefit, 1988. Internat. Coll. Surgeons fellow, 1982. Mem. AMA, ACP, Am. Fedn. for Clin. Rsch., Southern Med. Assn., Ill. State Med. Soc., Chgo. Med. Soc., Am. Acad. Med. Dirs., Nat. Acad. Arts and Scis., Am. Soc. Handicapped Physicians (bd. dirs., v.p.), Vestibular Disorders Assn. (bd. dirs., pub. rels. com., co-chmn. fundraising).

ENGELMAN, WAYNE, advertising executive; b. 1934. With Colle & McAvoy, Inc., Mpls., 1966—, officer, 1969—, sec., CFO. Office: Colle & McVoy Inc 8500 Mormandale Lake Blvd Minneapolis MN 55437*

ENGELMANN, PAUL VICTOR, plastics engineering educator; b. Ann Arbor, Mich., Jan. 15, 1958; s. Manfred David and Patricia (Park) E.; m. Martha Ann Heystek, Aug. 14, 1983 (dec. May 1996); 1 child, David. AS in Geology, Lansing (Mich.) C.C., 1980; BS in Indsl. Edn., Western Mich. U., 1982, MA in Vocat. Edn., 1984, EdD in Ednl. Leadership, 1988. Owner H.L. & S. Auto Restoration & Fabrication, Lansing, Mich., 1977-82; tchg. asst. dept. engring. tech. Western Mich. U., Kalamazoo, 1982-83, part time instr., 1983-87, instr., 1987-89, asst. prof. plastics, 1989-93, assoc. prof. dept. indsl. and mfg. engring., 1993—; prin. investigator Rsch. and Tech. Inst., Grand Rapids, Mich., 1988—; rschr. Robert Morgan & Co., Battle Creek, Mich., 1990-94; prin. investigator Copper Devel. Assn. Inc.; cons. plastics Parker Hannafin Corp., Ostego, Mich., 1990—; v.p. Western Mich. SPE Edn. Found., 1994—. Author (book) Manufacturing Technology, 1989; contbr. articles to profl. jours.; patentee in field. Pres. Plainwell (Mich.) Hist. Preservation Soc., 1990-91; bd. dirs. Pipp Found., 1992—, sec. 1992—. Presdl. scholar, 1982; recipient Protective Package of the Yr. award Children's Hosp. of Birmingham, 1990, Teaching Excellence award Western Mich. U., 1990. Mem. Soc. Plastics Engrs. (sr., past pres. 1992-93, pres. 1991-92, pres.-elect 1990-91, v.p. Western Mich. sec. 1989-90, sec. 1988-89, edn. chmn. 1985-88, Sectional award 1986, 87, 88, Best Paper award 1992, Outstanding Member award 1994). Methodist. Home: 311 E Chart St Plainwell MI 49080-1703 Office: Western Mich U Dept Indsl and Mfg Engring Kalamazoo MI 49008

ENGELS, KEVIN J., securities company official; b. Wichita, Kans., Feb. 17, 1966. Ops. mgr. B.C. Christopher Securities, Wichita, 1984-87, Am. Discount Securities, Wichita, 1987—. Office: Am Discount Securities 220 W Douglas Ave Ste 62 Wichita KS 67202-3178

ENGELS, THOMAS JOSEPH, sales executive; b. New Orleans, May 24, 1958; s. Ronald Henry and Sally (Jacobsen) E.; m. Tamara Lewis Engels, May 29, 1982; children: Kristen, Danielle. BS in Gen. Mgmt., Purdue U., 1980. Sales rep. Johnson & Johnson, New Brunswick, N.J., 1980-82, mgr., 1982-83; dist. sales mgr. Pepsi Cola U.S.A., Somers, N.Y., 1983-87; regional sales mgr. Rich Sea Pak Corp., St. Simons Island, Ga., 1988-89; cen. regional mgr. food svc. div. Sara Lee Bakery, Chgo., 1990-93; area mgr. Ctrl. Zone Sara Lee Bakery Food Svc., 1993-94, divsn. promotion mgr. East, 1995—. Mem. Substandard and Poors Investment Club (pres. Indpls. 1985-86), Sigma Nu. Roman Catholic.

ENGESSER, KAREN LYNNE SHARP, physical therapist; b. Bryan, Ohio, Jan. 9, 1945; d. Marion L. and Kathryn E. (Keep) Sharp; m. Daniel Joseph Engesser, June 21, 1975; children: J. Daniel, Matthew K., Katherine M. BS in Zoology, Ohio U., 1968; cert. in phys. therapy, Mayo Clinic, 1968. Staff phys. therapist Meth. Hosp., St. Louis Park, Minn., 1968-69; rehab. phys. therapist Younker Rehab. Ctr., Des Moines, 1969-70; dir. phys. therapy, dir. fed. grant Woodwood (Iowa) State Hosp. Sch., 1970-76; phys. therapist Area Edn. Agy. VI, Marshalltown, Iowa, 1979-91; staff phys. therapist Marshalltown Med./Surg. Ctr., 1991—; charter mem. Head Injury Support Group, Marshalltown. Clarinet player Marshalltown City Bd., 19779—, Marshalltown C.C., 1979—, also in Bryan, Ohio, Rochester, Minn., Ames, Iowa. Mem. Am. Phys. Therapy Assn., Iowa Phys. Therapy Assn. Republican. Roman Catholic. Home: 411 Park St Marshalltown IA 50158

ENGLAND, CHRISTOPHER MATTHEW, marketing information analyst; b. Columbus, Ohio, Jan. 22, 1968; s. David Leroy and Glenda Sue (Lane) E. BBA summa cum laude, Kent State U., 1990; MBA, Franklin U., 1995. Fin. transaction analyst Nationwide Ins., Columbus, Ohio, 1990-91, customer svc. analyst, 1991-95; mktg. info. analyst, Ohio, 1995—. Tech. sgt. USAFR, 1986-88. Mem. Fairfield County Young Republicans Club, Beta Gamma Sigma. Methodist.

ENGLAND, JAMES WESLEY, accountant; b. Detroit, Mar. 6, 1938. BBA, Ea. Mich. U., 1961. Chief acct. U. Mich., Ann Arbor, 1963-70; dir. fin. U. Mich. Hosp., Ann Arbor, 1970-75; assoc. adminstr. Chelsea (Mich.) Cmty. Hosp., 1975-85; v.p. Retirement Resources, Inc., Manchester, Mich., 1985—; pres. Products, Inc., Manchester, 1980—. 1st lt. U.S. Army, 1961-63. Mem. Healthcare Fin. Mgmt. Assn., Optimists (pres. 1980).

ENGLE, BARBARA LOUISE, state legislator; b. Berne, Ind., Sept. 11, 1945; d. Luther and Maxine (Moser) E. B in English, Ball State U., 1967; MEd, St. Francis Coll., 1971. Tchr. North Adams Cmty. Schs., 1967—; mem. Ind. Ho. of Reps. Divsn. leader United Way, Adams County, Ind., 1989-94. Recipient Pacesetter award Ind. State Tchrs. Assn., 1985. Mem. Decatur Bus. and Profl. Women. Republican. Mem. Ch. of Christ. Home: 916 Waynesboro Ave Decatur IN 46733-2624 Office: Ind State Ho of Reps State Capital Indianapolis IN 46204

ENGLE, PAUL E., book editor, educator; b. Buffalo, Aug. 19, 1942; s. George E. and Marion P. E.; m. Margaret Walker, Dec. 20, 1969; children: Christine, Heather. BA, Houghton (N.Y.) Coll., 1964; MDiv, Wheaton (Ill.) Coll. Grad. Sch., 1967; D Ministry, Westminster Theological Sem., Phila., 1977. Ordained min. Presbyn. Ch. Asst. min. The Blue Ch., Springfield, Pa., 1967-72; min. Evangelical Free Ch., Branford, Conn., 1972-77; sr. min. Village Ch. of Lincolnshire, Ill., 1977-86, Christ Ch., Grand Rapids, Mich., 1986-89; editor profl. books Baker Book House, Grand Rapids, 1990—; editl. dir. Baker Bytes, 1993—; vis. instr. Trinity Evangelical Divinity Sch., Deerfield, Ill., 1980-85, Reformed Theol. Sem., Jackson, Miss., 1990—, Knox Theol. Sem., Ft. Lauderdale, Fla., 1993—; vis. prof. Spring Arbor Coll., Grand Rapids, 1995. Author: (books) Discovering the Fullness of Worship, 1978, Worship Planbook, 1984, The Governor Drove Us Up the Wall, 1985, Guarding & Growing, 1989, Baker's Wedding Handbook, 1995, Baker's Funeral Handbook, 1996. Presbyn. Office: Baker Book House 6030 E Fulton Ada MI 49301

ENGLER, JOHN, governor; b. Mt. Pleasant, Mich., Oct. 12, 1948; s. Mathias John and Agnes Marie (Neyer) E.; m. Michele; children: Margaret Rose, Hannah Michelle, Madeleine Jenny; B.S. in Agrl. Econs., Mich. State U., 1971; J.D., Thomas M. Cooley Law Sch., 1981. Mem. Mich. Ho. of Reps., 1971-78; mem. Mich. Senate, 1979-90, Republican leader, 1983, majority leader, 1984-90; ; state senator, 1979-90; gov., 1990—. Del. White House Conf. on Youth, 1972; U.S. Trade Reps.' Intergovernmental Policy Adv. com., 1988, Intergovernmental Adv. Coun. on Edn., 1988. Bd. dirs. Mich. Spl. Olympics; chmn. Presdl. Scholars, 1991-92. Recipient Disting. Service to Agr. award Mich. Agr. Conf., 1974; named Legislator of Yr., Police Officers Assn. Mich., 1981; One of 5 Outstanding Young Men of Mich., Mich. Jaycees, 1983. Fellow State Bar Mich.; mem. Nat. Gov.'s Assn. (welfare reform task force 1993—, edn. goals panel 1993—). Republican. Roman Catholic. Club: Detroit Economic.*

ENGLISH, FLOYD LEROY, telecommunications company executive; b. Nicholas, Calif., June 10, 1934; s. Elvan L. and Louise (Corliss) E.; m. Wanda Parton, Sept. 8, 1955 (div. 1980); children: Roxane, Darryl; m. Elaine Ewell, July 3, 1981; 1 child, Christine. AB in Physics, Calif. State U., Chico, 1959; MS in Physics, Ariz. State U., 1962, PhD in Physics, 1965. Divsn. supr. Sandia Labs., Albuquerque, 1965-73; gen. mgr. Rockwell Internat.-Collins, Newport Beach, Calif., 1973-75; pres. Darcom, Albuquerque, 1975-79; cons in energy mgmt. and acquisitions Albuquerque, 1979-80; v.p. U.S. ops. Andrew Corp., Orland Park, Ill., 1980-82, pres., 1982—, COO, 1982-83, CEO, 1983—, also bd. dirs., 1994—; bd. dirs. Internat. Engring. Consortium. Contbr. articles to profl. jours. Bd. dirs. Ill. Math. and Sci. Acad. Fund for Advancement of Edn. 1st lt. U.S. Army, 1954-57; capt. Res., 1957-69. Mem. IEEE, Execs. Club of Chgo. (bd. dirs.). Republican. Presbyterian. Office: Andrew Corp 10500 W 153rd St Orland Park IL 60462-3071

ENGLISH, LAURA JANE, zoning coordinator; b. Berea, Ohio, Sept. 13, 1952; d. Donald Leo and Mary Jean (Vitek) Lamberton; m. Craig Scott English, Aug. 10, 1974. BA in Edn., Otterbein Coll., 1974. Agy. bookkeeper Lake County Comty. Svcs. Coun., Mentor, Ohio, 1982-86; office mgr. Tartan Marine Co., Grand River, Ohio, 1986-90; adminstrv. sec. Concord (Ohio) Twp., 1990-92, zoning sec., 1992-95, zoning coord., 1995—. Mem. AAUW (treas. Painesville, Ohio br. 1991—), Benevolent Bear Soc. of Western Res. Office: Concord Twp 7229 Ravenna Rd Concord OH 44077

ENGLISH, PHYLLIS JEAN, clinical psychologist; b. Detroit, Apr. 10, 1943; d. Sanders English and Bernice Rucker; m. John Bass Jr., June, 1960 (div.); children: Anthony, Wendy, Sherry Bass. BA, Concordia Coll., 1988; MSA, Cen. Mich. U., 1989; PhD, Union Inst. (Grad. Sch.), 1993; postgrad., Washtenaw C.C., 1995—. Psychology intern pvt. facility Leonia, Mich., 1991-92; psychology intern Huron Valley Men's Facility, Ypsilanti, Mich., 1992. Tutor Spanish-speaking students Milan (Mich.) Fed. Prison, 1991; parent mentor Cath. Social Svcs., Ann Arbor, 1980s. Mem. APA, Assn. for Advancement of Psychoanalysis, Mich. Psychoanalytic Soc., Mich. Neuropsychol. Soc. Home: 1457 Harry Ypsilanti MI 48198-6621

ENGSTROM, FREDERICK WILLIAM, psychiatrist; b. New Haven, Conn., June 21, 1948; s. William Weborg and Elizabeth Grace (Wulf) E.; m. Ellen Belle Urquhart, June 12, 1971; children: Carl Frederick, Anna Katherine. BA magna cum laude, Harvard U., 1970; MD, U. Rochester, 1974. Diplomate Am. Bd. Psychiatry and Neurology; cert. adminstrv. psychiatrist, 1988. Resident in psychiatry U. Colo., Denver, 1974-77; psychiatrist Park Nicollet Clinic, Mpls., 1977—, chmn. mental health dept., 1983-90; clin. assoc. prof. U. Minn., Mpls., 1977—; trustee Park Nicollet Clinic, 1990—, sec., 1992—, vice chair 1994—; trustee HealthSystem Minn., 1994—; lectr. in field. Mem. Am. Psychiatric Assn., Minn. Med. Assn. Office: Park Nicollet Clinic 3800 Park Nicollet Blvd Saint Louis Park MN 55416

ENK, SCOTT, editor; b. Milw., Apr. 9, 1958; s. Kenneth Benedict and Audrey Pearl (Szymanowski) E. BA in Mass Comm. and Econs. with distinction, U. Wis., Milw., 1981. Pers. asst. Fleet Mortgage Corp., Milw., 1982, foreclosure asst., 1983, pubs. designer, editor, writer, 1983-87; documentation editor, writer, tester Aardvark/McGraw-Hill, Milw., 1987-88; rsch./quality assurance editor Gareth Stevens, Inc., Milw., 1988-91; sr. editor Southea. Wis. Regional Planning Commn., Waukesha, 1992—; guest lectr. silent film history and women's roles in silent film Alverno Coll., Milw., 1991-93, 96. Editor, writer, rschr. reports, newsletters, manuals, children's books; contbr. articles, essays and editls. to various publs. Mem. West Suburban Milw. chpt. NOW, 1978—, sec., 1984-89, pres., 1987—, chairperson fundraising com., 1983-84; founder, pres. Greater Milw. chpt. Hear My Voice/Protecting Our Nation's Children (formerly DeBoer Com. for Children's Rights), 1993—; mem. Milwaukee County Hist. Soc., 1984—; officer Wis. Phi Beta Kappa Found., Inc. Recipient award in recognition of children's rights work United Foster Parents Assn. Greater Milw., 1995; journalism scholar Milw. profl. chpt. Soc. Profl. Journalists, 1979, Harry J. Grant Found., Milw., 1979-81. Mem. U. Wis. Milw. Alumni Assn. (Coll. Letters and Sci. scholar 1979), Mensa, Milw. 9 to 5, Nat. Model R.R. Assn., Phi Beta Kappa (bd. dirs. Greater Milw. assn. 1984—, sec. 1985-90, pres. 1990—, del. to nat. triennial coun. 1988, 91, 94), Phi Kappa Phi, Phi Alpha Theta, Sigma Epsilon Sigma, Phi Eta Sigma. Home: 3163 S 10th St Milwaukee WI 53215-4729

ENNES, MARK RAYMOND, financial consultant; b. Lebanon, Mo., Mar. 4, 1952. BA, Valparaiso (Ind.) U., 1974. Fin. cons., asst. v.p. Merrill Lynch, Merrillville, Ind., 1981—; continuing edn. instr. Purdue U. North Ctrl.; bd. dirs. Lake Tippecanoe Property Owners Inc., Leesburg, Ind. Bd. dirs., vice chmn. Valparaiso (Ind.) Lakes Area Conservancy Dist., 1989—; pres. Hillcrest Improvement Assn., Valparaiso, 1982—; mem., alumni chmn. cmty. campaign Valparaiso U., 1988—. Mem. Valparaiso U. Alumni Assn., Bond Club Chgo., Valparaiso Sunrise Kiwanis (past pres.). Lutheran. Office: Merrill Lynch 8585 Broadway # 590 Merrillville IN 46410-7064

ENNS, HARRY JOHN, state official. Former min. natural resources Man. Natural Resources Dept., Winnipeg, Can.; min. agr. Man. Agr. Dept., Winnipeg. Office: Man Agr Dept, Legislative Bldg-Rm 165, Winnipeg, MB Canada R3C 0V8

ENRIGHT, GEORGANN MCGEE, mental health nurse; b. Chgo., Nov. 8, 1943; d. George Daniel and Marjorie (Altenburg) McGee; m. John Joseph Enright, Apr. 8, 1967; children: Sean, Erin, Emily, Katherine. BSN cum laude, U. Mich, 1965; cert., Patricia Stevens Career Coll., 1966; postgrad., Edison State Community Coll.; MS, Wright State U., 1994. Cert. psychiat. nurse ANCC. Staff nurse, med. surg. U. Hosp., Ann Arbor, Mich., 1965-66; float nurse, med. surg. ICU Christ Community Hosp., Oak Lawn, Ill., 1966; staff nurse, med. surg. Saratoga Gen. Hosp., Detroit, 1967; med.-surg. float nurse, staff nurse neurosurgery and neurology Ohio State U. Hosp., Columbus, 1967-68; clin. nurse, team leader Planned Parenthood Miami Valley, Dayton, Ohio, 1970-71; float nurse, med. surg. pediatrics Stouder Hosp., Troy, Ohio, 1974-75; staff nurse adolescent and adult mental health unit Upper Valley Med. Ctr., Troy, 1983—; instr. Edison State C.C., Piqua, Ohio, 1990—, Sinclair C.C., Dayton, 1993—. Mem. Am. Psychiat. Nurses Assn., Ohio Psychiat. Nurses Network, Miami Valley Gerontol. Coun., Dayton Area Psychiatric Nurses Assn., Sigma Theta Tau, Phi Kappa Phi, Alpha Lambda Delta. Home: 103 S Monroe St Troy OH 45373-2932

ENRIGHT-SIDNEY, CATHERINE, chaplin; b. Greenwood, Miss., Oct. 14, 1939; d. Richard Enright and Arena (Moore) Howard; children: Carolyn, Theresa, Michelle, Kenneth. Min. New Hope Int. Ministry, 1987—. Recipient Black Excellent award Prison Ministry, 1994. Home: 9009 N 75th St Apt 07 Milwaukee WI 53223 Office: Benedict Criminal Justice 1015 N 9th St Milwaukee WI 53233

ENSLEN, RICHARD ALAN, federal judge; b. Kalamazoo, May 28, 1931; s. Ehrman Thrasher and Pauline Mabel (Dragoo) E.; m. Pamela Gayle Chapman, Nov. 2, 1985; children—David, Susan, Sandra, Thomas, Janet, Joseph, Gennady. Student, Kalamazoo Coll., 1949-51, Western Mich. U., 1955; LL.B., Wayne State U., 1958; LL.M., U. Va., 1986. Bar: Mich. 1958, U.S. Dist. Ct. (we. dist.) Mich. 1960, U.S. Ct. Appeals (6th cir.) 1971, U.S. Ct. Appeals (4th cir.) 1975, U.S. Supreme Ct 1975. Mem. firm Stratton, Wise, Early & Starbuck, Kalamazoo, 1958-60, Bauckham & Enslen, Kalamazoo, 1960-64, Howard & Howard, Kalamazoo, 1970-76, Enslen & Schma, Kalamazoo, 1977-79; dir. Peace Corps. Costa Rica, 1965-67; judge Mich. Dist. Ct., 1968-70; U.S. dist. judge Kalamazoo, 1979—, chief judge, 1995—; mem. faculty Western Mich. U., 1961-62, Nazareth Coll., 1974-75; adj. prof. polit. sci. Western Mich. U., 1982—. Co-author: The Constitution Law Dictionary: Volume One, Individual Rights, 1985; Volume Two, Governmental Powers, 1987, Constitutional Deskbook: Individual Rights, 1987. Served with USAF, 1951-54. Recipient Disting. Alumni award Wayne State Law Sch., 1980, Disting. Alumni award Western Mich. U., 1982; Outstanding Practical Achievement award Ctr. Pub. Resources, 1984; award for Excellence and Innovation in Alternative Dispute Resolution and Dispute Mgmt., Legal Program; Jewel Corp. scholar, 1956-57; Lampson McElhorne scholar, 1957. Mem. ABA (standing com. on dispute resolution 1983-90), Mich. Bar Assn., Am. Judicature Soc (bd. dirs. 1983-85), Sixth Cir. Jud. Coun. Office: US Dist Ct 410 W Michigan Ave Kalamazoo MI 49007-3746

ENSLEY, TOM MICHAEL, manufacturing engineer; b. Ft. Wayne, Ind., Apr. 6, 1957. Prin. designer Phillips Techs., Auburn, Ind., 1983-93; mgr.

design engring. Tri Tech Mfg. Inc., Ft. Wayne, 1993—. Mem. Son. of Am. Legion. Home: 8311 Santa Fe Trl Fort Wayne IN 46815-6637 Office: Tri Tech Mfg Inc 2728 Commercial Rd Fort Wayne IN 46809-2922

ENSLOW, ROGER DEMETRI, electrical engineer; b. Neosho, Mo., Jan. 28, 1962; s. Kenneth Wayne and Joyce Ann (Pittman) En.; m. Mary Ann Martin Enslow, Mar. 15, 1986; children: Benjamin, Christopher. BEE, U. Mo., 1985; MS in Engr. Mgmt., 1986. Quality engr. LaBarge Inc., Joplin, Mo., 1991-92; tchr. Electronics Crowder Coll., Neosho, Mo., 1992—; project engr. Eagle Picher Ind. Inc., Joplin, Mo., 1993—. Sgt. U.S. Army, 1987-91, Korea. Mem. IEEE,. Democrat. Home: 819 N High St Neosho MO 64850-1219 Office: Eagle Picher Ind Inc 1215 W B St Joplin MO 64801-2869

ENSMINGER, DALE, mechanical engineer, electrical engineer; b. Mt. Perry, Ohio, Sept. 26, 1923; s. Charles Henry and Mary Elpha (Koehler) E.; m. Lois Elizabeth Hamilton, Mar. 25, 1948; children: Martha Jean, Laura Lee, Charles Robert, Jonathan Dale, Mary Ann, Daniel Joseph. BSME, BSEE, Ohio State U., 1950, postgrad., 1950-53. Registered profl. engr., Ohio. Researcher Battelle Meml. Inst., Columbus, Ohio, 1950; prin. researcher Battelle Meml. Inst.; sr. researcher Battelle Columbus Labs., mgr. ultrasonics, sr. rsch. scientist, 1988—; cons. in field. Author: Ultrasonics, 1973, 2d edit. 1988; contbr. articles to profl. jours., chpts. to books; patentee in field; contbr., reviewer Am. Soc. Non-Destructive Testing Handbook, 1989—. Sec. Columbus Prison Assn., 1950—; dean, dir. Columbus Bible Inst., 1952—; mem. bd. Fundamental Bapt. Mission of Trinidad and Tobago. With U.S. Army, 1943-46. Recipient Cert. of Recognition, NASA, 1975. Mem. Acoustical Soc. Am., Soc. for Non-Destructive Testing, Ultrasonic Industry Assn. Home: 198 E Longview Ave Columbus OH 43202-1236 Office: Battelle 505 King Ave Columbus OH 43201-2696

ENTENZA, MATT, state legislator; b. Oct. 4, 1961; m. Lois Quam; 3 children. BA, Macalester Coll.; postgrad., Oxford (Eng.) U.; JD, U. Minn. Pvt. practice; rep. Dist. 64A Minn. Ho. of Reps., 1994—.

ENTRIKEN, ROBERT KERSEY, JR., retired newspaper editor, motorsport writer; b. Houston, Feb. 13, 1941; s. Robert and Jean (Finch) (stepmother) E.; married 1972 (div., 1982); 1 child, Jean Louise; m. Sandra Jo Miller, Mar. 4, 1989; children: Caitlyn Miller, Matthew Kersey; 1 adopted child, Stephanie Lynn; stepchild: Jared Ray Adamson. Student Sch. Journalism, U. Kans., 1961-69. Gen. assignment reporter Salina Jour., Kans., 1969-71, motorsport columnist, 1970-83, courts reporter, 1971-82, Sunday editor, 1972-75, spl. sects. editor, 1975-94, neighbors editor, 1982-95, TV editor, 1994-95; contbg. editor Sports Car Mag., Tustin, Calif., 1972—; motorsport columnist Motorsports Monthly, Tulsa, Okla., 1983-85; operator Ikke så Hurtig Racing; Contbr. Performance Racing Industry mag., Sports Car World mag, Car Collector mag., Parts & People mag., Kansas! mag., editor Kansas Motor Sports Ann. With USN, 1969-71, Guam. Mem. Am. Auto Racing Writers and Broadcasters Assn. (gen. v.p. 1982-86, Midwest v.p. 1980-82, chmn. All-Am. Team selections 1983—, chmn. Legends in Racing selections hall of fame 1989—), Soc. of Profl. Journalist Sigma Delta Chi, Sports Car Club Am. (Best Story award 1972, 73, 76-78, 83-87, 89, 92, Solo Cup nat. award 1981, England-Stipe award 1989, Nat. Solo I champion 1986, Road Racing Driver of the Year 1995, Solo Driver of Yr. Wichita Region 1976, 82, Solo II Champion, Kans. 1978, 84, Midwest div. 1984, regional exec. of Kans. Region, 1974, founding mem. Salina Region 1990, regional exec. Salina Region 1994, Midwest divsn. Mid-Am. pointskeeper 1974—, nat. pointskeeper 1995—). Avocations: sports car racing, autocrossing, skiing. Home: 2731 Scott Ave Salina KS 67401-7858 Office: The Salina Jour 333 S 4th PO Box 740 Salina KS 67402-0740

ENYEDY, GUSTAV, JR., chemical engineer; b. Cleve., Aug. 23, 1924; s. Gustav and Mary (Silay) E.; m. Zoe Agnes Zachlin, Aug. 25, 1956 (div.); children: Louise Elaine, Roseann Marie, Arthur Gustav, Lillian Alice, Edward Anthony; m. Barbara Martha Ludwig Holley, May 9, 1987. B.S. in Chem. Engring., Case Inst. Tech., 1950, M.S., 1955. Registered profl. engr., Ohio. Engr., Rayon Tech. div. E.I. duPont, Richmond, Va., 1950-51; project engr. Grasselli Chem. Div., Cleve., 1951-54; devel. engr. Diamond Alkali (Soda Products), Painesville, Ohio, 1954-60; process engr. Central Engring., Cleve., 1960-61; staff engr. research dept. Central Engring., Painesville, 1961-65; supr. computer services Central Engring., 1965-68; mgr. Diamond Shamrock Corp., Painesville, 1968-73; engring. cons., 1973-85; pres. PDQS, Inc., 1975—; lectr. chem. engring. Fenn Coll., Cleve., 1957-61, Cleve. State U., 1975-76. Contbr. articles to tech. jours., textbooks. Treas., cubmaster, chmn. Gates Mills Cub Scout Pack, 1970-71, 75-78. Served with AUS, 1943-46. Decorated Bronze Star medal, Combat Inf. badge. Fellow Am. Inst. Chem. Engrs., Am. Assn. Cost Engrs. (tech. v.p. 1966-68, pres. 1969-70, speakers' bur. program 1971-89, O.T. Zimmerman Founder's award and hon. life mem., 1992); mem. Tau Beta Pi, Pi Delta Epsilon. Home: 7830 Sugarbush Ln Gates Mills OH 44040-9317 Office: PDQS Inc RR 1 Gates Mills OH 44040-9801

ENZ, CATHERINE S., state legislator. Mem. Mo. Ho. of Reps., Jefferson City. Republican.

EOYANG, EUGENE CHEN, comparative literature educator; b. Hong Kong, Feb. 8, 1939; came to U.S., 1946; s. Thomas Ts'ao and Ellen Ying-ru (Ts'ao) E.; m. Patricia Chiu-yi Lee, Mar. 10, 1962; children: Christopher, Gregory. BA, Harvard Coll., 1959; MA, Columbia U., 1960; PhD in Comparative Lit., Ind. U., 1971. Editorial trainee Doubleday and Co., N.Y.C., 1960-62; editor Doubleday Anchor Books, N.Y.C., 1962-66; asst. prof. Ind. U., Bloomington, 1971-74, assoc. prof., 1974-80, prof. comparative lit., 1980—, assoc. dean rsch. and grad. devel., 1977-80, chmn. East Asian langs. and cultures, 1982-84, founder, dir. East Asian Summer Lang. Inst., 1984-89; trustee, sec.-treas. Kinsey Inst., Bloomington, 1982-93, chmn. bd., 1993-95; mem. com. on scholarly comm. People's Republic China, 1984-89. Author: The Transparent Eye, 1993, Coat of Many Colors, 1995; editor: Translating Chinese Poetry, 1995; translator, editor: Selected Poems of Ai Qing, 1982; co-founder, co-editor Chinese Lit.: Essays, Articles, Revs. (CLEAR), 1979—; major contbr.: Sunflower Splendor: Three Thousand Years of Chinese Poetry, 1975; also articles. Woodrow Wilson fellow, 1959-60, Title IV fellow NDEA, Washington, 1966-68, Fulbright-Hayes fellow, 1968-69, Alfred Hodder fellow Coun. on Humanities, Princeton U., 1974-75, Lilly Endowment Faculty Open fellow, 1981, Renditions Hon. fellow, 1994. Mem. MLA (adv. com. on fgn. langs. and lit. 1989-92), Am. Comparative Lit. Assn. (v.p. 1993-95, pres. 1995-97), Soc. for Comparative Study Civilization, Am. Coun. Learned Socs. (com. on studies Chinese civilization 1972-76). Office: Ind U Ballantine Hall 402 Bloomington IN 47405

EPP, MARY ELIZABETH, technologies consultant; b. Buffalo, Aug. 7, 1941; d. John Conrad and Gertrude Marie (Murphy) Winkelman; m. Harry Francis Epp, Aug. 31, 1963. BA in Math., D'Youville Coll., 1963; MS in Math., Xavier U., 1974, MBA in Fin., 1981, MBA in Mktg., 1987. Systems analyst GE, Evendale, Ohio, 1965-71, Palm Beach Co., Cin., 1972-73; hardware systems engr. Procter & Gamble, Cin., 1973-76; systems engr. CalComp Inc., Anaheim, Calif., 1980-84; software engr. SDRC Inc., Cin., 1984-86; advanced systems project mgr. SAMI/Burke Mktg., Cin., 1986-89; ptnr., dir. strategic planning Info. Advantage, Inc., Cin., 1989-91; internat. product control specialist Cincom Systems Inc., Cin., 1991-94; cons. Sybase, Inc., Cin., 1995—; cons. Shelley & Sands, Zanesville, Ohio, 1983-85. Contbr. articles to profl. jours. Mem. Fairfield Charter Rev. Commn., 1981-83. Mem. AAUW (br. treas. 1975-79, state women's chair 1979-80, state treas. 1980-82), NAFE, IEEE, Assn. Computing Machinery (treas. Cin. chpt. 1987-88, pres. 1988-89, program co-chair 1989-90), Nat. Computer Graphics Assn., Nat. Fedn. Music (Ohio fedn. music parade chair 1979-81.), Mercy Hosp. Aux. Club (treas. 1978-79), Musical Arts Club. Republican. Roman Catholic. Home: 4242 Stahlheber Rd Hamilton OH 45013-8911 Office: Sybase Inc Ste 550 625 Eden Park Dr Cincinnati OH 45202

EPPERSON, BRYAN KEITH, geneticist, educator; b. Fresno, Apr. 25, 1957; s. Edward Leo and Marianne (Schmall) E.; 1 child, Joseph Keith Epperson. BS, U. Calif., 1979, Phd, 1983. Postdoctoral assoc. U. Ga., Athens, 1983-84; postdoctoral geneticist U. Calif., Riverside, 1984-91, asst. rsch. geneticist, 1992-93; asst. prof. Mich. State U., 1994—; reviewer Princeton U. Press, 1992—; reviewer grant proposals for NSF, mem. panel, 1995; vis. prof. N.E. Forestry U. Harbin, China, 1995—. Reviewer for more than 20 jours.; author articles. Mem. rsch. scholar, 1975, Alumni scholar U. Calif., 1975, Calif. state scholar, 1975-79, Herbert-Kraft Meml. scholar, 1978; Jastro-Shields grad. rsch. fellow U. Calif., 1980; NIH grantee, 1993-96. Mem. European Soc. Evolutionary Biology, Soc. for the Study of Evolution, Genetics Soc. of Am., Nature Conservancy, Sigma Xi, Xi Sigma Pi. Office: Mich State U Dept Forestry East Lansing MI 48824

EPSTEIN, AVROM DAVID, physician, ophthalmologist; b. Brookline, Mass., Aug. 26, 1954; s. Bart Jacob and Judith Joy (Clayman) E.; m. Marcia Rosemary Kohn, June 15, 1986; children: Daniel Jay, Benjamin Meir, Leah Rachel. AB, Miami U., 1976; MD cum laude, Ohio State U., 1980. Diplomate Am. Bd. Ophthalmology, Am. Bd. Psychiatry and Neurology, Nat. Bd. Med. Examiners. Resident in internal medicine Rush-Presbyn.-St. Luke's Med. Ctr., 1980-81; resident in ophthalmology Mayo Grad. Sch. Medicine, 1981-84; resident in neurology Univ. Hosps. of Cleve., 1984-86; Heed/Knapp fellow in neuro-ophthalmology Wilmer Ophthal. Inst., Johns Hopkins U., Balt., 1986-88; asst. prof. depts. ophthalmology, neurology and surgery U. Ky. Coll. Medicine, Lexington, 1988-94; attending physician U. Ky. Med. Ctr., Lexington, 1988-94; attending physician Ohio State U. Hosps. and Clinic, Columbus, 1994—, asst. prof. depts. neurology and ophthalmology, 1994—; cons. VA Med. Ctr., Lexington, 1988-94, Ky. Commn. for Handicapped Children, 1992—. Contbr. chpts. to books, articles to profl. jours. Kenneth Wiseman scholar Ohio State U., 1979-80, Samuel J. Roessler Meml. med. scholar, 1979; Rawlings Four Star scholar Miami U., 1973-74; recipient grants. Fellow Am. Acad. Ophthalmology; mem. AMA, Am. Acad. Neurology, Soc. for Neurosci., Assn. for Rsch. in Vision and Ophthalmology, Ohio State Med. Assn., Ohio Ophthalmological Soc., Acad. Medicine Columbus and Franklin County, Alpha Omega Alpha, Phi Eta Sigma, Phi Sigma. Jewish. Home: 89 S Cassingham Rd Columbus OH 43209-1846 Office: Ohio State U Dept Neurology Means Hall Rm 465 1654 Upham Dr Columbus OH 43210-1250

EPSTEIN, ERWIN HOWARD, sociology and education educator; b. Chgo., Jan. 2, 1939; s. Louis Nathan and Charlotte (Kozin) E.; m. Barbara Myrna Robbin, Sept. 3, 1961; children: Jack R., Eric M., M. Avram. BA, U. Ill., 1960; MAT, U. Chgo., 1962, PhD, 1966. Tchr. Niles Twp. High Sch., Skokie, Ill., 1961-62; asst. prof. U. Wis., Madison, 1965-71; assoc. prof. U. Nebr., Kearney, 1971-73; prof. U. Mo., Rolla, 1973-91; dir. internat. studies Ohio State U., 1991-95; prof. edn., 1991—. Editor Comparative Edn. Rev., Chgo., 1988—; contbr. articles to profl. jours. Mem. adv. bd. ARC, Columbus, Ohio, 1994—; mem. adv. bd. UN-USA Assn., 1994—. Recipient Fulbright-Hays award Coun. for Internat. Exch., 1982-83, Acad. Specialist Grants U.S. Info Agy., 1984, 85, 87, Lourdes Casal award Latin Am. Studies Assn., 1985. Mem. World Council Comparative Edn. (pres. 1980-83), Comparative and Internat. Edn. Soc. (pres. 1981-82), Am. Sociol. Assn., Latin Am. Studies Assn., Am. Ednl. Research Assn., Caribbean Studies Assn., Rural Sociol. Soc. Democrat. Jewish. Office: Ohio State U Ramseyer Hall Comparative Edn Review Profl Devel Edn Columbus OH 43210

EPSTEIN, ROBERT MORRIS, history educator; b. Phila., Aug. 1, 1948; s. Irving Joseph and Estelle Evelyn (Taleb) E.; m. Jan Lelain Lorenzen, May 19, 1953. BA, Temple U., 1970, MA, 1973, PhD, 1981. Instr. history C.C. of Phila., 1978-79, Drexel U., Phila., 1979; vis. assoc. prof. history U.S. Army Command and Gen. Staff Coll., Ft. Leavenworth, Kans., 1981-84, prof. history Sch. Advanced Mil. Studies, 1984—. Author: Prince Eugene at War: 1809, 1984, Napoleon's Last Victory and the Emergence of Modern War, 1994. Mem. Soc. for Mil. History (Moncado prize 1992). Office: Sch Advanced Mil Studies Eisenhower Hall Fort Leavenworth KS 66027

EPSTEIN, WOLFGANG, biochemist, educator; b. Breslau, Germany, May 7, 1931; came to U.S., 1936, naturalized, 1943; s. Stephan and Elsbeth (Lauinger) E.; m. Edna Selan, June 12, 1961; children: Matthew, Ezra, Tanya. B.A. with high honors, Swarthmore Coll., 1951; M.D., U. Minn., 1955. Postdoctoral fellow in physiology U. Minn., Mpls., 1959-60; postdoctoral fellow Pasteur Inst., Paris., 1963-65; postdoctoral fellow in biophysics Harvard Med. Sch., 1961-63, research asso., then asso. in biophysics, 1965-67; asst. prof. biochemistry U. Chgo., 1967-73, asso. prof., 1973-79, prof., 1979-84, prof. dept. molecular genetics and cell biology, 1984—. Served with M.C. U.S. Army, 1957-59. Mem. AAAS, Am. Soc. for Biochemistry and Molecular Biology, Am. Soc. for Microbiology. Home: 1120 E 50th St Chicago IL 60615-2804 Office: 920 E 58th St Chicago IL 60637-1432

EPTING, C. CHRISTOPHER, bishop; b. Greenville, S.C.; m. Pam Flagg; children: Michael, Amanda. Grad., U. Fla., Seabury-Western Theol. Sem., Evanston, Ill., 1952; STM, Gen. Theol. Sem., N.Y.C., 1984. Formerly curate Holy Trinity Ch., Melbourne; vicar Ch. of St. Luke the Evangelist, Mulberry, Fla., 1974-78; founding vicar St. Stephen's Ch., Lakeland, Fla.; canon residentiary St. John's Cathedral, from 1978; rector St. Mark's Episc. Ch. and Sch., Cocoa, Fla.; bishop coadjutor, then bishop Episc. Diocese of Iowa, Des Moines, 1988—; formerly dean Inst. Christian Studies, St. Luke's Cathedral, Orlando, Fla. Address: Episc Diocese of Iowa 225 37th St Des Moines IA 50312-4305

ERBE, JANET SUE, medical surgical, orthopedics and pediatrics nurse; b. Hamilton, Ohio, Aug. 25, 1952; d. Robert A. and Evon R. (Walls) Schlotterbeck; m. Gene Erbe. ADN, Miami U., Hamilton, 1972; BS summa cum laude, Coll. Mt. St. Joseph, 1989. Cert. in neonatal resuscitation, BLSC. With; asst. nurse mgr. Ft. Hamilton-Hughes Hosp., Hamilton, 1972—. Mem. ANA, ONA (legiis. liason). Home: 549 Beeler Blvd Hamilton OH 45013 Office: 630 Eaton Ave Hamilton OH 45013-2767

ERBES, JOHN ROBERT, engineering executive; b. LaSalle County, Ill., Sept. 13, 1946; s. Robert William and Jeanette Marie (Brey) E. Cert. of Indsl. Engring. Tech., Allied Inst. Tech., 1966; BS in Gen. Engring., Kennedy Western U., Utah, 1993. Engring. project mgr. Methode Electronics, Inc., Carthage, Ill., 1977—. Vol. Reading is Fundamental, Bus. Ptnrs. Com., Boy Scouts Am. Recipient Awards of Merit, Boy Scouts Am., 1989. Mem. Soc. automotive Engrs., Soc. Plastics Engrs. Roman Catholic. Home: 1260 E County Road 1200 Warsaw IL 62379-3409 Office: Methode Electronics Inc 111 W Buchanan St Carthage IL 62321-1250

ERCK, ROBERT ALAN, metallurgist, researcher; b. Chgo., Oct. 11, 1954; s. Harold and Doris P. Erck. MS in Physics, U. Ill., 1979, PhD in Metallurgy, 1988. Metallurgist Argonne (Ill.) Nat. Lab., 1992—; faculty mem. Coll. of DuPage, Glen Ellyn, Ill., 1991—. Contbr. articles to profl. jours. Mem. Soc. Tribologist and Lubrication Engrs. (assoc. editor 1989—). Office: Argonne Nat Lab 9700 Cass Ave Lemont IL 60439-4838

ERDEL, SALLY ELIZABETH, nurse; b. Peoria, Ill., Mar. 28, 1952; d. Robert William and Mary Maxine (Vick) Birky; m. Timothy Paul Erdel, Aug. 28, 1977; children: Sarah Beth, Rachel Elaine, Matthew Robert. AA summa cum laude, Ft. Wayne Bible Coll., 1972; grad. with highest honor, West Suburban Hosp. Sch. Nursing, Oak Park, Ill., 1975; BSN with high honor, U. Ill. Med. Ctr., Chgo., 1977, MS, 1980. Staff nurse West Suburban Hosp., 1975-77; tchg. asst. U. Ill. Med. Ctr., 1980; staff nurse Highland Park (Ill.) Hosp., 1981-82; staff nurse Carle Found. Hosp., Urbana, Ill., 1982-87; mem. nursing faculty Bethel Coll., Mishawaka, Ind., 1994—; acting program dir. divsn. of nursing, Bethel Coll., Mishawaka, Ind., 1995—; staff nurse St. Joseph's Hosp., Mishawaka, Ind., 1994—; seminar/workshop spkr., 1982—; clin. nurse specialist, 1985—; campus nurse, Jamaica Theol. Sem., Kingston, Jamaica, 1988-93, lectr. abnormal psychology, 1992-93; thesis sec. Caribbean Grad. Sch. Theology, Kingston, Jamaica, 1988-93; nursing cons. Devel. and Behavioral Evaluation Svcs., South Bend, Ind., 1994; team mem. Med. Group Mission, Liberia, 1975; vol. clinic nurse St. Andrew's Settlement, Kingston, 1991-93; missionary World Partners, 1987-94; mem. instnl. animal care and use com. U. Notre Dame, 1996—. Mem. Cen. Ill. Oncology Nurses (co-editor newsletter 1983-87), Missionary Ch. Hist. Soc., Ill. Mennonite Hist. and Geneal. Soc., Ind. Nurses Assn. Home: 56111 Francis Ave Mishawaka IN 46545-7507 Office: Bethel Coll Divsn Nursing 1001 W Mckinley Ave Mishawaka IN 46545-5509

ERDMAN, PAMELA ANN, occupational therapist; b. Buffalo, N.Y., Mar. 16, 1962; d. Robert Stanley and Joan Marie (Bitka) Mazur; m. Gary William Erdman, May 13, 1989. BS in Occupational Therapy, U. Buffalo, 1985; M of Health Svcs. Adminstrn., Cardinal Stritch Coll., 1989. Cert. occupational therapist, Wis. Occupational therapist Jewish Vocat. Svcs., Milw., 1985-86; occupational therapist I, II Milw. County Mental Health Complex, Milw., 1986—, occupational therapist III, 1989-95; occupational therapist III/therapeutic case mgr., 1995—. Mem. NAFE, Wis. Occupational Therapy Assn. Home: 4134 W Thorncrest Dr Franklin WI 53132-9649 Office: Milw Mental Health Complex 9501 W Watertown Plank Rd Milwaukee WI 53226-3552

ERDMANN, AUGUST, protective services official. Now fire chief City of Milw. Office: Fire Dept 711 W Wells St Fl 3 Milwaukee WI 53233-1403

ERHARDT, PAUL WILLIAM, medicinal chemist; b. Mpls., Oct. 31, 1947; m. Judy M. Erhardt, Feb. 19, 1971; children: William J., Michael P., Tricia M., John M., Christine M. BA in Chemistry, U. Minn., 1969, PhD in Medicinal Chemistry, 1974. Postdoctoral fellow Drug Dynamics Inst. U. Tex., Austin, 1974-75; asst. prof. Northeastern U., Boston, 1975-76; rsch. scientist, group leader Am. Critical Care, McGaw Park, Ill., 1976-83; sect. head, asst. dir. Berlex Labs., Inc., Cedar Knolls, N.J., 1983-94; prof. medicinal chemistry, dir. Ctr. Drug Design and Devel. U. Toledo, 1994—. Contbr. over 50 articles to profl. jours. Mem. Am. Chem. Soc. Home: 5036 Fairway Ln Sylvania OH 43560-2227

ERHARDT, RON, state legislator; m. Jacquelyn. BBA, U. Minn., 1958, BA, 1959. State rep. Minn. Ho. Reps., Dist. 42A, 1991—; mem. govt. oper. com., com. & econ. devel.-internat. trade, tech. & econ. devel. divsn., regulated indsl. & energy & taxes coms., Minn. Ho. Reps. Home: 4214 Sunnyside Rd Minneapolis MN 55424-1114*

ERICKSON, CLARK ERWIN, lawyer, author; b. Ironwood, Mich., Mar. 23, 1948; s. Erwin Helge and Anna Marie (Ohman) E. BS, 1976, MBA, 1971; JD, U. Ill., 1976. Bar: Ill. 1976. Asst. states atty. County of Kankakee, Ill., 1976-92, states atty., 1992-95; cir. judge 21st cir. Ill. Supreme Ct., 1995—. Home: 2601 N Oakridge Dr Kankakee IL 60901 Office: Kankakee County States Atty 450 E Court Kankakee IL 60901

ERICKSON, CURTIS ALLEN, physician; b. Itazuke USAF Fukuoka, Japan, Sept. 1, 1960; s. Clark Allen and Jean Darlyn (Gann) E.; m. Susan V. Temple, May 24, 1986 (div. June 1991); m. Whitney Jay Norsworthy, Mar. 10, 1992. BA, Hendrix Coll., 1982; MD, U. Ark., 1986. Diplomate Am. Bd. Surgery. Surg. resident U. Ark. for Med. Scis., Little Rock, 1986-91; trauma surgeon Tucson (Ariz.) Med. Ctr., 1993-94; vascular surgery resident Med. Coll. of Wis., Milw., 1994—. Contbr. articles to profl. jours. Maj. U.S. Army, 1991-93. Marie Wilson Howelss Rsch. fellowship U. Ark., 1983. Fellow ACS (assoc., Ariz. chpt.); mem. AMA, Ariz. Med. Assn., Ark. Med. Soc., Alpha Chi.

ERICKSON, JUDITH BOWEN, sociologist; b. Peekskill, N.Y., July 13, 1934; d. Carl August and Virginia (Bowen) E. AB, Wheaton Coll., 1955; MA, U. Minn., 1968, PhD, 1975. Caseworker Spokane (Wash.) County Child Welfare, 1956-57; dist. dir. Mpls. Coun. Camp Fire, 1961-66; asst. prof. dept. sociology Macalester Coll., St. Paul, 1970-80; program assoc. NSF, Washington, 1978-80; vis. fellow Ctr. for the Study of Youth Devel., Boys Town, Nebr., 1980-82; assoc. prof. Ctr. for Youth Devel. and Rsch. U. Minn., St. Paul, 1982-89; dir., rsch. svcs. Ind. Youth Inst., Indpls., 1989—; mgr. Am. Inst. Holy Land Studies, Jerusalem, Israel, 1959-60; mem. task force Carnegie Coun. on Adolescent Devel., Washington, 1990-92; cons. Boy Scouts Am., Irving, Tex., 1986-96, Girl Scouts of the USA, 1990-96. Author: Directory of American Youth Organizations, 1983, 86, 89, 91, 93, 96; contbr. articles to profl. jours. Bd. dirs. Girl Scouts USA, St. Croix Valley, St. Paul, 1970-78; allocations vol. Mpls. Area United Way, 1987-89. Lilly Endowment grantee, 1985-89. Mem. AAAS, Am. Sociol. Assn., Am. Ednl. Rsch. Assn., Am. Evaluation Assn. Democrat. Office: Ind Youth Inst Ste 200 3901 N Meridian St Indianapolis IN 46208-4046

ERICKSON, LARRY ALVIN, electronics sales and marketing executive; b. La Crosse, Wis., May 13, 1950; s. Leslie Louis and Alida Lillian Erickson; m. Sharon Kay Bakke, June 5, 1973 (div. Dec. 1980); children: Melissa J., Amy J., Brian D.; m. Sherri Sue Hillberg, Sept. 10, 1983; children: Mark E., Stephanie L. Student, Winona (Minn.) State Coll., 1968-72, Austin (Minn.) Vo-Tech. Sch., 1988-89, Austin C.C., 1990-91. Driver, mechanic Preston (Minn.) Equipment, 1977-80; truck driver Internat. Transport, Rochester, Minn., 1980-81, Comml. Svcs., Storm Lake, Iowa, 1981-82; meat cutter Hormel, Austin, 1982-85; gen. mgr. McPherson Archery Co., Austin, 1985-89; substitute tchr. Austin Vo-Tech. Sch., 1989-90; bookkeeper Hanson Constrn., Lyle, Minn., 1990—; mgr. sales and mktg. LeRoy (Minn.) Products Corp., 1990—; v.p. Compact Cirs. Corp., Decorah, Iowa, 1996—; ind. sales rep. Tech. Tool, Austin, 1992; small bus. cons., 1992—. Dir. communion distbn. St. Olaf Luth. Ch., Austin, 1992. Recipient certificate of commendation Gov. State of Minn., 1987; named Outstanding Mem. of Month and Yr., Austin Jaycees, 1990. Mem. Am. Prodn. and Inventory Control Soc. (bd. dirs. 92), Minn. Archers Assn. (bd. dirs. 1989-91). Republican. Home: 206 15th St SE Austin MN 55912-4240 Office: Le Roy Products Corp Highway 56 And County Rd Le Roy MN 55951

ERICKSON, MARGARET ANN, physical therapist; b. Mt. Kisco, N.Y., Sept. 11, 1958; d. Elvin Eugene and Eleanor Victoria (Ashley) Shoop; m. Scott Carl Erickson, Jan. 1, 1992. BS in Phys. Therapy, U. Conn., 1980. Lic. phys. therapist, Ill. Phys. therapist St. Joseph's Hosp., Lowell, Mass., 1980-82, Swedish Am. Hosp., Rockford, Ill., 1982-84, Rockford Meml. Hosp., 1984-91; phys. therapist Rockford Clinic, 1991—, pre- and post-natal exercise class fitness instr., 1995—; phys. therapy tchg. asst. No. Ill. U., Dekalb, 1991—. Named Therapist of Yr., Rockford A.M. Ambucs, 1988. Mem. Am. Phys. Therapy Assn. (del. 1994). Office: Rockford Clinic 2300 N Rockton Ave Rockford IL 61103

ERICKSON, MARGARET KATHRYN, lawyer; b. Sioux Falls, July 29, 1954; d. Wendell Oliver and Kathryn Ann (Thorsgard) E. BA, Gustavus Adolphus Coll., 1978; JD, U. Minn., 1982. Bar: Minn. 1982, U.S. Dist. Ct. Minn. 1984. Tour guide Historic Fort Snelling/Minn. Hist. Soc., 1972-74; field rschr. State Hist. Preservation Office, Fort Snelling, 1977; rschr. and writer Minn. Hist. Soc., St. Paul, 1979; atty. So. Minn. Regional Legal Svcs., Worthington, 1983—; book critic Tempest Mag., Sioux Falls, 1990-92; adj. instr. Worthington (Minn.) c.C., 1986-87; judge Minn. Book Awards, St. Paul, 1992, 93, 94, 95, 96; co-leader Adult Gt. Books Discussion Group, Worthington, 1990—. Founding editor (newsletter) Placement Weekly, 1980-82; vocalist (quartet) The Waites, St. Paul, 1980-88. Del. Minn. Rep. Conv., Mpls., 1972, Dem.-Farmer-Labor Party, Rochester, 1988, Duluth, 1992; bd. dirs. Nobles County Hist. Soc., 1987—, Worthington Concert Assn., 1990—, Nobles Coun. Art Ctr., 1988—, v.p., 1992-93. Nat Merit scholarship Gustavus Adolphus Coll., 1972, R.A. Stone scholarship U. Minn. Law Sch., 1979-82. Mem. AAUW (br. pres. 1991-93), Minn. Bar Assn. (del. 1991-92, 94, 95, 96), Worthington Bus. and Profl. Women (v.p. 1990-91, Woman of Yr. award 1990). Lutheran. Home: 1100 6th Ave Worthington MN 56187-2204

ERICKSON, MARK H., stockbroker; b. Canton, Ohio, Nov. 27, 1962; m. Katrina Erickson. BA in Acctg., St. Ambrose Coll., Davenport, Iowa, 1985. Stockbroker E.F. Hutton, Peoria, Ill., 1986-90, A.G. Edwards & Sons Inc., Peoria, 1990—; bd. dirs. Raritan State Bank. Mem. Kiwanis, KC. Republican. Roman Catholic. Home: 10205 N Forrest Dr Peoria IL 61615-1351

ERICKSON, RICHARD LEE, engineering executive; b. Youngstown, Ohio, Jan. 3, 1938; s. Albin E. and Martha L. (Sandberg) E.; m. Jean A. Brickley, Sept. 10, 1960; children: Carolyn, Diane, David. AA, North Park Coll., 1957; BSEE, Northwestern U., 1959; MS in Engring. Adminstrn., Syracuse U., 1969. Devel. engr. Motorola Inc., Chgo., 1958-61; project engr., engring. mgr. GE Co., Syracuse, N.Y., 1961-71; Presdl. exch. exec. U.S. Dept. Transp., Washington, 1971-72; mgr. strategic planning GE Co., Erie, Pa., 1972-78; v.p. products planning Purolator Inc., Piscataway, N.J., 1978-79; dir. planning TRW Indsl. Products Group, Cleve., 1979-84; v.p. planning and devel. TRW Automotive Worldwide, Solon, Ohio, 1984-86; pres. Strategic Ptnrs., Inc., Shaker Heights, Ohio, 1987-94; mng. prin., chmn. The Allegheny Mktg. Group, Pitts., 1988-91; pres., CEO Akron Regional Devel. Bd., 1994—; dir. Albin E. Erickson Co., Youngstown, 1960-77. Sch. dir., Liverpool, N.Y., 1970-71; mem. Millcreek Twp. Planning Commn., Erie, 1975-78, chmn., 1978; mem. County Exec. Rep. com., Erie, 1973-75; chmn.

Redeemer Evang. Covenant Ch., Liverpool, 1969-71; chmn. Middle East Conf. Evang. Covenant Ch. Am., 1975-78; mem. World Missions Bd., 1973-78; deacon The Chapel, Beachwood, Ohio, 1982-84; dir. Greater Cleve. Habitat for Humanity, 1987-90; vol. coord. Prison Fellowship Northeastern Ohio, 1987-89; mem. Ohio Justice Fellowship Task Force, 1988—, chmn., 1989—; mem. adminstrv. coun. Ch. of the Savior, 1989-94; mem. Northern Ohio Dist. Export Coun., 1995—; trustee Akron Roundtable, 1994—, Summit Ednl. Partnership Found., 1994—, Akron Tomorrow, 1994—, Leadership Akron, 1994—, Inventure Place, 1995—, Downtown Akron Partnership, 1996—. Mem. IEEE, Pres.'s Exec. Exch. Alumni Assn., The Planning Forum (bd. dirs. Cleve. chpt. 1988—, v.p. comm. 1989-90, pres. 1990-92), Elfun Soc. (chpt. sec. 1974-75, vice chmn. 1975-76). Office: Akron Regional Devel Bd One Cascade Plz Akron OH 44308-1192

ERICKSON, ROBERT ANDERS, optical engineer, physicist; b. Benson, Minn., Aug. 6, 1962; s. Wilton Robert and Irene Dorothy (Fenstra) E.; m. Deborah Popovchak, June 18, 1994. BS in Physics, S.D. Sch. Mines and Tech., 1985; MS in Physics, U. Mo., St. Louis, 1989. Instr. physics S.D. Sch. Mines and Tech., Rapid City, 1984-85; optical software devel. engr., physicist McDonnell Douglas Corp., St. Louis, 1985—. Twin Cities scholar, 1981, Frank & Portia Vanlueve scholar, 1983. Mem. IEEE, Optical Soc. Am., Am. Inst. Physics, Sigma Pi Sigma (chpt. pres. 1984-85). Republican. Lutheran. Home: 3120 Wabash Pl Granite City IL 62040-5100 Office: McDonnell Douglas Corp Dept 312 MIC 1069253 PO Box 516 # 257 Saint Louis MO 63166-0516

ERICKSON, TIMOTHY C., financial advisor; b. Des Moines, June 28, 1945. BA, North Park Coll., Chgo., 1967; MBA, Loyola Coll., Chgo., 1971; CSP, Coll. Fin. Planning, Denver, 1985. Fin. advisor FSC Securities, Muskegon, Mich., 1988-95, Abbit Mgmt. Corp., Grand Haven, Mich., 1995—. Mem. Muskegon C. of C. Republican. Home: 1451 Brookwood Dr Muskegon MI 49441-5266 Office: FSC Securities Corp 950 W Norton Ave Ste 415 Muskegon MI 49441-4184

ERICKSON, W(ALTER) BRUCE, business and economics educator, entrepreneur; b. Chgo., Mar. 4, 1938; s. Clifford Eric and Mildred B. (Brinkmeier) E. BA, Mich. State U., 1959, MA, 1960, PhD in Econs., 1965. Rsch. assoc. subcom. on antitrust and monopoly U.S. Senate, 1960-61; asst. prof. econs. Bowling Green (Ohio) U., 1964-66; asst. prof. bus. and govt. Coll. Bus. Adminstrn., U. Minn., Mpls., 1966-70; assoc. prof. Coll. Bus. Adminstrn., U. Minn., 1971-75, prof. dept. mgmt., 1975—, prof., chmn. dept. mgmt., 1977-80, co-chmn., then chmn., 1988-92; bd. dirs. various bus. and venture capital orgns.; cons. rock salt antitrust cases for atty. gens. Mich., cons. rock salt antitrust cases for atty. gens. Calif., Ill., Wis., Minn.; cons. U.S. Justice Dept. Author: An Introduction to Contemporary Business, 4th edit., 1985, Government and Business, 1980; bd. editors Antitrust Law and Econs. Rev., Jour. Indsl. Orgn.; contbr. articles to profl. jours. Bd. dirs. Found. for Constl. Edn. and the Citizens League, 1991-92. Mem. Am. Econ. Assn., Royal Econ. Soc. Office: Carlson Sch Mgmt 271 19th Ave S Minneapolis MN 55455-0430

ERICKSON, WENDELL O., county commissioner, educator; b. Stanchfield, Minn., June 17, 1925; s. Raymond and Helen Sophia (Anderson) E.; m. Kathryn Thorsgard, May 30, 1953; children: Margaret, Kirsten, Charles, Anna, Hans. BS in Agr. and Edn., U. Minn., 1951, postgrad., 1963. State rep. Minn. Legislature, St. Paul, 1965-86; farm mgr. S.W. Tech. Coll., Jackson, 1968-85, 1985; farm landowner N.D. and S.D., 1972; neutral mediator Minn., 1988; county commr. Rock County, Hills, Minn., 1995—; adj. prof. S.W. U., Marshall, Minn., 1987; adv. bd. Minn. Acad. Excellence Found., St. Paul, 1993-95; commn. mem. Edn. Commn. of the States, Denver, 1967-71, 79-81; advisor on edn. Control Data Corp., Mpls., 1985-86. Chmn. edn. com. Minn. Legislature, St. Paul, 1985-86, chmn. edn. diu, appointments, 1979-81; chmn. stewardship com. Beth Luth. Ch. Staff sgt. U.S. Army, 1944-46. Named Hon. Am. Farmer, Future Farmers Am.; recipient 4-H Alumni award 4-H Clubs of Am. Mem. Am. Farm Bur., Minn. Assn. of Counties, Gideon's, U. Minn. Coll. Agr. Alumni Assn. (pres. 1990, Disting. Svc. award 1991). Republican. Home: 204 Elizabeth Ave Hills MN 56138 Office: Erickson Assocs Box 575 Hills MN 56138

ERICKSON, WHITNEY JAYE, critical care nurse; b. Williams AFB, Ariz., July 6, 1966; d. Morris Edward and Donna Sue (Wilson) Norsworthy; m. Curtis Allen Erickson, Mar. 10, 1992. ADN, Texarkana Coll., 1988; BSN, U. Ark. Med. Scis., 1991, MNSc, 1992; postgrad., Rush U., 1994—. Staff nurse med.-surg. Wadley Regional Med. Ctr., Texarkana, Tex., 1987-88; staff nurse burn/trauma Univ. Hosp., Little Rock, 1989-90; rsch. nurse coord. Dr. John Eidt, Little Rock, 1990-92; staff nurse ICU Sierra Vista (Ariz.) Community Hosp., 1992, Univ. Med. Ctr., Tucson, Ariz., 1993-94; rsch. asst., cons. Children's Hosp. Wis., Milw., 1995—. Mem. AACN, ANA, Am. Assn. Nurse Anesthetists, Am. Pain Soc., Ark. Nurses Assn., Sigma Theta Tau. Mem. RLDS Ch. Home: 7662 Camino Amistosopt 101 Tucson AZ 85750

ERICKSON-WEERTS, SALLY ANNETTE, dietetics educator; b. Phoenix, Oct. 18, 1952; d. Dennis Lee and Ann Marie (Conklin) E.; children: Matthew, Alexander, Kyle. BS, Mankato State U., 1973; MS, Kans. U., 1976. Registered dietitian, Minn. Clin. dietitian Saga Food Svc., Pitts., 1975-76; pub. health nutritionist Minn. Dept. of Health, Mpls., 1976-77; prof. Lakewood (Minn.) C.C., 1977-79; fed. nutritionist Indian Health Svcs./Pub. Health Svc., Anchorage, 1979-85; pvt. practice Mankato, Minn., 1986-89; pres. Dietary Care Systems, Inc., Mankato, Minn., 1989-92; asst. prof. Mankato State U., 1992—; cons. in field. Author: One Menu System, Nutritional Care System, Lite Weight, Diet Care Seminars, 1989-92. Mem. PEO, Am. Dietetic Assn. Office: Mankato State U Box 44/ PO Box 8400 Mankato MN 56002-0044

ERICSON, CONSTANCE MARIE, library director, elementary educator; b. Aledo, Ill., Dec. 25, 1953; d. Richard Leo and Shirley Gene (Stone) Baldwin; m. David Lee Bevard, Nov. 3, 1973 (div. Feb. 1980); 1 child, Christopher David; m. David Alan Ericson, June 21, 1992. AA, Carl Sandburg Coll., Galesburg, Ill., 1988; BA in Elem. Edn., Knox Coll., Galesburg, Ill., 1990. Cert. tchr. elem. edn., Ill. Tchr. King Sch., Galesburg, 1990-91; prevention specialist Housing Authority of Henry County, Kewanee, Ill., 1991-93; substance abuse counselor/prevention specialist Bridgeway, Inc., Galesburg, 1993-94; part-time tchr. Cooke Sch., Galesburg, 1995—; libr. dir. Galva (Ill.) Pub. Libr. Dist., 1994—. Mem. Ill. Libr. Assn., Vasa Lodge. Office: Galva Pub Libr Dist 120 NW 3d Ave Galva IL 61434

ERICSON, RICHARD CHARLES, social service agency executive; b. St. Paul, June 21, 1933; s. Rolph Christopher and Sonia Margaret (Carlson) E.; children: Lynn Ericson Starr, David Alan. BA, Roosevelt U., 1959; MA, U. Chgo., 1961. U.S. probation officer U.S. Probation Office, Chgo., 1960-61; juvenile probation officer Hennepin County Ct. Svcs., Mpls., 1961-62; asst. supr. Hennepin County Juvenile Detention Ctr., Mpls., 1962-63; asst. dir. Pres.'s Com. on Youth Crime, Charleston, W.Va., 1963-64; project coord. parolee rehab. project Mpls. Rehab. Ctr., 1964-67; pres. Minn. Citizens Coun. on Crime and Justice, 1967—; pres. Ericson Properties, Inc. Served with C.E., U.S. Army, 1954-56. Grantee in field. Mem. Nat. Coun. on Crime and Delinquency, Am. Correctional Assn., Rotary of Mpls. Contbr. articles on crime and justice to profl. jours. Office: 822 S 3rd St Ste 101 Minneapolis MN 55415-1260

ERIKSEN, PETER BENDTSEN, investment company executive; b. Chgo., Oct. 19, 1918; s. Jerry Leigh and Charlotte JoAnn (Kolter) R.; m. Vicki Lynn Tippett-Riness, Mar. 30, 1984; children: Cole Clayton, Grace Victoria. BS in Commerce, Northwestern U., 1939. Auditor Hart, Schaffner & Mary, Chgo., 1939-48; contr. Baskin's, Chgo., 1948-52; sr. v.p., sec., treas. Baker, Fentress & Co., Chgo., 1952-83. Bd. mem. N.W. Community Hosp., Arlington Heights, Ill., 1989—. Capt. U.S. Army, 1942-46. Republican. Episcopalian. Home: 207 S Kaspar Ave Arlington Heights IL 60005-1769

ERIKSSON, JAMES ERNEST, insurance agency executive; b. Hammond, Ind., Oct. 11, 1943; s. Carl Philip and Margaret Maria (Franzen) E.; m. Rachel Eve Beilman, Sept. 23, 1967; children: Rachel Christine, Kelly Elizabeth. Cert., Life Underwriters Tng. Council, Washington, 1985. Agt., agy. mgr. Met. Life Ins. Co., Gary, Ind., 1965-74, State Farm Ins. Co., Gary, 1974—. Bd. dirs. Miller Area Bus. Assn., Gary, 1974-87, Porter County Planning Commn., Valparaiso, Ind., 1988; mem. Porter Town Planning Commn., 1996—. Mem. Calumet Assn. Life Underwriters, N.W. Ins. Assn. Life. Underwriters Ill. (bd. dirs. 1994—), Ill. Gen. Agts. and Mgrs. Assn. (pres.), Exch. Club. Republican. Lutheran. Office: State Farm Ins Co 405 Johnson Rd Michigan City IN 46360

ERLANSON, DEBORAH MCFARLIN, state program administrator; b. Watertown, N.Y., Oct. 17, 1943; d. Raymond Thomas and Alberta Antoinette (Schultz) McF.; m. David Norman Erlanson, Sept. 10, 1966; 1 child, Joshua David. AA in Liberal Arts, Dutchess C.C., 1964; BA in Psychology, Am. Internat. Coll., 1966; MS in Edn., So. Ill. U., 1972. Coord. occupancy tng. Decatur (Ill.) Housing Authority, 1975-76, coord. target projects program, 1976-77, coord. spl. svcs., 1977-78, asst. dir. planning, 1978-82, dir. program devel., 1982—; speaker various convs., 1978—; cons. Piatt County Housing Authority, Monticello, Ill., 1985-89, Woodford Homes, Inc., Decatur, 1985-86. Mem. steering com. Near West Restoration and Preservation Soc., Decatur, 1985-86, bd. dirs., 1986—, v.p., 1992—; mem. steering com. Cmtys. in Partnership, 1991—, bd. dirs., 1993—; mem. Decatur Advantage 20/20, 1993, Macon County Literacy Coun., 1992-95; parent group counselor Macon County Parents Anonymous, Decatur, 1976-80; mem. health divsn. Decatur Coun. Cmty. Svcs., 1978-84; bd. dirs. YWCA, Decatur, 1992-95; mem. adv. bd. Ill. Housing Devel. Authority, 1993—. Mem. Nat. Assn. Housing/Redevel. Ofcls. (sr. v.p. 1995—, mem. nat. bd. govs. 1987—, mem. profl. devel. com. 1983-93, vice chariperson 1987-89, v.p. profl. devel. 1987-89, mem. task force on product devel. 1987, mem. task force on elderly housing issues 1990-91, profl. devel. trainer 1986—, mem. Award of Excellence jury 1991—, mem. task force on family self-sufficiency 1992-93, regional pres. 1993-95, Charles A. Thompson award 1991, mem. state exec. bd. 1983-93, state pres. 1984-87, William R. Hammond award 1993), Decatur Women's Network, Internat. City Mgmt. Assn. Home: 465 W Macon St Decatur IL 62522-3122 Office: Decatur Housing Authority 1808 E Locust St Decatur IL 62521-1565

ERNST, DANIEL PEARSON, lawyer; b. Des Moines, Sept. 30, 1931; s. Daniel Ward and Thea Elaine (Pearson) E.; m. Ann Robinson, April 14, 1956; children: Ellen, Daniel R., Ruth Ann. BA, Dartmouth Coll., 1953; JD, U. Mich., 1956. Bar: Iowa 1956, Ill. 1964, Mich. 1980. Assoc. Clewell Cooney & Fuerste, 1960-64; ptnr. Nelson Stapleton & Ernst, Stapleton & Ernst, Stapleton Ernst & Sprengelmeyer, East Dubuque, Ill., Nelson Stapleton & Ernst & Sprengelmeyer, Dubuque, Iowa, 1964-79; pvt. practice Dubuque, 1979-80; ptnr. Ernst & Cody, Dubuque, 1981-84, Daniel P. Ernst, P.C., Dubuque, 1984-90, Vincent Roth & Ernst, P.C., Galena, Ill., 1991; pub. defender State of Iowa, Dubuque, 1991—; U.S. trustee 1979-91. Capt. USAF, 1957-60. Mem. ABA, Iowa State Bar Assn. (bd. govs. 1985-89), Dubuque County Bar Assn. (2d v.p. 1979-80, 1st v.p. 1980-81, pres. 1981-82), Ill. State Bar Assn., Jo Daviess County Bar Assn., State Bar Assn. Mich., Grand Traverse-Leelanau-Antrim Bar Assn., Nat. Assn. Criminal Def. Lawyers, Nat. Legal Aid and Defenders Assn. Democrat. Office: 555 Fischer Bldg 909 Main Dubuque IA 52001

ERNST, GORDON EMERY, JR., librarian; b. Glendora, Calif., Dec. 31, 1959; s. Gordon Emery Sr. and Muriel Ruth (Appel) E. BA in History, Kent State U., 1982, MLS, 1985. Media cataloger U. Toledo, Ohio, 1985-87; monographic/audiovisual cataloger Northwestern U., Chgo., 1988-91; asst. head cataloging Western Mich. U., Kalamazoo, 1991—. Author: Robert Benchley: An Annotated Bibliography, 1995. Mem. ALA, Mich. Acad. Sci., Arts and Letters (chair libr. and info. sci. sect. 1993-94).

ERNST, RANDY F., stockbroker; b. Anamosa, Iowa, Feb. 18, 1950. BS, U. No. Iowa, 1973. Salesman Wilson & Co., Cedar Rapids, Iowa, 1973-76; account rep. IBM, Cedar Rapids, 1976-87; stockbroker Securities Corp. Iowa, Cedar Rapids, 1987—. Girl's basketball coach Linnmar Elem. Sch., Marion, Iowa, 1985-90. Mem. X-Club (bd. dirs. 1994—). Roman Catholic.

ERNST, TIMOTHY GEORGE, electrical engineer; b. Bellevue, Iowa, Apr. 29, 1959; s. George William and Joanne Marie (Daniels) E.; m. Jana Dee Stitzell, Nov. 3, 1990; children: Jeremy George, Cassandra Marie. BSEE, Iowa State U., 1981, MSEE, 1993. Registered profl. engr., Iowa. Staff engr. Burns & McDowell, Kansas City, Mo., 1981-85; engr., adminstrv. asst. Harlan (Iowa) Mcpl. Utilities, 1985-87; sr. protection engr. Iowa Power, Des Moines, 1987-95; co-owner, prin. engr. P&E Engring. Co., Carlisle, Iowa, 1995—; relay technician short course adv. com. Iowa State U., Ames, 1989-92; instr. personal computer adult edn. Waukee (Iowa) Cmty. Schs., 1989-90. Mem. IEEE, Power Engring. Soc. Home: 516 SE Diehl Ave Des Moines IA 50315 Office: P&E Engring Co 220 S 1st St Carlisle IA 50047

ERNSTER, R. GENE, manufacturing manager; b. Dubuque, Iowa, Sept. 21, 1942. Tech. engr. X-Cell-O Corp., Rockford, Ill., 1977-87; mfg. mgr. Genesis Systems, Davenport, Iowa, 1987—; advisor local electronics coll. Sgt. USAF, 1962-66. Office: Genesis Systems 4821 Tremont Ave Davenport IA 52807-1010

ERRION, JACK G., marketing professional; b. Jan. 28, 1928; s. Edgar J. and Marion F. Errion. BS, Bradley U., 1950. Writer, sales tng. mgr., promotion mgr. Wabco, Peoria, Ill.; indsl. writer, media cons. Caterpillar, Inc., Peoria; promotion mgr., dealer cons. Contbr. articles to profl. jours. DLR prom. constnt.-Africa, Mid. E. With U.S. Army, 1945-48. Home: 300 W Northridge Ln Peoria IL 61614

ERSTAD, LEON ROBERT, lawyer; b. Tyler, Minn., Aug. 3, 1947; s. Clifford and Josie (Dellberg) E.; m. Nancy Youel, July 19, 1969; children: Eric, Andrew, Jonathan. BSBA, U. Minn., 1969; JD cum laude, Temple U., 1976. Bar: Minn. 1976, U.S. Dist. Ct. Minn. 1976, U.S. Ct. Appeals (8th cir.) 1992, U.S. Supreme Ct. 1994. Ptnr. Chadwick, Johnson & Condon, P.A., Mpls., 1976-90, Erstad & Riemer P.A., 1990—; adj. instr. law William Mitchell Coll., St. Paul, 1985-94. Contbr. articles to profl. jours. Bd. dirs. Loring Nicollet Cmty. Ctr., Mpls., 1981-91, Minn. Returned Peace Corps Vols., Mpls., 1980-86, pres., 1980-81; trustee Lynnhurst Congrl. Ch., 1991-94, deacon, 1994—. Mem. ABA, Minn. State Bar Assn., Minn. Def. Lawyers Assn. Home: 4700 Dupont Ave S Minneapolis MN 55409-2324 Office: Erstad & Riemer PA 1000 Northland Plz Minneapolis MN 55431

ERTEL, GARY ARTHUR, accountant; b. Racine, Wis., Feb. 16, 1954; s. Arthur and Jean Ann (Potterville) E.; m. Judith Marie Vasy, Aug. 9, 1975; children: James Arthur, Emily Marie. BSBA in Acctg. cum laude, Drake U., 1975; MBA, Marquette U., 1984. CPA, Wis.; cert. cash mgr. Mem. staff Arthur Andersen & Co., Milw., 1975-77; mgr. Jezzo, Deppisch & Co., Cedarburg, Wis., 1978; gen. acctg. mgr. to asst. sec.-treas. and contr. Grede Foundries, Inc., Milw., 1978—. Mem. Amateur Radio Emergency Svc., Milw., 1984—; bd. dirs. Grace Evang. Luth. Ch., Milw., 1984-87, stewardship com., 1980-89. Mem. AICPAs, Wis. Inst. CPAs (chmn. acctg. careers com. 1979-87, bd. dirs. southeastern chpt. 1988, chmn. long-range planning com. 1987-90, sec.-treas. 1989-90, pres. 1991-93, fin. com. 1993-95, Svc. award 1989-94), Nat. Cash Mgmt. Assn. (edn. com. 1989—), Am. Foundrymens Soc. (treas. Wis. chpt. 1994-96), Wis. Cash Mgmt. Assn. (program com. 1985-87, v.p. 1987, pres. 1988, bd. dirs. 1989—), Risk and Ins. Mgmt. Assn., Western Raquet Club (fin. com. 1993—, bd. dirs. 1993—, v.p. 1995, pres. 1996). Home: 765 Talon Trl Brookfield WI 53045-6648 Office: Grede Foundries Inc 9898 W Bluemound Rd Milwaukee WI 53226-4319

ERTLE, WILLIAM JUSTIN, manufacturing company financial executive; b. Cleve., Jan. 24, 1968; s. John Beardsley and Mary Anne (Forristell) E. BSBA, Xavier U., 1995. Intern Von Lehman & Co., CPAs, 1988-89; intern Rockwell Laser Industries, Inc., Cin., 1989-91, bus. mgr., contr., treas., 1991—. Contbr. articles to profl. jours. Named to Outstanding Young Men Am., 1992. Mem. Am. Soc. Laser Medicine and Surgery, Laser Inst. Am. (chmn. sub-com. on laser eye protection, mem. steering com. Internat. Laser Safety conf.). Republican. Roman Catholic. Office: Rockwell Laser Industries 7754 Camargo Rd PO Box 43010 Cincinnati OH 45243

ERWIN, JUDY, state legislator; b. Detroit, 1950. BS, U. Wis.; MA, Nat. Coll. Edn., Evanston, Ill.; postgrad., Kennedy Sch. Govt., 1987. Formerly tchr. pub. schs.; mgmt. cons. Grant Thornton LPP; formerly dir. comms. staff Senate Dem. Staff; mem. from 11th dist. Ill. Ho. of Reps. Former del. Dem. Convs.; mem. Gov.'s Human Resource Task Force. Home: 1400 N State Pky Chicago IL 60610 Office: Ill Ho of Reps State Capitol Springfield IL 62706*

ERWIN, LINDA L., college administrator; b. Elwood, Ill., Feb. 25, 1948; d. Clifford Wilson and Cleo Lavonne (Fetz) Sheley; m. Alan Wayne Erwin, Aug. 31, 1975; children: Mark Alan, Daniel Brian. BA in Psychology, Taylor U., Upland, Ind., 1970; MA Student Pers. Admin. in Higher Edn., Ball State U., 1989. Social worker VA Hosp., Lexington, Ky., 1970-76; case worker Welfare Dept., Anderson, Ind., 1979-86; acad. advisor Ind. Wesleyan U., Marion, 1989-90; student svcs. mgr. Ivy Tech State Coll., Anderson, 1990—; mem. adv. bd. Anderson Area Vocat. Sch., 1994. Pub. rels. coord. Alexandria (Ind.) Band Boosters, 1995—; music libr. Alexandria Cmty. Band, 1992—. Mem. Assn. Christians in Student Devel., Ind. Coll. Pers. Assn., Nat. Assn. Student Pers., Nat. Coll. Student Devel. Baptist. Home: 117 Winding Dr Alexandria IN 46001

ERZEN, DEBORAH ANNE, materials engineer; b. Scranton, Pa., Apr. 21, 1971. BS in Materials Engring., Purdue U., 1993. Design engr. Bock Water Heaters, Detroit, Wis., 1996—. Mem. Am. Soc. Metallurgy, Mining, Minerals, and Materials Soc. Office: Welduction Corp 24492 Indoplex Cir Farmington Hills MI 48335

ESCH, RAYMOND GATES, lawyer; b. Akron, Ohio, May 31, 1940; s. Raymond Gates and Ruth (Durham) E.; m. Janet Louise Allen, June 17, 1962; children: Daniel Allen, Elizabeth Durham, Thomas Gates. BA, Ohio Wesleyan U., 1962; JD, U. Mich., 1965. Bar: Ohio 1965. Assoc. Fuller & Henry, Toledo, 1965-71, ptnr., 1971—; mng. ptnr. Fuller & Henry, 1984-87; spl. counsel to atty. gen. of Ohio, 1995—; mem. Bd. of Commrs. on Grievances and Discipline of Supreme Ct. of Ohio, 1996—. Exec. com. Lucas County Rep. Cen. Com., Toledo, 1991—; officer Toledo area coun. Boy Scouts Am., 1982-95; trustee Family Svc. N.W., Ohio, Toledo, 1983-89, chmn. 1986-88. Mem. ABA, Ohio Bar Assn., Toledo Bar Assn., Toledo Estate Planning Coun. Episcopalian. Home: 732 River Glen Maumee OH 43537-3743 Office: Fuller & Henry 1 Seagate Fl 17 Toledo OH 43604-1558

ESKEW, WAYNE R., portfolio manager; b. Gillett, Wyo., Dec. 1, 1961. BA, North Ctrl. Christian U., Mpls., 1985. Dir. devel. Youth in the City, Mpls., 1985-88; fin. cons. MTI Fin., Edina, Minn., 1988-90; v.p. Trend Capital Mgmt., Mpls., 1990—; mem. bd. Trend Capital, Mpls. Mem. bd. deacons ch., Eden Prairie, Minn., 1993—. Republican. Mem. Assembly of God Ch. Office: Trend Capital Mgmt 600 Highway 169 S Ste 950 Minneapolis MN 55426-1212

ESMAILI, MAHYAR, mechanical engineer; b. Tehran, Iran, Aug. 19, 1965; came to U.S., 1983.; BS in Nuclear Engring., U. Wis., 1989; MME, Ohio U., 1992. Mech. engr. Athens (Ohio) Mold & Machinery Corp., 1992-94; mech. engr. ATM engring. dept. InterBold, Canton, Ohio, 1994—. Mem. ASME. Office: PO Box 3091 5995 Mayfair Rd North Canton OH 44720

ESPAHBODI, HASSANALI, educator; b. Tehran, Iran, May 2, 1952; came to U.S., 1974; s. Gholamreza (Shokat Lashkar) and Ezzat (Khosraui) E.; m. Pouran Toluian Aug. 20, 1981; children: Sara, Sam. MBA, George Washington U., Washington, 1977; PhD, U. Ala., Tuscaloosa, 1981. CPA. Grad. tchg. asst. U. Ala., Tuscaloosa, 1979-81; asst. prof. Fla. Internat. U., Miami, Fla., 1981-83, Northeastern U., Boston, 1983-90; assoc. prof. Western Ill. U., Macomb, Ill., 1990-95; prof. Western Ill. U., Macomb, 1995—; editl. bd. Midwestern J. of Bus. and Econs. Contbr. articles to profl. jours. Grantee Ill. CPA Soc. Found., 1994. Mem. Am. Acctg. Assn., Am. Statis. Assn., Beta Gamma Sigma. Muslim. Home: 16 Briarbrook E Macomb IL 61455 Office: Western Ill Univ 1 University Cir Macomb IL 61455

ESPELAGE, HOWARD JOHN, police chief; b. Cin., June 14, 1929; s. Frank and Erma M. (Woefle) E.; m. Joan F. Espelage, May 2, 1953; children: David, Terry, Sandra. BS in Criminal Justice magna cum laude, U. Cin., 1974. Police capt. City of Cin. Police Dept., 1952-82; asst. police chief Green Twp., Cin., 1982-87; police chief City of Loveland, Ohio, 1988—. With USN, 1946-49, 50-51. Fellow FOP; mem. VFW. Home: 3751 Cartwheel Ter Cincinnati OH 45251 Office: Loveland Police Dept 120 W Loveland Ave Loveland OH 45140

ESPICH, JEFFREY K., state legislator; m. Sharon Espich; 2 children. BS, Ind. U. With Kozy Kourt Inc.; rep. Dist. 32 Ind. Ho. of Reps., 1972-91, rep. Dist. 82, 1991—, minority whip, asst. minority floor leader, mem. elec. and appropriations coms., ins. and corps. com., rds. and transp. com., ways and means com., mem. cts. and criminal code, ins. and corp., small bus. coms; bd. dirs. Old First Bank. Mem. Farm Bur., Bluffton C. of C. Home: 1250 W Hancock St Uniondale IN 46791*

ESPOSITO, STEVEN F., securities company executive; b. Chgo., Sept. 2, 1960; m. Heidi Motzqur, July 25, 1987; 1 child, Stephanie. BA, Bolling U., Chgo., 1983. Stockbroker PaineWebber, Chgo., 1983-85, Merrill Lynch, Northbrook, Ill., 1985-88; v.p. Prudential Securities Inc., Deerfield, Ill., 1988—. Deerfield Country Club. Republican. Roman Catholic. Office: Prudential Securities Inc 500 Lake Cook Rd Ste 100 Deerfield IL 60015-4922

ESPY, BEN, state senator, lawyer; m. Kathy Espy; children: Elizabeth, Amy, Laura, Lynette. BA, Ohio State U.; JD, Howard U. Bar: Ohio. Pvt. practice, Columbus, Ohio; mem. Ohio Senate, Columbus, 1993—. Councilman City of Columbus, 1982-92; mem. adv. bd. Cath. Diocese Found.; mem. Big Ten Adv. Bd. Commn. Named Outstanding Legislator of Yr., Franklin County Trial Lawyers Assn.; recipient Young Black Dem. recognition, Columbus Man of Yr. award Frank Loris Peterson Soc. Adventist Men, vol. svc. award Neighborhood House; named to Sandusky H.S. Athletic Hall of Fame, Carter G. Woodson Hall of Fame. Mem. ABA, Ohio Bar Assn., Columbus Bar Assn., Urban Christian Leadership Assn., Kappa Alpha Psi, Sigma Delta Tau. Democrat. Home: 1350 Brookwood Pl Columbus OH 43209-2813*

ESSAR, DAVID WILLIAM, biology professor; b. Kalamazoo, Mich., May 14, 1958; s. Kenneth George and Evelyn Irene (De Hollander) E. BS in Pharmacy with distinction, Ferris State Coll., 1981; MS in Pharmacy, U. Iowa, 1983, PhD in Microbiology, 1989. Rsch. microbiologist Biological Control Rsch. Unit USDA ARS, Pullman, Wash., 1989-92; asst. prof. Winona (Minn.) State U., 1992—; adj. prof. U. Wis. La Crosse, 1995—. Contbr. chpts. to books; contbr. articles to Jour. of Bacteriology. Tutor Winona Cmty. Edn. Adult Literacy Program, 1993—; vol. Women's Resource Ctr., 1995—. Recipient Bristol award Ferris State Coll., 1981; rsch. fellow NSF, 1980. Mem. Am. Soc. for Microbiology, Nat. Assn. of Biology Tchrs., Assn. for Biology Lab. Edn., Minn. Acad. of Sci. Home: 327 W Wabasha St Winona MN 55987 Office: Winona State U 215 Pasteur Hall Winona MN 55987

ESSEX, WANDA ELIZABETH, speech and language pathologist; b. Benham, Ky., Jan. 25, 1925; d. Nathaniel Otto and Elizabeth Marie (Ausmus) Irwin; children: Michael, Elane, Christopher. BS, U. Nebr., 1969, MA, 1973. Fingerprint classifier FBI, Washington, 1943-45; sec. Libr. of Congress, Washington, 1948-49; speech pathologist Ednl. Svc. Unit #6, Milford, Nebr., 1969, Fremont (Nebr.) Pub. Schs., 1969-92; pvt. practice speech pathology Lincoln, Nebr., 1993—; speech pathologist Meml. Hosp. Dodge County, Fremont, 1975-93, U. Nebr., Lincoln, 1994-96. Bd. dirs. Nebr. Stroke Found., sec. 1994. Recipient award of Excellence, Nat. Coun. for Better Hearing and Speech Month, 1988, 89. Mem. AAUW, Am. Speech-Lang. Hearing Assn. (continuing edn. award 1985, 89), Nebr. Speech-Lang. Hearing Assn. (chair better hearing and speech month 1993-96, chair Breakfast for Senators 1996, honors award 1985), Nat. Coun. Better Hearing and Speech Month (Nebr. co-chair 1988-95), Dodge County Stroke Club (project dir. 1987-94), Delta Kappa Gamma (v.p., pres.), Phi Delta Kappa.

ESSIG, GARTH FREDRIC, obstetrician gynecologist, medical educator; b. Longmont, Colo., Sept. 19, 1935; s. John F. and Bertha V. (Halstead) E.; m. Judith A. Stutsman, June 15, 1957 (div. Mar. 1975); children: Erik, Kurt, Gretchen, Christina; m. Marcia Stroud, Mar. 31, 1975; children: Christopher, Garth, Elisabeth. BS, De Pauw U., 1957; MD, Ohio State U., 1961. Intern

Springfield (Ohio) City Hosp., 1961-62; gen. med. officer USPHS, Philadelphia, Miss., 1962-64; resident ob-gyn. Ohio State U., Columbus, 1964-67, chief resident ob-gyn., 1967-68, from instr. to assoc. prof., 1968—; dir. ob-gyn. clerkships Ohio State U., 1968—; acting chmn. dept. ob-gyn. Ohio State U. Lt. comdr. USPHS, 1962-64. Fellow Am. Coll. Ob-Gyn., Am. Cancer Soc.; mem. Am. Assn. Profs. Gyn. and Obstetrics (Excellence in Tchg. award 1992), Ohio State Med. Assn., Columbus Acad. Medicine. Democrat. Roman Catholic. Office: Ohio State U 545 Means Hall 1654 Upham Dr Columbus OH 43210 also: Univ Ob-Gyn 3360 Tremont Rd Columbus OH 43221

ESSINGER, SUSAN JANE, special education educator; b. Paris, Ill., Oct. 7, 1952; d. Rex Milburn and Virginia Ellen (White) E. BS in Edn., Ea. Ill. U., Charleston, 1973; MS in Edn., Ind. State U., 1981; postgrad. Cert. learning disabilities, elem., educationally mentally handicapped with early childhood endorsement. Elem. tchr. Havana (Ill.) Sch. Dist., 1973-74; tchr. early childhood spl. edn. Paris Sch. Dist. 95, 1974—. Mem. NEA, Assn. for Edn. Young Children, Ill. Edn. Assn., Paris Tchrs. Assn., Coun. for Exceptional Children. Home: 1104 S Main St Paris IL 61944-2823 Office: Paris Sch Dist 95 S Main St Paris IL 61944

ESSLINGER, MARILYN ANN, city clerk; b. Rockford, Ill., Nov. 9, 1938; d. John D. and Vernette (Bouchard) Hoefle; m. William F. Esslinger, Feb. 8, 1957; children: William, Arden, James, David, Ann. Clk. Rock Island (Ill.) County. Home: 2902 56th St Ct Moline IL 61265 Office: County of Rock Island PO Box 5230 Rock Island IL 61204-5230

ESTEP, DENNIS ALAN, occupational medicine physician; b. Oklahoma City, Nov. 15, 1954; s. William H. and Lois (Porter) E.; m. Susan Allard, Jan. 23, 1993. BS, Okla. Christian U. Sci. & Arts, 1977; MS, Baylor U., 1982; DO, Okla. State U., 1989; MPH with honors, U. Okla., 1991. Cert. Am. Coll. Preventive Medicine Occupl. Medicine. Chemist Dow Chem. Co., Freeport, Tex., 1980-83; constrn. worker Nix Constrn., Albuquerque, 1983-84; intern Oak Hill Hosp., Joplin, Mo., 1989-90; resident occupational medicine U. Okla. Health Sci. Ctr.-Occupational Medicine, Oklahoma City, 1990-91, chief resident occupational medicine, 1991-92; adminstrv. dir., physician Occumed, Joplin, 1992-94, med. dir., 1994—; drug prevention program support team leader Coll. Osteo. Medicine, Okla. State U., 1987-88. Contbr. articles to profl. jours. Named Outstanding Young Men of Am., 1987; recipient ACT Acad. scholarship Okla. Christian U. Sci. and Arts, 1973-77, Grad. assistantship Baylor U., 1977-79, Robert A. Welch Found. Rsch. fellowship Baylor U., 1979-80. Fellow Am. Coll. Occupational and Environ. Medicine; mem. Okla. Coll. Occupational and Environ. Medicine, Okla. Osteo. Assn., Okla. State U. Alumni Assn. Office: OCCUMED Freeman Hosp 3315 Mc Intosh Cir Joplin MO 64804-3649

ESTEP, MARK RANDALL, secondary education educator, dairy farmer; b. Springfield, Mo., June 18, 1962; s. Wendall Eugene Estep and Martha Anne (Wheeler) Johns; m. Shawna Lea Dittmar, June 18, 1988; children: Cheyanne Elizabeth, Shelby Lea, Jamie Lee. BS in Edn., S.W. Mo. State U., 1990; MEd, U. Mo., 1996. Cert. secondary tchr., Mo. Supr. Harry Cooper Supply Co., Springfield, 1985-90; co-owner Shawn-Mar Dairy Farm, Marionville, Mo., 1986—; tchr. agriculture McDonald County Schs., Anderson, Mo., 1990-93, Marionville (Mo.) Schs., 1993—; advisor McDonald County Future Farmers Am., Anderson, 1990-93; advisor Marionville Future Farmers of Am., 1993—. Treas. McDonald County Fair Bd., Anderson, 1991-92; advisor Area 9 Future Farmers Am., 1995-96. Mem. Nat. Vocat. Assn., Mo. Vocat. Agr. Tchrs. Assn. (Outstanding Agr. Program award 1992-93), Area 9 Agr. Tchrs. Assn. (sec.-treas. 1995-96, v.p. 1996—), Mo. Ayrshire Assn. (pres. 1989-90). Home: PO Box 237 Marionville MO 65705-0237 Office: Marionville Future Farmers PO Box J Marionville MO 65705-0409

ESTERLINE, BRENDA LEE, elementary school educator, travel advisor; b. Indpls., Apr. 21, 1940; d. Earl Temple and Dallas Louise (Newman) Williamson; (div. 1976); children: Laura Lee, Jennifer Lynn. BS, Ball State U., 1962; MS, Butler U., 1969. Cert. tchr., Ind. Tchr. Pike Twp. Schs., Indpls., Ind., 1962-66, Washington Twp. Schs., Indpls., Ind., 1970-74, Orchard Country Day Sch., Ind., 1976-88; owner, mgr. The Gold Dust Emporium, Indpls., 1988-89; 4th grade tchr. St. Richard's Sch., Indpls., 1990-93; vacation reservation agt. Am. Trans Air Airlines, 1993-96; asst. tchr. handicapped children North Ctrl. H.S., 1995-96; leader ednl. tour Europe Am. Coun. for Internat. Studies, 1980, 85, 87; outdoor edn. experiences overnights Gnaw Bone Camp, Nashville, Ind., 1976-87. Sponsor Africa Christian Children's Fund, 1987-90. Mem. Psi Iota Xi.

ESTES, DOUGLAS LEE, motel owner; b. Oakland, Calif., Sept. 12, 1944; s. Elmer Leroy and Patricia Lillian (Hansen) E.; Justine Nell Pinard, Mar. 5, 1977; children: Jordan, Aaron, Natasha, Allison. BS in Bus. Adminstrn., U. S.D., 1966; MS, U. Wyo., 1971. Teaching asst. U. Wyo., 1969-70; devel. dir. Yankon Sioux Tribe, Wagner, S.D., 1970-71; price analyst Cost of Living Council, Washington, 1972-74; fin. analyst Fed. Energy Office, Washington, 1974-75; owner, mgr. Sands Motel, Wall (S.D.) Motel, Wall Super 8 Motel, 1975—; bd. dirs., treas. BED Co., Full House, Inc., S.D. Vending, Inc. Bd. dirs. S.D. Bldg. Authority, Pierre, 1983—; Rep. committeeman, Pennington County, 1978-86; mem. Black Hills Badlands and Lakes Assn., 1976—, bd. dirs., 1995—; bd. dirs. S.D. Tourism Adv. Bd., Pierre, 1980—; chmn. S.D. Mktg. Task Force, 1986-87. With U.S. Army, 1967-69. Mem. Am. Legion (post comdr. 1980-81), Wall C. of C. (bd. dirs. 1984—), Wall Hospitality Assn. (v.p. 1986, 87, 88), S.D. Innkeepers Assn. (bd. dirs.), Beta Gamma Sigma. Methodist. Office: Sands Motel 804 Glenn St Wall SD 57790

ESTES, ELAINE ROSE GRAHAM, retired librarian; b. Springfield, Mo., Nov. 24, 1931; d. James McKinley and Zelma Mae (Smith) Graham; m. John Melvin Estes, Dec. 29, 1953. BSBA, Drake U., 1953, tchg. cert., 1956; MSLS, U. Ill., 1960. With Pub. Libr. Des Moines, 1956-95, coord. extension svcs., 1977-78, dir., 1978-95, ret., 1995; lectr. antiques, hist. architecture, libraries; mem. conservation planning com. for disaster preparedness for libraries. Author bibliographies of books on antiques; contbr. articles to profl. jours. Mem. State of Iowa Cultural Affairs Adv. Coun., 1986-94, Nat. Commn. on Future Drake U., 1987-88; chmn. Des moines Mayor's Hist. Dist. Commn.; bd. dirs. Des Moines Art Ctr., 1972-83, hon. mem., 1983—; bd. dirs. Friends of Libr. USA, 1986-92, Henry Wallace Housing Found.; mem. Iowa Libr. Centennial Com., 1990-91; nominations rev. com. Iowa State Nat. Hist. Register, 1983-89; chmn. hist. subcom. Des Moines Sesequecentennial com., 1993, Iowa Sister State Commn., 1993-95; mem. 45th anniversary com. Des Moines Art Ctr., 1993; mem. com. 40th anniversary Drake U. alumni weekend; mem. Iowa Sesequecentennial July 4 com., 1996. Recipient recognition for outstanding working women - leadership in econs. and civic life of Greater Des Moines, YWCA, 1975, Disting. Alumni award Drake U., 1979, Woman of Achievement award YWCA, 1989, City of Des Moines Excellence in Hist. Preservation award, 1994. Mem. ALA, Iowa Libr. Assn. (pres. 1978-79), Iowa Urban Pub. Libr. Assn., Libr. Assn. Greater Des Moines Metro Area (pres., chmn. 1992), Iowa Soc. Preservation Hist. Landmarks (bd. dirs. 1969—), Terrace (Gov.'s Mansion) Soc. (v.p. 1991-93, pres. 1993—), Links Club, Quester's, Inc. Club (pres. 1982, state 2nd v.p. 1984-86), Iowa Antique Assn., Proteus, Rotary.

ESTKA, ROBERT J., marketing executive; b. Chgo., Ill., June 3, 1956. BS, U. Wis., 1978; MBA, Notre Dame U., 1992. Nat. sales mgr. Logo-7, Inc., Indpls., 1979-82; spl. markets mgr. Phillips Consumer Electronics, Knoxville, Tenn., 1982-93; pres. Spl. Markets Sales Co., Indpls., 1993—. Mem. AIM (assoc. incentive mfg. 1982-95), Incentive Mfg. Assn. Office: Spl Markets Sales Co 11715 Fox Rd 400 Ste 123 Indianapolis IN 46236-8424

ETLING, TERRY DOUGLAS, state agency administrator; b. Akron, Ohio, Jan. 24, 1943; s. Harold A. and Betty Jean (Newton) E.; m. Rosalind Joyce Gallogly, Dec. 26, 1966 (div. Mar. 1983); children: Allison Irene, Bret Newton. BS, Ohio State U., 1966; MEd, Kent (Ohio) State U., 1968. Vocat. rehab. counselor Apple Creek (Ohio) State Hosp., 1966-67, rehab. unit supr., 1967-69; coord. facility and program devel. Ohio Bur. Vocat. Rehab., Columbus, 1969-71; supr. rsch., planning and devel. div. Ohio Rehab. Svcs. Commn., Columbus, 1971-73, chief rsch., planning and devel. div., 1973-77, dep. adminstr., 1977-80, dir. bur. program support, 1980-91; retired Ohio Rehab. Svcs. Commn., 1991; cons. pvt. practice, 1991—; mgr. program devel. MEDVOC Mgmt., Inc., Columbus, 1992-93, dir. program devel., 1993—; mem. nat. adv. com. The Therapeutic Community of Upper Valley Med. Ctrs., J.M. Found. Search for Excellence in Vocat. Programs; mem. exec. com. chmn. standards com., trustee Commn. on Accreditation Rehab. Facilities, Tucson, 1985-89; chmn. Nat. State Facility Specialists Conf., Chgo., 1989; regional adv. coun. Rehab. Inst. Chgo. Rsch. and Tng. Ctr. in Prevention and Treatment of Spinal Cord Injury; dir. program devel. project boss Community Bankers Assn. Ohio, 1993—. Contbr. articles to profl. jours.; commentator for profl. papers Jour. of Rehab. Adminstrn., 1991—. Past pres. Assn. for Developmentally Disabled, Columbus, bd. dirs., 1977-88; ins. adv. coun. Good Samaritan Med. Ctr., Zanesville, Ohio, State Com. Purchase Products and Svcs. Severly Handicapped, 1977-88; chmn. Nat. Results Coun., Mpls., 1995—. Recipient Spl. Recognition award Commn. on Accreditation Rehab. Facilities, 1976, Meritorious Svc. award Ohio Industries for Handicapped, 1984, Disting. Svc. award Ohio Rehab. Counselors Assn., 1988. Mem. Council State Adminstrs. Vocat. Rehab. (mem. facility com.), Ohio Assn. Rehab. Facilities (agy. liaison to bd. dirs.), Nat. Rehab. Assn., Assn. for Developmentally Disabled (bd. dirs. 1987-88), SAR, Ohio State U. Alumni Assn., Union League Club, Delta Sigma Phi. Home: 733 NE 16th Terr Fort Lauderdale FL 33304-2940

ETTER, GREGG WAYNE, SR., police officer, educator; b. Hutchison, Kans., Oct. 17, 1952; s. Lendell Wayne and Imojean (Swearingen) E.; m. Pamela Lynn Scoggins, June 30, 1979 (div. Oct. 1989); children: Gregg Jr., Alexander P., Nicholas V.; m. Bonnie Lou Arnold, Dec. 10, 1991. B of Gen. Studies in Polit. Sci., Wichita State U., 1976, M in Adminstrn. Justice, 1981; diploma, USAF Air Command & Staff Coll., 1978. Lt. Sedgwick County Sheriff's Dept., Wichita, Kans., 1977—; instr., mem. AJ adv. com. Butler County C.C., El Dorado, Kans., 1991—. Unit comdr. Civil Air Patrol, Wichita, 1974-94. Mem. Am. Soc. Law Enforcement Tnrs., Kans. Peace Officers Assn., Kans. Sheriff's Assn., North Okla./South Kans. Peace Officers Assn., Am. Correctional Assn. Republican. Episcopalian. Office: Sedgwick County Sheriff'sDept 525 N Main Wichita KS 67203

ETTER, JOHN PHILLIP, police officer; b. Indpls., Feb. 9, 1953; s. Jerome J. and Phyllis E. (Safski) E.; m. Mindy S. Huffman, June 5, 1981. BS in Criminal Justice, Ind. U., 1976; postgrad., Northwestern U., 1989; student, FBI Nat. Acad., Quantico, Va., 1991. Patrolman Carmel (Ind.) Police Dept., 1976-85, lt., shift comdr., accident investigator, hostage negotiator, 1985-91, maj. tng. div., 1992—. Mem. FBI Nat. Acad. Assn., Fraternal Order of Police (pres. Carmel 1987-90), Serra Club (v.p. 1991), KC, Alpha Alpha Omega. Republican. Roman Catholic. Office: Carmel Police Dept 3 Civic Sq Carmel IN 46032

ETTINGER, JOSEPH ALAN, lawyer; b. N.Y.C., July 21, 1931; s. Max and Frances E.; children: Amy Beth, Ellen Jane. BA, Tulane U., 1954, JD with honors, 1956. Bar: La. 1956, Ill. 1959. Asst. corp. counsel City of Chgo., 1959-62; pvt. practice Chgo., 1962-73, 76—; sr. ptnr. firm Ettinger & Schoenfield, Chgo., 1980-92; sole practice Chgo., 1993—; assoc. prof. law Chgo.-Kent Coll., 1973-76; chmn. Village of Olympia Fields (Ill.) Zoning Bd. Appeals, 1969-76; chmn. panel on corrections Welfare Coun. Met. Chgo., 1969-76. Capt., Judge Adv. Gen. Corps, U.S. Army, 1956-59. Contbr. articles to profl. publs. Recipient Svc. award Village of Olympia Fields, 1976. Mem. Chgo. Bar Assn., Assn. Criminal Def. Lawyers (gov. 1970-72). Office: 33 N La Salle St Ste 2119 Chicago IL 60602-2606

ETTINGER, M(ARTHA) JEANNE, retired nurse; b. Granite City, Ill., July 11, 1924; d. John T. and Jennie Ethel (Bline) Liggett; m. Milton Gene Ettinger, June 26, 1957; children: Adrienne Sue Baranauskas, David Norman. Diploma, St. Luke's Sch. Nursing, 1946, U. Oreg., Portland, 1952. Surg. clin. instr. Providence Hosp. Sch. Nursing, Portland, Oreg., 1950-52; staff nurse VA Hosp., Long Beach, Calif., 1953-55; head bookkeeper Pan Loan Co., Mpls., 1955-56; indsl. nurse Napco, Mpls., 1956-57; exec. sec. Tri Mut. Inc., Mpls., 1978-79, purchasing agt., 1980-81; project coord. Stroke study Mpls. Med. Rsch. Found., Mpls., 1982-87. Precinct chair Rep. party, Plymouth, Minn., 1977-79, vice chair, 1979-81, state del., 1978—; pres. Hennepin County Rep. Women, Mpls., 1978-80, Minn. Fedn. Ind. Rep. Women, Mpls., 1990-94; exec. bd. dirs. Hennepin County Med. Ctr. Svc. League, 1991—, treas., 1993—. Mem. Aux. to Am. Acad. Neurology (hon. mem., pres. 1971-73, newsletter editor 1962-68), Hadassah (life). Jewish. Home: 15545 17th Pl N Minneapolis MN 55447-2402

ETZEN, JASON A., journalism and mass communication educator; b. Mason City, Iowa, Mar. 19, 1971; s. Keith Allen and Barbara Ann (Wilson) E. AA, North Iowa Area C.C., Mason City, 1991; BA, U. No. Iowa, 1994, MA, 1996. Reporter KIMT-TV3, Mason City, 1992, Mason City Globe Gazette, 1993-94; head boys tennis coach No. U. High Sch., Cedar Falls, Iowa, 1993-94; sports editor No. Iowan, Cedar Falls, 1993-94; pub. rels. dir. U.S. Table Tennis Assn., Colorado Springs, 1995; instr. journalism U. No. Iowa, Cedar Falls, 1994—; cons. Arrive Alive, Cedar Falls, 1995. Mem. Cedar Falls Pub. Utility Cable Com., 1994—. Recipient The Best award No. Iowan, 1994, Purple and Old Gold award U. No. Iowa, 1994. Mem. Soc. Profl. Journalists, Iowa Comm. Assn. Home: 694 3d Pl SE Mason City IA 50401

EUANS, ROBERT EARL, architect; b. Columbus, Ohio, July 6, 1941; s. William Weldon Euans and Hilda Aurelia (Daugherty) Roberts; m. Carol May Chamberlain, Dec. 18, 1964; children: Bradley James, Lori Ellen, Bryant Scott, Bruce Allen. BArch, Ohio State U., 1967. Registered architect, Ohio, Mich., Pa., Ind., Ill., Minn, Mo., Ky., Fla. Draftsman Blaw-Knox Corp., Pitts., 1967-68; chief draftsman Schofield & Assocs., Columbus, Ohio, 1968-70; project architect Karlsberger & Assocs., Columbus, 1970-74, dir. tech., 1974-77; pvt. practice architecture Columbus, 1977—. Mem. AIA (bd. dirs. Columbus chpt. 1984-86), Architects Soc. Ohio, Constrn. specification Inst. Lutheran.

EUBANK, GEORGE B., financial consultant; b. Corpus Christi, Tex., Aug. 17, 1951; divorced; children: Zachary, Maxamilon, Samantha. BBA, U. Tex., 1973. Fin. cons. Merrill Lynch, Kansas City, Mo., 1981—. Mem. Athletic Club. Libertarian.

EUBANKS-POPE, SHARON G., real estate entrepreneur; b. Chgo., Aug. 26, 1943; d. Walter Franklyn and Thelma Octavia (Watkins) Gibson; m. Larry Hudson Eubanks, Dec. 20, 1970 (dec. Jan. 1976); children: Rebekah, Aimée; m. Otis Eliot Pope, June 7, 1977; children: O. Eliot Jr., Adrienne. BS in Edn., Chgo. Tchrs. Coll., 1965; postgrad., Ill. Inst. Tech., 1967, John Marshall Law Sch., 1970, Governor's State U., 1975-76. Educator, parent coord. Chgo. Bd. Edn., 1965-77; owner, ptnr. Redel Rentals, Chgo., 1977—; realtor ERA Diversified Real Estate, Hazel Crest, Ill., 1990—; bd. dirs. Jack and Jill of Am. Found. Adminstrv. bd. St. Mark United Meth. Ch., Chgo., 1967, bd. trustees, 1988; com. chair Englewood Urban Progress Ctr., Chgo., 1973; coord., educator League Women Voters, Chgo. (Outstanding Community Law Class award 1975), 1975-76. Named Outstanding Sch. Parent Vol., Chgo. Bd. Edn., 1977; recipient Christian Leadership award United Meth. Women, Chgo., 1985. Mem. NAFE, NAACP, Am. Soc. Profl. and Exec. Women, Nat. Assn. Realtors, Greater South Suburban Bd. Realtors, Jack and Jill Am., Inc. (Chgo. chpt. journalist 1989-91, Midwestern region sec./treas. 1993-95, Mid-western regional dir. 1995—, founder Parents for Parity in Edn. 1992, pres. Eubanks-Pope constrn. 1993, parliamentarian of Parity 1991), Links, Inc., Jack & Jill of Am. Found. (bd. dirs. 1995—), Alpha Beta Gamma. Office: Redel Rentals 4338 S Drexel Blvd Chicago IL 60653-3536

EULBERG, GREG A., design engineer; b. Garnaville, Iowa, July 15, 1963. BS in Elec. Engring. Tech., DeVry Tech. Inst., Kansas City, Mo., 1984. Design engr. Rockwell Internat., Cedar Rapids, Iowa, 1984—. Home: 440 Quass Rd Robins IA 52328-9708 Office: Rockwell Internat 855 35th St NE Cedar Rapids IA 52402-3613

EULER, RUSSELL NELSON, mathematics educator, researcher; b. Maryville, Mo., May 18, 1950; s. Marion Francis and Dorris Lorraine (Strong) Groshong; m. Pamala Lea DeWar, Aug. 23, 1974; children: Karamaneh Elizabeth, Karissa Leighanne, Serena Nakale. BA, Mo. Western State Coll., St. Joseph, 1972; MA, U. Ala., 1972, U. Ky., 1977; PhD, U. Mo., 1982. With math. dept. Rockhurst Coll., Kansas City, Mo., 1979-81, Mo. Western State Coll., 1981-82; prof. math. N.W. Mo. State U., Maryville, 1982—. Contbr. numerous articles in profl. publs. Mem. Pi Mu Epsilon.

EUSTACHE, DANIEL LEE, secondary education educator; b. Troy, Ohio, July 4, 1943; s. Floyd Richard and Jeanette Elizabeth (Steinke) E.; m. Jeanette Lois Vagi, June 12, 1965. BSc, Ohio State U., 1965; MEd, Cleve. State U., 1973; postgrad., Western Wash. State Coll., Bellingham, 1973, U. Wyo., Debois, 1982. Tchr. vocat. agrl. Bradford (Ohio) H.S., 1965-66, No. Balt. (Ohio) H.S., 1966-67; tchr. sci., asst. prin. Cory-Rawson H.S., Cory, Ohio, 1967-68; tchr. sci. Parma City Schs., Parma, Ohio, 1968—; sci. dept. head Parma H.S., Parma, Ohio, 1973—; sci. curriculum devel., Parma city schs., 1973-95; owner, operator D.L. Builders, Hinckley, Ohio, 1976-87; facilator Regional Sci. Olympiad, Lorin, Ohio, 1989-94; presentor Ohio Acad. Sci. Symposium, 1971, State Sci. Conf., 1991. Author: DOE/SECO Workshop, 1991. Adv. bd. mem. CEI Energy, Cleveland, 1985-93. Jennings Found. Environ. grant, 1991; recipient Tchr. Achievement award, Parma PTA 1988, 90; named Outstanding Sci. Olympiad Coach, Lorain Ohio, 1991-94. Mem. NEA, N.E. Ohio Ed. Assn., Ohio Ed. Assn., Parma Edn. Assn. (rep. 1969-72). Home: 750 Center Rd Hinckley OH 44233-9479 Office: Parma Sr High Sch 6285 West 54th St Parma OH 44129

EUTSLER, THERESE ANNE, physical therapist; b. Jasper, Ind., Sept. 11, 1959; d. Joseph Martin and Viola Agnes (Rasche) Wagner; m. Mark Leslie Eutsler, Oct. 3, 1987. BS, Ind. U., 1982. Physicial therapist Reid Meml. Hosp., Richmond, Ind., 1982-84; physical therapist Cen. Convalescent Services, Crawfordsville, Ind., 1984-85, St. Elizabeth Hosp., Lafayette, Ind., 1985-86, 95—; clinical coord. St. Elizabeth Hosp., Lafayette, 1986-92; with Indsl. Rehab. of Crawfordville, 1992-94. Bd. dirs. Arthritis Found. Tippecanoe unit, Lafayette, 1986-89, John T. Conner Ctr. for U.S.-USSR Reconciliation, 1989—; del. Ind. State Dem. Conv., Indpls., 1988. Mem. Am. Phys. Therapy Assn. (Orthopedic sect., state ethics com. Ind. chpt.). Roman Catholic. Home: 207 Main St Linden IN 47955

EVANCHO, JOSEPH ANDREW, writer; b. Detroit, Sept. 16, 1929; s. Andrew and Clarinda Marie (Bonin) E.; m. Dorothy Marie Goodrich, Nov. 10, 1951; children: Robert Remington, Mary Katherine, Ann Marie, Joseph Hamilton. BS in Journalism, U. Detroit, 1960. Asst. dir. pub. rels. J.L. Hudson Co., Detroit, 1956-60; sr. writer Jam Handy Orgn., Detroit, 1960-66; copywriter J. Walter Thompson, Detroit, 1966-71; editor CECO Pub., Detroit, 1971-76; freelance writer Detroit, 1976-79; tech. comm. mgr. Kelsey Hayes Corp., Traverse City, Mich., 1979-82; creative dir. Beurmann-Marshall Corp., Lansing, Mich., 1983-88; freelance writer, mktg. cons. Westridge Enterprises, Traverse City, 1988—. Author: Bird Homes, 1990; editor: Fine Furniture & Furnishings Guide, 1995, Fishing Idaho, An Angler's Guide, 1995; assoc. editor: History of 352d Fighter Group of Eight Air Force During WWII, 1990. Tutor, Enterprise Learning Lab., Traverse City, 1989—. Staff sgt. USAF, 1950-53, Korea. Mem. Traverse City Exch. Club. Home and Office: 629 W 11th St Traverse City MI 49684-3149

EVANGELISTI, ROBERT, environmental engineer; b. Binghamton, N.Y., June 20, 1954; s. Louis and Pauline F. (Shupa) E.; m. Joan Glocka, May 24, 1980; 1 child, Anne M. B in Biology, U. Rochester, 1976; M of Engring., Cornell U., 1978. Profl. engr., Wis., Tex. Rsch. asst. Cornell U., Ithaca, N.Y., 1977; rsch. engr. Rexnord Environ. Rsch. Ctr., Milw., 1978-79; engr. ESEI, Milw., 1979, project mgr., 1979-81; environ. specialist BP America, Cleve., 1981-84; sr. environ. engr. BP Exploration, Inc., Houston, 1984-88, regulatory supr., 1988-89, mgr. health, safety & environment, 1989-90; mgr. environ. compliance Outboard Marine Corp., Waukegan, Ill., 1990—; tchr. environ. auditing U. Wis.-Extension, 1995—. Contbr. papers to profl. publs. Bd. dirs. Hunter's Pk. Cmty. Assn., Houston, 1990, deed com., 1988-90; mem. budget rev. com. City of Kenosha, 1995. Recipient Environ. scholarship U.S. EPA, 1976-77, Regent's scholarship N.Y. State Bd. Regents, 1972-76. Mem. ASTM, Inst. for Environ. Auditing, Water Environ. Fedn., Environ. Audit Roundtable, Fed. Environ. Tech., Environ. Audit Com. Home: 6903 5th Ave Kenosha WI 53143-5510 Office: Outboard Marine Corp 190 Sea Horse Dr Waukegan IL 60085-2141

EVANS, ANTON NELSON (TONY EVANS), marketing communications executive; b. Detroit, Nov. 27, 1941; s. Chester H. and Virginia M. (Nelson) E.; m. Linda Beth Swisher, June 19, 1965; children: Michael, Douglas, Elizabeth. BS in Indsl. Mgmt., Purdue U., 1963; MBA in Mktg., Xavier U., 1972. Various mktg. positions Frigidaire Div. GM, Dayton, Ohio, 1963-69; dist. mgr. Frigidaire Div. GM, Dayton, Cin., 1969-72; zone mgr. Frigidaire Div. GM, Dayton, 1972-74, cen. region merchandising mgr., 1974-76; nat. merchandising mgr. Frigidaire Div. GM, Dayton, 1976-79; v.p merchandising Frigidaire Co. WCI, Dayton, 1979-85; v.p. tng. and devel. WCI Major Appliance Group GM, Dublin, Ohio, 1985-89; dir. customer support and communications WCI Major Appliance Group GM, Dublin, 1989-91; dir. comms. Frigidaire Co., Dublin, 1991-95; v.p. comms. White Consol. Indsl., Cleve., 1996—; adj. assoc. prof. Wright State U., Dayton, 1980. Mem. Am. Mgmt. Assn., Assn. Home Appliance Mfrs. (chmn. communications com. 1992). Office: Frigidaire Co 6000 Perimeter Dr Dublin OH 43017-3233 also: White Consol Indsl 11770 Berea Rd Cleveland OH 44111

EVANS, ARTHUR BRUCE, Romance languages educator; b. Salem, Mass., Oct. 24, 1948; s. Richard Albert and Mary Kathleen (Meares) E.; m. Mary Agnes Bertha, July 4, 1970 (div. Sept. 1978); 1 child, Kelly Kristin Evans; m. Janice Elaine Lemmink, Apr. 26, 1986; 1 child, Seth Houston Mishler. BA, Tufts U., 1970; MA, Goddard Coll., Plainfield, Vt., 1972, Middlebury (Vt.) Coll., 1979; PhD, Columbia U., 1985. Lic. tchr., Vt. Teaching asst. Tufts U., Medford, Mass., 1969-70; tchr. Montpelier (Vt.) High Sch., 1970-78; adj. instr. Community Coll. Vt., Montpelier, 1974-75; preceptor French Columbia U., N.Y.C., 1981-83; asst. prof. DePauw U., Greencastle, Ind., 1985-90, assoc. prof. romance langs., 1990—, chmn. dept. romance langs., 1994—; cons. Heinle & Heinle Pubs., Boston, 1989, Nineteenth Century French Studies and other jours., 1988—. Author: Jean Cocteau, 1977, Jules Verne Rediscovered, 1988 (Eaton award U. Calif. 1990); contbg. editor: En Route!, 1985, On Philip K. Dick, 1992; co-editor Sci.-Fiction Studies, 1990—; contbr. articles to profl. jours. Mem. MLA, AAUP, Am. Assn. Tchrs. of French, Jules Verne Soc., Amnesty Internat. Home: 1006 S Locust St Greencastle IN 46135-2056 Office: East Coll L 06 DePauw U Greencastle IN 46135

EVANS, BRENT, state legislator. Mem. Mo. Ho. of Reps., Jefferson City. Republican.

EVANS, CHARLOTTE MORTIMER, communications consultant, writer; b. Newton, N.J., Nov. 26, 1933; d. Karl Otto and Wilhelmina (Otterbach) Pfau; student Douglass Coll., 1952-54; BS, RN, Columbia U. Presbyn. Hosp., 1957, postgrad., 1957-59; postgrad. NYU, 1959-60; MPA, Coll. of Notre Dame, 1979; m. John Atterbury Mortimer, Nov. 20, 1964; children: Meredith Elizabeth, Mandy Leigh; m. G. Robert Evans, Sept. 4, 1982. Spl. assignment nurse Columbia-Presbyn. Med. Center, N.Y.C., 1957-59; med. advt. copywriter Paul Klemtner & Co., N.Y.C., 1959-61, William Douglas McAdams Agy., N.Y.C., 1961-62; account exec. Arndt, Preston, Chapin, Lamb & Keen, N.Y.C., 1962-63; Rocky Mountain corr. Medical World News, Denver, 1963-64; owner Publicite, Denver; gen. mgr. Center Mktg. Assn., Palo Alto, Calif., 1964-66; freelance writer, pub. rels. and mgmt. cons., Woodside, Calif., 1966-85; pres. Communications for Youth, 1979—. Mem. Palo Alto-Stanford Hosp. Aux., 1968-72; pub. rels. assistance Peninsula Children's Ctr., Palo Alto, 1968-73, Triton Mus. Art, San Jose, Calif., 1966-70; chmn. citizens adv. com. San Mateo County Juvenile Social Svcs.; health component Early Childhood Com., Woodside Elem. Sch. Dist.; mem. adv. com. South County Youth and Family Svcs. Program; mem. Statewide Citizens Adv. Com. on Child Abuse and Neglect Ill. Dept. Children and Family Svcs., 1987—; past chair, mem., bd. dirs. ct.-apptd. spl. advocate program CASA-Kane County, 1989—; chair adv. com. to Congressman Dennis Hastert on Family and Child Legis., 1990—; bd. dirs. N.J. Jr. C. of C./UNICEF/African Project, 1960-61; mem. San Mateo County Mental Health Adv. Bd., Friends of Woodside Libr. Bd, 1983-85; mem. Rep. Senatorial Inner Circle, 1982—; vol. Nat. Com. for Prevention Child Abuse and Neglect, 1987—; acting chair, founder Chicagoland Media & Children Com., 1993—; adv. com. Our Children's Place, Kane County, 1995—. Home and Office: PO Box 710 Wayne IL 60184-0710

EVANS, CINDY L., investment company official; b. Columbus, Ohio, June 20, 1969. BS in Fin., Miami U., Oxford, Ohio, 1991. CSP Huntington Nat. Bank, Columbus, 1991-92, personal banker, 1992-94; compliance specialist

Huntington Investment Co., Columbus, 1994—. Office: Huntington Investment Co 41 S High St Columbus OH 43287

EVANS, DANIEL E., sausage manufacturing and restaurant chain company executive; b. 1936. With Bob Evans Farms Inc., Columbus, Ohio, 1957—, chmn. bd., sec. and CEO, also dir. Office: Bob Evans Farms Inc Box 07863 Sta G 3776 S High St Columbus OH 43207-4012

EVANS, DEANNA GENELLE, English language educator; b. Bastrop, Tex., Feb. 1, 1943; d. Armand and Helen Delmar; m. Neil K. Evans, Aug. 22, 1964 (div. Nov. 1983); children: Elizabeth, Henry, Margaret. BA, U. Pa., 1963; MA, U. Tex., 1966; PhD, Case Western Res. U., 1971. Cert. secondary English tchr., Ohio. Tchr. The Laurel Sch., Shaker Heights, Ohio, 1964-65; lectr. Cleve. State U., 1966, 71, adj. asst. prof., 1974-83; lectr. Cuyahoga C.C., Cleve., 1972, 83; prof. English Bemidji (Minn.) State U., 1983—, acting chmn. dept., 1989, 90, editor Calliope newsletter, 1984-95; hon. rsch. fellow U. Aberdeen, Scotland, 1992-93; conf. presenter in field; manuscript referee Studies in Scottish Literature, 1988—; cons., reader Houghton-Mifflin Co., 1991, 93. Contbr. articles and book revs. to profl. jours. Recipient best article award Minn. English Jour., 1986; grantee NEH, 1984, 85, Ford Found., 1991-92. Mem. MLA, New Chaucer Soc., Medieval Acad. Am., Nat. Coun. Tchrs. English, Medieval Assn. Midwest, Assn. Scottish Lit. Studies, Delta Omicron, Delta Phi Alpha, Phi Delta Gamma. Office: Dept English Bemidji State U Bemidji MN 56601

EVANS, DONALD LEROY, real estate company executive; b. Madison, Wis., Apr. 22, 1933; s. LeRoy E. and Pearl U. Evans. BS, U. Wis., 1959, MS, 1964. Staff appraiser Am. Appraisal Group, Milw., 1959-64; founder, pres. D.L. Evans, Inc., Madison, 1964—. Dir. U. Wis. Found.; trustee U. Wis. Rsch. Park. Served as sgt. U.S. Army, 1953-55, Korea. Recipient appreciation award, U. Wis. Real Estate Alumni Assn., 1979. Mem. Am. Soc. Appraisers (sr.; pres. 1968; Appreciation award 1968), Am. Soc. Real Estate Counselors, Am. Inst. Real Estate Appraisers (pres. 1972; Appreciation award 1972), Madison Bd. Realtors (bd. dirs. 1974-76; Appreciation award 1976). Republican. Lutheran. Club: Madison. Lodge: Rotary. Office: D L Evans Co Inc 6409 Odana Rd Madison WI 53719-1125

EVANS, GERALDINE ANN, academic administrator; b. Zumbrota, Minn., Feb. 24, 1939; d. Wallace William and Elda Ida (Tiedemann) Whipple; m. John Lyle Evans, June 21, 1963; children: John David, Paul William. AA, Rochester Community Coll., 1958; BS, U. Minn., 1960, MA, 1963, PhD, 1968. Cert. tchr., counselor, prin. and supt., Minn. Tchr. Hopkins (Minn.) Pub. Schs., 1960-63; counselor Anoka (Minn.) Pub. Schs., 1963-66; cons. in edn. Mpls., 1966-78; policy analyst Minn. Dept. Edn., St. Paul, 1978-79; dir. personnel Minn. Community Coll. System, St. Paul, 1979-82; pres. Rochester (Minn.) Community Coll., 1982-92; chancellor Minn. C.C. System, St. Paul, 1992-94; exec. dir. Ill. C.C. Bd., Springfield, 1994—. Consulting editor Cmty. Coll. Jour. of Rsch. and Practice, 1992-94. Vice chair, bd. dirs. Wayzata (Minn.) Sch. Bd., 1980-83; bd. dirs. Minn. Tech. Ctr., Rochester, 1991-92; sec.-treas. Coun. North Ctrl. Cmty. and Jr. Colls., 1990-92; moderator Mizpah United Ch. Christ, Hopkins, 1982; mem. Gov.'s Job Tng. Coun., St. Paul, 1983-94, chair, 1992-94; mem. ACE Commn. on Edn. Credit and Credentials, 1992—. Inst. Ednl. Leadership fellow, Washington, 1978-79. Mem. Nat. League Nursing (bd. assoc. degree accreditation rev. 1990-93, exec. com. 1993-96), Am. Assn. Cmty. Jr. Colls. (bd. dirs. 1984-87), North Ctrl. Assn. Cmty. and Jr. Colls. (evaluator). Congregationalist.

EVANS, JOHN THOMAS, logistics manager; b. Bloomington, Ill., Dec. 13, 1954; s. Hugh Bernard amd Merrillee (Gregg) E.; m. Paula Jayce Rickers, Feb. 12, 1977; children: Sean Thomas, Geoffrey Bernard. BA in psychology, Ill. Western U., 1977. Mgr., instr. Guitar World, Normal, Ill., 1977-90; transporter builder GATX Logistics, Inc., Normal, Ill., 1990-91, inventory control, 1991-92, edn. coord., 1991-95, mgr. engring. data, oper., 1995—. Mem. Am. Prodn. & Inventory Control Soc., Am. Soc. Tng. & Devel. Home: 910 W Taylor Bloomington IL 61701 Office: GATX Logistics Inc 2601 W College Ave Normal IL 61761

EVANS, LANE, congressman; b. Rock Island, Ill., Aug. 4, 1951; s. Lee Herbert and Joycelene (Saylor) E. B.A., Augustana Coll., 1974; J.D., Georgetown U., 1978. Bar: Ill. 1978. Mng. atty. Western Ill. Legal Assistance Found., Rock Island, 1978-79; mem. nat. staff Kennedy for Pres., Washington, 1978-80; atty., ptnr. Community Legal Clinic, Rock Island, Ill., 1981-82; mem. 98th-104th Congresses from 17th Ill. Dist., 1983—; mem. nat. security com., ranking minority mem. vets. affairs subcom. on compensation, pension, ins. and meml. affairs. Served with USMC, 1969-71. Mem. AmVets, Am. Legion, Marine Corps League, Vietnam Vets Ill. Democrat. Roman Catholic. Office: US Ho of Reps 2335 Rayburn Bldg Washington DC 20515-0005*

EVANS, MARGARET ANN, human resources administrator, business owner; b. Great Bend, Kans., Dec. 26, 1947; d. Freddy Florence and Peggy (Hawkins) Green; m. Carl Evans, Aug. 13, 1972; children: Carl André, Christopher Dion. B in Psychology, U. Mo., 1971, MPA, 1972. Pers. specialist Met. Jr. Coll., Kansas City, Mo., 1972-73; employee rels. specialist Amoco Oil Co., Kansas City, 1973-74; classification specialist Richards-Gebaur AFB, Mo., 1974-75; employee rels. officer Govt. Employee Hosp. Assn., Kansas City, 1977-84, mgr. pers., 1984-87, dir. human resources, 1987—; mem. pers. com. Sta. KKFI, Kansas City, 1989—; mem. cert. bd. Human Resource Inst., exam devel. dir., 1994-95, sec.-treas., 1995-96. Sec. and v.p. Booster Club, Hickman Mills High Sch., Kansas City, 1989—. Ford Found. fellow U. Mo., 1971; recipient Contbr. of Yr. award Human Resource Mgmt. Assn., 1992, Pres. award 1993, 1995; named One of Kansas City's 100 Most Influential Kansas Citians, 1996. Mem. NAFE, Soc. Human Resources Mgmt. (pers. rsch. com. Kansas City chpt. 1989—, nat. com. 1990—, sec.-treas. Mo. state coun. 1992-93, area IV bd. mem.), Pers. Mgmt. Assn. (co-chmn. coll. rels. 1981), Urban League, NAACP, Links, Inc., ASPA, ASTD, Alpha Kappa Alpha (chair midwestern regional conf., 1996, Outstanding Grad. Soror). Home: 10216 E 96th St Kansas City MO 64134-2309 Office: Govt Employee Hosp Assn 35 W 40th St Kansas City MO 64111-2219

EVANS, MARVIN PAUL, insurance operations administrator; b. Spanish Fork, Utah, June 7, 1953; s. Paul and Mabel Norma (Liechty) E.; m. Alice Paula Joyner, Feb. 13, 1975; children: Brian, Angela, Matthew, Sharla, Cory, Wesley. BS in Adminstrv. Office Mgmt., Brigham Young U., 1976, MS in Bus. Edn., 1978. Cert. adminstrv. mgr., Adminstrv. Mgmt. Soc. (now Inst. Cert. Profl. Mgrs.). Grad. asst. Brigham Young U., Provo, Utah, 1977-78; bus. analyst Kemper Nat. Ins., Long Grove, Ill., 1978-83, corp. ops. support mgr., 1983-86; div. ops. officer Kemper Nat. Ins., Syracuse, N.Y., 1986-94; continuous improvement officer Kemper Nat. Ins., Long Grove, 1994—. Co-author: The Administrative Manager, 1987. Bishop LDS Ch., Syracuse, 1986-92. Republican. Office: Kemper Nat Ins 1 Kemper Dr Long Grove IL 60049

EVANS, R. MARK, pharmacologist; b. Omaha, Sept. 10, 1953; s. Ralph Matthew and Joan Elizabeth (Maddrix) E.; m. Mary Margaret Vaux, Oct. 19, 1979; children: Andy, Adam, Audrey. BS in Biology, Bates Coll., 1975; PhD in Pharmacology, SUNY/Roswell Park Meml. Inst., Buffalo, 1980. Rsch. asst. Brookhaven Nat. Labs., L.I., N.Y., 1974; postdoctoral fellow dept. cell biology Baylor Coll. Medicine, Houston, 1980-81; postdoctoral fellow dept. pharmacology U. Tex., Houston, 1981-83; sr. scientist Lorillard Rsch. Ctr., Greensboro, N.C., 1983; sr. scientist AMA, Chgo., 1983-86, dir. biotech., 1986-91; sci. editor divsn. consumer affairs Am. Med. TV and AMA, Chgo., 1992-94; dir. devel. multimedia interactive continuing med. edn. AMA, Chgo., 1995—; adv. com. Biol. Scis. Curriculum Study, Colorado Springs, 1991-92; sec. health policy agenda and ref. com., ho. dels. AMA, 1987-91. Contbg. author to 6th and 7th edits. AMA Drug Evaluations, articles to profl. jours. Mem. Hinsdale (Ill.) Village Caucus, 1990—; coach Am. Youth Soccer Orgn., Hinsdale, 1987—, Hinsdale Little League, 1990-94, Boy Scouts Am., 1991—. Mem. AAAS, N.Y. Acad. Sci. Republican. Methodist. Home: 712 S Bruner St Hinsdale IL 60521-4337 Office: Am Med Assn 515 N State St Chicago IL 60610-4320

EVANS, RICHARD JAMES, mechanical engineer; b. Wabash, Ind., Nov. 26, 1960; s. Tommy Lewis and Joyce Anne (Leckrone) E.; children: Matthew Thomas, Kari Lynn, Jenna Marie. BSME, Rose-Hulman Inst. Tech., 1983; MBA with honors, Ind. U., 1993. Registered profl. engr., Ky., Ind.; cert. lighting efficiency profl. Sales engr. Johnson Controls, Inc., Indpls., 1983-90, sales team leader in healthcare mktg., 1990-93; br. mgr. Johnson Controls, Inc., Evansville, Ind., 1993-95, area installation mgr., 1995—. Active Sons of Am. Legion, Wabash, 1989—. Mem. ASHRAE (pres. ctrl. Ind. chpt. 1991-92, bd. dirs. 1992-93, Presdl. award of Excellence 1992), NSPE, Assn. Energy Engrs. (cert. energy mgr.), Am. Soc. Hosp. Engrs., Ind. Soc. Profl. Engrs., Ind. Soc. Hosp. Engrs., Beta Gamma Sigma. Home: 338 Brixham Ct Fishers IN 46038 Office: 1255 N Senate Ave Indianapolis IN 46202 Office: Johnson Controls Inc 1255 N Senate Ave Indianapolis IN 46202

EVANS, ROBERT A., manufacturing company executive; b. Gardner, Kans., June 24, 1959. Layout designer Balderson Inc., Wamego, Kans., 1978—. Office: Balderson Inc PO Box 6 Wamego KS 66547-0006

EVANS, ROBERT GEORGE, JR., retail and mail order executive; b. Wabash, Ind., May 6, 1953; s. Robert George and Helen (Kalb) E.; m. Leisa Marie Napier, June 13, 1987. Student, Ind. U., 1970-74; BSBA, Wesleyan U., 1993. Dir. computer services Ind. U. Northwest Campus, Gary, 1972-75; mgr. configuration planning CNA Ins., Chgo., 1975-79; mgr. tech. support Brylane/Ltd. Inc., Indpls., 1979-85, sr. mgr. tech. svcs., 1985-89; dir. MIS Lane Bryant/Ltd., Inc., Indpls., 1989-91; dir. Brylane/Ltd., Inc., Indpls., 1991-93; v.p. MIS Brylane, LP, Indpls., 1993—; pres. Tri-Star Consulting, Merrillville, Ind., 1983-86; cons., instr. Ind.-Purdue U. Indpls. Continuing Studies Program, 1980-83. Mem. Major of Indpls. Liaison for County Agys. and Twps., 1991. Republican. Methodist.

EVANS, ROBERT LEONARD, mathematical physiologist, educator; b. Duluth, Minn., May 30, 1917; s. John Leonard and Amy (Magnusson) E.; m. Frances Janet Bentley, Dec. 21, 1941 (dec. Nov. 1955); children: Amy Elizabeth, Thomas Randall, Julia May; m. Elsie Frances Hardy, Jan. 11, 1957. B of Chemistry, U. Minn., 1938, MS, 1939, PhD, 1951. Assoc. metallurgist U.S. Bur. Mines, Salt Lake City, 1940-44; rsch. assoc. Allegany Ballistics Lab., Cumberland, Md., 1944-45; from instr. math. and mechanics to asst. prof. physiology U. Minn., Mpls., 1945-63, assoc. prof. biometry and math. biology, 1963-70, lectr. physiology, 1970—. Author: Fall and Rise of Man If ...., 1973; editor, sect. author: Eight Writers Seeking Readers, 1985. Grantee Rockefeller Found., 1954-59, USPHS, 1958-68. Mem. AAAS (life), N.Am. Com. for Humanism, World Federalist Assn., Minn. Acad. Sci., Sigma Xi. Unitarian. Home and Office: Ste 503 2601 Kenzie Ter Minneapolis MN 55418-3262

EVANS, ROGER LYNWOOD, scientist, patent liaison; b. Ipswich, Suffolk, Eng., June 25, 1928; came to U.S., 1953; s. Evelyn Jesse and Ethel Jane (Woods) E.; m. Jane Adelaide Baird, Nov. 24, 1954 (div. 1976); children: Robert Malcolm Baird, Roderick Lawrence Woods, Alison Clare; m. Wendy Dorothy Grove, Apr. 11, 1977. BA in Natural Sci., Oxford (Eng.) U., 1953, MA, 1955, DPhil in Natural Sci., 1958; MS in Inorganic Chemistry, U. Minn., 1955. With chem. and radiopharm. R & D dept. 3M Co., St. Paul., 1958-77, patent liaison, 1977-91; developer intellectual property initiative, tech. devel. dept., 1992-93; cons. 3M, 1993—, program cons., 1995; originator 3M Richard G. Drew Creativity Award, 1970, program cons., 1995—. Founder, editor Newsletter of the Tech. Forum, 1971-93; inventor, writer, producer series of videos on intellectual property topics. Mem., chmn. Mendota Heights Planning Commn., 1962-68, Sunfish Lake Planning Commn., 1968-84, Dakota County Planning Commn., Minn., 1965-72. 2d lt. Brit. Army, 1946-49, Eng. Anglican. Home and Office: 9965 Rich Valley Blvd Inver Grove Heights MN 55077-4529

EVANS, SARA MARGARET, history educator; b. McCormick, S.C.; d. J. Claude and Maxilla (Everett) E.; m. Harry Chatten Boyte, June 5, 1966 (div. Aug. 1994); children: Craig Evans Boyte, Rachel Boyte Evans. BA, Duke U., 1966, MA, 1968; PhD in History, U. N.C., 1976. Instr. history dept. Duke U., Durham, N.C., 1974-75, U. N.C., Chapel Hill, 1975-76; asst. prof., then assoc. prof. history dept. U. Minn., Mpls., 1976-89, dir. ctr. for advanced feminist studies, 1987-90, prof., 1989—, chair history dept., 1991-94; mem. editorial bd. Feminist Studies, College Park, Md. Author: Personal Politics, 1979, Born for Liberty, 1989; co-author: Free Spaces, 1986, Wage Justice, 1989; cons. editor: Jour. Am. History, 1990-95. Kellogg Nat. fellow W. K. Kellogg Found., 1983-86; recipient Book award Policy Studies Orgn., 1990. mem. Orgn. Am. Historians (bd. dirs. 1991-94), Am. Studies assn. (bd. dirs. 1990-93), Am. Hist. Assn. Methodist. Office: U Minn History Dept 267 19th Ave S Minneapolis MN 55455-0499

EVANSON, BARBARA JEAN, middle school education educator; b. Grand Forks, N.D., Aug. 15, 1944; d. Robert John and Jean Elizabeth (Lommen) Gibbons; m. Bruce Carlyle Evanson, Dec. 27, 1965; children: Tracey, John, Kelly. AA, Bismarck State Coll., 1964; BS in Spl. and Elem. Edn., U. N.D., 1966. Tchr. spl. edn. Winship Sch., Grand Forks, 1966-67, Simle Jr. High, Bismarck, 1967-70; tchr. Northridge Elem. sch., Bismarck, 1980-86, Wachter Middle Sch., Bismarck, 1986—; workshop facilitator Brass Found., Chgo., 1990-96, Dept. Pub. Instrn., Bismarck, 1988—, Chpt. I, Bismarck, 1989—, McRel for Drug Free Schs., Denver, 1990—. Co-founder The Big People, Bismarck, 1978—; mem. task force Children's Trust Fund, N.D., 1984; senator N.D. Legislature, Bismarck, 1989-94; mem. N.D. Bridges Adv. Bd., 1991—, DPI English Adv. Com., 1993—; co-facilitator Lead Mid. Sch. for Carnegie, 1994—; bd. dirs. Caring for Children, 1993-94, N.D. Art Edn. Task Force, 1992-93, N.D. Health Adv. Coun., 1993-94, N.D. Tchr.'s Fund for Retirement. Recipient Gold award Bismarck Norwest Bank, 1985; named Tchr. of Yr., N.D. Dept. Pub. Instrn., 1989, Legislator of Yr., Children's Caucus, 1991, Outstanding Alumnae, Bismarck State Coll., 1991, Milken Nat. Tchr. of Yr., 1995-96. Mem. N.O.R.A., N.C.T.E., Nat. Edn. Assn., N.D. Edn. Assn., Bismarck Edn. Assn., N.D. Reading Assn., Alpha Delta Kappa. Home: 723 N Washington St Bismarck ND 58501-3622 Office: Wachter Middle Sch 1107 S 7th St Bismarck ND 58504-6533

EVANSON, ELIZABETH MOSS, editor; b. Dallas, Oct. 13, 1934; d. Clifton Lowther and Virginia (Spence) M.; m. Jacob T. Evanson, Apr. 8, 1958; children: Evan A., Virginia M. BA with high honors, Swarthmore Coll., 1956; MA, Columbia U., 1957. Ency. and book editor Columbia U. Press, N.Y.C., 1957-61; adminstrv. asst. New Haven (Conn.) Redevel. Agy., 1961-63; freelance editor Yale U. Press, New Haven, 1964-69; editor Ctr. for Studies of John Dewey, Carbondale, Ill., 1971-72, U. Wis. Press, Madison, 1975-80; editor Inst. for Rsch. on Poverty U. Wis., Madison, 1980—, conf. organizer, 1984—; asst. dir. pub. info. Inst. for Rsch. on Poverty, Madison, 1989—, sr. editor, 1986—. Translator: The French Revolution, 1962; contbr. articles and essays on poverty rsch. Mem. Acad. Staff Pub. Representation Orgn., Phi Beta Kappa. Unitarian. Office: Inst for Rsch on Poverty 1180 Observatory Dr Madison WI 53706-1320

EVENBECK, SCOTT EDWARD, university official, psychologist; b. Findlay, Ohio, Aug. 14, 1946; s. Benjamin F. and Norma H. (Kelley) E.; m. Elizabeth Ann Jones, Aug. 14, 1970 (div. July 1995); 1 child, Benjamin F. III. AB, Ind. U., 1968; MA, U. N.C., 1971, PhD, 1972. Asst. prof. psychology Ind. U.-Purdue U., Indpls., 1972-76, asst. dean Purdue U. Sch. Sci., 1977-79, assoc. dean, 1979-80, assoc. dir. adminstrv. affairs, assoc. prof. psychology, 1976—, assoc. dir. adminstrv. affairs, 1980-85, dir. continuing studies, 1985—, also assoc. dean Ind. U. Sch. Continuing Studies, 1985-88, assoc. dean of faculties, 1988-90, assoc. vice chancellor, 1990—; bd. dirs. Parent Info. Resource Ctr., 1977-85; exec. v.p. Assn. for Continuing Higher Edn., 1990-93, bd. dirs., 1993—. Contbr. articles in field to profl. jours. Mem. exec. com., asst. treas., v.p., pres. Am. Lung Assn. Cen. Ind., bd. dirs., 1985—, v.p. 1986; pres. Am. Lung Assn. Ind., 1988; mem. nat. coun. Am. Lung Assn., 1991-94; bd. dirs. Christamore House, 1985—; sec. Indpls.-Searborough Peace Games, 1977-80; mem. bd. Consortium Endowed Episcopal Parishes, 1992—, v.p., 1994-96, pres., 1996—; dep. gen. Espiscopal Ch. Convention, 1988, 91, 94, standing commn. on human affairs, 1995—; sec. Diocese Indpls., 1995—. USPHS trainee, 1968-72; Arthur R. Metz scholar Ind. U., 1964-68. Mem. APA, Nat. Coun. Univ. Rsch. Adminstrs. (mem. exec. com. 1979-80), Indpls. C. of C. (mem. exec. com. speaker's bur.), Masons. Republican. Episcopalian. Home: 5115 E 74th Pl Indianapolis IN 46250-2529 Office: 620 Union Dr Indianapolis IN 46202-5130

EVENS, MARY RUTH, tool room supervisor; b. Flint, Mich., May 26, 1947; d. Russell Dell and Mary Ruth (Ryman) Spickler; m. Robert G. Evens, Aug. 17, 1968; children: Michelle Jeanette Evens LaRose, Brian Craig. A in Mech. Tech., Mott C.C., Flint, Mich., 1978; B in Applied Sci., U. Mich., Flint, 1980. Cert. journeyman toolmaker. Skilled trades supr. Delphi Energy & Engine Mgmt. Sys., Flint, 1972—; toolmaker AC Spark Plug, Flint, 1972-80, skilled trades supr., 1981, cons., 1987-89; mfg. engr. AC Rochester, Flint, 1989-91. Mem. Am. Horse Show Assn., Internat. Arabian Horse Assn., Arabian Horse Assn. Mich., West Mich. Arabian Horse Assn. Roman Catholic. Office: Delphi Energy & EngineMgmt Sys 1300 N Dort Hwy Flint MI 48556

EVENS, MICHELLE JEANETTE, photographer; b. Flint, Mich., Nov. 20, 1964; d. Robert Gordon and Mary Ruth Evens; m. Clayton Richard LaRose, Sept. 28, 1991. Student, Lansing Community Coll., 1983-85. Real estate license, Fla. V.p. Magic Carpet, Lansing, Mich., 1990-95; owner Chelle Artist at Large, Lansing, 1992—. Freelance artist, photographer.

EVENS, RONALD GENE, radiologist, medical center administrator; b. St. Louis, Sept. 24, 1939; s. Robert and Dorothy (Lupkey) E.; m. Hanna Blunk, Sept. 3, 1960; children: Ronald Jr., Christine, Amanda. BA, Washington U., 1960, MD, 1964, postgrad. in bus. and edn., 1970-71. Intern Barnes Hosp., St. Louis, 1964-65; resident Mallinckrodt Inst. Radiology, St. Louis, 1965-66, 68-70; rsch. assoc. Nat. Heart Inst., 1966-68; asst. prof. radiology, v.p. Washington U. Med. Sch., 1970-71, prof., head dept. radiology, dir., 1971-72, Elizabeth Mallinckrodt prof., head radiology dept., 1972—, adj. prof. med. econs., 1988—; radiologist-in-chief Barnes Hosp., St. Louis, 1971—; radiologist-in-chief Children's Hosp., 1971—, pres., chief exec. officer, 1985-88; vice chancellor fin. Washington U., St. Louis, 1988—; mem. adv. com. on splty. and geog. distbn. of physicians Inst. Medicine, Nat. Acad. Scis., 1974-76, Hickey lectr., 1976, Carmen lectr. Calif. U., 1985, Kiewit lectr. Eisenhower Med. Ctr., 1986; Hornick lectr. U. Pitts., 1986; ann. orator Can. Radiol. Soc., 1984; Hodes lectr. Jefferson U., 1991—; Smith lectr. Royal Coll. Physicians, Edinburgh, 1992; Seaman lectr. Columbia Presbyn., 1992; dir. Boatmens Bank Inc., Mallinckrodt Group Inc., Right Choice Inc., Blue Choice, Inc.; chmn. bd. Med. Care Group St. Louis, 1980-86. Contbr. over 210 articles to profl. jours. Active Boy Scouts Am., 1975—; elder Glendale Presbyn. Ch., 1971-74, Kirkwood Presbyn. Ch., 1983-86. Served with USPHS, 1966-68. Advance Acad. fellow James Picker Found, 1970; recipient Disting. Svc. award. St. Louis C. of C., 1972; named Disting. Eagle Scout Nat. Coun., 1983. Fellow Am. Coll. Radiology (chair elect 1995); mem. AMA (editl. bd. JAMA), Mo. Radiol. Soc. (pres. 1977-78), Soc. Nuclear Medicine (trustee 1971-75), St. Louis Med. Soc., Mo. State Med. Assn., Soc. Chmn. Acad. Radiology Depts. (pres. 1979), Radiol. Soc. N.Am., Assn. Univ. Radiologists (pres. 1988), Am. Roentgen Ray Soc. (pres. 1989), Phi Beta Kappa, Alpha Omega Alpha (Sheard-Sanford award). Office: Washington U Mallinckrodt Inst Radiology 510 S Kingshighway Blvd Saint Louis MO 63110-1016

EVERETT, BILL D., electrical engineer; b. Sidney, Ohio, Nov. 30, 1968. A in Engring. Design, Ediston State C.C., 1991. Detail drafter PMI Foods, Troy, Ohio, 1989-91; design engr. A.O. Smith, Tipp City, Ohio, 1991-92, EMI Corp., Jackson City, Ohio, 1992—; tchr. physics World in Motion, Halston, Ohio, 1994. Mem. Alfa-Cmty. Ctr., Sidney, Ohio, 1995. Republican. Church of God. Office: EMI Corp 427 W Pike St Jackson OH 45334

EVERETT, GARRETT, veterinary clinic executive. Office: Wentzville Veterinary 602 E Pearce Wentzville MO 63385*

EVERETT, KAREN J., librarian; b. Cin., Dec. 12, 1926; d. Leonard Kelly and Kletis V. (Wade) Wheatley; m. Wilbur Mason Everett, Sept. 25, 1950; children: Karen, Jan, Jeffrey, Jon, Kathleen, Kerry, Kelly, Shannon. BS Edn. magna cum laude, U. Cin., 1976; postgrad., Coll. Mt. St. Joseph, 1981-86, Xavier U., Cin., 1985-87, U. Cin., 1982-85, Miami U., 1987. Libr. S.W. Local Schs., Harrison, Ohio, 1967—; dist. media coord. S.W. Local Schs., 1980—, dist. vol. dir., 1980—; cons. in field; lectr. in field. Contbr. articles to profl. jours. Pres. Citizens Adv. Coun., Harrison, Ohio, 1981-84, 88—, Citizens Adv. Coun., 1989; state chmn. supervisory div. Ohio Ednl. Libr./Media Assn.; mem. Ohio Ambulance Licensing Bd., 1991—. Named Woman of the Yr., Cin. Enquirer, 1978, Xi Eta Iota, 1979; named PTA Educator of the Yr., 1981, others. Mem. NEA, Ohio Ednl. Libr./Media Assn. (chair supervisory div. 1990—, bd. dirs. 1993-94), Ohio Edn. Assn., S.W. Local Classroom Tchrs. Assn., Hamilton County Geneal. Soc. (bd. dirs. 1992—). Home: 122 Westfield Dr Harrison OH 45030-1431

EVERETT, RONALD EMERSON, government official; b. Columbus, Ohio, Jan. 4, 1937; s. John Carmen and Hermione Alicia (Lensner) E.; BA, Ohio U., 1959; postgrad. Baldwin-Wallace Coll., 1962-63; grad. U.S. Army Command and Gen. Staff Coll., 1978, U.S. Army War Coll., 1984; cert. Inst. Cost Analysis, 1982; cert. profl. estimator; m. Nancy Helen Leibersberger, Aug. 10, 1963; children: Darryl William, Darlene Anne, John Lee (dec.). Reporter, Dun & Bradstreet, Cleve., 1960-66; program analyst Lewis Research Center, NASA, Cleve., 1967-70, contract price analyst and negotiator, 1970-85, chief contract support br., 1985-86; chief space systems br., 1986—. Served with inf. U.S. Army, 1960; col. USAR, ret. Decorated Legion of Merit, Meritorious Service medal with six oak leaf clusters, Army Commendation medal with oak leaf cluster; cert. cost analyst. Mem. Assn. Govt. Accts., Res. Officer Assn., Internat. Platform Assn., Am. Def. Preparedness Assn., Assn. U.S. Army, Am. Security Council, Army War Coll. Found. Republican. Mem. Reformed Ch. in Am. Home: 27904 Blossom Blvd North Olmsted OH 44070-1723 Office: 21000 Brookpark Rd Cleveland OH 44135-3127

EVERETT, WAYNE, marketing consultant; b. Winchester, Kans., Aug. 27, 1946. BS in Mktg., Mo. Western State Coll., 1972; MBA, U. Kansas City, 1979. Ctrl. buyer automotive Sears, Kansas City, Mo., 1972-77; nat. buyer automotive Coast to Coast, Minnetonka, Minn., 1980-86; pres. Retail Support, Eden Prairie, Minn., 1986—. With USN, 1963-67, Vietnam. Office: Retail Support Inc 6459 Pinnacle Dr Eden Prairie MN 55346-1904

EVERETT, WILLIAM ARLIE, musicology educator; b. El Paso, Tex., June 4, 1962; s. James Eugene and Jeanne (Swails) E. MusB in Music Theory, Tex. Tech U., 1984; MusM in Conducting and Music History, So. Meth. U., 1986; PhD in Musicology, U. Kans., 1991. Asst. prof. music Washburn U., Topeka, 1986—; condr. Topeka Youth Orch., 1986-90; presenter in field. Contbr. articles to profl. jours. Bd. dirs Topeka String Project, 1989-93, Topeka Chamber Music Series, 1989—. Washburn U. rsch. grantee, 1987, 89, 92, 93, 95; Steinhardt scholar U. Kans., 1988. Mem. Am. Musicol. Soc., Croatian Musicol. Soc., Soc. for Ethnomusicology, Sonneck Soc. for Am. Music (chmn. pub. rels. com. 1992-96, treas. 1996—), Coll. Music Soc., Am. String Tchrs. Assn. (bd. dirs. Kans. chpt. 1989-94), Am. Viola Soc., Kans. Music Educators Assn. Mennonite. Office: Washburn U 1700 SW College Ave Topeka KS 66621-0001

EVERHART, ROBERT PHILLIP (BOBBY WILLIAMS), entertainer, songwriter, recording artist, festival producer; b. St. Edward, Nebr., June 16, 1936; s. Phillip McClelland and Martha Matilda (Meyer) E.; m. Feb. 14, 1992 Sheila Dawn Armstrong. Student U. Nebr., 1959-62, A. in Radio-TV Iowa Western Coll., 1971, A. in Graphic Arts, 1974, diploma in Journalism London Sch. Journalism, 1983, spl. studies Mexican Indian culture U. Okla., 1990—. Disc jockey various stas., Omaha and Juneau, Alaska, 1959-63, songwriter Royal Flair Music, BMI Pub., Walnut, Iowa, 1964—; host prodr. (TV series) Old Time Country Music, (radio show) Old-Time Music Hour; rec. artist Folkways Records, N.Y.C., 1970—, Smithsonian Inst., Westwood Records, Wales, 1981—, Folk Variety Records, Europe, 1980—, Allied Records, Philippines, OGA Records, Austria, Prairie Music Records, Unltd. Prodns., internat. concert artist performing traditional Am. country and folk music; curator, owner Pioneer Music Instrument Mus., Mid-Am. Country Music Hall of Fame., Mid-Am. Old Time Fiddlers Hall of Fame, Capt.'s Quarters Bed & Breakfast, all located in Walnut, Iowa, Lawtell, La., and Vera Cruz, Mex., Oaktree Opera, Anita, Iowa; festival promoter Old-Time Country Music Contest and Pioneer Exposition, 1976—, Nat. Traditional Music Performer Awards, 1991—; pres. Nat. Traditional Country Music Assn., Inc., 1982—; regular performer La. Hayride, 1985—. Served with USN, 1954-59. Named to Profl. Musicians and Entertainers Club Iowa Hall of Fame, 1994, Country Music Showcase Internat. Hall of Fame, 1995; Ky.

col., 1995. Mem. Great Plains Old Time Music Assn., Acad. Country Music, Nat. Bluegrass Assn., Ill. Traditional Country Music Assn., Tri-State Bluegrass Assn., Ky. Cols., Internat. Bluegrass Music Assn., Profl. Musicians Club of Iowa, Midwest Producers Assn. (chmn.). Democrat. Lutheran. Club: Carribean. Editor, Tradition Country Music Mag., 1980—; author: Clara Bell, 1976, Hart's Bluff, 1977, Listen to the Mockingbird, 1995; (poetry) Silver Bullets, 1979, Savage Trumpet, 1980, Prairie Sunrise, 1982, Snoopy Goes to Mexico, 1983; (TV scripts) The Life of Jimmie Rodgers, 1984, Matecombe Treasure, 1984, The Ghost of Carl Herrmann, 1993; recs. include: Let's Go, Dream Angel, She Sings Sad Songs, Love to Make Love, Bad Woman Blues, Fishpole John, Time after Time, Street Sleepers, No One Comes Near, Berlin Folksinger. Avocations: scuba diving, traveling. Office: Walnut Country Opera House PO Box 438 Walnut IA 51577-0438 also: Nat Traditional Country Music Assn 203 Antique City Dr Walnut IA 51577

EVERILL, RICHARD HAROLD, computer information scientist; b. Rockford, Ill., Sept. 2, 1942; s. Kelsey William and A. Ruth (Padgett) E.; m. Deana Doris Baldwin, Mar. 20, 1965; children: James, Richard. BSEd, Ball State U., 1964. Programmer Arvin Industries, Columbus, Ind., 1966-67; programmer, analyst Ind. Lumberman's Ins., Indpls., 1967-68; dept. head Lear Siegler Inst., Indpls., 1968-71; tchr. Elwood (Ind.) Community Schs., 1971-73; systems analyst Essex Group, Logansport, Ind., 1973-75; programmer, analyst Essex Group, Ft. Wayne, Ind., 1976-77, N. Am. Van Lines, Ft. Wayne, 1977-79; programmer Internat. Harvester, Ft. Wayne, 1979-81; systems analyst GTE North, Ft. Wayne, 1981—; tchr. Ind. Vocational/Tech. Inst., Ft. Wayne, 1976-81; cons. R.H. Everill & Assocs., New Haven, Ind., 1979-81; participant company task force, GTE, Ft. Wayne. Mem. Masons, Order Ea. Star. Republican. Methodist. Office: GTE North Ste 300 6920 Pointe Inverness Way Fort Wayne IN 46804-7926

EVERIST, BARBARA, state legislator; b. Sioux Falls, S.D., July 6, 1949; d. F. M. and H. M. (Kobb) McBride; m. Thomas Stephen Everist Jr., 1968; children: Thomas Stephen III, Michael Clayton, Lacey Elizabeth. BA, U. Santa Clara, 1971; JD, U. S.D., 1990. Law clk. S.D. 2d Cir., 1990-91; state rep. S.D. Ho. Reps. Dist. 14, 1993-94; senator S.D. State Senate Dist. 14, 1995—; mem. Commerce, Judiciary and Taxation Coms.; atty., Sioux Falls, 1990—. Mem. S.D. State Bar Assn., Assn. Gifted and Talented (pres. 1985), Jr. League Sioux Falls (pres. 1980-81), Phi Alpha Delta, Pi Beta Phi. Home: 709 E Tomar Rd Sioux Falls SD 57105-7053 Office: SD House of Reps State Capitol Pierre SD 57501*

EVERSON, DIANE LOUISE, publishing executive; b. Edgerton, Wis., Mar. 27, 1953; d. Harland Everett and Helen Viola (Oliver) E. BS, Carroll Coll., 1975. Co-pub. Edgerton (Wis.) Reporter, 1976—; v.p. Silk Screen Creations, 1981—; bd. dirs. Inland Press. Pub. Career Directors newspaper, 1981—, Directions mag., 1981—, Career Waves Newsletter, 1989—, Coll. and Univs. Directories. Trustee Carroll Coll., 1987—; active ARC. Mem. Nat. Newspaper Assn. (regional bd. dirs.), Inland Press Assn. (bd. dirs. 1993—). Democrat. Lutheran. Home: 114 Kellog Rd Edgerton WI 53534-9352 Office: Directions Pub 21 N Henry St Edgerton WI 53534-1821

EVERT, RAY FRANKLIN, botany educator; b. Mt. Carmel, Pa., Feb. 20, 1931; s. Milner Ray and Elsie (Hoffa) I.; m. Mary Margaret Maloney, Jan. 2, 1960; children: Patricia Ann, Paul Franklin. B.S., Pa. State U., 1952, M.S., 1954; Ph.D., U. Calif. at Davis, 1958. Mem. faculty Mont. State U., 1958-60; mem. faculty U. Wis.-Madison, 1960—, prof. botany, 1966-77, prof. botany and plant pathology, 1977-88, Katherine Esau prof. botany and plant pathology, 1988—, chmn. dept. botany, 73-74/77-79/94—; vis. prof. U. Natal, Pietermaritzburg, S. Africa, winter, spring 1971, U. Göttingen, W.Ger., summer 1971, 74-75, summer 1988; mem. gen. biology and genetics fellowship rev. panel NIH, 1964-68, NSF Adv. Com. for Biol. Research Ctrs. Program, 1987-88; forensic plant anatomy cons. Co-author: Biology of Plants; sci. editor Physiol. Plantarum, 1983—; mem. editorial bd. Trees, 1991—, Internat. Jour. Plant Scis., 1991—; contbr. articles on food conducting tissue in higher plants and leaf structure-function relationships. Recipient Alexander von Humboldt award, 1974-75, Emil H. Steiger award for excellence in teaching U. Wis., 1981, Bessey Lectr. award Iowa State U., Ames, 1984, Benjamin Minge Duggar lectureship award Auburn U., 1985, Disting. Service citation Wis. Acad. Scis., Arts and Letters, 1985; Guggenheim fellow, 1965-66. Fellow Am. Acad. Arts and Scis., AAAS; mem. Bot. Soc. Am. (pres. 1986-87, Merit award 1982), Am. Inst. Biol. Scis., Wis. Acad. Scis., Arts and Letters, Am. Soc. Plant Physiol., Internat. Assn. Wood Anatomists, Deutschen Botanischen Gesellschaft, Golden Key Nat. Honor Soc., Sigma Xi, Phi Kappa Phi, Phi Sigma, Phi Epsilon Phi., Pi Alpha Xi. Home: 810 Woodward Dr Madison WI 53704-2238

EVISTON, MITCHELL D., agricultural products company executive; b. Wabash, Ind., Nov. 12, 1968; s. Michael P. and Kathy Dale (Chopson) E. B of Agrl. Econs., Purdue U., 1991. Ter. sales mgr. CIBA Seeds, Indpls., 1991-93; dist. sales mgr. CIBA Seeds, Bloomington, Ill., 1993, regional mgr., 1993—. Mem. Alpha Gamma Rho. Republican. Home: 53 Vermont Ave Bloomington IL 61701

EWALD, ROBERT FREDERICK, insurance association executive; b. Newark, May 5, 1924; s. Frederick J. and Florence M. (Reiley) E.; B.S. cum laude in Bus. Adminstrn., with spl. honors in Econs., Rutgers U., 1948; m. Jeanine Martinez, Jan. 3, 1976; children: Robert, Steven; children by previous marriage: William F., John C., George E. Asst. corp. auditor Prudential Ins. Co., Newark, Houston, Chgo., 1948-61; audit mgr. N.Y. Life Ins. Co., N.Y.C., 1962-64; treas. Mass. Gen. Life Ins. Co., Boston, 1965-68; adminstrv. v.p., controller Res. Life Ins. Co., Dallas, 1969-70; pres. Nat. Ben Franklin Life, Chgo., 1971-77; trustee, pres. Rockford (Ill.) Blue Cross Plan; pres., dir. Life Ins. Assos., Inc.; trustee Communities Health Plan, Inc., North Communities Health Plan, Inc., 1979-82; exec. dir. Ill. Life and Health Ins. Guaranty Assn., Chgo., 1984-92; exec. dir. Ill. HMO Guaranty Assn., Chgo., 1988-92; dir. emeritus Blue Cross and Shield Ill; dir. Guaranty Reassurance Corp., 1993-95, chmn. audit com., 1993-95; pres. Guaranty Systems Cons., LTD. Served with U.S. Army, 1943-46. Fellow Life Mgmt. Inst.; mem. Fin. Execs. Inst., Am. Arbitration Assn., Adminstrv. Mgmt. Soc., Mensa, Nat. Orgn. Life and Health Ins. Guaranty Assns. (emeritus dir., chmn. members coun. 1992-95, chmn. exec. com.). Home: 12 Wisner St Park Ridge IL 60068-3546

EWBANK, THOMAS PETERS, lawyer, retired banker; b. Indpls., Dec. 29, 1943; s. William Curtis and Maxine Stuart (Peters) E.; m. Alice Ann Shelton, June 8, 1968; children—William Curtis, Ann Shelton. Student Stanford U., 1961-62; A.B., Ind. U., 1965, J.D., 1969. Bar: Ind. 1969, U.S. Tax Ct., 1969, U.S. Dist. Ct. (so. dist.) Ind. 1969, U.S. Supreme Ct. 1974. CFA, cert. Trust & Fin. Advisor. Legis. asst. Ind. Legis. Council, 1966-67; estate and inheritance tax adminstr. Mchts. Nat. Bank, Indpls., 1967-69; assoc. Hilgedag, Johnson, Secrest and Murphy, Indpls., 1969-71; asst. gen. counsel Everett I. Brown Co., Indpls., 1971-72; with Mchts. Nat. Bank & Trust Co. (name changed to Nat. City Bank), Indpls., 1972-95, successively probate adminstr., head probate div., head personal account adminstrn. group in trust div., v.p. and sr. trust officer, sr. v.p., pres. Merchants Capital Mgmt., Inc., Ind., 1990-93; ptnr. Krieg DeVault Alexander & Capehart Law Firm, 1995—; asst. treas. Ruckelshaus for U.S. Senator Com., 1968; candidate for Ind. Legislature, 1970, 74. Fellow Ind. Bar Found. (life patron); mem. Estate Planning Council Indpls. (pres. 1982-83), Indpls. Bar Assn., Ind. Bar Assn., Indpls. Bar Found. (treas. 1976-81), Indpls. Soc. Fin. Anaylsts, Blue Key, Meridian Hills Country Club, Masons, Kiwanis (Circle K Internat. trustee 1963-64, pres. 1964-65, chmn. internat. com. 1988-90, George Hixson Diamond fellow), (treas. Indpls. club 1980-81, 84-85 designated a maj. builder 1983). Contbr. articles to profl. jours. Republican. Baptist. Home: 4516 Sylvan Rd Indianapolis IN 46208-2847 Office: One Indiana Sq Ste 2800 Indianapolis IN 46204-2017

EWERSEN, MARY VIRGINIA, retired secondary educator; b. Van Wert County, Ohio, June 7, 1922; B.S. in Elem. Edn., Bowling Green, 1966, Toledo and Ohio U. State U.; m. Herbert Ewersen (dec.); 2 children. Remedial reading tchr. Port Clinton (Ohio) City Schs., 1966-70, reading tchr. chpt. I/coord., 1970-94, ret. Cert. tchr. K-12, reading, Ohio. Mem. Internat. Reading Assn., Sandusky Choral Soc., Kappa Delta Pi. Author activity card set: From Hyperactive to Happy-Active in Limited Spaces, 1979; poet. Home: 1786 S Hickory Grove Rd Port Clinton OH 43452-9637 Office: 431 Portage Dr Port Clinton OH 43452-1724

EWERT, QUENTIN ALBERT, lawyer, consultant; b. Griggsville, Ill., Aug. 19, 1915; s. Albert Merritt and Anna Mabel (Beard) E.; m. Frances Norfleet, Dec. 25, 1941; children: David Norfleet, Gregory Albert, Catherine Ann, Mary Frances, Jane Cranston; m. Arlayne Joy Brown, May 1973 (div. June 1981). BA, Mich. State U., 1938; JD, U. Mich., 1946. Bar: Mich. 1946. Atty. Auto Owners Ins. Co., Lansing, Mich., 1946-47; ptnr. Ewert and Fagan, Lansing, Mich., 1947-48; sole practice Lansing, Mich., 1948-53; pres., bd. chmn. Guardsman Ins. Co., Pasadena, Calif., 1953-55; ptnr. Loomis, Ewert, Ederer, Parsley, Davis & Gotting, P.C., Lansing, 1955-87, of counsel, 1988—; owner, bd. chmn. Communications, Inc., Grand Rapids, Mich., 1972-87; cons. TIE/communications, Inc., Shelton, Conn., 1988-91. Met. area chmn. Rep. party, Lansing, 1952. Served to lt. cmdr. USNR, 1941-45. Mem. Kiwanis (Lansing), The Springs Country Club. Home (winter): 11 Mount Holyoke Dr Rancho Mirage CA 92270-3667 Office: Loomis Ewert Parsley Davis & Gotting 232 S Capitol Ave Ste 1000 Lansing MI 48933-1525

EWING, DAVID CHARLES, automobile dealership executive; b. Canton, Ohio, Sept. 27, 1942; s. Stanley Clement and Dolores Joan (Darr) E.; m. Penni Lynn West, Sept. 10, 1966; 1 child, Amy Lynn. BSBA, Bowling Green State U., 1964; MBA, Western Res. U., 1966. 2nd lt. USAR, 1966-72; mgr. truck sales Ewing Chevrolet, Canton, 1966-72, mgr. lease sales, 1972-75, mgr. new car sales, 1975-81, gen. mgr., 1981-88, pres., 1988—; owner, pres. Ewing Motors, Inc., Canal Fulton, Ohio, 1993—. Trustee Malone Coll., Canton, 1979-80; chmn. adminstrv. bd. Ch. of Saviour, United Methodist Ch., 1989-92, chmn. found., 1992—; dir. Canal Fulton C. of C., Ohio and Erie Canal Corridor Coalition. Mem. Greater Canton C. of C., Nat. Automobile Dealers Assn., Ohio Auto Dealers Assn., Brookside Country Club, Canton Club, Rotary (pres. Canton Club 1989-90, dist. gov. 1996-97), Elks, Alpha Tau Omega. Republican. Home: 2545 Glenmont Dr NW Canton OH 44708-1341 Office: 929 Cleveland Ave NW Canton OH 44702-1811 also: Ewing Motors Inc 321 S Canal St Canal Fulton OH 44614-1103

EWING, DONNA MARIE, business educator; b. McLean, Ill., Apr. 16, 1936; m. Nathaniel H. Ewing, Dec. 24, 1954; children: Nathaniel H. Jr., Cindy Marie. BS in Bus. Edn., Ill. State U., 1971, MS in Bus., 1975; EdD, U. Ill., 1991. Acctg. clk., exec. sec. Ill. Agrl. Assn., Bloomington, 1971-75; prof. secretarial sci. Ill. Cen. Coll., East Peoria, 1975—; cons. econ. edn. book Caterpillar. Mem. Nat. Bus. Edn. Assn., Assn. Records Mgrs. and Adminstrs. (chmn. scholarship com.), Ill. Bus. Edn. Assn., Ill. Vocat. Assn., Info. Processing Assn., Peoria Area Bus. Edn. Assn., Faculty Forum, Kappa Omicron Phi, Kappa Delta Pi, Delta Pi Epsilon (v.p.), Pi Omega Pi, Omicron Tau Theta, Phi Delta Kappa. Republican. Methodist. Club: Home Extension (Armington, Ill.). Home: PO Box 34 Armington IL 61721-0034 Office: Ill Cen Coll East Peoria IL 61635

EWING, MARY EILEEN, radiologic technologist; b. Morning Sun, Iowa, Aug. 26, 1926; d. Frank Leeman and Myrtle Marguerite (Mehaffy) Steele; m. Dean Willard Ewing, Mar. 29, 1952; children: John, Eileen, Diane, Denise. BS in Radiologic Tech., St. Louis U., 1948. Registered technologist. Staff technologist Mo. Pacific Hosp., St. Louis, 1948-52; staff technologist Blanchard Valley Hosp., Findlay, Ohio, 1968-69, asst. chief technologist, 1969-80, asst. dir. dept., 1980-90; clin. instr. Lima (Ohio) Tech. Coll., 1978-90; sec. N.W. Libr. Dist. Exec. Bd., 1988—. Library trustee McComb (Ohio) Pub. Libr., 1957—; pres. Libr. Bd., McComb, 1967—; elder ck. of session, 1994—. Mem. Am. Soc. Radiologic Techs., Ohio Soc. Radiologic Techs., World Orgn. China Painters, Internat. Porcelain Artists and Tchrs., Philomath Club (pres. 1958, 95), Mansfield China Painters, NSDAR (Ft. Findlay chpt. sec. 1993-94, regent 1995). Democrat. Presbyterian. Home: 103 W South St Mc Comb OH 45858

EWING, RAYMOND PEYTON, educator, author, management consultant; b. Hannibal, Mo., July 31, 1925; s. Larama Angelo and Winona Fern (Adams) E.; m. Audrey Jane Schulze, May 7, 1949; 1 child, Jane Ann. AA, Hannibal La-Grange Coll., 1948; BA, William Jewell Coll., 1949; MA in Humanities, U. Chgo., 1950. Mktg. mgmt. trainee Montgomery-Wards, Chgo., 1951-52; sr. editor Commerce Clearing House, Chgo., 1952-60; dir. corp. communications Allstate Ins. Cos. & Allstate Enterprises, Northbrook, Ill., 1960-85, dir. issues mgmt., 1979-85; pres. Issues Mgmt. Cons. Group, 1985—; assoc. prof., dir. grad. corp. pub. rels. program Medill Sch. Journalism Northwestern U., Evanston, Ill., 1986-89, prof., 1989-90; vis. prof., 1990-91; pub. rels. dir. Chicago Mag., 1966-67, book columnist, 1968-70; staff Book News Commentator, Sta. WRSV, Skokie, Ill., 1962-70. Author: Mark Twain's Steamboat Years, 1981, Managing the New Bottom Line, 1987, Handbook of Communications in Corporate Restructuring and Takeovers, 1992; contbr. articles to mags. Mem. Winnetka (Ill.) Libr. Bd., 1969-70; pres. Skokie Valley United Crusade, 1964-65; bd. dirs. Suburban Community Chest Coun., Onward Neighborhood House, Chgo.; mem. House Commerce Com., Pvt. Sector Foresight Task Force, 1982-83. Served with AUS, 1943-46, ETO. Mem. Pub. Rels. Soc. of Am. (accredited; Silver Anvil awards for pub. affairs, 1970, 72, for fin. rels. 1970, for bus. spl. events 1976, chmn. nat. pub. affairs sect. 1984), Publicity Club of Chgo. (v.p. 1967, bd. dirs. 1966-68; Golden Trumpet award for pub. affairs, 1969, 70, 72, 79, for fin. rels. 1970), Insurers Pub. Rels. Coun. (pres. 1980-81), Issues Mgmt. Assn. (founder, pres. 1981-83, chmn. 1983-84), Mensa, World Future Soc., U.S. C. of C. (trends and perspective coun.), U.S. Assn. for Club of Rome, Chgo. Poets and Writers Found. (pub. rels. dir. 1966-67), Union League (Chgo.).

EWING, THOMAS WILLIAM, congressman, lawyer; b. Atlanta, Ill., Sept. 19, 1935; m. Connie Lupo, 1981; children: Jane, Kathryn, Sam, Christine Lupo, John Lupo, Stephanie Lupo. BS, Millikin U., 1957; JD, John Marshall Law Sch., Chgo., 1968. Asst. state atty. Livingston County, 1968-73; ptnr. Satter Ewing Beyer & Spires, Pontiac, Ill., 1969-91; mem. Ill. Ho. of Reps., 1974-91, 102nd, 103rd and 104th Congresses from 15th Ill. Dist., 1991—; mem. agr. com. Ill. Ho. Reps., chmn. subcom. on risk mgmt. and specialty crops, subcom. on dept. ops., nutrition and fgn. agr., transp. and infrastructure com., aviation subcom., water resources and environment subcom., joint econ. com., former dep. minority leader, chmn. policy com., house revenue com., 1980, co-chmn. Ill. Econ. and Fiscal Commn., co-chmn. Legis. Space Needs Commn. Rep. precinct committeeman; del. Rep. Nat. Conv., 1980, 84, 88; committeeman 15th Congl. Dist., 1986-93. With U.S. Army, 1958, USAR, 1957-63. Recipient Best Legislator award Nat. Rep. Legislator of the Yr. award, 1982, Ill. Small Businessmen Assn., 1983, 85, 87, Friend of Agr. award Ill. Agrl. Assn., 1985, 87, 89, 91, Legislator of Yr. award Ill. Assn. Homes for the Aging, 1986. Mem. Livingston County Bar Assn., Pontiac C. of C. (past exec. dir., past pres.), Livingston County Farm Bur., Elks, Moose, Masons. Methodist. Home: 310 W Lincoln St Pontiac IL 61764 Office: US Ho of Reps 1317 Longworth HOB Washington DC 20515-1315*

EWING-WILSON, DEBORAH LOUISE, neurologist; b. Seattle, Aug. 6, 1955; d. Edwin Stanley Ewing and Mary Alice Castleman; m. Fredrick Paul Wilson, Sept. 25, 1982; children: Victoria, Katherine. BA, Wellesley Coll., 1978; DO, Chgo. Coll. Osteo. Medicine, 1983. Diplomate Am. Bd. Psychiatry and Neurology, Am. Bd. Electrodiagnostic Medicine; added qualifications in clin. neurophysiology. Intern Brentwood Hosp., Cleve., 1983-84; resident Cleve. Clinic Found., 1984-87; staff section neurology Ohio Permanent Med. Group, Cleve., 1987—, chief neurology, 1992—; staff Cleve. Clinic found., 1992—, Metrohealth St. Luke's Med. Ctr., Cleve., 1992-94; clin. prof. neurology Ohio U., Athens, 1989—. Contbr. articles to profl. jours. Fellow Am. Assn. Electrodiagnostic Medicine; mem. AMA, Am. Acad. Neurology, Am. Osteo. Assn., Ohio Osteo. Assn., Cleve. Acad. Medicine, Epilepsy Found. N.E. Ohio, Cleve. (mem. profl. adv. bd. 1991—). Episcopalian. Office: Ohio Permanente Med Group 3733 Park East Dr Cleveland OH 44122-4311

EXE, DAVID ALLEN, electrical engineer; b. Brookings, S.D., Jan. 29, 1942; s. Oscar Melvin and Irene Marie (Mattis) E.; m. Lynn Rae Roberts; children: Doreen Lea, Raena Lynn. BSEE, S.D. State U., 1968; MBA, U. S.D., 1980; postgrad. Iowa State U., 1969-70, U. Idaho, 1978-80. Registered profl. engr., Idaho, Oreg., Minn., S.D., Wash., Wyo., Utah, N.Y., Ind., Wis. Applications engr. Collins Radio, Cedar Rapids, Iowa, 1969-70; dist. engr. Bonneville Power Adminstrn., Idaho Falls, Idaho, 1970-77; instr. math U. S.D., Vermillion, 1977-78; CEO EXE Engring., Idaho Falls, Idaho, 1978-83, Bloomington, Minn., 1985—; safety mgr. CPT Corp., Eden Prairie, Minn., 1983-85; owner, chief exec. officer Exe Inc., Eden Prairie, 1983—; chmn. bd. Applied Techs. Idaho, Idaho Falls, 1979—; chmn., CEO Azimuth Cons., Idaho Falls, 1979-81; v.p. D & B Constrn. Co., Idaho Falls, 1980-83; bd. dirs., v.p., COO Nat. Multi-Housing Corp., 1989. Technical advisor Nat. Earth Day, 1991; apptd. Minn. State Bd. Profl. Engrs., 1991. With USN, 1960-64. Mem. IEEE, Am. Cons. Engrs., Nat. Soc. Profl. Engrs., Nat. Contrcts Mgrs. Assn., IEEE Computer Soc., Mensa, Am. Legion, VFW, Masons, Elks. Office: Exe Engring Inc 10740 Lyndale Ave S Minneapolis MN 55420-5615

EXON, J(OHN) JAMES, senator; b. Lake Andes, S.D., Aug. 9, 1921; s. John James and Luella (Johns) E.; m. Patricia Ann Pros, Sept. 18, 1943; children: Stephen, Pamela, Candace. Student, U. Omaha, 1939-41; LLD (hon.), Creighton U., 1991. Mgr. Universal Finance Corp., Nebr., 1946-53; pres. Exon's, Inc., Lincoln, Nebr., 1954-71; gov. State of Nebr., 1971-79; mem. U.S. Senate, Nebr., 1979-96; mem. Armed Svcs. Com., ranking Min. mem. of budget com., ranking Min. mem. commerce, sci. and transp. subcom. of consumer affairs, fgn. commerce and tourism. Active state, local, nat. Democratic coms., 1952—; del. Dem. Nat. Conv., 1964, 72, 74, 76, 88, 92; former Dem. nat. committeeman. Served with Signal Corps AUS, 1942-45. Mem. Am. Legion, VFW, Masons (33rd degree), Shriners, Elks, Eagles, Optimist Internat. Office: US Senate 528 Hart Senate Bldg Washington DC 20510

EYBEL, CARL EUGENE, cardiologist; b. Pana, Ill., Jan. 22, 1943; s. Carl Edward and Martha Elizabeth (Simpson) E.; m. Barbara Lee McDonald, Sept. 5, 1964; children: Angie Elizabeth, Max Andrew. BS, U. Ill., 1965; MS, U. Ill., Chgo., 1969, MD, 1969. Diplomate Am. Bd. Internal Medicine, Am. Bd. Internal Medicine subspecialty bd. in Cardiovascular Disease, Nat. Bd. Med. Examiners. Intern and resident in internal medicine Rush-Presbyn.-St. Luke's Med. Ctr., Chgo., 1969-72, fellow in cardiology, 1972-74; pvt. practice specializing in cardiovascular disease Chgo., 1974—; adj. attending Presbyn.-St. Luke's Hosp., 1972-74, asst. attending, 1976-81, assoc. attending, 1981-86, sr. attending, 1986—; instr. U. Ill. Coll. Medicine, 1969-72; asst. Rush Med. Coll., 1970-72, instr., 1972-76, asst. prof., 1976—. Contbr. articles to profl. jours. Maj. USAF, 1974-76. Decorated Air Force Commendation Medal. Fellow ACP, Am. Coll. Cardiology, Coun. on Clin. Cardiology of Am. Heart Assn., Soc. for Cardiac Angiography and Interventions; mem. AMA, Ill. Med. Soc., Chgo. Med. Soc., Chgo. Heart Assn., Am. Chem. Soc., Am. Oil Chemists Soc., Alpha Kappa Kappa. Home: 1711 Midwest Club Pky Oak Brook IL 60521-2588 Office: 1725 W Harrison St Ste 1138 Chicago IL 60612-3828

EYBERG, DONALD THEODORE, JR., architect; b. Mpls., July 8, 1944; s. Donald Theodore and Helen Irene (Young) E.; m. Sally Jo Birch, Dec. 30, 1967; children: Jon, Erin. Student, Mankato State U., 1962-64; BArch, U. Minn., 1968. Registered architect, Minn., Fla., Tex. Planner Midwest Planning and Rsch., Mpls., 1966-67; designer Matson-Wegleitner, Mpls., 1967-68; architect Ellerbe Assocs., Mpls., 1968-76, exec. architect, 1977-82, v.p., 1983—. Prin. works include Providence Civic Ctr., 1971, Dahlgren Hall U.S. Naval Acad., Annapolis, Md., 1973 (numerous awards), Rupp Arena/Hyatt Regency Hotel, Lexington, Ky., 1975 (numerous awards), Huntington (W.Va.) Civic Ctr., 1977, Charleston (W.Va.) Civic Ctr., 1980 (Merit award Athletic Bus. 1981), Hartford (Conn.) Coliseum, 1981 (numerous awards), Mpls. Coll. Art and Design, 1982, Children's Theater Co., Mpls., 1983, Mpls. Inst. Arts, 1984, Ocean Ctr., Daytona Beach, Fla., 1985, Manatee Ctr., Bradenton, Fla., 1985, Thirteen Hundred Biscayne Bldg. Study, Miami, 1985 (Minn. Paper Architect award AIA), Santa Clara (Calif.) Conv. Ctr., 1986, expansion, 1995, Mayo Civic Ctr., Rochester, Minn., 1986, Santa Clara Golf and Tennis Ctr., 1986 (Merit award Athletic Bus. 1988), Nat. Hockey Ctr., St. Cloud, Minn., Lawrence Joel Vet. Meml. Coliseum, Winston-Salem, N.C. (Merit award Athletic Bd. 1991), Hubert H. Humphrey Metrodome Expansion, Mpls., Austin (Tex.) Conv. Ctr., Reino Aventura Arena, Mexico City, Minn. Twins Baseball Club Office Expansion, Mpls., Summit Arena Expansion, Houston, 1993, Santa Clara (Calif.) Conv. Ctr. Expansion, Commonwealth Conv. Ctr. Expansion, Louisville, Miami Arena Expansion, Von Braun Conv. Ctr. Expansion, Aquatics Ctr. and Gymnasium U. Chgo., Payne Whitney Gym Planning Study and Renovation/Expansion, Yale U., Univ. Hall rebuild U. Va., Charlottesville, Springfield (Mass.) Civic Ctr. expansion and plaza, Walter A. Haas Jr. Pavilion, U. Calif., Berkeley, track/football stadium Claremont (Calif.) Coll., Target Ctr. Upgrades, Mpls. Track/Football stadium, fieldhouse St. Johns U., Collegeville Mn. Mem. AIA, Urban Land Inst., Minn. Soc. Architects (Merit award 1977), Nat. Coun. Archtl. Registration Bd., Mpls. Soc. Fine Arts., Nat. Fire Protection Assn. Home: 6600 Dakota Trl Minneapolis MN 55439-1119 Office: Ellerbe Becket 800 Lasalle Ave Minneapolis MN 55402-2006

EYRICH, ROBERT PAUL, real estate appraiser; b. Joliet, Ill., Feb. 2, 1938; s. Alfred N. Eyrich and Lenetta M. Zatteau; m. Carol A. Tutt, May 1962; children: Sue, Robert. BS, No. Ill. U., 1961. Lic. real estate appraiser, Ill. With dept. personnel and pub. rels. adminstrn. Joliet (Ill.) Fed. Bank, 1964-71; v.p. mortgage loan dept. 1st Savs. and Loan, Wilmington, Ill., 1971-78; owner Walsh Locker, Manhattan, Ill., 1978-88, Ind. Fee Appraiser, Manhattan, 1978—; appraiser Will County Supr. of Assess, Joliet, 1988-94. Clk. Manhattan Twp.; mem. bd. edn. Lincoln Way H.S. With USN, 1961-64. Mem. Internat. Assn. Assessing Officers, nat. Assn. if Ind. Fee Appraisers, Sports Car Club Am. (driver, steward 1975—), Lions Club. Home: 16252 S Creek Dr Manhattan IL 60442-9341

FABER, CURTIS W., banker; b. Mendota, Ill., Aug. 14, 1950; s. Warren P. and Velma M. (Wolf) F.; m. Julie Faber, May 30, 1981; children: Ann, Doug. BS, Ill. State U., 1977; postgrad., U. Wis., 1990. Vice pres. credit Prodn. Credit Assn., Bloomington, Ill., 1977-85; pres., CEO Farmers State Bank of Buffalo, Ill., 1986; exec. v.p. Logan County Bank, Lincoln, Ill., 1986-92; v.p., dir. Sublette (Ill.) Bank, 1992—. Mem. Elks (chaplin 1995—), Lions (v.p. 1995—), Moose. Republican. Methodist. Office: Sublette Bank PO Box 20 Sublette IL 61367

FABIAN, HEATHER LYNN, journalist; b. Titusville, Fla., May 28, 1969; d. Brian Paul and Dona Ceil (Becker) Dick. BA, Mich. State U., 1991. Edn. reporter The Doings Newspapers, Hinsdale, Ill., 1991-92; gen. assignment reporter Star Publs., Chicago Heights, Ill., 1992-93; account exec. S & S Pub. Rels., Northbrook, Ill., 1993-94; pub. affairs mgr. Ibbotson Assocs., Chgo., 1994—. Mem. Pub. Rels. Soc. Am., Women in Comms., Inc., Chgo. Women in Publishing. Home: 2741 Lake Dr Flossmoor IL 60422-2112

FABRIKANT, ILYA IOSIFOVICH, physics educator; b. Riga, Latvia, USSR, Feb. 15, 1949; came to U.S., 1988; s. Joseph and Sara (Khaikina) F.; m. Marina Sorkina, Oct. 30, 1981; children: Benjamin, Maya, Eva. MS, Latvian U., 1971; PhD, Inst. Physics, Riga, 1974. Jr. rsch. fellow Inst. Physics Latvian Acad. Scis., Riga, 1974-84, sr. rsch. fellow Inst. Physics, 1984-88; assoc. prof. physics U. Nebr., Lincoln, 1989-95, prof., 1995—; vis. scholar U. Chgo., 1988-89; vis. scientist Harvard U.-Smithsonian Ctr., Cambridge, Mass., 1989. Contbr. articles to Phys. Rev., Physics Reports, Jour. Physics B. NSF grantee, 1990—. Fellow Am. Phys. Soc. Office: U Nebr Dept Physics and Astronomy Lincoln NE 68588-0111

FADELY, JAMES PHILIP, admissions director, educator, writer; b. New Castle, Ind., Jan. 10, 1953; s. Harry Ellison and Viola May (Clapp) F.; m. Sally Jane Fehsenfeld, Aug. 16, 1975; 1 child, James Philip Jr. BA, Hanover Coll., 1975; MA, Ind. U., 1977, PhD, 1990. Tchr. Brookstone Sch., Columbus, Ga., 1975-76; tchr., adminstrv. asst. Savannah (Ga.) Country Day Sch., 1979-83; lectr. Ind. U., Indpls., 1984—; tchr., asst. headmaster St. Richard's Sch., Indpls., 1988-90, tchr., 1990-91, dir. admissions, tchr., 1991—; bd. dirs. Marion County-Indpls. Hist. Soc., English-Speaking Union Indpls. Br. Dem. nominee 6th Dist. of Ind. for Congress, 1990. Mem. Am. Hist. Assn., Ind. Assn. Hists., Ind. Hist. Soc. (grant 1991-94), Indpls. Lit. Club, Soc. Ind. Pioneers, Hanover Coll. Alumni Assn. (bd. dirs. 1985-88), Hanover Club Indpls. (bd. dirs. 1988—), Phi Delta Theta. Democrat. Roman Catholic. Home: 9146 Kenwood Dr Indianapolis IN 46260-1400 Office: St Richards Sch 3243 N Meridian St Indianapolis IN 46208-4645

FAETH, GERARD MICHAEL, aerospace engineering educator, researcher; b. N.Y.C., July 5, 1936; s. Joseph and Helen (Wagner) F.; m. Mary Ann Kordich, Dec. 27, 1959; children: Christine Louise, Lorraine Vera, Elinor Jean. BME, Union Coll., 1958; MS, Pa. State U., 1961, PhD, 1964. Instr. mech. engring. Pa. State U., University Park, 1958-59, research asst., 1959-64, asst. prof., 1964-68, assoc. prof., 1968-74, prof., 1974-85, prof. emeritus, 1985—; Modine prof., head gas dynamics labs. U. Mich., Ann Arbor, 1985—; vis. prof. Air Force Office Sci. Rsch., Washington, 1983-84; cons. GM, Warren, Mich., 1977—, Applied Rsch. Lab., Pa. State U., 1964-85; prof.-in-residence GM Inst., Detroit, 1983. Mem. editorial bd. Combustion Sci. and Tech., 1979—, Ann. Rev. Numerical Fluid Mechanics and Heat Transfer, 1985—, Atomization and Sprays, 1989—, Progress in Energy and Combustion Sci., 1991—; contbr. numerous articles to profl. jours. Rep. Precinct Chmn. Centre County, Pa., 1977-84; bd. dirs. Eagles Mere (Pa.) Assn., 1982-88, Eagles Mere Park Assn., 1978-85. Recipient Oustanding Engr. Alumnus Awd., 1990, PA State Univ. Alumni Assn. Fellow ASME (tech. editor 1981-84, sr. tech. editor 1985-90, Meml. award heat transfer divsn. 1988), AIAA (Propellants and Combustion award 1993), AAAS; mem. NAE, Combustion Inst. (dep. editor 1984-90, tech. editor 1990—, bd. dirs. 1988—), Am. Phys. Soc., Sigma Xi, Pi Tau Sigma, Phi Kappa Phi. Episcopalian. Home: 2665 Overridge Dr Ann Arbor MI 48104-4039 Office: U Mich 3000 FXB Bldg Ann Arbor MI 48109-2118

FAHEY, DAVID MICHAEL, history educator; b. Ossining, N.Y., May 18, 1937; s. Frederick John and Ester Marie (Drach) F.; m. Mary Julia Fuller, Feb. 6, 1988; 1 child, Juliana. BA, Siena Coll., 1959; MA, U. Notre Dame, 1961, PhD, 1964. From instr. to asst. prof. history Assumption Coll., Worcester, Mass., 1963-66; asst. prof. history Ind. U. NW, Gary, 1966-69; assoc. prof. history Miami U., Oxford, Ohio, 1969-81, prof. history, 1981—. Co-author: The English Heritage, 1978; author: Temperance and Racism: John Bull, Johnny Reb, and the Good Templars, 1996; editor: The Black Lodge in White America: "True Reformer" Browne and His Economic Strategy, 1994; editor: Alcohol in History (now Social History Alcohol Rev.), 1983-85, The Collected Writings of Jessie Forsyth, 1847-1937, 1988; contbr. articles to profl. jours. Mem. Alcohol and Temperance History Group (pres. 1986-88), Ohio Acad. History (exec. coun. 1989-91), Ohio Valley World History Assn. (exec. coun. 1992-95). Office: History Dept Miami U Oxford OH 45056

FAHIEN, ROSE MARIAN, small business owner; b. Union, Mo., June 28, 1933; d. William Henry and Ella Caroline (Kissling) Burmeister; m. Leonard August Fahien, June 21, 1958; children; Catherine Fahien Reuter, Lisa Fahien Uldrich, James Robert. BA, Washington U., 1955; student, U. Wis., 1956-57, Madison (Wis.) Tech. Coll., 1972. Cert. secondary tchr., Mo., Wis. Tchr. English Mehlville Jr. H.S., Lemay, Mo., 1955-57, Kirkwood (Mo.) H.S., 1957-60, 61-62, Ctrl. H.S., Madison, Wis., 1960-61; tchr., buyer Ch. Day Nurseries, Madison, Wis., 1971-75; Panhellenic advisor U. Wis., Madison, 1984-91; founder, owner Bog Lake Outfitters, La Pointe, Wis., 1989—; co-owner Trippers Too, Ltd., Madison, 1985—; customer sales rep. Lands' End, Cross Plains, Wis., 1990—. Author: Research Paper Manual for High School Students, 1959; editor newsletter U. League, 1978; contbr. articles to profl. jours. Pres. Shorewood Hills PTA, Madison, Bethel Luth. Ch. Women (pres., sec.), Shorehawk Sqaure Dancers, 1983; chairperson Van Hise-Shorewood Neighborhood Girl Scouts, 1977; bus. mgr. Midwest Assn. for Edn. Young Children. Mem. Attic Angel Assn. (expansion chair 1989-90, fin. com. 1993-95), PEO Sisterhood (pres. 1985), Civics Club, Univ. League (pres. 1981), Shorewood Garden Club (pres.). Lutheran. Home: 3212 Topping Rd Madison WI 53705

FAHRNBRUCH, DALE E., state supreme court justice; b. Lincoln, Nebr., Sept. 13, 1924; s. Henry and Bessie M. (Osborne) F.; m. Margaret L. Hunt, July 4, 1952; children: Rebecca Kay Fahrnbruch Braymen, Daniel D. (dec.). AD in Journalism, U. Nebr., 1948, BS in Law, 1950; JD, Creighton U., 1951; LLM, U. Va., 1986. Bar: Nebr. 1951, U.S. Ct. Appeals (8th cir.) 1969. City editor Jour. Newspapaer, Lincoln, 1951-52; asst., then dep. county atty. Lancaster County, Lincoln, Nebr., 1952-55; chief dep. county atty. Lancaster County, Lincoln, 1955-59; ptnr. Beynon, Hecht & Fahrnbruch, Lincoln, 1959-73; dist. judge Nebr. Lincoln, 1973-87; justice Nebr. Supreme Ct., Lincoln, 1987—. Office: Nebr Supreme Ct 2207 State Capitol Bldg Lincoln NE 68509

FAIBISCH, LOREN, psychologist; b. New London, Conn., Apr. 21, 1963; 1 child, Heather. BA, Columbia U., 1986; EdM, Harvard U., 1989, EdD, 1995. Counselor Boston English H.S., 1986-88; psychology clinician Dept. Social Svcs., Boston, 1989-90; psychology trainee Dimock Comm. Health Ctr., Roxbury, Mass., 1990-91; intern Boston City Hosp., 1989-91; tchg. fellow Harvard Grad. Sch., Cambridge, Mass., 1991-92; cons. U. Mass., Boston, 1993; fellow in disability study U. Minn., Mpls., 1995—; appointee to dean's com., Harvard Grad. Sch., Cambridge, Mass., 1991-92; counselor Women's Counseling Project, n.Y.C., 1985-86; adminstr./cons. Svcs. for Physically Disabled, Somerville, Mass., 1980—. Author: Harvard Alumni Bulletin, 1994, Inclusion in Education, 1994. Recipient grant for grad. women, Radcliffe, 1994, dissertation rsch. award Harvard Grad. Sch., 1994, APA dissertation rsch. award, 1993, Twitty-Milsap Sterban award, 1992. Mem. Soc. Disabilities Studies, APA, Soc. for Study of Psychol. Social Issues. Home: Apt #5-211 13055 Dahlia Cir Eden Prairie MN 55344

FAIER, JAMES MICHAEL, lawyer; b. Chgo., Jan. 2, 1960; s. Martin and Kathleen (Gindich) F. BA, Pomona Coll., Claremont, Calif., 1983; M. Pub. Policy, Harvard U., 1986; M.Mgmt., Northwestern U., Chgo., 1990, JD, 1990. Bar: Ill. 1990. Assoc. Boston Fin. Cons. Group, 1985-86, Mayer Brown & Platt, N.Y.C., 1989; ptnr. Faier & Faier, Chgo., 1990—. Bd. dirs. KAM/Isaiah Israel Congregation, Chgo., 1992—. Mem. ABA, Internat. Trademark Assn., Ill. Bar Assn., Chgo. Bar Assn., Choate Alumni Assn., Thistle Class Assn., Pomona Coll. Alumni Assn. (chmn. Chgo. chpt. 1990-93). Jewish. Office: Faier & Faier 566 W Adams St Chicago IL 60661

FAIFERLICK, JUSTIN MICHAEL, computer services company owner; b. Fort Dodge, Iowa, Jan. 26, 1969; s. Mark Matthew Faiferlick Sr. and Bonnie Lynn (Sime) Hefty; m. Deann Annette Maschino, June 6, 1992; 1 child, Kelsey Grace. AA in Airway Sci., C.C. of the Air Force, Maxell AFB, Ala., 1992; BS in Mgmt. and Computer Sci., Buena Vista Coll., 1995. Instr. Hemann Martial Arts and Fitness, Fort Dodge, 1984—; surveillance technician Air Nat. Guard, Fort Dodge, 1987—; supr. Fort Dodge (Iowa) Labs., 1990—; owner JDK Computer Svcs., Fort Dodge, 1993—. Mem. C. of C. (com. mem. small bus. devel. 1993—). Home: 710 S 19th St Fort Dodge IA 50501

FAILINGER, MARIE ANITA, law educator, editor; b. Battle Creek, Mich., June 29, 1952; d. Conard Frederick and Joan Anita (Lang) F.; children: Joanna, Kristina. BA, Valparaiso U., 1973, JD, 1976; LLM, Yale U., 1983; postgrad., U. Chgo., 1990. Bar: Ind. 1976, U.S. Dist. Ct. (no. dist.) Ind. 1976, U.S. Dist. Ct. (so. dist.) Ind. 1977, U.S. Ct. Appeals (7th cir.) 1979, Minn. 1984, U.S. Supreme Ct. 1980. Prof. of law Hamline U., St. Paul, 1983—, assoc. dean, 1990-93. Editor: Jour. of Law and Religion, 1988—; contbr. articles, book revs. to profl. publs. Bd. dirs. Crossroads Adoption Svc., Mpls., 1986—; treas. Am. Indian Rsch. and Policy Inst., 1993—; vice chair Church Innovations Inst. Mem. Minn. Women Lawyers (bd. dirs. 1989-90), Am. Assn. Law Schs. (chair poverty sect. 1984-88, exec. com. law and religion sect.), Ctrl. Minn. Legal Svcs. Bd., Nat. Equal Justice Libr. (bd. dirs. 1989—). Democrat. Mem. Evang. Luth. Ch. Am. Office: Hamline U Sch Law 1536 Hewitt Ave Saint Paul MN 55104-1205

FAIN, MIKE, judge; b. Miami, Fla., July 15, 1946; s. James Edward and Laura Bennett (Turner) F.; m. Valita R. Randolph, Dec. 22, 1994; children: Paul Augustus, James Marshall. BS in Polit. Sci., Yale U., 1968; JD, U. Pa., 1972. Bar: Ohio 1973, U.S. Dist. Ct. (so. dist.) Ohio 1973, U.S. Ct. Appeals (6th cir.) 1980. Assoc. Estabrook, Finn & McKee, Dayton, Ohio, 1973-77; ptnr. Bogin & Patterson, Dayton, 1977-87; judge Ohio Ct. Appeals (2d dist.), Dayton, 1987—; bd. commrs. character and fitness Ohio Supreme Ct., 1979-85; adj. prof. U. Dayton Law Sch., 1988-91. Chmn. various coms. Dayton United Way, 1983-85; gen. counsel Montgomery County Democratic Com., Ohio, 1982-86; chmn. criminal law & procedure com. Ohio Jud. Conf., 1991-94; mem. rules adv. com. Ohio Supreme Ct. , 1992—, chmn. appellate rules subcom., 1995—. With USNR, 1969-71. Recipient cert. of merit Epilepsy Found. Am., 1979, Am. Jurisprudence awards. Mem. Dayton Bar Assn., Ohio State Bar Assn., ABA (bench and bar rels. com. 1987—), Leadership Dayton Alumni Assn. (chmn. 1982). Methodist. Avocation: computer and non-computer simulations. Home: 1401 Yankee Vineyards Dayton OH 45458-3119 Office: Ohio Ct Appeals (2d dist) 41 N Perry St Dayton OH 45402-1431

FAINTER, LYNDA JEAN, organization executive; b. Galesburg, Ill., June 24, 1947; d. Bernard Joseph and Evelyn Margaret (Cheek) Wahl; m. July 1, 1967 (div. Sept. 1983); 1 child, Jeffrey Lee. AAS in Exec. Secretarial Sci., Carl Sandburg Coll., Galesburg, Ill., 1984. Typist Galesburg Register-Mail, 1966-67, Gates Rubber Co., Galesburg, 1969-71; program dir., sec. Sta. WHBF-TV, Rock Island (Ill.) Broadcasting Co., 1968-69; sec. to v.p. and pres. Huskee Bilt Constrn. Co., Monmouth, Ill., 1971-74; counselor, placement sec. Carl Sanburg Coll., 1978—; exec. dir. Quad City League Native Ams., Rock Island, 1990—; participant stage audience TV program Racism in Iowa, Iowa Pub. TV, 1993, 4-Font, Sta. WHBF-TV, Rock Island, 1992; mem. site coun. Job Tng. Partnership Act Native Am. Enhancement Program, Rock Island; mem. site coun. U.S. Dept. Labor Job Tng. Partnership Act program Native Am. Ednl. Svcs. Coll., Chgo., 1995—; spkr., presenter in field. Mem. Nat. Orgn. for Victim Assistance, Washington, 1990-92; dep. registrar Knox County Bd. Commrs., Galesburg, 1991-92; mem. Iowa Gov.'s Indian Leadership Adv. Coun., Des Moines, 1992—; founding mem. Am. Indian Coun. Ill., 1994—. Recipient award for presentation Western Ill. U., Ill. Bd. Edn. and Ill. Bd. Govs., 1991. Mem. NEA, Ill. Edn. Assn., Ill. Women in Govt., Internat. Platform Assn. Home: PO Box 275 Galesburg IL 61401 Office: Quad City League Native Ams 418 19th St Rock Island IL 61201-8123

FAIR, HUDSON RANDOLPH, recording company executive; b. Evanston, Ill., Aug. 15, 1953; s. Harry Joel Jr. and Virginia (Gauntlett F. BS in Speech, Northwestern U., 1976, MA in Speech, 1979. Mktg. rep. Calumet Refining Co., Chgo., 1975-78, Calumet Petro-Chems., Inc., Houston, 1977-78, Stellavox, S.A., Schaumburg, Ill., 1986-87, Nagra Magnetic Recorders, Inc., N.Y.C., 1987-91; pres. Ealing Mobile Recording, Ltd., Chgo., 1981—; cons. in field. prodr. over 90 classical albums, 1981—. Speech writer Rep. George Bush Presdl. Campaign, Chgo., 1979-80. Grantee Ill. Arts Coun., 1982-86, Nat. Endowment for Arts, 1986; recipient Chorus award Best Choral Recording, 1989. Mem. NARAS (bd. govs. 1991-95, 96—, nat. trustee 1991-95), Audio Engring. Soc., Engring. and Rec. Soc. (bd. dirs. 1987—, chmn. 1991-92). Republican. Episcopalian. Office: Ealing Mobile Rec Ltd 4906 N Talman Ave Chicago IL 60625-2722

FAIRCHILD, HENRY BRANT, III, manufacturing executive; b. Grand Rapids, Mich., May 15, 1945; s. Henry Brant and Leora Mary (Barnaby) F.; m. Marcia Jean Anderson, Jan. 9, 1979; children: Steven May, Timothy May. Student, Miami U., 1963-66; BS, Grand Valley State Coll., 1977. Mgr. Jack Loeks Theatres, Inc., Wyoming, Mich., 1970-77, Commonwealth Theatres, Kansas City, 1977-78; pres. Handy Wacks Corp., Sparta, Mich., 1978—. Mem. Kent County Rep. Com., Grand Rapids 1980-88. Mem. Mfrs. Reps. Am. (mem. adv. council 1985-87), Grand Rapids Econ. Club (dir.), Blytherfield Country Club. Office: Handy Wacks Corp 100 E Averill St Sparta MI 49345-1516

FAIRCHILD, JOHANNE WINDLE, biology and horticulture educator; b. Columbus, Kans., Apr. 22, 1940; d. John Curtiss and Maxine (McNeil) Windle; m. Francis Patrick Wynne, Sept. 4, 1965 (div. Feb. 4, 1986; children: Stephanie Michele, Francis Patrick, Rebecca Windle; m. Mahlon Lowell, Jan. 3, 1995. BS, U. Tulsa, 1962; MS, U. Mo., Kansas City, 1966; PhD in Entomolgoy, U. Mo., 1989. Rsch. technician U. Kans. Med. Ctr., Kansas City, 1964-65; grad. teaching asst. U. Mo., Kansas City, 1965-66; grad. teaching asst. U. Mo., Columbia, 1966-67, rsch. asst., 1966-67, 1970; instr. biology N.W. Mo. State U., Maryville, 1975, assoc. prof., 1978—; tchr. chemistry Maryville R-II H.S., 1976-77; cons. Soil Conservation Svc., Macon, Mo., 1992-94. Author: Tree Walk, 1995; contbr. articles to profl. jours. Choir 1st Unied Meth. Ch., Maryville, 1975—; mem. Maryville Tree Bd., 1990—. Recipient Teaching Award of Merit, Nat. Assn. Colls. and Tchrs. Agr., 1994. Mem. AAUW, Mo. Acad. Sci., Entomol. Soc. Am., Ctrl. States Entomol. Soc., Cosmopolitan Internat., Mortar Bd. Methodist. Home: 504 Highland Ave Maryville MO 64468 Office: NW Mo State U 800 University Dr Maryville MO 64468

FAIRCHILD, THOMAS E., federal judge; b. Milw., Dec. 25, 1912; s. Edward Thomas and Helen (Edwards) F.; m. Eleanor E. Dahl, July 24, 1937; children: Edward, Susan, Jennifer, Andrew. Student, Princeton, 1931-33; A.B., Cornell U., 1934; LL.B., U. Wis., 1938. Bar: Wis. 1938. Practiced Portage, Wis., 1938-41, Milw., 1945-48, 53-56; atty. OPA, Chgo., Milw., 1941-45; hearing commr. Chgo. Region, 1945; atty. gen. Wis., 1948-51; U.S. atty. for Western Dist. Wis., 1951-52; justice Supreme Ct. Wis., 1957-66, U.S. Ct. Appeals for 7th Circuit, 1966—. Dem. candidate Senator from Wis., 1950, 52. Mem. ABA, Wis. Bar Assn., Fed. Bar Assn., Milw. Bar Assn., 7th Cir. Bar Assn., Dane County Bar Assn., Am. Judicature Soc., Am. Law Inst., Phi Delta Phi, KP. Democrat. Mem. United Ch. of Christ. Office: US Courthouse Rm 2764 219 S Dearborn St Chicago IL 60604-1875

FAIRLEIGH, KENNETH FISHER, JR., electrical manufacturing company executive; b. Cleve., Dec. 4, 1955; s. Kenneth Fisher and Louise (Robertson) F.; m. LeAnn Isenberg, Mar. 22, 1986; children: Kenneth Fisher III, Philip Ryan. BS in Econs., Duke U., 1978; MBA, U. Dallas, 1986. Various sales positions GE, Cleve., 1980-88; region sales mgr. GE, Dallas, 1988-90; gen. mgr. consumer products divsn. Square D Co., Chgo., 1990-91; v.p. distbn. mktg. and sales Groupe Schneider, Chgo., 1991-92, v.p. channel mgmt., 1992-94, v.p. integrated customer svc., 1994, v.p. constrn./utility bus., 1995—. Home: 25649 Canyon Creek Ct Barrington IL 60010-1323 Office: Groupe Schneider-Square D 1415 S Roselle Rd Palatine IL 60067-7337

FAKES, MARY E. A., nurse; b. Sioux Falls, S.D., Sept. 4, 1962; d. Leslie L. and Kathryn A. (Nason) Lemme; m. James E. Fakes, Apr. 21, 1990; children: Katlyn Elizabeth, Moriah Eleanor. RN, Deaconess Sch. Nursing, 1983; BSN, Deaconess Coll., 1987. RN, Mo.; CEN; cert. trauma nurse specialist, BCLS instr., TNCC provider, ACLS affil. faculty, PALS, ENPC; cert. funeral dir., Mo. Charge nurse emergency dept. Alexian Bros. Hosp., St. Louis, 1983-87, St. Louis U. Hosp., 1986-89; occupational health nurse HealthLine, St. Louis, 1989-90; coord. emergency nursing programs, mem. continuing edn. faculty St. Louis C.C., 1990—; staff nurse practitioner emergency unit St. Louis Children's Hosp., 1991—; mem. faculty Jefferson Coll., Hillsboro, Mo., 1992—; mem. case rev. staff Midwest Med./Legal Svcs., Kirkwood, Mo., 1992—; funeral dir. Lemme Funeral Home, Festus, Mo., 1984-95. Bd. dirs. Greater St. Louis Soc. for Healthcare Edn. and Tng., 1992-93. Named Citizen of the Month, City of St. Louis, 1988; recipient cert. of recognition Mo. Nurse's Assn. 3d Dist., 1988, Gold medal Hosp. Assn. Met., 1988, S.I.S.H.E.T. award for audio visual presentation Pediatric Vascular Access, 1991. Mem. Emergency Nurses Assn., Greater St. Louis Soc. for Health Edn. and Tng. (bd. dirs. 1992—, pres. 1996). Home: 9 Cedarbrook Festus MO 63028-3730

FALBO, JEFFREY F., electrical engineer; b. Milw., Dec. 18, 1965. BSEE, Milw. Sch. Engring., 1988. Electronic design engr. Dukar Ltd., Milw., 1988—. Home: 8623 N 62nd St Milwaukee WI 53223-2808

FALCONE, CHARLES ANTHONY, electric utility executive; b. Flushing, N.Y., Mar. 21, 1942; s. Anthony J. and Mabel (Seymour) F.; m. Nola Elizabeth Maddox, Dec. 6, 1968; 1 child, Charles M. BS, Lehigh U., 1963; M. Elec. Engring., Rensselaer Poly. Inst., 1964, D. Engring., 1973. Engr. Am. Electric Power Svc. Corp., N.Y.C., 1964-70, sr. engr., 1970-73, staff engr., dir. load rsch., 1973-75; sr. energy economist Stanford Rsch. Inst., Menlo Park, Calif., 1975-76; dir. power supply and reliability U.S. Dept. Energy, Washington, 1976-79; exec. asst. Am. Electric Power Svc. Corp., N.Y.C., 1979-80; v.p. info. systems Am. Electric Power Svc. Corp., Columbus, Ohio, 1980-86, v.p. system transactions, 1986-94, sr. v.p. system power markets, 1994—. Contbr. articles and papers to profl. jours. Moderator First Bapt. Ch., White Plains, N.Y., 1985-93. Mem. IEEE (sr. mem.), Sigma Xi, Tau Beta Pi, Eta Kappa Nu, Pi Mu Epsilon. Home: 70 Drake Rd Scarsdale NY 10583-6447 Office: Am Electric Power Svc Corp 1 Riverside Plz Columbus OH 43215-2355

FALCONER, JUDITH ANN, occupational therapist, educator; b. Berwyn, Ill., July 2, 1952; d. Robert John and Marian Ann (Cavalier) F.; m. E. John Saliba, Feb. 15, 1992. BS in Occupl. Therapy, U. Ill., Chgo., 1975, MPH, 1981, PhD in Pub. Health, 1984. Occupl. therapist Mass. Rehab. Hosp., Boston, 1975-77, Valens (Switzerland) Clinic, 1977-78, London (Eng.) Hosp., 1978-80; tchg. asst. U. Ill., Chgo., 1980-81, rsch. asst., 1981-83; rsch. assoc. Northwestern U., Chgo., 1984-86, rsch. asst. prof., 1986-87, asst. prof., 1987-92, assoc. prof., 1992—. Mem. editl. bd. Am. Occupl. Therapy Jour., 1988-90, Occupl. Therapy Jour. Rsch., 1989-91, Arthritis Care Rsch., 1990-92, 95—; editl. bd. assoc. mem. Archives Phys. Medicine and Rehab., 1994—; contbr. articles to profl. jours. Rsch. grantee NIH, 1986-89, 94-96, Arthritis Found., 1986-89, 87-88, 95-96, Robert Wood Johnson Found., 1988-91. Mem. APHA, Am. Occupl. Therapy Assn., Assn. Health Svcs. Rsch., Am. Congress Rehab. Medicine, Arthritis Health Prof. (rsch. com. 1989-90, pub. com. 1994-95), Delta Omega. Office: Northwestern U Ste 1100 645 N Michigan Ave Chicago IL 60611

FALK, ALLAN, lawyer; b. Sioux City, Iowa, Jan. 18, 1947; s. Martin D. and Bernice C. (Goldstein) F. BA, Mich. State U., 1969; JD, Yale U., 1972. Bar: Mich. 1972. Rsch. atty. Mich. Ct. Appeals, Lansing, 1972-74, commr., 1974—; asst. prof. Mich. State U., East Lansing, 1973-74. Author: Spingold Challenge, 1988, Team Trial, 1992, Bridge Toolkit, 1992, Short Tall Bridge Tales, 1996. Bd. dirs. Common Cause of Mich., Lansing, 1990-95, Opera Guild of Greater Lansing, 1973-80, Greater Lansing Jewish Welfare Fedn., East Lansing, 1982—. Capt. U.S. Army, 1972-80. Recipient Romex award Internat. Bridge Press Assn., 1992; North Am. Bridge Champion Am. Contract Bridge League, 1994. Mem. State Bar of Mich. (mem. appellate ct. adminstrn. com. 1988-94, mem. ethics com. 1989—), Lansing Jewish Ednl. Soc. (bd. dirs. 1982—). Jewish. Home: 2010 Cimarron Dr Okemos MI 48864-3908 Office: Mich Ct Appeals 109 W Michigan Ave Lansing MI 48933

FALK, MARSHALL ALLEN, retired university dean, physician; b. Chgo., May 23, 1929; s. Ben and Frances (Kamins) F.; m. Marilyn Joyce Levoff, June 15, 1952; children: Gayle Debra, Ben Scott. B.S., Bradley U., 1950; M.S., U. Ill., 1952; M.D., Chgo. Med. Sch., 1956. Diplomate Am. Bd. Psychiatry. Intern Cook County Hosp., Chgo., 1956-57; resident Mt. Sinai Hosp., Chgo., 1964-67; gen. practice medicine Chgo., 1959-64; resident in psychiatry, faculty dept. psychiatry Chgo. Med. Sch., 1964-67, prof., acting chmn. dept. psychiatry, 1973-74, dean, 1974-92, v.p. med. affairs, 1981-82, exec. v.p., 1982-91, dean emeritus, emeritus prof. psychiatry, 1991—; med. dir. London Meml. Hosp., 1971-74; mem. cons. com. to commr. health City of Chgo., 1972-82; mem. Ill. Gov.'s Commn. to Revise Mental Health Code, 1973-77, Chgo. Northside Commn. on Health Planning, 1970-74, Ill. Hosp. Licensing Bd., 1981-91. Contbr. articles to profl. jours. Trustee John F. Kennedy Hosp., Atlanta, 1993-95, cons., 1991-92; trustee Quantum Found. for Health, Palm Beach, Fla., 1995—. Capt. AUS, 1957-59. Recipient Bd. Trustees award for rsch. Chgo. Med. Sch., 1963, Disting. Alumni award Chgo. Med. Sch., 1976, Alumnus of Yr. award Bradley U., 1990. Fellow Am. Psychiat. Assn., Am. Coll. Psychiatrists; mem. Ill. Coun. Deans (pres. 1981-83), Coun. Free Standing Med. Sch. Deans (bd. dirs. 1984-92, pres. 1989-91), Sigma Xi, Alpha Omega Alpha.

FALK, NANCY ELLEN AUER, religion educator; b. Bethlehem, Pa., Sept. 3, 1938; d. Allen Archibald and Pearl Emma (Kichline) Auer; m. Arthur Eugene Falk, Oct. 28, 1967; children: Indira Joy, Amelia Marie. BA, Cedar Crest Coll., 1960; MA, U. Chgo., 1963, PhD, 1972. Asst. prof. religion Western Mich. U., Kalamazoo, 1966-72, assoc. prof. religion, 1972-79, chair religion dept., 1972-75, prof. religion, 1979—; Fulbright lectr. Coun. for Internat. Exch. of Scholars, New Delhi, 1984-85. Co-editor: Unspoken Worlds, 1981, new edit., 1989; contbr. articles to profl. jours.; contbg. author encys. Am. Inst. Indian Studies sr. fellow, India, 1991-92. Mem. Am. Acad. Religion (assoc. dir. at large 1977-80), North Am. Assn. for the Study of Religion (steering com. 1989—). Office: Western Mich U Religion Dept Kalamazoo MI 49008

FALK, WANDA E., financial advisor; b. Munsengn, Germany, July 26, 1950; came to U.S., 1951.; BA, U. Minn., 1973. Broker Merrill Lynch, Grand Rapids, 1979-94; fin. advisor Dean Witter Reynolds, Grand Rapids, 1994—. Mem. Econs. Club. Republican. Roman Catholic. Office: Dean Witter Reynolds 300 Ottawa Ave NW Ste 100 Grand Rapids MI 49503-2314

FALKENBERG, MARY ELAINE, small business owner; b. Romeo, Mich., Jan. 10, 1940; d. Paul Emerson and Florence Irene (Joughin) Teal; m. Theodore Henry Falkenberg, June 19, 1965; children: Wendy Elaine, Amy Elizabeth, Theodore Paul. AB in Speech, Geography, Ctrl. Mich. U., 1962. Tchr. West Bloomfield (Mich.) H.S., 1962-63, Coopersville (Mich.) H.S., 1963-65; tchr. forensics Harbor Beach (Mich.) H.S., 1966-69; owner Falkenburg's Screenprinting & Honey, Harbor Beach; trustee Harbor Beach Sch. Bd., 1991-95. Mem. Mich. Beekeepers Assn. (sec., treas.), Harbor Beach Garden Club (v.p. 1993), Women's Club (program dir.), Luth. Women's Missionary League (pres., sec., treas.), Ladies of Zion (pres.), Evangelism (sec. 1994-95, pres. 1995-96), Jaycettes (pres., v.p., sec., treas., Spark Plug), Ski Club. Republican. Home and Office: 1205 S Klug Rd Harbor Beach MI 48441

FALLON, PATRICK R., advertising executive; b. 1946. With Leo Burnett, Chgo., 1967-69; with Stevson & Assocs., Mpls., 1969-76, v.p.; with Martin/Williams Advt., Mpls., 1976-81, v.p.; chmn. bd. dirs., CEO Fallon McElligott, Inc., Mpls., 1981—. Office: Fallon-McElligott Inc 901 Marquette Ave Ste 3200 Minneapolis MN 55402-3205*

FALLS, KATHLEENE JOYCE, photographer; b. Detroit, July 3, 1949; d. Edgar John and Acelia Olive (Young) Haley; m. Donald David Falls, June 15, 1974; children: Daniel John, David James. Student, Oakland Community Coll., 1969-73, Winona Sch. Profl. Photography, 1973-80; degree in photography, 1988, 90. Lic. ham radio-technician class. Printer Guardian Photo, Novi, Mich., 1967-69; printer, supr. quality control N.Am. Photo, Livonia, Mich., 1969-76; free lance photographer Livonia, 1969-76; owner, pres. Kathy Falls, Inc., Carleton, Mich., 1976—; instr. digital imaging Monroe County (Mich.) C.C., 1994—; instr. Monroe County Community Coll. Continuing Edn., 1981-83; nat. artisan judge Congl. High Sch. Art Competition, 1985—; owner Picture Perfect, Carleton, 1987; co-owner Haleys Gift Shoppe, Dundee, Mich., 1989. Author: (booklet) Emergency Photo-Retouching for Photographers, 1988; contbr. articles to profl. jours. Represented in spl. categories in the Nat. Loan Collection, Profl. Photographers Am., 1980, 81, 83, 87; represented in permanent Collections Monroe County Hist. Mus., Archives Notre Dame. Catechist St. Parick's Ch., Carleton, 1984-87; active Big Bros. and Big Sisters, Monroe, 1986-87; corr. sec. Monroe Women's Ctr., 1986-88; bd mem. Heartbeat, 1995; mem. Amateur Radio Emergency Svc. Recipient Photographic Craftsman degree, 1989, numerous awards granted by profl. photographic orgns. Mem. NAFE, Am. Soc. Photographers, Detroit Profl. Photographers Assn. (bd. dirs. 1987—, artisan chmn. 1981-82, Best of Show award 1981, 83), Profl. Photographers Mich. (artisian chairperson 1982-83, Best of Show award 1976, 81, Artist of Yr. 1980, 91), Profl. Photographers Am. (cert. profl. photog. specialist, photographic specialist degree 1988), Am. Photographic Artisans Guild (council mem., bd. dirs. 1987—, pres. 1992, Photographic Artisan degree 1989, Artisan Laurel degree 1991), Monroe County Fine Arts Council, Monroe C. of C. (chmn. council women bus. owners), Nat. Orgn. Women Bus. Owners, Profl. Photographers Am. (Photographic Craftsman degree 1990), Monroe County Radio Communications Assn., Toastmasters, Internat. Club. Democrat. Roman Catholic. Club: Monroe Camera. Home and Office: 10779 Swan Creek Rd Carleton MI 48117-9324

FALZONE, ANTHONY JOSEPH, research physicist; b. Rochester, N.Y., Oct. 11, 1942; s. Joseph Frank and Eva Helen (Paixao) F.; m. Rita Giuseppina Ganzini, Apr. 24, 1976; children: Sonia, Sergio, Fabio. MS, Kent State U., 1966; PhD, U. Queensland, Australia, 1981. Cert. quality engr. Physicist Xerox Corp., Webster, N.Y., 1966, U.S. Naval Rsch. Lab, Washington, D.C., 1967-68, U.S. Naval Observatory, Washington, D.C., 1968-77; tutor U. Queensland, Brisbane, Australia, 1977-81; rsch. assoc. U. Chgo., 1982-83; sr. r & d physicist Standard Oil/BP Research, Cleve., 1983-89; project leader BP Rsch., Cleve., 1990-91; quality mgr. BP Rsch. Cleve., 1991-92; pres. AJF and Assocs., 1992—; quality mgr. ABC Dispensing Technologies, Inc., Akron, Ohio, 1993—. Mem. PTA bd. St. Louis Sch.,

Cleveland Heights, 1989-91. Mem. Am. Phys. Soc., Am. Assn. Physics Tchrs., Am. Geophys. Union, Am. Soc. Quality Control, Sigma Xi. Home: 1373 Yellowstone Rd Cleveland OH 44121-1564

FANCHER, HERSHEL E., development engineer; b. Louisville, Dec. 9, 1969. BS, Rose-Hulman Inst., Terre Haute, Ind., 1992. Design engr. Zimmer Co., Warsaw, Ind., 1991-93; project engr. Law Cons./Engring., Louisville, 1993-94; devel. engr. Servend Internat. Inc., Sellersburg, Ind., 1994—. Mem. ASME. Home: 1524 Slate Run Rd New Albany IN 47150-6210 Office: Servend Internat Inc 2100 Future Dr Sellersburg IN 47172-1874

FANG, ZHAOQIANG, research physicist; b. Ya An, Sichuan, China, Oct. 28, 1939; came to U.S., 1985; s. Zhongdai Fang and Zhijing Zhang; m. Lei Shan; children: Bin Fang, Jing Shan. B in Semiconductor and Solid State Electronics, Tsinghua U., Beijing, China, 1963. Rsch. asst. Inst. Semicondrs. Chinese Acad. Scis., Beijing, 1963-79, rsch. assoc. Inst. Semicondrs., 1979-85; vis. scholar dept. elec. and computer engring. Carnegie Mellon U., Pitts., 1985-89; rsch. physicist, assoc. rsch. prof. dept. physics and Univ. Rsch. Ctr. Wright State U., Dayton, Ohio, 1989—; cons. for mfrs. of III-V compound semicondr. materials. Editor: VLSI Electronics-Micro-Structure Sciences (in Chinese), 1986; contbr. articles to profl. jours. Recipient Nat. Sci. and Tech. Achievement award Nat. Commn. for Sci. and Tech., Beijing, 1985. Mem. IEEE, Materials Rsch. Soc., Minerals, Metals and Materials, Chinese Profls. Club USA, Inc. Office: Wright State U Physics Dept 3640 Col Glenn Hwy Dayton OH 45435

FANNING, RONALD HEATH, architect, engineer; b. Evanston, Ill., Oct. 5, 1935; s. Ralph Richard and Leone Agatha (Heath) F.; m. Jenine Vivian Schnelle, Jan. 9, 1960; children: Anthony Lee, Traycee Anne. BArch, Miami U., Oxford, 1959. Registered arch. in 24 states, Nat. Coun. Archtl. Registration Bd.; registered engr. in 13 states Nat. Coun. Engring. Examiners. Chmn. of the bd. Fanning/Howey Assocs., Inc., Celina, Ohio, 1959--; mng. ptnr. Manning Partnership, Celina 1978—, FFH Ltd. Partnership, 1986-91. Chmn. Mercer County Young Reps., Celina 1962-65. Mem. NSPE, Am. Inst. Archs., Internat. Coun. Ednl. Facility Planners (Great Lake Regional Membership chmn.), Ohio Soc. Profl. Engrs., Ohio Soc. Archs., Soc. Mktg. Profl. Svcs., Fla. Ednl. Facilities Planners Assn., Buckeye Assn. Sch. Adminstrs. Methodist. Home: 422 Magnolia St Celina OH 45822-1254 Office: Fanning Howey Assoc Inc PO Box 71 Celina OH 45822-0071

FANTIN, ARLINE MARIE, state legislator; b. Hammond, Ind., Sept. 26, 1937. Ill. state rep. Dist. 29, 1995—. Office: 523 Burnham Calumet City IL 60409

FARBER, BERNARD JOHN, lawyer; b. London, Feb. 27, 1948; came to U.S., 1949; s. Solomon and Regina (Wachter) F.; m. Mary Lee Mueller, Feb. 14, 1987; children: Zachary, Anne. BS, U. of State of N.Y., Albany, 1978; JD, Ill. Inst. Tech., 1983. Bar: Ill. 1983, U.S. Dist. Ct. (no. dist.) Ill. 1983, U.S. Ct. Appeals (7th cir.) 1985, U.S. Tax Ct. 1986, U.S. Ct. Mil. Appeals 1986, U.S. Supreme Ct. 1987, U.S. Ct. Appeals (6th cir.) 1988, U.S. Ct. Appeals (4th cir.) 1989, U.S. Ct. Appeals (11th cir.) 1990. Instr. legal writing Chgo.-Kent Law Sch. Ill. Inst. Tech., 1983-85, computer rsch. atty., 1985-86, adj. prof. law, 1987—; legal editor Longman Fin. Svcs., Chgo., 1986-87; rsch. counsel publs. Ams. for Effective Law Enforcement, Chgo., 1987—; instr. Law Scholastic Aptitude Test; preparation course BAR/BRI, Chgo., 1984-88; pres. bd. dirs. Employment Rsch. Inst., Chgo.; v.p. Brickton Montessori Sch., Chgo., 1992-93; sec. bd. dirs., 1993-95. Mng. editor: Chgo.-Kent Law Rev., 1981-82, editor-in-chief, 1982-83; co-author: Protective Security Law, 1996; editor: (with others) Dow Jones-Irwin Handbook of Micro Computer Applications in Law, 1987, Illinois Law of Criminal Investigation, 1986; contbr. articles to profl. jours. Elected mem. Local Sch. Coun., Agassiz Elem. Sch., Chgo., 1996—. Mem. ABA, Ill. State Bar Assn., Chgo. Bar Assn., Sci. Fiction Rsch. Assn., Mensa. Home and Office: 1126 W Wolfram Rear Chicago IL 60657-4330

FARBER, PHIL A., photographer, lecturer; b. Chgo., Sept. 23, 1953; s. Irving A. and Naomi (Karlin) F.; m. Paul Farber; children: Melissa, Ashley. BA, U. Ill. Cert. photographer. Pres., CEO Farber Food Corp., Chgo., 1975-80; pres. Photo Images, Inc., Northbrook, Ill., 1980—. Recipient: Kodak Gallery award, Kodak, 1987,91; named Best Comml. Photographer, PPA, 1991, Top Ten Photographers of Ill., PPA, 1987. Mem. Wedding Photographers Internat. Home: 671 Academy Dr Northbrook IL 60062

FARIS, JAMES VANNOY, cardiology educator, hospital executive; b. Indpls., July 18, 1943; s. Vannoy and Maudeline (Freeman) F.; m. Jacqueline Claire Bexell, July 1, 1978; children: Nathan James, Jamie Lynn, Jenna Claire, Brittany Jean, James Vannoy III, Janessa Marie. AB, Ind. U., 1965, MD, 1968. Diplomate Am. Bd. Internal Medicine, Am. Bd. Cardiology. Intern, resident Ind. U. Med. Ctr., Indpls., 1968-71, asst. prof. medicine, 1976-80, assoc. prof. medicine, radiology, 1980—; chief of staff Richard L. Roudebush VA Med. Ctr., Indpls., 1983-95; asst. dean sch. medicine Ind. U., 1983-95. Served to maj. U.S. Army, 1971-73, Vietnam. Ind. Heart Assn. grantee. Fellow Am. Coll. Cardiology; mem. AMA, Ind. State Med. Assn., Alpha Omega Alpha, Alpha Epsilon Delta. Republican. Methodist. Avocations: snow skiing, tennis, water skiing.

FARKAS, JULIUS, chemist; b. Brownsville, Pa., Apr. 9, 1958; s. Julius and Marcella (Stanko) F. BA, Washington and Jefferson Coll., Washington, Pa., 1980; PhD, Pa. State U., University Park, 1985. Teaching/rsch. asst. Washington and Jefferson Coll., 1979-80; lab. technician Stauffer Chem. Co., Washington, 1979-80; teaching asst. Pa. State U., University Park, 1980-82, grad. rsch. assoc. rsch. & devel., 1981-85; assoc. B.F. Goodrich Co., Brecksville, Ohio, 1987—. Mem. Am. Chem. Soc., Am. Inst. Chemists, Soc. Plastics Engrs. Presbyterian. Office: BF Goodrich Co 9921 Brecksville Rd Brecksville OH 44141

FARLEY, BRUCE A., state legislator; b. L.A., Apr. 12, 1943; m. Karen Farley; 2 children. Student, DePaul U.; BA, Loyola U. Formerly mem. from 6th dist. Ill. Ho. of Reps.; mem. Ill. State Senate, 1992—. Home: 2434 W Berenice Ave Chicago IL 60618-3708*

FARLEY, DAVID E., stockbroker; b. Pontiac, Mich., Feb. 7, 1970. BA, U. N.D., 1992. Stockbroker Roney & Co., Petroskey, Mich., 1993—. Mem. Alumni U. N.D., Kiwanis Club. Republican. Roman Catholic. Home: 4910 Atkins Rd Petoskey MI 49770-9534 Office: Roney & Co 8 Pennsylvania Plz PO Box 806 Petoskey MI 49770

FARLEY, JOHN E., stockbroker; b. N.Y.C., Apr. 29, 1924. BA, Princeton U., 1949. Broker Roney & Co., Petoskey, Mich., 1950—. Staff sgt. USMC, 1942-46. Republican. Roman Catholic.

FARLEY, JOHN EDWARD, sociologist, educator, researcher; b. Waterloo, Iowa, Sept. 13, 1949; s. C. J. and Florenda (Schon) F.; m. Margi Wagner, Aug. 15, 1980 (div. 1991); 1 child, Megan S. BA in Polit. Sci. with high honors, Mich. State U., 1971; MA in Sociology, U. Mich., 1973, M in Urban Planning, 1975, PhD in Sociology, 1977. Asst. prof. So. Ill. U., Edwardsville, 1977-82, assoc. prof., 1982-86, prof., 1986—; vis. instr. Moorhead (Minn.) State U., 1976-77; mem. faculty senate So. Ill. U., Edwardsville, 1982-85, 92-96, pres., 1994-95. Author: Majority-Minority Relations, 1982, 3d edit., 1995, American Social Problems, 1987, 2d edit., 1992, Sociology, 1990, 3d edit., 1994; author, guest editor Internat. Jour. Mass Emergencies and Disasters, 1993; mem. editl. bd. Urban Affairs quar., 1989-92. Co-founder, pres. Met. St. Louis Equal Housing Opportunity Coun., 1992—; mem. steering com. OPIN Coalition, Edwardsville, 1994-95; Dem. campaign vol., various locations. Rsch. grantee NIMH, NSF; recipient Cmty. Svc. award Kimmel Leadership Ctr., 1995. Mem. ASA, Midwest Sociol. Soc. (chair exhibits and advt. com. 1993-95), Ill. Sociol. Assn., St. Louis Ski Club (trip dir. 1988-89, pres. 1992-93). Democrat. Roman Catholic. Office: So Ill U Sociology Dept Box 1455 Edwardsville IL 62026-1455

FARLEY, ROBERT HUGH, police detective, child abuse consultant; b. Chgo., Sept. 12, 1950; s. Hugh John and Dorothy Marie (Kennedy) F. BS in Edn., Chgo. State U., 1970; cert., Northwestern U., 1979, U. So. Calif., 1983, U. Louisville, 1979, 84; MS in Criminal Justice and Corrections, Chgo. State U., 1991. Cert. tchr., Ill. Patrolman Cook County Sheriff's Police Dept., Chgo., 1973-74, tactical officer, 1974-75, detective crimes against children, 1975—; detective Fed. Child Exploitation Strike Force, Chgo., 1988—; instr. cons. office of delinquency prevention U.S. Dept. Justice, 1986—; instr. Ill. Local Law Enforcement Tng. Bd., Springfield, 1984—, Fed. Law Enforcement Tng. Ctr., Glynco, Ga., 1986—, FBI Tng. Acad., Quantico, Va., 1994—; faculty Nat. Coll. Edn., Evanston, Ill., 1986—, Morain Valley Coll., Palos Hills, Ill., 1985—, Fox Valley Tech. Coll., 1994—. Contbr. articles to profl. jours. Mem. Ill. State Senate Com. on Teen Suicide Prevention, Cook County States Atty.'s Task Force on Sexual Molestation, Ill. Adv. Com. on Child Abuse and Neglect, Cook County Death Rev. Commn., Ill. Atty. Gen.'s Violence to Children Task Force, Cook County Forensic Interviewing Task Force. Recipient Law Enforcement award U. So. Calif., 1985, Superior Pub. Svc. award City of Chgo., 1986, Cook County State's Atty.'s Recognition award, 1988, U.S. Customs Svc. Recognition award, 1987, U.S. Postal Inspector Law Enforcement award, 1994, Am. Profl. Soc. on the Abuse of Children Law Enforcement award, 1995, Sons and Daus. of the Am. Revolution Law Enforcement medal, 1995; named Police Officer of Yr., Internat. Juvenile Officers Assn., 1991. Mem. Ill. Police Assn. (state exec. bd. 1983—, chmn. 1985—, Law Enforcement award for Bravery 1986), Ill Juvenile Officer Assn., South Suburban Juvenile Officer Assn., Fedn. of Police, Emerald Soc. of Ill., Ill. Art Therapy Assn., Am. Heritage Sertoma, Am. Profl. Soc. on the Abuse of Children, Internat. Soc. for Prevention of Child Abuse.. Office: Cook County Sheriffs Police Dept Spl Ops Unit 1401 Maybrook Dr Maywood IL 60153-2475

FARMAKIS, GEORGE LEONARD, education educator; b. Clarksburg, W.Va., June 30, 1925; s. Michael and Pipitsa (Roussopoulos) F.; BA, Wayne State U., 1949, MEd, 1950, MA, 1966, PhD, 1971; MA, U. Mich., 1978; postgrad. Columbia U., Yale U., Queens Coll. Tchr., audio-visual aids dir. Roseville (Mich.) Pub. Schs., 1951-57; tchr. Birmingham (Mich.) pub. schs., 1957-61; tchr. Highland Park (Mich.) Pub. Schs., 1961-90; substitute tchr. Grosse Pointe Pub. Schs., 1990—; lectr. Lawrence U., 1990—; lectr. Oakland County C.C., 1990-92; instr. Highland Park C.C., 1966-68, Wayne County C.C., 1969-70; assoc. mem. grad. faculty Coll. Edn. Wayne State U., 1988-89; founder Ford Sch. Math. High Intensity Tutoring Program, 1971; chairperson Highland Park Sch. Dist. Curriculum Coun. and Profl. Staff Devel. Governing Bd., 1979-82; pres. Mich. Coun. Social Studies, 1985-86; founder, dir. Mich. Social Studies Olympiad, 1987; founder, editor Mich. Social Studies Jour., 1986; participant ESEA Title I/Nat. Diffusion Network. Cpl., USNG, 1948-51. Author, translator: Letters of Nicholas Gysis 1842-1901; co-author: Michigan School Finance Curriculum Guide.; contbr. poems to books of poetry, articles to Focus jour. Recipient spl. commendation Office of Edn., 1978, Outstanding Svc. award Nat. Coun. Social Studies 1987, Presdl. award Mich. Coun. Social Studies 1988. Mem. Mich. Assn. Supervision and Curriculum Devel., Am. Hist. Assn., Nat. Council Social Studies (pres. SIG-CASE 1987-88, pres. JESIG, 1988-89), Am. Philol. Assn., Assn. Supervision and Curriculum Devel. (bd. dirs. Mich. 1983—), Internat. Reading Assn., U. Mich. Alumni Assn., Wayne State U. Coll. Edn. Alumni Assn. (bd. dirs. 1985—), Mich. Reading Assn., Masons (32 degree), Shriners, Phi Delta Kappa (Outstanding Educators award 1988). Greek Orthodox Home: 15215 Windmill Dr Macomb MI 48044-4929

FARMER, MIKE, state legislator; m. Jean Farmer. Sys. analyst; mem. Kans. State Ho. of Reps. Dist. 87.

FARMER, NANCY, state legislator; b. Jacksonville, Ill.. Student, Ill. Coll., 1979—. Exec. dir. Skinker-DeBaliviere Cmty. Coun.; state rep. dist. 64 Mo. Ho. of Reps.; mem. Woman's Polit. Caucus Mo. Ho. of Reps. Active Woman's Com. Forest Park, Rosedale Neighborhood Assn., mem. exec. com.; active West End Arts Coun. Mem. Ctrl. West End Assn., Women Legislators Mo. Home: 6026 Waterman Blvd Saint Louis MO 63112-1329 Office: Mo Ho of Reps State Capitol Building Jefferson City MO 65101-1556*

FARNEN, MARK EDWARD, economic development specialist; b. San Antonio, Jan. 11, 1957; s. John Kevin and Jane Carolyn (Paxson) F. Student, U. Mo., 1975-78, 82, 85, U. Mo., 1990—. Field organizer Carter Presdl. Campaign, Washington, 1979-80; advt. dir. The Mo. Times, Columbia, 1980-82; state dir. Mondale for Pres. Campaign, Little Rock, 1983-84; cons. Nat. Strategies and Mktg. Group, Washington, 1985; logistics dir. Hands Across Am., Little Rock, 1986; campaign mgr. Roehrick for U.S. Senate, Des Moines, Iowa, 1986; dep. campaign mgr. Gephardt for Pres., Des Moines, 1987-88; dir. Rural Vote '88, Mexico, Mo., 1988-89, Dept. Econ. Devel., Mexico, 1989-93; pres. Hawthorn Found., Jefferson City, Mo., 1993—; ptnr. Elvis Catering, 1992—; chmn. bd. Enterprise Devel. Corp., Columbia, 1995—. Columnist, contbr. Mid Missouri Mag., 1991-92; food critic Mid Missouri Bus. Jour., 1996—; host (TV show) Country Video Bullets, 1992. Bd. dirs. Mexico YMCA, 1991-92; adv. bd. Mo. Global Partnership, 1996—. Mem. Am. Econ. Devel. Coun., Mo. Indsl. Devel. Coun. (state sec. 1992—), Boone County Muleskinners, Audrain County Hist. Soc., Audrain County Dem. Club (v.p. 1988-89), Rotary Internat. (participant group study exch. 1989), Mexico Jaycees (v.p. 1990-91, Dir. of Yr., Outstanding Missourians 1992. Mid-Mo. Internat. Trade Club (treas. 1995—). Roman Catholic. Home: 1052 Boonville Rd Jefferson City MO 65109-0620

FARNEN, TED WILLIAM, state legislator; b. Mexico, Mo., Sept. 3, 1965; s. John Kevin and Jane Carolyn (Paxson) F. BJ, U. Mo., 1987. Reporter Sedalia (Mo.) Dem., 1987-89; comms. specialist Mo. Senate, Jefferson City, Mo., 1989-94; state rep. Mo. House, Jefferson City, Mo., 1994—; mem. adv. bd. Arthur Ctr., Mexico, 1995—. Mem. Audrain County Hist. Soc., Boone County Muleskinners, Mo. Alumni Assn., Travelers Protective Assn. Democrat. Roman Catholic. Home: 13 Wonneman Cir Mexico MO 65265 Office: Mo Ho of Reps State Capitol Jefferson City MO 65101

FARNSWORTH, WELLS EUGENE, biochemist, educator; b. Hartford, Conn., July 10, 1921; s. Francis Porter and Eleanor Adelaide (Wells) F.; m. Marjorie Ann Whyte, Sept. 15, 1945; children: Samuel Bartlett, Marjorie Wells. BS, Trinity Coll., Hartford, Conn., 1946; MA, U. Mo., 1949, PhD, 1951. Endocrinologist William Merrel Co., Cin., 1951-52; rsch. chemist VA Med. Ctr., Buffalo, N.Y., 1952-80; prof., chmn. biochemistry dept. Chgo. Coll. Osteo. Medicine, 1980-88, prof. of biochemistry, 1988-91; instr., assoc. prof. SUNY, Buffalo, 1952-80; adj. prof. of urology Northwestern U., Sch. Medicine, Chgo., 1991—. With U.S. Army 1942-46, ETO. Recipient Acad. Rsch. Enhancement award Chgo. Coll. Osteo. Medicine, 1987-89; grantee Pierre Fabre Inst., Castves, France, 1988-91. Mem. Endocrine Soc., Am. Physiol. Soc., Soc. Biochemistry and Molecular Biology. Office: 303 Chicago Ave 11715 Tarry Bldg Chicago IL 60611

FARQUHARSON, JOHN S., investment broker; b. Lafayette, Ind., Jan. 29, 1957; m. Kathy M. Gray, Oct. 10, 1986; children: John M., Elise G. BBA, Western Mich. U., 1980. Dist. sales mgr. Nat. Office Furniture, Jasper, Tenn., 1984-88; regional sales mgr. Globe Bus. Furniture, Nashville, 1988-92; investment broker A. G. Edwards & Sons Inc., Grand Rapids, Mich., 1992—. Mem. Rockford Rotary (bd. dirs. 1994—), Rockford C. of C. Republican. Roman Catholic. Home: 6077 Cannon Highland Dr NE Belmont MI 49306-9678 Office: A G Edwards & Sons Inc 50 Monroe Ave NW Ste 100 Grand Rapids MI 49503-2643

FARRALL, HAROLD JOHN, retired accountant; b. Harvard, Nebr., Mar. 25, 1918; s. John William and Olive Almira (Frazell) F. BSBA, Nebr. U., 1940. Clk. Bur. of Aeronautics, Washington, 1946-47; supr. acct. Bur. of Reclamation Region 7, Denver, 1948-72; accts. payable acct. Dutton-Lainson Co., Hastings, Nebr., 1974-85. Author: The Rise and Fall of the United States, 1990. With U.S. Army, 1941-45. Regents scholarship U. Nebr., 1936. Mem. DAV, VFW, Am. Legion, Ind. order of Odd Fellows, Fed. Govt. Accts. Assn., Mensa.

FARRAND, ROLLIN ELVIN, county engineer, civil engineer, consultant; b. Shipshewana, Ind., Oct. 17, 1928; s. Edward Doyle and Golda Marie (Lovell) F.; m. Patricia Ann Cook, June 2, 1951; children: Rollin E. Jr., Cynthia Carol Rowell, Leslie Marie Hill, Joel Edwin; m. Kathleen F. Cekanski, Dec. 2, 1977; 1 child, Kathleen Marie. BS in Civil Engring., Purdue U., 1950. Engr. U.S. Bur. Reclamation, Moses Lake, Wash., 1950-51; instrument man N.Y.C. RR Co., Indpls, 1953-56; project engr. CAA, Indpls, 1956-58; project engr. (engr. 2) Ind. State Hwy. Commn., Indpls, 1958-64, squad leader (engr. 3), 1964-68, group leader (engr. 4), 1968-70; dept. head Cole Assocs., Inc., South Bend, Ind., 1970-73; v.p. engring. Cole Assocs., Inc., 1977-92; city engr. South Bend, Ind., 1973-77; county engr. St. Joseph County, South Bend, Ind., 1993—. 1st lt. U.S. Army Engr. Corps., 1951-53. Home: 60895 Fir Rd Mishawaka IN 46544 Office: St Joseph County Dept Pub Works 227 W Jefferson Blvd South Bend IN 46601

FARRAR, ELIZABETH TURRELL, lawyer; b. Steubenville, Ohio, May 22, 1957; d. Ronald Sherman and Joanna Marguerite (Van Orden) Turrell. BA, Smith Coll., 1979; JD, U. Va., 1982. Bar: Ohio 1982, U.S. Dist. Ct. (so. dist.) Ohio 1983. Assoc. Vorys, Sater, Seymour and Pease, Columbus, Ohio, 1982-88, ptnr., 1989—; mem. registration adv. com. Ohio Div. Securities, 1990—; mem. gender fairness task force Ohio State Bar Assn./ Ohio Supreme Ct.-Lawyer and Workplace Lifestyle Com., 1991-93; counsel to bldg. code and standards com. of Ohio Mfrs. Assn., 1995—. Mem. Columbus Children's Hosp. Twig III, 1990, treas., 1995—; mem. Bexley (Ohio) Bd. Zoning Appeals, 1990—, Bexley Planning Task Force, 1995—. Dillard fellow U. Va., 1981-82; recipient Bus. First 40 under 40 award Bus. First and Morton's of Chgo., 1994. Mem. ABA (exec. com. young lawyers divsn. 1986-88), Ohio Bar Assn. (corps. com. 1991—), Columbus Bar Assn. (admissions com. 1986—, securities com. 1984—), U. Va. Alumni Club, Smith Coll. Alumnae Club (candidate chmn. 1984-87, pres. 1990—), Smith Coll. Class of 1979 (fund agt. and alumnae fund team coord. 1994—, treas. 1979-84). Republican. Episcopalian. Home: 2345 Brentwood Rd Columbus OH 43209-2103 Office: Vorys SaterSeymour and Pease 52 E Gay St Columbus OH 43215-3108

FARRELL, DANIEL GEORGE, safety administrator; b. Columbus, Ohio, Aug. 19, 1947; s. Ralph Charles and Rita Mary (Wells) F.; m. Sharon Lee Zeigler, July 8, 1972; children: Brent George, Bradley Kevin. BA, Otterbein Coll., 1969; MBA, U. Dayton, 1977. Cert. hazardous materials mgr. Inst. Hazardous Materials Mgmt. Sales rep. Mass. Mutual, Columbus, Ohio, 1970-72; planning adminstr., distbn. adminstr. GTE, Marion, Ohio, 1973-86; sect. supr. environ. compliance GTE, Westfield, Ind., 1986-94; sect. mgr. safety GTE, Westfield, 1994—; instr. Ind. Wesleyan, Marion, 1991—, Ind. Inst. Tech., Fort Wayne, 1992—. Mem. Ind. Soc. Hazardous Materials Mgmt. (ethics com. 1993—). Republican. Office: GTE 17845 N US 31 Westfield IN 46074

FARRELL, JEREMIAH LOUIS, retired psychologist; b. Green Bay, Wis., July 16, 1932; s. Thomas Robert and Lulu Dorothy (Fournier) F.; m. Jean Marian Lamine, June 25, 1960. BS, U. Wis., Stevens Point, 1957; MEd, U. Wis., Superior, 1959; EdD, U. Wyo., 1965. Lic. psychologist, Alaska; cert. tchr., Wis. Assoc. prof., dean of men U. N.D., Ellendale, 1965-67; psychologist intern VAMC, Milw., 1967-68; cons. psychologist VA, Sioux Falls, S.D., 1968-69, VACO, Washington, 1969-71, VA, Tomah, Wis., 1971-76; dir. mental health ctr. Mauneluk Assn., Kotzebue, Alaska, 1976-78; lead psychologist USAF, Elmendorf, Alaska, 1978-81; cons. psychologist VA Regional Office, Anchorage, 1981-82, USAF, Elemdorf, 1985; pvt. practice Anchorage, 1982-85; dir. drug treatment ctr. U.S. Army, Ft. Richardson, Alaska, 1985-90; vice-pres., mem. Alaska Coun. on Prevention of Alcohol and Drug Abuse, Anccrage, 1978-92. Bd. dirs. Kotzebue C.C., 1976-78. With USNR, 1949-50; with U.S. Army, 1952-54, Korea; with USAR/Alaska Army N.G., 1972-92. Mem. NRA (life), VFW (life), NEA (life), Am. Pers. and Guidance Assn. (life), Ret. Officers Assn. (life), Nat. Assn. Ret. Fed. Employees (life), Res. Officers Assn. (life), Alaska Army N.G. 3d Bn. (hon. life), Arctic Alaska Socuts (hon., life), Izaak Walton League (life), TROA (life). Roman Catholic. Home: 723 Sunset Beach Rd Suamico WI 54173

FARRELL, JIM, state legislator; b. Mar. 1, 1960; m. Donnal Luzaich; 2 children. BS, U. Minn., JD. State rep. Minn. Ho. Reps., Dist. 67A, 1990—; mem. coms. ins. & govt. coms., mem. com. & econ. devel.-tourism & small bus. divsn., econm. devel.-infrastructure & regulation fin., fin. inst. & ins. & labor-mgmt. rels. coms., Minn. Ho. Reps. Home: 407 State Office Building Bldg Saint Paul MN 55155-1201*

FARRELL, JOHN TIMOTHY, hospital administrator; b. St. Louis, Feb. 22, 1947; s. Michael James and Jane Frances (Lautenschlager) F.; m. Martha Anne Paynter, June 4, 1971; children: Kathleen Marie, Margaret Mary, Anne Elizabeth, John Timothy, Mary Ellen. B.A. in Philosophy, Cardinal Glennon Coll., 1969; postgrad., U. Mo., 1969-71; M.H.A., St. Louis U., 1973. Adminstrv. resident St. John's Mercy Med. Center, St. Louis, 1970-72, 73, exec. v.p., chief operating officer, 1979-86; pres., chief exec. officer St. John's Mercy Med. Ctr., St. Louis, 1986-95; pres., chief exec. officer St. John's Mercy Hosp., 1986-95, chmn. bd. trustees, 1991-95; asst. exec. dir. St. Mary's Hosp., Richmond, Va., 1973-74, assoc. exec. dir., 1974-76; adminstr. St. Francis Mercy Hosp., Washington, Mo., 1976-78, exec. v.p., 1978-95; chmn. bd., pres., CEO St. John's Mercy Health Sys., 1994-95; cons. health care St. Louis, 1995-96; v.p. employee benefits Anheuser-Busch Cos., Inc., St. Louis, 1996—; adj. faculty mem., designated preceptor Grad. Program in Hosp. and Health Adminstrn., Xavier U., Cin., 1989; pres. Mercy Doctors Bldg., Inc., 1986-93, Mercy Health Ventures, Inc., Edgewood Program, Inc.; mem. health adv. bd. Sisters of Mercy of the Union, Province St. Louis, 1976-79, mem. personnel com., 1978-79; mem. Catholic health care facilities com. Mo. Cath. Conf., Jefferson City, 1976-82, chmn., 1979-82, mem. health affairs task force, 1977-82; mem. adv. com. med. records technician program St. Mary's Coll., O'Fallon, Mo., 1978-79; mem. subcom. on svcs. pediatric tech. adv. group Health Systems Agy., 1978-79; mem. mental health task force St. Louis-Jefferson-Franklin Counties, Devel. Mental Health Facilities, 1977-79; mem. steering subcom. Health Systems Agy. Local Impact Com., 1979; Mercy Physicians Partnership; mem. shared svcs. coun. Sisters of Mercy Health Sys., St. Louis; adj. instr. health care adminstrn. Washington U. Sch. Medicine, St. Louis, 1985—; pres. bd. dirs. Area Rescue Consortium of Hosp., St. Louis, 1988, 91-92, sec., bd. dirs., 1989-94, v.p., treas., 1990; mem. steering com. Greater St. Louis Healthcare Alliance, 1993-95, mem. exec. com., 1993-95, mem. quality measurement com., 1992; cons. com. St. Louis Regional Hosp., 1992-93; program com. Coun. Tchg. Hosps., 1993-94; bd. mgrs. Unity Health Network, 1994-95; bd. dirs. Mercy Med. Group; trustee Mercy Health Plan, 1994—. Mem. mgmt. adv. com. Washington (Mo.) Sch. Dist., 1976-79; bd. dirs. St. Francis Mercy Hosp., 1979-82, Mercy Health Conf., 1982-84, Family Planning Coun. St. Louis, 1979-81, mem. personnel com., 1979-81, budget com., 1980; bd. dirs. Mercy Hosp., Mansfield, Mo., 1983-87, St. John's Regional Hosp., Springfield, Mo., 1987-94, Affiliated Hosp. Dialysis Ctr., St. Louis, 1986—, Midwest Stone Inst., 1987-92; mem. CEO coun., corp. ethics com. Sisters of Mercy Health Systems, St. Louis, 1987-89; pres., bd. dirs. Cath. Outreach Cmty. Program, 1992; bd. dirs. United Way Greater St. Louis, 1995—, chmn. hosp. sect. campaign, 1988, chmn. Health Svcs., 1994, mem. area wide rels. com., 1995—; bd. dirs., chmn. postgrad. conf. St. Louis U. Alumni; mem. Parish Coun. St. Genevieve DuBois, St. Louis, 1989-92, pres., 1991-92; mem. Brotherhood/ Sisterhood dinner com. NCCJ, St. Louis, 1990-94; bd. dirs. James Clinic Mercy Med. Group, Rolla, Mo., 1992-94, chmn. bd. dirs. Cath. Cmty. Svcs., 1992—; fundraising com. St. Louis County Police and Firefighter Meml., 1993; exec. com. Joint Hosp. Assn. Met. St. Louis and St. Louis Met. Med. Soc., 1991-93; bd. dirs. Priests Mutual Benefits Soc., 1996—. Mem. Am. Coll. Hosp. Adminstrs., Mo. Hosp. Assn. (chmn. bd. trustees 1993, chmn.-elect 1992, past chmn. 1994, trustee 1989, 91-95, chmn. coun. rsch. and policy devel. 1990, chmn. fin. and budget 1991, annual meeting com.), Hosp. Assn. Met. St. Louis (coun. on fin. 1979-81, chmn. environ. svcs. com. 1981-86, mem. coun. mgmt. svcs. 1981-86, physician rels. com. 1987-88, chmn. coun. on pub. policy and issues 1987-88, bd. dirs. sec. 1991, treas. 1992, vice chmn. 1993, chmn. 1994), Midwest Stone Inst. (pres. 1988-92, bd. dirs. 1988-93), St. Louis U. Sch. Pub. Health Alumni Assn. (pres. 1991-92), Shared Resources Enterprise (bd. dirs. 1990, treas. 1991, sec. 1992, vice chmn. bd. dirs. 1993, chmn. 1994), Mental Health Assn. (host Spirit of St. Louis com. 1990), Creve Coeur Squires. Home: 537 Meadow Creek Ln Saint Louis MO 63122-1656

FARRELL, KATHLEEN ELLEN, marketing, public relations executive; b. Breese, Ill., July 6, 1948. BA, So. Ill. U., 1971. Alumni dir. U. Mo., St. Louis, 1975-78; pres. Corp. Bd. Inc., St. Louis, 1980-86; v.p. The Farrell Group Inc., St. Louis, 1987—. Office: # 9 The Pines Ct Saint Louis MO 63141

FARRELL, LENORE EMMA, elementary education educator, guidance counselor; b. Eagle River, Wis., Feb. 16, 1918; d. Edward Burton and Emma Katherine (Schmidt) Croker; m. Emerson Ellsworth Farrell, Dec. 11, 1937; children: Sherilyn Dee, Michael Emerson. BE, U. Wis., Stevens Point, 1963; ME, U. Wis., Superior, 1968. cert. tchr.; lic. guidance counselor. Elem. sch. tchr. Sch. Dist. # 1 Northland Pines, Eagle River, 1936-38, 54-80; v.p., sec. Vilas County Tchrs. Assn., Eagle River, 1960-62, 70-74. Author, illustrator: (children's books) Skag the Lonesome Dinosaur, 1994, Skag Goes to the Dentist, 1994, Skag and the Bears, 1994, Skag at the Lake, 1994. sec. Eagle River Historical Soc., 1992-95. Recipient State Exhibit award Wis. Regional Art Program, U. Wis., 1995. Home: 3190 Valeria Rd Eagle River WI 54521

FARRELL, PHILIP M., physician, educator, researcher; b. St. Louis, Nov. 26, 1943; m. Alice Yeakle; children—Michael Henry, David Sean, Bridget Mary. A.B., St. Louis U., 1964, M.D., 1970, Ph.D., 1970. Diplomate Am. Bd. Pediatrics. Asst. prof. dept. child health Washington U., Washington, 1975; asst. prof. dept. pediatrics U. Wis., Madison, 1977-78, assoc. prof. pediatrics, 1978-82, prof. pediatrics, 1982—, chmn. dept. pediatrics, 1985—, affiliate scientist Wis. Regional Primate Research Ctr., 1978, affiliate faculty dept. nutrition scis., 1978, dir. Pediatric Pulmonary Specialized Ctr. of Research, 1981—, co-dir. Cystic Fibrosis Ctr., 1983—; sr. investigator pediatric metabolism br. Nat. Inst. Arthritis, Metabolism and Digestive Diseases NIH, Bethesda, Md., 1974-75, chief sect. on devel. biology and clin. nutrition Neonatal and Pediatric Medicine br. Nat. Inst. Child Health and Human Devel., 1975, chief Neonatal and Pediatric Medicine br., 1975. Editor: Lung Development: Biological and Clinical Perspectives, 1982. Avalon Found. scholar, 1965-67, Thurston Meml. scholar, 1966-70; Fogarty Internat. fellow, 1985. Mem. Am. Chem. Soc., Am. Acad. Pediatrics, Am. Coll. Nutrition, Soc. Pediatric Research, Am. Thoracic Soc., Soc. Exptl. Biology and Medicine, Perinatal Research Soc., Am. Inst. Nutrition, Am. Soc. Clin. Nutrition, Wis. Assn. Perinatal Care, Sigma XI, Phi Beta Kappa, Alpha Omega Alpha. Home: 2783 Marshall Pky Madison WI 53713-1022 Office: Univ Wis Dept Pediatrics 600 Highland Ave Madison WI 53792-0001

FARRELL, RICHARD F., investment company executive; b. Moline, Ill., Jan. 14, 1947. BBA, U. Notre Dame, 1969. Adminstr. Assn. Mgmt. Inc., Washington, 1969-70; mng. editor Nat. Tire Dealers Assn., Washington, 1970-71; owner, mgr. Farrell & Farrell, Moline, 1971-92; investment officer Robert W. Baird & Co. Inc., Moline, 1992—. Office: Robert W Baird & Co Inc PO Box 846 2020 52d Ave Moline IL 61266

FARRELL, ROBERT W., manufacturing company executive; b. Cin., Nov. 7, 1948. BA in Mfg. Engring., U. Cin., 1971, BA in Bus. Mgmt., 1974. Sr. mfg. engr. Campbell Hausfeld, Harrison, Ohio, 1972-75, Am. Power Equipment, Harrison, 1975-87; pres. All Craft Mfg. Co., Cin., 1987—; cons. Cin.Milacron, 1986—. Republican. Roman Catholic. Office: All Craft Mfg PO Box 58651 Cincinnati OH 45258-0651

FARRELL-DONALDSON, MARIE DELOIS, municipal official; b. Detroit, Aug. 10, 1947; d. Herman and Lorine (Carter) Morgan; m. Joseph C. Farrell, July 18, 1970 (div. 1974); 1 child, Piper; m. Clinton Lavonne Donaldson, Nov. 29, 1975; 1 child, Christia. BS, Wayne State U., 1969; cert. in govt., Harvard U., 1982; MS, Walsh Coll., 1992. CPA, Mich. (first Black female). Jr. acct. Iceman, Johnson and Hoffman, Ann Arbor, Mich., 1969-71; comptroller Model Neighborhood Devel., Detroit, 1972-74; pvt. practice acctg. Detroit, 1974-75; auditor gen. City of Detroit, 1975-84, ombudsman, 1984-95; dir. internal audit Detroit Bd. Edn., 1995—. Treas. Mich. Metro Girl Scouts Am., 1984—, United Community Svcs., Detroit, 1985-90; pres. Detroit chpt. Nat. Coun. Alcoholism, 1979-85. Named Michiganian Yr. Detroit News, 1982, Outstanding Young Working Woman Glamour Mag., 1985, Outstanding Alumni Wayne State U., 1985, Outstanding Pub. Servant, 1991, Wayne State U. Disting. Alumni, 1991. Mem. Nat. Assn. Black Accts. (bd. dirs.), Nat. Coun. Govt. Accts. (bd. dirs. 1979-82), Women's Econ. Club (pres. 1987-88), Mich. Assn. CPAs (bd. dirs. 1985-89),Links, Inc., Alpha Kappa Alpha. Methodist. Office: Detroit Bd Edn 5035 Woodward Ave Detroit MI 48202

FARRINGTON, THOMAS RICHARD, financial executive, investment advisor; b. Columbus, Ohio, Oct. 10, 1941; s. Robert Alexander and Catherine Ann (Lafferty) F.; m. Saundra Sue Birk, Dec. 9, 1989. BS in Engring., Ariz. State U., Tempe, 1969, postgrad., 1969-71. Fin. systems analyst Motorola, Phoenix, 1971-77; info. systems mgr. McDonnell Douglas, St. Louis, 1977-91; investment rep. Edward D. Jones & Co., St. Louis, 1991-93; pres. Heartland Fin. Svcs. Group, Inc., Cape Girardeau, Mo., 1993—; bd. dirs. Commonwealth Realty, Inc., Cape Girardeau. Served with USAF, 1961-65. Mem. Eta Kappa Nu, Phi Theta Kappa. Republican. Lutheran. Home: 229 Hillview St Cape Girardeau MO 63703-6327 Office: Heartland Fin Svcs Group 121 S Broadview St Cape Girardeau MO 63703-5760

FARRON, JOHN R., stockbroker; b. Detroit, Sept. 17, 1947; s. John R. and Betty M. (Nash) F.; m. Marcia A. Barnbrook, Nov. 7, 1991; 1 child, Kristina; children by previous marriage: Steven Rudolph, Matt Rudolph. BA, Eastern Mich. U., Ypsilanti, 1970, MA, 1972. Sales mgr. Chrysler Corp., Hyde Park, Mich., 1970-75; stockbroker Prudential Securities, South Bend, Ind., 1975-80; br. mgr. Raffenperger Huges, South Bend, 1990-91, R.W. Baird & Co., South Bend, 1991—. Dir. Project Future, South Bend, 1985—. Mem. South Bend C. of C. Republican. Roman Catholic. Home: 52070 Lake Shore Granger IN 46530 Office: Robert Baird & Co Inc 202 S Michigan St Ste 200 South Bend IN 46601-2006

FARROW, MARGARET ANN, state legislator; b. Kenosha, Wis., Nov. 28, 1934; d. William Charles and Margaret Ann (Horan) Nemitz; m. John Harvey Farrow, Dec. 29, 1956; children—John, William, Peter, Paul, Mark. Student Rosary Coll., 1952-53; B.S. in Polit. Sci., Marquette U., 1956, postgrad., 1975-77. Tchr., Archiodese of Milw., 1956-57; trustee Elm Grove Village, Wis., 1976-81, pres., 1981-86; mem. Wis. State Assembly, 1986-89, State Senate, 1989—. asst. majority leader, 1993—; chair com. on govt. effectiveness, 1995—, mem. joint com. on audit, 1995—, mem. joint legislative coun., 1993—, mem. com. on environ. & energy, 1993—, mem. joint survey com. on tax exemptions, 1995—, mem. com. on orgn., 1993—, mem. commn. on state human resources reform, 1995—, chair Wis. women's coun., 1991—, mem. Wis. glass ceiling commn., 1993—, mem. gov.'s clean air task force, 1993—, mem. low level radioactive waste coun., 1991—. Home: 14905 Watertown Plank Rd Elm Grove WI 53122-2332 Office: Wis State Capitol Senate House Madison WI 53702

FARRUG, EUGENE JOSEPH, SR., lawyer; b. Detroit, May 22, 1928; s. Michael and Bridget Mary (Foley) F.; m. Dolores Marie Augustine, Apr. 14, 1951; children: Elizabeth Marie Streit, Eugene Joseph Jr., Matthew Augustine, Pamela Ann, Bridget Louise, Donna Michele. BBA, U. Mich., 1950, JD, 1958. Bar: Ill. 1958, U.S. Dist. Ct. (no. dist.) Ill. 1958; U.S. Supreme Ct. 1980. With Lincoln-Mercury div. Ford Motor Co., Dearborn, Mich., 1950, Aircraft Engine div., Chgo., 1951; assoc. McKenna, Storer, Rowe, White & Farrug, Chgo., 1958-62, ptnr., 1962-92; of counsel, 1992—. Mem. Citizens of Greater Chgo., 1970-80, pres., 1976-79. Served with USN, 1951-55. McGreggor Fund scholar, 1946; Mich. Bd. Realtors scholar, 1949. Mem. Ill. Bar Assn., Chgo. Bar Assn., DuPage County Bar Assn., Am. Judicature Soc., Cath. Lawyers Guild, Trial Lawyers Club Chgo., Phi Alpha Delta. Lodge: Kiwanis (pres. 1964). Home: 206 N Lincoln St Hinsdale IL 60521-3441

FASANELLA, JOHN J., investment executive; b. Joliet, Ill., Aug. 7, 1947. BBA, Norvond U., 1969; MBA, Fla. State U., 1977. Sr. acct. Marine Trust Co., Milw., 1979-81; pres. Comty. Banks Trust Co., Madison, Wis., 1981-88; investment profl. Kemper Securities, Madison, 1988-93; v.p. investments retirement planning Dean Witter Reynolds, Madison, 1993—; bd. advisors 1st Nat. Bank & Trust, Madison. Dir. Children's Theater, Madison, 1988-93; fin. com. Middleton Outreach Ministry, Madison, 1992-95. Mem. Builder Assn., Middleton Optimist (bd. dirs. 1989-95), Middleton C. of C., Wis. Soc. Enrolled Agts., West Met. Bus. Assn. Roman Catholic. Home: 1309 N Westfield Rd Middleton WI 53562-3640 Office: Dean Witter Reynolds # 412 6510 Grand Teton Plz Madison WI 53719-1029

FASHING, ANNETTE LOUISE, elementary education educator, reading specialist; b. Chgo., Feb. 5; d. Alvin Christian David and Gertrude Alice (Reding) Lubker; m. Edward Michael Fashing, Jan. 29, 1959: children: Anita, Mary, Edward, James, John. BS, Mundelein Coll., 1959; MEd with distinction, DePaul U., 1979. Svc. rep. Ill. Bell Telephone Co., Chgo., 1959-60; organist-cantor Our Lady of Lourdes Ch., Chgo., 1960-83; tchr. Herzl Sch., Chgo., 1965-69, St. Joseph Sch., Chgo., 1969-70, Cathedral of the Holy Name, Chgo., 1970-71; reading specialist Chgo. Bd. of Edn., 1971-83, Boone County Region VI, Centralia, Mo., 1983—; dir. Writer's Anonymous, Centralia, 1990-92; tchr. confraternity of Christian doctrine Holy Spirit Ch., Centralia, 1991—, founder Singing with the Grandmas. Mem. Sturgeon (Mo.) Fair Bd., 1987-91; leader Holy Spirit Folk Group, Centralia, 1975—, 4-H, Sturgeon and Centralia, 1980-91;l bd. dirs., treas. Children's Ranch Inc., Sturgeon, 1989—. DePaul U. fellow, 1958; Mundelein Coll. scholar, 1955-58. Mem. Nat. Assn. Pastoral Musicians, Internat. Reading Assn., Am. Agrl. Movement, Mo. State Tchrs. Assn., Centralia Tchrs. Assn. (v.p. 1994, pres. 1995-96), Farm Bus. Roman Catholic. Home: RR 1 Sturgeon MO 65284-9801 Office: Chance Elem Sch 510 S Rollins St Centralia MO 65240-1563

FASHING, EDWARD MICHAEL, ranch owner, physical sciences educator; b. Chgo., Jan. 27, 1936; s. Michael George and Leontine (LeClercq) F.; m. Annette Louise Lubker, Jan. 29, 1959; children: Anita Fashing Kiska, Mary Fashing Schillig, Edward Jr., James, John. BS in Chemistry, Loyola U., Chgo., 1960; MS in Chemistry, DePaul U., 1968; postgrad., U. Mo., 1982-84. Cert. jr. coll. chemistry tchr., Ill. Instr. geology Triton Coll., River Grove, Ill., 1969-81; Simmental cattle and sheep rancher Cedar Ln. Farm, Sturgeon, Mo., 1973—; asst. prof. N.E. Mo. State U., Kirksville, 1981-82; chemistry asst. U. Mo., Columbia, 1982-84; instr. physics Columbia (Mo.) Coll., 1986. Writer, news commentator, show moderator, producer Farm Forum Sta. KOPN-Radio, 1985-89; freelance reporter, columnist, proof reader Am. Agr. Reporter, 1990—. Leader 4H, Sturgeon, 1974-84, 88; vol., creator posters Mo. Rural Crisis Ctr., Columbia, 1986—, bd. dirs., 1990-93; ch. cantor, lector; Dem. rep. 1988 Mo. State Conv., Am. Agrl. Movement Grassroots (publicity dir. 1985, demonstrator 1985, spokesman Chgo. demonstrations 1984, 85, 86), Nat. Farm Union, Am. Agr. Movement Inc. of Mo. (v.p. comms. 1991—), Farm Alliance of Rural Mo. (bd. dirs. 1986-88, 95), N.Am. Farm Alliance, Nat. Farmers Union (lobbyist 1990), Phi Delta Kappa (treas. Triton chpt. 1978). NSF grantee, 1966, 76. Mem. AAAS, Am. Chem. Soc., Am. Physics Tchrs., Mo. Acad. Sci., Ill. Acad. Sci., Am. Simmental Assn., Mo. Simmental Assn., Nat. Cattleman's Assn. Democrat. Roman Catholic. Home and Farm: Cedar Ln Farm RR 1 Box 286 Sturgeon MO 65284-9504

FASSLER, CRYSTAL G., marketing consultant; b. Marion, Ohio, Mar. 15, 1942; d. Lloyd C. and Iola M. (Runkle) Mahaffey; student public schs., Prospect, Ohio; m. Donald D. Fassler, May 6, 1960; 1 son, Curtis A. Media buyer H. Swink Advt., Marion, 1968-73; media buyer and planner Tracey Locke Advt., Columbus, Ohio, 1973-74, Lord, Sullivan & Yoder Advt., Marion, 1974-82; youth conselor State of Ohio Employment Services, Marion, 1982-83; nat. mktg. consultant WMRN-AM and FM, Marion, 1983-84, gen. mgr., 1985; gen. sales mgr. WRFD Radio, Columbus, 1986-90; gen. sales mgr. Stas. WMAN-AM and WYHT-FM, Mansfield, Ohio, 1990-92, media cons., Dimension Media Svcs., Marion, Ohio, 1992-93, cons., Credit Bur. Co., Marion, 1993-94, ptnr. Media Mktg. Strategies, 1994—. Home and Office: 1846 Smeltzer Rd Marion OH 43302-7352

FASSNACHT, DEBRA KERR, communications executive; b. Fairfax, Okla., Aug. 15, 1958; d. David Harold Kerr and Dixie (Lee) King; m. Harold John Fassnacht, Jr., July 5, 1980; 1 child, Anne Claire. BA in Journalism, U. Okla., 1980. Copy editor Okla. Daily Newspaper, Norman, 1978-80; staff writer Phillips Petroleum Co., Bartlesville, Okla., 1979; editorial asst. Gruy Petroleum Tech., Bartlesville, 1980-81, info. specialist, 1981-83, office mgr., 1983; pub. rels. coord. IIT Rsch. Inst., Bartlesville, 1983-85; pub. rels. mgr. IIT Rsch. Inst., Chgo., 1985-88, mgr. corp. comms., 1988-93; pub. rels. & mktg. mgr. John G. Shedd Aquarium, Chgo., 1993-94, communications dir., 1994-95, v.p. comm., 1995—; comm. dir. Nat. Atty.'s Comm. for Transplant Awareness, 1993—. Author, editor: IITRI: A Fifty Year Portrait, 1986; editor: Reservoir Characterization, 1985; author brochures; contbr. articles to mags. Pres. St. James Ch. Parish Coun., Bartlesville, 1984-85; sec. Concern (food pantry and svcs. for poor), Bartlesville, 1983-85; membership recruiter Bartlesville Area C. of C., 1984-85; lector, parish coun. mem. Old St. Mary's Ch., Chgo., 1991—; mem. Chgo. NOW. Mem. Pub. Rels. Soc. Am., Soc. Profl. Journalists, Am. Zoo and Aquarium Assn., Am. Assn. Museums, Am. Inst. Physics (pub. info. adv. com. 1990-93), Arts and Bus. Coun. (Chgo.), Gamma Phi Beta. Democrat. Roman Catholic. Office: John G Shedd Aquarium 1200 S Lake Shore Dr Chicago IL 60605-2435

FAST, KELLY, design engineer; b. Livingston, N.J., Mar. 25, 1968. BS in Mech. Engring., Cornell U., 1990. Tng. engr. mgmt. Auto. Product. Sys. Ingersoll Rand, Farmington Hills, Mich., 1990-91; design engr. Aro Corp.-Ingersoll Rand, Bryan, Ohio, 1990—, engr. mgmt. tng., 1991-93; design engr. Aro Corp.-Ingersoll Rand, Stemse, Ohio, Belgium, 1993-94; project engr. Aro Corp.-Ingersoll Rand, Bryan, Ohio, 1994-95. Patentee in field. Office: Ingersoll Rand Divsn Aro Corp 1 Aro Ctr Bryan OH 43506-1100

FATUM, SANDRA KAYE, nurse; b. Reed City, Mich., Nov. 19, 1965; d. Dennis Charles and Marlene Karon (Swanson) F. Lic. practical nurse, Mercy Sch. Practical Nursing, Cadillac, Mich., 1984; ADN, West Shore Community Coll., Scottville, Mich., 1986; BSN, Ferris State U., Big Rapids, Mich., 1989; MSN, Grand Valley State U., Allendale, Mich., 1993. RN, Mich.; cert. pediatric nurse; cert. ACLS, BCLS instr. Staff nurse Mecosta County Gen. Hosp., Big Rapids, Butterworth Hosp., Grand Rapids, Mich.; instr. pediatrics Southwestern Mich. Coll, Dowagiac. Home: 1347 Wayne St Niles MI 49120-1848

FATZINGER, DALE ROGER, geographer, educator; b. Allentown, Pa., Jan. 14, 1935; s. Charles Edward and Geraldine Katherine Fatzinger; m. Marie Margaret Sneddon, May 28, 1955 (div. Apr. 1978); children: Curt D., Eric W.; m. Susan Carol Edwards, June 1, 1979; children: (adopted) D. Grant Edwards, Gregory J. Edwards. BS, Kutztown State U., 1956; MS, U. Wis., 1958; PhD, Mich. State U., 1971. Prof. geography U. Wis., Platteville, 1957-59, 94-95, dean Coll. Arts and Scis., 1979-94, dean emeritus, 1995—. Author: A Historical Geography of Lead and Zinc Mining in Southwest Wisconson 1820-1920: A Century of Change, 1971. Scholarship U.S. Fulbright Commn., 1961; fellow NSF, 1963. Mem. Nat. Coun. Geog. Edn., Rotary Club Platteville (pres.), Phi Kappa Phi, Gamma Theta Upsilon, Kappa Delta Pi. Office: Univ Wis Platteville 244 Gardner Hall Platteville WI 53818

FAUBEL, GERALD LEE, agronomist, golf course superintendent; b. Normal, Ill., Feb. 14, 1941; s. Elmer Joseph and Agnes (Alexander) F.; m. Sally Sue Shook, Feb. 22, 1973; 1 child, Sarah. AAS, Iowa State U., 1963, MS, 1969. Golf course supt. Lawsonia Golf Course, Green Lake, Wis., 1962-63, South Hills Club, Fond du Lac, Wis., 1963-68, Saginaw (Mich.) Country Club, 1969—; pres. Exec. Golf Search, Inc.; dir. Mich. Turfgrass Found., Lansing, 1978-81, sec.-treas., v.p., 1982, pres., 1984. Mem. Parks commn. Saginaw (Mich.) Twp. 1972-78; mem. Valderrama (Spain) Scholarship Com., 1991—. Mem. Golf Course Supt. Assn. Am. (bd. dirs. 1985-92, sec.-treas. 1988, v.p. 1989, pres. 1990), U.S. Golf Assn., Mich. Assn. Agr. (exec. sec. 1991-94), Nat. Inst. Golf Mgmt. (bd. regents), Nat. Golf Found. Republican. Mennonite. Home: 699 Westchester Rd Saginaw MI 48603-6232

FAULKNER, ANITA L., stock brokerage executive; b. Kokomo, Ind., Mar. 14, 1949; d. Charles R. and Imogene (Smith) Hurd. Lic. series 7 Nat. Assn. Securities Dealers. Sec. Greeno Ins., Kokomo, K.J. Brown, Kokomo, 1980-87; v.p., stockbroker Smith Gaylor Investments Inc., Kokomo, 1987—. Lutheran. Office: Smith Gaylor Investments PO Box 4058 2713 Rockford Ln Kokomo IN 46904

FAULKNER, JOHN C., mathematics and data management consultant; b. Kenton, Ohio, Mar. 5, 1946; s. Carlos Ansley and Eleanor Jane (Machetanz) F.; m. Leah Peeples, Aug. 15, 1970; children: Scott, David. BS, The Citadel, 1968; MS, Tex. A&M U., 1972. Supr. Engring. Computer Ctr., Dearborn, Mich., 1973-84; chair geometry com. U.S. TGES/PDES Orgn. Nat. Inst. Standards, Gaithersburg, Md., 1989-91; sr. tech. devel. engr. SDRC, Milford, Ohio, 1984-86, mgr. math. group, 1989-94, dir. data mgmt., 1994-95, sr.tech. cons., 1995—. Author materials in field. Sunday sch. tchr. Milford United Meth. Ch., 1990-93; chmn. Tecumseh dist. Boy Scouts Am.

FAULS, THOMAS J., machinery executive; b. Detroit, Feb. 18, 1958. Student, Wayne State U., 1976-78. Pres. Perch Machinery Inc., Detroit, 1976—. Republican. Roman Catholic. Office: Perch Mfg Inc 19140 Mount Elliott St Detroit MI 48234-2723

FAUST, MARK JOSEPH, management consultant, speaker, trainer; b. Cin., Apr. 21, 1966; s. Robert Joseph and Mary Ann (Promberger) F.; m. Julie Ann Tuke, Apr. 28, 1990. Student, U. Cin., 1984. Registered profl. hynotherapist. Prin. Echelon, Cin., 1985-87; mgmt. cons. Executech Consultants Inc., Cin., 1987-89; prin. Echelon Mgmt., Cin., 1990—; speaker, guest instr. Univ. Cin. Author: The Principles of Top Echelon Performance, 1992; contbr. articles to profl. jours.; guest on several Cin. radio and tv programs. Mem. Nat. Rep. Com., 1982—, Rep. Hispanic Com., 1989-90, pres. coun. Ohio Buckeye Boys Scouts State; official of Hamilton County Rep. Party. Mem. ASTD, Internat. Platform Assn., Nat. Spkrs. Assn., Ohio Spkrs. Forum, Anderson Hills C. of C., Cin. Art Mus., Cin. Hist. Soc., Toastmasters Internat. (pres. 1989-90). Republican. Roman Catholic. Home: 888 Alnetta Dr Cincinnati OH 45230 Office: Echelon Mgmt 26 E 6th St # 800 Cincinnati OH 45202

FAUTH, JOHN J., venture capitalist. Chmn. Churchill Capital, Inc., Mpls. Office: Churchill Capital Inc 333 S 7th St Ste 2400 Minneapolis MN 55402*

FAWCETT, JAMES DAVIDSON, herpetologist, educator; b. New Plymouth, N.Z., Jan. 10, 1933; s. James and Edna Lola (Catterick) F.; B.Sc., U. N.Z., 1960; M.Sc., U. Auckland (N.Z.), 1964; Ph.D., U. Colo., 1975; m. Georgene Ellen Tyler, Dec. 21, 1968. Head dept. biology Kings Coll., Auckland, 1960; grad. demonstrator dept. zoology U. Auckland, 1961-62, sr. demonstrator, 1963-64; grad. asst. U. Colo., 1969-72; instr. biology U. Nebr., Omaha, 1972-75, asst. prof., 1975-81, asso. prof., 1981—. Recipient Great Tchr. award U. Nebr., 1981. Mem. Royal Soc. N.Z., N.Z. Assn. Scientists, Am. Soc. Zoologists, Soc. Systematic Zoology, Herpetologists League, Brit. Soc. Herpetologists, AAAS, Nebr. Herpetological Soc. (pres. 1979-80), Sigma Xi (pres. Omaha chpt. 1980-81), Phi Sigma. Contbr. articles to profl. jours. Home: 309 S 56th St Omaha NE 68132-3413 Office: U Nebr Biology Dept Omaha NE 68182

FAWELL, BEVERLY JEAN, state legislator; b. Oak Park, Ill., Sept. 17, 1930. BA, Elmhurst Coll., 1970; postgrad., No. Ill. U., 1974. Mem. Ill. Ho. of Reps., Springfield, 1981-83, Ill. Senate, Springfield, 1983—. Republican. Office: 213 Wesley Ste 105 Wheaton IL 60187

FAWELL, HARRIS W., congressman; b. West Chicago, Ill., Mar. 25, 1929; m. Ruth Johnson, 1954; children: Richard, Jane, John. Student, Naperville North Central Coll., 1949; LL.D., Chgo. Kent Coll. Law, 1952. Ptnr. Fawell, James & Brooks, Naperville, Ill., 1954-84; mem. Ill. Senate, Springfield, 1963-77; gen. counsel Ill. Assn. Park Dists., 1977-84; mem. 99th-104th Congresses from 13th Ill. dist., 1985—; mem. House Econ. and Edn. Opportunity Com., chmn. subcom. on employer-employee rels.; mem. House Sci. Com. Office: US Ho of Reps 2159 Rayburn Bldg Washington DC 20515

FAWELL, JEFFREY BRUCE, lawyer; b. St. Charles, Ill., June 5, 1952; s. Bruce Raymond and Beverly (Landon) F.; m. Blanche Hill, Aug. 21, 1983; children: Daniel, Timothy, Joseph. BA, North Ctrl. Coll., Naperville, Ill., 1974; JD, So. Ill. U., Carbondale, 1977. Bar: Ill. 1977. Dep. pub. defender DuPage County Pub. Defender's OFfice, Wheaton, Ill., 1977-83; ptnr. Fawell & Fawell, Wheaton, 1983—. Treas. Milton Twp. Rep. Orgn., Wheaton, 1988—. Mem. Nat. Assn. Criminal Def. Attys., Am. Immigration Lawyer's Assn., Ill. Attys. for Criminal Justice, Ill. Bar Assn., DuPage County Bar Assn. Office: Fawell & Fawell 2100 Manchester Rd Ste 101 Wheaton IL 60187

FAWKS, STEVEN W., dentist; b. Moberly, Mo., Dec. 5, 1952; s. Alfred E. and Viola Gennevieve (Buffington) F.; m. Dolores A. Mason, Oct. 23, 1953; children: Stephanie R., Angela M., Ryan P. BS in Biology, N.E. Mo. State U., 1975; DDS, U. Mo., Kanas City, 1979. Cert. gen. dentistry, Mo. Pvt. practice dentist Richmond, Mo., 1979—; pres. Lexington (Mo.) Dental Ctr., 1994—. Mem. bd. R XVI Sch. Bd., Richmond, 1991—, Richmond (Mo.) Little League, 1995. With Mo. Army Nat. Guard, 1971-77. Mem. ADA, Mo. Dental Assn., Greater Kansas City Dental Assn., Nat. Muzzleloading Rifle Assn. Office: 205 Spartan Dr Richmond MO 64085

FAXON, JACK, headmaster; b. Detroit, June 9, 1936; s. Morris Faxon and Pauline Krimsky. BS in Edn., Wayne State U., 1956, MEd, 1958; MA in History, U. Mich., 1963. Tchr. Detroit Pub. Schs., 1956-64; founder, headmaster Internat. Sch., Beverly Hills, Mich., 1968—; corp. dir. Cellex Bioscis. Corp. Inc., Mpls., 1988—; dir. Quest Biotech. Inc., Detroit, 1986—. Paintings exhibited in group shows at Wayne State U. (Arts award 1978), U. Mich., 1981; dancer The Nutcracker Ballet, Detroit Symphony Orch./Dance Detroit, 1979, 88-95; singer Die Fledermaus, Naughty Marietta, Mich. Opera Theater, 1976, 77, 78, 79, 94. Elected del. to Mich. Constnl. Conv., State of Mich., Lansing, 1961-62, elected rep. to State Ho. of Reps., Lansing, 1964-70, elected senator, Lansing, 1970-94; pres. pro tem Mich. Senate, Lansing, 1977-83; bd. dirs. Anti Defamation League, Friends of African Art, Detroit, 1987-91, Friends of Asian Art, Detroit Inst. Arts, 1984-91, Russian Am. Studio Theater, 1991—; bd. trustees Mich. Libr., Lansing, 1976-87; mem. Edn. Commn. of State, Denver, 1975-85, Mich. Hist. Soc., 1981-89, Mus. African Art, N.Y.C., 1993—. Recipient 1st pl. award Mich. Watercolor Soc., 1978, Citation of Merit, Wayne County Coun. on Smoking Health, 1981; Eagleton fellow Rutgers U., 1966. Mem. Founder Soc. Detroit Inst. Arts (life), Pres.'s Club (U. Mich.). Democrat. Office: The Internat Sch 32605 Bellvine Ter Beverly Hills MI 48025

FAY, LAURA ELIZABETH, financial analyst; b. Greater Geneva, Wis., July 12, 1960; d. Garfield James and Margaret Vee Coerper; m. Peter Carlyle Fay, Nov. 27, 1981. BSBA in Fin. and Banking, U. Wis., 1982; MBA, Keller Grad. Sch. Mgmt., Chgo., 1992, M Cert. in Human Resource Mgmt., 1994. Cert. paralegal, Ill. Corp. fin. analyst Superior Bank, Hinsdale, Ill., 1985-88; asst. v.p. compliance officer First Bank of Highland Park, Ill., 1989-91; asst. v.p. comml. lending Am. Nat. Bank & Trust Co., Waukegan, Ill., 1991-94, First Midwest Bancorp, Waukegan, Ill., 1994—; bd. dirs. ReBound, Inc., Waukegan. Mem. adv. bd. Salvation Army, Lake County, Ill., 1994—. Mem. Exch. Club. (pres.-elect), Lake County Alpha Chi Omega Alumnae (treas.). Republican. Lutheran. Home: 34615 N Hunt Club Rd Gurnee IL 60031

FAY, SISTER MAUREEN A., university president. BA in English magna cum laude, Siena Heights Coll., 1960; MA in English, U. Detroit, 1966; PhD, U. Chgo., 1976. Tchr. English, speech, moderator student newspaper, student council St. Paul High Sch., Grosse Pointe, Mich., 1960-64; chairperson English dept., dir. student dramatics, moderator student publs. Dominican High Sch., Detroit, 1964-69; co-dir. Cath. student ctr. Adrian (Mich.) Coll., 1969-71; instr. English Siena Heights Coll., Adrian, 1969-71; evaluators inst. criminal justice execs. U. Chgo., 1971-73; instr. English U. Ill., Chgo., 1971-74; dir. evaluation sch. new learning DePaul U., Chgo., 1974-75; fellow in acad. adminstrn. Saint Xavier Coll., Chgo., 1975-76, dean. grad. studies, 1979-83, dean continuing edn., 1976-83; asst. prof. No. Ill. U., Dekalb, 1980-83; pres. Mercy Coll. Detroit, 1983-90, U. Detroit Mercy, 1990—; v.p. VAUT Corp, bd. dirs. four inner city high schs., Archdiocese Chgo.; mem. exec. com. Assn. Mercy Colls.; adv. com. Adult Learning Svcs., The Coll. Bd., Met. Affairs Corp. of Detroit and S.E. Mich., cons. Nat. Assn. for Religious Women, 1974-75, North Cen. Assn. Colls. and Schs., evaluator commn. on higher edn.; trustee Rosary Coll., River Forest, Ill., New Detroit, Inc., 1993; emeritus mem. div. bd. Mercy Hosps. and Health Svcs. of Detroit; bd. dirs. Nat. Bank of Detroit., Detroit Econ. Growth Corp., 1992; mem. Nat. Commn. Ind. Higher Edn.; commr. North Centrl Assocs., Commn. on Instns. of Higher Edn., 1993. Asst. editor: (book rev.): Adult Education, A Journal of Research and Theory, 1971-74. Bd. dirs. United Way SE Mich., 1991, Assn. Catholic Colls. and Univs., 1992; Steering com. Metro Detroit GIVES; exec. com., edn. task force Detroit

Strategic Planning com., 1987; trustee Mich. Opera Theatre; bd. dirs. Greater Detroit Interfaith Round Table Nat. Conf. Christians and Jews, Inc., The Detroit Symphony; mem. Nat. Bipartisan Commn. on Ind. Higher Edn. in U.S., 1993. Mem. Am. Assn. Higher Edn., North Cen. Assn. (cons., evaluator commn. on higher edn.), Nat. Assn. Ind. Colls. and Univs. (bd. dirs.), Assn. Ind. Colls. and Univs. of Mich. (exec. com., chairperson), Am. Assn. Cath. Colls. and Univs., AAUW, Pi Lambda Theta. Office: U Detroit Mercy Office of the President 4001 W McNichols Rd Detroit MI 48219-0900*

FAY, PETER CARLYLE, mechanical engineer; b. Pitts., Nov. 2, 1958; s. Carlyle Waldie and Marjorie Ann (Sundquist) F.; m. Laura Elizabeth Coerper, Nov. 27, 1981. BSME, U. Wis., 1981; MBA, Northwestern U., 1992, M Human Resources Mgmt., 1994, postgrad., 1995. Registered profl. engr., Wis., Ill. Field engr. Schlumberger Wells Svcs., Laurel, Miss., 1981-83; tech. engr. Commonwealth Edison, Braidwood, Ill., 1983-84, startup test engr., 1984-85, hot functional dir., 1985-86, fuel load coord., 1986, startup test coord., 1986-88; supr. maintenance staff Commonwealth Edison, Zion, Ill., 1988-92; integrated assessment adminstr. Commonwealth Edison, Downers Grove, Ill., 1992—. Mem. ASME, Am. Nuclear Soc. Republican. Lutheran. Home: 34615 N Hunt Club Rd Gurnee IL 60031-2434 Office: Commonwealth Edison 1400 Opus Pl Downers Grove IL 60515-1198

FAZIO, ANTHONY LEE, investment company executive; b. Wheeling, W.Va., Jan. 27, 1937; s. Frank G. and Julia Louise (DeFillipo) F.; m. Faye Elizabeth Kelly, Sept. 3, 1964; children: Tracey Lee, Kelly Ann. BSEE, W.Va. U., 1959. Registered investment advisor, investment mgmt. cons., bus. mgmt. cons.; cert. fin. planner. With computer div. RCA, 1964-72, mgr. product mktg., 1970-71, mgr. systems planning, 1971-72; dir. bus. and product planning Univac, 1972-73, dir. product mktg. and bus./product planning N.Am., 1973-75, regional mgr., 1975-77; v.p. sales Sycor, Inc., Ann Arbor, Mich., 1977-78; v.p. sales No. Telecom Systems Corp., 1978-79, v.p. mktg., 1979-80; pres. Gibbs Irwin Investments Co., 1981-83; product procurement and due diligence officer Midland Mgmt. Corp., 1983-86; pres. Fazio Investments, Inc., 1986—. With U.S. Army, 1959-61. Mem. Inst. Cert. Fin. Planners, Minn. Soc. Inst. Cert. Fin. Planners (pres.-elect, bd. dirs.), Tau Beta Pi, Eta Kappa Nu. Republican. Home: 4770 Regents Walk Excelsior MN 55331-9209 Office: 4770 Regents Walk Ste 100 Excelsior MN 55331-9209

FAZIO, FAYE ELIZABETH, financial planner; b. Wheeling, W.Va., Dec. 11, 1946. Fin. cons. Fin. Network Investment Corp., Edina, Minn., 1986-90; para-planner Multi-Fin. Securities, Excelsior, Minn., 1990—. Republican. Methodist. Office: Multi-Fin Securities 4770 Regents Walk Excelsior MN 55331-9209

FAZIO, PETER VICTOR, JR., lawyer; b. Chgo., Jan. 22, 1940; s. Peter Victor and Marie Rose (LaMantia) F.; m. Patti Ann Campbell, Jan. 3, 1966; children: Patti-Marie, Catherine, Peter. AB, Holy Cross Coll., Worcester, Mass., 1961; JD, U. Mich., 1964. Bar: Ill. 1964, D.C. 1981, Ind. 1993, U.S. Dist. Ct. (no. dist.) Ill. 1965, U.S. Ct. Appeals (7th cir.) 1972, U.S. Supreme Ct. 1977, U.S. Ct. Appeals (D.C. cir.) 1988. Assoc. Schiff, Hardin & Waite, Chgo., 1964-70, ptnr., 1970-82, 84—; exec. v.p. Internat. Capital Equipment, Chgo., 1982-83, also dir., 1982-85, sec., 1982-87; bd. dirs. Planmetrics Inc., Chgo., 1984-92, Chgo. Lawyers Commn. for Civil Rights Under Law, 1976-82, co-chmn., 1978-80; bd. dirs. Seton Health Corp. No. Ill., Chgo 1987-90, vice chmn., 1989-90. Trustee Barat Coll., Lake Forest, Ill., 1977-82; bd. dirs. St. Joseph Hosp., Chgo., 1990-95, mem. exec. adv. bd. 1984-89, chmn., 1986-89; bd. dirs. Cath. Health Ptnrs., 1995—; dir. exec. com. Ill. Coalition, 1994—, Northwest Ind. Forum, 1994—. Mem. ABA (vice chmn. program com., chmn. corp. fin. com., mem. coun. 1991-94, sect. pub. utlity, transp. and comm. law), Ill. State Bar Assn., Chgo. Bar Assn., Fed. Bar Assn., Fed. Energy Bar Assn., Edison Electric Inst. (chmn. generation, transmission and environ. regulation subcom. legal com.), Am. Gas Assn. (mng. comm., legal sect.), Am. Soc. Corp. Secs., Nat. Health Lawyers Assn., Am. Acad. Hosp. Attys., Am. Soc. Law and Medicine, Met. Club (Chgo.), Econ. Club of Chgo. Office: Schiff Hardin & Waite 7300 Sears Tower 233 S Wacker Dr Chicago IL 60606-6306

FEAGIN, SUSAN LOUISE, philosophy educator; b. Bklyn., July 11, 1948; d. Roy Chester and Lillian Elizabeth (Joyner) F.; m. Gerald Cushing MacCallum, Jr., June 19, 1977 (dec.). BA, Fla. State U., 1969; MA, U. Wis., 1973, PhD, 1975. Lectr. U. Wis., Madison, 1975-76, vis. assoc. prof., 1990-91; asst. prof. Bowling Green (Ohio) State U., 1976-77; asst. prof. philosophy U. Mo., Kansas City, 1977-83, assoc. prof., 1983-96, prof., 1996—; panelist NEH, 1988. Author: Reading with Feeling: The Aesthetics of Appreciation, 1996; book rev. editor Jour. Aesthetics and Art Criticism, 1988-94; contbr. numerous articles and revs. to profl. jours. Recipient faculty rsch. award U. Kansas City Trustees, 1988; grantee NEH, summer 1983, rsch. grantee U. Mo., 1988, 93. Mem. Am. Soc. for Aesthetics (trustee 1988-91), Am. Philos. Assn., Internat. Assn. for Aesthetics, Ctrl. States Philos. Assn. (v.p. 1995, pres. 1996), Kansas City Area Philosophy Assn. (v.p. 1988-89, pres. 1989-90). Office: Dept Philosophy U Mo Kansas City MO 64110

FEAGLES, GERALD FRANKLIN, marketing executive; b. Kansas City, Kans., Dec. 8, 1934; s. George Joseph and Florence Ada (Johnson) F.; m. Eleanor Jean Holder, Aug. 31, 1957; 1 child, Gerald Franklin II. Student, Kansas City Jr. Coll., 1953-55. Mktg. and sales rep. Sears Roebuck and Co., Kansas City, 1963-70; br. mgr. SunarHauserman, Overland Park, Kans., 1970-86; mgr. bus. devel. govt. svcs. group The Austin Co., Kansas City, 1986-91; mgr. mktg. and indsl. divsn. Black & Veatch Architects & Engrs., Kansas City, 1991-93; mgr. ctrl. region Va. Metal Industries Inc., Orange, Va., 1994—. Com. chmn. Boy Scouts of Am. Kansas City, 1973. Mem. Kansas City C. of C., Constrn. Specifications Inst., Prodrs. Coun., Internat. Facility Mgmt. Assn., Assoc. Gen. Contractors, Soc. Am. Mil. Engrs. Office: Va Metal Industries 1702 N 155th St Basehor KS 66007-9394

FEARS, LILLIE MAE, journalism educator, mass media researcher; b. Holly Grove, Ark., Jan. 6, 1962; d. Willie Bert and Rebecca (Coleman) F. AA in Gen. Studies, Phillips County C.C., Helena, Ark., 1982; BS in Journalism, Ark. State U., 1984, MS in Mass. Comm., 1986; postgrad., U. Mo., 1993—. Instr. developmental studies Phillips County C.C., Helena, Ark., 1986-87, Philander Smith Coll., Little Rock, 1987-89; lectr. in journalism U. Ark., Little Rock, 1989; instr. in journalism Ark. State U., Jonesboro, 1990—. Mem. Soc. Profl. Journalists (bd. dirs. 1992-93), Internat. Comm. Assn., Assn. Edn. in Mass Comm. Home: 1305 Ashland Rd Apt A Columbia MO 65201 Office: U Mo Sch Journalism Columbia MO 65211

FEATHER, LISA KAY, physician assistant; b. Mt. Vernon, Ill., Sept. 14, 1963; d. Fred E. and D. June (McKinney) Bradford; m. Kenneth R. Feather, Oct. 2, 1981; children: Randall Ray, Brandi Jo. ADN, Frontier C.C., 1982; BSN, So. Ill. U., 1988; physician asst., U. N.D., 1996. Cert. CPR, Am. Heart Assn.; cert. ACLS instr., BTLS instr.; cert. trauma nurse specialist, emergency nurse. Staff RN ortho/neuro unit Good Samaritan Hosp., Mt. Vernon, Ill., 1982-85, staff RN emergency dept., 1985-88, staff RN ICU/CCU, 1988; PRN office nurse Drs. Sahni and Chow, Mt. Vernon, 1988-90; staff RN emergency dept., dir. emergency dept and Emergency Med. Svcs.coord. Good Samaritan Regional Health Ctr., Mt. Vernon, 1990-94; EMT lead instr. Rend Lake Coll., 1991. Mem. Ill. Coun. Nurse Mgrs., Emergency Nurse Assn., Sigma Theta Tau (Epsilon Eta). Office: Good Samaritan Regional Health Ctr 605 N 12th St Mount Vernon IL 62864-2857

FEATHERSTON, JAMES WILLIAM, freelance writer; b. Doniphan, Mo., July 3, 1923; s. Henry Marion and Etta Frances (Rideout) F.; m. Virginia Rae Frazer, Nov. 14, 1941 (div. Apr. 1966); children: Ronald, Helene, Jon; m. Donna Jean, June 28, 1990. Diploma, U.S. Army Command, Ft. Leavenworth, Kans., 1970. Officer USAF, England, 1944-45; sheriff Ripley County, Mo., 1948-52; conservation agt. Butler County, Mo., 1953-56; svc. rep. Blue Cross, Blue Shield, St. Louis, 1957-63; mgr. Unitog, St. Louis, 1964-83; herbalist, instr., writer. Author: Reflections, 1983, 2d edit., 1989; contbr. articles popular publs. Mem. VFW, Masons.

FEATHERSTONAUGH, HENRY GORDON, psychologist; b. San Diego, Nov. 11, 1917; s. Henry Stuart and Evelyn (Borrow) F.; BS, U. Calif., Berkeley, 1939; MS, Lehigh U., 1974; PhD, U. Mo., 1978; Diplomate Am. Bd. Sexology; m. Nancy Ellen Couper, July 28, 1946 (div.); children: Wendy, Rusby. Chemist, H.J. Heinz Co., Berkeley, Calif., 1938-40; dist. mgr. Union Carbide Corp., N.Y.C., 1945-73; geriatric svcs. coord. The Ctr. for Mental Health, Anderson, Ind., 1979-82; co-founder, pres. Living Skills Inst., Inc., Indpls., 1982—; lectr. in field. Exec. bd. Madison County Council on Aging, 1979—. Served with U.S. Army, 1941-43, USAAF, 1943-45; ATO, CBI. Decorated Air medal with oak leaf cluster, D.F.C.; Lehigh U. teaching asst. and tuition grantee, 1972-73; U. Mo. research grantee, 1974-78. Mem. APA, Ind. Counselors Assn. on Alcohol and Drug Abuse, Psi Chi, Phi Kappa Phi. Contbr. articles to profl. jours. Office: 8204 Westfield Blvd Indianapolis IN 46240-2366

FEDDERS, DON D., accounting executive; b. Orange City, Iowa, Apr. 8, 1943. CPA, Ill. Pres. Williams and Co., Cons., Sioux City, 1964—. Bd. dirs. Woodbury County Selective Svc. System, Sioux City, 1991—. Mem. AICPA (bd. dirs. 1988-93). Republican. Home: 3700 S Briar Path Sioux City IA 51104-1323 Office: Williams & Co Cons 814 Pierce St Sioux City IA 51101-1004

FEENEY, DON JOSEPH, JR., psychologist; b. Greenville, N.C., Jan. 17, 1948; s. Don Joseph Sr. and Louise (Saieed) F.; 1 child, Kelly Lynn. BA, Colgate U., 1971; MA, Gov.'s State U., 1973; PhD, Loyola U., Chgo., 1979. Registered psychologist, Ill., Ind.; cert. addictions counselor. Clin. dir. Champaign (Ill.) Coun. on Alcoholism, 1976-79; pvt. practice psychology, hypnotherapy, family services Downers Grove, Ill., 1979—; pvt. practice psychology, hypnotherapy and family svcs. Dangerous Drugs Com., Chgo., 1979-80; psychologist Tri-City Mental Health Ctr., East Chicago, Ind., 1980-82; psychologist alcohol treatment program Christ Hosp., Oak Lawn, Ill., 1982—; cons. Psychol. Cons. Svcs., Downers Grove, Ill., 1985—; chmn. adv. coun. on alcoholism Govs. State U., University Park, Ill., 1979-82; devel., presenter self-hypnosis and wellness programs on smoking, weight control and chem. abuse. Contbr. articles to profl. jours.; guest cons. to nat. talk shows, Oprah Winfrey, Jerry Springer, Jenny Jones, others. Fellow, Loyola U., 1976. Mem. APA, Ill. Psychol. Assn. Roman Catholic. Office: Psychol Cons Svcs 6900 Main St Ste 54 Downers Grove IL 60516-3455

FEENEY, WILLIAM S., financial advisor; b. Fargo, N.D., Sept. 3, 1961. BS, U. Colo., 1983. Fin. advisor Driscoll Bernam, Northbrook, Ill., 1985-90, Paine Webber, Northbrook, 1990—; mem. adv. bd. Nuvena Adv. Coun. Syndicate Mgmt., Chgo., 1992. Republican. Presbyterian. Office: Paine Webber 5 Revere Dr Northbrook IL 60062-1566

FEENSTRA, LAURENCE HENRY, physician; b. Grand Rapids, Mich., Aug. 27, 1927; s. Henry and Agnes (Hofstra) F. m. June Elaine Nykamp, Aug. 15, 1952; children: Richard D., Lori Beth, David Scott, Cheryl Sue. BS, Calvin Coll., Grand Rapids, 1949; MD, U. Mich., 1952. Diplomate Am. Bd. Internal Medicine, Am. Bd. Geriatrics. Mem. staff, cons. Buttwerworth Hosp., Grand Rapids, 1958—, chief internal medicine, 1971-75, program dir. internal medicine, 1971-90; mem. staff Blodgett Meml. Hosp., Grand Rapids, 1958-70, mem. courtesy staff, 1970—; mem. staff St. Mary's Hosp., Grand Rapids, 1958-70; clin. prof. medicine Mich State u., 1984—. Lt. M.C., USN, 1953-55. Fellow ACP; mem. AMA, Mich. State Med. Soc., Kent County Med. Soc., Mich. Athletic Club, East Hills Athletic Club. Home: 2137 N Cross Creek Dr SE Grand Rapids MI 49508 Office: Butterworth Hosp 100 Michigan St NE Grand Rapids MI 49503

FEFERMAN, MARTIN EARL, neurosurgeon; b. South Bend, Ind., July 21, 1922; s. Reuben and Bessie (Feldman) F.; m. Carol P. Feinberg, July 7, 1946; children:Betty, Peggy, John. BS, U. Mich., 1944, MD, 1946. Diplomate Am. Bd. Neurol. Surgery. Resident in neurosurgery U. Minn. Hosp., Mpls., 1946-52; chief neurosurgery Walter Reed Army Hosp., Washington, 1954-56; chief surgery St. Joseph's Hosp., South Bend, Ind., 1964; chief surgery Meml. Hosp., South Bend, 1967, assoc. dir. med. staff affairs and occupl. health, 1992—; pvt. practice South Bend, 1946—; cons. Surgeon Gen., U.S. Army, Washington, 1954-56; mem. credentials com. Ind. ACS, 1978-82; bd. dirs. Norwest Bank Ind., South Bend. Pres. Temple Bethel, South Bend, 1967-68; mem. Ind. Motor Vehicles Bd., Indpls., 1974-82; trustee St. Joseph County, St. Joseph, Ind., 1972-74, mem. econ. devel. bd.; bd dirs. Salvation Army, 1972-79. Capt. U.S. Army, 1954-56. Named Sagamore of the Wabash, Gov. Ind., 1974. Mem. Am. Assn. Neurosurgeons, Neurosurg. Soc. Am., Congress Neurol. Surgeons, Soc. Cons. Armed Forces. Republican. Jewish. Home: 17913 Ashmont Pl South Bend IN 46635 Office: Meml Office Plaza 707 N Michigan St South Bend IN 46601

FEHLBERG, BRENDA, investment company manager; b. Cedar Rapids, Iowa, July 23, 1964. Lic. prin. Nat. Assn. Securities Dealers. Trust sec. 1st Trust & Savs. Bank, Cedar Rapids, 1985-91; ops. mgr. Heartland Investment Assn., Cedar Rapids, 1991—. Vol. March of Dimes, Cedar Rapids, 1990—. Republican. Methodist. Office: Heartland Investment Assn PO Box 10167 4403 1st Ave S Cedar Rapids IA 52410

FEIBEL, FREDERICK ARTHUR, financial consultant; b. Chgo., Oct. 27, 1942; s. Fred and Emma Feibel; BSEE, Purdue U., 1964; MBA, Northwestern U., 1970; m. Marlene Ruth Edwards, Aug. 7, 1965; 1 son, Frederick Curtis. Project engr. Johnson Controls Corp., Milw., 1964-69; sr. mgmt. cons. Arthur Andersen & Co., Chgo., 1970-76; rep. pension fund evaluation A.G. Becker Securities Co., Chgo. 1976-77; spl. agt. Northwestern Mut. Life Ins. Co., Milw., 1977-82; pres. F.A. Feibel Fin. Assocs., Northbrook, Ill., 1982—. Chmn., Village of Northbrook Bicentennial Commn., 1975-76, Boy Scouts Am. Troop 67, 1990—, chmn.; v.p., Northbrook Civic Found., 1977, pres., 1978, also bd. dirs., life mem.; pres. Northbrook Hist. Soc., 1977, also bd. dirs.; deacon Northfield Cmty. Ch., 1978-81, asst. treas. 1986—. Recipient Disting. Svc. award State of Ill., 1976, Northbrook Civic Found., 1983, Civic Svc. award Northbrook B'nai B'rith, 1981-82, Disting. Svc. award Northbrook Civic Found., 1989; Vol. Initiative of Pvt. Sector Recognition award, Northbrook C. of C. and Industry, 1985, Vol. Appreciation award Northbrook Park Dist., 1987; named Northbrook Rotary Man of Yr., 1978-79, Hall of Fame Ill. Festival Assn., 1992; Mem. Am. Soc. CLU & ChFC, Greater North Shore Estate Planning Coun., Eta Kappa Nu, Tau Beta Pi. Home: 1342 Hillside Rd Northbrook IL 60062-4613 Office: FA Feibel Fin Assocs PO Box 355 Northbrook IL 60065-0355

FEICHTINGER, JOSEF, engineer; b. Altmuenster, Austria, Sept. 17, 1940; came to U.S., 1983.; Bachelor, Fed. Tech. Coll., Vienna, Austria, 1968. Chief engr. Clevel. Crane, Luxembourg, Luxembourg, 1969-84; mgr. mech. engring. Litton Industries, Florence, Ky., 1984—; engring. mgr. Mannesmann Demag MHC, Cleve., 1990—. Home: 8304 Pebble Creek Ct Chagrin Falls OH 44023-4865 Office: Mannesmann Demag MHC PO Box 39245 Cleveland OH 44139-0245

FEIGENHOLTZ, SARA, state legislator; b. Chgo., Dec. 11, 1956; d. Bernard and Florence (Buky) F. Student, Northeastern Ill. U. Ill. state rep. Dist. 12, 1995—; exec. dir. Cen. Lakeview Merchants Assn., 1993-94; former cons., Chgo. Mem. NOW, Nat. Coun. Jewish Women, Am. Jewish Coun. (gov. coun. 1994-95), Conf. Women Legislators, Phi Theta Kappa. Office: 1322 W Melrose St Chicago IL 60657

FEIKENS, JOHN, federal judge; b. Clifton, N.J., Dec. 3, 1917; s. Sipke and Corine (Wisse) F.; m. Henriette Dorothy Schulthouse, Nov. 4, 1939; children: Jon, Susan Corine, Barbara Edith, Julie Anne, Robert H. A.B., Calvin Coll., Grand Rapids, Mich., 1938; J.D., U. Mich., 1941; LL.D., U. Detroit, 1979, Detroit Coll. Law, 1981. Bar: Mich. 1942. Gen. practice law Detroit; dist. judge Ea. Dist. Mich., Detroit, 1960-61, 70-79, chief judge, 1979-86, sr. judge, 1986—; past co-chmn. Mich. Civil Rights Commn.; past chmn. Rep. State Central Com.; past mem. Rep. Nat. Com. Past bd. trustees Calvin Coll. Fellow Am. Coll. Trial Lawyers; mem. ABA, Detroit Bar Assn. (dir. 1962, past pres.), State Bar Mich. (commr. 1965-71). Club: University of Michigan. Office: US Dist Ct 851 Theodore Levin US Ct 231 W Lafayette Blvd Detroit MI 48226-2719

FEIN, ROGER GARY, lawyer; b. St. Louis, Mar. 12, 1940; s. Albert and Fanny (Levinson) F.; m. Susanne M. Cohen, Dec. 18, 1965; children: David I., Lisa J. Student Washington U., St. Louis, 1959, NYU, 1960; BS, UCLA, 1962; JD, Northwestern U., 1965; MBA, Am. U., 1967. Bar: Ill. 1965, U.S. Dist. Ct. (no. dist.) Ill. 1968, U.S. Ct. Appeals (7th cir.) 1968, U.S. Supreme Ct. 1970. Atty. div. corp. fin. SEC, Washington, 1965-67; ptnr. Arvey, Hodes, Costello & Burman, Chgo., 1967-91, Wildman, Harrold, Allen and Dixon, Chgo., 1992—, co-chair Corp., Securities and Tax Practice Group; mem. Securities Adv. Com. to Sec. State Ill., 1973—, chmn., 1973-79, 87-93, vice chmn., 1983-87, chmn. emeritus, 1994—; spl. asst. atty. gen. State of Ill., 1974-83, 85—; spl. asst. state's atty. Cook County, Ill., 1989-90; mem. Appeal Bd., Ill. Law Enforcement Commn., 1980-83; mem. lawyer's adv. bd. So. Ill. Law Jour., 1980-83; mem. adv. bd. securities regulation and law report Bur. Nat. Affairs Inc., 1985—; lectr., author on land trust financing, consumer credit and securities law. Mem. Bd. Edn., Sch. Dist. No. 29, Northfield, Ill., 1977-83, pres., 1981-83; mem. Pub. Vehicle Ops. Citizens Adv. coun., City Chgo., 1985-86; mem. Chgo. regional bd. Anti-Defamation League of B'nai B'rith, 1975-91, vice chmn. 1980-88 ; chmn. lawyers' com. for ann. telethon Muscular Dystrophy Assn., 1983; past bd. dirs. Jewish Nat. Fund., Am. Friends Hebrew U., Northfield Community Fund. Recipient Sec. State Ill. Pub. Svc. award, 1976, Citation of Merit, WAIT Radio, 1976, Sunset Ridge Sch. Community Svc. award, 1984; City of Chgo. Citizen's award 1986. Fellow Am. Bar Found., Ill. Bar Found. (bd. dirs. 1978-88, v.p. 1982-84, pres. 1984-86, chmn. Fellows 1983-84, chmn., past pres. adv. com. 1988-90, Cert. of Appreciation 1985, 86), Chgo. Bar Found.; mem. Decalogue Soc. Lawyers, ABA (state regulation of securities com. 1982—, Ill. liaison of com., ho. of dels. 1981-85), Ill. State Bar Assn. (bd. govs. 1976-80, del. assembly 1976-88, sec. 1977-78, cert. of appreciation 1980, 88, chmn. Bench and Bar com. 1982-83, chmn. Bench and Bar sect. coun. 1983-84, chmn. bar elections supervision com. 1986-87, chmn. assembly com. on hearings 1987-88, mem. com. on jud. appointments 1987-90), Chgo. Bar Assn. (mem. task force delivery legal svcs. 1978-80, cert. of appreciation 1976, chmn. land trusts com. 1978-79, chmn. consumer credit com. 1977-78, chmn. state securities law subcom. 1977-79), Standard Club, Legal Club Chgo., Tau Epsilon Phi, Alpha Kappa Psi, Phi Delta Phi. Office: Wildman Harrold Allen & Dixon 225 W Wacker Dr Ste 3000 Chicago IL 60606-1224

FEIN, THOMAS PAUL, software support specialist; b. Cin., Jan. 13, 1946; s. Harold Robert and Virginia May (Gray) F.; m. Linda Ann Stofle, Dec. 11, 1971. Student, Ohio State U., 1964-67, BBA, 1976. Programmer The Ohio Casualty Group, Hamilton, 1976, Am. Laundry Machinery, Cin., 1976; programmer/analyst Automated Data Systems, Cin., 1976-78, Savs. and Loan Data Corp., Cin., 1978-81; programmer/analyst Champion Internat. Corp., Hamilton, 1981-85, data security adminstr., 1985-89, pers. computer software analyst, 1990—. Bd. dirs. St. Raphael Social Svc. Agy., Inc. Mem. Cin. Personal Computer Users Group, Ohio State U. Alumni Assn. (life). Republican. Methodist. Lodges: Masons (local trustee 1982—, sec.-treas. 1982—, chmn. scholarship com. 1983-86), Order of Eastern Star. Home: 650 History Bridge Ln Hamilton OH 45013-3659 Office: Champion Internat Corp 101 Knightsbridge Dr Hamilton OH 45011-3166

FEINBERG, GLENDA JOYCE, restaurant chain executive; b. Louisville, Feb. 8, 1948; d. Harold and Winnie Esther (McIntosh) F.; divorced; 1 child, Anthony John. Student, Purdue U., 1967-68, Ind. U., 1977-79. Cert. in restaurant and personnel mgmt. Beverage mgr. Don Ce Sar Beach Hotel, St. Petersburg Beach, Fla., 1979-80; catering dir. Best Western-Skyway Inn, St. Petersburg, Fla., 1980-83; gen. mgr. Village, Inc., St. Petersburg Beach, 1983-86; banquet mgr. Tradewinds Resort Hotel, St. Petersburg Beach, 1986-87; exec. mgr. Ponderosa, Inc., Clearwater, Fla., 1987-90; food and beverage dir. Days Inn Island Beach Resort, St. Petersburg Beach, 1990-92; owner, mgmt. cons., pvt. caterer G.F. Sans, Marengo, Ind., 1992—. Bd. dirs. AIDS Coalitions Pinellas, 1990. Mem. NOW, World Wildlife Fedn., Nat. Geographic Soc., Greenpeace, Amnesty Internat., Environ. Def. Fund, Nat. Audubon Soc., Nat. Arbor Day Found. Democrat.

FEINBERG, RICHARD, anthropologist, educator; b. Norfolk, Va., Nov. 4, 1947; s. Isadore and Rose Selma (Hartmann) F.; m. Nancy Ellen Grim, Apr. 15, 1978; children: Joseph Grim-Feinberg, Kate Grim-Feinberg. AB, U. Calif., Berkeley, 1969; MA, U. Chgo., 1971, PhD, 1974. Asst. prof. anthropology Kent (Ohio) State U., 1974-80, assoc. prof., 1980-86, prof., 1986—; mem. editorial bd. Kent State U. Press, 1990-93. Author: Anuta: Social Structure of a Polynesian Island, 1981, Polynesian Seafaring and Navigation, 1988; editor: Politics of Culture in the Pacific Islands, 1995, Seafaring in the Contemporary Pacific Islands, 1995, Leadership and Change in the Western Pacific, 1996. Kent State Rsch. Coun. grantee, 1983, 88; Wenner-Gren Found. grantee, 1991. Fellow Am. Anthrop. Assn., Assn. for Social Anthropology in Oceania (newsletter editor 1986-90); mem. Polynesian Soc., Am. Ethnological Soc., Ctrl. States Anthrop. Soc. (bulletin editor 1994-96). Office: Kent State U Dept Anthropology Kent OH 44242

FEINGOLD, DANIEL LEON, anesthesiologist; b. Boston, May 19, 1958; s. Macey Gerson and Hélène Sultana (Benlolo) F. BS with distinction, U. Ill., Chgo., 1980; MD, U. Health Scis., Chgo. Med. Sch., 1984. Intern Weiss Meml. Hosp., Chgo., 1984-85; resident in anesthesiology U. Ill. Hosps. and Clinics, Chgo., 1986-89; anesthesiologist Hosp. Anesthesia Group, Chgo., 1989—. Contbr. articles to profl. publs. Mem. AMA, AAAS, Am. Soc. Anesthesiologists, Am. Soc. Regional Anesthesia, Ill. State Med. Soc. Home: PO Box 577429 Chicago IL 60657-7429 Office: PO Box 25678 Chicago IL 60625-0678

FEINGOLD, EUGENE NEIL, health services management and policy educator; b. Bklyn., Mar. 21, 1931; s. Paul and Rose Elaine (Brook) F.; m. Marcia Goldberg, Mar. 26, 1960; children: Eleanor, Ruth. AB in Chemistry, Cornell U., 1952; postgrad. pub. adminstrn., Syracuse U., 1952-53; MA in Politics, Princeton U., 1958, PhD in Politics, 1960; JD, U. Mich., 1992. Rsch. fellow Brookings Instn., Washington, 1959-60; instr. polit. sci. U. Mich., Ann Arbor, 1960-63, asst. prof., 1963-66, assoc. prof. med. care orgn., 1966-71, prof. health svcs. mgmt. and policy, 1971-90, prof. emeritus, 1990—, chmn. dept., 1971-77, assoc. dean Rackham Sch. Grad. Studies, 1977-84, acting dean, 1979-80; spl. rsch. fellow Nat. Ctr. for Health Svcs. Rsch. and Devel., 1970-71; vis. prof. social medicine and clin. epidemiology dept. St. Thomas's Hosp. Med. Sch., U. London, 1970-71; cons. numerous govt. agys., univs. and orgns., 1963—, including OEO, HEW, NSF, NIH, Pa. State U., N.D., Legal Svcs. Southeastern Mich., Mich. Gov.'s Task Force on Access to Health Care; mem. Mich. Med. Care Adv. Coun., 1988—; chmn. Program Dirs. in Health Adminstrn. at Schs. Pub. Health, 1976-77, also numerous others. Author: Medicare: Politics and Policy, 1966, also monographs; mem. editorial bd. Poverty and Human Resources, 1966-70, Med. Care Rev., 1968-77, 80-83, Internat. Jour. Health Svcs., 1974-75, Jour. Health Politics, Policy and Law, 1976-94, Jour. Pub. Health Policy, 1979-82, Med. Care, 1981-83; contbr. articles to profl. jours. Bd. dirs. Mich. ACLU, 1965—; bd. dirs. Mich. League for Human Svcs., 1980—, v.p., 1987-92, chair bd. dirs., 1992—. With U.S. Army, 1953-55. USPHS spl. rsch. fellow, 1970-71, NEH fellow, 1982. Fellow APHA (exec. bd. 1987-95, vice chmn. 1988-89, pres. 1993-94); mem. Mich. Pub. Health Assn. (bd. dirs. 1986-89). Home: 352 Hilldale Dr Ann Arbor MI 48105-1119 Office: U Mich Sch Pub Health Ann Arbor MI 48109

FEINGOLD, RUSSELL DANA, U.S. senator, lawyer; b. Janesville, Wis., Mar. 2, 1953; s. Leon and Sylvia (Binstock) F.; m. Susan Levine, Aug. 21, 1977; children: Jessica, Ellen; m. Mary Speerschneider, Jan. 21, 1991; stepchildren: Sam, Ted. B.A. with honors, U. Wis.-Madison, 1975; postgrad. Magdalen Coll., Oxford U., 1975-77; J.D. with honors, Harvard U., 1979. Bar: Wis. 1979. Assoc., Foley & Lardner, Madison, 1979-82, LaFollette, Sinykin, Anderson & Munson, Madison, 1983-85, Goldman & Feingold, 1985-88; mem. Wis. Senate, 1983-92, U.S. Senator, 1993—, mem. Judiciary Com. Fgn. Rels, 93—, Dem. Policy, 93—, Spl. Com. Aging, 93—. Wis. Honors scholar, 1971; Rhodes scholar, 1975. Mem. Phi Beta Kappa. Democrat. Jewish. Office: US Senate 502 Hart Senate Office Bui Washington DC 20510 Office: US Senators Office 8383 Greenway Blvd Middleton WI 53562-3506*

FEINSILVER, DONALD LEE, psychiatry educator; b. Bklyn., July 24, 1947; s. Albert and Mildred (Weissman) F. B.A., Alfred U., 1968; M.D., Autonomous U.-Guadalajara, Mexico, 1974. Diplomate Am. Bd. Psychiatry and Neurology, Am. Bd. Forensic Psychiatry. Intern in medicine L.I. Coll. Hosp., Bklyn., 1975-76; resident in psychiatry SUNY-Bklyn., 1977-78, chief resident, 1979; asst. prof. psychiatry and surgery Med. Coll. Wis., Milw., 1980-85, assoc. prof., 1985—; dir. psychiat. emergency service Milw. County Mental Health and Med. Complexes, 1980-88; dir. med.-psychiat. unit Milw.

Psychiat. Hosp./West Allis Meml. Hosp., 1988—. Contbr. articles to profl. jours.; editor: Crisis Psychiatry: Pros and Cons, 1982; mem. editorial bd. Psychiat. Medicine Jour., 1983—. Mem. Am. Psychiat. Assn., AMA, Am. Acad. Psychiatry and the Law, AAAS, Acad. Psychosomatic Medicine. Office: West Allis Psychiat Assocs 2424 S 90th St Milwaukee WI 53227-2417

FEIR, DOROTHY JEAN, entomologist, physiologist, educator; b. St. Louis, Jan. 29, 1929; d. Alex R. and Lillian (Smith) F. B.S., U. Mich., 1950; M.S., U. Wyo., 1956; Ph.D., U. Wis., 1960. Instr. biology U. Buffalo, 1960-61; mem. faculty St. Louis U., 1961—, prof. biology, 1967—; mem. tropical medicine and parasitology study sect. NIH, 1980-84. Editor Environ. Entomology, 1977-84; mem. editl. bd. Jour. Med. Entomology, 1995—. Fellow Entomol. Soc. Am. (hon., pres. 1989, Riley Achievement award north ctrl. br. 1993), Mo. Acad. Sci. (v.p. 1987-88, pres.-elect 1988-89, pres. 1989-90, Most Disting. Scientist award 1995); mem. AAAS, Am. Physiol. Soc., N.Y. Acad. Scis., Phi Beta Kappa, Sigma Xi. Office: St Louis U Dept Biology Saint Louis MO 63103

FEIST, WILLIAM CHARLES, consultant; b. St. Paul, Nov. 13, 1934; s. George Henry Martin and Mildred Catherine Feist; married Sept. 7, 1956 (widowed 1990); children: Grant William, Blake Edward; married, July 6, 1991. BS, Hamline U., 1956; PhD, U. Colo., 1961. Rsch. chemist Esso Rsch., Linden, N.J., 1960-64; rsch. chemist Forest Products Lab., Madison, Wis., 1964-83, project leader, 1983-92; rsch. chemist Forest Products Lab., Madison, 1992-94; cons., 1994—. Contbr. more than 185 articles to tech. and practical publs. Fellow Internat. Acad. Wood Sci.; mem. Am. Chem. Soc., Forest Products Soc.

FEISTER, JOHN BOOKSER, editor, journalist; b. Akron, Sept. 25, 1957; s. John Fanning and Alice Romayne (Lent) F.; m. Catherine Rose Bookser, June 7, 1980; children: Jesse, Scott, John. BA in Am. Studies, U. Dayton, 1979; MA in Humanities, Xavier U., 1983. Carpenter Frontier Housing, Inc., Morehead, Ky., 1979-80; supr., trainer Lansdowne Mental Health Ctr., Ashland, Ky., 1980-82; comms. dir. Southerners for Econ. Justice, Durham, N.C., 1983-89; editor, journalist St. Anthony Messenger, Cin., 1989—. Author: Radical Grace: Daily Meditations by Richard Rohr, 1994; prodr.: (video) Option for the Poor: The Southern Hearings, 1984; contbr. articles to mags. Bd. dirs. Covington (Ky.) Comty. Ctr., Commn. on Religion in Appalachia, Knoxville, Tenn., Cath. Com. Appalachia, Whitesburg, Ky.; mem. parish coun. St. Bernard Ch., Dayton, 1992-95. Mem. Cath. Press Assn. (1st pl., 3d pl. best article in gen. interest mag. 1995, 3d pl. best editl. 1990), Soc. Profl. Journalists, Cin. Editors Assn. (1st pl. writing award 1994, 95). Democrat. Roman Catholic. Office: St Anthony Messenger 1615 Republic St Cincinnati OH 45210

FEIT, MICHAEL, controller; b. Tarnopol, Poland, Sept. 8, 1928; came to U.S., 1949; s. Henryk and Anna (Taube) F.; m. Irene Mischel, Mar. 17, 1956; children: Elizabeth, Susan. BS cum laude, NYU, 1955, postgrad., 1956-57; postgrad., Boston U., 1958-59. CPA, Ma., Pa., Ill. Mgr. cost acctg. Microwave & Powertube div. Raytheon Co., Waltham, Mass., 1957-59; sr. cons. Price Waterhouse & Co., Boston, 1959-64; mgr. MIS Scott Paper Co., Phila., 1964-68; dir. MIS Admiral Corp., Chgo., 1968-70; contr. Superior Tea & Coffee Co., Chgo., 1971-76; contr., CFO Ride Corp., Chgo., 1977-78; contr. Bd. of Edn. City of Chgo., 1978-81; interim CFO Bd. of Edn. City of Chgo., 1980-81; contr., CFO The Lambs, Inc., Libertyville, Ill., 1981—. Mem. AICPA, Mass. Soc. CPAs (Silver medal 1961), Ill. Assn. Rehab. Facilities. Home: 1240 Park Ave W Highland Park IL 60035-2264 Office: The Lambs Inc PO Box 520 Libertyville IL 60048-0520

FELDBUSCH, MICHAEL F., engineering company executive; b. Evansville, Ind., Aug. 26, 1951; s. Ronald Farrell and Rita Carolyn (Snodgrass) F.; m. Lisa Ann McDowell, Feb. 14, 1986. AAS in architecture, ITT Tech. Inst., Indpls., 1971. Cert. profl. land surveyor, Ind., Ky., Fla. Engr. Lake States Engrng., Chgo., 1974, Mayfair Constrn., Detroit, 1975; surveyor Warrick County Planning Commn., Boonville, Ind., 1976, Warrick County, Boonville, 1977-85; pres., owner AES/Warrick Engrng., Newburgh, Ind., 1978—; pres. Warrick County Planning Commn., 1978, 85; chief surveyor Warrick County, 1985—; mem. Examinations for Profl. Surveyors com. Nat. Soc. Examiners Engrs. Surveyors; pro-tem law judge Bd. of Registrations for Land Surveyors. Del. Ind. Dems., Indpls., 1978, 82, 86; sec. Newburgh Youth Sports Assn., 1980-81; apptd. by gov. Evan Bayh to Ind. State Bd. Registration For Profl. Engrs. and Land Surveyors, 1990. Served with USAR, 1971-77. Recipient Edward Gesser Jr. Meml. award Newburgh Youth Sports Assn., 1986; named one of Outstanding Young Men Am., 1980, 81, 83-85. Mem. NSPE, Ind. Soc. Prof. Land Surveyors, County Surveyors Assn., Am. Congress on Surveying, Nat. Soc. Prof. Surveyors, Ind. Jaycees (Top 40 award, 1979). Lodge: Lions. Home: 9911 Powers Dr Newburgh IN 47630-8866 Office: AES/Warrick Engrng Inc 605 State St Newburgh IN 47630-1299

FELDHOUSE, LYNN ALEXANDRA, corporate philanthropist; b. Detroit, Mar. 5, 1951; d. Mack S. and Sophie F. (Gralewski) Cehanowicz; m. Robert W. Feldhouse, Dec. 4, 1976; 1 child, Katherine A. BS in Bus. Adminstrn., Wayne State U., 1981; postgrad., Okla. U., 1991—. Adminstr. Chrysler Corp. Fund, Highland Park, Mich., 1981-85, mgr., 1985-87, mgr., sec., 1987—. Bd. dirs. Citizens Scholarship Found. Am., St. Peter, Minn., 1989—, Conf. Bd., N.Y.C., 1996-97, Leadership Detroit, 1991—. Office: Chrysler Corp fund 485-02-46 1000 Chrysler Dr Auburn Hills MI 48326-2766

FELDHUSEN, HAZEL J., elementary education educator; b. Camp Douglas, Wis., Feb. 20, 1928; d. Vincent O. and Helen (Johnson) Artz; m. John F. Feldhusen, Dec. 18, 1954; children: Jeanne V., Anne M. B, U. Wis., 1965; M, Purdue U., 1968. Tchr. Suldal Sch., Mauston, Wis., 1947-50, Lake Geneva (Wis.) Schs., 1950-55, West Lafayette (Ind.) Schs., 1965-91; cons. World Conf., Hamburg, 1985, Juneau (Alaska) Schs., 1986, Connersville (Ind.) Schs., 1987, Vancouver (B.C., Can.) Schs., 1990, Norfolk (Va.) Schs., 1991, Taiwan Nat. U., 1992, U. New South Wales, Sydney, Australia, 1993, New Zealand Schs., Auckland, 1993; 2d Nat. Conf. Gifted, Taiwan, 1992. Author: Individualized Teaching of the Gifted, 1993. Mem. Tchr. of Yr. Com., West Lafayette, 1988. Recipient Outstanding Tchr. award Elem. Tchrs. Am., 1974, Appreciation award U. Stellenbosch, 1984, Appreciation award Australian Assn. for the Gifted, 1987; winner Golden Apple Tchg. award Greater Lafayette C. of C., 1989, Disting. Alumnus award Purdue U., 1996. Mem. NEA, Ind. State Tchrs. Assn., West Lafayette Edn. Assn. (Outstanding Achievement award 1984), Phi Delta Kappa, Delta Kappa Gamma (v.p 1983-85). Home: 2411 Trace 24 West Lafayette IN 47906-1887

FELDMAN, BRUCE ALAN, psychiatrist; b. St. Louis, Apr. 21, 1959; s. Jerome Stanley and Arlene (Greenberg) F.; m. Kathryn Matilda Estill, May 25, 1990. BA in Biology, U. Mo., Kansas City, 1982, MD, 1985. Diplomate Nat. Bd. Med. Examiners, Am. Bd. Psychiatry and Neurology. Resident in psychiatry So. Ill. U., Springfield, 1986-89, adminstrv. chief resident, 1988, geriatric psychiat. chief resident, 1989; pvt. practice Psychiat. Assocs., Springfield, 1990—; resident cons. psychiatrist Alzheimers Ctr. for Decatur, Ill., 1989, Alzheimers Ctr. and Memory Disorders Ctr., Springfield, 1989; cons. psychiatrist Taylorville (Ill.) Mental Health Ctr., 1990—, Country View Living Ctr., Decatur, 1990—, Jacksonville Terr. Nursing Home, 1990—, Walnut Ridge N.H., 1992—, Springfield Mental Health Ctr., 1992—; hosp. affiliate Drs. Hosp., 1990—, Meml. Med. Ctr., 1990—, St. Johns Hosp., 1990—, St. Vincent Meml. Hosp., 1990—, Passavant Hosp., 1990—; mem. utilization rev. com. Drs. Hosp., 1990-91, St. Johns Hosp., 1994—, pharm. & therapeutics com., 1992—; ltd. ptnr., owner Drs. Hosp., Springfield, 1990-94, Wentville, Mo., 1991—; bd. dirs. Ind. Physicians Network, Springfield; contbr. THA clin. studies SIU Alzheimers Clinic, 1989, Proscom Clin. Study, 1992. Mem. Jewish Fedn., Springfield, Ill., Temple Israel Synagogue, Springfield; exec. prodr., dir. Miss K.C. Pageant, 1981; mem. Nat. Rep. Congress com., 1988—, Rep. Nat. Candidate Trust, 1992—, Rep. Inner Circle, 1993—, Rep. Nat. Com., 1994—, Crescent Counties Found. for Med. Care, 1993—. Named to Rep. Nat. Hall of Honor, 1992; recipient Rep. Congl. Order of Liberty, 1993, Rep. Senatorial Medal of Freedom, 1994. Mem. AMA, Am. Psychiat. Assn., N.Y. Acad. Scis. (life), So. Med. Assn., Am. Assn. for Geriatric Psychiatry, Am. Geriatrics Soc., U.S. Senatorial Club, Bnai Brith (Emes chpt., former exec. bd. mem.), Delta Chi (past pres. Kansas City chpt. 1979, nat. v.p., chpt. advisor 1981-82, Alumnus of Yr. 1982). Republican. Office: Psychiat Assocs 1124 S 6th St Springfield IL 62703-2406

FELDMAN, EDWIN, health care executive, internist, cardiologist; b. Chgo., Nov. 29, 1924; s. Henry and Sarah (Weiss) F.; m. Sophia Athena Dussias, Nov. 22, 1950; children: Paul Keith, Michael Leslie. MD, The Chgo. Med. Sch., North Chicago, 1947. Diplomate Am. Bd. Internal Medicine. Fellow in cardiology Oak Forest (Ill.) Hosp., 1947-48; resident in internal medicine Ill. Masonic Med. Ctr., Chgo., 1949-52; pvt. practice specializing in internal medicine/cardiology Chgo., 1954—; med. dir. Ill. Masonic Med. Ctr., Chgo., 1972-82, v.p. med. affairs, 1982-90, sr. v.p. med. affairs, 1990—; assoc. dean Rush Med. Coll., Chgo., 1994—, exec. dir. med. programs, 1996—; mem. Chgo. Bd. of Health, 1979-80. Capt. M.C. U.S. Army, 1952-54. Mem. Masons (33 degree). Jewish. Home: Apt 19S 1110 N Lake Shore Dr Chicago IL 60611 Office: Ill Masonic Med Ctr 836 Wellington Chicago IL 60657

FELDMAN, HARRIS JOSEPH, radiologist, educator; b. Balt., Mar. 4, 1942; s. Charles William and Ruth (Emanuel) F. AB, Western Md. Coll., 1963; MD, U. Md., 1967. Diplomate Am. Bd. Radiology. Intern, Mercy Hosp., Balt., 1967-68; resident in radiology George Washington U. Hosp., Washington, 1968-71; staff radiologist U. Ill. Hosp., Chgo., 1973-77, Bethany Meth. Hosp., Chgo., 1977-87, Walther Meml. Hosp., Chgo., 1977-87, Weiss Meml. Hosp., Chgo., 1987-89, Lincoln West Hosp., Chgo., 1987-89, Holy Cross Hosp., Chgo., 1989—; cons. radiologist Langley AFB Hosp., 1972-73; asst. prof. Abraham Lincoln Sch. Medicine, U. Ill., Chgo., 1974-77, clin. asst. prof., 1977—. Served with M.C., USN, 1971-73. Mem. AMA, Ill. Med. Soc., Chgo. Med. Soc., Am. Coll. Radiology, Ill. Radiol. Soc., Chgo. Radiol. Soc., Radiol. Soc. N.Am. Home: 1339 N Dearborn St Chicago IL 60610 Office: Holy Cross Hosp Dept Radiology 2701 W 68th St Chicago IL 60629-1813

FELDMAN, LORI STRAUSS, marketing educator; b. Boston, Mar. 5, 1965; d. Bruce Paul Strauss and Judi (Schleimer) Strauss-Lipkin; m. Lawrence Eric Feldman, Oct. 15, 1989; 1 child, Jacob. BA, U. Mich., 1987, MBA, 1992, PhD, 1992. Asst. prof. Purdue U.-Calumet, Hammond, Ind., 1993—; vis. asst. prof. Purdue U. - Calumet, 1992-93. Contbr. articles to profl. jours. Fellow Albert Haring Symposium, Bloomington, Ind., 1990. Mem. Am. Mktg. Assn., Mktg. Mgmt. Assn., So. Mktg. Assn., Assn. Consumer Rsch., Acad. Mgmt., Beta Gamma Sigma, Mortar Bd., Golden Key. Home: 121 Hill Rd Willowbrook IL 60521 Office: Purdue Univ Calumet Dept Mgmt 2233 171st St Hammond IN 46323

FELDMAN, RUTH DUSKIN, writer; b. Chgo., June 13, 1934; d. Boris and Rita (Schayer) Duskin; m. Gilbert Feldman, June 14, 1953; children:Steven J., Laurie Nadine, Heidi Carolyn. BS, Northwestern U., Evanston, 1954. Tchr. Nichols Sch., Evanston, Ill., 1954-55, U.S. Army, Ft. Sheridan, Ill., 1964; tchr. and curriculum coord. Congregation Beth Or, Deerfield, Ill., 1970-80; corr. and staff writer Lerner Newspapers, Highland Park, Ill., 1973-81; creative editor Humanistic Judaism, Farmington Hills, Mich., 1983—; panel mem. Quiz Kids Radio & TV Program, Chgo., 1941-50; quizmistress Chgo. Sun-Times Quizdown, 1947-50; guest editor Mademoiselle mag. coll. bd., N.Y.C., 1952; freelance writer for mags. and newspapers, 1974—. Author: Chemi the Magician, 1947, Whatever Happened to the Quiz Kids, 1982 (Ind. Writers of Chgo. award 1983), Study Guide for Papala/Olds A Child's World, 1990, 93, 96; co-author: Rematch, 1989, Communicoding, 1989, Human Development, 4th edit., 1989, Adult Development and Aging, 1996. Madrikha (Jewish ceremonial officiant), 1993—. Named James Alton James scholar, Northwestern U., Evanston, 1953-54; recipient Benjamin Fine award for outstanding ednl. writing, Nat. Assn. Secondary Sch. Prins., 1983, Lowell Thomas award (runner-up), Soc. Am. Travel Writers, 1986. Mem. Am. Soc. Journalists and Authors, Authors Guild, Soc. Profl. Journalists, Nat. Writers Union, Soc. Midland Authors, Ind. Writers of Chgo., Soc. for Humanistic Judaism (leadership conf. of secular Humanistic Jews, N.Am. com. for humanism), Phi Beta Kappa. Home and Office: 935 Fairview Rd Highland Park IL 60035-3635

FELDMANN, JUDITH G., language professional, educator; b. Grenova, N.D., Feb. 10, 1938; d. Jule and Evelyn (Hagen) F.; children: Robert, Carole Elizabeth. BA magna cum laude, Minot State Tchrs. Coll., 1962; MA, Mich. State U., 1971; postgrad, U. Oslo, 1980, U. London, 1982, 85; postgrad., Western Mich. U., 1987, Eastern Mich. U., 1992-93, Harvard U., 1994. Cert. tchr., secondary adminstrn., Mich. English tchr. Minot Pub. Schs., N.D., 1961; english tchr. Charlotte Pub. Schs., Mich., 1962; grad. asst. instr. Mich. State Univ., East Lansing, Mich., 1963; reading specialist, English educator Jackson (Mich.) Pub. Schs., 1964-95. Mem. Internat. Reading Assn., Mich. Reading Assn., Assn. for Supervision and Curriculum Devl., Jackson Edn. Assn. (v.p.). Home: 2791 Brookside Blvd Jackson MI 49203-5532

FELDSTEIN, CHARLES ROBERT, fund raising consultant; b. Chgo., Nov. 9, 1922; s. Herman and Fannie (Frank) F.; m. Janice Josephson, Sept. 6, 1948; children: James Frank, Frances Emily, Thomas Mark. MA, U. Chgo., 1944. Dir. devel. U. Chgo., 1948-53; pres. C.R. Feldstein & Co., Chgo., 1953-88, chmn. bd., 1988—; pres. Charles Frank & Co. Antiquarians, Chgo., 1970—. Bd. dirs. Scholarship & Guidance, Chgo., United Charities, Chgo., Ragdale Found., Lake Forest. Mem. Am. Assn. Fund Raising Counsel (chmn. 1982-83), Standard Club, Cliff Dwellers, Attic, Harvard Club. Home: 680 N Lake Shore Dr Chicago IL 60611-4402 Office: 135 S La Salle St Chicago IL 60603-4105

FELDSTEIN, RICHARD, psychiatrist; b. July 6, 1945; m. Theresa Marie Pavelek, July 3, 1983; children: Rachel Elizabeth, David Alexander, Emily Rebecca. BA in English, Wayne State U., 1967, MD, 1971. Diplomate Am. Bd. Psychiatry and Neurology; lic. physician, Mich. Resident Detroit Psychiat. Inst./Wayne State U., 1971-74; mem. Psychiat. Ctr. Mich., Detroit, 1974-79; attending physician Detroit Meml. Hosp., 1976-79; clin. instr. dept. psychiatry Sch. Medicine, Wayne State U., Detroit, 1975-77; staff psychiatrist Adult Psychiat. Clinic, Detroit, 1974-75; attending psychiatrist Harper Hosp., Detroit, 1974-79, clin. dir. polydrug unit, 1974-75; pvt. practice Farmington Hills, Mich., 1979—; mem. staff Harper Hosp.; $D; mem. staff Detroit Riverview Hosp., Macomb Hosp. Ctr.; dir. dept. psychiatry Select-care Medextend, 1984-89; past cons. Carmel Hall Home for Aged, Dearborn Heights Human Svc. Ctr., Detroit Police Dept., HEAD Ctr., Metro Indsl. Clinic; cons. examiner Disability Determination Svc., State of Mich., 1985—; panel mem. Mich. Med. Arbitration, Am. Arbitration Assn., 1986—; cons. utilization rev. Pathway Rev. Systems, 1990—; psychiat. expert Social Security Adminstrn., U.S. HHS, 1990—. Mem. Am. Psychiat. Assn., Mich. Psychiat. Soc., Mich. State Med. Soc., Am. Acad. Psychiatry and the Law, Wayne County Med. Soc. Jewish. Office: Ste 240 32300 Northwestern Hwy Farmington Hills MI 48334-1567

FELDT, ALLAN GUNNAR, retired urban planner, educator; b. Tonawanda, N.Y., Apr. 20, 1932; s. Gunnar Axel and Alma Wilhelmina (Ahnberg) F.; m. Barbara Alice McVittie, Jan. 30, 1954; children: David, Linda, Laurie. BS in Physics, U. Mich., 1954, MA in Sociology, 1958, PhD in Sociology, 1963. Asst. prof. sociology Cornell U., Ithaca, N.Y., 1962-67, asst. prof. city planning, 1962-67, assoc. prof. city planning, 1967-71; assoc. prof. urban planning U. Mich., Ann Arbor, 1971-73, prof. urban planning, 1973-94; cons. DATUM, Bonn, Fed. Republic of Germany, 1970-72, Smith, Hinchman and Gryll, Detroit, 1976-80, Fred Moger Assocs., Chgo., 1979-85, Homer Hoyt Inst., Palm Beach, 1990-93, Coopers & Lybrand, N.Y.C., 1996; chair PhD program in urban planning U. Mich., 1972-74, MUP program in urban planning, 1985-86. Author: Community Land Use Game, 1971; editor: Papers on Simulation Gaming, 1965; contbr. chpts. to books and articles to profl. jours. Vice chair County Charter Commn., Tompkins County, N.Y., 1967-68; active City Planning Comm., Ithaca, 1964-67, chmn., Ann Arbor, 1985-89; alderman Common Coun., Ithaca, 1967-71. With U.S. Army, 1954-56. Recipient Excellence in Teaching award Sol King Fund, 1983, Disting. Svc. award U. Mich. Urban Planning Alumni, 1989, Disting. Planning Educator award Am. Collegiate Schs. of Planning, 1995; U. Mich. rsch. fellow, 1958-60, Population Coun. fellow, 1960. Mem. AAUP, North Am. Simulation and Gaming Assn. (bd. dirs. 1986-89), Mich. Soc. Planning Officials, Pottawattamie Land Trust (bd. dirs. 1990). Democrat. Home: 136 Gralake Ave Ann Arbor MI 48103-2021 Office: U Michigan Coll Architecture and Urb Plan Ann Arbor MI 48109

FELDT, ROBERT JUNIOR, retired conservationist; b. St. Ansgar, Iowa, Feb. 17, 1929; s. Robert Ferdinand and Laura Emma Louise (Schroeder) F.; m. Catherine Christina Dworshak. Farm ops., Iowa State U., 1950. Soil conservationist U.S. Soil Conservation Svc., Waterloo, Iowa, 1951-52, Waseca, Minn., 1952-53; work unit conservationist U.S. Soil Conservation Svc., Redwood Falls, Minn., 1953-67; dist. conservationist U.S. Soil Conservation Svc., Crookston, Minn., 1967-77; resource conservation and devel. coord. U.S. Soil Conservation Svc., Eau Claire, Wis., 1977-88; organizer Shiitake Growers Assn. Wis., Eau Claire; instr. U. Minn., Crookston, 1968-70, USAR, Fort McCoy, Wis., 1968-77. Prodn. asst. 20-minute film. Mem. Nat. Assn. Ret. Fed. Employees (life; chpt. pres. 1994-96), Ret. Officers Assn. (life; chpt. pres.), Soil and Water Conservation Soc. Am. (bd. dirs. 1986-87), Shiitake Growers Assn. Wis. (life; charter), Minn. Wheat Growers Assn. (charter), Minn. Inventors Congress (charter; pres. 1963-65, presdl. award 1964), Eau Claire Rod and Gun Club, Ruffed Grouse Soc., Nat. Wild Turkey Fedn., Elks, Beta Sigma Psi. Home and Office: 2360 E Kirk Dr Eau Claire WI 54701-9686

FELECIANO, PAUL, JR., state legislator; b. N.Y.C., 1942; m. V. Arlene Williams, 1966; children: Treven, Eric, Heather. AAS, N.Y.C. C.C., 1961. Kans. state rep., 1972-76, Kans. state senator Dist. 28, minority whip, former asst. senate Dem. leader, former ranking minority mem. com. and jud. com., former assessment and taxation com.; mem. comm. com. State-Fed. Assembly Nat. Conf. State Legisatures; mem. joint com. arts and cultural resources, investments pensions and benefits com.; mem. children and youth adv. com. Women's Correctional Task Force; mem. Kans. Coun. Employment and Tng.; mem. Gov.'s Task Force on Housing and Homeless, Washington; mem. force and policy alt. leader Ctr. Policy Alternatives; sec. Aircap Truck Plz., Inc.; v.p. Air Cap Motel, Inc.; pres. polit. affairs Nat. Telecom. Cons. Mem. Riverside Dem. Club. Mem. Am. Legion (Post 401, Wichita). Office: 815 Barbara St Wichita KS 67217-3115 also: State Senate State Capitol Topeka KS 66612*

FELGER, RALPH WILLIAM, educator, retired military officer; b. Hamilton, Ohio, Oct. 14, 1919; s. Edward Lewis and Blanche Esther (House) F.; m. Bernice Regina Moeller, Dec. 28, 1944; 1 child, Mary Karen. BA, Whitworth Coll., 1950; MBA, U. Denver, 1952; MS, Trinity U., 1954. Cert. instr. bus. and psychology, Calif. Commd. 2d lt. U.S. Army, advanced through grades to 1st lt., pers. tng. officer, 1942-46, relieved from active duty, 1946; commd. 1st lt. USAF, 1951, advanced through grades to col., edn. and pers. officer, 1951-67, ret., 1967; asst. prof. Bakersfield (Calif.) Coll., 1967-68; dean continuing edn. Lincoln Land C.C., Springfield, Ill., 1968-72; dir. corp. tng. Sangamo Electric Co., West Union, S.C., 1972-74; asst. campus dir. Ohio State U., Marion, 1974-79; asst. to v.p. Ohio State U., Columbus, 1979-83; exec. v.p. Internat. Mgmt. Inst., Westerville, Ohio, 1983-84; dir. continuing edn. N.Mex. Inst. Mining and Tech., Socorro, 1984-85; part-time cons. edn. and mktg. Midwest Human Resource Sys., Columbus, Ohio, 1985-89; acad. counselor Franklin U., Columbus, 1990-91; edn. program mgr. Jr. Achievement of Ctrl. Ohio, Columbus, 1991-92; v.p. Career Mgmt. Ctrs., Inc., Columbus, 1991-92; ret., 1992. Div. chmn. United Way, Springfield, 1972; mem. Police Human Rels. Com., Springfield, 1970-72; bd. dirs. ARC, Oconee, S.C., 1973; edn. chmn. Marion (Ohio) Econ. Coun., 1975-79, Marion County chpt. Am. Heart Assn., 1975-79. Decorated Legion of Merit, U.S. Joint Chiefs of Staff Badge, 3 USAF Commendation medals; recipient 2 commendations United Way Community Service. Mem. Pers. Mgrs. Club (v.p. 1972-74), U.S. Ret. Mil. Officers Assn., Am. Biog. Inst. (rsch. bd. advisors), Internat. Parliament for Safety and Peace, Delta Sigma Pi (life). Home: 2153 Olde Sawmill Blvd Dublin OH 43016-8221

FELICIANO, SANTIAGO, JR., lawyer; b. Y Auco, P.R., Nov. 24, 1951; came to U.S., 1952; s. Santiago Sr. and Cielo (Rodriquez) F.; m. Rosa Carrion, May 27, 1978; children: Judith M., Santiago R., Laura T., William G. BA in History, John Carroll U., 1973; JD, Cleve. Marshall Law Coll., 1976. Counsel Fedn. Cath. Cmty Svcs., Cleve., 1979-83; dir. legal office Cath. Diocese Cleve., 1984—. Bd. trustees mem. ARC, Legal Aid Soc., Woman's Law Fund, Citizens League Greater Cleve., Greater Cleve. Roundtable, Ohio Coll. Podiatric Medicine, Guidance Ctr., Vis. Nurses Assn., Cleve. Sight Ctr., Health Sys. Agy. North Ctrl. Ohio. Recipient Cert. Appreciation Supreme Ct. Ohio Bd. Commrs., 1988. Roman Catholic. Office: Diocese Cleveland Legal Office 1027 Superior Cleveland OH 44135

FELLAND, RICHARD A., electrical design engineer; b. Forest City, Iowa, Nov. 7, 1949. AAS, North Iowa Area Coll., 1969. Design engr. John Deere Product Engrng., Waterloo, Iowa, 1979—. Patent for Lever Actuated Switch Mechanism. Mem. United Meth. Ch., Waterloo, 1981—; coach Little League, Waterloo, 1990—. With U.S. Army, 1969-71. Mem. Soc. Automotive Engrs. Methodist. Home: 835 Rose Ln Waterloo IA 50702 Office: John Deere Foundry PO Box 2000 Waterloo IA 50704-2000

FELLINGHAM, DAVID ANDREW, retired mortgage banker; b. Chgo., Mar. 5, 1937; s. Warren Luther and Dorothy (Park) F.; m. Meredith Ann Hall, Nov. 25, 1965; children: Beth Park, Ruth More. AB, Ripon Coll., 1961; MBA, Ind. U., 1965; student, Dartmouth Coll., 1955-56. Credit adminstr. NBD Bank, N.A., Detroit, 1967-74, cash mgmt. mgr., 1978-80, energy div. comml. lender, 1980-86; regional comml. lending officer NBD Bank, N.A., Bloomfield Hills, Mich., 1986-87; comml. mortgage banker NBD Mortgage Co., NBD Bank, N.A., Troy, Mich., 1987-95; ret., 1996. 1st lt. U.S. Army, 1961-63. Mem. Mortgage Bankers Mich., Ripon Coll. Alumni Club.

FELLINGHAM, WARREN LUTHER, JR., banker; b. Chgo., Dec. 28, 1934; s. Warren Luther and Dorothy Eaton (Park) F.; m. Judith Cutler, Sept. 14, 1962; children; Warren III, Margo, Victoria. AB, Dartmouth Coll., 1956; MBA, Northwestern U., 1968. Cert. bank compliance officer. Auditing asst. The Northern Trust Co., Chgo., 1956-61, asst. cashier, 1962-71, 2d v.p., 1972-77, v.p., 1978—, consumer compliance officer, 1988—; pres. Chicagoland Compliance Assn., 1988—. Village pres., mayor Village of Golf, Ill., 1981-85, village trustee, clk., 1973-81; bd. dirs. United Way of Glenview-Golf, 1983-92. Recipient Dist. award of Merit, N.E. Ill. Coun. Boy Scouts of Am., 1989. Mem. Chicagoland Compliance Assn., Dartmouth Club of Chgo., Order of the Arrow. Home: 37 Overlook Dr Golf IL 60029 Office: The Northern Trust Co 50 S La Salle St Chicago IL 60603-1003

FELLNER, MICHAEL JOSEPH, government executive, educator; b. St. Paul, Minn., Aug. 10, 1949; s. Joseph George and Carol Marie (Bovy) F.; m. Carol Lois Archer, Oct. 14, 1972; children: Christopher Michael, Kimberly Ann. BS in Edn., U. Minn., Mpls., 1971; postgrad., U. Wis., La Crosse, 1972. Cert. Dept. Def. acquisition profl. Secondary sch. educator La Crescent (Minn.) Sch. Dist., 1971-72; contract price analyst Def. Contract Adminstrn. Svcs., Mpls., 1977-84, adminstrv. contracting officer, 1984-86, div. adminstrv. contracting officer, 1986—; mem. Dept. Def. Acqusition Corp.; mem. bd. advisors U. St. Thomas, St. Paul, 1988—. Mem. Jaycees, Richfield, Minn., 1978-79; coach St. Peter's Sch., Richfield, Minn., 1982-88; chmn. St. Peter's Ch., Richfield, 1983-84; CPR instr. ARC, Mpls., 1984-85. Named Civil Servant of Yr., Fed. Exec. Bd., Twin Cities, Minn., 1982, Disting. Employee of Yr., DCASR St. Louis, 1983. Fellow Nat. Contract Mgmt. Assn. (cert. profl. contract mgr. 1991, chmn. Mentor com., sec. 1982-83, treas. 1985-86, v.p. 1986-87); mem. Minn. Street Rod Assn. Republican. Roman Catholic. Home: 6633 4th Ave S Minneapolis MN 55423-2421 Office: Defense Plant Rep Office 2701 4th Ave S Minneapolis MN 55440-0524

FELLOWS, DALE RUSSELL, physical therapist, consultant; b. Mpls., Nov. 2, 1918; s. Ira Vance and Jessie May (Vogen) F.; m. Norma Jean Iseminger, July 10, 1942 (div. June, 1952); children: Russell, Leanne; m. Doris Arlene Mairose Fellows, Dec. 8, 1961. BA in Phys. Edn., Augustana Coll., 1950; cert. in phys. therapy, U. Iowa, 1951. Registered phys. therapist, AMA; lic. phys. therapist, S.D. Chief phys. therapist Sioux Valley (S.D.) Hosp.; phys. therapist VA Hosp., Hot Springs, S.D., Luth. Hosp., Hot Springs, S.D.; home phys. therapy care Hot Springs; cons. Luth. Hosp., Hot Springs. Sgt. Armed Forces, 1943-46, PTO. Mem. Am. Phys. Therapy Assn., DAV, Am. Legion. Home: 1046 Fresno Hot Springs SD 57747

FELSENTHAL, STEVEN ALTUS, lawyer; b. Chgo., May 21, 1949; s. Jerome and Eve (Altus) F.; m. Carol Judith Greenberg, June 14, 1970; children: Rebecca Elizabeth, Julia Alison, Daniel Louis Altus. AB, U. Ill.,

1971; JD, Harvard U., 1974. Bar: Ill. 1974, U.S. Dist. Ct. (no. dist.) Ill. 1974, U.S. Ct. Claims 1975, U.S. Tax Ct. 1975, U.S. Ct. Appeals (7th cir.) 1981. Assoc. Levenfeld, Kanter, Baskes & Lippitz Chgo., 1974-78, ptnr. Levenfeld & Kanter, Chgo., 1978-80; ptnr. Levenfeld, Eisenberg, Janger, Glassberg & Lippitz, Chgo., 1980-84; sr. ptnr. Sugar, Friedberg & Felsenthal, Chgo., 1984—; lectr. Kent Coll. Law, Ill. Inst. Tech., Chgo., 1978-80. Mem. ABA, Ill. State Bar Assn., Chgo. Bar Assn., Chgo. Coun. Lawyers, Harvard Law Soc. Ill., Phi Beta Kappa. Clubs: Standard, Harvard (Chgo.). Office: Sugar Friedberg & Felsenthal 30 N La Salle St Ste 2600 Chicago IL 60602-2505

FELSTEHAUSEN, HERMAN HENRY, natural resources-land planning educator; b. Clark, S.D., Feb. 24, 1936; s. Fred W. and Ena Lea (Fossum) F.; m. Geke de Vries; children: Deborah Felstehausen McClellan, Mark Harold. BS, S.D. State U., 1959; MS, U. Wis., 1960, PhD, 1964. Radio newscaster WNAX, Yankton, S.D., 1955-56, WHO, Des Moines, 1957; sci. editor U. Wis., Madison, 1961-62, asst. prof., 1964-69, asst. dir. Land Tenure Ctr., 1964-66; project dir. Land Tenure Ctr., Bogota, Colombia, 1966-69; assoc. prof. U. Wis., Madison, 1969-76, founder, 1st chair Land Resources Program, 1973-76, prof. natural resources and landscape architecture, 1976-95, prof. land use and environ. studies, 1996—; advisor on urban growth studies, Madison, 1970—, Mexican rural devel., Puebla, 1969, Europe-Albania land registration, 1994—, land use and environ. projects, Madison; lectr. architecture of Frank Lloyd Wright, Madison. Contbr. articles to profl. jours., manual in field. Fulbright fellow U.S.-Netherlands, 1962-63; Fulbright faculty fellow, 1978. Mem. Wis. Acad. Scis., Arts and Letters, Rural Sociol. Soc. Am., Agrl. History Assn., Phi Kappa Phi (Wis. pres.). Office: U Wis Agriculture Hall 1450 Linden Dr Madison WI 53706-1522

FELTEY, KATHRYN MARGARET, sociology educator; b. L.I., N.Y., Aug. 1, 1954; d. Donald Robert and Betty Jean (Monroe) F.; 1 child, Zachary Devlin Maher. BA in Sociology, Wright State U., Dayton, Ohio, 1978, MA in Applied Behavioral Scis., 1982; PhD in Sociology, Ohio State U., Columbus, 1988. Rsch. asst. dept. corrections State of Hawaii, Honolulu, 1974; asst. prof. sociology U. Akron, Ohio, 1988—; rsch. cons. Miami Valley Transit Authority, Dayton, 1981; rsch. cons. dept. black studies Ohio State U., Columbus, 1985, dept. ednl. policy, 1987; cons. Task Force on Homelessness, Akron, 1989—. Editor: (internat. newsletter) Network News, 1993—; contbr. articles to profl. jours. Bd. trustees Akron Citizen's Coalition for Emergency Shelter Svcs., Inc., 1990—. Ohio Bd. Regents grantee, 1988, N.E. Ohio Urban grantee, 1989, 90; Univ. Rsch. fellow, 1991. Mem. Am. Sociol. Assn., Sociol. for Women in Soc., Soc. for Applied Sociology, North Cen. Sociol. Assn., Project on Study of Gender and Edn. Office: U Akron Olin Hall Dept of Sociology Akron OH 44325-1905

FELTHOUSE, TIMOTHY ROY, research chemist; b. Berkeley, Calif., Sept. 25, 1951; s. James Whitman and Patricia Mae (Avrit) F. BS magna cum laude, U. Pacific, 1973; PhD, U. Ill., 1978. NSF rsch. participant Wash. State U., Pullman, 1972; rsch. asst. U. Pacific, Stockton, Calif., 1973; grad. tchg. rsch. asst. U. Ill., Urbana, 1973-78; rsch. assoc. Tex. A&M U., College Station, 1978-80; sr. rsch. chemist Monsanto Co., St. Louis, 1980-83, rsch. specialist, 1983-87, sr. rsch. specialist, 1987-88, assoc. fellow, 1988-92, fellow, 1992-93, Huntsman Specialty Chems. Corp., St. Louis, 1994-96; sr. rsch. assoc. Huntsman Corp., Austin, Tex., 1996—. Contbr. articles on chemistry to profl. jours. Calif. State scholar, 1969-73. Mem. Am. Chem. Soc. (news editor St. Louis 1981-82, sci. fairs chmn. St. Louis 1991, fin. com. chmn. 1995, analytical div. undergrad. award 1972), Am. Inst. Chemists, N.Y. Acad. Scis., Catalysis Soc., Phi Kappa Phi, Sigma Xi, Phi Lambda Upsilon. Republican. Methodist. Club: Monsanto-Catalysis (chmn. 1982-83). Office: Huntsman Corp 7114 N Lamar Blvd Bldg 38 Austin TX 78752

FELTON, PATRICIA ANN, nurse, hospital administrator; b. Birmingham, Ala., Nov. 10, 1949; d. Perry Lee and Frankie (Walton) Brown; m. Herman Felton, Jan. 28, 1971; children: Kenneth, Karla, Felicia. Assoc. Nursing Arts, Wayne County Community Coll., 1974; B Nursing Sci., Madonna Coll., 1981; M Adminstrn., Marygrove Coll., 1987; postgrad., Mercy Coll.; MBA, U. Detroit-Mercy, 1992. RN, Mich. Staff nurse oper. rm. Sinai Hosp., Detroit, 1980-82; asst. dir. Meharry Allied Health Learning Ctr., Detroit, 1982-84; dir. of nursing Universal Variable Staffing Systems, Detroit, 1982-83; clin. instr. Highland Pk. (Mich.) Community Coll., 1983-85, Mercy Coll., Detroit, 1983-85, Westland (Mich.) Med. Ctr., 1984-85; patient care educator staff devel. Grace Hosp., Detroit, 1985-87; dir. surg. svcs. Mercy Meml. Hosp., Monroe, Mich., 1988-91; dir. surg. svcs., anesthesia St. Luke's Hosp., Saginaw, Mich., 1991—; DON, chief nurse exec. Mercy Hosp. Detroit, Mich.; dir. nursing; cons. Kitch, Saurbier, Drutchas, Wagner and Kenney, P.C., Detroit, 1986-89. Mem. NAFE, Assn. Oper. Rm. Nurses, Black Nurses Assn., Wayne County Community Coll. Nurse Alumni (sec. 1984), Mich. Assn. Nurse Execs. Democrat. Baptist. Home: 25096 Lindenwood Ln Southfield MI 48034-6188 Office: Mercy Hosp Detroit 5555 Conner Ave Detroit MI 48213

FELTY, DONALD, SR., financial advisor; b. Oneida, Ky., Aug. 6, 1945; s. Woodrow and Glenna (Cunnigan) F.; m. Judith Lynn Stephenson, Nov. 26, 1968; children: Melissa Lynn, Donald Jr. BA, Georgetown (Ky.) Coll., 1967; MA, Miami U., Oxford, Ohio, 1972, PhD, 1992. CLU, ChFC, Am. Coll.; registered investment advisor, U.S. Securities Exch. Commn. With pub. rels. staff Easter Seal Soc., Atlanta, Ga., 1968-69; underwriter Reliance Ins. Co., Atlanta, 1969-70; dir. forensics, instr. Wright State U., Dayton, Ohio, 1972-73, Vanguard H.S., Ocala, Fla., 1973-76; spl. agt. Prudential Ins. Co., Cin., 1976-77; prin. Boone County Alternative Sch., Florence, Ky., 1977-80; ind. fin. advisor Donald Felty & Co., Cin., 1980—; adj. prof. Miami U., 1993—; regional coord. Ednl. Techs., Troy, Mich., 1993—. Co-author: (record/tape) The Making of a Speech, 1972; author, dir.: (video tape) Pensions for the Totally Confused, 1994; dir. (TV series) American Dreams, 1993-94. Mem. adv. bd. No. Ky. Mental Health Assn., Newport, 1976-77, Habitat for Humanity, Hamilton, Ohio, 1988-89, Boone County Planning and Zoning Commn., Burlington, Ky., 1983-84. Mem. Am. Soc. CLU, ChFC, Internat. Assn. Fin. Planning, Social Investment Forum, No. Ky. C. of C., Greater Cin. C. of C. Republican. Episcopalian. Home: 6981 Morris Rd Hamilton OH 45011-5423 Office: Capital Ctr 4858 Interstate Dr Cincinnati OH 45246

FELTZ, TODD A., financial planner; b. Sioux City, Iowa, Apr. 13, 1959. Student, Iowa State U., 1978-79. CFP. Dir. fin. planning Grandy-Pratt, Sioux City, 1980-89; v.p. Carson Feltz Retirement Planning, Omaha, 1989—; speaker Sta. KFAB-Radio, 1991-95. Republican. Roman Catholic. Office: Carson Feltz Retirement Pln 10855 W Dodge Rd Ste 100 Omaha NE 68154-2666

FEMENTIRA, DIOMEDES CALIO, geriatrics nurse; b. Corella, Bohol, The Philippines, Aug. 16, 1922; came to U.S., 1946; s. Juan and Regina (Calio) F.; m. Anne Katheryn Breitbach, Nov. 23, 1963 (dec. 1968); 1 child, Karen Renee; m. Ruby Eleanor Brown, Aug. 24, 1974. Student, So. Coll., Cebu City, The Philippines, 1941; cert. in practical nursing, Offalon Tech. Sch., St. Louis, 1971. Lic. practical nurse. Staff nurse Robert Koch Hosp., St. Louis, 1971-83, Oak Park Nursing Home, St. Louis, 1986-87, Marquette Manor, St. Louis, 1989-93; security officer Wells Fargo, St. Louis, 1987-89. Staff sgt. USN, 1946-54. Decorated Air Force Commendation medal, WWII Victory medal, Am. Def. medal, Asiatic Pacific Def. medal, Philippines Def. medal, Nat. Def. medal USAF; recipient Presdl. Unit citation S.A.C. 379th Bomb Wing. Mem. AARP, Ret. Enlisted Assn., Air Force Sgts. Assn., Non Commd. Officers Assn., Nat. Assn. for Uniformed Svcs., Am. Legion (adjutant 1978—). Democrat. Roman Catholic. Home: 2714 Hawson Dr Saint Louis MO 63125-4024

FENECH, JOSEPH C., lawyer; b. London, May 28, 1950; came to U.S., 1953; s. Carmel John and Elizabeth Frances (Borg) F.; m. Cynthia A. Rennie, June 14, 1980; children: Paul C., Peter J., Elizabeth F. BA with high honors, Mich. State U., 1972; JD, U. Mich., 1975. Bar: Mich. 1975, U.S. Dist. Ct. (ea. dist.) Mich. 1975, U.S. Ct. Appeals (6th cir.) 1977, Ill. 1980, U.S. Dist. Ct. (no. dist.) Ill. 1980, U.S. Dist. Ct. (ctrl. dist.) Ill. 1993, U.S. Dist. Ct. (ea. dist.) Wis. 1993, U.S. Ct. Appeals (7th cir.) 1980, U.S. Supreme Ct. 1993, U.S. Tax Ct. 1993. Law clk. Washtenaw Cir. Ct., Ann Arbor, Mich., 1975-76; asst. atty. gen. State of Mich., Detroit, 1976-80; labor rels. counsel McDonald's Corp., Oak Brook, Ill., 1980-82, sr. internat. atty., 1982-84; sr. mem. Fenech & Toussaint, P.C., Oak Brook, Ill., 1985—. Contbr. articles to profl. jours. Bd. dirs. Cath. Charities Diocese of Joliet, Ill.; mem. Family Focus, Mich., 1979-80, Internat. Found. Employee Benefit Plans, Brookfield, Wis., 1980-83, Chairman's Club Ctrl. DuPage Hosp., Tree of Life, Republican Campaign Coun., 1995; supt. adv. com. Naperville Cmty. Sch. Dist. 203. Named Regents scholar U. Mich., 1973, 74, 75, Trustees scholar Mich. State U., 1969-72. Mem. ABA, Ill. State Bar Assn., Mich. Bar assn., DuPage Estate Planning Coun., U. Mich. Lawyers Club, Ill. Bankers Assn., Ill. Mortgage Bankers Assn., Internat. Platform Assn. Am. Hosp. Assn. (sr. mem.), Am. Acad. Healthcare Attys. (sr. mem.). Office: Fenech & Toussaint PC 2 Mid America Plz Ste 924 Villa Park IL 60181-4719

FENG, ALBERT S., science educator, researcher; b. Bandung, Java, Indonesia, Feb. 10, 1944; s. Shu-San and Yi (Chow) F.; m. Phoebe Lifei Wang, Oct. 14, 1974; children: Jeffrey Thomas, Jacqueline A. BSEE, U. Miami, 1968, MSc, 1970; PhD, Cornell U., 1975. Reliability engr. Singer Corp. Kearfott Div., Little Falls, N.J., 1970; asst. rsch. neuroscientist U. Calif. at San Diego, La Jolla, 1974-76; postdoctoral fellow Washington U., St. Louis, 1976-77; asst. prof. U. Ill., Urbana, 1977-83, assoc. prof., 1983-89, prof., 1989—, head dept. molecular and integrative physiology, 1992—; mem. adv. bd. Parmly Hearing Inst., Chgo., 1982-88; mem. review panel NSF, Washington, 1986-88; chmn. neurosci. program U. Ill., Urbana, 1987-90; mem. hearing rsch. study sect. NIH, Washington, 1991-95, chmn., 1993-95. Contbr. articles to profl. jours. including Jour. Neurophysiology, Jour. Comparative Physiology, Science, Jour. Comparative Neurology, Hearing Research. Fellow AAAS; mem. Assn. for Rsch. Otolaryngology, Internat. Soc. Neuroethology (treas. 1992—), Soc. of Neurosci., Acoustical Soc. Am. Home: 1209 Wilshire Ct Champaign IL 61821-6916 Office: U Ill 405 N Mathews Ave Urbana IL 61801-2325

FENN, WILLIAM HARTLEY, health care administrator; b. Midland, Mich., Apr. 27, 1955; s. Howard Nathan and Mary Eleanor (Chesley) F.; m. Glynis Jennifer Cox, Jan. 21, 1978. AA in Liberal Arts, Thomas Edison Coll. of N.J., 1978; AAS in Emergency Medicine, Comm. Coll. of Air Force, Maxwell AFB, Ala., 1981; BS as Physician Assoc., U. Okla., 1981; BS in Bus., U. State N.Y., Albany, 1990; M Mgmt., Aquinas Coll., Grand Rapids, Mich., 1989. Cert. physician asst. primary care and surgery. Staff clinician Grand Valley Health Plan, Grand Rapids, 1985-87; dir. clin. svcs. Glenbeigh Regional Ctr., Grand Rapids, 1987-90; asst. clin. dir. Dept. Vets. Affairs, Gaylord, Mich., 1990-94; chmn., assoc. prof. physician asst. Western Mich. U., Kalamazoo, 1994—; owner cons. Renaissance Cons. Group, Gaylord, 1988-94; v.p., founder Western Mich. Addictionology Cons., Grand Rapids, 1987-90; adj. assoc. prof. Western Mich. U., Kalamazoo, 1986-94. Dir. Backdoor Theater, Wichita Falls, Tex., 1982-84; treas. Gaylord Area Coun. of Arts, 1991-94; trustee PA Found. of Mich., 1995—. Lt. col. USAF, 1975-85, Res., 1985-95. Fellow Am. Acad. Physician Assts., Mich. Acad. Physician Assts. (v.p. 1986-87), Vets. Affairs Physician Assts. (chief del. 1991-93, pres.-elect 1993); mem. DAV, Kiwanis (dir. Gaylord chpt. 1992-94). Episcopalian. Home: 2300 Ramblewood Dr Kalamazoo MI 49009-8914 Office: Western Mich Univ Physician Asst Dept Kalamazoo MI 49008-5138

FENNEMA, BETTY JANE, nurse; b. Chgo., Nov. 21, 1942; d. William Louis and Dorothy Helen (Swanson) Bertz; m. Eugene Raymond Fennema, Apr. 10, 1965; children: Paul Brett, Craig William. BS, Coll. St. Francis, Joliet, Ill., 1979; postgrad., Roseland Community Hosp. Sch., Chgo., 1964; MA, Govs. State U., 1990. Cert. childbirth educator, CPR instr., trainer, perinatal bereavement counselor. Staff nurse nursery St. Francis Hosp., Blue Island, Ill., 1964-67, asst. nurse nursery, 1967-75, head nurse post partum, 1975-80, coordinator edn., 1980-90; dir. Riverside Women and Family Ctr. Riverside Med. Ctr., Kankakee, Ill., 1990—. Mem. NAACOG, Am. Soc. Psychoprophylaxis Obstetrics, Lamaze, Internat. Childbirth Edn. Assn., Coun. Childbirth Edn. Specialists, Nat. Assn. Women's Health Profls., Kankakee County C. of C., Working Women's Coun., Zonta Internat.

FENNEMA, LEONARD K., engineer, design consultant; b. Grand Rapids, Mich., May 17, 1942. AS, Allied Tech., Chgo., 1961. Sales engr. Gen. Welders, Grand Rapids, Mich., 1987-88; sales engr. mgr. U.S. Engring., Grand Rapids, 1988—. Mem. Am Welding Soc. (bd. dirs.). Home: 2541 22nd St Hopkins MI 49328-9639 Office: US Engring 2530 Thornwood St SW Grand Rapids MI 49509-2149

FENTON, MARJORIE, university official, consultant; b. Warren, Ohio, Feb. 7, 1935; d. Leland Reed and Elma Arlene Titus; m. Harold W. Fenton, June 11, 1955 (div. Sept. 1984); children: Brian, Amy. BS in Edn., Kent State U., 1985, M in Edn. Adminstrn., 1988. Treas. Champion Local Sch. Dist., Warren, 1967-80, Trumbull County Joint Vocat. Sch. Dist., Warren, 1980-89; pres., cons. Sch. Mgmt. Svcs., Inc., Worthington, Ohio, 1989—; coord. Ashland U., Ohio, 1989—; cons. Ohio Dept. Edn., Columbus, 1980-84, 89—, Kemper Securities, Inc., 1993-94; trustee Champion Cmty. Sr. Housing, Inc., Warren, 1982-90, Trimble & Julian, Inc., 1996—. Mem. Trumbull County Bd. Edn., Warren, 1968-93. Recipient Exemplary Service to Edn. award Champion Local Schs., Warren, 1980. Mem. Ohio Assn. Sch. Bus. Ofcls. (state pres. 1979-80, state legis. chmn. 1980-89, Pres.'s Disting. Svc. award 1984, Recognition Outstanding Svc. 1985), Assn. Sch. Bus. Ofcls. Internat. (chair profl. devel. rsch. com.), Ohio Sch. Bds. Assn., Phi Delta Kappa.

FER, AHMET F., electrical engineer, educator; b. Ankara, Turkey, July 31, 1945; came to U.S., 1959; s. Muslih F. and Hayrunnisa (Gurkan) F.; m. Esther Elizabeth Horvath, Nov. 14, 1987; children: Danyal, Adam. BSEE, Mid. East Tech. U., 1967, MSEE, 1970; PhD, U. Birmingham, Birmingham, U.K., 1975. Asst. dept. chmn. elec. engring. dept. Mid. East Tech. U., Ankara, 1979-81, asst. prof., 1975-83, assoc. prof., 1983-84; exec. sec. Engring. Rsch. div. Sci. and Tech. Rsch. Coun., Ankara, 1984-85; assoc. prof. engring. and tech. Purdue U., Indpls., 1985-91, 95—; permanent cons. Technalysis, Inc., Indpls., 1989—. Co-author: Microwave Techniques, 1978; contbr. articles to profl. jours. Fund raiser Multiple Sclerosis Soc., Indpls., 1989-90; mem. electromagnetic wave propagation panel AGARD/NATO. Mem. IEEE, Instn. Elec. Engrs. Eng., Scientech Club. Home: 5223 Mosswood Dr Indianapolis IN 46254-9796 Office: Technalysis Inc 7120 Waldemar Dr Indianapolis IN 46268-2183

FERGUSON, JOHN ALLEN, organist, church musician, music educator; b. Cleve., Jan. 27, 1941; s. Allen Bebee and Nancy Sophie (Carlson) F.; m. Ruth Ann Hofstad, Aug. 22, 1971; 1 child, Christopher. MusB, Oberlin Coll., 1963; MA, Kent State U., 1965; D in Mus. Arts, Eastman Sch. Music, 1976. From instr to prof. music Kent (Ohio) State U., 1965-78; organist, choirmaster United Ch. Christ, Kent, 1963-78; music dir., organist Cen. Luth. Ch., Mpls., 1978-83; prof. organ and ch. music St. Olaf Coll., Northfield, Minn., 1983—; endowed chair in ch. music St. Olaf Coll., 1986; vis. prof. U. Notre Dame, Ind., Yale U.; organ cons. Coll. St. Thomas, St. Paul, 1985-86, Luth. Northwestern Seminary, St. Paul, 1985-87, Shrine of Snows, Bellville, Ill., 1987-90; ch. music cons. 1st Luth., Sioux Falls, S.D., 1986, Augustana Luth., Denver, 1986-87; lectr. in field; active various hymn festivals. Author: Walter Holtkamp Organ Builder, 1979, Guide to Planning for Worship Music, 1983; (mini-course) Creative Hymn Playing, 1986; co-author: Musician's Guide to Church Music, 1981; editor: Hymnal-United Ch. Christ, 1975; over 50 octavos in print; (CD) Te Deum, 1994, When In Our Music, 1994; contbr. articles to profl. jours. Named one of Outstanding Young Men of Am., Jaycees, 1976; Ford Found. Venture Fun grantee 1974, Am. Luth. Ch. grantee 1986. Mem. Am. Guild Organists (sec. com. profl. edn. 1980-90, gen. chmn. nat. conv. 1974, chmn. nat. improvisation competition 1988-89), Nat. Assn. Pastoral Musicians, Hymn Soc. Am., Choristers Guild (bd. dirs. 1989-93), Assn. Choral Dirs. of Am. Home: 820 Ivanhoe Dr Northfield MN 55057-1337 Office: St Olaf Coll Music Dept Northfield MN 55057

FERGUSON, JOHN DUNCAN, medical researcher; b. Saskatoon, Sask., Can., Aug. 20, 1929; s. George Alexander and Urdine (LeValley) F.; m. Tamara van den Bergh, Sept. 12, 1958. MA, U. Toronto, Ont., Can., 1956; PhD, Columbia U., 1966. Project dir. Bur. Applied Social Rsch., Columbia U., N.Y.C., 1958-64; asst. prof. Northeastern U., Boston, 1966-68; from assoc. prof. to prof. U. Windsor, Ont., 1968—; mem. assoc. med. staff Harper Hosp., Detroit, 1982. Author reports in field. Grantee Ont. Cmty. and Social Svcs. Ministry, 1991—. Presbyterian. Home: 1516 Iroquois Ave Detroit MI 48214 Office: U Windsor, Windsor, ON Canada N9B 3P4

FERGUSON, JOHN WAYNE, SR., librarian; b. Ash Grove, Mo., Nov. 4, 1936; s. John William and Eula Marie (Rogers) F.; m. Nancy Carolyn Southerland, Apr. 4, 1958; children: John Wayne Jr., Mark Warren, Steven Ward. BS, S.W. Mo. State Coll., 1958; MS, U. Okla., 1961. Libr. Springfield (Mo.) Pub. Libr., 1952-64; asst. dir. Jackson County Pub. Libr., 1964-65; dir. Mid-Continent Pub. Libr., 1965-81, 1981—; libr. Mid-Continent Pub. Libr., Independence, Mo. Bd. dirs. YMCA, Independence, 1969-89, Independence Regional Health Ctr., 1981-90. Capt. U.S. Army, 1959-65. Named Libr. of Yr. Libr. Jour. mag., 1993. Mem. Rotary (dist. govt. Independence chpt. 1986-87, pres. 1981-82). Home: 14504 E 43rd St S Independence MO 64055-4840 Office: Mid-Continent Pub Libr 15616 E 24 Hwy Independence MO 64050

FERGUSON, JULIE ANN, physical education educator; b. Maquoketa, Iowa, June 19, 1958; d. Donald Hayes and Bonnie Lea (Bullock) Maxey; m. John Stephan Ferguson, Aug. 10, 1985; children: Dawn Ann, John Ryan, John Scott. BS in Edn., U. Mo., 1980; MS in Athletic Adminstrn., U. Ill., 1982. Cert. tchr. Mo. Sub. tchr. Ritenour Dist., St. Louis, 1978-80; asst. women's basketball coach U. Ill., Champaign, 1980-82, instr. phys. edn., 1981-82, adminstrv. asst. Athletic Assn., 1982-83; dir. championships, supr. officials Big Eight Conf., Kansas City, Mo., 1983-90; instr. phys. edn Lee's Summit (Mo.) Sch. Dist., 1990—; speaker, clin. coord. Fellowship Christian Athletes, Kansas City, 1986; selection com. U. Mo., Kansas City, 1987, 88; scholar athlete Kansas City Star, 1989; coach, tour adminstr. Athletes in Action Basketball Team to China and Far East, 1984; tour adminstr. Big Eight Conf. Basketball Tour to Czechoslovakia, 1990. Deacon Lee's Summit Christian Ch., 1990-. Mem. U. Mo. Columbia Alumni Assn., U. Ill. Alumni Assn., Women's Basketball Coaches Assn., Am. Volleyball Coaches Assn., Coun. Collegiate Women Athletic Adminstrs., Fellowship Christian Athletes. Home: 4151 SE Paddock Cir Lees Summit MO 64082-4926

FERGUSON, PAMELA ANDERSON, mathematics educator, educational administrator; b. Berwyn, Ill., May 5, 1943; d. Clarence Oscar and Ruth Anne (Stroner) Anderson; m. Donald Roger Ferguson, Dec. 18, 1965; children: Keith, Amanda. BA, Wellesley Coll., 1965; MS, U. Chgo., 1966, PhD, 1969. Asst. prof. Northwestern U., Evanston, Ill., 1969-70, U. Miami, Coral Gables, Fla., 1972-77; assoc. prof. U. Miami, 1978-81, prof. math., 1981-91, dir. honors program, 1985-87, assoc. provost, dean Grad. Sch., 1987-91; pres. Grinnell Coll., Iowa, 1991—. Contbr. over 50 articles to refereed jours. Mem. Iowa Rsch. Coun., 1993—. NSF grantee. Mem. Am. Math. Soc., Am. Women in Math., Wellesley Club, Sigma Xi, Phi Beta Kappa, Omicron Delta Chi. Lutheran. Office: Grinnell Coll Office of the Pres 1121 Park St PO Box 805 Grinnell IA 50112-0805

FERGUSON, ROBERT P. (H-BOMB), musician, songwriter; b. Charleston, S.C., May 9, 1929; s. Lorenzo and Irene (Thomas) F.; m. Christine Marie Busemeyer, Sept. 24, 1988; 1 child, Robert Hamilton. Mem. Joe Liggins and the Honeydrippers; performer The Baby Grand Club, N.Y.C.; mem. Charlie Singleton and Orch., H-Bomb Ferguson and His Mad Lads, The Medicine Men; rec. artist with Derby Records, Atlas, Savoy Records, Earwig Music; musician, comedian at various clubs, N.Y.C., Cin., including Cotton Club, Apollo Theatre, others, at Chgo. Blues Fest, 1992, Mississippi Valley Blues Fest, Davenport, Iowa, 1994, numerous other blues music festivals. Composer various blues songs, including Slowly Goin' Crazy, My Brown Frame Baby, Bookies Blues, Tortured Love, Midnight Ramblin' Tonight, Mary Little Mary, Leavin You Tomorrow. Appeared in benefit concerts for musical colls. and sr. citizen groups, Cin. Recipient W.C. Handy award Nat. Blues Found., 1986, 89. Home and Office: 1646 California Ave Cincinnati OH 45237

FERGUSON, ROGER CLARK, computer science educator; b. Bay City, Mich., Jan. 21, 1959; s. Russell L. and Grace L. (Wieland) F.; married, 1985; 1 child, Ian. BSEE, Mich. Tech. U., 1982; MS in Computer Sci., Ctrl. Mich. U., 1987; PhD in Computer Sci., Wayne State U., 1992. Software engr. ABW, Ann Arbor, Mich., 1982-84; adj. faculty Ea. Mich. U., Ypsilanti, 1984-89; rsch. asst. Wayne State U., Detroit, 1989-92; pvt. computer cons. Plymouth, Mich., 1992—; prof. computer sci. Lawrence Tech. U., Southfield, Mich., 1992—. Author: (software) Build a Software Program to Sell, 1984; contbr. articles to profl. jours. Rumble fellow Wayne State U., 1989. Fellow IEEE Computer Soc., AEM Comm., Eta Kappa Nu. Home: 11969 Traiwood Plymouth MI 48170 Office: Lawrence Tech U 21000 Ten Mile Rd Southfield MI 48075

FERGUSON, RONALD JOSEPH, historian, educator; b. Bellevue, Ohio, Dec. 21, 1956; s. Ernest Joseph and Evelyn Y. (Garman) F.; m. Janet Roorda, Nov. 29, 1980; children: Aaron Joseph, Jennica Marie. BS in Edn., Bowling Green State U., 1979; MA, Wheaton Coll., 1982; MEd, U. Alta., 1991; PhD, Ohio State U., 1995. Regional rep. Pioneer Clubs Can., Inc., Burlington, Ont., 1983-86; dir. Christian edn. Beulah Alliance Ch., Edmonton, Alta., Can., 1986-88; asst. prof. Ball State U., Muncie, Ind., 1994—. 1st v.p. Nat. Fedn. Blind Ohio Parents Divsn., Columbus, 1995-96. Mem. History of Edn. Soc., Midwest History of Edn. Soc., Phi Kappa Phi, Phi Beta Delta. Home: 3463 Homecraft Dr Columbus OH 43224 Office: TC 823 Tchrs Coll Ball State Univ Muncie IN 47306

FERGUSON, SCOTT, mechanical engineer; b. Cin., Nov. 5, 1969. BSME, U. Cin., 1994. Mech. engr. Cin. (Ohio) Gear Co., 1991-94, Fujitec Am., Lebanon, Ohio, 1994—. Volleyball coach, Milford, Ohio, 1992-95. Mem. ASME. Home: 5575 Kay Dr Milford OH 45150-2875

FERGUSON, STEVEN MARK, business analyst; b. Galveston, Tex., Aug. 11, 1968; s. Earl Wilson and Bonnie Rose (Harrington) F.; m. Christine Marie Hobbs, June 27, 1992; 1 child, Justin Lee. BS in bus., Ea. Ill. U., 1990. Cert. pub. acct., Ill. Auditor Caterpillar, Inc., Decatur, Ill., 1990-91, staff acct., 1991-94, pricing analyst, 1994—. Sec. Health, Safety & Adminstrn. Com., Village Forsyth, Ill., 1993—; patrolman Decatur Aux. Police Dept., 1993—. Office: Caterpillar Inc 27th Perching Rd Box 1410 Decatur IL 62525

FERGUSON, TAMARA, clinical sociologist; b. The Hague, Netherlands; came to U.S., 1955; d. Simon and Sonia (Pokrowska) Van den Bergh; m. John D.A. Ferguson, Sept. 12, 1958. MA in Sociology, Columbia U., 1962, PhD, 1970. Asst. prof. U. Detroit, 1960-71; asst. prof., then assoc. prof. U. Windsor, Ont., Can., 1971-78; adj. assoc. prof. sociology Wayne State U. Med. Sch., Detroit, 1978—; assoc. med. staff dept. psychiatry Harper Hosp., Detroit, 1982—. Co-author: The Young Widow: Conflict and Guidelines, 1981; contbg. author: Clinical Sociology in Mental Health Setting, 1991, Qualitative Analysis in Human Sciences: New Perspectives in Methodology, 1996. 2d lt. Free French armed forces, 1944-45, ETO. Mem. Am. Sociol. Assn., Found. Thanatology, Sociol. Practice Assn. (bd. dirs.). Office: Harper Hosp Neuropsych Day Treatment Prog 50 E Canfield St Detroit MI 48201-1804

FERGUSON-RAYPORT, SHIRLEY MARTHA, psychiatrist, educator; b. Syracuse, N.Y., Mar. 9, 1923; married; 3 children. AB magna cum laude, Syracuse U., 1945, MD magna cum laude, 1947. Diplomate Am. Bd. Psychiatry and Neurology; cert. Nat. Bd. Med. Examiners; lic. psychiatrist, N.Y., Calif. Ohio. Rotating intern Jewish Hosp., Bklyn., 1947-48; intern in surgery and gynecology N.Y. Infirmary, N.Y.C., 1948-49, asst. resident in obstetrics, 1949-50; asst. resident in medicine and neurology 3d (NYU) divsn. Goldwater Meml. Hosp., N.Y.C., 1950-51; resident in neuropsychiatr U.S. VA Hosp., Lexington, Ky., 1951-53; sr. asst. resident Allan Meml. Inst. Psychiatry, Montreal, Can., 1953-54; rsch. fellow dept. psychiatry McGill U., Montreal, 1954-55; clin. fellow Allan Meml. Inst. Psychiatry, Royal Victoria Hosp., Montreal, 1954-55; staff psychiatrist Montreal Children's Hosp., 1955-56; rsch. assoc. dept. psychiatry Queen Mary VA Hosp., Montreal, 1956-57; psychiatrist Epilepsy Clinic Montreal Neurol. Inst., 1957-58; rsch. assoc. depts. neurol. surgery and neurology Columbia U., N.Y.C., 1958-60; Psyc Rsch Assoc Albert Einstein Coll Med Dept Neur Surg, N.Y.C., 1960-65; Asst Neur Columbia-Presby Med Ctr, N.Y.C., 1959-63; Post-Doctoral Fellow Albert Einstein Coll Med, N.Y.C., 1963-65; Asst Att Psyc Montefiore Hosp, Bronx, N.Y., 1965-68; Assoc Prof Psyc Med Coll Ohio,

Toledo, 1969-84; Act Staff Med Coll Ohio Hosp Div Psyc, 1969-93; Dir Toledo Mental Hlth Ctr Med Coll Unit, 1971-82; Assoc Prof Neuroscis Med Coll Ohio Sect Behav Neurol, 1976-84; Chrmn. dept. Psyc. Mercy Hosp, Toledo, OH, 1979-81; Head Sect. Neuropsyc Med Coll Ohio Dept Psyc, 1982-93; Prof Psyc & Neur Surg Med Coll Ohio, 1984-93, Prof Emerita Psyc, 1993; Hon. Staff Med Coll Ohio Hosp Div Psyc, 1993—; asst. vis. psychiatrist in neurol. surgery Bronx Mcpl. Hosp. Ctr., N.Y., 1960-68; vis. scientist Unite de Recherche sur l'Epilepsie, INSERM, Paris, 1986; adj. dept. psychiatry Mt. Zion Hosp. and Med. Ctr., San Francisco, Calif., 1968-69; rsch. fellow Montreal Neurol. Inst., Montreal, 1957-58; mem. adult svcs. com. Lucas County Mental Health Bd., 1991-92; psychiat. cons. Bapt. Hosp. of U. of Tenn., 1989. Bd. trustees Creative Arts Comty., Toledo, 1974-76; profl. adv. bd. Epilepsy Ctr. N.W. Ohio, 1981—; head injury adv. coun., head injury program Ohio Dept. Health, Divsn. Chronic Diseases, 1990-92. Rsch. grantee. Fellow Am. Psychiat. Assn. (life); mem. Am. Epilepsy Soc., Soc. Biol. Psychiatry, N.W. Ohio Psychiat. Assn. (exec. com. 1982—, pres. 1980-82), Acad. Medicine Toledo and Lucas County (comty. health com.), Ohio State Med. Assn., Ohio Psychiat. Assn. (membership com. 1980-83, pub. mental health com. 1980-81, 86—, liaison com. 1989-92), Assn. Acad. Psychiatry, Internat. Neuropsychol. Soc., Behavioral Neurology Soc., Am. Neuropsychiat. Soc., Sigma Xi, Alpha Omega Alpha, Phi Beta Kappa. Office: Med Coll Ohio Dept Psychiatry PO Box 10008 Toledo OH 43699-0008

FERINO, CHRISTOPHER KENNETH, computer information scientist; b. Chgo., May 25, 1961; s. Natale Ferino and Carol Marie Anderson; m. Anita Louise Vanderhoof, Oct. 19, 1985; children: Anthony Natale, Kenneth Allen. Student computer sci., acctg., Elgin Community Coll., 1978; student computer sci., McHenry County Coll., 1985. Cons. Lachman Assn., Inc., Westmont, Ill., 1979-80; AS/RS operator W.W. Grainger, Niles, Ill., 1980-82; mem. computer staff Paddock Publs., Arlington Heights, Ill., 1982-84; data processing coord. Power Systems, Schaumburg, Ill., 1984-85; dir. tech. svcs. Follett Software Co., Crystal Lake, Ill., 1985-88; tech. service dir. Follett Software Co., Crystal Lake, 1987-88; tech. editor MacGuide mag., 1988-89; pres. CKF Assoc., 1989—; cons. faculty Boston MacWorld Expn., 1988, 90, San Francisco, 1988, 89, 92, 93, 94. Tech. editor MacGuide Mag., 1988-89. Home and Office: 611 Anderson Dr Lake in the Hills IL 60102

FERKINGSTAD, SUSANNE M., cosmetics executive; b. Red Wing, Minn., Aug. 19, 1955; m. Steve Ferkingstad, Oct. 19, 1991. Diploma Cosmetology, Ritter St. Paul Coll., 1974; grad., Bruno's, 1978. Instr. Ritter's St. Paul Coll., 1974-75; asst. mgr., mgr. Scot Lewis Inc., Bloomington, Minn., 1975-79; edn. dir. My Kind of Place, St. Paul, 1979-80; pres., co-owner Someone's Looking (formerly Charpentier's Inc.), St. Paul, 1980-86, owner, 1986—; styles dir. women's sect. Minn. Cosmetology Edn. Com. Fundraiser, chairperson Battered Women's Shelter, St. Paul, 1984, Children's Home Soc., St. Paul, 1985; vol. St. Paul Food Shelves Food Dr., 1985, 88; vol., model United Arts Fashion Show, 1986; vol. fundraiser pub. TV Action Auction, Ronald McDonald House, Food Shelf Drives Someone's Looking, St. Paul, MS Walkathon, 1988. Recipient numerous hairstyling awards. Mem. Nat. Cosmetologists Assn., Minn. Hairdressers and Cosmetologists Assn., St. Paul Cosmetologists Assn. (dir. 1981-83, pres. 1983-85), Hair Am., Minn. Hair Fashion Com. Home: 3111 Drew Ave N Robbinsdale MN 55422-3247 Office: Someone's Looking Inc 141 4th St E Ste 125 Saint Paul MN 55101-1620

FERM, LOIS ROUGHAN, religious organization administrator; b. Buffalo, Feb. 5, 1918; d. Laurence Francis and Bertha Margaret Lucy (Jopp) R.; m. Robert O. Ferm, June 28, 1941 (dec. Mar. 1994); children: Lois Esther, Rebecca Ann, Paul Robert, Stephen John. BA, Houghton Coll., 1939; MA, U. Mich., 1955; PhD, U. Minn., 1972. Cert. tchr., N.Y. Tchr. Rushford (N.Y.) Cen. Sch., 1939-41; instr. library, sociology John Brown U., Siloam Springs, Ark., 1949-51; librarian Cuba (N.Y.) Cen. Schs., 1953-55; chmn. dept. edn. Houghton (N.Y.) Coll., 1955-57; instr. edn. U. Minn., Mpls., 1959-61, mgr. Coll. Edn. Library, 1961-64; personal asst. rsch., resource coord. Billy Graham Evangel. Assn., Mpls., 1973—. Pres. Riceville Property Owners Assn., Asheville, N.C., 1982, 83, 87, 88; active N.C. Arboretum Bd., 1992-96. Mem. Soc. Am. Archivists, Oral History Assn., Christian Women's Clubs, Pi Lambda Theta, Pi Alpha Theta. Republican. Baptist. Home: 27 Patriots Dr Asheville NC 28805-9730 Office: Billy Graham Evang Assn 1300 Harmon Pl Minneapolis MN 55403-1925

FERMANIAN, THOMAS WALTER, turfgrass scientist, educator; b. Milw., Apr. 22, 1950; s. Eleanor Vrana; m. Nancy Ann Mayer, May 20, 1972; children: Alysa, Jessica. MS, Okla. State U., 1978, PhD, 1980. Asst. prof. U. Ill., Urbana, 1980-96, assoc. prof. dept. natural resources & environ. scis., 1986—; vis. prof. George mason U., Fairfax, Va., 1988; mem. Intelligent Sys. Group Dept. Computer Sci., Urbana, 1983-96; advisor Ill. Turfgrass Found., Chgo. Author: Controlling Turfgrass Pests, 1987, Knowledge Engineering for Agriculture, 1989; contbr. articles to Agronomy Jour. Mem. IEEE, Am. Soc. Agronomy (Outstanding Paper award 1979), Am. Assn. for Artificial Intelligence, Am. Soc. for Hort. Scis. Home: 2048 County Road 125 E Mahomet IL 61853-8907 Office: U Ill 1102 Goodwin Ave Urbana IL 61801-4720

FERNÁNDEZ, OSCAR A., designer, graphic; b. Hoboken, N.J., Mar. 18, 1951; s. Santiago Oscar and Ana Emelia (Hernandez) F.; m. Stacy Lynn Russell, Apr. 13, 1973 (div. Aug. 1982); m. Michele Elizabeth Fadley, June 12, 1983; 1 child, Amber Kristina. BS in Art, Lamar U., 1973; MFA in Graphic Design, Yale U., 1976. Graphic designer Caudill Rowlett Scott, Houston, 1976-79; asst. prof. Mont. State U., Bozeman, 1979-81; assoc. prof. Ohio State U., Columbus, 1981-85; chmn. dept. graphic design Maine Coll. Art, Portland, 1985; assoc. prof. Columbus (Ohio) Coll. Art and Design, 1987-89, U. Cin., 1989-90; dir. design Wexner Ctr. for Arts, Columbus, 1990-92, Degnen Assocs., Columbus, 1992-93, Moorehead Design, Columbus, 1993—. Named Best of Show Columbus Soc. Creative Arts, 1993; recipient Award of Excellence Graphis Mag., 1989. Mem. Am. Inst. Graphic Arts (bd. dirs. 1993-95, Award of Excellence 1990), Am. Ctr. for Design (Award of Excellence 1989), Soc. Environ. Graphic Design, Columbus Soc. Comml. Arts. Home: 2884 Phoenix Ave Hilliard OH 43026 Office: Moorehead Design 88 E Broad St Ste 1920 Columbus OH 43215

FERNEAU, THOMAS E., insurance consultant; b. Omaha, Nebr., June 26, 1948; s. John and Emilie (Ludwig) F.; m. Nancy C. White, Feb. 9, 1980; children: Thomas A., Benjamin J. BA, U. Nebr., 1970, JD, 1972. Bar: Nebr., U.S. Dist. Ct. Nebr., U.S. Supreme Ct., Tax Ct. Ptnr. Ferneau & Sullen Law, Auburn, Nebr., 1972-76; assoc. Aten, Nobel & Ide Law, Holdrege, Nebr., 1976-77; atty. Phelps County Pub. Defender, Holdrege, 1978-80; assoc. Anderson, Ferneau & Anderson, Lincoln, Nebr., 1980-84; pvt. practice Lincoln, 1985—; pres. 1st Nebraska Securities, Inc., Lincoln, Market Advisors, Inc., 1st Insurance Group of Nebr., Inc., Lincoln.; lectr. in field of ins. and taxes. Sec. Nemaha County Devel. Corp., Auburn, 1974-75. With U.S. Army, 1969. Mem. Lions (sec./treas. 1977-78), Kiwanis, Nebr. State Bar Assn., Lincoln Bar Assn., Southeastern Nebr. Bar Assn. (sec./treas. 1973-74). Office: 650 J St #400 Lincoln NE 68516

FERNER, DAVID CHARLES, non-profit management and development consultant; b. Rochester, N.Y., Mar. 14, 1933; s. John Theodore and Dorothy Flora (Seel) F.; m. Ursula Milda Thieme, Sept. 6, 1958. BA, Amherst Coll., 1955; MEd, U. Rochester, 1957; postgrad., Columbia U., 1961. Dir. student activities U. Rochester, N.Y., 1956-58; asst. to provost Tchrs. Coll. Columbia U., N.Y.C., 1959-60; asst. dir. devel. St. Lawrence U., Canton, N.Y., 1961-62; dir. devel. Sarah Lawrence Coll., Bronxville, N.Y., 1962-66; cons., v.p. Frantzreb & Pray Assocs., Inc., N.Y.C., 1966-72; v.p., sec. Frantzreb & Pray Assocs., Inc., Arlington, Va., 1972-75; pres. Frantzreb, Pray, Ferner & Thompson, Inc., Arlington, 1975-77, David C. Ferner & Assocs., Annandale, Va., 1977-80; v.p., dir. devel. Minn. Orchestral Assn., Mpls., 1980-87; mng. ptnr. Currie, Ferner, Scarpetta & DeVries, Mpls., 1987—. Contbr. articles to profl. publs. Bd. dirs. Madeline Island Mus. Camp, Nat. Soc. Fundraising Execs. Minn. chpt. Amherst Coll. scholar, 1951-55. Mem. Nat. Soc. Fundraising Execs. (bd. dirs. Minn. chpt. 1995—), Coun. for Advancement and Support of Edn., Am. Symphony Orch. League, Opera Am. Home: 19025 Walden Trl Deephaven MN 55391-3544 Office: Currie Ferner & DeVries 1111 3rd Ave S Ste 460 Minneapolis MN 55404-1008

FERNG, DOUGLAS MING-HAW, infosystems executive; b. Anshan, Peoples Republic of China, Feb. 27, 1945; came to U.S., 1968; s. Jau-Tarng and Hwei-In (Chu) F.; m. Gloria K. Chao, Oct. 28, 1972; children: Jennifer, Albert. BS, Nat. Taiwan U., Taipei, 1967; M in Forestry, Yale U., 1970; MBA, U. Wash., Seattle, 1979. Sci. programmer Weyerhaeuser Co., Federal Way, Wash., 1970-72, computer analyst, 1972-77, forest economist, 1977-79; mgr. silvicultural econs. Champion Internat., Stamford, Conn., 1979-80, mgr. resource econs., 1980-83; mgr. bus. systems Champion Internat., Hamilton, Ohio, 1983-87, mgr. paper applications, 1987-93; dir. bus. info. svcs., 1993—. Served as 2d lt. Taiwan Army, 1967-68. Fellow Yale Univ., 1968-70. Mem. Paper Industry Mgmt. Assn., Assn. System Mgmt., Cin. Chinese Assn., Chinese Assn. of Fairfield County (v.p. 1981-83). Club: Cin. Yale. Office: Champion Internat 101 Knightsbridge Dr Hamilton OH 45011-3166

FERRALL, VICTOR EUGENE, JR., college administrator, lawyer; b. Urbana, Ill., July 31, 1936; s. Victor Eugene and Lucile Elizabeth (Hill) F.; m. Suzanne Elizabeth Lilly (div. 1985); children: Christopher Key, David Hill, Katherine Elizabeth; m. Linda K. Smith, 1987. AB, Oberlin Coll, 1956; student law, Harvard U., 1956-57; MA in Econs., Yale U., 1958, LLB, 1960. Bar: D.C. 1961, U.S. Supreme Ct. 1981. Atty. U.S. Dept. Justice, Washington, 1960-61; asst. to staff dir. antitrust and monopoly subcom. U.S. Senate, Washington, 1961-63; assoc. then ptnr. Koteen & Burt, Washington, 1963-75; ptnr. Jones, Day, Reavis & Pogue, Washington, 1975-79, Crowell & Moring, Washington, 1979-91; pres. Beloit (Wis.) Coll., 1991—. Contbr. articles to profl. jours.; editor: Yearbook of Broadcasting Articles (anthology edition), 1980. Trustee Olivet (Mich.) Coll., 1979-81. Mem. ABA, D.C. Bar Assn., Wis. Bar Assn., Nat. Assn. Ind. Colls. and Univs. (bd. dirs. 1993—). Democrat. Episcopalian. Home: 709 College St Beloit WI 53511-5509 Office: Beloit Coll 700 College St Beloit WI 53511-5509

FERRARI, LINDA JOY, nurse; b. Wausau, Wis., Aug. 28, 1960; d. Joel Darwin and Sharron (Junghans) Walter; m. Louis A. Ferrari Jr., Oct. 28, 1989; 1 child, Louis A. III. ADN, Rochester (Minn.) C.C., 1982. Cert. BLS, ACLS, CCRN, Wis. RN Theda Clark Regional Med. Ctr., Neenah, Wis., 1982-88; RN Door County Meml. Hosp., Sturgeon Bay, Wis., 1988—, supr., 1992-95; supr. Dorchester Nursing Ctr., 1989—; staff nurse Baylake Outpatient Surgery Ctr., 1994—; entrepreneur LJ Mktg. and Promotions, 1996—; entrepreneur L.J. Mktg. and Promotions, 1996—.

FERRARI, MICHAEL DAVID, financial planner, investment advisor; b. Washington, Mo., June 19, 1945; s. David D. and Alma (Farrell) F.; m. Jan Byrne, June 4, 1966; 1 child, Elizabeth A. BS, U. Miami, 1968. CLU; CFP. Asst. mgr. Conn. Gen. Life Ins. Co., Kansas City, Mo., 1968-78; agy. mgr. Equitable Iowa, Kansas City, 1979-83; pres. Ferrari Fin. Ins. and Investment Mgmt., Overland Park, Kans., 1982—; author, pub. Which Way the Market newsletter, 1982—. Contbr. articles to newspapers. Instr. adult edn. area colls., Kansas City, 1982—. Mem. Inst. CFPs, Toastmasters (best spkr. award). Republican. Home: 6619 W 69th St Shawnee Mission KS 66204-1442

FERRARI, MICHAEL RICHARD, JR., university administrator; b. Monongahela, Pa., May 12, 1940; s. Michael Richard and Lillian Ann (Cristina) F.; m. Janice Bjurstrom, Sept. 5, 1964; children: Elizabeth Anne, Michael, III. BA, Mich. State U., 1962, MA, 1963, DBA (Ford Found. fellow), 1968; D of Pub. Svc. (hon.), Bowling Green State U., 1991. Asst. to dean men U. Cin., 1965-66; asst. to dir. residence life, resident hall head advisor Mich. State U., 1966-68; acting chmn. dept. adminstrv. scis. Kent (Ohio) State U., 1970-71; mem. adminstrv. staff Bowling Green (Ohio) State U., 1971-73, v.p. resource planning, 1973-78, provost, exec. v.p., 1978-81, interim pres., 1981-82; vis. scholar U. Mich., 1982-83; prof. mgmt., provost Wright State U., Dayton, 1983-85; pres. Drake U., Des Moines, 1985—; bd. dirs. Norwest Bank Iowa, NA, Irish Life of N.Am., Hubbell Realty; mgmt. cons., 1968—. Author: Profiles of American College Presidents, 1970, Measuring the Quality of Universities, 1970, National Study of Student Personnel Manpower Planning, 1972. Bd. dirs. Greater Des Moines Com., Bus. and Econ. Devel. Council, Living History Farms of Iowa. Research fellow Am. Coll. Testing Program, 1970. Mem. Acad. Mgmt., Iowa Coordinating Coun. for Post-Secondary Edn. (chmn. 1988-89), Iowa Ind. Colls. and Univs., Mo. Valley Athletic Coun. of Pres.'s (chmn. 1986-87), Omicron Delta Kappa, Phi Kappa Phi, Beta Gamma Sigma, Pi Gamma Mu. Episcopalian. Home: 227 37th St Des Moines IA 50312-4305 Office: Drake U 25th University Ave Des Moines IA 50311

FERRARO, CHARLES DOMENIC, psychologist, educator; b. Cleve., Apr. 12, 1913; s. Ross and Mary (Cundra) F.; m. Alice Carolyn Nimrichter, Dec. 30, 1939 (div. Dec. 1965); children: Diane, Linda; m. Donna Joan Gamble, Apr. 12, 1966. AB, Ohio U., 1936; BS, Case Western Res. U., 1938, MA, 1953, PhD, 1957. Lic. psychologist, Ohio. Chief counselor John Carroll U., University Heights, Ohio, 1949-51, lectr. psychology, 1951-70, 81-86, assoc. prof., 1970-74, prof., chmn. psychology dept., 1974-78; placement officer NASA-Lewis Research Ctr., Cleve., 1951-70; pvt. practice counseling psychologist Lakewood, Ohio, 1953—. Bd. dirs., chmn., governance com. Far W. Mental Health Ctr., Westlake, Ohio, 1979-85. Recipient Career Service award Cleve. Fed. Exec. Bd., 1969, Fed. Service award Am. Soc. Pub. Adminstrn., 1969, Commendation cert. Pres. Nixon, 1970. Mem. Am. Psychol. Assn. (life), Ohio Psychol. Assn. (life). Home: 1550 Cedarwood Dr Cleveland OH 44145-1811 Office: 1550 Cedarwood Dr Apt C Cleveland OH 44145-1811

FERREIRA, DANIEL ALVES, secondary education Spanish language educator; b. Lisbon, Portugal, Feb. 24, 1944; came to U.S., 1959, naturalized, 1963; s. Manuel and Lourdes (Alves) F.; m. Cheryl R. Jann, July 1, 1978; children: Jeffrey, Douglas, Peter. BA, U. Ill., 1966, MEd, 1970; Diploma Superior, U. Salamanca, Spain, 1994. Cert. tchr., Ill. Tchr. Homewood-Flossmoor (Ill.) High Sch., 1966—; boys and girls Soccer Coach at Homewood-Flossmoor (Ill.). Bd. dirs. Grace Migrant Day Care Ctr., Park Forest, Ill., 1971-80. Named Chgo. Area Tchr. of Yr., U. Chgo., 1985. Mem. Am. Assn. Tchrs. of Spanish and Portuguese, Ill. High Sch. Soccer Coaches Assn., Nat. Soccer Coaches Assn. Am., Ill. Edn. Assn., NEA, Homewood-Flossmoor Edn. Orgn. (pres. 1981-82), Phi Delta Kappa. Home: 21343 Ginger Ln Frankfort IL 60423-9428 Office: Homewood Flossmoor High Sch 999 Kedzie Ave Flossmoor IL 60422-2248

FERREIRA, JO ANN JEANETTE CHANOUX, consumer electronics manufacturing executive; b. Melrose Park, Ill., Dec. 3, 1943; d. John W. and June B. Chanoux; BS, Purdue U., 1965, MS (NSF fellow), 1969; m. G. Dodge Ferreira, Apr. 21, 1979 (div. Dec. 1993). With systems devel. research IBM, San Jose, Calif., 1965-67; asst. dir. mgmt. info. systems edn. Union Carbide Corp., N.Y.C., 1969; mgmt. cons. Touche Ross & Co., N.Y.C., 1970-72, Peat Marwick Mitchell, N.Y.C., 1974-75; dir. corp. devel. strategy cons. A.T. Kearney-Mgmt. Cons., Chgo., 1975-83; dir. Computer Devel. Center, United Airlines, 1983-88; pres. WSG Designs Inc., Northbrook, Ill., 1988-92, Accorde-Moraine Consulting, Inc., 1992-93; gen. mgr. acoustic rsch. divsn. Internat. Jensen, Inc., Lincolnshire, Ill., 1993—, v.p. bus. plans and export ops., 1994—; lectr. Purdue U., 1969, 73-74; guest lectr. Northwestern U., 1981; gen. mgr. acoustic rsch. divsn., exec. asst. to pres. Internat. Jensen, Inc., 1993—. Mem. Inst. Mgmt. Cons. (cert. mgmt. cons.), Am. Arbitration Assn. Phi Kappa Phi. Contbr. articles to profl. publs.; speaker various groups. Office: Internat Jensen Inc 25 Tri State Internat Ctr Lincolnshire IL 60069

FERRELL, JAMES EDWIN, energy company executive; b. Atchison, Kans., Oct. 17, 1939; s. Alfred C. and Mabel A. (Samson) F.; m. Elizabeth J. Gillespie, May 10, 1959; children: Kathryn E., Sarah A. B.S. in Bus. Adminstrn., U. Kans., 1963. Pres. Ferrell Cos., Inc., Liberty, Mo., 1965—; chmn., chief exec. officer Gas Service Co., Kansas City, Mo., 1983-85; bd. dirs. United Mo. Bancshares, Kansas City, Ferrell Cos., Inc. Bd. dirs. Coun. Ind. Colls., 1988-91; trustee Kansas City Symphony, 1987—. Served to 1st lt. U.S. Army, 1963-65. Republican. Lutheran. Office: Ferrell Cos Inc 1 Liberty Plz Liberty MO 64068-2970

FERRELL, PAUL CLEVELAND, author; b. Morehouse, Mo., Aug. 17, 1943; s. Sherman Gentry and Virginia Irene (Brawley) F.; m. Wanda Darlene Jones, Nov. 27, 1963. Student, Mineral Area Jr. Coll., Flat River, Mo., 1965-66, U. Mo., S.E. Mo. State U. Registered technologist Am. Radiol. Soc. Radiologist, head dept. Madison Meml. Hosp., Fredericktown, Mo., 1965-66; ambulance attendant Pub. Emergency Svc., Sikeston, Mo., 1970-73; tchr. math. Sikeston Pub. Schs., 1978-80, vocat. instr., 1980-85; ghost writer Sikeston, 1981-84; author Bloomfield, Mo., 1985—; mem. adv. bds. Vocat. Edn., Sikeston, 1980-85; lectr. in math., health and philosophy. Author: Diet and the Cardiovascular Condition, 1995, others; ghost writer, editor: The Headlee Anthology, 1984; author cultural newsletter The Plow and the Stars, 1992-93; inventor game Choice and Chance, 1992. Served with USN, 1966-70, Vietnam. Mem. Am. Registry Radiol. Technologists. Office: The Plow and the Stars 21212 County Rd 510 Bloomfield MO 63825

FERRENBERG, WILLIAM A., mechanical engineer; b. Toledo, Ohio, Apr. 19, 1947. Assoc. Mech. Engrng. Tech., U. Toledo Cmty. Tech. Coll., 1982. Draftsman Haughton Elevator Co., Toledo, 1968-70; designer, sr. draftsman DeVilbiss Co., Toledo, 1970-74; mech. designer Textileather divsn. Gen. Tire & Rubber, Toledo, 1974-78; staff engr. Acklin Stamping divsn. Tecumseh Products, Toledo, 1978-79; project engr. Clarke Am. Lincoln, Bowling Green, 1979—; mem. steering com. Clarke Am. Lincoln, 1990—. Chmn. Zoning Com., Village of Holland, Ohio, 1982—. Republican. Roman Catholic. Home: 6962 Dunn Dr Holland OH 43528-8549 Office: Clarke Am Lincoln 1100 Haskins Rd Bowling Green OH 43402-9363

FERRIELL, PETER PAUL, federal agency administrator; b. Richmond, Ind., Oct. 17, 1955; s. Alton B. and Julia (Horrigan) F.; m. Linda Marie Moore, Sept. 4, 1981; children: Megan Marie, Daniel Richard. BS in Econs., and Agr., Wilmington Coll., 1978; MBA, U. Dayton, 1992. Agrl. mgmt. specialist, agrl. credit mgr. Farm Svc. Agy., Eaton, Ohio, 1978—. Mem. Nat. Assn. County Suprs., Ohio Assn. County Suprs. (dist. rep. 1988, v.p. 1990, pres., 1991, fin. com. 1992, Outstanding Mem. 1984), Delta Tau Alpha. Democrat. Roman Catholic. Home: 2341 Rosetta Dr Eaton OH 45320-9703 Office: Farm Svc Agy 1655 N Barrow St Eaton OH 45320-9703

FERRIS, JOSEPH EDWARD, electrical engineer; b. Jackson, Mich., Apr. 27, 1929; s. Harry R. and Caroline J. (Davis) F.; m. Jean Marie Kleps, Jan. 20, 1951; children: Noreen L., Wolcott, Cynthia E. Smith, Joseph E. Jr. BEEE, George Washington U., 1961. Engr. Melpar Inc., Falls Church, Va., 1955-61; sr. engr. Bendix Systems Div., Ann Arbor, Mich., 1961-63; research engr. U. Mich., Ann Arbor, 1963-84; pres. JEF Cons. Inc., Saline, Mich., 1984—, engr., 1979-84. Patentee broadband high gain antenna, millimeter wave microstrip antenna. Served to sgt. U.S. Army, 1952-55. Home: 3544 Weber Rd Saline MI 48176-9215

FERSHTMAN, JULIE ILENE, lawyer; b. Detroit, Apr. 3, 1961; d. Sidney and Judith Joyce (Stoll) F.; m. Robert S. Bick, Mar. 4, 1990. Student, Mich. State U., 1979-81, James Madison Coll., 1979-81; BA in Philosophy and Polit. Sci., Emory U., 1983, JD, 1986. Bar: Mich. 1986, U.S. Dist. Ct. (ea. dist.) Mich. 1986, U.S. Ct. Appeals (6th cir.) 1987, U.S. Dist. Ct. (we. dist.) Mich. 1993. Assoc. Miller, Canfield, Paddock and Stone, Detroit, 1986-89; assoc. Miro, Miro & Weiner P.C., Bloomfield Hills, Mich., 1989-92; pvt. practice, Bingham Farms, Mich., 1992—; adj. prof. Schoolcraft Coll., Livonia, Mich., 1994—; lectr. in field. Author: Equine Law & Horse Sense, 1996; contbr. article to Barrister Mag. Bd. dirs. Franklin Cmty. Assn., 1989-92, sec., 1991-92; mem. Franklin Planning Commn., 1993-94. Mem. ABA (planning bd. litigation sect. young lawyers divsn., honoree Barrister mag. 1995), FBA (courthouse tours com. Detroit chpt.), State Bar Mich. (exec. coun. young lawyers sect. 1989—, sec.-treas. bd. commrs. 1991-93, vice chmn. 1993-94, chmn. elect 1994-95, chmn. 1995—), Oakland County Bar Assn. (professionalism com. 1995—, Inns of Ct. com. 1995—), Markel Equestrian Safety Bd., Women Lawyers Assn. Mich., Soc. Coll. Journalists, Phi Alpha Delta, Omicron Delta Kappa, Phi Sigma Tau, Pi Sigma Alpha. Home: 31700 Briarcliff Rd Franklin MI 48025-1273 Office: 30700 Telegraph Rd Ste 3475 Bingham Farms MI 48025-4527

FERSTENFELD, JULIAN ERWIN, internist, educator; b. Des Moines, Sept. 5, 1941; m. Sharon Rukas, Mar. 8, 1975; children: Megan Ann, Adam Justin. B.A., U. Iowa, 1963, M.D., 1966. Intern Milwaukee County Gen. Hosp., Milw., 1966-67, resident in internal medicine, 1969-71, fellow in infectious diseases, 1972-73; instr. internal medicine Med. Coll. Wis., Milw., 1974-75, asst. prof. medicine, 1975-78, asst. clin. prof. medicine and family practice, 1978-83, assoc. clin. prof. family practice and medicine, 1983—, internal medicine dir. Waukesha family practice residency, 1978—; practice medicine specializing in infectious diseases, Milw., 1974—; mem. staff Waukesha Meml. Hosp. (Wis.), West Allis Meml. Hosp. (Wis.), Elmbrook Meml. Hosp., Brookfield, Wis., Froedtert Meml. Hosp., Milw. Served as capt. M.C., U.S. Army, 1967-69. Korea. Fellow ACP; mem. Wis. Thoracic Soc., Am. Fedn. Clin. Research, Phi Beta Kappa. Contbr. articles, abstracts to profl. jours.

FERWERDA, JAN ANNETTE, direct marketing consultant; b. Atlanta, Apr. 16, 1954; d. Charles Garvin and Sarah (Stark) Crawford; m. David Ferwerda; children: Rachelle, Hannah, Micaela. BFA, Memphis State Univ., 1986. Mgmt. U.S. Postal Svc., Memphis, 1975-85; acct. mgr. Malmo Adv. Direct, Memphis, 1986-88; dir., direct mktg. Walker & Assocs., Memphis, 1988-90; dir. new bus. Weinstock, White & Assocs., Memphis, 1990-91; acct. supr. NB Devel. A. Eicoff & Co., Chgo., 1992-93; direct mktg. cons. in pvt. practice Overland Park, Kans., 1993-96; program chairperson Memphis Direct Mktg., 1986-90. Bd. dirs. Jr. Women's Symphony Alliance, Kansas City. Mem. Am. Mktg. Assn. Home and Office: 15708 Beverly Overland Park KS 66223

FERZACCA, PAMELA ANN, elementary education educator; b. Detroit, Sept. 28, 1963; d. John Joseph and Lois Susan (Henson) F. BS, Grand Valley State Coll., Allendale, Mich., 1987. Cert. spl. edn. tchr. Substitute tchr. Almont (Mich.) Community Schs., 1987-88, bilingual tchr., 1988-90; 1st grade tchr. Almont Summer Migrant Edn. Program, 1988, tchr. kindergarten, 1989, 90, recruiter, 1990; tchr. 3d grade Almont Elem. Sch., 1990-94; tchr. educably mentally impaired Almont Jr./Sr. H.S., 1994-95; tchr. 3d grade Almont Elem. Sch., 1995—. Mem. Nat. Assn. Migrant Educators, Coun. Exceptional Children, Mich. Edn. Assn., Almont Edn. Assn. Democrat. Roman Catholic. Home: PO Box 120 132 S Main St Almont MI 48003 Office: Almont Elem Sch 401 Church St Almont MI 48003-1030

FERZACCA, WILLIAM, education educator, consultant; b. Iron Mountain, Mich., Apr. 26, 1927; s. William Olando and Santina Maria (Bruno) F.; m. Suzanne Rogers, Sept. 19, 1953; children: Steven, Matthew, Laurie. BA, Mich. State U., 1950, MA, 1957. Cert. Am. Bd. Med. Therapists. Desk clk. Huron Hotel, Ypsilanti, Mich., 1948-50; asst. mgr. in tng. Hotel LaSalle, South Bend, Ind., 1950-52; swing and asst. chef Midland (Mich.) Country Club, 1952-54; head tchr. Harding Day Nursery, Kalamazoo, 1954; group tchr. Nursery Found., St. Louis, 1954-56, Mich. State Faculty Nursery Sch., East Lansing, Mich., 1956-57; dir. Jewish Community Ctr., St. Louis, 1957-59, nat. cons. for headstart, 1960-63; tchr. Child Guidance Clinic, St. Louis, 1959-65; pres., ednl. and child devel. cons. Learning Cons., Inc., Clayton, Mo., 1963—; child devel. cons. Affton (Mo.) Lindbergh Early Childhood, 1992—, Edgewood children's Ctr., Webster Groves, Mo., 1965—, Clayton Pub. Schs., 1967-78, Mehlville (Mo.) Pub. Schs. Early Childhood, 1975—; tchr. evaluation and assessment of learning environment, com. early childhood Mo. Dept. Elem. and Secondary Edn., 1989—; mem. adj. faculty St. Louis U. Sch. Social Work, 1993—, masters of teaching program Webster U., 1992-95. Chair St. Louis County Family Svcs. Commn., 1985-94; reviewer Human Studies Com., St. Louis, 1986-94; bd. dirs. Nursery Found., St. Louis, 1987-89, Therapeutic Intervention Pre-sch., Ctr. for Holistic Health, 1992; mem. mental health disaster team ARC, Task Force Sudden Infant Death Syndrome Devel. Brochure. With USN, 1945-47. Mem. Am. Bd. Psychotherapists, Am. Ortho-Psychiat. Assn., St. Louis Assn. Early Childhood Edn. (pres. 1957-58), Mo. Assn. Children with Learning Disabilities (bd. dirs. 1986-89), Kappa Delta Phi. Democrat. Home: 7137 Princeton Ave Saint Louis MO 63130-2344 Office: Learning Cons Inc 35 N Central Ave Ste 202 Saint Louis MO 63105-3871

FESCO, EDWARD J., surgeon; b. Tarrytown, N.Y., July 10, 1930; s. John and Mary (Lantosh) F.; m. Anne E. Condron, June, 1956; children: Eileen, Mary, John, Nora, Carol, Beth. BS, Villanova U., 1952; MS in Anatomy, Northwestern U., Chgo., 1955, MD, 1956. Diplomate Am. Bd. Surgery. Pres., med. staff Ill. Valley Community Hosp., Peru, 1992—, med. dir., 1995—; gov. Ill. State Med. Ins. Exch., Chgo., 1992—; trustee Ill. State Med. Soc., Chgo., 1987—, pres., 1987-88; assoc. dir. Health Plan HMO Ctrl. Ill.,

Peoria, 1989-91. Bd. mem. Ill. Sch. Dist. #120, LaSalle, 1982—, pres., 1982-83. Capt. USAF, 1957 -61. Roman Catholic. Home: 709 3rd St La Salle IL 61301-2503 Office: 206 Marquette St La Salle IL 61301-2415

FESKE, JEFF E., tooling engineer; b. Centuria, Wis., Apr. 12, 1952. AD, River Falls State U., 1973. Foreman Northern Metals, Osceola, Wis., 1976-79; supr. Progressive Tool & Design, Dresser, Wis., 1979-87; tooling engr. West Industries, Inc., Hudson, Wis., 1987—. Vol. Local Shelters Food Share, 1992—.

FESKO, TIMOTHY, state legislator; m. Frankie Fesko; children: Heather, Donald, Timothy. BS, Ind. U., 1965. Ins. and real estate agt.; rep. dist. 15 Ind. Ho. of Reps., 1990—, mem. fin. insts. and rules and legis. procedures com., chmn. ins. and corp. coms. Past mem. econ. devel. com. N.w. Ind. Forum; coach Munster (Ind.) Little League; bd. dirs. Tradewinds Rehab. Ctr., Inc.; past dist. chmn. Boy Scouts Am.; bd. dirs. Munster H.S. Booster Club. Named Citizen of the Yr. Town of Munster, 1979; Paul Harris fellow Rotary. Mem. C. of C. (pres.), Rotary (past pres.), Pirates, Ind. U. Alumni Assn. Varsity Club, Delta Tau Delta, Delta Sigma Pi. Home: 1121 Holly Ln Munster IN 46321-3012*

FESLER, DAVID RICHARD, foundation director; b. Mpls., Sept. 21, 1928; s. John K. and Elsie L. Fesler; m. Elizabeth P.; children: Dael F. Zywiec, Nancy K., Janet C. B.B.A. with distinction, U. Minn., 1950. Pres. Lampert Yards, Inc., 1950-79; pres. Liberty State Bank, St. Paul, 1952-82, chmn. bd., 1982-85; treas. Mason City Builders Supply Co., Inc., 1972-85, The Sussel Co., Inc., 1975-79; pres. Wim Co., St. Paul, 1952-79, Liberty Agy., Inc., 1952-75; profl. vol. various orgns., 1960—. past pres., bd. dirs. Stout U. Found., Menomonie, Wis.; past bd. dirs., mem. fin. com., mem. exec. com. Shattuck St. Mary's Sch., Faribault, Minn., Inver Grove Heights (Minn.) Planning Commn., Indianhead coun. Boy Scouts Am., St. Croix Valley coun. Girl Scouts U.S., St. Paul Area YMCA, Family Svc. St. Paul Area, Edgcumbe Presbyn. Ch., Presbyn. Homes Minn., St. Paul Tech. Coll. Trust, U. Minn. Found., The Works, Mpls., Lyngblomston Found., Depot Found., Duluth, Minn.; mem. Minn. Planned Giving Coun. Mem. Nat. Soc. Fund Raising Execs. (Minn. chpt. Outstanding Vol. Fundraiser award, 1994), Rotary, Beta Gamma Sigma, Phi Delta Theta. Office: 1573 Selby Ave Ste 246 Saint Paul MN 55104-6328

FESSLER, JOYCE ANN, journalist; b. Richmond, Ind., Apr. 15, 1932; d. Olan Dale and Anna G. (Wilbur) Edwards; m. Walter George Fessler, Nov. 15, 1958 (dec. 1979); children: Joseph, MaryAnn, John, Teresa, Christopher, Catherine. BA, Marian Coll., 1953. Reporter Comml. Rev., Portland, Ind., 1953-54; reporter, editor Palladium-Item, Richmond, 1954-58, 72-90, part-time reporter, editor, 1958-72; regional reporter The Criterion, Indpls., 1954-80's. Mem. Soc. Profl. Journalists, Delta Epsilon Sigma. Republican. Roman Catholic. Home: 100 NW 6th St Richmond IN 47374-4044

FESSLER, PATRICIA LOU, library and media coordinator; b. Chgo., Dec. 1; d. Eugene Rickert and Dorothy May (Schmidt) McKeen; m. Kermit John Fessler, June 23, 1951; children: Barbara, Peter, James. BA, Cornell Coll., 1950; MS, Chgo. State U., 1970. Cert. tchr., supr., Ill. Tchr. phys. edn. Harlan (Iowa) Pub. Schs., 1950-51, Blue Island Community High Sch. Dist. # 218, Oak Lawn, Ill., 1960-63, 67-70; coord. library, media A.B. Shepard High Sch., Oak Lawn, Ill., 1971-93; mem. adv. coun. Grad. Sch. Libr. Scis. U. Ill., Champaign, 1977-80; mem. libr./media adv. coun. State Bd. Edn., Springfield, Ill., 1980-83. Deacon Palos Park (Ill.) Presbyn. Ch., 1991-93. Named as one of Those Who Excel Ill., State Bd. Edn., 1987. Mem. AAUW (edn. found. honoree 1992), Assn. for Ednl. Comms. and Tech. (bd. dirs. 1981-84, Spl. Svc. plaque 1989, bd. trustees 1984—, found. sec. 1988—), Ill. Ednl. Comms. and Tech. (pres. 1977-78, 80-82, Disting. Svc. award 1982-84, Meritorious Svc. award A.V. Am. 1983).

FESTA, ROGER REGINALD, chemist, educator; b. Norwalk, Conn., Sept. 6, 1950; s. Reginald and Rosemary (Chappa) F. BA in Biology and Chemistry magna cum laude, St. Michael's Coll., 1972; MA in Agr., U. Vt., 1979; cert. in Adminstrn., Fairfield U., 1981; PhD in Edn., U. Conn., 1982. Tchr. Cen. Cath. High Sch., Norwalk, 1975-79, Brien McMahon High Sch., Norwalk, 1979-82; asst. prof. chemistry Truman State U. (formerly Northeast Mo. State U.), Kirksville, 1983-89, dir. chem. communication devel. ctr., 1983-90, assoc. prof. of chemistry, 1989—, dean of frats., 1991-92, coach men's volleyball, 1991—, advisor Sigma Phi Epsilon, 1991—; adj. prof. U. Conn., 1983. Author: National Curriculum Development Programming for Teachers of High School Chemistry, 1981, Fairfield County High School Chemistry Curriculum Handbook, 1982. Sec. Diocese Bridgeport (Conn.) Edn. Assn., 1978-79, sci. cons. schs. office, 1979, exec. adminstr., 1979; bd. dirs. Norwalk Community Services Agy., 1980-81. Named one of Ten Outstanding Young Men of Mo., Mo. Jaycees, 1986. Fellow Am. Inst. Chemists (pub. edn. com. 1980-83, edn. editor The Chemist Jour. 1981—, mem. editl. bd. The Chemist 1981-86, bd. dirs. 1982—, chmn. nat. meetings com. 1982-91, history com. 1982—, archivist 1983, sec. 1991-93, pres.-elect 1994-95, pres. 1996—); mem. Am. Chem. Soc. (founding editor The Fairfield Chemist 1978-79, assoc. editor Jour. Chem. Edn. 1980-89, vice chmn. edn. com. Western Conn. sect. 1979-81, chmn. elect Mark Twain sect. 1985, chmn. 1986, exec. bd. 1984-95, program chair 1984-95), St. Louis Inst. Chemists (founder 1984, pres. 1985-87), Acad. Sci. St. Louis, Assn. Frat. Advisors, Coll. Frat. Editors' Assn., Kirksville Jaycees (bd. dirs. 1983-86, sec. 1984-85, chair ret. sr. vols. com. 1985-87), Delta Epsilon Sigma, Alpha Chi Sigma (assoc. editor The Hexagon 1984—), Lambda Chi Alpha (chancellor Truman State U. chpt. 1988-91, CEO House Corp. 1989-94), Order of Omega. Democrat. Roman Catholic. Home: 114 E Mcpherson St Kirksville MO 63501-3570 Office: Truman State U Dept Chemistry Kirksville MO 63501-4221

FETRIDGE, BONNIE-JEAN CLARK (MRS. WILLIAM HARRISON FETRIDGE), civic volunteer; b. Chgo., Feb. 3, 1915; d. Sheldon and Bonnie (Carrington) Clark; m. William Harrison Fetridge, June 27, 1941; children: Blakely (Mrs. Harvey H. Bundy III), Clark Worthington. Student, Girls Latin Sch., Chgo., The Masters Sch., Dobbs Ferry, N.Y., Finch Coll., N.Y.C. Bd. dirs. region VII com. Girl Scouts U.S.A., 1939-43, nat. program com., 1966-69, nat. adv. bd., 1972-85, internat. commr.'s adv. panel, 1973-76, Nat. Juliette Low Birthplace Com., 1966-69; bd. dirs. Girl Scouts Chgo., 1936-51, 59-69, sec., 1936-38, v.p., 1946-49, 61-65, chmn. Juliette Low world friendship com., 1959-67, 71-72; mem. Friends Our Cabana Com. World Assn. Girl Guides and Girl Scouts, Cuernavaca, Mexico, 1969—, vice chmn., 1982-87; founder, pres. Olave Baden-Powell Soc. of World Assn. Girl Guides and Girl Scouts, London, 1984-93, bd. dirs., 1984—, hon. assoc., 1987; asst. sec. Dartnell Corp, Chgo., 1981-91, sec., 1991—, bd. dirs. 1989—; vice chmn. Dartnell Found., 1990—; bd. dirs. Jr. League of Chgo., 1937-40, Vis. Nurse Assn. Chgo., 1951-58, 61-63, asst. treas., 1962-63; women's bd. dirs. Children's meml. Hosp., 1946-50; v.p. parents coun. Latin Sch., 1952-54, bd. dirs. alumni assn., 1964-69; Fidelitas Soc., 1979; women's bd. U.S.O., 1965-75, treas., 1969-71, v.p., 1971-73; women's svc. bd. Chgo. Area coun. Boy Scouts Am., 1964-70, mem. nat. exploring com., 1973-76; staff aide and ARC Motor Corps, World War II. Recipient Citation of Merit Sta. WAIT, Chgo., 1971, Juliette Low World Friendship medal Girl Scouts U.S.A., 1989; 1st recipient Medal of Recognition World Assn.Girl Guides and Girl Scouts, 1993; Baden-Powell fellow World Scout Found., Geneva, 1983. Mem. Nat. Soc. Colonial Dames Am. (life, Ill. bd. mgrs. 1962-65, 69-76, 78-82, v.p. 1970-72, corr. sec. 1978-80, 1st v.p. 1980-84, state chmn. geneal. info. svcs. com. 1972-76, corr. sec. 1978-80, hist. activities com. 1979-83, mus. house com. 1980-83, house gov. 1981-82), Chgo. Dobbs Alumnae Assn. (past pres.), Nat. Soc. DAR, Chgo. Geneal. Soc., Conn. Soc. Genealogists, New Eng. Hist. Geneal. Soc., N.Y. Geneal. and Biog. Soc., Newberry Libr. Assocs., Chgo. Hist. Soc. Guild, Casino Club, The Racquet Club Chgo., Union League. Republican. Episcopalian. Home: 2430 N Lakeview Ave Chicago IL 60614-2720

FETRIDGE, CLARK WORTHINGTON, publisher; b. Chgo., Nov. 6, 1946; s. William Harrison and Bonnie-Jean (Clark) F.; m. Jean Hamilton Huebner, Apr. 19, 1980; children: Clark Worthington, William Hamilton. BA, Lake Forest Coll., 1969; MBA, Boston Coll., 1971. Money market specialist Continental Ill. Nat. Bank, Chgo., 1971-73; with Dartnell Corp., Chgo., 1973—; sr. v.p. Dartnell Corp., 1977-78; pres., CEO Dartnell Corp., Chgo., 1978-95; chmn. bd., CEO Dartnell Corp., 1995—. Author: Office Administration Handbook, 1975. Trustee Lake Forest Coll., 1977-85, 91-95, Jacques Holinger Meml. Found., 1983-95, Dartnell Found., 1989—, Latin Sch. Chgo., 1990-94; internat. commr. Boy Scouts Am., 1992-95, mem. nat. exec. bd., 1986-96, mem. internat. com., mem. Chgo. coun.; pres. U.S. Found. Internat. Scouting 1991-95; chmn. 1200 Club Ill., Rep. candidate for Congress, 1972; del Rep. Nat. Conv., 1976; mem. pres.'s coun. Mus. Sci. and Industry, Chgo., 1986-94. Mem. Ill. Mfrs. Assn. (bd. dirs.), Latin Sch. Chgo. Alumni Assn., St. Andrews Soc. (bd. dirs.), Nat. Eagle Scout Assn. (chmn. 1985-88), Tau Kappa Epsilon. Republican. Episcopalian. Office: Dartnell Corp 4660 N Ravenswood Ave Chicago IL 60640-4510

FETSCH, MICHAEL FRANCIS, financial consultant; b. Gary, Ind., Sept. 3, 1952; s. Ralph M. Sr. and Charlotte B. (Klein) F.; m. Connie B. Long, July 4, 1976. Br. mgr. Walddell Reed, Kansas City, Mo., 1977-88; fin. cons., br. mgr. South Mall Securities, Dallas, 1988-89; co-owner 1st Pacific Capital, Wash., 1989-91; fin. cons., br. mgr. Fin. Network, Indpls., 1991—. Named Sagamore of Walbach, Gov. Ind., 1988. Mem. ADA (joint commn. on dental examination 1995—), Ind. Dental Bd. (bd. dirs. 1983-88), Pro Fed Credit Union (bd. dirs. 1994—), Inst. Fin Planners, Miata Club Am. Republican. Office: Fin Network Inv Corp # 100 5342 W Vermont St Indianapolis IN 46224-8841

FETT, PATRICIA DIANE, elementary education educator; b. Chgo., Sept. 14, 1958; d. William Leo and Patricia June (Cunradi) Kuhn; married; children: Jonathan, David; stepchildren: Ryan, Rob. BA, Concordia Tchr.'s Coll., River Forest, Ill., 1980; MEd, U. Ill., Chgo., 1987. Cert. elem. tchr., Ill., Wis. 1st grade tchr. Rhodes Sch., River Grove, Ill., 1980-82, kindergarten tchr., 1982-92; kindergarten tchr. New Holstein (Wis.) Elem. Sch., 1992-93; coord. of svcs. birth to three Fond du Lac County Dept. of Community Programs, Fond du Lac, Wis., 1993—; early interventionist U. Ill., Chgo., 1985-87; dir. dept. cmty. programs, Fond du Lac, Wis., 1994—. U.S. Dept. Edn. grantee, 1986. Mem. ASCD, Nat. Assn. Edn. of Young Children, Coun. for Exceptional Children. Lutheran. Home: 1802 Silver Moon Ln New Holstein WI 53061-1626 Office: Dept Community Programs 459 E 1st St Fond Du Lac WI 54935-4505

FETTEROLF, CHARLES E., account executive; b. Pottsville, Pa., Dec. 17, 1947. BS, Pa. State U., 1970; MBA, U. Ark., 1978. Commd. ensign U.S. Army, 1970, advanced through grades to lt. col.; acct. exec. Dean Witter Reynolds, Westlake, Ohio. Bd. dirs. Cleve. Air Show, 1995. Mem. Ret. Officers Assn. (bd. dirs. 1994-95), USO No. Ohio (bd. dirs. 1995). Roman Catholic. Office: Dean Witter Reynolds Gemini Towers 1991 Crocker Rd Westlake OH 44145-1962

FETTIG, JASON L., financial planner; b. Charlevoix, Mich., July 21, 1969. BA in Bus. Adminstrn., Mich. State U. Fin. planner Olde Discount Corp., Detroit, 1993—. Home: 417 Curry Ave Royal Oak MI 48067-1988 Office: Olde Discount Corp 751 Griswold St Detroit MI 48226-3224

FETZER, JAMES HENRY, philosopher, educator; b. Pasadena, Calif., Dec. 6, 1940; s. Henry Jr. and Eleanor Atwood (Waterhouse) F.; m. Janice Elaine Morgan, June 12, 1977. AB in Philosophy magna cum laude, Princeton U., 1962; MA in History and Philosophy of Sci., Ind. U., 1968, PhD in History and Philosophy of Sci., 1970; postgrad., Columbia U., 1968-69. Asst. prof. U. Ky., Lexington, 1970-77; vis. assoc. prof. U. Va., Charlottesville, 1977-78; vis. assoc. prof. U. Cin., 1978-79, vis. NSF rsch. prof., 1979-80; vis. lectr. U. N.C., Chapel Hill, 1980-81; vis. assoc. prof. New Coll. of U. South Fla., Sarasota, 1981-83, MacArthur vis. disting. prof. arts and scis., 1983-84, rsch. scholar, 1985-86; adj. prof. U. South Fla., Tampa, 1984-85; vis. prof. U. Va., Charlottesville, 1984-85; prof. philosophy U. Minn., Duluth, 1987-96, dept. chmn., 1987-96, disting. McKnight prof., 1996—; rsch. scholar New Coll. U. South Fla., Sarasota, 1985-86; postdoctoral fellow Wright State U., Dayton, Ohio, 1986-87; Landsdowne lectr. U. Victoria, Can., 1992. Author: Scientific Knowledge, 1981, AI: Its Scope and Limits, 1990, Philosophy and Cognitive Science, 1991, Philosophy of Science, 1993; co-author: Glossary of Cognitive Science, 1993, Glossary of Epistemology/Philosophy of Science, 1993; editor: Principles of Philosophical Reasoning, 1984, Sociobiology and Epistemology, 1985, Aspects of AI, 1988, Probability and Causality, 1988, Epistemology and Cognition, 1991, Foundations of Philosophy of Science, 1993; co-editor: Philosophy, Language, and AI, 1988, Philosophy, Mind, and Cognitive Inquiry, 1990, Definitions and Definability, 1991, Program Verification, 1993, Synthese, 1990—; founder, book series editor: Studies in Cognitive Systems, 1986—; founder, editor: Minds and Machines, 1989—. With USMC, 1962-66. Recipient Dickinson prize Princeton U., 1962, Medal of U. Helsinki, Finland, 1990. Mem. AAUP, AAAS, Am. Philos. Assn., Internat. Soc. for Human Ethology, Soc. for Machines and Mentality (founder), Philosophy of Sci. Assn., Assn. Computing Machiner, Human Behavior and Evolution Soc. Office: U Minn Dept Philosophy Duluth MN 55812

FEUERBORN, BILL, state legislator; m. Linda Feuerborn. Mem. Kans. State Ho. of Reps. Dist. 5.

FEY, SUZANNE JANE, management consultant; b. Hackensack, N.J., Sept. 25, 1955; d. Robert Paul and Mary Jane (Walko) Wederich; m. Fey, Sept. 1, 1984; children: Avery Jane, Zoe Leigh. BA in psychology, Coe Coll., Cedar Rapids, 1980, BA in Russian studies, 1980. Chief cons. Austin Lawler & Assoc., St. Charles, Ill., 1980-95; ops. cons. Fed. Reserve Bank of Cgo., Des Moines, Iowa, 1995—.

FIALA, DAVID MARCUS, lawyer; b. Cleve., Aug. 1, 1946; s. Frank J. and Anna Mae (Phillips) F. BBA, U. Cin., 1969; JD, Chase Coll., No. Ky. State U., 1974. Bar: Ohio 1974, U.S. Dist. Ct. (so. dist.) Ohio 1974, U.S. Tax Ct. 1974. Assoc. Benesch, Friedlander, Coplan and Aronoff, Cin., 1974-78, ptnr., 1979-92; ptnr. Rice & Fiala, 1992-94, sole practice, Cin., 1995—. lectr. Southwestern Ohio Tax Inst., 1978-79, 88, Cin. Bar Assn. Estate Planning Inst., 1989. Bd. dirs. Elkhorn Collieries. Trustee, sec. Sta. WCET-TV, Cin., 1983-87, auction chmn., 1979, chmn. 1987-90, trustee emeritus, 1990—; trustee Jr. Achievement Greater Cin., 1979-93, Mental Health Svcs. West, 1974-83, Contemporary Dance theatre, 1974-80. Mem. ABA, Ohio State Bar Assn., Cin. Bar Assn. (lectr. estate planning inst. 1989), Am. Culinary Fedn. Cin. (trustee 1985-90), Cincinnatus Assn.

FIALA, PAUL G., financial consultant; b. Davenport, Iowa, Aug. 10, 1945. BA in Econs., U. Iowa, 1970. Fin. cons. Merrill Lynch, St. Louis, 1970-74, E.F. Hutton, St. Louis, 1974-76; office mgr. Iowa City, 1976-80; fin. cons. Shearson Bros., Cedar Rapids, Iowa, 1980-90, A G Edwards & Sons Inc., Cedar Rapids, 1990—. With U.S. Army, 1966-70, ETO, Vietnam. Office: A G Edwards & Sons Inc PO Box 75010 425 2d St SE Cedar Rapids IA 52407

FICHTHORN, FONDA GAY, principal; b. Jamestown, Ohio, Sept. 4, 1949; d. Robert William and Evelyn Elizabeth (Schmitt) F. BS, Otterbein Coll., 1970; MEd, Wright State U., 1983. Cert. tchr., prin., supr., Ohio. Elem. tchr. Groveport (Ohio) Madison Schs., 1970-71; elem. tchr. Miami Trace Schs., Washington Court House, Ohio, 1971-92, prin., 1992—. Recipient Class Act award Sta. WDTN-TV, 1990. Republican. Home: 7313 State Route 729 NW Washington Court House OH 43160-9526 Office: Wilson Sch 1604 State Route 41 SW Washington Court House OH 43160-9789

FICKERT, KURT JON, writer, retired language educator; b. Pausa, Saxony, Germany, Dec. 19, 1920; came to U.S., 1926; s. Kurt Alfred and Martha Elsa (Searchinger) F.; m. Madlyn Barbara Janda, Aug. 6, 1946; children: Linda Mosbacher, Jon, Chris. AB, Hofstra U., 1941; MA, NYU, 1947, PhD, 1952. Instr., then asst. prof. Hofstra U., Hempstead, N.Y., 1948-53; asst. prof. Fla. State U., Tallahassee, 1953-54, Kans. State U., Ft. Hays, 1954-56; assoc. prof., then prof. Wittenberg U., Springfield, Ohio, 1956-86, ret., 1986; chairperson dept. langs. Wittenberg U., 1969-75. Author: To Heaven and Back, 1972, Hermann Hesse's Quest, 1978, Kafka's Doubles, 1979, Signs and Portents, 1980, Franz Kafka: Life, Work, Criticism, 1987, End of a Mission, 1993, Dialogue with the Reader, 1995; contbr. articles and poetry to lit. publs. Fullbright grantee, Germany, 1957, NEH grantee, U. Calif., Irvine, 1981; Fickert Lang. award established in his honor Wittenberg U., 1986. Lutheran. Home: 33 S Kensington Pl Springfield OH 45504-1030

FIDDICK, PAUL WILLIAM, broadcasting company executive; b. St. Joseph, Mo., Nov. 20, 1949; s. Lowell Duane and Betty Jean (Manring) F.; m. Julie Hanna Lorms, July 31, 1983; children: Lea Elizabeth, Hanna Manring. BJ, U. Mo., 1971. Account exec. Sta. KCMO-KFMU, Kansas City, Mo., 1971-72; account exec. Sta. WEZW, Milw., 1972-74, dir. sales mktg., 1974-76, v.p., gen. mgr., 1976-81; sr. v.p. Multimedia Broadcasting Co., Milw., 1981; pres. Multimedia Radio, Cin., 1982-86, Radio Group, Heritage Communications, Inc., Des Moines, 1986-87, Radio Group, Heritage Media Corp., Dallas, 1987—; bd. dirs. Nat. Assn. Broadcasters, Washington, 1994—, Radio Advt. Bur., N.Y.C., 1983—, chmn. 1993-94, mem. acad. staff U. Wis., Milw., 1978-81. Named one of 40 Most Powerful People in Radio, Radio Ink Mag., 1996, Fifth Estater, Broadcasting Mag., 1990, Up and Coming Radio Exec. of Yr., Radio Only Mag., 1983. Mem. Phi Eta Sigma, Kappa Tau Alpha. Office: Heritage Media Corp One Galleria Tower 13355 Noel Rd Ste 1500 Dallas TX 75240-6650

FIDLER, ALAN BANDELIN, retired physician; b. West Allis, Wis., June 30, 1922; s. Clarence Celester and Marie Rose (Bandelin) F.; m. Betty Mae Meyer, May 24, 1947; children: Susan Lynn Fidler Watson, Jahn Alan, Paul Robert. BS, U. Wis., 1944, MD, 1946. Diplomate Am. Bd. Radiology. Inern, resident Evangelical Deaconess Hosp., Milw., 1946-48, resident in gen. practice, 1950-51; resident in radiology Kansas City (Kans.) Rsch. Hosp., 1951-53; radiology practice Habbe, Wright, Schmidt & Fidler, Milw., 1953-57; with Milw. Radiologists, S.C., 1967-77, Radiation Oncology Assocs., S.C., Milw., 1977-88. Capt. U.S. Army, 1943-51. Fellow Am. Coll. Radiology; mem. AMA, Wis. State Med. Soc., Milwaukee County Med. Soc., Radiol. Soc. N.Am., Milw. Roentgen Ray Soc. (past pres.), Wis. Radiol. Soc., Nuclear Medicine Soc., Milw. Acad. Medicine. Home: N8398 Bell School Rd East Troy WI 53120

FIDLER, CAROL ANN, accountant; b. Sharon, Pa., Apr. 28, 1942; d. Thomas Daniel and E. Geraldine (Boyer) Bracken; m. Michael Lawrence Fidler, Aug. 23, 1969 (div. 1991); 1 child, Michael Lawrence Jr. Diploma, Akron City Hosp. Sch. Nursing, 1963; BS in Chemistry, Kent State U., 1967; MS in Preventive Medicine, Ohio State U., 1972, MBA, 1979. CPA, Ohio; RN, Ohio. Rsch. assoc. dept. preventive medicine Ohio State U., Columbus, Ohio, 1969-70; dir. Riverside Meth. Hosp. Sch. Nursing, Columbus, 1973-77; dir. nursing devel. Ohio Hosp. Assn., Columbus, 1977-79; sr. bus. analyst Borden Inc.-Chem. div., Columbus, 1979-81; fin. adminstr. Bank One, Columbus N.A., 1981-84; pres. Northwest Tax Svc., Columbus, 1984-86; sr. cons. Peat, Marwick, Mitchell, Columbus, 1985-86; sole practice acctg. Columbus, 1986-90; controller The Wood Co's., Columbus, 1987-88; co-owner Clem & Fidler CPAs, 1991-94; owner Carol A. Fidler & Assocs., CPAs, Columbus, 1994—; instr. Newton Becker CPA Rev., Columbus, 1988-90; dir., treas. Donovan Prodns. Inc., Columbus, 1989—; bd. dirs. Dominican Home Health Agy. Vol. Arthritis Assn., Columbus, 1978-84; treas. Northside Child and Family Devel. Ctr., Columbus, 1987-95, bd. dirs., 1986—. Mem. Ohio Soc. CPAs (chair MAP com. Columbus chpt. 1991-93, mem. 1992—, Cert. award 1986, Silver medal 1986), Inst. Mgmt. Accts. (dir. member attendance Columbus chpt. 1988-89, dir. tech. programs 1989-90, dir. student and acad. affairs 1990-91, dir. CMA program 1991-93, treas. 1993-95, lead instr. CMA rev. course 1991-94), Planning Forum (pres. Columbus chpt. 1986-87, v.p. fin. com. 1985-86, v.p. programs 1984-85, dir. 1987-90). Republican. Home: 4138 Winfield Rd Columbus OH 43220-4606

FIDLER, CHARLES ROBERT, electrical engineer; b. Park Ridge, Ill., July 7, 1964; s. Charles Ezra and Shirley Ann (Skerce) F.; m. Mary Beth Olson, Mar. 16, 1991; children: Ashley Paige, Charles Robert Jr. BSEE, Ill. Inst. Tech., 1986. Registered profl. engr., Ill. Student surface warfare officer sch., commd. ensign USN, Orlando, Fla., 1986; advanced through grades to lt. USN, 1990; student Navy nuclear power sch. USN, Orlando, 1986; student Navy nuclear prototype USN, Idaho Falls, Idaho, 1986-87; student surface warfare officer sch. USN, San Diego, 1987-88; anti-submarine warfare officer USS Cushing, San Diego, 1988-90; reactor plant shift supr. USS Enterprise, Norfolk, Va., 1990-91; prin. engr. ABB Impell Corp., Chgo., 1991-93; sr. engr. Vectra, Chgo., 1993-96; maintanence support supr. Nebr. Pub. Power Dist. Cooper Nuclear Station, 1996; sr. rector opr. cert. Cooper Nuclear Station, 1996. Contbr. articles to profl. jours. Lt. comdr. USNR, 1996. Mem. IEEE, Am. Nuclear Soc., Naval Inst., Naval Reserve Assn., Am. Soc. Naval Engrs., Midwest Cogeneration Assn. Home: 116 S Main St Rockport MO 64482 Office: Nebr Pub Power Dist Cooper Nuclear Station PO Box 98 Brownsville NE 68321

FIEBELMAN, KENNETH FRANKLIN, state representative; b. St. Louis, Dec. 19, 1941; s. Lawrence William Jacob and Cynthia Warfel Fiebelman. BS, U. Mo., Columbia. Tchr. Salem and St. Clair; tourism promoter Meramec Caverns; state rep. dist. 150 Mo. Ho. of Reps., 1985—; chmn. House Mines and Mining com.; mem. House Agri-Bus. Com., State Parks, Recreation and Natural Recources Com., Transp. Com. Author: A History and Genealogy of East Dent County Missouri Families; editor: Ozark Heritage, Vols. I, II and III, 1978, 80, Crawford County History, Vol. I, 1987—. Mem. Meramec Regional Planning Com., 1985—, Howes Mill Union Ch., Farm Bur., Mo., Dent County Mus. Bd., Dent County Home Care Adv. Commn. Recipient Outstanding Citizen award Salem C. of C., Outstanding Legislator award Meramec Regional Planning Comm., award for promoting tourism St. James, Mo. Mem. Mo. State Tchrs. Assn., Dent County Hist. Soc., Odd Fellows, Shriners, Masons, Cuba C. of C., Salem C. of C., Steelville C. of C., Crawford County Cattlemen's Assn., Dent County Cattelmen's Assn., Dent County Hist. Soc., Crawford Counsy Hist. Soc., Phelps County Hist. Soc., Reynolds County Hist. Soc., Davisville Hist. Soc., Mo. Hist. Soc., Nat. Riflemen's Assn., Fraternal Order of Eagles, ABC. Home: 1202 Gertrude St Salem MO 65560

FIEGEN, KRISTIE K., state legislator. State rep. S.D. Dist. 11; mem. Health and Human Svc. and Local Govt. Coms., S.D. Ho. Reps. Home: 6832 W Westminster Dr Sioux Falls SD 57106-3234 Office: SD House of Reps State Capitol Pierre SD 57501*

FIELD, EDWARD, journalist; b. Norfolk, Va.. BA in Modern History with honors, Oxford (Eng.) U. Midwest corr. The Economist, Chgo. Office: The Economist 360 N Michigan Ave Chicago IL 60601

FIELD, GILBERT VERN, information systems manager; b. St. Louis, Apr. 3, 1945; s. Bryon D. and Norma J. (Ashley) F.; m. Grace M. Williams, July 1, 1972; children: Gwen, Colleen, Jeffrey. BS in Indsl. Mgmt., Washington U. St. Louis, 1973; MBA in Corp. Resource Mgmt., Webster U., 1992. Adminstrv. supr. Mallinckrodt Chemistry, St. Louis, 1967-83; staff supr. Contel/GTE, Wentzville, Mo., 1984-92; mgr. info. systems The Western Group, St. Louis, 1993—. Sgt. U.S. Army, 1967-69. Office: The Western Group 1637 N Warson Rd Saint Louis MO 63132

FIELD, KAREN ANN, real estate broker; b. New Haven, Jan. 27, 1936; d. Abraham Terry and Ida (Smith) Rogovin; m. Barry S. Crown, June 29, 1954 (div. 1969); children: Laurie Jayne, Donna Lynn, Bruce Alan, Bradley David; m. Michael Lehmann Field, Aug. 10, 1969 (div. 1977). Student Vassar Coll., 1953-54, Harrington Inst. Interior Design, 1973-74, Roosevelt U., 1987—. Cert. residential specialist. Owner Karen Field Interiors, Chgo., 1970-86, Karen Field & Assocs., Chgo., 1980-81; pres., ptnr. Field-Pels & Assocs., Chgo., 1981-86; with top sales volume Sudler-Marling, Inc., 1989; sales broker Koenig & Strey, Inc., Chgo., 1989—; elected to Pres.'s Club, Koenig & Strey, Inc., 1996. Mem. Women's Coun. Camp Henry Horner, Chgo., 1960; bd. dirs., treas. Winnetka Pub. Sch. Nursery (Ill.), 1961-63; pres. Jr. Aux. U. Chgo. Cancer Rsch. Found., 1960-66, mem. exec. com. woman's bd., 1965-66; bd. dirs., sec. United Charities, Chgo., 1966-68, Victory Gardens Theatre, Chgo., 1979; co-founder, pres. Re-Entry Ctr., Wilmette, Ill., 1978-80; mem. br. Child Abuse Svcs., Chgo., 1981-89, Stop AIDS Real Estate Div., 1988, AIDS Walkathon Com., 1990; bd. dirs. The Chicago Ctr. for Self-Taught Art. Recipient Servian award Jr. Aux. of U. Chgo. Cancer Rsch. Found., 1966, Margarite Wolf award Women's Bd., U. Chgo. Cancer Rsch. Found., 1967, WAIT Woman of Day. Mem. Internat. Real Estate Fedn. (chmn. membership Chgo. chpt. 1994, bd. dirs. 1996), Chgo. Real Estate Bd., Chgo. Assn. Realtors, Chgo. Coun. Fgn. Rels., English Speaking Union (jr. bd. 1958-59), Carlton Club, Art Inst. Chgo., Field Mus., Chgo. Architecture Found., Presidents Club, Founders Club. Office: Koenig & Strey Inc 900 N Michigan Ave Chicago IL 60611-1542

FIELD, ROBERT EDWARD, lawyer; b. Chgo., Aug. 21, 1945; s. Robert Edward and Florence Elizabeth (Aiken) F.; m. Jenny Lee Hill, Aug. 5, 1967; children: Jennifer Kay, Kimberly Anne, Amanda Brooke. BA, Ill. Wesleyan U., 1967; MA, Northwestern U., 1969, JD, 1973. Bar: Ill. 1973, U.S. Dist. Ct. (no. dist.) Ill. 1974, U.S. Supreme Ct. 1979. Exec. dir. Winnetka Youth Orgn., Ill., 1969-73; assoc. Seyfarth, Shaw, Fairweather & Geraldson, Chgo., 1973-79, ptnr., 1979-93; ptnr. Field, Golan & Swiger, Chgo., 1993—; bd. dirs. Gt. Lakes Fin. Resources, Matteson, Ill., 1983—, vice chmn., 1988-91, chmn. 1991—; bd. dirs. Chgo. chpt. Ill. Wesleyan U. Assocs.; chmn. bd. dirs. 1st Nat. Bank of Blue Island, 1989—, Bank of Homewood, 1988—; bd. dirs. Winchester Mfg. Co., Wood Dale, Ill., 1980—; dir. Comml. Resources Corp., Naperville, Ill., 1984-93; dir., sec. Ellis Corp., Itasca, Ill., 1980—; chmn. bd. dirs. Community Bank of Homewood-Flossmoor, Ill., 1983-92, Bank of Matteson, Ill., 1992—; mem. State Banking Bd. Ill., 1993—. Family Svc. Ctrs. Cook County, Matteson, bd. dirs. 1979—, treas., 1981-82, pres. 1986-88, chmn., 1988-93; pres. Lakes of Olympia Condominium Assn., 1987-89; trustee Village of Olympia Fields, Ill., 1981-89, pres., 1991—; trustee Ill. Wesleyan U., 1990—, treas. 1994—; bd. dirs. Northwestern U. Sch Law Alumni Assn., 1990-94. Mem. ABA, Ill. Bar Assn., Am. Bankers Assn., Ill. Bankers Assn., United Meth. Bar Assn. (v.p. Chgo. chpt. 1989), Chgo. Bar Assn., Bankers Club of Chgo., Union League Club Chgo., Calumet Country Club. Republican. Home: 3424 Parthenon Way Olympia Fields IL 60461-1321 Office: Field Golan & Swiger 3 1st Nat Plz Ste 2100 Chicago IL 60602

FIELD, ROBERT STEVEN, investment advisor; b. Chgo., July 30, 1949; s. Marshall Harvey and Rita (Stock) F.; m. Ruth Ellen Teplinsky, Aug. 7, 1971; children: Lisa, David. BS in Acctg., Ind. U., 1971. CPA, Ill. Acct. Lester Witte & Co., Chgo., 1971-76; pres., CEO ACCI Fin. Svcs., Inc., Palatine, Ill., 1976—. Mem. AICPA, Ill. Soc. CPAs, Internat. Assn. Fin. Planning (bd. dirs. North Shore chpt. 1985—, pres. 1988-89), Internat. Assn. Registered Fin. Cons. (registered), Inst. Cert. Fin. Planners (cert.), B'nai Brith (pres. 1984-85), Kiwanis (bd. dirs. 1985-86). Home: 812 Downing St Northbrook IL 60062-3021 Office: ACCI Fin Svcs Inc Ste 814 800 E Northwest Hwy Palatine IL 60067-6514

FIELDBINDER, A. CHRISTINE, accountant, educator; b. Ft. Dodge, Iowa, Mar. 19, 1951; d. Max Eugene and Lougene Jewell (Heater) Powell; m. William Wright Fieldbinder, June 24, 1974; 1 child, Anna Christine. BBA, U. Iowa, 1972; MBA, Marquette U., 1987. Inventory analyst HON Co., Muscatine, Iowa, 1972-74; acct. Louis Allis, Milw., 1974-78; capital asset acct. Graber Co., Middleton, Wis., 1978; supr. acctg. Grede Foundries, Inc., Milw., 1979-82, supr. employee benefits, 1983-86, mgr. employee benefits, 1986-92; mgr. compensation, benefits Twin Disc, Inc., Racine, Wis., 1992-95; mgr. benefit sys. and fin. analysis Johnson Control, Inc., Milw., 1995—; adj. instr. Cardinal Stritch Coll., Milw., 1989—. Republican. Roman Catholic. Office: Johnson Controls Inc 5757 N Green Bay Ave Milwaukee WI 53209

FIELDER, CECIL GRANT, professional baseball player; b. L.A., Sept. 21, 1963; m. Stacey Granger; child, Prince. Student, U. Nev., Las Vegas. Baseball player Kansas City Royals, 1982-83, Toronto Blue Jays, Can., 1983-88, Hanshin (Japan) Tigers, 1988-90, Detroit Tigers, 1990—; player Venezuelan League in off-season. Player Am. League All-Star Team, 1990-91, 93, All-Star Team Sporting News, 1990-91; named twice Am. League Player of Week, Am. League Player of Month, Am. League Player of Yr. Sporting News, 1990; recipient Silver Slugger award, 1990, 91; ranked 1st in Am. League for home runs, 1990-91, 1st in Am. League for runs batted in, 1990-92. Office: Detroit Tigers Tiger Stadium Detroit MI 48216*

FIELDER, JAMES B., industrial paint company executive; b. Detroit, July 3, 1951; s. Richard Russell and Mary Jeanne (Carey) Longley; children: Denise Marie Rosiek, Sept. 13, 1980; 1 child, Elyssa Marie. BS, Western Mich. U., Kalamazoo, 1976. Electrocoat svc. rep. PPG, Detroit, 1977-81, electrocoat regional mgr., 1981-86; sales/mktg. mgr. Haden Tech. Svcs., Detroit, 1986-87; electrocoat svc. mgr. BASF, Detroit, 1987-88, electrocoat acctg. mgr., 1988-94, mgr. electrocoat sales/svc. N.Am./S.Am., 1995—. Author presentation E-Coat Changing Film Build Properties by Overfeed, 1988. Treas. Canterbury Commons, Farmington Hills, Mich., 1990—. Cpl. USMC, 1971-73, Vietnam. Mem. Detroit Golf Club. Home: 30150 Valley Side Dr Farmington Hills MI 48334 Office: BASF 2855 Coolidge Hwy Troy MI 48007

FIELDING, RONALD ROY, aeronautical engineer; b. Saskatoon, Sask., Can., July 24, 1961; s. Stanford R. and Helen A. (Rogers) F. BSc in Aero. Engring., Embry-Riddle Aero. U., 1986; BA, U. Sask., 1987. Cert. profl. engr. Assn. Profl. Engrs. of the Province of Manitoba. Material rev. bd. engr. Menasco Aerospace Ltd., Oakville, Ont., Can., 1987-89, test engr.-flight controls, 1989-90; target systems engr. Boeing Can. Tech. Ltd., Winnipeg, Manitoba, Can., 1990-93; engr. assembly tech. support unit Boeing Can. Tech. Ltd., Winnipeg, Man., Can., 1993-95, quality engr., 1995—. Named to Hon. Citizenship, Daytona Beach (Fla.) C. of C., 1986; recipient Sask. Proficiency award Sask. Govt., 1979. Mem. AIAA (treas. Prescott, Ariz. sect. 1984-86), Can. Aero. and Space Inst. (treas. Winnipeg br. 1991-93, chmn. 1994—), Am. Helicopter Soc., Boeing Engring. Social Club (activities dir. 1991-92), Alpha Eta Rho (treas. Pi Rho chpt. 1984-85). Home: 4310 193 Victor Lewis Dr, Winnipeg, MB Canada R3P 2A3 Office: Boeing Can Tech Ltd, Winnipeg Divsn 99 Murray Park, Winnipeg, MB Canada R3J 3M6

FIELDS, ERIC J., financial advisor; b. Evanston, Ill., Sept. 14, 1972. BS, U. Kans., 1994. Fin. advisor Olde Discount Corp., Glenview, Ill., 1994—. Office: Olde Discount Corp 1701 E Lake Ave Ste 100 Glenview IL 60025-2085

FIELDS, MATTHEW H., composer, educator, computer programmer; b. Milw., Dec. 15, 1961; s. Marshall G. and Natalie Ernestine (Krischer) F.; m. Amy Joanne Cannaday, Sept. 30, 1992. MusB in Composition, Oberlin Coll., 1985, BA in Mathematics, 1986; MA in Music, Leland Stanford Jr. U., 1987; DMA in Composition, U. Mich., 1991. Programmer, analyst U. Mich., Ann Arbor, 1992—. Composer: Vindication of Hypatia, 1988, Mount Washington Memories, 1990, The Winds of Springtime, 1990, Origami Symphony, 1991, String Quartet, 1991, Call of the Shofar, 1992, Winter Moonbronze, 1992, Summer Mischief, 1993, Rooster's Court Ball, 1993, Kabala, 1993, Crossroads, 1994, Music for Amy's Birthday, 1995, Sh'mah, 1995. Maile-Johnson fellow Stanford U., 1985-87, Regents fellow U. of Mich., 1987-90; Busoni Composers Competition first prize, 1991. Mem. ASCAP, Sigma Xi. Home: 1310 Packard Rd No 2 Ann Arbor MI 48104 Office: U Mich Med Ctr 1500 E Medical Way Ann Arbor MI 48109

FIELDS, RENEE CHRISTINE, outpatient mental health therapist; b. Wichita, Kans., Mar. 8, 1953; d. Ray and Rosella P. (Suelzle) Hodge; m. James A. Fields, May 19, 1979 (div. 1991); children: Lacy M., David N. BSW magna cum laude, U. Mo., St. Louis, 1979; MSW, U. Kans., 1986. Staff counselor Youth-in-Need, St. Charles, Mo., 1977-78; rsch. asst. psychology dept. U. Mo., St. Louis, 1978-79; adminstrv. asst. Clifton Monica House, Wichita, Kans., 1981-83; therapist Wichita Guidance Ctr., 1986—; pvt. practice Wichita, 1991—; coord. (dir.) Children of Divorce, Wichita, 1991—; hosp. screener Wichita Guidance Ctr., 1992—, mediator, 1986—; cons. Am. Home Health, Wichita, 1985-87; seminar presenter Wichita Bar Assn., 1991-96. U. Mo. acad. scholar, 1978. Mem. Assn. of Family and Conciliation Cts., Heart Land Mediators, Assn. for Infant and Toddler Mental Health. Office: Wichita Guidance Ctr 415 N Poplar St Wichita KS 67214-4529 also: 353 N Market Ste B Wichita KS 67202

FIENE, JEANNE RAE, education educator; b. Aurora, Ill., Aug. 17, 1960; d. Raymond Herman and Esther Minnie (Frank) F. B in Music Edn., Pittsburg (Kans.) State U., 1983, MusM, 1990; EdS, S.W. Mo. State U., 1992; PhD, U. Mo., 1995. Cert. tchr., cert. adminstr., Mo., Kans. Tchr. elem. and secondary music Unified Sch. Dist. 258, Cedar Vale, Kans., 1983-84; tchr. secondary math. Wheaton (Mo.) Dist. R-III, 1986-88, prin. h.s., 1988-92; grad. asst. U. Mo., Columbia, 1992-95, vis. asst. prof. edn., 1995—; presenter profl. confs.; mem. Satellite Acad., Jeff City, Mo., 1994-95. 1st Vet's. scholar Am. Legion Post 80, Downers Grove, Ill., 1978. Mem. ASCD, Nat. Assn. Secondary Sch. Prins., Mo. Assn. Secondary Sch. Prins., UCEA (grad. rsch. symposium award 1995), Phi Delta Kappa, Sigma Alpha Iota (Sword of Honor 1983). Lutheran. Office: Univ Mo 104 Hill Hall Columbia MO 65211

FIES, JAMES DAVID, elementary education educator; b. Chgo., May 19, 1950; s. Arthur Herbert Sr. and Ruth Paulina (Rehm) F.; m. Ruth Elaine Carlson, June 24, 1972; children: Samuel Jacob, Sarah Rae. BA, Purdue U., 1972, MS, 1975. Cert. elem. edn. tchr., Ind. Tchr. math. Morton Elem./Mid. Sch., Hammond, Ind., 1972-82, Eggers Elem./Mid. Sch., Hammond, 1982-88; tchr. math. Gavit Jr./Sr. High Sch., Hammond, 1988—, interim asst. prin., 1992; dept. chair Eggers Mid. Sch., 1983-86. Bldg. union rep. Hammond Tchrs. Fedn. Local 394, 1981-87; trustee Trinity Luth. Ch., Hammond, 1976-82, 86-87, bd. fin., 1993—. Mem. Nat. Coun. Tchrs. of Maths., Hammond Tchrs. Fedn., Am. Fedn. of Tchrs. Home: 544 Hickory Ln Munster IN 46321-2409

FIES, RUTH ELAINE, media specialist; b. Hammond, Ind., Oct. 13, 1949; d. Raymond O. and Elmyra C. (Papageorge) Carlson; m. James. D. Fies, June 24, 1972; children: Samuel Jacob, Sarah Rae. BA in edn., Purdue U., 1971, MS, 1974. Cert. elem. educator, ednl. media profl. K-12, Ind. Tchr. 5th grade Highland (Ind.) Sch. Dist., 1971-72; media specialist Cook County Sch. Dist. #149, Dolton, Ill., 1972-78, George Rogers Clark Middle/H.S., 1991—. Mem. Trinity Luth. Ch. Mem. Hammond Tchrs. Fedn. Home: 544 Hickory Ln Munster IN 46321 Office: George Rogers Clark Sch 1921 Davis Ave Whiting IN 46344

FIETSAM, ROBERT CHARLES, accountant; b. Belleville, Ill., Oct. 18, 1927; s. Celsus J. and Viola (Ehret) F.; BS, U. Ill., 1955; m. Miriam Runkwitz, Apr. 12, 1952; children: Robert C., Guy P., Nancy A., Lisa R. CPA, Mo., Ill. Claims adjuster Ely & Walker Dry Goods, St. Louis, 1947-48; acct. Price Waterhouse & Co., 1949-54; staff acct. J.W. Boyle & Co., East St. Louis, 1955-59; owner R.C. Fietsam, CPA's, Belleville, Ill., 1959-68; mng. ptnr. R.C. Fietsam & Co. CPA's, 1969—. Mem. Belle-Scott Com., 1979—; bd. dirs., pres. Belleville Center, Inc., 1980-81; mem. adv. bd. Masterworks Chorale, 1984—; mem. Ill. Pub. Accts. Registration Com., 1985-87; bd. dirs. Meml. Found., Inc., 1986-91, Bellville Hosp. Golf Classic, mem., 1983-91, chmn., 1986-91; Ill. Bd. Examiners, 1994—. council v.p., pres. St. Paul United Ch. of Christ., 1969-73. With USAF, 1951-53. Mem. AICPAs (coun. 1981-84, 85-90), Ill. CPA Soc. (pres. south chpt. 1972-73, Mr. Southern Chpt. award 1976, chpt. award 1976, state bd. dirs. 1979-81, sr. v.p. 1987-88, pres. 1988-89, bd. dirs. 1989-90, hon. mem. 1992, ICPAC PAC 1979-92, chmn. PAC 1989-92, Pub. Svc. award 1982-83), Mo. Soc. CPA's, U. Ill. Greater Belleville Illini Club (past pres.), Belleville C. of C. (pres. 1973-74), Belleville Jr. C. of C. (life, Key Man award 1959-60, Outstanding Citizen award 1976), Belleville Econ. Progress, Inc. (Ambassadors 1973—), U. of Ill. Found. (St. Louis Accountancy Com. 1991—), Lambda Chi Alpha Alumnae Assn., St. Clair Country Club. Optimists (Belleville Chpt. pres. 1979-80, Disting. Pres. award 1979-80, Optimist of Yr. Belleville, 1977, Ill. Dist. 1980), Elks. Home: 23 Persimmon Rdg Belleville IL 62223-3946 Office: 325 W Main St Belleville IL 62220-1505

FIGARD, STEVE DAVID, biochemist; b. Lancaster, Pa., Mar. 23, 1954; s. Glenn Leon and Jacqueline Mae (Steckler) F.; m. Renee Michelle Bartholomew, Mar. 21, 1981; children: Kristin Helen, Tracy Ellen. BA, Cornell U., 1976; MS, No. Ill. U., 1978; PhD, Fla. State U., 1984. Postdoctoral staff mem. Los Alamos (N.Mex.) Nat. Lab., 1984-86; biochemist Abbott Labs., North Chicago, Ill., 1986—; instr. biochemistry and organic chemistry Barat Coll., Lake Forest, Ill., 1991-93. Contbr. articles to profl. jours. Republican. Office: Abbott Labs Dept 7CB Bldg AP31 Abbott Park IL 60064

FIGGS, LINDA SUE, principal; b. Westhope, N.D., Dec. 19, 1946; d. Clifford James and Ethel Grace (Geise) Drake; m. Tom R. Figgs, Dec. 27, 1969. Student, Minot State U., 1964-66; B.Music Edn., U. Kans., 1968, M.Music Edn., 1972, EdD, 1978. Cert. secondary music tchr., ednl. adminstr., Kans., Iowa, Nebr., N.D. Music tchr. Jefferson County N. High Sch., Winchester, Kans., 1968-76, 89-91, supr. student tchrs., 1970-75; rsch. asst. to assoc. dean of edn. U. Kans., Lawrence; prin. McKinley Elem., Liberal, Kans., 1992-95, Maynard Elem., Emporia, Kans., 1995-96, Stanton Street Early Childhood Ctr., 1995-96; rsch. asst. Sch. Edn., U. Kans., Lawrence, 1977; piano tchr. Toon Shop, Atcison, Kans., Leavenworth, Kans.; music tchr. Little Flower Sch., Minot, N.D., Effingham, Kans.; mgr. music store, Effingham; sec. humanities Minot State U.; counselor Internat. Music Camp, Dunseith, N.D., Midwestern Music and Art Camp, Lawrence; summer counselor, unit leader Nat. Music Camp, Interlochen, Mich.; sponsor 5th grade Positive Peer Group; mem. edn. adv. panel TeleKansas Alliance; mem. U.S. D.480 Action Team Mem., McKinley Action Team Mem.; reader adv. bd. S.W. Daily Times; chmn. rural residency coordinating team Chamber Music Am. and NEA; mem. tech. com. for Unified Sch. Dist. 480 and McKinley Quality Performance Accreditation Team; elem. adminstrn. rep. Stakeholders Com., Sch. Site Coun., strategic planning teams Unified Sch. Dist., 1980, McKinley preassessment team, 504 team, intensive assistance team, skunk works, supervision, stakeholders, McKinley Drug Team; bd. dirs., patron, docent Baker Arts Ctr.; coord. ESL and migrant summer sch.; coord. for Unified Sch. Dist. 253 Migrant/ESL program, 1995—, Leadership Emoria, 1995—; 1st grade prin. rep. for Supt.'s Curriculum Coun. for Sci., elem. prin. rep. sci. com. Contbr. articles to profl. publs. Bd. dirs. Am. Youth Symphony Band and Orch., Nebr., 1970-76; music dir. United Meth. Ch., Atchison, 1988-92; mem. choir United Meth. Ch., Liberal, 1992-95; choir dir. 1st Christian Ch., Liberal, 1995, McKinley Elem. PTA, S.W. Kans. Humane soc.; bd. dirs. Cmty. Concert, 1994-95; vol. Mid Am. Air Mus.; mem. 500 Club, Leadership Liberal, 1995, Leadership Emporia, 1996, Maynard Elem. PTO, Maynard Elem. Sch. Site Coun., Flint Hills Humane Soc., SOS, Emporia Arts Coun., Emporia Area Friends of the Zoo; mem. bus. and edn. com. Emporia Area C. of C. Mem. ASCD, NEA, AAUW (edn. and scholarship com.), Nat. Assn. Elem. Sch. Prins., United Sch. Adminstrs., Kans. Assn. Sch. Adminstrs., Kans. ASCD, Kans. Assn. Elem. Sch. Prins., Kans. Edn. Assn., Nat. Mid. Sch. Assn., Kans. Assn. Mid Level Edn., Kans. Reading Assn., Knas. Reading Coun., Profl. Devel. Coun. (co-pres., insvc. com.), U. Kans. Alumni Assn. (life), S.W. Symphony Soc. (pres. 1993-95), Assn. Cmty. Art Agys. Kans., Emporia Area C. of C. (bus. edn. com.), Sigma Alpha Iota, Pi Kappa Lambda, Phi Delta Kappa. Presbyterian. Home: 1007 Dickinson Rd Effingham KS 66023 Office: Maynard Elem Sch 19 Constitution Emporia KS 66801

FILAN, JOHN B., finance company executive; b. Chgo., May 4, 1946; s. Patrick Joseph and Catherine Agatha (O'Brien) F.; divorced; 1 child, Sheila. BS, St. Joseph's Coll., 1967; MBA, U. Chgo., 1976. Mem. staff Price Waterhouse, Chgo., 1967-68; mkg. and sys. IBM, Chgo., 1968-72; asst. to gov. Office of The Gov., Springfield, Ill., 1973-76; ptnr., head consulting PTW, Ltd., Chgo., 1977—; isntr. St. Xavier's Coll., Chgo. U., U. Ill. Polit. dir., mem. issues com. Campaigns-Govt. and Sec. of State, Chgo., 1972-94; bd. dirs. Chgo. Bd. Edn., 1994-95.; mem. bd. Chgo. Area Campfire Boys and Girls; mem. Chgo. Coun. Fgn. Rels., Citizens Coun. Pub. Aid-Ill. Gen. Assembly; former chair Comptroller's Mcpls. Acct. Adv. Bd.; mem. Wisdom Bridge Theater Bd., Cir. Ct. Clks. Audit Guidelines Com. Mem. U. Chgo. Club (bd. dirs.), Chgo. Area Tech Assistance Providers.

FILCHOCK, ETHEL, education educator, poet. BS in Edn., Kent State U. Tchr. Cleve. Pub. Schs.; with EFC Creations, Solon, Ohio. Author: Voices in Poetics: Vol. 1, 1985 (Merit award), Hall of Fame: Ethel Filchock, Vol. 1, 1991 (book of poetry) Softer Memories Across a Lifetime, 1989, (poetryu chapbook) A Glimpse of Love, 1991; composer: Praise God, The Lord is Coming; lyricist: (songs) He Is Born, 1991, An Old-Fashioned Christmas, Let's Wave the Stars and Stripes Forever, 1991, Be There for Me Music of America, 1993, Christmas Joy, Happy Holidays, 1993, Beautiful Lady of Medugorje, 1993 (Harmonious Honor award), Christmas Joy, There is a Story, 1994, Hilltop Country, Love is Not a Game, 1994, High Country, Loving is Caring, 1995. Chmn. sch. United Way, 1985-86. Recipient Cert. of Achievement N.Y. Profl./Amateur Song Jubilee, 1986, Editor's Choice award Disting. Poets of Am., Outstanding Achievement in Poetry, Nat. Libr. of Poetry, 1993, Outstanding Poets of 1994, Interregnum Nat. Libr. of Poetry, Best Poets of 1995, Transformation, Nat. Libr. of Poetry, Editor's Choice award Outstanding Achievement in Poetry, Nat. Libr. of Poetry, 1995. Mem. NAFE, Am. Fedn. Tchrs. Roman Catholic. Club: Akron Manuscript.

FILICE, GREGORY ALAN, physician; b. Berkeley, Calif., Aug. 30, 1947; s. Gennaro August Jr. and Mae Merle (Molfino) F.; m. Amy Elizabeth Walker, Dec. 13, 1970; children: Ross Warren, Clara Elizabeth, Bradley Samuel. AB in Sociology, U. Calif., Berkeley, 1969; MD, Cornell U., 1973. Diplomate Am. Bd. Internal Medicine and Infectious Diseases. Intern, then resident U. Minn. Hosps., Mpls., 1973-75; resident U. Wash., Seattle, 1977-78; epidemiologist U.S. Ctrs. for Disease Control, Atlanta, 1975-77; fellow infectious diseases Sch. Medicine, Stanford (Calif.) U., 1978-80; staff physician Vet. Affairs Med. Ctr., Mpls., 1980—; chief infectious disease sect., 1992—; asst. prof. medicine U. Minn., Mpls., 1980-88, assoc. prof. medicine, 1988—. Contbr. articles to sci. jours., chpts. to books. Mem. St. Paul Pub. Schs. Bd. Edn., 1992—, chair, 1994-95. Mem. Democratic Farmer Labor Party. Office: Vet Affairs Med Ctr 1 Veterans Dr Minneapolis MN 55417-2300

FILLBROOK, THOMAS GEORGE, telephone company executive; b. Detroit, Jan. 3, 1949; s. John Moyle and Marie Evelyn (Pelto) F. BA, Wayne State U., 1970. Cert. tchr., Mich. Substitute tchr. Van Dyke Pub. Schs., Warren, Mich., 1971-73; mgr. Ameron, Okemos, Mich., 1973-74; salesman F&E Check Protector, Detroit, 1974-76; ops. mgr. Loss Prevention Inc., Royal Oak, Mich., 1976-78; svc. rep. Ameritech, Southfield, Mich., 1979—; actor/clown Clowning Around Entertainment, Romeo, Mich., 1958—; actor Holy Cow Show, WGPR Channel 62, Detroit, 1988; dir. Winter Magic, Harron Cable, Rome, 1991. Polit. and hist. columnist, polit. editor Mill Creek View Newspaper, Washington; mem. City of Hope 1994 Com. Mem. Rep. Nat. Com., Washington, Founders Soc., Detroit Inst. Arts. Recipient commendation Macomb County Bd. Commrs., 1991, 1st Place Clown Costume Competition and Group Act award Mich. State Fair and Exposition, 1995. Mem. Internat. Platform Assn., Finnish Ctr. Assn., Detroit Zool. Soc., Citizens Against Government Waste (charter), Elks (chmn. 1985). Episcopalian. Home: 54723 Shelby Rd Shelby Township MI 48316-1441

FILLICARO, BARBARA JEAN, business owner, consultant; b. Chgo.; d. Frank and Lillian (Kosach) F. Student, DePaul U., 1974-78, BA in Bus. Mgmt., 1978; desktop publishing cert., Coll. of DuPage, 1992. Exec. sec. Continental Bank, Chgo., 1962-68; supr. secretarial svcs. Morton Quality Products, Chgo., 1968-71; adminstrv. asst. Libby, McNeill & Libby, Chgo., 1971-76, purchasing agt., 1976-78; mktg. rep. TRW Fin. Systems, Orlando, Fla., 1978-82; dist. sales rep. Streamline Industries, N.Y.C., 1982-84; office automation specialist Microage Computer Stores, Lombard, Ill., 1984-86; applications software trainer, cons. Fillicaro & Assocs., Lombard, 1986—; mem. faculty Coll. of Du Page, Glen Ellyn, Ill., 1988—; multimedia tech. specialist St. Augustine Coll., Chgo., 1993-95, tech. mgr. 1995—; charter mem., chmn. advocacy com. DuPage County Women's Bus. Coun., 1992; spkr. Multimedia '95, Orlando, Fla. Mem. Art Inst., Chgo., 1975-78. Mem. Chgo. Orgn. Data Tng. Educators, Am. Mgmt. Assn., Women in Mgmt. (bd. dirs., program chmn. 1986-88), Am. Assn. Individual Investors, Assn. for Devel. of Desktop Pub. Technique, DePaul U. Alumni Coun., Zonta Internat. (charter mem., treas. 1979-80), Internat. Interactive Comm. Soc. Home and Office: 5108 W Winnemac Ave Chicago IL 60630-2330

FILMON, GARY ALBERT, Canadian provincial premier, civil engineer; b. Winnipeg, Man., Can., Aug. 24, 1942; s. Albert and Anastasia (Doskocz) F.; m. Janice Clare Wainwright, 1963; children—Allison, David, Gregg, Susanna. B.Sc. in Civil Engring., U. Man., 1964, M.Sc., 1967. Registered profl. engr. Municipal design engr. Underwood McLellan and Assocs., Winnipeg, 1964-67, br. mgr., Brandon, Man., 1967-69; v.p. Success Bus. Coll., Winnipeg, 1969-71, pres., 1971-81. City councillor Queenston Ward, City of Winnipeg, 1975-77, Crescent Heights Ward, City of Winnipeg, 1977-79; mem. legis. assembly River Heights Constituency, Man., 1979-81, Tuxedo Constituency, Man., 1981—, minister consumer and corp. affairs and environment Man. Govt., 1981, leader of the opposition, 1983-88, premier of Manitoba, 1988—; chmn. com. of works and ops. City of Winnipeg, 1977-79; dir. Winnipeg Jets Hockey Club, 1977-78. Mem. Assn. Profl. Engrs. (Province of Man.), Assn. Can. Career Colls. (pres. 1974-75), U. Man. Alumni Assn. (pres. 1974-75). Progressive Conservative. Anglican. Office: Man Legis Assembly, Legislature Bldg Rm 204, Winnipeg, MB Canada R3C 0V8

FINA, PAUL JOSEPH, lawyer; b. Chgo., Mar. 1, 1959; s. Paul Emil and Vera Christiane (Mutzbauer) F.; m. Robyn Leann Hughes, May 24, 1986. BA in Econs., U. Ill., 1982, MA, 1983; JD, DePaul U., Chgo., 1987. Bar: Ill. 1988, U.S. Dist. Ct. (no. dist.) Ill. 1990, U.S. Ct. Appeals (7th cir.) 1990, U.S. Supreme Ct. 1991. Assoc. Haskin, Taylor & McDonough, Wheaton, Ill., 1988-90, Komessar & Wintroub, Chgo., 1990-94; pvt. practice Law Office of Paul J. Fina, Chgo., 1994—; mem. bus. faculty Coll. of DuPage, Glen Ellyn, Ill., 1986—. Gen. counsel Housing Helpers, Inc., Riverside, Ill., 1991—. DePaul law grantee, 1985. Mem. ABA, Ill. BAr Assn., Assn. Trial Lawyers Am., DuPage County Bar Assn. (civil practice com.), Phi Alpha Delta. Roman Catholic. Home: 605 S Brainard Ave La Grange IL 60525-2744 Office: 30 N. LaSalle St Ste 1530 Chicago IL 60602

FINAISH, FATHI ALI, aeronautical engineering educator; b. Tripoli, Libya, July 22, 1954; came to U.S., 1981; s. Ali Finaish and Zuhra (Lamin) Mahfud; m. Deborah Lynn Demijohn, Dec. 28, 1984. BS in Aero. Engring., U. Al-Fateh, Tripoli, 1978; MS in Aerospace Engring., U. Colo., 1984, PhD in Aerospace Engring., 1987. Lic. pvt. pilot; FAA airframe and power plant cert. mechanic. Rsch. asst. U. Colo., Boulder, 1984-87, adj. asst. prof., 1987-88; asst. prof. aero. engring. U. Mo., Rolla, 1988-94, assoc. prof., 1994—; airworthiness engr. Dept. Civil Aviation, Tripoli, 1979-81; ground sch. instr. Tripoli Flight Ctr., 1980-81; rsch. fellow Naval Under Water Systems Ctr., Newport, R.I., 1991, NASA Langley Rsch. Ctr., Hampton, Va., 1992; lectr. various univs.; advisor Licking High Sch., St. James High Sch.; summer rsch. fellow U.S. Navy-Am. Soc. Engring. Edn., 1991, NASA-Am. Soc. Engring. Edn., 1992. Contbr. articles to profl. jours. Head coach Rolla Soccer Club. Grantee U. Mo., Rolla, 1988-92, U. Mo. Systems, 1991-92, U. Mo. Rsch. Bd., 1994-95, Office Naval Rsch., 1991, NASA, 1993-95. Mem. AIAA (sr., Outstanding Tchr. award U. Mo. chpt. 1993), ASEE, ASHRAE (grantee 1992-93). Office: U Mo Dept Mech Engring Rolla MO 65401

FINAN, JOHN, health facility administrator. Pres. Barnes Hosp., St. Louis. Office: Barnes Hosp One Barnes Hospital Plz Saint Louis MO 63110

FINAN, RICHARD H., state senator, lawyer; b. Cin., Aug. 16, 1934; m. Joan L. Finan, 1956; children: Patrick, Nancy, Julie, Michael. BS, U. Dayton; LLB, U. Cin. Bar: Ohio. Pvt. practice, Sharonville, Ohio; mem. Ohio Senate, Columbus, 1978—; asst. pro tem, chmn. ways and means com., Senate legis. ethics com., fin. com., commerce and labor com., rules com., reference and oversight com., joint legis. com. on fed. funds, welfare oversight com., taxation rev. com., mem. Rep. campaign com.; chmn. fed. budget and taxation com. Nat. Conf. State Legislators; bd. dirs. Franklin Savs. & Loan; arbitrator Hamilton County Ct. Common Pleas, Am. Arbitration Assn. Councilman Evendale Villae, Ohio, 1963-69, mayor, 1969-73; mem. Ohio Ho. of Reps., Columbus, 1973-78; exec. dir. Hamilton County Reagan-Bush Campaign, 1984; dir. Dole for Pres. Campaign, 1988; trustee U. Dayton; past trustee St. Rita's Sch. for Deaf; bd. dirs. Cath. Social Svcs. Southwestern Ohio, Carillon Funds, Rest Haven. Named Legislator of Yr., Ohio Trial Lawyers Assn., 1975, Twp. Clks. and Trustees Assn., 1976, Disting. Alumnus award U. Dayton, Andrew Carnegie award Oho Libr. Assn., 1993, Outstanding Merit award for statehouse preservation Ohio Hist. Soc. Mem. Ohio Bar Assn., Cin. Bar Assn., Sharonville Bus. Assn., U. Dayton Alumni Assn. (past pres. Cin. chpt.), U. Dayton Nat. Alumni Assn. (past pres.). Office: 3068 Stanwin Pl Cincinnati OH 45241-3360 also: 11137 Main St Cincinnati OH 45241-2614 also: 3457 Sherbrooke Dr Cincinnati OH 45241-3282*

FINCH, ROBERT JONATHAN, communications engineering consultant; b. Chgo., Sept. 21, 1955; s. Herman Manuel and Frances (Gutlow) F.; m. Gayle Deborah Falk, Mar. 28, 1991; 1 child, Layla Michelle. BA in Broadcast Mgmt., U. So. Calif., 1977. Engr.-in-charge LFI Prodns., Inc., Lafayette, Ind., 1990-92; comm. engring. cons., L.A., 1978-90, Lafayette, 1992—. Developer: ABC Hollywood's 1st satellite video-tape ctr., Saudi Arabia's 1st color TV studio, 1st digitally based pub. transponder in 2-way radio svc. in continental U.S., 1st large volume, pub. access and radio accessed computer database in U.S.; contbr. articles to publs. Mem. Tippecanoe Amateur Radio Assn. (trustee), Hollywood (Calif.) Magic Castle, Pasadena Casting Club (instr.). Home: 7530 Ridgeview Ln Lafayette IN 47905-9795

FINDER, KENNETH A., director of business development; b. Chgo., Nov. 15, 1949. BS, MIT, 1973, MS, 1973. Systems analyst Lulejian and Assocs., Falls Church, Va., 1973-75; dir. bus. devel. Teradyne, Deerfield, Ill., 1975—; mem. overseers coun. Internat. Engring. Consortium. Patentee telephone line testing; contbr. articles to profl. jours.

FINDER-STONE, PATRICIA ANN, registered nurse, nursing educator; b. Platteville, Wis., Jan. 27, 1929; d. Arthur Charles and Marcella Mary (Roseliep) Finder; m. Mark Henry Stone, Dec. 28, 1953; children: Teresa Kay Stone Gulyas, Susan Elizabeth Stone Crane, Mark Henry Jr., Matthew Riley. Grad., Columbia Sch. Nursing, 1950; BS, U. Wis., Green Bay, 1973; MS, U. Wis., Madison, 1975. RN; cert. in pub. health, Wis. Staff and adminstrv. nurse various hosps., 1980-95; dir. nurses San Luis Manor, Green Bay, 1967-68; asst. head nurse Bellin Meml. Hosp., Green Bay, 1968-69; instr. nursing Bellin Sch. Nursing, Green Bay, 1969-79; dir. Bellin Hospice Program, Green Bay, 1979-80; nursing cons. local law firms, Green Bay, 1984-87; instr. ADN program N.E. Wis. Tech. Coll., Green Bay, 1980—; vice chairperson Brown County Bd. of Health; mem. ethics com. St. Mary's Hosp., Green Bay, 1987—; mem. Wis. ethics com. network Med. Coll. Wis., Milw., 1988—; assoc. mem. Hastings Ctr. Inst. Soc., Ethics and Life Scis., N.Y., 1975—; assoc. mem. Wis. Health Decisions, Inc., 1991; chairperson bd. dirs., 1996. Bd. dirs., sec., pub. affairs chair Wis. divsn. Am. Cancer Soc., 1978—, bd. dirs., pres., pub. affairs chair Brown County unit, 1976—; bd. dirs. Greater Green Bay Cmty. Found., 1991—, Bay Area Cmty. Coun., 1992—; mem. adv. bd. Brown County Planning Commn., 1992—; mem. planning bd. United Way, 1992—; past bd. dirs. Northeastern Wis. Health Systems Agys., Wis. Health Policy Coun. Named Woman of the Yr. Green Bay YWCA, 1977; recipient Tchr. of the Yr. award Wis. Vocat. Assn., 1983, Nurses Leadership award Green Bay Nurses. Mem. LWV (bd. dirs. Greater Green Bay chpt. 1984—, pres. 1989-92, bd. dirs. Wis. 1992-94, action chairperson), AAUW (pres.-elect 1996), Wis. Nurses Assn. (chairperson legis. commn. 1985-94, ethics commr. 1994—, pub. policy commr. 1995—), Green Bay Dist. Nurses Assn. (bd. dirs., pres. 1992-94, co-chairperson legis. com. 1994—), Nat. League for Nursing, Wis. League for Nursing, Pi Lambda Theta, Sigma Theta Tau (v.p.), Phi Delta Kappa. Home: Crow's Nest No 57 985 N Broadway De Pere WI 54115-2659

FINDLEY, TROY RAY, state legislator. B in Polit. Sci., U. Kans., 1990. Active grocery/retail industry, 1982-92; county desk dir. Kans. Dem. Party, 1992-94; mem. Kans. State Ho. of Reps. Dist. 46.

FINE, DWIGHT LYLE, lobbyist; b. North Hopkins, Iowa, July 18, 1942; s. Orris Leroy and Ardith Claire (Lister) F.; m. Eva Louise Hargrove, Apr. 8, 1966; children: Marc, Aimee. AA, Southwest Bapt. U., 1962; BA, Ouachita Bapt. U., 1964, MA, 1964; MS, U. Mo., 1966. Budget analyst State of Mo., Jefferson City, 1965-66; adminstrv. asst. Dept. of Revenue, Jefferson City, 1967-69, Sec. of State, Jefferson City, 1970-72; campaign cons. Jefferson City, 1972-74; adminstrv. mgr. Auditors Office, Jefferson City, 1975-76; chief clk. House of Reps., Jefferson City, 1977-81; adminstrv. asst. Lt. Gov., Jefferson City, 1981-84; lobbyist Mo. Hosp. Assn., Jefferson City, 1985—. Office: PO Box 60 Jefferson City MO 65102

FINE, WILLIAM IRWIN, real estate developer; b. St. Paul, May 26, 1928; s. Adolph and Ida (Cohen) F.; m. Bianca M. Conti, Apr. 10, 1994. BLS, U. Minn., 1949, LLB, 1950. Bar: Minn. 1950, Tex. 1950. Asst. dist. atty. Dallas County, 1950-52; judge adv. gen. USAF, Keesler AFB, Miss., 1952-53; ptnr., founder Fine, Simon & Schneider, Mpls., 1953-69; pres., co-founder Fine Properties Corp., Chgo., 1969-71; mng. gen. ptnr., co-founder Fine Assocs., Mpls., 1972—; co-founder VISTA Sci., Inc., 1991, DYUAR, Inc., 1992; advisor Inst. Tech. U. Minn., Mpls., 1987—. Trustee Sci. Mus. Minn., St. Paul, 1989-94; co-founder/co-chmn. Theoretical Physics Inst. U. Minn., 1987; charter mem. indsl. liaison com. Materials Rsch. Lab. U. Chgo., 1993—. Mem. AAAS, Am. Inst. Physics. Office: Fine Assocs 1916 IDS Ctr Minneapolis MN 55402

FINEBERG, CHARLES M., computer engineer; b. St. Louis, Sept. 22, 1962; s. Mark S. and Barbara (Bass) F. BS, Washington U., BSEE. From programmer to prin. engr. internet connections Washington U., St. Louis, 1984—. Office: St Louis Internet Connect 710 N Tucker Ste 802 Saint Louis MO 63101

FINEGOLD, JORDAN, assistant attorney general; b. Boston, May 28, 1959; m. Amy D. Klaben, Mar. 1, 1986; children: Andrew, Joshua. BA, Williams Coll., 1981; JD, Northeastern U., 1986. Bar: Ohio 1986, U.S. Dist. Ct. (so. and no. dists.) Ohio 1986. Asst. atty gen. Atty. Gen. of Ohio, Columbus, 1986-89, 92—; assoc. Ulmer & Berne, Columbus, 1989-92; spl. asst. U.S. Atty, Columbus Ohio, 1994—. Mem. Ohio State Bar Assn., Columbus Bar Assn. Office: Atty Gen Ohio Health Care Fraud Sect 101 E Town St 5t Fl Columbus OH 43215

FINGER, STANLEY, psychology educator; b. Bronx, N.Y., May 11, 1943; s. Harry Finger and Beatrice Kaplowitz; m. Wendy Zien; children: Robert, Bradley. BA, Hunter Coll., 1964; MA, Ind. U., 1966, PhD, 1968. Prof., psychology dept. Washington U., St. Louis, 1968—; visiting prof. U. Gothenberg, Sweden, 1972, Clark U., Worcester, Mass., 1979, Cambridge U., Eng., 1987. Author: Brain Damage and Recovery, 1982; editor: Early Brain Damage, 1984, Brain Injury and Recovery, 1988, Origins of Neuroscience, 1993. Recipient Prin. Investigator award NIH, 1966-82, Miles Labs., 1986-93. Mem. AAAS, Internat. Neuropsychological Soc., Soc. Hist. Neurosci., Soc. for Neurosci. Office: Wash U Psychology Dept Saint Louis MO 63130

FINK, JOHN FRANCIS, newspaper editor; b. Ft. Wayne, Ind., Dec. 17, 1931; s. Francis Anthony and Helen Elizabeth (Hartman) F.; m. Marie Therese Waldron, May 31, 1955; children: Regina Marie, Barbara Ann, Robert Paul, Stephen Lawrence, Therese Rose, David Francis, John Noll. B.A., U. Notre Dame, 1953. Assoc. editor Our Sunday Visitor, Religious Pub. Co., Huntington, Ind., 1956-68; editor Family Digest, 1956-67, mktg. mgr., 1967-72, exec. v.p., 1972-76, pres., 1976-82, pub., 1982-84; chmn. Noll Printing Co., 1978-84; editor in chief The Criterion, Indpls., 1984—; bd. dirs. Center for Applied Research in the Apostolate, 1978-85, Internat. Cath. Orgns. Center, 1979-85; mem. Cath. Com. for White House Conf. on Families, 1980; mem. communications com. U.S. Cath. Conf., 1981-84. Author: Moments in Catholic History, 1992. Chmn. United Fund Drive, 1963; pres. United Way of Huntington County, 1973-74, bd. dirs., 1971-74; bd. dirs. YMCA, Huntington, 1966-78, Cath. Journalism Scholarship Fund, Founds. and Donors Interested in Cath. Activities, 1977-84; trustee Huntington Coll., 1978-81; bd. dirs. Huntington Coll. Found., 1977-84, pres. bd., 1978-81; bd. dirs. Huntington Med. Meml. Found., 1978-84. Served as 1st lt. USAF, 1954-56. Decorated knight of Malta, knight of Holy Sepulchre; recipient Disting. Svc. award Huntington Jaycees, 1960; named Chief of Flint Springs Tribe, 1971, St. Francis de Sales award Cath. Press Assn., 1981, award of yr. Notre Dame Club of Indpls., 1994. Mem. Internat. Fedn. Cath. Press Assn. (v.p. 1974-80, pres. 1980-86), Internat. Cath. Union of the Press (hon., coun. and bur. mem. 1974-86), Cath. Press Assn. (pres. 1973-75, dir. 1965-75), Indpls. Serra Club (pres. 1995-96).

FINK, THOMAS EDWARD, cosmetologist, manager; b. Columbus, Ohio, June 28, 1940; s. Thomas Austin and Louise Eva (Longworth) F.; children: Teresa, Thomas Jr., Troy, Tina, Tricia. Grad., Ohio State Cosmetology, 1959, Antoine of Paris, 1960, Pivot Point Internat., 1968, Dale Carnegie, 1970. Owner, pres. Greater Columbus Beauty Salons, Inc., Columbus, Ohio, 1962-80; co-owner, mgr. Robert Thomas Hair Designers of Naples, Fla., Fla., 1981-85; mgr. Dibela Ltd., Columbus, 1985—; styles dir., lectr. Ohio State Sch. Cosmetology, Columbus, 1960s; com. mem. Cit and State Hair Fashion Com., Columbus, 1960s; stylist Miss Ohio/Miss Am. Pageant, Columbus, 1966; head stylist Kenley Players, Columbus, 1960-79; competition judge, 1964—. Master mason Humboldt Lodge No. 476, Columbus, 1971—; 32nd degree mason Ancient Accepted Scottish Rite, 1971—; shriner Aladdin Temple, Columbus, 1971—; mem. Loyal Order Moose Lodge No. 11, Columbus, 1984—. Recipient Silver Guild award Hair Guild of Ohio, 1963, Outstanding Contbn. to the Art of Hair Color award Clairol, 1964. Mem. Nat. Hairdressers and Cosmetologists Assn., Columbus Computer Soc. Home: 828 Weldon Ave Columbus OH 43224-3902 Office: Dibela Hair Designers 5903 Karric Square Dr Dublin OH 43017-4244

FINK, THOMAS MICHAEL, lawyer; b. Huntington, Ind., Oct. 6, 1947; s. Francis Anthony and Helen Elizabeth (Hartman) F.; m. Sheila Ann Jeffers, Aug. 11, 1973; children: Mark, Matthew, Megan. BBA, U. Notre Dame, 1970; JD, Northwestern U., 1973. Bar: Ind. 1973, U.S. Dist. Ct. (no. dist.) Ind. 1973. Assoc. Barrett & McNagny, Ft. Wayne, Ind., 1973-78, ptnr., 1979—; mem., speaker Estate Planning Coun., Ft. Wayne, 1987—. Pres. Bishop Luers H.S. Bd. Edn., Ft. Wayne, 1992-93; bd. dirs., pres. Ft. Wayne Cmty. Found. Bus. Edn. Fund, 1990-93; bd. dirs., treas. Planned Giving Coun. N.E. Ind., 1995—. Mem. Ft. Wayne Country Club, Notre Dame Club of Ft. Wayne, Beta Gamma Sigma. Roman Catholic. Home: 1302 Sunset Dr Fort Wayne IN 46807-2952 Office: Barrett & McNagny 215 E Berry St Fort Wayne IN 46802-2705

FINKE, THOMAS SEDDON, lawyer; b. Chgo., Mar. 24, 1966; s. Kenneth Thompson and Deborah (Lanctot) F.; m. Lisa Anne Gollob, Oct. 9, 1993. BA, Claremont McKenna Coll., 1988; JD, MM, Northwestern U., 1992. Assoc. atty. Sidley & Austin, Chgo., 1992—. Mem., bd. dirs. Carol Gollob Found. for Breast Cancer Rsch., Chgo., 1992—. Office: Sidley and Austin One First National Plz Chicago IL 60022

FINKEL, BERNARD, public relations, fund-raising and association management executive, radio show host; b. Chgo., Nov. 12, 1926; s. Isadore and Sarah (Goldzweig) F.; m. Muriel Horwitz, Dec. 23, 1951; children: Phillip Stuart, Calvin Mandel, Norman Terry. Student Hebrew Theol. Coll., Chgo., 1939-44, Lewis Inst. Arts and Scis., Ill. Inst. Tech., Chgo., 1944-45, U. Ill.-Chgo., 1947-48; BS in Journalism, U. Ill., 1951. Reporter, rewriter Peacock Newspapers, Chgo., 1949, Defender Newspapers, Chgo., 1951, Chgo. North Side Newspapers, 1952; asst. dir. pub. relations Combined Jewish Appeal-Jewish Fedn. Met. Chgo., 1953; mng. editor Electric Appliance Service News, Chgo., 1954-57; asst. account exec. Burlingame-Grossman Advt., Chgo., 1957; account exec. Glassner & Assocs., Pub. Relations, Chgo., 1958-61; pub. relations cons. Bernard Finkel Communications, Chgo., 1961—; dir. devel. and pub. rels. Japanese Am. Svc. Com., 1981-89; nat. dir. of communications and donor rels. Little Brothers - Friends of the Elderly, Chgo., 1989-90; owner, producer, host weekly radio show Jewish Community Hour, Sta. WONX-AM, Evanston, Ill. Author: Life and the World, 1947. Mem. pub. relations and youth commns. Village of Skokie, 1964-65; v.p., coach Boys Baseball, Skokie, 1963-67; mem. adv. bd., chmn. pub. relations Chgo. Area Career Conf., 1961-62; pres. Acad. Assocs. of Ida Crown Jewish Acad., Chgo., 1973-75; v.p. Hillel Torah North Suburban Day Sch., 1965-66, Congregation Or Torah, Skokie, 1970-71; bd. dirs. Skokie Valley Traditional Synagogue, 1987—. Served with U.S. Army, 1945-46. Recipient awards for pub. service Jewish Community Hour, 1978, Chgo. Rabbinical Coun., Chgo. Bd. Rabbis, Council Traditional and Orthodox Synagogues of Greater Chgo., Midwest Region of Nat. Fedn. Jewish Men's Clubs, Israel Aliyah Ctr. of World Zionist Orgn., Religious Zionists of Chgo., B'nai B'rith Lodge of Survivors of Nazi Holocaust, others. Mem. Nat. Soc. Fund-Raising Execs., Pub. Rels. Soc. Am., Social Svc. Communicators, Publicity Club of Chgo. (profl. achievement awards). Home and Office: 3300 Capitol St Skokie IL 60076-2402

FINKEL, WARREN EDWARD, architect; b. Elyria, Ohio, Nov. 2, 1920; s. Edward Raymond and Hazel (Allen) F.; m. Doris Croyle, Nov. 4, 1977. Grad., Case Western Res. U., 1950. Registered architect Ohio, Mich., Fla., N.C. Architect Dalton-Dalton, Cleve., 1950, R.G. Wheeler, San Diego, 1951-52, Weinberg & Teare, Cleve., 1953-55; pres. Finkel & Knilans, Inc. Prin. works include: Oak Hills Country Club, Lorain, 1960, 1st Ch. of Christ, Scientist, Lorain, 1960, Lorain Cmty. Hosp., 1962, Lorain County C.C., 1964, 74, Firelands Retirement Ctr., 1965, Lorain County Red Cross Hdqrs., 1966, Lorain County Sch. for Retarded Children, 1967, Lorain Family YMCA, 1968, Lorain Cmty. Hosp., 1969, Lorain County C.C., 1970, Lorain City Hall, 1971, Elyria Savs. and Trust Bank, 1976, Fine Arts Ctr., 1977, Stark Tech., Coll., 1979, St. Joseph Hosp., 1981, Harshaw Chem. Co., 1981, Boy Scouts Am. Ctr., 1982, Advanced Tech. Ctr., 1984, TRW Nelson Div., 1986, R.W. Beckett Corp., 1987, Lorain County C.C. Fieldhouse, conferencing-classroom bldg., 1993, News Herald newspaper pub. plant, Mentor, Ohio, 1993. Mem. AIA, Architects Soc. Ohio, Lorain C. of C. (pres. 1967). Lodge: Masons. Home: 3761 E Lake Rd Lorain OH 44054-1058

FINKELMEIER, PHILIP RENNER, law librarian, lawyer; b. Cin., Sept. 5, 1914; s. Louis Philip and Lena (Renner) F.; m. Marion A. Oberling, June 24, 1936 (dec. Dec. 1990); children: Phyllis Rush Finkelmeier Head, Robert Louis. JD, No. Ky. U., 1940. Bar: Ohio 1940, U.S. Dist. Ct. (so. dist.) Ohio 1949, U.S. Ct. Appeals (6th cir.) 1967, U.S. Supreme Ct. 1968. Dep., hearing officer Ohio Indsl. Commn., 1941-48; ptnr. Hoover, Beall & Eichel, Cin., 1948-58; pvt. practice law Cin., 1958-68; ptnr. Louis J. Finkelmeier Jr., Cin., 1968-89; asst. libr. Cin. Law Libr. Ohio Ct. House, Hamilton County, 1989—. Ruling elder Immanuel Presbyn. Ch. Mem. ABA, Ohio Bar Assn. (workers' compensation com.), Cin. Bar Assn. (workers' compensation com.), Masons, Shriners. Home and Office: 5300 Hamilton Ave Apt 1700 Cincinnati OH 45224-3165

FINKLER, JOSEPH M., investment broker; b. Muskegon, Mich., Mar. 4, 1966. AAS, Muskegon Coll., 1990. Insp. Kaydon Corp., Muskegon, 1984-92; investment broker Kent King Securities, Grand Rapids, Mich., 1992-93, J.J.B. Hilliard W.L. Lyons Inc., Holland, Mich., 1994-95. Mem. MEGA. Republican. Roman Catholic. Office: JJB Hilliard WL Lyons Inc 36 W 8th St Holland MI 49423-3153

FINLEY, DENNIS HOWARD, vocational education educator; b. Massillon, Ohio, June 8, 1965; s. Donald Eugene Sr. and Linda Francis (Bullman) F.; m. Lori Ann Hisey, June 13, 1987; 1 child, Kyle David. Cert. in food tech., R.G. Drage Career Ctr., Massillon, 1983. Cert. tchr., vocat. instr. Quality control technician Superior's Brand Meats, Inc., Massillon, 1983-85; mgr. quality control Country Smoked Meats, Inc., Wooster, Ohio, 1985-89; tchr. meat-bakery and food sci. Wayne County Schs. Career Ctr., Smithville, Ohio, 1989—. Recipient Best of Best award div. vocat. edn. Kent State U., 1989; named Ohio Agrl. Sci. Tchr. of Yr., 1993, 95, silver medal Nat. Agr. Sci. Tchr. of Yr., 1994. Mem. Am. Vocat. Assn., Ohio Vocat. Assn., Wayne County Sch. Dist. Edn. Assn. (mem. exec. com.), ECO Food Dealers Assn., Ohio Assn. Meat Processors. Mem. Assembly of God Ch. Home: 150 Mill St N Dalton OH 44618-9402 Office: Wayne County Sch Career Ctr 518 W Prospect St Smithville OH 44677-9517

FINLEY, GARY ROGER, financial company executive; b. Gays, Ill., June 3, 1940; s. Fred Forrest and Dena Maxine (Jeffris) F.; m. Ardeth Kay Clawson, June 12, 1960; children: Deborah Finley Fisher, Shari Finley Swiger. AB, Lincoln (Ill.) Christian Coll., 1964; MA, Lincoln Christian Sem., 1971. Lic. commodities broker, securities broker. Ministry work Christian Ch. of Christ, Cen. and Western Ill., 1959-74; personnel counselor Jamar Personnel, Rock Island, Ill., 1974-75; sales and dept. mgr. Commodity Trend Svc., Davenport, Iowa, 1975-79; co-founder, co-owner Valley Commodities, Orion, Ill., 1979-83; sales rep. FGL Commodity Svcs., West Des Moines, Iowa, 1983-85; commodity pool operator pvt. practice, Orion, 1979-89; commodity broker, equity raiser Farmers Commodities Corp., Inc., West Des Moines, Iowa, 1987-93; pres. FCC Investments, Inc. and FCC Ultra, Inc., West Des Moines, 1990-93, also bd. dirs.; v.p., treas. The Com-Pac Corp., Davenport, Iowa, 1989-94; founder, pres. Finley Fin. Svcs., Inc., Gays, Ill., 1993—; co-owner, pres. Value Fuel, Inc., Gays, Ill., 1995—. Dir., assoc. Nat. Ch. Growth Rsch. Ctr., Washington, 1992—; elder Orion Christian Ch., 1986-91; v.p. Prayerhouse Warehouse Ministry, Des Moines, 1992—. Home and Office: Finley Fin Svcs Inc RR 1 Box 17 Gays IL 61928

FINLEY, PHILIP BRUCE, retired state adjutant general; b. White City, Kans., Mar. 25, 1930; s. Marshall Arthur and Zelma Rena (Krenkle) F.; m. Jacqueline Lou Thomas, May 23, 1952; children: Jeffrey Allen, Robin Lyn. BS, Kans. State U., 1951, MS, 1954. Commd. U.S. Army, 1951, advanced through grades to maj. gen., 1988; served in Kans. N.G., 1967-84; served with Res. Norton, Kans., 1954-67; high sch. tchr. Bird City, Kans., 1954-55, Norton, Kans., 1955-67; extension agt. Decatur County Agr. Extension Council, Oberlin, Kans., 1967-72; rural devel. specialist Kans. State U. Area Office, Colby, 1972-74; N.W. Area dir. Kansas State U. Agrl. Extension, Colby, 1974-86, assoc. head, 1986—; adjutant-gen. State of Kans., Topeka, 1987-90; retired, 1990. Mem. N.W. Kans. Planning and Devel. Group, Hill City, 1972-74, "Future Kans." Planning Commn., Topeka, 1985-86. Mem. 7th Div. Assn., VFW, Am. Legion, Phi Delta Kappa, Epsilon Sigma Phi. Republican. Methodist. Home: 685 S Court Ave Colby KS 67701-3411

FINN, DANIEL RUSH, economics and theology educator, former dean; b. Rochester, N.Y., Apr. 30, 1947; s. George Elwood and Ruth Mary (Schwenzer) F.; m. Nita Jo Rush, June 17, 1978; children: Jacob, Stephanie. BS, St. John Fisher Coll., 1968; MA, U. Chgo., 1975, PhD, 1977. Asst. prof. econs. and theol. ethics St. John's U., Collegeville, Minn., 1977-84, assoc prof., 1984-91, prof., 1991—, dean sch. of theology, 1984-89, William E. and Virginia Clemens chair econ. and liberal arts, 1989—, prof. econ. and theol. ethics, 1991; cons. on programs joining econs. and ethics, 1985—. Author: (with others) Toward Christian Economic Ethic, 1980, Just Trading: On the Ethics and Economics of International Trade, 1996. Mem. Assn. for Social Econs. (pres. 1986), Am. Econs. Assn., Soc. Christian Ethics (bd. dirs. 1988-92), Midwest Assn. Theol. Schs. (pres. 1985-87), Minn. Consortium of Theol. Schs. (v.p. 1987-89), History of Econs. Soc., Minn. Econ. Assn. Office: St Johns U Dept Econs Dept Econs Collegeville MN 56321

FINN, HAROLD R., state legislator; b. Oct. 27, 1948; m. Terit; 2 children. BA, U. Minn., 1971, JD, 1979. State senator Minn. State Senate, Dist. 4, 1991—; mem. tax 7 tax laws, environ. & natural resources & health & human svcs. coms., chmn. judiciary com., vice chmn. energy & pub. urilities com., Minn. State Senate. Sec., treas. Leech Lake Indian Reservation. Home: PO Box 955 Cass Lake MN 56633-0955*

FINNEGAN, FRANK ROMAN, investment broker; b. St. Louis, June 1, 1926. BA, St. Louis U., 1952. Investment broker Edward D. Jones & Co., St. Louis, 1953—. With USN, 1944-46. Republican. Roman Catholic. Office: Edward D Jones & Co 201 Progress Pky Maryland Heights MO 63043-3003

FINNEGAN, JAMES JOHN, JR., editor, publisher; b. Chgo., Dec. 21, 1948; s. James John and Carmen Maria (Carrasquillo Badillo) F.; m. Joan Karen Quinlan, June 26, 1971; children: James III, Erin, Byron. BA, De Paul U., 1973. Editor, asst. dir. Ill. Inst. Tech., Chgo., 1974-76; gen. mgr. Scroll Studio, Inc., Chgo., 1976-78; pres. Scribes, Inc., Riverside, Ill., 1978—; editor, pub. The Landmark newspaper, Riverside, 1985—. Bd. dirs. Riverside Arts Coun., 1986—, Riverside Little League, 1986-87, IHM High Sch., Westchester, Ill., 1986-88; commr. Riverside Hist. Commn., 1989-93; chmn. St. Mary Elem. Sch. Bd., Riverside, 1990-91; mem. Riverside Strategic Planning Task Force Com., 1995—. Mem. Frederick Law Olmstead Soc. (bd. dirs. 1987-94), Exec. Club of Chgo., Riverside Swim Club. Office: Scribes Inc Landmark Pub 355 E Burlington St Riverside IL 60546-2149

FINNEMORE, DOUGLAS KIRBY, physics educator; b. Cuba, N.Y., Sept. 9, 1934; s. David Jerome and Mildred (Bosworth) F.; m. Faith Romaine Watson, June 16, 1956; children: Martha, Susan, Sara. BS, Pa. State U., 1956; MS, U. Ill., 1958, PhD, 1962. Mem. faculty Iowa State U., Ames, 1962—; assoc. prof. physics Iowa State U., 1965-68, prof., 1968—, Disting. prof. sci. and humanities, 1987—, program dir. solid state physics, 1978-83, assoc. dir. Ames Lab, 1983-88, chair dept. physics and astronomy, 1994—; program dir. quantum solids and liquids program NSF, 1976-77; detailee U.S. Dept. Energy, 1993-94; vis. fellow U. Coll. Oxford, 1989. Fellow Univ. Coll. Oxford, 1989. Fellow Am. Phys. Soc.; mem. Sigma Xi. Home: 3312 Oakland St Ames IA 50014-3520

FINNERTY, MADELINE FRANCES, consulting firm owner; b. Stockbridge, Mass., Jan. 3, 1949; d. John James and Frances Finnerty. BA cum laude, Newton Coll. of Sacred Heart, Newton, Mass., 1971; MBA, Ashland U., 1984. From plant staff to gen. employee involvement mgr. Sprint United Tel. Co., Mansfield, Ohio, 1977-92; training and orgn. devel. mgr. Nat. Exchange Carrier Assn., Whippany, N.J., 1984-87; pres. Finnerty Internat., Ashland, Ohio, 1992—. Dir. Miss Ohio Pageant Festival, Mansfield, 1990; active mem. C. of C. Edn. Com., Mansfield, 1990-96. Mem. ASTD (pres. Mohican Valley chpt. 1984, regional coord. 1986-89, dir. women's network 1990-91, nat. nominating com. 1992-94, quality symposia adv. com. 1992-94), AAUW (program chair 1995—), North Ctrl. Ohio Employee Participation Coun., Ashland Area C. of C., Rotary Club Ashland. Office: Finnerty Internat 1046 Oak Hill Cir Ashland OH 44805-2947

FINNEY, JON PHILIP, county auditor; b. Fairfield, Iowa, Nov. 24, 1952; s. Raymond Verner and Nellie Gertrude (Horn) F.; m. Deborah Marie Noble, Sept. 24, 1983; children: Jonathan Andrew, Elizabeth Marie. BA, Iowa Wesleyan Coll., 1975. County auditor Van Buren County, Keosauqua, Iowa, 1976—; pres. 5th Dist. County Auditors Assn., S.E. Iowa, 1970s; state exec. bd. Iowa County Auditors Assn., 1970s; vice chair County Fin. Com., 1995—. Editor, contbr. VBC Annual Fin. Report, 1975—. Precinct committeeperson Van Buren County Reps., Keosauqua, 1984—; sec.-treas. Van Buren County Devel. Assn., Keosauqua, late 1970s; v.p. Douds (Iowa) Hist. Preservation Assn., Inc., 1977—; pres. Twin City Manor, Inc., Douds, early 1980s, Douds Cmty. Club, 1970-74; trustee, chair Heartland Ins. Risk Pool, 1991—, Christ United Meth. Ch., 1995—; dir. Van Buren Cmty. Sch. Bd. Edn., 1990—. Arthur Secor scholar Arthur Secor Found., 1971. Mem. Rotary (sec.-treas. Keosauqua chpt. 1979—), Knights of Pythias. Republican. Methodist. Home: RR 2 Box 168 Keosauqua IA 52565-9623 Office: Van Buren County PO Box 475 Keosauqua IA 52565-0475

FINNEY, THOMAS D., chiropractor; b. Bklyn., Dec. 3, 1959. AS with honors, Sauk Valley Coll., 1981; D Chiropractic, Palmer Coll. Chiropractic, 1984. Lic. Ill. Chiropractor Finney Chiropractic & Rehab. Ctr., Sterling, Ill., 1986—, Finney Chiropractic of Morrison, Ill., 1993—, Finney Chiropractic of Dixon, Ill., 1994—; chiropractic preceptor, 1993—; asst. instr. Palmer Coll., 1990—, instr. philosophy and comms. Chiropractic Technician Program, 1984. Mem. Am. Chiropractic Assn., Am. Chiropractic Assns. coun. on Sports Injuries & Physical Fitness, Ill. Prairie State Chiropractic Assn., Palmer Coll. Chiropractic Alumni Assn., Acad. Indsl. Health Cons., Found. Chiropractic Edn. and Rsch. Home: 604 W 4th St Sterling IL 61081 Office: Finney Chiropractic & Rehab Ctr 110 E Lynn Blvd Sterling IL 61081

FINSETH, TIM, state legislator; b. Jan. 7, 1964; m. Ruth Finseth; 1 child. AA, Northland C.C.; BA, Moorhead State U. Mgr. Marshall County Soil and Water Conservation Dist.; rep. Dist. 18 Minn. Ho. of Reps., 1993—.

FINTEL, ERIC D., electrical engineer; b. Bowling Green, Ohio, June 7, 1958. BSEE, Ohio State U., 1980. Software engr. McDonnell-Douglas, St. Louis, 1980-83; P.C. sys. supr. Glasstech, Inc., Perrysburg, Ohio, 1983—; cons. BF Sys., Perrysburg, 1990—. Co-patentee for glass positioner, safety monitor. Mem. coun. Village of Genoa, Ohio, 1992—; mem. Econ. Devel. Com. for Ottawa County, Ohio, 1992—. Mem. IEEE. Republican. Lutheran. Home: 204 E 11th St Genoa OH 43430-1412 Office: Glasstech Inc 995 4th St Perrysburg OH 43551-4369

FINTON, DAVID JON, computer scientist; b. L'Anse, Mich., July 3, 1960; s. David Carlisle and Karen Kay (Lundahl) F. BS in Math., Mich. State U., 1983; MS in Computer Sci., U. Wis., 1985. Teaching asst. dept. math. Mich. State U., East Lansing, 1979-83; lectr., teaching asst. dept. computer sci. U. Wis., Madison, Ill., 1983-90; software developer Sch. of Music U. Wis., Madison, 1992-94; software developer AT&T Bell Labs., Naperville, Ill., 1991-92; fellowship NASA, 1993-96. Mem. Pi Mu Epsilon. Baptist. Home: 425 Paunack Pl Apt 3D Madison WI 53705-2318 Office: U Wis Computer Scis Dept 1210 W Dayton St Madison WI 53706-1613

FINUCANE, RONALD CHARLES, history educator; b. L.A., Aug. 10, 1939; s. George Francis and Olivia (Tully) F.; m. Lynette Folken, 1987. BA in History, U. Nev., 1967; MA in History, Stanford U., 1968, PhD in History, 1972; postgrad., Oxford U., Eng., 1970. Cert. tchr., Calif. Rsch. fellow, lectr. Reading (Eng.) U. Medieval Ctr., 1973-77; lect. U. Maryland, Eng., 1972-82; vis. asst. prof. U. Puget Sound, Tacoma, Wash., 1983-85; asst. prof. Ga. So. Coll., Statesboro, 1985-88; assoc. prof., chair Benedictine Coll., Atchison, Kans., 1988-91; prof., chair Oakland U., Rochester, Mich., 1991—; dir. Oxford Rsch. Svcs., U.K. and Mich., 1976-91. Author: Miracles and Pilgrims, 1977, 2d edit., 1995, Appearances of the Dead, 1982, 2d edit.,

1996, Soldiers of the Faith, 1983. Recipient Rsch. award Am. Philos. Soc., 1973; Leverhulme Found. fellow, Oxford U., U.K., 1970-71; NEH grantee 1985, 87; Am. Coun. of Learned Socs. travel and rsch. grantee, Perugia, Italy, Vienna, Austria, Linköping, Sweden, 1987, 90, 93. Mem. Am. Hist. Assn., Medieval Acad Am. Office: Oakland Univ Dept History Rochester MI 48309

FIORITO, RICHARD JOSEPH, trucking executive; b. Chgo., Dec. 24, 1948; s. Joseph Dominick and Irene Mae (Page) F.; married, Oct. 26, 1970 (div. 1971); 1 child, Richelle; m. Patricia Maurer, Jan. 26, 1980; children: Christina, James. BA in Mgmt., U. Ill., Chgo. With Am. Truck Leasing Co., Chgo., 1966-71; owner J. Fiorito Leasing Ltd., Rosemont, Franklin Park, Ill., 1971—. Vol. Little League, Riverside, Ill., 1986—. With USAR, 1970-76. Democrat. Roman Catholic. Home: 366 Audubon Rd Riverside IL 60546

FIREBAUGH, EMILY ROULETTE, newspaper editor, publisher; b. Cape Girardeau, Mo., Sept. 8, 1941; d. Leon Roulette and Mary Jane (Benjamin) Brennecke; B.S. in Secondary Edn., Southeast Mo. State Coll., Cape Girardeau, 1963; Married; children—Kathryn Ryan, Art supr. Sikeston (Mo.) High Sch., 1963-66; elem. art supr. Fredericktown (Mo.) R-1 Sch. System, 1966-69; advt. mgr. Democrat-News, Fredericktown, 1968-79, editor-pub., 1979—; editor-pub. Press-Advertiser, Farmington, Mo., 1983—; pres. Mineral Area Pubs., Inc. Del., Mo. Democratic Conv., 1980, 84. Mem. Nat. Newspaper Assn., U.S. C. of C., Mo. Press Assn. (sec. 1982—, pres. 1984—), Mo. Dem. Editors Assn. (2d v.p. 1982—, pres. 1984—), Southeast Mo. Press Assn. (dir. 1981-82, pres. 1984—), Fredericktown C. of C. (dir. 1981-82), Mo. C. of C., Fredericktown Retail Mchts. Assn., Ironton Retailers Assn., Farmington C. of C. Roman Catholic. Clubs: Friday, Federated Women's. Office: PO Box 676 Farmington MO 63640*

FIRESTEIN, BETH ANN, psychologist; b. Houston, Nov. 20, 1957; d. Louis and Margaret (Furman) Firestein. BA, So. Meth. U., 1978; MA, U. Tex., 1982, PhD, 1987. Lic. clin. psychologist, Colo., Mo., Ill. Coord. women's svcs. So. Ill. U., Carbondale, 1986-96, counseling psychologist, 1986-96; pvt. practice Psychotherapy Assocs., Carbondale, 1989—; programs chair exec. com. Women's Caucus, Carbondale, 1988-89, co-chair, 1989-90; vis. scholar Colo. State U., 1994; chair Presdl.-Mayoral Task Force on Sexual Assault, 1992-96. Editor: Bisexuality: The Psychology & Politics of an Invisible Minority. Named Univ. Woman of Dinstinction, So. Ill. U., 1996. Mem. APA (Outstanding Rsch. Women and Gender Rsch. prize 1987), Assn. Women in Psychology, Nat. Assn. Women's Ctrs., Phi Kappa Phi, Kappa Delta Pi, Phi Beta Kappa. Office: So Ill U Counseling Ctr Carbondale IL 62901

FIRESTONE, JON, advertising executive; b. Washington, Nov. 21, 1944; s. John M. and Evelyn (Levin) F.; m. Jan Marie Bateman, Nov. 7, 1964; children: Jed, Johanna. BA, Mich. State U., 1966. Media planner Kenyon & Eckhardt, Detroit, 1966-69; media planner BBDO, N.Y.C., 1969-72, v.p., 1972-83, sr. v.p., 1983-87; pres., chief exec. officer BBDO, Mpls., 1987—; bd. dirs. Saga Communications. Bd. dirs. Minn. Taxpayers Assn., St. Paul, 1989—; mem. exec. com. Internat. Spl. Olympics, Mpls., 1989-91; mem. centennial com. Minn. State Parks, Mpls., 1990-91; mem. mktg. adv. com. U. Iowa. Mem. Am. Assn. Advt. Agys. (bd. govs. 1991—), Advt. Fedn. Minn. (bd. dirs. 1992—). Home: 12620 Bent Tree Rd Hopkins MN 55305-2851 Office: BBDO Mpls 900 Brotherhood Bldg 625 4th Ave S Minneapolis MN 55415-1624

FISCH, CHARLES, physician, educator; b. Nesterov (Zolkiew), Poland, May 11, 1921; s. Leon and Janette (Deutscher) F.; m. June Spiegal, May 23, 1943; children: Jonathan, Gary, Bruce. AB, Ind. U., 1942, MD, 1944; Dr. Medicine (hon.), U. Utrecht, 1983. Diplomate Am. Bd. Internal Medicine, Am. Bd. Cardiovascular Medicine (mem. 1977-82). Intern St. Vincent's Hosp., Indpls., 1945; resident internal medicine VA Hosp., Indpls., 1948-50; fellow gastroenterology Marion County Gen. Hosp., Indpls., 1950-51; fellow cardiology Marion County Gen. Hosp., 1951-53; asst. prof. medicine Ind. U. Med. Sch., 1953-59, asso. prof., 1959-63, prof., 1963—, Distinguished prof., 1975, dir. cardiovascular div., 1963-90; dir. Krannert Inst. Cardiology, 1953-90; mem. cardio-renal adv. com. HEW-FDA, 1973-77, 79—, Am. Heart Assn. Connor lectr., 1980; chmn. manpower rev. com. Nat. Heart, Lung and Blood Inst., 1985-89. Author: Electrocardiography of Arrythmias, 1989; co-editor Digitalis, 1969, Cardiac Electrophysiology and Arrythmias, 1991; contbr. articles to med. jours.; mem. editorial bd. Am. Heart Jour., 1967—, Am. Jour. Electrocardiology, 1967—, Coeur et Medicine Interne, 1970—, Am. Jour. Medicine, 1973—, Circulation, 1977—, Am. Jour. Cardiology, 1967—; assoc. editor Am. Jour. Cardiology, 1977—. Served to capt. M.C. AUS, 1946-48. Recipient James Herrick award, Am. Heart Assn. Fellow ACP, Am. Coll. Cardiology (pres. 1975-77, dir., chmn. publ. com. 1988-94, Gifted Tchr. award 1993), World Congress Cardiology (v.p. 1986); mem. Am. Fedn. Clin. Research, Central Soc. Clin. Research, Am. Physiol. Soc., Assn. Univ. Cardiologists, Assn. Am. Physicians. Home: 7901 Morningside Dr Indianapolis IN 46240-2526 Office: Ind U Med Ctr Krannert Inst Cardiology 1111 W 10th St Indianapolis IN 46202-4800

FISCHBEIN, LEWIS CONRAD, internist; b. Irvington, N.J., July 10, 1948; s. Martin Meyer and Naomi (Litzky) F.; m. Kathleen Gibbs, Dec. 31, 1981; 1 child, Benjamin Martin. AB, U. Rochester, 1970; MD, Washington U., 1974. Diplomate Am. Bd. Internal Medicine and Rheumatology. Intern and resident Barnes Hosp., St. Louis, 1974-77; rheumatology fellow Washington U., St. Louis, 1977-79; pvt. practice Barnes Hosp., 1979—; assoc. clin. prof. medicine Washington U., St. Louis, 1993—. Mem. ACP, Am. Coll. Rheumatology, St. Louis Met. Med. Soc., Phi Beta Kappa, Alpha Omega Alpha. Office: 16422 Barnes Hospital Plz Saint Louis MO 63110

FISCHER, ANDREW, mechanical designer; b. Detroit, Nov. 12, 1961. AD, McComb C.C., 1985. Mech. designer Reliance Industries, Detroit, 1985-88, Newman Engring. Products, Madison Heights, Mich., 1988-90, Precise Tech. & Elecs., Livonia, Mich., 1990—. Mem. McGraw-Hill Mech. Engring. Book Club. Republican.

FISCHER, BRUCE DOUGLAS, business educator, management consultant; b. Shelby, Mich., July 3, 1944; s. Henry and Dorothy (Prill) F.; 1 child, Laura Van Zoest. BS in Engring., Western Mich. U., 1967; MBA, U. Chgo., 1972; PhD, Northwestern U., 1987. Mgf. engr. Parker-Hannifin Corp., Des Plaines, Ill., 1969-70; mgmt. trainee Borg-Warner Corp., Chgo., 1972-73; assoc. A.T. Kearney, Inc., Chgo., 1973-76; cons. Bruce D. Fischer: Mgmt. Cons., Chgo., 1976—; asst. prof. Coll. Bus. and Mgmt. Northeastern Ill. U., Chgo., 1983-88; asst. prof. Coll. Engring. and Applied Scis. Western Mich. U., Kalamazoo, 1988-90; prof. Coll. Bus. and Pub. Adminstrn. Govs. State U., University Park, Ill., 1990—; bd. dirs. Naylor Pipe Co., Chgo. Contbr. articles to profl. jours. With U.S. Army, 1966-69. Mem. Acad. Mgmt., Internat. Modapts Assn. (bd. dirs.), Inst. Indsl. Engrs., Northwestern U. Alumni Assn., Chgo. Grad. Sch. Bus. Club. Home: 1744 N Wood St Chicago IL 60622-1356 Office: Govs State U Coll Bus and Pub Adminstrn University Park IL 60466

FISCHER, GUSTAV FRED, stockbroker; b. Lohman, Mo., July 8, 1938. Student, La Salle U., Chgo., 1968-69. Account clk. div. resources State of Mo., Jefferson City, 1960-67; owner, mgr. Lohman Milling Corp., 1967-82; stockbroker B.C. Christopher Securities, Jefferson City, 1983-86, A.G. Edwards & Sons Inc., Jefferson City, 1986—; bd. dirs. Farmers Bank Lohman. Pres. St. Paul's Luth. Ch., Lohman, Mo., 1991—. 2d class petty officer USN, 1956-59. Mem. Lions (treas., pres. Lohman). Republican. Home: 5105 Kautsch Rd Russellville MO 65074-2209 Office: AG Edwards & Sons Inc PO Box 1686 500 Broadway Jefferson City MO 65102

FISCHER, JAMES ADRIAN, clergyman; b. St. Louis, Oct. 15, 1916; s. John and Agnes (Henke) F. A.B., St. Mary's Sem., Perryville, Mo., 1941; S.T.L., Cath. U. Am., 1949; S.S.L., Pontifical Bib. Inst., Rome, Italy, 1951; LL.D. (hon.), Niagara U., 1968. Joined Congregation of Mission, 1936; ordained priest Roman Cath. Ch., 1943; prof. sacred scripture St. John's Sem., San Antonio, 1943-45; prof. sacred scripture St. Mary's Sem., Houston, 1951-56, Perryville, 1958-62; provincial Western province Vincentian Fathers, 1962-71, De Andreis Sem., Lemont, Ill., 1971-81; pres. Kenrick Sem., St. Louis, 1981-86, St. Thomas Sem., Denver, 1995—. Author: The Psalms, 1974, God Created Woman, 1979, How to Read the Bible, 1981, Priests, 1987, Looking for Moral Guidance, 1993. Chmn. bd. trustees De Paul U., Chgo., 1962-71. Mem. Cath. Bibl. Assn. (pres. 1976-77). Address: St Mary's of the Barrens 1701 W St Joseph St Perryville MD 63775

FISCHER, KEVIN J., service engineer; b. Antigo, Wis., Apr. 5, 1962. Svc. engr. Volm Bag Co., Antigo, Wis., 1980—. Vol. coach local high sch., 1985—. Home: 1215 Pine St Antigo WI 54409-1556

FISCHER, MARY ELIZABETH, library director; b. Buffalo, N.D., Feb. 14, 1935; d. Patrick Francis and Elizabeth Sarah (Laufenberg) Killoran; m. Clair Arthur Fischer, Sep. 27, 1952 (dec. Aug. 1967); children: Judith, Barbara, Veronica, Theresa, Ruth, Raymond, Linda, Rudolph; m. Donald Edward Anderson, Apr. 17, 1995. BS in Edn. summa cum laude, Valley City (N.D) State U., 1978. Librn. Valley City Barnes County Pub. Libr., 1978-88, libr. dir., 1988—, ADA promotor, 1990—. Columnist Valley City Times Record, 1978—. Active St. Catherine's Ch., Valley City, 1970-79; 4H leader Hobart Honeydews (5 yr. leadership pin 1975), Valley City, 1960-79; active local PTA, 1960-79; club and orgn. spkr.; active bible study, prayer groups; mem. Friends of the Libr. (facilitator, 1988—). Recipient various poetry awards, 1990—. Mem. N.D. Libr. Assn. Democrat. Roman Catholic. Home: 3120 113th R Ave RR3 Box 83 Valley City ND 58072 Office: Valley City Barnes CountyLibr 410 N Ctrl Ave Valley City ND 58072

FISCHER, PATRICIA ANN, middle school educator; b. Cleve., Apr. 11, 1951; d. Norman Stanley and Teresa (Domagalski) Michaels; m. David Leland Stroh, June 1, 1973 (div. June 1977); m. Lawrence Joseph Fischer, June 14, 1986. BA in Edn., Ohio No. U., 1973; MBA in Edn., Mt. St. Joseph Coll., Cin., 1986; postgrad., Miami U., Oxford, Ohio, 1985—, Ohio State U., 1988. Cert. K-8 tchr., 7-12 history tchr., Ohio. Mid. sch. tchr. St. Gerard Sch., Lima, Ohio, 1973-79, Our Lady of Rosary Sch., Cin., 1980-89; mid. sch. tchr. Little Flower Sch., Cin., 1989—, coord. sci., 1989—. Recipient award Project Bus., Cin., 1986, 87, 88, 89, Civic Achievement award Burger King Corp., Cin., 1990, 91, 92, Sci. Tchr. award NSTA, 1993, 20-Yr. award for Cath. educator Diocese of Cin., 1994. Mem. Nat. Cath. Edn. Assn., Ohio Edn. Assn., European Am. Study Ctr. Alumni Assn., Order Ea. Star, Alpha Omicron Pi. Roman Catholic. Home: 5450 Cecilia Ct Cincinnati OH 45247-7508 Office: Little Flower School 5555 Little Flower Ave Cincinnati OH 45239

FISCHER, ROBERT KEITH, retail company executive; b. Rapid City, S.D., Apr. 10, 1954; s. Samuel and Helen F.; m. Rita D. Miller, Apr. 25, 1976; children: Samuel, John, Maggie, Carrie, Abby. BBA, U. Nebr., 1975. Pres. Fischer Furniture, Rapid City, 1974—; Fischer Broadcasting, 1992-96. Deacon Calvary Bapt. Ch., Rapid City, 1978; chmn. West River Jack Kemp for Pres., 1988; precinct coord. Pennington County Rep. Party, 1989-91; alderman Rapid City Commn Coun., 1990-92; mem. platform com. S.D. Rep. Party, 1990, 92; del., mem. platform com. Rep. Nat. Conv., 1992; Penn County co-chair Phil Gramm for Pres., 1995. Mem. Coun. for Nat. Policy, S.D. Family Policy Coun. (pres. 1990-95). Southern Baptist. Office: Fischer Furniture Inc PO Box 523 Rapid City SD 57709-0523

FISCHMAR, RICHARD MAYER, resort executive, financial consultant; b. N.Y.C., Apr. 11, 1938; s. John B. and Sylvia (Moosnick) F.; m. Sandra P. Fensin, July 3, 1967; children: Brian, Laura. BS, U. Ill., 1959, MA, 1962. CPA, Ill. Sr. auditor L.K.H.&H., Chgo., 1962-66; contr. Lake States Engr., Park Ridge, Ill., 1966-68, New Communities Enterprises, Park Forest South, Ill., 1968-70; dep. dir. Ill. Drug Abuse Program, Chgo., 1970-71; dir. internal audit Ill. Dept. Labor, Chgo., 1971-73; contr. Ill. Dept. Employment Security, Chgo., 1973-78, D.L. Pattis Real Estate, Lincolnwood, Ill., 1978-86, Goodman Realty Group, Inc., Chgo., 1986-90, Harold J. Carlson, Rosemont, Ill., 1990-92; CFO L.J. Sheridan & Co., Chgo., Ill., 1992-94, Am. Resorts Internat., Oakbrook, Ill., 1994—; guest lectr. Mich. State U., Gov.'s State U. Author: (booklet) Bibliography of Management Services, 1972; contbr. articles to profl. jours. Mem. Ill. Soc. CPAs (real estate com., mgmt. adv. svcs. and constrn. com., entertainment and leisure industries coms.).

FISH, DAVID CARLTON, architect; b. Oceanside, Calif., Oct. 25, 1956; s. David and Agnes Lois (Noe) F.; m. Jamey Louise Burris, Mar. 14, 1980; children: Celeste Nicole, Jessica J., Carlton Neyle. AA, Mira Costa Coll., Oceanside, 1976; BArch, Calif. Poly. U., San Luis Obispo, 1983. Registered architect, Kans., Mo.; cert. Nat. Coun. Archtl. Registration Bds. Architect Seidler Owsley Assocs., Pittsburg, Kans., 1984-87, Architects Workshop, Pittsburg, 1990—; assoc. prof. constrn. engring. tech. Pitts. State U., 1993-95. Mem. Pittsburg Community Child Care Learning Ctr., 1985. Mem. AIA, Nat. Trust for Hist. Preservation, Kans. Soc. Architects. Democrat. Office: Architects Workshop 110 W 6th St Pittsburg KS 66762-3804

FISH, GARY WAYNE, computer company executive, consultant; b. Mpls., Jan. 28, 1949; s. Wayne Irving and Marquerite Effie (Blaska) F.; m. Shawn Ann McGovern, Mar. 22, 1975; children: Matthew Graham, Justin Ross, Aaron Patrick. BA, Berry Coll., 1973, MBA, 1976. Fiscal analyst Coosa Valley Area Planning and Devel. Com., Rome, Ga., 1977-80; fin. dir. Floyd County, Rome, Ga., 1980-81; bus. systems analyst Local Govt. Info. Systems, Mpls., 1981-84; corp. enrollment data adminstrn. Honeywell, Mpls., 1984-85; mgr. govt. contracts div. Analytical Technologies, Mpls., 1985-87; EDP search specialist CompuSearch, Mpls., 1987-88; account exec. Programming Alternatives, Mpls., 1988, Computer Power Group, Mpls., 1989; dir. corp. devel. Beau, Inc., Mpls., 1989—; bus. mgr. Julian Harrison, Inc., Rome, 1976-77; indsl. engr. Milliken, Spartanburg, S.C., 1976. Contbr. articles to profl. jours. Mem., v.p., treas. Minn. Marine Corps Family Coun., Mpls., 1989-92; mem. Mil. Order of the Purple Heart, Mpls., 1989-92; mem. Cap Unit Assn., 1992; gov., treas. Big Island Vets. Camp, Mpls., 1992; scoutmaster Boy Scouts Am., Troop 529, Mpls., 1992, charter orgn. rep., Troop 2406, Mpls., 1992. With USMC, 1967-69, Vietnam. Decorated Purple Heart, Vietnam Cross of Gallantry, Combat Action Ribbon; recipient cert. Dept. Vets. Affairs State of Minn., Cert. of Commendation, Gov. Arne H. Carlson, 1996. Mem. DAV, VFW, Data Processing Mgmt. Assn., Data Adminstrv. Mgmt. Assn., Assn. Systems Mgrs., DB/DC Users Group, IDMS Users Group, Sys. 38 Users Group, Mcpl. Fin. Officers Assn., Assn. MBA Execs., U.S. Naval Inst., 2d Marine Divsn. Assn. (treas. 1987-88), 1st Marine Divsn. Assn., Friends of the Boundary Waters Canoe Area Wilderness, Phi Alpha Theta (Omicron Epsilon chpt.). Lutheran. Home: 7464 Colfax Ave N Brooklyn Park MN 55444-2680 Office: Beau Inc PO Box 23 Chanhassen MN 55317-0023

FISH, GEORGE, writer; b. St. Louis, Dec. 27, 1946; s. George Thomas and Geraldine Ann (Sasek) F. Student, Mich. State U., 1965-72; AB in Econs., Ind. U., 1977; Cert. in Chinese, Washington U., St. Louis, 1970. Cert. paralegal. Freelance writer, 1981—; paralegal and legal writer/rschr., 1988—. Contbr. numerous articles to publs. including: The Guaridan, In These Times, Monthly Rev., Living Blues, Blues Access, Skeptical Inquirer, NUVO, others. Mem. Indpls. Peace and Justice Ctr.; former mem. Ind. Civil Liberties Union. Mem. Nat. Abortion and Reproductive Rights Action League, Blues Soc. Ind., Dem. Socialists Am., Coms. of Correspondence, Ctrl. Ind. Socialist Coalition. Home: 508 Jefferson Indianapolis IN 46201-3176

FISH, JAMES M., investment broker; b. Milw., Aug. 8, 1949. B Fin. and Mgmt., U. Wis., Milw., 1972. Investment broker Braun, Monroe, Milw., 1972-79; sales mgr. F H Hutton, Milw., 1979-88; investment broker A.G. Edwards & Sons Inc., Milw., 1988—. Mem. Athletic Club Milw. Office: AG Edwards & Sons Inc 700 N Water St Ste 540 Milwaukee WI 53202-4206

FISH, MICHELE LOYD, retailer; b. Belleville, Ill., Jan. 5, 1952; d. Delmer Edward and Patricia Ann (Marshall) Munie; m. Robert Wendelin Fish, May 25, 1973 (div. Feb. 1981). BS cum laude, U. Mo., 1973. Asst. buyer Famous-Barr, St. Louis, 1974-75, dept. mgr., 1975-76, buyer, 1976-81, store mgr., 1981-82; buyer Venture Stores, St. Louis, 1982-84, divsn. merchandise mgr., 1984-85, divsn. v.p., 1985-93; sr. v.p. Roman Co., St. Louis, 1993-94; sr. dir. frame buying LensCrafters, Cin., 1995; market rep. May Co., St. Louis, 1996—; adv. bd. dept. textile and apparel mgmt. U. Mo., Columbia, 1987-96, chair, 1988-90. Spl. venue mgr. Athlete's Village, U.S. Olympic Festival, 1994; dir. AMC Cancer Rsch. Ctr., 1986-96, also v.p., sec.; chair gifts Women's Event, 1988-94, chair gifts golf tournament, 1989-93, co-chair St. Louis Walks for Women, 1994, Together a Day of Caring, 1995; vol. Reach to Recovery, 1992-94; vol. coord. First Night St. Louis, 1994-96, bd. dirs. 1996—; bd. dirs. Talking Tapes for the Blind, 1996—. Recipient Torch of Liberty award Anti-Defamation League, 1990, Citation of Merit, U. Mo., 1992. Republican. Roman Catholic. Home: 82 E Sherwood Dr Saint Louis MO 63114

FISHEL, JAMES DEAN, telecommunications executive; b. Bedford, Ind., Aug. 30, 1953; s. Dale Fishel and Marilyn (Pruitt) Conrad. Student, Ball State U., 1972, Ivy Tech. Coll., 1977. Lic. real estate broker. Builder Fishel Builders, Jeffersonville, Ind., 1973-78; real estate broker Lamping Real Estate Broker, Clarksville, Ind., 1978-82; dir. east coast property TMC, Inc., Louisville, 1982-83; territorial mgr. TMC of Northwest Ind. (now Tri-Tel Communications), Munster, 1983—; also bd. dirs., mgr. TMC of Ill. and N.Mex.; gen. dir. PTI Khabouansk, Russia, 1992-93; telecoms. cons.; officer, dir. Tri-Tel of N.Mex., Ill., Ind., 1993; dir., v.p. Selltrax Inc., Munster, 1993—; owner, pres. Time Plus, Orlando, Fla., 1994—. Inventor IN-WATS service for resale carriers, 1985, nat. origination svcs. for regional inter-exch. carriers. Dir. Better Bus. Bur., Gary, Ind., 1987. Mem. C. of C. of U.S., Ind. C. of C., Hammond C. of C., South Bend C. of C., Chgo. C. of C., Orlando C. of C. Republican. Home: 4530 Pageant Way Orlando FL 32808-2731 Office: TMC of NW Ind 900 Ridge Rd Ste T Munster IN 46321-1722

FISHER, CARL A, hardware store owner; b. Mishawaka, Ind., May 30, 1938; s. Carl A. and Lillian Ruth (Greenwood) F.; m. Mary Catherine Koelndorfer, June 18, 1960; children: Heidi Christine Fisher Ragan, Greta Anne. BA in Acctg. and Mgmt., Ind. U., South Bend, 1968. Sec.-treas. Fisher Hardware Inc., South Bend, 1958-84, pres., 1984-95. Author: Poetic Insights, 1987, Beyond Relativity, 1989, River Park History, 1993, Greenwood Lineage and History, 1995. Rep. County Coun. candidate, St. Joseph County, Ind., 1976-80, South Bend 3d Dist. chmn., 1979-80. Mem. River Park Bus. Assn. (pres. 1986, v.p. 1993, dir. 1994-95), Lions (sec./treas. 1970-71). Home: 2624 Cypress Way South Bend IN 46615-2753 Office: Fisher Hardware Inc 2314 Mishawaka Ave South Bend IN 46615-2143

FISHER, CHARLES THOMAS, III, banker; b. Detroit, Nov. 22, 1929; s. Charles Thomas Jr. and Elizabeth Jane (Briggs) F.; m. Margaret Elizabeth Keegin, June 18, 1952; children: Margaret Elizabeth Jones, Curtis William, Charles Thomas IV (dec.), Lawrence Peter II, Mary Florence Hickey. AB in Econs, Georgetown U., 1951; MBA, Harvard U., 1953. C.P.A., Mich. With Touche, Ross, Bailey & Smart, Detroit, 1953-58; asst. v.p. Nat. Bank Detroit, 1958-61, v.p., 1961-66, sr. v.p., 1966-69, exec. v.p., 1969-72, pres., chief adminstrv. officer, 1972-82, chmn., pres., chief exec. officer, 1982—, bd. dirs.; pres., bd. dir. NBD Bancorp, Inc., 1973-82, chmn., pres., chief exec. officer, 1982-94; ret.; bd. dirs. GM, Am. Airlines, First Chgo. NBD Corp., NBD Bank Mich. Civilian aide to sec. army State of Mich., 1974-77; chmn. Mackinac Bridge Authority; past chmn. Detroit Renaissance, Inc., United Way Southeastern Mich. Named Detroit Young Man of Year Detroit Jr. Bd. Commerce, 1961. Mem. AICPA, Assn. Res. City Bankers, Mich. Assn. CPAs, Bloomfield Hills Country Club, Country Club of Detroit, Grosse Pointe Club, Detroit Athletic Club, Detroit Club, Yondotega Club. Office: 100 Renaissance Ctr Ste 2412 Detroit MI 48243-1102

FISHER, DAN, state legislator, bank executive; b. Tobias, Nebr., May 19, 1935; s. Leon and Nina (Bergocsen) F.; m. Mary Alice Jennings, Aug. 9, 1959; children: Dan Jennings, Mary Catherine Limbach, Amy Sue. BS in Econs., U. Nebr., 1963; MBA, U. Nebr., Kearney, 1990. Pres., CEO, dir. Crawford (Nebr.) State Bank, 1963-82, Dan Fisher Consulting, Grand Island, Nebr., 1983—, Gresham (Nebr.) State Bank, 1984-86, Jennings State Bank, Davenport, Nebr., 1985—, Lawrence (Nebr.) State Bank, 1986-89; state legislator Nebr., Lincoln; bd. dirs. State Bank of Bartley, Nebr., Petersburg (Nebr.) State Bank; adj. prof. U. Nebr., Kearney, 1990-92. Bd. dirs. Crawford Meml. Hosp., 1975-80. Named Boss of Yr. Jaycees, 1970. Mem. NRA, Am. Legion, Shriners, Masons, Rotary. Republican. Presbyterian. Home: 619 S Clay St Grand Island NE 68803-5844 Office: State Capitol Lincoln NE 68509

FISHER, EDWARD JOSEPH, JR., psychiatrist; b. Hammond, Ind., Nov. 12, 1945; s. Edward Joseph Sr. and Lillian Rose (Kasza) F.; m. Kay Keeler, April 24, 1971; children: Jason Anthony, Joshua Charles, Erin Jocelyn, Jonathan Edward; m. Karen Ann Poti, Dec. 24, 1990; 1 child, Jared Michael. AB in Zoology, Ind. U., 1968, MD, 1972. Diplomate Am. Bd. Psychiatry and Neurology, gen. psychiatry and child psychiatry, Am. Bd. Adolescent Psychiatry; lic. Ohio, Ky., Ind., Calif. Intern Cin. Gen. Hosp., 1972-73, resident, 1973-75; crisis intervention therapist U. Cin. Med. Ctr., 1974-76, fellow child and adolescent psychiatry, 1975-77; pvt. practice Cin., 1977—; cons. Longview State Hosp., Cin., 1976-77, Cin. Pub. Schs., 1976-77, Cen. Community Health Bd., Cin., 1977-81, Resident Home for Mentally Retarded of Hamilton County, Inc., Cin., 1977-81, Clermont County Community Mental Health Ctr., Batavia, Ohio, 1977-80, Adams/Brown County (Ohio) Residential Psychol. Svcs., 1978-80, Mental Health Svcs. NW, Forest Park, Ohio, 1979, Gen. Protestant Orphans Home, Cin. 1980, Straight, Inc., Milford, Ohio, 1982-84, Clermont County Diagnostic Ctr., Batavia, 1982-85, med. dir. dept. psychiatry adolescent divsn., Jewish Hosp., Cin., 1992—, also asst. med. dir. dept. psychiatry; asst. prof. psychiatry, U. Cin. Med. Ctr., 1992—. Bd. trustees mem. Cin. Speech and Hearing Ctr., 1976-77, bd. dirs. Tourette Syndrome Assn. Ohio, Inc., Milford, 1981-82. Mem. AMA, Am. Acad. Child and Adolescent Psychiatry, Am. Soc. Adolescent Psychiatry, Am. Psychiat. Assn., Am. Coll. Physician Execs., Ohio Psychiat. Assn. (econ. affairs coun. 1989-92), Ohio State Med. Assn., Cin. Coun. of Child and Adolescent Psychiatry, Acad. Medicine Cin., Cin. Psychiat. Soc. Office: 7438 Jager Ct Cincinnati OH 45230-4344

FISHER, ERMAN CALDWELL, corporate executive; b. Mt. Sterling, Ky., Oct. 10, 1923; s. Cato and Mattalean W. (Tyler) F.; cert. Highland Park Jr. Coll., 1947, Wayne State U., 1965, B.E. in Archtl. Engring., Detroit Inst. Tech., 1954; m. Ruby Nelson, June 28, 1947; children—Paul Cato, Nancy Carol. With Aero. Products, Inc., Detroit, 1943, Great Lakes Mut. Life Ins. Co., Detroit, 1946-48; prin. constrn. insp. City of Detroit Water Dept., 1948-68, supt. bldg. and grounds maintenance, 1968-74, supt. plant and mech. maintenance, 1974-75, mgr. plant, bldg. and mech. maintenance, 1975-77; dep. dir. Detroit Water and Sewage Dept., 1977-80, asst. dir. tech. support, 1980-81; dir. phys. plant Wayne State U., Detroit, 1980-83; gen. mgr. Central Installation Co., Fraser, Mich., 1984-88; ret., 1988. Bd. dirs. Shaw Coll., 1970-73; del. state conv. Republican party, 1954-55; now mem. Democratic State Central Com; vice chmn. transp. adv. commn., City of Glendale, Ariz., 1993. Served with U.S. Army, 1943-46. Recipient Edward Dunbar Rich Service award, 1974. Mem. Am. Pub. Works Assn. (past pres. Inst. Bldgs. and Grounds 1977-78, pres. Detroit Met. br., pres. Mich. State chpt. 1986-87, Samuel A. Greeley award 1985), Assn. Phys. Plant Adminstrs. Univs. and Colls., Phylon Soc. Wayne State U., NAACP (life), Am. Water Works Assn., Water Pollution Control Fedn., Engring. Soc. Detroit, Soc. Municipal Engrs., Mich. Assn. Phys. Plant Adminstrs., Detroit Retired City Employees Assn. (assoc. dir. 1980-87), Am. Legion Dept. Ariz., Valley of the Sun Duplicate Bridge Club, DupliatAlpha Phi Alpha (life). Club: Lions (charter). Office: 16505 E 13 Mile Rd Fraser MI 48026-2540

FISHER, GLENN DUANE, small business executive; b. Celina, Ohio, Jan. 29, 1947; s. Darrell Donald and Frankie Juanita (Engle) F; m. Linda Kay Brown, June 11, 1971; children: Lisa Marie, Jennifer Lynn, Jeffrey Robert. Student, Ohio State U., 1969; BS in Bus., Wright State U., 1972. Sr. acct. Howard, Beeler and Co. CPA's, Lima, Ohio, 1972-79; treas. Lima Flack Co., Lima, Ohio, 1979-84, owner, 1984—; owner, pres. Lima Flack Co. Celina, 1988—, Lima Scaffolding & Supply, 1988—, G & L Leasing Co., Elida, Ohio, 1989—, Fisher & Associated, Elida, Ohio, 1992—. bd. dirs., pres. Lima Noon Sertoma, Ohio, 1980-88. Recipient Svc. to Mankind award Wheel Chair Olympics, 1986. Mem. Am. Legion, Elks. Republican. Roman Catholic. Office: Lima Flack Co 1420 Elida Rd Lima OH 45805-1508

FISHER, JED FREEMAN, chemist; b. Yonkers, N.Y., Sept. 25, 1950; s. Harry Freeman and Lucy (Acker) F.; m. Joann Gurdak, Sept. 9, 1972; children: Matthew, Sally, Jane. BS, SUNY, Stony Brook, 1972; PhD, MIT, 1976; postdoctoral fellow, Harvard U., 1976-79. Asst. prof. chemistry U.

Minn., Mpls., 1979-85; scientist Pharmacia & Upjohn, Inc., Kalamazoo, 1985—. Contbr. 50 articles to profl. jours. Recipient DuPont Young Faculty award, 1980. Mem. AAAS, Am. Chem. Soc. (various offices Kalamazoo chpt.), Southwest Mich. Math and Sci. Alliance (exec. com.). Home: 20337 Moorepark Rd Three Rivers MI 49093-9668 Office: Pharmacia & Upjohn 7246 #209-701 Kalamazoo MI 49007-4940

FISHER, JOHN JAMES, advertising executive; b. St. Louis, Mar. 23, 1941; s. Benjamin Edwards Fisher and Beulah Fay (Tucker) Hughes; m. Beverly Firth Brown, June 7, 1962; children: John J. Jr., Jennifer Leigh. BBA in Mktg., Memphis State U., 1964. Sales rep. Pfizer Labs., Memphis, 1965-69; product mgr. Pfizer Labs., N.Y.C., 1969-71; account exec. L.W. Froelich Inc., N.Y.C., 1971-72; account supr. Lavey/Wolff/Swift Inc., N.Y.C., 1972-74, v.p., account supr., 1974-76, sr. v.p., dir. client svcs., 1976-78; exec. v.p. Frank J. Corbett Inc., Chgo., 1978-80, pres., 1980-91, chmn., chief exec. officer, 1991—; exec. v.p. Health and Med. Com., N.Y.C., 1986-92, chmn., CEO, 1993—. Contbr. articles to profl. jours. Chmn. Rep. Com., Weston, Conn., 1970-78; mgr. campaign state rep. and senator, Weston, 1974, congl. dist., Weston, 1977. Mem. Med. Mktg. Assn., Biomed. Mktg. Assn., Pharm. Advt. Coun., Midwest Pharm. Advt. Coun. (pres. 1984-85, Sweeny award 1985), Biltmore Country Club (Barrington, Ill.), N.Y. Athletic Club. Office: Frank J Corbett Inc 211 E Chicago Ave Chicago IL 60611-2616*

FISHER, JULIA KATHLEEN, library media specialist; b. Tribune, Kans., July 2, 1951; d. Lyle Lee and Ella Louise (Kinlund) Griffin; m. James Dale Fisher Jr., Aug. 11, 1977 (div. Jan. 1991); children: Sarah Kathleen, Benjamin James. BS in Edn., U. Colo., 1973; MS in Edn., Ft. Hays State U., Hays, Kans., 1976, Libr. Media Specialist, 1991. Cert. libr. media specialist K-12, cert. in elem. edn., lang. arts, social sci. and natural sci., Kans. Kindergarten screening coord. Greeley County Schs., Tribune, 1973-88, kindergarten tchr., 1973-89, libr. media specialist, 1990—; libr. media practicum supr. Ft. Hays State U., 1991. Pianist for children's choir United Meth. Ch., Tribune, 1980—, sec., 1994—; mem. Greeley County Hist. Soc., Tribune, 1995—. Named Ch. Woman of Yr., United Meth. ch., 1988; recipient scholarships. Mem. NEA, Greeley County Tchrs. Assn. (all offices), Kans.-NEA, Kans. Assn. Sch. Librs., Delta Kappa Gamma (all offices). Home: 3427 Woods Dr Manhattan KS 66502 Office: Manhattan H S East Campus 901 Poyntz Manhattan KS 66502

FISHER, LAWRENCE EDGAR, market research executive, anthropologist; b. Los Alamos, N.Mex., Jan. 13, 1946; s. Leon H. and Phyllis (Kahn) F.; m. Valerie Joseph, Mar. 25, 1979; children: Lael Sharon, Jonathan Daniel, Matthew Joseph. AB, U. Calif., Berkeley, 1968; MA, Northwestern U., 1969, PhD, 1973; cert. in bus. adminstrn., U. Pa., 1982. Postdoctoral fellow U. Chgo., 1973-74; asst. prof. U. Ill., Chgo., 1974-83; dir. Ethnographic Field Sch. Northwestern U., Evanston, Ill., 1975-78; vis. asst. prof. U. Mich., Ann Arbor, 1979-80; account exec., sr. account exec., dir. client svcs. MRCA Info. Svcs., Northbrook, Ill., 1983-88; group mgr. Burke Mktg. div. Control Data Corp., Chgo., 1988-89; dir. client svcs. Info. Resources, Inc., Chgo., 1989-90, v.p. client svcs., 1991-94, sr. v.p., 1994—; mem. external adv. bd. Grad. Sch. Bus. U. Wis., Madison, 1991—. Author: Colonial Madness, 1985; also numerous articles. Fellow Woodrow Wilson Found., 1972-73, NIH, 1973-74, NEH, 1975. Home: 324 S Euclid Ave Oak Park IL 60302-3508 Office: Info Resources Inc 150 N Clinton St Chicago IL 60661-1402

FISHER, MARK ROBERT, industrial sales and management executive; b. Denver, Oct. 8, 1950; s. Robert James and Louise (Bokan) F.; m. Katherine Elizabeth Hess, May 6, 1978; 1 child, Zachariah Mark. Profl. musician and entertainer pvt. practice, Denver, 1962-82, owner and mgr. thoroughbred horses, 1975-81; sales engr. Pipe Products Co., Denver, 1971-73, v.p., 1973-80; v.p. Excellent Sales Co., Denver, 1980-81; territory mgr. Keystone Sales, Denver, 1981-86; distributor sales mgr., regional mgr. Keystone Valve U.S.A., Houston, 1986-87; br. mgr. Keystone Sales, Lenexa, Kans., 1987-91, sales mgr. Midwest region, 1991-95; regional mgr. Performance Valve & Controls, Inc., Broken Arrow, Okla., 1995—; bd. mem., Excellent Sales, Denver, 1981-84; owner/mem., Colo. Racing Commn., Denver, 1977-80; mem., Rocky Mt. Plumbing & Heating Assn., Denver, 1971-83. Author: (book) Champagne Canyons, 1968; songwriter. Me. Oak Hill Homes Assn., Lenexa, Kans., 1988—; charter mem. Sons of Am. Legion, Golden, Colo., 1956-84. Mem. Instrument Soc. Am. (chpt. v.p. 1985-86, show chmn. 1983-85), 10-K Club, Club France, PGA Tour Ptnrs., U.S. Golf Assn., BMW CCA, Smithsonian Inst., Spotlighters.

FISHER, MARY BUCHER, technical editor; b. Columbus, Ohio, Jan. 9, 1937; d. Paul and Florence Hale (Burington) Bucher; m. J.R. Fisher, Mar. 22, 1991 (div. Mar. 1993); 1 stepchild, Patricia Diane Fisher Anderson. BA cum laude, Ohio State U., 1958, MA, 1973. Sec. Ohio State U., Columbus, 1958-60; editorial asst. Ohio State U. Press, Columbus, 1960-68; asst. editor Jour. Higher Edn., Columbus, 1968-72; pub. info. specialist Transp. Rsch. Ctr., East Liberty, Ohio, 1974; editor Apropos Nat. Ctr. on Ednl. Media and Materials for Handicapped, Columbus, 1974-77; sr. tech. writer-editor Battelle, Columbus, 1978-89; freelance tech. editor Columbus, 1990—; rep. Columbus Tech. Coun., 1987-88; mem. tech. comms. adv. bd. Columbus State C.C., 1991—. Contbr. feature articles to various nationwide mags. and Ohio newspapers. Co-founder Buckeye Singles Coun., Columbus, 1981, originator Nat. Singles Week, 1984; mem., treas., group rep., publicity chair various Twelve-Step Groups, Columbus, 1988—; sewing guild vol. Riverside Meth. Hosp., Columbus, 1994—. Mem. Soc. for Tech. Comm. (sr., editing awards 1981-90), Women in Comm., Inc. (Excellent Book Editing award 1984), Soc. for Profl. Journalists, Am. Mensa (membership chair Columbus area), Phi Beta Kappa, Zeta Tau Alpha. Methodist. Office: 100 Glenmont Ave Columbus OH 43214

FISHER, MERLE A., advertising executive; b. McKeesport, Pa., Apr. 2, 1952. V.p. Joshua Leigh Enterprises, Youngstown, Ohio, 1985—. Republican. Office: Joshua Leigh Enterprises 310 Churchill Hubbard Rd Youngstown OH 44505-1371

FISHER, PHILIP CLYDE, business administration educator; b. Spencer, Nebr., Aug. 7, 1938; s. Clyde Harold and Georgia Elizabeth (Carder) F.; m. Helen Jean Sire, Aug. 12, 1960; children: Rebecca Sue, Robert Clyde. BS summa cum laude, Wayne State Coll., 1968; MBA, U. S.D., 1969; PhD, Stanford U., 1979. Electronics technician RCA, Cherry Hill, N.J., 1961-66; from asst. prof. to prof. bus adminstrn. U. S.D., Vermillion, 1969-91, dir. bus. grad. programs, 1982-87, assoc. dean bus., 1988-90; pres. Vermillion Devel. Corp., 1990; dean of bus. U So. Ind., Evansville, 1991—; pres. Coun. on Higher Edn., Sioux Falls, S.D., 1981-82. Editor: Annual Advances in Case Research, 1987, Business Case Jour., 1993-94. With U.S. Army, 1958-61. Mem. Acad. of Mgmt., Midwest Bus. Adminstrn. Assn., Soc. Case Rsch. (pres. 1988-89), Met. Evansville C. of C. (bd. dirs. 1992—), Rotary, Beta Gamma Sigma. Democrat. Home: 811 SE 3rd St Evansville IN 47713-1142 Office: U So Ind 8600 University Blvd Evansville IN 47712-3534

FISHER, RALPH TALCOTT, JR., historian, educator; b. Washington, Apr. 5, 1920; s. Ralph Talcott and Margaret (Merriam) F.; m. Ruth Paroni Meads, Dec. 20, 1942; children: Ralph Talcott III, Margaret Manson, Albert Meads. BA, U. Calif., Berkeley, 1942, MA, 1948; cert., Russian Inst., Columbia U., 1950, PhD, 1955. Asst. in instrn., then asst. prof. history Yale U., New Haven, 1950-58; assoc. prof. history U. Ill., Urbana-Champaign, 1958-60, dir. Russian and East European Ctr., 1959-87, prof. history, 1960-88, prof. emeritus, 1988—; Bd. Dirs. U. Ill. Library Friends, Urbana-Champaign, 1992—; rsch. asst. Am. Mus. Natural History, N.Y.C., 1949; vis. lectr. Russian history U. Calif., Berkeley, 1954; disting. vis. prof. history Ariz. State U., 1990; trustee Russian Rev., 1979—. Author: Pattern for Soviet Youth, 1959; co-editor: Dictionary of Russian Historical Terms, 1970, Source Book for Russian History, 1972. Capt. inf., U.S. Army, 1942-46, CBI. Grantee, Social Sci. Rsch. Coun., 1951, Fulbright-Hays Found., 1964, Am. Coun. Learned Socs., 1965; Rockefeller Found. fellow, 1956. Mem. Am. Hist. Assn. (chmn. conf. Slavic and East European history 1969), Am. Assn. Advancement Slavic Studies (pres. 1979-80, Award for Disting. Contbns. to Slavic Studies 1995), Nat. Coun. Soviet and East European Rsch. (trustee 1978-83), Golden Bear Club, Phi Beta Kappa, Alpha Delta Phi. Congregationalist. Home: 2115 Burlison Dr Urbana IL 61801-6605 Office: U Ill Dept History 810 S Wright St Urbana IL 61801-3611

FISHER, ROBERT SYLVESTER, JR., corporate executive; b. Dayton, Ohio, Dec. 12, 1956. AA, Sinclair C.C., Dayton, 1977; BA, Kenyon U., 1979; MBA, Harvard U., 1983. Pres. Fisher's Concrete Slabs, Dayton, 1973-77; mfg. ops. Bendix Corp., Dayton, 1979-80; fin. analyst Bendix Corp., Detroit, 1980-81; mktg. svcs. mgr. Bendix Corp., Cleve., 1983-84; mktg. mgr. Advanced Robotics, Columbus, Ohio, 1984-85; mktg., sales mgr. Sensotec, Columbus, 1985-87; from strategic planning mgr. to assoc. dir. corp. devel. Eaton Corp., Cleve., 1987-92; plant mgr. Eaton Corp., Bethlehem, Pa., 1992-94; bus. unit mgr. Eaton Corp., Carol Stream, Ill., 1995—. Cons. Jr. Achievement, Cleve., 1990-91; mem. Lehigh County Human Svcs. Adv. Bd. Mem. Assn. for Corp. Growth, Bethlehem Area C. of C., Phi Beta Kappa, Phi Theta Kappa. Home: 4307 Clearwater Ln Naperville IL 60564-9999 Office: Eaton Corp 191 E North Ave Carol Stream IL 60188-9999

FISHER, ROBERT WARREN, accountant; b. Springfield, Ohio, Sept. 17, 1952; s. Carl Arthur and Frances (Runyan) F.; m. Elizabeth Ann Davies, Dec. 11, 1982; children: Katherine Marie, Anne Margaret, Andrew Robert. BA, Wittenberg U., 1974; MBA, U. Toledo, 1975. CPA; registered investment advisor. Mgr., acct. Price Waterhouse, Battle Creek, Mich., 1975-83, Deloitte, Haskins & Sells, Appleton, Wis., 1983-84; ptnr., acct. Wojahn & Fisher, S.C., Appleton, 1984-85; shareholder, v.p. Schumaker, Romenesko & Assocs., Appleton, 1985—; treas., bd. dirs. Wis. Bus. Devel. Fin. Corp., Madison, 1983—; ind. cons. to CPA firms. Mem. fin. com. St. Mary's Ch., 1986—, Appleton Cath. Edn. System, 1986-90; mem. com. St. Paul Home. Mem. AICPA (PCPS peer rev. com. 1991-95), Wis. Soc. CPAs (exec. com., quality rev. com. 1989-95, assn. chmn. 1991, chmn. 1992-94), Nat. Assn. Accts. (v.p. 1982), Appleton C. of C. (small bus. com. 1984—), Riverview Country Club (bd. dirs. 1986-96, treas. 1987-90, v.p. 1990-93, pres. 1993-94), KC, Rotary (membership dir. 1986, treas. 1988-94, Paul Harris fellow 1995). Home: 1027 E Rustic Rd Appleton WI 54911-8547 Office: Schumaker Romenesko & Assoc SC 2323 E Capitol Dr # 2459 Appleton WI 54911-8731

FISHER, TED ALAN, director of information services, consultant; b. Danville, Ill., Sept. 10, 1954; s. Theodore R. and Peggie L. (Johnston) F.; m. Suzanne M. McGraugh, Feb. 9, 1974; children: T.R., Jay M., Stacie L. Student, Danville Area C.C., Danville, Ill., 1985. Retail sales, estimator Voorhees Lumber Mart, Danville, Ill., 1972-82; computer mgr. Tandy Corp., Danville, 1982-84; systems mgr. Voorhees Lumber Mart, Danville, 1984-85; dir. info. svcs. Vermilion County, Danville, 1985—; Mem. Danville Art League adv. com., 1995. Mem. Danville Art League. Home: 123 Marlowe Danville IL 61832 Office: Vermilion County MIS 6 N Vermilion Rm 4 Danville IL 61832

FISHER, THOMAS GEORGE, lawyer, retired media company executive; b. Debrecen, Hungary, Oct. 2, 1931; came to U.S., 1951; s. Eugene J. and Viola Elizabeth (Rittersporn) F.; m. Rita Knisley, Feb. 14, 1960; children: Thomas G. Jr., Katherine F. Vaaler. B.S., Am. U., 1957, J.D., 1959; postgrad., Harvard U., 1956. Bar: D.C. 1959, Iowa 1977. Atty. FCC, Washington, 1959-61, 65-66; pvt. law practice Washington, 1961-65, 66-69; asst. counsel Meredith Corp., N.Y.C., 1969-72; assoc. gen. counsel Meredith Corp., Des Moines, 1972-76, gen. counsel, 1976-80, v.p. gen. counsel, 1980-94, corp. sec., 1988-94; comml. law liaison ABA Ctr. and East European Law Initiative, Krakow, Poland, 1994-95; atty. Legal Aid Soc. Polk County, 1996—. Contbr. articles to profl. jours. Bd. dirs. Des Moines Met. Opera Co., Indianola, 1980-94, pres., 1990-91; bd. dirs. Civic Music Assn., Des Moines, 1982-92, pres., 1987-88; chmn. legis. com. Greater Des Moines C. of C., 1976-77; bd. dirs. Legal Aid Soc. Polk County, 1986-93, pres., 1993; of counsel Legal Aid Soc. Polk County, 1996—. With U.S. Army, 1952-54. Mem. ABA, Iowa State Bar Assn. (chmn. corp. counsel subcom. 1979-82), Fed. Comms. Bar Assn., Polk County Bar Assn., Am. Corp. Counsel Assn., Com. Fgn. Rels., Counsel for Internat. Understanding (bus. adv. com. 1994), Embassy Club. Office: Legal Aid Assn 1111-9th St Ste 380 Des Moines IA 50314

FISHER, THOMAS SCOTT, career officer, broadcasting network operations officer; b. Madison, Wis., June 24, 1963; s. Gale Eugene Fisher and Claudia Jane Cloofelter Killinger; m. Andreina Louisa Zanier Fisher, Aug. 4, 1989; children: Thomas Junior, Maximilian Andreas. BA, U Minn., 1987; MA in Journalism, Marshall U., 1995. Commd. 2d lt. U.S. Army, advanced through grades to capt., 1996; airborne ranger A Co. 2d Bn., 75th Inf., Tacoma, Wash., 1981-83; platoon leader Canadian Army Trophy Team, 7th Corps, Bavaria, 1987-89; exec. officer B Co. 2-64 ARMOR, Scuwewfurt, Germany, 1989-90, bn. maintenance officer HQ, 1990; brigade asst. ops. officer 1st Brigade, 3 I.D., Scuwewfurt, Germany, 1990-91; co. comdr. A Co. 2-64 ARMOR, Schweisfurt, Germany, 1991-93; ops. officer Am. Forces Network, Frankfurt, Germany, 1996—. Co-author: (book) ...So Are They All, All Honorable Men, 1996, (screenplay) Storm In The Desert, 1995, Reoccurence, 1996. Decorated Army Achievement medal with two oak leaf clusters, 1983, Nat. Def. Svc. medal, 1990, Army Commendation medal, 1992, Meritorious Svc. medal, 1993. Mem. U.S. Armor Assn., Order of St. George (knight, bronze medallion 1993), World Martial Arts Fedn. (black belt). Baptist.

FISHER-ROSS, LISA LYNN, physical therapist; b. Cold Water, Kans., June 26, 1960; d. Gary Lee Fisher and Nira Mione (Campbell) Jones; m. Dale R. Ross, Mar. 31, 1984; children: Stacey E., Scott E. BS, U. Kans., 1982. Registered phys. therapist, Kans. Staff phys. therapist Bergan Mercy, Omaha, 1982-84; dir. phys. therapy Douglas County Hosp., Omaha, 1984-88, Meml. Hosp., McPherson, Kans., 1988—; clin. istr. Rockhurst Coll., Kansas City, Mo., 1984-99, U. Nebr., Omaha, 1984-88, Colby (Kans.) C.C., 1988—, Wichita State U., 1988—. Sun. sch. tchr. First United Meth. Ch., McPherson, 1991; troop leader Girl Scouts, McPherson, 1992-93, 94-95, svc. unit mgr., 1993—. Mem. Am. Phys. Therapy Assn., Kans. Phys. Therapy Assn. Methodist. Home: 425 Liberty Dr Mc Pherson KS 67460 Office: Meml Hosp 1000 Hospital Dr Mc Pherson KS 67460

FISHMAN, ARNOLD LAWRENCE, direct marketing consultant, publisher; b. Bklyn., Apr. 17, 1926; s. Harry and Dora (Rechter) F.; married Dec. 24, 1960; children: George, Hilary. BA, Queens Coll., 1947; MA, Columbia U., 1949; postgrad., New Sch. for Social Rsch., 1950-52, Asia Inst., 1953; MBA, NYU, 1964. Market rsch. analyst Mktg., Merchandising, Rsch. Inc., 1954-59; market research analyst Benton & Bowles, N.Y.C., 1960-62, IBM, Harrison, N.Y., 1962-66; dir. mgmt. scis. Miles Labs., Elkhart, Ind., 1966-68; dir. market planning Paramount Pictures, N.Y.C., 1968-70, Franklin Mint, Franklin Center, Pa., 1970-74, Citibank, N.Y.C., 1974-78; pres., cons. divsn. Maxwell Stroge Agy., Chgo., 1978-82; pres. Mktg. Logistics, Inc., Lincolnshire, Highland Pk, Ill., 1982—. Author: Annual Guide to U.S. Mail Order, 1982-96, Annual Mail Order 750, 1990-96, Annual Mail Order Sales Directory, 1990-96, Bus. Development Information Handbook of 150 Mail Order Markets, 1993, 94 Information Superhighway Marketplace Guide, Portable Mail Order Industry Statistics, Business Irwin, 1994, Gifts Mail Order Marketing Management, 1983, Financial Services Direct Response Marketing, 1983, Consumer High Technology Mail Order Marketing Management, 1984, Business to Business Mail Order Marketing Management, 1984, Retail Mail Order Marketing Management, 1986, Annual Guide to Telemarketing, 1987-92, Apparel Mail Order Marketing Management, 1987, Insurance Direct Response Marketing, 1987. Served with U.S. Army, 1944-46. Mem. Am. Mktg. Assn., Am. Statis. Assn., Ops. Research Soc., Chgo. Direct Mktg. Group (pres. Lincolnshire chpt. 1982-85). Jewish. Home: 1460 Cloverdale Ave Highland Park IL 60035-2817 Office: Mktg Logistics Inc 1460 Cloverdale Ave Highland Park IL 60035-2817

FISK, DWIGHT RODNEY, paper company executive; b. Taylor Falls, Minn., Nov. 5, 1925. BS, U. Wis., 1962. Process engr. Badger Ordnance Works, Baraboo, Wis., 1952-57; gen. converting supt. Thilmany Paper Co., Kaukauna, Wis., 1957-76; pres. Straubel Paper Co., Green Bay, Wis., 1976—. Contbr. articles to tech. publs.; patentee in engring. field. Republican. Office: Straubel Paper Co 995 Waube Ln Green Bay WI 54304-5530

FITES, DONALD VESTER, tractor company executive; b. Tippecanoe, Ind., Jan. 20, 1934; s. Rex E. and Mary Irene (Sackville) F.; m. Sylvia Dempsey, June 25, 1960; children: Linda Marie. B.S. in Civil Engring., Valparaiso U., 1956; M.S., M.I.T, 1971. With Caterpillar Overseas S.A., Peoria, Ill., 1956-66; dir. internat. customer div. Caterpillar Overseas S.A., Geneva, 1966-67; asst. mgr. market devel. Caterpillar Tractor Co., Peoria, 1967-70; dir. Caterpillar Mitsubishi Ltd., Tokyo, 1971-75; dir. engine capacity expansion program Caterpillar Tractor Co., Peoria, 1975-76, mgr. products control dept., 1976-79; pres. Caterpillar Brasil S.A., 1979-81; v.p. products Caterpillar Tractor Co., Peoria, 1981-85, exec. v.p., 1985-89; pres., chief opd. officer Caterpillar Inc., Peoria, 1989-90, chmn., chief exec. officer, 1990—, also bd. dirs.; bd. dirs. Mobil Corp., First Chgo. NBD Corp., Equip. Mfg. Inst., Ga.-Pacific Corp. Trustee Farm Found., 1985—, Meth. Med. Ctr., 1985—, Knox Coll., 1986—; mem. nat. adv. bd. Salvation Army, 1985—, adminstrv. bd. 1st United Meth. Ch., 1986—; bd. dirs. Valparaiso U., Keep Am. Beautiful; chmn. U.S.-Japan Bus. Coun. Mem. Agrl. Roundtable (chmn. 1985-87), SAE, ACTPN, Bus. Coun., Bus. Roundtable (policy com.). Republican. Clubs: Mt. Hawley Country, Creve Coeur. Office: Caterpillar Inc 100 NE Adams St Peoria IL 61629-0001*

FITTS, JANET SUE, trauma nurse coordinator, emergency room nurse, paramedic educator; b. Kansas City, Mo., Apr. 7, 1963; d. George Humphrey and Peggy Jean (Thompson) Jones; m. Thomas Allen Fitts, Oct. 14, 1989; children: Megan, Adam. BSN, St. Louis U., 1989; cert. EMT-paramedic, St. John's Mercy Med. Ctr., St. Louis, 1991. RN, Mo.; cert. CEN, BLS instr.-trainer, ACLS affiliate faculty, pediatric advaned life support provicer, neonatal advanced life support provider, pre-hosp. trauma life support instr., advanced burn life support provider; cert. trauma nurse specialist. Firefighter, nurse, paramedic Eureka (Mo.) Fire Protection Dist., 1988-95; neonatal-obstetrics nurse Met. Med. Ctr.-West, Des Peres, Mo., 1989-90; paramedic supr. Medcor, Inc., Eureka, 1989-94; paramedic Meramec Ambulance Dist., 1991-93; nurse emergency dept. St. John's Mercy Hosp., Washington, Mo., 1990—; trauma nurse coord. St. John's Mercy Hosp., Washington, 1994—; nurse emergency dept. Mo. Bapt. Med. Ctr., St. Louis, 1991-93; owner, educator Emergency Med. Svcs. Edn. Programs, Pacific, 1990—; paramedic instr. East Ctr. Coll., Union, Mo., 1990—; instr. emergency nursing Forest Park C.C., St. Louis, 1992—; community/outreach educator Eureka Fire Protection Dist., 1990-94, dir. CPR program, 1991-94. Contbr. articles to profl. jours. Named Student Nurse of Yr., Mo. Student Nurses' Assn., 1987-88. Mem. ANA, Mo. Nurses Assn. (membership com. 1990-91), Emergency Nurses Assn. (cert. trauma nurse core course provider), Nat. Assn. EMTs, Mo. Emergency Med. Svcs. Assn., Firefighters Assn. Mo., Am. Heart Assn. (coun. on cardiopulmonary and critical care), Sigma Theta Tau, Sigma Alpha Iota. Office: St John's Mercy Hosp 200 Madison Ave Washington MO 63090-3022

FITTS, THOMAS ALLEN, emergency nurse; b. Kirkwood, Mo., July 23, 1966; s. Robert Allen and Marian Catherine (Weber) F.; m. Janet S. Walker, Oct. 14, 1989; 1 child, Megan E. AAS, St. Louis Community Coll., 1987; student, Maryville Coll., 1987-90; BSN, Webster U., 1992; postgrad., Covenant Seminary, 1995. RN, Mo.; EMT, CEN, instr. BLS, ACLS. Emergency med. technician Meramec Ambulance Co., Pacific, Mo., 1984-87; staff nurse open heart surgery St. Lukes Hosps., St. Louis, 1987-90; staff nurse emergency rm. Deaconess Med. Ctr.-West, St. Louis, 1989—; PRN staff nurse Emergency Rm. St. Louis (Mo.) U. Med. Ctr., 1993-95; asst. patient care mgr. medicenter and emergency dept. Deaconess Med. Ctr.-Ctrl., St. Louis, 1994—; instr. dept. emergency/nursing continuing edn. St. Louis C.C., 1992—. Instr. CPR Franklin County ARC, 1986-88, vol. nurse, 1988—; firefighter, emergency med. technician Eureka (Mo.) Fire Protection Dist., 1987-93; instr. Am. Heart Assn., 1989—; bd. dirs. Catawissa (Mo.) Union Protestant Ch., 1988-92. Named one of Outstanding Young Men of Am., 1989, Outstanding Coll. Students of Am., 1989. Mem. Emergency Nurses Assn., Mo. Emergency Med. Svcs. Assn., Heritage Presbyn. Ch. Home: 1942 Kesha Ct Pacific MO 63069

FITZ, BROTHER RAYMOND L., university president; b. Akron, Ohio, Aug. 12, 1941; s. Raymond L. and Mary Lou (Smith) F. B.S. in Elec. Engring., U. Dayton, Ohio, 1964; M.S., Poly. Inst. Bklyn., 1967, Ph.D., 1969. Joined Soc. of Mary, Roman Catholic Ch., 1960; mem. faculty U. Dayton, 1968—, prof. elec. engring. and engring. mgmt., 1975—, exec. dir. Center Christian Renewal, 1974-79, univ. pres., 1979—. Author numerous papers, reports in field. Bd. dirs. various civic orgns. Recipient Disting. Alumnus award Poly. Inst. Bklyn., 1980. Office: U Dayton 300 College Park Ave Dayton OH 45469-0001*

FITZGERALD, CAROL E., state legislator. Mem. S.D. Ho. of Reps., mem. agr. and natural resources and judiciary coms.; rental mgr. *

FITZGERALD, DANIEL PETER, insurance company executive; b. Mpls., Aug. 29, 1959; s. John Thomas and Shirley (Galvin) F. BSBA, Drake U., 1981; MBA, Loyola U., Chgo., 1983. Systems analyst Rand McNally & Co., Skokie, Ill., 1981-83; systems cons. Rehab Group, Inc., 1983-84; assoc. Booz Allen & Hamilton, Chgo., 1984-86; asst. v.p. info. tech. dept. CNA Ins. Co., Chgo., 1986—. Bd. dirs. Chgo. Architecture Found., 1990-95; bd. dirs. Windy City Performing Arts, 1994—, chair, 1995—. Home: 3150 N Lake Shore Dr Apt 20C Chicago IL 60657-4803 Office: CNA Ins Co CNA Plaza Chicago IL 60685

FITZGERALD, FRANK MOORE, state legislator; b. Lansing, MI, Nov. 11, 1955; s. John W. and Lorabeth (Moore) F.; m. Ruth Davey, 1981; children: Ellen Lora, John Wesley. BA, Coll. William & Mary, 1979; MD, Thomas M. Cooley Law Sch., Lansing. Asst. prosecuting atty. Eaton County, MI, 84-86; rep. Mich. Dist. 71, 87—; asst. minority whip Mich. Ho. Reps., chmn. Rep. policy com., oversights & ethics com., spkr. pro tem. Author: Very Sincerely: A Remembrance of Gov. Frank D. Fitzgerald, 1985. Pres. Capitol Libr. Coop. Mem. Mich. Bar Assn., Eaton County Bar Assn., Grand Ledge Hist. Soc. Home: 430 W Jefferson St Grand Ledge MI 48837-1408 Address: PO Box 30014 Lansing MI 48909*

FITZGERALD, JAMES ALFRED, JR., sales and strategy consultant; b. Elgin, Ill., Nov. 21, 1956; s. James Alfred Sr. and Bernice Mildred (Mapes) F.; m. Kimberly Ellen Raitz, May 19, 1990. BS in Journalism, Bradley U., 1976; cert., Ctr. for Creative Leadership, 1989; cert. in mgmt., Pa. State U., College Park, 1990; cert., Ctr. for Creative Leadership, 1989; MBA, U. Minn., 1992. Sales rep. N.W. Airlines, Mpls., 1978-81; asst. mgr. N.W. Airlines, Manila, 1981-83, Taipei, Taiwan, 1983-84; mgr. Guam and Micronesia N.W. Airlines, Agana, Guam, 1984-85; sales mgr. N.W. Airlines, Mpls., 1985-86; sales mgr. So. Calif. and Latin Am. N.W. Airlines, L.A., 1986-88; dir. strategy and mktg. N.W. Airlines Cargo, St. Paul, 1988-92; aviation cons., owner mktg. co., Afton, Minn., 1992—; guest lectr. U. N.D., 1989-90. Mem. pub. rels. com. St. Joseph's Home for Children, Mpls., 1989; vol. Ch. of Guardian Angels, Lake Elmo, Minn., 1989; primary sponsor Cancerthon, Agana, 1985; organizer, mem. pub. rels. com. Walk for Hunger, Woodbury, Minn., 1990; coord. Internat. Spl. Olympics, 1991; bd. dirs. Athletes in Action Baseball Tournament, Agana, 1985, Park Grove Christian Ctr., 1994. Home and Office: 12631 15th St S Afton MN 55001-9747

FITZGERALD, JAMES FRANCIS, cable television executive; b. Janesville, Wis., Mar. 27, 1926; s. Michael Henry and Chloris Helen (Beiter) F.; m. Marilyn Field Cullen, Aug. 1, 1950; children: Michael Dennis, Brian Nicholas, Marcia O'Loughlin, James Francis, Carolyn Jane, Ellen Putnam. B.S., Notre Dame U., 1947. With Standard Oil Co. (Ind.), Milw., 1947-48; pres. F.-W. Oil Co., Janesville, 1950—, Total TV, Inc. (cable TV Systems), Wis., 1965-86; bd. dirs. Milw. Ins. Co., Bank One, Janesville N.A.; chmn. bd. Golden State Warriors, Oakland, Calif., 1986—, Total TV Calif., 1987—. Bd. govs., chmn. TV com. NBA; chmn. bd., pres. S.P.A.C.E. Inc. subs. Milw. Bucks NBA team, 1976-85; chmn. Greater Milw. Open (PGA Tournament), 1985, Notre Dame Bus. Adv. Coun., 1989—. Served to lt. (j.g.) USNR, 1944-46, 51-53. Mem. Chief Execs. Forum, World Bus. Coun., Wis. Petroleum Assn. (pres. 1961-62), Janesville Country Club, Castles Pines Golf Club, Vintage Club (pres. 1989-91), San Francisco Golf Club, El Dorado Country Club. Roman Catholic. Home and Office: PO Box 348 Janesville WI 53547

FITZGERALD, MICHAEL LEE, state official; b. Marshalltown, Iowa, Nov. 29, 1951; s. James Martin and Clara Francis (Dankbar) F.; m. Janet Roewe; children: Ryan, Chris, Erin, Bridie. B.B.A., U. Iowa, 1974. Campaign mgr. Fitzgerald for Treas., Colo., Iowa, 1974; market analyst Massey Ferguson, Inc., Des Moines, 1975-83; treas. State of Iowa, Des Moines, 1983—. Democrat. Roman Catholic. Office: Office of State Treas Capitol Bldg Des Moines IA 50319

FITZGERALD, PETER GOSSELIN, state senator, lawyer; b. Elgin, Ill., Oct. 20, 1960; s. Gerald Francis and Marjorie (Gosselin) F.; m. C. Nina Kerstiens, July 25, 1987; 1 child, Jake Buchanan. AB, Dartmouth Coll., 1982; cert. of attendance, Aristotelian U., Salonica, Greece, 1983; JD, U. Mich., 1986. Bar: Ill. 1986, U.S. Dist. Ct. (no. dist.) Ill. 1986. Assoc. Isham, Lincoln & Beale, Chgo., 1986-88; ptnr. Riordan, Larson, Bruckert & Moore, Chgo., 1988-92; mem. Ill. Senate, 1993—; counsel Harris Bankmont, Inc., 1992—; bd. dirs. Harris Bank Palatine N.A. Translator: Dartmouth Classical Jour., 1982. Pres. Young Rep. Orgn., Palatine, Ill., 1988; candidate for U.S. Ho. of Reps., 1991; bd. dirs. north ctrl. Ill. region Children's Home and Aid Soc. Rotary Found. internat. grad. scholar, 1982-83. Mem. Ill. State Bar Assn., Chgo. Bar Assn., Econ. Club Chgo., Inverness Golf Club, Union League Club, Meadow Club. Roman Catholic. Office: 117 W Slade St Palatine IL 60067-5096

FITZGERALD, SCOTT, state legislator; b. Nov. 16, 1963. Senator Wis. State Dist. 13; planning com. City of Juneau, Wis. Chmn. Dodge County (Wis.) Rep. Com. Address: 105 Leonard Ave Juneau WI 53039

FITZGERALD, THOMAS JOE, psychologist; b. Wichita, Kans., July 8, 1941; s. Thomas Michael and Pauline Gladys (Zink) F.; B.A., San Francisco State U., 1965; M.A., U. Utah, 1969, Ph.D., 1971. Dir. behavioral services programs VA Hosp., Topeka, 1971-73; pvt. practice as psychologist, Topeka, 1973-74, Prairie Village, Kans., 1974—; clin. instr. Menninger Sch. Psychiatry, Topeka, 1972-74; v.p. Preferred Mental Health Care Mgmt., Inc., 1986-90, pres., Preferred Mental Health, Inc., 1990—; sec.-treas. Kans. Bd. Psychologist Examiners, 1976-79, 79-80, chmn., 1980—, chmn. psychology examining com.; mem. Behavioral Scis. Regulatory Bd., 1980-82; pres. Psychol. Services Corp., Prairie Village, 1974—. Mem. Gov.'s Commn. on Criminal Adminstrn., 1974-76; vice-chmn. Gov.'s Com. on Med. Assistance, 1978-80; mem. Mid-Am. Health Systems Agy., 1979-82; mem. com. on utilization review orgns. Kansas Ins. Commr. Adv. Com., 1994—. Served with USMC, 1958-61. Mem. Kans. Psychol. Assn. (pres. 1980-81), Kans. Assn. Profl. Psychologists (pres. 1981-82, Outstanding Psychologist award 1979, 80, 81, 82), Greater Kansas City Soc. Clin. Hypnosis (pres. 1978-85). Office: Preferred Mental Health Inc 8220 Robinson St Overland Park KS 66204-3626

FITZPATRICK, CHRISTINE MORRIS, legal administrator, former television executive; b. Steubenville, Ohio, June 10. 1920; d. Roy Elwood and Ruby Lorena (Mason) Morris; student U. Chgo., 1943-44, U. Ga., 1945-46; m. T. Mallary Fitzpatrick, Jr., Dec. 19, 1942; 1 child, Thomas Mallary III. BA, Roosevelt U., 1947; postgrad. Trinity Coll., Hartford, Conn., 1970. Assoc. dir. Joint Human Rels. Project, City of Chgo., 1965-66; tchr. English, Austin Sch. for Girls, Hartford, 1966-70; promotion coord. Conn. Pub. TV, Hartford, 1971-72, dir. community rels., 1972-73, v.p., 1973-77; pub. rels./pub. affairs cons. Commonwealth Edison Co., Chgo., 1977-79; dir. spl. events Chgo. Public TV, 1979-84; v.p. Fitzpatrick Group, Inc., Chgo., 1986-88; adminstrv. dir. Fitzpatrick Law Offices, 1988-94, Fitzpatrick Eilenberg & Zivian, 1994-96; v.p. Pub. Rels. Clinic Chgo., 1980-81. Bd. advisers Greater Hartford Mag., 1975-77; bd. dirs. World Affairs Ctr., Hartford, 1975-77; mem. adv. coun. Am. Revolution Bicentennial Commn. Conn., 1975-77. Mem. Pub. Rels. Soc. Am. (dir. Conn. Valley chpt. 1976-77), Am. Women in Radio and TV (New Eng. chpt. pres. 1976-77), LWV (Chgo. chpt. pres. 1962-64, Hartford chpt. v.p. 1971-73). Home: 5518 S Harper Ave Chicago IL 60637-1830

FITZPATRICK, SEAN KEVIN, advertising agency executive; b. Atlanta, Sept. 28, 1941; s. J.J. and Roxane (Athanassiades) F.; m. Sue Ellen House; children: Seamus McGee, Elizabeth Christina, Samantha Louise. A.B., Hamilton Coll., 1963. Reporter Bloomington (Ind.) Daily Herald, 1964, Hearst Newspaper, Albany, N.Y., 1964; v.p., exec. creative dir. J. Walter Thompson Co., N.Y.C., Toronto and L.A., 1965-75; v.p. creative dir. Bing Crosby Prodns., Hollywood, Calif., 1976-77; creative dir. Columbia Pictures, Burbank, Calif., 1977-78; sr. v.p. creative dir. Dancer Fitzgerald Sample, Torrance, Calif., 1978-83; vice chmn., dir. creative svcs. Lintas: Campbell-Edward Co., Warren, Mich., 1983-89; vice chmn., worldwide creative dir. McCann-Erickson, 1989—. Developer movies Final Chpt. Walking Tall, 1976, Mean Dog Blues, 1976, The Great Santini, 1976-77; producer for TV Buford Pusser, Tennessee Sheriff, 1976; creator The Heartbeat of America, Today's Chevrolet. Recipient more than 300 advt. awards. Mem. ASCAP, Motion Picture Acad. Arts and Scis., Orchard Lake Country Club, Yale Club, Bloomfield Open Hunt Club, Delta Kappa Epsilon.

FITZPATRICK, VALDA, artist; b. Kulm, Poland, Aug. 6, 1941; came to U.S., 1960; d. Albinas Siugzda and Albina (Kahlau) Paliulis; m. Donald Gregory Fitzpatrick, Feb. 18, 1963; 1 child, Kelly O'Brian. BFA, Ohio State U., 1978, B Art Edn., 1980, M Art Edn., 1986; postgrad., Columbus Coll. Art and Design, 1993—. Art instr. Ohio State U., Marion, 1976-80, Cardington (Ohio) Schs., 1980-89; freelance artist, 1972—; cons. to art tchrs. Cardington Schs., 1980-89; presenter workshops Marion and Morrow County pub. schs.; organizer art oriented events Ohio State U., tchr. adult edn. classes, 1976-80; spkr. in field. One-woman show Toronto, Can., 1971-78, Ohio State U., Marion, 1974-79; group exhibitions at galleries in Cleve., Ohio, Chgo., Windsor, Can., 1974-80; commd. artworks for Dresser Industries, Marion, Marion Audio Visual Prodns., Time Tells., Inc., Cardington. Art tchr. for mentally retarded, Mt. Gilead, Ohio. Recipient Hon. Mention award Ohio State Fair, 1970, Most Popular Art Work award Greater Marion Arts Coun., 1975, L. & K. Purchase award, 1974, Profl. Divsn. Art award Greater Marion Arts Coun., 1975, Best of Show award Kiwanis of Palm Beach, Fla., 1989, 2d place award Kiwanis of Montgomery, 1993. Mem. Nat. Art Edn. Assn., Art Edn. Assn. Ohio., Am. Coll. Student Pers. Assn., Nat. Assn. Student Pers. Adminstrns. Home: 402 Elm Crest Dr Mount Gilead OH 43338

FITZPATRICK, WILLIAM ALLEN, pharmacist; b. Edwardsville, Ill., Jan. 1, 1942; s. Ray Allen and Irene Marie (Frey) F.; m. Sherrie Elaine Smith, Sept. 24, 1966(div. Jan. 1990); children: Julie Ann, Kelly Lynn, Cheri Elaine and Debbie Marie (twins), Jodi Leigh. BS, St. Louis Coll. of Pharmacy, 1965. Registered pharmacist, Mo., Ill.; lic. nursing home adminstr., Mo. Pres. Fitzpatrick Pharmacy, Ellisville, Mo., 1971—, Universal Packaging Sys., 1995—; v.p. Interlock Pharmacy Sys., 1989—; pres. Mo. State Bd. Pharmacy, 1991-96. Recipient Johnson & Johnson Leadership award, 1965. Mem. Nat. Assn. Bds. Pharmacy (mem. task force to study pharmacist workload 1994-95, past mem. task force therapeutic interchange, past mem. task force longterm care, past mem. pharmacy practice com.), Am. Soc. Cons. Pharmacists (past mem. orgnl. affairs coun.), Am. Soc. Hosp. Pharmacy, Am. Coll. Health Care Adminstrs., Am. Pharm. Assn., Nat. Assn. Retail Druggists (mem. longterm care com. 1994-95), Mo. Pharm. Assn. (chmn. longterm care com. 1990-95), St. Louis Pharmacist Assn., Acad. Gen. Practice of Pharmacy, Mo. Found. for Pharm. Care, St. Louis Coll. Pharmacy Alumni Assn., Mo. League Nursing Home Adminstrs., Mo. Health Care Assn., Mo. Assn. Homes for Aging, West County Kiwanis, Kappa Psi (exec. dir. 1971-73, nat. pres. 1974-79, Man of Yr. award 1971).

FITZSIMMONS, JOSEPH JOHN, publishing executive; b. Newark, Nov. 10, 1934; s. Joseph A. and Frances E. (Baume) F.; m. Nancy L. Lind, June 11, 1957; children: Joseph John, Michael, Patricia, Susan, Thomas. B.Chem. Engring., Cornell U., 1957. With Xerox Corp., Rochester, N.Y., 1957-65; v.p., gen. mgr. Xerox Univ. Microfilms, Ann Arbor, Mich., 1974-75; pres. Univ. Microfilms Internat., Ann Arbor, 1976—, pres., chief exec. officer, 1987-94; v.p. Bell and Howell Co., 1987—; chmn. Univ. Microfilms Internat., Ann Arbor, 1994-95, ret., 1995; bd. dirs. First of Am. Bank Corp., Bartech Inc. Gen. campaign chmn. Wastenaw United Way, 1977-78; mem. devel. com. St. Joseph's Hosp.; mem. adv. bd. for entrepreneurship Ea. Mich. Cen. U., 1986—; mem. adv. bd. U. Mich. Sch. Info. and Libr. Studies, U. Pitts. Sch. Libr. and Info. Sci. Mem. ALA, Info. Industry Assn. (bd. dirs. 1985, chmn. mktg. com. 1986, chmn. long range planning com. 1987, chmn. bd. elect 1988, chmn. 1989), The White House Conf. on Librs. and Info. Sci. (vice chmn. 1991). Roman Catholic. Home: 101 N Main St # 1005 Ann Arbor MI 48104

FITZWATER, RODGER L., state legislator. Mem. Mo. Ho. of Reps., Jefferson City. Democrat.

FIVECOATE, KEVIN, engineering company executive; b. Kokomo, Ind., July 22, 1967. Designer BMJ Mold and Engring., Kokomo, 1986—. Office: BMJ Mold and Engring PO Box 2676 Kokomo IN 46904-2676

FIZDALE, RICHARD, advertising agency executive; b. 1938. Copywriter BBDO Advt., 1967-68; copywriter Leo Burnett Co., Inc., Chgo., 1969-70, copy supr., 1970-72, assoc. creative dir., 1972-73, creative dir., 1973-74, v.p., 1974-78, v.p., exec. creative dir., 1978-79, sr. v.p., exec. creative dir., 1979, sr. v.p., mgr. creative ops., 1979-82, exec. v.p., dep. dir. creative svcs., 1982-85, pres., chief creative officer, bd. dirs., 1985-86, exec. com., 1986-87, pres., chief creative officer, 1987-92, chmn., CEO, chief creative officer, 1992-93, chmn., chief creative officer, 1993—. Office: Leo Burnett USA 35 W Wacker Dr Ste 2220 Chicago IL 60601*

FLAATEN, RUBY CHERYL, nurse manager; b. Mason City, Iowa, Dec. 12, 1944; d. Truman Almer and Truly Zeola (Ones) Flaaten. Diploma in nursing, Meth.-Kahler Sch. Nursing, 1965. Staff nurse Ear, Nose and Throat Rochester (Minn.) Meth. Hosp., 1965-67, asst. head nurse Ear, Nose and Throat, 1967-69; head nurse, nurse mgr. ear, nose and throat, plastic surgery, oral surgery, ophthalmology, gen. surgery Rochester (Minn.) Meth. Hosp./Mayo Med. Ctr., 1969—. Mem. ANA, Minn. Nurses Assn., 6th Dist. Minn. Nurses Assn. (sec.-treas., del.), Am. Orgn. Nurse Execs. (coun. nurse mgrs.), Minn. Orgn. Leaders in Nursing, Dist. F. Orgn. Leaders in Nursing, Oncology Nurse Soc., Am. Soc. Plastic and Reconstructive Surgery Nurses, Soc. Otorhinolaryngology and Head-Neck Nurses, Acad. Med.-Surg. Nurses, Meth.-Kahler Alumni Assn. (treas.), Sons of Norway. Republican. Lutheran. Home: 1929 3rd Ave NE Apt 4 Rochester MN 55906-4031

FLAHERTY, SUSAN SWEENEY, university educational foundation administrator; b. Council Bluffs, Iowa, Dec. 29, 1949; d. John Patrick Sr. (dec.) and Althea Charlotte (Rosmann) Sweeney; m. Luke Jospeh Flaherty, Dec. 29, 1972. BA, Benedictine Coll., 1972; MA, U. Iowa, 1984. Secondary sch. tchr. Kansas City (Kans.) Pub. Schs., fall 1972; installment loan clk. Hawkeye State Bank, Iowa City, 1973; asst. clk. Johnson County Clk. of Dist. Ct., Iowa City, 1973-77, dep. clk., 1977-79, clk., 1979-80; legal sec. Legal Svcs. Corp. of Iowa, Iowa City, 1981; adminstrv. assoc. Margolin & Assocs., Iowa City, 1981-86; rsch. asst. U. Iowa Found., Iowa City, 1987, rsch. coord., 1987-88, dir. devel. rsch. and records, 1989—; mem. faculty Internat. Nat. Soc. Fund Raising Exec. Conf., San Francisco, 1992, Coun. for Advancement and Support of Edn., Info. Mgmt. Summer Inst., Boulder, Colo., 1991; mem. guest faculty Big Ten Fund Raisers Inst., Mackinac Island, Mich., 1990. Mem. credentials com. Johnson County Dems. Orgn., Iowa City, 1980; mem. Johnson County LWV, Iowa City, 1979-80, Iowa City Craft Guild, 1978-79. Mem. Am. Prospect Rsch. Assn. (ethics task force com. 1991-92, Svc. award 1995), Univ. Athletic Club. Democrat. Roman Catholic. Office: U Iowa Found PO Box 4550 Iowa City IA 52245-4550

FLANAGAN, DAN M., manager, broker; b. Mt. Clemens, Mich., Nov. 9, 1970. BS in Psychology and Social Sci., Mich. State U., 1992. Mgr., broker Olde Discount Corp., Detroit, 1992—. Republican. Roman Catholic. Office: Olde Discount Corp 751 Griswold St Detroit MI 48226-3224

FLANAGAN, HARRY PAUL, publishing executive; b. Columbus, Ohio, Dec. 8, 1933; s. Hugh Anthony and Kathryn Marie (Sutherly) F.; m. Joan Dickas, June 23, 1956; children: Mary Beth, Kevin Hugh, Megan Joan. BS in Mktg., Ohio State U., 1956; Cert. in Mgmt., Capital U., Columbus, 1982, Adv. Mgmt. Cert., 1983. Pers. trainer For Lazarus Co., Columbus, 1960-61; supr. Wesleyan Press Co., Columbus, 1961-65; mgr. Xerox Ednl. Publs., Columbus, 1965-84; mgr. Field Publs., Columbus, 1984-89, ret., 1989; corp. dir. Highlights for Children, Columbus, 1989-94; ret., 1994—; pvt. practice bus. cons., freelance photographer Columbus, 1995—; pvt. practice cons., photographer, 1995—. Chmn. Christ the King Sch. Bd., Columbus, 1975-80, mem. parish coun., 1968-78, 91-94, pres., 1993-94, chmn. golden jubilee com., 1995-96; bd. dirs. Multiple Sclerosis Soc., Franklin County, Ohio, 1980-83. Recipient citation from Jr. Achievement, Columbus, 1966, Vol. award Ohio Ho. of Reps. Mem. Am. Mgmt. Assn., Fulfillment Mgrs. Assn., Techs. User Assn., Direct Mail Assn., Customer Svc. Coun. Roman Catholic. Home and Office: 1236 Haddon Rd Columbus OH 43209-2928

FLANAGAN, JOSEPH PATRICK, advertising executive; b. Chgo., Jan. 6, 1938; s. Charles Larkin and Helen Mary (Sullivan) F.; children: Charlotte Ahern, Joseph P. Jr., Michael S., Larkin S., Brian A. BA, Mich. State U., 1959; MBA, U. Chgo., 1961. Dist. mgr. sales Time mag., Pitts. and Chgo., 1961-69; gen. mgr. Ctr. Advanced Research in Design, Chgo., 1969-75; v.p., dir. client services BBDO, Chgo., 1975-77; sr. v.p. IMPACT subs. Foote, Cone & Belding Comm. Co., Chgo., 1977-85, pres., 1985—; corp. dir. sales promotion Foote, Cone & Belding Comm. Co., Chgo., 1987—; pres. Coun. of Sales Promotion Agys., 1986-89, also bd. dirs. Mem. governing bd. Chgo. Symphony Orch., 1974; v.p. Lyric Opera Guild, Chgo., 1974; trustee Loyola Acad.; bd. dirs. Court Theater; dir. arts and letters bd. Nat. Adv. Coun., Mich. State U. Named Sales Promotion Profl. of Yr., Coun. Sales Promotion Agys., 1989; recipient Disting. Alumni award Mich. State U., 1991. Mem. Am. Assn. Advt. Agencies (chmn. sales promotion com.), Exmoor Country Club (Highland Park, Ill.). Roman Catholic. Home: 1520 N State Pky Chicago IL 60610-1634 Office: IMPACT FCB Ctr 101 E Erie St Chicago IL 60611-2811

FLANAGAN, MICHAEL PATRICK, congressman, lawyer; b. Edgewater, Ill., Nov. 9, 1962; s. Michael and Rosemary F. BA in Polit. Sci., Loyola U., Chgo., JD. Bar: Ill. Mem. U.S. Ho. of Reps., Washington, 1994—; mem. Jud. Com., Govt. Reform and Oversight Com., VA Com. U.S. Ho. of Reps., vice-chmn. Jud. subcom. Constl. Law, vice-chmn. Govt. Reform and Oversight subcom. Govt. Mgmt., Info., & Tech.; part-time lawyer, Neiberg & Rojas, 1994. Vol. Howard Brown Health Ctr. Capt. U.S. Army, 1987-92, Persian Gulf. Republican. Office: US House Reps 1407 Longworth House Office Bldg Washington DC 20515*

FLANDERS, RAYMOND ALAN, governmental health agency administrator; b. Bangor, Maine, Jan. 4, 1929; s. Carroll Benjamin and Mary (Watson) F.; m. Anne-Liss Teisen; children: Molly Olivia and Michael Benjamin (twins). Student, Colgate U., 1948-50; BS, U. Miami, Fla., 1955; DDS, U. Md., 1959; MPH, U. Mich., 1979. Mem. faculty W.Va. U., Morgantown, 1964-65; program dir. Project Hope, Brazil, 1976-78; regional dental dir. Va. State Health Dept., Richmond, 1970-76, 79-85; mem. faculty Med. Coll. Va., Richmond, 1980-85; state dental dir. Ill. Dept. Health, Springfield, 1985—; mem. faculty Coll. Dental Medicine So. Ill. U., Alton, 1985—; cons. Project Esperanca, Amazon River, Brazil, 1981, Project HOPE/U.S.A.I.D., Grenda, West Indies, 1984, Project HOPE, Honduras, 1986, Am. Dental Assn., Brazil and Guyana, 1992. Contbr. articles to profl. jours. Served to capt. U.S. Army, 1946-47, 50-51, 60-63. USPHS fellow, 1978-79, Sec's. Excellence in Health Promotion award, 1990. Mem. ADA (Preventive Dentistry award 1983, Cmty. Preventive Dentistry award 1990, 95), Ill. Dental Assn., Am. Pub. Health Assn., Assn. State Territorial Dental Dirs., Am. Assn. Pub. Health Dentists, Ill. Pub. Health Assn. Office: 535 W Jefferson St Springfield IL 62702-5058

FLANERY, GAIL LINDEN, administrator; b. Ganado, Ariz., Nov. 6, 1938; d. Randolph and Ethel Marguerite (Linville) Denman; m. James Allen Flanery, Dec. 26, 1961; 1 child, Patrick Denman. BA, Calif. State U., 1961; MA, U. Md., 1973; PhD, U. Nebr., 1991. Primary tchr. 1st grade Reedley (Calif.) Pub. Schs., 1961-62, Santa Monica (Calif.) Pub. Schs., 1962-63, Teague Pub. Schs., Highway City, Calif., 1963-64, Bakersfield (Calif.) Pub. Schs., 1964-66; primary tchr. 2nd grade Lincolnwood (Ill.) Pub. Schs., 1966-70; primary tchr. 1st grade Parlier (Calif.) Pub. Schs., 1973-75; asst. project mgr. Answers for Child Care, Omaha, Nebr., 1984; child care coord. Region VII, U.S. Dept. of Labor Women's Bur., Omaha, Nebr., 1983-85; cons. Nebr. Dept. of Social Svcs., 1990-91; dep. dir. Voices for Children in Nebr., Omaha, 1992—. Vice chair infringement com. Citizens Action Assn., Omaha, Nebr., 1992—; founding bd. mem. Voice for Children in Nebr., 1986-89; treas. bd. Parent United, Omaha, 1983—; co-founder, pres. Legis. Coalition for Children, Omaha, 1979-85. Willis Moreland fellow U. Nebr., 1990, Regents fellowship, 1988, Senning Meml. fellowship, 1987, Chi Omega fellow Chi Omega Sorority, 1989,. Mem. Nebr. assn. for the Edn. of Young Children (pub. policy chair 1992—), Omaha Assn. for the Edn. of Young Children (bd. dirs., pub. policy chair 1992—), Nat. Soc. for Fund Raising Execs. Democrat. Presbyterian. Home: 314 S 68th Ave Omaha NE 68132 Office: Voices for Children Ste 103 7521 Main St Omaha NE 68127

FLANIGAN, ALAN WAYNE, designer; b. Uniontown, Pa., Apr. 15, 1955; m. Linda J. Robertson, July 23, 1983; children: Kiley, Brooke.; Student, Akron U., 1983-88. Designer Rotek, Inc., Aurora, Ohio, 1976-84, Ametek Inc., Kent, Ohio, 1984—. Office: Ametek Inc 627 Lake St Kent OH 44240

FLANNAGAN, WILLIAM MARVIN, JR., banker; b. Richmond, Va., Apr. 8, 1961; s. William Marvin and Joyce (Caldwell) F.; . Robin Jeanne Killeen, May 24, 1985. BA in Clin. Psychology, U. Mo., 1983, MBA in Fin., 1987. Comml. loan officer Boatmen's Nat. Bank, St. Louis, 1987-88, pvt. banking officer, 1988-91, v.p., mgr., 1992—; adv. bd. mem. Blue Cross and Blue Shield, St. Louis, 1991—. Alumni coun. U. Mo. Grad. Sch. of Bus., St. Louis, 1991—; mem. St. Louis Art Mus., 1987—, Mo. Bot. Garden, 1987—, United Way Found., 1987—. Mem. Am. Inst. Banking, Robert Morris Assocs., The Noonday Club, Alpha Sigma Phi Alumni. Republican. Presbyterian. Home: 823 Barbara Ann Ln Ballwin MO 63021-4203 Office: The Boatmen's Nat Bank One Boatmen's Plz 800 Market St # 200 Saint Louis MO 63101-2500

FLAPAN, JAN, civic worker; b. Dallas, Mar. 13, 1943; d. Joseph Lewis and Henrietta (Goodman) Ginsberg; m. William R. Flapan, Aug. 21, 1966; children: David, Deborah. BA, U. Iowa, 1965. Cert. 6-12 art and English tchr., Ill. Employment cons. Circle Pers., Chgo., 1965-66; wholesale advt. copywriter City Products, Des Plaines, Ill., 1966-67; tchr. art and social studies Sch. Dist. 59, Elk Grove, Ill., 1967-69; exec. dir. Rogers Park Family Network, Chgo., 1984-86. Fundraiser Ill. Women's Agenda, Chgo., 1988; mem. ad hoc task force Family/Med. Leave Act, 1991-92; co-chmn. Chgo. Com. Libr. Users, 1991-93; pres. Friends Northtown Pub. Libr., 1990-92; bd. dirs. Peterson Park Improvement Assn., 1989-92; mem. Chgo. adv. coun. coop. ext. svc. U. Ill., 19926; mem. local sch. coun. Solomon Sch., Chgo., 1991-93; cons. on fundraising, grant writing, advocacy and gen. orgn.; mem. Nat. Coun. Jewish Women; chair steering com. Progress Ill., 1993-94. Mem. LWV Ill. (v.p. 1990-93, Olive Greensfelder award 1992, chair local arrangements for 1996 nat. conv. in Chgo. 1995-96), ACLU, Nature Conservancy.

FLASKAMP, RUTH EHMEN STAACK, retired elementary education educator; b. Moline, Ill., Dec. 11, 1927; d. Henry Frederick and Tjiede Lena (Ehmen) Staack; m. Richard Kresse Flaskamp, June 10, 1950; children: Richard Henry, Thomas Marc. BA, Augustana Coll., 1949; MEd, Bowling Green State U., 1971. Tchr. elem. grades Lanark (Ill.) Consolidated Schs., 1949-50; tchr. elem. grades Sylvania (Ohio) City Schs., 1956-93, ret., 1993; field supr. Coll. Edn., U. Toledo, 1994—; field supr. Coll. of Edn., U. Toledo, Ohio, 1994—. Contbr. articles to profl. jours., various curriculum guides. Bd. dirs. Sylvania Pub. Libr., 1960-61; mem. ednl. adv. com. Toledo Edison, Toledo Zoo, 1986; active various polit. campaigns. Jennings scholar, 1982-83; recipient award for excellence in edn. NEA/Ladies Home Jour., 1990-91. Mem. NEA, Sylvania Edn. Assn. (sec. 1975-76, 89-90, pres. 1991), Ohio Edn. Assn. (rep.), N.W. Ohio Edn. Assn., Nat. Sci. Tchrs. Assn., Golden Emblem Club. Republican. Lutheran. Home: 6510 Cornwall Ct Sylvania OH 43560 Office: Sylvania Stranahan Sch 3840 N Holland Sylvania Rd Toledo OH 43615-1008

FLAUM, MORRIS AARON, hematologist, oncologist; b. Fed. Republic of Germany, Jan. 29, 1947; came to U.S., 1949; s. Jacob S. and Sara (Sissiski) F.; children: Alisa, Geoffrey. BS, U. Pitts., 1969; MD, U. Miami, Fla., 1974; MBA, Tulane U., 1990. Diplomate Am. Bd. Internal Medicine and Hematology. Intern Yale-New Haven (Conn.) Hosp., 1974-75, resident, 1975-77; clin. assoc. NIH, Bethesda, Md., 1977-79; physician St. Petersburg (Fla.) Med. Clinic, 1979-81; physician Ochsner Clinic, New Orleans, 1981-92, bd. mgmt., fin. com., 1987-92; chmn. dept. internal medicine St. Joseph Mercy Hosp., Ann Arbor, Mich., 1992—; chmn. quality assessment com. Ochsner Med. Inst., New Orleans, 1987-92. Author: (with others) Transplantation, 1991. Bd. dirs. Am. Cancer Soc., New Orleans, 1982-89; trustee Leukemia Soc. Am., La., 1990-92. Recipient Best in Specialty (hematology) award Detroit Monthly, 1995. Fellow Am. Coll. Physicians, mem. Am. Soc. Hematology (practice com.), Am. Soc. Clin. Oncology, Am. Coll. Physician Execs., So. Assn. Oncology (founding mem. 1988), Beta Gamma Sigma, Phi Kappa Phi, Alpha Omega Alpha. Jewish. Office: St Joseph Mercy Hosp 5333 Mcauley Dr Ste R-3009 Ypsilanti MI 48197-1014

FLECK, ALBERT HENRY, JR., insurance agency executive; b. Jasper, Ind., Aug. 4, 1929; s. Albert J. and Emily M. (Hopf) F.; m. LaVern C. Sermersheim, Oct. 8, 1953 (dec. 1980); children: Steven L., Jeffery E., Patrick J., Gregory K., Lisa A., Christopher A., Douglas G. Grad. high sch., Jasper. With Jasper Turning Co., 1952-56; pres. A.H. Fleck Agy., Inc., Jasper, 1956—. Clk. cir. ct. Dubois County, Jasper, 1971-78; councilman County of Dubois, Jasper, 1982-94. With U.S. Army, 1948-52, Korea. Mem. K.C., Jasper Civitan (pres. 1972-74), Am. Legion, Ind. Guard Res. (capt. 1987—). Democrat. Roman Catholic. Home and Office: AH Fleck Agy Inc 309 E State Road 164 Jasper IN 47546-9305

FLECK, DEBBORAH K., financial consultant; b. Springfield, Ill., Nov. 7, 1957; d. James L. and Nancy C. (Lock) F.; m. Edward L. Schainker, Dec. 1, 1988; 1 child, Jason D. Barnes. Portfolio mgr. First Nat. Bank & Trust, Springfield, Ill., 1981-87; fin. cons. Merrill Lynch, Springfield, 1987—. Fundraiser St. Johns Hosp., Springfield, 1994—. Mem. Country Club, Priority Prodrs. Club (priority prodr.). Republican. Roman Catholic. Home: 45 Vivian Ln Springfield IL 62707-8924

FLEENOR, GARY BRYCE, brokerage executive, councilman; b. Topeka, Sept. 27, 1942. Lic. series 7 Nat. Assn. Securities Dealers. Various positions to pres., ptnr. Capitol City Office Products, Topeka, 1960-87; v.p. investments Everen Securities Inc., Topeka, 1987—. Pres. Topeka Jaycees, 1969-70; mem. Topeka City Coun., 1985—; bd. dirs. Stormont-Vail Regional Med. Ctr., Topeka, 1989—, Topeka Conv. and Visitors Bur., 1987—; treas. Kans. Internat. Mus., Topeka, 1994—. With Army N.G., 1960-66. Mem. Optimists (pres. Topeka chpt. 1978-79). Republican. Office: Everen Securities Inc 534 S Kansas Ave Ste 1010 Topeka KS 66603-3432

FLEHARTY, MARY SUE, communication specialist; b. Lincoln, Nebr., Aug. 13, 1962; d. Joseph Patrick and Joy Lou (Harnish) Huntley; m. Bradley Daryle Osborne, Mar. 26, 1983 (div. June 1988); m. Terry Lester Fleharty, Aug. 13, 1990. Student, S.E. Comm. Coll., Lincoln. Loan processor Am. Charter Fed. Savings and Loan, Lincoln, 1981-84; pub. broadcast exchange operator, sec. Lincoln Clinic, P.C., 1989-91; PBX operator, sec. Woods Park Med. Mgmt. Inc., Lincoln, 1991-93; data reporting asst. Harris Tech. Group, Lincoln, 1993; lease coord. Progressive Lease, Inc., Lincoln, 1993; PBX comms. specialist Branker Buick, Lincoln, 1994—. Vol. ARC, Lincoln, 1977—, chmn., 1983-84, pres. Lincoln Fire Dept. Aux., 1993; cert. EMT. Named Outstanding Vol. ARC, 1985. Mem. NAFE, Jaycees. Republican. Presbyterian. Office: Branker Buick 421 N 48th St Lincoln NE 68504-3410

FLEISCHER, JOHN RICHARD, retired secondary education educator; b. Milw., Mar. 7, 1934; s. Ernest William and Ruth Ida (Braun) F.; m. Barbara Ann Seidel, June 11, 1955; children: Lisa (dec.), Kurt Richard. BS in Art Edn., U. Wis., Milw., 1960. Cert. art tchr., Wis. Art tchr. Kenosha (Wis.) Pub. Schs., 1960-62, Westosha High Sch., Salem, Wis., 1963-94; ret., 1994; art instr. adult classes Gateway Tech. Inst., Kenosha County, 1970-74, Kenosha Pub. Mus., 1961-62; speaker various community groups, S.E. Wis., 1960—; judge art shows, 1960—. Exhibited in group shows at Nat. Air and Space Mus., 1984, The Exptl. Aircraft Assn., 1980-86. With U.S. Army, 1957-59. Mem. NEA, Wis. Edn. Assn., Salem Cen. Edn. Assn. (pres. 1974-75), Lions Club of Greater Kenosha, Internat. Assn. Lions (dist. gov. 1978-79, Gov. award 1979), Westosha Lions Club (pres. 1973-74, Pres. award 1974). Home: 210 Walnut Rd Twin Lakes WI 53181-9367

FLEISCHMAN, STEPHEN, art center director; b. Newton, Mass., July 7, 1954; s. David and Dorothy (Myers) F.; m. Barbara Jane Katz, May 18, 1986; children: Daniel Katz Fleischman, Benjamin Katz Fleischman, Jacob Katz Fleischman. BS in Fine Arts, U. Wis., 1977, MA in Bus. Adminstrn., 1983. Gallery owner, studio potter Seattle, 1977-81; devel. asst. Madison (Wis.) Art Ctr., 1981-83; spl. asst. to dir. Walker Art Ctr., Mpls., 1983-86, dir. program planning, 1986-90; dir. Madison Art Ctr., 1991—. Bd. dirs. So. Theater, Mpls., 1988-90, Minn. Citizens for the Arts, Mpls., 1985-90, Cable Arts Consortium, Mpls., 1986-88, Madison CitiArts, 1991—; pres. adv. bd. Bolz Ctr. for Arts Adminstrn., U. Wis., 1995—. Mem. Rotary Internat. Office: Madison Art Ctr 211 State St Madison WI 53703-2214

FLEISCHMANN, SHIRLEY TINA, mechanical engineer, educator; b. Grand Rapids, Mich., July 4, 1953; d. William and Gay (Mulder) Hekman; m. Frederick Royal Fleischmann, Dec. 16, 1972; children: Eric Leon, Ian William, Eileen Claire, Ryan Frederick. BS in Physics, U. Md., 1975, MS in Physics, 1977, MS in Mech. Engring., 1979, PhD in Mech. Engring., 1982. Asst. prof. U.S. Naval Acad., Annapolis, Md., 1982-89; assoc. prof. Grand Valley State U., Allendale, Mich., 1989-95; prof. Seymour and Esther Padnos Sch. Engring. Grand Valley State U., Grand Rapids, Mich., 1995—; pres. Fleischmann & Assoc. Ltd., Alto, Mich., 1989—; dir. Design for Recycling Project, Grand Valley State U., Allendale, Mich., 1990-91. Contbr. articles to profl. jours. Mem. ASME, Soc. Mfg. Engrs., Soc. Automotive Engrs., Am. Soc. Engring. Edn., Sigma Xi. Republican. Christian Reformed. Home: 9033 Foecke Dr SE Caledonia MI 49316-9596 Office: Grand Valley State Univ Eberhard Ctr Grand Rapids MI 49504

FLEMING, MARGARET ANN, marketing executive; b. St. Louis, Mo., Apr. 7, 1947. BS in Math., Purdue U., 1965-69. Tchr. Brockton (Mass.) H. S., 1969-72, Lawrence Ctrl. H. S., Indpls., 1972-74; v.p. Luminatae, Inc., Indpls., 1980-90; pres. Bldg. Restoration Svcs., Inc., Indpls., 1990-93; v.p. Oracle Cons., Inc., Indpls., 1993—. Spkr. Girls, Inc., Indpls., 1994—; mem. Indpls. Symphony of Women's Group, 1976—. Recipient Edwin Guth award Illuminating Engring. Soc., 1984, 86, 87, 89. Republican. Protestant. Office: Oracle Consulting Inc 7002 N Graham Rd Ste 214 Indianapolis IN 46220-4050

FLEMING, MARIANNE HELEN, physical therapist; b. Milw., July 23, 1958; d. Ervin Anthony and Helen Therese (Romba) Bishop; m. Mikel Conn Fleming, Nov. 15, 1986; children: Angela Marie, Anthony Lewis, Daniel Joseph. BS in Phys. Therapy, Marquette U., 1980; MS, U. Ill., 1985. Phys. therapist St. Luke's Hosp., Milw., 1980-83; phys. therapist clin. coord. St. Elizabeth's Hosp., Danville, Ill., 1983-84; phys. therapist grad. asst. U. Ill., Urbana, 1984-85; phys. therapist Carle Found. Hosp., Urbana, 1985, indsl. rehab. clin. coord., 1985-86; asst. dir. phys. therapy Hosp. Svcs., Inc., Lafayette, Ind., 1986-91; phys. therapist Vita Care-Lafayette, Louisville, 1991-92; co-owner, phys. therapist Lafayette (Ind.) Rehab. Svcs., Inc., 1992—; ctr. clin. coord. edn. U. Indpls., 1994—, Ind. U., Indpls., 1994—. Daisy leader Sagamore Coun., Girl Scouts U.S.A., 1994-95. Mem. Am. Phys. Therapy Assn., Ind. Phys. Therapy Assn. Office: Lafayette Rehab Svcs Inc 200 Professional Ct Ste A Lafayette IN 47905

FLEMING, SCOTT THOMAS, commercial artist; b. Green Bay, Wis., June 17, 1961; s. Joseph Robert and Barbara Jean (Van Wagoner) F. Grad. high sch., Naperville, Ill. Draftsman, surveyor City of Naperville, 1978-80; comml. artist Lidejo Sales Promotion Agy., Lisle, Ill., 1984-88; art dir. Corp. Printing and Graphics, Downers Grove, Ill., 1988-90; computer artist SS&E Systems, Inc., Naperville, 1990-91, Sun Pubs., Naperville, 1991-93; comml. artist, owner Fleming Comml. Art (name changed to Infinite Design Solutions), Naperville, 1991—; graphic designer Teledec Internat., 1993—. Mem. Graphic Artist Guild. Roman Catholic. Home and Office: Fleming Comml Art 10 S Testa Dr Apt 301 Naperville IL 60540-4275

FLEMING, THOMAS MICHAEL, artist, educator; b. Phila, May 12, 1951; s. Thomas Joseph and Eleanor Virginia (Huston) F.; m. Kristin Karen Wigley, Oct. 29, 1977 (dec. Jan. 1980); m. Beverly Jean Folgert, Sept. 25, 1987. AA with honors, Harrisburg (Pa.) Community Coll., 1972; BFA with honors, Pa. State U., 1975; MFA, U. Minn., 1978. Art instr. U. Wis., Wausau, 1978-84, asst. prof., 1985-89, assoc. prof., 1990—; dir., co-founder SoHo Studio Ctr., N.Y.C.; pres. Art Shoot, N.Y.C.; artistic program cons. Anglo-American Workshops, N.Y.C., 1988-89; art. dir. :W/Co., Wis. Represented in permanent collections Musee Des Arts, Lausanne, Switzerland, Corning (N.Y.) Mus., Internat. Glasmuseum, Ebeltoft, Denmark. One of 100 Art Judges U.S. News and World Report's Best of America, 1990. Grantee U. Wis., 1981, 82, 84, 86, 87, 91, Wis. Arts Bd. Madison, 1985, 91. Mem. Glass Art Soc., Wis. Acad. Scis. Arts and Letters, Internat. Sculpture Assn., Wis. Painters and Sculptors, Artist Space N.Y. Home: 518 S 7th Ave Wausau WI 54401-5362 Office: U Wis Dept of Art 518 S 7th Ave Wausau WI 54401-5362

FLETCHALL, LYLE R., civil engineer; b. Duncombe, Iowa, June 16, 1929; s. Clyde H. and Evelyn Hildred (Rhodes) F.; m. Doris Fletchall, Apr. 3, 1955; children: Valli Jo, Vicki Raenae, Cheryl Ann, Cassandra Dee. BSCE, Iowa State U., 1954. Registered profl. engr., Minn., Wis. Pres. Associated Engrs., Inc., Ft. Dodge, Iowa, 1966-84; regional v.p. Ayres Assocs., Eau Claire, Wis., 1985-87; engr. City of Cedar Falls, Iowa, 1988—; pres. Iowa Engring. Soc., 1981-82; state bd. dirs. City Engrs. Coun., Des Moines, 1975-82. 1st lt. Corps of Engrs., 1954-56. Methodist. Home: RR 2 Fort Dodge IA 50501

FLETCHER, DAVID J., medical clinic administrator; b. Cleve., Sept. 30, 1954; s. Archie Eaton and Dorthy Jean (Heidloff) F.; m. Wanda, Mar. 22, 1978; children: Janine, Jeffrey. Student, U. Ill., 1976, Rush Med. Coll., Chgo., 1979, U. Calif., Berkeley, 1982. Asst. chief preventive medicine U.S. Army Madigan Army Med. Ctr., Tacoma, Wash., 1983-86; dir. DMH Corp. Health Services, Decatur, Ill., 1986-89, Midwest Occupational Health Assocs., Decatur, 1989—; faculty position U. Ill. Coll. medicine 1988, clin. asst. prof., dir. occupl. preventive medicine; clin. assoc. prof SIU Sch. Medicine, 1994. Author: David Bowie: Discography, 1979; Med. Sch. Mayhem, 1980; Contbg. editor Med. Self-Care, Men's Health, Geriatric Cons., 1982—; editor: Postgrad. Med., Jour. Series Health Promotion for Practitioners 1984-87; producer Bowiecon I; 1980 Floor Show 1980. Active Macon County Health Bd., 1990-95. Fellow Am. Coll. Preventive Medicine, Am. Coll. Occupl. Medicine; mem. AMA, Am. Tchrs. Preventive Medicine, Am. Pub. Health Assn., Ctrl. States Occupl. Medicine Assn. (bd. dirs. 1991-94, planning dir. 1992), Am. Coll. of Occupl. Environ. Medicine (exec. com. sect. of med. rev. officers 1995),. Mem. Soc. of Friends. Home: 160 John Dr Mount Zion IL 62549-1818 Office: Midwest Occupl Health Assoc Ste 200 1900 E Lake Shore Dr Decatur IL 62521-3809

FLETCHER, MARTIN EDWARD, electrical engineer, computer specialist; b. Fayetteville, Ark., Feb. 17, 1947; s. Donald Albert and Virginia Alice (Skillern) F.; m. Beverly Ann Sigler, Nov. 30, 1974; children: Cindy, Charles. BSEE, U. Ark., 1970. Reg. profl. engr. Ark. Computer specialist U.S. Army Corps of Engrs., Omaha, Nebr., 1970-79; systems engring. mgr. Lockheed Martin Astro Space, Omaha, 1980—. Mem. IEEE. Home: 104 Somerset Ave Council Bluffs IA 51503

FLETCHER, PHILIP B., food products company executive; b. 1933. BA, St. Lawrence U.; MBA, MIT, 1954. With ctrl. foundry divsn. Gen. Motors Corp., 1954-58; various mgmt. positions Campbell Soup Co., 1958-73; gen. mgr. ops. and agriculture H.J. Heinz USA, Inc., 1973-78; v.p. mfg. Heublein Co., 1978-82; pres. Banquet Foods Co., Omaha, 1982-84; corp. pres., COO ConAgra Inc., Omaha, 1982-92, CEO, 1992—, chmn., 1993—, also dir. Office: ConAgra Inc 1 Conagra Dr Omaha NE 68102-5094*

FLETCHER, THOMAS LINCOLN, electrical engineer; b. Columbus, Ohio, Apr. 12, 1958; s. Billie Lincoln and Jeanne Ann (Fawcett) F.; m. Diane Elizabeth Cattran, Feb. 23, 1985; children: David, Charles. BSEE, Ohio State U., 1980. Profl. engr. Ohio. Prin. rsch. scientist Battelle Meml. Inst., Columbus, 1980-92; pres. Advanced Engring. Concepts, Inc., Columbus, 1992—. Mem. IEEE, Nat. Soc. Profl. Engrs. Home: 1112 Broadview Ave Columbus OH 43212 Office: Advanced Engring Concepts 1504 W 1st Ave #302 Columbus OH 43212

FLICK, THOMAS MICHAEL, mathematics educator, educational administrator; b. Covington, Ky., July 14, 1954; s. Thomas Lawrence and Crystel (Moore) F.; m. Jeanne M. Moran, Nov. 23, 1991. BS, No. Ky. U., 1976, MA, 1981; MEd, Xavier U., 1977; PhD, Southeastern U., 1979; EdD, U. Sarasota, 1989. Cert. secondary tchr., Ohio, Ky. Assoc. vice prin., dean, chmn. math., prin. summer sch. Purcell Marian High Sch., Cin., 1977-89; asst. prof. Xavier U., Cin., 1989-95, assoc. prof., 1995—; lectr. astronomy Wilmington Coll., Ohio, 1977-78, engring. and nat. sci., U. Cin., 1979—. Author: Guidelines for Astronomy Courses, 1976, 78, (with J. Ventre & J. Boothe) Astronomy Teaching Handbook, 1992, Introduction to the Universe, 1991, 93; contbr. articles to profl. jours. Guest lectr. Cin. Nature Ctr., Milford, 1976—; chmn. edn. Astron. League, Washington; tchr. Super Saturday Program for Gifted and Talented., Cin., 1983; commn. mem. Archdiocese Cin., 1986. Recipient Ohio NSF Presdl. Award for Excellence in Math. Edn., 1986, Greater Cin. Found./GE grantee, 1987. Mem. Ohio Coun. Tchrs. Math. (contest coord. 1983—, Outstanding Math. Tchr. award 1982), Nat. Astron. League (v.p. 1980-82), Nat. Coun. Tchrs. Math, Math Assn. Am., Ohio Acad. Sci. (Jerry Acker Outstanding Math. Tchr. award 1986-87), Sigma Xi (Outstanding Math. Tchr. award 1985), Pi Mu Epsilon. Roman Catholic. Club: Midwestern Astronomers. Home: 1720 Monticello Dr Fort Wright KY 41011-3765 Office: Xavier U Dept Edn 3800 Victory Pky Cincinnati OH 45207-1035

FLICKINGER, THEODORE BLAIR, association administrator; b. Wooster, Ohio, May 15, 1944; s. Blair Lee and Geraldine (Baney) F.; m. Judith Bunn, Jan. 2, 1964; children: Brett, Amy. BS, Southern Ill. U., 1967, MS, 1968; PhD, Ohio State U., 1976. Supr. Wooster (Ohio) Park and Recreation Dept., 1960-61, Nat. Job Corps, OEO, Morganfield, Ky., 1967; cons., grad. asst. So. Ill. U., 1968; dir. West Frankfort (Ill.) Park District, 1968-69, Bexley (Ohio) City Parks and Recreation, 1968-73; prof. parks and recreation div. Ohio State U., 1973-77; regional dir. Great Lake Nat. Recreation and Parks Assn., Chgo., 1977-80; exec. dir. Ill. Assn. of Park Dists., Springfield, 1980-. Author: Guidelines for Parks and Recreation Boards, Excellence in Park and Recreation Systems, Parks and Recreation Concepts; contbr. several articles to jours. and mags. Mem. Dist. 214 Sch Bd., 1979—. Recipient Nat. Gold medal, 1973; named to Hall of Fame, Am. Park and Recreation Acad. Mem. Am. Park and Recreation Soc. (pres. 1988—), Am. Soc. Assn. Execs. (cert.). Home: 2315 S Willemore Ave Springfield IL 62704-4361 Office: Ill Assn of Park Dists 211 E Monroe St Springfield IL 62701-1126

FLINN, CHARLES GALLAGHER, lawyer; b. Ft. Lauderdale, Fla., Feb. 22, 1938; s. Robert Galloway and Gertrude (Gallagher) F. AB, Princeton U., 1959; LLB, U. Va., 1962; BD, U. London, 1980; ThM, Westminster Theol. Sem., 1994. Bar: Fla. 1962, Va. 1962, U.S. Supreme Ct. 1966, D.C. 1970; Ordained to ministry Episcopal Ch. as deacon, 1991, as priest 1992. Assoc. Charles B. Fulton, Esq., West Palm Beach, Fla., 1962-63; asst. counsel Office Gen. Counsel U.S. Dept. Navy, Washington, 1963-71; asst. commonwealth's atty. County of Arlington, Va., 1971-72, asst. county atty., 1972-75, dep. county atty., 1975-81, county atty., 1981-93; atty. Arlington Sch. Bd., 1981-93; curate Grace Episcopal Ch., Brunswick, Md., 1991-93; vicar Trinity Episcopal Ch., Monmouth, Ill., 1994—; Episcopal chaplain Monmouth Coll., 1994—. Mem. Va. Local Govt. Attys. Assn. (bd. dirs. 1988-92), Va. Coun. Sch. Bd. Attys. (dir.-at-large 1988-93), Princeton Club N.Y. Home: 620 E Broadway Monmouth IL 61462-1974

FLOM, EDWARD LEWIS, retired oil company official; b. Rock Island, Ill., Nov. 24, 1932; s. Lewis O. and Sara L. (Brodtkorb) F.; m. Beryl Light, July 6, 1968; children: Sharon, David. BSChemE, Ill. Inst. Tech., 1954; postgrad., Northwestern U., DePaul U., NYU. Sr. staff engr. Amoco Oil Co., Whiting, Ind., 1954-62; supr. econs. Amoco Internat. Oil Co., N.Y.C., 1963-68; gen. mgr. econs. Amoco Chem. Co., Chgo., 1969-75; mgr. industry analysis and forecasts Amoco Corp., Chgo., 1976-93. Bd. dirs. I Have A Dream Program, North Chicago, Ill., 1992—; mem. president's coun. Ill. Inst. Tech., Chgo.; elder Presbyn. Ch. Mem. Am. Petroleum Inst., Internat. Assn. Energy Econs., Phi Kappa Sigma (pres. ednl. fund).

FLOM, MARK ALAN, architect; b. Grand Forks, N.D., Aug. 23, 1955; s. Curtis Milton and Lois (Sondreal) F.; m. Laurie Ann Dukerschein, Nov. 12, 1988; children: Haley C., Anna K. BArch magna cum laude, Ariz. State U., 1978. Lic. architect Ill., Wis., Minn., Ga., Calif. Project designer Baker Assocs., Mpls., 1978-80, Loebl Schlossman & Hackl, Chgo., 1980-83; project architect Cooper Carry & Assocs., Atlanta, 1983-85; project mgr. ISD Inc., Chgo., 1985-86; sr. v.p. Chgo., 1986—. Mem. Santa Claus Anonymous, Chgo., 1982-83. Recipient travel/study prize to Oxford U., Ariz. State U., 1977. Mem. AIA (interiors com. 1985-86, design com. 1982-83), Internat. Coun. Shopping Ctrs., Tau Beta Pi, Phi Kappa Phi. Home: 2510 N Burling St Chicago IL 60614-2510 Office: Urban Retail Properties Co 900 N Michigan Ave Chicago IL 60611-1542

FLOOD, JOSEPH, physician, educator; b. Cleve., Aug. 8, 1952; s. Joseph John and Elsie (Carpenter) F.; m. Jeanne M. Likins, May 19, 1984. AS, Cuyahoga C.C., Cleve., 1973; BS, Baldwin-Wallace Coll., 1975; MD, Georgetown U., 1979. Chair dept. medicine Central Ohio Med. Group, Columbus, Ohio, 1987-92, 95—, v.p. med. affairs, 1992-94; clin. asst. prof. medicine Coll. Medicine Ohio State U., Columbus, 1986—; founder, dir. Arthritis Care Ctr., Grant Med. Ctr., Columbus, 1987—, chair dept. medicine, 1995—; bd. dirs. Ctrl. Ohio chpt. Arthritis Found., Columbus, 1986—. Fellow Am. Coll. Rheumatology; mem. Ohio State Med. Assn. (vice chair, group practice adv. com.), Acad. Medicine Columbus and Franklin County. Democrat. Roman Catholic. Office: Ctrl Ohio Med Group 497 E Town St Columbus OH 43215-4779

FLORA, JOHN GERALD, director public works, city engineer; b. Chgo., May 10, 1936; s. Rose C. Flora; m. Jan C. Kucienski, Aug. 8, 1959; children: John, Jolie. BS, Univ. Wis., 1960, Mo. Sch. Mines, 1964; MA, Pepperdine Univ., 1973; MS, Okla. State Univ., 1974. Co. comdr. 94th engr. BN Co. D, Germany, 1962-63; asst. S3 18th engr. Bde, 1965-66; dept. dir. USAES, Ft. Belvoir, Va., 1966-67; comdr. 13th engr. bn., Korea, 1967-68; engr. staff officer HQ USARPAC, Ft. Shafter, Hawaii, 1969-73; ops. officer USMA, West Point, N.Y., 1974-77; dir. faculty engr. Ft. McCoy US Army, Sparta, Wis., 1977-80; DPW/CE City of Fridley, Minn., 1980—. del. Minn. Pub. Works Assn., 1988-95, pres., 1986; region VI dir. APWA, 1995—. Decorated Bronze star, Korea; named Engr. of Yr., Minn. Pub. Works Assn., 1991, APWA Top Ten award, 1994. Mem. Lions Club, VFW, Am. Legion. Office: City of Fridley 6431 University Ave NE Fridley MN 55432-4383

FLORA, KENT ALLEN, small business owner; b. Urbana, Ill., Jan. 7, 1944; s. Loyal Lee and Ercel Hannah (Puzey) F.; m. Sharon Jean Bray, Dec. 31, 1974; children: Donald William, William Christopher, Brent Allyn. BS, U. Ill., 1966. Prodn. mgr. Flora Farms, Fairmount, Ill., 1961-70, owner, operator, 1970-89; nat. sales mgr. Marketmatic Ltd., Champaign, Ill., 1990-91; owner AmeriSpec Home Inspection Svc., Champaign, 1994-96; tech. staffing specialist Snelling Search, Champaign, Ill., 1996—; bd. dirs. Vermilion County Agrl. Extension Adv. Council, 1967-69; nat. pres. Am. Shropshire Registry Assn., 1972-73, nat. bd. dirs., 1965-73; pres. Ill. Shropshire Assn., 1970-72; bd. dirs. Ill. Purebred Sheep Breeder's Assn., 1965-70. Mem. Jamaica Unit Dist. #12 Bd. Edn., Sidell, Ill., 1981-90, v.p. bd. dirs., 1987-90, pres. citizen's adv. council, 1978-82; trustee Vance Twp., Fairmount, 1967-75, mem. Park Bd., 1977-81; mem. exec. com. Vermilion County Rep. Cen. Com., 1986-89; v.p. Vermilion County Merit Commn. for Law Enforcement, 1986-88, pres. 1988-89; pres. Vermilion County Chmn. Unit Am. Cancer Soc., 1972-73; Vermilion County campaign coordinator Mike Houston for Ill. State Treas., 1986; Ill. 19th Congl. Dist. del. Jack Kemp for Pres., 1988. Served to sgt. USAR. Named Outstanding Young Farmer Jaycees, Danville, Ill., 1972, Hon. Chpt. Farmer Jamaica Future Farmers Assn., 1985; recipient Centennial Farm award State of Ill., 1970. Mem. U. Ill. Alumni Assn., Chi Phi, Masons, Shriners. Presbyterian. Home and Office: 2606 Woodridge Rd Champaign IL 61821-7521

FLORA, VAUGHN LEONARD, state legislator; b. Quinter, Kans., Jan. 17, 1945; s. Leonard Henry and Billie Hazel (Leighton) F.; m. Rose Mary Owens, 1963; children: Troy Vaughn, Trent Leighton, Trina Rose. BS, Kans. State U., 1968; postgrad., Lincoln Grad. Sch., 1989. Pres. Topeka City Homes, 1993-94; mem. Kans. State Ho. of Reps. Dist. 57, 1995—. Precinct committeeman Ward 2 Precinct 6, 1988—; mem. Govs. Commn. on Housing, 1994—.

FLOREN, DAVID D., advertising executive. BA in Journalism, U. Minn. Copywriter, account svc. rep. GE; with Martin/Williams Advt., Mpls., chmn., CEO, chmn. mgmt. bd.; bd. dirs. Gold Greenlees Trott, London. Recipient Silver Medal award Am. Advt. Fedn., 1990. Mem. Am. Assn. Advt. Agys. (ctrl. region bd., nat. bd.). Office: Martin Williams Advt Inc 10 S 5th St Minneapolis MN 55402-1012

FLORENCE, PAUL SMITH, agronomist, business owner; b. Pickaway County, Ohio, June 8, 1931; s. Henry W. and Altia Marie (Hoffman) F.; m. Laura Lee Kimmins, Sept. 4, 1954; children: Michael A. Florence, Barbara (Florence) Akers. BS, Ohio State U., 1956. Rsch. project leader O.M. Scott & Sons Co., Marysville, Ohio, 1956-65; sales field coord. O.M. Scott & Sons Co., Marysville, 1965-72; tech. sales mgr. Robert Dye Seed Ranch, Pomeroy, Wash., 1972-76, Seaboard Seed Co., Bristol, Ill., 1976-82; owner Paul Florence Turfgrass, Marysville, Ohio, 1982—. Mem. Am. Sod Producers Assn. (dir. 1973, v.p. 1974), Ohio Sod Producers Assn., Kiwanis. Republican.

FLORESTANO, DANA JOSEPH, architect; b. Indpls., May 2, 1945; s. Herbert Joseph and Myrtle Mae (Futch) F.; m. Peggy Joy Larsen, June 6, 1969. BArch, U. Notre Dame, 1968. Designer, draftsman Kennedy, Brown & Trueblood, architects, Indpls., 1965-69, Evans Woolen Assn., architects, Indpls., 1966; designer, project capt. James Assos., architects and engrs., Indpls., 1969-71; architect, v.p. comml. projects Multi-Planners Inc., architects and engrs., 1972-73; pvt. practice architecture, Indpls., 1973—; pres. Florestano Corp., constrn. mgmt., Indpls., 1973—; co-founder, pres. Solargenics Natural Energy Corp., Indpls., 1975—; pres. Florestano Archery Co., 1985—, Star Archery Corp., Indpls., 1989—; prof. archtl. and constrn. tech. Ind. U.-Purdue U. at Indpls.; instr. in field. Tech. adviser hist. architecture Indpls. Model Cities program, 1969-70; mem. Hist. Landmarks Found. Ind., 1970-72; chmn. Com. to Save Union Sta., 1970-71, founder, pres. Union Sta. Found. Inc., Indpls., 1971—. Dep. commr. and tournament dir. archery Pan-Am. Games, Indpls., 1987. Recipient 2d design award Marble Inst. Am., 1967, 1st design award 19th Ann. Progressive Architecture Design awards, 1972; Design award for excellence in devel. Marriott Inn, Indpls., Met. Devel. Commn.-Office of Mayor, 1977; 1st place award design competition for Visitor's Info. Ctr., Cave Run, Lake, Ky., 1978; 2d design award 1st Ann. Qualified Remodeler, Nat. Competition for Best Rehab. Existing Structures in Am., 1979. Mem. U. Notre Dame Alumni Assn., Notre Dame Club Indpls., AIA (nat. com. historic resources 1974—, commn. on community svcs., Speakers Bur. Indpls. chpt. 1976—), Ind. Soc. Architects (chmn. historic architecture com. 1970—), Ind. Archery Assn. (founder, pres. 1985—, Overall Male State Champion 1987, 90, 94), No. Archery Assn. (bd. dirs., pres. 1987—), Internat. Archery Ctr. (founder, exec. dir. 1992—), Constrn. Specifications Inst., Constrn. Mgrs. Assn. Ind. (incorporator, dir. 1976—), World Archery Ctr. Home: 5697 Broadway St Indianapolis IN 46220-3072 Office: 6214 Carrollton Ave Indianapolis IN 46220-1925

FLORIAN, MARIANNA BOLOGNESI, civic leader; b. Chgo.; d. Giulio and Rose (Garibaldi) Bolognesi; BA cum laude, Barat Coll., 1940; postgrad. Moser Bus. Sch., 1941-42; m. Paul A. Florian III, June 4, 1949; children—Paul, Marina, Peter, Mark. Asst. credit mgr. Stella Cheese Co., Chgo., 1942-45; With ARC ETO Clubmobile Unit, 1945-47; mgr. Passavant Hosp. Gift Shop, 1947-49; pres., Jr. League Chgo., Inc., 1957-59; pres. woman's bd. Passavant Hosp., 1966-68; bd. dirs. Northwestern Meml. Hosp., 1974-81, mem. exec. com., 1974-79; pres. Women's Assn., Chgo. Symphony Orch., 1974-77, founder WFMT/CSO Radiothon, 1976; chmn. Guild Chgo. Hist. Soc., 1981-84, trustee Chgo. Hist. Soc., 1981-84; life trustee Orchestral Assn., v.p. 1978-82, vice chmn. 1982-86, mem. exec. com. 1978-87; mem. women's bd. U. Chgo.; mem. vis. com. dept. music U. Chgo., 1980-90; pres. bd. dirs. Antiquarian Soc. of Art Inst., 1989-91. Recipient Citizen Fellowship, Inst. Medicine Chgo., 1975, Presdl. Commendation for leadership and svc. Barat Coll., 1990. Clubs: Friday (pres. 1972-74), Contemporary; Winnetka Garden.

FLORY, BETSY J., educator; b. Grand Rapids, Oct. 16, 1936; Divorced; 2 children. AA, Grand Rapids C.C., 1957; AB, Calvin Coll., 1957; MA, U. Mich., 1987. Dem. nom. for Mich. House of Reps., 1978, Kent County Commn., 1982; Dem. candidate 3d dist. Mich. U.S. House of Reps., 1996. Congregationalist. Office: 309 Palmer NE Grand Rapids MI 49505*

FLORY, CLYDE REUBEN, JR., physician, clinical immunologist; b. Sellersville, Pa., Oct. 2, 1933; s. Clyde R. and Miriam Wagner (Hummell) F.; m. Karen Colleen McComb, Mar. 9, 1963; children: William, Robert, Timothy. BA in Chemistry, Lehigh U., 1955; MD, Johns Hopkins U., 1959. Diplomate Am. Bd. Allergy and Immunology. Intern Henry Ford Hosp., Detroit, 1959-60, resident, 1960-63, fellow dept. Allergy and Immunology, 1963-64; chief allergy subsection of medicine Ingham Med. Hosp., Lansing, Mich., 1974-95; assoc. clin. prof. Medicine Mich. State U., East Lansing, 1976—. Fellow Am. Coll. Chest Physicians (mem. Mich. chpt.), Am. Coll. Allergy, Asthma and Immunology, Am. Acad. Allergy, Asthma and Immunology; mem. AMA, Mich. Allergy Soc. (pres. 1983), Am. Thoracic Soc., Mich. Thoracic Soc., Mich. Soc. Internal Medicine, Mich. State Med. Soc. (continuing med. edn. com., legis. com.), Mich. Health Coun. (bd. dirs.), Asthma and Allergy Found. of Am. (Mich. chpt., bd. dirs.), Ingham County Med. Soc. (pres. 1987, del. 1989-94). Home: 1022 Whitman Dr East Lansing MI 48823-2450 Office: Allergy & Asthma Cons Mid-Mich 600 S Capitol Ave Lansing MI 48933-2308

FLORY, WENDY STALLARD, English language educator; b. Fulmer, Bucks, England, Nov. 14, 1943; came to U.S., 1965; naturalized, 1996; d. Frederick Clifford and Ethel (Smart) Stallard; m. David Allan Flory, July 3, 1966; children: Quentin Michael, Graham Stallard. BA in English with honors, London U., Bedford Coll., 1965; PhD in English, U. Tex., Austin, 1970. Asst. prof. English Rutgers U., Douglass Coll., New Brunswick, N.J., 1970-79, U. Pa., Phila., 1980-89; assoc. prof. Purdue U., West Lafayette, Ind., 1989-93, prof. English, 1993—. Author: Ezra Pound and The Cantos: A Record of Struggle, 1980, The American Ezra Pound, 1989. Fulbright grantee, 1965, Travel grantee, Am. Coun. Learned Socs., 1980; Rsch. fellow, AAUW, 1979-80, NEH, 1982-83. Mem. Modern Lang. Assn., The Melville Soc. Office: Purdue U Dept English West Lafayette IN 47907

FLOTEMERSCH, JANET SYLVIA, dietician; b. Cin., Dec. 11, 1929; d. Melville John and Irene Dewetta (Dreyer) Lehman; widowed; children: Janet, JoAnn, Harry, Joseph, Thomas. BS, Mt. St. Joseph Coll., 1952, MA, 1992. Registered dietician; lic. dietician, Ky. Food svc. dir. Ala. Poly. Inst., Auburn, 1952-55, Howard Simpson Clinic, Glascow, Ky., 1955-56; food svc. dir. Madison (Ind.) State Hosp., 1956-63, clin. dir., 1979-91; food svc. dir. King's Daus. Hosp., Madison, 1963-65, Carroll County Hosp., Carrollton, Ky., 1967-74; cons. to 8 health care ctrs. Ky., Ind., 1975-80; co-owner Dietetic Svcs. Am., Madison, 1980—; clin. dietician Lake Cumberland Regional Hosp., Somerset, Ky., 1990-92; ret., 1992; cons. Cumberland Manor, Parkers Lake, Ky.; speaker in field. Contbr. articles to profl. jours. Bd. dirs. Head Start, Carrollton; mem. entertainment com. Horse Show, Carrollton, Drama Club, Carrollton; sec. Peace & Justice Com., Somerset, 1993. Recipient Gov's. award State of Ind., 1987, Unifiber award Dow B. Hickam, Inc., 1988. Mem. Am. Dietetic Assn., South East Ind. Dietetic Assn. (pres. 1981-83), Ky. Dietetic Assn., Ind. Cons. Dietetic Assn., Ky. Cons. Dietetic Assn., Nat. Cons. Practice Group, Dieticians in Gen. Clin. Practice (area V coord. 1989). Home: 53 Woodson Bnd Bronston KY 42518 Office: Dietetic Svcs Am PO Box 321 Madison IN 47250-0321

FLOTRON, FRANCIS E., state legislator; b. St. Louis, Dec. 23, 1954; m. Anne Lewis, 1984. BS, Washington U., 1977. State rep. dist. 85 Mo. Ho. of Reps., 1982-88, asst. minority floor leader, 1987; state senator dist. 7, minority floor leader Mo. State Senate. Del. Mo. Rep. State Conv., 1976, 80—; treas., mem. exec. bd. St. Louis County Young Reps. Mem. St. Louis Soaring Soc., DeSmet Jesuit High Sch. Alumni Assn., Mo. Young Ams. for Freedom, St. Louis County Pachyderms, Kappa Sigma. Home: 13043 Olive St Rd Saint Louis MO 63141*

FLOTT, LESLIE WILLIAM, quality control professional; b. Chgo., Jan. 4, 1934; s. Leslie Steven and Edna Caloline (Smith) F.; m. Lynda Jean Wietzorek, Jan. 27, 1962; children: Robert Leslie, Daniel Norbert, Jonathon Paul. Student, U. Wis., 1958; PhB in Chemistry, Northwestern U., 1965; postgrad., J.B. Kushner Electroplating Sch., Evansville, Ind., 1966, Notre Dame U., 1972-73, Ind. U., 1983-85, Purdue U., 1983-85. Cert. wastewater treatment operator, Ind. Clk. The Chgo. Burlington, Quincy R.R., Cicero, Ill., 1956-57; inhalation therapist Oak Park (Ill.) Hosp., 1957-58; rsch.

technician The Richardson Co., Melrose Pk., Ill., 1958-62; with tech. sales-dept. Mobil Oil Corp., Skokie, Ill., 1962-66; supr., engr. C.T.S. Corp., Elkhart, Ind., 1966-69; project mgr., engr.air pollution control div. Wheelabrator-Frye Inc., Pitts., 1969-73; asst. plant mgr. Electrovoice div. Gulton Industries, Buchanan, Mich., 1973; supr., engr. Wabash (Ind.) Inc., 1973-75; ind. cons., 1975-81; supr. Anaconda-Ericson, Marion, Ind., 1978-82; mgr. Wayne Metal Protection Co., Fort Wayne, Ind., 1982—; sec. Mobile Ophthalmic Clinic Internat., Patna, Bihar, India, 1958-73; adj. faculty Ivy Tech. State Coll., 1986—, Ind. Inst. Tech., 1993—; speaker at confs. Columnist Metal Finishing mag., 1990—; contbr. articles to profl. jours. Mem. by-laws com. Greater Ft. Wayne Consensus Com., 1991-93; com. chmn., scout master, cub master, dist. commr., Boy Scouts Am., 1955-89, numerous other coun. positions; vol. instr. The Gabriel Richard Inst., Detroit, 1965-72; Eucharist minister, choir mem. Confraternity Christian Doctrine religious edn. St. Bernard Roman Catholic Ch., Wabash. With USAF, 1952-56. Recipient Sam Hanna award Ft. Wayne Tourism Bur. and Grand Wayne Ctr., 1991. Fellow Am. Soc. Quality Control (cert. quality engr., exam. proctor, chmn. midwest quality conf. com., v.p. confs., vice chmn. to exec. chmn., Forest R. Guimont award 1988); mem. Am. Soc. for Metals, Am. Electroplating Soc., Ind. Engrs. Soc. (legis. adv. com.), Ft. Wayne Engrs. Club (Citizen engr. 1988), KC (past grand knight, 4th degree, mem. Gibault Sch. envoy). Home: 1863 N Wabash St Wabash IN 46992-1214 Office: Wayne Metal Protection Co 1511 Wabash Ave Wabash IN 46992-1310

FLOWER, JOANN, state legislator; b. May 6, 1935; m. Paul Flower. BS, Johns Hopkins U. Kans. state rep. Dist. 47, 1996—, nurse, 1996—. Home: PO Box 97 Oskaloosa KS 66066-0097 Office: Kans State Senate State Capital Topeka KS 66612*

FLOWERS, CHARLES E., state legislator; m. Aleta Flowers; 3 children. Student, Huron Coll. Mem. S.D. State Senate, 1993—, mem. taxation, edn., local govt., transp. coms., mem. agr. and natural resources coms.; trucker and auction, real estate. Home: PO Box 156 Iroquois SD 57353-0156*

FLOWERS, DAMON BRYANT, architect, facility planner; b. Detroit, May 16, 1952; s. Marrell Curtis and Mattie (Rice) F.; m. Adria Faye Burrows, July 28, 1979; children: Lee, Dadria, Damon Bryant II. BS in Architecture, Lawrence Inst. Tech., 1974; BA in Liberal Arts, Cen. Mich. U., 1982; MS in Fin., Wayne State U., 1984; JD, Detroit Coll. Law, 1990. Bar: Mich. 1990; registered arch., Mich., Ill., Wis., Ohio. Architect Wayne State U., 1983-85; construction project mgmt. dir. St. Joseph Hosp. and Health Ctrs., 1985-91; v.p. ops. Argus & Assocs., 1991-94; dir. facilities devel. and ops. Washtenaw C.C., 1994—. Mem. AIA, APPA, BOCA, Constrn. Spec. Inst. Mem. African Methodist Episcopal Ch. Home: 22341 Avon Ln Southfield MI 48075 Office: Washtenaw CC Ann Arbor MI 48106

FLOWERS, MARY E., state legislator; b. July 31, 1951; married. Ed., Kennedy-King C.C., U. Ill. Mem. from 21st dist. Ill. Ho. of Reps., 1985—, now asst. majority leader, mem. appropriations and pub. utilities coms.; co-chmn. Il. Conf. Women Legis.; spokesperson Com. on Ins.; mem. Healthcare and Human Svcs. Com., Fin. Instns. Com., Consumer Protection Com. Recipient Black Rose award League of Black Women, 1988, Kizzy award Black Women Hall of Fame Found., 1990, Friend of Labor award AFL-CIO, 1990. Home: 2109 W 79th St Chicago IL 60620-4417 Office: Ill Ho of Reps State Capitol Springfield IL 62706*

FLOYD, WILLIAM SANFORD, gynecology and obstetrics educator; b. Detroit, Mar. 7, 1933; s. David G. and Ada (Levine) F.; m. Gayle Babette Floyd, June 27, 1976; children: Jered, Jennifer. BS, MIT, 1953; MD, Wayne State U., 1957. Diplomate Am. Bd. Ob-gyn. Intern Sinai Hosp., Detroit, 1957-58, resident ob-gyn., 1957-61; prof. ob-gyn. Wayne State U., Detroit, 1961—; resident in ob-gyn., 1958-61. Editor Oakland County Bull.; contbr. over 50 articles to profl. jours. Mem. ACS, ACOG, Am. Fertility Soc., Am. Assn. Prof. Gynecology and Obstetrics. Home: 1320 Ravenwicke Way Bloomfield Hills MI 48302-1966

FLUHARTY, CHARLES WILLIAM, policy research institute director, consultant, researcher; b. Wheeling, W.Va., Apr. 21, 1947; s. Irwin Adrian and Mary Elizabeth (Foster) F.; m. Marsha Jean Prospal, June 27, 1970; children: Matthew, Joshua, Megan. BA cum laude, U. Steubenville, Ohio, 1969; MDiv with distinctions, Yale U., 1973. Counselor Family Svc. Assn., Steubenville, 1973-77; instr./counselor The U. of Steubenville, 1974-78; prin. Fluharty Farms, Smithfield, Ohio, 1975-84; exec. v.p. Ind. Beef Coun./Beef Cattle Assn., Indpls., 1985-90; co-dir. Rural Policy Rsch. Inst. U. Mo., Columbia, 1990-92, dir. Rural Policy Rsch. Inst., 1992—; human resources cons., 1987—; presenter Congl. hearing/briefing testimonies. Author numerous rural policy rsch. publs., reports, briefings. Mem. Nat. Cattlemen's Assn. (exec. com. 1980-84, membership chmn. 1980-84, Outstanding Young Cattlemen Selection 1979), Am. Soc. Assn. Execs., Rural Sociol. Soc., Phi Beta Kappa, Alpha Chi. Office: U Mo Rural Policy Rsch Inst Mumford Hall Columbia MO 65211

FLUKE, WILLIAM ALBERT, pharmaceutical company safety manager, engineer; b. Lincoln, Nebr., May 24, 1942; s. William Jerome and Elizabeth (Cotta) F.; m. Constance Dianne Connelly, Sept. 10, 1966; children: Tiffany Lynn, Tanya Renee. BSEE, Duke U., 1970; diploma, DeVry Inst. Tech., Chgo., 1974. Registered profl. engr., N.C. Prodn. supr. Proctor & Gamble Co., Cin., 1970-71; safety engr. Proctor & Gamble Co., 1971-72; environ. engr. Merrell Nat. Labs., Cin., 1972-74; environ. engring. mgr. Merrell Nat. Labs., 1974-77, plant protection & safety mgr., 1977-80; mgr. safety, security Merrell Dow Pharms., Cin., 1980-83; mgr. safety, secuirty, environ. Marion Merrell Dow, 1983—, chmn. corp. safety com., 1992—; sec. Reading (Ohio) CAER, 1987—; instr. 1st aid/CPR ARC, Cin., 1978-81. Pres. Pleasant Run Farms Bowling League, Cin. 1983-86, Tri County Youth Soccer Assn., Cin. 1986-88, league dir. 1982-86; environ. chmn. Pleasant Run Farms Civic Assn., Cin., 1975-77. With USMC, 1963-67, Vietnam. Letter of Merit USMC; named Ky. Col. Commonwealth Ky., 1985. Mem. IEEE, Pleasant Run Farms Soccer Club (league rep. 1982-88). Republican. Presbyterian. Home: 12018 Freestone Ct Cincinnati OH 45240-1020 Office: Hoechst Marian Roussol 2110 E Galbraith Rd Cincinnati OH 45215

FLUSSER, JONATHAN SCOTT, SR., commercial banker; b. Waukegan, Ill., Sept. 2, 1965; s. Joseph Sidney and Leanne Elizabeth Flusser; m. Elizabeth Krauzcyk, May 7, 1994; 1 child, Jonathan Scott Jr. BA, U. Ill.; MBA, Northwestern U. V.p., divsn. head Am. Nat. Bank & Trust Co. Chgo., 1987-94; v.p., team leader Bank One, Chgo. NA, 1994—. Mem. No. Bus. Indsl. Coun., Chgo. Yacht Club (co-chmn. sponsorship com. 1994—, spl. regatta events 1995—, co-chmn. assocs. com. 1993—, sec./treas.). Congregational. Home: 1503 St Johns Ave Highland Park IL 60035 Office: Bank One Chgo NA 208 S LaSalle Chicago IL 60604

FLYGT, THOMAS REX, internist; b. Chandler, Ariz., Nov. 11, 1951; s. Helmer Harding and Gladys Nadene (Costain) F.; m. Charlene Donna Buchner, Aug. 21, 1976; children: Adrian Andrew, Austin Reed. BA, U. Wis., 1973; MD, Johns Hopkins U., 1977. Diplomate Am. Bd. Internal Medicine, Geriatrics. Intern, resident Ind. U. Med. Ctr., Indpls., 1977-81; physician Interstate Med. Ctr., St. John's Hosp., Red Wing, Minn., 1981-82, Baraboo (Wis.) Internal Medicine, St. Clare Hosp., 1982—; physician St. Mary's Regional Clinic, Baraboo, 1984—. Recorded with The Messengers gospel quartet, 1983— - Lighting the Road, Undivided, Let it Shine, The Invitation, Hearts Set Free. Fellow ACP; mem. AMA, Am. Soc. Internal Medicine, Soc. Gen. Internal Medicine, Wis. State Med. Soc., Sauk County Med. Soc. (pres. 1987), Baraboo Rotary Club (Rotarian of Yr. 1989, 95, Paul Harris Fellow 1990). Home: 1902 Jefferson St Baraboo WI 53913 Office: Baraboo Internal Medicine 637 15th St #300 Baraboo WI 53913

FLYNN, BARBARA LEE, librarian; b. Chgo., Oct. 3, 1943; d. Ralph W. and Sophie C. (Fritz) F. BA, Loyola U., 1969, MRE, 1984; MLS, Rosary Coll., 1971. Dir. film/video ctr. Chgo. Pub. Libr., 1979-93; dir. Park Forest (Ill.) Pub. Libr., 1993—. Contbr. articles to profl. jours. Bd. dirs. United Way, Park Forest. Mem. ALA (Ethnic Materials Round Table pres. 1995-96), Ill. Libr. Assn., Rotary Club. Office: Park Forest Pub Libr 400 Lakewood Park Forest IL 60466

FLYNN, CAROLYN, investment executive; b. Winchester, Mass., Nov. 2, 1960. BA, U. Calif., San Diego, 1987. Lic. series 7 securities. Jr. ptnr. Peterson Fin. Svcs., San Diego, 1988-91; investment exec. Piper Jaffray Inc., Ames, Iowa, 1991—; mem. adv. coun. Am. Inst. Bus., Des Moines, 1992—; advisor internship program Iowa State U., Ames, 1992—, Jr. Achievement, Ames, 1993—. Mem. Govt. Affairs Coun., Ames, 1992—, Jr. Achievement, Ames, 1993—. Mem. LWV, Country Club. Office: Piper Jaffray Inc 402 Main St Ames IA 50010-6150

FLYNN, PETER ANTHONY, lawyer; b. Bronxville, N.Y., July 23, 1942; s. Ralph Harold and Caroline (Lindberg) F. BA magna cum laude, Harvard U., 1963; LLB, Yale U., 1966. Bar: Ill. 1969, U.S. Dist. Ct. (no. and so. dists.) Ill. 1969, U.S. Ct. Appeals (7th cir.) 1969, U.S. Supreme Ct. 1976, U.S. Dist. Ct. (ea. dist.) Wis. 1980, U.S. Ct. Appeals (2d and 5th cirs.) 1980, U.S. Ct. Appeals (9th cir.) 1987. Asst. lect. law U. Ife, 1967-69; assoc. Jenner & Block, Chgo., 1969-75; ptnr. Cherry & Flynn, Chgo., 1976—. Mem. Olympia Fields Plan Commn., Ill., 1979-83, chmn., 1983-85; trustee Village of Olympia Fields, 1985-89; pres. Touchstone Theatre, 1990-93; active U.S. Peace Corps, 1967-69. Mem. ABA, Ill. Bar Assn., Am. Law Inst. Roman Catholic. Office: Cherry & Flynn 30 N La Salle St Ste 2300 Chicago IL 60602-2504

FLYNN, PETER FRANCIS, superintendent of schools; b. Poughkeepsie, NY, Mar. 26, 1940; s. Joseph C. and Helen R. (Cobey) F.; m. Joan Fausch, July 10, 1965; children: Kristin, Erin. BA in Polit. Sci., U. Bridgeport (Conn.), 1963; MA in Curriculum, Mich. State U., 1969, PhD in Tchr. Edn., 1971; cert. adminstrn., Pa. State U., 1975. Tchr. Regina Coeli Sch., Hyde Pk., N.Y., 1963-64, Eymard Preparatory Sch., Hyde Pk., 1964-65; tutor counselor, sr. instr. Rodman Job Corps Ctr., New Bedford, Mass., 1965-68; substitute language arts tchr. New Bedford Pub. Schs., 1968; grad. teaching asst. Coll. Edn. Mich. State U., East Lansing, 1969-71; asst. prof. elem. edn. Northeastern Ill. U., Chgo., 1971-73; program dir. Harrisburg (Pa.) Mid. Sch., 1973-75; asst. supt. schs. Harrisburg Sch. Dist., 1975-78; supt. schs. Scranton (Pa.) Sch. Dist., 1978-86, Davenport (Iowa) Community Sch. Dist., 1986-94, Fayette County (Ky.) Pub. Schs., 1994—. Past campaign chair United Way of the Quad Cities; hon. life mem. Pa. PTA. Mem. ASCD, Am. Assn. Sch. Adminstrs., Nat. Congress Parents and Tchrs. (hon. life), Urban Supts. Assn. Am. (regional v.p.), Rotary (bd. dirs.), Kappa Delta Pi, Phi Kappa Phi, Phi Delta Kappa (Educator of Yr. 1985). Office: Fayette County Pub Schs 701 E Main St Lexington KY 40502-1601

FLYNN, RAYMOND REGIS, press company executive; b. Steubenville, Ohio, July 2, 1921. BA in Econs., Notre Dame U., 1943. Rep. MacDonald Fluid Power, Rochester Hills, Mich., 1969-84; rep. Burton Press Co., Inc., Rochester Hills, 1969-84, pres., 1984—; pres. MacDonald Fluid Power, Rochester Hills, 1984—. Sgt. U.S. Army Infantry ETO, 1943-45. Decorated Bronze Star and other mil. awards. Mem. Soc. Mfg. Engrs., Am. LEgion, Saturday Club. Office: Burton Press Co Inc 2156 Avon Industrial Dr Rochester MI 48309-3610

FODREA, CAROLYN WROBEL, educational researcher, publisher, consultant; b. Hammond, Ind., Feb. 1, 1943; d. Stanley Jacob and Margaret Caroline (Stupeck) Wrobel; m. Howard Frederick Fodrea, June 17, 1967 (div. Jan. 1987); children: Gregory Kirk, Lynn Renee. BA in Elem. Edn., Purdue U., 1966; MA in Edn., U. Chgo., 1973; postgrad., U. Colo., Denver, 1986-87. Cert. elem. tchr., Ind., Ill. Tchr. various schs., Ind., Colo., 1966-87; founder, supr., clinician Reading Clinic, Children's Hosp., Denver, 1969-73; pvt. practice in reading rsch. clinic Denver, 1973-87, Deerfield, Ill., 1973—; creator of pilot presch.-kindergarten lang. devel. program Gary, Ind. Diocese Schs., 1987—, therapist lang. and reading disabilities, 1987—; pvt. practice Reading Clinic, Highland, Ind., 1987—, Deerfield, Ill., 1988—; founder Ctr. for Rsch. in Ednl. Ecology, Deerfield, Ill., 1989—; conducted Lang. Devel. Workshop, Gary, Ind. 1988; pres. Lang. Comm. Strategies for the 21st Century Corp. Cons. Firm; tchr. adult basic edn. Dawson Tech. Sch., 1990, Coll. Lake County, 1991, Prairie State Coll., 1991—, Chgo. City Colls., 1991, R.J. Daley Coll., 1991, Coll. DuPage, 1991—; condr. adult basic edn. workshops for Coll. of DuPage, R.J. Daley Coll., 1992, Ill. Lang. Devel. Literacy Program; tchr. Korean English Lang. Inst., Chgo., 1996. Author: Language Development Program, 1985, Presch. Kindergarten Lang. Devel. Program, 1988, A Multi-Sensory Stimulation Program for the Premature Baby in Its Incubator to Reduce Medical Costs and Academic Failure, 1986, Predicting At-Risk Babies for First Grade Reading Failure Before Birth, Oral Language Development Program, Grades 1 to Adult, 1988, 92; editor, pub.: ESL For Native Spanish Speakers, 1996, ESL for Native Korean Speakers, 1996. Active Graland Country Day Sch., Denver, 1981-83, N.W. Ind. Children's Chorale, 1988—. Mem. NEA, Am. Ednl. Rsch. Assn., Internat. Reading Assn., Am. Coun. for Children with Learning Disabilities, Assn. for Childhood Edn. Internat., Colo. Assn. for Edn. of Young Children, Infant Stimulation Edn. Assn., AAUW, NAFE, Nat. Assn. for Women in Career-North Shore, Art Inst. Chgo., Smithsonian Instn., Cousteau Soc., U. Chgo. Alumni Club (Chgo. area ann. fund, Pres. fund com. 1988—, numerous positions Denver area chpt. 1974-87). Roman Catholic. Office: Lang Comm Strategy 280 Crestwood Village Northfield IL 60093-3402

FODY, EDWARD PAUL, pathologist; b. Balt., June 11, 1947; s. Edward Paul and Frances Dorothy (Schultz) F.; m. Nancy June Keipe, July 19, 1974. BS, Duke U., 1969; MS, U. Wis., 1971; MD, Vanderbilt U., 1975. Diplomate Am. Bd. Pathology. Resident in pathology Vanderbilt U. Hosp., Nashville, 1975-78; fellow in chemistry U. Tex. Med. Sch., Houston, 1979-80, asst. prof. pathology, 1980-81; chief lab. VA Hosp., Little Rock, 1981-87; assoc. prof. pathology U. Ark. Med. Sch., Little Rock, 1981-87; dir. pathology Bethesda Hosp., Cin., 1987—. Editor, author: Clinical Chemistry, 1984, chpt. to book. Mem. Cin.-Kharkov Sister City Project, 1990. Fellow Coll. Am. Pathologists, Am. Soc. Clin. Pathologists; mem. AMA, Am. Assn. for Clin. Chemistry, Am. Soc. for Microbiology, Ohio Med. Assn., Cin. Acad. Medicine. Republican. Lutheran. Home: 7730 Coldstream Woods Dr Cincinnati OH 45255-5612 Office: Bethesda Hosp Dept Pathology 619 Oak St Cincinnati OH 45206-1613

FOERSTER, KENT, environmental scientist; b. Troy, N.Y., May 29, 1955; s. Bernd and Enell (Dowling) F.; m. Beth Regier Foerster, Dec. 22, 1979; children: Kelly Elizabeth, Anna Kathryn. BS in Polit. Sci. and Geography, Kans. State U., 1979; JD, Washburn U., 1989. Rsch. intern Alliance to Save Energy, Washington, 1978; adminstrv. asst. to commr., rschr. Kans. Corp. Commn., Topeka, 1979-84; exec. dir. Save the Tallgrass Prairie, Inc., Topeka, 1984-85; rschr. energy and utility Kans. Natural Resource Coun., Topeka, 1985-86; rschr. R&D adminstr. Kans. Elec. Utilities Rsch. Program, Topeka, 1986-88; rschr. free trade Washburn U. Sch. of Law, Topeka, 1988; pres. Prairie Assocs., Inc., Topeka, 1989-91; chief planning and grants Kans. Dept. Health & Environ., Topeka, 1991—. Editor: Mother Earth Handbook, 1993. Com. mem. College Hill Neighborhood Assn., Topeka, 1994—. Recipient Presdl. Environ. Action award White Ho., 1974, Environ. Citation Kans. chpt. Sierra Club, 1989-90. Mem. Solid Waste Assn. of the N.Am. (sec. Kans. chpt. 1992—), Nat. Recycling Coalition, Gamma Theta Upsilon, Phi Kappa Phi, Phi Sigma Alpha. Home: 1526 SW Mac Vicar Ave Topeka KS 66604 Office: Kans Dept of Health and Environ Forbes Field Bldg 740 Topeka KS 66620

FOERSTERLING, JAY, consultant; b. Elgin, Ill., Nov. 12, 1957; s. Vernon H. and Martha (Russell) F.; m. Donna Lynn Mueller, Dec. 5, 1987: 1 child, Peter Jay (dec.); stepchild, Tiffany N. Tate. BS, Utah State U., 1980, MBA, 1982, cert. Internat. Rels. Mktg. cons. Small Bus. Devel. Ctr., Logan, Utah, 1980-82; mgr. communications Tool & Die Inst., Park Ridge, Ill., 1983-85; mktg. coord. Spectrum Mfg., Wheeling, Ill., 1985-86; project mgr. Arthur Young/ Ernst & Young, Chgo., 1986-90; assoc. A.T. Kearney, Inc., Chgo., 1990-94; sr. mgr. McGladrey & Pullen, LLP, Davenport, Iowa, 1994—. Bd. dirs. Chgo. Archtl. Assistance Ctr., 1988—. Recipient Silver Trumpet award, Publicity Club of Chog., 1983. Mem. Am. Mktg. Assn. Office: McGladrey & Pullen LP 220 N Main St Ste 900 Davenport IA 52801

FOGAS, BRUCE SCOTT, psychologist, educator; b. Pensacola, Fla., Apr. 12, 1959; s. Ted Casler and Gretchen Elizabeth (Majercik) F.; m. Lauren Scott Mason, July 17, 1982 (div. Dec. 16, 1986); m. Karen Marie Hurst, July 6, 1991; children: Erik Peterson, Nicole Peterson, Andrew Fogas, Samuel Fogas. BA, Rutgers U., 1981; MA, Ariz. State U., 1986, PhD, 1990. Lic. psychologist. Rsch. assoc. Ariz. State U., Tempe, 1981-89; psychology intern U. N.C. Sch. Medicine, Chapel Hill, 1989-90; asst. prof. dept. psychology U. Idaho, Moscow, 1990-92; asst. prof. divsn. child and adolescent psychiatry U. S.D. Sch. of Medicine, Sioux Falls, 1992—, asst. prof. dept. pediatrics, 1994—; acting clin. dir. S.D. Univ. Affiliated Program, Vermillion, 1992-93, head psychology dept., 1993-95; dir.tng., 1994-95; lectr. WAMI Basic Med. Scis. program Wash. State U., Pullman, 1991-92; asst. prof. dept. psychology U. S.D., Vermillion, 1992—; pvt. practice Child and Family Enrichment Ctr., Moscow, Idaho, 1990-92, Univ. Physicians, Sioux Falls, 1992—; cons. Idaho Dept. Health and Welfare, Lewiston, 1991, Charter Hosp., Sioux Falls, 1993-94, Turning Point Youth Svc., Sioux Falls, 1994—, S.D. Dept. Edn., 1995, Children's Care Hosp. and Sch., 1995-96; mem. hosp. staff Sioux Valley Hosp., McKennan Hosp., Sioux Falls, 1992—, vice chair psychology sect., 1994—; workshop presenter in field. Contbr. articles to profl. jours. Mem. Sierra Club, San Francisco, 1988—, Wilderness Soc., Washington, 1989—. Grantee U. Idaho, 1992-93, U. S.D., 1993-94. Mem. APA, Assn. for Advancement of Behavior Therapy, Nat. Register of Health Svc. Providers in Psychology, S.D. Psychol. Assn. (mem.-at-large exec.com. 1996—, pres. divsn. profl. practice divsn. 1 1996-97), Psi Chi, Phi Kappa Phi. Home: 500 S Churchill Ave Sioux Falls SD 57103-2620 Office: U of South Dakota Divsn Child/Adol Psychiatry 1100 S Euclid Ave Sioux Falls SD 57105-0411

FOGEL, ROBERT WILLIAM, economist, educator, historian; b. N.Y.C., July 1, 1926; s. Harry Gregory and Elizabeth (Mitnik) F.; m. Enid Cassandra Morgan, Apr. 2, 1949; children: Michael Paul, Steven Dennis. AB, Cornell U., 1948; AM, Columbia U., 1960; PhD, Johns Hopkins U., 1963; MA, U. Cambridge, Eng., 1975, Harvard U., 1976; DSc, U. Rochester, 1987, U. de Palermo, Italy, 1994. Instr. Johns Hopkins U., 1958-59; asst. prof. U. Rochester, 1960-64; Ford Found. vis. research prof. U. Chgo., 1963-64, asso. prof., 1964-65, prof. econs., 1965-69, prof. econs. and history, 1970-75; prof. econs. U. Rochester, 1968-71, prof. econs. and history, 1972-75; Taussig research prof. Harvard U., Cambridge, Mass., 1973-74; Harold Hitchings Burbank prof. polit. economy, prof. history Harvard U., 1975-81; Charles R. Walgreen Disting. Svc. prof. Am. instns. U. Chgo., 1981—; Pitt prof. Am. history and insts. U. Cambridge, 1975-76; chmn. com. math. and statis. methods in history Math. Social Sci. Bd., 1965-72; rsch. assoc. Nat. Bur. Econ. Rsch., 1978—, dir. DAE program, 1978-91. Author: The Union Pacific Railroad: A Case in Premature Enterprise, 1960, Railroads and American Economic Growth: Essays in Econometric History, 1964, (with others) The Reinterpretation of American Economic History, 1971, (with others) Dimensions of Quantitative Research in History, 1972, (with S.L. Engerman) Time on the Cross: The Economics of American Negro Slavery, 1974, Ten Lectures on the New Economic History, 1977, (with G.R. Elton) Which Road to the Past? Two Views of History, 1983, Without Consent or Contract: The Rise and Fall of American Slavery, Vol. 1, 1989, (with others) Vols. 2-4, 1992. Gilman fellow, 1957-60, Social Sci. Rsch. Coun. fellow, 1960, Ford Found. Faculty Rsch. fellow, 1970; Faculty Rsch. grantee, 1966, NSF grantee, 1967, 70, 72, 75, 76, 78, 92, 93, Fulbright grantee, 1968, NIH grantee, 1991, 92, 93; recipient Arthur H. Cole prize, 1968; Schumpeter prize, 1971; co-recipient The Bancroft prize, 1975, Gustavus Myers prize, 1990; Nobel Prize in Econ. Sci., Nobel Foundation, 1993. Fellow Econometric Soc., Royal Hist. Soc., AAAS; corr. fellow Brit. Acad.; mem. Am. Econ. Soc., Royal Econ. Soc., Econ. History Assn. (trustee 1972-81, pres. 1977-78), Econ. History Soc., Am. Hist. Assn., Assn. Am. Historians, Social Sci. History Assn. (pres. 1980-81), Agrl. History Soc., Am. Acad. Arts and Scis., Nat. Acad. Scis., Population Assn. Am., Internat. Union for Sci. Study of Population, Phi Beta Kappa. Office: U Chgo Grad Sch Bus 1101 E 58th St Chicago IL 60637-1511

FOGELBERG, PAUL ALAN, continuing education company executive; b. St. Paul, May 18, 1951; s. Harry William and Dorothy Marie (Dokmo) F.; m. Melissa Rosanne Ormsbee, Oct. 1980; children: Emily Lauren, Julia Christine, Sara Ellen. BS, U. Minn., 1975; JD, Hamline U., 1978. Pub. affairs asst. The Pillsbury Co., Mpls., 1974-75; dir. Nat. Practice Inst., Mpls., 1978-81; CEO The Profl. Edn. Group, Inc., Minnetonka, Minn., 1981—. Mem. Hamline U. Pres. Club, Hamline U. Sch. Law Alumni Assn. (Disting. Svc. 1988, pres. 1985-86). Presbyterian. Office: The Profl Edn Group Inc 12401 Minnetonka Blvd Minnetonka MN 55305-3994

FOGERTY, JAMES EDWARD, archivist, state official; b. Mpls., Jan. 26, 1945; s. Robert P. and Ralpha Chamberlain (James) F. B.A., Coll. St. Thomas, 1968; M.L.S., U. Minn., 1972. Regional ctrs. dir. Minn. Hist. Soc., St. Paul, 1972-76, field dir., 1976-79, dep. state archivist, 1979-86, head aquisitions and curatorial dept., 1986—; sec.-treas. Midwest Archives Conf., Chgo., 1977-81, pres., 1983-85. Author: Collecting Phil Spector, 1991; editor: Oral History Collections of the Minnesota Historical Society, 1984; contbr. articles to Am. Archivist, Midwestern Archivist, History News, others. Fellow Soc. Am. Archivists; mem. Internat. Coun. Archives (U.S. rep., com. on oral sources), Oral History Assn., Midwest Archives Conf., Am. Assn. For State and Local History, Phi Alpha Theta. Office: Minn Hist Soc 345 Kellogg Blvd W Saint Paul MN 55102-1906

FOGLE, DENISE MARIE, computer consultant; b. Aurora, Ill., July 14, 1969; d. Donald Howard and Sharon Marie (Larson) F. BS in computer sci., Millikin U., 1991; MS in computer sci., Aurora U., 1995. Cons. Crowe Chizek and Co., Oak Brook, Ill., 1993—. Mem. Assn. Computing Machinery. Office: Crowe Chizek and Co One Mid Am Plaza Oak Brook IL 60522

FOGUS, KATHLEEN MARIE, nurse; b. Midland, Mich., Jan. 8, 1963; d. Kenneth Fredrick and Carolyn Hope (Southwell) Kareus; m. Brian Joseph Fogus, Aug. 6, 1988; children: Kenneth Joseph, Timothy Bryant. BS, No. Mich. U., Marquette, 1985. RN, Mich.; cert. Am. Bd. Quality Assurance and Utilization Rev. Physicians. Telemetry nurse St. Luke's Hosp., Saginaw, Mich., 1986; oncology nurse Mid Michigan Regional Med. Ctr., Midland, 1987; coronary/intensive care nurse St. Mary's Med. Ctr., 1988-89; utilization mgr. HealthPlus of Mich., Saginaw, 1989-96; quality assurance coord. Access Med. Group, Inc., 1996—. Active EPA, Saginaw, 1989—, United Way, 1994—. Home: 1797 N Hicks Rd Midland MI 48640-9472

FOLBERG, DONALD MOON, financial consultant; b. Milw., Feb. 8, 1940; s. Irving Israel and Sylvia Sybil (Goldberg) F.; m. Louetta Sheila Hartstein, Dec. 27, 1957 (div. 1973); children: Laura, Kenneth, Walter, Robert, Angelique; m. Suzanne Beatrice Moon, May 19, 1973; children: Elizabeth, Rachel. Student, Wayne State U., 1963-70, U. Wis. Ext., 1985-89; diploma, Life Underwriter Tng. Coun., 1992. CLU, ChFC, LUTCF. Sales mgr. Fahrnbacher Wholesale Toy Co., Dayton, Ohio, 1960-63; asst. state mgr. U-Haul of Mich., Redford, 1963-65; divsn. mgr. Detroit Wholesale Drug Co., 1965-70; pres., treas., CEO Picidilli Trading Co., Ltd., Chgo., Janesville, Wis., 1970-76; dist. agt. Prudential Ins. Co., Janesville, 1976-81; owner, operator Atwood Ins. Assn., Madison, Wis., 1982-89; mng. ptnr. Blue Ribbon Exposition Co., Madison, 1984-89; registered rep. Prudential Ins./Fin., Madison, 1989-94; pres., CEO DM Folberg Assocs., Ltd., Fort Atkinson, Wis., 1990—; mem. agt. adv. bd. Prudential Ins. Co., Madison, 1990-95. Mem. Madison Assn. Life Underwriters (edn. moderator 1979-95), Rock River Toastmasters (pres. 1993-94), Fort Atkinson Area C. of C., Jefferson Area C. of C., Fort Atkinson Rotary Club. Jewish. Home: 2706 Milwaukee St Madison WI 53704 Office: Folberg-Am Fin Group 509 McMillen St Fort Atkinson WI 53538

FOLEY, CASEY CHARLES, non-profit executive; b. San Francisco, May 2, 1958; s. William Joseph and Eunice Margaret (Bestwick) F. Student, Prince Georges Cmty. Coll., 1975, U. Md., 1975-76, Inst. for Devel. Enterprises, Honduras, Earlham Coll., 1983-86. Aquatic and water safety program dir. ARC, Alexandria, Va., 1974-79; adminstrv. mgr. Am. Soc. for Psychoprophylaxis, Washington, 1979-80; youth devel. advisor Peace Corps, Chile, 1981-82; micro-enterprise devel. advisor Peace Corps, Honduras, 1982-83; asst. to pres. Earlham Coll., Richmond, Ind., 1984; exec. dir. Urban Enterprise Assn. of Richmond, Ind., 1987-93; quality devel. mgr. Primex Platics Corp., Richmond, 1994; prin. Concept One Resource Developers, Richmond, 1987—; lead designer Whitewater Valley Brands Mktg. Assn., Boston, Ind., 1989-92; gov.'s del. Ind., Econ. Devel. Congress, Indpls., 1988-91; contbr. Zone Devel. Impact Study, New Sch. for Social Rsch., N.Y.C., 1992-93; neighborhood resource generation lead designer The Lilly Endowment, Indpls., 1990-93; originator, devel. agt. Richmond Farmers Market at the Depot, Richmond Homeowners Rehab. Loan Fund, Wayne County Expert Devel. Program; guest lectr. Purdue U. Sch. of Urban Design, Ind. U. East Ivy Tech U., Richmond Cmty. Sch. System, Greater Richmond Progress Com., Greater Lafayette Progress Com. Co-author: (devel. plan) Wayne County Overall Economic Development Plan, 1988, (master plan) City of Richmond Master Plan, 1990; producer: (video) The Enterprise Zone, 1993; contbr. articles to profl. jours. rep. Peace Corps Vol. Coun., Chile, U.S. Peace Corps, Washington, 1981; funding pres. Richmond Cmty. Devel. Corp., 1987; funding officer S.U.R.E., Inc., Richmond, 1988; devel. agt. Ind. Assn. Enterprise Zones, Evansville, 1993—. Recipient 1993 Ann. SURE award Sustainable Urban/Rural Enterprise, Inc., 1993; named Md. Senate scholar, 1976, Earlham Alumni scholar, 1983, 84, 85, Honor del. Model UN, 1986. Mem. Nat. Coun. Peace Corps Vets, Nat. Coun. for Urban Econ. Devel., Am. Assn. Enterprise Zones, Nat. Trust for Hist. Preservation, Nat. Assn. Neighborhoods, Co-op America, Peace Brigades Internat., Ind. Econ. Devel. Congress, Ind. Main St. Coun., Ind. Enterprise Zone Forum, Ind. Assn. for Cmty., Econ. Devel., Ind. Area Econ. Devel. Coun., U.S. Sustainable Enterprise Exch.

FOLEY, DEBORAH ANN, civil engineer; b. Salem, Mass., July 21, 1954; d. Philip Douglas and Claire Joanne (Simoneau) Hussey; children: Joseph William, Michael Thomas. BCE, U. N.H., 1976; MS mgmt. tech., Vanderbilt U., 1994. Registered profl. engr., Minn. Ensign Nat. Oceanic & Atmospheric Adminstrn., Rockville, Md., 1976-77; civil engr. Wilmington (N.C.) Dist. C.E., 1977-79; project engr. Toltz, King, Duvall, Anderson, Inc., St. Paul, 1979-81; civil engr., software devel. St. Paul Dist. C.E., 1981-83, hydraulic engr., 1983-85, project mgr., 1985-89, 1989—. Contbr. articles to profl. jours. Active Turtle Lake Sch. PTA, Shoreview, Minn., 1990-96. Mem. ASCE, Soc. Am. Mil. Engrs. (Tudor medal 1990), Order of Engrs. Office: St Paul Dist Corps Engrs 190 Fifth St Saint Paul MN 55101-1638

FOLEY, JAMES M., state legislator. State rep. dist. 81 Mo. Ho. of Reps. Home: 3274 Adie Rd Saint Ann MO 63074-3402*

FOLEY, JOHN MILES, English language and classical studies educator; b. Northampton, Mass., Jan. 22, 1947; s. Cornelius Burns and Eleanor Margaret (Broggi) F.; m. Anne Marie Conlisk, July 30, 1983; children: Elizabeth Anne, Isaac Michael. AB in Physics, Math., and Chemistry, Colgate U., 1969; MA in English Lit., U. Mass., 1971, PhD in English and Comparative Lit., 1974. Asst. prof. English Emory U., Atlanta, 1974-79; fellow Harvard U., Cambridge, Mass., 1976-77, 80-81; from assoc. prof. to prof. U. Mo., Columbia, 1981—, prof. English and classics, 1985—; vis. prof. U. Belgrade, Serbia, 1980. Author: The Theory of Oral Composition, 1988, Traditional Oral Epic, 1990, Immanent Art, 1991, The Singer of Tales in Performance, 1995, others; contbr. articles to profl. jours. Fellow Am. Folklore Soc., Russian Acad. Scis., Internat. Folklore Fellows (Finland); mem. MLA (exec. com. 1985-89, 87-91, 89-93). Office: U Mo Ctr for Studies in Oral Tradition 316 Hillcrest Hall Columbia MO 65211

FOLEY, LEO THOMAS, lawyer; b. Anoka, Minn., Oct. 25, 1928; s. John Edward and Anna Mathilda (Leubrecht) F.; m. Sally Lynn Werner, July 6, 1954 (dec. Aug. 1990); children: Jane Anne Foley Doyle, Nancy Lee Foley Nelson. BA, U. Minn., 1974; MA, Mankato State U., 1979; JD, William Mitchell Coll. Law, 1994. Cert. insdsl. security mgr. Security officer Fed. Cartridge Corp., New Brighton, Minn., 1952-54; maj. Minn. State Patrol, St. Paul, 1954-87; security mgr. Unisys, St. Paul, 1987-91; asst. Anoka County (Minn.) atty., 1994—. Bd. dirs. Citizens League, Mpls., 1972-76; mem., chmn. Planning Commn., Anoka, 1972—; mem., treas. Minn. Bicentennial Com. of U.S. Constn., St. Paul, 1984-91. With USN, 1947-52. Mem. ABA, ACLU, LWV, Minn. Bar Assn., Hennepin County Bar Assn., Minn. Justice Found., Am. Soc. for Indsl. Security, Wilderness Soc., Auditors Soc., Minn. Police and Peace Officers Assn. (life), Am. Legion, Common Cause, U. Minn. Alumni Assn., Sierra Club. Democrat. Mem. United Ch. of Christ. Home: 210 Yoho Dr Anoka MN 55303-1901

FOLEY, PATRICK J., judge; b. Dayton, Ohio, Sept. 12, 1932; s. Edward J. and Regina Ida Foley; m. Joan C. Wallace; children: Michael P., Daniel K. AS in Commerce, U. Notre Dame, 1955, JD, 1956. Atty. Dayton, 1959-90; twp. trustee Madison Twp., Montgomery County, Dayton, 1969-74; judge of county ct. Montgomery County, Huber Heights, Ohio, 1974-90; judge of common pleas ct. Montgomery County, Dayton, 1991—. Served to 1st lt. USAF, 1956-59. Recipient Disting. Jurist award Miami Valley Trial Lawyers, 1993. Mem. Ohio State Bar Assn. (com. on jud. adminstrn. and legal review 1988-95), Ohio Jud. Conf. (com. on legislation 1993-95), Archdiocese of Cin. (commn. on social action and world peace 1992-95, commn. on racism 1993-95). Democrat. Roman Catholic. Office: Common Pleas Ct 41 N Perry St Dayton OH 45422

FOLEY, SARA KAY, public relations executive; b. Des Moines, May 24, 1943; d. James and Mildred Margaret (Sandy) F.; m. Norman Gilbert Bezane, June 21, 1969; children: Foley, Conor. BS in Tech. Journalism, Iowa State U., 1965. Pub. rels. dir. Alliance of Businessmen, Chgo., 1969-70; pub. rels. mgr. Western Elec. Co., Chgo., 1966-73; publs. editor Ill. Bell Telephone Co., Chgo., 1973-74, Chgo. pub./comty. mgr., 1974-78, dist. pub. rels. and advt. mgr., 1978-83, comms. dir., 1985-92; advt. dir. Ameritech, Chgo., 1983-85; assoc. v.p. Loyola U., Chgo., 1992-93, v.p., 1993—. Bd.dirs. Publicity Club Chgo., 1970-73, Women's Aux. Sch. Art Inst., Chgo. Recipient Gold Quill award Internat. Assn. Bus. Commn., 1989. Mem. Pub. Rels. Soc. Am. (Silver Anvil award 1988, 91, 92). Home: 2609 N Southport Chicago IL 60614

FOLISI, JOSEPH CHARLES, accountant; b. Chgo., Sept. 22, 1948; s. Charles and Agnes (Battaglia) F. BBA, Loyola U., Chgo., 1971; MBA, DePaul U., Chgo., 1978. CPA; cert. fin. planner. Sr. mgr. Kpmg Peat Marwick, Chgo., 1971-79; ptnr. Folisi, Samz & Co., Schaumburg, Ill., 1979—. Trustee Twp. of Schaumburg, 1982—; contr. Rep. Orgn. Schaumburg Twp. Office: Folisi Samz & Co 1251 N Plum Grove Rd Schaumburg IL 60173-5603

FOLKERTS, KENNETH LEE, farmer, educator; b. Litchfield, Ill., July 12, 1950; s. Lester William and Hildegarde Christine (Haarstick) F.; m. Lucinda Marie DeBrun, Feb. 5, 1982; children: Megan LeAnn, Marissa Renee. BS with honors, Ea. Ill. U., 1972, MA with distinction, 1973. Grain sampler Rieke Elevator & Supply, Nokomis, Ill., 1968-73; map librarian Ea. Ill. U., Charleston, 1972-73; map editor Lincoln Lake Environ. Impact Study, Charleston, 1972-73; part-time instr. Lincoln Land C.C., Springfield, Ill., 1984—; supr. Rountree Twp., Nokomis, 1985—; farmer Harvel, Ill., 1973—; bd. dirs. Morrisonville (Ill.) Farmers Coop., 1974-87, pres., 1976-80. Contbr. poetry to mags. Mem. bd. edn. Panhandle Unit Sch. Dist. 2, Raymond, Ill., 1993—; treas. St. Raymond's Cath. Cemetery, 1991—. Recipient Golden Poet award World of Poetry, 1990. Mem. KC (dep. grand knight). Republican. Roman Catholic. Home: 13246 N 21st Ave Harvel IL 62538-9735

FOLLESE, CAROLYN J., stockbroker; b. Mpls., Oct. 9, 1938. Stockbroker Ingler & Budd, Edina, Minn., 1967-68, Summit Investment, Bloomington, Minn., 1988-94, Prin. Fin. (Hamilton/Hallum), Bloomington, 1994—. Office: Prin Fin Ste 1710 8500 Normandale Lake Blvd Bloomington MN 55437-3813

FOLLETT, JEFF L., design engineer; b. Webster City, Iowa, Oct. 30, 1954. AS, D-MACC, Ankenny, Iowa; BS in Engring. Owner Economy, Welding & Fabrication, Webster City, Iowa, 1978-85; design engr. Frigidaire Laundry, Webster City, Iowa, 1979—; mem. adv. bd. Am. Home Appliance Mfrs. Vol. local sch. Home: 214 Elm St Webster City IA 50595-2307 Office: Frigidare Laundry Products Engring 400 Des Moines St Webster City IA 50595-1407

FOLLETT, ROBERT JOHN RICHARD, publisher; b. Oak Park, Ill., July 4, 1928; s. Dwight W. and Mildred (Johnson) F.; m. Nancy L. Crouthamel, Dec. 30, 1950; children: Brian L., Kathryn R., Jean A., Lisa W. AB, Brown U., 1950; postgrad., Columbia U., 1950-51. Editor Follett Pub. Co., Chgo., 1951-55, sales mgr., 1955-58, gen. mgr. ednl. div., developer first multi-racial textbook program, first textbooks for disadvantaged, first beginning-to-read books, 1958-68, pres., 1968-78; chmn., dir. Follett Corp., 1979-94; pres. Alpine Guild, Inc., 1977—; dir. Assn. Am. Pubs., 1972-79; chmn. Sch. Pubs., 1971-73; dir. Ednl. Systems Corp.; mem. Ill. Gov.'s Commn. on Schs., 1972; pres. Alpine Rsch. Inst., Adv. Coun. on Edn. Stats., 1975-77; chmn. Book Distbn. Task Force of Book Industry, 1978-81; adv. coun. Krannert Sch. of Mgmt., 1988-93; chmn. Keystone Ranch Land Trust, 1994—. Author: Your Wonderful Body, 1961, What to Take Backpacking and Why, 1977, How to Keep Score in Business, 1978, The Financial Side of Book Publishing, 1982, rev. edit., 1988, Financial Feasibility in Book Publishing, 1988, rev. edit., 1996. Bd. dirs. Village Mgr. Assn., 1964-84, Cmty. Found. Oak Park and River Forest, 1959-86, Fund for Justice, 1974-77, For Character, 1983-93, Ctr. Book Rsch., 1985-88; trustee Inst. Ednl. Data Systems, 1965—; elected mem. Rep. State Com. from 7th dist. Ill., 1982-90, vice chmn., 1986-90; chmn. Ill. Reps. Strategic Planning Com., 1986-87; PResdl. Elector, 1988. Served in AUS, 1951-53. Mem. Chgo. Pubs. Assn. (pres. 1976-94), Mid.-Am. Pubs. Assn. (mng. dir., 1987-88, dir. 1988-93), Rocky Mountain Book Pubs. Assn., Am. Book Coun. (v.p. 1987-88), Ill. C. of C. (chmn. edn. com. 1977-79), Soc. Midland Authors, Sierra CLub, River Forest Tennis Club. Office: Alpine Guild Inc PO Box 4846 Dillon CO 80435-4846

FOLLICK, JOSEPH HOWARD, journalist; b. Terre Haute, Ind., Oct. 6, 1967; s. Jack Gerald and Mary Jo (Wheeler) F.; m. Karen Sue Sylvester, Sept. 9, 1995; children: Jacob Paul, Josie Rebecca. BA in English Lit., U. Cin., 1990. Mng. editor Daily Advocate, Greenville, Ohio, 1992-93; editorial writer Kokomo (Ind.) Tribune, 1993—; syndicated columnist Thomson News Svc., Kokomo, 1995—. Named Best Editorial Writer Hoosier State Press Assn., Indpls., 1992—, Best Columnist Ind. SPJ. Office: Kokomo Tribune 300 N Union Kokomo IN 46901

FOLSOM, LOWELL EDWIN, English language educator; b. Pitts., Sept. 30, 1947; s. Lowell Edwin and Helen Magdalene (Roeper) F.; m. Patricia Ann Jackson, Aug. 30, 1969; 1 child, Benjamin Bradford. BA, Ohio Wesleyan U., 1969; MA, U. Rochester, 1972, PhD, 1976. Chmn. English dept. Lancaster (Ohio) H.S., 1969-70, 71-72; instr. Eastman Sch. Music, Rochester, N.Y., 1974-75; vis. asst. prof. SUNY, Geneseo, N.Y., 1975-76; asst. prof. U. Iowa, Iowa City, 1976-82, assoc. prof., 1982-87, prof., 1987—, chair English dept., 1991-95; cons. Am. Coll. Testing Co., Iowa City, 1980—, Nat. Assessement of Ednl. Progress, Denver, 1980-84; dir. Walt Whitman Centennial Conf., Iowa City, 1992. Author: Walt Whitman's Native Representations, 1994 (Choice Best Acad. Book 1995); editor: Walt Whitman: The Centennial Essays, 1994, Walt Whitman: The Measure of His Song, 1981 (Choice Best Acad. Book 1982), Walt Whitman and the World, 1995; editl. bd. Walt Whitman Encyclopedia, 1994—. Recipient Rsch. award NEH, Washington, 1991-94; Rochester (N.Y.) Disting. scholar U. Rochester, 1995. Mem. MLA, Am. Lit. Assn., Am. Studies Assn., Whitman Scholars Assn. (dir. 1992—). Home: 739 Clark St Iowa City IA 52240 Office: Univ Iowa Dept English 308 EPB Iowa City IA 52242

FOLZ, CAROL ANN, financial analyst; b. Cedar Rapids, Iowa, Dec. 28, 1951; D. Glenn Frederick and Ruth Frances (McIntosh) Rullman; m. Donald Harold McElderry, Oct. 3, 1970 (div. 1981); m. David Charles Folz, Mar. 19, 1983. AA, St. Louis Community Coll., 1973, AS in Library Svcs., 1973; BSBA, U. Mo., St. Louis, 1980. Library asst. Bloomfield (Iowa) Pub. Library, 1968-70, Ferguson (Mo.) Pub. Library, 1972-77; payroll clk. U. Mo., St. Louis, 1977-79; sr. sec. U. Mo., 1979-80, acct., 1980-82, sr. acct., 1982; sr. fiscal analyst U. Mo., St. Louis, 1982-1989; payroll analyst Blue Cross and Blue Shield of Mo., St. Louis, 1990-91, sr. payroll acct., 1991; acct. Harris-Stowe State Coll., 1996—. Methodist.

FOLZ, KATHLEEN LOUISE, elementary education educator; b. Chgo.; d. Roman Louis and Dorothy Irene (Krueger) Salik; m. Thomas F. Folz. BS in Edn., Loyola U., Chgo., 1971. Tchr., fourth and fifth grades St. Veronica Sch., Chgo., 1971-73; tchr., first to third grades St. Robert Bellarmine Sch., Chgo., 1973-79; substitute tchr. St. Mary's Sch., Des Plaines, Ill., 1979-80, kindergarten and presch. tchr., 1980-86; kindergarten tchr. South Elem. Sch., Franklin Park, Ill., 1986-92, head tchr., 1989-90; first gr. tchr. South Elem. Sch., Franklin Park, 1992-93, tchr. 1st grade, 1992-93; tchr. kindergarten, 1993—; master tchr. Archdiocese of Chgo., 1982-86. Creator/tchr. kindergarten program, 1975, perceptual-motor program, 1976-95; sold 2 ideas (Spl. Spiders and Little Sprouts to The Mailbox mag., 1995, others.

FONNE, HIRAM A., dean; b. Hamelin, Germany, Apr. 1, 1932; came to U.S., 1969; s. Ichbin E. and Gretchen (Grimm) F.; m. Brunhilda Schwartzwald, Feb. 29, 1959; children: Fable, Hans. BA, U. Heidelberg, Germany, 1960; PhD, U. Heidelberg, 1964. Tchr. Ctr. for Creative Studies, Detroit, 1970-72; prof. Slippery Rock (Pa.) State Coll., 1972-75, Assumption Coll., Worcester, Mass., 1975-79, Converse Coll., Spartanburg, S.C., 1979-82; dean Mo. Inst. Tech., Kansas City, 1982—. Author: Modern American Hypocrites, 1985, Fool-Foist-Fleece, An Anthology, 1981, History of Mythology-Pinochio to Nixon, 1978. Capt. German Air Force, 1965-69. Mem. Am. Classical League, Authors League of Am., Mensa, Puppeteers of Am., Mendasity Guild (sgt. at arms 1983-86), Mo. Mimes, Rascals and Rogues Quartet. Republican. Lutheran.

FONTÁNEZ-PHELAN, SANDRA MARÍA, special education director, consultant; b. Las Piedras, P.R., June 1, 1952; came to U.S., 1955; d. Santos and Felicita (Velazquez) Fontánez; m. Patrick Mallon Phelan, July 23, 1983; children: Patrick Brandon, Cory Michael. Student, U. P.R., 1969-70; BA, U. Ill. at Chgo., 1973, MA in Edn., 1980; postgrad., So. Ill. U., Carbondale, 1986, Ill. State U., Normal, 1988—. Cert. tchr., adminstr., learning disabilities, behavior disorders, emotionally disturbed, educable mentally disabled, trainable mentally disabled, Spanish K-12, bilingual edn. and ESL tchr. Tchr. Spanish Chgo. Pub. Schs., 1974-77, tchr., counselor behavior disorders, 1977-80, tchr. home and hosp., 1980-81, resource tchr. bilingual learning disabilities, 1981, master tchr. bilingual spl. edn., 1981-83, ednl. diagnostician, 1983-85, dir. spl. edn., 1991—; tchr. communications Fermi Lab. Sci. and Engring. Program, Batavia, Ill., 1980; facilitator Chgo. Pub. Sch. Compliance and Due Process, 1985-89; grad. asst. Ill. State U., Normal, summer 1989; prin. John Hancock Elem. Sch., Chgo., 1989-91; dir. spl. edn. Chgo. Pub. Schs., 1991—; counselor Chgo. City Colls., 1982-85; hearing officer level I Ill. State Bd. Edn., Springfield, 1988—; cons. Bilingual and Spl. Edn. Issues, Chgo., 1988—; mem. adv. coun. Truman Coll., Chgo., 1988—; tchr. rep. U. Chgo. Mock Congress, Chgo., 1979, translator law offices, Chgo., 1979. Mem. adv. coun. Truman Coll., Chgo., 1988—, Dover St. Block Club, Chgo., 1983—, Sheridan Pk. Neighbors Assn., Chgo., 1983—, Our Lady of Lourdes Ch.-Womens Guild, Chgo., 1983—. Ill. Consortium for Ednl. Opportunity Ill. State U. fellow, 1989—; So. Ill. U. fellow, 1986. Mem. Nat. Conf. of P.R. Women (pres. 1990—), Ill. Coun. of Adminstrs. for Spl. Edn., Coun. for Exceptional Children, Chgo.'s Prin. Assn. (dist. 7 staff devel. 1989-90), Southwest Community Congress (edn. com. 1989-90), Nat. Assn. Bilingual Edn., Learning Disabilities Assn. Democrat. Roman Catholic. Office: Chgo Pub Schs 1819 W Pershing Rd Chicago IL 60609-2317

FONTES, WAYNE, professional football team head coach; b. New Bedford, Mass., Feb. 17, 1939; m. Evelyn; children: Mike, Scott, Kim. BA, Michigan St. Univ., 1962, MA, 1965. Defensive back N. Y. Jets; secondary coach, then defensive coord., then asst. head coach Tampa Bay Buccaneers, 1976-85; defensive coord., secondary coach Detroit Lions, from 1985, head coach, 1988—. Office: Detroit Lions 1200 Featherstone Rd Box 4200 Pontiac MI 48342

FOOTE, DAVID WARD, JR., insurance agency executive; b. Athens, Ohio, Feb. 26, 1958; s. David W. Sr. and Shirley I. (Harter) F.; m. Sue Ellen Maccombs, Oct. 9, 1983; children: Tessa, Shana, Kyle. Grad. high sch., Madison, Ohio. Dept. mgr. Sears & Roebuck, Mansfield, Ohio, 1977-78; asst. mgr. Sport & Toy City, Mansfield, 1978-79; owner, pres. David Foote Jr. Ins. Agy., Mansfield, 1979-82, Nelsonville, Ohio, 1982-83, Geneva, Ohio, 1983—. Treas. Ashtabula County Young Reps., 1990-93, Ashtabula County Concerts of Prayer, 1991—; bd. dirs. Leadership Ohio, 1992—. Mem. NRA, Ashtabula Life Underwriters (bd. dirs. 1984-85), Ashtabula Farm Bur., Life Underwriters Tng. Coun., Leadership Ashtabula, Civic Devel. Corp., Ducks Unlimited, Geneva C. of C. (v.p. 1987-89, pres. 1989-91), Jaycees (pres. Geneva chpt. 1985-86, named one of Outstanding Young Men of Am. 1982, 83, 90, Jaycee of Yr. 1984-85, Geneva's Citizen of Yr. 1991). Home: PO Box 567 Geneva OH 44041-0567 Office: PO Box 567 866 E Main St Geneva OH 44041-1334

FOOTE, SHERRILL LYNNE, retired manufacturing company technician; b. Marshalltown, Iowa, Apr. 19, 1940; d. Howard Raymond Ellis and Lois Ellen (Cooper) F.; m. Terry D. Downey, July 27, 1958 (div. 1978); children: Patrick L., Holly L. Harrelson; m. Frank H. Foote, Nov. 17, 1979 (div. 1989); stepchildren: Lauri K., Christopher R. Student, Marshalltown C.C., 1981—. Receptionist Drs. Long & Clawson, Marshalltown, 1958-59; clk. Fisher Controls, Marshalltown, 1963-73, cost estimating analyst, 1974-82, sr. cost estimator, 1982-95. Contbr. limericks Des Moines Register (Contest Winner), 1976, Marshalltown Times Rep., 1986. Mem. Mensa (contbr. Bull. Wordplay 1981—, limerick editor M-Pressions Ctrl. Iowa newsletter 1989-91, local sec. 1991-93). Democrat. Methodist. Home: 702 Ratcliffe Dr Marshalltown IA 50158-3453

FOOTE, THOMAS LYN, financial consultant; b. Bellefontaine, Ohio, July 16, 1947. BA, Ball State U., 1969. Tchr. Yorktown (Ind.) Mid. Sch., 1969-74; fin. cons. Prudential Securities Inc., Muncie, Ind., 1974-86, Raffensperger Hughes, Muncie, 1986—. Mem. ch. bd. High Street United Meth. Ch., Muncie, 1965—; chmn. bd. Sta. WIPB, Muncie, 1986—; vice chmn. Cambridge House, Muncie, 1990—; treas. Jr. Achievement, Muncie, 1990—. Mem. Kiwanis.

FORAKER, DAVID KENNETH, III, chemical engineer; b. Cedar Rapids, Iowa, May 27, 1969; s. David Kenneth and Karen (Boley) F. BS, Purdue U. Intern chemist, engr. Pum-Co., Inc., Springfield, Mo; dir.'s asst. The World Bank HSD, Washington; battery engr. Eagle-Picher Industries, Joplin, Mo.; TQM coord., R&D engr., space shuttle sry, RSS Battery Program; computer cons. Summerhouse RCFI, Walnut Shade, Mo. Contbr. articles to jours. and mags. Vol. sound tech., City of Lafayette, 1993-94. Recipient Bright Flight scholarship. Mem. AIChE, Electro Chem. Soc., Order of Engr. Office: Eagle Picher Industries C & Porter St Joplin MO 64802

FORAN, DAVID JOHN, public relations consultant; b. Milw., July 15, 1937; s. George Robert and Kathleen Terese (Melchior) F.; m. Donna Rae Skovira, June 11, 1960; children—Christopher G., Patrick D., Anne K., Mary E., Timothy M. B.S. in Journalism, Marquette U., 1959, postgrad. 1966-68. Reporter Catholic Herald Citizen, Milw., 1960, Milw. Jour., 1960-66; dir. news bur. Marquette U., Milw., 1966-74, assoc. dir. pub. relations, 1974-81, exec. dir., 1981-92, special asst. to v.p., 1992-93, instr. journalism, 1975-81; dir. pub. rels. & advtg. WMUS/WMVT-TV, Milw., 1994—; moderator TV program Sta. WTMJ, Milw., 1982-83. Past mem. bd. dirs. Wis. Heart Assn., past chmn. pub. rels. com.; chmn. adv. com. Walnut Improvement Counc.; past pres. Human Rels. Radio and TV Coun. of Milw. With U.S. Army, 1959, 61-62. Mem. Soc. Profl. Journalists-Sigma Delta Chi (past pres., chmn., dir. Milw. chpt.), Milw. Pen and Mike Club (past pres.), Milw. Press Club. Home: 209 W Lexington Blvd Milwaukee WI 53217-5017 Office: 1036 N 8th St Milwaukee WI 53233

FORBES, MILTON LESTER, biology educator, writer; b. Aruba, Netherlands Antilles, Dec. 14, 1930; s. Oliver Ferdinand and Hazel Alma (Walker) F.; m. Marcia June Boyer, Sept. 16, 1951; children: Pamella Diane Forbes Sullivan, James Alan, Stanley Lawrence, Brian Wayne. BA in Edn., U. No. Iowa, Cedar Falls, 1952, MA in education, 1953; PhD in Biol. Sci., Fla. State U., Tallahassee, 1962. Instr. biology Burlington (Iowa) High Sch., 1953-56, Ill. State U., Normal, 1956-57; assoc. prof. biology F. T. Nicholls State U., Thibodaux, La., 1960-63, Lamar U., Beaumont, Tex., 1963-70; prof. sci. U. of the Virgin Islands, St. Croix, 1970-91; writer Glenwood, Iowa, 1991—. Author: The Messiah, 1989, Out of the Mists of Time: Who Wrote the Bible and Why, 1992; contbr. articles to profl. jours. NSF grad. fellow, 1958-59. Mem. AAAS, Sigma Xi. Mem. Unitarian Universalist Ch.

FORBES-RICHARDSON, HELEN HILDA, state agency administrator; b. Detroit, July 26, 1950; d. Henry and Trunette (Adams) Forbes; m. Leon Richardson (div.); 1 child, Leon Ronald Jr. BA in Edn. and Human Svcs., U. Detroit, 1972; MPA, Harvard U., 1989. Cert. tchr. Mich. Substitute tchr. Detroit Bd. Edn., 1972-75; assistance payment worker State Dept. Social Svcs., Detroit, 1976-79, supr. assistance payment, 1979-85, section mgr., 1985—; adminstrv. asst. to chief dep. dir. Wayne County Dept. Social Svcs., Detroit, 1989-90; mem. case rev. com. Mich. Dept. Social Svcs. Gen. Assistance, 1985, 87, labor rels. subcom., quality initiative task force tng. com., 1985; co-chairperson quality initiative error reduction com. and conf. planning com.; mem. tng. com. quality initiative task force Mich. Dept. Social Svcs., 1984, client svc. subcom., 1989—, coord. employee recognition program, 1989-90, chmn. procedure com., Grand River Warren local office, 1990—, coord. state employee recognition program, Wayne County, 1980-90; chair security plan com. client info. system County of Wayne, 1989, mem. UAW Secondary Contract Negotiations Team, 1988; mem. conf. planning com. Mich. County Social Svcs. Assn., 1988; chairperson Grand River/Warren Procedures Com., 1990, employee recognition awards program level 1 Grand River/Warren Dept. Social Svcs., 1990; pres. Forbes-Richardson Ltd., 1990—, mgmt. cons., 1990; owner, editor Adams-Forbes Pub. Co., Detroit. Coordinator Social Svc. United Found. Dr., Lafayette local office 1985, Social Svc. Black United Fund Dr. 1987, speaker Nat. Polit. Congress Black Women, 1986; student project coord. Wayne County Community Coll., Wayne County Dept. Social Svcs., 1989; coord. scholarship project Mary Holmes Coll. Spirit of Detroit Leadership award, 1985. Mem. Am. Pub. Welfare Assn. (planning com. 1986), Am. Legion Aux. Office: Mich Dept Social Svcs 1200 6th St Detroit MI 48226

FORBIS, BRYAN LESTER, state agency administrator; b. Jefferson City, Mo., Aug. 14, 1957; s. Lewis Wagner and Thelma Rose (Thompson) F.; m. Mary Beth Dobbs, Nov. 1987. BA in Polit. Sci. with honors, U. Mo., 1979, MA in Polit. Sci., 1981. Rsch. asst. Mo. Office of Lt. Gov., Jefferson City, 1980; teaching asst. U. Mo., Columbia, 1980-81; mgmt. analysis specialist I, Mo. Div. Family Svcs., Jefferson City, 1981-83; mgmt. analysis specialist II, Mo. Div. Med. Svcs., Jefferson City, 1983-85; asst. to dir. Mo. Div. of Aging, Jefferson City, 1985-89, dir., 1992-93, special asst. to dir., 1996—; asst. dir. Mo. Dept. of Natural Resources, 1989, dir. program coordination, 1989-90, dir. policy devel., 1991-92; dep. dir. Mo. Div. Child Support Enforcement, 1993-95; spl. asst. Mo. Divsn. Aging, 1995—. Mem. Capital City Coun. on Arts, Jefferson City, 1985-89, Mo. Mansion Preservation Inc., Jefferson City, 1985-89; steering com. March of Dimes, Jefferson City, 1986; mem. Conservation Fedn. of Mo., 1992—; sec. U. Mo. Arts & Scis. Leaders, 1996—. Named One of Outstanding Young Men of Am., 1985, 86; curator scholar U. Mo., 1975, 77, 78, William Bradshaw scholar U. Mo., 1979. Mem. ASPA, Mo. Inst. Pub. Adminstrn., Acad. Polit. Sci., Capital Area Mo. U. Alumni Assn. (exec. asst., pres. bd. dirs., dist. bd. dirs. 1992—), Phi Beta Kappa, Pi Sigma Alpha, Omicron Delta Kappa. Republican. Lutheran. Club: Pachyderms (Jefferson City). Home: 935 Fairmount Blvd Jefferson City MO 65101-3544 Office: Mo Divsn Aging 615 Howertown Jefferson City MO 65109

FORBUSH, ALBERT H., company owner; b. Youngstown, Ohio, Jan. 11, 1955. Journeyman degree, Warren Harding, 1977. Journeyman machinist, Ohio. Machinist, foreman Machine Design Svc., Boardman, Ohio, 1973-83; machinist Hazenstab, Ellsworth, Ohio, 1984-89; owner Forbush Machine, Youngstown, Ohio, 1989—. Democrat. Presbyterian. Office: Forbush Machine 27 N West Ave Youngstown OH 44502-1329

FORCINIO, HALLIE EUNICE, editor; b. Cleve., Aug. 25, 1952; d. Quentin L. and Bertha W. (Bolman) Schirch; m. Robert K. Forcinio, Jan. 24, 1981. BA cum laude, Baldwin-Wallace Coll., Berea, Ohio, 1974. Traffic mgr. Jaeger Advt., Berea, 1975; editorial asst. Arthur G. McKee & Co., Cleve., 1975-78; comm. asst. Work Wear Corp., Cleve., 1978-82; assoc. editor HBJ Publs. (name now Advanstar Comm.), Cleve., 1982-84, mng. editor, 1984-91, editor in chief, 1991-92; freelance writer, editor Cleve., 1992—. Mem. Friends Cleve. Pub. Libr. Mem. Internat. Assn. Bus. Communicators (sec., editor, facilitator), Am. Soc. Bus. Press Editors, Inst. Packaging Profls. (sec., v.p. Cleve. chpt.), Internat. Packaging Press Orgn., Cleve. Zool. Soc., Cleve. Mus. Natural History, Kappa Phi (editor 1976-83, pres. 1983-87, 89-91). Republican. Lutheran.

FORD, CONSTANCE ELAINE, electroneurodiagnostic technician; b. Greenfield, Ohio, Aug. 27, 1938; d. Oram Clyde and Mabel Elizabeth (Byrd) Hardgrow; m. Donald Eugene Lowery (div.); children: Steven Dwayne Hardgrow, Barbara Joanne Lowery; m. David Melvin Ford; children: Leslie Rene Ford Lee, David Cabell Ford. Degree in mng. cosmetology, Poro

Sch., Columbus, Ohio, 1961. Beautician Ken's Hair Designs, Columbus, Ohio; nurses aid Ohio State U. Hosp., Columbus, psychiat. attendant, EEG technician; nurse Columbus; electroneurodiagnostic technician Neurol. Assocs., Inc., Columbus; polysomnographic technician Riverside Meth. Hosp., Columbus. Vol. Greenfield Hist. Soc., 1994—; treas. Ohio Soc. EEG Technicians; ambassador to China. Democrat. Ch. of Christ. Home: 116 S Wheatland Ave Columbus OH 43204 Office: Neurol Assocs Inc 931 Chatham Ln Columbus OH 43221

FORD, DAVID CLAYTON, lawyer; b. Hartford City, Ind., Mar. 3, 1949; s. Clayton I. and Barbara J. (McVicker) F.; m. Joyce Ann Bonjour, Aug. 22, 1970; children: Jeff, Matthew, Kelly, Andrew. BA in Polit. Sci., Ind. U., 1973; JD, Ind. U., 1976, MBA Internat. Trade, Ball State U., 1988. Bar: Ind. 1975, U.S. Dist. Ct. (so. dist.) Ind. 1976, U.S. Dist. Ct. (no. dist.) Ind. 1977, U.S. Tax Ct. 1988, U.S. Supreme Ct. 1983. City atty. City of Montpelier, Ind., 1977-79; town atty. Town of Shamrock Lakes, Ind., 1977—; gen. counsel, internat. trade dir. Ind. Farm Bur. Inc., 1988—; chief dep. prosecutor, Blackford County, 1979; pros. atty. 71st Jud. Cir., Blackford County, Hartford City, Ind., 1983-86; mem. com. on character and fitness State Bd. of Law Examiners. Rep. nominee for 19th Dist. Ind. State Sen., 1986, elected 1994, Ind. Agrl. Leadership Program, 1990-91; bd. dir. Blackford County Young Reps., 1977-82, pres., 1977-78; chmn. Town of Shamrock Lakes Rep. Com., 1983, Ind. Lawyers for Bush and Quayle, 1988; vice chmn. Blackford County Rep. Cen. Com., 1978-82, chmn. 1993—; precinct committeeman Blackford County, Licking 7, 1980—; mem. Ind. 10th Congl. Dist. Rep. Caucus, 1978-82, U.S. Edn. Appeals Bd., U.S. Dept. Edn., 1982-90, Nat. Def. Execs. Res. 1983—; former mem. bus. adv. com. to Congressman Dan Burton; chmn. bus., industries and devel. com. Ptnrs. of Ams., Ind. chpt., 1983-84; mem. Blackford County Bd. Aviation Commrs., 1977-83, pres., 1979-83; bd. dirs. Dollars for Scholars, Blackford County, 1977—, v.p., 1977—; mem. St. John's-Riedman Meml. Sch. Bd., 1978-82, pres., 1978-82; mem. Blackford County Sheriff's Merit Bd., 1981-82. Named Man of Yr. Hartford City C. of C., 1978, Sagamore of the Wabash, Gov. Otis Bowen, 1978; Hon. Sec. of State Edwin J. Simcox, 1981; participant Rotary group study exch. to São Paulo, Brazil, 1981; named Outstanding Young Man of Am. U.S. Jaycees, 1982. Mem. ABA, Assn. Trial Lawyers' Am., Ind. State Bar Assn., Blackford County Bar Assn., World Trade Club Ind., Mensa, Sigma Iota Epsilon. Home: 2776 S Angling Pike Hartford City IN 47348-9752 Office: 210 W Main St Hartford City IN 47348-2209

FORD, E(MMA) JANE, public relations executive; b. Anderson, Ind., Mar. 25, 1918; d. Kenneth E. and Emma (Thomas) Griffith. BGS, Ind. U.-Purdue U. at Indianapolis, 1982. Advt. dir. Farm Bur. Ins., Indpls., 1956-73; pub. relations dir. Brulin & Co., Indpls., 1973-76; pub. info. dir. Ind. Arts Commn., Indpls., 1976-79, Indpls. Art League, Indpls., 1982-84; ret., 1984—; talent coord., moderator Indy Internat. Cable TV, Indpls.; past vice chmn. Svc. Corps of Retired Execs. Author: (play) An Evening With Zane Gray, 1985; sculpture Indpls. Mus. Art. Guide Eiteljorg Mus. Am. Indian and Western Art; nat. chmn. ann. conv. Women's Overseas Svc. League, 1994. Named Ad Woman of Yr. Ad Club of Ind., 1961. Mem. AAUW (assoc. editor), Nat. Soc. Arts and Letters (pres. Indpls. chpt. 1996-97, Indpls. schs. poetry chair), Women in Comms. (past sec.), Women's Press Club Ind. (past sec.), Pub. Rels. Soc. Am. (accredited). Republican. Episcopal.

FORD, FREDERICK ROSS, university official; b. Kentland, Ind., Mar. 25, 1936; s. Merl Jackson and Marie Jeanne (Ross) F.; m. Mary A. Harrison, May 31, 1959; children—Lynne Elizabeth, Steven Harrison, Katherine Jeannette. B.S. in Mech. Engring., Purdue U., 1958, M.S., 1959, Ph.D., 1963. Asst. to bus. mgr. Purdue U., West Lafayette, Ind., 1959-61, asst. to v.p., treas., 1961-65, asst. bus. mgr., 1965-69, bus. mgr., asst. treas., 1969-74, exec. v.p., treas., 1974—; Lafayette, Circle Income Shares, Indpls.; trustee Tchrs. Ins. and Annuity Assn., N.Y.C., 1982—. Treas. capital funds found. United Way, Lafayette, 1984-85. Recipient Disting. Bus. Officer award, 1989. Mem. Council on Govtl. Relations (bd. mgmt. 1984-90), Nat. Assn. Coll. and Univ. Bus. Officers (bd. dirs. 1980-83, sec. 1982-83), Central Assn. Coll. and Univ. Bus. Officers (exec. com. 1976-81, pres. 1979-80), Lafayette C. of C. (pres. 1978-79; chmn. edn. relations com. 1984-85), Delta Upsilon. Republican. Presbyterian. Lodge: Rotary. Avocations: sailing; fishing. Home: 160 Creighton Rd West Lafayette IN 47906-2102 Office: Purdue U West Office Exec VP and Treas Hovde Hall Of Adminstr West Lafayette IN 47907

FORD, GARY HENRY, computer engineer; b. Chgo., Oct. 26, 1952; s. Andrew and Mary Ann (Stewart) F.; m. Marilyn Ellen Aspell, Sept. 22, 1984; children: Thomas Gary, Marissa Lyn. Cert., DeVry Tech. Inst., 1976. Customer engr. Calif. Computer Products, Anaheim, 1976, Incoterm, Northborough, Mass., 1977-79; field svc. engr. Honeywell Info. Systems, Indpls. and Chgo., 1979-81; sr. hardware engr. Automatic Data Processing, Hoffman Estates, Ill., 1981—. Charter mem. Statue of Liberty/Ellis Island Found., 1984—; mem. Nat. Rep. Congl. Com., 1988, Rep. Party, 1988. Mem. DeVry Inst. Alumni Assn., Heritage Found. Office: ADP 1950 Hassell Rd Schaumburg IL 60195-2308

FORD, GORDON BUELL, JR., English language, linguistics, and medieval studies educator, author, retired hospital industry financial management executive; b. Louisville, Sept. 22, 1937; s. Gordon Buell Sr. and Rubye (Allen) F. AB summa cum laude in Classics, Medieval Latin, and Sanskrit, Princeton U., 1959; AM in Classical Philology and Linguistics, Harvard U., 1962, PhD in Linguistics, 1965; postgrad., U. Oslo, 1962-64, U. Sofia, Bulgaria, 1963, U. Uppsala, Sweden, 1963-64, U. Stockholm, 1963-64, U. Madrid, 1963. Yeager, Ford, and Warren Found. Disting. prof. Indo-European, Classical, Slavic and Baltic linguistics, Sanskrit, and Medieval Latin Northwestern U., Evanston, Ill., 1965—; Lybrand, Ross Bros., and Montgomery Found. Disting. prof. English and linguistics U. No. Iowa, Cedar Falls, 1972—; sr. exec. v.p. for real estate fin. mgmt. Gorgay, Inc.-A Real Estate Co., Louisville, 1976-77; sr. exec. v.p. for reimbursement and rates accounting fin. mgmt. Humana, Inc., The Hosp. Co., Louisville, 1978-93; dir. Southeastern Investment Trust, Inc., Louisville, 1978-93; ret., 1993; rsch. prof. The Southeastern Investment Trust, Inc. Rsch. Found., Louisville, 1976—; vis. prof. Medieval Latin, U. Chgo., 1966—; vis. prof. linguistics U. Chgo., Downtown Ctr., 1966—; prof. English evening divs. Northwestern U., Chgo., 1968-69, prof. anthropology, 1971-72. Author: The Ruodlieb: The First Medieval Epic of Chivalry from Eleventh-Century Germany, 1965, The Ruodlieb: Linguistic Introduction, Latin Text with a Critical Apparatus, and Glossary, 1966, The Ruodlieb: Facsimile Edition, 1965, 3d edit. 1968, Old Lithuanian Texts of the Sixteenth and Seventeenth Centuries with a Glossary, 1969, The Old Lithuanian Catechism of Baltramiejus Vilentas (1579): A Phonological, Morphological, and Syntactical Investigation, 1969, Isidore of Seville's History of the Goths, Vandals, and Suevi, 1966, 2d edit. 1970, The Letters of Saint Isidore of Seville, 1966, 2d edit. 1970, The Old Lithuanian Catechism of Martynas Mazvydas (1547), 1971, others; translator: A Concise Elementary Grammar of the Sanskrit Language with Exercises, Reading Selections, and a Glossary (Jan Gonda), 1966, The Comparative Method in Historical Linguistics (Antoine Meillet), 1967, A Sanskrit Grammar (Manfred Mayrhofer), 1972; contbr. numerous articles to many scholarly jours. Appointed to Hon. Order Ky. Cols. (life). Mem. Linguistic Soc. Am. (life, Sapir life patron), Internat. Linguistic Assn., Societas Linguistica Europaea (charter, life), Am. Philol. Assn. (life), Classical Assn. Middle West and South (life), Medieval Acad. Am. (life), MLA (life), Am. Assn. Tchrs. Slavic and East European Langs., Am. Assn. Advancement Slavic Studies (life), Assn. for Advancement Baltic Studies (life), Inst. Lithuanian Studies (life), Tchrs. of English to Speakers of Other Langs. (charter, life), SAR (life), Princeton Club (N.Y.C., Chgo.), Princeton Alumni Assn. (Louisville), Harvard Club (N.Y.C., Chgo., Louisville, Lexington, Ky.), Pres.'s Soc. Bellarmine Coll. (life), Louisville Country Club, KC (life), Phi Beta Kappa (life). Baptist. Home: 3619 Brownsboro Rd Louisville KY 40207-1863 also: PO Box 2693 Clarksville Br Jeffersonville IN 47131-2693

FORD, JACK, state legislator; m. to Cynthia Ford; children: Ryan, Jessica, Jacqueline. BA, Ohio State U.; MPA, Univ. Toledo. Mem. Ho. of Reps., Columbus, Ohio, 1994—. past city councilman City of Toledo, former pres. Toledo coun.; instr. U. Tpoledo. Former mem. citizens' adv. bd. Toledo Mental Health Ctr.; chmn. bd. Cordelia Martin Mental Health Home, former pres. Mental Health Agy. Ins. Trust, pres. and founder Substance Abuse Svc.; current mem. Toledo Symphony Bd.

FORD, JEAN ELIZABETH, former English language educator; b. Branson, Mo., Oct. 5, 1923; d. Mitchell Melton and Annie Estella (Wyer) F.; m. J.C. Wingo, 1942 (div. 1946; m. E. Syd Vineyard, 1952 (div. 1956); m. Vincent Michel Wessling, Feb. 14, 1983 (div. Dec. 1989). AA in English, L.A. City Coll., 1957; BA in English, Calif. State U., 1959; MA in Higher Edn., U. Mo., 1965. Cert. English tchr. Dance instr. Arthur Murray Studios, L.A., 1948-51; office mgr. Western Globe Products, L.A., 1951-55; pvt. dance tchr., various office jobs L.A., 1955-59; social dir. S.S. Matsonia, 1959; social worker L.A. County, 1959-61; 7th grade instr. Carmenita Sch. Dist., Norwalk, Calif., 1961-62; English instr. Leadwood (Mo.) High Sch., 1962-63; dance instr. U. Mo., 1963-66, SW Mo. State U., 1966-68, NW Mo. State U., 1970-76, Johnson County Community Coll., 1976-77; tax examiner IRS, Kansas City, Mo., 1978-80; tax acct. Baird, Kurtz & Dobson, Kansas City, Mo., 1981; substitute tchr. various sch. dists., 1976-85; dance chmn. Mo. Assn. Health, Phys. Edn. and Recreation, 1965-66, 68-69, ctrl. dist. AAHPER, 1972-73; vis. author Young Author's Conf., Ctrl. Mo. State U., 1987, 88, 89; speaker Am. Reading Assn., Grandview, Mo., 1990; real estate sales agt., Kansas City, 1980-84; real estate sales broker, Mo. and Kans., 1990—; pvt. practice tax acct., dance tchr., 1984—. Author, pub.: Fish Tails and Scales, 1982, 2d edit., 1988. Mem. Village Presbyn. Ch., Prairie Village, Kans. Mem. Am. Contract Bridge League, Kansas City Ski Club. Democrat. Presbyterian. Home and Office: 9528 Manning Ave Kansas City MO 64134-2229

FORD, JERRY LEE, service company executive; b. Muncie, Ind., July 11, 1940; s. Robert Thomas and Thelma Adrien (Stricker) F.; m. Margaret Annette Bailey, Sept. 10, 1966; children: Duane A., Diana K., Brenda D. BS in Acctg., Ind. U., 1962. CPA, Ind. Sr. auditor Peat Marwick, Main, Indpls., 1964-67; contr. Georgia Kraft Co., Rome, Ga., 1967-71; asst. dir. acctg. Gen. Mills, Inc., Mpls., 1971-75, sys. contr. foods group; v.p. fin., contr. Ship N Shore subs. Gen. Mills, Inc., Phila., 1979-80; v.p. fin., treas. Poppin Fresh Pies divsn. Pillsbury Co., Mpls., 1980-81; v.p. fin. foods group Pillsbury Co., Mpls., 1981-84, v.p. adminstrn. svcs., 1984-87; COO, exec. dir. Lindquist & Vennum, Mpls., 1988-93; chief operating officer Comdisco Network Svcs., Minnetonka, Minn., 1994—; instr. Def. Contract Audit Agy. Exec. Program, Memphis 1987,. Co-author: Controllers Handbook, 1984, 92. Bd. dirs. Min. Acctg. Aid Soc., 1986-88, 90-94, Mpls. YMCA, 1974-78. Mem. Fin. Execs. Inst. (chpt. pres., nat. bd. dirs.), Inst. Mgmt. Accts. (nat. v.p. 1984-85), Inst. Cert. Mgmt. Accts. (cert., chmn. bd. dirs. 1982-84), Ind. U. Alumni Assn. (mem. exec. bd. Bloomington chpt. 1993—), N.W. Racquet Club. Republican. Methodist.

FORD, JOHN BATTICE, III, business executive; b. Detroit, July 3, 1924; s. John Battice and Katharine (Tanner) F.; m. Peggy Powers, July 12, 1980; 1 child, John Battice IV. BS, Yale U., 1949. Adminstrv. asst. Nat. Bank of Detroit, 1950-53; asst. treas. Huron Portland Cement Co., Detroit, 1953-58, treas., 1958-59; owner, pres. Tradco/Detroit, Inc., 1960-69; pres. H.M. Robins Co., 1961-67; pres. Gentrex, Inc., 1968-82; pres., owner John Ford & Assocs., 1982—. Bd. dirs. Cottage Hosp./Henry Ford Health System; past chmn. S.E. Mich. chpt. ARC; chmn. Friends of Riverside Theater, Vero Beach, Fla. Mem. Founders Soc. Detroit Inst. Arts, U.S. C. of C., Detroit Bd. Commerce. Episcopalian. Clubs: Yondotega, Country of Detroit; Grosse Pointe (Mich.); Circumnavigators, Little Harbor, Little Traverse Yacht, John's Island. Home: 43 De Petris Way Grosse Pointe MI 48236-3701 Office: John Ford & Assocs 19818 Mack Ave Grosse Pointe MI 48236-2506

FORD, LOUIS H., state legislator; b. Miss., Mar. 12, 1935. Mgr. Pest Control Co. State rep. dist. 58 Mo. Ho. of Reps., 1983—. Home: 3229 N 20th St Saint Louis MO 63107-3538*

FORD, MARY ALICE, city employee; b. Eudora, Ark., Apr. 24, 1932; d. Dave and Emma (Woodruff) Bess; m. Sanceola Ford, June 10, 1956; children: Michael Dennis, Ronald Kirby, Lisa Cassandra, Kimberly Corinta. Student, Kennedy-King Coll., Chgo., Wilson Jr. coll., Chgo., Columbia Coll., Chgo. Instr. merchandising Montgomery Ward, Chgo., 1947-53; keypunch operator U.S. Treasury Dept., Chgo., 1953-56; tchr. asst. Chgo. Pub. Schs., 1962-70; internat. teller Harris Bank, Chgo., 1978-84; elderly aide clk. City of Chgo., 1987—. Songwriter; clothing designer; poet. Treas. Mich. Ind. Cmty. Assocs., Chgo., 1988—; core team leader Greater Grand Crossing Organizing Com., Chgo., 1985—; pres. sick and shut-in com. St. James Luth. Ch., Chgo., 1985—. Recipient Golden Poets award World of Poetry, 1989, 90, Poet's award Internat. Soc. Poets, 1995, Neighborhood Garden award City of Chgo., 1994. Mem. Christian Women's Club. Home: 7708 S Michigan Ave Chicago IL 60619

FORD, QUENTIN K., manufacturing company executive; b. Chgo., Mar. 18, 1934. BSBA, Northwestern U., 1959. Pres. Mfg. Control Assocs., Inc., Palatine, Ill., 1975—. Contbr. articles to profl. jours.; inventor in field of distbn. requirements planning. Dist. chmn. Boy Scouts Am., Chgo., 1959-89; sr. layperson St. Phillips Episcopal, Palatine, 1947—. Fellow Am. Prodn. and Inventory Control Soc. (cert. practitioner inventory mgmt.); me. Assn. for Mfg. Excellence. Office: Mfg Control Assocs Inc 461 E Balsam Ln Palatine IL 60067-3776

FORD, THOMAS BRADY, architect, consultant; b. Columbus, Ohio, Nov. 9, 1952; s. Paul Joseph and Berenice Bridget (Brady) F.; m. Lori Ann Hart, Sept. 1, 1979; children: Hart Ashley Elizabeth, Paul Joseph J. BS in Architecture, Kent (Ohio) State U., 1980, BArch, 1981. Registered arch., Ohio, Ky., Pa., Mo., Wis., Ill., Mich., N.C.; cert. Nat. Coun. Archtl. Registration Bds. Intern arch. J.T. Brown, Solon, Ohio, 1981-82, R.A. Busser & Assocs., Archs., Columbus, 1982-84; constrn. adminstr. A.E.T. & P. Archs., Columbus, 1984-85, project arch., 1985-87, prin., 1987-89; arch., project adminstr. Office State Arch., Columbus, 1989—; sec. Capitol Square Rev. and Adv. Bd., Columbus, 1990—. Treas. Short North Bus. Assn., Columbus, 1983; chmn. Luminaries, League Against Child Abuse, Columbus, 1988; bd. dirs. Planned Parenthood Ctrl. Ohio, Columbus, 1989. Recipient Gov.'s All Star award State of Ohio, 1993. Mem. AIA (bd. dirs. Columbus chpt. 1987-92, pres. 1992-93), Nat. Trust for Hist. Preservation, Ohio Hist. Found., Columbus Mus. Art, Leo Yassenoff Jewish Ctr., Capital Club, Univ. Club Columbus. Republican. Roman Catholic. Home: 893 Francis Ave Columbus OH 43209 Office: Office of State Arch 30 E Broad St 35th Fl Columbus OH 43266-0403

FORD, WILLIAM CLAY, automotive company executive; b. Detroit, Mar. 14, 1925; s. Edsel Bryant and Eleanor (Clay) F.; m. Martha Firestone, June 21, 1947; children: Martha, Sheila, William Clay, Elizabeth. BS, Yale U., 1949. Sales and advt. staff Ford Motor Co., 1949; indsl. relations, labor negotiations with UAW, 1949; quality control mgr. gas turbine engines Lincoln-Mercury Div., Dearborn, Mich., 1951, mgr. spl. product ops., 1952, v.p., 1953, gen. mgr. Continental Div., 1954, group v.p. Lincoln and Continental Divs, 1955, v.p. product design, 1956-80; dir., 1948—, vice chmn. bd., 1980-89; mem. fin. com. Ford Motor Co., 1987—; pres., owner Detroit Lions Profl. Football Club. Chmn. emeritus Edison Inst.; hon. life trustee Eisenhower Med. Ctr. Mem. Soc. Automotive Engrs. (asso.), Automobile Old Timers, Econ. Club Detroit, Masons, K.T., Phelps Assn., Psi Upsilon. Office: Ford Motor Co Design Ctr PO Box 6012 Dearborn MI 48121-6012 also: Detroit Lions 1200 Featherstone Rd Pontiac MI 48342-1938

FOREMAN, JAMES LOUIS, retired judge; b. Metropolis, Ill., May 12, 1927; s. James C. and Anna Elizabeth (Henne) F.; m. Mabel Inez Dunn, June 16, 1948; children: Beth Foreman Banks, Rhonda Foreman Kressenberg, Nanette Foreman Love. BS in Commerce and Law, U. Ill., 1950, JD, 1952. Bar: Ill. Ind. practice law Metropolis, Ill.; ptnr. Chase and Foreman, Metropolis, until 1972; state's atty. State of Ill., Massac County; asst. atty. gen. State of Ill.; chief judge U.S. Dist. Ct. (so. dist.) Ill., Benton, 1979-92, sr. status, 1992—. Pres. Bd. of Edn., Metropolis. With USN, 1945-46. Mem. Ill. State Bar Assn., Metropolic C. of C. (past pres.). Republican. Home: 38 Hilanoa-East Dr Metropolis IL 62960-2533 Office: US Dist Ct 301 W Main St Benton IL 62812-1362

FOREMAN, JOHN RICHARD, newspaper editor; b. Decatur, Ill., Sept. 3, 1952; s. Forrest Earl and Susan Adelaide (Jenkins) F.; m. Sharon Ann Koeberlein, Sept. 21, 1973; children: Shannon Denise, Robert Forrest. BS, U. Ill., 1977. Reporter Champaign-Urbana (Ill.) News Gazette, 1977-81, city editor, 1981-85, mng. editor, 1985-87, editor-in-chief, 1987—; v.p. Profl. Impressions Media Group, Champaign, 1989—. Contbr. articles to profl. jours. Bd. dirs. Friends of Univ. Ill. Libr., Champaign, 1989-91; mem. Ill. Gen. Assembly Task Force on Access to Govt., 1991. Mem. Am. Soc. Newspaper Editors, Ill. Press Assn. (bd. dirs. 1989—, v.p. 1994—, James C. Craven award for freedom of press 1994), Ill. AP Editors Assn. (exec. com., pres. 1993), Mid-Am. Press Inst. (bd. dirs. 1991—, chmn. 1995), Soc. Profl. Journalists (state chmn. Project Sunshine). Office: The News-Gazette PO Box 677 15 E Main St Champaign IL 61820-3625

FORESMAN, JAMES BUCKEY, geologist, geochemist, industrial hygienist; b. Neosho, Mo., Apr. 8, 1935; s. Frank James and Helen Blackburn (Buckey) F.; m. Barbara Ellen Runkle, Aug. 13, 1961; children: James Runkle, Robert Buckey. BSBA, BS, Kans. State U., 1962; MS, U. Tulsa, 1970. Cert. petroleum geologist; cert. insp., mgmt. planner, contractor, supr. in asbestos control EPA. From geologist, geochemist to staff dir. geology N.Am.-S.Am. Phillips Petroleum Co., Denver, Midland, Tex., Bartlesville, Okla., 1962-83; petroleum cons. Bartlesville, 1983-84; v.p. Mopro, Inc., Lyons, Mich., 1985-87; indsl. hygienist, asst. dir. phys. plant Pittsburg (Kans.) State U., 1987—; geochemistry advisor Joint Oceanographic Instsn. for Deep Earth Sampling, 1974-75; ocean drilling advisor NSF, Washington, 1974-75; indsl. rep. for joint ventures with USSR, 1978; rep. Univ.-Indsl. Assoc. Programs, N.Y., Tex., Ariz., Mass., Calif., Cambridge (Eng.), 1981-83; citizen amb. programs Environ. Del. to Russia, Latvia, and Estonia, 1992. Contbr. articles to periodicals, jours., chpts. to books. Com. mem. Boy Scouts Am., Bartlesville, 1975-82; bd. dirs. U.S. Little League, Bartlesville, 1975; smoke jumper U.S. Dept. Agr., Forest Svc. Sgt. USMC, 1954-57, Korea. Recipient Disting. Svc. award City of Bartlesville, 1977. Mem. Am. Assn. Petroleum Geologists (founding mem. energy minerals divsn., charter mem. divsn. environ. geologists), Am. Soc. Safety Engrs., Am. Conf. Govtl. Indsl. Hygienists, Am. Indsl. Hygiene Assn. (bd. dirs., past pres.), Kiwanis. Republican. Presbyterian. Home: 1506 Woodland Ter Pittsburg KS 66762-5551

FORGUS, RONALD HENRY, psychology educator; b. Cape Town, Republic of South Africa, May 18, 1928; came to U.S., 1951; s. William and Marie (Kleinhans) F.; divorced; children: Michael, Sandra, Tristan, Kilian. BSc, McGill, Montreal, Can., 1950, Msc, 1951; PhD, Cornell U., 1953. Bd. cert. clinical psychology. Asst. prof. psychology U. Pa., Phila., 1953-58; from assoc. prof. and chairperson to prof. Lake Forest Coll., 1958-93, prof. emeritus, 1993—; vis. prof. Harvard U., Cambridge, Mass., 1965-66; pvt. practice. Author: Perception, 1966, Personality, 1979. Fellow NRC, 1951-53. Fellow APA (named Disting. Nat. Lect.), Chgo. Psychol. Assn., Am. Psychol. Soc. (exec. bd. 1990), Acad. Clinical Psychology. Democrat. Episcopalian. Home: 1008 Ibis Ct Bradenton FL 34209-7323

FORHART, DENNIS JAMES, automotive executive; b. Billings, Mont., Sept. 25, 1961; s. Al and Darlene Marie (Doig) F. BBA in Mktg., Tex. A&M U., 1986; MBA in Fin., Wash. U., 1990. Gen. mgr. Forhart Constrn., Hibbing, Minn., 1986-88; fin. analyst, contr. Mitsubishi Motor Mfg. of Am., Normal, Ill., 1990-92; sr. fin. analyst, corp. planning Diamond-Star Motors, Normal, Ill., 1992-93; br. mgr. traffic and customs Mitsubishi Motor Mfg. of Am., Normal, Ill., 1993—; cons. McDonald Douglas Corp., St. Louis, summer 1989, various residential constrn. projects. Mem. U.S. Power Squadron. Republican. Home: 507 N Fell Normal IL 61761 Office: Mitsubishi Motor Mfg Am 100 N Diamond Star Pky Normal IL 61761

FORLINI, FRANK JOHN, JR., cardiologist; b. Newark, Mar. 30, 1941; s. Frank Sr. and Rose Theresa (Parussini) F.; m. Joanne Marie Horch, July 19, 1969; children: Anne Marie, Victoria, Frank III, Anthony. BS in Biology, Villanova (Pa.) U., 1963; MD, George Washington U., 1967. Diplomate Am. Bd. Internal Medicine, Am. Bd. Cardiovascular Disease. Intern Bklyn.-Cumberland Med. Ctr., N.Y., 1967-68, resident in internal medicine, 1968-70; fellow in cardiology Inst. Med. Sci. Pacific Med. Ctr., San Francisco, 1970-72; practice medicine specializing in cardiology Rock Island, Ill., 1974—; sr. ptnr. Forlini Med. Speciality Clinic, Rock Island, 1974—; owner Forlini Farm and Forlini Devel. Enterprises; assoc. prof. pharmacy L.I. U., Bklyn., 1969-70; pres., CEO U.S. Oil & Transp. Co., Inc., 1966-89; pres. Profl. and Execs. Ins. Assocs., 1973-89, Profls. Assocs., 1973-89; med. and exec. dir. Cardiovasc. Inst. Northwestern Ill., 1984—; exec. dir., owner Franksoft Pub., 1988—; Shelter for Abused Women and Children, Rock Island, 1992-94, pres., chmn., 1994, chmn. capital campaign com., 1994; bd. dirs. Rescue Missions and Christian Family Care Ctr., 1992-94, pres., 1994. Contbr. articles to profl jours. Chmn. D.C. Young Reps., 1965-66; mem. exec. com. Rep. Ctrl. Com., Washington, 1965-66; mem. nat. com. Coll. Young Reps., 1965-66; mem. exec. com. Young Rep. State Ctrl. Com., Washington, 1965-66; mem. Physicians for Reagen-Bush, 1980, 84; vice chmn. Rock Island Reps., 1985-90, precinct committeeman, 1985-90, 92-93; dep. registrar County of Rock Island, 1985—; trustee South Rock Island Twp., Rock Island County, 1987—; trustee Twp. Intergovtl. Agy., 1993—, Friends of Twp. Govt. of Rock Island County, chmn., 1995—; mem. exec. com. Rock Island County Rep. Ctrl. Com., 1992-94; del. Ill. State Rep. Conv., 1992; pres. parish coun., extraordinary min., eucharist min. Roman Cath. Ch. Maj. USAF, 1972-74. Nat. Inst. Heart Disease NIH-USPHS grantee, 1964-66, 70-72; Fellowship of Cath. Scholars, 1994—. Fellow Am. Coll. Cardiology, N.Am. Soc. Pacing and Electrophysiology; mem. AMA, Ill. State Med. Soc., Rock Island County Med. Soc. (chmn. com. on ins. 1990—), Western Ill. Ind. Physicians Assn. (bd. dirs. 1995—, mem. exec. com. 1996—, sec. 1996—), Rock Island County Twp. Assn. (v.p. 1994, pres. 1994-95, mem. exec. com. 1994—), Soc. Cath. Social Scientists, Univ. Faculty for Life, KC (3d deg. 1994—). Office: 2508 25th St Ste B Rock Island IL 61201-5419

FORLOW, DAVID, stockbroker; b. Glasgow, Scotland, Aug. 5, 1963; came to U.S., 1966; s. John Kelly and Elizabeth Doherty (Mulholland) F.; m. Molly Ann Hickey, Aug. 25, 1990; 1 child, Ian. BS, Ill. State U., Normal, 1985. Broker R.W. Baird & Co., Chgo., 1986-88; mgr. investment dept. Comerica Bank, Skokie, Ill., 1988-93; stockbroker David Noyes & Co., Skokie, 1993—; mem. golden scale coun. Putnam, Boston, 1994—, Kemper (Asset Builders Coun.), Chgo., 1990—, AIM Family Funds, Houston, 1994—. Recipient Van Kampen Merritt Harbor Club award, Oakbrook Terrace, Ill., 1993-94. Mem. David A. Noyes Assocs. Club. Republican. Home: 4 Crows Nest Ct Grayslake IL 60030 Office: David A Noyes & Co 8707 Skokie Blvd Ste 100 Skokie IL 60077-2200

FORMAN, LINDA HELAINE, accountant; b. Chgo., July 15, 1943; d. Hymen and Rose (Klapman) Davis; divorced; children: David, Rachel. BBA, Loyola U., Chgo., 1969. CPA, Ill., Iowa. Ptnr., dir. health-care cons./employee benefits cons. depts. Gleeson, Sklar, Sawyers & Cumpata, LLP, Skokie, Ill., 1972—. Mem. AICPA (key person legis. contact 1994—), Ill. Soc. CPAs (v.p. 1995-96, bd. dirs. 1993-95, chairperson film subcom. 1984-86, mem. spkrs. bur. 1986-88, pub. svc. announcer 1988-90, chairperson pub. rels. com. 1990-92, mem. strategic planning com. 1992-93, participant legis. contact program 1993—, Jeanette Cochrane symposium com. 1996, com. structure task force 1996), Internat. Group Acctg. Firms (mem. healthcare and tax groups 1986—), Nat. Assn. Women Bus. Owners (bd. dirs. 1986-90, co-chairperson Pub. Affairs Day 1991-92, mem. pub. affairs com. 1990—, chairperson Holiday Event 1995, 96, mem. nat. healthcare task force 1993—), Destiny Inst. (mentor 1992-94), LaLeche League Internat. (Ill. state treas. 1974-76, budget chairperson 1992-93), Chgo. Ptnrs. Earned Income Credit (mem. founding com. 1994—), Small Bus. United of Ill. (bd. dirs. 1996). Jewish. Office: Gleeson Sklar Sawyers & Cumpata LLP 5550 Touhy Ave Ste 300 Skokie IL 60077-3254

FORMO, JEROME LIONEL, chemist; b. Mpls., Aug. 24, 1915; s. John Martin and Jennie Marie (Imsdahl) F.; m. Martha Winifred Helland, Aug. 12, 1939; children: David (dec.), Philip, Katherine Whitaker. BA in Chemistry, Math. and Music, Augsburg Coll., Mpls., 1937; postgrad., U. Minn., Mpls. Tchr. high sch. sci. Verndale, Minn., 1937-41; chemist Honeywell, Inc., Mpls., 1941-43, dir. plastics rsch., 1943-61; v.p. Plastics Corp. Am., 1961-62; cons. plastics, 1962-63; v.p. rsch. and devel. and engring. Plastics Inc., St. Paul, 1963-78; cons. in plastics Formo & Assocs., Roseville, Minn., 1978-93; mem. U.S. Dept. Commerce Trade Mission Team to Poland representing U.S. Plastics Industry, 1959; mem. Internat. Exec. Svc. Corps, Guatemala, 1988, 92, El Salvador, 1989. Regional corr. Plastic Trends, 1985-88; contbr. articles to profl. jours. Recipient Disting. Alumni award Augsburg Coll, Mpls. Fellow Am. Inst. Chemists; mem. Am. Chem. Soc. (emeritus), Soc. Plastics Engrs. (disting., pres. Upper Midwest sect., nat. pres. 1956), Soc. Plastics Industry (chmn. tech. confs. 1973, 79). Lutheran. Home: 500 W County Rd B Saint Paul MN 55113-6665

FORNATTO, ELIO JOSEPH, otolaryngologist, educator; b. Turin, Italy, July 2, 1928; came to U.S., 1953; s. Mario G. and Julia (Stabio) F.; m. Mary Elizabeth Pearson, Dec. 17, 1960; children: Susan, Robert, Daniel. MD, U. Turin, Italy, 1952. Diplomate Am. Bd. Otolaryngology. Intern Edgewater Hosp., Chgo., 1956-57; resident U. Ill., Chgo., 1953-56; chief otolaryngologist Elmhurst (Ill.) Clinic, 1958—; sr. otolaryngologist Elmhurst (Ill.) Meml. Hosp., 1964—; med. dir. Chgo. Eye Ear Nose Throat Hosp., 1966-69; clin. asst. prof. Loyola U., Chgo., 1967-87; bd. dirs. DuPage County unit Am. Cancer Soc., 1977-94; chmn. Elmhurst Clinic, 1980-89. Founder Centurion Club, Deafness Research Found., N.Y.C., 1960—. Recipient Disting. Svc. award Elmhurst Meml. Hosp., 1994. Mem. AMA, Ill. Med. Soc., Am. Acad. Facial Plastic and Reconstructive Surgery, Am. Acad. Otolaryngologic Allergy, Am. Acad. Otolaryngology and Head and Neck Surgery. Roman Catholic. Home: 200 W Jackson St Elmhurst IL 60126-4807 Office: Elmhurst Clinic 172 Schiller St Elmhurst IL 60126-2816

FORNAY, ALFRED RICHARD, publishing executive, editor; b. Cin.; s. Alfred H. Sr. and Marguertie (Weatherford) F. AAS, CUNY, SUNY Fashion Inst. Tech., 1971. Asst. ethnic mktg. mgr. Clariol Inc., N.Y.C., 1971-72; assoc. beauty editor Essence Mag., N.Y.C., 1973-74; tng. dir. Fashion Fair Cosmetics, Chgo., 1975-76, nat. beauty dir., 1977; internat. beauty dir. Fashion Fair Cosmetics, 1980-83; creative dir. polished amber collection Revlon Inc., 1978-80; beauty editor Ebony mag., N.Y.C., 1978-83; editor EM: Ebony Man mag., N.Y.C., 1984-87; contbg. fashion and beauty editor Bus. Week Careers Mag., N.Y.C., 1988—; cons. Beauty Fashion Mag., N.Y.C., 1989, Fashion Fair Cosmetics, Chgo., 1974—, Cover Girl Cosmetics, Noxell divsn. Procter & Gamble Co., Naomi Sims Cosmetics. Author: Fornay's Skin Care and Makeup Guide for Women of Color, 1989; fashion writer Bus. Week Career Mag. 1987. Bd. dirs. Boy's Choir of Harlem, N.Y.C., 1980-85, com. mem., 1986-88; mem. The Author's Guild, Inc. Mem. N.Y. Assn. of Black Journalists, Nat. Assn. of Black Journalists, Nat. Assn. of Mag. Editors, Author's Guild. Home: Grand Central Station PO Box 1321 New York NY 10163-1321 N.Y. Office: 17th Flr 1270 Ave of the Americas New York NY 10020

FORNES, CANDACE RAE, professional violist; b. Fargo, N.D., Dec. 1, 1964; d. Lawrence Robert and Delphine Mae (Stangler) F. MusB, Concordia Coll., Moorhead, Minn., 1988; postgrad., Moorhead State U., 1992—, U. Minn., 1994-96. Violist Fargo-Moorhead (Minn.) Symphony, 1982—; appointed prin. violist, 1992—; libr. Fargo-Moorhead (Minn.) Symphony, 1991—; violist Fargo (N.D.)-Moorhead Civic Opera Co., 1982—; violist Moorhead State U., 1991-92, Straw Hat Players, Moorhead, 1990—; string quartet guest artist Trollwood Fine Arts Park, Fargo, 1990—; tchr., Fargo, 1983—; originator, violist Fargo-Moorhead String Quartet, 1983—. Contbr. poem to Mists of Enchantment, 1996. String quartet violist Sr. Citizen's Ctr., Dilworth, Minn., 1990-91, Moorhead, 1990-91, New Horizons (Disabled Persons Ctr.), Fargo, 1992, Women of Today (Ronald McDonald House Benefit), Fargo and Moorhead, 1990. Recipient Dahl scholarship, 1994-96, Sigvald Thompson scholarship Fargo-Moorhead Symphony, 1989, 92, 3d pl. award Young Artists Solo Competition Fargo-Moorhead, 1983, 1st pl. award Moorhead State U. Concerto Competition, 1989, 92; named one of Outstanding Young Women of Am., 1991. Mem. Pi Kappa Lambda. Roman Catholic. Home: 1805 5th Ave S Fargo ND 58103-1426

FORNOFF, FRANK J(UNIOR), retired chemistry educator, consultant; b. Mt. Carmel, Ill., Mar. 29, 1914; s. Frank and Ada (Arnold) F. A.B., U. Ill., 1936; M.S., Ohio State U., 1937, Ph.D., 1939. Asst. prof. Lehigh U., Bethlehem, Pa., 1942-44; chem. engr. Western Electric Co., N.Y.C., 1944-45; asst. prof. chemistry Lehigh U., 1945-47, assoc. prof., 1947-53; assoc. prof. Kans. State U., Manhattan, 1953-56; lectr. Rutgers U., New Brunswick, N.J., 1956-84; sr. examiner Ednl. Testing Svc., Princeton, N.J., 1956-93, group head, 1956-83. Editor AP Chemistry newsletter, 1976-90; contbr. articles to profl. jours. Active Boy Scouts Am., Princeton, 1957-93. NRC fellow U. Calif., Berkeley, 1939-40; Procter and Gamble fellow Ohio State U., 1938-39. Mem. AAAS, Am. Chem. Soc. (chmn. local sect. assn. publs. 1960-70), Am. Soc. Engring. Edn., Nat. Sci. Tchrs. Assn., Nat. Council Measurements in Edn., N.J. Acad. Sci., N.Y. Acad. Sci. Methodist. Home: 110 E 7th St Mount Carmel IL 62863

FORNSHELL, DAVE LEE, educational broadcasting executive; b. Bluffton, Ind., July 9, 1937; s. Harold Christman and Mary Ann Elizabeth (Fox) F.; 1 child, John David; m. Delphia Crum, May 18, 1991. BA, Ohio State U., 1959. Continuity dir. Sta. WTVN-TV, Columbus, Ohio, 1959-61; traffic dir., asst. program mgr. Sta. WOSU-TV, Columbus, 1961-69; ops. mgr. Md. Center for Pub. Broadcasting, Balt., 1969-70; exec. dir. Ohio Ednl. TV Network Commn., Columbus, 1970—; pres. Ohio Radio Reading Services; dir., mem. exec. com. Central Ednl. Network, 1972—, chmn. bd. dirs., 1986—; mem. exec. com., chmn. Postsecondary Edn. Council of Central Ednl. Network; chmn. Ohio Postsecondary Telecommunications Council; mem. adv. com. Ohio State Awards. Pres. Landings Residents Assn., 1973; active March of Dimes, 4-H. Served with USAF, 1961-62. Recipient award Dayton Fedn. Women's Clubs, 1974. Mem. N.G. Assn., Ohio State U. Alumni Assn., Nat. Acad. TV Arts and Scis. (bd. govs. Columbus chpt. 1970—), Nat. Assn. Ednl. Broadcasters (chmn. state adminstrs. council), Broadcast Pioneers, Ohio State Awards Adv. Com., Health Scis. Communications Assn., Nat. Assn. TV Program Execs., Nat. Press Club, Am. Assn. Higher Edn., Alpha Epsilon Rho, Alpha Delta Sigma, Sigma Delta Chi. Clubs: University, Athletic (Columbus), Symposiarchs, Rotary. Home: 3388 Scioto Run Blvd Hilliard OH 43026-3002 Office: Ohio Ednl Broadcasting 2470 N Star Rd Columbus OH 43221-3405

FORREST, MELBA JUNE, real estate broker, appraiser, educator; b. Melbourne, Ark., Mar. 31, 1931; d. William Turner and Mamie Mae (Felts) Clem; m. Cloyce Byram Forrest, May 5, 1951; children: Ruth Ann, James Byram. BA, U. Wichita, 1957; MEd, Wichita State U., 1970. Cert. real estate appraiser, residential real property appraiser, Kans. Real estate assoc. Bond Realty Investment Corp., Wichita, 1976-79; pres. Forrest Properties, Inc., Wichita, 1979—; instr. Wichita Pub. Schs., 1957-66, 68-75, Minneha Sch. Dist., Wichita, 1962-66; speaker in field. Author: Narrative Appraisal Report Writing, 1987. Mem. Nat. Assn. Realtors, Kans. Assn. Realtors, Nat. Assn. Ind. Fee Appraisers (designated 1988, pres. Wichita chpt. 1988-90, Kansas State dir. 1990—, named Kansas Coord. of Yr. 1988, Kansa Ind. Fee Appraiser of Yr. 1989). Home: 25 Laurel Dr Wichita KS 67206-2542 Office: Forrest Properties Inc 25 Laurel Dr Wichita KS 67206-2542

FORRESTER, ALAN MCKAY, capital company executive; b. Cleve., Oct. 13, 1940; s. John Carens and Mary Ann (Bryan) F.; m. Donna Dee Forrester, June 1964 (div. 1976); children: Sheri Lynn, Stephan Alan; m. Nancy V. Sullivan (div. 1990). Bachelor in Civil Engring, Ohio State U., 1963, Masters in Bus. Adminstrn, 1963. Registered Profl. engr., CPA. Indsl. engr. E.I. DuPont de Nemours and Co., Virginia, 1964-66; mgr. program mgmt. support Tex. Instruments, Dallas, 1966-69; ptnr. Cons. Assocs. Inc., Dallas, 1969; v.p. fin. Medicus Systems Corp., Chgo., 1969-73, Acts Computing, Southfield, Mich., 1973-74; pres. Van Arnem Co., Mich., 1974-80, First Nat. Capital, Birmingham, 1980—, McDonnell Douglas Capital Corp., Troy, Mich., 1987-89; bd. dirs. First Nat. Capital Corp., Troy, First Nat. Capital Leasing Corp., Meresco Corp., Bloomfield Hills, Mich., First Nat. Energy Corp.; pres. Classic Investment Cars Corp., 1990—, The Forrester Group, 1992—, The Lewis Group, 1995—; exec. distbr. Interior Design Nutritionals, Bloomfield Hills, 1992—. Contbr. articles to profl. jour. Chmn. bd. trustees St. Joseph Mercy Hosp., Pontiac, 1988-89, vice chmn. bd. trustees, 1987, chmn. fin. com., 1985; trustee Sta. WTVS-TV, Detroit, 1982-88. Mem. AICPA, Internat. Assn. Fin. Planners, Am. Assn. Equipment Lessors, Computer Dealers and Lessors Assn., Oakland U. Pres. Club, Beta Theta Pi (v.p. 1962-64). Republican. Office: First Nat Capital Corp Classic Investment Cars 1672 Hamilton Bloomfield Hills MI 48302-0220

FORRESTER, ROSEMARY WELLINGTON, regional senatorial representative; b. Petoskey, Mich., Aug. 1, 1953; d. James Doud and Mary Margaret (Thompson) Wellington; m. Dan L., June 16, 1974; children: Jennifer Mary, Joshua Daniel. BS in Sociology, No. Mich. U., Marquette, 1977; postgrad., No. Mich. U., 1987—. Activities coordinator E.U.P. Mental Health Bd., Sault, Mich., 1978-80; client services asst. E.U.P. Mental Health Bd, Sault, 1980; assoc. dir. U.P. Health Systems Agy., Sault, 1980-82; U.P. field coordinator Riegle for Mich., Sault, 1982, Marquette, 1988; community educator Chippewa County Health Dept., 1983-84; legal asst. U.P. Legal Services, Sault, 1983-85; camp lic. cons. Mich. Dept. of Social Services, Mich., 1985-86; career cons. Six County Consortium for Employment, Marquette, 1985-92; regional rep. U.S. Senator Carl Levin, Escanaba, Mich., 1992—. Del. Mich. Dem. State Ctrl. Com., 1986-91; chair Marquette County Health Care Access project adv. com., 1987-90; publicity chair United Way Marquette County, 1987-89; mem. Marquette Women's Ctr. Life Skills adv. com., 1987-88; appointee Alger-Marquette Community Mental Health Bd., 1989-93; vice chmn., mem. fin. com. Marquette County Irwin for Congress, 1988, coord., 1988; mem. adv. bd. spl. projects No. Mich. U. Mem. Mich. Assn. Community Mental Health Bds. (del., legis. com.), U.P. Pers. Assn. Methodist. Home: 774 Lakewood Ln Marquette MI 49855-9518

FORRISTAL, THOMAS JOSEPH, pediatrician; b. Cleve., Sept. 11, 1932; m. Judith Forristal; children: Ellaine Herschede, Lynne Gallivan, Alison O'Neill. AB, Kent State U., 1960; MD, U. Cin., 1965. Intern Bethesda Hosp., Cin., 1965-66; resident Children's Hosp. Med. Ctr., Cin., 1966-68; pvt. practice Pediatric Assocs. Mt. Carmel, Inc., Cin., 1968—; staff physician Children's Hosp. Med. Ctr., Anderson Mercy Hosp., Cin., Christ Hosp., Cin.; prof. clin. pediatrics U. Cin.; pres. med./dental staff Children's Hosp. Med. Ctr., 1985; dir. pediatrics newborn nursery Our Lady of Mercy Hosp., Cin., 1974-91; co-chmn. Cin. Pediatic Hist. Com. With USAF, 1952-56. Mem. Cin. Pediatirc Soc., Cin. Med. Soc. (pres. 1981), Am. Acad. Pediatrics (exec. com. Ohio chpt.), Irish and Am. Pediatric Soc. Office: Pediatric Assocs Mt Carmel 4420 Aicholtz Rd Cincinnati OH 45245

FORSEE, SHERRI DAYLE, intensive care nurse; b. Alton, Ill., Apr. 17, 1954; d. Earl and Loveda (Crain) Robinson; m. Richard L. Forsee, June 29, 1974; children: Stephani, Amanda. ADN, Lewis & Clark Community Coll., 1976; BSN, McKendree Coll., 1983; MSN, So. Ill. U., 1991. CCRN. Staff nurse Alton (Ill.) Meml. Hosp., 1976-78, Decatur (Ill.) Meml. Hosp., 1978; staff nurse Wood River (Ill.) Twp. Hosp., 1979-86, Barnes Hosp., St. Louis, 1986, St. Louis U., 1986-87; instr. critical care Alton Meml. Hosp., 1987-91, clin. nurse specialist, ICU, 1991—; mem. faculty Lewis and Clark C.C., 1995—; spkr. in field. Author: Creating the Perfect ICU, 1993. Mem. AACN, Am. Heart Assn., Sigma Theta Tau. Home: 2347 Briarcliff Dr Alton IL 62002-6954 Office: Alton Meml Hosp 1 Memorial Dr Alton IL 62002-6722

FORSETH, LYNN MARIE, college administrator; b. Milw., Oct. 7, 1956; d. Jack Paul and Elizabeth Ann (Van Zeeland) Spridco; m. Michael Vernon Forseth, June 27, 1981; children: Nicole Anne, Rachel Marie. BS in Elem. Edn., U. Wis., 1978, MS in Continuing and Vocat. Edn., 1985; MS in Ednl. Psychology, U. Wis., Milw., 1992. Elem. tchr. New Berlin (Wis.) Pub. Schs., 1978, Mukwonago (Wis.) Pub. Schs., 1978; registration clk. Milw. Area Tech. Coll., 1978-79, student svcs. specialist, 1979-86, basic edn. instr., 1986, project coord., 1987-88, student svcs. adminstr., 1987—; Wis. Leadership Identification Program participant Wis. State Bd. Vocat., Tech. and Adult Edn., Madison, 1984-85. mem. ACA, Am. Vocat. Assn., Am. Assn. Women in C.C.s, Am. Coll. Counseling Assn., Nat. Assn. for Career Devel., Wis. Vocat. Assn. (state com. 1987-88), Milw. Vocat. Assn. (pres. 1987-88, bd. dirs. 1985-86, award of merit 1987), Sigma Epsilon Sigma, Pi Lambda Theta. Home: 2760 S 149th St New Berlin WI 53151-3702 Office: Milw Area Tech Coll 1200 S 71st St Milwaukee WI 53214-3110

FORST, EDMUND CHARLES, JR., communications educator, consultant; b. Chgo., June 25, 1961; s. Edmund Charles Sr. and Patricia Ann (Dopek) F. BA, Ea. Ill. U., 1983, MA, 1984; EdD, W. Va. U., 1994. Leader, mem. staff Neighborhood Boys Club, Chgo., summer 1975-84; instr. in communication DePaul U., Chgo., 1988-93; instr. Waubonsee C.C., Sugar Grove, Ill., 1993-94, dean comms. and humanities, 1994—; cons. communication for Leon Spinks, 1990. Contbr. articles to profl. jours. Euracharist minister Our Lady of Mercy, Chgo., 1989-90; bd. dirs. Neighborhood Boys Club, Chgo., 1988-92. Mem. Am. Ednl. Rsch. Assn., Speech Communication Assn., Ea. Communication Assn. Republican. Roman Catholic. Home: 2622 75th Ave 1E Elmwood Park IL 60635

FORSTER, PETER, electrical engineer; b. McHenry, Ill., July 14, 1967. BSEE, U. Wis., Platteville, 1992. Sr. assoc. engr. Marquip, Inc., Madison, Wis., 1992—. Mem. IEEE, Phi Kappa Phi. Office: Marquip Inc 1245 E Washington Ave Madison WI 53703-3040

FORSTER, PETER HANS, utility company executive; b. Berlin, Germany, May 28, 1942; s. Jerome and Margaret Hanson; m. Susan E. Forster. B.S., U. Wis., 1964; postgrad., Bklyn. Law Sch., Columbia U., 1972. Engr. trainee Wis. Electric Power Co., 1960-64; head regional planning Am. Electric Power Service Corp., 1964-73; atty. Dayton Power & Light Co., Ohio, from 1973, v.p. adminstrn., treas., 1977, v.p. fin. and adminstrn., 1977-78, v.p. energy resources, 1978-79, exec. v.p., 1980-81, exec. v.p., chief operating officer, 1981-82, pres., chief operating officer, 1982-84, pres., chief exec. officer, 1984-88, chmn., 1988—; chmn. Miami Valley Rsch. Found.; bd. dirs. Bank One, Dayton, Ohio. Bd. dirs. Amcast, Comair; trustee Med Am. Health Systems, F.M. Tait Found., Dayton Bus. Com., Arts Ctr. Found. Mem. Am. Bar Assn., Ohio Bar Assn., Dayton Bar Assn. Office: DPL Inc Courthouse Plz SW PO Box 1247 Dayton OH 45402-9792*

FORSYTH, DALE MARVIN, animal nutritionist, educator; b. Charles City, Iowa, Feb. 4, 1945; s. Wilbur Benjamin and Mabel J. (Winters) F.; m. Judi Helen Reynolds, May 28, 1967; children: Heather Nicole, Hilary Dawn. BS, Iowa State U., 1967; PhD, Cornell U., 1971. Asst. prof. Purdue U., West Lafayette, Ind., 1972-78, assoc. prof., 1978—. Author: (with others) Swine Nutrition, 1991; contbr. articles to Jour. Animal Sci. Grantee Lilly Endowment, 1974-76, Nat. Pork Producers, 1977-78, Agrimerica, 1987, BASF Corp., 1988, Eli Lilly & Co., 1991. Mem. Am. Soc. Animal Sci. Office: Purdue U Dept Animal Sci Lilly Hall # 1151 West Lafayette IN 47907-1151

FORSYTHE, PATRICIA HAYS, development professional; b. Curtis, Ark.; d. John Chambers and Flora Jane (Eby) Hays; m. Kurt G. Pahl, Dec. 15, 1962 (div. Dec. 1980); children: Thomas Walter, Susan Clara; m. Robert E. Forsythe, June 20, 1981; 1 child, Nathaniel Ryan. BA, Calif. State U., Los Angeles, 1974; MSLS, U. So. Calif., 1976. Asst. to dir. devel. office The Assocs., Calif. Inst. Tech., Pasadena, 1978-81; exec. dir. Iowa City Pub. Library Found., 1982-89; dir. devel. Hoover Presdl. Libr. Assn., West Branch, Iowa, 1989-94, exec. dir., 1994—. Contbr. articles to profl. jours. Recipient Outstanding Fund Raising Exec. award Ea. Iowa, 1990, honorary Paul Harris fellow, 1994. Mem. ALA, LWV (editor 1985-87), Nat. Soc. Fund Raising Execs. (bd. dirs. 1987-89, chmn. Ea. Iowa Philanthropy Day 1990-91, bd. dirs. Ea. Iowa chpt. 1986—), Iowa City C. of C., West Branch C. of C. (bd. dirs.), Iowa Life Shares Assn. (bd. dirs., pres. 1995-96), Libr. Adminstrn. and Mgmt. Assn., Women in Mgmt., Hancher Guild (audience devel. 1981-85, pres. 1985-86), Univ. Athletic Club, Rotary (program chair 1992-96z0. Congregationalist. Home: 1806 E Court St Iowa City IA 52245-4643 Office: Hoover Presdl Libr Assn PO Box 696 West Branch IA 52358-0696

FORTAE, MARY ANN, hospice nurse; b. Granite City, Ill., Sept. 11, 1951; d. Edward John and Pauline Gladys (Baczewski) Tutka; m. Jim Lee Fortae, Sept. 10, 1971; children: Edward, Darrell. ADN, Belleville (Ill.) Area Coll., 1986. RN, Ill. Staff nurse ICU, PRN Anderson Hosp., Maryville, Ill., 1986-92; staff nurse Aphoresis Dept. St. Louis U. Hosp., 1992-94; staff nurse Hospice of Madison County, Granite City, 1993—. Vol. Hospice of Madison County, 1990-93. Recipient award So. Ill. Health Edn. and Teaching Orgn., 1991. Mem. Internat. Assn. Near Death Studies. Home: PO Box 898 Collinsville IL 62234-0898

FORTEAU, EDWIN BRIAN, marketing advisor to small businesses; b. Wright Patterson AFB, Ohio, Oct. 21, 1960; s. Maxwell B. and Hulda E. (Pounder) F.; m. Michellé A. Spaulding, Aug. 7, 1992. Mfg.Engr., Ctrl. State U., Wilberforce, Ohio, 1984. In quality assurance Miller Brewing, Auburn, N.Y., 1984-89; pres. Hullwell & Assocs., Minnetonka, Minn., 1989-93, Chameleon Mktg., Minnetonka, Minn., 1993—; creator, lectr. sci. mktg. seminars. Creator, interviewer audiotape series Audio Interview Report, 1995; editor, pub. Chameleon Mktg. Letter; author reports and articles on advt. and mktg. Co-founder, exec. bd. dirs. Home-based Action Forum. Mem. Home Based Bus. Assn. Minn., Minn. Entrepreneurs Club, Wayzata Bus. Profls. Office: Chameleon Mktg 5001 Sparrow Rd Minnetonka MN 55345

FORTENER, ROGER GERARD, rehabilitation services professional; b. Coldwater, Ohio, July 30, 1957; s. Walter Raymond and Mary Louise (Knapke) F.; m. Jane Marie Frey, Oct. 1, 1988. B in Psychology, Ohio U., 1980; MPA, Bowling Green State U., 1988; MEd, U. Toledo, 1993, postgrad., 1993—. Youth counselor Western Ohio Youth Ctr., Troy, Ohio, 1980-81, Sherron's Group Homes, Dayton, Ohio, 1981-82; dir. Mercer County Residential, Celina, Ohio, 1983-86; clin. dir. Anne Grady Ctr., Holland, Ohio, 1986—; counselor trainee Ridgewood Manor, Maumee, Ohio, 1993—. Bd. dirs. Mercer County Drug and Alcohol Bd., Celina, 1985-86; treas. Walt Fortener State Rep., Mercer County, 1985. Mem. ACA, Civitan-Maumee Valley (pres.). Office: Anne Grady Ctr 1525 Eber Rd Holland OH 43528

FORTIN, CLAUDE JEAN, neurologist; b. Drummondville, Que., Can., Apr. 25, 1957; s. Rheaume and Rolande (Gendron) F.; m. Nancy Bridget Titone, May 21, 1981; children: Timothy, Matthieu, Melissa, Jennifer. BS in Biology magna cum laude, Loyola U., Chgo., 1979; MD, Loyola Stritch Med. Sch., Maywood, Ill., 1982. Diplomate Am. Bd. Psychiatry & Neurology, Am. Bd. Electroencephalography & Neurophysiology. Pvt. practice Springfield Clinic Neurosci. Inst., 1986—; clin. assoc. So. Ill. Med. Sch., Springfield, 1987—. Mem. AMA, Ill. State Med. Soc., Am. Acad. Neurology, Am. EEG Soc., Am. Acad. Physician Execs., Am. Assn. Electrodiagnostic Medicine. Roman Catholic. Office: Springfield Clinic Neurosci Inst 455 W Carpenter St Springfield IL 62702-4928

FORTINO, JOHN F., financial consultant; b. Grand Haven, Mich., Oct. 28, 1953. BS, BA, Grand Valley State Coll., Allendale, Mich., 1974. Asst. v.p. Merrill Lynch, Grand Haven, Mich., 1986—. Mem. Rotary Club. Office: Merrill Lynch 212 S Harbor Dr Grand Haven MI 49417-1372

FORTMAN, RICHARD ALLEN, publishing executive; b. Mpls., May 27, 1936; s. Leslie John and Helen Mary (Oltvedt) F.; m. Phyllis Naomi Mader, Sept. 14, 1963; children: Jill Leslie, Jared Richard. AA in Commerce, Graceland Coll., 1956; BS in Bus. Adminstrn., Central Mo. State U., 1960; MA in Religion, Park Coll., 1992. Buyer Jones Store Co., Kansas City, Mo., 1960-66; wage incentive engr. Western Elec. Co., Lee's Summit, Mo., 1966-70; dir. mktg. and merchandising Herald Pub. House, Independence, Mo., 1970-95; pubs. rep. Clark and Miles Pub., Inc., St. Paul, 1995—; bd. dirs. Santa Fe Day Care, Inc., Kansas City, Mo. Bd. dirs. YMCA, Independence, Mo., 1982-89; bd. dirs. Truman Ann. Concert, treas. 1994—. Mem. Independence C. of C. (bd. dirs., v.p. membership 1981-83, Disting. Svc. award 1981, Centurion award 1982). Republican. Mem. Reorganized Ch. of Jesus Christ of Latter-day Saints. Home: 14708 E 33rd St S Independence MO 64055-2520

FORTUNA, WILLIAM FRANK, architect, architectural engineer; b. Paris, Ill., Apr. 3, 1948; s. William F. Sr. and Mary O. (Komatz) F.; m. Gayle M. Meadors, June 11, 1983. BArch, U. Ill., 1972, MS in Archtl. Engring., 1973. Lic. arch., Ill., Wis., Iowa, lic. structural engr., Ill., lic. profl. engr., Wis., lic. archtl. engr. specializing in crisis mgmt., Nat. Coun. Examiners for Engring. and Surveying, Nat. Coun. Archtl. Registration Bds. Designer Unteed Associs. Ltd., Champaign, Ill., 1973-76; structural engr. Consoer Townsend, Chgo., 1976-79, Schmidt, Garden & Erikson, Chgo., 1979-83; sr. project structural engr. Skidmore Owings & Merrill, Chgo., 1983-87; pres. W.F. Fortuna Ltd., Archtl. Engring., Lake Bluff, Ill., 1987—; project engr. World Trade Ctr., Cairo; structural engr. exhbn. ctr. McCormick Place Annex, Chgo., United Airlines terminal O'Hare Airport, Bishop's Gate, London; contract adminstr. One and Two Prudential Plaza, Chgo. (SEAOI Best Structure award for tallest concrete bldg. in the world). Active mem. Illinois Emergency Mgmt. Agency. Mem. AIA, NCARB, Structural Engrs. Assn. Ill., Nat. Coun. Examiners for Engring. and Surveying, Am. Concrete Inst., Am. Inst. Steel Constrn., Chgo. Hist. Soc., Nat. Trust His. Preservation. Home: 530 E Prospect Ave Lake Bluff IL 60044-2616 Office: WF Fortuna Ltd Archtl Engr 28A E Center Ave Ste 2 Lake Bluff IL 60044

FORTUNATO, JOSEPH M., electrical engineering executive; b. Cleve., May 4, 1949. BSEE, Case Western Res. U., 1970. Engr., pres. IBIS Techs., Cleve., 1981—. Mem. IEEE. Republican. Roman Catholic. Office: IBIS Techs Inc 5545 Wilson Mills Rd Cleveland OH 44143-3269

FORTUS, JANET ANNE, special education educator; b. Middletown, Conn., Sept. 11, 1943; d. Henry Godfrey and Barbara Louise (Cryder) Derbyshire; m. Ralph Fortus, July 10, 1965; children: Richard, Laura. BA, Ohio Wesleyan U., 1965; MEd, Maryville U., St. Louis, 1983. Cert. tchr. learning disabled, behavior disordered, mentally handicapped, also secondary home econs., Mo. Spl. edn. tchr. Epworth Children's Home, Webster, Mo., 1985-87, St. Louis County Spl. Sch. Dist., Town and Country, Mo., 1980-85, 88—; mem. adv. bd. St. Louis Post Dispatch, 1989—; mem. family adv. coun. Life Skills, St. Louis, 1994—. V.p., bd. dirs., mem. Bel Canto Chorus, St. Louis, 1980—; charter mem. St. Louis Women's Chorale, 1995-96; mem. St. Louis Cmty. Leadership Program for Tchrs., 1994-95. Recipient computer edn. grants. Mem. Spl. Sch. Dist. NEA (bd. dirs. 1995-96, mem. nat. alternate NEA resolutions 1996—), Mo. Edn. Assn. (caucus for edn. of exceptional children, v.p. 1994-96, state resolutions com. 1993-96), Phi Delta Kappa. Presbyterian. Home: 13232 Damask Ct Saint Louis MO 63146

FOSBENDER, JULE JOANN, librarian; b. Paw Paw, Mich., Aug. 23, 1932; d. Harold L. and Grace (Weaver) Walmer; m. Conrad Fosbender, Feb. 12, 1954 (div. Aug. 1960); 1 child, Scott Carl. BA, Western Mich. U., 1954, MLS, 1972. Dir. Tecumseh (Mich.) Pub. Libr., 1954-67; bus./reference libr. Kalamazoo Pub. Libr., 1967-72; dir. Adrian (Mich.) Pub. Libr., 1972—; chair health adv. com. Lenawee Intermediate Sch. Dist., Adrian, 1984-91. Active Adrian Heritage Festival, City of Adrian, 1984—; worker Jerry Lewis Telethon, Adrian, 1985—. Recipient Spirit of Woodlands award Woodlands Libr. Coop., Albion, Mich., 1988, Cert. of Appreciation, Porter Edn. Ctr., Adrian, 1986, othres. Mem. ALA (chpt. pres. 1990-91), Mich. Libr. Assn. (pres. 1990-91, Libr. of Yr. 1994), Optimists. Office: Adrian Pub Libr 143 E Maumee St Adrian MI 49221

FOSDICK, HOWARD, computer scientist; b. Cin.. BA, Vanderbilt U.; MS, U. Ill., No. Ill. U. Pres. Fosdick Cons. Inc., Villa Park, Ill., 1987—. Author: VM Handbook, ISPF Dialog Manager, OSL Database Manager, PC/I Programming; contbr. over 150 articles to profl. publs. Mem. Internat. Database Users Group (founder, past pres.), Corp. Assn. Microcomputer Profls. (founder), Midwest Client/Server Users Group (founder, past pres.), Midwest Database Users Group (pres.). Office: Fosdick Cons Inc 49 N Princeton Ste 100 Villa Park IL 60181

FOSS, CHARLES R., transportation specialist; b. Chgo., Nov. 1, 1945; s. Raymond C. and Marilyn (Halas) F. Assoc. in Transp., Davenport Coll., 1973, B in Mktg., 1985, BS in Mgmt., 1994. Cert. purchasing mgr., Nat. Assn. Purchasing Mgmt.; cert. profl. mgr., Inst. Cert. Profl. Mgrs.; cert. transp. and logistics profl., Am. Soc. Transp. Logistics. Yardmaster Chesapeake and Ohio Ry., Benton Harbor, Mich., 1963-66; ticket agt. Chesapeake and Ohio Ry., Holland, Mich., 1969-71; freight agt., train dispatcher Penn Cen. Ry., Ft. Wayne, Ind., 1971-76; crew dispatcher Consol. Rail Corp., Grand Rapids, Mich., 1976-78; trainmaster Mich. No. Ry., 1978-85; customer service rep. Superior Brand Produce, Hudsonville, Mich., 1985; purchasing buyer U.S. Dept. Def., Dayton, Ohio, 1986-89; contract adminstr. U.S. Dept. Def., Grand Rapids, Mich., 1989-94; transp. specialist, ops. CSX Transp. Inc., Grand Rapids, 1994—; part-time sales rep. Foss Police Equipment and Communications, Battle Creek, Mich., 1978-85. Author: Evening Before The Diesel, 1980. Coord. Susquicentennial Commemorative Winchester Carbine, Byron Twp., Byron Ctr., Mich., 1985; hon. life mem. RR History Mus., Durand, Mich. With U.S. Army, 1966-69, Vietnam. Mem. NRA (life), Nat. Assn. Purchasing Mgmt. (cert. purchasing mgr.), Nat. Contract Mgmt. Assn., Am. Soc. Transp. and Logistics (cert. in transp.

and logistics mgmt.), Chgo. and North Western Hist. Soc. (contbr.), So. Mich. R.R. Soc. (contbr.), Am. Truck Hist. Soc. (life). Republican.

FOSS, RICHARD JOHN, bishop; b. Wauwatosa, Wis., Dec. 27, 1944; s. Harlan Funston and Beatrice Naomi (Lindaas) F.; m. Nancy Elizabeth Martin, June 21, 1969; children: Susan, John, Naomi, Elizabeth, Peter, Andrew. BA, St. Olaf Coll., 1966; MDiv, Luther Theol. Seminary, 1971; ThM, Luther N.W. Theol. Seminary, 1984. Ordained to ministry Luth. Ch., 1971. Pastor St. Andrews Ch. and Ch. of Christ the Redeemer, Mpls., 1971-77; assoc. pastor First Luth., Fargo, N.D., 1977-79; sr. pastor Prince of Peace Luth., Seattle, 1979-86, Trinity Luth., Moorhead, Minn., 1986-92; bishop Ea. N.D. Synod, Fargo, ND, 1992—. Soloist F-M Opera Co., Fargo, 1979; coach St. James Girls' Basketball Team, Settle, 1982-84; vol. Wash. State Patrol Crisis Chaplaincy, Seattle, 1983-86; bd. dirs. Discovery, Inc., Mpls., 1972-77, Highline Boys' and Girls' Club, Burien, Wash., 1980-81, Luth. Compass Ctr., Seattle, 1983-86, v.p., 1985-86; mem. Master Chorale, 1987—; bd. regents Concordia Coll., 1993—; bd. dirs. Daily Bread, 1991—, Luth. Social Svcs. of N.D., 1992—, Oak Grove Luth. H.S., 1990—, Luth. Resources Network, 1994—. Home: 1510 2nd St S Moorhead MN 56560-4014 Office: Ea ND Synod 1703 32nd Ave S Fargo ND 58103-5936

FOSTER, BILL L., state legislator. Mem. Mo. Ho. of Reps., Jefferson City. Republican.

FOSTER, DAVID RAYMOND, economic development organization administrator; b. Batu-Gajah, Malaysia, Nov. 17, 1948; s. William Harris Foster and Lila (Henderson) Henschel; m. Jean Marie McManama, Aug. 11, 1979; children: James David, Wesley Barett. BA in Geography, U. Wis.-Parkside, Kenosha, 1976; MS in Urban and Regional Planning, U. Wis., Madison, 1978; postgrad., U. Wis., Platteville, 1983-86. Econ. devel. planner Southwestern Wis. Regional Planning Commn., Platteville, 1978-83; econ. devel. mgr., coord. bus. and mktg. S.W. Wis. Tech. Coll., Fennimore, 1983-86; dir. econ. devel. Whitewater (Wis.) Community Devel. Authority, 1986-93; exec. dir. Coles Together, Mattoon, Ill., 1993—; bd. dirs. S.W. Wis. Pvt. Industry Coun., Dodgeville, 1984-86; adminstr. Whitewater Tax Increment Dists., 1982-93; chmn. S.W. Wis. Vocat. Edn. Assn. Tng. Com., Fennimore, 1987, Whitewater Downtown Revitalization Com., 1988-93; enterprise zone adminstr. Coles County, Ill.; bd. dirs., treas. Ea. Ill. R.R.; chmn. bd. dirs. Mattoon-Charleston Corridor Zoning Dist.; mem. adv. com. on curriculum devel. Lakeland Coll.; mem. Ill. Devel. Coun., Mid-Am. Econ. Devel. Coun., Am. Econ. Devel. Coun. Author: Southwest Wisconsin Industrial Recruitment Strategy, 1983, Overall Economic Development Strategy for Southwest Wisconsin, 1985; contbr. articles to profl. jours.; editor: (film) Whitewater-On the Edge, 1987. Chmn. Whitewater Downtown Revolving Loan Fund Com., 1991-92; chmn. missions com. Wesley United Meth. Ch., mem. ch. exec. com. Mem. Whitewater C. of C., Wis. Econ. Devel. Assn., Ying Yang Do Karate Assn. (sensei 1975—), Masons (master St. John's Lodge), Knights Templar (sir knight). Congregationalist. Home: 18 Robin Dale Cv Charleston IL 61920-9014 Office: 400 Airport Rd Mattoon IL 61938-9228

FOSTER, HATTIE A., business executive; b. Chgo., July 6, 1960. AA, Chgo. Coll. of Commerce, 1982. Legal sec. Schiff, Harten, Waite, Chgo., 1980-87; dir. adminstrn., pers. Aviation Resource Ptnrs., Inc., Chgo., 1988—. Mem. Bldg. Owners and Mgrs. of Oak Park. Democrat. Pentocostal. Office: Aviation Resource Ptnrs 407 S Dearborn St Ste 600 Chicago IL 60605-1115

FOSTER, JAMES FRANKLIN, professional sports management executive; b. Iowa; s. M. (Egerer) F.; m. Susan Jane Salsi, July 19, 1976. BGS, U. Iowa, 1972; postgrad. U. Pa., 1982. Retail advt. specialist Maytag Co., Newton, Iowa, 1972-78; founder, gen. mgr. Iowa Nite Hawks AAA Pro Football Club, 1974-78; founder, dir. Am. Pro Football Tour of Europe, 1977, 79; promotion mgr. NFL Properties, Inc., N.Y.C., 1979-82; asst. gen. mgr. Ariz. Wranglers Pro Football Club, U.S. F.L. Phoenix, 1982-83; exec. v.p. Chgo. Blitz Pro Football Club, U.S. F L., Chgo., 1983-84; v.p. Chgo. Sting Indoor soccer promotions-Burke Promo Mktg. Inc., 1984-85; founder, pres. Arena Football, Chgo., 1985-90, commr., 1985-92, spl. cons., 1992-94; mng. owner, team pres. Iowa Barn Stormers Arena Football Club, 1994—; bd. dirs. Greater Des Moines Sports Authority. Patent holder Arena Football, U.S. 1990, Can. 1992, Mex., 1993, Japan, 1995. Active YMCA; bd. advisors Greater Des Moines Jazz Festival. Recipient Golden Helmet Excellence awards Nat. Football League Properties, Inc., 1981, 82; named Minor Pro Football Exec. of Yr., Pro Football Weekly, 1976, No. States League Gen. Mgr. of Yr., AAA Football, 1976, League Exec. of Yr., 1995; named to Minor Pro Football Hall of Fame, 1982, Exec. of the Yr. award Arena Football League, 1995. Mem. Iowa State Hist. Soc., Antique and Classic Boat Soc., Boat Owners Assn. of U.S., Univ. Iowa Alumni Assn., Aircraft Owners and Pilots Assn., Nat. Iowa Lettermans Club, Nat. Assn. Railroad Passengers, Embassy Club (Des Moines). Democrat. Methodist. Home: 2800 Ridge Rd Des Moines IA 50312-4418 Office: 505 5th Ave Ste 1001 Des Moines IA 50309-2315

FOSTER, MARK GARDNER, retired physicist, educator; b. Winfield, Kans., Mar. 17, 1914; s. Everett Kin and Harriet (Gardner) F.; m. Louella Turney, June 29, 1939; children: Mary Ann, Charles, John. AB, Miami U., Oxford, Ohio, 1935; PhD, Calif. Inst. Tech., 1939. Physicist Champion Paper & Fiber Co., Hamilton, Ohio, 1939-41, U.S. Naval Ordnance Lab., Washington, 1941-45; dept. head Cornell Aero. Lab., Buffalo, 1945-56; prin. physicist Cornell Aero. Lab., Arlington, Va., 1957-60; dir. rsch. Crosley Div. AVCO Corp., Cin., 1956-57; prof. elect. enging. U. Va., Charlottesville, 1960-79, prof. emeritus, 1979—; cons. Nat. Def. Rsch. Coun., Washington, 1951, GE, Waynesboro, Va., 1966, U.S. Army Fgn. Sci. & Tech., Charlottesville, Va., 1969-76. Co-author (with others) McGraw Hill Sci. Encyclopedia, 1970. Participant Ret. Sr. Vol. Program, Charlottesville, 1979-81; vol. income tax aide, Bloomington, 1987-93. Mem. IEEE, Am. Phys. Soc., Phi Beta Kappa, Sigma Xi. Republican. Methodist. Home: 2455 Tamarack Trl Bloomington IN 47408

FOSTER, MICHAEL THOMAS, lawyer; b. La Porte, Ind., Feb. 14, 1951; s. Gerald Richard and Dolores (Pinkleman) F.; m. Myra Lynn; children: Michelle K., Jeffrey D., Steven T., Paul David Toller, Danielle L. BS, St. John's U., Collegeville, Minn., 1972; JD, U. Nebr., 1974. Bar: Nebr. 1975, Iowa 1978, Ill. 1985, Ind. 1990; CLU. Staff corp. atty. Lincoln (Nebr.) Libertylife Ins. Co., 1973-77; assoc. Qualley, Larson & Jones, Sioux City, Iowa, 1977-79; advanced mktg. specialist Allied Life Ins. Co., Des Moines, 1979-82; pvt. practice estate and bus. planning various locations, 1981—; adv. mktg. specialist Mut. Trust Life Ins. Co., Oakbrook, Ill., 1984-86; dir. adv. mktg. Zurich Am. Life Ins. Co., Schaumburg, Ill., 1986-87; estate and bus. planning specialist Prudential Life Ins. Co., Chgo. and Indpls., 1988-90; chartered fin. cons. Revision author: Estate Planning; contbr. articles to profl. jours. Mem. Chgo. Estate Planning Coun. Fellow Life Mgmt. Inst.; mem. Assn. Life Underwriters, ABA, Ill. Bar Assn., Iowa Bar Assn., Nebr. State Bar Assn., Ind. Bar Assn., Internat. Claims Assn. Office: 11711 N Meridian St Ste 360 Carmel IN 46032-4500 also: 1800 Broad St New Castle IN 47362-3925

FOSTER, NANCY BUSHNELL, genealogist; b. Chgo., June 20, 1925; d. Elbert Ernest and Dorothy Emma (Rising) Bushnell; m. Frank McEwen Foster, Jan. 22, 1955; children: Frank McEwen Jr., Abby Jean. BA, Lawrence U., 1946. Cert. geneal. record searcher Bd. Geneal. Cert. trustee Ohio Geneal. Soc., 1981-84. Author: Genealogical and Biographical Record of Frank and Alice Firbank Foster, 1990; editor: Every Name Index to History of Newspapers of Beaver County PA, 1992; contbr. articles to profl. jours. Mem. Daus. Founders and Patriots of Am. (Ohio pres. 1994-97), Soc. Mayflower Descendants (Ohio corr. sec. 1993-96), Daus. 1812 (chpt. pres. 1979-81), Colonial Dames 17th Century (Ohio pres. 1995-97), Daus. Am. Colonists (chpt. regent 1990-92). Home: 12145 Thames Pl Cincinnati OH 45241

FOSTER, PAMELA ANNE, adapted physical education educator; b. Oak Bluffs, Mass., Aug. 6, 1937; d. John Clayson and Mary Ford (Child) F. BS, Boston U., 1959; MS, Ind. U., Bloomington, 1962; Cert. in Bibl. Studies, Logos Bible Coll., Fla., 1986. Phys. Edn., Coaching, Devel./Adapted Phys. Edn. Tchr., outdoor edn. Cleveland Heights Sch., Cleveland Heights, Ohio, 1959-61; camp, conf. dir. YWCA, Mpls., 1962-63; instr. phys. edn. Northwestern Coll., Mpls., 1963-65; tchr. adapted phys. edn. and aquatics St. Paul Pub. Schs., St. Paul, Minn., 1965—; vol., coach Courage Ctr. Youth Sports, Minn.; team leader Jr. Nat. Wheel Chair Games, Tenn., 1988, Calif., 1989, Colo., 1990. Mem. adv. coun. Am. Lung Assn., St. Paul, 1977-92; faculty rep. Minn. Edn. Assn.; vol. helper The Box Project, Inc., Miss. Delta, 1990—, bd. dirs., 1994—. Recipient Nat. Thanks to Tchrs. award Apple Computer, Nat. Found. for Improvement Edn., Nat. Alliance Bus., Group W TV Sales, 1990, Golden Apple Achiever award Ashland Oil Co., 1990, Minn.'s Devel. Adapted Phys. Educator of Yr., 1990, George Hanson award Minn. Assn. Health, Phys. Edn., Recreation and Dance, 1990, Eleven Who Care Vol. Recognition, KARE II TV, 1990, 1,000 Hours Vol. award Courage Ctr., 1991, Am. Lung Assn. Ramsey County 15 Yr. Svc. award 1993, spl. recognition Sargent Coll. of Boston U. Alumni Assn., 1994. Mem. NEA, AAHPERD, Concerned Women of Am., Minn. Edn. Assn., Minn. Assn. Health, Phys. Edn. and Recreation, Nat. Wheelchair Athletic Assn., Minn. Aquatics Educators, People to People Internat. (mem. fitness del. citizen's amb. program Seattle chpt. to China 1991). Republican. Home: 6325 Pillsbury Ave Richfield MN 55423-1524 Office: Como Elem Sch 780 Wheelock Pky W Saint Paul MN 55117-4039

FOSTER, STEPHEN V., sales executive. V.p. Basic Mfrs. Sales Co., Toledo, 1963—. Republican. Methodist. Office: Basic Mfrs Sales Co PO Box 2947 Toledo OH 43606-0947

FOSTER, TONYA LEA, journalist; b. Belleville, Kans., Jan. 30, 1972; d. Anthony Baxter and Karen Dorthea (Coffey) F. AA, Cloud County C.C., Concordia, Kans., 1992; BS in Journalism/Mass Comms., Kansas State U., Manhattan, 1994. Reporter, designer Hays (Kans.) Daily News, 1994—. Mem. Soc. Profl. Journalists (v.p. chpt. 1993-94), Kans. State U. Alumni Assn. Democrat. Presbyterian. Home: 502 E 13th St Apt A Hays KS 67601 Office: Hays Daily News 507 Main St Hays KS 67601

FOSZCZ, JOSEPH L., editor; b. Chgo., Feb. 3, 1934. B, Ill. Inst. Tech., 1955. /engring. mgr. Symons Corp., Des Plaines, Ill., 1973-80; chief engr. Speedfam Corp., Des Plaines, Ill., 1980-87; sr. editor Plant Engring. Mag., Chgo., 1987—. Mem. ASME. Office: Plant Engring Mag 1350 E Touhy Ave Des Plaines IL 60018-3303

FOTA, FRANK GEORGE, artist; b. Northampton, Pa., Feb. 20, 1921; s. Frank Michael and Elizabeth Rose (Simko)F.; m. Christine June Ringwald, Oct. 18, 1947. Student, Chgo. Acad. of Fine Art, 1951-53. Artist Studio Maintained in Residence, S. Holland, Ill.; comml. artist, designer Triangle Outdoor Advt. Co., Chgo., 1956-61, Gen. Outdoor Advt. Co., Chgo., 1961-63; art dir. Triangle Outdoor Advt. Co., Chgo., 1963-83. Artist: (paintings) The Juniper Tree, 1971, Moab, Utah, 1974, Give Us This Day, Crete, Ill., 1972; exhibits include Wally Findlay Gallery, Chgo., 1953, 54, 55, Richard H. Love Gallery, Steger, Ill., Olympia Fields, Ill., Chgo., 1973, 74, 75, others. Mem., photographer Dolton (Ill.) Civic Assn., 1983-85. Roman Catholic. Clubs: Veteran of Foreign Wars, Dolton, Ill. (Trustee), Am. Legion, Riverdale, Ill. (Photog.). Home: 16748 Clyde Ave South Holland IL 60473-2611

FOTI, STEVEN M., state legislator; b. Oconomowoc, Wis., Dec. 3, 1958; married; 2 children. Student, U. Wis., Whitewater. Real estate sales agt. Oconomowoc; aide to Rep. James Sensenbrenner U.S. Ho. of Reps., Washington; mem. from dist. 33 Wis. State Assembly, Madison, 1982-92, mem. from dist. 38, 1993—. Mem. Jaycees, Lions, Elks. Home: 1117 Dickens Dr Oconomowoc WI 53066-4316*

FOUGHT, LORIANNE, chemist; b. Upper Darby, Pa., Oct. 5, 1962; d. Edwin Howard and Jeanette Marie Matthews; m. Daniel Lynn Fought, Jan. 22, 1990; children: Bethannie, Angelique, Daniel. BS, Pa. State U., 1985; MS, U. Ky., 1988, PhD, 1992. Rsch. aid Pa. State U., University Park, 1982-85; grad. rsch. asst. U. Ky., Lexington, 1985-91; chemist II Bayer Corp., Bayer Research Park, Kans., 1991-93; sci. and regulatory specialist Bayer Corp./Animal Health, Shawnee Mission, Kans., 1993—. Contbr. articles to profl. jours. Tchr. So. Hills United Meth. Ch., Lexington, 1989-90. Recipient dept. fellowship Dept. Plant Pathology, Univ. Ky., Lexington, 1985-91. Mem. Am. Phytopathol. Soc. (sec. grad. student com. 1990-91), AAAS, N.Y. Acad. Sci., Gamma Sigma Delta. Republican. Office: Bayer Corp Animal Health 9009 W 67th St Merriam KS 66202

FOULK, DOROTHY MARGARET, nurse; b. Springfield, Mo., June 18, 1946; d. Hugh Griff and Lillian M. (Pearson) DeBord; m. Gary Donald Foulk, May 22, 1964; children: Donald Ray, Laurene Ann. Student, SW Bapt. U., 1988-91; AS in Nursing, SW Mo. State U., 1990. RNC. Owner retail bus. Montier, Mo., 1968-89; nurse technician Ozark's Med. Ctr., West Plains, Mo., 1989, clin. coord. Neuro-Psych Unit, 1990—. Mem. NOW, Bus. and Profl. Women. Baptist. Home: Highway 60 Montier MO 65546 Office: Ozarks Med Ctr Neuro-Psych Unit 1103 Alaska St West Plains MO 65775-2001

FOURNELLE, RAYMOND ALBERT, engineering educator; b. St. Louis, Dec. 9, 1941; s. August Carl and Adella Emma (Fleer) F. BS in Metall. Engring., U. Mo., 1964, MS in Metall. Engring., 1968, PhD in Metall. Engring., 1971. Registered profl. engr., Wis. Rsch. engr. Shell Oil Co., Wood River, Ill., 1964-66; rsch. assoc. Northwestern U., Evanston, Ill., 1971-72; asst. prof. Marquette U., Milw., 1972-78, assoc. prof., 1978-86, prof., 1986—. Contbr. articles to profl. jours. 1st lt. U.S. Army, 1964-66, Fed. Republic Germany. Rsch. grantee NSF, 1975, 79, 86; Fulbright fellow U. Stuttgart (Germany), 1983-84, 90-91, Alexander von Humboldt fellow, 1985-88, Mac-Planck-Forschungspreis fellow, 1994. Mem. ASME, ASTM, AAUP, ASM Internat. (bd. rev. 1981—), Metall. Soc. AIME (com. mem.), Am. Ceramic Soc., Am. Soc. Engring. Edn. Home: 1129 N Jackson St Apt 1207 Milwaukee WI 53202-3208 Office: Marquette U Dept Mech/Indsl Engring PO Box 1881 Milwaukee WI 53201-1881

FOUSE, SARAH VIRGINIA, geriatrics nurse; b. Florence, Ala., Apr. 24, 1948; d. John E. and Violet (Chandler) Perkins; m. Alvin Fouse Jr., Feb. 9, 1967; children: Anthony, Alicia, Alvin III. LPN, Gateway Tech. Coll., 1975, ADN, 1984; BSN, Alverno Coll., 1987; MSN, U. Wis., Milw., 1992. Cert. psychiat.-mental health nurse; cert. gerontology nurse. Staff nurse VA Med. Ctr., North Chicago, Ill., LPN, nursing asst., head nurse, adminstrv. clin. nurse specialist, mental health clin. coord., 1995—. Mem. ANA, Kans. Nurses Assn., Wis. Nurses Assn., Kenosha-Racine Nurses Assn., Milw. Assn. Black Nurses, Sigma Theta Tau. Home: 1900 21st St Racine WI 53403

FOUSHI, JOHN ANTHONY, cost engineer; b. Chicago Heights, Ill., June 13, 1928; s. John Anthony Sr. and Clara (Bachtle) F.; m. Betty L. Schofield, Oct. 21, 1950; children: John H., Debora A., David A. BSME, Ill. Inst. Tech., 1950. Supervising cost engr. Inland Steel Co., East Chicago, Ind., 1950-85; cons. Foushi & Assocs., Chicago Heights, 1985—. Sch. bd. mem. Bd. Edn. Sch. Dist. #170, Chicago Heights, 1968-84. Cpl. U.S. Army, 1951-53. Recipient medal of merit for cmty. svc. George M. O'Brien 4th Congl. Dist. Ill., Chicago Heights, 1984. Mem. AACE Internat. (cert. cost engr., life mem., pres. 1981-82, award of merit 1995). Home: 839 Campbell Ave Chicago Heights IL 60411

FOUST, THOMAS A., information scientist, minister; b. Aaron, Mo., Oct. 29, 1930; s. Albert Elmer and Aletha Inez (Broddle) F.; m. Mary Rosalie Kessler, July 16, 1955 (div. Feb. 1984); children: Thomas R., Nancy K., Janett L., Timothy A., Christie C. BA, Bethany Nazarene Coll., 1952; BTH, Nazarene Theol. Sem., 1955; MPA, U. Kans., 1979. CCP. Min., pastor, 1956—; from tax examiner/auditor to mgr. tech. svcs. Kans. Dept. Revenue, Topeka, 1961—. Republican. Office: Kans Dept Revenue Topeka KS 66612

FOUTY, MARVIN FRANCIS, land surveyor, land developer, real estate broker; b. Lansing, Mich., Oct. 5, 1936; s. John Watkins and Dorothy Marie (Sollid) F.; m. Margaret Ann Buxton, Jan. 5, 1957 (div. 1993); children—Katherine, Elizabeth, Cynthia, Nancy. A.A. magna cum laude, Lansing Community Coll., 1964; BA Mich. State U., 1968. Registered land surveyor, Mich., Ind. Technician Mich. Hwy. Dept., Lansing, 1960-65; jr. engr. City of East Lansing, Mich., 1965-71; surveyor Polaris Assocs., Inc., Lansing, 1971-74, Kyes Assocs., Inc., Okemos, Mich., 1974-77; owner, mgr. Fouty & Assocs., Haslett, Mich., 1977—; v.p. Keystone Devel. Corp., Houghton Lake, Mich., 1978-87; sec. Sandstone Devel. Corp., Okemos, 1983-87; pres. Sandyoak Venture Inc., 1987-93. Dir. Mich. Surveyors Mus. and Found. Fellow Mich. Soc. Registered Land Surveyors (pres. Central chpt. 1982, state bd. dirs. 1984-88), Am. Congress Surveying and Mapping; mem. Mich. Assn. of Professions, Mensa, Intertel, Phi Theta Kappa. Avocations: travel, computers. Home: 4345 Courtside Dr Williamston MI 48895-1449 Office: 160 E Grand River Ave Ste A Williamston MI 48895

FOWLER, CARL, retired educator, boxing statistician; b. St. Louis, Mar. 19, 1939; s. Cornelius and Esther (Laten) F.; m. Grace Hicks, Apr. 12, 1967 (div. Feb. 1976); children: Kinmberly, Maya; m. Marlis Lorraine Tennon, Aug. 22, 1978; 1 child, Ingrid. BS, Lincoln U., Jefferson City, Mo., 1963; MS, Govs. State U., Chgo., 1975, postgrad. Lic. pvt. investigator. Tchr. Chgo. Bd. Edn., 1965-93. Author: Boxing for Boxers, 1982; inventor computerized statis. data base system for boxing. Served with U.S. Army, 1963-65. Recipient Cert. of Merit, ARC, St. Louis, 1960. Home: 1545 W 120th St Chicago IL 60643

FOWLER, CAROL HELEN, acquisitions consultant; b. Parma, Ohio, July 29, 1954; d. Adelbert C. and Gloria Carol (Larsen) F. BS in Edn., Slippery Rock (Pa.) State U., 1975. Tchr. Fayette County Schs., Fayetteville, W.Va., 1975-76, Shaler Area Sch. Dist., Glenshaw, Pa., 1976-80; support rep. Diacon Systems, Cleve., 1980-81; supr. services Columbus, Ohio, 1981-82; mgr. conversion Pro-Computer Systems, Columbus, 1982-83; specialist bus. accounts Digital Equipment Corp., Columbus, 1983-87; cons. software licensing Stow, Mass., 1987-88; software licensing program mgr. Maynard, Mass., 1988-90; proposal devel. mgr. Novi, Mich., 1990-93; acquisition cons. Elk Grove Village, Ill., 1993—. Office: Digital Equipment Corp 100 NW Point Blvd Elk Grove Village IL 60007-1018

FOWLER, DEAN ROBERT, business consultant; b. Niagara Falls, N.Y., Mar. 18, 1949; s. Arthur Robert and Winifred Fowler; m. Marjorie G. Fowler, June 27, 1970; children: Keith Robert, Paul Kennith. BA magna cum laude, St. Lawrence U., 1971; MA, Claremont Grad. Sch., 1972, PhD, 1975. Cert. marriage and family therapist, Wis., cert. mgmt. cons. Instr. Calif. State Poly. Inst., Pomona, 1973-75; lectr. U. Calif., Riverside, 1974-76; assoc. prof. Marquette U., Milw., 1976-83; chmn. Exec. Com., Brookfield, Wis., 1983-90; pres., owner Pilgrim Place Psychol. Svcs., Inc., Elm Grove, Wis., 1991—; owner Dean Fowler Assocs., Elm Grove, 1987—; mgmt. track chairperson Family Firm Inst., Boston, 1994-95. Author: (assessment tool) Family Bus. Assessment Tool, 1995, (newsletter) Crossroads. Strategic planner Washington Park Devel. Corp., Milw., 1987; active Future Milw., 1985; sect. leader Milw. Symphony Orch. Chorus, 1976-91; mem. human rsch. rev. com. Wis. Med. Coll., Wauwatosa, 1978-82. NEH grantee, 1980-81. Mem. Am. Assn. for Marriage and Family Therapy, Soc. for Profls. in Dispute Resolution, Inst. Mgmt. Cons. (pres. Wis. chpt. 1992-93), Phi Beta Kappa. Office: 740 Pilgrim Pkwy # 300 Elm Grove WI 53122

FOWLER, DOUGLAS TODD, lawyer; b. Parma, Ohio, Sept. 13, 1969; s. Loren and Ann Louise F. BA in Comms., Coll. Wooster, 1991; JD, Case We. Reserve U., 1994. Bar: Ohio; lic. radio operator, FCC. Legal intern Canton City (Ohio) Law Dept., 1992; pvt. practice Canton, Ohio, 1995—. Author: If Baseball Integrated Earlier, 1994; creator: (comic strip) The Reynolds, 1995; contbr.to Family Circul comic strip. Vol. Wayne County Big Brothers & Big Sisters, Wooster, Ohio, 1989-91, Canton Baptist Temple, 1995—; participant various charity talent shows, Wooster, Cleve., 1987-94. Mem. Student Pub. Interest Law Fellowship, Fraternal Order of Eagles, Phi Alpha Delta, Lambda Pi Eta.

FOWLER, ELIZABETH ANN, occupational therapist; b. Orange, N.J., July 10, 1940; d. Walter Edwin and Emily (Parker) F.; 1 child, Dendy Rae. BS in Psychology, Old Dominion U., 1964; MS in Occupl. Therapy, Va. Commonwealth U., 1969. Occupl. therapist coord. pulmonary & amputee units Moss Rehab. Hosp., Phila., 1969-71; student coord. clin. edn. Magee Rehab. Hosp., Phila., 1971-72; clk. coord., instr. U. Pa., Phila., 1972-73; coord. therapy svcs. Montgomery County Sch. Physically Handicapped, Norristown, Pa., 1973-75; dir. occupl. therapy Bryn Mawr Hosp. Rehab Ctr., Malvern, Pa., 1975-79, Heatherband Rehab Ctr., Columbia, Pa., 1979-82; pvt. practice York, Beaver Falls, Pa., 1982—; asst. prof. Kent State U., East Liverpool, Ohio, 1991-94, dir. occupl. therapy program, 1994—; mem. Pa. Commn. Edn., 1981—; mem. profl. adv. bd. Vis. Nurse, Westchester, Pa., 1973-75, York, 1979-91, Red Lion, Pa., 1979-91; mem. patient care com. Pa. Soc. Am. Assn. Respiration Therapy, York, 1981-85; lectr. in field. Mem. planning com. Bryn Mawr Hosp. Rehab. Ctr., 1978-79; mem. med. adv. bd. VNA, York, 1979-91, Beaver Falls, 1991-93; mem. utilization rev. coms., York, Red Lion, 1979-91. Mem. Am. Occupl. Therapy Assn., Pa. Occupl. Therapy Assn., Ohio Occupl. Therapy Assn., World Fedn. Occupl. Therapy. Home: 407 Rohrmann Rd Darlington PA 16115 Office: Kent State U 400 E 4th St East Liverpool OH 43920

FOWLER, GEORGE SELTON, JR., architect; b. Chgo., Jan. 20, 1920; s. George Selton and Mabel Helena (Overton) F.; m. Yvonne Fern Grammer, Nov. 25, 1945; 1 child, Kim Ellyn. Cert. Hamilton Coll., 1944; B.S., Ill. Inst. Tech., 1949, postgrad. city and regional planning, 1968; cert. Elec. Assn. Ill., 1976. Registered architect, Ill., Ohio. Co-founder, pres. The Modern Arts Press, Chgo., 1946; instr. archtl. and related engring. subjects Am. Sch. and Tech. Soc., Chgo., 1948-65; urban planner Chgo. Land Clearance Commn., 1949-50; liaison architect Chgo. Housing Authority, 1950-68, chief design-tech. div., 1968-80, dir. dept. engring., 1980-84; prin. George S. Fowler, Architect, Chgo., 1984—; treas., bd. dirs. Chgo. Housing Authority Credit Union, 1963-65; architect, community planner and cons. Interconco., 1965-66; cons. in field. Author: (text book study guide) Reinforced Concrete Design, 1959. Patentee. Subcommittee chmn. Mayor's Adv. Commn. to Revise the Bldg. Code, 1986—; founder, pres. EFCO, Chgo., 1988—. Served with C.E., U.S. Army, 1942-46. Recipient Citation for Residential Devel., Mayor Richard J. Daley, Chgo., 1960, Black Achievers of Industry Recognition award YMCA, Chgo., 1977; Kappa Alpha Psi grantee, 1936. Mem. Architects in Industry, Nat. Assn. Housing and Redevelopment Officials, Internat. Platform Assn., Inventors Coun. of Chgo. Home and Office: 8209 S Rhodes Ave Chicago IL 60619-5005

FOWLER, JACK W., printing company executive; b. 1931; B.S., East Tenn. State U., 1957. Plant estimator, salesman Kingsport Press, 1952-65; western sales mgr.-books Plimpton Press, 1965-67; v.p. mktg. J.W. Clement, 1967-69; v.p., gen. sales mgr. Arcata Graphics, 1969-71; with W.A. Krueger Co., Scottsdale, Ariz., 1971—, v.p. mktg. books and related products, 1971-72, v.p., gen. sales mgr., 1972-73, group v.p. books and related products, then group v.p. mag. and comml. products, 1973-76, sr. v.p. ops., then pres. and COO, 1976-78, pres., CEO, 1978—, also dir. Office: W A Krueger Co 1 Pierce Pl Ste 800 Itasca IL 60143-1253

FOWLER, STEPHEN EUGENE, retired military officer, human resources executive; b. Pilot Point, Tex., Dec. 10, 1940; s. Stephen Lafette and Virginia (Whitten) F.; m. Patricia Ann Chichilla, July 16, 1966 (div. May 1982); children: Shannon Jean Al-Qutub, Brittany Michelle; m. Cristine Ann Buttafoco, May 25, 1985; 1 child, Beth Ann Skamser. BA, U. North Tex., 1966; MA, Ball State U., 1974. Commd. 2d lt. USAF, 1966, advanced through grades to lt. col., 1982; chief airman support assignment Hdqrs. USAF Europe, Ramstein AB, Fed. Republic of Germany, 1973-76; chief, sec. police, intelligence and OSI Air Force Mil. Personnel Ctr., Randolph AFB, Tex., 1976-79, chief Air Force Classification and Control Sect., 1979-81; comdr. 3537th Recruiting Squadron, Sumter, S.C., 1981-84; chief airman assignments Hdqrs. Strategic Air Command, Offutt AFB, Nebr., 1984-86; chief inspections and inquiries 55th Wing, Offutt AFB, Nebr., 1986-92; mgr. human resources Pamida, Inc., Omaha, 1994—. Mem. Omaha Sister City Assn.; vol. tchr. non-profit agy.; mem. pvt. industry task force State of Nebr. Decorated Republic of Vietnam Cross of Gallantry; named Admiral (mythical) Nebr. Navy, Gov. Orr, State of Nebr. Mem. Pi Sigma Alpha. Republican. Office: Pamida Inc 8800 F St Omaha NE 68127-1507

FOX, DONALD LEE, mental health counselor, consultant; b. Seymour, Ind., Sept. 9, 1948; s. John L. and Thelma P. (Engel) F.; m. Patricia L. Sain, Aug. 26, 1978; children: Ashley M., Aimee E. BA, Ind. U., Indpls., 1978; MS, Ind. State U., 1979. Cert. clin. social worker, social worker, marriage and family therapist. Coord. mental health Cath. Social Svcs., Indpls., 1979-85; coord. psychiat. assessment Valley Vista Hosp., Greenwood, Ind., 1985-

86; clin. dir. Pathways, Speedway, Ind., 1986—; lectr., cons. Butler U., Indpls., 1988-89; adj. prof. U. Indpls., 1990—; cons. Wayne Twp. Vol. Fire Dept., Indpls., 1984—, La Porte (Ind.) Child Welfare Dept., 1988—. Pres., CEO Five Stop of Ind.: A Program for Youth, Inc., 1987-92. Mem. APA (assoc.), AACD, Am. Mental Health Counselors Assn. (nat. conf. com. 1990), Ind. Assn. Counseling and Devel. (conf. chmn. 1989), Ind. Mental Health Counselors Assn. (pres.-elect 1989-91, pres. 1991-92, Outstanding Svc. award 1989), Soc. Personality and Social Psychology (assoc.). Roman Catholic. Home: 730 Greenlee Dr Indianapolis IN 46234-2237

FOX, MICHAEL, state legislator, underwriting consultant; b. Hamilton, Ohio, Dec. 15, 1948; m. Mary Ann Fox; children: Ryan, Ashley. BS in Edn. in Polit. Sci., Miami U., Oxford, Ohio, 1971. Asst. to sec. of agr. USDA, Washington, 1973; spl. asst. to Senator Robert Taft, Jr. of Ohio, U.S. Senate, Washington, 1973-74; mem. Ohio Ho. of Reps., Columbus, 1975—; underwriting cons., Hamilton. Mem. Butler County Youth Svc. Bur. Named Legislator of Yr., Ohio Vocat. Edn. Assn., 1988; recipient leadership award Middletown Sch. Dist., 1989, President's award, Ohio. Mem. Butler County trustees Assn., Fraternal Order Police, Hamilton O'Tucks, Ky. Cols., Elks, Delta Tau Delta. Republican. Home: 5881 Fairham Rd Hamilton OH 45011-2034*

FOX, PATRICIA SAIN, academic administrator; b. Indpls., Jan. 8, 1954; d. Thomas Troy and Faye Melba (Martinez) Sain; m. Donald Lee Fox, Aug. 26, 1978; children: Ashley Marie, Aimee Elizabeth. BS in Acctg., Ind. U., 1980; MBA, Butler U., 1985. Adminstrv. asst. Sch. Engring. and Tech. Ind. U.-Purdue U., Indpls., 1980-83, asst. to the dean Sch. Engring. and Tech., 1983-86, asst. dean Sch. Engring. and Tech., 1986—; cons. Gene Glick Mgmt. Co., Indpls., 1986-87. Eucharistic minister St. Christopher Ch., Speedway, Ind., 1987—. Mem. Am. So. for Engring. Edn. Roman Catholic. Office: Ind U-Purdue U Sch Engring & Tech 799 W Michigan St Indianapolis IN 46202-5195

FOX, SHARON ELIZABETH, political scientist, educator, researcher; b. Holden, Mass., Mar. 30, 1970; d. Peter Edmund Fox and Nancy Charlotte (Lindberg) Seremeth. BA, DuQuesne U., 1991; PhD, U. Ill., 1996. Rsch. specialist Inst. for Devel. Disabilities, Chgo., 1992; rsch. asst. Great Cities Inst., Chgo., 1995—; instr., rsch. asst. U. Ill., Chgo., 1993-95; asst. project dir. Ill. Voter Project, Chgo., 1993-95; cons. Polit. Data Program, Chgo., 1993, Womens Self Employment Project, Chgo., 1994, NBC News/WMAQ Election Coverage, Chgo., 1994-95, Westside Local Intergy. Coun. for Early Intervention, Chgo., 1994. Contbr. articles to profl. jours. Fellow, Robert Corley Scholar U. Ill., 1994. Mem. Am. Polit. Sci. Assn., Midwest Polit. Sci. Assn., Ill. Polit. Sci. Assn., Soc. Women Internat. Polit. Economy, Pi Sigma Alpha. Home: Apt 703 4600 N Clarendon Ave Chicago IL 60640 Office: U Ill Dept Polit Sci M/C 276 1007 W Harrison St Chicago IL 60607

FOX, WILLIAM RICHARD, retired physician; b. Bozeman, Mont., Oct. 12, 1915; s. William Edward Fox and Anah Grace Bump; m. Esther Viola Jorgenson, Aug. 15, 1948 (dec. 1985); 1 child, Susan Jane Fox. MD, U. Manitoba, Can., 1941. Intern St. Joseph Hosp., St. Paul, 1940-41; staff Good Samaritan Hosp, Johnson Clinic, 1941-85; pub. health officer Pierce County, 1948-85; surgeon Gt. No. Ry., 1950-70. Past pres. Rugby Econ. Devel. Assn. Recipient N.D. Physicians Community and Profl. Svc. award, 1984. Mem. Union Hills County Club (Sun City Ariz.), Mason (past master), Shriners, Elks.

FOXWORTH, JOHN EDWIN, JR., automotive executive, philatelist; b. Bishopville, S.C., Apr. 6, 1932; s. John Edwin and Myrtle V. (Stuckey) F.; m. Virginia I. Davis, Dec. 21, 1952; children: John David, Brenda Gayle, Donald Edwin. BA in Journalism, U. S.C., 1957, MBA in Mgmt., 1976. Staff reporter The State newspaper, Columbia, S.C., 1955-58; pub. rels. writer S.C. State Hwy. Dept., Columbia, 1958-60; dist. sales mgr. Chevrolet Motor divsn. GM, Athens, Ga. and Knoxville,, Tenn., 1960-69; asst. zone bus. mgr. Chevrolet Motor divsn. GM, Charlotte, N.C., 1969-70, zone bus. mgr., 1970-72; dealer mgmt. cons. Chevrolet Motor divsn. GM, Charlotte and Atlanta, 1972-76; asst. nat. bus. mgr. Chevrolet Motor divsn. GM, Detroit, 1976-81; asst. nat. sales fin. adminstrn. mgr. Chevrolet Motor divsn. GM, Warren, Mich., 1981-85, mgr. nat. bus. mgmt. adminstrn., 1985-93, nat. bus. mgr., 1993—; trustee Am. Philatelic Rsch. Libr., State College, Pa., 1969-81, trustee, pres., 1985-95. Editor stamp column Detroit News and Free Press, 1985-94, The Eccentric Newspapers, Birmingham, Mich., 1995. Mem. Citizens Stamp Adv. Com., U.S. Postal Svc., Washington, 1984-90; bd. trustees Woodlawn Ch. God, Royal Oak, Mich., 1989-91, 95—, vice chmn., 1989-91, 96. With USN, 1951-53. Recipient Phoenix award Phoenix Philatelic Soc., 1969. Mem. Am. Philatelic Soc. (life, bd. dirs. 1969-85, pres. 1977-81, editor pres.'s column Am. Philatelist mag. 1977-81, chmn./writer news bur. com. 1962-77, pres. Writers Unit 30 1975-76, mem. Luff awards com. 1987—, chmn. com. 1993—, John N. Luff award 1983), Am. Tropical Assn. (life), Bur. Issues Assn., Internat. Philatelic Press Club, Am. Assn. Philatelic Exhibitors (nat. accredited philatelic judge 1974—, internat. accredited judge 1980—), Coun. Philatelic Orgns. (founder, pres. 1979-85), Full Gospel Bus. Men's Fellowship (life mem., v.p. South Oakland County chpt. 1981-85). Republican. Home: 2560 Lone Pine Rd West Bloomfield MI 48323-3615 Office: Chevrolet Motor Divsn Mail Code 480 205 329 PO Box 9065 Warren MI 48090-9065

FOY, EDWARD DONALD, investment advisor; b. Omaha, June 2, 1952; s. Donald Edward and Eloise Annette (Knudson) F.; m. Kathleen Joyce Sykora, Oct. 1, 1971; children: Becky Jo, Stacy Ann, Cindy Lee. BS cum laude, Dana Coll., Blair, Nebr., 1974. Pharm. sales rep. Schering-Plough, Inc., Lincoln, Nebr., 1974-80; account exec. Dain Bosworth, Inc., Lincoln, 1980-84, E.F. Hutton & Co., Inc., Lincoln, 1984-87; prin. Investment Advisors, Lincoln, 1987—; gen. securities prin. FFP Securities, Inc., Chesterfield, Mo., 1989—, registered agt. FFP Adv. Svcs., Inc., Chesterfield, 1990—; regional v.p. 1st Fin. Planners, Inc., Chesterfield, 1991—, mem. adv. bd., 1990—. Vocalist A Song with Class, Lincoln, 1987-91; soloist St. John's Ch., Lincoln, 1986—, chmn. fin. com., 1989-91, sponsor godparent program, 1988-92; pres. Meadowlane Area Residents Assn., Lincoln, 1990. Republican. Roman Catholic. Office: Investment Advisors 12501 Holdrege St Lincoln NE 68527-9430

FRAGOLA, TERESA T. (TERRY), financial consultant; b. Des Plaines, Ill., Jan. 2, 1965. BA, Wheaton Coll., Norton, Mass., 1988. Fin. cons. Merrill Lynch, Chgo., 1991—. Home: 1262 Saint Johns Ave Highland Park IL 60035-3425 Office: Merrill Lynch 141 W Jackson Blvd Ste 290 Chicago IL 60604-2905

FRAHM, SHEILA, senator, lieutenant governor, former state legislator; b. Colby, Kans., Mar. 22, 1945; m. Kenneth Frahm; children: Amy, Pam, Chrissie. BS, Ft. Hays State U., 1967. Mem. bd. edn. State of Kans., 1985-88; mem. Kans. Senate, Topeka, 1988-94, senate majority leader, 1993-94; lt. gov. State of Kans., 1995-96; U.S. senator from Kans., 1996—. Mem. AAUW (Outstanding Br. Mem. 1985), Thomas County Day Care Assn., Shakespeare Fedn. Women's Clubs, Farm Bur., Kans. Corn Growers, Kans. Livestock Assn., Rotary (Paul Harris fellow 1988). Republican. Address: 6005 SW 39th St Topeka KS 66610-1369 Office: US Senate 141 Hart Senate Office Bldg Washington DC 20410

FRAKER, ANNE TURNER, research consultant; b. Shelbyville, Ind., Aug. 22, 1946; d. Otis Atlee and Dorothy Alice (Turner) Fraker; m. Rupert A.D. Wentworth, July 25, 1992. BS in Edn., Ind. U., 1968, MS in Edn., 1970, postgrad., 1975-78; postgrad., Christian Theol. Sem., Indpls., 1984-85. Tchr. 4th grade Franklin (Ind.) Community Schs., 1968-69; tchr. 3rd grade Monroe Gregg Schs., Monrovia, Ind., 1970-72; customer svc. rep. Blue Cross/Blue Shield, Indpls., 1974-75; adminstrv. asst. African Studies Program, Bloomington, Ind., 1975-80; cons. Gen. Bd. Ch. and Soc., Washington, 1980-82; project coord. Project on Religion and Am. Life, Indpls., 1983-85; project adminstr. Project and Ctr. on Religion and Am. Culture, Indpls., 1986-90; cons. Lilly Endowment, Indpls., 1986-90; rsch. cons. Ctr. on Philanthropy, Indpls., 1990-92; project dir. Robert K. Greenleaf Ctr., Indpls., 1992—; cons. United Meth. Com. on Relief, N.Y.C., summer 1988, Francis Pinter Pubrs., Oxford, Eng., 1979. Co-editor Seeker and Servant, 1996, Seeker and Servant, 1996; editor: Religion and American Life: Resources, 1989; contbr. articles to profl. jours. Bd. dirs. CROP regional adv. com. Ch. World Svc., Indpls., 1990-93; chmn. environ. task force 1st United Meth. Ch., 1986-93, convenor immediate needs task force, 1992—; del. South Ind. United Meth. Conf., Bloomington, 1988—, mem. dist. coun. on ministries and coms., 1981—, mem. Commn. on Status and Role of Women, 1993—; membership chmn. LWV, Bloomington, 1977-78; bd. dirs. Cmty. Kitchen of Monroe County. Mem. Am. Soc. Ch. History (Women's Caucus convenor 1988-90), Pi Lambda Theta. Home: 4450 N Benton Ct Bloomington IN 47408-9501

FRAMPTON, ELON WILSON, microbiologist; b. N.Y.C., July 27, 1924; s. Elon Wilson and Anna (Callahan) F.; m. Priscilla Burhans, Aug. 16, 1958; children: Richard, Gail. BA, Syracuse U., 1949; MS, Northwestern U., Evanston, Ill., 1951; PhD, U. Ill., 1959. Postdoctoral fellow, rsch. assoc. U. Tex.-M.D. Anderson Hosp. and Tumor Inst., Houston, 1959-62, asst. biologist, asst. prof., 1962-66, assoc. biologist, assoc. prof., 1966-69; assoc. prof. No. Ill. U., DeKalb, 1969-90; prof. emeritus, 1990; rsch. microbiologist, cons. Gycor-Internat., Ltd., Bridgeview, Ill., 1990-93; cons. R&F Labs., Bridgeview, Ill., 1993—. Contbr. articles to profl. jours. With U.S. Army, 1943-46; ETO. USPHS postdoctoral trainee, 1959-60; AEC grantee, 1962-68. Mem. AAAS, Am. Soc. Microbiology, Radiation Rsch. Soc., Ill. Soc. Microbiology, Sigma Xi. Home: 119 Stoney Creek Rd De Kalb IL 60115-1022 Office: R&F Labs 7510 W 99th Pl Bridgeview IL 60455-2404

FRAMPTON, RICHARD KEITH, state agency administrator, finance specialist; b. Houston, Jan. 28, 1960; s. Elon W. and Priscilla (Burhans) F. BA in Econs., U. Ill., 1982; MPA, No. Ill. U., 1985. Student intern Ill. Devel. Fin. Authority, Chgo., 1984-85, program asst., 1985-86, asst. program adminstr., 1986-89, program adminstr., 1989-92, sr. program adminstr., 1992—. Vol. WBEZ-FM, Chgo., 1996—. Mem. Ill. Devel. Coun., 545-7 Condo Assn. Office: Ill Devel Fin Authority Ste 5310 Sears Tower 233 South Wacker Chicago IL 60606

FRANAHO, SUSAN M., theater administrator; b. Sept. 30, 1946; m. Frank Franaho; 1 child, Nico. BFA in Music, Stephens Coll., 1967; postgrad., U. Mo., Kansas City, 1967-68, So. Ill. U., Edwardsville, 1968-69. Dental office mgr., 1971-74, freelance singer, actress, voice instr., 1069-82; mgr., performer Lyric Opera Group, 1977-82; tour coord. Lyric Opera, Kansas City, 1980-82; dir. outreach Kansas City Symphony and Lyric Opera, Kansas City, 1982-83; asst. mgr. Kansas City Symphony, 1983-84, ops. mgr., 1984-86, gen. mgr., 1986—. Mem. artistic adv. bd. Imagination Celebration; mem. adv. coun. Arts for Lifelong Learning; mem. regional amenities task force Mid-Am. Regional Coun., 1987—; cantor Christ the King Ch., 1988—; chmn. Bi-State Cultural Dist. Planning Com., 1990; mem. ad hoc touring com. Mo. Arts Coun., 1990; mem. planning panel Nat. Arts Stabilization Fund, N.Y., 1992; mem. city-wide strategic planning task force Focus Kansas City, 1993; mem. music adv. panel Mo. Arts Coun., 1993—. Mem. Nat. Endowment for Arts (orchestra panel 1991, 93, challenge panel 1992), Am. Arts Alliance, Am. Coun. for Arts, Am. Symphony Orchestra League (group II orchestra chair, policy com. A, Nat. Issues Task Force 1992), Am. Guild Musical Artists (local delegate 5 yrs.), Mo. Citizens for Arts, Cultural Alliance Greater Kansas City, Actors Equity, Ctrl. Exchange, Stephens Coll. Alumni Assn. (bd. dirs., nat. v.p. 1974-76). Office: Kansas City Symphony Lyric Theatre 1020 Central St Kansas City MO 64105-1620

FRANCIS, KENNETH ALLEN, protective services official; b. St. Joseph, Mo., Sept. 6, 1946; s. Harry K. and Marguerite A. (Cornell) F.; m. Linda Pat Guile Leverach, June 10, 1966 (div. Mar. 1, 1984); children: Harry, Leigh, David; m. Patricia A. Marrota Francis, Sept. 4, 1987; 1 child, Patrick. Capt. Gladstone (Mo.) Pub. Safety,, 1967-73; chief of police City of Weston, Mo., 1973-74, City of Trenton, Mo., 1974-76; dir. pub. safety City of Sikeston, Mo., 1976-80, City of Gladstone, Mo., 1980-86, City of Gardner, Kans., 1987—; pres. Mo. Police Chief Assn., Jefferson City, Mo., 1981-82, Johnson County Police Chiefs, Olathe, Kans., 1990, FBI Nat. Acad. Assn., Kans., W. Mo., 1985; adv. mem. Johnson County C.C., Overland Park, Kans., 1989—. Treas., sec., 1990-91, pres., 1993, Lions Club, Gardner, Kans. Recipient Award of Valor United Frateral Firefighters, Kansas City, Mo., 1970, Cert. Appreciation Am. Legion, Johnson County, Kans., 1993; named Outstanding Officer Jaycees, Sikeston, Mo., 1977. Mem. Johnson County Police Chiefs. Internat. Police Chiefs, FBI Nat. Acad. Assn., Kans. Police Chiefs Assn., Mo. Police Chiefs Assn. Home: 735 Colleen Dr Gardner KS 66030 Office: Gardner Dept Public Safety 440 E Main Gardner KS 66030

FRANCIS, PAUL WILLIAM, retired broadcast executive; b. St. Louis, July 28, 1933; s. William Paul Francis and Elsie Scott; m. Merideth McKelvy, June 7, 1957 (dec. May 1989); 1 child, Gail Francis Periman. B Journalism, U. Mo., 1958. Reporter Record News, Wichita Falls, Tex., 1958-59; assoc. Sunday editor Kansas City (Mo.) Star, 1959-74; advt./pub. rels. exec. H&R Block, Inc., Kansas City, 1974-76; dir. comms. KCPT Pub. TV, Kansas City, 1976-95; ret., 1995. Pres. Nat. Coun. on Alcoholism, Kansas City, 1985; mem. Mayor's Cable TV Access Bd., Independence, Mo., 1986-90; chmn. Bd. Zoning Adjustment, Jackson County, Mo., 1987-91; mem. Tax Increment Commn., Jackson County, 1993-94; mem. Mayor's Media Adv. com., Independence, 1993—; bd. dirs. Citizens for Effective Leadership, Independence, 1994—. Sgt. U.S. Army, 1953-55. Named Outstanding Lobbyist, Am. Pub. TV Stas., 1995. Mem. Soc. Profl. Journalists, Kansas City Press Club (pres.-elect 1996). Democrat. Methodist. Home: 3912 S Stayton Ave Independence MO 64055

FRANCIS, RICHARD T., electrical engineer; b. St. Joseph, Mo., Mar. 11, 1946. BS, Mo. Western State U., 1975, BSBA, 1977. Sr. technician Greb Exray Co., Lenexa, Kans., 1972-74; project engr. Gray Automotive Products Co., St. Joseph, Mo., 1974—. Patentee in Lifting Equipment for Auto Industry, Wheel Life Systems-Commercial Vehicles. Staff sgt. USAF, 1966-70.

FRANCK, ARDATH AMOND, psychologist; b. Wehrum, Pa., May 5, 1925; d. Arthur and Helen Lucille (Sharp) Amond; m. Frederick M. Franck, Mar. 18, 1945; children—Sheldon, Candace. B.S. in Edn., Kent State U., 1946, M.A., 1947; Ph.D., Western Res. U., 1956. Cert. high sch. tchr., elem. supr., sch. psychologist, speech and hearing therapist. Instr., Western Res. U., Cleve., summer 1953, U. Akron, 1947-50; sch. psychologist Summit County Schs., Ohio, 1950-60; cons. psychologist Wadsworth Pub. Schs., Ohio, 1946-86; dir. Akron Speech & Reading Ctr., Ohio, 1950—; pres. Twirling Unlimited; cons., dir. Hobbitts Pre-Sch., 1973-88. Author: Your Child Learns, 1976. Pres. Twirling Unltd., 1982—. Mem. Am. Speech and Hearing Assn., Internat. Reading Assn., Ohio Psychol. Assn., Mensa, Soroptimist (Akron). Home: 631 Ghent Rd Akron OH 44333-2629 Office: Akron Speech & Reading Ctr 700 Ghent Rd Akron OH 44333-2632

FRANCKE, MELVIN L., electrical designer; b. Iron Mountain, Mich.. Sr. elec. designer Alkar divsn. DEC Internat., Inc., Lodi, Wis., 1969—. With U.S. Army, 1966-69, Vietnam. Mem. Exptl. Aircraft Assn. Lutheran. Office: Alkar divsn DEC Internat 932 Development Dr Lodi WI 53555-1300

FRANCKO, DAVID ALEX, botany educator, administrator, researcher; b. Cleve., Aug. 15, 1952; s. Alex Frank and Marie (Novak) F.; m. Diana Whitmer, June 14, 1975; children: Tyler W., Amy W. BS in Biology, Kent State U., 1974, MS, 1977; PhD in Botany, Mich. State U., 1980. Postdoctoral rsch. assoc. Kellogg Biol. Station Mich. State U., Hickory Corners, 1980-81; asst. prof. botany Coll. Arts & Scis. Okla. State U., Stillwater, 1981-85, assoc. prof., 1985-89, prof., dir. rsch., 1987-90; prof., chair dept. botany Miami U., Oxford, Ohio, 1990—; cons. S.R. Taylor and Assocs., Bartlesville, Okla., 1987, Two Herons Environ./Edn. Cons. Co., 1994. Author: To Quench Our Thirst, 1983; contbr. numerous articles to profl. jours. Named Outstanding Young Man Am. U.S. Jaycees, 1983; NSF rsch. grantee, 1980-94, sci. edn. grantee, 1988-90. Mem. AAAS, Internat. Soc. Theoretical and Applied Limnology, Am. Soc. Limnology and Oceanography, Bot. Soc. Am., Botanical Soc. Am., Internat. Assn. Great Lakes Rsch., Sigma Xi. Roman Catholic. Office: Miami Univ Dept Botany Oxford OH 45056

FRANG, JERRY LEE, mathematics educator; b. Rockford, Ill., June 19, 1946; s. Emery Winger and Ruby Louise (Barnett) F.; m. Martha Nell Zuroske, Oct. 23, 1971; 1 child, Corey Allen. AS, Rock Valley Coll., 1974; BS, No. Ill. U., 1975, MS, 1980. Tchr. Sch. Dist. 205, Rockford, Ill., 1978-82, Rock Valley Coll., Rockford, Ill., 1982—. Author: Study Guide for Plane Trigonometry, 1980, 2d edit., 1984, 3d edit., 1989, 4th edit., 1993. Mem. Tech-Prep Adv. Com. Rockford, Ill., 1990—. Sgt. U.S. Army, 1968-70, Vietnam. Decorated Bronze Star, Army Commendation medal. Mem. Optimists (charter, Rock Valley club, sec.-treas. 1990-92). Home: 5509 Ponderosa Dr Rockford IL 61107-1783 Office: Rock Valley Coll 3301 N Mulford Rd Rockford IL 61114-5640

FRANK, DEBRA WILSON, retail manager and trainer; b. Seattle, Nov. 14, 1961; d. Melvin Edmond W. and Deanna May Sanner; m. Thomas S. Frank, Aug. 6, 1994. BA in Bus. Adminstrn. cum laude, U. Wash., 1984. Asst. buyer, dept. mgr. Frederick & Nelson, Seattle, 1985-86; gen. mgr. Borders Book Shop, Indpls., 1986-87; regional mgr. Borders Book Shop, Ann Arbor, Mich., 1987-89, v.p. ops., 1989-92, mgmt. trainer, 1993—. Pres. Brownstones Condominium Assn., Ann Arbor, 1992-93. Mem. Am. Soc. Tng. & Devel., Phi Beta Kappa, Beta Gamma Sigma.

FRANK, JOACHIM RHEINHARD, engineer; b. Wolfsburg, Germany, Feb. 19, 1949; came to the U.S., 1976; s. Erich H. and Margarete Helen (Dehmel) F.; m. Gertraude Gehrmann, Mar. 23, 1973; children: Mark, Eric. BS in Mech. Engring., Th Tech. U., Braunschweig, Germany, 1973. Plant mgr. Nat. Prodn. Sys., Los Nietos, Calif., 1978-85; product mgr. Guehring Inc., Sussex, Wis., 1985-91; engr. Grob Sys., Bluffton, Ohio, 1992-94; engr., plant mgr. Modern Tool & Die J & M Tooling, Akron, Ohio, 1994—. Contbr. articles to profl. jours. With German Army, 1967-68. Republican. Lutheran. Home: 14506 W Sprague Rd Middlebrg Hts OH 44130-6907 Office: Modern Tool & Die J & M Tooling 1246 Princeton St Akron OH 44301-1168

FRANK, JOHN V., foundation executive; b. Cleve., Oct. 14, 1936; s. Paul A. and Frances (Halbert) F. Student Babson Coll., 1956-57; BBA, U. Miami-Fla., 1960. Mgmt. trainee Nat. City Bank, Cleve., 1960-62; investment analyst officer First Nat. Bank, Akron, 1962-70, asst. trust officer, 1970-73, trust officer, 1973-80, v.p., trust officer, 1980-81; pres. Summit Capital Mgmt. Co., Akron, 1982—. Treas., Fairlawn Heights Assn., Inc., Akron, 1971—; pres. Ohio Ballet, 1973-74; trustee Howland Meml. Fund, Akron, 1974—; pres., trustee Burton D. Morgan Found., Akron, 1976—; councilman City of Akron, 1978—; trustee Akron Art Mus., 1976-83, pres., 1979-81; trustee Akron City Hosp. Found., 1980-83, 1992, Summa Health Systems Found., 1992—; mem. Coun. on Founds. Com. on Legis. and Regulations, 1990-94; nat. steering com. Coll. Wooster, 1992—; mem. 50th anniversary com. UN, Grace Cathedral Ch., San Francisco, 1993-95, St. Paul's Episc. Ch.; bd. overseers Blossom Music Ctr., 1996; trustee Arkon Rural Cemetery, 1994—. 1st lt. USAR, 1963-69. Mem. Cleve. Soc. Security Analysts. Republican. Episcopalian. Clubs: Portage Country; Hillsboro (Hillsboro Beach, Fla.). Avocation: art collecting. Office: Burton D Morgan Found PO Box 1500 Akron OH 44309-1500

FRANK, KRISTY LOUISE, English educator; b. Oshkosh, Wis., June 29, 1942; d. Allan Theodore and Marian Virginia (Johnson) F.; married, Oct. 8, 1977, widowed, Jan. 1991. Student, Oshkosh State Coll., 1961-64; BA in English, U. Wis., Milw., 1967, MS in Ednl. Adminstrn. and Supervision, 1984; teaching cert., Marquette U., 1969. Tchr. English and Holocaust studies Juneau High Sch., Milw. Pub. Schs., 1967—; instr. in Holocaust studies McPherson Coll., Milw., 1993—. Active Simon Wiesenthal Ctr., Planned Parenthood, Raoul Wallenberg Com. Coun. for Basic Edn./Nat. Endowment for Arts fellow, 1987—; Honeywell grantee, 1987; recipient Gold Tchr. award Ameritech-Wis. Bell, 1992, Holocaust Teaching award Yom Hashoah Commemeration Com., 1992. Mem. NOW, ACLU, Milw. Tchrs. Assn. (v.p. 1993—, mem. various coms., bldg. rep., field staff mem.), Nat. Fedn. Interscholastic Spirit, Am. Soc. for Vad Vashem, U. Wis.-Milw. Alumni Assn. Democrat. Home: 3216 S 124th St West Allis WI 53227 Office: Juneau High Sch 6415 W Mount Vernon Ave Milwaukee WI 53213-4025

FRANK, LOWELL C., mechanical engineer; b. Pitts., June 28, 1929. BSME, Armour Inst., 1954. Indsl. engr. Formold Plastics, Inc., Blue Island, Ill., 1960-67; midwest sales mgr. Heil Co., Milw., 1967-76; pres., CEO Progressive Devel., Heartland, Wis., 1976-93; dir. engring. Galland Henning NoPak, Milw., 1994—; cons. FrankLogic, Okauchee, Wis., 1993—. Holder 6 patents for rotary dehydration system; contbr. articles to profl. mag. Sgt. U.S. Army, 1950-52, Korea. Mem. Masons. Office: Galland Henning NoPac PO Box 343917 Milwaukee WI 53234-3917

FRANK, PAUL WILBUR, social worker; b. Amery, Wis., Oct. 5, 1947; s. Wilbur Raymond and Harriet Josephine (Sukow) F. BA magna cum laude, Augsburg Coll., 1969; MS in Social Work, U. Wis., 1975, MA in Pub. Policy and Adminstrn., 1975. Lic. ind. clin. social worker, Minn. Psychiat. aide Met. Med. Ctr., Mpls., 1972-73; social worker III Crow Wing County Social Svc. Ctr., Brainerd, Minn., 1976-78; supr. social svcs. Wright County Human Svcs. Agy., Buffalo, Minn., 1978-79; coord. tng. and placement Mo. Epilepsy Fedn., St. Louis, 1979-80; med. social worker Met. Med. Ctr., Mpls., 1980-82, counselor employee assistance program, 1981-87; mgr. employee assistance program Met.-Mt. Sinai Med. Ctr. (formerly Met. Med. Ctr.), Mpls., 1987-90, mgr. Behavioral Health Access Ctr., 1989-90; employee assistance program mgr. Health East St. Joseph's Hosp., St. Paul, 1990-93; employee assistance program counselor, mktg. rep. Behavioral Health Svcs., Inc., Mpls., 1993—. With U.S. Army, 1969. Grantee, scholar U. Wis., 1973-74. Mem. NASW, Acad. Cert. Social Workers, Employee Assistance Profls. Assn., Minn. Social Svc. Assn. (Minn. employer assistance program adminstrs. and counselors), Mental Health Assn. Minn. Home: 2548 83rd Ave N Brooklyn Park MN 55444-1504

FRANK, ROBERT THOMAS, sporting goods manufacturing company executive; b. Wichita Falls, Tex., May 13, 1949; s. William James and Lela Mae (Birdette) Nolen; m. Teresa Mae Nicholson, Mar. 5, 1983; children: Brandy Nichole, Travis Nolen. AS, Okla. Mil. Acad., Claremor, 1969; BS in Indsl. Engring., U. Tex., Arlington, 1974; MBA, So. Meth. U., 1977. Plant supt. Lee Apparel Co., St. Joseph, Mo., 1980-84, Stevenson, Ala., 1984-86; supt. Costa Rica ops. Lee Apparel Co., San Jose, 1986-88; v.p. ops. Marcade Group, N.Y.C., 1988-90, Umbro Internat., Greenville, S.C., 1990-93; v.p. mfg. Rawlings Sporting Goods, Fenton, Mo., 1993—; mem. adv. bd. Costa Rican Indsl. Coun., San Jose, 1987; mem. U.S. Apparel Industries Coun., Washington, 1991. Pres. elect Rockwood Sch. Dist. PTO, Fenton, 1994-95; bd. trustees First Bapt. Ch., Fenton, 1995—. Republican. Baptist. Office: Rawlings Sporting Goods 1859 Intertech Dr Fenton MO 63026

FRANK, STEPHEN IRA, political science educator; b. Seattle, Oct. 14, 1942; s. Nancy Ann (Schwartz) Frank; m. Barbara Ann Covey; 1 child, Thomas Aaron. BS in Edn., History and Polit. Sci., Cen. Mich. U., 1966, MA in Polit. Sci., 1969; PhD in Polit. Sci., Wash. State U., Pullman, 1976. Tchr. social sci. Clarkston (Mich.) High Sch., 1967-69; instr. in polit. sci. Gogebec Community Coll., Ironwood, Mich., 1967-69, Lamar U., Beaumont, Tex., 1975-76; prof. polit. sci. N.E. La. U., Monroe, La., 1976-78, St. Cloud (Minn.) State U., 1978—; co-dir., founder St. Cloud State U. Survey. Contbr. articles to profl. jours. Mem. Am. Polit. Sci. Assn., Am. Assn. Pub. Opinion, Nat. Assn. Prelaw Advisors, Midwest Prelaw Advisors Assn., St. Cloud State U. Faculty Assn. (pres. 1993-94), Phi Kappa Delta. Office: St Cloud State U Dept Polit Sci 319 Brown Hall Saint Cloud MN 56301-4444

FRANK, THOMAS PAUL, medical equipment manufacturing company executive; b. Appleton, Wis., July 8, 1956; s. Paul J. and Irene (Small) F.; widower; children: Aaron, Rachel. AAS with honors, Fox Valley Coll., 1977; BS in Biomed. Engring. with honors, Milw. Sch. Engring., 1980; postgrad., Temple U., 1984-85; MBA, Ohio State U., 1990. Registered profl. engr., Wis. Biomed. engring. intern VA Hosp., Wood, Wis., 1979-80; devel. engr. Microswitch div. Mpls.-Honeywell, Inc., Freeport, Ill., 1980-82; dir. transducer devel. Ametek Controls Div., Feasterville, Pa., 1982-85; dir. R&D Medex, Inc., Dublin, Ohio, 1985-86; corp. v.p. R&D Medex, Inc., Dublin, 1986—; mem. editorial bd. Jour. Clin. Engring., AAMI Blood Pressure Monitoring and Standardization Com.; bd. dirs. Ctrl. Ohio Credit Union. Patentee: holds six U.S. patents for med. devices with patents pending on another 3; contbr. articles to profl. jours. Mem. IEEE (medicine and biology soc.), Assn. Advancement Med. Instrumentation. Republican. Roman Catholic. Office: Medex Inc 6750 Shier-Rings Rd Dublin OH 43017

FRANKE, MARIPAT KEMPS, chemical engineer; b. Appleton, Wis., Nov. 12, 1960; d. Ralph Edward and Mary Lee (Marciniak) Kemps; m. Mark Steven Franke. BA in Math. and Physics, Coe Coll., Cedar Rapids, Iowa, 1983; MS in Chem. Engring., Inst. Paper Sci. and Tech., 1987. Rsch. technician Kimberly Clark Corp., Neenah, Wis., 1984-85; process engr. Kimberly Clark Corp., Memphis, 1987-88, area process engr., 1988-90. Dance instr. YMCA, Neenah, 1996—; fundraising chairperson Coolidge Sch. PTO. Mem. TAPPI, Paper Industry Mgmt. Assn., LaLeche League, Profl. Women's Assn., Mortar Board, Sigma Phi Sigma, Delta Delta Delta. Home: 548 E Peckham Rd Neenah WI 54956-4220

FRANKE, RICHARD JAMES, investment banker; b. Springfield, Ill., June 23, 1931; s. William George and Frances Marie (Brennan) F. BA, Yale U., 1953; MBA, Harvard U., 1957. With John Nuveen & Co., Chgo., 1957—, v.p., 1965-69, exec. v.p., 1969-74, chief adminstrv. officer, 1970-74, pres., 1974-89, chief exec. officer, 1974—, chmn., 1988—, also dir., 1969—; vice chmn. Yale Corp., 1987-94, chmn., 1994—. Chmn. investment com. Yale U.; mem. Pres.'s Com. on the Arts and Humanities; trustee Chgo. Symphony Orch.; trustee U. Chgo.; bd. dirs. Lyric Opera, Newberry Libr. 1st lt. U.S. Army, 1953-55. Office: John Nuveen Co 333 W Wacker Dr Chicago IL 60606-1218

FRANKER, STEPHEN GRANT, investment executive; b. Spencer, Iowa, July 29, 1949; s. Oscar Grant and Betty Jean (Greenwaldt) F.; m. Dianne Alice Russell, Aug. 24, 1970; children: Derek, Leah. BA, U. No. Iowa, 1971. CPA, Iowa. Staff acct. McGladrey, Hansen, Dunn & Co., CPA's, Mason City, Iowa, 1971-75; audit supr. Clinton, Iowa, 1975-76; contr. 1st Fed. Savs. & Loan Assn., Spirit Lake, Iowa, 1976-82, pres., 1982-83; v.p. NW Fed. Savs. Bank, Spencer, 1983-90; investment exec. Piper Jaffray, Inc., Storm Lake, Iowa, 1990—. Republican. Lutheran. Home: 503 9th St Spirit Lake IA 51360-1701 Office: Piper Jaffray Inc 4 E 4th St Spencer IA 51301

FRANKING, HOLLY MAE, software publisher; b. Washington, D.C., May 13, 1944; d. Nelson W. and Dorothy Elizabeth (O'Connor) F.; m. John Robert Slegman, Aug. 16, 1986. BA in English, Mt. St. Mary's Coll., 1967; MA in English, Loyola U., L.A., 1970; MA in Philosophy, U. Kans., 1986, PhD in English, 1988. Cert. preschool, kindergarten, grades 1-12, adult tchr., Calif., jr. coll. tchr., Calif. Grade 3 tchr. Valley Sch., L.A., 1968-69; grade 4 tchr. St. Elizabeth Sch., Van Nuys, Calif., 1970-72, grades 5,6 tchr., vice prin., 1972-77; grades 7, 8 tchr. St. Mel Sch., Woodhills, Calif., 1977-78, Woodland Hills, Calif., 1978-79; grades 7, 8 tchr. St. Elizabeth Sch., Van Nuys, Calif., 1978-82; grades 10-12 tchr. Taft High Sch., L.A., 1982-83; pres., co-founder, software pub., author Diskotech, Inc., Prairie Village, Kans., 1987—; faculty rep. for sch. bd. St. Elizabeth Sch., Van Nuys, 1973-78. Author: (computerized video novel) Negative Space, 1990, CD-ROM version, 1995, Dr. Franking's Language Lessons, 1990; editor: Mae Franking's "My Chinese Marriage," 1991; pub.: How to Be Happily Employed in the 1990s, 93, Martensville Nightmare CD-ROM, 1996; author, pub. software; pub. PCcards (1st multimedia greeting cards 1992); book reviewer Kansas City Star newspaper, 1994. Democrat. Home: 6240 Rosewood Shawnee Mission KS 66205 Office: Diskotech Inc 7930 State Line Rd Ste 210 Prairie Village KS 66208-3704

FRANKL, DONALD T., company president; b. Algona, Iowa, Mar. 28, 1952. BSBA, U. S.D., 1975. Agrl. cons. Agrl. Consultant Svcs., Sioux City, Iowa, 1975-90; pres. Internat. Industries Inc., Sioux City, Iowa, 1990—. Patent for Aeration Device, Solid Separation. Mem. St. Peter's Parish, Jefferson, S.D., 1970-95; pres., bd. dirs. McCook Lake (S.D.) Recreation Assn., 1975-87; past mem. Isaac Walton League, McCook Lake. Republican. Roman Catholic. Office: Internat Industries Inc 713 Market Sioux City IA 51103-4350

FRANKLIN, BENJAMIN BARNUM, dinner club executive; b. Topeka, Kans., Nov. 7, 1944; s. Charles Benjamin and Margaret Lavona (Barnum) F. BA in Speech, U. Colo., 1967. With Associated Clubs, Inc., Topeka, 1967—, v.p., 1972-83, pres., 1983—; lectr., 1969-76; trustee Capper Found, 1994—, John Austin Cheley Found., 1995—. Honoree, Benjamin Barnum Franklin Day, Lima, Ohio, June 11, 1983. Editor, pub. newsletter The Dinner Gong. Chmn. steering com. Capper Found. for Crippled Children, Topeka. Mem. Kans. Soc. Assn. Execs., Nat. Speakers Assn. (chmn. chpt. 1982-83), Internat. Platform Assn. (gov. 1975—), SAR, Topeka Sales and Mktg. Execs. (bd. dirs. 1985—), Explorers Club, Am. Alpine Club, Knife and Fork Club (internat. v.p. 1991—), Internat. Knife and Fork Club (pres. 1994—), Topeka Knife and Fork Club, Met. Dinner Club (pres. 1983—), Exec. Dinner Club (pres. 1983, lectr. 1969-76), Rotary (bd. dirs. 1975-78, Paul Harris fellow), Friends of Libr., Sigma Phi Epsilon. Republican. Presbyterian. Contbr. articles to profl. publs. Office: 1 Townsite Plz Ste 315 Topeka KS 66603-3406

FRANKLIN, BRUCE WALTER, lawyer; b. Ellendale, N.D., Feb. 26, 1936; s. Wallace Henry and Frances (Webb) F.; m. Kristy Ann Jones, Feb. 7, 1944; children—Kevin, Monica, Taylor. Student, U. Mich., 1954-56; grad. Eastern Mich. U., 1957; LL.B., Detroit Coll. Law, 1962. Bar: Mich. 1963. Sole practice, Troy, Mich., from 1962; mng. ptnr. Franklin, Bigler, Berry & Johnston, P.C., Troy; now mng. ptnr. Franklin & Leonard, P.C., Troy. Past chmn. Mich. Young Reps. Chmn. United Meth. Retirement Cmtys.; pres., CEO Landward III Devel. Corp. Served with U.S. Army. Office: 2701 Troy Center Dr Ste 201 Troy MI 48084-4741

FRANKLIN, CLIFFORD, state legislator. Elec. engr.; mem. Kans. State Ho. of Reps. Dist. 23.

FRANKLIN, DOUGLAS E., publishing executive; b. 1957. Grad., U. Dayton, 1979. Staff acct. Dayton (Ohio) Newspapers, 1979, asst. contr., 1980, 1986-90; with Springfield (Ohio) Newspaper, 1981-83; bus. mgr. Longview Newspaper, Tex., 1983-86; with Dayton (Ohio) Daily News, 1990—, exec. v.p., gen. mgr. Office: Dayton Daily News 45 S Ludlow St Dayton OH 45402-1810*

FRANKLIN, FREDERICK RUSSELL, retired legal association executive; b. Berlin, Mar. 20, 1929; s. Ernest James and Frances (Price) F.; AB, Ind. U., 1951, JD with high distinction, 1956; m. Barbara Ann Donovan, Jan. 26, 1952; children: Katherine Elizabeth, Frederick Russell. Bar: Ind. 1956. Trial atty. criminal div. and ct. of claims sect., civil div. U.S. Dept. Justice, Washington, 1956-60; gen. counsel Ind. State Bar Assn., Indpls., 1960-67; dir. continuing legal edn. for Ind., adj. prof. law Ind. U., Indpls., 1965-68; staff dir. profl. standards ABA, Chgo., 1968-70, legal edn. and admissions to the bar, 1972-92, Sr. lawyers div., 1988-93; retired 1993. exec. v.p. Nat. Attys. Title Assurance Fund, Inc., Indpls., 1970-72. Trustee, Olympia Fields (Ill.) United Meth. Ch., 1980-84; treas. bd. dirs. Olympia Fields Pub. Libr., 1984-91; mem. Olympia Fields Pub. Safety Bd., 1983-92. Served to capt. USAF, 1951-53. Fellow Ind. Bar Found. (life), Found. Fed. Bar Assn. (life), Ind. State Bar Found. (life); mem. ABA (coun. sr. lawyers divsn. 1993—, bar admissions com. 1993—), Ind. Bar Assn., Ill. Bar Assn., Fed. Bar Assn. (officer, found. bd. dirs. 1974—, historian 1979—, treas. sr. lawyers divsn. 1993-95, sec. 1995—, nat. coun., nat. v.p. 1967-69, chpt. pres. 1965-66, chmn. admission to practice and recert. com. 1980-82, bd. dirs. Chgo. chpt. 1984-93), Nat. Orgn. Bar Counsel (pres. 1967), Kiwanis, Elks, Order of Coif, Phi Delta Phi. Home: 7788 N Lakeview Dr Unionville IN 47468-9729

FRANKLIN, JOSEPH EARL, furniture and bedding components company executive; b. Norfolk, Va., Dec. 24, 1953; s. Joseph Emmett Jr. and Alida Moore (Piver) F.; m. Marymarie Baker, June 19, 1976; children: Andrew Joseph, Timothy Crell, Maryann. BS in Acctg., Va. Poly. Inst. and State U., 1976. Staff acct. The Lane Co., Altavista, Va., 1976; office mgr. and acct. The Lane Co., Rocky Mount, Va., 1976-78; mgr. cost acctg. Action Industries divsn. Lane Co., Tupelo, Miss., 1978-79, asst. dir. fin. and adminstrn., 1979-81; divsn. contr. Leggett & Platt, Inc., High Point, N.C., 1981-88, adminstrv. mgr. S.E. divsn., 1988-90; mfg. sys. project mgr. corp. staff Leggett & Platt, Inc., Carthage, Mo., 1990—. Asst. cubmaster Boy Scouts Am., Lexington, N.C., 1987-89, cubmaster, 1989-93, dist. chmn., 1996—, dist. chmn. Big Three Dist., 1996—; sec. bd. trsutees, chmn. parsonage com. Shiloh United Meth. Ch., 1989-92, mem. nominations, fin. and parsonage coms., mem. adminstrv. coun., 1989-93. Mem. Am. Prodn. and Inventory Control Soc., Inst. Mgmt. Accts. Republican. Home: 721 Jennison Pl Carthage MO 64836-3322 Office: Leggett & Platt Inc PO Box 757 Carthage MO 64836-0757

FRANKLIN, MARCIA RUTH, information systems professional; b. Birmingham, Ala., Oct. 5, 1961; d. Royce Eugene and Roberta Ivon (Bishop) F. BS, Bob Jones U., 1983, MS, 1985, MA, 1988. Instr. math. Bob Jones U., Greenville, S.C., 1983-86, host sys. operator, 1986-88; computer programmer Langford Computer Svcs., Columbus, Ind., 1989-90; info. sys. supr. Tobar, Inc., Columbus, 1990—. Editor: (syllabus) Math. Reasoning, 1986; (book) Shepherds or Nomads?: When Preachers Look for Greener Grass, 1990; author: (play) Bound Feet, Bound Souls, 1988. Republican.

FRANKLIN, MARGARET LAVONA BARNUM (MRS. C. BENJAMIN FRANKLIN), civic leader; b. Caldwell, Kans., June 19, 1905; d. LeGrand Husted and Elva (Biddinger) Barnum; m. C. Benjamin Franklin, Jan. 20, 1940 (dec. 1983); children: Margaret Lee (Mrs. Michael J. Felso), Benjamin Barnum. B.A., Washburn U., 1952; student, Iowa State Tchrs. Coll., 1923-25, U. Iowa, 1937-38. Tchr. pub. schs. Union, Iowa, 1925-27, pub. schs., Kearney, Nebr., 1927-28, Marshalltown, Iowa, 1928-40; advance rep. Redpath-Vawter-Chautauquas, 1926, Associated Chautauquas, 1927-30. Mem. Citizens Adv. Com., 1965-69; mem. Stormont-Vail Regional Ctr. Hosp. Aux.; bd. dirs. Marshalltown Civic Theatre, 1938-40, pres. 1938-40; bd. dirs. Topeka Pub. Libr. Found., 1984-92; mem. Park Ave. Christian Ch., N.Y.C.; 1st sec. beautification com. City of Topeka, 1951. Recipient Waldo B. Heywood award Topeka Civic Theatre, 1967, Vol. Svc. award Topeka Pub. Libr., 1991. Mem. DAR (state chmn. Museum 1968-71), AAUW (50+ Yr. mem.), Gemini Group of Topeka, Topeka Geneal. Soc., Topeka Civic Symphony Soc. (dir. 1952-57, Svc. Honor citation 1960), Doll Collectors Am., Shawnee County Hist. Soc. (dir. 1963-75, sec. 1964-66), Stevengraph Collectors Assn., Friends of Topeka Public Libr. (dir. 1970-79, Disting. Svc. award 1980), PEO Sisterhood, Philanthropic and Ednl. Orgn. (pres. chpt. 1956-57, coop. bd. pres. 1964-65, chpt. honoree 1969), Native Sons and Daus. Kans. (life), Nonoso, Topeka Stamp Club, Western Sorosis Club (pres. 1960-61), Minerva Club (2d v.p. 1984-85), Woman's Club (1st v.p. 1952-54), Knife and Fork Club, Alpha Beta Gamma. Republican.

FRANKLIN, MARY ROSE, women's health nurse; b. Cleve., Sept. 30, 1958; d. Thomas Matthew and Mary Jane (Franklin) Callaghan; m. Paul Francis Franklin, June 9, 1979. BSN, Case Western Res., 1980, MSN, 1986. C.N.M., A.C.N.M., Ohio. Dir. family planning Free Med. Clinic of Greater Cleve., Ohio, 1980-83; staff RN Mt. Sinai Med. Ctr., Cleve., 1983-86; nurse midwife MetroHealth Med. Ctr., Cleve., 1986-90, MetroHealth Clement Ctr., Cleve., 1990-94; dir. nurse midwifery practice Doctors Hosp., Massillon, Ohio, 1994—; vol. Free Med. Clinic of Greater Cleve., Ohio, 1983—; clin. instr. Schs. of Medicine and Nursing, Case Western Res. U., Cleve., 1986—; mem. Coun. on Practice Greater Cleve. (Ohio) Nurses Assn., 1987-90. Recipient Rsch. grant Alumni Assn. Frances Payne Bolton Sch. Nursing, Cleve., 1988. Mem. ANA, Assn. Women's Health, Obstetric and Neonatal Nurses, Nat. Assn. Reproductive Health Profls., Am. Coll. Nurse Midwives, Am. Nurse Midwives (No. Ohio chpt. co-chair 1989-92), Ohio Coalition Nurses (specialty certification), Jacobs Inst. Women's Health, Sigma Theta Tau. Home: 2600 Yellow Creek Rd Akron OH 44333-2322 Office: 434 Lake Ave NE Massillon OH 44646-4352

FRANKLIN, RICHARD, state representative; b. Milan, Mo., July 15, 1934; m. Joyce Ann Fishback; children: James, Elizabeth. BS, Mo. State U., 1956; MA, U. Mo., 1963; postgrad., Ctrl. Mo. State U., 1972—. Prin. Ft. Ossage High Sch. State rep. dist. 53 Mo. Ho. of Reps., mem. edn. com., retirement com., chmn. appropriations-edn. com., banking com. Mem. Masons, Shriners, Kiwanis. Home: 18005 Cheyenne Dr Independence MO 64056-1981 Office: 18005 Cheyenne Independence MO 64056*

FRANKLIN, RONALD VINCENT, technology company executive; b. Indpls., Sept. 6, 1952; s. Ronald and Doris Elizabeth (Watkins) F.; m. Deborah Vivian Young, Feb. 21, 1974; children: Dawn Rachelle, Kelle Michelle. Student, Ind. U., 1970-74, U. Ill., 1984, U. Mo., 1985. Employment counselor City of Indpls., 1976-78; br. mgr. Household Internat., Indpls., 1978-81, Security Pacific Bank, Kokomo, Ind., 1981-82; sr. fin. examiner Indpls. Dept. Fin. Instns., 1982-88; fin. analyst Marion County Auditor's Office, Indpls., 1988-91; pres. Franklin Technologies, Indpls., 1983—, Environ. Tng. Svcs., Inc., Inpls., 1995—; cons. Cmty. Action Against Poverty, Inpls, 1992—, Mozel Sanders Homes, Indpls, 1992—; mem. Pub. Housing Bd. Commrs., Indpls., 1992—; treas. Urban Enterprise Assn. Developer fin. software products. Asst. twp. chmn. Lawrence Twp. Reps., Indpls., 1988—; founding mem. Kiwanis Club of Lawrence, Indpls., 1989; bd. dirs. Weed 'n' Seed Youth Program, Indpls., 1992, Homeless Vets. Ind.; city-county councillor-at-large Marion County/Indpls.; active Mayor's Commn. on African-Am. Males. Mem. Lawrence Twp. Rep. Club, Govt. Fin. Officers Assn., Black Rep. Coun., Young Reps. for Change. Methodist. Home: 6218 Albury Dr Indianapolis IN 46236-8204 Office: Franklin Technologies 3805 N Dearborn St Indianapolis IN 46205

FRANKLIN, SHIRLEY MARIE, marketing consultant; b. Kansas City, Mo., Apr. 13, 1930; d. Eric E. and Marie M. (Kilpatrick) Snodgrass; div. 1967; 1 child, Scot Wesley. BA, State U. Iowa, 1952; MS, Simmons Coll., 1954; MA, Kans. U., 1974. Cert. tchr., Kans., Mass., N.J., Ariz., Calif. Tchr., adminstr. various schs., 1952-76; gifted student program designer Leavenworth County (Kans.) Pub. Schs., 1976-77; sales cons., mgr. Sealight Co., Inc., Kansas City, Mo., 1978-82; dir. chain sales Haagen Dazs Ice Cream Co., Teaneck, N.J., 1982-87; program dir. case space mgmt. Ice Cream Industry, 1986-88; prin. Shirley Franklin Consulting, Basehor, Kans., 1987—; apptd. U.S. brands dir. Mövenpick Co., Zurich, Switzerland, 1990—; mktg. cons. Franklin & Assocs., 1994—; speaker at dairy industry meetings, seminars. Contbr. articles to profl. jours. and mags. Foster parent World Vision, Pasadena, Calif., 1986—; mem. nat. com. steering com. U.S. Congress Arts Caucus, Washington, 1988, 89; vol. ct. appointed spl. advocate for children in trouble, Kans., 1994; apptd. City Planning Commn., 1996—. Recipient Excellence in Sales Promotions award Dairy and Food Industries Supply Assn. Mem. Internat. Ice Cream Assn. (mktg. coun. 1979—), Delta Delta Delta. Republican. Episcopalian. Home and Office: 3741 N 155th St PO Box 233 Basehor KS 66007-9205

FRANKS, HERBERT HOOVER, lawyer; b. Joliet, Ill., Jan. 25, 1934; s. Carol and Lottie (Dermer) F.; m. Eileen Pepper, June 22, 1957; children: David, Jack, Eli. BS, Roosevelt U., 1954; postgrad., Am. U., 1960. Bar: Ill. 1961, U.S. Dist. Ct. (no. dist.) Ill. 1961, U.S. Supreme Ct. 1967. Ptnr. Franks & Gerkin (formerly Franks & Filler), 1985—; chmn. Wonder Lake State Bank, Ill., 1979—, First Nat. Bank, Marengo, Ill., 1976-84, mem. exec. com., 1976—; vice chmn. hotel mgmt. orgn. Bricton Group, Park Ridge, Ill., 1992—. Bus. editor Am. U. Law Rev. 1959, 60. State pres. Young Dems. of Ill., 1970-72; trustee Hebrew Theol. Coll., Skokie, Ill., 1974—; trustee, sec. Forest Inst. Profl. Psychology, Wheeling, Ill., 1979-91; chmn. Forest Hosp., Des Plaines, 1980-88. With U.S. Army, 1956-58. Fellow Ill. State Bar (bd. govs. 1994—); mem. Ill. Trial Lawyers (mem. bd. 1975-92, treas. 1985-87), Sigma Nu Phi (pres. 1980-82). Lodges: Masons, Shriners. Home: 19324 E Grant Hwy Marengo IL 60152 Office: Franks & Gerkin 19333 E Grant Hwy Marengo IL 60152-9439

FRANTZ, DEAN LESLIE, psychotherapist; b. Beatrice, Nebr., Mar. 27, 1919; s. Oscar C. and Flora Mae (Gish) F.; m. Marie Flory, Aug. 31, 1940; children: Marilyn, Shirley, Paul. BA, Manchester (Ind.) Coll., 1942; MDIV, Bethany Theol. Sem., Oak Brook, Ill., 1945; Diploma, C.G. Jung Inst. Zurich, 1977. Assoc. prof. Bethany Theol. Sem., 1957-64; dir. ch. rels. Manchester Coll., North Manchester, Ind., 1964-72; pvt. practice Jungian analyst Ft. Wayne, Ind., 1977—. Author: Meaning for Modern Man in the Paintings of Peter Birkhauser; editor: Barbara Hannah: The Cat, Dog, and Horse Lectures, and the Beyond, 1992. Mem. Internat. Assn. Analytical Psychology, Assn. Grad Analytical Psychologists. Home: 3831 Evergreen Ln Fort Wayne IN 46815-4707

FRANTZE, DAVID W., lawyer; b. Kansas City, Mo., Jan. 28, 1955; s. James W. and Margaret M. (Pursley) F.; m. Geri L. Sexton, July 28, 1979; children: Kevin, Lisa, Christopher, Timothy. BA, Avila Coll., 1976; JD, U. Mo., Kansas City, 1981. V.p. Stinson, Mag & Fizzell, P.C., Kansas City, 1981—. Bd. dirs. Kansas City Spirit, Inc., 1986-88, pres., 1988, mem. adv. coun., 1989—; bd. dirs. Kansas City Neighborhood Alliance, 1987—, chmn., 1994—, Kansas City Riverfront, Inc., 1991-94; bd. counselors Avila Coll., 1989—; trustee Mid-Am. chpt. Leukemia Soc. Am., 1992—; mem. Civic Coun. Kansas City, 1995—. Mem. ABA, Mo. Bar Assn., Kansas City Met. Bar Assn. (chmn. real estate law com. 1992), Lawyers Assn. Kansas City. Roman Catholic. Home: 11812 Central St Kansas City MO 64114-5536 Office: Stinson Mag & Fizzell 1201 Walnut St Ste 2600 Kansas City MO 64106-2136

FRANTZEN, JEFFREY ALAN, civil engineer; b. Webster City, Iowa, Nov. 2, 1953; s. Karl Herman and Mildred Bernice (Skola) F.; m. Naomi Louise Henry, Apr. 25, 1982; children: Avery Jamison, Charles August, Nathan Daniel Graff. BSCE, U. Nebr., Omaha, 1977; MSCE, Kans. State U., 1990. Registered profl. engr., Kans. Engr. in tng. Kans. Dept. Transp., El Dorado, 1977-78; found. engr. Kans. Dept. Transp., Topeka, 1978-83, soils engr., 1983-90, rsch. devel. engr., 1990, dist. materials engr., 1990—. Author: Transportation Research Record, 1983. Mem. Soc. for Exptl. Mechs., N.Y. Acad. Sci. Office: Kans Dept Transp 121 W 21st St Topeka KS 66612

FRANZ, DANIEL THOMAS, financial planner; b. Dayton, Ohio, Jan. 30, 1949; s. Albin Benedict and Monica Elizabeth (Moeller) F.; m. Sally Ann Stickley, Oct. 11, 1968; children: Amanda Marie, Stephanie Ann. BS, Charleston So. U., 1971, postgrad., 1975; postgrad., S.C. State U., 1974. Cert. fin. aid adminstr., fin. planner. Coach, admissions officer Bapt. Coll., Charleston (S.C.) So. U., 1971-72; dir. fin. aid Bapt. Coll., Charleston, S.C., 1972-76; pvt. practice fin. planning Greenville, Ohio, 1977—; cons. S.C. Bapt. Conv., Columbia, 1974-76, U.S. Office Edn., Atlanta, 1974-76, Corning Glass Works, Greenville, 1984—, Franklin-Monroe High Sch., Pitsburg, Ohio, 1985—, United Telephone Co., Bellefontaine, Ohio, 1986—. Bd. dirs. Darke County Supts. Roundtable, Greenville, 1983—, Darke County Widows Assn., 1984-86; mem., chmn. bd. dirs. S.C. Com. Higher Edn., Columbia, 1974-76, Darke County Mental Health Clinic, 1984-90; bd. dirs. Coun. on Rural Svcs. Programs, 1991—; chmn. bd. dirs. Ch. of the Transfiguration Cath. Ch., West Milton, Ohio, 1978-82. Mem. Inst. Cert. Fin. Planners, Internat. Assn. Fin. Planners, Nat. Assn. Life Underwriters, Miami Valley Assn. Life Underwriters, S.C. Assn. Student Fin. Aid Adminstrs. (bd. dirs. 1971—), Darke County C. of C. (bd. dirs. 1993—), Lions. Republican. Office: Fin Achievement Svcs PO Box 657 5116 Childrens Hm Bradford Rd Greenville OH 45331-9327

FRANZ, RAYMOND ANDREW, electronic engineer; b. Goessel, Kans., July 7, 1956; s. Arthur and Hilda F. BA in Indsl. Tech. cum laude, Wichita State U., 1988. FCC lic. Elec. engr. Moridge Mfg., Moundridge, Kans., 1990—. Fundraiser Big Bros./Big Sisters, 1992-94. Mem. Phi Kappa Phi. Office: Moridge Mfg Co PO Box 810 Moundridge KS 67107-0810

FRAPPIER, CARA MUNSHAW, school social worker; b. Grand Rapids, Mich., Feb. 13, 1942; d. Carroll Lambert and Ruth (Switzer) Munshaw; m. Calvin Leslie Frappier, July 30, 1966; 1 child, Arielle. BA, Mich. State U., 1963, MA, 1966, MSW, 1973. Lic. social worker, marriage and family counselor, Mich.; diplomate in clin. social work. Elem. tchr. Lansing (Mich.) Pub. Schs., 1963-65; sch. social worker Ingham Intermediate Sch. Dist., Mason, Mich., 1965—; bd. dirs. profl. staff assn. Ingham Intermediate Pub. Schs., 1981-85; founding mem. Family Therapy and Consultation Program for Sch. Social Workers. Mem. Nat. Assn. Social Workers, Am. Assn. Marriage and Family Counselors, Am. Orthopsychiat. Assn., Mich. Sch. Social Workers Assn. Democrat. Home: 5706 Bearcreek Dr Lansing MI 48917-1400 Office: Ingham Intermediate Sch Dist 2630 W Howell Rd Mason MI 48854-9329

FRASE, CHARLES FREDERICK, marketing professional; b. Barberton, Ohio, Nov. 28, 1961; s. Harold Wesley and Joseba Ann (Miller) F. Student, Hobe Sound (Fla.) Bible Coll., 1990, 92. Pres. Frase Mktg., Doylestown, Ohio, 1990—; distbr. Watkins, Doylestown, 1993—. Inventor Amirrorcan. Mem. Baberton Wesleyan Meth. Ch., Loyal Oak Community Ch., Nat. Right to Life Com., Inc. Recipient O.W.E. award, 1983. Republican. Home and Office: 13870 S Hametown Rd Doylestown OH 44230-9577

FRASER, DONALD MACKAY, former mayor, former congressman, educator; b. Mpls., Feb. 20, 1924; s. Everett and Lois (MacKay) F.; m. Arvonne Skelton, June 30, 1950; children: Thomas Skelton, Mary MacKay, John DuFrene, Lois MacKay (dec.), Anne T. (dec.), Jean Skelton. BA cum laude, U. Minn., 1944, LLB, 1948. Bar: Minn. 1948. Ptnr. Lindquist, Fraser & Magnuson (and predecessors), 1948-62; Minn. State senator, 1954-62; sec. Senate Liberal Caucus, 1955-62; mem. 88th-95th Congresses from 5th Dist. Minn., mem. fgn. affairs com., chmn. subcom. on internat. orgn., mem. budget com.; mayor City of Mpls., 1980-93; mem. study and rev. com. Dem. Caucus; mem. Commn. on Role and Future Presdl. Primaries, 1976; adj. prof. law and pub. affairs U. Minn., Mpls.; Vice chmn., dir. Mpls. Citizens Com. on Pub. Edn., 1950-54; Sec. Minn. del. Democratic Nat. Conv., 1960; chmn. Minn. Citizens for Kennedy, 1960; mem. platform com. Dem. Nat. Conv., 1964, mem. rules com., 1972, 76; vice chmn. Com. Dem. Selection Presdl. Nominees, 1968; chmn. Democratic Study Group Congress, 1969-71, Commn. on Party Structure and Del. Selection Dem. Party, 1971-72; 1st Am. co-chmn. Anglo-Am. Parliamentary Conf. on Africa, 1964; mem. U.S. del. 7th spl. session and 30th session UN Gen. Assembly, 1975; Congl. adviser to U.S. del. to UN Conf. on Disarmament, 1967-73, to U.S. del. to 3d Law of Sea Conf., 1972, to UN Commn. on Human Rights, 1974. Chair health com. U.S. Conf. Mayors; bd. dirs. Mpls. United Way, 1986-93; co-chair Ctr. for Internat. Policy, 1976—; co-founder, pres. Dem. Farmer-Labor Edn. Found.; initiated numerous youth programs such as Transitional Work Internship Program, Youth Work Internship Program, Neighborhood Early Learning Ctrs., Youth Coordinating Bd., Youth Trust. Lt. (J.G.) USNR, 1944-46. Recipient 1st Minn. Internat. Human Rights award, 1985, Disting. Svc. award Mpls. United Way, 1992. Mem. Mpls. Fgn. Policy Assn. (pres. 1952-53), Citizens League Greater Mpls. (sec. 1951-54), Minn. Bar Assn., Hennepin County Bar Assn., Ams. for Dem. Action (nat. chmn. 1973-76), Dem. Conf. (nat. chmn. 1976-78), U. Minn. Law Alumni Assn. (dir. 1958-61), Univ. Dist. Improvement Assn. (pres. 1950-52), Nat. League of Cities (2d v.p. 1991, 1st v.p. 1992, pres. 1993), Minn. Advocates for Human Rights (co-founder, bd. dirs. 1982-93), League of Minn. Cities (bd. dirs. 1991-93).

FRASER, JOHN G., marketing professional; b. Chgo., Aug. 6, 1938; s. William Leo and Alice Anna (Schulz) F.; 1 child, Alexander. AB, U. Ill., 1963, MA, 1965, PhD, 1968. Asst. prof. Carleton U., Ottawa, Can., 1967-68, U. Ky., Lexington, 1968-72, U. Wis., Milw., 1972-74; mktg. rep. Control Data Corp., Milw., 1974-76; dir. rsch. First Wis. Corp., Milw., 1976-78, v.p., group product mgr., 1978, v.p., dir. mktg., 1984; pres. Fraser Mktg., Milw., 1988—. With USN, 1956-59. Office: 2302 E Marion St Shorewood WI 53211-2058

FRASER, MALCOLM JAMES, JR., biological sciences educator; b. Troy, N.Y., Oct. 20, 1952; s. Malcolm James and Rose-Marie Evelyn (Jordan) F.; Tresa Marie Strauss; children: Steven James, Nicholas Alan, Mark Evan. BS, Wheeling (W.Va.) Coll., 1975; MS, Ohio State U., 1979, PhD, 1981. Postdoctoral fellow Pa. State U., State College, 1981; postdoctoral assoc. Tex. A&M U., College Station, 1981-83; asst. prof. U. Notre Dame, Ind., 1983-89, assoc. prof., 1989—; cons. Am. Biogenetic Scis., Notre Dame, 1985-92, scientific adv. bd., 1986-92. Contbr. articles to profl. jours. Asst. coach Irish Youth Hockey League, South Bend, Ind., 1990-91; den leader Boy Scouts Am., South Bend, 1989—. Recipient Rsch. Career Devel. award NIH, 1991-96, rsch. grantee, 1985-89, 90-95, U.S. Dept. Agriculture, 1984-87, 88-91. Mem. AAAS, Am. Soc. for Virology, Tissue Culture Assn. (chmn. invertebrate div. 1990-92). Office: U Notre Dame Biol Scis Notre Dame IN 46556

FRASER, STANLEY CHARLES, credit union executive; b. Cairo, Ill., Nov. 6, 1951; s. Frederick Howard Jr. and Elizabeth Ann (Musgroves) F.; m. Alice Lynne Rohrer, Aug. 30, 1985; children: Sara, Matthew, Douglas, Nicholas, Jonathan. BA, So. Ill. U., 1976. Loan officer Bank of De Soto, Ill., 1977-79; asst. v.p. Charter Bank, Sparta, Ill., 1979-83; loan officer 1st Nat. Bank and Trust, Carbondale, Ill., 1983-85; chief exec. officer Ill. State Police Fed. Credit Union, Springfield, 1985—. Candidate Jackson County Clk., Murphysboro, Ill., 1974; bd. dirs. Jackson County Mental Health Bd., Murphysboro, 1980, Am. Cancer Soc., Carbondale, 1984; treas. Rochester New Ch. Devel.; youth baseball coach; asst. cubmaster Boy Scouts Am.,

1994-95. Named one of Outstanding Young Men of Am. U.S. Jaycees, 1974. Mem. Credit Union Execs. Soc. (Ill. Exec. of Yr. award 1989, 92), Ill. Credit Union Found. (bd. dirs. 1989-90, vice-chmn. 1991, chmn. 1992, 93; fundraising chmn. 1994-96), Ill. Police Offiers Meml. com., Sangamon Valley Chpt. Credit Unions (chmn. 1992), Shriners, Masons, Scottish Rite. Republican. Presbyterian. Home: PO Box 20641 Springfield IL 62708-0641 Office: Ill State Police Fed Credit Union 201 E Adams St Ste 150 Springfield IL 62701-1122

FRASIER, RALPH KENNEDY, lawyer, banker; b. Winston-Salem, N.C., Sept. 16, 1938; s. LeRoy Benjamin and Kathryn O. (Kennedy) F.; m. Jeannine Quick, Aug. 1981; children: Karen D. Frasier Alston, Gail S., Ralph Kennedy Jr., Keith Lowery, Marie Kennedy, Rochelle Doar. BS, N.C. Cen. U., Durham, 1963, JD, 1965. Bar: N.C. 1965, Ohio 1976. With Wachovia Bank and Trust Co., N.A., Winston-Salem, N.C., 1965-70; v.p., counsel Wachovia Bank and Trust Co., N.A., 1969-70; asst. counsel, v.p. parent co. Wachovia Corp., 1970-75; v.p., gen. counsel Huntington Nat. Bank, Columbus, Ohio, 1975—; sr. v.p. Huntington Nat. Bank, 1976-83, sec., 1981—, exec. v.p., 1983—, cashier, 1983—; v.p. Huntington Bancshares Inc., 1976-86, gen. counsel, 1976—, sec., 1981—; sec., dir. Huntington Mortgage Co., Huntington State Bank, Huntington Leasing Co., Huntington Bancshares Fin. Corp., Huntington Investment Mgmt. Co., Huntington Nat. Life Ins. Co., Huntington Co., 1976-88; v.p., asst. sec. Huntington Bank N.E. Ohio, 1982-84; asst. sec. Huntington Bancshares Ky., 1985—; sec. Huntington Trust Co., N.A., 1987—, Huntington Bancshares Ind., Inc., 1986—, Huntington Fin. Services Co., 1987—. Bd. dirs. Family Svcs. Winston-Salem, 1966-74, sec., 1966-71, 74, v.p., 1974; chmn. Winston-Salem Transit Authority, 1974-75; bd. dirs. Rsch. for Advancement of Personalities, 1968-71, Winston-Salem Citizens for Fair Housing, 1970-74, N.C. United Community Svcs., 1970-74; treas. Forsyth County (N.C.) Citizens Com. Adequate Justice Bldg., 1968; trustee Appalachian State U., Boone, N.C., 1973-83, endowment fund, 1973-83, Columbus Drug Edn. and Prevention Fund, Inc., 1989-92; trustee, vice chmn. employment and Edn. Commn. Franklin County, 1982-85; mem. Winston-Salem Forsyth County Sch. Bd. Adv. Coun., 1973-74, Atty. Gen's Ohio Task Force Minorities in Bus., 1977-78; bd. dirs. Inorads Columbus, Inc., 1986-95, Greater Columbus Arts Coun., 1986-94, Columbus Urban League Inc., 1987-94, vice chmn., 1990-94, Ohio Bd. Regents, 1994—; trustee Riverside Meth. Hosp. Found., 1989-90, Grant Med. Ctr., 1990-95, Grant/Riverside Meth. Hosps., 1995—; dir. Cmty. Mutual Ins. Co., 1989-92, mem. audit com., 1989-92; trustee N.C. Ctrl. U., 1993—, vice-chmn., 1993-94, chmn. 1995—; mem. Ohio Bd. Regents, 1987-96, vice-chmn., 1993-95, chmn., 1996—; trustee Nat. Jud. Coll., 1996—. With AUS, 1958-60. Mem. ABA, Nat. Bar Assn., Ohio Bar Assn., Columbus Bar Assn. Office: Huntington Nat Bank Huntington Ctr 41 S High St Ste 3412 Columbus OH 43287-0001

FRATESCHI, LAWRENCE JAN, economist, statistician, educator; b. Chgo., Oct. 7, 1952; s. Lawrence and Olga (Los) F. BS in Math. and Psychology, U. Ill., Chgo., 1975, MA in Econs., 1979, MS Pub. Health in Biostats. and Epidemiology, 1990, PhD in Econs., 1992. Teaching asst. dept. math, lectr. dept. info. and decision scis. U. Ill., Chgo., 1978-80, rsch. assoc. epidemiology and biostatistics Sch. Pub. Health, 1989-90; statistician Argonne (Ill.) Nat. Labs., 1980-81; asst. prof. econs. and stats. Coll. of DuPage, Glen Ellyn, Ill., 1981-86, assoc. prof., 1986-90, prof. econs., stats., 1990—; rsch. prof. epidemiology and biostats. Sch. Pub. Health U. Ill., Chgo., Ill., 1993—. Contbr. articles to profl. publs. Mem. Am. Econ. Assn., Am. Statis. Assn., Am. Pub. Health Assn., Soc. Epidemiologic Rsch., Midwest Econs. Assn., Ill. Econs. Assn., Ill. Pub. Health Assn., Phi Eta Sigma, Phi Kappa Phi, Delta Omega. Office: Coll of DuPage 22nd and Lambert Rd Glen Ellyn IL 60137

FRAUENS, MARIE, editor, researcher; b. Kansas City, Mo., July 10, 1902; d. Frank Henry and Amanda Margaret (Stansch) F. AA, Kansas City (Mo.) Jr. Coll., 1921; BJ, U. Mo., 1924; MA, Columbia U., 1947; postgrad., Naval Res. Officers Sch., Washington, 1955-64, Indsl. Coll. Armed Forces, 1964. Instr. swimming, Kansas City, 1919-21; rschr. Mo. State Hist. Soc., 1922-24; teaching prin., dir. extra curricular newspaper and dramatics club Wardell (Mo.) High Sch., 1924-27; math. editor Row Peterson and Co., Evanston, Ill., 1927-35; chief editor high sch. program McGraw-Hill Book Co., N.Y.C., 1935-43; commd. lt. (j.g.) USNR, 1943, advanced through grades to permanent commn. as lt. comdr., 1949, liaison officer U.S. Navy-U.S. Armed Forces Inst., 1943-44, tng. officer Bur. Ordnance, 1944-47; tech. writer Naval Res. Tng. Publs. Project, 1947-49; ret. from Res., 1965; tng. dir. John I. Thompson and Co., Washington, 1949-57; tech. writer Dept. Navy, Washington, 1957; adminstrv. officer Office of Sec. Def., Washington, 1958-69; freelance editor, rschr., Washington, 1969-86, Kansas City, Mo., 1986—, messages of Gov. Ky. to gen. assembly for Ky. Hist. Soc., 1974-76; editor The Machine Gun, Vol. II, Part VII for Lt. Col. George Chinn, USMC, 1952; editor reports for, also exec. sec. Spl. Com. Adequacy of Range Facilities, Dept. Def., 1958; completed authentic restoration of 1882 town house on Capitol Hill, 1980. Active first aid, health courses ARC, 1917-18; girls' advisor YWCA, Kansas City, 1921; counselor Chgo. settlement house, 1930-35; active Red Cross Fund, D.C., 1949; mem. bd. dirs. Naval Gun Factory Welfare and Recreation Assn., 1947-49; mem. work group to develop Interagy. Sci. and Engring. Exhibit The Vision of Man, Office Sec. Def., 1963-65. Decorated mil. medals. Mem. Naval Res. Assn., Ret. Officers Assn., Res. Officers Assn., Naval Order U.S., Am. Def. Preparedness Assn., Union Cemetery Hist. Soc., Nat. Trust Hist. Preservation, Pi Gamma Mu. Contbr. to Commn. Implications of Armed Services Ednl. Programs. Author manuals, pamphlets in field of naval ops. Avocation: genealogical and historical rsch. Home and Office: 435 W 10th St Kansas City MO 64105-2221

FRAUTSCHI, WALTER ALBERT, contract and publications printing company executive; b. Madison, Wis., Dec. 4, 1901; s. Emil John and Ida (Parman) F.; m. Dorothy Jones, Aug. 10, 1927; children: John Jones, Walter Jerome. B.A., U. Wis., 1924. Chmn. emeritus bd. Webcrafters, Inc., Madison, 1959—. Campaign chmn. Madison United Givers Fund, 1938; trustee, pres. Wis. Alumni Research Found.; chmn. Vilas Estate Fund, 1972, Madison Civic Center Campaign, 1976; Chmn., trustee Brandenburg Found. (merged with Madison Rotary Found.). Mem. Wis. Acad. Sci., Arts and Letters, Wis. Alumni Assn. (pres. 1948), Sigma Nu, Sigma Delta Chi, Phi Kappa Phi. Presbyn. (trustee). Club: Rotarian (pres. Madison 1955). Home: Wynfield Home 413 S Yellowstone Dr Madison WI 53719

FREBORG, LAYTON W., state legislator; m. Delilah Freborg; 4 children. Gen. contractor, state rep., 1973-81, state senator dist. 8, 1985—; chmn. edn. and natural resources com. N.D. State Senate. Chmn. N.D. State Rep. Com. (mem. edn. and agr. com.); mem. Underwood Sch. Bd. (pres. 14 yrs.). Mem. Farm Bur., Turtle Lake Civic Club, Underwood Civic Club, Underwood C. of C. Republican. also: State Senate State Capital Bismarck ND 58505*

FRED, MICHAEL E., financial consultant; b. Niles, Mich., July 5, 1958. BA, Ball State U., Muncie, Ind., 1982. Fin. cons. Edward Jones, Elkhart, Ind., 1983-84; asst. v.p. Merrill Lynch, South Bend, Ind., 1984—. Mem., chmn. Pastor Perrish Com., South Bend, 1994—. Mem. Moose, Kiwanis. Republican. Methodist. Home: 51893 Stoney Creek Dr Elkhart IN 46514-5809 Office: Merrill Lynch 404 S Columbia St PO Box 4013 South Bend IN 46699

FREDERICK, JOHN, food products executive; b. 1915. Grad., U. Ky., 1938. Ptnr. Creighton Bros., Warsaw, Ind., 1938—; ret. Office: Creighton Bros LP 4217 E Old Rd 30 Warsaw IN 46580*

FREDERICK, JOHN EDGAR, chemistry educator; b. Thursday, W.Va., Aug. 10, 1940; s. Orlan Leonard and Mildred (Maston) F.; m. Anne Elizabeth Zsilli, Mar. 21, 1970; 1 child, Ann-Catherine. BS in Chemistry, Glenville (W.Va.) State Coll., 1960; PhD in Phys. Chemistry, U. Wis., 1964. Postdoctoral fellow Stanford Rsch. Inst., Menlo Park, Calif., 1964-66; assoc. prof. chemistry and polymer sci. U. Akron, Ohio, 1966—. Office: Univ Akron Inst Polymer Sci Akron OH 44325-3909

FREDERICK, LLOYD RANDALL, soil microbiologist; b. Shannon, Ill., Aug. 5, 1921; s. Elmer Lewis and Ina Hattie (Hendricks) F.; m. Shirley Althea Miller, Oct. 20, 1943; children: June Ann, Mary Lou, David Randall. BS, U. Nebr., 1943; PhD, Rutgers U., 1950. Asst. prof. soil microbiology Purdue U., West Lafayette, Ind., 1949-55; prof. soil microbiology Iowa State U., Ames, 1955-78; sr. soil microbiologist U.S. Agy. Internat. Devel., Washington, 1978-89; cons. Cambridge, Iowa, 1989—; cons. W.R. Grace & Co., Princeton, Ill., 1966-70, Rsch. Seeds, St. Joseph, Mo., 1970-74. Author (with others): Methods of Soil Analysis, 1985; contbr. articles to profl. jours. Pres. Collegiate Meth. Credit Union, Ames, 1962-71; lay speaker United Meth. Ch., Iowa, 1960-75. Soil Sci. Soc. Am. fellow, 1961; Fulbright scholar, 1962. Mem. Am. Soc. Agronomy (fellow 1961). Republican. Home and Office: 119 8th St Cambridge IA 50046-1015

FREDERICK, RANDALL DAVIS, state legislator; m. Cindy Abraham; 3 children. Student, S.D. State U., 1974-76. Mem. S.D. Ho. of Reps., 1989-92, mem. appropriations com., 1992-93, mem. taxation and transp. coms., 1992—, chmn. appropriations com., 1994—, co-chmn. joint appropriations com., 1994—; farmer, Hayti, S.D., 1976—. Home: RR 1 Box 106 Hayti SD 57241*

FREDERICK, RAYMOND JOSEPH, sales engineering executive; b. Chgo., Oct. 27, 1948; s. Clarence W. and Lorraine T. (Frey) F.; m. Doreen Lynne Thompson, Nov. 7, 1970; children: Victoria Lynne, Steven, Joseph. Student, U. Ill., Chgo., 1966-68, Tri-State Coll., Angola, Ind., 1968-69; BSEE, Chgo. Tech. Coll., 1974. Technician, jr. engr. Rauland-Borg Corp., Chgo., 1970-74, assoc. engr., 1974-75, design engr., 1975-78, application engr., 1978-79, sales engr., 1979-81, product mgr., 1981-83; sales engr. Nichimen Am. Inc., Chgo., 1983-87; mgr. sales engring. Nichimen Am. Inc., Farmington Hills, Mich., 1987—. Pres. Westgate Civic Assn., Farmington Hills, 1989—. Mem. Soc. Automotive Engrs., Intelligent Vehicle Hwy. System Am., Nat. Assn. Broadcasters. Roman Catholic. Home: 30180 Richmond Hl Farmington Hl MI 48334-2335 Office: Nichimen Am Inc Ste 155 32000 Northwestern Hwy Farmington Hills MI 48334

FREDERICK, RONALD DAVID, aerospace engineer; b. Dayton, Ohio, Feb. 17, 1966; s. Ronald Richard and Judith Anne (Echle) F. BS in Aerospace Engring., U. Cin., 1989; MS in Aerospace Engring., U. Dayton, 1992. Aerospace engr. ASC/AMD USAF, Wright Patterson AFB, Ohio, 1989—. Mem. AIAA. Republican. Roman Catholic. Office: ASC/ENFT ASC/ENFT Wright Patterson AFB OH 45433

FREDERICK, VIRGINIA FIESTER, state legislator; b. Rock Island, Ill., Dec. 24, 1916; d. John Henry and Myrtle (Montgomery) Heise; B.A., U. Iowa, 1938; postgrad. Lake Forest Coll., 1942-43, LLD, 1994; m. C. Donnan Fiester (dec. 1975); children—Sheryl Fiester Ross, Alan R., James D.; m. Kenneth Jacob Frederick, 1978. Free-lance fashion designer, Lake Forest, Ill., 1952-78; pres. Mid Am. China Exchange, Kenilworth, Ill., 1978-81; mem. Ill. Ho. of Reps., Springfield, 1979-95, asst minority leader, 1990-95. Alderman, first ward Lake Forest, 1974-78; del. World Food Conf., Rome, 1974; mem. Ill. Commn. on Status of Women subcom. pensions and employment, 1976-79; co-chmn. Conf. Women Legislators, 1982-85; bd. trustees Lake Forest Coll., 1995; city supr. City of Lake Forest, Ill., 1995-96. Named Chgo. Area Woman of Achievement, Internat. Orgn. Women Execs., 1978. Recipient Lottie Holman O'Neal award, 1980, Jane Addams award, 1982, Outstanding Legislator award Ill. Hosp. Assn., 1986, VFW Svc. award, 1988, Joyce Fitzgerald Meml. award, 1988, Susan B. Anthony Legislator of the Yr. award, 1989, award Delta Kappa Gamma, 1991, Outstanding Legislator award, 1995, Svcs. for Srs. award, Ill. Dept. Aging, 1991, Ethics in Pols. award, Rep. Women's Club, 1992, Woman of Achievement award YWCA North Eastern Ill., 1994, Ill. Women in Govt. award, 1994. Mem. LWV (local pres. 1958-60, state dir. 1969-75, mem. nat. com. 1975-76), AAUW (local pres. 1968-70, state pres. 1975-77, state dir. 1963-69, mem. nat. com. 1967-69, Legislator of Yr. award 1993), UN Assn. (dir.), Chgo. Assn. Commerce and Industry (dir.). Methodist. Home: 1290 N Western Ave Lake Forest IL 60045-1317

FREDERICKS, MARSHALL MAYNARD, sculptor; b. Rock Island, Ill., Jan. 31, 1908; s. Frank A. and Frances Margaret (Bragg) F.; m. Rosalind Bell Cooke, Sept. 9, 1943; children: Carl Marshall and Christopher Matzen (twins), Frances Karen Bell, Rosalind Cooke, Suzanne Pelletreau. Student, John Huntington Poly. Inst., Cleve.; grad., Cleve. Sch. Art, 1930; student, Heimann Schule, Schwegerle Schule, Munich, Germany, Academie Scandinav, Paris, France; pvt. studies, Copenhagen, Rome and London, Carl Milles' Studio, Stockholm, Sweden; student, Cranbrook Acad. Art; 3 hon. doctorate degrees in fine arts. Faculty Cleve. Sch. Art, 1931, Cranbrook Sch., Bloomfield Hills, Mich., 1932-38; Kingswood Sch., Cranbrook, 1932-42, Cranbrook Acad. Art, Bloomfield Hills, Mich., 1932-42. Local, nat., internat. exhbns. art since 1928 include, Carnegie Inst., Pitts., Cleve. Mus., Pa. Acad., Chgo. Art Inst., Whitney Mus. Am. Art Nat. Invitational, Detroit Art Inst., Denver Mus., Phila. Internat. Invitational, N.Y. World's Fair Am. art exhbn., Modern Sculpture Internat. Exhbn. Detroit, Internat. Sculpture Show Cranbrook Mus., AIA, Nat. Sculpture Soc., Archtl. League of N. Y., Mich. Acad., Brussels, Belgium, Port of History Mus. Phila. Nat. Sculpture Soc. Exhbn.; others; commns. include Vets. Meml. Bldg, Detroit, adminstrn. bldg. war meml., U. Mich., Louisville Courier-Jour. Bldg, Jefferson Sch., Wyandotte, Mich., Holy Ghost Sem., Ann Arbor, Mich.; State Dept. Fountain, Washington, Cleve. War Meml. Fountain, Milw. Pub. Mus. Sculpture, N.Y. World's Fair permanent sculpture, Fed. Bldg. sculpture, Cin., Community Nat. Bank, Pontiac, Mich., Sir Winston Churchill Meml., Freeport, Bahamas; union bldg., Freeport, Bahamas; J.L. Hudson's Eastland, Northland, and Flint (Mich.) Mall, Two Sister fountain, Cranbrook, Michigan, Dallas Library sculpture, Henry Ford Meml., Dearborn, Mich., Oakland U., Saints and Sinners Fountain, Midland Center for Arts, Crittenton Hosp., Rochester, Fgn. Ministry Copenhagen, Freedom of the Human Spirit, Shain Park, Birmingham, Mich., 1986, Leaping Gazelle Her Majesty Queen Margrethe II Denmark, Marselisborg Castle, 1990, Wings of the Morning Kirk in the Hills, Bloomfield Hills, Mich., 1986, Gazelle & Thinker, Millesgarden, Lidingo, Sweden, 1992, God the Father and the Rainbow Fountain, Stockholm, 1995; portrait commns. include Willard Dow, Midland, Mich., George G. Booth Meml., Cranbrook, Mrs. Horace Rackham Meml, Pres. John F. Kennedy, Yoshita, others; works included numerous museums, pvt., civic collections. Mem. Pres.'s Com. for Employment of Handicapped; mem. Gov.'s State Capitol Com.; co-founder, dir. DIADEM Program for Internat. Exchange of Handicapped.; trustee Am.-Scandinavian Found., People-to-People Program, Inc. Served with C.E. U.S. Army, 1942-44; lt. col. 20th bomber command; 8th Air Force 1944-45, Okinawa. Decorated knight Order of Dannebrog, also officer 1st class, comdr. Order Dannebrog (Denmark); knights cross 1st class Order of St. Olav (Norway), comdr. Order of the North Star (Sweden); recipient 1st prize Cleve. Mus. Art, 1931, Anna Scripps Whitcomb prize Detroit Inst. Arts, 1938, 1st prize internat. exhbn. Dance Internat., Rockfeller Ctr., N.Y.C., 1st prize Barbour Meml. nat. competition, medal Mich. Inst. Architects, gold medal Archtl. League of N.Y., Golden Plate award Am. Acad. Achievement, silver medal Am. Scandinavian Found., citation Mich. Assn. Professions, Nat. Soc. Interior Designers, Internat. Com. of Internat. Ctr. Disabled, U. Detroit, Pres.'s Cabinet award U. Detroit, 1973, 1st prize NAD 160th Ann. Exhbn., 1985, Am. Soc. Landscape Architects award, 1987, Ellis Island Medal of Honor, 1993, Internat. Achievement award Gov. Mich., 1993; Marshall M. Fredericks Sculpture Gallery named in his honor Saginaw Valley State U., other Am. and fgn. awards and decorations. Fellow Internat. Inst. Arts and Letters, Royal Soc. Arts, Nat. Sculpture Soc. (Henry Hering medal, Herbert Adams Medal, Medal of Honor 1985, bd. dirs., 1st v.p. Brookgreen Gardens); mem. Mich. Soc. Architects (hon.), Federation Internationale de la Medaille, AIA (fine arts gold medal 1952, Gold Medal), St. Dunstans Dramatic Guild, Mich. Acad. Sci., Arts and Letters (gold medal honor 1953), Nat. Acad. Design (academician, Agop Agopoff award 1987), C. of C., Am. Soc. Interior Designers, Mich. Assn. Professions, Nat. Soc. Interior Designers, Beta Sigma Phi, Alpha Beta Delta. Clubs: Royal Swedish Yacht, Orchard Lake Country; Architectural League N.Y. (N.Y.C.); Prismatic (Detroit); Royal Norwegian Yacht, Royal Danish Yacht. Studio: 4113 N Woodward Ave Royal Oak MI 48073-6450 also: E Long Lake Road Bloomfield Hills MI 48304

FREDERICKS, SHARON KAY, nurses aide; b. Grand Rapids, Mich., July 12, 1942; d. Leroy and Edith Luella (Crawford) F. Cert. in Interior Decorating, LaSalle U., 1975; AAS, Community Svc. Asst., Kalamazoo Valley Coll., 1982; assoc. paralegal studies, Internat. Corr. Schs., Scranton, Pa., 1991; AAS in Bus. Mgmt., Davenport Coll., 1995, student, 1994—. Cashier Goodwill Industries, Battle Creek, Mich., 1963; dishwasher Woolworths, Kalamazoo, 1963; nurses aide Mary L. Bocher, Kalamazoo, 1964-69, Sisters St. Joseph, Nazareth, Mich., 1976—; kitchen aide Saga Foods, Kalamazoo Valley C.C., 1981-82, Saga Foods, Nazareth Coll., 1983-84. Vol. Portage Ctrl. Jr. and Sr. High Sch., 1961-62, Bronson Meth. Hosp., Kalamazoo, 1961-62; vol. nurse aide ARC, 1964-69, Bloodmobiles, 1970-75, Borgess Med. Ctr., 1977; sec.-treas. 3d Order St. Francis Secular, 1976-79, pres., dir. pres. pub. rels. and bulls., 1979-81; participant neighborhood watch Vine Neighborhood, Kalamazoo, 1985-88; vol. Cath. Family Svcs., 1991—; vol., adminstrv. aide, Kalamazoo, 1991—; vol. monitor Kalamazoo Women's Festival, 1991, 92. Thomas F. Reed Jr. scholar Davenport Coll.; recipient John Edgar Hoover gold medal, 1991; named vol. of month, Kalamazoo Regional Psychiat. Hosp., July 1976; named vol. of week Catholic Family Svcs., Sept. 13, 1993, Oct. 1995. Mem. Nat. Spl. Child Advocates. Roman Catholic. Home: 2310 Inverness Ln Apt 204 Kalamazoo MI 49001-1459

FREDERICKSON, DENNIS RUSSEL, senator, farmer; b. Morgan, Minn., July 27, 1939; s. Louis Bernard and Mary (Kragh) F.; m. Marjorie Davidson, July 15, 1961; children: Kari, Karl, Disa. BS, U. Minn., 1961. Farmer Morgan, 1967—; commr. Redwood County, Minn., 1973-80; mem. Minn. Senate, St. Paul, 1981—, asst. minority leader, floor leader; past bd. dirs. Redwood Electric Coop. Author: (with others) The Fairy Tale Grim of Prince Perp, 1986. Served to lt. comdr. USN, 1962-67. Mem. Farm Bur., S.W. Farm Mgmt. Assn., Council for Agr. Sci. and Tech. Republican. Lutheran. Home: 4 Sunrise Dr New Ulm MN 56073-3615 Office: Minn Senate State Office Bldg Rm 143 Saint Paul MN 55155-1201

FREDLAND, RICHARD ALAN, political science educator; b. Pitts., Nov. 18, 1937; s. Jay and Lillian (Johnson) F.; m. Dorane Lowman, June 12, 1964; children: Valita, Rick. BA in Govt., Wofford Coll., 1958; MA, Am. U., 1965, PhD in Internat. Rels., 1970. Tchr. Blue Ridge Sch., Hendersonville, N.C., 1958-64; rsch. asst. to Congressman John Ashbrook Washington, 1960; tchr. Landon Sch., Bethesda, Md., 1964-66; instr. So. Ill. U., Edwardsville, Ill., 1966-67; prof. Ind. U., Indpls., 1970—, pres. faculty coun., 1992-94. Author: Africa Faces the World, 1990; editor, author: Integration and Disintegration in East Africa, 1985, African International Organizations, 1990. Mem. Africa Studies Assn., Phi Beta Kappa. Methodist. Office: Ind U 425 University Blvd Indianapolis IN 46202

FREDRICKSON, LEIGH HARRY, wetland ecologist, educator; b. Sioux City, Iowa, Mar. 13, 1939; s. Harry T. and Fern Elizabeth (Happel) F.; m. Judith Carolyn Stotts, July 18, 1965; children: Nicole, Jill. BS in Fish and Wildlife Mgmt., Iowa State U., 1961, MS in Zoology, 1963, PhD in Zoology, Ecology, 1967. Asst. prof., assoc. prof., now prof. wetland ecology U. Mo.-Columbia, Puxico, 1967—, also dir. Gaylord Meml. Lab., 1967—; cons. Kans. Biol. Survey, Lawrence, 1985-86, Calif. Dept. Water Resources, Sacramento, 1987-91, U.S. Forest Svcs., Harrisburg, Ill., 1989-90, The Nature Conservancy, Kans., 1992—, Grasslands Water Dist., Los Banos, Calif., 1992-95. Editor Procs. 1988 N.Am. Wood Duck Symposium, 1990. Recipient Silver Eagle award U.S. Fish and Wildlife Svc., 1991, Profl./Tech. award Ducks Unltd., 1996. Mem. Wildlife Soc. (E. Sidney Stephens award Mo. chpt. 1985, Mgmt. Excellence award S.E. sect. 1990, award of merit North Ctrl. Sect. 1991). Presbyterian. Home: 27196 County Rd 267 Puxico MO 63960-9747 Office: U Mo Columbia Gaylord Meml Lab RR 1 Box 185 # U Puxico MO 63960-9686

FREDRICKSON, LOLA JEAN, communications company executive; b. Mpls., Feb. 8, 1945; d. Clifford James Byron and Ardythe (Ellen) F. BS in Applied Art and Design, U. Minn., 1969, MS in Plant Scis. and Chemistry, 1969; MMI, Carlson Sch. of Mgmt., 1990. Editorial asst. dept. econs. U. Minn., Mpls., 1965-70; mem. faculty, rsch. asst., student advisor U. Minn., 1973-80; mgr. documentation control EG&G Idaho, Inc. at Idaho Nat. Engring. Lab., Idaho Falls, 1980-81; mgr. tech. publs. and indsl. security EG&G Washington Analytical Svcs. Ctr., Inc., Newport, R.I., 1981-84; tech. communications con. Mpls. and St. Paul, 1984-85; owner, pres. Fredrickson Communications, Inc., Mpls., 1985—; speaker in field. Contbr. numerous articles to profl. publs. Founder, pres., bd. dirs. Advantage Communications, Inc., 1986-91. Mem. Soc. for Tech. Communications, Mpls. Women's Rotary (bd. dirs. 1993—), Mpls. Women's Club, Gamma Sigma Delta. Office: Fredrickson Communications 119 N 4th St Ste 513 Minneapolis MN 55401-1792

FREDRICKSON, SHARON WONG, accountant; b. Cleve., Nov. 24, 1956; d. Jack Don and Fung Suey (Chow) Wong; m. Brant M. Fredrickson, Mar. 19, 1988; children: Eric Brant, Saul Wong. BS in Acctg. summa cum laude, Case Western Res. U., 1978, MBA, 1987. CPA, Ohio. Acct. Price Waterhouse, Cleve., 1978-81, sr. acct., 1981-84; acctg. rsch. and planning analyst BP Am., Inc. (formerly Standard Oil Co.), Cleve., 1984-85, sr. fin. analyst rsch. and devel. acctg., 1985-88, bus. analyst, regional ctr. fin. reporting, 1989-93; fin. reporting analyst BP Oil Co., 1994-96. Bus. advisor Inroads Cleve., Inc., 1982-84. Mem. Inst. Mgmt. Accts., Am. Inst. CPAs, Am. Woman's Soc. CPAs (Northeastern Ohio affiliate pres. 1985-86, v.p. 1984-85, sec. 1983-84), Ohio Soc. CPAs (state bd. dirs. 1985-86, 88-89, sec. Cleve. chpt. 1987-88, chpt. bd. dirs. 1986-87), Young Profls. Cleve. (trustee 1984-85).

FREDRICKSON, WILLIAM ROBERT, trading company executive; b. Chgo., Sept. 2, 1960; s. Robert Arnold and Mary Eileen (Cleary) F. Student, Wabash Coll., Crawfordsville, Ind., 1979, Purdue U., West Lafayette, Ind., 1980-82, 90, Ind. U./Purdue U., Indpls., 1984, 87. Rschr. in amino acids Ind. U./Purdue U., Indpls., 1984-85; rsch. in HIV antivirals Fredrickson & Strecker Trading Co., Indpls., 1987—; cons. in fields of mktg. and mgmt. Author: The Tree of Life, 1994, Genesis, 1994; composer: (anthology of music) Believe, 1995; 1 patent pending. Republican. Home and Office: Fredrickson & Strecker 5461 N Illinois St Indianapolis IN 46208

FREEBORN, JOANN LEE, state legislator; m. Warren S. Freeborn Jr. Kans. state rep. Dist. 107, 1996—, farmer, tchr., 1996—. Home: RR 2 Box 59 Ames KS 66931*

FREEBURG, AMY L., stockbroker; b. Grand Haven, Mich., June 19, 1966. B Fin. and Sci., Grand Valley State U., Alandale, Mich., 1989. Stockbroker Merrill Lynch, Grand Rapids, 1988—. Active Arthritis Found., Grand Rapids, 1993—, Vision Enrichment, Grand Rapids, 1992. Mem. Western Mich. Soc. Fin. Analysts, Grand Rapids Jaycees. Office: Merrill Lynch Frey Bldg 300 Ottawa Ave NW Grand Rapids MI 49503-2304

FREED, JOHN BECKMANN, history educator; b. N.Y.C., Feb. 6, 1944; s. John A. and Lilly B. (Beckmann) F.; m. Susan Mary Anderson, Jan. 5, 1980; 1 child, Jenny Clare. AB, Cornell U., 1965; PhD, Princeton U., 1969. Asst. prof. Ill. State U., Normal, 1969-75, assoc. prof., 1975-82, prof., 1982-91, disting. prof. history, 1991—, chair dept. history, 1994—. Author: Friars and German Society, 1977, Counts of Falkenstein, 1984, Noble Bondsmen, 1995. Mem. Am. Hist. Assn., Am. Cath. Hist. Assn. Medieval Acad. Am. Office: Ill State U Dept History Normal IL 61790

FREEDMAN, ERIC, journalist; b. Brookline, Mass., Nov. 6, 1949; s. Morris and Charlotte (Nadler) F.; m. Mary Ann Sipher, May 24, 1974; children: Ian Sipher, Cara Sipher. BA, Cornell U., 1971; JD, NYU, 1975. Bar: N.Y. 1976, Mich. 1985. Congl. aide U.S. Rep. Charles Rangel, Washington and N.Y.C., 1971-76; reporter Knickerbocker News, Albany, N.Y., 1976-84, Detroit News, Lansing, Mich., 1984-95; adj. faculty Mich. State U. Author: Pioneering Michigan, 1992, On the Water, Michigan, 1992, Michigan Free, 1993, Great Lakes, Great National Forests, 1995; contbr. numerous articles to profl. jours. Co-treas. Okemos (Mich.) High Sch. Band Boosters. Recipient Merit citation Am. Judicature Soc., Journalism awards AP, Pulitzer prize for beat reporting, 1994. Mem. Am. Soc. Writers on Legal Subjects, Investigative Reporters and Editors, State Bar Mich. (journalism award), N.Y. State Bar Assn. (journalism awards), Ingham Country Bar Assn., Lansing Area Folksong Soc. (bd. dirs.). Home and Office: 2698 Linden Dr East Lansing MI 48823-3814

FREEDMAN, RONALD, sociology educator; b. Winnipeg, Man., Can., Aug. 8, 1917; came to U.S., 1924, naturalized, 1930.; s. Isador and Ada

(Greenstone) F.; m. Deborah Gail Selin, May 4, 1941; children: Joseph Selin, Jane Ilene. BA, U. Mich., 1939, MA, 1940; PhD, U. Chgo., 1947. Mem. faculty U. Mich., Ann Arbor, 1946—; prof. sociology U. Mich., 1954—, Roderick D. McKenzie prof. sociology, 1979-87, now Roderick D. McKenzie prof. emeritus; rsch. assoc. Survey Rsch. Ctr., 1954-70; dir. Population Studies Ctr., 1962-71; co-dir. Taiwan Population Studies Ctr., 1962-64; cons. to Taiwan govt., 1962-88; mem. tech. adv. com. 1970 Census of Population, 1965, Pres.'s Adv. Com. on Population and Family Planning. Author: The Sociology of Human Fertility, 1960, (with others) Family Planning, Sterility and Population Growth, 1959, Principles of Sociology, 1952, Family Planning in Taiwan, 1969; also articles and monographs. With USAAF, 1942-45. Recipient award excellence on teaching U. Mich. Class of, 1952, Disting. Faculty Svc. award U. Mich., 1970, Taeuber award, 1981; Guggenheim fellow, 1957-58; Fulbright fellow, 1957-58; fellow Center for Advanced Study in Behavioral Scis., 1970; Lady Davis fellow and Einstein fellow Hebrew U., 1987. Fellow Am. Acad. Arts and Scis., U.S. Nat. Acad. Sci., Am. Statis. Assn.; mem. NAS, Population Assn. Am. (pres. 1964-65), Internat. Union Study Population (v.p. 1966-67), Am. Sociol. Assn., Sociol. Rsch. Assn., Phi Beta Kappa. Home: 2125 Nature Cove Apt 206 Ann Arbor MI 48104

FREEHILL-DAVIS, THERESE ROSE, physical therapist; b. Fairbury, Ill., Dec. 22, 1953; d. Joseph A. and Wilma Jean (Metz) Freehill; m. Stanley Eugene Davis, Nov. 14, 1978; children: Michael Eugene, Jeremy Wright. BS in Phys. Therapy with honors, U. Ill., Chgo., 1977. Lic. phys. therapist, Ill.; cert. specialist in neurologic phys. therapy, Am. Bd. Phys Therapy Specialists. Staff phys. therapist Mt. Sinai Med. Ctr., Chgo., 1977-78, U. Ill. Med. Ctr., Chgo., 1978, Mercy Hosp., Urbana, Ill., 1978-79; sr. phys. therapist Burnham Hosp., Champaign, Ill., 1979-84; asst. dir. phys. therapy Americana Healthcare Ctr., Urbana, 1984-86; mgr. therapy svcs. Carle Found. Hosp., Urbana, 1986—; guest instr. phys. therapy Bradley U., Peoria, Ill., 1994-95. Cub scout leader, Troop 25, Boy Scouts Am., Mahomet, Ill., 1988-90, 91-93, sec. com., 1990-91; sacrificial giving com. Our Lady of the Lake Ch., Mahomet, 1994-95. Mem. Am. Phys. Therapy Assn., Ill. Phys. Therapy Assn. (del. to state assembly 1987-89, 95-96, sec. 1982-84, chair edn. com. ctrl. dist. 1984-87, geriatric task force 1986-87, peer rev. task force 1992-95). Roman Catholic. Home: 706 Hilltop Ct Mahomet IL 61853 Office: Carle Found Hosp 611 W Park St Urbana IL 61801

FREEHLING, HAROLD GEORGE, JR., respiratory therapist, consultant; b. Benton Harbor, Mich., Nov. 20, 1947; s. Harold George and Wilma Louise (Backus) F.; m. Janet Louise Peppel, June 10, 1971; children: Wendy Brooke, Joel Zachary, Bret Jeromy, Melissa Bethann. AS, Lake Mich. Coll., 1972; Diploma in Respiratory Therapy, U. Chgo., 1977; B in Liberal Studies, Bowling Green State U., 1978; M Health Care Adminstrn., Cen. Mich. U., 1987. Dir. respiratory care O.E. Meyer Co., Sandusky, Ohio, 1974-84; mgr. support svcs. O.E. Meyer Co., Sandusky, 1984—; bd. dirs., 1989-93; clin. evaluator Calif. Coll. of Helath Sci., Nature City, 1981—; chmn. Firelands Coll. Respiratory Care Adv., Huron, Ohio, 1984—; cons. Ohio Bd. Regents, Columbus, 1986. Pres. Erie County Cancer Svcs., 1990, 94. With USN, 1967-70, Vietnam. Recipient Ed Ruff Community Svc. award, Am. Lung Assn., South Shore, Milan, Ohio, 1987, Disting. Alumnus/Alumna award Bowling Green State U. Firelands Coll., 1993. Mem. Am. Assn. Respiratory Care (cert. tech., registered respiratory therapist), Ohio Soc. Respiratory Care (sec. 1986), Ohio Thoracic Soc., Ohio Assn. Med. Equipment Svcs. (sec. 1991-92, treas. 1992-93, v.p. 1994-96, pres. 1996), Erie County Health Planning Assn. Home: 154 Fairway Cir Norwalk OH 44857-1970 Office: O E Meyer Co PO Box 479 Sandusky OH 44871-0479

FREEMAN, ARTHUR J., physics educator; b. Lublin, Poland, Feb. 6, 1930; s. Louis and Pearl (Mandelbaum) F.; m. Rhea B. Landin, June 21, 1952 (div. 1991); children: Jonathan (dec.), Seth, Claudia, Sarah; m. Doris Caro, Mar. 1991. B.S. in Physics, Mass. Inst. Tech., 1952, Ph.D., 1956. Instr. Brandeis U., 1955-56; solid state physicist Army Materials Research Agy., Watertown, Mass., 1956-62; instr. Northeastern U., 1957-59; assoc. lab. dir., leader theory group Francis Bitter Nat. Magnet Lab., Mass. Inst. Tech., 1962-67; prof. physics Northwestern U., Evanston, Ill., 1967-83; Morrison prof. physics Northwestern U., 1983—, chmn. dept. physics, 1967-71; cons. Argonne Nat. Lab., Los Alamos Nat. Lab., Lawrence Livermore Nat. Lab. Editor: Hyperfine Interactions, 1967, The Actinides: Electronic and Related Properties, Handbook on the Physics and Chemistry of the Actinides, Internat. Jour. Magnetism, 1970-75, Jour. Magnetism and Magnetic Materials, 1975—; mem. editl. adv. bd. Computational Materials Sci., 1992, Jour. Computer-Aided Materials Design, 1993; contbr. numerous articles to tech. lit. Guggenheim fellow, 1970-71; Fulbright-Hays fellow, 1970-71; Alexander von Humboldt Stiftung fellow 1977-78; 1st recipient medal Materials Rsch. Soc., 1990, award in magnetism Internat. Union Pure and Applied Physics, 1991. Fellow Am. Phys. Soc.; fgn. mem. Acad. Natural Scis. Russia, Russian Acad. Scis., Polish Acad. Scis. Home: 2739 Ridge Ave Evanston IL 60201 Office: Northwestern Univ Dept Of Physics Evanston IL 60208-3112

FREEMAN, BRYANT C., foreign language educator; b. Richmond, Va., June 26, 1931; s. Loomin Oscar Jr. and Virginia Bourke (Oliver) F.; m. Stephanie Lynn Smith; 1 child, Timothy Oliver Freeman. BA with honors, U. Va., 1953; MA, Yale U., 1954, PhD, 1961. Instr. French Yale U., New Haven, Conn., 1955-59; asst. prof. French U. Va., Charlottesville, 1961-66, assoc. prof. French, 1966-71; prof. French U. Kans., Lawrence, 1971—, chmn. dept. French, Italian, 1971-76, prof. African Studies, 1989—; dir. Inst. of Haitian Studies, 1992—; United Nations observer Haiti, 1993-94; cons. on Haiti U.S. Dept. Justice, 1988—, U.S. Immigration and Naturalization Svc., 1991-92; lectr. Kans. Com. on the Humanities, 1991—; cons. on Haitian Creole, Ind. U., 1991—; UN adviser, Haiti, 1995. Author: Chita Pa Bay: Readings in Haitian Creole, 1984, Survival Creole, 1990, Haitian-English Medical Dictionary, 1992, and others. Woodrow Wilson fellow Yale U., 1953-55, Yale U. fellow, 1953-55, Fulbright scholar Paris, 1959-61. Mem. Modern Lang. Assn. Am. (life), Am. Assn. Tchrs. French (life), Haitian Studies Assn. (bd. dirs.), Soc. for Caribbean Linguistics, Assn. Internationale d'Etudes Créoles, Lawrence Symphony Orch., Alvamar Country Club, Phi Beta Kappa. Office: U Kans Haitian Studies Dept French University KS 66045

FREEMAN, CATHERINE ELAINE, educator; b. Independence, Kans., Oct. 18, 1956; d. John R. and Irma J. (Simmons) F. BA, Pitts. State U., 1978, MS, 1979, EdS, 1985; PhD, U. Tulsa, 1990; student, Oxford U., Eng., 1993. Residence hall dir. Pitts. State U., 1979-80; counselor, coord. orientation Mo. So. State Coll., Joplin, 1980-85, dir. coll. orientation and patron's scholarship coord., 1985-88; teaching asst. U. Tulsa, 1988-90; assoc. prof. of edn., dir. spl. projects Mo. So. State Coll., Joplin, 1990—, asst. dir. honors program, 1992-93; intern Okla. State Regents for Higher Edn., Oklahoma City, summer 1989, Pres.'s Office, U. Tulsa, 1988-89. Contbr. articles to profl. jours. First v.p. Mo. So. Women's Club, 1982-83; team capt., vol. Mo. So. State Coll. Fundraising Phon-a-Thon, 1982-88, 90—; team capt. United Way Mo. So. State Coll., 1991—; mem. S.W. Mo. Cmty. Band. Mem. Am. Ednl. Rsch. Assn., Nat. Assn. Student Pers. Adminstrs., Omicron Delta Kappa (faculty sec. 1987-88, 92—, Outstanding Faculty Sec. Province XI 1994, faculty province dir. 1995—), Phi Delta Kappa. United Methodist. Office: Missouri So State College 3950 Newman Rd Joplin MO 64801-1512

FREEMAN, CHARLES E., state supreme court judge; m. Marylee Voelker; 1 child, Kevin. BA in Liberal Arts, Va. Union U., 1954; JD, John Marshall Law Sch., 1962, LLD (hon.), 1992. Bar: Ill. 1962. Pvt. practice, 1962-76; pvt. practice, Cook County, Chgo., Ill., 1962-76; asst. state's atty. Cook County, 1964; asst. atty. gen., then asst. state's atty. Cook County, Chgo., 1964; asst. atty. Bd. Election Commrs., Chgo., 1964-65; mem. Ill. Indsl. Commn., Chgo., 1965-73, Ill. Commerce Commn., Chgo., 1973-76; judge law and chancery divsns. Cook County Circuit Ct., Chgo., 1976-86; judge Appellate Ct. Ill., 1986-90; justice Ill. Supreme Ct., 1990—. First African-Am. to swear in a Mayor city Chgo., to serve on Ill. Supreme Ct., 1990; leader in case disposition by published opinion, 1988, 89; recipient cert. Achievement, Internat. Christian Fellowship Missions, Earl B. Dickerson award Chgo. Bar Assn., Merit award Habilative Systems, award Statesmanship, Monarch Awards Found. of Alpha Kappa Alpha. Mem. ABA (cert. Recognition, task force opportunities minorities in jud. adminstrn. divsn. and comsn. opportunities minorities in profession), Am. Judges' Assn., Ill. State Bar Assn., Ill. Jud. Coun. (Kenneth Wilson Meml. award, Meritorious Svc. award), Ill. Judges' Assn., Cook County Bar Assn. (Kenneth E. Wilson award, Cert. Merit, Ida Platt award, Presdl. award, Jud. award), Du Page County Bar Assn. Office: Supreme Ct Ill 160 N La Salle St 20th Fl Chicago IL 60601

FREEMAN, CORWIN STUART, JR., investment adviser; b. Elmhurst, Ill., July 31, 1947. AA in Edn., Waubonsee Community Coll., Sugar Grove, Ill., 1971. CLU; cert. estate counselor, investment advisor. Ins. salesman Hatcher & Assoc., Geneva, Ill., 1971-80; pres. Valley Estate Planners Ltd., Elgin, Ill., 1980—; chmn. Leaders Coun. Can. Life Assurance Co., 1988; mem. agts. coun. Delta Life and Annuity Co., 1993-95. With USMC, 1965-68, Vietnam. Named to Million Dollar Round Table, 1982—, life and qualifying mem., 1996, Ct. of Table Status, 1988. Fellow Life Underwriter Tng. Coun.; mem. Nat. Tax Sheltered Annuity Assn. (charter mem. 1991-93), Elgin Area Life Underwriters (past pres. 1987-88), Ill. Life Underwriters Assn. (bd. dirs. 1991-93, region III v.p.). Home and Office: Valley Estate Planners Ltd 14 N 555 Tyrrell Rd Elgin IL 60123 also: 150 Terrane Ridge Peachtree City GA 30269

FREEMAN, GREGORY BRUCE, newspaper columnist; b. St. Louis, Aug. 18, 1956; s. Frederic William and Doris (Bradley) F.; m. Elizabeth Louise Johnson, July 7, 1979; 1 child, William Gregory. BA in Spanish, Washington U., 1978. Reporter, assoc. editor St. Louis Am., 1977-78; reporter Oakland Press, Pontiac, Mich., 1978-79, Belleville (Ill.) News-Dem., 1979-80; reporter St. Louis Post-Dispatch, 1980-86, asst. city editor, 1986-90, polit. editor, 1990-92, columnist, 19889—; bd. dirs. St. Louis Journalism Found., 1984—, St. Louis Journalism Rev., 1982—; regional dir. Nat. Assn. Black Journalists, 1986-91; past fellow Multicultural Mgmt. Program, 1987. Mem. Fordyce Group, St. Louis, 1990; co-founder Bridges Across Racial Polarization, St. Louis, 1993; past participant Leadership St. Louis, 1984-85. Recipient award Mo. Assn. for Social Welfare, 1991, Guardian Angel award Family Svcs. Network, 1995. Mem. Soc. Profl. Journalists (pres. St. Louis chpt. 1990), Greater St. Louis Assn. Black Journalists (pres. 1982, 88-89, Journalist of Yr. 1987), Press Club Met. St. Louis (chmn. 1995—). Office: St Louis Post-Dispatch 900 N Tucker Blvd Saint Louis MO 63101

FREEMAN, JOHN F., state legislator; b. Ann Arbor, MI, May 13, 1957. BS, U. Mich.; JD, U. Detroit. Bar: Mich. Rep. Mich. Dist. 34, 1993—; cmty. organizer Assn. Cmty. Orgns. for Reform Now; atty. O'Connor & Youmans, Detroit. Home: 28342 Dartmouth St Madison Heights MI 48071-4506 Address: PO Box 30014 Lansing MI 48909-7514*

FREEMAN, J.P. HAWK, underwater exploration, security and transportation executive, educator; b. Berkley, Calif., Feb. 21, 1951; d. Gilbert Richard and Rachael Mary (Kim) (Leaney) F.; m. B.M. McGlynn Freeman, Febr. 9, 1974; 1 child, Jennifer Patricia (dec.). BA, Davis & Elkins Coll., W.Va., 1973; grad., USAF Air Weapons Controller Sch., Tyndall AFB, Fla., 1973, USAF Air Command and Staff Coll., 1982, U.S. Marine Corps and Staff Coll., 1982; M in Aviation Mgmt., Embry-Riddle Aeronautical U., Daytona Beach, Fla., 1986, postgrad., 1986; grad., USAF Air War Coll., Montgomery, Ala., 1988. Cert. EMT. Mem. 56th spl. ops. rescue for Southeast Asia NKP Royal Thai Air Force Base, 1974, 75; chief wing radar standardization/evaluation RAF, Alconbury, England, 1980-83; commdr. joint U.S. forces Operation Raleigh, 1986; support chief of staff Hdqs. NORAD, Colorado Springs, Colo., 1987-89; dep. base commdr. NATO Hdqs. Allied Forces No. Europe, Norway, 1989-91; chief airport mgmt. divsn. Whiteman AFB, Knob Noster, Mo., 1991-93; dir. spl. projects USAF Acad. Hosp., Colorado Springs, 1993-94; systems performance specialist Colo. Sport & Spine Rehab., Colorado Springs, 1994-95; dir. FLEET International Explorations and Svcs. Co., Colorado Springs, 1995—; spl. adv. for anti and counter terrorist security Internat. Olympic Games, Oslo, Norway, 1994; designer Automated Provider Credentialing System USAF Acad. Hosp., USAF Acad., Colo., 1993-94; spl. adv. comms. NATO German High Commd., 1980. Poet, poems included in numerous anthologies. Acheivement: first woman named dir. FLEET International Explorations and Services Co. Mem. bd. dirs. Johnson County (Mo.) United Way, 1991-93; surgery life support specialist ARC, USAF Acad. Hosp., 1993-95; mem. nat. scholarship com. Red River Valley Fighter Pilots Assn., 1993—; hosp. vol., med. technician, provider credentialing system designer, oral surgery life support system specialist. Recipient 52 awards and decorations including Defense Meritorious Svc. medal with 1 oak leaf cluster, Meritorious Svc. medal with 2 oak leaf clusters, Joint Svc. Commendation medal with 1 oak leaf cluster, Air Force Commendation medal, Armed Forces Expeditionary medal with 2 bronze stars, 2 Humanitarian Svc. medals, 2 Kuwait Liberation medals, 2 Southwest Asia medals; named Admintrsn. Officer of Yr. USAF, 1986; named one of the six top Support Officers USAF, 1986-87. Mem. Air Force Assn., Assn. of Old Crows, Alpha Phi Omega, Iota Beta Sigma. Mem. Anglican Ch. Home: 4861 Chaparral Rd Colorado Springs CO 80917 Office: FLEET Internat Explorations & Svcs Co PO Box 14192 Colorado Springs CO 80914

FREEMAN, MARY LOUISE, state senator; b. Willmar, Minn., Oct. 21, 1941; d. James Martin and Luella Anna (Backlund) Hawkinson; m. Dennis Lester Freeman, June 10, 1962; children: Mark D., Sara L., Cary D., Maret S. BA, Gustavus Adolphus Coll., 1963. Substitute tchr. Arrowhead Edn. Assn., Storm Lake, Iowa, 1982-93; tchr., cons. Midwest Power, Des Moines, 1991-94; mem. Iowa Senate, Des Moines, 1994—; mem. early childhood intervention com., 1994—, mem. disaster prevention svcs. com., 1994—. Del. alt. Rep. Nat. Conv., Kansas City, 1976; active Midwest-Can. Relations Co., 1994—. Mem. Am. Legis. Exch. Coun., Nat. Coun. State Govt. Lutheran. Home: 311 E Lakeshore Dr Storm Lake IA 50588-2539 Office: Iowa State Senate State Capitol Des Moines IA 50319*

FREEMAN, SANDRA MARLENE, publishing executive; b. Chgo., July 28, 1956; d. Albert and Zola Lee (Phillips) Gildersleeve; m. Larry Dobie Freeman, Mar. 1, 1952; 1 child, Lawrence Isaac Kenyatta. BA in Sociology/Anthropology, Earlham Coll., 1979; MS in Criminal Justice, Chgo. State U., 1986. Cert. tchr. secondary and primary, Chgo. Adminstrv. asst. Mendil Prep., Chgo., 1979; profl. asst., fin. aid advisor Chgo. State U., 1980, 81-86; counsel, asst. project coord. Truman and Loop City Colls., Chgo., 1980, 81; supr. office ROTC Chgo. State U., 1986—; adv. bd. mem. Jessie Houston Correctional Ctr., Chgo., 1990—. Author: (book of poems) Butterflies, 1991, Caged Bird, 1991, Living, Loving, and Learning, 1993, Life, 1995. Recipient Poet of Yr. Internat. Black Writers Conf., 1991, Charles Browning award, 1988, Golden Poetry award World of Poetry, 1987, 88, 89, 90, McDonald's Literary Achievement award finalist, 1988, Kool Achievers award nomination, 1987, John F. Kennedy Profile in Courage award nomination, 1990, Negro Women Nat. Coun. award finalist, 1994. Mem. Internat. Soc. Poets. Baptist. Home: 8300 S Throop Chicago IL 60620

FREESE, STEPHEN J., state legislator; b. Dubuque, Iowa, Mar. 16, 1960; s. Joseph and Rowetta (Johnson) F.; m. Dawn Fredse; 1 child, Marie. BS, U. Wis., Platteville, 1982. Asst. to chmn. 3d Dist. Rep. Com., Wis., 1981-82; sales rep. Tegler's Inc., 1982-91; mem. from dist. 51 Wis. State Assembly, Madison, 1990—, vice chmn. Rep. caucus, 1993-94, spkr. pro tempore, 1995—. Supr. Town of Jamestown, Wis., 1980-94; mem. Grant County Bd. Suprs., 1982-92; mem. Wis. Fedn. Young Reps.; mem. Wis. State Rep. Com.; chmn. Grant County Rep. Com., 1983—. *

FREIER, TOM D., state legislator; m. Melinda Freier; 2 children. Student, Valley City (N.D.) State Coll. Owner restaurant Linton, N.D.; fin. planner Linton; state rep. dist. 28, 1991—; mem. appropriations com., edn. and environ. com., asst. majority leader N.D. Ho. Reps. Bd. dirs. Linton Indsl. Devel. Corp., N.D. Credit Union; former pres. Linton City Coun. Mem. N.D. Hosp. Assn., Linton C. of C., Lions, Elks. Republican. Home: PO Box 368 Linton ND 58552-0368*

FREIJ, BISHARA JOUDEH, pediatrician, consultant; b. Jerusalem, Palestine, Aug. 30, 1954; came to U.S., 1980; s. Joudeh Bishara and Artimis (Simeriotis) F.; m. Marina S. Glagolev, Oct. 1, 1989; 1 child, Joudeh. BS, Am. U., 1972-75; MD, Am. U. of Beirut, 1975-80. Diplomate Am. Bd. Pediatrics, Am. Bd. Pediatric Infectious Diseases. Intern, resident pediatrics Georgetown U. Med. Ctr., Washington, 1980-83; fellow pediatric infectious diseases U. Tex. Southwestern Med. Sch., Dallas, 1983-85; vis. fellow NIH, Bethesda, Md., 1985-87; asst. prof. pediatrics Georgetown U. Sch. Medicine, Washington, 1987-90; chief pediatric infectious diseases William Beaumont Hosp., Royal Oak, Mich., 1990—; clin. assoc. prof. peidatrics Wayne State U. Sch. Medicine, Detroit, 1991—. Editor: Infectious Complications of Pregnancy, 1988; author of more than 20 books chpts.; contbr. 30 articles to profl. jours. Mem. AAAS, Am. Soc. Microbiology, Am. Fedn. Clin. Rsch., Infectious Disease Soc. Am., Soc. Epidemiologic Rsch., N.Y. Acad. Scis., Arab Am. Med. Assn. Office: William Beaumont Hosp 3535 W 13 Mile Rd Royal Oak MI 48073-6700

FREITAG, FREDERICK GERALD, osteopathic physician; b. Milw., Feb. 12, 1952; s. Frederick August and Shirley June (Siewert) F.; m. Lynn Nadene Stegner, Sept. 10, 1977; children: Crescentia Adella, Abigail Amadea, Genevieve Angelica. BS in Biochemistry, U. Wis., 1974; DO, Chgo. Coll. Osteopathic Medicine, 1979. Intern Brentwood Hosp., Warrensville Heights, Ohio, 1979-80, resident in family practice, 1980-81; dir., physician Twinsburg (Ohio) Family Clinic, 1981-83; assoc. prof. family medicine Coll. Osteo. Medicine, Ohio U., Warrensville Heights, 1982-83; mem. staff Diamond Headache Clinic, Chgo., 1983-86, assoc. dir., 1986—; attending staff mem. Louis A. Weiss Meml. Hosp., Chgo., 1983-93; attending staff Columbus Hosp., 1993—; mem. Janssen Rsch. Coun.; sec. Diamond Headache Rsch. and Edn. Found.; vis. lectr. dept. family medicine Chgo. Coll. Osteo. Medicine, 1985—; clin. assoc. dept. medicine Pritzker Sch. Medicine U. Chgo., 1989-93; editorial bd. Headache Quar., 1991—; chmn. instnl. rev. bd. Louis A. Weiss Meml. Hosp., 1991-93. Contbr. articles and abstracts to profl. jours., chpts. to books. Bd. dirs. Nat. Headache Found. Fellow Am. Assn. for Study of Headache; mem. AMA, Am. Coll. Gen. Practioners in Osteo. Medicine, Am. Osteo. Assn., Am. Soc. Clin. Pharmacology and Therapeutics (vice chmn. headache sect. 1995-96), Ill. Assn. Osteo. Physicians and Surgeons, Ill. Med. Soc., Internat. Assn. Study Pain, Am. Pain Soc., Nat. Headache Found., Chgo. Med. Soc. (speakers bur.), German Wine Soc. (past pres. Chgo. chpt.), U. Wis. Alumni Assn. Lutheran. Home: 931 Clinton Pl River Forest IL 60305-1503 Office: The Diamond Headache Clinic 467 Deming Pl Ste 500 Chicago IL 60614

FRELS, LOIS MARIAN PARNELL (MRS. CALVIN EDWIN FRELS), nursing educator; b. Geneseo, Ill., Nov. 20, 1929; d. Floyd Vinton and Mary Jane (Davis) Parnell; m. Calvin Edwin Frels, Oct. 28, 1950; children: Mark Edwin, Arlan James. RN, Moline (Ill.) Pub. Hosp., 1950; student pub. Health U. Minn., Loyola U., Chgo., 1951-54; BNS, Augustana Coll., Rock Island, Ill., 1959; MA, U. Iowa, 1964; diploma for testing, Marianne Frostic Ctr. Ednl. Therapy, Los Angeles, 1969; PhD, U. Minn., 1977. Nurse East Moline Elem. Schs., 1951-54; pub. health work East Moline Vis. Nurses Assn., 1955-57; sch. nurse, project dir., nurse cons. United Twp. High Sch., East Moline, 1957-67; instr. psychology Blackhawk Jr. Coll., Moline, part time 1966-68; tchr., dir. gifted program Silvis (Ill.) Elem. Schs., 1968; counselor Pleasant Valley (Ia.) H.S., 1969-70; asst. prof. Pub. Health Nursing Marycrest Coll., Davenport, Iowa, 1970-73; chmn. nursing div. Iowa Wesleyan Coll., Mt. Pleasant, 1973-76; dir. div. nursing Bradley U., Peoria, Ill., 1976-88, prof. emeritus, 1988—; pres. Frels & Assocs., 1991—; project dir. Nursing Edn. Anesthesia Requirements and Mobility between NAFTA countries; mem. coun. on accreditation Nurse Anesthetics Edn. Programs, 1994—, Riverdale Unit 100 Bd. Edn., Port Byron, Ill., 1964-67, 68-73; bd. govs. Trinity Coll. Nursing, Moline, Ill., 1994—; chmn. Rock Island County Fact Finding Com. White House Conf. Children and Youth, 1970, Ill. Com. of Nursing, 1982-88; organizer Little White House Conf. Children and Youth, Rock Island County, 1969; del. Nat. White House Conf. on Children and Youth, 1970; 2d v.p. Rock Island Country Welfare Council, 1968-70; mem. adv. bd. Ill. Dept. Pub. Health, 1987—; mem. Bylaws com. Nat. Council State Bds. of Nursing, 1986-88; mem. Ill. Sch. Health Adv. com. Ill. Dept. Pub. Health; trustee Riverdale Found., 1991—; pres. Riverdale Edn. Found., Port Byron, Ill., 1994—; mem. Ill. Coalition for Access to Health Care Planning Com.; adv. Am. Farm Bur. Rural Health And Safety Com., 1991-94; mem. Nat. Republican Party, 1994—, nat. policy forum health care reform, 1993—. Author: History of MPHS of N, 1990. Bd. dirs. Opportunity Mentally Handicapped. Recipient Mergen award Bradley U. Instrn., 1985, Disting. Svc. award Ill. Sch. Health Assn., 1995, Disting. Alumni award Trinity Nursing Alumni Assn., 1995; grantee Western Ill. U., 1968; Nurse traineeship grantee, 1973. Fellow Am. Sch. Health Assn. (disting. service award 1978); mem. Nat. League Nursing (MRACLN Disting. Service award 1987, chmn. sch. nurse subcom.), Ill. League Nursing (pres. 1983-87), Iowa Citizens League for Nursing (pres. 1975-77), Ill. Nurses Assn., Am. Sch. Health Assn., Ill. Sch. Health Assn. (mem. rural health force farm bur. 1988-94—), Nat. Nurse Cons. Assn. (bd. dirs. 1991-93), Ill. Assn. Sch. Nurses (Annual award 1989, Lois Frels Rsch. award named in her honor 1991), Am. Sch. Health Assn. (gov. coun. 1989-91), Royal Soc. Health (London, Eng.), Lt. Gov.'s Rural Affairs Coun. (rural health task force 1991-93), Ill. Lincoln Series (gov. 1994—), Phi Kappa Phi, Sigma Theta Tau, Pi Lambda Theta. Editorial bd. Jour. Sch. Health, 1988-92. Republican. Home: 25329 1st Ave N Hillsdale IL 61257-9628

FREMON, DAVID KENT, writer, consultant; b. Chgo., Feb. 17, 1949; s. William Joe and Irene (McGoldrick) F.; m. Sonja Yap Pacana, June 24, 1988; 1 child, Kent Joseph; children from previous marriage: Palomila, Karl, Tommy. BA, Lawrence U., 1970. Ind. writer, 1986—; cons. Chgo. Bd. Edn., 1991-92. Author: Chicago Politics Ward by Ward, 1988, The Trail of Tears, 1994, The Negro Baseball Leagues, 1994, Running Away, 1996; author media sect.: Restoration '89, 1991. Recipient Hispanic Journalism award Cermak Rd. C. of C., 1990, Investigative Journalism award Chgo. Electric Options Campaign, 1991, Spur award Western Writers Am., 1995; named best local polit. columnist New City Poll, 1993. Mem. St. Louis Browns Fan Club, Merrie Gangsters Lit. Soc. Mem. United Ch. of Christ. Home: 4451 N Rockwell St Chicago IL 60625-3018

FRENCH, DIANE LYNN, health facility administrator; b. Flint, Mich., Aug. 15, 1948; d. Robert Emory and Barbara Jane (Becker) Lyons; m. Patrick Raymond Mehall, Dec. 27, 1968 (div. 1981); children: Matthew Patrick, Todd David; m. Jeffrey Stewart French, Apr. 9, 1988. ADN, Mott Community Coll., 1968; BS, BA, Aquinas Coll., 1985; MPA, Western Mich. U., 1990. Charge nurse Fenton (Mich.) Extended Care, 1969; office nurse Buchanan and Martin Assn., Fenton, 1969-70; staff nurse William Beaumont Hosp., Royal Oak, Mich., 1974-75; staff nurse St. Mary's Hosp., Grand Rapids, Mich., 1977-78, edn. coord., 1979-80, home care coord., 1981-85, nurse mgr., 1985-89, dept. mgr., 1989-94; adminstr. ops. Mich. Kidney Ctr., Southfield, Mich., 1994—; mem. adv. bd. Amicare Home Health, Grand Rapids, 1989-94, Juvenile Diabetes Assn., Grand Rapids, 1991-94. Mem. Mich. scientific adv. bd. Nat. Kidney Found., 1995-96. Recipient Distinguished Svc. award Nat. Kidney Found. Mich., 1992; grantee Mich. Dept. Pub. Health, 1981-82. Mem. Nat. Renal Adminstrs. Assn., Am. Nephrology Nurses Assn. (pres. Mich. chpt. 1979, 85, sec.-treas. 1992-94, 96-97, cert. nephrology nurse 1992), Soc. Human Resource Mgmt., Mich. Orgn. Nurse Execs. Republican. Home: 7430 Cherry Valley Caledonia MI 49316 Office: 23077 Greenfield Rd Ste 104 Southfield MI 48075-3744

FRENCH, JAY MICHAEL, oil company financial analyst, consultant; b. Moline, Ill., Aug. 8, 1963; s. Harold E. and Marjorie J. (Hollister) F. BS in Computer Engring., U. Ill., 1985, MBA, 1988. Mktg. analyst McDonnell Douglas, St. Louis, 1983-87; tech. analyst Amoco, Chgo., 1988-91, fin. analyst, 1992—. Mem. INFORMS.

FRENCH, MICHAEL FRANCIS, non-profit education agency administrator; b. La Crosse, Wis., July 25, 1948; s. Albert Frank Jr. and Kathryn Patricia (MacKoske) F.; m. Janet Alan Streeter Head, Nov. 26, 1991. BS in Edn., U. Wis., 1972. Cert. emergency med. technician. Tng. coord. emergency med. svcs. Wis. Dept. Health and Social Svcs., Madison, 1975-80, tng. dir. emergency med. svcs., 1980-84, chief emergency med. svcs., 1984-90; co-dir. Mo. Rural AHEC Kirksville (Mo.) Coll. Osteo. Medicine, 1990—, adj. instr. community health, 1990—; emergency med. svcs. cons., Kirksville, 1984—; founding mem. Continuing Edn. Coordinating Bd. for Emergency Med. Svcs., Inc., Kirksville, 1992. Author: (tng. curriculum) EMS Instructor Training Course-U.S. Dept. Transportation, 1985; editor newsletter, editor-in-chief publs. Nat. Assn. Emergency Med. Technicians, 1983-91; author book chpts. V.p., pres. bd. dirs. Adair County Ret. Sr. Vol. Program, Kirksville, 1992-95. Recipient Lunda Trauma award Am. Trauma Soc., 1982, Svc. awards Nat. Coun. State EMS Tng. Coords., 1982, 83, A. Roger Fox Founders award Nat. Assn. Emergency Med. Technicians, 1989, others. Mem. ASTM, ASCD, ASTD, APHA, Nat. Rural Health Assn., Mo. Rural Health Assn. (bd. dirs. 1995-96, pres.-elect 1996—), Mo. PEW Health Professions Partnership (chair exec. com. 1994-95), Mo. Pub. Health Assn.,

Wis. Emergency Med. Tech. Assn., Profl. Emergency Educators Assn., Mensa. Office: Mo Rural AHEC Program 800 W Jefferson St Kirksville MO 63501-1443

FRENCH, WILLIAM CULLEN, theology educator; b. Washington, Mar. 24, 1951; s. John Lawrence and Alice Beauregard (Diamond) F. BA, Dickinson Coll., 1973; MDiv, Harvard U., 1977; PhD, U. Chgo., 1985. Tchr. Nat. Children's Ctr., Washington, 1973-74, Willibrord Cath. High Sch., Chgo., 1978-79; asst. prof. Loyola U. of Chgo., 1985-90, assoc. prof., 1990—; chair Shalom Edn., Chgo., 1982-83, Chgo. Ctr. Peace Studies, 1994—, Loyola Peace Studies program dir., bd. mem. Peace Mus., 1996—. Contbr. articles to profl. jours. and editorials to Chgo. Tribune. Mem. Amnesty Internat., Chgo., 1988. Mem. Am. Acad. Religion (chair ecology consultation 1987), Coll. Theology Soc. (Best Article award 1990), Soc. Christian Ethics. Democrat. Office: Loyola U of Chgo 6525 N Sheridan Rd Chicago IL 60626-5311

FRENCL, REBECCA LYNN, writer; b. Chgo., Oct. 29, 1974; d. Thomas James and Della Rose (Marino) F. AA, Morton Coll., Cicero, Ill., 1994; attending, Northeastern Ill U., Chgo., 1994—. Freelance author Commonwealth Pub., Inc., Edmonton, Alberta, Canada, 1996—. Author: (book) Bonds of Blood, Bonds of Steel, 1996; assoc. editor: Morton Coll. Literary Mag., 1992; editor: St. Pius X Chronicle, 1995—. Vol. Spl. Olympics, Riverside-Brookfield, 1991; chair public relations Phi Theta Kappa Honors Soc. Morton Coll., 1992-94; fin. sec. Catholic Order of Foresters St. Procopius Court, 1993. Mem. Catholic Order of Foresters, Phi Theta Kappa. Roman Catholic.

FRENZER, PETER FREDERICK, insurance company executive; b. Omaha, Aug. 19, 1934; s. William J. and Ruth E. (Berliner) F.; m. Mary Virginia Yates, June 1, 1957; children: Peter, Michelle M., Christopher P., Jennifer S., Paula B. B.S. summa cum laude, Creighton U., 1956; student, Creighton U. Coll. Law, 1956-57; LL.B. cum laude, William Mitchell Coll. Law, 1961; LLD (hon.), Otterbein Coll., 1988. C.P.A., Nebr. Investment analyst, cost acct. Prudential Ins. Co., Mpls., 1957-62; v.p. securities, 2d v.p., analyst United Benefit Life Ins. Co., Omaha, 1962-74; v.p. investments Heritage Securities Inc., Columbus, Ohio, 1974-81; v.p. securities investment Nationwide Ins. Cos., Columbus, 1977-81; exec. v.p. investments Nationwide Ins. Enterprise, Columbus, 1981-95, exec.. v.p., 1995—; pres. Nationwide Corp., 1990—; pres., COO, bd. dirs. Nationwide Life Ins. Co, Nationwide Life & Annuity Ins. Co., 1991—; chmn. Nationwide Investing Found., Fin. Horizons Investment Trust, Nationwide Tax Free Fund, Neckura Holding Co.; pres. Assn. Ohio Life Ins. Cos. Trustee Ohio State U. Hosps.; mem. adv. bd. Alliance for the Mentally Ill of Ohio; mem. dean's adv. coun. Fisher Coll. of Bus., Ohio State U.; bd. dirs. Life and Health Ins. Med. Rsch. Fund. Capt. U.S. Army, 1957. . Mem. ABA, Nebr. Bar Assn., Minn. Bar Assn., Assn. for Investment Mgmt. and Rsch. Roman Catholic. Office: Nationwide Mut Ins Co 1 Nationwide Plz Columbus OH 43215-2423

FRERER, RONALD KENT, customer service representative, owner; b. Cathage, Mo., Dec. 11, 1959; s. Victor F. and Mildred M. (Corumn) F.; m. Deborah J. Reed Woodridge, Feb. 15, 1984; children: Amy (Nikki), Trevor A.; m. Nancy J. Gentry, July 2, 1994; children: Megan E., Amanda M. BSBA in business, Mo. So. State, Joplin, 1993. Customer svc. rep. Southwestern Bell Tel., Nevada, Mo., 1979-82; customer svc. technician Southwestern Bell Tel., Lamar, Mo., 1982-94, Webb City, Mo., 1994—; v.p. Comm. Workers, Am. Local 6313, Joplin, Mo., 1987—; owner Courteys Ct. Apts., Angel Estate Mobile Home Park, Burton County Mini-Storage. Pulpit com. mem. Calvary Bapt. Ch., Carthage, Mo., 1995—. Baptist. Home: Rt 4 Box 504-1 Carthage MO 64836

FRERICHS, DONALD L., state legislator; b. Ocheyedan, Iowa, Jan. 3, 1931; m. Dianne R. Rickbeil, 1951; children: Craig D., Scott R., Krista B. BA, Mankato State U., 1954. Supr. Rochester Twp., 1968-81; state rep. Minn. Ho. Reps., Dist. 31A, 1981-96; pres. Bio-Conversion Inc.; mem. econ. devel. infrastructure and regulation fin., transp. & transit, transp. fin. and ways and means coms., Minn. Ho. Reps.; CFO Irish Holdings, Inc. Home: 2233 Brook Lane SW Rochester MN 55902 Office: 247 State Office Bldg Saint Paul MN 55155*

FRESHWATER, PAUL ROSS, consumer goods company executive; b. Columbus, Ohio, Aug. 16, 1941; s. Fayne F. and Lillian (Ross) F.; m. Robertine Ann Nekervis, June 14, 1964; 1 child, Ross Foley. BArch, Ohio State U., 1964; SM in Mgmt., MIT, 1968. Brand asst., mgr. Procter & Gamble, Cin., 1968-74, asst. to v.p., 1974-80, mgr. spl. projects, 1980-83, mgr. issues analysis, 1983-89, regional pub. affairs mgr., 1989—; treas., dir. The Film House, Inc., Cin., 1986—; treas. Ohio Alliance for Environ., Columbus, 1986-89; founding mem. Ohio Issues Scanning Network, Akron, 1988-89; founding bd. dirs., vice chair So. States Waste Mgmt. Coalition, Atlanta, 1992—; chair So. States Energy Bd. Assocs., Atlanta, 1994—. Editor Kennedy Heights Community News, 1973-75; editor-in-chief The Ohio State Engr., 1961-62. V.p., dir. Charter Com. of Greater Cin., 1979—; pres., mem. Kennedy Hts. Cmty. Coun., Cin., 1973— (Citizen of Yr. 1977); founding mem. Neighborhood Support Program Rev. Bd., Cin., 1980-82; high adventure exploring chmn. Dan Beard coun. Boy Scouts Am., Cin., 1983—. Lt. Civil Engring. Corp, USNR, 1964-66. Named Citizen of Yr., Kennedy Hgts. Cmty. Coun., 1977; recipient Silver Beaver award Boy Scouts Am., 1992. Mem. Calumet Theater Soc., Keweenaw County Hist. Soc., Buick Club Am., Miscowaubik Club Calumet, Lit. Club Cin., Ohio Soc. Colonial Wars, Sigma Phi Epsilon (pres. Ohio Gamma Alumni Corp. 1970-71). Office: The Procter & Gamble Co 1 Procter Gamble Plz Cincinnati OH 45202

FRESTEDT, JOY LOUISE, cytogeneticist and molecular biologist; b. Oak Park, Ill., Jan. 31, 1959; d. James Albert Machnicki and Wanda Louise (McConnaughhay) Katzman; m. Robert LeVance Frestedt, Aug. 8, 1987; 1 child, Megan Marie. BA, Knox Coll., 1980; PhD, U. Minn., 1996. Cytogeneticist Ill. Masonic Med. Ctr., Chgo., 1980-81; med. tech., asst. scientist, rsch. asst. U. Minn., Mpls., 1981-89, 91-96; cancer rsch. scientist III Roswell Park Cancer Inst., Buffalo, 1989-90; grad. fellow Sci. Mus. Minn., St. Paul, 1993-95; grants reviewer U. Minn., 1994; mem. exec. bd. Grad. Women in Sci., 1994-2003, pres., 1996—; exec. bd. Minn. Acad. Sci., St. Paul, 1994-96. Adv. bd. Operation Smart, YWCA, St. Paul, 1994-96. Mem. AAAS, Coalition of Women Grad. Students, Preparing Future Faculty, Am. Assn. Cancer Rsch., Assn. Molecular Pathology, Am. Soc. Investigative Pathology, Am. Soc. Leukocyte Biology. Home: 5727 W 42d St Saint Louis Park MN 55416-3101

FREY, HARLEY HARRISON, JR., anesthesiologist; b. Toledo, Feb. 22, 1920; s. Harley Harrison and Mina Rosina (Wiedemann) F.; m. Jane Luceia Murray, Aug. 28, 1944 (dec. 1964); children: Richard E., Martha J., Thomas C.; m. Emma Jean Hamilton, Apr. 15, 1966; 1 stepchild, Rick A. Gregory. BS, U. Toledo, 1942; MD, U. Cin., 1945. Diplomate Am. Bd. Anesthesiology. Intern Akron City Hosp., Ohio, 1946-49; fellow anesthesia U. Minn., Mpls., 1950; hon. mem. staff St. Elizabeth Hosp. Med. Ctr., Lafayette, Ind., 1950—, Lafayette Home Hosp., 1950—. Bd. dirs. Lafayette Symphony Orch., 1952-54; counselor, committeeman Lafayette coun. Boy Scouts Am., 1955-63; ruling elder Presbyn. Ch., 1964-67, active deacon, 1991-94; bd. dirs. Lafayette Citizens Band, 1996—. Fellow Am. Coll. Anesthesiology; mem. Am. Soc. Anesthesiology (bd. dirs. 1965-74), Ind. Soc. Anesthesiology (pres., bd. dirs. 1961-74, Disting Svc. award 1992), Ind. State Med. Soc. (Cert. Distinction 1995), Tippecanoe County Med. soc. (pres. 1961), Rotary (bd. dirs. 1992-95) Lafayette Country Club (bd. dirs. 1963-65). Home and Office: 3513 Creek Ridge Lafayette IN 47905-5619 Office: 2323 Ferry St Ste 209 Lafayette IN 47904

FREY, JUDITH LYNN, elementary education educator; b. Ashland, Ohio, Sept. 10, 1956; d. Lloyd Baeder and Norma Claire (Hostetler) Wygant; m. Daniel K. Frey, Nov. 21, 1981; children: Jennifer Lynn, Lynnette Danielle. BS in Edn., Otterbein Coll., 1978. Elem. remedial reading tchr. Norwalk (Ohio) City Schs., 1978-79; elem. remedial reading tchr. Bucyrus (Ohio) City Schs., 1979—, kindergarten tchr., 1981-87. Co-dir. Holy Trinity Cath. Ch. Pre-Sch. Religion, Bucyrus, 1987-92; co-leader Girl Scout Daisy Troop, Bucyrus, 1991-92. Mem. Internat. Reading Assn. (Crawford County chpt., bldg. rep. 1991-94). Home: 9940 County Highway 134 Nevada OH 44849-9763 Office: Lincoln Elem Sch 170 Plymouth St Bucyrus OH 44820-1627

FREY, MARGO WALTHER, career counselor, columnist; b. Watertown, Wis., July 1, 1941; d. Lester John and Anabel Marie (Bergin) Walther; m. James Severin Frey, June 29, 1963; children: Michelle Marie Frey Loberg, David James. BA in French, Cardinal Stritch Coll., 1963; MS in Counseling and Guidance, U. Wis., Milw., 1971; EdD in Adult Edn., Nova U., 1985. Nat. bd. cert. career counselor. Acad. counselor biology dept. Ind. U., Bloomington, 1975-76; dir. career planning and placement Cardinal Stritch Coll., Milw., 1977-89; pres. Career Devel. Svcs., Inc., Milw., 1989—; weekly columnist Milw. Sentinel, 1994-95. Mem. Bloomington (Ind.) women's commn. com. on employment assessment Displaced Homemakers Task Force, 1975. Named to Practitioner's Hall of Fame, Nova U., 1985. Mem. ASTD (bd. dirs. 1992), Wis. Career Planning and Placement Assn. (bd. dirs. 1987), Wis. Assn. Adult and Continuing Edn. (bd. dirs. 1983-85), Milw. Coun. Adult Learning, Human Resource Mgmt. Assn., Tempo (bd. dirs. 1995—).

FREY, NEAL, religious educator; b. Kings County, N.Y., Apr. 27, 1948; s. Henry Nicholas and Vesta Wilhamina (Honore) F.; m. Constance Dian Miles, Dec. 22, 1973; children: Joel Andrew, Heather Rebecca. AAS, Aidrondack C.C., Glens Falls, N.Y., 1972; BS, SUNY, Buffalo, 1974; MA, Assemby of God Sem., Springfield, Mo., 1983; ThM, Orland (Fla.) Sem., 1981. Assoc. mgr. A&ET, N.Y.C., 1965-72; dept. mgr. Kleinhan Store, Buffalo, 1973-74; assoc. pastor Creekside Gospel Temple, Amherst, N.Y., 1974-77; head dept. bus. Sherman (N.Y.) H.S., 1978-80; pastor Sherman Assembly of God Ch., 1977-82; asst. prof. Micronesian Bible Coll., Agana, Guam, 1984-88, pres., 1988-93; asst. prof. Evangel Coll., Springfield, Mo., 1993-95; prof. theology Caribbean Sch. Theology, Springfield, 1995—, also bd. dirs. Bd. dirs. Micronesian Sch. Theology, 1984-92, Creekside Gospel Temple, Amherst, 1974-77. With USN, 1969-71. Republican. Home: 1340 Bonaire Springfield MO 65803 Office: Caribbean Sch of Theology PO Box 2084 Springfield MO 65801

FREY, PAUL HOWARD, chemical engineer; b. Gilman, Ill., Feb. 12, 1922; s. Carl Fredrick and Doretta Mary (Koritz) F.; m. Patricia Anne Leonard, Oct. 6, 1942; children: Paul H. Jr, Elizabeth Ann. BSChE, U. Ill., 1943. Registered profl. engr., Ill. Tech. advisor Manhatten Dist. (Atom Bomb Project) Union Carbide Corp., Tonawanda, N.Y., 1943-46, rsch. and devel. engr., 1946-49; project engr. Union Carbide Corp, Chgo., 1960-80, engring. mgr., 1980-86; plant engr. U.S. Reduction Co., East Chicago, Ind., 1949-54; project and sales engr. Sunbeam Corp., Chgo., 1954-58; plant mgr. Detinning Corp., Chgo., 1958-60; owner Freytone Co., Spooner, Wis., 1986—. Inventor/patentee in field. Leader Citizens for Improved Edn., LaGrange, Ill., 1967-69; mem. vestry St. Alban's Epis. Ch., 1993—. Mem. AIChE, Lions (Lion Tamer officer Spooner chpt., 1992—), Jaycees (Key award Hammond, Ind. 1951), Waukegan Yacht Club (bd. dirs. to commodor 1976-82), No. Ill. Venture Assn. (various officers to commodore 1974-78). Home and Office: N5683 Tanglewood Dr Spooner WI 54801

FREY, ROBERT MARK, lawyer; b. Osceola, Iowa, Jan. 13, 1954; s. Robert B. and Patricia A. (Meacham) F.; m. Mona K. Walden-Frey, June 9, 1979; 1 child, Hannah Song-Yee. BA, U. Iowa, 1976, MA, 1979; MA, U. Calif., Davis, 1981; JD, Hamline U., 1988. Bar: Minn. 1988, U.S. Dist. Ct. (fed. cir.) Minn. 1990. Community educator VISTA, Norfolk, Nebr., 1976-77; rsch. asst. U. Calif., Davis, 1980; teaching asst. U. Iowa, Iowa City, 1978-79, U. Calif., Davis, 1980-81; grievance counselor Madison (Wis.) Tenant Resource Ctr., 1982-84; legal aide Koritzinsky, Neider, Langer, and Roberson, Madison, Wis., 1983-84; immigration atty. Mpls., St. Paul, 1989—; consulting atty. Minn. Advocates for Human Rights, Mpls., 1992—, direct svc. atty., 1989—; team tchr. law and justice St. Paul Acad., 1993; tchr. constl. law Breck Sch., 1993.civ. Contbr. articles and working papers to profl. publs. Vol. Minn. Advocates for Human Rights, 1988—. Mem. Minn. State Bar Assn. (immigration law sect. and human rights com.), Am. Immigration Lawyers Assn., Immigration Lawyers on the Web, Ramsey County Bar Assn., Iowa Archaeol. Soc., Phi Beta Kappa, Phi Eta Sigma. Unitarian. Office: PO Box 120351 Saint Paul MN 55112-0016

FREY, STACEY JANE, elementary education educator; b. Springfield, Ohio, Mar. 30, 1955; d. Royal Desmer and Elizabeth Jane (Moon) F. BS in Elem. and Spl. Edn., Miami U., Oxford, Ohio, 1977; MS in Edn. Administrn., U. Dayton, 1980. Cert. elem. tchr., Ohio. Tchr. East Elem. Sch., Fairborn, Ohio, 1977—; mem. Fairborn Schs. Academic Coun., 1985-88, Tchr.-In-Space Program, 1985-86, East Sch. Inclusion Team, Fairborn, 1994-95. Author poems. Vol. Spl. Olympics, Greene County, 1983, 84; mem. tchr. edn. adv. bd. Wright State U., 1988-89. Recipient Golden Apple Achiever award Ashland Oil Co., 1989. Mem. NEA, Ohio Edn. Assn., Fairborn Edn. Assn., Phi Delta Kappa (pres. 1991-92). Methodist.

FREYMILLER, MARY JEAN, archives curator; b. Muscoda, Wis., May 11, 1933; d. Frank John and Delia Mary (Bremmer) Sikhart; m. John J. Karasek, Sept. 13, 1952 (div. July 1964); children: Jean M. Ward, Susan L. French, Kevin J. (dec.), Deborah A. Childs; m. Rudolph Benjamin Freymiller, Dec. 10, 1971 (dec. Nov. 1989). Student, U. Wis., Platteville, 1977. Legal sec. McIntyre & Kinney, Lancaster, Wis., 1951-57; stenographer II Employment Rels. Bd., Madison, Wis., 1957-58, Textbook Ctr. Wis. State Coll., Platteville, Wis., 1961-62, 63-65; libr. tech. Karrmann Libr. U. Wis., Platteville, Wis., 1965-82; archives curator U. Wis., Platteville, 1982—. Trustee, treas. St. Mary's Ch. Coun., Fennimore, Wis., 1991-96; rep. Wis Coun. on Local History. Mem. Nat. Geneal. Soc., Midwest Archives Conf., Wis. State Geneal. Soc., Lower Wis. River Geneal. and Hist. Rsch. Ctr., Grant County Geneal. Soc., Grant County Hist. Soc., Iowa County Hist. Soc., Grant County Rep. Women, Lead Region Hist. Trust, U. Wis. Archives Coun. Roman Catholic. Home: 1420 Madison St Fennimore WI 53809-1935 Office: U Wis 1 University Plz Platteville WI 53818-3012

FRIAS, RAFAEL, state legislator. BA, U. Ill., Chgo. Mem. Chgo. Police Dept.; mem. from 1st dist. U.S. Ho. of Reps. Founder United Neighbors Improving the Environment. Home: 3637 S Maplewood Ave Chicago IL 60632-1022*

FRICK, ARTHUR CHARLES, art educator; b. Milw., Oct. 15, 1923; s. Arthur Clement and Nola Ann (Mangum) F.; m. Fay Arrieh, June 11, 1948 (div. 1966); children: Arthur James Frederick, Sumaya; m. Aida Moukheibir, June 7, 1968; children: Nola Ann, Delia Anne. BS in Art, U. Wis., Milw., 1948; postgrad., Ox-Bow, Saugatuck, Mich., 1948-49; MS in Art, U. Wis., 1949; postgrad., Escuela de Pintura y Escultura, Mex., 1950-51; Art Student's League of N.Y., 1994-95. Instr. Berea (Ky.) Coll., 1949-50, Stephens Coll., Columbia, Mo., 1951-56; prof., chmn. dept. fine arts Am. U. Beirut, Lebanon, 1957-76; prof., chmn. dept. art Wartburg Coll., Waverly, Iowa, 1976-95; prof. emeritus, 1995—; instr. U. Wis., Madison, 1949, Ox-Bow, Saugatuck, Mich., 1949-51, 54-56; vis. prof. Am. Coll., Lugano, Switzerland, U. Wis., Green Bay, 1967-68, U. Wis., Milw., 1972-73; curator Mooney Print Collection, Charles City, Iowa, 1996; cons., lectr. various countries, orgns. Exhbns. include Art Inst. Chgo., 1950, City Art Mus., St. Louis, 1955-57, Cleve. Mus. Art, Sursock Mus., Beirut, Palais de UNESCO, Lebanon, numerous others; co-author: Graphic Arts Processes, 1957; contbr. articles to profl. jours. pres. League Milw. Artists, 1949-51. Rsch. grantee Am. U. Beirut, 1960-61, 63-64, 67-68, 70-72, 74-75, Rockefeller Found., 1963-64, 66-68, Harvard U., 1960-61, Wartburg Coll. 1980. Mem. VFW, Coll. Art Assn. Am., Mid-Am. Coll. Art Assn., Mid-West Art History Soc. Mid-West Fedn. Chaparral Poets, Iowa Watercolor Soc., Iowa Poetry Assn., Waterloo Art Assn., Am. Legion. Republican. Methodist. Home: 212 2nd Ave NW Waverly IA 50677-2502

FRICK, GENE ARMIN, university administrator; b. Huntingburg, Ind., Oct. 13, 1929; s. Armin John and Naomi S. (Kemp) F.; m. Barbara Sue Partenheimer, Feb. 12, 1955; children: David Alan, Barbara Jean. BS in Acctg., Butler U., 1951. Acct. Huntingburg Machine Works, 1947-51; auditor Army Audit Agy., Louisville, 1952-53; property acct. E.I. DuPont, Louisville, 1954; acting internal auditor Purdue U., West Lafayette, 1955-57, contract adminstr., 1957-76, dir. contracts, 1976-93, dir. emeritus, 1993—; treas. Purdue Calumet Devel. Found., East Chicago, Ind., 1955-57; sec., treas. East Chicago Housing Corp., 1955-57; mem. com. on contracts Coun. Govt. Rels., Washington, 1975-82, com. on costing, 1982-84, bd. dirs., 1978-84; lectr. Nat. Grad. U., 1976-80. Cpl. U.S. Army, 1951-53. Named Outstanding Regional Dir., Toastmaster Internat., 1978, Ky. Col., 1989, Sagamore of the Wabash, State of Ind., 1993. Mem. Am. Assn. Investors, Elks, Lafayette Country Club, John Purdue Club, Sigma Nu (pres. housing corp. 1977-87). Republican. Home: 2166 Tecumseh Park Ln West Lafayette IN 47906-2182 Office: Purdue U Hovde Hall West Lafayette IN 47905

FRICK, JAMES WILLIAM, university administrator, consultant; b. New Bern, N.C., Aug. 5, 1924; s. Odo Aloysius and Mary Elizabeth (Cox) F.; m. Bonita Charlotte Torbert, Mar. 26, 1951 (div. 1984); children: Michael, Terence, Thomas, Theresa, Kathleen; m. Karen Ann Fogle, Oct. 13, 1984. BS in Commerce, U. Notre Dame, 1951, PhD in Edn., 1973, LLD, 1983. Project dir. U. Notre Dame, Ind., 1951-56, regional dir., 1956-61, exec. dir., 1961-65, v.p., 1965-83, trustee, 1983-84, asst. to pres., 1983-87, v.p. emeritus, 1987—; pres. James W. Frick Assocs., Inc., South Bend, Ind., 1983—; chmn. exec. com. Soc. Bank Ind., South Bend, 1967-92; dir. W.R. Grace Co., Inc., N.Y.C., 1984—, Grace Found., 1984—, Magic Circle Energy Corp., Oklahoma City, 1983-91; pres., exec. dir. Community Found., St. Joseph County, Ind., 1992-94; bd. dirs. Ind. Dept. Fin. Instns., 1983-84. Contbr. chpts. to books, articles to profl. jours. Chmn. United Way St. Joseph County, 1970, Project Future, South Bend, 1982-87; exec. com. Fin. Devel. Council Nat. Urban Coalition, Washington, 1975; nat. devel. council Assn. Am. Colls., Washington, 1978-80. Served to lt. (j.g.) USN, 1942-46. Recipient James E. Armstrong award U. Notre Dame, 1978; named Knight of Malta, Cath. Ch., 1981, Profl. of Yr. Ind. Coun. Fund Raising Exec., 1985. Mem. Council Advancement and Support Edn. (pres. 1971-72, Ashmore award 1982), Assn. Governing Bds. (devel. adv. council 1982-89), Assn. of Devel. Officers of Urban U.; Knights of Malta (bd. councillors 1990—), Phi Delta Kappa. Roman Catholic. Clubs: Marco Polo (N.Y.C.). Avocations: operas; symphonies; reading; historical novels; walking. Office: James W Frick Assocs 875 Key Bank Bldg South Bend IN 46601

FRICK, JOHN WILLIAM, health industry executive; b. St. Charles, Mo., Sept. 11, 1951; s. William Lee and Dorothy Ann (Hollingsworth) F.; m. Karen Elizabeth Gercken, Sept. 12, 1987; children: Kathryn Anne, Kerry Kathleen, John William Frick II. Student, U. Mo., Columbia, 1972; BS in Pharmacy, U. Mo., Kansas City, 1975. Lic. pharmacist. Mgr. Adam's Drug, Kansas City, Mo., 1972-77; sec., treas. Drug Depot of Blue Springs (Mo.), Inc., 1978-89; pres. Sam's Prescription Shop, Raytown, Mo., 1983—; pres., founder Home Health Depot, Inc., Kansas City, 1984-92; dir. pharmacy Two Rivers Psychiat. Hosp., Kansas City, 1986—; CEO MedFlex, 1991-93; regional mgr. Curaflex Health Svcs., Inc., 1992-94; pres., CEO Innovative Pharm. Svcs., Inc., 1992—; mem. profl. rels. staff Coram Healthcare Inc. Profl. Rels., 1994—. Mem. Greater Kansas City Sports Commn., 1986—; adv. mem. St. Joseph Health Care Ctr., 1986—; mem. Spl. Olympics Com., 1988—. Republican. Lutheran. Office: Innovative Ventures 10 E 9 St Ste G-2 Lawrence KS 66044

FRICKE, THOMAS FREELAND, lawyer; b. Bryn Mawr, Pa., Jan. 4, 1943; s. John Emory and Katherine Reed (Gessner) F.; m. Nancy Wilson Mills. BA, U. Pa., 1966; JD, Temple U., 1973. Bar: Pa. 1973. Assoc. Wright, Spencer, Manning & Sagenderph, Norristown, Pa., 1973-74; div. counsel Pantry Pride, Inc., Phila., 1974-81; gen. counsel Time-Out Family Amusement Ctrs., Inc., Fairfax, Va., 1982-90; counsel Edison Bros. Stores, Inc., St. Louis, 1990-94; pvt. practice law St. Louis, 1995—. Exec. com. 5th ward Rep. party, Phila., 1976-79; bd. dirs. Green Hedges Sch., Vienna, Va., 1986-90. 1st lt. U.S. Army, 1966-69. Mem. Internat. Assn. Leisure Def. Attys., Internat. Family Entertainment Ctr. Assn. (chmn. govt. rels. com.). Episcopalian. Home: 4563B Laclede Ave Saint Louis MO 63108

FRIDLEY, RUSSELL WILLIAM, historian; b. Oelwein, Iowa, Mar. 21, 1928; s. Lloyd and Laura (Tift) F.; m. Metta Holtkamp, Feb. 26, 1954; children—Scott, Nancy, Jane, Susan, Elizabeth, Jennifer. B.A., Grinnell Coll., 1950; M.A., Columbia U., 1953; Litt.D. (hon.), Concordia Coll., Moorhead, Minn., 1980; L.H.D. (hon.), Gustavus Adolphus Coll., 1985. Asst. dir. Minn. Hist. Soc., St. Paul, 1953-54; dir. Minn. Hist. Soc., 1954-86; v.p. Grinnell (Iowa) Coll., 1966; vice chmn. Nat. Adv. Council on Hist. Preservation, 1967-70; dir. Div. Edn. and Pub. Programs, Nat. Endowment for Humanities, 1968-69; chmn. Minn. Humanities Com., 1970-78; dir. Northwood Inst. Margaret Chase Smith Library Ctr., Skowhegan, Maine, 1987-88, Minn. Labor History Ctr., 1994—. Author: Minnesota: A State That Works. Mem. Nat. Mus. Act Adv. Coun., 1976-79, Quetico-Superior Found., Mpls., 1967-88; mem. coun. Hubert H. Humphrey Inst. Pub. Affairs, U. Minn., 1978=87; trustee James J. Hill Reference Libr., St. Paul, 1980-88, Charles A. Lindbergh Fund, N.Y.C., 1981-88, Am. Folklife Ctr. Libr. of Congress, Washington, 1986-89, Norwegian-Am. Hist. Assn., Northfield, Minn., 1987-94, Sigurd F. Olson Environ. Inst., Northland Coll., Ashland, Wis., 1987-90. Served with U.S. Army, 1946-48, PTO. Mem. Am. Assn. Museums (dir. 1969-72), Am. Assn. State and Local History (pres. 1966-68), Nat. Conf. State Hist. Pres. Officers (v.p. 1977-79). Home: 740 Amber Dr Shoreview MN 55126-4101 Office: Minn Labor History Ctr 443 Lafayette Rd N Saint Paul MN 55155-4301

FRIDRICK, M. ROGENE, gerontology educator, retired social worker; m. John Stephen Fridrick; children: Stephen J., Christine F. Olinsky, Thomas P., George M. Baughman. BS, Bowling Green (Ohio) State U., 1952; MSPH, U. Toledo, 1979; MSASS, Case Western Res. U., Cleve., 1988. Cert. mental health profl. Nat. Coun. Cert. Activity Profl.; lic. social worker. Program dir. Metro YMCA Greater Toledo; activity dir. 1 PR-Mktg.-SS Bowling Green Manor, HCF, Inc.; ret.; ret. social worker, adminstrv. dir. Mercy L.T.C.F., Dayton; dir. Prime Time Adult Day Care YWCA, Dayton, Ohio; sr. therapist, sr. adult treatment svc. Eastway-Life Span, Dayton; part-time faculty gerontology Sinclair Community Coll.-Allied Health and Human Svcs. Contbr. articles to profl. jours. Active NAACP. Mem. NASW, Gerontol. Soc. Am., Nat. Activity Professor Assn., Miami Valley Gerontol. Assn. Home: 428 Elm Grove Dr Dayton OH 45415-2936

FRIDY, JOHN ALBERT, mathematics educator; b. Lancaster, Pa., Sept. 30, 1937; s. Wayne Charles and Helen (Garman) F.; m. Sylvia Ann Guyer, Mar. 27, 1959 (div. July 1971); children: Linda, Jay; m. Carol Sue Govedich, Dec. 28, 1971; children: Jeremy, Susan. BS, Pa. State U., 1959, MA, 1961; PhD, U. N.C., 1964. Part-time instr. U. N.C., Chapel Hill, 1961-64; asst. prof. of math. Rutgers U., New Brunswick, N.J., 1964-67; assoc. prof. Kent (Ohio) State U., 1967-74, prof., 1974—. Author: Introductory Analysis: Theory of Calculus, 1987; contbr. over 30 math. rsch. articles to profl. publs. Mem. Am. Math. Soc., Math. Assn. Am., Am.Fedn. Musicians, Pi Mu Epsilon. Republican. Office: Kent State U Dept Math and Computer Sci Kent OH 44242

FRIED, JEREMY STEVEN, forester, educator; b. Santa Monica, Calif., Feb. 27, 1961; s. Burton David and Sally Rachel (Goldstein) F.; m. Kathleen Gay Tully, Jan. 16, 1994. BS in Forestry, U. Calif., Berkeley, 1982, PhD of Wildland Resource Sci., 1992; MS in Forest Mgmt., Oreg. State U., 1985. Lab. asst. II Dept. Forestry U. Calif., Berkeley, 1980-82; specialist forest inventory So. Pacific Land Co., Grass Valley, Calif., 1982-83; grad. rsch. asst. Dept. Forest Mgmt. Oreg. State U., Corvallis, 1983-85; rsch. assoc. Environ. Internship Program, San Francisco, 1985-86; assoc. specialist, postgrad. rschr. Dept. Forestry U. Calif., Berkeley, 1986-92; asst. prof. Dept. Forestry Mich. State U., East Lansing, 1992—; cons. Calif. Dept. Forestry and Fire Protection, Sacramento, 1992—, Sierra Now/The Wilderness Soc., San Francisco, 1992, EA Engring, Walnut Creek, Calif., 1993-94. Contbr. articles to profl. jours. Mem. Soc. Am. Foresters (working group chair-elect 1995-96), Am. Soc. Photogrammetry and Remote Sensing, Am. Econs. Assn., Phi Beta Kappa, Xi Sigma Pi (Outstanding Achievement award 1982). Office: Mich State U Dept Forestry 126 Natural Resources East Lansing MI 48824

FRIED, JOEL ROBERT, chemical engineering educator; b. Memphis, Dec. 9, 1946; s. Samuel J. and Mathilda (Kleinman) F.; m. Ava S. Krinick, June 8, 1969; children: Marc S., Aaron M. BS, Rensselaer Poly. Inst., 1968, 71, ME, 1972; MS, U. Mass, 1975, PhD, 1976. Mem. assoc. rsch. staff GE, Schenectady, N.Y., 1972-73; sr. rsch. engr. Monsanto Co., St. Louis, 1976-78; asst. prof. chem. engring. U. Cin., 1978-83, assoc. prof. chem. engring., 1983-90, dir. grad. studies, 1986-90, dir. polymer rsch. ctr., 1989-92, prof. chem. engring., 1990—; acting dir. membrane ctr., 1994; dir. Ohio Molecular Computation and Simulation Network and Ctr. Computer-Aided Molecular Design, 1995—; pres. Polymer Rsch. Assocs., Inc., Cin., 1984—; Jr. Morrow rsch. chair U. Cin., 1980. Author: Polymer Science and Technology, 1995; contbr. articles to sci. jours. Jr. M. Recipient Faculty Achievement award,

1994; Jr. Morrow rsch. chair U. Cin., 1980; USAF summer faculty rsch. fellow, 1981, 93, 94. Mem. Am. Chem. Soc., Am. Inst. Chem. Engrs., Soc. Plastics Engrs. Office: U Cin Dept Chemical Engineering Cincinnati OH 45221-0171

FRIEDEL, HELEN BRANGENBERG, counselor, therapist; b. Kampsville, Ill., May 16, 1938; d. Carl Morris and Martha Marie (Zipprich) Brangenberg; m. John Laverne Friedel; children: Vincent Joseph, John Francis. BS, So. Ill. U., 1969, MS, 1973. Lic. profl. counselor, Mo. Educator Archdiocese of St. Louis, 1956-87; counselor Diocese of Belleville, Waterloo, Ill., 1988-89, Christian Bros. H.S., St. Louis, 1989—; pvt. practice Florissant, Mo., 1987—. Mem. parents adv. bd. St. Louis Prep. Sem., Florissant, 1973-79; youth moderator Sacred Heart Parish, Florissant, 1967-71, lector and eucharistic min. Mem. ACA, Mo. Counseling Assn. (bd. dirs. 1986-88, 90-93, sec. 1990, pres. 1992, legis. chair 1992-93, Kitty Cole Human Rights award 1993), St. Louis Counseling Assn., Mo. Multicultural Counselors, Mid Rivers Counseling Assn. (pres. 1986), Am. Sch. Counselors Assn., Mo. Sch. Counselors Assn., St. Louis Learning Disabilities Assn. (bd. dirs. 1994), Kappa Delta Pi. Roman Catholic. Home: 425 Saint Marie St Florissant MO 63031-5830 Office: Christian Bros Prep HS 6501 Clayton Rd Saint Louis MO 63117-1705

FRIEDEWALD, ROBERT A., securities broker; b. St. Louis, Jan. 14, 1934. BS, St. Louis U., 1959. Securities broker Edward D. Jones & Co., St. Louis, 1961—. With U.S. Army, 1953-55. Mem. Yacht Club. Office: Edward D Jones & Co 201 Progress Pky Maryland Heights MO 63043-3003

FRIEDLAENDER, FRITZ JOSEF, electrical engineering educator; b. Freiburg/Breisgau, Germany, May 7, 1925; came to U.S., 1947, naturalized, 1953; s. Ludwig and Frieda (Murzynski) F.; m. Gisela Triebe, Aug. 7, 1969; 2 children. BS, Carnegie Inst. Tech., 1951, MS, 1952, PhD, 1955; Dr.-Ing. (E.h.), Ruhr-Universität Bochum, Germany, 1992. Asst. prof. Columbia, 1954-55, Purdue U., West Lafayette, Ind., 1955-59; assoc. prof. Purdue U., 1959-62, prof. elec. and computer engring., 1962—; guest prof. Max-Planck Institut Metallforschung, Tech. U. Stuttgart, Fed. Repubic Germany, 1964-65; Humboldt award and guest prof. Institut für Werkstoffe der Elektrotechnik, Ruhr-Universität, Bochum, West Germany, 1972-73; Japan Soc. for Promotion Sci. fellow and guest prof. Nagoya U., summer 1980; guest prof. U. Regensburg (Fed. Republic Germany), 1981-82; Meyerhoff vis. prof. Weizmann Inst. Sci., Rehovot, Israel, Jan.-June 1990; cons. Gen. Electric Corp., Ft. Wayne, Ind., 1956-58, Components Corp., Chgo., 1959-61, Lawrence Radiation Lab., U. Calif. at Livermore, 1967-69, P.R. Mallory & Co., 1974-78, Oakridge Nat. Lab., 1979-82. Adv. editor Jour. Magnetism and Magnetic Materials, 1975—; co-editor Magnetic Separation News, 1983-91, Magnetic and Electrical Separation, 1991—; mem. editorial bd. Proc. IEEE, 1975-78; contbr. articles to profl. jours. Fellow IEEE (revs. editor trans. Magnetics 1965-67, editorial bd. jour. 1968—, chmn. awards Magnetics Soc. 1966-74, 85—, achievement award Magnetics Soc. 1986, chmn. Intermag 1975, London, program co-chmn. Intermag 1978, Florence, Italy, v.p. Magnetics Soc. 1975-76, pres. 1977-78, chmn. Central Ind. sect. 1979-80, J. Fred Peoples award 1989, disting. lectr. 1991-93, IEEE Magnetics Soc.), fellow Am. Phys. Soc.; mem. Am. Soc. Engring. Edn., Arbeitsgemeinschaft Magnetismus, Sigma Xi, Phi Kappa Phi, Tau Beta Pi, Eta Kappa Nu, Beta Sigma Rho. Home: 150 Colony Rd West Lafayette IN 47906-1209 Office: Purdie U Sch Elec Engring Elec Engring Bldg West Lafayette IN 47907-1285

FRIEDLAND, ROBERT PAUL, medical researcher, neurologist, educator; b. N.Y.C., Dec. 4, 1948; separated with two children. BS in Biology, CCNY, 1969; MD, CUNY, 1973. Diplomate Nat. Bd. Med. Examiners; cert. Am. Bd. Psychiatry and Neurology. Fellowship in neurology Boston (Mass.) U. Sch. Medicine, 1970; intern Beth Israel Hosp., N.Y.C., 1973-74; neurology resident, chief resident Mt. Sinai Sch. Medicine, N.Y.C., 1974-77; NIH rsch. fellow, assoc. dept. neurology Albert Einstein Coll. Medicine, N.Y.C., 1977-78; clin. fellow dept. neurology Jacobi Hosp., Bronx, 1977-78; asst. prof. neurology in residence U. Calif., Davis, 1978-85, assoc. prof. neurolog in residence, 1985; dir., founder No. Calif. Alzheimer's Disease Ctr. U. Calif. Davis, Herrick Hosp. and Health Ctr., Berkeley, 1985; clin. dir. Alzheimer Ctr., U. Hosps. of Cleve., Ohio, 1990-94; assoc. prof. dept. neurology, psychiatry and radiology Case Western Res. U. Sch. Medicine, 1990—; staff neurologist VA Med. Ctr., Martinez, Calif., 1978-85; asst. chief neurol. svc., 1978-84; attending neurologist Highland Gen. Hosp., Oakland, Calif., 1979-85; guest scientist Donner Lab., U. Calif., Berkeley, 1979-85, chief neurologist rsch. medicine group, 1982-85; chief brain aging and dementia sect. Lab. of Neuroscis., Nat. Inst. Aging, NIH, 1986-90, dep. clin. dir.; clin. prof. Georgetown U., 1988-90, others. Editor: The Selected Papers of Morris B. Bender, 1983; Editorial bd.: Alzheimer's Disease: An Internat. Jour., 1985—; contbr. chpts. to books and articles to profl. jours. Recipient S. Horowitz award Mt. Sinai Sch. Medicine, 1994. Fellow Am. Acad. Neurology (steering com., rsch. subcom. geriatric neurology sect., L. McHenry award 1990); mem. Am. Neurol. Assn., Internat. Soc. Cerebral Blood Flow and Metabolism, Soc. for Neurosci., Behavioral Neurology Soc. Home: 3588 Lynnfield Shaker Heights OH 44122 Office: Case Western Res Sch Medicine 2074 Abington Rd Cleveland OH 44106-2602

FRIEDLANDER, DANIEL SIMON, public relations executive; b. Chgo., Apr. 11, 1933; s. Leo and Ann (Simon) F.; m. Shirley Tishcott, Sept. 16, 1959; children: Janet, Alan, Shirley. B in Journalism, U. Colo., 1955. Asst. city editor City News Bur., Chgo., 1958-59; editor AP, Chgo., 1959; editor, night Chgo. Am., 1959-61; pub., owner Warren-Newport Press, Waukegan, Ill., 1960-63; editor Metalworking News, Chgo., 1961-69; pres. Friedlander Comm., Bannockburn, Ill., 1969—. Recipient State of Ill. Proclamation for Contbns. to Journalism, 1994. Mem. Chgo. Press Vets (sec. 1991-96, Contbn. to Chgo. Journalism award 1993, Spl. award 1994), Chgo. Newspaper Reporters, South-Ctrl. Lake County C. of C. (pres., newsletter editor, 1st Spl. award), Chgo. Headline Club (dir., officer). Office: Friedlander Comm Ltd 2203 Lakeside Dr Bannockburn IL 60014

FRIEDLANDER, JOSEPH DAVID, environmental administrator, ecologist; b. San Francisco, May 24, 1955; s. Walter Jay and Florence Zelma (Eastburn) F.; m. Janelle Kathleen Durick, Dec. 16, 1979; children: Elizabeth Jo, Thomas Walter. BA in Landscape Arch., U. Calif., Berkeley, 1977; MS in Range Sci., Colo. State U., 1980. Landscape arch. Mits Kawamoto and Assocs., Omaha, 1977-79; environ. specialist N.Am. Coal Corp., Bismarck, N.D., 1980-83; sr. environ. specialist Coteau Properties Co., Beulah, N.D., 1983-89, environ. mgr., 1989—; mem. adv. com. N.D. State U. Land Reclamation Rsch. Ctr., Mandan, 1990—. Contbr. articles to profl. jours. Recipient Disting. Svc. award for regulatory program Lignite Energy Coun., 1994. Mem. Soil and Water Conservation Soc. (profl. soil erosion and sediment control specialist), Am. Soc. for Surface Mining and Reclamation (nat. exec. bd. dirs. 1991-93), Soc. for Ecol. Restoration, Soc. for Range Mgmt., Hazen C. of C. (exec. bd. dirs. 1992-94).

FRIEDLANDER, PATRICIA ANN, marketing executive; b. Chgo., May 9, 1944; d. James Farrell and Therese Mary (Pfeiler) Crotty; m. Daniel B. Friedlander, July 3, 1971 (div. Apr. 1978); children: Michael Derek, David Colin; m. Denis R. Johnson, Feb. 24, 1994. BA, Cardinal Stritch Coll., 1966; MA, U. Wis., Milw., 1968; postgrad., U. Chgo., 1968-69, U. London, 1968—. Instr. U. Wis., Milw., 1966-68, Chgo. State U., 1968-71, Argo Community High Sch., Summit, Ill., 1971-73, Park Dist., Park Forest South, Ill., 1973-77; counselor Will County Mental Health Clinic, Park Forest South, 1977-78; sales rep. Prentice-Hall, Inc., Englewood Cliffs, N.J., 1978-84; nat. sales mgr. Dow Jones-Irwin, Homewood, Ill., 1984-87; dir. mktg. Nat. Textbook Co., Lincolnwood, Ill., 1987-88; mgr. mktg. Scott Foresman & Co., Glenview, Ill., 1988-90; corp. advt. dir. Giltspur, Inc., Itasca, Ill., 1990-96; dir. Mktg. Comms. Exhibitgroup/Gitspur, Roselle, Ill., 1996—; dir. Printer's Row Bookfair, Chgo., 1985; pub. cons.; spkr. and author in trade show and pub. field; mem. Ctr. for Exposition Rsch. Den mother Cub Scouts Am., Park Forest South, 1981-84. Mem. Bus. Mktg. Assn., Am. Book Travelers, Midwest Book Travelers (pres. 1983-87), Chgo. Book Clinic, Chgo. Women in Pub., Am. Mgmt. Assn., Am. Mktg. Assn., Health Care Conv. & Exhibitors Assn., Internat. Exhibitors Assn. (del.), Exhibit Designers and Prodrs. Assn. (del.), Computer Exhibit Mgrs. Assn. Home: 2320 W Farwell Ave Chicago IL 60645-4735 Office: Exhibit Group/Giltspur 200 N Gary Ave Roselle IL 60172

FRIEDMAN, ARNOLD EDWARD, computer scientist; b. Pawtucket, R.I., July 14, 1949; s. Arnold and Mary (Fine) F.; m. Joy Carol Pell, June 26, 1977 (div. Mar. 1981); m. Shelly Rae Caren, Dec. 8, 1991. AB, Brown U., 1971; PhD, U. Chgo., 1993. Computer coord. dept. math. U. Chgo., 1987—. Mem. Sigma Xi. Office: U Chgo Dept Math 5734 S University Ave Chicago IL 60637-1514

FRIEDMAN, BERNARD ALVIN, federal judge; b. Detroit, Sept. 23, 1943; s. David and Rae (Garber) F.; m. Rozanne Golston, Aug. 16, 1970; children: Matthew, Megan. Student, Detroit Inst. Tech., 1962-65; JD, Detroit Coll. Law, 1968. Bar: Mich. 1968, Fla. 1968, U.S. Dist. Ct. (ea. dist.) Mich. 1968, U.S. Ct. Mil. Appeals 1972. Asst. prosecutor Wayne County, Detroit, 1968-71; ptnr. Harrison & Friedman, Southfield, Mich., 1971-78, Lippitt, Harrison, Friedman & Whitefield, Southfield, 1978-82; judge Mich. Dist. Ct. 48th dist., Bloomfield Hills, 1982-88; U.S. dist. judge Ea. Dist. Mich., Detroit, 1988—. Lt. U.S. Army, 1967-74. Recipient Disting. Service award Oakland County Bar Assn., 1986. Office: US Dist Ct US Courthouse Rm 235 231 W Lafayette Bvld Detroit MI 48226-2719

FRIEDMAN, BRUCE HOWARD, psychologist, researcher; b. Cleve., Jan. 10, 1957; s. Seymour and Elinor June (Yosowitz) F. BA in Psychology, Case Western Reserve U., 1985; MS in Psychology, Pa. State U., 1989, PhD in Psychology, 1992. Postdoctoral fellow U. Pitts., 1992-94; rsch. assoc. Washington U., St. Louis, 1994-95; lectr. Washington U., 1994-95; rsch. fellow Found. Creativity and Idiodynamics, St. Louis, 1994-95; facilitator U. Pitts., 1994; instr. Pa. State U., University Park, 1985-92. Contbr. articles to profl. jours. Postdoctoral tng. fellow, NIH, 1992-94. Mem. APA, Am. Psychol. Assn., Soc. Psychophysiol. Rsch., Midwestern Psychol. Soc., Inst. Noetic Scis. Home: 327 N Taylor Ave #103 Saint Louis MO 63108 Office: Washington U Dept Psychology Box 1125 1 Brookings Dr Saint Louis MO 63130

FRIEDMAN, ERNEST HARVEY, physician, psychiatrist; b. Cleve., Jan. 8, 1931; s. Sol and Ann (Nittskoff) F.; m. Anita Rose Bogdanow, Oct. 26, 1962; children: Rachel Samantha, Sarah Ann, Eric Daniel, Jessica Emily. BS, Case Western Res. U., 1952; MD, Ohio State U., 1956. Diplomate Am. Bd. Psychiatry and Neurology. Intern U. Ill. Hosps., Chgo., 1956-57; psychiat. resident U. Hosps. of Cleve., 1957-60; clin. instr. Case Western Res. U., Cleve., 1974-86, asst. clin. prof., 1983—; vis. psychiatrist Mt. Sinai Hosp., Cleve., 1963-70, sr. vis. psychiatrist, 1970—; pvt. practice psychiatry, medicine Cleve., 1962—; owner, computer mfr. Voxaflex Co., East Cleveland, Ohio, 1986—; mem. courtesy staff Laurelwood Hosp., Willoughby, Ohio, 1991—; mem. courtesy staff Huron Hosp., East Cleveland, Ohio, 1971—; chmn. ad hoc com. on stress Am. Heart Assn., Cleve., 1977; cons. psychiatrist Nat. Exercise and Heart Disease Study, Washington, 1972-75. Mem. editorial bd. Heart and Lung, 1974-80; patentee computer software and hardware. Served as lt. comdr. M.C., USNR, 1960-62. Grantee-in-aid Am. Heart Assn., Cleve., 1964, 65, 75. Fellow Am. Psychiat. Assn. Jewish. Office: Voxaflex Co 1831 Forest Hills Blvd Cleveland OH 44112-4313

FRIEDMAN, GARY SETH, physician, educator; b. Bklyn., May 17, 1953; s. Joel and Delia (Rubin) F. BA, Columbia Coll., 1974; MD, SUNY, 1978. Asst. prof. neurology U. Olka., Okla. City, 1989-91; asst. prof. and chief neuroehabilitation U. S. Ala., Mobile, 1991-93; asst. prof. neurol, chief inpatient svcs. divsn. neurology U. Mo., Columbia, 1993-95. Fellow Am. Bd. Physical Medicine & Rehab., Am. Bd. Psychiatry & Neurology. Democrat. Jewish. Office: Harry S Truman VA Hosp 800 Hospital Dr Columbia MO 65201 Home: 3711 Sardis Ct Columbia MO 65203-5373 Office: U Mo Columbia Divsn Neurology M741-HSC One Hosp Dr Columbia MO 65212

FRIEDMAN, JAMES DENNIS, lawyer; b. Dubuque, Iowa, Jan. 11, 1947; s. Elmer J. and Rosemary Catherine (Stillmunkes) F.; m. Kathleen Marie Maersch, Aug. 16, 1969; children: Scott, Ryan, Andrea, Sean. AB in Polit. Sci., Marquette U., 1969; JD, U. Notre Dame, 1972. Bar: Wis. 1972, U.S. Supreme Ct. 1978, U.S. Ct. Appeals (D.C. cir.) 1973, U.S. Ct. Appeals (7th cir.) 1976, U.S. Ct. Appeals (6th cir.) 1989. Pvt. practice law Milw., 1972-81; ptnr. Quarles & Brady, Milw., 1981—; presenter in field; mem. legis. coun. spl. study com. on regulation of fin. instns. State of Wis., 1986-87. Mng. Editor: Notre Dame Law Review, 1971-72; contbr. articles to profl. jours. Alderman 4th and 7th dists. Mequon, Wis., 1979-85, pres. common coun., 1980-82; bd. dirs. Weyenrg, Pub. Libr. Found. Inc., 1983—, pres., 1984—; bd. dirs. Ptnrs. Advancing Values in Edn. Inc., 1987—; bd. visitors Marquette U. Ctr. for Study of Entrepreneurship, Milw., 1987-95; bd. dirs. Ozaukee Family Svcs., 1983—, sec., 1993—; bd. dirs. Notre Dame Club of Milw., 1984-88, sec., 1978, v.p., 1986-88; chair attys. unit United Way Fund Dr. Greater Milw., 1987; mem. St. James Ch., Mequon. Mem. ABA (savs. instns. and banking law coms. sect. bus. law), State Bar Wis. (internat. transactions sect. bd. dirs. 1984—, sec. and chair-elect 1988-89, chair 1989-90, del. to ABA Ho. of Dels. 1980-82, standing com. on adminstrn. justice and judiciary 1979-81, legal edn. and bar admissions com. 1984-89, com. on minority lawyers 1992—, bd. dirs. Young Lawyers divsn. 1978-82, chmn. YLD bar admission standards and requirements com. 1979), Milwaukee Bar Assn., Wis. Acad. Trial Lawyers (bd. dirs. 1980-82), Wis. League Fin. Instns. Ltd. (attys. com.), Sigma Phi Epsilon, Milw. Country Club. Roman Catholic. Office: Quarles & Brady 411 E Wisconsin Ave Milwaukee WI 53202-4409

FRIEDMAN, RICHARD LEE, lumberyard owner; b. Hammond, Ind., Jan. 28, 1950; s. Arthur and Ida (Ander) F.; m. Carol Smulevitz, May 28, 1972; children: Brett Joseph, Joshua David. BA, Ind. U., 1972. Pers. cons. Murphy Employment Svc., Wheaton, Ill., 1973-74; pers. mgr. Warshawsky and Co., Chgo., 1974-76; pers. mgr. controls div. Singer Co., Crystal Lake, Ill., 1976-79; mgr., owner State Lumber Co., Inc., Calumet City, Ill., 1979—, pres., 1995—. Bd. dirs. Ind. Jewish Hist. Soc., 1987—, pres., 1995—. Named Vol. of Yr. N.W. Ind. Jewish Fedn., 1985. Mem. B'nai B'rith (mem. internat. cabinet 1987-91, pres. Ind. state assn. 1990-91, dist. leadership chmn. 1992-93, AZA advisor youth orgn. 1985—, internat. bd. govs. 1992-94, dist. pres. 1993-94, Man of Yr. 1987). Democrat.

FRIEDMAN, STEPHEN BELAIS, real estate development consultant; b. Phila., Dec. 17, 1945; s. Alfred Henry and Sylvia (Sclar) F.; m. Cynthia Swan, May 24, 1974 (div. 1984); 1 child, Benjamin Belais; m. Anita Cross, Aug. 7, 1988. BA, Goddard Coll., 1968; MS in Urban Planning, U. Wis., Madison, 1971. Planner Kendree & Shepherd Planning Consultants, Phila., 1968-69; planning analsyt Wis. Dept. Local Affairs and Devel., Madison, 1970-71; planning analyst dept. adminstrn. Wis. State Planning Office, Madison, 1971-76; sr. rsch. assoc. Am. Planning Assn., Chgo., 1976-78; prin. counselor Real Estate Rsch. Corp., Chgo., 1978-81; from assoc. to prin. real estate adv. svcs. Laventhol & Horwath, Chgo., 1981-90; pres. S.B. Friedman & Co., Chgo., 1990—. Author: (with others) Practice of Local Government Planning, 2d edit., 1988; contbr. articles to profl. jours. Mem. Met. Planning Coun., 1978—, chair infrastructure subcom., 1983); mem. transp. com. Civic Fedn., 1994—; trustee Emanuel Congregation, 1991-94. Mem. Am. Planning Assn. (v.p. Chgo. chpt. 1986-88), Am. Inst. Cert. Planners (counselors of real estate, 2nd vice chair of Midwest chpt. 1996), Urban Land Inst. (asst. chair Chgo. Dist. coun. 1995—), Lambda Alpha (land econs. soc., pres. Ely chpt. 1989, internat. bd. govs., scribe, treas. 1990-95). Jewish. Office: SB Friedman & Co Ste 1007 221 N LaSalle St Chicago IL 60601

FRIEDMAN, VICTOR ALLEN, linguist, eduator; b. Chgo., Oct. 18, 1949; s. Norman Benjamin and Lorraine (Weisman) F. BA, Reed Coll., 1970; MA, U. Chgo., 1971, PhD, 1975; golden plaque (hon.), U. Skopje, Macedonia, 1991. From asst. prof. to prof. U. N.C., Chapel Hill, 1975-93; prof. U. Chgo., 1993—; cons. Internat. Rsch. and Exch. Bd., 1981—; mem. joint com. on Eastern Europe Am. Coun. Learned Socs., 1992—, fellow, 1986. Author: Grammatical Categories of the Macedonian Indicative, 1977; translator: Macedonian Historical Phonology, 1983; contbr. numerous articles to profl. jours. Fellow NEH, 1980-81; recipient Medal Peoples Republic Bulgaria, 1982. Mem. Am. Com. Slavists (v.p. 1994—), Am. Assn. Southeast European Studies (pres. 1990-92, Soc. Albanian Studies (v.p. 1978-81), Bulgarian Studies Assn. (nominating com. 1984-90), Macedonian Acad. Arts and Scis. Jewish.

FRIEDRICH, CHARLES WILLIAM, corporate executive; b. Elgin, Ill., Aug. 30, 1943; s. Charles Kenneth and Veronica Elizabeth (Sharpe) F.; BA, Parsons Coll., 1967; student Loras Coll., 1961-63; m. Janet Lee West, June 20, 1970; children: Joan Elizabeth, Charles Kenneth II. Salesman, Bendix Corp., South Bend, Ind., 1967; safety dir., asst. personnel mgr. Nat. Castings div. Midland Ross, Cicero, Ill., 1968-69; personnel mgr. Continental Tube Co. div. Hofmann Industries, Bellwood, Ill., 1969, asst. indsl. relations mgr., 1970, Midwest dir. indsl. relations Hofmann Industries, 1971-73; dir. indsl. relations, gen. mgr. Lemont Shipbuilding and Repair Co. (Ill.), 1973-75; indsl. relations exec. Modern Mgmt. Methods, Inc., Deerfield, Ill., 1975-77; pres. Standard Cons. Services Co., Inc., Hinsdale, Ill., 1977-88; chmn. bd. dirs., pres. B.I. Industries, Inc., Brulé Pollution Control Co., Radiant Products Co., Brulé C.E. & E., Inc., 1986—; past Ill. Pres., Burr Ridge (Ill.) Park Dist. Bd.; scoutmaster Boy Scouts Am., 1982-88; past treas. Palisades Sch. Dist. Mem. Packard Automobile Classics Club (pres. 1996—), Antique Automobile Club Am., Kiwanis, Alpha Phi Omega. Club: K.C. (former grand knight, trustee Mayslake council). Home: 10s431 Glenn Dr Burr Ridge IL 60521-6859 Office: 13920 Western Ave Blue Island IL 60406-3213

FRIEDRICH, ROSE MARIE, travel agency executive; b. Chgo., May 17, 1941; d. Theodore A. and Ann Bernadine (Coppoth) Dlugosz; m. Gerhard K. Friedrich, Apr. 18, 1964; 1 child, Alan C. Cert. travel agt. Travel cons. Chgo. Motor Club, 1959, Drake Travel, Chgo., 1960-65; mgr. 1st Nat. Travel, Arlington Heights, Ill., 1969-71, Total Travel, Palatine, Ill., 1971-76; owner, pres. Travel Bug Ltd., Lake Zurich, Ill., 1977-89; owner Travel Edn. Concepts, Inc., Palatine, Ill., 1987-91, Am. Inst. Travel, Inc., Lake Zurich, Ill., 1987-91, Group Travel Specialists, Inc., Lake Zurich, 1988-91; editor, pub. Christian Times, 1992—; advisor Coll. Lake County, Grayslake, Ill., 1985-90; ind. cons., writer. Author: (books) Travel Career Textbook, 1980, Guide to Tour Organizing, 1984, Build Profits Through Group Travel, 1984, Independent Travel Agent, 1986. Sec., bd. dirs. Candlewick Lake Assn., 1992—. Mem. Inst. Cert. Travel Cons. (chmn. edn. forum 1981-84, appreciation award 1984), Soc. Travel and Tourism Educators, State of Ill. Council Vocat. Edn. (mem. Career Guidance Consortium, Appreciation award 1986), Lake Zurich C. of C. (pres. 1984-85). Republican. Roman Catholic. Home: 904 Candlewick Dr NE Poplar Grove IL 61065-8918 Office: Christian Times PO Box 249 Poplar Grove IL 61065-0249

FRIEND, HELEN MARGARET, chemist; b. Lyndon, Ohio, Jan. 30, 1931; d. Maurice Chapman and Margaret (Beath) Mossbarger; m. William Warren Friend, Oct. 9, 1982. BA in Chemistry, Coll. of Wooster, 1953. Rsch. chemist Union Carbide Co., Cleve., 1953-56, asst. patent coord. battery products div., 1956-59, patent coord., 1959-86; patent coord. Eveready Battery Co., Westlake, Ohio, 1986-90, tech. patent assoc., 1990-95; ret., 1995; mng. editor JEC Press-Internat. Battery Materials Assn., Cleve., 1978—. Mng. editor Progress in Batteries and Battery Materials, 1978-96; JEC Battery Newsletter, 1987—; tech. editor Electrochem. Soc. Japan, U.S. br., 1975—. Mem. Am. Chem. Soc., Phi Beta Kappa. Presbyterian. Home: 576 Buckeye Dr Sheffield Lake OH 44054-1615

FRIEND, ROBERT NATHAN, financial counselor, economist, market technician; b. Chgo., Feb. 2, 1930; s. Karl D. and Marion (Wollenberger) F.; AB, Grinnell Coll., 1951; MS, Ill. Inst. Tech., 1953; m. Lee Baer, Aug. 12, 1979; children: Karen, Alan. With K. Friend & Co., Chgo., 1953—, v.p., early 1960's, 1st v.p., 1964—, dir. merger activities with Standard Oil Co. (Ind.), trustee employees' benefit trust, 1958—; active Friend Fin. Svcs. Admissions; cons. Grinnell Coll., Ill. Inst. Tech., 1968-70; Alumni career counselor Ill. Inst. Tech.; bd. dirs. Nat. Anorexia Nervosa & Associated Disorders Assn. Fellow So. Finance Assn., Southwestern Fin. Assn., Acad. Internat. Bus., Am. Acad. Polit. and Social Sci., Am. Assn. Individual Investors, Vintage Soc., Renaissance Soc., Sarah Siddons Soc., Art Inst. Chgo. (life), Chgo. Council Fgn. Relations, Am. Econ. Assn., Ea. Fin. Assn., Market Techicians Assn., Acad. Polit. Sci., Phi Kappa Phi; mem. Seed Savers Exch. (contbg. assoc.). Clubs: Carlton, Yale. Home: 1300 N Lake Shore Dr Chicago IL 60610 Office: 223 W Jackson Blvd Chicago IL 60606

FRIEND, WILLIAM C., state legislator; m. Ann friend. BA, U. Indpls. Auditor; rep. Dist. 23 Ind. Ho. of Reps., 1992—, mem. agr. and rural devel., county and twp. coms., mem. family and children, ways and means coms.; owner/farmer Friend Farms. Trustee Allen Twp.; mem. coun.-at-large Miami County; contr. Miami County Solid Waste Dist.; mem. Farm Bur., Grissom Cmty. Redevel. Authority. Mem. Ind. Auditors Assn., Miami County Pork Prodrs., Peru C. of C., Scottish Rite. Home: RR 2 Box 314 Macy IN 46951-9582*

FRIGGE, THOMAS RICHARD, food products executive; b. Piqua, Ohio, Sept. 18, 1952; s. Edward L. and Charlotte J. (Williams) Frigge; m. Rebecca J. Poock, June 26, 1971. BS in Restaurant Mgmt., Ohio State, 1977, MS in Food Tech., 1981. Chemist, product testing lab Burger King Corp., Miami, Fla., 1982-83; product inspection supv. Burger King Corp., Columbus, Ohio, 1983-85; test kitchen mgr. Burger King Corp., Miami, Fla., 1985-88, ops. QA mgr., 1988-89; nat. account dir. Gojo Industries, Akron, Ohio, 1989—. Inventor Microwave Barrier Tech., 1989, Handwashing Compliance Measurement Technology, 1995. Mem. Internat. Assn. Milk, Food and Environ. Sanitarians, Inst. Food Tech., Conf. for Food Protection, Mensa. Home: 1115 Broadway St Piqua OH 45356-1703

FRIGGENS, THOMAS GEORGE, state official, historian; b. Pontiac, Mich., July 12, 1949; s. Francis G. and Jane E. (Pettit) F.; m. Mary T. Bahra. BA, Albion Coll., 1971; MA, Wayne State U., 1973. Contract historian Mich. Dept. Natural Resources, Fayette, 1973; site historian 07 Mich. Dept. State, History Div., Fort Wilkins Hist. Complex, Copper Harbor, 1974-75, site historian 09, 1975-76, site historian 11, 1976-80, site historian VII, 1980-85; site historian VII Dept. State, Bur. History, Mich. Iron Industry Mus., Negaunee, 1985-87, regional historian VII, 1987-92, regional historian VII supr., 1992—; cons. St. Louis County Hist. Soc., Duluth, Minn., 1985, 86. Contbr. articles to jours. in field. Active Hist. Soc. Mich., bd. dirs., 1984-90; active Copper County Heritage Coun., pres., 1982-83; bd. dirs. Marquette County Hist. Soc., 1992—; mem. Mich. Hist. Preservation Network. Recipient Roy W. Drier award Houghton County (Mich.) Hist. Soc., 1987, Merit award Hist. Soc. Mich., 1983, Disting. Svc. award, 1983. Mem. Am. Assn. State and Local History, Nat. Trust for Hist. Preservation, Phi Alpha Theta. Office: Mich Iron Industry Mus 73 Forge Rd Negaunee MI 49866-9532

FRINGS, MANFRED SERVATIUS, philosophy educator; b. Cologne, N. Rhine, Germany, Feb. 27, 1925; came to U.S., 1958; U.S. citizen.; s. Gottfried and Maria (Over) F.; m. Karin Frambach, Dec. 30, 1985; 1 child. PhD, U. Cologne, North Rhine, 1953; postgrad., Staatsexamen, 1956. Sch. master German Higher Edn., North Rhine, 1956-58; asst. prof. philosophy U. Detroit, 1958-62; assoc. prof. philosophy Duquesne U., Pitts., 1962-66; prof. philosophy DePaul U., Chgo., 1966-92, prof. emeritus, 1992—; dir. Max Scheler Archives, Albuquerque; guest prof. U. Cologne, 1979, 83; guest lectr. U. Mainz, Freiburg, Germany, 1980-81; pres. Max Scheler Gesellschaft, 1993—. Author: Max Scheler: A Concise Introduction, 1965, 2d edit., 1995, Person and Dasein, 1969, Philosophy of Prediction and Capitalism, 1987, The Mind of Max Scheler, 1996; editor: The Collected Works of Max Scheler; co-editor: Heidegger/Gesamtausgabe, 1976-82; mem. adv. bd. Jour. Mus. Rsch., 1980—; contbr. over 100 articles to profl. jours. and mags. including Chinese, French, German and Japanese translations. Fulbright grantee, 1958, Deutsche Forschungsgemeinschaft of Germany grantee, 1972, 79, 82, 87 Thyssen Found. of Germany grantee, 1983. Mem. Brit. Soc. Phenomenology (corr. 1975-96), Heidegger Conf. in Am. (initiator), Max Scheler Soc. (pres. 1993—). Roman Catholic. Home: 11809 San Francisco Dr NE Albuquerque NM 87122-1095

FRINK, BRIAN LEE, artist, educator; b. Ft. Lee, Va., Sept. 22, 1956; s. Joseph Lee and Darlene Jean (Ratcliff) F.; m. Denise Ellen Neushwander; children: Blake, Annakeiko. BFA, Ill. State U., 1979; MFA, U. Wis., 1988. Assoc. prof. art Mankato (Minn.) State U., 1989—; vis. lectr. U. Wis., Madison, 1989. Exhibited in group shows at Mpls. Inst. of Art, Mpls. Coll. Art and Design, Carolyn Ruff Gallery, Mpls. Nat. Endowment for Arts individual fellow, 1993, Minn. State Arts Bd. individual fellow, 1993, 95, McKnight fellow McKnight Corp., 1992. Home: 923 Baker Ave Mankato MN 56001 Office: Mankato State U Box 42 Mankato MN 56002

FRISBIE, MARLENE ANN, business executive; b. Chgo., Aug. 25, 1955; d. George Francis and Marian (Senics) Andrasco; m. Hugh David Frisbie, Aug.

19, 1978; children: Brandon Hugh, Catherine Marie. BS, U. Ill., 1977; MBA, DePaul U., 1983. CPA, Ill. Audit supr. Coopers & Lybrand, Chgo., 1977-83; sr. fin. acct. FMC Corp., Chgo., 1983-85; mgr. external reporting GATX Corp., Chgo., 1985-88; v.p., controller Iverson Perennial Gardens, Inc., Long Grove, Ill., 1989-95; pres., owner Prairie Haven, Ltd., Long Grove, Ill., 1995—. Treas. Village of Cary, Ill., 1979-83. Named Young Career Woman Met. Bus. and Profl. Women, 1984. Mem. AICPA, Chgo. Soc. Women CPAs (bd. dirs. 1982-85), Am. Soc. Women CPAs, Ill. CPA Soc., AICPA. Office: Prairie Haven Ltd 2787 RFD Long Grove IL 60047

FRISBIE, RICHARD PATRICK, communications consultant, author; b. Chgo., Nov. 27, 1926; s. Chauncey Osborn and Pearl Genevieve (Harrison) F.; m. Margery Rowbottom, June 3, 1950; children: Felicity, Anne Celeste, Thomas, Ellen, Paul, Patrick, Teresa, Margaret. BA, U. Ariz., 1948. Writer, editor Chgo. Daily News, 1948-55; copy chief Tempo, Inc., Chgo., 1956-57, Cunningham & Walsh, Chgo., 1958-61, Hill, Rogers, Mason & Scott, Chgo., 1961-63; creative dir. Campbell-Ewald Co., Chgo., 1964-66; editor-in-chief Chgo. Mag., 1971-73; owner Frisbie Comms., Chgo., 1966—; exec. sec. Nat. Satellite Cable Assn., Chgo., 1982-83. Author: Family Fun and Recreation, 1964, How to Peel a Sour Grape, 1965, Who Put the Bomb in Father Murphy's Chowder, 1968, It's a Wise Woodsman Who Knows What's Biting Him, 1969, Basic Boat Building, 1979; author: (with wife Margery) The Do-It-Yourself Parent, 1963. Trustee Arlington Heights (Ill.) Meml. Libr., 1967—, treas., 1971-73, pres., 1973-79, v.p. and sec., 1993—; dir. North Suburban Libr. System, Wheeling, Ill., 1976-77, treas., 1978, pres., 1979-81; dir. Ill. Ctr. for the Book, Chgo., 1989-93, pres., 1991-92. Served with USN, 1945. Recipient Best Mag. Article award Cath. Press Assn., 1957. Mem. Am. Libr. Assn., Ill. Libr. Assn., Authors Guild, Soc. Midland Authors (pres. 1985-88), Chgo. Pres Vets., Internat. Press Club Chgo. Democrat. Roman Catholic. Home: 631 N Dunton Ave Arlington Heights IL 60004 Office: Frisbie Comms 111 E Wacker Dr Chicago IL 60601

FRISK, RUTH DAVIS, retired educator; b. Roseville, Ill., Feb. 11, 1916; d. George Francis and Ruth (Stanley) Davis; m. John A. Frisk, Feb. 2, 1947; 1 child, Judith Frisk Baamonde. BS in Edn., U. Ill., 1942. Speech and English tchr. Rock Island (Ill.) H.S., 1942-47; English tchr. Geneseo (Ill.) H.S., 1948-49; speech and English tchr. Westerfield H.S., Kewanee, Ill., 1956-61, Galva (Ill.) H.S., 1961-78; mem. Am. Cancer Soc. Speakers' Bur., 1949-58; presenter in field. S.C.A.N. coord., women's com. Henry County Farm Bur., Cambridge, Ill., 1978—, speakers' bur., 1989—; columnist Henry County Farmer, Cambridge, 1989—; ct. observer MADD, Cambridge, 1991—. Recipient Mem. of Yr. award Henry County Women's Com. Henry County Farm Bur., 1990-91. Mem. AAUW, Ill. Retired Tchrs., Kappa Delta Pi, Delta Kappa Gamma. Lutheran. Home: 10740 E 1500 St Cambridge IL 61238

FRISMAN, ROGER LAWRENCE, industrial sales executive; b. Cleve., Apr. 30, 1952; s. Al and Elsie (Joseph) F. BA, Kent State U., 1974. Sales rep. Lawyers Title Ins. Corp., Cleve., 1977-80, sales mgr., 1980; asst. v.p. sales Midland Title Security, Cleve., 1983-84, sr. v.p. comml. indsl. sales, 1984-90, sr. v.p., mgr. home builder dept., 1990—; bd. dirs. Ohio Home Builders Assn., mem. exec. com. Advisor YMCA Youth Gov., Stow, 1974; chmn. Nat. Assn. Home Builders Assoc., Build Pac, Wash., 1988—, chmn., 1995, com. vice-chmn., 1996. Recipient Affiliate of the Yr. award Bldg. Industry Assn., 1986, Affiliate of the Yr. award Ohio Home Builders Assn., 1985. Mem. Cleve. Bldg. Industry Assn., Cleve. Bd. Realtors (Affiliate of Yr. award 1982), Mortgage Bankers Assn. Apartment and Home Owners Assn. (Affiliate of Yr. award 1984), Nat. Assn. Home Builders Soc. (assoc.). Jewish. Home: 725 Village Club Rd Northfield OH 44067-2333 Office: Midland Title Security Inc 1 Erieview Plz Cleveland OH 44114-1715

FRITZ, JACQUELYNN, medical surgical nurse; b. Youngstown, Ohio, Nov. 29, 1953; d. Louis and Elverna Anna Christina (Poese) F. Diploma in Nursing, Immanuel Hosp., Omaha, 1975; B Gen. Studies, U. Nebr., Omaha, 1988. Staff nurse med./surg. Immanuel Med. Ctr., Omaha, 1975-79, staff nurse orthopedics, 1979-80; staff nurse ICU St. Joseph Hosp., Omaha, 1980-82, staff nurse pulmonary endocrine, 1982-84, staff nurse progressive care, 1984-86, staff nurse telemetry/stepdown, 1986-95, mem. computer charting implementation com., 1995—; mem. nurse practice com. St. Joseph Hosp., 1991-92, recruitment and retention com., 1990-93; presenter critical care classes, 1988-90, mem. critical care edn. com., 1994; presenter computer orientation classes. Mem. Disaster Action Team ARC, Omaha, 1991, disease health svcs. com., 1992; active Omaha Symphony Guild, 1994—. Named one of Outstanding Young Women Am., 1978, 82. Mem. ANA, Nat. League for Nursing. Democrat. Home: 2730 Read St Omaha NE 68112-3122 Office: St Joseph Hosp 601 N 30th St Omaha NE 68131-2137

FRITZ, JOCK THANE, radio executive; b. Detroit, Apr. 27, 1952; s. Charles Dean and Barbara Jean (Campbell) F.; m. Patricia Anne Doyle, Sept. 12, 1975; children: Jennifer, Laura, Matthew, Nicholas. BA in Bus., We. Mich. U., 1975. Account exec. WKBD Kaiser Broadcasting, Detroit, 1976-78; sales mgr. WKBD Field Broadcasting, Detroit, 1979-82; gen. sales mgr. WKBD Cox Broadcasting, Detroit, 1983-90; v.p. sales WXYT, WMXD Fritz Broadcasting, Detroit, 1991-94, pres., gen. mgr., 1992—; pres., CEO Fritz Broadcasting, Detroit, 1994—. Mem. Mich. Assn. Broadcasters, Detroit Radio Advt. Group, Adcraft Club Detroit. Republican. Presbyterian. Office: Fritz Broadcasting 5455 Corp Dr Ste 120 Troy MI 48098

FRIZZELL, DAVID NASON, state legislator; m. Valda Frizzell. BA, Loyola U.; postgrad., Ind. Christian U. Cert. fundraising exec. Fundraising exec.; rep. dist. 93 Ind. Ho. of Reps., 1992—, mem. election and apportionment, family and children coms., mem. ways and means, urban affairs coms., chmn. commerce and econ. devel. Pres. Greater Indpls. Rep. Fin. Com.; mem. variance bd. City of Indpls.; bd. dirs. Ind. Opera Theatre, Inc., ARC, Johnson County, Ind.; past pres. Nat. Kidney Found. of Ind.; past chmn. devel. Alzheimer's Assn. Ind. Mem. Nat. Soc. Fundraising Execs. Home: 8310 Hill Gail Dr Indianapolis IN 46217-4813*

FRIZZELL, LINDA DIANE BANE, exercise physiologist; b. Council Bluffs, Iowa, May 6, 1950; d. Howard Austin and Dorothy (Eyberg) Bane; m. Richard J. Frizzell, Sept. 5, 1971; children: William, Michelle, Audra, Austin. Cert. athletic trainer, John F. Kennedy Coll., 1970; BA, Parsons Coll., 1972; postgrad., U. Iowa, 1973; MS, Bemidji State U., 1988; PhD, U. N.D., 1991. Lic. phys. edn. tchr., coach, adaptive phys. edn. tchr., Minn.; cert. auto mech., nursing asst.; trained medication aide; water safety instr.; life guard tng. instr.; cert. leisure profl.; qualified mental retardation profl.; cert. personal trainer, CPR, first aid instr. Mgr. swimming pool, dir. swimming lessons Town of Oakland (Iowa), 1971; head cross country, men and women's track and field, asst. coach women's basketball, dir. women's instramurals, phys. edn. instr. Parsons Coll., Fairfield, Iowa, 1972-73; mgr. parts and svc. head mech. Winebrenner Ford, Walker, Minn., 1974-76; tchr., coach Laporte (Minn.) Sch., 1976-81; coach Cass Lake (Minn.) Sch., 1981-85; grad. asst. coach men and women track and field Bemidji (Minn.) State U., 1987; community edn. instr., mem. adv. bd. Walker (Minn.)-Hackensack Schs., 1987-90; mgr. warranty parts and svc. Walker Electric & Hardware, 1987-90; recreation dir. Town of Walker, 1991; therapeutic recreation specialist Ah-Gwah-Ching (Minn.) SNF, 1987-91; grad. rsch. asst. Bureau Ednl. Svcs., U. N.D., Grand Forks, 1989-91; exec. dir. tng. facility developmentaly disable adults Deer River Hired Hands, 1991-92; cons. Bush Grant Study, U. N.D.; presenter at AAHPERD nat. conv. (conf. scholarship 1990, 91, 95); adj. prof. Bemidji State U., 1993—; ind. cons. excercise physiology, rehabilitative therapy, leisure edn., health edn., 1991—; tribal health planner. Leech Lake Reservation, 1993—; speaker for various nat. orgns. on adult aging, devel. and exercise, and innovations in health care and education for rural areas. Designed and copyrighted a wellness circuit for older adults; contbr. articles in field. Minn. rep. to Coun. on Aging and Adult Devel.; active mem. Nat. Minority Involvement Com.; mem. Gov.'s Task Force on Health Promotion and Phys. Fitness for Srs. Grantee Indian Health Svc.-Tribal Mgmt., 1994, State Minn. Cmty. Health Ctr., 1994, Bur. Primary Healthcare/Maternal & Child Health Sch. Based Health Clinic & Wellness Program, 1994. Mem. Am. Assn. Leisure and Recreation (mem. com. on aging), Am. Coll. Sports Medicine (profl., govt. affairs com., Minn. rep.), Nat. Assembly Sch. Based Health Ctrs. (co-chair health edn. sect., sect. rep. to exec. com.), Am. Assn. Health Edn. (govs. task force on health promotion and phys. fitness for srs.).

FROCK, JEFF L., mechanical design engineer; b. Covington, Ohio, Mar. 24, 1966. A.Mech. Engring., ITT, Dayton, 1986. Tool designer Aronca, Middletown, Ohio, 1986-87; mech. designer PMI Food Equip., Troy, Ohio, 1987-90, Miller Automation, Troy, 1990—; cons. in field. Mem. Eagles. Office: Miller Automation 1314 Barnhart Rd Troy OH 45373-9510

FROELKER, JIM, state legislator; b. Gerald, Mo., Aug. 9, 1949; m. Terry S. Hempelmann, 1974; children: Chad, Becky. Grad., United Electronic Inst., Louisville. Quality control inspector. Rep. com. mem. Boone Twp.; state rep. dist. 111 Mo. Ho. Reps., mem. agrl. bus., elec. com., local govt. com. Mem. Mo. State Sch. Bd. Assn., Cattleman's Assn., C. of C. Home: RR 2 Box 262ab Gerald MO 63037-9652 Office: 7437 Hwy H Gerald MO 63037*

FROGGE, WILLIAM FRANCIS, retired communications company executive; b. St. Louis, Apr. 24, 1915; s. William Francis and Anna Ellen (White) F.; m. Alice Ellen Rich, July 28, 1934; children: Frances Mae, Dorothy Evelyn, William Eugene, Steven Douglas. BS, U. Wash., 1953; MS, Newark Inst. Tech., 1969. Engr. AT&T, St. Louis, 1953-55; sr. engr. AT&T, Kansas City, Mo., 1955-58; mem. tech. staff Bell Tel. Labs., Merrimac Valley, Mass., 1958-60, Holmdel, N.J., 1961-64; supervising engr. AT&T, Bedminster, N.J., 1964-78, ret., 1978. Patentee, NORAD switcher, switch encoder, pvt. line and digital data testing devices. Mem. Math. Assn. Am., N.Y. Acad. Scis. Baptist. Home: 3015 Nanette Dr RR 2 Box 457 Saint Joseph MO 64506

FROHLICHSTEIN, ALAN, retinal angiographer; b. Fort Wayne, Ind., Oct. 31, 1953; s. Ben and Juliana Rose (Levey) F.; m. F. Diane Willett, Sept. 2, 1984. BFA, Ohio U., 1975; AS, Rochester (N.Y.) Inst. Tech., 1976, BS, 1977; cert. completion, Rsch. and Holographic Ctr., Chgo., 1983. Intern U. Chgo., 1976; med. photographer Luth. Gen. Hosp., Niles, Ill., 1977-80; cert. retinal angiographer Wilder & Vygantas MD, Ltd., Niles, 1980-84, C.M. Vygantas MD, Ltd., Des Plaines, Ill., 1984-89; pres. Retinal Angiography Svcs., Morton Grove, Ill., 1989—; adj. faculty Triton Coll., River Grove, Ill., 1988—; lectr. Joint Commn. on Allied Pers. in Ophthalmology; instr. Soc. of Ophthalmic Med. Assts. in Chgo. Ann. Rev. Course, 1991—. Contbg. editor: Jour. Ophthalmic Photography, 1988—; contbr. articles to profl. jours., jour. cover; inventor anaglyphic stereo projection sys. for ophthalmology. Recipient Med. Edn. award Biol. Photographic Assn., 1992. Fellow Soc. Ophthalmic Med. Assts. in Chgo.; mem. Ophthalmic Photographers Soc. (bd. dirs. 1994—, v.p. 1984-86, chmn. sci. exhibit 1988-89, ethics com. 1990—, cert. pres. Chgo. chpt. 1981—, workshop instr. 1983—), Fine Arts Rsch. and Holographic Ctr. Alumni Assn. (charter v.p. 1990—), Mensa, Am. Acad. Ophthalmology (Honor award 1993).

FROLIO, JEFFREY LYNN, photojournalist, musician; b. Omaha, July 10, 1958; s. Joseph Sebastian and Clella Grace (Giberson) F.; m. Marianne Hartman, Oct. 15, 1982; children: Nicole Jo, David Jeffrey, Carly Anne. BA, U. Nebr., Omaha, 1982. Photojournalist KSFY-TV, Sioux Falls, S.D., 1982-84, KETV-TV, Omaha, 1984—; keyboard player Bakersfield Band. Author: (melodrama plays) Egad, You Cad, 1992, Dazed in Florence, 1993, Rock Bottom, 1994. Bd. dirs. Florentine Players, Omaha, 1992. Recipient Janus award Mortgage Bankers Assn., 1986; named best actor Florentine Players, 1979, 88, 89, 90, 92, 93. Mem. Nebr. News Photographer Assn. (runner-up Nebr. News Photographer of the Year, 1992), Omaha Press Club. Office: KETV-Pulitzer Broadcasting 2665 Douglas St Omaha NE 68131

FROM, ARTHUR HARVEY LEIGH, cardiologist, educator; b. South Bend, Ind., Oct. 1, 1936; s. Irving and Sanda Ruth (Kornberg) F.; m. Suzanne Paine, May 1, 1962. AB, Ind. U., 1958, MA, 1960; MD, Ind. U., Indpls., 1961. Diplomate Am. Bd. Internal Medicine. Intern, resident in medicine U. Minn. Hosp., Mpls., 1961-64; NIH trainee in cardiovascular disease U. Minn. Hosp./C.T. Miller Hosp., St. Paul and Mpls., 1964-66; asst. prof. medicine U. Minn., Mpls., 1968-76, assoc. prof., 1976-88, prof., 1988—; cardiologist U. Minn. Health Sci. Ctr., Mpls., 1968-76, Mpls. VA Med. Ctr., 1976—. Contbr. articles to profl. publs. including Jour. Biol. Chemistry, Jour. Molecular and Cellular Cardiology, Biochemistry, Circulation Rsch. Sr. asst. surgeon, USPHS, 1966-68. Grantee NIH, 1976, 90, 91, 94, VA, 1977—. Mem. Internat. Soc. Cardiac Rsch., Am. Physiol. Soc., Am. Fedrn. Clin. Rsch., Am. Heart Assn., Soc. Gen. Physiologists, Phi Beta Kappa, Alpha Omega Alpha. Office: Mpls VA Med Ctr 1 Veterans Dr Minneapolis MN 55417-2300

FROMM, HAROLD, English language educator; b. N.Y.C., July 19, 1933; m. Gloria Glikin, Mar. 25, 1970 (dec. Nov. 1992). BA, CUNY, 1954; MA, Columbia U., 1956; PhD, U. Wis., 1962. Instr. English Oakland U., Rochester, Mich., 1960-62; asst. prof. English Wayne State U., Detroit, 1962-67, Bklyn. Coll., 1968-70; assoc. prof. English Ind. U. Northwest, Gary, 1970-80; vis. prof. English U. Ill., Chgo., 1994—; advisory bd. Assn. for Study of Lit. and Environment, 1992—. Author: Bernard Shaw and the Theater in the Nineties, 1967, Academic Capitalism and Literary Value, 1991; co-editor: The Ecocriticism Reader, 1996; mem. editl. bd. Inerdisciplinary Studies in Lit. and Environ., 1995—. Mem. MLA, Midwest Modern Lang. Assn., Am. Studies Assn. Home: 678 Shoreline Rd Barrington IL 60010

FROSETH, GLEN, state legislator; m. Donna Froseth; 4 children. Newspaper pub., state rep. dist. 6, 1993—; mem. industry, bus. and labor com., polit. subdivsns. com. N.D. Ho. Reps. Mem. N. Dak. Newspaper Assn. (past pres.), Lions, Eagles. Home: PO Box 894 Kenmare ND 58746-0894*

FROSS, LYNDELL RAY, financial consultant; b. Quincy, Ill., Sept. 21, 1955. Sales rep. Modern Bus. Sys., Quincy, 1981-84; fin. cons. Paine Webber, Quincy, 1984-85, Smith Barney Inc., Quincy, 1985—. Bd. dirs. United Way, Quincy, 1995—; fin. com., bd. dirs. Luth. ch., 1995—; fundraiser YMCA, Quincy, 1995—. Mem. Kiwanis, Jaycees. Lutheran. Home: 112 Spring Lake Est Quincy IL 62301-9694 Office: Smith Barney Inc 418 Maine St Quincy IL 62301-3930

FROST, BRIAN E., stockbroker; b. Lancaster, N.H., Mar. 4, 1950. BA, Union Coll., Schenectady, N.Y., 1972; MBA, Ind.U., 1977. Stockbroker Raffensperger Hughes & Co., Indpls., 1988-91, The Ohio Co., Indpls., 1991—. Active Children's Mus., Zoo, Indpls. Mem. Indpls. Athletic Club. Democrat. Methodist. Office: The Ohio Co 251 E Ohio St Ste 900 Indianapolis IN 46204-2133

FROST, BRIAN REGINALD THOMAS, materials scientist; b. London, Sept. 6, 1926; s. Reginald E. and Beatrice A.E. (Cope) F.; m. Pamela C. Heath, June 5, 1954; children: Carol M., Timothy J. BS, U. Birmingham, Eng., 1947, PhD, 1949; MBA, U. Chgo., 1974. Chartered engr., U.K. Scientist A.E.R.E Harwell, Eng., 1947-69; assoc. dir. materials sci. div. Argonne (Ill.) Nat. Lab., 1969-73, dir. materials sci. divsn., 1973-84, dir. tech. transfer ctr., 1985-90, sr. tech. advisor, 1990—; mem. Nat. Materials Adv. Bd., 1982-88. Author: Nuclear Fuel Elements, 1982; co-author: Nuclear Reactor Materials, 1959; editor: Nuclear Materials, 1993. Fellow Brit. Inst. Metals, Am. Nuclear Soc., Am. Soc. for Metals. Home: 1311 Marcey Ave Wheaton IL 60187-9054 Office: Argonne Nat Lab 9700 Cass Ave Argonne IL 60439-4803

FRUCHTER, ROSALIE KLAUSNER, elementary school educator; b. Bklyn., May 1, 1940; d. Marcus and Sarah (Twersky) Klausner; m. Marvin Fruchter, Aug. 15, 1970; children: Marcus, Alexander. BA, Bklyn. Coll., 1960; MA, Nat. Louis U., Evanston, Ill., 1988; postgrad., U. Chgo., 1962-65. Tchr. William H. Ray Sch./Chgo. Bd. Edn., 1961—; cons. math project U. Chgo., 1985-87; presenter in field. Contbr. to math book: One Minute Math, 1990. Bd. dirs. Jewish Community Ctr. of Hyde Park, Chgo., 1978-84, Congregation KAM Isaiah Israel, Chgo., 1984-91, 93—; co-founder Nurit chpt. Hadassah, Hyde Park, 1980; mem. Hyde Park Neighborhood Club, Chgo., 1975—; mem. adv. bd. Humana Michael Reese Hyde Park HMO. Recipient Kate Maremont award Chgo. PTA, 1980, award Chgo. Found. for Edn., 1994; Chgo. Found. for Edn. grantee, 1990, 92, 93, 94, Oppenheimer grantee, 1991. Mem. ASCD, Nat. Coun. Tchrs. Math., Nat. Coun. Tchrs. English, Acad. Econ. Edn., Ill. Sci. Tchrs. Found., Chgo. Tchrs. Union, Internat. Reading Assn., Ill. Resource Coun., Pi Lambda Theta. Democrat. Home: 5434 S Hyde Park Blvd Chicago IL 60615-5802

FRUITT, TRACY L., stockbroker; b. Muncie, Ind., Aug. 28, 1961. BS in Acctg., Ball State U., 1984. Asst. store mgr. KMart, Ind., 1984-89; stockbroker Edward D. Jones & Co., Indpls., 1989-93, Raffensperger Hughes, Muncie, 1993—. Muncie Small Bus. Coun., 1995—. Republican. Methodist.

FRY, CHARLES GEORGE, theologian, educator; b. Piqua, Ohio, Aug. 15, 1936; s. Sylvan Jack and Lena Freda (Ehle) F. BA, Capital U., 1958; MA, Ohio State U., 1961, PhD, 1965; BD, Evang. Lutheran Theol. Sem., 1962, MDiv, 1977; DMin, Winebrenner Theol. Sem., 1978. Ordained to ministry Lutheran Ch. U.S.A, 1963. Pastor St. Mark's Luth. Ch. and Martin Luther Luth. Ch., Columbus, Ohio, 1961-62, 63-66; instr. Wittenberg U., 1962-63; instr. Capital U., 1963-75, asst. prof. history and religion, 1966-69, assoc. prof., 1969-75; theologian-in-residence North Community Luth. Ch., Columbus, 1971-73; assoc. prof. hist. theology, dir. missions edn. Concordia Theol. Sem., Ft. Wayne, Ind., 1975-84; sr. minister First Congl. Ch., Detroit, 1984-85; Protestant chaplain St. Francis Coll., Fort Wayne, 1982-92; prof. philosophy and theology Luth. Coll. of Health Professions, Ft. Wayne, 1992—; interim min. Arbor Grove Congl. Ch., Jackson, Mich., 1980, First Presbyn. Ch., Huntington, Ind., 1988-89, St. Luke's Luth. Ch., Ft. Wayne, 1989-90, Mt. Pleasant Luth. Ch., 1990-91, St. Mark's Luth. Ch., 1990-91, Mt. Zion Luth. Ch., Ft. Wayne, 1991-93; interim min. Cmty. Christian Ch., New Carlisle, Ind., 1993-94, First Luth. Ch., Stryker, Ohio, 1994-95, Zion Luth. Ch., West Jefferson, Ohio, 1994-96; vis. prof. Damavand Coll., Tehran, 1973-74, bd. dirs., 1976-94; vis. prof. Ref. Bible Coll., 1975-80, Concordia Luth. Sem. at Brock U., summers 1977, 79, St. Francis Coll., 1980-82, Wheaton Coll., 1987-88; vis. scholar Al Ain U., United Arab Emirates, 1987; theologian-in-residence, tchg. theologian Queentown Luth. Ch., Singapore, 1991; adj. faculty history Ind. U./Purdue U., Ft. Wayne, 1982—, Luth. Coll. Health Profls., Ft. Wayne, 1992—, Columbus, 1992—, Winebrenner Theol. Sem., Findlay, Ohio, 1992. Author books including Age of Lutheran Orthodoxy, 1979, Lutheranism in America, 1979, Islam, 1980, 2d edit. 1982, The Way, The Truth, The Life, 1982, Great Asian Religions, 1984, Francis: A Call to Conversion, 1988, Brit. edit., 1990, The Middle East: A History, 1988, Congregationalists and Evolution: Asa Gray and Louis Agassiz, 1989, Pioneering a Theology of Evolution: Washington Gladden and Pierre Teilhard de Chardin, 1989, Avicenna's Philosophy of Education: An Introduction, 1990, Explorations in Protestant Theology, 1992, others. Bd. dirs. Luth. Liturgical Renewal, 1983-90, 94—; v.p. Internat. Luth. Fellowship, 1995—. Recipient Praestantia award Capital U., 1970, Concordia Hist. Inst. citation, 1977; Regional Coun. for Internat. Edn. rsch. grantee, 1969; Joseph J. Malone post-doctoral fellow, Egypt, 1986, Maline post-doctoral fellow, United Arab Emirates, 1987. Fellow Brit. Interplanetary Soc.; mem. Am. Hist. Assn., Am. Acad. Religion, Mid. East Inst. Gen. Soc. War of 1812 (compatriot 1994—, chaplain Ohio chpt. 1996—), Ohio Soc. (chaplain 1996—), Phi Alpha Theta. Democrat. Home: 158 W Union St Circleville OH 43113-1965 Office: Luth Coll Health Professions 3024 Fairfield Ave Fort Wayne IN 46807-1604

FRY, CRAIG R., state legislator; b. Mishawaka, Ind., Oct. 6, 1952; s. Harold L. and Sonna Kay (wilson) F.; m. Carol Sue Granning, 1973; children: Courtney Lynn, Lucas Craig. Student, Ball State U., 1970, 72, Ind. U., South Bend, Ivy Tech. Coll. Bus. agt. N.E. Indt. Coun. of Carpenters, 1988—, svc. rep.; rep. Dist. 5 Ind. Ho. of Reps., 1988—, mem. age and aging com., environ. affairs com., mem. fin. inst. com.; chmn. ins. and corps., small bus. and labor coms., ranking minority mem.; exec. dir. apprenticeship tng. Ivy Tech. State Coll. Pres. Carpenters #413, 1988; mem. Healthy Mothers/Healthy Babies; mem. Mishawaka/Penn Dem. Club.; mem. Penn Twp. Adv. Bd., 1987-88; mem. rules com. Ind. and Nat. Dem. Conv. Home: 637 Bay View Dr Mishawaka IN 46544-4157*

FRY, JONATHAN BRADFORD, software engineer; b. Owosso, Mich., Aug. 4, 1944; s. Halleck Duncan and Anne Margaret (King) F.; m. Kathleen Fern Legan, Apr. 2, 1966; children: Denise Marie Fry Sacks, David Halleck, Patrick Joseph, Melissa Sue. BS, U. Akron, 1967, MS, 1974. Programmer U. Akron, Ohio, 1971-75; software engr. SPSS, Inc., Chgo., 1975—. Capt. U.S. Army, 1968-70, Vietnam. Mem. Assn. Computing Machinery, Computer Soc. of IEEE. Democrat. Mem. Disciples of Christ. Office: SPSS Inc 444 N Michigan Ave Chicago IL 60611

FRY, PHILIP MICHAEL, business student; b. Kittery, Maine, Dec. 5, 1965; s. Philip Francis Jr. and Maureen Leona (Shea) F.; m. Jenni Lynne Bodey, June 22, 1991. AB in Math., Harvard U., 1988; postgrad., U. Chgo., 1995—. Cons. Oracle Corp., Cin., 1988-94, instr., 1994-95. Mem. Math. Assn. Am. Home: 5140 S Hyde Park Blvd #21-D Chicago IL 60615

FRY, ROY H(ENRY), librarian, educator; b. Seattle, June 16, 1931; s. Ray Edward and Fern Mildred (Harmon) F.; m. Joanne Mae Van de Guchte, Sept. 12, 1970; 1 child, Andrea Joy. BA in Asian Studies, U. Wash., 1959, BA in Anthropology, 1959; MA in Libr. Sci., Western Mich. U., 1965; MA in Polit. Sci., Northeastern Ill. U., 1977; archives cert. U. Denver, 1970; advanced studies program cert. Moody Bible Inst., 1990. Cert. tchr., Wash.; cert. pub. libr., N.Y.; cert. Med. Libr. Assn. Libr. and audio-visual coord. Zillah (Wash.) Pub. Schs., (Wash.), 1960-61; librarian Mark Morris High Sch., Longview, Wash., 1961-64; evening reference libr. Loyola U. of Chgo., 1965-67, head reference libr., 1967-73, bibliog. svcs. libr., 1973-74, head circulation libr., 1974-76, coord. pub. svcs., 1976-85, gov. documents libr., 1985-91, teaching asst. in anthropology, 1966-67, instr. libr. sci. program for disadvantaged students, 1967, 68, univ. archivist, 1976-78, bibliographer for polit. sci., 1973-91, instr. corr. study div., 1975-85; ind. libr. cons., 1991-94; ref. asst. Trinity Evang. Divinity Sch., Deerfield, Ill., 1994—. Mem. Niles Twp. Regular Republican Orgn., Skokie, Ill., 1982—, sec. 1986—; mem. Skokie Caucus Party, 1981—; vol. Deputy Registration Officer, 1986—; mem. Skokie Traffic Safety Commn., 1984—, Skokie 4th July Parade com., 1986—; election judge, Niles Twp., 1983—. With USNR, 1951-52. Mem. Nat. Librs. Assn. (founding mem., bd. dirs. 1975-76), Asian/Pacific Am. Librs. Assn. (founding mem.), Chgo. Area Theol. Librs. Assn., Pacific N.W. Libr. Assn., Chgo. Area Archivists (founding mem.), Midwest Archives Conf. (founding mem.), ALA, Assn. Coll. and Rsch. Librs., Ill. Prairie Path Assn., Royal Can. Geog. Soc., Skokie Hist. Soc. (recording sec. 1986—), Ballard Hist. Soc. (Seattle), Macon County Hist. Soc. (Decatur, Ill.), Nat. Right to Life Com., Ill. Fedn. For Right to Life, Am. Legion, VFW, Korean War Vets. Assn., Pi Sigma Alpha. Republican. Evangelical Free. Home: 10059 Frontage Rd # D Skokie IL 60077-1006 Office: Trinity Evang Divinity Sch Rolfing Meml Libr 2065 Half Day Rd Deerfield IL 60015-1241

FRYCZKOWSKI, ANDRZEJ WITOLD, ophthalmologist, educator, business executive; b. Mstyczow, Poland, Oct. 10, 1939; came to U.S. 1981; s. Jan and Anna (Kugler) F.; m. Hanna B. Bruszewska, Dec. 27, 1962; children: Krzysztof J., Piotr T. MD, U. Lodz, Poland, 1962, PhD, 197l; DSc, U. Bydgoszcz, Poland, 1995. Fellow cornea and external eye disease dept. ophthalmology U. Ghent, Belgium, 1975-76; intern U. Lodz, resident in gen. ophthalmology, 1964-66, fellow in ophthalmology, 1966-70, instr., then asst. prof. anatomy, 1958-64, asst. prof., then assoc. prof. ophthalmology, 1964-73; cons. in ophthalmology Inst. Hygiene and Epidemiology, Warsaw, Poland, 1973-76; assoc. prof. Mil. Med. Acad., Warsaw, 1976-80; rsch. fellow dept. ophthalmology U. N.C., Chapel Hill, 1981-84; chief ophthalmology Kino Hosp., Tucson, 1984-85; rsch. assoc. prof. U. Ariz., Tucson, 1984-87; vis. assoc. prof. ophthalmology Ohio State U., Columbus, 1987-88, asst. prof., 1988-91, assoc. prof., 1991—; vis. assoc. prof. U. Ghent (Belgium), 1975-76; pres. Al-Bio-Cosmetics, Inc., Tucson, 1986-88, Frysko Enterprises, Inc., 1990—, Friendly Help, Inc., 1991-94; over 200 invited lectures in field. Contbr. over 200 articles to med. jours., including Archives Ophthalmology, also chpts. to books, poems to various publs.; reviewer sci. jours.; inventor refractive sutures and vacuum corneal trephanon. V.p. Chopin Assn., Tucson, 1985-87. Recipient bronze medal Francois Assn., Ghent, 1980, lst photography award Assn. Scanning Electron Microscopy Microbeam Analysis, 1984. Fellow AAUP, Am. Acad. Ophthalmology, Assn. for Rsch. in Vision and Ophthalmology; mem. AMA, Rsch. to Prevent Blindness, Inc. Home: 895 Dennison Ave Columbus OH 43215-1321 Office: Ohio State U Dept Ophthal 456 W 10th Ave Columbus OH 43210-1240

FRYDMAN, PAUL, real estate broker and developer; b. Yedlinsk, Poland, July 20, 1906; came to U.S., 1933; s. Chaim Jacob and Masha Rachel (Rosenbaum) F.; m. Sarah Weisman, Sept. 11, 1932; children: Harold, Joseph, Gloria, Ronald. Student pub. schs., Poland. Lic. real estate broker and developer, Ohio. Owner street produce bus., Dayton, Ohio, 1934-39, wholesale and retail produce store, Dayton, 1939-48; ptnr. Dybvig & Frydman Realtors, Dayton, 1953-76, Frydman & Assocs., Realtors, Dayton, 1976—; comml. indsl. cons ., Dayton, 1953—. Active numerous civic orgns., including pres. Beth Jacob Synagogue, Dayton, 1958-59; mem. bldg. com., 1981; chmn. Holocaust Meml. Com., Dayton, 1976-80; former bd. dirs. Jewish Fedn. Greater Dayotn, hon. life mem.; gen. chmn. Bonds for Israel, 1968-69; chmn. United Jewish Appeal and Israel Emergency Fund, 1970-71; mem. U. Dayton President's Club, 1974—; active Coun. for Retarded Children Montgomery County; former mem. bldg. com. Hillel Acad. Dayton; mem. Simon Wiesenthal Rsch. Found. Recipient numerous awards, including citation Jewish Community Coun., 1965, tribute Zionist Orgn. Am., 1964, Disting. Svc. award State of Israel Bonds, 1968, David Ben Gurion award, 1973, proclamation Gov. of Ohio, 1984, Mayor, 1984; named hon. citizen Boys Town, 1961; Hillel Acad. bldg. dedicated in name Paul and Sarah Frydman, 1973. Mem. Beth Abraham Synagogue (hon. life), Bar Ilan U. Israel in Fla., Telshe Yeshiva U. Cleve., Covenant House Dayton, Weismann Inst. Israel, Hadassah Hosp. Israel, Shaare Zedek Hosp. Israel, Zionist Orgn. Am., Dayton Area Bd. Realtors, Covenant House Dayton (hon. life), Yeshivot Bnei Akiva, Israel, Red Magen David for Israel, Diskin Orphan Home of Israel, Friends of Israel Disabled War Vets., Gen. Israel Orphans Home for Girls, Home of the Sages of Israel, Keren-Or, Israel, Ner Israel Rabbinical Coll. Balt., Yeshiva U. N.Y. Office: 7271 N Main St Ste 5 Dayton OH 45415-2541

FRYER, ROBERT SAMUEL, state agency administrator, consultant; b. Vandergrift, Pa., Dec. 20, 1931; s. Samuel Henderson Jr. and Mary Florence (Goldsborough) F.; m. D. Carole Carriere, Oct. 19, 1968. BA in Philosophy and History, Roberts Wesleyan Coll., 1956; MDiv, N.Y. Theol. Sem., 1959; MFA, Columbia U., 1964; postgrad., Syracuse U., 1967-69. Ordained to ministry United Presbyn. Ch. USA, 1960. Asst. min. First Presbyn. Ch., Hackensack, N.J., 1960-62; asst. min. First Presbyn. Ch., Ridgewood, N.J., 1962-63, assoc. min., 1963-65; mgr. Abercrombie & Fitch Co., N.Y.C., 1966-67; dir. comm. Synod of N.Y. United Presbyn. Ch. USA, Syracuse, 1967-68; min. First Presbyn. Ch., Chittenango, N.Y., 1970-73; from dir. alumni rels., assoc. devel. officer to dir. pub. rels. Bloomfield (N.J.) Coll., 1973-77; from dir. pub. and instr. rels. to dir. pub. affairs N.J. Inst. Tech., Newark, 1977-83; dir. comm. Ind. Corp. Sci. and Tech., Indpls., 1984-91; from mgr. outreach and market devel. to mgr. pub. affairs Ind. Bus. Modernization and Tech. Corp., Indpls., 1991—; cons. comm. and info. U.S. AID, Washington, United Arab Rep. of Egypt, Min. of Sci. and Tech., Sci. and Tech. Cooperation project, Cairo, Internat. Devel. and Energy Assoc., Washington, 1990—; chmn. State of Ind. Quality Improvement Award task force, 1996—; team leader Pan Am. Congress of Evangelism, Caracas and Venezuela, 1956; sec.-treas. Ministerial Assn., Hackensack, 1961-62; leader Trailblazers canoe exploration, no. Que. Province, French Can., 1966; chmn. Pub. Housing Coun., Madison County, N.Y., 1970-73; founder, chmn. mng. bd. dirs. Tech. and Soc. Mag., 1981-83; founder, editor CST News, 1984-91; participant U.S. Senate hearings on FDA Reform, 1996; chmn. State Ind. quality Improvement award task force, 1996—. Founder, editor: CST News, 1984-91, BMT News, 1992; contbr. articles to profl. jours. Leader Trailblazers Canoe Exploration, No. Que. Province, Can., 1966; bd. dirs. The Frost Valley YMCA Assn., Montclair, N.J., 1965-68, United Fund, Bloomfield, 1973-77; fin. devel. cons. Englewood (N.J.) Plaza for the Performing Arts, 1965-67; mem. U.S. Bicentennial Com., Bloomfield, 1975-77; mem. exec. com. Newark Black Film Festival, 1979-83; chmn. United Way, Newark, 1980-81; mem. adv. bd. Ind. Sister Cities, Inc., Indpls., 1989—. Recipient McGraw-Hill Excellence award, 1975. Mem. Alpha Kappa Sigma. Office: Ind Bus Modern & Tech Corp One N Capital Ave Ste 925 Indianapolis IN 46204-2242

FRYMAN, DAVID TRAVIS, professional baseball player; b. Lexington, Ky., Mar. 25, 1969. With Detroit Tigers, 1987—. Recipient Silver Slugger award, 1992; mem. Sporting News All-Star Team, 1993, Am. League All-Star Team, 1992-93, 94, 96. Office: Detroit Tigers Tiger Stadium Detroit MI 48216*

FUCHS, ELAINE V., molecular biologist, educator; b. Hinsdale, Ill., May 5, 1950; d. Louis H. and Viola L. (Lueck) F.; m. David T. Hansen, Sept. 10, 1988. BS in Chemistry with honors, U. Ill., Urbana, 1972; PhD in Biochemistry, Princeton U., 1977. Postdoctoral fellow dept. biology MIT, 1977-80; asst. prof. U. Chgo., 1980-85, assoc. prof., 1985-88, prof. dept. molecular genetics and cell biology, 1989—, Amgen prof. basic scis., 1993—, investigator, Howard Hughes Med. Inst., 1988—. Assoc. editor Jour. Cell Biology, 1993—, mem. editorial bd., 1988—; contr. numerous articles to profl. jours. Recipient R.R. Benesely award Am. Assn. Anatomists, 1988, Searle Scholar award Chgo. Cmty. Trust, 1981-84, Presdl. Young Investigator award NSF, 1984-89, NIH Merit award, 1993, Wm. Montagna award Soc. Investigative Dermatology, 1995. Fellow Am. Acad. Arts and Scis.; mem. Inst. Medicine of NAS, Am. Assn. Cell Biology, Am. Assn. Biol. Chemists, Phi Beta Kappa. Office: U Chgo Howard Hughes Med Inst Dept Molecular Genetics 5841 S Maryland Ave Rm 314N Chicago IL 60637-1463

FUCHS, JOHN MICHAEL, librarian; b. Pitts., July 4, 1945; s. John Joseph and Dolores Marie (Miskinis) F.; m. Kathryn Jeanne Bosworthick, June 17, 1967; 1 child, Linda. BS in Econs., John Carroll U., 1967; MLS, U. Pitts., 1977. Mgmt. trainee Chem. Bank, N.Y.C., 1972; asst. buyer J.C. Penney Co., Inc., N.Y.C., 1973-75; libr. Pikes Peak Libr. Dist., Colorado Springs, Colo., 1977-81; interim libr. dir. Pikes Peak Community Coll., Colorado Springs, 1981-84; dir. Berkshire Athenaeum, Pittsfield, Mass., 1984-91, Carmel Clay Pub. Libr., Carmel, Ind., 1991—; bd. dirs., treas. Pittsfield Community TV, 1986-91; bd. dirs. Literacy Vols. Berkshire County, Pittsfield, 1984-91. Contbr. book revs. to libr. jours. and articles to newsletter. Mem. Pittsfield Cable Commn., 1985-91; treas. Carmel Arts Coun., 1993—. Mem. ALA, Pub. Libr. Assn., Ind. Pub. Libr. Assn. (pres. 1995—), Ind. Libr. Fedn. Roman Catholic. Home: 13735 Roswell Dr Carmel IN 46032-5129 Office: Carmel Clay Pub Libr 515 E Main St Carmel IN 46032-2258

FUDGE, MARY ANN, vocational school educator; b. Traverse City, Mich., July 21, 1947; d. Thomas C. and Mildred M. (Garey) Moran; m. Lew Fudge, June 28, 1969; children: Brian M., Cheryl M. BS, Cen. Mich. U., 1969; MA, Ea. Mich. U., 1975. Jr. high sch. tchr. math. St. Charles (Mich.) Schs., 1969-71; mid. sch. tchr. Gallatin County Schs., Bozeman, Mont., 1972-73; substitute tchr. Lincoln Consol. Schs., Ypsilanti, Mich., 1973-77; tchr. adult edn. Benton Harbor (Mich.) Area Schs., 1980-82; instr. math. Southwestern Mich. Coll., Dowagiac, 1983-84; high. sch. tchr. math. Coloma (Mich.) Pub. Schs., 1984-86; tchr. adult edn. math. Van Buren Vocat.-Tech. Ctr., Lawrence, Mich., 1982-83, math. cons., coord., 1986—. Dep. clk. Hagar Twp., Riverside, Mich., 1987-88. Mem. Nat. Coun. Tchrs. Math., Mich. Coun. Tchrs. Math. Roman Catholic. Home: 25403 63rd Ave Mattawan MI 49071-9523 Office: Van Buren Intermediate Sch Dist 701 S Paw Paw St Lawrence MI 49064-9507

FUGER, JOHN A., stockbroker; b. Detroit, Feb. 20, 1962. BA, Aquinas Coll., Grand Rapids, Mich., 1985. Stockbroker Robert Baird, Grand Rapids, 1985-91, Smith Barney Inc., Grand Rapids, 1991—; dir., sec.-treas. Fuller Labs., Detroit. Republican. Roman Catholic. Office: Smith Barney Inc 99 Monroe Ave NW Ste 200 Grand Rapids MI 49503-2639

FUGER, THEODORE HALL, JR., investment analyst; b. Detroit, July 3, 1930; s. Theodore Hall Fuger. BA, Yale U., 1953; MBA, U. Mich., 1958. Investment analyst Nat. Bank Detroit, 1958-65, OK Kent Bank, Grand Rapids, Mich., 1965-70, Robert Burnham, Grand Rapids, 1970-75, Buys, McGregor Capital, Grand Rapids, 1976-88, Robert Baird & Co. Inc., Grand Rapids, 1988—. Lt. USN, 1953-56. Mem. Univ. Club, Spring Lake Yacht Club. Republican. Roman Catholic. Office: Robert W Baird & Co Inc 333 Bridge St NW Ste 1000 Grand Rapids MI 49504-5356

FUJII, SAMUEL TOSHIMI, engineering manager; b. Lihue, Hawaii, Mar. 4, 1942; s. Toshio and Mitsue Fujii; m. Sheila Storts, Mar. 19, 1970; 1 child, Stephen P. BSME, Ohio State U., 1971. Mech. tester Batelle Meml. Inst., Columbus, Ohio, 1966-70; mgr. application engring. Denison Hydraulics, Inc., Marysville, Ohio, 1972—. With USAF, 1962-66.

FUKUI, YOSHIO, biology educator; b. Shinagawa, Tokyo, Japan, Jan. 4, 1942; came to U.S., 1985; s. Shizuo and Momoko (Utsumi) F.; m. Yumiko Osawa, Mar. 12, 1978; children: Ibuki, Maya. BA, Internat. Christian U., 1966; MS, Osaka (Japan) U., 1969, PhD, 1972. Rsch. assoc. prof. Osaka U., 1972-74, asst. prof., 1974-77; rsch. assoc. Princeton (N.J.) U., 1977-78; assoc. prof. Osaka U., 1978-85; vis. assoc. prof. Northwestern U., Chgo., 1985-89, assoc. prof. cell, molecular, structural biology (tenured), 1989—; prof. cell biology, Yamada exch. scientist Yamada Sci. Found., Osaka, 1978; Yoshida exch. visitor Yoshida Chem. Found., Tokyo, 1983. Contbr. articles to profl. jours. including Nature, Jour. Cell Biology, Internat. Rev. Cytology. Recipient Matsunaga Rsch. award Matsunaga Meml. Found., Tokyo, 1976; rsch. grantee NIH, 1988—. Mem. Cooperation of Marine Biol. Lab. (Woods Hole, Mass.), Am. Soc. for Cell Biology, Soc. Advancement of Sci., N.Y. Acad. Scis. (elected), Japan Soc. for Cell Biologist (Tokyo). Office: Northwestern Med Sch 303 E Chicago Ave Chicago IL 60611-3008

FULGENZI, BENJAMIN, computer software executive, consultant, marketing professional; b. Arkansas City, Kans., Oct. 27, 1925; s. Benjamin and Daisy June (Logan) F.; m. Betty Jean Ehman, Sept. 24, 1943 (dec. Nov. 1982); children: Sheila Ann, Benjamin III; m. Susan Anne Power, May 29, 1985. Student, Okla. A&M Coll., 1946-47, U. Miami, 1947-51. Internat. lic. coord. ACF Industries, Houston, 1961-64; mgr. export sales Comml. Filters Div. Carborundum Co., Lebanon, Ind., 1964-71; v.p., chief exec. officer Systems Mfg. Corp., Indpls., 1972-76, also bd. dirs.; v.p., chief exec. officer SMC Pneumatics, Inc., Indpls., 1977-86, also bd. dirs.; pres. B. Fulgenzi & Co., Indpls., 1972—; pres., chief exec. officer Software Job Shop, Inc. With USN, 1941-46, PTO. Mem. Data Processing Mgmt. Assn., Ind. C of C., Internat. Wang Users Group, Am. Prodn. and Inventory Control Soc., Am. Legion. Republican. Home: 8461 Westport Ln Indianapolis IN 46234-2144 Office: B Fulgenzi & Co d/b/a/Fulpower Data Sys 5726 Professional Cir 106 Indianapolis IN 46241-5023

FULGONI, GIAN MARC, market research company executive; b. Crickhowell, Brecon, England, Jan. 24, 1948; came to U.S., 1970; s. Romeo and Maria F. B.Sc. in Physics (with honors), Manchester U., 1969; M.A. in Mktg., Lancaster U., 1970. Exec. v.p. Mgmt. Sci. Assocs., Inc., Pitts., 1970-81; pres. Info. Resources, Inc., Chgo., 1981-89, CEO, 1986—, vice chmn., 1989-90, chmn., 1991-95; bd. dirs. Platinum Tech., Inc. Mem. Young Pres. Orgn. Mem. Am. Mktg. Assn. Home: 65 E Bellevue Pl Chicago IL 60611-1114 Office: Info Resources Inc 150 N Clinton St Chicago IL 60661-1402

FULLER, HARRY LAURANCE, oil company executive; b. Moline, Ill., Nov. 8, 1938; s. Marlin and Mary Helen (Ilsley) F.; m. Nancy Lawrence, Dec. 27, 1961; children: Kathleen, Laura, Randall. BSChemE, Cornell U., 1961; JD, DePaul U., 1965. Bar: Ill. 1965. With Standard Oil Co. (and affiliates), 1961—, sales mgr., 1972-74, gen. mgr. supply, 1974-77; exec. v.p. Standard Oil Co. (Amoco Oil Co. div.), Chgo., 1977-78; pres. Amoco Oil Co., Chgo., 1978-81; exec. v.p. Standard Oil Co. of Ind. (now Amoco Corp.), Chgo., 1981-83; pres. Amoco Corp., Chgo., 1983-91, chmn., pres., CEO, COO, 1991—, also dir.; bd. dirs. Chase Manhattan Corp., Chase Manhattan Bank N.A., Abbott Labs., Motorola, Inc. Bd. dirs. Chgo. Rehab. Inst.; trustee Northwestern U., Orchestral Assn. Mem. Am. Petroleum Inst. (bd. dirs.). Republican. Presbyterian. Clubs: Mid-Am, Chgo. Golf, Chicago. Office: Amoco Corp 200 E Randolph St Chicago IL 60601-6436

FULLER, JACK WILLIAM, writer, newspaper executive; b. Chgo., Oct. 12, 1946; s. Ernest Brady and Dorothy Voss (Tegge) F.; m. Alyce Sue Tuttle, June 2, 1973; children: Timothy, Katherine. B.S., Northwestern U., 1968; J.D., Yale U., 1973. Bar: Ill. 1974. Reporter Chgo. Tribune, 1973-75, Washington corr., 1977-78, editorial writer, 1978-79, dep. editorial page editor, 1979-82, editorial page editor, 1982-87, exec. editor, 1987-89, v.p. and editor, 1989-93, pres., CEO, 1993—, pub., 1994—; spl. asst. to atty. gen. U.S. Dept. Justice, Washington, 1975-77. Author: Convergence, 1982 (Cliff Dwellers award 1983), Fragments, 1984 (Friends of Am. Writers award 1985), Mass, 1985, Our Fathers' Shadows, 1987, Legends' End, 1990, News Values, 1996. Bd. dirs. McCormick Tribune Found., InternAm. Press Assn.; mem. Pulitzer Prize Bd.; trustee U. Chgo. With U.S. Army, 1969-70. Recipient Gavel award ABA, 1979, Pulitzer prize for editl. writing, 1986. Fellow Am. Acad. Arts and Scis.; mem. Am. Soc. Newspaper Editors, InterAm. Press Assn. (exec. com.). Office: Chgo Tribune Co PO Box 25340 435 N Michigan Ave Chicago IL 60611-4001

FULLER, JACQUALYN GIST, speech language clinician; b. Madison, S.D., June 16, 1942; d. John David and Sylvia Louise Gist; m. Anthony Peter Fuller, Sept. 12, 1964; children: John-Ernest Brook, Jason Peter, Justin Thad, Alecia Elizabeth. BA, U. S.D., 1965. Speech therapist Yankton (S.D.) Pub. Schs., 1965-68, Chamberlain (S.D.) Pub. Schs., 1968-71; retailer In Phoebes Closet, Lead, S.D., 1984-88; speech/lang. clinician Black Hills Spl. Svcs. Coop., Lead, 1988—. City commr. City of Lead, 1981-89, mayor, 1991-93; bd. dirs. Govs. Bd. of Econ. Devel., 1987—; bd. dirs., pres. Hist. S.D. Found., Rapid City, 1983-89, S.D. for the Arts, Deadwood, 1987-93. Mem. PEO (chpt. L), Beta Sigma Phi. Republican. Methodist. Home: 11 Glendale Dr Lead SD 57754-1525

FULLER, LEE DENNISON, nursing educator, therapist; b. Oceana County, Mich., June 7, 1910; s. Arthur Oglethorpe and Georgina Katrina (Dennison) F.; m. Kathryn A. Ochsner, Mar. 6, 1992. Diploma in nursing, McLean Hosp., 1932; BS, N.Y.U., 1949, MA, 1950; EdD, Ind. U., 1970. RN, Mass., Ind. Staff nurse N.Y. State Psychiat. Inst., N.Y.C., 1944-52; dir. in-service edn. Jacksonville (Ill.) State Hosp., 1953-55; edn. cons. Ind. Dept. Mental Health, Indpls., 1955-60; prof. nursing Ind. U., Indpls., 1955-80, prof. emeritus, 1980—; pvt. practice psychotherapy Bloomington, Ind., 1982—; cons. Reid Meml. Hosp., Richmond, Ind., 1973-74, 77, Ind. State Prison, Mich. City., Ind., 1973, Psychodrama Ind. Meth. Ch., 1979-81, Marion (Ind.) Vets. Hosp., 1977-83; adj. staff therapist South Cen. Community Mental Health Ctr., Bloomington, 1975-85. Leader Boy Scouts U.S., Belmont, Mass., 1932-36, N.Y.C., 1944-48; layreader Trinity Epsicopal Ch., N.Y.C., 1943-52, Jacksonville, 1953-54, Bloomington, 1956-65; donor Lee Dennison Fuller award in Rsch. Grad. Dept. Psychiatric-Mental Health Nursing, Ind. U.; mem. sr. coun. Ind. U.-Purdue U. at Indpls. Recipient Disting. Service award to Non-Mem. Ind. U. Nurses Alumni Assn., 1981, Disting. Svc. award Bloomington Mental Health Ctr., 1985. Mem. ANA (pres. dist. 16 1968-72, Lit. award, cert. clin. specialist in adult psychiat. nursing 1981-92), Am. Group Psychotherapy Assn., Am. Soc. Group Psychotherapy and Psychodrama, Am. Assn. Marriage and Family Therapy (clin. mem.), Tri-State Group Psychotherapy Assn. (pres. 1978-79, Presdl. award 1979), Oceana County Hist. Soc. (v.p. 1988-93, pres. 1994—), Ruby Creek Conservation Club (pres. 1988-90), Kappa Delta Pi, Phi Delta Kappa, Sigma Theta Tau. Home: 11710 Wayside Ave Louisville KY 40243-1449

FULLER, RICHARD MILTON, physics educator; b. Crawfordsville, Ind., July 23, 1933; s. Harold Q. and Charlotte Mae (Gohl) F.; m. Judith Wheaton, Aug. 28, 1955; children: Cynthia, Christopher, Janet. BA, DePauw U., 1955; MA, U. Minn., 1960; PhD, Mich. State U., 1965. From instr. to asst. prof. Alma (Mich.) Coll., 1958-68; from assoc. prof. to prof. Gustavus Adolphus Coll., St. Peter, Minn., 1968—; vis. prof. U. Mo., Rolla, 1966, 67, Hamline U., St. Paul, 1982, 85, Jilin U. Tech., Chaugchun, Peoples's Rep. China, 1988-89. Author: (text book) Physics: Including Human Applications, 1978, (lab. book), 1978; editor: Bang: The Evolving Cosmos, 1994 (nobel conf. XXVII). Recipient Edgar M. Carlson award for Teaching, 1971. Mem. AAAS, Am. Assn. Physics Tchrs., Am. Physical Soc., Fedn. Am. Scientists, Sigma Xi. Methodist. Home: 723 Upper Johnson Cir Saint Peter MN 56082-1143 Office: Gustavus Adolphus Coll Saint Peter MN 56082

FULLER, STEVEN CRAIG, dentist; b. Des Moines, Apr. 21, 1961; s. Richard Jasper and Sharon (Kay) F. BS, U. Iowa, 1983, DDS, 1990. Asst. orgn. dir. Rep. State Cen. Com., Des Moines, 1983; asst. mgr. Hal's Sportswear, Des Moines, 1983-84; sales assoc. Younkers of Iowa, Des Moines, 1984-85; dentist Fuller Assocs., Des Moines, 1991—, Park Ave., Des Moines, 1991-93; dental asst. Richard J. Fuller DDS, Des Moines, 1978-89. Bd. dirs. East High Booster Club, Des Moines, 1990, v.p., 1992-96, Grant Park Christian Ch., Des Moines, 1982—, trustee, 1991—, chmn. of elders, 1996, Greater East Side Devel., Des Moines, 1991—; dir. Iowa AAU Regional and State Basketball Tournament, co-chmn., 1995—; co-chmn. Basketball Iowa AAU. Mem. ADA, Iowa Dental Assn., Des Moines Dist. Dental Soc., Acad. Gen. Dentist, East High Alumni Assn., U. Iowa alumni Assn., Kiwanis, Shriners. Office: Fuller Assocs 2822 E 29th St Des Moines IA 50317-8720

FULLER, WILLIAM RICHARD, mathematics educator; b. Indpls., Oct. 27, 1920; s. Cyrus Holbrook and Gladys Beulah (Whelan) F.; m. Louella Myers Peterson, Apr. 23, 1943; children: William Richard Jr., Theodore Daniel, James Holbrook. BS, Butler U., 1948; MS, Purdue U., 1951, PhD, 1957. Instr. Butler U., Indpls., 1948-49; teaching asst. Purdue U., West Lafayette, Ind., 1949-51, instr., 1954-57, from asst. to full prof., 1957-59; dept. head Purdue U., West Lafayette, 1959-61, 62-63, assoc. dean, 1963-75; chanceller North Cen. Purdue U., Westville, Ind., 1978-82; emeritus prof. Purdue U., West Lafayette, 1991—; mathematician Indpls. Naval Avionics Facility, 1951-54; cons. U.S. Naval Avionics Facility, Indpls., 1958-59, RCA Svc. Co., Cape Canaveral, Fla., 1959, GE, 1961. Author: Fortran for Use in a Calculus Courses, 1977. Bd. dirs., pres. Lafayette Symphony, Inc., 1970-80, Ptnrs. of Ams., Lafayette, 1988—. 1st lt. F.A., U.S. Army, 1942-46, ETO. Decorated Bronze Star; recipient AMOCO undergrad. tchg. award, 1976, Gaucho medal State of Rio Grande do Sul, Brazil, 1990; named Sagamore of Wabash, Gov. of Ind., 1978. Mem. Rotary (pres. Lafayette chpt. 1991-92). Office: Purdue U West Lafayette IN 47907-1395

FULRATH, ANDREW WESLEY, financial planner, charitable gift planner; b. Rockford, Ill., Jan. 31, 1967; s. Lee Eldon and Susan Mae (Leonard) F.; m. Janelle Ann Edson, Aug. 19, 1989. BA with honors, Trinity Coll., Deerfield, Ill., 1989; Cert. profl. edn., Nat. Endowment for Fin. Edn., Coll. Fin. Planning, Denver, 1995; MA in Religion, Trinity Evangelical Divinity Sch., Trinity Internat. U., 1996. CFP. Assoc. dir. alumni Trinity Coll., Deerfield, 1989-90, assoc. dir. devel., 1990-91, dir. devel., 1991-93; dir. gift planning svcs. Trinity Internat. U., Deerfield, 1993—; tutor Trinity Coll., Deerfield, 1987-89, yearbook advisor, 1990-92; vol. St. matthew Luth. Home, 1995. Author, editor newsletter Options, 1994—. Recipient Am. Bible Soc. Outstanding Scholar award, 1989, Lilly Endowment Fund Raising Effectiveness scholarship, 1991. Mem. Coun. for Advancement and Support of Edn. Republican. Office: Trinity Internat U 2065 Half Day Rd Deerfield IL 60015-1238

FULTON, DARRELL NELSON, information systems specialist; b. Urbana, Ill., Nov. 11, 1946; s. Arthur Nelson and Mabel Rose (Felix) F.; m. Janet Marie Arndt, Dec. 28, 1968; children: Michael Nelson, Kevin James, Steven Lloyd. BBA, U. Iowa, 1968; MS, Air Force Inst. Tech., 1969; MA, U. Pa., 1975, PhD, 1975. CPA, Iowa. Commd. 2d lt. USAF, 1968; logistics officer Air Force Inst. Tech., Wright-Patterson AFB, Ohio, 1968-69; advanced through ranks to maj. Air Force Inst. Tech., 1978; logistics programmer U.S. Air Force Security Svc., Kelly AFB, Tex., 1969-72; assoc. prof. Air Force Inst. Tech., Wright-Patterson AFB, 1975-78, dep. dir. resource mgmt., 1978-80; computer systems mgr. C.H. Dean & Assocs., Dayton, Ohio, 1980-84, dir. info. systems, 1987-89, asst. v.p. info. systems, 1989-92, v.p., 1992—, mem. exec. com., 1995—; assoc. prof. acctg. U. Dayton, 1984-87; mem. investment com. Dean Investment Assocs., 1995—; cons. D.N. Fulton Cons., Huber Heights, Ohio, 1975-80, 84-87. Author: Defense Resource Management Systems, 1976-78; contbr. articles to The Basic-2 Report. Treas. Huber Heights Amateur Baseball Assn.; chief umpire Huber Heights Umpire Assn.; umpire Amateur Softball Assn.; commr. Huber Heights Amateur Baseball; mgr., treas. Huber Heights Little League; registered umpire Little League Baseball, Inc.; chmn., bd. trustees Aldersgate United Meth. Ch. Named Vol. of Yr. Huber Heights Little League, 1995. Mem. Nat. Assn. Sports Ofcls., Macintosh Computer Users Group, Rotary, Am. Legion. Office: CH Dean & Assocs 2480 Kettering Tower Dayton OH 45423

FULTON-CALKINS, PATSY JO, educational administrator, writer; b. Ft. Worth, Sept. 14, 1934; d. Roy and Thyra Pearl (Smith) LaFaver; m. Stanley R. Fulton (div. June 1987); 1 child, Paul Alan Foust. BBA, North Tex. State U., 1965, MEd., 1969, PhD, 1975. Tchr. Irving (Tex.) High Sch., 1965-70; instr. Mountain View Coll., Dallas, 1970-77; div. chairperson Cedar Valley Coll., Lancaster, Tex., 1977-80, v.p. instr., 1980-82; v.p. instr. El Centro Coll., Dallas, 1982-84; pres. Brookhaven Coll., Dallas, 1984-91; chancellor Oakland Community Coll., Bloomfield Hills, Mich., 1991—; bd. dirs. Town North Bank, Dallas; cons. Evergreen Coll., Washington, 1987—. Author: Exploring Human Relations, 1982, General Office Procedures for College, 1983, Procedures for the Professional Secretary, 1985, General Office Procedures and Technology for Colleges, 1994, Procedures for the Office Professional, 1995' contbr. articles to profl. jours. Mem. Tex. Jr. Coll. Tchrs. Assn., Am. Mgmt. Assn., Tex. Bus. Edn. Assn. (sec. 1974, historian 1975, treas. 1976), Metrocrest and Farmers Branch C. of C. (chmn. bd. 1984—), Bookhaven Country Club, Beta Gamma Sigma, Delta Pi Epsilon (treas. 1975). Democrat. Baptist. Office: Oakland Community Coll George Bee Adminstrn Ctr 2480 Opdyke Rd Bloomfield Hills MI 48304-2223

FULTON-MARTINEZ, KATHLEEN, insurance company official; b. Kansas City, Kans., Sept. 20, 1960; d. Clarence Davy Crockett and Shirley Frances Fulton; m. Daryl Gerard Martinez, May 14, 1994. BA in Bus., Baker U., 1994. Ins. processor Mut. Benefit Life Ins. Co., Kansas City, Mo., 1978-81; lab. technician II, U. Kans. Med. Ctr., Kansas City, 1981-87; office rep. Mid-Am. Cardiology, Kansas City, Mo., 1987-88; ins. claims rep. Blue Cross Blue Shield Kansas City, 1988-93, electronic media claims ins. field rep., 1993—; cons., Kansas City, 1992—. Com. asst. League Dem. Women Voters, Kansas City, 1982, 84, 90. Mem. NAFE, Am. Bus. Women's Assn., Phi Theta Kappa. Methodist. Office: Blue Cross Blue Shield Kansas City 2301 Main St Kansas City MO 64108-2423

FULTZ, JOHN HOWARD, elementary school educator; b. East Liverpool, Ohio, Mar. 4, 1949; s. John C. and Irene (Christy) F.; m. Sandra Liebhart, 1975. BS in Edn., Kent State U., 1971, MEd, 1976. Cert. tchr., Ohio. Laborer Union Labor Local 809, Steubenville, Ohio, 1967-71; clk. Montgomery Ward, East Liverpool, 1967-71; tchr., tutor Wellsville (Ohio) Schs., 1968-70; tchr. Kent (Ohio) City Schs., 1971—; chmn. curriculum adv. com. Kent City Schs., 1982. Editor monthly publ. for pub. speakers Phantastic Phunnies, 1978-91. Active Make-A-Wish Found., Cleve., 1989—, Rails to Trails Conservation, Washington, 1992—, Spl. Olympics Ohio, Columbus, 1991—, No. Ohio chpt. Leukemia Soc. Am., 1995—; vol. Meml. Sloan Kettering Cancer Found., N.Y.C., 1991—. Martha Holden Jennings Found. scholar, Cleve., 1972; recipient Coast to Coast marathon award Mercedes-Benz Co., 1991, Vol. award Meml. Sloan Kettering Cancer Found., 1991-93, Leukemia Soc. Am., 1995. Mem. ASCD, Fraternal Order of Police, Masons (brother), Kent State Alumni and Blue and Gold Club, U.S. Athletics Congress, Ohio Athletics Congress, N.Y.C. Road Runners Club, Erie (Pa.) Road Runners Club, Summit Athletic Club, Scotish Rite, Phi Delta Kappa, Kappa Sigma. Home: 1450 Loop Rd Kent OH 44240-4619 Office: Kent City Schs/Franklin 6662 Cleveland Canton Rd Kent OH 44240

FULWEILER, HOWARD WELLS, language professional; b. Media, Pa., Aug. 26, 1932; s. Howard Wells and Mary Louise (Boyles) F.; m. Sally Starr Nichols, Dec. 28, 1953; children—Peter, John, Mary, Ann. Grad., Kent Sch., 1950; BA, U. S.D., 1954, MA, 1957; PhD, U. N.C., 1960. Teaching fellow U. S.D., 1956-57; teaching fellow U. N.C., 1957-59, 59-60; asst. prof. U. Mo. at Columbia, 1960-64, assoc. prof., 1964-70, prof. English, 1970—, chmn. dept., 1967-71. Author: Letters from the Darkling Plain, 1972, Here a Captive Heart Busted, 1993; contbr. articles profl. jours. Served to lt. AUS, 1954-56. Mem. Modern Lang. Assn. Am., Midwest Modern Lang. Assn., AAUP. Democrat. Episcopalian. Home: 601 S Greenwood Ave Columbia MO 65203-2768

FUMAGALLI, MARK LEONARD, oil company executive; b. Joliet, Ill., Sept. 25, 1951; s. Leonard J. and Ann C. (Tusek) F.; m. Jan. 8, 1977; children: Matthew, Michael. AA, Joliet (Ill.) Jr. Coll., 1974; BA, Lewis U., Lockport, Ill., 1978. With Uno-Ven Co., Lemont, Ill. Sec., Shorewood (Ill.) Homeowners Assn., 1981-83; mem. Troy Sch. Bd., Shorewood, 1987—. Republican. Home: 303 Greenfield Rd Shorewood IL 60435 Office: Uno-Ven Co 135th and New Ave Lemont IL 60439

FUNAHASHI, AKIRA, physician, educator; b. Chingtao, China, Mar. 5, 1928; came to U.S., 1969; s. Shikanosuke and Masu (Yoshida) F.; m. Masako Kinukawa, Oct. 21, 1956; children: Yuri, Tadashi, Kenji. MD, Kyushu U., Fukuoka, Japan, 1954, PhD, 1959. Diplomate Am. Bd. Internal Medicine. Intern Kyushu U. Hosp., Fukuoka, Japan, 1954-55, resident, 1955-59; resident U. Cin. Hosps., 1964-66; chief of medicine Japan Bapt. Hosp., Kyoto, 1960-67, chief of staff, 1967-69; assoc. prof. medicine Med. Coll. Wis., Milw., 1977-83, fellow, 1969-70; chief pulmonary function lab. VA Med. Ctr., 1972-94; prof. Med. Coll. Wis., Milw., 1983-94; dir. Hakuju Med. Clinic, Arlington Hts., Ill., 1994—; cons. in field. Contbr. articles to profl. jours. Fulbright Found. scholar, 1964-66. Fellow Am. Coll. Chest Physicians (pres. Northland chpt. 1977-78), Am. Coll. Physicians. Home: 348 S Royal Ridge Dr Anaheim Hills CA 92807-4050 Office: Japan Internat Med Clinic Ste 750 1140 W La Veta Ave Orange CA 92668

FUNDINGSLAND, LYNN OMAR, county official; b. Minot, N.D., Sept. 3, 1948; s. Dale Gorman and Mable (Rasmussen) F.; m. Suzanne, June 10, 1984 (div. Oct. 1990). BA in Art, Humboldt State U., 1976; MA in Community Planning, N.D. State U., 1979. Energy coord. SEND Community Action Agy., Fargo, N.D., 1977-78; city planner Lake Agazzis Regional Coun., Fargo, N.D., 1979-80; asst. city planner City of Moorhead, Minn., 1981-82; exec. dir. Becker County HRA, Detroit Lakes, Minn., 1982—; housing cons. MMCDC, Detroit Lakes, 1992, Star Devel., Mahnomen, Minn., 1992; housing com. mem. Minn. NAHRO, 1990-92. Author: ND Wind Resources, 1979. Pres. Gallery 4, Moorhead, 1987; coord. Earth Day, Fargo, 1978; bd. dirs. Becker County Econ. Devel. Coun., Detroit Lakes, 1992. With USMC, 1966-69. Recipient Nat. Merit award Nat. Assn. Housing and Redevel. Ofcls., 1992, Publ. grant U.S. Dept. Energy, 1979, Scholarship award Fargo Archtl. Assn., 1977. Mem. Nat. Assn. Housing and Redevel. Ofcls., N.W. Minn. Housing Partnership (bd. dirs.). Office: Becker County HRA PO Box 982 803 Rooseveldt Ave Ste 303 Detroit Lakes MN 56502

FUNG, KWOK K., electronic engineer, research manager; b. Hong Kong, Hong Kong, Aug. 15, 1953; came to U.S., 1974; BS, BA, U. Mich., 1976, 77, MS, 1978. Rsch. asst. U. Mich., Ann Arbor, 1978-79; advanced rsch. mgr. Tyler Refrigeration Corp., Niles, Mich., 1979—. Inventor: two patents in comml. refrigeration. Mem. IEEE, ASHRAE, Tau Beta Pi, Eta Kappa Nu, Pi Tau Sigma. Office: Tyler Refrigeration Corp 1329 Lake St Niles MI 49120-1235

FUNK, DAVID ALBERT, law educator; b. Wooster, Ohio, Apr. 22, 1927; s. Daniel Coyle and Elizabeth Mary (Reese) F.; children—Beverly Joan, Susan Elizabeth, John Ross, Carolyn Louise; m. Sandra Nadine Henselmeier, Oct. 2, 1976. Student, U. Mo., 1945-46, Harvard Coll., 1946; B.A. in Econs., Coll. of Wooster, 1949; M.A., Ohio State U., 1968; J.D., Case Western Res. U., 1951, LL.M., 1972; LL.M., Columbia U., 1973. Bar: Ohio 1951, U.S. Dist. Ct. (no. dist.) Ohio 1962, U.S. Tax Ct. 1963, U.S. Ct. Appeals (6th cir.) 1970, U.S. Supreme Ct. 1971. Ptnr. Funk, Funk & Eberhart, Wooster, Ohio, 1951-72; assoc. prof. law Ind. U. Sch. Law, Indpls., 1973-76, prof., 1976—; vis. lectr. Coll. of Wooster, 1962-63; dir. Juridical Sci. Inst., Indpls., 1982—. Author: Oriental Jurisprudence, 1974, Group Dynamic Law, 1982; (with others) Rechtsgeschichte und Rechtssoziologie, 1985, Group Dynamic Law: Exposition and Practice, 1988; contbr. articles to profl. jours. Chmn. bd. trustees Wayne County Law Library Assn., 1956-71; mem. Permanent Jud. Commn., Synod of Ohio, United Presbyn. Ch. in the U.S., 1968. Served to seaman 1st class USNR, 1945-46. Harlan Fiske Stone fellow Columbia U., 1973; recipient Am. Jurisprudence award in Comparative Law, Case Western Res. U., 1970. Mem. Assn. Am. Law Schs. (sec. comparative law sect. 1977-79, chmn. law and religion sect. 1977-81, sec.-treas. law and society sci. sect. 1983-86), Japanese-Am. Soc. Legal Studies, Law and Society Assn., Am. Soc. for Legal History, Societe Jean Bodin, Pi Sigma Alpha. Republican. Office: Ind U Sch Law 735 W New York St Indianapolis IN 46202-5222

FUNK, HOWARD G., research and development consultant; b. Algona, Iowa, Apr. 5, 1940. B, U. Iowa, 1963. Factory mgr. Liquid Carbonic Corp., Oconto, Wis., 1970-83; chief engr. Kelvinator Comml. Products, Manitowoc, Wis., 1983-89; mgr. rsch. & devel. Manitowoc Equipment Corp., 1989—; mem. tech. bd. Lakeshore Tech. Coll., Cleveland, Wis., 1985—. Asst. scout master Boy Scouts Am., Oconto, 1979-83. Sgt. U.S. Army, 1964-70. Mem. ASME, ASHRE, Am. Soc. Quality Control.

FUNK, JAMES WILLIAM, JR., insurance agency administrator, business owner; b. Vincennes, Ind., May 31, 1947; s. James William and Elizabeth (Bauer) F.; m. Janis Burrell, Aug. 11, 1973; children: Christopher James, Kelly Elizabeth. BA, Butler U., Indpls., 1969. Cert. ins. counselor, 1991. Mem. campaign staff U.S. Senator Birch Bayh, Indpls., 1968; bus. cons. Dun & Bradstreet, Inc., Indpls., 1969-71; dir. ops. Terry Properties Inc., Springfield, Ill., 1971-72; personnel mgr. Am. Underwriters, Inc., Indpls., 1972-73, adminstrv. asst. to pres., 1973-75, asst. sec., 1975-78, v.p. pub. rels., 1978-79; adminstrv. mgr. Affiliated Agys., Inc., Indpls., 1979-93; ind. agent, v.p., sec. Ctrl. Ins. Assocs., Inc., 1993—; owner Bauer Bros. Exploration Co. Sec., treas. Cen. N. Civic Assn., Indpls., 1976, pres., 1977-78; bd. dirs. Ind. Amateur Baseball Assn., 1993—. Active Bishop Chaters High Sch. PTO, 1995—. Mem. Ind. Soc. Chgo., Ind. Ins. Agts. Ind. (mem. agy.-co. rels. com., Ins. Agt. of Yr. 1990), Profl. Ins. Agts. Ind. (v.p., 1984-85, pres. 1986-87, chmn. legis. com., treas. polit. action com., bd. dirs. 1982-83), Indpls. Children's Mus., Indpls. Zool. Soc., Preussian Benefit Soc., Heimaths Benefit Soc., Butler Univ. Pres.'s Club, K.C. Roman Catholic.. Home: 2799 Circle Ct Carmel IN 46032-9526 Office: 3520 E 96th St Ste A-2 Indianapolis IN 46240-3734

FURLONG, PATRICK DAVID, educator, researcher; b. Cleve., Sept. 27, 1948; s. Harold Joseph and Jean Ann (Blair) F. BS magna cum laude, Lake Erie Coll., Painesville, Ohio, 1975. Staff psychometrist VA Med. Ctr., North Chicago, Ill., 1975-78; psychometrist Northwestern U., Chgo., 1978-80; counselor/coord. vets. affairs Columbia Coll., Chgo., 1980-81; assoc. coord. internat. edn. Roosevelt U., Chgo., 1981-84; dir. accreditation Nat. Commn. on Correctional Health Care, Chgo., 1984-85; sch. counselor/coord. student support svcs. United Edn. and Software, Chgo., 1985-87; psychometrist Northwestern U., Chgo., 1987—; asst. adminstr. Assessment Systems, Inc., Chgo., 1993-94; ctr. dir. Sylvan Learning Systems, Inc., Chgo., 1994—. With USN, 1967-71, Vietnam. Decorated Navy Achievement medal with combat V. Mem. AACD, APA, Ill. Psychol. Assn., Psi Chi. Home: 1233 W Winnemac Ave Chicago IL 60640-2911

FURNEY, LINDA JEANNE, state legislator; b. Toledo, Sept. 11, 1947; d. Robert Ross and Jeanne Scott (Hogan) F. BS in Edn., Bowling Green State U., 1969. Tchr. Washington Local Schs., Toledo, 1969-72, Escola Americano do Rio de Janiero, 1972-74; asst. mgr. banquets Holiday Inn, Perrysburg, Ohio, 1976-77; tchr. Springfield Schs., Holland, Ohio, 1977-83; council mem. City of Toledo, 1983-86; mem. Ohio State Senate, Columbus, 1987—; minority whip. Pres. Ohio NOW, 1979-81; Dem. precinct committeewoman Toledo, 1980-90; mem. Toledo Bd. Edn., 1982-83. Congregationalist. Home: 2626 Latonia Blvd Toledo OH 43606-3620 Office: State House Senate Columbus OH 43215

FURNWEGER, KAREN, science and environmental writer, editor; b. Chgo., Aug. 16, 1951; d. Edward Irving and Beatrice Loraine (Rathz) F. BA in English, U. Ill., Chgo., 1972. Freelance writer Chgo., 1971-74; supr. publ. prodn. Commuter, Inc., Chgo., 1973-88; co-editor Compass Chgo. Audubon Soc., 1985-90; publs. coord. John G. Shedd Aquarium, Chgo., 1988—; freelance lectr., Chgo., 1988—; mem. seminar planning com. Nat. Mus. Pub., 1995; Great Lakes regional coord. Ctr. for Marine Conservation's Internat. Coastal Cleanup, 1991-93; docent Lincoln Park Zoo, Chgo., 1978-83, 85-89; tutor Chgo. Literacy Vols., 1985; active Help Endangered Animals-Ridley Turtles, Houston and Chgo., 1986—; vol. Caribbean Conservation Corp., Tortuguero, Costa Rica, 1988; judge nat. newsletter competition Nat. Audubon Soc. Recipient 3d prize newsletter competition Nat. Audubon Soc., 1989; Cert. of Distinction for brochure design, 1991, 1st prize acad. jour. Chgo. Women in Pub., 1993, 2d prize individual writing Chgo. Women in Pub., 1993; cert. of merit Printing Industries Am., 1991. Mem. Am. Zoo and Aquarium Assn., Nat. Assn. Sci. Writers, Chgo. Herpetological Soc. (bd. dirs. 1989-90), Chgo. Audubon Soc. (bd. dirs. 1985-94, Excellence in Writing award. 1989). Office: John G Shedd Aquarium 1200 S Lake Shore Dr Chicago IL 60605-2435

FURSTE, WESLEY LEONARD, II, surgeon, educator; b. Cin., Apr. 19, 1915; s. Wesley Leonard and Alma (Deckebach) F.; m. Leone James, Mar. 28, 1942; children: Nancy Dianne, Susan Deanne, Wesley Leonard III. A.B. cum laude (Julius Dexter scholar 1933-34); Harvard Club scholar 1934-35), Harvard U., 1937, M.D., 1941. Diplomate: Am. Bd. Surgery. Intern Ohio State U. Hosp., Columbus, 1941-42; fellow surgery U. Cin., 1945-46; asst. surg. resident Cin. Gen. Hosp., 1946-49; sr. asst. surg. resident Ohio State U. Hosps., 1949-50, chief surg. resident, 1950-51; limited practice medicine specializing in surgery Columbus, 1951—; instr. Ohio State U., 1951-54, clin. asst. prof. surgery, 1954-66, clin. assoc. prof., 1966-74, clin. prof. surgery, 1974-85, clin. prof. emeritus, 1985—; mem. surg. staff Mt. Carmel Med. Center, chmn. dept. surgery, 1981-85, dir. surgery program, 1981-82; mem. surg. staff Children's, Grant Med. Ctr., Univ., Riverside, Meth. Hosps., St. Anthony Med. Ctr., Park Med. Ctr. (all Columbus); surg. cons. Dayton (Ohio) VA Hosp., Columbus State Sch., Ohio State Penitentiary, Mercy Hosp., Benjamin Franklin Hosp., Columbus; regional adv. com. nat. blood program ARC, 1951-68, chmn., 1958-68; invited participant 2d Internat. Conf. on Tetanus, WHO, Bern, Switzerland, 1966, 3d, São Paulo, Brazil, 1970, 4th, Dakar, Sénégal, 1975, 5th, Ronneby Brunn, Sweden, 1978, 6th, Lyon, France, 1981, 7th, Copanello, Italy, 1984, 8th, Leningrad, USSR, 1987, 9th, Granada, Spain, 1991; invited rapporteur 4th Internat. Conf. on Tetanus, Dakar, Sénégal, 1975; mem. med. adv. com. Medic Alert Found. Internat., 1971-73, 76—, bd. dirs., 1973-76; Douglas lectr. Med. Coll. of Ohio, Toledo; founder Digestive Disease Found. Prime author: Tétanos; Tetanus: A Team Disease; contbg. author: Advances in Military Medicine, 1948, Management of the Injured Patient, Immediate Care of the Acutely Ill and Injured, 1978, Anaerobic Infections, 1989, Procs. of Internat. Confs. in Switzerland, Brazil, Sweden, Sénégal, France, Italy, USSR, Current Therapy in Emergency Medicine, Surgical Infectious Diseases (4 edits.), Currenty Emergency Therapy, Surgical Infections, Current Diagnosis (multiple edits.), Current Therapy (multiple edits.), Surgical Infections, 5 Minute Clinical Consult, 3 edits., Medical Microbiology and Infectious Diseases, editor Surgical Monthly Review; contbr. articles to profl. jours. Mem. Ohio Motor Vehicle Med. Rev. Bd., 1965-67; bd. dirs. Am. Cancer Soc. Franklin County, pres., 1964-66. Served to maj., M.C. AUS, 1942-46, CBI, 1951-53. Recipient China Liberation medal, 2 commendations for surg. service in China U.S. Army; cert. of merit Am. Cancer Soc.; award for outstanding achievement in field clostridial infection dept. surgery Ohio State U. Coll. Medicine, 1984, Outstanding Service award, 1985; award for outstanding and dedicated service Mt. Carmel Med. Ctr., 1985; award for over 25 yrs. service St. Anthony Med. Ctr., U.S.A. Nat. Softball Champion for age group, 1992, 96. Mem. AMA, AAAS, APHA, Cen. Surg. Assn., Surgical Infection Soc., Internat. Biliary Assn., Shock Soc., Soc. Am. Gastrointestinal Endoscopic Surgeons (com. on stds. of practice, resident and fellow edn., com. legis. review), Soc. Surgery of Alimentary Tract, A.C.S. (gov.-at-large, chmn. Ohio com. trauma; nat. subcom. prophylaxis against tetanus in wound mgmt., Ohio chapter Disting. Service award 1987; regional credentials com.), Am. Assn. Surgery of Trauma, Ohio Surg. Assn., Columbus Surg. Assn. (hon. mem.; pres. 1983), Am. Trauma Soc. (founding mem., dir.), Ohio Med. Assn., Acad. Medicine Columbus and Franklin County (Award of Merit for 17 yrs. service, chmn. blood transfusion com., 50 Year Svc. award), Acad. Medicine Cin., Am. Med. Writers Assn., Grad. Surg. Soc. U. Cin., Robert M. Zollinger Surg. Ohio State U. Surg. Soc., Mont Reid Grad. Surg. Soc., Am. Geriatrics Soc., N.Y. Acad. Scis., Assn. Program Dirs. in Surgery, Assn. Physicians State of Ohio, Collegium Internationale Chirurgiae Digestivae, Assn. Am. Med. Colls., Internat. Soc. Colon and Rectal Surgeons, Soc. Internat. de Chirurgie, Am. Assn. Sr. Physicians, Société Internationale sur le Tétanos, Am. Physicians Art Assn., China-Burma-India Vets., Assn. Columbus Basha (vice comdr. 1992-93, comdr. 1993-94, V-J Day coord., surgeon gen. 1994-96), Am. Legion NW Post # 443, Am. Med. Golfing Assn., Internat. Brotherhood Magicians, Soc. Am. Magicians, N.Y. Cen. System Hist. Soc., U.S. Squash Racquets Assn. (mem. ranking com.), Am. Platform Tennis Assn., Columbus Squash Racquets Assn. (bd. dirs.), Am. Legion. Presbyterian. Home and Office: 3125 Bembridge Rd Columbus OH 43221-2203

FUSSICHEN, KENNETH, computer scientist; b. Bklyn., Aug. 3, 1950; s. Lorenzo Anthony and Sue (Treppiedi) F.; m. Bobbie J. Ezra, May 18, 1974; children: Matthew, David, Vanessa, Natalie. AS in Data Processing, San Antonio Coll., 1975; BS in Bus., Ind. U., Indpls., 1980; MS in Mgmt., Ind. Wesleyan U., 1991. Programmer, analyst Computer Mgmt. Systems, Indpls., 1976-81; sr. programmer, analyst Jefferson Nat. Life, Indpls., 1981-84; project leader HAS (Healthcare Adminstrv. Systems), Inc., Indpls., 1984-87; sr. computer scientist Computer Scis. Corp., Indpls., 1987-92, Dayton, 1992—; assoc. prof. computer scis. Ind. U./Purdue U., Indpls., 1981-88; tech. advisor U.S. del. Internat. Stds. Orgn. on Ada 95 and Info. Systems, 1992-94. Info. Systems mgr. Cerebral Palsy Support Group, Indpls., 1987-89; computer cons. United Cerebral Palsy Ctrl. Ind., 1984-85; participant Ada 95 Lang. Rev., 1990-95. Mem. IEEE, Assn. Computing Machinery, Indpls. Computer Soc. (pres. 1989-90). Home: 130 Massie Dr Xenia OH 45385-3740

FYLER, CARL JOHN, dentist; b. Spearville, Kans., May 14, 1921; s. John Henry and Helen Elsie (Parthie) F.; m. Marguerite E. Burris, Feb. 14, 1946. DDS, U. Mo., 1950. Practice dentistry Topeka, Kans., 1950-92; ret., 1992. Author: Staying Alive. Served to maj. USAF, 1942-46, ETO. Decorated Purple Heart, 5 Air Medals, Distinguished Flying Cross, E.T.O medal with 3 battle stars, Prisoner of War medal. Mem. ABA (life), Kans. Dental Assn., Shawnee County Dental Assn., Internat. Fedn. Dentists, Am. Ex-Prisoners of War (nat. dir. 1974-85, nat. jr. vice comdr. 1984-85), Kans. Ex-Prisoners of War (Gov.'s adv. com. 1978-86), 303d H.B.G. Assn. (pres. 1987-89), Eighth Air Force Hist. Soc. (bd. dirs. 1989-92, heavy bomb group), Mil. Order of World Wars (pres. Topeka chpt. 1996—), Distinguished Flying Cron Soc., Am. Legion, D.A.V., V.F.W., Am. Vets. Republican. Presbyterian. Home: 300 SW Yorkshire Rd Topeka KS 66606-2260

GAAR, MARILYN AUDREY WIEGRAFFE, political science educator; b. St. Louis, Sept. 22, 1946; d. Arthur and Marjorie Estelle (Miller) W.; m. Norman E. Gaar, Apr. 12, 1986. AB, Ind. U., 1968, MA, 1970, MS, 1973. Mem. faculty Stephens Coll., Columbia, Mo., 1971-73, Johnson County C.C., Overland Park, Kans., 1973—; interviewer Fulbright Hayes Tchr. Exch. fellowship candidates, Kansas City, Mo., 1982-92; mem. state selection com. Congress Bundestag Youth Exch. Program, Kans., 1985; pres. faculty del. Kans. Assn. C.C.s, 1984-85; gov.'s appointee, admissions interviewer, mem. selection palen Sch. Medicine U. Kans., 1991-95, mem. admissions criteria and admissions process rev. com., 1992. Author: Profile of Kansas Government, 1990; contbg. editor to instr.'s manual Am. Democracy (by Thomas Patterson). Pres. LWV Johnson County, 1987-89, prodr. 1990 Candidates Forum, mem. governing bd., 1993-95; mem. Johnson County Elder Net Coalition, 1988; mem. governing bd. Johnson County Mental Health Ctr., 1981-86, chmn., 1985-86; vol., translator Russian Refugee Resettlement Program of Jewish Family and Children Svcs., Kansas City, 1979-81; alt. mem. Rep. Party State Com., Kans., 1984-86; chmn. Rep. Party City Com., Shawnee, Kans., 1982-86; bd. dirs. Substance Abuse Ctr., Johnson County, 1983-85; treas. Heart of Am., Japan Am. Soc., 1979; program chmn. Kans. Fedn. Rep. Women, 1984-87; hon. dir. Rockhurst Coll., Kansas City; bd. dirs. Huntington Farms Homes Assn., Leawood, Kans., 1993-95. Grantee Europaische Akademie, West Berlin, 1984, 92, Fulbright Hayes, The Netherlands, 1982, Japan, 1975; univ. fellow NEH, 1990. Mem. C.C. Humanities Assn., Kans. Polit. Sci. Assn., Internat. Rels. Coun., People to People, Soc. Fellows, Nelson-Atkins Mus. Arts, Mus. Contemporary Art L.A., Norton Simon Mus., Friends of Huntington Libr., Dobro Slovo Nat. Slavic Honor Soc., Phi Beta Kappa, Phi Sigma Alpha. Episcopalian. Office: Johnson County C C 12345 College Blvd Shawnee Mission KS 66210-1283

GAAR, NORMAN EDWARD, lawyer, former state senator; b. Kansas City, Mo., Sept. 29, 1929; s. William Edward and Lola Eugene (McKain) G.; student Baker U., 1947-49; A.B., U. Mich., 1955, J.D., 1956; children: Anne, James, William, John; m. Marilyn A. Wiegraffe, Apr. 12, 1986. Bar: Mo. 1957, Kans. 1962, U.S. Supreme Ct. 1969. Assoc. Stinson, Mag, Thomson, McEvers & Fizzell, Kansas City, 1956-59; ptnr. Stinson, Mag & Fizzell, Kansas City, 1959-79; mng. ptnr. Gaar & Bell, Kansas City and St. Louis, Mo., Overland Park and Wichita, Kans., 1979-87, ptnr. Burke, Williams, Sorensen & Gaar, Overland Park, Kans., L.A., Camarillo, Fresno and Costa Mesa, Calif., 1987-96; shareholder McDowell, Rice, Smith & Gaar, Kansas City, Mo., Kansas City and Overland Park, Kans., 1996—; mem. Kans. Senate, 1965-84, majority leader, 1976-80; mem. faculty N.Y. Practising Law Inst., 1969-74; adv. dir. Panel Pubs., Inc., N.Y.C. Mcpl. judge City of Westwood, Kans., 1959-63, mayor, 1963-65. Served with U.S. Navy, 1949-53. Decorated Air medal (2); named State of Kans. Disting. Citizen, 1962. Fellow Am. Coll. Bd. Counsel; mem. ABA, Am. Radio Relay League, Nat. Assn. Bond Lawyers, Calif. Assn. Bond Lawyers (charter), Flying Midshipmen Assn., Assn. Naval Aviators, Antique Airplane Assn., Exptl. Aircraft Assn., People to People. Republican. Episcopalian. Club: Woodside Racquet. Office: McDowell Rice Smith & Gaar 7101 College Blvd Ste 200 Overland Park KS 66210-1879

GABER, ELSIE JEAN KINS, university counselor; b. Iron Mountain, Mich., Oct. 31, 1952; d. Verle Willard and Ada Emily (Parr) Kins; m. Ron Gaber, Aug. 14, 1976. BA in English and Psychology, Ea. Ill. U., 1973, MS in Ednl. Counseling, 1974; specialist in ednl. adminstrn., N.E. Mo. State U., 1986; PhD in Adminstrn. and Mgmt., Walden U., 1994. Asst. hall dir. Ea. Ill. U., Charleston, 1973-74; hall dir. Ball State U., Muncie, Ind., 1974-76; career specialist Kirksville (Mo.) Coll. Osteo. Medicine, 1976-80; counselor N.E. Mo. State U., Kirksville, 1980-96; asst. v.p. for instnl. support staff svcs. Kirksville Coll. Osteopathic Medicine, 1996—. Chairperson univ. campaign United Way, 1987, chairperson county campaign United Way, 1980; pres. Univ. (Dames) League, 1982. Recipient Outstanding Women Leader award Women of Today-Kirksville, 1991, Women of Today-State of Mo., 1991, Nat. Residence Hall Hon. William O-Donnell Lee advising award, 1990. Mem. Nat. Peer Helpers Assn. (founding bd. dirs. 1988), Freshman Yr. Experience, Rotary (pres. 1990-91, chmn. 6050 Ambassadorial Scholar 1993-95, Paul Harris fellow 1990), Phi Delta Kappa (pres. 1977-78). Office: Kirksville Coll Osteo Med Kirksville MO 63501

GABLE, JOHN STARRETT, marketing professional; b. Chgo., Apr. 29, 1946; s. Clyde A. and Virginia R. (Starrett) G.; m. Elizabeth Boquin, June 8, 1976; children: Mark, Nicole. B Mech. Engring., Gen. Motors Inst., Flint, Mich., 1967; MBA, Harvard U., 1969. Mgr. design control GMIC Argentina, Buenos Aires, 1972-73; asst. to mng. dir. GM Locomotives Ltd., Sao Paulo, Brazil, 1974-76; mgr. Electro-Motive Div., GM South Africa, Port Elizabeth, 1977-78; pres. Terex do Brazil, Ltd., Belo Horizonte, Brazil, 1979-83; gen. sales mgr. export locomotives Electro-Motive Divsn. GMC, LaGrange, Ill., 1984-85, gen. dir. locomotive Bsns unit, 1985-87; gen. dir. bsns units GMC, LaGrange, 1988-89, gen. dir., engring. Electro-Motive Divsn., 1990-91; gen. dir. Bsns devel. GMC, LaGrange, Ill., 1992-94; exec. dir. EMD svcs. and bus. devel. GMC, LaGrange, 1995—; bd. dirs. Railway Supply Assn., Chgo. Mem. pastoral search com. Union Ch. Hinsdale, Ill., 1991-92; village trustee Village of Hinsdale; bd. dirs. Respite House. Baker scholar Harvard U., Boston, 1969, Sobey scholar Gen. Motors Inst., Flint, Mich., 1967. Office: GMC/Electro-Motive Div La Grange IL 60525

GABLE, KAREN ELAINE, health occupations educator; b. Des Moines, Nov. 12, 1939; d. John E. and Mabel I. (Davis) Clay; m. Robert W. Gable, Jr., Feb. 4, 1961; children: Susan Kay, Barbara Lynne, R.J. Kent. AS, Ind. U., Indpls., 1969, BS in Edn., 1976, MS in Edn., 1979, EdD, 1985. Registered dental hygienist, Ind.; cert. dental asst., Ind. Clin. instr. dental hygiene program Sch. Dentistry, Ind. U., 1977, asst. prof., coord./program dir. health occupations edn. Sch. Medicine, 1977-81, asst. prof. Sch. Edn., 1981-94, assoc. prof. health scis. edn. Sch. Allied Health & Medicine, 1994—. Contbr. articles to profl. jours. Recipient Disting. Dental Hygiene Alumna award Ind. U. Sch. Dentistry. Mem. Assn. Health Occupations Tchr. Educators (treas., pres.), Ind. Allied Health Assn. (pres.-elect, pres.), Ind. Health Occupations Assn. (pres.-elect, pres.), Ind. Dental Hygienists Assn. (sec.), Ind. Vocat. Assn. (Outstanding Svc. awards), Am. Vocat. Assn. (mem. profl. devel. com.), AVA/Health Occupations Edn. Policy Bd., Phi Delta Kappa, Kappa Delta Pi, Sigma Phi Alpha.

GABLE, ROBERT WILLIAM, JR., aerospace engineer; b. Clarinda, Iowa, Nov. 20, 1939; s. Robert William and Elsie Pearl (Stone) G.; m. Karen Elaine Clay, Feb. 4, 1961; children: Susan, Barbara, Robert. BS, Iowa State U., 1963. Engr. Boeing, Seattle, 1963; engr. GM, Indpls., 1964-71, Phoenix, 1971-73; engr., project mgr. GM, Indpls., 1973-93; systems engr. Allison Engine Co., 1993-94; tech. control officer, bus. mgr. Allison Advanced Devel. Co., 1995—. Home: 460 N County Road 450 E Danville IN 46122-8020 Office: Allison Advanced Devel Co Speed Code X12 PO Box 7162 Indianapolis IN 46206-7162

GABRICK, ROBERT WILLIAM, secondary education educator; b. Mpls., Nov. 11, 1940; s. Michael Jr. and Helen Marie (Lendt) G.; children: Brad William, Ross Michael. BS, U. Minn., 1962, postgrad., 1962, 63; MEd, Macalester Coll., 1969; postgrad., U. Wis., River Falls, 1968-69, 71, 84, U. Va., 1988, UCLA, summer 1990, U. Minn., 1991, U. Mass., 1995. Cert. social studies tchr. Tchr. River Falls, Wis., 1962-70, White Bear Lake (Minn.) Schs., White Bear Lake, Minn., 1970-84, 87—; social studies curriculum leader White Bear Lake (Minn.) Schs., 1994—; tchr. Blaine (Minn.) Sr. High Sch., 1984-87; cons. teaching Ednl. Growth, 1974—; reviewer, panelist tchr. scholar program NEH, 1989, mem. summer seminar, 1993; cons. Ednl. Testing Svc., Tex. Assessment of Acad. Skills, Austin, summer, 1990; adj. faculty history U. Minn., 1989—; reviewer, panelist innovative projects tech. U.S. Office Edn., 1993; reviewer mem. Minn. State rev. com. Nat. Stds. Civics and Govt., 1993-94; reviewer panelist NEH, Humanities Focus grant, 1995; judge Nat. History Day nat. competition, 1996. Author: Humanities Focus grant: Victorian America: The Birth of Modern American Culture, 1860-1915, 1995-96. Scholar Am. Studies Inst., COE Found., 1965, NDEA Fgn. Policy Inst., U. Wis., 1968, Inst. for Staff Devel., White Bear Lake Schs., 1972, 73, Minn. History Teaching Alliance, 1987-88, Monticello-Stratford Hall Seminar for Tchrs., summer 1988; Allen J. Ellander fellow Close-Up Program, 1973; nat. fellow for ind. study humanities Coun. for Basic Edn., 1988, Montpelier Program Nat. Trust for Hist. Preservation fellow, 1989, Ctr. for Civic Edn./UCLA fellow, 1990; grantee NEH, 1989, 90, Minn. Humanities Commn., 1990-91, Bill of Rights Summer Inst., U. Minn., 1991, Bill of Rights Edn. Collaborative, 1991-92, NEH Summer Inst., 1992, 94, 95, 96. Mem. NEA, ASCD, Assn. Tchr. Educators, Orgn. Am. Historians (presenter ann. mtg. 1995), Nat. Coun. Social Studies, Nat. Coun. History Educators, Wis. Assn. Tchr. Educators (exec. bd. 1984-90, pres. 1989-90), St. Croix Valley Assn. Tchr. Educators (pres. 1984-86, 95—), Minn. Assn. History Educators (v.p. 1994—), Minn. Edn. Assn., Phi Delta Kappa (chpt. pres. 1986-88). Home: 424 165th Ave Somerset WI 54025-7011 Office: White Bear Lake Pub Sc White Bear Lake MN 55110

GABRIEL, LARRY E., state legislator; b. Philip, S.D., Oct. 10, 1946; s. Floyd O. and Tressa (Coleman) G.; m. Charlotte Ann Burns, 1967; children: Malynda Sue, Jeffrey Allen. BS, S.D. State U., 1970. Mem. Haakon County Commn., S.D., 1974-82; mem. S.D. Ho. of Reps., 1985-92, 93—, asst. majority whip, chmn. taxation com., mem. local govt. com., mem. legis. procedure and state affairs com.; rancher Cottonwood, S.D., 1970—. Mem. S.D. Stockgrower's Assn. (dir. 1982). Home: HC 3 Cottonwood SD 57775*

GABRIELSEN, CAROL ANN, employment consulting company executive; b. Oak Park, Ill., Aug. 8, 1951; d. George Kenneth and Mary Jo (Martin) G.; foster children: Sean, Nathan Zachary. Student, Harper Jr. Coll., 1970-71. Regional mgr. Reed Roberts Assn., Ill., Wis., Pa., 1972-79; account rep. The Gibbens Co., Schiller Park, Ill., 1980-81; CEO Unemployment Consultants, Inc., Arlington Heights, 1981-94; tech. advisor Gov. Edgar Unemployment Task Force, 1990-96. Author: Manufacturer's Guide to the New Unemployment Law, 1987, rev. edit., 1992. Vol. Bush/Quayle campaign, Arlington Heights, 1988; chairwoman golf outing Spl. Leisure Svcs. Found., 1992-95; legis. com. Greater Ohare Assn., 1992-96. Mem. Assn. Unemployed Tax (v.p. 1989, pres. 1990), Ill. Mfrs. Assn., Employers Assn. Ill., Our Lady of the Wayside Alumni Assn. (pres. 1990-92), Arlington Heights C. of C. (bd. dirs. 1987-92, v.p. 1991), Arlington Heights Rotary (chair youth exch. 1987-94, chair membership com. 1994-95, GSE sect. chair, 1995). Roman Catholic. Office: Unemployment Consultants 1020 S Arlington Heights Rd Arlington Heights IL 60005-3108

GACH, MARTIN G., electronic design engineer, software engineer; b. St. Joseph, Mo., Aug. 23, 1962. BSEE, DeVry, Kansas City, Mo., 1983. Software and hardware design engr. Boeing Co., Wichita, Kans., 1983-89; electronic design engr. Allen Bradley Co., Cleve., 1989—. Office: Allan Bradley 747 Alpha Dr Cleveland OH 44143-2124

GADKE, KAREN, biomedical communications and clinical research consultant; b. Wincheringen, Rhineland, Germany, Sept. 26, 1934; came to U.S., 1961; d. Johann and Klara (Lang) Lippert; m. William Lutz, July 14, 1959 (div. 1968); 1 child, Mark; m. Richard E. Gadke, July 24, 1976; 1 adopted child, Cheryl Gadke Starnes. Diploma Interpreter/Translator, Industrie und Handelskammer, Koblenz, Germany, 1960; journalism diploma, Werner Welz Sch. Journalism, Hameln, Germany, 1961; BS, Columbia Pacific U., San Raphael, Calif., 1989, MS, 1990; PhD, Greenwich U., Hilo, Hawaii, 1991. Rsch. asst. G.D. Searle & Co., Skokie, Ill., 1966-76; pres. Willowcreek Med. Comm. Cons., Capron, Ill., 1976—; paramedic, firefighter Long Grove (Ill.) Fire Dept., 1976-79. Author: Understand Arrhythmias, Save Your Heart, 1979, Illnesses and Emergencies in Dogs--A Guide to Quick Assessment, 1986; author 1/2 hour audio tape: Feeding of the Working Dog, 1986. Mem. spkr.'s bur. Lake County Heart Assn., 1976-79; mem. nutrition/wellness com. U. Ill. Extension Svc., Boone County, Ill., 1992-94; assoc. bd. dirs. Boone County Soil and Water Conservation Dist., 1994, publicity chairperson; vol. mental health worker Janet Wattles Inst., Rockford, Ill. Mem. ASCPA, Humane Soc., Winnebago County, Internat. Wolf Ctr. Republican. Home and Office: 8132 Hunter Rd Capron IL 61012-9724

GADOLA, PAUL V., federal judge; b. 1929. AB, Mich. State U., 1951; JD, U. Mich., 1953. Diplomate Nat. Bd. Trial Advocacy; Bar: Mich. Atty. Hoffman and Rubenstein, Flint, Mich., 1955-60; pvt. practice Flint, 1960-88; judge U.S. Dist. Ct. (ea. dist.) Mich., Detroit, 1988—; mem. bd. dirs. Mackinac Ctr. for Pub. Policy Rsch.; past trustee, chmn. bd. dirs. Mott Coll. With U.S. Army, 1953-55. Fellow Am. Trial Lawyers Found. (life), Roscoe Pound Found. (life), Mich. State Bar Found.; mem. Mich. State Bar Assn., U. Mich. Alumni Assn., Mich. State U. Alumni Assn., Soc. Irish/Am. Lawyers (pres.), Hannah Soc. and Pres.'s Club of Mich. State U., Federalist Soc., Flint Coll. and Cultural Fund Committed of Sponsors, Phila. Soc., Econ. Club of Detroit. Address: US Customs Regulatory Audit 211 W Fort St Ste 1400 Detroit MI 48226-3211

GADZIOLA, JEAN ZEUN, microbiologist, database coordinator; b. Balt., Sept. 16, 1938; d. Stanley Louis Zeun and Dorothy Louise (Greer) Benbow; m. David S. Gadziola, Apr. 4, 1958; children: Elaine, Bruce. Med. technologist, Am. Coll. Clin. Pathology, Chgo., 1972; BS, Ball State U., 1972, MS, 1975. Rsch. asst. Johns Hopkins U., Balt., 1958-68; med. technologist Ball Meml. Hosp., Muncie, Ind., 1972-75, Ball Meml. Hosp./Pathologists Associated, Muncie, 1976-93; database coord. Pathologists Associated, Muncie, 1993—. Pres. Am. Heart Assn., Muncie, 1993-95. Office: Pathologists Associated 2401 University Ave Muncie IN 47303

GAERTIG, JANET L., marketing professional; b. Milw., Apr. 28, 1957. Lic. life ins. agt. V.p. M.J. Mktg. Cons., Inc., Brookfield, Wis., 1986—, Mktg. Affiliates Inc., Brookfield, 1989—; co-owner B.A.J., Inc., Milw., 1994—. Coach Milw. Kitchen Soccer Club, Brown Deer, Wis., 1988—; den leader Cub Scouts of Milw., 1990—; mem. Brown Deer Home Sch. Assn., 1983—. Mem. Life Underwriters, Wis. Health Underwriters, Nat. Liquor Beverage Assn., Wis. Restaurant Assn. Lutheran. Office: 2525 N 124th St # H Brookfield WI 53005-4676

GAERTNER, DONELL J., library director; b. St. Louis, Sept. 30, 1932; s. Elmer Henry and Norine Helen (Colomb) G.; m. Darlene Oberbeck, Mar. 17, 1956; children: Karen Elaine, Keith Alan. A.B. in Econs., Washington U., 1954; M.L.S., U. Ill., 1955. Adminstrv. asst. St. Louis County Library, 1957-64, asst. dir., 1964-68, dir., 1968—. Bd. dirs. Emmaus Homes Inc. (for adult mentally retarded). Served to 1st lt. U.S. Army, 1955-57. Mem. ALA, Mo. Library Assn., Spl. Library Assn., Phi Beta Mu, Omicron Delta Gamma. Mem. United Church of Christ. Lodges: Masons, Order Eastern Star. Office: St Louis County Libr 1640 S Lindbergh Blvd Saint Louis MO 63131-3501

GAETA-HARPER, THERESA, psychotherapist; b. Altoona, Pa., July 6, 1955; d. Joseph D. and Anna M. (Malfara) Gaeta; m. Kevin W. Harper, Oct. 16, 1982. BA in Psychology, St. Francis Coll., 1977; grad. cert., Roosevelt U., 1986, MA in Clin. Psychology, 1989. Clinically cert. substance abuse counselor. Clin. therapist Family Guidance Ctr., Chgo., 1985-86, counseling coord., 1986-87, dir., clin. therapist, 1987-89; pvt. practice psychotherapy Chgo., 1989-91; mgr. vol. dept., clin. therapist Howard Brown Health Ctr., Chgo., 1989-96; cons., psychotherapist Rush Presbyn.-St. Luke's Med. Ctr., 1995—; seminar and workshop trainer, educator Howard Brown Health Ctr., Chgo., 1989-96, nat. trainer and educator, 1991-94. Producer video Active Duty, 1992. Vol. Guild for the Blind, Chgo., 1990-94, Cris Radio, Chgo., 1987-88; bd. dirs. Lakeview Mental Health Ctr., Chgo., 1989-91. Recipient Friend for Life award Howard Brown Health Ctr., 1992, Hon. Recognition PWA Support award, 1991; finalist Internat. Health and Med. Film Festival, 1994. Mem. ACA, Am. Mental Health Counselors, Midwestern Psychol. Assn., Coalition Ill. Counselors. Democrat. Roman Catholic.

GAEUMAN, JOHN VICTOR, physician, educator; b. Newberry Springs, Calif., Mar. 7, 1932; s. William F. and Marjorie Belle (Egley) G.; m. Ruth E. Farnsworth, Dec. 17, 1955; children: William, David, Suzanne, Dawn. AB, Oberlin Coll., 1954; MD, Ohio State U., 1958, MS, 1961. Diplomate Am. Bd. Internal Medicine, Am. Bd. Preventive Medicine, also cert. in aerospace medicine. Chief spl. env. medicine N.Am. Aviation, Downey, Calif., 1965-68; fellow pulomonary medicine U. So. Calif. Lavina Hosp., Altadena, 1968-69; resident in internal medicine Huntington Meml. Hosp., Pasadena, Calif., 1969-71; pvt. practice Sterling, Colo., 1971-79; dir. Giacomini Cardio Pulmonary Lab. High Plains Rehab. Facility, Sterling, 1971-79; assoc. prof. clin. preventive medicine and internal medicine Ohio State U., Columbus, 1979-95, med. dir. employee health svcs., 1995—. Fellow Am. Coll. Preventive Medicine; mem. ACP, Aerospace Med. Assn., Ctrl. Ohio Indsl. Hygiene Assn., Am. Coll. Occupational and Environ. Medicine. Office: Employee Health Svcs Rm 2110 UHC 456 W 10th Ave Columbus OH 43210

GAGE, KENNETH DONALD, railroad electronics technician, publisher, singer; b. Aurora, Ill., May 29, 1969; s. Kenneth Eugene Gage and Christine Anne (Skeris) Sims. Cert. electronic warfare, Keesler AFB Tech. Sch., Biloxi, Miss., 1989; student, U. Md. European Divsn., Germany, 1991. Electronics technician USAF, Ramstein AFB, Germany, 1989-92; mem. electronics signal dept. Chgo. and Northwestern R.R. Travel Crew, Ill., Iowa, Wis., 1993—; pub. IZM Enterprises, Maple Pk., Ill., 1992—; recording artist C9C, Maple Pk., Ill., 1993—; cons. musical arrangements PSI-Labs. Technologies Ctr., Maple Pk., 1993—. Author: (short stories) Red, 1994; editor, pub. (mag.) Diabolical Creations, 1993—; ghostwriter, ghost editor, 1992—; contbr. art (periodical) The Nose, 1994; vocalist and musician Church of the 9 Candles, 1993—. Sgt. USAF, 1988-92. Libertarian. Office: IZM Enterprises PO Box 353 Maple Park IL 60151-0353

GAGE, LOIS WAITE, nursing educator; b. Ipswich, Mass., Mar. 8, 1922; d. Roy Appleton and Mary Agnes (Surrette) Waite McGregor; children: Nancy Marie Gage-Lindner, John Barry. Diploma, St. Elizabeth Sch. of Nursing, Brighton, Mass., 1943; BS, Simmons Coll., 1949; MA, Columbia U., 1957; PhD, U. Mich., 1972. RN, Mass., Mich. Assoc. dir. primary care community medicine U. Mich., Ann Arbor, 1973-83; assoc. prof. Psychiatry-Mental Health Nursing Wayne State U., Detroit, 1963-73; supr. of pub. health nursing Health Dept., Pitts., 1952-55; prof. emerita Nursing U. Mich., Ann Arbor, 1991; cons. WHO, Pan-Am. Health Orgn., 1980, 85, 86, 87, 88. Contbr. numerous articles and rsch. to profl. jours. Lt. j.g. USNCR, 1944-46. Recipient Sarah Goddard Power award Acad. Women's Caucus, 1996. Fellow Am. Acad. Nursing, APHA (chmn. mental health sect., Mental Health Sect. award); mem. ANA, AAUP (steering com.), Mich. Nurses Assn., Nat. League for Nursing, Sigma Theta Tau (Excellence in Nursing award), Pi Lambda Theta, Kappa Delta Pi. Home: 423 Sumark Way Ann Arbor MI 48103-6613 Office: U Mich Sch Nursing #3342 400 N Ingalls Ann Arbor MI 48109-0482

GAGLIARDI, PAT, state legislator; b. Dec. 14, 1950; married; children: Adele, Lisa, Laura, Michelle.; BA, Lake Superior State Coll., 74. Commr. Chippewa County, Mich.; rep. Mich. Dist. 107, 1983—; Dem. floor leader Mich. Ho. Reps., vice chmn. house oversight com., capitol com., legis. coun. com. Named legis. of yr. 1991 Police Officer Assn. Mich., 1992 Mich. Assn. State & Federal Program Specialists; recipient disting. govt. award Upper Peninsula Cmty. Edn. Assn., disting. alumni award Lake Superior State U. Mem. Lions, Drummond Island C. of C., Am. Diabetes Assn., Moose, Elks, Christopher Columbus Soc. Home: PO Box 191 Drummond Island MI 49726-0191*

GAGNE, PATRICIA C., insurance company executive; b. Lewiston, Maine, Sept. 6, 1959. Dir. mktg. Benefit Adminstrn. of Am., Inc., Des Moines, 1983-90; v.p. Claim Technologies, Inc., Des Moines, 1990—. Bd. dirs. Des Moines Birth Place, 1990-92; H.S. youth min. St. Pius, Des Moines, 1985—. Mem. Assn. of Health Care Internal Auditors (bd. dirs. 1994—). Office: 100 Court Ave Ste 306 Des Moines IA 50309-2200

GAIL, SANFORD R., lawyer; b. Chgo., July 24, 1943. BS, U. Ill., 1965; JD, De Paul U., 1968; LLM in Taxation, John Marshall Law Sch., 1974. Bar: Ill. 1968, D.C. 1982, Fla. 1984; U.S. Dist. Ct. (no. dist.) Ill. 1968; U.S. Ct. Appeals (7th cir.) 1972, (D.C. cir.) 1974; U.S. Supreme Ct. 1974; U.S. Tax Ct., 1971; CPA Ill. Ptnr. Bell, Boyd & Lloyd, Chgo. Mem. ABA (real property sect.), AICPA, Ill. Soc. CPA, Chgo. Bar Assn. (real property sect.), The D.C. Bar, The Fla. Bar. Office: Bell Boyd & Lloyd Ste 3200 70 W Madison St Chicago IL 60602-4205

GAILEY, JOAN DALE, business management educator; b. Beaver Falls, Pa., May 10, 1940; d. Irvin D. and Elizabeth Jane (Hollander) Anderson; m. Ronald L. Gailey, Aug. 15, 1957; 1 child, Ronald. BSBA, Geneva Coll., 1975; MBA, Youngstown State U., 1980; PhD, U. Pitts., 1987. Libr. tech. Community Coll. Beaver County, Monaca, Pa., 1969-74; customer liaison, floor supr. LTV Steel, Aliquippa, Pa., 1975-79; instr. Youngstown (Ohio) State U., 1980-83; asst. prof. bus. mgmt. Kent State U., East Liverpool, Ohio, 1984-91, assoc. prof. bus. mgmt., 1992—; cons. in bus. mgmt., 1988—; dir. Kent State East Liverpool Bus. Resource Ctr. Abstract editor: Interface, 1994, 95; contbr. articles to profl. jours. Mem. Rochester (Pa.) Area Planning Commn., 1989, Rochester Area Mktg. Com., 1990; tutor Adult Lit. Coun., Monaca, 1984-91; mem. adv. bd. Ret. Sr. Vol. Program, Lisbon, Ohio, 1990, vice chair, 1993—, facilitator Columbiana County Mini-Loan Fund, 1994—. Recipient Kent State Teaching Devel. award, 1990, Kent State Profl. Devel. award, 1992. Mem. Am. Ednl. Rsch. Assn. (editor newsletter 1993-94, program chair 1992), Midwest MLA, Ohio Bus. Tchrs. Assn., Humanities and Tech. Assn., Assn. for Bus. Communication, Alpha Mu (Outstanding Mktg. Tchr. 1983). Office: Kent State U 400 E 4th St East Liverpool OH 43920-3402

GAINES, ROBERT DARRYL, lawyer, food services executive; b. Kansas City, Mo., May 27, 1951; s. Ralph Robert and Betty June (Crawford) G.; m. Shanette Carrol Kirch, Aug. 14, 1977; 1 child, Ariel Kirch. BA, U. Ariz., 1972; MBA, Mich. State U., 1973; JD, U. Mo., Kansas City, 1983. Bar: Mo. 1983, Ariz. 1983. Pvt. practice law Kansas City, 1983—; pres. Colony Lobster Pot Co., Kansas City, 1984—, Colony Pla Co., Kansas City, 1985—. Mem. ABA, Mo. Bar Assn., Ariz. Bar Assn., Kansas City Bar Assn., Nat. Restaurant Assn., Mo. Restaurant Assn., Citizen's Assn. of Kansas City, Phi Delta Phi (treas. 1982-83). Avocations: flying, racquetball. Home: 11201 Madison Kansas City MO 64114 also: 8821 State Line Rd Kansas City MO 64114

GAINES, TYLER BELT, lawyer; b. Omaha, Oct. 21, 1924; s. Francis S. and Dorothy Tyler (Belt) G.; m. Elizabeth Bush Caldwell, Feb. 24, 1951; children: Katherine C., Elizabeth D., David T., Sarah B., Mary C.; m. Agneta Margareta Anderhagen, Nov. 27, 1977; stepchildren: Anna C., Anders C. Student Yale U., 1942-43, U. Omaha, 1946; LLB, Nebr. U., 1949. Bar: Nebr. 1949, U.S. Supreme Ct. 1964, U.S. Ct. Appeals (8th cir.) cir.) 1953, U.S. Dist. Ct. Nebr. 1949, U.S. Tax Ct. 1970. Ptnr., Gaines, Mullen, Pansing & Hogan and predecessor firms, Omaha, 1960—. Mem. Brownell Talbot Sch. Bd., 1964-75, pres., 1968-72; bd. dirs. Gilbert and Martha Hitchcock Found., 1970—, Kirkpatrick Charity Found., 1991—. Served with USNR, 1943-45. Mem. ABA, Am. Coll. Probate Counsel, Nebr. Bar Assn., Omaha Bar Assn. (pres. 1982-83). Republican. Episcopalian. Clubs: Omaha Country, Omaha. Office: Gaines Mullen Pansing & Hogan 10050 Regency Cir Omaha NE 68114-3732

GAINES, WILLIAM CHESTER, journalist; b. Indpls., Nov. 1, 1933; s. Philip Damon and Georgia Agnes (Smith) G.; m. Nellie Gilyan; children: Michael, Michelle, Matthew. BS in Broadcasting, Butler U., 1956. Announcer Sta. WCTW Radio, New Castle, Ind., 1952-54, Sta. WINN Radio, Louisville, 1954-56; TV announcer Sta. WKZO-TV, Kalamazoo, 1958-59; reporter Sta. WWCA Radio, Gary, Ind., 1959-60, Sta. WJOB Radio, Hammond, Ind., 1960-63; pres. Sta. WAMJ Radio, South Bend, Ind., 1983—; from reporter to investigative reporter Chgo. Tribune, 1963—; instr. Columbia Coll., Chgo., 1974-88. Recipient Pulitzer prize in Journalism, Columbia U., N.Y.C., 1976, 1988, Peter Lisagor award Chgo. Headline Club, 1986, 87. Office: Chgo Tribune 435 N Michigan Ave Chicago IL 60611-4001

GAIPA, NANCY CHRISTINE, pharmacist; b. Benton Harbor, Mich., Oct. 11, 1949; d. Frank Thomas and Anne Marie (Scardina) G. BS, Marygrove Coll., Detroit, 1971; BS in Pharmacy, Wayne State U., 1992; postgrad. in Cons. Pharmacy, Ferris State U., 1996. Registered pharmacist, Mich.; cert. secondary educator, Mich. Educator Regina High Sch., Harper Woods, Mich., 1971-88; staff pharmacist Perry Drugs, Northville, Mich., 1993, Meijers, Inc., Westland, Mich., 1993—. Vol. Detroit Welfare Reform Coalition, 1989-91, Maral, Southfield, Mich., 1991. State of Mich. scholar, 1967-71. Mem. NOW, Detroit Area Women's Network, Am. Pharm. Assn., Mich. Pharmacists Assn., Golden Key Nat. Honor Soc., Iota Gamma Alpha, Rho Chi. Office: Meijers Inc Westland MI

GALA, RICHARD ROBERT, physiology educator; b. Bayonne, N.J., July 2, 1935; s. Stephen Francis and Jennie (Matusweicz) G.; m. Anita Louis Diliddo, June 19, 1960 (div. Mar. 1976); children: Leslie Beth, Richard Robert; m. Callie Hoxie, June 3, 1995. BS, Rutgers U., 1957; student, U. Maine, 1957-58; PhD, Rutgers U., 1963. Rsch. asst. Rutgers U., New Brunswick, N.J., 1958-60, grad. assc., 1960-63; rsch. assoc. U. Louisville (Ky.), 1963-65; asst. prof. physiology Boston U., 1965-69, assoc. prof., 1969-70; assoc. prof. Wayne State U., Detroit, 1971-76, prof., 1976—; vis. scientist Nat. Inst. Rsch. in Dairying, Shinfield, Eng., 1978-79, Nat. Inst. Allergy and Infectious Diseases, NIH, Bethesda, Md., 1991-92, Nat. Inst. Allergy and Infectious Diseases, NIH, Bethesda, Md., 1995-96; cons. Rorer Group, Inc., Fort Washington, Pa., 1987-89, Delagrange Pharm., Paris, 1989. Mem. editorial bd. Procs. of the Soc. for Exptl. Biology and Medicine, 1977-88, Neuroendocrinology, 1988-91; contbr. more than 140 articles to publs. Recipient Disting. Fgn. Scholar award Taiwan nat. Sci. Coun., Tiapai, 1988, Vis. Fgn. Scholar award Meiji U., Kawasaki, Japan, 1988. Mem. AAAS, Am. Physiol. Soc., Soc. Experimental Biology and Medicine, Soc. Study of Reprodn., Endocrine Soc., British Endocrine, Soc. for Neurosci., Sigma Xi. Home: 2909 Bamlet Rd Royal Oak MI 48073-2978 Office: Wayne State U Sch Medicine Dept Physiol 540 E Canfield St Detroit MI 48201-1928

GALBRAITH, RUTH ELLEN, family nurse, patient care coordinator; b. Winner, S.D., Nov. 25, 1959; d. Richard J. and Maxie K. (Novotny) Nelson; m. Gary Lee, June 20, 1987; children: Kelsey Rae, Grant Michael, Calli Nicole. BA in Psychology, U. S.D., 1982, ADN, 1984; BSN, Regnets Coll., 1989; MSN, S.D. State U., 1993. Cert. nurse practitioner. Nurse practitioner Winner Regional Healthcare Ctr., 1984—; also edn. coord., asst. dir. nursing Winner (S.D.) Regional Healthcare Ctr.; clin. instr. U. S.D., Vermillion, 1991—. Named Outstanding Young Woman of Am., 1991. Mem. Am. Heart Assn., S.D. Nurses Assn. (steering com. for S.D. pain initiative), S.D. Nurses Assn., Sigma Theta Tau. Republican. Home: HC 57 Box 22 Ideal SD 57541-9200 Office: Winner Regional Healthcare Ctr 745 E 8th St Winner SD 57580-2677

GALE, PAMELA LYNN BECKMAN, organization executive; b. Columbus, Ohio, Nov. 4, 1945; d. Fred N. Beckman and Alice Aileen (Cardwell) Beckman-Davis; m. Marshall Paul Gale, June 6, 1971; children: Dawn Michele, Derek Matthew. Student, U. Fla., 1962-64; BA in Pers. Adminstrn., U. Kans., 1989. Flight attendant TWA, Chgo. and N.Y.C., 1965-67; tng. specialist TWA, Kansas City, Mo., 1967-75; exec. dir. Downtown Overland Park, Inc., Kans., 1990-94; exec. dir. Heart of Am. chpt. Cystic Fibrosis Found., Overland Park, 1994—. Religious educator Temple B'nai Jehudah, Kansas City, 1980-92, Congregation Beth Toran, 1994-96, co-chmn. entertainment Welcome Home Troops parade City of Overland Park, 1991. Recipient creative teaching award Cen. Agy. for Jewish Edn., Kansas City, 1988. Mem. Hadassah (past pres.), Nat. Coun. Jewish Women, Beth Shalom Sisterhood, B'nai B'rith Women, Golden Key. Democrat. Office: Cystic Fibrosis Foundation 5750 W 95th St #214 Overland Park KS 66207

GALEHOUSE, DANIEL CHRISTIAN, physicist, researcher; b. Doylestown, Ohio, Aug. 12, 1949; s. Howard James and Shirley Rita (Pernettas) G.; m. Donna Christina Moon, June 24, 1971; children: Benjamin, James, Peter. SB, MIT, 1970; PhD, U. Calif., Berkeley, 1978. Sr. engr. Polaroid Corp., Waltham, Mass., 1978-80; design physicist Gen. Electric, Twinsburg, Ohio, 1980-81; asst. prof. U. Akron, Ohio, 1982-84, 87-88, 1996—; ind. cons., researcher, 1984-86, 88—; instr. Kent (Ohio) State Univ., 1986. Contbr. articles to Internat. Jour. Theoretical Physics, Astrophys. Jour. NSF fellow, 1970-73. Mem. Lions (pres. 1988-89). Republican. Methodist. Home: 15764 Galehouse Rd Doylestown OH 44230-9309

GALEWSKI, MICHAEL H., mechanical designer; b. Winona, Minn., Jan. 28, 1949. Student, Winona State U., 1968. Parts mgr., mech. designer Abrasive Engring. and Mfg., Olathe, Kans., 1973—. With USN, 1964-73, Vietnam. Republican. Office: Abrasive Engring & Mfg 540 E Highway 56 Olathe KS 66061-4640

GALINSKY, DENNIS LEE, radiation oncologist, educator; b. Des Moines, Sept. 16, 1948; s. Sam and Joyce Geraldine (Givant) G.; m. Daryl Lee Goldstein, Nov. 9, 1975; children: Dana Lauren, David Lawrence. BS, Drake U., 1970; MD, U. Iowa, 1974. Diplomate Am. Bd. Radiology. Intern U. Ariz., Tucson, 1974-75, resident in radiation oncology, 1975-77; resident in radiation oncology U. Minn., Mpls., 1977-78; assoc. attending physician Evanston (Ill.) Hosp., 1978-80; dir. radiation oncology Copley Meml. Hosp., Aurora, Ill., 1980-89, U. Ill. Hosp., Chgo., 1991-93, DuPage Oncology Ctr., Winfield, Ill., 1993; assoc. prof. Rush U., Chgo., 1994—, 1994—; pvt. practice, Chgo., 1978; clin. assoc. Northwestern U., Evanston, 1978-80; co-dir. rev. course Osler Inst., Lisle, Ill., 1991; presenter Internat. Congress Radiology, 1989, European Soc. Radiation Oncology, 1990. Contbr. articles to med. jours. Bd. dirs. Congregation Beth Shalom, Naperville, Ill., 1984-85; mem. Dist. 27 Sch. Bd., Northbrook, Ill., 1990—. Graneee NSF, 1968. Mem. AMA, Am. Coll. Radiation Oncology (vice chmn. 1991-92), Chgo. Met. Area Radiation oncology Soc. (pres. 1987-88), Beta Beta Beta.. Office: Nuclear Oncology SC 6929 W Ogden Ave Berwyn IL 60402

GALITZ, LAURA MARIA, secondary education educator; b. Chgo., Apr. 16, 1951; d. John Anthony and Barbara Jean (Bunche) Lauzon; m. Richard Allen Galitz, June 17, 1973; children: Melissa Jean, Kimberly Anne. BS in Biology, DePaul U., 1973. Cert. tchr., Ill. Tchr. St. Viator H.S., Arlington Heights, Ill., 1973-76; sales rep. E.R. Squibb & Sons, Princeton, N.J., 1976-77; fin. analyst Motorola, Inc., Schaumburg, Ill., 1978-81; substitute tchr. Palatine, 1990; substance abuse prevention coord. Lake Zurich (Ill.) Schs., 1991-94; tchr. earth sci. and chemistry Grant Cmty. H.S., Fox Lake, Ill., 1994—. Bd. dirs. Lake Zurich Mid. Sch.-North PTO, 1991—, sec., 1994-95, pres., 1995—; music parent coord. Seth Paine Sch. PTO, 1993-94, vol. coord., 1992-93; vol. coord. Thomas Jefferson Sch. PTA, 1985-90; vol. tchr. Palatine and Lake Zurich Schs., 1989—; project co-dir. Ela Area Cmty. Partnership, Lake Zurich, 1991; referendum co-chmn. Citizens for New Schs., 1990-91, head spkrs. com., 1991; dep. registrar Lake County, Ill. Co-recipient Partnership award Lake County Fighting Back Project, 1991. Office: Grant Cmty HS 285 E Grand Ave Fox Lake IL 60020-1634

GALL, BETTY BLUEBAUM, office services executive; b. Williamson, W.Va., June 11, 1944; d. Thomas Jefferson Bluebaum and Ollie Mae (Moore) Bluebaum Walker; Charles B. Walker (stepfather); 1 child, Thomas Ethan. Ptnr., dir. Chicagoland Register, dating service, Chgo., 1974-84; cooking instr. Elizabeth Benson Internat. Cooking Lessons, 1978-84; owner Ethnic Party People Catering, 1981-92, Phone-A-Friend Dating Service, Chgo., 1984-90, Betty Gall Office Svcs., Chgo., 1991—. Mem. comm. dept. Little City Found., 1989-91. Home: 6314 N Troy St Chicago IL 60659-1414

GALL, HELEN LOUISE, elementary education educator, retired; b. Port Huron, Mich., Jan. 27, 1930; d. James Stanley and Marguerite Elizabeth (Fuerst) Burns; m. George Thomas Gall, Jly 19, 1952; children: Peggy Eileen, Kirk Patrick. AA, Community Coll. Port Huron, 1949; BA, Western Mich. U., 1951; MA, Eastern Mich. U., 1978; cert. in reading, Mich. State U. Cert. elem. tchr., Mich. Tchr., rep. sch. Port Huron Area Sch. Dist., 1953-58; tchr. Port Huron, Mich., 1961-93; ret., 1993; mem. Port Huron Edn. Assn. negotiating team for tchr. contracts, 1971, 88. Vol. fundraiser Port Huron Hosp., participant Health O'Rama and Festival of Trees Christmas project; vol. fundraiser Mercy Hosp., 1986—; troop leader Girl Scouts U.S., Kalamazoo, 1950-51, Port Huron, 1959-62; chmn. scholarship com. League Cath. women, 1995-96, advisor to scholarship com., workshop participant, bd. dirs., 1994-96; tchr. catechism chs. Port Huron, 1963-72; mem. parish coun. St. Stephen's Cath. Ch., 1973-81, chair fin. bd. ecumenical ministers, 1980-96, sponsor, instr. adult edn., 1986-91; charter mem. St. Christopher Cath. Ch., Marysville, Mich.; mem. caucus Dave Bonior Commn.; precinct del. Dem. Com., 1987—, liaison, 1992-93; active appeal dr. Cath. Svcs. Archdiocese of Detroit, 1988-96; mem. Port Huron Area Sch. Millage Com., 1988-93, St. Clar Coun. Sr. Citizens; cand. County Commr. St. Clair County, 1994; mem. Am. Assn. Ret. Persons/Port Huron Coun. on Aging, 1994—; vol. steering com. Comprehensive Cmty. Health Models, St. clair County; vol. Sr. Ctr.; vol. chairperson 50th H.S. Class Reunion, 1997. Mem. AAUW, Md. Assn. Ret. Sch. Pers. (life, scholarship com. 1994-95), Port Huron Edn. Assn. (exec. bd. 1980-93, treas., pres. vice chair Coun. on Polit. Affairs, rep. on millage proposals-legis. on Ptrns. in Edn Reform at state level in Lansing, rep. nat. NEA convs.), Cath. Social Svcs. Assn. (life), League of Cath. Women St. Clair County (chmn. Christmas project 1995), Black River Boat Club (exec. bd., treas. 1974-88), Am. Legion Women's Aux. Home: 3212 Waldheim Dr Port Huron MI 48060-2320 Office: 2588 Michigan Rd Port Huron MI 48060-2446

GALL, PATIENCE BETH, elementary education educator; b. Battle Creek, Mich., July 9, 1936; d. Richard Bernhart and Martha Helen (Luedders) Hervig; m. Bruce John Gall, Mar. 18, 1967; children: Bethann, John. BA in Edn., U. Mich., 1958. Cert. tchr., Minn. Tchr. Mpls. Pub. Schs., 1958-70, 79—. Dir. Christian edn. Osseo (Minn.) United Meth. Ch., 1979-84; dir. Osseo Sch. Bd., Maple Grove, Minn., 1979—, chair, 1983-84, 89-90, 95-96; crew dir. U.S. Dept. Census, Mpls., 1979, with census crew, 1980; chairperson com. to elect state sen., Minn., 1972—; leader Girl Scouts U.S.A., Maple Grove, 1979-88; sch. bd. liaison PTA, Maple Grove, 1975-78. Recipient Leadership award Greater Mpls. coun. Girl Scouts U.S.A., 1987, Sch. Bd. Mem. of Yr. award Minn. Sch. Bds. Assn., 1993. Mem. Phi Kappa Phi, Delta Kappa Gamma. Home: 8123 Maple Ln N Maple Grove MN 55311-2203

GALLAGHER, DAVID ALDEN, research engineer; b. Chgo., Apr. 20, 1949; s. Carson Alden and Carolyn (Treutler) Moss; m. Eileen Mary Reminiec Gallagher, July 29, 1972; children: Drew Brook, Melissa Mary. BS in Physics, U. Ill., Chgo., 1971; MS in Physics, Urbana, 1973, PhD in Physics, 1978. Engr. specialist sr. Northrop Grumman, Rolling Meadows, Ill., 1977—. Contbr. chpt. to book, articles to profl. jours. Trombone player in ch. orch. Arlington Heights (Ill.) Evang. Free Ch., 1989—. Mem. Am. Phys. Soc. Home: 715 E Charles Arlington Heights IL 60004 Office: Northrop Grumman ESID-EIWS 600 Hicks Rd Rolling Meadows IL 60008

GALLAGHER, JOHN ROBERT, JR., county official; b. Berwyn, Ill., May 6, 1941; s. John Robert and Marion Catherine (Banker) G. AB in Govt., Georgetown U., 1963; MA in Pub. Adminstrn., Govs. State U., University Park, Ill., 1977; grad., Armed Forces Staff Coll., 1974; grad. Econ. Devel. Inst., U. Okla., 1985. Adminstrv. asst. City of Joliet, Ill., 1977-78, asst. personnel dir., 1978-79, dep. city mgr., 1979-82; devel. dir. County of Will, Joliet, 1982-86, personnel dir., 1986-92, dep. county adminstr., 1989-92; county adminstr. County of Whiteside, Morrison, Ill., 1992—; instr. polit. and mil. sci. U. Conn., West Hartford, 1970-72; cons. Joliet, 1977-92, Sterling, Ill., 1992—. Mem. citizens adv. bd. No. Ill. RTA Met. Rail, Chgo., 1987-92. With USNG, 1959-61, 84-91, USAR, 1961-63, 75-84, U.S. Army, 1963-75; brig. gen. N.G. ret. Mem. Am. Soc. for Pub. Adminstrn., Internat. City Mgmt. Assn., Ill. City Mgmt. Assn., Will County Mgrs. and Adminstrs. Assn., Assn. U.S. Army, Soc. 1st Inf. Div., 2d U.S. Inf. Regt. Assn., Am. Legion, VFW, Georgetown U. Alumni Assn., Governors State U.

Alumni Assn., U. Okla. Alumni Assn. Roman Catholic. Office: County of Whiteside 200 E Knox St Morrison IL 61270-2809

GALLAGHER, KENT GREY, theater arts educator, real estate developer; b. Oak Park, Ill., Nov. 9, 1933; s. Charles Joseph and Lucile Catherine Bianca (Nussle) G.; m. Sandra Rae Hamblin, Aug. 31, 1957 (div. 1975); children: Geoffrey Kent, Douglas Grey, Bradford Dean; m. Sonja Eileen Newland, Jan. 30, 1976; children: Justin Blake, Andrew Anthony. B.A., Carleton Coll., Northfield, Minn., 1957; M.A., Ind. U., 1960, Ph.D., 1962. Prof., dir. theatre Ball State U., Muncie, Ind., 1962-66; dir. theatre Wash. State U., Pullman, 1966-76, grants adminstr., 1973-75; chmn. theatre arts Tex. Christian U., Ft. Worth, 1976-80; prof. No. Ill. U., DeKalb, 1980—, chmn. theatre arts, 1980-84, asst. to dean, grants and devel. adminstr., 1984-88; evaluator NEH, Washington, 1976-82; cons. N. Fort Worth Devel. Corp., 1977-80, Arts V, DeKalb, 1984-86, Preserve the Egyptian Theatre Found., DeKalb, 1982-84; realtor, Geneva, Ill., 1987-88, 96—, Wayne, Ill., 1988-95; prin. Fountains of Glendale Heights Ltd., Wayne Adv. Corp., Wayne Partnership Ltd. Producer Walla-Walla Outdoor Drama, 1969-71, Granbury Opera House, Tex., 1977-80, Ft. Worth Shakespeare in Park, 1978-80; founder, producer Ill. Stage Co., Woodstock, DeKalb, 1984. Author: Foreigner in American Drama, 1966; (film) The Bariloche Connection, 1979. Dir. numerous TV, film and stage prodns. Contbr. articles to profl. publs. Pres. ACLU, Pullman, 1968-70, bd. dirs., 1969-71. Prodn. cons. Ft. Worth Council Chs., 1976-80. Served with U.S. Army, 1953-55. Edwards fellow, 1961-62; Woodrow Wilson fellow, 1967; London prof. Northwest Interinstnl. Council, 1972; recipient Kennedy Ctr. Medallion, 1980. Mem. Am. Theatre Assn. (bd. dirs. 1968-76), Am. Coll. Theatre Festival (bd. dirs. 1972-76), Tex. Coll. Theatre Festival (bd. dirs. 1978-80), Northwest Drama Conf. (pres. 1973-74), Ill. Theatre Assn., Nat. Assn. Realtors, Ill. Assn. Realtors, Alpha Psi Omega. Avocations: sailing, skiing. Home: 1128 Brentwood Pl Geneva IL 60134-1628 Office: No Ill U Dept Theater Arts De Kalb IL 60115 also: Wayne Partnership 32W 273 Army Trail Rd Wayne IL 60184

GALLAGHER, PAULA MARIE, real estate appraiser; b. Omaha, Nov. 10, 1959; d. Kenneth Leroy and Phyllis Virginia (Stopak) G. Diploma, Nebr. Coll. Bus., 1978-79; student, Met. Tech. Community Coll., Omaha, 1979-81, U. Nebr., Omaha, 1981-85, 91, Coll. St. Mary, Omaha, 1986-90; BS, Bellevue U., 1993. Lic. real estate appraiser and broker, Nebr. Legal sec. McCormick Cooney Mooney & Hillman P.C., Omaha, 1979; word processor Firstier Bank, Omaha, 1979-83, staff asst., 1983-84; appraiser trainee Morrissey Appraisal Svcs., Omaha, 1985-88, real estate appraiser, 1988—; residential mem. Am. Inst. Real Estate Appraisers. Mem. Appraisal Inst. (sr. residential appraiser), Am. Bus. Women's Assn. (rec. sec. 1984-85, treas. 1988-89, Women of Yr. award 1989), Omaha Women's C. of C. (pres.-elect 1996—, mem. edn. com. 1990-92, mem. fin. com. 1991, dir. cmty. recognition 1992, dir. edn. 1993, chmn. fin. style show 1995). Roman Catholic. Home: 10321 N 186th Ave Bennington NE 68007-6165 Office: Morrissey Appraisal Svcs 11314 Davenport St Omaha NE 68154-2630

GALLAMORE, BETTY LOU, nurse; b. Poplar Bluff, Mo., Nov. 23, 1951; d. Virgil Luther and Alta Elaine (Dickerson) Groves; m. James Dewey Gallamore, June 27, 1970 (div. 1979); 1 child, Deborah Lynn; m. Jerry L. Capes, May 28, 1988 (div. 1993). AAS, Belleville Area Coll., Ill., 1979; BSN, St. Mary Coll., Leavenworth, Kans., 1987; MS in Nursing, U. Mo., Kansas City, 1991. RN, Kans.; cert. ARNP; clin. nurse specialist in gerontology. Office nurse Met. Orthopedics Ltd., St. Louis, 1973-81; dir. nursing Gardner (Kans.) Skilled Facility, 1982-84; staff nurse Bethany Med. Ctr., Kansas City, Kans., 1984-88; staff nurse-ICU Munson Army Hosp., Ft. Leavenworth, 1985-88; nurse coordinator VA Hosp., Leavenworth, 1988-90; staff nurse Bethany Med. Ctr., Kansas City, Kans., 1989-93, Trinity Luth. Hosp., Kansas City, Mo., 1990-95; edn. coord. Kansas City Presbyn. Manor, 1991-95; nurse Coffeyville (Kans.) Regional Med. Ctr., 1993-95; nurse Mercy Hosp., Independence, Kans., 1993-94, traveling nurse, 1995—; conductor workshop in field; affiliate faculty U. Mo., Kansas City, 1992—. Mem. ANA, AACN, Kans. Nurses Assn., Eagles, Nightingale Nursing Honor Soc. (fellow in nursing sci.), Sigma Theta Tau. Home: 201 Kroeger Ave Dupo IL 62239

GALLAS, MARTIN HANS, librarian; b. Berlin, Nov. 23, 1947; came to U.S., 1953; s. Ernst Gallas and Kate Lesser; m. Myoung Ok Lee, Dec. 23, 1977; children: Monica, Matthew. AA, Springfield (Ill.) Coll., 1971; AB, U. Ill., 1973, MLS, 1974. Reference libr. Starved Rock Libr. System, Ottawa, Ill., 1979-81; libr. dir. Springfield Coll., 1974-79, Oakland City (Ind.) U., 1981-86, Ill. Coll., Jacksonville, 1986—. Chmn. Sangamon Valley Acad. Libr. Consortium, 1977-79, 92—. With U.S. Army, 1965-68. Office: Ill Coll Schewe Libr 1101 W College Ave Jacksonville IL 62650-2212

GALLE, EDWARD LOUIS, retired food processing research engineer; b. Arkansas City, Kans., Nov. 27, 1927; s. Kurt Raphael and Louisa Marie (Epp) G.; m. Genevieve Violet Goff, June 6, 1948; children: Pamela Jean, John Edward, Diana Marie, Judith Rose. BS in Milling Tech., Kans. State U., 1950. Sr. rsch. engr. The Pillsbury Co., Mpls., 1951-89; tech. cons. Compatible Tech., Inc., Mpls., 1992—. Patentee process for pasteurizing flour, process for simulated nutmeat, process for coating foods, method for producing nut-like texture, other processes and methods. Served with USN, 1945-46, PTO. Presbyterian. Home: 2755 N Dellwood Roseville MN 55113

GALLIGAN, FRANK DANIEL, automotive company executive; b. Bronx, N.Y., Apr. 15, 1938; s. Frank A. and Mary G. (Moran) G.; B.S., U. Scranton, 1960; grad. exec. devel. program U. Ill., 1975; m. M. Elizabeth Jordan, Oct. 14, 1961; children—Michael F., Eileen M., Paul F. Vice pres. mktg. Toledo Tools Co., 1971-74; nat. sales mgr. AP Parts Co., Toledo, 1974-77; v.p. McQuay-Norris, Inc., St. Louis, 1977-84; exec. v.p., dir. Delta Inc. of Ark., Jonesboro, 1984-87 ; v.p., dir. Delta Group Inc., 1984-87, World Motor Cons., Inc., 1987-94, pres., 1994—, chmn.; pres. Galligan Mktg., 1991—. Pres., Brightwaters Acres Civic Assn., 1965-66, Indsl. Products div. Delta Consol. Industries; mem. bus. adv. com. Lucas County Port Authority, 1976-77. Mem. Automotive Parts and Accessories Assn. (dir. 1990—), Automotive Service Industries Assn. (mem. young exec. nat. bd. dirs. 1977-78). Republican. Roman Catholic. Club: Glen Echo Country (bd. govs., pres. 1987) (St. Louis), Innsbrook Estates Country.

GALLINA, CHARLES ONOFRIO, nuclear scientist; b. New Brunswick, N.J., Oct. 10, 1943; s. Matthew Salvatore and Mary (Piazza) G.; m. Ellen Mary Romano, Oct. 10, 1976; children: Mary Catharine, Matthew Charles, Maria Christine. BS, Fordham U., 1965; MS, Rutgers U., 1967, PhD, 1971. Environ. radiation specialist Consol. Edison N.Y., N.Y.C., 1971-72; radiation specialist AEC, Newark, 1972-73; sr. radiation specialist Nuclear Regulatory Commn., King of Prussia, Pa., 1973-76, sr. duty officer, 1973-82, investigation specialist, 1976-80, coord. emergency preparedness, 1980-82; sr. emergency preparedness engr. Tera Corp., King of Prussia, 1982; sr. radiol. engr. Hydro Nuclear Svcs., Marlton, N.J., 1982-84, dir. tech. mktg., 1984-85; mgr. bus. devel. Westinghouse Electric Corp., Moorestown, N.J., 1985-87; mgr. tech. program devel. Westinghouse Radiological Svcs., Moorestown, N.J., 1987-89; sr. nuclear scientist Dept. Nuclear Safety State of Ill., Springfield, 1990—; pres., CEO Springfield Stopp, Inc., 1994—; exec. cons. Profl. Nuclear Assocs., Springfield, Ill., 1990—; mem. bd. sci. and policy advisors Am. Coun. on Sci. and Health, 1991—; spl. tech. cons. to U.S. Def. Nuclear Agy.; tech. expert in area of emergency preparedness, radiation safety environ. monitoring and reactor health physics. Tech. reviewer, contbr. Radiation Protection Management Mag., Health Physics Soc. Jour.; contbr. articles to Health Physics Soc. Jour. Pres. Providence Force Condominium Assn., 1973-77; pres., CEO STOPP (Stop Planned Parenthood) of Ill., Inc., 1993—. AEC fellow, 1968-70, USPHS fellow, 1967, fellow Fed. Water Pollution Control Assn., 1971. Mem. Am. Nuclear Soc. (vice chmn., chmn.-elect Midwest Ill. chpt. 1991-93), Delaware Valley Soc. Radiation Protections, Health Physics Soc. (charter mem. Prairie State chpt. 1990—, bd. dirs. Prairie State chpt. 1993—), Am. Coun. of Sci. and Health (bd. sci. and policy advisors 1991—). Home: 3505 Bluff Rd Springfield IL 62707-9674 Office: 1035 Outer Park Dr Springfield IL 62704-4462

GALLINAT, MICHAEL PAUL, fisheries biologist; b. Flint, Mich., Nov. 1, 1962; s. Paul John Richard and Myrna Mae (Dingman) G.; m. Carol Ann Koshko, Sept. 8, 1989; children: Nathan Michael, Adam Andrew. BS in Fisheries and Wildlife Mgmt., Lake Superior State U., Sault Ste. Marie, Mich., 1985; MS in Fisheries Biology, Ball State U., 1987. Grad. rsch. asst. Ball State U., Muncie, Ind., 1985-87; pvt. aquatic contractor, Flushing, Mich., 1987-88; rsch. asst. U. Mich., Ann Arbor, 1988; fisheries biologist, program adminstr. Red Cliff Band of Lake Superior Chippewa, Bayfield, Wis., 1988—; mem. Wis. Coastal Mgmt. Coun., Madison, 1991—, Native Peoples Fisheries Com., 1990-92; adj. mem. Lake Superior Tech. Com., 1988—, mem. steelhead, walleye and brook trout subcoms.; adj. faculty Envirovet Program U. Ill., 1991—. Mem. Am. Fisheries Soc., Sigma Xi (assoc.). Home: 1012 3rd Ave W Ashland WI 54806-3107 Office: Red Cliff Fisheries Dept PO Box 529 Bayfield WI 54814-1167

GALLINOT, RUTH MAXINE, educational consultant; b. Carlinville, Ill., Feb. 16, 1925; d. Martin Mike and Augusta (Kumpus) G. BS, Roosevelt U., Chgo., 1971, MA with honors, 1974; PhD, The Union Inst., Cin., 1978. Adminstrv. asst., exec. sec. Karoll's Inc., Chgo., 1952-66; asst. dean Cen. YMCA Community Coll., Chgo., 1966-81, dir. life planning inst., 1979-80; pres. Gallinot & Assocs., Chgo., St. Louis and Bethalto, Ill., 1980—; mem. task force Office Sr. Citizens and Handicapped, City of Chgo., 1971-79; mem. criteria and guidelines com. Internat. Assn. for Continuing Edn. and Tng., 1983-86, survey and rsch. com., 1984-88; team chair accreditation evaluation team Accrediting Commn. Ind. Colls. and Schs., Washington, 1983-88; instr. Grad. Sch., USDA, 1984—, Coun. Rehab. Affiliates, Chgo., 1985—. Developer leisure time adult edn. series for elderly Uptown model cities area dept. human resources City of Chgo., 1970; editor: Certified Professional Secs. Rev., 1983; reporter Greater Alton Pub. Co., 1987-89; contbr. articles to profl. jours. Chmn. Commn. Status of Women in State of Ill., 1963-68; del. White House Conf. on Equal Pay, 1963, White House Conf. on Civil Rights, 1965, City of Chgo. White House Conf. on Info. and Library, 1976, State of Ill. White House Conf. Info. Services and Library Services, 1977; life mem. Mus. Lithuanian Culture, Chgo., 1973—; pub. mem. Fgn. Service Selection Bd. U.S. Dept. State, 1984; bd. dirs. Luths. for Chgo., 1978-83, also founding member; member adv. edn. com. Chgo. Commn. Human Relations, 1968-75 fundraising chmn. Bethalto (Ill.) Sr Citizens new bldg. furnishings, 1990-91, pres. 1995—. Recipient Leadership in Civic, Cultural and Econ. Life of the City award YWCA, Chgo., 1972, Achievement in Field Edn. award Operation P.U.S.H., Chgo., 1975. Mem. Profl. Secs. Internat. (past pres., ednl. cons. 1980-84), Edn. Network Older Adults (v.p., sec. 1979-86), Nat. Assn. Parliamentarians (Ill. and Chgo. chpts.), Literacy Coun. Chgo. (bd. dirs. 1979-86), Zonta of Alton (treas. Chgo. club 1965-66). Lutheran. Home and Office: Gallinot & Assocs 210 James St Bethalto IL 62010-1318

GALLOPOULOS, NICHOLAS EFSTRATIOS, chemical engineer; b. Athens, Apr. 5, 1936; came to U.S., 1953; s. Efstratios C. and Lucia N. (Romanides) G.; m. Mary Frances Veale, Oct. 25, 1958; children: Gregory S., Lucia Anne. BS in Chem. Engring., Tex. A&M U., 1958; MS in Chem. Engring., Pa. State U., 1959. Tech. specialist Humble Oil & Refining Co. (Exxon), Houston, 1967-68; rsch. engr. Gen. Motors Rsch. Labs., Warren, Mich., 1959-67, 68-75, asst. dept. head fuels and lubricants, 1975-85, head dept. environ. sci., 1985-89, head dept. engine rsch., 1989—; mem. Coordinating Rsch. Coun., Atlanta, 1974-89. Author: Future Automotive Fuels, 1977; contbr. chpts. to books, articles to Sci. American, Indsl. and Engring. Chemistry. Mem. Econ. Devel. Corp., Rochester Hills, Mich., 1978-91; mem., chmn. Planning Commn., Rochester Hills, 1982-92. Mem. AAAS, Soc. Automotive Engrs., Am. Chem. Soc., Sigma Xi. Home: 1565 Hampstead Ln Rochester Hills MI 48309-2948 Office: Gen Motors Rsch Box 9055 30500 Mound Rd Warren MI 48092-2031

GALLOWAY, DANIEL LEE, investment executive; b. Columbia, Mo., Apr. 16, 1958; s. Robert Eugene and Lilie Ann (Riechard) G.; m. Wanda Sue Wegener, June 22, 1979; 1 child, Rob. BA, William Jewell Coll., Liberty, Mo., 1979; postgrad., Wolfson Coll., Cambridge, Eng., 1979-80. Asst. to pres. Galloway Limestone Co., Inc., Bowling Green, Mo., 1980-81; v.p. Galloway Limestone Co., Inc., 1981-90; pres., investment adviser Galloway & Galloway, Inc., 1989—; bd. dirs. MCM Savs. Bank, FSB; treas., chair fin. com. bd. dirs. Hannibal Regional Healthcare Sys., 1994—; cons. Cecil C. Daffron & Assocs., Bowling Green, 1987-90, 95. Bd. dirs. Mo. State Sch. Bds. Assn. Region 6, 1989, 90; sec. Bowling Green R-1 Sch. Bd., 1989-92, First Presbyn. Ch. Bd. of Session, 1983-86; diaconate First Christian Ch., Hannibal, 1995—; mem. steering com. Hannibal Accelerated Mid. Sch. Program, 1995—. Mem. Mo. Limestone Producers Assn. (bd. dirs. 1982-85), Mo. State Sch. Bd. Assn. (edn. com. 1989-90). Home: 15 Riverpoint Rd Hannibal MO 63401-2019 Office: Galloway & Galloway Inc PO Box 350 215 W Church St Bowling Green MO 63334-1524

GALLOWAY, DAVID N., state legislator. Constable White Lake Twp., Mich., 1986-88, trustee, 1989-92; mem. Oakland County Cmty. Devel. Com.; mem. dist. 44 Mich. State Ho. of Reps., 1993—; police officer Pontiac, Mich.; owner Master Clean Equip Co.; real estate broker, owner Realty Group, Inc. Mem. Fraternal Order of Police, Lions Club, Waterford Pontiac Elks Club, Waterford Eagles, Waterford Optimist Club. Home: 9575 Steepholow Dr White Lake MI 48386-2370 Address: PO Box 30014 Lansing MI 48909-7514*

GALLUCCI, JOHN P., stockbroker; b. Chgo., Aug. 2, 1967. BS in Econs., Elmhurst Coll., 1993. Lic. series 7, 63 Nat. Assn. Securities Dealers. Stockbroker Chatfield Dean Investment Bankers, Chgo., 1992-93, Olde Discount Corp., Parkridge, Ill., 1993—. Home: 1030 S May St Chicago IL 60607-4265

GALLUPPI, THOMAS LAWRENCE, healthcare executive; b. Chgo., Feb. 22, 1954; s. Albert J. and Virginia R. (D'Antonio) G. BA, Ill. Inst. Tech., 1976; MBA, Roosevelt U., 1979. CPA, Ill. Acct. Chgo. Osteopathic Med. Ctr., 1977-79; acctg. mgr. Resurrection Med. Ctr., Chgo., 1979-85; sr. v.p., CFO Vis. Nurse Assn. Chgo., 1985-95; sr. assoc. Curran Care, 1996—; treas., bd. dirs. Ill. Home Care Coun., Chgo., 1993—, chmn., bd. trustees worker's compensation trust, 1994—. Mem. AICPA, Am. Coll. Healthcare Execs., Ill. CPA Soc. Home: 6324 W 60th St Chicago IL 60638 Office: Curran Care 7222 W Cermak Ste 601 North Riverside IL 60546

GALOWICH, RONALD HOWARD, real estate investment executive, venture capitalist; b. Peoria, Ill., Feb. 18, 1936; s. Louis J. and Leah (Kahn) G.; m. Eleanor Bernstein, June 16, 1957 (div. Aug., 1977); children: Jeffrey, Robert, Pamela; m. Susan E. Loggans, Sept. 11, 1977 (div. Apr. 1988). BS in Commerce and Law, U. Ill., 1957, JD, 1959. Bar: Ill. 1959, U.S. Supreme Ct. 1963. Pres. Twin Oaks-Burr Oaks Realty, Joliet, Ill., 1961-81; ptnr. Galowich & Galowich, Joliet, Ill., 1960-81; dir. real estate ops. Pritzker & Pritzker, Chgo., 1981-90; chmn. Madison Realty Group, Inc., Chgo., 1985—, Madison Group Holdings, Inc., Chgo., 1990—; co-founder, chmn. CEO Madison Info. Technologies, Inc. (formerly RBG Corp.), Chgo., 1994—; co-founder, exec. v.p., sec., gen. counsel HealthCare COMPARE Corp., Downers Grove, Ill., 1982—; commr. Ill. Supreme Ct., 1968-70. Fellow Am. Judicature Soc., Ill. Bar Found.; mem. ABA, Ill. Bar Assn., Urban Land Inst. Jewish. Home: 1248 N Astor St Chicago IL 60610-2308 Office: Madison Group Holdings Inc 200 W Madison St Chicago IL 60606-3414

GALVAN, MARY THERESA, economics and business educator; b. Rockford, Ill., Dec. 19, 1957; d. Dino F. and Ida M. Dal Fratello; m. John D. Galvan, June 27, 1987; children: Marie K., John M., Kathleen T. BA, Rockford Coll., 1979; MA, No. Ill. U., 1981, PhD, 1988. Instr. No. Ill. U., DeKalb, 1979-81; asst. prof. Rockford Coll., 1981-87; assoc. prof. bus. and econs. St. Xavier Coll., Chgo., 1987-92; assoc. prof. mktg. North Ctrl. Coll., Naperville, Ill., 1992—, dir. Ctr. for Rsch., 1994—; chmn. grad. studies com. North Ctrl. Coll., 1996—; cons. Fed. Res. Bank Chgo., 1988—. Lector, St. Elizabeth Seton Parish, Naperville, 1987—, pres. Women's Network. Earhart Found. fellow, 1988; Hegelar Carus scholar, 1987.. Mem. AAUW, Am. Econs. Assn., Am. Mktg. Assn., Am. Statis. Assn. (v.p. 1994—), Western Econs. Assn. Internat., Midwest Bus. Adminstrn. Assn., Midwest Econs. Assn., Phi Delta Kappa, Omicron Delta Epsilon. Office: North Ctrl Coll 30 N Brainard St Naperville IL 60540-4607

GALVEZ, ANGEL, physician; b. Barcelona, Spain, May 15, 1959; came to U.S., 1983; s. Francisco and Julia Galvez; m. Esperanza Garcia, Sept. 10, 1983; children: Carlos, Daniel. MD, U. Barcelona, 1982, PhD, 1991. Diplomate Am. Bd. Internal Medicine, Am. Bd. Med. Oncology. Rsch. fellow Mt. Sinai Hosp., N.Y.C., 1983-86; resident in internal medicine L.I. Coll. Hosp., N.Y.C., 1986-89; hematology-oncology fellow St. Luke Roosevelt Hosp., N.Y.C., 1989-92; attending physician Hosp. De Terrasa, Barcelona, 1992-94, Ill. Masonic Med. Ctr., Chgo., 1994—. Mem. AMA, Ill. Med. Soc., Chgo. Med. Soc.

GALVIN, MATTHEW REPPERT, psychiatry educator; b. Seattle, July 24, 1950; s. Ralph B. and Virginia (Reppert) G.; m. Deborah Ann Chernin, Dec. 22, 1979; children: Joseph, Sarah. AB with honors, Ind. U., 1975, MD, 1979. Diplomate Am. Bd. Adolescent Psychiatry, Am. Bd. Psychiatry and Neurology. Asst. prof. Ind. U. Med. Ctr., Indpls., 1984-95, clin. assoc. prof., 1995—; staff psychiatrist Larue Carter Meml. Hosp., Indpls., 1984-88, assoc. dir. youth svcs., 1988, acting dir., 1988-90; child psychiatrist Riley Child Psychiatry Svcs., Indpls., 1990—; asst. dir. psychiatric svcs. children and adolescents Ind. U. Hosps. Author: Ignatius Finds Help, A Story about Psychotherapy, 1988, Otto Learns About Medicine, A Story About Grown-ups Helping Children, 1988, Clouds and Clocks, A Story for Children Who Soil, 1989; co-author: Sometimes Y, A Story for Families with Gender Identity Issues, 1993; contbr. articles to profl. jours. With M.C., U.S. Army, 1970-73, Vietnam. Fellow Am. Psychiat. Assn.; mem. Am. Acad. Child Adolescent Psychiatry, Am. Soc. Adolescent Psychiatry, Nat. Alliance Against Mental Illness (affiliate), Ind. Coun. Child and Adolescent Psychiatry (treas. Indpls. chpt. 1986-89, pres. elect 1989-90, pres. 1990-91). Office: Ind U Child and Adolescent Psychiatry Svcs 702 Barnhill Dr Indianapolis IN 46202-5128

GALVIN, PAT G., state legislator; m. Carol Galvin; 2 children. Student, Barber Coll. Barber; rep. Dist. 33 N.D. Ho. of reps., mem. human svcs., natural resources coms. Mem. Hazen City Commn., Hazen City Sch. Bd. With N.D. N.G. Mem. Am. Legion, Eagles. Home: 621 Third Ave NW Hazen ND 58545

GALYSH, ROBERT ALAN, information systems analyst; b. Cleve., Apr. 4, 1954; s. Fred Theodore and Jennie Catherine (Masiglowa) G.; m. Nanette Marie Kappus, Mar. 3, 1984; children: Joanna Marie, Matthew Glenn. BA in Econs., Cleve. State U., 1976, MA in Econs., 1982. Savs. officer Cleve. Fed. Savs., 1977-79; asst. v.p. systems, procedures analyst Continental Fed. Savs. (formerly Cleve. Fed. Savs.), Cleve, 1979-84; data processing officer, mgr. systems and procedures Continental div. Dollar Bank FSB, Cleve, 1984-86; systems analyst Cleve. Met. Gen. Hosp., 1986-87, sr. systems analyst, 1987-90; project leader info. systems MetroHealth System (formerly Cleve. Met. Gen. Hosp.), 1990-95, group mgr. info. svcs., 1995—; cons. on microcomputer installations and applications, Cleve., 1984—. Mem. Nat. Warplane Mus. Mem. Gt. Lakes Hist. Soc., Omicron Delta Epsilon. Presbyterian. Home: 26602 Sudbury Dr North Olmsted OH 44070-1844

GAMBLE, DOUGLAS IRVIN, state official, educator; b. Wheeling, W.Va., Dec. 27, 1953; s. Wiley Irvin and Myrtle Stewart (Yeater) G.; m. Lois Winifred Betz, June 26, 1976; children: Rebekah Winifred, Mary Amelia, Martha Suzanne, Rachel Emma, Michael Irvin, Katrina Ruth. Student, Archtl. Assn. Sch. Architecture, London, 1975; B in Environ. Design, Miami U., Oxford, Ohio, 1976; MArch, U. Ill., 1979. Lic. asbestos worker, insp., mgmt. planner and supr. Draftsman G.T. Hardwick & Assocs., Champaign, Ill., 1976-77, Glenn G. Frazier & Assocs., Urbana, Ill., 1977; rsch. asst. Small Homes Coun.-Bldg. Rsch. Coun., Urbana, 1977-79; archtl. designer Carl Fischer & Assocs., Springfield, Ill., 1979-80; archtl. programmer Sarti-Huff Archtl. Group, Springfield, 1980-82, Huff Archtl. Group, Springfield, 1982-86; project mgr. Capital Devel. Bd. State of Ill., Springfield, 1986—; instr. Parkland Coll., Champaign, 1978-79, U. Ill. Midwest Tng. Ctr., Chgo., 1987—, Lincoln Land Coll, Springfield, 1991—. Testifier elem. and secondary edn. com. on asbestos Ill. Senate, 1984; v.p. Faith Luth. Ch., Springfield, 1988-89. Miami U. rsch. grantee, 1975. Mem. AIA (assoc.), Constrn. Specificiations Inst. (pres. Cen. Ill. chpt. 1990-92, membership chair North Cen. region 1992-93, dir. North Cen. region 1996—, mem. nat. spkrs. bur. 1988—, Pres. cert. of appreciation Cen. Ill. chpt. 1988, North Cen. region mem. commendation award 1989, Inst. Commendation award 1990, North Cen. Region Dirs. Cert. award 1991), Nat. Asbestos Coun. (spkr. nat. conv. 1992), On My Own Time Art Competition, Geneal. Inst. Mid-Am., Nat. Geneal. Soc., Ill. State Geneal. Soc., Springfield Civil War Roundtable, Hon. Order Ky. Cols. Home: 1425 Whittier Ave Springfield IL 62704 Office: Ill Capital Devel Bd 3d Fl 401 S Spring St Springfield IL 62706

GAMER, ROBERT EMANUEL, political science educator; b. Champaign, Ill., Apr. 26, 1938; s. Carl Wesley and Alice Clara (Michael) G.; m. May Lim Tay, Mar. 15, 1980; stepson, Keith Buchanan. BA, Monmouth (Ill.) Coll., 1960; PhD, Brown U., 1965. Asst. lectr. U. Singapore, 1964-65, lectr., 1965-68; asst. prof. polit. sci. U. Mo., Kansas City, 1968-72, assoc. prof., 1972-77, prof., 1977—, chmn. dept., 1981-83; vis. lectr. AID, Harpers Ferry, W.Va., 1984; vis. prof. Hangzhou (China) U., 1989, Shanghai U., 1993. Author: Politics of Urban Development in Singapore, 1972, The Developing Nations, 1976, 2d edit., 1982, Governments and Politics in a Changing World, 1994. Nat. trustee Interfuture N.Y.C., 1982-84; mem. Mo. selection com. Harvard U. Program for Sr. Execs. in State and Local Govt., Jefferson City, 1983-85; bd. dirs. Edgar Snow Meml. Fund, 1992—; policy analysis panelist Truman Scholars Leadership Week, Liberty, Mo., 1996—. Mem. Am. Polit. Sci. Assn., Blue Key, Phi Beta Kappa, Alpha Tau Omega. Methodist. Home: 5605 Kenwood Ave Kansas City MO 64110-2729 Office: U Mo Dept Polit Sci Kansas City MO 64110

GAMM, CAROL AMY, counselor; b. Louisiana, Mo., May 20, 1967; d. Wayne Eldon and Georgia Mae (Finley) G. BS, N.E. Mo. State U., 1989, MA in Counseling, 1993. Counselor asst. acad. planning svcs. N.E. Mo. State, Kirksville, 1986-88; peer counselor Career Planning Ctr., N.E. Mo. State U., Kirksville, 1988-89; psychology advisor social sci. div. N.E. Mo. State U., Kirksville, 1991-92; program asst. Ruth Jensen Village Residential Svcs. Inc., Bowling Green, Mo., 1989-90, program specialist, 1990, residential coord., 1990-91; community support worker Preferred Family Health Care, Inc., Kirksville, 1992; community integration provider Marion County Svcs. for the Developmentally Disabled, Hannibal, Mo., 1992; intern with v.p. for acad. affairs N.E. Mo. State U., 1992-93; qualified mental retardation profl. Baker Mgmt., Kirksville, Mo., 1993-94; counselor Mo. Vocat. Rehab., Kirksville, 1994—. Mem. Am. Counseling Assn., The Boomerang Kids, Inc. (bd. dirs.), N.E. Mo. State U. Alumni Assn., Region II Planning and Coord. Coun. for Devel. Disabilities (bd. dirs., treas. 1996—), Psi Chi. Home: 712 E Pierce Apt B Kirksville MO 63501

GAMMELL, WAYNE WILLIAM, title company executive; b. Dayton, Ohio, Mar. 2, 1940; s. Willard DeWitt and Violet Gay (McNew) G.; m. Gail Louise Martin, Apr. 28, 1962; children: Jeffrey Wayne and Susanne Louise. Engring. student, U. Dayton, 1958-61. Lic. title ins. agt., real estate agt. Escrow officer, title examiner Lawyers Title Ins., Dayton, 1961-67; escrow officer Ohio Title Corp., Dayton, 1967-69; v.p., mgr. Louisville Title, Dayton, 1969-73; owner, pres., chmn. bd. Mid Am. Land Title Agy., Inc., Dayton, 1973—; bd. dirs. Olympic Title Ins. Co., Dayton. Asst. treas. Centerville (Ohio) Schs. Levy Renewal, 1975; charter mem. Rep. Presdl. Task Force. Served with Air NG, 1962-68. Named to Dayton Mortgage Bankers Hall of Fame, 1990. Mem. Dayton Area Bd. Realtors, Mortgage Bankers Assn. (sec., bd. dirs. 1980-84, named to Hall of Fame Dayton chpt. 1990), Dayton Title Underwriters (pres. 1982-83), Miami Valley Land Title Assn. (pres. 1992—), South Dayton C. of C., Nat. C. of C., Am. Bus. Club. Republican. Lutheran. Club: Am. Bus. Home: 6311 Marshall Rd Dayton OH 45459-2236 Office: Mid Am Land Title Agy Inc 761 Miamisburg-Centerville Dayton OH 45459

GAMSKY, NEAL RICHARD, university administrator, psychology educator; b. Menasha, Wis., Feb. 17, 1931; s. Andrew P. and Lillian G.; m. Irene Janet Jimos, Aug. 16, 1956; children—Elizabeth, Patricia. BS, U. Wis., 1954, MS, 1959, PhD, 1965. Counselor, Appleton Pub. Schs. (Wis.), 1959-62; ednl. and counseling cons. Wis. Div. Mental Hygiene, 1967. dir. ednl. services Wis. Diagnostic Ctr., Madison, 1962-67; dir. rsch. pupil pers. svcs. Coop. Edn. Svc. Agy., Waupun, Wis., 1967-70; dir. student counseling ctr. Ill. State U., Normal, 1970-73, v.p. student affairs, prof. psychology, 1973-91; Served with U.S. Army, 1954-56. Mem. Am. Psychol. Assn., Am. Assn. Counseling and Devel., Nat. Assn. Student Pers. Adminstrs., Am. Assn. Higher Edn., Am. Coll. Pers. Assn., Am. Orthopsychiat. Assn. Author: (with G.F. Farwell and B. Mathieu-Coughlan) The Counselor's Handbook, 1974; contbr. 26 articles in field to profl. jours.

GANAWAY, NORMA JEAN, vocational counselor; b. South Bend, Ind., Apr. 9, 1927; d. Welvin Sr. and Alphia (Bond) G. Grad., Thomas Comml. Sch., 1947; cert. in bus., Ind. U., 1980, cert. in supervisory devel., 1980. Sec. to contr. Robertson's Dept. Store, South Bend, 1947-62, sec. to divsnl. mgr. mdse., 1962-68; dir. Urban Tech. Asst. Project, South Bend, 1971; asst. dir. Neighborhood Assn. Model Cities, South Bend, 1971-74; client svc. specialist CETA Program, South Bend, 1974-83; vocat. counselor Workforce Devel. Svcs. No. Ind., South Bend, 1983-94. Sec. Sunday Sch. Pilgrim Bapt. Ch., 1942-43, 50, pres. fellowship club, 1968-69, active red circle; bd. dirs. St. Joseph County YWCA, 1968-71, chmn. Y teenage com 1969-70; bd. dirs., pub. rels. com. Campfire Girls, 1969, 2d v.p., 1972; sec. bd. dirs. Hansel Ctr. Neighborhood Svcs., 1972-73; nat. bd. dirs. YWCA of U.S.A, N.Y.C., 1973-76; apptd. by mayor Commn. Status of Women, 1975, 76; housing commr. City of South Bend Pub. Housing, 1991—; active, past bd. dirs. South Bend Urban League; Rep. committeewoman, South Bend; dir. dist. # 2 St. Joseph County Rep. Women, 1994—. Recipient Woman of Yr. award South Bend-Mishawaka C. of C., 1970, Counselor award Ind. Vocat. Tech. Coll., 1990, Woman of Yr. award Ind. State Women in the NAACP, 1995, NAACP Midwest Region III, 1995, Svc. award East Chgo. br. NAACP, 1995, Appreciation award Order Ea. Star, 1993-95; Ganaway scholarship named in her honor, Workforce Devel. Svcs., 1993. Mem. NAACP (nat. life; state chair 1969—, Ind. conf., Achievement award 1990) Sorelle Entre Nous Club (pres., organizer 1951—, chair Ebony Fashion Show 1992), Order Ea. Star (grant chpt. Ind., dist. dep. grand matron 1968, Dist. Yr. award 1988-91, exec. dir. pub. rels. 1993-94, appreciation placque grand chpt. 1993-95), Imperial Ct. Daus. Isis (illustrious commandress 1962, imperial NAACP coord. 1967-89, Community Leader Am. award 1971). Home: 214 Birdsell St South Bend IN 46628-2107

GANDURSKI, RONALD EDWARD, manufacturing executive; b. Chgo., July 6, 1941; s. Louis Edward and Gladys Elaine (Wichman) G.; m. Mary Ann Swiatek, Apr. 11, 1964; children: Thomas, James. BSME, Ill. Inst. Tech., 1964, BSEE, 1970; MBA, U. Chgo., 1974. Design engr. Link Belt div. FMC, Chgo., 1964-73, prodn. mgr., 1973-76; prodn. mgr. Signode, Bridgeview, Ill., 1976-79, plant mgr., 1979-89; v.p. mfg. Leighton Industries, Cicero, Ill., 1990-91; mfg. mgr. Summit Industries, Chgo., 1992-93; dir. mfg. Quam-Nichols Co., Chgo., 1995—. Home: 10605 S Lockwood Oak Lawn IL 60453-5177 Office: Quam-Nichols Co 234 E Marquette Rd Chicago IL 60637

GANESH, OREKONDE, physician; b. Davangere, Mysore, India, Oct. 19, 1941; came to U.S., 1967; d. Bakkappa and Muppama Orekonde; m. Dakshayeni Ganesh, Dec. 8, 1967; children: Nisha, Nina, Nitya. MD, U. Mysore, 1964. Diplomate Am. Bd. Psychiatry and Neurology. Intern K.R. Hosp. U. Mysore, 1964-65, Meml. Hosp., R.I., 1967-68; resident in internal medicine V.S. Gen. Hosp., Gujarat, India, 1965-67; resident in psychiatry Northville (Mich.) State Hosp., 1968-71; pres. Quality Med. Clinics P.C., Southfield, Mich., 1977—; pres. Geno Pharms., Inc., Southfield, 1990—; pres. Greater Detroit Hosp. Inc., Quality Med. Plan. Mem. Nat. Geno Scis. (pres. 1980—), Am. Psychiatric Assn., Am. Sch. Health Assn., Oakland County Med. Soc., Mich. State Med. Soc., AMA, Am. Sch. Tropical Medicine, Am. Coll. Internat. Physicians, Am. Diabetes Assn. Home: 2003 Wickford Ct Bloomfield Hills MI 48304-1088 Office: 28165 Greenfield Rd Southfield MI 48076-3063

GANG, STUART WORTHINGTON, advertising and public relations company executive; b. N.Y.C., Oct. 18, 1928; s. James Gang and Sylvia (Weitz) Dudovitz; m. Marjorie Paul, Aug. 15, 1979. BA, U. Minn., 1951. News reporter Sta. KSTP-TV, Mpls., 1951-55, Sta. WCCO-TV, Mpls., 1956-57; asst. news dir. Sta. WTCN-TV, Mpls., 1955-56; coord. Minn. Pvt. Coll. TV, Mpls., 1957-59; owner, mgr. Stu Gang & Assocs., St. Paul, 1959-72, pres., 1979-86; v.p. Gang & Withy, Inc., St. Paul, 1972-79; chmn., CEO, Gang Carlson Cunico Inc., St. Paul, 1987—. Co-inventor med. instrument. V.p. Humane Soc. Ramsey County, St. Paul, 1979-86; bd. dirs. Vision Found., U. Minn., Mpls., 1989-94; dist. supr. Ramsey County Soil and Water Conservation, 1995—. Mem. Pub. Rels. Soc. Am. (Classic award 1984), Masons (master 1992, grand orator St. Paul 1989-92), Shriners (cert. of honor 1988), Rotary (bd. dirs. St. Paul 1989-92). Home: 1355 Colonial Dr Roseville MN 55113-4242 Office: Gang Carlson Cunico Inc 405 Sibley St Saint Paul MN 55101-1900

GANOCY, CARL PAUL, city manager; b. Uniontown, Pa., Mar. 21, 1946; s. Louis and Mary Ann (Salansky) G.; m. Regina Kay Spies, July 27, 1974; 1 child, Heather Ann Ganocy Gittins. BS in Biology, U. Akron, 1976. Water plant operator City of Ravenna (Ohio), 1986-87, water plant chemist, 1987-89, water plant asst., 1989-94, utilities dir., 1994—. Vol. lake monitoring program N.E. Ohio Four County Regional Planning and Devel. Orgn. (NEFCO), Akron, 1987—; mem. environ. resources tech. adv. com., 1995. With USN, 1965-71. Recipient 5-Yr. Excellence award N.E. Ohio Four County Regional Planning and Devel. Orgn., 1992. Mem. Am. Water Works Assn., Water Environment Fedn., Ohio Lake Mgmt. Soc., N.Am. Lake Mgmt. Soc., Am. Legion. Democrat. Home: 5237 Camp Rd Ravenna OH 44266 Office: City of Ravenna 210 Parkway Ravenna OH 44266

GANSKE, J. GREG, congressman, plastic surgeon; b. New Hampton, Iowa, Mar. 31, 1949; s. Victor Wilber and Mary Jo (O'Donnell) G.; m. Corrine Mikkelson, 1976; children: Ingrid, Briget, Karl. BA, U. Iowa, 1972, MD, 1976. Diplomate Am. Bd. Plastic Surgery, Am. Bd. Surgery. Intern in gen. surgery U. Colo. Med. Ctr., Denver, 1976-78; resident in gen. surgery U. Oreg. Health Sci. Ctr., Portland, 1978-81, chief resident in gen. surgery, 1981-82; resident in plastic surgery Harvard Med. Sch., Boston, 1982-84; chief resident plastic surgery Brigham and Women's Hosp. and Children's Hosp., 1983-84; pvt. practice plastic/reconstructive surgeon Des Moines, 1984-94; mem. U.S. Ho. Reps., Washington, 1994—; mem. staff Iowa Luth. Hosp., Iowa Meth. Med. Ctr., Mercy Hosp. Med. Ctr., Vets. Hosp., Charter Cmty. Hosp., Des Moines Gen. Hosp. Lt. col. M.C., USAR, 1984—. Fellow ACS, Am. Soc. Plastic and Reconstructive Surgeons; mem. AMA, Am. Assn. Plastic Surgeons, Iowa Med. Soc., Polk County Med. Soc., Iowa Soc. Plastic and Reconstructive Surgeons, Am. Assn. Hand Surgery, Midwestern Assn. Plastic Surgeons, Am. Soc. for Surgery of the Hand, Iowa Acad. Surgery, Am. Cleft Palate-Craniofacial Assn. Republican. Roman Catholic. Home: 5206 Waterbury Rd Des Moines IA 50312 Office: US Ho of Reps 1108 Longworth HOB Washington DC 20515

GANT, RON (RONALD EDWIN GANT), professional baseball player; b. Victoria, Tex., Mar. 2, 1965. With Atlanta Braves, 1983-94, Cin. Reds, 1994—. Mem. Nat. League All-Star Team, 1992; named to Sporting News All-Star team, 1991, recipient Silver Slugger award, 1991. Office: Cin Reds 100 Riverfront Stadium Cincinnati OH 45202*

GANTZ, BRUCE JAY, otolaryngologist, educator; b. N.Y.C., May 18, 1946; m. Mary Katherine DeJong; children: Ellen Katherine, Jessica Rose, Jay Alexander. BS in Gen. Sci., U. Iowa, 1968, MD, 1974, MS in Otolaryngology, 1980; fellow neurotology, U. Zürich, Zurich, 1981-82. Asst. prof. dept otolaryngology U. Iowa Coll. Medicine, Iowa City, 1980-84, assoc. prof., 1984-87, prof., 1987—; interim head dept. otolaryngology head & neck surgery U. Iowa Hosps. & Clinics, Iowa City, 1993-95, head dept. otolaryngology head & neck surgery, 1995—; mem. adv. bd. Deafness Research Found. Sci., 1988—. Mem. editl. bd. Am. Jour. Otology, Laryngoscope, Skull Base Surgery, Operative Techniques in Otolaryngology-Head and Neck Surgery, Anales De Otolarnolaringo-logica Mexicana; contbr. articles to profl. jours. Recipient Tchr.-Investigator Devel. award Pub. Health Svc., 1981-86, Program Project award NIH, 1985—; clin. rsch. ctr. grantee NIDCD, 1990, 95. Mem. AMA, Assn. for Rsch. in Otolaryngology (pres. 1995), Deafness Rsch. Found. (state chmn. 1985—), Am. Acad. Otolaryngology-Head and Neck Surgery, Soc. Univ. Otolaryngologists, Am. Neurotology Soc. (v.p. 1994-96, pres.-elect 1996—), Am. Otological Soc., Collegium Oto-Rhino-Laryngologicum Amictuae Sacrum. Office: U Iowa Hosps & Clinics 450 Newton St Iowa City IA 52242

GANTZ, RICHARD ALAN, museum administrator; b. Ft. Wayne, Ind., July 28, 1946; m. Ruth Ann Kennell; 1 child, Sally Elizabeth. BS in Edn. with honors, Ball State U., 1968; MA, George Washington U., 1971; PhD, Ind. U., 1986. Social studies tchr. Ft. Wayne (Ind.) Community Schs., 1969-73; Nat. Park Svc. seasonal hist. Homestead Nat. Monument, Beatrice, Nebr., 1972; assoc. instr. Ind. U., Bloomington, 1975-76; asst. state hist. preserv. officer dept. natural resources State of Ind., 1976-90, asst. dir. divsn. mus. and memls., 1978-81, acting dir., 1982-83, dir. divsn. hist. preservation and archeology, 1981-90, acting dir. divsn. state mus. and hist. sites, 1989, dir. divsn. state mus. and hist. sites and Ind. State Mus., 1990—; mem. adj. faculty history dept. Butler U., Indpls., 1988—; mem. steering com. Dept. Commerce Heritage, Tourism and Edn., 1991—; mem. project com. Ind. Heritage Trust, 1992—; chmn. Ind. Hist. Exchange Coun., 1984—, Ind. Hist. Bridge Com., 1984-90. Contbr. articles to profl. jours. Active Ind. Main St. Coun., 1986—. Mem. Orgn. Am. Hists., Nat. Trust Hist. Preservation, Ind. Assn. Hists., Ind. State Mus. Soc., Assn. Ind. Mus., Midwest Mus. Conf. Office: Ind State Mus & Hist Sites 202 N Alabama St Indianapolis IN 46204-2101

GANTZ, SUZI GRAHN, special education educator; b. Chgo., May 17, 1954; d. Robert Donald and Barbara Edna (Ascher) Grahn; m. Louis Estes Gantz, July 11, 1976; children: Christopher, Joshua. BS in Edn. of Deaf and Hard of Hearing, U. Ill., 1976. Tchr. A.G. Bell Sch., Chgo., 1976-80, 88—; sales asst. Bob Grahn & Assocs., Chgo., 1982-84; with sales dept. Isis/My Sisters Circus, Chgo., 1984-86; interpreter Glenbrook North High Sch., Northbrook, Ill., 1986-87; interpreter, aide Lake Forest (Ill.) Dist. 67, 1987-88. Mem. Northbrook Citizens for Drug and Alcohol Alliance, 1988—; cubmaster Boy Scouts Am., Northbrook, 1990-93. Mem. Ill. Tchrs. of the Hearing Impaired, A.G. Bell Soc., Coun. on Exceptional Children. Home: 485 Laburnum Dr Northbrook IL 60062-2259 Office: AG Bell Sch 3730 N Oakley Ave Chicago IL 60618-4813

GAPPA, JUDITH M., university administrator. Student, Wellesley Coll., 1957-60; BA in Music, George Washington U., 1968, MA in Musicology, 1970; EdD in Ednl. Adminstrn., Utah State U., 1973; cert. Inst. for Ednl. Mgmt., Harvard U., 1980. Lectr. George Washington U., Washington, 1968-69; dir. fine arts program The York Sch., Monterey, Calif., 1970; adminstrv. asst. dean's office coll. edn. Utah State U., Logan, 1971-72, adminstrv. intern to dir. gen. edn. & provost, 1972-73; program cons. Western Interstate Commn. for Higher Edn., Boulder, Colo., 1973; coord. affirmative action program Utah State U., Logan, 1973-75, dir. affirmative action/equal opportunity programs, asst. prof., 1975-77, 78-80, project dir., 1979-81; sr. staff assoc. Nat. Ctr. for Higher Edn. Mgmt. Systems, Inc., Boulder, 1977-78; assoc. v.p. for faculty affairs, dean of faculty, prof. San Francisco State U., 1980-91; sr. assoc. Am. Assn. Higher Edn., 1995—; v.p. for human rels., prof. Purdue U., West Lafayette, Ind., 1991—; served on numerous coms., couns. Utah State U., San Francisco State U.; cons. Assn. Governing Bds., 1994, U. Mich., Duluth, 1992, Calif. State U. Human Resources Mgmt. Office, 1992, Am. U., Washington, 1987, No. Rockies Consortium for Higher Edn. Conf., 1985, So. Utah State Coll., 1982, Nat. Ctr. for Rsch. in Vocat. Edn., 1980-81, Hood Coll., 1982-84, Am. Insts. for Rsch. in Behavioral Scis., 1980-81; condr. workshops on edn. Co-author: The Invisible Faculty, 1993; contbr. numerous articles to profl. jours. Grantee Lilly Endowment, 1995, United Techs. Corp., 1992, TIAA-CREF/Lilly Endowment, 1990, Calif. State U., 1985, San Francisco State U., 1981, HEW, 1979-81, Nat. Inst. Edn., 1977, Utah State U., 1977, Fed. workshop grant, 1976, State of Utah, 1975, 76. Mem. Western Assn. Schs. & Colls. (accreditation team mem. Calif. State U.-L.A. 1990), Am. Assn. for Higher Edn. (sr. assoc. Washington chpt. 1995—), Assn. for Study of Higher Edn. (nat. adv. bd. ASHE-ERIC Higher Edn. Report Series 1990-91, nominating com. 1986-87, program com. for 1986 nat. conf., membership com. 1982-84, conf. com. 1983), Am. Coun. on Edn. Nat. Identification Program (No. Calif. state coord. 1988-91). Office: Purdue Univ VP Human Rels 1075 Hovde Hall West Lafayette IN 47907-1075

GARASIMOWICZ, GREGORY ALEXANDER, mechanical engineer; b. Bridgeport, Conn., Sept. 4, 1949. BSME, Northeastern U., 1972; postgrad., Marquette U., 1991—. Sr. product engr. Bear Automotive, New Berlin, Wis., 1975-90, J&L Fiber Svcs., Waukesha, wis., 1990—. Patentee clip-engine analizer probe, extended outer ring for refiner plate; patents pending in field. Troop committeeperson Boy Scouts Am., Mukwonago, Wis. Mem. ASME, Rotary, Tau Beta Pi, Pi Tau Sigma. Home: S 84 W 30298 Hickory Ln Mukwonago WI 53149 Office: J&L Fiber Svcs 831 Progress Ave Waukesha WI 53186-5926

GARBACZEWSKI, DANIEL FRANK, restaurateur; b. Chgo., Sept. 4, 1950; s. Daniel Jacob and Sophie Evelen (Kurranty) G.; m. Dawn Marie Ciciora, May 7, 1983. AA, No. Ill. U., 1970; cert. recording engr., Inst. Audio Research, 1974. V.p. Garbaczewski Corp., Chgo., 1979-89, pres., 1989—; treas., chief exec. officer Gemtech Packaging Inc., Chgo., 1990—; pres. Fantasy Food Corp., Chgo., 1985—; v.p. Dynamic Design Products, 1990. Bd. dirs. Am. Cancer Soc., 1993. Republican. Roman Catholic. Home: 13713 Cavecreek Ct Lockport IL 60441-8653 Office: Chesdan Restaurant 4465 S Archer Ave Chicago IL 60632-2845

GARBER, DAVID J., sports association executive, marketing consultant; b. Stevens Point, Wis., Apr. 23, 1949; s. Ben and Audrey C. (Pickard) G.; m. Ann Wilcox, Sept. 23, 1978. BS in History, U. Wis., Stevens Point, 1971. Casualty processing mgr. Sentry Ins., A Mut. Co., Stevens Point, 1974-76; asst. v.p. Sentry Assurance Internat., Inc., Stevens Point, 1976-82; gen. mgr. Permanent Life Assurance Co., Johannesburg, South Africa, 1979; mktg. mgr. Sentry Travel Guard Ins., Stevens Point, 1982-85; v.p. Market Sq. Communications Inc., Stevens Point, 1985—; exec. dir. U.S. Curling Assn., Stevens Point, 1985—. Editor: U.S. Curling News, 1991—. Divsn. head United Way of Stevens Point, 1989; pub. rels. person Boy Scouts Am., Samoset Coun., Stevens Point, 1989; head coach U.S. Army Wrestling Team, 1974. 1st lt. U.S. Army, 1971-73. Fellow Life Mgmt. Inst.; mem. Wis. State Curling Assn. (sec. 1990-92, v.p. 1992-94), Stevens Point Curling Club (pres. 1984-86). Office: US Curling Assn PO Box 866 1100 Center Point Dr Stevens Point WI 54481

GARBER, SAMUEL BAUGH, lawyer, retail company executive; b. Chgo., Aug. 16, 1934; s. Morris and Yetta G.; m. Marietta C. Bratta; children: Debra Lee, Diane Lori. JD, U. Ill., 1958. MBA, U. Chgo., 1968. Bar: Ill., 1958. Ptnr. Brown, Dashow and Langluttig, Chgo., 1960-62; corp. counsel Walgreen Co., 1962-69; v.p., gen. counsel, exec. asst. to the pres. Carlyle & Co., 1969-73; dir. legal affairs Stop & Shop Co., Inc., 1973-74; gen. counsel Goldblatt Bros., Inc., 1974-76; v.p., sec., gen. counsel Evans, Inc., 1976—; prof. mgmt. DePaul U., 1975—; instr. grad. sch. bus. U. Chgo., 1993—. Dir. BBB of Chgo. and No. Ill. With U.S. Army, 1958-60. Mem. ABA, Am. Arbitration Assn. (arbitrator 1993—), Nat. Retail Fedn., Ill. Retail Mchts. Assn., Carlton Club, East Bank Club. Home: 2626 N Lakeview Ave Chicago IL 60614-1839 Office: Evans Inc 36 S State St Chicago IL 60603-2602

GARBER, SHELDON, hospital executive; b. Mpls., July 21, 1920; s. Mitchell and Esther (Amdur) G.; BA, U. Minn., 1942; postgrad. U. Chgo., 1952-53; m. Elizabeth Sargent Mason, May 16, 1949 (div. May 1983); children: Robert Michael, Daniel Mason, Sarah Sargent; m. Joellen Palmer Prullage, July 21, 1985. Reporter, editor U.P.I., Mpls., Chgo., Springfield, Ill., 1938-58; dir. media services U. Chgo., 1958-64; asso. dir. communication Blue Cross Assn., Chgo., 1964-69; pres. Sheldon Garber Assocs., Inc., 1969—; exec. v.p. Charles R. Feldstein & Co., 1969-73; v.p. philanthropy and communication Rush-Presbyn.-St. Luke's Med. Center, Chgo., 1973-88, sec. bd. trustees, 1976-92; exec. v.p. Orthopaedic Rsch. and Edn. Found., 1981-92, cons. Shedd Aquarium, Chgo., Cardinal Glennon Children's Hosp., St. Louis, Parkinson's Disease Soc. Am., Cook-Fort Worth (Tex.) Children's Med. Ctr., Univ. Chgo. Med. Ctr., Thoracic Surg. Found. Rsch., Edn., Chgo. Zool. Soc. (Brookfield Zoo), Dermatology Found., Commn. on Drug Safety, Joint Commn. for Accreditation of Healthcare Orgns., Ill. Math. and Sci. Acad., Great Books Found., Am. Assn. U. Programs in Hosp. Adminstrn., Am. Nurses Found., Am. Acad. Pediatrics, Sigma Theta Tau, Henry Ford Health Care Corp.; mem. faculty Inst. on Indsl. and Tech. Communications, Colo. State U., Fort Collins, 1970. Adv. bd. Internat. Inst. Edn.; trustee Citizens Information Service; mem. bd. Nat. Soc. Fund Raisers, 1974-77. Served to 1st lt. C.E., AUS, 1942-46, 50-52. Am. Soc. Hosp. Pub. Relations Dirs., AAAS, Nat. Assn. Sci. Writers, Am. Med. Writers Assn., Inst. Medicine Chgo., Sigma Delta Chi.

GARBERDING, LARRY GILBERT, utilities companies executive; b. Albert City, Iowa, Oct. 29, 1938; s. Gilbert D. and Lavern Marie (Specketer) G.; m. Elizabeth Ann Hankens, Aug. 20, 1961; children: Scott Richard, Kathryn Ann, Michael John. BS, Iowa State U., 1960. CPA, Nebr. Ptnr. Arthur Andersen & Co., Chgo., 1960-71; chief fin. officer Kans.-Nebr. Natural Gas Co., Inc., Hastings, Nebr., 1971-81; chief fin. officer Tenn. Gas Transmission, Houston, 1981-83, exec. v.p., 1983-87; pres. Tenn. Gas Mktg., Houston, 1987-88, NICOR Inc., Naperville, Ill., 1988-90; exec. v.p., chief fin. officer Detroit Edison Co., 1990—. With U.S. Army, 1961. Mem. AICPA. Republican. Lutheran. Office: The Detroit Edison Co 2000 2nd Ave Detroit MI 48226-1203

GARBO, BERNARD, publisher, fiduciary consultant; b. Witzenhausen an der Werra, West Germany, Apr. 26, 1956; 1 ward, Daniel Brandon Brewer. BA in Polit. Sci., U. Ill., 1978. Nat. trust examiner Office of Comptroller of Currency, U.S. Treasury, Chgo., 1978-83; sr. cons. Fiduciary Consultants, Chgo., 1984—; pub., sr. editor A.M. Pub., Inc., Trust Regulatory News, Chgo., 1992—. Pres. Ill. Found. for the Arts, Chgo., 1984-87; mem. Joseph Jefferson Awards Com., Chgo., 1989-94; pres. Child's Play Touring Theater, Chgo., 1988-91; mem. Com. for the Future of Ill., Springfield/chgo., 1991-92. Office: AM Pub Inc PO Box 1110 Chicago IL 60690-1110

GARCIA, EDWINA, state legislator; b. Dec. 8, 1944; m. Joe Garcia; 1 child. BA, U. Minn., 1979. City councilman City of Richfield (Minn.), 1986-90; state rep. Minn. Ho. Reps., Dist. 63B, 1990—; mem. higher edn. & redistricting coms., mem. health & human svc.-human svc. fin. divsn., housing & transp. & transit coms., Minn. Ho. Reps. Mem. LWV, VFW Aux. Home: 6732 18th Ave S Richfield MN 55423-2738 Office: Minn Ho of Reps State Capital Building Saint Paul MN 55155-1606*

GARCIA, JESUS G., state legislator; b. Apr. 12, 1956. BA, U. Ill., Chgo., 1980. Paralegal Legal Assistance Found., 1977-80; asst. dir. Little Village Neighborhood Housing Svc., 1980-84; dep. commr. Dept. of Water, 1984-86; alderman City of Chgo., 1986-92; mem. Ill. State Senate, 1993—; chmn. aviation com., mem. budget and govt. ops. com., mem. edn. com., mem. fin. com. Home: 4226 W 25th Pl Chicago IL 60623-3607*

GARCIA, JOHN GILBERT, state legislator; b. Houston, Nov. 1, 1928; s. Anastacio R. and Ruth (Reyne) G.; m. Dolores Elaine Hanthorne, 1950; children: Gaye (Garcia) Huss, Thomas C., John Gilbert, Jr., Bruce alle, Marcia Sue (Garcia) Fraver. H.s. grad., Gibonsburg, Ohio. Mem. Ohio Ho. of Reps., Columbus; chmn. Coun. of Neigborhood Assns., Inc., 1962—; mem. adv. com. Toledo Urban Renewal, 1962-73; pres. Northwest Ohio Rep. Hispanic Assembly, 1989—;mem. Ohio local Selective Svc. Bd. No. 76, 1991—. Chmn. East Toledo Family Ctr., Inc., 1971-85, East Toledo Against Drugs, 1987—, Citizen Participation Forum, 1991—. Named Outstanding Athlete, Toledo Times, 1950; recipient Citizenship award Sertoma Club of Toledo, 1973. Mem. Glass Workers Union Local 9 (chmn. COPE 1965), Eagles (trustee Arie 197 1991—), Masons, Scottish Rite, Shriners. Office: Ohio Ho of Reps State House Columbus OH 43215

GARCIA, WILMA THACKSTON, English language and literature educator; b. Detroit, Jan. 11, 1933; d. James Bruce Thackston and Gertrude (Epps) Thackston Molinar; div.; children: Lorraine Garcia-McGlynn, Sally, Catherine Garcia-Lindstrom, John, Martha Garcia-Carr, Joseph, Rachel Garcia-Bieszak, William. A in Liberal Arts, Oakland C.C., Bloomfield Hills, Mich., 1971; BA in English, Oakland U., 1973, MA in English, 1975; PhD in English and Folklore, Wayne State U., 1983. Cert. secondary tchr., Mich. From spl. instr. to assoc. prof. Oakland U., Rochester, Mich., 1976—; speaker in field. Author: Mothers and Others, 1985; contbr. articles to profl. jours. Recipient Meritorious Alumni award Oakland C.C., 1986, Headliner award Women of Wayne State U., 1987; honoree Wonder Woman award Pontiac Women's Survival Ctr., 1989. Mem. NOW, ACLU, Mich. Coll. English Assn. (past. pres., bd. dirs., Disting. Svc. award 1992), Coll. English Assn. (bd. dirs. 1991-94), Nat. Coun. Tchrs. English. Home: 656 W Hazelhurst Ferndale MI 48220 Office: Oakland U 510 Wilson Hall Rochester MI 48309-4401

GARCIAGODOY, JUANITA, Mexican studies educator; b. Mexico City, Mar. 10, 1952; d. Jorge and Marilyn (Wiese) G.; m. George Anthony Rabasa, Aug. 8, 1981. BA, Macalester Coll., 1974; M Theol. Studies, Harvard U., 1976; PhD, U. Minn., 1994. Tchr. Am. H.S., Mexico City, 1977-81, U. of Americas, Mexico City, 1977-78; tchr. women's studies U. Minn., Mpls., 1991, 93; instr. Spanish Macalester Coll., St. Paul, 1984—; cons. on translations into Spanish, Voice Plus, Actors Plus, White Bear Lake, 1993—; presenter, lectr. in field. Mem. MLA, L.Am. Studies Assn., N.Am. Catalan Studies. Home: 110 Bank St SE 303 Minneapolis MN 55414-3902

GARD, JOHN, state legislator; b. Milw., Aug. 3, 1963; m. Cathy Zeuske; 2 children. BA, U. Wis., La Crosse, 1986. Mem. from dist. 89 Wis. State Assembly, Madison, 1987—, mem. joint com. rev. adminstrv. rules, mem. tourism and recreation conf., mem. select com. welfare reform, chmn. assembly welfare reform com. Mem. KC, Ducks Unltd., Sportsmen's Club, Lions. Office: PO Box 1119 481 Aubin St Peshtigo WI 54157*

GARDANO, JOSEPH, landscaping company executive. Pres. Unico Landscaping Inc. Office: Unico Landscaping Inc 5115 S Hoyne Chicago IL 60647*

GARDAPHE, FRED LOUIS, English language educator; b. Chgo., Sept. 7, 1952; s. Fred William and Anna Julianna (Rotolo) G.; m. Katharine Teeter, June 12, 1976 (div. 1978); m. Susan Rose Stolder, Sept. 18, 1982; children: Frederico Carmen, Marianna Carmen. AA, Triton Coll., 1973; BS in Edn., U. Wis., 1976; MA, U. Chgo., 1982; PhD, U. Ill., 1993. Cert. tchr. secondary edn. Instr. Sun Prairie (Wis.) High Sch., 1976-77, Mason City (Iowa) High Sch., 1977-78; instr., counselor Prologue High Sch., Chgo., 1978-81; teaching asst. Italian dept. U. Chgo., 1981-82; prof. English Columbia Coll., Chgo., 1982—; freelance writer ednl. and comml. media, Chgo., 1980—. Auythor: Italian Signs, American Streets, 1996, Italian Signs and Dagoes Read, 1996; assoc. editor: Fra Noi Newspaper, Northlake, Ill., 1985—; co-editor: From the Margin: Writings in Italian Americana, 1991; editor: New Chicago Stories, 1990, Italian American Ways, 1989; co-editor: Voices in Italiana Americana Jour., 1990—, The Italian American Writer, 1995; contbr. articles, short stories and critical essays to publs. in field. Bd. dirs., pres. Prologue Learning Ctr., Chgo., 1989—; bd. dirs. Fra Noi Newspaper, 1991—, Ill. Ethnic Coalition, 1995—; v.p. Young Dems. of Proviso Twp., Melrose Park, Ill., 1970-71. Recipient Fondazione Giovanni Agnelli dissertation prize, 1994. Mem. MLA, Soc. for Study of Multi-Ethnic Lit. of U.S., Am. Assn. Italian Studies, Nat. Writers Union, Am. Italian Hist. Assn., Italian Cultural Ctr. Roman Catholic. Office: Columbia Coll Dept English 600 S Michigan Ave Chicago IL 60605-1996

GARDINER, JOHN ANDREW, political science educator; b. Niagara Falls, N.Y., July 10, 1937; s. William Cecil and Anne Charlotte (Hicks) G.; m. Jane Enstrom, Nov. 6, 1993; children: Margaret, Allison, Barrett. BA, Princeton U., 1959; MA, Yale U., 1962; LLB, Harvard U., 1963, PhD, 1966. Bar: Mass. 1963. Asst. prof. U. Wis., Madison, 1965-68; assoc. prof. SUNY, Stony Brook, 1968-69; chief rsch. planning Nat. Inst. Justice, Washington, 1969-71, dir. rsch. ops., 1971-73, asst. dir., 1973-74; prof. polit. sci. U. Ill., Chgo., 1974—, head dept. polit. sci., 1974-76, dir. office social sci. rsch., 1987—, acting assoc. dean Liberal Arts and Scis., 1991-92. Author: Fraud Control Game, 1984, Decisions for Sale, 1978, Politics of Corruption, 1970, Traffic and the Police 1969; contbr. articles to profl. jours. V.p. Ill. Citizens for Better Care, Chgo., 1988-90; rsch. dir. Chgo. Ethics Project, 1986-88. Rsch. fellow Am. Judicature Soc., 1985-86. Mem. Am. Polit. Sci. Assn., Law and Soc. Assn., Phi Beta Kappa. Office: U Ill Office Soc Sci Rsch M/C 307 1007 W Harrison St Chicago IL 60607-7136

GARDINER, ORMSIN SORNMOONPIN, mathematics educator, physicist, electrical engineer; b. Potaram, Thailand, Apr. 7, 1934; d. Charoen and Kasorn Sornmoonpin; m. Harry Walter Gardiner, Mar. 9, 1968; children: Alisa Jarin, Alan Verason, Alexina Tippa, Aldric Harin. BSc with honors, Chulalongkorn U., Bangkok, 1957; MSc, U. Manchester Inst. Sci. Tech., Eng., 1966. Tchr. Govt. Secondary Sch., Potaram, 1952-53; instr. Chulalongkorn U., Bangkok, 1957-62, sr. lectr., assoc. dean women's dorm, 1966-68; asst. engr. George Kent Co., Ltd., Luton, Eng., 1963; part-time lectr. Coll. St. Teresa, Winona, Minn., 1972-76; engr. EMD Assocs., Winona, 1978-81; instr., now asst. prof. math. Winona State U., 1983—. Contbg. author: Women in Thailand, 1991, The Asian American Experience, 1994. Mem. IEE, Math. Assn. Am. Home: Garvin Heights RR 5 Box 23 Winona MN 55987-9700 Office: Winona State U Dept Math 322 Gildemeister Hall Winona MN 55987

GARDNER, CARYN SUE, lawyer; b. Queens, N.Y., Mar. 9, 1960; d. Louis Arthur and Rhoda (Madonick) G. BA in Environ. Sci. and Urban Planning, SUNY, Binghamton, 1982; JD, DePaul U., 1985. Bar: Ill. 1985, U.S. Dist. Ct. (no. dist.) Ill. 1987, U.S. Ct. Appeals (7th cir.) 1987. Assoc. Rivkin, Radler, Dunne & Bayh, Chgo., 1985-86, Rudd & Kim, Schaumburg, Ill., 1986-87, Schain, Firsel & Burney, Schaumburg, 1987-92, Bickley & Bickley, Schaumburg, 1992-93, Bickley, Hart & Gardner, Schaumburg, 1993—; asst. instr. Harper Coll., Palatine, Ill., 1987-92, prof., 1992—; atty. Assn. Condominium, Townhouse and Homeowners Assns., Schaumburg, 1987, Assn. Condominium Edn., South Barrington, Ill., 1990—. Mem. ABA, Chgo. Bar Assn. Office: Bickley Hart & Gardner 117 E Schaumburg Rd Schaumburg IL 60194

GARDNER, COLLEEN, investment company executive; b. Albia, Iowa, Sept. 17, 1933. Legal asst. Don Payer Atty., Ames, Iowa, 1970-77; real estate agt. Century 21 Gray, Ames, 1977-82; investment exec. Piper Jaffray Inc., Ames, 1982—. Republican. Home: 3120 Grove Ave Ames IA 50010-4722 Office: Piper Jaffray Inc PO Box 72 402 Main St Ames IA 50010

GARDNER, EVELYN MAE, librarian; b. Omaha, June 24, 1944; d. Kenneth Alix and Flossie Eva (Lamphear) JOnes; m. Dave G. Gardner, July 20, 1972 (dec. 1983). BA in Edn., U. Nebr., 1985; MLS, U. Mo., 1986. Acquisitions/serials libr. Creighton U. Law Libr., Omaha, 1986-87, tech. svcs. libr., 1987-93, head tech. svcs., 1993—. Mem. ABWA (sec. Omaha chpt. 1974-75, v.p. 1975-76, pres. 1976-77, 86-87), Am. Assn. Law Librs., Nebr. Libr. Assn. Office: Creighton U Law Libr 2500 California Plz Omaha NE 68178-0340

GARDNER, GARY EDWARD, lawyer; b. Windsor, Ont., Can., Oct. 21, 1952; s. Edward Thomas and Antonionette Ursla (Urbanski) G.; m. Sheila Mary Hand, Oct. 5, 1984. BA, Mich. State U., 1975; JD, U. Detroit, 1981. Mktg. officer Ford Motor Co. Australia, Melbourne, 1975-77; analyst Ford Motor Co., Dearborn, Mich., 1977-79; asst. to gen. counsel Ford Motor Co. Australia, Melbourne, 1979-80; assoc. James R. Shively, P.C., Detroit, 1980-82; instr. law Detroit Coll. of Bus., Dearborn, Mich., 1982-84; ptnr. Shively, McCloskey, Corriveau & Gardner, Mich., 1984-86; pvt. practice Dearborn, 1986-90; ptnr. Gardner & Doyle, 1990-94, Gary Edward Gardner, P.C., Dearborn, Mich., 1995—; atty. pvt. practice, 1995—. Candidate Judge of Ct. of Appeals S.E. Mich., 1988; candidate Judge 19th Dist. Ct., 1992, 94. Mem. ABA, Mich. Bar Assn. (com. domestic violence 1993-96), Dearborn Bar Assn. (pres. 1996—), Fairlane Club, Detroit Coll. Rugby Club, Kiwanis Club Dearborn. Republican. Roman Catholic. Home: 246 River Ln Dearborn MI 48124-1047 Office: 25121 Ford Rd Dearborn MI 48128-1058

GARDNER, HAROLD WAYNE, research biochemist; b. Carlisle, Pa., June 19, 1935; s. Edward Jacob and Mildred Isabel (Brougher) G.; m. Arlene Patricia Howsley, Dec. 24, 1960 (div. 1975); children: Scott Edward, Brooke Maureen, Kelly Micheen, Michael Paul; m. Cheryl D. Pauli, Feb. 12, 1981; 1 child, Bryce Andrew. BS, Pa. State U., 1957, MS, 1963, PhD, 1965. Assoc. biochemist Pineapple Rsch. Inst., Honolulu, 1965-66; postdoctoral fellow UCLA, 1966-67; rsch. chemist Nat. Ctr. Agrl. Utilization Rsch., USDA, Peoria, Ill., 1967—. Assoc. editor Lipids; contbr. more than 80 articles to profl. jours., chpts. to books. Prairie ecologist Cen. Ill. Nature Conservancy. Lt. (j.g.) USNR, 1958-61. Recipient classic citation Inst. for Sci. Info., 1989. Mem. Am. Soc. Biochemistry and Molecular Biology, Am. Chem. Soc., Am. Soc. Plant Physiologists, Am. Oil Chemists Soc., Oxygen Radical Soc. Home: RR 1 Box 168A Brimfield IL 61517-9801 Office: Nat Ctr Agrl Util Rsch Peoria IL 61604

GARDNER, HOWARD GARRY, pediatrician, educator; b. Gary, Ind., Oct. 5, 1943; s. Oscar and Anita (Arenson) G.; m. Judith (Green), June 21, 1986; children: Molly, Joseph. BA, Ind. U., 1965, MD, 1968. Intern, then resident St. Louis U., 1969-73; pvt. practice Hinsdale (Ill.) Pediatrics, 1973-79, DuPage Pediatrics, Darien, Ill., 1979—; attending staff Hinsdale Hosp., 1973—, Loyola U. Med. Ctr., Maywood, Ill., 1973—; courtesy staff Childrens Meml. Hosp., Chgo., 1988—; clin. prof. Dept. Pediatrics Loyola U. Sch. of Medicine, Maywood, 1983—; past-chmn. Dept. of Pediatrics Hinsdale Hosp., 1983-85; med. adv. bd. YMCA of the USA, Chgo., 1989—. Editorial adv. bd. Pediatric News, 1990—; contbr. articles to profl. jours. Co-chmn. med. adv. bd. DuPage Easter Seal Ctr., Villa Park, Ill.; bd. dirs. Loyola Ronald McDonald House; co-founder, past pres. Ill. Child Passenger Safety Assn.; pediatric program dir. Des Plaines Valley Health Ctr., Argo, Ill.; mem. med. adv. bd. Pathways Awareness Found.; officer, steering com. DuPage Interagy. Coun. on Early Intervention. Lt. USN, 1969-71. Recipient Outstanding Clin. Tchr. award Loyola Med. Sch., 1978, Tchr. of Yr. Hinsdale Hosp. Family Practice Residency, 1981, Chgo. Caring Physician's award Met. Chgo. Health Care Coun., 1987, Buckle Up Am.! award Ill. Coalition for Safety Belt Use, 1991, Parent and Child Edn. Soc. 20th Anniversary Achievement award, 1992. Fellow Am. Acad. Pediat. (past pres. Ill. chpt., mem. nat. nominating com., Pisani Pediatrician of Yr. award 1986); mem. Chgo. Pediat. Soc. (past pres., Archibald Hoyne Pediatrician of Yr. 1994), Ill. Maternal and Child Health Coalition (bd. dirs.). Democrat. Jewish. Office: DuPage Pediatrics 1306 Plainfield Rd Darien IL 60561-5038

GARDNER, JOLENE S., resource center director; b. Emmetsburg, Iowa, Sept. 16, 1944; d. Merlyn Ordean and Pearle Sylvania (Jacobson) Larson; m. George Gardner, Feb. 23, 1975 (div. Jan. 1985). BS, Northwestern U., 1966; MA, Loyola/Mundelein U., 1991; PhD, Union Grad. Inst., 1995. Cert. Reiki master/tchr.; cert. focusing trainer. Pres. Larson & Assocs., Chgo., 1966-68; singer, pianist Pat O Brien's, New Orleans, 1967; primary and secondary sch. tchr. Chgo. Pub. Schs., 1968; traffic mgr. Post Keyes Gardner, 1969-70; account asst. Campbell-Mithun, 1970-71; buyer Montgomery Ward, 1971-76; sr. v.p. Rubloff, Inc., 1976-87; pres. Jody Gardner and Assocs., 1987-95; dir. Women's Place Resource Ctr., 1994-95; bd. dirs. Limina, Oak Park, Ill. Mem. Assn. for Humanistic Psychology, Assn. for the Study of Dreams, Mandala Assn., Univ. Club. Home: 340 Barry St Chicago IL 60657

GARDNER, JOSEPH HENRY, engineer; b. Princeton, Ind., Nov. 19, 1935; s. Joseph Franklin and Lillie Ellen (Wolfe) G.; m. Judith Lee Casebier, June 24, 1956; children: Brett Alan, Gary Joseph. AS in Mech. Engring., U. Evansville, 1972, BBA, 1975, AS in Acctg., 1976, A in Elect. Engring., 1980, BS in Engring. Mgmt., 1982, BS in Indsl. Engring., 1986. Registered profl. engr., Ind. Design engr. Hansen Mfg. Co., Inc., Princeton, Ind., 1962-68, project engr., 1968-73, asst. chief engring., 1973-87, mgr. design engring., 1987—. Treas. Princeton Community High Sch. Band Boosters, 1981-82. Mem. IEEE, NSPE, ASME (sec.-treas. local chpt. 1988-89), Am. Soc. Quality Control (cert. reliability engr., cert. quality engr.), Soc. Mfg. Engrs. (cert., chmn. attendance 1984-85). Republican. Mem. Ch. of Nazarene. Home: RR 4 Box 350 Princeton IN 47670-9412 Office: Hansen Mfg Co Inc 901 S 1st St Princeton IN 47670-2369

GARDNER, RANDALL, state legislator, realtor; b. Bowling Green, Ohio, Aug. 20, 1958; s. Dallas E. and Velma (Brownson) G.; m. Sandra Kay Ford; children: Brooks, Christine, Austin. BS, Bowling Green State U., 1981, MA, 1987. Journalist Daily Sentinel-Tribune, Bowling Green, 1981-86; tchr. Otsego (Ohio) Local Schs., 1981-86; realtor, Bowling Green; mem. Ohio Ho. of Reps., Columbus, 1985—, now asst. minority whip. Pres. Wood County Young Reps. Club, 1976-80; co-chmn. 5th Dist. Reagan for Pres. Com., 1980; dist. del. Rep. Nat. Conv., 1980, 84; vice chmn. Wood County Bd. Elections, 1982-85; exec. com. Wood County Rep. Com., 1982-86. Recipient Watchdog of Treasury award; Jennings scholar. Mem. Ohio Assn. Election Ofcls., Ohio Edn. Assn., Wood County Hist. Soc., Wood County Farm Bur., Legis. Exch. Coun., Sons Am. Legion, Omicron Delta Kappa. Home: 14900 Mitchell Rd Bowling Green OH 43402-8900*

GARDNER, ROBERT JOSEPH, general and thoracic surgeon; b. Barrington, Ill., Dec. 26, 1924; s. Anthony Joseph and Elizabeth Caroline (Jurs) G.; m. Mary Rickley, June 26, 1948; children: Susan Elizabeth, Nancy Gardner Hargrave, Julie Gardner Withrow. Student, Ill. Inst. Tech., Chgo., 1942-44; BS, Wash. State U., 1947; MD, Northwestern U., Chgo., 1951. Intern Cook County Hosp., Chgo., 1951-52; pvt. gen. med. practice Menomonie (Wis.) Clinic, 1952-58; surg. resident Northwestern U. Hosps., Chgo., 1958-62; staff surgeon Fairmont (W.Va.) Clinic, 1962-68; fellow thoracic surgery W.Va. Med. Ctr., Morgantown, 1968-69, instr. surgery, 1969-70, asst. prof. surgery, 1970-72, assoc. prof. surgery, 1972-75, prof. surgery, 1975-78; staff surgeon St. Joseph's Community Hosp., West Bend, Wis., 1978-95; ret.; retired, 1995. Contbr. articles to profl. jours., chpts. to books. Ensign, USNR, 1944-46; PTO. W.Va. Heart Assn. grantee, 1968-73. Fellow ACS; mem. AMA, Wis. Med. Soc., Wis. Surg. Soc., Cen. Surg. Assn., Soc. Thoracic Surgeons, Am. Assn. Thoracic Surgeons. Home: 844 W Badger Ln West Bend WI 53095-4502

GARDNER, ROBERT MEADE, building contractor; b. Portsmouth, Ohio, Aug. 12, 1927; s. David Edward and Mary Petrea (Gableman) G.; m. Ruth Sieker, Aug. 8, 1952; children: Leslie, Robert Jr., Stephen, Lorianne. BA, Ohio Wesleyan U., 1951. Engr. J.A. Jones, Charlotte, N.C., 1944; v.p. D.E. Gardner Co., Columbus, Ohio, 1951-55; pres. The Gardner Co., Columbus, Ohio, 1955-92, chmn., 1993—; Dir. Builders Exchange, Columbus, 1959-60; officer Young Pres.' Orgn. Cen. Ohio, 1969-79. Mem. Athletic Bd. Ohio Wesleyan U., Del., 1965—, mem. Alumni Bd., 1969—; mem. Columbus Bldg. Code Commn., 1974, World Pres. Orgn., Columbus, 1980—; officer Upper Arlington (Ohio) Booster Assn., 1974; pres. Vision Ctr. Ctrl. Ohio, Columbus, 1981, Ohio Valley Tennis Assn., 1977-78; bd. dirs. Jazz Arts Group, Columbus, 1989-95, First Cmty. Village, 1988—. Named to Athletic Hall of Fame Ohio Wesleyan U.; recipient Disting. award Phi Gamma Delta, Medick award, Vision Ctr. Cen. Ohio, Gillespie award Ohio Valley Tennis Assn. Mem. World Pres. Orgn. (chpt. chmn. 1996), Scioto Country Club (bd. dirs.), Athletic Club, Racquet Club, Players Club. Home: 4500 Dublin Rd Columbus OH 43221-5006 Office: 1350 W 5th Ave Columbus OH 43212

GARDNER, RUSSELL ROOSEVELT, small business owner; b. Denver, Aug. 10, 1929; s. Thor Marthens and Margaret (Roosevelt) G.; m. Patricia Purviance, June 20, 1953 (div. 1976); children: Susan, Jeffrey, David; m. Barbara Jean Robinson, Sept. 20, 1980. BA in History, Dartmouth Coll., 1951. Sales rep. Elgin (Ill.) Nat. Watch Co., 1951-63; regional mgr. Bulova Watch Co., N.Y.C., 1963-74; regional v.p. Gordon B. Miller Co., Cin., 1974-76; founder, pres., CEO Gardner & Geldmacher, Inc., Schaumburg, Ill., 1976—. Pres. Arlington Heights (Ill.) Youth Athletic Assn., 1974. Home: 326 Indian Point Barrington IL 60010 Office: Gardner & Geldmacher Inc 2207 N Hammond Dr Schaumburg IL 60173

GARDNER, THOMAS JOSEPH, vocational educator; b. Mpls., Dec. 5, 1957; s. Herman Harold and Emily Josephine (Konicek) G.; m. Deloris Ruby Ames, Oct. 28, 1989; children: Jodi, Domine, Desirae, Virginia, Stephen. Degree in auto tech., Bemidji Tech., 1985; BS in Vocat. Edn. magna cum laude, Bemidji State U., 1994. Cert. vocat. tchr., Minn. Svc. tech. Maneches Auto, Fosston, Minn., 1982-87; shop mgr. Stinars Nursery, Bagley, Minn., 1987-92; automotive educator ISD # 2022, Bemidji, Minn., 1992—; indsl. tech. educator ISD # 31, Bemidji, 1994—. Pres. Clearwater County 4-H, Minn., 1972-76; sch. bd. dir. ISD # 162, Bagley, 1992—; dir. Pine to Prairie Governing Bd., Red Lake Falls, Minn., 1993—, cooperative bd., 1993-94. Staff sgt. U.S. Army, 1976-82. Decorated Commendation medal, Aircrew badge, Air assault badge. Mem. Am. Legion, Minn. Citizens Concerned for Life (treas. 1982—). Republican. Lutheran.

GARFIELD, JOAN BARBARA, statistics educator; b. Milw., May 4, 1950; d. Sol. L. and Amy L. (Nusbaum) G.; m. Michael G. Luxenberg, Aug. 17, 1980; children: Harlan Ross and Rebecca Ellen (twins). Student, U. Chgo., 1968; BS, U. Wis., 1972; MA, U. Minn., 1978, PhD, 1981. Assoc. prof. ednl. psychology Coll. Edn., U. Minn., Mpls., 1981—, coord. rsch. and evaluation The Gen. Coll., 1984-87. Mem. Am. Ednl. Rsch. Assn., Math. Assn. Am., Nat. Coun. Tchrs. of Math., Internat. Assn. for Statis. Edn., Am. Statis. Assn., Internat. Study Group on Learning Probability and Stats. (sec. 1987-95). Jewish. Office: U Minn Dept Edn Psychology 332 Burton Hall Minneapolis MN 55455

GARFIELD, NANCY ELLEN, marketing and advertising professional; b. Cin., Sept. 18, 1954; d. M. Robert and Pegge (Gerber) G. BA in Econs., Rollins Coll., 1976; MBA, Xavier U., 1980. Mktg. svcs. specialist Am. Standard, Inc., Cin., 1977-81; mktg. specialist F.H. Lawson Co., Cin., 1982-83; dir. mktg. Talsol Corp./Mar-Hyde subs. RPM Inc., Cin., 1983-88; mktg. and advt. cons. Cin., 1988—. Mgmt. advisor Cin. Jr. Achievement, 1978-81; bd. dirs. Cin. sect. mem. Nat. Clun. Jewish Women, 1992—, v.p. cmty. svc. 1993-95, pres. 1995-96; mem. Cin. Civic Confedn., 1991—; mem. recruitment com. Big Bros./Big Sisters Assn. Cin., 1992—. Mem. Losantiville C. of C. (ltd. bd. dirs. 1986-89, pres. 1989), Cin. Indsl. Advertisers, Chi Omega.

GARFIELD, PHYLLIS H., international program administrator, educational consultant; b. Columbus, Nebr., Aug. 21, 1950; d. Carl and Wilma (Phillips) Rafferty; m. Alan J. Garfield, Sept. 2, 1979; children: Eliot, Margaret, Carolan. AA, Platt C.C., Columbus, Nebr., 1972; BA, Midland Luth. Coll., Fremont, Nebr., 1974; student, Phillips U., Marburg, Germany, 1973-74; postgrad., Creighton U., 1975-79. Asst. to dean of students Marycrest Coll., Davenport, Iowa, 1980-83; cons. and v.p. Digigraphic Systems, Inc., Davenport, 1985—; internat. travel advisor Digigraphic Systems, Inc., Meenaleck, Ireland, 1992—; internat. study advisor Teikyo Marycrest U., Davenport, 1981—. Pres. Temple Emanuel Sisterhood, Davenport, 1993—. Fulbright fellow, Marburg, 1973-74. Home: 34 Oak Ln Davenport IA 52803-3124 Address: Meenaleck Letterkenny, County Donegal Ireland

GARFINKLE, DAVID, physics educator; b. N.Y.C., Apr. 1, 1958; s. Norton and Vivienne (Feigenbaum) G.; m. Kimberly L. Eddy, Aug. 1995. BA, Princeton U., 1980; PhD, U. Chgo., 1985; postgrad., Washington U., St. Louis, 1985-87, U. Fla., Gainesville, 1987-89, U. Calif., Santa Barbara, 1989-91. Asst. prof. physics Oakland U., Rochester, Mich., 1991-95, assoc. prof., 1996—. Contbr. articles to profl. jours. Office: Oakland U Dept Physics Rochester MI 48309

GARG, UMESH, physicist, educator; b. Bikaner, Rajasthan, India, Mar. 29, 1953; came to U.S., 1974; s. Shiv Nandan and Shakuntala (Mittal) G.; m. Anita Padhye, Dec. 28, 1980; children: Noopur Neha, Neehar Nimesh. BS, Birla Inst. Tech. and Sci., Pilani, India, 1972, MS, 1974; MA, SUNY, Stony Brook, 1975, PhD, 1978. Teaching asst. SUNY, Stony Brook, 1974-75, rsch. asst., 1975-78; rsch. assoc. Tex. A&M U., College Station, 1978-82; asst. prof. U. Notre Dame, Ind., 1982-87, assoc. prof., 1987-93; prof. U. Notre Dame (Ind.), 1994—; cons. Tex. A&M U., 1982-83; vis. scientist Bhabha Atomic Rsch. Ctr., Bombay, India, 1985-87; vis. prof. Vrije U., Amsterdam, 1988-89; chmn. nominating com. nat. Superconducting Cyclotron Lab. Users' Group, E. Lansing, Mich., 1984. Editor: Symposium of Northeastern Accelerator Personnel, 1987. Vice pres. India Assn. Tex. A&M, College Station, 1981. Mem. Am. Phys. Soc., Am. Chem. Soc. (program com. divsn. nuclear physics), Indian Physics Assn. (pres. U.S. chpt. 1986, chmn. nominating com. 1992—), Sigma Xi. Hindu. Office: Univ Notre Dame Physics Dept Notre Dame IN 46556

GARMAN, TERESA AGNES, state legislator; b. Ft. Dodge, Iowa, Aug. 29, 1937; d. John Clement and Barbara Marie (Korsa) Lennon; m. Merle A. Garman, Aug. 5, 1961; children: Laura Ann Garman Hansen, Rachel Irene Garman Coder, Robert Sylvester, Sarah Teresa Garman Powers. Grad. high sch., Ft. Dodge. With employee relations dept. 3M Co., Ames, Iowa, 1974-86; mem. Iowa Ho. of Reps., Des Moines, 1986—. Asst. majority leader, mem. platform com., del. Rep. Nat. Conv., 1988, del., mem. platform com., 1992; mem. Iowa Rep. Ctrl. Com. Mem. Rep. Farm Policy Coun., Story County Rep. Women, Story County Pork Prodrs., Farm Bur., Story City C. of C., Nev. C. of C. Roman Catholic. Home: RR 2 Ames IA 50010-9802 Office: State Capitol Des Moines IA 50319*

GARN, GLENN, engineering manager; b. Manton, Mich., Feb. 24, 1944. AS, R.E.T.S., Flint, Mich., 1971. Prodn. line worker GM, Flint, 1967-68; from engr. to engring. mgr. Owosso (Mich.) Corp., 1968—. Sgt. U.S. Army, 1965-67. Republican. Lutheran. Office: Owosso Co 201 S Delaney Rd Owosso MI 48867-9100

GARNER, JIM D., state legislator, lawyer; b. Coffeyville, Kans., June 14, 1963; s. Wayne W. and Carol L. (Adey) G. AA with honors, Coffeyville C.C., 1983; BA in History with distinction, U. Kans., 1985, JD, 1988. Bar: Kans. 1988. Jud. clk. for Dale E. Saffels U.S. Dist. Judge, Kans., 1988-90; atty. Hall, Levy, Lively, DeVore, Belot and Bell, Coffeyville, 1990-92; pvt. practice Coffeyville, 1992—; mem. Kans. Ho. of Reps., 1991—; ranking Dem. on judiciary com.; mem. house rules com., select com. on juvenile justice; mem. Coun. on the Future of Post Secondary Edn.; served on select com. investigating investment practices Kans. Pub. Employees Retirement Sys.; mem. joint com. on congl. legis. and jud. reapportionment; mem. criminal law adv. com. Kans. Jud. Coun.; mem. assembly on fed. issues Nat. Conf. of State Legislatures; mem. Program for Emerging Polit. Leaders, Darden Sch. of Bus., U. Va., 1994, Bowhay Inst. for Legis. Leadership Devel., Coun. of State Govts., U. Wis., 1995. Active cmty. adv. com. Youth and Bus. Tng. Program; bd. dirs. Hospice Care Inc., Coffeyville; mem. task force Coffeyville C.C. Honors Program; leadership Coffeyville Class of 1995. Mem. Kans. Bar Assn., Order of Coif, Phi Alpha Theta, Phi Kappa Phi, Coffeyville Lions Club. Home: 601 E 12th St Coffeyville KS 67337-6615 Office: PO Box 538 121 W 8th St Coffeyville KS 67337-0538

GARNETT, JESS, state legislator. Home: PO Box 801 West Plains MO 65775-0801*

GARRETSON, JAMES DEHART, secondary education educator; b. Rushville, Ind., Feb. 20, 1942; s. Donald Dehart and Marjorie Naomi (Mattox) G. BSEd, Ball State Tchrs. Coll., 1964; MA, Ball State U., 1969. Cert. secondary tchr., Ind. Social studies tchr. Carmel (Ind.) H.S., 1964—, social studies dept. chmn., 1969—; nat. chain account coord. Heartland Industries, Carmel, 1985-90; mem. Ctr. for Study of the Presidency, 1984-95, Carmel Clay Faculty Coun., 1964-73; speaker in field. Author: (textbook) State and Local Government in Indiana, 1985, 89, 93; author: (novel) The Deadwood Conspiracy, 1996; contbr. articles to profl. publs. City councilman, Carmel, 1975-87; mem. Young Reps. of Ind., 1974; v.p. bd. trustees Ball State U., Muncie, Ind., 1977-90. Recipient Sagamore of the Wabash award Govt. Otis Bowen, Indpls., 1980, Gov. Robert Orr, 1989; named Outstanding Secondary Tchr. of Yr., Carmel Clay Edn. Found., 1977; named Young Rep. of Yr., Ind., 1974. Mem. Ball State Alumni Assn. (Beany award 1983). Home: 55 York Dr Carmel IN 46032

GARRETT, DAVID L., manufacturing company executive; b. Strawn, Kans., June 16, 1938; s. Lester Dale and Emma (Dornes) G.; children: Lisa, Denise, Michelle, Angela. Mem. R&D devel. staff Bettcher Industries, Birmingham, Ohio, 1970-81; plant mgr. J.A. Compressor, Grove, Okla., 1981-87; mgr. C&C dept. Fay Tool & Die, Orlando, Fla., 1987-91; gen. foreman Ellsworth (Kans.) Mfg., 1991-93; owner Garrett Machine, Fairbury, Nebr., 1993—. Patentee cut resistant glove for meat cutters. Pres. PTO, Norwalk, Ohio. Recipient Suggestion award Ford Motor Co., 1966. Lutheran. Home: 910 9th St Fairbury NE 68352-2024 Address: 1018 W Elm St #A Salina KS 67401-2516

GARRETT, EUGENE AMUSSEN, retired marketing professional; b. Santa Monica, Calif., Aug. 15, 1920; s. Eugene Claude and Emma Mae (Amussen) G.; m. Mary Ann Norstad, Jan. 31, 1948; Robert Eugene, Chrisanne Norstad, Stephen Norstad, Eugene Norstad, Suzanne Norstad Wheatland. AA, Santa Monica (Calif.) Coll., 1942; student, Occidental Coll., 1946-47. Corp. mktg. mgr. Liquid Carbonic Corp., Chgo., 1948-87. Author: (book) A Postal History of the Japanese Occupation of the Philippines, 1991 (7 gold medals 1991); editor philatelic jours., 1986—; author numerous articles, studies, 1976—. With U.S. mil., WWII. Mem. Internat.Philippine Philatelic Soc. (pres. 1985—), U.S. Possessions Philatelic Soc. (pres. 1994—), Internat. Soc. for Japanese Philately (bd. dirs. 1988—). Home: 446 Stratford Ave Elmhurst IL 60126-4123 Office: Liquid Carbonic Industries 810 Jorie Blvd Oak Brook IL 60521-2216

GARRETT, MARILYN RUTH, nurse; b. Columbia, Mo., Mar. 28, 1957; d. Charles Filmore and Mable Ruth (Rice) Pasley; m. Donald Burce Garrett, June 9, 1983 (div. Mar. 1994); children: Patrick Bryan, Christopher Ryan. ADN, Cen. Meth. Coll., 1985. Cert. psychiat. and mental health nurse. Staff nurse Fulton (Mo.) State Hosp., 1985, clin. nursing supr., 1989-91, overall nursing supr., 1991-92, nurse educator, nursing edn. and staff devel., 1992-94, psychosocial rehab. tng. specialist, 1994—; instr. CPR, 1987—; aggressive mgmt. tng. instr., 1990—; chair nurse recruitment and retention com., Mo., 1991-93. Mem. vol. task force team Callaway County unit Am. Cancer Soc.; mem. panel Smoking Cessation Group for County Health Svcs., 1993. Named Employee of the Month State of Mo., Dept. Mental Health, 1991. Home: 1015 Bluff St Fulton MO 65251-2320 Office: Fulton State Hosp 600 E 5th St Fulton MO 65251-1753

GARRETT, NORMAN ANTHONY, business education educator; b. San Diego, Aug. 30, 1947; m. Margaret Ann Florence, Dec. 11, 1970; children: Rachel, Ethan, Joshua, Aaron, Emily. BA, Brigham Young U., 1971; MA, Ariz. State U., 1975, EdD, 1986. High sch. tchr. Tolleson (Ariz.) Union High Sch., 1973-80; systems engr. Electronic Data Systems, Phoenix, 1980-83; acad. computing specialist Ariz. State U., Tempe, 1983-84; assoc. dir. Ariz. State U. Computer Inst., Tempe, 1984-86; instr. South Mountain Community Coll., Phoenix, 1986-89, assoc dean instrn., 1989-90; assoc. prof. bus. edn./ adminstrv. info. systems Eastern Ill. U., Charleston, 1990-95, prof., 1995—. Author: Great Bread Machine Recipes, 1992, Quick and Delicious Bread Machine Recipes, 1993, Advanced Microcomputer Applications, 1994, Favorite Bread Machine Recipes, 1994; contbr. numerous articlesto profl. jours. 1st lt. USAF, 1972-73. Mem. Nat. Bus. Edn. Assn., Office Systems Rsch. Assn., Ill. Bus. Edn. Assn., Internat. Soc. Tech. in Edn., Internat. Assn. for Computer Info. Systems. Office: Ea Ill U Bus Edn and Adminstrv Info Systems Charleston IL 61920

GARRETT, PAUL WILLIAM, retired management executive; b. Harrisville, W.Va., Oct. 16, 1921; s. Grover C. and Sarah Ann (Six) G.; m. Mary Evelyn, Mar. 26, 1943; children: Robert Eugene, David Roger, Patricia Ann. AS, Salem Tech. Sch., 1948. Pres. Garrett Cons. Inc., Columbiana, Ohio, 1965-87, ret., 1987. Patentee in field. Mem. local sch. bd.; vol. Santa local children's hosp.; vol. local church. With U.S. Army, 1943-44. Mem. Masons. Home: 358 Kingwood Dr Columbiana OH 44408-1106

GARRICK, GEORGE R., marketing professional; b. Cleve., July 17, 1952; s. Richard and Lin Garrick; m. Laine Garrick, Oct. 26, 1991. BS in Engring., Purdue U., 1975, BS in Math., 1976, MS in Mgmt., 1976. V.p. mktg. Mgmt. Sci. Assocs., Chgo., 1976-81; v.p. mktg. Info. Resources, Inc., Chgo., 1981-83, sr. v.p. mktg., 1984-85, exec. v.p. region mgr., 1986-88, pres., CPG div., 1989-91, pres. European info. svcs., 1992—. Office: Information Resources 150 N Clinton St Chicago IL 60661-1402

GARRIER, JO ANN ROSS, college program administrator; b. Cedar Rapids, Iowa, Sept. 15, 1960; d. James Robert and Mildred Arlene (Platner) Ross; m. Randall Lee Garrier, July 23, 1983. BS, Iowa State U., 1982; MS, Kans. State U., 1991. Sales assoc. Neiman-Marcus, Dallas, 1982-83; bookkeeper Western Kans. Found., Garden City, 1983-89; grant coord. Garden City Community Coll., 1989—. Bd. dirs. Finney County United Way, Garden City, 1991—, Family Crisis Svcs., Garden City, 1986—; grant proposal writer March of Dimes, Garden City, 1990-92. Mem. AAUW, Women Work, Phi Upsilon Omicron, Kappa Omicron Nu. Office: Garden City CC 801 Campus Dr Garden City KS 67846-6333

GARRIGAN, KRISTINE OTTESEN, English literature educator; b. Alameda, Calif., Nov. 16, 1939; d. Harold and Leah Martha (Osborne) Ottesen; m. Richard Thomas Garrigan, Dec. 26, 1962; 1 child, Michael Osborne. Student, Stanford U., 1956-58; BA with highest honors, Denison U., 1960; MA, Ohio State U., 1964; PhD, U. Wis., 1971. Instr. U. Wis. Extension, Madison, 1968-78; vis. asst. prof. Denison U., Granville, Ohio, 1978-79; asst. prof. English DePaul U., Chgo., 1981-84, assoc. prof., 1984-90, prof., 1990—. Author: Ruskin on Architecture, 1973, Victorian Art Reproductions, 1991; editor: Victorian Scandals, 1992; contbr. articles and revs. to profl. jours. Mem. MLA, Midwest Victorian Studies Assn. (exec. sec. 1984-88, exec. bd. 1995—), Historians Brit. Art, Assn. Lit. Scholars & Critics, Virginia Woolf Soc., Rsch. Soc. for Victorian Periodicals, Ruskin

Assn., African Lit. Assn. Home: 920 Romona Rd Wilmette IL 60091-1222 Office: DePaul U Dept English 802 W Belden Ave Chicago IL 60614-3214

GARRIGAN, WILLIAM HENRY, III, firefighter, paramedic; b. Evergreen Park, Ill., Apr. 5, 1954; s. William Henry Jr. and Mary Jane (O'Connell) G.; m. Melissa Ann Vaughan, Aug. 2, 1980; children: William, Vaughan. AA, Coll. of DuPage, Glen Ellyn, Ill., 1975; grad. paramedic tng., Loyola Med. Ctr., Maywood, Ill., 1976; student, No. Ill. U., 1976-77; BS, So. Ill. U., 1987. Cert. instr. CPR, Am. Heart Assn.; adv. cert. fire fighter III; cert. fire apparatus engr.; cert. fire svc. instr. I. Firefighter/paramedic North Palos (Ill.) Fire Dept., 1977-78; firefighter/paramedic Oak Brook (Ill.) Fire Dept., 1979—, asst. coord. emergency med. svcs., 1983-87, coord. emergency med. svcs., 1987—; mem. edn. com. for paramedic edn. Village of Downers Grove, Ill., 1990—; mem. safety com. Village of Oak Brook, 1987—; mem. ambulance report com. Good Samaritan Hosp., Downers Grove, 1988—. ACLs provider Heart Assn. South Cook County, Ill., 1986—; active Quigley South High Sch. Alumni Assn., 1972—. Recipient acknowledgement of contbn. Dept. Pub. Health, State of Ill., 1987, recognition and appreciation of dedication and svc. Village of Oak Brook, 1989. Mem. Nat. Assn. EMTs, Ill. Profl. Firefighters Assn., North Palos Firemen's Assn. (pres. 1982-84, Outstanding Svc. award 1988), Profl. Assn. Specialty Divers, Dive Rescue Inc. Internat., Phi Kappa Sigma Alumni Assn. Republican. Roman Catholic. Office: Oak Brook Fire Dept 1212 Oak Brook Rd Oak Brook IL 60521-2203

GARRIONE, ROBERT MICHAEL, clergy member; b. Salina, Kans., Feb. 24, 1950; s. Alfonso Jacob and Josephine Patricia (Mason) G. B in Humanities, Holy Apostles Coll. Sem., Cromwell, Conn., 1985; BTh, Pontifical U. St. Thomas, Rome, 1987-88; MDiv, St. Joseph Seminary, Yonkers, N.Y., 1985-89; postgrad., Am. Isnt. Holistic Theology, Birmingham, Ala., 1994—. Assoc. pastor Our Lady of Guadalupe Parish, Holbrook, Ariz., 1989-91, St. Mary of The Angels Parish, Pinetop, Ariz., 1991; pastor St. Bonaventure Parish, Thoreau, N.Mex., 1991-93, St. Thomas Parish, Garden City, Kans., 1995—. Mem. Charles F. Menninger Soc. Episcopalian. Office: St Thomas Parish 710 N Main Garden City KS 67846

GARRISON, CHARLES EUGENE, automotive executive; b. New London, Conn., Apr. 9, 1943; s. Charles Westel and Thelma Rae (Coleman) G.; m. Trudy Elisabeth Thorburn, Aug. 26, 1967 (div.); children: Matthew Charles, Mark Andrew; m. Beverley Halcyone Watkins, Apr. 19, 1991. BA, Mich. State U., 1965, MBA, 1966. Supr. service garage and motor pool Mich. State U., East Lansing, 1972, mgr. automotive services dept., 1972—; co-owner The Latest Scoop, 1980—; fleet mgmt. instr. various agys., 1985—; cons. in field, 1985—. Elder Holt Presbyn. Ch., 1975-77, mem. various coms., 1977-85; divsn. coord. United Way, 1972-73; mem. East Lansing Mass Transit com., 1972-75; judge Ingham County Fair, 1977-80. Capt. USAF, 1967-72. Recipient Vol. Achievement award United Way, 1984, 85, Cost Reduction Incentive award Nat. Assn. Coll. and Univ. Bus. Officers, Gov. Mich. Energy Mgmt. award, 1988, Spl. Energy Innovation award U.S. Dept. of Energy, 1990. Mem. Nat. Assn. Fleet Adminstrs., Big Ten Transp. Assn., U. Club. Mich. State U. (bd. dirs., pres. 1986-94), Kiwanis (Internat. Diamond Single Svc. award 1982, Mich. dist. Disting. Pres. award 1982, Outstanding Bull. Editor 1983, sec. 1995—). Lodge: Kiwanis (Internat. Diamond Single Service award 1982, Mich. dist. Disting. Pres. award 1982, Outstanding Bulletin Editor 1983). Home: 3730 Lott Ave Holt MI 48842-9414 Office: Mich State U Automotive Svcs Stadium Rd East Lansing MI 48824

GARRISON, LARRY RICHARD, accounting educator; b. Kansas City, Mo., Jan. 10, 1951; s. Robert Milton and Virginia Claire (Huntington) G.; m. Sheila Caroline Murry, Aug. 10, 1973. BBA, Cen. Mo. State U., 1973; MS in Acctg., U. Mo., 1982; PhD, U. Nebr., 1986. CPA, Mo. Mgr. Garrison & Co., CPAs, Kansas City, 1973-79; controller G.F. & F. Enterprises, Kansas City, 1979-82; instr. U. Nebr., Lincoln, 1983-86; assoc. prof. U. Mo., Kansas City, 1986—; exec. dir. Tax Policy Rsch. Project. Contbr. articles to profl. jours. Recipient Disting. Teaching award U. Nebr., 1984-85. Mem. Am. Inst. CPA's, Am. Taxation Assn., Mo. Soc. CPA's, Am. Acctg. Assn., Beta Alpha Psi, Beta Gamma Sigma. Office: U Mo 5100 Rockhill Rd Kansas City MO 64110-2446

GARRISON, LAWRENCE DUANE, air force officer; b. Altadena, Calif., May 12, 1930; s. Clarence Cecil and Edna Ione (Bill) G.; m. Evelyn Smith, Oct. 21, 1955; children—Lawrence D., Kenneth A., Julie K. B.Mgmt., Ind. U., 1957; postgrad., Air Force Command and Staff Coll., 1965—, Indsl. Coll. of Armed Forces, 1968. Commd. U.S. Air Force, 1950, advanced through grades to maj. gen., 1980; squadron pilot, asst. prof. aerospace studies (U. N.C.), Chapel Hill, 1962-65; insp. Tactical Air Command, Langley AFB, Va., 1971-72; squadron comdr. F-4 Squadron, RAF Sta. Alconburg, U.K., 1975-77; wing comdr. Pilot Tng. Wing, Laughlin AFB, Tex., 1980-81; dir. maintenance and supply hdqrs. Pilot Tng. Wing, Washington, 1981—; air dep. to comdr. NATO, Oslo, No. Europe; now comdr. Def. Constrn. Supply Ctr., Columbus, Ohio. Decorated D.S.M., D.S.C., D.F.C. with 2 oak leaf clusters, Legion of Merit, Air medal (6). Mem. Air Force Assn., Airpower Hist. Assn., Daedalians. Club: Rotary. Home: Quarters 120 DCSC 3990 E Broad St Columbus OH 43213-1152 Office: Rickenbacker Internat Airport 2365 Fred Haise Ave Columbus OH 43217-5500*

GARRISON, PAUL CORNELL, retired office products company executive; b. Marietta, Ohio, June 18, 1935; s. William John and Alice Ray (Wilson) G.; m. Carole Virginia Whinery, July 3, 1960; children: Kristin, Holly, Craig, Kelee. Student, Ohio State U., 1953, Marietta Coll., 1958. V.p. Garrison Brewer Co., Marietta, 1955-64, pres., 1965-93; dir. of design Garrison Brewer Co. Div. of Stationers, Inc., 1992-93; v.p. Innerspace Interiors, Inc., Marietta, 1980-88. Pres. Eve, Marietta, 1982-85, YMCA, 1974-76; chmn. Marietta Com., 1986, United Way Campaign, 1986. With U.S. Army, 1957-61. Republican. Presbyterian.

GARRISON, WILLIAM LLOYD, cemetery executive; b. Ridgway, Pa., Dec. 26, 1939; s. Lloyd and Mary Rebecca (Morrow) G.; m. Mary Jo Florio, May 30, 1964; children: David, Mark. BA in Psychology, Ohio Wesleyan U., 1962; postgrad., Garrett Theol. Sem., 1962-63, U. Pa., 1963-64; MSW, Fla. State U., 1967; MS in Mgmt., Case Western Res. U., 1976. Caseworker Mpls. Ct. Chgo., 1963-64, United Cerebral Palsy Assn., Phila., 1964-65; psychiat. social worker Bellefaire, Shaker Heights, Ohio, 1967-74; dir. pers. and tng. Ctr. Human Services, Cleve., 1974-81, dir. resource devel., 1981-83; exec. dir. Cleve. Soc. for the Blind, 1983-85, Cleve. Eye Bank, 1983-85; exec. v.p. Lake View Cemetery Assn., Cleve., 1985-87, pres., 1987—; v.p. Lake View Cemetery Found., Cleve., 1988—; adj. prof. Sch. Applied Social Sci., Case Western Res. U., 1974-80; v.p. E.A. Mabry Inc., Akron, Ohio, 1970—; chmn. agri-bus. adv. com. Cleve. Pub. Schs., 1990—, bus. adv. directorate, 1991—. Dist. cub scout chmn. Boy Scouts Am., 1979-81, dist. chmn., 1981-84, scoutmaster, 1983-87, mem. exec. bd., 1981—, asst. coun. commr., 1984-87, v.p. Boy Scouting, 1987-89, scoutmaster to world jamboree in Australia, 1988, coun. commr., 1989-92, area v.p., 1992-95, area pres., 1995—, region exec. com., 1995—, mem. nat. coun., 1989—; mem. pers. com. Lake Erie coun. Girl Scouts U.S., 1982-89; mem. Big Bros., Cleve., 1968-73; pres. Mayfield Heights Homeowners Assn., 1974-84, Cuyahoga County Reach Out Counseling Svcs., trustee, 1977-95, pres., 1991-95; bd. dirs. Garfield Meml. United Meth. Ch., 1979-81; mem. del. assembly United Way Svcs. of Cleve., 1987-95; trustee Alta House Comty. Ctr., 1994, Ctr. for Families and Children, 1995—. Recipient Dist. award Merit Boy Scouts Am., 1980, Silver Beaver award, 1984, Silver Antelope award, 1994; Menninger Found fellow. Mem. NASW, Acad. Cert. Social Workers, Soc. Human Resource Mgmt., Pers. Accreditation Inst., Am. Cemetery Assn., Ohio Assn. Cemetery Supts. and Ofcls. (exec. bd. 1992—, v.p. 1993, pres.-elect 1994, pres. 1995—), Greater Cleve. Cemetery Assn. (pres. 1987-90), Nat. Eagle Scout Assn., Greater Cleve. Pers. Coun., Social Agys. Employee Union (pres. 1970-73), Greater Cleve. Growth Assn., St. Luke's Hosp. Assn., Cleve. U. Cir. Inc., Am. Field Svc., Cleve. Playhouse Club, Rotary (trustee Cleve. club 1993-96, v.p. 1996, pres.-elect 1996-97), Delta Tau Delta, Phi Mu Alpha. Office: Lake View Cemetery Assn 12316 Euclid Ave Cleveland OH 44106-4313

GARSCADDEN, ALAN, physicist; b. Glasgow, Scotland, June 10, 1937; came to U.S., 1962; s. Andrew and Sarah Florence (Black) G.; m. Avril Margaret Thompson Garscadden, Jan. 24, 1962; children: A. Graeme, A.K. Neil, A.K. Gael, A.E. Hilary. BS (hon.), Queens U., Belfast, Ireland, 1958; PhD in Physics, 1962. Rsch. physicist Aerospace Rsch. Labs, Wright-Patterson AFB, 1962-73; lab. dir., 1973-75; rsch. physicist Aero Propulsion & Power Divsn., 1975-91; assoc. chief scientist, 1991-94; chief scientist Wright Lab., 1995—. Contbr. articles to profl. jours. Commr. Planning Commn., Village of Yellow Springs, 1985-96. Fellow Am.. Phys. Soc.; mem. IEEE (sr.). Office: WL/CA Wright Laboratory USAF Wright Patterson AFB OH 45433

GARTNER, DANIEL LEE, computer information executive; b. Newark, Ohio, Jan. 24, 1945; s. Harold Jerome and Hazel Marie (Wright) G.; m. Holly L. Hanbaum, July 31, 1993; 1 child, Sarah Marie. Student, Ohio State U., 1967-74; BA, Park Coll., 1978; MS, USAF Inst. Tech., 1982. Computer programmer USAF, Newark AFB, 1974-78, computer systems analyst, 1978-82, chief info. ctr., 1981-82, chief customer support div., 1988-92, chief office staff support, 1992—; adj. prof. logistics and computers Park Coll., Newark, 1986-91; cons. pvt. sector, Newark, 1983—. Designer 1st broadband local area network, 1st info. ctr. Air Force Logistics Command. Adv. Boy Scouts Am., Newark AFB, 1984-86; active Big Bros. and Big Sister, Newark AFB, 1986; bd. dirs. Newark YMCA, Licking County Planning Commn.; 1st chmn. Licking Park Dist., 1990-91. Mem. Newark C. of C. (mem. leadership tomorrow 1986). Home: 1500 Londondale Pkwy Newark OH 43055-9999 Office: DSDC-DX Columbus OH 43213-1152

GARTNER, JESSIE LEE, emergency nurse; b. St. Paul, Kans., Feb. 7, 1940; d. Herbert Lee and Lela V. (Shouse) Moore; m. Billy C. Couey, June 18, 1960 (dec. Feb. 1981); m. Gary E. Gartner, Dec. 10, 1988. AAS with honors, Coffeyville C.C., 1986; ADN with honors, Labette County C.C., 1987; postgrad., Oxford U., 1991; BSN, Mo. Southern State Coll., 1992; MSN, U. Mo., Kansas City, 1996. Cert. emergency nurse. Clk.-typist Pittsburg (Kans.) State U., 1957-62, Jayhawk Distbrs., Independence, Kans., 1962-64; office mgr., asst. compt. Starcraft Corp., Independence, 1964-74; bookkeeper, parts sales rep. O'Malley Equipment, Independence, 1975-77; sec. Guaranty Performance, Independence, 1977-78; sec., bookkeeper Independence Community Coll., 1978-81; paramedic Coffeyville (Kans.) Regional Med. Ctr., 1981-87; clin. nurse St. John Regional Med. Ctr., Joplin, Mo., 1987—; CPR instr. Coffeyville Regional Med. Ctr., 1984-87; TNCC instr. St. John Regional Med. Ctr., 1991—; vol. asst. Kans. Bd. of Emergency Medicine, Coffeyville, 1981-87. Vol. Nat. Multiple Sclerosis Found., Joplin, 1989-91, Over 60 Olympics, Joplin, 1990, Spl. Olympics State Bowling Tournament, 1993. Mem. Emergency Nurses Assn. (trauma com., treas. 1994—), Nursing Honor Soc., Order Ea. Star (past matron, Grand Chpt. Page award 1962, 91, chmn. state nursing com. 1994), St. Johns Hundred Club. Home: 415 S Connor Ave Joplin MO 64801-2927 Office: St John Regional Med Ctr 2700 Mc Clelland Blvd Joplin MO 64804-1623

GARTNER, MICHAEL GAY, editor, television executive; b. Des Moines, Oct. 25, 1938; s. Carl David and Mary Marguerite (Gay) G.; m. Barbara Jeanne McCoy, May 25, 1968; children: Melissa, Christopher (dec.), Michael. BA, Carleton Coll., 1960; JD, NYU, 1969; LittD (hon.), Simpson Coll., 1984; LLD (hon.), James Madison U., 1989; LittD (hon.), Grand View Coll., 1990. Bar: N.Y., Iowa. With Wall St. Jour., N.Y.C., 1960-74, page one editor, 1970-74; exec. editor Des Moines Register and Tribune, 1974-76, editor, 1976-82, editorial chmn., 1982-85, v.p., 1975-76, exec. v.p., 1977, pres., chief operating officer, 1978-85; editor Courier-Jour. and Louisville Times, 1986-87; gen. news exec. Gannett Co., 1987-88; pres. NBC News, 1988-93; editor, co-owner Ames (Iowa) Daily Tribune, 1986—; dir., co-owner McCoy Broadcasting Co. Syndicated Columnist on lang., 1978—; columnist USA Today. Hon. trustee Simpson Coll.; mem. Pulitzer Prize Bd., 1982-92, chmn., 1991-92. Mem. ABA, Iowa Bar Assn., Assn. Bar City N.Y., Am. Soc. Newspaper Editors (pres. 1986-87), Wakonda Club, Garden of Gods Club. Home: 5315 Waterbury Rd Des Moines IA 50312-1923 also: 366 W 11th St New York NY 10014-6225 Office: 317 5th St Ames IA 50010-6101

GARTON, ROBERT DEAN, state senator; b. Chariton, Iowa, Aug. 18, 1933; s. Jesse Glenn and Ruth Irene (Wright) G.; m. Barbara Hicks, June 17, 1955; children: Bradford, Brenda. BS, Iowa State U., 1955; MS, Cornell U., 1959. Pers. rep. Cummins Engine Co., Columbus, Ind., 1959-61; owner Garton Assocs., mgmt. cons., Columbus, 1961—; mem. Ind. Senate, 1970—, minority caucus chmn., 1976-78, majority caucus chmn., 1978-80, pres. pro tempore, 1980—; mem. exec. com. Nat. Conf. State Legislatures, 1989-92; chmn. Mid-West Conf. State Legislatures, Coun. State Govts., 1984-85, mem. governing bd., 1985—; bd. dirs. Monroe Guaranty Ins. Co. Chmn. Ind. Civil Rights Commn., 1969-70; mem. exec. com. Nat. Fedn. Young Republicans, 1966; bd. dirs. Ind. Econ. Devel. Coun., Rural Water System, Columbus, 1969—. Served with USMCR, 1955-57. Named Hon. Citizen Iowa, 1962, Tenn., 1977; winner internat. speech contest Toastmasters, 1962; recipient Disting. Service award Jr. C. of C. Columbus, 1968, Guardian of Small Bus. award Nat. Fedn. for Ind. Bus., 1990, 93, 94, Lee Atwater Leadership award Nat. Rep. Legislator Assn., 1991, United Sr. Action Legis. Leadership award, 1994; named One of 5 Outstanding Young Men in Ind., 1968, Man of Yr., Ind. Rep. Mayor's Assn., 1991. Mem. Beta Theta Pi. Lodge: Rotary. Office: 530 Franklin St Columbus IN 47201-6214

GARTRELL, RICHARD BLAIR, travel marketing association executive; b. Oakland, Calif., Dec. 7, 1940; s. Thorold Ivan Lance and Phyllis May (Smith) G.; children: Diane Lillian, Lance Richard. BS, San Francisco State U., 1964, MS, 1969; postgrad., U. Nebr., 1970-80. Cert. Assn. Exec., Cert. Tour Planner. Grad. asst. speech dept. San Francisco State U., 1968-69; asst. prof. speech communication Doane Coll., Crete, Nebr., 1969-76; dir. divsn. travel & tourism Nebr. Dept. Econ. Devel., Lincoln, 1976-80; pres., CEO Ann Arbor (Mich.) Conf. & Visitors Bur., 1981-89, Newport Beach (Calif.) Conv. & Visitors Bur., 1989-94, Chgo. Southland Conv. & Visitors Bur., Olympia Fields, Ill., 1994—; lectr. in field. Author: Destination Marketing for Convention and Visitor Bureaus, 1988; contbr. articles to profl. jours. and trade publs. Lt., USN, 1963-68. Recipient Outstanding Svc. award Nebr. Speech Communication Assn., Lincoln, 1978; named Outstanding Young Coll. Speech Tchr. Nebr. Speech Communication Assn., 1972, Outstanding Pub. Sector Mem. Nat. Tour Assn., Lexington, 1987, Vic HArtley Assn. Exec. of Yr. So. Calif. Soc. Assn. Execs., Pasadena, 1993. Mem. Ill. travel & Tourism Assn. (bd. dirs. 1995—). Presbyterian. Office: Chgo Southland Conv & Visitors Bur 20200 Governors Dr Ste 202 Olympia Fields IL 60461

GARVER, FREDERICK MERRILL, industrial engineering executive; b. Indpls., Mar. 25, 1945; s. Clyde Louis and Elizabeth Kemp (Finch) G.; m. Ruth Sikkema, Nov. 8, 1969. BS, Western Mich. U., 1967; postgrad., Grand Valley State U., 1976-77; MS, Western Mich. U., 1990. Cert. mfg. engr. Methods analyst Boeing Co., Seattle, 1968-69; indsl. engr. Wolverine World Wide, Inc., Rockford, Mich., 1969-72; mgr. indsl. engring. Leigh Products Inc., Coopersville, Mich., 1972-77; dir. indsl. engring. Integrated Metal Techs., Spring Lake, Mich., 1977-79; mgr. mfg. engring. Haworth Inc., Holland, Mich., 1979-88, Hart & Cooley, Inc., Holland, 1988-92; mfg. engr. Trumark Inc., Lansing, Mich., 1992-94; sr. adv. process engr. Walker Mfg. Inc., Grass Lake, Mich., 1994—. Mem. Inst. Indsl. Engrs. (sr.), Soc. Mfg. Engrs. (sr., ad hoc govt. relations com.), Chem. Coaters Assn., Assn. Bus. Advocating Tariff Equity, Assn. Finishing Processes, Jaycees (treas. Ithaca, Mich. chpt. 1971-72). Republican. Mem. Reformed Church of America. Home: 9466 Tannis Rd Clarksville MI 48815-9727 Office: Walker Mfg Inc 3901 Willis Rd Grass Lake MI 49240

GARVEY, MARY ANNE, lawyer; b. Cleve., Apr. 4, 1955; d. John Joseph and Anna May (Simonetti) G. BA, John Carroll U., 1977; JD, Case Western Res. U., 1980. Bar: Ohio 1980, U.S. Dist. Ct. (no. dist.) Ohio 1982. Trial atty. U.S. Dept. of Labor, Cleve., 1981—. Mem. Marinello Endowment Fund Com., Cleve., 1985—; vol. Playhouse Sq. Assn., Cleve., 1981—; class agt. Case Western Res. Law Sch., Cleve., 1983—, bd. govs.; sec. Vol. Lawyers for the Arts, 1982—; v.p. North Coast Ballet Theatre, Cleve., 1985—; pres. North Coast Ballet Theatre, 1988—. Mem. ABA, Cleve. Bar Assn. Club: John Carroll U. Cleve. Alumni (sec.). Office: US Dept of Labor 1240 E 9th St Cleveland OH 44199-2001

GARWOOD, DOUGLAS LEON, agricultural scientist; b. Taylorville, Ill., Feb. 8, 1944; s. Harold Leslie and Lillian (Kerns) G.; m. Alice Elizabeth Stout, Aug. 25, 1973; children: Mark, Karen. BS in Agr., U. Ill., 1966, MS in Agronomy, 1968; PhD in Genetics, Pa. State U., 1973. Instr. Pa. State U., University Park, 1972-73, asst. prof., 1973-77, assoc. prof., 1977-80; mgr., sec., treas., dir. Garwood Seed Co., Stonington, Ill., 1980—; mem. rsch. com. Golden Harvest Seeds, Bloomington, Ill., 1981—, mem. mktg. com., 1988—, mem. customer svc. com., 1992—, dir., treas., chmn. mktg. com., 1994—; treas. Seed Engrs. Inc., 1993—. Co-author: Starch Chemistry and Technology, 1984. Mem. Am. Soc. Agronomy, Crop Sci. Soc. Am., Am. Soc. Horticulture Sci., Nat. Sweet Corn Breeders Assn., Sigma Xi, Alpha Zeta, Gamma Sigma Delta, Phi Kappa Phi, Phi Eta Sigma. Republican. Baptist. Office: Garwood Seed Co 1929 N 2050 E Rd Stonington IL 62567-5306

GARZA, MELITA MARIE, journalist; b. Madrid, Oct. 19, 1959; came to U.S., 1961; d. Carlos Mario and Linda Rose (Caballero) G. BA, Harvard U., 1983; postgrad., Poynter Inst. Reporter, writer L.A. Times, 1984-85, Milw. Jour., 1986-89, Chgo. Tribune, 1989—; discussion leader Am. Press Inst., Reston, Va., 1995; spkr., instr. Wilmington (Del.) Writers Workshop, 1995. Bd. dirs. SciTech mus., Aurora, Ill., 1991—; mem. com. on fgn. rels. Chgo. Coun. on Fgn. Rels., 1991—. Named one of top 20 young people in U.S. newspaper industry Newspaper Assn. Am., 1993, one of 100 Women Making a Difference Today's Chgo. Women, 1996; recipient Excellence in Journalism award Ill. Coalition for Immigrant and Refugee Protection, 1995, Cardinal's Comm. award for Profl. Excellence Archdiocese of Chgo., 1996. Mem. Nat. Assn. Hispanic Journalists (v.p. bd. dirs. 1989-94, Pres.' award 1994), Internat. Women's Media Found., Harvard Club of Chgo. (v.p. 1993-94), Radcliffe Club of Chgo. (pres. 1993-94). Roman Catholic. Office: Chgo Tribune 435 N Michigan Ave Chicago IL 60611

GASH, LAUREN BETH, lawyer, state legislator; b. Summit, N.J., June 11, 1960; d. Ira Arnold and Sondra Regina (Stetin) G.; m. Gregg Allen Garmisa, June 12, 1983; children: Sarah, Benjamin. BA in Psychology, Clark U., 1982; JD, Georgetown U., 1987. Bar: Ill. 1989. Projects dir. U.S. Senator Alan Dixon, Washington, 1981-83; statewide constituency coord., dir. Women for Simon, U.S. Senator Paul Simon, Chgo., 1990; aide State Rep. Grace Mary Stern, Highland Park, Ill.; atty. Prairie State Legal Svcs., Waukegan, Ill.; mem. Ill. State Bar Assn. Com. on Community Involvement, Springfield. Mem. women's health adv. bd. Highland Park Hosp., southeast adv. bd Coll. Lake County, JUF govt. agencies divsn. campaign cabinet, Highland Park 2000 com., human needs subcom. Women in Law as 2d Career grantee; recipient Disting. Svc. award Ill. Com. for Honest Govt., 1996, Best Legis. Record Voting award Ind. Voters Ill., 1996. Mem. Formerly Employed Mothers at the Leading Edge (co-founder North Shore chpt.), Chgo. Women in Govt. Rels., Women Employed, Ravinia PTA (bd. dirs., polit. action chair), Com. for Interdist. Cooperation, North Shore Synagogue Beth El (social action com.) LWV (bd. dirs. Highland Park chpt., bd. dirs. Lake County chpt.). Home: 1299 Lincoln Ave South Highland Park IL 60035-3400 Office: 108 Wilmot Rd Ste 210 Deerfield IL 60015-5117 also: 2098-M Stratton Bldg Springfield IL 62706

GASKILL, SAM, state legislator. Mem. Mo. Ho. of Reps., Jefferson City. Republican.

GASPER, DAVID ANTHONY, computer software executive; b. Dayton, Ohio, Aug. 14, 1956; s. William Bickford and Marie Elizabeth (Shroyer) G.; m. Theresa, Apr. 24, 1993; 1 child, Laura Katherine. B.S., Wright State, 1978; M.B.A., U. Dayton, 1984. Programmer NCR, Dayton, Ohio, 1978-79; programmer-analyst Mead Corp., Dayton, 1979-80; systems analyst Source Data Systems, Dayton, 1980-83; pres. Gasper Corp., Dayton, 1983—, chmn. CEO Devlpmnt. Comm. Dayton area Chamber of Comm., 1996—. Vol. Dayton Area Cancer Assn., 1987. Named Exec. of Yr., 1995. Roman Catholic. Avocation: basketball. Office: Gasper Corp 1430 Oak Ct Ste 314 Dayton OH 45430

GASPER, RUTH EILEEN, real estate executive; b. Valparaiso, Ind., July 16, 1934; d. Reuben John and Effie (Wesner) Tenpas; m. Ralph L. Gasper, May 25, 1957. Student Purdue U., 1952-56; BA, Govs. State U., 1982. Analyst computer systems Leo Burnett Advt., Chgo., 1958-69; nat. adminstr. registrars Sports Car Club Am., Denver, 1977-79; pres. Ainslie, Inc., Chgo., 1982—; mem. North River Commn. Housing Com., Chgo., 1982-83, fin. com. Mayor's Task Force on Homelessness City of Chgo. Area coordinator Concerned Action Party, Lansing, Ill., 1977; chief race registrar Ind. Northwest Region Sports Car Club Am., 1969-80. Mem. Chgo. Property Owners Assn., Single Room Operators Assn. (co-founder, treas.), Albany Park C. of C., Condominium Assn. (sec. Fantasy Island II), Single Room Housing Assistance Corp. (co-founder, treas.). Avocations: sports car racing, classical music.

GASS, KENNETH CHRISTIAN, communications executive; b. Milw., Oct. 10, 1948; s. Kenneth Erwin and Jeanette Lucille (Momblow) G.; m. Lauralee Ann Theune, Sept. 8, 1973; children: Todd Christian, Kevin Michael, Lindsey Victoria, Damien Kenneth, Joshua Steven, Karly Samantha. AAS, Milw. Area Tech. Coll., 1977; BA in Geology, U. Wis., 1979. Mfg. chemist W.H. Brady Co., Milw., 1979-86; supplier quality engr. Serigraph Inc., West Bend, Wis., 1986-88; process engring. mgr. Colt Industries, Necedah, Wis., 1988-90; quality assurance engr. Alcoa, Rantoul, Ill., 1991-92; plant mgr. Dunhill Software Svcs., Plover, Wis., 1993-95; facilitator Internat. Orgn. for Standardization AT&T, Viroqua, Wis., 1995—; cons., owner Specialized Quality Publs., La Crosse, Wis., 1991—. Author: The Procedural System, 1995; contbr. articles to profl. jours. Activist Wis. Citizens Concerned for Life, Milw., 1980; charter mem. Nat. Mgmt. Assn. Kettle Moraine Chpt., Tomah, Wis., 1988. Adoption of co-authored proposal (opinion no. 1216) Internat. Commn. on Zool. Nomenclature, London, 1982. Mem. Am. Soc. Quality Control, Paleontol. Soc. Home: 921 11th St S Wisconsin Rapids WI 54494 Office: AT&T Global Info Sys 1201 N Main St Viroqua WI 54665

GAST, HARRY T., JR., state legislator; b. St. Joseph, Mich., Sept. 20, 1920; s. Harry T. Sr. and Fern (Shearer) G.; m. Vera Jean Warren, 1944; children: Barbara Gast Moray, Linda, Dennis. Student, Mich. State U., 1939-41. Treas, then supervisor Lincoln Twp., 1946-70; rep. Mich. Dist. 43; sen. Mich. State Senate Dist. 20, Mich. State Senate Dist. 22, 1995—; county supervisor Berrien County, Mich., 1965-69; mem. Berrien County Bd. Pub. Works, Berrien County Bd. Health, 1965-70. Mem. Lions, Farm Bur., Jaycees (hon.), Mich. United Conservation Clubs. Office: 5165 Lincoln Ave Saint Joseph MI 49085-9738 Address: State Senate 5165 Lincoln Ave Saint Joseph MI 49085*

GAST, LINDA KAY, accountant, financial executive; b. San Antonio, Apr. 15, 1949; d. Jerry Joseph and Dolores Mae (McCurry) Rasmussen; m. Steven Alan Schwartzberg, Apr. 19, 1970; m. Johnny R. Gast, Jan. 8, 1994; 1 child, Laurie Rachelle; stepchildren: Laura Lee, Stacy Jo, Josh Daniel. BS, Lindenwood Coll., 1987. CPA, Mo. Office mgr. Coopers & Lybrand, St. Louis, 1982-84; controller The Type House, Inc., St. Louis, 1984-86; cons. Arthur Young & Co., St. Louis, 1986-87; v.p. fin. Amedco Health Care, Inc., Wright City, Mo., 1987-90; CFO RAPCO Internat., Inc., Jackson, Mo., 1990-94, exec. v.p., CFO, 1995—, CEO, 1996—; bd. dirs. RAPCO Holding Co. Pres. bd. trustees Congregation B'nai Torah, St. Charles, Mo., 1987-90; bd. dirs. Hidden Valley, Burfordville, Mo. Mem. Wright City C. of C., Beta Sigma Phi (v.p. St. Peters, Mo. chpt. 1988-89, Woman of Yr. 1988-89). Home: 241 Clay Ln Whitewater MO 63785-6051

GASTON, HUGH PHILIP, marriage counselor, educator; b. St. Paul, Sept. 12, 1910; s. Hugh Philander and Gertrude (Heine) G.; BA, U. Mich., 1937, MA, 1941; postgrad. summers Northwestern U., 1938, Yale U., 1959; m. Charlotte E. Clarke, Oct. 1, 1945 (dec. 1960); children: Trudy E. Gaston Crippen, George Hugh. Counselor, U. Mich., Ann Arbor, 1936; tchr., counselor W. K. Kellogg Found., Battle Creek, Mich., 1937-41; tchr. spl. edn., Detroit, 1941; instr. airplane wing constrn. Briggs Mfrs. Co., Detroit, 1942 (rep. Mich. Indstrl. Tng. Coun.); psychologist VA, 1946-51; chief VA guidance ctr. U. Mich., 1949-51; with Mich. State VA Guidance Ctr, 1951; sr. staff asso. Sci. Rsch. Asso., Chgo., 1951-55; marriage counselor Cir. Ct., Ann Arbor, 1955-60; pvt. practice marriage counseling, Ann Arbor, 1955-90; educator 14 different courses Ea. Mich. U., 1963-80; former chief Guidance Ctr., V.A. Grad. Ctr. U. Mich. and Mich. State U.; lectr., Ea. Mich. U., Ypsilanti, 1964-67, asst. prof., 1967-81; mem. Study Group for Health Care of Elderly, China, USSR, 1983, Profl. Study Group on Family Affairs, USSR, 1986. Acting postmaster, Ann Arbor, 1960-61. Chief insp. U.S. Army Engrs. Civil Svc., 1930-35, Monroe, Mich. and Toledo, Ohio, 1930-35, insp. Livingston Channel, Detroit; chmn. Wolverine Boys State, Am. Legion,

1957-86; chmn. com. on Christian marriage Presbyn. So. Mich., 1962-69; mem. exec. com., legis. agt., chmn. legis. com. Mich. Coun. Family Rels., 1972-74; bd. dirs. Internat. Parents Without Partners, 1968-69, 1st pres. Mich. chpt. 38, 1961; bd. dirs. Ann Arbor Sr. Citizens, 1982-85, Washtenaw County Coun. Alcoholism, 1982-84. Served with U.S. Army, 1943-46. Decorated Purple Heart (2), Bronze Star; Medallion of Nice (France); named Citizen of Year, Am. Legion, 1968, Single Parent of Yr. Parents Without Ptnrs. chpt. 38, 1978, Patriot of Yr. State of Mich., Mil. Order of Purple Heart, 1987-88. Mem. Am. Assn. Marriage Counselors, Am. Personnel and Guidance Assn., Nat. Vocat. Guidance Assn., D.A.V. (past comdr. local chpt. 13), Am. Soc. Tng. Dirs., Mich. Indsl. Tng. Coun. (charter), SAR (past pres.), U. Mich. Band Alumni Assn. (pres. 1957-58), Mil. Order Purple Heart (nat. exec. com. 1977-82, 1st comdr. chpt. 459 Mich., state comdr. Mich. 1984-85, nat. historian 1981-85), Rotary (Paul Harris fellow 1989), Phi Delta Kappa (past pres. U. Mich., 50 yr. mem.). Address: 513 4th St Ann Arbor MI 48103-4817

GASTON, KARL KUNTIS, newspaper publisher; b. Corning, Kans., July 6, 1929; s. Karl Howard and Edna Alice (Wadleigh) G.; m. Dorothy Anne Buckley, May 31, 1953; children: Kurtis A., Kent H., Kale B. BJ, Kans. State U., 1955. News editor Belleville (Kans.) Telescope Weekly, 1955-65; pub. Ellsworth (Kans.) Reporter, 1965—, Sterling (Kans.) Bull., 1973—, Wilson (Kans.) World and Marquette (Kans.) Tribune, 1974—, Rice County Monitor-Jour., Little River, Kans., 1975—, Kanhistique Monthly, Ellsworth, Kans., 1976, Kans. Works, Ellsworth, 1988—. Mayor City of Ellsworth, 1967-71; pres. South Cen. Econ. Devel. Dist., Wichita, Kans., 1986; media advocate U.S. SBA; active North Ctrl. Kans. Regional Planning Commn.; econ. com. Ellsworth County. Capt. U.S. Army, 1951-53. Recipient Sweepstakes award Better Newspaper, Kans., 1975-84. Mem. Kans. Press Assn. (pres. 1976), Ellsworth C. of C., Kans. C. of C., U.S. C. of C. Republican. Methodist. Home: 311 E 10th St Ellsworth KS 67439-2314 Office: Ellsworth Reporter 220 Court Ave Ellsworth KS 67439-3512

GASTON, MACK CHARLES, naval officer; b. Dalton, Ga., July 17, 1940; s. John H. and Mildred Felicia (Gillard) G.; m. Lillian Juanita Bonds, Aug. 15, 1965; 1 child, Sonja Marie. BS in Comml. Electronics, Tuskegee U., 1964; diploma, Naval Command and Staff Coll., Newport, R.I., 1977; cert., Indsl. Coll. Armed Forces, Washington, 1983; MBA, Marymount U., 1984. Commd. ensign USN, 1964, advanced through grades to rear adm., 1990; electronic and combat info. officer USS Buck, San Diego, 1965-67; chief engr. USS O'Brien, Long Beach, Calif., 1967-69; engr. nuclear safety Destroyer Squadron 5, San Diego, 1969-71; personal aide to dir. Navy Rsch., Test and Evaluation, Washington, 1971-73; assignment officer Bur. Naval Pers., Washington, 1973-74; exec. officer USS Conyngham, Norfolk, Va., 1974-76; comdg. officer USS Cochrane, Pearl Harbor, Hawaii, 1977-79, USS Cone, Charleston, S.C., 1981-82; dir. navy equal opportunity, spl. asst. to chief Naval Pers. for Equal Opportunity, Washington, 1984-85; comdg. officer USS Josephus Daniels, Norfolk, 1986-88; dir. manpower and pers. readiness for comdr. in chief Atlantic Command, Washington, 1988; mem., fellow Chief of Naval Ops. Strategic Study Group, Washington, 1988-89; dir. surface warfare manpower and tng. Office Chief of Naval Ops., Washington, 1989-90; comdr. field command Def. Nuclear Agy., Albuquerque, 1990-92; comdr. Naval Tng. Ctr., Great Lakes, Ill., 1992—. Speaker, councilor chs., community groups, Navy League, others; chmn. Drug Edn. Youth; bd. dirs. United Way Lake County, Ill., No. Ill. Coun. on Alcohol and Substance Abuse, USO of Ill., Lake County Econ. Devel. Commn. Recipient Pres.'s award Nat. Image Inc., 1992, Mass. Bay Area Navy League Coun. Dalton Baugh award, 1993, Wilkins Meritorious Svc. award NAACP, 1994, Kemper Humanitarian Svc. award No. Ill. Coun. Alcohol and Substance Abuse, 1994; inducted into Dalton Edn. Hall of Fame, 1990; portion of North Dalton By-Pass Hwy. named The Admiral Mack Gaston Pkwy., 1992. Mem. Nat. Naval Officer Assn. (life), Fed. Exec. Bd. (policy bd. 1990), U.S. Naval Inst., Naval Order of U.S., Surface Navy Assn., Nat. Mil. Family Assn., Am. Legion, Tin Can Sailors, Inc., Ret. Officers Assn., Naval Meml. Found., Nat. Strategy Forum, Flag & Gen. Officer's Mess, Navy Club of U.S. Office: Office of Comdr Naval Tng Ctr Great Lakes IL 60088-5000

GATES, CHARLES R., college administrator; b. Sanger, Calif., Mar. 12, 1943; s. Charles Elmer and Elizabeth A. (Senior) G.; m. Julie M. Gates, May 10, 1982; children: Darlene Canale, Ranell Bond. BS, Barclay Coll., Haviland, Kans., 1995. Regional sales mgr. Gulf Devel., Torrence, Calif., 1971-77; sales mgr. Lakeside Printing, Skaniatelas, N.Y., 1977-79; v.p. mktg. Century Pub., Post Falls, Idaho, 1979-81; classified dir. Coeur d'Alene (Idaho) Press, 1981-83; v.p. mktg. Better Homes, Ceour d'Alene, 1983-86; v.p. devel., coll. adminstr. Barclay Coll., Haviland, 1988-95; dir. stewardship Back to the Bible, Lincoln, Nebr., 1995—; seminar presenter Barclay Coll., Haviland, 1988-95; fin. counsel Christian Fin. Concepts, Gainesville, Ga., 1982—. Writer news articles Kiowa County Signal, 1990-95; author, articles writer Barclay Progress, 1988-95. Chair fin. com. Mid-Am. Yearly Meeting of Friends, Wichita, Kans., 1992-95; mem. City Coun., Haviland, 1994, 95. Sgt. USMC, 1963-68. Mem. Christian Stewardship Assn. Republican. Home: 437 NW 15th Lincoln NE 68528 Office: Back to the Bible PO Box 82808 Lincoln NE 68501

GATES, MARTINA MARIE, food products company executive; b. Mpls., Mar. 19, 1957; d. John Thomas and Colette Clara (Luetmer) G. BSBA in Mktg. Mgmt. cum laude, Coll. St. Thomas, 1984, MBA in Mktg., 1987. Tchrs. asst. Mpls. Area Vocat. Tech. Inst., Mpls., 1978-79; sec., regional sales mgr. Internat. Multifoods, Mpls., 1979, sec. bakery mix, mktg. mgr., 1979-80, sec., v.p. sales and new bus. devel., 1980, customer svc. rep. regional accounts, 1980-81, customer svc. rep. nat. accounts, 1981-82, credit coordinator indsl. foods div., 1982-85, asst. credit mgr. consumer foods div., 1985, advt./sales promotion mgr. indsl. foods div., 1985-86, asst. credit mgr. fast food and restaurant div., 1986-87, dir. devel. USA and Can. franchise area, 1987-89; dir. franchise devel. FIRSTAFF, Inc., Mpls., 1989-90; dir. adminstrn. Robert Half Internat., Inc., Mpls., 1990-94; dir. client svcs. The NPD Group, Inc., Chgo., 1994—. Vol. seamstress Guthrie Theater Costume Shop, Mpls., 1975—; alumni mem. New Coll. Student Adv. Council St. Thomas, St. Paul, 1984—; vol. Mpls. Aquatennial, 1987. Mem. Omicron Delta Epsilon.

GATTON, CARL GROVER, environmental technologist; b. Louisville, June 5, 1942; s. Carl Grover and Elaine Myrtle (Eldridge) G.; m. Linda Joyce Poston, June 3, 1961 (div. Sept. 1969); children: Carla J. Phelps, Mark A., Rebecca D.; m. Mary Jo Owens, June 9, 1971; children: Eric R., Steven C. BS in Environ. Sci., The Union Inst., 1995. Cert. lab. analyst, class IV, Ohio. Chemist Louisville Ext. Water Dist., 1960-63; engring. technician GE Co., Louisville, 1963-69, equipment engr., 1969-79, quality control engr., 1979-83, mgr. quality control, 1983-85; mgr. indsl. electronics Xetron Corp., Cin., 1985-91, City of Hamilton, 1991—. Patent for Leak Testing by Gas Flow Signature Analysis. Pres. Fairdale (Ky.) Jaycees, 1963-65. Recipient Edwina B. Gantz scholarship The Union Inst., 1993. Mem. Water Environment Fedn. Home: 6518 Liberty Fairfield Rd Hamilton OH 45011 Office: City of Hamilton 2451 River Rd Hamilton OH 45015

GATTSHALL, WANDA G., physical therapist assistant; b. Cedar Rapids, Ind., Aug. 19, 1965; d. Betty Lou (Evens) Thompson; m. John W. Gattshall, Sept. 1, 1984; children: Melinda Elizabeth, Heather Michelle. AAS, Colby C.C., 1986, AS, 1986. Cert. by Kans. State Bd. of Healing Arts. Phys. therapist asst. Onaga (Kans.) Cmty. Hosp., Inc., 1986-87, Meml. Hosp., Manhattan, Kans., 1987-88, 95—; dir. phys. therapy Comanche County Hosp., Coldwater, Kans., 1988-89, Edward County Hosp., Kinsley, Kans., 1989-90, Kiowa County Meml. Hosp., Greensburg, Kans., 1990-93; phys. therapist asst. St. John's Regional Health Ctr., Salina, Kans., 1993—. Mem. Am. Phys. Therapy Assn., Phi Theta Kappa. Republican. Baptist. Home: 410 NE 9th Abilene KS 67410

GAUGER, MICHAEL THOMAS, historian, editor; b. Milw., Aug. 23, 1961; s. Donald Melvin and Barbara (Falteisek) G. BA in Journalism, U. Wis., Milw., 1983, MA in History, 1988. Sports copy editor The Milw. Jour., 1989-95; copy editor The Milw. Jour. Sentinel, 1995—; freelance editor, writer, historian, 1988—. Mem. U. Wis. Milw. Alumni Assn., Phi Beta Kappa (bd. govs. Greater Milw. Assn. 1988—), Phi Alpha Theta. Home: 2896 S Wentworth Ave Milwaukee WI 53207

GAUGER, MICHELE ROBERTA, photographer, studio administrator, corporate executive; b. Elkhorn, Wis., Feb. 28, 1949; d. Robert F. and Christiane J. (Guiffaut) Marszalek; m. Richard C. Gauger, May 3, 1969 (div.). Student U. Wis., Superior, 1967-69, U. Wis., Whitewater, 1978-80, Winona Sch. Profl. Photography-Chgo., 1984-91; Degree in Photographic Craftsmenship, Profl. Photographers of Am., 1990, MA in Photography, 1994. Wedding photographer Fossum Studio, Elkhorn, 1973-78; owner Photography by Michele, Whitewater, 1978-81; pres., photographer, mgr., Michele Inc. of Wis., Whitewater, 1981—, Foxes Reg., 1987; speaker Wedding Photographers Internat. Conv., Las Vegas, Nev., 1987, 89, Nashville, 1988, 93, Tenn. Profl. Photographers Assn., Nashville, 1987, Twin Cities Profl. Photographers, Mpls., 1987; lectr. Supra Color Seminar, Mpls., 1987, 89, San Francisco Profl. Photographers Assn., 1988, Monterey Profl. Photographers Assn., Nev. Profl. Photographers Assn., 1989, Mich. Profl. Photographers Assn., 1989, 94, Wis. Profl. Photographers Assn., 1993, 94, N.J. Profl. Photographers, Assn., 1995. Contbr. articles to profl. jours.; works exhibited Chinese Nat. Gallery, Beijing, 1987, 88, 89, 91, 94, 95. Mem. Nat. Arbor Found, Nebr., 1984—. Recipient 1st place Wedding Photography award Internat. Wedding Photography, 1983, 84, 87, 88 (two awards), 89, 91, 96, 2nd place award, 1985, 96, Grand award, 1988; named to Wis. Ct. Honor, 1991, 96. Mem. Profl. Photographers Am. (Natl. Loan Collectional 1984), Exhibited Chinese Nat. Gallery, Beijing, China (2d place award 1988, Bronze medal 1989), Wis. Profl. Photographer Assn., Wedding Photographer Internat., Winona Sch. Profl. Photography Alumni Assn., Whitewater C. of C. Republican. Roman Catholic. Avocations: world travel, big game hunting, horseback riding, cooking. Home: RR 2 Whitewater WI 53190-9802 Office: Michele Inc RR 2 Whitewater WI 53190-9802

GAULKE, EARL H., religious publisher and editor, clergyman; b. Milw., July 18, 1927; s. Albert and Olga (Reinhardt) G.; m. Margaret Elaine Preuss, Aug. 5, 1951; children: Cheryl, Stephen. BS in Edn., Concordia U., River Forest, Ill., 1950; BA, MDiv, Concordia Sem., St. Louis, 1956; MA, Washington U., St. Louis, 1965, PhD, 1970; DD, Concordia U., Irvine, Calif., 1995. Ordained minister Lutheran Ch., 1956. Prin., tchr. Pilgrim Luth. Sch., Santa Monica, Calif., 1950-52; tchr., dept. head Detroit Luth. High Sch., 1956-57; assoc. pastor Faith Luth. Ch., L.A., 1957-58; editor bd. of parish svcs., 1958-75; dir. editorial svcs. Luth. Ch.-Mo. Synod, St. Louis, 1975-92; v.p. editl. Concordia Pub. House, St. Louis, 1992—; vis. instr. Washington U., U. Mo., St. Louis, Concordia Sem., Concordia Coll., Mpls.; rsch. assoc. Ctrl. Lab. (CEMREL), St. Louis, 1967-68. Author: You Can Have A Family, 1975, First Chance for the Church, 1978; contbr. articles to profl. jours. Recipient Epphatha award Detroit Inst. for Deaf, 1992. Mem. Am. Edn. Assn., Luth. Edn. Assn. (exec. editor 1978-79, Christus Magister 1989). Home: 2447 Camberwell Ct Des Peres MO 63131-2118 Office: Concordia Pub House 3558 S Jefferson Ave Saint Louis MO 63118-1329

GAULT, STANLEY CARLETON, manufacturing company executive; b. Wooster, Ohio, Jan. 6, 1926; s. Clyde Carleton and Aseneth Briton (Stanley) G.; m. Flo Lucille Kurtz, June 11, 1949; children: Stephen, Christopher, Jennifer. BA, Coll. of Wooster, 1948. With GE (and subs.), 1948-79; v.p. and group exec. maj. appliance bus. group GE (and subs.), Louisville, 1970-77; v.p. and sector exec. consumer products and svcs. sector GE (and subs.), Fairfield, Conn., 1977; sr. v.p., sector exec. GE (Indsl. Products and Components sector), 1977-79; vice chmn. bd. Rubbermaid Inc., Wooster, Ohio, 1980, chmn. bd., chief exec. officer, 1980-91, co-chmn. bd., 1992—, now bd. dirs.; chmn. bd., chief exec. officer Goodyear Tire & Rubber Co., Akron, 1991—; bd. dirs. Avon Products, Inc., Internat. Paper Co., PPG Industries, Inc., The Timken Co., N.Y. Stock Exch., Rubbermaid, Inc.; mem. Adv. Com. on U.S. Trade Policy and Negotiations, 1987. Trustee Coll. of Wooster, chmn. bd., 1987—. With USAAF, 1944-46. Mem. NAM (bd. dirs., chmn. bd. 1986-87). Republican. Methodist. Office: Goodyear Tire & Rubber Co 1144 E Market St Akron OH 44316-0001*

GAUNCE, MICHAEL PAUL, insurance company executive; b. Paris, Ky., Oct. 17, 1949; s. Paul D. and Mary E. (Gardner) G. BA, U. Ky., 1971. Cert. Life Underwriters Tng. Coun. Agt., mgr. Equitable Life of N.Y., Lexington, Ky., 1972-74; agt., regional mgr. Assn. Ins. Marketers, Inc., Indpls., Cin., South Bend, Ind., 1974-77; pres., chmn. Ins. Corp. Am., Indpls., 1977—; chmn. bd. Argent Ins. Corp., Indpls., Alternative Healthcare Marketers, Inc., Indpls.; dir., past chmn. Brokers Ins. Corp., Indpls.; dir. Brokers Ins. Corp. Tenn., Nashville, Brokers Ins. Agy., Atlanta; dir., Brokers Ins. Corp., Ky., Agy. Mgmt. Corp., Indpls.; cons. adv. bd. Blue Cross/Blue Shield, Indpls., 1982-89; mem. adv. bd. Acordia, Inc., Indpls., 1996—. Active Rep. Nat. Com. Mem. Ind. Assn. Employee Benefit cons. (pres. 1984-88), Elks, Greenwood C. of C., Franklin C. of C., Seymour C. of C. Republican. Office: Ins Corp Am 5140 Commerce Cir Indianapolis IN 46237

GAUTHIER, JIM, marketing executive; b. Dayton, Ohio, May 18, 1954. V.p. Afsco, Milw., 1978-87, Rowe Mktg. Group Inc., Chgo., 1987—. Active City of Hope, 1994—. Mem. Hardware Assn. Chgo., Housewares Assn. Chgo. Roman Catholic. Office: Rowe Mktg Group Inc 727 N Hudson Ave Ste 201 Chicago IL 60610-3423

GAUTHIER, MARY ELIZABETH, librarian, researcher, secondary education educator; b. Tudor, Alta., Can., May 17, 1917; d. Harold Bertram and Mary Evelyn (Foley) Bliss; m. Louis Lyons Gauthier, May 31, 1947 (dec. 1976). PhB, Northwestern U., 1970; MA in Edn., Lewis U., 1976; EdD, Pacific States U., London, 1979. Clk. LaGrange (Ill.) Pub. Libr., 1956-57; package libr. AMA, Chgo., 1958-60; staff libr. Duff, Anderson & Clark, Chgo., 1960-63; libr./tchr. Fremont Sch. Dist. 79, Mundelein, Ill., 1970-75; substitute tchr. Valleyview Sch. Dist. 365-U, Romeoville, Ill., 1978-89; dormitory dir./tchr. Project Upward Bound, Romeoville, Ill., 1984-94, enrichment studies, 1991-94; ind. researcher South Bend, Ind., 1990-94; instr. Joliet (Ill.) Jr. Coll., 1986-89; cons. Wash. High Sch.; bd. of advisors Ivy Tech. Coll., Southbend, 1993. Contbr. monograph and articles to profl. jours.; author: Some Basic Principles of New Scientific Attitudes in Education, 1980. Active Manor Pk. Community Assn., Ottawa, Can., 1953. With RCAF, 1943-45. Recipient Gold medal Internat. Symposium on the Mgmt. of Stress, Monte Carlo, 1979; grantee Ill. State Bd. Edn., 1985, Ind. U. South Bend, 1992. Mem. AAAS, N.Y. Acad. Scis.

GAUTSCH, KAY ANNE, physical therapist; b. Racine, Wis., Mar. 16, 1942; d. Albert Joseph and Margaret Dorothy (Claussen) Troestler; m. James Patrick Gautsch, Sept. 2, 1972; children: Laura Kay, Julie Ann. BS in Phys. Therapy magna cum laude, Marquette U., 1966. Lic. phys. therapist, Wis. Staff phys. therapist St. Luke's Hosp., Racine, Wis., 1966-67; phys. therapy cons. St. Catherine's Infirmary, Racine, Wis., 1966-77; phys. therapy dept. head St. Mary's Med. Ctr., Racine, Wis., 1967-72, staff phys. therapist, 1972-79; staff phys. therapist Inst. of Phys. Medicine & Rehab., Peoria, Ill., 1979-82; staff phys. therapy rehab. unit Sacred Heart Hosp., Eau Claire, Wis., 1984—, mem. head injury com., 1993—; clin. instr. phys. therapy Marquette U., Milw., U. Wis., Madison and La Crosse, 1984—. Mem. St. Patrick's Congregation. Mem. Am. Phys. Therapy Assn. (Wis. chpt.), Young Persons Stroke Club (facilitator, organizer 1988—). Roman Catholic. Home: 811 Taft Ave Eau Claire WI 54701 Office: Sacred Heart Hosp 900 W Clairemont Ave Eau Claire WI 54701

GAVIN, MARY JANE, medical, surgical nurse; b. Prairie Du Chien, Wis., Sept. 1, 1941; d. Frank Grant and Mary Elizabeth Wolf; m. Alfred William Gavin, Nov. 9, 1963; children: Catherine Heidi Elizabeth, Carl Alfred Eric. Student, North Cen. Coll., Naperville, Ill., 1959-61; BS, RN, U. Wis., 1964; postgrad., Deepmuscle Tng. Ltd., 1980; postgrad. in deep muscle therapy. RN, Wis. Staff nurse U. Wis. Hosps., Madison; RN home response VA, Milw. Unit chair Badger Girls State, 1991—; mem. Wis. Am. Legion Aux.; mem. task force for handicapped Eastside Wis. Evang. Luth. Ch., Madison, 1993. U. Wis. scholar. Mem. Monona Grove Am. Legion Aux. (pres. Unit 429). Home: 702 Fairmont Ave Madison WI 53714-1424

GAW, ROBERT STEVEN, lawyer, state representative; b. Moberly, Mo., July 7, 1957; s. William Robert and Julia Marie (Bentley) G.; m. Fannie Beth Bowdish, Aug. 18, 1990. BS in Physics summa cum laude, N.E. Mo. State U., 1978; JD, U. Mo., 1981. Bar: Mo. 1981. Atty. State of Mo., Jefferson City, 1982-84, James Wheeler, Keytesville, Mo., 1984, City of Moberly, Mo., 1985-92, Schirmer & Gaw, Moberly, 1984-94, Schirmer, Suter & Gaw, 1994—; elected spkr. Mo. House of Reps., 1996. State rep. Dist. 22, Mo., 1993—; chmn. Dem. Ctrl. Com., Randolph County, Mo., 1984-89; bd. dirs. Am. Diabetes Assn., Randolph County, 1990—; mem. com. Huntsville (Mo.) Horse Show, 1980's—, Mo. Children's Svcs. Commn., KIDS COUNT adv. com., Mo. Bar Commn. Children & the Law. Recipient award Am. Cancer Soc., 1993, award United Way; nominee Truman scholarship N.E. Mo. State U., 1977, Charles Dick Medal of Merit Nat. Guard Assn. of the U.S., 1995. Mem. Mo. Bar Assn., Randolph County Bar Assn. (pres. 1984—), Moberly Area C. of C. (bd. dirs. 1991—), Moberly Rotary Club. Methodist. Office: Mo Ho of Reps State Capitol Building Jefferson City MO 65101-1556

GAY, ALEDA SUSAN, mathematician, educator; b. Frederick, Okla., Oct. 25, 1951; d. Paul W. and Evelyn (Tefertiller) G. BS, Okla. State U., 1973, MS, 1975, EdD, 1990. Cert. tchr., Okla. Tchr. math. Stillwater (Okla.) Pub. Schs., 1973-83; math. specialist Okla. Dept. Edn., Oklahoma City, 1983-89, computer cons., 1984-89; instr. Okla. State U., Stillwater, 1988-90; asst. prof. math. edn. U. Kans., Lawrence, 1991—; cons. math. textbook Houghton Mifflin, 1985-86; presenter panelist at profl. confs.; presenter workshops. Co-author: Principal Resources in Secondary Mathematics, 1985; developer high sch. algebra curriculum syllabus; contbr. articles to profl. jours. Mem. Assn. State Suprs. Math. (sec. 1988-90), Okla. Coun. Tchrs. Math. (v.p. 1982-84, rep. to Nat. Coun. Tchrs. Math. 1985-90, Outstanding Svc. award 1990), Math. Assn. Am., Nat. Coun. Suprs. Math., Kans. Assn. Tchrs. Math. (v.p. colls.), Assn. Math. Tchrs. Educators (bd. dirs.), Phi Delta Kappa. Office: U Kans Dept Curriculum and Instrn 202 Bailey Hall Lawrence KS 66045-2340

GAY, DAVID EARL, experimental chemist; b. Decatur, Ind., Nov. 10, 1944; s. Robert Earl and Miriam Evelyn (Haley) G.; m. Peggy Ann Sheets, Sept. 2, 1966 (div. Oct. 1981); children: Jeffery David, Christopher David; m. Lou Ann Gluesenkamp, Apr. 22, 1989; 1 child, Robert William. BS, Ball State U., 1967. Process engr. Delco Remy Div., GMC, Anderson, Ind., 1970-76, sr. chemist, 1976-89; sr. exptl. chemist Delphi Automotive Sys., Indpls., 1989—; analytical liaison Delco Remy div. GMC; analytical liaison GM, Delco Remy, Anderson, 1978-89; chmn. Local Hazardous Material Com., Indpls., 1986—; hygiene officer M.G. Corp., Indpls., 1989—. Inventor in field; contbr. articles to profl. jours. Dir. volleyball program YMCA, Anderson, 1982-86, Anderson Park Dept., 1982-86; vol. St. John's Hosp., Anderson, 1987-90; pres. Social Health Ctrl. Ind., Indpls., 1990—. Named Vol. of Yr., YMCA, Anderson, 1985; recipient Paper of Yr. award Metal Powder Internat. Fedn., 1995. Mem. Am. Chem. Soc., Am. Soc. Metals, Sigma Xi. Presbyterian. Home: 12310 E 131st St Noblesville IN 46060-9312 Office: Delphi Automotive Sys 2401 Columbus Ave Anderson IN 46018

GAY, KATHLYN RUTH, author; b. Zion, Ill., Mar. 4, 1930; d. Kenneth Charles and Beatrice (Anderson) McGarrahan; m. Arthur L. Gay, Aug. 28, 1948; children: Martin, Douglas, Karen. Student, No. Ill. U., DeKalb, 1947-50. Author more than 70 books including: Caution: This May Be An Advertisement - Teen Guide to Advertising, 1992, Global Garbage: International Trade in Toxic Waste, 1992, Church and State, 1992, Day Care: Looking for Answers, 1992, The Right-to-Die, 1993, Breast Implants: Making Safe Choices, 1993, Getting Your Message Across, 1993, Rainforests of the World, 1993, Pregnancy: Private Decisions, Public Debates, 1994, The New Power of Women in Politics, 1994, Pollution and the Powerless: The Environmental Justice Movement, 1994, I Am Who I Am: Speaking Out About Multiracial Identity, 1995, Keep the Buttered Side Up: Food Superstitions from Around the World, 1995, Voices From the Past (series on America's wars), 1995, Rights and Respect, 1995, The Not-So-Minor Leagues, 1996, The Information Superhighway, 1996, Saving the Environment, Debating the Costs, 1996, Encyclopedia of North American Eating and Drinking Traditions, Customs and Rituals, 1996. Recipient various book awards. Home and Office: 3121 Ezekiel Ave Zion IL 60099

GEAKE, RAYMOND ROBERT, state senator; b. Detroit, Oct. 26, 1936; s. Harry Nevill and Phyllis Rae (Fox) G.; B.S. in Spl. Edn., U. Mich., 1958, M.A. in Guidance and Counseling, 1959, Ph.D. in Edn. and Psychology, 1963; m. Carol Lynne Rens, June 9, 1962; children—Roger Rens, Tamara Lynne, William Rens. Coordinator child devel. research Edison Inst., Dearborn, Mich., 1962-66; dir. psychology dept. Plymouth (Mich.) State Home and Tng. Sch., Mich. Dept. Mental Health, 1966-69; pvt. practice ednl. psychology, Northville, Mich., 1969-72; mem. Mich. Ho. of Reps., 1973-76, Mich. Senate, 1977—; adj. asst. prof. edn./psychology dept. Madonna Coll., Livonia, Mich., 1984-86. Trustee-at-large Schoolcraft Community Coll., 1969-72, chmn. bd. trustees, 1971-72; vice chmn. nat. adv. com. on mental health and illness of elderly HEW, 1976-77; vice chmn. human svcs. com., assembly fed. issues Nat. Conf. State Legislatures, 1994-95. Recipient Recognition award Found. for Improvement of Justice, 1993. Fellow Mich. Psychol. Assn.; mem. NEA (life), APA, Mich. Soc. Geneal. Research. Republican. Rotarian. Co-author: Visual Tracking, a Self-instruction Workbook for Perceptual Skills in Reading, 1962. Office: Mich Senate PO Box 30036 Lansing MI 48909-7536

GEARHART, MARILYN KAYE, mathematics and biology educator; b. Tucson, Apr. 11, 1950; d. Raymond Fred and Joan Gazelle (White) Hagerty; m. Lon David Gearhart, Mar. 22, 1975; children: Amanda Kaye, Shannon Leigh. BA in Elem. Edn. with dis, Manchester Coll., 1972; MS in Elem Edn. summa cum, Ind. U., 1976; BS in Math. with high hon, Tri-State U., 1985; postgrad., Ind. U., 1983-89. Substitute tchr. South Bend (Ind.) Community Sch. Corp., 1971-72; tchr. DeKalb County Ea. Community Sch. Dist., Butler, Ind., 1972-77; founder, tchr. Pleasant View Christian Early Learning Ctr., Angola, Ind., 1981-85; also bd. dirs. Pleasant View Christian Early Learning Ctr., Angola; micro computer tchr. Purdue U., Ft. Wayne, Ind., 1984; substitute tchr. Met. Sch. Dist. Steuben County, Angola, 1985; tchr. math. and biology DeKalb County Cen. United Sch. Dist., Auburn, Ind., 1985--. Author: (textbook) The Impossibility of Achieving and Maintaining an Utopia, 1971. Sponsor freshman class DeKalb H.S., 1987-89, sophomore class, 1989-96, Students Against Drunk Driving, Auburn, 1985-90, Butler Elem. Little Hoosiers, 1973-77; mem. attendance and gifted and talented coms. DeKalb H.S., 1989-90; coach Acad. Decathlon and Hoosier Acad. Super Bowl, 1989—, Hoosier Spell Bowl, 1993—; leader Girl Scouts U.S., 1986-91, mem., coord. product sales Svc. Unit, 1989-90; del. Rep. State Conv., 1996. Dir's. award Jr. Hist. Soc., 1981-85; maths. and sci. scholars Tri-State, 1985; grantee Tchrs. Retng. Fund. Ind.-State, 1983-85. Mem. NEA, AAUW (treas. 1987-89), Dekalb High Sch. Band and Show Choir Parents, Beta Beta Beta. Mem. Christian Ch. Home: 910 Duesenberg Rd Auburn IN 46706-3223 Office: DeKalb High Sch County Rd 427 Waterloo IN 46793

GEBHARD, ROGER LEE, medical educator, researcher; b. Sioux City, Iowa, Jan. 30, 1945; s. Kenneth C. and Pauline E. (Glantz) G.; m. Gloria J. Brisson, Sept. 10, 1966; children: Kristin H., Roger K. BA, U. Minn., 1966, MD, 1969. Diplomate Am. Bd. Internal Medicine. Resident in medicine Columbia-Presbyn. Hosp., N.Y.C., 1969-71; clin. assoc. NIH, Bethesda, Md., 1971-73; med. resident Stanford (Calif.) U., 1973-74, fellow in gastroenterology, 1974-76; prof. medicine U. Minn. VA Hosp., Mpls., 1977—. Contbr. articles to profl. jours. Bd. dirs. Celiac Sprue Assn. U.S., Omaha, 1989—. Lt. comdr. USPHS, 1971-73. Grantee DVA, 1977—. Fellow ACP; mem. Am. Gastroenterologic Assn., Am. Soc. for Gastrointestinal Endoscopy, Am. Assn. Study Liver Disease, Am. Physiol. Soc. Office: Mpls VA Hosp One Vets Dr111-D Minneapolis MN 55417

GECK, FRANCIS JOSEPH, furniture designer, educator, author; b. Detroit, Dec. 20, 1900; s. Jacob C. and Anna Mary (Angermeyer) G.; m. Evelyn Marie Sturdyvin, July 22, 1937 (dec.). Diploma, N.Y. Sch. Fine and Applied Art, 1924; MFA in Interior Design, Syracuse U., 1946. Instr. N.Y. Sch. Fine & Applied Art, Paris, 1924-27; interior architect and designer William Wright Co., Detroit, 1927-30; interior architect, consultant T. Eaton Co., Toronto, 1930; prof. interior design U. Colo., Boulder, 1930-69; dir. exhibits Boulder Hist. Soc., 1944-58; curator of exhibits U. Colo., 1947-57; dir. exhibits Pioneer Mus., Boulder, Colo., 1958-79; design cons. Mullins Plastics, 1969-71. Author: French Interiors and Furniture: Gothic through Louis XVI, 9 vols., 1982-96; designer 17 pvt. offices in Fisher Bldg. Recipient Honorable Mention award Fla. Internat. Art Exhbn., Lakeland, 1952, Grumbaker Award of Merit, 1952, Gold Award Winner Am. Artists Profl. League, 1953, Silver medal Accademia Internazionale di Letters-Arti-

Scienze, 1970, Cert. of Merit Benedictine Art award, 1971. Home: 18360 Martin Rd Roseville MI 48066-4805

GEDULD, HARRY MAURICE, humanities educator; b. London, Mar. 3, 1931; came to the U.S., 1962; s. Sol and Ann (Berliner) G.; children: Marcus, Daniel. BA, Sheffield U., 1953, MA, 1954; PhD, London U., 1961. Instr. in English Ind. U., Bloomington, 1962-63, asst. prof., 1963-65, assoc. prof., 1965-69, prof. in English, 1969-73, prof. in comparative lit., 1973-96, chair comparative lit., 1990-96, prof. Western European studies, 1980-96, prof. emeritus comparative lit., Western European studies, 1996—. Author: Birth of the Talkies, 1975, Prince of Publishers, 1969, Film Guide to Henry V, 1973; editor: Definitive Time Machine, 1987. Office: Ind U Comparative Lit Bloomington IN 47405

GEE, ELWOOD GORDON, university administrator; b. Vernal, Utah, Feb. 2, 1944; s. Elwood A. and Vera (Showalter) G.; m. Elizabeth Dutson, Aug. 26, 1968 (dec. Dec. 1991); 1 dau., Rebekah. B.A., U. Utah, 1968; J.D., Columbia U., 1971, Ed.D., 1972. Asst. dean U. Utah, Salt Lake City, 1973-74; jud. fellow U.S. Supreme Ct., Washington, 1974-75; assoc. dean Brigham Young U., Provo, Utah, 1975-79; dean W.Va. U., Morgantown, 1979-81, pres., 1981-85; pres. U. Colo., 1985-90, Ohio State U., Columbus, 1990—. Author: Education Law and Public Schools, 1978, Law and Public Education, 1980, Violence, Values and Justice in American Education, 1982, Fair Employment Practice, 1982. W.K. Kellogg fellow, 1971-72; Mellon fellow, 1977-78. Mem. ABA, Adminstrv. Conf. U.S., Phi Delta Kappa, Phi Kappa Phi. Mem. LDS Ch. Home: PO Box 3600 Columbus OH 43210-0600 Office: Ohio State U 205 Bricker Hall 190 N Oval Mall Columbus OH 43210-1358

GEE, PHYLLIS ANN, critical care nurse; b. Cin., July 27, 1964; d. Albert Thomas and Catherine Ann (Kersker) Veith; m. Ricky Leroy Gee, Jan. 26, 1986 (div. June 1988); 1 child, Justin Thomas; m. Michael Edward Leder, Feb. 1, 1991 (div. Aug. 1992); 1 child, Jonathan David. Cert. in diversified health occupations, Warren County Career Ctr., Lebanon, Ohio, 1982; diploma, Community Hosp. Sch. Nursing, Springfield, Ohio, 1985. RN, Ohio; cert. ACLS. Nursing asst. III pulmonary ICU Community Hosp., Springfield, 1983-85; staff nurse, charge nurse ICU Clermont Mercy Hosp., Batavia, Ohio, 1985-89; staff nurse ICU Upjohn Agy. Univ. Hosp., Cin., 1991; staff nurse cardiovascular ICU The Christ Hosp., Cin., 1989—. Tchr. Sunday sch. True Faith Holiness Ch. of God, South Lebanon, Ohio, 1990-95; vol. Goshen (Ohio) Libr., 1992-93. Mem. AACN. Office: The Christ Hosp 2139 Auburn Ave Cincinnati OH 45219-2906

GEE, ROBERT LEROY, agriculturist, dairy farmer; b. Oakport Twp., Moorhead, Minn., May 25, 1926; s. Milton William and Hertha Elizabeth (Paschke) G.; m. Mae Valentine Erickson, June 18, 1953. B.S. in Agronomy, N.D. State U., 1951, postgrad., 1955; postgrad., Colo. A&M U., 1954. Farm labor controller Minn. Extension Service, Clay County, 1944-45, county 4-H agt., 1951-57; rural mail carrier U.S. Postal Service, Moorhead, Minn., 1946-47; breeder registered shorthorn cattle and registered southdown sheep Moorhead, Minn., 1950-63; owner, operator Gee Dairy Farm (Oak Grove Farm), Moorhead, Minn., 1957—; asst. prof. status U. Minn., 1951-57; bd. dirs. Red River Valley Fair, West Fargo, N.D., 1960-86, Minn. Dairy Promotion Bd., St. Paul, 1968-69; bd. dirs. Red River Valley Devel. Assn., Crookston, Minn., 1973—, v.p., 1992—; bd. dirs. Red River Milk Producers Pool, Minn., N.D., 1963-78, treas., 1968-78; bd. dirs. Cass Clay Creamery Inc., Fargo, N.D., 1969—, chmn. bd., 1982-85, 92—, v.p., 1990-91; bd. dirs. U.S. Meat Animal Rsch. Ctr., Clay Ctr., Nebr., 1970; mem. Nat. Dairy Promotion Bd., Washington, 1984-88. Treas. Oakport Twp., 1974-82, supr., 1986—, v.p., 1987—; mem. Clay County Planning and Zoning Commn., 1991, v.p., 1992—, zoning commr., 1991, vice chmn., 1992-96, chmn., 1996—; mem. Clay County Bd. Adjustment, 1995, chmn., 1996. With USN, 1945-46. Recipient Grand Champion Farm Flock award Man. Expn., 1960, Clay County's Outstanding Agriculturist award, 1996; named Clay County King Agassiz, Red River Valley Winter Shows, 1966, Grand Champion forage exhibit Red River Valley Winter Shows, 1979, 82; co-recipient Clay County Dairy Farm Family of Yr. award Red River Valley Dairymen's Assn., 1979. Mem. Minn. Milk Producers Assn. (bd. dirs., treas. 1978-88, 93—), Minn. Assn. Coops. (bd. dirs. 1984—), State Coop. Assn. (dairy council 1975—), Am. Farm Bur. Fedn., Nat. Farmers Union, Kragnes Farmers Elevator Assn., Red River Valley Livestock Assn., Am. Shorthorn Breeders Assn., Am. Southdown Breeders Assn., Holstein-Friesian Assn. Am. Republican. Mem. United Ch. of Christ. Club: Agassiz (v.p. 1979-81, pres. 1981-82) (Moorhead). Home and Office: RR 1 Box 118 Moorhead MN 56560-9729

GEESAMAN, DONALD FRANKLIN, physicist; b. Balt., Dec. 26, 1949; s. Franklin Quinton and Mildred Elizabeth (Snyder) G.; m. Janis Arlene Graner, June 19, 1974; children: Megan, Matthew. BS, Colo. Sch. Mines, 1971; PhD, SUNY, Stony Brook, 1976. Postdoctoral fellow Argonne (Ill.) Nat. Lab., 1976-78, asst. physicist, 1978-81, physicist, 1981-91; sr. physicist, 1991—; mem. Nuclear Sci. Adv. Com., 1989-92; bd. dirs. Lampf Users Group, Los Alamos, N.Mex., 1985-86; program adv. com. ICUF, Bloomington, Ind., 1985-88, MIT BATES, Cambridge, 1989-93; bd. dirs. CEBAF Users Group, Newport News, Va. Editorial bd. Phys. Rev. C, 1987-89; editor proceedings various meetings, workshops; contbr. articles to profl. jours. Fellow AAAS, Am. Phys. Soc. Office: Argonne Nat Lab 9700 Cass Ave Lemont IL 60439-4803

GEHM, DAVID EUGENE, construction and environmental management executive; b. St. Louis, Nov. 15, 1952; s. John Francis and Rosemary Helen (Krupp) G.; m. Victoria Lynn Renken, Mar. 7, 1992. Cert. civil engring. tech., St. Louis Community Coll. Florissant Valley, 1973. Quality control inspector Fla. Testing and Engr., Ft. Lauderdale, 1973-76; surveyor Wunderlich Co., Union, Mo., 1976-77; quality control inspector The Binkley Co., Warrenton, Mo., 1977-78, Daniel Internat., Fulton, Mo., 1978-79; project mgr. Booker Assocs., Inc., St. Louis, 1979-86; pres. GEHM Corp., Boonville, Mo., 1986—. Mem. Nat. Inst. Cert. Engring. Techs., Inst. Cert. Engr. Techs., Tau Alpha Pi, Sons of the Am. Legion. Home: 16975 Holliday Cir Boonville MO 65233-9802 Office: 1480 Ashley Rd Boonville MO 65233-0065

GEHR, THOMAS YEATS, JR., railway industry executive; b. Michigan City, Ind., Nov. 23, 1953; s. Thomas Yeats and Marie V. Gehr; m. Joan Valentine Miller, Sept. 4, 1982; children: Samantha Kientzy, Kelly Valentine. Student Purdue U., Research Inst. Am. Operator, Automation Industries/Sperry Rail Service, Danbury, Conn., 1974-75; sales rep. Esco Equipment Service Co., Palatine, Ill., 1975-81, v.p. sales, 1981—, treas., asst. sec., dir., 1986—, pres. 1993—; pres., treas., chmn. bd. dirs. Associated Signal Co., 1993; Mem. Am. Ry. Engring. Assn.(committeeman 1993—), Roadmaster and Maintenance of Way Assn., NRC Assn. (committeeman), AWS (committeeman), New Eng. Ry. Assn., Am. Short Line Ry Assn. Met. Ry. Assn. (exec. com. 1984—).

GEHRES, CLINT EDWIN, mechanical engineer; b. Van Wert, Ohio, Mar. 29, 1968. A in Mech. Engring., Interstate Tech, Fort Wayne, Ind., 1988. Designer Mim Industries Inc., Miamisburg, Ohio, 1990—. Office: Mim Industries Inc 4301 Lyons Rd Miamisburg OH 45342

GEHRING, DONALD D., education educator; b. Trenton, N.J., Oct. 9, 1937; s. Philip F. and Elsie E. (Jackson) G.; m. Bettie Groover, Aug. 6, 1960; children: Lisa Seger, David. BS, Ga. Inst. Tech., 1960; MEd, Emory U., 1966; EdD, U. Ga., 1971. Asst. to dean men Emory U., Atlanta, 1962-66; dir. housing West Ga. Coll., Carrollton, 1966-69; dean student devel. Mars Hill (N.C.) Coll., 1971-78; prof. higher edn. U. Louisville, 1978-91; prof. Bowling Green State U., 1991—; tchr. People's Republic China, El Salvador. Editor Coll. Student Affairs Jour.; contbr. numerous articles to profl. jours. Founder Assn. Student Jud. Affairs. Lt. USN, 1960-62. Recipient S. Earl Thompson award Assn. Coll. and Univ. Housing Officers, Outstanding Tchr. Sch. Edn. award. Mem. Nat. Assn. Student Pers. Adminstrn. (Outstanding Contbr. to Lit. or Rsch. award, Excellence as Grad. Faculty Mem. award), Am. Coll. Pers. Assn. (sr. scholar), Assn. Student Jud. Affairs (Disting. Svc. award), Am. Assn. for Higher Edn., So. Assn. for Coll. Student Affairs (past pres., Melvene Hardee and H. Howard Davis awards). Office: Bowling Green State U Rm 330 Edn Bldg Bowling Green OH 43403

GEHRING, FREDERICK WILLIAM, mathematician, educator; b. Ann Arbor, Mich., Aug. 7, 1925; s. Carl E. and Hester McNeal (Reed) G.; m. Lois Caroline Bigger, Aug. 29, 1953; children: Kalle Burgess, Peter Motz. BSE in Elec. Engring., U. Mich., 1946, MA in Math, 1949; PhD (Fulbright fellow) in Math, Cambridge U., Eng., 1952, ScD, 1976; PhD (hon.), U. Helsinki, Finland, 1977, U. Jyväskylä, Finland, 1990. Benjamin Peirce instr. Harvard U., Cambridge, Mass., 1952-55; instr. math. U. Mich., Ann Arbor, 1955-56, asst. prof., 1956-59, assoc. prof., 1959-62, prof., 1962-96, T.H. Hildebrandt prof. math., 1984-96, prof. emeritus, 1996; chmn. dept. math. U. Mich., 1973-75, 77-84, disting. univ. prof., 1987—; hon. prof. Hunan U., Changsha, People's Republic of China, 1987; vis. prof. Harvard U., 1964-65, Stanford U., 1964, U. Minn., 1971, Inst. Mittag-Leffler, Sweden, 1972, Mittag-Leffler, Sweden, 1990; Lars Onsager prof. Norwegian Tech. Hochschule, Norway, 1995; chair program in Geo Function Theory, MSRI, 1986. Editor Duke Math. Jour., 1963-80, D. Van Nostrand Pub. Co., 1963-69, North Holland Pub. Co., 1970—, Springer-Verlag, 1974—; editl. bd. Procs. Am. Math. Soc., 1962-65, Ind. U. Math. Jour., 1967-75, Math. Revs., 1969-75, Bull. Am. Math. Soc., 1979-85, Complex Variables, 1981—, Mich. Math. Jour., 1989, Annales Academiae Scientiarum Fennicae, 1996; contbr. numerous articles on rsch. in pure math. to sci. jours. With USNR, 1943-46. Decorated Comdr. Finnish White Rose, 1986; NSF fellow, 1959-60; Fulbright fellow, 1958-59; Guggenheim fellow, 1958-59; Sci. Research Council sr. fellow, 1981; Humboldt fellow, 1981, 88; Finnish Acad. fellow U. Helsinki, 1989. Mem. NAS, Am. Acad. Arts and Scis., Assn. Women in Math., Math. Assn. Am., Am. Math. Soc. (coun. 1980-83, trustee 1983-93), Inst. for Math. and Its Applications (gov. 1981-84), Swiss Math. Soc., Finnish Math. Soc., London Math. Soc., European Math. Soc., Finnish Acad. Sci., German Math. soc., Royal Norwegian Soc. Scis. and Letters. Home: 2139 Melrose Ave Ann Arbor MI 48104-4067

GEHRKE, JOAN SMITH, public relations director; b. Lincoln, Nebr., Oct. 11, 1947; d. Leo Weber and Frances Loretto (McEvoy) Smith; m. William J. Gehrke, Apr. 8, 1972; children: William J. Jr., Michael E., Joseph M. BA in Polit. Sci. magna cum laude, Creighton U., 1969. Mgmt. intern NASA, Washington, 1969-70, budget analyst, 1970-72; asst. to bus. mgr. Calif. State U., San Francisco, 1972-73; wage and compensation analyst Nat. Bank of Detroit, 1974-75; dir. cmty. rels. PVS Chems., Inc., Detroit, 1993—. Dep. campaign mgr. Nicholson for U.S. Senate, Inc., Roseville, Mich., 1995-96; vice chmn. Metro Matrix Human Svcs., Detroit, Detroit Sci. Ctr.; bd. dirs. United Way Cmty. Svcs., Detroit. Recipient Heart of Gold, United Way S.E. Mich., 1993, Spirit of Detroit, Detroit City Coun., 1993, Mich. Senate and House Resolution, Mich. Legislature, 1994. Mem. Detroit Area Grantmakers, Jr. League Detroit (pres. 1987-88), Greater Detroit C. of C. (bus. contbrns. com.), Women's Econ. Club, Holley Ear Inst. (adv. coun. 1995—), Sigma Gamma (adv. bd.). Republican. Roman Catholic.

GEHRKE, KAREN MARIE, accountant; b. Gaylord, Minn., Apr. 12, 1940; d. Stanley Henry and Frieda Marie (Hammel) Ostermann; m. Orville Raymond Gehrke, Oct. 21, 1961 (div. Aug. 1994); children: Kimberly, Karla, Kent. Grad. high sch., Gaylord, 1958. Inspector Fingerhut Mfg., Gaylord, 1959-60; rewinder 3M, Hutchinson, Minn., 1960-61; packer 3M, Hutchinson, 1971-72; sec. Boehmke Ins. Agy., Gaylord, 1961-63, Law Office of H.A. Knobel, Gaylord, 1964-68; teller First State Fed. Savs. and Loan, Hutchinson, 1969; sec. Wally's Tire Shop, Hutchinson, 1970, Lyle R. Jensen, CPA, Hutchinson, 1974-84; owner Karen M. Gehrke L.P.A., Hutchinson, 1984—. Mem. Nat. Assn. Female Execs., Nat. Soc. Pub. Accts., Minn. Assn. Pub. Accts., Hutchinson Area C. of C.

GEIB, GEORGE WINTHROP, history educator; b. Buffalo, Oct. 31, 1939; s. Irving G. and Jessie A. (Hammond) G.; m. Mirian K. Orelup, Aug. 17, 1973; children: Helen K., Geoffrey W. BA, Purdue U., 1961; MA, U. Wis., 1963, PhD, 1969. Prof. history Butler U., Indpls., 1965—. Author: Indianapolis: Hoosier Circle City, 1981, Lives Touched by Faith, 1987 (IRHA Best Book 1991), Indianapolis First, 1990. Pres., mem. Indpls. Civilian Fire Merit Bd., 1980-87, Indpls. Hist. Preservation Com., 1989—; Presdl. elector from Ind. U.S. Electoral Coll., 1984; mem. Marion County Sheriff's Pension Bd., Indpls., 1987—, Ind. Constitution Bicentennial Com., Indpls., 1987-91; bd. dirs. Ind. Humanities Coun., Indpls., 1980-85, Ind. Ass. Historians, Indpls., 1989-91. Fellow Woodrow Wilson Found., 1961, Henry Vilas, 1964, English Speaking Union, 1979; Jenn Rsch. grantee Jenn Found., 1987, C-SPAN ednl. grantee, 1995. Fellow Ind. Policy Rev. (sr.); mem. Ind. Acad. of the Social Scis. (bd. dirs. 1991). Republican. Presbyterian. Office: Butler U Dept History 4600 Sunset Ave Indianapolis IN 46208-3443

GEIER, JAMES AYLWARD DEVELIN, manufacturing company executive; b. Cin., Dec. 29, 1925; s. Frederick V. and Amey (Develin) G.; children: Deborah Anne, James Develin, Aylward Whittier. Student, Williams Coll., 1947-50; hon. doctorate, U. Cin., Wilmington Coll., Cin. Tech. Coll. With Cin. Milacron Inc., 1951—, v.p., 1964, dir., 1966, exec. v.p., 1969, pres., chief exec. officer, 1970-90, chmn. exec. com., 1991—; bd. dirs. Clark Equipment Co., USX Corp., BDM Holdings, Inc. Mem. Labor-Industry Coalition for Internat. Trade; commr. Hamilton County Park Dist.; trustee Cin. Mus. Natural History, Rensselaer Poly. Inst., 1987—; mem. Kenton County Airport Bd.; pres. Children's Home Cin., 1990—. With USAAF, 1944-46. Mem. Assn. Mfg. Tech. (chmn. 1988-89), Mgmt. Execs. Soc. (exec. com., chmn. 1991—), U.S. C. of C. (bd. dirs.), Comml. Club, Commonwealth Club, Queen City Club, Camargo Club. Republican. Office: 455 Delta Ave Ste 108 Cincinnati OH 45226-1127

GEIGER, HAROLD STEPHEN, television producer; b. Houma, La., Apr. 17, 1957; s. Emanuel B. and Selma C. Geiger. B in Journalism, U. Mo., 1977. Reporter, announcer Sta. KHOM-FM, Houma, 1973-75; producer, reporter Sta. KFRU-AM, Columbia, Mo., 1977; reporter KPLC-TV, Lake Charles, La., 1978; producer, assignment editor KATC-TV, Lafayette, La., 1979-82; producer KHOU-TV, Houston, 1982-87, KTVI-TV, St. Louis, 1988—. Recipient award for best newscast UPI La., 1980. Mem. Soc. Profl. Journalists, Internat. Brotherhood Electrical Workers. Jewish. Home: 605 Clara Ave Apt 108 Saint Louis MO 63112-1934 Office: KTVI-TV 2 5915 Berthold Ave Saint Louis MO 63110

GEIGER, TERRY, state legislator. Rep. Mich. State Dist. 87, 1995—. Address: PO Box 30014 Lansing MI 48909-7514

GEIMAN, J. ROBERT, lawyer; b. Evanston, Ill., Mar. 5, 1931; s. Louis H. and Nancy O'Connell-Crowe G.; m. Ann L. Fitzgerald, July 29, 1972; children: J. Robert, William Patrick, Timothy Michael. BS, Northwestern U., 1953; JD, Notre Dame U., 1956. Bar: Ill. 1956, U.S. Ct. Appeals (7th cir.) 1956, U.S. Supreme Ct. 1969. Assoc. Eckert, Peterson & Lowry, Chgo., 1956-64; Peterson & Ross Peterson, Lowry, Rall, Barber & Ross, Chgo., 1964-70; ptnr. Peterson & Ross, Chgo., 1970—; mem. com. on civil jury instructions Ill. Supreme Ct., 1979-81. Case editor Notre Dame Law Rev., 1956. Bd. advisors Cath. Charities of Archdiocese of Chgo., 1973—. Fellow Internat. Acad. Trial Lawyers, Am. Coll. Trial Lawyers, Ill. Bar Found.; mem. ABA (aviation com., tort and ins. practice sect. 1980—), Ill. Bar Assn. (sec. 1969-70, sec. bd. govs. 1969-71), Chgo. Bar Assn. (aviation law com. 1970-73), Bar Assn. of 7th Fed. Ct. (meetings com. 1968-70, vice chmn. membership com. 1973-75), Soc. Trial Lawyers Cath. Lawyers Guild of Chgo. (bd. advisors 1973—), Law Club Chgo., Chgo. Athletic Assn. (pres. 1973), Mid-Am. Club, Mich. Shores Club (Wilmette). Republican. Office: Peterson & Ross 200 E Randolph St Ste 7300 Chicago IL 60601-6436

GEIS, PHILIP ANTHONY, microbiologist; b. El Paso, Tex., Oct. 31, 1948; s. Robert William and Virginia Luella (Taylor) G. BA in Microbiology, U. Tex., 1975, PhD of Microbiology, 1981. Microbiologist, sect. head Procter & Gamble Co., Cin., 1981—; com. mem. Chem. Specialties Mfrs. Assn., Washington, 1988—; chair preservation com. Cosmetic Toiletry Fragrance Assn., Washington, 1985—. Contbr. chpts. in books and articles to profl. jours. Judge sci. fair Walnut Hills, Madiera, Kings Mill, Cin., Mason, Ohio, 1985—; mem. Hamilton County Solid Waste Visioning Com., Cin., 1991. With U.S. Army, 1971. Recipient Commendation medal U.S. Army. Mem. Am. Soc. Microbiology (reviewer continuing edn. program 1982—), Ohio Acad. Science, Soc. Indsl. Microbiology (assoc. editor newsletter 1982—), Mensa, Theta Xi, Phi Eta Sigma. Home: 8226 Baytree Ct West Chester OH 45069

GEISEL, MICHAEL OLIVER, city official; b. St. Louis, Nov. 5, 1959; s. Oliver Arthur James Geisel and Wanda Lee Geisel Cunningham; m. Sandra Ann McKay, May 28, 1982; children: Lindsay Kaitlin, Jordan Alexandra. BSCE, U. Mo., Rolla, 1982; MBA, U. Mo., St. Louis, 1993. Registered profl. engr., Mo. Jr. engr. Ga. Power Co., Waynesboro, 1983-84; civil engr. City of St. Charles, Mo., 1984-86; engring. and ops. adminstr. City of Maryland Heights, Mo., 1986-88; asst. city engr. City of Chesterfield, Mo., 1988-94, dir. pub. works, city engr., 1994—. Mem. ASCE, NSPE, Am. Concrete Inst., Inst. Traffic Engrs., Am. Pub. Works Assn.,Mo. Soc. Profl. Engrs. Home: 1114 Athena Way Saint Peters MO 63376 Office: City of Chesterfield 922 Roosevelt Pkwy Chesterfield MO 63017

GEISENDORFER, JAMES VERNON, author; b. Brewster, Minn., Apr. 22, 1929; s. Victor H. and Anne B. (Johnson) G.; student Augustana Coll., 1950-51, Augsburg Coll., 1951-54, Orthodox Luth. Sem., 1954-55; BA, U. Minn., 1960; LLD, Burton Coll. and Sem., 1961; m. Esther Lillian Walker, Sept. 23, 1949; children: Jane, Karen, Lois. Grain buyer Pillsbury Mills, Inc., Worthington, Minn., 1947-48; hatchery acct., Worthington, 1949-50; night supr. Strutwear, Inc., Mpls., 1951-52; dispatcher Chgo. and North Western Ry., 1953-54; office mgr. Froedtert Malt Corp., Mpls., 1955-56, Nat. Automotive Parts Assn., 1957-60; sr. creative writer Brown & Bigelow, St. Paul, 1960-72; religious rschr., writer, 1972—; rsch. cons. Inst. for the Study of Am. Religion; mem. panel of reference Chelston Bible Coll., New Milton, Eng. Recipient Amicus Poloniae medal Polish Ministry of Culture and Edn., 1969. Mem. AAAS, Am. Acad. Religion, Acad. Ind. Scholars, Wis. Evang. Luth. Synod Hist. Inst., Augustana Hist. Soc., Ea. Territorial Hist. Soc. (charter), Medieval Acad. Am., Renaissance Soc. Am., Wis. Acad. Scis., Arts and Letters, N.Y. Acad. Scis., Aristotelian Soc., Hegel Soc. Am., Sixteenth Century Studies Conf., Acad. Polit. Sci., Internat. Soc. for Comparative Study of Civilizations, Collingwood Soc., Internat. Assn. Greek Philosophy, Boethius Soc., Brit. Soc. Philosophy Religion, Inst. Interdisciplinary Rsch. Lutheran. Author: (with J. Gordon Melton) A Directory of Religious Bodies in the United States, 1977; Religion in America, 1983, Religion USA, 1989; mem. editorial bd. Biog. Dictionary of American Cult and Sect Leaders; contbr. articles to books and periodicals; cons. editor Directory of Religious Organizations in the United States, 1977. Address: 1001 Shawano Ave Green Bay WI 54303-3020

GEISENHEIMER, NORMAN KENNETH, sales, marketing, manufacturing executive; b. Milw., June 16, 1940. BS, Milw. Sch. Engring., 1968. Mgmt. positions Allen Bradley Co., Milw., 1964-77; br. mgr. Sumer Inc., Brookfield, Wis., 1977-91; v.p. Control Products, Grafton, Wis., 1991—; pres. Electronic Reps. Assn., Milw., 1980-84. With U.S. Airforce, 1958-62. Office: Control Products Corp 1000 Hickory St Grafton WI 53024-1128

GEISLER, HANS EMANUEL, gynecologic oncologist; b. Ratibor, Germany, Apr. 5, 1935; came to U.S., 1938; s. Harry and Marianne C. (Barthel) G.; m. Margaret Ann Colglazier; children: Dorothy Marianne, Kathleen Marie, Stephan Harry, Suzanne Joan, John Patrick. HAB, Xavier U., 1955; MD, Loyola U., Chgo., 1959. Cert. Am. Bd. Ob-Gyn., Gynecologic Oncology. Pvt. practice specializing in gynecologic oncology and surgery Indpls., 1965—; asst. prof. ob-gyn. Ind. U. Med. Ctr., Indpls., 1967-84, dir. gynecol. tumor svc., 1967-70, clin. assoc. prof. ob-gyn., 1984-90, clin. prof. ob-gyn, 1990—; dir. gynecol. oncology Meth. Hosp., Indpls., 1970-72, 85-91; dir. gynecol. oncology div. St. Vincent Hosp., Indpls., 1972—, chmn. cancer com., 1985—, dir. oncology program, 1985-88. Contbr. articles to profl. jours. Mem. Marion County Cancer Soc., Indpls., profl. edn. com. Am. Cancer Soc., Indpls., Fire Merit Bd. Indpls., Com. to Select Police Chief, Indpls., 1975; pres. St. Luke Parish Coun., 1988-90; mem. Archdiocesan Pastoral Coun., 1991-94. Decorated knight Equestrian Order of Holy Sepulchre of Jerusalem; named Disting. Physician, St. Vincent Hosp. and Health Ctrs., 1996. Mem. AMA, Ind. Med. Soc., Med. Soc. Indpls., Am. Coll. Ob-Gyn., Soc. Gynecol. Oncologists, Ctrl. Assn. Ob/Gyn, Continental Gynecol. Soc. (pres.), Soc. Meml. Gynecol. Oncologists (pres.), Am. Assn. Pro-Life Ob/Gyn (bd. dirs.), Am. Assn. for Med. Ethics, European Soc. Gynecol. Oncologists, Internat. Soc. Gynecol. Oncologists. Republican. Roman Catholic. Home: 10609 Winterwood Carmel IN 46032-8258 Office: 8424 Naab Rd Indianapolis IN 46260-1954

GEIST, JILL MARIE, medical writer; b. Oak Park, Ill., Nov. 11, 1959; d. Raymond Joseph and Julia Thersa Weiner; children: Samantha Rae, Jacob Lee. Student, Coll. of Lake County, Grayslake, Ill., 1982-86. Line worker Zenith Microcircuits, Elk Grove, Ill., 1978, inspector, 1978, prodn. screen specialist, 1978-79, group leader screen print, 1979-80, process control inspector, 1980-81, engring. technician, 1981-83; engring. specialist Abbott Labs., Abbott Park, Ill, 1983-89, process devel. engr., 1989-93; new product coord. Abbott Labs., Abbott Park, Ill., 1993-95, med. writer, 1995—. Patentee in field. Pres., co-founder Abbott Parent Network, Abbott Park, Ill., 1989-91, pres. emeritus, 1992. Office: Abbott Labs D-7B4AP6A-2 100 Abbott Park Rd Abbott Park IL 60064-3501

GEISTFELD, RONALD ELWOOD, dental educator; b. St. James, Minn., Nov. 9, 1933; s. Victor E. and Viola (Becker) G.; m. Lois N. Tolzman Wilkens, June 15, 1955 (div. June 1974); m. Annette L. Swenson, Jan. 14, 1977; children: Shari, Mark, Steven, Ann, Leah, Erik. AA, Bethany Jr. Coll., 1952; BS, U. Minn., 1954, DDS, 1957. Pvt. practice dentistry Northfield, Minn., 1959-72; clin. asst. prof. dentistry U. Minn. Sch. Dentistry, Mpls., 1969-72, assoc. prof., 1972-82, chmn. dept. operative dentistry, 1978-87, prof., 1982—; dental cons. Hennepin County Med. Ctr., Mpls., 1975-96, VA Hosp., Mpls., 1977-96, VA Hosp., St. Cloud, Minn., 1978-96, Human Performance and Informatics Inst., Atama, Japan, 1990-95, K-9 Dental Sys. Quidnunc Australia Pty. Ltd., 1994-95, Metro Dental Group, Mpls., 1995—, VGM Expert Systems, 1996—, The Dentists Ins. Co., 1995—; mem. resource faculty for Bush faculty devel. program on excellence and diversity in teaching U. Minn., 1993-94. Pres. PTA, Northfield, 1965, Arts Guild, Northfield, 1968; bd. dirs., chairperson Rice County Health and Sanitation Bd., Faribault, Minn., 1966-74; bd. dirs. Northfield Bd. Edn., 1969-74; pres. Roseville Luth. Ch., 1987-88. Capt. U.S. Army, 1957-59. Am. Coll. Dentists fellow, 1972. Mem. Am. Dental Assn. (chairperson operative dentistry sect. 1979-80, curriculum cons. 1981-88, grants and spl. projects request evaluator 1988-92, Am. fund for Dental Health, edit. review bd. JADA 1992-96), Minn. Dental Assn. (ethics com. 1969-76, chairperson sci. and ann. sessions com. 1984-86, spkr. house del. 1992-96, del. to ADA 1992-96, bd. dirs. 1992-96), Mpls. Dist. Dental Soc. (program chairperson 1978-79, peer rev. com. 1988-92, bd. dirs. 1979-80, 87-89, MDA del. 1989-92), Minn. Acad. Restorative Dentistry (pres. 1979-80), Minn. Acad. Gnathological Rsch. (pres. 1986-87), Am. Assn. Dental Schs. (chairperson operative dentistry sect. 1984-85, edit. rev. bd. 1984-88), Acad. Operative Dentistry (exec. council 1978-81, rsch. com. 1987-89), Am. Acad. Gold Foil Operators, Northfield C. of C. (treas. and chairperson 1968-70), Delta Sigma Delta, Omicron Kappa Upsilon (Theta chpt.). Lodge: Rotary (pres. Northfield 1972-73). Home: 740 River Dr Apt 21D Saint Paul MN 55116-1037 Office: U Minn Sch Dentistry 8-450 Moos Tower 515 Delaware St SE Minneapolis MN 55455-0348

GELBER, BRIAN, commodities trader; b. 1954. With Thomson Mc Kinnon Securities, Chgo., 1975-82; with Gelber Group Inc., Chgo., 1982—, pres. Office: Gelber Group Inc 141 W Jackson Blvd Ste 1 Chicago IL 60604*

GELDIEN, JUDITH RUTH MOTTER, elementary educator; b. Ravenna, Ohio, June 3, 1944; d. Theodore James and Lois Ethel (McHenry) Motter; m. Robert James Geldien, Aug. 29, 1964; children: Christopher Scott, Wendy Lynne. BS, Ind. U., Ft. Wayne, 1980, MS, 1983; postgrad., Ball State U., 1991-95. Elem. tchr. East Allen County Schs., New Haven, Ind., 1981—; tchr. Sci. Day Camp, 1992—; mem. Enriching Activities for Creative Sciencing, 1994—. Mem. subcom. Dist. Planning Commn., East Allen County Schs., New Haven, 1991-92; vol. Sci. Ctrl., 1990—. Mem. NEA, Internat. Reading Assn., Hoosier Assn. Sci. Tchrs. (presenter convs. 1992-95), East Allen County Schs. Assn., Ind. Educators Assn., East Allen Educators Assn. (bldg. rep. 1987-89, 92—), Delta Kappa Gamma (chmn. attendance 1987-89, treas. 1989—). Republican. Home: 3914 Scarborough Dr New Haven IN 46774-2710 Office: Monroeville Elem Sch 401 Monroe St Monroeville IN 46773-9306

GELFAND, IVAN, investment advisor; b. Cleve., Mar. 29, 1927; s. Samuel and Sarah (Kruglin) G.; m. Suzanne Frank, Sept. 23, 1956; children: Dennis Scott, Andrew Steven. BS, Miami U., Oxford, Ohio, 1950; postgrad., Case Western Res. U., 1951; grad., Columbia U. Bank Mgmt. Program, 1968; certs., Am. Inst. Banking, 1952-57. Acct. Cen. Nat. Bank Cleve., 1950-53, v.p., mgr. bank and corp. investments, 1957-75; chief acct. Stars & Stripes newspaper, Darmstadt, Germany, 1953-55; account exec. Merrill, Lynch, Pierce, Fenner & Smith, Inc., Cleve., 1955-57; chmn., CEO Gelfand, Quinn & Assos., Inc., Cleve., 1975-83; v.p., mng. dir. Prudential-Bache Securities, Inc., 1983-85; pres. Lindow, Gelfand and Quinn, Inc., 1976-83; co-editor Gelfand-Quinn/Liquidity Portfolio Mgr. Newsletter, 1978-81, Gelfand-Quinn Analysis/Money Market Techniques, 1981-84; money market columnist Nat. Thrift News, 1976-78, guest money market columnist, 1982-85; pres. Ivan Gelfand & Assocs., Inc., 1985-90; sr. v.p. Prescott, Ball & Turben, Inc., 1986-88; v.p., dir. fixed income investments Roulston & Co., 1988-90; chief exec. officer Gelfand Ptnrs. Asset Mgmt., Cleve., 1990—; instr. investments adult divsn. Cleve. Bd. Edn., 1956-58, Am. Inst. Banking, 1958-68; talk show host Sta. WERE, Cleve., 1993-95; lectr. econs., fin. instn. portfolio mgmt., cash mgmt., 1972—; guest lectr., spkr. nat. and local TV and radio stas. Mem. investment com. United Torch Cleve., 1972-74; study-rev. team capt. Lake Erie Regional Transp. Authority, 1973-77; trustee Mt. Sinai Med. Ctr., Cleve., 1983-92, 93-96, treas., 1986-89, chmn. investment com., 1989-92; trustee Cleve. Coll. Jewish Studies, 1988-93; mem. bond com. Jewish Cmty. Fedn., Cleve., 1979-91, fin. com., 1981-85, trustee, 1986-89, 90-92; mem. Cuyahoga County Rep. Fin. Com., 1978-82, exec. com. Cuyahoga County Rep. Orgn., 1982—; trustee Nat. Multiple Sclerosis Soc., Cleve. Ctr. No. Ohio Reg., 1991-96, Laurelwood Hosp., Cleve., 1994—. With AUS, 1945-47. Mem. Nat. Assn. Bus. Econs., Cleve. Soc. Security Analysts, Les Politiques, Oakwood Club, Union Club, Cleve. Econ. Club (pres. 1991-92), Thursday Econ. Club, Masons. Home: 2900 Alvord Pl Cleveland OH 44124-4702 Office: Gelfand Ptnrs Asset Mgmt Ohio Savs Plz 1801 E 9th St Cleveland OH 44114-3101

GEMBOLIS, DON, manufacturing engineer; b. Toledo, Ohio, June 5, 1952. BS, Toledo U., 1978. Mfg. engr. Parker Hannifin Filter Mfg., Metamora, Ohio, 1977—. Office: Parker Hannifin Filter Mfg 16810 Fulton Co Rd 2 Metamora OH 43540

GEMIGNANI, ROBERT BALDO, marketing director; b. Hancock, Mich., Sept. 4, 1948; m. June Lorene Harris; children: Karrie, Amy, Dominic. BSEE, Mich. Tech. U., 1970, MS in Bus. Adminstrn., 1971. Sales engr. Cooper Industries, Raleign, N.C., 1975-79; product mktg. mgr. Cooper Industries, Zanesville, Ohio, 1980-85; dist. mgr. Cooper Industries, Columbus, Ohio, 1986-89; dir. mktg. Reliable Power Products, Chgo., 1990—. V.p. Pirana Swim Club, Zanesville, 1983-84, pres., 1984-85. Mem. IEEE, Nat. Elec. Mfrs. Assn., Can. Elec. Assn., Nat. Ski Patrol. Home: 2118 University Dr Naperville IL 60565 Office: Reliable Power Products 11411 Addison St Franklin Park IL 60131

GEMMELL-AKALIS, BONNI JEAN, psychotherapist; b. Lansing, Mich., Mar. 11, 1950; d. James Stewart Gemmell and Alpha Alice (Hackenberg) Vanden Bosch; m. Thomas Joe Akalis, Dec. 14, 1974 (div. Sept. 94); children: Scott Aaron, Ty Alexander, Zachary Alan. BS, Ctrl. Mich. U., 1972, MA, 1974. Ltd. lic. psychologist; cert. social worker. Clin. psychologist, sr. mental health therapist Lincoln Ctr. for Emotionally Disturbed Children & Youth, Lansing, 1974-77; outpatient psychologist Grand Rapids (Mich.) Child Guidance Clinic, 1978-81; pvt. practice Grand Rapids Psychiat. Svcs., 1981-88; pvt. practice Associated Therapists, Inc., Grand Rapids, 1988—, pres., 1989-90. Grad. fellow Ctrl. Mich. U., 1972-73. Mem. Mich. Psychoanalytic Coun., Mich. Women Psychologists, Mich. Assn. Profl. Psychologists, Am. Group Psychotherapy Assn. (founder nat. registry 1996), Grand Rapids Area Psychology Assn., Psi Chi. Home: 632 Duxbury Ct SE Grand Rapids MI 49546-9605 Office: Psychol Svcs 1025 Spaulding Ste B Grand Rapids MI 49546

GENDLER, ALAN M., stock brokerage executive; b. Cleve., Feb. 21, 1943. BS in Mktg. and Econs., Miami U., Oxford, Ohio, 1965. 1st v.p. Merrill Lynch, Pepper Pike, Ohio, 1971—. With Ohio N.G., 1965-71. Republican. Jewish. Office: Merrill Lynch 30100 Chagrin Blvd Pepper Pike OH 44124-5705

GENDREAU, MARGOT LYNN, lobbyist; b. Deer Park, N.Y., Feb. 19, 1952; d. Raymond and Helen Louise (Schmidt) G. Pharmacy Technician, Baylor U., 1973-74; BFA, U. Mo., 1981. Registered pharmacy technician. Chief pharmacy tech. Columbia Regional Hosp., Columbia, Mo., 1976-77, Ellis Fischel State Cancer Hosp., Columbia, Mo., 1977-79; pharmacy tech. Harry S. Truman VA Hosp., Columbia, 1981-82; profl. products rep. Hoffman-La Roche, Nutley, N.J., 1982-86; profl. products rep. Boehringer-Ingelheim Pharm. Inc., Columbia, Mo., 1986-88, mgr. state govt. affairs, 1988—, mgr. managed healthcare svcs., 1995—. Bd. dirs. Abuse Assault Rape Crisis Ctr., Columbia, 1981; Mem. Health Care Task Force, 1991—, Am. Legion Exch. Coun., Washington, 1991—, Mo. Dem. Party, 1993—, Mo. C. of C., 1993—, Tex. C. of C., Austin, 1993—. With U.S. Army, 1973-75, USAR, 1976-82. Named Traveler of Yr., Mo. Pharmacy Assn., 1988. Mem. Am. Legis. Exch. Coun., Kans. Parmacy Assn., Midwest Pharmacy Technicians Assn. (pres. 1980), Mo. Pharm. Travelers Assn. (pres. 1985-86), sec./treas. 1986—), Pharm. Mfrs. Assn. (chairperson Kans. task force 1991-93, S.D. task force). Roman Catholic. Office: Boehringer Ingelheim Pharm PO Box 10230 Columbia MO 65205-4003

GENNICK, JONATHAN GEORGE, information systems consultant; b. Detroit, Nov. 15, 1961; s. George and Beverly Ann (Ellis) G.; m. Donna Ruth Todd Gennick, Sept. 4, 1983; 1 child, Jennifer Lynn Gennick. BA, Andrews U., Berrien Springs, Mich., 1984. Programmer analyst Interlink, Inc., Berrien Springs, Mich., 1984-87, Andrews U., Berrien Springs, Mich., 1988-90; analyst Dow Chemical, Midland, Mich., 1990-93; cons. Solutions Consulting, St. Louis, 1993, Computer Horizons, Troy, Mich., 1993-94, Midland, Mich., 1994, KPMG Peat Marwick UP, Detroit, 1994—. Youth group leader Harbor Lights Pathfinder Club, Benton Harbor, Mich., 1987-90. Recipient Best Dealer Tip award Xerox Ventura Pub., 1987. Mem. Digital Equipment Computer User Soc.

GENOWAYS, HUGH HOWARD, systematic biologist, educator; b. Scottsbluff, Nebr., Dec. 24, 1940; s. Theodore Thompson and Sarah Louise (Beales) G.; m. Joyce Elaine Cox, July 28, 1963; children: Margaret Louise, Theodore Howard. AB, Hastings Coll., 1963; postgrad. U. Western Australia, 1964; PhD, U. Kans., 1971. Curator The Mus., Tex. Tech U., Lubbock, 1972-76, lectr. Mus. Sci. Program, 1974-76; curator Carnegie Mus. Natural History, Pitts., 1976-86; dir. U. Nebr. State Mus., Lincoln, 1986-94; chair mus. studies program U. Nebr., 1989-95, prof. state mus., 1986—, prof. biol. scis., 1987—, prof. mus. studies, 1990—. Author, editor: Mammalian Biology in South America, 1982; Natural History of the Dog, 1984; Contributions in Vertebrate Paleontology, 1984; Species of Special Concern in Pennsylvania, 1985; Current Mammalogy, 1987, 90; Biology of the Heteromyidae, 1993, Storage of Natural History Collections: A Preventive Conservation Approach, 1996. Packmaster, Allegheny Trails coun. Boy Scouts Am., 1981-83, asst. scoutmaster, 1983-86. Grantee, Fulbright, 1964, NSF, 1977-86, R.K. Mellon Found., 1981-86, Smithsonian Fgn. Currency Program, 1983-84, Inst. Mus. Svcs., 1989-95. Mem. Am. Soc. Mammalogists (pres. 1984-86, C. Hart Merriam award 1987, editor Spl. Pubs. 1995-96), Southwestern Assn. Naturalists (pres. 1984-85), Am. Assn. Museums, Nebr. Mus. Assn. (pres. 1990-92, 1st Hugh H. Genoways Achievement award 1994), Assn. Systematics Collections (bd. dirs. 1993-94), Nat. Inst. for Conservation Cultural Property (bd. dirs. 1993-94), Soc. Conservation Biology, Sociedad Argentina para Estudio Mamiferos, Lincoln Attractions and Mus. Assn. (chair 1987-94), Soc. Systematic Biologists, Rotary (bd. dirs. Lincoln N.E. club, 1990-92). Office: U Nebr-Lincoln State Mus W436 Nebraska Hall Lincoln NE 68588-0514

GENRICH, JUDITH ANN, real estate executive; b. Milw., Mar. 10, 1949; d. Einar and Eleanor Svea (Russell) Barnes; m. Nathan Mark Genrich, Oct. 23, 1971; children: Krista Svea, Erik Leif. BA, Gustavus Adolphus Coll., 1970; grad., Wis. Sch. Real Estate, Milw., 1979; postgrad., Carroll Coll., 1980, U. Wis., 1978-80, 92. Tchr. Oak Grove Middle Sch., Bloomington, Minn., 1970-71, Mukwonago (Wis.) High Sch., 1971-72; sales mgr. Lincoln Park Homes, West Allis, Wis., 1972-73, v.p., 1973-74, pres., 1974—; chmn. Mfrd. Housing Subdivision Sec., Madison, 1978-80; sec. Southeastern Wis. Housing, Milw., 1981-82, treas., 1982-84. Bd. dirs. Waukesha YMCA, 1985-87, v.p. 1987-89; bd. dirs. YMCA Heritage Found., 1994—; bd. dirs. Waukesha County United Way, 1984-87; mem. alumni bd. Gustavus Adulphus Coll., St. Peter, Minn., 1974-80; trustee The Cooper Inst., Naples, Fla., 1987-93, mem. adv. bd., 1993—. Recipient Dedicated Svc. award Wis. Mfrd. Housing, 1975-84, 88. Mem. West Allis C. of C., Wis. Mfrd. Housing Assn. (bd. dirs. 1975-80), Ind. Bus. Assn. Wis. (trustee University Lake 1991—), Merrill Hills Country Club (chair golf 1991), Milw. Women's Dist. Golf Assn. (bd. dirs. 1993, v.p. 1994, pres. 1995-96), Vasa Lodge, Eagle Creek Country Club, Chenequa Country Club. Republican. Lutheran. Home: 5219 State Road 83 Hartland WI 53029-9306

GENTRY, FRANK D., electrical engineer; b. Dayton, Ohio, Jan. 26, 1961. ASEET, Sinclair C.C., Dayton, 1985; BSEE, Wright State U., Dayton, 1990. Controls engr. Interphase, Centerville, Ohio, 1985-86; applications engr. All-Phase, Dayton, 1987-91; controls engr. Prodn. Design Svc., Dayton, 1991—. Republican. Baptist. Office: Prodn Design Svcs Inc 401 Fame Rd Dayton OH 45449-2314

GENTSCH, TED P., project engineer; b. Bronxville, N.Y., June 13, 1955. Student, U. Akron, 1973-77. SIS engr. Akron (Ohio) Air Products, 1981-82; design engr. Akron (Ohio) Welding and Spring, 1982-89; project engr. Linden Industries Inc., Peninsula, Ohio, 1989—; past pres. Akron (Ohio) Auto CAD Users Group, 1988-89. Staff sgt. USAF, 1977-81. Office: Linden Industries Inc 4020 Bellaire Ln Peninsula OH 44264-9786

GEO-KARIS, ADELINE JAY, state legislator; b. Tegeas, Greece, Mar. 29, 1918; student Northwestern U., Mt. Holyoke Coll.; LLB, DePaul U. Bar: Ill. Founder Adeline J. Geo-Karis and Assocs., Zion, Ill.; former mcpl., legis. atty. Mundelein, Ill., Vernon Hills, Ill., Libertyville (Ill.) Twp., Long Grove (Ill.) Sch. Dist.; justice of peace; former asst. state's atty.; mem. Ill. Ho. of Reps., 1973-79; mem. Ill. Senate, 1979—, asst. majority leader, 1992—; mayor, City of Zion, Ill. Served to lt. comdr. USNR., Res. ret. Recipient Americanism medal DAR; named Woman of Yr. Daughters of Penelope, Outstanding Legislator Ill. Fedn. Ind. Colls. and Univs., 1975-78, Legis. award Ill. Assn. Park Dists., 1976. Sponsor Guilty but Mentally Ill Law. Greek Orthodox. Office: Ill State Senate State Capitol Springfield IL 62706

GEOPPINGER, JAMES CARL, pharmacist; b. Cin., Aug. 3, 1940; s. Edwin John and Catherine Teresa (Tallon) G.; m. Judy Delle Lansdowne, Aug. 1, 1964; children: Carl E., John R., Teresa M., Catherine L. BS in Pharmacy, U. Cin., 1968. Registered pharmacist, Ohio, Ky., Ind. Staff pharmacist SuperX Drugs, Cin., 1968-69, store mgr., 1969-79, pharmacist, dist. supr., 1979-89; ops. mgr. Hook-SuperX, Inc, Cin., 1989-94; P.A.L. trainer Revco Drugs, 1994, regional pharmacy supr., 1995—; clin. instr. U. Cin. Coll. Pharmacy, 1987-94. Dir. Crimestoppers Greater Cin., 1981-90, treas., 1981-84. Named Citizen of Day Sta. WLW, 1981, Kentucky Col., 1987. Mem. Am. Pharm. Assn., Ohio State Pharm. Assn. (legis. com. 1990-94), Hamilton County Pharm. Assn. (treas. 1987, pres. 1990), Nat. Assn. Retail Druggists (Leadership award 1991), U. Cin. Alumni Assn. (trustee 1990—, v.p. 1993, pres. 1994-95). Roman Catholic. Office: 13 Mary St Cincinnati OH 45216

GEORGE, DAVID BRUCE, hotel executive; b. Wichita, Kans., Feb. 28, 1944; s. Harold R. and Helen V. (Gray) G.; m. Leslie A. Blake, Aug. 14, 1965 (div. Nov. 1980); children: David Blake, Alison Ann; m. Helen Angela Linn, Sept. 2, 1988; stepchildren: Andrew Ferguson, Ian Ferguson. BSBA, Kans. State U., 1966. With Target Stores, Inc., 1966-74; personnel mgr. Target Stores, Inc., Houston, 1969-71; ops. mgr. Target Stores, Inc., Clinton, Iowa, 1971-74; pres., chief operating officer Local Loan Co., Wichita, 1974-81; gen. mgr. Residence Inn Co., Tulsa, 1981-85; v.p. ops. TMH Hotels, Inc., Wichita, 1985—; bd. dirs., chmn. Local Loan Co., Wichita; gen. ptnr. DG Properties, L.P., Wichita, 1986—; mem. com. for operating stds. and procedures Residence Inn by Marriott, Bethesda, Md., 1988—. Co-chmn. United Way, Clinton, 1973. Mem. Nat. Pawnbrokers Assn., Tulsa Hotel and Motel Assn. (v.p. 1983), Jaycees (pres. Clinton chpt. 1974, Outstanding Pres. 1974), Optimists (v.p. Wichita chpt. 1977), Phi Delta Theta. Republican. Methodist. Home: 133 N Fountain St Wichita KS 67208-3831 Office: TMH Hotels Inc 250 N Water St Ste 325 Wichita KS 67202-1216

GEORGE, DEBORAH ANN, physical therapist, educator; b. Mayfield Heights, Ohio, Aug. 1, 1957; d. John George and Charlene B. (Kasher) Nemunaitis; m. Lawrence Daniel George, June 7, 1986; children: Elisabeth Marie, Sarah Kathlene. BS in Phys. Therapy, Cleve. State U., 1979; MS in Edn./Rsch., Ohio State U., 1984. Phys. therapist Sunny Acres SNF, Warrensville Heights, Ohio, 1979-81; phys. therapist, clin. instr. Euclid (Ohio) Gen. Hosp., 1981-82; part-time phys. therapist Patrick Mahoney, Inc., Columbus, Ohio, 1982-83; asst. prof., acad. coord. clin. edn. Ohio U., Athens, 1984-86; phys. therapy coord. head injury program, wheelchair clinic St. Francis Health Care Ctr., Greensprings, Ohio, 1986-94; asst. prof. acad. coord. clin. edn. U. Findlay, Ohio, 1994—. Editor, author (booklet) Family Book for the Brain Injury Survivor, 1993. Girl scout leader Girl Scouts Am., Seneca County, Ohio, 1994—. Mem. Am. Phys. Therapy Assn. (chairperson of edn. 1980-81, chairperson student component 1984-86), Sheltering Arms Hops. Found., Inc., Am. Phys. Medicine and Rehab. Assn., Nat. Head Injury Found. (mem. adv. bd. 1990-93), Northwest Ohio Clin. Edn. Consortium (founder, sec.), Phi Kappa Phi. Democrat. Roman Catholic. Office: Univ Findlay 1000 N Main St Findlay OH 45840

GEORGE, DONALD RICHARD, retired principal; b. Coffeyville, Kans., Oct. 1, 1926; s. Murl C. and Georgia M. (Leib) G.; m. Zepha Lowry, June 5, 1949; children: Donna L. Kellison, David L., Mary M. Tribby. BS in Edn., Pitts. State U., 1960; MS in Edn., Emporia State U., 1965. Tchr., asst. prin. Hugoton (Kans.) Elem. Sch., 1954-75; prin. Nelson Elem. Sch., Haysville, Kans., 1975-80; prin. W.D. Munson Primary Sch., Mulvane, Kans., 1980-93, ret., 1993. IDEA Kettering Found. fellow, 1978-83. Mem. Nat. Assn. Elem. Sch. Prins., Kans. Assn. Elem. Sch. Prins., United Sch. Adminstrs. Kans., Lions, Phi Delta Kappa. Mem. Ch. of God. Home: 713 Tristan Dr Mulvane KS 67110-1212

GEORGE, GARY MARK, pastor; b. Dover, Ohio, Feb. 10, 1957; s. L. Mark and Gaynalee Ethel (Stonebraker) G.; m. Lorraine Renee Baab, July 30, 1980; children: G. Mark, Michael Wayne. BS cum laude, Asbury Coll., 1979; MDiv, Ashland (Ohio) Theol. Sem. Ordained elder United Methodist Ch. Dir. youth ministry Scott Meml. United Meth. Ch., Cadiz, Ohio, 1979-80; pastor Dellroy (Ohio) United Meth. Ch., 1980-83; assoc. pastor Dueber United Meth. Ch., Canton, 1983-86; pastor Mt. Zion United Meth. Ch., Canton, 1986-91; sr. pastor Christ United Meth. Ch., Newcomerstown, Ohio, 1991—; mem. Bd. Ordained Ministry, North Canton, 1992—; chmn. Cambridge (Ohio) Dist. Com. for Ordained Ministry, 1992—; mem. Bd. Ch. & Soc., North Canton, 1990-92. Treas. Newcomerstown Acad. Boosters, 1993—; adv. bd. Gordon DeMarco Found., Newcomerstown, 1994—. Mem. Newcomerstown Ministerial Assn. (pres. 1994—), Phi Alpha Theta. Office: Christ United Meth Ch 648 Oak St Newcomerstown OH 43832

GEORGE, GARY RAYMOND, state senator; b. Milw., Mar. 8, 1954; s. Horace Raymond and Audrey C. (Chevalier) G.; BBA, U. Wis., 1976; JD, Mich. Law Sch., 1979; children: Alexander, Daniel Raymond. With Tax Dept., Arthur Young & Co., Milw., 1979-81; Wis. State senator from 6th Senate Dist., Madison, 1981—. Democrat. Roman Catholic. Office: 1100 W Wells St Apt 1711 Milwaukee WI 53233-2326

GEORGE, RANDY W., executive, manager; b. Columbus, Ohio, June 24, 1964. BSEE, DeVry, Columbus, 1988; MBA, Capital U., 1994. Sales, driver Clever Lumber, Mt. Vernon, Ohio, 1982-85; comms. group mgr. Eaton, Inc., Westerville, Ohio, 1985—. Home: 58 S Grove St Westerville OH 43081 Office: Eaton Inc 173 Heatherdown Dr Westerville OH 43081

GEORGE, THOMAS JOHN, municipal official; b. Ravenna, Ohio, Apr. 26, 1951; s. Emil and Wilma (Thomas) G.; m. Jean Finlin, Apr. 18, 1980; children: Meghan Frances, Timothy John. BA in Journalism, Ohio State U., 1973. Dep. dir. Ohio Bur. Motor Vehicles, Columbus, 1983-85; pres. TJMT Inc., Lakewood, Ohio, 1985-91; councilman City of Lakewood, Ohio, 1988—; bd. dirs. Aaccess, Cleve.; mem. Energy Environ. and Natural Resources Com., Washington, 1995. Mem. Greater Cleve. Suburban Coun. Assn., 1991—; bd. trustees Lakewood (OH). Mem. Greater Cleve. Suburban Coun. Assn., 1991—; trustee Lakewood Hosp., 1993—; dem. vice chair Cuyahoga County, Cleve, 1993—; pres. Cosmopolitan Dem. League, Cuyahoga County, Cleve., 1993—. Home: 1063 Rosalie Ave Lakewood OH 44107-1240 Office: Ohio Atty Gen 615 W Superior Cleveland OH 44113

GEORGIANA, JOHN THOMAS, electrical engineer; b. Gibbstown, N.J., June 5, 1942; s. Andrew Michael and Loretta Shirley (Cassidy) G.; m. Dorothy A. Cameron, June 30, 1963 (div. 1983); children: Lori Alice, Maria JoAnn, Andrew Michael. BS in Elec. Engring., Drexel U., Phila., 1966; MBA, Webster U., Webster Groves, Mo., 1989, postgrad., 1989—. Registered profl. engr., Tex. Power engr. Texaco, Inc., Westville, N.J., 1966-68; project engr. Owens Corning Fiberglass, Barrington, N.J., 1968-70; elec. engr., project engr. Pepperidge Farm/Campbell Soup, Norwalk, Conn., 1970-77, asst. mgr. new plant devel., 1975-76, mgr. maintenance engring., 1976-77; mgr. project engring. The Great Atlantic and Pacific Co., Montvale, N.J., 1977-82; major projedct engr. Interstate Brands Corp., Kansas City, Mo., 1982-83; project engr. Anheuser Busch/Campbell Taggart, St. Louis, 1983-89, Anheuser Busch/Metal Container, St. Louis, 1989-91; sr. equipment engring proposal coord. The Pritchard Corp., Kansas City, Kans., 1991—. Pres. PTA, Gibbstown, N.J., 1971-72. Mem. IEEE. Home: 13305 W 78th Pl Lenexa KS 66216-3025 Office: The Pritchard Corp 10950 Grandview St Overland Park KS 66210-1505

GEPHARDT, RICHARD ANDREW, congressman; b. St. Louis, Jan. 31, 1941; s. Louis Andrew and Loreen Estelle (Cassell) G.; m. Jane Ann Byrnes, Aug. 13, 1966; children: Matthew, Christine, Katherine. B.S., Northwestern U., 1962; J.D., U. Mich., 1965. Bar: Mo. 1965. Ptnr. Thompson & Mitchell, St. Louis, 1965-76; alderman 14th ward City of St. Louis, 1971-76; mem. 96th-104th Congresses from 3d Mo. dist., 1979—; Dem. leader. Dem. committeeman 14th ward, St. Louis, 1968-71; pres. Children's Hematology Rsch. Assn., St. Louis Children's Hosp., 1973-76; candidate for Dem. nomination for Pres. of U.S., 1987-88. Mem. Mo. Bar Assn., St. Louis Bar Assn., Am. Legion, Young Lawyer's Soc. (chmn. 1972-73). Club: Mid-Town (St. Louis). Lodge: Kiwanis. Office: US Ho of Reps 1226 Longworth HOB Washington DC 20515-2503 also: Office of Dem Leader H-204 The Capitol Washington DC 20515-6502*

GERALDSON, RAYMOND I., JR., lawyer; b. Racine, Wis., Oct. 19, 1940; s. Raymond I. Sr. and Evelyn (Thorpe) G.; m. Melinda Paine, June 13, 1964; children: Amy, Raymond I. III. BA, DePauw U., 1962; JD, Northwestern U., 1965. Bar: Ill. 1965, D.C. 1966, U.S. Dist. Ct. (no. dist.) Ill. 1967. Ptnr. Pattishall, McAuliffe, Newbury, Hilliard & Geraldson, Washington, 1965-67, Chgo., 1967—; adj. prof. John Marshall Law Sch. 1978—; lectr. in field. Contbr. articles on trademark law to profl. jours. Trustee Kendall Coll., 1985—, chmn., 1990—. Mem. ABA, Ill. State Bar Assn. (coun. sect. intellectual property law 1978-82, chmn. 1980-81), Chgo. Bar Assn., 7th Crct. Intellectual Property Law Assn. Chgo. (bd. dirs. 1984-86, 92-93, pres. 1991-92), Internat. Trademark Assn. (bd. dirs. 1985-87), Am. Intellectual Property Law Assn., Lawyers for Creative Arts (hons. coun. 1994—, bd. dirs. 1974-94, pres. 1976-78), Legal Club Chgo., Law Club Chgo., Econ. Club Chgo., Sunset Ridge Country Club, Union League Club of Chgo., Sigma Chi. Office: Pattishall McAuliffe Newbury Hilliard & Geraldson 311 S Wacker Dr Ste 5000 Chicago IL 60606-6618

GERBERRY, RONALD V., state legislator; b. Youngstown, Ohio, Jan. 10, 1953; s. Edward S. and Erma (Timko) G.; m. Kathryn M. Schrum, 1976; children: Deanna Lynn, Ronald Vincent Jr., Daniel Schrum. AB, Youngstown State U., 1975. Tchr. social studies Beaver Local Sch. Dist., Columbiana County, Ohio, 1978-79; with Trumbull County (Ohio) J.V.S., 1978-81, Hubbard Exempted Village Schs., Trumbull County, 1981-82; mem. Ohio Ho. of Reps., Columbus, 1982, now asst. minority whip. Mem. Austintown (Ohio) Bd. Edn., 1974-82, v.p., 1977, pres., 1978, 81. Named hon. county supt. Ohio County Sypts. Assn., Legislator of Yr. Ohio Assn. Elem. Sch. Adminstrs., Educator of Yr., Mahoning County Elem. Sch. Adminstrs., Legislator of Yr. Ohio Acad. Trial Lawyers, 1996. Democrat. Home: 2940 Whispering Pines Dr Canfield OH 44406-9628*

GERDES, NEIL WAYNE, library director; b. Moline, Ill., Oct. 19, 1943; s. John Edward and Della Marie (Ferguson) G. A.B., U. Ill., 1965; B.D., Harvard U., 1968; M.A., Columbia U., 1971; M.A. in L.S., U. Chgo., 1975; DMin, U. St. Mary of the Lake, 1994. Diplomate; Ordained to ministry Unitarian Universalist Assn., 1975. Copy chief Little, Brown, 1968-69; instr. Tuskegee Inst., 1969-71; library asst. Augustana Coll., 1972-73; editorial asst. Library Quar., 1973-74; librarian, prof. Meadville Theol. Schs., Chgo., 1973—; library program dir. Chgo. Cluster Theol. Schs., 1977-80; dir. Hammond Library, 1980—; prof. Chgo. Theol Sem., 1980—. Mem. exec. bd. Sem. Coop. Bookstore, Chgo., 1982—, Ctr. for Religion and Psychotherapy, Chgo., 1984—, Ind. Voters of Ill., 1986-89, Hyde Park-Kenwood Cmty. Orgn., Chgo., 1988-89; pres. Hyde Park-Kenwood Interfaith Coun., 1986-90; chair libr. coun. Assn. Chgo. Theol. Sch., 1984-88, 96—; trustee Civitas Dei Found., 1994—. Mem. ALA, Am. Theol. Library Assn., Chgo. Area Theol. Library Assn., Unitarian Universalist Mins. Assn. (sec., treas. nat. body 1990-94), Assn. Liberal Religious Scholars (sec., treas. 1975—), Phi Beta Kappa. Office: Chgo Theol Sem Hammond Libr 5757 S University Ave Chicago IL 60637-1507

GERDES, RALPH DONALD, fire safety consultant; b. Cin., Aug. 11, 1951; s. Paul Donald and Jo Ann Dorothy (Meyer) G. BArch, Ill. Inst. Tech., 1975. Registered architect, Ill. Architect Schiller & Frank, Wheeling, Ill., 1976; sr. assoc. Rolf Jensen & Assocs., Inc., Chgo., 1976-84; pres. Ralph Gerdes & Assocs., Inc., Indpls., 1984-88, chmn., 1988—; lectr. Purdue U., Ind. U., Ill. Inst. Tech., Butler U., Ball State U.; bd. dirs. Ind. Fire Svcs. Inst. Co-author: Planning and Designing the Office Environment, 1981. Recipient Joel Polsky prize Am. Soc. Interior Designers, 1983. Mem. ASHRAE, AIA (bldg. performance and regulations com. liaison to Nat. Fire Protection Agy.), Soc. Fire Protection Engring. (assoc., exec. com. Ind. chpt. 1992—, pres. 1995-96), Nat. Fire Protection Assn. (tech. coms.), Bldg. Ofcls. and Code Adminstrs., Internat. Conf. Bldg. Ofcls., Ind. Fire Safety Assn. (bd. dirs. 1986-92, 94-95, pres. 1989-91), Archs. and Engrs. Bldg. Ofcls. (bd. dirs. 1994-96, Ind. code devel. com.), Ind. Assn. Bldg. Ofcls., Ind. Soc. for Hosp. Engring., Maple Creek Country Club. Roman Catholic. Home: 556 Lockerbie Cir N Indianapolis IN 46202-3600 Office: 127 E Michigan St Ste 400 Indianapolis IN 46204-1518

GERDIN, BARRY F., JR., stockbroker; b. Pittsfield, Mass., Jan. 14, 1967; s. Barry F. and Annalee (Byers) G. BS, U. Mo., Columbia, 1991. Stockbroker Cutter & Co., Chesterfield, Mo., 1991—. With USAF, 1985-89. Mem. Broker Club. Office: Cutter & Co 15510 Olive Blvd Ste 204 Chesterfield MO 63017-0710

GERDINE, LEIGH, retired academic administrator; b. Sheyenne, N.D., June 22, 1917; s. O. E. and Margaret E. (Mattson) G.; m. Alice Strauch Meyer, Nov. 21, 1961. AB, U. N.D., 1938, MusD (hon.), 1989; MusB (Rhodes scholar), Oxford (Eng.) U., 1941, postgrad., 1946-48; PhD, U. Iowa, 1941; HHD (hon.), Washington U., St. Louis, 1979; LHD (hon.), Tarkio Coll., 1984, Webster U., 1990; HHD (hon.), U. N.D., 1990. Asst. prof. music Miss. State Coll. for Women, Columbus, 1941-42; assoc. prof., exec. sec. dept. music Miami (Ohio) U., 1948-50; prof., chmn. dept. music Washington U., St. Louis, 1950-70; pres. Webster U., St. Louis, 1970-90, pres. emeritus, 1990—; chmn. bd. dirs. Block Partnership, Inc., 1968-70; program annotator St. Louis Symphony Orch., 1950-66, acting mgr., 1965-67; trustee Gateway Found., 1993—. Translator: Phrasing and Articulation (by Hermann Keller), 1965, The Well-Tempered Clavier (by Hermann Keller), 1976, New Music with Thirty-One Notes (by Adriaan Fokker), 1975; pub. orchestrations Brahms sonatas, realizations of Handel violin sonatas, Bach flute sonatas; original work: Violin Concerto, 1996. Bd. dirs. St. Louis Symphony Soc., Opera Theatre St. Louis; chmn. emeritus bd. Sheldon Arts Found., St. Louis Cmty. Found., Ranken Tech. Coll. With USAAF, 1942-46, ETO. Decorated Bronze Star medal, Croix de Guerre France, Nat. Medal of Arts, 1989; recipient St. Louis award, 1989, Right Arm of St. Louis award Regional Commerce and Growth Assn., 1989; hon. fellow Lincoln Coll., Oxford U., 1991. Home: 801 S Skinker Blvd Apt 14B Saint Louis MO 63105-3228 Office: Exec Office Bldg Ste 1504 515 Olive St Saint Louis MO 63101-1849

GEREMIA, FRANK V., computer company executive; b. 1948. With Kemper Clearing Corp., Milw., 1987—; with Beta Systems Inc., Brookfield, Wis., 1987—, chmn., CEO. Office: Beta Systems Inc 350 N Sunny Slope Rd Brookfield WI 53005*

GERGIS, SAMIR DANIAL, anesthesiologist, educator; b. Beni-Suef, Egypt, Sept. 24, 1933; came to U.S., 1968; s. Danial and Hekmat (Assaad) G.; m. Dorothy K. Auen, June 16, 1973 (div. 1983); 1 child, Michael. M.B., Ch. B., Cairo U., 1954, D.A., 1957, D.M., 1958, M.D. in Anesthesia (Ph.D.), 1962; D.A., U. Copenhagen, 1963. Intern Cairo U. Hosp., 1955-56, resident, 1957-59; instr. dept. anesthesia U. Iowa Coll. Medicine, Iowa City, 1968-69, asst. prof., 1969-72, assoc. prof., 1972-76, prof., 1976—. Fellow Am. Coll. Anesthesiology; mem. AAAS, Am. Soc. Anesthesiologists, Internat. Anesthesia Rsch. Soc., N.Y. Acad. Scis., Am. Soc. Pharmacology and Exptl. Therapeutics, Soc. Exptl. Biology and Medicine, Nat. Soc. Med. Rsch., Soc. for Neurosurgery, Anesthesia and Neurologic Supportive Care Assn., Assn. Anesthesia Clin. Dirs., Am. Soc. Clin. Pharmacology, Assn. Univ. Anesthesiologists. Coptic Orthodox Christian. Home: 1019 Sunset St Iowa City IA 52246-4938 Office: U Iowa Dept Anesthesia Coll Medicine Iowa City IA 52242

GERHARDSTEIN, SAMUEL EDWARD, state agency administrator; b. Bellevue, Ohio, Jan. 6, 1956; s. Rodger Ambrose and Irene May (Griffin) G.; m. Charlotte Ebsen, Nov. 11, 1976 (div. 1986); children: Natalie Alice, Sonja Michelle; m. Brenda Leah Vickery, Jan. 17, 1992. BA in Polit. Sci. and Econs., Bowling Green State U., 1982, MPA, 1987. Legis. aide Ohio State Senate, Columbus, 1983-85; rsch. asst. Bowling Green (Ohio) State U., 1986-87; emergency preparedness rep. Toledo Edison, 1987-91; legis. liaison Dept. Adminstrv. Svcs., Columbus, 1991-93; dir. legis. affairs Pub. Utilities Commn. Ohio, Columbus, 1993-95; mgr. govtl. affairs Columbia Gas Ohio, Columbus, 1995—; mem. Edn. Tech. Equity Commn., Columbus, 1993-95, Ohio Sch. Net Interagy. Adv. Com., Columbus, 1994-95, Ottawa County 800 MHz Radio Adv. Bd., Port Clinton, Ohio, 1989-91. Chmn. Sandusky county Taft for Sec. of State, Bellevue, 1990; prin. Rep. Senate Campaign Com., Columbus, 1984. Sgt. USAF, 1974-78. Mem. Elks, Am. Legion, Am. Mensa. Roman Catholic. Home: 1721 Drew Ave Columbus OH 43235 Office: Columbia Gas Ohio 200 Civic Ctr Dr Columbus OH 43215

GERHART, PAUL F., business educator. AB in Econs., Princeton U., 1964; MBA in Labor & Indsl. Rels., U. Pa., 1966; PhD, U. Chgo., 1973. Asst. prof. Inst. Labor & Indsl. Rels., U. Ill., Urbana, 1969-77; assoc. prof. then prof. indsl. rels. Case Western Res. U., Cleve., 1977—, mem. exec. MBA program faculty, 1980—; mem. indsl. rels. staff Tex. Instruments, Dallas, Pa. Railroad, Phila., Lebanon (Pa.) Steel Foundry, 1962-66; rsch. assoc. Brookings Instn. Studies of Unionism in Govt., 1968-69; labor mgmt. rels. specialist U.S. Fed. Labor Rels. Coun., Washington, 1974-75; vis. asst. prof. indsl. rels. U. Chgo., 1975-76; vis. prof. U. Glasgow, vis. lectr. Catholic U., Lueven, Belgium, vis. scholar Arbetslivscentrum, Stockholm, 1984; vis. assoc. prof. Cornell U., 1990; book reviewer, rschr. in field. Contbr. articles to profl. jours. Trustee Luth. Med. Ctr., Cleve., 1983—; mem. exec. com. Fairview Gen. Hosp., Cleve., 1989-90, trustee, 1990—, chair quality assurance com., 1994—; program advisor Cmty. Re-Entry Program for Ex-Offenders, 1984-87; mem. grievance panel State of Ill., 1976-77; chmn. grievance procedure com. Civil Svc. Commn., Urbana, Ill., 1973-74. Joseph Wharton scholar, 1964-66; Ford Found. fellow, 1966-68. Mem. Am. Econs. Assn., Nat. Acad. Arbitrators (chair internat. studies com.), Internat. Indsl. Rels. Assn., Indsl. Rels. Rsch. Assn., Soc. Advancement Socio-Econs., Beta Gamma Sigma.

GERHOLD, PETER KARL, real estate executive; b. Vienna, Austria, Apr. 1, 1958. BA in Fin. and Econs., Loyola U., 1981. Asst. v.p. Deutsche Bank, N.Y.C., 1984-85; v.p. Palmer Group, Chgo., 1985-88; pres. Equity Resources Ltd., Chgo., 1988—. Mem. Exec. Club of Chgo., German C. of C., Am. c. of C. Office: Equity Resources Ltd 130 N Franklin St Ste 800 Chicago IL 60606-1815

GERIKE, ERNEST LUTHER, clergyman; b. Tripp, S.D., Nov. 13, 1917; s. Henry Frederick William and Clara Wilhelmina (Bornhoeft) G.; m. Vera Martha Roschke, June 11, 1944; children: Mary Ann Richard, James Walter, Kenneth John. BA, Concordia Sem., St. Louis, 1940, MDiv, 1944. Ordained to ministry, Luth. Ch. Pastor St. Paul Luth. Ch., East St. Louis, Ill., 1944-49, St. Andrew Luth. Ch., St. Louis, 1949-61; head pastor Trinity Luth. Ch., Bloomington, Ill., 1961-85, paster emeritus, 1985—; supply pastor Cen. Ill. Area, 1985—; advisor So. Ill. Luth. Women's Missionary League, East St. Louis, 1948, 49; v.p., bd. dirs. Cen. Ill. Dist. of Luth. Ch.-Mo. Synod, Springfield, 1964-85. Contbr. articles to profl. jours. Chmn. bd. dirs. Mid-Ill. Area Health Planning, Bloomington, 1984; com. mem. McLean County United Way, Bloomington, 1982-92. Mem. McLean County C. of C. (hosp. clergy staff liaison 1989-93), Kiwanis. Republican. Home: 711 S Cottage Ave Unit 106 Normal IL 61761-4337 Office: Trinity Luth Ch 801 S Madison St Bloomington IL 61701-6464

GERINGER, GERALD GENE, state legislator; m. Dorothy M. Geringer. Kans. state rep. Dist. 65, 1996—; health care cons., 1996—. Office: Southwest Medical Ctr W 15th St Liberal KS 67901*

GERLITZ, CURTIS NEAL, business executive; b. Wichita, Kans., Jan. 26, 1944; s. Gustav Albert and Elna (Olsgaard) G.; m. Audrey Jean D'Almaine, Oct. 6, 1973. BSBA, U. Minn., 1966; MBA, No. Ill. U., 1990. Purchasing agt. I. S. Berlin Press, Chgo., 1973-75; asst. purchasing agt. Daubert Chem. Co., Oak Brook, Ill., 1975-78; purchasing mgr. IBG Internat., Wheeling, Ill., 1978-86; dir. purchasing Advance Process Supply Co., Chgo., 1986-91; pres. Selectech, Mount Propsect, Ill., 1991—. Decorated Purple Heart. Mem. Nat. Assn. Purchasing Mgmt., Purchasing Assn. Chgo., Mfrs. Agts. Nat. Assn., United Assn. Mgrs. Reps. (mem. nat. bd. advisors 1994—), Beta Gamma Sigma, Sigma Iota Epsilon. Home: 404 S Helena Ave Mount Prospect IL 60056-2854 Office: Selectech Internat Inc 800 W Central Rd Mount Prospect IL 60056-2382

GERMAN, KRISTI LYNN, bank officer, small business owner; b. Yankton, S.D., Apr. 15, 1967; d. Harvey Clifford and Opal O. (Behrens) Stout; m. Thomas Allen German, June 27, 1992. BS, Wayne State Coll., 1989. Asst. bank examiner Fed. Deposit Ins. Corp., Sioux City, Iowa, 1989-93; compliance officer First State Bank, Ida Grove, Iowa, 1993—; pres. Hearts Afire, Inc., Holstein, Iowa, 1996—. Mem. Ida Grove C. of C. (bd. mem. 1994-95). Home and Office: 5139 210th St Holstein IA 51025

GERMANN, RICHARD PAUL, pharmaceutical company chemist, executive; b. Ithaca, N.Y., Apr. 3, 1918; s. Frank E.E. and Martha Minna Marie (Knechtel) G.; m. Malinda Jane Plietz, Dec. 11, 1942; 1 child, Cheranne Lee. Student (lab. asst.), U. N.Mex., summers 1938, 39; student (meteorology), Calif. Inst. Tech., 1939; BA, Colo. U., 1939, postgrad., 1940-41; student, Western Res. U. (Naval Rsch. fellow), 1941-43, Brown U., 1954. Chief analytical chemist Taylor Refining Co., Corpus Christi, 1943-44; rsch. devel. chemist Calco Chem. div. Am. Cyanamid Co., 1944-52; devel. chemist charge pilot plant Alrose Chem. Co. div. Geigy Chem. Corp., 1952-55; new product devel. chemist, rsch. div. W.R. Grace & Co., Clarksville, Md., 1955-60; chief chemist soap-cosmetic div. G.H. Packwood Mfg. Co., St. Louis, 1960-61; coord., promoter chem. product devel. Abbott Labs., North Chicago, Ill., 1961-71; internat. chem. cons. to mgmt., 1971-73; pres. Germann Internat. Ltd., 1973-82, Ramtek Internat. Ltd., 1973—; real estate broker, 1972-90; cons. major Japanese chem. cos., 1971—, dept. chemistry Bowling Green (Ohio) State U., 1988. Author: Science's Ultimate Challenge - The Re-evaluation of Ancient Occult Knowledge, Decontamination of Plant Wastes - An Overview; patentee in U.S. and fgn. countries on sulfonamides, vitamins, detergent-softeners and biocides. Rep. Am. Inst. Chemists to Joint Com. on Employment Practices, 1969-72; vestryman St. Paul's Episc. Ch., Norwalk, Ohio, 1978-81, chmn. adminstrn. and long-range planning commn., 1980-81, The Ch. of Light; trustee Svcs. for the Aging, Inc., 1982-94, treas., 1992-93, pres., 1994; mem. nutritional coun. Ohio Dist. Five Area Agy. on Aging, 1983-84; sr. adv. Ohio Assn. Ctrs. for Sr. Citizens, Inc., 1982—; bd. dirs. Christie Lane Industries, 1981—, chmn., 1988—; mem. com. Huron County Disaster Svcs. Agy., 1987-89. Fellow AAAS, Am. Inst. Chemists (chmn. com. employment rels. 1969-72), Chem. Soc. (London); mem. Am. Chem. Soc. (councilor 1971-73, chmn. membership com. chem. mktg. and econs. div. 1966-68, chmn. program com. 1968-69, del. at large for local sects. 1970-71, chmn. 1972-73, chmn. Chgo. program com. 1966-67, chmn. Chgo. endowment com. 1967-68, dir. Chgo. sect. 1968-72, chmn. awards com. 1972-73, sec. chem. mktg. and econs. group Chgo. sect. 1964-66, chmn. 1967-68), Internat. Sci. Found., Sci. Rsch. Soc. Am., Comml. Chem. Devel. Assn. (chmn. program com. Chgo. conv. 1966, mem. fin. com. 1966-67, ad hoc com. of Comml. Chem. Devel. Assn. and Chem. Market Rsch. Assn. 1968-69, co-chmn. pub. rels. Denver conv. 1968, chmn. membership com. 1969-70, mem. directory com. 1967-68, employment com. 1969-70), Nat. Security Indsl. Assn. (com. rep. ocean sci. tech. com., maintenance adv. com., tng. ad. com. 1962-70), Midwest Planning Assn., Am. Assn. Textile Chemists and Colorists, Am. Pharm. Assn., Midwest Chem. Mktg. Assn., Am. Mgmt. Assn., N.Y. Acad. Scis., Internat. Platform Assn., Am. Meteorol. Soc., Water Pollution Control Fedn., Lake County Bd. Realtors, World Future Soc., Midwest Planning Assn., Am. Fedn. Astrologers, Washington Astrological Assn. (v.p. 1959-60), Ancient Astronaut Soc., Am. Philatelic Soc., Firelands Stamp Club (v.p. 1996—), Am. Numismatic Assn., Am. Rose Soc., AARP (pres. Huron county Firelands chpt. #4110 1986-88, chmn. legis. com. 1988-90, active project vote), Chemists Club (N.Y.C., Chgo.), Torch Club, Toastmasters, Lions (sec. Allview, Md. 1956-57), Kiwanis, Masons, (32nd degree), Knights Templar, Rotary, Gamma Delta (pres. Cleve. chapt. 1941-42), Sigma Xi, Alpha Chi Sigma (chmn. profl. activities com. 1968-70, pres. Chgo. chpt. 1968-70). Home and Office: 6 Vinewood St Norwalk OH 44857-1919

GERMANO, CARMEN PETER, retired piezoelectric engineer, consultant; b. Cleve., Aug. 5, 1924; s. Anthony and Rosaria (Sava) G.; m. Joan Carol Lawrence, Jan. 10, 1959; children: Julie M., Peter C., Sara L., Jean M. Germano Wright, Joan C. Germano Cuva, Maria L., Ann M. Germano Ivanovics. BSEE, Northwestern U., 1950; MS in Physics, John Carroll U., 1952. Engr. Clevite Corp., Cleve., 1950-54; sect. head Clevite Rsch. Ctr., then Clevite Electronic Components, Cleve., 1954-59; sr. engr. Clevite Electronic Rsch., Cleve., 1959-61; sect. head Clevite Electronic Components, Bedford, Ohio, 1961-68, Piezoelectric divsn. Gould Inc., Bedford, 1968-70, Piezoelectric divsn. Vernitron, Bedford, 1970-76, Channel Products, Inc., Chagrin Falls, Ohio, 1976-78; chief engr. Channel Products, Inc., Chesterland, Ohio, 1978-86; sr. staff engr. Channel Products, Inc., Chesterland, 1986-91, ret., 1991; piezoelec. engring. cons. Cleve., 1991—; mem. piezo ceramic standards com. Mil. Standards, Bur. Ships, 1984-85; presenter at profl. confs. Contbr. articles to tech. jours. Sgt. U.S. Army, 1943-46, CBI. Mem. IEEE (sr. mem., vice chmn. Cleve. profl. group on audio 1955-56, chmn. 1956-57), Acoustical Soc. Am. Roman Catholic. Home and Office: 5046 Fairlawn Rd Cleveland OH 44124-1125

GERMANOTTA, JEFFREY STEVEN, investment banker; b. Milw., June 30, 1958; s. Louis Robert and Marily Jean (Robinson) G.; 1 child, Daniel Scott. BBA, U. Wis., Milw., 1980; MBA, Marquette U., 1989. Credit analyst First Wis. Nat. Bank, Milw., 1981, comml. loan officer, 1982-83, comml. banking asst. v.p., 1984-85; corp. banking group asst. v.p. Bank One, Milw. N.A., Milw., 1985-86; corp. planner Banc One Wis. Corp., Milw., 1986-87; v.p. corp. fin. Bank One Milw., N.A., 1987-89, v.p. and mgr. capital markets div., 1989-94; investment banker Robert N. Baird & Co. Inc., Equity Rsch., Brookfield, Wis., 1994—.

GERNAAT, JOHN, state legislator; m. Karen; four children. Student, Davenport Coll. Rep. Mich. Dist. 102, 1993—; ch. coun. Congressman Camp agrl. adv. com., Bill Schuette agrl. adv. com.; treas. late Sid Ouwinga Campaign com.; vice chair comms. com. Mich. Ho. Reps., 1993—, vice chair tax policy com., 1993—, transp., agriculture & forestry com., 1993—; owner, operator Dairy Beef Farm & Cash Crop. Named outstanding citizen of yr. Farm Bur.; recipient Missaukee Soil Conservation award. Mem. Jr. Achievement., McBain C. of C., McBain Downtown Devel. Auth. (treas.). Home: 10104 S Blodgett Rd Mc Bain MI 49657-9415 Address: 10104 S Blodget McBain MI 49657*

GERNTHOLZ, GERELD FELIX, farmer, state representative; b. Valley City, N.D., Sept. 7, 1936; s. Felix Alfred and Nellie Theresa (Thompson) G.; m. Marian Joyce Huether, June 28, 1959; children: Gregory, Beth, Steven. BS, N.D. State U., 1959. Mem. N.D. Ho. of Reps., 1984—; bd. dirs. Norwest Bank, Nat. Assn., Valley City, N.D., N.D. Winter Show, Valley City; mem. house appropriations com. N.D. Ho. of Reps., Bismarck, 1985—, chair govt. ops. sect. appropriations com., 1991—. Chmn. 24th Dist. Rep. Com., Valley City, 1983-84, mem. exec. com., 1982—; bd. dirs. Bethel Luth. Ch. Col. U.S. Army, N.D. N.G., 1957-94. Decorated Legion of Merit; recipient Outstanding Agriculturist award N.D. State U. Alumni Assn., 1985, N.D. Centennial Farm award Greater N.D. Assn., 1989, Charles Dick medal of merit N.G. Assn. U.S., 1993; named An Outstanding Young Farmer, Jaycees, 1967. Mem. Nat. Farmers Orgn. (county pres. 1965—), N.G. Assn. U.S., N.D., Bames County Agrl. Improvement Assn., Valley City Area C. of C., Valley City State Univ. V-500 Club. Home: 2734 105th Ave SE Sanborn ND 58480-9743

GERRISH, WAKEFIELD E., investment broker; b. Clinton, Ind., July 11, 1931. Student, Waubash Coll., 1949-51; BS in Bus., Ind. U., 1953; post-grad., Sch. Warton, 1981-84. CFP. Investment broker Dupont Corp., Terre Haute, Ind., 1960-70; mgr. Hilliard-Lyons, Terre Haute, 1973-85; investment broker Shearson-Lehman-Hutton, Terre Haute, 1985-90, AG Edwards and Sons, Terre Haute, 1990—. With U.S. Army, 1950-54, Korea. Methodist. Home: 2 Chickadee Ln Terre Haute IN 47803 Office: AG Edwards and Sons Inc 1 South 6th St Terre Haute IN 47807

GERS, HARVEY, marketing professional; b. St. Louis, May 27, 1947; s. Bernard S. and Jean (Brody) G.; m. Susan Lynn Kozloff, June 6, 1971; children: Andrew S., Jeffrey B. BA, Washington U., St. Louis, 1969, MBA, 1971. Engring. asst. Brasch Mfg. Co., St. Louis, 1966-70; mgmt. trainee Fed. Res. Bank St. Louis, 1971-72; sr. site selection analyst May Dept. Stores Co., St. Louis, 1972-76; sr. mktg. analyst Am. Investment Co., Clayton, Mo., 1976-79; sr. fin. analyst ITT Comml. Fin. Corp., Clayton, 1979-93, mgr. mktg. rsch., 1994-95; dir. mktg. planning and analysis Deutsche Fin. Svcs., St. Louis, 1995—; pres. Computer Support Corp., St. Louis 1985; cons. Sr. Mgmt. Svcs., St. Louis 1986-88. Co-developer automated comml. bankruptcy prediction sys., 1986, physician referral sys., 1987, expert credit sys., 1988, preliminary design of bankruptcy predictor using neural networks, 1992. Mem. Mo. Real Estate Brokers Assn. (former), Mystery Club. Home: 14945 Manor Ridge Dr Chesterfield MO 63017-7712 Office: Deutsche Fin Svcs 655 Maryville Centre Dr Saint Louis MO 63141

GERSHON, WILLIAM I., copywriter, voiceover actor, communications executive; b. Chgo., Apr. 12, 1934; s. Irving and Ruth (Gershbein) G.; m. Matilda (Marion) K. May, June 29, 1957. Grad., Wright Jr. Coll., Chgo., 1954; BA in Speech and English, Roosevelt U., 1956. Classical music dir., announcer Sta. WNIB-FM, Chgo., 1955-57; writer H. Epstein Advt., Chgo., 1956-59; asst. to copy chief Walgreen Co., Deerfield, Ill., 1959-61; advt. mgr. Lyon & Healy, Inc., Chgo., 1961-63; writer/account mgr. Garfield-Linn & Co., Chgo., 1963-78, v.p., 1978-82; sr. writer Abelson-Taylor, Inc., Chgo., 1983-84; owner Bill Gershon Mktg. Communications, Skokie, Ill., 1982—. Creator of the name Expocenter for Chgo.'s Apparel Ctr. Exposition Hall; voiceover actor; children's book narrations My Own Noah's Ark, My Own Nativity; sales tng. modules, employee tng. modules Nat. Edn. Tng. Group; radio and TV commls. Mem. Independent Writers of Chgo. Office: Bill Gershon Mktg Comm 9828 Crawford Ave Skokie IL 60076-1107

GERSON, GARY STANFORD, rabbi; b. Ypsilanti, Mich., June 17, 1945; s. Bernard and Ruth Edith (Levin) G.; m. Carol Roberts, Oct. 12, 1969; children: Jordana, Jessica. BA magna cum laude, Western Mich. U., 1967; MA in Religion, Temple U., 1976; grad., Reconstructionist Rabbinical Coll., 1976; MA in Psychology, Temple U., 1977; Dr. Ministry, Chgo. Theol. Seminary, 1984. Ordained rabbi, 1976. Rsch. fellow U. Pa., 1969, teaching asst., 1972; teaching asst. Temple U., Phila., 1974-75; rabbi Temple Brith Achim, King of Prussia, Pa., 1974-78; asst. rabbi Temple Beth Israel, Chgo., 1978-79; rabbi Oak Park (Ill.) Temple B'nai Abraham Zion, 1979—; psychologist Benjamin Rush Ctr. for Mental Health and Mental Retardation Svcs., Phila., 1977-78. Contbr. articles to profl. jours. Mem. adv. bd. Ctr. for Jewish-Christian Studies, Chgo., 1985—, Nat. Abortion rights Action League, Ill., 1985—, Ctr. for Ch.-State Studies, Chgo., 1986—, Cmty. Response, 1989—; chmn. Religious Coalition for Abortion Rights policy coun., 1984-88; active Justice Campaign, 1985, ACLU, Ill., 1979—; bd. dirs. Jewish Fedn. Met. Chgo., 1995—, Anti-Defamation League, 1994—. Fulbright grantee, 1967, Hebrew U. fellow, 1969-70, Dropsie U. fellow, 1970-71. Mem. Chgo. Assn. Reform Rabbis (v.p. 1987-91, pres. 1991-93), Cen. Conf. Am. Rabbis (exec. bd. 1991-93), Chgo. Bd. Rabbis (exec. com. 1983—), Union Am. Hebrew Congregations (exec. com. Gt. Lakes region 1991-93), Olin-Sang-Ruby Union Inst. (bd. govs. 1990, chmn. rabbinic adv. com.), United Jewish Appeal (rabbinic cabinet 1980—), Oak Park-River Forest Comty. of Congregations (v.p. 1994-96, pres. 1996—), Omicron Delta Kappa. Office: Oak Park Temple Bnai Abraham Zion 1235 N Harlem Ave Oak Park IL 60302-1377

GERSON, LOWELL WALTER, epidemiologist, educator; b. N.Y.C., Sept. 26, 1942; s. Jack J. and Sylvia (Berliner) G.; m. Francine Linda Goldstein, Aug. 16, 1964; children: Stacey, Jeremy. BA, Western Res. U., 1964, MA, 1966; PhD, Case-Western Res. U., 1970. Asst. prof. sociology John Carroll U., University Heights, Ohio, 1968-70; asst. prof. med. sociology Meml. U. Newfoundland, St. John's, Can., 1970-74, assoc. prof. epidemiology, 1975; assoc. prof. epidemiology McMaster U., Hamilton, Ont., Can., 1975-78; assoc. prof. epidemiology Northeastern Ohio U. Coll. Medicine, Rootstown, 1978-82, prof., assoc. dir. divsn. cmty. health, 1982—; standing chair on pub. policy Can. Pub. Health Assn., Ottawa, Ont., 1974-78; mem. Mayor's Adv. Bd. for Emergency Med. Svcs., 1979-82. Author: Profiles of Nursing Care, 1975; editor: Patterns of Health: Rural and Urban, 1975; contbr. articles, papers, abstracts to profl. publs. Trustee Weathervane Playhouse, Akron, Ohio, 1981-90; adv. bd. Adolescent Svcs. Network, Akron, 1985—. Grantee So. Australia Health Commn., 1986, Robert Wood Johnson Found., 1989-90, 90-91, Bruce A. Mansfield Found., 1990-91, John A. Hartford Found., 1993. Mem. AAAS, APHA, Ohio Pub. Health Assn. (governing coun. 1992—, chair planning com. 1993 annual meeting), Assn. Tchrs. Preventive Medicine, Internat. Epidemiology Assn., Soc. Epidemiologic Rsch., Ohio Acad. Family Practice (rsch. com. 1982—), Soc. for Acad. Emergency Medicine (geriatic emergency medicine task force 1991—, pub. health and edn. com. 1994—). Home: 7385 Lacosta Dr Hudson OH 44236-1804 Office: Northeastern Ohio Univ Coll Medicine PO Box 95 Rootstown OH 44272-0095

GERSTNER, ROBERT WILLIAM, structural engineering educator, consultant; b. Chgo., Nov. 10, 1934; s. Robert Berty and Martha (Tuchelt) G.; m. Elizabeth Willard, Feb. 8, 1958; children: Charles Willard, William Mark. B.S., Northwestern U., 1956, M.S., 1957, Ph.D., 1960. Registered structural and profl. engr., Ill. Instr. Northwestern U., Evanston, Ill., 1957-59; research fellow Northwestern U., 1959-60; asst. prof. U. Ill., Chgo., 1960-63; asso. prof. U. Ill., 1963-69, prof. structural engring., architecture, 1969-92, prof. emeritus, 1992—; structural engr. cons., 1959—; mem. State of Ill. Structural Engring. Bd., 1992-94. Contbr. articles to profl. jours. Pres. Riverside Improvement Assn., 1973-77, 79-82. Mem. AAUP, ACLU, ASCE, Am Concrete Inst., Am. Soc. Engring. Edn., Structural Engrs. Assn. Ill. (bd. dirs. 1986-89, 92-94, sec. 1989-91, pres. 1991-92). Home: 2628 W Agatite Ave Chicago IL 60625-3011

GERTH, SHARON ANN, adult health nurse, educator; b. Boulder, Colo., Feb. 18, 1947; d. Robert John Sr. and Theresa Ann (Mozier) Seager; m. Aug. 29, 1970 (div. Jan. 1974); m. Frederick A. Gerth, June 4, 1977. BSN, So. Ill. U., 1970; MEd, U. Ill., 1976; MSN, Ind. U., Indpls., 1980, DNS, 1992. Staff nurse Christian Welfare Hosp., East St. Louis, 1970; staff nurse Lawrence and Meml. Hosp., New London, Conn., 1970-71, instr. Sch. Nursing, 1971-72; staff nurse, charge nurse Carle Found. Hosp., Urbana, 1973; coord., developer practical nursing program Parkland Coll., Champaign, Ill., 1973-79, nursing instr., 1973-80, nursing instr. ADN program, 1980-94; dept. chair/nursing Parkland Coll., Champaign, 1994—; adj. faculty U. Ill., Urbana-Champaign, 1991—; affiliate mem. nursing and patient care com. Carle Hosp., Urbana, 1991—. Host family program for fgn. students, U. Ill., Urbana, 1981—. Mem. ANA, Am. Ednl. Rsch. Assn., Ill. Vocat. Assn., Nat. League for Nursing (coun. of assoc. degree programs, nursing informatics, rsch. in nursing edn. Ill. chpt.), Ill. Nurses Assn., Sigma Theta Tau, Kappa Delta Pi, Pi Lambda Theta, Phi Delta Kappa. Office: Parkland Coll 2400 W Bradley Ave Champaign IL 61821-1806

GERTZ, ELMER, lawyer, author, educator; b. Chgo., Sept. 14, 1906; s. Morris and Grace (Grossman) G.; m. Ceretta Samuels, Aug. 16, 1931 (dec.); children: Theodore, Margery Ann Hechtman; m. Mamie L. Friedman, June 21, 1959; 1 child, Jack M. Friedman. Ph.B., U. Chgo., 1928, J.D., 1930. Bar: Ill. 1930. Formerly assoc. firm McInerney, Epstein & Arvey, Chgo.; sole practice Chgo.; asst. to masters in chancery Jacob M. Arvey, Samuel B. Epstein, 1930-43; atty. for Nathan Leopold in successful parole procs., 1957-58; atty. various censorship litigations including Tropic of Cancer, 1962-64, atty. for Jack Ruby in setting aside death sentence, other capital cases; counsel commn. to investigate disorders in Chgo. during, spring, summer 1968; prof. John Marshall Law Sch., 1970—; mem. mission to USSR, Comm. Soviet Jewry, 1981; successful plaintiff in landmark libel case Gertz vs. Robert Welch, Inc., 1969-83; adj. prof. John Marshall Law Sch. Author: (with A.I. Tobin) Frank Harris: A Study in Black and White, 1931, The People vs. The Chicago Tribune, 1942, (play) Mrs. Bixby Gets a Letter, 1942, Joe Medill's War, 1946, American Ghettos, 1946, A Handful of Clients, 1965, Moment of Madness: The People vs. Jack Ruby, 1968, foreword Tropic of Cancer On Trial, 1968, For the First Hours of Tomorrow, 1971, To Life, 1974 (Friends of Lit. award), rev. and enlarged edit. 1990, Henry Miller: Years of Trial and Triumph: The Letters of Henry Miller and Elmer Gertz, 1978, German edit., 1980, Odyssey of a Barbarian, 1979, (with Joseph Pisciotte) Charter for a New Age, 1983, (with Edward Gilbreth) Quest for a Consitution: A Man Who Wouldn't Quit, 1985, Gertz v. Robert Welch, Inc.-The Story of a Landmark Libel Case, 1992, others; editor: Short Stories of Frank Harris, 1975; contbr. to Henry Miller and the Critics, 1963, Mass Media and the Law, 1969; author articles in various periodicals and encys. Dir. pub. rels. Ill. Police Assn., 1934; mem. exec. com. Ill. Com. Equal Job Opportunity ; mem. nat., Chgo. adv. bd. commn. on law and social action Am. Jewish Congress; chmn. soldier vote com. Profl. and Bus. People, 1944; mem. law and order com. Chgo. Commn. on Human Rels., 1945; v.p. Ill. Freedom to Read Com.; chmn. Vets. Housing Com., 1945-47; mem. Mayor's Housing Com., 1946-48, legal chmn., 1946-47; mem. Chgo. Com. on Housing Action, 1947-49; adv. com. Chief Justice Mcpl. Ct. Chgo., 1950-51; pres. Greater Chgo. coun. Am. Jewish Congress, 1959-63; elected del. 6th Ill. Constl. Conv., 1969-70; chmn. conv. Bill of Rights com., 1969-70; bd. dirs. Jackson Park Hosp.; pres. Blind Svc. Assn., 1988-92; trustee Belefaire; nat. bd. trustees City of Hope; mem. Auditorium Theatre Coun. Recipient Golden Key award City of Hope, 1966; award Ill. div. A.C.L.U., 1963, 74; award U. Chgo. Alumni Assn., 1959; State of Israel Prime Minister's medal, 1972; selected for Chicagoland honor roll Chgo. Council Against Discrimination, 1946, 47, Hadassah, 1975, Educator of Year award, 1975, Disting. Svc. award Kagan Home for the Blind, Bill of Rights Bicentennial award IVI-IPO, Constl. Rights Found. Bill of Right in Action award, Jackson Pk. Hosp., Chgo. Bar Assn.; Elmer Gertz Day in Ill. proclaimed in his honor by Gov. Edgar, Elmer Gertz Day in Chgo. proclaimed by Mayor Richard M. Daley and City Coun., numerous other awards. Mem. Pub. Housing Assn. (founder, counsel, pres. 1943-49), Civil War Round Table (founder, exec. com., pres., hon. life), Adult Edn. Council Chgo. (sec., pres.), Shaw Soc. (founder, pres., exhibit chmn. Shaw Centennial 1956, Darrow Centennial 1957), ABA., Fed. Bar Assn., Chgo. Bar Assn. (chmn. legal edn. com. 1970-71,chmn. civil rights com. 1978-79), Ill. State Bar Assn. (sr. counsellor, chmn. civil rights com. 1979-80), Bar Assn. 7th Circuit, Am. Judicature Soc., Decalogue Soc. Lawyers (mgr., pres., editor Jour.), First Amendment Lawyers Assn. (pres. 1978-79, chmn. 1979-80), Soc. Midland Authors (award 1969, sec. 1976), Authors Guild, Appellate Lawyers Assn. Ill. Clubs: Chicago Literary (v.p. 1968-69, 1978-79, pres. 1979-80), Cliff Dwellers, Caxton Club. Home: 6249 N Albany Ave Chicago IL 60659-1401 Office: 315 S Plymouth Ct Chicago IL 60604-3907

GERVAIS, VICKII, midwife; b. Chgo., Apr. 29, 1963; d. William Joseph and Jerre Su (Hilliard) Schmidt; 1 child, Nicholas Philip Rock. Cert., Casa de Nacimiento, 1991. Lic. midwife, Tex., N.Mex. Apprentice midwife Blessed Transitions, Chgo., 1988-90; intern midwife Casa de Nacimiento, El Paso, Tex., 1990, staff midwife educator, 1990-91; owner, midwife Traditional Midwifery Svc., Chgo., 1991—; tchr. Casa de Nacimiento, El Paso, 1991—; pres. Ill. Alliance Midwives, 1995—. Editor Mother's Underground, 1989-91. Mem. Midwives Alliance N.Am., Ill. Alliance of Midwives. Home and Office: Traditional Midwifery Svc 2322 N Newland Chicago IL 60635

GERY, MICHAEL E., state legislator; m. Carolyn Gery. BA, Purdue U.; MAT, Ind. U. Tchr.; senator Dist. 22 Ind. State Senate, 1974—, mem. commerce and consumer affairs com., ranking minority mem. fin. com. and natural resources com. Mem. United Teaching Profls., Phi Gamma Delta. Office: 530 Robinson St West Lafayette IN 47906-2739 also: State Senate State Capital Indianapolis IN 46204*

GESLER, DONNA MARIE, newsletter editor, consultant; b. Detroit, June 11, 1940; d. John Edward and Loretto Marie (Snyder) Kennedy; m. William G. Gesler, Aug. 1, 1959; children: Marvin, Alexander, William III, Rebecca. AA, Wayne County C.C.; BA, Ea. Mich. U., 1978; MBA, Mich. State U., 1984. CPIM. Sr. demand/supply specialist Unisys, Plymouth, Mich., 1989-91; sr. ops. specialist GE Med. Systems, Novi, Mich., 1991-94; cons. Gesler & Assocs., Northville, Mich., 1994—; adj. faculty Ctrl. Mich. U., Troy, 1987—. Editor, cons. (newsletter) Productivity News. Dep. registrar of voters Twp. of Nankin, 1962. Mem. Am. Prodn. Inventory Control Soc., Soc. Logistics Engrs., Prodn. Ops. Mgmt. Soc., NAFE. Home: 19471 Scenic Harbour Dr Northville MI 48167 Office: PO Box 79 Northville MI 48167

GETZ, JAMES EDWARD, legal association administrator; b. Shelbyville, Ill., June 8, 1950; s. William Forrest and Betty Jean (Mitchell) G.; m. Rita Genevieve Boyd, June 16, 1973; children: Christopher Brandon, Sarah Lynne. BS in Edn., Eastern Ill. U., 1972, MA, 1974. Grad. asst. Political Sci. Dept. Eastern Ill. U., Charleston, 1972-73; tchr. Plano (Ill.) Community Schs., 1973-74; conservation police officer Ill. Dept. Natural Resources, Office Law Enforcement, Springfield, Ill., 1974-77; region IV Ops. supr. Ill. Dept. Natural Resources, Office Law Enforcement, Springfield; region IV comdr. Ill. Dept. Conservation Div. Law Enforcement, Springfield, 1980-82; deputy chief Ill. Dept. Natural Resource, Office Law Enforcement, 1982-86; region II comdr. Ill. Dept. Natural Resource, Office Law Enforcement, Springfield, 1986-90; Lake Mich. enforcement ops. comdr. Ill. Dept. Natural Resources divsn. Law Enforcement, Springfield, 1990—; boating law adminstr. State Ill., 1984-86; chmn. several coms. Nat. Assn. State Boating Law Adminstrs.; mem Nat. Boating Safety Adv. Coun. U.S. Coast Guard; pres. Conservation Police Lodge #146, Fraternal Order Police, 1993—. Author: Illinois Public Act 84-515, 1985; Illinois Public Act 85-147, 1987. Mem. Nat. Marine Mfr. Assn. Boat Cert. Com., Gt. Lakes Fisheries Commn. Law Enforcement Com. (vice chmn. 1986-90, chmn. 1990-92), Am. Boat & Yacht Coun. (bd. dirs.). Home: 1709 N Orleans St Mc Henry IL 60050-3885 Office: Ill Dept Natural Resources 701 N Point Dr Winthrop Harbor IL 60096-1351

GEVITZ, NORMAN JAN, medical historian, educator; b. N.Y.C., June 29, 1948; s. Joseph and Evelyn (Machacek) G.; m. Melanie Palczynski, Sept. 21, 1973; 1 child, Kathryn. BA, NYU, 1970, MA, 1971; PhD, U. Chgo., 1980; LHD (hon.), Coll. Osteo. Medicine of Pacific, Pomona, Calif., 1991, Kirksville Coll. Osteo. Medicine, 1996; LLD (hon.), Phila. Coll. Osteo. Medicine, 1995. Asst. prof. sociology Ill. Inst. Tech., Chgo., 1980-85; asst. prof. history of medicine Coll. Medicine, U. Ill., Chgo., 1985-91, assoc. prof., 1991-96, prof., 1996—. Author: The D.O.'s: Osteopathic Medicine in America, 1982; editor: Other Healers: Unorthodox Medicine in America, 1988, (with B. Barzansky) Beyond Flexner: Medical Education in the 20th Century, 1992; mem. editorial bd.: Jour. Med. Humanities, 1990—. Recipient Phillips medal pub. svc. Ohio U. Coll. Osteo. Medicine, 1995, Walter Patenge medal pub. svc. Mich. State U. Coll. Osteo. Medicine. Mem. Am. Assn. History of Medicine (chmn. com. on edn. 1991-92), Am. Inst. History of Pharmacy, History of Sci. Soc., Soc. Med. History Chgo. (pres. 1986-90). Office: U Ill Coll Medicine Dept Med Edn 808 S Wood St Rm 976 Chicago IL 60612-7300

GEYER, SIDNA PRIEST, secondary and business education educator; b. Anderson, Ind., Dec. 9, 1943; d. James Dale and Lavada Belle (Lantz) Priest; m. James Eugene Geyer, Aug. 29, 1965; children: Jonathan Andrew, Susan Leigh. BS in Edn., Ball State U., 1969; MS in Edn., U. Wis., Oshkosh, 1975; EdS, U. Wis., Stout, 1980. Cert. secondary tchr., post-secondary tchr., Wis.; lic. supr., coord., counselor, Wis. Tchr. 6th grade St. Mary's Sch., Charlotte, Mich., 1966-67; tchr. bus. edn. Oak Hill High Sch., Converse, Ind., 1969-70, Stockbridge (Wis.) High Sch., 1970-72; tchr. bus., counselor Fox Valley Tech. Coll., Appleton, Wis., 1972-83, assoc. dean bus. edn., 1983-87; tchr. bus., English, computer sci. Baraboo (Wis.) Sr. High. Sch., 1988-90; dir. continuing edn. and performing arts U. Wis. Ctr. Baraboo-Sauk County, 1990-95; mgr. edn. outreach program U. Wis., LaCrosse, 1995-96; assoc. dean bus. occ. Blackhawk Tech. Coll., 1996—; evaluator bus. edn. U. Wis., Stout, 1981, N.E. Wis. Tech. Coll., Green Bay, 1985; mem. bus. adv. com. Brillion (Wis.) High Sch., 1983-87; mem. state-wide task force on develop curriculum for a sex equity course VTAE staff, 1983. Bd. dirs. Baraboo Literacy Coun., 1990-93; mem. bd. Baraboo Cmty. Scholarship Corp., 1993-94; mem. aux. bd. St. Clare Hosp., 1991-95. Mem. ASTD, AAUW (bd. dirs. 1971-95), Wis. Vocat. Assn. (mem. awards com.), Wis East Ctrl. Assn. Vocat. Edn. (treas. 1984), Eomen in Mgmt. (mem. edn. com.), Notrh Ctrl. Assn. (bus. edn. evaluator 1984, 07—), Wis. Assn. Adult and Cntinuing Edn. (bd. dirs. 1993-94), Nat. U. Continuing Edn. Assn. Methodist. Home: 2210 Holiday Dr Janeville WI 53545 Office: Univ Wisconsin 221C Morris Hall La Crosse WI 54601

GHERITY, JAMES ARTHUR, economics educator; b. Highland Park, Mich., Dec. 19, 1929; s. James Arthur and Florence Dorothy (Van Winkle) G.; m. Ermadell Marie Borsky, June 18, 1955; children: Christopher William, Shawn Patrick. BA, Wayne State U., 1951; MA, U. Mich., 1952; PhD, U. Ill., 1958. Instr., lectr., asst. prof. Mich. State U., Lansing, 1955-61; asst. prof. SUNY, Buffalo, 1961-64; from assoc. prof. to prof. No. Ill. U., DeKalb, 1964-67, prof., 1967—. Editor: Economic Thought, 1965; contbr. articles to profl. jours. 1st lt. USAR, 1953-57. Mem. History of Econs. Assn., Veblen Soc., Adam Smith Soc. Home: 9020 Baseline Rd Kingston IL 60145 Office: No Ill U Dept Econs De Kalb IL 60113

GHERTY, JOHN E., food products and agricultural products company executive; b. 1944; married. BBA, U. Wis., 1965, JD, 1968, MA, 1970. Lawyer corp. law dept. Land O' Lakes Inc., Arden Hills, Minn., 1970-79, asst. to pres., 1979-81, group v.p., 1981-89, pres., CEO, 1989—; bd. dirs. Recovery Engring., Mpls.; bd. dirs., mem. exec. com. CF Industries, Long Grove, Ill. Bd. dirs. Grad. Inst. Coop. Leadership. Mem. Nat. Milk Producers Fedn. (bd. dirs.), Nat. Coun. Farmer Coops. (bd. dirs.), Minn. Bus. Partnership (bd. dirs.), Nat. Parenting Assn. (bd. dirs.). Office: Land O'Lakes Inc PO Box 116 Minneapolis MN 55440-0116 Office: 4001 Lexington Ave N Saint Paul MN 55126-2934

GHILARDUCCI, AUGUST CHRISTOPHER, financial and business consultant; b. Evergreen Park, Ill., June 6, 1960; s. August Francis and Marie Antoinette (Angelastro) G.; m. Beth Ann Conroy, Nov. 17, 1984; children: Kelsey Ann, Dominick August. BS, St. Joseph's Coll., 1982; postgrad., 1988—. Br. mgr. Met. Life Ins. Co., Oak Park, Ill., 1982-86; CFO Mid Rite Entertainment Group, West Chicago, 1994—, Ind. Telecom., Palos Hills, Ill., 1993—; fin. and bus. cons. Westchester Fin. Assoc., Oak Brook, Ill., 1986—. Mem. alumni bd. dirs. St. Joseph's Coll., Rensselaer, Ind., 1990-92; mem. com. Term Limit Ill., Du Page County, 1993-94. Mem. Nat. Assn. Life Underwriters, Gen. Accts. and Mgmt. Assn. (bd. dirs. 1984—), Internat. Assn. Fin. Planners. Republican. Roman Catholic. Home: 241 Massel Ct Bensenville IL 60106 Office: Westchester Fin Assocs Inc 1550 Spring Rd Ste 310 Oak Brook IL 60521

GHOSH, KANCHAN, electrical engineer, researcher; b. N.Y.C., Mar. 4, 1966; s. Binayak and Manjula (Banerjee) G. BE, Jadavpur U., India, 1984-88; MS, La. State U., 1988-90; PhD, Ill. Inst. Tech., 1996. Teaching asst. La. State U., Baton Rouge, 1988-90; engr. Commonwealth Edison Co., chpt.), Power Engring. Soc., We. Soc. Engrs. Home: 513 W Saint Charles Rd # D Elmhurst IL 60126-3145

GIANAKOS, PATRICIA ANN, social worker; b. Warren, Ohio, Oct. 14, 1948; d. Jimmie Lambros and Julie (Mougianis) G. BA in Pre-Profl. Social Work, Kent State U., 1970. Lic. social worker. Aid for aged workers Trumbull County Human Svcs. Dept., Warren, 1970-71, social svc. worker, 1971-88, adult svcs. worker, 1988—, mem. excellence com., 1991, 93, contbg. editor County Line newsletter, 1991—, mem. awards com., 1991-93, chmn. awards com., 1993—; mem. Trumbull County Task Force on Wellness in Later Yrs., Warren, 1991-92. Vol. St. Demetrios Festival, Warren, 1979—; mem. Dem. Nat. Com., Warren, 1992—, Ladies Philoptochos Soc., Warren, 1979—; co-founder, adviser Sr. Citizens Orgn. St. Demetrios Ch., Warren, 1979—. Mem. ACA, NASW, Am. Bus. Women's Assn., Assn. for Adult Devel. and Aging, Nat. Com. for Prevention of Elder Abuse. Greek Orthodox. Home: 1786 Dodge Dr NW Warren OH 44485-1823 Office: Trumbull Cou Human Svcs 150 S Park Ave Warren OH 44481-1018

GIANCOLA, DENNIS JAMES, marketing professional; b. Youngstown, Oct. 22, 1952; s. Dante J. and Mary (Pierko) G.; children: Angela M., Deanna M. BE in Metallurgy, Youngstown State U., 1975; MBA, Baldwin Wallace, Berea, 1980. Chartered Indsl. Gas Cons. Sr. melter Youngstown Sheet and Tube Co., 1974-77; ind. sales rep. E. Ohio Gas Co., Cleve., 1977-81, heat treating specialist, 1981-87, new technology specialist, 1987-89; mktg. specialist CNG Energy Co., Cleve., 1989-90; pres. H.P. Techs., Inc., Cleve., 1984—. Met. Resources, Inc., 1993-94, Heat Treating Network, 1987-94. Contbr. articles to profl. jours. chmn. Zoning Com., Brunswick Hills, 1986. Recipient Technical Achievement Cleve. Technical Socs., 1987, Hall of Flame Am. Gas Assn., Wash., 1987. Mem. Heart Assn. Fund, Brunswick Sch. Levy, ASM Internat. (chmn. Cleve. chpt. 1988-89), Youngstown State U. Alumni Assn. (chmn. 1990-92).

GIANITSOS, ANESTIS NICHOLAS, surgeon; b. Chios, Greece, Aug. 31, 1961; came to U.S., 1966; s. Dimitrios and Soultani (Zannikos) G.; m. Laurie S. Hallmark. BA, Boston U., 1983, MD, 1987. Physician U. Wis. Hosp., Madison, 1987-92; pres. Tricorp Informational Svcs., Williams Bay, Wis., 1989—; staff urologist Riverview Clinic, Janesville, Wis., 1992—; pres. Geneva Mktg. Systems, Lake Geneva, Wis.; cons. Rural Wis. Hosp. Coop., Sauk City, 1989-93. Contbr. articles to profl. jours. Mem. Am. Assn. Clin. Urologists, Am. Urologic Assn., Wis. Med. Soc. Republican. Greek Orthodox. Home: 1237 Geneva National Ave W Lake Geneva WI 53147-5009 Office: Riverview Clinic/Dean Med Ctr 580 N Washington Janesville WI 53545

GIANNAMORE, DAVID MICHAEL, electronics engineer; b. Steubenville, Ohio, May 25, 1956; s. Robert Anthony and Marjorie Irene (Smith) G.; m. Tracy Lynn Rayburn, Apr. 3, 1982; children: Cynthia Marie, Robert Joseph. AAS in Electronic Engring., Jefferson County Tech. Inst., 1977. Video tech. Sta. WSTV-TV, Steubenville, 1977; svc. tech. TCI of Ohio, Steubenville, 1978-80; cable splicer Gen. Telephone Ohio, Cadiz, 1980-81; customer svc. rep. Ohio Power Co., Steubenville, 1981-84; svc. engr. Warner Amex, Columbus, Ohio, 1985-86; tng. instr. Liebert Customer Svc and Support, Worthington, Ohio, 1986-90, tng. instr., supr., 1990-93, project mgr., 1993-95, quality mgr., 1995—. Mem. Am. Soc. for Quality Control, Assn. for Svc. Mgmt. Internat. Office: Liebert Customer Svc Suppor Ste 100 250 E Wilson Bridge Rd Worthington OH 43085

GIANNETTO-ADAMS, JUDY MARIA TERESA, magazine editor; b. Bristol, Eng., Mar. 18, 1968; d. Carmelo and Maria Pierina (Gianella) Giannetto; m. Craig Russell Adams, Feb. 27, 1993. BA in English, Theatre, Film and Art History with distinction, U. Kans., 1992. Asst. editor, circulation asst. Am. Art Rev., Leawood, Kans., 1993-94; assoc. editor Kansas City Mag., Overland Park, Kans., 1994-95, mng. editor, 1995—; mng. editor Where Kansas City, 1995—; cons. dept. comm. Avila Coll., Kansas City, Mo., 1995. Mem. Soc. Profl. Journalists, Nat. Trust (U.K.), Golden Key. Office: Abarta Metro Pub Kansas City 7007 College Blvd Overland Park KS 66211

GIANNOPOULOS, JOANNE, pharmacist, consultant; b. Chgo.; m. James Giannopoulos, July 16, 1972; children: Alexandra, Andronike. BS in Pharmacy, U. Ill., Chgo., 1967, PharmD, 1988; MBA, Rosary Coll., River Forest, Ill., 1985. Asst. dir. pharmacy N.W. Hosp., Chgo., 1969-85; dir. pharm. svcs. and lab. Forest Health Sys., Des Plaines, Ill., 1990-91; dir. pharm. Rehab. Inst. Chgo., Northwestern U., 1991-94, clin. pharmacist coord., 1994—. Mem. Plato Sch. Bd., Chgo., 1988-93. Mem. Ill. Pharmacists Assn. (hosp. ednl. com. mem.). Office: Rehab Inst Chgo 345 E Superior St Chicago IL 60611-3015

GIBANS, NINA FREEDLANDER, special projects director; b. Cleve., July 30, 1932; d. Samuel Oscar and Adeline (Kaden) Freedlander; m. James David Gibans, July 16, 1955; children: David Myer, Jonathan Samuel, Amy Gibans McGlashan, Elisabeth. Student, Wellesley (Mass.) Coll., 1950-52; BA, Sarah Lawrence Coll., Bronxville, N.Y., 1954; MA, Case Western Res. U., 1966. Instr. Cleve. Mus. Art, 1966-72; dir. Cleve. Area Arts Coun., 1972-79; prin. Nina Gibans Cons. Inc., Cleve., 1979—; mem. faculty Capital U., Cleve., 1984—; cons. Cleve. Children's Mus., 1985, dir. community rels., 1986-94, spl. projects 1995—. Author: The Community Arts Council Movement: History, Opinions and Issues, 1982. Trustee, pres. Cleve. Artists Found., 1989—; trustee Citizens' League, 1987-94, Fairmount Theatre of the Deaf, Friends of Shaker Square, 1986-94. Recipient Arts Mgmt. award Bus. and Arts Coun., Inc., 1974; grantee H V Kaltenborn Found., 1981, AHS Found., 1981, Harry and Emma Fox Found., 1982. Mem. Am. Assn. Mus., Am. Coun. of the Arts. Home: 13800 Shaker Blvd Cleveland OH 44120-1584 Office: Cleve Children's Mus 10730 Euclid Ave Cleveland OH 44106-2200

GIBBONS, DONA LEE, principal; b. San Diego, Mar. 22, 1949; d. Donald Leland and Joan Elaine (Gray) Riley; children: Lee, Nicole. BA, U. Mo., Kansas City, 1972, MA, 1988, EdS, 1989. Vol. U.S. Peace Corps, Micronesia, 1972-74; tchr. Koror Palan Dept. Edn., Micronesia, 1974-80; tchr. bilingual edn. Kansas City (Mo.) Sch. Dist., 1983-84, tchr. gifted program, 1984-87, instnl. asst., 1987-88, prin., 1988—; prin. Maplewood Elem. Sch. North Kansas City Sch. Dist., Kansas City, Mo., 1995—; mem. dist. adv. com. Kansas City Schs., 1992—. Mem. ASCD, Nat. Assn. Elem. Sch. Prins., Advocates of Lang. Learning, Nat. Assn. Yr. Round Edn., Fgn. Lang. Assn. Mo., Mo. Assn. Elem. Sch. Prins., North Kansas City Prins. Assn., Clay-Platte Prins. Assn. Roman Catholic. Home: 3735 Kimstin Cir Blue Springs MO 64015-4577 Office: Maplewood Elem Sch 6400 NE 52d St Kansas City MO 64119

GIBBONS, LARRY V., laboratory director; b. Harrisburg, Ill.; s. Jesse I. and Oma M. (Tison) G.; m. Ann Wilson, Aug. 21, 1954; children: Valerie, Lisa, Cathy, Grant. AB, Washington U., St. Louis, 1954; MS, So. Ill. U., 1958, PhD, 1970. Rsch. supr. UMC Industries, Ferguson, Mo., 1959-63; spacecraft and design scientist McDonnell-Douglas, St. Louis, 1963-68; assoc. dir. rsch. Intersci. Rsch. Inst., Champaign, Ill., 1968-70; rsch. dir. Unidynamics, Phoenix, 1970-71; pres. Applied Rsch. and Devel. Labs., Inc., Mt. Vernon, Ill., 1971—; pres. Ill. State Acad. Sci., Springfield, Rend Lake Coll. Found. Mt Vernon. Recipient Indsl. Appreciation award City of Mt. Vernon, 1993. Mem. Am. Chem. Soc., AAAS, Air Pollution Control Assn., Sigma Xi. Home: Rte 5 Box 316 Mount Vernon IL 62864 Office: Appld Rsch & Devel Labs Inc Rte 15 East Mount Vernon IL 62864

GIBBONS, MICHAEL EUGENE, investment banker; b. Cleve., Apr. 10, 1952; s. Eugene Vernon and Elizabeth Ann (Barron) G.; m. Diane West; children: Megan E., Caitlin E., Connor A., Ryan E., Michael H. AB, Kenyon Coll., 1974; MSM, Case-Western Res. U., 1975; JD, Cleve. State U., 1982. Ptnr. McDonald & Co. Securities, Cleve., 1975-83, sr. v.p., 1983-85; prin. No. Lake Properties Inc., Cleve., 1982—; exec. v.p. Underwood-Newhaus & Co., Houston, 1985-87, also bd. dirs., 1985—, pres., chief exec. officer, 1987-89; pres., chief exec. officer Brown, Gibbons & Co., Inc., Cleve., 1989—.

GIBBONS, MICHAEL RANDOLPH, lawyer; b. Kirkwood, Mo., Mar. 24, 1959; s. Michael and Folsta Sara (Bailey) G.; m. Elizabeth Weddell O'Neill, Jan. 30, 1988; children: Danny, Meredith. BA, Westminster Coll., 1981; JD, St. Louis U., 1984. Bar: Mo. 1984. Assoc. Michael Gibbons, Kirkwood, 1984-86; ptnr. Gibbons and Gibbons, Kirkwood, 1986—; state rep. 94th Dist. Mo., 1992—. Mem. coun. City of Kirkwood, 1986-92; dep. mayor, 1990-92; mem. Bonhomme Twp. Rep. Club, v.p., 1985-87, bd. dirs.; vestry mem. Grace Episcopal Ch., Kirkwood, 1986-88. Mem. Bar Assn. of Met. St. Louis, Kirkwood C. of C. (bd. dirs. 1986-88), Kiwanis (pres. Kirkwood chpt. 1986-87). Republican. Home: 651 Pearl Ave Kirkwood MO 63122-2721 Office: Gibbons & Gibbons PC Kirkwood MO 63122

GIBBS, ARLAND LAVERNE, real estate agent; b. New Lyme, Ohio, July 24, 1916; s. Myrl DeForest and Freda Amber (Ritter) G.; m. Winifred Imogene Willard, Apr. 13, 1941; children: Marjorie Ann Gibbs Flock, Suzanne Elizabeth Gibbs Wludyga. Student, Youngstown State U., 1985. Owner, operator Gibbs Bakery Delivery Svcs., Ashtabula County, Ohio, 1937-40; grinder Lake City Malleable, Ashtabula, Ohio, 1943; sales agt. Town & Village Ins. Svc. Inc. of Columbus, Ohio, 1940-81; owner, operator retail flea market "I Saw It Here", Jefferson, Ohio, 1981-95; realtor Joan Curtis Realty, Ashtabula, 1992-96. Pres. Ashtabula County Hist. Soc., 1982-84. Sgt. armored inf. U.S. Army, 1941-43. Named Citizen of Yr., Jefferson Area C. of C., 1983. Mem. SAR (pres. Northeastern Ohio chpt. 1996), DAV (life), Am. Legion (life), Masons (master 1950-80, high priest), Order Ea. Star (50 yr. membership award 1991). Republican. Methodist. Home: 206 S Chestnut St Jefferson OH 44047-1315

GIBBS, LINDA ANN, bookstore manager; b. Omaha, Nebr., Jan. 23, 1958; d. Walter John and Marion Ellen (Weinfurtner) G. BA in Art, Coll. of Saint Mary, 1980. Bookstore asst. Coll. of Saint Mary, Omaha, Nebr., 1980-91, bookstore mgr., 1991—; enrollment retention com. Coll. of Saint Mary, 1992—, registration com., 1992—. Mem. Gamma Phi Sigma. Democrat. Roman Catholic. Office: Coll of Saint Mary 1901 S 72nd St Omaha NE 68124

GIBBS, VIRGINIA GAYLE, Spanish language and literature educator; b. Salt Lake City, Dec. 11, 1944; d. Richard Sincoe and Margaret (Stadden) G. BA, U. Wis., 1967; MA, NYU, 1985; PhD, U. Minn., 1989. Asst. prof. Spanish U. Wis., Green Bay, 1985-87, La Crosse, 1987-89; assoc. prof. Spanish Luther Coll., Decorah, Iowa, 1989—. Author: Las Sonatas de Valle Inclan, 1989; editor curriculum materials for teaching about Latin Am.; author articles. Founder Winneshiek County Animal Welfare League, Decorah, 1995. Mem. AAUP (chpt. pres. 1993-95), North Ctrl. Coun. Latin Americanists (pres. 1991-92), Assn. Tchrs. of Spanish and Portuguese, Sigma Delta Pi. Office: Luther Coll 700 College Dr Decorah IA 52101

GIBERMAN, ALEXANDER, engineering director; b. Kiev, Ukraine, Nov. 9, 1947; came to U.S., 1988; B, State U. Russia, 1969; M, Bransk U., 1971. Design engr. Universal Automatic Corp., Des Plaines, Ill., 1989-92, engring. mgr., 1992—. Patentee in field. Vol. Jewish United Fund, 1993—. Home: 9326 Murray Ct Morton Grove IL 60053-1658

GIBLIN, LOUIS, stockbroker; b. Omaha, Neb., Nov. 1, 1944; s. Richard and Mary (Mahoney) G.; m. Janis Schoblocher, May 20, 1977; 1 child, Marijo. AB, Creighton U., 1966; MBA, U. Chgo., 1968; cert. in investment mgmt., Princeton U., 1986. Asst. sec. No. Trust. Co., Chgo., 1968-73; v.p. MGIC Investment Corp., Milw., 1973-85; 1st v.p. Smith Barney Harris Upham and Co., Milw., 1985—; chmn. fin. analyst seminar Northwestern U., Evanston, Ill., 1990; adj. faculty U. Wis., Milw., 1985—; adviser Financiers U. Wis., Milw., 1986—; exam grader Inst. CFAs, 1986—; fin. svcs. vol., corp. cons. Skoda Koncern, Czech Republic, 1993—. Founder Joint Univ./Soc. Scholarship program, CFA exam, 1988; trustee St. Stephen's Ch., Milw., 1989—; chmn. investment com., mem. fin. com. & ops. com. United Way, Milw.; mem. Oak Creek (Wis.) Housing Authority, City of Oak Creek Cost Reduction Com., Oak Creek Econ. Devel. Authority; mem. Creighton U. Alumni Senate, 1991—; mem. adv. com. Creighton U.; bd. dirs. Creighton U. Alumni, 1993. Pulitzer Prize nominee, 1985. Mem. Internat. Soc. Fin. Analysts (charter), Internat. Inst. Forecasters, N.Y. Soc. Security Analysts, Nat. Assn. Bus. Economists, Nat. Options and Futures Soc. (bd. dirs. 1986—), Deutsch-Amerikanischer Nat. Kongress, North Atlantic Cultural Exchange League, Internat. Inst. Am. Host, Milw. Investment Analysts Soc. (bd. dirs. 1988—), Fin. Analysts Fedn. (bd. dirs. 1991—), Milw. Investment Analysts Soc. (pres. 1989-90), Mensa. Home: 7468 S Logan Ave Oak Creek WI 53154-2234

GIBSON, BENJAMIN F., federal judge; b. Safford, Ala., July 13, 1931; s. Eddie and Pearl Ethel (Richardson) G.; m. Lucille Nelson, June 23, 1951; children: Charlotte, Linda, Gerald, Gail, Carol, Laura. B.S., Wayne State U., 1955; J.D. with distinction, Detroit Coll. Law, 1960. Bar: Mich. 1960. Acct. City of Detroit, 1955-56, Detroit Edison Co., 1956-61; asst. atty. gen. Mich., 1961-63; asst. pros. atty. Ingham County, Mich., 1963-64; pvt. practice law Lansing, Mich., from 1964; prof. Thomas Cooley Law Sch., 1979; judge U.S. Dist. Ct. Western Dist. Mich., Grand Rapids, 1979—, chief judge U.S. Dist. Ct., 1991-95;; bd. dirs. Cooley Law Sch.; adj. prof. Cooley Law Sch. Mem. United Way Project Blueprint; met. bd. dirs. YMCA. Mem. Fed. Bar Assn., Mich. State Bar Assn., Grand Rapids State Bar Assn., Black Judges of Mich., Floyd H. Skinner Bar Assn., Fed. Judges Assn., Sigma Pi Phi. Club: Peninsular Club. Office: US Dist Ct 616 Fed Bldg 110 Michigan St NW Grand Rapids MI 49503-2313

GIBSON, FLOYD ROBERT, federal judge; b. Prescott, Ariz., Mar. 3, 1910; s. Van Robert and Katheryn Ida G.; m. Gertrude Lee Walker, Apr. 23, 1935; children: Charles R., John M., Catherine L. A.B., U. Mo., 1931, LL.B., 1933. Bar: Mo. 1933. Practiced law Independence, 1933-37, Kansas City, 1937-61; mem. firm Johnson, Lucas, Bush & Gibson (and predecessor), 1954-61; county counselor Jackson County, 1943-44; judge U.S. Dist. Ct. (we. dist.) Mo., 1961-65, chief judge, until 1965; judge U.S. Ct. Appeals (8th cir.), Kansas City, Mo., 1965—, chief judge, 1974-80; former chmn. bd. Mfrs. & Mechanics Bank, Kansas City, Mo., Blue Valley Fed. Savs. & Loan Assn.; mem. Nat. Conf. Commrs. Uniform State Laws, 1957—, Jud. Conf. U.S., 1974-80; chmn. Chief Judges Conf., 1977-78; bd. mgrs. Coun. State Govts., 1960-61; pres. Nat. Legis. Conf., 1960-61. Mem. Mo. Gen. Assembly from 7th Dist., 1940-46; mem. Mo. Senate, 1946-61, majority floor leader, 1952-56, pres. pro tem, 1956-60; del. Nat. Democratic Conv., 1956, 60; Mem. Mo. N.G. Named 2d most valuable mem. Mo. Legislature Globe Democrat, 1958, most valuable, 1960; recipient Faculty-Alumni award U. Mo., 1968; citation of merit Mo. Law Sch. Alumni, 1975; Spurgeon Smithson award Mo. Bar Found., 1978. Fellow ABA (adv. bd. editors Jour., chmn. jud. adminstrn. div. 1979-80, chmn. conf. sect. 1980-81, chmn. appellate judges conf. 1973-74, mem. ho. of dels.); mem. Fed. Bar Assn., Mo. Bar, Kansas City Bar Assn. (Ann. Achievement award 1980), Lawyers Assn. Kansas City (past v.p., Charles Evans Whittaker award 1985), Mo. Law Sch. Found. (life), Mo. Acad. Squires, Order of Coif, Phi Delta Phi, Phi Kappa Psi (Man of Yr. 1974). Democrat. Roman Catholic. Clubs: University, Carriage, Mercury. Home: 411 W 46th Ter Apt 1201 Kansas City MO 64112-1437 Office: US Ct Appeals 8th Cir 837 US Courthouse 811 Grand Blvd Kansas City MO 64106-1904

GIBSON, GEORGE EDWARD, retired lawyer; b. Grove, Okla., Aug. 19, 1909; s. Warren Delmar and Mabel Mae (Faris) G. AB, U. Okla., 1934; LLB, George Washington U., 1937. Bar: Mo. With IRS, 1938-53; asst. counsel in-charge IRS, St. Louis, 1946-51, dist. counsel, 1952; assoc. Stinson, Mag & Fizzell, Kansas City, Mo., 1953-56, ptnr., 1956-74, cons. ptnr., 1974-92. With USN, 1943-46. Mem. ABA, Kansas City Bar Assn., Lawyers Assn. Kansas City, Order of Coif, Phi Delta Phi, Pi Kappa Alpha. Democrat. Episcopalian. Home: 221 W 48th St Kansas City MO 64112-2413 Office: Stinson Mag & Fizzell PC PO Box 41925 1201 Walnut St Kansas City MO 64141-0079

GIBSON, GREGORY JAMES, elementary school custodian; b. St. Charles, Mo., June 6, 1958; s. James Orland and June Eleanor (First) G. Grad. high sch., Overland, Mo., 1976. Chief storeskeeper Electronic & Space Corp., Emerson Electric Co., St. Louis, 1982-90, ESCO, St. Louis, 1990-94, Govt. Property Adminstrn. Gen. Stores; with Winfield Reorganized Sch. Dist. R-IV, 1994—; owner GG Enterprises, Annada, Mo., 1994—. Roman Catholic. Home: RR1 Box 87B Annada MO 63330-9711

GIBSON, JANET MARIE, psychology educator; b. Phila., July 23, 1959; d. Howard Walter and Elinor Marie (Heil) G. BA, Temple U., 1981; MA, Rice U., 1987, PhD, 1990. Asst. prof. memory and cognition Grinnell (Iowa) Coll., 1989-95, assoc. prof., 1995—. Ad hoc reviewer Memory & Cognition, 1990—; contbr. articles to profl. jours. Am. Women in Sci. scholar, 1987-88; Rice U. fellow, 1984-85. Mem. APA, Am. Psychol. Soc., Midwest Psychol. Assn., Psychonomic Soc., Soc. for Judgment and Decision Making. Roman Catholic. Office: Grinnell Coll Dept Psychology Grinnell IA 50112

GIBSON, JOHN ROBERT, federal judge; b. Springfield, Mo., Dec. 20, 1925; s. Harry B. and Edna (Kerr) G.; m. Mary Elizabeth Vaughn, Sept. 20, 1952 (dec. Aug. 1985); children: Jeanne, John Robert; m. Diane Allen Larrison, Oct. 1, 1986; stepchildren: Holly, Catherine. AB, U. Mo., 1949, JD, 1952. Bar: Mo. 1952. Assoc. Morrison, Hecker, Curtis, Kuder & Parrish, Kansas City, Mo., 1952-58, ptnr., 1958-81; judge U.S. Dist. Ct. (we. dist.) Mo., 1981-82, U.S. Ct. Appeals (8th cir.), Kansas City, 1982-94; sr. judge U.S. Ct. Appeals (8th cir.) Kansas City, Kansas City, 1994—; mem. Mo. Press-Bar Commn., 1979-81; mem. com. on adminstrn. of magistrate sys. Jud. Conf. U.S., 1987-91, mem. security, space and facilities com., 1995—. Vice chmn. Jackson County Charter Transition Com., 1971-72; mem. Jackson County Charter Commn., 1970; v.p. Police Commrs. Bd., Kansas City, 1973-77. Served with AUS, 1944-46. Recipient Citation of Merit award U. Mo. at Columbia Sch. of Law, 1994. Fellow Am. Bar Found.; mem. ABA, Mo. State Bar (gov. 1972-79, pres. 1977-78; Pres.' award 1974, Smithson aard 1984), Kansas City Bar Assn. (pres. 1970-71), Lawyers Assn. Kansas City (Charles Evan Whittaker award 1980), Fed. Judges Assn. (bd. dirs. 1991—), Phi Beta Kappa, Omicron Delta Kappa. Presbyterian. Office: US Ct Appeals 8th Cir 851 US Courthouse 811 Grand Blvd Kansas City MO 64106-1904

GIBSON, PATRICIA ANN, health care administrator; b. Joplin, Mo., Nov. 14, 1942; d. Arrell Morgan and Dorothy (Deitz) G. BA in English, U. Okla., 1963, MLS, 1966, PhD in Edn., 1977. English tchr. Norman (Okla.) Pub. Schs., 1963-65; pub. svcs. librarian U. Okla. Health Scis. Ctr., Oklahoma City, 1966-68, serials librarian, 1971-72, dir. media prodn., 1972-77; coord. library svcs. Okla. Regional Med. Program, 1968-70; head reference dept. Wichita State U., 1978-80; mgr. library devel. DataPhase Systems, Inc., Kansas City, Mo., 1980-82; v.p. program adminstrn., libr. dir. Am. Acad. Family Physicians Found., Kansas City, 1982—; cons. Am. Coll. Cardiology Library, 1986-87. Contbr. articles to profl. jours. Chmn. regional screening com. Am. Field Svc., Kansas City, 1987-89; bd. dirs. Midwest Ear Inst., 1993—. Kellogg Found. grantee, 1987-88. Mem. Med. Libr. Assn. (disting. mem. Acad. Health Sci. Librs., chmn. med. libr. edn. sect. 1989-90, med. soc. librs. sect. 1991-92), Kansas City Met. Libr. Network (pres. 1986, sec. 1987-89), Health Scis. Libr., Group Greater Kans. City (pres. 1992—), Nat. Network Med. Librs. (regional adv. com. midcontinental region 1991—, regional adv. com. 1994—). Democrat. Presbyterian. Office: Am Acad Family Physicians Found 8880 Ward Pkwy PO Box 8418 Kansas City MO 64114-0418

GIBSON, ROBERT REED, electrical engineer; b. Chgo., Apr. 28, 1951; s. William Godfrey and Harriet Edith (Page) G.; m. Linda Marie Lederer, Dec. 15,1973; children: Robert Jr., Peter, Elizabeth, Andrew, Stephen. Regional customer svc. mgr. Halcyon, Oak Brook, Ill., 1977-80; sr. systems engr. General Data Comm., Oak Brook, 1980-83; sr. applications engr. Codex, Schaumburg, Ill., 1983-87; consulting systems engr. Network Equipment Techs., Itasca, Ill., 1987-91, regional NMS specialist, 1993—; systems engr. Netrix Corp., Downers Grove, Ill., 1991-92. Leader Blackberry Rangers, Elburn, IL 1992—; active 4-H Club. With U.S. Navy, 1970-76. Mem. IEEE, St. Charles (Ill.) Morning Kiwanis Club (disting. club pres. 1994). Republican. Roman Catholic. Home: 3N216 Echo Valley Rd Elburn IL 60119-9526 Office: NET 500 Park Blvd Ste 1000 Itasca IL 60143-2608

GIBSON, ROGER FLETCHER, JR., philosopher, educator; b. St. Louis, Feb. 21, 1944; s. Roger Fletcher Gibson Sr. and Virginia (Melton) Sloane; m. Joyce Ann O'Neill, June 12, 1965 (div. 1981); 1 child, Georgia Alexandra; m. Sharon Ann Haverinen, Mar. 23, 1984. BA, NE Mo. State U., 1971; MA, U. Mo., 1973, PhD, 1977. Asst. prof. Kans. State U., Manhattan, 1978-79, Whittier (Calif.) Coll., 1979, We. Ill. U., Macomb, 1980-81, 83-84, Lindenwood Coll., St. Charles, Mo., 1981-83; from asst. prof. to prof. Washington U., St. Louis, 1985—. Author: The Philosophy of W.V. Quine, 1982, Enlightened Empiricism, 1988; editor: Perspectives on Quine, 1990. With USMC, 1962-66, Vietnam. Fellow NEH 1984-85. Mem. Am. Philos. Assn. Home: 192 Hastings Way Saint Charles MO 63301-5510 Office: Washington U Philos Dept One Brookings Dr Saint Louis MO 63130

GIBSON, SHERI JO, clinical nurse specialist, family nurse practitioner; b. Wagner, S.D., Sept. 28, 1959; d. John Berton and Elaine Ella (Mazourek) Weber; m. David John Gibson, Dec. 31, 1982; children: Daniel, Taylor. BSN, S.D. State U., 1981; MSN, Ariz. State U., 1989; FNP, S.D. State U., 1995. RN, S.D.; cert. nurse practitioner ANCC; CCRN; cert. case mgr. Ins. Rehab. Specialists Commn.; cert. ACLS provider and instr., pediatric advanced life support provider, diabetes team instr. Nurse technician cardiovascular ICU St. Mary's Hosp., Rochester, Minn., 1980; staff nurse McKennan Hosp., Sioux Falls, S.D., 1981-83, staff nurse ICU, 1983-84; staff nurse special care unit Valley Lutheran Hosp., Mesa, Ariz., 1984-87, 1988, adminstrv. coord., 1985-88, clin. nurse specialist critical care, 1988-91; clin. nurse specialist, dir. ctr. case mgmt. Sioux Valley Hosp., Sioux Falls, 1991—; chair Diabetes Team, 1986-88; adj. faculty Coll. Nursing Ariz. State U., 1991-92; presenter, rschr. in field. Mem. ANA, S.D. Nurses Assn., Sigma Theta Tau. Home: 1005 E Plum Creek Rd Sioux Falls SD 57105-7050 Office: Sioux Valley Hosp PO Box 5039 1100 S Euclid Ave Sioux Falls SD 57117-5039

GIBSON, TIM G., investment broker; b. South Bend, Ind., Mar. 19, 1952. BS, King Coll., 1974. V.p. investments A. G. Edwards & Sons Inc., Ft. Wayne, Ind., 1985—. Mem. ch. coun. Trinity English Luth., Ft. Wayne, 1993—. Mem. Press Club, Rotary (bd. dirs. 1990—). Republican. Home: 3306 Rockwood Dr Fort Wayne IN 46815-6139 Office: A G Edwards & Sons Inc 333 E Washington Blvd Fort Wayne IN 46802-3123

GIDWITZ, GERALD, hair care company executive; b. Memphis, 1906; married; 5 children. PhB, U. Chgo., 1927. Chmn. bd., chmn. exec. com. Helene Curtis Industries, Inc., Chgo. Trustee Roosevelt U., Auditorium Theatre Coun.; bd. dirs. Chgo. Crime Commn., Jamestown Found. Mem. Ill. Mfg. Assn. (past bd. dirs.). Office: Helene Curtis Industries Inc 325 N Wells St Chicago IL 60610-4705

GIDWITZ, RONALD J., personal care products company executive; b. Chgo., 1945. Grad., Brown U., 1967. With Helene Curtis Industries, Inc., Chgo., 1968—, pres., 1979—, CEO, 1985—; bd. dirs. Continental Materials Corp., Am. Nat. Can Co., Mus. Sci and Industry. Bd. dirs. Field Mus. Nat. History, Lyric Opera Chgo.; chmn. bd. trustees City Colls. Chgo.; mem. nat. bd. dirs., gov. Boys and Girls Club Am. Mem. Chicagoland C. of C. Office: Helene Curtis Industries Inc 325 N Wells St Chicago IL 60610-4705

GIEBNER, CARA RAE, trade association administrator; b. Cleve., Sept. 29, 1940; children: Catherine, Elaine, Christopher. BS, Ohio U., 1960. Exec. sec. Marcus Advt., Cleve., 1969-75; with personnel dept. Van Dorn Plastics, Strongsville, Ohio, 1975-80; exec. v.p. Suspension Specialists Assn., Medina, Ohio, 1980—; exec. sec. Heavy Duty Reps. Assn., Medina, 1986—. Newsletter editor Van Dorn Plastics Press, 1975-80, Svc. Specialists Assn., 1981—, Gerspacher, 1981-85. Mem. Sales and Mktg. Execs. Cleve., Cleve. Area Meeting Planners, Fleet Maintenance Coun. of N.E. Ohio, Greater Cleve. Soc. Assn. Execs., Medina County Bd. Realtors, Alpha Delta Pi. Home and Office: 4015 Marks Rd Apt 2B Medina OH 44256-8316

GIELOW, THOMAS CHRISTOPHER, software engineer; b. St. Louis, Dec. 25, 1964; s. George Thomas and Carol Ann (Przyzycki) G.; m. Tracy Thompson, May 14, 1993; children: Kenneth Shane, Chad Sinjin, Curt Simon, Karch Christian. BS in Computer Sci., U. Mo., 1990. Programmer Def. Mapping Agy., St. Louis, 1984-88, Conter Customer Support, St. Louis, 1988-90; mgr. software engring. Demand Mgmt., Inc., St. Louis, 1990—; cons. Gielow Cons., St. Louis, 1990—. Mem. IEEE Computer Assn., Assn. Computing Machinery. Republican. Roman Catholic. Home: 330 Shadwell Dr St Louis MO 63125 Office: Demand Mgmt Ste 600 7911 Forsyth Blvd Saint Louis MO 63105

GIER, AUDRA MAY CALHOON, environmental chemist; b. Bella Vista, Peru, Aug. 21, 1940; came to U.S., 1944; d. Nathan Moore and Olivia Cleo (Hite) Calhoon; m. Delta Warren Gier, Apr. 4, 1968. BA, Austin Coll., 1962; MS in Chemistry, Kans. State Coll., 1964; MA in History of Sci., U. Wis., 1974; postgrad., York U., Toronto, Can., 1974-79. Food technologist Midwest Rsch. Inst., Kansas City, Mo., 1963-64; chemist Mobay (formerly Chemagro), Kansas City, 1964-67; instr. chemistry St. Andrews Presbyn. Coll., Laurinburg, N.C., 1967-68; chemist Cardinal Chem. Co., Columbia, S.C., 1968; asst. prof. chemistry Lea Coll., Albert Lea, Minn., 1969-72; psychology intern emergency unit Thistletown Regional Centre for Children & Adolescents, Toronto, Ont., Can., 1975-77; assoc. prof. chemistry Cleveland Chiropractic Coll., Kansas City, 1979-84; adj. faculty Pk. Coll., Parkville, Mo., 1982-92; environ. chemist, quality assurance specialist Ecology & Environ., Inc., Overland Park, Kans., 1987-95; pres. Delta and Assocs., Inc., Kansas City, 1988-92; co-founder, v.p. Midwest Sci. Found., Kansas City, 1990—; mem. adj. faculty Donnelly Coll., 1992-94, dean adminstrn. health scis. program, 1992—; mentor tng. program Option Inst. and Fellowship, Sheffield, Mass., 1994—. Author: Highlights of Organic Chemistry, 1985; co-editor: (with D.W. Gier) History and Directory of Chemical Education, 1974, (with D.W. Gier) Peace is Something Speshl; co-inventor, co-patentee acetylenic ketones as herbicides. Mem. adv. bd. Kansas City Interfaith Peace Alliance, 1980-95, bd. dirs., 1982-85, pres., 1985-86; bd. dirs. Prairie Star Dist./Unitarian-Universalist Midwest (Upper), 1985-91; co-chair Bragg Symposium on Humanism, Kansas City, 1980-90; chair Social Responsibility Com., Prairie Star Dist. UUA, 1986-91; mem. N.Am. Com. for Humanism and Fellowship of Religious Humanists. Recipient Social Justice award Social Justice Com. Prairie Star Dist, 1985; named Woman of Yr., 1982, Humanist of Yr., 1987, All Souls Unitarian Ch., Kansas City. Mem. NAFE, AAUW, ACLU, DAR, NARAL, Am. Chem. Soc., Am. Soc. for Quality Control (cert.), Inst. for Soc. Ethics and Life Scis., Midwest Bioethics Ctr., Planned Parenthood, Assn. for Quality and Participation, Habitat for Humanity. Democrat. Home: 421 W 99th St Kansas City MO 64114-3908

GIES, FREDERICK JOHN, education educator; b. Chgo., Sept. 4, 1938; s. Leo M. and Gertrude E. (Demmer) G.; m. Margaret Meads, May 30, 1964; children: Frederick Meads, Edward Michael, Nicholas John, Maria Louise. BA, DePaul U., 1960; MEd, U. Mo., 1964, EdD, 1970. Cert. secondary English and Latin tchr., h.s. prin. Assoc. prof., assoc. dir. U. Mo., Columbia; prof., dean Seattle U. Sch. Edn.; prof., dean Coll. Edn. and Behavioral Scis., Northwestern State U.; prof. ednl. leadership, former dean Wright State U. Coll. Edn. and Human Svcs., Dayton, Ohio; Editor, pub. Record in Ednl. Leadership, Nat. Forum Applied Ednl. Rsch. Jour.; mem. editl. bd. Teaching Edn.; mem. editl. rev. Jour. Ednl. Pub. Rels.; contbr. over 200 publs., grants, tech. reports. Editor: Record in Ednl. Leadership, Nat. Forum Applied Ednl. Rsch. Jour.; mem. editl. bd. Teaching Edn., AASA Profl., Jour. Ednl. Pub. Rels.; contbr. over 200 publs., grants, tech. reports. Former site dir. Nat. Network for Ednl. Renewal; chmn. bd. trustees Dayton Area Higher Edn. Consortium; chmn. bd. Leadership Svcs. Internat., Dayton. Recipient numerous rsch. grants. Home: 3672 Northern Dr Dayton OH 45431-3129 Office: Wright State U Kettering Ctr Dayton OH 45435

GIESEN, FRANCIS GREGORY, newspaper editor; b. Nashville, May 28, 1971; s. Frank Hartman and Mary Margaret (Gerouard) G.; m. Brenda A., Apr. 27, 1996. BA in Journalism, Marquette U., 1992. Intern Eagle River (Wis.) County News Review, 1987-89; sports editor Associated Press, Milw., 1990-92, Marquette U., Milw., 1990; editor Clintonville (Wis.) New Gazette, 1992—, St. James (Minn.) New Dealer, 1995—. Roman Catholic. Home: 131 9th Ave Apt 6-A Saint James WI 56081

GIESEN, MARY MARGARET, performing arts company administrator; b. Superior, Wis., Nov. 8, 1933; d. Joseph Edward and Edna Anne (Hicks) Girouard; m. Frank Hartman Giesen, Aug. 13, 1955; children: David, Stephen, Robert, Tracy, Mary Patrice, F. Gregory. Student, Coll. St. Scholastica, Duluth, Minn., U. Wis., Superior. Adminstrv. asst. No. Suburban Synagogue Beth El, Highland Park, Ill., 1955-56; educator St. Joseph Sch., Nashville, 1965-71; gen. mgr. Lucius Woods Performing Arts Ctr., Inc., Solon Springs, Wis. Bd. dirs. Infant-Welfare Soc. Soc., 1986-87, Diocese of Superior Pastoral Bd., 1992—, Lucius Woods Performing Arts Ctr., Solon Springs, 1994-96; mem. bd. edn. Sch. Dist. Solon Springs, Wis., 1992—, pres., 1994-95; mem. governing bd. Douglas County Hist. Soc., 1995—. Home: PO Box 4 Solon Springs WI 54873-0004

GIESLER, ROBERT ALVIN, small business owner; b. Elmore, Ohio, Sept. 15, 1929; s. Alvin Albert and Edna Amanda (Moellman) G.; m. Aug. 18, 1950; children: Terrance, Timothy, Thomas, Todd. Student, U. Toledo, 1948-49. Gen. mgr. Farmers Elevator Co., Elmore, 1949-61; asst. dist. sales mgr. Ralston Purina, Defiance, Ohio, 1961-63; dist. sales mgr. Ralston Purina, Wooster, Ohio, 1963-65, Elmore, 1965-67; mgr. Ralston Purina, Sebawing, Mich., 1967-69; product mgr. poultry Ralston Purina, St. Louis, 1969-70, product mgr. hog chows, 1970-71; area dir. ops. Ralston Purina, Sioux City, Iowa, 1971-75, Lafayette, Ind., 1975-80; pres. All Seasons Marine I, South Haven, Mich., 1980—; chmn. adv. coun. Marine Assocs., Chgo., 1989-92. Author training handbook: Hog Production, 1971. Pres., bd. dirs. Bd. Pub. Utilities, Elmore, 1953-61; pres. Elmore Businessmen's Assn., 1952-53. With U.S. Army, 1949-52. Named to Mich. Boating Industry Hall of Fame, 1994. Mem. West Mich. Marine Assn. (dir., pres. 1982-84, Outstanding Leadership award 1984), Mich. Boating Industry Assn. (dir. 1983-89, chmn. 1986-89), Marine Retailers Am. (exec. com., dir. 1990-95, Legis. award 1991), Marine Operators Assn. Am. (pres. 1992-95), U.S. Yacht and Racing Assn., South Haven Yacht Club (commodore 1987-88). Democrat. Office: All Seasons Marine PO Box 431 234 Black River St South Haven MI 49090-0431

GIESSER, NANCY LYNNE, nursing educator; b. Cleve., Apr. 4, 1942; d. Robert Raymond and Blanche Bernice (Buchholzer) G. BA, Baldwin Wallace Coll., 1966; MEd, Kent State U., 1971. Staff nurse Fairview Gen. Hosp., Cleve., 1963-66, head nurse orthopedic unit, 1966-68, instr. Sch. Nursing, 1968-78, coord., 1975-78; asst. dir. nursing Lorain (Ohio) Community Hosp., 1978-80; instr. pediatric nursing Cleve. Met. Gen. Hosp. Sch. Nursing, 1980, lead instr. medicine and surgery, 1980-82, asst. dir., curriculum coord., 1982-85; dir. Sch. Nursing MetroHealth Med. Ctr., 1985, Cleve.; instr. continuing edn. Cleve. State U., 1976-79. Mem. adv. com. Project Ladders in Nursing Careers, 1988-93. Mem. ANA, Nat. League for Nursing, Ohio Citizens League Nursing (bd. dirs. 1988—), Nursing Edn. Coun., Ohio Coun. Hosp. Based Sch. Nursing, Greater Cleve. Nursing Roundtable (sec.-treas.), Greater Cleve. Hosp. Assn. (exec. nursing com.), N.E. Ohio League for Nursing (pres. 1995—). Republican. Home: 25118 Carey Ln North Olmsted OH 44070 Office: Met Health Med Ctr Sch Nursing 1803 Valentine Ave Cleveland OH 44109-1930

GIFFEN, LAWRENCE EVERETT, SR., family physician, anesthesiologist, historian; b. Jefferson City, Mo., Jan. 30, 1923; s. Fred Lemon and Angeline Henrietta (Patterson) G.; m. Mary Opal McKnight, Oct. 15, 1947 (div. Mar. 1950); 1 child, Lawrence Everett Jr.; m. Jerena East, June 17, 1955; children: Michael Gregory, Jerena Ann. DO, Kirksville Coll. Osteo Medicine, 1945; BS in Biology, Lincoln U., 1960; BA in History, U. Md., 1981; MS in Criminal Justice, Cen. Mo. State U., 1980; MA in History, Lincoln U., 1987; postgrad., U. Mo. Diplomate Am. Osteo. Bd. Anesthesiology, Am. Bd. Family Practice. Intern Brighton Med. Ctr., Portland, Maine, 1945-46; practice gen. medicine Chamois, Mo., 1946-50; resident in anesthesiology Art Ctr. Hosp., Detroit, 1950-51; practice gen. medicine and anesthesiology Jefferson City, Mo., 1951-80, 83—; med. examiner Jefferson City, 1968-80. Contbr. articles to profl. and hist. jours. Comdr. USNR, 1980-83; ret. 1991. Fellow Am. Osteo. Coll. Anesthesiologists (pres. 1962), Am. Osteo. Coll. Surgeons (hon.), Am. Acad. Family Physicians; mem. AMA, Mo. State Med. Soc., U.S. Naval Inst., Am. Assn. History Medicine, Am. Hist. Assn., Orgn. Am. Historians, Masons. Republican. Presbyterian. Home and Office: 1606 Hayselton Dr Jefferson City MO 65109-1212

GIFFIN, JASON S., investment broker; b. Wichita, Kans., Mar. 23, 1964. BS, Emporia State U., 1987. Investment broker Shearson Lehman, Wichita, 1989-90; br. mgr. Powell Disatterfield, Wichita, 1990-92; investment broker A. G. Edwards & Sons Inc., Wichita, 1992—. Office: A G Edwards & Sons Inc PO Box 47430 # 300 201 N Main Wichita KS 67201

GIFFORD, JOHN IRVING, retired agricultural equipment company executive; b. Lockport, N.Y., July 23, 1930; s. John Jacob and Carrie (McAdam) G.; m. Sara Jane Bauer, Jan. 28, 1955; children: John Hutchins, James Scott. BS, Purdue U., 1952, MS, 1956. Sales trainee Am. Nat. Foods, Inc., L.A., 1956; economist Deere & Co., Moline, Ill., 1956-65; personnel adminstr. Deere & Co., Moline, 1965-70, mgr. data svcs., 1970-96; stats. cons., 1996—. Bd. dirs., Rock Island (Ill.) sect. Easter Seal Found., 1981-87; v.p. coun., St. John Luth. Ch., Rock Island, 1981-82; pres., Rock Island Little League, 1981-82; v.p. Babe Ruth Baseball, Rock Island, 1983. 1st lt. U.S. Army, 1952-54, Korea. Recipient Leadership recognition Equipment Mfrs. Inst. Mem. Am. Agrl. Econs. Assn., Nat. Assn. Bus. Econs., Equipment Mfrs. Assn., Farm and Indsl. Equipment Inst., Constrn. Industry Mfrs. Assn., Outdoor Power Equipment Inst., Engine Mfrs. Assn., Internat. Farm Tractor Com., Internat. Harvesting Equipment Com. (chmn. statistics com. 1994-95).

GIGLIO, NICKI SUE, critical care nurse, administrator; b. Terre Haute, Ind., Apr. 2, 1951; d. James Dean and Doris Marie (Campbell) G. Student, Ind. U., 1969-71, Ind. State U., 1971-74; diploma, St. Anthony Hosp. Sch. Nursing, Terre Haute, 1974. Cert. emergency nurse, ACLS. Clinician, emergency dept. Humana Hosp., San Antonio, 1983-84; staff nurse emergency dept. Mary Immaculate Hosp., Newport News, Va., 1985-87, St. Mary's Hosp., Richmond, Va., 1987-88; house supr. Iroquois Meml. Hosp., Watseka, Ill., 1988—. Mem. ANA, ARC, Emergency Nurses Assn., Ill. Orgn. of Nurse Leaders, Bus. and Profl. Women's Assn., Watseka Bus. and Pofl. Women's Orgn., Delta Theta Tau. Home: 559 N 6th St Watseka IL 60970

GIHL, NICHOLAS T., company executive; b. DuQuoin, Ill., Nov. 7, 1956. BSEE, Purdue U., 1979. Exec. v.p. Total Control Products, Melrose Park, Ill., 1982-93, pres., 1993—. Patentee in Diagnostic System Machine Control. Mem. IEEE, Assn. Computing Machinery. Republican. Office: Total Control Products 2001 N Janice Ave Melrose Park IL 60160

GILB, CORINNE LATHROP, history educator; b. Lethbridge, Alta., Can., Feb. 19, 1925; d. Glen Hutchison and Vera (Passey) Lathrop; m. Tyrell Thompson Gilb, Aug. 19, 1945; children: Lesley Gilb Taplin, Tyra. BA, U. Wash., 1946; MA, U. Calif., Berkeley, 1951, law student, 1950-53; PhD, Harvard U., 1957. History lectr. Mills Coll., Oakland, 1957-61; prof. humanities San Francisco State U., 1964-68; rsch. assoc. U. Calif., Berkeley, 1953-68; prof. history Wayne State U., Detroit, 1968-94, co-dir. Liberal Arts Urban Studies program, 1976-86; dir. planning City of Detroit, 1979-85; spl. cons. Calif. Legislature, 1963, 64; vis. scholar Hooer Instn., Stanford U., fall 1993; UN Nongovtl. Orgn. rep. Internat. Orgn. for Unification of Terminological Neologisms, 1995—. Author: Conformity of State to Federal Income Tax, 1964, Hidden Hierarchies, 1966, numerous chpts. in books; contbr. articles to profl. jours. Vol. writer Silicon Valley Global Trading Ctr., 1995-96. Guggenheim fellow, 1957; grantee Social Sci. Rsch. Coun. Mem. Internat. Soc. Comparative Study of Civilizations (exec. coun., 1st v.p. 1995—), No. Calif. World Affairs Coun., various acad. assns. Presbyterian.

GILBERT, BRUCE FREDERIC, small business owner; b. Whitehall, Wis., Dec. 23, 1932; s. Frederic and Louise (Hahn) G.; m. Ellen Foster Strachan, June 28, 1968; children: James, Eric, Heidi, Sarah. BS, Marquette U., Milw., 1958. Pres., founder Cedar Lake Sand and Gravel, Hartford, Wis., 1962—; dir., founder, sec. Dodge Concrete, Inc., Watertown, Wis. Contbr. articles to profl. jours. Recipient ABC (Associated Builders and Contractors Assn.) High Stds. award, 1990. Mem. Assoc. Bldrs. and Contrs. of Wis. (dir. 1992), Aurora Rd. Businessman's Assn. (pres, dir. 1995—), Safari Club (dir. 1987—), Bean Club. Republican. Lutheran. Office: Cedar Lake Sand and Gravel 5189 Aurora Rd Hartford WI 53027-9550

GILBERT, GLENN GORDON, linguistics educator; b. Montgomery, Ala., Sept. 17, 1936; s. William H. and Margaret (Christensen) G.; m. Erika Wrede, Aug. 8, 1964 (dec. Nov. 1993); children: Alexander Martin, Christa Selene; m. Sharon Wright Pape, July 23, 1994. AB in German Lang. and Lit., U. Chgo., 1957; postgrad., U. Frankfurt, Fed. Republic Germany, 1957-59; Diplôme de la Langue Française with honors, Sorbonne, U. Paris, 1960; PhD in Linguistics, Harvard U., 1963. Instr. Germanic langs. and lits. U. Tex., Austin, 1963-66, asst. prof. Germanic langs., 1967-70; vis. asst. prof. linguistics Can. Summer Sch. Linguistics, U. Alta., Edmonton, summer 1966; Fulbright lectr. linguistics U. Marburg, Fed. Republic Germany, 1966-67; assoc. prof. So. Ill. U., Carbondale, 1970-74, prof., 1975—, chmn. dept. linguistics, 1987-89; Fulbright lectr. linguistics U. Mainz, Fed. Republic Germany, 1973-74; Z.W.O. research fellow in creole langs. U. Nijmegen, The Netherlands, 1984-85; active numerous univ. linguistics coms. and councils; bd. dirs., mem. editorial bd., Ill. bus. rep. Papers in Linguistics, 1979-87; pres. Linguistic Research Inc., 1983-87. Founder, editor Journal of Pidgin and Creole Languages, 1985—; author: Linguistic Atlas of Texas German, 1972; editor: (books) Texas Studies in Bilingualism, 1970, The German Language in America, 1971, Pidgin and Creole Languages: Essays in Memory of John E. Reinecke, 1987; co-editor (with Jacob Ornstein) Problems in Applied Educational Sociolinguistics, 1978; editor and translator: Pidgin and Creole Languages: Selected Essays by Hugo Schuchardt, 1980; editor: (book series) Studies in Ethnolinguistics, 1993—; contbr. numerous articles to profl. jours. and chpts. to books in field; also reviews. Translator, interpreter various community orgns. NDEA fellow in Swedish, Harvard U., 1961-63; research grantee U. Tex.-Austin, 1963-70, Nat. Carl Schurz Meml. Fund, 1968, So. Ill. U.-Carbondale, 1970-84, NEH, 1981, Am. Philos. Soc., 1982; numerous invited lectures. Mem. Soc. Caribbean Linguistics, Soc. for Pidgin and Creole Linguistics. Home: 166 Union Grove Rd Carbondale IL 62901 Office: So Ill U Dept Linguistics Carbondale IL 62901

GILBERT, HAROLD FREDERICK, publishing executive, art lecturer; b. Elyria, Ohio, Nov. 9, 1916; s. Fred Earl and Hazel Mildred (Tooth) G.; m. Alice Myers, Aug. 11, 1943; children: Kenneth F., Marcia A. Student, Cleve. State U. (formerly Fenn Coll.), 1935-51, Harvard U., 1944. Owner Gilbert Printing Svc., Lakewood, Ohio, 1930-46; pres. Gilbert Pub. Co., Cleve., 1946—; sec.-treas. Madison Press, Lakewood, Ohio, 1975-91; prin. Gilbert Religious Publs., Lakewood, 1984—; trustee Lakewood Hosp. Found., 1992—. Trustee John Bruere Scholarship Fund, Cleve., 1985-90, Calvary Presbyn. Ch., Cleve, 1968-88, Cleve. Ctr. Contemporary Art, 1985-94; treas. Neighbors Organized for Action in Housing, Cleve., 1969-72; col. Confederate Air Force, 1990—. 1st lt. USAAF, 1942-46 PTO. Decorated Bronze Star; Endowment fellow Cleve. Mus. Art, 1984—, 1st charter fellow U. of World, 1989—; recipient Disting. Alumni Hall of Fame award Lakewood H.S., 1994. Fellow Inst. Modern Russian Culture (life); mem. N.Y. Ctr. Sys. Hist. Soc. (life), San Francisco Cable Car Gripman (hon.), East African Wildlife Soc. (life) Masons (George Washington Plaque 1983), Scottish Rite. Home: 1063 Kirtland Ln Lakewood OH 44107-1423 Office: Gilbert Pub Co 15624 Detroit Ave Cleveland OH 44107-3708

GILBERT, HOWARD ALDEN, economics educator; b. Spokane, Wash., Feb. 1, 1935; s. Alden Phineas and Hester Anne (Warner) G.; m. Lucille Dorothy Weaver, June 28, 1957; children: Douglas Alden, Daniel William, Dawnna Faye Gilbert Berndt, Debra Anne Gilbert La Croix. BA, Cen. Bible Inst., Springfield, Mo., 1957; BS, Wash. State U., 1961, MA, 1962; PhD, Oreg. State U., 1967; postgrad., Vanderbilt U., 1971. Asst. prof. S.D. State U., Brookings, 1966-70, assoc. prof., 1970-76, prof., 1976—; expert witness retained by various attys. Mem. Am. Agrl. Econs. Assn., Am. Econs. Assn., Am. Sci. Affiliation, Western Agrl. Econs. Assn., Western Econs. Assn., Mensa (pres. S.D. chpt. 1989-91, v.p. 1992-94, 96—), Mortar Bd., Phi Kappa Phi (pres., v.p., sec., marshall), Pi Gamma Mu (sec., v.p., pres.), Gamma Sigma Delta (treas., pres.), Alpha Zeta, Omicron Delta Epsilon, Lambda Chi Alpha (head advisor, order of merit, Alumni Hall of Fame). Democrat. Wesleyan. Home: 605 9th St Brookings SD 57006-1335

GILBERT, MICHAEL D., stockbroker; b. Omaha, Nov. 21, 1949. AA in Law Enforcement, Kirkwood C.C., 1979. Lic. series 7. Trooper State Troopers, Iowa City, 1973-88; stockbroker Edward D. Jones & Co., Altoona, Iowa, 1988—. Mem. Students Against Drunk Driving. 1st sgt. USAR, 1968-71. Decorated Purple Heart (2), Silver Star. Mem. Church of Christ. Office: Edward D Jones & Co PO Box 20 # G 100 8th St SE Altoona IA 50009

GILBERT, RICHARD A., investment consultant; b. Jersey City, June 28, 1941. BA in Bus., Miami U., Oxford, Ohio, 1962. Sr. v.p. Prescott Ball & Turben, Cleve., 1962-91; investment cons. Kemper Securities Inc., Westlake, Ohio, 1991—.

GILBERT, RUBY, state legislator; m. Booker Gilbert. Kans. state rep. Dist. 89, 1993—. Home: 2629 N Erie St Wichita KS 67219-4739 Office: Kans Ho of Reps State Capitol Topeka KS 66612*

GILBERT, SAMUEL LAWRENCE, business owner; b. Chgo., Mar. 3, 1950; s. Robert Augustus and Ruby Elizabeth (Gammon) G.; m. Sharon Faye Warner, Nov. 3, 1972 (div. Oct. 1984); children: Shaundra, Shari, Sharita. AA in Health Care, Malcolm X Coll., Chgo., 1969; cert. in acctg., Bryant Stratton Coll., Chgo., 1989. Mail/shipping coord. Natural Gas Pipeline Co. Am., Chgo., 1970-82; mailroom asst. IBM Corp., Chgo., 1982-83; CEO Genesis Comics Group, Inc., Chgo., 1986-94; chmn., pub., CEO Genesis Pub., Ltd., Chgo., 1994—. Deacon Christ the King Temple Ch., Chgo., 1985-87; asst. pastor Greater Holy Rock MBC, Chgo., 1988-92, St. Titus MBC, Chgo., 1994—; assoc. min. Greater New Mt. Carmen, Chgo., 1992-94. Mem. Am. Mgmt. Assn., Rsch. Inst. Am. Democrat. Baptist. Home and Office: Genesis Comics Group Inc 2631 S Indiana Ave Apt 1410 Chicago IL 60616-2832

GILBERT, VINCENT NEWTON, publisher; b. Chgo., Dec. 7, 1955; s. Herman Cromwell and Ivy Newton (McAlpine) G.; m. Denise Sharon Rawlings, Aug. 15, 1982; children: Diona Vinise, Vincent Newton II. BA in Polit. Sci., Ind. U., 1978; JD, John Marshall Law Sch., 1983. Dir., Maple Park Strong Ctr., Chgo., 1976; terr. mgr. Carnation Co., Chgo., 1978-81; sales dir. Path Press, Chgo., 1982—; exec. v.p. CDM Transp. Svc., Inc., Chgo., 1984-86; dir. consumer edn. dept. of consumer svcs., Chgo., 1987-88; dist. dir. Office of Congressman Gus Savage, Chgo., 1988—; apptd. to Small Bus. Utility Advocate State of Ill., 1992—. Speech writer Savage for Alderman campaign, Chgo., 1983; area coord. Savage for Congress campaign, Chgo., 1982, Washington for Mayor campaign, Chgo., 1983; vice chmn. Danny Davis for Mayor campaign, 1991. Mem. Student Bar Assn., Black Am. Law Student Assn. Methodist. Office: James R Thompson Ctr 100 W Randolph St Ste 3-400 Chicago IL 60601-3219

GILBERTSON, ERIC RAYMOND, academic administrator, lawyer; b. Cleve., Mar. 5, 1945; s. Ewald R. and Esther V. (Johnson) G.; m. Cynthia F. Forrest, Jan. 25, 1974; children: Sara, Seth. BS, Bluffton Coll., 1966; MA in Econs., Ohio U., 1967; JD cum laude, Cleve. State U., 1970; DLitt (hon.) U. Mysore, Karnataka, India, 1993. Bar: Ohio 1970, Vt. 1984, U.S. Dist. Ct. (no. and so. dists.) Ohio 1971, U.S. Supreme Ct. 1981. Instr. econs. Kent State U., Ohio, 1969-70; law clk. Supreme Ct. of Ohio, Columbus, 1970-71; asst. atty. gen. State of Ohio, Columbus, 1971-73; exec. asst. to pres. Ohio State U., Columbus, 1973-79; assoc. Vorys, Sater, Seymore & Pease, Columbus, 1979-81; pres. Johnson State Coll., Vt., 1981-89, Saginaw Valley State U., University Center, Mich., 1989—; Bd. dirs. Bay County Alliance for Schs., Consortium for Internat. Earth Scis. Info. Network; mem. Midland County Econ. Growth and Devel. Corp.; trustee Saginaw Gen. Hosp. Contbr. articles to profl. jours. Mem. Am. Coun. Edn. Leadership Commn., Am. Assn. State Colls. and Univs. (com. on policies and purposes), Saginaw County C. of C., Torch Club, Saginaw Club, Bay City Country Club. Home: 7371 Glen Eagle Dr Bay City MI 48706-9316 Office: Saginaw Valley State U University Center MI 48710

GILBERTSON, JILL STENSLAND, banker; b. Rochester, Minn., Mar. 16, 1960; d. Milton C. and Jacqueline (I.) S.; m. David T. Gilbertson, Sept. 2, 1990; 1 child, Jena. BSBA cum laude, U. Wis., Menomonie, 1982; postgrad., U. St. Thomas, 1993—. With 1st Bank, Austin, Minn., 1980, Vermillion (Minn.) State Bank; Hudsons, Mpls.; officer Met. Fed. Bank, Mpls., 1987-89, area sales mgr., 1989-90, mgr., asst. v.p., 1990-93. Mem. C. of C., N.W. Racquet Club. Lutheran.

GILBERTSON, STEVEN E(DWARD) SATYAKI, real estate broker, guidance counselor; b. Winona, Minn., Nov. 5, 1951; s. Conrad Orville and Lorraine Kristina (Munson) G.; m. Jayne Ann Rock, June 13, 1992. BA, U. Minn., Morris, 1974; MS, Winona State U., 1982. Math tchr. Winona Pub. Schs., 1974-76, Owatonna (Minn.) Pub. Schs., 1976-77; tie gang laborer Milw. Railroad, Winona, 1978; spl. edn. tchr. Winona Heights Acad., 1978-79; math tchr. Rushford (Minn.) Pub. Schs., 1980-81, Gale Ettrick Trempealeau Sch., Galesville, Wis., 1981-82; salesperson Winona Realty, 1983-86, broker, 1993—; broker S.G. Realty, Winona, 1986-93; tchr. elem. phys. edn. St. Francis Sch., Rochester, Minn., 1993; spl. edn. tchr. Austin Pub. Schs., 1994—; mem. edn. com., multiple listing svc. com. Multiple Listing Svc., Winona, 1988-90, 93. Fundraiser YMCA, Winona, 1990; mem. focus group Winona County Chem. Abuse Prevention Task Force, 1991-93; facilitator Course in Miracles Study Group, Winona, 1991-93; creator Adult Children Anonymous, Emotions Anonymous (Winona chpt.), 12-Step Groups, 1990. Mem. Minn. Assn. Realtors, Sons of Norway, Westfield Golf Club (men's league champion 1987, 89). Home: 234 15th Ave SE Rochester MN 55904-4731

GILBRIDE, KATHLEEN SUE, business analyst; b. Racine, Wis., Oct. 24, 1952; m. Kevin J. Gilbride, Sept. 16, 1987. BS, Winona State U., 1977. Classroom tchr. Austin (Minn.) Pub. Schs., 1977-83; classroom tchr. Gale-Ettrick Trempeauleau, Galesville, Wis., 1983-85; software instr. Bankers Systems, Inc., St. Cloud, Minn., 1985-89; software tng. supr. Bankers Systems, Inc., St. Cloud, 1990-92, project mgr., 1992—. Author: (instrnl. workbook) Software, 1989, (instrnl. video) Software, 1990. Co-leader Girl Scouts U.S., St. Cloud, 1992, svc. unit mgr. 1993-96, coun. trainer, 1995-96, bd. dirs Land of Lakes coun., 1995—, 3rd v.p. bd. dirs. 1996—. Recipient Outstanding Vol. award Girl Scouts U.S., 1995; LWV scholar, 1970. Office: Bankers Systems Inc 1457 Saukview Dr Saint Cloud MN 56301

GILCHREST, THORNTON CHARLES, retired association executive; b. Chgo., Sept. 1, 1931; s. Charles Jewett Gilchrest and Patricia (Thornton) Thornton; m. Barbara Dibbern, June 8, 1952; children: Margaret Mary, James Thornton. B.S. in Journalism, U. Ill., 1953. Cert. tchr., Ill. Tchr. pub. high sch. West Chicago, Ill., 1957; exec. dir. Plumbing-Heating-Cooling Info. Bur., Chgo., 1958-64; asst. to pres. A.Y. McDonald Mfg. Co., Dubuque, Iowa, 1964-68; exec. dir. Am. Supply Assn., Chgo., 1968-77, exec. v.p., 1977-82; exec. v.p. Nat. Safety Coun., Chgo., 1982-83, pres., 1983-95; chmn. Internat. Safety Coun., Chgo., 1992; pres. Nat. Safety Coun. Found. for Safety and Health, 1986. Bd. dirs. Prevent Blindness Am., 1993. With USN, 1953-55. Mem. Am. Soc. Assn. Execs., Chgo. Soc. Assn. Execs. Methodist.

GILDENBLATT, ROSLYN WARSHOFSKY, nursing administrator; b. N.Y.C., Aug. 2, 1925; d. Isadore and Ida (Rosen) Warshofsky; m. Jule Gildenblatt, May 29, 1949; children: Stuart Alan, Daryl Lee, Nancy Gildenblatt Kahn. Diploma, RN, Jewish Hosp. Cin., 1947; BS in Psychology cum laude, Xavier U., 1970, MEd, 1972; postgrad., U. Cin., 1973, 74, 75. RN, Ohio. Supr. surg. areas The Jewish Hosp., Cin., 1961-68, asst. dir. nursing svc., 1968-78; dir. patient care Bethesda Hosp., Cin., 1979-80; supr. nursing svc. phys. therapy and respiratory therapy EPP Meml. Hosp., Cin., 1980-87, acting dir. nursing svc. phys. therapy & respiratory therapy, 1987-88; ret., 1988; vol. nurse ARC. Bd. dirs., sec. Jewish Nat. Fund, Cin., 1987—; bd. dirs., donor chair, life mem. Na' Amat U.S.A., Cin., 1990—, fundraising chair, 1990-93, pres., 1994-96. Mem. ANA, NLN, HAdassah (life), Isaac M. Wise Temple Sisterhood (life), Na'Amat (life). Jewish.

GILDING, RONALD EDWIN, electrical engineer; b. Quincy, Mich., Oct. 24, 1926; s. Orville Brice Gilding and Edna Mildred (Cook) Bottesi; m. LaVonne Marie Swanson (div.); m. Ruth Elenore Huse, Mar. 6, 1982. BS, Milw. Sch. of Engring., 1952. Registered profl. engr., Wis., Ohio. Power distrn. engr. Commonwealth Edison Co., Chgo., 1952-54, Consumers Power Co., Jackson, Mich., 1955-56; electrical engr. I Lakehead Pipe Line Co., Superior, Wis., 1956-67; prin. engr. Programmed & Systems Co., St. Paul, 1967-69; electrical project mgr. Commonwealth Electric Co., St. Paul, 1969-72; electrical engr. Gilbert/Commonwealth Co., Jackson, Mich., 1973-80; sr. electrical engr. Davy McKee Co., Cleve., 1980-82, Engring. Sci. Co., Cleve., 1982-86, MK Ferguson Co., Cleve., 1986-91; ptnr. engr. Garrett & Clemmer, Inc., Chagrin Falls, Ohio, 1996—; cons. BAT Assocs., Cleve., 1992-95, Westinghouse Electric Co., Orlando, 1994. Mem. IEEE. Home: 5411 Belvoir Blvd South Euclid OH 44121 Office: Garrett & Clemmer Inc PO Box 23472 Chagrin Falls OH 44023

GILES, CALVIN LAMONT, state legislator; b. Chgo., July 10, 1962. Ill. state rep. Dist. 8, 1995—. Office: 5255 W North Ave Chicago IL 60639

GILES, CONRAD LESLIE, ophthalmic surgeon; b. N.Y.C., July 14, 1934; s. Irving Samuel Giles and Victoria Ampole; m. Marilyn Toby Schwartz, June 20, 1955 (div. 1978); children: Keith Martin, Suzanne Speer, Kevin William, Brian Alan; m. Lynda Fern Schenk, Nov. 26, 1978; stepchildren: Jared Schenk, Jamie Schenk. MD, U. Mich., 1957, MS, 1961. Diplomate Am. Bd. Ophthalmology. Clin. assoc. NIH, Bethesda, Md., 1961-63; clin. asst. prof. Wayne State U. Sch. Medicine, Detroit, 1965-72, clin. assoc. prof. ophthalmology, 1973-89, clin. prof. ophthalmology, 1989—; chief ophthalmologist Children's Hosp. Mich., 1985—. Contbr. articles to med. jours. Active Jewish Welfare Fedn., Detroit, 1981-86, pres. 1986-89; bd. govs. Jewish Agy. for Israel, 1995—. Fellow Am. Acad. Ophthalmology; mem. AMA, Mich. State Ophthal. Soc., Coun. Jewish Fedns. (v.p. 1992-95, treas. 1995-96, pres. 1996—), United Jewish Appeal (nat. vice chmn. 1992—), Mich. Jewish Conf. (pres. 1992-95). Avocations: golf, tennis, skiing. Home: 6300 Westmoor Rd Bloomfield Hills MI 48301-1359 Office: 4400 Town Ctr Southfield MI 48075-1601

GILES, HOMER WAYNE, lawyer; b. Noble, Ohio, Nov. 9, 1919; s. Edwin Jay and Nola Blanche (Tillison) G.; m. Marcia Ellen Hurt, Oct. 3, 1987; children: Jay, Janice, Keith, Tim, Gregory. A.B., Adelbert Coll., 1940; LL.B., Western Res. Law Sch., 1943, LL.M., 1959. Bar: Ohio 1943. Mem. firm Davis & Young, Cleve., 1942-43, William I. Moon, Port Clinton, Ohio, 1946-48; pres. Strabley Baking Co., Cleve., 1948-53; v.p. French Baking Co., Cleve., 1953-55; law clk. 8th Dist Ct. Appeals, Cleve., 1955-58; ptnr. Kuth & Giles, Cleve., 1958-68, Walter, Haverfield, Buescher & Chockley, Cleve., 1968—; pres. Clinton Franklin Realty Co., Cleve., 1958—, Concepts Devel., Inc., 1980—; sec. Holiday Designs, Inc., Sebring, Ohio, 1964—; trustee Teamster Local 52 Health and Welfare Fund, 1950-53; mem. Bakers Negotiating Exec. Com., 1951-53. Contbr. articles to profl. publs.; editor: Banks Baldwin Ohio Legal Forms, 1962. Troop com. chmn. Skyline council Boy Scouts Am., 1961-63; adviser Am. Security Council; trustee Hiram House Camp, Florence Crittenton Home, 1965; chmn. bd. trustees Am. Econ. Found., N.Y.C., 1973-80, chmn. exec. com., 1973-80; mem. Heritage Found. Served with AUS, 1943-46, ETO. Mem. Am. Bar Assn., World Law Assn. (founding), Am. Arbitration Assn. (nat. panel), Com. on Econ. Reform and Edn. (life), Inst. Money and Inflation, Speakers Bur. Cleve. Sch. Levy, Citizens League, Pacific Inst., Phila. Soc., Aircraft Owners and Pilots Assn., Cleve. Hist. Soc., Mus. Modern Art, Met. Mus., Mercantile Libr., Delta Tau Delta, Delta Theta Phi. Unitarian. Clubs: Cleve. Skating, Cleve. Econ., Harvard Bus., The City, Cleve. City, Cleve. Econs. Home: 2588 S Green Rd Cleveland OH 44122-1534 Office: Am Econ Found 1215 Terminal Tower Cleveland OH 44113*

GILES, ROBERT HARTMANN, newspaper editor; b. Cleve., June 6, 1933; s. Robert Hamilton and Grace (Hartmann) G.; m. Nancy May Morgan, Feb. 6, 1960; children: David Morgan, Megan Elisabeth, Robert Hamilton II. BA, DePauw U., 1955, D Journalism (hon.), 1996; MS, Columbia U., 1956; Doctorate of Journalsim (hon.), DePauw U., 1996. Reporter Newport News Daily Press, 1957-58; reporter Akron (Ohio) Beacon Jour., 1958-63, editorial writer, 1963-65, city editor, 1966-68, mgt. editor, 1968-69, mng. editor, 1969-73, exec. editor, 1973-76; spl. lectr. Sch. Journalism, U. Kans., 1976-77; exec. editor Gannett Rochester (N.Y.) Newspapers, 1977-81, editor, 1981-86; v.p., exec. editor Detroit News, 1986-89, editor, pub., 1989—; pres. Media Mgmt. Books Inc. Author: Newsroom Management: A Guide to Theory and Practice. Trustee William Allen White Found., U. Kans., 1978—. With AUS, 1956-58. Nieman fellow Harvard, 1965-66; co-recipient Pulitzer prize for local reporting, 1971, Scripps-Howard 1st Amendment award, 1978. Mem. AP Mng. Editors Assn. (pres. 1988), Am. Soc. Newspaper editors (bd. dirs., treas. 1994, v.p. 1995, pres. 1996), Soc. Profl. Journalists, Found. Am. Comm. (co-chmn.), Accrediting Coun. for Edn. in Journalism and Mass Comm. (pres. 1992—), Alpha Tau Omega. Office: Detroit News 615 W Lafayette Blvd Detroit MI 48226-3124

GILGEN, ALBERT RUDOLPH, psychologist, educator; b. Akron, Ohio, Sept. 19, 1930; s. Albert and Jeannette (Rufer) G.; m. Carol E. Keyes, 1954; children: James D., Jeanne Elizabeth, Albert P. AB in Chemistry, Princeton U., 1952; MA in Psychology, Kent State U., 1963; PhD in Psychology, Mich. State U., 1965. Lic. psychologist, Wis. Asst. then assoc. prof. Beloit (Wis.) Coll., 1965-73; prof., head of dept. U. No. Iowa, Cedar Falls, 1973-93. Author: American Psychology Since World War II, 1982; editor: Contemporary Scientific Psychology, 1970, Chaos Theory in Psychology, 1995; co-editor: International Handbook of Psychology, 1987, Post-Soviet Perspectives on Russian Psychology, 1996; contbr. numerous articles to profl. jours. USN, 1952-55. Fulbright Exchangelectr. U. Coll. Galway, Ireland, 1971-72. Fellow APA, Am. Psychol. Soc.; mem. AAAS, Fulbright Alumni Assn. Home: 1107 Washington St Cedar Falls IA 50613-3069 Office: Univ No Iowa Dept Psychology Cedar Falls IA 50614

GILHAUS, BARBARA JEAN, secondary education home economics educator; b. Hindsboro, Ill., Aug. 30, 1940; d. Garold Wayne and Lois Marie (Gaede) Farthing; m. Robert Lee Gilhaus, Sept. 28, 1963; 1 child, Gregory Lee. BS in Edn., Ea. Ill. U., Charleston, 1962; postgrad., Ill. State U., 1975-85, No. Ill. U., 1978. Tchr. home econs. and consumer edn. Heritage High Sch., Broadlands, Ill., 1962-93; consumer edn. cons. Ill. State Bd. Edn., Springfield, 1976-80; mem. Ill. White House Conf. on Children, 1980; chair, mem., sec. Edn. Svc. Ctr. 13, Rantoul, Ill., 1985-91. Author booklet and consumer edn. articles; participant radio program In the Consumer Interest, 1975. Chair Homer (Ill.) Zoning Bd. Appeals, 1980—; active in voter registration Champaign County, Urbana, Ill., 1980—. Recipient Ednl. Excellence award Ill. State Bd. Edn., 1985, award Ill. Ho. of Reps., 1985, Educator's award Champaign/Ford County, 1989. Mem. NEA, Ill. Edn. Assn. (bd. dirs. 1982-88), Ill. Consumer Edn. Assn. (bd. dirs., sec., treas., Gladys Bahr award 1985), Ill. Vocat. Home Edn. Tchrs. Assn., Heritage Edn. Assn. (all offices). Methodist. Home: 607 W 4th St Homer IL 61849-1017

GILJOHANN, PETER T., finance company executive; b. Herkimer, N.Y., Dec. 26, 1952. Sales mgr. Equity Enterprises, Wauwatosa, Wis., 1981-89; pres. Prime Fin. Svcs., Inc., Wauwatosa, 1989—. Publisher, editor: Prime Times newspaper, 1989—; contbr. numerous articles to newspaper. Leader Cub Scouts Am., Brookfield, Wis., 1994-95; coach Elmbrook (Wis.) Youth League girls basketball, 1994—; tchr. Sundaysch., 1994—. Salesman of the Year award Equity of Enterprises, 1983, 85. Mem. practitioner Internat. Assn. for Fin. Planning; mem. Nat. Assn. of Mortgage Brokers. Evangelical.

GILKES, ARTHUR GWYER, lawyer; b. Bronxville, N.Y., Feb. 6, 1915; s. Arthur Burton and Frances (Gwyer) G.; m. Ann Fullan, Feb. 26, 1942; children: Arthur Gwyer Jr., Ann Colwell Gilkes Liu, Judith Porter Gilkes Benson, Jane Scott Gilkes Strassgütl. A.B., Princeton U., 1939; LL.B., NYU, 1947. Assoc. Pennie, Edmonds, Morton & Barrows, N.Y.C., 1945-49; ptnr. Adams, Forward & McLean, N.Y.C., 1949-54; gen. mgr. patents and lic. dept., gen. patent atty. Standard Oil Co. (Ind.), Chgo., 1954-80; of counsel Leydig, Voit & Mayer, Ltd., Chgo., 1980—; pres., dir. Mid-Century Corp., 1967-74. Served with USN, 1942-45. Mem. ABA, Am. Intellectual Property Law Assn., Intellectual Property Assn. Chgo., Assn. of Bar. of City of N.Y., Internat. Intellectual Property Assn., Am. Judicature Soc., Assn. Corp. Patent Counsel, Univ. Club, Racquet Club, Glen View Club, Princeton, Nassau, Northeast Harbor Fleet, The Country Club of Fla., Ocean Club of Fla., The Pot and Kettle. Home: 6 Country Rd E Village Of Golf FL 33436 Office: 2 Prudential Plz Ste 4900 Chicago IL 60601

GILL, BERNARD IVES, librarian; b. Rockford, Ill., May 16, 1921; s. Richard Hackett and Floss Adeline (Campbell) G.; m. Dorothy Marie Hovde, Aug. 24, 1949; 1 son, Brian Hovde. Student, Beloit Coll., 1939, 42; B.A., U. Ill., 1943, M.S., 1949; grad. student, U. Minn., 1962, 63-64. Tchr. Bensenville, Ill., 1946-47; head librarian Moorhead (Minn.) State U., 1950-80. Served with USNR, 1943-46. Mem. NEA, ALA, AAUP. Methodist. Home: PO Box 325 Hillsboro ND 58045-0325

GILL, CHUCK S., stockbroker; b. Virginia, Minn., Mar. 19, 1955. BA in Fin., St. Cloud (Minn.) State U., 1980. Stockbroker Engler Budd, Mpls., 1984-88, Carig-UM, Bloomington, Minn., 1988-93, Summit Investment Corp., Bloomington, 1993—. Republican. Lutheran. Home: 14270 Cobbler Ave Rosemount MN 55068-7127 Office: Summit Investment Corp 3800 W 80th St Ste 200 Bloomington MN 55431-4417

GILL, SUZANNE, software publisher; b. Quincy, Ill., June 30, 1941; d. Harry J. and Anne (McDonnell) Lutz; m. James H. Gill, June 25, 1966 (div.); children: Michael, Brian, Molly. BS, Fontbonne Coll., St. Louis, 1963; MS, U. Mich., 1967. Tchr., librarian Parkway Sch. Dist., St. Louis, 1963-66; coordinator LTA Program U. Toledo, Cuyahogha Community Coll. (Cleve.), St. Louis Community Coll., 1967-84; pres. Info. Resources Cons., St. Louis, 1977—. Author: File Management and Information Retrieval Systems, 1981, 2d edit., 1988, 3d edit., 1993; contbr. numerous mag. articles; developed numerous software programs, 1984-88. Mem. Kirkwood Hist. Soc. Mem. Mo. Sch. Libr. assn., Mo. Libr. Assn., Chesterfield Hist. Soc., Am. Legion Aux. Republican. Roman Catholic. Home and Office: 1556 Walpole Dr Chesterfield MO 63017-4615

GILL, W(ALTER) BRENT, lawyer; b. Bedford, Ind., May 23, 1950; s. Jim and Barbara Dean (Medlock) G.; m. Marina Mae Floyd, May 18, 1974; children: Keenan Shane, Trevor Floyd, Bryce Bennett. BS in Edn., Ind. U., 1976; postgrad., Ohio No. U., 1976-77; JD cum laude, Ind. U., Indpls., 1979; diploma, Nat. Inst. for Trial Advocacy, Boulder, Colo., 1983. Bar: Ind. 1980, U.S. Dist. Ct. (so. dist.) Ind. 1980, U.S. Dist. Ct. (no. dist.) Ind. 1990, U.S. Ct. Appeals (7th cir.) 1992; cert. civil trial advocate. Law clk. Ind. Jud. Ctr., Indpls., 1977-78, Ind. Ct. Appeals, Indpls., 1978-80; atty. Goebel & Gill, Indpls., 1980-82, Montgomery, Elsner & Pardieck, Seymour, Ind., 1982-85, Pardieck, Gill & Vargo, Seymour, 1985—. With U.S. Navy, 1969-71. Fellow Roscoe Pound Found., Ind. Coll. of Trial Lawyers; mem. ABA, Ind. Bar Assn., Jackson County Bar Assn. (pres. 1987-88), Assn. Trial Lawyers Am. (in state del. 1996—), Ind. Trial Lawyers Assn. (bd. dirs. 1988—, exec. com. 1995—). Home: 2993 N County Rd 400 E Seymour IN 47274 Office: Pardieck Gill & Vargo 100 N Chestnut St Seymour IN 47274-2102

GILL, WILFRED GEORGE, financial executive; b. Akron, Ohio, Nov. 9, 1912; s. Lemmen Cecil and Nellie (Berlitz) G.; widowed; children: Don B., Lesley K., Nancy E., Sherry Lee. Student, Wayne U. Registered rep., fin. cons. Inspector Retail Credit Co., Akron, Detroit, 1934-41; scheduler Standard Steel Spring, Detroit, 1941-43; salesman Bostitch Stapling, Detroit, 1943-54, Goodbody & Co., Royal Oak, Mich., 1954-64; v.p., mgr., sales W.E. Hutton, Royal Oak, Troy, Mich., 1964-74; salesman Loed-Rhoades, Troy, 1974-75; v.p. mgr. White Weld, Troy, 1975-77; v.p., salesman Paine Webber, Troy, 1977-91; fin. cons. Merrill Lynch, Bloomfield Hills, Mich., 1991-94. Mem. Securities Traders, Detroit Athletic Club, Birmingham Optimist (past pres., lt. gov.). Republican. Roman Catholic. Home: 2828 Bacon Ave Berkley MI 48072-1071

GILLAN, JEFFREY SCOTT, news anchor; b. Milw., June 1, 1957; s. Theodore Edward and Siegrid Helene (Burst) G. AB in Am. Govt., Georgetown U., 1979; MA in Journalism, Am. U., 1985. Gen. assignment reporter Sta. KFSM-TV, Ft. Smith, Ark., 1986-87; weekend news anchor Sta. WSLS-TV, Roanoke, Va., 1987-90; weeknight news anchor Sta. WKOW-TV, Madison, Wis., 1990—. Vol. intensive care nursery Meriter Hosp., Madison, 1991—; cons. Madison AIDS Support Network, 1992; bd. dirs. New Harvest Found. Recipient John Merriman award Writers Guild Am., 1985, 1st place for enterprise-investigative story AP, Ark., 1987. Mem. Kappa Tau Alpha. Office: Sta WKOW-TV 5727 Tokay Blvd Madison WI 53719-1219

GILLEN, JOHN E., financial manager; b. Ludington, Mich., Nov. 24, 1932. BA, Mich. U., 1954. Owner Marina Glenn Lake, Glenn Lake, Mich., 1970-80; br. mgr. E. F. Hutton, Traverse City, Mich., 1980-84, A. G. Edwards & Sons Inc., Traverse City, 1984—; bd. dirs. Old Mission Conservatory, Traverse City. 1st. lt. USAF, 1954-57. Mem. Elks, Country Club. Republican. Episcopalian. Office: A G Edwards & Sons Inc Delta Ctr 415 Munson Ave Traverse City MI 49686-3059

GILLESPIE, GARY DON, physician; b. Jackson, Mich., Apr. 23, 1943; s. Harold Don and Marion Estella (Diemer) G.; m. Nancy Bliven Hinkle, June 29, 1969 (div. July 1980; children: Brian James, Julie Elizabeth; m. Elaine Marie Beard, July 25, 1984. BS, U. Mich., 1966, D of Medicine, 1971. Diplomate Am. Bd. Family Practice. Intern Edward W. Sparrow Hosp., Lansing, Mich., 1971-72, resident in family practice, 1971-74; physician Dept. Family Practice, USN Med. Corps., Orlando, Fla., 1974-76; pvt. practice Okemos, Mich., 1976—; chmn. continuing edn., dept. family practice Edward W. Sparrow Hosp., 1976-91; asst. clin. prof. dept. family practice Mich. State U. Coll. Medicine, East Lansing, 1981—. Lt. comdr. USN, 1974-76. Mem. AMA, Am. Acad. Family Physicians, Am. Bd. Family Practice, Mich. Acad. Family Physicians (treas. Capitol chpt. 1982-92). Republican. Office: 1745 Hamilton Rd # 340 Okemos MI 48864-1810

GILLESPIE, J. MARTIN, sales and distribution company executive; b. Detroit, Sept. 27, 1949; s. John Martin and Shirley Ann (Rees) G.; BBA, Xavier U., 1971; MBA, U. Mich., 1973; m. Jeannette Downes, Sept. 27, 1975; children: Heather, Tara. Account exec. Foote Cone & Belding, Chgo., 1973-76; account supr., 1976-77; mktg. mgr. Hansen Corp., Walled Lake, Mich., 1977-80, gen. mgr., 1980-82; chmn., chief exec. officer Hansen Mktg. Services, Inc., Walled Lake, 1982—. Recipient Merit award Nat. Alliance Businessmen, 1973. Mem. Assn. MBA Execs., Am. Mgmt. Assn., Nat. Acad. TV Arts and Scis., Nat. Assn. Credit Mgmt., Nat. Bldg. Materials Distbn. Assn. (chmn. govt. rels. com.), Alpha Kappa Psi. Home: 3792 W Pembroke Rd Bloomfield Hills MI 48302-1445 Office: Hansen Mktg Svcs Inc PO Box 638 1000 Decker Rd Walled Lake MI 48390

GILLESPIE, JOANN MARIE, ecologist, educator; b. Hilbert, Wis., Feb. 11, 1929; d. Roy Peter and Olive Lois (Elmergreen) Madler; m. Calvin J. Gillespie, Sept. 8, 1953 (dec.); children: Paula S., Chris H. BS, St. Mary of the Woods Coll., 1951, LittD, 1995; MEPD, U. Wis. Rsch. chemist U.S. Vets. Hosp., Milw., 1953-58, L.I. Jewish Hosp., New Hyde Park, N.Y., 1958-60; tchg. naturalist Wehr Nature Ctr., Milw., 1976-79; dir. WMAS Sanctuary Monastery Lake, Franklin, Wis.; lectr., spkr. in field. Contbr. articles to profl. jours. Bd. dirs. Womens Club. Mem. Restoration/Mgmt. Soc., Audubon Soc., Friends of the Bonner Bot. Gardens, Soc. of Wetlands Scientists, Soc. of the State Wetlands Mgrs. Roman Catholic. Home: Box 523 S 75 N 20755 Field Dr Muskego WI 53150 Office: Country Wetlands Nursery and Cons Ltd Muskego WI 53150

GILLETTE, KENNETH E., stockbroker; b. Dayton, Ohio, June 27, 1953. BS, Wright State U., Dayton, 1979. Lic. series 7 Nat. Assn. Securities Dealers. Investment mgr. PaineWebber Inc., Cin., 1980—. Republican. Home: 5668 Brookstone Dr Cincinnati OH 45230-3587 Office: PaineWebber Inc 312 Walnut St Ste 3300 Cincinnati OH 45202-4061

GILLILAND, MARCIA ANN, nurse clinician, infection control specialist; b. Kansas City, Mo., Sept. 15, 1949; d. Robert Joseph and Mary Agnes (Paup) Caton; m. John Lee Gilliland, Mar. 28, 1974 (dec. Oct. 1983); children: Marcella Lyn, John Patrick, Devon Marie. ADN, Kansas City C.C., 1979; BSN, Webster U., 1990. RN, Kans. Staff nurse U. Kans. Med. Ctr., Kansas City, 1979-84, infection control coord., 1984—, facilitator HIV/AIDS wellness group, 1991—; community health nurse Cath. Charities, Kansas City, 1980-82; pres., owner Kansas City Total Image, Overland Park, Kans., 1981-83. Active Rep. Committeewoman, Overland Park, Kans., 1994; Rep. candidate Overland Park City Coun., Kans., 1995. Mem. Nat. Speakers Assn., Assn. Profls. in Infection Control and Epidemiology (pres. Kansas City chpt., 1993-94), Assn. Nurses in AIDS Care. Republican. Home: 9430 Riggs St Overland Park KS 66212-1443 Office: U Kans Med Ctr 3901 Rainbow Blvd Kansas City KS 66160-0001

GILLIS, KEITH A., process engineer; b. East Chicago, Ind., May 14, 1961. B, Purdue U., 1983. Indsl. engr. Frito Lay, Denver, 1983-86; staff engr. Gen. Mills, Cedar Rapids, Iowa, 1986-92; sr. process engr. Square D Co., Cedar Rapids, Iowa, 1992—. Youth advisor NAACP, Cedar Rapids, 1990—. Baptist. Home: 1631 21st St NW Cedar Rapids IA 52405-1469

GILLISPIE, HAROLD LEON, tax consultant; b. Levant, Kans., May 11, 1933; s. Harold Leon and Agnes Anne (Dryden) G. BA in Bus. Adminstrn., Kans. Wesleyan U., 1955. Youth dir. Cen. YMCA, Des Moines, 1957-61;

exec. dir. West Des Moines br. YMCA, 1961-65; exec. dir. Aurora Br. YMCA, Denver, 1965-69; exec. dir. YMCA, McCook, Nebr., 1969-75, Junction City, Kans., 1975-79; owner H & R Block Franchise, Manhattan, Kans., 1979-91; proofreader text H & R Block, Kansas City, Mo., 1986-92. Bd. dirs. Flint Hills Breadbasket, Manhattan, Kans., 1982-89, treas., 1987; bd. dirs. Big Bros. Big Sisters, Manhattan, 1981-85, pres., 1983-85; pres. Downtown Manhattan, Inc., 1986; bd. dirs. Manhattan Main Street, 1986-89; bd. dirs. Ecumenical Campus Ministry, Kans. State U., 1995—, chmn., 1996—. Republican. Presbyterian. Home: 710 Bertrand St Manhattan KS 66502-5156

GILLMOR, KAREN LAKO, state legislator, strategic planner; b. Cleve., Jan. 29, 1948; d. William M. and Charlotte (Sheldon) Lako; m. Paul E. Gillmor, Dec. 10, 1983; children: Linda D., Julie E., Paul M. BA cum laude, Mich. State U., 1969; MA, Ohio State U., 1970, PhD, 1981. Asst. to v.p. Ohio State U., Columbus, 1972-77, spl. asst. dean law, 1979-81; asst. to pres. Ind. Cen. U., Indpls., 1977-78; rsch. asst. Burke Mktg. Rsch., Indpls., 1978-79; v.p. pub. affairs Huntington Nat. Bank, Columbus, 1981-82; fin. cons. Ohio Rep. Fin. Com., Columbus, 1982-83; chief mgmt. planning and rsch. Indsl. Commn. Ohio, Columbus, 1983-86; mgr. physician rels. Univ. Hosps., Columbus, 1987-91; cons. U.S. Sec. Labor, Washington, 1990-91; mem. Regional Bd. Rev., Industrial Commn., Ohio, 1991-92; assoc. dir. Ctr. Healthcare Policy and Rsch. Ohio State U., 1991-92; mem. Ohio General Assembly, 1993—; legis. liaison Huntington Bancshares, Ohio, Ohio State U., Columbus. Grantee Andrew W. Mellon Found. 1978, Carnegie Corp. 1978; named Outstanding Freshman Ohio Legislator, Ohio, 1994, Bulldog of the Treasury; recipient Pres. award Ohio State Chiropractic Assn., 1994, Pub. Svc. award Am. Heart Assn., 1995, Nat. Freshman Legislator of Yr., 1995. Mem. Women in Mainstream, Women's Roundtable, Ohio Fedn. Rep. Women, Am. Assn. Higher Edn., Coun. Advancement and Support Edn., DAR, Phi Delta Kappa. Methodist. Clubs: University (Columbus). Office: The Statehouse Columbus OH 43215-4276

GILLMOR, PAUL E., congressman, lawyer; b. Tiffin, Ohio, Feb. 1, 1939; s. Paul Marshall and Lucy Jeannette (Fry) G.; m. Karen Lee Lako, Dec. 10, 1983; children: Linda Dianne, Julie Ellen, Paul Michael, Connor Sheldon, Adam William. B.A., Ohio Wesleyan U., Delaware, 1961; J.D., U. Mich, 1964; LL.D. (hon.), Tiffin U., Ohio, 1985. Bar: Ohio, 1965. Mem. Ohio Senate, 1967—, minority leader, 1978-81, 83-85, pres., 1981-83, 85-88; mem. 101st-104th Congresses from 5th Ohio dist. 101st-103rd Congresses from 5th Ohio dist., Washington, D.C., 1989—; assoc. firm Tomb and Hering, Tiffin, 1967-88; bd. dirs. Old Fort Banking Co., Ohio, Dealers Alliance Corp., Columbus, Thermocolor Corp. Pres. Ohio Electoral Coll., Columbus, 1984. Served to capt. USAF, 1965-67. Recipient Gov.'s award, Ohio, 1980; Phillips medal of pub. service Ohio U. Coll. Osteopathy, 1981; Exec. Order, Ohio Commodores Assn., 1981; Disting. Citizen award Med. Coll. Ohio, 1982; named Legislator of Yr., Ohio VFW, 1994. Mem. ABA, Ohio State Bar Assn., Nat. Republican Legislators Assn. (named Outstanding Legislator of Yr. 1983). Methodist. Office: US Ho of Reps Office House Mems 1203 Longworth Washington DC 20515

GILLMOR, VERLA JANE, communication consultant; b. Kansas City, Mo., Oct. 11, 1943; d. Veryl Leroy and Eleanor (Harvey) Thurman; m. Reidar S. Martinson, Nov. 13, 1965 (div. Dec. 1988); 1 child, Lisa Martinson; m. George Wellington Gillmor, Apr. 17, 1993; stepchildren: Jennifer, Alex. BA in English Lit., Wheaton (Ill.) Coll., 1965. Lic. 1st class radio engr., FCC. Radio news anchor and reporter Sta. WBBM, Sta. WMAQ, Sta. WGN, and Sta. WCFL, Chgo., 1976-88; dep. dir. media rels. and dir. spokesperson tng. Hill & Knowlton, Chgo., 1988-91; media rels. mgr. Luth. Gen. Health Sys., Park Ridge, Ill., 1991-94; comm. cons., writer Skokie, Ill., 1994—; speaker in field. Press sec. Gottleib For Mayor Campaign, Chgo., 1991; mem. pub. rels. task force Opportunity, Internat., Oak Brook, Ill., 1993—; mem. journalism task force Mercy Ships, Internat., Lindale, Tex., 1995. Recipient Superior Achiever award Sta. RKO Radio, 1977, Cmty. Affairs Programmer of Yr., 1978; Outstanding Contrbn. to Dental Edn., Chgo. Dental Soc., 1978, Crusader for Edn., Knights of Dabrowski, 1979. Mem. Nat. Writers Union, Soc. Profl. Journalists, Chgo. Headline Club (bd. dirs. 1983-89). Presbyterian.

GILL THOMPSON, NORMA N., home healthcare executive; b. Akron, Ohio, June 26, 1920; Richard Nottingham and Esther (Mullennax) Day; m. Edward Grover Gill, Sept. 5, 1938 (dec. 1974); children: Marilyn A., David E., Sally J. Thompson; m. Herbert George Thompson, Oct. 1, 1983. Cert. in enterostomal therapy, Cleve. Clinic Found., 1958. Dir. R.B. Turnbull Jr., M.D. Sch. Enterostomal Therapy Cleve. Clinic Found., 1961-78, coord. enterostomal therapy, 1978-81; v.p. Worldwide Home Health Care Ctr., Inc., Akron, 1981—, Worldwide Home Health Ctr., Akron, 1996—; cons. Akron City Hosp., St. Thomas Hosp. Med. Ctr., Children's Hosp. Med. Ctr. Akron, Cuyahoga Falls (Ohio) Gen. Hosp.; lectr. on ostomy care; cons. in establishing enterostomal therapy schs., Eng., Australia, Germany, France, Sweden, India, Japan, Brazil, Argentina, Peru, Chile; 1st dir. Rupert B. Turnbull Sch. of Enterostomal Therapy, Cleve. Clinic Found., 1961; lectr. to colon-rectal surgeons and enterostomal therapy nurses, Tokyo, Shanghai, China, Hangzhou, China, 1994-95; spkr. in field. Author: Ostomy Series, 1990, rev. 1995 and ednl. materials; contbr. numerous articles on ostomy-related topics to various publs.; editor World Coun. of Enterostomal Therapists Jour., 1982-84, 84-86; editl. bd. Am. Urol. Assn., 1982-83, 83-85. Recipient Rupert B. Turnbull Spl. Recognition award Cleve. Clinic Found., 1988. Mem. Internat. Ostomy Assn. (profl. adv. bd. 1980-83, 83-85), Wound, Ostomy and Continence Nurses (hon.; Pres.'s aard 1993), United Ostomy Assn. (enterostomal therapist 1990-91), Akron Ostomy Assn., Am. Urol. Assn., Ileitis and Colitis Found., French Assn. Stoma Therapy (hon. pres.), World Coun. Enterostomal Therapists (founder 1975, hon. 1984, Norma N. Gill Found. established 1980). Democrat. Methodist. Office: Worldwide Home Health Ctr 926 E Tallmadge Ave Akron OH 44310-3562

GILMAN, DONALD W., JR., French language educator; b. Newport News, Va., Feb. 24, 1945; s. Donald W. and Bernice M. (Vest) G. AB, U. N.C., 1967, PhD, 1976; AM, Harvard U., 1970. Instr. Christopher Newport Coll. Coll. of William and Mary, Newport News, 1968-70; asst. prof. Ball State U., Muncie, Ind., 1974-79, assoc. prof., 1979-87, prof. French, 1987—; mem. NEH summer inst. Yale U., 1989, NEh summer seminar U. Ill., Champaign, 1980. Co-editor: Dialogues, 1986; editor: Everyman and Company, 1989; contbr. articles in French, Italian and Neo-Latin to profl. publs. Fellow Woodrow Wilson Found., 1967-68, Newberry Libr., 1983-84; grantee U. B.C., Can., 1981, Cen. Mich. U., 1981, 83, U. Toronto, 1988, Learned Socs. Can., 1991, Ctr. Nat. de la Recherche Scientifique, 1991. Mem. Phi Beta Kappa. Roman Catholic. Home: 3825 N Lakeside Dr Muncie IN 47304-6350 Office: Ball State U Dept Mod Langs Classic Muncie IN 47306

GILMAN, SID, neurologist; b. L.A., Oct. 19, 1932; s. Morris and Sarah Rose (Cooper) G.; m. Carol G. Barbour. B.A., UCLA, 1954; M.D., 1957. Intern UCLA Hosp., 1957-58; resident in neurology Boston City Hosp., 1960-63; from instr. to assoc. in neurology Harvard Med. Sch., 1965-68; from asst. prof. to prof. neurology Columbia U., N.Y.C., 1968-76; H. Houston Merritt prof. neurology, 1976-77; prof., chmn. dept. neurology U. Mich., Ann Arbor, 1977—; cons. VA Hosp., Ann Arbor, 1977—; mem. peripheral and ctrl. nervous sys. drugs adv. com. FDA, 1983-85, 86-87, 90-94, chmn., 1996—; adj. attending neurologist Henry Ford Hosp., Detroit; mem. chronic disease adv. com. Mich. Dept. Pub. Health, 1988-94; mem. neurol. sci. rsch. and tng. com. NIH, mem. neurol. disorders program project B com., mem. sci. programs adv. com. Nat. Inst. Neurol. Diseases, Communicative Disorders and Stroke, 1982-84, mem. nat. adv. neurol. disorders and stroke coun., 1994—; dir. Mich. alzheimer's Disease Rsch. Ctr., 1991—; mem. rsch. adv. coun. United Cerebral Palsy Found.; mem. sci. adv. coun. Nat. Ataxia Found., Nat. Amyotrophic Lateral Sclerosis Found., Inc.; mem. profl. adv. bd. Epilepsy Found. Am.; mem. rsch. adv. com. Nat. Multiple Sclerosis Soc., 1986-90; mem. exec. bd. Nat. Coalition for Rsch., 1989-95, Nat. Found. for Brain Rsch., 1989-95; mem. rsch. adv. com. Dana Alliance. Author: (with J.R. Bloedel and R. Lechtenberg) Disorders of the Cerebellum, 1981, (with S.W. Newman) Manter and Gatz's Essentials of Clinical Neuroanatomy and Neurophysiology, 9th edit., 1996, (with J.C. Mazziotta) Clinical Brain Imaging: Principles and Applications, 1992; mem. editl. bd. Exptl. Neurology, Current Opinion in Neurology and Neurosurgery, Neurology, Annals Neurology, Jour. Neuropathology and Exptl. Neurology, Neurobase Arbor Pub. Co.; editor-in-chief Contemporary Neurology Series, 1995—, Neurology Network Commentary, 1996—; contbr. articles to profl. jours. With USPHS, 1958-60. Recipient Lucy G. Moses prize Columbia U., 1973, Weinstein Goldenson award United Cerebral Palsy Assn., 1981, UCLA Alumni Profl. Achievement award, 1992, UCLA Med. Alumni Profl. Achievement award, 1992. Mem. AAAS, Am. Neurol. Assn. (1st v.p. 1985-86, pres.-elect 1987-88, pres. 1988-89), Mich. Neurol. Assn. (pres. 1987-88), Soc. Clin. Investigation, Am. Physiol. Soc., Am. Assn. Neuropathologists, Soc. Neurosci., Am. Acad. Neurology (vice chmn. geriatric neurology subcom. 1992—, chmn. 1994-96, chmn. Decade of Brain com. 1990-95), Am. Epilepsy Soc., Assn. Rsch. in Nervous and Mental Disease, Inst. Medicine, Nat. Acad. Scis., Phi Beta Kappa, Alpha Omega Alpha. Home: 3411 Geddes Rd Ann Arbor MI 48105-2518 Office: U Mich Dept Neurology Ann Arbor MI 48109

GILMAN, TERRY RAY, state agency administrator; b. Joplin, Mo., Aug. 26, 1954; s. Clifford Ted and M.L. "Betty" (Bowyer) G.; m. Mary Ann Lundy, Dec. 23, 1972; children: Kimberly Dawn, Terran D. "Trip". AS in Radiation Tech., Okla. State U., 1977, BS, 1978. Supervising engr. Commonwealth Edison, Chgo., 1975-90; cons. United Energy Svcs. Corp., Albuquerque, 1990-95; dist. coord. S.W. Mo. Solid Waste Mgmt. Dist., Mt. Vernon, Mo., 1995—. Mem. Mo. Waste Control Coalition, Nat. Recycling Coalition, Mo. Recycling Assn. (bd. dirs. 1995—). Home: 18829 Beech Rd Diamond MO 64840

GILMER, DONALD H., state legislator; b. Battle Creek, Mich., Nov. 29, 1945; s. Howard N. and Genevieve (Raymer) G.; m. Lynn A. Weimeister; children: Laura, Steven, Jason. Student, Mich. State U., 63-65, Western Mich. U., 1966. Vice chair, then chair Kalamazoo (Mich.) County Bd. Commrs., 1973-74; mem. Mich. Agrl. Labor Commn., 1975-77; rep. Mich. Dist. 63, 1977—; chmn. appropriations com. Mich. Ho. Reps. Recipient citizenship award Am. Legion, 1963—. Mem. Mich. Farm Bur., Mich. Horticulture Soc., Kiwanis (v.p. 1971), Jaycees (impact award 1977), Assn. Retarded Citizens, Urban League. Home: 7021 N 46th St Augusta MI 49012-9230 Address: 7021 N 46th St Augusta MI 49012*

GILMORE, HELEN CAROL, computer specialist, executive; b. Trenton, N.J.; d. Louis Alfred and Catherine (Peto) Fennimore; m. Lester Wayne Gilmore, Oct. 18, 1963; 1 child, Matthew Todd. Student, Purdue U., 1977-78, St. Mary-of-the-Woods Coll., 1980-85. Stenographer USAF, McGuire AFB, N.J., 1958-63; investigative recorder USAF, McGuire AFB, 1963-65; assoc. realtor Faherty Real Estate, Bordentown, N.J., 1969-74; asst. terminal mgr. G&G Tank Co., Inc., Columbus, N.J., 1974-76; adminstrv. asst. to assoc. dean Krannert Grad. Sch. Mgmt., Purdue U., West Lafayette, Ind., 1976-78; cons. Secs., Inc., Oak Brook, Ill., 1979; adminstrv. asst. to dir. materials Amphenol N.Am., Bunker Ramo Corp., Broadview, Ill., 1979-80; inventory specialist, product planner Amphenol N.Am., Bunker Ramo Corp., Broadview, 1980-81; system analyst Eastman Kodak Co., Oak Brook, Ill., 1981-85; applications engr. Eastman Kodak Co., Oak Brook, 1985-87; sr. system engr. NBI, Inc., Chgo., 1987, mgr. tech. support, 1988; tng. devel. mgr. Crawford & Assocs., Chgo., 1988-89; regional systems cons. Xyvision Inc., Chgo., 1990-91; owner Image Dynamix, Chgo., 1990—; mgr. nat. programs application engring. Frame Tech. Inc., Oak Brook, Ill., 1991-93; dir. tech. svcs. ArborText Inc., Ann Arbor, Mich., 1993—. Mem. N.J. Assn. Realtors, Am. Bus. Women's Assn. (chpt. v.p. 1979), Nat. Assn. Female Execs., Soc. Office Automation Profls. (charter), Am. Prodn. and Inventory Control Soc. Office: 1000 Victors Way Ann Arbor MI 48108-2743

GILMORE, HORACE WELDON, federal judge; b. Columbus, Ohio, Apr. 4, 1918; s. Charles Thomas and Lucille (Weldon) G.; m. Mary Hays, June 20, 1942; children—Lindsay Gilmore Feinberg. A.B., U. Mich., 1939, J.D., 1942. Bar: Mich. bar 1946. Law clk. U.S. Ct. Appeals, 1946-47; practiced in Detroit, 1947-51; spl. asst. U.S. atty., Detroit, 1951-52; mem. Mich. Bd. Tax Appeals, 1954; dep. atty. gen. State of Mich., 1955-56; circuit judge 3d Jud. Circuit, Detroit, 1956-80; judge U.S. Dist. Ct., 1980—; adj. prof. law Wayne State U. Law Sch., 1966-82; lectr. law U. Mich. Law Sch., 1969-90; faculty Nat. Coll. State Judiciary, 1966-83; mem. Mich. Jud. Tenure Commn., 1969-76; chmn. Mich. Com. to Revise Criminal Code, 1965-82, Mich. Com. to Revise Criminal Procedure, 1971-79; trustee Inst. for Ct. Mgmt. Author: Michigan Civil Procedure Before Trial, 2d edit, 1975; contbr. numerous articles to legal jours. Served with USNR, 1942-46. Mem. ABA, State Bar Mich., Am. Judicature Soc., Am. Law Inst., Nat. Conf. State Trial Judges. Office: US Dist Ct 867 US Courthouse 231 W Lafayette Blvd Detroit MI 48226-2719

GILMORE, JUNE ELLEN, psychologist; b. Middletown, Ohio, Oct. 22, 1927; d. Linley Lawrence and Elizabeth Kathleen (Barker) Wetzel; m. John Lester Gilmore, July 6, 1945; children: John Lester Jr., Michael Edward. BS, Miami U., Oxford, 1961; MS, Miami U., 1964. Lic. psychologist, Ohio. Intern in psychology Hamilton (Ohio) City Schs., 1963-64; psychologist Talawanda, Shiloh, Trenton Schs., Butler County, Ohio, 1964-66, Franklin (Ohio) City Schs., 1966-72, Wapakoneta (Ohio) City Schs., 1972-76, Cin. City Schs., 1978-86; pvt. practice psychology, 1975—; planner, evaluator Warren/Clinton Counties Mental Health Bd., Ohio, 1986-88; adj. instr. Wright State U., Dayton, Ohio, 1989-90. Co-author: Summer Children-Ready or not for School, 1986, The Rape of Childhood--No Time to be a Kid, 1990. Sec. Tri County Drug Coun., Lima, Ohio, 1975; chmn. Auglaize County Social Svcs., Wapakoneta, 1973-75; bd. dirs. Butler County Alcohol and Drug Addiction Svcs. Bd., 1990—, sec., 1992-94. Mem. Ohio Sch. Psychologists Assn. (exec. bd. 1982-86), Southwestern Ohio Sch. Psychologist Assn. (pres.), Southwest Council Exceptional Children (Pres.), Nat. Assn. Sch. Psychologists, Ohio Psychol. Assn., Butler County 648 Mental Health Bd. (bd. dirs. 1978-86, pres. 1983-84). Republican. United Methodist. Home and Office: 6120 Michael Rd Middletown OH 45042-9402

GILMORE, KATHI, state treasurer; b. Dec. 23, 1944; m. Richard Gilmore; children: Suzi, Barb, Jeff, Amy. Mem. N.D. Ho. of Reps. from Dist. 6; treas. State of N.D., 1993—; mem. Bd. Tax Equalization, State Hist. Bd., State Investment Bd., Tchrs. Fund for Retirement Bd., State Canvassing Bd., Bd. of Univ. and Sch. Lands. Mem. Nat. Conf. State Liquor Adminstrs., Nat. Assn. State Treas. (pension com., employee suggestion incentive com.), State Gov. Nat. Coms. (chmn. retirement and investment office internal audit com.), Assn. Securities Profls. (hon. co-chair pension fund conf. 1994), Task Forces Orgnl. Planning and Coordinating Com. 1993). Democrat. Presbyterian. Office: State Treasurer 600 E Boulevard Ave Bismarck ND 58505-0660

GILMORE, MICHAEL CLINTON, health services executive; b. Lafayette, Ind., Sept. 26, 1954; s. John William and Betty Ruth (Hollis) G.; m. Terrie Lynn Schreiver, Apr. 28, 1984. Cert. nursing with honors, Ind. Vocat. Tech. Coll., 1982. LPN, Ind. Staff nurse St. Vincent Hosp. and Heathcare Ctr., Indpls., 1982-87, chief orthop. technologist, 1987-90; patient rep. Thera-Kinetics, Inc., Mt. Laurel, N.J., 1990-91; pres. Health Tech. Assocs., Indpls., 1991—; rsch. asst. total joint patient edn. program St. Vincent Hosp. and Healthcare Ctr., Indpls., 1990-91. Sponsor, Explorer Post 384, Boy Scouts Am., Indpls. With U.S. Army, 1972-75. Mem. ASTM (com. F-32 on search and rescue), Nat. Assn. Orthopedic Technologists (mem.-at-large), Nat. Assn. Orthopaedic Nurses, Nat. Assn. for Search and Rescue, Zulu Land Search and Rescue Assn. (dir.), Ind. Search and Rescue Assn. (exec. dir.). Presbyterian. Office: Health Tech Assocs PO Box 68805 Indianapolis IN 46268

GILMORE, PHYLLIS, state legislator; m. Kenneth Gilmore. Social worker; mem. Kans. State Ho. of Reps. Dist. 27.

GILMORE, ROBERT WITTER, foundation administrator; b. College Corner, Ohio, Sept. 6, 1933; s. Robert Foster and Frances Elizabeth (Witter) G.; m. Sara Louise McIntosh, Dec. 23, 1956; children: Susan Lynne, Robert Riley, Christopher Edwin. EdB, Miami U., Oxford, Ohio, 1955; M in Social Work, Ohio State U., 1957. Exec. dir. United Way, Massillon, Ohio, 1960-64, St. Joseph, Mo., 1964-69, Dayton, Ohio, 1969-78, Cin., 1978-88; ret. United Way, 1988, cons., 1988—. 1st lt. U.S. Army, 1957-60. Named Man Of Yr. Jr. C. of C., St. Joseph, 1967. Mem. Assn. Cert. Profl. Social Workers (cert.), Queen City Club, Rotary, Masons, Sigma Chi. Home: 6424 Butler Israel Rd College Corner OH 45003

GILMORE, RODNEY SCOTT, electrical engineer; b. Kansas City, Miss., Apr. 5, 1965; s. Richard G. Mervin and Huberta May (Vanderue) G.; m. Patricia Darleen Scanlan, Feb. 26, 1993. BSEE, Central Miss. State, Warrensburg, 1991. Registered profl. engr. Sales engr. Northern Telecom, Overland Park, Kans.; NTSII translations Sprint, Overland Park, Kans.; analyst I Sprint, Gardner, Kans.; installer-tester Northern Telecom, St. Louis, installer; materials handler Northern Telecom; cons. Sprint, Overland Park. Republican. Christian. Home: 1010 NW Maple Lees Summit MO 64063

GILPATRIC, LAWRENCE, hospitality management educator; b. Bridgeport, Conn., Aug. 3, 1948; s. Ralph Edwin and Doris Rose (McCormack) G.; m. Suzanne Bronstein, Aug. 10, 1975; children: Rebecca Lynn, Jeremy Todd, Brendan Scott. AS, Manchester Community Coll., 1978; BS, Charter Oak Coll., 1990; MS, Cen. Conn. State U., 1991; sixth yr. cert., So. Conn. State U., 1994. Cert. hotel adminstr., foodsvc. mgmt. profl. Exec. chef Holiday Inns, Bridgeport and New London, Conn., 1971-73; chef mgr. Szabo Food Svc., Hartford, Conn., 1973-74; chef instr. Assoc. Restaurants of Conn., Hartford, Conn., 1974-77; exec. chef Burning Tree Country Club, Greenwich, Conn., 1977-79; pres. Stowe's Pilot House Restaurant, West Haven, Conn., 1979-81; exec. chef Coveleigh Club, Rye, N.Y., 1981-84; gen. mgr. H. B. Brownson Country Club, Huntington, Conn., 1984-88; asst. prof. Gateway Community-Tech. Coll., New Haven, 1987-95; asst. prof., coord. hospitality mgmt. U. Akron, Ohio, 1995—; interim gen. mgr. Winged Foot Golf Club, Mamaroneck, N.Y., 1991; satirical columnist Naugatuck Daily News, 1993-94; mgr. Copper Valley Club, Cheshire, Conn., 1994—. Lector St. Vincent Ferrer Ch., Naugatuck, Conn., 1990—. With USMC, 1966-69. H. J. Heinz Grad. fellow The Edn. Found. of Nat. Restaurant Assn., 1991; recipient Silver Plate scholarship Nat. Inst. Foodservice Industry, 1977, Excellence in Edn. award, 1991. Home: 312 W Maple St Hartville OH 44632-9689 Office: U Akron 102 Gallucci Hall Akron OH 44325-7907

GILZOW, H(OMER) FLOYD, JR., educational administrator; b. Springfield, Mo., Aug. 15, 1950; s. Homer Floyd and E. Jeane (Moseley) G.; m. Becky L. Goodwin, June 7, 1969; children: Paul F., Joshua F., Timothy A. Grad. in theology, Bapt. Bible Coll., 1971. News dir. KWFC Radio, Springfield, Mo., 1969-71, news editor, 1974-79; minister of youth Calvary Bapt. Ch., Bellflower, Calif., 1971-74; purchasing dir. Greene County, Springfield, 1979-81, dep. clk., 1981-85; dep. sec. State of Mo., Jefferson City, 1985-93; dir. Walton Regional Literacy Ctr., asst. to pres. S.W. Bapt. U., Bolivar, Mo., 1993-94, v.p. for adminstrn., 1994—. Chmn. allocation com. Jefferson City United Way, 1989-90; cubmaster Boy Scouts Am., Springfield, 1981-84; chmn. Environ. Adv. Bd., Springfield, 1977-79; committeeman Greene County Reps., Springfield, 1980-85; exec. dir. Gov.'s Adv. Coun. on Literacy, 1988; treas. Mo. Citizens for Life, 1989-92; del. White House Conf. on Librs. and Info. Svcs.; mem. State Coun. Prison Fellowship, 1993—, chair coun., 1996—; mem. Polk County Telecommunications Resource Com., 1994—. Named one of Outstanding Young Men Am., 1985-86; recipient First Place Coverage award Assoc. Press, Kansas City, 1970.

GIMMARRO, STEVEN PAUL, financial planning executive; b. Kansas City, Mo., Sept. 4, 1959; s. Jasper Michael and Vesta Katherine (Crumm) G.; m. Vicki Annette Beard, June 2, 1984; children: Michael Steven, Jonathan Milton, Daniel Paul. Grad. high sch., Independence, Mo. Store mgr. Weiss-Neuman Shoe Co., St. Louis, 1977-81; agt. Allstate Ins. Co., Independence, 1981-82, Bob Raga Ins. Agy., Independence, 1982-84, State Mut. Ins. Agy., Independence, 1984-85; pres. First Fin. Group, Independence, 1985—, Blue Springs, Mo., 1988—. Home: 211 NW Leann Dr Blue Springs MO 64014-1548 Office: First Fin Group PO Box 1238 Blue Springs MO 64013-1238

GIN, JACKSON, architect; b. Chgo., June 11, 1934; s. Frank Tsue and Jennie Shee (Pang) G.; m. Jayne Ping Kan, Oct. 5, 1963; children: Paul L., Michael F., Daniel. BA, U. Ill., 1958. Designer Milton M. Schwartz, Architects, Chgo., 1958-60; project architect Greenberg & Finfer, Architects, Chgo., 1960-62, Hausner & Macsai, Architects, Chgo., 1962-67; project architect, ptnr. Dubin, Dubin, Black & Moutoussamy, Architects, Chgo., 1967-77; prin., pres. Mann, Gin, Ebel & Frazier, Ltd., Architects-Engrs., Chgo., 1977—. Trustee Chinese Christian Union Ch., 1968-70; bd. dirs. Neighborhood Redevel. Assistance, 1972-74; mem. Euclid-Lake Assn., Mount Prospect, Ill. Mem. AIA, Chinese Am. Civic Fedn. Club: Builders of Chgo. Home: 1332 N Peachtree Ln Mount Prospect IL 60056-1826 Office: Mann Gin Ebel & Frazier Ltd 30 S Michigan Ave Chicago IL 60603-3201

GINGERICH, JAMES A., financial consultant; b. Valparaiso, Ind., Jan. 28, 1952. BS, Ind. State U., 1974. Asst. v.p. Bank of Ind., Merrillville, 1974-80; fin. cons. Merrill Lynch, Merrillville, 1980—. Bd. dirs. alumni adv. bd. Ind. State U., Merrillville, 1993—. Mem. Kiwanis (past pres.). Republican. Mennonite. Office: Merrill Lynch 8585 Broadway # 590 Merrillville IN 46410-7064

GINI, MARIA LUIGIA, computer science educator; b. Milan, July 30, 1946; came to U.S., 1982; d. Carlo and Iolanda (Ferrari) G.; m. Daniel L. Boley, Oct. 16, 1982. D Physics, U Milan, 1972. Rsch. assoc. Politecnico, Milan, 1973-76, sr. rsch. assoc., 1978-82; vis. rsch. assoc. Stanford (Calif.) U., 1976-77; asst. prof. computer sci. U. Minn., Mpls., 1982-88, assoc. prof., 1988—. Author: Robotics (in Italian), 1982 (trans. into French and English); contbr. articles on robotics to sci. jours. Leader nat. level Girl Scout Assn., Italy, 1971-72. Grantee AT&T Found., GTE, 1984, 87, NSF, 1985, 88, 90, 92, 93, IBM, 1986, Morse grantee U. Minn., 1986. Mem. Assn. for Computing Machinery, Am. Assn. for Artificial Intelligence, Computer Profls. for Social Responsibility. Office: U Minn 4-192 EE/CSCI 200 Union St SE Minneapolis MN 55455-0154

GINSBERG, MYRON, computer scientist; b. Brockton, Mass., May 3, 1943; s. Frank and Evelyn Hazel (Spekin) G.; m. Judith Beverly Rosenbaum, Nov. 19, 1989; 1 stepchild, Ellen Joy Schoenfeld. BA in Math., Boston U., 1965; MA in Math., Clark U., 1967; PhD in Computer Sci., U. Iowa, 1972. Instr. dept. computer sci. U. Iowa, Iowa City, 1969-72; from asst. prof. to assoc. prof. computer sci. So. Meth. U., Dallas, 1972-77, 77-79; NASA/ASEE rsch. fellow NASA Langley Rsch. Ctr, Hampton, Va., summer 1979; assoc. sr. rsch. scientist GM Rsch. Labs., Warren, Mich., 1979-81; sr. rsch. scientist GM Rsch. Labs, Warren, Mich., 1981-82, staff rsch. scientist, 1982-92; cons. systems engr. EDS Advanced Computing Ctr., GM NAO Rsch. & Devel. Ctr., Warren, 1992—; mathematician U.S. Army Ballistics Rsch. Lab., Aberdeen Proving Ground, MD., summers, 1964-67; data systems analyst NASA Electronics Rsch. Ctr., Cambridge, Mass., summers, 1968-69; adj. assoc. prof. U. Mich., Ann Arbor, 1990; editorial bd. ComputinSystems in Engring., 1988-93; adv. bd. Cray Rsch. Fortran, 1991-92; grant review panelist NSF, 1992-93; GM/EDS rep. to Supercomputing Automotive Applications Partnership, 1992-94; founder and first chmn. of AUTOBENCH Project of U.S. Coun. for Automotive Rsch., 1995—. Editor: Supercomputers in the Auto Industry, 1985, Automotive Applications of Supercomputers, 1988, High-Speed and Large-Scale Computing: A Panoramic View, 1988, Automotive Applications of Vector/Parallel Computers: State-of-the-Art, 1992; contbr. articles to profl. jours. Grantee Mobil Oil Found., 1975, U.S. Army C.E., 1977-78, NSF, 1983-84, 77-79, Alfred P. Sloan Found., 1975-78; recipient award for excellence in oral presentation Soc. Automotive Engrs., 1985, 86, 87, Disting. Speaker plaque, 1988, Forest R. McFarland award, 1994. Fellow Assn. for Computing Machinery (lectr., bd. dirs. SIGNUM 1976-80 editor-in-chief SIGNUM newsletter 1976-80); mem. IEEE, IEEE Computer Soc. (lectr.), ASME (lectr.), Soc. for Indsl. and Applied Math. (lectr., spl. group on supercomputing), Soc. Automotive Engrs. (lectr.), Sigma Xi (lectr.). Office: EDS Advanced Computing Ctr GM NAO R & D Ctr Bldg 1-6 30500 Mound Rd Warren MI 48090-9055

GINTOFT, ETHEL MARGARET, journalist; b. Milw.; m. Bruno Gintoft (dec.); children: Bruce J., Robert A. AB in Journalism summa cum laude, Marquette U., 1946, MA in Journalism, 1966; LHD (hon.), Mt. Mary Coll., 1991; LLD (hon.), Cardinal Stritch Coll., 1991. Adminstrv. asst. to dean dept. journalism Marquette U., Milw., 1962-65, instr. in journalism, 1971-79; assoc. editor Cath. Herald, Milw., 1965-81, exec. editor, assoc. pub., 1981—. Bd. dirs. Sch. Sisters of St. Francis Found., Milw., 1989-94, Villa Clement, Inc., Milw., 1982-86; mem. adv. coun. to dean Coll. Comm., Marquette U.

Recipient Headliner award Women in Comm., Achievement award YMCA, 1979, Byline award Marquette Coll. Journalism, 1983. Mem. Cath. Press Assn. U.S. and Can. (pres. 1979-81, v.p. ednl. grants com., St. Francis de Sales award), Soc. Profl. Journalists (pres. Milw. chpt. 1974-75), Journalism Alumni Assn. Marquette U. (pres. 1970), Milw. Press Club Found. (pres. 1993-96). Office: Cath Herald 3501 S Lake Dr Saint Francis WI 53235-0913

GIOIA, ANGELO JOSEPH, marketing executive, underwriter; b. Bklyn., Sept. 4, 1951; s. Vito and Ann (Seminerio) G.; m. Carole Louise Zambuto; children: Evan, Brian, Gregory. BBA, Coll. Ins., N.Y.C., 1974. Branch mgr. Am. Internat. Group, San Francisco, 1978-80; v.p. assn. group Inapro, N.Y.C., 1980-84; div. mgr. Delaney Mgmt. Co., N.Y.C., 1984-85; v.p., dir. mktg. Rollins, Burdick & Hunter, Inc., Chgo., 1985-88; pres. Gioia, Miller & Young & Assocs., Inc., Oak Brook Terr., Ill., 1988; v.p., dir. mktg. Kirke Van Orsdel, Inc., Chgo., 1988-89; v.p., profl. liability div. mgr. Avreco, Inc., Chgo., 1989-93; ptnr. Rigdon, Powers & Gioia, Ltd., Lisle, Ill., 1993—. Coach, mgr. Wheaton (Ill.) Youth Baseball, 1987—. Mem. Profl. Liability Underwriting Soc. (founder 1986, trustee 1986—, pres. 19990-91). Republican. Roman Catholic. Home: 1049 Dorset Dr Wheaton IL 60187-8023

GIOIOSO, JOSEPH VINCENT, psychologist; b. Chgo., Mar. 6, 1939; s. Vincent James and Mary (Bonadonna) G.; B.A., DePaul U., 1962, M.A., 1963; Ph.D. summa cum laude, Ill. Inst. Tech., 1971; m. Patricia A. Aksamit, June 30, 1990; children by previous marriage: Joseph, Randy Marie, Danielle; stepchildren: Josephine Anne, Jennifer Marie Cammarata. Psychologist, Sch. Assn. for Spl. Edn. in DuPage County, Wheaton, Ill., 1964-67; pvt. practice as clin. psychologist, Chgo. and Downers Grove, Ill., 1966—; clin. psychologist J.J. McLaughlin, M.D., Profl. Corp., Chgo., 1970-92. Founder dept. psychology Ill. Benedictine Coll., Lisle, 1968, chmn. dept. psychology, prof., dir. testing, 1968-71; cons. psychologist Chicago Ridge (Ill.) Sch. Dist. 127 1/2, 1973-76, Cath. Charities Counseling Service, Chgo., 1963-66, St. Laurence High Sch., Oak Lawn, Ill., 1963-64, Oak Lawn-Hometown Sch. Dist. No. 123, 1967-68, Addison (Ill.) Sch. Dist. 4, 1969-72; vis. prof. psychology Inst. Mgmt., Lisle, 1968-69, George Williams Coll., Downers Grove, 1970-71; chief psychologist Valley View Sch. Dist. 365U, Bolingbrook, Ill., 1971-73; dir. Pub. Program for Exceptional Children, Lisle, 1969-71; mem. Nat. Register Health Service Providers in Psychology, 1975—. Bd. dirs. Ray Graham Assn. for Handicapped, DuPage County, Ill., 1970-73; adv. bd. Care and Counseling Center DuPage County, 1977—; founder Aquinpsy Human Svcs. Ctr., 1987. DePaul U. publ. grantee, 1959-61, Fitzgerald Bros. Found. grantee, 1969-71. Fellow Ctr. for the Study of Great Ideas, Chgo., 1994—; mem. AAAS, Am., Midwestern, Ill. psychol. assns., Soc. Pediatric Psychology, Alpha Phi Delta. Author: Completion Intelligence Test, 1963, Children's Emotional Symptoms Inventory, 1979; contbr. articles to profl. jours. Home and Office: 6900 Main St Downers Grove IL 60516-3454

GIOVANNI, ROBERT WILLIAM, sales executive; b. St. Louis, Aug. 2, 1946; s. William J. Hulsey, Nov. 7, 1969 (dec. Apr. 1977); m. Bonny J. McNelly, Feb. 9, 1991; children: Michelle, Donald, Matthew. BS in Mktg., St. Louis U., 1969. Store mgr. Firestone Tire, St. Louis, 1969-72; sales rep. Bell & Howell Co., St. Louis, 1972-77; br. mgr. Am. Air Filter, St. Louis, 1977-83, Cummins-Allison Corp., St. Louis, 1983-85; dist. sales mgr. Kent Industries, St. Louis, 1986-90; br. mgr. Rochester Midland, St. Louis, 1990-94; dist. sales mgr. UZ Engineered Products, St. Louis, 1994—. With U.S. Army Res., 1969-74. Home and Office: 4208 Ashwick Saint Louis MO 63128

GIRARD, G. TANNER, state environmental officer; b. Jacksonville, Fla., May 15, 1952; s. Gerald Joseph and Paula Jean (Tanner) G.; m. Suellen Hill, Aug. 14, 1976; children: Anne Rachel, Justin Porter. BS, Principia Coll., 1974; MS, U. Cen. Fla., 1976; PhD, Fla. State U., 1979. Tchr., rsch. asst. U. Cen. Fla., Orlando, 1974-1975; tchr. asst. Fla. State U., Tallahassee, 1976-1977; prof. biology Principia Coll., Elsah, Ill., 1977-92; mem. Ill. Pollution Control Bd., Jerseyville, 1992—; vis. prof. U. del Valle de Guatemala, 1988; dir. field study programs Mex., Guatemala, Costa Rica. Contbr. articles to profl. jours. Ornithologist Bartram Trail Canoe Expdn., Ga. and Fla. Bicentennial Commns., 1975; mem. Riverbend in 90's, Alton, Ill., 1989-92, Ill. Nature Preserves Commn., Springfield, Ill., 1987-94, chmn., 1989-92; organizer Mississippi River Conf., Alton, 1984-86; del. Gov.'s Environ. Forum, Springfield, 1986; dir. Ill. Audubon Soc., Wayne, Ill., 1983-92, pres., 1985-89; mem. Gov.'s Sci. Adv. Com., Ill., 1991—. Mem. Am. Ornithologists Union, Am. Inst. Biol. Scis., Nat. Assn. Biology Tchrs., Fla. Ornithological Soc., Ill. Acad. Scis., Natural Lands Inst. Mem. Christian Sci. Ch. Home: 13 Spring Valley Est Grafton IL 62037-9727 Office: Pollution Control Bd 110 S State St Jerseyville IL 62052-1853

GIRARD, JIM, state legislator; b. Marshall, Minn., June 12, 1953; s. Louis Felix and Beatrice (Barnady) G.; m. Becky; children: Chrsitine Marie, Ryan James. BS, Dakota State U., 1975, MS, 1971. Chmn. Lyon County Rep. Com., 1987-88; mem. Minn. State Rep. Ctrl. Com., 1987-89; state rep. Minn. Ho. Reps., Dist. 21A, 1989—; mem. agrl. capital investments, fin. inst. & ins. & Tex. coms., Minn. Ho. Reps.; agrl. rep. Western Bank & Trust, 1977—; nutritionist Feeders Choice Foods, 1977-79; owner Girard Farms, 1979—. Recipient Key Press award Minn. Jaycees, 1983, Disting. Svc. award Marshall Area Jaycees, 1984. Mem. Marshall Area C. of C. (chmn. agrl. com. 1987-88), Minn. Park Producers Assn. (legis. chmn. exec. com. 1986-89), Minn. Farm Bur., Alpha Gamma Rho. Home: RR 1 Box 111 Lynd MN 56157-9729*

GIRVIN-QUIRK, SUSAN, nursing administrator; b. Owensboro, Ky., Dec. 9, 1950; d. William Fred and Anna (Tillotson) G.; m. Thomas Michael Quirk; 1 child, Thomas Matthew. BSN, U. Ky.; MS in Nursing, Ind. U. Adminstr. Am. Transitional Hosps., Indpls. Mem. ANA, Am. Assn. Neurosci. Nurses, Am. Mgmt. Assn., Sigma Theta Tau.

GISLASON, ERIC ARNI, chemistry educator; b. Oak Park, Ill., Sept. 9, 1940; s. Raymond Spencer and Jane Ann (Clifford) G.; m. Nancy Brown, Sept. 11, 1962 (dec. June 1994); children: Kristina Elizabeth, John Harrison. BA summa cum laude, Oberlin Coll., 1962; PhD, Harvard U., 1967. Postdoctoral fellow U. Calif-Berkeley, 1967-69; asst. prof. chemistry U. Ill., Chgo., 1969-73; assoc. prof. U. Ill.-Chgo., 1973-77, prof., 1977—; acting head chemistry dept. U. Ill., Chgo., 1993-94, head chemistry dept., 1994—; vis. scientist FOM Inst. Atomic and Molecular Physics, Amsterdam, 1977-78; prof. associé U. Paris South, 1985. Contbr. articles to profl. jours. Recipient Silver Circle Teaching award U. Ill., 1982, Excellence in Teaching award U. Ill., 1990. Mem. Am. Chem. Soc. (vis. assocs. program), Am. Phys. Soc., Phi Beta Kappa, Sigma Xi. Congregationalist. Home: 7227 Oak Ave River Forest IL 60305-1935 Office: U Ill-Chgo Chemistry M/C 111 Rm 4500 845 W Taylor St Chicago IL 60607-7061

GISSELQUIST, JOEL M., stockbroker; b. Sioux City, Iowa, Sept. 18, 1954. BA, Augusberg Coll., 1977; postgrad., U. Wis., 1979. Asst. v.p. mktg. Merrill Lynch Pvt. Client Group, Edina, Minn., 1979—. Nat. merit scholar Augusberg Coll., 1972. Office: Merrill Lynch Pvt Client Gp # 100 3400 W 66th St # 100 Edina MN 55435-2111

GISSLER, SIGVARD GUNNAR, JR., journalism educator, former newspaper editor; b. Chgo., July 2, 1935; s. Sigvard Gunnar Sr. and Louisa (Anderson) G.; m. Mary Catherine Engman, Oct. 23, 1954; children—Gary, Glenn, Gregory. B.A. in Am. Civilization, Lake Forest Coll., 1956; Student, Northwestern U., 1958-61; LLD (hon.), Lake Forest Coll., 1991. News editor Independent Register, Libertyville, Ill., 1958-59; exec. editor News-Sun, Waukegan, Ill., 1963-67; editorial writer Milw. Jour., 1967-77, editorial page editor, 1977-84, assoc. editor, 1984-85, editor, 1985-93; v.p. Jour. Communications, Milw., 1987-93, also bd. dirs.; sr. v.p. Jour./Sentinel Inc., Milw., 1987-93, also bd. dirs.; vis. prof. dept. comms. Stanford U., 1993; assoc. prof. grad. sch. journalism Columbia U., 1994—. Recipient disting. svc. citation Lake Forest Coll., 1977, Pub. of Yr. award Wis. Newspaper Assn., 1987, 91, 92; journalism fellow Stanford U., 1976, sr. fellow Freedom Forum Media Studies Ctr. Columbia U., 1993-94. Mem. Am. Soc. Newspaper Editors, Internat. Press Inst., Pulitzer Prize Jury, Phi Beta Kappa. Home: 101 W 79th St Apt 6D New York NY 10024-6478

GIUNTA, JOSEPH, conductor, music director; b. Atlantic City, May 8, 1951; m. Cynthia Reid, June 5, 1982. MusB in Theory, Northwestern U., 1973, MusM in Conducting, 1974; DFA (hon.), Simpson Coll., 1986. Condr., music dir. Waterloo/Cedar Falls Symphony and Chamber Orch. of Iowa, 1974-89; music dir. Des Moines Symphony Orch., 1989—; guest condr. numerous symphonies, orchs. including Chgo. Symphony, London Philharm., Philharmonia Orch. of London, Minn. Orch., Indpls. Orch., Phoenix Symphony, Fla. Symphony, Akron (Ohio) Symphony, Syracuse (N.Y.) Symphony, R.I. Philharm. Recipient Helen M. Thompson award; named Outstanding Young Condr. in U.S., 1984. Mem. Phi Mu Alpha, Pi Kappa Lambda. Office: Des Moines Symphony 221 Walnut St Des Moines IA 50309-2101

GIVAN, RICHARD MARTIN, state supreme court justice, retired; b. Indpls., June 7, 1921; s. Clinton Hodell and Glee (Bowen) G.; m. Pauline Marie Haggart, Feb. 28, 1945; children: Madalyn Givan Hesson, Sandra Givan Chenoweth, Patricia Givan Smith, Elizabeth Givan Whipple. LL.B., Ind. U., 1951. Bar: Ind. 1952. Partner firm Bowen, Myers, Northam & Givan, 1960-69; justice Ind. Supreme Ct., 1969-74, chief justice, 1974-87, assoc. justice, 1987-95; ret.; dep. put. defender Ind., 1952-53; dep. atty. gen., 1953-54; dep. pros. atty. Marion County, 1965-66; ret., 1995; mem. Ind. Ho. Reps., 1967-68. Served to 2d lt. USAAF, 1942-45. Mem. Ind. Bar Assn., Indpls. Bar Assn., Ind. Soc. Chgo., Newcomen Soc. N.Am., Internat. Arabian Horse Assn. (past dir., chmn. ethical practices rev. bd.), Ind. Arabian Horse Club (pres. 1971-72), Lions, Sigma Delta Kappa. Mem. Soc. of Friends. Home: 6690 S County Road 1025 E Indianapolis IN 46231-2495

GIVENS, DOUGLAS RANDALL, archaeologist, educator; b. St. Louis, May 4, 1944; s. Glenn Stuart and Helena Katherine (Neff) G.; m. Linda Louise West, Mar. 29, 1969; 1 child, Clayton West. BA, So. Ill. U., 1972, MA, 1972; PhD, Washington U., 1986. Instr. anthropology St. Louis Community Coll.-Meramec, St. Louis, 1973-75, asst. prof. anthropology, 1975-78, assoc. prof. anthropology, 1978-88, prof. anthropology, 1988—; adj. prof. anthropology U. Mo., St. Louis, 1989—. Editor Bull. of History of Archaeology, 1991—; assoc. editor obituaries/history of archaeology Am. Antiquity, 1990-94; author: Alfred Vincent Kidder and the Development of Americanist Archaeology, 1992; contbr. articles to profl. jours. With USAF, 1967-70. Wenner-Gren Found. for Anthropol. Rsch. grantee, 1990-91, 93-94. Fellow Am. Anthropol. Assn.; mem. Soc. Am. Archaeology (mem. task force on curation 1992—), History of Sci. Soc., Internat. Soc. for the Study of Time, Mo. Archaeol. Soc., AAAS, Brit. Assn. for Advancement of Sci. Office: Saint Louis CC Dept Anthropology 11333 Big Bend Rd Saint Louis MO 63122-5720

GIVRAY, HENRY STEVEN, association management services executive; b. Athens, Greece, July 16, 1953; came to U.S., 1960; s. Jacques Leon and Stavroula (Georgiou) G.; m. Deborah Ratelle, Sept. 9, 1978 (div. Sept. 1982); m. Jannine Smith, July 25, 1987; stepchildren: Kerry, Kristina. BS, Cornell U., 1975, M in Engring., 1976; MBA, U. Chgo., 1982. Internal cons. Xerox Corp., Rochester, N.Y., 1976-78; systems cons. Ernst & Young (formerly Ernst & Whinney), Cleve., 1978-80; sr. ops. rsch. analyst Amoco Oil Co., Chgo., 1980; cons., cons. mgr., sr. mktg. rep. Interactive Data Corp., Chase Econometrics, Chgo., 1980-83; acct. exec., prin., sr. v.p. Smith, Bucklin & Assocs., Chgo., 1983—. Featured in book, Second to None, by Charles Garfield, 1991. Mem. Chgo. Club Execs., Cornell Club Chgo. Home: 2030-A N Sedgwick St Chicago IL 60614 Office: Smith Bucklin & Assocs 401 N Michigan Ave Chicago IL 60611-4212

GJOVIG, BRUCE QUENTIN, manufacturing consultant; b. Crosby, N.D., Mar. 24, 1951; s. Ronald Daniel and Agnes (Smedberg) G.; children: Mike Mohn, Todd Chaffee. BA, BS, U. N.D., 1974. Rsch. chemist Man-in-the-Sea Project, Grand Forks, N.D., 1975-76; campaign advisor Elkin for Gov. Com., Bismarck, N.D., 1976; exec. officer Grand Forks Bd. Realtors, 1977-81; devel. officer U. N.D. Found., 1981-84; founder, dir. Ctr. for Innovation & Bus. Devel., Grand Forks, 1984—; bd. dirs. 1st Seed Capital Co., Grand Forks, Ask-Me Multimedia Sys., Inc., Brooklyn Park, Minn., Microdose Internat., Grand Forks, Eide Helmeke, Fargo, SBIR Project West, Phoenix; founder, chmn. N.D. Entrepreneur Hall of Fame, 1985—; founder Rural Tech. Incubator, 1994—. Editor: The Business Plan: Step-by-Step, 1988, The Marketing Plan: Step-by-Step, 1990; author, editor: Boxcar of Peaches: Nash Finch Co., 1990, Pardon Me, Your Manners are Showing!, 1992; contbr. articles to profl. jours. Founder, sponsor 67th Patent & Trademark Depository Libr., 1991—. Named Friend of Sml. Bus., Fargo C. of C., 1988; named U. N.D. Outstanding Greek Alumnus, 1990, Outstanding Svc. award, U. N.D. Alumni Assn., 1984, others. Mem. Assn. Univ. Tech. Mgrs., Assn. Univ. Related Rsch. Pks., Univ. Small Bus. Tech. Consortium (state dir. 1986-90), Alumni Inter-Fraternity Coun. (chmn. 1982-86, 90-95, Outstanding Alumnus 1990), Rotary, Delta Tau Delta. Republican. Episcopalian. Home: Condo # 31 2501 26th Ave S Grand Forks ND 58201-6478 Office: Ctr Innovation & Bus PO Box 8372 100 Harrington Grand Forks ND 58202-8372

GLABE, ELMER FREDERICK, food scientist; b. Chgo., Apr. 3, 1911; s. Fred John and Holdina (Jennrich) G.; m. Marjorie Browne; children: John E., Lynne Glabe Mueller, David H. BS in Chemistry, Ill. Inst. Tech., 1942. Analytical chemist W.E. Long Co., Chgo., 1929-38; research chemist, tech. dir. Stein Hall and Co., Chgo., 1938-45; founder, pres. Food Tech., Inc, Chgo., 1946—, Food Tech. Lab. and Food Tech. Products, Northbrook, Ill. Author numerous tech. papers in food sci.; patentee (110) in field. Recipient Hon. Membership and Outstanding Svc. award Am. Coun. Independent Labs., Victor Marx award Am. Soc. Bakery Engrs., 1991. Mem. Am. Chem. Soc. (50 yr. award), Am. Assn. Cereal Chemists (50 yr. award), Inst. Food Technologists (50 yr. award). Lutheran. Office: 3000 Dundee Rd Ste 204 Northbrook IL 60062-2432

GLADDEN, DEAN ROBERT, arts administrator, educator, consultant; b. Columbus, Ohio, Dec. 27, 1953; s. Cyril Robert and Eileen (Faulkner) G.; m. Jane Frances Tellers, Aug. 27, 1953; children: John Dean, Catherine Eileen. B in Music Edn., Miami U., Oxford, Ohio, 1976; MS in Urban Arts Mgmt., Drexel U., 1978. Exec. dir. Council for Arts of Greater Lima, Ohio, 1977-80, Arts Comm. Greater Toledo, 1980-82; dir. devel. and adminstrn. Great Lakes Theater Festival, Cleve., 1982-86; assoc. mng. dir. The Cleve. Play House, 1986, mng. dir., 1987—; cons. Ohio Arts Coun., Cleve., 1977—, chmn. sponsor/touring panel, 1981-83; adj. assoc. prof. U. Akron, Ohio, 1984-87; mem. adv. com. Mandel Sch. of Non-Profit Mgmt., Case Western Res. U., Cleve. Author booklets on the econs. of arts in Ohio, 1981, 83, 85, 87, 89, 91, 93. Mem. League Resident Theatres (mem. exec. com.), Ohio Concerned Citizens for the Arts (v.p.), Rotary. Episcopalian. Home: 3605 Ingleside Rd Cleveland OH 44122-5003 Office: The Cleve Play House 8500 Euclid Ave Cleveland OH 44106-2032

GLADSTONE, LEE, psychiatrist, addictionist; b. Chgo., May 22, 1914; s. Maurice and Sadie (Siegel) G.; m. Gertrude Hope Fremmel; children: Evan-Lorna. Student, U. Ill., 1936; BS, MD, Chgo. Med. Sch., 1940. Cert. by Am. Soc. Addictive Medicine, 1986. Intern Meml. Hosp., Harvey, Ill., 1940-42; resident psychiatry Northwestern Meml. Hosp., 1967-70; pvt. practice Chgo., 1946—; dir. McHenry Med. Group and Hosp., McHenry, Ill., 1947-67; dir. psychiat. day hosp. Northwestern Meml. Hosp., Chgo., 1971-72, dir. alcoholism treatment program Inst. of Psychiatry, 1975-80, med. dir. chem. dependence program Inst. Psychiatry, 1988-90; med. dir. Amethyst Group, Chgo., 1988—; assoc. Northwestern U. Chgo., 1972—, prof. emeritus, 1990—; dir. Foxfire Partial Hosp. Program, Summit, Ill., 1974—; dir. Martha Washington Hosp., Chgo., 1982-88. Contbr. articles to profl. jours. Med. adv. bd. Ill. Dept. Alcoholism and Substance Abuse, 1986—; mem. HEW's Nat. Adv. Coun. on Alcohol Abuse and Alcoholism, 1980-83; adv., bd. Alcoholism Treatment Licensure Program Ill. Dept. Mental Health, 197780; bd. dirs. Head Start, McHenry, Ill., 1966-67; founder, bd. dirs. McHenry Hosp., 1958-71. With U.S. Army, 1941-46. Recipient Francis J. Gerty award Ill. Dept. Mental Health, 1978; fellow Dingleton (Scotland) Hosp., 1970; Lee Gladstone Fellowship in Addiction Medicine named in his honor Northwestern Med. Sch., 1992. Mem. Am. Soc. Addictive Medicine (nat. com. nicotine cessation 1989—), Ill. Med. Soc. (impaired physicians com. 1982-85), Am. Acad. Clin. Psychiatrists, Am. Psychiat. Assn., Wilderness Soc., Sierra Club, Nature Conservancy. Office: The Amethyst Group 233 E Erie St Chicago IL 60611-2926

GLANCY, ALFRED ROBINSON, III, public utility company executive; b. Detroit, Mar. 14, 1938; s. Alfred Robinson and Elizabeth A. (Tant) G.; m. Ruth Mary Roby, Sept. 15, 1962; children: Joan C., Alfred R. IV, Douglas Roby, Andrew Roby. BA, Princeton U., 1960; MA, Harvard U., 1962. Vice pres. corp. planning Am. Nat. Gas Service, Detroit, 1976-79; econ. and fin. planning staff Mich. Consol. Gas Co., Detroit, 1962-64, supr. econ. studies and rates, 1965-67, mgr. econ. and fin. planning dept., 1967-68, treas., 1969-72, v.p., treas., 1972-73, v.p. customer and mktg. services, 1976-79, v.p. mktg./dist. ops., 1979-81, sr. v.p. mktg./customer services, 1981-83, sr. v.p. utility ops., 1983-84, chmn., chief exec. officer, 1984-92; chmn., pres., CEO MCN Corp., 1992—; bd. dirs., exec. com. UNICO Properties, Inc., Seattle; bd. dirs. Ga., MLX Corp., Detroit, NBD Bank, Mich. Chmn. Detroit Symphony Orch., Detroit Renaissance Inc., exec. com.; past chmn. Detroit Med. Ctr., New Detroit, Inc.. Mem. Princeton Club Mich., Country Club of Detroit, Detroit Club. Republican. Office: MCN Corp 500 Griswold St Detroit MI 48226-3700

GLANVILLE, JOYCE M., stockbroker; b. Eindhoven, The Netherlands, Aug. 20, 1937; d. Gerard A. and Jannett H. (Rooseboom) Jonkers; m. David Glanville, May 5, 1979; children: Jerry, Steve, Jeannie, Rick; stepchildren: Adam, Jason, Ryan. Stockbroker Prescott Ball Rosen, Grand Rapids, Mich., 1988-90, Kemper/Prescott, Grand Rapids, 1990-92; v.p., stockbroker Dean Witter Reynolds, Grand Rapids, 1993—. Advisor Hospice, Grand Rapids, 1993—. Office: Dean Witter Reynolds 300 Ottawa Ave NW Ste 600 Grand Rapids MI 49503-2310

GLANZ, BARBARA ANNE, author, speaker, consultant; b. Harlan, Iowa, May 24, 1943; d. Wayne Robert and Gertrude Lucille (Anderson) Bauerle; m. Charles William Glanz, June 25, 1966; children: Garrett Wayne, Gretchen Margaret, Erin Adah. BS in Edn., U. Kans., 1965; MS in Adult Continuing Edn., No. Ill. U., 1980. Cert. secondary edn. tchr., Ill. English tchr. Lyons Twp. High Sch., LaGrange, Ill., 1965-69, ESL instr. adult evening sch., 1973-78; instr. English Coll. of DuPage, Glen Ellyn, Ill., 1977, 81-83; ESL instr. Argonne (Ill.) Nat. Lab., 1982-86; showroom mgr. The Paige Collection, Chgo., 1983-86; ind. contractor communications seminars Western Springs, Ill., 1984-87; platform instr. The Grammar Group, Chgo., 1987-88; mgr. tng. Kaset Internat., Tampa, Fla., 1988-90, dir. quality in tng., 1990-93; pres. Barbara Glanz Comm., Inc., Western Springs, Ill., 1994—; presenter Instructional Systems Assn., Sunset Beach, Calif., 1991, Coun. on Licensing, Enforcement and Regulation, Lexington, Ky., 1991, Am. Cancer Soc., Tampa, 1991, Nat. Soc. for Performance and Instrn., Washington, 1992, ASTD, Alexandria, Va., 1990, 92, 93-96; with Kaset Internat., Tampa, Fla., 1989-94, Nationwide Ins. Co., Columbus, Ohio, 1992, Inc, Mag., Miami, Fla., 1993; Best of Am. Conf, Tampa, Fla., 1993-94, 25th Anniversity New Zealand Inst. of Travel and Tourism, Rotorua, 1993, Hawaiian Electric Co., Honolulu, 1993, Internat. Quality and Productivity Ctr. Conf., Chgo. and San Francisco, 1993-95, Chgo. Soc. Assn. Execs., 1994, NAWBO, 1994, Meeting Planners Internat., Mich., 1994, Nat. Commerce Bank Svcs., Women's Jewelry Assn., Hellenic Inst. Mgmt., 1995, State of Mich., 1996, Rockwell Internal, 1996, Am. Farm Bur., 1996, APAC Telesvcs., 1996, Ill. Dept. Pub. Health, 1996, N.W. Pub. Power Assn., 1996, U.S. Dept. Energy, 1996, Nat. Assn. Svc. Mgrs., 1996, and others. Author: Facilitating vs. Teaching, 1989, The Creative Communicator: 399 Tools to Communicate Commitment without Boring People to Death, 1993, Building Customer Loyalty, 1994, 49 Creative Ways to Get Your Ideas and Values Across, 1994, Care Packages for the Workplace-Dozens of Little Things You Can Do To Regenerate Spirit at Work, 1996; (bus. TV and video series) Masters on Motivation, 1994, The Evolving Workplace, 1996; contbr. articles to profl. jours. and bus. mags. Chmn., founder intergenerational sharing program Field Park PTO, Western Springs, 1976-78, ways and means and social chmn., 1975, 79-81, officer, 1982-83, 86; chmn., bd. trustees, choir, adult edn. co. Village Ch., Western Springs, 1982, 85-88. Mem. NAFE, ASTD (presenter internat. conf.), Nat. Spkr.'s Assn., Profl. Spkrs. of Ill. (bd. dirs.), Nat. Soc. for Performance and Instrn., Kappa Delta Pi, Gamma Phi Beta (alumnae, Honor Initiate award 1962, Outstanding Sr. Woman 1965). Home and Office: Barbara Glanz Comm Inc 4047 Howard Ave Western Springs IL 60558-1215

GLANZMAN, JOYCE C., investment broker; b. Quincy, Ill., June 1, 1942. Nurse Sunset Nursing Home, Quincy; investment broker Edward D. Jones, Quincy, 1984-93, A.G. Edwards & Sons Inc., Quincy, 1993—. Mem. NAFE, Am. Bus. Women, Fine Arts Soc., Quincy Preserves, Quincy Symphony, Eagles Aux. Roman Catholic. Office: AG Edwards & Sons Inc 3325 Maine St Quincy IL 62301-4438

GLASER, GARY A., bank executive. Grad., Baldwin-Wallace, Case Western Res. U. With Nat. City Corp., 1967-84; pres., CEO Nat. City Bank, Columbus, Ohio, 1984—. Office: Nat City Bank 155 E Broad St Columbus OH 43215*

GLASSCOCK, KENTON, state legislator; m. Kick Glasscock. BA, Kans. State U., 1976. Kans. state rep. Dist. 62, 1991—, mem. taxation and energy and natural resources com., mem. joint com. on adminstrv. rules and regulations; pres. Kans. Lumber Homestore. Home: PO Box 1307 Manhattan KS 66502-0014*

GLASSHEIM, ELIOT ALAN, grants officer; b. N.Y.C., Feb. 10, 1938; s. Raymond S. and Edith (Ruthizer) G.; m. Patricia Sanborn, July 20, 1969 (div. Feb. 1979); children: Eagle, Don; m. Dyan Rey, Feb. 14, 1996. BA, Wesleyan U., 1960; MA, U. N.Mex., 1966, PhD, 1972. Copy boy, book reviewer Wash. Post, 1960-61; editorial proofreader Wall St. Jour., N.Y.C., 1962-64; mgmt. trainee Accessory Fashions, N.Y.C., 1964-66; asst. prof. English Augusta (Ga.) Coll., 1968-70; postdoctoral fellow U. N.D., Grand Forks, 1971-73; state rep. N.D. State Legis., Grand Forks, 1975-76, 93—; dir. devel. N.D. Mus. Art, Grand Forks, 1993—; owner used bookstore Dr. Eliot's Twice Sold Tales, Grand Forks, 1992—; dir. Population/Food Fund, Grand Forks, 1977-79; housing coord., grantswriter N.D. Migrant Coun., Grand Forks, 1979-81. Editor: Population and Food Issues, 1977, 78; author: (poems) The Restless Giant, 1968. Exec. dir. Quad County Cmty. Action Agy., Grand Forks, 1981-87; field rep., office mgr. Sen Quentin Burdick, Grand Forks, 1987-92; city councilman Grand Forks City Coun., 1982—; mem. planning com. Grand Forks Planning and Zoning Commn., 1984—; founder, dir. Red River Valley Habitat for Humanity, Grand Forks, 1988—; chmn. Dist. 17/18 Dems., Grand Forks, 1980-81. Mem. Kiwanis. Jewish. Home: 619 N 3rd St Grand Forks ND 58203-3203 Office: ND Mus Art PO Box 7305 Grand Forks ND 58202-7305

GLASSMEYER, JAMES MILTON, aerospace, computer, and electronics engineer; b. Cin., Mar. 31, 1928; s. Howard Jerome and Ethel Marie (Nieman) G.; m. Anita Mary Tschida, Apr. 21, 1979. Student, U. Cin., 1947-49; BSEE with spl. honors, U. Colo., Boulder, 1958; MS in Aeronautics and Astronautics, MIT, 1960. Commd. 2d lt. USAF, 1950, advanced through grades to lt. col., 1971; astron. engr. Air Force Space Systems Div. Hdqrs. USAF, L.A., 1960-64; astronautical engr. and astronautics intelligence analyst Air Force Rocket Propulsion Lab USAF, Edwards AFB, Calif., 1967-73; ret. USAF, 1973; aerospace, computer, and electronics rsch. and analysis and analysis, 1973—. Contbr. articles to jours. in field. Recipient Air Force Inst. Tech. scholarship, U. Colo., 1956-58, MIT, 1958-60, Am. Rocket Soc. Grad. Student Nat. 1st Pl. award, MIT, 1960, USAF Master Missileman badge, Air Force Rocket Propulsion Lab., 1970. Mem. AIAA, IEEE, Air Force Assn., Planetary Soc., Ret. Officers Assn., Tau Beta Pi (1st grand prize Greater Interest in Govt. Nat. Essay Contest 1957), Eta Kappa Nu, Sigma Tau, Sigma Gamma Tau, Sigma Xi. Roman Catholic. Home: 61 Brookhill Woods Ln Tipp City OH 45371-1951 Office: PO Box 84 Tipp City OH 45371-0084

GLATZ, CHRISTINE ELIZABETH, association administrator; b. Chgo., Sept. 2, 1961; d. Donald Henry and Evelyn Mildred (Jurich) May; m. Fred John Glatz Jr., Oct. 5, 1985; 1 child, Katlyn Elizabeth. BS in Mktg., DePaul U., 1985. Exec. sec. 1st Nat. Bank Chgo., 1981-84, office mgr., 1984-86, records mgr., 1986-88, project mgr., 1988-90; assn. mgr. Mgmt. Svcs., Frankfort, Ill., 1990—. Editor: (newsletter) Chgo., 1994. Bd. mem. Lincoln-Way High Sch. Bd. Edn., New Lenox, Ill., 1993—; vol. March of Dimes, Chgo., 1992—; corr. sec. Frankfort Square Homeowners Assn., 1990—; founder Farm Brook Terrace Homeowners Assn., Frankfort, 1990-92; co-chair Citizens for Lincoln-Way, New Lenox, 1992; mem. Supt.'s Adv.

Coun., Frankfort, 1991-93. Mem. Assn. Records Mgrs. and Adminstrs. (pub. rels. chair 1986-87, Rookie of Yr. 1987, sec./treas 1987-88, Cert. of Accomplishment 1988, v.p. membership 1988-90, Joseph Jurich Meml. award 1990), Internat. Facility Mgmt. Assn. (adminstrs. 1993—, Chpt. of Yr. 1994), Pi Sigma Epsilon (membership chair 1982-83, v.p. 1983-84, seminar chair, region v.p. 1986-87, Rookie of Yr. 1987). Republican. Roman Catholic. Home: 20400 Green Meadow Ln Frankfort IL 60423

GLAW, JOHN P., manufacturing engineer; b. Chgo., Apr. 10, 1949; s. John and Ursula (Methner) G.; m. Milica Saric, Nov. 7, 1970; children: Jason T., Kirsten A. BSME, Midwest Coll. Engring., Lombard, Ill., 1984. From technician to project engr. Borg Warner Corp., Des Plaines, Ill., 1969-87; from engr. to sr. engr. II Sundstrand Aerospace, Rockford, Ill., 1987—. Team mem. Sch. Dist. # 15 Planning Team and Gifted Program, McHenry, Ill., 1993—; advancement chmn. Boy Scout Troop 459, McHenry, 1992—. Mem. Soc. Mfg. Engrs. Roman Catholic. Home: 6104 Chickaloon Mc Henry IL 60050

GLAZE, TIM LEON, electronics engineer; b. Dayton, Ohio, Jan. 1, 1951; s. Ralph Charles and Christine (Shingledecker) G. BSEE, GM Inst., Flint, Mich., 1974; MSEE, U. Dayton, 1981. Assoc. engr. Delco Products, Dayton, 1974-77, project engr., 1978-81, systems engr., 1982-85; supr. Electronic Data Systems, Dayton, 1986-89, engring. S.E., 1990-95; site rep. ORC, 1995—; mem. ORSC survey team Electronic Data Systems, Dayton, 1992-93, chmn. ORSC quality award and recognition team, 1992-93; quality advisor EDS Ohio Regional Support Ctr., 1993—. Mem. steering com. dean engring. U. Dayton, 1992—. Mem. IEEE (chmn. Dayton chpt. 1988), Nat. Aerospace and Electronics Cond. (bd. dirs. 1992-95), miami Valley Cmputeing Socs. (bd. dirs. 1988—), Riverbend Art Ctr. (3rd place award 1990), Dayton Art Inst., Dayton Philharm. Home: 3735 Crosswood Dr Beavercreek OH 45430-1607

GLAZIER, STEPHEN DAVEY, anthropologist, theologian; b. New London, Conn., June 10, 1949; s. David Arthur and Betty (Davey) G.; m. Rosemary Custer, Sept. 24, 1976; 1 child, Catherine Marie. AB, Eastern Coll., 1971; MDiv, Princeton Theol. Sem., 1974; MA, U. Conn., 1976, PhD, 1981. Postdoctoral rsch. Yale U., New Haven, Conn., 1981-82; asst. prof. Trinity Coll., Hartford, Conn., 1982-83, Conn. Coll., New London, 1983-84; assoc. prof. Wayland Bapt. U., Plainview, Tex., 1984-86, Westmont Coll., Santa Barbara, Calif., 1986-88; dept. chmn. Kearney (Ncor.) State Coll., 1988-91; assoc. prof. U. Nebr., Kearney, 1991-94, prof., grad. faculty fellow, 1994—. Author: Marchin' the Pilgrims Home, 1983; editor: Caribbean Ethnicity Revisited, 1985, Anthropology of Religion, 1996; book rev. editor Anthropology of Consciousness. Summer fellow U. Calif., Yale U., Princeton U., U. Colo., U. Mich., Haverford Coll., 1986, 88, 89, 90, 91, 92, 95, 96, Mellon fellow Rice U., 1987; recipient Rsch. Svc. Coun. awards, 1990, 92. Fellow Am. Anthrop. Assn.; mem. Am. Folklore Soc., Northeast African Am. Religious History Group, Mid-West Sociol. Assn. (endowment coun. 1991-96), V.I. Archaeol. Soc. (pubs. bd. 1976-92), Soc. for Sci. Study of Religion (exec. coun. 1991-94). Republican. Baptist. Office: U Nebr Dept Sociology Anthrop Kearney NE 68849

GLEASON, CAROL ANN, mental health nurse, educator; b. Fairfield, Iowa, Mar. 6, 1945; d. Maurice Alvin and Geraldine (Cook) Crist; m. Michael Gleason Jr., Nov. 26, 1966 (div. Nov. 1980); children: Daniel Lee, Raymond Joe, Christopher John, Crystal Dawn. ADN, Indian Hills Coll., 1977; AS in Adminstrn., Des Moines Area Coll., 1982; BSPA in Health Care, St. Joseph's, 1985; cert. nurses aides edn., U. Iowa, 1989. Lic. nursing home adminstr., Iowa; cert. psychiat. and mental health, gerontology ANA. Staff night charge nruse Mahaska Manor Nursing Home, Oskaloosa, Iowa, 1977; dir. nursing Tower Park Nursing Home, Oskaloosa, 1977-78; dir. nursing Pleasant Park Nursing Home, Oskaloosa, 1978-85, adminstr., 1985-86; staff nurse ICU-CCU Ottumwa (Iowa) Regional Hosp., 1986; psychiat. nurse Knoxville (Iowa) Vets. Hosp., 1986—; coord., instr. Iowa Ednl. inst., Oskaloosa, 1987—; cons. Tower Park Nursing Home, Oskaloosa, 1985-87, Siesta Park Nursing Home, 1985-87, Mahaska Manor, 1993-95. Mem. NAFE, Am. Fedn. Govt. Employers. Democrat. Roman Catholic. Home: Box 155 Rt 1 220 Keomah Village Oskaloosa IA 52577

GLEASON, DARLENE HARRIETTE, retired personnel director; b. Wichita, Kans., Apr. 18, 1933; d. John Wilbur and Mildred Catherine (Zogleman) Garnett; m. Orval Lee Gleason, Nov. 22, 1953; children: Michael Lee, Michelle Catherine Gleason Wolf. AA in Elem. Edn., Wichita State U., 1952. Tchr. Ellsworth (Kans.) Elem. Sch., 1952-53; bookkeeper Wichita Fin. & Thrift, 1953-56; with payroll Coleman Co., Wichita, 1957-58, Aircapitol Mfg., Wichita, 1961-62; acctg. technician Dept. Air Force, Wichita, 1964-67; staffing asst. U.S. Office Pers. Mgmt., Wichita, 1967-76, pers. staffing specialist, 1976-88, supervisory pers. staffing specialist, 1988-94. Fin. sec. S.W. Presbyn. Ch., Wichita, 1963-81, elder, 1970, trustee, 1971-73, 80-82, 89-91, chmn. bd. trustees, 1973, 81, 82, 91.

GLEASON, DAVID, state legislator; m. Bonnie Gleason; 2 children. Student, S.D. State U. Mem. S.D. Ho. of Reps., mem. health and human svc. and judiciary coms.; pers. officer. Home: PO Box 15 Claire City SD 57224-0015*

GLEASON, GERALD WAYNE, retired lawyer; b. Springfield, Mo., May 22, 1911. A.B., Drury Coll., 1933; postgrad U. Mo., 1938. Bar: Mo. 1938. Asst. pros. atty. Greene County (Mo.), 1947-48, 50-51; city atty. Springfield, 1952-56; acting city mgr. Springfield, 1953; mcpl. judge, Springfield, 1956-73; ptnr. Tucker & Gleason, Springfield, 1938-87, ret., 1988 Served to capt. U.S. Army, 1941-45, ETO. Mem. Greene County Bar Assn., Mo. Bar Assn., Exch. Club.

GLEASON, LINDA MARY, geriatrics nurse; b. Baldwin, Wis., July 3, 1956; d. George Christian and Mary Agnes (Geraghty) Hop; m. James John Gleason, Sept. 23, 1978; 4 children. Student, U. Wis., Eau Claire, 1974-75, Augsburg Coll., 1975-76; diploma in nursing, Abbott Northwestern Sch. Nursing, 1978; student, U. Wis., River Falls, 1993-94. Staff nurse Baldwin Community Meml. Hosp., 1978-79; dir. nursing Glenhaven, Inc., Glenwood City, Wis., 1979-80; staff nurse Am. Heritage Care Ctr., Hammond, Wis., 1980-84, insvc. dir., 1984-88, staff nurse, 1988-94, nurse mgr., 1994, dir. nursing, 1994—. Treas. Local Minn. Student Nurse's Assn., Mpls., 1977-78; religious edn. tchr. St. Patrick's Cath. Ch., Erin, Wis., 1987-88; co-leader jr. Girl Scout troop 1117 St. Croix Valley coun. 476 Girl Scouts U.S., Baldwin, 1990-94; tchr.'s aide, vol. Greenfield Elem., Baldwin, 1989-94, vol. presch. screening, 1989-94. Recipient Outstanding Leader award Girl Scouts U.S.A. Coun., 1992. Roman Catholic. Home: 1380 9th Ave Baldwin WI 54002-9375

GLEDHILL, ROGER CLAYTON, statistician, engineer, mathematician, educator; b. Parkersburg, W.Va., July 14, 1943; s. Arthur Clayton and Frances Marie (Freeman) G.; m. Barbara Louise Baker, June 12, 1965; children: Diane Michelle, David Arthur. BBA, Miami U., Oxford, Ohio, 1965; MA, U. Mass., 1972; MS, PhD, Va. Poly. Inst. and State U., 1976. Assoc. prof. statistics Ea. Mich. U., Ypsilanti, 1976—. Author: Numerical Methods, 1993; contbr. articles to profl. publs. Ford Found. fellow, 1975. Mem. Mensa, Alpha Iota Delta, Phi Kappa Phi, Alpha Pi Mu, Pi Mu Epsilon, Omicron Delta Epsilon, Alpha Kappa Psi, Tau Beta Phi, Beta Gamma Sigma, Tau Kappa Epsilon. Office: Ea Mich Univ Owen Hall Ypsilanti MI 48197

GLEICHERT, GREGG CHARLES, human resources executive; b. Danville, Pa., Aug. 9, 1948; s. James Elder and Nancy Ann (Cocheville) G.; m. Jacqueline Carol Lacy, Dec. 20 (div.); 1 child, Christine; m. Ann Marie Curran, July 26; 1 child, Kathryn. BS in Econs., Drury Coll., Springfield, Mo., 1974. Employment rep. Zenith Radio Corp., Springfield, 1972-74, employee svcs. mgr., 1974-76; exec. mgr. Sellner Mfg. Co., Faribault, Minn., 1976-80; dir. personnel Jerome Foods, Faribault, 1980-84; dir. compensation Jerome Foods, Barron, Wis., 1984-86, v.p. human resources, 1986-92, v.p. adminstrn., 1992-95; exec. v.p., sec.-treas., 1995—; bd. dirs. Wis. Agri-bus. Coun.; v.p. Turkey Promotion Coun. Bd. dirs. Minn. Turkey Promotion Coun., v.p.; bd. dirs. Wis. Agri-Bus. Coun.; registered lobbyist, Minn., Wis., 1991—. Mem. Soc. Internat. Benefit Found., Soc. Human Resources, Wis. Mfrs. and Commerce (human resources adv. coun., co-chair environ. work group), Minn. Turkey Growers Assn. (v.p., bd. dirs., mem. environ. work group, legis. affairs com.), Nat. Turkey Fedn. (bd. dirs.), Wis. Poultry Consortium (bd. dirs.). Office: Jerome Foods Inc 34 N 7th St Barron WI 54812-1231

GLEICHMAN, JOHN ALAN, safety and loss control executive; b. Anthoney, Kans., Feb. 11, 1944; s. Charles William and Caroline Elizabeth (Emch) G.; m. Martha Jean Cannon, July 1, 1966; 1 son, John Alan Jr. BS in Bus. Mgmt., Kans. State Tchrs. Coll., 1966. Cert. hazard control mgr.; cert. safety profl.; cert. safety exec. Office mgr. to asst. supt. Barton-Malow Co., Detroit, 1967-72, safety coord., 1972-76, corp. mgr. safety and security, 1976-89, dir. corp. safety and loss control, 1989—; instr. U. Mich., Wayne State U., 1977-81, Lawrence Technological U., 1994—; mem. constrn. safety standards commn. adv. com. for concrete constrn. and steel erection Bur. of Safety and Regulations, Mich. Dept. Labor, 1977—; rep. constrn. standards com. Am. Nat. Standards Inst., 1984—. Author: (with others) You, The National Safety Council, and Voluntary Standards, 1981, Construction Accident Analysis: The Inductive Learning Approach, 1991. Instr. multi media first aid ARC, 1976-89; past trustee Apostolic Christian Ch., Livonia, Mich. Recipient Safety Achievement awards Mich. Mut. Ins. Co., 1979-83; Cameron award Constrn. sect. Indsl. div. Nat. Safety Coun., 1982, 1987. Mem. Mich. Safety Conf. (pres. 1984-85), Am. Soc. Safety Engrs. (pres. Detroit chpt. 1982, nat. adminstr. constrn div. 1988-89, bd. dirs. 1988-90, Safety Prof. of Yr. 1984) Nat. Safety Coun. (chmn. tech. rev. constrn. sect. indsl. div. 1980-84, chmn. standards com. indsl. div. 1983-85, chmn. assn. com. indsl. div. 1985-86, dir. tech. support com. indsl. div. 1986-87, dir. sects. group indsl. div. 1987-89, chmn. elect indsl. div. 1989-90, chmn. 1990-91, bd. dirs. 1987-92, Disting. Svcs. to Safety award, 1993), Am. Arbitration Assn. (panel arbitrators 1985). Office: Barton Malow Co 27777 Franklin Rd Ste 800 Southfield MI 48034-8258

GLEISS, HENRY WESTON, lawyer; b. Detroit, Nov. 22, 1928; s. George Herman and Mary Elizabeth (Weston) G.; m. Joan Bette Christopher, July 23, 1955; children—Kent G., Keith W. B.A., Denison U., 1951; J.D., U. Mich., 1954. Bar: Mich. 1955, U.S. Dist. Ct. (ea. dist.) Mich. 1955, U.S. Dist. Ct. (we. dist.) Mich. 1960, U.S. Ct. Appeals (6th cir.) 1964, U.S. Supreme Ct. 1967. Sole practice, Benton Harbor, Mich., 1957-61; ptnr. Globensky, Gleiss, Bittner & Hyrns, P.C., St. Joseph, 1961—; spl. asst. atty. gen. Mich., 1960—. Officer Jaycees, Mich.; bd. dirs. United Fund. Served with U.S. Army, 1955-57. Mem. ABA, Mich. Bar Assn., Berrien County Bar Assn. (pres. 1974), Assn. Trial Lawyers Am., Twin Cities C. of C. (v.p. 1975). Congregationalist. Clubs: Kiwanis, Moose (Benton Harbor); Economic of S.W. Mich.; Elks (St. Joseph). Home: 1224 Miami Rd Benton Harbor MI 49022-5616 Office: 610 Ship St PO Box 290 Saint Joseph MI 49085

GLENN, CLAUDIA ANN, physical therapist; b. Chgo., Apr. 3, 1955; d. George Raymond and Charlotte Rose (Menkick) Chambers; m. John Riley Glenn, Aug. 28, 1976; children: Elise Kristine, Daniel Chambers. BS in Phys. Therapy with honors, U. Ill., 1978; postgrad., Inst. Phys. Therapy, St. Augustine, Fla., 1993—. Lic. phys. therapist, Ill. Staff phys. therapist Marianjoy Rehab. Hosp., Wheaton, Ill., 1978-80, St. Therese Med. Ctr., Waukegan, Ill., 1980-82; home health, nursing home phys. therapist Excellcare, Prospect Heights, Ill., 1986-90; staff phys. therapist Condell Med. Ctr., Libertyville, Ill., 1982-86, from staff phys. therapist to clin. skills coord., 1990—. Vol. Copeland Family Assn., Copeland Sch., Libertyville, 1987-95; vol. parent ednl. program Family Network, Copeland and Highland Schs., 1994; mem. liturgy team St. Mary of Vernon Ch., Prairie Creek, ill., 1986-92, co-coord. Eucharistic min., 1994—. Mem. Am. Phys. Therapy Assn. (dist. rep. 1978—), Am. Acad. Orthopedic Manual Phys. Therapists, Ill. Phys. Therapy Assn. (dist. rep. 1995), Mortar Bd. Office: Condell Med Ctr Centre Club 200 W Golf Rd Libertyville IL 60048

GLENN, JOHN HERSCHEL, JR., senator; b. Cambridge, Ohio, July 18, 1921; s. John Herschel and Clara (Sproat) G.; m. Anna Margaret Castor, Apr. 1943; children: Carolyn Ann, John David. Student, Muskingum Coll., 1939-42, B.Sc., 1962; naval aviation cadet, U. Iowa, 1942; grad. flight sch., Naval Air Tng. Center, Corpus Christi, Tex., 1943, Navy Test Pilot Tng. Sch., Patuxent River, Md., 1954. Commd. 2d lt. USMC, 1943, assigned 4th Marine Aircraft Wing, Marshall Islands campaign, 1944, assigned 9th Marine Aircraft Wing, 1945-46; with 1st Marine Aircraft Wing, North China Patrol, also Guam, 1947-48; flight instr. advanced flight tng. Corpus Christi, 1949-51; asst. G-2/G-3 Amphibious Warfare Sch., Quantico, Va., 1951; with Marine Fighter Squadron 311, exchange pilot 25th Fighter Interceptor Squadron USAF, Korea, 1953; project officer fighter design br. Navy Bur. Aero. Washington, 1956-58; astronaut Project Mercury, Manned Spacecraft Center NASA, 1959-65; pilot Mercury-Atlas 6, 1st orbital space flight launched from Cape Canaveral, Fla., Feb. 1962; ret. as col., 1965; v.p. corp. devel. and dir. Royal Crown Cola Co., 1966-74; pres. Royal Crown Internat.; U.S. senator from Ohio, 1975—; mem. Spl. Com. on Aging, Armed Svcs. Com., Senate Dem. Tech. and Comm. Com., Intelligence Com.; ranking minority mem. Govtl. Affairs Com.; vice-chmn. Senate Dem. Policy Com. Co-author: We Seven, 1962; author: P.S., I Listened to Your Heart Beat. Made first supersonic transcontinental flight, July 16, 1957; trustee Muskingum Coll. Decorated D.F.C. (six), Air medal (18); recipient Astronaut medal USMC, Navy unit commendation, Korean Presdl. unit citation, Disting. Merit award Muskingum Coll., Medal of Honor N.Y.C., Congl. Space Medal of Honor, 1978, Centennial awd., Nat. Geographic Soc., 1988, other decorations, awards and hon. degrees. Mem. Soc. Exptl. Test Pilots, Internat. Acad. of Astronautics (hon.). Democrat. Presbyterian. Office: US Senate 503 Hart Senate Bldg Washington DC 20510

GLENN, MICHAEL T., investment company executive; b. Detroit, Mar. 19, 1949; s. James M. and Bettye J. (Neal) G.; m. Nancy Jean Ollila, Nov. 202, 1982; children: Nicole Ollila, Jessica Taylor, Christopher Michael. BBA, Western Mich. U., 1971, MA with honors, 1974, EdD, 1979. Cert. tchr., Mich. Asst. prof. Western Mich. U., Kalamazoo, 1974-81; project mgr. orgn. devel. Kellogg Co., Battle Creek, Mich., 1981-86; mgr. mgmt. devel. Batesville (Ind.) Casket Co., 1986-87; dir. ednl. svcs. Good Samaritan Hosp., Cin., 1987-90; dir. tng. and devel. Fidelity Investments, Cin., 1990—; dir. Consumer Educators Mich., Lansing, 1979; cons. Xavier U., Cin., 1989, Am. Heart Assn., Columbus, Ohio, 1988. Author newsletter Students As Consumers, 1978. Vol. Am. Cancer Soc., Cin., 1988-90. Scholar State of Mich., 1967. Mem. ASTD, Delta Pi Epsilon, Pi Omega Pi, Phi Chi Theta (faculty advisor 1979-80). Lutheran.

GLENN, RUSSELL DAVID, electrical engineer; b. Granite City, Ill., Aug. 4, 1961; s. Donald Lloyd and Mildred Elma (Knobeloch) G.; m. Ellen Kay Glenn, Sept. 17, 1988. BSEE, So. Ill. U., 1983; MSEE, Purdue U., 1985; PhDEE, Ohio U., 1995. Part-time instr. Tri-Cities Tech. C.C., Blountville, Tenn., 1986; elec. design engr. Tex. Instruments Indsl. Controls Divsn., Johnson City, Tenn., 1985-91; rsch. asst. Ohio U., Athens, 1991-95; sr. devel. engr. Demino Control Systems, Glen Carbon, Ill., 1995—. Contbr. articles to profl. jours. Mem. Athens Ch. of Christ, 1991—, Grace Fellowship Ch., Johnson City, 1985-91. Presdl. scholar So. Ill. U., 1979; Purdue Grad. Instr. fellow Purdue U., 1983, Stocker fellow Ohio U., 1991-93; named Eagle Scout Boy Scouts Am., 1978. Mem. IEEE. Home: 6 Stone Ct Highland IL 62249 Office: Domino Control Systems 19 Kettle Run Dr Glen Carbon IL 62034

GLENNEN, ROBERT EUGENE, JR., university president; b. Omaha, Mar. 31, 1933; s. Robert E. and La Verda (Elledge) G.; m. Mary C. O'Brien, Apr. 17, 1958; children: Maureen, Bobby, Colleen, Billy, Barry, Katie, Molly, Kerry. A.B., U. Portland, 1955, M.Ed., 1957; Ph.D., U. Notre Dame, 1962. Asst. prof. U. Portland, 1956-60; asst. prof., assoc. prof. Eastern Mont. Coll., Billings, 1962-65; assoc. dean U. Notre Dame, South Bend, Ind., 1965-72; dean, v.p. U. Nev.-Las Vegas, 1972-80; pres. Western N.Mex. U., Silver City, 1980-84, Emporia (Kans.) State U., 1984—; bd. dirs. Emporia Enterprises; cons. HEW, Washington, 1964-84. Author: Guidance: An Orientation, 1966. Contbr. articles to profl. jours. Pres. PTA, South Bend, Ind., 1970-71; bd. trustees Am. Coll. Testing Corp., Iowa City, 1977-80; chmn. Kans. Regents Coun. of Pres., 1986-87, 92-93, 95-96. Recipient award of excellence Nat. Acad. Advising Assn., Disting. Alumnus award U. Portland, 1993, Kans. Master Tchr. award, 1994; named Coach of Yr., Coach and Athletic mag., 1958, Pub. Administr. of Yr., 1994, Athletic Hall of Fame, Portland, 1995; Rotary Paul Harris fellow, 1995, Ford Found. fellow, 1961-62. Mem. Kans. C. of C. (bd. dirs.), Emporia C. of C. Regional Devel. Assn. (bd. dirs., Bank IV), Am. Personnel and Guidance Assn., Am. Assn. State Colls. and Univs. (chair pres's. commn. on tchr. edn.), Am. Assn. Higher Edn., Nev. Personnel and Guidance Assn., Assn. Counselor Educators and Suprs., Am. Assn. Counseling and Devel., Nat. Assn. Student Personnel Adminstrs. Republican. Roman Catholic. Office: Emporia State U Office of Pres 1200 Commercial St Emporia KS 66801-5057

GLENNER, RICHARD ALLEN, dentist, dental historian; b. Chgo., Apr. 14, 1934; s. Robert Joseph and Vivian (Prosk) G.; BS, Roosevelt U., 1955; BS in Dentistry, U. Ill., 1958, DDS, 1959; m. Dorothy Chapman, July 13, 1957; children: Mark Steven, Alison, Scott Jay. Gen. practice dentistry, Chgo., 1962—; cons. on dental history to Smithsonian Instn. Nat. Mus. Dentistry, ADA, various corps., libraries, univs., museums, dental jours., Dr. Samuel D. Harris Nat. Mus. Dentistry; dental rschr. Nat. Park Svc., Nat. Mus. Health and Medicine, 1993—. lectr. in field. Served to capt. AUS, 1960-62. Mem. ADA, Ill. Dental Assn., Chgo. Dental Soc., Assn. Mil. Surgeons U.S., Am. Acad. History of Dentistry (historian 1984, chmn. Smithsonian Instn. adv. group 1987, Hayden-Harris award 1983, columnist The Bull. of the History of Denistry 1989—, editorial bd. The Bull. of the History of Dentistry, 1993—, hist. display com. 1993—, pub. com., 1993—, Hayden-Harris award com. 1995-96), Fed. Dentaire Internationale, Lindsay Soc. Great Britain, Ill. State Dental Soc. (history com.), The Pierre Fauchard Acad., Am. Med. Writers Assn., Sci. Instrument Soc., Jewish War Vets. U.S.A, Alpha Omega. Author: The Dental Office: A Pictorial History; co-author The American Dentist: A Pictorial History, A Visit to the Dentist: Then & Now; appeared in PBS video Scientific American Frontiers; cons. editor A Bicentennial Salute to Am. Dentistry, 1976; contbr. articles on dental history to profl. jours.; film maker The Dental Office. Home: 6715 N Lawndale Ave Lincolnwood IL 60645-3711 Office: 3414 W Peterson Ave Chicago IL 60659-3447

GLESER, GOLDINE COHNBERG, psychologist; b. St. Louis, June 15, 1915; d. Julius and Lena (Goldberg) Cohnberg; m. Sol Morris Gleser, June 4, 1936; children: Leon Jay, Malcolm Anthony, Judith Augusta. AB, Washington U., 1935, MS in Math., 1936, postgrad., 1936-38, PhD in Psychology, 1950. Instr. math. Washington U., St. Louis, 1947-49, rsch. asst. psychol. svcs., 1949-50; rsch. asst. to assoc. Washington U. Coll. Medicine, St. Louis, 1950-54; asst. to assoc. prof. U. Cin. Coll. Medicine, 1956-64; rsch. asst. to assoc. prof. U. Ill., Urbana, 1957-63; prof. psychology U. Cin., 1964-79, dir. psychol. div. dept. psychiatry, 1967-79, prof. emerita, 1979—; cons. Dept. Edn., U. Ill., 1951-55, Malcolm Bliss Rsch. Lab., Washington U., 1954-56, Traumatic Stress Study ctr., U. Cin., 1981-91; cons. on evaluation Shiawassee County Community Mental Health Ctr., Ososso, Mich., 1972-85; mem. adv. com. on clin. drug evaluation NIH, Washington, 1960-61, reviewer devel. behavioral sci. rsch. grants, 1972-75; mem. joint com. to revise edn. and psychol. test standards APA/AERA, 1981-83. Author: (with Cronbach) Psychological Tests and Personnel Decisions, 1965, (with Gottschalk) Measurement of Psychological States, 1969, (with others) The Dependability of Behavioral Measurements, 1972, Prolonged Psychosocial Effects of Disaster, 1981, (with Ihilevich) Evaluating Mental-health Programs: The Progress Evaluation Scales, 1982, Defense Mechanisms: Their classification, correlates and measurement with the Defense Mechanisms Inventory, 1986, Defenses in Psychotherapy: The Clinical Application of the Defense Mechanisms Inventory, 1991, The Defense Mechanisms Test, 1968, others. Grantee Found. Fund for Rsch. in Psychiatry, U. Cin., 1959-65, NIMH, 1975-77; recipient Rieveschl award U. Cin., 1979, Lifetime Achievement award Ohio Women in Psychology, 1988, award for Traumatic Stress Studies, 1990. Fellow APA (rep. to coun. 1976-78, award 1985), Am. Statis. Assn., Am. Psychol. Soc., Ohio Psychol. Assn.; mem. Midwest Psychol. Assn., Cin. Psychol. Assn. (pres. 1957-58, 65-66, award 1988), Psychometric Soc. (trustee 1966-69), Soc. of Multivariate Exptl. Psychology (pres. 1977-78). Home and Office: 3604 Lansdowne Ave Cincinnati OH 45236-3008

GLESSNER, JAMES ROGER, retired orthopedic surgeon; b. Balt., May 26, 1924; s. James R. and Margaret Hoskins (Evans) G.; m. Wilhelmina Johanna Schaefer, March 24, 1946; children: James R. III, Robert S. BS, Franklin and Marshall, Lancaster, 1941-45; MD, Univ. Pa., Phila., 1944-47. Lic. MD, Mich., Diplomate Am. Bd. Orthopedic Surgery. Orthop. surgeon Henry Ford Hosp., Detroit, 1953-54, Middleton, Conn., 1954-60, UCLA, L.A., 1960-61, Grand Rapids, Mich., 1961-94. Contrb. articles to profl. jours. Capt. U.S. Army, 1951-53, Korea. Decorated Bronze Star medal. Fellow Am. Acad. Orthop. Surgeons, Am. Coll. Surgeons, Internat. Coll. Surgeons,; mem. Midwest Orthop. Assn., Clinical Orthop. Assn. Democrat. Protestant. Home: 5089 S. Quail Crest SE Grand Rapids MI 49546 Office: 309 Jefferson SE Grand Rapids MI 49503

GLEUE, LORINE ANNA, elementary education educator; b. Lucas, Kans., Feb. 12, 1926; d. Otto Martin and Bertha Marie (Luker) Becker; m. Fred Christoph Gleue, June 12, 1947; children: David Jean, Steven Randolph, Paul Frederick. Assoc., Cloud County Community Coll., 1969; BS in Edn., Ft. Hays (Kans.) State Coll., 1971; MS in Elem. Edn., Ft. Hays State U., 1977; reading specialist degree, Kans. State U., 1984. Cert. tchr., Kans. Elem. tchr. Coffey County, Kans., 1944-47; librarian Belleville (Kans.) Pub. Library, 1960-67, Carnegie Free Pub. Library, Concordia, Kans., 1967-68; elem. tchr. Chester, Nebr., 1971-72, Washington (Kans.) Unified Sch. Dist. #222, 1972-75; Chpt. I program instr. Washington, Kans., 1975-87; tchr. Republic County Schs., Mankato, and USD #333, Concordia, 1987—; Producer, co-owner Gleue's-On-The-Go Shows, Flying Carpet Story Hours, Lorine's Letter Writing Svc. to Shut-ins and Small Fry, Mother's Mender, Gleue-Gomoll Home-Loomed Rag Rugs; co-owner, developer Acres for Wildlife Resource Ctr., Belleville. Published poet; contbr. articles to profl. jours. Mem. book selection com. Kans. State Reading Circle, Topeka, 1979-81. Recipient Golden Poet award 3rd Ann. Poetry Conv., Las Vegas, 1987, World of Poetry Golden Poet award, 1988, 89, 90, 91, 92; third place award Poetry Rendezvous, 1991, Best of Fair and Blue Ribbon awards, 1993, Celebrate Literacy award Internat. Reading Assn., 1993. Mem. Kans. Authors Club, Kans. Reading Assn., Internat. Soc. of Poets, Thunderbird Coun., Fort Hays Alumni Assn. (life), Washington Sign Lang. Club.

GLIEBERMAN, HERBERT ALLEN, lawyer; b. Chgo., Dec. 6, 1930; s. Elmer and Jean (Gerber) G.; m. Evelyn Eraci; children—Ronald, Gale, Joel. Student, U. Ill., 1947, Roosevelt U., 1948-50; J.D., Chgo. Kent Coll. Law, 1953. Bar: Ill. 1954, D.C. 1987. Pvt. practice Chgo., 1954—; lectr. Chgo. Kent. Coll. Law, Ill. Inst. Continuing Legal Edn. Author: Some Syndromes of Love, 1965, Know Your Legal Rights, 1974, Confessions of A Divorce Lawyer, 1975, Closed Marriage, 1978, Four Weekends to an Ideal Marriage, 1981; former host 2 radio shows for NBC Sta. WMAQ: Ask the Lawyer, Law and Controversy. Former trustee Chgo. Kent. Coll. Law; former bd. dirs. Chgo. Coun. on Alcoholism. Mem. Am. Acad. Matrimonial Lawyers (cert. of appreciation 1967), Decologue Soc. Lawyers (cert. of appreciation 1965, 66, 68), Assn. Trial Lawyers Am. (cert. of appreciation 1973), Ill. Trial Lawyers Assn. (cert. of appreciation 1974), ABA, Ill. State Bar Assn., Chgo. Bar Assn. Jewish (bd. dirs., pres. Temple). Home: 180 E Pearson St Chicago IL 60611-2130 Office: 19 S La Salle St Chicago IL 60603-1401

GLOBOKE, JOSEPH RAYMOND, accountant; b. Kansas City, Kans., Mar. 9, 1955; s. Anthony Joseph and Loretta Margaret (Bartkoski) G.; m. Debra Ruth Neumann, Nov. 13, 1982; children: Theresa Renee, Michael Richard, William Robert. BSBA, Rockhurst Coll., 1977. CPA, Mo., Kans. Intern Ernst & Whinney, Kansas City, Mo., 1976-77; staff acct. Troupe Kehoe Whiteaker & Kent, Kansas City, 1977-84, mgr., 1984-88; sr. acct. Kennedy & Coe, Salina, Kans., 1988-91; audit supr. Robert Garrison & Assocs., Grandview, Mo., 1991-93; sr. staff acct. Logan & Schmidt, Kansas City, Kans., 1993-96; mgr., 1996—. Bd. dirs., treas. Children's Mus. of Kansas City; mem. Cub Scouts. Mem. AICPA, Kans. Soc. of CPA, K.C. Roman Catholic. Home: 15601 Ann Ave Belton MO 64012-1459 Office: Logan & Schmidt 1300 N 78th St Ste 100 Kansas City KS 66112-2406

GLOE, DONNA, critical care nurse; b. Moberly, Mo., Apr. 24, 1951; d. James F. and E. Emogene (Semones) Osborn; m. Lloyd R. Gloe, Feb. 14, 1975; children: Darin Robert, Leslie Renee. BA, U. Mo., 1973; MEd, Lincoln U., Jefferson City, Mo., 1977; diploma, St. John's Sch. Nursing, Springfield, Mo., 1983; BSN, S.W. Bapt. U., 1991; EdD, Nova Southeastern U., 1996. Cert. critical care nurse.; cert. nursing staff devel. and continuing edn. Family therapist Burrell Mental Health Ctr., Springfield; edn. coord., staff nurse surg. ICU St. John's Regional Health Ctr., Springfield; adj. faculty S.W. Bapt. U., 1992. Contbr. articles to profl. jours.; author video. Mem. AACN, Nat. Nursing Staff Devel. Orgn., Mo. Assn. Hosp. Educators, Am. Nursing Credentialing Ctr. (mem. nursing staff devel. and continuing edn.). Home: HC 88 Box 4 Marshfield MO 65706-9005

GLOVER, ALBERT DOWNING, retired veterinarian; b. Newark, Mo., Dec. 4, 1907; s. Albert D. and Mattie O. (Downing) G.; m. Mildred Elva Haselwood; children: Allen, Gary, Janet. BS in Agr., U. Mo., 1932; DVM, Colo. State Coll., 1936. Former chmn. City Coun., Canton, Mo., other civic activities. Mem. Mo. VMA (pres. 1951, legis. commn.), AVMA (v.p. 1952), Mo. Vet. Examining Bd., Am. Legion (past comdr.), Shriners, others. Home: 806 Lewis St Canton MO 63435-1449

GLOVER, JAMES TODD, manufacturing company executive; b. Aberdeen, S.D., Apr. 30, 1939; s. Fay and Vi (Bruns) G.; m. Joann Elizabeth House; children: Jason, Jeffrey, Jamie. Student, S.D. State U.; BS in Math., No. State Coll., Aberdeen, 1961. Inside sales engr. Aberdeen Ops. Safeguard, 1961-64, asst. sales engr., 1965-67, mktg. mgr., 1968-72, gen. mgr., 1973-77; v.p. ops. Safeguard PowerTech Systems, Aberdeen, 1978-83, exec. v.p., 1984-85, pres., 1986-89; pres., chief exec. officer, chief ops. officer, dir. Hub City, Inc., Aberdeen, 1989—; officer Safeguard Sci. Co., Inc.; v.p. corp. devel. Regal-Beloit (Wis.) Corp., 1990-93; v.p. HQ Cos., Mpls., 1993—, gen. mgr. Pixall Ltd. Partnership, Clear Lake, Wis., 1993—. Bd. mem. S.D. Swimming Assn.; S.D. Dist. Export Council. Export Devel. Authority; bd. dirs. No. State Found., James River Water Devel.; bd. mem., chmn. James River Water Devel. Dist. Recipient Ernie Gunderson award S.D. Swimming Assn. Mem. Power Transmission Distbrs. Assn. (past bd. dirs., past chmn. allied adv. bd.), Power Transmission Rep. Assn. (past bd. dirs., past chmn. allied adv. bd.), Aberdeen C. of C., S.D. Mfrs. Assn. (past dir.). Republican. Roman Catholic. Office: Pixall Ltd Partnership 100 Bean St Clear Lake WI 54005-9999

GLOVER, ROB W., stockbroker; b. Peoria, Ill., May 3, 1947; m. Barbara Glover; children: Lindsey, Timothy. Student, U. Colo., 1965-67; BS in Edn., Ill. State U., 1971; postgrad., Coll. Fin. Planning, 1989—. LUTC, CFP. Driving instr. Sears Easy Method Driving, 1972; ins. profl. Spangler & Assocs., Bloomington, 1973-78; br. mgr. E. F. Hutton, Bloomington, 1978-88; assoc. v.p. investments A. G. Edwards & Sons Inc., Bloomington, 1988—; instr. adult edn. investments, 1985—. Mem. Normal Rotary Club. Lutheran. Office: A G Edwards & Sons PO Bpx 1587 Bloomington IL 61702

GLOWER, DONALD DUANE, university executive, mechanical engineer; b. Shelby, Ohio, July 29, 1926; s. Raymond W.W. and Irva (Scheerer) G.; m. Betty Stahl, June 18, 1953; children: Donald, Michel, Leilani, Jacob. BS, U.S. Mcht. Marine Acad., 1946, Antioch Coll., 1953; MS, Iowa State U., 1958, PhD, 1960; M of Pub. Svc., U. Rio Grande, 1992. Engring. officer Grace Lines, Inc., San Francisco, 1947-49; research engr. Battelle Meml. Inst., Columbus, Ohio, 1953-54; asst. prof. Coll. Engring., Iowa State U., 1954-58, 60-61; mem. research staff Sandia Corp., Albuquerque, 1961-63; head radiation effects dept. Gen. Motors Corp., Milw., 1963-64; prof., chmn. dept. mech. and nuclear engring. Ohio State U., 1964-76, dean Coll. Engring., 1976-90, v.p. univ. com. and devel., 1990-92; Honourable prof. Xidian U., Xian, China, 1992; bd. dirs. Chipworks Inc., Internat. Techne Group Inc., Superconductive Components, Inc., Transp. Rsch. Ctr. of Ohio; mem., vice chmn. Ohio Power Siting Bd., 1990; mem. Internat. Cons. Bd. S.E. U., Nanjing, China, 1991. Author: Graphical Theory and Application, 1957, Basic Drawing and Projection, 1957, Working Drawings and Applied Graphics, 1957, Experimental Reactor Analysis and Radiation Measurements, 1965. Bd. dirs. Indsl. Tech Enterprise Bd. Ohio, 1982-89, Orton Found., 1976-90; trustee U. Rio Grande. Recipient Outstanding Bus. Achievement award U.S. Mcht. Marine Acad., 1961; Outstanding Profl. Achievement award Iowa State U., 1979; spl. citation Ohio Senate and Ho. of Reps., 1985; named Tech. Person of Yr., Columbus Tech. Council, 1986. Fellow Am. Nuclear Soc.; fellow ASME; mem. Am. Soc. Engring. Edn. (Donald E. Marlowe award 1987), Ohio Acad. Sci., Argonne Univs. Assn., Sigma Xi, Tau Beta Pi, Texnikoi.

GLOYD, LAWRENCE EUGENE, diversified manufacturing company executive; b. Milan, Ind., Nov. 5, 1932; s. Oran C. and Ruth (Baylor) G.; m. Delma Lear, Sept. 10, 1955; children: Sheryl, Julia, Susan. BA, Hanover Coll., 1954. Salesman Shapleigh Hardware, St. Louis, 1956-60, W. Bingham Co., Cleve., 1960-61; salesman Amerock Corp., Rockford, Ill., 1961-68, regional sales mgr., 1968-69, dir. consumer products mktg., 1969-71, dir. merchandising, 1971-72, dir. mktg. and sales, 1972-73, v.p. mktg. and sales, 1973-81, exec. v.p., 1981-82, pres., gen. mgr., 1982-86; v.p. Hardware Products Group, Anchor Hocking Corp., Lancaster, Ohio, 1983-86; pres., chief oper. officer CLARCOR, Rockford, Ill., 1986-95, chmn. bd., CEO, 1995—, also bd. dirs.; bd. dirs. AMcore Fin. Inc., Rockford, Thomas Industries Inc., Louisville, G.U.D. Holdings Ltd., Melbourne, Australia, Woodward Gov. Co., Rockford, Ill.; past. chmn. bd. trustees Rockford Coll.; mem. Middle West adv. bd. Liberty Mut. Ins. Co.; chmn. SwedishAm. Corp. Bd. dirs. Coun. of 100; bd. dirs. Ill. Coun. on Econ. Edn.; nat. bd. dirs. Big Bros./Big Sisters. Mem. Am. Hardware Mfrs. Assn., Ill. Mfrs. Assn., Nat. Assn. Mfrs., Hardware Group Assn., Pres. Assn., Masons. Republican. Office: CLARCOR PO Box 7007 2323 6th St Rockford IL 61125

GLUKLICK, EDWARD, construction executive; b. Toronto, Ont., Can., Oct. 23, 1921; came to U.S., 1925; s. Samuel and Annie (Freed) G.; m. Shirley Lee Belkin, Nov. 18, 1945; children: Peter, Daniel, Karen. Grad., Cass Tech. H.S., Detroit, 1939. Cert. builder, Mich.; arbitrator, AAA; environ. inspector, environ. assessment assoc., Ariz. Salesman various cities, 1939-42; pres. Gluck Constrn. Co., Huntington Woods, Mich., 1945-77; v.p. Fogel and Assoc. of Mich., Detroit, 1975-90; pres. Gluck Group, Inc., Oak Park, Mich., 1990—; cons. various surety cos., 1954—; lect. Chgo. Bar Assn., Mich. State Bar, Nat. Assn. Minority Contractors, Profl. Edn. Assn., 1972-90. Contbr. articles to profl. jours.; composer classical piano music. Served to 1st lt. USAF, 1944-45. Mem. ABA (surety-fidelity com.). Office: Gluck Group 13705 W 11 Mile Rd Oak Park MI 48237

GLYNN, NATALIE JO, physical therapist, athletic trainer, emergency medical technician; b. Ft. Gordon, Ga., Aug. 7, 1966; d. Paul Michael Nourie and Sharon Ann (Doris) Kent; m. Douglas Paul Glynn, Sept. 14, 1991. AA, Kaukaku (Ill.) C.C., 1986; BS in Phys. Therapy, U. Health Sci., Chgo. Med. Sch, 1990. Lic. EMT, Ill. Phys. therapist, athletic trainer Dreyer Med. Clinic, Aurora, Ill., 1990—. Mem. Am. Phys. Therapy Assn., Nat. Athletic Trainers Assn. Roman Catholic.

GNAT, RAYMOND EARL, librarian; b. Milw., Jan. 15, 1932; s. John and Emily (Syperko) G.; m. Jean Helen Monday, June 19, 1954; children—Cynthia, Barbara, Richard. B.B.A., U. Wis., 1954, postgrad., 1959; M.S., U. Ill., 1958; M.P.A., Ind. U., Indpls., 1981. Page Milw. Pub. Library, 1950-53, jr. librarian, 1954, librarian, 1958-63; circulation asst. U. Ill., 1956-57, serials cataloger, 1957-58; asst. dir. Indpls.-Marion County Pub. Library, 1963-71, dir., 1972-94; Exec. dir. Ind. Nat. Library Week, 1965. Served with AUS, 1954-56. Mem. ALA, Ind. Library Assn. (pres. 1980), Bibliog. Soc. Am. Clubs: Literary, The Portfolio. Home: 8246 Shadow Cir Indianapolis IN 46260-2761

GNIRK, LLOYD ALLEN, clergyman, educational administrator; b. Norfolk, Nebr., June 5, 1952; s. Lloyd William and Betty (Reuter) G. BA in French, U. St. Thomas, St. Paul, 1974; MDiv, St. Paul Sem., 1978; MS in Secondary Adminstrn., Creighton U., 1984. Cert. tchr. and adminstr., Nebr.; ordained priest Roman Catholic Ch., 1978. Assoc. pastor St. Patrick Parish, Fremont, Nebr., 1978-81; tchr./campus ministry Bergan High Sch., Fremont, 1978-81; pres. St. Joseph High Sch., Omaha, 1983-89; tchr. Roncalli High Sch., Omaha, 1981-83, pres., 1989—. Mem. Mayor's Clergy Adv. Bd., Omaha, 1991—, chmn., 1993-95. Recipient Outstanding Devel. award Archdiocese of Omaha, 1991. Mem. Nat. Cath. Edn. Assn. (regional assoc. 1990—), Rotary Club Omaha (bd. dirs. 1992-95, sec. 1993-94). Democrat. Home: 4102 S 13th St Omaha NE 68107-2315 Office: Roncalli High Sch 6401 Sorensen Pky Omaha NE 68152-2241

GNODTKE, CARL F., state legislator; b. Jan. 2, 1936; m. Mary Jane Frame; children: Julie, Jacquie, Calvin, Lora, Charles (dec.). Rep. Mich. Dist. 43, 1978-92, Mich. Dist. 78, 1993—; commr. Berrien County, Mich., drain commr.; twp. officer; bd. dirs. Berrien County Parks and Recreation Commn., Bd. Pub. Works; mem. conservation com. Mich. Ho. Reps., recreation & environ. com., pub. health com., towns and counties com., minority vice chmn. agrl. com., vice chmn. labor com., bus. & fin. com., conservation, environ. & great lakes affairs com.; dir. Galien River Soil Conservation Dist.; bd. dirs. Berrien County Econ. Devel. Corp.; farmer. Mem. Farm Bur. Home: 12211 Baldwin Rd Sawyer MI 49125-9135*

GO, ROBERT A., management consultant; b. July 29, 1955; s. Michael and Sabina (Tan) G. BS, U Detriot, 1977; MBA, U. Santa Clara, 1981. Nat. ptnr. Deloitte & Touche (formerly Touche Ross & Co.), Detroit, 1977—; Contbr. articles to profl. jours. Mem. Health Care Fin. Mgt. Assn., Am. Hosp. Assn., Renaissance Club. Office: Deloitte & Touche 600 Renaissance Ctr 10th Fl Detroit MI 48243

GOAR, JAMES VERNON, JR., real estate broker; b. Kirklin, Ind., Dec. 30, 1919. AB, Earlham Coll., Richmond, Ind., 1946; MBA, Harvard U., Boston, 1948. Asst. bus. mgr. Richmond In Palladium-Item, Ind., 1948-50; ptnr. J.V. Goar & Son, Frankfort, Ind., 1950-55; owner Goal Assocs., Realtors, Frankfort, Ind., 1955—. Capt. U.S. Army AC, 1941-45. Home: 451 S Harrison St Frankfort IN 46041-2406

GOCIAL, TAMMY MARIE, educational administrator; b. Chgo., June 9, 1965; d. Guenther and Amelia Louise (Santos) G. BSEd, Northwestern U., 1986; MA, Bowling Green State U., 1989; postgrad., St. Louis U., 1994—. Asst. dir. student activities Lorain County C.C., Elyria, Ohio, 1986-87; coord. Student Wellness Ctr. Bowling Green (Ohio) State U., 1987-88; coord. student activities Washington U., St. Louis, 1988-91; coord. wellness programs Maryville U., St. Louis, 1991-93; asst. to v.p. for student svcs. Webster U., St. Louis, 1993-95, asst. dean students, 1995—; cons. Northeastern U., Boston, 1989, Webster U., St. Louis, 1991, St. Louis C.C., 1991. Vol. crisis counselor Women's Resource Ctr., YWCA, St. Louis, 1989-94; vol. judge Nat. Sr. Olympics, St. Louis, 1990; tng. facilitator A World of Difference, St. Louis, 1991-95. Mem. ACA, APA, AAUW (Career Devel. grantee 1995-96), Am. Coll. Pers. Assn. (stnding com. directorate 1990-94, planning com. nat. conv. 1989), Mo. Coll. Pers. Assn. (exec. com. 1989-95, pres. 1992-95). Home: 6509 Laconia Dr Saint Louis MO 63123-2619 Office: Webster Univ 470 E Lockwood Ave Saint Louis MO 63119-3141

GOCKLEY, BARBARA JEAN, corporate professional; b. Pitts., July 26, 1951; d. William Ervin and Dorothy Marie (Wolf) Cain; m. William Lee Gockley, Mar. 29, 1975 (div. Aug. 1989); children: Ervin Cain, Marianne Cain, William Cain, Malinda Cain. Student, Indiana U. Pa., 1969-71, Thomas Edison State Coll., 1986-88; BA in Bus. Mgmt. and Mktg. Mgmt., Alvernia Coll., 1993. Cert. in purchasing mgmt. Asst. materials mgr. Redman Mobile Homes, Ephrata, Pa., 1972-75; mgr. inventory control Gym-Kin, Inc., Reading, Pa., 1975-77; supr. prodn./inventory control Wyomissing Converting, Reading, 1979-82; mgr. prodn./inventory control Dorma Door Controls, Inc., Reamstown, Pa., 1982-85, project mgr., 1985-86; materials mgr. Powder Coatings Group-Morton Internat., Reading, 1986-94; dir. purchasing Dexter Corp., Waukegan, Ill., 1994—; dir. programs Congress for Progress Inc., 1984-88, vice chmn., 1988-89, chmn., 1989-90; dir. programs Pansophic/ASD User Group Internat. Conf., 1991, 92; instr. Berks Campus, Pa. State U., Reading, 1985-86. Dir. Reinholds (Pa.) PTA, 1978-81; bd. dirs. Cocalico Sch. Bd., Denver, Pa., 1985-89. Mem. Am. Prodn. and Inventory Control Soc. (cert. prodn. and inventory mgmt., treas. Schuylkill Valley chpt. 1981-82, pres. 1982-84, dir. membership region IX 1985-86, asst. v.p. 1987, v.p. 1988-89, Internat. Vol. Svc. award 1986), Nat. Assn. Purchasing Mgrs., Assn. Mfg. Excellence, NAFE, Am. Bus. Women's Assn., Soc. Mfg. Engrs., Mothers of Twins Club (nominating chmn. Lancaster, Pa. 1977-78). Republican. Presbyterian. Office: Dexter Corp East Water St Waukegan IL 60085

GODDARD, LINDA ANN, insurance company official; b. Chgo., Nov. 30, 1953; d. John Joseph and Rose Marie (Mungovan) West; m. Gregory M. Goddard, Feb. 6, 1993. AAS, Southwest Coll., 1973. Asst. to pres. Brokers Risk Placement Svc., Chgo., 1979-80; with CNA Ins., Chgo., 1980—; staff asst. to pres. comml. ops. dept. CNA Ins. Cos., Chgo., 1984—. Roman Catholic. Home: 11106 S Lawler Ave Worth IL 60482-2236 Office: CNA Ins Cos CNA Plz # 40S Chicago IL 60685

GODDARD, SANDRA KAY, elementary education educator; b. Steubenville, Ohio, Oct. 31, 1947; d. Albert Leonard and Mildred Irene (Hill) G. BS in Edn., Miami U., Oxford, Ohio, 1969; MEd, Miami U., 1973. Tchr. elem. grades Gregg Elem.-Edison Local Schs. Dist., Hammondsville, Ohio, 1969—; mem. curriculum and textbook com. Jefferson County Schs., Steubenville, 1994-95; active Spl. Olympics, 1992, 93; presenter in field. Publicity chmn., rec. sec., box office chmn. Steubenville Players, 1981-83; mem. Edison Local Adv. Coun. on Drug Edn., 1987—; mem. Edison Local Curriculum Instrn. Com., 1993—; state judge Ashland Oil Tchr. Achievement awards, 1988-90; regional and state judge Odyssey of the Mind, 1992—, bd. dirs. region XI, 1993-94, regional dir. Region XI, 1994—, state bd. dirs. Ohio Odyssey of the Mind, 1994—; exec. com. Gregg Elem. PTO, 1990-92; instr. 1st aid and cmty. CPR, ARC, 1990—, instr.-trainer 1993—, county disaster team. Martha Holden Jennings scholar, 1972-73; minigrantee Jefferson County Schs., 1991, 94. Mem. NEA (del. to rep. assembly 1979, 85, 86, 87, 88), Ohio Edn. Assn. (exec. com. 1983-89, pres.'s cabinet 1985-87, appeals bd. 1994—), Ea. Ohio Edn. Assn. (pres. 1978-79, exec. com. 1983-89), Edison Local Edn. Assn. (pres. 1974-75, v.p. 1986-88, 89-91, exec. com. 1991-94, mem. negotiation's team 1987, 90, 93), Ohio Valley UNISERV Coun. (treas. 1986-92), Delta Kappa Gamma (legis. chair 1990-92). Democrat. Methodist. Home: 200 Fernwood Rd Apt 11 Steubenville OH 43952-9200 Office: Gregg Elem Sch RR 1 Bergholz OH 43908-9801

GODFREY, JOYZELLE EFFIE, economic development and small business consultant; b. Ft. Thompson, S.D., Jan. 18, 1942; d. Lawrence Michael and Nina Mae (Menzie) Gingway; m. Gene Rilling, Sept. 1963 (div. May 1970); children: Rodney, Mike, Neil, Nicolle, Yvette; m. Jerry Dean Godfrey, Sept. 1985 (div. Nov. 1993). BS, Black Hill State U., 1973; MPA, U. S.D., 1985. Mgr. Lakota Devel. Coun. St. Joseph's Indian Sch., Chamberlain, S.D., 1989—; small bus. cons. to Native Am. enterpreneurs. Author of poetry and short stories. Humanities scholar. Mem. Lambda Iota Tau Soc. Home: PO Box 257 Fort Thompson SD 57339-0257 Office: PO Box 440 Fort Thompson SD 57339

GODOLLEI, RUTHANN, artist, educator; b. South Bend, Ind., Mar. 9, 1958; d. Paul B. and Lois (Tenbeig) G. BFA, Ind. U., 1981; MFA, U. Minn., 1984. Printing mgr. Schmitt Music Co., Mpls., 1983-85; head screen printer Vermillion Editions Ltd., Mpls., 1985; lectr. art U. Minn., Mpls., 1987-90; lectr. art Macalester Coll., St. Paul, 1986-91, asst. prof. art, 1991—; mem./curator Rifle Sport Alternative Art Gallery, Mpls., 1986-89; columnist CAKE mag., Mpls., 1993—; lectr./spkr. in field. Solo exhbns. include Art Ctr. of Winona, Minn., 1995, Coll. St. Benedict, St. Joseph, Minn., 1995; group shows include Peninsula Fine Arts Ctr., Newport News, 1995, "Under Pressure," juried nat. show, Mesa, Ariz., 1995. Main organizer Quasi-ann. Auto Art Show, 1986—. Recipient Beller award MTN Network Cable TV, Mpls., 1987; Forecast, Inc. and City of St. Paul Installation grantee, 1987, Film in the Cities/Am. Film Inst. grantee, 1985. Mem. AAUP, Coll. Art Assn. Office: Macalester College 1600 Grand Ave Saint Paul MN 55105

GODWIN, DAVID FRANK, editor; b. Dallas, Jan. 21, 1939; s. Cyril Oliver and Serena Lily (Paige) G. BJ, U. Tex., 1961. Reporter Killeen (Tex.) Daily Herald, 1963-64; depts. editor Gulf Pub. Co., Houston, 1964-66; tech. editor ITT Fed. Electric (NASA contract), Houston, 1966-71; typesetter various orgns. Dallas, Houston, Atlanta, 1971-90; sr. editor Llewellyn Publs., St. Paul, 1990-95; exec. editor Galde Press, St. Paul, 1995—. Author: Light in Extension, 1992, Godwin's Cabalistic Encyclopedia, 1979, 89, The Truth About Cabala, 1995, How to Choose Your Own Tarot, 1995; contbr. articles to Dragon and Fate mags. Staff sgt. U.S. Air N.G., 1962-68. Mem. Masons (master St. Paul lodge # 3 1996). Home: 17110 Hershey Ct Lakeville MN 55044-9041 Office: Galde Press Inc PO Box 460 Lakeville MN 55044

GOEBEL, DAVID MAXWELL, career officer; b. Glen Ridge, N.J., Oct. 6, 1939; s. Maxwell Henry and Ruth (Fenton) G.; m. Earline Shane Berry, June 13, 1964; children: Karen Elizabeth, Thomas Matthew. BS, U.S. Naval Acad., 1962; MS, MIT, 1965, MS in Nuc. Engring., 1966. Commd. ensign USN, 1962, advanced through grades to rear adm.; ops. officer USS Kamehameha, Groton, Conn., 1970-74; exec. officer USS Lafeyette, Groton, 1974-78; ops. officer USS Benjamin Franklin, Groton, 1978-81; comsublant rep. Portsmouth (N.H.) Naval Shipyard, 1981-83; sr. mem. nuc. propulsion examining bd. Atlantic Fleet, Norfolk, Va., 1983-85; comdr. Submarine Squadron 14, Holy Loch, Scotland, 1985-87; dep. dir. strategic submarine divsn. Office of CNO, Washington, 1987-89, force level plans officer, 1991-92; dir. internat. negotiations Office of CJCS, Washington, 1989-91; comdr. Submarine Group 2, Groton, 1992-94; plans and policy officer U.S. Strategic Command, Omaha, 1994—. Trustee Mystic (Conn.) Marinelife Aquarium, 1983—; mem. gov. bd. Cardinal Spellman Sch., Omaha, 1995—. Decorated various milit. awards. Mem. Elks. Home: Quarters 12 Offutt AFB NE 68113 Office: US Strategic Command SAC Blvd Offutt AFB NE 68113

GOEBEL, RICHARD ALAN, veterinarian; b. Wabash, Ind., Mar. 16, 1944; s. Meredith Clair and Lavonne Eileen (Leyman) G.; m. Michele J., June 18, 1966; Heidi C., Ross C., Heather E. DVM, Purdue U., 1968. Ptnr. Hafner Vet. Clinic, Huntington, Ind., 1968-69; dir. Monrovia (Calif.) Animal Hosp., 1970-77, Magrane Animal Hosp., Mishawaka, Ind., 1979—, Maplecrest Animal Hosp., Goshen, Ind., 1984-88; veterinarian Potawatami Zoo, South Bend, Ind., 1982-85; chmn. bd. Animal Emergency Clinic, Inc., South Bend, 1983-84; dir. vet. teaching hosp. Purdue U. Sch. Vet. Medicine, W. Lafayette, Ind., 1988—. Edit. cons. Jour. Am. Animal Hosp. Assn., 1982-85. Moderator Jefferson Brethren Ch., Goshen, 1983-84, deacon, 1985-87. Mem. AVMA, Am. Animal Hosp. Assn. (area dir. 1985-88, regional dir. 1988-94), Assn. Avian Veterinarians, Am. Assn. Veterinary Clinicians, Vet. Mgmt. Group I, Michiana Vet. Med. Assn. (treas. 1984, sec. 1985, v.p. 1986, pres. 1988), West Ctrl. Ind. Vet. Med. Assn., Ind. Vet. Med. Assn. (non-practice award 1992, Veterinarian of Yr. 1995), So. Calif. Vet. Med. Assn., Dean's Club, Pres.'s Coun., Calif. Vet. Med. Assn. (chmn. ho. of dels. 1976), Purdue Vet. Alumni Assn. (pres. 1985-86), World Small Animal Vet. Assn., Phi Zeta, Alpha Zeta, Gamma Sigma Delta. Republican. Presbyterian. Office: Magrane Animal Hosp 2324 Grape Rd Mishawaka IN 46545-3006 Office: Purdue U Vet Teaching Hosp Veterinary Teaching Hosp 1249 Lynn Hall West Lafayette IN 47907

GOEDDE, TONY G., registrar; b. Lima, Ohio, Nov. 19, 1964; s. Norman B. and Angela I. (Schmenk) G.; m. Allison M. Arico, Sept. 16, 1995. BS in Edn., Bowling Green State U., 1987, MA, 1989. Registrar U. of Findlay, Ohio, 1989—. Home: 900 Laurel Ln Findlay OH 45840

GOEGLEIN, GLORIA J., state legislator; b. Ft. Wayne, Ind., Jan. 13, 1931; d. Alton F. and Nellie I. (Black) Woods; m. Leonard O. Goeglein, Oct. 17, 1954; children: Julia, Chris, Mark. Auditor Allen County, Ind., 1979-86; purchasing dir. City of Ft. Wayne, 1988-90; mem. Ind. Ho. of Reps., Indpls., 1990—; mem. Ways and Means Com., 1993-95, Govtl. Affairs Com., 1991-94, Cities and Town Com., 1991-92, Autism Commn., 1991-94, Local Govt. Fin. Study Commn., 1991-94, Mental Health Commn., 1994—, chair, 1996; mem. Interim Study Com. on State Govt. Mgmt. Issues, 1994, Local Govt. Com., 1995—, chair, 1996; mem. Ind. Adv. Commn. on Intergovernmental Rels., 1995—, Interim Study Com. on State Mgmt. Issues, 1995, Families, Children and Human Affairs Com., 1996, Mental Health Practices Study Com., chair, 1996; mem. Interim Study Com. on Procurement Law, 1996. Mem. Allen County Coun., 1974-78, v.p., 1975-78. Home: 9339 Maysville Rd Fort Wayne IN 46815-5820

GOEL, ASHOK KUMAR, electrical engineering educator; b. Kaithal, Haryana, India, Sept. 4, 1953; came to U.S., 1977; s. Daya Nand and Kamal Goel; m. Sangita Gupta, Feb. 14, 1982; children: Sumeet Kumar, Rachna Shikha. BS with honors, Panjab U., Chandigarh, India, 1972, MS with honors, 1973; MPhil, CUNY, 1982; PhD, Johns Hopkins U., 1987. Asst. prof. Mich. Technol. U., Houghton, 1987-91, assoc. prof., 1991—; mem. summer internat. engring. program Oxford U., 1995; faculty Oreg. Grad. Inst. of Sci. and Tech., 1996. Author: High-Speed VLSI Interconnections, 1994, John Wiley & Sons, Inc.; contbr. numerous papers to profl. jours. Recipient Rsch. Initiation award NSF, 1987; rsch. grantee USAF Office of Sci. Rsch., 1990, GM Rsch. Labs., 1991, NSF, 1993; faculty rsch. grantee Wright-Patterson AFB, 1990, Griffiss AFB, 1991, U.S. Army Missile Command, 1992. Mem. IEEE, Am. Soc. for Engring. Edn., Internat. Soc. Computers and their Applications, Internat. Assn. Math. and Computer Modeling, Sigma Xi. Office: Mich Technol U Dept Elec Engring Houghton MI 49931

GOERS, SARAJANE, community education nurse; b. Clinton, Iowa, Apr. 5, 1946; d. Charles Maurice and Sarah Mardelle (Nichols) Cavanagh; m. Donald Fred Goers, Sept. 22, 1972 (dec. Mar. 1991); children: Christine M., Sarah E., Donald E. Diploma, Mercy Sch. Nursing, Iowa City, 1966; student, U. Iowa, 1969-71. RN, Ill., Iowa. Staff Mercy Hosp., Clinton, 1964-66, staff, nursing relief supr., 1966-68; staff, nursing relief supr. U. Iowa Hosp. Clinics, Iowa City, 1968-69, head nurse, 1969-71; with surg. intensive care Rockford (Ill.) Meml. Hosp., 1971-74, head nurse, 1974-77; patient edn./nursing supr. Freeport (Ill.) Meml. Hosp., 1977-90, RN community edn./svc., 1990—. Advisor Stephenson County Sr. Ctr., Freeport, 1991—. Mem. Am. Lung Assn. (bd. dirs. 1988—), Am. Cancer Soc. (bd. dirs., prevention early detection chair, reach/recovery trainer 1980—), Am. Bus. Woman's Assn. (sec. 1987-90, pres. 1993, Woman of Yr. 1992), Am. Ostomy Assn., Am. Diabetes Assn., Quota Club Internat. (rec. sec.). Home: 22 N Stewart Ave Freeport IL 61032-3754 Office: Freeport Meml Hosp 1045 W Stephenson St Freeport IL 61032-4864

GOETSCH, ROBERT GEORGE, state legislator; b. Juneau, Wis., Aug. 5, 1933; 010s. Elmer Allen and Dorothy (Stein) G.; m. Carolyn Helen Koboski, 1974; children: Chad Evan, Shana Renee. BS, U. W. Madison, 1975. Farmer Juneau; mem. from dist. 39 Wis. State Assembly, Madison, 1982—. Exch. del. to Rhodesia, Internat. Farm Youth Exch., 1962-63; county supr., Dodge County, Wis., 1972-83; chmn. Town of Oak Grove, Wis., 1971-82. Mem. Nat. Farmers Orgn., Am. Legion, Elks, Phi Kappa Phi. Home: N6485 High Point Rd Juneau WI 53039-9750*

GOETTSCHE, JIM J., manufacturing engineer; b. Grand Island, Nebr., July 22, 1943. Pres., owner Goettsche Electronics, Grand Island, Nebr., 1969-79; mgr. R & D Chief Industries, Grand Island, Nebr., 1979-90; gen. mgr. Greystone Inc., Columbus, Nebr., 1990—. Dr. chmn. United Way, Columbus, Nebr. Mem. Soc. Mfg. Engrs. (chmn. 1974-94). Roman Catholic. Office: Greystone Incorp PO Box 904 4530 19th St Columbus NE 68601-2954

GOETZ, MICHAEL BLAINE, aircraft company executive; b. Sault St. Marie, Mich., Jan. 12, 1937; s. Charles Alexander and Leone Mae (Firkus) G.; m. Patricia Margaret Goll, Aug. 17, 1958; children: Michael, David, Susan, Brian. BS in Aero. Mech. Engring., St. Louis U., 1959; M in Engring. Adminstrn., George Washington U., 1967; student, Air U., 1978. Lic. comml. pilot single and multi engine; cert. flight instr.; cert. engine and airframe mechanic; cert. aviation ground instr. Commd. 2d lt. USAF, 1959, advanced through grades to col., 1978; aircraft maintenance officer 78th Fighter Group, Hamilton AFB, Calif., 1959-62; missile launch ops. officer ICBM 1st Strategic Missile Divsn., Vandenberg AFB, Calif., 1962-64; missile range ops. officer Air Force Western Test Range, Vandenberg AFB, 1964-66; air force plant rep. for engine devel. GE Co., Evendale, Ohio, 1971-73; prof. dept. head of aero. studies Mich. Technol. U., Houghton, 1973-78; dir. strategic engines program office Aero. Sys. Divsn. WPAFB, Dayton, Ohio, 1978-80; dep. dir. materials lab. Wright Aero. Labs. WPAFB, Dayton, 1980-83; ret. USAF, 1983; regional mgr. Great Lakes Region Raytheon Aircraft Corp. Beechcraft/Hawker, Dayton, 1983-95; dir., treas. Beech Mil. Regional Office Inc., Wichita, 1993-95; bd. advisors Wright State U. Coll. Bus., Dayton, 1989-95; treas., dir. Beech Aircraft Mil. Regional Offices, Inc., Dayton, 1993-95. Bd. advisors airport users group Lewis A. Jackson Regional Airport, Xenia, Ohio, 1994-95. Decorated Legion of Merit, USAF, 1983; recipient Guiding Light award Air Force Wright Aero. Labs., 1986. Mem. AIAA, SAE Engring. Soc., Nat. Aviation Hall Fame, Exptl. Aircraft Assn. (Spark Plug award 1970), Am. Def. Preparedness Assn., U.S. Naval Inst. Republican. Roman Catholic. Home: 3101 Maginn Dr Beavercreek

OH 45434-5835 Office: Beech Aircraft Corp Wright Point Office Park 5200 Springfield Pike Dayton OH 45431-1265

GOETZ, RAYMOND, law educator, labor arbitrator; b. Rockford, Ill., May 14, 1922; s. Fred J. and Irma W. (Rathke) G.; m. Elizabeth Morey, Apr. 24, 1951; children: Raymond, Sibyl Goetz Wescoe, Thomas, Victoria, Steven, Morey. JD, U. Chgo., 1950, MBA, 1963. Bar: Ill. 1950, Kans. 1966. Assoc. Seyfarth, Shaw, Fairweather & Geraldson, Chgo., 1950-57, ptnr., 1957-66; prof. law U. Kans., Lawrence, 1966-87, prof. emeritus, 1987—; permanent umpire Ford Motor Co. and UAW, Detroit, 1984-89; salary arbitrator Major League Baseball, N.Y.C., 1984-91; mem. arbitration panel AT&T, Communications Workers Am., 1988-96. Trustee Village of Northfield (Ill.), 1955-57, Kans. Pub. Employees Retirement System, Topeka, 1968-76. Lt. (j.g.) USNR, 1943-47, PTO. Mem. ABA (sec. sect. labor law 1977-78, neutral co-chmn. com. on labor arbitration 1980-83), Nat. Acad. Arbitrators (bd. govs. 1992-95), Indsl. Rels. Rsch. Assn. (exec. bd. Kansas City chpt. 1968—), Am. Arbitration Assn. (labor arbitrator 1967-96). Office: U Kans Sch Law Lawrence KS 66045

GOETZ, ROBERT J., chemical engineer; b. St. Louis, June 22, 1962. Student, U. St. Louis, 1980-82; BSChemE, U. Mo., Rolla, 1984. Quality control mgr. Raskas Dairy, St. Louis, 1984-90; project engr. Dairy Svs. and Mfg. Inc., St. Louis, 1990—; tech. com. Nat. Conf. Interstate Milk Shipment, Ames, Iowa, 1993. Mem. St. Margaret Mary Ch., St. Louis, 1984—, coach soccer and softball, 1991—. Mem. AIChE. Roman Catholic.

GOETZ, WILLIAM G., state legislator; b. Hazen, N.D., Jan. 6, 1944; s. Otto E. and Elfrieda (Knoop) G.; m. Marion R. Schock, 1970; children: Marcia, Paul, Mark. AA, Bismarck Jr. Coll., 1964; BA, Minot State Coll., 1966; MA, U. N.D., 1967. Asst. mgr. Medora divsn. Gold Seal Co., 1963-70; dean sch. bus. and adminstrn. Dickinson State U., 1967; state rep. dist. 37, 1975-90, state senator, 1990—; chmn. Rep. Ho. Caucus; asst. majority leader, vice chmn. fin. and tax. com. N.D. Ho. Reps., 1975-90; asst. minority leader; mem. appropriations com., asst. majority leader N.D. State Senate, 1990—. Chmn. dist. 37 Rep. com., 1976—, mem. exec. com.; appointed by pres. to Nat. Coun. for Edn. Rsch. and Improvement. Recipient Pub. Svc. award N.D. Lignite Coun. Mem. Greater N.D. Assn. (formerly bd. dirs., Educator of Yr.), Nat. Conf. State Legislators. Republican. Home: 251 Allen St Dickinson ND 58601-4042*

GOFF, WILMER SCOTT, photographer; b. Steubenville, Ohio, July 11, 1923; s. Floyd Orville and Ellen Armenia (Funk) G.; m. Mary Elizabeth Fischer, Dec. 7, 1950; children: Carolyn, Christopher. BFA with honors, Ohio U., 1949. Photographer Columbus (Ohio) Dispatch, 1949-52, Warner P. Simpson, Columbus, 1952-53; owner Willy Goff Photo Studio, Grove City, Ohio, 1954-59; photographer N.Am. Rockwell, Columbus, 1953-70; supr. Transp. Rsch. Ctr. Ohio, East Liberty, 1970-89; adult edn. instr. photography Upper Arlington and Worthington Schs., 1989-95; photography instr. Columbus Coll. Art and Design, 1949-71; photography judge Ohio State Fair, 1966-68; judge Greater Columbus Film Festival, 1970-72; photographer John Glenn campaign, 1974. One man shows include 100 print exhibit Southern Hotel, Columbus, 1953. Recipient Public's Choice award Columbus Art Gallery, 1958, Photo-Pictoral 1st Pl. award Dix Newspapers, 1960, Best of Show award Balloon Show Competition, 1985. Mem. Aircraft Camera Club (pres. 1954-55), Grove City Camera CLub (pres. 1959-60). Republican. Roman Catholic. Home: 6110 Darby Ln Columbus OH 43229-2628

GOFORTH, MARY ELAINE DAVEY, secondary education educator; b. Barnesville, Ohio, Sept. 9, 1922; d. Frederick Richard and Lola (Knox) Davey; m. Richard Eugene Goforth, Sept. 9, 1944; 1 child, Diane Lynell Goforth-Ohning. B.M.Ed., Oberlin Coll., 1944; MA in Edn., Coll. of Mt. St. Joseph, 1987. Cert. edn. Music tchr. Leipsig, Ohio, 1944-45, Perry Local, 1945-47; English tchr. Ohio No. Univ., 1946; English and music tchr. Perry Sch., Lima, Ohio, 1945-47; English tchr. Stone Creek, Ohio, 1947-51, Barnesville, Ohio, 1952-53, Tuscarawas, Ohio, 1957-59; English tchr. Conotton Valley Sch., Bowerston, Ohio, 1960-62; English tchr. New Philadelphia, Ohio, 1964-68, Indian Valley, Midvale, Ohio, 1973-88, Indian Valley, Gnadenhetten, Ohio, 1988-93. Author poems. Pres. New Philadelphia (Ohio) Tchrs.' Assn., 1967. Named Indian Valley Tchr. of Yr., 1985, Candidate for Ohio Tchr. of the Yr., 1985; Martha Holden Jennings scholar, 1985. Home: 2123 E High Ave New Philadelphia OH 44663-3323

GOGOLA, FRANK XAVIER, JR, information technology executive, consultant; b. Berwyn, Ill., Nov. 27, 1956; s. Frank Xavier and Ann (Ganas) G.; m. Elena Fratto Gogola, Oct. 6, 1990; children: Frank Xavier III, Joseph Vincent. BS, No. Ill. U., DeKalb, 1978; MBA, Loyola U. Chgo., 1989. Cert. network engr. Acct. exec. Republic Printing, Geneva, Ill., 1979-80; acct. Mid Am. Fed. Savings Bank, Clarendon Hills, Ill., 1980-84; controller Maywood (Ill.) Park Trotting Assn., 1985-88; office/lan mgr. Koppers Industries, Stickney, Ill., 1988-89; mgr. Info. Tech. The Ednl. Found. of the Nat. Restaurant Assn., Chgo., 1990—; customer adv. bd. Digital Consulting Andover, Mass., 1992; career cons. network Loyola U., Chgo., 1992—; bus. adv. coun. Program Able, Chgo., 1993—. Recipient Small Bus. Adminstrn. Excellence in Consulting award, 1978. Mem. Network Profls. Assn., Data Processing Mgmt. Assn., Computer Security Inst. Office: Ednl Found of the National Restaurant Assn 250 S Wacker Dr Ste 1400 Chicago IL 60606

GOH, ANTHONY LI-SHING, business owner, consultant; b. Cleve., Apr. 14, 1954; s. Albert Goh and May C. (Chang) Wong; m. Renee Jean Kropat, Oct. 3, 1981; children: Anthony Tian-Fenn, Andrew Li-Shing. BS in Elec. Engring., U. Mich., 1975; MBA, U. Dayton, 1982. Sales engr. Toledo Scale, Mpls., 1975-76; application engr. Toledo Scale, Columbus, Ohio, 1976-77; product specialist Toledo Scale, Columbus, 1977-78, product mgr., 1978-80; internat. mktg. mgr. Toledo Scale, Benecia, Calif., 1980-82, modifications mgr., 1983; mktg. mgr. heavy capacity Toledo Scale, Columbus, 1984-86; v.p., gen. mgr. Ricton Corp., Columbus, 1987-92; owner Li-Shing Enterprises, Westerville, Ohio, 1992-95; product mgr. Mettler-Toledo, 1995—; industry rep. Nat. Bur. Standards, Washigton, 1984-85; distributors coun. Mitel Trillium Phone Systems, Boca Raton, Fla., 1990-91. Mem. Nat. Assn. Telecommunications Dealers (ethics com. 1990). Home: 89 W College Ave Westerville OH 43081-2031

GOHEEN, JANET MOORE, counselor, sales professional; b. Everett, Mass., Sept. 29, 1945; d. Franklin Pierce and Virginia Louise (Murphy) Moore; m. Peter Arthur Goheen, Apr. 2, 1967; children: Kevin Murphy Moore Goheen, Andrew Hudson Moore Goheen. BA, Ohio Wesleyan U., 1967; MS, U. Bridgeport, 1979. Cert. profl. guidance counselor, Ohio. Tchr. English Nordinia Hills High Sch., Macedonia, Ohio, 1967-69, White Plains (N.Y.) High Sch., 1969-71, Hudson (Ohio) High Sch., 1982-83; tchr. emotionally disturbed Palisades Learning Ctr., Paramus, N.J., 1986-87; sales cons. The Longaberger Co., Dresden, Ohio, 1983-84, br. advisor, 1984-90, regional advisor, 1990—; middle sch. counselor Hudson Middle Sch., 1988—; tchr. ESL Hitchcock Presbyn. Ch., Scarsdale, N.Y., 1976-79, Aurora (Ohio) City Schs., 1979-81, Hudson Local Schs., 1980-82. Mem. Jr. League of Scarsdale, 1976-79, Jr. League of Akron, 1979-82, Jr. League No. N.J., Ridgewood, 1983-85; mem. alumni bd. dirs. Ohio Wesleyan U., Delaware, Ohio, 1990-93. Mem. Am. Sch. Counselors Assn., Ohio Sch. Counselors Assn., Kappa Kappa Gamma, Kappa Delta Pi. Home: 97 Manor Dr Hudson OH 44236-3406 Office: Hudson Middle Sch 77 N Oviatt St Hudson OH 44236-3043

GOLBERG, LARRY, insurance company executive; b. Beloit, Wis., Dec. 16, 1931; s. Morris and Ronia (Baskin) G.; m. Nancy Louise Reinicke, Apr. 30, 1956 (div. Dec. 10, 1986); children: Susan L., Gail A., Karen L. BA, Beloit Coll., 1954; MA, Ind. U., 1955. CLU Am. Coll. Life Underwriters, Pa. Asst. mgr. pub. rels., advt. Prudential Ins., Chgo., 1958-66; dir. distbn. CNA Ins., Chgo., 1966-80; owner Lawrence Golberg Gen. Ins., Evanston, Ill., 1980-82; v.p. First Penn Pacific Life Ins. Co., Oak Brook, Ill., 1982-87; mgr. mktg. devel. Zurich Am. Ins. Co., Schaumburg, Ill., 1987—. Trustee Oakton C.C. Dist. 535, 1993—. With U.S. Army, 1956-58. Home: 711 S River Rd #717 Des Plaines IL 60016-4772 Office: Zurich Am Ins Co 1400 American Ln Schaumburg IL 60196

GOLD, DON, magazine editor, author; b. Chgo., Mar. 13, 1931; s. Sidney and Bess (Seidler) G.; divorced; children: Tracy, Paul; remarried Patricia McNabb, 1992. BS in Journalism, Northwestern U., 1952, MS in Journalism, 1953. Mng. editor Down Beat mag., Chgo., 1956-59, Travel and Leisure mag., N.Y.C., 1975-77; assoc. editor Playboy mag., Chgo., 1959-62, mng. editor, 1980-84; assoc. editor Saturday Evening Post, Curtis Pub. Co., N.Y.C., 1962-68, asst. mng. editor Ladies'Home Jour., 1962-68, mng. editor Holiday mag., 1962-68; head lit. dept. William Morris Agy., N.Y.C., 1968-73; editor-in-chief Chicago mag., 1984-87; journalism dept. Columbia Coll., Chgo., 1989-96. Author: Letters to Tracy, 1972, Bellevue, 1975, The Park, 1978, Until the Singing Stops, 1979, The Priest, 1981, Zoo, 1988; contbr. articles to mags., including N.Y. Times Sunday Mag., N.Y. Times Book Rev., Harper's, Holiday, Travel and Leisure, Cosmopolitan, Reader's Digest, Ladies' Home Jour., Playboy. With U.S. Army, 1953-55. Mem. ASME, PEN, Authors Guild. Home: 2423 Thayer St Evanston IL 60201-1495

GOLD, MICHAEL, materials engineer; b. New York, Oct. 21, 1938; s. Murray Abraham and Celia Calfin (Donner) G.; m. Sue Ann Shaffer, May 28, 1967; children: Rebecca Donner Gold Anderson, Daniel Murray, Marjorie Ann. BS in physics, Yale U., New Haven, 1960, ME in metallurgy, 1962; postgrad, Cornell U., Ithaca, 1965. Mgr., materials tech. Babcock & Wilcox, Barberton, Ohio, 1965—. Author (with others): STEAM It's Generation and Use, 1992; patentee non-welded tube support; contbr. articles to profl. jours. Recipient Cert. of Service award, 1984, Cert. of Acclamation, 1992, ASME. Fellow ASME (chmn. subcommittee II on materials main com., exec. com.), mem. ASTM, ASM Internat., Yale Club of New York City, Berlin Yacht Club, US Sailing, Flying Scot Sailing Assn., U.S. Amature Ballroom Dancing Assn. Democrat. Jewish. Home: 8757 Lynn Park St NE Alliance OH 44601 Office: Babcock & Wilcox PO Box 351 Barberton OH 44203-0351

GOLDBERG, BOB, management information systems director, consultant; b. Chgo., Jan. 6, 1964; s. David and Barbara G. Dir. MIS PC Distributing, Elmhurst, Ill., 1983-88, Crane Plumbing, Elmhurst, 1988—; pres. RJ Svcs., Morton Grove, Ill., 1991—; adv. P. Rosenberg & Sons, Chgo., 1995—. Sec. bd. dirs. Niles Twp. Shelter Workshop, Skokie, Ill., 1993—. Recipient Standing Expert medal 22 Rifle NRA, 1980-82, 2d Degree Black Belt Tai Kwan Do, 1987—. Mem. North Shore Corvette Club (mem. bd. govs. 1983—). Home: 7228 Lake St Morton Grove IL 60053

GOLDBERG, EDWARD JAY, orthopaedic surgeon; b. Chgo., Dec. 30, 1957; s. Sheldon Norman and Edith (Goldstein) G.; m. Jamie Kim Schoonover, Sept. 13, 1992; 1 child, Sarah. BS, Tulane U., 1979; MD, U. Ill., Chgo., 1983. Diplomate Am. Bd. Orthopaedic Surgeons. Intern U. Ill., 1983-84, resident in orthopaedic surgery, 1984-88; orthopaedic surgeon Midwest Orthopaedics, Chgo., 1989—; asst. prof. dept. orthopaedic surgery Rush Med. Ctr., Chgo., mem. orthopaedic selection com., 1992—. Author: Lumbar Spinal Stenosis, 1991. Mem. AMA, Chgo. Med. Soc., Ill. State Med. Soc., Chgo. Botanic Gardens. Office: Midwest Orthopaedics 1725 W Harrsion Ste 1063 Chicago IL 60612

GOLDBERG, KENNETH PAUL, information specialist; b. Rochester, N.Y., Jan. 13, 1949; s. Morris and Miriam Ruth (Manson) G.; m. Lillian Esther Weil, Dec. 26, 1976; children: Rachel Celia, Aaron Samuel. BA cum laude, Syracuse U., 1970; MA, SUNY, Binghamton, 1972; MLS, Syracuse U., 1973. Pub. svcs. libr. Cleve. Inst. Art, Cleve., 1973-81; tech. editor Am. Soc. Metals, Metals Park, Ohio, 1981-82; analyst Mkt. Rsch. Svcs., Cleveland Heights, Ohio, 1982-83; instr. Cuyahoga C.C., Cleve., 1982-83; info. specialist, Intergovtl. Rev. coord. N.E. Ohio Areawide Coordinating Agy., Cleve., 1983—; instr. Capital Univ., Cleve., 1983-87; archtl. and hist. tour guide, lectr. pub. and pvt. orgns., Ohio, 1975—; instr. architecture and local history, local adult ednl. programs, Cleve., 1978—; exterior archtl. color cons. Author (with others), editor Guide to Cleveland Architecture, 1990, 96; contbr. Habitat newspaper, 1985-90, Focus in the Heights, 1993—. Mem. Cleveland Heights Landmark Commn., 1990—, Cleveland Heights Cmty. Improvement Awards Com., 1989—, Cleveland Heights Hist. Soc., 1996—; Resource Guide to Humanities cons. State Libr. of Ohio, 1979; mem. N.E. Ohio Govt. Documents Interest Group, 1991—; cons. Ohio Hist. Soc., Columbus, 1992—; trustee Park Synagogue Couples Club, 1980-87. Mem. Western Res. Hist. Soc., Soc. Archtl. Historians (pres., v.p., sec., treas., trustee 1974— Cleve. chpt.). Home: 3412 Ormond Rd Cleveland Heights OH 44118 Office: NE Ohio Areawide Coord Agy Atrium Office Pla 668 Euclid Ave Cleveland OH 44114-3000

GOLDBERG, MARSHALL ROBERT, former diplomat, former tax administrator; b. Chgo.; s. Philip and Bertha (Appelman) G.; m. Joyce Goldberg, June 26, 1948; children: Jeffrey Leonard, David Martin, Philip Ross. Student, U. Ill.; BSC, Roosevelt U., 1948; MSE, Northeastern Ill. U. Diplomat Nat. Soc. Pub. Accts., Chgo., IAAI, Chgo.; technician ARRL, Highland Park, Ill.; spl. agt. tax fraud Ill. Dept. Revenue, Springfield, Ill., chief fraud audit group; dist. tax adminstr. Ill. Dept. Revenue, Ill., Lake, Kane, McHenry Counties; assoc. lectr. ICPA, Chgo., 1970-82, IBA/ABA, Chgo.; lead instr. Ill. Dept. Revenue, Springfield/Chgo., 1970-84; lectr. AMA, Martinique. Asst. scoutmaster Boy Scouts Am., Northbrook, Ill., 1958-62; chpt. founder B'nai B'rith, Northbrook, 1972; organizer Congregation Beth Shalom, 1978. Recipient Appreciation award Boy Scouts Am., 1962, Appreciation award Congregation Beth Shalom, 1978. Mem. Nat. Soc. Pub. Accts., Am. Acctg. Assn. Jewish. Home: 301 Southgate Dr Northbrook IL 60062-4816

GOLDBERG, NORMAN ALBERT, music publisher, writer; b. Belleville, Ill., Mar. 11, 1918; s. Charles S. and Bessie (Tenenbaum) G.; m. Ruth E. Rodenberg, Dec. 29, 1940; children: Marcia Lee, Marc Edwin. BS, U. Ill., 1939, M in Music, 1942. Instr. U. Ill., Urbana, 1939-41; mem. faculty State U. Iowa, Iowa City, 1941-42, Mo. High Sch., Univ. City, 1944-48; owner Baton Music Co., St. Louis, 1948-73; pres. Magnamusic-Baton Inc. (name now MMB Music), St. Louis, 1964—, G. Henle, USA, 1981-86, Norruth Music, Inc., 1985—; pub. Internat. Jour. Arts Medicine; pres. Contemporary Arts Corp., St. Louis, 1993—; edn. com. St. Louis Symphony. Composer various works for alto and bass clarinets; arranger various symphony orchs. and bands. Bd. dirs. Internat. Assn. Music for Handicapped, Provo, Utah, St. Louis Conservatory and Sch. for the Arts (now St. Louis Symphony), 1991-94, Rhythm for Life, 1992—, Music Brain Info. Ctr., 1992—. With U.S. Army, 1943. Mem. Music Industry Conf. (bd. dirs. 1972-84, past pres. 1982-84, Outstanding Svc. award 1986), Univ. City C. of C. (past pres. 1971), Am. Assn. Music Therapy (bd. dirs. 1988—), Jewish War Vets. (past dep. comdr. 1953), Univ. Ill. Alumni Assn. (bd. dirs. 1990-96, chair constituents com. 1994-96), Am. Orff-Schulwerk Assn. (life, bd. dirs. 1970-75), St. Louis chpt. ADSA (life), Music Educators Nat. Conf. (exec. bd. 1982-84), Internat. Soc. for Music in Medicine, Internat. Arts Medicine Assn. (bd. dirs. 1990—, St. Louis Symphony Edn. Com. 1994—), B'nai El Cong. (life, past pres.), Phi Mu Alpha, Rotary (past pres. 1967-78, Univ. City chpt.), Shriners, Mason. Democrat. Jewish. Home: 790 Dielman Rd Saint Louis MO 63132-3520 Office: MMB Music Inc Contemporary Arts Bldg 3526 Washington Ave Saint Louis MO 63103-1019

GOLDBERG, VICKI COMM, employment services executive; b. Chicago, Ill., Oct. 21, 1945; d. Julius and Esther (Kennon) Comm; m. Sheldon Goldberg, Aug 16, 1970; children: Felicia, Sharisse. BA in Psychology, Northeastern Ill. U., 1967. Lic. employment counselor, Ill.; cert. teacher, Ill. Elem. sch. tchr. Sch. Dist. 21, Wheeling, Ill., 1967-70; community svc. rep. Welcome Wagon, Memphis, 1977-80; mktg. rep. McDonald's Corp., Oakbrook, Ill., 1980-83; staff supr. Debbie Temps, Niles, Ill., 1983-85; day care ctr. dir. Kinder Care, Palatine, Ill., 1985-86; office mgr. Casey Svcs. Inc., Des Plaines, Ill., 1986-89; regional mgr. Profl. Resources Internat., Oakbrook Terrace, Ill., 1989-92; mgr. acctg. ops. Kelly Temp. Svcs., Downers Grove, Ill., 1992—; guest facilitator Northeastern Ill. U., Elmhurst Coll., Ill. Dept. Employment Securities, Ill. CPA Soc., Inst. Mgmt. Accts., U. Ill. Chgo. Advisor Morton Grove (Ill.) Pk. Dist., 1981; columnist Vol. Svcs. of Skokie (Ill.) Valley, 1988-94. Mem. Nat. Assn. Pers. Cons., Nat. Assn. Job Search Trainers. Office: Kelly Temp Svcs 4711 Golf Rd Ste 915 Skokie IL 60076-1247

GOLDBERGER, ARTHUR EARL, JR., industrial engineer, executive. BS in Systems Engring., U. Ariz., 1974, BS in Indsl. Engring., 1975; MS in Indsl. Engring., Tex. A&M U., 1977, postgrad., 1991—. Cert. Novell engr.; registered profl. engr., Ky., Tex., Mo., Ariz., Fla. Gen. engr. DARCOM/RRAD, Texarkana, Tex., 1975-77; mgr. DARCOM/AVSCOM, St. Louis, 1977-81; div. dir. prodn. improvement McDonnell Douglas, St. Louis, 1981-90; pres. Spectrum Techs., Inc., St. Louis, 1990—; chmn. CAD/Expert System Tool Design, Seattle, 1991; internat. cons. in field. Author: Real Leadership, 1993; contbr. articles to profl. jours. Bd. dirs. Engrs. Club St. Louis, 1978, Nat. Com. on U.S. Competitiveness, Washington, 1989—; mem. Scientific Olympiad, Mo., 1989. Recipient Quality Leadership award McDonnell Douglas Corp., 1988. Mem. IEEE (chmn. 1987-88, vice chmn. vehicle tech. soc. conf. 1991, Leadership award 1988), Inst. Indsl. Engrs., Soc. Mfrg. Engrs., Alpha Pi Mu.

GOLDEN, BRIAN MICHAEL, marketing executive; b. Phila., June 17, 1966; s. Harry Raymond and Natalie Carol (Alessio) G.; m. Karen Ann Hewes, Oct. 21, 1989; 1 child, Sean Ryan. BSBA, Villanova U., 1988; MBA, Loyola Coll., 1990; JD, Fordham U., 1994. Mktg. assoc. Archtl. Brands Mgmt., Wayne, Pa., 1987-88; mktg. rep. U.S. Gypsum Co., Balt., 1988-91; mktg. adminstrn. mgr. U.S. Gypsum Co., Boston, 1991-92, Stony Point, N.Y., 1993-94; mktg. svcs. mgr. Nat. Accts. /East, Chgo., 1995—. Mem. New Eng. Law Rev., 1992. Recipient Am. Jurisprudence award-torts Lawyers Coop. Pub., 1990. Mem. ABA (contbr. to law revs.).

GOLDEN, ELOISE ELIZABETH, community health nurse; b. Hope, Ind., Nov. 20, 1938; d. John M. and Hazel E. (Gosch) Holder; m. Don Golden, Aug. 2, 1959; children: David, Susanne. Diploma, Ball State U., 1959. RN. Office nurse Columbus, Ind.; staff nurse Pub. Health Dept. Bartholomew County, Columbus; parish nurse, clinicare staff nurse, housecall coord. Bartholomew County Hosp., Columbus, intake coord. Hospice, 1991—. Lutheran. Home: 11635 E 600 N Hope IN 47246

GOLDEN, RUSSELL L., plant superintendent; b. Mentone, Ind., Aug. 4, 1959. Plant supr. Kessington Machine Products, Granger, Ind., 1979—. Coach Boys Little League, Osceola, Ind., 1983-86. Office: Kessington Machine Products PO Box 370 Granger IN 46530-0370

GOLDEN, STEVE M., financial consultant; b. Detroit, Apr. 11, 1953. BA in Bus. Adminstrn., Mich. State U., 1975. Pres. Land Data Network, Southfield, Mich., 1988-92; fin. cons. Smith Barney Inc., Southfield, 1992—; pub. Land Data Director of Vacant Land, 1989. Creator online computer sys. Land Data Computer Network, 1989. Mem. Wabeek Country Club. Jewish. Office: Smith Barney Inc 2000 Town Ctr Ste 1800 Southfield MI 48075-1151

GOLDENHERSH, LAURI DAVIDIAN, musician, educator; b. Loma Linda, Calif., Aug. 1, 1968; d. James Lowell and Marilyn Rae (Hopkins) Davidian; m. Andrew Stephen Goldenhersh, Mar. 16, 1994. BA in Music, Washington U., St. Louis, 1992, MM in Vocal Performance, 1995. Instr. Paulin Ctr. for the Creative Arts, Angwin, Calif., 1989-90; soloist Christ Ch. Cathedral, St. Louis, 1992-94; grad. asst. Washington U., 1992—; soloist Temple Israel, St. Louis, 1993—, Episcopal Ch. of the Holy Communion, St. Louis, 1995—; benefits adminstr. St. Louis Bread co., 1994—. Mem. Human Resources Mgmt. Assn. Greater St. Louis, Inc., Am. Kantorei, Midwest Lyric Opera, Golden Key, Phi Beta Kappa. Seventh-Day Adventist. Home: 6031A Waterman Blvd Saint Louis MO 63112

GOLDFARB, BERNARD SANFORD, lawyer; b. Cleve., Apr. 15, 1917; s. Harry and Esther (Lenson) G.; m. Barbara Brofman, Jan. 4, 1966; children—Meredith Stacey, Lauren Beth. A.B., Case Western Res. U., 1938, J.D., 1940. Bar: Ohio bar 1940. Since practiced in Cleve.; sr. ptnr. firm Goldfarb & Reznick, 1967-95; ptnr. Goodman Weiss Miller Goldfarb, Cleve., 1996—; spl. counsel to atty. gen. Ohio, 1950, 71-74; mem. Ohio Commn. Uniform Traffic Rules, 1973—. Contbr. legal jours. Served with USAAF, 1942-45. Mem. Am., Ohio, Greater Cleve. bar assns. Home: 39 Pepper Creek Dr Pepper Pike OH 44124 Office: Goodman Weiss Miller & Goldfarb 100 Erieview Plz 27th Fl Cleveland OH 44114

GOLDFARB, MARVIN AL, retired civil engineer; b. Memphis, Tenn., Dec. 12, 1928; s. Al Bohne and Melba (Pollock) G.; m. Lorene Shelton, June 13, 1965 (div. 1974); children: David Al, Julie Lin. BSCE, U. Tenn., 1950; MS in Engring. Mgmt., U. Mo., 1971. Registered profl. engr., Ala., Mo. Field engr. Inter-Am. Geodetic Survey, Panama, 1950-53; engr., supr. Rust Engring. Co., Birmingham, Ala., 1956-64; engr., prin. Monsanto Co., St. Louis, 1964-90, ret., 1990. Author: An Owner's Approach to Project Scheduling, 1975. Chmn. troop com. Boy Scouts Am., 1980—; councilman City of Maryland Heights, Mo., 1985-86, mem. Planning and Zoning Commn., chmn., 1986—. Mem. Mo. Soc. Profl. Engrs. (pres. 1985-86), Profl. Engrs. Industry (regional vice chmn. 1980-82), Am. Legion (comdr. post 213 1991-93). Jewish. Home: 1474 Glenmeade Dr Maryland Heights MO 63043-2928

GOLDGAR, ARNOLD BENJAMIN, lawyer; b. Princeton, N.J., Jan. 15, 1957; s. Bertrand Alvin and Corinne Cohn (Hartman) G.; m. Marcia Beth Weinstein, June 14, 1981; children: Sarah Rachel, Leah Hartman. AB magna cum laude, Brown U., 1979; JD, Northwestern U., 1982. Bar: Ill. 1982, U.S. Dist. Ct. (no. dist.) Ill. 1982, U.S. Ct. Appeals (7th cir.) 1985, U.S. Dist. Ct. (ctrl. dist.) Ill. 1989, U.S. Dist. Ct. (ea. dist.) Wis. 1991, U.S. Supreme Ct. 1991. Assoc. Keck, Mahin & Cate, Chgo., 1982-88, ptnr., 1988-95; asst. atty. gen., civil appeals bur. State of Ill., Chgo., 1995—; arbitrator Cook County Mandatory Arbitration Program, Chgo., 1990-95. Mem. editorial bd. Jour. Criminal Law and Criminology Northwestern U., 1981-82. Vol. atty. Chgo. Vol. Legal Svcs. Found., 1984—; mem. vol. panel U.S. Ct. Appeals (7th cir.), 1992-95; mem. Jud. Adv. Coun. Pro Bono Appeals Program, 1993-95; mem. civil rights com. Anti-Defamation League, Chgo., 1986—, mem. exec. com. regional bd., 1987—. Recipient Disting. Svc. award Chgo. Vol. Legal Svcs. Found., 1986. Mem. ABA (litigation sect., appellate practice com.), Ill. State Bar Assn., Chgo. Bar Assn., 7th Cir. Bar Assn., Appellate Lawyers Assn. Ill. (bd. dirs. 1996—), Brown U. Club Chgo., Phi Beta Kappa. Home: 2765 Quail Ln Northbrook IL 60062-7629 Office: 100 W Randolph 12th Fl Chicago IL 60601

GOLDGAR, CORINNE HARTMAN, marketing coordinator; b. Nashville, June 14, 1928; d. Arnold and Mabel (Cohn) Hartman; m. Bertrand A. Goldgar, Apr. 6, 1950; children: Arnold Benjamin, Anne Hartman Goldgar. BA, Vanderbilt U., 1950. Asst. circulation libr. Clemson (S.C.) Coll. Libr., 1950-52; tchr. Prince George County Pub. Schs., Petersburg, Va., 1952-54; sr. asst. acquisitions dept. Princeton (N.J.) U. Libr., 1954-56; exec. asst. Transit Commn., Appleton, Wis., 1974-77; coord. grants and info. Valley Transit, Appleton, 1978-83, mktg. coord., 1984—; mem. adv. com. Transit Mgmt. Ctr., U. Wis., Milw., 1983-85. Editor, writer, designer (on-bd. newsletter) Rider's Digest, 1983—, Dept. of Pub. Works Newsletter Apple Source, 1992-96, Red Cross Outagmie County chpt. newsletter Vol. Views, 1995—; editor, writer (booklet) This is Appleton, 3d edit., 1966, Public Education in Appleton, 1969. Member Mayor's Com. on Urban Transp. Svc., Appleton, 1972, Gov.'s Com. on Urban Mass. Transp., Madison, 1972-73, Transit Commn., Appleton, 1973. Mem. LWV (pres. Appleton chpt. 1971-73), Women in Mgmt. (pres. Fox Cities chpt. 1988-89), Wis. Urban Transit Assn. (bd. dirs. 1981-83), Phi Beta Kappa. Home: 914 E Eldorado St Appleton WI 54911-5536 Office: Valley Transit 801 Whitman Ave Appleton WI 54914-4649

GOLDIN, MARTIN BRUCE, financial executive, consultant; b. Teaneck, N.J., May 18, 1938; s. Arthur Daniel and Shirley Edith (Holland) G.; m. Joyce Anne Rossin, Aug. 22, 1960; children: Melissa Beth, Julie Amber, Kevin James, Sabrina Nicole. BBA, U. Miami, 1960; postgrad., Detroit Coll. Law, 1967. Fin. analyst Chrysler Corp. Detroit, London, Eng., 1967-70; chief fin. officer Chrysler de Mex., Mexico City, 1971-77, Chrysler Australia Ltd., Adelaide, 1978-80, Internat. Harvester De Mex., Mexico City, 1980-85; compt. Citicorp Diners Club, Denver, 1985-87; chief fin. officer, exec. v.p. Citicorp Diners Club, Chgo., 1988—; fin. cons. Rossin-Goldin, Detroit, 1960—, La Torre de Acapulco (Mex.), 1980-88. Home: 3775 Whirlaway Dr Northbrook IL 60062-6313 Office: Citicorp Diners Club 8430 W Bryn Mawr Ave Chicago IL 60631-3415

GOLDMAN, ARTHUR JOSEPH, research and development executive; b. N.Y.C., Aug. 14, 1934; s. Henry Julius and Lottie (Schumer) G.; m. Joan Marilyn Broder, Jan. 27, 1957; children: Jeffrey Howard, Rona Beth. B-

ChemE cum laude, CCNY, 1957; MChemE, NYU, 1961, PhD, 1966; MBA, U. Chgo., 1980. Sr. engr. NDA/United Nuclear Corp., White Plains, N.Y., 1957-66; project mgr. Esso Math and Systems Inc., Florham Park, N.J., 1966; v.p., tech. dir. Nuclear Tech. Corp., White Plains, 1967-70; dir. fuel mgmt. svcs. S.M. Stoller Corp., N.Y.C., 1971; v.p. applied scis. Transfer Systems Inc., North Haven, Conn., 1972; assoc. div. dir. Argonne (Ill.) Nat. Lab., 1973-92, dir. quality mgmt., 1992-95, deputy chief ops. officer, 1995—; adj. assoc. prof. NYU, N.Y.C., 1966-71. Contbr. articles to profl. jours. Mem. sch. bd., Oak Park, Ill., 1975-78. Mem. Am. Nuclear Soc., Beta Gamma Sigma. Office: Argonne Nat Lab 9700 Cass Ave Lemont IL 60439-4803

GOLDMAN, DONA LU, writer, retired educator; b. Princeton, Ind., Sept. 14, 1928; d. Irvin and Georgia Fern (Battles) G. AB, Ind. U., 1950, MAT, 1960. Cert. tchr., Ind. Tchr. Hammond (Ind.) City Schs., 1950-52, 53-62, Fulton County Schs., Akron, Ind., 1952-53; Fulbright tchr. U.S. Govt., Bergamo, Italy, 1962-63; tchr. Hammond City Schs., 1963-86; substitute reference libr. Hammond Pub. Libr., 1986—. Author: Dandelion Soul, 1994; contbr. to Bitterroot, Am. Goat, Voices Internat., Skylark, Taste of Poetry. Mem. AAUW, Poets Club of Chgo., Hemlock Soc., Ind. Ret. Tchrs. Assn. Presbyterian. Home: 2311 Hampton Dr Apt 15 Highland IN 46322

GOLDMAN, JACK LESLIE, health professions educator; b. Chgo., Nov. 20, 1935; s. Mandel and Katherine (Kaplan) G. BA, BS, U. Chgo., 1958; MS, Loyola U., 1963, PhD, 1966. Lectr. chemistry Mundelein Coll., Chgo., 1963-65; head phys. chemistry Velsico Corp., Chgo., 1966-67; head natural scis. Shimer Coll., Mt. Carroll, Ill., 1967-71; lectr. chemistry Loyola U., Chgo., 1972-82; lectr. natural scis. Roosevelt U., Chgo., 1980-83; lectr. math. Loyola U., Chgo., 1982-87, dir. health professions, 1987-95; cons. Cardinal Newman Coll., Detroit, 1975-76. Fellow Am. Inst. Chemists. Mem. AAAS, Park Ridge Ctr., Hastings Inst., Nat. Assn. Advisors to the Health Professions. Jewish.

GOLDMAN, RACHEL BOK, civic volunteer; b. Phila., Mar. 28, 1937; d. W. Curtis and Nellie Lee (Holt) Bok; m. James Nelson Kise, Dec. 20, 1958 (div. May 1974); children: Jefferson B, C. Curtis; m. Allen S. Goldman, Nov. 28, 1981; stepchildren: Jonathan, Benjamin Allen, Adam Louis. Student, Sweet Briar (Va.) Coll., 1955-57; BA in Art History, U. Pa., 1977. Bd. dirs. Arts Exchange mag., 1977-79, chmn. bd. dirs., 1977-79. Mem. collector's circle Pa. Acad. Fine Arts, 1983-85, exhbn. selection com. Morris Gallery, 1979-82; mem. Rittenhouse Sq. Women's Com. Pa. Orchestra, 1979-85; mem. Indian com. Pa. Yearly Meeting, 1971-75; mem. ladies' com. Powel House, 1965-69; founder, pres. Friends of Curtis Inst. Music, 1982—, chmn. 1982-85; bd. dirs. Mary Louis Curtis Bok Found., 1982—, The Curtis Inst. Music, 1982—, The Buten Mus., 1982-84, Brady Cancer Rsch. Inst. 1983—, Settlement Music Sch., 1984-87, The Phila. Award, 1970—, Elfreth's Alley Assn., 1962-65, sec. 1963-65; bd. dirs. The Am. Found., 1955-83, sec.-treas., 1980-83; bd. dirs. The Community Sch. of Phila., 1971-74, chmn. bd. dirs., co-founder, adminstr.; bd. dirs. Women in Transition, 1973-78, div. counselor, 1974-76; bd. dirs. Friends of Phila. Mus. Art, 1977-83, sec., 1979-81, program chmn., 1981-82, co-chmn., 1982-83; bd. dirs. Samuel Yellin Found., 1977-86, co-founder, sec., 1977-84; mem. com. Soc. for Contemporary Art, Art Inst. Chgo., 1988-90, exhibitrix-selection subcom., 1987-88; collectors' group Mus. Contemporary Art, Chgo., 1986-92; bd. dirs. Art Resources in Teaching (A.R.T.), 1987-93, Craniofacial Ctr., 1989-95, AboutFace, 1993-95, Bay Chamber Concerts Inc. 1993—. Democrat. Clubs: Camden Yacht (Maine), Cosmopolitan of Phila. (house com. 1981-84).

GOLDRING, NORMAN MAX, advertising executive; b. Chgo., June 22, 1937; s. Jack and Carolyn (Wolf) G.; m. Cynthia Lois Garland, Dec. 20, 1959; children: Jay Marshall, Diane. BS in Bus., Miami (Ohio) U., 1959; MBA, U. Chgo., 1963. Advt. account mgr. Edward H. Weiss & Co., Chgo., 1959-61; sr. v.p., dir. mktg. svcs. Stern, Walters & Simmons, Inc., Chgo., 1961-68; chmn. Goldring & Co., Inc., Chgo., 1968-89; pres., CEO CPM, Inc., 1969-93, chmn., 1994—; pres. CPO Inc., 1994—; dir. Creative Works, Inc.; instr. mktg. and advt. mgmt. Roosevelt U., 1965-68. Mem. editorial bd. Jour. Media Planning. Commr. Ridgeville Park Dist., Evanston, Ill., 1971-75, pres. 1974-75; bd. dirs., v.p. Mus. Broadcast Comm., 1983-92; dir. Chgo. Chamber Musicians 1988—; dir. Chgo. Metro History Fair, 1990. Mem. Am. Mktg. Assn. (speaker), Advt. Coun. Inc. (Midwest adv. bd. 1983-90), Am. Mgmt. Assn. Home: 855 Beverly Pl Lake Forest IL 60045-3901 Office: CPM Inc 515 N State St Chicago IL 60610-4320

GOLDSEN, BRUCE I., radio executive; b. Norwalk, Conn., Aug. 5, 1959; s. Leonard and Esther (Rosenfeld) G.; m. Susan Eva Szanti, Sept. 15, 1984; 1 child, David Tyler. BA, Western Conn. State U., 1981. Music dir. Sta. WRKI, Danbury, Conn., 1981-83; program dir. Sta. WINE, Danbury, 1983-85, Sta. WTFM, Kingsport, Johnson City, Tenn., 1986-87, Sta. WIVY-FM, Jacksonville, Fla., 1987-90; v.p., gen. mgr. Sta. WABJ/WQTE, Adrian, Mich., 1990—; v.p. Sta. WMXE, Hudson and Hillsdale, Mich., 1995—. Mem. Dem. Town Com., Weston, Conn., 1982-83; bd. dirs. Lewanee United Way and Vol. Ctr., 1992—, ann. campaign co-chair, 1992-94, pres. 1995-96; bd. dirs. Croswell Opera House, 1995—. Mem. Mich. Assn. of Broadcasters (bd. dirs. 1993—), Adrian Rotary Club (bd. dirs. 1996—). Office: Sta WABJ/WQTE 121 W Maumee St Adrian MI 49221-2019

GOLDSEN, SUSAN EVA, radio station executive; b. Montgomery, Ala., Jan. 26, 1963; d. Joseph and Susan (Elek) Szanti; m. Bruce Goldsen, Sept. 15, 1984; 1 child, David. BBA, Western Conn. State U., 1984. Dir. coop. advt. Stas. WINE-WRKI, Danbury, Conn., 1984-85; account exec. Sta. WINE-WRKI, Danbury, Conn., 1989-90; pers. cons. Bailey Employment, Ridgefield, Conn., 1985-86; computer operator AFG Industries, Kingsport, Conn., 1986-87; account exec. Sta. WIVY, Jacksonville, Fla., 1987-89; v.p., gen. sales mgr. Sta. WABJ-WQTE, Adrian, Mich., 1990—, WMXE, Hudson/Hillsdale, Mich., 1995—. Bd. dirs. Adrian Symphony, 1991—, pres., 1995-96; bd. dirs. Lenawee County Agr. Soc., Adrian, 1991—; bd. dirs. Downtown Adrian Assn., 1990-92, v.p., 1992—; mem. pres.'s cabinet Lenawee chpt. United Way, 1990—, campaign co-chair, 1992-94, bd. dirs. Hillsdale chpt., 1995—. Mem. Lenawee County C. of C. (chmn. pres.'s cabinet 1992—), Hillsdale County C. of C., Zonta (sec. Adrian 1990-95, pres. 1995—). Home: 915 Riverside Ave Adrian MI 49221-1447 Office: Stas WABJ-WQTE 121 W Maumee St Adrian MI 49221-2019

GOLDSMITH, ETHEL FRANK, medical social worker; b. Chgo., May 31, 1919; d. Theodore and Rose (Falk) Frank; m. Julian Royce Goldsmith, Sept. 4, 1940; children: Richard, Susan, John. BA, U. Chgo., 1940. Lic. social worker, Ill. Liaison worker psychiat. consultation service U. Chgo. Hosp., 1964-68; med. social worker Wyler Children's Hosp., Chgo., 1968—. Treas. U. Chgo. Service League, 1958-62, chmn. camp Brueckner Farr Aux., 1966-72; pres. Bobs Roberts Hosp. Service Commn., 1962; bd. dirs. Richardson Wildlife Sanctary, 1988—; mem. Field Mus. Women's Bd., 1966—; bd. dirs. Hyde Park Art Ctr., 1964-82, Chgo. Commons Assn., 1967-77, Alumni Assn. Sch. Social Service Adminstrn., 1976-80, Self Help Home for Aged, 1985—. Recipient Alumni Citation Pub. Service, U. Chgo., 1972. Mem. Phi Beta Kappa. Home: 5631 S Blackstone Ave Chicago IL 60637-1827 Office: Wyler Hosp Dept Social Svc 5841 S Maryland Ave Chicago IL 60637-1463

GOLDSMITH, JANET JANE, pediatric nurse practitioner; b. creston, Iowa, Mar. 3, 1942; d. Paul William and Mary Lucille (Crow) Schafroth; m. Olin Russel Goldsmith, Aug. 31, 1963; children: Rodney, Scott, Kristen. Diploma, Iowa Meth. Hosp. Sch. Nursing, Des Moines, 1963; PNP, U. Iowa, 1982; BSN, Graceland Coll., Lamoni, Iowa, 1984. Cert. pediatric nurse practitioner. Staff nurse Rosary Hosp., Corning, Iowa, 1963-66, 71-72; sch. nurse Corning Commun. Schs., 1966-67; area adminstr., occupant protection program adminstr. Iowa Gov.'s Traffic Safety Bur., Des Moines, 1985—; clin. instr. Southwestern Commun. Coll., Creston, Iowa, 1970, adj. faculty, 1985-86; part-time health/handicap coord. Matura-Head Start, Creston, 1973-81; part-time pediatric devel. nurse Child Diagnostic and Planning Svc., Creston, 1975-81; part-time pediatric nurse practitioner, physician's office, Lenox, Iowa, 1982-84, Otologic Med. Svcs., Iowa City, 1982-87, Taylor County Pub. Health, Bedford, Iowa, 1982-87; numerous state and nat. motor vehicle injury presentations. Author booklets, tng. video, articles, tng. curricula. Recipient Recognition of Accomplishment award Gov. of Iowa, 1989. Mem. Iowa Pub. Health Assn. (exec. bd., legis. com.) Nat. Assn. Pediatric Nurse Assocs. and Practitioners (pub. rels. com.), Iowa Nurses Assn. (local treas., state policy com.), Iowa Assn. Nurse Practitioners (constn. and by-laws chmn., pres.), Iowa Traffic Control and Safety Assn. (bd. dirs., treas., sec., v.p., pres.). Methodist. Home: 2650 Hwy 34 Prescott IA 50859 Office: Gov's Traffic Safety Bur 307 E 7th St Des Moines IA 50319-0248

GOLDSMITH, MARK SARGENT, urban conservation specialist; b. Milledgeville, Ga., Feb. 7, 1963; s. Herbert P. and Mary E. (Demaree) G.; m. Wendy E. Minnis, Oct. 24, 1987; 1 child, Grayson N. BS in Natural Resources, Environ. Sci., Purdue U., 1986. Erosion control specialist Hoham, Smith & Co., Auburn, Ind., 1987-88, Geo-Synthetics, Inc., Waukesha, Wis., 1988; geo-synthetics/ erosion control specialist Culverts Plus, Inc., Bedford, Ind., 1989-91; urban conservation specialist Ind. Dept. Natural Resources, divsn. soil conservation, Indpls., 1992—. Vice chmn. Pearl Park Com., Madison, Ind., 1993—. Recipient cert. appreciation USDA Soil Conservation Svc., Columbus, Ind., 1992. Home: 624 E Second St Madison IN 47250 Office: Ind Dept Natural Resources Divsn Soil Conservation 2600 N State Hwy 7 North Vernon IN 47265

GOLDSMITH, MICHAEL R., tool design supervisor; b. Heidelburg, Germany, June 1, 1957; came to U.S., 1958; Student, U. Upper Iowa, 1993—. Head greenskeeper Foursome Golf Course, Oelwein, Iowa, 1972-79; tool designer E&M Tool, Waterloo, Iowa, 1979-82; tool design supr. Viking Pump, Inc., Cedar Falls, Iowa, 1982—. Vol. Jr. Achievement, Cedar Falls, 1983—. Mem. Soc. Mfg. Engrs. Lutheran. Office: Viking Pump Inc PO Box 8 Cedar Falls IA 50613-0008

GOLDSMITH, STEPHEN, mayor; b. Indpls., Dec. 12, 1946; s. Joseph F. and Marjorie (Holmes) G.; m. Margaret McDaniel, June 15, 1988; children: Reid, Elizabeth, Devereaux, Olivia. A.B., Wabash Coll., 1968; J.D., U. Mich., 1971. Bar: Ind. 1972, U.S. Dist. Ct. (so. dist.) Ind. 1972, U.S. Ct. Apls. (7th cir.) 1974, U.S. Supreme Ct. 1977. Dep. corp. counsel City of Indpls., 1974-75, chief trial dept., 1976-78; assoc. Barnes, Hickam, Pantzer & Boyd, Indpls., 1971-78; pros. atty. Marion County, Indpls., 1979-90; with Dann, Pecar, Newman, Talesnick & Klieman, 1990-91; mayor City of Indpls., 1991—; asst. prof. Ind. U., 1989—. Assoc. editor U. Mich. Law Rev., 1970-71. Mem. adv. bd. justice stats. U.S. Dept. Justice, Washington, 1982-84, Criminal Law Study Commn., Indpls., 1980-88; chmn. Gov.'s Task Force to reduce Drunk Driving, 1983-85, Gov.'s Task Force on Child Support; v.p. Crossroads council Boy Scouts Am., 1984; Atty. Gens. Adv. Bd. on Missing Children; co-chmn. Pres.'s Commn. on Model State Drug Laws, 1992-93; mem U.S. Environ. Fin. Adv. Bd., 1992-93. Served with USAR, 1968-74. Rsch. fellow Kennedy Sch. of Govt. Harvard U., 1989. Mem. Ind. Pros. Attys. Assn. (pres. 1983-84), Nat. Dist. Attys. Assn. Republican. Office: Office of Mayor 2501 City-County Bldg 200 E Washington St Indianapolis IN 46204-3307*

GOLDSTEIN, ALFRED GEORGE, retail and consumer products executive; b. N.Y.C., Sept. 22, 1932; s. Milton and Pauline M. G.; m. Hope D. Perry, July 5, 1959; children: Mark, Robert. A.B., CCNY, 1953; M.S., Columbia U., 1954. With Sears, Roebuck & Co., Chgo., 1956-79, v.p. mdse, group nat. mdse. mgr., 1976-79; sr. v.p. consumer bus. Am. Can Co., Greenwich, Conn., 1979-81, sr. v.p. waste recovery bus., 1981-82, exec. v.p. plastics packaging bus., 1982-83, pres. splty. retailing sector, 1983-87; pres. splty. merchandising and direct mktg. group, Sears Logistics Svc. Sears, Roebuck & Co., Chgo., 1987-93; bd. dirs. Sears Mdse. Group, Sears Can., Ltd.; former vice chmn., CEO, bd. dirs. Fingerhut Corp.; chmn. bd. dirs. Pickwick Internat.; chmn., CEO, Musicland Group; bd. dirs. Gender Mountain Corp., 1994. Exec. editor: Internat. Jour. Addictions, 1975-80. Trustee Archeus Found.; bd. dirs. United Negro Coll. Fund, 1991—, Columbia U. Grad. Sch. Bus. Alumni Assn., 1980-85, Am. Can Co. Found.; mem. mktg. com. bd. trustees Art Inst., Chgo., 1988—; mem. adv. bd. J.L. Kellogg Sch. Mgmt. Ctr. Study Ethical Issues in Bus., Northwestern U., 1992—, Gozuieta Bus. Sch. Ctr. Leadership and Career Studies, Emory U., 1990—; bd. dirs. Art Americana, 1996. With AUS, 1954-56. Mem. Am. Arbitration Assn. (arbitrator).

GOLDSTEIN, JULIUS LESTER, biomedical engineer, consultant; b. Bklyn., July 9, 1935; s. Benjamin and Dorothy (Steinberg) G.; m. Batya Abramson, June 17, 1962; children: Hillel N., Miriam D., Naama L., Avi D. BEE, Cooper Union, 1957; MEE, Poly. Inst. Bklyn., 1960; PhD, U. Rochester, 1965. Postdoctoral fellow Inst. for Perception Rsch., Eindhoven, The Netherlands, 1965-66; rsch. assoc., Lab. Psychophysics Harvard U., Cambridge, Mass., 1966-68; asst. prof. elec. engring. MIT, Cambridge, 1968-71, assoc. prof. elec. engring., 1971-73; dir. biomed. engring. Tel Aviv U., Israel, 1973-76; chmn. dept. electronics Tel Aviv U., 1976-78, assoc. prof., 1973-82, prof. elec. engring., 1982-90; vis. prof. Johns Hopkins U., Balt., 1986-88; rsch. prof. Ctrl. Inst. for the Deaf, St. Louis, 1988—; pres. Israel Soc. for Med. and Biomed. Engrs., Tel Aviv, 1975-77; dir. biomed. engring. program Tel Aviv U., 1973-76; cons. Digital Speech Systems, Tel Aviv, 1984-86, Models of Human Hearing, AT&T Bell Labs., Murray Hill, N.J., 1991—. Contbr. articles profl. jours. Achievements include the discovery and formulation of math models of basic principles of auditory signal processing, including nonlinear cochlear sound analysis, detection of signal peaks and intervals, and central processing in pitch perception. Bd. dirs. Epstein Hebrew Acad., St. Louis, 1991-94; organizer, symposium chmn. Assn. for Rsch. in Otolaryngology 17th Midwinter meeting, 1994. Recipient NIH grant MIT, 1972, Johns Hopkins U., 1986-88, U.S./Israel Binational Fund grant, 1977-80, NIH-NIDCD grant Ctrl. Inst. for the Deaf, 1990-95. Fellow Acoustical Soc. Am., Collegium Oto-Rhino-Laryngologicum Amicitae Sacrum, 1980; mem. IEEE (sr.). Office: Ctrl Inst for the Deaf 818 S Euclid Ave Saint Louis MO 63110-1504

GOLDSTEIN, MARC L., water purification company administrator; b. Springfield, Mass., Oct. 24, 1950; s. Selden E. Goldstein and Iris (Leavitt) Krintzman; m. Jeanine M. Goldstein, May 24, 1984. BA, U. Vt., Burlington, 1973. Purchasing clk. Mass. Wholesale Drug Co., Springfield, 1973-78; sales mgr. FIPCO Products, West Springfield, Mass., 1978-84, Am. Pump Co., West Springfield, 1984-88; nat. sales mgr. Osmonics, Minnetonka, Minn., 1988-91, nat sales mgr./Mace, 1991-92, dist. mgr., 1992—. Home: 187 Quinnchtok Rd Longmeadow MA 01106 Office: Osmonics Inc 5851 Clearwater Dr Minnetonka MN 55343

GOLDSTEIN, MARGARET HARDY, political scientist; b. Springfield, Mass., Apr. 22, 1933; d. Philip Campbell and Marjorie (Waterhouse) Hardy; m. Willie Goldstein, Nov. 29, 1969; children: Kenneth T., Sophie. BA in Polit. Sci., Dickinson Coll., 1955. In customer svc. sector ins. industry, 1955-69; relocation rep. City of Chgo., Dept. Urban Renewal, 1969-72. Author: The Selfishness System: Why Society is Overwhelmed with Problems, 1994. Chairperson local sch. coun. Cregier Vocat. High Sch., Chgo., 1991-93. Mem. World Federalist Assn. (pres. Chgo. chpt. 1993—), LWV (v.p. 1979-80, bd. dirs., 1982-85, chair internat. rels. com. 1982-85, 94—). Democrat. Home: 6542 N Seeley Ave Chicago IL 60645

GOLDSTEIN, PAUL H(ENRY), ophthalmologist, educator; b. Chgo., May 20, 1936; s. Alex and Leah (Swabsky) G.; m. Marilyn Gail Holtzman, Sept. 4, 1960; children: Todd, Jordan, Karen, Ross. BS, U. Ill., 1956; MD, U. Ill., Chgo., 1960. Diplomate Am. Bd. Ophthalmology. With basic and clin. sci. ophthalmology Harvard Med. Sch., 1961-62; intern Cook County Hosp., Chgo., 1960-61, resident, 1962-64; pvt. practice Milw., 1965—; asst. clin. prof. Med. Coll. of Wis., Milw., 1965—; chief of ophthalmology Sinai-Samaritan Med. Ctr., Milw., 1989—. Mem. Milw. Ophthal. Soc. (pres. 1973), Alpha Omega Alpha. Office: Eye Physicians Assn 2901 W Kinnickinnic River Pky Milwaukee WI 53215-3660

GOLDSTEIN, RICHARD JAY, mechanical engineer, educator; b. N.Y.C., Mar. 27, 1928; s. Henry and Rose (Steierman) G.; m. Barbara Goldstein; children: Arthur Sander, Jonathan Jacob, Benjamin Samuel, Naomi Sarith. BME, Cornell U., 1948; MS in Mech. Engring., U. Minn., 1950, MS in Physics, 1951, PhD in Mech. Engring., 1959; DSc (hon.), Israel Inst. Tech., 1994. Instr. U. Minn., Mpls., 1948-51, instr., rsch. fellow, 1956-58, mem. faculty, 1961—, prof. mech. engring., 1965—, head dept., 1977—, James J. Ryan prof., 1989—, Regents' prof., 1990—; devel. rsch. engr. Oak Ridge Nat. Lab., 1951-54; sr. engr. Lockheed Aircraft, 1956; asst. prof. Brown U., 1959-61; vis. prof. Technion, Israel, 1976, Imperial Coll., Eng., 1984; cons. in field, 1956—; chmn. Midwest U. Energy Consortium; chmn. Council Energy Engring. Research; NSF sr. postdoctoral fellow, vis. prof. Cambridge (Eng.) U., 1971-72; Prince lectr., 1983, William Gurley lectr., 1988, Hawkins Meml. lectr., 1991; disting. lectr. Pa. State U., 1992. Editorial adv. bd. Experiments in Fluids, Heat Transfer-Japanese Rsch., Heat Transfer-Soviet Rsch., Bull of the Internat. Centre for Heat andMass Transfer, Internat. Archives of Heat and Mass Transfer; hon. editorial adv. bd. Internat. J. Heat and Mass Transfer, Internat. Communications in Heat and Mass Transfer. 1st U.S. Army lt. AUS, 1954-55. Recipient NASA award for tech. innovation, 1977, MUEC Dist. Svc. award, 1986, George Taylor Alumni Soc. award, 1988, A.V. Lykov medal, 1990, Max Jakob Meml. award ASME/AICE, 1990, Nusselt-Reynolds prize, 1993, Dr. Scientiarum Honoris Causa award Technion-Israel Inst. Tech., 1994; NATO fellow, Paris, 1960-61, Lady Davis fellow Technion, Israel, 1976. Fellow AAAS, ASME (Heat Transfer Meml. award 1978, Svc. award 1978, Centennial medallion 1980, BEG v.p. 1984—, 50th anniv. award of heat transfer divsn. 1988, sr. v.p. 1989-93, hon. mem. 1992, BOG 1993—, pres. 1996—), Assembly for Internat. Heat Transfer Confs. (pres. 1986-90), Internat. Ctr. for Heat and Mass Transfer (exec. com. 1985—, chmn. 1992), Am. Phys. Soc., Japan Soc. Promotion of Sci.; mem. Am. Phys. Soc., Am. Soc. Engring. Edn., Minn. Acad. Sci., Nat. Acad. Engring., Nat. Acad. Engring.-Mex. (corr. 1991), Golden Key Nat. Honor Soc., Sigma Xi, Tau Beta Pi, Pi Tau Sigma. Home: 520 Janalyn Cir Minneapolis MN 55416-3327 Office: U Minn Dept Mech Engring 111 Church St SE Minneapolis MN 55455-0150

GOLDWASSER, JUDITH WAX, writer; b. Detroit, June 29, 1944; d. Reuben D. and Rena (Krause) Wax; m. James Stephen Goldwasser, Sept. 15, 1968; children: Amy Lynne, Lawrence Lanter. BA cum laude, U. Mich., 1966. Reporter Detroit Free Press, 1966-70; freelance writer local and nat. mags., 1970—; assoc. editor Cranbrook Quar. Cranbrook Ednl. Community, Bloomfield Hills, Mich., 1980-81; pres., owner Wordwatch, Birmingham, Mich., 1984—. Co-author: Unstuck for Words, 1993; contbr. articles to profl. jours. Recipient (with others) Pulitzer Prize, 1968, 1st pl. United Found. Writing awards, 1988, External Pub. Affairs and Spl. Events Writing awards Internat. Assn. Bus. Communicators/Detroit Renaissance, 1993, Nat. Pub. Rels. Campaign and Sales/Promotional Writing award Internat. Assn. Bus. Communicators, 1994. Mem. Cranbrook Writers Guild (bd. dirs.), Internat. Assn. Bus. Communicators (membership chair Detroit chpt.), Phi Beta Kappa, Phi Kappa Phi, Phi Sigma Iota. Jewish. Office: Wordwatch 3683 Quail Hollow Bloomfield Hills MI 48302-9999

GOLIN, MILTON, editor, publisher, writer; b. Oak Park, Ill., Apr. 2, 1921; s. Joseph and Rose (Stein) G.; m. Carol Florence Thurnau, Dec. 12, 1975; 1 child, James Milton. Student, Wright City Coll., 1939-41, Central YMCA Coll. (name changed to Roosevelt U.), 1941-42. Founding radio-TV news editor City News Bur. Chgo., 1949-56; asst. editor Jour. AMA, 1956-59; founding editor Medicine at Work, 1956-67; asst. to pres. Pharm. Mfrs. Assn., Washington, D.C., 1960-67; founding editor Ob-Gyn. News, Pediatric News, Diagnosis News, Washington, D.C., 1966-67, Med. Group News, Adolescent Medicine, CME Today, Surgery Update, Chgo., 1968-89; editor, publisher Computers and Medicine, Med. Software Resources Directory, Chgo., 1982—; instr. creative writing Chgo., 1947-48; speaker, cons. in field. Contbr. more than 200 articles to profl. jours. Co-founder Park Forest (Ill.) Civic Music Assn., dir. pub. rels., 1953-56. Served to 1st lt. USAF, 1942-46. Decorated Air medal with four oak leaf clusters; recipient Nation's First Met. Area Broadcast News Svc. Citation award Editor and Pub., 1954. Mem. AAAS, Assn. Sci. Writers, Am. Med. Writers Assn., Am. Assn. Journalists and Authors, Sigma Delta Chi. Republican. Presbyterian. Office: PO Box 11147 Chicago IL 60611-0147

GOLL, PAULETTE SUSAN, secondary education educator; b. Cleve., June 5, 1947; d. Ferdinand Paul and Lillian Clarice (Mehalko) G. BA in English, Cleve. State U., 1969, MEd, 1974; MA in English, U. Bridgeport, Conn., 1979; PhD in English, Case Western Res. U., 1987. Cert. secondary tchr., English tchr., asst. supr., secondary prin., Ohio. Part-time instr. U. Bridgeport, 1978-79, Case Western Res. U., Cleve., 1985-87; tchr. English, Cleve. Pub. Schs., 1969—, chmn. dept., coord. Ohio Proficiency Test, 1991—; advisor Students Against Drunk Drivers, 1985-86; coord. project success Lincoln-West H.S., Cleve., 1987-90. Co-author: Shakespearean Comedies, 1985. Mem. com. on human rels. Cleve. Partnerships, 1989-92; co-chmn. High Schs. for Future, 1985-86; liaison MetroHealth/Lincoln-West Partnership, 1989-92. Named Master Tchr., Martha Holden Jennings Found., 1988; recipient Congl. Commendation Mary Rose Oaker, 1988, Award of Excellence, Rotary, 1989; NEH fellow, 1985, NEH Ind. Studies in Humanities fellow, 1993; Jennings scholar, 1985, 88. Mem. ASCD (presenter), Nat. Coun. Tchrs. of English, North Cen. Assn. (chairperson vis. team 1991, 93), Phi Delta Kappa (v.p. programs 1993). Republican. Roman Catholic. Home: 4907 Parkway Dr Garfield Heights OH 44125-1725 Office: Lincoln-West High Sch 3202 W 30th St Cleveland OH 44109-1506

GOLLER, SUE LYNNE, government consultant, researcher; b. Jefferson City, Mo., Oct. 22, 1961; d. David Rudolph and Dorothy Eda (Linhardt) G. BSBA, U. Mo., 1984. CPA, Mo. Staff Mo. Rep. party, Jefferson City, 1981; intern U.S. Senator John Danforth, Washington, 1983; staff Hansen-Beck and Co. CPAs, Columbia, 1984; auditor Mo. State Auditor's Office, Jefferson City, 1984-86; spl. asst. to state treas. State of Mo., Jefferson City, 1986-88; adminstrv. asst. to Rep. floor leader Mo. Ho. of Reps., Jefferson City, 1988-90, 92-94, adminstrv. asst. Rep. caucus, 1990-92; 1988-90, 92-94; prin. Sue L. Goller and Assocs., 1995—. Mem. NAFE, Am. Assn. Profl. Cons., Mo. Soc. CPAs, Assn. Govt. Accts., Jaycees, Mystical Seven, Omicron Delta Kappa. Lutheran. Office: Sue L Goller and Assocs 1600 Wooded Hills Ln Jefferson City MO 65109

GOLLHOFER, DAVID LEE, manufacuturng executive; b. St. Louis, Aug. 16, 1935. Prodn. mgr. Zero Corp., Burbank, Clearwater, Calif/Fla., 1974-86, Sign Co., St. Louis, 1986-88; v.p. mfg. Hawkeye Steel, Inc., Houghton, Iowa, 1988—. Mem. Soc. Mfg. Engrs. (sr.). Office: Hawkeye Steel Co Inc PO Box 2000 Hwy 16 W Houghton IA 52631

GOLOSCHOKIN, ALEXANDER ISAAC, electrical engineer; b. Leningrad, USSR, Apr. 25, 1965; came to U.S., 1989; s. Isaac Gregory and Miriam (Joffey) G.; m. Irena Michelle Eydel, Aug. 29, 1986. MS in Elec. Engring., Leningrad Poly. Inst., 1988. Rsch. engr. Leningrad State Rsch. Facility of Electro Machinery, 1988-89; assoc. engr. Indpls. Power & Light Co., Inc., 1990-92, substa. design engr., 1992-94, lead engr., 1994-95, indsl. sales cons., 1995—. Mem. IEEE. Office: Indpls Power & Light Co PO Box 1595 One Monument Cir Indianapolis IN 46206-1595

GOLTZ, SONIA MAY, management educator; b. Penang, Malaysia, Apr. 15, 1959; came to U.S. 1962; d. Charles Robert and Yolanda Azara (Pereira) G.; m. James Earle Northey Jr., Feb. 14, 1982; children: Jacob Will, Madeline Marie. BA, U. Indpls., 1982; MS, Purdue U., 1985, PhD, 1987. Asst. prof. mgmt. U. Notre Dame, Ind., 1987-95; assoc. prof. Mich. Technol. U., Houghton, 1996—. David Ross Summer fellow, 1986, 87; recipient Jesse Jones Faculty Rsch. award, 1990-91. Mem. APA, Am. Psychol. Soc., Acad. Mgmt., Soc. Indsl. and Orgnl. Psychology. Home: 609 Sibley St Houghton MI 49931 Office: Mich Tech U Sch Bus 1400 Townsend Ave Houghton MI 49931

GOLUBSKI, JOSEPH FRANK, pathologist, physician; b. Cleve., Apr. 30, 1953; s. Joseph John and Rita Dolores (Krysinski) G.; m. Wanda Beth Kalencki, Nov. 11, 1983; children: Anne Elise, Joseph Edward. BA, Ohio Wesleyan U., 1975; MS, Cleve. State U., 1976; DO, U. Health Scis., Kansas City, Mo., 1980. Diplomate Am. Bd. Pathology; cert. med. rev. officer, Am. Assn. of Med. Rev. Officers. Intern Brentwood Hosp., Warrensville Heights, Ohio, 1980-81, chmn. pathology dept., 1987-88; resident in pathology Naval Regional Med. Ctr., Portsmouth, Va., 1981-85, mem. staff, head of autopsy svc. and clin. chem., 1985-87; assoc. pathologist Sheboygan (Wisc.) Meml. Med. Ctr., 1988—; cons. pathology Naval Hosp. Guantanamo Bay, Cuba, 1985-87, asst. clin. prof. pathology Ea. Va. Med. Sch., Norfolk, 1985-87. Comdr. USNR-IRR (Ind. Ready Res.), 1990—. Hall undergrad. fellow in chem. Ohio Wesleyan U, 1974. Fellow Am. Coll. Pathologists, Am. Soc. Clin. Pathologists; mem. AMA, Am. Osteo. Assn., Wis. Med. Assn., Sheboygan County Med. Soc. (sec.-treas. 1992—), Farmer's and Sportsman's Conservation Club (bd. dirs. 1990), Sheboygan Falls Conservation Club, Sheboygan Yacht Club. Home: 2232 N 7th St Sheboygan WI 53083-4923 Office: Sheboygan Meml Med Ctr 2629 N 7th St Sheboygan WI 53083-4932

GOLUSIN, MILLARD R., obstetrician/gynecologist; b. Detroit, Feb. 14, 1947; s. Raddie and Joan (Lalich) G.; m. Yvonne Marie Cronovich, Sept. 29, 1974; children: Milan, Marko, Matthew. BS with honors, Wayne State U., 1968, MS, 1970, MD, 1975. Diplomate Am. Bd. Obstetrics and Gynecology. Intern, then resident William Beaumont Hosp., Royal Oak, Mich., 1975-78; practice medicine specializing in obstetrics and gynecology Village Gynecologic and Obstetric Assocs., P.C., Southfield and Troy, Mich., 1978-92; pvt. solo practice specializing in obstetrics and gynecology Troy, Mich., 1992—; mem. quality assurance com. William Beaumont Hosp., Royal Oak, Mich., 1979—, mem. gynecol. quality assurance com., 1993—. Trustee United Beaumont Physicians Group, 1993—. Served with U.S. Army, 1969-71. Fellow ACOG; mem. Am. Soc. Reproductive Medicine, Mich. State Med. Soc., Am. Inst. Ultrasound Medicine, Serbian Singing Soc., Ravanica (musical dir. 1967—, pres. 1981-82). Republican. Serbian Eastern Orthodox. Office: 1050 Wilshire Dr Ste 100 Troy MI 48084-1526

GOMBERG, SAMUEL HARRIS, social studies educator; b. St. Louis, Apr. 29, 1946; s. Ben and Ida Gomberg; widowed. BA, U. Wis., 1968, MA, 1969; PhD, Carnegie-Mellon U., 1987. Tchr. Downers Grove (Ill.) H.S., 1969—. Mem. ASCD, NCSS, Assn. of Moral Edn. (workshop leader cons., 1978—), Phi Delta Kappa, Pi Sigma. Office: South High Sch 1436 Norfolk Downers Grove IL 60516

GOMBERT, RICHARD WILLIAM, information systems professional; b. Cuyahoga Falls, Ohio, Dec. 7, 1957; s. William Richard and Florence Elizabeth (Kline) G.; m. Kelly Diana Watts, Oct. 3, 1992; 1 child, Katherine Diana. BS, Kent State U. Programmer, operator Consol. Data Processing, Cleve., 1980-82; programmer Zeta Systems, Inc., Akron, Ohio, 1983-84; programmer, system adminstr. Computer Svcs. Group, Akron, 1992-93; programmer Richard L. Young & Assocs., Akron, 1993; system developer, integrator Midrange Computer Solutions, Cleve., 1993—. Programmer, co-author: (game) Trailblazer, 1983. Mem. Cleve. Area Lotus Notes Users Group, IEEE (assoc.), HP Users Group. Home: 1359 Niagara Ave Akron OH 44305 Office: Midrange Computer Solutions 1015 Euclid Ave Ste 500 Cleveland OH 44115

GOMER, ANNE OLAH, mathematics educator; b. Pitts., Oct. 18, 1928; d. John Stephen and Marie Catherine (Kosco)'Olah; m. Robert Gomer, Jan. 31, 1955; children: Richard H., Maria. BS, U. Ill., Chgo., 1974, MS, 1977. Vis. lectr. U. Ill., 1977-82; lectr. math. De Paul U., Chgo., 1982—. Mem. Math. Assn. Am., Assn. Women in Math. Home: 4824 S Kimbark Ave Chicago IL 60615-1916 Office: De Paul U 2219 N Kenmore Ave Chicago IL 60614-3504

GOMES, EDWARD CLAYTON, JR., construction company executive; b. Terre Haute, Ind., Nov. 15, 1933; s. Edward Clayton Sr. and Jewel Margaret (James) G.; m. Pamela Thompson, Jan. 11, 1958; children: Hilary T., Valerie C. BBA, Washington U., St. Louis, 1955, MBA, 1968. Pres. Mo. Petroleum Products Co., St. Louis, 1969-80; pres., CEO Lionmark Constrn. Cos., St. Louis, 1980—; bd. dirs. Martin K. Eby Constrn., Inc., Wichita, Magna Bank, St. Louis, Rightchoice Managed Care, Inc., 1994—; internat. dir. Young Pres.'s Orgn., N.Y.C., 1975-80; trustee Blue Cross Blue Shield Mo., 1991-94. Bd. dirs. Acad. of Sci., St. Louis, 1977-80; trustee St. Louis Art Mus., 1988-92, The Hawthorne Found., Jefferson City, Mo., 1983-86; commr. St. Louis Sci. Ctr., 1980-83. Mem. World Bus. Coun., Chief Execs. Orgn. (bd. dirs.), Whittemore House, St. Louis Club, Beta Gamma Sigma. Episcopalian. Office: Lionmark Inc 1620 Woodson Rd Saint Louis MO 63114-6129

GONDER, SHARON, special education educator; b. Princeton, Mo., Aug. 1, 1943; d. Raymond Dale and V. Juanita (Wharton) Hagan; m. Glen William Gonder, Oct. 18, 1985; 1 child, Patricia; stepchildren: Gil, Gailen, Gary, Geoffrey, Gregory, Douglas. BS in Edn., U. Mo., 1968, MEd in Spl. Edn., 1971; MEd in Counseling, Lincoln U., Jefferson City, Mo., 1978. Cert. elem. edn., behavioral disorders, learning disabilities, mentally handicapped, orthopedic handicapped, counseling, psychol. exam., adaptive phys. edn.. Instr. Mental Health Ctr., Columbia, Mo., 1969-71; diagnostician staffing coord. Non-Pub. By-Pass Program, Jefferson City, 1976-89; psychol. examiner Disabilities Determ, Dept. Elem. and Sec. Edn., Jefferson City, 1981-84; coord. Project Lift-Up Lincoln U., Jefferson City, 1984-86; diagnostician Metro Bus. Coll., Jefferson City, 1987-89; tchr., psychol. examiner Jefferson City Pub. Schs., 1968—; program cons. Lincoln U., Jefferson City, 1980—, adj. prof., 1985—; sec. Osage Bend Pub. Co., 1989—; bd. dirs. Ednl. Resources Info. Ctr. Leader 4-H, Jefferson City, 1978-81; non-registered lobbyist Mo. State Tchrs. Assn., 1987—; deacon, tchr. Sunday sch. First Christian Ch., 1985—; mem. task force to establish area at risk programs Jefferson City C. of C., 1993—. Named Mo. State Spl. Edn. Tchr. of Yr., Mo. Fedn. Coun. for Exceptional Children, 1991. Mem. Coun. for Exceptional Children (legis. chmn., sec.-treas. subdivsns. learning disabilities and mentally retarded 1988-95, bd. rep. Mo. coun. 1973-88, state fedn. pres. 1984-86, internat. del. 1974, 85, non-registered lobbyist 1983—), Internat. Spl. Disabilities Assn. (chpt. pres., exec. bd. dirs. 1975—), Delta Kappa Gamma (spkr. nat. circuit 1991—, author nat. publs. 1992—, bd. dirs. Ednl. Resource Info. Ctr. 1993—). Home: 213 Belair Dr Jefferson City MO 65109-0703 Office: Jefferson City Pub Schs 315 E Dunklin St Jefferson City MO 65101-3128

GONGWER, JUDITH MARLENE BECK, obstetrical nurse; b. Archbold, Ohio, Aug. 25, 1957; d. Lowell Eugene and Marlene Fay (Wyse) Beck; m. Stephen Alan Gongwer, Aug. 15, 1981. BSN, Goshen Coll., 1979. RN, Ind. Staff nurse in obstetrics Goshen (Ind.) Gen. Hosp., 1979-86, staff nurse in oper. rm., 1986-87, dir. obstetrics, 1987-95; nurse mgr. Fairhaven Physicians, Inc., Goshen, 1995—. Mem. adv. com. Parents As Tchrs., Goshen, 1993-95; puppy raiser Leader Dogs for Blind, Rochester, Mich. Mem. Am. Women's Health Obstetrics and Neonatal Nursing, Am. Orgn. Nurse Execs., North Cen. Ind. Nursing Honor Soc. Mennonite. Home: 28239 County Road 26 Elkhart IN 46517-9786 Office: Fairhaven Physicians Inc 301 Westward Rd Goshen IN 46526

GONNERING, RUSSELL STEPHEN, ophthalmic plastic surgeon; b. Milw., Nov. 21, 1949; s. Russell Richard and Virginia Mary (Mlinar) G.; m. Sandra Lynne Brubaker, Aug. 6, 1971; children: Julie Kathleen, Stephen Russell, Scott Duncan. Student, U. Vienna, Austria, 1969-70; AB in History cum laude, Boston Coll., 1971; MD, Med. Coll. Wis., 1975. Diplomate Am. Bd. Ophthalmology; lic. physician, Wis. Intern St. Luke's Hosp., Milw., 1975-76; fellow in ophthalmic plastic and reconstructive surgery U. Wis., Madison, 1980-81, asst. clin. prof. dept. ophthalmology, 1981-92, assoc. clin. prof. dept. ophthalmology, 1992-96; clin. prof. dept. ophthalmology, 1996—; resident in ophthalmology Med. Coll. Wis., Milw., 1977-80, asst. clin. prof. dept. ophthalmology, 1985—; ophthalmologist Children's Hosp. Wis., Milw., St. Joseph's Hosp., Milw.; ophthalmologist St. Luke's Hosp., Milw., chief ophthalmologist, 1983-92; pvt. practice Ophthalmic Plastic & Reconstructive Surgery, 1981—; rsch. assoc. in corneal physiology Med. Coll. Wis., 1976-77; rsch. advisor to fellowship in ophthalmic plastic and reconstructive surgery U. Wis., Madison, 1983—. Author: (with others) Infections of the Eye and Ocular Adnexa, 1986, Oculoplastic, Orbital and Reconstructive Surgery, 1988, Oculoplastic and Orbital Emergencies, 1990; sect. editor: Principles and Practice of Ophthalmic Plastic and Reconstructive Surgery, 1995; contbr. numerous articles to profl. jours.; presenter in field. Fellow ACS, Am. Acad. Ophthalmology (basic and clin. sci. course com. 1986-92, chmn. 1988-92, Honor Award 1990, Ruedemann lectr. 1994), Am. Soc. Ophthalmic Plastic and Reconstructive Surgery (editl. bd. 1987—, edn. com. 1988—, vice chmn. edn. com. 1995—, Marvin H. Quickert award 1982, Rsch. award 1982); mem. AMA, Internat. Soc. for Orbital Disorders, European Soc. Ophthalmic Plastic and Reconstructive Surgery, Internat. Dacryology Soc., Assn. for Rsch. in Vision and Ophthalmology, Med. Soc. Wis., Milw. County Med. Soc. (del. to state med. soc. 1987-90, bd. dirs. 1989-94, Dirs. citation 1994), Milw. Acad. Medicine, Milw. Ophthalmol. Soc. (treas. 1989-90, sec. 1990-91, v.p. 1991-92, pres. 1992-93), Am. Soc. Ocularists (med. adv. bd. 1987—), Nat. Soc. to Prevent Blindness (med. adv. bd. Wis. chpt. 1987-88). Office: Oculoplastic & Orbital Cons 2600 N Mayfair Rd Ste 950 Milwaukee WI 53226-1307

GONZALEZ, JUDYTH L. BETZ, speech communication educator; b. Anchorage, Dec. 3, 1947; d. Richard Earl and V. Lavelle (Bailey) Betz; m. Luis Gonzalez-Becerra, Aug. 1, 1970; children: Amanda, Elizabeth. BA, Oral Roberts U., 1970; MA, So. Nazarene U., 1981. Instr. adult basic edn. San Antonio, 1971-73; instr. Kenai (Alaska) Peninsula C.C., 1973-74; tchr. h.s. Christian Schs. of Alaska, Anchorage, 1974-76; tchr. East Park Christian Sch., Anchorage, 1976-77; tchr. bilingual resource Anchorage Sch. Dist., 1978-80; instr. Oklahoma City Southwestern Coll., 1980-81, 82-83, Yukon (Okla.) H.S., 1981-82; instr. ESL Tex. Wesleyan Coll., Ft. Worth, 1990; instr. speech comm. Delta Coll., University Center, Mich., 1991—. Mem. Internat. Listening Assn., Speech Comm. Assn., C.C. Humanities Assn. Office: Delta Coll University Center MI 48710

GONZALEZ, SISTER PAULA, futurist, educator, environmentalist; b. Albuquerque, Oct. 25, 1932; d. Hilario Chavez and Emilia Anna (Sanchez) G. BA, Coll. Mt. St. Joseph, Cin., 1952; MS, Cath. U. Am., 1962, PhD, 1966. Joined Sisters of Charity of Cin., Roman Cath. Ch., 1954. Instr. sci. Regina Sch. Nursing, Albuquerque, 1952-54; tchr. biology Seton High Sch., Cin., 1955-60; assoc. prof. biology Coll. Mt. St. Joseph, 1965-70, prof., 1970—; freelance futurist, educator, environmentalist, lectr., condr. workshops, cons.; founder, pres. EarthConnection, 1992—. Asst. editor Nursing Mgmt. Jour., 1985—. Fellow USPHS, 1961-65. Mem. Alt. Energy Assn. (pres. 1988-90), Union Concerned Scientists, Inst. Noetic Scis. Office: EarthConnection 370 Neeb Rd Cincinnati OH 45233-5101

GONZALEZ, SERGIO ANTONIO, economist; b. LaPaz, Bolivia; s. Walter and Nelly Esther (Sfeir) G. AB in Econs. with honors, Harvard U., 1988; MS in Acctg., U. Ill., 1990. CPA, Ill. Auditor Arthur Andersen & Co., Chgo., 1990-92, Premark Internat., Inc., Deerfield, Ill., 1992-95; sr. auditor R.R. Donnelley & Sons Co., Chgo., 1995—. Recipient Sci. award Bausch & Lomb. Mem. AICPA, Am. Prodn. and Inventory Control Soc. Roman Catholic.

GONZALEZ, WILLIAM G., hospital administrator, educator; b. Hackensack, N.J., Mar. 28, 1940; s. William G. and Blanche Irene (Saffery) G.; m. Shirley Ann Mos, Aug. 15, 1964; children: Dana Lynn, Liane Renee. BA, Rutgers U., 1964; MBA, Cornell U., 1966; cert., Sloan Inst. Hosp. Adminstrn., 1966; MPA, NYU, 1980. Bus. adminstr. U. Calif.-San Francisco Med. Ctr., 1966-68, asst. dir., various positions, 1968-74; dep. dir. Capital Dist. Psychiat. Ctr., Albany, N.Y.,, 1974-79; instr. Albany Med. Coll., 1974-79; adj. asst. prof. SUNY-Albany, 1978-79; dir. U. Calif.-Irvine Med. Ctr., Orange, 1979-85; sr. lectr. Grad. Sch. Mgmt. and Calif. Coll. Medicine, U. Calif., Irvine, 1980-85; bd. dirs. Hosp. Coun. So. Calif., 1983-85; pres., chief exec. officer Butterworth Health Corp. and Butterworth Hosp., Grand Rapids, Mich., 1985—; adj. prof. health svcs. adminstrn. Mich. State U. Coll. Human Medicine, 1985—; mem. gov.'s Task Force on Access to Health Care, 1987-89; mem. nursing task force Joint Commn. on Accreditation Health Care Orgns., 1988-90; trustee Mich. Hosp. Assn., 1990—; chmn. M in Mgmt. adv. coun. Aquinas Coll., Grand Rapids, 1992-95; bd. dirs. Grand Rapids Area Med. Edn. Ctr., chmn., 1995—; mem. accreditation coun. grad. med. edn., Am. Hosp. Assn., coordinating Com. on Med. Edn.; regent ACHE Area B., Mich., 1994—. Bd. dirs. Grand Rapids Pub. Edn. Fund, 1993—; bd. dirs. Old Kent Bank, 1994—; active Health Professions Coun., San Francisco, 1971-74; active Planned Parenthood-World Population, Alameda Calif. and San Francisco, 1972-74; mem. coun. of dels. sect. on met. hosps. Gov.'s Coun., 1989-92; mem. regional policy bd. AHA, 1990-93. Served with M.C. U.S. Army, 1961-64. William Stout scholar, 1964; Alfred P. Sloan scholar, 1964-65; N.Y. State Regents scholar, 1964-65; Rotary Internat. exchange fellow in hosp. adminstrn. Australia, summer 1982.

GOOCH, NANCY JANE, realtor, mortgage executive; b. Ann Arbor, Mich., Dec. 19, 1941; d. Donald B. and Marjorie (Gilchrist) G. BA, Western Mich. U., 1963; MA, Ea. Mich. U., 1987. Lic. real estate broker, Fla., Mich. Tchr. Broward County Schs., Ft. Lauderdale, Fla., 1968-73; v.p. Chinelly Real Estate, Inc., Miramar, Fla., 1973-83; closing exec. Cenville Devel. Co., Hollywood, Fla., 1983-85; mortgage originator Empire of Am., Southfield, Mich., 1987-90; dir. Am. Mortgage Tng. Co., Garden City, Mich., 1990—; founder First Fin. Mortgage Corp. Editor Bridlepath mag., 1983-84, The Saddlebred Mag., 1989-95; contbr. numerous articles to various publs. Pres. Broadway Area Neighborhood Assn., Ann Arbor, 1985-86. Recipient honors S. Fla. Trail Riders Broward County, 1983. Mem. Wayne-Oakland Bd. Realtors, Am. Saddlehorse Assn. (bd. dirs. Mich. chpt. 1990-95, sec. 1994-95), Women's Econ. Club. Republican. Office: First Fin 346 N Lafayette South Lyon MI 48178

GOOCH, U. L., state legislator; m. Augusta Gooch. Kans. state senator Dist. 29, 1993—. Address: 985 S Range Ave Colby KS 67701-3504*

GOOD, ARTHUR JAMES, business executive; b. Columbus, Ohio, May 19, 1952. BBA, Ohio U., 1974. V.p. A Good Co., Pickerington, Ohio, 1974—; pres. Video Masters, Inc., Pickerington, 1974—. Vol. Boy Scouts Am., Brice, Ohio, 1990—. Office: A Good Co PO Box 213 Pickerington OH 43147-0213

GOOD, NANCY SUSAN, health system administrator; b. Detroit, Mar. 22, 1940; d. Stanley Edward and Sybyl Delores (Adams) G.; m. James Anthony Waters, Oct. 25, 1958 (div. Sept. 1985); children: James A., Dawn Lisa, Kathleen, Christine. BGS, Wayne State U., 1988. Cert. fund raising exec. Rsch. coord. Cranbrook Ednl. Community, Birmingham, Mich., 1983-84; dir. devel. The Adventure Sch. (now Eaton Acad.), Birmingham, 1984-85; devel. officer Wayne State U. Sch. Medicine, Detroit, 1985-89; assoc. dir. devel. U. Detroit, 1989-90; dir. adminstrv. svcs. philanthropy and market communications Henry Ford Health Sys., Detroit, 1990-94, dir. development Western Wayne region, 1994—; cons. Southeastern Mich. Hospice Found., Southfield, 1986, Wayne State U., 1989-90; bd. dirs. Techniques for Effective Alcohol Mgmt. (TEAM) Mich. Mem. NAFE, Nat. Soc. Fundraising Execs., Coun. for Advance and Support of Edn., Assn. for Healthcare Philanthophy, Am. Prospect Rsch. Assn. (bd. dirs. Mich. chpt., membership chmn. 1989-91), Women's Econ. Club, Rotary, Planned Giving Roundtable. Roman Catholic. Office: Henry Ford Health Sys 1 Ford Pl Detroit MI 48202-3450

GOOD, SHELDON FRED, realtor; b. Chgo., June 4, 1933; s. Joseph and Sylvia (Schwartz) G.; student Drake U., 1951; children: Steven, Todd; m. Susan Forman, Dec. 22, 1990. BBA, U. Ill., 1955. Sales mgr. Baird & Warner Real Estate, Chgo., 1957-65; chmn. Sheldon F. Good & Co. Realtors, Chgo., 1965—; guest lectr. Northwestern U., U. Chgo., U. Calif., Wharton Grad. Sch., U. Pa., Stanford U., Vanderbilt U., U. Ill.; staff instr. Central YMCA City Coll., Chgo.; cons. in field. Chmn. United Settlement Appeal, Chgo., YMCA Edn. Libr. Drive, Chgo., Chgo. Jewish United Fund. Bd. dirs. Child, Inc.; pres. Gastrointestinal Research Found., U. Chgo., 1979; chmn. Realtors Hall of Fame. Served with AUS, 1955-57. Recipient Levi Eshkol Premier medal State Israel, 1967, Crown of A Good Name award Jewish Nat. Fund, 1972, Chgo. Realtor of Yr. award, 1991; named one of 10 outstanding young men Chgo., 1968. Mem. Chgo. Real Estate Bd. (treas., pres. 1988-89), Nat. Assn. Real Estate Bds., Nat. Assn. Realtors (chmn. nat. auction com. 1990, RTC task force), State of Ill. Internat. Real Estate Fedn. (FIABCI exec. com., pres. 1991, pres. FIABCI-USA, 1994-95, world pres.- elect FIABCI-Internat., 1995-96, world pres. 1996—), Chgo. Better Bus. Bur., Chgo Assn. Commerce and Industry, Alpha Epsilon Pi, Lambda Alpha, Omega Tau Rho. Club: Bryn Mawr Country (pres. 1988), Hundred of Cook County (bd. dirs.). Author: How to Sell Apartment Buildings; Techniques of Investment Property Exchanging; How to Lease Suburban Office Buildings; The Real Estate Auction as a Marketing Tool. Home: 180 E Pearson St Chicago IL 60611-2130 Office: 333 W Wacker Dr Chicago IL 60606-1218

GOOD, TIMOTHY JAY, medical equipment services company executive; b. Lima, Ohio, May 3, 1947; s. Marion Edward and Erma Mae (Sibold) G.; m. Ruth Ann Wray, July 22, 1967; children: Lucinda, Kelley, Ryan, Evan, Andrew. Student, Sinclair Community Coll., Dayton, Ohio, 1976-78, Ohio U., 1976-80, BioSystems Inst., Phoenix, 1982-86. Cert. cardiopulmonary technologist; cert. respiratory therapy technician; cert. pulmonary function technician; registered cardiopulmonary technologist. Asst. dir. respiratory therapy Bethesda Hosp., Zanesville, Ohio, 1968; dir. respiratory therapy Mount St. Mary Hosp., Nelsonville, Ohio, 1968-75, Hocking Valley Hosp., Logan, Ohio, 1972-81, Med. Ctr. Hosp., Chillicothe, Ohio, 1975-78; pres. Cardiopulmonary Care, Inc., Logan, 1976—, Patient Evaluation Services, Logan, 1986-95; cons. respiratory therapy S.E. Ohio Tb Hosp., Nelsonville, 1970-72, Ohio Lung Assn., 1978; mem. adv. com. and clin. faculty Shawnee State Coll., Portsmouth, Ohio, 1976-78; affiliate med. staff Hocking Valley Cmty. Hosp., Logan, Ohio, 1992—, Drs. Hosp., Nelsonville. Pres. Hocking County (Ohio) Heart Asn., 1977; trustee Green Twp. (Ohio), 1980-82; chmn. Hocking, Vinton and Athens Counties (Ohio) Mental Health Bd., 1986, Hocking County Regional Planning Commn., 1986; mem. adv. coun. Faith Builders Ednl. Programs, Guys Mill, Pa., 1988—. Mem. Am. Assn. Respiratory Care (bd. dirs. 1982-84), Nat. Soc. Cardiopulmonary Technologists, Nat. Assn. Med. Equipment Suppliers, Ohio Soc. Respiratory Care (pres. 1978). Republican. Mennonite. Lodge: Kiwanis (pres. Logan chpt. 1986—). Home: 3290 Stoney Hill Rd SW Lancaster OH 43130-8594 Office: 450 State Rte 664 N Logan OH 43138

GOODALE, JOANN OLSON, rehabilitation nurse; b. Huron, S.D., Mar. 6, 1937; d. Robert H. and Maxine (Biggerstaff) Olson; m. Eugene Clark Goodale, Dec. 15, 1957; children: Diane Kay Goodale Renz, Julie Ann, Michael Eugene. BSN, S.D. State U., 1959; MS in Rehab. Adminstrn. Mgmt., Depaul U., 1987. TN, S.D., Va., Ohio, Ill.; cert. ins. rehab. specialist, rehab. nurse, case mgr. Pvt. duty nurse U.S. Mil. Hosp., Madrid, Spain, 1959-60; staff nurse, acting head nurse No. Va. Hosp., Arlington, 1961-63; staff nurse, charge nurse, hosp. relief supr., employee health, staff devel. Kettering (Ohio) Meml. Hosp., 1965-75; rehab. nurse, case mgr. Liberty Mutual Ins. Co., Peoria, Ill., 1981-92; program dir. Midwest Acquired Brain Injury Rehab. Ctr. Meth. Med. Ctr., Peoria, Ill., 1992-94; mem. ins. adv. com. Rehab. Inst. Chgo., 1990-92. Mem. Pekin (Ill.) Mayor's Adv. Com. for Persons with Disabilities, 1992-95; mem. adult Christian edn. com. 1st Presbyn. Ch., Pekin, 1985-87. Mem. AAUW, Occupational Health Nurses Ill., Assn. Rehab. Nurses. Presbyterian. Home: 614 Washington St Pekin IL 61554-4238

GOODCHILD, ROSINA ANN, community health nurse; b. Streator, Ill., Nov. 28, 1963; d. David Floyd and Reita Mae (Keith) Allen; m. Robert Joseph Goodchild, June 4, 1988; children: Christopher Robert, Matthew James, Nathan Charles. AAS in Nursing, Ill. Valley Community Coll., 1984; BSN, Bradley U., 1988. RN, Ill. Camp nurse, counselor YMCA/CETA, Streator, 1983; pvt. duty nurse Streator, 1982-85; staff nurse emergency/trauma dept. St. James Hosp., Pontiac, Ill., 1984-88; charge nurse, preceptor ARC, Peoria, Ill., 1988-94; immunization nurse La Salle County Health Dept., Ottawa, Ill., 1992-94; mem. nursing adv. com. Heart of Ill. Blood Svcs., ARC, 1985-88. Spl. events coord. Village of Grand Ridge, Ill., 1995—; feature and staff writer for "Round the Ridge," 1995—; youth choir dir., 1995—. Mem. ANA, Ill. Nurses Assn., Emergency Nurses Assn. Home: PO Box 233 400 Sylvan Ave Grand Ridge IL 61325-0233

GOODE, JAMES FRANCIS, history educator; b. Hyannis, Mass., May 29, 1944; s. Charles Edward and Mary Blake (Childs) G.; m. Virginia Lawson Dixon, Jan. 20, 1972; children: Matthew Lawson, Zachary James. BS, Georgetown U., 1966; MA, U. Mass., 1968; diploma in edn., Mitchell Coll., Bathurst, N.S.W., Australia, 1976; PhD, Ind. U., 1984. Vol. Peace Corps, Iran, 1968-71; instr. U. Mashhad, Iran, 1971-73; tchr. Convent of Sacred Heart, Sydney, Australia, 1974-78; editorial asst. Am. Hist. Rev., Bloomington, Ind., 1981-84; instr. in history U. Ga., Athens, 1984-86; prof. history Grand Valley State U., Allendale, Mich., 1986—. Author: U.S. and Iran, 1946-51, 1989; contbr. articles to profl. publs. Fellow NEH, 1985, Nat. Coun. on U.S.-Arab Rels., 1987, 90, 94. Mem. Soc. for Historians of Am. Fgn. Rels., Soc. Iranian Studies, Mich. Com. on U.S.-Arab Rels. (dir. 1993—), Phi Kappa Phi. Office: Grand Valley State U Dept History Allendale MI 49401

GOODE, WAYNE, state senator, corporate executive; b. St. Louis, Mo., Aug. 20, 1937; s. Peter Wayne and Helen Celeste (McManus) G.; m. Jane Margaret Bell, July 27, 1963; children: Peter Wayne III, Jennifer Jacquelyn. BS in Banking and Fin., U. Mo., 1960. Mem. Mo. Ho. of Reps., Jefferson City, 1962-82, Mo. State Senate, Jefferson City, 1984—; pres. Aspen Group Inc., St. Louis, 1972—. Former mem. dean's coun. Sch. Bus. and Pub. Adminstrn. U. Mo., Confluence St. Louis Conf. on Edn.; bd. dirs. St. Louis Art Mus.; chmn. Commerce Consumer Protection and Environ., vice chmn. Interstate Coop., Ways and Means; mem. Appropriations Edn., Pub. Health and Welfare. Lt. U.S. Army, 1960-61. Recipient numerous awards including V.I.P. award Advt. Club, Recognition Meritorious Svc. award St. Louis Indsl. Rels. Assn., Disting. Svc. award Mo. Assn. for Children with Learning Disabilities, Outstanding Contribution in Improving Mental Health Care award Mental Health Assn., 1980 Globe Dem. award; named Conservation Legislator of Yr. Mo. Conservation Fedn., 1st Ann. Friend of Edn. Mo. NEA, Outstanding Legislator Mo. Assn. Pub. Employees, One of Ten Best Legislators St. Louisan Mag., Among Best and Brightest Columbia (Mo.) Daily Tribune, 1983 Ten Best Legislators Mo. Times. Home: 7231 Winchester Dr Saint Louis MO 63121-2623 Office: State Senate 334 E State St Jefferson City MO 65101-3021

GOODELL, JOHN DEWITTE, electromechanical engineer; b. Omaha, Nebr., Sept. 20, 1909; s. Edwin Dewitte and Vera May (Watts) G.; m. Bernadette Michel, Apr. 27, 1943; children: Mary, Greg, Thomas, Caroline, Daniel. Cons. engr. N.Y.C., 1931-41; tech. dir. U.S. Army Detroit Signal Lab., 1941-43; dir. engring. Minn. Electronics, St. Paul, 1946-57; mgr. new product design CBS Lab., Stamford, Conn., 1957-60; dir. engring. Robodyne, U.S.Industries, Silver Spring, Md., 1960-61; corp. tech. dir. U.S. Industries, N.Y.C., 1962-63; producer Goodell Motion Pictures, St. Paul, 1964-75; cons. engr. New Product Design, St. Paul, 1976-90; exhibit prototyper Sci. Mus. of Minn., St. Paul, 1990-93; dir. engring. Tomorrow's World, St. Paul, 1993—. Author: The World of Ki, 1967; writer, dir. (motion picture) Always a New Beginning, 1973, (acad. nominated best documentary 1973), (TV documentary) Wisdom and Change, 1992; dir. Challenge for Tomorrow, 1964 (indsl. Oscar); inventor: automatic mail handler, automatic manipulator, magnetic pulse controlling device, conditioned reflex teaching machines and others, 1954—; editor Jour. of Computing Systems, 1965-70. With U.S. Navy, 1943-46, S. Pacific. Recipient Master Design award, Product Engring., 1962. Mem. IEEE (sr.), Soc. Motion Picture and TV Engrs. Home: 751 Mt Curve Blvd Apt 5 Saint Paul MN 55116-1113

GOODHEW, HOWARD RALPH, JR., wholesale executive; b. Manitowoc, Wis., Aug. 28, 1923; m. Marie Walter; five children. Grad. high sch. Various positions including credit mgr., br. store supr. Ridge Co., Inc., South Bend, Ind., 1940-46, sec., 1946-56, pres., 1956-86, chmn. bd. dirs., 1986—; supt. South Bend Water Works, 1964-66, South Bend Utilities, 1966-68; bd. dirs. Nat. Bank & Trust Co., South Bend, First Interstate Bank of South Bend, Ind.; sec., dir. H.J. Schrader Co., 1963-69, Grunow Authorized Svc., Inc., 1966-69, pres. St. Joe Sales Co., 1949-55, P.B.M. Inc., 1968-79; chmn. bd. St. Joe Distbg. Co., 1984—; pres. HRG Inc., 1980—; pres., chmn. bd., nat. pronto dir. Distbrs. Assn., 1991—. Mem. South Bend Crime Commn., 1974—; pres. Better Bus. Bur. South Bend-Mishawaka, 1961-62, 74-75; mem. adv. bd. Adrian Coll. Found., 1958-75; deacon 1st Presbyn. Ch., South Bend, 1963-66, trustee, 1967-76; bd. dirs. United Community Svcs. of St. Joseph County, Inc., 1966-70; mem. bd. mgrs. community planning div. United Community Svc., 1965-70; bd. dirs. Meml. Hosp. South Bend, 1969, chmn. bldg. com., 1960-72; bd. dirs. South Bend Community Sch. Corp., 1969-73, pres., 1971-72; mem. Ind. Wage Adjustment Bd., 1969-74; fin. chmn. Ind. Rep. 3d Dist., 1964-70; fin. chmn. South Bend City Rep. Com., 1963, 67, St. Joseph County Rep. Com., 1964, 65, 70; mem. St. Joseph County Rep. Adv. Bd., 1964—; primary candidate for mayor of South Bend, 1963, 71, 83; dir., chmn. bd. dirs. Nat. Pronto, 1984—; v.p. South Bend Urban Enterprise Assocs., 1986—; chmn. Local Property Tax Control Bd. Ind. State, 1981-91; pres. South Bend Mid. Schs. Bldg. Corp., 1974—, South Bend Pub. Libr. Leasing Corp., 1981—, Brethern Care South Bend, Inc., 1974-83, St. Joseph County Parks Found., 1991; numerous other civic activities. Served with U.S. Army, World War II. Decorated Bronze Star. Recipient GEORGE award Mishawaka Enterprise-Record newspaper, 1975, Sagamore of the Wabash award Ind. Govs., 1976, 84; Rotary Community Service award, 1983. Mem. Automotive Svc. Industries Assn., South Gateway Improvement Assn. (pres. 1984—), Distbrs. Inst., South Bend-Mishawaka Area C. of C. (dir. 1968-84, v.p. 1970, 82), Rotary. Home: 59090 Goodhew Dr South Bend IN 46614-4119 Office: 1535 S Main St South Bend IN 46613-2207

GOODIN, DAVID LYNN, power systems engineering; b. Fargo, N.D., Oct. 21, 1961; s. Lawrence Dalphin and Mary Agness (Smith) G.; m. Patricia Jayne Redfield, Sept. 17, 1983; children: Michaela Leigh, Alayna Lynn,

Stephanie Kay. BSEE with honors, N.D. State U., 1983. Registered profl. engr., N.D. Electric engr. Mont.-Dakota Utilities Co., Dickinson, N.D., 1983-86, Glendive, Mont., 1986-89; electric supt. Mont.-Dakota Utilities Co., Williston, N.D., 1989-93; electric sys. supr. Mont.-Dakota Utilities Co., Bismarck, N.D., 1993—. Resident bus. leader Bus. Challenge-Greater N.D. Assn., Dickinson, 1990-92; vol. volleyball/basketball YMCA, Bismarck, 1993—; ch. coun. chmn. Gloria Dei Luth., Williston, 1993; bd. mem. MDU Employees Fed. Credit Union, 1988-89. Mem. IEEE, Toastmasters Internat. (v.p. edn. 1995—), Lions Internat., Toastmasters Club (pres. 1996—). Republican. Lutheran. Home: 2103 Thompson St Bismarck ND 58501

GOODMAN, DONALD JOSEPH, dentist; b. Cleve., Aug. 14, 1922; s. Joseph Henry and Henrietta Inez (Mandel) G.; BS, Adelbert Coll., 1943; DDS, Case-Western Reserve U., 1945; m. Dora May Hirsh, Sept. 18, 1947; children: Lynda (Mrs. Barry Allen Levin), Keith, Bruce; m. Ruth Jeanette Weber, May 1, 1974. Pvt. practice dentistry, Cleve., 1949-86; lectr. in field. With Dental Corps, USNR, 1946-48. Mem. Am. Acad. Gen. Dentistry, ADA Ohio State Dental Assn., Cleve. Dental Soc., Fedn. Dentaire Internationale, Cleve. Council on World Affairs, Greater Cleve. Growth Assn., Council of Smaller Enterprises, Phi Sigma Delta, Zeta Beta Tau, Alpha Omega. Clubs: Masons (32 deg.), Shriners, Travelers' Century (Gold award), Circumnavigators. Home: 29099 Shaker Blvd Cleveland OH 44124-5022

GOODMAN, GARY ALAN, lawyer; b. Memphis, Nov. 27, 1947; s. Louis H. and Margie (Evensky) G.; m. Teresa E. Berry, July 2, 1987. AB, Cornell U., 1969; JD, Columbia U., 1972. Bar: N.Y., 1973, U.S. Dist. Ct. (so. dist.) N.Y., 1973, Ill. 1979, U.S. Dist. Ct. (no. dist.) Ill. 1979, U.S. Cir. Ct. (2d cir.), U.S. Cir. Ct. (7th cir). Assoc. Sullivan & Cromwell, N.Y.C., 1972-79; ptrn., gen. counsel Winston & Strawn, Chgo., 1979—. Home: 219 E Lake Shore Dr Chicago IL 60611-1352 Office: Winston & Strawn 35 W Wacker Dr Chicago IL 60601-1614

GOODMAN, HUBERT THORMAN, psychiatrist, consultant; b. Oklahoma City, Mar. 5, 1933; s. Hubert Thorman and Belle (Wilkonson) G.; m. Doris Alene Knight, Feb. 1, 1957 (div. 1975); children: Mark, Martha Harris, Mary, Carmen Lugo, Valerie Freeman; m. Paulette Sue Freeman, Oct. 28, 1988. MD, Ind. U., 1957. Diplomate Am. Bd. Forensic Examiner, Am. Bd. Forensic Medicine; sr. disability analyst, diplomate Am. Bd. Disability Analysts. Intern Riverside Hosp., Toledo, 1957-58; resident in pub. health Miss. Dept. Health, Jackson, 1958-60; resident in psychiatry Cen. Ohio Psychiat. Hosp., Columbus, 1960-63; Ctrl. Ohio Psychiat. Hosp.; officer Pub. Health Svc., Jackson, 1958-60; pvt. practice Columbus, 1964—; clin. asst. prof. psychiatry Ohio State U., 1972-91; cons. Dept. Mental Health, 1990-95, Peer Rev. Sys. Ohio, 1990—. Contbr. articles to profl. jours. Capt. USPHS, 1958-60. Recipient Felix Underwood award Miss. Med. Assoc., 1963. Mem. AMA, Am. Psychiat. Assn., Ctrl. Ohio Med. Assn., Ohio State Med. Assn., Ctr. Ohio Psychiat. Assn. Home: 4770 Dierker Rd Columbus OH 43220-2985 Office: 4700 Reed Rd Columbus OH 43220-3074

GOODMAN, MORRIS, anatomy educator; b. Milw., Jan. 12, 1925; s. Benjamin and Sara (Bratt) G.; m. Selma Kessler, Apr. 5, 1946; children: Louise, Julia, David. BS, U. Wis., 1948, MS, 1949, PhD, 1951. Rsch. assoc. U. Ill. Coll. Medicine, Chgo., 1952-54, Detroit Inst. Cancer Rsch., 1954-58; sr. investigator immunology Lafayette Clinic, 1958-65; rsch. assoc. prof. Wayne State U., Detroit, 1960-66, prof. dept. anatomy, 1966—; dir. rsch. Plymouth (Mich.) State Home, 1966-72; mem. adv. panel for systematic biology, div. biol. and med. scis. NSF, 1969-72; Disting. vis. scholar Christ's Coll., Cambridge U., Eng., 1984; von Hofsten Meml. lectr. U. Uppsala, Sweden, 1987. Editor: Molecular Anthropology, 1976, Macromolecular Sequences in Systematic and Evolutionary Biology, 1982; co-editor: Jour. Human Evolution, 1971-77, editor, 1972; mem. editorial bd. Human Biology, 1974, Advances in Primatology, 1975, Jour. Molecular Evoluation, 1975, Molecular Biology and Evolution, 1983; editor in chief Jour. Molecular Phylogenetics and Evolution, 1991; contbr. articles to profl. jours. Mem. rsch. com. Mich. Assn. for Retarded Citizens, 1981—; bd. dirs. Voice of Reason, 1982—. With USAF, 1943-45; ETO. Recipeint Disting. Grad. Faculty award Wayne State U., 1986, Gershenson Disting. Faculty Fellow award, 1986, Sigma Xi Faculty Rsch. award, 1989-90 Lawrence M. Weiner award Wayne State U. Sch. Medicine Alumni Assn., 1995; grantee NSF, NIH; pres. Wayne State U. Acad. of Scholars, 1991. Fellow Am. Acad. Arts & Scis.; mem. Soc. Systematic Zoology, Am. Assn. Anatomists, Soc. for Study Evolution, Genetics Soc. Am., Am. Naturalist Soc. Home: 24211 Oneida St Oak Park MI 48237-1749 Office: Wayne State U Sch Medicine 540 E Canfield St Detroit MI 48201-1928

GOODMAN, MYRNA MARCIA, school nurse; b. Bklyn., Mar. 5, 1936; d. Louis and Anna R. (Bernowitz) Sheinberg; m. Stanley M. Goodman, June 30, 1957; children: Farrell Jay, Blayne Barrie, Devin Josh, Danica Janine. Diploma, L.I. Coll. Hosp., Bklyn., 1956; B in Elected Studies, Thomas More Coll., 1980; postgrad., Xavier U., 1984-86. Cert. sch. nurse, Ohio. Sch. nurse, supr. health and wellness svcs. L.I. Coll. Hosp., 1956-58; nurse, office mgr. Pediatric Assocs. of Fairfield (Ohio), Inc., 1962-72; nurse Fairfield City Sch. Dist., 1972-89, dir. health svcs., 1989-92, supr. health and wellness svcs., 1992—, sch. nurse Kindergarten Ctr., 1995; sch. nurse Kindergarten Ctr.; sec. Fairfield City Safety Coun., 1987-90; mem. Intervention Team for At-Risk Students, 1987-90, 95-96, Del. to Study Sch. Health, Australia, 1989; keynote spkr. Ohio Comprehensive Sch. Health Conf., 1991; conf. spkr. Ohio Assn. Health, Phys. Edn., Recreation and Dance, 1990, Nat. Sch. Bds. Assn., 1993. Mem. adv. coun. on drug free schs. and cmty. Butler County Mental Health Assn., 1988; chmn. sch. site com. Am. Heart Assn., 1981, coord. heart-at-work program; chmn. employee wellness com., spkr. del. assembly Ohio affiliate, 1992, pres., 1995, co-pres. Hamilton-Fairfield div., 1995, mem. adv. com. for county practical nurse program, 1994-95; pres. Fairfield Tempo Club, 1976; com. mem. Fairfield Sister City Program; mem. Modern Music Masters, 1976; mem. adv. coun. Daytime Ctr. for Girls; bd. dirs. Greater Hamilton Safety Coun., 1988; mem. adv. com. Fairfield Pub. Presch.; chmn. adv. com. Fairfield Schs. Food Svc. Recipient Outstanding Svc. award Fairfield Cen. Sch., 1974, 77, 78, 89, Letters of Recognition for Outstanding Svc. to Fairfield Sch. Dist. Supt., 1980, 86, 89, 90, March of Dimes, Am. Lung Assn., 1980, Am. Heart Assn., 1988, 89, 90, Hall of Fame award Am. Heart Assn., 1992, co-recipient Cert. of Appreciation, Am. Heart Assn. Sch. Site Task Force, 1992. Mem. NEA, ASCD, Ohio Edn. Assn., Ohio Assn. Sch. Nurses (conf. speaker 1993), S.W. Ohio Sch. Nurses Assn. (sec. 1987-90), Am. Sch. Health Assn., Nat. Assn. Sch. Nurses, Parents and Tchrs. for Children, Ohio Assn. Secondary Sch. Adminstrs., Nat. Assn. Secondary Sch. Adminstrs. Home: 5180 Suwannee Dr Fairfield OH 45014-2482 Office: Fairfield City Sch Dist 211 Donald Dr Fairfield OH 45014-3006

GOODMAN, NANCY JANE, small business owner; b. Monett, Mo., May 9, 1946; d. William F. and Audie L. (Stolle; m. Douglas L. Goodman, May 9, 1969; children: Kelly, Gregory, Kristi, Anthony, Richard. Student, Drury Coll., Springfield, Mo., 1969-70, Crowder Coll., Neosho, Mo., 1991-93. Lic. real estate salesperson, Mo., notary public. Supr. Family Svcs., Aurora, Mo., 1972-87; exec. sec. Little Tikes Toy Co., Aurora, 1987-90, buyer, 1990—; pres., owner DJ's Catering, Aurora, 1991—. Author: South American Travel, 1985. Area rep. Am. Intercultural Students, Aurora, 1989—. Named to Outstanding Young Women of Am., 1984. Mem. NAFE, Am. Purchasing Soc., Optimist Club (charter pres., lt. gov. Western Mo. dist. 1996—), Phi Theta Kappa. Home: 519 W College St Aurora MO 65605-2833

GOODNESS, RICHARD GRAYSON, sales executive; b. Huntingburg, Ind, Mar. 29, 1955; s. Joseph Kulamanu and Doris Elaine (Koehler) G.; m. Diane Mary Oeding, Oct. 13, 1984; children: Mariah Leilani, Guy Kulamanu, Jud Keaka. BA, Middle Tenn. State Univ., 1978. Sales training, mgt. Jasper (Ind.) Engines & Transmissions, 1979—. City councilman City of Jasper, 1992—; v.p. Dubois County Child Abuse Prevention Coun. Republican. Methodist. Office: Jasper Engines & Transmissions 815 Wernsing Rd Jasper IN 47546-8141

GOODNO, KEVIN P., state legislator; b. Oct. 22, 1962; m. Linda. BA, Concordia Coll., 1985. State rep. Minn. Ho. Reps., Dist. 9A, 1991—; mem. regulated industry com., tax com., labor mgmt. rels. com., gov.'s jobs & tng. coun., state coun. vocat. tech. edn., advantage Minn., Minn. Ho. Reps. Mem. Moorhead C. of C., Ducks Unltd. Home: 806 3rd St S Moorhead MN 56560-3314*

GOODRIDGE, ALAN GARDNER, research biochemist, educator; b. Peabody, Mass., Apr. 2, 1937; s. Lester Elmer and Gertrude Edith (Gardner) G.; m. R. Ann Funderburk, Aug. 19, 1960; children—Alan Gardner Jr., Bryant C. B.S. in Biology, Tufts U., 1958; M.S. in Zoology, U. Mich., 1963, Ph.D. in Zoology, 1964. Rsch. fellow dept. biochemistry Harvard Med. Sch., Boston, 1964-66; asst. prof. physiology U. Kans. Med. Ctr., Kansas City, 1966-68; assoc. prof. Banting and Best dept. med. rsch. U. Toronto, Ont., Can., 1968-76; prof. Banting and Best dept. med. rsch. U. Toronto, 1976-77; prof. pharmacology and biochemistry Case Western Res. U., Cleve., 1977-87; prof., head dept. biochemistry U. Iowa, 1987—. Assoc. editor Jour. Biol. Chemistry, 1990—, Ann. Rev. of Biochemistry, 1994—, Jour. Lipid Rsch., 1995—; contbr. numerous articles to profl. jours. Served with USN, 1958-61. Grantee Med. Rsch. Coun. Can., 1968-77, NIH, 1966-68, 77—; Josiah Macy Jr. faculty scholar, 1975-76, USDA, 1986-90, 93—. Mem. AAAS, Am. Soc. Biochemistry and Molecular Biology, Thyroid Assn., Assn. Med. and Grad. Sch. Depts. Biochemistry (treas. 1990-92, pres.-elect 1993, pres. 1994). Home: 3005 Dubuque St NE Iowa City IA 52240-7990 Office: U Iowa Dept Biochemistry Iowa City IA 52242

GOODRIE, JOANN ILENE, human services administrator; b. Beach, N.D., Mar. 22, 1940; d. Harold and Garnet Esther (Hathaway) Feldhusen; m. Robert Montgomery Zoller, May 28, 1965 (div. Aug. 1974); children: Jason, Jennifer; m. Leo Dean Goodrie, June 7, 1986. BA, Jamestown Coll., 1963; postgrad., U. S.D., 1965, U. Minn., 1971. Resident dir. Mouse River Players, Minot, N.D., 1971-78; coord. devel. and pub. rels. Northeast Human Svcs., Grand Forks, N.D., 1978-80; adminstrv. officer, dir. program devel. U. N.D., Grand Forks, 1980-88; cons., 1988-91; dir. devel. and human resources Ctrl. Minn. Mental Health, St. Cloud, 1991—; cons. Wright County Human Svcs., Buffalo, Minn., 1993—. Editor N.D. Family Practice Quar., 1981-85. Mem. Ctrl. Minn. Planned Giving Coun., St. Cloud Human Svcs. Coun., C. of C., Order Ea. Star. Democrat. Office: Ctrl Minn Mental Health Ctr 1321 N 13th St Saint Cloud MN 56303

GOODSTEIN, SANDERS ABRAHAM, scrap iron company executive; b. N.Y.C., Oct. 3, 1918; s. Samuel G. and Katie (Lipson) G.; m. Rose Laro, June 28, 1942; children: Peter, Esther, Jack, Rachel. Student, Wayne State U., 1934-36; AB, U. Mich., 1938, MBA, 1939, JD, 1946; postgrad., Harvard, 1943. Bar: Mich., 1946. Sec. Laro Coal & Iron Co., Flint, Mich., 1946-60, pres., 1960—; owner, operator Paterson Mfg. Co., Flint, 1953—; gen. ptnr. Indianhead Co., Pontiac, Mich., 1955-70, pres., 1965-70; sec. Amatac Corp., Erie, Pa., unitl 1969; chmn. bd. Gen. Foundry & Mfg. Co., Flint, 1968—, pres., 1970—; pres. Lacron Steel Co., Providence, 1975-80, ETL Corp., Flint, 1983-91, Can. Blending and Processing, Windsor, 1988—; mem. corp. body Mich. Blue Shield, 1970-76. Served to lt. comdr. USNR, 1942-46. Mem. Fed. Bar Assn., Am. Bar Assn., Bar Mich., Am. Pub. Works Assn., Am. Foundrymen's Soc., Order of Coif, Beta Gamma Sigma, Phi Kappa Phi. Jewish. Home: 2602 Parkside Dr Flint MI 48503-4662 Office: 4296G W Pierson Rd Flint MI 48504-1337

GOODWIN, CHARLES PEMBERTON, athletic trainer; b. Camp Lejune, N.C., Mar. 25, 1966; s. Joel Sexton and Mary Ellen (Pemberton) G.; m. Bonnie Marie Campbell, July 13, 1991; 1 child, Amanda Pemberton. BA in Health/Phys. Edn., Furman U., Greenville, S.C., 1988; MS, U. Fla., 1991. Cert. athletic trainer. Asst. athletic trainer Coast Guard Acad., New London, Conn., 1991-93; head athletic trainer Muskingum Coll., New Concord, Ohio, 1993—. Mem. Nat. Athletic Trainers Assn., Am. Coll. Sports Medicine (cert.), Ohio Athletic Trainers Assn. (lic., mem. pub. reis. 1994-96). Democrat. Methodist. Office: Muskingum Coll. Athletic Dept New Concord OH 43762

GOODWIN, GRETA HALL, state legislator; m. James G. Goodwin. Kans. state rep. Dist. 78, 1993—, legal asst., 1996—. Home: 420 E 12th Ave Winfield KS 67156-3721 Office: Kans Ho of Resp State Capitol Topeka KS 66612*

GOODWIN, STEPHEN BRUCE, plant pathologist; b. Bethlehem, Pa., Oct. 27, 1958; s. Bruce Kesseli and Joan (Horton) G. BS summa cum laude, Duke U., 1981; PhD, U. Calif., Davis, 1988. Postdoctoral assoc. Cornell U., Ithaca, N.Y., 1987-91, rsch. assoc., 1991-95; USDA rsch. plant pathologist, adj. asst. prof. Purdue U., West Lafayette, Ind., 1995—. Contbr. articles to profl. jours. Mem. Genetics Soc. Am., Am. Phytopathol. Soc., Soc. for Study of Evolution, Phi Beta Kappa. Office: Dept of Botany/Plant Path 1155 Lilly Hall Purdue Univ West Lafayette IN 47907

GOODYEAR, JULIE ANN, marketing and fundraising specialist; b. Lafayette, Ind., Dec. 10, 1956; d. Charles Robert and Leona Mae (Widmer) Stroop; m. Michael Clark Goodyear, May 31, 1986; children: Elizabeth, Katharine, (twins) Charles and David. BA, Purdue U., 1983; MA, U. N.D., 1985. Asst. mktg. dir. Mo. Repertory Theater, Kansas City, 1985-88; dir. mkg. and pub. rels. Northlight Theater, Chgo., 1988-91; membership mgr. Chgo. Bot. Gardens, Glencoe, Ill., 1991-92; mgr. rel. mktg. Evanston (Ill.) Hosp. Corp., 1992-93, sr. devel. officer, 1993—. Active Dawes Elem. Sch. PTA, Evanston, 1992—; pres. Ctrl. Evanston ChildCare Parents Bd., 1993-94. Design winner for poster Saks 5th Ave., 1986. Mem. Nat. Soc. Fundraising Execs., Assn. Healthcare Philanthropy, Jr. League of Evanston-North Shore. Home: 1804 Cleveland St Evanston IL 60202

GOOGINS, LOUISE PAULSON, financial planner; b. Iola, Wis., June 14, 1941; d. Walter August and Helen Veronica (Waldoch) Paulson; m. James R. Googins, June 19, 1965 (div. 1978); children: Michael James, Shane Paul. BS, Stevens Point State U., 1963; MA, U. Wis., 1976, Coll. Fin. Planning, Denver, 1984. Recreational therapist Cen. Wis. Colony, Madison, Wis., 1966-69; tchr. mentally retarded Madison Schs., Madison, 1969-71; supr. student tchrs. U. Wis., Madison, 1972-76; tchr. learning disabled Monona, Wis., 1976-78; rep. FPC Secs. & Charter Securities, Madison, 1978-83; prin., pres. Googins & Co. Inc., Madison, 1983—. Bd. dirs. REBOS House, Madison, 1982-95, pres. 1987-90. Mem. Inst. CFPs, Madison South Rotary (bd. dirs. 1993—, sgt. at arms 1990-91, pres.-elect 1996—). Office: Googins & Co Inc 437 S Yellowstone Dr Madison WI 53719-1096

GOOLD, FLORENCE WILSON, occupational therapist; b. Chgo., Aug. 26, 1912; d. Frank Elmer and Marie Louise (Walker) Wilson; m. Robert Charles Goold, Dec. 28, 1938; children: Frances Louise Goold Felty, Nancy Jean Gould Magurno, Elizabeth Jane Ill, Robert Charles, Jr. Student, U. Wis., 1934; BA, Boston Sch. Occupational Therapy, 1936. Occupational therapist Ypsilanti (Mich.) State Hosp., 1936-40, Michael Reese Hosp., Chgo., 1940-42, DuPage County Easter Seal Ctr., Villa Park, Ill., 1959-62; dir. occupational therapy Hinsdale (Ill.) Sanitarium and Hosp., 1962-71, Marianjoy Rehab. Hosp., Wheaton, Ill., 1971-73, Cen. DuPage Hosp., Winfield, Ill., 1972-73, Royal Oak Convalescent Home, Oak Park, Ill., 1973, Highland House Nursing Home, Downers Grove, Ill., 1973-75, St. Charles Med. Ctr., Aurora, Ill., 1975-78, Westmont (Ill.) Health Ctr., 1978-80, Americana Health Care Ctr., Naperville, Ill., 1981-84, Med. Pers. Pool, Chgo., 1985-89, Midwest Rehab. Svcs., Hinsdale, 1986-95. Pres. bd. dirs. DuPage County Easter Seal Ctr., Villa Park, 1942-59; bd. dirs. Community Adult Day Care, Downers Grove, 1985-95. Named Citizen of Yr., Downers Grove, 1987. Mem. PEO, Am. Occupational Therapy Assn., Ill. Occupational Therapy Assn. (past pres., Occupational Therapist of Yr. 1988), Phi Mu. Episcopalian. Home: 6582 Willowwood Ct Downers Grove IL 60516-3045 Office: Ill Occupational Therapy Assn 715 Lake St Ste 710 Oak Park IL 60301-1416

GOOLDY, PATRICIA ALICE, elementary education educator; b. Indpls., Nov. 23, 1937; d. Harold Emanuel and Emma Irene (Wade) VanTreese; m. Walter Raymond Gooldy, May 4, 1968. BS, U. Indpls., 1959; MS, Butler U., 1963. Tchr. Franklin Twp. Cmty. Schs., Indpls., 1959-68, 72—, USA Dep. Schs., Bad Kreznack, Germany, 1969-72; co-owner Ye Olde Genealogie Shoppe, Indpls., 1972—; lectr. in field. Author: 21 Things I Wish I'd Found, 1984; editor: Indiana Wills to 1880: Index to Indiana Wills, 1987; co-editor: Indiana Manual For Gen, 1991, Illinois Manual For Gen, 1994. Mem. Franklin Twp. Geneal. Soc. (founder), Ind. Geneal. Soc. (chartered). Office: Ye Olde Genealogie Shoppe PO Box 39128 Indianapolis IN 46239

GOONEWARDENE, HILARY FELIX, retired entomology professor, consultant; b. Colombo, Sri Lanka, Apr. 9, 1925; came to U.S., 1958; s. Hector Felix and Rosalind Christina (Kahawita) G.; m. Rosemarie Eileen Goonewardene, Dec. 24, 1955; children: Julie Karen, Howard Michael, David Reed. BSc, U. Sidney, 1953; B of Agrl. Sci., U. New Zealand, 1957; MSc, Rutgers U., 1960, PhD, 1961. Pres. Internat. Club, U. Sydney (Australia), 1950-52, Rutgers U., 1960-61; rsch. asst. Commonwealth Sci. and Indsl. Rsch. Orgn., Canberra, Australia, 1952-53; crop protection officer Coconut Rsch. Inst., Lunuwila, Sri Lanka, 1956-58; rsch. asst. Rutgers U., New Brunswick, N.J., 1958-61; tech. dir. PPG Industries, Moorestown, N.J., 1961-63; head pesticides rsch. Smith, Kline & French, Phila., 1963-64; rsch. entomologist USDA, Moorestown, 1965-72, Wooster, Ohio, 1972-74; rsch. entomologist USDA, West Lafayette, Ind., 1974-88, collaborator ARS, 1988-91; cons. facilities mgmt. div. Marriott Corp., Washington, 1988—; cons. agrl. pesticides rsch. and devel. PPG Industries, Moorestown, 1963; cons. facilities mgmt. Sandoz Corp. Hanover, N.J., 1964, UNICCO, Boston, 1992—, Morrison-Crothall, Media, Pa., 1993; cons. insect rearing Gardens Alive, Lawrenceburg, Ind,. 1994—; adj. prof. Ohio State U., 1972-74, Ohio Agrl. R & D Ctr., 1972-74, Purdue U., 1974-88, emeritus prof, 1988—. Patentee in field. Mem. AAAS (emeritus), Entomol. Soc. Am. (emeritus), Am. Hort. Soc. (emeritus), Am. Pomological Soc., Ind. Acad. Sci., 20th Century Jr. League (Palmerston, N.Z. chmn. 1954), Sigma Xi. Episcopalian. Home: 630 Eden St West Lafayette IN 47906-1528

GOOSEY, THOMAS H., packaging technician; b. Moberly, Mo., Oct. 18, 1953; s. Alfred Harold and Margaret Arlene (Newbrough) G.; m. Deborah Diane Rollins, July 8, 1978; 1 child, Megan. Student, SMU, 1973. Pkg. technician, CAD tech. Fasco Industries Inc., Ozark, Mo., 1976—. Mem. Bible study dir., First Bapt. Ch., Ozark, 1986. With USN, 1975-77. Republican. Baptist. Home: 241 Utah Dr Ozark MO 65721-8161 Office: Fasco Industries Inc 1600 W Jackson St Ozark MO 65721-9156

GOOSSEN, DUANE, state legislator; b. Newton, Kans., Aug. 21, 1955; s. Henry W. and Edna M. (Ensz) G.; m. Rachel Waltner. BA, Bethel Coll., 1978. Councilman Goessel, Kans., 1979-83; Kans. state rep. Dist. 70, 1983—, contractor; bd. dirs. Goessel Devel. Corp. Bd. dirs. Bethesda Hosp. and Home, 1980—, Bethel Coll., 1984—. Mem. Lions. Home: PO Box 97 Goessel KS 67053-0097*

GOPON, LEON MICHAEL, insurance company executive; b. Oak Park, Ill., Aug. 25, 1941; s. Leon George and Genevieve S. (Pustelnik) G.; m. Sharon Carol Iwanski, Mar. 12, 1943; 1 child, Gregory Brian. Student, Northwestern U., Evanston, Ill., 1959-60; BS in Indsl. Edn., U. Ill., 1965. Indsl. arts tchr. Chgo. Pub. Schs., 1965; systems analyst Allstate Ins., Northbrook, Ill., 1969-72, systems supr., 1972-75, systems project mgr., 1975-79, sr. systems project mgr., 1979-94; cons., 1994-95; dir. ops. United Equitable Ins. Co., Lincolnwood, Ill., 1995—. Commr. Buffalo Grove Youth Commn., 1981-86; mem. Ill. USAF Acad. Selection Panel, Congressmen Porter and Hyde, 1988—; admissions liaison officer USAF Acad., Chgo., 1986-92. Lt. col. USAF/USAFR, ret., 1965-93. Fellow Life Mgmt. Assn., Atlanta, 1984; health ins. assoc. Health Ins. Assn. Am., Washington, 1990. Mem. Res. Officers Assn. (life), Buffalo Grove Jaycees (pres. 1981, 88, Internat. Senator 1983), U. Ill. Alumni Assn. (life). Office: United Equitable Ins Co 7373 N Cicero Ave Lincolnwood IL 60646

GORCHEFF, NICK A., controller; b. Salem, Ohio, Sept. 20, 1958; s. Albert N. and Jean A. (Felger) G. BS, Youngstown State U., 1981. Acct., computer programmer RE Gibson Contractor Inc., Lisbon, Ohio, 1981-85; v.p., contr. The Traichal Construction Co., Niles, Ohio, 1985—; officer Plant Indsl. Sales Co., 1989-92; v.p. Fowler Ctr. A & C Inc., 1989-91; pres. Austintown Mgmt. Corp., 1991—; v.p., treas. Royal Palms Mgmt. Inc., 1995—; v.p. Cloud 9 Limousine Inc., 1996—. Home: 447 E Beacon Dr Youngstown OH 44515-4064 Office: The Traichal Constrn Co PO Box 70 Niles OH 44446-0070

GORDER, WILLIAM E., state legislator; m. Marlene Gorder; 4 children. BA, U. N.D., MEd. Tchr., farmer, state rep. dist. 16, 1981—; Vice chmn. natural resources com.; mem. edn. and human svcs. com. N.D. Ho. Reps. Mem. Grafton C. of C., Grafton Gideon Camp, Walsh Hist. Soc., Farm Bur., Am. Legion. Republican. Home: 1345 Lawler Ave Grafton ND 58237-1764*

GORDON, ALICE JEANNETTE IRWIN, secondary and elementary education educator; b. Detroit, Mar. 18, 1934; d. Manley Elwood and Jeannette (Coffron) Irwin; m. Edgar George Gordon, Feb. 4, 1967; children: David Alexander, John Scott. BA in Elem. Edn., Mich. State U., 1956; MA in Child Devel., U. Mich., 1959, EdS in Ednl. Psychology, 1967, MA in Reading, 1990. Cert. K-12 tchr., Mich. Elem. tchr. Detroit Pub. Schs., 1956-67, reading tchr., 1967-68; secondary tchr. English and reading Parchment Pub. Schs., 1989-94; secondary reading specialist Kalamazoo Pub. Schs., 1994—; reading supr. Western Mich. U., Kalamazoo, 1992-95. Mem. alumni bd. Mich. State U. Coll. Edn., 1990—; chmn. Century Ball, Nazareth Coll., Kalamazoo, 1987; co-chmn. Evening of Nte, Kalamazoo Symphony, 1989; precinct del. Kalamazoo Rep. Com., 1989, 92; mem. spelling and adult learner Mich. Adult Edn. Practitioner Inquiry Project, 1994, 95. Fellow U. Mich., 1963, 66; coop. learning grantee Mich. Dept. Edn., 1990. Mem. Internat. Reading Assn., Mich. Reading Assn., Homer Carter Reading Assn., P.E.O., Jr. League, Lawyers Wives Auxillery, Kappa Delta Pi, Phi Delta Kappa, Alpha Omega Pi. Presbyterian. Home: 4339 Lakeside Dr Kalamazoo MI 49008-2802 Office: Loy Norrix HS 606 E Kilgore Rd Kalamazoo MI 49008-3610

GORDON, AUDREY KRAMEN, university administrator; b. Chgo., Nov. 18, 1935; d. Edward J. and Anne (Levin) K.; children: Bradley, Dale, Holly. BS with highest distinction, Northwestern U., 1965, MA, 1967, postgrad., 1971; MA, U. Chgo., 1970; PhD, U. Ill., Chgo., 1991. Cert. in clin. pastoral edn. Lectr. Northwestern U., Evanston, Ill., 1966-74; vis. asst. prof. Beloit (Wis.) Coll., 1974-75; research specialist U. Ill., Chgo., 1983-86, dir. continuing edn. Sch. Pub. Health, 1986-91, lectr. community health scis., 1988-91, dir. coll. advancement Sch. Pub. Health, 1991-92; coord./counselor Jewish Hospice, Chgo., 1984-89; asst. prof. community health scis. Sch. Pub. Health U. Ill., Chgo., 1992—; sr. rsch. specialist Ctr. for Pub. Health Practice, Sch. Pub. Health, U. Ill., 1992—; lectr. Loyola U. Stritch Sch. Medicine, Maywood, Ill., 1982—; pres. Rainbow Hospice Orgn., 1984-88, mem. profl. adv. bd., 1988—. Co-author: They Need To Know: How To Teach Children About Death, 1979; co-editor: Hospice and Cultural Diversity, 1995. Recipient Northwestern Univ. Alumni Merit award, 1993. Mem. APHA, Ill. Pub. Health Assn., Ill. Hospice Orgn. (pres. 1989-90), Nat. Hospice Orgn. (coun. of profls.), Alpha Sigma Lambbda, Alpha Kappa Lambda, Delta Omega.

GORDON, CRAIG JEFFREY, oncologist, educator; b. Detroit, Feb. 10, 1953; s. Maury Allen and Shirley Phoebe (Jacoby) G.; m. Susan Ann Blase, Aug. 3, 1980; children: Sari, Scott, Brittany. BS, Oakland U., 1978; DO, U. Osteopathic Medicine and, Health Scis./Des Moines, 1983. Diplomate Am. Bd. Internal Medicine, Am. Bd. Med. Oncology. Intern-chief Botsford Gen. Hosp., Farmington Hills, Mich., 1983-84, resident, 1984-87; fellow in hematology and oncology Wayne State Univ. (affiliated Hosp.'s Prog.), Detroit, 1987-90, fellow-chief, 1989-90; clin. asst. prof. dept. medicine Wayne State U., Detroit, 1990—; dir. divsn. hematology and oncology Botsford Hosp., Livonia, Mich., 1992—; med. dir. Angela Hospice, 1993—; mem. extrarenal transplantation com. Mich. Dept. Pub. Health; physician advisor Gilda's Club Mich. Contbr. articles to profl. jours. Named Intern of the Yr. Botsford Hosp. Staff, 1984, Resident of the Yr., 1985-87; clin. fellow Am. Cancer Soc., 1987-90. Fellow Am. Coll. Osteo. Internists; mem. AAAS, Am. Osteopathic Assn., Am. Coll. Osteopathic Internists, Assn. Adminstrs. and Cancer Execs., Mich. Assn. Osteopathic Physicians and Surgeons, Assn. Cancer Execs., So. Med. Assn., S.W. Oncology Group, Am. Soc. Clin. Oncologists, Oakland County Osteo. Assn. Office: Botsford Gen Hosp Ste 300 28595 Orchard Lake Rd Farmington Hills MI 48334

GORDON, EDWARD EARL, management consultant; b. Evergreen Park, Ill., Feb. 28, 1949; s. Earl and Estelle (Biehn) G.; m. Elaine Huarisa, Aug. 6, 1983. BA in History, Edn., DePaul U., 1971, MA in History, 1972; postgrad., U. Chgo., 1972-73; PhD in History of Edn./Psychology, Loyola U., 1988. Founding pres. Imperial Edn. Corp., Oak Lawn, Ill., 1968—; exec.

dir. North Am. Inst. for Tng. and Ednl. Rsch., 1972—; arbitrator Am. Arbitration Assn., Chgo., 1973—, Coun. Better Bus. Burs., Chgo., 1977—, Ill. Bd. Edn., 1986—; lectr. Sch. Edn., DePaul U., Chgo., 1979-92, instr. dept. history, 1989-91; mem. adv. coun. U. Ill., Chgo., 1989—; adj. prof., dir. grad. program in tng. and devel. Roosevelt U., Chgo., 1990-91; instr. adult corp. instrn. mgmt. program Loyola U., Chgo., 1992—; mem. Conf. Bd. Bus. Edn. Conf., 1996; keynote spkr. Partnerships in Learning at Work program U. B.C., Vancouver, Can., 1990, Workplace Tng. Inst. VI, Kans. State U., Kansas City, 1995, R.R. Personnel Assn. 43d Ann. Conf., Palm Beach, Fla., 1995, Corp. Univ. Forum, Chgo., 1996, Measuring Performance and Profit for Workforce Edn. Programs, Palm Springs, Calif., 1996; presenter profl. confs. Author: Educators' Consumer Guide to Private Tutoring Services, 1989, Centuries of Tutoring: A History of Alternative Education in America and Western Europe, 1990, Closing the Literacy Gap in American Business: A Handbook for Trainers and Human Resources Development Specialists, 1991, The Need for Work Force Education, 1993, FutureWork: The Revolution Reshaping American Business, 1994, Ethics for Training and Development, 1995, Enhanceing Learning in Training, 1996, Opportunities in Training and Development Careers, 1996; contbr. articles to profl. jours.; mem. editl. adv. bd., columnist Corp. Univ. Forum Mag., 1995—. Bd. dirs. Ill. Literacy Resource Devel. Ctr., BBB of Chgo. and No. Ill., 1996—; mem. bus.-edn. partnerships bd. Ill. Bd. Edn., 1995—; mem. Pvt. Industry Coun. of Cook County, 1994—. Mem. ABA, ASTD (pres.-elect. Chgo. chpt. 1989-90, dir. manuscript rev. bd. 1988—), Orgnl. Devel. Network, Am. Ednl. Rsch. Assn., Am. Hist. Assn., Internat. Reading Assn., Am. Mgmt. Assn.(presenter New Strategic Corp. Model 1993), Am. Man. Assn., Nat. Soc. Perform and Instrn., Midwest History of Edn. Soc. (pres.), Phi Delta Kappa (pres. DePaul U. chpt. 1986-88). Roman Catholic. Office: Imperial Edn Corp 10341 Lawler Ave Oak Lawn IL 60453

GORDON, ELLEN RUBIN, candy company executive; d. William B. and Cele H. (Travis) Rubin; m. Melvin J. Gordon, June 25, 1950; children: Virginia, Karen, Wendy, Lisa. Student, Vassar Coll., 1948-50; B.A., Brandeis U., 1965; postgrad., Harvard U., 1968. With Tootsie Roll Industries, Inc., Chgo., 1968—, corp. sec., 1970-74, v.p. product devel., 1974-76, sr. v.p., 1976-78, pres., COO, 1978—, also dir.; v.p., dir. HDI Investment Corp.; bd. dirs. CPC Internat., Inc.; mem. coun. on divsn. biol. scis. and Pritzker Sch. Medicine U. Chgo. Mem. adv. coun. J.L. Kellogg Grad. Sch. Mgmt. at Northwestern U., Stanford U. Grad. Sch. Bus.; mem. bd fellows Harvard U. Med. Sch.; mem. univ. resources and overseers com. Harvard U.; trustee, mem. Com. for Econ. Devel., Northwestern U. Assocs.; active Pres. Export Coun. Recipient Kettle award, 1985. Mem. Nat. Confectioners Assn. (bd. dirs.). Office: Tootsie Roll Industries Inc 7401 S Cicero Ave Chicago IL 60629-5818

GORDON, HOWARD LYON, advertising and marketing executive; b. Chgo., Oct. 8, 1930; s. Milton Arthur and Bess Z. (Ginsburg) G.; BS, U. Ill., 1953; MS, Northwestern U., 1954, MBA, 1962; m. Lois Jean Kaufman, Aug. 21, 1955; children: Carolyn Ann, Leslie Meredith. Mktg. rsch. mgr. Marsteller Inc., advt., Chgo., 1960-68, v.p. mktg. services Marsteller Inc. and Burson Marsteller, Chgo., 1968-76; dir. client service Britt and Frerichs Inc., mktg. research and advt. cons., Chgo., 1977-78, sr. v.p., 1978—, prin., 1979—, ptnr., 1986—; lectr. advt. and mktg. Northwestern U., 1963—, vis. prof. Medill grad. studies in advt., 1981—; advt. prof. in residence No. Ill. U., DeKalb, 1974-76; lectr., seminar leader Am. Mgmt. Assn., 1965-72; bd. dirs. Bus. Advt. Rsch. Coun., 1985—, chmn. life style rsch. com. Advt. Rsch. Found., 1985—; bd. dirs. Advt. Rsch. Found., Media Comm. Coun.; mem. alumni awards com. Medill Sch. Northwestern U., 1986, fund-raising com. Kellogg Grad. Sch. Northwestern U., 1986—. Co-author: Marketing Manager's Handbook, 3d edit., 1994; contbr. articles to profl. publs. Regional chmn. Crusade of Mercy, Evanston, Ill., 1969; founding dir. Alumni Assn. Medill Sch., 1984—; adv. council athletic dept., Northwestern U., 1985—. With AUS, 1954-56. Recipient award Dept. Def., 1956, Alumni Award Northwestern U., 1989. Mem. Am. Mktg. Assn. (dir., v.p. mktg. mgmt.), Northwestern U. Faculty, Kellogg Alumni Assn. (program com., exec. bd. dirs.), Direct Mktg. Assn., Assn. Consumer Rsch., Sigma Delta Chi. Contbr. articles to profl. publs. and mktg. texts. Office: 400 E Randolph Dr Chicago IL 60601-7329

GORDON, IRVING MARTIN, osteopathic physician; b. Canton, Ohio, Aug. 10, 1926; s. Harry and Sarah (Axelrod) G.; m. Roberta Levine, Feb. 12, 1956; children: Ellen, Nina, Bruce, Roger. BA, Case Western Res. U., 1949; BS, Kent State U., 1950; DO, Chgo. Coll. Osteo. Medicine, 1954. Lic. osteo. physician, Ohio, S.C.; cert. in family practice Am. Bd. Family Practitioners in Osteo. Medicine and Surgery. Intern, Detroit Osteo. Hosp., 1954-55; locum tenens, Fort Lee, N.J., 1955-56; gen. practice osteo. medicine, Massillon, Ohio, 1957-63, Gordon & Sharkis, 1963-70, Gordon, Sharkis & Larusso, Inc., 1970-71; pres. Perry Family Practice Ctr., Inc., 4 physician group; gen. practice family medicine Perry Family Practice Ctr., Inc., Massillon, 1972—; clin. asst. prof. family practice Ohio U. Coll. Osteo. Medicine, 1977—; lectr. Chgo. Coll. Osteo. Medicine, 1980, 81; lectr. Howard U. Hosp., Washington, and Grandview Hosp., Dayton, Ohio, Ohio U. Coll. Osteo. Medicine, 1984, Des Moines Gen. Hosp., 1984, Botsford Hosp., Farmington, Mich., 1985. Trustee Wooster Eight County Health Systems Agy. (Ohio), 1975-81; mem. pres.'s adv. bd. Stark Tech. Coll., Canton, 1980—, trustee, 1983—, found. trustee, 1982, bd. dirs., pres. bd. trustees, 1992-94; mem. annual fund-raising com. United Jewish Appeal, 1970—, fin. com. Temple Israel, 1979—; founding mem., trustee Doctors Hosp. Stark County (Ohio), 1963—, chief of staff, 1969, 70, mem. fin. com., chmn. community affairs com., mem. steering com. 25th-anniversary gala 1988-91, post-grad. edn. com., 1992—; emeritus mem. bd. trustees Drs. Hosp. Served to cpl. USAF, 1945-46. Fellow Am. Coll. Family Practice; mem. AMA, Am. Osteo. Assn., Ohio Osteo. Assn., Akron-Canton Acad. Osteo. Medicine and Surgery (pres. 1974-75), Ohio Soc. Am. Coll. Gen. Practitioners Osteo. Medicine and Surgery (pres. 1981-82), Stark County Med. Soc., Ohio Med. Assn. Clubs: Canton, Glenmoor Country (fin. com. 1991—), Nat. Amateur Radio Relay League, Med. Amateur Radio Council (founding mem.), Canton. Lodges: Masons, Shriners. Office: 4125 Lincoln Way E Canton OH 44646

GORDON, JESSE EMMANUEL, retired psychology educator; b. N.Y.C., Jan. 13, 1930; s. Harry and Sophie (Pais) G.; m. Anitra Sisholle, Mar. 8, 1956; children: Scott, Jessani, Erica. BS, NYU, 1950, MA, 1951; PhD, Pa. State U., 1956. Asst. prof. U. Wis., Madison, 1955-57, Mont. State U., Missoula, 1957-59; prof. U. Mich., Ann Arbor, 1959-93, prof. emeritus, 1993—; pres. Manpower Sci. Svcs., Ann Arbor, 1968-88. Pres. Jewish Cmty. Ctr., Ann Arbor, 1993, Jewish Cultural Soc., Ann Arbor, 1995; bd. dirs. Mich. League Human Svcs., Lansing, 1995. Capt. U.S. Army, 1951-61. Fulbright scholar, Germany, 1962-63. Fellow APA. Democrat. Home: 1300 Chalmers Rd Ann Arbor MI 48104 Office: U Mich Frieze Bldg Ann Arbor MI 48109

GORDON, JOHN SIESEL, art college administrator, sculptor; b. Milw., Nov. 16, 1946; s. Myron L. and Ruth Peggy (Siesel) G. BA, Antioch Coll., Yellow Springs, Ohio, 1970; MFA, Claremont Grad. Sch., 1973. Instr. art Mt. St. Mary's Coll., L.A., 1973; asst. prof. U. So. Calif., L.A., 1973-79, assoc. prof., 1979-87, 89-91, dean fine arts, 1981-87; v.p. acad. affairs Calif. Coll. Arts and Crafts, Oakland, 1987-88; dean fine arts and cultural studies Inst. Am. Indian Arts, Santa Fe, N.Mex., 1991-93; v.p. for acad. affairs Kansas City (Mo.) Art Inst., 1993—; cons. Los Angeles County Transp. Com., L.A., 1990—; grants panelist arts div. State of N.Mex., Santa Fe, 1991. One man shows include Shidoni Contemporary Gallery, Tesuque, N.Mex., 1991, Jan Weiner Gallery, Kansas City, 1994; group shows include N.Mex. Mus. Fine Arts, Santa Fe, 1991, Sena Gallery, Santa Fe, 1991, Charlotte Jackson Gallery, 1993. Mem. L.A. Mayor's Task Force on Arts, 1988; bd. dirs. Sta. KUNM-FM, U. N.Mex., Albuquerque, 1991; juror Taos (N.Mex.) Arts Festival, 1992; trustee Santa Fe Chamber Music Festival, 1991-92; mem. steering com. Friends Contemporary Art, Santa Fe, 1991-92; mem. adv. bd. Kansas City Ctr. for Design Rsch. and Edn., 1995—; mem. Mayor's Task Force on Race Rels., 1996. Recipient mayor's cert. of appreciation City of L.A., 1984; fellow Nat. Endowment for Arts, 1976. Mem. Coll. Art Assn., Nat. Assn. Schs. Art and Design.

GORDON, LARRY DAVID, professional sports team owner, broadcast executive; b. Maynooth, Ont., Can., July 19, 1938; s. David M. and Mary Kathleen (Hickey) G.; m. Judith Ann Sharp, Feb. 14, 1963 (div. June 1974); children: Lawrence D., David M., James R. BSBA cum laude, U. Rochester, N.Y., 1962; LLB, LaSalle U., 1966. Mktg. dir. Boston Bruins Hockey Club, 1967-72, Cleve. Pro Sports, Inc., 1972-74; exec. dir. World Hockey Assn., Toronto, Ont., Can., 1974-78; gen. mgr. Edmonton (Alta.) Oilers Hockey Club, 1978-80; pres., owner Wichita (Kans.) Wind Hockey Club, 1980-83, Mont. Magic Hockey Club, Billings, 1983-84, Muskegon (Mich.) Lumberjack Hockey Team, 1984-92, Cleve. Lumberjacks Hockey Team, 1992—; owner Civic Arena Mgmt. Corp.; mng. ptnr. Sta. WLCS-FM; cons. Can. Govt. Sports Ministry, Ottawa, Ont., Can., 1974-78, A.A.U. Winter Games, Muskegon, 1986-92; bd. dirs. Amateur Sports Coun., Muskegon. Pres. Muskegon County Am. Cancer Soc., 1988-92; bd. dirs. Muskegon Visitor and Conv. Bur., 1985-92, Econ. Growth Alliance, Muskegon, 1988-92, Muskegon C. of C., 1985-88, Amicare Home Health Svcs., 1988-92, YFCA, 1989-92; mem. drug enforcement adv. bd.; trustee Shoes for Kids, Cleve., 1993—. Sgt. USMC, 1957-58. Mem. World Hockey Assn. (gov. 1978, Exec. of Yr. 1975, 78), Internat. Hockey League (gov. 1984—, Exec. of Yr. 1985, 89, chmn. bd. dirs. 1995—), Nat. Hockey League (gov. 1979), Century (bd. dirs. Muskegon chpt. 1989-91), Grand Haven (Mich.) Country Club (bd. dirs. 1986-92), Elks (3d chair 1969-70). Republican. Roman Catholic. Office: Cleve Lumberjacks One Center Ice 200 Huron Rd E Cleveland OH 44115-1006

GORDON, LINDA, history educator; b. Chgo., Jan. 19, 1940; d. Bill and Helen (Appelman) G.; m. Allen Hunter; 1 child, Rosa Gordon Hunter. BA in History magna cum laude, Swarthmore Coll., 1961; MA in History and Russian Studies, Yale U., 1963, PhD in History with distinction, 1970. Prof. history U. Mass., Boston, 1968-84; prof. history U. Wis., Madison, 1984-90, Florence Kelley prof. history, 1990—, Vilas disting. rsch. prof., 1993—; vis. prof. U. Amsterdam, 1984; cons. and lectr. in field. Author: Woman's Body, Woman's Right: A Social History of Birth Control in America, 1976, paperback edit., 1977, 2d rev. edit., 1990, Cossack Rebellions: Social Turmoil in the Sixteenth Century Ukraine, 1983, Heroes of Their Own Lives: The Politics and History of Family Violence, Boston 1880-1960, 1988 (AHA Joan Kelly prize, Wis. Libr. Assn. award 1988), paperback edit., 1989, Brit. edit., 1989, Pitied But Not Entitled: Single Mothers and the History of Welfare, 1994 (winner Berkshire prize, 1995, Gustavus Myers human rights award, 1995). NIMH rsch. grantee, 1979-82, Am. Coun. Learned Socs. travel grantee, 1980; Guggenheim fellow, 1983-84, Bunting Inst. fellow Radcliffe, 1983-84, Am. Coun. Learned Socs./Ford Found. fellow, 1985, Harry Frank Guggenheim Found. fellow, 1987; recipient Antonovych prize, 1983, Bird Meml. Lectureship, U. Maine, 1986, Am. Philos. Soc. Rsch. award, 1988-89. Mem. Presdl. Adv. Coun. on violence against women, Am. Hist. Assn. (jour. editl. bd. 1990-93), Orgn. Am. Historians (exec. bd. 1991-94, mem. editl. bd. jour. 1994-97), Inst. for Rsch. on Povety (exec. com. 1990-95). Jewish. Office: Dept History U Wis Madison WI 53706

GORDON, ROBERT JAMES, economics educator; b. Boston, Sept. 3, 1940; s. Robert Aaron and Margaret (Shaughnessy) G.; m. Julie S. Peyton, June 22, 1963. A.B., Harvard U., 1962; M.A., Oxford U., Eng., 1969; Ph.D., MIT, 1967. Asst. prof. econs. Harvard U., 1967-68; asst. prof. U. Chgo., 1968-73; prof. econs. Northwestern U., Evanston, Ill., 1973—, Stanley G. Harris prof. social scis., 1987—; chair econs. dept. Northwestern U., Evanston, 1992—; rsch. assoc. Nat. Bur. Econ Rsch., 1968—; mem. Brookings Panel Econ. Activity, 1970—; co-chmn. Internat. Seminar Macroecons., 1978-94; mem. exec. com. Conf. Rsch., Income and Wealth, 1978-83; mem. panel rev. productivity measures NAS, 1977-79; cons. bd. govs. Fed. Res. Sys., 1973-83, U.S. Dept. Treasury, 1967-80; mem. Nat. Commn. on CPI, 1995—. Author: Macroeconomics, 1978, 6th edit., 1993, Milton Friedman's Monetary Framework, 1974, Challenges to Interdependent Economies, 1979, The American Business Cycle: Continuity and Change, 1986, The Measurement of Durable Goods Prices, 1990, International Volatility and Economic Growth, 1991, Economics, 1994; editor Jour. Polit. Economy, 1970-73. Marshall fellow, 1962-64; fellow Ford Found., 1966-67; grantee NSF, 1971—; fellow Guggenheim Meml. Found., 1980-81; rsch. fellow German Marshall Fund, 1985-86. Fellow Econometric Soc. (treas. 1975—); mem. Am. Econ. Assn. (bd. editors 1975-77, mem. exec. com. 1981-83), Phi Beta Kappa. Office: Northwestern U Dept Econs Evanston IL 60208

GORDON, RONALD F., mechanical engineer; b. Crestline, Ohio, Feb. 26, 1962; s. Robert E. and Leona M. (Vogt) G.; 1 child, Ryan. A in Mech. Tech., No. Control Tech. Coll., 1992. Engr. lab. asst. Warren Rupp, Mansfield, Ohio, 1980-82; time keeper Warren Rupp, Mansfield, 1982-86, machinist, 1986-94; mechanic M H Crane Sys. Inc., Galion, Ohio, 1994—; farmer, Crestline, 1990-94. Trustee Crawford County Farm Bur. Trustees, Ohio, 1993—. Mem. KC. Roman Catholic. Home: 3300 State Route 61 Crestline OH 44827-9755

GORDON, SANDY GALE COMBS, medical surgical nurse, community health nurse; b. Lafollette, Tenn., Sept. 8, 1950; d. Wise and Edna Leona (Boshears) Combs; m. Ralph William Gordon, Aug. 30, 1975. Diploma, Middletown Hosp., 1971. RN, Ohio. Pub. health nurse Bur. Pub. Health, Middletown, Ohio, 1979-82; staff nurse Middletown Hosp., 1971-79. Named Internat. Women of Yr., 1994-95. Mem. Middletown Hosp. Alumni Assn. Home: 1107 Ellen Dr Middletown OH 45042-3341

GORDON, THELMA HUNTER, state official. Sec. Aging Dept., Topeka. Office: Aging Dept 915 SW Harrison St Rm 150-S Topeka KS 66612-1500*

GORE, ALVIN E., stockbroker; b. Tampa, Fla., Oct. 8, 1942. BS, Fla. State U., 1969; profl. designation, Am. Coll., 1983. Stockbroker Prudential Ins., Ft. Wayne, Ind., 1970-83, Elkhart, Ind., 1983—; account exec. Employers of Warsaw (Ind.) Ins., 1973-76. With USAF, 1963-67. Mem. Warsaw Optimists. Republican. Lutheran. Office: Prudential Securities Inc PO Box 1066 # 10 4215 S 2d St Elkhart IN 46515

GORE, DAVID LEE, lawyer; b. Horry County, S.C., Dec. 17, 1937; s. Samuel and Sadie (Anderson) G.; m. Mary Letha Andrews, Nov. 26, 1960; children: David Lee Jr., Sheila. BA, Allen U., 1959; MEd, S.C. State Coll., 1966; JD, Howard U., 1969. Bar: S.C. 1970, Ill. 1976, Pa. 1971. Tchr. St. Helena High Sch., Beaufort, S.C., 1959-60, Palmetto High Sch., Mullins, S.C., 1963-66; legal asst., chmn. NLRB, Washington, 1969-70; asst. gen. counsel United Steelworkers Am., Pitts., 1970-81; dist. counsel United Steelworkers Am., Chgo., 1982—. Sgt. U.S. Army, 1960-63. Mem. Ill. Bar Assn., Phi Alpha Delta. Democrat. Baptist.

GORE, DONALD RAY, orthopedic surgeon; b. Michigan City, Ind., Mar. 13, 1936; s. Clarence Bernard and Susan Leone (Fuller) G.; m. Jacqueline Marie Kraabel, Aug. 25, 1956; children: Donald, Daniel, Jennifer, Elizabeth. BS, U. Ill., 1958, MD, 1960; MS, Marquette U., 1967. Cert. Am. Bd. Orthopaedic Surgery. Intern Milw. County Gen Hosp., 1960-61; resident gen. surgery Marquette U. Sch. Medicine, Milw., 1961-64, resident orthopaedic surgery, 1964-67; fellow Biomechanics Lab U. Calif., San Francisco, 1967-68; practice medicine specializing in orthopaedic surgery Sheboygan (Wis.) Orthopaedic Assocs., S.C., 1968—; clin. prof. dept. orthopaedic surgery Med. Coll. Wis., Milw., 1980—; staff St. Nicholas Hosp., Sheboygan, Sheboygan Meml. Hosp.; cons. surgery Wood (Wis.) VA Hosp., 1970—; asst. instr. dept. surgery Med. Coll. Wis., 1964-68, clin. instr. dept. surgery, 1969-72, asst. clin. prof., 1972-73, assoc. clin. prof., 1973-80; research assoc. VA Med. Ctr., Milw., 1970—, co-investigator kinesiology research lab., 1970-84. Mem. bd. editors Jour. Orthopaedic Surg. Techniques, 1985—; contbr. articles to profl. jours. Served to capt. USAF, 1962-63. Fellow Am. Acad. Orthopaedic Surgeons (bd. councilors 1985—); mem. AMA, Mid-Am. Orthopaedic Soc., Clin. Orthopaedic Soc., Wis. Orthopaedic Soc. (pres. 1982-84), Milw. Orthopaedic Soc., Wis. Arthritis Found. (bd. dirs. 1974-82), Sierra Cascade Trauma Soc., Cervical Spine Research Socs. Republican. Lutheran. Home: 2528 N 3rd St Sheboygan WI 53083-5007 Office: Sheboygan Orthopaedic Assocs SC 2920 Superior Ave Sheboygan WI 53081-1944

GORES, GARY GENE, credit union executive; b. Wildrose, N.D., Mar. 7, 1940; s. Orville Jerome and Irene Constance G.; m. Gail H. Gores, 1963 (div. Dec. 1989); m. Terre Jenice, June 29, 1991; children: Leslie, Christopher, Brent, Brandon, Aaron. AA, Grays Harbor Coll., Aberdeen, Wash., 1961; BA in Bus., Seattle U., 1969. V.p. 7 Up Bottling Co., Aberdeen, 1955-69, Capitol Savs. & Loan, Olympia, Wash., 1970-75; CEO Wash. State Employees Credit Union, Olympia, 1975-83; br. mgr. Nat. Consumer Coop. Bank, Seattle, 1983-86; CEO Chetco Fed. Credit Union, Brookings, Oreg., 1986-89; pres. Gt. Am. Herb Co., Olympia, 1989-90; pres., CEO Ohio Credit Union League & Svc. Corp., Columbus, 1990—. Pres. Capitol Area Assn. Performing Arts, Olympia, 1975-86; dist. chair Boy Scouts Am., Brookings, Oreg., 1987-89. With U.S. Army, 1962-68. Home: 7042 Shady Nelms Dr Dublin OH 43017-3030

GORHAM, EVILLE, ecologist, biogeochemist; b. Halifax, N.S., Can., Oct. 15, 1925; s. Ralph Arthur and Shirley Agatha (Eville) G.; m. Ada Verne MacLeod, Sept. 29, 1948; children: Kerstin, Vivien, Jocelyn, James. BSc in Biology with distinction, Dalhousie U., 1945, MSc in Zoology, 1947, LLD (hon.), 1991; PhD in Botany, U. London, Eng., 1951; DSc (hon.), McGill U., 1993. Lectr. botany U. Coll., London, Eng., 1951-54; sr. sci. officer Freshwater Biol. Assn., Ambleside, Eng., 1954-58; lectr., asst. prof. botany U. Toronto, 1958-62; assoc. prof. botany U. Minn., Mpls., 1962-65; prof. U. Minn., 1966-84, head dept., 1967-71, prof. ecology, 1975-84, Regents prof. ecology and botany, 1984—; prof., head dept. biology U. Calgary, Alta., Can., 1965-66; mem. for Can., Internat. Commn. on Atmospheric Chemistry and Radioactivity, 1959-62; mem. vis. panel to rev. toxicology program NAS-NRC, 1974-75, mem. com. on inland aquatic ecosys. water sci. and tech. bd., 1994-96; mem. coordinating com. for sci. and tech. assessment environ. pollutants Environ. Studies Bd., 1975-78; mem. com. on med. and biologic effects of environ. pollutants Assembly Life Scis., 1976-77; mem. com. on atmosphere and biosphere Bd. Agr. and Renewable Resources, 1979-81; mem. panel on environ. impact diesel impact study com. NAE-NRC, 1980-81; mem. U.S.-Can.-Mex. joint sci. com. on acid precipitation Environ. Studies Bd., NAS-NRC, Royal Soc. Can., Mex. Acad. Scis., 1981-84; mem. health and environ. rsch. adv. com. U.S. Dept. Energy, 1992-94. Mem. editl. bd. Ecology, 1965-67, Limnology and Oceanography, 1970-72, Conservation Biology, 1987-88, Ecol. Applications, 1989-92, Environ. Revs., 1992—; contbr. articles on limnology, ecology, and biogeochemistry to profl. jours. Bd. dirs. Acid Rain Found., 1982-87, sec. treas. 1982-84. Named Royal Soc. Can. rsch. fellow State Forest Rsch. Inst., Stockholm, Sweden, 1950-51; grantee NSF, AEC, NIH, ERDA, NASA, Dept. of Energy, NRC Can., Environment Can., Office Water Resources Rsch, Dept. Interior, Andrew W. Mellon Found., N.Y.C.; recipient Regents medal U. Minn., 1984. Fellow AAAS, Royal Soc. Can., Am. Acad. Arts and Scis.; mem. NAS, Am. Soc. Limnology and Oceanography (G. Evelyn Hutchinson medal 1986), Ecol. Soc. Am., Internat. Assn. Theoretical and Applied Limnology, Soc. Wetland Scientists, Swedish Phytogeog. Soc. (hon.), Gown in Town Club. Home: 1933 E River Ter Minneapolis MN 55414-3673

GORMAN, GERALD WARNER, lawyer; b. North Kansas City, Mo., May 30, 1933; s. William Shelton and Bessie (Warner) G.; m. Anita Belle McPike, June 26, 1954; children: Guinevere Eve, Victoria Rose. A.B. cum laude, Harvard U., 1954, LL.B. magna cum laude, 1956. Bar: Mo. 1956. Assoc. firm Dietrich, Tyler, Davis, Burrell & Dicus, Kansas City, 1956-62; ptnr. Dietrich, Davis, Dicus, Rowlands, Schmitt & Gorman, 1963-90; dir. Slagle, Bernard & Gorman, P.C., 1990—; bd.dirs. Musser-Davis Land Co., Curry Investment Co. Bd. govs. Citizens Assn. Kansas City, 1962—; trustee Harvard/Radcliffe Club Kansas City Endowment Fund, chmn. bd., 1977-83, Kansas City Mus., 1967-82, Avondale Meth. Ch., 1969-92, Citizens Bond Com. of Kansas City, 1973—, chmn. 7th jud. cir. citizens com., 1982-84; chmn. Downtown Coun. Allis Plaza Reconstrn., 1983-85; bd. dirs. Spofford Home for Children, 1972-77, Clay County Econ. Devel. Commn., 1989-94, mem. exec. com., 1991-93. With U.S. Army, 1956-58; capt. USAR, 1958-64. Mem. Lawyers Assn. Kansas City (exec. com. 1968-71), ABA, Mo. Bar Assn., Kansas City Bar Assn., Clay County Bar Assn., Harvard Law Sch. Assn. Mo. (pres. 1973), Harvard Club (pres. 1966), Univ. Club (bd. dirs. 1983-86, 88-93, pres. 1990-91), Kansas City Club (bd. dirs. 1993—), 611 Club (bd. dirs. 1987-91, pres. 1990), Old Pike Country Club, River Club. Republican. Home: 917 E Vivion Rd Kansas City MO 64118 Office: 4600 Madison Ave Ste 600 Kansas City MO 64112-3012

GORMAN, JOSEPH TOLLE, corporate executive; b. Rising Sun, Ind., 1937. BA, Kent State U., 1959; LLB, Yale U., 1962. Assoc. Baker, Hostetler & Patterson, Cleve., 1962-67; with legal dept. TRW Inc., Cleve., 1968-69, asst. sec., 1969-70, sec., 1970-72, v.p. sr. counsel automotive worldwide ops., 1972-73, v.p., asst. gen. counsel, 1973-76, v.p., gen. counsel, 1976-80, acting head communications function, 1978, exec. v.p. indsl. and energy sector, 1980-84, exec. v.p., asst. pres., 1984-85, pres., chief operating officer, 1985-88, chmn., pres., chief exec. officer, 1988-91, chmn. and chief exec. officer, 1991—, also bd. dirs., 1984—; bd. dirs. Aluminum Co. Am., Procter & Gamble Co.; mem. adv. bd. BP Am. Inc.; bd. dirs. U.S.-China Bus. Coun.; mem. Bd. of the Prince of Wales Bus. Leaders Form; mem. hon. com. Fedn. Internat. des Soc. d'Ingenieurs des Tech. de l'Automobile; chmn. Def. Industry Initiative Steering Com.; chmn. Internat. Trade and Investment task force; mem. strengthening of Am. Initiative Ctr. for Strategic and Internat. Studies; mem. Conf. Bd., Bus. Coun., Trilateral Commn., Bus. Roundtable's Policy Com., Coun. on Fgn. Rels., Pres.'s Export Coun., Coun. on Competitiveness. Trustee Cleve. Tomorrow, Mus. Arts Assn., Cleve. Inst. Art, United Way Svcs., Cleve. Clinic Found., Com. for Econ. Devel.; mem. Ohio Gov.'s Edn. Mgmt. Coun.; bd. overseers Amos Tuck Sch. Bus. Adminstrn., Dartmouth Coll.; chmn. Leadership Clevel.; be. mem. The New Am. Schs. Devel. Corp., The Bus.-Higher Edn. Forum. Recipient Japan Prime Minister's Trade award, 1994. Office: TRW Inc 1900 Richmond Rd Cleveland OH 44124-3719

GORMAN, KAREN MACHMER, optometric physician; b. Poughkeepsie, N.Y., June 4, 1955; d. James Andrew and Joan (Benton) Machmer; m. D.L. McCartney III, Aug. 16, 1976 (div. June 1982); m. N. David Gorman, Oct. 16, 1985; 1 stepchild, Danette Y. Gorman. BS in Optometry, U. Houston, 1976, OD, 1978; therapeutic pharm. lic., U. Mo., St. Louis, 1993. Diplomate Nat. Bd. Examiners Optometry; lic. optometrist, Colo., Mo., Tex. Pvt. practice Dallas, 1978-83, 1984-85, Hurst, Tex., 1984-85, St. Joseph, Mo., 1986—; charter mem. optometric adv. panel Pearle, Inc., 1991-93; lectr. on eyecare to community groups; free-lance journalist St. Joseph News-Press, Benson (N.C.) Rev. Contbr. poetry to lit. jours. including Nat. Libr. of Poetry and Typo mag., articles to profl. jours. including St. Joseph News Press and Benson (N.C.) Review; lead actress (play) None Come Back Innocent, Robidoux Resident Theatre, St. Joseph, 1990, Hay Fever, 1991, The Best Man, 1992, Wedded But No Wife, 1993, Mousetrap, 1993, Diary of Anne Frank, 1994, Death and the Maiden, 1995, Veronica's Room, 1996. Vol. Dallas Humane Soc., 1981, YWCA Women's Abuse Shelter; patron Robidoux Resident Theatre, St. Joseph, 1988-92, Ice House Theatre, St. Joseph, Kemper Albrecht Art Mus., St. Joseph, St. Joseph Animal Shelter; sponsor, coach, cheerleader and drill team Mo. Western State Coll., St. Joseph, 1985-86; legis. corr. Humane Soc. U.S., 1990-92; mem. Nat. Soc. Newspaper Columnists. Recipient Optometric Recognition awards Pearle, Inc., 1986-90; U. Houston scholar, 1972-76. Mem. U. Houston Alumni Assn., CWENS, Nat. Assn. Newspaper Columnists, St. Joseph Lit. Guild, Tau Sigma.

GORMAN, STEPHEN THOMAS, state legislator; b. Fargo, N.D., Dec. 4, 1924; m. Mary K. Sullivan Johnson; 3 children. Student, St. John's U., Collegeville, Minn., N.D. State Sch. Sci., Wahpeton. Chmn. Knight Printing Co., ret.; state rep. dist. 46, 1987—; vice chmn. fin. and taxation com.; mem. natural resources com., appropriations com., edn. and environ. divsn. com. N.D. Ho. Reps. Recipient Silver Metal award Advtg. Fedn. Fargo/Moorhead, Disting. Svc. award Jaycees. Mem. Fargo C. of C., Elks, Rotary, K.C., Am. Legion. Republican. Home: 810 Southwood Dr Fargo ND 58103-6020*

GORODY, ANTHONY WAGNER, geologist, geochemist, consultant; b. Zurich, Switzerland, Oct. 13, 1949; came to U.S., 1960; s. Antal Gorody and Denise (Wagner) Lohman; m. Adele Caldara, June 27, 1981. BA, Rutgers U., 1971; MS, PhD, Rice U., 1980. Cert. profl. geologist. Rsch. asst. Lamont-Doherty Geol. Obs., Palisades, N.Y., 1972-75; asst. curatorial rep. Scripps Inst. Oceanography, La Jolla, Calif., 1975-76; sr. rsch. advisor Tex. Ea. Corp., Houston, 1980-86; prin. project mgr. Gas Rsch. Inst., Chgo., 1986-94; pres. Universal Geosci. Cons., North Riverside, Ill., 1994—; cons. orgns. including Hanna Mining Co., Cookeville, Tenn., 1977-80, Amax Coal Co., Gillette, Wyo., 1987-90, Amoco, 1995, Lone Star Gas, 1995, Emerald Gas Co., 1995, S.W. Rsch. Inst., STA Argonne Nat. Labs., 1995. Mem. Meals on Wheels, Chgo., 1989—. Grantee Am. Assn. Petroleum Geologists,

1979. Mem. AAAS, Am. Geophys. Union, Soc. Petroleum Engrs., Am. Assn. Petroleum Geologists, Am. Inst. Profl. Geologists, Am. Statistical Assn. Office: Universal Geosci Cons Inc 7222 W Cermak Rd Ste 701 North Riverside IL 60546-9999

GORRELL, LARRY W., stockbroker; b. Quincy, Ill., July 4, 1947; s. Robert M. and Lucille (Wagner) G.; m. Lynn Shanks, June 25, 1972; children: Laura J., Nathan T. BS, Culver-Stockton Coll., 1969; MBA, NYU, 1971. Stockbroker Reinholdt & Gardner, St. Louis, 1971-75; stockbroker, 1st v.p. Everen Securities, Inc., Quincy, 1975—. Trustee, chmn. bus. affairs Culver Stockton Coll., 1982—; treas. Quincy Sch. Dist., 1984—; trustee, chmn. fin. Quincy Symphony Orch. Assn., 1984-94; trustee chair Bus. and Fin. Sunset Home, 1988—; mem., bd. chair Disciples of Christ Ch., 1994—. Mem. Scottish Rite (33d deg.). Home: 2300 York St Quincy IL 62301-4360 Office: Everen Securities 535 Maine St Quincy IL 62301-3950

GORSALITZ, JEANNINE LIANE, elementary school educator; b. Appleton, Wis., Sept. 22, 1939; d. Gustav Herman and Viola Rachel (Wiedenhaupt) G. BS, Dr. Martin Luther Coll., 1961; MA, U. Wis., Oshkosh, 1969. Cert. elem. tchr., Wis. Tchr. Palos Luth. Sch., Palos Heights, Ill., 1959-60; tchr., prin. St. Peter's Luth. Sch., Freedom, Wis., 1960-65; tchr. Grace Luth. Sch., Neenah, Wis., 1965-68, Gegan Elem. Sch., Menasha, Wis., 1968-93, Butte des Morts Elem. Sch., Menasha, 1993—; coord. elem. social studies Menasha Schs., 1988—; advisor Wis. Coun. for Local History, Madison, 1987—; lectr. Sch. Edn., U. Wis. Author/co-author ednl. curriculum (various awards). Vol. 1st Responder, Ellington, Wis., 1981-86, ARC, 1988—; block capt. Neighborhood Watch, Neenah, 1989—; active State Hist. Soc., Madison. Recipient Outstanding Contbn. award State Hist. Soc., 1980, Excellence in Edn. award U.S. Sec. Edn., Washington, 1989, Excellence award Nat. Coun. Econs., N.Y.C., 1990. Mem. Nat. Fedn. Tchrs., Nat. Coun. for Social Studies, Wis. Fedn. Tchrs., Wis. Coun. for Social Studies, Wis. Coun. for Environ. Edn., Wis. Coun. for Econ. Edn., Kiwanis. Lutheran. Home: 440 E Peckham St Neenah WI 54956-4168 Office: Butte des Morts Elem Sch 501 Tayco St Menasha WI 54952-2732

GORSKI, CHRIS, engineering consultant; b. Milw., Jan. 24, 1962. Head engrng. Master Circuits, Kokomo, Ind., 1984—. Coach Little League Baseball. Office: Master Circuits 424 N Apperson Way Kokomo IN 46901-4736

GORSKI CROISSANT, KATHLEEN, occupational therapist; b. Cleve., July 27, 1958; d. Michael Robert and Marian Frances (Doubrava) G.; m. Ronald B. Croissant, Apr. 1993; children: Deandra Croissant, Kevin Croissant. AAS, Cuyahoga Community Coll., Cleve., 1981; BS, Ea. Mich. U., 1983. Reg. occupational therapist; cert. aerobics instr., personal trainer. Activity dir. Dover Nursing Home, Westlake, Ohio, 1981-82; staff therapist U. Hosps. of Cleve., 1984-86, sr. therapist, 1986-87, clin. specialist, 1989-90, clin. mgr., 1990-95; pres. Kathleen Gorski Rehab., Westlake, Ohio, 1989—, Fairview Health Sys., Cleveland, 1995—; occupational therapist UPS, Cleve., 1987-89. Named Outstanding Clinician, Cleve. Dist. O.T. Assn., 1988; recipient Humanitarian award Ea. Mich. U., 1983. Mem. Cleve. Dist. Occupational Therapists Assn., Ohio Occupational Therapists Assn., Am. Occupational Therapists Assn. Republican. Roman Catholic. Office: Fairview Health Sys 18101 Lorain Ave Cleveland OH 44111

GORTE, PAUL MICHAEL, land use planner; b. Detroit, May 4, 1951; s. David Alex and Joyce Elaine (Duttweiler) G.; m. Suzanne Kathleen Coutts, June 16, 1973; children: Brandon Michael, Christopher Michael. BA with high honors, Mich. State U., 1973, M of Urban Planning, 1977. Cert. planner, Am. Inst. Cert. Planners. City planner City of Rock Springs, Wyo., 1977; transp. planner Capital Region Planning Commn., Baton Rouge, 1977-80; planner City of Joliet, Ill., 1980-82, prin. planner, 1982-86; dir. planning County of Will, Joliet, 1986-90; cmty. devel. dir. Village of Bolingbrook, Ill., 1990—; chmn. intergovtl. cooperation working group Northeastern Ill. Planning Commn., Chgo., 1993-94, mem. land use/transp. task force, 1994—; mem. Gov.'s Flood Control Task Force, Chgo., 1988. Supervising mgr. (land use plan) Will County Land Resource Mmgt. Plan, 1990; project mgr. (rehab. study) Joliet Union Sta. Restoration and Adaptive Reuse Plan, 1981; author (transp. plan) Transp. for the Elderly and Handicapped in the Baton Rouge Metro. Are, 1979. Cubmaster Pack 33, Joliet, 1986-87; asst. coach Bolingbrook (Ill.) Youth Baseball League, 1994, head coach, 1996; asst. coach Bolingbrook Barons Travelling Baseball, 1995; soccer coach Joliet Park Dist. Soccer, 1987-89; asst. football coach Bolingbrook Trojans, 1995.. Mem. Am. Planning Assn., Phi Beta Kappa, Phi Kappa Phi. Office: Village of Bolingbrook 375 Briarcliff Rd Bolingbrook IL 60440

GOSCHKA, MICHAEL JOHN, state legislator; b. Saginaw, Mich., Oct. 21, 1953; s. Arthur Clarence and Ethel Marie (Alden) G.; m. Maryann Louise Sielaff, 1979. Student, Delta Coll., 1972, Cornerstone Coll., 1974-77. Forklift operator Dow Corning Corp., 1984-92; rep. Mich. Dist. 94, 93—; vice chmn. tourism & recreation com. Mich. Ho. Reps., 1993—, agriculture & forestry com., 1993—, edn. com., 1993—, mental health com., 1993—, house oversight com., 1993—, ethics com., 1993—, tax policy com., 1995—. Exec. com. Saginaw County Rep. Com., 1982—, del. to state, 1982—, rep. precinct, 1982—. Mem. Mich. Farm Bur., Sons Am. Legionnaires, Saginaw Right to Life. Home & Office: 16393 W Schroeder Rd Brant MI 48614-9788 Address: 16393 Schroeder Rd Brant MI 48614*

GOSHORN, LARRY FREDERICK, aerospace industry administrator, consultant; b. Ft. Wayne, Ind., Feb. 13, 1951; s. Eugene Frederick and Marjorie Ellen (Jackson) G.; m. Allison Jan Lowery, Nov. 24, 1973 (div. 1986); m. Susan Mary Hannie, Aug. 29, 1992. AS in Elec. Engrng. Tech., Alpena Coll., 1974; BS in Mgmt. Sci., Purdue U., 1992. Avionics technician Ft. Wayne Avionics, 1974-75; test supr., quality engr., then prodn./materials mgr. ITT Aerospace/Communications, Ft. Wayne, 1975-82, test mgr. spl. programs, 1982-83, mgr. spl. program, 1983-91, program mgr., 1991-92, test mgr. space systems, 1992-94, sr. program mgr. space systems, 1994—; mem. adv. com. Purdue Sch. Bus. and Mgmt., Ft. Wayne, 1990—. Sgt. USAF, 1970-74. Mem. Am. Prodn. and Inventory Control Soc. Office: ITT Aerospace Comm PO Box 3700 Fort Wayne IN 46801-3700

GOSLIN, GERALD HUGH, concert pianist, teacher; b. Detroit, Jan. 7, 1947; s. Hugh Jennings and Helen Margaret (Senauit) G.; m. Margaret Louise Babineau, May 20, 1983 (div. July, 1992). Music maj., Wayne State U., Detroit, 1966-69. Music tchr. Peralta Music, Farmington, Mich., 1965-80, Hammell Music, Livonia, Mich., 1980-83; adj. prof. of music Oakton C.C., Farmington Hills, Mich., 1983—; choir master and organist Cmty. Congl. Ch., Lathrup Village, Mich., 1994—; host The Piano Hour Station: WHND-AM, Oak Park, Mich., 1985; recitalist Allen, Rodgers and Baldwin organs, Detroit, Calif., 1975—, Rodgers & Allen Organs, Detroit, 1995—. Block capt. Rogers Park Residents Assn., Redford, 1995—. Mem. Detroit Fedn. of Musicians Local #5, Am. Choral Dir. Assn., Am. Guild of Organists. Congregationalist. Home and Office: 19782 Olympia Redford MI 48240-1334

GOSLING, DAVID, architect, urban design educator; b. Manchester, Eng., Sept. 14, 1934; came to U.S., 1989; s. John Arthur and Clara Novello (Shaw) G.; m. Miriam Caetano De Deus Vieira, Mar. 10, 1965; children: Maria-Cristina, Ana-Lucia, Stephen. BA, U. Manchester, Eng., 1956; MArch, MIT, 1958; MCP, Yale U., 1960; PhD, Sheffield (Eng.) U., 1986. Registered architect, Ohio, U.K. Sr. asst. architect Manchester City Architect Dept., 1960-62; assoc. ptnr. Leach, Rhodes & Walker, Architects, Manchester, 1962-65; dep. chief architect Runcorn (Eng.) New Town Devel. Corp., 1965-68; chief architect Irvine (Scotland) New Town Devel. Corp., 1968-73; prof., dean architecture Sheffield (Eng.) U., 1973-89; prof. U. Cin., 1989—; dir. Ctr. for Urban Design, DAAP, U. Cin., 1989-96; city planning commr. City of Cin., 1996—; tech. expert Ministry of Overseas Devel., Rio De Janeiro, 1973, Ministry of the Interior, Brasilia, 1976-77; planning cons. Cent. Bank of Barbados, Bridgetown, 1977-78; ptnr. Saudi-European Assocs., Ministry of the Interior, Saudi Arabia, 1981-84; urban design cons. London Docklands Devel. Corp., London, 1980-88. Co-author: The Design and Planning of Retail Systems, 1976, 77, 79, 84, Concepts of Urban Design, 1984, 85, Gordon Cullen: Visions of Urban Design, 1996; chief editor: Irvine New Town Plan, 1971; assoc. editor 3rd World Planning Rev., 1979-89. Staff rep. Nat. Whitley Coun., London, 1966-68; chmn. Brit. New Towns Tech. Officers Com., London, 1968-70; chmn., trustee North Sheffield Housing Assn., 1975-89; city planning commr. City of Cin., 1996—. Recipient Pub. Realm Design award Progressive Architecture, 1992, DAAP award for outstanding rsch. U. Cin., 1993-94; Commonwealth (Harkness) fellow Harkness Found., 1957-59, Leverhulme sr. fellow Leverhulme Trust, 1980, Quantas Disting. scholar Australian U., 1984, State of Ohio eminent scholar in urban design, 1989—, Graham Found. (Chgo.) fellow for advanced studies, 1994. Fellow Royal Soc. Arts, Inst. Urban Design (N.Y.); mem. AIA, Royal Inst. Brit. Architects (chmn. accreditation bd. 1983-88, Rsch. award 1994), Royal Town Planning Inst., Royal Incorp. Architects (Scotland). Roman Catholic. Home: 1 Rawson Woods Cir Cincinnati OH 45220-1130 Office: Ctr for Urban Design DAAP U Cin PO Box 210016 Cincinnati OH 45221

GOSNELL, THOMAS CHARLES, former mayor; b. London, Ont., Can., Apr. 7, 1951; s. James Fredrick and Evelyn Winnifred (Head) G.; m. Laurel Joanne Strople, Apr. 17, 1986; children: Craig, Jennifer. BA in Polit. Sci. and History, U. Western Ont., 1974. Pres. Gosnell Paving Stone, Inc., London, 1978; alderman City of London, 1978-85, mayor, 1985-95; with Goswell Passmore & Co., London, Ont., Can., 1995—; chmn. bd. of control City of London; mem. ex-officio devel. adv. bd. planning com., environment and transp. com., community and protective svcs. com., hydro electric com. City of London, London Police Svcs. Bd. Mem. diaster and emergency co-ordinating com., liaison com. City of London/Middlesex County; bd. dirs. London Pub. Library, Western Fair Assn., London; bd. govs. U. Western Ont., Can. Mem. Fedn. Can. Municipalities (big city mayor's caucus), Assn. Municipalities of Ont. Office: Gosnell Passmore & Co, 300-252 Pall Mall St, London, ON Canada N6A 5P6

GOSS, DAVID ARTHUR, optometry educator, researcher; b. Joliet, Ill., July 22, 1948; s. Arthur L. and Virginia A. Goss; m. Dawn A. Goss. BA in Biology, Ill. Wesleyan U., 1970; BS in Optometry, Pacific U., Forest Grove, Oreg., 1972, OD, 1974; PhD in Physiol. Optics, Ind. U., 1980. Optometrist Drs. Lande & Crouch, Storm Lake, Iowa, 1974-75; assoc. instr. optometry Ind. U., Bloomington, 1976-79, rsch. assoc., 1979-80; asst. prof. optometry Northeastern State U., Tahlequah, Okla., 1980-85, assoc. prof., 1985-89, prof., 1989-92; prof. Ind. Univ., Bloomington, 1992—; mem. working group on myopia prevalence and progression NRC, 1984-87. Author: Ocular Accommodation Convergence and Fixation Disparity, 1986, 2d edit., 1995; editor: Eye and Vision Conditions in the American Indian, 1990; contbr. articles to profl. jours. Grantee, Am. Optometric Found., 1985-87, Nat. Eye Inst., 1987-88, Okla. Ctr. for Advancement Sci. and Tech., 1989-91, faculty of yr. rsch. and scholarly activity Northeastern State U., Tahlequah, Okla., 1990-91. Fellow Am. Acad. Optometry; mem. Am. Optometric Assn. (mem. rev. bd. jour. 1988-94, rev. panel, clin. Practice Guideline on Comprehensive Adult Eye Examination, 1993-94, cons. editor jour. 1994—), Assn. Optometric Educators (pres. 1988-90), Optometric Hist. Soc. (newsletter editor 1996—), Optical Soc. Am., Assn. for Rsch. in Vision and Ophthalmology, Sigma Xi. Office: Sch of Optometry Indiana Univ Bloomington IN 47405

GOSS, GEORGE ROBERT, chemist; b. Kewaunee, Ill., Dec. 16, 1952; s. Robert George and Maribelle (Boultinghouse) G.; m. Susan Gwen Esposito, Aug. 25, 1975 (div. Sept. 29, 1989); children: Robert J., Thomas P., Phillip M. BS in Biology, Western Ill. U., 1974, MS in Chemistry, 1979, MS in Botany, 1982; PhD in Chemistry, Loyola U., Chgo., 1994. Chemist Kalo Ag Chemicals, Inc., Quincy, Ill., 1978-80, rsch. mgr., 1980-84; chief chemist Oil-Dri Corp. Am., Chgo., 1984-87, tech. dir., 1987—. Mem. ASTM (chairperson task group 1984-96), Am. Chem. Soc. Home: 7400 36th Ave Kenosha WI 53142

GOSS, RICHARD HENRY, lawyer; b. Worcester, Mass., Oct. 24, 1935; s. George Lee and Marion Bernadine (Henry) G.; children: Margaret Elizabeth, Richard Henry Eric, Emily Charlotte; m. Eleanor Kirsten Berg, Nov. 28, 1971. Student, Mich. State U., 1952-54; BA in Econs., Clark U., 1956; JD, Northwestern U., 1959. Bar: Ill. 1959, U.S. Supreme Ct. 1970. Asst. cashier Nat. Blvd. Bank of Chgo., 1959-61; v.p. Paul D. Speer & Assocs. Inc., Mcpl. Fin. Cons., Chgo., 1962-68; mng. ptnr. Chapman and Cutler, Attys. at Law, Chgo., 1968-95. Bd. dirs. Japan Am. Soc. Chgo., 1987-96, v.p., chmn. mem. com., 1988-90; chmn. bd. dirs. Brays Island Plantation Colony, Inc., 1995—. Mem. ABA, Chgo. Bar Assn. (chmn. com. on local govt. 1978-80), Pub. Securities Assn. (com. on fed. legislation and regulation 1982-93), Govtl. Fin. Officers Assn. U.S. and Can. (lectr. 1972-79), Sunset Ridge Country Club (chmn. skeet and trap com. 1986-88), Northbrook Sports Club (bd. dirs. 1985-90), Hanover (Ill.) Farm Hunt Club (sec. 1979-83), Chgo. Athletic Assn. (entertainment com. 1979-81), Michigan Shores Club. Republican. Episcopalian. Home: Brays Island Plantation 24 Pocataligo Pl Sheldon SC 29941

GOSSELL, TERRY RAE, advertising agency executive, small business owner; b. Rockford, Ill., Jan. 24, 1947; d. Virgil Houston and Wilma Beatrice (Cox) Pierce; m. Ronald Richard Gossell, Mar. 3, 1979 (div. Apr., 1983); children: Cameo Ann Elliott, Ronica Rae. Grad. high sch., Loves Park, Ill.; arts cert., U. Kans., 1962. Artist Rockford (Ill.F) Silk Screen Process, 1967-72, Grocery Co-op Advt., Ocala, Fla., 1973-74; art dir. Carlson & Co. Advt., Rockford, Ill., 1975; co-owner R.S.S.P. Graphics & Typesetting, Rockford, 1975-76; owner Graphic Comm., Inc., Rockford, 1976-79, T.R. Gossell Advt., Rockford, 1979-82; owner The Gossell Agy., Phoenix, 1982-88, Rockford, 1988—. Author, artist: (comic book) The Gang from Carl Hayden High Sch., 1986-87. Advisor No. Ill. Advt. Coun. Explorer Post #423, Rockford, 1990-92. Recipient Merit and 1st Place awards Rockford Advt. Club, 1978, 79, 1st Place award of Excellence, Nat. Assn. Pers. Cons., San Diego, 1985, Cert. of Merit, BMA Tower awards, 1994. Mem. Am. Advt. Fedn., No. Ill. Advt. Coun. (pres. 1992-94, merit, 1st and 2nd pl. awards 1980, 81, 91, 93, 94, 95). Democrat. Lutheran. Office: The Gossell Agy 5002 Sherwood Forest Rd Rockford IL 61109-2735

GOSSETT, KATHRYN MYERS, language professional, educator; b. Baltimore, Ohio; d. Charles Edgar and Vera Mae (Good) Myers; m. William Thomas Gossett, June 30, 1984. BA summa cum laude, Ohio U., 1931, MA, 1936. Cert. tchr., Ohio, Pa., Mich. Latin and English tchr. Beccaria Twp. High Sch., Coalport, Pa., 1931-32; French, Latin and English tchr. Buford (Ohio) High Sch., 1932-36; tchr. fgn. langs. Oak Hill (Ohio) High Sch., 1936-42; critic tchr. Ohio U. and Athens High Sch., 1942-43; English and Spanish tchr. Eastern High Sch., Lansing, Mich., 1943-45; French tchr. Kingswood/Cranbrook Pvt. Sch., Bloomfield Hills, Mich., 1945-55, chmn. fgn. lang., 1955-75; Fulbright tchr. Lycée de Jeunes Filles, Annecy, France, 1953-54. Contbr. articles to profl. jours. Decorated chevalier des Palmes Academiques (France); recipient Cranbrook Founders medal, 1976; U. Besancon (France) scholar. Mem. AAUW, Am. Assn. Ret. Persons, Eastern Star, Bloomfield Hills Country Club, The Ocean Club of Fla. (Ocean Ridge), The Little Club (Gulf Stream, Fla.), The Village Club (Bloomfield Hills), Phi Beta Kappa. Republican. Episcopalian. Home: 1276 Covington Rd Bloomfield Hills MI 48301-2365

GOSSLING, JENNIFER, microbiologist; b. Welwyn Garden City, England, July 25, 1934; came to U.S., 1962; d. Richard S. and Millicent E. (Hodson) Sayers; m. William Frank Gossling, Nov. 3, 1956. BA, Cambridge (Eng.) U., 1955; PhD, W.Va. U., 1973. Asst., instr. U. Manchester, Eng., 1966-69, W.Va. U. Med. Ctr., Morgantown, 1969-73, Med. Col.. Ohio, Toledo, 1975; postdoctoral scholar Dental Rsch. Inst., U. Mich., Ann Arbor, 1978-79; mem. staff Indiana (Pa.) Hosp., 1979-80; med. technologist Jewish Hosp. of St. Louis, 1980—; asst. prof. Sch. of Dental Medicine, Washington U., St. Louis, 1981-91, St. Louis Coll. Pharmacy, 1993-95; Contbr. to Bergey's Manual of Systematic Bacteriology, Vol. 3, 1989.

GOTFRYD, WILLIAM TED, lawyer; b. Chgo., Oct. 5, 1955; s. Ted Joseph and Cecelia (Blazejewski) G.; m. Diane Cooper, May 9, 1992. BS, Loyola U. Chgo., 1977, JD, 1980. Bar: Ill. 1980, U.S. Dist. Ct. (no. dist.) Ill., U.S. Ct. Appeals (3d, 7th cirs.). Assoc. Susan E. Loggans & Assocs., Chgo., 1981; ind. cons. Chgo., 1981-82; assoc. Sloan & Assocs., P.C., Chgo., 1982-88; counsel Pedersen & Houpt, Chgo., 1988-93; prin. William T. Gotfryd & Assocs., Chgo., 1993—; panel chmn. inquiry bd. Atty. Registration and Disciplinary Commn., Ill. Supreme Ct., 1991-93, panel chmn. hearing bd., 1993-96; dir. spl. projects Inst. for Consumer Antitrust Studies, Sch. Law Loyola U. Mem. Chgo. Bar Assn., 7th Cir. Bar Assn. Home: 1451 W Wrightwood Ave Chicago IL 60614-1121 Office: William T Gotfryd & Assocs 180 N LaSalle St Ste 2002 Chicago IL 60601-2701

GOTSDINER, MURRAY BENNETT, lawyer; b. Des Moines, Jan. 2, 1953; s. harold B. and Shirlee Ann (Gorshel) G.; m. Debora Zadina, Feb. 5, 1972; children: Alexander, Erik, Elizabeth. BA, Drake U., 1975, JD, 1979. Bar: Iowa 1980, Tex. 1989, U.S. Dist. Ct. Iowa, 1980, U.S. Ct. Appeals (8th cir.), 1982, U.S. Supreme Ct. 1983. Ptnr. Cook, Gotsdiner McEnroe & McCarthy, Des Moines, 1980—. Mem. Iowa Bar Assn., Tex. Bar Assn., Polk County (Iowa) Bar Assn., Des Moines Club. Republican. Jewish. Home: 13211 Sunset Cir Clive IA 50325-8805 Office: Cook Gotsdiner McEnroe 601 Locust St Apt 1300 Des Moines IA 50309-3751

GOTSHALL, MARK EDWARD, employee assistance executive; b. Cin., Dec. 4, 1960; s. Raymond E. and Delores M. A. (Kuehm) G. AA, William Rainey Harper Coll., Palatine, Ill., 1981; BS, Carroll Coll., Waukesha, Wis., 1984; MA, Ctrl. Mich. U., 1992. Cert. chem. dependency counselor; lic. profl. counselor, Mich.; registered social worker. Child care worker St. Rose Residence, Milw., 1984; group home counselor DePaul Rehab. Hosp., Milw., 1984; counselor Mercy Health Ctr., Dubuque, Iowa, 1984-88; family counselor extended care program St. Luke's Hosp., Cleve., 1988-89; clin. supr. Bay Haven Chem. Dependency Programs, Bay City, Mich., 1990-91, integrated care mgr., 1991-93; employee assistance counselor Health Mgmt. Sys. Am., East Pointe, Mich., 1994-95; regional supr. G.A.P., 1995—. Mem. Nat. Assn. Alcoholism and Drug Abuse Counselors. Methodist. Home: 3427 Canal Ave SW Apt 8 Grandville MI 49418-1555

GOTTLANDER, ROBERT JAN LARS, dental company executive; b. Bohuslan, Sweden, Sept. 5, 1956; came to U.S., 1986; s. Jan H. K. and Ragnhild S.E. (Rutgerson) G.; m. Eva L.M. Svenson, July 4, 1987; children: Daniel J.R., Magdalena A.E. Student, Kongahalla Coll., Sweden, 1975; candidate of odontology, U. Gothenburg, Sweden, 1976, DDS, 1980. Dentist Swedish Health Care, Trollhattan, Sweden, 1980-82; asst. prof. dept. orthodontics Community Dentistry, Trollhattan, 1982-84; mgr. tng. and edn. Nobelpharma AB, Gothenburg, 1984-85, product mgr., 1985; v.p., mgr. edn. and product Nobelpharma USA Inc., Waltham, Mass., 1986-87, v.p. profl. affairs, 1987-88; v.p., gen. mgr. Nobelpharma USA Inc., Chgo., 1988—; pres. V-Dal Union of Dentists, Trollhattan, Sweden, 1982-84; chmn. V-Dal Dental Soc., Sweden, 1983-84, sec. 1981-82. Lt. Swedish Royal Navy, 1976-79. Mem. AMA, Swedish Dental Soc., Swedish Orthodontic Soc.; affiliate mem. ADA, Acad. of Osseointegration. Lutheran. also: Exec Place 1 777 Oakmont Ln Ste 100 Westmont IL 60559-5511

GOTTRON, FRANCIS ROBERT, III, small business owner; b. Youngstown, Ohio, Dec. 26, 1953; s. Francis R. Jr. and Norma J. (Giba) G.; m. Joyce L. Garling, Nov. 25, 1975. BSBA cum laude, Youngstown State U., 1978. With Commonwealth Land Title Youngstown, Inc., 1972-87, Lender's Svc., Inc., 1979—, Title Agy. Michaels, 1984—; examiner delinquent tax Mahoning County Prosecutor's Office, 1989—; owner, prin. Mahoning County Recorder's Office, Youngstown, 1978—; examiner Fed. Title Agy., 1982—; pres. M&G Title Search Inc.; appraiser Probate Ct., 1989—. Democrat. Lutheran. Home: 9165 New Rd North Jackson OH 44451-9707 Office: PO Box 268 Youngstown OH 44501-0268

GOTTSCHALK, ALFRED, college chancellor; b. Oberwesel, Germany, Mar. 7, 1930; came to U.S., 1939, naturalized, 1945; s. Max and Erna (Trum-Gerson) G.; m. Deanna Zeff, 1977; children by previous marriage: Marc Hillel, Rachel Lisa. AB, Bklyn. Coll., 1952; MA with honors, Hebrew Union Coll.-Jewish Inst. Religion, 1957; PhD, U. So. Calif., 1965, STD (hon.), 1968, LLD (hon.), 1976; LLD (hon.), U. Cin., 1976, Xavier U., 1981, Mt. St. Joseph Coll., 1995, No. Ky. U., 1996; DHL (hon.), U. Judaism, 1971, Jewish Theol. Sem., 1986, Bklyn. Coll., 1991, Trinity Coll., 1996; LittD (hon.), Dropsie U., 1974, St. Thomas Inst., 1982; D Religious Edn. (hon.), Loyola-Marymount U., 1977; DD (hon.), NYU, 1985. Ordained rabbi, 1957;. Dir. Hebrew Union Coll., Jewish Inst. Religion, L.A., 1957-59, dean, 1959-71, prof. Bible and Jewish intellectual history, 1965—, pres., 1971-95, chancellor, 1996—; hon. fellow Hebrew U., Jerusalem, 1972, Oxford Ctr. for Hebrew and Jewish Studies, 1994. Author: Your Future as a Rabbi-A Calling that Counts, 1967, (translator) Hesed in the Bible, 1967, The Man Must be the Message, 1968, Jewish Ecumenism and Jewish Survival, 1968, Ahad Ha-Am, Maimonides and Spinoza, 1969, Ahad Ha-Am as Bible Critic, 1971, A Jubilee of the Spirit, 1972, Israel and the Diaspora: A New Look, 1974, Limits of Ecumenicity, 1979, Israel and Reform Judaism: A Zionist Perspective, 1979, Ahad Ha-Am and Leopold Zunz: Two Perspectives on the Wissenschaft Des Judentums, 1980, Hebrew Union College and Its Impact on World Progressive Judaism, 1980, Diaspora Zionism: Achievements and Problems, 1980, What Ecumenism Means to a Jew, 1981, Introduction: Religion in a Post-Holocaust World, 1982, Problematics in the Future of American Jewish Community, 1982, Introduction to the American Synagogue in the Nineteenth Century, 1982, A Strategy for Non-Orthodox Judaism in Israel, 1982, Our problems and Our Future: Jews and America, 1983, From the Kingdom of Night to the Kingdom of God: Jewish Christian Relations and the Search for Religious Authenticity after the Holocaust, 1983, The Making of a Contemporary Reform Rabbi, 1984, Is Yom Kippur Obsolete?, 1985, Ahad Ha-am: Confronting the Plight of Judaism, 1987, To Learn and To Teach, Your Future as a Rabbi, 1988, Preface to Gezer V: The Field I Caves, 1988, The American Reform Rabbinate Retrospect and Prospect, A Personal View, 1988, The German Pogrom of November 1938 and the Reaction of American Jewry, 1988, Building Unity in Diversity 1989, Ahad Ha'am and the Jewish National Spirit (Hebrew), 1992; contbr. to Studies in Jewish Bibliography, History, and Literature, 1971, The Yom Kippur War: Israel and the Jewish People, 1974, The Image of Man in Genesis and the Ancient Near East, 1976, The Public Function of the Jewish Scholar, 1978, The Reform Movement and Israel: A New Perspective, 1978, The Use of Reason in Maimonides--An Evaluation by Ahad Ha-Am, 1993; also numerous articles to profl. jours. Mem. Pres. Johnson's Com. on EEO, 1964-66, Gov.'s Poverty Support Corps Program, 1964-66, Pres.'s Commn. on Holocaust, 1979, U.S. Holocaust Meml. Coun., 1980-92, 96— (exec. com., 1980-87, chmn. edn. com., 1987-88, chmn. acad. com., 1988—, chmn. com. on conscience, 1996—); chmn. N.Am. Assocs. Internat. Ctr. Univ. Teaching of Jewish Civilization, 1982-93, Am. Sch. Oriental Rsch., Albright Inst. Archaeol. Rsch.; bd. govs. Oxford Ctr. for Hebrew and Jewish Studies, 1995. Recipient award for contbns. to edn. L.A. City Coun., 1971, Human Relations award Am. Jewish Com., 1971, Tower of David award for cultural contbn. to Israel and Am., 1972, Gold medallion Jewish Nat. Fund, 1972, Alumnus of Yr. award Bklyn. Coll., 1972, Myrtle Wreath award Hadassah, 1977, Brandeis award Z.O.A., 1977, Nat. Brotherhood award NCCJ, 1979, Alfred Gottschalk Chair in Communal Svc. HUC, 1979, Jerusalem City of Peace award 1988, Defender of Jerusalem award honoree, 1990, Isaac M. Wise award, 1991, Heritage award Jewish Club of 1933, 1991, Nat. award NCCJ, 1994, ShanAcad. Social Scis. award, 1994, others; grantee State Dept./Smithsonian Instn., 1963, 67. Mem. AAUP, NEA, Union Am. Hebrew Congregations and Ctrl. Conf. Am. Rabbis (exec. com.), Soc. Study Religion, Am. Acad. Religion, Soc. Bibl. Lit. and Exegesis, Internat. Conf. Jewish Communal Svc., Israel Exploration Soc., So. Calif. Assn. Liberal Rabbis (past pres.), So. Calif. Jewish Hist. Soc. (hon. pres.), World Union Jewish Studies (internat. coun.), World Union Progressive Judaism (v.p.), Coun. for Initiatives in Jewish Edn. (bd. dirs.). Home: 2401 Ingleside Ave Apt 12G Cincinnati OH 45206-2157 Office: Hebrew Union College Jewish Inst 3101 Clifton Ave Cincinnati OH 45220-2404

GOTTSCHALK, JOHN E., newspaper publishing executive; b. 1943. Pub. Sidney (Nebr.) Newspaper, 1966-74; with Omaha World Herald Co., 1975—, now pres., CEO. Office: Omaha-World Herald Co World-Herald Sq Omaha NE 68102*

GOUDY, JAMES JOSEPH RALPH, electronics executive, educator; b. Bloomfield, Iowa, Nov. 3, 1952; s. Charles Jacob and Marjorie Ethel (Morten) G.; m. Diane Marie Guenther, Nov. 24, 1978; children: Megan Joanne, Monica Victoria, Mitchell Thaddeus. BS, Wayne State Coll., 1976; AAS, Indian Hills C.C., Ottumwa, Iowa, 1978; MA, N.E. Mo. State U., 1980; BA, Iowa Wesleyan Coll., 1986. Cert. engrng. technician Nat. Inst. Certification Engrng. Technicians. Sr. electronic comm. cons. ANR Pipeline Co., Fairfield, Iowa, 1978—, instr. high tech., 1987—; sr. electronics technician ANR Pipeline Co., Birmingham, Iowa, 1991—; owner Advanced Tech. Cons., 1993—; temp. instr. Wayne (Nebr.) State Coll., 1976-77; instr.

VA program Indian Hills C.C., Ottumwa, 1978, mem. high tech. programs adv. com., 1992—; instr. Iowa Wesleyan Coll., Mt. Pleasant, 1986. Bd. dirs. Wapello County Agrl. Fair, Eldon, 1988—, Ottumwa Area Translator Sys.; participant Nat. Runners Health Study, U. Calif. Mem. IEEE, Masons, Shriners, Order Ea. Star, Toastmasters, Optimists. Home: 702 S 32nd St Fairfield IA 52556-9688 Office: ANR Pipeline Co PO Box 9 Birmingham IA 52535-0009

GOUDY, JOSEPHINE GRAY, social services administrator; b. Des Moines, Nov. 30, 1925; d. Gerald William and Myrtle Maria (Brooks) Gray; BA, State U. Iowa, 1953, MSW, 1966; m. John Winston Goudy, June 5, 1948; children: Tracy Jean, Paula Rae. Clin. social worker, Iowa, Ill.; Diplomate in Clin. Social Work. Child welfare supr. Iowa Dept. Social Svcs., 1960-68; psychiat. social worker Community Mental Health Ctr. Scott County (Iowa), 1966-71; social work instr. Palmer Jr. Coll., Davenport, Iowa, 1967-70; psychiat. social worker, chief social svcs. Jacksonville (Ill.) State Mental Hosp., 1971-74; coord. community mental health outpatient services McFarland Mental Health Ctr., Springfield, Ill., 1974; exec. dir. Macoupin County Mental Health Ctr., Carlinville, Ill., 1974—; chmn. Human Svcs. Edn. Coun., Springfield, 1979-81; bd. mem. Alzheimer's Disease and Related Disorders Assn., Springfield Ill. Area Chpt., past exec. Davenport Community Welfare Coun.; adj. prof. dept. psychiatry So. Ill. U., Carbondale. Mem. Nat. Assn. Social Workers (Social Worker of Yr. Central Ill. area 1983), Acad. Cert. Social Workers, AAUW (br. pres. 1964-66, mem. state bar 1966-68, br. grantee 1975), Internat. Fedn. U. Women, U. Iowa Alumni Assn., Bus. and Profl. Women (Woman of Yr. 1983), Delta Kappa Gamma, Kappa Delta Pi. Republican. Methodist. Club: Carlinville Women's (pres. 1975-77). Home: 364 W Tremont St Waverly IL 62692-1073 Office: 100 N Side Sq Carlinville IL 62626-1748

GOUGEON, JOEL, state legislator; b. Bay City, Mich., Jan. 13, 1943; m. Kaye; 1 child, Amy. Grad., Gen. Motors Inst., 1966. Commr. Bay City Bd. Commrs., 1984-90; senator Mich. State Dist. 34, 1993—; chmn. agriculture and forestry com. Mich. State Senate, local govt. com., urban affairs com. Mem. Bay City Lions, Bay County Crime Stoppers, Elks, Am. Legion, Vietnam Vets, John Glenn Boosters. Address: 241 Donahue Beach Bay City MI 48706

GOUIN, WARNER PETER, project engineer; b. International Falls, Minn., Sept. 14, 1954; s. Joseph Andre and Rose Marie (Grandaw) G.; m. Judith Ann Nelson, Aug. 25, 1979; 1 child, Nicole Renee. AA, Rainy River Community Coll., 1974; BS Mgmt., St. Cloud State U., 1979; BSEE, N.D. State U., 1985, MS in Indsl. Engring. and Mgmt., 1987. Cert. systems integrator. Purchasing/prodn. contr. Plastech Rsch., Inc., Rush City, Minn., 1979-80; inventory supr. Aero Systems Engring., St. Paul, 1980-81; grad. asst. N.D. State U., 1985-87; elec. engr. Marvin Windows, Warroad, Minn., 1987-93; systems integrator MIS dept. Marvin Windows, Warroad, 1993-95, systems engr., automation systems acquisition, 1995—; project mgmt. trainer Process Re-Engring., Total Quality Mgmt., Warroad, Minn., 1992-95. Scoutmaster Boy Scouts Am., Warroad, 1989-91. Mem. Office Automation Soc. Internat. (editor 1989-90), Soc. Mfg. Engrs. Office: Marvin Windows PO Box 100 Warroad MN 56763-0100

GOULD, PHILLIP LOUIS, civil engineering educator, consultant; b. Chgo., May 24, 1937; m. Deborah Paula Rothholtz, Feb. 5, 1961; children: Elizabeth, Nathan, Rebecca, Joshua. BS, U. Ill., 1959, MS, 1960; PhD, Northwestern U., 1966. Structural designer Skidmore, Owings & Merrill, Chgo., 1960-63; prin. structural engr. Westenhoff & Novick, Chgo., 1963-64; NASA trainee Northwestern U., Evanston, Ill., 1964-66; asst. prof. civil engring. Washington U., St. Louis, 1966-68, assoc. prof., 1968-74, prof., 1974—, chmn. dept. civil engring., 1978—, Harold D. Jolly prof. civil engring., 1981—; vis. prof. Ruhr U., Fed. Republic Germany, 1974-75, U. Sydney, Australia, 1981, Shanghai Inst. Tech., Peoples Republic of China, 1986; dir. Earthquake Engring. Rsch. Inst., exec. coun. Internat. Assn. for Shelland Spatial Structures, pres. Great Lakes chpt. Earthquake Engring. Rsch. Inst. Author: Static Analysis of Shells: A Unified Development of Surface Structures, 1977, Introduction to Linear Elasticity, 1984, Finite Element Analysis of Shells of Revolution, 1985, Analysis of Shells and Plates, 1987; co-author: Dynamic Response of Structures to Wind and Earthquake Loading, 1980; co-editor: Environmental Forces on Engineering Structures, 1979, Natural Draught Cooling Towers, 1985; editor: Engineering Structures, 1979—. Dir. Earthquake Engring. Rsch. Inst., 1993-95; mem. Mo. Seismic Safety Commn. Recipient Sr. Scientist award Alexander von Humboldt Found., Fed. Republic Germany, 1974-75. Fellow ASCE (bd. dirs. St. Louis sect. 1985-87, Otto Nutli award); mem. Am. Soc. Engring. Edn., Internat. Assn. Shell Structures, Structural Engrs. Assn. Ill., Mo. Soc. Profl. Engrs. (Outstanding Engr. in Edn. award), Civil Engring. Alumni Assn. U. Ill., Urbana-Champaign (Disting. Alumnus award). Home: 102 Lake Frst Saint Louis MO 63117-1303 Office: Washington U Dept Civil Engring Box 1130 Saint Louis MO 63130

GOULDEY, GLENN CHARLES, manufacturing company executive; b. N.Y.C., July 28, 1952; s. George Howard and Jeannette Ruth Williamson; m. Leslie Jeanne Ruth, Oct. 2, 1982; children: Jeremy Charles, Nicholas Glenn, Alexander James George. BS in Bus., Trenton State Coll., 1976; postgrad. Portland State U., 1980; MBA Rider U., 1981; postgrad. Dartmouth Coll., 1994-95. Cert. in purchasing mgmt. Purchasing Mgrs. Assn. Sr. planner Eaton Corp., Flemington, N.J., 1975-77, pricing mgr., distbn., 1977-79, inventory control mgr., 1979-80, materials mgr., purchasing, Beaverton, Oreg., 1980-81, mfg. and materials mgr., 1981-83, mktg. and materials mgr., 1983-87, plant and gen. mgr., 1987-88, v.p. sales and mktg., Carol Stream, Ill., 1988-89, mgr. ops. div., 1989-93, gen. bus. mgr., 1993-95, pres., gen. mgr., LECTRON Products Divsn./EATON, Rochester Hills, Mich., 1995—; bd. advisors Oakland U. Bus. Sch. Patentee in field. Mem. Am. Prodn. Inventory Control Soc. (cert. in prodn. and inventory control), Nat. Youth Sports Coaches Assn. (cert.), Soc. Automotive engrs. Internat. Republican. Lutheran. Office: Lectron Products Eaton Corp 1400 S Livernois Rochester Hills MI 48308

GOULET, KEVIN, marketing professional; b. Evergreen Park, Ill., Sept. 10, 1963; s. Lawrene Earl and Sharon Rose (Cook) G.; m. Cynthia Ruth Mann, June 4, 1988; children: Christopher Ryan, Colin Michael. BSEE, U. Ill., 1985; postgrad., Northwestern U., 1994. Project engr. Underwriters Labs., Inc., Northbrook, Ill., 1985-88; liaison engr., product engr., product mgr., mktg. mgr.q ONEAC Corp., Libertyville, Ill., 1988-94; dir. mktg. Ameritech Cellular Svcs., Hoffman Estates, Ill., 1995—. Contbr. articles to engring. publs. Mem. IEEE, Am. Mktg. Assn., McHenry County Defenders. Home: 3312 Ramsgate Ln Mc Henry IL 60050-1638 Office: Ameritech Cellular Svcs 2000 W Ameritech Ctr Dr Hoffman Estates IL 60195-5000

GOVE, PETER CHARLES, special education educator; b. St. Louis, Oct. 13, 1954; s. Clem Charles and Adelaide (Bockhorst) G. AS, George Washington U., 1992; BS in Edn. cum laude, Lincoln U., 1994. Laborer Kingsford Charcoal Co., Belle, Mo., 1973; x-ray aide Charles E. Still, Jefferson City, 1974-76; substitute tchr. Linn (Mo.) RII H.S., 1993, East Elem. Sch., Waynesville, Mo., 1994; substitute tchr. South Callaway RII Sch., Mokane, Mo., 1994, tchr. H.S. learning disabled, 1994—; asst. audio visual Lincoln U., Jefferson City, Mo., 1994. Troop leader Boy Scouts Am., Beaufort, S.C., 1986-89. With USN, 1977-89. Mem. Coun. for Exceptional Children, Disabled Am. Vets, Nat. Order Trench Rats, Am. Legion, Phi Alpha Theta. Home: PO Box 79 1114 Jefferson St Linn MO 65051

GOVINDJEE, biophysics and biology educator; b. Allahabad, India, Oct. 24, 1933; came to U.S., 1956, naturalized, 1972; s. Vishveshvar Prasad and Savitri Devi Asthana; m. Rajni Varma, Oct. 24, 1957; children: Anita Govindjee, Sanjay Govindjee. BSc, U. Allahabad, 1952, MSc, 1954; PhD, U. Ill., 1960. Lectr. botany U. Allahabad, 1954-56; grad. fellow U. Ill., Urbana, 1956-58; research asst. U. Ill., 1958-60, USPHS postdoctoral trainee biophysics, 1960-61, mem. faculty, 1961—, assoc. prof. botany and biophysics, 1965-69, prof. biophysics and plant biology, 1969—, disting. lectr. Sch. Life Scis., 1978. Author: Photosynthesis, 1969; editor: Bioenergetics of Photosynthesis, 1975, Photosynthesis: Carbon Assimilation and Plant Productivity, Energy Conversion by Plants and Bacteria, 2 vols., 1982 (Russian transl. 1987), Light Emission by Plants and Bacteria, 1986, Excitation Energy and Electron Transfer in Photosynthesis, 1989, Photosynthesis: From Photoreactions to Productivity, 1993, Hist. Corner: Photosynthesis Rsch., 1989—; guest editor spl. issue Biophys. Jour., 1972, Photochemistry and Photobiology, 1978; editor-in-chief Photosynthesis Rsch., 1985-88; series editor: Advances in Photosynthesis, vol. 1, 1994, vol. 2, 1995, vols. 3, 4, and 5, 1996; contbr. articles to profl. jours., also Sci. Am. Fulbright scholar, 1956-61, 96-97. Fellow AAAS, NAS (India); mem. Am. Soc. Plant Physiologists, Biophys. Soc. Am., Am. Soc. Photobiology (coun. 1976, pres. 1981), Internat. Photosynthesis Soc. (exec. com., publ. com. 1995-98), Sigma Xi. Home: 2401 Boudreau Dr Urbana IL 61801-6655

GOWARD, RUSSELL, state legislator; b. St. Louis, Aug. 25, 1935; s. William and Zenobia (Askew) G.; m. Dolores Jean Thornton, 1957; children: Russell II, Monika. Cert., Hubbard's Bus. Coll., 1959; student, Harris Tchrs. Coll. Divsn. leader 21st Ward Dem. Orgn., Mo., 1963-65; rep. Mo. State Ho. Reps. Dist. 60, 1967—; pres., treas. Goward's & Assocs., Inc., 1967—. Active Boy Scouts Am. Decorated Nat. Def. Svc. Ribbon, European Occupl. medal. Mem. Masons. Home: 5000 Tyus Ct Saint Louis MO 63115-1553*

GOWEN, NANCY ADELE, vocational education educator, consultant; b. New Brunswick, N.J., Apr. 20, 1934; d. William Rogers and Rose Elizabeth (Muha) Applegate; m. Richard Joseph Gowen, Dec. 28, 1955; children: Jeffrey, Cindy, Elizabeth, Susan, Kerry Beth. BS in Edn., Kean Coll., 1955; MA in Edn., U. Colo., 1972. Tchr. Madison Sch., Rahway, N.J., 1955-56, Little Folks Pre-Sch., Colorado Springs, Colo., 1968-69, USAF Acad. Pre-Sch., Colo., 1973-74, 75-77; coord., tutor Giles Edn. Ctr., Colorado Springs, 1977-78; head tchr., then edn. coord. Head Start, Rapid City, S.D., 1979-84; instr. Western Dakota Vocat. Inst., Rapid City, 1988—; ind. edn. cons. Rapid City, 1988—; cons. Rapid City Regional Hosp., 1988-89; instr. Black Hills State U., Spearfish, S.C., 1990; project dir. Pre-Sch. Readiness Program Project 2000, 1992-95; presenter workshops on creative dramatics, computers in early childhood, parental images in children's lit., discipline, growth and devel.; ct. apptd. spl. advocate. Bd. dirs. Mayor's Task Force on Child Care, Rapid City, 1988-90, pres., 1989-90; bd. dirs. Rapid City Arts Coun., 1990-93, Mus. in Motion, Rapid City, 1989—; adv. com. Luth. Social Svcs., Rapid City, 1990-96. Recipient Svc. award S.D. Assn. Young Children, 1993. Mem. AAUW (equity chair 1991-92, membership v.p. 1993-95), Assn. Edn. Young Children (pres. Black Hills chpt. 1990-91, S.D. chpt. 1985-89, bd. dirs., sec. Midwestern unit 1987-93), Positive Parents Network (1990-91), Delta Kappa Gamma.

GOWEN, RICHARD JOSEPH, electrical engineering educator, academic administrator; b. New Brunswick, N.J., July 6, 1935; s. Charles David and Esther Ann (Hughes) G.; m. Nancy A. Applegate, Dec. 28, 1955; children: Jeff, Cindy, Betsy, Susan, Kerry. BS in Elec. Engring., Rutgers U., 1957; MS, Iowa State U., 1961, PhD, 1962. Registered profl. engr., Colo. Research engr. RCA Labs., Princeton, N.J., 1957; commd. USAF; ground electronics officer Yaak AFB, Mont., 1957-59; instr. USAF Acad., 1962-63, research assoc., 1963-64, asst. prof., 1964-65, assoc. prof., 1965-66, tenured assoc. prof. elec. engring., 1966-70, tenured prof., 1971-77, dir., prin. investigator NASA instrumentation group for cardiovascular studies, 1968-77; mem. launch and recovery med. team Johnson Space Ctr., NASA, 1971-77; v.p., dean engring., prof. S.D. Sch. Mines and Tech., Rapid City, 1977-84, pres., 1987—; pres. Dakota State U., Madison, 1984-87; prin. investigator program in support space cardiovascular studies NASA, 1977-81; co-chmn. Joint Industry, Nuclear Regulatory IEEE, Am. Nuclear Soc. Probabilistic Risk Assessment Guidelines for Nuclear Power Plants Project, 1980-83; mem. Dept. Def. Software Engring. Inst. Panel, 1983; bd. dirs. ETA Systems, Inc., St. Paul, Minn., 1983-89, Data Max, Inc. Contbr. articles to profl. jours.; patentee in field. Bd. dirs. St. Martins Acad., Rapid City, S.D. Bd. dirs. St. Martins Acad., Rapid City, S.D., Greater Rapid City Econ. Devel. Partnership, 1991—, Data Max Inc. Fellow IEEE (Centennial Internat. pres. 1984, USAB/IEEE Disting. Contbns. to Engring. Professionalism award 1986); mem. Am. Assn. Engring. Socs. (chmn. 1988), Rotary, Sigma Xi, Phi Kappa Phi, Tau Beta Phi, Eta Kappa Nu, Pi Mu Epsilon. Roman Catholic. Home: 1609 Palo Verde Dr Rapid City SD 57701-4461 Office: SD Sch Mines & Tech Office of Pres Rapid City SD 57701

GOWER, CINDY ELAINE, electronic technician; b. Springfield, Ohio, Nov. 27, 1960; d. James K. Lones and Catherine May (Dellinger) Oldfield; m. George W. Gower Jr., July 11, 1981 (div. 1986); children: Natasha May, Matthew W. AAS, Columbus State C.C., 1993. Owner, assembler Qaulity First Assembly & Fabrication, Columbus, Ohio, 1993-94; HVAC electronic control tech. Creative Control Designs, Inc., Columbus, 1993—; owner Gower's Tax Svc., Grove City, Ohiuo, 1992—; tax cons. H&R Block, Inc., Gove City, 1993; tech. writer Creative Control Designs, team leader, VAV coord.; bus. cons. K.I.D.S., Hillard, Ohio, 1993, Oldfield's Odds & Ends, 1989—. Mem. Federated Tax Profession, Nat. Assn. Tax Profls., WIBC. Republican.

GOZA, FRANKLIN WILLIAM, sociology educator; b. Peoria, Ill., July 19, 1955; s. Franklin Delano Roosevelt and Zona Ann (Challe) G.; m. Lynn Louise Tratnik, Nov. 8, 1986; children: Angelica L., Olivia C. BA magna cum laude, U. Wis., 1980, MS, 1983, PhD, 1987. Vis. prof. demography Fed. U. Minas Gerais, Belo Horizonte, Brazil, 1987-89; asst. prof. sociology Bowling Green (Ohio) State U., 1989-94, assoc. prof., 1994—. Rockefeller Found. fellow, 1987-89; sr. Fulbright scholar Brazil, 1992-93. Mem. Am. Sociol. Assn., Population Assn. Am., Brazilian Population Assn., Phi Kappa Phi, Sigma Delta Pi. Office: Bowling Green State U Dept Sociology Bowling Green OH 43403

GOZON, JOZSEF STEPHAN, engineering educator; b. Öcsény, Hungary, Nov. 16, 1933; came to U.S., 1979; s. Jozsef and Erzsebet (Grof) G.; m. Jolan Szabo, May 10, 1958 (dec. 1972); m. Julianna Teleki, Nov. 18, 1972; children: Eszter Julianna, Peter Richard. BS, Coll. Mining, Sopron, Hungary, 1958; D of Tech., Tech. U., Miskolc, Hungary, 1967; PhD in Mining, Mining Inst. Moscow, 1967; PhD in Tech. Sci., Acad. Scis., Budapest, Hungary, 1967. Registered profl. engr. Asst. lectr. Tech. U., Miskolc, 1958-60, lectr., 1964-69, assoc. prof., 1969-73, 75-79; assoc. prof. Coll. Petroleum and Mining, Tripoli, Libya, 1973-75; assoc. prof. mining engring. Ohio State U., Columbus, 1979-82, prof., 1982—; rsch. fellow Geothermal Lab., Miskolc, 1960-64; pres. Mining Tech. and Measurement Inc., Columbus, 1985-95; v.p. GCK Corp., 1991—; cons. in field. Author: Use of Geothermal Energy, 1965, Mining Machines, 1968; editor Internat. Jour. Surface Mining, 1987-90. Active Forest Park Civic Assn., Columbus, 1980-95. Mem. Am. Soc. Mining Engrs., Hungarian Soc. Mining Engrs. (vice chmn. 1977-79), Am. Soc. Engring. Edn. Roman Catholic. Home: 3246 Foxcroft Dr Lewis Center OH 43035-9338 Office: Ohio State Univ Dept Civil Engring 2070 Neil Ave Columbus OH 43210-1275

GRABER, ROBERT BATES, anthropologist; b. Lansing, Mich., Apr. 30, 1950; s. Virgil Rich and Evelyn Louise (Scarff) G.; m. Rosanna Ruth Stoltzfus, June 18, 1972; children: Kathryn Elizabeth, Karen Marie. BA, Ind. U., 1973; MS, U. Wis., 1976, PhD, 1979. Scientific aide Milw. Pub. Mus., 1975-76; teaching asst. U. Wis., Milw., 1976-77, univ. fellow, 1977-78; asst. prof. of anthropology and sociology Millsaps Coll., Jackson, Miss., 1979-81; asst. prof. of anthropology and sociology Truman State U. (formerly Northeast Mo. State U.), Kirksville, 1981-86, assoc. prof., 1986—, prof., 1993—; adv. bd. Thomas Jefferson U. Press, Kirksville, 1987—. Author: A Scientific Model of Social and Cultural Evolution, 1995, Valuing Useless Knowledge, 1995; co-editor: Circumscription and the Evolution of Society, 1988; contbr. articles to profl. jours. Fellow Am. Anthropol. Assn.; mem. Soc. for Am. Archaeology, Phi Kappa Phi, Phi Beta Kappa (pres. N.E. Mo. Assn. 1992-93). Office: Truman State Univ Divsn Social Sci Kirksville MO 63501

GRABINSKI, C. JOANNE, gerontologist, educator; b. Bend, Oreg., Dec. 8, 1941; d. Jack George and Helen Margaret (Thomsen) Huffman; m. Roger Neil Grabinski, Aug. 13, 1966; 1 child, Lawrence Neil. BS, MS in Home Econ. Edn., Oreg. State U., 1963, 68; MA in Ednl. Adminstrn./Cmty. Leadership, Ctrl. Mich. U., 1976, MA in Family Rels., 1980; postgrad., Mich. State U., 1982-87. Dept. chair, tchr. home econs. Oakridge (Oreg.) Jr./Sr. High Sch., 1963-67, Briggs Jr. High Sch., Springfield, Oreg., 1967-68; prof. home econs. Lane C.C., Eugene, Oreg., 1968-69; residence hall dir., assoc. dir. Western Mich. U., Kalamazoo, 1970-72; dir., spl. interest coord. Mt. Pleasant (Mich.) Pub. Schs., 1976-77; money mgmt. counselor Coop. Ext. Svc./DSS, Mt. Pleasant, 1977-78; asst. prof. ednl. adminstrn./community leadership Ctrl. Mich. U., Mt. Pleasant, 1976, 77, asst. prof. home econs., 1980-86, dir./asst. prof. interdisciplinary gerontology program, 1984-91; pres., cons. cjgGERONTOLOGY, Mt. Pleasant, 1991—; project dir. Region 7 Alzheimer's Disease and Related Conditions Caregiver Edn. Project, Mich. Dept. Mental Health, Ctrl. Mich. U., 1986-91; adj. prof. gerontology Western Mich. U., Kalamazoo, 1992-94; continuing edn. rep., lectr. gerontology Ea. Mich. U., 1992-96, continuing edn. coord.-gerontology Ea. Mich. U., 1996—; Ea. Mich. U. Elderwise liaison, 1995—. Editorial bd. AGHE Exchange, 1988-91, asst. editor, 1988-91; contbr. articles to profl. jours. Bd. dirs. Hospice of Cen. Mich., Mt. Pleasant, 1986-89, Cen. Mich. U. Dames, 1974-78, pres., 1976-77; bd. dirs. Mt. Pleasant Welcome Wagon Newcomers Club, 1972-76, pres., 1974-75; team mem. Bldg. Ties, Isabella County, Mich., 1983-84. Marie Dye Grad. fellow Mich. Home Econ. Assn., 1983; named Outstanding Faculty Mem., Ctrl. Mich. U. Mortar Bd. Mem. Am. Soc. on Aging, Gerontol. Soc. Am., Nat. Coun. on Aging, Mich. Coun. on Family Rels. (bd. dirs. 1984-87), Nat. Coun. Family Rels., Assn. Gerontology Higher Edn. (instnl. rep.), Kappa Omicron Nu, Omicron Nu, Kappa Omicron Phi, Phi Delta Kappa. Democrat. Lutheran. Home: 310 Apricot Ln Mount Pleasant MI 48858-6156 Office: cjgGERONTOLOGY PO Box 868 Mount Pleasant MI 48804-0868

GRABLE, R(EGINALD) HAROLD, psychologist; b. Putnam County, Ind., Sept. 22, 1917; s. Reginald R. and Cecil Ruth (Jones) G.; AB, U. Kans., 1938, tchr.'s diploma, 1940; MA, U. Minn., 1949; m. Elizabeth Hannah Baird, Aug. 17, 1946; children: Celia, Nancy, Daniel. Group leader occupational coders Nat. Roster Sci. and Specialized Personnel, Washington, 1940-42; vocat. counselor U. Minn., Mpls., 1947; clin. psychologist trainee VA Hosp., St. Paul, 1947-49; chief clin. psychologist Willmar (Minn.) State Hosp., 1949-51, Winnebago (Wis.) State Hosp., 1951-61; clin. psychologist West Shore Mental Health Clinic (formerly Hackley Adult Mental Health Clinic), Muskegon, Mich., 1961-82; clin. psychologist Kalamazoo Regional Psychiat. Hosp., 1983-85; pvt. practice, Willmar, Minn., 1949-51, Oshkosh, Wis., 1951-61, Spring Lake, Mich., 1961—; instr. extension div. U. Wis., 1956-61; mem. profl. adv. bd. Wis. Council Mentally Retarded Children, 1956-61. Contbr. articles to profl. jours. First aid instr. ARC, 1963-79; exec. bd. Grand Valley council (name now West Mich. Shores council) Boy Scouts Am., 1966-76, dist. chmn., 1968-70, commr., 1972-90; various offices PTA, 1953-78, Vols. in Probation; elder, Muskegon Christian Ch. (Disciples of Christ), 1966—, chmn. bd. 1970-73, mem. regional bd. dirs. 1988—. With AUS, 1942-46. Decorated Combat Infantry Badge; recipient Silver Beaver award Boy Scouts Am., 1981, Dist. award of Merit, 1977, cert. Appreciation Second Amendment Found., Alumnus of Notable Achievement award U. Minn.; lic. psychologist, Mich. Mem. APA, Nat. Register Health Svc. Providers in Psychology, Mich. Assn. Children with Learning Disabilities, The Writers (pres. 1991—), VFW (life, commdr. polar bear post 3734 1992-93, Disting. Svc. Citation), Rotary. Home and Office: 717 Summer St Spring Lake MI 49456-1964

GRABNER, CAREN SUE, food service manager; b. Longview, Tex., Feb. 11, 1955; d. Keith C. and Patricia (Kuhn) Shaffer; m. Michael A. Grabner, Oct. 7, 1978 (div. Nov. 1989). Grad. high sch., Ft. Wayne, Ind. Exec. mgr. Ponderosa, Ft. Wayne, 1972-79; gen. mgr. Sizzler Steak House, Ft. Wayne, 1980-83; mgr. Pizza Hut, Ft. Wayne, 1984-86; sr. mgr. Burger King, Ft. Wayne, 1986-87; mgr. Ponderosa, Ft. Wayne, 1987-88; gen. bus. mgr. Taco Bell, Inc., Grand Rapids, Mich., 1988—.

GRABOSKY, TERRI JO, artist; b. Waukegan, Nov. 20, 1949; d. Joseph Vincent and Margaret D. (Schroeder) Morrissey; m. Hugh Francis Grabosky, July 23, 1985. BA in Art, Art Edn., Carthage Coll., Kenosha, 1972, MEd in Creative Arts, 1984. Art teacher Jefferson J.H.S., Waukegan, 1974-79, Jack Benny Ctr. for the Arts, Waukegan, 1976-77; itinerant art teacher Waukegan Dist. #60, 1979-80; visual art specialist Cooke Magnet Sch., Waukegan, 1980-89; art tchr. Glencoe (Ill.) Sch. Dist., 1989—; presenter, State Gifted Convention, Chgo., 1981, State Convention of Ill. Music Edn. Assn., Springfield, 1982, Related-Arts Programs, 1981-87. Presenter BASIC workshop Sch. Art Inst., chgo., 1985; panelist State Art Region 1 Conf. Columbia Coll., 1987. Named Tchr. of the Yr., Waukegan Public Sch., Dist #60, 1984. Mem. Ill. Alliance for Arts Edn., Nat. Art Edn., Assn., Ill. Art Edn., Assn., Am. Craft Coun., Pi Lambda Theta. Episcopalian. Office: South Sch 266 Linden Ave Glencoe IL 60022-2165

GRACE, MARK EUGENE, professional baseball player; b. Winston-Salem, N.C., June 28, 1964. Student, Saddleback C.C., San Diego State U. First baseman Chgo. Cubs, 1985—; mem. Nat. League All-Star Team, 1993. Recipient Golden Glove award, 1992-93; named Sporting News Rookie Player of Yr., MVP Ea. League, 1987; assist leader for 1st basemen, 1990-92; ranked 1st in Nat. League for put-outs, 1991-92. Office: Chgo Cubs Wrigley Field 1060 W Addison St Chicago IL 60613-4305*

GRACE, RICHARD EDWARD, engineering educator; b. Chgo., June 26, 1930; s. Richard Edward and Louise (Koko) G.; m. Consuela Cummings Fotos, Jan. 29, 1955; children: Virginia Louise, Richard Cummings (dec.). BS in Metall. Engring., Purdue U., 1951; PhD, Carnegie Inst. Tech., 1954. Registered profl. engr., N.J. Asst. prof. Purdue U., West Lafayette, Ind., 1954-58, assoc. prof., 1958-62, prof., 1962—, head sch. materials sci. and metall. engring., 1965-72, head div. interdisciplinary engring. studies, 1970-82, head freshman engring. dept., asst. dean engring., 1981-87, v.p. for student services, 1987-95, dir. undergrad. studies program, 1995—; cons. to Midwest industries. Contbr. articles to profl. jours. Pres. Lafayette Symphony Found. Bd., 1993-95. Named Sagamore of Wabash, Gov. of Ind., 1995. Fellow Am. Soc. Metals (tchr. award 1962), Am. Soc. Engring. Edn. (Centennial medallion 1993), Accreditation Bd. Engring. and Tech. (past dir. and officer engring. edn. and accreditation com., related engring. com., Grinter award 1989); mem. AAUP, Minerals, Metals and Materials Soc. (bd. dirs. 1987-90), Lafayette Country Club, Rotary, Elks, Sigma Xi, Tau Beta Pi, Omicron Delta Kappa, Phi Gamma Delta. Home: 2175 Tecumseh Park Ln West Lafayette IN 47906-2118 Office: Purdue U Undergrad Studies Program 1073 Student Health Ctr West Lafayette IN 47907-1073 Office: Purdue Univ Undergrad Studies Program 1073 Student Health Ctr West Lafayette IN 47907-1073

GRACEY, ROBERT WILLIAM, account executive, minister; b. Steubenville, Ohio, Aug. 11, 1941; s. Robert S. and Mary O. (Barnett) G.; m. Patricia J. Zapka, Aug. 29, 1964; children: R. Stephen, Jonathan B. BA, Davis & Elkins Coll., 1963; MDiv, Pitts. Theol. Sem., 1966, postgrad., 1968-70; postgrad., Coll. Fin. Planning, 1991-93. CFP; cert. hotel adminstr.; registered rep.; lic. ins. agt. Pastor, dir. Clay County Larger Parish, Manchester, Ky., 1966-68; pastor Union First Presbyn. Ch., Cowansville, Pa., 1968-78; caseworker Family Counseling Ctr., Kittanning, Pa., 1970-78; gen. mgr. Quality Inn/Royle, Kittanning, 1978-84; mgr. Wheeling (W.Va.) Country Club, 1984-87; investment exec. Legg Mason Wood Walker, Inc., Wheeling, 1987-93; acct. exec. The Ohio Co., Martins Ferry, Ohio, 1993—; supply preacher Presbytery of Upper Ohio Valley, Wheeling, 1985—. Trustee Presbyn. Homes, Inc., Camp Hill, Pa., 1992-96; chair ch. and cmty. com. Presbytery of Upper Ohio Valley, 1989-91, sec. com. on ministry, 1995; chair Mission Support and Adv. Coun., Mark H. Kennedy Park, Community Home Care and Hospice; mem. Flood Relief Network of Upper Ohio Valley, Wheeling, 1990-91; bd. dirs., sec.-treas. B.O.L.T., Inc., Weirton, W.Va., 1990-94. Named Mgr. of Yr. Aladdin Food Mgmt. Svcs., Inc., Wheeling, 1987. Mem. Brooke County Geneal. Soc., Cumberland Trail Geneal. Soc., Tuscaraurus County Geneal. Soc., Geneal Soc. Southwestern Pa., Minig Your History Found., Rotary Internat. (pres. Weirton club 1994-95, dir.-at-large, Rotarian of Yr. 1990, Paul Harris Fellow), Internat. Platform Assn., Weirton C. of C. Republican. Home: 1 Echo Ln Wheeling WV 26003-5799 Office: The Ohio Co care Citizens Bank 4th and Hickory Sts Martins Ferry OH 43935

GRACY, JANINE LOUISE, director health education, educator; b. Wellington, Kans., Nov. 3, 1962; d. Eldon Bruce and Helen Louise (Metscher) Gracy; children: Andrew Bradford, Ashlynn Louise. BS in Edn., U. Kans., 1985, MS in Edn., 1991. Cert. health edn. specialist, Kans. Instr. pub. health U. Kans., Lawrence, 1985-87, dir. health edn., 1987—; instr. Peer Health Advisor Orgn., Lawrence, 1985—; mem. adv. bd. project COPE (Comprehensive Orgn.-wide Prevention Edn. for Healthcare Students) U. Kans. Med. Ctr., Kansas City, 1993; advisor in field. Mem. Douglas County AIDS Svc. Provider Com., Lawrence, 1988—; mem. adv. coun. Douglas

County AIDS Project, 1988-95, mem. exec. bd., 1995—; chmn. gov. bd. Campus Ministry, 1993-95. Recipient Outstanding Greek Alumni award U. Kans., 1992, Order of Omega Outstanding Faculty award, 1994. Mem. AAHPERD, AAUW, Assn. for Advancement in Health Edn., Nat. Assn. Student Pers. Adminstrs. (presenter 1994), Am. Coll. Health Adminstrs. (presenter 70th ann. meeting 1992), Delta Delta Delta (Theta Omega House Corp. pres. 1989—, State of Kans. conv. spkr. 1995, nat. conv. spkr. 1996). Methodist. Home: 904 Prescott Dr Lawrence KS 66049-3665 Office: U Kans Watkins Health Ctr Student Health Svcs Lawrence KS 66045

GRAD, EDWARD ALPHONSE, family practice physician; b. Cin., July 22, 1930; s. Edward and Anna (Brandt) G.; m. Page C. Haisley, May 21, 1960; children: Denise, Michele. BS, U. Cin., 1952, MS, 1953, MD, 1959. Diplomate Am. Bd. Family Practice. Pvt. practice Cin., 1961-75; physician occupl. medicine Procter & Gamble, Cin., 1975-89, Cin., 1990—. With U.S. Army, 1953-55. Fellow Am. Acad. of Family Practice, Am. Acad. of Occupl. Medicine; mem. Western Ohio Occupl. Med. Assn., Ohio State Med. Assn., Am. Acad. of Family Practice, Am. Coll. Occupl. Medicine. Republican. Presbyterian. Home: 4651 Day Rd Cincinnati OH 45252-1807

GRADDY, WILLIAM EDWARD, english professor; b. Evansville, Ind., Apr. 16, 1944; s. William H. and Juanita (McDonald) G.; m. Julia H. Lane, Oct. 10, 1944. BA (honors), So. Ill. U., Carbondale, 1965, MA, 1968, PhD, 1975. Asst. prof. Trinity Coll., Deerfield, IL, 1973-75, assoc. prof., 1976-85, prof., 1986—. Contbr. articles to profl. jours. Recipient Tchg. Excellence and Campus Leadership Award, Sears-Roebuck Found., 1990. Mem. Nat. Coun. of Tchrs. of English. Office: Trinity Internat. Univer. 2065 Half Day Rd Deerfield IL 60015

GRADE, LORNA J(EAN), medical writer & editor, medical business manager; b. Milw., May 7, 1954; d. William H. and Carol A. (Kaczmarowski) Momberg; m. Scott F. Grade, Aug. 16, 1986; children: Aaron D. Hendrix, Anna T., Elena D. BA in Bus. and Communications, Alverno Coll., 1981. Supr. med. records Mt. Sinai Med. Ctr., Milw., 1974-79; mgr. cardiovascular disease sect. U. Wis. Med. Sch., Milw., 1980-89; freelance med. writer, Milw., 1989—; mgr. Definitive Health Svcs. Inc., Winter Park, Fla., 1992—, Milw., 1992—; mgr. Heart Study Ctr., Winter Park, Fla., 1981-89, Mobile Cardiovascular Testing, Milw., 1985-89, Mobile Diagnostic Svcs., Milw., 1987-89, Met. Imaging Ctr., 1988-89. Co-editor 4 med. ednl. newsletters; contbr. articles to profl. jours. Roman Catholic. Home: 413 E Birch Ave Milwaukee WI 53217-5168

GRADELESS, DONALD EUGENE, secondary education educator; b. Warsaw, Ind., Apr. 17, 1949; s. Harmon Willard and Donna Maxine (Mort) G. BS in Acctg., U. Wis., Stevens Point, 1972; MS in Teaching, U. Wis., Eau Claire, 1975; PhD in Edn., Pacific Western U., 1988. Cert. in data edn. Tchr. high schs. Racine, Wis., 1972-77; mgr. constrn. Computer Control Corp., Milw., 1977; indsl. engr. Weatherhead div. Dana Corp., Columbia City, Ind., 1977-78; instr. bus. edn. Elmbrook pub. schs., Brookfield, Wis., 1978—; coordinator instructional data processing Racine Unified Schs., 1973-77. Author geneal. books. Fellow Am. Coll. Genealogists; mem. NEA, NRA (golden eagles, life mem.), SAR (sec., host. 1977, registrar 1975-76, publs. chmn. 1975-77, pres. 1976-77, 95-96, Nat. Soc. Mem. awards 1976-78, Silver Good Citizenship edal 1978, mem. Ind. soc.), S.R. (chmn. 1975-79, pres. 1979-83, registrar 1979-82, 84-87, sec. 1983—, Gen. Pres.'s Spl. Commendation award 1985, Outstanding Svc. award 1982, mem. various state bds. mgrs.), Nat. Bus. Edn. Assn., Wis. Bus. Edn. Assn., Children Am. Revolution (sr. registrar 1976-77, 80-83, sr. v.p. 1984-86, sr. pres. 1986-90, hon. sr. state pres. 1990—), Sons and Daus. of Pilgrims (counselor 1979-80, 2d dep. govs. 1989-90, 1st dep. gov. 1990-92, gov. Wis. 1992—), Soc. Colonial Wars (dep. sec. Wis. chpt. 1978-79, registrar 1994-96, lt. gov. 1975-77), Studebaker Family Nat. Assn. (life mem.), Soc. of the War of 1812 (v.p. 1994-95, pres. 1995—, life mem.), Huguenot soc. (registrar 1975-77, chaplain 1993—), Wis. State Old Cemetery Soc., U.S. Postal Svcs. Racine (customer adv. com. 1992—), Mensa, Whitley County Hist. Soc., Soc. Ind. Pioneers, Sons of Union Vets of Civil War, Children Am. Revolution, Nat. Officers Club (patron award 1993), Delta Phi Epsilon. Lodge: Masons (32 degree), K.T. Home: 1721 Edgewood Ave Racine WI 53404-2306 Office: Brookfield Ctrl High Sch 16800 Gebhardt Rd Brookfield WI 53005-5137

GRADWOHL, DAVID MAYER, anthropology educator; b. Lincoln, Nebr., Jan. 22, 1934; s. Bernard Sam and Elaine (Mayer) G.; m. Hanna Rosenberg, Dec. 29, 1957; children: Steven Ernst, Jane Mayer Nash, Kathryn Mayer. BA in Anthropology and Geology, Nebr. U., 1955; postgrad., Edinburgh (Scotland) U., 1955-56; PhD in Anthropology, Harvard U., 1967. Instr. anthropology Iowa State U., Ames, 1962-66, asst. prof., 1966-67, assoc. prof., 1967-72, coord. anthropology, 1968-75, chair Am. Indian studies program, 1981-85, prof. anthropology, 1972—; asst site supr. Winchester (Eng.) Excavations Com., 1965; advisor Nat. Register Hist. Sites, Des Moines, 1969-88, Office of State Archaeologist, Iowa City, 1983—; commr. Ames Hist. Preservation Commn., 1988-91. Co-author: The Worlds Between Two Rivers, 1987, Exploring Buried Buxton, 1990; co-author (audio visual programs) Blacks and Whites in Buxton, 1986, Iowa's Indian Heritage, 1972. With U.S. Army, 1957-59. Fulbright fellow U.s. Ednl. Commn., Edinburgh, 1956; recipient Faculty Citation, Iowa State Alumni Assn., Ames, 1980, Charles Irby Disting. Svc. award Nat. Assn. Ethnic Studies, 1990, Career Achievement award for undergrad. teaching AMOCO, 1992. Fellow Am. Anthropol. Assn., Assn. Iowa Archaeologists (chair 1977-78), Nebr. Assn. Profl. Archaeologists; mem. Soc. Am. Archaeology, Soc. Hist. Archaeology, Nebr. Jewish Hist. Soc., Nebr. State Hist. Soc., Plains Anthropol. Soc. (bd. dirs. 1987-90), Nat. Assn. Ethnic Studies (mem. editorial bd. 1987—), Iowa Archaeol. Soc. (mem. editorial bd. 1992—). Democrat. Jewish. Home: 2003 Ashmore Dr Ames IA 50014-7804 Office: Iowa State U Dept Anthropology Ames IA 50011

GRADY, FRANCIS XAVIER, lawyer; b. Cleve., Nov. 17, 1957; s. John J. and Mary Veronica (Carey) G.; m. Donita Marie Labas. BS in Internat. Politics magna cum laude, Georgetown U., 1980; cert. advanced European studies, Coll. Europe, 1981; JD, Ohio State U., 1984. Bar: Ohio 1984, D.C. 1985. Atty. FDIC, Washington, 1984-86; assoc. Muldoon, Murphy & Faucette, Washington, 1986-87, Hahn, Loeser & Parks, Cleve., 1987-90; of counsel Seeley, Savidge & Aussem, Cleve., 1990-94; ptnr. Grady & Assocs., Cleve., 1994—. Author: The New CRA: A Practical Guied to Compliance; contbr. articles to profl. jours. Mem. Am.'s Cmty. Bankers. Roman Catholic. Office: Grady & Assocs Ste 620 1468 W 9th St Cleveland OH 44113-1220

GRADY, JOSEPH PATRICK, real estate professional; b. Canton, Ohio, June 12, 1958; s. Robert Emmett and Mildred Sara (Sharrock) G. BA in Polit. Sci., Ohio State U., 1979; cert. in real estate, Malone Coll., 1986, 89. Lic. real estate broker, Ohio. Front office supr. Hyatt Regency Columbus, Ohio, 1979-81; customer svc. agt. Western and Piedmont Airlines, L.A. and Canton, 1981-84; pub. rels. dir., bus. coord. North Canton (Ohio) C. of C., 1985-86; broker, owner Re/Max Xpress, North Canton, 1986-95; broker/realtor Re/Max Ptnrs., 1995-96, Good Real Estate Edn. Enterprises, 1996—; chmn. St. Hope Housing Bd., 1991; bd. dirs. Canton Tele. Credit Union; instr. in real estate Malone Coll. Stark County Rep. precinct com. 1983-90; councilman at large City of North Canton, 1985-91; concert chmn. Ohio State U. Marching Band, 1987; Meml. Day parade chmn. City of North Canton, 1990. Recipient Disting. Svc. award North Canton Jaycees, 1995; named Ohio Realtor/Salesperson of Yr., 1995. Mem. Nat. Assn. Realtors (Realtor-Broker of Yr. 1993, Realtor Salesperson of Yr. 1995), Ohio State U. Alumni Assn., Stark County Assn. Realtors (chmn. edn. com.), Leadership Canton Alumni Assn., Ohio Assn. Realtors (pres. club. 1988-94, edn. com. 1991-93, vice chmn. edn. com. 1994-95, presdl. blue ribbon task force com., state trustee 1993-95), North Canton C. of C. (bd. dirs. 1987-90, chmn. cmty. recognition dinner), Ohio State U. Alumni Club Stark County (bd. dirs., pres. 1986-88). Home: 710 Ruth Ave SW North Canton OH 44720-2973 Office: Good Real Estate Edn 710 Ruth SW North Canton OH 44720

GRADY, WILLIAM EARL, marketing executive; b. Wichita, Kans., Oct. 31, 1953; s. Jack L. and Helen May (Curfman) G. BS, Avila Coll., 1973. Mktg. profl. Am. Lining Co., Mission, Kans., 1973-80, v.p., 1980—; lectr. in field. Recipient Outstanding Svc. award U. Mo. at Kansas City, Squire Single Achiever award Squire Newspaper. Home: 4837 Booth St Shawnee Mission KS 66205-1830

GRAEBER, CLYDE D., state legislator; b. Aug. 29, 1933; m. Pauline Graeber. BA, U. Tulsa, 1954, JD, 1959. City commr. Leavenworth, Kans., 1978-84, mayor, 1983-84; Kans. state rep. Dist. 41, 1985—, chmn. Rep. House Caucus, lawyer, banker, 1996—. Mem. Am. Legis. Exch. Coun., Okla. Bar Assn. Home: 2400 Kingman St Leavenworth KS 66048-4230*

GRAEF, LUTHER WILLIAM, civil engineer; b. Milw., Aug. 14, 1931; s. John and Pearl (Luther) G.; BCE, Marquette U., 1952; MCE, U. Wis., 1961; m. Lorraine Linnerud, Sept. 18, 1954; children—Ronald, Sharon, Gerald. Registered profl. engr., Wis., Colo. Engr., C.W. Yoder & Assocs., cons. engrs., Milw., 1956-61; ptnr. Graef Anhalt Schloemer, cons. engrs., Milw., 1961-67; chmn. bd. Graef Anhalt Schloemer Assocs., Inc., Milw., 1967—; mem. accreditation bd. for engring. and tech., 1989-95. Active Boy Scouts Am.; chmn. bd. assessment, City of Milw., 1962-89; bd. dirs. Luther Manor. 1st lt. AUS, 1953-56. Named Disting. Marquette U. alumnus, 1982, Wis. Profl. Engr. of Yr., 1983. Mem. ASCE (sect. pres. 1968, nat. bd. dirs., 1989-92, nat. v.p. 1993-95), Nat. Soc. Profl. Engrs., Wis. Soc. Profl. Engrs., Cons. Engrs. Coun. Wis. (pres. 1973-75), Engrs. Scientists Milw. (pres. 1975). Home: 8503 Country Club Dr Franklin WI 53132-2710 Office: Graef Anhalt Schloemer 345 N 95th St Milwaukee WI 53226-4441

GRAF, JUDITH ANN, communications executive; b. Chgo., Sept. 19, 1946; d. John Anthony and Marie Evelyn (Noethe) G. AB, Washington U., St. Louis, 1968; MA, Fairfield (Conn.) U., 1980; MBA, U. Conn., Stamford, 1982. Pub. rels. specialist Japan Trade Ctr., Chgo., 1968-73; community rels. mgr. GE Capital Corp., Stamford, 1975-78, employee rels. mgr., 1978-82, mktg. rep., 1982-83, bus. devel. officer, 1984-87; account supr. Hill & Knowlton, Inc., N.Y.C., 1988-89; v.p. mktg. Swiss Bank Corp., N.Y.C., 1989-90; v.p., mgr. corp. comms. First Chgo. NBD Corp. (formerly First Chgo. Corp.), 1990—. Mem. Women in Mgmt. (dir. 1983-84), Nat. Investor Rels. Inst., Chgo. Pub. Rels. Forum, Speechwriter's Forum. Office: First Chgo NBD Corp Ste 0359 First Nat Plz Chicago IL 60670

GRAF, KARL ROCKWELL, nuclear engineer; b. San Diego, Apr. 19, 1940; s. Frederic August and Beatrice (Rockwell) G.; m. Nancy Ann Scott, June 9, 1962; children: Robin Elizabeth, Scott Frederic. BS, U. S. Naval Acad., 1962. Submarine officer USN, 1962-84; sr. mgmt. cons. Advanced Sci. and Tech. Assn., Solana Beach, Calif., 1984; dir. nuclear support Ill. Power Co., Decatur, 1985, dir. ops. monitoring, 1986-89, dir. quality assurance, 1990-92, dir. engring. projects, 1992-94; leader life cycle mgmt., 1994—; dep. comdr., readiness and tng. officer, Submarine Squadron One, USN, Pearl Harbor, Hawaii, 1982-84; founder life cycle mgmt. program Clinton Nuc. Power Sta. Author: Monitoring Manual, 1986. Exec. dir. St. John's Luth. Ch., 1995—; chmn. zoning bd. Village of Forsyth, Ill., 1988—, chmn. long-range plan com., 1989-92. Mem. Am. Nuclear Soc., Am. Soc. for Quality Control, U.S. Submarine League, Ret. Officers Assn. Home: 736 Weaver Rd Forsyth IL 62535-9777 Office: Ill Power Co 500 S 27th St Decatur IL 62521-2200

GRAF, MARJORIE ANN, advertising executive; b. Denver, Nov. 27, 1945; d. William Robert and Lena Mae (Grisham) Rafferty; m. Thomas Charles Graf, May 20, 1967; children: Chris, Chad, Shaunna, Carey. Grad. high sch., Clarksville, Ind., 1963. Order wireroom controller Stein Bros. & Boyce, Louisville, 1963-64; exec. sec. GE, Louisville, 1964-68; receptionist Wood Personnel, Louisville, 1973-74; billing clk., receptionist Drs. Perlstein & Perlstein, Louisville, 1974-76; inventory programmer Bryant Horton, Louisville, 1976-78; acctg. programmer U. Louisville, 1978-83, program analyzer, 1983-89; v.p. TMG, Inc., Greenville, Ind., 1989—, Graf Enterprises Inc. Sec. St. Mary's Navilleton, Ind., 1989-90. Democrat. Roman Catholic. Home: 8592 Rufing Rd Greenville IN 47124-9609 Office: TMG Inc PO Box 392 New Albany IN 47151-0392

GRAF, MELVIN WILLIAM, telecommunications executive; b. Mpls., Dec. 21, 1955; s. Saul and Ada (Strimling) G.; m. Miriam Graff; children: Aaron, Lelana. BSBA, U. Minn., 1978. Pres. Network Properties Corp., Mpls., 1978-82; acctg. mgr. Republic Airlines, Mpls., 1982-84; account exec. Am. Savs., Stockton, Calif., 1984-85; pres., chief exec. officer Travel Network Inc., Mpls., 1985-89; chief exec. officer Intelliphone, Inc., Mpls., 1989—. Mem. Sigma Alpha Mu. Home: 3104 Sheffield Cir Minnetonka MN 55305 Office: Intelliphone Inc 6801 Wayzata Blvd Saint Louis Park MN 55426-1715

GRAF, MICHAEL F., stockbroker; b. Grand Rapids, Mich., July 28, 1950. BS, Ea. Mich. U., 1972; MA, Mich. State U., 1976. Prin. elem. schs. Edmoore, Mich., 1977-83; stockbroker E.F. Hutton, Grand Rapids, 1983-90, A. G. Edwards & Sons Inc., Grand Rapids, 1990—. Office: A G Edwards & Sons Inc # 100 50 Monroe Ave NW Grand Rapids MI 49503-2643

GRAFF, RICHARD THOMAS, manufacturing executive; b. Toledo, Oct. 17, 1953; s. Hugh Reddington and Mary Kathleen (Oberhausen) G.; m. Lori S. Olson, July 15, 1953; children: Sarah, Rebecca. BS in Journalism, Kent State U., 1974, MBA, 1975. Cert. CFPIM. Mktg. rsch. assoc. Firestone Tire & Rubber, Akron, Ohio, 1976-81; dir. of mktg. Copeland Elec. Corp., Humboldt, Tenn., 1981-82, mgr. info. systems, 1983-84, materials mgr., 1985-86; plant mgr. Emerson Motor Co., Humboldt, 1987-94; v.p. ops. Electromech. Technologies, Cin., 1994—. Chmn. Humboldt Indsl. Coun., 1992; chmn. campaign United Way, West Tenn., 1992-94. Mem. Am. Prodn. & Inventory Control Soc. (v.p. edn. 1987-88, W. Tenn. chpt. bd. dirs. 1987-93).

GRAFF, ROBERT ALAN, computer consultant; b. Detroit, Nov. 13, 1953; s. Jack and Irene Bertha (Horowitz) G.; m. Karen Elaine Morgan, Dec. 21, 1985; 1 child, David. BS in Physics, Wayne State U., 1976, MS in Computer Engring., 1981. Office automation specialist Burroughs Corp., Detroit, 1977-78; optical engr. Energy Conversion Devices Co., Troy, Mich., 1978-80; ind. contract programmer Southfield, Mich., 1981; sr. programmer/analyst Comprehensive Health Planning Coun. Southeastern Mich., Detroit, 1981-86; pres., computer cons. Data Concepts, Bloomfield Hills, Mich., 1983—; adj. instr. Walsh Coll., 1987—, Detroit Coll. Bus., 1990—; instr. U. Detroit, 1994—. Contbr. articles for devel. custom software for acctg. oriented micro computer applications and network analysis; custom tng. on software products; topical computer topics. Mem. Assn. Computing Machinery, IEEE, Nat. Computer Soc. Democrat. Jewish. Office: Data Concepts 984 S Reading Rd Bloomfield Hills MI 48304-2044

GRAFING, KEITH GERHART, marketing representative, consultant; b. Hibbing, Minn., Mar. 23, 1942; s. Gerhart and Wilhelmine Emilia (Knittel) G.; m. Edith Ione Miessler, Dec. 22, 1964. MusB, Bethany Coll., 1964; MusM, U. Mo., Kansas City, 1968, D of Mus. Arts, 1972, MA, 1983, PhD, 1991. Tchr. Winona (Minn.) Pub. Schs., 1964-65; prof. St. Paul's Coll., Concordia, Mo., 1965-68, Concordia Coll., Milw., 1968-69, Met. C.C., Kansas City, Mo., 1972-92; cons. U. Mo., Kansas City, 1992-95; mktg. rep. John Hancock Fin. Svcs., Overland Park, Kans., 1995—. Contbr. articles to profl. jours. Bd. dirs. Westport Ministry and Housing, Kansas City, Mo., 1994—; chmn. U. Mo. Alumni Alliance (4 campuses), 1989-91. Doctoral fellow Kansas City Assn. Trusts and Founds., 1970-72. Mem. U. Mo.-Kansas City Alumni Assn. (pres. 1981-82), Pi Lambda Theta (pres. Hearland region 1992-93). Episcopalian. Home: 4545 Wornall Rd Kansas City MO 64111

GRAHAM, CHRISTOPHER, lawyer; b. Dayton, Ohio, Jan. 28, 1946; s. Thomas D. and Christine (Wood) G.; m. Marsha Carol Gum, Aug. 24, 1968; children: Christiana, Elizabeth, Margaret. BSBA, U. Mo., 1968, JD, 1971; LLM in Taxation, Georgetown U., 1973. Law clk. Mo. Supreme Court, Jefferson City, Mo., 1971-72; ptnr. Graham and Graham, Jefferson City, 1975—. City atty. City of Jefferson, 1977-81, state rep. Gen. Assembly, 1983-91. Col. JAGC U.S. Army Res. Mem. ABA, Mo. Bar Assn., Fla. Bar Assn., Lions, Arts Council (pres. 1976-77). Democrat. Home: 1204 Major Dr Jefferson City MO 65101-3660 Office: Graham and Graham 304 E High St Box 746 Jefferson City MO 65102

GRAHAM, DAVID B., JR., stockbroker; b. Washington, Ind., Apr. 23, 1966; s. David B. Sr. and Stuart (Smith) G.; m. Carol V. Voor, Sept. 11, 1993. BA, Purdue U., 1988. Broker Chgo. Bd. Trade, 1989-90; stockbroker Merrill Lynch, South Bend, Ind., 1990-92, Norwest Investment Svcs. Inc., South Bend, 1993—. Mem. Nat. Assn. Bus. Ecology. Republican. Roman Catholic. Office: Norwest Investment Svcs 112 W Jefferson PO Box 1512 South Bend IN 46634

GRAHAM, DEAN C., financial consultant; b. Detroit, May 31, 1963. BS in Mktg., Mich. State U., 1986. Fin. cons. Merrill Lynch, Detroit, 1986—. Republican. Lutheran. Office: Merrill Lynch 200 Renaissance Ctr Ste 3000 Detroit MI 48243-1302

GRAHAM, DIANE E., newspaper editor; b. Gary, Ind., June 29, 1953; d. William M. and Mary Jane (Shreve) G.; m. Daniel Kevin Miller, Oct. 18, 1986. Bachelor's degree, Drake U., 1974. Reporter Des Moines Tribune, 1974-78; reporter Des Moines Register, 1978-84, bus. editor, 1984-86, dep. mng. editor, 1986-95, mng. editor, 1995—; pres. Iowa Freedom of Info. Coun., Des Moines, 1992-93; chair adv. bd. Drake U. Sch. Journalism, Des Moines, 1995—. Davenport fellow for bus./econ. reporting U. Mo., 1983. Office: Des Moines Register 715 Locust St Des Moines IA 50309

GRAHAM, DONALD D., manufacturing executive; b. O'Niell, Nebr., Apr. 21, 1934. BS, BA, Creighton U., 1958. CPA, Nebr. Pvt. practice as tax cons. Omaha, 1957-76; CEO Omni, Omaha, 1985—, Meylan Enterprises, Omaha, 1987—. Patentee equipment for specialty computerized cleaning. Active Bendictine Coll. Coun. 1960-90, Douglas County Rep. Com., Omaha, 1970-95, Nebr. Rep. Com., Lincoln, 1970-95; pres. adv. coun. Creighton U., 1990-95. With U.S. Army, 1953-55. Mem. Old Mill Bus. Ctr. Assn. (pres.). Roman Catholic. Office: Old Mill Bus Ctr Assn 10828 Old Mill Rd Omaha NE 68154-2608

GRAHAM, DONALD JAMES, food technologist; b. York, N.Y., Sept. 24, 1932; s. Howard Alexander Graham and Naomi Irene (Fletcher) Graham Horgan; m. Dorothy Jane Schroeder, Jan. 1, 1965; children: Christopher Howard, Jonathan Edward. AAS, N.Y. State Agrl. Tech. Inst., 1952; BS with honors, Mich. State U., 1958, MS, 1959; postgrad., Oreg. State U., 1959-62. Profit planning dir. Green Giant Co., LeSueur, Minn., 1962-67; dir. tech. svc. Green Giant of Can., Windsor, Ont., 1967-77; dir. quality assurance William Underwood Co., Westwood, Mass., 1977-83; internat. tech. dir. Pet, Inc., St. Louis, 1983-87; sr. food technologist, food sanitation cons., lectr., fellow Sverdrup Corp., St. Louis, 1988—; faculty, com. mem. Food Processors Inst., Washington, 1980-92. Contbr. articles to tech. publs. Troop com. chmn. Boy Scouts Am., Medfield, Mass., 1979-82, treas., Chesterfield, Mo., 1984-89; mem. Minn. Rep. Com., 1965-67. Sgt. U.S. Army, 1952-54, Korea. Mem. Inst. Food Technologists, Internat. Assn. Milk, Food and Environ. Sanitarians, Inst. Thermal Processing Specialists (bd. dirs. 1980-82), Mo. Food Processors Assn. (bd. dirs. 1992—, pres. 1994, 95), Am. Soc. Quality Control, Alpha Zeta (chancellor Kedzie chpt. 1957-58). Home: 14318 Aitken Hill Ct Chesterfield MO 63017-2820 Office: Sverdrup Corp 801 N 11th St Saint Louis MO 63101-1015

GRAHAM, HAROLD STEVEN, lawyer; b. Kansas City, Mo., Feb. 1, 1950; s. Martie Sydney and Elsie Helen (Bradford) G.; m. Deborah Ruth Glick, Apr. 8, 1973; children: Elizabeth, Jonathan, Joshua, Lauren. BS with distinction, U. Wis., 1972; JD, U. Chgo., 1976. Bar: Mo. 1976. Assoc. Lathrop, Koontz & Norquist, Kansas City, 1976-81; mem. Lathrop & Norquist, L.C., Kansas City, 1982-95, Lathrop & Gage L.C., Kansas City, 1996—. Active Kansas City Tomorrow Alumni Assn. Year X; bd. dirs. Hyman Brand Hebrew Acad., Kansas City, 1985—; bd. dirs. Beth Shalom Synagogue, Kansas City, 1983-88, Jewish Community Campus, 1992—. Mem. ABA (sect. on real property and trust law, mem. Forum on Affordable Housing), Mo. Bar Assn. (property law com.), Am. Soc. for Technion. Office: Lathrop & Gage LC 2345 Grand Blvd Ste 2600 Kansas City MO 64108-2603

GRAHAM, JAMES MILLER, physiology researcher; b. St. Louis, Oct. 16, 1945; s. Alvin Rudd and Edrie (Miller) G.; m. Linda Kay Edwards, May 3, 1969; children: Michael Edwards, Melissa Edwards. MA, U. Mich., 1968, PhD, 1979. Postdoctoral scholar environ. engring. U. Mich., Ann Arbor, 1979-80; lectr. zoology U. Wis., Madison, 1981-82, rsch. assoc. physiology, 1983-88, lectr. botany, 1987-88, physiology researcher, 1988—; reviewer Phycological Soc. Am., Jour. Great Lakes Rsch., Microbial Ecology. Contbr. chpt. to Periphyton of Freshwater Ecosystems, 1983; contbr. articles to profl. jours. With U.S. Army, 1969-72. Mem. Am. Soc. Limnology and Oceanography, Am. Inst. Biol. Scis., Phycological Soc. Am., Soc. Protozoologists, Phi Beta Kappa, Sigma Xi. Office: U Wis Dept Physiology 1300 University Ave Madison WI 53706-1510

GRAHAM, JAMES R., financial planner; b. Fredrick Town, Mo., May 2, 1935; m. Virginia L. Schwaner, June 5, 1955; children: Bradley, Lisa, Nancy. BS, U. Mo., Rolla, 1957. CFP. Divsn. mgr. Southwestern Bell, St. Louis, 1960-90; fin. planner FFP Sec/1st Fin. Planners, Chesterfield, Mo., 1990—. Capt. U.S. Army, 1957-60, res., 1960-67. Recipient Chgo. Tribune award ROTC. Home: 14425 Valley Meadow Ct W Chesterfield MO 63017-9631 Office: FFP Sec/1st Fin Planners # 250 500 Chesterfield Ctr Chesterfield MO 63017-4823

GRAHAM, JAMES, state legislator; b. Ironton, Mo., June 22, 1960. AA, Mineral Area Coll.; degree, Mo. FFA State Farmer. State rep. Dist. 106 Mo. State Congress, 1991—; mem. agr. appropriations com., correctional insts. com., mines and mining com.; cattle farmer. Mem. NRA, Marcus Lodge 110 AF&AM (master), Optimist Club, C. of C. *

GRAHAM, JOHN THOMAS, history educator; b. Brookfield, Mo., Mar. 28, 1928; s. Thomas Patrick and Zona (Dunnington) G.; m. Alsacia Alsy Izurieta; 1 child, Monica Marie. BA with honors, Rockhurst Coll., 1952; PhD in European History, St. Louis U., 1957. Instr.-asst. prof. history St. Ambrose Coll., Davenport, Iowa, 1957-61; asst. prof. Gonzaga U., Spokane, Wash., 1961-66; asst. prof. U. Mo., Kansas City, 1966-74, assoc. prof., 1974-95, prof., 1995—. Author: Donoso Cortes: Utopian Romanticist and Political Realist, 1974 (award 1974), A Pragmatist Philosphy of Life in Ortega y Gasset, 1994. With U.S. Navy, 1946-48. Mem. Am. Assn. of Univ. Profs., Consortium on Revolutionary Europe. Democrat. Roman Catholic. Home: 2000 W 95th St Leawood KS 66206

GRAHAM, JOHN W., advertising executive; b. 1946. With Richfield (Ohio) Properties, 1969-83; with Nationwide Advt. Svc., Cleve., 1983—, now pres., COO. Office: Nationwide Advt Svc Inc 1228 Euclid Ave Ste 600 Cleveland OH 44115-1831*

GRAHAM, LESTER LYNN, radio executive; b. Carlinville, Ill., Aug. 16, 1960; s. Lyndal L. and Betty L. (Cottingham) G.; m. Evelyn Elaine Epperson, Aug. 4, 1979; children: Joshua Nathanael, Alayna Renee. AAS, Lewis & Clark Coll., 1985. News dir. Metroplex Comm. WBGZ, Alton, Ill., 1985; news dir. Midwest Comm. WPMB WKRV, Vandalia, Ill., 1986-87; news dir. Seith-Serafin Comm. WSDR WSSQ, Sterling, Ill., 1987-88; news dir. No. Ill. U. WNIU WNIJ, Rockford, Ill., 1988-94; news dir. U. of Mo.-St. Louis KWMU, 1994—. Recipient Nat. Individual Achievement award UPI 1990, John Stewart Meml. Broadcasting award Lewis and Clark Coll., 1985. Mem. Pub. Radio News Dirs. Inc. (Nat. Spot News Coverage award 1990, 1994, Nat. Use of Medium award 1991, Nat. Breaking News Coverage award 1994), Radio and TV News Dirs. Assn. (News Series Documentary award 1992, Spot News award 1994, Use of Sound award 1994), Ill. News Broadcasters Assn. (bd. dirs.), Lewis and Clark Radio Adv. (bd. dirs.). Home: 211 Jefferson St Brighton IL 62012-1335 Office: KWMU 8001 Natural Bridge Rd Saint Louis MO 63121-4401

GRAHAM, PARKER LEE, II, computer systems manager; b. Shelby, Ohio, Aug. 6, 1957; s. Parker Lee, Sr. and Shelvy Jean (Schwall) G.; m. Renee Marie MacCartney, Sept. 4, 1976; children: Tella Marie, Kami Nicole. Grad. high sch., Shelby. Parts insp. Essex Wire, Lexington, Ohio, 1974-76; supr. shipping dept. Supreme Distbr., Detroit, 1978-79; driver Everett Delivery Service, Detroit, 1979-81; field supr. Wesco Energy Systems, Warren, Mich., 1981-82; mgr. shipping Kemar Inc., Sterling Heights, Mich., 1982-84; pres., chief exec. officer Metro Cartage Co., Romulus, Mich., also bd. dirs., 1984-90; salesman Swad Chevrolet, Columbus, Ohio, 1991-92; computer systems mgr. MBA Mktg. Corp. dba "Just for Feet", Dublin, Ohio, 1992-93;

customer edn. specialist CAM Data Systems, Inc., Fountain Valley, Calif., 1993-96; sys. adminstr. Donatos Pizza, Inc., Columbus, 1996—.

GRAHAM, WILLIAM B., pharmaceutical company executive; b. Chgo., July 14, 1911; s. William and Elizabeth (Burden) G.; m. Edna Kanaley, June 15, 1940 (dec.); children: William J., Elizabeth Anne, Margaret, Robert B.; m. Catherine Van Duzer, July 23, 1984. SB cum laude, U. Chgo., 1932, JD cum laude, 1936; LLD, Carthage Coll., 1974, Lake Forest Coll., 1983; LLD (hon.), U. Ill., 1988; LHD, St. Xavier Coll. and Nat. Coll. Edn., 1983. Bar: Ill. 1936. Patent lawyer Dyrenforth, Lee, Chritton & Wiles, 1936-40; mem. Dawson & Ooms, 1940-45; v.p., mgr. Baxter Internat., Inc., Deerfield, Ill., 1945-53, pres., 1953-71; CEO Baxter Internat., Inc., Deerfield, 1960-80; chmn. bd. Baxter Internat., Inc., Deerfield, Ill., 1980-85, sr. chmn., 1989-95, chmn. emeritus, 1995—; prof., chair Weizmann Inst. Sci., Rehoboth, Israel, 1978; lectr. U. Chgo., 1981-82. Chmn. bd. dirs. Lyric Opera Chgo.; bd. dirs. Big Shoulders, Wendy Will Care Fedn., Chgo. Hort. Soc.; trustee Orchestral Assn., U. Chgo., Evanston (Ill.) Hosp.; past pres. Cmty. Fund of Chgo. Recipient V.I.P. award Lewis Found., 1963, Disting. Citizen award Ill. St. Andrew Soc., 1974, Decision Maker of Yr. award Am. Statis. Assn., 1974, Marketer of Yr. award AMA, 1976, Found. award Kidney Found., 1981, Chicagoan of Yr. award Chgo. Boys Club, 1981, Bus. Statesman of Yr. award Harvard Bus. Sch. Club Chgo., 1983, Achievement award Med. Tech. Svcs., 1983, Disting. Fellows award Internat. Ctr. for Artificial Organs and Transplantations, 1982, Chgo. Civic award DePaul U., 1986, Internat. Visitors Golden Medallion award U. Ill., 1988, Chgo. medal U. Chgo., 1992, Laureate award Lincoln Acad. Ill., 1992, Lyric Opera Carol Fox award, 1992, Good Scout award N.E. Coun. Boy Scouts Am., 1993, Making History award Chgo. Hist. Soc., 1996; recognized for pioneering work Health Industry Mfrs. Assn., 1981; inducted Jr. Achievement Chgo. Bus. Hall of Fame, 1986, Modern Healthcare Hall of Fame, 1994. Mem. Am. Pharm. Mfrs. Assn. (past pres.), Ill. Mfrs. Assn. (past pres.), Pharm. Mfrs. Assn. (past chmn., award for spl. distinction leadership 1981), Chgo. Club (past pres.), Commonwealth Club, Comml. Club, Indian Hill Club, Casino Club, Old Elm Club, Seminole Club, Everglades Club, Bath and Tennis Club, Links Club, Phi Beta Kappa, Sigma Xi, Phi Delta Phi. Home: 40 Devonshire Ln Kenilworth IL 60043-1205 Office: Baxter Internat Inc 1 Baxter Pky Deerfield IL 60015-4625

GRAHAM, WILLIAM FRED, religious studies educator; b. Columbus, Oct. 31, 1930; s. William Fred and Serena (Clark) G.; m. Marjory Jean Garrett, Aug. 12, 1953; children: Terese L., Bonny, Marcy Jean Graham Murphy, Geneva S. Graham Looker. AB, Tarkio Coll., 1952; BD, Pittsburgh Theol. Sem., 1955; ThM, Louisville Presbyn. Sem., 1958; PhD, U. Iowa, 1965. Pastor Bethel Presbyn. Ch., Waterloo, Iowa, 1955-61, instr., 1963; assoc. prof. Mich. State U., E. Lansing, 1963-74, prof., 1974-93, ret., 1993. Author: The Constructive Revolutionary, 1971, reprinted, 1987, Picking Up the Pieces, 1975; editor: Later Calvinism, 1994. Grantee Travel to Collections Grant Nat. Endowment for the Humanities, Scotland, 1985, Fin. Grant Am. Philosophical Soc., Scotland, 1987. Mem. 16th Century Studies Soc. (pres. 1988-89), The Calvin Studies Soc., Am. Soc. for Ch. History, Phi Kappa Phi (pres. 1987, 91). Office: Mich State U Dept Religious Studies East Lansing MI 48824

GRAMS, BETTY JANE, minister, educator, writer; b. Lead, S.D., Mar. 13, 1926; d. Harold C. and Elizabeth Amanda (Vaughn) Haas; m. Monroe David Grams, May 1, 1949; children: MonaRe' Grams Shields, Rocky Vaughn, Rachel Jo Grams Schaible. Student, North Cen. Bible Coll., 1945-48, Diploma in Theology, 1963; BA in Edn. and Theology, Assemblies of God Theol. Sch., 1978. Ordained to ministry Assemblies of God, 1957. Asst. pastor local ch. Huron, S.D., 1948-49; co-pastor local ch. Cataract, Wis., 1949-51; missionary to Latin Am. Assemblies of God Ch., Springfield, Mo., 1951—; sec. women's orgn. Assemblies of God, various South Am. countries, 1972-77, missionary educator, Bolivia, Argentina, 1951-91; prof. North Cen. Bible Coll., Mpls., 1963-64, 68-70; speaker Pentecostal Fellowship of N.Am., 1st Hispanic Congress, Can. Author: Women of Grace, 1978, Families Can Be Happy, 1981, Solving Ministry's Toughest Problems, 1985, Familia, Fe, y Felicidad, 1985, Ministering Through Music, 1990; (music theory) Ministrando Con Musica, 1960—; contbr. articles to various publs. Musician, dir. choirs, Bolivia and Argentina. Home: 6161 Manchester Ln Davie FL 33331-2970 Office: Assemblies of God 1448 N Boonville Ave Springfield MO 65802-1806

GRAMS, RODNEY D., senator, former congressman; b. 1948. Student, Anoka-Ramsey Jr. Coll., Brown Inst., Minneapolis, Minn., Carroll Coll., Helena, Mont. Engring. cons. Orr-Schelen Mayeron & Assoc., Mpls.; anchor, producer Sta. KFBB-TV, Great Falls, Mont., Sta. WSAU-TV, Wausau, Wis., Sta. WIFR-TV, Rockford, Ill., Sta. KMSP-TV, Mpls.; mem. 103d Congress from 6th Minn. Dist., 1993-94; U.S. Senator Minn., 1995—; pres., CEO Sun Ridge Builders. Republican. Office: US Senate 261 Dirksen Senate Office Bldg Washington DC 20510

GRAMZA, RICHARD L., transportation executive; b. Manistee, Mich., Mar. 18, 1953. BS in Biology, San Diego State U., 1977. Owner Shawnee Transp. Co., Kansas City, Kans., 1980-88; v.p. Bauer & Gramza Inc., Olathe, Kans., 1988—. Author: (computer program) TMS-90, 1990. With USN, 1970-74. Office: Bauer & Gramza Inc 748 N Persimmon Dr Olathe KS 66061-5965

GRANATO, GREGORY A., stockbroker; b. Chgo., Feb. 20, 1967. BA, DePaul U., 1991. Asst. to v.p. Lehman Bros., Chgo., 1989-91; stockbroker David A. Noyes & Co., Chgo., 1991—. Mem. Assocs. Club. Republican. Roman Catholic. Office: David A Noyes & Co # 610 208 S La Salle St Chicago IL 60604-1005

GRANBERG, KURT, state legislator, lawyer; b. Breese, Ill., June 16, 1953; s. Marnen George and Agnes Mary (Vahlkamp) G. B.S., U. Ill.-Chgo., 1975; postgrad. Sangamon State U., 1975-76; J.D., Ill. Inst. Tech., 1980. Bar: Ill. 1980, U.S. Dist. Ct. (so. dist.) Ill. 1983. Legis. intern. Ill. Ho. of Reps., Springfield, 1975-76, mem. staff, 1975-77; assoc. James Donnewald Law Office, Breese, 1980-83; asst. pub. defender Clinton County, Ill., 1981-83; ptnr. Donnewald & Granberg, Breese, 1983—; spl. asst. atty. gen. State of Ill., Breese, 1983—; registered lobbyist, Breese, 1984—; mem. Ill. Ho. of Reps., 1986—, asst. Dem. leader. Mem. fin. com. Ill. Inst. Tech.-Chgo. Kent. Sch. Law, 1979-80; Democratic precinct committeeman, Carlyle, Ill., 1982-84; mem. Clinton County Bd., Carlyle, 1984—, Carlyle Lake Adv. Com.; bd. dirs. Central Comprehensive Mental Health Ctr., Centralia, Ill., 1984—. Mem. Ill. Bar Assn., ABA, Clinton County Bar Assn., Jaycees, Carlyle Bus. and Profl. Assn. Roman Catholic. Lodges: K.C., Optimists. Home: 850 4th St Carlyle IL 62231-1516 Office: Donnewald & Granberg 550 N 2nd St Breese IL 62230-1650

GRANGE, WILLIAM MARSHALL, actor, educator; b. Cin., Jan. 8, 1947; s. James Michael and Roberta Ferne (Smith) G.; m. Willa Bradford, Nov. 18, 1987; children: Leah Holt, George Haydon. Student, Heidelberg U., Fed. Republic Germany, 1968-69; BA, U. Toledo, 1970; MFA, Columbia U., 1972; PhD, Ind. U., 1981. Actor with Ala. and N.Y. Shakespeare Festivals, Light Opera of Manhattan, Performing Arts Repertory Theatre, Nat. Theatre Co., 1971-75; actor Mark I Dinner Theatre, Lakeland, Fla., 1984; dir. with Labor Theater, South Shore Music Circus, Antique Festival Theatre, 1975-76; chmn. dept. theater Fla. Southern Coll., 1981-87, Marquette U., Milw., 1987—. Author: (essays) Magill's Critical Survey of Drama, 1986, Zeitschrift für Anglistik und Amerikanistik, 1987, Theatre Survey, 1987, Essays in Theatre, 1988, New England Theatre Jour., 1990, Partnership in The German Theatre, 1991, On-Stage Studies, 1994, The Theatre of the Third Reich, 1995, Brecht Unbound, 1995, Comedy in the Weimar Republic, 1996. Doctoral fellow German Acad. Exchange Service, Bonn, Fed. Republic Germany, 1979-80. Mem. Actors Equity Assn., Am. Soc. for Theatre Rsch., Internat. Brecht. Soc. Republican. Office: Marquette U 13th and Clybourn Sts PO Box 1881 Milwaukee WI 53201-1881

GRANGER, PHILIP RICHARD, minister; b. Detroit, June 19, 1943; s. Myrl Richard and Alvirta May (Kling) G.; m. Karen Elizabeth Draper, Feb. 20, 1965 (div. 1972); children: Mark, Leslie; m. Susan Kay Alderfer, Mar. 4, 1973; children: Randall, Candace. AA, Jackson Jr. Coll., 1963; BA, MBA, Mich. State U., 1965, 67; MDiv, No. Bapt. Theol. Sem., Lombard, Ill., 1978; D of Ministry, Oral Roberts U., 1986. Ordained deacon United Meth. Ch., 1977, ordained elder, 1980; CPA, Mich. Audit staff, cons. Ernst & Ernst, Detroit, 1967-71; mem. contrs. staff Assocs. Corp., South Bend, Ind., 1971-73; v.p., contr. 1st Fed. Savs. and Loan, Chgo., 1973-76; pastor Mokena (Ill.) United Meth. Ch., 1976-82; dir. fin. No. Ind. Conf. United Meth. Ch., Marion, 1982-86; sr. pastor St. Lukes United Meth. Ch., Kokomo, Ind., 1986-89, Trinity United Meth. Ch., Huntington, Ind., 1989-94; dist. supt. Kokomo (Ind.) Dist. United Meth. Ch., 1994—; mem. adj. faculty Huntington Coll., 1990-94; new life missioner Gen. Bd. Discipleship, Nashville, 1980—; bd. dirs. Good News, Wilmore, Ky., Samaritan Ctr., Inc., Huntington, Found. for Mission and Ministry, Inc., Marion. Author: Discerment Planning, 1986. Founding mem. Tri-Village Crisis Intervention Ctr., Mokena, 1978-81; treas. Village of Mokena, 1978-82; bd. dirs. Mental Health Assn. Ill., Chgo., 1974-75. Mem. Am. Assn. Christian Counselors, Rotary Internat., Delta Sigma Pi, Beta Gamma Sigma, Beta Alpha Psi. Home: 2936 Bagley Dr W Kokomo IN 46902-3281 Office: Kokomo Dist United Meth Ch PO Box 326 Bunker Hill IN 46914-0326

GRANNAN, WILLIAM STEPHEN, safety engineer, consultant; b. Detroit, Nov. 10, 1929; s. William Stephen and Rose Marie (Gebel) G.; m. Mary Suzanne Malasky, Apr. 8, 1961; children: William Bernard, Douglas Andrew, John Charles. BS in Fire Protection and Safety Engring., Ill. Inst. Tech., 1952. P.E. Cert. Safety Engrs., Calif. Fire ins. rater Ins. Svcs. Office, Detroit, 1952-54 1956-60; sales field rep. Springfield Fire Ins., Detroit, 1960-63, Aetna Life & Casualty Co., Detroit, 1963-66; mgr. property loss control Amerisure Co., Detroit, 1966-92; sr. cons. Crawford Risk Control Svcs., Southfield, Mich., 1993—; cons. pub. safety, commn. arson prevention Greater Detroit C. of C., 1986-93. Apptd. Bldg. Bd. Appeals City of Plymouth, 1994—. Mem. Engring. Soc. Detroit (industry amb. com. 1970—), Nat Fire Protection Assn., Soc. Fire Protection Engrs., Cert. Safety Profls., Safety Coms. Assoc. Gen. Contrs. Am., Am. Legion (Livonia, Mich.), Am. Assn. Ret. Persons. Unitarian. Home: 117 N Holbrook St Plymouth MI 48170-1441

GRANT, EDWARD ROBERT, chemistry educator; b. Tacoma, Sept. 23, 1947; s. Melven Edwin and Estelle Muriel (Gleuck) G.; m. Catherine Janine Carey, Aug. 10, 1980; children: Alexander Edward, Janine Catherine. BA in Chemistry, Occidental Coll., 1969; PhD in Chemistry, U. Calif., Davis, 1974. Asst. prof. Cornell U., Ithaca, N.Y., 1977-83; assoc. prof. Cornell U., Ithaca, 1983-86; prof. chemistry Purdue U., West Lafayette, Ind., 1986—, assoc. head dept. chemistry, 1989—; vis. prof. Laboratoire Photophysique Moleculaire, Universite de Paris-Sud, 1991; vis. prof. Technische Universitat Munchen, 1992-93. Contbr. numerous articles to profl. jours. Recipient Nobel Laureate Signature award, 1986, Humbuldt Rsch. award for sr. U.S. scientists, 1992; Fulbright sr. scholar, 1988. Fellow Am. Phys. Soc. Office: Purdue U Dept Chemistry West Lafayette IN 47907

GRANT, JILL, state legislator; m. William D. Grant Jr. Mem. Kans. State Ho. of Reps. Dist. 55; atty.

GRANT, JOHN THOMAS, retired state supreme court justice; b. Omaha, Oct. 25, 1920; s. Thomas J. and Mary Elizabeth (Smith) G.; m. Marian Louise Saner, Dec. 27, 1947; children: Martha Grant Bruckner, John P., Susan J., Joseph W., Timothy K. LLB, JD, Creighton U., 1950. Bar: Nebr. 1950. Sole practice law Omaha, 1950-74; judge State Dist. Ct., Omaha, 1974-83; justice Nebr. Supreme Ct., Lincoln, 1983-92. Served with Signal Corps, U.S. Army, 1942-45, PTO. Home: 912 S118 Plz Omaha NE 68154

GRANT, JUDITH IVERSEN, family health nurse, nursing administrator; b. Sioux City, Iowa, Mar. 30, 1952; d. Harry Andrew and Gertrude Roberta Iversen; m. George Alexander Grant, June 21, 1979 (dec. Feb. 1989); 1 child, Tyler Ross. BSN, Marquette U., 1974; postgrad., U. San Francisco, 1990-93. Cert. pub. health nurse, Calif.; lic. residential care facility for elderly, Calif.; adminstr. cert. RCFE and pub. health. Staff RN, relief supr. Midwest Med. Placement Agy., Milw., 1974-75; nursing supr. Marion Heights, Inc., Milw., 1975-76; patient care coord. Milw. Psychiat. Hosp./Dewey Ctr., Wauwatosa, Wis., 1976-77; RN, staff relief Med. Pers. Pool, Profl. Nurses Bur., Stat Nursing Svcs., San Francisco, 1977-89; asst., acting nurse mgr. Pacific Med. Ctr., San Francisco, 1979-84; staff devel. instr., clin. cons. San Francisco (Calif.) Gen. Hosp. Med. Ctr., 1984-85, adminstrv. nursing supr., 1985-89; RN neonatal ICU Children's Hosp./Pediatric Trauma Ctr., Oakland, Calif., 1986-87; nursing supr. Children's Hosp./Pediatric Trauma Ctr., Oakland, 1987-88; RN per diem U. Calif. San Francisco, 1984-88; pvt. practice North Sioux City, S.D., 1988—; cons., ind. nurse Marin County, Calif., 1979-84; co-coord. for group formation Bay Area Adminstrv. Nursing Suprs., 1986-87; postgrad. rsch. asst. pediat. pain study U. Calif.-San Francisco, Sch. Nursing, 1987; pvt. practice nurse cons., San Francisco, 1990-94; coord. cmty. edn., dir. Silver Advantage/Older Adult Svcs., Marian Health Ctr., Sioux City, Iowa, 1994—; nursing instr., cons. Morningside Coll., Sioux City, 1994—. Author (with others) Siouxland: An Anthology, 1995, Capturing Our Heritage, Vol. 1, 1996. Vol. Jerry Brown for Pres./We the People, San Francisco, 1991—; mem. Nat. Wildlife Fedn., Washington, 1991—; dir. Senior Writer Project, 1996; parish dir. Cath. of the Epiphany, Sioux City, Iowa; founder, exec. dir. Caring 4 U, 1996—. Grantee Iowa Humanities Bd. Mem. Nat. Wellness Assn., Nat. League for Nursing (coun. for nursing ctrs., coun. for nursing practice, coun. for the study for rsch. in nursing edn., coun. for nursing informatics, coun. cmty. health svcs.), Nat. Assn. Neonatal Nurses, Neonatal Nurses No. Calif., Iowa Nurses Assn., Neonatal Nurses of Iowa, Calif. Nurses Assn. (named expert nurse 1991), World Affairs Coun. No. Calif., The Smithsonian Assocs., Jr. League, Nat. Trust for Hist. Preservation, Siouxland Writer's Project. Roman Catholic. Home: 4303 W 19th St Sioux City IA 51103 Office: PO Box 1458 North Sioux City SD 57049-1458

GRANT, MICHAEL PETER, electrical engineer; b. Oshkosh, Wis., Feb. 26, 1936; s. Robert J. and Ione (Michelson) G.; m. Mary Susan Corcoran, Sept. 2, 1961; children: James, Steven, Laura. B.S., Purdue U., 1957, M.S., 1958, Ph.D., 1964. With Westinghouse Research Labs., Pitts., summers 1953-57; mem. tech. staff Aerospace Corp., El Segundo, Calif., 1961; instr. elec. engring. Purdue U., West Lafayette, Ind., 1958-64; sr. engr. Combustion Engring. Corp., Columbus, Ohio, 1964-67, mgr. advanced devel. and control systems, 1967-72, mgr. control and info. scis. div., 1972-74, asst. gen. mgr. indsl. systems div., 1974-76, mgr. system design, 1976-87; v.p., chief scientist SynGenics Corp., Columbus, 1987—; dir. Nat. Ctr. for Mfg. Scis., Ann Arbor, MIch., 1987-95. Contbr. articles to profl. jours.; holder 8 patents in field of automation. Mem. IEEE, Sigma Xi, Eta Kappa Nu, Pi Mu Epsilon, Tau Beta Pi. Home: 4461 Sussex Dr Columbus OH 43220-3857

GRANT, PAUL BERNARD, industrial relations educator; b. Chgo., Mar. 18, 1931; s. Paul B. and Catherine (Flyke) G.; m. Madeleine Grant, Aug. 15, 1959; children: Maura, Elizabeth, Paul, Francis, Timothy. BS, Loyola U., Chgo., 1952; MS, Inst. Indsl. Rels., Chgo., 1954. Asst. prof. Loyola U., Chgo., 1959-89, assoc. prof. indsl. rels., 1989—, asst. v.p., 1977-85, dir. employee rels., 1967-76, sec. retirement com., 1967-95; expert witness Employment Matters, Chgo., 1993—; expert witness Employment Matters, Chgo., 1993—; labor arbitrator Am. Arbitration Assn., Chgo., 1972—, Fed. Mediation Conciliation Svc., Washington, 1976—, Ill. Labor Rels. bd., Chgo., 1984—, Ill. Ednl. Labor Rels. Bd., Chgo., 1987—, Nat. Mediation Bd., Chgo., Washington, 1988—, Ctr. for Employment Dispute Resolution, 1993—; U.S. del. N.Am. Agreement on Labor Cooperation, 1993—. Author: Cutting Health Care Costs, 1987. Sgt. U.S. Army, 1954-56. Mem. Soc. Profls. in Dispute Resolution, Indsl. Rels. Rsch. Assn., Am. Legion. Roman Catholic. Home: 3300 W Rance Ter Lincolnwood IL 60645-3831 Office: Inst Indsl Rels 820 N Michigan Ave Chicago IL 60611-2103

GRANT, PHYLLIS MOORE, elementary education educator; b. Gordonsville, Ala.; d. William Jr. and Milie James (Black) Moore; m. James Grant, Sept. 5, 1970 (div. July 1987; children: Valarie Joy, Anne Sajo. BS in Music Edn., Ala. State U., Montgomery, 1964; MA in Elem. Edn., Eastern Mich. U., 1972, MA in Music Edn., 1978; EdS, Oakland U., Rochester, Mich., 1980; MA in Ednl. Adminstrn., Eastern Mich. U., 1992. Cert. elem. and secondary tchr., Mich. Sec. Alpha Alpha chpt. Gamma Phi Delta Sorority Alpha Alpha chpt., Montgomery, 1964-67; union rep. Huron Valley Assn., Milford, Mich., 1986-90; sec. Ala. State U. Alumni, Detroit, 1992—; test coord. Huron Valley Schs./Oxbow Elem. Sch., White Lake, Mich., 1990—; tchr. Huron Valley Sch. Dist., Highland, Mich., 1967—; tutor-tchr. Marygrove Coll., White Lake, 1967—. Sunday sch. tchr. Dexter Ave. Bapt. Ch., Detroit, 1977—, pianist, 1985—, dir., 1987—, coord. Sunday sch. programs, 1988—. Mem. ASCD, AAUW, Mich. Edn. Assn. (Svc. award 1986, 88), Huron Valley Edn. Assn. (Merit award 1974, 77), Nat. Staff Devel. Coun., Gamma Phi Delta sorority (Alpha Theta chpt.). Home: 27076 Aberdeen Southfield MI 48076-9999 Office: Huron Valley Schs 100 Oxbow Lake Rd White Lake MI 48386-2621

GRANT, ROBERT ALLEN, federal judge; b. Marshall County, Ind., July 31, 1905; s. Everett F. and Margaret E. (Hatfield) G.; m. Margaret Anne McLaren, Sept. 17, 1933; children—Robert A., Margaret Ann Soderberg. A.B., U. Notre Dame, 1928, J.D., 1930. Bar: Ind. bar 1930, U.S. Supreme Ct. bar 1940. Practiced in South Bend, Ind.; dep. pros. atty. St. Joseph County, 1935-36; mem. 76th-80th congresses from 3d Ind. Dist.; U.S. dist. judge No. Dist. Ind., 1957—, chief judge, 1961-72, sr. judge, 1976—; judge Temporary Emergency Ct. Appeals, 1976-93. Mem. nat. coun. representing No. Ind. Boy Scouts Am., 1967. Mem. ABA, Ind. Bar Assn., SAR, Masons (33 deg.), K.T., Shriners, Rotary, Elks, Order DeMolay (internat. supreme coun., past grand master), Columbia Club (Indpls.), Union League Club (Chgo.). Republican. Methodist. Home: 234 Ashbury Ct South Bend IN 46615-2695 Office: 308 Fed Bldg 204 S Main St South Bend IN 46601-2122

GRANTHAM, PAMELA MAAS, prosecutor; b. Des Moines, Feb. 12, 1962; d. Jack L. and Patty Ann (Hummel) Maas; m. Daniel Glen Grantham, Sept. 22, 1990. BA, U. Mich., 1984; JD, Wayne State U., 1987. Bar: Mich. 1987. Case worker Consumer Protection Clinic, Washington, 1983; law clk. to. Hon. Norman Barnard Oakland County Probate Ct., Pontiac, Mich., 1985; asst. prosecuting atty. Oakland County Prosecutor's Office, Pontiac, Mich., 1987—; chief prosecutor's office child sexual assault sect. Oakland County, Pontiac, Mich.; faculty advisor Nat. Coll. Dist. Attys., Houston, 1991; lectr. Oakland Police Acad., Auburn Hills, Mich., 1989—; co-chair investigative subcom. Oakland County Task Force on Child Sexual Assault, 1993-94. Nominating com. North Oakland coun. Girl Scouts U.S.A., Pontiac, 1990-92, bd. dirs., 1992-94; care house com. Child Abuse and Neglect Coun., 1992—; bd. dirs. Child Abuse and Neglected Coun., 1993—. Ida & Benjamin Alpert Found. scholarship, 1986. Mem. ABA, Mich. Bar Assn., Oakland County Bar Assn., Pros. Attys. Assn. Mich. (lectr. 1989—), Nat. Dist. Attys. Assn., U. Mich. Alumni Assn. Office: Oakland County Pros Office 1200 N Telegraph Rd Pontiac MI 48341-1032

GRANTS, VALDIS, engineering manager; b. Liepaja, Latvia, Mar. 5, 1942; came to U.S., 1949, naturalized, 1955; s. Karlis Valdemars and Meta Mudite (Greenvalds) G.; m. Yvette Marie Guhl, June 18, 1966; children: Kristine Marie, Carl Raymond. BS in Sci. Engring., U. Mich., 1964, BS in Engring. Maths., 1965, MS in Elec. Engring., 1967. Rsch. engr. U. Mich., Ann Arbor, 1965-70; sr. design engr. Info. Instrn., Inc., Ann Arbor, 1970-71, Allen-Bradley Co., Highland Heights, Ohio, 1971-76; engring. supr. Allen-Bradley Co., Highland Heights, 1976-77, engr. mgr., 1977-95; mgr. product safety Rockwell Automation/Allen-Bradley, Mayfield Heights, Ohio, 1995. Patentee in field. Mem. IEEE, Tau Beta Pi, Eta Kappa Nu, Phi Kappa Phi. Office: Rockwell Automation/Allen-Bradley 1 Allen-Bradley Dr Mayfield Heights OH 44124-6118

GRAPNER-MITCHELL, PAMELA KAY, primary education educator; b. Celina, Ohio, Nov. 28, 1946; d. Eldon Leroy and Mildred Katherine (Koldewey) Grapner; m. E. Eldon Mitchell, July 18, 1992. BS in Edn., Capital U., 1969; MEd, Nat. Lewis U., 1991. Cert. elem. tchr. Tchr. Columbus (Ohio) State Inst., 1970-72, West Jefferson (Ohio) Schs., 1972-74; with Dept. of Def. Schs., 1974-79, Okinawa, Japan, 1974-76, Bremerhaven, Germany, 1976-79; tchr. ethnic dancing, 1980-81; tchr. Keflavik, Iceland, 1981-82, Kitzingen, Germany, 1982-93, Schweinfurt, Germany, 1993-96, Kaiserslauten, Germany, 1996—; tchr. gifted children Camp Enquire, Celina, Ohio, 1985-88. Contbr. articles to profl. jours. Performer ethnic folk dance Community Arts Coun., Celina, 1978; guest folk dance artist Jay County Coun., Portland, Ind., 1979, Pkwy. Elem., Rockford, Ohio, 1979. Mem. NEA, Ohio Edn. Assn., Overseas Edn. Assn., Kitzingen Edn. Assn. Home: 630 N Buckeye St Celina OH 45822-1511

GRASSI, NICK J., business executive; b. Cleve., Nov. 27, 1945. BA, John Carroll U., 1971. With sales dept. Hanna Chem. Coating, Columbus, Ohio, 1979-91; v.p. Well Remember Co. Inc., Novelty, Ohio, 1991—. Mem. Chesterland C. of C. (trustee 1993—), Rotary (pres. Burton club 1980-95).

GRASSLEY, CHARLES ERNEST, senator; b. New Hartford, Iowa, Sept. 17, 1933; s. Louis Arthur and Ruth (Corwin) G.; m. Barbara Ann Speicher; children: Lee, Wendy, Robin, Michele, Jay. BA, U. No. Iowa, 1955, MA, 1956; postgrad., U. Iowa, 1957-58. Farmer; instr. polit. sci. Drake U., 1962, Charles City Community Coll., 1967-68; mem. Iowa Ho. of Reps., 1959-75, 94th-96th Congresses from 3d Iowa Dist.; U.S. senator from Iowa, 1981—. Mem. Am. Farm Bur., Iowa Hist. Soc., Masons, Pi Gamma Mu, Kappa Delta Pi. Republican. Baptist. Office: US Senate 135 Hart Senate Bldg Washington DC 20510

GRATZ, WILLIAM W., state legislator. State rep. Dist. 113 Mo. State Congress, 1993—. *

GRAU, THOMAS PAUL, marketing executive; b. Middleton, N.Y., July 29, 1960; s. John Wesley Jr. and M. Jeanne (Manouse) G.; m. Kathryn Ann Grau. Student, SUNY, New Paltz, 1978-79, BS, 1982. Home sys. sales cons. Computer Emporium, Middletown, 1982-84; asst. mgr. Orange Micro Inc., Santa Clara, Calif., 1984-85; product mgr. C. Itoh Digital Products, Inc., Torrance, Calif., 1985-87; mktg. mgr. NEC Techs., Inc., Wood Dale, Ill., 1987—. Republican. Home: 4724 Roslyn Rd Downers Grove IL 60515-5810 Office: NEC Techs Inc 1255 N Michael Dr Wood Dale IL 60191-1019

GRAUER, DOUGLAS DALE, civil engineer; b. Marysville, Kans., June 27, 1956; s. Norman Wayne and Ruth Ann (Schwindaman) G.; m. Bette Lynn Bohnenblust, Aug. 16, 1980; children: Diana Kathryn, Laura Jaclyn. Student, Baker U., 1976; BSCE, Kans. State U., 1979. Registered profl. engr., Kans., Okla. Pipeline engr. Cities Service Pipeline Co., Shreveport, La., 1979-80; products terminal engr. Cities Service Co., Braintree, Mass., 1980-81; project engr. Cities Service Co., Tulsa, 1981-83; staff engr. Cities Service Oil and Gas Corp., Tulsa, 1983-85; asst. products pipeline and terminal supt. Nat. Coop. Refinery Assn., Blue Rapids, Kans., 1985-90, supt. products pipeline and terminal, 1990—. Mem. ASCE, NSPE, Nat. Assn. Corrosion Engrs., Kans. Engring. Soc., Chi Epsilon. Republican. Home: 1116 Keystone Rd Marysville KS 66508-8771 Office: Nat Coop Refinery Assn PO Box 158 Blue Rapids KS 66411-0158

GRAVES, CAROL KENNEY, construction company executive; b. Boise, Idaho, May 3, 1937; d. Elmer Kenney and M. Elizabeth (Rogers) Kenney Stolquist; m. Philip L. Graves, Aug. 6, 1955; children: Steven P., Kenton L., Cynthia M. Owner Carols, Peoria, Ill., 1975-78; realtor Clifton-Strode E.R.A., Peoria, 1978-83; pres. Little Red Hen Outlets Inc., Peoria, 1983-87, Asbestos Enviro-Clean Inc., Bartonville, Ill., 1988-93; pres. Enviro-Care Ins., Inc., 1988-93, Twice Over Clean, Inc., 1993—. Rep. precinct committeeperson, Peoria, 1983—, funds dir. YWCA, Oconomowoc, Wis., 1965; active Girl Scouts U.S., Ill., 1963—; mem. Kickapoo Twp. Assn., bd. dirs., 1984-88. Mem. Downtown Bus. Assn. (bd. dirs., pres. 1987-90), Heart of Ill. Food Svc. Assn., Nat. Radon Assn., Midwest Asbestos Coun., Nat. Lead Abatement Coun., Nat. Asbestos Coun., Profl. Assn. for Asbestos Control, Nat. Lead Assn., Steel Structures Painting Coun., Nat. Air Duct Cleaners Assn. (cert.), Nat. Assn. Demolition Contractors, Ctrl. Ill. Builders Contractor Assn. Roman Catholic. Office: Twice Over Clean Inc 4405 Enterprise Dr Bartonville IL 61607-2756

GRAVES, JAMES FRANCIS, microbiologist, educator; b. Council Bluffs, Iowa, Nov. 24, 1951; s. James Wallace and Patty Jean (Ferguson) G. BA, U. Mo., 1974, PhD, 1978. Postdoctoral fellow U. N.C., Chapel Hill, 1978-82; rsch. assoc. U. Va., Charlottesville, 1982-85; scientist Ind. U., Indpls., 1985-87; asst. prof. microbiology U. Detroit Mercy, 1987-93; assoc. prof. U. Detroit, 1993—. Contbr. articles to profl. jours. Mem. Am. Soc. Microbiology. Office: U Detroit Mercy Dept Biology 4001 W Mcnichols Rd Detroit MI 48221-3038

GRAVES, JERRELL LOREN, demographic studies researcher; b. Humansville, Mo., Feb. 10; s. Loren Silas and Edith Lucille (Childress) G. AA, San Jose City Coll., 1986. Lic. gen. contractor, Calif. Farm laborer Guy McDaniel, Bolivar, Mo., 1952-54; laborer Standard Milk Co., Bolivar, 1952-55; constrn. worker Local Union # 676, Springfield, Mo., 1957-59; wood worker Bolivar Wood Products, 1959-61; rschr. life cycles and coop. living, coord. S.W. Dem. Studies, Half Way, Mo., 1961—; instr. hatha yoga San Jose City Coll., 1973. coord. Caring and Sharing, San Jose, 1977-81, San Jose Coop., Inc., 1985-87; vol. Getting out the Vote Friends of John Vasconselles, San Jose, 1980. Mem. ACLU, UN Assn. U.S.A., World Federalists Assn., Common Cause, Greenpeace, Self-Realization Fellowship, Internat. Platform Assn., Rosicrucian. Home and Office: SW Demographic Studies 4280 Hwy P Half Way MO 65663

GRAVES, KATHRYN LOUISE, dermatologist; b. Kansas City, Kans., Mar. 9, 1949; d. Jack Clair and Ruth Marjory (Prentice) Schroll; m. Jeffery Jackson Graves, Mar. 31, 1973; children: Jeffery Justin, Jonathon Tyler, Kathryn Camille. BA, U. Kans., 1971; MD, U. Kans., Kansas City, 1974. Diplomate Am. Bd. Dermatology. Intern St. Lukes Hosp., Kansas City, 1975-76, resident in internal medicine, 1976; resident dermatology Sch. Medicine U. Kans., Kansas City, 1976-79; dermatologist Hutchinson (Kans.) Clinic P.A., 1979—; mem. med. staff Hutchinson Hosp., 1979—. Fellow Am. Acad. Dermatology; mem. AMA, Kans. Dermatology Soc., Kans. Med. Assn., Reno County Med. Assn., Hutchinson C. of C., Gamma Phi Beta (standards chair 1973—). Republican. Methodist. Home: 211 Countryside Dr Hutchinson KS 67502-4457 Office: Hutchinson Clinic 2101 N Waldron St Hutchinson KS 67502-1131

GRAVES, MAUREEN ANN, counselor; b. Sioux City, Iowa, July 10, 1946; d. Jack Milford and Elizabeth Mildred (St. George) Dryden; m. Thomas Darrel Graves, Oct. 9, 1965; children: Michael James, Lorrie Michelle. Grad., Gestalt Inst. Iowa, 1980. Cert. drug and alcohol counselor, Nebr.; cert. profl. asst., U. S.D.; cert. hypnotherapist. Counselor Siouxland Coun. on Alcoholism and Drug Abuse, Sioux City, 1979-81; counselor, co-founder New Hope Alcohol and Addiction Ctr., South Sioux City, Nebr., 1981—; cons. St. Luke Hosp. Addiction Ctr., Sioux City, 1987—; trainer Va. Satir-Internat. Tng. Inst., Crested Butte, Colo., 1988-89. Vol. co-facilitator Siouxland Coun. on Alcoholism and Drug Abuse, Sioux City, 1976-79; mem. exec. team couple World Wide Marriage Encounter, N.E. Nebr., 1979-82; trainer Va. Satir-Internat. Tng. Inst., Crested Butte, Colo., 1992; co-leader Satir Family Camp, San Jose, 1992, 93, 94, 95, 96; mem. Avanta Governing Coun., 1994-95. Mem. Avanta Network, Am. Mental Health Counselors Assn., Moscow Inst. for Profl. Devel. of Psychologists and Social Workers (founding), AACD. Roman Catholic. Home: 424 W 16th St South Sioux City NE 68776-2233 Office: New Hope Alcoholism & Addiction Ctr Inc PO Box 35 South Sioux City NE 68776

GRAVES, SAM, state legislator. State rep. Dist. 4 Mo. State Congress, 1993-94, state senator Dist. 12, 1995—. *

GRAVES, VASHTI SYLVIA, computer analyst, consultant; b. Detroit, Mar. 22, 1967; d. James Graves and Sandra Horne Mcleod Graves Lewis. Student computer programming, Cass Tech. Sch., Detroit, 1981-85; BS in Computer Info. Systems, DeVry Inst. Tech., Chgo., 1988. Gen. officer worker Lenzip Mfg. Co., Chgo., 1985-86; programmer Safer Found., Chgo., 1986-89; programmer, user systems analysts Am. Automotive Assn., Dearborn, Mich., 1989-94; project adminstr. Comerica, Auburn Hills, Mich., 1994—; cons. GSA Advt., Chgo., 1988; owner, cons. Maze Advisors, Detroit, 1993; patron Internat. Inst. Active Alliance Française of Mich., 1995. Home: 99 Roanoke Ln Rochester Hills MI 48309

GRAVES, WILLIAM JOSEPH, state agency administrator; b. Greenville, Ohio, Feb. 3, 1950; s. M. Joseph and Cecilia A. (Batty) G.; m. Teresa Ann Speelman, July 9, 1982. BA in Geography, Ohio State U., 1976, MS in City and Regional Planning, 1983, MSCE, 1983, MA in Pub. Adminstrn., 1986. Cert. planner, econ. devel. profl., mediator. Devel. specialist Ohio Dept. Devel., Columbus, 1981-84, 86-89, program mgmt. supr., 1989-93, mgr. office of housing and cmty. partnerships, 1993—; project engr. Ohio Dept. Transp., Columbus, 1984-86; mem. adv. bd. Ohio Bus. Retention and Expansion, Columbus, 1990-94; bd. dirs. Downtown Ohio, Inc., Wooster; chair paperwork reduction task force HUD, Washington, 1990. Active Grandview Heights (Ohio) Zoning Bd., 1990-93; bd. dirs. Leadership Columbus, 1990-95, House of Hope, Inc., Columbus, 1994-95; vol. mediator Franklin County Small Claims Ct., Columbus, 1991-95. Mem. Soc. for Am. City and Regional Planning History, Am. Planning Assn. (sec. Ohio chpt. 1990-91), Am. Inst. Cert. Planners, Ohio Planning Conf., Pi Alpha Alpha, Phi Kappa Phi. Home: 5226 Lola Way Columbus OH 43235 Office: Ohio Dept Devel Office Housing Cmty Partner 77 S High St 24th Fl Columbus OH 43215

GRAVES, WILLIAM PRESTON, governor; b. Salina, Kans., Jan. 9, 1953; s. William Henry and Helen (Mayo) G.; m. Linda Richey, Apr. 1990; 1 child, Katie. BBA, Kans. Wesleyan U., Salina, 1975; postgrad., U. Kans., 1978-79. Dep. asst. sec. of state State of Kans., Topeka, 1980-85, asst. sec. of state, 1985-87, sec. of state, 1987-95; gov. State of Kans., 1995—; mem. Competitiveness Policy Coun. Mem. Kans. Cavalry; trustee Kans. Wesleyan U., 1987—; bd. trustes Sunflower State Games. Named Outstanding Young Alumnus, Kans. Wesleyan U., 1978, to Athletic Hall of Fame, 1986; named Outstanding Young Kansan, Salina Jaycees and Kans. Jaycees, 1986. Mem. Kans. C. of C. and Industry. Republican. Methodist. Office: Office of Gov 2nd Fl State Capitol Topeka KS 66612

GRAY, AUDREY NESBITT, elementary education educator; b. Kalamazoo, Mich., Feb. 5, 1920; d. Walter Hale and Hazel Violet (Wriglesworth) Nesbitt; m. Llewellyn Wallace Gray, Apr. 22, 1943; children: Susan Nesbitt Moffitt, Deborah Llewellyn Gray-Oliver, Gretchen Clarke Shannon. BS, Western Mich. U., 1943. Cert. elem. edn. tchr., Mich. Tchr. Three Rivers (Mich.) Pub. Schs., 1943-45; tchr. music Schoolcraft (Mich.) Pub. Schs., 1945-46; tchr. Comstock (Mich.) Pub. Schs., 1963-83, ret., 1983; bd. dirs. Mich. In Action for Drug Free Youth; mem. cons. team Drug Edn. Curriculum Guide, 1971, adv. com. Gov. Conf. Drug Free Schs. and Communities, 1990, steering com. for Med., Ednl., Legal Law Enforcement, State Bar Mich., 1991—, Mich alliance Drug Free Schs. and Communities, 1990-91; innovator, dir., advisor cmty. story hour program Juvenile Detention Facilities, Mich., 1993. Mem. Forum for Kalamazoo County, 1986—, Greater Kalamazoo Consortium, 1990—; mem. steering com. Nat. Issues Forum, Kalamazoo, 1989—; bd. dirs. Kalamazoo Area Families in Action, 1986-87; mem. State Bar of Mich. Task Force on Substance Abuse, 1991—; dir. Cmty. Story Hour Program, Kalamazoo County Juv. Home, 1993—. Recipient Top Tchr. award Grade Tchr. Mag., 1967, First Tchr. Appreciation award Nat. Honor Soc. Comstock High Sch., 1990. Mem. AAUW, Am. Lawyers Aux. (chair drug awareness com. 1990—, coun. state affiliates 1989-90, 91—, 2d v.p., 1991, pres., 1993), Gov.'s Conf. on Drug Free Schs. and Communities (adv. mem.), Mich. Lawyers Aux. (pres. 1987-88, drug awareness chair, 1989, co-chair statewide No Drug Use rally 1989), Kalamazoo Lawyers Aux. (pres., 1970-71, 88-89),. Republican. Presbyterian. Home: 1442 Prospect Hl Kalamazoo MI 49006-4446

GRAY, CARL THOMAS, architect; b. Montclair, N.J., June 14, 1943; s. Earl Boone and Mary (Dunlap) G.; m. Janet Ann Rulli, Oct. 23, 1976; children: Randall Joseph, Brian Thomas. BArch, Miami U., Oxford, Ohio, 1967. Registered architect, Minn. Archtl. designer Fisk Rhinehart, Cin., 1971-72, Toltz, King, Douvau & Anderson, St. Paul, 1973-74, Steenberg Constrn. Co., St. Paul, 1975-80, Milo Architects and Engrs., St. Paul, 1980-82; pvt. practice architecture St. Paul, 1983-89; architect U.S. Army C.E., 1989—. Prin. projects include Comstock Hall Rennovation U. Minn., 1986-88, St. Paul Flood Wall, 1991-95. Mem. Sci. Mus. St. Paul. Served with U.S. Army, 1967-70. Mem. AIA, Minn. State Assn. Architects. Republican. Roman Catholic. Home: 261 Summit Ave Saint Paul MN 55102-2150

GRAY, CARLOS GIBSON, restaurateur, seedsman, entertainer, producer; b. Shelbyville, Ind., Sept. 5, 1937; s. Gibson Tull and Edna Frances (Wicker) G.; m. Elizabeth Vivian Stickrod, Aug. 30, 1959 (div. 1971); children: Carla Elizabeth Christine Gray Stokes, Zarrell Thomas Gibson Gray; m. Carolyn June Breeden, 1971. BSEE, Purdue U., 1960. Cert. secondary tchr., Ind. Math. tchr. Reynolds (Ind.) High Sch., 1960-61, Jefferson High Sch., Lafayette, Ind., 1961-63, Warren Ctrl. High Sch., Indpls., 1963-64; systems engr. IBM, Indpls., 1964-67, mktg. rep., 1967-69; asst. v.p., data processing mgr. Aero Mayflower Transit Co., Indpls., 1969-74; asst. v.p. application devel. Ind. Nat. Bank, Indpls., 1974-76; co-owner Gray's Seed, Inc., Fairland, Ind., 1976—; owner Boggstown Inn and Cabaret-TDCC, Corp., Boggstown, Ind., 1984—; co-owner Jacray Corp., 1994—; data processing cons. Meth. Hosp., Indpls., 1968, Ford Motor Corp., Dearborn, Mich., 1967, Army, Naval Class of Indsl. Coll. Nat. Security, Indpls., 1967. Ragtime music video and audio cassettes This is Boggstown, 1986; prodr., dir. Ragtime Lil & Banjo-Banjo, Branson, Mo., 1994—. Active Hoosier Internat. Ragtime Soc. (developed home for preservation and promotion of Am.'s ragtime music), Boggstown, 1986. Mem. Fretted Instrument Guild Am., Exptl. Aircraft Assn., Purdue Pilots, Inc. (pres. 1959-60). Home: PO Box 103 Boggstown IN 46110-0103 Office: 6895 W Boggstown Rd Boggstown IN 46110-9732

GRAY, CHARLES MELVIN, economist, educator, consultant; b. Texarkana, Ark., Oct. 16, 1944; s. Charles Read and Marjorie Gayle (Twyman) G.; m. Virginia Sue Hickman, June 10, 1967; 1 child, Brian Charles. BA, Hendrix Coll., Conway, Ark., 1966; AM, Washington U., St. Louis, 1968, PhD, 1978. Economist Fed. Res. Bank, St. Louis, 1969-71; instr. Transylvania U., Lexington, Ky., 1971-73; economist Fed. Res. Bank, Mpls., 1973-74; dir. Community Devel. Corp., Mpls., 1974-75; economist, rsch. analyst State of Minn., St. Paul, 1975-79; prof. econs. U. St. Thomas, St. Paul, 1979—; cons. Econ. Cons. Svcs., St. Paul, 1980-87, Univ. Rsch. Consortium, Mpls., 1987—; dir. faculty devel. U. St. Thomas, 1987-90; vis. prof. U. Oslo, 1985, U. N.C., 1993-94. Author, editor: The Costs of Crime, 1979; co-author: Economics of Art and Culture, 1993. Chair bd. Caravan Dance Co., St. Paul, 1976-79; trustee Unity Ch., St. Paul, 1990-93, chair, 1991-93. Blandin Found. faculty fellow, 1986; Nat. Inst. Justice rsch. grantee, 1977-78. Mem. Am. Econ. Assn., Am. Law and Econs. Assn., Midwest Econs. Assn., Nat. Assn. Forensic Economists, Assn. for Cultural Econs. Democrat. Unitarian. Home: 1776 Pinehurst Ave Saint Paul MN 55116-2117 Office: U St Thomas 1000 Lasalle Ave Minneapolis MN 55403-2005

GRAY, EDMAN LOWELL, metal distribution company executive; b. Youngstown, Ohio, Feb. 13, 1939; s. Everett Lippincott and Martha Milligan (Reynallt) G.; m. Virginia Corwin Van Kirk, Dec. 23, 1967; children: David Edman, Elizabeth Louise (dec.). BA, Yale U., 1961. Salesman Procter and Gamble Co., N.Y.C., 1961, Ward Steel Svc. Co., Dayton, Ohio, 1965-75; v.p. Ward Steel Service Co., Dayton, Ohio, 1975-80, pres., 1980—. Elder Westminster Presbyn. Ch., Dayton, 1978-81, trustee, 1991-94; trustee Children's Med. Ctr., Dayton, 1987-93, Silver Bay (N.Y.) YMCA, 1992—, Daybreak, Dayton, 1992—; vol. Big Bros./Big Sisters of Dayton, 1992—; vol. Montgomery County Juvenile Ct., 1994—. With USN, 1961-65. Mem. Steel Svc. Ctr. Inst. (pres. Cin. chpt. 1979-80, nat. com. chmn. Cleve. 1987-95), Yale Club (pres. 1980-83), Yale Alumni Assn. (chmn. bd. sch. com. Dayton 1983-89), Rotary. Republican. Office: 3050 Dryden Rd Dayton OH 45439-1620

GRAY, HANNA HOLBORN, history educator; b. Heidelberg, Germany, Oct. 25, 1930; d. Hajo and Annemarie (Bettmann) Holborn; m. Charles Montgomery Gray, June 19, 1954. AB, Bryn Mawr Coll., 1950; PhD, Harvard U., 1957; MA, Yale U., 1971, LLD, 1978; LittD (hon.), St. Lawrence U., 1974, Oxford (Eng.) U., 1979; LLD (hon.), Dickinson Coll., 1979, U. Notre Dame, 1980, Marquette U., 1984; LittD (hon.), Washington U., 1985; HHD (hon.), St. Mary's Coll., 1974; LHD (hon.), Grinnell (Iowa) Coll., 1974, Lawrence U., 1974, Denison U., 1974, Wheaton Coll., 1976, Marlboro Coll., 1979, Rikkyo (Japan) U., 1979, Roosevelt U., 1980, Knox Coll., 1980, Coe Coll., 1981, Thomas Jefferson U., 1981, Duke U., 1982, New Sch. for Social Research, 1982, Clark U., 1982, Brandeis U., 1983, Colgate U., 1983, Wayne State U., 1984, Miami U., Oxford, Ohio, 1984, So. Meth. U., 1984, CUNY, 1985, U. Denver, 1985, Am. Coll. Greece, 1986, Muskingum Coll., 1987, Rush Presbyn. St. Lukes Med. Ctr., 1987, NYU, 1988, Rosemont Coll., 1988, Claremont U. Ctr. Grad Sch., 1989, Moravian Coll., 1991, Rensselaer Poly. Inst., 1991, Coll. William and Mary, 1991, Centre Coll., 1991, Macalester Coll., 1993, McGill U., 1993, Ind. U., 1994, Med. U. of S.C., 1994; LLD (hon.), Union Coll., 1975, Regis Coll., 1976, Dartmouth Coll., 1978, Trinity Coll., 1978, U. Bridgeport, 1978, Dickinson Coll., 1979, Brown U., 1979, Wittenburg U., 1979, Dickinson Coll., 1979, U. Rochester, 1980, U. Notre Dame, 1980, U. So. Calif., 1980, U. Mich., 1981, Princeton U., 1982, Georgetown U., 1983, Marquette U., 1984, W.Va. Wesleyan U., 1985, Hamilton Coll., 1985, Smith Coll., 1986, U. Miami, 1986, Columbia U., 1987, NYU, 1988, Rosemont Coll., 1988, U. Toronto, Can., 1991; LDH, U. Del., 1994, Haverford Coll., 1995, Tulane U., 1995; LLD, Harvard U., 1995; LHD, McGill U., 1993, Macalester Coll., 1993, Ind. U., 1994, Med. U. S.C., 1994, Haverford Coll., 1995, Tulane U., 1995; LLD, Harvard U., 1995. Instr. Bryn Mawr Coll., 1953-54; teaching fellow Harvard, 1955-57, instr., 1957-59, asst. prof., 1959-60, vis. lectr., 1963-64; asst. prof. U. Chgo., 1961-64, asso. prof., 1964-72; dean, prof. Northwestern U., Evanston, Ill., 1972-74; provost, prof. history Yale U., 1974-78, acting pres., 1977-78; pres. U. Chgo., Ill., 1978-93; prof. dept. history U. Chgo., 1978—, Harry Pratt Judson disting. svc. prof. history, 1994—; bd. dirs. Cummins Engine Co., J.P. Morgan & Co., Morgan Guaranty Trust Co., Atlantic Richfield Co., Ameritech; fellow Center for Advanced Study in Behavioral Scis., 1966-67, vis. scholar, 1970-71; vis. prof. U. Calif., Berkeley, 1970-71. Editor: (with Charles Gray) Jour. Modern History, 1965-70; contbr. articles to profl. jours. Mem. Nat. Coun. on Humanities, 1972-78; trustee Yale Corp., 1971-74, Com. on Econ. Devel., Bryn Mawr Coll., Howard Hughes Med. Inst., Marlboro Sch. Music; bd. dirs. Andrew W. Mellon Found.; mem. bd. regents The Smithsonian Instn. Decorated Grosse Verdienstkreuz (Germany); fellow Newberry Libr., 1960-61, hon. fellow St. Anne's Coll., Oxford (Eng.) U., 1978—; Fulbright scholar, 1950-51; recipient Grad. medal Radcliffe Coll., 1976, Yale medal, 1978, Medal of Liberty award, 1986, Medal of Freedom, 1991, Frontrunner award Sara Lee, 1991, Laureate Lincoln Acad. Ill., 1988, Charles Frankel prize, 1993, Centennial medal Harvard U., 1994; Disting. Svc. award in edn. Inst. Internat. Edn., 1994. Fellow Am. Acad. Arts and Scis.; mem. Renaissance Soc. Am., Am. Philos. Soc. (Jefferson medal 1993), Nat. Acad. Edn., Coun. Fgn. Rels. Chgo., Coun. on Fgn. Rels. N.Y. (bd. dirs.), Phi Beta Kappa (vis. scholar 1971-72). Office: U Chgo Dept History 1126 E 59th St Chicago IL 60637-1580

GRAY, JAMES PATRICK, business executive, consultant; b. Yonkers, N.Y., Oct. 27, 1958; s. James and Joan Frances (Saverese) G.; m. Lucy Marie Simoncic, July 26, 1985. BIE, Cleve. State U., 1982; MBA, Case Western Reserve U., 1987. Indsl. engr., project mgr. TRW, Inc., Cleve., 1980-87; gen. mgr., dir. engring. Ajax Mfg., Cleve., 1988-92; prin. J. P. Gray & Assocs., Chesterland, Ohio, 1991—; v.p. bus. devel. The Mentor Group, Mentor, Ohio, 1993-95; sr. cons. Kavon Internat., Inc., Mentor, 1993—; cons. Cleve. Coun. Smaller Enterprises, 1987—. Mem. Inst. Indsl. Engr. (sr.), Soc. Mfg. Engrs. (sr.), Am. Soc. Quality Control. Office: 12275 Bean Rd Chardon OH 44024

GRAY, JOHN F., mechanical engineer; b. Cambridge, Ohio, May 19, 1951; s. Stewart Bruce and MIldred Pauline (Rose) G.; m. Phyllis Carol Ann Engelbert, June 16, 1973; children: Kevin John, Kelly Ann, Eric Michael. BSME, Ohio State U., 1973; MSME, Rochester Inst. Tech., 1977. Rsch. engr. Kodak Co., Rochester, N.Y., 1973-78; tech. cons. Structural Dynamics Rsch. Corp., Cin., 1978-80; mgr. tech. support SDRC, Cin., 1980-85, IBM tech. mgr., 1985-94; pres. Gray & Assocs., 1994—; sr. cons. Internat. Technigroup Inc., 1995—. Pres. Clough Pike Elem. PTO, Cin., 1984, Glen Este Mid. Sch. PTO, 1986-88; mem. West Clermont Bd. Edn., Cin., 1990—, v.p. 1992, pres. 1993. Recipient Achievement award Ohio Sch. Bds. Assn., 1995. Home: 945 Locust Ln Cincinnati OH 45245-1313

GRAY, MARK WILLIAM, lawyer; b. Indpls., Oct. 19, 1916; s. Mark Roy and Elsie (Wegener) G.; m. Mary Sue Spilman, Aug. 2, 1940 (dec. 1963); m. Mary Neal, Dec. 21, 1963; children: Carolyn Lee, Mark William Jr. BS in Bus., Ind. U., 1938, JD, 1940. Bar: Ind. 1940, U.S. Dist. Ct. Ind. 1940, U.S. Supreme Ct. 1953; CPCU, 1952. Pvt. practice Indpls., 1940-42; ptnr. Kightlinger & Gray and predecessor firms, Indpls., 1946—. Mem., pres. Indpls. Sch. Bd., 1965-69; commr. Marion County Election Bd., Indpls., 1950-64; bd. dirs., officer Indpls. Conf. and Visitors Assn., 1947—; chmn. bd. Brebeuf Prep. Sch., 1982-86. Capt. inf. AUS, 1942-46, ETO. Mem. ABA, Internat. Assn. Def. Counsel, Fedn. Ins. and Def. Counsel, Ind. Bar, Indpls. Bar Assn., Masons (33 degree). Democrat. Methodist. Office: Kightlinger & Gray 151 N Delaware St Indianapolis IN 46204-2526

GRAY, MEL, professional football player; b. Williamsburg, Va., Mar. 16, 1961. Student, Coffeyville Jr. Coll., Purdue U. With L.A. USFL, 1984-85, New Orleans Saints, 1986-88; kick returner, wide receiver Detroit Lions, 1989—. Voted to Pro Bowl, 1990, 91, 92; named kick returner The Sporting News NFL All-Pro team, 1986, 90, 91, 93, punt returner The Sporting News NFL All-Pro team, 1987, 91, 92. Office: Detroit Lions 1200 Featherstone Rd Pontiac MI 48342-1938*

GRAY, STEPHEN THOMAS, newspaper editor; b. Ypsilanti, Mich., Dec. 17, 1950; s. Grattan and Amy Louise (Thomas) G.; m. Cynthia Joy Rowland, May 28, 1976; children: Benjamin Rowland, Matthew Rowland. BS in Journalism, Northwestern U., 1972. Reporter Monroe (Mich.) Evening News, 1972-75, city editor, 1975-78, exec. editor, 1978-80, editor, 1980—. Mem. Hist. Marker Trail Com., Monroe, 1970—. Mem. Inland Press Assn. (bd. dirs. 1991—), Mich. AP Editorial Assn. (bd. dirs. 1983-91, pres. 1989, numerous awards for columns and editorials 1979—), Mich. Press Assn. (bd. dirs. 1987—, pres. 1995—), Monroe Golf and Country Club. Christian Scientist. Office: Monroe Evening News 20 W 1st St PO Box 1176 Monroe MI 48161

GRAY, VIRGINIA HICKMAN, political science educator; b. Camden, Ark., June 10, 1945; d. George Leonard and Ethel Massengale (Bell) Hickman; m. Charles Melvin Gray, Oct. 16, 1944; 1 child, Brian Charles. BA with honors, Hendrix Coll., 1967; MA, Washington U., St. Louis, 1969, PhD, 1972. Asst. prof. polit. sci. U. Ky., Lexington, 1971-73; from asst. prof. to assoc. prof. U. Minn., Mpls., 1973-83, prof., 1983—, chairperson dept. polit. sci., 1985-88; guest scholar Brookings Inst., Washington, 1977-78; vis. prof. U. Oslo, 1985, U. B.C., 1992, U. N.C., 1993-94; NSF vis. prof. for women, 1993-94. Co-author: The Organizational Politics of Criminal Justice, 1980, Feminism and the New Right, 1983, Politics in the American States, 1983, 6th edit., 1995, American States and Cities, 1991, The Population Ecology of Interest Representation, 1996. Bd. dirs. Group Health Inc., 1992-98. Fellow Woodrow Wilson Found., 1970, NDEA, 1969-70; grantee Swedish Bicentennial Found., 1985; recipient rsch. assistantship NSF, 1968-69. Mem. Am. Polit. Sci. Assn. (coun. 1991-92), Midwest Polit. Sci. Assn. (coun. 1984-86), Policy Studies Orgn. (coun. 1977-79). Democrat. Unitarian. Home: 1776 Pinehurst Ave Saint Paul MN 55116-2117 Office: U Minn Dept Polit Sci 1414 Soc Sci Bldg Minneapolis MN 55455

GRAYSON, DAVID S., paper company executive; b. Binghamton, N.Y., Oct. 16, 1943; s. Milton M. and Helen A. (Oretskin) G.; m. Wendy W. Grayson (div. June 1986); children: Natalie, Marc, Dana. BS, Coll. Forestry, Syracuse, N.Y., 1965; MS, Rensselaer Poly., 1967. Various positions Riegel Paper div. James River Co., Milford, N.J., 1967-80; sales mgr. Kerwin Paper, Appleton, Wis., 1980-81; pres., founder Am. Fine Paper, Appleton, 1981—. Mem. Moses Montifiore Temple Bd., Appleton, 1983-86. Jewish. Home: 1401 S Nicolet Rd Appleton WI 54915-8226 Office: Am Fine Paper PO Box 2638 Appleton WI 54913-2638

GRAYSON, PAULA S., biofeedback clinician, mental health nurse; b. Louisville, Ky., Nov. 20, 1953; d. Paul and Joan Lee (Schoenbachler) Dickerson; m. W. Paul Grayson, July 29, 1978; children: Alaina Brock, Benton Paul,. Nursing ad., Jefferson C.C., U. Ky., Louisville, 1973; BA in Psychology, U. Mo., Kansas City, 1988, MA in Psychology, 1991. Cert. Biofeedback Clinician, Biofeedback Certification Inst. Am.; RN, Ky. Nurse med., surg., ICU St. Joseph's Infirmary, Louisville, Ky., 1973-75; recovery room nurse Louisville Gen. Hosp., 1975-77; ICU supr. Charity Hosp., New Orleans, 1977-79; mgr. surg. ward City of Memphis Hosp., 1979-81; prn. float, supr. Trinity Luth. Hosp., Kansas City, Mo., 1981-89; mental health nurse Trinity Luth. N., Kansas City, 1992-94; clinician Biofeedback North, Kansas City, Mo., 1994; biofeedback clinician, 1994—. Mem. Assn. Applied Psychophysiology and Biofeedback, Psi Chi. Episcopalian. Office: Biofeedback North Ste H 3805 N Oak Kansas City MO 64116

GRAZIANO, CHARLES DOMINIC, pharmacist; b. Cariati, Italy, June 28, 1920; s. Frank Dominic and Marianna (Bambace) G.; student Dowling Jr. Coll., 1939, 40; B.S. in Pharmacy, Drake U., 1943; m. Corrine Rose Comito, Feb. 5, 1950; children—Craig Frank, Charles Dominic II, Marianne, Kimberly Rose, Mark, Suzanne. Pharamacist Kings Pharmacy, Des Moines, 1946-47; partner Bauder Pharmacy, Des Moines, 1948-61, owner, 1962—. Mem. Des Moines Art Center. Served with AUS, 1943-45; ETO. Decorated Bronze Star. Named Drake U. Parent of the Year, 1983-84. Mem. Des Moines C. of C., Nat. Assn. Retail Druggists, Iowa, Polk County pharm. assns., St. Vincent de Paul Soc., Am. Pharm. Assn., Phi Delta Chi. Roman Catholic. Office: 3802 Ingersoll Ave Des Moines IA 50312-3413

GREB, RICHARD HAROLD, writer; b. Chgo., Feb. 11, 1945; s. Marcus and Rose (Berman) G.; m. Sue Amberson, Dec. 7, 1980. BS in Chemistry, Ill. Inst. Tech., Chgo., 1967. Reporter Lerner Newspapers, Chgo., 1967-68; reporter/deskman AP, Chgo., 1968-72; copy editor/makeup editor Chgo. Tribune, 1972-75; reporter/deskman Reuters News Svc., Chgo., 1976-83; subeditor/chief subeditor fin. Reuters News Svc., Hong Kong, 1983-86; chief subeditor commodities/fin. Reuters News Svc., London, 1986-88; Midwest news editor Reuters News Svc., Chgo., 1988; ind. writer, 1988—. Editor: The Orders of Change: Building Value-Driven Organizations, 1995. Mem. Ind. Writers Chgo. (publicity chair 1989-93, dir. 1990-95, v.p. 1992-93, pres. 1993-94, parliamentarian 1994-95), Chgo. Speechwriters Forum (pres. 1991—), Pub. Rels. Soc. Am. (Chgo. chpt. newsletter editor 1989-90, mem. internat. com. 1991—, Greater O'Hare chpt. sec. 1992-93, dir. 1993—, pres.-elect 1996), Am. Contract Bridge Assn. (life master).

GREELEY, ANDREW MORAN, sociologist, author; b. Oak Park, Ill., Feb. 5, 1928; s. Andrew T. and Grace (McNichols) G. A.B., St. Mary of Lake Sem., 1950, S.T.L., 1954; M.A., U. Chgo., 1961, Ph.D., 1961. Ordained priest Roman Cath. Ch., 1954. Asst. pastor Ch. of Christ the King, Chgo., 1954-64; program dir. Nat. Opinion Research Ctr., Chgo., 1961-68; dir. Ctr. for Study Am. Pluralism, from 1973; lectr. sociology U. Chgo., 1963-72; prof. sociology U. Ariz., Tucson, from 1978, now adj. prof.; prof. social sci. U. Chgo., 1991—; cons. Hazen Found. Commn. Syndicated columnist People and Values; guest columnist Chgo. Sun Times, 1985—; Author: The Church and the Suburbs, 1959, Strangers in the House, 1961, Religion and Career, 1963, (with Peter H. Rossi) Education of Catholic Americans, 1966, Changing Catholic College, 1967, Come Blow Your Mind With Me, 1971, Life for a Wanderer: A New Look at Christian Spirituality, 1971, The Denominational Society: A Sociological Approach to Religion in America, 1972, Priests in the United States: Reflections on A Survey, 1972, That Most Distressful Nation, 1972, New Agenda, 1973, Jesus Myth, 1971, Unsecular Man, 1974, Ethnicity in the United States: A Preliminary Reconnaissance, 1974, Ecstasy: A Way of Knowing, 1974, Building Coalitions: American Politics in the 1970's, 1974, Sexual Intimacy, 1975, Denomination Society, 1975, The Great Mysteries: An Essential Catechism, 1976, The Communal Catholic: A Personal Manifesto, 1976, Death and Beyond, 1976, The American Catholic: A Social Portrait, 1977, The Making of the Popes, 1978, 79, The Magic Cup: An Irish Legend, 1979, Women I've Met, 1979, Why Can't They Be Like Us?, 1980, Death In April, 1980, The Cardinal Sins, 1981, Religion: A Secular Theory, 1982, Thy Brother's Wife, 1982, Ascent Into Hell, 1983, Lord of the Dance, 1984, Virgin & Martyr, 1985, Piece of My Mind on Just About Everything, 1985, Happy are the Meek, 1985, The Magic Cup, 1985, God Game, 1986, Happy Are the Clean of Heart, 1986, Patience of a Saint, 1987, Rite of Spring, 1987, Angels of September, 1986, Happy Are Those Who Thirst For Justice, 1987, The Final Planet, 1987, Angel Fire, 1988, (photography) Andrew Greeley's Chicago, 1989, Love Song, 1989, St. Valentine's Night, 1989, The Bible and Us, 1990, The short stories All About Women, 1990, (photography) The Irish, 1990, The Catholic Myth: The Behavior and Beliefs of American Catholics, 1990, The Cardinal Virtues, 1990, Faithful Attraction: Discovering Intimacy, Love, and Fidelity in American Marriage, 1991, The Search for Maggie Ward, 1991, An Occasion of Sin, 1991, Happy Are the Merciful, 1992, Wages of Sin, 1992, Fall from Grace, 1993, Sacraments of Love: A Prayer Journal, 1994, others; contbr. articles to profl. jours. Recipient Cath. Press Assn. award for best book for young people, 1965, Thomas Alva Edison award for radio broadcast, 1963, C. Albert Kobb award Nat. Cath. Edn. Assn., 1977. Mem. Am. Sociol. Assn., Soc. for Sci. Study Religion, Religious Research Assn.

GREEN, ALLISON ANNE, retired secondary education educator; b. Flint, Mich., Oct. 5, 1936; d. Edwin Stanley and Ruth Allison (Simmons) James; m. Richard Gerring Green, Dec. 23, 1961 (div. Oct. 1969). BA, Albion Coll., 1959; MA, U. Mich., 1978. Cert. tchr., Mich. Tchr. phys. edn. Southwestern High Sch., Flint, 1959-62; tchr. math. Harry Hunt Jr. High Sch., Portsmouth, Va., 1962-63; receptionist Tempcon, Inc., Mpls., 1963-64; tchr. phys. edn. and math. Longfellow Jr. High Sch., Flint, 1964-81, tchr. math., 1981-92, tchr. lang. arts and social studies, 1986-87. Mem. Fair Winds council Girl Scouts U.S., 1943—, leader Lone Troop, Albion, Mich., 1957, sr. tchr. aide adviser, 1964-67; mem. Big Sisters Genesee and Lapeer Counties, 1964-68; mem. adminstrv. bd. Court St. United Meth. Ch., vice chmn. 1995, chmn. 1996—, treas. edn. work area, mission commn., sec. council on ministries, mem. worship com. United Meth. Women Soc. Christian Service, also chmn. meml. com. Mem. NEA, Mich. Edn. Assn., Mich. Assn. Mid. Sch. Educators, United Tchrs. Flint (bldg. rep.), Delta Kappa Gamma (treas. 1982-88, profl. affairs chmn. 1978-80, legis. chmn. 1980-82, pres. 1988-90), Alpha Xi Delta (pres. Flint, alumnae, v.p., treas., corp. pres. Albion Coll. alumnae dir. province 1972-77, Outstanding Sr. Albion Coll. 1959), Embroiderers Guild Am. (sec. 1977-80, maps rep. 1980-82), Phi Delta Kappa (historian 1985-91, treas. 1991-92). Home: 1002 Copeman Blvd Flint MI 48504-7326

GREEN, CALVIN, electrical engineer; b. Middletown, Ohio, Mar. 2, 1951; s. Andrew and Lula Mae (Jones) G.; m. Susie Louise Raby, Jan. 19, 1974 (div. Oct. 1983). AD in Archtl. Tech., ITT Tech. Inst., Dayton, Ohio, 1971; BS in Engring., Wright State U., 1981. Registered profl. engr., Ohio; radiologic technologist, Ohio. X-ray technician Greene Meml. Hosp., Xenia, Ohio, 1976-81; engr. Ohio Edison Co., Akron, 1981—. Bus. advisor, mentor Inroads, N.E. Ohio, 1991—. Sgt. USAF, 1971-76, Korea. Recipient Salute to Black Engrs. award Nat. Tech. Assn., 1992; named Significant African-Am. Male, Black Women's Caucus, Akron, 1994. Mem. NSPE (bd. dirs. Akron Dist. 1994), NAACP. Home: 1414 Gurley Cir Akron OH 44310

GREEN, DAVID, manufacturing company executive; b. Chgo., Mar. 22, 1922; s. Harry B. and Carrie (Scheinbaum) G.; m. Mary I. Winton, June 15, 1951; children: Sara Edmond, Howard Benjamin, Jonathan Winton. BA in Econs., U. Chgo., 1942, MA in Social Scis., 1949. Mgr., Toy Co., Chgo., 1949-54; founder, chmn., pres. Quartet Mfg. Co., Skokie, 1954—; pres. Colleague, Inc., Booneville, Miss., 1967-87; chmn. bd. and cons. DG Group, Chgo., 1977—; chmn. Quartet Ovonics, 1986—. Spl. cons. to White House-Trade Expansion Act, Washington, 1962; chmn. Winnetka Caucus (Ill.), 1971; chmn. Ill. state Dan Walker for Gov., 1972, 76; spl. asst. to Gov. for intergovtl. relations, Ill., 1973-76; mem. U. Chgo. pres.'s coun., pres.'s circle Chgo. Botanic Garden, playwright's circle Stratford Festival; founder dir. circle Steppenwolf Theatre Co. governing mem. Chgo. Symphony Orchestra. Served with U.S. Army, 1942-45, PTO. Recipient 1st Non-Smoking Office Bldg. award Skokie Clean Air Coalition, 1987, Sustaining fellow Art Inst. Chgo. Mem. Nat. Office Products Assn., Wholesale Stationers' Assn. (Office Product Mfr. of Yr. award 1989, 93, 94), Chgo. Soc. of Clubs. Clubs: Metropolitan (Chgo.); Pelican Bay (Naples, Fla.). Home: 969 Tower Manor Dr Winnetka IL 60093-1937 Office: Quartet Mfg Co 5700 Old Orchard Rd Skokie IL 60077-1036

GREEN, DAVID FERRELL, law enforcement official; b. Sioux Falls, S.D., Nov. 13, 1935; s. John C. and Mary A. (Meyer) G.; m. Renata M. Kappenman, Apr. 15, 1961; children: Tobin L., Anthony F., Thomas D. BA summa cum laude, Augustana Coll., Sioux Falls, 1980; MPA Univ. S.D., 1992; grad. FBI Nat. Acad., 1972; Juvenile Officers Inst., 1966. Cert. police officer; cert. police firearms instr. Dispatch dept. mgr. Sioux Falls Argus Leader, S.D., 1954-58; with Sioux Falls Police Dept., 1958-88, patrol officer, 1958-63, sgt., 1963-68, lt., 1968-71, capt., 1971-82, chief, 1982-88; exec. dir. Mid-State Organized Crime Info. Ctr., Springfield, Mo., 1988—; mem. NCIC Policy Bd. Justice Dept., Washington, 1976-78; mem. NCIC North Central Group, 1978-88, State Juvenile Task Force; vice chmn. Gov.'s Police Task Force S.D., 1979-81. Bd. dirs. Vol. Nat. Ctr. for Citizen Involvement, Washington, 1978-81, St. Therese Sch. Bd., Sioux Falls, pres., 1973-74; pres. Vol. Action Ctr., Sioux Falls, 1979-80; treas. found. bd. Little Flower Sch. Served with USNR, 1953-61. Recipient J. Edgar Hoover award Justice Dept., 1972; Jaycees Officer Yr. award Sioux Falls Jaycees, 1972; named to Augustana Coll. Honor Soc., 1980. Mem. Fraternal Order of Police (trustee 1971-83, chmn. bd. trustees 1979-83, Outstanding Service award 1983). Republican, Am. Legion., Elks, K.C. Roman Catholic. Office: Mid States Orgn Crime Info Ctr 4 Corporate Ctr Ste 205 Springfield MO 65804

GREEN, DAVID WILLIAM, chemist, educator; b. Hudson, Mich., Nov. 19, 1942; s. Francis Harger and Dorotha Louise (Onweller) G.; m. Mary Sarah McCullough, July 8, 1967; children: Laura, Brenda, Mark, Brian, William. BA, Albion Coll., 1964; PhD, U. Calif., Berkeley, 1968; MBA, U. Chgo., 1985. Instr. U. Calif., Berkeley, 1968; rsch. assoc. U. Chgo., 1968-71; asst. prof. Albion (Mich.) Coll., 1971-75; chemist Argonne (Ill.) Nat. Lab., 1975-82, mgr. analytical chemistry, 1982—; prof. chemistry Coll. DuPage, Glen Ellyn, Ill., 1991-93. Editor Mng. the Modern Lab, 1995—, mem. editl. bd., 1994—. Pres. Dist. 58 Bd. Edn., Downers Grove, Ill., 1976-79. Mem. Analytical Lab. Mgrs. Assn. (pres. 1986-87, treas. 1989). Home: 5625 Carpenter St Downers Grove IL 60516-1356 Office: Argonne Nat Lab 9700 Cass Ave Argonne IL 60439-4803

GREEN, DEBORAH PARKHURST, librarian; b. Moline, Ill., Nov. 24, 1954; d. James Edward and Judith Irene (Larson) Parkhurst; m. Leon Charles Green, July 11, 1981. BA, Augustana Coll., Rock Island, Ill., 1976; MLS, U. Ill., 1980. Children's libr. East Moline (Ill.) Pub. Libr., 1981-82; children's svcs. head Rock Island Pub. Libr., 1982-83, children's/ext. svcs. head, 1983-85; br. libr. II Tampa Hillsborough County Pub. Libr. System, Ruskin, Fla., 1985-86; br. libr. II Tampa Hillsborough County Pub. Libr. System, Tampa, Fla., 1986, coord. children's svcs./libr. III, 1987-88; coord. children's svcs. Iowa City (Iowa) Pub. Libr., 1988—; workshop/panel presenter various assns. Ill. State Libr. scholar, 1979, Honor scholar Augustana Coll., 1975, U. Ill. honor scholar, 1980. Mem. ALA, Iowa Libr. Assn., Nat. Assn. for Edn. of Young Children, Nat. Storytelling Assn. Democrat. Home: 312 Kimball Rd Iowa City IA 52245-5825 Office: Iowa City Pub Libr 123 S Linn St Iowa City IA 52240-1803

GREEN, DENNIS S., broadcast executive; b. Coral Gables, Fla., June 9, 1965; s. Milton S. and Harriet (Plotkin) G. BA in Comm. and Polit. Sci., Ind. U., 1986; MS in Sports Mgmt., U. Ill., Chgo., 1992. Sports dir., cmty. affairs prodr. Gables City Network, Coral Gables, Fla., 1986-91; freelance sportscaster Sta. WLRN-TV, Miami, Fla., 1987-91, Sunshine Network, Orlando, Fla., 1988-91; sports info. asst. U. Ill., Chgo., 1991-93; dir. corporate devel. Mid-Continent Conf., Naperville, Ill., 1992-94; dir. affiliate rels./ops. Ill./Wis. Radio Network, Chgo., 1994—. Contbr. articles to mags. Jr. bd. dirs. Mus. Broadcast Comm., Chgo., 1994—. Mem. Ill. Broadcasters Assn. (assoc.), Wis. Broadcasters Assn. (assoc.), Nat. Assn. State Radio Networks. Home: 3732 N Pine Grove Ave #1-BC Chicago IL 60613-4131 Office: Ill Radio Network 430 E Erie St Ste 505 Chicago IL 60610

GREEN, DIANA BEESLEY, athletic company executive; b. Garden City, Kans., July 13, 1951. BS in Child and Family Devel., Kans. State U., 1973. Sr. dir. ops. Golf Course Supervision Assn. Am., Lawrence, Kans., 1975-93; v.p. St. Andrews Corp. Inc., Lawrence, 1993—. Contbr. articles to profl. jours. Mem. Am. Soc. Assn. Execs. (Internat. Achievement award 1993), U.S. Golf Assn. Republican. Methodist. Office: Saint Andrews Corp Inc PO Box 3407 Lawrence KS 66046-0407

GREEN, DONALD EDWARD, sociology educator; b. Muskogee, Okla., Nov. 10, 1955; s. William Lovell and Ouida Jewel (Ratliff) G.; m. Cheryl Denise Johnson, May 31, 1986; children: Tyler Johnson, Ashley Carlynn. BA in Sociology, U. Okla., 1978, MA in Sociology, 1979; PhD in Sociology, U. Minn., 1986. Instr. sociology U. Minn., Mpls., 1983-86, St. Cloud (Minn.) State U., 1986; asst. prof. U. Wis., Milw., 1986-93, assoc. prof., 1993—, chairperson dept. sociology, 1995—, chmn. instnl. rev. bd. for protection human subjects, 1991-92; manuscript reviewer Criminology, 1991-92. Co-editor: American Indians: Social Justice and Public, 1991; contbr. articles to profl. jours., chpts. to books. Mem. mktg. adv. bd. Milw. Indian Health Ctr., 1988-89; mem. workforce diversity task force Pub. Policy Forum, Milw., 1992; bd. dirs. Milw. Indian Econ. Devel. Agy., 1988—, vice chmn., 1991-92, chairperson, 1992-93; mem. adv. bd. Strength of Nations Project. Mem. Am. Sociol. Assn. (minority fellow 1980-85), Am. Soc. Criminology, Soc. for Study Social Problems (election com. 1989-90), Am. Indian C. of C. Wis. (bd. dirs. 1991, vice chmn. 1991), Phi Kappa Phi.

GREEN, DONALD EDWARD, dean; b. Wellington, Tex., Apr. 15, 1936; s. Lewis and Margaret Christene (Schoonover) G.; m. Ozella Marie Crawford, Sept. 7, 1956 (dec. May 1987); children: Kelly Don, Kevin Dale; m. Florence Elenor Huntt, July 28, 1988. BA, Abilene (Tex.) Christian U., 1958; MA, Tex. Tech U., 1959; PhD, U. Okla., 1969. Prof. Okla. Christian Coll., Oklahoma City, 1962-65, 68-69; prof. Cen. State U., Edmond, Okla., 1969-82, chmn. dept. history and geography, 1982-90; dean liberal arts Chadron (Nebr.) State Coll., 1990—; chmn. bd. Westerners Internat., Oklahoma City, 1988-90, bd. dirs. Okla. Hist. Soc., Oklahoma City, 1979-82, 84-90. Author: Land of Underground Rain, 1973 (Tex. Inst. Letters, 1974), The Creek People, 1973, Fifty Years of Service to West Texas Agriculture, 1977, Panhandle Pioneer, 1979 (Okie award, 1980), A Centennial History of the Oklahoma State University College of Agriculture, 1991; editor: Rural Oklahoma, 1977. Mem. Western History Assn., Indian Terr. Posse Westerners Internat. (sheriff 1984-85), Mari Sandoz Soc. (chmn. bd. dirs. 1991—), Phi Alpha Theta. Democrat. Home: 1190 Parkwood Rd Rapid City SD 57701-5342 Office: Chadron State College Office of Dean of Liberal Arts Chadron NE 69337

GREEN, FRANK EARL, civil engineer; b. Joplin, Mo., Nov. 24, 1931; s. Lloyd Cuthbertson and Gladys Alberta (Kennedy) G.; m. Joan Imogene (Wheeler),July 25, 1953; children: Kevin Joe, Keely Sue Green Hotchkiss. BS in Math., S.W. Mo. State U., 1953; BSCE, Kans. State U., 1958. Registered profl. engr., Mo., land surveyor, Mo. Hwy. designer Mo. Hwy. and Transp. Dept., Kansas City, 1958-61, sr. hwy. designer, 1962-65, dist. hwy. design engr., 1966-96; retired, 1996. Mem. adminstrv. coun., usher, mem. Grandview (Mo.) United Meth. Ch., 1970—. With Army Corps. of Engrs., 1953-55. Mem. ASCE (life, bd. dirs. Kansas City sect. 1987-91, sec.-treas. and pres.-elect 1992, pres. 1993), Nat. Soc. Profl. Engrs. (life), Mo. Soc. Profl. Engrs. (bd. dirs. Western chpt. 1985-91). Republican. Home: 5608 E 100th Ter Kansas City MO 64137-1312

GREEN, GEORGE HAROLD, JR., lawyer, consultant, researcher; b. Omaha, Apr. 8, 1956; s. George Harold and Harriet Rose (Lilly) G.; m. Carle Lynn Krumme, May 6, 1995. BS, U. Nebr., 1978, JD, 1983. Bar: Nebr. Store mgr., dir. B & R Stores, Inc., Lincoln, 1978-94; plain clothes security guard Wells Fargo Security Svcs., Lincoln, 1990; uniformed security guard Corp. Security, Lincoln, 1994—; trainor, pub. speaker Lincoln and Nebr. Jr. C. of C., 1989—. Vol. worker Capital Humane Soc., Lincoln, 1994; lector Springfield and Lincoln Catholic Chs., 1972-76. With US Army ROTC, 1974-76. Recipient Jaycee of Month award, 1988, Jaycee of Quarter award, 1989, Tenth Degree Jaycee award, 1992. Mem. Lincoln Stamp Club, Lincoln Jr. C. of C. (membership & growth dir. 1989-90, individual devel. v.p. 1990-91, adminstrv. v.p. 1993-94, parliamentarian 1994—, state dir. 1995-96, pres. 1996—), Nebr. Jr. C. of C. (individual devel. v.p. 1991-92, parliamentarian 1992-93), Jr. Chamber Internat. Home: 3630 S 56th St Lincoln NE 68506-4535

GREEN, HAROLD DANIEL, dentist; b. Scranton, Pa., Feb. 4, 1934; s. Harold Charles and Viola Mildred (Brown) G.; m. Cornelia Ann Ellis, Aug. 1, 1959; children: Scott Alan, Mary Ann. BA, Beloit Coll. (Wis.), 1956; DDS, Northwestern U., 1960. Gen. practice dentistry, Beloit, Wis., 1964—; dir. Beloit Savs. Bank, chmn. trust com., 1989—; mem loan com. Blackhawk State Bank, mem. fin. com., 1993. Contbr. articles to profl. jours. Active Wis. div. Am. Cancer Soc., 1964-75; 1st pres., co-organizer Citizen's Council Against Crime, Beloit; past officer, chmn. membership Beloit YMCA; pres. Beloit Brewers, chmn. bd., 1988-91, class A midwest league affiliate of Milw. Brewers baseball team, 1986-87; chmn. Student Achievers Program, Wis., No. Ill.; mem. adv. bd. Salvation Army; chmn. Beloiters for Coun.-Mgr., 1989; stateline chmn. Student Achiever Program, 1988, 93; bd. dirs. Greater Beloit Found., 1989—; chmn. nominating com. Greater Beloit Community Trust, Inc., 1991,93; chmn. adminstrv. bd., chmn. Council of Ministries, First United Methodist Ch., Beloit, pastor parish rels., 1995—; chmn. ann. dinner, bd. dirs., nominating com., fundraising, pub. speakers Beloit Crime Stoppers, 1993—, chmn., 1995-96; chmn. facilities study com. Sch. Dist. Beloit, 1991—; chmn. Eagle Scout bd. rev. Sinnisippi coun. Boy Scouts Am., 1995-96. Recipient award for creativity in dentistry Johnson & Johnson Co., 1970; 3 citations for Community Service United Givers Fund, 1970-75; Disting. Sevice citation Greater Beloit Assn. Commerce. Fellow Acad. Gen. Dentistry, Internat. Coll. Dentists. (Wis. editor), Am. Acad. Dental Practice Adminstrn. (past chmn. profl. liaison; mem. ADA (chmn. council on dental practice 1982-84), Wis. Dental Assn. (pres. 1979-80, trustee 1968-74), Wis. Dental Assn. Found., Rock County Dental Soc. (pres. 1976), Wis. Council of Professions (bd. dirs. 1974-80, pres. 1973-75), Chgo. Dental Soc., Greater Milw. Dental Assn., Fedn. Dentaire Internationale, Pierre Fauchard Acad., Am. Acad. History of Dentistry, Lions (beloit programs, 1993—, past pres.)Delta Sigma Delta. Avocations: cycling, golf, basketball, running, fishing. Home: 2207 Collingswood Dr Beloit WI 53511-2332 Office: 419 Pleasant St Beloit WI 53511-6249

GREEN, HENRY LEONARD, physician; b. Detroit, Apr. 9, 1931; s. Albert and Fanya (Newman) G.; m. Loretta Laurie Teplitz; children: Toby, Jennifer, Cheryl, Joseph. BA with distinction, U. Mich., 1951, MD, 1955. Cert. Am. Bd. Internal Medicine in internal medicine and cardiology. Intern Detroit Receiving Hosp., 1955-56; resident internal medicine Henry Ford Hosp., Detroit, 1956-59, resident cardiology, 1959-61; pvt. practice Southfield, Mich., 1963—; dir. cardiac care unit surveillance project, 1969-74; attending physician Sinai Hosp. of Detroit, 1963—, Providence Hosp., Southfield, 1963—; clin. assoc. prof. Wayne State U. Sch. Medicine, Detroit; attending physician William Beaumont Hosp., 1995; dir. pacemaker clinic Providence Hosp.; mem. adv. and exec. coms. Inter-Soc. Commn. for Heart Disease Resources, N.Y.C., 1968-84. Author various med. software programs; contbr. articles to med. jours.; author various oral presentations nat. and local med. meetings. Lt. comdr. USN, 1961-63. Recipient Grand award Mich. Hosp. Assn., Detroit, 1973. Fellow ACP, Am. Coll. Cardiology, Am. Heart Assn., Mich. Heart Assn. (assoc. Coun. on Clin. Cardiology); mem. Phi Beta Kappa, Alpha Omega Alpha. Office: 22250 Providence Dr Ste 600 Southfield MI 48075-6214

GREEN, JAMES MURNEY, software products executive; b. Evanston, Ill., May 28, 1944; s. Harold Elmer and Helen Elizabeth (DeLong) G. BSBA, Northwestern U., 1966; M Mgmt., Kellogg Grad. Sch. Mgmt., Evanston, 1973. Circulation mgr. Packaging Mag., Chgo., 1963-66; systems analyst Dow Chem., Pitman Moore div., Indpls., 1967-69; group leader Systems Dynamics, Inc., Indpls., 1969-71; v.p. Info. Dynamics Inc., Indpls., 1971-73; pres. Green & Assocs. Ltd., Indpls., 1973-86, The Generic Software Pl., Indpls., 1986-89; CEO Software Testing Labs., Indpls., 1989—; twice featured in Entrepreneur Mag., 1987, 88; guest speaker Shareware Industry Conf., 1992-94. Co-developer RSAC computer software rating sys. Mem. Assn. Shareware Profls. (meetings chmn. 1992—), Shareware Trade Assn. and Resources (pres. 1994-95). Home: 7916 Hunters Path Indianapolis IN 46214-1535 Office: Software Testing Labs PO Box 19771 Indianapolis IN 46219-9771

GREEN, JERIE IRELAND, editor, reporter, freelance writer; b. Cleve., Mar. 6, 1950; d. Thurman James and Lenore Joyce (Pollack) Ireland; m. Mark Wayne Stacks, Mar. 27, 1971 (div. 1974); m. Donald Timothy Green, Dec. 28, 1977; children: KAthy, Jonathan, Christopher, Corey. Student, Emory and Henry Coll., 1968-72, Cuyahoga Community Coll., 1970-78. Freelance writer Madison, Ohio, 1977—; reporter Lake County Telegraph, Painesville, Ohio, 1979-82; reporter Western Res. Bus. Rev. (name changed to Bus. Rev. N.E. Ohio, 1989), Willoughby, Ohio, 1982-86, editor, 1988-89; reporter Lake County News Herald, Willoughby, 1988; editor City to Country Guide, Willoughby, 1989—, Lake County Bus. Jour., Willoughby, 1991—. Contbr. articles to Cleve. mag., Ohio mag., Dog Fancy mag., Mktg. Today, Legal Econs., also others. Recipient 2d place award UPI-Ohio, 1979, AP-Ohio, 1980, Ohio Newspaperwomen's Assn., 198l. Democrat. Unitarian. Office: The Lake County Bus Jour 4772 E 355th St Willoughby OH 44094-4632

GREEN, JERRY HOWARD, investment banker; b. Kansas City, Mo., June 10, 1930; s. Howard Jay and Selma (Stein) G.; BA, Yale U., 1952. m. Betsy Bozarth, July 18, 1981. Pres., Union Chevrolet, 1955-69, Union Securities, Inc., Kansas City, 1969—, Union Bancshares, Inc., Kansas City, 1969-76; chmn. Union Bank, Kansas City, 1976—, Budget Rent-A-Car Mo., Inc., 1961—, Budget Rent-A-Car Memphis, Inc., Budget Rent-A-Car Wichita, Kans., Broadway Ford, Inc., Kansas City, 1989—; pres. Pembroke Bancshares, Kansas City, 1983—; chmn., bd. dirs. Citizens Bank So. Mo., Ava, 1980—, Broadway Ford, Inc., Kansas City; bd. dirs. Century City Artists Corp., L.A. Bd. dirs. Jackson County Pension Plan Com.; bd. dirs., chmn. bd. Mo. Higher Education Loan Authority, 1987—; chmn. bd. Mo. Valley Bawcshares, Mountain Grove, Mo.; chmn. Yale Class of 1952 Reunion Gift. 1st lt. USAF, 1952-55. Mem. Am. Bankers Assn., Yale Alumni Assn. (bd. dirs.). Republican. Clubs: Kansas City, Oakwood Country, Saddle and Sirloin, University. Home: 5200 Belleview Ave Kansas City MO 64112-2336 Office: Union Bank 12th And Wyandotte Kansas City MO 64105

GREEN, JOHN LAFAYETTE, JR., education executive; b. Trenton, N.J., Apr. 3, 1929; m. Harriet Hardin Hill, Nov. 8, 1962; 1 child, John Lafayette III. BA, Miss. State U., 1955; MEd, Wayne State U., 1971; PhD, Rensselaer Poly. Inst., 1974. Asst. to treas. Internat. Paper Co., 1955-57; mem. faculty U. Calif., Berkeley, 1957-65; v.p. U. Ga., Athens, 1965-71, Rensselaer Poly. Inst., Troy, N.Y., 1971-76; exec. v.p. U. Miami, 1976-80; sr. v.p. U. Houston, 1980-81; pres. Washburn U., Topeka, Kans., 1981-88; exec. dir. Assn. Collegiate Bus. Schs. and Programs, Overland Park, 1988-95; pres, CEO Internat. Fedn. for Bus. Edn., Overland Park, Kans., 1992—; chmn. bd. dirs. Strategic Planning/Mgmt. Assocs., Inc., Overland, Kans., 1981—; past pres. Kansas City chpt. Planning Forum, past pres. Topeka and Kansas City chpts. Author: Budgeting, 1967, (with others) Cost Accounting, 1969, Administrative Data Processing, 1970, Strategic Planning, 1980, Strategic Planning: A System for Businesses, 1986, A Strategic Planning System for Higher Education, 1987, Strategy Development and Implementation for Banks, 1988. Bd. dirs. Boy Scouts Am., Topeka, 1983-85. With U.S. Army 1951-53. Recipient Disting. Kansan of Yr. in Pub. Adminstrn. award Topeka Capital Jour., 1984, Kans. Pub. Adminstr. of Yr. award Am. Soc. Pub. Adminstrn., 1984, Disting. Exec. award Mktg. Exec. Kans., 1984, Edn. Leader's Hall of Fame award, 1995. Mem. AAUP, Conf. Bd., Am. Mgmt. Assn., Fin. Execs. Inst., Demographics Inst., Masons, Shriners, Royal Order of Jesters, Phi Delta Kappa, Beta Alpha Psi, Phi Kappa Phi, Pi Kappa Alpha, Delta Sigma Pi. Republican. Presbyterian. (elder, deacon). Home: 12018 Connell Dr Overland Park KS 66213-2526 Office: 7007 College Blvd Ste 420 Overland Park KS 66211-1524

GREEN, JOSEPH H., small business owner; b. Wheeling, W.Va., Sept. 13, 1946. BS, Ohio U., 1968; MS, Wheeling Coll., 1978. Owner, mgr. Shamrock Conduit Products Inc., Barnesville, Ohio.

GREEN, JOYCE, book publishing company executive; b. Taylorville, Ill., Oct. 22, 1928; d. Lynn and Vivian Coke (Richardson) Reinerd; m. Warren H. Green, Oct. 8, 1960. AA, Christian Coll., 1946; BS, MacMurray Coll., 1948. Pres. Warren H. Green, Inc., St. Louis, 1992—; exec. dir. Affirmative Action Assn. Am., 1977—; pres. InterContinental Industries, Inc., 1980—; chief exec. officer Pubs. Svc. Ctr. Mem. St. Louis C. of C., Jr. League Club, Media Club, Mo. Athletic Club, Media Club. Democrat. Methodist. Home: 12120 Hibler Rd Saint Louis MO 63141-6615 Office: 8356 Olive Blvd Saint Louis MO 63132-2814

GREEN, KEVIN H., financial consultant, lawyer; b. Chgo., May 25, 1958. JD, Northwestern Ill. U., 1983. CPA, CFP. Atty. Met. Structures, Chgo., 1986-93; fin. cons. Smith Barney Inc., Northbrook, Ill., 1993—. Bd. dirs. K.I.D.S.S., Chgo., 1992—, Resource Com. of Jewish Elderly, Chgo., 1991—. Mem. Chgo. Soc. Inst. Fin. Planners, Rotary. Office: Smith Barney Inc 57th Fl 5 Revere Dr Fl 57 Northbrook IL 60062-1566

GREEN, LINDA LOU, museum curator, educator; b. Springfield, Mo., Nov. 12, 1949; d. Kenneth Lee and Nell Maureen (McDaniel) G.; divorced; 1 child, James Anthony Gott. BA in Art History, S.W. Mo. State U., 1987; MA in Art History, U. Iowa, 1990. Tchg. asst., curatorial asst. Art Mus. U. Iowa, Iowa City, 1988-90, tchg. asst. Sch. Art and Art History, 1988-90; lectr. Tex. Tech U., Lubbock, 1990, S.W. Mo. State U., Springfield, 1990-91; asst. curator, collections Saginaw (Mich.) Art Mus., 1991; curator of edn. Paris Gibson Square Mus., Great Falls, Mont., 1992; asst. dir. Muscatine (Iowa) Art Ctr., 1992—; cons. Native Am. Art Springfield Art Mus., 1989; mus. del. Sister Cities Internat., Moscow and Kislovodsk, Russia, 1994; arts educator Leadership Muscatine, 1994—; art pals coord. Yamanashi Japan Iowa Sister States, 1995-96. Performer (video) Amerindian Beadwork from the Deadrick Collection, 1989; author: (poetry) Writers on the Avenue, 1993, Lyrical Iowa, 1994. Chmn. social issues com., mem. stavropol steering com. Iowa Sister States, Des Moines, 1994—; bd. dirs., v.p. Sister Cities Assn., Muscantine, 1993—; bd. edn. Muscantine Cmty. Schs., 1993-94. Mem. Am. Assn. Mus., Iowa Global Edn. Assn., Iowa Assn. Dispute Resolution, Iowa Mus. Assn. (chmn. edn. com. 1992—), Sister Cities Assn. (pres. 1996), Muscatine LWV (bd. dirs. 1995—), Mus. Edn. Roundtable. Office: Muscatine Art Ctr 1314 Mulberry Ave Muscatine IA 52761

GREEN, MARSHA LYNN, legal assistant; b. Phoenix, Mar. 3, 1952. Sec., receptionist Alexander, Noerper, Thomas, St. Louis, 1973-74; legal asst. Edward D. Jones & Co., St. Louis, 1978—. Vol. Girl Scouts U.S.A., St. Louis, 1988—. Democrat. Roman Catholic. Office: Edward D Jones & Co 12555 Manchester Rd Saint Louis MO 63131-3716

GREEN, MARY ELOISE, nutrition and food management educator; b. East Liberty, Ohio, June 10, 1903; d. Milton M. and Sylvia M. (Creviston) G. BS, Ohio State U., 1928, MS, 1933; PhD, Iowa State U., 1949. Elem. tchr. Perry Twp. Sch., East Liberty, 1923-26; high sch. tchr. Monroe Twp. Sch., West Liberty, Ohio, 1928-37, Brown Twp. Sch., Kilbourne, Ohio, 1937-39; instr. Ohio Wesleyan U., Del., 1937-39; from instr. to prof. Ohio State U., Columbus, 1939-72, prof. emeritus, 1972—. Fellow AAAS; mem. Am. Dietetic Assn., Am. Assn. Family and Consumer Scis., Inst. of Food Technologists, Pi Lambda Theta, Sigma Delta Epsilon, Iota Sigma Pi, Kappa Omicron Nu, Am. Assn. Univ. Women, Order of Eastern Star. United Methodist. Home: 116 W Como Ave Columbus OH 43202-1028

GREEN, MIKE, state legislator; b. Risco, Miss., Sept. 28, 1948. Student, Flint Jr. Coll., 1966-68. Tool and die worker; mem. from dist. 84 Mich. State Ho. of Reps., Lansing, 1995—, vice chmn. agr. com., mem. human svc. and transp. coms. Address: PO Box 300014 Lansing MI 48909-7514

GREEN, PHILLIP MICHAEL, neurologist, gerontologist; b. Washington, Apr. 20, 1944; s. Samuel and Ann Jeanette (Ralston) G.; children: Joshua, Adrian, Matthew, Ryan; m. Sharon Grace Green, Sept. 17, 1994. BS, U. Wis., 1965; MD, U. Md., 1969; MPA, Western Mich. U., 1989, Cert. in Gerontology, 1989. Diplomate Am. Bd. Psychiatry and Neurology (examiner 1979—), Am. Bd. Neurophysiology. Rotating intern Washington U. Hosps., St. Louis, 1969-70; resident in psychiatry U. Wis., Madison, 1970-71; resident in neurology Barnes Hosp. Group Washington U., 1971-74; staff neurologist Marshfield (Wis.) Clinic, 1976-82, EEG fellow, 1978-79, chmn. dept. neurology, 1981-82; neurologist Kalamazoo Neurology, 1982—; chmn. dept. geriatric medicine, dir. geriatric medicine Borgess Med. Ctr., Kalamazoo, 1987—; instr. VA Physician's Asst. Program, St. Louis, 1972-74, Sch. Phys. Therapy and Occupational Therapy, Sch. Medicine Washington U., 1973-74; asst. clin. prof. medicine and neurology Eastern Va. Med. Sch., 1975-76; clin. asst. prof. neurology U. Wis., Madison, 1977-82, clin. assoc. prof., 1982; clin. assoc. prof. medicine Mich. State U., Lansing, 1983—; adj. assoc. prof. gerontology Western Mich. U., 1984—. Contbr. numerous articles to profl. jours. Served to lt. commdr. USN, 1974-76. Recipient William G. Birch Ednl. Excellence award Physicians Assistance Program, 1984, V.K. Volk award Mich. Soc. Gerontology, 1986. Fellow Am. Acad. Neurology, Am. EEG Soc. (ethics and legal rels. com. 1979—, vice chmn. 1980—); mem. Am. Epilepsy Soc., Am. Geriat. Soc., Mich. Neurol. Soc., Mich. State Med. Soc., Kalamazoo Acad. Medicine, Wis. Neurol. Soc., Alzheimer's Disease and Related Disorders Soc. (bd. dirs. 1986—), Kalamazoo Valley Parkinsons Soc. (bd. dirs. 1985—). Democrat. Unitarian. Office: Kalamazoo Neurology 1717 Shaffer St Kalamazoo MI 49001-1647

GREEN, ROBERT DOUGLAS, engineer; b. Decatur, Ill., Oct. 29, 1946; s. Robert Eugene and Inez Gevrne (Marlow) G.; m. Jennifer Mary Bruenig, Mar. 15, 1970 (div. Jan. 1990); children: William Douglas, Ann Marie; m. Margaret Ela, June 18, 1993. Registered profl. engr., Wis.; lic. comml. pilot. Commd. officer U.S. Army C.E., 1967-73; pilot, comdr. Wis. N.G., 1973-81; project engr. Oscay Mayer & Co., 1977-81; base civil engr. Volk Field Air N.G. Base, 1981-88, comdr., 1988-94; mgr. dept. mil. facilities svcs. Mead & Hunt, Inc., Madison, Wis., 1994—. Mem. Reedsburg Lions Club (pres. 1985-94), Reedsburg Country Club (bd. dirs.). Republican. Home: 1136 College Ave Baraboo WI 53913 Office: Mead & Hunt Inc 6501 Watts Rd Madison WI 53719-2700

GREEN, ROBERT F., automotive company executive; b. Mansfield, Ohio, Feb. 21, 1964. Student, Hobard Welding Sch., Troy, Ohio, 1982. Welding supr. HS Automotive, Mansfield, 1984—. Mem. Lincoln Hts. Christian Union, Mansfield, 1979—. Home: 1502 Reiser Dr Mansfield OH 44905-2239 Office: HS Automotive 912 Hanna Rd Mansfield OH 44906-4600

GREEN, RUTH MILTON, retired college administrator, consultant; b. Sioux City, Iowa, Feb. 29, 1924; d. John and Myrtle Alma (Phipps) Milton; m. Robert Wood Green, Dec. 31, 1943 (dec. July 1989): children: Robert William, Sandra Lou Green Montignani. Student, Morningside Coll., 1943-45. Registrar East High Sch., Sioux City, Iowa, 1943; acct. Buehler Bros., Iowa City, 1947-49; asst. dir. tchr. placement Morningside Coll., Sioux City, 1951-55, mem. staff registrar's office, 1960-65, asst. to registrar, 1965-70, dir. spl. project funding, 1971-81, dir. Title III Strengthening Devel. Institutions program, 1975-84, v.p. instl. research, planning and spl. projects, 1984-94; ret., 1994; asst. to prin. Ames (Iowa) High Sch., 1955-59; pvt. cons. for edn. and non-profit agys. in spl. project funding. Pres. First Congregational Ch., Sioux City, 1980; co-chair City Hall Site Selection Com., Sioux City, 1991-93; mem. Main St. Energy Greenway Com., co-chair fundraising com.; bd. dirs. Siouxland Mental Health Agy., 1983-89, v.p. bd. dirs., 1995; bd. dirs. Mary Treglia Community House, Waco, pres. bd. dirs., 1995 . Named Woman of Excellence Women Aware, 1986. Mem. PEO. Democrat. Home: 3801 6th Ave Sioux City IA 51106-2826

GREEN, RUTHANN, marketing and management consultant; b. Streator, Ill., July 14, 1935; d. John Joseph and Edna Marie (Peters) G. BS in Edn., U. Ill., 1957. Elem. tchr. Jefferson Sch., Davenport, Iowa, 1957-59; tchr. Hinsdale (Ill.) Jr. High Sch., 1959-62; ednl. cons. Harcourt Brace & World, Chgo., 1962-63; exec. sec. Everpure, Inc., Oakbrook, Ill., 1963-68; ednl. cons. Houghton Mifflin Co., Europe, 1968-69, Palo Alto, Calif., 1969-77; sr. mktg. mgr. Houghton Mifflin Co., Boston, 1977-87; v.p., nat. sales mgr. Riverside Pub. Co., Chgo., 1987-89; v.p., dir. mktg. McDougal, Littell & Co., Evanston, Ill., 1990-92; v.p., gen. mgr. Open Court Pub. Co., Chgo., 1992-94; pres. Peters & Green, Inc., Chgo., 1994—. Author: WSIL: Why Should I Listen, 1987, 93. Mem. Chicagoland Radio Info. Svc., Inc. Recipient Svc. award Am. Arbitration Assn., 1987, Golden Reel of Excellence Internat. TV Assn., 1983. Mem. Am. Mktg. Assn., Nat. Assn. Women Bus. Owners, Internat. Reading Assn., U.S. Bd. on Books for Young People, People for Am. Way, Common Cause, Am. Arbitration Assn. Home and Office: 1310 N Ritchie Ct Apt 21A Chicago IL 60610-2178

GREEN, SALLY JANE, surgical nurse; b. Sullivan, Ind., Mar. 18, 1954; d. Herman A. and Norma (Hassinger) Smith; children: Paul Robert, William Allan, Catherine Claire. ADN, Vincennes U., 1974. RN, Ind.; cert. ACLS, CPR instr., ARC. Staff nurse St. Anthony Hosp., Terre Haute, Ind., 1974-75; office coord. Jones Clinic, Munster, Ind., 1975-79; staff nurse St. Margaret Hosp., Hammond, Ind., 1979-81; office mgr. for pvt. practice physician Hammond, 1979-81; dir. surg. svcs. Terre Haute Regional Hosp., 1981—; mem. computer task force com. HealthTrust, Inc., Nashville, 1991. Fellow Assn. Oper. Rm. Nurses (cert.). Home: 1253 Clover Ct Terre Haute IN 47802-9352

GREEN, SCOTT W., financial advisor; b. Biloxi, Miss., June 23, 1966. BA, Miami U., Oxford, Ohio, 1988. Fin. advisor Prudential Securities Inc., Cin., 1991—. Bd. dirs. Meml. Cmty. Ctr., Cin., 1995—. Republican. Episcopalian. Office: Prudential Securities Inc 525 Vine St Ste 1900 Cincinnati OH 45202-3124

GREEN, TIMOTHY P., state legislator; b. North Saint Louis, Mo., June 29, 1963; m. Lisa Ann Green, 1990. BBA, U. Mo. St. Louis. State rep. Dist. 73 Mo. State Congress; mem. appropriations health and mental health com., ins. com., munic com.; vice chmn. labor com.; constrn. electrician. *

GREEN, VINCENT SCOTT, writer; b. Wichita, Kans., Dec. 16, 1953; s. Edgar T. and Peggy Jo Green; m. Mary C. Hutton, Nov. 24, 1978; children: Molly, Maggie. B of Gen. Studies, U. Mich., 1975; JD, Washburn U., 1978; MFA, U. Va., 1988. Bar: Kans. 1978, S.D. 1990. Author: The Price of Victory, 1992, Extreme Justice, 1995. Capt. U.S. Army, 1978-83. Recipient Emerging Artist grant S.D. Arts Coun., 1990. Mem. Phi Beta Kappa. Democrat. Home and Office: RR 1 Box 290 Vermillion SD 57069-9547

GREENBERG, EVA MUELLER, librarian; b. Vienna, Austria, July 19, 1929; came to U.S., 1939; d. Paul and Greta (Scheuer) Mueller; m. Nathan Abraham Greenberg, June 22, 1952; children: David Stephen, Judith Helen, Lisa Pauline. AB, Harvard/Radcliffe Coll., 1951; MLS, Kent State U., 1975. Head reference McIntire Libr., Zanesville, Ohio, 1978; with Lorain (Ohio) Pub. Libr., 1978-81; head reference Elyria (Ohio) Pub. Libr., 1981-82; reference libr. adult svcs. Cuyahoga County Pub. Libr., Strongsville, Ohio, 1983-89; head adult svcs. Oberlin (Ohio) Pub. Libr., 1989—. Contbr. articles to profl. jours. Grantee Ohio Humanities Coun. for Pub. Programs. Mem. ALA, Ohio Libr. Assn. (coord. community info. task force). Home: 34 S Cedar St Oberlin OH 44074-1520 Office: Oberlin Pub Libr 65 S Main St Oberlin OH 44074-1603

GREENBERG, HARRY SETH, neurologist, educator; b. Bklyn., Sept. 28, 1946; s. Milton and Bertha (Bernstein) G.; m. Anne Ferris, Sept. 2, 1989. BA, Cornell U., 1968; MD, SUNY, 1973. Diplomate Am. Bd. Psychiatry and Neurology; lic. physician, Calif., Mich., N.Y. Intern medicine Upstate Med. Ctr., SUNY, Syracuse, 1973-74; resident neurology Stanford (Calif.) U. Med. Sch., 1974-77; fellow neuro-oncology Meml. Sloan-Kettering Cancer Ctr., N.Y.C., 1977-79; fellow neurology N.Y. Hosp., Cornell U., N.Y.C., 1978-79; asst. prof. neurology U. Mich., Ann Arbor, 1979-85, assoc. prof. neurology, 1985-91, prof., 1991—, neurology prof. surgery sect. neurosurgery, 1991—; dir. neuro-oncology program U. Mich. Cancer Ctr., 1987—; cons. U. Mich. Neurofibromatosis Ctr., 1985; cons. VA Med. Ctr., Ann Arbor, 1980—, vis. prof., 1990—; speaker various confs. throughout U.S., Europe, Japan. Editl. bds., reviewer Annals of Neurology, 1982—, Neurology, 1984—, Cancer Treatment Reports, 1984—, Jour. Neuro-Oncology, 1985—, Jour. Clin. Oncology, 1985—, N.Y. State Jour. Medicine, 1986—, Neurosurgery, 1988—, Molecular Medicine, 1995, Epilepsia, 1995, Cancer, 1995; assoc. editor Neurobase, 1993—; contbr. articles to profl. jours., chpts. to books. Bd. dirs. U. Mich. Slusser Gallery, Ann Arbor, 1987—; bd. dirs. Ann Arbor Art Assn., 1990—, v.p. bd. dirs., 1993. Henry Viets scholar Nat. Myasthenia Gravis Found., 1970—; grantee NIH, Nat. Cancer Inst., U. Mich. Cancer Ctr. Support, 1988—, NIH, 1988—, NIH, Nat. Cancer Inst., 1992—, NIH, 1992. Fellow Am. Acad. Neurology; mem. Am. Fedn. Clin. Rsch., Am. Neurol. Assn. (membership adv. com. 1995), Am. Soc. Clin. Oncology, Am. Soc. Neurol. Investigation (Midwest councilor 180-86), S.W. Oncology Group, Mich. Neurol. Assn. (program chmn. 1979-86, v.p. 1993-95, pres. 1995—), Am. Assn. Neurosurgeons/Congress Neurol. Surgeons (joint tumor sect.), Mich. Cancer Ctr. (program dir. neuro-oncology), N.Y. Acad. Scis., Am. Brain Tumor Assn. (sci. adv. bd. 1994—). Home: 2611 Wylie Rd Dexter MI 48130-9781 Office: U Mich Dept Neurology 1914/0316 Taubman Ann Arbor MI 48109

GREENBERG, PATRICIA THOMAS, educational administrator; b. Corsicana, Tex., Mar. 14, 1959; d. Robert S. and Jettie (Schmidt) Thomas; m. Sanford Greenberg, May 20, 1994. BA, U. Tex., 1981; MEd, U. North Tex., 1992. Program officer Inst. Internat. Edn., Washington, 1993-94; sr. field rep. Inst. Internat. Edn., Chgo., 1994—. Mem. NAFSA: Assn. Internat. Educators, Phi Beta Kappa. Office: Inst Internat Edn 401 N Wabash # 722 Chicago IL 60611

GREENBERG, STEPHEN ROBERT, retired pathology educator; b. Omaha, May 5, 1927; s. Nathan Henry and Ruth (Levey) G.; m. Constance Bettine, June 4, 1952; children: Andrew Eugene, Nathan Henry. BS, St. Louis U., 1951, MS, 1952, PhD in Pathology, 1954. Asst. in pathology Clarkson Hosp., Omaha, 1954-55; instr. pathology Chgo. Med. Sch., 1955-57, assoc. in pathology, 1957-62, asst. prof., 1962-69, assoc. prof. pathology, 1969-93; lectr. Cook County Grad. Sch. Medicine, Chgo., 1973—. Contbr. over 150 articles to profl. jours. Forensic Scis. Found. grantee, 1988-91. Fellow Inst. of Medicine of Chgo.; mem. Am. Soc. Clin. Pathologists, Am. Acad. Forensic Scis., Am. Assn. Clin. Anatomists, Internat. Acad. Pathology, Masons (33 deg.). Republican. Hebrew.

GREENBERG, STEVE, brokerage house executive. Pres. Alaron Trading Corp., Chgo. Office: Alaron Trading Corp 822 W Washington St Chicago IL 60607*

GREENBLATT, DEANA CHARLENE, elementary education educator; b. Chgo., Mar. 13, 1948; d. Walter and Betty (Lamasky) Beisel; BEd., Chgo. State U., 1969; MA in Guidance and Counseling, Roosevelt U., 1973; m. Mark Greenblatt, June 22, 1975. Tchr., counselor Chgo. Pub. Schs., 1969-75, City Colls. of Chgo. GED-TV, 1976; tchr. Columbus (Ohio) Pub. Schs., 1976-86; tchr. Chgo. Pub. Schs., 1993—; participant learning exchange, Chgo. Active B'nai B'rith; vol. Right-to-Read, Columbus; mem. Community Learning Exchange, Acad. Yr. in U.S.A. Com. Counselor, 1989—. Columbus. Cert. tchr. K-9, Ill., Ohio; cert. personnel guidance, Ill., Ohio; cert. Chgo. Bd. Edn. Mem. Am. Personnel and Guidance Assn., Internat. Platform Assn., B'nai B'rith Women Club (chpt. v.p.). Democrat. Home: 3820 W Touhy Ave Lincolnwood IL 60645-1026

GREENBURG, BARRY HOWARD, lawyer; b. Chgo., Oct. 12, 1937; s. Julius Nelson and Bertha (Wolf) G.; m. Cynthia Dalbey, May 30, 1975; 1 child, Jennifer Joanna. Bachelor's degree, U. Ill., 1959; LLB, DePaul U., 1963. Bar: Ill. 1963. Assoc. Sennett, Levin, Craine & Stride, Chgo., 1963-64, Anthony Lazzara & Assocs., Chgo., 1964-65, Haft, Shapiro & Haft, Chgo., 1965-66; counsel City of Chgo./Corp. Counsel, 1966-77; ptnr. Fisch, Lansky & Greenburg, Chgo., 1977-90, Greenburg & Hermann, Chgo., 1990—; cons. U.S. EPA, Washington, 1974-77, Chgo. Dept. Environ. Control, 1977-79; dir. WBBS TV-Channel 60, Chgo., 1976-85; guardian ad litum com. Cir. Ct. of Cook County. Bd. dirs. Jane Adams Hull House, Chgo., 1985-86. Mem. ABA, Ill. Bar Assn. (family law com.), Ill. Trial Lawyers Assn. Office: Greenburg & Hermann 161 N Clark St Ste 2828 Chicago IL 60601

GREENE, CHARLES W., financial advisor; b. Akron, Ohio, Sept. 11, 1953. BA, Notre Dame U., 1975. Acct. Edward Hines Lumber, Chgo., 1975-88; fin. advisor Smith Barney Inc., Milw., 1988—. Mem. Kiwanis. Republican. Roman Catholic. Home: S 108 W 34612 S Shore Dr Mukwonago WI 53149 Office: Smith Barney Inc 411 E Wisconsin PO Box 2065 Milwaukee WI 53201

GREENE, CHRISTOPHER WILLIAM, marketing professional; b. Tampa, Fla., Dec. 17, 1957; s. Theodore William and Shelia (Mobley) G.; m. Dianne Magdelyn Wisneski, Apr. 16, 1983; children: Jessica Julianna, Theodore Chesley. BS in Park Adminstrn., Recreation, Western Ky. U., 1980. Sales rep. instnl. div. Procter & Gamble Distbg. Co., Louisville, 1980-81; ter. mgr. consumer products div. Beecham Products, St. Louis, 1981-83; owner, pres. C.W. Sweeps Residential and Comml. Bldg. Maintenance, St. Louis, 1983-84; regional mgr. consumer products div. J. Strickland & Co., St. Louis, 1984-88; pres., owner Chris Greene Assocs. Midwest Mktg., Cons./Mfrs. Rep., St. Louis, 1988—. Vol. Spl. Olympics, St. Louis, 1981-84, St. Joseph's Cath. Ch., Cottleville, Mo., 1990—. Named Amb. of Good Will Gov. of Ky., 1980; recipient cert. of appreciation Spl. Olympics of Ky., 1979, 80, Big Bros. and Big Sisters of Bowling Greene, Ky., 1980, Western Ky. Student Vol. Bur., 1980. Mem. Sales and Mktg. Execs. St. Louis, Regional Commerce and Growth Assn. St. Louis, Pi Kappa Alpha. Office: Chris Green Assocs 12 Plaza 94 Saint Peters MO 63376-7405

GREENE, FORD C., health care products executive; b. Orlando, Fla., Feb. 17, 1955. AS, Calif. Coll. Health Scis., 1982. Cert. respiratory therpay technician; lic. respiratory care practitioner Ohio. Staff therapist Valley View Hosp., Ada, Okla., 1972-77; dir. respiratory svcs. Mercy Hosp. Anderson, Cin., 1978-92; pres. Greene Respiratory Svcs., Milford, Ohio, 1991—; cons. Respiratory Cons. Okla., Ada., 1973-76; v.p. sales and mktg. Anderson Med. Equipment, Milford, 1994—. Councilman Village of Chilo, Ohio, 1982-95. Mem. Am. Assn. Respiratory Care, Greater Respiratory Care Mgrs. Assn. Cin. (chmn. 1988-89). Republican. Baptist. Office: Greene Respiratory Svcs 817 Us 50 Milford OH 45150-9513

GREENE, VICTOR ROBERT, history educator; b. Newark, Nov. 15, 1933; s. Jerome Harold and Sally (Colt) G.; m. Laura Judith Offenhartz; children: Jessica, Geoffrey. BA cum laude, Harvard U., 1955; MA, U. Rochester, 1960; PhD, U. Pa., 1963. Asst., assoc. prof. Kans. State U., Manhattan, 1963-71; assoc. prof., prof. U. Wis., Milw., 1971—; mem. history com. Statue of Liberty-Ellis Island Com., 1989-90; mem. planning com. Harvard Encyclopedia of Am. Ethnic Groups, 1971-79. Author: Slavic Community on Strike, 1968, For God and Country, 1975, Immigrant Leaders, 1987, A Passion for Polka, 1992. Recipient summer rsch. grant NEH, 1967, Nat. Humanities Inst. fellowship Yale U., 1975-76, sr. Fulbright award Fed. Rep. of Germany, 1980-81, Fulbright grant U.K., 1990, NEH sr. fellowship, 1987-88. Mem. Immigration History Soc. (pres. 1985-88, editor 1968-71). Office: U Wis-Milw History Dept Milwaukee WI 53201

GREENFIELD, JANE WEISS, library director; b. N.Y.C., Oct. 5, 1941; d. Harry and Ruth (Goldstein) Weiss; m. Robert M. Greenfield, June 4, 1967; children: Elaine, Elliott. BA, U. Rochester, 1963; MLS, Simmons Coll., 1964. Adult svcs. libr. N.Y. Pub. Libr., 1964-67; asst. dir. Cook Meml. Libr., Libertyville, Ill., 1968-70; from reader's advisor to coord. adult svcs. Evanston (Ill.) Pub. Libr., 1975-87; exec. dir. Highland Park (Ill.) Pub. Libr., 1987—. Mem. Highland Park Sister City Found., 1994—; chair Coll. of Lake County S.E. Adv. Com., 1994—. Mem. ALA (Libr. Adminstrn. and Mgt. Assn. staff devel. com. 1983-84, pers. adminstrn. sect. 1986-87, edtl. adv. com. 1990-94, publ. com. 1994—, ALA interlibr. loan com. 1980-84, Libr. Orgn. and Mgmt. sect.). Home: 2627 Reese Ave Evanston IL 60201 Office: Highland Park Pub Libr 494 Laurel Ave Highland Park IL 60035

GREENFIELD, JOHN CHARLES, bio-organic chemist; b. Dayton, Ohio, 1945; s. Ivan Ralph and Mildred Louise (House) G.; m. Liga Miervaldis, aug. 2, 1980; children: John Hollen, Mark Richard. BS cum laude, Ohio U., 1967; PhD, U. Ill., 1974. Instr. sci. area h.s. Dayton, 1968-71; grad. rsch. asst. U. Ill., 1971-74; postdoctoral rsch. fellow Swiss Fed. Inst. Tech., Zurich, 1975-76; rsch. chemist infectious diseases rsch. Upjohn Co., Kalamazoo, 1976-82, sr. rsch. scientist drug metabolism rsch., 1982-93; sr. project mgr. Upjohn Labs., Kalamazoo, 1993-95, Pharmacia & Upjohn Inc., Kalamazoo, 1995—; lectr. in field. Contbr. articles to sci. jours.; patentee in field. Adult leader Boy Scouts Am. Am.-Swiss Found. for Sci. Exchange fellow, 1975; NSF-NATO postdoctoral fellow, 1975-76. Mem. AAAS, Am. Chem. Soc. (chmn. Kalamazoo sect. 1994, Disting. Svc. award 1996), N.Y. Acad. Scis., Internat. Soc. for Study of Xenobiotics, Internat. Isotope Soc., Am. Assn. Pharm. Scientists, Sigma Xi, Phi Eta Sigma, Blue Key, Phi Lambda Upsilon, Delta Tau Delta. Home: 6695 East Ave Richland MI 49083-9729 Office: Pharmacia & Upjohn Inc 7000 Portage Rd Kalamazoo MI 49001

GREENFIELD, LEE, state legislator; b. Bklyn., July 29, 1941; s. Solomen and Edith (Herschman) G.; m. Marcia Greenfield, Nov. 25, 1965. BS in Physics, Purdue U., West Lafayette, Ind., 1963; postgrad., U. Minn., 1963-73. Instr. applied math. U. Minn., Mpls., 1964-73; prin. asst. Hennepin County Bd. Commrs., Mpls., 1975-77; mgmt. analyst Office of Planning & Devel., Hennepin County, Mpls., 1977; rep. Minn. No. of Reps., St. Paul, 1979—; mem. steering com. Reforming State Group, N.Y.C., 1993-94, chmn., 1994—. Bd. dirs. Twin City Cmty. Program for Affordable Health Care, Mpls., 1982-84, Arthritis Found., Mpls., 1988-90, Freeport West, Mpls., 1982—, Ams. for Dem. Action, Mpls., 1979—, v.p., 1976-78. Recipient Dwight V. Dixon award Mental Health Assn. Minn., 1994. Mem. Mental Health Assn. Minn. (Disting. Svc. award 1987), Planned Parenthood of Minn. (Pub. Svc. award 1993). Mem. Democratic-Farmer-Labor Party. Jewish. Office: Minnesota House of Reps State Capitol Saint Paul MN 55155

GREENGUS, SAMUEL, academic administrator, religion educator; b. Chgo., Mar. 11, 1936; s. Eugene and Thelma (Romirowsky) G.; m. Lesha Bellows, Apr. 30, 1957; children: Deana, Rachel, Judith. Student, Hebrew Theol. Coll., Chgo., 1950-58; MA, U. Chgo., 1959, PhD, 1963. Prof. semitic langs. Hebrew Union Coll.-Jewish Inst. Religion, Cin., 1963-89, Julian Morgenstern prof. bible and near eastern lit., 1989—, dean rabbinic sch., 1979-84, dean Cin. campus, 1985-87, dean sch. grad. studies, 1985-90, dean faculty, 1987—, v.p. for Acad. affairs, 1990—; vis. lectr. U. of Dayton, Ohio, 1964-69, Leo Baeck Coll., London, 1976-77; area supr. Tel Gezer Excavation, Israel, 1966-67; mem. bd. editors Hebrew Union Coll. Ann. Author: Old Babylonian Tablets from Ishchali and Vicinity, 1979, Studies in Ishchali Documents, 1986; mem. bd. editors Zeitschrift fur Altorientalische und Biblische Rechtsgeschichte; contbr. articles to profl. jours. Mem. Cin. Community Hebrew Schs. Bd., 1970-75; mem. vis. com. Sch. for Creative and Performing Arts, Cin., 1980-82; chmn. acad. officers, Greater Cin. Consortium Colls. and Univs., 1984-85, mem. exec. com., 1989—. Am. Council Learned Socs. fellow, 1970-71, Am. Assn. Theol. Schs. fellow, 1976-77. Mem. Am. Oriental Soc., Assn. Jewish Studies, Soc. Bibl. Lit., Phi Beta Kappa. Jewish. Office: Hebrew Union Coll Jewish Inst Religion 3101 Clifton Ave Cincinnati OH 45220-2404

GREENHILL, H. GAYLON, academic administrator. Chancellor U. Wis., Whitewater. Office: U Wis-Whitewater Office of Chancellor 800 W Main Whitewater WI 53190

GREENKORN, ROBERT ALBERT, chemical engineering educator; b. Oshkosh, Wis., Oct. 12, 1928; s. Frederick John and Sophie (Phillips) G.; m. Rosemary Drexler, Aug. 16, 1952; children: David Michael, Eileen Anne, Susan Marie, Nancy Joanne. Student, Oshkosh State Coll., 1951-52; B.S., U. Wis., 1954, M.S., 1955, Ph.D., 1957. Postdoctoral fellow Norwegian Tech. Inst., 1957-58; rsch. engr. Jersey Prodn. Rsch. Co., Tulsa, 1958-63; lectr. U. Tulsa, 1958-63; assoc. prof. theoretical and applied mechanics Marquette U., Milw., 1963-65; assoc. prof. chem. engring. Purdue U., Lafayette, Ind., 1965-67, prof., head chem. engring. dept., 1967-72, asst. dean engring., 1972-76, assoc. dean engring., dir. engring. expt. sta., 1976-80, v.p., assoc. provost, 1980-86; v.p. programs Purdue Rsch. Found., 1980-94, v.p. rsch., 1986-92, v.p. rsch., dean grad. sch., 1993-94, spl. asst. to the pres., 1994—, v.p. spl. programs, 1994; R. Games Slayter disting. prof. chem. engring., 1995—; rsch. coord. Ind. Pollution Prevention Inst., 1994—; dir. Tech. Assistance Program, 1996—. Author: (with D.P. Kessler) Transfer Operations, 1972, (with K.C. Chao) Thermodynamics of Fluids: An Introduction to Equilibrium Theory, 1975, (with D.P. Kessler) Modeling and Data Analysis for Engineers and Scientists, 1980, Flow Phenomena in Porous Media, 1983; contbr. articles to profl. jours. Served with USN, 1946-51. Decorated D.F.C., Air medal with two oak leaf clusters; recipient Fellow Members awd., Am. Soc. for Engineering Education, 1992. Fellow AIChE, Am. Soc. Engring. Edn.; mem. AAAS, Soc. Petroleum Engrs., Am. Chem. Soc., Am. Geophys. Union, Sigma Xi, Phi Eta Sigma, Tau Beta Pi, Phi Gamma Delta. Roman Catholic. Home: 151 Knox Dr West Lafayette IN 47906-2147

GREENLEE, MICHAEL LARRY, tax specialist; b. Wichita, Kans., Dec. 15, 1954; s. Dale E. and Mary F. (Gebhardt) G.; m. Marcia A. McHugh, Sept. 30, 1978; children: Laura, Elizabeth, Amber. BBA, Wichita State U., 1976. Cert. internal auditor Inst. Internal Auditors. Operational auditor Cessna Aircraft Co., Wichita, 1976-80; sr. operational auditor The Boeing Co., Wichita, 1980-83, tax mgr., 1983-92, mgr. tax/fin. acctg., 1993—. Mem. Boeing Mgmt. Club (treas. 1986-92, pres. 1993-94), Amateur Softball Assn. (treas. 1994-96), Wichita Ofcls. Assn. (bd. mem. 1991), Kans. C. of C. and Industry, Wichita C. of C. Republican. Roman Catholic. Home: 11710 First Wichita KS 67212 Office: The Boeing Co PO Box 7730 K11-14 Wichita KS 67277

GREENOUGH, WILLIAM TALLANT, psychobiologist, educator; b. Seattle, Oct. 11, 1944; s. Harrison and Maryon C. (Whitten) G.; 1 dau., Jennifer Anne. B.A., U. Oreg., 1964; M.A., UCLA, 1966, Ph.D., 1969. Instr. U. Ill., Urbana-Champaign, 1968-69; asst. prof. U. Ill., 1969-73, assoc. prof., 1973-77, chair neural and behavioral biology program, 1977-87, prof. psychology, cell and structural biology, 1978—; assoc. dir. Beckman Inst. for Advanced Sci. and Tech., 1987-91; vis. prof. psychobiology U. Calif., Irvine, 1972; vis. prof. psychology U. Wash., 1975-76; program chmn. Winter Conf. on Brain Rsch., 1984-85, conf. chair, 1994-95; panel mem. integrative neural sys. NSF, 1987-91; dir. NSF Ctr. of Neurobiology of Learning and Memory, 1989-94; v.p., exec. com. Forum on Rsch. Mgmt., Fed. Behavioral, Psychol. and Cognitive Scis., 1991-93; mem. sci. adv. bd. Am. Psychol. Assn. Sci. Directorate; mem. NSF Biol. Sci. Directorate Adv. Com. Editor: (with R.N. Walsh) Environments as Therapy for Brain Dysfunction, 1976, (with J.M. Juraska) Developmental Neuropsychobiology, 1987; co-editor jour. Neurobiol. Learning and Memory, 1984—; contbr. numerous articles to profl. jours. Cattell Found. fellow, 1975-76; USPHS and NSF grantee, 1969—; U. Ill. sr. scholar, 1985-88. Fellow AAAS, APA, Am. Psychol. Soc. (William James Fellow award), Soc. Exptl. Psychology; mem. NAS, Soc. Neurosci. (councilor 1990-94), Soc. Devel. Neurosci., Soc. Devel. Psychobiology (bd. dirs. 1977-80), Sigma Xi. Home: 1002 S Busey Ave Urbana IL 61801-4029 Office: U Ill Beckman Inst 405 N Mathews Ave Urbana IL 61801-2325

GREENSPAN, DANIEL S., molecular biologist; b. Jersey City, Aug. 31, 1951; s. Aaron and Doris (Greenspan) G. BA, NYU, 1974, MS, 1978, PhD, 1981. Postdoctoral fellow dept. human genetics Yale U., New Haven, 1981-84, rsch. scientist, mem. faculty, 1984-86; asst. prof. pathology U. Wis., Madison, 1986-92, assoc. prof., 1992—. Contbr. articles to profl. jours. Arthritis Found. fellow, 1984-87; prin. investigator NIH. Mem. Am. Soc. Biochemistry and Molecular Biology, N.Y. Acad. Scis., Am. Soc. Microbiology, Am. Soc. Human Genetics, Sigma Xi. Jewish. Avocations: sailing, scuba diving. Office: U Wis Dept Pathology 470 N Charter St Madison WI 53706-1509

GREENSTEIN, JULIUS SIDNEY, zoology educator; b. Boston, July 13, 1927; s. Samuel and Helen (Shriber) G.; m. Joette Mason, Aug. 23, 1954; children: Gail Susan, Jodi Beth, Jay Mason, Blake Jeffrey, Joette Elise. BA, Clark U., 1948; MS, U. Ill., 1951, PhD, 1955; postgrad., Harvard U., 1966. Mem. faculty U. Mass., Amherst, 1954-59; faculty Duquesne U., Pitts., 1959-70, chmn. dept. biol. scis., 1961-70, prof., 1964-70; prof., chmn. dept. biology State SUNY, Fredonia, 1970-74, acting dean arts and scis., 1973-74; dean math. and natural scis. Shippensburg (Pa.) U., 1974-80; also dir. Ctr. for Sci. and the Citizen; pres. Ctrl. Ohio Tech. Coll., 1980-94, pres. emeritus, 1994—; dean, dir. Ohio State U., Newark, 1980-94, prof. zoology, 1980—; vis. lectr. Am. Inst. Biol. Scis., 1966-76; disting. vis. prof. USAF Acad., 1994-95. Author: Contemporary Readings in Biology, 1971, Readings in Living Systems, 1972; spl. editor Internat. Jour. Fertility, 1958-69, Contraception, 1970-77; columnist Newark Advocate, 1981-93, Licking Countian, 1993-94; contbr. articles to profl. jours. Mem. Carnegie Civic Symphony Orch.; mem. sci. adv. bd. Human Life Found.; trustee Licking Meml. Hosp., Licking County Symphony Orch.; mem. campaign cabinet United Way Licking County; exec. bd. Cen. Ohio Rural Consortium and Pvt. Industry Coun.; mem. higher edn. panel Am. Coun. on Edn., labor com. Higher Edn. Coun. Ohio. Served in armored div. AUS, World War II. Recipient Wisdom award honor, 197O. Mem. AAAS, Am. Assn. Acad. Deans, Am. Assn. Univ. Admintrs., Am. Assn. Anatomists, Am. Inst. Biol. Scis., Internat. Fertility Assn., Am. Soc. Zoologists, Am. Fertility Soc., Soc. Study Fertility (Eng.), Coun. Biol. Editors, Pa. Acad. Sci. (editorial bd. 1963-70), N.Y. State Acad. Sci., Soc. Study Devel. Biology, Ohio Assn. Regional Campuses (vice chair 1988-89, chair 1989-90, pres.), North Cen. Assn. Colls. and Schs. (cons., evaluator), Newark C. of C., Rotary, Sigma Xi. Home: 1284 Howell Dr Newark OH 43055-1742 Office: Ohio State U at Newark University Dr Newark OH 43055-1797

GREENSTREET, ROBERT CHARLES, architect, educator; b. London, June 8, 1952; s. Joseph Philip Henry and Joan (Dean) G.; m. Karen Eloise Holland, Sept. 6, 1975. Diploma in architecture, Oxford Poly. Inst., 1976, PhD in Architecture, 1983. Registered architect, Eng. Vis. asst. prof. Kans. State U., 1978-79; asst. prof. U. Kans., 1979-80; vis. prof. Ball State U.,

Muncie, 1980-81; assoc. prof. U. Wis., 1981—, asst. vice chancellor, 1985-86, chmn. dept. architecture, 1986-90, dean Sch. Architecture and Urban Planning, 1990—. Author, co-author 7 books; contbr. more than 100 articles to profl. jours. Fellow Royal Soc. Arts; mem. AIA (assoc.), Royal Inst. Brit. Architects, Wis. Soc. Architects, Chartered Inst. Arbitrators, Faculty, Architects and Surveyors; mem. Am. Arbitration Assn., Assn. Collegiate Schs. of Architecture (pres. 1995-96). Anglican. Office: U Wis Dept Architecture PO Box 413 Milwaukee WI 53201-0413

GREENWALD, DOROTHY I., art educator; b. Harrison, Ark., Sept. 22, 1920; d. George W. and Caroline (Brown) Neal; student Sch. of Cosmetology, Miami, Okla., 1938-39, Craft Students League, N.Y.C., 1958-62; m. Harry Greenwald, Apr. 17, 1949. Owner, operator beauty salon and ladies ready to wear stores, 1940-58; instr. ceramic dept. Craft Student League, N.Y.C., 1962-80, Queens Museum Sch. of Art, Flushing, N.Y., 1980—; past chmn. Craft Students League of YWCA of N.Y.; chmn. crafts dept. Rockland Ctr. for Arts, West Nyack, N.Y.; pres., treas. Greenwald Electro-Mech. Cons., Inc., Whitestone, N.Y. Recipient awards Rockland Center for Art, 1972, L.I. Guild of Craftsmen, 1972, Artist-Craftsmen N.Y., 1975. Mem. World Craft Council, Am. Craft Council, Artist-Craftsmen N.Y. (pres. 1972-75), L.I. Guild of Craftsmen. Republican. Home: 12 James River Rd Kimberling City MO 65686-9702

GREENWALD, JEFFREY S., stockbroker; b. Phila., June 12, 1949. BS, U. Cin., 1971. Stockbroker Ohio Co., Cin., 1985-89, Kemper Securities, Cin., 1989-93, PaineWebber Inc., Cin., 1993—. Republican. Jewish. Office: PaineWebber Inc 312 Walnut St Ste 3300 Cincinnati OH 45202-4061

GREENWALT, MARY SUSAN, counselor; b. St. Louis, Dec. 26, 1946; d. LeGrand West and Susan Frances (Frier) Wheeler; m. Allen Duane Greenwalt, Apr. 11, 1992; stepchildren: Scott Harrison, Emily Megan. BS, So. Ill. U., 1968, MS, 1972; MBA, St. Louis U., 1982. Tchr. Lindbergh Sch. Dist., St. Louis, 1968-79, counselor, 1979—. Stage mgr. V-P Fair, St. Louis, 1984-93; vol. St. Louis Nursery Found. Book Fair, 1985-93. Recipient Tuition grant for women MBA students IBM, 1977. Mem. NEA, Mo. Edn. Assn., Lindbergh Edn. Assn. (pres. 1982-83), Am. Counseling Assn., Mo. Sch. Counselors Assn., St. Louis Suburban Sch. Counselors Assn. (Elem. Counselor of Yr. 1993), Jr. League St. Louis, Alpha Gamma Delta (St. Louis Alumnae Club). Republican. Methodist. Home: 14 Girard Dr Saint Louis MO 63119-4802 Office: Crestwood Elem Sch 1020 S Sappington Rd Saint Louis MO 63126-1005

GREENWOOD, DAVID WILBUR, elementary education educator; b. Bethesda, Ohio, Aug. 25, 1948; s. Wilbur Lewis and Helen M. (Breedlove) G.; m. Jeanette Ann Cheney, Apr. 17, 1976. BS in Edn., Ohio U., 1970. Cert. tchr., Ohio. Tchr. Cambridge (Ohio) City Schs., 1970—. Mem. NEA, Ohio Edn. Assn., Cambridge Edn. Assn. Methodist. Home: 9426 E 77 Dr Cambridge OH 43725-9656 Office: Park Elem Sch 150 Highland Ave Cambridge OH 43725-2573

GREENWOOD, DONALD THEODORE, retired aerospace engineering educator; b. Clarkdale, Ariz., Dec. 8, 1923; s. Arthur Irving and Elizabeth Alma (Swanson) G.; m. Esther Marie Harju, Mar. 17, 1951; children: Anne Elizabeth, Brian William. BSMechE, Calif. Inst. Tech., 1944, MS in Physics, 1948, PhDEE, 1951. Engr. Engring. Research Assocs., St. Paul., 1946-47; teaching fellow Calif. Inst. Tech., Pasadena, 1948-51; head analog computation Lockheed Aircraft Corp., Burbank, Cal., 1951-56; lectr. U. So. Calif., 1954-56; mem. faculty U. Mich., Ann Arbor, 1956-94, prof. aerospace engring., 1963-94, prof. emeritus, 1994—; vis. prof. U. Calif., San Diego, 1969-70. Contbr.: Computer Handbook, 1962, Classical Dynamics, 1977, Principles of Dynamics, 1988. Served with USNR, 1943-46. Mem. AAAS, Am. Inst. Aero. and Astronautics, ASME, Sigma Xi, Tau Beta Pi. Presbyterian. Home: 1630 Hanover Rd Ann Arbor MI 48103-5911

GREENWOOD, TIM, state legislator, lawyer; m. Linda J. Greenwood; children: Kelly, Katharine. BA, Denison U., 1971; JD, U. Toledo, 1978. Bar: Ohio 1978. Ptnr. Spengler & Nathanson, Toledo, Spengler, Nathanson, Heyman, McCarthy & Durfee, Toledo; mem. Ohio Senate, Columbus, 1994—. Mem. Ho. Ho. of Reps., Columbus, 1989-92, 93-94; active United Way, Toledo-Northwestern Ohio Foodbank. Named Freshman Legislator of Yr., 1990. Mem. Ohio Bar Assn., Toledo Bar Assn., Toledo Jr. Bar Assn. (pres.), Sylvania C. of C., Legis. Exch. Coun. Republican. Home: 4325 Mockingbird Ln Toledo OH 43623-3218*

GREER, CARL CRAWFORD, petroleum company executive; b. Pitts., June 12, 1940; s. Joseph Moss and Gene (Crawford) G.; m. Jerrine Ehlers, June 16, 1962 (div.); children: Caryn, Michael, Janet; m. Patricia Taylor, Feb. 4, 1989. B.S., Lehigh U., 1962; Ph.D., Columbia U., 1966. Assoc. in bus. Columbia U., 1964-66, asst. prof. banking and finance, 1966-67; retail mktg. mgr. Martin Oil Service Inc., Alsip, Ill., 1967-68; exec. v.p. Martin Oil Service Inc., 1968, pres., dir., 1968-76, chmn. bd., pres., 1976—; pres., dir. Martin Mktg. Corp. GP Martin Oil Mktg. Ltd., 1982, MEMCO Mgmt. Corp. GP Martin Exploration Mgmt. Co., 1985; bd. dirs. Fin. Assocs., Inc., Colo. Energy Corp. Mem. Beta Theta Pi, Tau Beta Pi, Beta Gamma Sigma, Omicron Delta Kappa. Presbyterian.

GREER, K. GORDON, banker; b. Tulsa, Oct. 28, 1936; s. H.K. and Afton (Goodman) G.; m. Nancy Lang, Nov. 22, 1958; children—Keith G., Scott A. B.S. in Banking and Fin., Okla. State U., 1958; postgrad. Grad. Sch. Banking, U. Wis.-Madison, 1964-67. Pres. Liberty Nat. Bank, Oklahoma City, 1958-84; chief exec. officer The First Nat. Bank and Trust Co., Tulsa, 1984—, pres., from 1984, now also chmn., dir. Served with Air Force N.G., 1958-64. Named to Hall of Fame, Bus. Adminstrn. Sch. Okla. State U., 1984. Mem. Am. Bankers Assn., Okla. Bankers Assn. (pres. 1983-84), Assn. Res. City Bankers. Democrat. Methodist. Clubs: So. Hills Country, Tulsa (Tulsa).

GREER, THOMAS H., newspaper executive; b. Nashville, July 24, 1942; s. Thomas H. and Eliza (Scruggs) G.; m. Shirley K. Greer, Aug. 5, 1967; children: Kasey Lynn, Janna Whitney. BA in Polit. Sci., Dillard U., 1963. News/sports reporter Trenton (N.J.) Evening Times, 1965-73; news reporter The Plain Dealer, Cleve., 1973-75, sports editor, 1983-86, mng. editor, 1986-89, exec. editor, 1989-92; v.p., sr. editor The Plain Dealer, 1992—; sports writer, columnist Phila. Daily News, 1977-80; sports columnist N.Y. Daily News, 1980-83; judge Scripps-Howard Founds. Walker Stone/Editl. Writing award, 1993; nominating jury mem. Pulitzer Prize, 1989-90. Bd. dirs. Greater Cleve. Roundtable, TV Sta. WVIZ, Cleve., Bus. Volunteerism Coun., ARC, Cleve., Cuyahoga Plan, Plain Dealer Credit Union, Performing Arts League. Named Paul Miller Disting. Journalism Lectr., Oklahoma State U., 1993. Mem. Am. Press Inst., Nat. Assn. Minority Media Execs. (bd. dirs.), Freedom Forum's Adv. Coun. for Sports Journalism, Am. Soc. Newspaper Editors, Nat. Assn. Black Journalists, AP Mng. Editors Assn., AP Sports Editors' Assn., Cleve. Press Club, Omega Psi Phi. Office: Plain Dealer 1801 Superior Ave E Cleveland OH 44114-2107

GREGG, GINA KAY, crisis care manager behavioral health; b. Kansas City, Mo., Feb. 1, 1963; d. Elbert Eugene and Judy Kay (Pugh) Nichols; m. Gerard Joseph Gregg, May 29, 1982; children: Zachariah, Austin, Dalton. BSN, Rockhurst-Rsch. Coll. Nursing, Kansas City, 1985. RN, Mo.; CEN; cert. trauma nurse core curriculum. Staff nurse Rsch. Med. Ctr., Kansas City, 1985-86; staff nurse, relief supr. Springfield (Mo.) Gen. Hosp., 1986-87; asst. dir. Sunshine Home Health Care, Springfield, 1987; staff nurse Cox Med. Ctr., Springfield, 1988-91, St. Joseph Health Ctr., Kansas City, 1991-92, St. John's Regional Health Ctr., Springfield, 1987-93, Bates County Meml. Hosp., Butler, Mo., 1992; case mgr. Home Health Plus, Kansas City, 1992-93; clin. supr. Kaiser-Permanente, Kansas City, 1993-95, MBC Iowa, 1995—. Democrat. Home: 6045 Colt West Des Moines IA 50266

GREGG, JAY MASON, geology educator; b. Pitts., Jan. 24, 1951; s. Jay Buell and Patricia Louise (Mason) G.; m. Elizabeth Michelle Prudot, Sept. 3, 1977; children: Patricia Michelle, Nicholas Mason, Jay William. BS in Geology and Biology, Bowling Green State U., 1974; MS in Geology, Okla. State U., 1976; PhD in Geology, Mich. State U., 1982. Assoc. geologist Sun Exploration and Prodn. Co., Midland, Tex., 1976-78; sr. rsch. geologist St. Joe Minerals Corp., Viburnum, Mo., Tucson, 1982-87; prin. scientist Westinghouse Hanford Co., Richland, Wash., 1987-88; asst. prof. geology U. Mo., Rolla, 1988-91, assoc. prof. geology, 1991-95; prof., 1995—. Co-editor SEPM Spl. Publ. on Basin-Wide Diagentic Patterns; mem. editl. bd. Soc. of Econ. Geologists 75th Anniversary Volume. Fulbright scholar U. Coll., Dublin, 1995-96. Mem. AAAS, Geol. Soc. Am., Soc. Econ. Paleontologists and Mineralogists, Soc. for Sedimentary Geology, Sigma Xi. Democrat. United Methodist. Home: 1321 Woodlawn Dr Rolla MO 65401-2591 Office: U Mo 125 Mcnutt Hall Rolla MO 65401

GREGG, JOHN BAILEY, surgery educator, researcher; b. Sioux Falls, S.D., June 5, 1922; s. John B. and Anna Elida (Bailey) G.; m. Pauline Benfer Snyder, June 29, 1946: children: Michele Lee, John Benfer, Stewart David, Rebecca Jo Anderson. BA, Iowa U., 1943, MD, 1946; DSc (hon.), U. S.D., 1989. Diplomate Am. Bd. Otolaryngology. Asst. prof. otolaryngology U. Iowa Hosps., Iowa City, 1959-60; prof. anthropology U. Tenn., Knoxville, 1972—; chmn. div. otolaryngology Sch. of Medicine U. S.D., Sioux Falls, 1968-72, vis. prof. Sch. of Medicine, 1972-75, dir. specialties of surgery Sch. Medicine, 1972-88; cons. VA Hosps, Iowa City and Sioux Falls, 1946-79, USPHS Indian Hosps., Rosebud, Pine Ridge and Wagner, S.D., 1956-75, U. S.D. Speech & Hearing Clinic, Vermillion, 1960—; dir. med. svcs. S.D. Dept. Health, 1982-84, dir. Div. Pub. Health, 1983-84. Author: Dry Bones, 1987, 2d rev. edit., 1989; author: (with others) Benigh Diseases of the Esophagus, 1982; contbr. over 200 articles to profl. jours. Speaker Ho. of Dels., S.D. State Med. Assn., Sioux Falls, 1973-75. Lt. (j.g.) USNR, 1942-49. Mem. Sioux Falls Elks, Sioux Falls Rotary. Republican. Episcopalian. Home: 2807 S Phillips Ave Sioux Falls SD 57105-4829

GREGG, ROBERT LEE, pharmacist; b. White River, S.D., Mar. 2, 1932; s. C.W. and Margaret (Maguire) G.; m. Julie D. Tyler, June 7, 1956; children: Allen, Mark, Susan. BS, S.D. State U., 1958. Registered pharmacist, S.D. Owner, mgr., pharmacist Kennebec (S.D.) Drug, 1958-79, Gregg Drug, Chamberlain, S.D., 1978—; mem. adv. coun. Coll. Pharmacy, S.D. State U., Brookings, 1985—; pres. S.D. Bd. Pharmacy, Pierre, 1992-93. Former sec. Indsl. Devel. Corp., Kennebec, S.D.; pres. Lake Francis Case Devel. Corp., Chamberlain, 1984-85. With Med. Svc. Corps, U.S. Army, 1953-55, Korea. Mem. S.D. Pharm. Assn. (pres. 1985-86, Bowl of Hygeia award 1992), Nat. Assn. Retail Druggists, Chamberlain C. of C., NRA (life), VFW (life, quartermaster Kennebec 1965-76, Outstanding Post Quartermaster award 1965), Am. Legion (life), Am. Quarter Horse Assn., S.D. Trail Riders (bd. dirs. 1986—), KC (4th degree). Republican. Roman Catholic. Home: PO Box 459 220 N Grace St Chamberlain SD 57325-1002 Office: PO Box 459 200 N Main St Chamberlain SD 57325-1326

GREGOR, HAROLD LAURENCE, artist, educator; b. Detroit, Sept. 10, 1929; s. Robert McKay and Annie Cameron (Malcolm) G.; m. Sandra Gardner, 1964 (div. 1977); children: Kathy L., Matissa S.; m. Marlene Pierce Rittenhouse, May 30, 1987. BS, Wayne State U., 1951; MS, Mich. State U., 1953; PhD, Ohio State U., 1960. Asst. prof. art San Diego State U., 1960-62, Purdue U., West Lafayette, Ind., 1963-66; assoc. prof., head dept. art Chapman Coll., Orange, Calif., 1966-70; Disting. prof. art Ill. State U., Bloomington-Normal, 1970-95; curator and/or juror numerous shows. Exhibited in one-man shows at Richard Gray Gallery, Chgo., 1983, 86, 88, 90, 91, 93, 95-96, Tibor DeNagy Gallery, N.Y.C., intermittently 1977-91, Nancy Lurie Gallery, Chgo., 1974, 76, 80, 81, 83, Sherry French Gallery, N.Y.C., 1993, Elliot Smith Gallery, St. Louis, 1995, retrospective show at Lakeview Mus. Art, Peoria, Ill., 1985, Rockford Art Mus., 1993; exhibited in numerous group shows: represented in collections at AT&T, Amoco Corp., Denver Art Mus., Hallmark Corp., others; painter murals Ill. State Libr., 1991; author articles. Grantee NEA, 1973, 86; recipient Burlington-No. award, 1989, Watercolor USA Purchase award, Visual Arts fellowship NEA, 1993-94. Mem. Watercolor Honor Soc. Home: 107 W Market St Bloomington IL 61701-3917 Office: G&H Studios PO Box 3246 Bloomington IL 61701

GREGOR, MARLENE PIERCE, primary education educator, elementary science consultant; b. Oak Park, Ill., Apr. 22, 1932; d. Kenneth Bryant and Dorothy (Bloeser) Pierce; m. G. Ray Timmons, Aug. 1, 1953 (div. 1972); children: Gregg R., Todd P., Wendy S. Timmons McGuire; m. Norman Rittenhouse, 1972 (div. 1976); m. Harold Laurence Gregor, May 30, 1987. BS in Elem. Edn., U. Ill., 1953; MS in Elem. Edn., Ill. State U., 1974, postgrad., 1975-91. Tchr. 2d grade Wethersfield Community Unit Schs., Kewanee, Ill., 1953-54; primary tchr. Fairbury (Ill.) Cropsey Schs., 1965-84, Prairie-Cen. Community Unit #8 Schs., Fairbury, 1984-91; ret. Prairie-Ctr. Community Unit # 8 Schs., Fairbury, 1991; item writer Stanford Achievement Test Psychol. Corp., San Antonio, 1989, sci. assessment Ill. State Bd. Edn., Springfield, 1987-88; grant reader Ctr. Sci. Literacy, Springfield, 1991-93; textbook reviewer The Wheetley Co., Wilmette, Ill., 1994-95. Author: (with others) Horizons Plus Science Stories-Grade 2, 1992, Toys That Teach Science, 1993, Celebrating Science, 1990, Award Winning Nutrition Education Lessons and Units, 1994; mem. sci. tchrs. writing team Ill. State U., 1992; contbr. articles and stories to various publs. Bd. dirs. Friends of the Arts Ill. State U., Normal, 1980-86, 92—, v.p., 1994-96; mem. Bloomington Mayoral Downtown Commn., 1993—, sec., 1994-96, chair pro tem, 1996—; mem. adv. bd. Kid's Crossing Mus., 1993-95; mem. steering com. Downtown Heritage Festival, Bloomington, 1995, 96, Ill. State U. Fell Arboretum, 1994—, co-chair edn. subcom., 1995—; mem. Leadership McLean County Class of 1996; bd. trustees Ill. Symphony Orch., 1996—. Named Outstanding Tchr. Sci. NSF-Ill. State U., 1985, Honors Sci. Tchr. Ill. State U., 1985, 86, 87; Chpt. II Mini grantee Edn. Svc. Ctr. #13, 1985-90; recipient Creative Nutrition award Nutrition and Edn. Tng. Ctr., 1989. Mem. ASCD, NEA, Nat. Sci. Tchrs. Assn. (presenter conv. 1985, 87), Coun. for Elem. Sci. Internat., Ill. Edn. Assn. (Tchr. Excellence award 1989), Ill. Ctr. Sci. Literacy (adv. mem. 1991-93), Ill. Sci. Tchrs. Assn. (sec. 1989-93, Presdl. Excellence Sci. Tchg. award 1991, State Finalist), Delta Kappa Gamma (v.p. chpt. 1990-92). Presbyterian. Home: 107 W Market St Bloomington IL 61701-3917

GREGOR, WILBUR RAY, writer; b. Cedar Rapids, Iowa, Aug. 16, 1923; s. Aldrich Owen and Albia Mary (Moses) G.; m. Lucille Roberts, Dec. 15, 1947 (div. June 1968); children: Stephen, David, Robert, Ann; m. Dianne Jean Probst, June 20, 1980. BA, Coe Coll., 1948. Cert. property casualty underwriter. Prin. Buffalo Center (Iowa) H.S.; pers. adminstr., edn. adminstr. Sentry Ins. Co., Santa Barbara, Calif.; dir. edn. Iowa Nat. Mutual Ins., Cedar Rapids, 1977-79, Ind. Ins. Agts. Am., West Des Moines, Iowa, 1979-90; writer Montezuma, Iowa, 1990—; cons. Ind. Ins. Agts. Am., West Des Moines, 1990-92; substitute tchr. Montezuma H.S., 1992—. Author: Interlang: Hidden Horizon, 1995. 1st lt. USAF, 1942-45. Mem. Lake Ponderosa Assn. (bd. dirs.). Home: 350 Hillcrest Ridge Montezuma IA 50171

GREGORICH, PENNY DENISE, production procurement analyst; b. Newark, Ohio, May 27, 1968; d. William Raymond and Ethel Faye (Wineman) G. AS in Office Adminstrn., Ctrl. Ohio Tech. Coll., 1989, AS in Bus. Mgmt., 1991; student, Otterbein Coll., 1991—. Sec./clk. Rockwell Internat., Newark, 1985-86, accounts receiveable coll. co-op., 1987-89, inventory control specialist, 1989-90, purchasing buyer/analyst, 1990-92, material procurement analyst, 1992—; bookkeeper's asst. Spenley Newspapers/Fostoria Times Rev., Newark, 1986-87. Licking County Joint Vocat.-Tech. Sch./Coop. Office Edn. historian, 1985-86; driver participant Miss Ohio Parade, Mansfield, 1990. Mem. NAFE, Assoc. Humane Soc., Capital Area Humane Soc., Licking County Humane Soc., Ctrl. Ohio Tech. Coll. Alumni Assn., Phi Theta Kappa. Office: Rockwell Internat Rt 79 Heath OH 43056-1440

GREGORY, KARL DWIGHT, economist, educator, consultant; b. Detroit, Mar. 26, 1931; s. Bertram Vincent and Sybil Louise (Wynter) G.; m. Tenicia Ann Banks, June 7, 1959; children: Karin Diane, Sheila Therese, Kurt David. BA, Wayne State U., 1952, MA, 1957; PhD, U. Mich., 1962. Fiscal economist Office of Mgmt. and Budget, Washington, 1961-64; prof. Wayne State U., Detroit, 1960-61, 64-68; prof. Oakland U., Rochester, Mich., 1968-96, disting. prof. emeritus, 1996—; bd. dirs. Detroit Econ. Growth Corp., United Am. Health Care, Detroit Barden Communications, Inc., Detroit br. Chgo. Fed. Res. Bank; chmn. bd., interim CEO Greater Detroit Bidco, Inc.; mem. coun. econ. advisors Gov. Engler of Mich., 1992-96; cons. UN Devel. Program, Beijing, People's Republic of China, 1991; chief organizer, dir. First Ind. Nat. Bank Detroit, 1968-81, interim pres., 1980-81; vis. prof. SUNY, Buffalo, 1975; vis. scholar, mem. exec. staff U.S. Congl. Budget Office, Washington, 1975-76; chmn. bd., chief exec. officer Accord, Inc., Detroit, 1969-71. Author (with others) State of Black Michigan, 1984-87, 91; contbr. articles to pubns. Trustee Episcopal Diocese of Mich., Detroit, 1981-83, 84-87, 90-92; mem. Gov.'s Entrepreneurial Commn., Lansing, Mich., 1984-88, Regional Devel. Initiative S.E. Mich. Coun. Govts., 1990-91, Gov.'s Task Force on Tourism, Lansing, 1986-89; bd. dirs., v.p. United Way S.E. Mich., Mich. Ctr. High Tech., 1991-95. 1st lt. U.S. Army, 1953-56. Recipient rsch. award Detroit chpt. NAACP, 1987, entrepreneurial awards Small Bus. Adminstrn., 1989, Mich. Dept. Commerce, 1992. Mem. Am. Econ. Assn., Nat. Econ. Assn., Oakland County Bus. Consortium, Detroit Urban League (bd. dirs.), Minority Tech. Coun. Mich. (bd. dirs.), Coms. of New Detroit, Inc., Econ. Club Detroit (v.p.). Home: 18495 Adrian St Southfield MI 48075-1803 Office: Sch Bus Oakland U Rochester MI 48309

GREGORY, MARIAN FRANCES, educator, counselor; b. Gary, Ind., Apr. 24, 1919; d. August Robert and Agnes Mae (Sturgess) Kuhn; m. Robert Wayne Gregory. BS in Edn., Ind. U., 1941; MA in Counseling, Columbia U., 1960. Elem. tchr. Bremen (Ind.) Schs., 1941-46; elem. tchr. Gary Pub. Schs., 1947-56, tchr. remedial reading, 1956-68; elem. prin. Spaulding and Lincoln schs., Gary, 1968-74; student tchr. cons. Ind. U., Bloomington, 1974-90; sec. Heritage Motors, Hammond, Ind., 1974. Author articles on genealogy. Mem., poll watcher LWV, Hammond, 1980-95; mem. Master Gardners Purdue U., Crown Point, Ind., 1977—; elder Presbyn. Ch. Mem. AAUW (pres. 1956-57), DAR, Bus. and Profl. Women's Club (pres. 1957-87), N.W. Ind. Women's Club (1st v.p. 1994-96), Delta Kappa Gamma, Kappa Kappa Kappa. Home: 2238 Ridge Rd Highland IN 46322-1562

GREGORY, PATRICIA JEANNE, corporate relations director; b. St. Louis, Feb. 13, 1951; d. Kenneth Robert and Mary Jane (Gibbs) Reilly; m. Mark Hitchcock Gregory, Apr. 20, 1985; children: Martin Hitchcock Gregory, Michael Wilford Gregory. BA, U. Mo., St. Louis, 1975; MS, U. Mo., 1978; PhD, U. Vt., 1986. Rsch. technician Washington U. Sch. Medicine, St. Louis, 1972-79; rsch. assoc. Univ. Coll., London, 1979-81; postdoctoral fellow U. Chgo., 1986-88; asst. chmn. Biochemistry Northwestern U., Evanston, Ill., 1988-92; dir. corp. and found. rels. Washington U. Sch. Medicine, St. Louis, 1992—; dir. minority recruitment for the life scis., Northwestern U., Evanston, 1988-92; assoc. dir. Ctr. for Biotech., Northwestern U., Evanston, 1990-92. Contbr. articles to profl. jours. Recipient Curator's Scholar award U. Mo. Bd. Curators, 1969, fellow Acad. Leadership Program, Com. on Instl. Cooperation, Urbana, Ill., 1990. Home: 404 Edgewood Dr Clayton MO 63105-2016 Office: Wash U Sch Medicine 4444 Forest Park Blvd Saint Louis MO 63108-2292

GREGORY, SAMUEL BAILEY, JR., financial advisor, financial planner; b. Altoona, Pa., May 11, 1930. BA, Ind. U., 1951. CFP. Ptnr. Gregory Assocs., Ft. Wayne, Ind., 1951—, Gregory & Zent Inc., Ft. Wayne, 1988—. Bd. dirs. Allen County Park Bd., 1994—; fundraiser Heart Assn. Recipient Nat. Quality award Million Dollar Round Table, 1954—. Mem. Internat. Fin. Planners, CLU Soc., Ft. Wayne Underwriters (past pres.), Sertoma Club, Ft. Wayne C. of C. Republican. Lutheran. Office: Gregory & Zent Inc PO Box 11207 4011 W Jefferson Fort Wayne IN 46856

GREGORY, THOMAS BRADFORD, mathematics educator; b. Traverse City, Mich., Dec. 13, 1944; s. Philip Henry and Rhoda Winslow (Hathaway) G.; m. Deirdre Dianne Mason, July 15, 1995. BA, Oberlin (Ohio) Coll., 1967; MA, Yale U., 1969, M of Philosophy, 1975, PhD, 1977. Lectr. Ohio State U., Mansfield, 1977-78, asst. prof. math., 1978-84, assoc. prof. math., 1984—. Reviewer: Math. Revs., 1984—; contbr. articles to profl. jours. Active Mansfield (Ohio) Symphony Chorus, 1977—, Presbytery Youth Ministries Com., New Philadelphia, Ohio, 1980-87, Ohio State U. Community Singers, Mansfield, 1985—; mem. Presbyn. Biblical Authority task force, 1994-95. Comdr. USNR, 1969—. Fellow NSF, Washington, 1967; hon. fellow U. Wis., Madison, 1987-88, 92. Mem. Am. Math. Soc. (translator 1974-82), Ohio Coun. Tchrs. Math., Am. Soc. Naval Engrs., Naval Inst., Res. Officers Assn., Naval Res. Assn., Navy League, Phi Beta Kappa, Sigma Xi. Republican. Home: 411 Overlook Rd Mansfield OH 44907-1533 Office: Ohio State U 1680 University Dr # 0 15 Mansfield OH 44906-1547

GREGORY, VANCE PETER, JR., chemist; b. Jacksonville, Fla., Sept. 7, 1943; s. Vance Peter and Roberta Marie (White) G.; m. Sharon Keilman, Apr. 27, 1990. BA, Vanderbilt U., 1965. Tech. svc. chemist CPC Internat., Argo, Ill., 1966-74; project chemist Uarco, Inc., Barrington, Ill., 1974-86; mgr. R & D Weber Marking Systems, Arlington Heights, Ill., 1986; plant chemist Wallace Computer Svcs., Streetsboro, Ohio, 1986-88; sr. project chemist Wallace Computer Svcs., Bellwood, Ill., 1988—. Mem. Historic Sites Commn., Glen Ellyn, Ill., 1985. Mem. Am. Chem. Soc., Tech. Assn. Pulp and Paper Industries. Home: 2286 Durham Dr Wheaton IL 60187-8818 Office: Wallace Computer Svcs 10 Davis Dr Bellwood IL 60104-1047

GREILING, MINDY, state legislator; b. Feb. 1948; m. Roger Greiling; 2 children. BA, Gustavus Adolphis Coll.; MEd, U. Minn. State rep. Minn. Ho. Reps., Dist. 54B, 1993—. Office: Minn Ho of Reps State Capitol Building Saint Paul MN 55155-1606*

GREIM, JEFFREY B., company executive; b. Huntington, Ind., Aug. 25, 1950. Student, Tri State U., 1972. Tool-maker Essex Internat., Auburn, Ind., 1974-78, Wheel-tek Inc., Fremont, Ind., 1985-86; pres. CNC Pattern Inc., Fremont, 1987—. Republican. Office: CNC Pattern Inc 7800 Norris Van Gilder Rd Fremont IN 46737

GREINEDER, JUERGEN KURT, surgeon; b. Berlin, Germany, June 2, 1937; came to U.S., 1965; s. Kurt Herbert and Renee (Chaoul) G.; m. Kathleen Marie Schmidt, Sept. 11, 1983; children: Kurt J., Walther J., Erik J. MD, Ludwig-Maximilians U., Munich, Germany, 1964. Diplomate Am. Bd. Surgery, Am. Bd. Thoracic Surgery. Instr. in surgery Albert Einstein Coll. Medicine, Bronx, N.Y., 1975-78; asst. attending surgeon Bronx Municipal Hosp. Ctr., 1975-78; vis. instr. surgery Albert Einstein Coll., 1978-82; surgery thoracic, vascular, gen. pvt. practice, N.Y., 1978-85, Quincy, Mass., 1985-94; Gregory, S.D., 1994—. Contbr. articles to profl. jours. Fellow Am. Coll. Surgeons. Lutheran. Office: 400 Park Ave Gregory SD 57533-1202

GREIS, GORDON P., tool and die maker; b. Milw., Nov. 28, 1955. Apprentice Tool and Die Maker, Milw. Tech. Coll., 1975. Tool and die maker Ak Kraussel Tool and Mfg., Milw., 1973-81, Gordon Tool, Milw., 1981-89, Moraine Precision, Hartford, 1989—. Lutheran. Office: Moraine Precision 509 Pine St # A Hartford WI 53027-1031

GRENDELL, DIANE V., state legislator, lawyer, nurse; m. Tim Grendell; children: James, Kate. Grad. in nursing, St. John's Coll.; JD, Cleve. Marshall Coll. Law; postgrad., Baldwin Wallace Coll. Bar: Ohio; RN, Ohio. Mem. Ohio Ho. of Reps., Columbus. Recipient Seven Seals award, Wilson achievement award. Mem. Ohio Bar Assn., Ohio Nurses Assn., Chester C. of C., Chester and Geauga County Hist. Soc., Farm Bur. (chmn.), Sierra Club. Republican. Home: 7413 Tattersall St Chesterland OH 44026-2036 Office: OH House of Reps State House Columbus OH 43215*

GRESLEY, STEPHEN CLARK, aerospace executive; b. Ft. Wayne, Ind., Sept. 7, 1940; s. Paul Wilson and June H. (Harvey) G.; m. Edith Irene Green, July 27, 1963; children: Jill Elizabeth, Jennifer Helen. BS in Indsl. Econs., Purdue U., 1962; MS, Indsl. Coll. Armed Forces, Washington, 1977. Commd. USAF, 1962, advanced through grades to maj., 1972, ret., 1982; exec. v.p. No. Ind. Savs. Assn., Chesterton, Ind., 1982-84; program mgr. CAI div. Recon-Opitcal, Inc., Barrington, Ill., 1984-87, Smiths Industries, Grand Rapids, Mich., 1987-96; ret., 1996; Mem. Pvt. Industry Coun., Porter County, Ind., 1983-84. Mem. fin. com. First United Meth. Ch., Grand Rapids, Mich., 1990-92. Decorated D.F.C., Air medal with 14 oak leaf clusters, Meritorious Svc. medal. Mem. Masons, Scottish Rite, Shriners. Republican. Methodist. Home: 2375 Oak Ridge Trl NE Grand Rapids MI 49505-9729

GRETHEN, CHERYL ANN, artist; b. Emmetsburg, Iowa, Apr. 1, 1953; d. Norman D. and Emilie M. (Kruml) Clark; m. David J. Grethen, Sept. 2, 1972; 1 child, Christopher J. Artist Elegant Expressions, Mallard, Iowa.

Mem. Am. Craft Coun., Sterling Who's Who Exec. Club, Assn. Crafts and Creative Industries. Roman Catholic. Office: Elegant Expressions PO Box 237 Mallard IA 50562

GREVE, DIANA LEE, community health nurse; b. Lima, Ohio, Feb. 10, 1949; d. Lee and Betty (Hedrick) Kinstle; m. Lawrence J. Greve, Feb. 1, 1969; children: Brian, Scott, Matthew, Bradley. ADN, Lima Tech. Coll., 1983; BSN, Bowling Green State U., 1989; MSN, Med. Coll. Ohio, Toledo, 1993; family nurse practitioner postgrad cert., Ind. Wesleyan Coll., 1995. Cert. in community health nursing. Staff nurse ob.-gyn. Van Wert (Ohio) County Hosp.; hospice coord. Van Wert Area Vis. Nurse Assn.; instr. Luth. Coll. of Health Professions, Ft. Wayne, Ind.; Wright State U., dayton, Ohio; clin. nurse specialist Joint Twp. Dist. Meml. Hosp., St. Marys, Ohio; adj. faculty Med. Coll. Ohio and Wright State U. Bd. dirs. Van Wert Cancer Soc.; mem., educator St. Marys Bereavement Com., Van Wert. Mem. Am. Coll. Nurse Practitioners, Oncology Nursing Soc., Midwest Nursing Rsch. Soc., Ohio Nurses Assn., Van Wert Area Nurses Assn., Sigma Theta Tau. Home: 1056 Mockingbird Ln Van Wert OH 45891-2642

GREVE, GUY ROBERT, lawyer; b. Bay City, Mich., Oct. 25, 1947; m. Nancy Lisbeth Mueller, Sept. 21, 1991; 1 child, Tyler James. BA, U. Mich., 1970; postgrad., U. Kent, Canterbury, Eng., 1974; JD, Detroit Coll. of Law, 1975. Bar: Mich. 1975, U.S. Dist. Ct. (ea. dist.) Mich. 1975. Ptnr. Patterson & Greve, Bay City, 1975-78; asst. atty. City of Bay City, 1975-76, atty., 1976-78; sole practice Bay City, 1978—. Numerous one man photography exhbn. Bd. dirs. Women's Crisis Ctr., Bay City, 1977-79, Am. Cancer Soc., 1975—, pres. 1982-83; pres. Muse-Hopper Mobile Mus., Eastern Mich., 1980-82. Named Disting. Alumnus Handy H.S., 1985; recipient Disting. Svc. award Bay City Jaycees, 1981. Mem. ABA, ATLA, Mich. Bar Assn., Mich. Bar Found., Bay County Bar Assn. (bd. dirs. 1994-96, Liberty Bell chmn. 1994-96), Mich. Trial Lawyers Assn., Bay Area C. of C., Studio 23 (hon. life), U. Mich. Alumni Club (Bay City chpt. pres. 1994-96), Saginaw Bay Yacht Club, Optimists (pres. Bay City 1979-80, lt. gov. Mich. 1985-86, chair new club bldg. 1986-87, chmn. club svcs. 1989-90, internat. conv. com. 1997). Home: 2300 Nurmi Dr Bay City MI 48708-6872 Office: PO Box 851 919 Washington Ave Bay City MI 48707

GREVE, LUCIUS, II, metals company executive; b. St. Paul, July 23, 1915; s. Joseph and Lillian (King) G.; m. Marguerita Philippa Buller Colthurst, Aug. 31, 1940; children: Lucius Richard, Guy Robert. Salesman Electric Auto-Lite Co., Detroit, 1934-42; methods engr. Electric Auto-Lite Co., Bay City, Mich., 1944-45; project engr. Electric Auto-Lite Co., Bay City, 1944-45, with sales dept., 1946-49; pres. L. Greve Sales Co., Bay City, 1949—; exec. v.p. Graphic Metals Co., 1962—, dir., chmn. fin. com., 1962—; pres. Montezuma Mining Co., 1963—. Mem. Sch. Sites Com., 1952, Sch. Citizens Com., 1957; sec. Saginaw Bay Assn., 1957. Mem. U.S. Power Squadron, Saginaw Bay Yacht Club (dir. 1961, comdr. 1965), Bay City Country Club, Great Lakes Crusing Club. Home: 194 Athlone Bch Bay City MI 48706-1179 Office: PO Box 331 Bay City MI 48707-0331 also: # 7 Blvd de Belgique, Monte Carlo Monaco

GREW, KIMBERLY ANN, social service administrator; b. Saginaw, Mich., Nov. 25, 1962; d. Chester Joseph and Ruth Irene (Kemmerling) G. AA, Delta Coll., University Center, Mich., 1981; BA, Saginaw Valley State U., 1983, MA, 1987; Cert. Paralegal Studies with distinction, Am. Inst. Paralegal Studies, Detroit, 1988. Lead tchr. Child & Family Svcs., Bay City, Mich., 1986-87; legal advocate/counselor Saginaw County (Mich.) Sexual Assault Ctr., 1987-88; specialized foster care worker Family & Children's Svc. Midland, Mich., 1989-90; asst. payments V Saginaw County Dept. Social Svcs., 1990-92, welfare svcs. specialist-foster care, 1992—. Editor/chmn. cookbook: Edible, Palatable, Delights, 1985. Mem. Child Abuse and Neglect Coun. Saginaw, Midland Art Coun.; membership com., nominations com. Saginaw Social Svc. Club, 1988—, sec., 1989-90, nominations com. 1991-92; vol. Bay City (Mich.) YWCA, Saginaw Vet. Hosp.; bd. dirs. Bay City Crime Stoppers, 1987—, treas., 1989-95; mem. Midland Ctr. for Arts, 1990—, Bay County Selective Svc. Bd., 1995—; contbg. mem. This Close for Cancer Rsch. Mem. AAUW (v.p. 1986-88, pres. 1988-90), Am. Soc. Criminology, Am. Criminal Justice Soc., Legal Assts. Assn. Mich., Mil. Order Purple Heart Aux. (v.p. 1987—), Saginaw Valley State U. Alumni Bd. (rec. sec. 1993-94, v.p. 1994-95), Phi Alpha Delta, Sigma Beta Phi (rec. sec. Xi Beta Delta chpt. 1990-92, Pledge of Yr. 1990, Perceptor 1993-95, kappa master 1995—, Bay County human svcs. com. 1996—). Democrat. Baptist. Home: 3329 W Douglas Dr Bay City MI 48706-1223

GREWELL, JOHANNE H. FAIRS, high school library media specialist; b. Pittsfield, Mass., June 30, 1938; d. John H. and Eleanor (Brooks) Fairs; m. Donald Robert Grewell, Aug. 5, 1961 (div. Feb. 1970); 1 child, Dawn Rebecca. BS in Edn., Ea. Ill. U., Charleston, 1960; MS in LS, U. Ill., 1965. Cert. in h.s. teaching, instructional materials, Ill. Tchr. English, 10th grade Mattoon (Ill.) H.S., 1960-64; tchr. lang. arts, 8th grade Ctrl. Jr. H.S., Mattoon, 1964-66; 1st asst. cataloger Ea. Ill. U., 1966-71; media specialist Armstrong Jr. H.S., Jacksonville, Ill., 1971-77; libr. media specialist Peoria (Ill.) H.S., 1977—; instr. media/libr. svcs. Ill. Ctrl. Coll., East Peoria, 1978-95; mem. subcom. on sys. Ill. State Libr. Adv. Coun., Springfield, 1994—; cons. Libr. Book Selection Svc., Bloomington, Ill., 1992—. Costume chmn. for numerous plays in cmty. theaters. Mem. ALA, Am. Assn. Sch. Librs., Ill. Sch. Libr. Media Assn. (bd. dirs., past pres.), PEO, Delta Kappa Gamma. Office: Peoria HS 1615 N North St Peoria IL 61604

GREWELL, JUDITH LYNN, automotive executive; b. New Orleans, Aug. 27, 1945; d. Raymond Walter and Dorothy Marie (Reymann) Potratz; m. John Nolting Grewell, Aug. 28, 1964; children: Patricia Lynn, Amy Elizabeth. BA with honors, Wayne State U., 1972; MA with honors, Oakland U., 1976. Cert. prodn. and inventory mgmt. Supr. mfg. Chevrolet-Pontiac-GM of Can. div., Pontiac, Mich., 1978-80, purchasing agt., 1980-82, trainer, organizational cons., 1982-84; supr. systems tng. Electronic Data Systems Div., Troy, Mich., 1985-86, supr. tech. tng. devel., 1986-88, supr. tng. and communications, 1988-89, prin. sr. cons. divsn., 1989-95, client server program dir., 1995—; head trainer UAW-GM Nat. Workshop, Black Lake, Mich., 1983. Contbg. editor Univ. Assocs. Handbook of Structured Experiences, 1985. Mem. Am. Prodn. and Inventory Control Soc., Pi Lambda, Phi Upsilon Omicron. Republican. Presbyterian. Home: 27085 Winchester Ct Farmington Hl MI 48331-3686 Office: 800 Tower Dr Troy MI 48331

GREY EAGLE, SANDRA LEE, special education educator; b. Sidney, Mont., Sept. 22, 1952; d. Donald Merl and June Dorothy (Burman) Radke; m. Benedict Matthew Grey Eagle, Sept. 19, 1978; children: Jason Wade, Justin Michael. BS cum laude, Black Hills State Coll., Spearfish, S.D., 1973; MA, Goddard Coll., Plainfield, Vt., 1979. Tchr. Sky Ranch (S.D.) for Boys, 1974, learning disabilities specialist, 1974-78, acting prin., 1978, dir. spl. edn., 1980-89; spl. educator/house parent Vision Quest Program, Tucson, Ariz., 1978; ednl. diagnostian Cheyenne River Sioux Tribe, Eagle Butte, S.D., 1978-79; spl. educator Timber Lake (S.D.) Pub. Sch., 1979-80; dir. spl. edn. N.W. Area Schs. Edn. Coop., Lemmon, S.D., 1989—; ednl. specialist Office Spl. Edn., Pierre, S.D., 1989—; mediator ednl. disputes Office Spl. Edn., Pierre, 1989—; mem. adv. bd. State Wide Systems Change, Pierre, 1991—; cons., mem. Collaborative Effective Edn. Design, 1991—. Chmn. Harding County Horse Show, Camp Crook, S.D., 1984-91, Dakota Family Horse Club Show, Haynes, N.D., 1992—; conf. chmn. Correctional Edn. Assn., Balt., 1988, dir. region IV, 1986; bd. mem. Live Ctr. Adjustment Tng. Ctr. for Developmentally Disabled, 1995. Mem. Coun. for Exceptional Children (Outstanding Adminstrs. S.D. fedn. 1994), Am. Coun. Rural Spl. Edn. Home: HC 5 Box 308 Haynes ND 58639-8768 Office: NW Area Schs Ednl Coop 11 4th St E Lemmon SD 57638-1524

GRIDER, KATHY JILL, medical record professional; b. Painesville, Ohio, Apr. 30, 1954; d. Roy Emerson and Norma Jean (Whipple) Burkholder; m. Gary Snider, Sept. 1970 (div. 1980); children: Erin S., April Dawn; m. Stephen E. Prater, May 1981 (div. 1989); 1 child, Jonathan Evan; m. Dwight D. Grider, Oct. 1, 1989. BS in Med. Records Adminstrn., Ind. U., 1982; MBA, Ind. Wesleyan U., 1990. Registered records adminstr., Am. Health Info. Mgmt. Assn. Coding rev. supr. St. John's Med. Ctr., Anderson, Ind., 1982-84; dir. med. records New Castle (Ind.) State Hosp., 1984-85, Cmty. Hosp., Anderson, 1985-89; v.p., ptnr. Svc. Enterprises, Inc., Anderson, 1989-90; area mgr., COO Smart Corp., Pendleton, Ind., 1989-93; exec. adv. coun. Smart Corp., Torrance, Calif., 1991-92; pres. Dictation Svcs. Inc., 1993—; v.p., co-owner Midwest Med. Copy Svc., Inc., Pendleton, Ind., 1993—; with AMMCORP, Pendleton; instr. Ind. U., Indpls., 1991. Mem. Am. Med. Record Assn., Ind. Med. Record Assn. (mem. pub. rels. com. 1988-89, officer, exec. bd. 1988—, chmn. continuing edn. 1989-91, chmn. nominating and credentials com. 1980-90), Ind. Health Info. Mgmt. Assn. (v.p. 1993-94), Ctrl. Ind. Med. Record Assn. (officer, exec. bd. 1987-89). Democrat. Methodist. Office: AMMCORP Records Mgmt PO Box 308 PO Box 308 Pendleton IN 46064

GRIESHEIMER, JOHN ELMER, state representative; b. St. Clair, Mo., July 19, 1952; s. Elmer Augustus and Mary (Middleton) G.; m. Rita Ann Maune, June 15, 1974; children: Sean, Aaron, Michelle. Cert. auto mechanics, East Cen. Coll., Union, Mo., 1971, AAS, 1973. Councilman ward II City of Washington, Mo., 1982-88; county commr. Franklin County, Union, Mo., 1989-92; state rep. State of Mo., Jefferson City, 1993—; chmn. Solid Waste com., 1984-88; vice chmn. East Ctrl. Solid Waste Task Force Waste com., 1990-92. Bd. dirs. Washington Lions Club; adv. bd. dirs. 4 Rivers Vo-Tech. Sch., Washington, Mo. Mem. KC (4th degree). Republican. Roman Catholic. Home: 33 Oxford Dr Washington MO 63090-4609 Office: State of Mo State Capitol Building # PO Jefferson City MO 65101-1556

GRIEVE, PIERSON MACDONALD, specialty chemicals and services company executive; b. Flint, Mich., Dec. 5, 1927; s. P.M. and Margaret (Leamy) G.; m. Florence R. Brogan, July 29, 1950; children: Margaret, Scott, Bruce. BSBA, Northwestern U., 1950; postgrad., U. Minn., 1955-56. Staff engr. Caterpillar Tractor Co., Peoria, Ill., 1950-52; mgmt. cons. A.T. Kearney & Co., Chgo., 1952-55; pres. Rap-in-Wax, Mpls., 1955-62; exec. AP Parts Corp., Toledo, 1962-67; pres., CEO Questor Corp., Toledo, 1967-82; CEO Ecolab Inc., St. Paul, 1983—, also chmn. bd. dirs.; bd. dirs. St. Paul Cos. Inc., Norwest Corp., Meredith Corp., US West Inc., Waldorf Corp., Meredith Corp.; chmn. Minnegasco. Chmn. Met. Airport Commn., State of Minn.; mem. adv. coun. J.L. Kellogg Grad. Sch. Mgmt., Northwestern U.; chmn. bd. overseers Carlson Sch. Mgmt., U. Minn.; bd. dirs. Guthrie Theatre; bd. trustees St. Thomas U. With USNR, 1945-46. Mem. Chevaliers du Tastevin, Minn. Club (St. Paul), Mpls. Club, Beta Gamma Sigma (dirs. table). Episcopalian. Clubs: Minn. (St. Paul); Mpls. Office: Ecolab Inc Ecolab Ctr Saint Paul MN 55102

GRIFFIN, ANITA JANE, elementary education educator; b. East Chicago, Ind., Dec. 16, 1945; d. John Tatu and Alfreda (Kaspick) Granger; m. Joseph Raymond Griffin, June 14, 1969; children: Jason David, Jennifer Sue. BA, Purdue U., Hammond, Ind., 1969, MS, 1972. Tchr. 2d grade Dist. 158, Lansing, Ill., 1969-73; tchr. 6th grade sci. Lake Cen. Sch. Corp., St. John, Ind., 1983, tchr. 6th grade English, 1984, tchr. 5th grade, 1985—; advisor, coach Sci. Club, 1992-94; mem. core team Integrated Learning System Computer Tech., 1992—; faculty advisor Star Lab. Program, 1988—; coord. Artist in Residency Program, 1993; mem. Peifer Sch. Parent's Adv. Com., 1991-94, prin.'s selection com., 1993, performance bd. accreditation team, 1993-94; advt. mgr. Lake Ctrl. Hockey Club, 1991-92. Editor newspaper on staff devel. Success Connection, 1988—. Mem. pastoral adminstrv. bd. Meth. Ch., Dyer, Ind., 1988-90. Mem. AAUW, NEA, ASCD (conv. presenter 1988), Ind. Tchrs. Assn., Peifer Home and Sch. Assn. (treas. 1990-91), Kappa Kappa Kappa (chpt. pres. 1990-91). Office: Lake Cen Sch Corp Peifer Sch 1824 Cline Ave Schererville IN 46375-2260

GRIFFIN, DEBORAH JOYCE, psychiatric-mental health nurse; d. Oscar and Constance (Mason) G. BSN, U. Mich., 1979, MS of Nursing, 1985. RN, Mich. Staff nurse, oper. rm. nurse U. Mich. Hosp., Ann Arbor, 1980-86; clin. nurse specialist Detroit Receiving Hosp., 1986-87; adult, adolescent psychiat. and substance abuse nurse Samaritan Hosp., Detroit, 1987-88; oper. rm. nurse Henry Ford Hosp., Detroit, 1988; clin. nurse specialist, adult mental health Heritage Hosp., Taylor, Mich., 1988-91; mgr. care mental health and substance abuse Value Behavioral Health, Southfield, Mich., 1991—. Mem. ANA (cert. clin. nurse specialist in adult psychiat. mental health nursing). Office: Value Behavioral Health Ste 600 One Towne Sq Southfield MI 48076

GRIFFIN, JAMES ANTHONY, bishop; b. Fairview Park, Ohio, June 13, 1934; s. Thomas Antohny and Margaret Mary (Hanousek) G. B.A., Borromeo Coll., 1956; J.C.L. magna cum laude, Pontifical Lateran U., Rome, 1963; J.D. summa cum laude, Cleve. State U., 1972; Dr. Humanities (hon.), Ohio Dominican Coll., 1994. Ordained priest Roman Catholic Ch., 1960, bishop, 1979; asso. pastor St. Jerome Ch., Cleve., 1960-61; sec.-notary Cleve. Diocesan Tribunal, 1963-65; asst. chancellor Diocese of Cleve., 1965-68, vice chancellor, 1968-73, chancellor, 1973-78, vicar gen., 1978-79; pastor St. William Ch., Euclid, Ohio, 1978-79; aux. bishop Diocese of Cleve.; vicar of western region Diocese of Cleve., Lorain, Ohio, 1979-83; bishop Diocese of Columbus (Ohio), 1983—; mem. clergy relations bd. Diocese of Cleve., 1972-75, mem. clergy retirement bd., 1973-78, mem. clergy personnel bd., 1979-83. Author: (with A.J. Quinn) Thoughts for Our Times, 1969, Thoughts for Sowing, 1970, (with others) Ashes from the Cathedral, 1974, Sackcloth and Ashes, 1976, The Priestly Heart, 1983, Reflections on the Law of Love, 1991, Summary of the New Catholic Catechism, 1994. Bd. dirs. Holy Family Cancer Home, 1973-78; trustee St. Mary Sem., 1976-78; bd. dirs., mem. pension com. Cath. Cemeteries Assn., 1978-83; bd. dirs. Meals on Wheels, Euclid, 1978-79; vice-chancellor Pontifical Coll. Josephinum, 1983—; bd. dirs. Franklin County United Way, 1984-90; chmn. bd. govs. N.Am. Coll., Rome, Italy, 1984-88; chmn. Mayor's Coun. on Youth, 1986-90; treas. Cath. Relief Svc. Bd., 1988-91, pres., 1991-96; co-chair Columbus Cmty. Rels. Commn., 1992-95. Decorated Knight of the Holy Sepulchre, 1993; recipient Human Rights award Anti-Defamation League B'nai B'rith, 1987, Gov.'s award State of Ohio, 1994, Jessing award Pontifical Coll., 1993. Mem. Am. Canon Law Soc., Columbus Bar Assn. (chmn. jud. advt. com. 1987-91, Liberty Bell award 1989).

GRIFFIN, MAX EUGENE, pediatrician; b. Montpelier, Ohio, June 20, 1924; s. Paul Edward and Vera Elizabeth (Borton) G.; m. Frances Barbara Rachkaitis, June 10, 1950; children: Constance Ann Griffin Spradling, Paula Marie Griffin Davis, Gregory Max. BS, U. Chgo., 1945, MD, 1947; MS in Pediatrics, U. Pa., 1955. Lic. physician, Ohio; diplomate Am. Bd. Pediatrics. Intern (rotating) St. Vincent's Hosp., Toledo, 1947; pediatric resident Children's Hosp. Med. Ctr., Akron, Ohio, 1948-51; pvt. practice pediatrics Barberton, Ohio, 1953-70; dir. ambulatory pediatrics Children's Hosp. Med. Ctr., Akron, Ohio, 1970-90, chmn. dept., 1980-85; assoc. prof. pediatrics Northeastern Ohio Univs. Coll. of Medicine, Rootstown, 1978-85, prof. pediatrics, 1985-91, emeritus prof. pediatrics, 1991—. Capt. M.C., U.S. Army, 1951-53. Recipient Disting. Svc. award Children's Hosp. Med. Ctr., 1990. Fellow Am. Acad. Pediatrics (exec. bd. Ohio chpt. 1976-81, Ohio Pediatrician of the Yr. 1985); mem. Summit County Med. Soc., Ambulatory Pediatric Assn., Am. Acad. History of Medicine, Ohio Acad. Med. History, Am. Philatelic Soc. Republican. Roman Catholic. Home: 42 Elmdale Ave Akron OH 44313

GRIFFIN, MICHAEL J., state legislator; b. Jackson, Miss., May 12, 1933; m. Janet Stark; children: Margaret, John, Martin, Michael, Robert, Gerald, Maureen. BA, Jackson C.C., 1959. City commr. Jackson, 1967-73; rep. Mich. Dist. 50, 1972-92, Mich. Dist. 64, 1993—; alt. chmn. joint com. on adminstrv. rules Mich. Ho. Reps., legis. coun., corps. & fin. com., tourism, fisheries, and wildlife com.; product mgr. Rhemm Mfg. Home: 505 N Elm Ave Jackson MI 49202-3507 Address: PO Box 30014 Lansing MI 48909-7514*

GRIFFIN, PATRICK J., bonds sales professional; b. Detroit, Sept. 6, 1946. BS in Econs., Mich. State U., 1969; postgrad., U. Detroit, 1970. Sales profl. Detroit Bank and Trust, 1970; mcpl. bonds profl. Drexel, Hairman Ripley, Detroit, 1970-73, Halsey Stewart, Detroit, 1973-78, Manley Bennet, Detroit, 1978-88; bonds sales profl. Kemper Securities, Detroit, 1988—. Chmn. of bd. Leader Dogs for Blind, Detroit, 1977—; past treas., pres. Grosse Pointe Farms Schs. Mem. Detroit Bond Club, Ducks Unltd., Gamma Alpha Mu. Republican. Roman Catholic. Home: 74 Lewiston Rd Grosse Pointe MI 48236-3613 Office: Kemper Securities Inc # 300 440 E Congress St Detroit MI 48226-2917

GRIFFIN, PAUL R., religious studies educator; b. Bridgeport, Ohio, Feb. 27, 1944; s. Joseph S. and Sarah J. (Robinson) G.; m. Barbara Diane Crockett; children: Jevon, Felicia. BA, Wright State U., 1973; MDiv, United Theol. Sem., Dayton, Ohio, 1976; PhD, Emory U., 1983. Assoc. prof. Payne Theol. Sem., Wilberforce, Ohio, 1979-83; dean, prof. Payne Theol. Sem., Wilberforce, 1983-88; assoc. prof. Wright State U., Dayton, 1992—; founder, dir. Nat. Conf. on The Future of Shape of Black Religion, Dayton, 1988—. Author: The Struggle For a Black Theology of Education, 1993—. Mem. Am. Soc. Ch. History, Am. Acad. Religion, Soc. Study of Black Religion. Home: 1913 N Longview St Dayton OH 45432 Office: Wright State U 3640 Colonel Glenn Hwy Dayton OH 45435-0001

GRIFFIN, ROBERT PAUL, former state supreme court justice and US senator; b. Detroit, Nov. 6, 1923; s. J.A. and Beulah M. G.; m. Marjorie J. Anderson, 1947; children—Paul Robert, Richard Allen, James Anderson, Martha Jill. AB, BS, Central Mich. U., 1947, LLD, 1963; JD, U. Mich., 1950, LLD, 1973; LL.D., Eastern Mich. U., 1969, Albion Coll., 1970, Western Mich. U., 1971, Grand Valley State Coll., 1971, Detroit Coll. Bus., 1972, Detroit Coll. Law, 1973; L.H.D., Hillsdale (Mich.) Coll., 1970; J.C.D., Rollins Coll., 1970; Ed.D., No. Mich. U., 1970; D. Pub. Service, Detroit Inst. Tech., 1971. Bar: Mich. 1950. Pvt. practice Traverse City, Mich., 1950-56; mem. 85th-89th congresses from 9th Dist. Mich., Washington, 1957-66; mem. U.S. Senate from Mich., Washington, 1966-79; counsel Miller, Canfield, Paddock & Stone, Traverse City, 1979-86; assoc. justice Mich. Supreme Ct., Lansing, 1987-95. Trustee Gerald R. Ford Found. Served with inf. AUS, World War II, ETO. Named 1 of 10 Outstanding Young Men of Nation U.S. Jaycees, 1959. Mem. ABA, Mich. Bar Assn., D.C. Bar Assn., Kiwanis.

GRIFFIN, SHEILA MB, electronics marketing executive; b. Chgo., June 17, 1951; d. George Michael and Frances Josephine (Sheehan) Spielman; m. Woodson Jack Griffin, Dec. 30, 1972; children: Woodson Jack, II, Kelly Sheehan. BS, U. Ill., 1975, MBA, 1979. Personal banking rep. Am. Express Banking, Boeblingen, Fed. Republic Germany, 1973-74; market rsch.analyst Market Facts, Chgo., 1975-77; mgr. strategic rsch. Motorola, Inc., Schaumburg, Ill., 1977-83, mgr. mktg. resource, 1985-88, mgr. spl. projects Corp. Strategy Office, 1988-89, dir. corp. advt. worldwide, 1989-93, dir. bus. assessment corp. strategy office, 1993-94, dir Global Applied Market rsch. consumer business office, 1994-96, dir. multimedia strategy office; gen. mgr. mktg. rsch. and info. Ameritech Mobile Communications, Inc., Schaumburg, 1983-85. Trustee (founding), Ill. Math. and Sci. Acad., 1985—. Mem. U. Ill. Chgo. MBA Alumni Assn. (founder, pres. 1984-86), U. Ill. Alumni Assn. (bd. dirs. 1984-86, Disting. Alumni 1985, Constituent Leadership award 1989). Home: 3017 Glen Eagles Ct Saint Charles IL 60174-8832 Office: Motorola Inc 1303 E Algonquin Rd Schaumburg IL 60196-4041

GRIFFITH, DENISE IRENE, school administrator; b. DeKalb, Ill., Apr. 14, 1954; d. Don Rae and Eva Joan (Cogswell) Sheriff; m. Cary Johns Griffith, May 20, 1976 (div. Dec. 1990); children: Nicholas, Noah; m. Dennis James Maher, Mar. 6, 1993. BA in Elem. Edn. and Spl. Edn., U. Iowa, 1976; MA in Ednl. Psychology, U. Minn., 1985. Cert. elem. tchr., learning disabilities and trainable educable retarded tchr., Minn. Spl. edn. tchr. Stuart (Iowa)-Menlo Schs., 1976-78; learning disabilities tchr. IHM Sch., St. Paul, 1978-80; program specialist Regional Resource Ctr. U. Minn., Mpls., 1980-82; MIS specialist, spl. edn. tchr. Mpls. Pub. Schs., 1982-88, spl. edn. supr., 1990-91; IBM/Macintosh trainer Microwar X Tng. Ctr., Minnetonka, Minn., 1988-91; tech. dir. Rosemount (Minn.)-Apple Valley-Eagan Schs., 1991—; mem. Minn. Telecomms. Coun., St. Paul, 1995—; mem. adv. coun. Minn. Internet INFORUMS, Roseville, Minn., 1993—. Mem. Phi Beta Kappa, Phi Kappa Phi. Home: 14016 Daytona Way Rosemount MN 55068 Office: Sch Dist 196 14445 Diamond Path Rosemount MN 55068

GRIFFITH, DONALD KENDALL, lawyer; b. Aurora, Ill., Feb. 4, 1933; s. Walter George and Mary Elizabeth Griffith; m. Susan Smykal, Aug. 4, 1962; children: Kay, Kendall. Grad. in History with honors, Culver Mil. Acad., 1951, BA, U. Ill., 1955, JD, 1958. Bar: Ill. 1958, U.S. Supreme Ct. 1973. Assoc. Hinshaw & Culbertson, Chgo., 1959-65, ptnr., 1965—; spl. asst. atty. gen. Ill., 1970-72; lectr. Ill. Inst. Continuing Legal Edn., 1970—. Trustee, Lawrence Hall Youth Svcs., 1967—, v.p. for program, 1969-74; bd. dirs. Child Care Assn. Ill., 1970-73; mem. Lake Forest High Sch. Bd. Edn., 1983-84. 2d lt. USAF, 1956. Fellow Am. Acad. Appellate Lawyers; mem. ABA (chmn. appellate advocacy com., tort and ins. practice sect. 1983-84), Ill. Bar Assn., Chgo. Bar Assn., Appellate Lawyers Assn. Ill. (pres. 1973-74), Def. Rsch. Inst., Ill. Def. Counsel, Chgo. Trial Lawyers Club, Alpha Chi Rho (chpt. pres.), Phi Delta Phi. Club: University of Chgo., Knollwood. Mem. editorial bd. Ill. Civil Practice After Trial, 1970; co-editor The Brief, 1975-83; contbg. author Civil Practice After Trial, 1984, 89; contbr. article to legal jour. Office: Hinshaw & Culbertson 222 N La Salle St Ste 300 Chicago IL 60601-1005

GRIFFITH, JAMES DAVID, lawyer; b. Evanston, Ill., Aug. 28, 1929; s. Wendell Crabtree and Mary Griffith; m. Elizabeth Meyer, Sept. 21, 1957 (div. July 1987); children: Ian Hunt, Alison Gail. BA, DePaul U., 1951; JD, Northwestern U., Chgo., 1953. Bar: Ill. 1956. Assoc. Campbell, Clithero & Fischer, Chgo., 1956-63; ptnr. Graham, Stevenson & Griffith, Chgo., 1963-67; prin. Auker & Griffith, Ltd., Chgo., 1969-79; pvt. practice, Chgo., 1967-69, 80—; magistrate Village of Glenview, Ill., 1961-65. Founder, pres. Com. on Lake Michigan Pollution, Wilmette, Ill., 1967-69, Fifth Percent, Chgo., 1991—; pres. Lake Michigan Fedn., Chgo., 1973-74, 92-94; pres. Glenview Civic Party, 1981. With U.S. Army, 1954-56. Mem. Nat. Strategy Forum, Chgo. Coun. on Fgn. Rels., Sheridan Shore Yacht Club (Wilmette, commodore 1970). Home: 1527 Pebble Creek Dr Glenview IL 60025 Office: 77 W Washington St Ste 508 Chicago IL 60602

GRIFFITH, VAUGHN A., program manager farm machinery company; b. Pitts., Aug. 13, 1947. BS, BA, U. No. Iowa, 1973. Materials mgr. John Deere Co., Woodridge, N.J., 1987-89; quality assurance mgr. John Deere Co., Woodridge, 1989-91; program mgr. John Deere Co., Waterloo, Iowa, 1991—; mem. Am. Nat. Stds. Inst. Bd., 1980-94, bd. dirs. Y14 com., 1980-85, B-46 com., 1979-94. Co-inventor 2 patents. Vol. Local Arbor Founds.; pres. tech. bds. Mem. Soc. Mfg. Engrs., Soc. Automotive Engrs., Am. Soc. Quality Control (cert. quality control profl.).

GRIFFITHS, ROBERT PENNELL, banker; b. Chgo., May 6, 1949; s. George Findley and Marion E. (Winterrowd) G.; m. Susan Hillman, Jan. 31, 1976. BA, Amherst Coll., 1972; MS in Mgmt., Northwestern U., 1974. Comml. banking officer No. Trust Co., Chgo., 1978-80, 2d v.p., 1980-83, v.p., 1983-85; sr. v.p. comml. lending UnibancTrust Co., Chgo., 1985-88; pres., chief exec. officer Old Kent Bank (formerly Ill. Regional Bank of Naperville, Ill.), 1988-90; sr. v.p. Old Kent Bank-Chgo., 1991-92; sr. v.p. UnibancTrust/Hawthorne (merged into Old Kent Bank of Naperville), 1987-89; pres., COO, Uptown Nat. Bank of Chgo., 1993—. Mem. Univ. Club (Chgo.), Onwentsia Club. Home: 691 Rockefeller Rd Lake Forest IL 60045-3141 Office: Uptown Nat Bank 4753 N Broadway St Chicago IL 60640-4907

GRIFFITHS, THOMAS M., stockbroker; b. Mpls., Dec. 1, 1942. BA, Mankato State U., 1964, MA, 1967. Tchr. Mpls. Pub. Schs., 1967-81; stockbroker Summit Investment, Bloomington, Minn., 1981—. Dir. Nat. Luth. Choir, Bloomington, 1985-90. Republican. Office: Summit Investment Corp # 200 3800 W 80th St Bloomington MN 55431-4420

GRIGGS, JOHN ROBERT, financial and consumer credit services executive; b. Franklin, N.J., Oct. 19, 1949; s. Frank E. and Verna L. (Geddes) G.; m. Sally Shutt, June 15, 1974; children: Brian, Dan, Carole. BS in Acctg., U. Tulsa, 1971, MBA, 1973. Cert. fin. and ops. prin. Nat. Assn. Securities Dealers, consumer credit exec. Fin. analyst Citicorp Person to Person, St. Louis, 1974, dir. fin. planning and analysis and various positions, 1975-78, chief of staff, 1978-79; sr. area mgr. Citicorp Person to Person, Seattle, 1979; area v.p. Citicorp Acceptance Co., Seattle, 1979-82; v.p., chief fin. officer, treas. Citicorp Acceptance Co., St. Louis, 1982-85; v.p. ops. Citicorp Acceptance Co., Atlanta, 1985-86; v.p., gen. mgr. Household Fin. Svcs., Chgo., 1986-91, sr. v.p., 1991-93; exec. v.p., CFO, treas., dir. Hamilton Investments, subs. Household Internat., Chgo., 1993-94; v.p. Household Internat., Prospect Heights, Ill., 1994-96; sr. v.p. nat. ops. mgr. Banc One Credit Corp., Columbus, Ohio, 1996—; chmn., bd. dirs. Consumer Credit Counseling Svc. Greater Chgo. (cert. consumer credit exec.). Coach Little League baseball,

St. Louis, Atlanta, Chgo.; advisor Cub Scouts, Atlanta; trustee, treas. Homeowner's Assn., St. Louis; mem., bd. dirs., treas. Barrington (Ill.) Youth Baseball. Mem. Am. Fin. Svcs. Assn. (bd. dirs., exec. com.), Nat. Second Mortgage Assn. (bd. dirs., exec. com.), Internat. Credit Assn., Alpha Phi Omega, Omicron Delta Kappa, Beta Gamma Sigma. Office: Banc One Credit Corp Ste 110 2400 Corporate Exchange Dr Columbus OH 43231

GRIGGS, KAREN, university educator, technical writer; b. Ft. Wayne, Ind., Nov. 4, 1946. BA, Purdue U., 1972, PhD, 1994; MSEd, Ind. U., Ft. Wayne, 1986. Instr. Purdue U., West Lafayette, Ind., 1987-93; asst. prof. James Madison U., Harrisonburg, Va., 1995-96; vis. asst. prof. No. Ill. U., DeKalb, 1994-95. Mem. Girl Scout coun., Ft. Wayne, 1972-78; editor Ind. divsn. Izaak Walton League Am., Gaithersburg, Md., 1983-92, regional gov. 1985-78, environ. health and air com. 1986—, tech. adv. com. 1996—. Grantee M.W. Pollution Prevention Conf. Environ. Def. Fund, 1991, 92. Mem. Soc. Tech. Comm., Assn. Bus. Comm., Rhetoric Soc. Am., Nat. Coun. Tchrs. Eng., Coll. Composition and Comm. Conf., Speech Comm. Assn. Home: 635 County Rd 35 Ashley IN 46705

GRIGGS, LEONARD LEROY, JR., federal agency administrator; b. Norfolk, Va., Oct. 13, 1931; s. Leonard LeRoy and Mary (Blair) G.; m. Denise Ziegler, Mar. 18, 1977; children: Margaret Rosalyn, Virginia Lorraine Williams, Julia Blair Pey, Deborah Branham Taylor. B.S., U.S. Mil. Acad., 1954; M.S. in Aero. Engring., Air Force Inst. Tech., 1960; M.S. in Internat. Affairs, George Washington U., 1967; disting. grad., Naval War Coll., 1967, Army War Coll., 1971. Registered profl. engr., Mo. Commd. 2d lt. U.S. Army, 1954; advanced through grades to col. USAF, 1970; served in Vietnam, ret., 1977; dir. Lambert St. Louis Internat. Airport, 1977-87; v.p. Ross & Baruzzini, Inc., 1987-89, Bangort Bros. Constrn. Co., St. Louis and Denver, 1989—; asst. adminstr. for airports FAA, Washington, 1990-93; airport dir. St. Louis Internat. Airport, 1993—; adj. prof. St. Louis U. Bd. dirs. USO, St. Louis/Lambert. Decorated Silver Star, D.F.C. with 4 oak leaf clusters, Bronze Star, Meritorious Service medal, Air medal with 22 oak leaf clusters, Purple Heart, Air Force Commendation medal with 2 oak leaf clusters, Army Commendation medal; Medal of Honor; Medal of Gallantry (Vietnam); recipient Aviation Engring. Safety award FAA, 1979. Mem. Airport Operators Coun. Internat., Am. Assn. Airport Execs., Profl. Engring. Soc. St. Louis, Order of Dadelians, St. Louis Air Force Assn., Engr. Club, Mo. Athletic Club, Army Navy Club, Univ. Club., Order DeMolay. Home: 1609 Tradd Ct Chesterfield MO 63017-5627 Office: Lambert-St Louis Intl Airport PO Box 10212 Lambert Airport MO 63145

GRIGGS, RUTH MARIE, retired journalism educator, writer, publications consultant; b. Linton, Ind., Aug. 11, 1911; d. Roy Evans Price and Mary Blanche (Hays) P.; m. Paul Philip Griggs, Aug. 4, 1940. BS, Butler U., 1933; postgrad. U. So. Calif., 1938, Northwestern U., 1939; MA, U. Wyo., 1944. Cert. tchr. journalism, English, speech, bus. edn. Travel writer Indpls. Star, 1927-37; summer reporter Worthington Times, Ind., 1928-33; journalism, speech tchr. Warren Cen. High Sch., Indpls., 1937-37; tchr. bus. edn., journalism Greene Twp. High Sch., South Bend, Ind., 1937-38; tchr. journalism, English, bus. edn Howe High Sch., Indpls., 1938-46; tchr. journalism Butler U., Indpls., 1946-48, evenings 1972-76; dir. publs. Broad Ripple High Sch., Indpls., 1948-77; summer journalism workshop instr. numerous univs. 1949-80. Author: History of Broad Ripple, 1968; co-author: Handbook for High School Journalism, 1951; Teacher's Guide to High School Journalism, 1965, Marquette Memoirs, 1996. Dow Jones Newspaper Fund fellow U. Minn., 1967; named Nat. Journalism Tchr. of Yr. Wall Street Jour., 1968, Woman of Achievement Woman's Press Club of Ind., 1984; recipient Rabb award Women's Press Club of Ind., 1988, Disting. Alumni award Butler U. Alumni Bd., 1989. Mem. AAUW, DAR, Journalism Edn. Assn. (v.p., pres. 1963-69, Towley award 1965), Women in Communications (pres. Indpls. 1969-70, Wright award 1969, Kleinhenz award 1978), Nat. Fed. Press Women (youth projects bd. 1979-87, Recognition award 1991), Columbia Scholastic Press Assn. (Gold Key award 1964, Golden Crown 1975, life mem. 1977), Ind. High Sch. Advisers Assn. (pres. 1972, Sengenberger award 1965), Delta Zeta (Ind. Woman of Yr. 1984). Republican. Presbyterian.

GRIMALDI, JACK, investment company official; b. Bklyn., Feb. 24, 1955. BS in Bus., Ind. State U., 1978; MA in Econs., Ball State U., 1982. Investment broker K.J. Brown & Co., Muncie, Ind., 1982-87; money mgr. Smith Gaylor Investments Inc., Muncie, 1987—. Republican.

GRIMES, HUGH GAVIN, physician; b. Chgo., Aug. 19, 1929; s. Andrew Thomas and Anna (Gavin) G.; m. Rose Anne Leahy, Aug. 21, 1954; children—Hugh Gavin, Paula Anne, Daniel Joseph, Sarah Louise, Nancy Marie, Jennifer Diane. Student, Loyola U., 1947-50; B.S., U. Ill., 1952, M.D., 1954. Diplomate Am. Bd. Ob-Gyn. Intern St. Joseph Hosp., Chgo., 1954-55; resident in ob-gyn St. Joseph Hosp., 1955-58; practice medicine specializing in ob-gyn Chgo., 1960—; lectr., asst. clin. prof. Stritch Sch. Medicine, Loyola U., Chgo.; active staff St. Joseph Hosp., Chgo., also v.p. med. staff, 1977-78, pres. staff, 1979-80; asst. prof. clin. ob-gyn Northwestern U. Med. Sch., 1980—. Contbr. articles to profl. jours. Trustee Regina Dominican High Sch. Served to capt. M.C., AUS, 1958-60. Fellow Am. Coll. Ob-Gyn., Chgo. Gynecol. Soc.; mem. Am. Cancer Soc. (mem. profl. edn. com. Chgo. unit), Am. Soc. Reproductive Medicine, Cath. Physicians Guild, Assn. Am. Physicians and Surgeons, Am. Soc. Colposcopy and Colpomicroscopy, Am. Assn. Gynecologic Laparoscopists, Assn. Art Inst. Chgo., Assn. Field Mus., Assocs. Smithsonian Instn., Pi Kappa Epsilon. Office: Ste 304 2800 N Sheridan Rd Chicago IL 60657-6156

GRIMES, MARGARET WHITEHURST, medievalist, educator; b. New Bern, N.C., Oct. 12, 1917; d. Robert Emmet and Margaret Edna (Ervin) Whitehurst; m. Alan Pendleton Grimes, May 16, 1942; children: Margaret, Alan P. Jr., Katherine E., Peter E. BA, U. N.C., 1938; MA, Mich. State U., 1967, PhD, 1969. Instr. Mich. State U., E. Lansing, 1969-71; asst. prof. humanities asst. prof. humanities, E. Lansing, 1971-75; assoc. prof. Mich. State U., E. Lansing, 1975-80, prof., 1980-86, prof. emeritus, 1986—; chmn., organizer Medieval Studies Consortium, Mich. State U., E. Lansing, 1991—. Contbr. articles to profl. jours.; presenter to medieval studies groups. Mem. Medieval Assn. Midwest, Dante Soc. Am., Medieval Acad. Am., Mich. State U. Dante Soc. (chmn., founder 1985). Democrat. Home: 728 Lantern Hill Dr East Lansing MI 48823-2828 Office: Mich State U Ctr Integrative Studies Linton Hall East Lansing MI 48824

GRIMES, MARILYN JANE LARSEN, nursing administrator; b. Pierre, S.D., July 28, 1933; d. Hans and Selma (Rappana) Larsen; m. Walter W. Grimes, June 5, 1955; children: Mark W., Christine E., Paul C. Diploma, Sioux Valley Hosp. Sch., Sioux Falls, S.D., 1954; BS in Nursing, U. Ill., Chgo., 1971, MS in Nursing, 1973. Cert. clin. specialist psychiat./mental health. Supervisory nurse Ill. Psychiat. Inst., Chgo., 1973-78; assoc. adminstr. Ill. Nurses Assn., Chgo., 1978-81; clin. nurse cons. II U. Ill. Hosp., Chgo., 1981—; vol. Human Rights Authority, Ill. Commn. Guardianship and Advocacy. Recipient Constituent Leadership award U. Ill. Alumni Assn., 1985. Mem. ANA, Midwest Nursing Rsch. Soc., Ill. Nurses Assn., Chgo. Nurses Assn., U. Ill. Coll. Nursing Alumni Assn. (pres., bd. dirs., loyalty award 1978), Nat. Assn. Perinatal Addiction Rsch. and Edn., Sigma Theta Tau.

GRIMES, MARK PARKER, research and development engineer; b. Des Moines, Oct. 10, 1951; s. Charles Marion and Faye Louise (Francisco) G.; m. Karen Anne Babcock, May 9, 1973; 1 child, Patrick Philip. BSEE, Iowa State U., 1981. Chief technician Heritage Comms., Des Moines, 1973-74; radar flight test engr. McDonnell Douglas, Edwards AFB, Calif., 1981-82; radar cross sect. measurement engr. McDonnell Douglas, Palmdale, Calif., 1982-83; instrumentation radar sys. design engr. McDonnell Douglas, St. Louis, 1983-91, sr. project engr., 1991-95, prin. investigator, 1996—; treas., chief engr. LoCat, Inc., St. Louis, 1990—; cons. in field, Mo., Fla., Calif., 1990—. Civil engring. officer Mo. Air N.G., St. Louis, 1984-91, svcs. ops. officer, 1991—. Capt. Air N.G., 1970—. Mem. IEEE, N.G. Assn. of U.S., McDonnell Douglas Amateur Radio Club. Home: 5206 Sun Lake Dr Saint Charles MO 63301 Office: McDonnell Douglas Aerospace MC 0642201 PO Box 516 Saint Louis MO 63166-0516

GRIMES, RONALD L., religion educator; b. San Diego, May 19, 1943; arrived in Can., 1974; s. Milton L. and Joyce Nadine (Williams) G.; m. Susan L. Scott, Aug. 18, 1984; children: Cailleah, Bryn. BA, Ky. Wesleyan Coll., 1964, HLD (hon.), 1984; MDiv, Emory U., 1967; PhD, Columbia U./Union Theol. Sem., 1970. Asst. prof. religion Lawrence U., Appleton, Wis., 1970-74; assoc. prof., then prof. religion Wilfrid Laurier U., Waterloo, Ont., Can., 1974-84, prof., 1984—. Author: Symbol and Conquest, 1976, 2d edit. 1992, Beginnings in Ritual Studies, 1982, 2d edit., 1994, Ritual Criticism, 1990, Reading, Writing and Ritualizing, 1992, Marrying & Buying, 1995; mem. editl. bd. Anthropology of Consciousness, 1992—, Spotlight on Teaching, 1993—; founding editor Jour. of Ritual Studies, 1986—. Mem. Am. Acad. Religion, Am. Anthropol. Assn. Home: 127 Dunbar Rd S, Waterloo, ON Canada N2L 2E8 Office: Wilfrid Laurier U, Dept Religion and Culture, Waterloo, ON Canada N2L 3C5

GRIMM, GLENN ALAN, real estate company executive, consultant; b. East Cleveland, Ohio, Apr. 19, 1951; s. Billy Ray Grimm and Freda Imogene (Hendrickson) Sonnie; m. Darlene Anne DiNardo, May 13, 1972; children: Joel Matthew, Leah Anne, Jacob William. Student, United Electronics Inst., Akron, Ohio, 1969-71, DeVry Isnt. Tech., Chgo., 1972-75; EMT, Cuyahoga Community Coll., 1975. Lic. fgn. real estate, pvt. pilot, radio-telephone. Electronics technician Warner & Swasey Co., Cleve., 1973-74; pres. Glendan Distbg. Inc., Chardon, Ohio, 1979-80; v.p. Convenient Food Mart Inc. #3-074, Rocky River, Ohio, 1982-86, Convenient Food Mart Inc #3-035, North Olmsted, Ohio, 1982-87; sr. sales mgr. Sunbelt Mktg., Norwalk, Ohio, 1989—; v.p. John Glenn Corp., Chesterland, Ohio, 1991—; pres. Convenient Food Mart Inc. #3-056, Mayfield Heights, Ohio, 1974-92; bus. cons. Priority Mgmt., 1992—. Treas. Vietnam Vets. Am., Geauga County, Ohio, 1988-92; treas. West Geauga Recreation Coun., Chesterland, Ohio, 1986-88; mem. Speakers Bur., Mothers Against Drunk Drivers, Cleve., 1983-92. Sgt. U.S. Army, 1971-73. Mem. SAR, Convenient Food Mart Owners Coun. (bd. mem. 1986—). Pentecostal. Home and Office: 11455 Rust Dr Chesterland OH 44026-1530

GRIMM, RICHARD CHARLES, marketing and finance educator, researcher; b. Youngstown, Ohio, Sept. 8, 1962; s. Richard Abtil and Barbara Ann (Hudock) G.; m. Janine Ross, Sept. 12, 1987. BSBA, Youngstown State U., 1988, MBA, 1995; postgrad., Kent State U. Fin. cons. Merrill Lynch, Youngstown, Ohio, 1988-89; investment exec. Paine Webber, Youngstown, 1990-91; fin. cons. Wheat First Butcher & Singer, Youngstown, 1992; exec. v.p. MDH Investment Mgmt., East Liverpool, Ohio, 1993; rsch. asst. fin. Youngstown State U., 1993-94; teaching fellow fin. Kent (Ohio) State U., 1994—. Scholar Youngstown State U. Found., 1993-94. Mem. Doctoral Students Mgmt. Assn., Phi Kappa Phi. Home: 3332 Estates Cir Youngstown OH 44511-2024

GRINDBERG, TONY, state legislator; m. Vanessa Grindberg; 1 child. Student, N.D. State Coll. Sci., Wahpeton, Moorehead State U. Dir. Interstate Bus. Coll.; state senator dist. 41, 1993—; vice chmn. edn. com.; mem. govt. and vet. affairs com. N.D. State Senate. Mem. Midwestern Bus. Coll. Assn. (pres.), Rotary. Republican. *

GRIPPANDO, MARK, information systems specialist; b. Blue Island, Ill., Apr. 8, 1965; s. Joseph T. and Patricia (Hannagan) G.; m. Amy Louise Ransdell, June 30, 1990; children: Anthony P., Brian J. BS in Acctg., U. Ill., 1987, MS in Computer Sci., 1988. Advanced sys. engr. Electronic Data Sys., Troy, Mich., 1988-94; from prin. cons. to sr. prin. cons. ORACLE Corp., Dallas, 1994—. Recipient Hero award Carnegie Found., 1991. Mem. Assn. Internat. CPAs., U. Ill. Young Commerce Alumni. Home: 376 N Kenilworth Elmhurst IL 60126

GRISHAM, GEORGE ROBERT, mathematics educator; b. Wheeler, Miss., Nov. 30, 1930; s. George B. and Maggie (Oakley) G.; m. Garnette S. Swinney, May 28, 1955; children: Deborah K. Grisham O'Neal, Jennifer L. Grisham Cichowski. BS, Miss. State U., 1952, MEd, 1956. Cert math. tchr., K-14 gen. supervision, Ill.; cert. math. tchr., Tex. Tchr. Streator (Ill.) Twp. High Sch., 1956-68; prof. math. Ill. Cen. Coll., East Peoria, Ill., 1968-86, chmn. dept., 1981-86; tchr. N.E. Ind. Sch. Dist., San Antonio, 1986-87; asst. prof. Bradley U., Peoria, Ill., 1987-92; ret., 1992. Author algebra study guides; editor The Math Connexion, 1972-75. Bd. dirs. Am. Field Svc., Morton, Ill., 1972. Comdr. USNR, 1952-54, Korea. Named Tchr. of Yr., Peoria Savs. and Loan Assn., 1972. Mem. Math. Assn. Am., Nat. Coun. Tchrs. Math. (conv. chmn. Peoria 1980), Ill. Coun. Tchrs. Math. (pres. 1976, co-chmn. conv. 1989), Ill. Math. Assn. C.C.'s (life, pres. 1981), Res. Officers Assn. (life), Moose, Elks. Democrat. Presbyterian. Home: 22 Maple Ridge Dr Morton IL 61550-1152

GRISMORE COWLES, MARY, government executive; b. Apr. 27, 1941; m. William J. Cowles, Aug. 31, 1990; children: Kevin Grismore, Lynn Burns, Robert Grismore, Tina Scarbrough. BA in Bus., U. Ill., Springfield, 1995. Pub. affairs profl. Sundstrand, Rockford, Ill., 1978-83; adminstr. Sec. of State, Springfield, Ill., 1983-95; exec. Gov.'s Office, Springfield, 1995—; tech. advisor Ill. Dept. Aging, Springfield, 1990-95; bd. dirs. Ill. Alliance on Aging, Springfield; chmn. Ill. Congl. Dist., Rockford, 1980-83. Editor: Springfield Historical Cookbook, 1995. Active Big Brother/Big Sister, Springfield, 1984-89; literacy tutor Ill. Literacy Program, Springfield, 1985-88; ombudsman Ill. Aging, Springfield, 1990-95; bd. dirs. Rep. Club, Springfield, 1992-95. Recipient Civic award Ill. Coalition on Aging, 1994; R. M. Farley scholar U. Ill., 1995, 96. Presbyterian. Home: 5218 S 2d St Springfield IL 62703 Office: State of Ill Off of Gov Springfield IL 62703

GRISOLIA, SANTIAGO, biochemistry educator; b. Valencia, Spain, Jan. 6, 1923; s. Santiago and Concepcion (Garcia) G.; m. Frances Lena Thompson, Aug. 16, 1949; children: James S., William F. BA, Nat. Inst., Cuenca, Spain, 1939; postgrad., Med. Sch., Madrid, 1940-41; MD, Med. Sch., Valencia, 1944; D Medicine and Surgery, U. Madrid, 1949; Hon. Degree in Medicine, U. Salamanaca, Spain, 1968, U. Valencia, 1973; Hon. Degree in Chemistry, U. Barcelona, Spain, 1972, U. Madrid, 1973; Hon. Degree in Med. Surgery, U. Siena, Italy, 1980; Hon. Degree in Biol. Sci., U. Leon, Spain, 1982; Hon. Degree in Med. Oncology, U. Basque Country, Bilbao, Spain, 1988; Hon. Degree in Med. Surgery, U. Florence, Italy, 1988; Hon. Degree in Politecnic U., U. Valencia, 1991. Asst. prof. Med. Sch., U. Valencia, 1944-45; fellow in pharmacology NYU, N.Y.C., 1946; vis. asst. prof. U. Chgo., 1946-47; rsch. assoc., asst. prof. physiology and chemistry Med. Sch., U. Wis., Madison, 1947-54; assoc. prof., then prof. medicine and biochemistry Med. Sch., U. Kans., Kansas City, 1954-62, chmn. biochemistry dept., 1962-73, disting. prof. biochemistry, 1973-95; disting. prof. emeritus U. Kans., Kansas City, 1995—; prof. Inst. Investigation Cytology, Valencia, 1977-92, disting. prof., 1992—; sec., pres. sci. com. Found. for Advanced Studies, Valencia, 1978—; pres. coord. com. human genome project UNESCO, Paris, 1988—; cons. GLAXO Labs., Madrid, 1980—, Sigma Tau Labs., Madrid, 1988—; organizer symposia in field; dir. summer course on human genetic map Complutense U., El Escorial, Spain, 1989, 90, Menendez y Pelayo U., Santander, Spain, 1990; com. mem. UNESCO Internat. Bioethics Com., 1993—; disting. prof. U. Las Palmas, Canary Islands, 1993; presenter summer courses in human genome aids, aging U. Menendez Pelayo, La Coruna, Spain, 1993, 94, 95; pres. jury DuPont Sci. Prize, Spain; adv. bd. mem. Fundacion Banco Bilbao Fizcaya and Colegio Libre de Emeritos; sci. advisor Pres. of Generalidad, Valencia, 1995; v.p. bd. Hosp. Concepcion, Madrid; pres. consejo de cultura, Generalidad, Valencia, 1996; rschr. in field. Contbr. articles to profl. publs.; co-editor various books in field. Pres. bd. dirs. Multiple Sclerosis Found., Madrid, 1990. Recipient Gold medal lecture Cuenco Villoro Found., 1975, Paul Harris award Rotary Internat., 1988, Rotary Flame award Valencia Centro Club, 1989, Grand Crosses King of Spain, in agr., 1982, health, 1984, edn., 1987, civil merit, 1993, Sci. award Principe de Asturias Found., 1990, Disting. Svc. Citation U. Kans., 1991. Mem. Am. Soc. Biol. Chemists (mem. various coms.), Spanish Soc. Biochemistry (hon.), Spanish Soc. Physiology (hon.), Internat. Soc. Neurochemistry, Royal Acad. Medicine Belgium (fgn. hon. mem.), Royal Acad. Pharmacy (corr. academician, Madrid), Internat. Soc. Clin. Enzymology (hon.), Academia Patavina (Italy, corr. mem.), Royal Acad. Medicine Valencia and Rome (hon. mem.), Coll. of Physicians (hon. mem.), Royal Acad. Scis. (Madrid, corr. mem.), Academia Gallega de Ciencias (Santiago de Compostela, corr. mem.), Sigma Xi, Alpha Omega Alpha (hon.), Academie de Honor, Real Academia de Doctores. Office: U Kans Med Ctr Deans Office 3901 Rainbow Blvd Kansas City KS 66160-0001 also: Fundacion Valenciana, de Estudios, Avanzados Pintor Lopez 7, 46003 Valencia Spain

GRISWOLD, DANIEL R., investment company executive; b. Onekma, Mich., Feb. 22, 1960. B Fin., Fair State U., Big Rapids, Mich., 1983. Lic. series 7 Nat. Assn. Securities Dealers. Stockbroker Rodman Renshaw, Chgo., 1987-88; v.p. Kemper Securities, Chgo., 1988-93, Dean Witter Reynolds, Grand Rapids, Mich., 1993—. Home: 7409 Decosta Dr NE Rockford MI 49341-9392 Office: Dean Witter Reynolds 300 Ottawa Ave NW Ste 600 Grand Rapids MI 49503-2310

GRISWOLD, FRANK TRACY, III, bishop; b. Bryn Mawr, Pa., Sept. 18, 1937; s. Frank Tracy Jr. and Luisa Johnson (Whitney) G.; m. Phoebe Wetzel, Nov. 27, 1965; 2 children. AB, Harvard U., 1959; attended, Gen. Theol. Sem., 1959-60; BA, Oxford U., 1962, MA, 1966. Ordained to ministry Episcopal Ch. as deacon, 1962, as priest, 1963. Bishop coadjutor Diocese of Chgo., 1985-87, bishop, 1987—; dep. to gen. conv.; former chmn. Pa. Liturgical Commn. Chair Standing Liturgical Commn., Episcopal Ch. U.S.; co-chair Anglican-Roman Catholic Dialogue U.S. Office: Diocese of Chgo 65 E Huron St Chicago IL 60611-2728

GRISWOLD, GREG, small business owner; b. Madison, Wis., May 10, 1954. BS in Horticulture, U. Wis., 1976. Founder Computer Components Inc., Middleton, Wis., 1986—. Office: Comco Holding Ltd 3202 W Beltline Hwy Middleton WI 53562

GRISWOLD, PAUL MICHAEL, clinical psychologist, consultant; b. Milw., Sept. 26, 1945; s. Willard Matthew and Evelyn (Haerle) G.; m. AnnMari Gerardine La Valle, Aug. 2, 1969; children: Matthew Paul, Jennifer Jean. BA, Marquette U., 1967, MS, 1969; PhD, Kent State U., 1972. Sr. staff psychologist Wis. Div. Corrections, Milw., 1972-83; pvt. practice clin. and cons. psychology Menomonee Falls, Wis., 1973—; lectr. Mount Mary Coll., Milw., 1973-78; faculty Wis. Sch. of Profl. Psychology, Milw., 1981—; cons. Ethan Allen Sch. Wis. Div. Corrections, Wales, Wis., 1984—. Contbr. articles to profl. jours. Mem. Am. Psychol. Assn., Wis. Psychol. Assn., Milw. Area Psychol. Assn. Home: 1366 County Hwy J Hubertus WI 53033-9426 Office: Clin Psychology Assocs W156 N8327 Pilgrim Rd Menomonee Falls WI 53051-3776

GRITZNER, CHARLES FREDERICK, geography educator; b. Fremont, Mich., June 6, 1936; s. Charles F. and Laura E. (Chamberlain) G.; m. Wilma J. Little, Aug. 26, 1956 (div. 1972); children: Lori Sue, Lynn Allison; m. Janet Hazen Bigbee, Mar. 4, 1972. BA, Ariz. State U., 1958; MA, La. State U., 1960, PhD, 1969. Asst. prof. E. Carolina Coll., Greenville, N.C., 1960-62, assoc. prof., 1970-73; instr. La. State U., Baton Rouge, 1962-70; vis. assoc. prof. U. Mont., Missoula, 1973-75, Oreg. Coll. Edn., Monmouth, 1975-76; assoc. prof. U. Houston, 1976-79; prof. geography S.D. State U., Brookings, 1980—, Disting. prof., 1993—; coord. S.D. Geographic Alliance. Author geography texts and trade books; contbr. articles to profl. jours. Coord. S.D. Geog. Alliance, S.D. State Geography Bee; mem. Social Sci. Edn. Consortium. Recipient Disting. Svc. award Assn. S.D. Geographers & Planners, 1982; recipient numerous grants. Mem. AAAS, Am. Geog. Soc., Assn. Am. Geographers, Nat. Coun. for Geographic Edn. (exec. dir. 1977-80, pres. 1986, Disting. Teaching award 1983), S.D. Social Studies Coun. (pres. 1984-85, Outstanding Social Studies Educator 1984, 91), Nat. Coun. for Social Studies. Democrat. Soc. of Friends. Home: 1011 7th Ave Brookings SD 57006-1313 Office: SD State U Dept Geography Brookings SD 57007

GROAT, LINDA NOEL, architectural educator; b. Stamford, Conn., Aug. 18, 1946; d. Everett Linwood and Vivian (Smith) G.; m. Lawrence K. Stern, Apr. 29, 1979; 1 child, Laura Linwood. BA, Conn. Coll., 1968; MA in Teaching, Yale U., 1969; MFA, Calif. Inst. Arts, 1972; MS, U. Surrey, 1979, PhD, 1985. Designer Charles Moore Assocs., New Haven, 1969-70, McCue Boone Tomsick Architects, San Francisco, 1974-77; cons. Kaplan, McLaughlin, Diaz Architects, San Francisco, 1979-80; asst. prof. U. Wis., Milw., 1980-86, assoc. prof., 1986-87; assoc. dean Coll. Arch. and Urban Planning U. Mich., Ann Arbor, 1987-92, assoc. prof, 1987—; faculty assoc. Ctr. for Rsch. on Learning and Tchg., 1996-97. Mem. editl. bd. Jour. Archtl. Edn., 1989-95, Jour. Environ. Psychology, Jour. Archtl. and Planning Rsch. Mem. Nat. Trust for Hist. Preservation, Washington, 1983—, Nat. Mus. Women in the Arts, Washington, 1987—. Recipient Environ. Graphics award Print Casebooks, 1979; design rsch. grantee Nat. Endowment for the Arts, 1982, 92, Graham Found. for Advanced Studies in Fine Arts, 1991. Mem. AIA (assoc.), Internat. Assn. for Study People and Their Phys. Surroundings, Assn. Collegiate Sch. Architecture (east ctrl. region dir. 1992-95), Environ. Design Rsch. Assn., Nat. Assn. for Women in Edn. Office: U Mich Coll Architecture & Urban Planning 2000 Bonisteel Dr Ann Arbor MI 48109-2069

GROAT, PAMELA FERNE, school librarian; b. Kalamazoo, Mich., Sept. 17, 1949; d. Jay J. and Margaret Ann (Jones) G. BA, Western Mich. U., 1971, MS in Librarianship, 1973. Substitute media specialist St. Charles (Mich.) Cmty. Schs., 1974; dist. libr. Baldwin (Mich.) Cmty. Sch., 1974—; del. White House Conf. on Librs., Lansing, Mich., 1990; advisor Lake County Regional Ednl. Materials Ctr. II, Traverse Bay Area Intermediate Sch. Dist., Traverse City, Mich., 1974. Mem. ALA, NEA, AAUW, Mich. Edn. Assn. (rep. to regional coms. 1974), Baldwin Edn. Assn. (pres., v.p., sec., bldg. rep.), Mich. Assn. for Media in Edn. (regional chair, bd. dirs.), Lake County Hist. Soc. (charter mem.). Democrat. Methodist.

GROBSCHMIDT, RICHARD A., state legislator; b. Milw., May 3, 1948; married; 1 child. BS, U. Wis., Oshkosh, 1972; MS, U. Wis., Milw., 1979. Polit. sci. tchr. South Milwaukee H.s., 1972-85; mem. from dist. 21 Wis. State Assembly, Madison, 1984-05, mem. from 7th senate dist., 1995—, chmn. adminstrv. rules com. and retirement com. Mem. Milw. Hist. Soc., Nature Conservancy. Home: 1513 Mackinac Ave South Milwaukee WI 53172-3045*

GROCE, JOAN ALICE, retired social services professional; b. Carey, Ohio, June 17, 1930; d. Willie Edward and Hazel Alice (Wentling) Cole; m. John Wesley Groce, Mar. 21, 1959; children: Alisa Marie, Daniel Walter. BA in Religion, Ohio Wesleyan U., 1952; MA in Guidance and Counseling, Ball State U., 1958. Dir. Christian edn. Westwood Meth. Ch., Cin., 1952-56, St. Andrews United Meth. Ch., Findlay, Ohio, 1957-59; tchr. Tiffin (Ohio) City Schs., 1959-60, Heidelberg Coll., Tiffin, 1960-62; dir. info. ctr. Tiffin-Seneca United Way, 1978-86; case mgr., dir. nat. program for vols. for mentally ill Sandusky Valley Ctr., Tiffin, 1987-92; ret., 1992. Pres. Seneca County Cmty. Coun., Tiffin, 1980-82; pres. Habitat for Humanity, Tiffin, 1986-88; trustee Sandusky Valley Ctr.; bd. dirs. Tiffin-Seneca Day Care Ctr., 1993—. Recipient Cmty. Citizen award VFW, 1989. Mem. LWV, Heidelberg Cmty. Club. Democrat. Mem. United Ch. of Christ. Home: 250 Riverside Dr Tiffin OH 44883-1606

GROCHOWSKI, MARY ANN, psychotherapist; b. Milw., Oct. 8, 1944; d. Leonard Edward and Mary (Hitti) Rebatzke; m. James Allen Grochowski, Jan. 27, 1968; children: Bradley, Brandon. BA, Marquette U., 1966; MSW, U. Wis., Milw., 1968. Cert. social worker; lic. ind. clin. social worker. Psychotherapist L.A. Child Guidance Clinic, 1968-70, Milw. Children's Hosp., 1970-74; psychotherapist Family Social & Psychotherapy Svcs., Milw., 1972-74, 79-93, clinic dir., 1986-93; psychotherapist Apogee-Winston Clinic, Inc., Milw., 1993—; chair adv. coun. Family Social & Psychotherapy Svcs., Milw., 1987-90; mem. bd. Children's Legal Action Fund, Milw., 1989; active Nat. Clin. Adv. Bd. Apogee, 1994—. Contbr. articles to jours. Mem. NASW, Am. Profl. Soc. on Abuse of Children, Internat. Soc. Study of Dissociation, Eye Movement Desensitization and Reprocessing Internat. Assn. (charter). Roman Catholic. Office: Apogee Winston Clinics Inc 7330 W Layton Ave Milwaukee WI 53220-0800

GRODELL, FREDERICK CHARLES, III, electrical engineer; b. Cleve., May 19, 1954; s. Frederick C. and Beryldene Ruth (McCoy) g.; m. Theresa Ann Sabo Grodell, Nov. 8, 1980. BSEE, Case Western Reserve U., 1976, MEE, 1980, D in Electrical Engring., 1996. Fgn. exchange student AFS-India, Goa, India, 1971; design engr. R & D Oerlikon-Motch Corp., Euclid, Ohio, 1978-82; elec. engr., configuration mgmt. Van Dorn DeMag Corp., Cleve., 1983—. Republican. Roman Catholic. Office: Van Dorn DeMag Corp 11792 Alameda Dr Cleveland OH 44136-3011

GROENERT, CHARLES R., architectural engineer, executive; b. Indpls., Ind., Jan. 17, 1962. A in Archtl. Engring., ITT, 1982. Supr. Ctrl. Hardware, St. Louis, 1980-87; v.p. Buckner Glen Group Ltd., Inc., Indpls., 1987—. Methodist. Office: Buckner Glen Group Ltd Inc 5525 S Meridian St Indianapolis IN 46217-3748 Home: 6234 Wilshire Dr Indianapolis IN 46259

GROESCH, JOHN WILLIAM, JR., marketing research consultant; b. Seattle, Nov. 22, 1923; s. John William and Jeanette Morrison (Gilmur) G.; B.S. in Chem. Engring., U. Wash., 1944; m. Joyce Eugenia Schauble, Apr. 25, 1948; children—Sara, Mary, Andrew. Engr., Union Oil Co., L.A., 1944-48, corp. economist, L.A., 1948-56, chief statistician, 1956-62, mgr., 1962-68, mgr., Schaumburg, Ill., 1968-90; exec. v.p. Performance Systems, Inc., Barrington, Ill., 1990—. Bd. dirs. Mt. Prospect (Ill.) Boy Scouts Am., 1977-88, 94-95, adv. bd., 1989-94, 96—, v.p., 1979, 82-85; commr. 1980-81, mem. OakBrook (Ill.) East Cen. Region, 1984-88; treas. Scout Cabin Found., Barrington, 1977—. Served with USN, 1944-47. Mem. West Coast Mktg. Research Council (chmn. 1969), Am. Petroleum Inst. (chmn. com. 1970-72), Am. Mktg. Assn. (emeritus). Lodge: Mason. Home: 17 Shady Ln Barrington IL 60010-3634 Office: PO Box 56 Barrington IL 60011-0056

GROETHE, REED, lawyer; b. Indpls., Mar. 21, 1952; s. Alfred Philip and Kathryn (Skerik) G.; m. Nancy Jayne Radefeld, June 2, 1974; children: Jacob Peter, Eric Alfred. BA, St. Olaf Coll., 1974; JD, U. Chgo., 1977. Bar: Wis. 1977. Law clk. to judge U.S. Ct. Appeals (5th cir.), Montgomery, Ala., 1977-78; assoc. Foley & Lardner, Milw., 1978-86, ptnr., 1986—. Pres. Bay Shore Luth. Ch., Whitefish Bay, Wis., 1985-89. Mem. ABA (tax sect.), Nat. Asn. Bond Lawyers, Wis. Bar Assn. Lutheran. Office: Foley & Lardner 777 E Wisconsin Ave Milwaukee WI 53202-5302

GROFF, SUSAN CAROLE, elementary education educator; b. Marshalltown, Iowa, Feb. 16, 1954; d. Ernest Jerome and Alice Marjorie (Harmon) G.; m. Wayne A. Van Arendonk, Aug. 14, 1994. BS, Iowa State U., 1976; MS in Edn., U. Kans., 1981; edn. specialist, U. Iowa, 1984. Resource rm. aide Pinckney Elem., Lawrence, Kans., 1976-77; tchr. spl. edn. Booth Elem., Wichita, Kans., 1977-78; tchr. resource rm. Clinton (Iowa) Community Schs., 1978-80; tchr. spl. edn. Henry Sabin Elem., Clinton, 1980-83; cons. No. Trails Area Edn. Agy., Clear Lake, Iowa, 1984-86; tchr. resource rm. Tomiyasu Yr.-Round Sch., Las Vegas, Nev., 1986-88, 90-92; tchr. elem. edn. Tomiyasu Yr.-Round Sch., Las Vegas, 1988-90, 92-94; cons. Heartland Area Edn. Agy., Johnston, Iowa, 1994-96; tchr. spl. edn. Haysville (Kans.) Middle Schs., 1996—; student tchr. supr. U. Iowa, Iowa City, 1983, grad. asst., 1984. Treas. U.S. Rep., Iowa, 1974-75. Recipient Excellence in Edn. award Clark County Sch. Dist., Las Vegas, 1992. Mem. Iowa State Edn. Assn., Iowa State Cons. Assn., Coun. for Exceptional Children, U. Iowa Alumni Assn. (life), Iowa State U. Alumni Assn. (life), U. Kans. Alumni Assn. Democrat. Jewish. Home: 2359 N Parkridge Ct Wichita KS 67212

GRONEMUS, BARBARA, state legislator; b. Nov. 21, 1931; d. Erwin J. and Irene (Resch) Barry; m. Lambert N. Gronemus, 1949; children: Michelle (Mrs. Jerome J. Carroll), Jacqueline (Mrs. Eric Baken), Margaret Susan (Mrs. David Williams). Former dir. nursing home activity; mem. from dist. 91 Wis. State Assembly, Madison, 1982—, mem. state affairs, small bus. coms., 1993, mem. agr. com., 1983—, vice chmn., 1985, chmn. subcom. on swing psuedorabies, 1985, vice chmn. commerce and consumer affairs, 1983, mem. excise/fees, tourism, recreation & forest productivity, 1985, mem. Minn.-Wis. boundary commn. legis. adv. com., 1983—, chmn. agr., forestry and rural affairs coms. Chmn. Trempealeau County Dem. Com., 1981-82, 3d Congl. Dist. Dem. Com., 1982-83. Mem. Am. Legion, Farmers Union, Whitehall Women's Club, Whitehall Rod and Gun Club, Trempealeau County Homemakers Club. Home: 1634 West St Whitehall WI 54773-9505 Office: Wis House of Reps Office of House Mems Madison WI 53702*

GRONICK, PATRICIA ANN JACOBSEN, school system administrator; b. Madison, S.D., May 1, 1930; d. Jay C. and Lauretta (Lynch) Jacobsen; m. Joseph Gronick, Aug. 12, 1950; 1 child, Joseph Patrick Michael. BS, Pa. State U., 1952; MEd, Kent State U., 1970; postgrad., John Carroll U., 1972—. Home economist to dir. regional home econs. West Pa. Power Co., Pitts., 1952-61; dir. nat. home econs. Cleve. Range Co., 1961-70; coord. mktg. edn. Beachwood, Mayfield, Richmond Heights, Orange, Chagrin Falls, West Geauga, Aurora and Solon Sch. Systems, Ohio, 1969—; coord. distributive edn. Mayfield, Richmond Heights, Orange, Bratenahl, and Beachwood Sch. Systems, Ohio, 1970—; cons. photog. food layouts, 1960-61. Recipient Excel award, 1968-93, Mktg. award Ohio State Dept., 1983, 88, 93 Svc. award, Voc. Ednl. Plannint Dist., Mayfield, 1988, Award for Ednl. Excellence, 1988, VIP award, 1988, Consortium award of Appreciation, 1993. Mem. Cleve. Social Health and Welfare Assn., Am. Home Econs. Assn., AAUW, Elec. Women's Round Table, Internat. Fedn. Univ. Women, Cath. Daus. Am., Home Economists in Bus., Woman's Club (rec. sec. Cleve. 1962, parliamentarian 1965-66), Isabella Guild (officer 1985-89), Delta Kappa Gamma. Home: 880 Haywood Dr Cleveland OH 44121-3404 Office: Beachwood High Sch 25100 Fairmount Blvd Cleveland OH 44122-2250

GRONNER, MARK I., investment consultant; b. Chgo., July 17, 1951. BA in Econs., Rutgers U., 1973; MBA, CUNY, 1975. Hosp. mgr. Med. Ctr., Cleve., 1975-83; investment mgr. Merrill Lynch, Pepper Pike, Ohio, 1983-85; investment cons. McDonald & Co. Securities Inc., Pepper Pike, 1985—. Trustee Diabetes Assn. of Greater Cleve., 1993—.

GROSKY, WILLIAM IRVIN, computer science educator; b. Gulfport, Miss., Aug. 4, 1944; s. Daniel and Irene (Schreibman) G.; m. Roslyn Dorothy Balgley, Sept. 12, 1965; children: Sara Beth, Seth Israel. BS, MIT, 1965; MS, Brown U., 1968; PhD, Yale U., 1971. Asst. prof. computer scis. Ga. Inst. Tech., Atlanta, 1971-76; assoc. prof. Wayne State U., Detroit, 1976-87, prof., 1987—, chair, 1995—; program evaluator Computing Scis. Accreditation Bd., N.Y., 1989—; cons. UN Indsl. Devel. Orgn., Vienna, Austria, 1989-91; presenter, lectr. profl. seminars and confs., including 10th Ann. Internat. Workshop on Multimedia Info. Sys. and Hypermedia, 1995, IEEE Conf. on Data Engring., 1991, NSF, San Francisco, 1992. Mem. editl. rev. bd. Jour. Database Adminstrn., 1989—; assoc. editor IEEE Multimedia and Pattern Recognition; contbr. numerous articles to profl. publs. Grantee Ford Motor Co., Dearborn, Mich., 1990-95, U.S. Army, 1994. Mem. IEEE (co-editor computer spl. issue jour. Dec. 1989), Assn. Computing Machinery. Office: Wayne State U Computer Sci 431 State Hall 5143 Cass Ave Detroit MI 48202-3929

GROS LOUIS, KENNETH RICHARD RUSSELL, university chancellor; b. Nashua, N.H., Dec. 18, 1936; s. Albert W. and Jeannette Evelyn (Richards) Gros L.; m. Dolores K. Winandy, Aug. 28, 1965; children: Amy Katherine, Julie Jeannette. BA, Columbia U., 1959, MA, 1960; PhD, (Knapp fellow), U. Wis., 1964. Asst. prof. Ind. U., Bloomington, 1964-67, assoc. prof. English and comparative lit., 1967-73, prof., 1973—, assoc. chmn. comparative lit. dept., 1967-69, assoc. dean arts and scis., 1970-73, chmn. dept. English, 1973-78, dean arts and scis., 1978-80, v.p., 1980-88, chancellor, 1988—; v.p. acad. affairs, 1994—; bd. dirs. Anthem, Inc.; exec. coun. acad. affairs Nat. Assn. Univ. and Land Grant Colls., 1986—, bd. dirs. Bd. dirs. Editor Yearbook of Comparative and Gen. Lit., 1968—, Vol. I: Literary Interpretations of Biblical Narratives, 1974, Vol. II, 1982; contbr. articles to profl. jours. Bd. dirs. Assoc. Group, 1983-95, Anthem Blue Cross and Blue Shield, 1995—; mem. Ind. Com. Humanities, chmn., 1980-81; chmn. Com. on Instnl. Coop., 1986—; mem. Nat. Commn. on Libr. Preservation and Access, 1986-93; vice chmn., bd. dirs. Ctr. for Rsch. Librs., 1986—, chmn. bd. dirs., 1987-88. Recipient Disting. Teaching award Ind. U., 1970. Mem. MLA, Nat. Coun. Tchrs. English, AAUP, Phi Beta Kappa. Home: 1119 E 1st St Bloomington IN 47401-5005 Office: Ind U Bryan Hall Rm 100 Bloomington IN 47405

GROSS, CHARLES ROBERT, personnel executive, legislator, appraiser; b. St. Charles, Mo., Aug. 20, 1958; s. Jack Robert and Margaret Ellen (Stumberg) G.; m. Leslie Ann Goralczyk, May 27, 1984; 1 child, Megan Marie. BS in Pub. Adminstrn., U. Mo., 1981, MPA, 1982. Personnel mgr. Army and Air Force Exch. Svc., various cities, 1983-89; personnel/safety dir. Ever-Green Lawns Corp., St. Charles, 1989-92; state rep. Mo. Legislature, Jefferson City, 1993—; real estate appraiser, 1994—. Pres. St. Charles County Young Reps., 1990-92. Mem. Kiwanis, Pacaderms, Alpha Kappa Psi (life). Lutheran. Home: 3019 Westborough Ct Saint Charles MO 63301-4550

GROSS, DELBERT L., state legislator; b. Jan. 20, 1950; m. Jo Ann Gross. BS, Kans. State U., 1973. Kans. state rep. Dist. 111, 1996—. Mem. sch. bd. Hays, Kans., 1982-86. Mem. KC, Eagles. Home: 2405 Indian Trl Hays KS 67601-2331*

GROSS, KELLY LYNN, physical therapist assistant, aerobics instructor; b. Columbia City, Ind., Oct. 22, 1966; d. Paul Lawrence and Meredith Ann (Clark) Walker; m. Luther Alton Gross, Mar. 19, 1988; children: Cameron Jay, Haleigh Laine. AS, Vincennes U., 1987. Cert. CPR Nat. Dance and Exercise Instrs. Tng. Assn. Phys. therapy asst. Toledo Hosp., 1987-88, Luth. Hosp., Ft. Wayne, Ind., 1988-89; phys. therapy asst., co-ctr. coord. clin. edn. Associated Phys. Therapists, Inc., Ft. Wayne, Ind., 1989—, clin. instr., 1990—; aerobics instr., Churubusco, Ind., 1994—. Vol. Youth for Christ, Ft. Wayne, Whitley County Child Abuse Prevention Coun.; tchr. Bible sch. and Sunday sch. Mem. Am. Phys. Therapists Assn. (assoc.). Methodist. Home: 8810 E 700 N Churubusco IN 46723 Office: Associated Phys Therapists 1234 E DuPont Fort Wayne IN 46825

GROSS, MARY ELIZABETH, pharmacy manager, educator; b. Chgo., Nov. 20, 1957; d. Henry Thomas and Patricia (Kloska) G. BS in Pharmacy, Drake U., 1980; PharmD, U. Utah, 1982. Lic. pharmacist; cert. in gerontology. Resident in clin. pharmacy U. Utah, Salt Lake City, 1980-82; asst. prof. clin. pharmacy Sch. Pharmacy W.Va. U., Charleston, 1982-84, asst. prof. pharmacology Sch. Medicine, 1982-84; asst. prof. clin. pharmacy, clin. pharmacist Drake U. Coll. Pharmacy & Health Scis./Mercy Hosp. Med. Ctr., Des Moines, 1984-89, assoc. prof. clin. pharmacy, clin. pharmacist, 1989-93; mgr. pharmacy, assoc. prof. clin. pharmacy Mercy Hosp. and Drake U., Des Moines, 1993—; cons. pharmacist Madrid (Iowa) Home for the Aging, 1989-92; faculty assoc. W.Va. U. Gerontology Ctr., Morgantown, 1983; cons. pharmacist Iowa long-term care coordinating unit Case Mgmt. Project for the Frail Elderly, Crossroads of Iowa, 1991—. Author, editor monograph; contbr. articles to profl. jours. Mem. task force Dept. Elder Affairs, Des Moines, 1989—; mem. Health Older People Adv. Coun., Des Moines, 1985-86; chmn. Cancer Pain Relief Initiative, 1995—. Recipient State of Iowa Gov.'s Vol. award, 1991, Merck Clin. Pharmacy award U. Utah, 1982; grantee in field. Mem. Am. Assn. Colls. Pharamcy (profl. affairs com. 1992-93), Iowa Soc. Hosp. Pharmacists (chmn. nominations com. 1990-91, computer com. 1988-89, pres. 1989-90, key mem. 1990-94, Hosp. Pharmacist of Yr. award 1988), ASCP (edn. affairs coun. 1994-95, nat. LTC task force on pharmacy stds. 1996—), Am. Soc. Hosp. Pharmacists (commn. on therapeutics 1995—). Office: Mercy Hosp Med Ctr Pharmacy Dept Des Moines IA 50314

GROSS, STANLEY MERHL, chiropractor; b. Breese, Ill., June 27, 1953; s. Walter Frank and Priscilla Dean (Myers) G.; m. Katherine Ferlisi, June 27, 1993; children: Timothy, Carisa, Geno, Zachary, Jason. BS in Biomed., Washington U., St. Louis, 1982; PhD, Harvard U., 1983; BS in Biology, Logan Coll., Chesterfield, Mo., 1986, D Chiropractic, 1988. Diplomate Advanced Chiropractic Technique; cert. acupuncture Community Chiropractic Ctr. Pvt. practice, chief staff Community Chiropractic Ctr., O'Fallon, Mo., 1988—; instr., lectr. Logan Coll. Chiropractic, Chesterfield, Mo., 1988—. Author: Bio-Synergistic Integration, 1984. Dir. Ankylosing Spondytitis Assn., St. Louis, 1988—; alderman ward II, St. Paul, Mo., 1993—. Recipient Star Scholarship Logan Alumni Assn., Chesterfield, 1987. Mem. Acad. Advancement Sci., Am. Chiropractic Assn., Toastmasters Internat. (Most Able award 1992). Home and Office: 1002 Mueller Rd O'Fallon MO 63366

GROSS, THEODORE LAWRENCE, university administrator, author; b. Bklyn., Dec. 4, 1930; s. David and Anna (Weisbrod) G.; m. Selma Bell, Aug. 27, 1955 (dec. 1991); children: Donna, Jonathan; m. Marion Simon, 1992. BA, U. Maine, 1952; MA, Columbia U., 1957, PhD, 1960. Prof. English CCNY, 1958-78, chmn. dept., 1970-72, assoc. dean and dean humanities, 1972-78, v.p. instl. advancement, 1976-77; provost Capitol Campus, Pa. State U., Middletown, 1979-83; dean Sch. Letters and Sci. SUNY Coll., Purchase, 1983-88; chmn. SUNY-Purchase Westchester Sch. Partnership, 1984-88; pres. Roosevelt U., Chgo., 1988—; vis. prof., Fulbright scholar, Nancy, France, 1964-65, 68-69, Dept. State lectr., Nigeria, Israel, Japan, Austria. Author: Albion W. Tourgée, 1964, Thomas Nelson Page, 1967, Hawthorne, Melville, Crane: A Critical Bibliography, 1971, The Heroic Ideal in American Literature, 1971, Academic Turmoil: The Reality and Promise of Open Education, 1980, Partners in Education: How Colleges Can Work with Schools to Improve Teaching and Learning, 1988; also essays, revs.; editor: Fiction, 1967, Dark Symphony: Negro Literature in America, 1968, Representative Men, 1969, A Nation of Nations, 1971, The Literature of American Jews, 1973; gen. editor: Studies in Language and Literature, 1974, America in Literature, 1978. With AUS, 1952-54. Grantee, Rockefeller Found., 1976-77, Am. Coun. Learned Socs. Mem. MLA, PEN, Nat. Coun. Tchrs. of English (chmn. lit. com.), Century Assn., Univ. Club. Home: 1515 N Astor St Chicago IL 60610-1655

GROSSKREUTZ, JOSEPH CHARLES, physicist, engineering researcher, educator; b. Springfield, Mo., Jan. 5, 1922; s. Joseph Charles and Helen (Mobley) G.; m. Mary Catherine Schubel, Sept. 7, 1949; children—Cynthia Lee, Barbara Helen. B.S. in Math., Drury Coll., 1943; postgrad., U. Calif.-Berkeley, 1946-47; M.S., Washington U., St. Louis, 1948, Ph.D. in Physics, 1950. Research physicist Calif. Research Corp., La Habra, 1950-52; asst. prof. physics U. Tex.-Austin, 1952-56; research scientist Nuclear Physics Lab., Austin, 1952-56; sr. physicist Midwest Research Inst., Kansas City, Mo., 1956-59, prin. physicist, 1959-63, sr. adviser, 1963-67; prin. advisor Midwest Research Inst., Kansas City, 1967-71; chief mech. properties sect. Nat. Bur. Standards, Washington, 1971-72; mgr. solar programs Black & Veatch Cons. Engrs., Kansas City, Mo., 1972-77, mgr. advanced tech. projects, 1979-88, project engr. design/constrn. solar thermal test facility, 1975-77; ret., 1988; research prof. physics U. Mo., Kansas City, 1989—; 1st dir. rsch. Solar Energy Rsch. Inst., Golden, Colo., 1977-79; spl. cons. NATO, 1967. Contbr. articles to profl. jours. Served to lt. USN, 1943-46. Recipient Disting. Service award Drury Coll., 1959; Washington U. fellow, 1948-49. Fellow Am. Phys. Soc., ASTM (dir. 1977-80, Merit award 1972); mem. Sigma Xi, Sigma Pi Sigma. Methodist. Home: 4306 W 111th Ter Shawnee Mission KS 66211-1702 Office: U Mo Physics Dept Kansas City MO 64110

GROSSMAN, KENNETH CEDRIC, health facility director; b. Chgo., Sept. 8, 1945; s. Walter Frederick and Frances (Kumskis) G.; m. Kathleen Cohan (div. 1980); children: Karina, Cynthia, Kristina, Kassandra; m. Jane Alta DeYoung, Oct. 14, 1983. Student, Ea. Mich. U., 1963-64, U. Nebr., 1966-71, U. Chgo., 1983-84; BA, Am. Inst. Hypnotherapy, 1989, PhD, 1990; CBA, U. Ill., Chgo., 1991. Cert. clin. hypnotherapist Nat. Bd. Hypnotherapy and Hypnotic Anesthesiology. Pres. Alpine Corp., Omaha, 1970-80; exec. dir. Am. Inst. Smoking Cessation, Hinsdale, Ill., 1980—. Served to sgt., USAF, 1962-66. Mem. Am. Assn. Counseling & Devel., Soc. of Group Behavioral Hypnotherapists (pres. 1990-91), Profl. Hypnotherapists, Specialists in Group Work, Nat. Speakers Assn., Profl. Speakers of Ill. Office: Am Inst Smoking Cessation PO Box 11 Hinsdale IL 60522-0011

GROSSMAN, LISA ROBBIN, clinical psychologist, lawyer; b. Chgo., Jan. 22, 1952; d. Samuel R. and Sarah (Kruger) G. BA with highest distinction and departmental honors in Psychology, Northwestern U., 1974, JD cum laude, 1979, PhD, 1982. Bar: Ill. 1981; registered psychologist, Ill. Jud. intern, U.S. Supreme Ct., Washington, 1975; pre-doctoral psychology intern Michael Reese Hosp. and Med. Center, Chgo., 1979-80; therapist Homes for Children, Chgo., 1980-83; psychologist Psychiat. Inst., Cir. Ct. Cook County, Chgo., 1981-87; pvt. practice, 1984—; invited participant workshop HHS, Rockville, Md., 1981. Contbr. articles to profl. jours. Mem. ABA, Am. Psychol. Assn. (com. on legal issues 1992-95, com. on profl. practice and stds. 1996-99, state leadership organizing com. 1996-98), Ill. Psychol. Assn. (pres. 1995-96), Chgo. Assn. for Psychoanalytic Psychologists (parliamentarian 1982), Ill. State Bar Assn., Chgo. Bar Assn., Soc. Personality Assessment, Mortar Bd., Phi Beta Kappa, Shi-Ai, Alpha Lambda Delta. Office: 500 N Michigan Ave Ste 1520 Chicago IL 60611-3703

GROSZ, ALBERT MICK, sales executive; b. Minot, N.D., Oct. 18, 1946; s. Robert J. and Emma (Wagner) G.; m. Mary Mitchell, Nov. 29, 1974; children: Michael, Marcus. BS, N.D. State U., 1969. Social studies tchr. Turtle Lake (N.D.) Pub. Sch., 1969-72; farmer Baldwin, N.D., 1974-77; contractor Turtle Lake, 1977-84; chem. sales exec. AGri Bus. Products, Turtle Lake, 1984—. Rep. N.D. Gen. Assembly, Bismarck, 1991, 93; bd. dirs. Turtle Lake-Mercer Sch. Dist., 1981-90, pres., 1983-90; dir. West River Telephone Coop, Hazen, N.D., 1985—. Sgt. U.S. Army, 1972-74. Decorated Commendation medal. Republican. Home: 480 Becker St Turtle Lake ND 58575 Office: Agri Bus Products PO Box 535 Turtle Lake ND 58575-0535

GROTELUESCHEN, RALPH D., manufacturing company executive; b. Columbus, Nebr., Feb. 8, 1941; s. Harold W. and Dorothy M. (Dirks) G.; m. Norma J. Monson, June 25, 1965; children: Amy D., Renee L., Mark A. BS, U. Nebr., 1963; MS, U. Wis., 1965, PhD, 1967. Scientist Deere & Co., Moline, Ill., 1967-70, mgr. environ. control, 1970-77, 78-84; dir. safety and environment Deere & Co., Moline, 1984-86, dir. safety standards and environment, 1986—; policy analyst U.S. EPA, Washington, 1977-78; mem. environ. study com. Iowa Bus. Coun., Des Moines, 1990-91; environ. stewardship Nat. 4-H, Beltsville, Md., 1990-94. Bd. dirs. The Nature of Ill. Found., Chgo., 1990—; trustee Foundry Edn. Found., Des Plaines, Ill., 1985—; mem. East Moline (Ill.) Bd. Edn., 1980-90, pres., 1985-89; bus. mgr. East Moline Youth Baseball, 1991-93, commr., 1994. Mem. Am. Soc. Agronomy, Am. Foundrymen's Soc. (chmn. environ.), Bus. Roundtable (environ. subcom.). Lutheran. Home: 706 27th Ave Ct East Moline IL 61244-3247 Office: Deere & Co John Deere Rd Moline IL 61265

GROTHAUS, PAMELA SUE, marketing professional; b. Alameda, Calif., Mar. 25, 1958; d. Michael James and Patricia Ann (Owsley) Spillers; m. David Michael Grothaus, June 3, 1977; children: Shannon Marie, Matthew David. Student, Webster U., Webster Groves, Mo., 1984-86, Cen. Mo. State U., 1976-77, St. Louis Community Coll., 1981-83. With U.S. Civil Svc., K.I. Sawyer AFB, Mich., 1979-80; adminstrv. asst. Mo. Dept. Consumer Affairs, Jefferson City, Mo., 1980-81; adminstrv. coord. Baur Properties, Inc., St. Louis, 1981-82; account exec. Atkinson Group Inc., St. Louis, 1982-87; advt. coord. Eveready Battery Co., St. Louis, 1987; advt. officer Mercantile Bancorporation, Inc., St. Louis, 1987-88; copywriter, sr. account exec. Wilson Sculley Assoc. Inc., 1989-91; mktg. mgr., copywriter Nehmen-Kodner, Inc., St. Louis, 1991-92; dir. mktg. and creative svcs. AdSell, St. Louis, 1993-94; account supr. Wilson Sculley Assocs., St. Louis, 1994-95, Clarion Direct, St. Louis, 1995—. Fitness instr. YMCA, Webster Grove, 1988-89. Mem. Direct Mktg. Assn. St. Louis (pres., bd. dirs. 1995). Republican. Roman Catholic. Home: 105 Waterford Dr Labadie MO 63055

GROTHEER-RIDINGS, PATRICIA, nurse; b. Pittsburg, Kans., Oct. 21, 1964; d. Arthur G. and Charlene Alva (Wingblade) G. BS in Nursing, Pitts. State U., Kans., 1989. Nurse's aide Med. Lodge South, Pitts., Kans., 1983-84; asst. Shield's Adult Care Home, Pitts., Kans., 1985; nursing asst. Mount Carmel Med. Ctr., Pitts., Kans., unit clerk, pediatrics dept., 1988-89; nursing intern St. Luke's Hosp., Kansas City, Mo., 1988; nurse Shawnee Mission (Kans.) Med. Ctr., 1989—; nurse telemetry unit St. John's Regional Med. Ctr., Joplin, Mo., 1990-92, ICU nurse, 1992—; acute dialysis nurse Four State Regional Dialysis, Joplin, 1994—. Veta Teaschner scholar, 1987, Pitts. Ladies Aux. scholar, 1988.

GROTHER, DAVID MICHAEL, computer company executive; b. Decatur, Ill., July 10, 1946; s. Carl William and Emily Francis (Montgomery) G.; m. Nancy Flaxman, Jan. 26, 1968 (div. 1976). BS in Math., U. Ill., 1967, MS in Computer Sci., 1969. Computer programmer U. Ill. Illiac IV Project, Urbana, 1966-70, U. Ill. Ctr. for Advanced Computation, Urbana, 1970-75, Army Corps of Engrs., Champaign, Ill., 1975-76, Associated Computer Consultants, Santa Barbara, Calif., 1976-79; computer cons. Urbana, 1979-83; pres. GCOM, Inc., Urbana, 1983—; cons. Bklyn. Children's Museum, 1971, U. Mex., Mexico City, 1977; vis. lectr. U. Alaska, Fairbanks, 1972; guest speaker IBM Europe User's Group, Sevilla, Spain, 1984. Contbr. articles to profl. jours. James scholar U. Ill., 1964. Mem. Assn. for Computing Machinery, IEEE, Mensa, Phi Kappa Phi. Democrat. Office: GCOM Inc 1800 Woodfield Dr Savoy IL 61874

GROTHMAN, GLENN, state legislator; b. July 3, 1955. BA, U. Wis. Tax & estate planning atty.; assemblyman Wis. State Dist. 59, 1993—. Active Washington County Vol. Ctr. Mem. Washington County Bar Assn., Kiwanis, Moose. Address: 111 S 6th Ave West Bend WI 53095

GROTZINGER, LAUREL ANN, university librarian; b. Truman, Minn., Apr. 15, 1935; d. Edward F. and Marian Gertrude (Greeley) G. BA, Carleton Coll., 1957; MS, U. Ill., 1958, PhD, 1964. Instr., asst. libr. Ill. State U., 1958-62; asst. prof. Western Mich. U., Kalamazoo, 1964-66; assoc. prof. Western Mich. U., 1966-68, prof., 1968—, asst. dir. Sch. Librarianship, 1965-72, chief rsch. officer, 1979-86, interim dir. Sch. Libr. and Info. Sci., 1982-86, dean grad. coll., 1979-92, prof. univ. libr., 1993—. Author: The Power and the Dignity, 1966; mem. editl. bd. Jour. Edn. for Librarianship, 1973-77, Dictionary Am. Libr. Biography, 1975-77, Mich. Academician, 1990—; contbr. articles to profl. jours. Trustee Kalamazoo Pub. Libr., 1991-93, v.p., 1991-92, pres., 1992-93. Mem. ALA (sec.-treas. Libr. History Round Table 1973-74, vice chmn., chmn.-elect 1983-84, chmn. 1984-85, mem.-at-large 1991-93), Spl. Librs. Assn., Assn. Libr. Info. Sci. Edn., Mich. acad. Sci., Arts and Letters (mem.-at-large, exec. com. 1980-86, pres. 1983-85, exec. com. 1990-94, pres. 1991-93), Internat. Assn. Torch Clubs (v.p. Kalamazoo chpt. 1992-93, pres. 1993-94, exec. com. 1989-95), Phi Beta Kappa (pres. S.W. Mich. chpt. 1977-78, sec. 1994—), Delta Phi Mu, Phi Delta Epsilon, Alpha Beta Alpha, Delta Kappa Gamma (pres. Alpha Psi chpt. 1988-92), Phi Kappa Phi. Home: 2729 Mockingbird Dr Kalamazoo MI 49008-1626

GROVE, HELEN HARRIET, historian, artist; b. South Bend, Ind.; d. Samuel Harold and LaVerne Mae (Drescher) Grove; grad. Bayle Sch. Design, Meinzinger Found., 1937-39, Washington U., 1940-42; spl. studies, Paris, France. Owner studios of historic research and illustration, St. Louis, Chgo., 1943—; dir. archives, bus. history research Sears, Roebuck & Co., 1951-67; research for Northwestern U., Chgo.-Sears Roebuck & Co., art Lawrence U., Appleton, Wis. Home: 6326 N Clark St Chicago IL 60660-1215 Studio: 6328 N Clark St Chicago IL 60660-1215

GROVE, MYRNA JEAN, elementary education educator; b. Bryan, Ohio, Oct. 24, 1949; d. Kedric Durward and N. Florence (Stombaugh) G. Student, Bowling Green State U., 1970-71; BA in Edn., Manchester Coll., 1971; postgrad., U. No. Colo., 1974-76, Purdue U., 1977, St. Francis Coll., Ft. Wayne, Ind., 1986, Coll. Mount St. Joseph, Ohio, 1986. Cert. elem. tchr., Ohio. Tchr. elem. sch. Bryan City Schs., 1972—. Author: Asbestos Cancer: One Man's Experience, 1995; editor newspaper column Education Today, 1975-82, newsletter N.W. Ohio Emphasis, 1981-83 (award 1981). Dir., violinist Bryan String Ensemble, 1981—; organist Trinity Episc. Ch., Bryan, 1979-89; active Lancaster Mennonite Hist. Soc., Hans Herr Found.; trustee Bryan Area Cultural Assn., 1984-89; bd. dirs. William County Cmty. Concerts; regional docent P. Buckley Moss. Jennings scholar Martha Holden Jennings Found., Bowling Green State U., 1982-83. Mem. NEA (Ohio del., state contact 1986-87), Nat. Assn. Gifted Children, Am. Booksellers' Assn. (assoc. mem.), Writers Info. Network, Ohio Edn. Assn. (presenter 1984, del. global issues 1986, sec. N.W. Ohio Tchrs. Uniserv. 1975-78), Ohio Assn. Gifted Children, Bus. and Profl. Women Ohio (individual devel. com. 1986-90, speaking skills cert. 1987), N.W. Ohio Manchester Coll. Alumni Assn. (past pres.), Bryan Edn. Assn. (exec. com., pres. 1985-86), P. Buckley Moss Soc., Trees of Life (v.p. 1994—, reg. moss docent), Alpha Delta Kappa (pres. 1996—), Alpha Mu.

GROVE, RICHARD CHARLES, power tool company executive; b. Bethlehem, Pa., Aug. 13, 1940; s. Dale Addison and Mary Elizabeth (Ripple) G.; m. Cynthia Ann Dimmick, Dec. 7, 1963; 1 child, Jeffrey. BEE, Cornell U., 1962; MBA, U. Pitts., 1967. Mgmt. cons. Touche Ross & Co., Detroit, 1967-72; mgr. bus. planning Amstar Corp., N.Y.C., 1972-75; treas. Spreckels Sugar div. Amstar Corp., San Francisco, 1975-82; treas. Amstar Corp., N.Y.C., 1983-84; v.p., controller Amstar Corp., Stamford, Conn., 1985-88, v.p., chief fin. officer, 1988-89; sr. v.p. Esstar Inc., New Haven, 1989, exec. v.p., dir., 1995; exec. v.p. Milw. Electric Tool Corp., 1990-91, pres., chief exec. officer, 1991—. Mem., bd. regents Milw. Sch. Engring. Served to 1st lt. U.S. Army, 1964-66. Mem. Blue Mound Golf and Country Club, Country Club of Darien (Conn.). Republican. Office: Milw Electric Tool Corp 13135 W Lisbon Rd Brookfield WI 53005-2550

GROVENDER, GLADYS LOVERN, archivist consultant; b. Mpls., May 14, 1921; d. Eddie nd Anna Olina (Grinden) Setran; m. Harold William Grovender, May 29, 1941; children: Steven Leroy, Suzan Ardelle, William Harold, John Edward. Choir dir. Luth. Ch. of the Ascension, Burnsville, Minn., 1964-68, organist, 1965-68; archivist, historian Minn. south dist. Luth. Women's Missionary League, 1974-78; archivist, historian Minn. south dist. Internat. Luth. Women's Missionary League, 1979-93, archivist, historian, cons., 1993—. Producer geneal. quar. Grawunder/Graffunder Connection; contbr. articles to profl. jours. Mem. com. on awards Concordia Hist. Inst., Luth. Ch.-Mo. Synod, St. Louis, 1980—, bd. govs., 1987—, mem. conf. archives and history, 1977—, rep.-at-large, 1979-95, mem. centennial history com. Minn. south dist., 1982; bd. dirs. Metro Luth., Mpls., 1985-93, sec., 1988-91, v.p., 1991-92, archivist, historian, 1992-93. Home and Office: 13108 Penn Ave S Burnsville MN 55337-2015

GROVER, JOHN WAGNER, physician; b. Moorefield, W.Va., June 21, 1927; s. Leon Rex Sr. and Evalyn Dechant (Wagner) G.; m. Philippa Eby, Apr. 5, 1952; children: Jessica Louise, Amy Rose, Ava Elizabeth. BA, Harvard Coll., 1952, MD, 1956. Diplomate Am. Bd. Ob-Gyn. Intern in surgery Mass. Gen. Hosp., Boston, 1956-57, ob-gyn., 1964-79; rsch. fellow USPHS, Cambridge, Eng., 1959-61; resident in ob-gyn. Boston Hosp. for Women, 1961-64, ob-gyn., 1964-79; resident Mass. Gen. Hosp., Boston, Ill., 1957-59; assoc. clin. prof. ob-gyn. Pritzker Sch. Medicine U. Chgo., 1992—; chmn. data com. U. Ill. Perinatal Network, Chgo., 1979-89. Author: VD-The ABC's, 1972, (with others) The Gentle Birth Book, 1979. Mem. Govs. Commn. on Status of Women, Boston, 1975. With USN, 1945-49. USPHS postgrad. fellow, Eng., 1959-61, Josiah Macy Found. fellow, 1956-64; recipient scholarship Pepsi-Cola, 1949-52. Fellow ACOG; mem. Mass. Med. Soc., Chgo. Gynecol. Soc., Boston Obstet. Soc. Democrat. Episcopalian. Home: 1420 Pleasant Ln Glenview IL 60025-1843 Office: Luth Gen Hosp 1775 Dempster St Park Ridge IL 60068-1143

GROVER, KAREN A., designer; b. Dubuque, Iowa, Feb. 12, 1948. BS in Art Edn., U. Wis., Platteville, 1966-70; A, Rock Valley Jr. Coll., Rockford, Ill., 1980-82. Designer Abar Ipsen, Cherry Valley, Ill., 1980-94, Warner Electric, Marengo, Ill., 1994—. Mem. Am. Soc. Metals. Methodist. Office: Warner Electric LM/E 1300 W State St Marengo IL 60152

GROVES, SHARON SUE, elementary education educator; b. Springfield, Mo., Apr. 25, 1944; d. William Orin Jr. and Ruth M. (Jones) Hodge; m. Donald L. Groves, July 20, 1963. BA, Drury Coll., 1966, MEd, 1969. Cert. life elem. tchg.; Psychol. Examiners Cert. Adminstrn. Elem. tchr. Springfield Pub. Schs., 1966—; asst. instr. individual testing Drury Coll., Springfield, 1969-76; asst. instr. enhancing math. S.W. Mo. State U., Springfield, 1991-94; sr. leader MAP 2000 (Mo. Assessment Project) Class I. Author: Modeling Effective Practices: Geometry and Computation. Active Springfield's Curriculum Coun.; mem. Tchg. Cadre, Strategic Planning Team; hon. life mem. PTA; chmn. adminstrv. coun. Hood United Meth. Ch.; children's coord., math. workshops.; sr. leader Mo. Assessment Project, 1993—. Recipient Extra Mile award, 1989; named Fremont Tchr. of the Yr., 1988, 93. Mem. ASCD, Internat. Reading Assn., Assn. for Childhood Edn., Nat. Coun. Tchrs. Math., Mo. Coun. Tchrs. Math., Mo. State Tchrs. Assn. (pres. S.W. dist., Educator of Yr. 1989, Leader of Yr. 1990), Springfield Edn. Assn. (pres.), Delta Kappa Gamma (1st v.p.). Home: 8076 W Farm Rd 144 Springfield MO 65802-9555

GROWE, JOAN ANDERSON, state official; b. Mpls., Sept. 28, 1935; d. Lucille M. (Brown) Johnson; children: Michael, Colleen, David, Patrick. B.S., St. Cloud State U., 1956; cert. in spl. edn., U. Minn., 1964; exec. mgmt. program State and local govt., Harvard U., 1979. Tchr. elem. pub. schs. Bloomington, Minn., 1956-58; tchr. for exceptional children elem. pub. schs. St. Paul, 1964-65; spl. edn. tchr. St. Anthony Pub. Schs., Minn., 1965-66; mem. Minn. Ho. of Reps., 1973-74; sec. of state State of Minn., St. Paul, 1975—; mem. exec. coun. Minn. State Bd. Investment. Mem. Women Execs. in State Govt., Women's Campaign Fund, Women's Polit. Caucus, Minn. Women's Econ. Roundtable; candidate U.S. Senate, 1984; bd. dirs. Greater Mpls. coun. Girl Scouts U.S., Wayside House. Recipient Minn. Sch. Bell award, 1977, YMCA Outstanding Achievement award, 1978, Disting. Alumni award St. Cloud State U., 1979, Charlotte Striebel Long Distance Runner award Minn. NOW, 1985, The Woman Who Makes a Difference award Internat. Women's Forum, 1991, Esther V. Crosby Leadership award Greater Mpls. Girl Scout Coun., 1992. Mem. Nat. Assn. Secs. of State (pres. 1979-80), Minn. Equal Rights Alliance, LWV. Roman Catholic. Office: Sec of State's Office 100 Constitution Ave Rm 180 Saint Paul MN 55155

GRUBB, FLOYD DALE, state legislator; b. June 26, 1949. BS, Purdue U., 1985. Agrl. economist, cash grain commodity broker; rep. Dist. 42 Ind. Ho. of Reps., mem. agr. com., chmn. Fin. Inst.; vice chmn. pub. health com.; farmer. Precinct committeeman, 1968—; chmn. Dem. Caucus, Ind. Named Outstanding Freshman House Dem., 1988. Mem. Am. Legion (adj. and comdr.), Nat. Fedn. Ind. Bus., Purdue U. Alumni Assn., Harry Truman Club, Ferguson Club. Home: 515 8th St Covington IN 47932-1416*

GRUBBS, PAULETTE DENISE, information engineer; b. Dayton, Ohio, Oct. 31, 1950; d. Morris and Lois Smyth; children: Djuan, Myesha. AA, Cuyahoga C.C., 1981; BA, Capital U., 1987; MS, Ctrl. Mich. U., 1990. Sec. to controller Woodruff Hosp., Cleve., 1973-79; dist. office pers. clk. Ohio Bell, Cleve., 1979-82; sec. Wright-Patterso AFB, Dayton, 1983, Sinclair Coll., 1984-86; mortgage loan processor Citfed Mortgage Corp., Dayton, 1986; sec. to br. chief DSCSMA, Dayton, 1986-87; legal asst. Office Gen. Counsel, 1987-91; computer systems programmer analyst Def. Electronics Supply Ctr., Dayton, 1986-94; software engr. Sci. Applications Internat. Corp., Dayton, 1994—; sr. info. engr. Maden Tech., Dayton, 1995—. Home: 1434 Academy Pl Dayton OH 45406

GRUBBS, STEVEN ERIC, state representative; b. Hill City, Kans., Oct. 20, 1964; s. Herman Lee and Joyce Marie (Godwin) G.; m. Kelli Rene Jacque, May 21, 1988; children: Justin, Erica. BBA, U. Iowa, 1989, JD, 1994. State rep. State of Iowa, Des Moines, 1991—, chmn. edn. com. ho. of reps. Recipient Guardian of Small Bus. award Nat. Fedn. Ind. Bus., 1992. Republican. Home: 5524 Appomattox Rd Davenport IA 52806-2351 Office: Iowa House Reps Des Moines IA 50319*

GRUBE, ALLEN D., mechanical engineer; b. Foldwater, Ohio, Dec. 17, 1958. AA in Mech. Engring., ITT, 1980. Mech. engr. CTS, Berne, Ind., 1980-92, Micro Precision, Berne, Ind., 1992—. Mem. Sons of Am. Legion. Roman Catholic. Office: Micro Precision 525 Berne St Berne IN 46711-1246

GRUBER, JOHN EDWARD, editor, railroad historian, photographer; b. Chgo., May 18, 1936; s. Edward David and Leah Elizabeth (Diehl) G.; m. Bonnie Jean Barstow, May 12, 1962; children: Richard J., Timothy J. BA in Journalism, U. Wis., 1959, postgrad., 1981-84. Editor, writer U. Wis., Madison, 1960-95; editor Vintage Rails, Waukesha, Wis., 1995—. Author: Focus on Rails, 1989, (pamphlet) Madison's Pioneer Buildings, 1987; also articles; contbr. photographs to Trains mag., 1960—. Dir. Historic Madison, Inc., 1981-89. Recipient Nat. Award in R.R. History for photography Rwy. and Locomotive Hist. Soc., 1994; James J. Hill rsch. grantee Hill Reference Libr., 1986. Mem. Mid-Continent Railway Hist. Soc. (bd. dirs. 1984-87, 88—, pres. 1988-89, sec. 1990-95, v.p. 1995—, editor Mid-Continent Railway Gazette 1982—). Home: 1430 Drake St Madison WI 53711-2211 Office: Pentrex Pub Pentrex Waukesha WI 53180-3790

GRUBER, LOREN CHARLES, English language educator, writer; b. Carroll, Iowa, Sept. 17, 1941; s. Maurice Deputy and Harriett Helen (Brynteson) G.; m. Irene Ellen Olson, Mar. 5, 1967 (div. 1980); children: Elizabeth Gruber Shinall, Stephen, Margaret; m. Meredith Adair Crellin, Jan. 22, 1983. BA, Simpson Coll., 1963; MA, Western Res. U., 1964; PhD, U. Denver, 1972. English instr. Grove City (Pa.) Coll., 1964-66, Simpson Coll., Indianola, Iowa, 1966-69; teaching asst. U. Denver, 1968-69, teaching fellow, 1969-70; from asst. to assoc. prof. Simpson Coll., Indianola, 1970-82; chief exec. cons. Stanley, Barber, Southard, Brown and Assocs., San Diego, 1982-83; account exec. Sta. KJEM-AM and K-95-FM, Bentonville, Ark., 1983-87; mgr., news dir. Sta. KQIS-FM, Clarinda, Iowa, 1987-89; asst. prof. English N.W. Mo. State U., Maryville, 1989-93, interim dir. composition, 1992-93; prof. English and Mass Comm. Mo. Valley Coll., 1993—; reviewer Choice, Middletown, Conn., 1973-82. Gen. editor In Geardagum Series, 1974-82, 91-92; bibliographer Neuphilologische Mitteilungen, Helsinki, Finland, 1978-82; bus. mgr. Laurel Rev., 1989-93; contbr. articles to profl. jours., magazines. Founding pres. Indianola Writers Workshop, 1972; sec. Indianola Fine Arts Commn., 1973; state del. Iowa Rep. Party Conv., Des Moines, 1976, 80, 88; hon. mem. 4-H, Page County, Iowa, 1988; bd. dirs. Writers Hall of Fame, 1995—; founder Marshall area chpt. Writers' Hall of Fame, 1996—. Mem. Medieval Acad. Am. (life, mem. endowment capaign com. 1995—), Soc. for Advancement Scandinavian Studies (life), Soc. for New Lang. Study (exec. sec. 1973-82, 91-92), Mo. Writers Guild (bd. dirs. 1992—, editor News 1992-94, 2nd v.p. 1993-94, 1st v.p. 1994-95, pres. 1995-96), Iowa Poetry Assn. (pres. 1980-82, 88-92), Bentonville/Bella Vista Ark. Kiwanis (pres. 1985-86, lt. gov.'s award 1986, Merit and Spl. award 1986), Clarinda Iowa Rotary (pres. pro-tem 1989), Mo. Writers' Guild (charter). Republican. Episcopalian. Home: PO Box 217 Marshall MO 65340-0217 Office: Mo Valley Coll Dept Of English Marshall MO 65340

GRUBICH, DONALD NICHOLAS, retired association administrator; b. Buhl, Minn., Feb. 1, 1934; s. Nick and Sophia (Smilanich) G.; m. Claire Ann DeLano, Oct. 12, 1974; children: Leah, Nicole. AS, Virginia (Minn.) Jr. Coll., 1953; BBA in Indsl. Adminstrn., U. Minn., 1955. Mining engr. Iron Range Resources and Rehab. Bd., Hibbing, Minn., 1956-71; research supr. Iron Range Resources and Rehab. Bd., Eveleth, Minn., 1971-90, adminstrv. mgr., 1990-91; ret., 1991; organizing chmn. 6th Internat. Peat Congress, Duluth, Minn., 1980. Mem. Arrowhead Regional Devel. Commn., Duluth, 1984-86; bd. dirs. Mt. Iron (Minn.) Bd. Edn., 1981-84. Mem. Internat. Peat Soc. (U.S. coun. 1978-90, v.p. 1990—, U.S. nat. com. sec.-treas. 1982—), Minn. Peat Assn. (bd. dirs. 1984-87, 89-91). Democratic Farmer Labor Party. Serbian Orthodox. Lodges: Masons, Shriners, Elks. Home: 10105 White City Rd Britt MN 55710-8278

GRUENER, JENNIFER LEE, accountant; b. Ft. Worth, Feb. 13, 1967; d. Randall Dean and Judith Lea Wakefield Williams; m. Robert Anton Gruener, Aug. 11, 1990; 1 child, Evan Anthony. BS, S.W. Mo. State U., 1990. Cert. mgmt. acct., govt. fin. mgr. Acct. PSC Acctg. and Tax Svc., Springfield, Mo., 1985-88, RMS Co., Springfield, 1989-91, Kirkpatrick, Phillips & Miller, CPAs, Springfield, 1988-89; plant acct. City Utilities of Springfield, 1991-95, fin. analyst, 1996—; bd. dirs. Center City Care Corp. Mem. Inst. Mgmt. Accts., Assn. Govt. Accts. (dir. edn. 1993-94, treas. 1996). Office: City Utilities of Springfield 301 E Central St Springfield MO 65802-3834

GRUENWALD, BARBARA SAVAGE, secondary school art educator, art coordinator; b. Washington, Nov. 12; d. Robert Arnold and Betty Lois Savage; m. Kirk Rodger Gruenwald, 1 child, Kent Thomas. Student, U. Conn., 1970-73; BFA, Ea. Mich. U., 1976; MPA, Wayne State U., 1984; postgrad.; Ed Specialist in Edn. Leadership, Wayne State U., 1995. Cert. elem. and mid. sch. tchr., cert. tchr. elem. and secondary art; cert. tchr. secondary social scis. and polit. sci. Client cost control coord. Young & Rubicam, Detroit, 1974; layout artist Crowley Milner & Co., Detroit, 1977; tchr. art Grosse Pointe (Mich.) Pub. Sch. System, 1977-87, secondary art dept. chair, 1987—; ad hoc com. h.s. of future, 1986; Grosse Pointe Pub. Sch. Sys. tchr. rep. Idea Conf., Seattle, 1989; mem. tchr. adv. group, Grosse Pointe, 1985-87; juror Grosse Pointe Artists Assn., 1980, The Art Studio, Detroit, 1992, Art on the Pointe, 1993, 94, mem. h.s. restructuring team, 1993. Artist posters and advt. materials. Mem. Founders' Soc., Detroit Inst. Art; asst. Cub den leader Boy Scouts Am., 1987. Presdl. Mgmt. Internship finalist Office Pers. Mgmt., U.S. Govt., Washington, 1985. Mem. ASCD, AAUW, Mich. Edn. Assn., Delta Kappa Gamm (scholarship chairperson 1994-96). Office: Grosse Pointe Pub Sch System 11 Grosse Pointe Blvd Grosse Pointe MI 48236-3711

GRUHN, ROBERT STEPHEN, parole officer; b. N.Y.C., Dec. 9, 1938; s. Jerome and Beatrice (Fuchs) G.; m. Shirley Darlene Brayfield, Sept. 14, 1984. BS, NYU, 1961; MA in Criminology, Sam Houston State U., 1975; AB in Legal Studies, Drury Coll., 1987. Cert. criminal investigator. Collection mgr. Sears, Roebuck & Co., Albuquerque, 1961-64; adjuster Gen. Adjustment Bur., Albuquerque, 1964-65; indsl. engr. LTV Aerospace Corp., Dallas, 1965-66; agy. sec. Am. Nat. Ins., Dallas, 1966-72; parole officer Tex. Bd. Parole, Dallas and Houston, 1974-80, Mo. Bd. Parole, Springfield, 1980—; with Springfield Police Dept. Tng. Acad. Facility, 1984—. Author Collision Course, 1984. Bd. dirs. Wayback Halfway House, Dallas, 1977-80; chmn. Gang Task Force, Springfield, 1992—, So. Mo. Fugitive Task Force, Springfield, 1992—; bd. dirs. youth svcs. Mo. Dept. Corrections, 1993—; sr. v.p. One Missong Link, Mission Children Non-Profit ORgn., 1994—, active P.E.A.C.E. Project, Springfield, 1994—. Recipient commendation cert. N.Y. Police Dept., 1961, Cert. of Achievement in Extremism and Terrorism, Mo. Dept. Corrections, 1986, Cert. of Achievement in Satanism and the Occult, Mo. Dept. Corrections, 1989, Cert. of Achievement in Dangerous Gangs, 1989, Cert. Achievement, Mid States Organized Crime Info. Ctr., 1990, Cert. of Appreciation, U.S. Treasury Dept., 1992. Mem. Am. Mgmt. Assn. (internat. v.p. 1971-74), Soc. for Advt. Mgmt. (sec. 1968-71, pres. 1971-72), Soc. for Advancement of Mgmt. (Profl. Achievement award 1972), Mo. Corrections Assn., Midwest Gang Investigations Assn., Mu Gamma Tau. Home: 2214 E Nora St Springfield MO 65803-4952 Office: 149 Park Central Sq Rm 232 Springfield MO 65806-1315

GRULIOW, AGNES FORREST, artist, educator; b. Davenport, Iowa, July 5, 1912; d. James Lindsay and Agnes (Johnston) F.; m. Leo Gruliow, Sept. 25, 1945; children: Frank Forrest, Rebecca Agnes Lindsay. BA, Antioch Coll., Yellow Springs, Ohio, 1938; student, Art Student League, N.Y.C., 1963-66. Resident dir. Am. Peoples Sch., N.Y.C., 1937-41; asst. nat. sec. Nat. Fedn. Settlements, N.Y.C., 1941-43; assoc. pers. dir.,asst. prof. Antioch Coll. Extramural Sch., Yellow Springs, 1943-45; index designer, editor Current Digest of Soviet Press, Washington and N.Y.C., 1949-53; freelance editor N.Y.C., 1954-57; tchr. art City & Country Sch., N.Y.C., 1966-68; hostess Am. Friends Svc. Com. Internat. Seminar, Oestgeest, The Netherlands, 1960, Poughkeepsie, N.Y., 1961; sr. vis. fellow Woodrow Wilson Found., 1977-80; proprietor art studio N.Y.C., 1961-69, Worthington, Ohio, 1970-72; art therapy asst. Harding Hosp., Worthington, 1970-72. One-woman show at Antioch Coll., 1967. Pres. Columbia U. Greenhouse Nursery Sch., N.Y.C., 1954-59; bd. mem. Open Door Day Care Ctr., N.Y.C., 1954-59; mem. founding and adv. bd. East Harlem Tutoring Program, N.Y.C., 1965-73; mem. bd. Columbus Area Internat. Program, 1970-72, 79-87, sec., 1981, pres., 1982-85, chair adv. bd., 1983-87; del. Nat. Bd. Coun. Internat. Programs, Cleve., 1981-83; mem. bd. Cmty. Svc., Inc., Yellow Springs, 1981—. Mem. Am. Assn. Slavic Studies, Columbus Coun. World Affairs, Columbus Meml. Soc., Columbus Mus. Art, Ohio Hist. Soc., South Ctrl. Ohio Preservation Soc., UNA, UNICEF, World Federalist Assn. Ctrl. Ohio (membership sect. 1987-94), Crichton Club (Columbus), Order Easter Star. Home: 163 E Lane Ave Columbus OH 43201

GRULIOW, LEO, journalist, translator, educator; b. Bayonne, N.J., May 27, 1913; s. George and Rebecca (Kagan) G.; m. Agnes Johnston Forrest, Sept. 25, 1945; children: Frank Forrest, Rebecca. Trainee to mng. editor The N.Y. Democrat, N.Y.C., 1929-32; rewrite N.Y.C. Bur. Federated Press, 1931-32; makeup editor, reporter Moscow Daily News, 1933-38; corr. Transradio Press Svc., Washington, N.Y.C., 1939-41; rsch. dir. Russian War Relief, Inc., N.Y.C., 1942; rep. in the U.S.S.R. Russian War Relief, Inc., Moscow, 1943-45; founder, editor The Current Digest of the Soviet Press, Washington, 1949; editor at Columbia U. The Current Digest of the Soviet Press, N.Y.C., 1950-69; editor at Ohio State U. The Current Digest of the Soviet Press, Columbus, 1969-78; editor emeritus The Current Digest of the Post-Soviet Press, Columbus, 1979-92; fgn. corr. The Christian Sci. Monitor, Moscow, 1972-75; overseas corr. The Saturday Evening Post, Moscow, 1975; U.S. lecture tours, 1946-48; lectr. on translation, Columbia U., N.Y.C., 1952-54; mem. bd. advisors, English translation, Great Soviet Ency., 30 vols., Macmillan Ednl. Corp., N.Y.C., 1974-78; adj. prof. Inst. Higher Internat. Studies, Geneva, 1959-60; disting. guest prof. Monterey Inst. Internat. Studies, Calif., 1984-85; Woodrow Wilson sr. vis. fellow at various colls. in the U.S., 1974-80; evaluator of Russian programs Radio Liberty-Bd. for Internat. Broadcasting, 1960, 64, 84, 86; lectr. Antioch Coll., N.Y.C. campus and Yellow Springs, Ohio, 1961-65; chmn. Am. Friends Svc. Com. seminars, Oestgeest, Netherlands, 1960, Poughkeepsie, N.Y., 1961; mem. U.S. dels. to UNESCO Internat. Journalism Conf., Strasbourg U., France, 1959, to Darmouth XI Conf., Riga, 1977; participant U.S.-Soviet Writers' Confs., Moscow, 1977, 90, N.Y.C., 1987, Washington, 1989; del. to Budapest forum Helsinki pact signatory countries, 1985. Author: (in Time-Life series The Great Cities) Moscow, 1976, (with Boris Streinikov and Vasily Peskov) As Others See Us, 1974; contbr. chpts. to books, articles to profl. jours.; translator Soviet Views on the Post-War World Economy, 1948, The Varga Debates, 1947-48, Alexandrov on Marxist Philosophy, 1949; introduction, editor, Current Soviet Policies I, 1953, II, 1957, III, 1960, (with Charlotte Sajkowski) IV, 1962, Babi Yar (Antoly Kuznetsov), 1966; translator under pseudonym Rebecca Frank: The Cancer Ward (Aleksandr I. Solzhenitsyn) 1968; translator: A Taste of Liberty (Bulat Okudzhava), 1986; translator (with Rebecca Gruliow) Lysenko and the Tragedy of Soviet Science, (Valery N. Soyfer), 1994; mem. editl. bd. of book, translator of short stories, The Human Experience, 1989; weekly TV commentator ABC-TV network, N.Y.C., 1953-54, Can. Broadcasting Corp. radio and TV network, N.Y.C., Toronto, 1955-58. Trustee Antioch Coll., 1961-67. NEH fellow, 1975; recipient Soviet medal for civilian relief work during WWII, 1945, Poynter fellowship award for journalism, Yale U., 1979. Mem. UN Assn. (former bd. dirs.), Am. PEN, Am. Assn. Advancement of Slavic Studies (award for disting. contrbn. 1978), Columbus Coun. on World Affairs (former bd. dirs.), Ctrl. Ohio World Federalist Assn. (bd. dirs.), Columbus Meml. Soc. (past pres.), Crichton Club. Home: 163 E Lane Ave Columbus OH 43201 Office: The Current Digest of the Post-Soviet Press 3857 N High St Columbus OH 43214

GRUMBO, HOWARD, state legislator; m. Joyce Grumbo; 3 children. BS, U. N.D.; MA, Long Beach State U. Tchr., ret., state rep. dist. 27, 1991—; mem. industry, bus. and labor com., transp. com. N.D. Ho. Reps. Mem. Pk. Bd. Commn.; chmn. Cmty. Devel. Corp. Mem. Lions. Democrat. Home: PO Box 435 Lidgerwood ND 58053-0435*

GRUNDBERG, BETTY, state legislator, property manager; b. Woden, Iowa, Feb. 16, 1938; d. Edwin and Eva Ruth Meyer; m. Arnie Grundberg, Dec. 31, 1960; children: Christine, Julie, Michael, Susan. BA, Wartburg Coll., 1959; MA, U. Iowa, 1969; postgrad., Drake U. Cert. tchr. Property mgr. and renovator Des Moines, 1973—; with Des Moines Sch. Bd., 1975-90; legis. State of Iowa, Des Moines, 1993—. Active LWV, Des Moines, 1972—. Republican. Home and Office: 224 Foster Dr Des Moines IA 50312-2540

GRUNDHOFER, JOHN F., banking executive; b. L.A., 1939. Student, Loyola U., 1960, U. So. Calif., 1964. Formerly with Wells Fargo & Co., San Francisco, also vice chmn.; now chmn., pres., chief exec. officer First Bank System, Inc., Mpls., 1990—, also dir. Office: First Bank System 601 Second Ave S Minneapolis MN 55402*

GRUNDY, ROY RAWSTHORNE, marketing educator; b. Hackensack, N.J., Feb. 4, 1930; s. Albert Victor Rawsthorne and Ann Beatrice (Nelson) G.; m. Priscilla Ann Noble, June 17, 1961; children: John, Christopher, William. BS, Ill. Inst. Technology, 1952; MBA, Roosevelt U., 1965; EdD, No. Ill. U., 1989. Lic. real estate broker. Lab. technician Container Labs., Chgo., 1955-57; advt. rep. Miller Freeman Pubs., Chgo., 1957-59; sales mgr. Celanese Corp. Am., Chgo., 1959-65; gen. mgr. Intec Inc., Chgo., 1965-70; prof. mktg. Coll. DuPage, Glen Ellyn, Ill., 1970—; vis. prof. Brit. Inst. Mgmt., Oxford U., 1972, Queensland U. Tech., Brisbane, Australia, 1990, Park Lane Coll., Leeds, Eng., 1992, Inst. for Entrepreneurship, Zholtye Vody, Ukraine, 1994, WSI-Inst. Mgmt. and Mktg., Koszalin, Poland, 1995, Ctr. for Citizens Initiatives, Voronezh, Russian Fedn., 1996; pres. Rawsthorne Rsch. and Assocs., Naperville, 1970—. Contbr. articles to profl. jours. Mem. Sch. Bd. Dist. 203, Naperville, 1976-79, Transp. Adv. Bd., 1970-75, Cable TV Com., 1970-76, Zoning Bd. Appeals, 1982-84; mem. secondary edn. adv. com. Congressman Fawell's 13th Congl. Dist. Fellow Dept. Energy, Solar Energy Rsch. Inst., 1979. Mem. Ill. Community Coll. Faculty Assn. (rep. 1987-88), Am. Mktg. Assn., Mktg. Educators Group Eng., Rotary (sec. 1985-87), Delta Sigma Phi. Republican. Mem. United Ch. Christ. Home: 512 Bayberry Ln Naperville IL 60563-2826 Office: Coll DuPage Dept Mktg Glen Ellyn IL 60137

GRUNWALD, ARNOLD PAUL, communications executive, engineer; b. Berlin, Dec. 7, 1910; came to U.S., 1952, naturalized, 1957; s. Richard Michael and Hedwig (Bamann) G.; m. Grete Marie Gwinner, Dec. 29, 1945; children: Eva Dubowski, Peter. Degree in physics and math., Univ., Munich, 1933; degree in engring., Tech. Univ., Munich, 1945. Chief engr., gen. mgr. Wehoba GmbH, Weilheim, Germany, 1946-49; engr. Capital Engring. Co., Chgo., 1952-58; assoc. engr. Argonne (Ill.) Nat. Lab., 1958-77, chmn. Argonne Senate, 1971-72; cons., pres. Rsch. for Braille Communication, Chgo., 1977—; cons. Am. Found. for Blind, N.Y.C., 1973-76, divsn. for blind Libr. Congress, Washington, 1970; cons. engr. Chisholm, Boyd & White, Chgo., Ethicon Inc., Chgo.; participant internat. confs. on engring., social and ethical issues. Contbr. articles to profl. jours. V.p., edn. chmn. Parents of the Blind, Chgo., 1957-67; group discussion leader World Federalists, Chgo.; lectr. Union of Concerned Scientist, Argonne; ptnr. Pub. Citizen Ptnrs. Recipient Letter of Commendation, Pres. U.S., 1976, One of 100 Most Significant Products award Indsl. Rsch. mag., 1969; Hew grantee U.S. Dept. Health, Edn. and Welfare, 1969-75, grantee State of Ill., 1992-93. Mem. Fedn. Am. Scientists, Nat. Found. of the Blind, Sigma Xi. Home: 18135 Martin Ave Homewood IL 60430-2136

GRUYS, ROBERT IRVING, physician, surgeon; b. Silver Creek, Minn., Oct. 15, 1917; s. Herman and Dorothy (Vondergon) G.; m. Cornelia Mol, June 30, 1943 (div. 1976); children: Kathy, Robert, William, John. B in Medicine, U. Minn., 1946, MD, 1947. Gen. surgery resident Wayne County Gen. Hosp., Detroit, 1948-49, Mpls VA Hosp., 1958-62; postgrad. Cook County Gen. Hosp., Chgo., 1957, 63, 64, Mayo Clinic, Rochester, Minn., 1949-58, U. Minn., 1958-68, 70-75; physician, surgeon Watkins Clinic, Wells, Minn., 1949-58, 63-67, 70-75, Ganado Presbyn. Hosp., Ariz., 1953-57, Southwest Clinic, Edina, Minn., 1967-68, Chiayi Christian Hosp., Taiwan, 1968-70, Estes Park Med. Clinic, Colo., 1975-79, St. Cloud VA Med. Ctr., 1979—; mem. staff Wells Community Hosp., 1951-75, Meth. Hosp., Mpls., 1967-68, Mt. Sinai Hosp., Mpls., 1967-68, North Meml. Hosp., Mpls., 1967-76, Fairview Southdale Hosp., Mpls., 1967-68, Met. Med. Ctr., Mpls., 1967-76, Elizabeth Knutson Meml. Hosp., Estes Park, Colo., 1975-79, Weld County Gen. Hosp., Greeley, Colo., 1976-79, St. Cloud VA Med. Ctr., 1979-94; prin. physician chem. dependence alcoholic unit, 1981-94. Mem. Am. Soc. Abdominal Surgeons, Internat. Coll. Surgeons, Christian Med. Soc., AMA, Physicians Serving Physicians in Minn., Stearns-Benton County Med. Soc., Internat. Doctors in Alcoholics Anonymous, Mission Aviation Fellowship, Pilots for Christ Internat., Alpha Omega Alpha. Lodge: Masons. Mem. Reformed Ch. Avocations: flying, country-western music. Home and Office: 2100 Pleasant Ave Saint Cloud MN 56303-0223

GRZEBIENIAK, JOHN FRANCIS, psychologist; b. New Castle, Pa., Jan. 9, 1949; s. John and Helen (Mielcuszny) G.; married; children: Anna Helen, Sarah Mary, Andrew John. BA, Youngstown (Ohio) State U., 1970, MS in Edn., 1974; PhD, U. Pitts., 1982. Lic. psychologist, Ohio, Pa.; cert. chem. dependency counselor. Substance abuse counselor, mental health counselor Columbiana County Mental Health Counseling Ctr., 1974-82, intern in psychology, 1982-84; cons. psychologist Diagnostic and Evaluation Clinic, Youngstown, 1985—; staff psychologist Columbiana County Mental Health Ctr., 1984-95, sr. psychologist, 1995—; cons. psychologist Beaver (Pa.) Valley Psychol. Svcs., 1988-90; adj. prof. dept. psychology Kent (Ohio) State U., 1989—. Mem. APA. Roman Catholic. Office: Columbiana County Mental Health Ctr 40722 State Route 154 Lisbon OH 44432-8500

GSCHNEIDNER, KARL ALBERT, JR., metallurgist, educator, editor, consultant; b. Detroit, Nov. 16, 1930; s. Karl and Eugenie (Zehetmair) Gschneidner; m. Melba E. Pickenpaugh, Nov. 4, 1957; children: Thomas, David, Edward, Kathryn. BS, U. Detroit, 1952; PhD, Iowa State U., 1957. Mem. staff Los Alamos Sci. Lab., 1957-62, sec. chief, 1961-62; vis. asst. prof. U. Ill., Urbana, 1962-63; assoc. prof. materials sci. and engring. Iowa State U., Ames, 1963-67, prof., 1967-79, Disting. prof., 1979—, metallurgist, 1963-67, sr. metallurgist, 1967—, dir. Rare-earth Info. Ctr., 1966-96; vis. prof. U. Calif.-San Diego, La Jolla, 1979-80; cons. Los Alamos Nat. Lab., 1981-86,

Teltech, 1987—. Author: Rare Earth Alloys, 1961, Scandium, 1975, others; editor: (22 vol. book) Handbook on the Physics and Chemistry of Rare Earths, 1978-95, Industrial Applications of Rare Earth Elements, 1981; contbr. numerous chpts. in books and articles to profl. publs. Recipient William Hume-Rothery award AIME, Warrendale, Pa., 1978, Burlington No. award for Excellence in Rsch., Iowa State U., 1989; co-recipient Outstanding Sci. Accomplishment in Metallurgy and Ceramics award Dept. Energy, Washington, 1982, Frank H. Spedding award Rare Earth Rsch. Confs., 1991, Russell B. Scott Meml. award Cryogenic Engr. Conf., 1995. Fellow Minerals, Metals and Materials Soc., Am. Soc. for Materials Internat.; mem. AAAS, Am. Chem. Soc., Am. Crystallographic Assn., Materials Rsch. Soc., Am. Phys. Soc., Iowa Acad. Sci., Materials Rsch. Soc. India (hon.). Roman Catholic. Office: Iowa State U Ames Lab Ames IA 50011-3020

GUBOW, DAVID M., state legislator. AB, U. Mich.; JD, U. Detroit. Mem. dist. 35 Mich. Ho. of Reps., 1985—; majority whip, chmn. mental health com., vice chmn. judiciary com., mem. pub. health com., pub utilities com., taxation com., also atty. Mem. State Bar Mich., Oakland County Bar Assn. (past chmn.), Judicial Conf. of 6th Cir. (life), Jewish Cmty. Coun., Jewish Welfare Fedn. Home: 26728 York Rd Huntington Woods MI 48070-1358 Address: PO Box 30014 Lansing MI 48909-7514*

GUCCIONE, JOYCE E., securities company executive; b. Chgo., June 23, 1954. CFP, Coll. Fin. Planning, Denver, 1994. V.p. Prin. Fin. Securities Inc. (formerly Hamilton Investments), Gurnee, Ill., 1990—. Contbr. articles to mags. Mem. adv. bd. Ill. Coll. Accts. Network, 1993—; mem. Nat. Ctr. for Women and Retirement Rsch., L.I. U., 1995—. Roman Catholic. Office: Prin Fin Securities Inc 5101 Washington St Gurnee IL 60031

GUDGEON, RICHARD GENE, assistant translation editor; b. Amarillo, Tex., Nov. 28, 1954; s. Lyle Hart and Betty Marie (Floyd) G.; m. Kay Loraine Pritzlaff, May 28, 1983; children: Michael Paul, Sarah Elizabeth. BA with distinction, U. Wisc., 1977, MA, 1978; MDiv, Bethany Lutheran Theol. Sem., 1986; D of Ministry, Colgate Rochester Div. Sch., 1991. Hebrew instr. Concordia Theol. Sem., Fort Wayne, Ind., 1978-84; pastor Indian Landing Luth. Ch., Rochester, N.Y., 1985-87, Redeemer Luth. Ch., Scottsville, N.Y., 1985-88; student chaplain Cornell U., Ithaca, N.Y., 1988-89; asst. translation editor, lect., Novell Network supr. God's Word to the Nations Bible Soc., Cleve., 1989-94; project coord. Gods Word to the Nations Bible Soc., Cleve., 1994—, God's Word Complete Concordance, 1996; beta testor for three software products; creator God's Word to Nats. Bible Soc. William F. Vilas fellow Regent of U. Wisc., 1977-78. Mem. Soc. Bibl. Lit., Evang. Theol. Soc., North East Ohio Novell Users Group, Luth. Soc. for Missiology. Lutheran. Office: Gods Word to Nations Bible Soc 22050 Mastick Rd Cleveland OH 44126-3162

GUDIN, CASIMIR CONTSANTINE, electrical engineer; b. Cleve., Oct. 19, 1942; s. Alphonse and Mary G. (Zarzycki) G.; m. Donna R. Howe, Sept. 19, 1970; children: Cherie Ann, Robert Andrew. BS, Cleve. State U., 1979. Sr. engring. technician Centerior Electric, Cleve., 1968-78, assoc. engr., 1979-84, advanced engr., 1985-93; contract engr. TAD Energy Svcs., Cleve., 1993-94; prin. engr. Commonwealth Edison, Chgo., 1994—. Mem. IEEE, Cleve. Toastmasters (pres. 1974-84).

GUDMUNDSON, BARBARA ROHRKE, ecologist; b. Chgo.; d. Lloyd Ernest and Helen (Bullard) Rohrke; m. Valtyr Emil Gudmundson, June 14, 1951 (dec. Dec. 1982); children: Holly Mekkin, Martha Rannveig. BA, U. Tenn., 1950; MA, Mankato State Coll., 1965; PhD, Iowa State U., 1969. Microbiologist Hektoen Inst. & Ill. Ctr. Hosp., Chgo., 1950-52; immunologist Jackson Meml. Lab., Bar Harbor, Maine, 1952-54; dist. ecologist Corps of Engrs., St. Paul, 1971-72; sr. ecologist North Star Rsch. Inst., Mpls., 1972-76; staff engr. Met. Waste Control Commn., St. Paul, 1976-77; pres., prin. ecologist Ecosystem Rsch. Svc./Upper Midwest, Mpls., 1978—; pvt. practice as cons. ecologist, Des Moines and Mpls., 1968-70; mem. Citizens League Task Force on the Mississippi Riverfront, 1973-74; mem. adv. com. Mpls. Lakes Water Quality, Mpls., 1974-75; field ecologist Mississippi River Canoe Expdn., Coll. of the Atlantic, Bar Harbor, 1979. Author: V. Emil Gudmundson: Icelandic Canadian Unitarian, A Personal Biography, 1991; editor-in-chief The Icelandic Unitarian Connection, 1984; contbr. articles to profl. jours. Mem. from 61st dist. Dem.-Farmer-Labor Ctr. Com., Minn., 1978-80; mgr. Minnehaha Creek Watershed Dist., Hennepin & Carver Counties, Minn., 1979-83; mem. Capital Long-Range Improvements Com., Mpls., 1981; mem. steering com. Nokomis East Neighborhood Assn., 1995—. River Basin Ecology grantee Iowa Acad. Scis., Cedar Falls, 1976, Mississippi River Ecology grantee Freshwater Biol. Rsch. Found., Navarre, Minn., 1979, Fulbright Sr. Rsch. grantee USA/Iceland Fulbright Commns., Washington, Reykjavik, 1986, 92; recipient Anita Hill Courage and Justice award, 1994. Mem. NOW (Minn. state bd. 1979—), Ecol. Soc. Am. (pres. Minn. chpt. 1971-75), Geol. Soc. Minn. (pres. 1981), Phycological Soc. Am., Internat. Assn. Diatom Rsch., Sigma Xi, Phi Kappa Phi, Sigma Delta Epsilon-Grad. Women in Sci. (nat. membership com. 1990-93, chmn. 1991-93). Unitarian Universalist. Home: 5505 28th Ave S Minneapolis MN 55417-1957 Office: Ecosystem Rsch Svc/Upper Midwest PO Box 17102 Minneapolis MN 55417-0102

GUE, CHARLES SYLVESTER, JR., stockbroker; b. Germantown, Md., Nov. 4, 1935. BS in Agr., U. Md., 1962; DVM, U. Ga., 1960; MPH, U. Minn., 1966. Field vet. Va. Dept. Agr., Warrenton, 1961-64; vet. epidemiologist USDA, Roseville, Minn., 1964-67, regional epidemiologist, 1968-86; stockbroker, br. mgr. Fahnestock & Co., Inc., Jefferson City, Mo., 1986—. Mem. Nat. Assn. Fed. Vets. (Dr. Daniel E. Salmon award 1965). Presbyterian. Home: RR 1 Box 291 Russellville MO 65074-9452 Office: Fahnestock & Co Inc 118 E High St Jefferson City MO 65101

GUEGOLD, WILLIAM KENT, music educator; b. Cambridge, Ohio, Feb. 28, 1953; s. Walter William and Nancy Ann G.; m. Judith Anne Kenreich, Mar. 22, 1975; children: Nathan, Anna, Meghan, Bethany. BMus, Capital U., Columbus, Ohio, 1975; MMus, Kent State U., 1981, PhD in Music, 1989. Dir. bands Painesville (Ohio) City Schs., 1975-79; mktg. rep. Guegold Constrn., Cambridge, Ohio, 1979-81; asst. dir. bands Kent (Ohio) State U., 1986-87; coord. of music edn. U. Akron, Ohio, 1991—. Author: (book) 100 Years of Olympic Music, 1996. Mem. Ohio Music Edn. Assn. (pres. 1995-96). Office: Univ of Akron Sch of Music Akron OH 44325-1002

GUERRERO-ANDERSON, ESPERANZA, management consultant; b. Managua, Nicaragua, Dec. 22, 1944; came to U.S., 1978; d. Julian Napoleon Guerrero and Gertrudis Mairena. BA in Bus. Adminstrn., Universidad Centro, Nicaragua, 1969; MS in Mgmt. Info. Systems, U. Mpls., 1973; postgrad., Hubert H. Humphrey Inst., 1986-87, Yale U., 1989. Assoc. dir. and prof. of fin. and acctng. Centro de Estudios Superiores, Nicaragua, 1966-69; group head Banco Cent. de Nicaragua, 1970-79; founding ptnr. Consultores Interamericanos, Nicaragua, 1975-79; mgmt. cons. Touche Ross and Co., Atlanta; internat. banking officer First Bank Mpls., 1980-81; pres. chief exec. officer, Chief oper. officer Met. Econ. Devel. Assn., 1981-89; pres., chief exec. officer Milestone Growth Fund, 1990—; adv. U.S. SBA, Mpls.; bd. dirs. Milestone Growth Fund, Mpls., Nat. City Bank. Active Mpls. United Way, Norstar Guarantee, Minn. Internat. Ctr., Walker Art Ctr., Ctr. of Am. Expt. Mem. Nat. Assn. Small Investment Cos., Nat. Assn. Investment Cos. Roman Catholic. Office: Milestone Growth Fund Plaza VII 45 S 7th St Ste 2326 Minneapolis MN 55402-1617

GUEST, BUDDY ROSS, geography educator; b. Republican City, Nebr., Apr. 11, 1920; s. Hezekiah H. and Florice W. (Camp) G.; children: Marian T. Guest Drewitz, Christopher R. BA, Nebr. Wesleyan U., 1942; MA, U. Nebr., 1947; PhD, U. Chgo., 1951. Lectr. geography Rutgers U., New Brunswick, N.J., 1950-51; rsch. analyst Dept. of Air Force, Washington, 1951-58; prof. geography No. Ill. U., DeKalb, 1958-84, prof. emeritus, 1984—. Col. USAF, 1942-80. Salisbury fellow U. Chgo., 1948-50; recipient Citation Air Force Assn., Chgo., 1962. Mem. Assn. Am. Geographers, Ill. Geog. Soc. (pres., v.p., sec. 1967-77, editor bull. 1967-71, Disting. Geog. Educator 1979), U.S.-China Friendship Assn. (pres., v.p. 1987—), No. Ill. U. 21+ Club (chmn. 1987-90). Methodist. Home: 417 N 2nd St # 8 De Kalb IL 60115-3288

GUFFIN, JAN ARLEN, secondary education educator; b. Rush County, Ind., May 11, 1938; s. James Lowell and Helen Lorene (Whitinger) G. BS in Edn., Ind. U., 1963, MAT in English, 1966; PhD, Duke U., 1975. Cert. in English and edn., Ind. Adminstrv. trainee Am. Fletcher Nat. Bank, Indpls., 1957-62; tchr. English Shortridge H.S., Indpls., 1964-65; tchr. English North Ctrl. H.S., Indpls., 1966-86, chmn. dept., 1977-89, coord. internat. baccalaureate, 1986-94, curriculum coord., 1989-94; chmn. dept. English, coord. global scholars program Park Tudor Sch., Indpls., 1994—; chair Advanced Placement test devel. com. The Coll. Bd., N.Y.C., 1975-77, chair English adv. bd., 1977-79; seminar leader Coll. Bd. and U.S. Dept. State, Taipei, Taiwan and U.S., 1980-90; cons. dept. English, Culver (Ind.) Mil. Acad., 1992. Cons. editor The Clearinghouse, 1979&; asst. editor Jour. of Teaching Writing, 1980—; author articles. Mem. edn. bd. North United Meth. Ch., Indpls., 1980-83; mem. adv. bd. Arts, Ind., Indpls., 1993—, Gov.'s Scholar Acad., Indpls., 1985-86; external examiner Internat. Baccalaureate, N.Y.C., 1994—. Recipinet E.H. Kemper-McComb award Ind. Coun. Tchrs. English, 1986. Mem. ASCD, Nat. Coun. Tchrs. English, Ind. Tchrs. of Writing (exec. bd. 1976-79, treas. 1977-79), Ind. Commn. for Humanities, Phi Beta Kappa, Phi Delta Kappa. Democrat. Office: Park Tudor Sch 7200 N College Ave Indianapolis IN 46240-3016

GUIDO, FRANK, engineer; b. Windsor, Ont., Can., Nov. 22, 1967; came to U.S., 1991; B, Ferris State U., 1993. Mold maker Genisis, Windsor, Ont., Can., 1989-92; proposals engr. Heller Machine Tools, Elk Grove Village, Ill., 1992—. Office: 950 Morse Ave Elk Grove Village IL 60007-5108

GUILFOYLE, JAMES JOSEPH, financial executive, accountant; b. Trenton, N.J., Mar. 11, 1956; s. James Clarence and Eleanor Josephine (Zientek) G.; m. LuAnn Calabro, Sept. 18, 1982. BS, Fordham U., 1978; MBA candidate, U. Detroit Mercy. CPA, N.J. Cost acct. Triangle Industries, New Brunswick, N.J., 1978-79; consolidations acct. Wheelabrator-Frye Inc., Belle Mead, N.J., 1979-81, cost acct., 1981-82; asst. controller Wheelabrator subs. Airpol, Englewood, N.J., 1982-83; gen. acctg. mgr. U.S. Lines, Cranford, N.J., 1983-84; controller PRC Mgmt. Co. Inc., West Long Branch, N.J., 1984-86; asst. v.p., chief fin. officer Tryon Equities Corp., Charlotte, N.C., 1987-88; sr. staff asst. fin. acctg. and reporting GM, Detroit, 1988-95, employment cost analysis and health care initiatives team, 1995—. Mem. AICPA, Mich. Assn. CPA's, N.J. Soc. CPA's, Inst. Mgmt. Accts. Roman Catholic. Home: 2563 Wenona Dr Wixom MI 48393-2157 Office: GM 3044 W Grand Blvd Ste 13115 Detroit MI 48202-3091

GUILIANO, GARY, mechanical engineer; b. Hamilton, Ohio, Dec. 26, 1966. BS in Mech. Engring., U. Cin., 1991. Cert. in fluid power mechanics. Project engr. Buschman Conveyors, Cin., 1988—. Republican.

GUILLORY, JEFFERY MICHAEL, lawyer; b. Kansas City, Mo., July 26, 1966; s. Glenford Lee and Brenda Charlene (Thomas) G.; m. Leanna Carol Rainbolt, Aug. 10, 1991. Student, Mo. So. State Coll., Joplin, 1984-86; BA in Polit. Sci., Ctrl. Meth. Coll., Fayette, Mo., 1988; JD, U. Ark., 1991. Bar: Mo. 1991, U.S. Dist. Ct. (we. dist.) Mo. 1991, U.S. Supreme Ct. 1994. Law clk. Hall, Wright & Baker, P.A., Fayetteville, Ark., 1989-91; assoc. atty. Law Office of Allan C. Wilcox, Joplin, 1991-92; ptnr. Wilcox & Guillory, Joplin, 1992-95; assoc. atty. Roberts, Fleischaker, Williams, Wilson & Powell, Joplin, 1995—. Chmn. adminstr. bd. Christ's Cmty. United Meth. Ch., Joplin, 1993-95, youth counselor, 1992—; asst. scoutmaster Boy Scouts Am., Joplin, 1991—. Mem. ABA, Assn. Trial Lawyers Am., Mo. Bar Assn., Mo. Assn. Trial Lawyers, Jasper County Bar Assn. Office: Roberts Fleischaker et al 418 Wall St PO Box 996 Joplin MO 64802

GUINTHER, CHRISTINE LOUISE, special educator education; b. Chgo., Oct. 27, 1949; d. William Joseph and Olga (Sandul) Bacha; m. Paul H. Demper, July 22, 1972 (div. 1987); m. William Robert Guinther, June 25, 1988. BS in Edn., Ill. State U., 1971; MA in Exceptional Child Edn., Ohio State U., 1974. Cert. tchr., Mo. Resource tchr. for learning disabled students Palatine (Ill.) Community Consol. Sch. Dist. #15, 1971-72, Scioto-Darby City Schs., Hilliard, Ohio, 1972-76, Francis Howell Sch. Dist., St. Charles, Mo., 1976—. Mem. NEA (human rels. com. 1987-93, bd. dirs. 1993—), ACLU, ASCD, Nat. Staf devel. Coun., AAUW, Mo. NEA (bd. dirs. 1985-91, human rels. com. 1983—, exec. com. 1993—), Francis Howell Edn. Assn. (pres. 1981-82), NMSA, Delta Kappa Gamma. Methodist. Home: 161 Castlewood Rd Ballwin MO 63021-7217

GULDA, EDWARD JAMES, automotive executive; b. Detroit, Oct. 28, 1945; s. Alfred and Lucy Irene (Ball) G.; m. Nancy Mary Greenlee, Nov. 28, 1964; children: Kimberly Sue Marsh, Nicholas Edward. BS in Aerospace Engring., U. Mich., 1968, MBA, 1979. Systems engr. LTV Aerospace Corp., Sterling Heights, Mich., 1966-72; mgr. systems engring. Ford Motor Co., Dearborn, Mich., 1972-78; mgr., prodn. plan. Rockwell Internat. Corp., Dearborn, Mich., 1978-79; dir. prod. plan. Rockwell Internat. Corp., Troy, Mich., 1979-80, dir. mkt. electronics, 1980-81; gen. mgr. auto electronics Rockwell Internat. Corp., Troy, 1981-84, v.p. rsch. and engring., 1984-85; pres. ITT Teves Am., Troy, 1985-87; group v.p. engring. ITT Auto, Inc., Troy, 1987-88; pres., chief exec. officer Dayton Walther (Varity) Corp., Dayton, Ohio, 1988-89; pres. Varity Brake Group Kelsey-Hayes Brake Group N.Am., Romulus, Mich., 1989-94; pres. Kelsey-Hayes Co., Romulus, Mich., 1994-95; chief exec. Kelsey-Hayes Co., Livonia, Mich., 1995; CEO Opal Mgmt. Group, Troy, Mich., 1996—. Mem. Soc. Automotive Engrs., Engring. Soc. Detroit, MENSA, Birmingham Country Club. Office: Kelsey-Hayes Corp 38481 W Huron River Dr Romulus MI 48174-1158

GULICK, PETER GREGORY, medical educator; b. Youngstown, Ohio, July 12, 1950; s. Peter and Sophie (Kudera); m. Charlotte Ann Chubick, July 21, 1973; children: Gregory, Jeff, Laurie, Scott. BS in Biology and Chemistry, Mt. Union Coll., 1972; DO, Chgo. Osteo. Coll., 1976. Diplomate Am. Bd. Osteo. Examiners. Intern Detroit Osto. Hosp., 1976-77; internal medicine resident Cleve. Clinic Found., 1977-80; infectios disease fellow Cleve. Clinic Found, 1981-83, med. oncology fellow, 1983-84; med. oncology fellow Roswell Park Meml. Inst., Buffalo, 1980-81; clin. assoc. primary care Cleve. Clinic Found, 1983-84; asst. prof. medicine Mich. State U., East Lansing, 1984-90, assoc. prof. medicine, 1990—; rsch. instr. medicine, SUNY, Buffalo, 1980-81; instr. biology Cleve. State U., 1982-83; dir. med. edn. Lansing (Mich.) Gen. Hosp., 1987-92, assoc. dir. med. edn., 1992—. Author: Clinics of North America, 1983. Mem. Mich. State AIDS Task Force, Lansing, 1986, Mich. State Breast Cancer Task Force, 1986, Lansing area AIDS Network, 1988. Mem. AMA, Am. Osteo. Assn., Mich. Assn. Osteo. Physicians, Am. Microbiology Assn., Am. Fedn. Clin. Rsch., Am. Coll. Physicians, Infectious Disease Soc. Am., Am. Microbiology Assn. Democrat. Roman Catholic. Home: 1839 Pine Knoll Dr Okemos MI 48864-3802 Office: Mich State U Coll Medicine Dept Internal Medicine B318 W Fee Hall East Lansing MI 48824-1315

GULLESON, PAM, state legislator. Home: PO Box 215 Rutland ND 58067-0215 Office: ND Hos of Reps State Capitol Bismarck ND 58505*

GULLET, LEON ESTLE, retired cartographer; b. St. Clair, Mo., June 15, 1930; s. Estle Reece and Gertie Ethel (Maupin) G.; m. Willodean House, June 27, 1959 (dec. Nov. 1983). AA, Jeff City Jr. Coll., 1950; BS, S.W. Mo. State U., 1953. Cartographic aid Aero. Chart & Info. Ctr., St. Louis, 1955-57, cartographer, 1957-78; sr. cartographer Def. Mapping Aerospace Ctr., St. Louis, 1978-85; ret., 1985. Author: Life's Greatest Decision, 1995, After Life's Greatest Decision, 1996; composer hymns; author one-act plays; editor ch. history First Bapt. Ch., St. Clair, Mo., 1922-92; writer Franklin County Bapt. Camp History 1947-93; chmn. com. that compiled ops. manual for Franklin County Bat. Assn.; contbr. articles to profl. jours. Music dir. First Bapt. Ch., St. Clair, 1967-76, 83-85, chmn. constn. and by-laws com., 1995-96, chmn. ch. history com., 1995—; chair ops. manual compilation com. Franklin County Bapt. Assn., 1994. With U.S. Army, 1953-55. Decorated Nat. Def. Svc. medal, Army of Occupation medal. Democrat. Home: 615 E Gravois Ave Saint Clair MO 63077-1609

GULLICK, RICHARD WARREN, environmental engineer, scientist; b. Syracuse, N.Y., July 10, 1958; s. Herbert Durant and Shirley Vernon (Whittemore) G. BS in Environ. Sci., Mich. State U., 1980; MS in Pub. Health in Environ. Mgmt. and Protection, U. N.C., 1983; postgrad., U. Mich., 1989—. Environ. chemist O'Brien & Gere Engrs., Inc., Syracuse, 1983-86; environ. scientist Wehran Engring., Middletown, N.Y., 1987-89; rsch. asst. dept. civil and environ. engring. U. Mich., Ann Arbor, 1989—. Mem. ACS (div. analytical chemistry and environ. chemistry), Water Pollution Control Fedn., Am. Water Works Assn., Clay Mineral Soc. Office: Dept Civil-Environ Engring 181 EWRE Bldg Ann Arbor MI 48109-2125

GULLIKSON, ANGELA KATHLEEN, quality management analyst; b. Aberdeen, S.D., Nov. 30, 1936; d. Albert H. and Winifred K. (Smith) G. Nursing diploma, Presentation Sch. Nursing, Aberdeen, 1957; student, SUNY, Albany, 1984—, U. Wis., 1984—. Cert. healthcare quality profl. Healthcare Quality Cert. Bd. Staff nurse Gettysburg (S.D.) Hosp., 1957-58, Mercy Hosp., Toledo, 1959-61; staff nurse William S. Middleton Meml. Vets. Hosp., Madison, 1961-69, head nurse, 1969-87, quality mgmt. analyst, 1987—. Mem. Nat. Assn. for Healthcare Quality, Wis. Assn. for Healthcare Quality, City-Wide Quality Assurance Assn. (chairperson 1990-91). Home: 722 Sauk Ridge Trl Madison WI 53705-1157 Office: Wm S Middleton Meml Vets Hosp 2500 Overlook Ter Madison WI 53705-2254

GULLING, NICK, state legislator. Student, San Diego City Coll., Ind. U., U. Va.; grad., FBI Acad. Sheriff Hancock County, Ind., 1982-90; spl. investigator Gov. Otis Bowen, State of Ind.; jail comdr. Hancock County; rep. Dist. 53 Ind. Ho. of Reps., 1992—, mem. familty and children, cts. and criminal codes com., mem. pub. health com., chmn. pub. safety com. organizer/advisor Hancock County Youth Coun.; bd. dirs. Ind. Juvenile Justice Task Force; mem. Adult Literacy Coalition, Farm Bur. With USAR. Mem. Greenfield C. of C., FOB, Kiwanis. Home: 1640 E Rd 300 N Greenfield IN 46140*

GULSON, DELORIS ANNE, reading specialist; b. Sioux Falls, S.D., Aug. 10, 1940; d. Alden LeRoy and Wava DeLoris (McCain) Eisland; m. George Arthur Gulson, Aug. 17, 1968; 1 child, James Andrew. Student, Gen. Beadle Coll., Madison, S.D., 1960; BS, Sioux Falls Coll., 1968; MS, U. S.D., 1982, adminstrv. endorsement, 1992, EdS in Adminstrn., 1993. Lic. reading specialist, mid. sch., adminstrn. Jr. high tchr. Brandon (S.D.) Valley Schs., 1960-67; jr. high tchr. Sioux Falls (S.D.) Pub. Schs., 1968-91, mid. sch. tchr., 1991-94; staff devel. dir. Sioux Falls Pub. Schs., 1995—; adult instr. Sioux Falls Tchr. Insvc. Program, 1992; cons. S.D. Curriculum Coalition, 1989—. Author curriculum devel. model, 1989, policy for selection and rev. of materials, 1990. Pres. Minnehaha County (S.D.) Libr. Bd., 1991-92. Mem. NEA, ASCD, S.D. Edn. Assn., S.D. Reading Coun. (pres. 1989), S.D. Mid. Level Educators Nat. Staff Devel. Coun., Delta Kappa Gamma (pres. 1990-94). Home: 400 E Pine Lake Dr Sioux Falls SD 57103

GUMNIT, ROBERT JEROME, healthcare executive, epilepsy researcher; b. Pitts., July 4, 1931; s. Herman P. and Sara S. Gumnit; m. Grace P. Lotke, June 14, 1957 (dec. May 1984); children: Daniel, Ruth, Stephen; m. Frances H. Graham, June 7, 1986. BA, Swarthmore Coll., 1953; MD, U. Pa., 1957. Diplomate Am. Bd. Clin. Neurophysiology, Am. Bd. Psychiatry and Neurology. Rsch. asst. dept. psychology Swarthmore Coll., 1952-53; rsch. asst. dept. neurophysiology Inst. of Living, Hartford, Conn., 1954; rotating intern U. Ill. Rsch. and Ednl. Hosps., Chgo., 1957-58; clin. assoc. sect. behavioral scis. Clin. Neuropharmacology Rsch. Ctr., NIMH, 1958-60; clin. assoc. br. electroencephalography NINDB, 1960-61; fellow dept. neurology State U. Iowa, Iowa City, 1961-64; asst. prof. neurology U. Minn., Mpls., 1964-67, assoc. prof., 1968-71, prof., 1971-86, clin. prof. neurology and neurosurgery, 1986—; head dept. neurology St. Paul Ramsey Hosp., 1964-82; dir. U. Minn. Epilepsy Clin. Rsch. Ctr., Mpls., 1974—; pres. MINCEP Epilepsy Care, Mpls., 1986—. Author: Epilepsy, A Handbook for Physicians, 1981, 2d edit., 1995; editor: Intensive Neurodiagnostic Monitoring, 1987, Living Well with Epilepsy, 1991, Your Child and Epilepsy, 1995; contbr. chpts. to books, numerous articles to profl. jours. Bd. dirs. St. Paul Chamber Orch., 1967-91, treas., 1985-90. Capt. USPHS, 1958-61. Named Amb. for Epilepsy, Epilepsy Internat., Copenhagen, 1980. Fellow Am. Acad. Neurology; mem. AMA, Nat. Assn. Epilepsy Ctrs. (pres. 1987—), Am. EEG Soc. (pres. 1983-84), Am. Neurol. Assn., Am. Epilepsy Soc. (pres. 1980). Office: MINCEP Epilepsy Care 5775 Wayzata Blvd Minneapolis MN 55416-1222

GUNARATNE, DHAVALASRI SHELTON ABEYWICKREME, communications educator, journalist; b. Weligama, Sri Lanka, Jan. 22, 1940; came to U.S., 1966; s. Don William Abeywickreme and Keliduwa Widanagamage (Ariyawathie) G.; m. Chia Yoke-Sim, Sept. 11, 1976; children: Junius Asela, Carmel Maya. BA in Econs., U. Ceylon, Peradeniya, 1962; MA in Journalism, U. Oreg., 1968; PhD in Mass Comm., U. Minn., 1972. Journalist Assoc. Newspapers Ceylon Ltd., Colombo, Sri Lanka, 1962-67; asst. prof. Cen. Mo. State U., Warrensburg, 1972-73, U. Fla., Gainesville, 1973; lectr. U. Sains Malaysia, Penang, 1974-76; lectr. I Ctrl. Queensland U., Rockhampton, Australia, 1976-85; prof. comm. Moorhead (Minn.) State U., 1985—; writer The Daily News, Longview, Wash., summer 1989; cons. World Assn. for Christian Comm., London, summer 1990, Assoc. Newspapers Ceylon Ltd., summer 1991; adviser NEA Libr., Washington, Polish Press Rsch. Ctr., Cracow, Poland, 1976—. Author: The Taming of the Press in Sri Lanka, 1975, Modernization and Knowledge, 1976; co-author: Global Communication and Dependency; rev. editor Jour. of Internat. Communication, 1994—. Fellow World Press Inst., 1967, Inst. World Affairs, 1970; grants Am. Soc. Newspaper Editors, 1989, 91. Mem. Soc. Profl. Journalists (adviser 1988-91), Asian Mass Comm. Rsch. and Info. Ctr., Assn. for Edn. in Journalism and Mass Comm., Internat. Comm. Assn., Kappa Tau Alpha. Buddhist. Home: 3215 Village Green Dr Moorhead MN 56560-5411 Office: Moorhead State U 1104 7th Ave S Moorhead MN 56563-0001

GUND, CHRISTOPHER MICHAEL, computer scientist; b. St. Louis, Apr. 23, 1968; s. Robert Louis and Patricia Ann (Bresnahan) G. BS, U. Mo., St. Louis, 1991; postgrad., Washington U., St. Louis, 1991-92, 95—. Cons. Suburban Psychiat., St. Louis, 1988-89; lab. cons. U. Mo., St. Louis, 1991; audit intern Citicorp Mortgage, St. Louis, 1989-91; computer programmer/analyst Data Rsch. Assocs., St. Louis, 1991-92; cons. Dill and Assocs., St. Louis, 1988-89, Stockell Info. Systems, St. Louis, 1992—. Mem. Assn. Computing Machinery. Roman Catholic. Home: 2918 Ridgeview Dr Saint Louis MO 63121-4542

GUND, GEORGE, III, financier, professional sports team executive; b. Cleve., May 7, 1937; s. George and Jessica (Roesler) G.; m. Mary Theo Feld, Aug. 13, 1966; children: George, Gregory. Student, Western Res. U., Menlo (Calif.) Sch. Bus. Engaged in personal investments San Francisco, 1967—; cattle ranching Lee, Nev., 1967—; partner Calif. Seals, San Francisco, 1976-77; pres. Ohio Barons, Inc., Richfield, 1977-78; chmn. bd. Northstar Fin. Corp., Bloomington, Minn., from 1978; formerly chmn. bd. Minn. North Stars, Bloomington; chmn., co-owner San Jose Sharks, NHL, San Jose, CA, 1991—; dir. Ameritrust Cleve.; vice-chmn. Gund Investment Corp., Princeton, N.J.; chmn. North Stars Met Center Mgmt. Corp., Bloomington; v.p. hockey Sun Valley Ice Skating, Inc., Idaho. Chmn. San Francisco Internat. Film Festival, 1973—; mem. sponsors council Project for Population Action; adv. council Sierra Club Found.; mem. internat. council Mus. Modern Art, N.Y.C.; collectors com. Nat. Gallery Art; bd. dirs. Calif. Theatre Found., Bay Area Ednl. TV Assn., San Francisco Mus. Art, Cleve. Health Museum, George Gund Found., Cleve. Internat. Film Festival, Sun Valley Center Arts and Humanities, U. Nev. Reno Found., Sundance Inst. Served with USMCR, 1955-58. Clubs: Calif. Tennis (San Francisco), University (San Francisco), Olympic (San Francisco); Union (Cleve.), Cleve. Athletic (Cleve.), Kirkland Country (Cleve.), Rowfant (Cleve.); Ranier (Seattle). Office: 1821 Union St San Francisco CA 94123-4307 also: Nationwide Advt Svc 1228 Euclid Ave Ste 600 Cleveland OH 44115*

GUND, GORDON, advertising executive; b. Cleve., Oct. 15, 1939; s. George and Jessica (Roesler) G.; m. Llura Liggett; children: Grant Ambler, Gordon Zachary. BA, Harvard U., 1961; DPubSvc (hon.), U. Maryland, 1980; DHL, Whittier Coll., 1993; LLD (hon.), U. Vt., 1994. Pres., chmn., CEO Gund Investment Corp., Princeton, N.J.; gen. ptnr. GUS Enterprises; prin. owner Cleve. Cavaliers, NBA, 1983—; chmn. Nationwide Advt. Svc. Inc.; co-owner San Jose Sharks, NHL, 1990—; mem. bd. govs. NHL, NBA; bd. dirs. Kellogg Co., Corning Inc. Co-founder The Found. Fighting Blindness, 1971, also chmn.; pres., trustee Gund Collection of Western Art; mem. Nat. Adv. Eye Coun., 1980-84. also: Nationwide Advt Svc 1228 Euclid Ave Ste 600 Cleveland OH 44115

GUNDELFINGER, RALPH MELLOW, retired insurance company executive; b. St. Louis, Apr. 10, 1925; s. Thomas Christopher and Janet Lea (Aal) G.; m. C. Maxine Gundelfinger, Aug. 18, 1946 (dec. Sept. 1983); m. Stella Marie Gundelfinger, May 28, 1989; children: Kevin, Christa Lynn. BA, U. Mo., 1950. Claim supr. Zurich Ins. Co., Kansas City, Mo., 1950-54; claim mgr. Tri-State Ins. Co., Kansas City, 1954-64, Gulf Ins. Co., Kansas City, 1964-66; regional claim mgr. Argonaut Ins. Co., Kansas City, 1966-80; v.p. Hosp. Svcs. Group, Kansas City, 1980-91; media profl. ins. specialist E & O Profls., Kansas City, 1991-94; pres. Kansas City Claims Coun., 1978-79; lay lectr. U. Mo. Law Sch., Kansas City, 1982, 83. State chmn. Young Rep. Mo., Kansas City, 1950; v.p. Kansas City Opera Guild, 1989; bd. mem. Kansas City Lyric Opera, 1990. With USMC, 1943-45, PTO. Named Compagnon de Bordeaux, Le Grand Conseil L'Acad. du Vin, 1976. Mem. Chaine de Rotisseurs (charge de presse 1990—), Order de Mondial (sec. 1991—).

GUNDERSON, SCOTT L., state legislator; b. Oct. 10, 1956. Supervisor Town of Waterford, Wis.; assemblyman Wis. State Dist. 83; owner Gundy's Liquor & Sport. Mem. Wind Lake C. of C. (past pres.), Waterford Lions, Wings Over Wis. Commn. Address: 28918 Kramer Dr Waterford WI 53185

GUNDERSON, STEVE CRAIG, congressman; b. Eau Claire, Wis., May 10, 1951; s. Arthur E. and Adeline C. G. BA, U. Wis., 1973. Mem. Wis. Assembly, 1974-79; legis. dir. Rep. Toby Roth, 1979; mem. 97th-104th Congresses from 3d Wis. dist., 1981—; chmn. agrl. subcom. on livestock, dairy and poultry, mem. econ. and ednl. opportunity com.; Dir. spl. projects Gov. Dreyfus of Wis. campaign, 1978. Mem. Lions (Pleasantville chpt.). Republican. Lutheran. Office: US Ho of Reps 2185 Rayburn HOB Washington DC 20515*

GUNDRY, JO ANN, mental health services professional; b. Minot, N.D., Apr. 11, 1945; d. James Edwin and Agnes Lucy (Gervais) G. BA, Mary Coll., 1971; MA, U. N.D., 1977, PhD, 1980. Lic. consulting psychologist. Tchr. St. Leo's Sch., Minot, 1966-67, 70-71, Colegio de las Hermanas Benedictinas, Bogota, Colombia, 1967-70, Little Flower Sch., Minot, 1971-75, St. Mary's Sch., Malta, Mont., 1975-76; elem. sch. counselor Grand Forks (N.D.) Pub. Schs., 1979-80, 81-82; mental health therapist Cath. Charities, Crookston, Minn., 1980-81, Counseling Assocs., Bemidji, Minn., 1983; psychologist, dir. outpatient svcs. program Hiawatha Valley Mental Health Ctr., Winona, Minn., 1983-90; pvt. practice, 1991—. Mem. APA, Minn. Psychol. Assn. Democrat. Roman Catholic. Office: PO Box 872 Winona MN 55987-0872

GUNDY-REED, FRANCES DARNELL, librarian, healthcare manager; b. Muskegon, Mich., Aug. 19, 1947; d. Joseph Leo and Olaverne (Mathis) Merle; m. Russell Norman Gundy, Sept. 18, 1965 (div. 1985); 1 child, Raymond Joseph; m. Robert A. Reed, Aug. 26, 1995. AS, Aquinas Coll., 1988, BA, 1991; MLS, Wayne State U., 1993. Owner, pres. Helpmates, Inc., Muskegon, 1992—. Active Mich. Strategic Planning Com., Muskegon Cmty. Health Project. Mem. ALA (nat. chair grassroots com., Specialized Svcs. Coordination com.), AAUW, Nat. Assn. for Self-Employed, AMBUCS (2d v.p.), Network Small Bus. Owners, Intellectual Freedom Roundtable, Libr. Info. and Tech. Assn., Assn. Libr. Collections and Tech. Svcs., Mich. Libr. Assn., Pub. Libr. Assn., Women's Divsn. C of C (bd. dirs.), Women's Expo. (bd. dirs.). Home: 629 Fruitvale Rd Montague MI 49437

GUNN, MARY ELIZABETH, retired English language educator; b. Great Bend, Kans., July 21, 1914; d. Ernest E. and Elisabeth (Wesley) Eppstein; m. Charles Leonard Gunn, Sept. 13, 1936 (dec. Apr. 1985); 1 child, Charles Douglas. AB, Ft. Hays State U., 1935, BS in Edn., 1936, MA, 1967. Tchr. English Unified Sch. Dist. 428, Great Bend, 1963-80; tchr. English Barton County C.C., Great Bend, 1977-84, tchr. adult edn., 1985-87, tchr. ESL, 1988-94; ret., 1994. Conf. Am. Studies fellow De Pauw U., 1969; recipient Nat. Cmty. Svc. award DAR, 1996. Mem. AAUW (Outstanding Mem. 1991), NEA, Bus. and Profl. Women (Woman of Yr. 1974), Kans. Adult Edn. Assn. (Master Adult Educator 1986), Kans. Assn. Tchrs. English, PEO, Delta Kappa Gamma, Alpha Sigma Alpha. Democrat. Mem. United Ch. of Christ. Home: 3009 16th St Great Bend KS 67530-3705

GUNN, RUSSELL CLIFTON, financial services company executive; b. St. Louis, Nov. 27, 1948; s. Robert Funn and Myrtle (Foster) Wells; m. Gwendolyn K. Fletcher, May 26, 1969; children: Gwendolyn C., Grenetta, Russell II. Student, Forest Park C.C., 1970-72. Pres. Gunn's Diversified Fin. Svc., St. Louis, 1989—. Fundraiser, organizer Normandy Twp. Regular Dem. Club, 1991-93; pres. Northwoods 2d Ward Civic Orgn., 1989-91, Normandy Jr. High PTA, St. Louis, 1987-89; chair fundraising Normany High Marching Band, 1986-92. Recipient Disting. Svc. award City of Northwoods, 1990, Outstanding Pub. Svc. award U. Mo., 1993, Outstanding Achievement award Normandy Community Forum, 1992. Mem. Life Underwriters Assn. African Methodist Episcopalian. Home: 6723 Maryellen St Northwoods MO 63121-3134 Office: Gunns Diversified Fin Svc 7309 Natural Bridge Rd # 201 Saint Louis MO 63121-5025

GUNNER, LAWRENCE GEORGE, dentist; b. Murdo, S.D., Feb. 20, 1939; s. Carl Sigurd and Emily Josephine (Legner) G.; m. Nancy Kay McNamara, Sept. 15, 1962; children: Pamela Lynn, Philip Donald (dec.), Eric Christopher, Andrea Burdae. Student, S.D. Sch. of Mines & Tech., Rapid City, 1957-58; BS, U. of S.D., Vermillion, 1958-60; DDS, U. of Minn., Mnpls., 1960-64. Pvt practice Martin, S.D., 1966—; pres. U. Minn. Sch. Dentistry, 1963. Party chmn. Bennett County Rep., 1980-86; chmn. Med. Devel. Crop., 1972-82; bd. dirs. Bennett County Meml. Hosp., 1976-82; commr. S.D. Game, Fish and Parks Commn., 1987-91. Recipient Oral Diagnosis award of Excellence U. of Minn. Sch. of Dentistry, 1964, S.D. Sportsmans of the Yr., 1996. Mem. ADA, Am. Orthodontic Soc., Acad. Gen. Dentistry, Gen. Practice Acad. Orthodontics, S.D. Dental Assn., Black Hills Dental Assn., Am. Assn. Orthodontics, Internat. Assn. Orthodontics. Republican. Home: 204 Hwy 73 Box G Martin SD 57551 Office: 406 3d Ave S Martin SD 57551

GUNTER, G. JANE, state legislator; 3 children. Grad. high sch. Rep. Dist. 7 N.D. Ho. of Reps., mem. human svcs. and polit. subdivsn. coms. Mem. Gov.'s Coun. Human Resources, Com. Children and Youth. Home: PO Box 449 Towner ND 58788

GUNTER, RANDEL HARLAN, advertising agency executive; b. Moline, Ill., Apr. 25, 1961; s. Robert Harlan and Corinne Faye (Ensminger) G.; m. Lucinda Pollpeter, Dec. 29, 1984; 1 child, Trevor Maxfield. V.p., account dir. Comm. Network Advt., Davenport, Iowa, 1989-90; pres. Gunter Advt. Design, Moline, Ill., 1990-95; creative dir. Orion Advt., Madison, Wis., 1995—. Contbr. articles to profl. jours. Bd. dirs., leader Boy Scouts Am. Recipient Print Mag. citation of design excellence Print Regional Design Ann., 1993. Mem. Quad City Advt. Fedn. (bd. dirs. 1987—, best of show Addy 1992, other Addys 1987—), Am. Advt. Fedn. (nat. Addy 1988). Democrat. Office: Orion Advt 330 S Whitney Way Madison WI 53719

GUPTA, SURAJ NARAYAN, physicist, educator; b. Haryana, India, Dec. 1, 1924; came to U.S., 1953, naturalized, 1963; s. Lakshmi N. and Devi (Goyal) G.; m. Letty J.R. Paine, July 14, 1948; children: Paul, Ranee. M.S., St. Stephen's Coll., India, 1946; Ph.D., U. Cambridge, Eng., 1951. Imperial Chem. Industries fellow U. Manchester, Eng., 1951-53; vis. prof. physics Purdue U., 1953-56; prof. physics Wayne State U., Detroit, 1956-61, Distinguished prof. physics, 1961—; researcher on high energy physics, nuclear physics, relativity and gravitation. Author: Quantum Electrodynamics, 1977. Fellow Am. Phys. Soc., Nat. Acad. Scis. of India. Home: 30001 Hickory Ln Franklin MI 48025-1566 Office: Wayne State U Dept Physics Detroit MI 48202

GURAK, LAURA JEAN, communication educator, computer consultant; b. Troy, N.Y., Oct. 22, 1958; d. Carl J. and Eileen M. (Bragin) G. BA, Coll. St. Rose, Albany, N.Y., 1989; MS, Rensselaer Poly. Inst., 1990, PhD, 1994. Teaching asst. Rensselaer Poly. Inst., Troy, 1989-94; asst. prof. dept. rhetoric U. Minn., Mpls., 1994—; cons. on database design and info. devel. to various software cos., 1990—. Author: Persuasion in Cyberspace; contbr. numerous articles to profl. jours.; author book chpts., conf. procs. Mem. MLA, IEEE-Profl. Comm. Soc., Soc. for Tech. Comm. (Outstanding Article award 1993), Assn. for Computing Machinery, Assn. Tchrs. Tech. Writing, Speech Comm. Assn. Office: Univ Minn Dept Rhetoric/Coll Agrl 1364 Eckles Ave Saint Paul MN 55108

GURD, ALAN R., surgeon; b. Belfast, No. Ireland, U.K., Oct. 9, 1940; s. Robert and Evelyn (Ferguson) G.; m. Ruth K. Imrie, Sept. 15, 1966; children: Andrew, Alan, Colin, David, Jennifer. MBBCh, Queens U., Belfast, 1964, MCh, 1969. Registrar gen. surgery Royal Victoria Hosp., Belfast, 1964-69; registrar orthopaedic surgery Musgrave Park Hosp., Belfast, 1969-73; fellow pediat. orthopaedics Hosp. Sick Children, Toronto, Can., 1973-74; staff orthopaedic surgeon Royal Victoria Hosp., Belfast, 1974-76; staff orthopaedic surgeon Cleve. Clinic, 1976—, bd. govs., 1994—. Co-author: Trauma Care, 1981, Problematic Musculositieetal Injuries in Children, 1983, Pediatric Fractures, 1994. Fellow Royal Coll. Surgeons, Am. Assn. Orthopaedic Surgeons; mem. Am. Acad. Pediatricians, British Orthopaedic Assn. Home: 17754 Lost Trail Chagrin Falls OH 44023 Office: Cleve Clinic Found A51 Euclid Ave Cleveland OH 44195

GURNETT, DONALD ALFRED, physics educator; b. Cedar Rapids, Iowa, Apr. 11, 1940; s. Alfred Foley and Velma (Trachta) G.; m. Marie Barbara Schmitz, Oct. 10, 1964; children: Suzanne, Christina. B.S. in Elec. Engring., U. Iowa, 1962, M.S. in Physics, 1963, Ph.D. in Physics, 1965. Prof. physics and astronomy U. Iowa, Iowa City, 1965-75, 76-79, 80—; rsch. scientist Max-Planck Inst., Garching, Fed. Republic Germany, 1975-76; vis. prof. UCLA, 1979-80; mem. space physics com. Nat. Acad. Sci., Washington, 1975-78, mem. com. on solar terrrestrial research, 1976-79, mem. com. on planetary and lunar exploration, 1982-85. Recipient Alexander von Humboldt Found. award, 1975, Disting. Sci. Achievement award NASA, 1981, Space Act award NASA, 1986, Sci. Achievement medal Gov. of Iowa, 1987, Disting. Iowa Scientist award Iowa Acad. Sci., 1989, Marion L. Huit award U. Iowa, 1990, Iowa Bd. Regents award for faculty excellence, 1994. Fellow Am. Geophys. Union (assoc. editor Jour. Geophys. Rsch. 1974-77, Fleming medal 1989), Am. Phys. Soc. (award for excellence in plasma physics 1989); mem. Internat. Union Radio Sci. (Dellinger gold medal 1978), Soaring Soc. Am. (Iowa State gov. 1983-86). Home: 6 Durham Ct Iowa City IA 52240-2832 Office: U Iowa Dept Physics and Astronomy 715 Van Allen Hall Iowa City IA 52242-1403

GURNEY, PAMELA KAY, social services official; b. Joliet, Ill., Sept. 25, 1948; d. Wayne Franklin and Charlotte Marie (Geissler) G. BA, Coll. St. Francis, 1971. Tchr. Joliet Pub. Schs., 1971-73; field dir. Trailways coun. Girl Scouts U.S., Joliet, 1973-76; dir. adult devel. Mich. Waterways coun. Girl Scouts U.S., Port Huron, 1976-80; dir. adult devel. Irish Hills coun. Girl Scouts U.S., Jackson, Mich., 1980-88; planning specialist for community svc. Northeastern Ill. AAOA (formerly Region Two Area Agy. on Aging), Kankakee, 1989—; adv. bd. Kankakee chpt. Alzheimer's Disease and Related Disorders. Trainer Trailways coun. Girl Scouts U.S.; chairperson child care bd., chmn. ch. and soc. com., former tchr. Sunday sch., former leader youth group Asbury United Meth. Ch., Kankakee; mem. svc. team Kankakee Girl Scouts. Mem. Nat. Assn. Nutrition and Aging Svcs. Programs. Home: 1090 S Nelson Ave # 8 Kankakee IL 60901-5675 Office: Northeastern Ill AAOA PO Box 809 Kankakee IL 60901-0809

GURNIS, MICHAEL CHRISTOPHER, geological sciences educator; b. Boston, Oct. 22, 1959; s. George Albert and Barbara (Dempsey) G. BS, U. Ariz., 1982; PhD, Australian Nat. U., Canberra, 1987. Rsch. fellow in geophysics Calif. Inst. Tech., Pasadena, 1986-88, assoc. prof. geophysics, 1994—; asst. prof. geol. scis. U. Mich., Ann Arbor, 1988-93, assoc. prof., 1993—; assoc. dir. Seismological lab. Seismological Lab., Calif. Inst. Tech., Pasadena, 1995—. Recipient Presdl. Young Investigator award NSF, 1989, fellowship David and Lucile Packard Found., 1991. Fellow Am. Geophys. Union (Macelwance medal 1993), Geol. Soc. Am. (sr., Donath medal 1993). Office: Calif Inst Tech Seismol Lab Pasadena CA 91125

GURNITZ, ROBERT NED, steel industry company executive; b. N.Y.C., Dec. 1, 1938; s. Meyer and Beatrice G.; m. Ellen M. Gurnitz, Sept. 3, 1961; children: Allison D., Karen L. SB, MIT, 1960, SM, 1961, PhD, 1966. V.p., gen. mgr. Rockwell Internat. Corp., Troy, Mich., 1966-85; div. pres. Bethlehem (Pa.) Steel Corp., 1985-88; pres. Webcraft Technologies, Inc., North Brunswick, N.J., 1988-90; pres., CEO, chmn. bd. Northwestern Steel and Wire Co., 1991—. Mem. Soc. Automotive Engrs., Sigma Xi, Steel Mfrs. Assn. Home: 5011 Parliament Pl Rockford IL 61107-5007 Office: 121 Wallace St Sterling IL 61081-3558

GUSE, CAROL ANN, educational consultant; b. Ft. Wayne, Ind., Oct. 28, 1952; d. Lloyd Ervin and Clara Louise (Romine) Ramel; m. Daniel Richard Guse, Sept. 16, 1972; children: Melissa Ann, Andrea Elizabeth. Grad. magna cum laude, Ind. U., 1979, postgrad., 1996. Taxpayer svc. rep. IRS, Ft. Wayne, Ind., 1976-81; corp. sec. The Video Shoppe, Inc., 1982-89; pvt. practice tax acct. Speaking of Taxes, Ft. Wayne, Ind.; distributor. Success Motivation Inst., Ft. Wayne, Ind., 1989-91; pres. Guse & Assocs., Inc., Ft. Wayne, Ind., 1989—; pub. speaker pvt. practice, Ft. Wayne, Ind., 1989—; edn. cons. Ft. Wayne Community Schs., Ft. Wayne, Ind., 1991—; pres. SIRIUS Readers Inc., Ft. Wayne, Ind., 1992—, SIRIUS Corp., Ft. Wayne, Ind., 1992—, School and Family Partnership Svcs., 1994—. Author: Developing the Reading Habit in Your Child is Easy as A-B-C, 1992, Children First Newsletter, 1992, A SIRIUS Reader Handbook, 1994, Building Partnerships Between School and Home, 1994, Building Partnerships in Your School Community, 1995. Mem. Aldersgate United Meth. Ch., Ft. Wayne, Ind., 1984—, Internat. Reading Assn., Ft. Wayne, 1990—, Sch. Am. Registered Reader, 1990—; candidate Ft. Wayne Cmty. Schs. Bd. of Trustees, 1988, 90; edn. commn. chmn. Ind. PTA, 1993-95, state legis. coord., 1991-93; mem. WPTA-TV Cmty. Adv. Bd., 1992-93, WFWA-TV Cmty. Adv. Bd., 1992—, Allen County Collaborative for Edn., 1992-93, Ft. Wayne C. of C. Parental Involvement Task Force, 1991-93, Paul Douglas Teacher Scholarship Adv. Bd., Ind. Dept. Edn., 1992-93; pres. Ft. Wayne PTA Coun., 1992—; mem. Children's TV Ascertainment Com., 1992—; mem. Ind. Dept. Edn. Read-Aloud Adv. Com., 1993—; co-chair Parent Action Panel-Leadership Roundtable Violence & Youth, 1994—. Recipient Superior Performance award U.S. Dept. Treasury, Ft. Wayne, 1978, Advocates for Children award Nat. PTA, Ind. PTA, Ft. Wayne PTA Coun., 1990-92, Nat. Reading Lit. award Nat. PTA, 1992, Celebrate Reading/Literacy award Internat. Reading Assn., 1992, "15 Who Care" Vol. of the Yr. award, 1992, YWCA Tribute to Women of Achievement award, 1993; named Outstanding Mega Skills Vol., Allen County C. of C., 1995; nominee Sara Lee Frontrunner award, 1993; grantee Allen County Local Edn. Fund, 1994. Mem. Pleasant Ctr. Elem. PTA, Avalon Summersports Club, Ind. U. Alumni Assn., Friends of Allen County Pub. Libr. United Methodist. Home: 5304 Cresthill Dr Fort Wayne IN 46804 Office: SIRIUS Corp 5304 Cresthill Fort Wayne IN 46804

GUSEK, TODD WALTER, food scientist; b. St. Louis Park, Minn., Oct. 24, 1959; s. Walter Thomas and Mary Virginia (Dustin) G.; m. Christine LaVerne Olson, Aug. 1, 1987; children: Lyndsay Christine, Anna Virginia. BS, U. Minn., 1983; PhD, Cornell U., 1990. Rsch. food scientist Gen. Mills, Inc., Mpls., 1990-94; sr. rsch. scientist Cargill, Inc., Mpls., 1994—; cons., expert Teltech, Inc., Bloomington, Minn., 1988—. Contbr. articles to profl. jours.; patentee in field. Fulbright rsch. scholar to India (Mysore), 1991; recipient rsch. awds. Am. Chem. Soc., Inst. Food Technolgists, Procter & Gamble, Biotechnology Rsch. Soc.,Flegenheimer Found. Mem. Inst. Food Techs., Sigma Xi, Phi Kappa Phi. Mem. Christian Ch. Home: 3240 Yates Ave N Crystal MN 55422-2615 Office: Cargill Inc PO Box 5699 Minneapolis MN 55440

GUSKIN, ALAN E., university president; b. Bklyn., Mar. 22, 1937; s. David N. and Frances (Midler) G.; m. Lois La Shell, 1990; children from previous marriage: Sharon, Andrea. BA with honors, Bklyn. Coll., 1958; PhD, U. Mich., 1968; LHD (hon.), Saybrook Inst., 1989. Instr., Peace Corps. vol. Chulalongkorn U., Thailand, 1961-64; dir. of selection VISTA, 1964-65; asst. dir. Ctr. for Research on the Utilization of Scientific Knowledge, Inst. for Social Research, 1968-69; lectr. dept. of psychology and residential coll. U. Mich., 1968-71, dir. ednl. change team, Sch. of Edn., 1969-71, assoc. prof. edn., 1971; provost Clark U., Worcester, Mass., 1971-73, acting pres., 1973-74, prof. sociology and edn., 1973-75; chancellor, prof. edn. U. Wis.-Parkside, Kenosha, 1975-85; pres., prof. Antioch Coll. and Antioch U., Yellow Springs, Ohio, 1985-94; chancellor, Disting. univ. prof. Antioch U., 1994—. Author: (with Samuel Guskin) A Social Psychology of Education, 1970; editor New Directions on Teaching and Learning, The Administrator's Role in Effective Teaching, 1981; contbr. numerous articles and reports to profl. jours. Chmn. bd. Coun. on Adult and Experiential Learning, 1993-95. Mem. Am. Assn. Higher Edn. Office: Antioch U Office of Chancellor Yellow Springs OH 45387

GUSS, EMILY RENEE, librarian; b. Ensley, Ala., June 22, 1953; d. Charles Wimberly and Mary Emily (Gaines) G.; 1 child, Richard Darnell Guss. BA, Rosary Coll., River Forest, Ill., 1975; MLS, U. Mich., 1977; Specialist Cert., U. Wis., 1988. Regional libr. dir., br. mgr. various librs. Chgo. Pub. Libr., 1977—; program co-chmn., 2nd Nat. Conf., Black Caucus of ALA, 1993-94. Worker Harold Washington Mayoral Campaign, Chgo., 1983, 87; vol. voter registrar various orgns. Mem. ALA, Delta Sigma Theta (co-chair of arts and letters com. 1985-87). Office: Chicago Public LibrarySystem Carter G Woodson Regional Libr 9525 S Halsted St Chicago IL 60628

GUST, JOYCE JANE, artist; b. Milw., June 5, 1952; d. Walter F. and Jane A. (Klappa) Stoelzel; m. Wayne C. Fitzner, Feb. 13, 1971 (div. 1979); 1 child, Mark Wayne; m. Melvin. R. Gust, June 24, 1983. BS, Marquette U., 1981; postgrad., U. Wis., Oshkosh, 1985-90. Registered med. technolgosit. One woman shows include Pinecotheca Gallery, Waupun, Wis., 1993, Blatz Gallery, Milw., 1994, Lazarro Signature Gallery Fine Art, Stoughton, Wis., 1994, Constance Lindholm Fine Art, Milw., 1995, Artworks Gallery, Green Bay, 1995; two person shows include Capitol Civic Ctr., Manitowoc, Wis., 1992; represented in group shows at Signature Gallery, Stoughton, 1989, 91, Cudahy Gallery of Milw. Art Mus., 1989-92, Allen Priebe Art Gallery, Oshkosh, Wis., 1990, Jura Silverman Gallery, Spring Green, Wis., 1990, Chimerical Gregg Art Gallery, La Puente, Calif., 1990, Peltz Gallery, Milw., 1991-92, Ariel Gallery, N.Y., 1990, Neville Mus., Green Bay, 1992, John Michael Kohler Art Ctr., Sheboygan, Wis., 1993, Paine Art Mus., Oshkosh, 1996, others; represented in permanent collections Carroll Coll. Art Mus., Waukesha, Wis., Very Special Arts Wis. Permananet Wis. Artists Collection, Madison, Neville Pub. Mus., Green Bay, Sister Kenny Inst., Mpls., Aid Assn. for Lutherans Ins., others; featured artist Artworks Gallery, Green Bay, 1993. Recipient Jurors award 1st Ann. Wis. Artists Exhbn., 1992, purchase awards Parkside Nat. Print Exhbn., 1993, Galex Nat., Galesburg, Ill., 1993. Very Spl. Arts Wis. Purchase award, 1994, 96, 1st Pl. Internat. Award in Drawing, Sister Kenny Inst., 1995. Mem. Wis. Painters and Sculptors (Jurors award 1992), Wis. Women in The Arts. Home and Studio: 7064 Jacobson Dr Winneconne WI 54986-9764

GUSTAFON, DEBORAH, financial services company executive; b. Westbrook, Minn., July 25, 1963. BA in Sociology, Gustavus Adolphus Coll., 1985. Pres. Bridgewater Fin. Group, Inc., Plymouth, Minn., 1985—. Contbr. articles to profl. jours. Mem. adv. bd. Mpls. Econ. Devel. Co., 1994—; chairperson Vadnais Heights (Minn.) Econ. Devel. Corp., 1992-95, active, 1985—. Mem. Minn. Banker Assn. Colls., Econ. Devel. Assn. Minn., Twin West C. of C. (Karen Gibbs Women of Achievement award 1984). Lutheran. Office: Bridgewater Fin Group Inc 4025 Lancaster Ln N Minneapolis MN 55441-1700

GUSTAFSON, DAN, state legislator. State rep. Dist. 67 Mich. Ho. of Reps., 1993—. Home: 4648 Sandstone Dr Williamston MI 48895-9433*

GUSTAFSON, DAVID HAROLD, retired research chemist; b. Ft. Wayne, Ind., Dec. 7, 1935; s. Harold and Georgana (Rodebaugh) G.; m. Ermalou Rodda, Aug. 2, 1957 (div. Apr. 1975); 1 child, Derek William; m. Audrey Sophia Hecker, Nov. 18, 1978 (dec. May 1992); m. Elizabeth Jane Harris, Nov. 5, 1994. BS, Purdue U., 1957; PhD, U. Ill., 1961. Rsch. chemist Procter & Gamble Co., Cin., 1961-64; analytical chemist William S. Merrell Co., Cin., 1964-79; adminstrv. asst. Merrell Dow Rsch. Ctr., Cin., 1979-81; sr. analytical chemist Merrel Dow Rsch. Inst., Cin., 1981-88, sr. rsch. chemist, 1988-91; sr. assoc. chemist Marion Merrell Dow Inc., Cin., 1991-93; ret., 1993. Mem. Winton Woods (Ohio) Bd Edn., 1985—, pres., 1987-89; mem. Gt. Oaks Joint Vocat. Bd. Edn., Hamilton County, Ohio, 1989—. Mem. Am. Chem. Soc., N.Y. Acad. Scis., Sigma Xi, Phi Lambda Upsilon.

GUTERMUTH, SCOTT ALAN, accountant, pharmaceutical company executive; b. South Bend, Ind., Nov. 24, 1953; s. Richard H. and Barbara Ann (Bracey) G. BS in Bus., Ind. U., 1976. CPA, Ind. With Coopers & Lybrand, Indpls., 1976-83, supervising auditor, 1980-83, audit mgr., 1983; v.p., contr. Society Nat. Group, Indpls., 1983-89; v.p., CFO Am. Svc. Life Ins. Co., 1989-90; CFO Quad Pharms., Inc., 1990—; instr., nat. update analyst Becker CPA Rev. Course, 1980—. Advisor Jr. Achievement; mem. Marion County Rep. Com., 1978—, Rep. Nat. Com., 1972—. Fellow Life Mgmt. Inst.; mem. AICPA, Nat. Assn. Accts., Ins. Acctg. and Statis. Assn., Ind. Assn. CPAs (ins. com. 1984—), Life Mgmt. Inst. (assoc.). Methodist. Home: 3132 Sandpiper South Dr Indianapolis IN 46268-3229 Office: 5140 W 79th St Indianapolis IN 46268-1603

GUTHRIE, DIANA FERN, nursing educator; b. N.Y.C., May 7, 1934; d. Floyd George and A. May (Moler) Worthington; m. Richard Alan Guthrie, Aug. 18, 1957; children: Laura, Joyce, Tammy. AA, Graceland Coll., 1953; RN, Independence (Mo.) Sanitarium, 1956; BS in Nursing, U. Mo., 1957, MS in Pub. Health, 1969; EdS, Wichita State U., 1982; PhD, Walden U., 1985. RN, Mo., Kans.; lic. profl. counselor, Kans.; cert. in stress mgmt. edn.; cert.clin. hypnosis; lic. holistic nursing; cert. healing touch; advanced RN practitioner; registered marriage and family therapist. Instr. red cross U.S. Naval Sta., Sangley Point, Philippines, 1961-63; acting head nurse newborn nursery U. Mo., Columbia, 1963-64, birth defect nurse dept. pediatrics, 1964-65, nursing dir. clin. research ctr., 1965-67, research asst., 1967-73; asst. then assoc. prof. Sch. Medicine U. Kans., Wichita, 1974-85, prof. nursing, 1982—, diabetes nurse specialist Sch. Medicine, 1973—; nurse cons. diabetes Mo. Regional Med. Program, Columbia, 1970-73; nat. advisor Human Diabetes Ctr. for Excellence, Lexington, Ky., 1982-90, Phoenix, 1983-92, Charlottesville, Ky., 1990-95. Author: Nursing Management of Diabetes, 3d edit. 1991, The Diabetes Source Book, 1990, rev. edit., 1995; contbr. articles to profl. jours. Mem. health adv. bd. Mid-Am. All Indian Ctr., Wichita, 1978-80; bd. dirs. Wichita Urban Indian Health Clinic, 1980-82; trustee Graceland Coll., Lamoni, Iowa, 1996—. Recipient Explemprary Recognition award Epsilon Gamma chpt. Sigma Theta Tau, 1996. Fellow Am. Acad. Nursing; mem. ANA, APHA, Am. Diabetes Assn. (affiliate bd. dirs. 1979-83, pres. Kans. affiliate 1980-81, 90-91, Outstanding Educator award 1979), Am. Assn. Diabetes Educators (cert., Disting. Svc. award 1984), Am. Assn. Med. Psychotherapists (profl. adv. bd. 1985—), Sigma Theta Tau (exemplar recognition award Epsilon chpt. 1996). Democrat. Mem. Reorganized LDS Ch.

GUTHRIE, MICHAEL STEELE, magnetic circuit design engineer; b. Murray, Ky., Nov. 22, 1954; s. Steele G. and Lunelle (Holmes) G. BS in Physics, Murray State U., 1976. Engr. quality control & mfg. Allegheny Ludlum, Princeton, Ky., 1977-79; engr. applications & design Hitachi Magnetics Corp., Edmore, Mich., 1979-86; engr. applications & design Delco Remy div. GM, Anderson, Ind., 1986-91; regional mgr. applications engring. Stackpole Magnetic Systems, Kane, Pa., 1991—, Carbone of Am., Farmville, Va., 1991—. Co-author: Rapidly Solidified Alloys, 1993. Mem. IEEE, Magnetics Soc., Am. Phys. Soc., Clan Guthrie, Ky. Cols. Home and Office: 9055 Ravinewood Ln South Lyon MI 48178-9373

GUTIERREZ, LUIS V., congressman, elementary education educator; b. Chgo., Dec. 10, 1956. BA magna cum laude in English, Northeastern Ill. U., 1976. Social worker Ill. Dept. Children and Family Svcs.; adminstrv. asst. Mayor's Subcom. on Infrastructure, 1984-85; alderman for 26th ward Chgo., 1986-93; pres. Pro Tempore, 1992; mem. 103d-104th Congresses from 4th Ill. Dist., 1993—; mem. banking and fin. svcs. com.; chmn. Housing, Land Acquisition and Disposition com., 1989-93. Democrat. Office: US Ho of Reps 408 Cannon HOB Washington DC 20515*

GUTIERREZ, PAMELA JEAN HOLBROOK, nurse, clinical perfusionist; b. Maryville, Mo., Jan. 13, 1956; d. John Peter and Doris Ladene (Allen) Curry; m. Mark Lee Gutierrez, Dec. 9, 1978. Student, U. Nebr., 1973-93, Nebr. Meth. Sch. Nursing, 1976; BSN, U. State N.Y., 1989; grad. Clin. Perfusionist, U. Nebr., 1992-94. RN, cert. perfusion scis. Charge nurse ICU

St. Joseph's Hosp., Omaha, 1976-80, staff nurse emergency dept., 1980-81, flight nurse Life Flight, 1981-91, charge and staff nurse emergency dept., 1991-94; project nurse, rsch. asst. dept. surgery Creighton U., 1978-79; mem. PACU staff, nurse, clin. perfusionist Immanuel Med. Ctr., Omaha, 1994—; trauma nurse core course instr. emergency dept. Nurse's Assn., Neonatal Advanced Cardiac Life Support, 1990, Am. Heart Assn.; pediatric advanced life support instr.; advanced cardiac life support instr. Am. Heart Assn., 1985—; paramedic cert., pre-hosp. trauma life support instr. Nat. Assn. Emergency Med. Technicians and Paramedics, 1982. Contbr. articles to profl. jours. Mem. AACN, Nat. Flight Nurses Assn., Nat. Emergency Med. Svcs. Pilots Assn., Emergency Nurses Assn. Roman Catholic. Home: 4207 Woolworth Ave Omaha NE 68105-1752

GUTKE, JEFFREY ALAN, Spanish language educator; b. Chgo., Nov. 19, 1968; s. Earl George and Linda May (Hlavac) G. BA, No. Ill. U., 1991, MA in Spanish, 1993. Instr. No. Ill. U., DeKalb, 1991-93, Kishewaukee C.C., Malta, Ill., 1992-93; Spanish tchr. Thornton Fractional North H.S., 1993-94, Woodland Mid. Sch., 1994—; mem. Grad. Adv. Coun., DeKalb, 1991-92. Vol. Transitional Program of Instrn., DeKalb, 1992-93. Mem. Ill. Coun. on Teaching Fgn. Langs., Sigma Delta Pi (pres. 1991-93), Phi Sigma Iota (sec. 1991-93).

GUTMAN, RUTH LOUISE, real estate broker; b. Picher, Okla., Mar. 12, 1925; d. James Kendridge and Ella MAdeline (Chapin) Ruark; m. Kenneth Carter Gutman, May 30, 1921; children: Gregory, David P. BS with high honors, Okla. State U., 1947. Lic. real estate broker; grad. Realtors Inst. Lab. tech. Okla. Health Dept., Oklahoma City, 1947-49; virologist Abbott Labs., North Chicago, Ill., 1949-52; substitute tchr. Waukegan (Ill.) Jr. High Sch., 1962-65; real estate sales Barnet & Co., Waukegan, 1972-75; real estate broker Callahan Blandings Schaper, Inc., Waukegan, 1975—. Active Waukegan Sch. Bd., 1965-70, Waykegan Unit Sch. Dist. 60 Bd., 1970-75, Waukegan Coun. Race & Religion, 1965-69. Mem. AAUW (life mem., pres. 1964-67), NOW, ACLU, LWV (pres. 1988-91), Nat. Assn. Realtors, Ill. Assn. Realtors, Lake County Assn. Realtors, Urban Symphony Bd., Multi Million Dollar Club, Kappa Alpha Theta. Democrat. Home: 96 Mariposa Ave Waukegan IL 60087-4036 Office: Callahan Blandings Schaper Inc 830 W Glen Flora Ave Waukegan IL 60085-1839

GUTOWICZ, MATTHEW FRANCIS, JR., radiologist; b. Camden, N.J., Feb. 23, 1945; s. Matthew F. and A. Patricia (Walczak) G.; m. Alice Mary Bell, June 27, 1977; 1 child, Melissa. BA, Temple U., 1968; DO, Phila. Coll. Osteo. Medicine, 1972. Diplomate Am. Bd. Radiology, Am. Bd. Nuclear Medicine. Intern Mercy Hosp., Denver, 1972-73; resident in diagnostic radiology Hosp. of U. Pa., Phila., 1973-76, fellow in nuclear medicine, 1976-77; chief dept. radiology and nuclear medicine Fisher Titus Med. Ctr., Norwalk, Ohio, 1977—; pres. Firelands Radiology, Inc., Norwalk, 1977—. Republican. Roman Catholic. Home: 23 Patrician Dr Norwalk OH 44857-2463

GUTOWSKI, ANTHONY LOUIS, marketing consultant; b. St. Louis, Aug. 27, 1953; s. Louis Anthony and Elizabeth Marie (Nowak) G.; m. Alicia Gayle Townsend, Aug. 18, 1990; 1 child, Anthony L. III. BSBA, Tarkio Coll., 1980. Sales rep. H.B. Fullen Co., Omaha, 1979-85, Chem-Trend, Inc., Memphis, 1985-88; product mgr. Chem-Trend, Inc., Howell, Mich., 1989-92, mktg. mgr., 1993, mktg. mgr. North Am., 1994; v.p. sales and mktg. Huron Technologies, Inc., Ann Arbor, Mich., 1994—. With U.S. Army, 1976-77. Mem. North Am. Die Cast Assn. (membership chair 1991-92, Svc. award 1992), KC. Roman Catholic. Home: 716 W Washington Howell MI 48843 Office: Huron Technologies Inc 3729 Track Ctr Dr Ann Arbor MI 48108

GUTSTEIN, SOLOMON, lawyer; b. Newport, R.I., June 18, 1934; s. Morris Aaron and Goldie Leah (Nussbaum) G.; m. Carol Feinhandler, Sept. 3, 1961; children: Jon Eric, David Ethan, Daniel Ari, Joshua Aaron. AB with honors, U. Chgo., 1953, JD, 1956. Bar: Ill. 1956, U.S. Dist. Ct. (no. dist.) Ill. 1957, U.S. Ct. Appeals (7th cir.) 1958, U.S. Ct. Appeals (5th cir.) 1971, U.S. Supreme Ct. 1980; Rabbi, 1955. Assoc., Schradzke, Gould & Ratner, Chgo., 1956-60; ptnr. firm Schwartz & Gutstein, Chgo., 1961-65, Gutstein & Cope, Chgo., 1968-72, Gutstein & Schwartz, Chgo., 1980-83, Gutstein & Sherwin, Chgo., 1983-85; ptnr. Arvey, Hodes, Costello & Burman, 1991-92, Tenney & Bentley, 1992—; spl. asst. atty. gen. State of Ill., 1968-69; adj. prof. law, John Marshall Law Sch., 1993—; lectr. bus. law U. Chgo. Grad. Sch. Bus., 1973-82; lectr. in field, real estate broker. Author: Illinois Real Estate, 2 vols., 1983, rev. ann. updates, 1984-95, Judaism in Art (The Windows of Shaare Tikvah), 1995; co-author: Construction Law in Illinois, annually 1980-84; contbr. chpt. to Commercial Real Estate Transactions, 1962-76. Assoc. editor U. Chgo. Law Rev., 1954-56; editorial adviser Basic Real Estate I, also Advanced Real Estate II, 1960s-70s.; author: Analysis of the Book of Psalms, 1962; cons. Ill. Real Property Svc., Bancroft Whitney Co., 1988-89; contbr. articles to profl. publs. Mem. Cook County Citizens Fee Rev. Com., 1965; alderman from 40th ward Chgo. City Council, 1975-79; mem. govt. affairs adv. com. Jewish Fedn., 1984-94. Fuerstenberg scholar U. Chgo., 1950-56; Kosmerl fellow U. Chgo., 1953-56. Mem. Chgo. Bar Assn., Ill. State Bar Assn., Decalogue Soc. Lawyers (25 yr. cert. 1982). Lodge: B'nai B'rith. Office: Tenney & Bentley 111 W Washington St Chicago IL 60602

GUTTORMSON, MARK STEVEN, financial planner; b. Minot, N.D., Feb. 11, 1961; s. Clarence Ohio and Lilas Mae (Waswick) G.; m. Penny Colleen Wastweet, Apr. 28, 1984; children: Nicolas Arlan, Alexa Kaye, Skylar Elija (dec.), Marissa Amber, Brianna Danielle. Grad. high sch., Makoti, N.D., 1979. Ins. agt. C.A. Spletstoser, Minot, 1982-83; gen. agt. Blue Cross, Minot, 1984-85; gen. agt., dist. mgr. Red River Brokerage, Fargo, N.D., 1985-87; owner Consol. Ins. Agy., Minot, 1985-91; nat. mktg. mng. gen. agt. Investors LIfe of Nebr., 1990—; owner Consol. Fin. Svcs., Minot, 1991-95; ptnr. Fin. Advantage Brokerage Svcs., Inc., Minot, 1995—. Sponsor Youth for Christ, Minot, 1990—; active N.D. Family Alliance, Turtle Lake, 1990—, Rep. cen. com., Minot, 1990—, N.D. C. of C.; creator family farm transfer program. Named Outstanding New Agent Specialized Mktg., 1983, 1st runner up Agt. Yr. Fin. Dynamics, 1987; recipient Pres.'s cup Fin. Dynamics, 1987, Personal Prodn. Achievement award Banner Life Ins., 1995; appointed to Chmn.'s Inner Circle Fin. Dynamics, 1989. Mem. N.D. Farm Bur. Mem. Pentecostal Ch. Home: 1301 SW 10th St Minot ND 58701 Office: 17 S Main St Minot ND 58701

GUYON, JOHN CARL, university administrator; b. Washington, Pa., Oct. 16, 1931; s. Carl Alexander and Sara Myrle (Bumgarner) G.; m. Elizabeth Joyce Smith, Nov. 12, 1955; children—Cynthia Joan, John Carl, II. B.A., Washington and Jefferson Coll., 1953; M.S., Toledo U., 1958; Ph.D., Purdue U., 1961. Mem. faculty U. Mo., 1961-71, prof. chemistry, chmn. dept., 1970-71; prof. chemistry, chmn. dept. Memphis State U., 1971-74; dean Coll. Sci., So. Ill. U., Carbondale, 1974-75; dean Coll. Sci., So. Ill. U. (Grad. Sch.), assoc. v.p. research, 1976-80, v.p. acad. affairs and research, from 1980; pres. So. Ill. U., 1987-95, chancellor, 1996—. Author: Aanlytical Chemistry, 1965, Qualitative Analysis, 1966, Solution Equilbria, 1969; also articles, abstracts.; Gen. editor: Instrumental Methods of Analysis. Served with AUS, 41954-56. Eli Lilly Co. fellow, 1959-61; Owens Ill. Co. fellow, 1958; Jesse W. Lazear scholar, 1953. Mem. Am. Chem. Soc., AAAS, Phi Beta Kappa, Sigma Xi, Phi, Lambda Upsilon. Office: So Ill U Anthony Hall Office of Chancellor Carbondale IL 62901

GUZAK, DEBRA ANN, special education educator; b. Blue Island, Ill., Jan. 11, 1963; d. Robert Joseph and Angeline (Kozak)G. BS in Edn., Ea. Ill. U., 1985; MEd, U. Ill., 1993; postgrad., U. Wis., Whitewater, U. Manosh, Frankston, Australia. Cert. tchr., early childhood edn., Ill. Spl. edn. tchr. Southwest Cook County Coop., Oak Forest, Ill., 1985; early childhood specialist Sunnybrook Sch. Dist. # 171, Lansing, Ill., 1985—, intern in administrn., 1992-93; pvt. tutor, Lansing, 1985—; track coach Heritage Mid. Sch., Lansing, 1990—. Editor: Share a Story, 1992. Vol. Little City, Paletine, Ill., 1986—, Orland Park (Ill.) Spl. Recreation; fundraiser Misericordia/Heart of Mercy, Chgo., 1986—; steering com. Young Hearts Am. Heart Assn., Chgo., 1987-91; co-chmn. fashion show seating com. Ronald McDonald House, Chgo., 1994, 95. Grantee Ill. State Bd. Edn., 1990; recipient Educator of Yr. award Lansing Rotary, 1996. Mem. Assn. Supervision and Curriculum Devel., Coun. Exceptional Children (divsn. early childhood, svc. award 1981-86), Ind. Order Foresters. Republican. Roman Catholic. Home: 3205 186th St Lansing IL 60438-3233

GUZMAN, LAURA A., mortgage company executive; b. Detroit, May 8, 1960. Student, Henry Ford Coll. With svc. dept. First Dearborn (Mich.) Bank, 1981-84, mortgage closer, 1987-89; mortgage closer Liberty Mortgage, Southfield, Mich., 1984-87, MLA, Inc., Southfield, 1989-90; v.p. Eagle Mortgage Svc. Inc., Ann Arbor, Mich., 1990-94, pres., 1994—. Mem. Mortgage Bankers Assn. Roman Catholic. Office: Eagle Mortgage Svcs Inc 4125 Jackson Rd Ann Arbor MI 48103-1827

GWALTNEY, THOMAS MARION, education educator, researcher; b. Sikeston, Mo., Sept. 17, 1935; s. Thomas Marion and Niva (Kem) G.; m. Dolores Doreen Barrow, Dec. 23, 1962; children: Anne Elise, Karen Lee, Kristen Diane. BS, S.E. Mo. State U., 1957; MS, So. Ill. U., 1959, PhD, 1963; BA, Ea. Mich. U., 1979; postdoctoral studies, U. Mich., Harvard U. Cert. elem. and secondary tchr., Mich.; cert. adminstr. Tchr. Wyatt (Mo.) Elem. Sch., 1955-56; jr. high tchr. Scott County Sch. Dist., Sikeston, 1957-58; elem. supr. Scott County Sch. Dist., Benton, 1958-60; vis. lectr. So. Ill. U., Carbondale, 1960-63; asst. prof. edn. No. Mich. U., Marquette, 1963-64; prof. Ea. Mich. U., Ypsilanti, 1964—, assoc. dean grad. sch., 1989-90, honors advisor, 1984—, cons., 1986—, coord. grad. advising, 1992—, coord. social founds. program, 1995-96; edni. cons. Computing and Ednl. System, Dallas, 1969-70, World Coll., 1986, cons., 1987-89; vis. prof. U. Autònoma Met., Mexico City, 1990—, sr. Fulbright lectr., rschr., 1990-91; vis. prof. sch. langs. and sch. sociology U. Autònoma de Querètaro, Mex., 1994, presenter, 1993, 94; mem. Fulbright Selection Com., U.S. Embassy, Mex. City, 1990-91; rschr., tchr. edn. U.S., Russia, 1991-93; vice chair Collegium for Advanced Studies, 1992-93, chair, 1993-95, bd. dirs., 1995—; vis. prof. Escuela de Idiomas U. Autònoma de Querètaro, Mex., 1993; cons. Field-Intensive Tchr. Tng. Bilingual Program, 1988—; cons. rschr. and supr. bilingual edn. spl. transition project Ea. Mich. U., Farmington Pub. Schs., U.S. Dept. Edn., 1993-94; invited lectr. (in Spanish) Fundaciòn Gran Mariscal de Ayachucho, Venezuela, 1994; vis. prof. Escuela de Idiomas and Escuela de Sociologiá, 1994; presenter internat. meeting Kappa Delta Pi, 1995. Author: EDUSIM: Educational Simulation, 1972, Teaching Cultural Foundations, Handbook for Freshman, 1979; editor: Orientation Course, 1984, Teacher and Educational Foundations; book reviewer Houghton Mifflin Co., 1994-95; contbr. articles to profl. jours. Active desegregation bd. Ypsilanti Pub. Schs., 1975-76, campaign organizer, 1983-84; cons. Latin-Am. Initiative, 1989-90. Recipient Disting. Faculty award Ea. Mich. U., 1984-87, award Collegium for Advanced Studies, 1986—, Excellence in Higher Edn. Tchg. award State of Mich., 1990, Alumni Assn. Excellence in Teaching award Ea. Mich. U., 1993, Excellence award Mich. Assn. Governing Bds., 1996. Mem. AAUW, Am. Assn. Tchrs. Am. Edn. Studies Assn., Spanish and Portuguese, Coun. Grad. Schs., Mich. Assn. Staff Devel. and Sch. Improvement (exec. bd. 1992—), Mich. Assn. for Bilingual Edn., Mich. Assn. Bilingual Edn. Advocates, Hist. Soc. Mich., Mich. Ethnic Heritage Found., Mich. One Rm. Sch. Assn. (exec. bd. 1993—), Detroit Inst. Arts (founder's soc. 1982—), Fulbright Assn., Southeastern Mich. Fulbright Assn. (bd. dirs. 1993—), Soc. Profl. of Edn., Phi Delta Kappa, Phi Kappa Phi, Kappa Delta Pi (Mich. area rep. 1990—, internat. com. 1992—, L.Am. rep. 1992—, co-founder first L.Am. chpt. in Mex., 1994, Honor Key 1992, Queré taro Quo Mex. chpt. 1994, installing officer 1994, internat. constn. and bylaws com. 1994—, lectr. internat. convocation 1995). Baptist. Home: 833 Cornell Rd Ypsilanti MI 48197-2006 Office: Ea Mich U Dept Tchr Edn 714G Pray-Harrold Hall Ypsilanti MI 48197-2212

GWATKIN, RALPH BUCHANAN LLOYD, biologist; b. Newport, Gwent, Wales, May 23, 1929; came to U.S., 1959; s. Ralph Lloyd and Ada Alexandra (Lennie) G.; m. Selma Lila Schatz, June 20, 1954; children: Sharon, Nadine, David. MA, U. Toronto (Can.), 1951; PhD, Rutgers U., 1954. Rsch. assoc. U. Toronto, 1956-61, Wistar Inst., Phila., 1956-61; asst. prof. vet. sch. U. Pa., Phila., 1962-66; from asst. dir. to dir. Merck Inst., Rahway, N.J., 1967-80; vis. prof. Dartmouth Coll., Hanover, N.H., 1980-81; prof. McMaster U. Med. Sch., Hamilton, Ont., Can., 1982-85; dir. Cleve. Clinic Found., 1986-89; pres. ReproGene, Beachwood, Ohio, 1990—; adj. prof. reproductive biology Case Western Res. U. Med. Sch.; founder, chair Gordon Conf. on Fertilization, Holderness, N.H., 1974; mem. reproductive biology study sect. NIH, Washington, 1980. Author: Fertilization Mechanisms, 1977; editor-in-chief: Molecular Reprodn. and Devel.; editor: Manipulation of Mammalian Development, 1986, Genes in Mammalian Reproduction, 1993; mem. editorial bd.: Developmental Biology: A Comprehensive Synthesis, 1982—; contbr. articles to profl. jours. Recipient Rsch. Career Devel. award NIH, 1964, Rubin award Am. Fertility Soc., 1967, Rsch. award Pacific Coast Fertility Soc., 1973; rsch. grantee NIH, NSF, MRC. Mem. Soc. Study Reproduction, Am. Soc. Cell Biology. Office: ReproGene 25460 Bryden Rd Cleveland OH 44122-4164

GWILLIM, RUSSELL ADAMS, manufacturing company executive; b. Passaic, N.J., May 4, 1922; m. Elda E. Gwillim; children: Joanne, Linda, Cynthia. BS, MIT, 1948. Sales engr. CR Industries, Elgin, Ill., 1948-58, gen. sales mgr., 1958-64, v.p. mktg., 1964-65, exec. v.p., 1965-69, pres., 1969-84; chmn. bd. Safety-Kleen Corp., Elgin, 1974-90, chmn. emeritus, 1990—; bd. dirs. Safety-Kleen Corp., Elgin. Chmn. United Way of Elgin, 1980; bd. dirs. Elgin Assn. Commerce, 1978, Ill. C. of C., 1979; mem. adv. bd. St. Joseph Hosp., Elgin, 1984. Served with U.S. Army, 1942-46, PTO. Presbyterian. Clubs: Butler Country (Oak Brook, Ill.); Medinah Country (Itasca, Ill.) (bd. dirs. 1976—). Office: Safety-Kleen Corp 1000 N Randall Rd Elgin IL 60123-2318

GWINN, ROBERT P., publishing executive; b. Anderson, Ind., June 30, 1907; s. Marshall and Margaret (Cather) G.; m. Nancy Flanders, Jan. 20, 1942 (dec. 1989); 1 child, Richard Herbert. PhB, U. Chgo., 1929. With Sunbeam Corp., Chgo., 1936-51, gen. sales mgr. elec. appliance div., 1951-52, v.p., dir., 1952-55, pres., chief exec. officer, 1955-71, chmn. bd., chief exec. officer, 1971-82, also bd. dirs.; chmn. bd., chief exec. officer Ency. Britannica, Inc., Chgo., 1973-93, chmn. emeritus, 1993—; chmn. bd., CEO Titan Oil Co., Riverside; chmn. bd. S.A. King Corp.; bd. dirs. Continental Assurance Co., Continental Casualty Co., NCA/Fin. Corp., Inst. for Philos. Rsch., Alberto-Culver Corp. Trustee Chgo. Zool. Soc., U. Chgo., The Orchestral Assn.; mem. Citizens Adv. Com., Chgo.; bd. fellows Harvard Med. Sch., James Madison Coun., Libr. of Congress. Mem. Soc. Chgo., Internat. Food and Wine Soc. Chgo., Mid. Am. Club, Elec. Mfrs. Club (hon.), Comml. Club Chgo., Casino Club, Execs. Club, Bird Key Yacht Club, Riverside Golf Club, U. Chgo. Club, Alpha Sigma Phi. Office: 1 Riverside Rd Riverside IL 60546

GYLLANDER, NIKKI K., human services administrator; b. East Chicago, Ind., Mar. 9, 1946; d. Nick and Olga (Karchut) Migas; children: Grant, Greg. BSSW, No. Mich. U., 1972; MPA, U. Wis., Oshkosh, 1988; postgrad., Wis. State U., Whitewater. Cert. adminstrv. cons., surveyor Commn. on the Accreditation of Rehab. Facilities. Human svcs. dir. LaCrosse County, LaCrosse, Wis.; dep. dir. Sheboygan County Unified Bd., Sheboygan, Wis.; program coord. Florence County Combined Svcs., Florence, Wis. Author: Preventive Programs for Youth. Chair United Way Campaign. Mem. Wis. Cos. Human Svcs. Assn. (bd. dirs.), LaCrosse C. of C., Avant, Rotary (Paul Harris fellow). Office: PO Box 4002 La Crosse WI 54602-4002

GYOPOS, ROBERT WILLIAM, stockbroker; b. Budapest, Hungary, Feb. 27, 1944; came to U.S., 1957.; BS, Wayne State U., 1966, MBA, 1969. Broker Bank Commonwealth, Detroit, 1966-70, Arthur Anderson, Detroit, 1970-72; salesman Clark Equipment, Bucanan, Mich., 1972-80; self-employed South Bend, Ind., 1980-90; stockbroker City Securities Corp., South Bend, 1990—. Contbr. articles to profl. jours. Republican. Home: 5533 Reilgh Dr South Bend IN 46614 Office: City Securities Corp 112 W Jefferson Blvd Ste 304 South Bend IN 46601-1909

GYURO, PAULA CANDICE, financial planner; b. Phillipsburg, N.J., May 23, 1947; d. Alfred Eugene Gyuro and Pauline Johanna (Tinnes) Caldwell. BA, Ohio Wesleyan U., 1969; MBA, Xavier U., 1984. CFP. Events coord. The Nestle Co., Marysville, Ohio, 1969-73; sr. technologist R&D The Kroger Co., Cinti, Ohio, 1973-88; personal fin. advisor Am. Express Fin. Advisors, Inc., Cinti, 1989—. Mem. Inst. CFPs, Miami Valley Soc. Inst. CFPs. Office: Am Express Fin Advisors Inc 11590 Century Blvd Ste 214 Cincinnati OH 45246-3317

HAACK, RICHARD WILSON, retired police officer; b. Chgo., July 7, 1935; s. Arthur Frank and Mildred Ann (Meyer) H.; m. Ruth Marie Tietz, May 27, 1972; children: Laura Marie, Karl Richard. Grad., Cook County (Ill.) Sheriff's Police Acad., 1967; AS, Triton Coll., 1973; cert. Chgo. Police Acad., 1974; BA, Lewis U., 1975; MA, Northeastern Ill. U., 1979; BS in Bus. Adminstrn., Elmhurst Coll., 1982. Shipping clk. Am. Furniture Mart, Chgo., 1955-60; quality control insp. Nat. Can Co., Chgo., 1961-67; police officer Northlake Police Dept. (Ill.), 1967-92, watch comdr. patrol div., 1978-85, dept. chief of police, 1986-87, in-svc. tng. coord., 1991-92; retired, 1992; realtor Internat. Realty World-Norton & Assocs., 1984-87. Recipient John Edgar Hoover Meml. Gold medal, 1987. Mem. Bill Bruce fundraising com. Aid Assn. Luths., Christ Evang. Luth. Ch., Northlake, 1981-82, mem. Gala Variety Show, 1982, chmn. evang. bd., 1981-85, ch. rep. Internat. Luth. Laymen's League, 1984—, pub. rels. dir., usher, 1973-85, dir. Project Compassion, 1983-85; ombudsman No. Ill. dist. Luth. Ch.-Mo. Synod, 1984-85; choir Apostles Luth. Ch., 1985-87, membership chmn. Redeemer Luth. Ch. Men's Club, 1995—; dir., emcee German-Am. Police Assn. Oktoberfest, 1980—, chmn. entertainment, 1984—; coach Northlake Little League baseball team, 1985. Served with USMC, 1952-55, Korea, with res. 1955-60. Recipient numerous letters of commendation, competitive shooting awards. Mem. NRA, Internat. Assn. Chiefs of Police, Ill. Police Assn., Fraternal Order Police (sec.-treas. Perri-Nagle Meml. Lodge 18, 1977-85), St. Jude Police League, Nat. Police Officers Assn., Internat. Police Assn. (life), German/Am. Police Assn. (bd. dirs. 1980—), Combined Counties Police Assn., Internat. Juvenile Officers Assn., Ill. Juvenile Officers Assn., Emerald Soc. Ill. Irish/Am. Police Assn., Northeastern Ill. U. Alumni Assn. (bd. dirs. 1980-86), Am. Polit. Sci. Assn., Schwaben Verein, N.W. Real Estate Bd., Leyden Real Estate Bd. (inner circle 1984-87), Sharkhunters, Internat. Platform Assn., Realtors Polit. Action Com. Ill. (inner circle 1984-87), Am. Legion, Ret. and Disabled Police of Am., Kaire Ind. Distbr., Svc. Corps Ret. Execs., S.C.O.R.E., Die Hard Cub Fans, Moose Lodge. Republican. Contbr. law enforcement articles to profl. publs.; author Ency. Am. Judiciary. Home: 244 E Palmer Ave Northlake IL 60164-1735 Office: 55 E North Ave Northlake IL 60164-2518

HAACKE, E(WART) MARK, physicist, consultant; b. Toronto, Jan. 24, 1951; came to U.S., 1978; s. Ewart Mortimer and Helena Doris (Davies) H.; m. Linda T. Clarke, July 19, 1975; children: Bryon C., Daniel C. PhD, U. Toronto, 1978. Postdoctoral fellow Case Western Res. U., Cleve., 1978-80, instr., 1980-81, rsch. assoc., 1981-83, asst. prof., 1985-89, assoc. prof. dept. radiology physics and biomed. engring., 1989-93; rsch. geophysicist Gulf R&D Corp., Pitts., 1981-83; imaging physicist Picker Internat., Cleve., 1983-85; prof. dept. radiology Washington U., St. Louis, 1993—; pres. E. M. Haacke, Rsch. and Consulting Svcs., St. Louis, 1983—. Contbr. articles to profl. jours., chpts. to books, genealogical articles; co-editor MRA: Concepts and Applications, 1992. Grantee NASA, 1987-91, Whitaker Found., 1989-91, NIH, 1991-95. Mem. Assn. Med. Physicists (Sylvia Sorken Greenfield award 1990), Soc. Magnetic Resonance Imaging (pres. 1991-92), Soc. Magnetic Resonance (pres. 1993-94), Rittenhouse Family Assn. (co-editor newsletter, pres. 1988-95). Office: Mallinckrodt Inst Radiology 510 S Kingshighway Blvd Saint Louis MO 63110-1016

HAAG, DONALD RICHARD, director facilities and services; b. Kansas City, Mo., Nov. 9, 1943; s. William Anthony and Georgia Katherine (Vogeli) H.; m. Barbara Louise Krause, May 4, 1973; children: Marcella Ann, Eric Frederick, Michael Richard, Peter Joseph. BS, St. Benedict's Coll., 1965. Counterperson Leo's Ice Cream Parlor, Leavenworth, Kans., 1957-60; inventory clk. McCormick Payton Moving Co., Leavenworth, Kans., 1965; sales Montgomery Ward, Leavenworth, Kans., 1959, 60-66; mailroom clk. Armed Forces Ins., Ft. Leavenworth, Kans., 1966-67, mail and supplies clk., 1967-72, dep. dir., 1972-84, dir. supplies, svcs., 1984-91, dir. facilities, svcs., 1991—; CEO Allied Svcs., Inc., Leavenworth, 1975—; sec., steering com. INSERV, Inc., Leavenworth, 1987—; treas. Henry Leavenworth Chpt., Assn. U.S. Army, 1978—. Sch. bd. mem. Leavenworth Pub. Schs., 1991—, pres. 1996—; dep. chmn. Community Devel. Block Grant Bd., Leavenworth, 1988—; appt. mem. Mayor's Traffic Corridor Study Com., Leavenworth, 1985-86; mem. Boy Scouts of Am., den leader, cubmaster 1987-89, 90—, fundraiser, 1990-91; mem. Muncie Sch., PTO, v.p., 1988-91. Recipient Cert. of Appreciation, Boy Scouts of Am., 1987-89, Salvation Army, 1986, Appreciation Plaque, Life Master Am. Contract Bridge League, 1976, Cert. of Appreciation, Muncie Elem. Sch., 1990, Coaches award Parks/Recreation Dept., 1991-92. Republican. Roman Catholic. Home: 2205 Wilson Ave Leavenworth KS 66048-4641 Office: Armed Forces Ins 550 Eisenhower Rd Leavenworth KS 66048-4969

HAAG, JOEL EDWARD, architect; b. Wayne, Nebr., June 30, 1962; s. Robert James and Shirley Ann (Krutz) H. BS, N.E. Mo. State U., 1984; BArch, U. Kans., 1986. Registered architect, Mo. Architect Hollis & Miller Group, Prairie Village, Kans., 1986-90, Tognascioli, Gross, Kautz Architects, Inc., Kansas City, Mo., 1991-92; engr., structural design draftsman Borton Inc., Hutchinson, Kans., 1992-93; registered architect Mann & Co., Hutchinson, Kans., 1993—; co-chmn. Archtl. Explorer Post, Kansas City, Mo., 1989-92. Trustee Redeemer Luth. Ch., Lawrence, Kans., 1987-88; mem. choir Bethany Luth. Ch., Overland Park, Kans., 1989-92; chmn. Hutchinson Landmarks Commn., 1995—. Mem. Reno Choral Soc., Kans. Mennonite Men's Chorale, Optimists. Home: 1010 N Washington St Hutchinson KS 67501-4456 Office: Mann & Co 335 N Washington St Ste 110 Hutchinson KS 67501-4861

HAAKENSON, PHILIP NIEL, pharmacist, educator; b. Hatton, N.D., Apr. 15, 1924; s. Martin Selmer and Theodora H.; m. Eldora Ida Robinson, June 19, 1950; children: Mary Kim, Martin Niel. BS in Pharmacy, N.D. State U., 1950, MS in Pharmacy, 1965; PhD in Pharmacy Adminstrn., U. Wis., 1972. Owner Portland (N.D.) Drug, 1950-60, Hatton Drug, 1956-60; asst. prof. pharmacy adminstrn. N.D. State U., Fargo, 1961-65, assoc. prof., 1965-70, prof., 1970-87, prof. emeritus, 1987—, dean sch. of pharmacy, 1970-80; dir. Pharmacy Continuing Edn., 1982-87; vis. prof. Univ. Mont. Sch. Pharmacy, 1987-88, Univ. Man. (Can.), 1988-95. Editor Nodak Pharmacist, 1962-74, 1982-87. Mgmt. counselor Svc. Corps Ret. Execs. Assn. Served with USN, 1942-45. Mem. Am. Assn. colls. of Pharmacy, N.D. Pharm. Assn. (recipient Bowl of Hygiea 1979), Am. Pharm. Assn., Kappa Psi (named Outstanding Alumni 1974, Pharmacist of Yr. 1977), Sigma Xi. Republican. Lutheran. Lodges: Lions, Masons, Shriners. Home: 210 28th Ave N Fargo ND 58102-1624 Office: Sch of Pharmacy Nd State U Fargo ND 58105 also: Svc Corps of Ret Execs Assn Box 3086 Rm 225 Main PO Bldg Fargo ND 58108-3086

HAAN, STEPHEN M., investment broker; b. Grand Rapids, Mich., Feb. 9, 1959; m. Carol S. Elenbaas, Oct. 12, 1984; 1 child, Ethan. BA, Calvin Coll., Grand Rapids, 1981. Investment broker Primus Investment, Grand Rapids, 1983-89, Centennial Securities, Grand Rapids, 1989-93, Anderson & Co. Inc., Grand Rapids, 1993—. Chmn. bd. deacons Hagger Park Ref. Ch., Grand Rapids, 1990-93. Republican. Office: Anderson & Co Inc 2025 E Beltline Ave SE Ste 203 Grand Rapids MI 49546-7630

HAAS, BILL, state legislator; b. June 25, 1949; m. Joenie Haas; 2 children. AA, U. Minn. Employee benefits broker; rep. Dist. 48A Minn. Ho. of Reps., 1994—.

HAAS, JONATHAN STUART, financial company executive; b. Harrison, N.Y., Apr. 8, 1950; s. Adrian L. and Millicent Rochelle (Trachtenberg) H.; m. Linda Sue Lyons, July 13, 1981; children: Michael Lee, Jennifer Lyn. AS in Psychology, Stetson U., DeLand, Fla., 1973; BS in Psychology magna cum laude, Magnosenic Sem., Orlando, Fla., 1973, MS in Counseling, 1975. Cert. leasing profl. Br. mgr. Gen. Fin. Corp., Orlando, 1976-80; collection mgr. All Am. Equipment & Leasing, Sanford, Fla., 1980-83; dist. sales mgr. Capital Assocs., Pompano Beach, Fla., 1983-85; regional mgr. Eaton Fin. Corp., Framingham, Mass., 1985-87; dir. mktg. Copelco Credit Corp., Maywood, N.J., 1987; field sales mgr. Lowe's Cos., Orlando, 1987-88; asst. v.p. The CIT Group/Datronics, Schaumburg, Ill., 1988-92; v.p. MetroLease, Inc., Rolling Meadows, Ill., 1992-94; pres. Triad Cons. Network, Ltd., Chgo., 1992—, Genesis Fin. Svcs., Inc., Hoffman Estates, Ill., 1995—; instr. sales tng. Granieri & Assocs./Top Gun, 1990—; pres. Genesis Fin. Svcs., Inc., 1995—; spkr. industry topics various orgns., 1989—. Author newspaper column The Monitor, 1991—. Pres. P.T.A., Kissimmee, Fla., 1989, 90. Regents scholar State Bd. Edn., N.Y., 1969. Mem. Nat. Assn. Equipment Lease Brokers, Western Assn. Equipment Lessors (regional chmn., chair cert. com. 1988—, bd. dirs., chair program com., now United Assn. Equipment Leasing), Ea. Assn. Equipment Lessors (ethics com. 1991—), Equipment Leasing Assn. (midwest regional com.),. Office: Triad Cons Network Ltd 275 Cascade Dr Crystal Lake IL 60012-3345

HAAS, KELLEY WEYFORTH, marketing and communications company executive; b. St. Louis, July 27, 1964; d. Francis Griffin Jr. and Mara (Kelley) Weyforth; m. Timothy John Haas, June 27, 1987. BSBA, U. Kans., 1986. Bookkeeper Mktg. Resources, Inc., Overland Park, Kans., 1983-84, prodn./traffic asst., 1984-85, media buyer, planner, 1985-86, coord. tng. programs, 1986-87, traffic mgr., 1987-89; sr. account. exec. Mktg. Resources Am., Inc., Overland Park, 1989-91, account supr., 1991-92, v.p., account supr., 1992-93, v.p. mktg. svcs., 1993-94, sr. v.p. mktg. svcs., 1994-95; sr. v.p. COO Mktg. Resources Am. Inc., Overland Park, 1995—; also bd. dirs., mem. exec. com. Mktg. Resources Am., Inc., Overland Park. Mem. Advt. Club Kansas City, Bus. Mktg. Assn. Office: Mktg Resources Am Inc 10551 Barkley St Overland Park KS 66212-1812

HAAS, MARILYN ANN, real estate broker; b. Belleville, Ill., Jan. 13, 1941; d. Oscar Henry and Edna Mary (Ernst) Rensing; m. Larry Allan Haas, June 28, 1961; children: Jeffery L., Cynthia L., Gregory A., Jeanine K. Student, Belleville Area Coll.; grad., Realtors Inst. Ill., 1980. Lic. real estate broker, Ill. Residential saleswoman Crown Realty, Belleville, 1974-77, Century 21 AG Realtors, Belleville, 1977-78; sales mgr., broker Century 21 Blankenship, Fairview Heights, Ill., 1978-79, comml. saleswoman, 1980-82; relocation coord. Century 21 Belscott, Belleville, 1979-80; comml. saleswoman Century 21 Battoe, Belleville, 1982-84; residential-comml. saleswoman Eckert & Assoc. Realtors, Belleville, 1984-86; residential saleswoman Camelot Realty, B, 1986—. Bd. dirs. St. Clair County Citizens for Devel. Disabled, 1987. Mem. Nat. Assn. Realtors, Ill. Assn. Realtors (co-chmn. coms. 1980-85, Realtors Active in Politics award 1985, Million Dollar Prodn. award), Belleville Bd. Realtors (bd. dirs. 1980-85, sec. 1985, Realtor Assoc. of Yr. award 1982), So. Ill. Real Estate Exchangors (bd. dirs. 1982-87, sec. 1987). Roman Catholic. Home: 8700 Concordia Rd Belleville IL 62223-6949 Office: Camelot Realty 5812 N Illinois St Fairview Heights IL 62208-3505

HAAS, SUZANNE NEWHOUSE, management consultant, human resources specialist; b. Akron, Ohio, Feb. 7, 1945; d. Earl Wallace and Bernice (Pikoski) Newhouse; m. Raymond John Haas, Feb. 8, 1975; children: Monique, John, Alexander. BA in Psychology, Kent (Ohio) State U., 1984, BA in Bus. Adminstrn., 1985; MA in Indsl. Psychology, Cleve. State U., 1991. Asst. dept. head Green Cross Gen. Hosp., Cuyahoga Falls, Ohio, 1966-73; customer svc. rep. Ohio Bell Telephone Co., Akron, 1973-75; job analyst McKinley Life Care, Canton, Ohio, 1988; mgmt. cons. Paragon Human Resource Systems, Canton, 1989—; rsch. asst. N.E. Ohio U. Coll. of Medicine, Rootstown, 1990-93; site coord. Vanderbilt U. Inst. Mental Health Policy, Nashville, Tenn., 1993—; rsch. site coord. Vanderbilt U., Nashville, 1993—. Mem. APA, ASTD, Am. Psychol. Soc., Acad. Mgmt., Ohio Psychol. Assn. Republican. Roman Catholic. Home: 115 48th St NW Canton OH 44709-1418 Office: Paragon Human Resource Sys 115 48th St NW Canton OH 44709-1418

HAAS, SYLVIA See TEMLITZ, SYLVIA

HABAK, PHILIP ANTOINE, cardiologist; b. Cairo, Sept. 24, 1937; came to U.S., 1965; s. Antoine and Jeanette (Saydi) H.; m. Hermina Geels, Feb. 7, 1970; children: Patricia J., Glenn E. MB, BCh, Ain Shams U., Cairo, 1963. Diplomate Am. Bd. Internal Medicine, Am. Bd. Cardiology. Intern Cook County Hosp., Chgo., 1965-66; resident in internal medicine U. Iowa, Iowa City, 1966-69, fellow in cardiology, 1971-73; resident in internal medicine Ain Shams U., 1969; assoc. cardiovascular div. U. Iowa Hosp., 1973-74; pvt. practice, Davenport, Iowa, 1975—; clin. asst. prof. dept. internal medicine U. Iowa, 1977—. Maj. M.C., U.S. Army, 1969-70, Korea. Fellow ACP, Am. Coll. Cardiology (gov. Iowa chpt. 1996-99, pres. Iowa chpt. 1996-99); mem. AMA, Am. Heart Assn. (fellow coun. on clin. cardiology), Iowa Heart Assn., Iowa Med. Soc., Scott County Med. Soc. Office: Cardiovascular Medicine PC 1230 E Rusholme St Ste 305 Davenport IA 52803-2400

HABASEVICH, ROBERT ALLAN, healthcare executive; b. Linden, N.J., Jan. 18, 1947; s. Andrew L. and Julia (Levonick) H.; m. Judith Russ, Oct. 1, 1988; 1 child, Andrew W. BA, Va. Mil. Inst., 1969; BS, Med. Coll. of Va., 1971; MS, Boston U., 1977. Phys. therapist Yale/New Haven (Conn.) Med. Ctr., 1971-74; dir. rehab. U. Conn., Farmington, 1975-78, Brigham & Womens Hosp., Boston, 1978-83; pres. Mass Bay Rehab., Duxbury, Mass., 1983-84; dir. phys. therapy Moss Rehab. Hosp., Phila., 1985-87; adminstr. Moss Rehab. Inc., Phila., 1987-89; v.p. Sigmedics Inc., Northfield, Ill., 1990-95; dir. ops. Chgo. Medirisk, Inc., Atlanta, 1996—; adv. bd. Jimmie Heuga Ctr., Beaver Creek, Colo., 1984-85; profl. adv. com. Plymouth County Nursing Assn., 1982-85. Author: (with others) Multiple Sclerosis-A Rehab Approach to Management, 1991; contbr. articles to profl. jours. Adv. com. Delaware Valley Multiple Sclerosis Soc., Phila., 1987-90. Mem. Am. Phys. Therapy Assn. (legis. amb. Pa. chpt. 1988-90), Am. Congress of Rehab. Medicine. Home: 401 Beech Dr Glenview IL 60025

HABEGGER, CYNTHIA A., nursing administrator; b. Van Wert County, Ohio, Dec. 14, 1953; d. Palmer Paul and Donna Jean (Hertel) Johnson; m. Alan Duane Habegger, Oct. 13, 1979; children: Duane Alan, Rebekkah Ann. ADN, Purdue U., Ft. Wayne, 1985, AD in Supervision, 1991; BSN, Luth. Coll. Health Profls., Ft. Wayne, 1994. RN, Ind.; lic. supr. Staff nurse Swiss Village, Berne, Ind., 1985-87; staff nurse med.-surg. unit Caylor Nickel Clinic, Bluffton, Ind., 1987-88; DON geriatric Decatur (Ind.) Community Care, 1988; charge nurse Cooper Community Care Corp., Bluffton, 1988; psychiat. staff nurse and charge nurse Caylor Nickel Clinic, Bluffton, 1988-92; ADON Meadowvale Nursing Home, Bluffton, 1992-93; intermittent RN Vis. Nurse Svc. and Hospice, Fort Wayne, Ind., 1993-94; instr. nursing Ivy Tech State Coll., 1994-95; DON, ExtendaCare of Bluffton (Ind.), 1995—. Home: 665 High St Berne IN 46711-1320 Office: ExtendaCare of Bluffton 1001 S Clark Ave Bluffton IN 46714

HABEN, JOHN WILLIAM, funeral director; b. Evanston, Ill., Oct. 11, 1956; s. R. William and Barbara A. (Wilson) H.; m. Mary Anne McNulty, Nov. 28, 1981; children: John W. Jr., Peter W., Clare M., William D., Thomas E., Nicholas R. BS in Bus., Miami U., Oxford, Ohio, 1978; diploma in mortuary sci., Worsham Coll., 1979. Intern, apprentice Haben Funeral Home, Skokie, Ill., 1979-80, lic. funeral dir. and embalmer, 1980—, sec., treas., 1982-92, pres., 1992—. Mem. steering com. Skokie Centennial Celebration, 1987, 88; bd. dirs. Skokie Hist. Soc., 1988-91; active Young Families Task Force, Skokie, 1988-89; commr. zoning bd. appeals Village of Skokie, 1989-94; bd. dirs., pres., mem. steering com. 125th Anniversary St. Peter Ch. Sch., 1995—. Named One of Outstanding Young Men of Am., 1985. Mem. Nat. Funeral Dirs. Assn., Nat. Selected Morticians, Ill. Funeral Dirs. Assn., Funeral Dirs. Svcs. Assn. (bd. dirs. 1982), Skokie C. of C. (bd. dirs. 1989-93, pres. 1992), Luxembourg Brotherhood of Am. (officer 1994—), KC, Rotary (bd. dirs. Skokie chpt. 1987-91), Evanston Golf Club (fin. com. 1990-93), Evanston Golf Club (house com. 1996—). Roman Catholic. Home: 8051 Lincoln Ave Skokie IL 60077-3612 Office: Haben Funeral Home 8057 Niles Center Rd Skokie IL 60077-2506

HABERLY, H. PAUL, JR., investment broker; b. May 19, 1939; m. Carol Haberly; children: Jim, Andy. BS, U. Miami, 1962; MS, U. Washington, Chgo., 1970. Lic. series 7, 6. Loan officer 1st Fed. Savs. and Loan, Ft. Wayne, Ind., v.p. ops., sr. v.p. adminstrn., pres. N.E. ins. divsn., v.p. N.C. enterprises; investment broker Shearson Lehman Huton, Ft. Wayne, 1984-89, Roney & Co., Ft. Wayne, 1989—; lectr. investment seminars. Contbr. United Way, Ft. Wayne; brokers chair Fine Arts, Ft. Wayne. Mem. Rotary. Home: 4424 Brixworth Ct Fort Wayne IN 46835-4609 Office: Roney & Co 202 W Berry St Ste 105 Fort Wayne IN 46802-2242

HABERMANN, JAMES HERBERT, retired pathologist; b. Cassville, Wis., June 18, 1926; s. Matthew Herbert and Clara Cordelia (Reilly) H.; m. Helen Audrey Howe, June 14, 1952; children: Thomas, Patrick, Michael, Jane, Mary Ann. MD, Marquette U., Milw., 1952. Diplomate in anat. and clin. pathology Am. Bd. Pathology. Family practice physician Mt. Calvary, Wis., 1953-60; resident in pathology Denver Gen. Hosp., 1960-64; dir. labs. Mercy Hosp. and Luth. Hosp. (merged into Trinity Hosp.), Ft. Dodge, Iowa, 1964-77; staff pathologist Freeman Hosp., Joplin, Mo., 1977-80, St. John's Med. Ctr., Joplin, 1980-91; pres. bd. dirs. Trinity Regional Hosp., Ft. Dodge, 1973-77; chief of staff St. John's Med. Ctr., Joplin, 1984-85. 1st lt. U.S. Army, 1944-47, Germany. Fellow Am. Soc. Clin. Pathologists, Coll. Am. Pathologists. Roman Catholic. Home: 2111 E 36th St Joplin MO 64804

HABERSTROH, RICHARD DAVID, insurance agent; b. St. Louis, Mar. 21, 1943; s. Richard J. and Helen M. (Jones) H.; m. Patricia Steinlage, Aug. 22, 1964; children: Michelle, Stacy, Richard David. BA, S.E. Mo. State U., Cape Girardeau, 1965. CLU. Ins. agt. Constitution Life, Chgo., 1963-70; gen. agt. Monarch Life, Springfield, Mass., 1971-78; pres. Richard D. Haberstroh, CLU, Inc., St. Louis, 1978—; bd. mem. Jefferson Bank, St. Louis, Family Physician Health Svc. Corp. of Ind., Ind. Acad. Family Physicians; cons. Purdue U. Ins. Mktg. Inst., West Lafayette, Ind., 1992, dir. Contbr. articles to profl. jours. Bd. mem., chmn. United Cerebral Palsy, 1982. Mem. St. Louis Assn. Life Underwriters (bd. mem. 1992), Gateway Chpt. Nat. Speakers (pres. 1987), King's Men (bd. mem. 1978—), Million Dollar Round Table (life). Republican. Roman Catholic. Office: Richard D Haberstroh CLU 1023 Executive Parkway Dr Ste 2 Saint Louis MO 63141-6323

HABLUTZEL, PHILIP NORMAN, law educator; b. Flagstaff, Ariz., Aug. 23, 1935; s. Charles Edward and Electa Margaret (Cain) H.; m. Nancy Zimmerman, July 1, 1980; children: Margo Lynn, Robert Paul. BA, La. State U., 1958; postgrad., U. Heidelberg, Fed. Republic Germany, 1959-60, 62-64; MA, U. Chgo., 1960, JD, 1967. Bar: Ill. 1967, U.S. Dist. Ct. (no. dist.) Ill. 1967, U.S. Supreme Ct. 1995. Rsch. atty. Am. Bar Found., Chgo., 1967-68, sr. rsch. atty., 1968-71; asst. prof. law Chgo.-Kent Coll. Law, Ill. Inst. Tech., 1971-73, assoc. prof., 1973-79, prof., 1979—, dir. grad. program in fin. svcs. law, 1985—; dir. student exch. program with U. Darmstadt, Germany, 1994—; co-dir. Ann. conf. on Not-for-Profit Orgns., Chgo., 1984—; chair Conf. on Derivative Fin. Products, 1995; sr. Fulbright prof. U. Mainz, Germany, 1993; lectr. banking law U. Torcuato di Tella, Buenos Aires, 1995; cons. OEO Legal Svcs. Program, 1967-69; pres., trustee Chgo. Sch. Profl. Psychology, 1979-83; instr. course on profl. responsibility Chgo. Merc. Exch., 1990-93; reporter Ill. sect. state's com. on revision of not-for-profit corp. act, 1984-87; reporter Ill. sect. of state's corp. laws adv. com., 1986-89, mem., 1989—. Author: (with R. Garrett, W. Scott) Model Business Corporation Act Annotated, 2d edit., 3 vols., 1971, (with J. Levi) Model Residential Landlord-Tenant Code, 1969, International Banking Law, 2 vols., 1994. Mem. Adv. com. Scouting for People with Disabilities, Chgo. area Boy Scouts Am., 1988-92. Rotary Found. Advanced Study fellow, 1959-60. Fellow Chgo. Bar Found. (life), Ill. Bar Found., Ill. Bar Assn.; mem. ABA (chmn. subcom. on adoption of Uniform Trade Secrets Act 1984-86, com. on consumer fin. svcs. 1989—, ad hoc com. on Ctrl. and Ea. European Law Initiative 1991-95), Ill. State Bar Assn. (uniform comml. code revision com. 1989—, coun., sect. comml. banking and bankruptcy law 1990-96, sec. 1991-92, vice chmn. 1992-93, chmn. 1993-94), Chgo. Bar Assn. (chmn. com. on sci., tech. and law 1971-72, sec. corp. law com. 1986-87, vice-chmn. corp. law com. 1987-88, chmn. corp. law com. 1988-89, task force state takeover legis. 1987-89, joint com. banking act revisions 1988-90, chair ann. seminar on forming and Ill. Corp. 1990—). Republican. Presbyterian. Office: 565 W Adams St Chicago IL 60661-3691

HABUSH, ROBERT LEE, lawyer; b. Milw., Mar. 22, 1936; s. Jesse James and Beatrice (Liebenberg) H.; m. Miriam Lee Friedman, Aug. 25, 1957; children: Sherri Ellen, William Scott, Jodi Lynn. BBA, U. Wis., 1959, JD, 1961. Bar: Wis. 1961, U.S. Dist. Ct. (ea. and we. dists.) Wis. 1961, U.S. Ct. Appeals (7th cir.) 1965, U.S. Supreme Ct. 1986. Pres. Habush, Habush, Davis & Rottier, S.C., Milw., 1961—; lectr. U. Wis. Law Sch., Marquette U. Law Sch., State Bar Wis., other legal orgns. Author: Cross Examination of Non Medical Experts, 1981. Contbr. articles to legal jours. Served to capt. U.S. Army, 1959-75. Mem. ABA, Wis. Bar Assn., Wis. Acad. Trial Lawyers (pres. 1968-69), ATLA (bd. govs. 1983-86, pres. 1986-87, mem. Nat. Coll. Advocacy), Internat. Acad. Trial Lawyers (bd. dirs. 1983-87, 91-92), Am. Bd. Trial Advocates, Am. Inns of Court, Internat. Soc. Barristers, Inner Circle Advocates, Am. Soc. Writers on Legal Subjects, Nat. Bd. Trial Advocates, Trial Lawyers for Pub. Justice, Roscoe Pound Found., Scribes. Office: Habush Habush Davis & Rottier 777 E Wisconsin Ave Milwaukee WI 53202-5302

HACAULT, ANTOINE JOSEPH LEON, archbishop; b. Bruxelles, Man., Can., Jan. 17, 1926; s. Francois and Irma (Mangin) H. B.A., U. Man., 1947; theol. student, St. Boniface Maj. Sem., 1947-51; S.T.D., Angelicum U., Rome, 1954; D.C.L. honoris causa, St. John's Coll., Winnipeg, Man., 1977; D.L.L. honoris causa, U. Man., 1989. Ordained priest Roman Cath. Ch., 1951; chaplain St. Boniface Sanatorium, 1954; prof. theology St Boniface Maj. Sem., 1954-64; dir. diocesan rev. Les Cloches de Saint Boniface, 1961; former personal theologian to archbishop of St. Boniface; also council expert 2d Vatican Ecumenical Council, 1962-65; bishop titular of Media; aux. bishop of St. Boniface, 1964-72; coadjutor bishop, 1972-74; archbishop St. Boniface, 1974—; rector Coll. St. Boniface, 1966-69; mem. Pontifical Coun. for Promoting Christian Unity, Rome, 1976-89; pres. Western Cath. Conf. Bishops, 1988-92. Address: Archevêché de Saint Boniface, 151 Ave de la Cathedrale, Saint Boniface, MB Canada R2H 0H6

HACHTEN, RICHARD ARTHUR, II, hospital administrator; b. L.A., Mar. 24, 1945; s. Richard A. and Dorothy Margaret (Shipley) H.; m. Jeanine Hachten, Dec. 12, 1970; children: Kristianne, Karin. BS in Econs., U. Calif.-Santa Barbara, 1967; MBA, UCLA, 1969. Mgmt. intern TRW Systems Group, Redondo Beach, Calif., 1969-72; adminstrv. asst. Methodist Hosp., Arcadia, Calif., 1972-73, asst. adminstr., 1973-74, assoc. adminstr., 1974-76, v.p. adminstrn., 1976-80, exec. v.p., adminstr., 1980-81, pres., adminstr., 1981-84; CEO Tri-City Hosp. Dist., Oceanside, Calif., 1984-91; pres. Bergan Mercy Health Sys., Omaha, 1991-95, Algent Health, Omaha, 1996—; instr. health care mgmt. Pasadena (Calif.) City Coll. Bd. dirs., pres. Hospice of Pasadena, Inc.; bd. dirs. ARC, Arcadia, Mercy Housing Midwest, Omaha. Mem. Am. Coll. Healthcare Execs., Hosp. Council San Diego and Imperial Counties (chmn., bd. dirs.), Nebr. Assn. Hosp. and Health Sys. (bd. dirs., chmn. dist. 1), Calif. Assn. Hosps. and Health Sys. (bd. dirs.), Beta Gamma Sigma. Republican. Methodist. Club: Rotary. Home: 2676 S 96th Cir Omaha NE 68124-1949 Office: Alegent Health 1010 N 96th St Ste 200 Omaha NE 68114

HACKBARTH, TOM, state legislator; b. Dec. 28, 1951; m. Mary Hackbarth; 3 children. Student, North Hennepin C.C. Rep. Dist. 50A Minn. Ho. of reps., 1994—.

HACKEL, MARY ROEPER, counselor, placement coordinator; b. Streator, Ill., Dec. 4, 1933; d. Henry Edward and Clara Marcella (Horan) Roeper; m. William K., Feb. 11, 1956; children: William Andrew, Elizabeth Ann. BA in Elem. Edn., Harris Tchrs. Coll., 1960; MA Edn. in Guidance and Counseling, U. Mo., 1973. Admitting sec. Barnes Hosp., St. Louis, 1952-53; research tech. Wash. U. Sch. Medicine, St. Louis, 1952-53; elem. tchr. St. Louis County Schs., 1955-58, St. Louis Pub. Schs., 1959-65; placement specialist St. Louis Community Coll. Meramec, 1973-76; counselor Notre Dame High Sch., 1980-85; research field tech. U. Mo., Columbia, 1986; counselor Jobs Partnership Ctr., Kirkwood, Mo., 1986-89; pres. publ. div. Riverbend, St. Louis, 1987—. Mem. Friends of Gov., Jefferson City, 1987, Rep. Nat. Com., Wash., 1986—; supporter Citizens for Senator, St. Louis, 1975. Roman Catholic. Home: 4904 Sherborne Dr Saint Louis MO 63128-2737

HACKER, DAVID WILLSON, newspaper correspondent and staff writer; b. Ft. Wayne, Ind., June 2, 1928; s. George Frank and Kathryn Wilding (Willson) H.; m. Pauline Lynch, June 26, 1949 (div.); 1 child, Holly; m. Barbara Davidsmeyer, June 20, 1968; children: Sandy, Jonathan, Sarah. Student, U. Chgo., 1944-46, Ind. U., 1951; AB in Sociology and Psychology, Hanover Coll., 1952; postgrad., Harvard U., 1952-53. Reporter, sports editor Jonesboro (Ark.) Evening Sun, 1953; reporter Ark. Gazette, Little Rock, 1954-55, Louisville Times, 1955-62; writer Nat. Observer, Washington, 1961-77; vis. prof. Kans. State U., Manhattan, 1977-81; writing coach Kansas City (Mo.) Times, 1981, Wichita (Kans.) Eagle-Beacon, 1986-87; editor Manhattan Mercury, 1981-86; staff writer, no. corr. Detroit Free Press, 1993-95; contbg. editor, columnist Prime Time News & Observer, Traverse City, 1994—; writing, coach; lectr. Author: Mudbath, 1986, The Quilted Eye: Stories from a Compassionate Reporter, 1987, Leonard Mikowski Is Full of Baloney--And Other Michigan Stories, 1987; editor: Who Governs Kansas, 1981, North America's Third Coast: Reflections of 50 Years of the Great Lakes. Staff sgt. U.S. Army, 1946-49. Recipient Paul Myhre award U. Mo., 1981, Best Newspaper in Kans.-Mo. award Kansas City (Mo.) Press Club, 1983; co-recipient Pulitzer prize for local reporting, 1982; fellow Internat. Press Inst., South Africa, 1958. Unitarian. Home and Office: 1039 W Long Lake Rd Traverse City MI 49684-9268

HACKER, STEVEN D., information systems consultant. BS in Computer Sci., N.W. Mo. State U., 1986. Software engr. Perceptronics, Inc., Leavenworth, Kans., 1986-89; dir. info. svcs. Kennedy Ctr., Washington, 1989-94; info. systems cons. McKnight Consulting Group, Inc., Cleve., 1994—. Office: McKnight Consulting Group Inc Bond Court Bldg Cleveland OH 44114

HACKETT, BARBARA (KLOKA), federal judge; b. 1928. B of Philosophy, U. Detroit, 1948, JD, 1950. Bar: Mich. 1951, U.S. Dist. Ct. (ea. dist.) Mich. 1951, U.S. Ct. Appeals (6th cir.) 1951, U.S. Supreme Ct. 1957. Law clk. U.S. Dist. Ct. (ea. dist.) Mich., 1951-52; chief law clk. U.S. Ct. Appeals, Mich., 1965-66; asst. pros. atty. Wayne County, Mich., 1967-72; pvt. practice law Detroit, 1952-53, 72-73, Frasco, Hackett & Mills, 1984-86; U.S. magistrate U.S. Dist. Ct. (ea. dist.) Mich., Detroit, 1973-84, judge, 1986—; mem. Interstate Commerce Commn., 1964. Trustee U. Detroit, 1983-89, Mercy High Sch., Farmington Hills, Mich. 1984-86, Detroit Symphony Orch., Orch. Hall Assocs., Detroit Sci. Ctr., United Community Svcs. Recipient Pres.'s Cabinet award U. Detroit Mercy, 1991. Mem. ABA (spl. ct. judge discovery abuse com. 1978-79, com. on cts. in cmty. 1979-84), Am. Judicature Soc., Fed. Bar Assn. (sec. 1981-82), Fed. Judges Assn., Nat. Assn. Women Judges, Nat. Dist. Attys. Assn., Nat. Assn. R.R. Trial Counsel, State Bar Mich., Women Lawyers Assn. Mich. Pros. Attys. Assn. Mich. (Disting. Svc. award 1971), Oakland County Bar Assn., U. Detroit Law Alumni Assn. (officer 1970-75, pres. 1975-77, Alumni Tower award 1976), Women's Econ. Club (bd. dirs. 1975-80, pres. 1980-81, named Detroit's Dynamic Women 1992), Econ. Club Detroit (bd. dirs. 1979-85, 88—), Phi Gamma Nu. Office: US Dist Ct 718 Theo Levin Courthouse 231 W Lafayette Blvd Detroit MI 48226-2719

HACKETT, WESLEY PHELPS, JR., lawyer; b. Detroit, Jan. 3, 1939; s. Wesley P. and Helen (Decker) H.; m. Linda Carol Hackett, Oct. 30, 1964; children: Kelly D. Hackett Pell, Robin C. BA, Mich. State U., 1960; JD, Wayne State U., 1968. Bar: Mich. 1968, U.S. Dist. Ct. (we. dist.) Mich. 1971, U.S. Ct. Appeals (6th cir.) 1972, U.S. Dist. Ct. (ea. dist.) Mich. 1972, U.S. Supreme Ct. 1972, U.S. Ct. Mil. Appeals 1991. Law clk. Mich. Supreme Ct., Lansing, 1968-70; ptnr. Brown & Hackett, Lansing, 1971-73; pvt. practice Lansing, 1973-84; ptnr. Starr, Bissell & Hackett, Lansing, 1984-87; pvt. practice East Lansing, Mich., 1987—; adj. prof. Thomas M. Cooley Law Sch., Lansing, 1973—; instr. Lansing C.C., 1981—. Author: Evidence: A Trial Manual for Michigan Lawyers, 1981, Hackett's Evidence: Michigan and Federal, 2d edit., 1995; co-author: Hiring Legal Staff, 1990. Mem. City of East Lansing Planning Commn., 1969-72; bd. dirs. St. Vincent Home for Children, Lansing, 1974-82. 1st lt. USAF, 1961-65. Fellow Coll. Law Practice Mgmt.; mem. ABA (sec. gen. practice sect. 1990-91, vice-chair 1991-92, chair-elect 1992-93, chair 1993-94), State Bar Mich. (chair legal econs. sect. 1990-91). Office: 1650 Kendale Blvd Ste 105 East Lansing MI 48823-2076

HACKL, DONALD JOHN, architect; b. Chgo., May 11, 1934; s. John Frank and Frieda Marie (Weichmann) H.; m. Bernadine Marie Becker, Sept. 29, 1962; children: Jeffrey Scott, Craig Michael, Cristina Lynn. BArch., U. Ill., 1957, MS in Architecture, 1958. With Loebl Schlossman & Hackl Architects, Chgo., 1963—, assoc., 1967-74, exec. v.p., dir., 1974, pres., dir., 1975—; prof. architecture Internat. Acad. Architecture, Sofia, Bulgaria; mem. Nat. Coun. Archtl. Registration Bds., 1986—; bd. dirs. Chgo. Bldg. Congress, 1983—, v.p., 1985—; design juries include: Reynolds Metals, Western Mont. Regional Design, Am. Inst. Steel Constrn., Precast Concrete Inst., Okla. Soc. Architects; chmn. Ariz. Soc. Architects, Midwest Design Conf., 1983; design critic dept. arch. U. Ill., 1975-76, 81; vis. critic sch. architecture U. Notre Dame, 1977, 78, 80, 82; adj. prof. Kent Coll. Law, Ill. Inst. Tech., 1983—; cons. Pub. Svcs. Adminstrn., Washington, 1974-76. Prin. works include Water Tower Place, Chgo., 1976, King Faisel Specialist Hosp. and Rsch. Ctr., Riyadh, Saudi Arabia, 1978, Household Internat. Hdqrs., Prospect Heights, Ill., 1978, Shriners Hosp. for Crippled Children, Chgo., 1979, Square D Co. Hdqrs., Palatine, Ill., 1979, West Suburban Hosp., Oak Park, Ill., 1981, Allstate Pla. West, Northbrook, Ill., 1981, 89, Sears Roebuck & Co. stores of future concept, 1985-89, Ford City Shopping Ctr. Redevel., Chgo., 1989, Commerce Clearing House, Riverwoods, Ill., 1986, Physicians' Pavilion Greater Balt. Med. Ctr., 1987, Two Prudential Plaza, Chgo., 1990, City Place, Chgo., 1990, 350 N. LaSalle, Chgo., 1990, Infinitec, Assistive Tech. Application Ctr. for United Cerebral Palsy Assn., Chgo., 1992, Shenzhen AVIC Plaza Bldg., Shenzhen, China, 1993, Ill. State U. Biol. and Chemistry News Scis. Lab. Bldg., Normal, 1995, Old Orchard Shopping Ctr. Redevel., Skokie, Ill., 1994, Sun Comml. City, Changchun, China, 1995, Shekou Harbor Bldg., Shenzhen, 1995, East Shanghai Film and TV Ctr., Hdqrs. for Almacenes Paris LTDA, Santiago, Chile, 1996. Mem. Met. Am. Cancer Crusade, 1973; life trustee West Suburban Hosp., 1983—, mem. exec. com., 1986-87; vice chmn. North Ctrl. Coll., 1990—; mem. Pres.'s Coun. U. Ill. Found.; mem. curricula adv. com. Dept. Architecture, U. Ill.; bd. dirs. World Trade Ctr., Chgo., 1995—. Fellow AIA (treas. Chgo. chpt. 1977-78, exec. com. 1978-81, v.p. 1981, pres. 1981, bd. dirs. Chgo. AIA Found. 1981-83, bd. dirs. Chgo. Archtl. Assistance Ctr., nat. v.p. 1985, 1st v.p. 1986, nat. pres. 1987, chmn. design com. 1985, exec. com. 1985-87, bd. dirs. 1981-84, documents com. 1974-79, chmn. 1980, exec. com. AIA Svc. Corp. 1983-84, chmn. internat. com. 1987—), fellow Royal Archtl. Inst. Can. (hon.), fellow Colegios Architectos Mexicanos (hon.), Internat. Acad. Architecture (hon.); mem. Union Internat. Archs. (bd. dirs., del. 1987—, 1st v.p. 1990—, coun. 1987-96), Union Bulgarian Archs. (hon.), Soc. Cuban Archs., Japan Inst. Archs. (hon.), Colegio Arquitectos Cochabamba (Bolivia), Colegios Arquitectos Espana, Chgo. Assn. Commerce and Industry, Greater North Michigan Ave. Assn., Art Inst. Chgo., Tavern Clubs, Carlton Club, Econ. Club, Lake Zurich Club. Office: Loebl Schlossman and Hackl Inc 130 E Randolph Dr Ste 3400 Chicago IL 60601-6313

HACKLER, RONALD ERVIN, chemist; b. Louisville, Oct. 5, 1940; s. Sheldon Vernon and Mary Honora (Sims) H.; m. Elinor Louise Chatfield, May 30, 1961; children: Pamela Kay, Jeffrey Mark. MS, U. Ill., 1964; PhD, Pa. State U., 1970. Organic chemist Eli Lilly and Co., Indpls., 1964-67; sr. organic chemist Eli Lilly and Co., Greenfield, Ind., 1969-73, rsch. scientist, 1973-89; tech. leader entomology chemists DowElanco, Greenfield, 1990-92; advisor DowElanco, Indpls., 1993—. Contbr. chpts. in books. Pres. Citizens for Decency Through Law of Cen. Ind., Indpls., 1984—. Mem. Am. Chem. Soc., Ind. Acad. Scis., Entomol. Soc. Am. Mem. Christian Ch. Office: DowElanco 9410 Zionsville Rd Indianapolis IN 46268-1054

HACKMAN, EDWARD MARTIN, hospital administrator; b. Beardstown, Ill., Mar. 16, 1943; s. Edward William and Mary Frances (Martin) H.; m. Judith Anne Prichard, Dec. 22, 1972; children: Anne, Scott, Jennifer. BA, Ill. Coll., 1966; MA, Sangamon State U., 1974, U. Nebr., 1975; PhD, U. Nebr., 1979. Cert. biomed. communications specialist. Tchr. Sch. Dist. 114, Jacksonville, Ill., 1966-73; faculty U. Nebr., Lincoln, 1974-75; dir. edn. Mercy Hosp., Mason City, Iowa, 1975-80; v.p. acad. affairs Meth. Hosp., Indpls., 1980-86; COO Lapeer (Mich.) Regional Hosp., 1986-89; pres. Manning (Iowa) Gen. Hosp., 1989-90; pres., CEO Atchison (Kans.) Hosp. Assn., 1990—. Bd. dirs. Ind. Lung Assn., Indpls., 1985, United Way of Lapeer, 1988; active Boy Scouts Am. Nat. Libr. of Medicine fellow, 1974. Mem. Am. Coll. Healthcare Execs., Kans. Hosp. Assn., Rural Healthcare Assn., Am. Hosp. Assn., Am. Acad. Med. Adminstrs., Am. Coll. Managed Care Adminstrs., Rotary (bd. dirs. 1989), Atchison C. of C. (bd. dirs. 1992). Presbyterian. Office: Atchison Hosp 1301 N 2nd St Atchison KS 66002-1297

HACKNEY, HOWARD SMITH, retired county official; b. Clinton County, Ohio, May 20, 1910; s. Volcah Mann and Gusta Anna (Smith) H.; B.S. cum laude, Wilmington Coll., 1932; m. Lucille Morrow, June 28, 1933; children: Albert Morrow, Roderick Allen, Katherine Ann Luby. Farmer, Wilmington,

Ohio; farm reporter Agrl. Adjustment Adminstrn., Wilmington, 1934-40, committeeman, 1940-52, office mgr., 1952—, county exec. dir. Agrl. Stblzn. and Conservation Service, 1961-88. Treas., dir. Clinton County Community Action Council; treas. Clinton County Council Chs.; dir. Ohio Pork Producers Coun.; trustee mem. agrl. adv. com. Wilmington Coll.; trustee Clinton County Hist. Soc. Named to Ohio State Fair Hall of Fame, 1983, Swine Hall of Fame, 1986. Mem. Nat. Assn. Stblzn. and Conservation Service Office Employees (awards 1970, state, regional legis. cons., Agriculturist of Yr. 1987), AAAS, Soil Conservation Soc. Am., Farmers Union, Ohio Duroc Breeders Assn. (pres., dir.), Ohio Acad. Sci., Ohio Acad. History, Ohio Hist. Soc., Grange, Ohio Southdown Breeders Assn., Clinton County Farm Bur. (sec., dir.), Clinton County Agrl. Soc. (treas., dir., award 1975), Clinton County Lamb and Fleece Improvement Assn. (dir.), Clinton County Hist. Soc., Delta Theta Sigma (hon.), Masons. Republican. Quaker. Home: 2003 Inwood Rd Wilmington OH 45177-9424

HADAS, JULIA ANN, social services administrator; b. Rome, Ga., May 23, 1947; d. Robert Franklin and Myrtle Julia (Patrick) Richmond; m. John R. Hadas, Apr. 22, 1967 (div.); children: Kevin, Brian. BS magna cum laude, No. Mich. U., 1972, MA, 1977. Cert. social worker; lic. profl. counselor. Placement worker adult community Mich. Dept. Social Svcs., Marquette, 1976-80, supr. vol. svcs., 1980-86, supr. children svcs., 1986-93; dir. Marquette Local Office, 1993—. Chair Parent Adv. Coun. Marquette Area Pub. Schs., 1984-85, Upper Peninsula Children's Coalition, 1986—; adv. bd. Student Vol. Orgn. No. Mich. U., 1984-85; sec., pers. com. Women's Ctr. Named one of Outstanding Young Women in Am., 1982. Mem. Childbirth Edn. Assn. (pres. 1975-76), Mich. Assn. Vol. Adminstrs., Zonta (pres. Marquette chpt. 1982-83). Episcopalian.

HADDAD, FREDDIE DUKE, JR., hospital development administrator; b. Charleston, W.Va., Oct. 18, 1952; s. Freddie Duke Haddad Sr. and Betty Jane (Perry) Campbell; m. Cynthia Ann LaMaster, July 17, 1976; children: Freddie Duke III, Shannon Lynn. BS, W.Va. U., 1974; MPA, W.Va. Grad. Coll., 1976; EdD, W.Va. U., 1986. Grad. asst. W.Va. Grad. Coll., Charleston, 1974-75; assoc. dir. devel. U. Louisville, Ky., 1975-77; dir. alumni affairs Fla. Internat. U., Miami, 1977-79; dir. alumni/devel. U. Charleston, W.Va., 1979-81; pvt. practice bus. cons. Charleston, 1981-82; dir. alumni/devel. Butler U., Indpls., 1982-89; dir. devel. St. Vincent Hosp. Found., Indpls., 1989—; adj. prof. Nova U., Ft. Lauderdale, Fla., 1978-79; cons. in field. Contbr. articles to profl. jours. Mem. parish coun. St. George Orthodox Ch., Indpls., 1990-93; mem. com. Red Cross Awards Program, Indpls., 1991—; sec., v.p. Lawrence Twp. Babe Ruth League, Indpls., 1991-93; bd. dirs. Lawrence Twp. Edn. Found., Indpls., 1994—. Named Ky. Col., Gov. Ky., Frankfort, 1976, Outstanding Young Men of Am., 1986, Outstanding West Virginian, Gov. W.Va., Charleston, 1994. Mem. Nat. Soc. Fund Raising Execs. (cert. fund raising exec., bd. mem. 1990-95, v.p., pres.-elect Ind. chpt. 1992-94, pres. Ind. chpt. 1995—, Pres.'s award 1993), Assn. Healthcare Philanthropy (Jour. award 1993), W.Va. U. Alumni Assn. (mountaineer amb. 1991—). Office: St Vincent Hosp Found 2001 W 86th St Indianapolis IN 46240

HADDAD, GLADYS MARYLIN, American studies educator, author, consultant; b. Cleve., Sept. 12, 1930; d. Fred and Rose (Amor) H. BA, Allegheny Coll., Meadville, Pa., 1952; BFA, Lake Erie Coll., Painesville, Ohio, 1974; MA, Case Western Res. U., 1961, PhD, 1980. Tchr. South Euclid-Lyndhurst (Ohio) Schs., 1952-60, Cleveland Heights (Ohio) Schs., 1960-63; prof., adminstr. Lake Erie Coll., 1963-89, Western Res. Hist. Soc., Cleve., 1989—; prof., adminstr. Am. studies Case Western Res. U., Cleve., 1990—; founder, dir. Western Res. Studies Symposia, 1985—; scholar, cons., planner Ohio Humanities Coun., 1984—. Author, editor: Ohio's Western Reserve: A Regional Reader, 1988, Anthology of Western Reserve Literature, 1992; editor: Western Reserve Studies: A Jour. of Regional History and Culture, 1984—; producer (video) Samuel Mather: Vision, Leadership, Generosity, 1994, Samuel and Flora Stone Mather: Partners in Philanthropy, 1995. Dir. Lake Erie Coll. Press, 1982-89; pres. trustees, Music and Performing Arts at Trinity Cathedral, inc., 1994—. Recipient Achievement award No. Ohio Live, Cleve., 1990, award Am. Assn. for State and Local History, 1988. Mem. Am. Studies Assn., Gt. Lakes Am. Studies Assn. (sec.-treas., v.p. 1985-94), Ohio Hist. Soc., Western Res. Hist. Soc., Western Res. Archtl. Historians (bd. dirs.), Women Historians of Greater Cleve. (pres. 1987-87), Lake County Hist. Soc. (trustee 1984-92), Fortnightly Mus. Club (bd. dirs., v.p. 1992—, trustee women in history project 1996). Episcopalian. Home: 1640 S Belvoir Blvd Cleveland OH 44121-3769 Office: Case Western Res U Dept American Studies Cleveland OH 44106

HADDAD, INAD, physician; b. Beirut, Lebanon, June 2, 1953; came to U.S., 1978; s. Andraos Y. and Juliette H. Student, St. Joseph U., 1971-74, U. Paris, 1975-78. Physician Emma L. Bixby Hosp., Adrian, Mich., 1981—, chmn. dept. medicine, 1986, dir. critical care unit, 1985-87, chief of med. and dental staff; chief med. dental staff Bixby Med. Ctr., 1988; bd. dirs., founder Cardiac Rehab. Clinic Adrian, 1986-94. Chmn. Lanawee County Dem. Party, 1991—. Named Dem. of Yr., Lenawee County Dem. Party, 1990. Mem. AMA, Mich. State Med. Soc., Lenawee County Med. Soc. (pres. 1991), Lenawee C. of C. (bd. dirs. 1989-95), Mich. Doctors Polit. Action Com. (bd. dirs.), Am. Soc. Internal Medicine, Mich. Soc. Internal Medicine. Roman Catholic. Home: 415 Meadowbrook Dr Adrian MI 49221-1319 Office: 4204 W Maple Ave Adrian MI 49221-1382

HADDEN, PHILLIP GREGORY, retail business owner; b. Urbana, Ill., Nov. 5, 1946. BS in Edn., Ea. Ill. U., 1969; MEd, Loyola U., 1974. Cert. state tchr., cert. adminstr. K-12, gen. adminstr., Ill., cert. h.s., Ill.; grad. Realtors Inst., Ill. Tchr. jr. h.s. math./sci. Oak Park (Ill.) Elem. Schs., 1970-76; real estate sales assoc. Quinlan & Tyson Real Estate, Evanston, Ill., 1976-80; sales mgr., owner Hadden Jewelry, Atwood, Ill., 1980—; v.p. At the Woods Corp., Atwood, 1994—. Recipient Gov.'s Home Town award, 1994. Office: Hadden Jewelry 111 N Main PO Box 887 Atwood IL 61913

HADDOCK, FRED T., astronomer, educator; b. Independence, Mo., May 31, 1919; s. Fred Theodore Sr. and Helen (Sea) H.; m. Margaret Pratt, June 24, 1941 (div. Sept. 1976); children: Thomas Frederick, Richard Marshall. SB, MIT, 1941; MS, U. Md., 1950; DSc (hon.), Rhodes Coll., 1965, Ripon Coll., 1966. Physicist U.S. Naval Rsch. Lab., Washington, 1941-56; assoc. prof. elec. engring. and astronomy U. Mich., Ann Arbor, 1956-59, prof. elec. engring., 1959-67, prof. astronomy, 1959-88, emeritus prof., 1988—; lectr. radio astronomy Jodrell Bank U. Manchester, Eng., 1962; vis. assoc. radio astronomy Calif. Inst. Tech., 1966; vis. lectr. Raman Inst., Bangalore, India, 1978; sr. cons. Nat. Radio Astron. Obs., W.Va., 1960-61; founder, dir. U. Mich. Radio Astron. Obs., 1961-84. Author: (chpts. in books) Space Age Astronomy, 1962, Radio Astronomy of the Solar System, 1966; contbr. articles to prof. jours. and publs. Mem. Union Radio Sci. Internat., nat. chmn. commn. on radio astronomy, 1954-57; trustee Associated Univs., Inc., 1964-68; prin. investigator, five Orbiting Geophys. Observatories, 1960-74, and Interplanetary Probe 9, 1964-77; co-investigator on Voyager planetary probes, 1970-86, NASA, Washington; mem. astronomy adv. panel NSF, Washington, 1957-60, 63-66. With USN, 1944-45. Fellow IEEE (life), Am. Astron. Soc. (v.p. 1961-63); mem. Internat. Astron. Union (commn. on radio astronomy 1948—), NAS (adv. panel astronomy facilities 1962-64), AIA (hon. mem. Huron Valley chpt. 1980—), Sigma Xi (past pres. U. Mich. chpt. 1956—). Home: 3935 Holden Dr Ann Arbor MI 48103-9415 Office: U Mich Astronomy Dept Ann Arbor MI 48109

HADDOCK, GERALD HUGH, geology educator; b. Neosho, Mo., Mar. 7, 1929; s. Hugh Ransom and Orpha Florene (Vaughan) H.; m. Faith Elizabeth Winsor, Aug. 23, 1960; children: Mary, Ralph, Frances. BS in Geology, Wheaton Coll., 1956; MS in Geology, Wash. State Coll., 1959; PhD in Geology, U. Oreg., 1967. Instr. geology to prof. Wheaton Coll., Ill., 1959—; emeritus prof., 1991. Served with USN, 1948-52, Korea. Mem. Geol. Soc. Am. Baptist. Home: 339 E Jefferson Ave Wheaton IL 60187-4209 Office: Wheaton Coll Dept Geology Wheaton IL 60187

HADIPRIONO, FABIAN CHRISTY, engineering educator, researcher; b. Cirebon, Java, Indonesia, Oct. 6, 1947; came to U.S., 1976; s. Robertus Sudarjo and Wertriani (Yoyoh) H. BCE, MCE, Parahyangan U., 1973; MS, U. Calif., Berkeley, 1978, M of Engring., 1980, DEng, 1982. Registered profl. engr., Ohio. Project engr. various design and constrn. cos., SE Asia, 1965-75; project mgr. Phoenix Inc., Jakarta, Indonesia, 1974-75; engr., asst. bd. dirs. Mahkota Group, Indonesia, 1975-77; instr., teaching assoc. U. Calif., Berkeley, 1981-82; asst. prof. civil and constrn. engring. and mgmt. Ohio State U., Columbus, 1982-89, assoc. prof. civil engring., constrn. engring. and mgmt., 1989—, 1989-95; prof. civil and constrn. engring. and mgmt. Ohio State U., Columbus, 1995—; tech. cons. various attys. at law for forensic engring. cases, 1984—; advisor to numerous constrn. cos. and univs. in Indonesia, 1984—. Contbr. more than 160 articles to profl. jours.; presenter in field. Recipient Dale Carnegie Human Rels. award, 1976, Rsch. award Ohio State U. Coll. Engring., 1989, Lichtenstein Meml. award 1989; Ohio State U. grantee, 1985, 86, U.S. Army C.E. grantee, 1986, USAF fellow and grantee, 1986, Newhouse Found. fellow U. Calif., Berkeley, 1978, Harry H. Hilp fellow U. Calif., Berkeley, 1981, Robert B. Rothchild Jr. fellow U. Calif., Berkeley, 1982. Fellow ASCE; mem. NSPE, ASME, Internat. Assn. Bridge and Structural Engring., Am. Concrete Inst., Archtl. and Engring. Roman Catholic. Home and Office: Ohio State U 2070 Neil Ave Columbus OH 43210-1226

HAEBERLE, ROSAMOND PAULINE, retired educator; b. Clearwater, Kans., Oct. 23, 1914; d. Albert Paul and Ella (Lough) H. BS in Music Edn., Kans. State U., 1936; MusM, Northwestern U., 1948; postgrad., Wayne State U., 1965, 65, 66. Profl. registered parliamentarian. Tchr. sch. dist., Plevna, Kans., 1936-37, Esbon, Kans., 1937-41, Frankfort, Kans., 1941-43, Garden City, Kans., 1943-44; music supr. sch. dist., Waterford Twp., Mich., 1944-47; tchr. sch. dist., Pontiac, Mich., 1947-80; ret. sch. dist., Pontiac, 1980. Bd. dirs., ho. chmn. Pontiac-Oakland Symphony; adv. coun. Waterford Sr. Citizens, chmn., 1990-93; pres. Oakland County Pioneer and Hist. Soc., 1992-94. Recipient Tchrs. Day award Mich. State Fair, 1963. Mem. AAUW (founds. chair Pontiac br.), Mich. Fedn. Music Clubs (state pres. 1993-95, pres. Tuesday musicale of Pontiac 1984-86), Mich. Fedn. Bus. and Profl. Womens Club (Woman of Achievement award dist. IX 1994), Mich. DARS (state parliamentarian), DAR (Gen. Richardson chpt., regent 1983-85, libr. and parliamentarian, pres. 1983-85, Excellence in Cmty. Svc. award 1995), Waterford-Clarkston Bus. and Profl. Womens Club (bylaws and parliamentarian), Pontiac Area Ret. Sch. Pers. (parliamentarian, pres. 1981-84), Mich. Assn. Retired Sch. Pers. (Disting. Svc. award 1994), Detroit Coll. Womens Club, Mich. Registered Parliamentarians, Eastern Star, Zeta Tau Alpha, Mu Phi Epsilon, Beta Sigma Phi (life). Republican. Methodist.

HAEBERLE, WILLIAM LEROY, corporate director, business educator, entrepreneur; b. Marion County, Ind., May 19, 1922; s. Louis Leroy and Marjorie Ellen (Jared) H.; BS, Ind. U., 1943, MBA, 1947, DBA, 1952; m. Yvonne Carlton, June 17, 1947; children: Patricia, William C., David C. Mem. faculty Ind. U., Bloomington, 1946—, prof. mgmt., 1963—; pres., dir. Nat. Entrepreneurship Found., 1982; bd. dirs. Ind. Inst. for New Bus. Ventures, Inc., 1988-91; dir. Martin Engring. Co., InterArt Holding Corp., Taylor Newcomb Industries Co., Inc., Syndicate Sales, Inc., Nor-Cote Internat., Inc., Impact Forge, Inc., St. Elmo, Inc. Capt. U.S. Army, 1943-46; lt. col. USAFR, 1947-82. Recipient Entrepreneur of Yr. award Ernst & Young, 1989, Entrepreneur of Yr., Inst. Hall of Fame. Mem. VFW, Air Force Assn., Res. Officers Assn., Am. Legion, Met. Club, Sigma Alpha Epsilon. Home: 1213 S High St Bloomington IN 47401-6109

HAENICKE, DIETHER HANS, university president; b. Hagen, Germany, May 19, 1935; came to U.S., 1963, naturalized, 1972; s. Erwin Otto and Helene (Wildfang) H.; m. Carol Ann Colditz, Sept. 29, 1962; children: Jennifer Ruth, Kurt Robert. Student, U. Gottingen, 1955-56, U. Marburg, 1957-59; Ph.D. magna cum laude in German Lit. and Philology, U. Munich, 1962; DHL (hon.), Cen. Mich. U., 1986. Asst. prof. Wayne State U., Detroit, 1963-68; assoc. prof. Wayne State U., 1968-72, prof. German, 1972-78, resident dir. Jr. Year in Freiburg (Ger.), 1965-66, 69-70, dir. Jr. Year Abroad programs, 1970-75, chmn. dept. Romance and Germanic langs. and lits., 1971-72, assoc. dean Coll. Liberal Arts, 1972-75, provost, 1975-77, v.p., provost, 1977-78; dean Coll. Humanities Ohio State U., 1978-82, v.p. acad. affairs, provost, 1982-85; pres. Western Mich. U., Kalamazoo, 1985—; asst. prof. Colby Coll. Summer Sch. of Langs., 1964-65; lectr. Internationale Ferienkurse, U. Freiburg, summers 1961, 66, 67. Author: (with Horst S. Daemmrich) The Challenge of German Literature, 1971, Untersuchungen zum Versepos des 20. Jahrhunderts, 1962; editor: Liebesgeschichte der schonen Magelone, 1969, Der blonde Eckbert und andere Novellen, 1969, Franz Sternbalds Wanderungen, 1970; contbr. articles to acad. and lit. jours. Fulbright scholar, 1963-65. Mem. MLA, AAUP, Am. Assn. Tchrs. of German, Mich. Acad. Arts and Scis., Phi Beta Kappa. Office: Western Mich U Office of Pres Kalamazoo MI 49008-5134*

HAERTEL, CHARLES WAYNE, minister; b. Stevens Point, Wis., May 20, 1937; s. George Henry and Eva Georgia (Kingsland) H. BA, St. Olaf Coll., 1960; BD, Luther Theol. Sem., 1965; STM, Wartburg Sem., 1977; D Ministry, McCormick Sem., 1988; postgrad., Luth. Sch. Theology, 1994-95; cert. multicultural ministry, 1995. Ordained to min. Evang. Luth. Ch. Am., 1965. Pastor Our Saviour's Luth. Ch., Almira, Wash., 1965-68, St. Jacob's Luth. Ch., Jackson Center, Ohio, 1968-72, Immanual Luth. Ch., Salem, Ohio, 1972-76, Zion Luth. Ch., Bridgewater, S.D., 1976-85, Cedar Valley-Looney Valley Luth. Parish, Houston, Minn., 1985-93, East Chain Luth. Ch., Blue Earth, Minn., 1993—; Emeu Mideast Tour, 1996; rep. nat. Am. Luth. Ch. Conv., Sioux Falls (S.D.) Conf., 1984-85; host refugee families Luth. Social Svcs., Sioux Falls, 1984. Mem. Peace and Justice Ctr., 1977-83; bd. dirs. Wellspring Wholistic Care Ctr., Freeman, S.D., 1980-85, M-2 State Penitentiary Visitation Program, 1980-85; mem. Alban Inst., Rochester (Minn.) Symphony Choral; bd. dirs. Houston County Minn. Child Abuse Prevention Program, 1989-92, Luth. Campus Ministry, Winona State U., 1986-93; camping staff Holden Village, Wash., 1993; Laubach reading tchr., Fairmont, Minn., 1993—; sec. Improved Muslim/Christian Rels. Chgo., 1994—; bishop liaison rep. Dodmoa, Tanzania, 1996; choral dir. Scouting scholar Luth. Brotherhood, St. Olaf Coll., 1956, McCormick scholar, 1982; grantee Shaloam Continuing Edn. Program, 1980-82. Mem. NAACP, McCook County (S.D.) Clergy (pres. 1982-83), So. Ea. Minn. Mission Ptnrs. (mem. com., editor mission newsletter 1988-93, Synod conf. vice dean 1994), Amnesty Internat., Sierra Club, Luth. Ch. Network, Nat. Geog. Toastmasters (pres. LaCrosse area club 1989-90, local area and divsn. gov. 1990—), Am. Philatelic Soc., Muslim/Christian Conf. Chgo. (sec.), Able Toastmaster (Bronze, Disting. Toastmaster award 1991), Kiwanis (pres. Jackson Center club 1969-70), Eagle Scout Assn. Office: Oshigambo, PO Bag 2026, Ondangwa Namibia

HAESSLY, JACQUELINE, peace and family life education specialist, writer, consultant; b. Milw., Feb. 18, 1937; d. Jerome Francis and Janice (Ball) H.; m. Daniel G. DiDomizio, July 8, 1972; children: Michael, Ernest, Randolph, Francis, Kristyn. LPN, Sacred Heart Sch. Practical Nursing, Milw., 1958; student Alverno Coll., 1958-67; BS in Edn. U. Wis., 1971, MS in Edn., 1976, BA Cardinal Stritch Coll., 1992, postgrad. Union Inst. Cin., 1991—. Staff nurse various local hosps., Milw., 1959-72; founder, dir. Milw. Peace Edn. Resource Ctr., 1974—; founder, pres. Peacemaking Assocs., Milw., 1983—, Creative Playtime, Milw., 1985—; cons., facilitator bus. and profl. orgns., 1974—; organizer prodn. Peace Child, Milw., 1985; cons. U. Wis., Milw., 1983—; chmn. Internat. Yr. of the Family state conf., 1993; coord. Internat. Yr. of the Family, Wis., 1994. Co-author: When the Canary Stops Singing: Women's Perspectives for Transforming Business, publs. (books) Peacemaking: Family Activities for Justice and Peace, 1980, Peacemaking Activity Book for Children, 1984, Gentle Gifts, 1985, What Shall We Teach Our Children?, 1986, Learning To Live Together, 1989, Spirit & Power To Heal a Hurting World, 1992, Promise & Possibility: Reflections on the 1994 Internat. Yr. of Family, 1994, The New Entrepreneurs: Business Visionaries for the 21st Century, 1994, Soul Work: A Corporate Challenge in Rediscovering the Soul of Business, 1995. Contbr. numerous articles to profl. publs. Bd. dirs. Milw. Mental Health Agy., 1975-78; coord. food policy conf. The Peace Ctr., Milw., 1975-77; mem. peace studies task force Milw. Pub. Schs., 1983—; conf. Peace Rsch. Edn. & Devel.; chmn. peace studies com. Parent Tchr. Council, Milw., 1983-86; del. Internat. Year of family, Family Life Edn. Peace Seminar, Costa Rica, 1992, del. World Congress on Family, 1992; del. UN 1994 Inaugeral of Internat. Yr. of the Family, Malta Conf., 1993. Mem. NAFE, Fellowship of Reconciliation (mem. bd., chmn. com. 1980-84), Nat. Speakers Assn., Nat. Coun. Family Rels., Consortium Study War, Peace & Global Cooperation, Wis. Speakers Assn., Parenting for Peace and Justice (mem. bd. 1981-84), Wis. Writer's Council, Nat. Writer's Club, Nat. Profl. Speakers Assn., Wis. Profl. Speakers Assn., Nat. Assn. Mediation Edn., Nat. Orgn. Women Bus. Owners. Roman Catholic. Avocations: sailing, swimming, hiking, mysteries.

HAGAN, ROBERT F., state legislator; m. Michele Hagan; children: Jennifer, Kristen, Thomas, James, Natalia. Engr. locomotive CSX Transp.; state rep. Dist. 53 Ohio State Congress, 1993—; vice chmn. Transp. and Urban Affairs com.; mem. commerce com., labor com., health and retirement com., human resources com. Trustee Northside Citizens Coalition. Named Pub. Ofcl. of Yr. Nat. Assn. Steel Workers Ohio, 1990, Ohioan of Yr. OCSEA, 1990, Legislators of Yr. Ohio Counseling Assn., 1991; recipient Legis. Leadership award Ohio Coalition for Edn. Handicapped Children, 1990, Legis. award Assn. Ohio Health Commrs., 1992. Mem. Nat. Fedn. Blind (chmn.), Steelworkers Oldtimers Club, Citizens League, United Transp. Union Local 604, Sierra Club. *

HAGAN-HARRELL, MARY M., state legislator; b. Cape Girardeau, Mo.; m. Stan Harrell. BS, Southeast Mo. State U.; MLS, George Peabody U. Committeewoman Ferguson Twp., 1972-89; state rep. Dist. 75 Mo. State Congress, 1986—; vice chmn. retirement com.; mem. appropriations, edn. and transp. com., govt. ogrn. com., edn. elem. and secondary com., labor com., joint coms. pub. employees retirement; sec. St. Louis County Dem. Ctrl. Com., 1976-89; tchr., libr., ret. Mem. NEA, Nat. Orgn. Women Legislators, Women Polit. Caucus, Mo. Orgn. Women Legislators, Mo. Sch. Librs. Assn., Downettes Charitable Club. Office: Mo Ho of Reps State Capitol Building Jefferson City MO 65101-1556*

HAGEL, WILLIAM CARL, metallurgical consultant; b. Pitts., Apr. 5, 1927; s. William and Mabel Florence (Geary) H.; m. Mary Ellen Roosa; children: Lisa Christine, Karen Andrea, Juliana Margaret. B in Metall. Engring., Cornell U., 1951; MS, PhD in Metallurgy, Carnegie-Mellon U., 1954. Metallurgist GE Co. Rsch. Lab., Schenectady, N.Y., 1954-66; prof., chmn. metallurgy dept. U. Denver, Colo., 1966-70; mgr. materials devel. GE Aircraft Engines, Evendale, Ohio, 1970-72; mgr. advanced materials Kelsey-Hayes R & D, Ann Arbor, Mich., 1972-73; mgr. R&D Climax Molybdenum Co. Mich., Ann Arbor, 1973-84; pres. Arbormet Ltd., Ann Arbor, 1984—; disting. vis. prof. Minas Inst. Tech., Minas Gerais, Brazil, 1969. Co-editor: The Superalloys, 1972, Superalloys II, 1987; contbr. articles to profl. jours.; patentee in field. Chair adv. bd. Northside Cmty. Ch., Ann Arbor, 1993-94. With USN, 1945-46. Fellow Am. Soc. for Metals, Am. Inst. for Chemists; mem. Am. Inst. Mining and Metall. Engrs., Am. Ceramic Soc., Electrochem. Soc., N.Y. Acad. Sci., Sigma Xi, Phi Kappa Phi. Home: 685 Skynob Dr Ann Arbor MI 48105

HAGEMEIER, JUANITA ELIZABETH, human services administrator; b. Kirkwood, Mo., June 30, 1933; d. Raliegh Anless and Dollie Elizabeth (Shelby) Gray; m. Leland William Hagemeier, Nov. 18, 1950; children: Dora, Delores, Shane, Susan. Asst. ind. living Disabled Citizens Alliance for Independence, Viburnum, Mo., 1980-84, asst. dir., 1984-87, exec. dir., 1987—; mem. Crawford County Bd. for People with Devel. Disabilities, 1991—; mem. Mo. Ind. Living Coun. finance com. Recipient Nat. Disting. Svc. award Nat. Disting. Exec. Coun., 1987. Mem. Nat. Coun. for Ind. Living, Assn. Programs for Rural Ind. Living, Nat. Rehab. Assn., Mo. Rehab. Assn., Vocat. Rehab. Ind. Living Coun. (exec. com.), Viburnum C. of C. Lutheran. Home: HC 88 Box 8269 Steelville MO 65565-9307

HAGEN, BRUCE, state agency administrator; b. Grand Harbor Twp., N.D., June 21, 1930; s. Ernest W. and Mildred T. (Bryn) H.; m. Sylvia Bergstrom, Dec. 28, 1968 (div.); children: Jennifer, Marin. BA, U. N.D., 1953, MA in Govt. and Econs., 1955; postgrad., U. Wis., 1955-56. Dep. registrar N.D. Dept. Motor Vehicles, Bismarck, 1961; commr. N.D. Pub. Svc. Commn., Bismarck, 1961—; farmer, Benson and Ramsey Counties, N.D., 1957—. Editl. adv. bd. Elec. Jour.; advisor The KMB Video Jour. Chmn. N.D. Commn. on Rev. Martin Luther Kind Jr. Holiday, 1985; chairperson UN Day Commn., N.D., 1986, 87; chmn. Am. Cancer Soc. Fund Drive for State Agys., 1994. Mem. Nat. Assn. Regulatory Utilities Commrs., N.D. State Intermodal Transp. Team (chmn. 1985-92), N.D. Lignite Rsch. Coun. (exec. com. 1987—), FCC Joint Bd., Mid-Am. Regulatory Commrs., Upper Gt. Plains Transp. Inst. (adv. com. 1985—). Democrat. Lutheran. Office: ND Pub Svc Commn State Capital Fl 12 Bismarck ND 58505

HAGEN, RICHARD E. (DICK), state legislator; b. Pine Ridge, S.D., Aug. 16, 1937; m. Mona Hagen; children: Shagne, Winona. Mem. S.D. Ho. of Reps., 1982-92, 93—, mem. health and human svc. com. and local govt. com.; painter, carpenter. Mem. Shannon County Sch. Bd. Home: PO Box 3 Pine Ridge SD 57770-0003*

HAGER, GREGORY MICHAEL, library director; b. Washington, Pa., Sept. 28, 1966; s. Steven Paul and Ann (Florian) Hurst; m. Tina Noel Grant, Aug. 17, 1991. BS with honors, Rio Grande (Ohio) Coll., 1988; MLS with honors, Ind. U., 1989. Cert. profl. libr. Reference and audiovisual libr. Branch Dist. Libr. Sys., Coldwater, Mich., 1989-93; adult svc. libr. Willard Libr., Evansville, Ind., 1993-94, dir., 1994—. Bd. dirs. Westside Improvement Assn., Evansville, 1994—, Repertory People of Evansville, 1994—; mem. Museum Guild, Evansville, 1994—, Jacobsville Neighborhood, Evansville, 1994—, Leadership Evansville, 1995—. Mem. ALA, Ind. Libr. Fedn., Culver Neighborhood Assn., Kiwanis (bd. dirs.). Home: 1402 SE 2d St Evansville IN 47713 Office: Willard Libr 21 1st Ave Evansville IN 47710

HAGER, HENRY BRANDEBURY, journalism educator; b. Sept. 12, 1926; s. John Franklin and Henryetta (Brandebury) H.; m. Laura Lee Price; children: John, Jenny Ellen. BA, Yale U., 1951. Mgr. pub. rels. Willow Run Airport, Ypsilanti, Mich., 1952-53; writer Friends Mag., Detroit, 1953-54; copy chief, sales promotion Campbell-Ewald Co., Detroit, 1954-59; copywriter McManus John & Adams, Bloomfield Hills, Mich., 1959-60; copy chief Batten, Barton, Durstine & Osborn, Detroit, 1960-63; creative supr. Campbell-Ewald Co., 1963-69; group historian, cons. The Parsons Group, Brimingham, Mich., 1969-70; v.p., assoc. creative dir. Young & Rubicam Co., Inc., Detroit, 1970-85; asst. prof. emeritus U. Mo. Sch. Journalism, Columbia, 1985—; mem. adv. bd. Mo. Review, Columbia, 1996—; faculty adv. bd. Mo. Honors Coll., 1992—. Author: (novel) Fireball, 1963. Sgt. U.S. Army, 1945-46. Mem. Elizabethan Club. Democrat. Episcopalian. Home: 5300 S Hwy 163 Columbia MI 65203 Office: Univ Mo Sch. Journalism Columbia MO 65205

HAGG, REXFORD A., state legislator; m. Cindy Hagg; 1 child. Student, Nebr. U., S.D. State U. Mem. S.D. Ho. of Reps., 1993—, vice chmn. judiciary com., mem. legis. procedure and taxation coms.; atty. Home: 1721 West Blvd Rapid City SD 57701-4555*

HAGGANS, JAMES MICHAEL, architect, university planning services director; b. Nevada, Mo., Apr. 29, 1948; s. Homer Wesley and Margret Susan H.; m. Kathryn Cecile Taylor, Sep. 6, 1975; children: John Matthew, Katherine Forsythe. B Environ. Design, U. Kans., 1970; MArch, SUNY, Buffalo, 1972. Registered architect. Sr. rsch. assoc. AIA Rsch. Corp., Washington, 1974-79; project architect Hawkweed Group, Soldiers Grove, Wis., 1979-80; dir. planning and devel. U. Mo., Columbia, 1980-86; dir. planning svcs. U. Ariz., Tucson, 1986-88, assoc. v.p. facilities, 1988-91; sr. v.p. Hellmuth, Obata & Kassabaum, St. Louis, 1991—; adj. prof. Coll. Architecture, U. Ariz., Tucson, 1988-91; mem. Mo. State Energy Futures Coalition, Jefferson City, 1994—; project mgr. rsch. project Bldg. Energy Performance Stds., 1978. Author: (book sect.) APPA Handbook, 1994. United Way campaign chair U. Ariz., Tucson, 1989; sr. warden St. Michael & All Angels, Tucson, 1989-91; jr. warden Trinity Episcopal Ch., St. Louis, 1994—. Mem. AIA, ASHRAE (mem. stds. com. 1984-89), Soc. Coll. and Univ. Planners, Assn. Phys. Plant Adminstrs., Assn. Univ. Architects (assoc.). Episcopalian. Office: Hellmuth Obata & Kassabaum Inc 211 N Broadway Saint Louis MO 63102-2733

HAGGARD, FORREST DELOSS, minister; b. Trumbull, Nebr., Apr. 21, 1925; s. Arthur McClellan and Grace (Hadley) H.; m. Eleanor V. Evans, June 13, 1946; children—Warren A., William D., James A., Katherine A. A.B., Phillips U., 1948; M.Div., 1953, D.D. (hon.), 1967; M.A., U. Mo., 1960. Ordained to ministry Christian Ch., 1948; minister Overland Park (Kans.) Christian Ch., 1953—; pres. Kansas City Area Ministers Assn., 1959, Kans. Christian Ministers Assn., 1960; mem. adminstrn. com., gen. bd. Christian Ch., 1968-72; pres. World Conv. Chs. of Christ (Christian/Disciples of Christ), 1975—; chmn. Grad. Sem. Council, Enid, Okla., 1970; pres.

Nat. Evangelistic Assn., 1972; pres. bd. dirs. Midwest Counseling Ctr., Kansas City, 1987—. Author: The Clergy and the Craft, 1970, also articles. Pres. Johnson County (Kans.) Mental Health Assn., 1962-63; mem. coun. Boy Scouts Am., 1964-69; bd. dirs. Kans. Home for Aged, 1960-65, Knas. Children's Svc. League, 1964-69, Johnson County Mental Health Ctr., 1991—; pres. bd. dirs. Kans. Masonic Home, 1974-75; bd. dirs. Kans. Masonic Found., 1970—; trustee Nat. Properties Christian Ch., 1987—. Mem. Masons (grand master Kans. chpt., chaplain gen. Grand chpt. Royal Arch Internat. 1975—, Grand Cross Supreme coun. 33d degree 1989, Disting. Svc. medal 1991). Mem. Masons (grand master Kans., chaplain gen. Grand chpt. Royal Arch Internat. 1975—, Grand Cross Supreme Coun. 33rd degree 1989, pres. Philolethes Soc. 1994—). Home: 6816 W 78th Ter Shawnee Mission KS 66204-3121 Office: 7600 W 75th St Shawnee Mission KS 66204-2853

HAGGARD, JOAN CLAIRE, church musician, piano instructor, accompanist; b. Ann Arbor, Mich., July 7, 1932; d. Clifford Buell and Bertha (Woodhurst) Wightman; m. Harold Wallace Haggard, June 30, 1956; children: Alan C., Stephen T., John A., Marian E. BA, Carleton Coll., 1954; postgrad., Ecole des Beaux Arts, Fontainebleau, France, 1954, U. Mich., 1954-55; A., Am. Guild Organists, 1980. Cert. pvt. piano tchr. Organist, choir dir. St. Paul's Episc. Ch., Riverside, Ill., 1955-59; dir. of music St. Andrew's Episc. Ch., Livonia, Mich., 1960-72; organist Christ Episc. Ch., Dearborn, Mich., 1973-83; dir. of music St. Philip's Episc. Ch., Rochester, Mich., 1983-92; organist, music coord. 1st United Meth. Ch., Farmington, Mich., 1992—; pvt. piano tchr., Livonia, 1960—; piano instr. Southfield (Mich.) Sr. Adult Ctr., 1992—; accompanist Creative and Performing Arts High Sch., Livonia, 1987-90; accompanist many solo instrumental and vocal performances, 1959—. Editor Livonia Youth Symphony Soc. newsletter, 1972-77; contbr. articles to profl. jours. Pres. Livonia Youth Symphony Soc., 1973-76; program dir. Episcopal Diocese Mich. Jr. Choir Camp, 1981-84, 87-89; coord. daily worship Triennial Conv. Episcopal Ch., Detroit, 1988. Mem. Am. Guild Organists (dean Detroit chpt. 1976-79, gen. chmn. nat. conv. 1986, councillor Region V 1986-92), Nat. Guild Piano Tchrs. (judge piano auditions 1987—), Music Tchrs. Nat. Assn., Assn. Anglican Musicians, Hymn Soc. in the U.S. and Can., Assn. Diocesan Liturgy and Music Commns., Music Commn. Episcopal Diocese Mich. (chmn. 1980-81), Piano Tchrs. Forum (Livonia area, pres. 1995—), Friend of Arts, SAI, PEO. Home: 33974 N Hampshire St Livonia MI 48154-2722

HAGGERTY, JOHN RICHARD, civil engineer; b. Royal Oak Twp., Mich., Nov. 23, 1925; s. Harold Edward Patrick and Grace Guenivierre (Walter) H.; m. Joan Catherine Silverness, July 20, 1947; children: Patrick Alan, Timothy Robin, Christopher Lee, Kevin Peter. BSCE, U. Wis., 1947, MSCE, 1950. Registered profl. engr., Mich. Civil engr. City of Flint, Mich., 1947-49; rsch. asst. U. Wis., Madison, 1949-50; pub. health engr. Wis. Bd. Health, Madison, 1950-56; prin. engr. Mich. Office of Hosp. Constrn., Lansing, 1956-63; project mgr., rsch. coord. Smith, Hinchman & Grylls Assoc., Detroit, 1963-73; planning dir. Pontiac (Mich.) Gen. Hosp., 1973-79; dir. health industry sales Cunningham-Limp, Birmingham, Mich., 1979-81; facilities dir. New Ctr. Hosp., Detroit, 1982-85, Modern Engring. Co., Warren, Mich., 1985-88; sr. engr. Hubbell, Roth & Clark, Bloomfield Hills, Mich., 1988-92; constrn. salesperson Beresh & Riedel, Inc., Gen. Contrs., Livonia, Mich., 1992-93; ret. Mich., 1993—; mem. hosp. adv. com. Mich. Fire Safety Bd., Lansing, 1956-63; mem. hosp. infection com. Mich. Health Commn., 1962-63. Author: Optimum Use of Hospital Project Information, Computerization, 1971; contbr. articles to profl. Jour. Am. Soc. of Fire Protection Engrs., Jour. Am. Hosp. Assn., Jour. Mich. Hosp. Assn. Chmn. Parks and Recreation Bd., Beverly Hills, Mich., 1969-79; mem. Village Coun., Beverly Hills, 1988-92; active Boy Scouts Am., 1958-81; tchr. Sunday sch., 1958—; deacon, elder, chmn. prop. care Presbyn. Ch. Mem. ASCE (life, chmn. various coms. 1948-93), Toastmasters Internat. (club sec.), NRA (life), Optimists Internat. (life, local pres., lt. gov. 1974-76), Beta Theta Pi (life). Home: 18242 Dunblaine Ave Beverly Hills MI 48025-3112

HAGGLUND, CLARANCE EDWARD, lawyer, publishing company owner; b. Omaha, Feb. 17, 1927; s. Clarance Andrew and Esther May (Kelle) H.; m. Dorothy Souser, Mar. 27, 1953 (div. Aug. 1972); children: Laura, Bret, Katherine; m. Merle Patricia Hagglund, Oct. 28, 1972. B.A., U. S.D., 1949; J.D., William Mitchell Coll. Law, 1953. Bar: Minn. 1955, U.S. Ct. Appeals (8th cir.) 1974, U.S. Supreme Ct. 1963. Diplomate Am. Bd. Profl. Liability Attys. Ptnr. Hagglund & Johnson and predecessor firms, Mpls., 1973—; mem. Hagglund & Weimer, P.A.; pres. Internat. Control Sys., Inc., Mpls., 1979—, Hill River Corp., Mpls., 1976—; gen. counsel Minn. Assn. Profl. Ins. Agts., Inc., Mpls., 1965-86; CFO, Pro-Trac, software for profl. liability ins. industry. Contbr. articles to profl. jours. Served to lt. comdr. USNR, 1945-46, 50-69. Fellow Internat. Soc. Barristers; mem. ABA, Minn. Bar Assn. (state bd. specialization), Lawyers Pilots Bar Assn., U.S. Maritime Law Assn. (proctor), Acad. Cert. Trial Lawyers Minn. (dean 1983-85), Nat. Bd. Trial Advocacy (cert. in civil trial law, bd. dirs.), Douglas Amdahl Inns of Ct. (pres.), Ill. Athletic Club (Chgo.), Edina Country Club (Minn.), Calhoun Beach Club (Mpls.). Roman Catholic. Home: 3168 Dean Ct Minneapolis MN 55416-4386 Office: 5101 Olson Memorial Hwy Ste 4000 Golden Valley MN 55422-5149

HAGIE, ALAN B., electrical design engineer; b. Ames, Iowa, Aug. 6, 1967. BA, Buena Vista Coll., 1992. Design engr. Hagie Mfg., Clarion, Iowa, 1992—. Republican. Unitarian. Office: Hagie Mfg Central Ave PO Box 273 Clarion IA 50525

HAGLE, ANDREW J., state legislator; m. JoAnn; three children. Mem. City Coun.; N.D. State rep. Dist. 23, 1993—; owner Cafe & Dairy Store; commr. Griggs Co.; mem. human svc. and polit. subdivns. coms. Recipient Excellence in County Govt. award, 1990. Mem. Elks. Home: PO Box 608 Cooperstown ND 58425-0608*

HAGLER, ALVIN RUSSELL, physicist, educator; b. Gleason, Tenn., Mar. 19, 1934; s. Noah Russell and Mary Vivian (Fodge) H.; m. Anna Augusta Christine Jorgensen, May 4, 1953; children: Rodney, Pamela, Gary. BS, Mich. State U., 1961, MS, 1965. Prof. physics GMI Engring. and Mgmt. Inst., Flint, Mich., 1961—; cons. Bear Archery Co., Gainesville, Fla., GMC; radon measurement specialist Radon Detection Sys., Boulder, Colo., 1991—. Contbr. articles to profl. jours. Chmn. archery competition Flint Olympian Games, 1993, 94, 95, Littel Meml. award, 1990. Recipient Gov.'s Twenty award Mich. Police Combat Pistol Assn., 1992, 93, 94. Mem. Am. Assn. Radon Scientists and Technologists, Health Physics Soc. (Mich. chpt.), Internat. Bear Assn. Home: 12166 W Bristol Rd Lennon MI Office: GMI Engring & Mgmt Inst 1700 W 3d Ave Flint MI 48504

HAGLER, DONALD JOSEPH, pediatric cardiologist; b. East St. Louis, Ill., Dec. 14, 1943; s. Raymond H.; m. Sharon J. Danaher, May 24. 1985; children: Donald, Thomas, Catherine, Michael. MD, St. Louis U., 1968. Diplomate Am. Bd. Pediatrics, Sub-Bd. Pediatric Cardiology. Intern St. Louis U., 1968-69, resident in pediatrics, 1969-70; fellow in pediatric cardiology UCLA Med. Ctr., 1972-73, Grad. Sch. Mayo Clinic, Rochester, Minn., 1973-74; assoc. cons. in pediatric cardiology Mayo Clinic, Mayo Found., Rochester, 1974-75, cons. in pediatric cardiology, 1975; asst. prof. pediatrics grad. sch. medicine Mayo Clinic, Rochester, 1976, assoc. prof., 1980, prof., 1987—; co-dir. Cardiac Cathetenization Lab., 1992. Served to capt. USNR. Fellow Am. Coll. Cardiology, Am. Acad. Pediatrics; mem. Soc. Pediatric Echocardiography (pres. 1987-89), Am. Heart Assn., Alpha Omega Alpha. Home: 2540 Summit Dr NE Rochester MN 55906-2847 Office: Mayo Clinic 200 1st St SW Rochester MN 55905-0001

HAGLUND, BERNICE MARION, elementary school educator; b. Negaunee, Mich.; d. Paul and Bernice Cody; m. Charles Haglund; children: Christopher C., Mary. BA, No. Mich. U., 1971, MA, 1978. Tchr. Arnold Elem. Sch., Mich. Center Schs., Mich.; social sec., v.p., pres. Mich. Ctr. Jr. Child Study Group, 1979-83, com. mem. sci. com., dept. head to curriculum counsel, 1993—. V.p., treas., social sec. Commonwealth Wives, Jackson, 1971-82. Mich. State grantee U.S. Optical soc., 1993. Mem. AAUW (sec. social edn. area), ASCD, Bus. and Profl. Women (sec. 1969-71, coord. study group 1972—, sec., social, contact edn. chair, woemn's issues), Orton Soc. (workshop trainer), Mich. Dyslexia Inst., Mich. Sci. Tchrs. Assn., Nat. Sci. Tchrs., Acad. Orton Gillingham, Phi Delta Kappa. Roman Catholic. Home: 1840 Noon Rd Jackson MI 49201-9154

HAGMAN, HARLAN LAWRENCE, education educator; b. DeKalb, Ill., Sept. 8, 1911; s. Gus Carl and Emily Sophia (Peterson) H.; m. Mary Anna Cassels, May 23, 1943; children: William Gordon, Richard Harlan, Jean Cassels, Thomas Lawrence; foster children: James Evanson, Donald Jones. EdB, No. Ill. U., 1936; MA, Northwestern U., 1939, PhD, 1947. Formerly tchr. pub. schs., prin. and supt.; instr. Northwestern U., 1940-41; assoc. prof. Drake U., Des Moines, 1947-49; prof. edn. Drake U., 1949-50, dean coll. edn., 1950-57; prof. edn. Wayne State U., 1957-60, dean adminstrn., 1960-72; prof. higher edn., 1972—; Moderator fgn. policy radio broadcasts, nat. network. Author: A Handbook for the Schoolboard Member, 1941, The Administration of American Public Schools, 1951, (with Alfred Schwartz) Administration in Profile for School Executives, 1955, Administration of Elementary Schools, 1956, September Campus, 1977, Bright Michigan Morning: The Years of Governor Tom Mason, 1981, The Academic Life, 1983, A Seasonal Present and Other Stories, 1989, (with Howard Snyder) Second Balcony, 1990, Nathan Hale and John Andre: Reluctant Heroes of the American Revolution, 1991; editorial cons., McGraw-Hill Book Co., Internat. City Mgrs. Assn.; editor: We Hold These Truths: The Collected Sermons of Rt. Rev. Richard Emrich; contbr. to: Am. Peoples Ency.; also contbr. to ednl. jours.. Bd. dirs. Youth for Understanding, Internat. Edn. Exchange. Served as lt. comdr. USNR, World War II. Mem. Players Club, Circumnavigators Club. Home: 1017 Kensington Ave Grosse Pointe MI 48230-1402 Office: Wayne State U Dept of Education Detroit MI 48202

HAGOOD, HENRY BARKSDALE, real estate developer; b. Wilson, N.C., Aug. 19, 1942; s. Emmett Baker and Aurelia (Muir) H.; m. Theresa Holder, Nov. 26, 1989. BA in Pre-Law, Mich. State U., 1965. Chmn., pres., CEO Barksdale Mgmt. Co.; developer Millender Ctr. Assoc., Detroit; devel. mgr. Signet Devel. Co., Detroit; dir. bus. devel. Walbridge Aldinger, Detroit; mayor's exec. liaison Detroit Housing Dept., Detroit; adminstrv. asst. contracts and grants Detroit Water & Sewer Dept.; dir. City Planning & Devel., Detroit; exec. asst. Mayor's Office, Detroit; v.p. The Farbman Real Estate Group, Southfield, Mich., 1994—; pres. H.B. Hagood & Assocs.; real estate broker, pres. H2 Devel. Corp., 1996—. Bd. dirs. Highland Park Bd. Dirs., Franklin Wright Settlement, YMCA. Recipient Outstanding Svc. award Area Coun. of the Citizens Dist. Coun., Detroit Neighborhood Non-Profit Housing Corp., Bd. recognition Univ. Citizen Dist. Coun., Disting. Svc. award S.E. Mich. Bldg. Assn., 1992. Mem. Econ. Devel. Corp., Downtown Devel. Authority, Detroit Econ. Growth Corp. Exec. Com. Office: H2 Devel Corp 1322 Broadway Detroit MI 48226

HAGSTEN, IB, animal scientist, educator; b. Assens, Denmark, May 18, 1943; came to U.S., 1971, naturalized, 1980; s. Kresten and Marie (Jakobsen) H.; m. Patricia Ellen Dettman, July 13, 1968; children: Ellen Marie, Scot (dec.), Lisa R. BA in Agr., Bygholm Landbrugskole, Horsens, Denmark, 1965; BS, Royal Danish Agr. U., Copenhagen, 1971; MS, Purdue U., 1973, PhD, 1975. Cert. animal scientist; diplomate Am. Coll. Animal Nutrition. Farm laborer, foreman various livestock farms, Denmark, Eng., Germany, Can., 1958-65; teaching asst. Royal Danish Agr. U., 1969-70; rsch. assoc. Nat. Danish Rsch. Found., Copenhagen, 1971; cons. nutritionist M.D. King Milling Co., Pittsfield, Ill., 1976-77; acting product mgr. Am. Hoechst Corp., Somerville, N.J., 1978, tech. specialist, 1977-83; profl. sales rep. Hoechst-Roussel Agri-Vet. Co., Gladstone, Mo., 1983-89, tech. svc. specialist, 1989-90, sr. profl. svc. specialist, 1990—; cons. Shell Farm, Inc., Ørum, Denmark, 1970-71, Agri-Bus. Tng. and Devel., Inc., Roswell, Ga., 1979-95, Nat. Renderer's Assn., Hong Kong, 1989, USDA Trade Mission, Moldova; adj. prof. Rutgers U., New Brunswick, N.J., 1981-84, U. Mo., Columbia, 1990—; pres. Personal Growth Alternatives, 1982—. Author: Energy Metabolism Evaluations, 1971; contbr. articles to profl. jours. and popular publs. Bd. dirs. MACOS handicapped support group, Macomb, Ill., 1976-77; co-chair Cmty. Hunger Walks (CROPú, Western N.J., 1978-82; mem. family curriculum bd. Lopatcong Twp. Sch., Phillipsburg, N.J., 1982; vice moderator Pilgrim Presbyn. Ch., Phillipsburg, 1980-83, elder, 1979-83, Gashland Presbyn. Ch., Gladstone, 1990-93; regional exec. bd. mem. United Marriage Encounter, Mo., Kans., 1983-95; bd. dirs. Gashland Christian Presch., 1991-93; mem. Core of Advocates, Coll. Vet. Medicine Kans. State U.; bd. dirs. Heartland Presbyn. Pro-Life, 1994-97. Sgt. Danish King's Royal Guard, 1959-61. Mem. Danish Soc. Animal Sci., Am. Soc. Agrl. Cons. (bd. dirs. 1978-81, 92-94, 95-97, chmn. ethics com. 1992-94, Disting. Svc. award 1980), Am. Soc. Agrl. Cons. Internat. (charter), Nat. Feed Ingredient Assn., Am. Registry Profl. Animal Scientists (chmn. ethics) com. 1982-85, cert.), Greater Kansas City Scandinavian Club (bd. dirs. 1992-96). Republican. Home and Office: Hoechst-Roussel Agri-Vet Co 7212 N Woodland Ave Kansas City MO 64118-2263

HAGSTROM, ALAN JOHN, religious association administrator; b. Oak Park, Ill., Mar. 30, 1945; s. Clarence Irving Edward and Frances Margaret (Jackson) H.; m. Nancy Susan Keen, June 22, 1968; children: Paul Alan, Karen Kristin, Sarah Elizabeth. BA, Carleton Coll., 1967; MDiv, Chgo. Theol. Sem., 1971; D of Ministry, United Theol. Sem., 1983. Ordained to ministry Meth. Ch., 1968, 71; endorsed chaplain United Meth. Divsn. Chaplains. Asst. min. Christ Congl. Ch., Chgo., 1968-69, 70-71; min. Calais-Woodbury (Vt.) Parish, 1969-70, 71-73; assoc. min. Pine Grove United Meth. Ch., Albany, N.Y., 1973-74; min. United Meth. Chs., Grantsburg, Siren, Lewis, Wis., 1974-79; dir. Ctr. Church Educators, St. Paul, 1978-81; chaplain St. Croix Chaplaincy Assn., Stillwater, Minn., 1981-85, chaplain dir., 1985—; assoc. min. First United Mech. Ch., Stillwater, 1982-85; edn. cons. Wis./ Minn. Conf. United Meth. Ch., Stillwater, 1978-85; adv. bd. chair Lakeview Hospice, Stillwater, 1988-92; chair St. Croix Valley Health Care Ethics Com., Stillwater, 1993—. Contbr. articles to profl. jours. Mem., bd. dirs. St. Croix Area United Way, Stillwater, 1987-89, chair Kay Clint fund, 1990-91. Recipient Spirituality and Family Project award Bayport Found., Stillwater, 1992, Margaret Rivers Found., Stillwater, 1992; named Employer of Yr., Am. Cancer Soc., St. Paul area, 1994. Fellow Coll. Chaplains; mem. Nat. Hospice Orgn., Minn. Hospice Orgn. (ethics com. chair 1993—), Assn. Clin. Pastoral Edn., St. Croix Valley Ministerial Assn. Office: St Croix Chaplaincy Assn 927 W Churchill St Stillwater MN 55082

HAHN, EUGENE HERMAN, state legislator; b. Milw., July 21, 1929; s. L. Herman and Julia (Senft) H.; m. Lorraine Closs, 1949; children: Jeffrey, Robert, Eugene Jr., Andrew. Student, U. Wis., 1947-48. Town assessor Town of Cambria, Wis., 1957-61; county supr., 1972-91; mem. from dist. 47 Wis. State Assembly, Madison, 1991—; dir. Fed. Land Bank, Sauk, Columbia, Dane, Adams, Juneau, Marquette, Green Lake, Wis., 1973-88. Committeeman Farmers Home Adminstrn., Columbia and Marquette Counties, 1969-72; chmn. county bd., Cambria, 1986-88. Mem. Wis. Farm Bur. Home: W3198 Old B Rd Cambria WI 53923-9757*

HAHN, H. MICHAEL, advertising executive; b. Huron, Ohio, June 15, 1928; s. Herbert Henry and Florence (Hast) H.; m. Jacqueline Williams, Sept. 22, 1956; children: Bruce Williams, Timothy Ross. BA in English, Psychology, Western Res. U., 1951; hon. humanities degree, Tokyo U., 1953. Acct. exec. Howard Swink, Advt., Marion, Ohio, 1954-59; exec. v.p. Jaqua Advt., Grand Rapids, Mich., 1959-68, Norman Navan Advt., Grand Rapids, 1968-83; pres., owner Strategic Mktg., Grand Rapids, 1984—; speaker to schs., colls., Mich., 1959—; cons. Gen. Assembly, Presbyn. Ch. (USA), western Mich., 1980—. Sgt. maj. U.S. Army, 1951-54, Korea. Presbyterian. Office: Strategic Mktg Inc 3445 Lake Eastbrook Blvd SE Grand Rapids MI 49546-5943

HAHN, JAMES HENRY, engineering educator; b. East Prairie, Mo., June 28, 1936; s. Henry I. and Elanora C. (Scheeter) H.; m. Mary JoAnn Becker, June 30, 1959; children: William, Robert, Stephen, Mary Jo, David. BS in elec. engring., Mo. Sch. Mines and Metallurgy, 1959; MS, U. Pitts., 1965; PhD, U. Mo., Rolla, 1977. Sr. engr. Westinghouse Electric, Balt., 1959-66; engring. specialist Monsanto Co., St. Louis, 1966-71; v.p. R&D Interface Tech. Inc., St. Louis, 1972-85; assoc. prof. elec. engring. U. Mo., Rolla, 1985-90, interim dir. Engring. Edn. Ctr., 1990-95; dir. Engring. Edn. Ctr., 1995—; cons. Monsanto Co., Roush Sci., St. Louis, Sprengnether Instrument Co., St. Louis, 1972-94, Smartone Inc., N.Y.C., 1993-94. Editor: Tech. Soc. Newsletter, 1993-95; contbr. articles to profl. jours. vol. Vols. in Tech. Assistance, 1980-95. Recipient Outstanding Engr. in Edn. award Mo. Soc. Profl. Engrs., St. Louis, 1994. Mem. IEEE (sr., regional treas. 1987, regional sec. 1990, award of honor St. Louis sec. 1993, mem. continuing edn. com. ednl. activities bd. 1995—). Home: 2 Hawthorne Estates Town and Country MO 63131 Office: U Mo-Rolla Engring Edn Ctr 8001 Natural Bridge Rd Saint Louis MO 63121

HAHN, LEWIS EDWIN, philosopher, retired educator; b. Swenson, Tex., Sept. 26, 1908; s. Edwin D. and Ione (Brewster) H.; m. Elizabeth Herring, June 30, 1932 (dec. 1991); children: Helen Elizabeth, Mary, Sharon; m. Mary Anne King, Sept. 1, 1992. BA, U. Tex., 1929, MA, 1929; PhD, U. Calif., 1939. Teaching fellow U. Calif., 1931-34; instr. philosophy U. Mo., Columbia, 1936-39, asst. prof., 1939-46, assoc. prof., 1946-49; vis. lectr. Princeton U., 1947; prof. philosophy Washington U., St. Louis, 1949-63, chmn. dept., 1949-63, assoc. dean Grad. Sch. Arts and Scis., 1953-54, dean Grad. Sch. Arts and Scis., 1954-63; research prof. philosophy So. Ill. U., Carbondale, 1963-77; prof. emeritus So. Ill. U., 1977—; vis. prof., editor So. Ill. U. (Library Living Philosophers), 1981—; disting. vis. prof. Baylor U., 1977, 79, 80; Mem. U.S. Nat. Commn. UNESCO, 1965-67. Author: A Contextualistic Theory of Perception, 1942, (with others) Value: A Cooperative Inquiry, 1949; co-author: Guide to the Works of John Dewey, 1970; editor: Library of Living Philosophers, 1981—; co-editor: The Philosophy of Gabriel Marcel, 1984, The Philosophy of W.V. Quine, 1986, The Philosophy of G.H. von Wright, 1989, Charles D. Tenney's Discovery of Discovery, 1991; editor: The Philosophy of Charles Hartshorne, 1991, The Philosophy of A.J. Ayer, 1992, The Philosophy of Paul Ricoeur, 1995, The Philosophy of Paul Weiss, 1995. Recipient Disting. Svc. award So. Ill. U., 1993. Fellow AAAS; mem. Am. Philos. Assn. (exec. bd. 1950-54, 70-73, chmn. com. placement, available pers. 1951-54, sec.-treas. West div. 1949-51, sec.-treas. 1960-66, com. on internat. coop. 1967-80), AAUP, Am. Soc. Aesthetics, S.W. Philos. Soc. (pres. 1955), Mo. Philos. Assn. (pres. 1949-50), So. Soc. for Philosophy and Psychology (pres. 1958-59), Ill. Philosophy Conf. (pres. 1969-71), Phi Beta Kappa. Home: 1951 N Reed Station Rd Carbondale IL 62901-9625

HAHN, SANGMAN, mechanical engineer; b. Seoul, Korea, Apr. 3, 1951; came to U.S., 1978; s. Jongsoo Hahn and Soonjung Suh. BSME, Seoul Nat. U., 1973; MSME, U. Tex., 1980. Engr. Daewoo Heavy Industries, Seoul, 1976-78; rsch. asst. engr. U. Tex., Austin, 1979-80; advanced project engr. Delco Electronics Corp., Kokomo, Ind., 1980—. Patentee (3) in field. Prin. Korean Sch. of Indpls., 1992-93. With Korean Army, 1973-76. Home: 3243 Eden Way Carmel IN 46033-3073 Office: Delco Electronics Corp 1 Corp Dr Kokomo IN 46904

HAHN, STEPHEN FRANK, polymer chemist; b. Midland, Mich., Apr. 19, 1960; s. James Richard and Sally Ann (Robbins) H.; m. Laura Ellen Kersten, Aug. 7, 1982; children: James Robert, Emily Kersten, Katherine Elaine. BS in Chemistry, Mich. Tech. U., 1982; MS in Chemistry, Cen. Mich. U., 1990. Chemist Cen. Rsch., Dow Chem. Co., Midland, 1982-84; rsch. chemist Cen. Rsch., Dow Chem. Co., Midland, Mich., 1984-88, sr. rsch. chemist, 1988-91; project leader Dow Chem. Co., Midland, 1991—; instr. organic chemistry Mid-Mich. C.C., Harrison, 1990—. Contbr. articles to profl. jours. Named Inventor of the Yr., Dow Chem. Cen. Rsch., 1990. Mem. Am. Chem. Soc., Soc. for Advancement of Materials and Process Engring., Sigma Xi. Office: Dow Chemical Co 1776 Bldg Midland MI 48674

HAHN, TANYA K., investment banker; b. Columbus, Ohio, Feb. 17, 1959; d. Charles E. and Caroletta (Francis) Werner; m. Eric P. Hahn, Oct. 5, 1985; children: Joshua, Katherine. BSBA in Fin., Miami U., Oxford, Ohio, 1981; MBA in Fin., Rochester Inst. Tech., 1988. CPA; cert. gen. securities rep. Sr. tax acct. KPMG Peat Marwick, Columbus, Ohio, 1979-83; tax and life ins. acct. State Auto Ins., Columbus, Ohio, 1983-84; sr. tax acct. Schlegel Corp., Rochester, N.Y., 1984-86; mgr. internal audit Citibank/Citicorp, Rochester, N.Y., 1986-91; controller, mgr. fin. analysis Citibank, Rochester, N.Y., 1991-93; investment banker pub. fin. McDonald & Co. Securities, Inc., Columbus, 1993—. Mem. AICPA, Ohio Soc. CPAs, Beta Alpha Psi. Methodist. Office: McDonald Co Securities Inc 10 W Broad St Columbus OH 43215-3418

HAIDOSTIAN, ALICE BERBERIAN, concert pianist, civic volunteer and fundraiser; b. Highland Park, Mich., Sept. 21, 1925; d. Harry M. and Siroun Vartabedian Berberian; m. Berj H. Haidostian, Oct. 1, 1949; children: Cynthia Esther Haidostian Wilbanks, Christine Rebecca Haidostian Garry, Dicran Berj. MusB, U. Mich., 1946, MusM, 1949. Pvt. piano tchr., 1946-48; tchr. music Detroit Pub. Sch., 1953; dir. The Haidostians vocal trio, 1959-71; dir. Youth Choral Group Cultural Soc. Armenians from Istanbul, 1965-72; chmn. adv. coun. Armenian Studies Program, U. Mich., 1984—. Active 1st profl. prodn. Armenian nat. opera Anoush, Mich. Opera Theatre, 1981-82; dir. (vocal trio) The Haidostians, 1959-71, Youth Choral Group of Cultural Soc. Armenians from Istanbul, 1965-72. Active Centennial Celebration U. Mich. Sch. Music, Detroit, 1980; organist, choir dir. Armenian Congl. Ch. Detroit, 1946-48; mem. Westminster Ch. Detroit Chancel Choir, 1965-80, Armenian Gen. Benevolent Union Alex Manoogian Sch., 1981-91, Detroit chpt. core group com., 1992—, chmn. Marie Manoogian group, 1993—; mem. Detroit Symphony Orch., 1986-88, bd. dirs. Hall Vol. Coun., 1994-96; mem. Detroit Women's Symphony Orch., Mich. Opera, Mich. Opera Theatre, Oakway Symphony Orch., Save Orch. Hall, Women's Divsn. Project Hope, 1964—, pres. 1995-96;pres. Detroit Armenian Women's Club, 1964-65, 73-75. Recipient Spirit of Detroit award, 1980, Heart of Gold award United Found. City Detroit, 1981, Nat. Svc. citation U. Mich. Alumnae Coun., 1980, Disting. Alumni Svc. award U. Mich., 1981, Magic Flute award Internat. Found. Mozarteum, Salzburg, Austria, 1989; named Armenian Mother of Yr., Internat. Inst. Detroit, 1981. Mem. Detroit Assn. Univ. Mich. Women (pres. 1969-71), Mich. Fedn. Music Clubs, Mich. State Med. Soc. Aux., Pro Mozart Soc. Greater Detroit (pres. 1982—), Pro Musica Detroit (sec. 1969-90, 1st v.p. 1990—), Tuesday Musicale Detroit (pres. 1970-72), Univ. Mich. Alumni Assn. (chmn. alumnae coun. 1977-79), Univ. Mich. Sch. Music Alumni Soc., Women's Assn. Detroit Symphony Orch. (pres. 1986-88). Home: 6838 Valley Spring Dr Bloomfield Hills MI 48301-2845

HAIFLICH, STEVAN RICHARD, minister; b. Bluffton, Ind., July 13, 1948; s. Richard Edward and Dorma Mae (Hoopingarner) H.; m. Cynthia Ann Harris Morphett, May 29, 1970 (div. June 1976); m. Shirley Lorraine Newnam, Dec. 31, 1992; children: Philip Todd, Andrew James. BA, Taylor U., 1970; MDiv, Asbury Theol. Sem., 1974. Cert. rural chaplain Rural Chaplains Assn. Dir. Calaski Fellowship Parish, Science Hill, Ky., 1974-77; asst. supt. United Meth. Mountain Mission, Jackson, Ky., 1977-81; pastor Main St. United Meth., Redkey, Ind., 1981-86; dir. Huntington County South Parish, Warren, Ind., 1986-91; pastor Maple Grove/Norris Chapel United Meth. Chs., Auburn, Ind., 1991—; chairperson Ind. Rural Justice Network, Indpls., 1986-91; exec. com. Rural Chaplains Assn., Columbus, 1988-94; sec. North Ctrl. Jurisdiction Town and Country Assn., 1988-93, pres., 1993—; adj. staff Ctr. for Town & Rural Min., Columbus, Ohio, 1990-93. Active Union Twp. Bd., DeKalb County, Ind., 1995. Mem. King Lodge Free & Accepted Masons. Democrat. Home: PO Box 6118 2008 Fairview Dr Auburn IN 46706

HAIMOWITZ, MORRIS LOEB, social psychologist; b. N.Y.C., June 5, 1918; s. Samuel and Frieda (Paster) H.; m. Natalie Reader, Dec. 31, 1948; children: Carla Elizabeth, Myrna Susan, Louise Ellen. BA with high honors, U. Fla., 1941, MA, 1942; PhD, U. Chgo., 1951. Cert. tchg. mem. Internat. Transactional Analysis Assn. Instr. Chgo. City Coll., 1951-53; prof. N.Y. State Tchrs. Coll., New Paltz, 1954-55; mem. staff Nat. Tng. Labs., Bethel, Maine, 1955; dir. Human Rels. Tng. U. Chgo., 1955-57; prof. Chgo. TV Coll., 1957-67; dir. human rels. Chgo. Bd. Edn., 1962-67; dir. adult edn. Chgo. City Coll., 1969-71; pres. Haimowoods Inst., Evanston, Ill., 1971—; cons. 50 hosps., univs., sch. systems, U.S., Mexico, Switzerland, Australia, others. Co-author: Human Development, 1960, revised, 1966, 73, Suffering is Optional, 1978, Human Relations Problems, 1961, 62, 65, author: Child Psychology, 1957, 63, 65, 72; contbr. articles to profl. jours. Bd. mem. Chgo. Boys Clubs, 1968-89; v.p. State of Ill. Com. on Day Care, 1965-68; pres. Evanston Human Rels. Assn., 1963-65. 1st lt. AC, 1942-46, ETO, PTO. Recipient Stone Brandzel, Chgo. Action People award. Mem. Internat. Transactional Analysis Assn. (bd. mem. 1966-77), Chgo. Transactional Analysis Assn. (pres. 1965-74), Chgo. Ednl. Dirs. Assn. (pres. 1965-67), Chgo. Vegetarian Assn. Home and Office: 1101 Forest Ave Evanston IL 60202-1407

HAINES, DAVID L., electrical engineer; b. Des Moines, Aug. 1, 1936. BSEE, Purdue U., 1971. Elec. engr. Wavetek, Beach Grove, Ind., 1972, Hurco, Indpls., 1973, Delco, Kokomo, Ind., 1974—. Patentee in field. With USMC, 1956-58.

HAINES, JOSEPH E., state legislator; b. Greene County, Ohio, Sept. 30, 1923; m. Joy Haines; children: Thomas, Thaddeus, Jonathan, Barbara. BS, Ohio State U., 1949. Chmn. then commr. Greene County, 1968-76; state rep. Dist. 75 Ohio State Congress, 1981-92, state rep. Dist. 74, 1993—; farmer; mem. agr. and natural resources com., fin. and appropriations com., energy and environ. com., fin. inst. com., rules com., hwy. and hwy. safety com., reference com. Mem. Nat. Assn. County Commrs. (chmn.), SW Dist. County Commr. Assn. (chmn.), Ohio Shorthorn Breeders (past pres.), Farm Bur., Kiwanis (past pres.), YMCA (bd. dirs.). *

HAIR, ROBERT EUGENE, editor, writer, historian; b. Winamac, Ind., Apr. 11, 1921; s. Charles Franklin and Lucy Agnes (Zellers) H.; m. Marian Martha Emerson, Dec. 11, 1949; children: Donald Edward, Martha Anne. AB, DePauw U., Greencastle, Ind., 1942; postgrad., U. Mich., Ann Arbor, 1943-44, 46-54. Newspaper writer and editor; editor Mich. Dept. Health, Lansing, 1956-60; asst. editor Encyclopedia Britannica, Chgo., 1960-64; exec. editor Battelle Rsch. Outlook, Columbus, 1964-69; editor Cordis Corp., Miami, 1969-80. Author: (books) Sturgis, Michigan: Its Story to 1930, 1992, Sturgis, Michigan: 1930-1945, 1996; contbr. articles to profl. jours. Pres. Civic Auditorium Bd., Sturgis, 1994, St. Joseph County Hist. Soc., Centreville, Mich., 1995; v.p. Sturgis Hist. Soc., Mich., 1996, Centennial Celebration Com., Sturgis, 1996. Mem. Am. Med. Writers Assn., Soc. Profl. Journalists, Masonic Blue Lodge, Sturgis Exchg. Club (pres. 1951-52), Lambda Chi Alpha. Republican. Presbyterian. Home: 428 Mortimer St Sturgis MI 49091

HAIRSTON, ELAINE HAYDEN, state college and university board of regents; b. Zanesville, Ohio, Oct. 28, 1943; d. James Gilbert and Geraldine (Kinsel) Hayden: m. George Watt Hairston, Dec. 21, 1968; children: Amy, Scott. BA, Ohio State U., 1966, MA, 1967, PhD, 1970; D in Pub. Svc. (hon.), Rio Grande (Ohio) Coll., 1986, Lake Erie Coll., 1990; LHD (hon.), Youngstown State U., 1992, Muskingum Coll., 1993. Asst. dir. computer assisted instrn. project Ohio State U., Columbus, 1970-71, assoc. dir. affirmative action program, 1971-74, asst. v.p. for registration svcs., 1976-78; dir. spl. programs Ohio Bd. of Regents, Columbus, 1979-84, acad. vice chancellor, 1984-90, chancellor, 1990—; bd. dirs. The Huntington Nat. Bank, Columbus, 1990—; chair coun. on coll. level svcs. The Coll. Bd., N.Y.C. Bd. trustees Columbus Sch. Girls, 1989—; bd. dirs. I Know I Can, 1991—; found. bd. Franklin County Acad. medicine, 1993—. Mem. State Higher Edn. Exec. Officers (pres. elect 1995-96, pres. 1996—), Phi Beta Kappa. Office: Ohio Bd of Regents 30 E Broad St 36th Fl Columbus OH 43266

HAIRSTON, JAY TIMOTHY, college administrator; b. Welch, W.Va., Dec. 3, 1956; s. John Thomas and Marion Naomi (Teal) H.; m. Sylvia Marie Borden, Sept. 10, 1983; children: Jay Timothy II, Jharie Danielle, Jason Danté. BA, Ohio Wesleyan U., 1978; MS, Bowling Green State U., 1982. Asst. dir. Upward Bound/Talent Search Bowling Green (Ohio) State U., 1982-84, assoc. dir. coll. access program, 1984-85; dir. EMCEC (cultural ctr.) U. No. Iowa, Cedar Falls, 1985-88; dir. student activities/acad. and cultural events series Baldwin-Wallace Coll., Berea, Ohio, 1988-95; dir. acad. and cultural events series Baldwin-Wallace Coll., 1996—; prof. Baldwin-Wallace Coll., Berea, Ohio, 1992—; tchr. Upward Bound program U. No. Iowa and Bowling Green State U., summers 1980-85; cons. on multiculturalism U. No. Iowa, Cedar Falls, Baldwin-Wallace Coll., Berea, Berea Pub. Schs., 1985—, It's Your Move conf. NCCJ, Cleve.; grant writer U. No. Iowa, Cedar Falls, Baldwin-Wallace Coll., Berea, 1986—; cons. gospel music workshops, guest artist Bowling Green State U., Eng., Sweden, Norway. Dir./founder (Gospel musical group) The Krooners, 1979—; artist, songwriter, musician, producer (Gospel recording-solo album) I'm Going On, 1990, 91; songwriter/vocalist (Gospel recording with choir) Jesus Never Fails, 1989; dir., artist, producer (Gospel recording with choir) We Should Pray, 1980; artist, grant writer (Gospel music demo tape) Creative Artists' Grant, 1987 (Iowa Arts Coun. award); cast mem. Glories of Gospel, 1992—; recorded with Glories of Gospel: Live, 1994. Dir. Berea Cmty. Mass Choir, 1995—; min. of music Faith Tabernacle United Holy Ch., Cleve., 1988-94; dir., musician United Faith Ch. of Christ, Cleve., 1988-92; cons., mem. presenting touring panel Ohio Arts Coun., 1991-94. Recipient Iowa Bus. and Profl. award Minority Leadership Agenda Com., Cedar Falls/Waterloo, 1988, Outstanding Adminstr. award Omicron Delta Kappa, 1991, Faculty Excellence award Student Senate, 1990, Adminstrv. Excellence award Student Senate, 1994; grantee Gospel Music Workshops, U. No. Iowa and Baldwin-Wallace Coll.; named Outstanding Young Man Am., Jaycees, 1981, 86, 92. Mem. Nat. Assn. Campus Activities, Nat. Hairston Clan, Inc., Ohio Coll. Pers. Assn, Kappa Alpha Psi (treas. 1985-86). Holiness. Home: 131 Jacob St Berea OH 44017-2013 Office: Baldwin Wallace Coll ACES Office 275 Eastland Rd Berea OH 44017-2005

HAJEK, ROBERT J., SR., lawyer, real estate broker, commodities broker, nursing home owner; b. Berwyn, Ill., May 17, 1943; s. James J., Sr., and Rita C. (Kalka) H.; m. Maris Ann Enright, June 19, 1965 (div. Oct. 1991); children: Maris Ann, Robert J., David, Mandie; m. DeLana S. Tieken, Sept. 16, 1995. BA, Loras Coll., 1965; JD, U. Ill., 1968. Bar: Ill. 1968, U.S. Tax Ct. 1970, U.S. dist. ct. (no. dist.) Ill. 1971, U.S. Ct. Appeals (7th cir.) 1972, U.S. Supreme Ct. 1972. Lic. real estate broker, Ill., Nat. Assn. Securities Dealers; registered U.S. Commodities Futures Trading Commn. ptnr. Hajek & Hajek, Berwyn, Ill., 1968-76; pres., bd. chmn. Hajek, Hajek, Koykar & Heying, Ltd., Westchester, Ill., 1976-85; pres., chief exec. officer Land of Lincoln Real Estate, Ltd., Glendale Heights, Ill., 1985-89, also bd. dirs.; ptnr., owner Camelot Manor Nursing Home, Streator, Ill., 1978—, Ottawa (Ill.) Care Ctr., 1981—, Glenwood House Nursing Home, Streator, Ill., 1988—, Sullivan House Nursing Home, Ottawa, Ill., 1991—, Law Centre Bldg., Westchester, 1976-91; exec. v.p., gen. counsel Ottawa Long Term Care, Inc.; owner Garfield Ridge Real Estate, Chgo., 1973-78, Centre Realty, Westchester, 1976-85; ptnr. Westbrook Commodities, Chgo., 1983; v.p., bd. mem., gen. counsel DeHart Gas and Oil Devel., Ltd., 1970-73; prin. Northeastern Okla. Oil and Gas Prodn. Venture, Tulsa, 1982—; exec. v.p., gen. counsel Garrett Plante Corp., 1978—; bd. dirs. Land of Lincoln Savs. and Loan, 1981-89, Home Title Services of Am., Inc., 1981-89, Land of Lincoln Ins. Agy., Inc., 1981-89, Medema Builders, Inc., 1983-88, Ptnrs. of Ill., Inc., 1984-89, The Ill. Co., 1984-88, Ill. Co. Properties, Inc., subs. of Ill. Co., 1984-87, Ottawa Long Term Care, Inc., 1982—, Garrett Plante Corp., 1978—, St. Mary's Living Square Chgo., 1985-92. Sr. boys' basketball coach Roselle Recreation Assn., Ill., 1981-83. Mem. ABA, Ill. Bar Assn., Nat. Assn. Realtors, Ill. Assn. Realtors, Northwest Suburban Bd. Realtors, Ill. Health Care Assn., Phi Alpha Delta. Republican. Episcopalian. Clubs: Amateur Radio, No. Ill. DX Assn.

HAKALA, JUDYTH ANN, data processing executive; b. Manistee, Mich., Sept. 19, 1955; d. John Emil and Reta Mae (Crain) H. BS, Taylor U., Upland, Ind., 1977. Cert. prodn. and inventory control. Tech. dir. Bowling & Rixom, Traverse City, Mich., 1981-82; programmer Systems for Profit, Inc., Grand Rapids, Mich., 1982-84, programmer, analyst, 1984-88, systems mgr., 1988-89; cons. Competitive Solutions, Inc., Grand Rapids, Mich., 1989-92, dir. of cons., 1992-96, design analyst, 1996—; ind. cons., 1981—. Mem. activist Right to Life Mich., Grand Rapids. Mem. Am. Prodn. and Inventory Control Soc., Finnish-Am. Soc. (membership com. 1988—, chmn. publicity com., 1989-92, sec. 1992—). Republican. Baptist. Home: 3024 Woodbridge Dr SE Grand Rapids MI 49512-5639 Office: Competitive Solutions Inc 3940 Peninsular Dr SE Grand Rapids MI 49546-6107

HAKES, WANDA FAYE, retired nursing educator; b. Narka, Kans., Apr. 14, 1930; d. John and Margaret Elizabeth (Holan) Chaloupka; m. Lester B. Hakes, Sept. 16, 1951; children—Anita Lytle, Frederick, Daniel, Carol Rohlfing. RN, St. Elizabeth Hosp. Sch. Nursing, 1950. RN, Nebr., Kans. Charge nurse St. Elizabeth Hosp., Lincoln, Nebr., 1950; staff nurse St. Joseph Hosp., Concordia, Kans., 1952-58, Gelvin-Haughey Clinic, Concordia, 1958-65; supr. Mennonite Hosp., Beatrice, Nebr., 1966-72; nursing instr. S.E. C.C., Beatrice, 1972-92, asst. to the instr. fundamentals nursing lab., 1992-93. Active adult edn. chmn. Gage County unit Am. Cancer Soc. Mem. Nat. Vocat. Assn., Nebr. Vocat. Assn., S.E. Nebr. League Nursing (sec.), Nat. League Nursing, S.E. C.C. Beatrice Campus Faculty Assn., League Nursing and Vocat. Assn., Beatrice Bus. and Profl. Women's Club.

HAKIM, ALI AIMAN, urologist; b. Medina, Saudi Arabia, Sept. 15, 1927; came to U.S., 1955; s. Kaid Yassin and Sauad Mustafa Hakim; m. Carolyn Mary Miller, Dec. 29, 1964; children; May Hakim, Brian, Jonathan. MD, U. Alexandria, Egypt, 1951; PhD, U. Minn., 1966. Diplomate Am. Bd. Urology. Clin. dir. dept. urology St. Paul Ramsey Hosp., 1962-67; asst. prof. in surgery U. Minn. Med. Sch., Mpls., 1964-68; pvt. practice Mpls., 1968—. Contbr. articles to profl. jours. Office: Hakim Urology Clinic 918 Metropolitan Med Bldg 825 S 8th St Minneapolis MN 55404

HALASA, ADEL F., chemist; b. Madaba, Jordan, Dec. 24, 1933; came to U.S., 1952; s. Farhan and Kathrin H.; m. Ofelia Vinlauan, Feb. 2, 1955; children: Malu, Marni, Mikel. BSc, Okla. U., 1955; MS, Butler U., 1958; PhD, Purdue U., 1964. Group leader Firestone Tire and Rubber Co., Akron, Ohio, 1965-68, assoc. scientist, 1968-74, sr. rsch. assoc., 1974-79; dir. Kuwait Inst. Sci. Rsch., 1979-84; R&D fellow Goodyear Tire and Rubber Co., Akron, 1984—. Contbr. articles to tech. publs. Area dir. Akron Anti Discrimination Coun., 1989. Recipient Disting. Inventor of Yr. award, IPO, 1993, Disting. award Akron Coun. Engrs. and Sci. Socs., 1993; named to Inventor Hall of Fame, 1993, Goodyear Coop. Inventor of Yr., 1993. Fellow Am. Inst. Chemists, N.Y. Acad. Scis.; mem. AAAS, Am. Chem. Soc. (chmn. Akron sect. 1967, chmn. APLG 1968, Local Sect. Svc. award 1995), Sigma Xi. Eastern Orthodox. Home: PO Box 825 Bath OH 44210-0825 Office: Goodyear Tire and Rubber Co 142 Goodyear Blvd Akron OH 44305-3375

HALBACH, MICHAEL J., stockbroker; b. Washington, Aug. 17, 1941. BS, U. Ill., 1970, MS, 1972. Agt. Continental Grain, Decatur, Ill.; stockbroker Smith Barney Inc., Decatur, 1984—. With U.S. Army, 1961-64. Roman Catholic. Home: 1002 Shurts St Urbana IL 61801-6863 Office: Smith Barney Inc 3090 N Main St Decatur IL 62526-2301

HALDAR, FRANCES LOUISE, business educator, accountant, treasurer; b. Mineola, N.Y., July 2, 1948; d. Alfred Karl and Gudrun Maria (Lucks) Loschen; m. Kali S. Haldar, Feb. 29, 1972; children: Neil Alexander, Monica Joyce. AA, The Ohio Sate U., 1985, BSBA in Acctg. summa cum laude, 1989, MBA, 1991. Adminstrv. asst. Pam Am. World Airways Inc., N.Y.C., 1968-73; acct., treas. K.S. Haldar, MD, Inc., Mansfield, Ohio, 1978—; adj. prof. bus. to assoc. prof., then assoc. prof. acctg. N. Ctrl. Tech. Coll., Mansfield, 1991—, acad. advisor, 1991—, assoc. prof. bus., 1993-96, assoc. prof. acctg., 1996—. Mem. Am. Acctg. Assn., Phi Kappa Phi, Beta Gamma Sigma, Golden Key Soc. Office: N Ctrl Tech Coll PO Box 698 Mansfield OH 44901-0698

HALE, CHARLES ADAMS, history educator; b. Mpls., June 5, 1930; s. Lloyd and Elizabeth (Adams) H.; m. Lenore Briggs Rice, Sept. 6, 1952; children: Elizabeth Adams, Charles Rice, Roger Rice, Caroline Hale-Coldwell. BA, Amherst Coll., 1951; MA, U. Minn., 1952; PhD, Columbia U., 1957. Instr. U. N.C., Chapel Hill, 1956-57; asst. prof. Lehigh U., Bethlehem, Pa., 1957-62, Amherst (Mass.) Coll., 1962-66; asst. prof. U. Iowa, Iowa City, 1966-68, assoc. prof., 1968-70, prof., 1970—, chair dept. history, 1977-80; vis. assoc. prof. Stanford (Calif.) U., 1967; vis. prof. El Colegio Mex., 1991, U. Wash., Seattle, 1995; bd. editors Hispanic Am. Hist. Review, 1970-75, mem. adv. bd., 1977-83, 90-95; pres. Conf. Latin Am. History, 1979. Author: Mexican Liberalism in the Age of Mora, 1821-1853, 1968, The Transofrmation of Liberalism in Late Nineteenth Century Mexico, 1989, (with others) Cambridge History of Latin America, 1986; contbr. articles to profl. jours. Named to Orden Mexicana del Aguila Azteca, 1983; Am. Coun. Socs., Social Sci. Rsch. Coun. grantee, 1962-63, 65-66, 76-77; John Simon Guggenheim Meml. Found. fellow, 1973-74, NEH fellow, 1969-70, 92; recipient May Brodbeck award in Humanities U. Iowa, 1986. Mem. Acad. Mex. History, Phi Beta Kappa. Democrat. Congregational. Home: 250 Black Springs Cir Iowa City IA 52246 Office: U Iowa Iowa City IA 52242

HALE, DAVID CLOVIS, former state representative; b. Sacramento, Aug. 14, 1964; s. Clovis Ray and Judy Garland (Lee) H.; m. Shannon Lynn Ruyle, June 19, 1993. BA in Social Sci., Cedarville Coll., 1986; M in internat. bus., St. Louis U., 1995. Asst. mgr. Assocs. Fin. Corp., Fairborn, Ohio, 1986-87; br. fin. rep. Am. Family Fin. Svc., St. Louis, 1987-88; state rep. State of Mo., Jefferson City, 1989-94; mgr. external affairs AT&T Wireless Svcs., St. Louis, 1995—. Mem. Am. Legis. Exch. Coun. Health Care Task Force, 1989-93, Trade, Travel and Tourism Task Force, 1993-94, Missourians First Task Force, 1992-94; allocator United Way, 1990-93; active First Evang. Free Ch., St. Louis. Mem. World Affairs Coun. (bd. dirs.), St. Louis World Trade Club St. Louis. Home: 2065 Wealdwood Ct Kirkwood MO 63122 Office: AT&T Wireless Svcs 1111 Woods Mill Rd Chesterfield MO 63017

HALE, EDWARD BOYD, physics educator, scientist; b. Washington, July 16, 1938; s. Charles Mansel and Annabel (Boyd) H.; m. Barbara Anne Nelson, May 30, 1963. BS in Elec. Engring., U. Md., 1960; PhD, Purdue U., 1968. Research assoc. U. Rochester, N.Y., 1968-69; asst. prof. U. Mo., Rolla, 1969-74, assoc. prof., 1974-82, prof. physics, sr. investigator Materials Research Ctr., 1982-88, prof. physics, assoc. dir., 1988-92, chmn. physics, 1992—. Contbr. articles, papers to profl. lit. Mem. Am. Phys. Soc., Am. Assn. Sci., Am. Vacuum Soc., Am. Assn. Physics Tchrs., Mo. Acad. Sci. (advisor prize winning physics students). Home: 611 W 9th St Rolla MO 65409-2946 Office: U Mo Physics Dept Rolla MO 65401-0249

HALE, ROGER LOUCKS, manufacturing company executive; b. Plainfield, N.J., Dec. 13, 1934; s. Lloyd and Elizabeth (Adams) H.; m. Sandra Johnston, June 10, 1961 (div.); children: Jocelyn, Leslie, Nina, Deirdre; m. Eleanor L. Hall, Nov. 24, 1989. BA, Brown U., 1956; MBA, Harvard U., 1961. With Tennant Co., Mpls., 1961—; pres. Tennant Co., 1975—, CEO, 1976—, also bd. dirs.; bd. dirs. 1st Bank System; bd. dirs., vice-chmn. Dayton Hudson Corp. Chmn. Neighborhood Employment Network, 1980; bd. dirs., vice chmn. Pub. Radio Internat., 1990, Walker Art Ctr., 1970-88, 91—; chmn. Minn. Bus. Partnership, 1993-95. Named Exec. of Yr., Corp. Report mag., 1988, Exec. of Yr., Fin. World mag., 1990; recipient Mpls. Spl. Recognition award for Svc. to City of Mpls., 1993. Office: Tennant 701 Lilac Dr N Minneapolis MN 55422-4611

HALES, PATRICIA LOUISE, secondary education educator; b. Gary, Ind., Feb. 8, 1955; d. Robert Eugene and Mary Mildred (Reha) H. MusB in Voice Performance, Ind. U., 1977, MusM in Vocal Pedagogy, 1978. Substitute tchr. Merrillville (Ind.) Community Sch. Corp., 1978-82; accompanist, dir. asst. Pierce Jr. High Sch., Merrillville, 1978-83, Merrillville High Sch., 1978-83; pvt. voice instr. Gary, 1978-83; adj. instr. Ind. U. N.W., Gary, 1983-92; asst. prof. music Ind. U. N.W., 1992—; music dir. Highland (Ind.) Parks Dept., 1986-91, Whiting (Ind.) Community Showcase, 1988-91, Purdue U. Calumet, Hammond, Ind., 1988-90, Crown Point (Ind.) Playmakers, 1989-91. Soloist, pianist, organist, Grace Bapt. Ch., Gary, 1968—; mem. Coun. for Arts, Gary, 1989-90. Mem. Nat. Assn. Tchrs. Singing, Nat. Assn. Rec. Arts & Scis., N.W. Ind. Excellence in Theatre Found. (Outstanding Vocal Direction of a Musical award 1993, 94), Psi Kappa Lambda, Mu Phi Epsilon (chorister, pres., chaplain, Sterling Achievement award 1977). Office: Ind Univ NW 3400 Broadway Gary IN 46408-1101

HALEY, DAVID, state legislator; m. Michelle Haley. Kans. state rep. Dist. 34; pub. affairs cons. Address: 936 Cleveland Ave Kansas City KS 66101

HALEY, DAVID ALAN, preferred provider organization executive; b. St. Louis, Aug. 29, 1943; s. John David and Helen Ermyl (Richardson) H.; m. Donna Lee Davis, Nov. 24, 1965; children: Trisha Lynn, Jason Alan, Eric Nathan. BA, So. Ill. U., Edwardsville, 1966; MPH magna cum laude, UCLA, 1971. Adminstrv. asst. Kaiser Found. Hosp., Panorama City, Calif., 1971; assoc. adminstr. Our Lady of Lourdes Hosp., Pasco, Wash., 1971-74, Garfield Hosp., Monterey Park, Calif., 1974-75; assoc. exec. dir. Gen. Hosp., Ft. Walton Beach, Fla., 1976-79; v.p. ops. Our Lady of the Lake Regional Med. Ctr., Baton Rouge, 1979-88; pres. Phoenix Connection, Baton Rouge, 1988-89; CEO Gibson Gen. Hosp., Princeton, Ind., 1989-93; pres., CEO Four States Physicians Assn., Joplin, Mo., 1993-94; exec. dir. MedQuest Health Resources, Inc., 1995—; mem. Four Rivers Comprehensive Health Planning Agy., Richland, Wash., 1972-74; treas. S.E. Wash. State Hosp. Coun., Pasco, 1973, v.p. 1974; corp. mem. Mid La. Health Systems Agy., Baton Rouge, 1979-82; gubernatorial appointee La. Statewide Health Coord. Coun., Baton Rouge, 1984, Ind. Healthcare Facility Adminstrn. Bd., Indpls., 1991-93; sec.-treas. S.W. Ind. Hosp. Coun., Evansville, 1992-93. Served with USNR, 1967-69. USPHS fellow, 1969-71. Fellow Am. Coll. Healthcare Execs.; mem. Healthcare Fin. Mgmt. Assn., La. Hosp. Assn. (council on planning, 1984-87), Ind. Hosp. Assn. (mem. coun. pub. rels. 1992-93), Vis. Nurse Assn. Southwestern Ind. (bd. dirs. 1992-93), La. Assn. Bus. and Industry (health care council 1987). Republican. Lodge: Kiwanis. Home: 21408 Old N Church Rd Frankfort IL 60423 Office: MedQuest Health Resources Inc 20060 Governors Dr Ste 102 Olympia Fields IL 60461

HALEY, JOHNETTA RANDOLPH, musician, educator, university administrator; b. Alton, Ill., Mar. 19; d. John A. and Willye E. (Smith) Randolph; children from previous marriage: Karen, Michael. MusB in Edn., Lincoln U., 1945; MusM, So. Ill. U., 1972. Vocal and gen. music tchr. Lincoln High Sch., E. St. Louis, Ill., 1945-48; vocal music tchr., choral dir. Turner Sch., Kirkwood, Mo., 1950-55; vocal and gen. music tchr. Nipher Jr. High Sch., Kirkwood, 1955-71; prof. music Sch. Fine Arts, So. Ill. U., Edwardsville, 1972—, dir. East St. Louis Campus, 1982—; adjudicator music festivals; area music cons. Ill. Office Edn., 1977-78; program specialist St. Louis Human Devel. Corp., 1968; interim exec. dir. St. Louis Council Black People, summer 1970. Bd. dirs. YWCA, 1975-80, Artist Presentation Soc., St. Louis, 1975, United Negro Coll. Fund, 1976-78; bd. curators Lincoln U., Jefferson City, Mo., 1974-82, pres., 1978-82; chairperson Ill. Com. on Black Concerns in Higher Edn.; mem. Nat. Ministry on Urban Edn., Luth. Ch.-Mo. Synod, 1975-80; bd. dirs. Council Luth. Chs., Assn. of Governing Bds. of Univs. and Colls.; mem. adv. council Danforth Found. St. Louis Leadership Program, nat. chmn. Cleve. Job Corps, 1974-78; trustee Stillman Coll; pres. congregation St. Philips Luth. Ch.; bd. dirs. Target 2000; mem. Ill. Aux. Bd., United Way, v.p. East St. Louis Community Fund, Inc. Recipient Cotillion de Leon award for Outstanding Community Service, 1977, Disting. Alumnae award Lincoln U., 1977, Disting. Service award United Negro Coll. Fund, 1979, SCLC, 1981; Community Service award St. Louis Drifters, 1979, Disting. Service to Arts award Sigma Gamma Rho, Nat. Negro Musicians award, 1981, Sci. Awareness award, 1984-85, Tri Del Federated award, 1985, Martin Luther King Drum Maj. award, 1985, Bus. and Profl. Women's Club award, 1985-86, Fred L. McDowell award, 1986, Vol. of Yr. award Inroad's Inc., 1986, Woman of Achievement in Edn. award Elks, 1987, Woman of Achievement award Suburban Newspaper of Greater St. Louis and Sta. KMOX-Radio, 1988, Love award Greeley Community Ctr., Sammy Davies Jr. award in Edn., 1990, Yes I Can award in Edn., 1990, Merit award Urban League, 1994, Legacy award Nat. Coun. of Negro Women, 1995; named Disting. Citizen, St. Louis Argus Newspaper, 1970, Dutchess of Paducah, 1973. Mem. Council Luth. Chs., AAUP, Coll. Music Soc., Music Educators Nat. Conf., Ill. Music Educators Assn., Nat. Choral Dirs. Assn., Assn. Tchr. Educators, Midwest Kodaly Music Educators, Nat. Assn. Negro Musicians, Jack and Jill Inc., Women of Achievement in Edn., Friends of St. Louis Art Mus., The Links, Inc., Las Amigas Social Club, Alpha Kappa Alpha (internat. parliamentarian, Golden Soror award 1995), Mu Phi Epsilon, Pi Kappa Lambda. Lutheran. Home: 230 S Brentwood Blvd Clayton MO 63105-1602 Office: So Ill U PO Box 1606 Edwardsville IL 62026-1500

HALEY, PAT, state legislator; m. Irene Haley; 3 children. Student, U. Minn., St. John's U. Mem. S.D. Ho. of Reps., 1993—, mem. commerce and state affairs com. Writer and pub. Home: 766 Utah Ave SE Huron SD 57350-2906*

HALEY-OLIPHANT, ANN ELIZABETH, science educator; b. Centerville, Ind., Jan. 29, 1957; d. William Howard and Shirley Anne (Wilson) Haley; m. Robert Charles Oliphant, Apr. 14, 1979; children: Kristen Rae, Matthew Adler. MEd, U. Cin., 1987, EdD, 1989. Sci. tchr. Hazelwood (Mo.) West Jr.-Sr. High Sch., 1979-81, Kings Mills (Ohio) local schs., 1987-92; instnl. coord. Mo. Botanical Garden, St. Louis, 1981-82; grad. rsch. asst. U. Cin., 1983-87, adj. instr., 1986; adj. instr. Miami U., Oxford, Ohio, 1986, vis. asst. prof., 1992-95; project dir. Miami U., Ohio's NSF State Systemic Inst. in Math. and Sci., 1993-94; asst. prof. Miami U., Oxford, Ohio, 1995—; chair secondary sci. Nat. Bd. Profl. Tchg. Stds., 1991—; evaluator, cons. GE Aircraft Engines, Evendale, Ohio, 1987-91; cons. Biol. Sci. Curriculum Study, Colorado Springs, 1990—. Recipient Ohio Tchr. of Yr. award Chief State Bd. Supts., 1990, Presdl. award for excellence in math. and sci. teaching NSF/NSTA, 1991. Mem. AAAS (evaluator, author), Nat. Assn. Rsch. in Sci. Teaching, Am. Edn. Rsch. Assn., Nat. Sci. Tchrs. Assn. Home: 1323 Chaucer Pl Maineville OH 45039-9136 Office: Miami U 467 McGuffey Hall Oxford OH 45056

HALFHILL, ROBERT WAKEFIELD, volunteer association executive; b. Lexington, Ky., Sept. 20, 1940; s. Robert E. and Louise (Gann) H. BA, U. Ky., 1963. Treas. Student Mobilization Com. to End War in Vietnam, Mpls., 1966-67, FREE: Gay Liberation of Minn., Mpls., 1969-73; sec.-treas. Minn. Com. for Gay Rights, Mpls., 1976-78; treas. Gay Pride Com., Mpls., 1979-83; sec.-treas. ACT-UP Gay Liberation Front Minn., Mpls., 1989-95. Contbr. short stories to mags. Home: 125 Oak Grove Apt 41 Minneapolis MN 55403-4308 Office: ACT-UP Gay Liberation Front PO Box 50201 Loring Sta Minneapolis MN 55405

HALFOND, IRWIN, history educator; b. N.Y.C., Nov. 14, 1944; s. Bernard and Bertha Halfond; m. Susan Bolef, June 15, 1973 (div. Dec. 1982); children: Scott, Brie; m. Joyce Kramer, Aug. 19, 1988. BA, NYU, 1966; MA in History, Temple U., 1967, PhD in History, 1974. Teaching asst., adj. Temple U., Phila., 1967-73; assoc. prof. history, chair social sci. divsn. Livingstone Coll., Salisbury, N.C., 1974-81, Eureka (Ill.) Coll., 1981-82; prof. history, chair humanities divsn. McKendree Coll., Lebanon, Ill., 1988—; faculty cons. advanced placement exam Ednl. Testing Svc., Princeton, N.J., 1995; faculty assessment coord. McKendree Coll., Lebanon, Ill., 1992—; advisor McKendree History Soc., 1988—; book reviewer in field. Study grantee NEH, 1993, Summer Seminar grantee, 1993. Mem. Am. Hist. Assn., Masons. Home: 4633 Maryland Ave Saint Louis MO 63108 Office: McKendree Coll Humanities Divsn 701 College Rd Lebanon IL 62254

HALGREN, LEE A., academic administrator. V.p. acad. and student affairs State Coll. Colo., Denver, 1995—. Office: The State Coll Colo 1580 Lincoln St Ste 750 Denver CO 80203-1509

HALIFAX, ROBERT WILLIAM, manufacturing engineer; b. Port Huron, Mich., Apr. 4, 1954. A, Lansing (Mich.) C.C., 1987. Product design engr. Toledo Communtator Co., Owosso, Mich., 1976-94; mgr. divsn. Resinoid Commutators, Heath, Ohio, 1994—. Vol. tchr. Adult Edn. Computers; vol. Job Fair Local High Sch. With U.S. Army, 1972-76. Republican. Office: Resinoid Communtators 1930 James Pky Heath OH 43056-1031

HALIKAS, JAMES ANASTASIO, medical educator, psychiatrist; b. Bklyn., Nov. 26, 1941; s. Peter Simon and Olga Peter (Vavayianni) H.; BS (N.Y. State Regents scholar), Bklyn. Coll., 1962; MD, Duke U., 1966; m. Anna May Van Der Meulen, Aug. 20, 1967; children: Peter Christopher, Anna Catherine. Intern, Barnes Hosp., St. Louis, 1966-67; resident psychiatry Barnes/Renard hosps., Washington U. Sch. Medicine, St. Louis, 1967-70; rsch. fellow alcoholism and drug abuse Sch. Medicine, Washington U., St. Louis, 1969-70, instr. psychiatry, 1970-72, asst. prof., 1972-77, mem. com. on admissions, 1975-77; assoc. prof. psychiatry U. Louisville Sch. Medicine, 1978, dir. div. social and community psychiatry, 1978; assoc. prof. psychiatry Med. Coll. Wis., Milw., 1978-84, dir. div. alcoholism and chem. dependency, 1978-84, mem. human rsch. rev. com., 1981-84; prof. psychiatry, dir. psychiat. residency tng. U. Minn. Med. Sch., Mpls., 1984-90, mem. com. on the use of human subjects in rsch., 1985—, co-dir. chem. dependency treatment program U. Minn. Hosps. and Clinics, 1984-89, dir. 1989—, mem Coun. on Med. Edn., 1991—; asst. psychiatrist Barnes, Renard and Affiliated hosps., 1970-77; cons. Malcolm Bliss Mental Health Ctr., St. Louis, 1970-77; dir. psychiat. divs. Webster Coll. Student Health Svc., Webster Groves, Mo., 1973-75; dir. Grace Hill Settlement House Psychiatry Clinic, St. Louis, 1973-77; clin. instr. dept. psychiatry Mo. Inst. Psychiatry, U. Mo., St. Louis, 1972-74; mem. profl. adv. com. Judevine Ctr. for Autistic Children, St. Louis, 1975-77; psychiat. rsch. cons. Reproductive Biology Rsch. Found., Masters and Johnson Inst., St. Louis, 1975-77. Mem. Mo. Gov.'s Adv. Council on Alcoholism and Drug Abuse, 1974-75; exec. com. Drug and

Substance Abuse Council Met. St. Louis, 1973-77, pres., 1971-72; chmn. Children's Mental Health Svs. Council Met. St. Louis, 1973-74; host Sta. KMOX-TV weekly TV series Trips, 1971; adviser on drug abuse St. Louis County Juvenile Ct., 1970-72; mem. adv. bd. Drug Crisis Intervention Unit, St. Louis, 1971-77; mem. St. Louis Youth Ctr. profl. adv. com. Mo. Dept. Mental Health, 1977; adv. on drug abuse Drug Info. Ctr., St. Louis, 1970-74, Human Devel. Corp., St. Louis, 1970-73, Alliance for Regional Community Health, 1972-74; med. dir. for alcoholism svcs. Jefferson County Alcoholism and Drug Abuse Ctr. for Treatment and Rsch., Louisville, 1978; exec. and med. dir. River Region Mental Health-Mental Retardation Bd., Ky. Region VI Community Mental Health System, Louisville, 1978; bd. dir. Wis. Alcoholism and Drug Abuse Rsch. Inst., Milw., 1978-84; sr. Scientist U. Wis., Milw., 1978-84; attending psychiatrist, dir. med. edn. DePaul Rehab. Hosp., Milw., 1978-84; dir. rsch. and edn. in chem. dependency, sr. attending psychiatrist Milwaukee County Mental Health Complex, Milw., 1978-84, dir. psychiat. supervision div. long term care, 1983-84, dir. outpatient clinic, 1984, also chmn. or co-chmn. various coms.; sci. dir. DePaul Hosp. Found., Milw., 1978-84; assoc. psychiatrist U. Louisville Affiliated Hosps., 1978; attending psychiatrist Milw. Psychiat. Hosp., 1978-84, Columbia Hosp., Milw., 1980-84; attending psychiatrist U. Minn. Hosps. and Clinics, 1984—, Met. Med. Ctr., Mpls., 1985—; mem. planning com. Am. Med. Soc. on Alcoholism, 1977-78, mem. program com., 1983—, chmn. com. on med. edn., 1981—, mem. cert. com., 1985—, chmn. fellowship com., 1985—, Wis. state chmn., 1979-84; psychiat. cons. Social Security Disability Determination Svc., 1984-87, Minn. Security Hosp., 1985-88, Moose Lake Regional Treatment Ctr., 1988—, Sandstone Fed. Correctional Inst., 1988-90; mem. Wis. Alcohol and Drug Abuse Adv. Com., HHS, 1981-84, St. Paul Mayor' Anti Drug Task Force, 1988-91; mem. Nat. Alcoholism Forum, 1978; co-chmn. clin. rsch. task force Nat. Drug Abuse Conf., Seattle, 1978; mem. Mental Health Assn. Louisville, 1978, Louisville Council on Alcoholism, 1978; cons. Midwestern Area Alcohol Edn. and Tng. Program, 1976-77. Bd. dirs. Mental Health Ast. Louis, 1973-77, chmn. St. Louis State Hosp. human research com., 1976-77; bd. dirs. Tellurian South Community, Inc., Madison, 1980—; mem. exec. council DePaul Rehab. Hosp., 1979-84; mem. med. appeals bd. Div. Motor Vehicles, State of Wis., 1980-84; mem. City of Mequon Bd. Appeals, 1980-84; mem. profl. adv. bd. Lactation Inst., L.A., 1981—; mem. dist. study and adv. council Moundsview Sch. Dist., 1987-88; also cons. Recipient NIMH Psychiatry Career Tchr. award in narcotics, drug abuse and alcoholism, 1972-75; diplomate Am. Bd. Psychiatry and Neurology, Nat. Bd. Med. Examiners. Mem. Am. Psychiat. Assn. (mem. Task Force on Substance Abuse Edn. in Psychiatry, 1985-87, task force postgrad. psychiatric edn. 1988—), Eastern Mo. Psychiat. Soc., Ky. Psychiat. Assn., Wis. Psychiat. Assn., Minn. Psychiat. Soc. (mem. com. on quality assurance and standards, 1987-89), Am. Psychopathol. Assn., Assn. for Med. Edn. and Rsch. in Substance Abuse, N.Y. Acad. Scis., AAAS, Ky. Med. Assn., Rsch. Soc. on Alcoholism, Assn. for Acad. Psychiatry, Am. Acad. Clin. Psychiatrists (bd. dirs. 1984-90, chmn. med. edn. com. 1984-90), Am. Assn. Dirs. of Psychiatric Residency Tng. (treas. 1987-89, chmn. liaison com. 1989-92), Soc. Biol. Psychiatry, Am. Acad. Psychiatrists in Alcoholism and Addictions (Midwest regional dir. 1990—), Am. Med. Assn., Am. Soc. Clin. Pharmacology and Therapeutics, Kappa Nu. Greek Orthodox. Contbr. numerous articles to profl. jours. Home: 22 Hill Farm Cir Saint Paul MN 55127-2007 Office: U Minn Dept Psychiatry PO Box 393 Minneapolis MN 55440-0393

HALIW, ANDREW JEROME, III, lawyer, engineer; b. Ansbach, Fed. Republic of Germany, Aug. 8, 1946; came to U.S., 1950; s. Ilko and Sophie (Kindrat) H.; children: Larissa Andrea, Andrea Stephanie. BEE, Wayne State U., 1968, JD, 1972; postgrad. in Fin., U. Mich., 1993—. Bar: Mich. 1973, U.S. Dist. Ct. (ea. dist.) Mich. 1973, U.S. Supreme Ct. 1982, Mich. (6th cir.) 1986; lic. profl. engr., Mich.; registered patent & trademark atty. Divisional elec. engr. J & L div. LTV, Warren, Mich., 1968-72; ptr. bd. dirs. Sullivan & Leavitt P.C., Northville, Mich., 1972-79, ptnr., 1979-91, also bd. dirs.; ptnr. Haliw, Siciliano & Mychalowych, P.C., Farmington Hills, Mich., 1991—; bd. dirs. Am. Supplier Inst., Dearborn Mich.; chmn. Advanced Systems and Designs, Inc., Dearborn; vice chmn. ASI Internat. Atty. Ukrainian Cultural Ctr., Warren, 1984; del., dist. dir. Farmington Hills Reps., 1990—; chair Zoning Bd. Appeals, Farmington Hills. Mem. ABA, Detroit Bar Assn., Oakland County Bar Assn., Detroit Engring. Soc. (dist. bd. dirs.). Republican. Eastern Catholic. Home: 38250 9 Mile Rd Northville MI 48167-9014 Office: Haliw Siciliano et al Ste 350 37000 Grand River Farmington Hills MI 48335

HALL, ALAN CRAIG, library director; b. Marietta, Ohio, Mar. 9, 1954; s. Harry Edward and Flossie June (Heddleston) H.; m. Barbara Ann Metzger, May 23, 1981; 1 child, Shawn Alan. BS in Edn., W.Va. U., 1976; MLS, Case Western U., 1977. With circulation dept. Washington County Pub. Libr., Marietta, Ohio, 1970-75; with govt. documents dept. Freiberger Libr., Cleve., 1976-77; dir. Delphos (Ohio) Pub. Libr., 1977-83, Pub. Libr. of Steubenville and Jefferson County, 1983—; cons. Morgan County Libr., McConnelsville, Ohio, 1992-93, Barnesville (Ohio) Pub. Libr., 1991; chair Ohio Libr. Coun., Columbus, 1994. Author: Mariett's Innkeeper, 1991; editor: The Papers of A.T. Nye, 1975, Abandoned Underground Coal Mines of Jefferson County, 1991, Richmond, Ohio Cemetery Book, 1995; compiler Historic Pages Series, 1975-76; contbr. articles to profl. publs. Chairperson Ohio Humanities Coun., Steubenville, 1991; pres. Ret. Sr. Vol. Program, Steubenville, 1989-90; ruling elder Starkdale Presbyn. Ch., 1985-88, 94—. Mem. ALA, Jefferson County Hist. Soc., Steubenville Lions Club (pres. 1986-87), Ohio Libr. Assn. (pres. 1992-93, Libr. of Yr. 1989). Office: Pub Libr Steubenville & Jefferson County 407 S 4th St Steubenville OH 43952

HALL, BYRON CARLYLE, JR., physics educator, philosopher, researcher; b. Cin., Oct. 28, 1937; s. Byron C. Sr. and Mary Alice H. BS in Physics with high honors, U. Cin., 1959; MA in Physics, Johns Hopkins U., 1966; postgrad., Boston U. and St. Louis U., 1970-75. Instr. physics Towson (Md.) State Coll., 1966-69; tchr. physics and chemistry Cardinal Gibbons H.S., Balt., 1969-70; tchr. physics John F. Kennedy H.S., Manchester, Mo., 1975-78; chair dept. math. Louisville Collegiate Sch., 1978-80; instr. physics Talladega (Ala.) Coll., 1980-82; instr. electronics ITT Tech. Inst., Dayton, Ohio, 1983-90; instr. physics Sinclair C.C., Dayton, 1991—; cons. Higher Edn., Inc., Boston, 1971-72. Editor, pub.: (jour.) Constructive Conservative, 1968-70; contbr. articles to profl. jours. State chmn. Young Ams. for Freedom, Md., 1967-69; bd. dirs. Dayton Right to Life, 1991-94. Mem. Am. Assn. Physics Tchrs. (mem. So. Ohio sect.), Am. Philos. Assn., Phi Beta Kappa. Office: Sinclair C C 444 W 3d St Dayton OH 45402

HALL, CAROL LYNN, purchasing agent; b. Evansville, Ind., Dec. 10, 1947; d. Lynn Elder and Mildred K. (Wulf) H. BA in Bus. Edn., U. Evansville, 1969. Tchr. high sch. bus. North Montgomery Sch. Corp., Linden, Ind., 1969-70; purchasing agt. Brown & Hubert, Inc., 1971—. Chairperson pastor-parish com. Wesley United Meth. Ch., Evansville, 1987-94; sec.-treas. Priscilla Circle, sec. bd. trustees, 1989-95. Office: Brown & Hubert Div Lensing Wholesale 306 N 7th Ave Evansville IN 47710-1024

HALL, CHARLES ADAMS, infosystems specialist; b. Damoh, India, Aug. 6, 1949; s. Keith Burckle and Virginia (Bevan) H.; m. Nancy Louise Dahl, June 7, 1980; 1 child, Loren Jarrett. BA, Hiram (Ohio) Coll., 1972; AA, Ind. Vocat. Tech. Coll., 1983. Programmer Superior Supply, Inc., Marion, Ind., 1983-85, data processing mgr., 1985-89, dir. mgmt. info. systems, 1990-92; systems adminstr. Hi-Way Dispatch, Marion, 1992—; programmer Freel & Mason, Marion, 1985; programmer, chief programmer Bruce, Hall & Assocs., Marion, 1986-88. Developer computer game. Sec., treas. bd. dirs. Health Environ. for All Life, Marion, 1988—. With U.S. Army, 1973-76. Mem. Christian Ch. (Disciples of Christ). Office: PO Box 896 Marion IN 46952-0896

HALL, DAVID MCKENZIE, marketing and management educator; b. Gary, Ind., June 21, 1928; s. Alfred McKenzie and Grace Elizabeth (Crimiel) H.; m. Jaqueline Virginia Branch, Apr. 30, 1960; children: Glen D., Gary D. BA, Howard U., 1951; MS, N.C. Agrl. Tech. State U., 1966. Enlisted USAF, 1951; advanced through grades to brig. gen.; chief social actions Hdqrs. Mil. Airlift Command, Scott AFB, Il., 1972-1974; dep. base comdr. 375th Air Base Group, Scott AFB, 1974-75, base comdr., 1975-76; dir. data processing Air Force Logistics Command, Wright-Patterson AFB, Ohio, 1976-77, comptr., 1977-83; ret. USAF, 1983; dir. data processing Delco-Remy div. GM, Anderson, Ind., 1983-85; regional mgr. Electronic Data Systems, Anderson, 1985-88, Saginaw, Mich., 1988-93; prof. mgmt. and mktg. Northwood Univ., Midland, Mich., 1993—. Mem. nat. bd. dirs. Boy Scouts Am. Brig. Gen. USAF, 1951-83. Recipient Hon. Citizenship East St. Louis, Ill., 1975, Key to City Gary Ind., 1981. Mem. NAACP, Saginaw Cmty. Found., Cmty. Affairs Com., Prince Hall Masons, Kappa Alpha Psi. Methodist. Home: 49 W Hannum Blvd Saginaw MI 48602-1938 Office: Northwood U J-9 3225 Cook Rd Midland MI 48640

HALL, DONALD VINCENT, social worker; b. Ft. Dodge, Iowa, June 13, 1955; s. John William and Helen Evelyn (Swanson) H.; m. Marla Jo Adamson, May 28, 1977; children: Lucas William, Jessica Lauren. BSW, U. Iowa, 1977; MSW, U. Kans., 1979. Cert. clin. social worker; lic. social worker, Iowa; diplomate bd. clin. social work; qualified clin. social worker. Social worker Heartland Edn. Agy., Johnston, Iowa, 1979-91, facilitator conflict resolution and concensus decision making, cons. long range planning, presenter workshops, 1989—; pvt. practice clin. social worker, psychotherapist children, individauls, couples, families, groups Counseling and Assessment Svcs., P.C., 1991—; participant Des Moines Family Therapy Tng. Inst., 1991—. Bd. dirs. Johnston (Iowa) Community Sch., 1984-90, pres. bd., 1987-90. Presbyterian (ordained elder). Home: 6845 NW Beaver Dr Johnston IA 50131-1245 Office: Counseling and Assessment Svcs PC 2404 Forest Dr Des Moines IA 50312-5400

HALL, GLENN ALLEN, lawyer, state representative; b. Pekin, Ill., Oct. 22, 1955; s. Gerald Eugene and Vinetta Bell Hall; m. Mary Melodie Hall, Dec. 30, 1978; children: Kimberly, Jaired, Ellie, Chava, Justice. BS in Edn., U. Mo., 1980; JD, Regent U., 1989. Bar: Mo. 1989. Atty. Glenn Allen Hall, Atty. at law, Kansas City, Mo., 1989—; state rep. State of Mo., 1993—. Author: No Justice in the Land, 1993. Bd. dirs. Rep. Club Greater Kansas City, 1992-95; elder Metro Vineyard Fellowship Christian Ch., Kansas City, 1992-93. Office: 740 NW Blue Pky Lees Summit MO 64086-5713*

HALL, HANSEL CRIMIEL, communications executive; b. Gary, Ind., Mar. 12, 1929; s. Alfred McKenzie and Grace Elizabeth (Crimiel) H. BS, Ind. U., 1953; LLB, Blackstone Sch. Law, 1982. Officer, IRS, 1959-64; gasoline svc. sta. operator, then realtor, Chgo., 1964-69; program specialist HUD, Chgo., 1969-73, dir. equal opportunity, St. Paul, 1973-75, dir. fair housing, Indpls., from 1975; human resource officer U.S. Fish and Wildlife Service, Twin Cities, Minn.; cons. in civil rights; pres. bd. dirs. Riverview Towers Cooperative Assn., Inc.; 1984-87; pres, CEO Crimiel Communications, Inc, 1988—; CFO, treas. Korean War Vets. Edn. Grant Corp., 1996—; del. U.S. Parliamentarian to Russia and Czechoslovakia, 1992; bd. dirs. Nat. Korean War Vets. Assn., 1992. Served with USAF, 1951-53; Korea. Recipient Ambassador For Peace cert. Korean Vets. Assn., 1991, Korean Svc. medal Rep. of Korea, 1991. Mem. NAACP (Golden Heritage life mem.), Res. Officers Assn., Am. Inst. Parliamentarians, Nat. Assn. Parliamentarians, Ind. U. Alumni Assn.; Omega Psi Phi. Club: Toastmasters DTM (past area gov.).

HALL, HOMER L., journalism educator; b. Reeds, Mo., June 11, 1939; s. Columbus Terry and MArgie (Fain) H.; m. Lea Ann (Watson), Sept. 4, 1960; children: Lynlea, Ashley. BS in Edn., U. Mo., 1960; MS in Edn., U. Kans., 1965; postgrad, various insts. Tchr. North Kirkwood (Mo.) Jr. High, 1963-68, 70-73, Shawnee Mission, Kans., 1968-69; reporter Sedalia (Mo.) Democrat, 1969; tchr. Sedalia High Sch., 1969-70, Kirkwood High Sch., 1973—; dir. journalism workshops Ball State U., Muncie, Ind., 1983-85, 87; tchr. summer journalism workshops, Mo., Ill., Tex., Ind., Calif., Wash., R.I., Iowa, Hawaii, Ariz., Kans., Oreg. Author: (textbooks) Junior High Journalism, 1969, rev. edit., 1993, Senior High Journalism, 1985, rev. edit., 1993, Yearbook Guidebook, 1981, rev. 4 times; contbr. numerous articles to journalism publs. Tchr. Sunday sch. Kirkwood Baptist Ch., 1982—, deacon, 1985—. Served to 1st lt. U.S. Army, 1961-63. Named Mo. Journalism Tchr. of Yr., Mo. Interscholastic Press Assn., 1973, Mo. Tchr. of Yr., Mo. Dept. of Edn., 1979, Merit medal Journalism Edn. Assn., 1979, Nat. Journalism Tchr. of Yr., Dow Jones Newspaper Fund, 1982; recipient Gold Key award Columbia Scholastic Press Assn., 1982, Pioneer award Nat. Scholastic Press Assn., 1982, Horace Mann award Mo. Nat. Edn. Assn., 1983, Scholastic Journalism award Ball State U., 1993, Nat. Yearbook Adviser of Yr. award, 1996; named to Scholastic Journalism Hall of Fame, Okla. U., 1992. Mem. Mo. Journalism Edn. Assn. (past pres.), Kirkwood Community Tchrs. Assn. (past pres.), Sponsors of Sch. Publs. Greater St. Louis (sec., past pres.), Nat. Journalism Edn. Assn. (sec., cert. commn. chair, v.p., Carl Towley award), Phi Delta Kappa. Home: 1027 Romine Kirkwood MO 63122-2452 Office: Kirkwood High Sch 801 W Essex Ave Saint Louis MO 63122-3608

HALL, JAMES ROBERT, secondary education educator; b. Salem, Ill., Dec. 24, 1947; s. James Wesley and Patricia Joyce (Ellis) H. B.S., U. Ill., 1970. Cert. secondary tchr., Ill. Tchr. Murphysboro High Sch., Ill., 1970—. Author, compiler: (tng. man.) Key Club Faculty Advisors, 1975. Sunday sch. tchr. United Methodist Ch., Murphysboro, 1973-76, youth dir., 1973-76, mem. council on ministries, 1984—, trustee, 1984—; founder, dir. Christian Lay Council Youth Coffeehouse, 1973-75; mem. Murphysboro Recreation Bd., 1974-76, pres. 1975-76; community amb. So. Ill. U. Area Services, 1975—; bd. dirs. Murphysboro Heart Fund, 1973-76, co-chmn., 1975-76; chmn. Murphysboro Muscular Dystrophy Assn., 1971-74; counsellor Little Grassy Youth Ch. Camp, 1973; steering com. Murphysboro Apple Festival, 1975—, exec. com., 1983—; bd. dirs. Murphysboro United Way, 1978-83, Murphysboro Sr. Citizens Council, 1980-83, Resource Reclamation, Inc., 1979-85; vice chmn. Murphysboro Swimming Pool Project Commn., 1983-84, chmn., 1984-88; active Murphysboro Tourism Commn., 1995—. Named one of Outstanding Young Men of Am., 1975, 84; recipient Citizenship award Sta. WTAO Radio, 1983, 84, Ann. Community Service award Modern Woodmen Am., 1982, Citizen of Yr. award Murphysboro C. of C., 1984, Disting. Educator award Phi Delta Kappa, 1991. Mem. NEA, Ill. Edn. Assn., Murphysboro Edn. Assn. Clubs: Key (advisor 1972—, adminstr. Ill.-Eastern Iowa dist. 1985-, Key Club Internats 1996), Kiwanis (pres. 1977-78, lt. gov. dist. div. 1984-85, chmn. spl. club services Ill.-Eastern Iowa dist. 1984-85, Mid. Sch. Builders Club advisor 1993—, cert. trnr. 1993—, gov.-elect 1995-96, gov. 1996—, Dr. Luis V. Amador medallion 1995). Avocations: collecting books and plates; bowling; tennis. Home: 28 Candy Ln Murphysboro IL 62966-2953 Office: Murphysboro H S 16 Blackwood Dr Murphysboro IL 62966

HALL, JOAN B., small business owner; b. Evanston, Ill., July 22, 1926; d. Frederick Joseph and Mona La Mothe (Gunn) Brockhoff; m. Frank Braden Hall, May 11, 1957; children: Braden, Scott. Student, Northwestern U., 1944-46. Adminstrv. asst. Walgreen Co., Chgo., 1948-49, NBC, Chgo., 1949-52, A.C. Nielsen Co., Chgo., 1952-57; pres. Joan B. Hall & Assoc., Park Ridge, Ill., 1980—; supr. Maine Twp., Park Ridge, 1989-93. Trustee Oakton C.C., Des Plaines, Ill., 1985—, chairwoman bd. trustees, 1993-94; chairwoman Cook County Suburban Rep. Orgn., 1981-90; committeewoman Maine Twp. Rep. Orgn., Des Plaines, 1969-76, 81-90; fundraisesr United Fund Heart Fund, Park Ridge, 1981-92, Cancer Fund, Maine Twp. Recipient Outstanding Govt. Ofcl. award Pvt. Industry Coun., 1991, Rep. Woman of Yr. award, 1993-94. Mem. Assn. Women Entrepreneurs, Internat. Group Agys. and Burs. (bd. govs.), City Club Chgo. Republican. Home: 2904 Scottlynne Dr Park Ridge IL 60068-2855

HALL, LYDIA JANE, geriatrics nurse; b. Ravenwood, Mo., Mar. 4, 1939; d. George G. and Lydia G. (Lambert) Griffin; m. Clifford Ray Hall, Sept. 18, 1987; children: Ray Ballin, Ronald Ballin, Janet Goad, Julia Newton. Assoc. Nursing, Butler County Community Coll., Eldorado, Kans., 1983; student, Arkansas City Community Coll., 1984, Kans. Newman Coll., Wichita, 1985. Staff nurse Arkansas City Meml. Hosp., 1983-85, St. Joseph Med. Ctr., Wichita, Kans., 1985-86, Heritage House, Winfield, Kans., 1986; evening and night charge nurse Health Concepts IV-Cedar Vale (Kans.) Regional Hosp., 1986-87, 88-89; staff nurse St. Luke's Hosp., Wellington, Kans., 1988, Augusta (Kans.) Med. Complex, Inc., 1989; night charge nurse Cumbernauld Village, Winfield, Kans., 1990; DON Grouse Valley Manor, Dexter, Kans., 1991—. Mem. sch. bd. Unified Sch. Dist. 462, Burden, Kans., 1975-79; mem., chmn. Cowley County Spl. Edn. Bd., 1975-79. Home: 1021 E 2nd Ave Winfield KS 67156-2302

HALL, MARI, agricultural company executive. With Pioneer Hi-Bred Internat., Des Moines. Office: Pioneer Hi-Bred Internat 11280 Aurora Ave Des Moines IA 50322-7905

HALL, MARION TRUFANT, botany educator, arboretum director; b. Gorman, Tex., Sept. 6, 1920; s. Frank Marion and Nora Gertrude (Wharton) H.; m. Virginia Riddle, Nov. 9, 1944; children: Susan, Alan Lee, John Lane. BS, U. Okla., 1943, MS, 1947; PhD, Washington U., St. Louis, 1951; DSc (hon.), North Central Coll., Ill., 1977. Ranger Nat. Park Service, Dept. Interior, 1942; instr. botany U. Okla., 1946-47; curator Bebb Herbarium, 1949; field botanist, instr. Tex. Nature Camp, Nat. Audubon Soc., Kerrville, Tex., 1948; grad. asst. zoology, teaching fellow Washington U., 1948-50; spl. lectr. genetics and evolution Henry Shaw Sch. Botany, 1952; botanist Cranbrook Inst. Sci., Bloomfield Hills, Mich., 1950-56; acting dir. Cranbrook Inst. Sci., 1955-56; prof., head dept. botany Butler U., 1956-62; vis. prof. botany U. Okla., 1962; dir. Stovall Mus. Sci. and History, 1962-66; dir. Morton Arboretum, Lisle, Ill., 1966-90, dir. emeritus, 1990—; prof. botany, acting dir. U. Mich. Bot. Gardens, 1963-64; prof. horticulture U. Ill., Urbana; adj. prof. biology No. Ill. U.; cons. Mich. Dept. Conservation, Handbook Biol. Materials for Museums, also cons. on conservation issues, open space preservation & mgmt., vegetational analysis, land use rating. Contbr. numerous research articles to profl. jours. Bd. dirs. Joyce Found., Chgo. Henrietta Heerman scholar Washington U., 1951; recipient award for professionalism Am. Assn. Bot. Gardens and Arboreta Inc., citation for svcs. to U.S. govt. Inst. Mus. Svcs., Alumni Achievement award U. Okla., 1953, Liberty Hyde Bailey medal for outstanding achievement in Am. horticulture Am. Hort. Soc., 1990, Hutchinson medal for outstanding svc. to horticulture, 1990; NSF grantee. Fellow Ind. Acad. Sci., Cranbrook Inst. Sci.; mem. Ecol. Soc. Am., Asa Gray Meml. Assn., Mich. Natural Areas Coun., Okla. Acad. Sci., Mich. Bot. Club (past pres. Detroit), Phi Beta Kappa, Sigma Xi, Phi Sigma. Home and Office: 1885 Southcliff Dr Maryville TN 37803-7524

HALL, PATRICIA ANN, educational administrator; b. Ind., July 29, 1939. BSN, Ind. U., 1962; MA, Ball State U., 1985. RN, Mich., Ind. Dean occupational studies Lake Mich. Coll., Benton Harbor, Mich., 1986—; Title III grant coord., 1992-95. Mem. Am. Assn. Women in Community and Jr. Colls. Leaders Program, 1989. Mem. Mich. Occupational Dean's Adminstrv. Coun. (pres. 1991-93), Nat. Coun. Occupational Edn. (rep. Region X). Home: 2511 Essex Ct Saint Joseph MI 49085-2703

HALL, PATRICIA MARIE, special education administrator; b. Streator, Ill., Mar. 9, 1956; d. Norman Ronald and Catherine (Grako) H. BS in Edn., Ill. State U., Normal, 1977, MS in Edn., 1990. Ednl. Adminstrn.. Spl. Edn., Visually Impaired, Elem. Edn., Early Childhood Spl. Edn. Spl. edn. tchr. Regional Ednl. Svc. Agency, Channahon, Ill., 1978-89, cord. visually impaired programs, 1989-92; coord. visually impaired program So. Will County Office of Spl. Edn., 1992—. Mem. Assn. for Edn. and Rehab. of Blind and Visually Impaired, Coun. for Exceptional Children, Kappa Delta Pi, Kappa Delta Epsilon. Roman Catholic. Home: 1017 Pearson Dr Joliet IL 60435-3255 Office: So Will Co Office Spl Edn Ste K 707 W Jefferson St Shorewood IL 60431

HALL, PAUL JAMES, JR., sales executive; b. Streator, Ill., Dec. 2, 1945; s. Paul James and Ruth Margret (Beall) H.; m. Joyce Lynn Patterson, Aug. 16, 1969; 1 child, Derek Jason. AA, Ill. Cen. Coll., 1971; BS in Econs., Ill. State U., 1973. Parts and svc. salesman Caterpillar Tractor Co., Peoria, Ill., 1973-81; dir. sales and mktg. Applied Learning, Naperville, Ill., 1981-89; sales mgr. TII Tech. Edn. Systems, Palatine, Ill., 1989—; mem. adv. com. Nat. Ctr. Mfg. Scis., Ann Arbor, Mich., 1992. Pres. Morton (Ill.) Little League, 1971-73; mem. adminstrv. bd. Frankfort (Ill.) United Meth. Ch., 1988-90, pres. Men's Club, 1986-90; mem. Dist. 161 Sch. Bd., 1989—; bd. dirs. Am. Cancer Soc., Frankfort, 1990-92. With USMC, 1966-69, Vietnam. Decorated Silver Star, Bronze Star, Purple Heart with 3 oak leaf clusters. Mem. ASTD (bd. dirs. Chgo. 1990-92) , VFW, DAV, N.Am. Fishing Club, Moose. Republican. Home: 411 Spruce Dr Frankfort IL 60423-8622

HALL, TIMOTHY, state legislator; b. Omaha, Mar. 8, 1956; m. Susa Jo Riha, 1981; children: Annie, Tim, Mike. Student, Drake U., U. Nebr., Omaha. Dir. pub. affairs Mut. Protective & Medico Life Ins. Co.; mem. from dist. 7 Nebr. State Senate, Lincoln, 1984—, past chmn. revenue com., mem. banking, comml. and ins. coms., com. on credentials, chmn. exec. bd. judiciary com. Office: Nebr State Senate State Capitol Rm 2010 Lincoln NE 68509*

HALL, TODD ANTHONY, research and development engineer; b. Louisville, Apr. 29, 1964; s. David B. and Judy (Wallace) H.; m. Jill Marie Puffer, Jan. 28, 1988; 1 child, Alexander David. BS in Engring. Sci., U. Louisville, 1988. R&D engr. Cook, Inc., Bloomington, Ill., 1988—. Patentee in field. Mem. ASME, NSPE. Home: 3952 Tulipwood Ct Bloomington IN 47404 Office: Cook Inc PO Box 489 Bloomington IN 47402

HALL, TONY P., congressman; b. Dayton, Ohio, Jan. 16, 1942; m. Janet Dick, 1973; children: Jyl, Matthew. Student, Ohio State U.; AB, Denison U., 1964; LLD (hon.), Asbury Coll., Eastern Coll. Vol. Peace Corps, Thailand, 1966-67; mem. Ohio Ho. of Reps., 1969-72, Ohio Senate, 1973-78, 96th-103rd Congresses from 3d Ohio dist., Washington, D.C., 1979—. Founder, mem. steering com. Congl. Friends of Human Rights Monitors; mem. bd. mgrs. Air Force Mus. Found.; trustee Holiday Aid; mem. adv. com. Emergency Resource Bank; chmn. Dem. Caucus Task Force on Hunger. Recipient Disting. Svc. Against Hunger award Bread for the World, 1984, 87, Tree of Life award Jewish Nat. Fund, 1986, Golden Apple award Nat. Assn. Nutrition and Aging Svcs. Programs, 1986, Freedom award Asian Pacific Am. C. of C., 1986, Presdl. End Hunger award, 1988, Silver Anniversary award NCAA, 1989, Silver World Food Day medal Food and Agriculture Orgn. of UN, Ptnrs. award Oxfam Am., 1992. Mem. Nat. Assn. Women, Infants & Children (Leadership award 1991). Democrat. Office: 1432 Longworth House Ofc Washington DC 20515-0005

HALL, TRACY LYNN, physician; b. Belleville, Ill., Apr. 28, 1963; d. Norman Keith and Joyce Ann (Greenhill) H. AS, Kaskaskia Coll., Greenville, 1983; BA, Greenville Coll., 1985; DO, Kirksville Coll. Osteo. Med., 1989. Diplomate Am. Bd. Family Practice. Cert. ACLS, BLS, neonatal resucitation. Intern Westview Osteopathic Hosp., Indpls., 1989-90; resident in family practice So. Ill. U., Belleville, 1990-92; physician McCracken-Dawdy Family Practice, Greenville, Ill., 1992—; clin. asst. prof. medicine U. Ill., Chgo., So. Ill. U. Medicine, Springfield. Mem. AMA, Am. Osteo. Assn., Am. Assn. Family Practice, Am. Coll. Family Practitioners, Christian Med. and Dental Soc., Am. Acad. Osteo. Sports Medicine, Ind. Assn. Osteo. Physicians, Fellowship Christian Athletes. Office: McCracken Dawdy Family Practice 201 Health Care Dr Greenville IL 62246-1155

HALL, WILLIAM EDWARD, educator; b. McGregor, Iowa, Aug. 19, 1907. BA, Williamette U., 1930; MA, Ohio State U., PhD. Registered clin. physcologist, Nebr. Prof. physcology U. Nebr., Lincoln, 1944-68; founder sch. human resource inst. U. Lincoln, 1944-68; cons. Physcological Selection, Atlanta, 1976—. Contbr. articles to profl. jours. Mem. AAAS. Republican. Methodist. Home: 2820 S 80th St Omaha NE 68124

HALL, WILLIAM GLENN, state government administrator; b. Springfield, Ill., Dec. 23, 1945; s. William Thompson and Alice Louise (Hester) H.; m. Imogene Greene Hall, Nov. 25, 1967 (div. Jan. 1987); children: Nicholas, Andrew. BA, U. Ill., Urbana, 1970; MA, U. Ill., Springfield, 1974. Asst. dir. City Day Sch. of Springfield, 1972-76, Planning Consortium for Children's Svcs., Springfield, 1976-77; assoc. dir. govt. affairs Ill. Alcoholism and Drug Dependence Assn., Springfield, 1977-79; chief, human resources unit Ill. Ho. of Rep., Springfield, 1979-84; dep. dir. Ill. Dept. Children and Family Svcs., Springfield, 1984-89; assoc. dir. Ill. Dept. Alcoholism and S.A., Springfield, 1989-91; exec. dir. Ill. Econ. and Fiscal Comm., Springfield, 1991—; adj. faculty Lincolnland C.C., Springfield, 1975-77, U. Ill., Springfield, 1991—. Mem. Springfield Human Rels. Comm., 1973. Mem. Nat. Conf. of State Legislators, Am. Pub. Welfare Assn., Nat. Assn. Bus. Economists. Office: Ill Econ and Fiscal Commn 703 Stratton Bldg Springfield IL 62706

HALLBERG, GAY ROBB, clinical psychologist; b. Mpls., Feb. 25, 1937; d. Gordon Gay and Dorothy (Mack) Robb. BA, Antioch Coll., 1959; MA, U. Minn., 1966; PhD, Union Inst., 1992. Lic. psychologist; lic. sch. psychologist; clin. psychologist. Psychologist Mpls. Rehab. Ctr., 1983-70; sch. psychologist II Mpls. Pub. Schs., 1970—; pvt. practice Mpls., 1977—; presenter in field. Co-author: How to Adopt from Europe, Asia and the South Pacific; contbr. articles to profl. jours. Bd. dirs. Adoptive Families of Am., 1974-79. Mem. APA, Minn. Soc. Clin. Hypnosis, Nat. Assn. Sch. Psychologists, Minn. Assn. Scy. Psychologists, Minn. Psychol. Assn., Internat. Sch. Psychologists Assn., Internat. Sch. Psychology Assn. (membership co-chair 1994—), Coun. Exceptional Children.

HALLER, ARCHIBALD ORBEN, sociologist, educator; b. San Diego, Jan. 15, 1926; s. Archie O. and Eleanor (Brizzee) H.; m. Hazel Laura Zimmerman, Feb. 15, 1947 (dec. 1985); children: Elizabeth Ann, Stephanie Lynn Bylin, William John; m. Maria Camila Omegna Rocha, Apr. 12, 1986 (div. 1987); m. Maria Cristina Del Peloso, Sept. 16, 1989; stepchildren: Graziella, Camila. B.A., Hamline U., 1950; M.A., U. Minn., 1951; Ph.D. (Univ. fellow), U. Wis., 1954. Assoc. prof., then prof. sociology Mich. State U., East Lansing, 1956-65; postdoctoral rschr. U. Wis., Madison, 1954-56, vis. prof., 1964-65, prof. sociology and rural sociology, 1965-94, emeritus prof., prin. investigator Brazil projects, 1994—; affiliated faculty Indsl. Rels. Rsch. Inst., U. Wis., Madison, 1965-94, Inst. Environ. Studies, U. Wis., Madison, 1990-94; Fulbright prof. sociology Rural U. of Brazil, 1962, U. Sao Paulo, 1974, 87-90, Fulbright travel grantee Univs. Sao Paulo, Brasilia, Pernambuco, Paraiba, and Ceara, Brazil, 1979; vis. prof. Brigham Young U., Provo, Utah, 1973; disting. vis. prof. rural sociology Ohio State U., 1982-83; vis. fellow Australian Nat. U., 1981; cons. Fed. U., Pernambuco, 1994, UNESCO, 1989; cons. on Amazonian rsch. Govt. of Brazil, 1991—; cons. on nat. social change Govt. of Brazil, 1994—; also others; organizer symposia on Brazil. Author: The Occupational Aspiration Scale: The Occupational Aspiration Theory, Structure and Correlates, 1963, 71, The Socioeconomic Macroregions of Brazil--1970, 1983; co-editor (with R.M. Hauser et al) Social Structure and Behavior: Essays in Honor of William Hamilton Sewell, 1982; editor spl. issues Luso-Brailian Rev.; author rsch. monographs and tech. articles; contbr. articles to profl. jours.; contbr. to theories of societal status allocation of the demographic structure of societal inequality and the socioeconomic development regions of Brazil. Mem. Mich. Com. on Mental Health Policies, 1961-62, Nat. Exec. Res., 1959-62; mem. sociology fellowship panel Coun. on Internat. Exch. Scholar, 1977-81. With USNR, 1943-46. Decorated with Order of Merit, Govt. of Brazil, 1981. Fellow AAAS, Am. Sociol. Assn.; mem. Internat. Rural Sociol. Assn., Internat. Sociol. Assn., L.Am. Rural Sociol. Assn., Midwest Sociol. Assn., Sociol. Rsch. Assn., L.Am. Studies Assn., N.Y. Acad. Scis., Rural Sociol. Soc. (pres. 1970-71, rep. AAAS 1973-86, Disting. Rural Sociologist 1990), Univ. Club, Sigma Xi, Gamma Sigma Delta, Phi Beta Kappa. Home: 529 Edward St Madison WI 53711-1207 Office: U Wis Coll Agr and Life Sci Brazil Projects Dept Rural Sociology Madison WI 53706

HALLETT, ROBERT STEVEN, minister, church fund raising executive; b. Millville, N.B., Can., Aug. 12, 1946; came to U.S., 1967; s. James Bleanis and Dorothy Margaret (Knox) H.; m. Carol Ruth Walker, Aug. 9, 1969; children: Stephanie, Heather, Robert Mark. Diploma, Bethany Bible Coll., 1967; BA in Theology, Ind. Wesleyan U., 1969; postgrad., Anderson Sch. Theology, 1969-71; MDiv, Asbury Theol. Sem., 1974. Ordained to Gospel ministry Wesleyan Ch., 1970. Min., evangelist Wesleyan & Friends Chs., Wis. & Ind, 1969-85; pub. rels. rep. Emery-Pratt Co., Owosso, Mich., 1977-79; sales rep. Dunn Water Conditioning, Marion, Ind., 1984-85; sr. cons. Cargill Assocs., Inc., Ft. Worth, 1985-89; planned giving rep. Wheaton (Ill.) Coll., 1989-90; pres., founder TLC Ministries, Inc., Dillsboro, Ind., 1990—; cons. in ch. fund raising. Contbg. author Wesleyan Advocate. V.p., sec., treas. Upland (Ind.) Area Ministrial Assn., 1981-84; zone ministrial chmn. Ind. North Dist., The Wesleyan Ch., 1979-81, Wis. Dist., 1974-76; camp bd., bd. ministrial standing Wis. Dist., 1974-76. Home and Office: 11279 US Hwy 50 Dillsboro IN 47018-8413

HALLSTRAND, SARAH LAYMON, denomination executive; b. Nashville, Oct. 25, 1944; d. Charles Martin and Lillian Christina (Stenberg) Laymon; m. John Peter Hallstrand, July 6, 1974; 1 child, Lillian Johanna. BA cum laude, Fla. So. Coll., 1966; ThM, Boston U., 1971; D of Ministry, McCormick Theol. Sem., 1985; grad., Coll. for Fin. Planning, Denver, 1990. Ordained Am. Baptist Ch., 1976. Dir. Christian edn. Trinity United Meth. Ch., Bradenton, Fla., 1968-70, Univ. United Meth. Ch., Syracuse, N.Y., 1971-73; assoc. min. First Bapt. Ch., Syracuse, 1973-78; pastor Oneida (N.Y.) Bapt. Ch., 1978-80; midwest rep. Mins. and Missionaries Benefit Bd., Am. Bapt. Chs., Oak Park, Ill., 1981—; leader retirement planning seminars Am. Bapt. Assembly, Green Lake, Wis., 1985—; mem. rep. Midwest Commn. on the Ministry, Valley Forge, Pa., 1985—; adj. prof., pastoral care McCormick Theol. Sem., Chgo., 1986—; adj. prof. retirement planning The Divinity Sch., Rochester, N.Y., 1994; vis. scholar Am. Bapt. Bd. Ednl. Ministries, Valley Forge, 1986-87; bd. dirs. Midwest Career Devel. Svc., Chgo., 1987—, chair, 1993—; bd. dirs. The Gathering Place Retreat Ctr., Gosport, Ind., 1988-95; mem. program com. and women in ministry rep. Roger Williams Fellowship, 1988-95; mem. nat. continuing edn. team Am. Bapt. Chs., Valley Forge, Pa., 1991—; conf. leader for women's spiritual renewal weekends; speaker in field. Contbg. author: Songs of Miriam: A Women's Book of Devotions, 1994; contbr. articles to profl. jours. Mem. Am. Bapt. Chs. Mins. Coun., Inst. Cert. Fin. Planners (cert.), Internat. Soc. Retirement Planners, Alpha Gamma Delta. Democrat. Office: Mins and Missionaries Benefit Bd PO Box 549 Oak Park IL 60303-0549

HALLWAS, JOHN EDWARD, English language educator; b. Waukegan, Ill., May 24, 1945; s. Emil Ferdinand and Ruth Edna (Wells) H.; m. Garnette Verna Stockstad, Jan. 3, 1965; children: John Darrin, Evan Bradley. BS in Edn., Western Ill. U., Macomb, 1967, MA, 1968; PhD, U. Fla., 1972. Grad. asst. Western Ill. U., Macomb, 1967-68, prof. English dept., 1970—. Author: Western Illinois Heritage, 1983, Illinois Literature: The 19th Century, 1986, Macomb: A Pictorial History, 1990, Spoon River Anthology: An Annotated Edition, 1992, others; editor Western Ill. Regional Studies, 1978-92; co-editor: Tales From Two Rivers book series, 1981—, Prairie State Books, 1987—; newspaper columnist Macomb Jour., 1981-84, Jacksonville (Ill.) Jour. Courier, 1984-85, 87-88. NDEA fellow U. Fla., Gainesville, 1968-70; recipient Faculty Svc. award Nat. U. Continuing Edn. Assn., 1981, Alumni Achievement award Western Ill. U., Macomb, 1983, MidAm. award, Soc. for Study of Midwestern Lit., 1994; named faculty lectr. Western Ill. U., Macomb, 1983, Disting. prof., 1992. Mem. Soc. for Study Midwestern Lit., Ill. State Hist. Soc. (adv. bd. 1990—), McDonough County Hist. Soc. (pres. 1981-83), Phi Beta Kappa, Phi Kappa Phi. Home: 8 Hickory Bow Macomb IL 61455-1018 Office: Western Ill U Libr Macomb IL 61455

HALPERIN, RICHARD GEORGE, data processing executive; b. Chgo., Apr. 5, 1948; s. Robert Charles and Phyllis Dorothy (Jewel) H.; m. Carolyn A'Della Bacino, Oct. 5, 1974; children: Nicole, Heidi, Erik. BSBA, Northwestern U., 1970. Mktg. mgr. IBM, Des Plaines, Ill., 1970-79; nat. sales mgr. Kast Metals, Shreveport, La., 1979-83; area dir. Wang Labs., Rolling Meadows, Ill., 1983-85; v.p. sales and svcs. System Software Assoc., Chgo., 1985-89; sr. v.p. Software Group XL Datacomp, Hinsdale, Ill., 1989-91; pres. Ex, Inc., Chgo., 1991-92; pres., CEO JBA Internat., Inc., Birmingham, Eng., 1992—, also bd. dirs.; bd. dirs. JBA Internat., Birmingham, Genesis, Glenview, Ill., Advanced Graphical Applications, Schaumburg, Am. Indian Svcs., Phoenix, Alliance, Anderson Cons., Chgo.; partnership CADDO Petroleum, Shreveport, La., 1981-86, BLM, Shreveport, 1981—. Named Top Dist. Mgr., Wang, Chgo., and Rome, 1984. Mem. Internat. Soc. Philos. Enquiry, Data Processing Mgrs. Assn., Info. Tech. Assn. Am., Northwestern Club of Chgo., Delta Upsilon, N Club Mens. Address: 641 Golf Rd Crystal Lake IL 60014-5650

HALPERN, JACK, chemist, educator; b. Poland, Jan. 19, 1925; came to U.S., 1962, naturalized; s. Philip and Anna (Sass) H.; m. Helen Peritz, June 30, 1949; children: Janice Henry, Nina Phyllis. BS, McGill U., 1946, PhD, 1949; DSc (hon.), U. B.C., 1986, McGill U., 1997. Postdoctorate overseas fellow NRC, U. Manchester, Eng., 1949-50; instr. chemistry U. B.C., 1950, prof., 1961-62; Nuffield Found. traveling fellow Cambridge (Eng.) U., 1959-60; prof. chemistry U. Chgo., 1962-71, Louis Block prof. chemistry, 1971-83, Louis Block Disting. Service prof., 1983—; vis. prof. U. Minn., 1962, Harvard, 1966-67, Calif. Inst. Tech., 1968-69, Princeton U., 1970-71, Max. Planck Institut, Mulheim, Fed. Republic Germany, 1983—, U. Copenhagen, 1978; Sherman Fairchild Disting. scholar Calif. Inst. Tech., 1979; guest scholar Kyoto U., 1981; Firth vis. prof. U. Sheffield, 1982, Phi Beta Kappa vis. scholar, 1990; R.B. Woodward vis. prof. Harvard U., 1991; numerous guest lectureships; cons. editor Macmillan Co., 1963-65, Oxford U. Press; cons. Am. Oil Co., Monsanto Co., Argonne Nat. Lab., IBM, Air Products Co., Enimont, Rohm and Haas; mem. adv. panel on chemistry NSF, 1967-70; mem. adv. bd. Am. Chem. Soc. Petroleum Research Fund, 1972-74; mem. medicinal chemistry sect. NIH, 1975-78, chmn., 1976-78; mem. chemistry adv. council Princeton U., 1982—; mem. univ. adv. com. Ency. Brit., 1985—; mem. chemistry vis. com. Calif. Inst. Tech., 1991—; chmn. German-Am. Acad. Coun., 1993—. Assoc. editor: Inorganica Chimica Acta, Jour. Am. Chem. Soc.; co-editor: Collected Accounts of Transition Metal Chemistry, vol. 1, 1973, vol. 2, 1977, Procs. NAS, Oxford Univ. Press, Internat. Series Monographs on Chemistry; mem. editl. bd. Jour. Organometallic Chemistry, Accounts Chem. Rsch., Catalysis Revs., Jour. Catalysis, Jour. Molecular Catalysis, Jour. Coord. Chemistry, Gazzetta Chimica Italiana, Organometallics, Catalysis Letters, Kinetics and Catalysis Letters; contbr. articles to Ency. Britannica, rsch. jours. Trustee Gordon Rsch. Confs., 1968-70; bd. govs. David and Arthur Smart Mus., U. Chgo., 1988—; bd. dirs. Ct. Theatre, 1989—. Recipient Young Author's prize Electrochem. Soc., 1953, award in catalysis Noble Metals Chem. Soc., London, 1976, Humboldt award, 1977, Richard Kokes award Johns Hopkins U., 1978, Willard Gibbs medal, 1986, Bailar medal U. Ill., 1986, Wilhelm von Hoffman medal German Chem. Soc., 1988, Chem. Pioneer's award Am. Inst. Chemists, 1991, Paracelsus prize Swiss Chem. Soc., 1992, Robert A. Welch award, 1994, Henry J. Albert award Internat. Precious Metals Inst., 1995, award in Organometallic Chem. Am. Chem. Soc., 1995. Fellow AAAS, Royal Soc. London, Am. Acad. Arts and Scis., Chem. Inst. Can., Royal Soc. Chemistry London (hon.), N.Y. Acad. Scis., Japan Soc. for Promotion Sci.; mem. NAS (fgn. assoc. 1984-85, mem. coun. 1990—, chmn. chemistry sect. 1991-93, v.p. 1993—), Am. Chem. Soc. (editl. bd. Advances in Chemistry series 1963-65, 78-81, chmn. inorganic chemistry 1985, award in inorganic chemistry 1968, award for disting. svc. in advancement of inorganic chemistry 1985, award in organometallic chemistry 1995), Max Planck Soc. (sci. mem. 1983—), Art Inst. Chgo., Renaissance Soc. (bd. dirs. 1985—), New Swiss Chem. Soc. (Paracelsus prize 1992), Sigma Xi. Home: 5630 S Dorchester Ave Chicago IL 60637-1722 Office: U Chgo Dept Chemistry Chicago IL 60637

HALPIN, MARY ELIZABETH, psychologist; b. Oak Park, ILl., June 4, 1951; d. Thomas Joseph and Rita Helen (Foley) H. BA, Marquette U., 1973, MEd, 1975, PhD, 1983. Lic. psychologist, Ill., Calif. Staff psychologist Milw. Children's Hosp., 1975-83; postdoctoral intern El Dorado County Mental Health Ctr., Placerville, Calif., 1983-84; psychologist Inst. for Motivational Devel., Lombard, Ill., 1985-88; psychologist, founder, gen. ptnr. Assocs. for Adolescent Achievement, Deerfield, Ill., 1989-94; psychologist pvt. practice, 1995—; appeared on Oprah Winfrey Show, 1995. T.v. appearance Oprah Winfrey Show, 1995. Chmn., mem. peer rev. com. Charter Barclay Hosp., Chgo., 1991-93. Mem. APA, AAUW, Ill. Psychol. Assn. (standing hearing panel ethics com. 1993, pub. rels. com. 1994). Office: 420 Lake Cook Rd Ste 109 Deerfield IL 60015-4914

HALSEMA, BARBARA ANN, geriatrics nurse; b. Keosawqua, Iowa, Dec. 18, 1959; d. Harold Lee and Mary Ann (Felty) Holsapple; m. Howard Lee Halsema, Apr. 18, 1984 (dec. Apr. 1994); children: Timothy Lee, Jaime Liann, Chad Moore. Student, Cen. Mo. State U., 1980-82, St. Luke's Sch. Nursing, St. Louis, 1982-83; AAS in Nursing, Parkland Coll., Champaign, Ill., 1984. RN, Ill.; cert. rehab. nurse, Ill.; bd. cert. disability analyst. Nurse psychiat. ICU St. Mary's Hosp., Decatur, Ill., 1984-92; DON Imboden Creek Living Ctr., Decatur, 1992-94, Ea. Star Nursing Home, Macon, Ill., 1994-96; br. mgr. Shaw Group, Decatur, 1996—; nurse cons. group home for devel. disabled. Recipient cert. of recognition Mental Health Assn. Macon County. Mem. Phi Eta Sigma. Home: 505 S Wall St Macon IL 62544-9602 Office: Shaw Group 3003 Pershing Ct Decatur IL 62526

HALSEY, JOHN ROBERT, archaeologist; b. L.A., Dec. 23, 1943; s. Norman E. and Harriett Elaine (Niemann) H.; m. Linda Ann Britton, Sept. 5, 1967; 1 child, Norman Edgar. BA in Anthropology, U. Mich., 1965, MA in Anthropology, 1967; PhD in Anthropology, U. N.C., 1976. Dir. salvage archaeology State Hist. Soc. Wis., Madison, 1969-76; state archaeologist Mich. Dept. State, Lansing, 1976—; rotating chair Underwater Salvage & Preserve com., Mich., 1980—, Conf. Mich. Archaeology, 1976—. Author: Beneath the Inland Seas-Michigan's Underwater Archaeological Heritage, 1990; contbr. articles to profl. jours. Recipient Disting. Alumni award Wayne Meml. H.S., 1979. Office: Mich Hist Ctr Dept State 717 W Allegan Lansing MI 48918

HALSO, ROBERT, real estate company executive. Pres. Pulte Homes of Michigan. Office: Pulte Homes of Michigan 315 S Woodwork Ste 204 Royal Oak MI 48067*

HALSTED, JUDITH ANN WYNN, educational consultant; b. Adrian, Mich., June 12, 1940; d. George Howard and Ruth Marian (Shriver) Wynn; m. David Wright Halsted, June 24, 1961; children: David George, Mark Jonathan. Student, Ohio Wesleyan U., 1958-60; BA, Mich. State U., 1962; MS, U. Ill., 1970. Cataloger Episcopal Sem. So. Austin, Tex., 1970-74; libr. Jr. High, Traverse City, Mich., 1975-77; libr. Pathfinder Sch., Traverse City, Mich., 1974-86, tchr. Latin, 1976-84, gifted program dir., 1977-82; tchr. external edn. N.W. Mich. Coll., Traverse City, Mich., 1985—; prin. Halsted Acad. Advisors, Traverse City, Mich., 1985—; cons. in field. Author: Guiding Gifted Readers, 1988, Some of My Best Friends Are Books, 1994; contbr. articles to profl. jours. Pres. Unitarian Universalist Fellowship, Traverse City, 1987-88, chair bldg. com., 1990-92; bd. dirs. LWV, 1988-91, chair libr. action com., 1989—; bd. dirs. AuSable River Property Owners Assn., 1992—, pres., 1994—; co-chair Citizens for Libraries, 1995—. Mem. ACA, Nat. Assn. for Gifted Children, Nat. Assn. Coll. Admission Counseling, Ind. Ednl. Cons. Assn., Mich. Alliance for Gifted Edn., Mich. Assn. Coll. Admission Counselors. Unitarian. Office: Halsted Academic Advisors 934 E 8th St Traverse City MI 49686-2750

HALTERMAN, MARTHA LEE, social services administrator, counselor; b. Poole, Ky., Feb. 4, 1940; d. Byron Lee and Mary Helen (Reinhardt) Melton; m. John David Halterman Jr., Apr. 26, 1968; 1 child, Rebecca Marie. B in Psychology and Sociology, Henderson (Ky.) C.C., 1975, Brescia Coll., 1977; M in Psychology, U. Evansville, Ind., 1980; cert. in mgmt., U. So. Ind., 1990. Cert. clin. social worker, social worker, marriage and family therapist, intervention tng. I and II, Am. Mgmt. Assn., dir. Rainbow for All Children. Office cashier J. J. Newberry Co., Henderson, 1958-63; regional trainer, office cashier C.I.T. Fin. Corp., Henderson, 1965-74; intern Redbanks Nursing Home, Henderson, 1975; dir. counseling and family svcs. Cath. Charities Bur., 1978—; supr. family & children svcs. Cath. Charities Bur. Family Life Diocese of Evansville, 1985-94; counseling and family svcs. dir., 1994—; coord. family life Cath. Charities Bur. Family Life Diocese of Evansville, 1987-94, coord. total svcs., 1993-94. Diocesan rep. Ind. Pro-Life Task Force, Indpls., 1987-94; sec. Domestic Violence Task Force, Evansville, 1980-88; bd. dirs. v.p. Birthright, Evansville, 1983-94; mem. Green River Regional Mental Health and Mental Retardation Bd., Owensboro, Ky., 1990-94. Mem. Evansville Psychol. Assn., Am. Assn. Marriage and Family Therapy (clin.). Roman Catholic. Home: 117 N Bobolink Run Henderson KY 42420-4701 Office: Cath Charities 123 NW 4th St Rm 603 Evansville IN 47708-1717

HALVA, ALLEN KEITH, legal publications consultant; b. Willow River, Minn., Jan. 23, 1913; s. Edward and Frances R. (Allen) H.; m. Julia M. Halva, Oct. 25, 1941; children—Barbara Jo Halva Kachmarzinski, Kurt Edward. Student Pasadena Jr. Coll. and Los Angeles City Coll., 1931-32; LL.B. cum laude, Calif. Assoc. Colls., 1935; LL.M., Los Angeles U. Applied Edn., 1950, S.J.D., 1951. Bar: Calif. 1936, Minn. 1941. With West Pub. Co., 1942-82; law book editor; ret.; legal publs. cons. Active Children's Home Soc., Sr. Coalition. Mem. State Bar Calif., Minn. State Bar Assn., Ramsey County Bar Assn., Am. Judicature Soc., Am. Security Council, Nat. Taxpayers Union, Am. Assn. Retired Persons, Am. Diabetes Assn., Met. Sr. Fedn. Presbyterian. Club: Hospitaller Order of St. John of Jerusalem. Home: 253 Warwick St Saint Paul MN 55105-2452

HALVERSON, HAROLD WENDELL, state legislator; b. Burke, S.D., Nov. 24, 1926; s. Reuben Arnold and Viola (Hauge) H.; m. Marie Christina Vosika, 1948 (dec.); children: James Arnold, Marilyn Marie, Cindy Lou, John Edward. Grad. high sch., Burke, S.D. Mem. S.D. Ho. of Reps., 1971-72; mem. S.D. State Senate, 1977-90, 92—, mem. judiciary, health and human svc. coms., mem. legis. procedure and state affairs com., pres. pro tempore, 1990—, minority leader, 1990—; fieldman Mo. Valley Mut. Ins., Burke, 1957-59; asst. claims supr. Milbank Mut. Ins. Co., 1959-60, 60-66, agy. dir., 1966—, bd. dirs., v.p., 1969-85; ins. exec. Mem. Gregory and Grant County Rep. Com., S.D.; mem. S.D. State Rep. Ctrl. Com., 1975—; chmn. bd. visitors Dakota Midwest Cancer Inst., McKennan Hosp. Mem. Mason (worshipful master Milbank chpt.), Eastern Star, Am. Legion (past comdr.), Commerce and Cmty. Club, Dale Carnegie Club. *

HAM, GEORGE ELDON, soil microbiologist, educator; b. Ft. Dodge, Iowa, May 22, 1939; s. Eldon Henry and Thelma (Ham) H.; m. Alice Susan Bormann, Jan. 11, 1964; children: Philip, David, Steven. BS, Iowa State U., 1961, MS, 1963, PhD, 1967. Asst. prof. dept soil sci. U. Minn., St. Paul, 1967-71, assoc. prof., 1971-77, prof., 1977-80; prof., head dept. agronomy Kans. State U., Manhattan, 1980-89; assoc. dean Coll. Agr., assoc. dir. Kans. Agr. Expt. Sta., 1989—; bd. dir. Kans. Crop Improvement Assn., Manhattan, Kans. Fertilizer and Chem. Inst., Topeka, Kans. Crops and Soils Industry Coun., Manhattan; cons. Internat. Atomic Energy Agy., Vienna, Austria, 1973-79. Assoc. editor Agronomy Jour., 1979-84. Contbr. articles to profl. jours. and biol. nitrogen fixation rsch. Asst. scoutmaster Indianhead coun. Boy Scouts Am., St. Paul, 1977-80; pres. North Star Little League, St. Paul, 1979-80. Sgt. U.S. Army, 1963-69. Fellow AAAS, Am. Soc. Agronomy, Soil Sci. Soc. Am.; mem. Crop Sci. Soc. Am. Sigma Xi, Gamma Sigma Delta, Phi Kappa Phi. Home: 2957 Nevada St Manhattan KS 66502-2355 Office: Kans State U Agr Expt Sta 113 Waters Hall Manhattan KS 66506-4000

HAMADA, ROBERT S(EIJI), economist, educator; b. San Francisco, Aug. 17, 1937; s. Horace T. and Maki G. H.; m. Anne Marcus, June 16, 1962; children: Matthew, Janet. BE, Yale U., 1959; SM, MIT, 1961, PhD, 1969. Economist Sun Oil Co., Phila., 1961-63; instr. U. Chgo., 1966-68, asst. prof. fin., 1968-71, assoc. prof., 1971-77, prof., 1977-89, Edward Eagle Brown prof., 1989-93, Edward Eagle Brown Disting. Svc. prof., 1993—, dir. Ctr. for Rsch. in Security Prices, 1980-85, dir. Ctr. Internat. Bus. Edn. and Rsch., 1992-93; dep. dean for faculty Grad. Sch. Bus. U. Chgo., 1985-90, dean, 1993—; vis. prof. univs. including London Grad. Sch. Bus. Studies, 1973, 79-80, UCLA, 1971, U. Wash., Seattle, 1971-72, U. B.C., Vancouver, Can., 1976; bd. dirs. A.M. Castle & Co., No. Trust Corp.; pub. dir. Chgo. Bd. Trade; cons. numerous fin. instns., banks, mfg., mgmt. cons., acctg. and law firms. Past assoc. editor: Jour. Fin., Jour. Fin. and Quantitative Analysis, Jour. Applied Corp. Fin.; cons. editor: Scott, Foresman & Co. fin. series; contbr. numerous articles to profl. jours. Bd. dirs. numerous neighborhood non-profit orgns., including Hyde Park Neighborhood Club, Chgo., Harper Ct. Found., Chgo., Hyde Park Co-op., U. Chgo. Lab Schs. Recipient First Outstanding Tchr. award Grad. Sch. Bus., U. Chgo., 1970, McKinsey Teaching prize, 1981; named to 8 Outstanding Bus. Sch. Profs., Fortune Mag., 1982; Sloan Found. fellow, 1959-61, Ford Found. fellow, 1963-65, Standard Oil Found. fellow, 1965-66; MIT scholar, 1959-61, Yale scholar, 1955-59. Mem. Am. Fin. Assn. (bd. dirs. 1982-85), Econometric Soc., Nat. Bur. Econ. Rsch. (bd. dirs., mem. investment and exec. coms.), Am. Econ. Assn. (investment com.), Inst. Mgmt. Scis. (investment com.), Tau Beta Pi. Office: U Chgo Grad Sch Bus 1101 E 58th St Chicago IL 60637-1511

HAMADE, THOMAS ALI, chemical engineering educator; b. Bint Jubail, Lebanon, July 4, 1952; came to U.S., 1971; s. Hajj Ali Mohammad and Hajjah Sikni (Machlab) H.; m. Lorri A. Basil, Sept. 15, 1977; children: Leila, Mohammad, Nadia, Hana, Fatimah, Mariam. BA in Chemistry, U. Detroit, 1975; MS in Phys. Chemistry, Wayne State U., 1978, PhDChemE, 1982. Qualified environ. profl. Rsch. asst. Wayne State U., Detroit, 1976-82; rsch. engr. Am. Filtrona, Richmond, Va., 1983-85; assoc. prof. U. Detroit Mercy, 1986—, chmn., 1989-93; environ. cons., Rochester, Mich., 1986; pres. Quantum Electronics Inc., Farmington Hills, Mich., 1986—. Contbr. articles to profl. jours. Trustee Mich. Edn. Coun.; bd. dirs. Mich. Islamic Acad., Ann Arbor, 1987-88. Rsch. grantee Fed. Mogul, 1987, EPA, 1994. Mem. AAAS, Am. Chem. Soc., Am. Inst. Chem. Engrs., Engring. Soc. of Detroit. Office: PO Box 19900 4001 W McNichols Rd Detroit MI 48219-0900

HAMANN, DERYL FREDERICK, lawyer, bank executive; b. Lehigh, Iowa, Dec. 8, 1932; s. Frederick Carl Hamann and Ada Ellen (Hollingsworth) Hamann Geis; m. Carrie Svea Rosen, Aug. 23, 1954 (dec. 1985); children: Karl E., Daniel A., Esther Hamann Brabec, Julie Hamann Bunderson; m. Eleanor Ramona Nelson Curtis, June 20, 1987. AA, Ft. Dodge Jr. Coll., Iowa, 1953; BS in Law, U. Nebr., 1956, JD cum laude, 1958. Bar: Nebr. 1958, U.S. Dist. Ct. Nebr. 1958, U.S. Ct. Appeals (8th cir.) 1958. Law clk. U.S. Dist. Ct. for Nebr., Lincoln, 1958-59; ptnr. Baird, Holm, McEachen, Pedersen, Hamann & Strasheim, Omaha, 1959—; chmn. adv. com. Supreme Ct. Nebr., Omaha, 1986-95; chmn. bd. or chmn. exec. com. seven Midwestern Cmty. Banks. Past pres. Omaha Estate Planning Coun. Mem. Nebr. Bar Found. (pres. 1981-86), Nebr. Assn. Bank Attys. (pres. 1985-86). Republican. Lutheran. Office: Great Western Securities Inc 10834 Old Mill Rd Omaha NE 68154

HAMANN, JAMES, manufacturing engineer; b. Scott, Iowa, Jan. 13, 1951. MBA, Iowa State U., 1974. Supr. French & Hecht, Walcot, Iowa, 1974-77; mfg. engr. Bendix Litton, Davonport, Iowa, 1978-91, Marley Pump, Davonport, 1991-93; MRB rep. McDonnell Douglas, Iowa, 1989-91. Home: 3215 S 25th Ave Eldridge IA 52748-9306

HAMANN, NORMAN LEE, SR., architect; b. Gypsum, Ohio, Jan. 27, 1936; s. Leonard Roland and Agatha Gertrude (Bowen) H.; m. Berta Steigenberger, July 25, 1959 (dec.); children: Norman L. Jr., Yvonne Marie Hamann-Moulton, Richard John, Robert James, Thomas M.A.; m. Laura Anne Maxson, March 13, 1993. BA in Architecture, U. Mich., 1959. Registered architect Mich., Ind., Mass., Ill., Fla. Designer, draftsman Louis C. Kingscott & Assocs., Inc., Kalamazoo, Mich., 1960-63; project architect Richard Prince Architect, Kalamazoo, 1963-66; assoc., project architect Noordhoek & Scurlock, Architects, Kalamazoo, 1966-68; assoc. G.E. Diekema & Assocs., Kalamazoo, 1968-77; v.p. Diekema/Hamann/Architects, Inc., Kalamazoo, 1977-90, pres., 1990—; appt. to Mich. Bd. Architects by Gov., 1992. Prin. works include West Mich. Cancer Ctr., Kalamazoo, Mich. State U. Kalamazoo Ctr. for Med. Studies, Univ. Med. Ctr., Kalamazoo, Sheraton Hotel, Kalamazoo, Emergency Svcs. Facility, City of Galesburg, Mich., Community Libr., Parchment, Mich., Argos East Office Bldg., Kalamazoo. Mem. Interfaith Forum on Religion, Art and Architecture, Comstock Twp. Zoning Bd., 1963-71, Comstock Twp. Bldg. Bd. Appeals, 1967—, Comstock Twp. Planning Commn., 1971-85, Comstock Zoning Bd. Appeals, 1975-81, 82-88; bd. dirs. Cath. Family Svcs., Kalamazoo, 1983-87, Mich. Archtl. Found., Detroit, 1984-89; v.p., bd. dirs. Comstock Community Ctr. Mem. AIA (sec. western Mich. chpt. 1979-80, v.p. western Mich. chpt. 1981, pres. western Mich. chpt. 1983, bd. dirs. 1984-85, Mem. of Yr. 1985), Mich. Soc. Architects (bd. dirs. 1984-88, sec. 1985, v.p. 1986, pres. 1987, Gold medal award 1990). Office: Diekema/Hamann/Architects 5106 Lovers Ln Kalamazoo MI 49002-1558

HAMBLET, MICHAEL JON, lawyer, city official, former state official; b. Rapid City, S.D., Aug. 10, 1940; s. Herbert F. and Helen F. (Tice) H.; m. Maureen Anne Murphy, Nov. 26, 1966 (div. May 1986); children: Tracy Anne, Michael Jon; m. Mary K. Harvick, Aug. 12, 1995. B.A., U. Ill., 1962; m. Mary Katherine Harvick, Aug. 12, 1995; J.D., U. Mich., 1965. Bar: Ill. 1965. Assoc. Mayer, Brown, Chgo., 1965-69; ptnr. Herrick, NcNeill, McElroy & Peregrine, Chgo., 1969-78, 82-83, Greenberg, Keele, Lunn & Aronberg, Chgo., 1979-81; Hamblet, Casey, Oremus, & Vacin (formerly Mathewson, Hamblet & Casey), Chgo., 1983—; mem. Ill. State Bd. Elections, Chgo. and Springfield, 1978—, chmn., 1979-81, 83-85, vice chmn., 1981-83; commr. Chgo. Bd. Elections, 1987-90, chmn. 1990—; mem. Ill. Bldg. Authority, Chgo., 1973-78, chmn., 1977-78. Mem. Cook County Econ. Devel. Adv. Com., 1982-87. Home: 1322 N Sutton Pl Chicago IL 60610-2008 Office: Hamblet Casey Oremus Vacin 75 E Wacker Dr Chicago IL 60601-3708

HAMBLEY, DELBERT EUGENE, real estate developer; b. Allegan County, Mich., July 28, 1933; s. George Verne Sr. and Ruth Irene (Sharp) H.; m. Shirley Ann Garn, Dec. 20, 1952; children: Colleen Sue, Michael Eugene, Sharon Ann. BA, Greenville Coll., 1953; MEd, Western Mich. U., 1960. Tchr. Sheridan (Mich.) H.S., 1953-57, Plainwell (Mich.) Jr. H.S., 1957-59; prin. East Cooper Elem. Sch., Kalamazoo, 1959-61; tchr. Portage (Mich.) Pub. Schs., 1961-88; builder, apartment mgr. Kalamazoo, 1958-91; developer Hambley-Beyer Devel., Kalamazoo, 1993—. Plat com. mem. Tex. Township, Kalamazoo, 1994—. Republican. Mem. Free Methodist Ch. Home and Office: 5957 Woodsong Way Kalamazoo MI 49009-8206

HAMBURG, ROGER PHILLIP, political science and public affairs educator; b. Davenport, Iowa, June 19, 1934; s. Abe and Geraldine (Wulp) H.; m. Sally Schulman, Aug. 29, 1959; children: Phillip, Ruth, Joel. AB, U. Mich., 1956; AM, U. Chgo., 1958; PhD, U. Wis., 1965. Asst. prof. Eastern Wash. U., Cheney, 1965-66, Marquette U., Milw., 1966-69, U. Wis.-Parkside, Kenosha, 1969-71; assoc. prof. dept. polit. sci. Ind. U., South Bend., 1971-79, prof., 1979-92; prof. sch. pub. and environ. affairs Ind. U., South Bend, 1992—; program dir. Michiana World Affairs Coun., South Bend, 1991—. With USAR, 1961-62. Home: 1922 Briarway South Bend IN 46614-1630 Office: Indiana U 1700 Mishawaka Ave South Bend IN 46634-1408

HAMEISTER, LAVON LOUETTA, farm manager, social worker; b. Blairstown, Iowa, Nov. 27, 1922; d. George Frederick and Bertha (Anderson) Hameister; B.A., U. Iowa, 1944; postgrad. N.Y. Sch. Social Work, Columbia, 1945-46, U. Minn. Sch. Social Work, summer 1952; M.A., U. Chgo., 1959. Child welfare practitioner Fayette County Dept. Social Welfare, West Union, Iowa, 1946-56; dist. cons. services in child welfare and pub. assistance Iowa Dept. Social Welfare, Des Moines, 1956-58, dist. field rep., 1959-64, regional supr., 1964-65, supr., specialist supervision, adminstrn. Bur. Staff Devel., 1965-66, chief Bur. Staff Devel., 1966-68; chief div. staff devel. and tng. Office Dep. Commr., Iowa Dept. Social Services, 1968-72, asst. dir. Office Staff Devel., 1972-79, coordinator continuing edn., 1979-86; now mgr. Hameister Farm, Blairstown, Iowa. Active in drive to remodel, enlarge Oelwein (Iowa) Mercy Hosp., 1952; active in devel. mental health ctrs. in N.E. Iowa in 1950's. Mem. Bus. and Profl. Women's Club (chpt. sec. 1950-52), Am. Assn. U. Women, Nat. Assn. Social Workers (chpt. sec.-elect 1958-59), Am. Pub. Welfare Assn., Iowa Welfare Assn., Acad. Cert. Social Workers. Lutheran.

HAMEL, LOUIS REGINALD, systems analysis consultant; b. Lowell, Mass., July 23, 1945; s. Wilfred John and Angelina Lucienne (Paradis) H.; AA, Kellogg Community Coll., 1978; m. Roi Anne Roberts, Mar. 24, 1967 (dec.); 1 child, Felicia Antoinette; m. Anne Louise Staup, July 2, 1972; children: Shawna Michelle, Louis Reginald III. Retail mgr. Marshalls Dept. Stores, Beverly, Mass., 1972-73; tech. service rep. Monarch Marking Systems, Framingham, Mass., 1973-74; employment specialist Dept. Labor, Battle Creek, Mich., 1977-78; v.p. corp. Keith Polygraph Cons. and Investigative Service, Inc., Battle Creek, Mich., 1978-79; indsl. engr., engine components div. Eaton Corp., Battle Creek, Mich., 1979-82; tooling and process engr. Kelley Tech. Services, Battle Creek, Mich., Clark Equipment Inc., 1983-84; tooling and mfg. engr., mfg. mgr. Trans Guard Industries Inc., Angola, Ind., 1983-85; facilitator employee involvement, safety dir., workers compensation adminstr., tng. dir. Wohlert Corp., Lansing, Mich., 1985—; systems analysis cons., 1975—. Mem. Calhoun County Com. on Employment of Handicapped, Battle Creek, Mich., 1977-78; mem. Capital Area Labor Mgmt. Com., 1986—. With USN, 1963-71, Vietnam. Recipient Services to Handicapped award Internat. Assn. Personnel in Employment Security, Mich. chpt., 1978. Mem. VFW, Nat. Geog. Soc., Mich. Assn. Concerned Vets. (dir.), Nat. Assn. Concerned Vets. Democrat. Roman Catholic. Home and Office: 12240 Assyria Rd Bellevue MI 49021-9607

HAMELMANN, NORMA RUTH, secondary education educator; b. Alton, Ill., June 14, 1944; d. Robert LeeRoy and Doris Mae (Schwensen) H. BS in Math. Edn., So. Ill. U., 1967, MS in Math. Edn., 1974. Cert. secondary tchr., 6-12, Ill. Tchr., math. Roxana (Ill.) Jr. High, 1967-78, Roxana Jr.-Sr. High, 1978-85, Roxana High Sch., 1985—. Mem. NEA, Nat. Coun. Tchrs. Math., Ill. Edn. Assn., Ill. Coun. Tchrs. Math., Roxana Edn. Assn. (2d v.p. 1972-73), Women of Moose (recorder Alton 1991-94, treas. 1994-95, star recorder chmn. 1995-96), Zonta (treas. Alton-Wood River 1987-89, 2d v.p. 1993-94, 1st v.p. 1994-95, pres. 1995-96). Home: 404 Main St Alton IL 62002-1746

HAMERSLEY, SHARON LEE, academic advisor, church musician; b. Eustis, Fla., Oct. 13, 1947; 1 child. BA, Ohio State U., 1969, MA, 1970. Acad. advisor Ohio State U., Columbus, 1977—, asst. to chair undergrad. recruitment steering com., 1990-93, trainer sexual harassment workshop, 1995—, trainer new academic advisors, 1995—. Mem., chair social ministry com. Holy Trinity Luth. Ch., Columbus, 1992—; prse. congl. organist, choir dir. com., chair del. U. Luth. Chapel, Columbus, 1968-92. Mem. ASTD, Nat. Assn. Advisers in the Health Professions, Ohi State U. Alumni Assn. Office: Ohio State U 164 W 17th Ave Columbus OH 43210

HAMES, GARY LAWRENCE, insurance company executive; b. N.Y., Oct. 26, 1945; s. Lambert Lewis and Gloria Marion (McNally) H.; m. Deborah Lynne Sales, Nov. 28, 1970; children: Jason, Indy, Kristin. BS in Phys. Edn., U. Fla., 1969. Agt. Northwestern Mut. Life, Denver, 1973-78, dir. agy. devel., 1978-80; asst. regional dir. Northwestern Mut. Life, Milw., 1980-85; gen agt. Northwestern Mut. Life, ShawneeMission, Kans., 1985—. Pres. Northwestern Group Mktg. Svcs. of Kansas City, Inc., 1986-88; bd. dirs. GAMC, 1988—, pres. 1991—. Sgt. USAF, 1969-73. Recipient Gen. Agts. Achievement award, 1991. Mem. Gen. Agt. and Mgrs. Assn. (bd. dirs. 1988, Mgmt. award 1986-93), Nat. Assn. Life Underwriters (Quality award 1973-88), Kansas City C. of C., Gen. Agts. Assn. (exec. sec., treas. Northwestern Mutual Life 1993-96). Republican. Lutheran. Home: 12810 Walmer St Overland Park KS 66209-3611 Office: Northwestern Mut Life 4330 Shawnee Mission Pky Shawnee Mission KS 66205-2507

HAMILL, ROBERT L., biochemical research advisor; b. Youngstown, Ohio, Mar. 13, 1927; s. James Edwin and Jane Marie (Hope) H.; m. Meritta Ann Floyd, June 27, 1953 (div. 1975); children: Sebette Ann, Sheree Hope Hamill; m. Beverly Ann Pruett, Sept. 25, 1976. Student, Youngstown (Ohio) State U., 1947-48; BS in Chemistry, Ohio U., 1950; MS in Biochemistry, Mich. State U., 1953, PhD, 1955. Rsch. asst. Mich. State U., E. Lansing, 1950-55; sr. biochemist Lilly Rsch. Labs., Indpls., 1955-64, rsch. scientist, 1964-69, rsch. assoc., 1969-83, rsch. advisor, 1983-91; chmn. Intersci. Conf. on Antimicrobial Agts. and Chemotherapy. Editor Jour. Antibiotics, 1975-91, Antimicrobial Agents and Chemotherapy, 1975-85; contbr. numerous articles to profl. jours.; holder of over 70 patents in field. Served with USN, 1945-47, 51-53. Mem. AAAS, Am. Chem. Soc., Am. Soc. Microbiology, N.Y. Acad. Scis., Soc. for Indsl. Microbiology, Sertoma Club, Phi Beta Kappa, Alpha Chi Sigma. Republican. Presbyterian. Home: 617 Brookview Dr Greenwood IN 46142-1802

HAMILTON, DARRIN TOD, city prosecutor; b. Des Moines, Dec. 18, 1965; s. Douglas J. and Betty J. (Hess) H.; m. Mary I. Probst, June 18, 1994. BS, U. Iowa, 1987; JD, Drake U., Des Moines, 1990. Bar: Iowa, 1990. Libr. aide Drake Law Libr., Des Moines, 1987-88; law clk. Ronald L. Wheeler, Des Moines, 1988; adminstrv. law intern Iowa Civil Rights Commn., Des Moines, 1989; prosecutor intern Warren County Attys. Office, Indianola, Iowa, 1989; law clk. Iowa Dept. Justice, Des Moines, 1989-90, G. Richard Apland, Ankeny, Iowa, 1990; asst. city atty./dir. human rels. commn. City of Council Bluffs, Iowa, 1990—. Bd. dirs. Regional Exec. Coun. on Civil Rights, Inc., Kansas City, Mo., 1990—, Cmty. Housing Resource Bd., Inc., Council Bluffs, 1991-93; mem. Mayor's Task Force on Youth, Council Bluffs, 1991—, Human Svcs. Adv. Coun., Council Bluffs, 1991—. Fellow Internat. Assn. Lions Club; mem. ABA, Iowa Bar Assn., Iowa Assn. Human Rights Agencies (dir. 1990—). Office: City of Council Bluffs Legal Dept 209 Pearl St Council Bluffs IA 51503

HAMILTON, DUANE LEE, health care executive; b. Greenville, Ohio, Dec. 22, 1954; s. Eldean Lee and Mary Louise (Strobel) H.; m. Deborah Jean Greenwood, Oct. 15, 1983; children: Andrew, Austin, Bryce, Claire. BS, Bowling Green State U., 1977; MS, So. Ill. U., 1979. Asst. residence hall mgr. Purdue U., West Lafayette, Ind., 1979-83; asst. dean students Culinary Inst. Am., Hyde Park, N.Y., 1983-88; dir. residential svcs. Oberlin (Ohio) Coll., 1988-93; facilty svcs. dir. Kendal at Oberlin, 1993—. Home: 363 S Professor St Oberlin OH 44074

HAMILTON, JAMES EUGENE, publishing executive, writer; b. Springfield, Mo., Dec. 30, 1947; s. Harold Eugene and Hazel (Daly) H.; m. Deann Joy Galbavy, Mar. 6, 1971 (div. Sept. 1994); children: Angela (dec.), Melissa; m. Martha Jo Glazier, Dec. 9, 1995. BA, Southwest Mo. State U., 1975. Editor SMSU Southwest Standard, Springfield, Mo., 1970-71, Seymour Johnson Scope, Seymour Johnson AFB, N.C., 1971-74, Bolivar (Mo.) Herald Free Press, 1976-77; pub., editor Buffalo (Mo.) Reflex, 1978—. Author: River of Used To Be, 1994. Pres. Dallas County Fair, Buffalo, 1985. Mem. Nat. Assn. Ag. Journalists, Mo. Writers Guild, Western Writers Am., Ozark Press Assn. (pres. 1994), Ozark Writers League (pres. 1994-96), Buffalo (Mo.) Kiwanis (pres. 1981), Buffalo (Mo.) C. of C. (pres. 1981, 92). Office: Buffalo Reflex PO Box 770 Buffalo MO 65622

HAMILTON, JAMES JOSEPH, orthopedic surgeon, educator; b. Chgo., Dec. 10, 1945; s. Gene Charles and Eleanor (Fordon) H.; m. Linda Kay Ziemer, Nov. 10, 1979; children: Elizabeth, Andrew, Peter. BA, Northwestern U., 1967; MD, Med. Coll. Wis., 1971, MS, 1976. Intern in surgery Parkland Hosp., Dallas, 1971-72; resident Med. Coll. Wis., Milw., 1972-76; chmn. dept. orthopaedic surgery. Author 3 books on orthopedic surgery; contbr. articles to profl. jours. Mem. advisor Nat. Ski Patrol, Midwest region, 1968—. Maj. U.S. Army, 1976-80. Recipient Outstanding Community Svc. ARC, 1990. Fellow ACS, Am. Acad. Orthopaedic Surgeons (councilor 1989-94); mem. AMA, Acad. Orthopaedic Soc., Mo. State Orthopaedic Assn. (pres. 1988-89), Mid. Ctr. States Orthopaedic Soc. Office: Truman Med Ctr 2301 Holmes St Kansas City MO 64108-2640

HAMILTON, JEAN CONSTANCE, judge; b. St. Louis, Nov. 12, 1945; d. Aubrey Bertrand and Rosemary (Crocker) H. A.B., Wellesley Coll., 1968; J.D., Washington U., St. Louis, 1971; LL.M., Yale U., 1982. Bar: Mo. 1971. Atty. Dept. of Justice, Washington, 1971-73, asst. U.S. atty., St. Louis, 1973-78; atty. Southwestern Bell Telephone Co., St. Louis, 1978-81; judge 22d Jud. Circuit, State of Mo., St. Louis, 1982-88; judge Mo. Ct. Appeals (ea. dist.), 1988-90; U.S. dist. judge U.S. Dist. Ct. (ea. dist.) Mo., 1990—, chief judge, 1995—. Mem. ABA, Bar Assn. Met. St. Louis, Women Lawyers Assn. Met. St. Louis, Nat. Assn. Women Judges, Am. Law Inst. Episcopalian. Office: US Court and Custom House 1114 Market St Fl 1 Saint Louis MO 63101-2043

HAMILTON, LEE HERBERT, congressman; b. Daytona Beach, Fla., Apr. 20, 1931; m. Nancy Ann Nelson, Aug. 21, 1954; children: Tracy Lynn, Deborah Lee, Douglas Nelson. AB, DePauw U., 1952, hon. degree; scholar, Goethe U., Germany, 1952-53; JD, Ind. U., 1956; hon. degree, Hanover Coll., Detroit Coll. Law, Ball State U., U. S. Ind., Wabash Coll., Union Coll., Ind. U., Am. Univ., Marian Coll., Suffolk U. Mem. 89th-104th Congresses from 9th Dist. Ind., Washington, 1965—; ranking minority mem. House com. internat. rels.; former chmn. select. com. to investigate covert arms transactions with Iran U.S. Congress, mem. joint econ. com., former chmn. fgn. affairs com., former co chair Joint com. Orgn. Congress, former chmn. Ho. intelligence com., former chmn. Ho. com. investigate Oct. surprise; v.p. congrl. del. to U.S. Group Interparliamentary Union. Democrat. Office: US House of Reps 2314 Rayburn House Office Bldg Washington DC 20515

HAMILTON, MARK ALAN, electrical engineer; b. Amarillo, Tex., Aug. 19, 1960; s. Larry Don and June Rae (Jones) H. BSEE, Kans. State U., 1984. Electronics engr. U.S. Army Comm.-Electronics Command, Ft. Monmouth, N.J., 1984-90, U.S. Army CECOM, Ft. Leavenworth, Kans., 1990—. Mem. Tau Beta Pi, Eta Kappa Nu. Roman Catholic. Home: 1434 Columbia Ave Leavenworth KS 66048-3140

HAMILTON, RANDALL L., personnel administrator; b. Cleve., Aug. 21, 1947. BA, Ohio U., 1969. Credit analyst Union Commerce Bank, Cleve., 1969-74; pers. dir. B.F. Goodrich, Cleve., Columbus, Ohio, 1983-85; sales pers. mgr. Premier Ind. Corp., Cleve., 1974-83; v.p. Copeland/Wilcox Inc., Columbus, 1986—; mem. Bus. Adv. Coun., Columbus, Ohio, 1992-95. Tutor Dublin City Schs., Columbus, 1994—; girls soccer coach Dublin Youth Assn., Columbus, 1992. Mem. Dublin C. of C., Allied Therapy Assn. (bd. dirs. 1994—), Columbus Area Profl. Resource (past pres. 1994). Methodist. Office: Copeland Wilcox Inc 3011 Bethel Rd Ste 201 Columbus OH 43220-2272

HAMILTON, RICHARD ALFRED, university administrator, educator; b. Pitts., Dec. 22, 1941; s. Robert Curtis and Dorothy Katherine (Sexauer) H.; BA, Otterbein Coll., 1965; MBA, Bowling Green State U., 1968; D in Bus. Adminstrn. (Univ. fellow 1968-71, Marathon Oil Co. dissertation fellow 1972), Kent State U., 1973. Prodn. rate analyst dept. indsl. engring. RCA, Findlay, Ohio, 1966-67; computer sys. analyst dept. market rsch. Marathon Oil Co., Findlay, 1967-68; tchg. fellow Coll. Bus. Adminstrn. Kent State U., 1968-71; assoc. prof. direct mktg. U. Mo., Kansas City, 1971—; pres. Mission Woods Cons., Inc., 1977—; cons. U.S. Senate Permanent Subcom. on Investigation, 1973-74, Midwest Rsch. Inst. and Office of Tech. Assessment of U.S. Congress, 1974-75; spkr. to profl. orgns. Recipient Cray Faculty award U. Mo., 1987; Robert B. Clarke Outstanding Direct Mktg. Educator award Direct Mktg. Ednl. Found., 1994. Mem. Am. Mktg. Assn., Direct Mktg. Assn., Beta Gamma Sigma. Methodist. Author: (with David R. Bywaters) How to Conduct Association Surveys, 1976, Tourism U.S.A.-Marketing Tourism, Vol. 3, 1978; Quantitative Direct Response Market Segmentation, 1989, Readings and Cases in Direct Marketing, NTC Business Books, Helzberg Diamonds-A Retailer's Use of Direct Marketing to Generate Store Traffice, 1995; contbr. articles to profl. jours. Home: 5306 Mission Woods Rd Shawnee Mission KS 66205-2008 Office: U Mo Bloch Sch Adminstrn Kansas City MO 64110

HAMILTON, ROBERT APPLEBY, JR., insurance company executive; b. Boston, Feb. 20, 1940; s. Robert A. and Alice Margaret (Dowdall) H.; m. Ellen Kuhlen, Aug. 13, 1966; children: Jennifer, Robert Appleby III, Elizabeth. Student Miami U. (Ohio), 1958-62. With Travelers Ins. Co., Hartford, Conn., Portland, Maine and Phila., 1962-65; with New Eng. Mut. Life Ins. Co., various locations, 1965-90, regional pension rep., Boston, 1968-71, regional mgr., Chgo., 1972-83, sr. pension cons., 1983-90; mktg. and fin. cons. Snowbeck Enterprises, Inc., Geneva, Ill., 1990—. Producer Sta. WCTV; mem. Republican Town Com., Wenham, Mass., 1970-72, Milton Twp., Ill., 1973-75; mem. Wenham Water Commn., 1970-72. C.L.U.; chartered fin. cons. Mem. Midwest Pension Conf. (chmn. 1989-90), Am. Soc. Pension Actuaries (assoc.), Am. Soc. C.L.U.s, Am. Assn. Fin. Planners, Profit Sharing Council Am., Chgo. Coun. Fgn. Rels., Alpha Epsilon Rho. Republican. Home: 2 S 110 Hamilton Ct Wheaton IL 60187 Office: Snowbeck Enterprises Geneva IL 60134

HAMILTON, THOMAS WOOLMAN, publishing company executive; b. Somerville, N.J., Aug. 25, 1948; s. John Wesley and Evelyne (Woolman) H.; m. Nancy Beth Familo, June 10, 1970; children: Susan Elizabeth, Catherine Anne. BA, Denison U., 1970; MBA, Rollins Coll., 1972. V.p. Continental Bank, Cleve., 1972-76; exec. v.p., gen. mgr. Am. Lawyers Co., Cleve. and N.Y.C., 1976—. Contbr. articles to profl. jours. Active Rep. Nat. Com.; bd. dirs. Morris Weissance Found., 1979—. Capt. USAF, 1972. Mem. Comml. Law League Am. (bd. dirs. 1983-86, bd. dirs. fund for pub. edn. 1986-89), Am. Comml. Collectors Assn., Assn. Lawlist Pubs. (pres. 1982-83, 89-90), Greater Cleve. Growth Assn., Westwood Country Club, Cleve. Yachting Club, Midday Club. Office: Am Lawyers Co 853 Westpoint Pky Cleveland OH 44145-1532

HAMILTON, VIRGINIA MAE, mathematics educator, consultant; b. Winchester, Ind., Apr. 15, 1946; d. Charles and Mildred Alene (Horseman) Campbell; m. William Earl Hamilton, Dec. 27, 1974; 1 child, Michelle Annette. BS in Math., Ball State U., 1968, MA in Math., 1974. Math. tchr. Osborn High Sch., Manassas, Va., 1968-71; grad. asst., math. Ball State U., Muncie, Ind., 1971-74, math. tchr., 1977-87, dir. testing and placement, dir. Math. Learning Ctr., 1984-87; math. tchr. WesDel High Sch., Gaston, Ind., 1974-76; math. prof. Shawnee State U., Portsmouth, Ohio, 1987—; cons. placement testing several univs., Calif., Ind., Ohio, 1986—; cons. in-svc. Scioto County Schs., Portsmouth, 1989—; mentor-tchr. Minority Edn. Advs., Muncie, 1985-87; presenter Ohio Acad. Sci., Portsmouth, 1988—; assessment chair nat. project to reform Devel. Math., 1992—; bd. dirs. Project Discovery South Region, 1993—, steering com., 1994—; spkr. at various confs. on math. and assessment. Author: Testbank for Fundamentals of Mathematics, 1989, Testbank for Elementary Algebra, 1989, Testbank for Intermediate Algebra, 1990, Prepared Tests for Elementary Algebra, 1990, (computer software) Dose Calc, 1984, Arithmetic Skill Builder, 1987, Instructors Manual and Testbank for Intermediate Algebra, 1995; editor: (testbanks) Keedy-Bittinger Worktext Trilogy, 1986, Intermediate Algebra, 1986. Mem. NEA, Nat. Coun. Tchrs. Math., Nat. Assn. Devel. Educators (chmn. com. on math. placement 1990—, co-chair math SPIN 1994—), Math. Assn. Am., Ohio Coun. Tchrs. Math., South Ctrl. Ohio Coun. Tchrs. Math. (bd. dirs. 1993—), Ohio Assn. Devel. Educators (chmn. spl. interest group 1989—, treas. 1992—, Svc. award 1992), Ohio Edn. Assn., Am. Math. Assn. 2-Yr. Colls., Am. Assn. Higher Edn. Office: Shawnee State U 940 2nd St Portsmouth OH 45662-4347

HAMILTON, WILLIAM MILTON, manufacturing executive; b. Phila., Feb. 5, 1925; s. Louis Valentine and Elsie Marie (Walter) H.; m. Edith Marie Busey, June 9, 1947; children: Barbara Marie, William Milton Jr., Patricia Ann. B.S. in Indsl. Mgmt., Ga. Inst. Tech., 1947. Asst. br. mgr. Swift & Co., Atlanta, 1947-48; treas. R.K. Price Co., Fayetteville, Ga., 1954-55; br. mgr. N.Y. Wire Cloth Co., Atlanta, 1955-56; from ops. mgr. to pres. Premier Indsl. Corp., Cleve., 1956-91, also bd. dirs.; dir., cons. Premier Indsl. Corp., 1991-96; spl. asst. to chmn., 1996—. Served to lt. USN, 1943-46, 48-54. Mem. Elyria Country Club (Ohio), Jonathan Landing Golf Club (Fla.). Methodist. Home: 2222 Pebblebrook Cleveland OH 44145-4378 Office: Premier Indsl Corp 4500 Euclid Ave Cleveland OH 44103-3736

HAMLIN, ROBERT J., stockbroker; b. St. Paul, Jan. 6, 1943; m. Judith I. Neuman, Feb. 8, 1964; children: David, Roberta, Ted, Andrew, Laura. Asst. v.p. 1st Bank Sys., Mpls., 1963-75; with lease divsn., accounts receivable, inventory purchasing Space Ctr. Co., St. Paul, 1975-81; stockbroker Dain Bosworth Inc., Edina, Minn., 1983—. Mem. Pro Life Activists, 1988—. Recipient award Youth Hockey. Republican. Roman Catholic. Home: 824 3rd Ave S South Saint Paul MN 55075-3007 Office: Dain Bosworth Inc Ste 250 6600 France Ave S Edina MN 55435-1800

HAMLIN, ROGER EUGENE, urban planning educator, economic and financial analyst; b. Oklahoma City, July 6, 1945; s. George Benjamin and Olive Ruth (Bettgar) H.; m. Patricia Ann Edwards, June 1, 1968; children: Eric, Amanda. BA, Hamilton Coll., 1967; M of Regional Planning, Syracuse U., 1971, PhD, 1973. Planner Ottawa Regional Planning Commn., Port Clinton, Ohio, 1967, A.J. Reed Planning Cons., Syracuse, N.Y., 1967-68, N.Y. Office Planning Services, Syracuse, 1968; investment programmer Ministry Housing and Urban Devel., Santiago, Chile, S.A., 1968-70; instr. Univ. Coll., Syracuse, 1970-71; legis. asst. N.Y. Senate, Albany, 1971-72; adminstr., asst. prof. Community Planning and Devel. Program Columbus (Ga.) Coll., 1972-74; prof., program dir. Mich. State U., East Lansing, 1974—; pres., chmn. bd. Proaction Inst., Inc., East Lansing, 1978—, Transnovo, Inc., East Lansing, 1980—; treas., bd. dirs. Red Cedar Cert. Devel. Corp., East Lansing, 1982—; asst. treas., bd. dirs. East Lansing Housing Corp., 1992—; co-chair Japanese nat. rsch. com. on pub./pvt. partnerships Housing and Urban Devel. Corp. of Japan, 1988-90; mem. water quality task force Tri-County Regional Planning Commn., Lansing, 1977; vis. prof. Tokyo Sci. U., Japan, 1991; chairperson econ. devel. response team State of Mich., 1993-94. Author: Design for the Delivery of Human Resource Services, 1979, Hydropower Redevelopment, 1983, Wind Power Development, 1983, Financing Dam Safety Programs, 1984, Guide to Graduate Education in Urban and Regional Planning, 3d edit., 1978, Creating an Economic Development Action Plan, 1990. Mem. adv. com. on health status Mich. Mid-South Health System Agy., Mason, Mich., 1977, East Lansing Transp. Commn., 1984-90. Recipient Trade Union Leadership Commn. Jack Edwards award, Detroit, 1980, White House Recognition award, Washington, 1980, Nat. Recognition award Am. Inst. Cert. Planners, 1993. Mem. Am. Planning Assn. (sec. Mich. chpt. 1977, Univ. liaison officer 1988—, Nat. Planning award 1992), Am. Chi Psi, Phi Beta Delta. Home: 1240 Marigold Ave East Lansing MI 48823-5157 Office: Transnovo Inc 1451 E Lansing Dr PO Box 6672 East Lansing MI 48826-6672

HAMLIN, TOM, radio and television sportcaster, realtor; b. West Middletown, Ohio, Aug. 20, 1930; s. Harlin and Martha (Selby) H.; m. Phyllis Ann Hazelwood, June 20, 1953; children: Margo Ann, Thomas Charles. BA in Journalism, Ohio Wesleyan U., 1951. Sports dir. Sta. WLOK-AM-TV, Lima, Ohio, 1953-54, Sta. WMAN, Mansfield, Ohio, 1954-56, Stas. WAPI-AM and WABT-TV, Birmingham, Ala., 1956-60, Sta. WHIO-AM-TV, Dayton, Ohio, 1960-77, Sta. WKEF-TV, Dayton, 1979-85; freelance TV and radio announcer Voice of Ohio State football network, Fla., 1973-75, Tampa Bay Bucs network, and midwest, 1976-77; freelance t.v. and radio sports announcer, 1977—; game analyst NCAA finals Sports Network Inc., 1963; Rose Bowl play-by-play announcer NBC Radio, 1974, 75. Bd. dirs. Greater Dayton Humane Soc., 1968-95, v.p., 1984-86. With USMC, 1945-46. Named Ala. Sportscaster of Yr. Nat. Sportswriters-Sportscasters Assn., 1959, Citizen of Yr., Dayton Jaycees, 1968; nominated Ohio Sportscaster of the Yr. Mem. Ohio Sportscasters Assn. (pres. 1966-67), Dayton Area Bd. Realtors, Agonis Club (pres. 1991-92). Presbyterian. Home: 401 Canterbury Dr Dayton OH 45429-1441 Office: Big Hill Realty Corp 5580 Far Hills Ave Dayton OH 45429-2228

HAMM, THOMAS DOUGLAS, archivist, history educator; b. New Castle, Ind., Jan. 8, 1957; s. James Stewart and Lois Diane (Knotts) H.; m. Mary Louise Reynolds, May 12, 1984. BA, Butler U., 1979; MA, Ind. U., 1981, PhD, 1985. Editorial asst. Jour. Am. History, Bloomington, Ind., 1981-84; vis. asst. prof. Ind. U., Indpls., 1985-87; archivist, assoc. prof. history Earlham Coll., Richmond, Ind., 1987—; cons. Conner Prairie, Noblesville, Ind., 1990—, Historic Landmarks of Ind., Indpls., 1992—, Henry County Hist. Soc., New Castle, 1985—. Author: Transformation of American Quakerism, 1988 (Brewer prize 1987), God's Government Begun, 1995; editorial bd. Ind. Mag. of History, 1990-93; book rev. editor Quaker History, 1990—; contbr. articles to profl jours. Exec. com. Ind. Yearly Meeting of Friends, Muncie, 1992-93; chmn. geneal. pub. com. Ind. Hist. Soc., Indpls., 1992-95, mem. libr. com., 1995—. Recipient O'Kell Teaching prize Ind. U., 1981; Butler U. scholar, 1978; Phi Kappa Phi grad. fellow, 1979; Ind. Hist. Soc. rsch. fellow, 1982. Mem. Orgn. Am. Historians, Am. Hist. Assn., Am. Soc. Ch. History, Conf. of Quaker Historians and Archivists (convener 1988-90), Ind. Assn. Historians (exec. bd. 1990-92, pres.-elect 1995, pres. 1995-96), Ind. Assn. Archivists (exec. com. 1992—), Soc. Ind. Archivists (pres. 1994-95), Ind. State Libr. and Hist. Bd. Democrat. Soc. of Friends. Home: PO Box 410 Spiceland IN 47385-0410 Office: Earlham Coll Library Richmond IN 47374

HAMM, VERNON LOUIS, JR., management and financial consultant; b. East St. Louis, Ill., Mar. 14, 1951; s. Vernon Louis and Colleen Ann Hamm; B.S., Murray (Ky.) State U., 1973; M.B.A., St. Louis U., 1975; postgrad. Stanford U., 1975. Jr. exec. corp. accounts Brown Group, Inc., St. Louis, 1973-75; group supr. APC Skills Co., Palm Beach, Fla., 1975-77; account mgr. Inst. Mgmt. Resources, Los Angeles, 1977-78; dir. mgmt. devel. Naus & Newlyn, Inc., Paoli, Pa., 1978-82; pres. Mgmt. Alternatives Ltd., 1982—; mgmt., fin. and energy cons., 1975—; bd. dirs. Ryan's Family Steakhouses, Inc., Psychosystems Mgmt. Corp., N.Y.C., MAL Ventures, Detroit. Mem. Am. Soc. for Tng. and Devel., Am. Prodn. and Inventory Control Soc., Murray State U. Alumni Assn. Contbr. articles to profl. publs.

HAMMEL, ERNEST MARTIN, medical educator, academic administrator; b. Ashtabula, Ohio, May 2, 1939; s. Eugene Christian and Etna Maria (Costas) H.; m. Martha Lorene Hertzer, Dec. 16, 1961; children: Eric John, James Martin. BS, Heidelberg Coll., 1962; MPH, U. Mich., 1966, PhD, 1976. Program developer Mich. Assn. Regional Med. Programs, East Lansing, 1973-74, asst. dir. ops., 1975-76; exec. dir. OHEP Ctr. for Med. Edn., Southfield, Mich., 1976—; adj. faculty depts. cmty. and family medicine, Wayne State U. Sch. Medicine, Detroit, 1993—; adj. faculty, health svcs. adminstrn. Cen. Mich. U. Extended Degree Programs, Mt. Pleasant, 1980—; co-dir. SAVE100 Pharmacy Initiative of WSU-OHEP Consortium Quality, Cost-Effective Med. Care Program, 1995—. Trustee Kenny Mich. Rehab. Found., Rochester Hills, 1984-88; chmn. program consultation and continuing med. edn. devel. CME Accreditation Com. Mich. State Med. Soc.,

Lansing. Behavioral Sci. fellow U. Mich., 1969-70, Behavioral Sci. Rsch. fellow, 1971-72; grad. student Rsch. grantee Rackham Sch. Grad. Studies, U. Mich., 1972; Pub. Health Svc. trainee U. Mich., 1965-66, 70-71, 72-73; contract Nat. Ctr. for Health Svcs. R&D, 1973. Mem. Assn. Am. Med. Colls., Am. Pub. Health Assn., Assn. Health Svcs. Rsch., Assn. for Hosp. Med. Edn., Assn. Tchrs. Preventive Medicine, Mich. Assn. for Med. Edn. (pres. 1995—), Mich. Pub. Health Assn. U. Mich. Alumni Assn., Heidelberg Fellows. Contbr. articles to profl. publs. Editor several med. care orgn. publs. Office: OHEP Ctr for Med Edn 21415 Civic Center Dr Ste 301 Southfield MI 48076-3954

HAMMEL, HAROLD THEODORE, physiology and biophysics educator, researcher; b. Huntington, Ind., May 8, 1921; s. Audry Harold and Ferne Jane (Wiles) H.; m. Dorothy King, Dec. 29, 1948; children: Nannette, Heidi. BS in Physics, Purdue U., 1943; MS in Physics, Cornell U., 1950, PhD in Zoology, 1953. Jr. physicist Los Alamos (N.Mex.) Lab., 1944-46, staff physicist, 1948-49; from instr. to asst. prof. U. Pa., Phila., 1953-61; assoc. prof., fellow John B. Pierce Lab. Yale U., New Haven, 1961-68; prof. Scripps Instn. of Oceanography U. Calif., San Diego, 1968-88, emeritus prof., 1988—; adj. prof. physiology and biophysics Ind. U., Bloomington, 1989—; fgn. sci. mem. Max Planck Inst. for Physiol. & Clin. Rsch., 1978—; U.S. sr. scientist Alexander von Humboldt Found., 1981. Author: (with Scholander) Osmosis and Tensile Solvent, 1976; contbr. over 200 articles to profl. jours. Fellow AAAS; mem. Am. Phys. Soc., Am. Physiol. Soc., Am. Soc. mammology, Norwegian Acad. Sci. & Letters. Democrat. Home: 1605 Ridgeway Dr Ellettsville IN 47429-9474 Office: Ind U Med Scis Program Bloomington IN 47405

HAMMER, DAVID LINDLEY, lawyer, author; b. Newton, Iowa., June 6, 1929; s. Neal Paul and Agnes Marilyn (Reece) H.; m. Audrey Lowe, June 20, 1953; children: Julie, Lisa, David. BA, Grinnell Coll., 1951; JD, U. Iowa, 1956. Bar: Iowa 1956, U.S. Dist. Ct. (no. dist.) Iowa 1959, U.S. Dist. Ct. (so. dist.) Iowa 1969, U.S. Supreme Ct. 1977, Ill. Ptnr. Hammer, Simon & Jensen, Dubuque, Iowa, Galena, Ill.; mem. grievance commn. Iowa Supreme Ct., 1973-85, mem. adv. rules com., 1986-92. Author: Poems From the Ledge, 1980, The Game is Afoot, 1983, For the Sake of the Game, 1986, The 22nd Man, 1989, To Play the Game, 1990, Skewed Sherlock, 1992, The Worth of the Game, 1992, The Quest, 1993, My Dear Watson, 1994, The Before Breakfast Pipe, 1995. Bd. dirs. Linwood Cemetery Assn., 1973—, pres., 1983-84; bd. dirs., past pres. Finley Hosp., hon. dir.; bd. dirs. Finley Found., 1988-95; past campaign chmn., past pres. United Way; past bd. dirs. Carnegie Stout Pub. Libr. Served with U.S. Army, 1951-53. Fellow Am. Coll. Trial Lawyers; mem. ABA, Young Lawyers Iowa (past pres.), Iowa Def. Counsel Assn. (pres. 1991-92, del. to Def. Rsch. Inst. 1992-93), Assn. Def. Trial Attys. (exec. coun. 1983-86, past chmn. Iowa chpt.), Iowa State Bar Assn. (past chmn. continuing legal edn. com.), Iowa Acad. Trial Lawyers, Dubuque County Bar Assn. (past pres.), Baker St. Irregulars. Republican. Congregationalist. Office: Cycare Plz Ste 190 Dubuque IA 52001

HAMMER, JOHN HENRY, II, hospital administrator; b. Bartlesville, Okla., Dec. 27, 1943; s. John Henry and Lucy (Macias) H.; BA, St. Joseph's Coll., 1966; student U. Md. (Europe), 1968-69; MBA, U. Ill., 1984; m. Maria Lynn Adams; children: John Henry, Erica. Project mgr. Econ. & Manpower Corp., N.Y.C., 1971-73; asst. dir. human resources St. Catherine Hosp., East Chicago, Ind., 1974-80, pres. Employees Credit Union, 1974-80; dir. pers. Lakeview Med. Ctr., Danville, Ill., 1980-84, v.p., 1984-88, v.p. United Samaritans Med. Ctr., Danville, Ill., 1988-95; bd. dirs. East Cen. Ill. Health Systems Agy., East Cen. Ill. Health Planning Orgn., Vermilion Area Cmty. Health Ctr. Chmn. De La Garza Career Ctr. Program Com., 1974-80, bd. dirs. Jr. Achievement of Danville, 1990—, vice chmn., 1991, chmn. 1993—. Capt. USAF, 1967-71, to lt. col. USAFR, 1974—. Mem. Ind. Soc. Hosp. Personnel Adminstrn. (chmn. 1976-77, dir. 1977-79, pres. 1979-80), Am. Coll. Healthcare Execs., Rotary (bd. dirs. 1990—, pres. 1991) Roman Catholic. Office: 218 Ellsworth Westville IL 61883

HAMMER, JOYCE MAE, gifted and talented education educator; b. Milw., May 21, 1933; d. George and Sara (Arne) Leviton; children: Deborah, Lori. BS, U. Ill., 1954; MA, Northwestern U., 1958, postgrad., 1974-78; postgrad., Nat. Coll. Edn., Evanston, Ill., 1986-89, Aurora U., 1990-92, 95. Tchr. math. Fairview Sch., Skokie, Ill., 1957-65, Arie Crown Sch., 1967-72, Fairview South Sch., 1972-77; elem. tchr. gifted math. edn., coord. gifted edn. Fairview South Sch., Skokie, 1978—. Recipient Those Who Excel award; grantee. Mem. Nat. Coun. Tchrs. Math., Ill. Coun. Tchrs. Math., Ill. Assn. for Gifted Children, Phi Delta Kappa.

HAMMER, PATRICK, scuba diving educator; b. Cork, Ireland, Apr. 28, 1953; s. Rudy and Gloria Hammer; m. Sherry Lange, Jan. 9, 1991. Student, U. Wis., Lacrosse, 1972-73, Moraine Valley Coll., 1973. Master instr. Profl. Assn. Diving Instrs., Santa Ana, Calif., 1973-74, 77; with emergency med. planning dept. State of Oreg., 1989—; developer Medic First Aid Tng. Program. Author: Art of Skin Diving, 1992, Wrecks of Lake Michigan, 1990, Retail Scuba Operation Manual, 1989, Diver's Log Book, 1988, Scuba Life, 1988. Mem. Diver Alert Network, Alsip C. of C., Our World Under Water (bd. dirs. 1992-95, corp. sponsor). Republican. Roman Catholic. Home and Office: 12003 S Cicero Ave Alsip IL 60658

HAMMER, ROBERT EUGENE, psychologist; b. Faribault, Minn., Aug. 7, 1931; s. Rolf Walter and Verona (Bakken) H.; m. M. Kitti Nations, Apr. 30, 1967 (div. Jan. 1988); children: Gregory Clay, Cynthia Beth; m. Bonnie Jo French, Nov. 12, 1988. BS in Counseling Psychology, U. Houston, 1959, MA, 1963; PhD in Spl. Edn. Adminstrn., U. Iowa, 1970. Lic. psychologist, Iowa; cert. health svc. provider in psychology. Tchr. educable mentally retarded Houston Ind. Sch. Dist., 1961-63; testing supr. U. Houston Counseling Ctr., 1963-65; child psychologist Mental Health Inst., Independence, Iowa, 1965-67, dir. adolescent treatment unit, 1969-74, dir. psychol. svcs., 1969-89, dir. adolescent treatment unit, 1989—; rsch. dir. Iowa Div. State Mental Health Resources; pvt. practice counseling and cons. psychologist, 1974—. Bd. dirs. Iowa Nursing Found.; vol. fireman; mem men's gospel quartet United Parish Ch. Served with USAF, 1950-53. Mem. Am. Psychol. Assn., Nat. Assn. Rural Mental Health, Am. Soc. Quality Control, State Mental Health Dirs. Assn., Iowa Psychol. Assn., Houston TKE Alumni Assn., SPEBSQSA, U.S. Chess Fedn., Evaluation Network, Am. Legion, Lions, Masons. Contbr. articles to profl. jours. Home: 120 2nd St S Coggon IA 52218-9616 Office: Mental Health Inst PO Box 111 Independence IA 50644-0111

HAMMERSLEY, MARSHALL LESTER, financial consultant; b. Chgo., Apr. 16, 1935. BA with honors, U. Ill., 1956; MBA, U. Chgo., 1977. CPA, CFP. Auditor Arthur Andersen & Co., Chgo., 1956-59; fin. exec. Brunswick Corp., Chgo., 1959-68; fin. cons. Coopers & Lybrand, Chgo., 1968-71; treas. Hirsh Co., Chgo., 1971-75, Century Am., Chgo., 1975-85; v.p. Smith Barney, Northbrook, Ill., 1985—. With USAR, 1957. Mem. Rotary (past treas. found. 1986—). Jewish. Home: 233 Greenleaf Ave Wilmette IL 60091-1907 Office: Smith Barney Inc 5 Revere Dr Northbrook IL 60062-1566

HAMMERSTROM, BEVERLY SWOISH, state representative; b. Mineral Wells, Tex., Mar. 28, 1944; d. William Graham and Marjorie Wirth (Lillis) Swoish; m. Don Preston Hammerstrom, June 25, 1966 (div. Oct. 1976); children: Todd Preston, Rory Scott. BA, Adrian Coll., 1966; MPA, U. Toledo, 1994. Cert. mcpl. clk. Tchr. Geneva (N.Y.) Pub. Schs., 1966-69; substitute tchr. Darien (Wis.) Pub. Schs., 1970-71; tchr. Bedford Coop. Nursery Sch., Lambertville, Mich., 1975; retail mgr., buyer Gallerie, Toledo, 1975-78, Personal Touch, Toledo, 1978-80; clk. Bedford Township, Temperance, Mich., 1980-92; state rep. State of Mich., Lansing, 1993—; bd. dirs. Family Med. Ctr., Temperance; emergency mgmt. bd. Washtenaw County, Ypsilanti, Mich., 1993—, Monroe (Mich.) County, 1993—. Mem. IIMC Found. (bd. dirs. 1996), Mich. Assn. Clks. (life, pres. 1990-91), Am. Legis. Exch. Coun. (transp. task force), Coun. State Govt. (med. policies com., del. 1995—), Women in Govt. Republican. Roman Catholic. Home: 1183 Oakmont Dr Temperance MI 48182-9563 Office: Mich Ho Rep PO Box 30014 Lansing MI 48909-7514

HAMMOCK, PERRY T., foundation executive; b. Lebanon, Ind., Apr. 26, 1953; s. Gordon L. and Glinda M. (Jones) H.; m. Melanie C. Myers, July 1, 1984; 1 child, Emily. BA, Purdue U., 1975, MA, 1977. Dir. devel. Ivy Tech. State Coll., Indpls., 1981-86; exec. dir. Ivy Tech. Found., Indpls., 1986—. Mem. family ministries commn. St. Luke's Meth., Indpls., 1994-95. Mem. Nat. Soc. Fund Raising Execs. (cert.), Nat. Coun. Resource Devel. Office: Ivy Tech Found 1 W 26th St Indianapolis IN 46206-1763

HAMMOND, EDWARD H., university president; b. McAllen, Tex., May 4, 1944; s. Will J. and Bergit A. (Lund) H.; m. Vivian hammeke, Aug. 26, 1967; children: Kelly Edvidge, Lance Edward, Julie Marie. BS in Speech, Kans. State Tchrs. Coll., 1966, MS, 1967; PhD, U. MO., 1971. Asst. dir. of field svcs. Kans. State Tchrs. Coll., Emporia, 1966-67; dir. student affairs Purdue U. North Cen. campus, Westville, Ind., 1967-68; counselor housing office U. Mo., Columbia, 1969-70; asst. dean of students So. Ill. U., Carbondale, 1970, asst. to pres. for student rels., 1970-73; v.p. student affairs Seton Hall U., S. Orange, N.J., 1973-76, U. Louisville, 1976-87; pres. Fort Hays State U., Hays, Kans., 1987—; chair bd. trustees Boost Alcohol Consciousness Concerning the Health of U. Students of the U.S. Inc., 1987-93; trustee The Lincoln Found., 1979-87; mem. Inter-Assn. Task Force on Coll. Alcohol Abuse and Misuse, 1984—; vis. faculty mem. Ind. U., Bloomington, 1972-83; cons. in field. Contbr. articles to profl. jours. NDEA fellow U. Mo., 1968-70. Mem. Am. Coun. on Edn., Am. Assn. State Colls. and Univs., Am. Assn. Univ. Adminstrs., Nat. Assn. Student Pers. Adminstrs. (nat. pres. 1983, John Jones award 1986), Kans. C. of C. and Industry (bd. dirs. 1990—), Pi Kappa Delta, Sigma Phi Epsilon. Office: Fort Hays State U 600 Park St Hays KS 67601-4009

HAMMOND, HAROLD LOGAN, pathology educator, oral and maxillofacial pathologist; b. Hillsboro, Ill., Mar. 18, 1934; s. Harold Thomas and Lillian (Carlson) H.; m. Sharon Bunton, Aug. 1, 1954 (dec. 1974); 1 child, Connie; m. Pat J. Palmer, June 3, 1986. Student Millikin U., 1953-57, Roosevelt U., Chgo., 1957-58; DDS, Loyola U., Chgo., 1962; MS, U. Chgo., 1967. Diplomate Am. Bd. Oral and Maxillofacial Pathology. Intern, U. Chgo. Hosps., Chgo., 1962-63, resident, 1963-66, chief resident in oral pathology, 1966-67; asst. prof. oral pathology U. Iowa, Iowa City, 1967-72, assoc. prof., 1972-80, assoc. prof., dir. surg. oral pathology, 1980-83, prof., dir., 1983—; cons. pathologist Hosp. Gen. de Managua, Nicaragua, 1970-90, VA Hosp., Iowa City, 1977—. Cons. editor: Revista de la Asociation de Nicaragua, 1970-71, Revista de la Federacion Odontologica de Centroamerica y Panama, 1971-77. Contbr. articles to sci. jours. Recipient Mosby Pub. Co. Scholarship award, 1962. Fellow AAAS, Am. Acad. Oral and Maxillofacial Pathology; mem. Am. Men and Women of Sci., N.Y. Acad. Scis., AAUP, Internat. Assn. Oral Pathologists, Internat. Assn. Dental Rsch., Am. Dental Assn., Am. Assn. for Dental Rsch. Avocations: collecting antique clocks, collecting gambling paraphernalia, collecting toys. Home: 1732 Brown Deer Rd Coralville IA 52241-1157 Office: U Iowa Dental Sci Bldg Iowa City IA 52242-1001

HAMMOND, THOMAS, quality engineer; b. May 9, 1961; s. Robert Neil and Margaret Madelyn (Foster) H.; m. Maureen Anne Callaghan, May 17, 1985; children: Catherine, Ian. BBA, Western Mich. U., 1985. Quality mgr. Hascall Steel Co., Grandville, Mich., 1990-94, The Deck Co., Grand Rapids, Mich., 1994; quality engr. Pridgeon & Clay Inc., Grand Rapids, 1995—. Mem. Nat. Orgn. Quality Profls. Mem. Congl. Ch. Home: 874 Aberdeen St NE Grand Rapids MI 49505-3872

HAMMOND BLACK, MERYL JEAN, accountant; b. Cin., Nov. 15, 1944; d. John Green and Elizabeth Martina (Berling) H.; m. Ronald Lee Black Sr., Feb. 24, 1980 (div. Aug. 1984); 1 child, Daryl Lee. Student, U. Cin., 1964-69. With Ohio Navy, Cin. Mem. coun. Village of Fairfax, Ohio, 1966-70; sec. Fairfax Bus. Men's Assn., 1966; advisor to teen group, Fairfax, 1969; active Mariemont PTA, 1985-88; dir. olympic funding, 1990. Mem. U. Cin. Alumni. Home: 3708 Germania St Cincinnati OH 45227-3506

HAMMONS, BRIAN KENT, lawyer, business executive; b. Wurzburg, Federal Republic Germany, Mar. 6, 1958; came to U.S. 1958; s. R. Dwain and Donna G. (Carender) H.; m. Kimberly M. Pflumm, July 26, 1980; children: April Michelle, David Dwain, Adam Carender. BS summa cum laude, S.W. Mo. State U., Springfield, 1980; JD cum laude, So. Meth. U., Dallas, 1985. Bar: Mo. 1985. Exec., treas., v.p. Hammons Products Co., Stockton, Mo., 1980-86; exec. v.p., sec. Hammons Products Co., 1987—; assoc. Stinson, Mag & Fizzell, Kansas City, Mo., 1986-87. Mem. Stockton Airport Bd., 1987-89, Stockton City Coun., 1989-91. Mem. ABA, Mo. Bar Assn., Masons (sec. 1980-81), Lions (pres. 1990-91), Leadership Mo., Phi Delta Phi. Republican. Methodist. Office: Hammons Products Co 105 Hammons Dr Stockton MO 65785*

HAMMONS, R. DWAIN, food products executive; b. 1933. BS in Bus., Southwest Mo. State U., 1956. With Hammons Products Co., Stockton, Mo., 1958—, now pres. With U.S. Army, 1956-58. Office: Hammons Products Co 105 Hammons Dr Stockton MO 65785*

HAMPE, WILLIAM CARL, information services administrator; b. Chgo., Feb. 27, 1953; s. Charles Otto and Ruth Marjorie (Keller) H.; m. LuAnn Curtis, May 31, 1980; children: Susan, Andrew. BS in Elec. Engring., Ill. Inst. Tech., Chgo., 1974, MS in Chem. Engring., 1978. Devel. engr. UOP Inc., McCook, Ill., 1974-77; automation engr. UOP Inc., Des Plaines, Ill., 1977-83; group leader-automation Signal Cos., Des Plaines, 1982-84; mgr. Allied-Signal Inc., Des Plaines, 1985-92; dir. info. svcs. World Relief Corp., Wheaton, Ill., 1993—; cons./trainer Flex Execs., 1992—; cons. HTS Inc., 1991. Treas. India Rural Evang. Fellowship, Park Ridge, Ill., 1994—, Asia Evang. Ministries, 1993—; chmn. mission bd. South Park Ch., Park Ridge, 1982-83, chmn. local ministries bd., 1985-86, fin. sec., 1991-93. Mem. IEEE, IEEE Computer Soc. Evangelical Christian. Home: 1300 S Fairview Park Ridge IL 60068 Office: World Relief Corp 450 E Gundersen Dr Carol Stream IL 60188

HAMPEL, ROBERT EDWARD, advertising executive; b. Cin., Apr. 29, 1941; s. John Edward and Ruth Elizabeth (Pister) H.; m. Nanci Jean Nau, Aug. 24, 1963; 1 child, Jeffrey Braam. BBA, U. Cin., 1964; MBA, U. Evansville, 1980. Asst. account mgr. Procter and Gamble, Balt., 1965; corp. forecaster Procter and Gamble, Cin., 1966-68; asst. contr. Keller-Crescent Co., Evansville, Ind., 1968-71; dir. mgmt. info. svcs. Keller-Crescent div. Am. Standards, Evansville, 1971-76, exec. v.p. fin., 1976-85, sr. exec. v.p., 1985-86; sr. exec. v.p., sec., treas., CFO Keller-Crescent Co., Inc., Evansville, 1987—, bd. dirs.; bd. dirs. Hahn, Inc. Pres. Jr. Achievement of S.W. Ind., Evansville, 1976-77, Evansville Philharm., 1981-82; pres. United Way of S.W. Ind., 1988-89; bd. dirs. Evansville Mus. Arts and Scis., 1988—, treas., 1987-88. Mem. Nat. Assn. Accts. (pres. Evansville chpt. 1980-81, nat. bd. dirs. 1984-85, nat. com. 1985-87). Home: 6633 Old Stonehouse Dr Newburgh IN 47630-1785 Office: Keller-Crescent Co Inc 1100 E Louisiana St PO Box 3 Evansville IN 47701*

HAMPER, ROBERT JOSEPH, marketing executive; b. Chgo., May 20, 1956; s. Robert William and Barbara Jean (Schreiber) H. BSBA with honors, Ill. State U., 1977, MBA with honors, 1979. Fin. mgr. Ill. Bell, Chgo., 1979-82; staff mgr. AT&T, Basking Ridge, N.J., 1982-84; mem. tech. staff Bell labs., Homedale, N.J., 1983-84; staff mgr. mktg. and fin. analysis Ill. Bell, Chgo., 1984-85; dir. stragetic planning Ill. Bell/Ameritech Corp., Chgo., Ill., 1987-90; pres. R.J. Hamper Strategic Bus. Cons., River Forest, Ill., 1981—; dir. strategic planning Ill. Bell/Ameritech Corp., Chgo., 1987-90; mgr. investment fund Strategic Bus. Cons., River Forest, Ill., 1990—; asst. prof. fin. and mktg. Rosary Coll., River Forest, 1990—; adj. prof. fin. Loyola U., Chgo., 1988—; seminar presenter in field; career counselor, 1985—. Author: Developing a Profitable Marketing Plan: Text and Cases, 1987, Marketing and Planning Forms, 1987, Strategic Market Planning, 1990, 92, 94, 95, Handbook for Proposal Writing, 1995; contbg. author: College Business Math, 1995; contbr. articles to profl. jours. Leader Boy Scouts Am., Park Forest, Ill., 1979-83; canvassor Park Forest Dem. Com., 1983-85. Mem. Am. Mktg. Assn. (exec.), Am. Mgmt. Assn., Fin. Mgmt. Assn., Am. Fin. Assn., Am. Hosp. Assn., Maywood Sportsmen Club. Home and Office: 730 Clinton Pl River Forest IL 60305-1914

HAMPTON, DORIAN SHERARD, clinical educator; b. Chgo., Nov. 7, 1959; s. Dwaine and Dolores Christina (Rhodes) H.; m. Regina Lynn May, June 11, 1983; children: Timothy Sherard, Joshua Sherard. AA, Olive-Harvey Coll., 1978; BS, Loyola U., 1983; MS, Nat. Louis U., 1991. Cert. respiratory tech. St. Joseph Hosp., Chgo., 1984—; registered respiratory therapist Mercy Hosp., Chgo., 1986—; cert. pulmonary function tech. South Chgo. Cmty. Hosp., 1991—; registered pulmonary function technologist Trinity Hosp., Chgo., 1995—, perinatal pediatric respiratory specialist, 1995—; procedural lab cons. Rush-Presbyn.-St. Lukes Hosp., Chgo., 1995. Assoc. min. Grace Apostolic Ch., Chgo., 1989—. 1st lt. U.S. Army. Mem. Am. Assn. Respiratory Care, Ill. Soc. Respiratory Care, Loyola U. Alumni, Nat.-Louis U. Alumni, Masons.

HAMPTON, GLEN RICHARD, environmental engineer; b. Detroit, June 11, 1948; s. LaVerne P. and Virginia M. (Hubbard) H.; BS in Engring., Mich. Tech. U., 1973; m. Jane E. Fenlon, Jan. 30, 1981; children: Sarah Lynn, Melanie Anne. Project engr. Granger Engring., Inc., Cadillac, Mich., 1973-79; exec. v.p., dir. Chippewa Architects & Engrs., Inc., Kincheloe and St. Ignace, Mich., 1979-82; constrn. mgr. J.H. Granger and Assocs., St. Ignace, Mich., 1983-89, v.p., bd. dirs., 1989-95; prin., dir. engring. Mitchell and Assocs., Gaylord, Mich., 1996—; cons. constrn. engring., environ. engring., civil engring., pollution control and solar energy. Pres. Moran Twp. Sch. Bd., 1992—; chmn. Moran Twp. Planning Commn., 1989—. Registered profl. engr., Mich., Ky., Minn., Wis. Recipient Nat. Honor award Am. Cons. Engrs. Coun., 1990. Mem. Nat. Soc. Profl. Engrs., Mich. Soc. Profl. Engrs., ASCE (pres. N.W. Mich. chpt. 1980-82), Mich. Water Pollution Control Fedn., Mich. Soc. Civil Engrs., Nature Conservancy (dir. Mich. chpt. 1980-88). Club: Kiwanis. Home: 208 Smith Rd Saint Ignace MI 49781

HAMPTON, MICHAEL R., investment company executive; b. Sikeston, Mo., Aug. 27, 1948. Mgr. Fitton Cunningham Lauzon, Madison, N.J., 1979-80; v.p., br. mgr. Prudential Securities, Grand Rapids, Mich., 1980—. Fin. com. Ruth Lully Ctr., Indpls., 1986-90; mem. devel. com. Right Place, 1991—; chmn. Jefferson Awards Selection, Grand Rapids, 1991—; bd. dirs. West Mich. coun. Boy Scouts Am., Grand Rapids, 1991—, Ednl. Forest Hills Found., 1991—. Mem. C. of C. (advisor, CEO 1991—), Rotary (advisor 1991—, bd. dirs., Paul Harris fellow 1987). Baha'i. Office: Prudential Securities Inc 99 Monroe Ave NW Ste 101 Grand Rapids MI 49503-2639

HAMRE, GARY LESLIE WILLIAM, entrepreneur; b. Mpls., July 28, 1939; s. Hiram O. and Mayme R. (Sorensen) H.; m. Margaret Ann Renshaw, July 14, 1958 (div. 1981); children: Jeffrey A.C., Cheryl L., Dayna L.; m. Karen Sue Link, Nov. 30, 1984. BA, U. Minn., 1966; postgrad., Ohio State U., 1978. Lic. real estate sales cons. Area mgr. Union Oil Co. Calif., Mpls., 1963-71, Columbus, Ohio, 1971-78; pres. G.L.W.H. Ent., Inc., Ohio, 1978—; owner 76 Halfway House Truck Stop, 1978-90; sales cons. comml. real estate, 1990—. Dep. sherif Franklin County Sheriff's Office, Columbus, 1977—; sustaining mem. Rep. Nat. Com., Washington, 1981—; bd. dirs., com. chmn. Am. Diabetes Assn., 1988-91. Mem. Nat. Restaurant Assn., Ohio Restaurant Assn., Ctrl. Ohio Restaurant Assn. (bd. dirs. 1984-92, pres. 1990, chmn. bd. 1991), Nat. Assn. Truckstop Operators (assignment com. 1986-90), Sales and Mktg. Execs. Internat., Nat. Fedn. Ind. Businessmen, U.S. C. of C., Columbus c. of C., Sales Execs. Club, Lions (pres. Powell, Ohio 1986-87, Lion of Yr. 1985-86, zone chmn. 1987-88, Melvin Jones fellow 1991, dist. 13F gov. 1990-91, chmn. state constn. and by-laws 1993-96), Masons, Shriners (provost), Moose. Lutheran. Home: 879 Bluffway Dr Columbus OH 43235-1729

HAMZAEE, REZA GHOLI, economics educator; b. Arak, Iran, July 5, 1951; came to the U.S., 1974; s. Gholamali and Nosrat (Saberi) H.; m. Diana Riazi, Sept. 21, 1979; 1 child, Maanie. BS, Nat. U. Iran, 1973; MA, U. Calif., 1977; PhD, Arizona State U., 1985. Tchr. Varjavand High Sch., Tehran, 1971-72; acct. Pars Indsl. Group, Tehran, 1973-74; econs. instr. Ariz. State U., Tempe, 1981-84; asst. prof. econ. Mo. Western State Coll., St. Joseph, 1984-88, assoc. prof. econs., 1988-92, prof., 1992—; prof. Walden U., 1992—; elected chairperson dept. bus. and econs. Mo. Western State Coll., 1990; prof. Walden U., 1992—; cons. editor Nat. Social Sci. Jour., 1991; cons. in field. Mem. nat. bd. referees Nat. Social Sci. Jour., cons. editor, 1991—; contbr. articles to profl. jours. Grad. scholar Ariz. State U., 1984; recipient Jesse Lee Myers Excellence in Teaching award, 1990, Burlington No. Faculty Achievement award 1991. Mem. Western Econ. Assn., Ea. Econ. Assn., Nat. Social Sci. Assn., Assn. Global Bus. Office: Mo Western State Coll Dept Econ 4525 Downs Dr Saint Joseph MO 64507-2246

HAN, XIANMING LANCE, physicist; b. Xinfeng, Jiangxi, China, May 3, 1963; came to U.S., 1983; s. Xipei and Fumei (Liu) H.; m. Hong Zeng, June 26, 1988. BS, U. Sci. and Tech. China, Hefei, 1982; MS, U. Colo., 1986, PhD, 1989. Rsch. asst. joint inst. for lab. astrophysics U. Colo., Boulder, 1983-89; asst. prof. physics dept. U. Idaho, Moscow, 1989-91; asst. prof. physics dept. Butler U., Indpls., 1991-96, assoc. prof., 1996—; PhD comprehensive exams com. dept. physics U. Colo., Boulder, 1986-88; computer networking com. dept. physics U. Idaho, Moscow, 1989-90. Contbr. articles to Phys. Review A, Jour. of the Optical Soc. of Am. B. U. Colo. fellow, 1984-86. Mem. Am. Phys. Soc. Office: Butler Univ Dept Physics 4600 Sunset Ave Indianapolis IN 46208-3443

HANAN, MICHAEL CLARK, administrator; b. Sioux City, Iowa, Dec. 29, 1957; s. Glen Dellmar and Janet Ann (Eaton) H.; m. Karen Louise Segelstrom, June 21, 1980; 1 child, Michael. BA in Biology, St. Cloud State U., 1980. Registered environ. health specialist. Environ. health specialist Stearns County, St. Cloud, Minn., 1980-87; dir. dept. solid waste Otter Tail County, Fergus Falls, Minn., 1987—. Com. chmn. Ducks Unltd., Fergus Falls, 1990-94; pres. Minn. Hunting Retriever Assn., Fergus Falls, 1989-94. Mem. Minn. Solid Waste Adminstrn. Assn. (pres. 1992, adv. coun. 1983-94, adv. com. 1988-94). Home: Rt 1 Box 94 Elizabeth MN 56533 Office: Dept Solid Waste 121 Junius Ave W Fergus Falls MN 56537

HANARD, MARCEL ROGER, II, research engineer; b. Manage, Belgium, Mar. 4, 1939; arrived in U.S., 1961; s. Marcel R. and Marie-Therese (Festré) H.; m. Patricia Byrum, Apr. 19, 1964; children: Marcel III, Samantha, Brendan, Dominic. Bachelor's degree, Ecoles Industrielles, Louviere, Belgium, 1960. Structural design engr. Ark. Foundry Co., Little Rock, 1961-64; tool engr., methods supr. John Deere Dubuque Tractor Works, Dubuque, Iowa, 1964-66; prodn. supr., supt. Caterpillar Inc., Gosselies, Belgium, 1966-70; engr. mfg. R&D Caterpillar Inc., East Peoria, Ill., 1970-89; project mgr. rsch. Caterpillar Inc. Tech. Ctr., Mossville, Ill., 1989—; chmn. Ill. Internat. Grinding Conf., Cin., 1992; com. mem. nat. codes and stds. Am. Soc. Mech. Engrs., Washington, 1984—. Mem. Soc. Mfg. Engrs. (cert., chmn. 1980-81, com. mem. internat com. abrasive cutting process 1982—), STLE. Roman Catholic. Home: 1023 Hiawatha Ct Dunlap IL 61525

HANARD, PATRICIA ANN, clinical nurse specialist; b. Searcy, Ark., Dec. 19, 1943; d. Claudis E. and H. Frances (Stringfellow) Byrum; m. Marcel Roger-Andre Hanard II, Apr. 19, 1964; children: Marcel III, Samantha, Brendan, Dominic. AAS, Ill. Cen. Coll., 1971; BS with honors, Coll. St. Francis, Joliet, Ill., 1985; MLS, Bradley U.; MSN in Pub. Health Nursing, U. Ill., 1996. RN, Ill;. cert. family nurse practitioner; cert. in reproductive endocrinology and infertility; registered med. lab. technician. Nurse emergency rm. Proctor Hosp., Peoria, Ill.; head nurse, mgr. office Midwest Med. Svcs., Peoria; head nurse ob/gyn Coll. Medicine U. Ill., Peoria; clin. nurse specialist, office mgr. Fertility and Reproductive Medicine Ctr. of Ctrl. Ill. Capt. USAR. Mem. AWHONN, Am. Fertility Soc., Am. Med. Technologists, Ill. State Assn. Med. Technologists, Alpha Chi Omega, Phi Theta Kappa, Phi Kappa Phi, Sigma Theta Tau. Home: 1023 W Hiawatha Ct Dunlap IL 61525-9543

HANCOCK, ALBERT SIDNEY, JR., engineering executive; b. Chickasha, Okla.; s. Albert Sidney and Grace Ora (Liles) H.; m. Lillian May Shields; children: Craig Sidney, Curt Eric, Kevin Jay. Chief engr. Silent Sioux Mfg. Corp., Orange City, Iowa; pres. B&M Mfg. Corp., Orange City; pres., founder Hi-Precision Mfg. Co., Inc., Orange City; ops. mgr., projectile and tool design divsn. S&W Ammunition Co., Orange City; owner Hancock Engring., Orange City, 1958—. Inventor in field. Chmn. Planning and Zoning Com., Orange City; dir. Orange City Devel. Corp. Mem. ASM, ASTM, ARA (life), Soc. Mfg. Engrs. (sr.), Am. Def. Preparedness Assn. (life), Nat. Reloading Mfrs. Assn., VFW, Elks, Shriners, Flying Fez. Home: 501 3rd St NE Orange City IA 51041-2123 Office: Hancock Engring PO Box 226 Orange City IA 51041-0226

HANCOCK, DORIS COLLEEN, critical care nurse; b. Kansas City, Kans., Nov. 9, 1948; d. Joseph C. and Shirley Mavis (Darling) Stephens; m. Shaun W. Kelly, June 15, 1974 (div. 1983); children: Colleen, Casandra, Shannon; m. DeVerre Hancock, Feb. 14, 1994. AA, Kansas City Community Jr. Coll, 1968; BSN, Kans. U., 1973; Nurse Practitioner, Wichita State U., 1980; postgrad., Kans. U., 1988-89, Hays U., 1991. Cert. cardiovascular technologist. Nurse ICU Kans. U. Med. Ctr., Kansas City, Kans., 1970-73; urology CCU nurse Wadsworth VA Hosp., Leavenworth, Kans., 1973-75; charge supr. and ICU LaBette County Hosp., Parsons, Kans., 1976-79; med. surg. instr. LaBette County Community Jr. Coll., Parsons, Kans., 1975-76; adult care nurse practitioner Dr. D. Pauls, Parsons, Kans., 1977-82; home health nurse Upjohn Home Health, Topeka, 1984-85; nurse ICU telemetry Meml. Hosp., Topeka, 1981, 84-85; nurse ICU emergency Meml. Hosp., Manhattan, Kans., 1984-85; nurse ICU, CCU, cardiac care lab, emergency room St. Francis Hosp., Topeka, 1981-90; nurse ICU Colmery O'Neil VA Hosp., Topeka, 1990-95; nurse in spl. procedures, cardiac catheterization lab. Lawrence (Kans.) Meml. Hosp., 1994—; nurse cardiac catheterization lab. Lawrence Meml. Hosp., 1994—; mem. infection control com. Elm Haven Nursing Home, Parsons, 1981-82; bd. dirs. Nursing Home, Parsons, 1981-82; founder, advisor Diabetes Assn., Parsons, 1980-83; instr. in field. Mem. Jaycees, Parsons, 1980-82. Recipient Scholarship, Kans. Heart Assn., 1966, Outstanding Young Woman of Am. award, 1981. Mem. AACN (cert.), Am. Heart Assn. Democrat. Home: 2626 SE Tidewater Dr Topeka KS 66605-2359

HANCOCK, JAMES BEATY, interior designer; b. Hartford, Ky.; s. James Winfield Scott and Hettie Frances (Meadows) H.; BA, Hardin-Simmons U., 1948, MA, 1952. Head interior design dept. Thornton's, Abilene, Tex., 1945-54; interior designer The Halle Bros. Co., Cleve., 1954-55; v.p. Olympic Products, Cleve., 1955-56; mgr. interior designer Bell Drapery Shops of Ohio, Inc., Shaker Heights, 1957-78, v.p., 1979—; lectr. interior design, Abilene and Cleve.; works include 6 original murals Broadway Theater, Abilene, 1940, mural Skyline Outdoor Theatre, Abilene, 1950, cover designs for Isotopics mag., 1958-60. Mem. Western Reserve Hist. Soc., Cleve. Mus. Art, Decorative Arts Trust. Served with AUS, 1942-46. Recipient 2d place award for oil painting West Tex. Expn., 1940, hon. mention, 1940. Mem. Abilene Mus. Fine Arts (charter), Cleveland Circle of the Decorative Arts Trust (charter mem.). Home and Office: 530 Sycamore Dr Cleveland OH 44132-2150

HANCOCK, MEL, congressman; b. Cape Fair, Mo., Sept. 14, 1929. BS, S.W. Mo. State Coll., 1951. Chmn. bd. dirs. Fed. Protection Inc.; with Internat. Harvester Co.; mem. 101st-104th Congresses from 7th Mo. Dist., 1989—; mem. ways and means com. Chmn. Taxpayer's Survival Assn. With USAF, USAFR. Mem. Nat. Rifle Assn. (life), Farm Bur., Am. Legion. Republican. Mem. Ch. of Christ. Office: US Ho of Rep 438 Cannon HOB Washington DC 20515-2507*

HAND, RAYMOND W., state legislator; b. Uhrichsville, Ohio, Sept. 9, 1928; m. Carole Smiley. BS, Ohio State U., 1953, LLB, JD, 1955. Mem. Mo. Ho. of Reps., Jefferson City, 1986—; atty., cons., St. Louis. Republican. Home: 545 Gascony Way Saint Louis MO 63122-1460*

HANDEL, DAVID JONATHAN, health care administrator; b. N.Y.C., Jan. 2, 1946; s. Milton M. and Ruth (Stamer) H.; m. Julia Elizabeth Noll, June 26, 1971; chldren: Daniel, Jennifer. BS, Cornell U., 1966; MBA, U. Chgo., 1968. Assoc. planning coordinator for health scis. Northwestern U., Chgo., 1970-73, adminstr. Northwestern U. Med. Clinics and Med. Assocs., 1973-76; dir. planning and implementation Mid-Ohio Health Planning Fedn., Columbus, Ohio, 1976-79; assoc. hosp. adminstr. Vanderbilt U. Hosps., Nashville, 1979-82, assoc. dir. ops., 1982-85; dir. Ind. U. Hosps., Indpls., 1985—; bd. dirs. U. Hosp. Consortium, Chgo., Ind. Hosp. Assn.; v.p. United Hosp. Svcs., Indpls., 1986-88, pres., 1989-90. Contbr. articles to profl. jours. Sr. asst. health svcs. officer USPHS, 1968-70. Fellow Am. Coll. Health Care Execs. Office: Ind U Med Ctr 5550 N University Blvd Indianapolis IN 46202-5262

HANDLER, AUDREY SOLOMON, artist, educator; b. Phila., Dec. 9, 1934; d. Harry and Dorie (Wein) Solomon; m. Joel Handler, July 11, 1954 (div. 1969); children: Stephen, Adam, Frances. BFA, Boston U., 1956; MS, U. Wis., 1967, MFA, 1970. Sr. rsch. fellow Royal Coll. Art, London, 1967-68; instr. Penland (N.C.) Sch. Crafts, 1971-85, Hunterdon Art Ctr., Clinton, N.J., 1972, Haystack Mt. Sch. Crafts, Deer Isle, Maine, 1973, Archie Bray Found., Helena, Mont., 1975, U. Wis. Extension, Madison, 1984, Madison Area Tech. Coll., 1973-93; bd. mem. Nat. Coun. on Edn. and the Ceramic Arts, 1973-74, Glass Art Soc., 1976-80; del. conf. World Crafts Coun., Kyoto, Japan, 1978; mem. Wis. Gallery Artist Adv. Bd., Milw. Mus. Art, 1980-81. Represented in permanent collections at Greenville (S.C.) County Art Mus., Lannan Found., Palm Beach, Fla., Lobmeyr Mus., Vienna, Austria, Corning (N.Y.) Mus. of Glass, Ebeltoft (Denmark) Glass Mus., Charles A. Wustum Mus., Racine, Wis., Am. Crafts Mus., N.Y.C. Recipient Juror's award 46th Wis. Designer-Craftsmen, Milw., 1966, Artists Exhbn. award Madison Art Ctr., 1970, Juror's award 59th Wis. Designer-Craftsmen, Milw., 1971, Art Scholarships City of Phila., 1951-56, Royal Coll. Art, London, 1967-68; Nat. Endowment Arts grantee, 1977-78, 81. Mem. Glass Art Soc. (hon. mem. 1994, bd. dirs. 1976-80). Democrat. Jewish. Home: 105 S Rock Rd Madison WI 53705-4636 Office: Handler Glass 7560 Marsh View Rd Verona WI 53593

HANDLER, DOUGLAS PERRY, economist; b. Phila., Oct. 17, 1957; s. Robert and Claire (Fischer) H.; m. Allison Joy Rubin, Mar. 31, 1984; children: Phillip, Daniel. AB, Dickinson Coll., 1978; MA, Georgetown U., 1981. Economist Bd. Govs., Fed. Res. Bd., Washington, 1982-85; dir. short-term forecasting WEFA Group (formerly Wharton Econometrics), Phila., 1985-87; mgr. econometric analysis Dun & Bradstreet Corp., N.Y.C., 1987-95; dir. rsch. A.C. Nielsen, Schaumburg, Ill., 1995—; mem. econ. adv. bd. N.Y.C. OMB, 1993—; mem. Coun. on Credit Risk, N.Y.C., 1989—; mem. indsl. roundtable Fed. Res. Bank Chgo., 1995—. Contbr. articles to Stern (NYU) Bus. Econs., Confedn. Svc. Industries, Comml. Lending Rev. Mem. Nat. Assn. Bus. Economists (fin. roundtable (sec./treas. 1988—), N.Y. Assn. Bus. Economists, Econ. Club Conn. (program chmn. 1987-88, membership chmn. 1988—), Nat. Bus. Econ. Issues Coun. Office: A C Nielsen 150 N Martingale Rd Schaumburg IL 60173-2076

HANDRICK, JOSEPH W., state legislator; b. Nov. 2, 1965. BA, U. Wis. Assemblyman Wis. State Dist. 34, 1994—; mem. Oneida County, Wis. Mem. Wis. Equal Rights Coun. Mem. Minocqua Lakes Improvement Assn. (bd. dirs.). Address: 514 Chicago Ave Minocqua WI 54548

HANDWERGER, STUART, pediatrics educator; b. Balt., Dec. 10, 1938; s. Joseph and Lillie (Baum) H.; m. Roberta Ann Blaker; children: David, Rachel. BA, Johns Hopkins U., 1960; MD, U. Md., 1964. Intern in pediatrics Albert Einstein Coll. of Medicine, Bronx, 1964-65; resident in pediatrics Mt. Sinai Hosp., N.Y.C., 1965-66; clin. assoc. NIH, Bethesda, Md., 1966-68; fellow in endocrinology Harvard U., Boston, 1968-71; asst. prof. pediatrics Duke U., Durham, N.C., 1971-75, assoc. prof. pediatrics, 1975-81, prof. pediatrics, 1982-90; prof. pediatrics U. Cin., 1990—; mem. study sect. NIH, Bethesda, 1978-85; nat. adv. coun. Nat. Inst. of Child Health and Devel., Bethesda, 1988-92; adv. bd. Barbara Davis Diabetes Ctr., Denver, 1984-94. Editor: Trophoblast Cells, 1993. Lt. comdr. USPHS, 1966-68. Mem. Endocrine Soc., Am. Pediatric Soc., Soc. for Pediatric Rsch., Am. Fedn. for Clin. Rsch., Am. Soc. of Clin. Investigation, Am. Assn of Physicians. Democrat. Jewish. Home: 7150 Fair Oaks Dr Cincinnati OH 45237 Office: Children's Hosp 3333 Burnet Ave Cincinnati OH 45229

HANDWERKER, A. M., retired transportation executive; b. Chgo., Mar. 15, 1928; s. Fred and Celia H.; m. Betty Jean Ellingson, Nov. 28, 1948; children: Michael L., Sharon J. Behtash, Nancy G. Karam, James A. BS in Indsl. Engring., Ill. Inst. Tech., 1950. With Chgo. & North Western Transp. Co., Chgo., 1950-88, v.p. rates and divs., 1980-85, v.p. corp. analysis, 1985-88; vol. Citizen's Dem. Corps, Bulgaria privatization, 1993; inspector Chinese railroads People to People, 1963. Author: (with others) A Guide to Railroad Cost Analysis, 1964. Chgo. Jaycees scholar Ill. Inst. Tech., 1946. Mem. Ops. Rsch. Soc. Am., Inst. Mgmt. Sci., Soc. for Advancement Mgmt., Am. Ry. Engring. Assn., Cost Analysis Orgn., Am. Statis. Assn., Soc. Indsl. and Applied Maths., Transp. Rsch. Forum, Am. Math. Soc., Math. Assn. Am., Alpha Pi Mu. Repubican. Methodist. Club: Union League of Chgo. (bd. dirs. Civic and Arts Found. 1987). Avocations: travel, tennis. Office: Union Pacific Railroad Co 1416 Dodge St Omaha NE 68179

HANDWERKER, SY, public relations executive; b. Chgo., Apr. 5, 1933; s. Alex and Bella (Schwartzberg) H.; m. Marilyn Iris Parker, Aug. 6, 1961; chidren: Jaye, Dana, Steven. BS in Journalism, U. Ill., 1954; postgrad., U. DePaul Coll. Law, 1954-56. Reporter, editor City News Bur. Chgo., 1952-54; asst. dir. athletic publicity U. Ill., Chgo., 1954-59; publicist Balaban & Katz, Chgo., 1959-60; account exec. Aaron D. Cushman & Assocs., Chgo., 1960-64, Cooper, Burns & Golin, Chgo., 1964-67; v.p. Bernard E. Ury Assocs., Chgo., 1967-69; pres. The Hanlen Orgn., Inc., Chgo., 1970—. Bd. dirs. FREE, Chgo., Maot Chitim, Chgo.; chmn. U. Ill./Chgo. Athletic Alumni and Hall of Fame, 1990-92. With U.S. Army, 1956-58. Mem. Pub. Rels. Soc. Am., Publicity Club Chgo. (pres. 1990, bd. dirs., Golden Trumpet award 1980, 87, 88, Shaugnessy award 1979), Chgo. Newspaper Reporters Assn., Press Vets. Assn., Headline Club. Home: 1637 Sherwood Rd Highland Park IL 60035-2260 Office: Penthouse 300 400 Central Ave Northfield IL 60093

HANDY, WILLIAM TALBOT, JR., bishop; b. New Orleans, Mar. 26, 1924; s. William Talbot Sr. and Dorothy Pauline (Pleasant) H.; m. Ruth Odessa Robinson, Aug. 11, 1948; children—William Talbot III (dec.), Dorothy D. Handy Davis, Stephen Emanuel, Mercedes Handy Cowley. Student, Tuskegee U., 1940-43; B.A., Dillard U., 1948, LL.D. (hon.), 1981; M.Div., Gammon Theol. Sem., 1951; S.T.M., Boston U., 1952; DD, Cen. Meth. Coll., 1991. Ordained to ministry United Meth. Ch., 1949, consecrated bishop, 1980. Pastor Newman Meth. Ch., Alexandria, La., 1952-59; pastor St. Mark Meth. Ch., Baton Rouge, 1959-68; pub. rep. Meth. Pub. House, Nashville, 1968-70; v.p. pers. svc. United Meth. Pub. House, Nashville, 1970-78; dist. supt. Baton Rouge-Lafayette dist. United Meth. Ch., 1978-80; bishop Mo. area United Meth. Ch., St. Louis, 1980-92; bishop in residence U. Meth. Ch., Nashville, 1993—; interim dir. The Mission Resource Ctr., Atlanta, 1992; vis. Arthur J. Moore prof. Evangelism Candler Sch. Theol., Atlanta, 1993-94; mem. exec. com. Gen. Bd. Publ., Nashville, 1988-92. Chmn. sibcom. on voting rights U.S. Commn. on Civil Rights, 1959-68; mem. mayor's biracial adv. com. La. Adv. Com., Baton Rouge, 1965-66; Golden Heritage life mem. NAACP, 1971; chmn. bd. trustees Gammon Theol. Sem., Atlanta, 1990-94, St. Paul Sch. Theology, Kansas City, Mo., 1980-92, Interdenominational Theol. Ctr., Atlanta, 1990-93; bishop in residence Meml. United Meth. Ch. Mem. Masons (33 degree).

HANEY, SEAN T., mechanical engineer; b. Dover, Del., June 2, 1967. BS in Mech. Engring., Ohio State U., 1991. Mech. engr. Honda R&D, Raymond, Ohio, 1992-93, Interbold, Canton, Ohio, 1993—. Office: PO Box 3091 Canton OH 44720-8091

HANGARTNER, THOMAS NIKLAUS, medical physicist, educator; b. Brunnen, Switzerland, Aug. 9, 1949; came to U.S., 1985; s. Josef Paul and Gertrud Maria (Bärlocher) H.; m. Elisabeth Ruth Everts, Oct. 18, 1975; 1 child, Lilian Regina. Diploma in phys. ETH, Swiss Fed. Inst. Tech., Zurich, 1975, Dr. Sc. nat., 1978. Rsch. assoc. Swiss Fed. Inst. Tech., 1978-79; rsch. assoc. U. Alta., Edmonton, Can., 1979-80, asst. prof. biomed. engring., 1981-82, assoc. prof., 1982-85; assoc. prof. biomed. engring., medicine and physics Wright State U., Dayton, Ohio, 1986-94, prof., 1994—; reviewer NIH, Washington, 1986—. Contbr. articles to profl. publs. Capt. Swiss Army, 1983—. Alta. Heritage Found. for Med. Rsch. scholar, 1981, 83, 86; recipient cert. of merit Radiol. Soc. N.Am., 1989. Mem. Am. Assn. Physicists in Medicine (mem. diagnostic radiology com. 1988-92). Home: 1000 Van Eaton Rd Xenia OH 45385-9341 Office: Wright State U Biomed Imaging Lab 1 Wyoming St 504 East Bldg Dayton OH 45409-2722

HANGER, WILLIAM SHERWOOD, university administrator; b. Welch, W.Va., Nov. 18, 1945; s. Robert Judy and Ellen (Hesket) H.; m. Nancy Stranahan, Apr. 22, 1967; children: Elizabeth Evans, Jill Ellen. AB in Polit. Sci., Miami U., Oxford, Ohio, 1968, MEd in Ednl. Adminstrn., 1972; cert., Inst. Ednl. Mgmt., Harvard U., 1974. Asst. registrar Miami U., Oxford, 1968-69, asst. to provost, 1970-74, asst. provost, 1975-82; v.p. Transylvania U., Lexington, Ky., 1983; dir. instnl. rels. Miami U., Oxford, 1984—; exec. dir. Ohio Student Loan Commn. State of Ohio, Columbus, 1988; chmn. steering com. faculty exch. program Ohio Coll. Assn., 1974-78; cons. Cleve. Commn. of Higher Edn., 1975, Exxon Found., 1978; del. Assn. of Am.'s Pub. TV Stas., 1979-82, 84-94, 95—; chmn. Greater Cin. Consortium of Colls. and Univs. Cable TV Policy Com., 1980-82; vice chmn. Chancellor Ohio Bd. of Regents Com. on Hither Edn. Telecoms.; sec. Greater Dayton Pub. TV, Inc., 1986—, treas., 1984-86, mem. exec. com., 1984—, trustee, 1976-82, 84-94, 95—; chmn. Inter U. Coun. Legis. Officers, 1986-88. V.p. Oxford chpt. NAACP, 1976-78, membership co-chmn., 1972-76; mem. Oxford Citizens Adv. Com., 1973-75; mem. fin. affairs com. Oxford City Coun., 1982; bd. dirs. Oxford Community Improvement Corp., 1982; mem. Oxford City Coun., 1982; bd. dirs. Oxford Adv. Welfare Svc., 1984-85. Recipient Nat. award Assn. Am.'s Pub. TV Stas., 1991; named Miami U. PArents of Yr., 1990. Mem. Assn. Internat. des Etudiants et Scis. Economiques et Commerciales, Ohio C. of C. (mem. edn. com. 1989—, pub. affairs com. 1994—), Oxford Tomahawk Club (past res.), Omicron Delta Kappa. Office: Miami U 201 Roudebush Hall Oxford OH 45056

HANGSLEBEN, JOHN WILLIAM, personnel specialist; b. Belleville, Ill., Dec. 6, 1959; s. Harold William and Isabel Hope (Martinez) H. AA, Belleville Area Coll., 1980; BA, So. Ill. U., Edwardsville, 1983, MPA, 1988. Selling specialist J.C. Penney Co., Fairview Heights, Ill., 1979-87; grad. asst. dept. pub. adminstrn. So. Ill. U., Edwardsville, 1987; adminstrv. intern Pub. Wks. Dept., Alton, Ill., 1988; civilian personnelist Aviation & Troop Command, St. Louis, 1989—; adj. faculty Nat. Louis U., St. Louis, 1988—. Recipient Operation Desert Storm commendation. Mem. Inst. for Mgmt. Scis., Am. Soc. for Pub. Adminstrn. Democrat. Home: 1006 Caroline Ave O'Fallon IL 62269

HANILAND, JEFFREY S., instrument company executive; b. Sioux City, Iowa, May 30, 1954. B, U. Minn., 1980; MBA, U. St. Thomas, 1989. Mgr. mktg. Honeywell Corp., Plymouth, Minn., 1980-93; pres. Seitz Stainless, Avon, Minn., 1994—. Mem. Instruments Soc. Am. Office: Seitz Stainless 17578 400th St Avon MN 56310-9735

HANISCH, KATHY ANN, psychologist; b. Spencer, Iowa; d. Gordon Lee and Carol Jean (Richards) H. BA, U. No. Iowa, 1985; MA, U. Ill., 1988, PhD, 1990. Grad. asst. Dept. Psychology, U. Ill., Champaign, 1985-90; psychology prof. Iowa State U., Ames, 1990—; cons. in field, 1988—. Contbr. articles to Jour. Applied Psychology, The Indsl.-Orgnl. Psychologist, Ergonomics, Jour. Vocat. Behavior, Current Directions in Psychol. Sci., Pers. Psychology and chpts. to books. Mem. APA, Am. Psychol. Soc., Soc. for Indsl. and Orgnl. Psychology (Ghiselli award 1989), Phi Kappa Phi. Home: 1420 Illinois Ave Ames IA 50014-3761 Office: Iowa State U W212 Lagomarcino Hall Ames IA 50011

HANKE, KARL WILLIAM, III, insurance company executive; b. Frankfurt, Fed. Republic of Germany, Feb. 16, 1958; came to U.S., 1960; s. Karl W. and Barbara R. (Favory) H.; m. Miriam Elizabeth Schubkegel, Oct. 28, 1979; children: Karl W. IV, Luke T., Audra F., Maranda E.; m. P.J. Walker, Dec. 31, 1993. Student, Western Ill. U., 1978-80. Registered fraternal ins. counselor. Laborer McGraw Edison Co., Macomb, Iowa, 1977-78; owner, operator Simrock Western Ill. U., East Iowa U., Macomb, 1979-80; dist. rep. Modern Woodmen Am., Macomb, 1980-84; dist. mgr. Modern Woodmen Am., Peoria, Ill., 1984-86, agy. mgr., 1986-96; owner, operator PIPCO Fin. Investment Firm, Blue Springs, Md., 1996—. Bd. dirs. Full Employment Coun. Greater Kansas City, 1992—. Fellow Fraternal Ins. Counselors (pres. Mo. 1993); mem. Kansas City Life Underwriters Assn. (LUPIC chmn. bd. dirs. 1993, 94), Life Underwriters Assn. (bd. dirs. 1985-86, Nat. Quality award 1985-89, Nat. Sales Achievement award 1985-89), Am. Heart Assn. Blue Springs (dir. 1988), Million Dollar Round Table, Gen. Agy. Mgrs. Assn., Blue Springs C. of C. (Blue Blazer 1986—), Kansas City C. of C. Republican. Lutheran. Office: PIPCO Fin 901 NW Vesper St Blue Springs MO 64015-3735

HANKINS, MARIE GARNER, chemistry educator; b. Magee, Miss., Dec. 27, 1943; d. Alfred Jesse and Albert Naydell (Herrington) Garner; m. Warren Mason Hankins, Oct. 19, 1962; children: Kimberly Keenan, Warren Tracy, Corinda Marie, Launa Darlene. BA, King Coll., 1965; PhD, U. Va., 1969. Vis. asst. prof. U. Evansville, Ind., 1969-70; tchr. Reitz Meml. High Sch., Evansville, 1974-75, Mater Dei High Sch., Evansville, 1975-83, Evansville Day Sch., 1984-85; asst. prof. chemistry U. So. Ind., Evansville, 1985-88, assoc. prof., chair chemistry dept., 1988—; cons. NASA/Am. Soc. Engring. Edn., Huntsville, Ala., 1975. Author: Introductory Chemistry, 1974; co-author NASA/ASEE and EDRA/ASEE publs.; contbr. articles to profl. publs. Coach Ind. Youth Soccer Assn., Evansville, 1976-79, state coach, 1986-87; soccer coach Mater Dei High Sch., 1978-84. Gov.'s fellow U. Va., 1970, summer fellow NASA/ASEE, 1974, ERDA/ASEE, 1976, U. So. Miss., 1991. Mem. Am. Chem. Soc. (chair local chpt. 1989-90, 93-94, councilor 1994—, task force for undergrad. programming 1993-95, com. on pub. rels. 1995—), Ind. Acad. Sci. Mem. United Ch. of Christ. Office: U So Ind 8600 University Blvd Evansville IN 47712-3534

HANKIS, ROY ALLEN, interior designer; b. Greenville, Mich., May 24, 1943; s. John LeRoy and Nila A. (Taylor) H. Interior design diploma Kendall Sch. Design, 1964; student Cranbrook Acad. Art, 1971. Dir. design, contract design firms, Grand Rapids and Detroit, Mich., 1964-73; owner, designer Roy Allen Hankis Interiors, Troy, Mich., 1974—; instr. interior design Henry Ford C.C., Dearborn, Mich., 1981—; trustee JONIRO Investment Co., Southfield, Mich., 1981—; set designer Lexington Village Players, 1991—. Patentee in field. Participating designer Detroit Symphony ASID Showhouse, Bloomfield Hills, Mich., 1985, 91, 93, Best of Detroit Design Live Mich. Design Ctr., 1992, 93, Health House, 1995; mem. founder's soc. Detroit Inst. of Arts, 1988—; designer Birmingham Jr. League-Mich. Design Ctr. Celebrity Room for Mich.'s first lady, 1985. Mem. Am. Soc. Interior Designers (dir. Mich. chpt. 1974, treas. 1992-93), Christian Bus. Men's Com. Detroit., Rotary, Detroit Yacht Club. Baptist. Home and Office: PO Box 99280 Troy MI 48099-9280

HANLEY, MICHAEL JOSEPH, state legislator; b. Saginaw, Mich., Dec. 9, 1955; s. Richard Albert and Doreen Ann (Goodrow) H.; m. Susi Arndt. BA summa cum laude, Western Mich. U., 1987. Mayor pro tem Saginaw, 1991-93; rep. Mich. State Dist. 95, 1995—; Saginaw City Coun., 1987-93; vice chair urban policy com. Mich. Ho. Reps., 1995—, human svcs. com., minority whip; apptd. Darden Emerging Polit. Leaders Program. Mem. NAACP. Address: State Capitol Lansing MI 48913

HANLEY, THOMAS PATRICK, obstetrician, gynecologist; b. St. Louis, Apr. 16, 1951; s. Thomas P. and Virginia Barbara (Lydon) H.; m. Patricia Ann McHargue, Dec. 27, 1975; children: Colleen, Thomas III, Timothy, Matthew. BA, St. Louis U., 1973, MD, 1977. Diplomate Am. Bd. Ob-gyn. Intern St. Louis U., 1977-78, resident, 1978-81; practice medicine speciailizing in ob-gyn St. Louis, 1981—; pres. med. staff St. Mary's Health Ctr., 1993; mem. staff Mo. Bapt. Hosp., Deaconess Hosp.; assoc. clin. prof. St. Louis U. Med. Sch., 1983—; mem. exec. com. St. Louis Med. Group, 1995—. Mem. AMA (Physicians Recognition award 1981—), Am. Coll. Ob-Gyn. (Physicians Excellence award 1986, 89, 92, 95), Gynecol. Laser Soc., St. Louis Gynecol. Soc. (pres. 1989-90), St. Louis Met. Med. Soc., West Borough Country Club. Republican. Roman Catholic. Office: 1035 Bellevue Ave Ste 208 Saint Louis MO 63117-1846

HANLON, DIANE WIEMER, administrative assistant; b. Pitts., Nov. 4, 1948; d. Robert C. and Dolores C. (Charlton) Wiemer; m. Roger L. Hanlon; 1 child, Mark Allan. Student, Bowling Green State U., 1966-67, Cleve. State U., 1968-74, 90-91. Sec. phys. plant, student life, Coll. Edn. Cleve. State U., 1969-74, adminstrv. asst. to chmn. dept. history, 1974-92; adminstrv. asst. to Women's Comprehensive Program, 1992—; freelance editing, indexing, proofreading, reading, 1992—; owner Streamers. Editor 2 cookbooks. V.p. ways and means, libr. aide, head room mother St. Justin Martyr Elem. Sch. Parent's Club, 1981-86; chair fundraising, chair social activities Gilmour Acad. Women's Club, 1988—; tchr. 1st aid and babysitting clinics ARC, 1984-86; vol. tchr., treas., sec., pres. laides com. West End YMCA, Willoughby, 1977-83, bd. dirs., 1979. Mem. Copywriter's Coun. Am. Office: Cleve State U E 24th St Cleveland OH 44115

HANN, ALAN FREDERICK, banker; b. Rapid City, S.D., Feb. 2, 1946; s. Mathew R. and Etta E. (Weiss) H.; m. Mary Kay Crider, Aug. 23, 1969; 1 child, Jennie Kay. BS in Metall. Engring., S.D. Sch. Mines and Tech., Rapid City, 1969. Engr. IBM Corp., Boulder, Colo., 1969-74; CEO First State Bank, Buffalo, S.D., 1974-88, Liberty Nat. Bank, Dickinson, N.D., 1988-95; pres. Norwest Bank, Dickinson, 1995—; bd. dirs. Pioneer Bank & Trust Belle Fourche, S.D., Liberty Nat. Bank, dickinson; bd. dirs., chmn. bd. First Nat. Bank, Bowman, N.D. Mem. Rotary. Home: 587 Park St Dickinson ND 58601-3848 Office: Norwest Bank 115 1st Ave W Dickinson ND 58601-5105

HANNA, DONALD EUGENE, academic administrator; b. Garden City, Kans., Aug. 20, 1947; s. Joseph Walkup and Iris Anzina (Brown) H.; m. Karna Ostrum; children: Jason Dean, Elizabeth Courtney. BA in Anthropology and History, U. Kans., 1969; MS in Edn., SUNY, Buffalo, 1974; PhD in Adult and Continuing Edn., Mich. State U., 1978. With Tchr. Corps, Lackawanna, N.Y., 1971-72, Peace Corps, Afghanistan, 1972-74; acad. advisor, instr. Mich. State U., East Lansing, 1974-77; asst. prof. adult, higher and continuing edn. U. Ill., Urbana-Champaign, 1979-83, asst. head div. extramural courses, 1977-79, head div. extramural courses, 1979-83; prof. adult and continuing edn. Wash. State U., Pullman, 1983-93, dir. continuing edn. and pub. svc., 1983-85, acting vice provost extended univ. svcs., 1985-87, assoc. vice provost extended univ. svcs., 1987-93; chancellor U. Wis. Ext., Madison, 1993—; cons. in field; co-organizer Internat. Telecomm. Symposium, 1990; bd. dirs. S.W. Wash. Joint Ctr. for Edn., 1985-87; founding mem. Ea. Wash. Area Health Edn. Ctr., 1986; sec. Nat. Univs. Degree Consortium, 1989-92. Contbr. articles to profl. publs., chpts. to books. Kellogg Found. fellow, 1987-90; recipient numerous grants. Mem. Western Ednl. Telecom. Coop. (steering com. 1988-91), Nat. U. Continuing Edn. Assn. (bd. dirs. 1984-86), Wash. Higher Edn. Telecom. System (sec. bd. dirs. 1985-89). Home: 2379 N Pleasant View Cir Lodi WI 53555 Office: U Wis Ext 432 N Lake St Rm 527 Madison WI 53706-1415

HANNA, JAMES LEANORD, financial consultant; b. San Antonio, Tex., Feb. 27, 1955. BS, U. Ala., 1977. Prodn. mgr. Pennwalt Corp., Calumet City, Ill., 1977-83; asst. v.p. Merrill Lynch, Chgo., 1983—. Mem. Union League Club. Office: Merrill Lynch # 290 141 W Jackson Chicago IL 60604

HANNA, MARSHA L., artistic director; b. Tiffin, Ohio, Nov. 27, 1951; d. Willis Leondadis and Frances Lucille (Neeley) H. BS, Bowling Green State U., 1980. Drama specialist City of Dayton, Ohio, 1975-80; gen. mgr. Illumination Theatre, 1978-85; product analyst Mead Data Ctrl., 1980-86; instr. Sinclair C.C., 1986—; freelance stage dir., 1986—; resident dir. Human Race Theatre Co., 1986—, artistic dir., 1990—. Dir.: That Championship Season, 1975, Dandelion Wine, 1978, Animal Farm, 1980, Equus, 1981, Beyond Therapy, 1983, The Diviners, 1984, Amadeus, 1985, The Fantasticks, 1986, Getting Out, 1987, Orphans, 1988, Fool for Love, 1989, A Shayna Maidel, 1990, A Christmas Carol, 1991, Steel Magnolias, 1992, The Elephant Man, 1993, Closer Than Ever, 1993, The Good Times Are Killing Me, 1994, Cloud Nine, 1995, Three Tall Women, 1996. Office: The Human Race Theatre Co 126 N Main St Ste 300 Dayton OH 45402

HANNA, SUZANNE LOUISE, nurse; b. Mankato, Minn., Aug. 31, 1953; d. Frank Edward and Phyllis Ruth (Moeller) Wilkins; m. Thomas Ray Hanna, Sept. 15, 1973; children: Elizabeth Amy, Joseph Ryan, Thomas Wilkins. Diploma in nursing with highest honors, Iowa Western C.C., Council Bluffs, 1991. RN, Iowa; cert. provider ACLS, Am. Heart Assn. Exec. sec. First Nat. Bank, Mpls., 1971-72, Nat. Bank of Am., Salina, Kans., 1972; receptionist The Evening Sentinel, Shenandoah, Iowa, 1972-73; ins. sec. Wilson Ins. Agy., Shenandoah, 1973-79; med./surg. staff nurse Shenandoah Meml. Hosp., 1980-81; office nurse Dr. Floyd A. Jones, Shenandoah, 1983-95; clin. nurse Great Plains Physician Group, Omaha, Nebr., 1995—; emergency rm. nurse Shenandoah Meml. Hosp., 1992-95; bd. dirs. Ag-Pro Corp., Shenandoah; co-chairperson family life com., 1989-90. Alt. Rep. Page County Convs., 1988, 92; active ladies guild St. Mary Ch., Shenandoah,

1986—, mem. parish coun. bd., pres. parish coun., 1989-92, instr. religious edn., 1988-90, mem. choir, 1991—, organist, song leader, 1992—; bd. dirs. Shenandoah Music Assn., 1995—; mem. local Am. Legion Aux., 1994—. Mem. Beta Sigma Phi (pres. 1979-80). Roman Catholic. Home: 1302 Johnson Dr Shenandoah IA 51601-2606 Office: 300 Park Ave Shenandoah IA 51601-2351 also: 300 Pershing Ave Shenandoah IA 51601-2355

HANNCKEN HENRY, JUDITH CURTIS, education educator; b. Toledo, Mar. 9, 1943; d. Charles Edward and Helen Mac (Burpe) Hanncken; m. Raymond S. Hanry Jr., June 25, 1988. B of Edn., U. Toledo, 1965; MEd, Bowling Green State U., 1967; PhD, U. Toledo, 1975. Tchr. English Whitmer High Sch., Toledo, 1965-66; grad. asst. Bowling Green (Ohio) State U., 1966-67; prof. gen. edn. U. Toledo, 1967—. Author: Write Right: A Guide, 1981. Mem., v.p. Toledo Athletic Commn., 1989—. Mem. Nat. Coun. Tchrs. English, Midwest Regional Con. English in Two-Yr. Coll. (chair 1975-83, sec. 1987-90), Ohio Assn. Two Yr. Colls. (mem. editorial bd. jour. 1987—), Women of Moose. Office: U Toledo 2801 W Bancroft St Toledo OH 43606

HANNINGTON, MARY LEE, production company executive; b. Detroit, July 18, 1960; d. Ian and Bernice (Sumiec) H. BFA, Mich. State U., 1982. Database program design and tng. profl. Bus. Computer, Southfield, Mich., 1983-86; animator, producer Geoffrey & Jeffrey, Farmington, Mich., 1987-89; exec. producer The Big Picture, Farmington, 1989-91; owner, creative dir. Rivet Films, Inc., Detroit, 1991—. Exec. prodr. (TV) Litter Pigs, 1988 (BDA Bronze award); exec. prodr., animator (TV) Jacobson's, 1990 (Silver Caddy); animator on computer (video for Chevy) Milton (N.Y. Film Festival Bronze); illustrator: Don't Stand Too Close to a Naked Man (by Tim Allen), 1994. Mem. Founders Soc. D.I.A., Detroit, 1990—, Nat. Mus. of Women in Art, Washington, 1991—. Recipient Mobius award, 1996. Mem. Internat. Platform Assn., Detroit Producers Assn. Office: Rivet Films Inc 230 E Grand River Ave Fl 6 Detroit MI 48226-2107

HANOVER, R(AYMOND) SCOTT, physical education trainer; b. Des Moines, June 10, 1964; s. Norman E. and Jo Ann (Taylor) H.; m. Marla J. Boicourt, Apr. 23, 1988. BA, Grand View Coll., 1986. Staff writer, news asst. Des Moines Register, 1985-90; sch. dir. Missouri Valley sect. USTA, Kansas City, Mo., 1990—; chmn., pub. rels. com. Mo. Valley Tennis Assn., Kansas City, 1989-90; corr. tennis, 1990—. Editor U.S. Profl. Tennis Assn. Missouri Valley divsn. newsletter, 1992-95. Recipient Svc. award Nebr. AHPERD, 1991. Mem. AAHPERD, Kans. and Mo. AAHPERD, Iowa Park and Recreation Assn., U.S. Tennis Assn., U.S. Profl. Tennis Registry, Grand View Alumni Coun. (pres. 1988-90). Office: USTA Missouri Valley Sect 801 Walnut St Ste 100 Kansas City MO 64106-1823

HANRATH, LINDA CAROL, librarian, archivist; b. Chgo., Aug. 22, 1949; d. John Stanley and Victoria (Fraint) Grzesiakowski; m. Richard Alan Hanrath, Nov. 1, 1980; 1 child, Emily. BA in History, Rosary Coll., 1971, MA in Library Sci., 1974. Tchr. social studies Notre Dame High Sch., Chgo., 1971-75; outreach libr. Indian Trails Pub. Libr., Wheeling, Ill., 1975-76, Arlington Heights (Ill.) Meml. Libr., 1976-78; corp. libr. William Wrigley Jr. Co., Chgo., 1978—. Mem. Spl. Librs. Assn. (chmn. libr. jobline com. 1981-83, 86-87, food agrl. and nutrition divsn. 1988-89, sec. Ill. chpt. 1984-86, pres.-elect 1993-94, pres. Ill. chpt. 1994-95), Assn. Records Mgrs. and Adminstrs., Soc. Am. Archivists, Midwest Archives Conf., Beta Phi Mu. Home: 715 E Devon Ave Roselle IL 60172-1461 Office: William Wrigley Jr Co 410 N Michigan Ave Chicago IL 60611-4211

HANREDDY, JOSEPH, stage director; b. Los Angeles, Oct. 18, 1947; s. Harvey Joseph and Geraldine (Powers) H. BA, San Jose State U., 1969, MA, 1970. Artistic dir. Ensemble Theatre Project, Santa Barbara, Calif., 1979-85, Madison Repertory Theatre, 1987-1993, Milw. Repertory Theater, 1993—; dir. San Diego Repertory Theatre, 1986, Cider Mill Playhouse, Binghamton, N.Y., 1985—, Santa Barbara Repertory Theatre, 1985. Office: Milwaukee Repertory Theatre 108 E Wells St Milwaukee WI 53202*

HANSEN, CARL G., electrical engineer; b. Millington, Tenn., Apr. 22, 1951. BS in Elec. Engring., U. Minn., 1974. Sr. design engr. Alliant Tech-Systems, Hopkins, Minn., 1986—. Mem. U.S. First, Nashua, N.H., 1994—; tutor Alliant Tchrs. Acad., Hopkins, 1995—. Mem. IEEE. Home: 4065 Raspberry Ridge Rd NE Prior Lake MN 55372-1125 Office: Alliant Tech-Systems 600 2d St NE Hopkins MN 55343

HANSEN, CARL R., management consultant, b. Chgo., May 2, 1926; s. Carl M. and Anna C. (Roge) H.; m. Christia Marie Loeser, Dec. 31, 1952; 1 child, Lothar. MBA, U. Chgo., 1954. Dir. market rsch. Kitchens of Sara Lee, Deerfield, Ill., Earle Ludgin & Co., Chgo.; svc. v.p. Market Rsch. Corp. Am., 1956-67; pres. Chgo. Assoc. Inc., 1967—. Chmn. Ill. adv. coun. SBA, 1973-74; mem. exec. com. Ill. Gov.'s Adv. Coun., 1969-72; resident officer U.S. High Commn. Germany, 1949-52; vice chmn. Rep. Cen. Com. Cook County; chmn. Cook County Young Reps., 1957-58, 12th Congl. Dist. Rep. Orgn., 1971-74, 78-82, Suburban Rep. Orgn., 1974-78, 82-86; del. Rep. Nat. Conv., 1968, 84, 92; chmn. Legis. Dist. Ill., 1964—; del. Rep. State Conv., 1962-96; Elk Grove Twp. Rep. committeeman, 1962—; pres. John Ericsson Rep. League Ill., 1975-76; Rep. presdl. elector Ill., 1972; chmn. Viking Ship Restoration Com., mem. Cook County Bd. Commrs., 1970, 74—, chmn. legis. com., adminstrn. com.; mem. bd. dirs. Nat. Assn. Counties; mem. Am. Scandinavian Found. 1st lt. AUS, 1944-48, maj. Res. Mem. Am. Mktg. Assn., Am. Statis. Assn., Nat. Assn. Counties (dir.), Res. Officers Assn., Chgo. Hist. Soc., Planning Forum, Am. Legion, VFW, Dania Soc., Sons of Norway, Swedish Am. Hist. Soc., Lions, Masons, Shriners. Home: 110 S Edward St Mount Prospect IL 60056-3414 Office: 118 N Clark St Chicago IL 60602-1304

HANSEN, CHERRY ANN, special education educator; b. Jackson, Minn., Nov. 9, 1951; d. Marlo Argene and Mary Ellen (Walsh) Fisher; m. Paul Herbert Hansen, June 26, 1977; children: Angela, Rachel. BA, U. No. Iowa, 1974; MA, Drake U., 1994. Lic. tchr., Iowa. Tchr. behaviors Council Bluffs (Iowa) C.C., 1974-79, 86-91; tchr. adult edn. Iowa Western C.C., Council Bluffs, 1982-86; tchr. behavior disorders Loess Hills Area Edn. Agy. # 13, Council Bluffs, 1991—; lead tchr. AEA 13, 1994-96. Mem. Nat. Tchrs. Assn. (exec. v.p.), Coun. for Exceptional Children, Council Bluffs Tchrs. Assn.

HANSEN, CLAIRE V., financial executive; b. Thornton, Iowa, June 3, 1925; s. Charles F. and Grace B. (Miller) H.; m. Renee C. Hansen, Aug. 17, 1946; children: Charles James, Christopher David, Peter Chrissis. B.Sc., U. Notre Dame, 1947; M.B.A., Harvard U., 1948. Chartered fin. analyst. With Salk, Ward & Salk, Inc.; v.p. Salk Inst. Agency, 1954-59; with Duff, Anderson & Clark, Chgo., 1959-67; v.p., dir. Duff, Anderson & Clark, 1967-71; dir. Duff and Phelps, Inc., 1972-88; exec. v.p. Duff & Phelps, 1973-75, pres., chief exec. officer, 1975-84, chmn., chief exec. officer, 1984-87; chmn., bd. dirs. Duff & Phelps Utilities Income, Inc., Chgo., 1987—. Bd. dirs. Chgo. Lung Assn., 1962-80, pres. 1973-75; bd. dirs. Am. Lung Assn., 1971-83, Ctr. Religion and Psychotherapy in Chgo., 1979-83; trustee Glenwood Sch. for Boys, 1974-95, chmn., 1983-87; bd. dirs. Auditorium Theatre Coun., 1983-88, treas., 1987-88; bd. dirs. Schwab Rehab. Hosp., 1978-82, pres., 1980-82; bd. dirs. Pelican Bay of Naples Found. Inc., 1992—, treas., 1992-95, pres., 1996—. Mem. Inst. Chartered Fin. Analysts, Mid-Am. Club, Univ. Club, Chgo. Club, Olympia Fields Country Club, Club Pelican Bay, Hole-in-the-Wall Golf Club. Republican. Episcopalian. Home: 5601 Turtle Bay Dr Apt 2001 Naples FL 33963-2703 Office: 55 E Monroe St Ste 3800 Chicago IL 60603

HANSEN, DAVID RASMUSSEN, federal judge; b. 1938. BA, N.W. Mo. State U., 1960; JD, George Washington U., 1963. Asst. clk. to minority House Appropriations Com. Ho. of Reps., 1960-61; adminstrv. aide 7th Dist. Iowa, 1962-63; pvt. practice law Jones, Cambridge & Carl, Atlantic, Iowa, 1963-64; capt., judge advocate General's Corps U.S. Army, 1964-68; pvt. practice law Barker, Hansen & McNeal, Iowa Falls, Iowa, 1968-76; ptnr. Win-Gin Farms, Iowa Falls, 1971—; judge Police Ct., Iowa, 1969-73, 2d Jud. Dist. Iowa Dist. Ct., 1976-86, U.S. Dist. Ct. (no. dist.) Iowa, Cedar Rapids, 1986-91, U.S. Ct. Appeals (8th cir.), Cedar Rapids, 1991—. Office: US Courthouse 101 1st St SE Cedar Rapids IA 52401-1230

HANSEN, DONALD MARTY, journalist, accountant; b. Elmhurst, Ill., July 6, 1935; s. Donald Joseph Hansen and Vivian Leona (Bourgart) Guthrie; m. Rose Ann Baumeister, Aug. 12, 1961 (div.); children: Teresa Lynn, Donna Louise, David Lawrence, Daniel Leonard. Assoc. in Acctg., Racine Tech., 1971. Drill press operator J.I. Case Co., Racine, Wis., 1964-70; acct. Scott Petersen Meat Co., Chgo., 1974-95, Crosby Freezer, Inc., Chgo., 1995—; editor, pub. Don Hansen's Nat. Weekly Football and Basketball Gazettes, Brookfield, Ill., 1987—; stringer Football News, Detroit, 1981—, The Sporting News, St. Louis, 1987—, USA Today, Arlington, Va., 1987—; mem. Melberger award selection com. Downtown Wilkes-Barre Touchtown Club, 1993—; mem. com. for NCAA Divsn. III Player of the Yr., John Gagliardi award, 1993—. Contbr. acticles to profl. jours. Originator, promoter, operator annual summer wrestling tournament Oak Park-River Forest (Ill.) H.S., 1978-80. With USN, 1952-54. Recipient Leadership trophy Chase Park (Chgo.), 1947, Celebrity Cert. of Appreciation ARC, 1992, Statistician of the Yr. Oak Park-River Forest H.S., 1981. Mem. CO-SIDA Coll. Sports Info. Dirs. Am. Republican. Mem. Assembly of God Ch. Home: 8802 45th Pl Apt 11 Brookfield IL 60513-2563 Office: Don Hansen's Nat Weekly Football Gazette PO Box 514 Brookfield IL 60513-0514

HANSEN, H. JACK, management consultant; b. Chgo., Mar. 28, 1922; s. Herbert Christian John and Laura Elizabeth (Osterman) H.; m. Joan Dorothy Norum, Nov. 28, 1980; children: Marilyn Joan, Gail Jean, Mark John, Jacquelyn Lee. BS in Mech. Engring., Ill. Inst. Tech., 1944; cert. mgmt. cons.; Mech. and indsl. engr. Harper Wyman Co., Chgo., 1944-51; chief plant indsl. engr. Shakeproof div. Ill. Tool Works, Des Plaines, 1951-53; cons., prin. A.T. Kearney & Co., Chgo. and N.Y.C., 1953-71; pres. H.J. Hansen Co., Elburn, Ill., 1971—; commr., planning commn. Village of Elburn, 1995—; acting mfg. engring. mgr. European oper. Hobart Corp., 1974-78; owner, mgmt. cons. Hansen Mgmt. Search Co., Mt. Prospect, 1980-93. Pioneered the use of Should Cost studies for the U.S. Def. Dept., conceptulized and devel. the procedure for gain sharing productivity improvement; active turn-around consulting, 1992—. Pres. Good Sheperd Luth. Ch., Des Plaines, 1988-90, pres. Men's Club, 1987-90. With AUS, 1945-46. Mem. Inst. Mgmt. Cons. (founding), Methods-Time Measurement Assn. (dir. 1964-70, pres. 1967-68), Am. Arbitration Assn., Soc. Advancement Mgmt. (past dir.), Coun. for Internat. Progress in Mgmt. (past dir.), Found. Internat. Progress in Mgmt. (past dir.). Office: H J Hansen Co 317 Prairie Valley St Elburn IL 60119-8977

HANSEN, JOHN HERBERT, university administrator, accountant; b. Milw., Mar. 20, 1945; s. John Herbert and Elsie F. (Patri) H.; m. Christina Ann Laniey, Sept. 5, 1970. BBA, U. Wis., 1969; M in Acctg., U. Ill., 1973. CPA, Wis. Assoc. v.p. fin. Marquette U., Milw., 1973—. With USAF, 1970-73. Mem. Am. Inst. CPA's, Milw. Bond Club. Republican. Club: Merrill Hills Country. Office: Marquette U PO Box 1881 Milwaukee WI 53201-1881

HANSEN, KATHRYN GERTRUDE, former state official, association editor; b. Gardner, Ill., May 24, 1912; d. Harry J. and Marguerite (Gaston) Hansen; BS with honors, U. Ill., 1934, MS, 1936. Sec., U. N.C., 1936-37; sec., U. High Sch., U. Ill., 1937-44; Personnel asst. U. Ill., Urbana, 1944-46, supr. tng. and activities, 1946-47, personnel officer, instr. psychology, 1947-52, exec. sec. U. Civil Service System Ill., also sec. for merit bd., 1952-61, adminstrv. officer, sec. merit bd., 1961-68, dir. system, 1968-72; lay asst. firm Webber, Balbach, Theis and Follmer, P.C., Urbana, Ill., 1972-74. Bd. dirs. U. YWCA, 1952-55, chmn., 1954-55; bd. dirs. Champaign-Urbana Symphony, 1978-81; sec. Presbyn. Women 1st Presbyn. Ch., Champaign, 1986-90, mem. coordinating team, 1986-91. Mem. Coll. and Univ. Personnel Assn. (hon., life mem., editor jour. 1955-73, newsletter, internat. pres. 1967-68, nat. publs. award named in her honor 1987, Ill. State award 1996), Annuitants Assn. State Univs. Retirement System Ill. (state sec.-treas. 1974-75), Pres.'s Council U. Ill. (life), U. Ill. Alumni Assn. (life), Friends of the Library (bd. dirs. 1987-91), U. Ill. Found., Nat. League Am. Pen Women, AAUW (state 1st v.p. 1958-60, hon., life), Secretariat U. Ill. (life, named scholarship 1972—), Grundy County Hist. Soc. (life), Delta Kappa Gamma (state pres. 1961-63), Phi Mu (life), Kappa Delta Pi, Kappa Tau Alpha. Presbyterian. Clubs: Fortnightly (Champaign-Urbana), U. Ill. Women's Club, Evening Etude-Mozart Club (hon.). Lodge: Order Eastern Star. Author: (with others) A Plan of Position Classification for Colleges and Universities; A Classification Plan for Staff Positions at Colleges and Universities, 1968; Grundy-Corners, 1982; Sarah, A Documentary of Her Life and Times, 1984, Ninety Years with Fortnightly, Vols. I and II, an historical compilation, 1986, Whispers of Yesterday, 1989, Through the Years with the Champaign-Urbana Business and Professional Women's Club, 1912-1993, 1993, My Heritage, 1995; editor: The Illini Worker, 1946-52; Campus Pathways, 1952-61; This is Your Civil Service Handbook, 1960-67; author, cons., editor publs. on personnel practices. Home: 1004 E Harding Dr Apt 307 Urbana IL 61801-6346

HANSEN, LORRAINE SUNNY SUNDAL (SUNNY HANSEN), counselor, educator; b. Albert Lea, Minn.; d. Rasmus O. and Cora B. Sundal; m. Tor Kjaerstad Hansen, Dec. 15, 1962; children: Sonja, Tor S. BS, U. Minn., 1951, MA, 1957, PhD, 1962; postgrad., U. Oslo, Norway, 1959-60. Nat. cert. counselor; cert. career counselor. English tchr. St. Louis Park, Minn., 1951-53, Lab. Sch. U. Chgo., 1953-54; tchr. English and journalism Univ. High Sch., U. Minn., Mpls., 1954-57, counselor, dir. counseling, 1957-70; asst. prof., assoc. prof., prof. ednl. psychology U. Minn., Mpls., 1962—; founder, dir. project BORN FREE; cons. schs. and colls.; lectr. throughout U.S. and 16 countries; dir. workshops on career devel. and career counseling, gender roles, integrative life planning; co-dir. MICI Internat. Counseling Inst., 1989, 91, 93, 95. Author: Career Guidance Practices in School and Community, 1970, An Examination of Concepts and Definitions of Career Education, 1976, Integrative Life Planning, 1987, (with others) Educating for Career Development, 1975, 80, Career Development and Planning, 1982, Eliminating Sex Stereotyping in Schools, 1984; editor: Career Development and Counseling of Women, 1978, Career Patterns of Selected Women Leaders, 1987, Integrative Career Planning, 1994, (with others) Growing Smart: What's Working for Girls in Schools, 1995, Gender vs. a Factor in Multicultural Counseling, 1995, Career Development Gender and Issues in U.S., 1993, Integrative Life Planning, 1995; mem. editl. bd. Internat. Jour. Advancement Counseling, 1980-88 (lectr. 15 countries), Minn. Jour. for Counseling and Human Devel., 1984-95. Fulbright scholar U. Oslo, 1959-60; named Outstanding Leader in Edn. Mpls. YWCA, 1984; recipient Career Devel. Profl. Award S.E. Minn. chpt. ASTD, 1986. Fellow APA; mem. AAUW, Am. Coun. Assn. (pres.-elect 1988-89, pres. 1989-90, Best Video award 1980, Nat. Profl. Devel. award 1995), Minn. Psychol. Assn., Minn. Assn. for Counseling and Devel. (recipient cert. recognition 1976, Nat. Disting. Achievement award 1990), Am. Sch. Counselors Assn., Am. Coll. Pers. Assn., Am. Coll. Counselors Assn., Assn. for Counselor Edn. and Supervision (Nat. Disting. Mentor award 1985), Nat. Career Devel. Assn. (pres.-elect 1984-85, pres. 1985-86, Eminent Career award 1990), Am. Counseling Assn. (Prof. Dev. award 1995), Minn. Career Devel. Assn. (pres. 1982-83, Rsch. award 1980, Outstanding Achievement award 1986), Internat. Assn. Ednl.-Vocat. Guidance, Internat. Round Table for Advancement of Counseling (exec. coun., v.p. 1986-88), Assn. for Multicultural Counseling and Devel., Assn. for Adult Devel. and Aging, Minn. Women's Consortium, Upper Midwest Norwegian-Am. C. of C. (pres., bd. dirs. 1988—), Phi Delta Kappa, Chi Sigma Iota. Democrat. Congregationalist. Office: U Minn Dept Ednl Psychology 139 Burton Hall 178 Pillsbury Dr SE Minneapolis MN 55455-0296

HANSEN, MARION JOYCE, nursing administrator; b. Wadena, Minn., Oct. 20, 1951; d. Charles R. and Dorothy M. (Hennen) Hillig; m. Keith Hansen, June 2, 1979; children: Adam, Angela, John James, Jason. Diploma, St. Luke's Hosp. Sch. Nursing, Duluth, Minn., 1972; BS, Moorhead State U., 1991. Lic. nursing home adminstr. Staff RN ICCU Tri-County Hosp., Wadena, 1972-74, house supr. ICCU, staff RN, edn. dir., ICCU coor., 1974-89, asst. adminstr.; dir. of nursing Elders' Home, Inc., New York Mills, Minn., 1989-96; contr. risk mgr. Elders' Home, 1996—; claims coord. workers compensation; chair nursing program adv. com., Northwest Tech. Coll. Mem. Nat. Assn. Dirs. Nursing Assn. Long Term Care, Minn. Dirs. Nursing Assn. Long Term Care, Am. Cancer Soc. (comms. chair, past pres.). Home: RR 1 Box 430 Sebeka MN 56477-9708

HANSEN, MIRIAM BRATU, English language educator; b. Offenbach, Germany, Apr. 28, 1949; came to U.S., 1977; d. Arthur E. and Ruth (Theiner) Bratu; m. Michael Geyer, Aug. 2, 1991. PhD, Johann-Wolfgang-Goethe U., Frankfurt, Germany, 1975, Staatsexamen, 1976. Lectr. Yale U., New Haven, 1980-82; asst. prof. Rutgers U., New Brunswick, N.J., 1982-88, assoc. prof., 1988-89; prof. English U. Chgo., 1989—, dir. Film Studies Ctr., 1989—; Ferdinand Schevill Disting. Svc. prof. in humanities, 1995—. Author: Babel and Babylon: Spectatorship in American Silent Film, 1991; co-editor New German Critique, Cornell U., 1984—. Am. Coun. Learned Socs. fellow Yale U., 1977-79, Andrew Mellon faculty fellow Harvard U., 1985-86, Alexander von Humboldt Found. fellow, Frankfurt, 1989-90, 93-94. Mem. MLA, Soc. Cinema Studies (exec. coun. 1987-90). Office: U Chgo Dept English 1050 E 59th St Chicago IL 60637-1512

HANSEN, OLE VIGGO, chemical engineer; b. Detroit, May 6, 1934; s. Oluf Viggo and Carrie Alma (Wary) H.; m. Shirley Elizabeth Ford, Dec. 29, 1966; 1 child, Victoria Louisa. BSChemE, Wayne State U., 1956; equivalent of BS in Meteorology, Tex. A & M Univ., 1958. Registered profl. engr., Mich. Engr. tech. svcs. 3M Co., Detroit, 1956-57; chem. engr. Fisher Body div. Gen. Motors, Detroit, 1960-64; mgr. mktg. Monsanto Co., St. Louis and Australia, 1964-76; dir. tech. mktg. Beltran Assocs., Inc., N.Y.C., 1976-78; leader mist eliminator profit ctr. Koch Engring. Co., Inc., Wichita, Kans., 1978—; bd. dirs. Divmesh of Canada, Ltd., Calgary, Alta., 1984-85. Contbr. articles to profl. jours.; patentee in field. Served to capt. USAF, 1956-60. Mem. Am. Inst. Chem. Engrs. (session chmn. nat. meeting 1980), Am. Meteorol. Soc., Soc. Automotive Engrs. Australasia. Home: 7800 Killarney Pl Wichita KS 67206-1633 Office: Koch Engring Co Inc 4111 E 37th St N Wichita KS 67220-3203

HANSEN, OWEN PETER, newspaper editor; b. Ogden, Utah, Aug. 30, 1931; s. Peter and Anna Margaret Hansen; m. Claire Lou Tribe, Aug. 30, 1953; children: April Luria, Heidi Warren, Hope Gustavson. BS, U. Utah, 1958. Reporter UPI News Svc., Salt Lake City, 1956-57; with The Reporter, Lebanon, Ind., 1958—, editor, 1978—. Editor: Comedy and Comment newsletter, 1990-92. Councilman, commr. Boone County, Ind., 1970-78; pres. Lebanon Utility Bd., 1975-94. With USAF, 1950-54. Mem. Jaycees (pres. 1965-67). Republican. Home: 2019 Elizaville Rd Lebanon IN 46052 Office: The Lebanon Reporter 117 E Washington St Lebanon IN 46052

HANSEN, RANDALL LEE, business executive; b. Lake View, Mich., Aug. 30, 1951. BSBA, Ctrl. Mich. U., 1977; JD, Thomas Cooley U., 1980. Atty., land man Lansing, Mich., 1980-85; pres. Elexco, Marysville, Mich., 1985—. Mem. State Bar of Mich. (oil and gas com.). Republican. Office: Elexco Land Svcs Inc PO Box 313 Marysville MI 48040-0313

HANSEN, SANDRA KAY, head librarian; b. Tea, S.D., Mar. 24, 1940; d. Albert Victor and Anna Marie (Andersen) H.; m. Gene Hansen, Aug. 21, 1973; children: Michael, Teresa. Student, Sioux Falls Coll., Sioux Falls, 1959-60, Sinte Gleska Coll., Winner, 1980-81; Assoc., No. State Coll., Aberdeen, 1993. County libr. Tripp County Libr., Winner, S.D., 1980—. Mem. Tripp County Dem., Winner, Bapt. Hosp. Aux., Winner, Am. Legion Aux., Winner; bd. dirs. So. Plains Mental Health - Adult Counciling Guidance Ctr., 1991-93; chmn. Libr. Carnivals Benefit, Winner, 1988-90; benefit chmn. Friends of the Libr. Orgn., Winner, 1994-95; vol. United Meth. Ch., Winner, 1973—; hostess Christian Women's Club, Winner, 1990—, Sunshine Bible Group, Winner. Recipient S.D. Literacy award S.D. Reading Coun., Winner, 1986. Mem. Winner Women's Club, Bus. and Profl. Women, Epsilom Sigma Alpha (secretary 1978—). Democrat. Methodist. Home: 501 W 9th St Winner SD 57580 Office: Tripp County Libr 442 Monroe Winner SD 57580

HANSEN, TODD RANDALL, small business owner, educator; b. Chgo., Mar. 11, 1965; s. Richard Brydon H. and Lynn (Gray) Miller. BA, The Am. U., 1986, MA, 1988; JD, George Mason Sch. Law, 1993. Runner, trade clk. Chgo. Bd. Trade, 1983; telecommunicator Tel Ac, Washington, 1984-86; investigator Merit Protective Svc., Washington, 1986; athletic dir. Alice Deal Jr. H.S., Washington, 1987-89; police officer US Capitol Police, Washington, 1987-93; owner Hansen's Hobbies, Wilmette, Ill., 1994—; Chmn. bd., Capital Investment Enterprise, Del., 1991—. Del. 10th congressional dist. Rep. Party, 1994. Republican. Home: 1187 Wilmette Ave Ste 145 Wilmette IL 60091 Office: Hansen's Hobbies 631 Green Bay Rd Wilmette IL 60091

HANSEN, WENDELL JAY, clergyman, gospel broadcaster; b. Waukegan, Ill., May 28, 1910; s. Christian Hans and Anna Sophia (Termansen) H.; m. Bertelle Kathryn Budman, Mar. 9, 1933 (dec. Jan. 6, 1956); 1 child, Sylvia Marie; m. Eunice Evaline Irvine, Nov. 2, 1957; 1 child, Dean. Grad. Cleve. Bible Coll., 1932; A.B., William Penn Coll., 1938; postgrad. Gletch Berg Skule, Switzerland, 1939; MA, U. Iowa, 1940, PhD, 1947. Ordained to ministry Recorded Friends, 1936, Evang. Reformed Ch., 1944; pastor chs., Grinnell, Iowa, Mpls. and Iowa City, 1934-47; evangelist with talking and performing birds, 1946—, past mgr. gospel radio stas. Two Rivers, Wis., Menomonie, Wis., Peru, Ind., Wabash, Ind., East St. Louis, Ill., Indpls., 1952—; pres., chmn. of bd. WESL Inc., East St. Louis, 1962—, cons. radio and TV, 1970—; appointed adv. com. to Indpls. Prosecutor, 1986. Appeared on Fuji Network, Tokyo and Channel X, London. Dir. St. Paul Inter-racial Work Camp, 1939; chmn. Minn. Joint Refuge Com., 1940-41. Recipient honor citation Nat. Assn. Broadcasters, 1980; Boss of Yr. award Hamilton County Broadcasters, 1979, award Boys Town, 1983, award Women of Faith, St. Louis, 1984. Mem. Internat. Platform Assn., Internat. Assn. Christian Magicians, Ind. Bird Fanciers, East St. Louis C. of C. (bd. dirs. 1981-86), Pi Kappa Delta. Republican. Quaker. Club: Ind. Pigeon (best exotic bird award 1969, 75, 80). Lodge: Kiwanis. Contbr. articles to popular mags.

HANSEN, WILLIAM ANTHONY, computer educator; b. Chgo., July 14, 1948; s. Edgar C. and Dorothy C. (Neubauer) H.; m. Sandra L. Stuebner, Aug. 23, 1969; children: Susan, Elizabeth, Kathryn, David. BS, Ill. Inst. Tech., 1970; MS, Northwestern U., 1971, PhD, 1974. Trainer Abbott Labs., North Chicago, Ill., 1972-74; assoc. prof. Wilkes Coll., Wilkes-Barre, Pa., 1974-76; oper. sys. prod. mgr., quality assurance mgr. Deltak, Inc., Oak Brook, Ill., 1976-80; pres. Hansen Tng. Sys., Inc., Barrington, Ill., 1980—; sec.-treas. Manta Techs., Inc., Barrington, 1994—. Author, editor numerous self-study course books, 1976-95; contbr. over 20 articles to profl. publs. Pres., sec. bd. dirs. Chevior Hills Homeowner's Assn., 1985—; planning commr. Village of Inverness, Ill., 1994—. Home and Office: Manta Techs Inc 1981 Abbotsford Dr Barrington IL 60010

HANSEN-RACHOR, SHARON ANN, conductor, choral music educator; b. Omaha, Nebr., Aug. 22, 1954; d. Joseph Anthony Busch and Helen Marie Prokop Krustev; m. David John Rachor, May 27, 1991; 1 stepchild, Stephanie Rachor. BM, U. Nebr., Omaha, 1975; MM, U. Nebr., Lincoln, 1978; postgrad., U. Ill., 1981-82; DMA, U. Mo., Kansas City, 1986. Pub. sch. music tchr. Millard and Springfield (Nebr.) schs., 1975-83; grad. teaching asst. U. Ill., 1981-82, U. Mo., Kansas City, 1983-86; assoc. prof. choral music and conducting U. No. Iowa, Cedar Falls, 1986-94; assoc. prof. choral music and conducting, dir. choral activities U. Wis., Milw., 1994—; vis. prof. orchestral studies U. Regensburg, Germany, 1993; cons. in field. Contbr. articles to profl. jours.; mem. editl. bd. Choral Jour. U. No. Iowa grantee, Amsterdam, 1991, Stuttgart, Germany, 1993-94; Kemper fellow U. Mo., Kansas City, 1986. Mem. Am. Choral Dirs. Assn., Internat. Fedn. Choral Music, Gachinger Kantorei Stuttgart, Phi Kappa Lambda, Mu Phi Epsilon, Pi Kappa Pi, Alpha Lambda Delta. Home: 4340 N Woodburn Shorewood WI 53211 Office: U Wis Milw Dept Music Fine Arts Music Box 413 Milwaukee WI 53201

HANSL, NIKOLAUS RUDOLF, neuropharmacologist; b. Neustadt, Austria, Oct. 24, 1923; came to U.S., 1946; s. Rudolf Franz and Luise (Fulop) H.; div.; 1 child, Liesl Marie. MS, Vienna U., 1946, PhD, 1946. Asst. prof. Cheighton U., Omaha, 1952-54; chief biochem. dir. labs. Chronic Disease Rsch. Inst., Buffalo, 1954-57; asst. dir. rsch. Sahyun Labs., Santa Barbara, Calif., 1957-64; prof. Creighton U., 1967-85; pres. Pacific Rsch. Labs., Omaha, 1964—. Author: Biochemistry for Pharmacology, 1976; patentee in field. Mem. Santa Barbara Rsch. Coun., 1958-70. Rsch. fellow Harvard U., Cambridge, Mass., 1948-49, McGill U., Montreal, Que., Can., 1951-52. Mem. AAAS, Am. Chem. Soc., Nebr. Acad. Scis. (chmn. biology-medicine sect. 1975-77), N.Y. Acad. Scis., Rho Chi, Sigma Xi. Roman Catholic. Home: 7815 Pine Cir Omaha NE 68124

HANSLER, STEPHEN PAUL, social worker; b. Cleve., May 18, 1960; s. Richard L. and Wanda A. (Hegner) H.; m. Susan M. Kerrigan, July 8, 1989; children: Jennifer Michelle, Leah Margaret. BA, Ithaca (N.Y.) Coll., 1982; MSW, Rutgers U., 1984. Coord. N.J. Coalition for the Homeless, New Brunswick, N.J., 1982-83, Middlesex County Community Housing Resource Bd., New Brunswick, 1983-84; exec. dir. Maximum Ind. Living, Cleve., 1984—; mem. ad hoc com. on HUD Restructuring, Washington, 1995; mem. Ohio Ind. Living Coun., 1990-92; mem. Ohio Gov.'s Coun. on Poeple with Disabilities, Columbus, 1990-93; mem. adv. com. Access Guide to Cleve., 1986-88, Transp. Coalition for Disabled Riders, Cleve., 1985-92; presenter in field. Trustee Ithaca Coll., 1980-82; coun. mem. Hope Luth. Ch., Cleveland Heights, 1988-92. Lutheran. Home: 1223 Quilliams Rd Cleveland OH 44121-1837 Office: Maximum Independent Living 11607 Euclid Ave Cleveland OH 44106-4348

HANSMEIER, BARBARA JO, elementary education educator; b. Jacksonville, Ill., Aug. 1, 1954; d. Samuel Farrell and Harriett Josephine (Moss) H. BA, Ill. Coll., 1976; MS in Elem. Edn., So. Ill. U., Edwardsville, 1993. Cert. tchr., Ill. Tchr. 4th and 5th grades Jacksonville Sch. Dist. 117, 1977-78, tchr. 3d grade, 1978-81; head counselor summer enrichment program for the gifted MacMurray Coll., Jacksonville, 1981-85; tchr. 1st grade Jacksonville Sch. Dist. 117, 1981—; tchr. 1st, 2d and 3d grades MacMurray Coll., Prairie Scholars, Jacksonville, 1988—, chaperone, tour leader, summers, 1986-87, 90. Mem. Jacksonville Art Assn., 1990—; exec. bd. Women's Crisis Ctr., Jacksonville, 1990-95; lifetime mem. aux. Passavant Area Hosp.; mem. Grace United Meth. Ch. Mem. NEA, ASCD, DAR, Ill. Edn. Assn., Jacksonville Edn. Assn., Phi Delta Kappa (sec. 1991-93), Delta Kappa Gamma (chmn. fin. com. 1988—). Methodist. Home: 3 Baldwin Rd Jacksonville IL 62650-2721 Office: Franklin Elem Sch 352 Franklin St Jacksonville IL 62650-2924

HANSON, BRUCE EUGENE, lawyer; b. Lincoln, Nebr., Aug. 25, 1942; s. Lester E. and Gladys (Diessner) H.; m. Peggy Pardun, Dec. 25, 1972 (dec. Nov. 1989). BA, U. Minn., 1965, JD, 1966. Bar: Minn. 1966, U.S. Dist. Ct. Minn. 1966, U.S. Tax Ct. 1973, U.S. Ct. Appeals (8th cir.) 1973, U.S. Ct. Appeals (fed. cir.) 1983, U.S. Supreme Ct. 1970. Shareholder, Doherty, Rumble & Butler, P.A., St. Paul, 1966—. Dir. Am. Saddlebred Horse Assn.; bd. trustees, chair United Hosp., 1996—. Mem. ATLA, Ramsey County Bar Assn., Minn. State Bar Assn., Am. Acad. Healthcare Attys., Minn. Soc. Hosp. Attys., North Oaks Golf Club, Order of Coif, Phi Delta Phi. Home: 23 Evergreen Rd Saint Paul MN 55127-2077 Office: Doherty Rumble & Butler 2800 Minn World Trade Ctr Saint Paul MN 55101

HANSON, DAVID BIGELOW, construction company executive, engineer; b. Cambridge, Mass., Feb. 24, 1946; s. David B. Jr. and Kathleen M. (Roscoe) H.; m. Colleen Marie Barrett, Oct. 31, 1969; children: Matthew Joseph, Joshua David. BS in Civil Engring., U. Mass., 1968; postgrad., Templeton Coll., 1989. Supt. Bechtel Corp., San Francisco, 1968-71; project engr. Dwight Bldg. Co., Hamden, Conn., 1971-74; cost engring. mgr. HBE Corp., St. Louis, 1974-79, dir. project devel., 1979-81, v.p., 1982-84; v.p. Bassett Constrn. Co., Pueblo, Colo., 1981-82; dir. procurement and estimating Turner Internat. Industries, Inc., N.Y.C., 1984-85, v.p. procurement and estimating, 1986, v.p., gen. mgr., 1986-89; v.p., gen. mgr. Healthcare div. Turner Constrn. Co., N.Y.C., 1989-91; v.p., gen. mgr. Turner Constrn. Co., Detroit, 1991-95; sr. v.p. Walbridge Aldinger Co., Detroit, 1995—; bd. dirs. Met. Realty Corp., 1994—. Mem. adv. bd. Regional Alliance for Minority and Women Businesses, N.Y.C., 1989-91; bd. dirs. Boys Hope, 1994—. Mem. ASCE, NSPE, Assn. Gen. Contractors (internat. constrn. com. 1987-89, chmn. Detroit EEO com. 1992—, bd. dirs. Detroit chpt. 1994-95), Constrn. Innovation Forum (bd. dirs. 1992-95, mem. exec. com. 1993-95), Engring. Soc. Detroit, Greater Detroit C. of C. (bd. dirs. 1993—), Assn. of African Am. Bus. and Contractors (adv. bd. dirs. 1993—), Detroit Golf Club, Econ. Club of Detroit. Office: Walbridge Aldinger Co 613 Abbott St Detroit MI 48226-2522

HANSON, DORIS J., state legislator; b. Oct. 24, 1925. Student, U. Wis. Former bus. mgr., now v.p. real estate co.; mem. from dist. 48 Wis. State Assembly, Madison, 1992—. Former sec., now pres. Village of McFarland, Wis.; former chairwoman Dane County Regional Airport Commn. Home: 6214 South Ct Mc Farland WI 53558-9497*

HANSON, DUDLEY MODAHL, federal agency administrator, civil engineer; b. LaCrosse, Wis., Jan. 20, 1941; s. Gordon Sacia and Lillian Marguerite (Modahl) H.; m. Barbara Jean All, May 28, 1965; children: Kristin, Joel, Meredith, Melanie. BSCE, U. Iowa, 1964, MS, 1968; MPW, U. Pitts., 1970. Registered profl. engr., Ill., Iowa. Civil engr. US Army Corp. Engrs., Rock Island, Ill., 1964-66, 1969-73, structural engr., 1966-69, chief resources mgt., 1973-76, chief program mgt., 1976-80, asst. chief engring., 1980-86, chief planning, 1986—; pres., sole owner Flaherty, Hanson & Baer P.C., Davenport, Iowa, 1976—, ptnr. Hanson and Beasley, 1980-84. Dir. Miss. Valley coun. Girl Scouts U.S., Iowa and Ill., 1993-94; active City Mgr. Screening Com., 1972, various ad hoc sch. bd. coms., 1975-90. Mem. ASCE (chpt. pres. 1973-74), Soc. Am. Mil. Engrs. (chpt. pres. 1978-79), Propeller Club of Quad Cities (past pres. 1980-81, 95-96), Rotary Club of Davenport (program chmn. 1994-96). Home: 3812 N Thornwood Davenport IA 52806 Office: US Army Engr Dist Rock Island PO Box 2004 Rock Island IL 61204-2004

HANSON, FLOYD BLISS, applied mathematician, computational scientist, mathematical biologist; b. Bklyn., Mar. 9, 1939; s. Charles Keld and Violet Ellen (Bliss) H.; m. Ethel Louisa Hutchins, July 27, 1962; 1 child, Lisa Kirsten. BS, Antioch Coll., 1962; MS, Brown U., 1964, PhD, 1968. Space technician Convair Astronautics, San Diego, 1961; applied mathematician Arthur D. Little, Inc., Cambridge, Mass., 1961; physicist Wright-Patterson AFB, Dayton, Ohio, 1962; assoc. research scientist Courant Inst., N.Y.C., 1967-68; asst. prof. U. Ill., Chgo., 1969-75, assoc. prof., 1975-83, prof., 1983—, assoc. dir. Lab. for Advanced Computing, 1990—; faculty rsch. participant Argonne (Ill.) Nat. Lab., 1985-87, faculty rsch. leave, 1987-88, rsch. assoc., 1988—; vis. prof., divsn. applied math. Brown U., 1994; mem. vis. faculty Sch. Civil & Environ. Engring., Cornell U., 1995. Assoc. editor-in-chief Applied and Computational Control Signals and Circuits, 1996—; author: (with others) Control and Dynamical Systems: Advances in Theory and Applications, 1996; contbr. articles in field to profl. jours. NSF rsch. grantee, 1970-83, 88—, NSF equipment grantee, 1973; Nat. Ctr. for Supercomputer Applications Computer grantee, 1986—; supercomputer grantee Los Alamos Nat. Lab., 1990—, Cornell Theory Ctr., 1993-95, Pitts. Supercomputer Ctr., 1993—. Mem. Soc. Indsl. and Applied Math., Computer Soc. of IEEE, Control Soc. of IEEE, Resource Modeling Assn. Home: 5435 S East View Park Chicago IL 60615-5915 Office: U Ill Dept Math Stats & Computer Sci M/C 249 851 Morgan St Rm 322 Seo Chicago IL 60607-7045

HANSON, GARY LEE, financial company executive; b. Watertown, Minn., Mar. 13, 1962. BA, St. Cloud (Minn.) State U., 1987. Stockbroker Merrill Lynch, St. Paul, 1987-90; v.p. Prin. Fin. Securities (a mem. of the Prin. Fin. Group), Bloomington, Minn., 1990—. Mem. Elks. Republican. Lutheran. Office: Prin Fin Ste 1710 8500 Normandale Lake Blvd Bloomington MN 55437-3813

HANSON, GEORGE ERIC, financial planner; b. Lansing, Mich., Apr. 6, 1960. Operation Degree, U. Mich., 1984. Cert. Dale Carnegie instr., stockbroker. Prodn. control mgr. Tri Cast Inc., Fruitport, Mich., 1984-87; instr., sales rep. Ralph Nichols, Detroit, 1987-94; fin. planner Anderson & Co., Grand Rapids, Mich., 1994—. Mem. Grand Rapids C. of C. Republican. Office: Anderson & Co Inc 2025 E Beltline Ave SE Ste 203 Grand Rapids MI 49546-7630

HANSON, HEIDI ELIZABETH, lawyer; b. Portsmouth, Ohio, Nov. 13, 1954. BS, U. Ill., 1975, JD, 1978. Bar: Ill. 1978, U.S. Dist. Ct. (no. dist.) Ill., U.S. Ct. Appeals (7th cir.). Atty. water, air and land pollution divs. Ill. EPA, Springfield, Ill., 1978-85; atty. water pollution div. Ill. EPA, Maywood, Ill., 1985-86; assoc. Ross & Hardies, Chgo., 1987-89, ptnr., 1990-94; founder H.E. Hanson Law Offices, Western Springs, Ill., 1994—. Mem. Chgo. Bar Assn., Air and Waste Mgmt. Assn., Indsl. Water, Waste and Sewer Group. Office: 4721 Franklin Ave Ste 1500 Western Springs IL 60558-1720

HANSON, JOHN ELBERT, chemistry educator; b. Toledo, Mar. 5, 1935; s. John E. and Ruth S. (Fike) H.; m. Esther Ruth Johnson, June 13, 1959; children: Heidi, Heather. AB, Olivet Nazarene Coll., 1957; PhD, Purdue U., 1964. Chemistry educator Olivet Nazarene U., Kankakee, Ill., 1961—; rsch. assoc. U. Chgo., 1975; vis. prof. U. Wis., Madison, 1984-85. Mem. bd. auditors Bourbonnais Twp., Kankakee County, Ill., 1970-72; election judge City of Bourbonnais, 1988. Mem. Am. Chem. Soc. (sec., chair Joliet, Ill. chpt. 1976), Ill. State Acad. Sci. Democrat. Office: Olivet Nazarene U Dept of Chemistry Kankakee IL 60901

HANSON, KAREN, philosopher, educator; b. Lincoln, Nebr., Apr. 11, 1947; d. Lester Eugene and Gladys (Diessner) H.; m. Dennis Michael Senchuk, Aug. 22, 1970; children: Tia Elizabeth, Chloe Miranda. BA summa cum laude, U. Minn., 1970; MA, Harvard U., 1980, PhD, 1980. Lectr. to assoc. prof. Ind. U., Bloomington, 1976-91, prof. philosophy, 1991—, adj. prof. Am. studies, women's studies, and comparative lit., 1991—; mem. governing bd. Ind. U. Inst. for Advanced Study, Bloomington, 1992-95; mem. editorial bd. Peirce Edition Project, Indpls., 1982-89, 90—. Author: The Self Imagined, 1986; co-editor: Romantic Revolutions, 1990; assoc. editor Jour. Social Philosophy, 1982-86; edtl. bd. Philosophy of Music Edn. Rev., 1992—; edtl. cons. Am. Philos. Quar., 1995—; contbr. articles to profl. books and jours. Del. Am. Coun. Learned Socs., 1993— (exec. com., 1994—); officer John Dewey Found., 1989—. Office of Women's Affairs disting. scholar, 1995. Mem. Am. Philos. Assn. (exec. officer 1986-91, program com. 1984-91, nominating com. 1993-94, 95—), Am. Soc. for Aesthetics (program com. 1989-90), Soc. for Women in Philosophy, Phi Beta Kappa (exec. com. Gamma of Ind. chpt. 1993—, officer 1995—). Home: 1606 S Woodruff Ln Bloomington IN 47401-4448 Office: Ind U Dept of Philosophy Sycamore 026 Bloomington IN 47405

HANSON, LYLE, state legislator; m. Betty; two children. BS, U. N.D.; MS, Moorehead State U. N.D. State rep. Dist. 48, 1979—; substitute tchr.; mem. edn. and natural resources coms.; Dem. caucus leader. Recipient Legis. Conservationist of Yr. award N.D. Wildlife Fedn., 1981, Jamestown United Sportsman of Yr., 1994; named to Ofcls. Hall of Fame. Mem. United Sportsman, Elks, Eagles, Safari Club Internat., N.D. Wildlife Fedn., Found. for N.Am. Wild Sheep. Home: 337 15th Ave NE Jamestown ND 58401-3830*

HANSON, MONTE RAY, lawyer; b. Aberdeen, S.D., June 3, 1956; s. Glenn J. and Doris Hanson; m. Deborah Grant, May 27, 1978; children: Erik, Karin. BA cum laude, Augustana Coll., Sioux Falls, S.D., 1978; MBA, U. S.D., Vermillion, 1983; JD with honors, U. S.D., 1983. Bar: Iowa 1983, S.D. 1983, U.S. Dist. Ct. (no. and so. dists.) Iowa 1983, U.S. Ct. Appeals (8th cir.) 1984. Assoc. Brown, Winick, Graves, Donnelly, Baskerville & Schoenebaum, Des Moines, 1983-87; v.p., asst. corp. counsel Western Surety Co., Sioux Falls, 1987-89, corp. counsel, 1989—; v.p. client counseling bd. U. S.D., 1981-82, pres. client counseling bd., 1982-83. Mem. ABA (sect. on bus. law), Am. Corp. Counsel Assn., State Bar S.D., Iowa State Bar Assn., S.D. 2d Jud. Cir. Bar Assn., Woodlake Athletic Club, Thomas Sterling Honor Soc., Beta Gamma Sigma. Republican. Lutheran. Office: Western Surety Co PO Box 5077 Sioux Falls SD 57117-5077

HANSON, PAULA E., state legislator; b. Jan. 21, 1944; m. Jim Hanson; 3 children. Mem. Minn. State Senate, 1992—, mem. various coms. Democrat. Home: 2428 Bunker Lake Blvd NE Ham Lake MN 55304-7129 Office: Minn State Senate State Capital Building Saint Paul MN 55155-1606

HANSON, ROBERT ARTHUR, retired agricultural equipment executive; b. Moline, Ill., Dec. 13, 1924; s. Nels A. and Margaret I. (Chapman) H.; m. Patricia Ann Klinger, June 25, 1955. B.A., Augustana Coll., Rock Island, Ill., 1948. Various positions Deere & Co., Moline, 1950-62; gen. mgr. Deere & Co., Mexico, 1962-64, Spain, 1964-66; dir. mktg. overseas Deere & Co., 1966-70, v.p. overseas ops., 1972, sr. v.p. overseas div., 1973, dir., 1974—, exec. v.p., 1975-78, pres., 1978-85, chief oper. officer, 1979-82, chief exec. officer, 1982-89, chmn., 1982-90. With USMCR, 1943-46. Mem. Bus. Coun. Home: 2200 29th Avenue Court Dr Moline IL 61265-6926 Office: Deere & Co John Deere Rd Moline IL 61265-6785

HANSON, ROBERT EUGENE, state official; b. Jamestown, N.D., Aug. 26, 1947; s. Louis J. and Kathlene A. (Wilmart) H.; m. Melody R. McFall, May 11, 1974; children: Jason Paul, Jamie Beth, Kristen Anne. BSBA, N.D. State U., 1968. Campaign scheduler N.D. Dem.-Non-Partisan League Party, Bismarck, 1968-70, campaign mgr., 1970; legis. aide Dem.-Non-Partisan League Legislators, Bismarck, 1971; youth coordinator State of N.D., Bismarck, 1971, dep. state treas., 1973-79, state treas., 1979-80, 85-92, state tax commr., 1993—; also manpower planner N.D. Employment Security Bur.; spl. asst. Office N.D. Gov., Bismarck, 1971-73; chmn. State Investment Bd., 1979-80, vice chmn., 1985-92; sales tax supr. N.d. State Tax Dept., 1981-84; treas. Multi-State Tax commn., 1993, vice chair, 1993-95, chair, 1995—. Vice chmn. ctrl. regional conf. Nat. Conf. State Liquor Adminstrs., 1975, exec. sec.-treas., 1976-79, v.p., 1979-80, chmn., 1985-86; chmn. Vets. Day, 1977, U.S. Savs. Bond., N.D., 1978; mem. state bd. dirs. N.D. PTA; chmn. bd. dirs. N.D. Easter Seal Soc., 1982-83; dem. candidate for State Pub. Svc. Commr., 1978; mem. adv. bd. N.D. State U. Coll. Bus. Adminstrn., 1992—; mem. adv. com. Agent Orange project N.D. Vietnam Vet.'s Children's Assistance Program, 1992—. Served with U.S. Army, 1968-70. Decorated Bronze Star with oak leaf cluster; recipient Pi Omega award, 1968, Disting. Svc. award N.D. Vets. Svc. Officers Assn., 1988, Freedoms Found. award, 1969. Mem. VFW, Nat. Assn. State Treas. (Disting. Svc. award Midwest region 1992, chair Midwest region 1986-88, 91-92, legis. com. 1987-92, pension com. 1989-92), Coun. State Govts. (OPAAC com. 1991-92), Am. Legion, Am. Vets., Vietnam Vets. Am., Nat. Conf. Pub. Employees Retirement Systems (exec. com. 1990-92), Internat. War Vets. Alliance, N.D. Vietnam Vets. (adv. bd. children's assistance program 1992—), Sons of Norway, KC, Blue Key, N.D. Century Club, Sigma Nu. Roman Catholic. Home: 304 Teton Ave Bismarck ND 58501-2664 Office: Office of State Tax Commr State Capitol 600 E Boulevard Ave Bismarck ND 58505-0599

HANSON, RONALD TILFORD, mental health counselor, psychotherapist, pastor; b. Bettendorf, Iowa, Apr. 25, 1949; s. Dale J. and Britonia Jane (Tilford) H.; m. Lona Lee Christopherson, Aug. 30, 1969; children: Sheri Lee, Ronald Timothy. BA, Colo. Christian U., 1971; MDiv, Denver Sem., 1974; postgrad., Trinity Evang. Div. Sch., Deerfield, Ill., U. Colo., Marycrest Coll., Western Ill. U., U. Iowa. Ordained to ministry Conservative Bapt. and Bapt. Gen. Conf., 1974. Youth dir. Edgewater (Colo.) Bapt. Ch., 1968-69; jr. high youth pastor Immanuel Bapt. Ch., Denver, 1969-71; assoc. pastor South Suburban Christian Ch., Littleton, Colo., 1971-73; sr. pastor Green Gables Chapel, Lakewood, Colo., 1973-82, Pleasant View Bapt. Ch., Bettendorf, Iowa, 1982-87; pvt. practice marriage, family and mental health therapy Bettendorf, 1987—; mem. adj. faculty Colo. Christian U., 1975-82, Denver Sem., 1979-82, Moody Bible Inst., 1984-85, Oakland City Coll., 1985-86, Trinity Evang. Div. Sch., 1988-89; speaker to chs., marriage and family seminars, Iowa, Ill.; cons., Iowa, Ill. Bd. dirs. Tri-Mark of Rockies, Denver, 1984—; trustee Colo. Christian U. Recipient cert. of appreciation Pleasant Valley Community Sch. Dist., Bettendorf, 1990. Mem. AACD, Am. Mental Health Counselors Assn., Am. Assn. Christian Counselors. Office: 2550 Middle Rd Ste 300 Bettendorf IA 52722-3287

HANTHORN, DENNIS WAYNE, performing arts association administrator; b. Lima, Ohio, Dec. 21, 1951; s. Floyd Wilber and June J. (Rummel) H.; m. Rebecca R. Hackler, Aug. 2, 1975; children: Rachel R., Micah A, Hanna. BS in Music Edn., Southwest Mo. State, Springfield, 1975; MusM in French Horn, U. Wis., 1977. Instr. U. Ala., 1978-79; gen. mgr. Cin. Chamber Orch., 1980-82; founder, dir. Queen City Brass, 1979-83; mng. dir. Dayton (Ohio) Opera, 1982-89; gen. dir. Florentine Opera Co., Milw., 1989—. Home: N75w5434 Georgetown Dr Cedarburg WI 53012-1557 Office: Florentine Opera Co 735 N Water St Ste 1315 Milwaukee WI 53202-4106

HANUS, JEROME, archbishop; b. May 26, 1940. Attended, Conception Sem., Mo., St. Anselm U., Rome, Italy, Princeton Theol. Sem., Princeton U. Ordained priest Roman Cath. Ch., 1966. Abbot Conception Abbey, 1977-87; pres. Swiss Am. Benedictine Congregation, 1984-87; bishop Diocese of St. Cloud, Minn., 1987-94; archbishop Dubuque, Iowa, 1995—. Office: PO Box 479 Dubuque IA 52004-0479

HANZAK, JANICE CHRISMAN, accountant; b. Cleve., Mar. 20, 1944; d. William Patrick and Helen (Mulvich) Chrisman; m. Henry Stanley Hanzak, July 18, 1964; 1 child, Kevin. BBA, Ursuline Coll., 1979. CPA, CFP; cert. mgmt., cert. valuation analyst. Clk. Prudential Ins. Co., East Cleveland, Ohio, 1962-63; bookkeeper White Motor Co., Cleve., 1963-68; CPA, tax mgr. Heiser & Assocs., Willoughby, Ohio, 1974-85; CPA, tax supr. Bond Sippola & DeJoy, Willoughby, 1985-91; CPA, pres. J.C. Hanzak & Co., Willoughby Hills, Ohio, 1991—; tax cons. Lake County Realtors Assn., Mentor, Ohio, 1992; speaker seminars in field. Treas. Highland Heights (Ohio) Mayoral Com., 1983; mem. Highland Heights Legis. Com., 1982, St. Paschal Bull. Com., Highland Heights, 1978; charter mem. Willoughby Hills Bus. Assn., 1992; founding pres. Network Profls. of Lake County, 1993; pres. Lake County Estate Planning Coun., Mentor, 1990-92; v.p. Women Bus. Owners of Western Res., Mentor, 1990-92; exec. bd. Ursuline Coll., Pepper Pike, Ohio. Recipient scholarship Bus. and Profl. Women's Assn., Washington, 1973. Mem. AICPA, Ohio Soc. CPAs, Am. Women's Soc. CPAs, Tax Club of Cleve., Internat. Bd. CFPs, Wildwood Yacht Club, Entrepreneurial Roundtable Assn. (founding mem.). Roman Catholic. Office: JC Hanzak & Co 2860 Bishop Rd Wickliffe OH 44092

HAQUE, MALIKA HAKIM, pediatrician; b. Madras, India; came to U.S., 1967; d. Syed Abdul and Rahimunisa (Hussain) Hakim; MBBS, Madras Med. Coll., 1967; m. C. Azeez Haque, Feb. 5, 1967; children: Kifizeba, Masarath Nashr, Asim Zayd. Diplomate Am. Bd. Pediatrics. Rotating intern Miriam Hosp., Brown U., Providence, 1967-68; resident in pediatrics Children's Hosp., N.J. Coll. Medicine, 1968-70; fellow in devel. disabilities Ohio State U., 1970-71; acting chief pediatrics Nisonger Ctr., 1973-74; staff pediatrician Children and Youth Project, Children's Hosp., Columbus, Ohio, also clin. asst. prof. pediatrics Ohio State U., 1974-80; clin. assoc. prof. pediatrics Ohio State U., 1981—, clin. assoc. prof. dept. internat. health Coll. Medicine, 1993—; pediatrician in charge cmty. pediatrics and adolescent svcs. clinics, Columbus Children's Hosp., 1982—, dir. pediatric acad. assoc., Columbus Children's Hosp., Ohio State U., 1992—; cons. Central Ohio Head Start Program, 1974-79; med. cons. Bur. Rehab. and Devel. Disabilities for State of Ohio, 1990—. Contbr. articles to profl. jours. and newspapers. Charter mem. Rep. Presdl. Task Force, 1982—, Nat. Rep. Senatorial Com., 1985—, U.S. Senatorial Club; charter founder Ronald Reagan Rep. Ctr.; trustee Asian Am. Health Alliance Network, Columbus, 1994—. Recipient Physician Recognition award AMA, 1971-86, 88-91, 92—, Gold medals in surgery, radiology, pediatrics and ob/gyn; Presdl. medal of Merit, 1982. Fellow Am. Acad. Pediatrics; mem. Islamic Med. Assn., Am. Assn. of Physicians of Indian Orgin, Ambulatory Pediatric Assn., Cen. Ohio Pediatric Soc. Muslim. Research on enuresis. Home: 5995 Forestview Dr Columbus OH 43213-2114 Office: 700 Childrens Dr Columbus OH 43205-2666

HARBAGE, PETER TODD, political organization worker; b. Tucson; s. Robert C. and Pamela H. BA, U. Mich., 1993, M of Pub. Policy, 1995. Rsch. asst. Inst. Social Rsch., Ann Arbor, Mich., 1991-92; intern policy asst. White House, Washington, 1993; field dir. Levin for Congress, Warren, Mich., 1994; teaching asst. U. Mich., 1995; web master Mich. Dem. Party, Lansing, Mich., 1995—. Co-author: Beyond NIMBY, 1995; editor-in-chief Mich. Jour. Polit. Sci., 1990-93. Chair Coll. Dems., Ann Arbor, 1994-95; treas. ACLU, Ann Arbor, 1991-93; mem. exec. bd. Coll. Dems. Mich., Lansing, 1995—; fundraiser Kildee for Congress, 1996—. Grad. fellow U. Mich., 1993; recipient J.E. Hogetts award Jour. Can. Pub. Adminstrn., 1995, Bryan award U. Mich. Dept. Polit. Sci., 1993. Mem. Pi Sigma Alpha, Phi Kappa Phi, Sigma Iota Rho (pres. 1991—), Phi Beta Kappa. Democrat. Home: 24890 Ravine Ct Farmington Hills MI 48335 Office: Mich Dem Party 606 Townsend Lansing MI 48916

HARBERGER, ARNOLD CARL, economist, educator; b. Newark, July 27, 1924; s. Ferdinand C. and Martha (Bucher) H.; m. Ana Beatriz Valjalo, Mar. 15, 1958; children: Paul Vincent, Carl David. Student, Johns Hopkins U., 1941-43; MA, U. Chgo., 1947, PhD, 1950; Doctor honoris causa, U. Tucuman, 1979, Cath. U. Chile, 1988, Tech. U. Cen. Am., 1989. Asst. prof. polit. economy Johns Hopkins U., 1949-53; asso. prof. econs. U. Chgo., 1953-59, prof., 1959—, chmn. dept., 1964-71, 75-80, Gustavus F. and Ann M. Swift disting. svc. prof., 1977-91, prof. emeritus, 1991—, dir. Ctr. Latin Am. Econ. Studies, 1965-92; vis. prof. MIT (Ctr. Internat. Studies), New Delhi, 1961-62, Econ. Devel. Inst., IBRD, 1965, Harvard U., 1971-72, Princeton U., 1973-74, UCLA, 1983, 84, U. Paris, 1986; prof. econs. UCLA, 1984—; cons. IMF, 1950, 89, U.S. Pres.'s Materials Policy Commn., 1951-52, U.S. Treasury Dept., 1961-75, Com. Econ. devel., 1961-78, Planning Commn., India, 1961-62, 73, Pan Am. Union, 1962-76, Dept. State, 1962-76, Cen. Bank, Chile, 1965-70, Dominican Republic, 1989, Nicaragua, 1990, China, 1995, Planning Dept., Panama, 1963-77, Colombia, 1969-71, Nicaragua, 1990; cons. Ford Found., 1967-77, Planning Commn., El Salvador, 1973-75, Budget and Planning Office, Uruguay, 1974-75, Can. Dept. Regional Econ. Expansion, 1975-77, Fin. Ministry, Bolivia, 1976, Mex., 1976—; cons. Can. Dept. Employment and Migration, 1980-82, Indonesian Ministry Fin., 1981-82, 86, Can. Dept. Fin., 1982-88, Can. Dept. Industry, Sci. and Tech., 1991—, Chinese Ministry Fin., 1983; ministry fin., Malawi, 1988, Venezuela, 1989, Colombia, 1991, 94; mem. internat. adv. coun. Inst. Internat. Studies, Stanford U., 1991—; v.p., chmn. adv. coun. Inst. for Policy Reform. Author: Project Evaluation, 1972, Taxation and Welfare, 1974; Editor: Demand for Durable Goods, 1960, The Taxation of Income from Capital, 1968, Key Problems of Economic Policy In Latin America, 1970, World Economic Growth, 1985; contbr. sci. papers to profl. jours. and govt. publs. With AUS, 1943-46. Guggenheim fellow; Fulbright scholar; faculty rsch. fellow Social Sci. Rsch. Coun.; Ford Found. faculty rsch. fellow, 1968-69. Fellow Econometric Soc., Am. Acad. Arts and Scis.; mem. Am. Econ. Assn. (mem. exec. com. 1970-72, v.p. 1992, pres.-elect 1996), Western Econ. Assn. (v.p. 1987-88, pres. 1989-90), Royal Econ. Soc., Nat. Tax Assn., NAS, Phi Beta Kappa. Home: 136 Buckskin Rd Bell Canyon CA 91307-1125 Office: UCLA 8283 Bunche Hall 405 Hilgard Ave Los Angeles CA 90024-1477

HARBIN, MICHAEL ALLEN, religion educator, writer; b. Vincennes, Ind., May 24, 1947; s. Hugh Allen and Norma June (Palmer) H.; m. Esther Marie Rinas, May 31, 1971; children: Athena Colleen, Heidi Elizabeth, Douglas Allen. BS, U.S. Naval Acad., 1969; ThM, Dallas Theol. Sem., 1980, ThD, 1988; MA, Calif. State U., Carson, 1993. Instr. Dallas Bible Coll., 1984-86; freelance writer Garland, Tex., 1986-93; fleet plans officer USN, Yokosuka, Japan, 1990-91; mem. elder bd. South Garland Bible Ch., Garland, Tex., 1981-93, chmn. elder bd., 1982-86; mem. elder bd. Upland Evangelical Mennonite Ch., 1995—; vis. prof. Taylor U., 1993—. Author: To Serve Other Gods, 1994; contbr. articles to profl. jours. Del. 16th Senatorial Dist. Rep. Conv., Dallas, 1990, 92; alt. del. State Rep. Conv., Ft. Worth, 1990. Fellow Inst. of Bibl. Rsch.; mem. Soc. Bibl. Lit., Bibl. Archaeol. Soc., Bible Sci. Assn. (cons. spkr.), Evang. Theol. Soc., Am. Legion, Near Ea. Archaeol. Soc. Home: 703 W South St Upland IN 46989

HARBISON, PATRICK LEWIS, music educator; b. Jeffersonville, Ind., Feb. 21, 1955; s. Lewis Joseph and LaVon (Darneal) H.; m. Kristin Berkman, Apr. 12, 1980; children: William Patrick, Alissa. BMusEd, U. Louisville, 1977; MMus in Jazz Studies, Ind. U., 1987. Instr. of music Ind. U. Southeast, New Albany, 1977-78, Bellarmine Coll., Louisville, 1977-78; artist-in-residence Elkhart (Ind.) Comm. Schs., 1980-82; assoc. instr. music Ind. U., Bloomington, 1982-84; faculty Jamey Aebersold Summer Jazz Workshop, various locations, 1976—; assoc. prof. U. Cin. Coll.-Conservatory of Music, 1984—; artist, cons. E.K. Blessing Co., Elkhart, 1984-95; artist/clinician Selmer/Bach Corp., Elkhart, 1995—; active as freelance jazz and comml. trumpet performer in Cin. area; guest soloist and condr. univ. and h.s. jazz programs nationwide; presenter major jazz festivals and pub. radio broadcasts. Asst. editor: Internat. Trumpet Guild Jour., 1990-91; trumpet soloist: (recordings) Reactivation - The PsychoAcoustic Orchestra, Supreme Thing - The PsychoAcoustic Orchestra, In a Whirl - The College-Conservatory of Music Faculty Jazz Septet, Struttin' - David Baker's 21st Century Bebop Band, R.S.V.P. - David Baker's 21st Century Bebop Band,

Sophisticated Lady - Sheryl Shay, Concerto for Flute, String Quartet, and Jazz Band; publs. include 20 Authentic Bebop Jazz Solos, 1989, Technical Studies for the Modern Trumpet, 1983, rev. 1988, Miles Davis Solos, 1981; contbr. articles to profl. jours. Faculty advisor InterVarsity Christian Fellowship, U. Cin., 1993—. Mem. AAUP, Am. Fedn. Musicians, Music Educators Nat. Conf., Ohio Music Educators Assn., Internat. Trumpet Guild, Internat. Assn. Jazz Educators (vp. Ohio unit 1994—). Home: 3079 Hoock Ct Cincinnati OH 45239 Office: Univ Cincinnati Cincinnati OH 45221-0003

HARBRON, GARRETT LEE, educational association executive; b. Clinton, Iowa, May 21, 1940; s. Ralph Thomas Harbron and Maxine Eleanor (Welch) Harbron Loeber; m. Margaret Lucille Pierce, June 2, 1962 (div. 1989); children: Garrett L. Jr., Brendon C., Jennifer L. BS, Anderson Coll., 1966; MA, Ball State U., 1969. Cert. secondary tchr., Ind. Tchr. math. Wendell Willkie H.S., Elwood, Ind., 1966-69, North Ctrl. H.S., Indpls., 1969-89; pres. Ind. State Tchrs. Assn., Indpls., 1989-95; tchr. math. Phoenix Sch., Indpls., 1995-96; dir. Ind. State Tchr.'s Assn. Fin. Svcs. Corp., 1996—. Mem. NEA (mem. Washington polit. action com. coun. 1989-95), Washington Twp. Edn. Assn. (pres. 1977-78). Office: Ind State Tchrs Assn 150 W Market St Ste 830 Indianapolis IN 46204-2815

HARBRON, THOMAS RICHARD, computer science educator; b. Clinton, Iowa, Dec. 16, 1937; s. Ralph Thomas Harbron and Maxine Eleanor (Welch) Loeber; m. Jean Phillips, June 6, 1964; children: Paul, Elizabeth, Benjamin. BSEE, Iowa State U., 1960, MSEE, 1961. Engr. Deere & Co., Moline, Ill., 1957-60; prof. computer sci. Anderson (Ind.) U., 1961—, dir. Computing Ctr., 1965-92. Author: File Systems: Structures and Algorithms, 1988. Warning officer Madison County Emergency Mgmt., Anderson, 1973—. Mem. IEEE, Assn. Computer Machinery, Eta Kappa Nu. Mem. Ch. of God. Office: Anderson U 1100 E 5th St Anderson IN 46012

HARD, CAROL DUBOVICK, investment company executive; b. Virginia, Minn., July 21, 1957; d. Joseph P. and Irene J. Dubovick; m. Garrett L. Hard, June 26 1982. BA, Augsburg Coll., Mpls., 1979. Lic. securities prin.; registered rep. Editor Conklin Co., Mpls., 1979-80; mgr. pub. rels. Mpls. Comm. Ctr., 1980-82; mgr. pub. rels. and prodn. Mohawk Advt., Mason City, Iowa, 1982-84; registered rep., ltd. ptnr. Edward D. Jones & Co., Appleton, Wis., 1984-90; v.p. mktg. AAL Capital Mgmt. Corp., Appleton, 1990-93; dir. mut. funds Bartlett & Co., Cin., 1993—. Bd. dirs. Outagamie County chpt. ARC, Appleton, 1987-93, chmn. bd., 1991-92. Mem. Internat. Assn. for Fin. Planning (pres., bd. dirs. Appleton 1990-93), Investment Co. Inst. (nat. com. 1990—), Nat. Investment Co. Svc. Assn. Home: 6201 Tanager Dr Apt 210 Burlington KY 41005-9240 Office: Bartlett & Co 36 E 4th St Cincinnati OH 45202-3811

HARDEN, MARY LOUISE, human resources management specialist; b. Natchez, Miss., Mar. 27, 1942; d. John Charles and Dorothy Louise (Reynolds) Brown; m. Billy Gene Redd, Mar. 12, 1957 (div. 1961); children: Andre Ranier, Allison Lawanda, Robin Yvette; m. Percy Lawrence Harden Jr., Aug. 31, 1968; children: Darrell Lawrence, Craig Robison. Student, Ball State U., 1975-76, Ind. U., Purdue U., 1983-88; BSBA, Ind. Wesleyan U., 1989; postgrad., U. S.C., 1990; MA, Ball State U., 1995. Editor-in-chief U.S. Army Fin. and Acctg. Ctr., Indpls., 1974-81, pers. mgmt. specialist, 1981-87, pub. affairs officer, 1987-91; personnel mgmt. specialist Def. Fin. and Acctg. Svc., 1991—; fed. women's program mgr. U.S. Army Fin. and Acctg. Ctr., Indpls., 1981-85; course mgr. Dept. Army, Indpls., 1982-85. Bd. dirs. Nat. Coalition of 100 Black Women, Indpls., 1986—, Indpls. YWCA, 1989—; minority advisor United Way of Cen. Ind., Indpls., 1985—. Named Madame C.J. Walker Outstanding Woman of Yr., Ctr. for Leadership Devel. and Indpls. C. of C., 1988. Fellow Dept. Def. Exec. Leadership Program; mem. Federally Employed Women (bd. dirs. 1978—), Am. Soc. Mil. Comptrs., Fed. Exec. Assn. (Fed. Employee of Yr. award 1978). Presbyterian. Office: Def Fin and Acctg Svc Human Resources Plan & Devel DFAS-HQ/HP Indianapolis IN 46249-2501

HARDENBURGER, JANICE, state legislator; m. William Hardenburger. Kans. state senator Dist. 21, 1993—, farm ptnr., 1996—. Home: RR 1 Box 78 Haddam KS 66944-9764*

HARDER, ELAINE RENE, state legislator; b. Windom, Minn., Dec. 27, 1947; d. Russell Jacob and Eunice Rupp; m. Ronald Dale Harder, 1970; children: Graydon, Nicole. BS, Mankato State U., 1970. Tchr. secondary sch., owner sml. bus., sales rep.; rep. Dist. 22B Minn. Ho. of Reps., 1995—; life and heatlh ins. profl. 4-H youth devel. agt. U. Minn. Ext. Svc. AAUW, Minn. Assn. Life Underwriters, Minn. Home Econ. Assn., Jackson C. of C., Kiwanis, Phi Upsilon Omicron, Delta Clovia.

HARDER, HENRY LOUIS, literature educator; b. Van Buren, Ark., Oct. 8, 1936; s. August Maxwell and Nadean Ann (Crawley) H.; m. Ramona Frances Johnson, Dec. 20, 1960; children: Karen Elaine, Monica Frances, Kenneth John, Stephen Henry, David Thomas. BA, Subiaco Coll., 1958; MA, U. Ark., 1961; PhD, U. Md., 1970. Instr. US Naval Acad., Annapolis, Md., 1965-69; asst. prof. Anne Arundel C. C., Arnold, Md., 1969-70; asst. prof. Mo. So. State Coll., Joplin, 1970-73, assoc. prof., 1973-80, prof., 1980—. Contbr. chpt. to book, articles to profl. jours. Mem. bd. med. ethics com., St. John's Regional Med. Ctr., Joplin, Mo., 1992—. Mem. Am. Assn. U. Profs. (chpt. pres. 1974), Medieval Acad. Am., Internat. Arthurian Soc., New Chaucer Soc., Medieval Assn. Midwest (pres. 1977). Home: 3119 W 27 St Joplin MO 64804 Office: Mo So State Coll Dept English 3950 E Newman Rd Joplin MO 64801

HARDER, ROBERT CLARENCE, state official; b. Horton, Kans., June 4, 1929; s. Clarence L. and Olympia E. (Kubik) H.; m. Dorothy Lou Welty, July 31, 1953; children: Anne, James David. AB, Baker U., Baldwin, Kans., 1951; MTh, So. Meth. U., 1954; ThD in Social Ethics, Boston U., 1958; LHD (hon.), Baker U., 1983, Ottawa U., 1991. Ordained to ministry Meth. Ch., 1959; pastor East Topeka Meth. Ch., 1958-64; mem. Kans. Ho. of Reps., 1961-67; rsch. assoc. Menninger Found., Topeka, 1964-65; instr. Washburn U., Topeka, 1964, 68, 69; dir. Topeka Office of Econ. Opportunity, 1965-67; tech. asst. coordinator Office of Gov. of Kans., 1967-68; dir. community resources devel. League of Kans. Municipalities, 1968-69; dir. Kans. Dept. Social Welfare, Topeka, 1969-73; sec. Kans. Dept. Social Welfare, 1973-87; projects adminstr. Topeka State Hosp., 1987-89; adj. prof. pub. adminstrn. Kans. U., 1987-95, instr. Sch. Social Welfare, 1971-87; cons. Menninger Topeka, 1991-92; sec. Kans. Dept. Health and Environment, 1992-95. Contbr. articles to profl. jours. Recipient Disting. Svc. award East Topeka Civic Assn., 1963, Romana Hood award, 1965, Cert. of Recognition, State of Kans., 1979, 87, Spl. Commendation award Kans. Senate, 1987, Spl. Commendation, Kans. Ho. of Reps., 1987; named Outstanding Pub. Ofcl. of the Yr., 1987. Mem. Am. Soc. Public Adminstrs. (Public Adminstr. of Yr. Kans. chpt. 1980), Am. Public Welfare Assn., Kans. Health Care Commn., Kans. Conf. Social Welfare (Outstanding Person of Yr. 1987). Democrat.

HARDIN, CLIFFORD MORRIS, retired university chancellor, cabinet member; b. Knightstown, Ind., Oct. 9, 1915; s. James Alvin and Mabel (Macy) H.; m. Martha Love Wood, June 28, 1939; children: Susan Carol (Mrs. L.W. Wood), Clifford Wood, Cynthia (Mrs. Robert Milligan), Nancy Ann (Mrs. Douglas L. Rogers), James. BS, Purdue U., 1937, MS, 1939, PhD, 1941, DSc (hon.), 1952; Farm Found. scholar, U. Chgo., 1939-40; LLD, Creighton U., 1956, Ill. State U., 1973; Dr. honoris causa, Nat. U. Colombia, 1968; DSc, Mich. State U., 1969, N.D. State U., 1969, U. Nebr., 1978, Okla. Christian Coll., 1979. Instr. U. Wis., 1941-42, asst. prof. agrl. econs., 1942-44; assoc. prof. agrl. econs. Mich. State Coll., 1944-46, prof., chmn. agrl. econs. dept., 1946-48, dir. expt. sta., 1949-53, dean agr., 1953-54; chancellor U. Nebr., 1954-69; sec. U.S. Dept. Agr., Washington, 1969-71; vice chmn. bd., dir. Ralston Purina Co., St. Louis, 1971-80; dir. Center for Study of Am. Bus., Washington U., St. Louis, 1981-83, scholar-in-residence, 1983-85; cons., dir. Stifel, Nicolaus & Co., St. Louis, 1980-87; bd. dirs. Gallup, Inc., Lincoln, Nebr., Halifax Corp., Alexandria, Va.; bd. dirs. Omaha br. Fed. Res. Bank of Kansas City, 1961-67, chmn., 1962-67. Editor: Overcoming World Hunger, 1969. Trustee Rockefeller Found., 1961-69, 72-81, Winrock, Internat., Morrilton, Ark., 1984-94, Am. Assembly, 1975—, U. Nebr. Found., 1975—; mem. Pres.'s Com. to Stregthen Security Free World, 1963. Mem. Assn. State Univs. and Land-Grant Colls. (pres. 1960, chmn. exec. com. 1961).

HARDIN, MARTHA LOVE WOOD, civic leader; b. Muncie, Ind., Aug. 13, 1918; d. Lawrence Anselm and Bonny Blossom (Williams) Wood; m. Clifford Morris Hardin, June 28, 1939; children: Susan Hardin Wood, Clifford Wood, Cynthia Hardin Milligan, Nancy Hardin Rogers, James Alvin. Librarian U. Chgo., 1939-40. Co-author Genealogy: Ancestors of Lawrence Anselm Wood, Genealogy Ancestors of Bonny Williams Wood; contbr. articles to profl. jours. Chmn. Nebr. Heart Fund, 1967; vol. worker Lincoln Gen. Hosp., 1965, Clarkson Hosp., 1966; hon. chmn. Symphony Ball, Washington, 1970; mem. met. bd. YWCA, Washington, 1969-71, St. Louis, 1973-95; mem. Women's Com. of Pres.'s Com. on Employment of Handicapped, 1970-91, permanent mem. bd., 1970—; bd. dirs. St. Louis Speech and Hearing Clinic, St. Louis Met. YWCA, Cen. Inst. Deaf, St. Louis, 1986-92; co-chmn. nat. fund-raising campaign U. Nebr. Found., 1977-80. Mem. DAR, PEO, St. Louis Geneal. Soc., Mortar Bd., Old Warson Country Club, St. Louis Club, Wednesday Club, Phi Beta Kappa, Pi Beta Phi.

HARDIN, PAUL G., broker; b. Columbus, Ohio, Nov. 14, 1961. BA, So. Ill. U., 1986. Broker Edward D. Jones & Co., Jerseyville, Ill., 1988—. Mem. Rotary, Lions, Jerseyville C. of C. Republican. Roman Catholic. Office: Edward D Jones & Co PO Box 89 308 S State Jerseyville IL 62052

HARDING, CLIFFORD VINCENT, III, pathologist, cell biologist, immunologist; b. Arlington, Va., Jan. 31, 1957; s. Clifford Vincent Jr. and Drusilla (Van Hoesen) H.; m. Mina Kay Chung, 1983; children: Clifford Vincent IV, Andrew Richard. AB magna cum laude, Harvard U., 1979; MD, PhD in Cell Biology, Washington U., St. Louis, 1985. Diplomate Nat. Bd. Med. Examiners. Resident in pathology Washington U., 1985-89, chief resident, 1989-90, asst. prof., 1990-93; asst. prof. pathology Case Western Reserve U., Cleve., 1993-96, assoc. prof. pathology, 1996—. Mem. editl. bd. Advances in Anatomic Pathology; contbr. articles and abstracts to med. jours. Mem. AAAS, Am. Assn. Immunologists, Am. Soc. Cell Biology, Am. Assn. Pathologists, Phi Beta Kappa. Office: Case Western Res Univ Dept Pathology 2085 Adelbert Rd Cleveland OH 44106

HARDING, G. HOMER, former state official; s. Guy Ula and Rose Marie (Kleepsie) H.; m. Patricia Binkley, 1947; children: Teresa Lynn Harding Retrum, Barbara Jane Harding Roenhorst, Steven Guy, William Homer. BS, U. S.D. Sen. dist. 19 State of S.D., minority leader, 1975-76, majority leader, 1977-88, state treas., 1990-94; cons. Pierre, S.D., 1995—; bd. dirs. First Nat. Bank, Pierre, S.D.; mem. Small Bus. Adv. Coun. Former mem. Pierre Sch. Bd., Bus. Adv. Coun. U. S.D. With U.S. Army, World War II, Korean War; brig. gen. S.D. N.G. Decorated Meritorious Svc. medal. Mem. VFW, Pierre C. of C., Lions, Masons, Elks. Methodist. Home and Office: 314 Mary Ln Pierre SD 57501

HARDING, RICK PETER, environmental engineering executive; b. Watertown, N.Y., Mar. 21, 1949; s. Richard Thomas and Beverly Jane (Barber) H.; m. Andrea Lee Frazer, Oct. 4, 1987. BA, SUNY, Oswego, 1971; PhD, Colo. State U., 1985. Rsch. asst. Atomic Energy Commn., Rochester, N.Y., 1971-73; rsch. assoc. U.S. Energy Devel. Agency, Rochester, 1973-78; project coord. Dept. of Radiology and Radiation Biology, Ft. Collins, Colo., 1978-82; Radiobiologist/health physicist, dir. environ. affairs Nuclear Metals, Inc., Concord, Mass., 1982-85; corp. health/safety officer, sr. project mgr. Goldberg-Zoino Assocs. of N.Y., Buffalo, 1985-88; asst. prin., v.p., regional mgr. GZA GeoEnviron., Inc., Livonia, Mich., 1988-92; prin., sr. v.p., regional mgr. GZA GeoEnviron., Inc., Livonia, 1992-94; pres., sr. prin. Integrated Environ., Inc., Farmington Hills, Mich., 1994—; presenter annual meeting Radiation Rsch. Soc., Mpls., 1981, Salt Lake City, 1982, Nat. Water Well Assn. Tech. Divsn. Regional Ground Water conf., Newton, Mass., 1984, Health Physics Soc., Denver, 1981, Colo. Springs, Colo., 1985, Dept. Def. Tng., Aberdeen Proving Ground, Md., 1985. Contbr. articles to profl. jours. Nat. Cancer Inst. fellow, 1978-82; named Young Scientist of Year, Radiation Rsch. Soc., 1981, 82, 83; recipient Quality award Chrysler Corp., 1992, Gold Pentastar, 1993. Mem. N.Y. Acad. Scis., Health Physics Soc., Sigma Xi. Office: Integrated Environ Inc 21435 Gill Rd Farmington Hills MI 48335

HARDISTY, WILLIAM LEE, English language educator; b. Creston, Iowa, Feb. 14, 1946; s. Ernest Dale and Velda Marie (Schaffer) H.; m. Bernadine Maxine Reimers, July 30, 1967; children: Lance William, Chad Eugene. AA, Creston (Iowa) C.C., 1964; BS, N.W. Mo. State U., Maryville, 1967, MA, 1972; postgrad., U. No. Iowa, Cedar Falls, 1988-96. Cert. tchr., Iowa, Mo. Instr. Iowa Western Coll., Council Bluffs, 1987—; chmn. lang. arts A-H-S-T H.S., Avoca, Iowa, 1967—; drama dir. A-S-T High Sch., Avoca, Iowa, 1967-92; presenter Iowa Tchrs. English, Des Moines, 1991-95, Iowa Conservation Edn. Coun., Ames, 1995, Iowa State Edn. Assn., 1982-95. Mem. dist. com. Mid-Am. coun. Boy Scouts Am., 1984-96; chmn. Rep. Party Knox Twp., Avoca, 1988-96; pres. Iowa Assn. County Conservation Bds., Des Moines, 1990; pres. Pott count R.E.A.P. Bd. Council Bluffs, 1992; elder Presbyn. Ch., 1969-96; exec. bd. Southwest Uniserv Unit, 1995-96. Mem. NRA (life), NEA (life), Nat. Coun. Tchrs. English (life), Pheasants Forever (bd. dirs. 1990-91), Iowa State Edn. Assn., Southwest Uniserv Unit (exec. bd. 1994-96), Phi Delta Kappa. Home: 107 Jaycee St Avoca IA 51521-5030 Office: A-H-S-T High Sch 300 Grant St Avoca IA 51521

HARDY, DAVID G., transportation executive; b. Kansas City, Mo., Jan. 31, 1952. AA, Lonview C. C., Lee's Summit, Mo., 1975; cert. transp., U. Kansas City, 1977. Driver Exhibitors Film Delivery, North Kansas City, Mo., 1974-81; v.p. Sandusky Traffic Counselors, Kansas City, 1982—. Mem. Nat. Assn. Freight Transp. Conss. Republican. Roman Catholic. Office: Sandusky Traffic Counselors 1003 Walnut St Ste 400 Kansas City MO 64106

HARDY, JAMES E., stockbroker; b. St. Louis, July 12, 1944. BS, Southeast Mo. U., 1968, Am. Inst. Banking, 1972; BA, Coll. Fin. Planning, 1987. Asst. v.p. United Mo. Bank, Kirkwood, 1968-71; v.p. Merrill Lynch, Chesterfield, Mo., 1972—. Bd. dirs. Therapeutic Horsemanship, St. Louis, 1989-90. Winn Smith fellow Merrill Lynch, 1979—. Mem. Chesterfield Rotary (founder), Chesterfield C. of C. (bd. dirs. 1981-91), Kirkwood C. of C. (bd. dirs. 1969-71), Rotary (Paul Harris fellow 1994), U.S. Pony Club (dist. commn. 1982-83), Bridlespur Foc Hunt Club (bd. dirs. 1989-92), St. Louis Polo Team, Charles E. MErrill Cir. Republican. Roman Catholic. Office: Merrill Lynch 16100 N Outer 40 Chesterfield MO 63017-1784

HARDY, RAYMOND REED, psychology educator; b. McKeesport, Pa., Apr. 2, 1944; s. James Wesley Hardy and Mary Virginia (Shaw) Shultz; m. Jill Lynn Hutchins, Dec. 27, 1967; children: Adam James, Lissa Ellen. BA, Clarion State U., 1967; MA, W.Va. U., 1973, PhD, 1974. Asst. prof. psychology St. Norbert Coll., De Pere, Wis., 1974-89; assoc. prof. psychology St. Norbert Coll., De Pere, 1989—; pres., CEO Share Wright, Inc., De Pere, Wis., 1983—. Author, developer (computer program) Behavior Analysis: A Computer-Based Tutorial, 1995; contbr. articles to profl. jours. Clk. Fox Valley Soc. of Friends, Green Bay, Wis., 1994—. Sgt U.S. Army, 1967-69, Vietnam. Named Tchr. of Yr. W. Va. U. Parents Assn., Morgantown, 1974. Mem. Midwestern Psychol. Assn., Assn. for Behavior Analysis, Animal Behavior Soc. Democrat. Office: St Norbert Coll Psychology Dept De Pere WI 54115

HARDY, RICHARD EVAN, human service professional, consultant; b. Inglewood, Calif., Sept. 21, 1952; s. Heber Albert and Myra Joy (Johnson) Hardy; m. Julie Kaye Despain, Mar. 27, 1980; children: Melina Mae, Jonathan Richard, Melissa Ann, Michelle Kaye. BA, Brigham Young U., 1981, MA, 1984. Rehab. evaluation profl. Utah Bd. Edn., Salt Lake City, 1985; sys. analyst/trainer GM/EDS, Warren, Mich., 1985-87; process and specifications analyst/trainer CDI Transp./Modern Engring., Troy, Mich., 1987-88; employment profl., multi-state regional mgr. LDS Employment and Rehab. Svc., Farmington Hills, Mich., 1988—; sr. officer Ameramedic, Sterling Heights, Mich., 1986-88; cons. and lectr. in field. Co-author: ASBYU History 1978-1979, 1979; author manuals. Bd. dirs. Bloomfield Hills Family History Ctr., 1990-91; vice chmn. Adv. Com. for Disabled People, Troy, 1992-93; co-founder Metro Detroit Employment Svc., 1992-94; active Boy Scouts Am., 1990. Served with U.S. Army, 1972-75, Army N.G., 1981-83, Air N.G., 1983-87. Mem. Greater Detroit Employment Opportunity Assn. (treasury chair 1991—), Nat. Rehab. Assn., Nat. Rehab. Counseling Assn., Mich. Rehab. Counseling Assn., Vocat. Evaluators and Work Adjustors Assn. Mormon.

HARDY, RICHARD J., political scientist, educator; b. Burlington, Iowa, July 7, 1948; s. Eldon L. and Ann (Nicol) H.; m. Linda Marie Nuss, Aug. 18, 1968; children: Amanda Marie, Thomas R. AA, Southeastern C.C., Burlington, 1968; BA with honors, Western Ill. U., Macomb, 1970; MA, U. N.D., Grand Forks, 1972; PhD, U. Iowa, 1978. Vis. asst. prof. No. State Coll., Aberdeen, S.D., 1972-74; tchr. St. John's Sch., Burlington, 1975; grad. tchr. U. Iowa, Iowa City, 1976-78; asst. prof. U. Mo., Columbia, 1978-83, assoc. prof. polit. sci., 1985—; vis. asst. prof. Duke U., Durham, N.C., 1984. Author: (h.s. textbook) Government in America, 1995, (coll. textbooks) Missouri Government and Politics, 1995, Perspectives in American Government, 1995. Rep. nominee for U.S. Congress from 9th Dist. Mo., 1992; state bd. dirs. Missourians for Ltd. Terms, 1991-95, Missourians for Fair Elections, 1993-95; mem. Transitional Housing Authority, Columbia, 1995. Mem. Nat. Fedn. Pachyderms. Methodist. Home: 4106 S Wappel Dr Columbia MO 65203

HARDY, WILLIAM ROBINSON, lawyer; b. Cin., June 14, 1934; s. William B. and Chastine M. (Sprague) H.; m. Barbro Anita Medin, Oct. 11, 1964; children: Anita Christina, William Robinson Jr. AB magna cum laude, Princeton U., 1956; JD, Harvard U., 1963. Bar: Ohio 1963, U.S. Supreme Ct. 1975. Life underwriter New Eng. Mut. Life Ins. Co., 1956-63; assoc. Graydon, Head & Ritchey, Cin., 1963-68, ptnr., 1968—; mem. panel comml. and constrn. industry arbitrators Am. Arbitration Assn., 1972—, mem. panel large complex case program, 1993—; reporter joint com. for revision of rules of U.S. Dist. Ct. for So. Dist. Ohio, 1975, 80, 83, mem., 1990—. Bd. dirs. Cin. Union Bethel, 1968—, pres., 1977-82; bd. dirs. Ohio Valley Goodwill Industries Rehab. Ctr., Cin., 1970—, pres., 1981-92; mem. Cin. Bd. Bldg. Appeals, 1976—, vice chmn., 1983, chmn., 1983—; pres. Hamilton County (Ohio) Alcohol and Drug Addiction Svcs. Bd., 1990-92. Capt. USAR, 1956-68; maj. gen. Ohio Mil. Res., insp. gen., 1988-89, TJAG, 1989-93, dep. comdr., 1993-96m, comdr., 1996—. Recipient award of merit Ohio Legal Ctr. Inst., 1975, 76. Mem. ABA, AAAS, Ohio Bar Assn., Cin. Bar Assn., Assn. Trial Lawyers Am., Ohio Acad. Trial Lawyers, 6th Cir. Jud. Conf. (life), Ohio Soc. Colonial Wars (gov. 1979), Phi Beta Kappa. Mem. Ch. of Redeemer. Club: Princeton (N.Y.C.). Home: 1339 Michigan Ave Cincinnati OH 45208-2701 Office: Graydon Head & Ritchey PO Box 6464 Cincinnati OH 45201-6464

HARE, LEROY, JR., pharmaceutical company executive; b. Topeka, Nov. 1, 1955; s. LeRoy and Carol Darlene (Johnson) H.; m. Margaret Ann Burke, Dec. 30, 1982; children: Susan Audrey and Sarah Jean (twins). Student, Kans. State U., 1974-76; BBA, Washburn U., 1978. Book buyer Palmer News, Inc., Topeka, 1978-81; store mgr. Town Crier Book Store, Topeka, 1980-81; field sales rep. USV Labs., Topeka, 1981-84; field sales rep. Glaxo Inc, Topeka, 1985-90, field sales trainer, 1988-90, regional sales trainer, 1989-90, mem. profl. devel. program, 1989, managed care area account mgr., 1990-94; dist. sales mgr., 1994-95; co-founder Info Tec, LLC, DAPS, 1995-96; acct. mgr. Networks Plus, Prairie Village, Kans., 1996—; account mgr. Networks Plus, 1996—, dist. sales mgr., 1996—. Author sales tng. manual. Mem. adv. panel Marian Clinic, Topeka, 1989-94, Black Health Care Coalition, 1994-95.

HARF, PATRICIA JEAN KOLE, syndicated columnist, educational consultant, lecturer; b. Berea, Ohio, Oct. 14, 1937; d. Paul Frederic and Mena (Labordes) Kole; m. Fredric Henry Harf, June 21, 1969. BS in Edn., Baldwin-Wallace Coll., Berea, Ohio, 1959; MS in Edn., U. Akron, 1966; Dr. in Edn., Ariz. State U., 1972; PhD, London Inst. Applied Rsch., 1995; HHD, World Acad., 1994; PhD, London Inst. Applied Rsch., 1995. Rsch. Ednl. Rsch. Coun. Am., 1967-69; tchr. Berea City Schs., Cleve. and Parma, Ohio, 1969-73; asst. prof. Cleve. State U., 1975—; corr., columnist, freelance writer, syndicated columnist Chronicle-Telegram, Elyria, Ohio, 1986-89; owner Harf's Comms. Inc., Berea, Ohio, 1993—; ednl. cons. State of Ohio; syndicated columnist Universal Press, Cleve. Plain Dealer; diagnostician of reading difficulties; cons. learning disabilities; guest lectr.; TV guest appearances. Author teaching materials and tchr. and children's texts; contbr. articles to profl. jours. ; also advisor to book pubs. and magazines. Pres. Berea Hist. Soc., World Found. Successful Women; mem. Cleve. Orch. Women's Com.; advisor Cleve. Radio and TV Coun.; tutor Project Learn, Cleve.; mem. Berea Rep. Precinct Com.; founder Preventive Parenting; dep. senator Internat. Parliament Safety & Peace Italy. Named Intellectual Woman of Yr., 1991-92, Emminent fellow in Universe of Mankind, 1994, Ohio Ednl. Woman of Yr., Ohio Educator of Yr. and Outstanding Educator, Outstanding Citizen Berea C. of C., Ohio Edn. Woman of Yr., 1991, Most Admired woman of Yr., 1993, Lifetime Fellow and Hon. Prof. Australian Inst. for Coordinated Rsch., 1995; recipient Women's Inner Cir. of Achievement award, 1992, Woman of Yr. commemorative medal Order of Internat. Fellowship, 1994, Excellence in Journalism award 1990-93, World Lifetime Achievement award, 1996; named baroness Royal Order Bohemian Crown, 1994. Mem. NEA, NOW, Soc. Profl. Journalists (Excellence in Journalism award 1990), Berea C. of c. (Outstanding Citizen 1965), Berea Hist. Soc., Berea Bus. and Profl. Women, Internat. Reading Assn. (cons. and writer for reading tchrs.), Ohio Edn. Assn. (Woman of Yr. in Comms. 1991), Internat. Platform Assn., World Found. of Successful Women, Nat. Assn. Women, Profl. Educators Assn., Learning Disability Assn., Nat. Assn. Psychologists, Ohio Assn. Psychologists, Nat. Assn. Women in the Arts, Western Res. Rep. Women's Assn., Kiwanis (sec., v.p.), Berea Rep. Club (Mayoral Volunteerism award 1987), Press Club of Cleve. Republican. Methodist. Home: 323 Westbridge Dr Berea OH 44017-1562

HARGROVE, MIKE (DUDLEY MICHAEL HARGROVE), professional baseball team manager; b. Perryton, Tex., Oct. 26, 1949; m. Sharon Rupprecht, Dec. 12, 1970; children: Kimberly Denise, Melissa Kathryn, Pamela Christine, Andrew Michael, Cynthia Michelle. BS in Phys. Edn. and Social Scis., Northwestern Okla. State U. Baseball player Tex. Rangers, 1974-78, San Diego Padres, 1979; baseball player Cleve. Indians, 1979-85, coach minor league team, 1986, mgr. minor league team, 1987-89, coach, 1990-91, mgr., 1991—. Named Am. League Rookie of Yr. Baseball Writers' Assn. Am., 1974, Am. League Rookie Player of Yr. Sporting News, 1974; named to All-Star team, 1975, Am. League Mgr. of Yr. Sporting News, 1995. Office: Cleveland Indians 2401 Ontario St Cleveland OH 44115-4003*

HARIED, JAMES ANDREW, business development executive; b. Aurora, Ill., Jan. 7, 1956; s. John Caspar and Margaret O'Brien (Matthews) H.; m. Vida Ann Mueller, July 7, 1984; children: James Andrew Jr., Alexander Mueller, Julia Margaret. BS in Nuclear Engring., U. Ill., 1979. Rsch. engr. Union Carbide, Nuclear Safety Info. Ctr., Oak Ridge, Tenn., 1979-81; regional sales mgr. Energenics, Aurora, Ill., 1982-84; v.p. sales Energenics, Lombard, Ill., 1985-90; pres. Energenics, Naples, Fla., 1991-92; mgr. bus. devel. Rust Environment and Infrastructure, Chgo., 1992—. Bd. dirs. Hinsdale Swim Club; deacon Cmty. Presbyn. Ch. Mem. Kiwanis. Republican. Presbyterian. Office: Rust Environ and Infrastructure 3121 Butterfield Rd Oak Brook IL 60521

HARINCK, JOHN GORDON, sales executive, hydraulics engineer; b. Detroit, Sept. 6, 1939; s. Peter Gordon and Mary Alice (Hooper) H.; m. Dorothy Elizabeth Wallace, Nov. 17, 1959 (div. Feg. 1984); children: Jeffery John, Elizabeth Mary, Pamela Ann, Timothy Alan, Shannon Elizabeth; m. Sally Ann Sperry, Feb. 9, 1985. BSME, Lawrence Inst. Tech., Southfield, Mich., 1965. Applications engr. Vickers, Inc., Troy, Mich., 1960-67; sales engr., sales supr., product mgr., gen. sales mgr. Eaton Corp., Marshall, Mich., 1967-74; Midwest regional mgr. Pall Corp., Glen Cove, N.Y., 1974-78; account mgr., branch mgr. Fauver Co., Inc., Madison Heights, Mich., 1978-84; nat. accounts mgr., regional mgr., Double A Products Co. Vickers, Inc., Troy, Mich., 1984—. Mem. Jaycees, Marshall, 1967-72. Mem. Engr. Soc. of Detroit, Nat. Fluidpower Assn., Fluid Power Soc., Soc. Automotive Engrs., Moose. Republican. Episcopalian. Home and Office: 281 Parkshore Dr Battle Creek MI 49017

HARIRI, V. M., arbitrator, mediator, lawyer, educator. BS, Wayne State U.; JD, Detroit Coll. Law; LLM, London Sch. Econs. and Polit.Sci.; diploma arbitration, Reading (Eng.) U. Pvt. practice internat. and domestic bus. law Northville, Mich.; drafting com. Republic of Kazakhstan Code on Arbitration Procedure, Free Econ. Zone Legislation, Republic of Belarus.

Fellow Chartered Inst. Arbitrators (mem. exec. com. N.Am. br., co-founder); mem. ABA, IBA, Am. Soc. Internat. Law, Am. Arbitration Assn., London Ct. Internat. Arbitration, World Jurist Assn., Mich. Trial Lawyers Assn. Office: 325 N Center St Ste E3 Northville MI 48167-1244

HARKIN, THOMAS RICHARD, senator; b. Cumming, Iowa, Nov. 19, 1939; s. Patrick and Frances H.; m. Ruth Raduenz, 1968; children: Amy, Jenny. BS, Iowa State U., 1962; JD, Cath. U. Am., 1972. Mem. staff Ho. of Reps. Select Com. U.S. Involvement in S.E. Asia, 1970; mem. 94th-98th Congresses from 5th Iowa Dist., mem. sci. and tech. com., mem. agr., nutrition and forestry coms.; U.S. Senator from Iowa, 1984—; mem. Dem. Steering Com.; ranking minority mem. Appropriations Subcom. on Labor, Health and Human Svcs and Edn.; ranking minority mem. Subcom. on Disability Policy; ranking minority mem. Agr., Nutrition, and Forestry subcom. on Rsch., Nutrition, and Gen. Legis.; mem. Small Bus. Com.; prin. author Ams. with Disabilities Act. Co-author: (with C.E. Thomas) Five Minutes to Midnight: Why the Nuclear Threat is Growing Faster than Ever, 1990. Dem. candidate for Presidency of U.S., 1992. Served with USN, 1962-67. Named Outstanding Young Alumnus Iowa State U. Alumni Assn., 1974. Democrat. Office: US Senate 531 Hart Senate Bldg Washington DC 20510*

HARKINS, RICHARD WESLEY, marine engineer, naval architect; b. Duluth, Minn., Oct. 11, 1946; s. Wesley Ray and Vivian G. (LaBrosse) H.; m. Deborah Ann deGonzaque, Aug. 17, 1974; children: Ryan Wesley, Blair Ashley, Danielle Ashley. BS, U.S. Mcht. Marine Acad., Kings Point, N.Y., 1971; MSE in Naval Architecture and Marine Engring., U. Mich., 1976. Registered profl. engr., Ohio. 3d asst. engr. Hanna Steamship Corp., Cleve., 1971; 1st asst. engr. Poling Transp. Corp., N.Y.C., 1971-72; engr. Ingalls Shipbuilding Co., Pascagoula, Miss., 1972-74; fleet supt. Interlake Steamship Co., Cleve., 1976-94; v.p. ops. Lake Carriers' Assn., Cleve., 1994—. Author: (tech. paper) Investigation of Fuel Injection Cavitation, 1985 (Best Paper of 1985 Soc. Naval Architects and Marine Engrs.). Mem. Soc. Naval Architects and Marine Engrs. (ship machinery com. 1985, chmn. diesel panel 1985—, chmn. papers com. 1985-87, local sect. rep. 1985-87). Roman Catholic. Home: 2771 Hampton Rd Cleveland OH 44116-2548 Office: 614 Superior Ave W Ste 915 Cleveland OH 44114-3401

HARKNA, ERIC, advertising executive; b. Tallinn, Estonia, June 24, 1940; came to U.S., 1947; s. Erich K. Harkna and Adelaide Mender; children: Britt, Kristiana, Christian Erik; m. Tonise Paul. B.A., Colgate U., 1962; M.B.A., Columbia U., 1964. Account exec. Benton & Bowles, N.Y.C., 1965-68; v.p., account supr. Kenyon & Eckhart, N.Y.C., 1969-71; v.p., account supr. BBDO, Inc., N.Y.C., 1973-74, v.p., mgmt. supr., 1974-76, sr. v.p., dir., 1977-82; exec. v.p., dir., 1979-82; pres., dir. BBDO, Inc., Chgo., 1982-84, pres., chief exec. officer, 1984-93; sr. v.p. BBDO Worldwide, Chgo., 1993—; chmn. ann. awards dinner Advt. Age, 1987; chmn. Media Subcom., Chgo. Bd. dirs. United Cerebral Palsy Found., Chgo., 1982-94, Friends of Prentice Hosp.; v.p. nat. fund raising exec. com. Juvenile Diabetes Found. Internat., 1987-95, bd. dirs., 1990-96, internat. long range planning com. 1995; bd. dirs. Chgo. Coun. Profl. Psychology, 1991-96, Mus. Broadcast Commn., 1992. Colgate U. Norwegian Study grantee, 1961; recipient Internat. Bus. award Columbia U., 1964. Mem. Am. Assn. Advt. Agys. (regional bd. govs. 1994), Am. Mktg. Assn., Chgo. Coun. Fgn. Rels., Chgo. Advt. Club, Chgo. Econs. Club, Lake Shore Soc. Clubs, Execs. Club Chgo., N.Y. Athletic Club (N.Y.C.), N.Y. A.C. Yacht Club (Pelham), Chgo. Estonia House, Chgo. Yacht Club, 410 Club (founder, bd. dirs., bd. govs.). Office: BBDO Worldwide Inc 410 N Michigan Ave Chicago IL 60611

HARKRADER, ALAN DALE, JR., photojournalist; b. Chgo., June 27, 1928; s. Alan Dale and Barbara Ann (Fiedler) H.; m. Mary Ellen Wheeler, July 17, 1954; children: Alan Dale III, Mark Eugene. BS in Journalism, Bradley U., 1954, MA in Fine Art, 1974. Staff photographer Morning Star, Peoria, Ill., 1952-54, Herald and Rev., Decatur, Ill., 1954-56; staff photographer Jour. Star, Peoria, 1956-91, ret., 1991. With U.S. Army, 1946-47, 50-52, Korea. Mem. Nat. Press Photographers Assn. (regional bd. dirs. 1965, Mellor award 1965, McLaughlin award 1969), Ill. Press Photographers Assn. (life, pres. 1960, Ill. Photographer of Yr. award 1958, 60, 62, 63, 65). Democrat. Roman Catholic. Home: 1712 E Shady Oak Dr Peoria IL 61614

HARLAN, JERRY WALLACE, electrical engineer; b. Wheeling, W.Va., Apr. 23, 1946; s. Frenzie H. and Bertha M. (Lucey) H.; m. Connie Marie Saunier, June 10, 1972; children: Mike, Jennifer, Jeff, Melissa. BSEE, W.Va. U., 1969. Elec. engr. RCA Radar Systems, Moorestown, N.J., 1969-70, AEP Svc. Corp., Canton, Ohio, 1970-75; elec. engr. Controlled Power Corp., Canton, 1975-77, regional sales mgr., 1977-84, nat. sales mgr., 1984-93, v.p. ops. mfg. and engring., 1995—; mktg. mgr. Powercon Corp., Severn, Md., 1993-95; exec. mgmt. staff Controlled Power Corp., 1995—. Mem. IEEE. Republican. Roman Catholic. Home: 1778 Cadbury Ave NW Massillon OH 44646 Office: Controlled Power Corp 1501 Raff Rd Canton OH 44710

HARLAN, NORMAN RALPH, construction executive; b. Dayton, Ohio, Dec. 21, 1914; s. Joseph and Anna (Kaplan) H.; Indsl. Engring. degree U. Cin., 1937; m. Thelma Katz, Sept. 4, 1955; children: Leslie, Todd. Chmn. Am. Constrn. Corp., Dayton, 1949—, Harlan, Inc., realtors; owner Norman Estates, Inc. Mem. Dayton Real Estate Bd., Ohio Real Estate Assn., Nat. Assn. Real Estate Bds., C. of C., Pi Lambda Phi. Home: 303 Glenridge Rd Kettering OH 45429-1631 Office: Am Constrn Corp 2451 S Dixie Dr Dayton OH 45409-1861

HARLAN, THOMAS N., marketing executive. Sales mgr. Ingham Internat., Mpls., 1984-86; owner Trade Link Internat., Mpls., 1986-88; sales mgr. Phoenix Internat., Mpls., 1988-89, C.H. Robinson, Mpls., 1990-92; pres. Harlan & Assoc., Mpls., 1990—. Republican. Roman Catholic. Office: Harlan & Assoc P O Box 26324 Minneapolis MN 55426-0324

HARLAN, TIMOTHY, state legislator. Mem. Mo. Ho. of Reps., Jefferson City. Democrat.

HARMAN, MIKE, real estate broker, small business owner; b. Troy, Kans., Aug. 27, 1952; m. Sue Harman; 2 children. Libertarian candidate for U.S. House 7th Dist., Mo., 1996. Office: 675 E 380th Rd Dunnegan MO 65640*

HARMON, HARRY ALAN, marketing educator; b. St. James, MO, Aug. 22, 1944; s. Harry and Catherine Mary (Brount) H.; m. Judy Sharon Murray, July 3, 1974. BS, BA, Ctrl. Mo. State, 1989, MBA, 1990; D in Bus. Adminstrn., La. Tech. U., 1993. Gen. mgr. Mo. Oxygen, Sedalia, 1963-80; customer svc. mgr. Broderick & Bascom, Sedalia, Mo., 1980-87; tchg. asst. La. Tech., Ruston, 1990-92; prof. of mktg. Ctrl. Mo. State U., Warrensburg, 1992—. Mem. editorial bd. So. Bus. Review, 1993, 94; contbr. articles to profl. jours. With U.S. Army, 1966-68. Mem. Am. Mktg. Assn., Acad. Mktg. Sci., Phi Kappa Phi (hon.), Beta Gamma Sigma (hon.). Republican. Baptist. Home: 1400 Timber Ridge Dr Sedalia MO 65301 Office: Central Missouri State University College of Business Warrensburg MO 64093

HARMON, LONNIE GALE, aerospace company business manager; b. Wood River, Ill., Dec. 21, 1957; s. Robert Gale and Lola May (Bean) H.; m. Kimberly Vincenza Signorello, Sept. 2, 1977; children: Natalie Suzanne, Nathan Robert. BBA, So. Ill. U., 1978, MBA, 1984. Bus. mgr. McDonnell-Douglas Corp., St. Louis, 1978—; pres. Equi-Share Cons. Inc., Wood River, Ill., 1986; proprietor K & L Vending, Wood River, Ill., 1992-93. Sec. Roxana (Ill.) Cmty. Unite Sch., 1985-93, fin. com. chair, 1987-93; deacon, treas. First Bapt. Ch., Roxana, 1982—; candidate for cir. clk. Rep. Party, Madison County, Ill, 1992, precinct committeeman, 1992; mem. United Way Fund Distbn. Com., 1993-94. Recipient Level II Cert. of Achievement, Ill. Assn. Sch. Bds., 1992, Level I Cert. of Achievement, Ill. Assn. Sch. Bds., 1991; named one of Outstanding Young Men ofAm., 1988, 92. Mem. NRA, Nat. Sch. Bds. Assn. Republican. Baptist. Home: 1549 Esther Ave Wood River IL 62095-2225 Office: McDonnell-Douglas Corp PO Box 516 Saint Louis MO 63166-0516

HARMON, ROY, plant manager gear company; b. La Plata, Mo., Aug. 28, 1938. Plant mgr. St. Louis Gear Co., Keokuk, Iowa, 1960—; quality control mgr. St. Louis Gear Co., Keokuk, 1977—. With U.S. Army, 1957-60. Office: St Louis Gear Co PO Box 880 Keokuk IA 52632-0880

HARMON, TIM JAMES, construction executive; b. Evanston, Ill.; s. James Richard Harmon and Muriel Joan (Schneider) Mortell; m. Debra Moore, 1975 (div. 1977); m. Maribeth Bailey, Dec. 20, 1980; 1 child, Avraham. G-rad. high sch., Indpls. Pres. Emmanuel Hot Line Inc., Indpls., 1969-71; pres., owner Ginkomyer Bros. Inc., Indpls., 1972-75; mgr. Tech. 300 Near Eastside Multi-Svc. Ctr., Indpls., 1975-76; owner, ptnr. Earth Garden Cafe Inc., Indpls., 1977-81; owner Tim J. Harmon Builder, Indpls., 1979-86, Cottage Home Antiques, Indpls., 1986—; pres., owner Restoration Svcs., Indpls., 1986—; pres. Cottage Home Neighborhood Assn., 1984-85, 89-90, bd. dirs., 1984-86, 89-91. Mem. Near Eastside Cmty. Orgn., VISTA adv. com., 1988—; bd. dirs. Mayor's Drug Abuse Task Force, 1972-73, Rehab Resource, 1989-90; precinct chair Dem. Com., 1988-91; bd. dirs. Amazing Space, 1993-95. Democrat. Mem. Christian Ch. Office: Tim & Billy's Salvage Store 970 Fort Wayne Ave Indianapolis IN 46202-3334

HARMONY, MARLIN DALE, chemistry educator; b. Lincoln, Nebr., Mar. 2, 1936; s. Philip and Helen Irene (Michal) H. A.A., Kansas City (Mo.) Jr. Coll., 1956; B.S. in Chem. Engring., U. Kans., 1958; Ph.D. in Chemistry, U. Calif.-Berkeley, 1961. Asst. prof. U. Kans., Lawrence, 1962-67, assoc. prof., 1967-71, prof., 1971—; chmn. U. Kans., 1980-88; panel mem. NRC-Nat. Bur. Standards., 1969-78; mem. review panel NSF, 1977, 92. Author: Introduction to Molecular Energies and Spectra, 1972; contbg. editor: Physics Vade Mecum, 1981; mem. editorial bd. Structural Chemistry; contbr. articles to profl. jours. Postdoctoral fellow NSF Harvard U., 1961-62. Fellow AAAS; mem. Am. Chem. Soc., Am. Phys. Soc., Sigma Xi, Alpha Chi Sigma, Phi Lambda Upsilon, Tau Beta Pi. Democrat. Home: 1033 Avalon Rd Lawrence KS 66044-2505 Office: U Kans Dept Chemistry Lawrence KS 66045

HARMS, NANCY ISABEL FITCH, entrepreneur; b. Hartford, Conn., May 8, 1939; d. William Grant II and Anna Emmons Burns (Jarrett) Fitch; m. Tancrede Alfred LaMontagne, Apr. 1, 1962 (div. Apr. 1964); m. Ricardo Moraga Lucero, Oct. 11, 1969 (div. May 1970); m. Allan Wayne Harms, Jan. 19, 1974 (dec. Apr. 1996). AA, Med. Sec., Va. Intermont Coll., Bristol, 1959; AA in English Lit., U. Bridgeport, 1965, BS in Secondary Edn., 1968; postgrad., Ariz. State U., 1970. Passenger agt., stewardess UAL, Newark, 1960-62; med. sec. Sherman Neurosurg. Group, Bridgeport, Conn., 1965-67; tchr. reading, math. and sci. Juliette Low Elem. Sch., Elk Grove, Ill., 1968; tchr. English and biology North High Sch., Phoenix, 1968; grad. asst. in L.S. Lab. Ariz. State U., Tempe, 1969-70; tchr. lang. arts Gemini Sch., Niles, Ill., 1970-71; supr. campus svcs. William Rainey Harper Coll., Palatine, Ill., 1972-77; owner Harmony Corner Homespun Shop, Rogersville, Mo., 1982-85, Snack Shop, Rogersville, Mo., 1977—; elem. substitute tchr. Springfield (Mo.) Pub. Schs., 1991-94. Contbg. editor: Quilt/Harris Publs., 1978-93; contbr. articles to profl. jours. Mem. AAUW (chair status of women 1973-75), Ozarks Geneal. Soc., Colonial Dames XVII, DAR, NRA, Greater Ozarks Colony of the Soc. Mayflower Descs. in State of Mo. (founding gov.), Order Ea. Star, Piecemakers Quilt Guild, Am. Quilters Soc., Roy Rogers Club. Home: 5055 S State Highway Rogersville MO 65742-8920 Office: The Snack Shop Junction Hwys 60 # 125 Rogersville MO 65742

HARMSEN, LEROY JOHN, business executive; b. Rock Rapids, Iowa, Sept. 10, 1957. BS in Constrn. Engring., Iowa State U., 1979. Project engr. Story Constrn. Co., Ames, Iowa, 1979-83; v.p. Stecker-Harmsen, Inc., Ames, 1983—. Republican. Home: RR 1 Kelley IA 50134-9801 Office: PO Box 884 Ames IA 50010-0884

HARNED, ROGER KENT, radiology educator; b. Madison, Wis., June 19, 1934; s. Lewis Boyer and Ermil Amelia (Caldwell) H.; m. Jacquelyn Sue Heal, Aug. 29, 1959; children: Roger Kent II, Jennifer Marie. BS, U. Wis., 1956; MD, U. Va., 1961. Am. Bd. Radiology. Intern Milw. County Gen. Hosp., 1961-62; resident in radiology Deaconess Hosp., Milw. Children's Hosps., 1964-67; instr. dept. radiology Sch. Medicine U. Va., Charlottesville, 1967-68; from asst. to assoc. prof. radiology Sch. Medicine U. Nebr., Omaha, 1969-79, prof. radiology, 1979-96, prof. emeritus, 1996—; cons. physician Omaha Vets. Hosp., 1969—; grad. faculty U. Nebr., Omaha, 1972—; peer rev. various med. jours. Contbr. articles on gastrointestinal radiology to profl. jours. Fellow Am. Coll. Radiology (emeritus, Armed Forces Inst. Pathology disting. scientist 1987-88); mem. Radiol. Soc. N.Am., Nebr. Radiol. Soc. (pres. 1982-83), Soc. Gastrointestinal Radiologists (pres. 1987-88). Presbyterian. Home: 12624 Martha St Omaha NE 68144-2626 Office: U Nebr Med Ctr Dept Radiology 600 S 42nd St Omaha NE 68105-1002

HARNEY, JOYCE ANN, nursing educator, administrator; b. Columbus, Ind., Apr. 2, 1952; d. John B. and Joan G. (Meredith) Redmon; m. Eugene Harney, Aug. 17, 1979; 1 child, Timothy Eugene. Degree in practical nursing, Bartholomew County Sch., 1971; BSN, Ind. U., Indpls., 1987, MS in Nursing, 1992. RN, Ind.; BLS, BLS instr., ACLS. Practical nurse Bartholomew County Hosp., Columbus, 1971-87; critical care nurse Richard Roudebush VA Hosp., Indpls., 1987-90; nursing instr. Ivy Tech. State Coll., Columbus, 1988—, dir. nursing dept. practical nursing, 1992—, dir. health and human svcs., 1995—. Item writer Nat. Coun. State Bds. of Nursing, 1993, 94, 95. Vol. ARC, Columbus, 1987—, Ind. AIDS Task Force, Ind. Dept. Health, 1991, 92, AIDS Support Group Bartholomew County Health Dept. Mem. ANA, Sigma Theta Tau. Home: 2589 N Talley Rd Columbus IN 47203-9169 Office: Ivy Tech State Coll 4475 Central Ave Columbus IN 47203-1868

HAROLD, KATHLEEN T., elementary education educator; b. Oak Park, Ill., Sept. 6, 1963; d. James Joseph Neville and Joan Esther (O'Keefe) Bartys; m. Mark Russell Harold, June 9, 1991; 1 child, Neil Austin Harold, May 10, 1996. BS in Edn., Bradley U., Peoria, Ill., 1985; MEd in Language and Literacy, Nat.-Louis U., Evanston, Ill., 1996. Cert. tchr., Ill. Tchr. 3d grade St. Thecla Elem., Chgo., 1985-87; tchr. 2d grade Avon Sch. Dist. # 47, Lake Villa, Ill., 1987-89; tchr. 1st grade Grayslake (Ill.) Sch. Dist. # 46, 1989-96. Mem. Ill. Whole Lang., Ill. Reading Coun., Whole Lang. Umbrella. Home: 400 Somerset Ln Vernon Hills IL 60061 Office: Woodview Elem Sch 340 Allegheny Ln Grayslake IL 60030

HARPER, GARY LEE, small business owner, educator; b. Oakland City, Ind., May 25, 1937; s. Hallie Hansel and Annabell (Dishon) H.; m. Margaret Earl McConnell, Dec. 29, 1964. BS, Oakland City U., 1964; MS, U. Evansville, 1974. Instr. Carnegie Coll., Cleve., 1959-60; chemist Whirlpool Corp., Evansville, Ind., 1966-68; tchr. North Gibson Schs., Princeton, Ind., 1970-75; owner Oaks Printing Co., Oakland City, 1976-86; instr. Oakland City (Ind.) U., 1989—. Publisher, editor Pike-Gibson Shopper, 1978-81. Pres. United Way of Gibson County, 1985; bd. dirs. United Way of Ind., Indpls., 1986-92, Oakland City U., Found., 1983; rep. Rep. State Conv., Indpls., 1984-86; with Gibson County Found., 1995—; elected city coun. mem. Oakland City, 1996—. Served with U.S. Army, 1964-66. Recipient Vol. award United Way, 1985; named Future Ind. Leader Pub. Service Ind., 1984. Mem. NEA, Ind. State Tchrs. Assn., Kiwanis (pres. Oakland City 1983-84, 93-94, lt. gov. Ind. 1986-87), Elks, Shriners, Eagles, Oakland City U. Alumni Assn. Republican. Methodist. Home and Office: 831 W College St Oakland City IN 47660-1023

HARPER, JOAN DIANE, obstetric nurse; b. St. Louis, Nov. 12, 1942; d. John Henry and Connie Buren (Eagen) Henrichs; m. Edward Alben Harper, Mar. 2, 1963; children: Kim Diane, Laura Ann. Diploma, St. Luke's Hosp. Sch. Nursing, St. Louis, 1963; BS in Health Arts, Coll. of St. Francis, Joliet, Ill., 1985. Childbirth educator San Jose (Calif.) Unified Sch. Dist., 1974-75; pvt. practice childbirth edn. St. Louis, 1976-83; nursing instr. St. Luke's Hosp. Sch. Nursing, St. Louis, 1964-66; office nurse, clinician for pvt. physician St. Louis, 1966-74; staff nruse St. John's Mercy Med. Ctr., St. Louis, 1975-84, mgr. maternal/child edn., 1984—. Recipient Cert. of Leadership YWCA, St. Louis, 1990. Fellow Am. Coll. Childbirth Educators; mem. Am. Soc. for Psychoprophylaxis in Obstetrics (cert.), NAACOG (cert. inpatient obstet. nursing), Gateway Aspo/Lamaze (bd. dirs.). Presbyterian. Home: 1800 Kehrswood Dr Chesterfield MO 63005-4462 Office: St John's Mercy Med Ctr 615 S New Ballas Rd Saint Louis MO 63141

HARPER, JOHN VINCENT, management consultant; b. Detroit, Apr. 22, 1947; s. Archibald Leonard and Georgia Florence (Hall) H.; m. Cornishaisly Chakawoneni Matowe, Sept. 8, 1979. BS in Engring., U. Mich., 1969, JD, 1973. Bar: Mich. Asst. pros. atty. Washtenaw County Prosecutor's Office, Ann Arbor, Mich., 1974; labor counsel Kellogg Co., Battle Creek, Mich., 1974-80, dir. pers. svcs., 1981-84; pres., CEO Managing Decisions, Inc., Battle Creek, 1984—; bd. dirs. Battle Creek Gas Co. Trustee Battle Creek Health System, 1990-94, Kellogg C.C., Battle Creek, 1982-90; active Mich. Job Tng. Coordinating Coun., Lansing, 1983-90, Local Govt. Rev. Bd., Lansing, 1989-90; commr. City of Battle Creek, 1979-82. 1st lt. U.S. Army, 1969-71, South Vietnam. Mem. Nat. Bar Assn., Mich. State Bar Assn., Assn. for Psychol. Type, Minority Bus. Owners of Battle Creek (pres. 1990—), Kiwanis Internat. Office: Managing Decisions Inc 18 Michigan Ave W Battle Creek MI 49017-3604

HARPER, JOSEPH J., social welfare specialist; b. Centreville, Ill., Nov. 25, 1960; s. Joseph and Betty V. (Argus) H. BBA with honors, McKendree Coll., 1984; MBA, Fontbonne Coll., 1992; MSW, Washington U., 1993. Lic. clin. social worker. Prodn. ops. staff Gen. Motors Corp., Wentzville, Mo., 1985-94; supr. child care svcs. Call for Help, Inc., Edgemont, Ill., 1993-94; child welfare specialist II Ill. Dept. Children and Family Svcs., Belleville, 1994—. Mem. NASW, Ill. Coun. on Tng. Roman Catholic. Office: Ill Dept Children & Family 12 N 64th St Ste 1 Belleville IL 62223

HARPER, MARGARET EARL, English language educator; b. Princeton, Ind., July 28, 1924; d. Earl F. and Gertrude (Williams) McConnell; m. Gary Lee Harper, Dec. 29, 1964. AB, Ind. U., 1946, M of Comml. Sci., 1947, PhD, 1963; BS, Oakland City Coll., 1956. Assoc. prof. English, dir. dramatics Oakland City (Ind.) Coll., 1947-60, prof. English, dir. dramatics, 1960-65, 69—; dean Sch Arts & Scis. Oakland City (Ind.) U., 1995; vis. prof. Univ. Md. Overseas Campus, Ramstein, Germany, 1965-66, Evansville (Ind.) Coll./Univ. Evansville, 1966-67. Author: William Warren II: The Boston Comedian, 1963, Centennial Moments, 1985, The English Story, 1993, The History of Drama at Oakland City College: 100 Years Plus, 1996; contbr. articles to profl. jours. Named Alumnus of Yr., Oakland City (Ind.) Coll., 1978, Tchr. of Yr., 1984, Disting. Prof. English, 1996. Mem. AAUP, DAR, Nat. Coun. Tchrs. of English, Nat. Trust for Hist. Preservation, Irish Wolfhound Club Am., Order Ea. Star, Ind. Univ. Alumni Assn., Oakland City Coll. Univ. Alumni Assn., Delta Kappa Gamma, Theta Sigma Phi, Kappa Kappa Kappa, Alpha Psi Omega, Alpha Phi Gamma (nat. exec. sec. 1957-64). Republican. Home: 831 W College St Oakland City IN 47660-1023 Office: Oakland City U 143 N Lucretia St Oakland City IN 47660-1099

HARPER, NELSON OWEN, pianist, educator; b. Dayton, Ohio, Apr. 20, 1953; s. Nelson Napoleon and Donna Mae (Allison) H. MusM, Ohio State U., 1978, D in Mus. Arts, 1992. Faculty pianist Jefferson Acad. Music, Columbus, Ohio, 1979-86; mem. adj. piano faculty Denison U., Granville, Ohio, 1986-92; orchestral pianist Pro Musica Chamber Orch., Columbus, 1989—; prof. piano Ohio State U., Columbus, 1991—; vis. asst. prof. music Antioch Coll., Yellow Springs, Ohio, 1984. Pianist various recs., including: Music of Ernest Bloch, 1978, Music of Wilfred Josephs, 1986, Music of John Ireland, 1994, Music of William Mathias, 1995, Music of Lennox Berkeley, 1995, Music of Frederick Delius, 1996, Vienna Modern Masters. Vol. AIDS Svc. Connection, Columbus, 1995. Mem. music Tchrs. Nat. Assn., Am. Fedn. Musicians. Office: Ohio State Univ Sch Music 1866 College Rd Columbus OH 43210

HARPER, OLIVER WILLIAM, III, investment company executive, consultant; b. Chgo., Nov. 25, 1953; s. Oliver William and Pauline W. (Simpson) H.; children: Oliver W., Julia D. BA, U. Ill.-Chgo., 1978, MBA U. Chgo., 1993. Agt., Occidental Life of Calif., 1979; registered rep. Lincoln Nat. Life Ins. Co., Ft. Wayne, Ind., 1979-80; agt., registered rep. Penn Mut. Life Ins. Co., Phila., 1980-85; dir. employee benefit div. Penn Fin. Group, Chgo., 1981-85; CEO, exec. v.p. Corp. Plan Cons., Inc., 1985-95; pres. Benefit Premium Claims Admins., Inc., 1993-95. Pres., trustee Employers Svc. Assn.; mng. adminstr.; Mem. Internat. Soc. Cert. Employee Benefit Specialists, Profl. Assn. Diving Instr., Chgo. Assn. Life Underwriters, Nat. Assn. Life Underwriters, Notaries Assn. Ill., U. Ill. Alumni Assn., Underwater Explorers Soc. Episcopalian. Club: Masons.

HARPER, PAIGE ANN JAMES, consultant; b. Little Rock, July 27, 1946; d. J.A. James and Mary E. (Baxley) Dorsett; 1 child, Jason. BA in Psychology, English, U. Ark., 1977; MS in Mgmt., Ind. Wesleyan U., 1993. Sr. cons. Dun & Bradstreet Corp., 1977—. Recipient Regional Citation award Dun & Bradstreet, 1983, 85, 86, 88; Presdl. Citation award 1984. Home: 7062 Canvasback Dr #2309 Fishers IN 46038-2451

HARR, MILTON EDWARD, civil engineering professor, engineering consultant; b. Chelsea, Mass., Oct. 19, 1925; s. Hyman and Ann (Kristal) H.; m. Florence Solomon, May 19, 1945; children: Faith, Karen, Robert. BS, Northeastern U., Boston, 1949; MS, Rutgers U., 1955; PhD, Purdue U., 1958; Docteur Honoris Causa, U. Brussels, 1987. Engr. Bureau of Reclamation, Provo, Utah, 1949, State Hwy. Dept., Beverly, Mass., 1949-53; asst. instr. Rutgers U., New Brunswick, N.J., 1953-55; instr. Purdue U., West Lafayette, Ind., 1955-58; asst. prof. Purdue U., West Lafayette, 1958-60, assoc. prof., 1960-72, prof., 1972—; cons. Bendix Corp., South Bend, Ind., Bougainville Copper Ltd., New Guinea, Brown and Root, Houston, Sandia Nat. Labs, Albuquerque, and many others; lectr. at many numerous colls. and univs. Author: Groundwater & Seepage, 1962, Foundations of Theoretical Soil Mechanics, 1966, Mechanics of Particulate Media, 1977, Reliability in Civil Engineering, 1987; editorial bd. Applied Ocean Research, 1978—, Internat. Jour. for Numerical and Analytical Methods in Geomechanics, 1978—; contbr. articles to profl. jours.; patentee in field. Bd. dirs. Ind. Joint Hwy. Research Project, 1969-72; adv. panel Am. Assn. State Hwy. Ofcls.; mem. Hwy. Research Bd. Com. on Stresses in Earth Masses, NASA Aeronautics Adv. Com., 1977-81, Task Force on Railway Maintenance Com., Transp. Research Bd., 1978-82, U.S. Com. on Large Dams; chmn. Track Structure Systems Design Com., 1976-79, Pavement Design Div. of HRB, 1964-70. Served with USN, 1943, ETO, with USMC, 1944-45, PTO. Recipient U.S. Sr. Scientist award Alexander von Humboldt Orgn., Bonn, Germany, 1983, Bechtel award Bechtel Engring. Co., Houston, 1983, G. Ernest Brooks award ASCE-Cleve. sect., Cleve., 1987; named Shaw Lectr., N.C. State U., 1984. Fellow Am. Soc. Civil Engrs.; mem. Ind. Acad. Sci., Third Marine Div. Assn., chi Epsilon, Sigma Xi, Elks. Home: 2201 Indian Trail Dr West Lafayette IN 47906-2106 Office: Purdue U 1284 Civil Engring Bldg West Lafayette IN 47907

HARRE, ALAN FREDERICK, university president; b. Nashville, Ill., June 12, 1940; s. Adolph Henry and Hilda (Vogt) H.; m. Diane Carole Mack, Aug. 9, 1964; children: Andrea Lyn, Jennifer Leigh, Eric Stephen. BA, Concordia Sr. Coll., 1962; MDiv, Concordia Sem., St. Louis, 1966; MA, Presbyn. Sch. Christian Edn., Richmond, Va., 1967; PhD, Wayne State U., 1976. Ordained to ministry Luth. Ch. Asst. pastor St. James Luth. Ch. of Grosse Pointe, Grosse Pointe Farms, Mich., 1967-73; asst. prof. theology Concordia Tchrs. Coll., Seward, Nebr., 1973-78, asst. to pres., 1981, assoc. prof. theology, 1978-84, dean student affairs, 1982-84, acting pres., 1984; pres. Concordia Coll., St. Paul, 1984-88, Valparaiso (Ind.) U., 1988—; bd. dirs. Minn. Pvt. Coll. Coun., St. Paul, 1984-88, Northwest Ind. Forum, Merrillville, 1989—. Author: Close the Back Door, 1984. Bd. dirs. Munster Med. Rsch. Found.; mem. Midway Civic and Commerce Assn., St. Paul, 1984-88. Mem. AAUP, Am. Assn. Higher Edn., Luth. Ednl. Conf. N.Am., Nat. Assn. Ind. Colls and Univs. (bd. dirs.), Ind. Colls. of Indiana (bd. dirs.), Valparaiso C. of C., Columbia Club (Indpls.), Union League Club (Chgo.), Rotary. Home: 3900 Hemlock St Valparaiso IN 46383-1814 Office: Valparaiso University Office of the President Valparaiso IN 46383-9978

HARRI, TAMMY ANN, data processing executive; b. Milw., June 14, 1962. AA, ITT Tech. Inst., 1982. Proofreader Moore Bus. Forms, Angola, Ind., 1983-88; photo lab. tech. Abramas Aerial Survey, Lansing, Mich., 1988-90; bus. mgr. Statimate Systems Inc., Lansing, 1990-94; ptnr. PC Plus Inc., Lansing, 1994—. Author: (tng. manuals) Working in Teams, 1994, Supervisor Workshop, 1995, TQM, 1994. Active Am. Heart Assn., 1994—. Mem. Nat. Assn. Small Bus., Lansing C. of C. Lutheran. Office: PC Plus LLC 4601 W Saginaw Hwy Ste I Lansing MI 48917-2741

HARRIGAN, RICHARD GEORGE, salesperson; b. Joliet, Ill., Feb. 12, 1952; s. William Francis and Margaret (Ruettiger) H.; m. Patricia Rae Bowman, Aug. 12, 1989; children: Michelle Freeman, Kimberly Freeman; children from a previous marriage: Jennifer Harrigan, Michelle Harrigan, Richard Harrigan, Sarah Harrigan, Samantha Harrigan. AS in Heating and

Refrigeration, Joliet Jr. Coll., 1980. Salesman G.W. Berkheimer, Gary, Ind., 1978-92; owner, operator East-West Ent., Hobart, Ind., 1992—. Mem. IBR, NHAW. Roman Catholic. Home: 780 Water St Hobart IN 46342-5142 Office: East-West Ent PO Box C Hobart IN 46342-0016

HARRIMAN, RICHARD LEE, performing arts administrator, educator; b. Independence, Mo., Sept. 10, 1932; s. Walter S. and M. Eloise (Faulkner) H.; AB, William Jewell Coll., 1953, LittD (hon.), 1983. MA, Stanford U., 1959. Instr., asst. prof. English U. Dubuque, Iowa, 1960-62; asst. prof. English, William Jewell Coll., Liberty, Mo., 1962, acting head English dept., 1965-69, dir. fine arts program, 1965—, asso. prof., 1966—. Treas. Kansas City Arts Council, 1980, sec., 1981; sec. Kansas City Am. Arts Festival, 1988-89. Served with, AUS, 1953-55. Woodrow Wilson fellow, 1957. Mem. MLA, AAUP, Shakespeare Assn. Am., Assn. Performing Arts Presenters (nat. exec. bd. 1975-78), Lambda Chi Alpha, Sigma Tau Delta, Alpha Psi Omega. Methodist. Home: 1043 E Hwy H Apt 3 Liberty MO 64068

HARRINGTON, KENNETH ALAN, communication company executive; b. Bennington, Vt., Nov. 24, 1948; s. Gerald Fred and Gertrude (Scott) H.; m. Lea Michelle Luchetti, Sept. 26, 1981; children: Mattison, Gabriel, Lucas, Parker. BSBA, U. Vt., 1970; MBA in Mktg. and Fin., U. Pa., 1978. Sales rep. N.Y. Tele. and AT&T, N.Y.C., 1970-76; assoc., cons. Booz Allen & Hamilton, N.Y.C., 1978-81; dir. strategy Plessey, N.Y.C., 1981-83; v.p. internat. Plessey Peripheral Systems, Irvine, Calif., 1983-86; pres. Spitz Inc., Chaddsford, Pa., 1986-89; v.p. market strategy UNISYS, Blue Bell, Pa., 1989-92; sr. v.p. mktg. and strategy JWP Info. Svcs., Canton, Mass., 1992-93; v.p., gen. mgr., officer Consol. Comm., Inc., St. Louis, 1993—. Bd. dirs., tech. com. MICDS, 1994—; mem. long range planning com. Fair St. Louis, 1995; bd. dirs. AIM High, 1995; advisor West End Cmty. Ctr., 1995; bd. govs. Vol. 5, 1994—; bd. dirs. Walden Sch., Swarthmore, Pa., 1991-92. Office: Consol Comm Inc 540 Maryville Centre Dr Saint Louis MO 63141-5828

HARRINGTON, LARRY THOMAS, industrial professional; b. Kansas City, July 22, 1952; s, Charles Fred and Jessie Claire (Zabel) H.; m. Karen Lynn Schmidt Harrington, Dec. 19, 1972; children: Shawn, Sheila. AA in Tool and Die Design, Southeast C.C., Milford, Nebr., 1972. Owner L&K Machine, Western, Nebr., 1972—; asst. instr. Tri County H.S., DeWitt, Nebr., 1988—. Mem. Assn. Blacksmith, Welders and Machinists. Lutheran. Office: L&K Machine 206 W Railroad Western NE 68464

HARRINGTON, LUCIA MARIE, elementary education educator; b. Marquette, Mich., May 19, 1947; d. Eugene and Saima (Bentti) Latvala; m. Warren Henry Harrington, June 21, 1969; children: Robert Joseph, Christen Marie. BS with high honors, No. Mich. U., 1969. Cert. tchr., Mich. Tchr. Marquette Area Pub. Schs., 1969-70, 71-73, 75-76, 82-95, Ysleta Ind. Schs., El Paso, Tex., 1970-71; substitute tchr. Schaumburg (Ill.) and Clear Lake (Iowa) Schs., 1973-75; tchr. 2d grade Whitman Elem. Sch., Marquette, 1996—; instr. Aerobic Dancing, Inc., Marquette, 1980-82; participant Gessell Sch. rEadines and Devel. Placement, 1985, Mich. Model Comprehensive Sch. Health Edn., 1987—, Essential Elements Effective Instrn., 1988, Lions/Quest Skills for Growing, 1990, Dyslexia Outreach Program Seminar, 1992; supr. student tchrs. 1988-96; mem. Marquette-Alger Reading Coun.; state presenter, trainer writing workshops. Named Elem. Tchr. of Yr., Kiwanis, 1991, Marquette Area Pub. Schs. Outstanding Educator, 1994. Mem. NEA, Mich. Edn. Assn. (cert. of merit), Mich. Coun. Tchrs. of Math., Upper Peninsula Reading Assn. (hospitality chair 1990-96), Mich. Reading Assn., Coop. Team Learning Initiative Group, Internat. Platform Assn., Mich. English Lang. Arts Framework Project (presenter), Marquette City Edn. Assn., Phi Delta Kappa. Lutheran. Home: 1705 West Ave Marquette MI 49855-1555 Office: Marquette Area Pub Schs Whitman Elem Sch 1400 Norway Ave Marquette MI 49855-2651

HARRINGTON, MICHAEL FRANCIS, paper and packaging company executive; b. Butte, Mont., Aug. 6, 1940; s. Bernard Michael and Ruth Ann (Mullane) H.; m. Beverly Elaine Oswood, Dec. 30, 1967; children: Michael, Moria, Kevin. BS, Gonzaga U., Spokane, 1964, MBA, 1971; postgrad., Stanford U., 1985. Indsl. rels. rep. Kaiser Aluminum, Spokane, 1965-69; region indsl. rels. rep. Gen. Inst. Corp., Post Falls, Idaho, 1969-72; region employee rels.mgr. Boise Cascade Corp., Medford, Oreg., 1972-75; div. employee rels. mgr. Boise Cascade Corp., Boise, Idaho, 1975-81, corp. dir. labor rels., 1981-91; v.p. human resources Jefferson Smurfit Corp., St. Louis, 1991—; mem. adv. bd. Gonzaga U. Sch. Bus., 1990—. Bd. dirs. Laumeier Sculpture Garden, St. Louis, 1995—, St. Joseph Sch. for Deaf, St. Louis, 1994—. Mem. Labor Policy Assn., Am. Forest and Paper Assn. (bd. dirs., chmn. employee rels. com. 1988—). Republican. Roman Catholic. Office: Jefferson Smurfit Corp 8182 Maryland Ave Saint Louis MO 63105

HARRINGTON, NANCY, state legislator. Mem. Kans. State Senate Dist. 26, 1995—.

HARRINGTON, RICHARD J., newspaper publishing executive; b. 1938. Pres., CEO Thomson Newspapers, Inc., Des Plaines, Ill. Office: Thomson Newspapers Inc 3150 Des Plaines Ave # 2 Des Plaines IL 60018-4205

HARRINGTON, WILLIAM RICHARD, investment broker; b. Cairo, Ill., Mar. 15, 1955; s. William Harrington and Betty (Trickey) Burns; m. Julie Ann Flamm, July 22, 1978; children: Jessica, Stephanie. BS, Murray (Ky.) State U., 1977. Broadcast mgmt. various cos., 1977-91; investment broker A.G. Edwards & Sons Inc., Decatur, Ill., 1991—. Referee H.S. Basketball, 1992—. Mem. Rotary Club of Met. Decatur (pres.-elect 1995-96, sgt.-at-arms 1994-95). Office: AG Edwards & Sons Inc 2884 N Monroe St Decatur IL 62526

HARRIS, ALBERTA O. ARMSTRONG, critical care nurse, administrator; b. St. Joseph, La., Nov. 20, 1930; d. Willie C. and Louida (Morris) Armstrong; m. David Harris Jr., May 7, 1950; children: Willie Wynn, David Jr., Marvin L., Beverly J., Danna, Jack, Gwendolyn. ADN, Lorain County Community Coll., Elyria, Ohio, 1972; BSN, BGSU, Huron, Ohio, 1986. Cert. critical care nurse. Staff nurse, med. ICU VA Med. Ctr., Cleve.; clin. nursing supr. Lorain (Ohio) Community Hosp.; charge nurse neurosurgery VA Med. Ctr., Cleve.; preceptor emergency room CVAMC, 1991—, edn. coord. Home: 4236 Leavitt Rd Lorain OH 44053-2343

HARRIS, BERNARD LESLIE, mechanical engineer; b. London, May 2, 1932; s. Mark Lenard and Ester (Fife) H.; m. Hermione Dora Round, Apr. 2, 1956; children: Jonathon Paul, Christopher Neil. BSME, London U., 1953. Registered profl. engr., Mo., Tex., Europe. Tech. apprentice and jr. engr. Handley Page Ltd., London, 1948-54; engr. Boeing Co., Seattle, 1958-61; sr. engr. Chrysler Co., New Orleans, 1961-68, Gen. Dynamics, Ft. Worth, 1968-74; chief engr. Silver Dollar City, Branson, Mo., 1974-79; cons. engr. in pvt. practice Branson, 1979—. Contbr. articles to profl. jours.; patenteein field. Lt. Royal Army, 1954-57. Mem. Nat. Soc. Profl. Engrs., Instn. of Prodn. Engrs. Episcopalian. Home: 270 Lone Pine Rd Branson MO 65616 Office: Allison Transmission MS K4 PO Box 894 Indianapolis IN 46206

HARRIS, BILL, state legislator; m. Mary C. Harris; children: Billy M. Jr., Lonny E., Scott, Sherry. Student, U. Ariz. Auto dealer, bus. owner Ashland, Ohio; mem. Ohio State Ho. Reps., Columbus; vice chmn. Buick Nat. Dealers' Coun. Trustee Samaritan Hosp., Ashland. Mem. Ohio Automobile Dealers Assn. (trustee), Ashland Area C. of C.

HARRIS, BOB L(EE), educational administrator; b. Chesapeake, Ohio, Mar. 7, 1938; s. Hiram Hurston and Emma Louise (Bevans) H.; m. Beverly Sue Fuller, June 17, 1959; children: Robert Todd, Amy Beth Harris Bane. Cert. cadet, Rio Grande Coll., 1957, BS in Elem. Edn., 1965; M of Ednl. Adminstrn., Marshall U., 1975, cert. postmasters supt., 1981. Tchr. Chesapeake East Elem. Sch., 1957-58, 60-71, occupational work adjustment coord., 1971-74; tchr. Chesapeake West Elem. Sch., 1958-60, asst. prin., 1974-75, prin., 1975—. Mem., asst. PTA, Chesapeake, 1975—. Mem. Ohio Assn. Elem. Sch. Adminstrs. (regional coord. intervention assistance team 1983, Hall of Fame Sch. 1992), Ohio Assn. Track and C.C. Coaches (dist. rep. 1964-75, 81-88, ofcl., interpreter local rules 1964-90, Hall of Fame inductee 1982), Athletic Congress (ofcl. 1980—). Republican. Mem. Ch. of Christ. Home: 98 Township Rd 1364 Chesapeake OH 45619-9513 Office: Chesapeake Elem Sch 11359 County Rd 1 Chesapeake OH 45619-9786

HARRIS, BRIAN M., broker; b. Smyrna, Tenn., Nov. 21, 1967. BSBA, U. Ark., 1991. Broker Edward D. Jones & Co., La Crosse, Wis., 1991—, A. G. Edwards & Sons Inc., La Crosse, 1994—. Mem. La Crosse C. of C., Kiwanis, Optimist Club Internat. (bd. dirs. 1993—). Republican. Roman Catholic.

HARRIS, BRUCE WAYNE, writer, gold mining consultant; b. San Antonio, Nov. 19, 1953; s. John Earnest and Elsie Kathrine (Martis) H.; m. Sharon Lynn Huddleston, Apr. 4, 1978 (div. Dec. 1983). Studied guitar with Russel Rakestraw, Dallas, 1976-82. Owner Heavy Metal Mining Co., Springfield, Mo., 1988—, Vacation Branson Mag., Springfield, Mo., 1994—; topographer, graphic artist, cartographer Vacation Branson, Springfield, Mo. Author: Gold Miner's Handbook, 1994, Modern Gold Dredging, 1995. With U.S. Army, 1971-74. Mem. Apple Squires of the Ozarks (reference libr. chmn. 1994—), Branson (Mo.) County C. of C. Office: Heavy Metal Mining Co PO Box 8256 Springfield MO 65801-8256

HARRIS, CHAUNCY DENNISON, geographer, educator; b. Logan, Utah, Jan. 31, 1914; s. Franklin Stewart and Estella (Spilsbury) H.; m. Edith Young, Sept. 5, 1940; 1 child, Margaret (Mrs. Philip A. Straus, Jr.). AB, Brigham Young U., 1933; BA, Oxford U., 1936, MA, 1943, DLitt, 1973; postgrad., London Sch. Econs., 1936-37; PhD, U. Chgo., 1940; DEcon (honoris causa), Catholic U., Chile, 1956; LLD (honoris causa), Ind. U., 1979; DSc (honoris causa), Bonn U., 1991, U. Wis., Milw., 1991. Instr. in geography Ind. U., 1939-41; asst. prof. geography U. Nebr., 1941-43; asst. prof. geography U. Chgo., 1943-46, assoc. prof., 1946-47, prof., 1947-84, prof. emeritus, 1984—, dean social scis., 1955-60, chmn. non western area programs and internat. studies, 1960-66, dir. ctr. for internat. studies, 1966-84, chmn. dept. geography, 1967-69, Samuel N. Harper Disting. Svc. prof., 1969-84, spl. asst. to pres., 1973-75, v.p. acad. resources, 1975-78; del. Internat. Geog. Congress, Lisbon, 1949, Washington, 1952, Rio de Janeiro, 1956, Stockholm, 1960, London, 1964, New Delhi, 1968, Montreal, 1972, Moscow, 1976, Tokyo, 1980, Paris, 1984, Sydney, Australia, 1988, Washington, 1992; v.p. Internat. Geog. Union, 1956-64, sec.-treas., 1968-76; mem. adv. com. for internat. orgns. and programs Nat. Acad. Scis., 1969-73, mem. bd. internat. orgns. and programs, 1973-76; U.S. del. 17th Gen. Conf. UNESCO, Paris, 1972; exec. com. div. behavioral scis. NRC, 1967-70; mem. coun. of scholars Libr.of Congress, 1980-83, Conseil de la Bibliographie Géographique Internationale, 1986—. Author: Cities of the Soviet Union, 1970; editor: Economic Geography of the U.S.S.R, 1949, International List of Geographical Serials, 1960, 71, 80, Annotated World List of Selected Current Geographical Serials, 1960, 64, 71, 80, Soviet Geography: Accomplishments and Tasks, 1962, Guide to Geographical Bibliographies and Reference Works in Russian or on the Soviet Union, 1975, Bibliography of Geography, Part I, Introduction to General Aids, 1976, Part 2, Regional, vol. 1, U.S., 1984, A Geographical Bibliography for American Libraries, 1985, Directory of Soviet Geographers 1946-87, 1988; contbr. Sources of Information in the Social Sciences, 1973, 86, Encyclopedia Britannica, 1989; contbg. editor: The Geog. Rev., 1960-73, Soviet Geography, 1987-91, Post-Soviet Geography, 1992—; contbr. articles to profl. jours. Life mem. vis. com. U. Chgo. Libr. Recipient Alexander Csoma de Körösi Meml. medal Hungarian Geog. Soc., 1971, Lauréat d'Honneur Internat. Geog. Union, 1976; Alexander von Humboldt Gold Medal Gesellschaft für Erdkunde zu Berlin, 1978; spl. award Utah Geog. Soc., 1985; Rhodes scholar, 1934-37. Fellow Japan Soc. Promotion of Sci.; mem. Assn. Am. Geographers (sec. 1946-48, v.p. 1956, pres. 1957, Honors award 1976), Am. Geog. Soc. (coun. 1962-74, v.p. 1969-74; Cullum Geog. medal 1985), Am. Assn. Advancement Slavic Studies (pres. 1962, award for disting. contbns. 1978), Am. Acad. Arts and Scis., Social Sci. Rsch. Coun. (bd. dir. 1959-70, vice-chmn. 1963-65, exec. com. 1967-70), Internat. Coun. Sci. Unions (exec. com. 1969-76), Internat. Rsch. and Exchs. Bd. (exec. com. 1968-71), Nat. Coun. Soviet and East European Rsch. (bd. dir. 1977-83), Nat. Coun. for Geog. Edn. (Master Tchr. award 1986); hon. mem. Royal Geog. Soc. (Victoria medal 1987), Geog. Socs. Berlin, Frankfurt, Rome, Florence, Paris, Warsaw, Belgrade, Japan, Chgo. (Disting. Svc. award 1965, bd. dir. 1954-69, 82-90), Polish Acad. Scis. (fgn. mem.). Home: 5649 S Blackstone Ave Chicago IL 60637-1871 Office: U Chgo Com on Geog Studies 5828 S University Ave Chicago IL 60637-1583

HARRIS, DAVID PHILIP, crisis management executive; b. Boston, June 23, 1937; s. David Henry and Edith Endicott (Young) H.; m. Uta Maria Kallina, Sept. 9, 1967; children: Kristian Alexander, Thomas Cameron. BS in Sci., U. Rochester (N.Y.), 1959; MBA, U. Pa., 1963. Auditor Touche, Ross et al, Boston, 1960-61; asst. contr. Kendall Co., Chgo., Charlotte, N.C., 1963-65; mgr. internal cons. Dart Industries, Stamford, Conn., 1965-67; asst. contr. Achushnet Co., New Bedford, Mass., 1967-70; asst. treas. Bell & Howell Co., Chgo., 1970-73; v.p., treas. CFS Continental, Inc., Chgo., 1973-78; pres., chief exec. officer Harris Devel. Co., Lake Forest, Ill., 1975—; chmn., CEO Amtec Devel. Co., Highland Park, Ill., 1978-83; affiliate Morris Andersen & Assocs., Glenview, Ill., 1984-93; bd. dirs. Juvenile Shoe Corp., Aurora, Mo., Intellimedia Corp., Benton Harbor, Mich.; exec. v.p., dir. STS Cons. Ltd., Deerfield, Ill., 1995—. Treas., dir. Lake Forest Symphony Assn., 1983-88, Touchstone Theatre, Chgo., 1987-90; mem. engring. com. Beach Restoration Project, Lake Forest, 1987-88, long term plan com., Lake Forest, 1991—; bd. dirs. Zoning Bd. Appeals, Lake Forest, 1988-93; fin. planning advisor Lake Forest Sch. Dist. 67, 1992—; dir. rsch. Lake Forest Civic Fedn., 1992—. Mem. Fin. Mgrs. Assn. Chgo. (sec. 1972-91, pres. 1988-89), Tower Club. Republican. Presbyterian.

HARRIS, DONALD WAYNE, research scientist; b. Ft. Scott, Kans., Sept. 23, 1942; s. Carl Raymond Harris and Kathryn Francis (Peare) Hayes; children: Daniel Duane (dec. 1994), Sheila, Lynette, Crystal Ann. BS, U. Mo., 1966, PhD, 1974. From scientist to mgr. carbohydrate polymer rsch. Clinton (Iowa) Corn Processing Co., 1974-84; sr. rsch. scientist AE Staley Mfg. Co., Decatur, Ill., 1984-92; rsch. fellow AE Staley Mfg. Co., Decatur, 1992—. Patentee in field; contbr. articles to profl. jours. With U.S. Army, 1968-70. Mem. Am. Chem. Soc., Am. Assn. Cereal Chemists, Phi Lambda Upsilon. Office: A E Staley Mfg Co 2200 E Eldorado St Decatur IL 62521-1578

HARRIS, EARL L., state legislator; m. Donna J. Harris. Student, Purdue U., Ill. Inst. Tech. With Ky Package Store; rep. Dist. 12 Ind. Ho. of Reps., 1981-91, rep. Dist. 2, 1991—, mem. commerce com., govt. affairs com., aged and aging com., mem. ins. com., corp. and small bus. com.; chmn. ways and means com. Mem. NAACP; past pres. Chgo. Black Coalition, Chgo. Homeowners Assn., Sunnyside Homeowners Assn.; chmn. African-Am. Leadership Forum; mem. N.W. Urban League. Home: 4114 Butternut St East Chicago IN 46312-2914*

HARRIS, EUGENE WHITNEY, financial company executive; b. St. Louis, Sept. 3, 1964; s. Whitney Robson and Jane (Freund) H.; m. Deborah Bernheimer, May 28, 1989. BS in Indsl. Engring., Stanford U., 1986; MBA, MIT, 1990. Assoc. cons. Bain & Co., Boston, 1986-88; bus. mgr. Monsanto Co., St. Louis, 1990-94; v.p. Eidelman Finger & Co., St. Louis, 1994—. Office: Ste 511 225 S Meramec Saint Louis MO 63105

HARRIS, FRANCES ALVORD (MRS. HUGH W. HARRIS), retired radio and television broadcaster, consultant; b. Detroit, Apr. 19, 1909; d. William Roy and Edith (Vosburgh) Alvord; m. Hugh William Harris, Sept. 24, 1932; children: Patricia Anne (Mrs. Floyd A. Metz), Hugh William, Robert Alvord. AB, Grinnell Coll., 1929; LHD (hon.), Ferris State Coll., 1980. With advt. dept. Himelhoch Bros. & Co., Detroit, 1929-31; broadcaster as Julia Hayes Robert P. Gust Co., 1931-34; tng. and pers. dept. Ernst Kern Co., 1935-36; broadcaster as Nancy Dixon Young & Rubicam, Inc., 1939-42; women's editor Sta. WWJ, Detroit, 1943-64, Sta. WWJ-TV, 1947-64; spl. features coord. Sta. WWJ-TV-AM-FM, 1964-74; treas. I.C. Harris & Co., Detroit, 1963-82, pres., chief exec. officer, 1982-84, chmn. bd., 1984-85; creator 1st ct. show Traffic Ct., 1949. Author, editor: Focus: Michigan Women, 1977. Mem. exec. bd. Wayne County chpt. Mich. Soc. for Mental Health, 1953-63; chmn. Mental Health Week, 1958-59; mem. Wayne County Commn. on Aging, 1975-85, chmn., 1976-77; publicity com. YWCA, 1945, 2d v.p., 1963; mem. publicity com. Tri-County League for Nursing, 1956-61; publicity chmn. Met. Detroit YWCA Bd. Dirs., 1961-66, exec. com., 1962-67; campaign dist. chmn. United Found., 1959, unit chmn., 1960-61, chmn. speakers bur., 1974; exec. bd. United Fund. Women's Orgn., 1962-64; governing bd. United Community Svcs. Women's Com., 1961-66; bd. dirs. United Community Svcs., 1964-67; bd. dirs. Homemaker Svc. Met. Detroit, pres., 1969-70, co-founder, 1965; bd. dirs. Vis. Nurse Assn., pres., 1974-76; bd. dirs. Camp Fire Girls of Detroit, mem. nat. coun., 1967-72, mem. nat. bd., exec. com., 1970-72, pres., 1978-80; bd. dirs. Well Being Svc. Aging, 1969-74, Sr. Ctr., 1971-76, Friends Detroit Pub. Libr., 1972—, Friends Children's Museum, 1972-74, 83—; trustee Detroit Com. Alcoholism, 1961-64; mem. Mayor's Com. for Freedom Festival, 1959, chmn. women's activities, 1965; mem. Mayor's Com. for UN Week, 1959; mem. Gov's. Commn. Status of Women, 1962-69, Mich. State Women's Commn., 1969-77; mem. nat. coun. Homemaker Svc., 1970-73; mem. adv. com. to trustees Grinnell Coll.; mem. bd. control Ferris State Coll., 1968-78; mem. def. adv. com. Women in the Svcs., 1970-73, chmn., 1973; program chmn. Met. Detroit YMCA, 1973-75; sec.-treas. Mich. Assn. Governing Bds. State Colls. and Univs., 1975, v.p., 1976-77, pres., 1977-78; bd. dirs. United Community Svcs., Detroit, 1973-75, mem. assembly, 1984-90; mem. communications com. local congregation and Episc. Diocese of Mich., 1965-66. Recipient Grinnell Coll. Alumni award, 1959, Mental Health Soc. Mich. award, 1958, Theta Sigma Phi Headliner award for Mich., 1951, nat., 1952, Heart of Gold award, 1976, Women's Advt. Club of Detroit Civic award, 1957, Gov. award NATAS, 1987, Mich. award NATAS, 1994; named Advt. Woman of Year, Detroit, 1958, 73, Soroptimist Woman of Yr., 1965, Fran Harris Day in her honor, Detroit, 1960, Vol. State of Mich., 1975; inducted into the Mich. Jouralism Hall Fame, 1986, Mich. Women's Hall of Fame, 1988; commendation service award Mich. Assn. Bus. Owners; 1st woman comml. newscaster, Detroit, 1943. Mem. Am. Women in Radio and TV (pres. Detroit chpt. 1957-58, gen. chmn. nat. conv. 1966, Outstanding Community Svc. award 1972, Life Achievement award 1991), Women's Advt. Club of Detroit (pres. 1959-60, mem. bd. 1974-77), UN Assn. U.S.A. (dir. Detroit chpt. 1962-65, Mich. div. bd. 1963-65), Advt. Fedn. (nat. v.p. women's activities 1964-67), Nat. Fedn. Press Women (hon.), 1973, Women in Communications (pres. Detroit 1950-51; del. to Asian-Am. Women in Broadcasting Conf. 1966, nat. 1st v.p. 1968-71, nat. pres. 1971-73, chmn. Communications Conf. Ams., 1968, del. III World Congress Women Journalists 1973), Women's Econ. Club (charter mem., dir. 1975-82, membership chmn. 1975, program chmn. 1976, pub. rels. co-chmn. 1977, treas. 1978, sec. 1979, 1st v.p. 1980, pres. 1981), Pi Epsilon Delta. Home: 34601 Elmwood St Apt 241 Westland MI 48185-3079

HARRIS, GREGORY, computer scientist, researcher; b. Cambridge, Mass., Nov. 21, 1954; s. James Lee and Claudine (Maroni) H.; m. Marcia Anne Murphy, Aug. 28, 1992 (div. Sep. 1993). BS in Computer Sci., Yale U., 1976; MS in Computer Sci., Carnegie-Mellon U., 1983. Rsch. asst. in artificial intelligence Bolt, Beranek & Newman, Cambridge, Mass., 1973-77, Xerox PARC, Palo Alto, Calif., 1979-80; rsch. programmer computer sci. dept. Carnegie-Mellon U., Pitts., 1981-82; rsch. asst. in imaging, psychiatry rsch. dept. U. Iowa Hosps. and Clinics, Iowa City, 1991—. Programmer and designer in field; contbr. articles to profl. jours. Active Alliance for the Mentally Ill, Johnson county, Iowa, 1986—. Recipient Nelson Urban award Mental Health Assn., 1993. Mem. Computer Soc. of IEEE, Am. Assn. for Artificial Intelligence, Assn. for Computer Machinery. Home: 315 Ferson Ave Iowa City IA 52246-3511

HARRIS, JAMES HOWARD, marketing executive; b. Chgo., Aug. 27, 1961; s. Thomas L. and JoAnn Harris; m. Lynn Chudacoff, Sept. 17, 1989. BA with honors, U. Mich., 1983; M in Mgmt., Northwestern U., 1985. Account exec. DDB Needham Worldwide, Chgo., 1985-88; pres. James Harris Entertainment Mktg., Chgo., 1988-89; mgr. bus. devel. and new products Miller Brewing Co., Milw., 1989-92; ptnr. Thomas L. Harris & Co., Highland Park, Ill., 1992—. Office: Thomas L Harris and Co Ste 280 600 Central Ave Highland Park IL 60035-3257

HARRIS, JAMES MELVIN, real estate appraiser; b. Ogallala, Nebr., May 23, 1929; s. Frank Henry and Vera Ford (Jeffery) H.; m. Patricia Lynne Gass, June 8, 1985; children: Philip James, Marcia Ellen Harris Jensen. 1st lt. U.S. Army, 1948-70; chief appraiser Mut. Bldg. & Loan, N. Platte, Nebr., 1970-83, Comml. Fed. Savs. & Loan, N. Platte, 1983-84; owner Jim Harris Appraiser Svc., N. Platte, 1984—. Republican. Home: 1201 S Carr North Platte NE 69101 Office: Jim Harris Appraisal Svcs 120 S Dewey PO Box 1422 North Platte NE 69103

HARRIS, JIM R., business executive; b. Dover, Ohio, June 29, 1951. BS, Babson Coll., 1973; AS, Kent State U., 1983. Prodn. mgr. Shelter-Rite Corp., Millersburg, Ohio, 1978-80; prodn./warehouse mgr. Aamco Transmissions, New Philadelphia, Ohio, 1980-87; pres. Coshocton (Ohio) Industries, Inc., 1987—. Bd. dirs. local country club; vol. Easter Seals, United Way. Recipient Harry Humphries scholarship, Babson Coll. Methodist. Office: Coshocton Industries Inc 605 N 15th St Coshocton OH 43812-1473

HARRIS, JOAN WHITE, foundation officer, arts administrator; b. New Haven, Mar. 9, 1931; d. Louis and Martha (Rahm) White; m. Gerald Baumann Frank, Feb. 12, 1953 (div. 1974); children: Daniel Bruce, Jonathan White, Louise Blanche; m. Irving Brooks Harris, June 19, 1974. BA, Smith Coll., 1952. Editorial asst. Oxford U. Press, N.Y.C., 1952-53, Ency. Brit., Chgo., 1953-54; TV producer, Chgo., 1976, 78, 80; pres. Chgo. Opera Theater, 1977-84, chair, 1984-87, bd. dirs., 1975-80; panelist, cons. Nat. Endowment for the Arts, 1980—; chair nat. bd. Aspen Music Festival, Colo., 1984-85, trustee, 1990—; mem. adv. bd. U.S.-China Arts Exchange, 1985-93. Pres. Harris Found., Chgo., 1976—; bd. dirs./trustee Mus. Contemporary Art, Chgo., 1976—, vice chmn., 1989—, Hampshire Coll., Amherst, Mass., 1977-84, Chgo. Symphony Orch., 1978—, Nat. Inst. Music Theater, Washington, 1982-87, Ind. Sector, Washington, 1983-89; pres. Ill. Art Alliance, 1990—; pres. Chgo. Music and Dance Theater, 1992—; trustee Columbia Coll., 1994—; bd. dirs. Ill. Ctr. for the Book, 1990-94, Northwestern Program for Performing Artists, 1986—, Am. coun. for the Arts, 1990-94, Nat. Cultural Alliance, 1991—, Sculpture Chgo., 1991—, Chgo. Inst. Architecture & Urbanism, 1992-94; commr. cultural affairs City of Chgo., 1987-89; pres. Ill. Arts Alliance, 1990—, Chgo. Music & Dance Theater, 1992. Clubs: Arts, Saddle and Cycle, Lake Shore, Standard (Chgo.), Lotos (N.Y.C.). Home and Office: Harris Found Ste 400 2 N LaSalle St Chicago IL 60602-3703

HARRIS, JOHN CHESTER, educational charity administrator, book editor, screen writer, movie script writer; b. Idaho City, Idaho, Oct. 29, 1953; s. John Chester Harris and Helena Monica (Crawley) Duerr. Founder The Scroll People Inc., Chgo., 1992—; also bd. dirs. Lance cpl. USMC, 1970-74. Democrat. Office: The Scroll People Inc PO Box 268093 Chicago IL 60626-8093

HARRIS, JOSEPH MCALLISTER, chemist; b. Pontiac, Ill., July 27, 1929; s. Fred Gilbert and Catherine Marguerite (McAllister) H.; m. Margot Jeanette L'Hommedieu, Feb. 17, 1952; children: Timothy, Kaye, Paula, Bruce, Anne, Martha, Rebecca. BA, Blackburn Coll., Carlinville, Ill., 1952; postgrad., So. Ill. U., 1953-54, U. Ill., 1956-61. Technician Olin Ind., Inc., Energy, Ill., 1953-54; quality control staff Union Starch and Refining Co., Granite City, Ill., 1954; rsch. asst. Ill. State Geol. Survey, Urbana, 1954-61; chemist II Water Pollution Control Bd., Annapolis, Md., 1961-63; phys. chemist Ball Bros. Rsch., Inc., Muncie, Ind., 1963-66; engr. Radio Corp. Am., Marion, Ind., 1966-70; chemist OA Labs., Inc., Indpls., 1973-86; chemist OA Labs. & Rsch., Inc., Indpls., 1986-93, cons., 1993—. Bd. dirs. Tri-County Hearing Assn. for Children, Muncie, 1967-70. Mem. Am. Chem. Soc., AAAS, Soc. Applied Spectroscopy. Republican. Presbyterian. Home: 800 E Washington St Muncie IN 47305-2533

HARRIS, JOYCE D., stockbroker; b. Ravenna, Ohio, June 16, 1946. Student, Kent State U., 1965-66. Sales asst. Merrill Lynch Pierce Fenner & Smith, Akron, Ohio, 1966-70, 80-81, 82-86; adminstrv. asst. Am. Sch. Health Asst., Kent, Ohio, 1978-80; sec. to dir. microbiology and immunology Northeastern Ohio Univs. Coll. Medicine, Rootstown, 1981-82; stockbroker Butler Wick & Co., Kent, 1986—. Mem. Kent C. of C. (bd. dirs. 1986-92), Kent Club, Kiwanis (bd. dirs. Kent 1988—).

HARRIS, K. DAVID, justice; b. Jefferson, Iowa, July 29, 1927; s. Orville William and Jessie Heloise (Smart) H.; m. Madonna Theresa Coyne, Sept. 4, 1948; children: Jane, Julia, Frederick. BA, U. Iowa, 1949, JD, 1951. Bar: Iowa 1951, U.S. Dist. Ct (so. dist.) Iowa, 1958. Sole practice Harris & Harris, Jefferson, 1951-62; dist. judge 16th Judicial Dist., Iowa, 1962-72; justice Iowa Supreme Ct., Des Moines, 1972—. Served with U.S. Amry, 1944-46, PTO. Mem. VFW, Am. Legion, Rotary. Roman Catholic. Office: Iowa Supreme Ct State Capitol Bldg Des Moines IA 50319

HARRIS, MARILYN LOUISE, educator; b. Hutchinson, Kans., July 29, 1950; d. Willard E. Wallace and Ruby V. (Coffey) O'Mara; m. Robert B. Harris, Mar. 6, 1982; children: Matt, Ted, Emily. BS, U. Nebr., 1971, MEd, 1975, PhD, 1984. Cert. elem. tchr., counselor, adminstr., Nebr. Elem. tchr. Lincoln (Nebr.) Pub. Schs., 1973-74, elem. counselor, 1974-77, elem. coord., 1977-82, staff devel. instr., 1982-83; grad. asst. U. Nebr., Lincoln, 1982-83, supr. student tchrs., 1985-87; dir. corp. tng. and devel. Harris Labs., Lincoln, 1987—; bd. dirs. Nebr. Job Tng. Coun., Lincoln, 1988-91. Bd. dirs. ARC, Lincoln, 1989-91, Jr. League Lincoln, 1989-92, Lincoln Cmty. Playhouse, 1988-91, Lincoln Children's Mus., 1987-92, 1st Plymouth Ch. Bd. Music/Fine Arts, Lincoln, 1990-92; bd. dirs. St. Elizabeth Cmty. Health Ctr., Lincoln, 1989—, bd. sec., 1991-92, bd. vice chairperson, 1992-95, bd. pres., 1995—; pres. St. Elizabeth Aux., Lincoln, 1989-91; mem. devel. com. Lincoln Pub. Schs. Found., 1989—, found. chairperson, 1995—; mem. adv. com. Inst. Lifelong Learning, Nebr. Wesleyan U.; mem. adult basic studies adv. com. S.E. C.C.; mem. planning com. Sisters of Charity, Cin., 1993—; bd. dirs. Nebr. Pub. TV, 1993, Nebr. Arts Coun., 1993—. Mem. ASTD (sec. 1988-89, pres. 1990-91), Phi Delta Kappa. Republican. Home: 2829 S 31st St Lincoln NE 68502-5201 Office: Harris Labs PO Box 80837 Lincoln NE 68501-0837

HARRIS, R(ICHARD) STEVEN, data processing executive, consultant, educator; b. Kansas City, Kans., Aug. 3, 1949; s. George Joseph and Bonnie Jean (Knecht) H.; m. Phyllis Lea Stopp, Aug. 29, 1970; children: April Lea, Steven Erhardt. BA magna cum laude, Knox Coll.; MS in Edn., Western Ill. U.; postgrad., Columbia Pacific U. Cert. secondary tchr., sch. guidance counselor, Ill.; cert. vocat. and tech. adult edn. tchr., Wis. Sci. tchr., counselor Brimfield (Ill.) High Sch., 1972-74, grad. of five factories, Galesburg, Ill., 1971-72, 74-80; plant mgr. Jacobson Barrel Corp., Milw., 1980-82; ind. systems cons. Milw. area, 1982-84; programmer Effective Mgmt. Systems, Milw., 1984-85; systems and programming tchr. Milw. Bus. Tng. Inst., 1985-86; programmer, customer support analyst, software package quality assurance specialist Systems For Profit, Inc., Milw., 1986-89; mgr. MIS Gendex Corp., Milw., 1989; ind. cons./contract programmer Milw., 1989-90, 91-92; staff analyst, cons. CAP Gemini Am., Milw., 1990-91; bus. math. systems and programming tchr. Milw. Area Tech. Col., 1987-91; sr. systems and tech. cons. Chaney Systems, Inc., New Berlin, Wis., 1992-95; sr. cons., founder JōB Sys. LLC, Oak Creek, Wis.; cons. New Resources Corp., 1995—. Pastor Covenant Apostolic Ch. Greater Milw. area, 1991—. Fellow Am. Prodn. and Inventory Control Soc. (fellow cert. inst. Milw. 1985-87); mem. Creation Sci. Soc. Milw (program chmn. 1985-86), Creation Rsch. Soc. (life), Creation Social Sci. and Humanities Soc. (voting), Inst. Cert. Computer Profls. (cert. data processor, cert. bus., sci. and operating systems computer programmer, charter mem., voting mem.), Assn. Systems Mgmt. (cert. systems profl.), Soc. Data Educators (cert.), Phi Beta Kappa. Mem. Covenant Apostolic Ch. Home and Office: 10853 S Nicholson Rd Oak Creek WI 53154-7015

HARRIS, ROBERT A., retired music educator; b. Rich Hill, Mo., May 8, 1928; s. Archie L. and Edith Jeannette (Bailey) H. AA in Music, Joplin Jr. Coll., 1948; MusB, Kans. State Tchrs. Coll., 1950, MS in Edn., 1953; student, Rosina Lhevinne. Pianist, organist 1st United Meth. Ch., Carthage, 1946—; pvt. tchr. piano Carthage, Mo., 1947—; tchr. music, choir dir. Coll. Our Lady of the Ozarks, Carthage, 1949-53, 55-57; prof. music Mo. So. State Coll., Joplin, 1971-95; adjudicator Am. Coll. Musicians; presenter piano and organ recitals. Cpl., chaplain's asst. U.S. Army, 1953-55. Mem. Nat. Guild Piano Tchrs., Mo. State Tchrs. Assn., Nat. Fedn. Music Clubs (local v.p.), Fellowship of United Methodists in Worship and Music, Music Tchrs. Nat. Assn., Mo. State Tchrs. Assn., Mo. Federated Music Club (ch. musician yr. 1993).

HARRIS, ROBERT EDWARD, comedian, history educator; b. Willoughby, Ohio, Oct. 15, 1963; s. James Robert and Freda Virginia (Arnett) H. BS in elec. engring., applied physics, Case Western Reserve U., 1984. Internat. engring. specialist Harris Corp., Rochester, N.Y., 1984; design engr. Neotek Corp., Chgo., 1984-87; stand-up comedian, 1987—; host, exec. producer "Bob" WJW-TV8 New World Comms., Cleve., 1995—; guest host Sta. WWWE, 1995; vis. history lectr., 1992—. Author: (poetry) Dial-A-Poem Chicago, 1986, (CD/ROM) Encyclopedia of the JFK Assassination, 1994; columnist Nat. Lampoon Mag., 1987-89, Z Mag., 1995—, Funny Times Mag., 1995—; writer, performer True Love and Other Subversive Arts, Cleve. Pub. Theatre, 1995. Recipient One of Cleve. Most Interesting People award Cleve. Mag., 1995; nominee Speaker Yr. award Campus Activities Today Mag., 1992, 93, 95; poetry grantee Ill. Arts Coun., 1986. Mem. ACLU, Amnesty Internat., Common Cause, Pub. Citizen. Office: PO Box 170 Willoughby OH 44094

HARRIS, ROBERT FRANK, federal official; b. Brownsville, Pa., Nov. 10, 1951; s. Edgar Allen and Shirley Ann (Hartley) H.; children: Brian Robert, Bethany Kristin. AA, L.A. C.C., 1981; BS, Drury Coll., Springfield, Mo., 1983; MS, Ctrl. Mo. State U., Warrensburg, 1985. Case mgr. U.S. Bur. Prisons, Springfield, 82—; adj. prof. Drury Coll., Springfield, 1985—; hostage negotiator U.S. Bur. Prisons, Springfield, 1990—; spkr. on gangs, violence and ritualistic crime, 1990—. Author: Citizen Information on Gangs, 1993. Mem. Am. Correctional Assn., Am. Criminal Justice Assn., Police Marksman Assn., Hostage Negotiators Am., Mo. Corrections Assn. (bd. dirs. 1990-92), Drury Criminal Justice Soc. (facility advisor 1994—). Office: US Bur Prisons 1900 W Sunshine Springfield MO 65808

HARRIS, RONALD WILLIAM, commodities trader; b. Orange, Tex., Mar. 14, 1952; s. Harold Abraham Harris and Mary (Gaspar) Fohrman; m. Joan Fuetterer, Feb. 27, 1982 (div. July 1988); 1 child, Julie Ann. B in Fin., North Tex. State U., 1976; Securities Diplomas, Wall Street Inst., Salt Lake City, 1984. Registered broker. Broker Woodstock Commodities, Chgo., 1976-78, Fox Investment Group, Chgo., 1978—; TV commentator Commodity Update WCIV-TV, Chgo., 1982. Author: (commodity trading system) The Ron Harris Program, 1988. Tennis champion Chgo. Sun-Times Regional, Chgo., 1980, table tennis champion, So. Ill. U., Carbondale, 1971. Office: Rosenthal-Fox Div Ste 1800 A 141 W Jackson Blvd Chicago IL 60604-3002

HARRIS, SHARI LEA, mathematics educator; b. Macon, Mo., May 17, 1964; d. Walter Edward and Darlene (Tipton) H. BSE in Math. Edn. cum laude, N.E. Mo. State U., 1986; MS in Applied Math., U. Mo., 1991. Cert. secondary math. tchr., Mo. Cons. micromputer lab. Northeast Mo. State U., Kirksville, 1982-84, tutor coll. algebra, 1984-85, instr. math. lab., 1985; teaching asst. U. Mo., Columbia, 1986-87, 89-91; math. tchr. Highland High Sch., Ewing, Mo., 1987-88; substitute tchr. Quincy (Ill.) Sr. High Sch., 1988-89; math. tchr. Kemper Mil. Acad., Boonville, Mo., 1990; instr. math. S.E. Mo. State U., Cape Girardeau, 1991—. John J. Pershing scholar Northeast Mo. State U., Kirksville, 1982-86. Mem. Math. Assn. Am., Nat. Coun. Tchrs. of Math., Kappa Mu Epsilon, Alpha Phi Sigma.

HARRIS, SHIRLEY, elementary, secondary and adult education educator; b. Chgo., Aug. 14, 1945. BA in Psychology, Nat. Lewis U., 1985; MS in Edn., Chgo. State U., 1993. Cert. in curriculum and instr., psychology. Legal sec. Friedman/Rochester, Chgo. and Portland, Oreg., 1974; supr., clerical positions Model Citie, Chgo. and Portland, Oreg., 1973-75; bd. sec. Portland Comm., 1976-78; tchr., clerical positions Portland O.C., 1975-76; tchr., juvenile/youth counselor Yaun Youth Ctr., Portland, 1978-80; pres. Flexible Temps, Chgo., 1980—; cons. in field, Chgo., 1983; typing tchr., Chgo., 1983; pers. recruiter, Chgo., 1974-75. Contbr. poetry to anthologies. Bd. dirs. Operation Probe, Chgo., 1990-93. Mem. NAFE, ASCD, Internat. Platform Assn. Baptist. Home: 653 N Lockwood Chicago IL 60644

HARRIS, STANLEY FRANCIS, management educator, consultant; b. Detroit, Nov. 30, 1938; s. Lorenzo Francis and Estelle Agatha (Roos) H.; m. Janice Lee Boundy, Feb. 3, 1962; children: Jeffrey Allan, James Edward, Donald Kenneth, Douglas Norman. BIE, GM Inst., Flint, Mich., 1961; MBA, Wayne State U., 1967, PhD, 1989. Cert. mfg. engr., sch. bd. mem. Engring. and prodn. supr. GM, Detroit, 1961-68; asst. prof. Lawrence Tech. U., Southfield, Mich., 1968-88; dir. admissions Lawrence Technol. U., Southfield, Mich., 1975-84, acad. planning adminstr., 1984-85, chmn. MBA program, 1991-92, assoc. prof., 1988—, dir. Coll. Mgmt. Leadership Ctr., 1990-92; work systems analysis cons. Eonic, Inc., Detroit, 1977-80; edn. program coord. Consulting Engrs. Coun. Mich., Lansing, 1991-92. Trustee Sch. Dist. City Royal Oak (Mich.) Sch. Bd., 1982-95, treas., 1985-89, sec., 1989-91, v.p., 1991-92, pres. 1992-93, 94-95. Recipient award of distinction Mich. Assn. Sch. Bds., 1991; Wayne State U. scholar, 1982. Mem. Acad. Mgmt., Soc. Mfg. Engrs., Engring. Soc. Detroit, F. & A., Masons, Sigma Iota Epsilon. Lutheran. Home: 3608 Mark Orr Rd Royal Oak MI 48073-2295 Office: Lawrence Technol U Coll Mgmt 21000 W 10 Mile Rd Southfield MI 48075-1051

HARRIS, THOMAS L., public relations executive; b. Dayton, Ohio, Apr. 18, 1931; s. James and Leona (Blum) H.; m. JoAnn K. Karch, Apr. 14, 1957; children: James Harris, Theodore Harris. B.A., U. Mich., 1953; M.A., U. Chgo., 1956. Exec. v.p. Daniel J. Edelman Inc., Chgo., 1957-67; v.p. pub. rels. Neddham Harper & Steers, Chgo., 1967-72; pres. Foote Cone & Belding Pub. Rels., Chgo., 1973-78; pres. Golin-Harris Communications Inc., Chgo., 1978-89, also vice chmn.; adj. prof. Medill Sch. Journalism, Northwestern U., Evanston, Ill., 1987—; mng. ptnr. Thomas L. Harris & Co., Highland Pk., Ill., 1992—. Served with U.S. Army, 1953-55. Mem. Public Relations Soc. Am. Home: 241 Melba Ln Highland Park IL 60035-1904 Office: Thomas L Harris & Co 600 Central Ave Highland Park IL 60035-3211

HARRIS, VAL EDWARD, financial consultant; b. Marion, Ind., Feb. 14, 1942; m. Eleanor Y. Saba, Aug. 20, 1966; children: Dawn Floyd, Diane Borgard. BA cum laude, Wabash Coll., 1964; BDiv, So. Meth. U., 1967. Registered fin. cons. Pastor Grace United Meth., Anderson, Ind., 1967-69, Immanuel & Faith United Meth. Chs., South Bend, Ind., 1969-75, Forest Park United Meth. Ch., Ft. Wayne, Ind., 1975-79, Daleville (Ind.) United Meth. Ch., 1979-83, Grace United Meth. Ch., Kokomo, Ind., 1983-89; fin. broker 1st Affiliated Securities, Elwood, Ind., 1989-90, Spelman & Co., Inc., Kokomo, Ind., 1990—; bd. dirs., pres./treas. Action Inc., St. Joseph County, South Bend, Ind., 1970-72. Chmn. gift planning com., chmn. edn. com. Grace United Meth. Ch., Kokomo, 1990—; mem. YMCA. Mem. Lions, Phi Beta Kappa. Republican. Office: Spelman & Co Inc PO Box 749 1213 E Hoffer Kokomo IN 46903-0749

HARRIS, VICTORIA FRENKEL, English language educator; b. Chgo., May 7, 1945; d. Leon and Faye (Velen) Frenkel; m. Charles B. Harris, Mar. 16, 1968; children: Kymberly Lynn, Gregory Paul. BA in English, Ill. State U., 1970, MA in English, 1972; PhD in English, U. Ill., 1977; postdoctoral student, U. Calif., Irving, 1979. Asst. prof. English Ill. State U., Normal, 1977-82, assoc. prof., 1982-92, prof. English, lit. theory, poetry, 1992—. Author: The Incorporative Consciousness of Robert Bly, 1992; contbg. author: Walking Swiftly, 1992; contbr. articles to profl. jours., chpts. to books. Resident Ragdale Ctr., Lake Forest, Ill., 1990, Vt. Studio Ctr., Johnson, 1992. Mem. MLA, Midwest MLA, Assn. Depts. English, Coll. English Assn. Democrat. Jewish. Office: Ill State Univ English Dept 4240 Adlai E Stevenson Hall Normal IL 61790-4240

HARRIS-CLINE, DIANE, history and classical archaeology educator; b. Austin, Tex., May 11, 1961; d. Robert Sidney and Sandra Lou (Robbins) H.; m. Eric H. Cline; 1 child, Hannah. BA in Classics, Stanford U., 1983; MA in Classical Archaeology, Princeton U., 1990, PhD in Classical Archaeology, 1991. Instr. history of Ancient Greek Art and Archaeology St. John's U., Athens, Greece, 1988, 89; vis. instr. history Portland (Oreg.) State U., 1990-91; assoc. prof. history Calif. State U., Fresno, 1991-95; asst. prof. classical archeology classics dept. U. Cin., 1995—; vis. assoc. prof. U. Cin., 1994-95; cons. Harper Collins Pubs., 1994, Prentice-Hall Pubs., 1992; lectr. in field. Author: The Inventory Lists of the Parthenon Treasures, 1991, The Treasures of the Parthenon and Erechtheion, 1995; contbr. articles to profl. jours. Advisor, founder Hillel of Calif. State U.-Fresno, 1991-94. Fulbright scholar to Greece, 1987-88; NEH travel grantee, summers 1992, 94, Calif. State U.-Fresno rsch. grantee, 1992-93, 93-94, 94—, Portland State U. grantee, 1990-91; Hencken Prize Travel grantee, 1989, Spears Travel grantee, 1986, Spears and Berry Funds grantee, 1985; Doreen C. Spitzer fellow, 1988-89, Princeton U. fellow, 1983-87, Seeger fellow, 1986. Mem. Archaeol. Inst. Am. (bd. dirs., v.p., San Joaquin Valley chpt. 1991—), Am. Philol. Assn. (Women's Classical Caucus), Inst. for Classical Studies (London), Fulbright Alumni Assn., Fresno County Archaeol. Soc. (bd. dirs. 1991—, co-v.p. programming 1994—), Calif. Classical Assn. (so. sect.), Classical Assn. Pacific N.W., Assn. Ancient Historians, Am. Classical League, Am. Hist. Assn., Alumni Assn. of Am. Sch. Classical Studies in Athens (nat. nominating com. 1990-91). Democrat. Jewish. Home: 3543 Ruther Ave Cincinnati OH 45220 Office: U Cin Blegen Libr ML0226 Cincinnati OH 45221-0226

HARRISON, BEATRICE MARIE BINION, business educator, small business owner; b. Detroit, Sept. 10, 1958; d. Lamar Clinton Sr. and Mildred Arretta (Blount) Binion; m. Albert Willard Harrison III, Feb. 7, 1981; 1 child, Sophia Marie. BA in Psychology, Mich. State U., 1980; postgrad., Wayne State U., 1980-81, 92—, U. Mich., Dearborn, 1982-83, Ea. Mich. U., 1988; MA in Human Resource Mgmt. magna cum laude, Marygrove Coll., 1990. Cert. counselor. Bookkeeper City Nat. Bank, Detroit, 1977; asst. sec. Mich. State U., East Lansing, 1979; co-ptnr., pers. & customer rels. mgr. Cordové Rental Co., Holly, Mich., 1980-83; counselor CBN, 700 Club Inc., Royal Oak, Mich., 1983-84; substitute tchr. Pontiac (Mich.) Sch. Dist., 1984-86; admissions adminstr., counselor Jordan Coll., Detroit, 1986-88; assoc. dir. undergrad. admissions Marygrove Coll., Detroit, 1988-90; v.p. ops., dir. human resources Harrison & Harrison Designs, Inc., West Bloomfield, Mich., 1987-92; account exec. Mgmt. Recuriters, Inc., Livonia, Mich., 1992-93; univ. instr. Wayne State U., Detroit, 1993—, Detroit Coll. Business, 1995—; mem. Echoes of Gt. Lakes Mutual Life Ins. Co., 1986—. Block chief Southfield (Mich.) Neighborhood Watch, 1983-84; vol. fund raiser Echoes of Great Lakes Mut. Life Ins. Co., 1986-8, Sta. WDIV-TV Easter Seal Telethon, 1988; team capt. fund raiser Alberta T. Williams for U.S. Congress Campaign, 1990; mem. cmty. and corporate affairs com. No. Br. YWCA of Met. Detroit, 1989-90, mem. nominating com., 1990-91, 92-93, bd. dirs., 1st vice chair, 1993-95; active Mich. Senator Jackie Vaughn III Re-election Com., 1984-86, Detroit Inst. Arts Founder Soc., NAACP. Mem. NAFE, AAUW, Am. Sociol. Assn., Am. Mgmt. Assn., Nat. Adj. Faculty Guild, North Ctrl. Sociol. Assn., Nat. Coun. on Family Rels., Top Ladies of Distinction Club (Cité d'etroit chpt.). Roman Catholic. Home: 5658 Drake Hollow Dr E West Bloomfield MI 48322-1272 Office: Wayne State U Dept Sociology Detroit MI 48202 also: Detroit Coll Bus Mgmt Dept Dearborn MI 48126 also: Harrison & Harrison Designs Inc PO Box 251131 West Bloomfield MI 48325-9998

HARRISON, FRANK JOSEPH, lawyer; b. Streator, Ill., Dec. 5, 1919; s. Frank Joseph and Nell (Webb) H.; m. Shirley Anne Summerhays, Dec. 30, 1950; children: Ellen Harrison Greinacher, Paul, Janice Harrison Tienhaara, Mark. AB, U. Chgo., 1941, JD, 1947; LLM, Harvard U., 1947. Bar: Ill. 1942. Atty. Chgo. Title and Trust Co., 1948-51, Pub. Housing Adminstrn., Chgo., 1951-53; pvt. practice Streator, 1953—; city atty. City of Streator, 1965-71, 73-87; twp. atty., 1990—; sr. law clk. Ill. Appellate Ct. 3d. Dist., Ottawa, 1971-76; atty. Streator Twp. High. Sch., 1975-83. Compiler, editor: Streator Mcpl. Code of 1968, 1968. Sgt. Signal Intelligence Svc. AUS, 1942-46, PTO, 1st lt. JAGC, 1949. Mem. ABA, Ill. Bar Assn., La Salle County Bar Assn., Streator Bar Assn. (pres. 1986-96). Presbyterian. Home: 135 W 1st St Streator IL 61364-1241 Office: 114 N Bloomington St Streator IL 61364-2208

HARRISON, HERM L., electrical engineer; b. Cin., June 10, 1967. BS, Purdue U., 1988. Engr. Foster Transformer Co., Cin., 1989—; mem. adv. bd. Butler County Joint Vocat. Electronics Program, 1995—. Mem. IEEE, Soc. Automotive Engrs. Office: Foster Transformer Co 3820 Colerain Ave Cincinnati OH 45223-2571

HARRISON, JOSEPH WILLIAM, state senator; b. Chgo., Sept. 10, 1931; s. Roy J. and Gladys V. (Greenman) H.; B.S., U.S. Naval Acad., 1956; postgrad. Ind. U. Law Sch., 1968-70; m. Ann Hovey Gillespie, June 9, 1956; children—Holly Ann, Tracy Jeanne, Thomas Joseph, Amy Beth, Kitty Lynne, Christy Jayne. Asst. to pres. Harrison Steel Castings Co., Attica, Ind., 1960-64, sales research engr., 1964-66, asst. sec., 1966-69, sec., 1969-71, v.p., 1971-84, dir., 1968-84, mem. Ind. Senate, 1966—, majority leader, 1980—. Mem. Attica Consol. Sch. Bd., 1964-66, pres., 1966-67. Served with USN, 1956-60. Mem. Am. Legion, Sigma Chi. Republican. Methodist. Lodges: Elks, Eagles. Home: 504 E Pike St Attica IN 47918-1524 Office: PO Box 409 Attica IN 47918-0409 also: State Senate State Capital Indianapolis IN 46204

HARRISON, KARÉN ANN, library director; b. Toronto, Ont., Can., Mar. 28, 1947; d. Donald Sidney and Irene Victoria (Aberdeen) Wodlinger; m. John L. Harrison, June 6, 1970 (div. 1988). BA, U. Western Ont., 1968; MLS, U. Toronto, 1972. Community svcs. libr. Toronto Pub. Libr., 1968-71; asst. libr. Mohawk Coll. Libr., Hamilton, Ont., 1972-73; libr. Brantford (Ont.) Pub. Libr., 1973-74, Delhi (Ont.) Pub. Libr., 1974-86; coord field svc. Ontario Libr. Svc.-Trent, Richmond Hill, 1986-88; dir. Parkland Regional Libr., Lacombe, Alberta, Can., 1988-91; chief libr. Thunder Bay (Ont.) Pub. Libr., 1992—. Bd. dirs. Thunder Bay Symphony, 1992-95. Mem. ALA, Can. Libr. Assn. (v.p./pres.-elect 1995—), Ont. Libr. Assn. Office: Thunder Bay Pub Libr, 285 Red River Rd, Thunder Bay, ON Canada P7B 1A9

HARRISON, KEVIN D., design engineer; b. Cin., Feb. 7, 1961. BSEE, U. Cin., 1984; BA in Bus. Mgmt., Wilmington (Ohio) Coll., 1995. Comms. specialist Mobile Comms., Cin., 1984-87; design engr. Xetron Corp., Cin., 1987—.

HARRISON, LARRY EDGAR, electrical engineer; b. Osakis, Minn., June 30, 1940; s. Frank Reed and Lucy Catheryn (Meyer) H.; m. Roberta Carol Soelberg, Sept. 14, 1968; children: Laura Lea, Brian Fredric. B of Elec. Engring., U. Minn., 1964. Registered profl. engr., Minn. Substation engr. No. States Power, Mpls., 1964-69, control sys. engr., 1969-75; elec. engr. Coop. Power, Eden Prairie, Minn., 1975-79, mgr. telecomms., 1979—. Mem. IEEE (sr.), Radio Club of Am., Masons (Master Compass lodge # 160). Republican. Evangelical Christian.

HARRISON, MICHAEL JAY, physicist, educator; b. Chgo., Aug. 20, 1932; s. Nathan J. and Mae (Nathan) H.; m. Ann Tukey, Sept. 1, 1970. A.B., Harvard, 1954; M.S., U. Chgo., 1956, Ph.D., 1960. Fulbright fellow and H. Van Loon fellow in theoretical physics U. Leiden, Netherlands, 1954-55; NSF fellow U. Chgo., 1957-59; research fellow math. physics U. Birmingham, Eng., 1959-61; asst. prof. Mich. State U., East Lansing, 1961-63; assoc. prof. Mich. State U., 1963-68, prof., 1968—, faculty grievance officer, 1972-73, dean Lyman Briggs Coll., 1973-81, adj. prof. community health scis., 1988-93, adj. prof. internal medicine and epidemiology, 1993—; vis. research physicist Inst. Theoretical Physics, U. Calif., Santa Barbara, 1980-81; with Air Force Cambridge Research Center, summer 1953, M.I.T. Lincoln Lab., summer 1954, RCA Sarnoff Lab., summers 1961-63; physicist Westinghouse Labs., summer 1956; cons. RCA Lab., 1961-64, United Aircraft Co., 1964-66, U.K. Atomic Energy Authority, Harwell Lab., summer 1960, Thailand project in Bangkok, Mich. State U.-AID, summer 1968; vis. research affiliate theoretical biology and biophysics, Los Alamos Nat. Lab., 1987-88. Contbr. articles to U.S., fgn. profl. jours. Am. Council on Edn. fellow U. Calif., Los Angeles, 1970-71. Fellow Am. Phys. Soc.; mem. AAUP (chpt. treas. 1966-67), N.Y. Acad. Scis., Harvard Club of Ctrl. Mich. (pres. 1988-93), Rotary, B'nai B'rith, Phi Beta Kappa, Sigma Xi. Jewish. Home: 277 Maplewood Dr East Lansing MI 48823-4746 Office: Mich State U Physics Dept East Lansing MI 48824

HARRISON, PATRICK WOODS, lawyer; b. St. Louis, July 14, 1946; s. Charles William and Carolyn (Woods) H.; m. Rebecca Tout, Dec. 23, 1967; children: Heather Ann, Heath Aaron. BS, Ind. U., 1968, JD, 1972. Bar: Ind. 1973, U.S. Dist. Ct. (so. dist.) Ind. 1973, U.S. Dist. Ct. Nebr. 1982, U.S. Supreme Ct. 1977. Assoc. Goltra, Cline, King & Beck, Columbus, Ind., 1972-73; ptnr. Goltra & Harrison, Columbus, 1973-78; sole practice Columbus, 1979-80; ptnr. Cline, King, Beck and Harrison, Columbus, 1980-85, Beck & Harrison, Columbus, 1985—; Ind. Jud. Nominating Commn. nominee Ind. Supreme Ct., 1984. Served with U.S. Army, 1968-70. Fellow Ind. Trial Lawyers Assn. (bd. dirs. 1984); mem. Am. Trial Lawyers Assn. Republican. Lutheran. Home: 14250 W Mount Healthy Rd Columbus IN 47201-9309 Office: Beck & Harrison 320 Franklin St Columbus IN 47201-6732

HARRISON, RICHARD PAUL, JR., university program administrator; b. Pitts., Sept. 19, 1960; s. Richard Paul and Carol Ann (Hutter) H. BS in Journalism, Ohio U., 1982. Leadership cons. Phi Kappa Tau Nat. Frat., Oxford, Ohio, 1982-84, dir. alumni devel., 1984-85; asst. dir. Ohio U. Alumni Assn., Athens, 1985-88, assoc. dir., 1988-94, dir. alumni rels., exec. dir., 1994—; chmn. standing com. on Greek Life, Ohio U., 1988-93; advisor Sr. Class Coun., 1989-94; advisor Phi Kappa Tau, 1985—. Capt. divsn. Unit Way Athens County, 1988-92; Athens County Rep. Central Com., 1996—, Athens Found.; pres. Greek Alumni Advisors Com., Ohio U., 1988—; mem. Trustees Acad. Ohio U. Recipient Outstanding Adminstr. award Ohio U., 1989, Outstanding Young Men of Am. award, 1982,83, 84, 87, 88, 90, 92; named Frat. Advisor of Yr., 1986, 87, 88, 90, 92, 93, 95. Mem. Am. Soc. Assn. Execs., Coun. for Advancement and Support Edn., Assn. Frat. Advisors, Rotary, Green and White Club, Phi Kappa Tau (nat. coun.), Alumni Dirs. State Univs. of Ohio Orgn. (pres. 1995—). Methodist. Home: 67 Franklin Ave Athens OH 45701-1726 Office: Ohio U Alumni Assn PO Box 869 Athens OH 45701-0869

HARRISON, STEVEN W., business executive; b. Plymouth, Wis., June 22, 1955. BBA, U. Wis., Eau Clare, 1978; MBA, U. Chgo., 1993. CPA, Wis. V.p. ConsIn Components Corp., Sheboygan, Wis., 1978—; adminstrv. mgr., contr. Old Wis. Sausage Co., Sheboygan, 1979—; pres. Innovative Moving Systems, Lewiburg, Wis., 1993—. Vol., bd. dirs. R.C.S., Sheboygan, 1993—; pres. Sheboygan Area Youth Soccer Orgn., 1987—. Named Outstanding Vol. of Yr. Sheboygan Area Sch. Bd., 1993. Mem. AICPA, Nat. Accg. Assn., Ducks Unltd. (treas. 1990—), Elks Club, Jaycees (pres. 1986-87, Outstanding Young Wisconsinite 1987), State of Wis. Jaycees (regional dir. 1988-89). Republican. Roman Catholic.

HARRISON, WILLIAM J., engineering manager; b. Centerville, Iowa, Feb. 15, 1930; s. William B. and Edith (Stewart) H.; m. Janet E. Wilkerson, Sept. 4, 1955; children: William, Erin. Supr. engring. Maytag & Admiral Products, Newton, Iowa, 1987-91, mgr. engring., 1991-95; ret., 1995. Pres. Optimist Internat., 1970, past disting. pres. Newton chpt. Sgt. U.S. Army, 1949-51. Recipient Iowa Gov. Vol. award, 1983, Silver Beaver award Boy Scouts Am. Mem. ASME. Republican.

HARROFF, WILLIAM CHARLES BRENT, artist; b. Elkhart, Ind., Nov. 20, 1953; s. Walter Edward and Elma Lucille (Bowers) H. BA, Purdue U., 1978; MLS, Ind. U., 1981; Diploma, Internat. Sommerakademie, Salzburg, Austria, 1983. Cert. profl. libr. Architecture libr., faculty mem. Okla. State U., Stillwater, 1981-84; asst. prof. Internationale Sommerakademie für Bildende Kunst, Salzburg, Austria, 1984, 85; vis. artist, lectr. Madison County Arts Coun., Edwardsville, Ill., 1985-90; staff writer, illustrator Art St. Louis, 1986-91; libr., faculty mem. So. Ill. U., Edwardsville, 1985-91; artist self-employed Edwardsville, 1985—; bd. dirs. Madison County Arts Coun., 1987-91, St. Louis Vol. Lawyers and Accts. for the Arts, 1991—. Contbr. articles to profl. jours. Competition finalist The Artist's Mag., 1991; grantee Artists Space, 1989, Ill. Arts Coun., 1988, 90, 92; Regional Artists Project grantee Nat. Endowment for Arts, 1993; Art Matters Inc. fellow, 1992; Ragdale Found. resident, 1995; Nat. Endowment for Arts fellow, 1995. Mem. Ctr. for Book Arts, Chgo. Artists' Coalition. Home: 453 Cass Ave Edwardsville IL 62025

HARROLD, LESLIE STUART, pathologist; b. Springfield, Ohio, Feb. 13, 1948; d. Bruce D. and Geraldine M. (Simons) H. AB, Ind. U., 1970; MD, Thomas Jefferson U., 1974. Diplomate Am. Bd. Internal Medicine, Anatomic and Clin. Pathology. Intern, then resident Akron (Ohio) City Hosp., 1974-79; emergency rm. physician Massillon (Ohio) Cmty. Hosp., 1979-80; resident SUNY, Syracuse, 1980-82; pathologist Union Hosp., Dover, Ohio, 1982—, chief pathology, 1994—; med. dir. Hospice of Tuscarawas County, Dover, 1988—. Office: Union Hosp 659 Boulevard Dover OH 44622

HARSTAD, CARL LESLIE, consultant, writer; b. Cass Lake, Minn., Mar. 11, 1942; s. Lester Marvin Harstad and Leola (Patnaude) Fischer. BA, U. Minn., 1971, MA, 1976. Area editor Faribault (Minn.) Daily News, 1971-72; staff writer Sun Newspapers, Wayzata, Minn., 1973-75; freelance writer Mpls., 1975-77; mgmt. info. systems supr. Hennepin County Govt., Mpls., 1977-83; cons. computer mgmt. info. systems Mpls., 1983-85; tech. support and ops. supr. Angiomedics, Plymouth, Minn., 1985-87; mgr. St. Paul Software, 1988-89; mng. editor Chisago Co. Press, Lindstrom, Minn., 1989-90; CEO C. Harstad Cons., St. Louis Park, Minn., 1990—; v.p. Hwang and Harstad, St. Louis Park, 1996—. Served with USN, 1961-65, Vietnam. Decorated Gallantry Cross Color (South Vietnam). Recipient Fire Photography award Minn. Fire Chiefs Assn., 1972; NSF scholar, 1959, St. Cloud State U. Alumni scholar, 1960. Mem. Soc. Profl. Journalists (bd. dirs. 1974-75), Investigative Reporters and Editors, Minn. Astron. Assn. (sec. 1979-80, pres. 1980-81, editor newsletter 1975-84, 87-94), Am. Meteorol. Soc., Am. Legion, Sierra Club, Amnesty Internat., China Rights Forum. Lutheran. Office: C Harstad Consulting PO Box 26709 Saint Louis Park MN 55426-0709

HART, CECIL WILLIAM JOSEPH, otolaryngologist, head and neck surgeon; b. Bath, Avon, Eng., May 27, 1931; came to U.S., 1957.; s. William Theodore Hart and Paulina Olive (Adams) Gilmer; m. Brigid Frances Molloy, June 15, 1957 (dec. Nov. 1984); children: Geoffrey Arthur, Paula Mary, John Adams; m. Doris Crystel Katharina Alm, Mar. 14, 1987; children: Kristen-Linnea Alm, Erik Alm, Britt-Marie Alm. BA, Trinity Coll., Dublin, Ireland, 1952, MB, BCH, BAO, 1955, MA, 1958. Diplomate Am. Bd. Otolaryngology. Intern Dr. Steevens Hosp., Dublin, Ireland, 1956, Little Co. Mary Hosp., Evergreen Park, Ill., 1957; mem. staff Little Co. Mary Hosp., 1958-59; resident in otolaryngology U. Chgo. Hosp. and clinic, 1959-62; instr. U. Chgo. Med. Sch., 1962-64, asst. prof., 1964-65; practice medicine specializing in otolaryngology Chgo., 1958—; mem. staff Northwestern Meml. Hosp., 1972—, Rehab. Inst. Chgo., 1965—, Children's Meml. Hosp., 1972—, Little Co. of Mary Hosp., 1977-94, LaGrange (Ill.) Community Meml. Hosp., 1977-94; tchg. assoc. Cleft Palate Inst., 1968, dir. otolaryngology, 1969-92; asst. prof. dept. otolaryngology-head and neck surgery Northwestern U. Med. Sch., 1965-75, assoc. prof., 1975-92, prof., 1992—; lectr. dept. otorhinolaryngology Loyola U., 1972; med. adv. bd. So. Hearing and Speech Found., Nat. Inst. of Deafness and Other Communicative Disorders, 1989-95. Producer videos, movie; contbr. numerous articles to profl. jours. and mags.; also guest appearances various radio and TV talk shows. NIH fellow U. Chgo., 1962-63; NIH grantee, 1985-88. Fellow Am. Neurotology Soc. (pres. 1974-75, chmn. editorial review & publ. com. 1978-79, constn. and bylaws com. 1979—), Am. Acad. Otolaryngology-Head and Neck Surgery (chmn. subcom. on Equilibrium 1980-86, computer com. 1987-90), ACS, Inst. Medicine Chgo., Soc. for Ear, Nose and Throat Advances in Children; mem. AMA, Brit. Med. Assn., Ill. State Med. Soc., Chgo. Med. Soc., Am. Cleft Palate Assn., Am. Council Otolaryngology, Am. Otological Soc., Chgo. Laryngological and Otological Soc. (v.p. 1975-76), Northwestern Clin. Faculty Med. Assn. (vice chmn. 1976-78, pres. 1979-81), Barany Soc., Royal Soc. Medicine, Irish Otolaryngological Soc., So. Hearing and Speech Found (med. adv. bd.), Chgo. Hearing and Balance Assn. (pres.), Sigma Xi. Roman Catholic. Office: 707 N Fairbanks Ct Chicago IL 60611-3042

HART, CLIFFORD HARVEY, lawyer; b. Flint, Mich. Nov. 12, 1935; s. Max S. and Dorothy H. (Fineberg) H.; m. Alice Rosenberg, June 17, 1962; children: Michael F., David E., Steven A. AB, U. Mich., 1957, JD, 1960. Cert. civil trial advocate, Nat. Bd. Trial Advocacy. Bar: Mich. 1960, U.S. Dist. Ct. (ea. and we. dists.) Mich. 1962. Assoc. Stevens & Nelson, Flint, Mich., 1960-62; ptnr. White, Newblatt, Nelson & Hart, Flint, 1962-64; with Dean, Dean, Segar, & Hart, P.C., and predecessor firms Leitson, Dean, Dean, Segar & Hart, Dean, Dean, Segar, Hart & Shulman, P.C., Flint, 1965-95; Dean, Dean, Segar & Hart, P.C., 1995—; adj. assoc. prof. Flint sch. mgmt. U. Mich., 1972—; lectr. Inst. Continuing Legal Edn., Mich.; lectr. Mich. Jud. Inst. Pres. Vis. Nurse Assn., Flint, 1967; pres. Temple Beth El, 1973-75; trustee United Way Genesee County, 1981—; chmn. bd. United Way Genesee County, 1990-91; sec. 1988-89, chmn. bd. dirs. Genesee County and Lapeer County, 1990-91; chair adv. bd. U. Mich., Flint, 1988-93. Faculty mem. Inst. Continuing Legal Edn., Ann Arbor, Mich., 1984—. Fellow Mich. Bar Found., Roscoe Pound Found.; mem. ABA, Mich. State Bar Assn. (chmn. Negligence Law sect. 1981-82, rep. assembly 1975-81), Mich. Trial Lawyers Assn. (pres. 1977-78, lectr.), Genesee County Bar Assn. (pres. 1975-76), ATLA (bd. govs. 1979—, lectr., home office and budget com. 1980-84, 87-89, chair 1989—, exec. com. 1984-85, 90-93, chmn. elections com. 1984-87, nat. parliamentarian 1990-91, nat. treas. 1991-92), Am. Judicature Soc., Nat. Bd. Trial Advocacy (cert. 1980, 85). Democrat. Lodge: B'Nai B'rith (past pres.). Office: Dean Dean Segar & Hart PC 120 E First St Ste 1616616 Flint MI 48502-1957

HART, ELSIE FAYE, elementary education educator; b. Shelbyville, Ill., Oct. 15, 1920; d. James Ray and Maude May (Allison) Cain; m. Harold Delbert Bible, June 15, 1941 (div. Apr. 1948); children: Gary H., Rex. E. (dec.); m. Frederick Christopher Hart, July 28, 1950 (dec. Dec. 1994); children: Susan Hart Eichman, Pamela L. Elem. teaching cert., Ea. Ill. U., 1942; BS in Edn., No. Ill. U., 1968; postgrad., Rockford Coll., 1972-73. Cert. elem. tchr., Ill. Tchr. Findlay (Ill.) Elem. Sch., 1942-47; tchr. Winnebago County Schs., Rockford, Ill., 1948-52, Rockford Parochial Schs., 1957-63; tchr. Rockford Pub. Schs., 1964-82, substitute tchr., 1982—. Author: The On and the Under Dog, 1992; contbr. articles to profl. jours. Pres. Assn. for Childhood Edn. Internat., Rockford, 1968-76; sec.-treas. Ill. Assn. for Supervision & Curriculum Devel., Rockford, 1970-80; mem. NEA, Ill. Edn. Assn., Rockford Edn. Assn., 1964-82; mem. Rockford Art Assn., 1968, Beta Sigma Phi, Rockford, 1950, Rockford Creative Dramatics Assn., 1968, Mauh-Nah-Tee See Country Club, Rockford, 1982; vol. tchr. Rockford Parochial schs. Recipient Cert. of Commendation in recognition of meritorious svc. Ill. Supt. Pub. Instrn., 1974; nominated Ill. Retired Tchrs. Hall of Fame. Mem. AAUW (historian Rockford chpt. 1970—), Ill. Ret. Tchrs. Assn., Winnebago/Boone Ret. Tchrs. Assn., Women of the Moose, Holy Family Women's Guild, Rockford Women's Club (sec. 1970, publicity com. 1971, membership com. 1972, ways/means com. 1988-91, bd. dirs. 1993-94, long-range planning com. 1994—, program com. 1994-95, dir. 1995-98), Nat. Women's Hall of Fame. Republican. Roman Catholic. Home: 1507 Al Crest Rd Rockford IL 61107-2125

HART, GEORGE ZAVEN, state legislator; b. Detroit, May 13, 1927. AA, Henry Ford C.C.; BA, Wayne State U., 1952. City councilman Dearborn, Mich., 1957-71; county commr. Wayne County, Mich., 1972-78; state senator Dist. 10 Mich. State Senate, 1978-82, 87-94, state senator Dist. 6, 1995—; chmn. Com. on Transp. & Tourism, Spl. Com. on Sports Violence Mich. State Senate; mem. Mcpl. & Election Com., Consumer Affairs Com., State Affairs, Transp. & Tourism Com., Local Govt. & Vet. Com., Energy Com. Mich. State Senate. Recipient Steering Wheel award Automobile Clubh, 1981. Mem. Am. Legion, Mason, Moose, Kiwanis, Goodfellows, Pulaski Civic Orgn. Address: 4200 Roemer St Dearborn MI 48126-3421 Office: State Senate State Capital Lansing MI 48909*

HART, JAMES HARLAN, retired emergency medicine physician; b. Hamilton County, Ill., Dec. 16, 1934; s. Gleason and Elizabeth Jane (Smith) H.; m. Sharon Lenore Darr, Sept. 20, 1937; m. 2d, Lora Rae Barnett, May 9, 1955; children: Shane, Kyle, Raelene. BS, Southwestern State U., Weatherford, Okla., 1963; MD, Okla. U., 1968. Intern, Mercy Hosp., Oklahoma City, 1968-69; resident in ob-gyn St. Anthony Hosp., Oklahoma City, 1969-72; practice medicine specializing in ob-gyn, Woodriver, Ill., 1972-77; practice medicine specializing in emergency medicine, Lincoln, Ill., 1977-80; emergency medicine physician St. Elizabeth Hosp., Danville, Ill., 1980-89; med. dir. emergency svc., 1980-89; emergency medicine physician, Danville, Ill., 1980-89; med. dir. urgent care clinic Community Hosp., Williamsport, Ind., 1989-92; dir. emergency med. dept., Williamsport Community Hosp., 1991; med. dir. emergency med. technicians program, 1989; clin. assoc. prof. U. Ill. Med. Sch., Urbana; ret. 1994. Served with U.S. Army, 1957-59. Mem. AMA, Am. Coll. Emergency Physicians, Ill. State Med. Soc., Ind. State Med. Soc., Warren County Ind. Med. Soc., Vermillion County Med. Soc. Republican. Home: RR 2 Williamsport IN 47993-9802

HART, JAY ALBERT CHARLES, real estate broker; b. Rockford, Ill., Apr. 16, 1923; s. Jabez Waterman and Monty Evangeline (Burgin) H.; student U. Ill., 1941-42, U. Mo., 1942-43, U. Miami (Fla.), 1952-56, Rockford Coll., 1961-62; m. Marie D. Goetz, July 16, 1976; children—Dale M. (dec. 1995), Jay C.H. Exec. v.p. Hart Oil Co., Rockford, 1947—; pres. Internat. Service Co., Pompano Beach, Fla., 1952-58; v.p. Ipsen Industries, Inc., Rockford, 1958-61; owner Hart Realtors, Rockford, 1961-86; owner Hart & Assocs., Rockford, 1987—; pres. Rock Cut Corp., 1978—; sec. Intra World, Inc., 1981-83; lectr. in field; trustee, sr. analyst Anchor Real Estate Investment Trust, Chgo., 1971-80. Dir. Winnebago County (Ill.) CD, 1975; dep. coordinator Winnebago County (Ill.) ESDA, 1976-86. Chmn. Rock River chpt. ARC, 1973, nat. nominating com., 1971, disaster chmn. Illiana div., 1972-80; bd. counselors Rockford Coll., 1974-80; emergency coordinator 9th Naval dist. M.A.R.S., USN, 1960-68, civilian adv. council, 1968-78, Ill. area coordinator, 1986-87, lifetime assoc. mem., 1987; net ops. officer 4th region Navy-Marine Corps MARS, 1988-89. Office mgr. Citizens for Eisenhower, Chgo., 1952. Served with USAAF, 1943-46. Mem. Rockford Air Guild (pres. 1974, 76-77), Rockford Art Guild (dir.), Exptl. Amateur Radio Soc. (pres. 1960-80), Nat. Assn. Real Estate Appraisers, Soc. Indsl. and Office Realtors, Nat. Assn. Rev. Appraisers and Mortgage Underwriters, Nat. Assn. Realtors, Phi Eta Sigma. Mason (Shriner). Clubs: Univ., City. Author: Real Estate Buyers and Sellers Guide, 1961. Paintings in pvt., pub. collections; illustrations in numerous publs. Home and Office: Hart and Assocs 2406 East Ln Rockford IL 61107-1116

HART, JEFFREY ALLEN, political scientist, educator; b. New Kensington, Pa., Dec. 29, 1947; s. Edwin and Enez (Blumm) H.; m. Joan Goldhammer, June 9, 1969; 1 child, Zachary. BA, Swarthmore Coll., 1969; PhD, U. Calif., Berkeley, 1975. Asst. prof. Princeton (N.J.) U., 1973-80; assoc. prof. Ind. U., Bloomington, 1980-86, prof., 1986—; profl. staff mem. Pres.' Commn. for Nat. Agenda for the Eighties, Washington, 1980-81; internal contractor office tech. assessment U. S. Congress, Washington, 1985-86; contractor Nat. Ctr. for Mfg. Scis., Ann Arbor, Mich., 1988-89. Author: The New International Economic Order, 1983, Interdependence in the Post-Multilateral Era, 1986, Rival Capitalists, 1992, The Politics of International Economic Relations, 5th edit., 1996. Co-chair Monroe County Cmty. Campaign for Riley Children's Hosp., Bloomington, 1991-93. Paul Henry Spaak fellow for U.S.-European affairs Boas Found., 1982-83. Mem. Am. Polit. Sci. Assn., Internat. Studies Assn., Phi Beta Kappa. Democrat. Jewish. Office: Ind U Dept Polit Sci Bloomington IN 47405

HART, JOHN MARCUS, electronics company executive; b. Anderson, Ind., Oct. 21, 1920; s. William Lloyd and Theresa E. (Cook) H. Student, Purdue U.; grad., Nat. Radio Inst. Corr. Sch., Wilcox Sch. for ILS, Kansas City, Mo. Pres. Mobile Electronics Inc., Anderson, 1958—. Patentee in field. Served with U.S. Navy, 1944-45, PTO. Mem. Masons. Office: Mobil Electronics 5300 Alex Pike Anderson IN 46012

HART, JOSEPH KIRWIN, advertising executive; b. N.Y.C., Oct. 13, 1934; s. Edward Remington and Katharine (Kirwin) H.; m. Rosalie Palazzolo, Apr. 30, 1966; children: Joseph Jr., Brian Francis. BS, Georgetown U., 1956. V.p. Ross Roy Advt., Detroit, 1968-79, Meldrum and Fewsmith, Detroit, 1979-83, McCann Erickson Advt., Troy, Mich., 1983-87, Cahners Pub. Co., West Bloomfield, Mich., 1987—. Served to lt. USN, 1957-60. Recipient Hall of Fame award TF Club, 1992, Presdl. award Reed Publ. USA, 1994; named Achiever of Yr., Advt. Pub., 1991, Salesman of Yr., Plant Engring. Mag., 1992-93, Nat. Sales Mgr., 1995. Mem. Bus. Profl. Advt. Assn. (cert. bus. communicator, bd. dirs. 1981—, Advt. Man of Yr. 1983, Leadership Excellence award 1992, Internat. Edn. award 1992, Achivement award Detroit chpt. 1980-95). Roman Catholic. Home: 5781 Plumcrest Dr West Bloomfield MI 48322-1728 Office: Cahners Pub Co 29777 Telegraph Rd Ste 2447 Southfield MI 48034-7651

HART, MARY, educator; b. Dawson, Ga., May 18, 1929; d. Qualis and Leaner (Countryman) Williams; m. James Hart, Sept. 20, 1952; children: Patricia Hart Purnell, James Jr. Nurse St. Barnard Hosp., Chgo., 1957-69; tchr. Chgo. Pub. Schs., 1969-80, 84—. Author: (poems) My Special Prayer, 1982, The Unseen World, 1988, 91, 93 (award 1990), The Light 1 and 2, 1983 (award 1983), Jesus Is Already There, 1983 (award 1987), Jesus Is On His Way, 1983 (award 1983), You Don't Have To Go Looking for Jesus, 1983, When You Are Through Going Around Circles, 1983, Jesus Know's You By The Way You Walk, 1983. Recipient award of merit cert. World of Poetry, 1987, Golden Poet award World of Poetry, 1987, Cert. of Merit Talent & Associated Cos., 1983, Silver Poet award World of Poetry, 1990. Home: 10115 S Bensley Ave Chicago IL 60617-5350

HART, MILDRED, counselor; b. Ever, Ky., Apr. 7, 1937; d. Dewey Otis and Malta Virginia (Adams) Cooper; m. Joseph Paul Surace, Oct. 26, 1956 (dec. Jan. 1966); children: Marisa Surace Craig, Vincent, Angela, Stephen (dec. 1994); m. James Robert Hart, June 26, 1994. BS in Edn., Ohio State U., 1974, MA in Guidance-Counseling, 1976. Cert. elem. and secondary tchr., secondary prin., supr., Ohio; lic. profl. counselor, Ohio. Sec. H.G. Snyder & Assocs., accts., Columubus, Ohio, 1958-63; tchr. Columbus Pub. Schs., 1974-79, counselor, 1977—, chmn. student svcs. dept., 1985—; adjustor Bancohio Nat. Bank, Columbus, 1985-93. Author: (booklet) College Handbook for Independence High School Students, 1988. Leader Girl Scouts U.S., Columbus, 1969-73. Mem. NEA, Ohio State U. Alumni Assn., Nat. Honor Soc., Pi Lambda Theta (sec. Cen. Ohio chpt. 1985—), Phi Kappa Phi. Democrat. Roman Catholic. Home: 2328 Sedgwick Dr Columbus OH 43220-5431 Office: Independence High Sch 5175 Refugee Rd Columbus OH 43232-5352

HART, MYRNA JEAN, art gallery and gift shop owner; b. Kansas City, Kans., Jan. 20, 1942; d. George Allen and George Ellen (Doak) Epps; m. Lawrence Eugene Hart, Aug. 31, 1963; children: Denise, Kimberly, Lawrence Eugene. Grad. high sch., 1959. Unit head acctg. dept. Fed. Res. Bank, Kansas City, Mo., 1963-67; 1040 processor IRS, Kansas City, Mo., 1967-70; account rep. Burlington No. R.R., St. Paul, 1970-86; owner Hart's Afro-Am. Art, St. Paul, 1986—; art cons. on spl. project United Way, Mpls., 1994; art cons. Rochester (Minn.) Schs., 1993. Action Abundant Life Christian Ch., 1989—, Urban League, St. Paul, 1994. Recipient Martin Luther King Arts award City of St. Paul, 1993, Small Bus. of Yr. award YMCA, 1993, The Quality Commendation award Gov. of Minn., 1993, Vol. Svcs. award Abundant Life Christian Ch., 1995. Office: Hart's Afro-Am ARt 474 S Hamline Saint Paul MN 55105

HART, PAMELA HEIM, banker; b. Chgo., July 14, 1946; d. Gordon Theodore and Leah Almira (Gardner) Heim; m. William Richard Hart, July 8, 1972 (div. 1979); 1 child, Elizabeth Alyson. BA, DePauw U., 1968; MA in Teaching, Washington U., St. Louis, 1970; M in Mgmt., Purdue U., 1982. Chartered bank auditor; cert. bank compliance officer. Tchr. history University City (Mo.) High Sch., 1969-74; teaching asst. Purdue U., Hammond, Ind., 1980-82, guest faculty, 1983-84; auditor Continental Bank NA, Chgo., 1984-86, legal and regulatory compliance specialist, 1986-88, asst. auditor, 1988-92, sr. portfolio risk analyst, 1992-94; with asset securitization group Bank of Am. (formerly Continental Bank NA), Chgo., 1994—; v.p. Capital Raising Products, 1994—. Trustee Forest Ridge Acad., Schererville, Ind., 1987-88; mem. vestry St. Paul Episc. Ch., Munster, Ind., 1982-92; active LWV. Mem. Chartered Bank Auditors Assn., Chicagoland Compliance Assn. (bd. dirs., treas. 1987-88), Cert. Bank Compliance Officer Assn. (exam. com. mem. 1992-95), P.E.O. Home: 8936 Southmoor Ave Hammond IN 46322-1808 Office: Bank of Am 231 S La Salle St Chicago IL 60604-1407

HART, RENEE ANN, food microbiologist, researcher; b. Lincoln, Nebr.; d. Wendell M. and Norma M. Hart. BS in Biology, Nebraska Wesleyan U., 1980; MS in Vet. Sci., U. Nebr., 1983; PhD, Kans. State U., 1992. Lab asst. Nebraska Wesleyan U., Lincoln; grad. asst. U. Nebr., Lincoln; grad. rsch. asst. Kans. State U., Manhattan, rsch. asst.; cons. Pizza Hut, Wichita, 1988, Excell Corp., Schulyer, Nebr., 1992; asst. dir. workshop, Monterrey, Mex., 1992; presenter 7th Internat. Congress on Rapid Methods and Automation in Microbiology and Immunology, London, 1993. Co-author: (with others) Seafood Quality Determination, 1986, Meat Safety, 1993; contbr. articles to profl. jours. Recipient scholarship Nebr. Wesleyan U., R. Robinson award Kansas City Inst. Food Technologists, 1990. Mem. Inst. Food Technologists (corr. sec., com. chair), Am. Soc. Microbiology, Nebr. Acad. Sci., Internat. Assn. Milk, Food and Environ. Sanitarians, Am. Dairy Sci. Assn. (student), Coun. for Agrl. Sci. and Tech., Beta Beta Beta, Gamma Sigma Delta, Sigma Xi (travel award), Phi Tau Sigma (assoc. mem.). Office: Kans State U Dept Anim Sci 1600 Midcampus Dr Manhattan KS 66506

HART, SHARON YVONNE, academic adminstrator; b. Saginaw, Mich., Aug. 7, 1956; d. David Allen Hill and Janice Rae (Dezelsky) Jaynes; m. Daniel Gerald Bintz, Jan. 18, 1991. BS, Mich. State U., 1978; MS, Ind. State U., Terre Haute, 1983; PhD, U. Ill., 1995. Instr. IVY Tech. Coll., Terre Haute, 1983; asst. state coord. expanded food and nutrition edn. program U. Ill., Urbana, 1983-86; dir. rsch. evaluation Chgo. City-Wide Coll., 1986-90; adminstrv. dean Madison (Wis.) Area Tech. Coll., 1990-96; v.p. acad. affairs Northcentral Tech. Coll., Wausau, Wis., 1996—; cons., evaluator Am. Coun. Edn., Washington, 1991—, North Cen. Assn. Colls./Schs., Chgo., 1989—. Author: Household Resources and their Changing Environment: A Case Study of Gujurat, India, 1987. Recipient Fulbright/Hayes scholar to India, 1985, Doctoral scholarship Am. Home Econ. Assn., 1985. Mem. Am. Tech. Edn. Assn. (trustee), Am. Vocat. Assn., Wis. Vocat. Assn., Nat. Coun. Occupl. Edn., Phi U. Honor Soc., Omicron Tau Theta. Office: Northcentral Tech Coll 1000 W Campus Dr Wausau WI 54401-1899

HARTENBACH, STEPHEN CHARLES, small business owner; b. St. Louis, Oct. 9, 1943. Student, Rockhurst Coll., 1961-62, St. Louis U., 1964-67. Salesman Revere Copper and Brass, N.Y.C., 1969-72; pres. Hartenbach Interiors, St. Louis, 1972-75; pres. and chmn. bd. dirs. Hartenbach Carpet and Gallery, St. Louis, 1975—. Alderman City of Sunset Hills, Mo., 1979-83, 87-89. 1st lt. U.S. Army, 1964-68. Mem. Am. Soc. Appraisers (assoc.), Regional Commerce and Growth Assn., Down St. Louis, Inc., Mo. Athletic Club, Elks. Republican. Roman Catholic. Office: 1408 Hanley Industrial Ct Saint Louis MO 63144-1916

HARTER, ROGER KARR, retired telephone compnany official; b. Normal, Ill., Dec. 12, 1923; s. Omar Newton and Helena (Karr) H.; m. Claire Phyllis Caverly; children: Deborah, Duncan, Malcolm, Penelope. AA, St. Petersburg Jr. Coll., Fla., 1938-40; BA, Swarthmore (Pa.) Coll., 1940-42; MA, Harvard U., 1948; student, U. Mich., 1949-51. Staff asst. New England Telephone and Telegraph Co., Boston, 1948-49; staff supr. Mich. Bell Telephone Co., Detroit, 1949-51, Am. Telephone and Telegraph Co., N.Y.C., 1951-58; gen. staff supr. Mich. Bell Telephone, Detroit, 1958-80. Sec., pres. Southfield (Mich.) Symphony Assn., 1960-80. Col. USMC, 1943-46, USMCR, 1946-83. Mem. Res. Officers Assn. of U.S. (state pres. 74-75), Navy League of U.S. (nat. dir., nat. historian, state and region pres. 1964—), Mich. State Assn. of Parliamentarians (pres. 1994-96). Republican. Presbyterian. Home: 1060 Puritan Birmingham MI 48009

HARTKE, CHARLES A., state legislator; b. Effingham, Ill., May 7, 1944; m. Kathy Hartke; 2 children. Farmer; mem. from 108th dist. Ill. Ho. of Reps., 1985—; vice chmn. agr. com.; chmn. counties and twps. com.; mem. appropriations com., elem. and secondary edn. com., transp. and motor vehicles com., children com., econ. devel. and legis. info. system com., pub. safety and infrastructure appropriations coms., vets. affairs com. *

HARTLEY, DAVID, state legislator; b. Dec. 16, 1942; m. Vicki Hartley. BA, U. Louisville, postgrad.; JD, Capital U. Law Sch. State rep. Dist. 62 Ohio State Congress, 1973-92, state rep. Dist. 73, 1993—; chmn. agr. and natural resources com., Clark County Dem. exec. com.; mem. adv. com. Ohio State Dept. Pub. Welfare Svc.; bd. dirs. Ohio Environ. Coun.; lawyer. Mem. UAW, AAUP, Civital, Bd. Project Women. *

HARTLEY, JAMES MICHAELIS, aerospace systems, printing and hardwood products manufacturing executive; b. Indpls., Nov. 25, 1916; s. James Worth and Bertha S. (Beuke) H.; m. E. Lea Cosby, July 30, 1944; children: Michael D., Brent S. Student Jordan Conservatory of Music, 1934-35, Ind. U., Purdue U., Franklin Coll. With Arvin Industries, Inc., 1934-36; founder, pres. J. Hartley Co., Inc., Columbus, Ind., 1937—; founder, pres. Hartley Group, 1989—. Inventor of and patent on a prerotation system for transport-size aircraft landing gear. Pres. Columbus Little Theatre, 1947-48; founding dir. Columbus Arts Guild, 1960-64, v.p., 1965-66, dir., 1971-74; musical dir., cellist Guild String Quartet, 1963-73; active Indpls. Mus. of Art; founding dir. Columbus Pro Musica, 1969-74; dir. Regional Arts Study Commn., 1971-74; v.p. Ind. Coun. Rep. Workshops, 1965-69, pres., 1975-77; pres. Bartholomew County Rep. Workshop, 1966-67. Served with USAAF, 1942-46. Mem. AAAS, Am. Legion (life), NAM, Nat. Fedn. Ind. Bus., N.Y. Acad. Scis., Planetary Soc., Air Force Assn., Nat. Space Soc., U.S. C. of C., Phi Eta Sigma (honoris causa). Achievements include invention, patent prerotation system for transport-size aircraft landing gear. Office: J Hartley Co Inc 101 N National Rd Columbus IN 47201-7848

HARTLEY, TERRY L., management consultant; b. Kawkawlin, Mich., Feb. 6, 1947; s. Robert John Hartley and Elizabeth Louise (Morrill) Trace; m. Lynn Helen Kitchen, July 5, 1969; children: Jill Ann, Jena Kaye, Lauren Nichole. BS, Ferris State Coll., Big Rapids, Mich., 1969; MBA, Cen. Mich. U., 1975. Terminal mgr. Ryder Truck Lines, Saginaw, Mich., 1974-79; corp. traffic dir. Ryder Truck Lines, Jacksonville, Fla., 1979-82; v.p. pricing Helms Express, Irwin, Pa., 1982-84; dir. pricing Con-Way Cen. Express, Ann Arbor, Mich.; mem. bd. govs. Mich. Trucking Assn., mem. motor carrier adv. com. Transp. div. Ill. Commerce Commn.; speaker in field. Contbr. articles to profl. jours. Republican. Presbyterian. Office: Con Way Cen Express 4880 Venture Dr Ann Arbor MI 48108-9559

HARTMAN, DAVID ELLIOTT, psychologist; b. N.Y.C., Jan. 9, 1954; s. Harry Wilson and Marian Phyllis (Milchin) H.; m. Roberta Maller; children: Sarah Beth, Adam Maller. AB, Vassar Coll., 1975; MA, Princeton U., 1978; PhD, U. of Ill., Chgo., 1982. Diplomate Am. Bd. Profl. Neuropsychology; lic. psychologist, Ill. Intern Michael Reese Hosp.; asst. coordinator in emergency psychiatry Northwestern U. Hosp., Chgo., 1982; dir. psychology tng. Lincoln Park Clinic at Columbus Hosp., Chgo., 1982-92; dir. neuropsychology Rush Presbyn. St. Lukes Hosp. Isaac Ray Ctr., Rush Human Performance Lab., Chgo., 1992—; adj. asst. prof. psychology U. Ill. Med. Ctr., Chgo., 1984—. Author: Neuropsychological Toxicology, 1988, 2d edit., 1995; mem. editl. bd. Archives Clin. Neuropsychology, 1990-91; contbr. numerous articles to profl. jours. Fellow NIMH. Fellow Nat. Acad. Neuropsychology, Am. Coll. Profl. Neuropsychology; mem. APA, Ill. Psychol. Assn. (past clin. chmn.), Phi Beta Kappa. Office: Rush Presbyn St Lukes Hosp Isaac Ray Ctr Rm 021 1702 W Polk St Chicago IL 60612-4315

HARTMAN, HERBERT ARTHUR, JR., oncologist; b. Halstead, Kans., Aug. 8, 1947; s. Herbert Arthur and Margrete Laverne (Schroeder) H.; m. Cynthia Craig, Dec. 26, 1971; m. April Craig, Herbert Arthur III. BA in Chemistry, U. Kans., 1969, MD, 1973. Diplomate Am. Bd. Internal Medicine, Am. Bd. Med. Oncology. Resident internal medicine U. Nebr. Med. Ctr., Omaha, 1973-76, fellow in med. oncology, 1976-78; oncologist Radiologic Ctr. Inc., Omaha, 1978-79, Sole Proprietorship, Omaha, 1979-80, Oncology Assocs., Omaha, 1980—; chmn. dept. medicine Immanuel Med. Ctr., Omaha, 1988-90; clin. assoc. prof. internal medicine U. Nebr. Med. Sch., 1979—. Contbr. articles to med. jours. Pres. Nebr. Cancer Soc., 1991. Fellow Am. Coll. Physicians; mem. AMA, Am. Soc. Internal Medicine, Am. Soc. Clin. Oncology, Nebr. Med. Assn. (bd. dirs. 1989-95), Metro Omaha Med. Soc. (exec. com. 1987), N.Y. Acad. Scis., Mensa. Republican. Episcopalian. Home: 6211 Chicago St Omaha NE 68132-2727 Office: Oncology Assocs PC Meth Cancer Ctr 8303 Dodge St Ste 225 Omaha NE 68124-0639

HARTMAN, JAMES ROBERT, public health sanitarian; b. Barberton, Ohio, May 14, 1951. BS in Microbiology, Ohio State U., Columbus, 1975, MS in Preventive Medicine, 1992. Registered sanitarian, Ohio. Sanitarian Columbus Health Dept., Columbus, 1979—. Mem. Internat. Assn. of Milk, Food and Environ. Sanitarians, Inst. of Food Technologists. Office: Columbus Health Dept Environmental Health 181 Washington Blvd Columbus OH 43215

HARTMAN, LENORE ANNE, physical therapist; b. Cleve., May 27, 1938; d. Howard Andrew and Emma Elizabeth (Beck) H. BS in Agriculture, Ohio State U., 1960, MS in Agriculture, 1963; postgrad., Kans. State U., 1963-67; cert. in phys. therapy, U. Kans., 1968. Staff phys. therapist R.J. Delano Sch. for the Handicapped, Kansas City, Mo., 1969-74; chief phys. therapist Children's Mercy Hosp., Kansas City, 1974-78; relief staff Mass Gen. Hosp.,

Boston, 1969-70; staff phys. therapist Menorah Med. Ctr., Kansas City, 1979-87; clin. instr. phys. therapy St. Louis U., 1974-78, U. Ky., 1974-78, U. Mo., Columbia, 1973-78, U. Kans. Med. Ctr., Kansas City, 1974-87; mem. med. adv. com. Hospice Care of Mid Am., Kansas City, 1984-87; staff phys. therapist S.W. Gen. Hosp., 1992—; phys. therapy cons. Rocky River Riding Therapeutic Riding Program, 1994—; chapel organist St. Luke's Hosp., Kansas City, 1978-87. Contbr. articles to profl. jours. Ohio del. Internat. Farm Youth Exch., Brazil, 1962. Mem. Internat. Farm Youth Exch. Assn. (life), Am. Phys. Therapy Assn. (del. to nat. 1975-76), Mo. Phys. Therapy Assn. (chmn. northwest dist. 1974-76), Am. Guild of Organists (chmn. profl. concerns com. Greater Kansas City chpt. 1983), Japan Am. Soc., Ohio State U. Alumni Assn. (life), Ohio Phys. Therapy Assn., Cleve. All-Breed Tng. Club, Western Res. Kennel Club, Pembroke Welsh Corgi Club of Western Res., Am. Morgan Horse Assn., N.Am. Riding Assn. for Handicapped, U.S. Dressage Fedn., North Ohio Dessage Assn., Omicron Delta Epsilon, Phi Delta Gamma. Office: Southwest Gen Health Ctr Dept Physical Therapy Middleburg Heights OH 44130

HARTMAN, MARIE SUZANNE, special education educator; b. Peoria, Ill., Mar. 30, 1964; d. Robert Norman and Marie Eunice (Grimm) Taufer; m. James Frederick Hartman, June 9, 1985; children: Perri Marie, Nathan James, Jacey Gail. BS, Ill. State U., Normal, 1985, MS in Edn., 1992. Tchr. learning disabled Deer Creek (Ill.) Sch., 1985-90; substitute tchr. Woodford County (Ill.) Schs., 1990-93; after-sch. remedial tchr. Congerville (Ill.) Sch., 1993-94; sub-lectr. Ill. State U., Normal, 1992—, rschr., 1993—; lectr. tchr. in-svcs., various sch. dists. in Ill., 1995—; mem. bd. human rights A.C. Home for Handicapped, Morton, Ill., 1991—. Republican. Apostolic Christian.

HARTMAN, ROBERT J., aluminum company executive; b. Buffalo, Jan. 30, 1951; s. Robert Turner and Mary Ann (Love) H.; m. Cindy Ann Duhlman, Nov. 13, 1976; 1 child, Cayle. BS, Penn. State U., State College, 1973. CPA, Penn. Sr. acct. Coopers & Lybrand, Pitts., 1973-76; contr./CFO Wachter Assoc., Pitts., 1976-79; project leader/audit supr./audit mgr. National Steel, Pitts., 1980-85; audit mgr. Quanex Corp., Houston, 1985-87, asst. contr., 1987-93; group contr./CFO Nichols-Homeshield, Davenport, Iowa, 1993—. Sargeant-E5 USMC, 1970-73. Mem. Penn. Inst. of CPA's, Am. Inst. of CPA's. Home: 2967 Crow Creek Rd Bettendorf IA 52722 Office: Nichols-Homeshield 201 W Second St # 420 Davenport IA 52801

HARTMAN, ROBERT RAY, retired physician, medical consultant; b. Jacksonville, Ill., Feb. 17, 1914; s. Ray Adam and Blanche Margaret (Perry) H.; m. Beatrice Hayes, Feb. 20, 1937; children: Linda Skop, Suzanne Verticchio. AB, Ill. Coll., 1935; BM, Northwestern U., Chgo., 1940, MD, 1941; LLD (hon.), Ill. Coll., 1986. Intern St. Louis City Hosp., 1939-40, resident in ob-gyn, 1940-43; practice medicine specializing in ob-gyn Jacksonville, 1946-85; chief of staff Passavant Hosp., Jacksonville, Ill., 1955, 66; assoc. clin. prof. ob-gyn So. Ill. U., Springfield, 1976-87; cons. Ill. Dept. Pub. Aid, 1974-85, Ill. Dept. Pub. Health, Springfield, 1972-74, Ill. Maternal Welfare Com., 1954-84, chmn., 1964-74; chmn. Ill. Maternal Welfare Com., 1964-74; sec. bd. trustees Ill. Coll., Jacksonville, 1963-86. Contbr. articles to profl. jours. Mem. Jacksonville Planning Com., 1959-67, chmn., 1962-67; mem. Jacksonville Mayor's Flood Control Com., 1978-82; mem. Morgan County Bd. Health, Jacksonville, 1960-85, pres., 1968-80; mem. Ill. Com. To Rewrite and Revise Pub. Aid Code, Springfield, 1978-81; trustee emeritus Ill. Coll., Jacksonville, 1986—. Capt. U.S. Army, 1943-46. Recipient cert. of appreciation Morgan-Scott Med. Soc., 1979. Fellow ACOG; mem. ACS, AMA (alt. del. 1976-82), Internat. Coll. Surgeons, Ill. Ob-Gyn. Soc. (pres. 1965-66), Ill. Med. Soc. (trustee 1975-84m, v.p. 1977, chmn. bd. trustees 1978-80), Am. Assn. Med. Assistance (nat. physician adv. 1982-84), The Club (assoc.), Elks, Masons, Rotary (pres. 1951, Paul Harris fellow 1982). Republican. Mem. United Ch. of Christ. Home: 5B Justin Dr Jacksonville IL 62650-2757

HARTMAN, STEVE EUGENE, civil engineer; b. Orrville, Ohio, May 19, 1958; s. Carl Edgar and Charolette Florence (Hartsfield) H.; m. Molly Kathleen Raiff, July 31, 1982; children: Zachary, Kathleen. BSCE, U. Dayton, 1981. Registered profl. engr., Ohio. Staff engr. City of Orrville (Ohio), 1981—. Dir. 4th of July tournament YMCA, Orrville, 1993—; corp. bd. dirs. Boys and Girls Club, Orrville. Mem. Wayne County Ofls. Assn., Ohio Soc. Profl. Engrs., Wayne County Umpires Assn. (pres. 1989—). Office: City of Orrville 207 N Main St Orrville OH 44667

HARTMAN-ABRAMSON, ILENE, adult education educator; b. Detroit, Nov. 8, 1950; d. Stuart Lester and Freda Vivian (Nash) Hartman; m. Victor Nikolai Abramson, Oct. 24, 1941. BA, U. Mich., 1972; MEd, Wayne State U., 1980, PhD in Higher Edn., 1990. Cert. continuing secondary tchr., Mich. Program developer and instr. William Beaumont Hosp., Royal Oak, Mich., 1972-74; vocat. counselor for emigres Jewish Vocat. Svc. and Cmty. Workshop, Detroit, 1974-81; program developer and cons. Detroit Psychiat. Inst., 1982; instr. for foreign students Oakland C.C., Farmington Hills, Mich., 1983—, acad. coord. overseas info. program, 1995—; mem. adv. bd. Mich. Dept. Edn., Detroit, 1981; lectr. Internat. Conf. Tchrs. English to Speakers of Other Langs., 1981; guest presenter Wayne State U., Lawrence Tech. U., 1991, U. Mich. Anxiety Disorders Program, 1993; presenter rsch. presentations Nat. Coalition for Sex Equity in Edn., Ann Arbor, Mich.; presenter at seminar on learning anxiety Interdisciplinary Studies program Wayne State U., 1995; chair profl. stds. and measures com. Mich. Devel. Edn. Consortium; mem. rehab. adv. coun. State of Mich. Contbr. articles to prof. jours. Am. Arabic and Jewish Friends, Detroit, 1988—, Orgn. for Rehabilitation Through Training, 1986—, Wayne State U., Alumni Assn., 1990—. Mem. Am. Anthropol. Assn., Am. Mensa Ltd. (rsch. rev. com.), Math. Assn. Am., Nat. Assn. Fgn. Student Affairs, Mich. Coun. on Learning for Adults, Assn. for Women in Math., TESOL, Nat. Assn. for Devel. Edn. Jewish. Office: Oakland Community Coll 27055 Orchard Lake Rd Farmington Hills MI 48334

HARTMANN, CHARLES JOHN, JR., law educator; b. St. Louis, Jan. 22, 1938; s. Charles John and Laura Marie (Schack) H.; m. Mary Lou Smith Gordon, Feb. 1, 1978 (div. June 1988); m. Bahar Bahramian, Oct. 17, 1992. AB in Econs., Washington U., St. Louis, 1959; JD, U. Mo., 1966. Bar: Mo. 1966. Asst. dir. student affairs for men U. Mo., Columbia, 1961-66; dir. residence programs Washington U., St. Louis, 1966-68; dean of students Georgetown U., Washington, 1968-70; exec. asst. to the pres. Wright State U., Dayton, Ohio, 1970-72, from asst. prof. to assoc. prof. to prof., 1972—. Contbr. articles to profl. jours. Bd. dirs. Salvation Army, Dayton, 1985-91. Rsch. fellow Inst. Advanced Legal Studies, London, 1992. Mem. ACLU, Friends of Inst. of Advanced Legal Studies (London), Dayton Racquet Club. Democrat. Lutheran. Home: 710 Irving Ave Dayton OH 45409 Office: Wright State U Dept Mgmt Dayton OH 45435

HARTMANN, RICHARD PAUL, accountant; b. Terre Haute, Ind., Sept. 4, 1934; s. Albert and Therese (Diekhoff) H.; m. Marcia Jean Von Blon, June 16, 1956; children: Richard Paul Jr., Jeffrey Bryan, Roger Alan. BA, Capital U., 1956; student Officers Candidate Sch., Newport, R.I., 1956, U.S. Naval War Coll., 1969; postgrad. Xavier U., 1964-65, U. Dayton, 1965-66. CPA, Ohio, 1969. Sr. staff acct. Battelle & Battelle, CPAs, Dayton, Ohio, 1960-69; owner, mgr. Richard P. Hartmann, CPA, Kettering, Ohio, 1970—. Mem. City Coun. Kettering, 1977-89; vice mayor City of Kettering, 1985-87, mayor, 1989—; treas. Holiday at Home, Inc., 1974-87; pres. Holiday at Home, 1989-90; mem. pres.'s council Capital U.; treas. Capital U. Alumni Bd., 1967-68; mem. Congrl. screening coms. USN Acad.; treas. S.W. Ohio dist. Evang. Luth. Ch. Am., Ohio, 1987-94; bd. dirs. Kettering Community Improvement Corp., 1972-90. retired Capt. USNR, 1956-87. Recipient Community Svc. award, Kettering, 1978, 79. Mem. AICPA, Ohio Soc. CPA's, Kettering C. of C. (past pres.), Naval Inst., Nat. League Cities, U.S. Conf. Mayors, Ohio Conf. Mayors, Mont Co. mayors and mgnrs. (pres 1995-96), Naval War Coll., Naval Res. Assn., U.S. Navy League (v.p. 1986), Miami Valley (Ohio) Mil. Affairs Orgn. (charter). Republican. Lutheran. Club: Exchange (Kettering pres. 1978-79). Office: 3560 Marshall Rd Kettering OH 45429-4916

HARTMUS, JOHN A., systems engineer; b. Highland Park, Mich., Apr. 5, 1961; s. John A. Jr. and Anita M. (Sutton) H.; m. Lucinda J. Guajardo, June 18, 1993. BEE cum laude, GM Inst., Flint, Mich., 1984; M in Computer Sci., Oakland U., 1988; MBA, U. Mich., 1992, JD, 1992. Engr.-in-tng., Mich. Reliability engr. GM/Cadillac, Detroit, 1979-85; telecomms. engr. GM/EDS, Warren, Mich., 1985-87; data systems engr. AT&T, Southfield, Mich., 1987-89; prin. bus. cons. Honeywell, Mpls., 1992-95; implementation mgr. Ryder Dedicated Logistics, Ann Arbor, Mich., 1995; systems engr. Advanced network Solutions, Bloomfield Hills, Mich., 1995—; computer cons. Mem. State Bar of Mich. Office: Advanced network Solutions Ste 202 1760 S Telegraph Bloomfield Hills MI 48302

HARTNETT, BARBARA MARY, college program director; b. Chgo., Dec. 5, 1946; d. Matthew Walter Witczak and Mary Ann Tomaszkiewicz; m. Michael Warren Hartnett, June 16, 1968. BS, U. Ill., Champaign, 1968; MS, Ill. State U., 1974; EdD, No. Ill. U., 1994. Tchr. spl. edn., elem. edn. Peoria (Ill.) Pub. Schs., 1968-72; prof. psychology Ill. Ctrl. Coll., Peoria, 1973-90, dir. corp. and cmty. edn., 1990-95. V.p. bd. dirs. Planned Parenthood, Peoria, 1992-94; founding mem. Peoria Area Women's Fund, 1995; co-chair Peoria Women's Coalition, 1993-95; mem. Peoria Area Labor Mgmt. coun., 1994-95, Ill. Intergenerational Coun., 1992-95; active United Way, Ctr. Prevention Abuse, LWV, YWCA. Recipient Appreciation award Women's Chautauqua Com. Ill. Ctrl. Coll., 1992, Boss of Yr. award Am. Bus. Women, Peoria, 1991, Retention Excellence award Nat. conf. Student Retention, 1989. Mem. Am. Assn. Women in Cmty. Colls. (pres. Ill. chpt. 1993-96), Nat. Assn. Women in Edn., Am. Assn. Cmty. Colls., Nat. Coun. Cmty. Svc. and Continuing Edn. Democrat. Office: Ill Ctrl Coll Perley Campus 115 SW Adams Peoria IL 61602

HARTNETT, D. PAUL, state legislator; b. Sioux City, Iowa, Sept. 29, 1927; m. Marjorie Sheehan, 1951; children: Debbie (Mrs. Burchard), Cindy (Mrs. Spagnola), Marcy (Mrs. Closner), Joan, Michael. BA, Wayne State Coll., 1951, MS, 1958; PhD, U. Nebr., 1966. H.S. tchr., coach, adminstr. Nebr.; coll. prof.; mem. from 45th dist. Nebr. State Senate, Lincoln, 1984—, chmn. urban affairs com., mem. gen. affairs com., natural resources com., mem. edn. com. of the states, mem. exec. bd. Past mem. Bellevue Sch. Bd. Mem. C. of C., Eagles, KC, Phi Delta Kappa. Office: Nebr State Senate State Capitol Rm 2108 Lincoln NE 68509*

HARTSAW, WILLIAM O., mechanical engineering educator; b. Tell City, Ind., Oct. 17, 1921; s. William A. and Hazel (Barr) H.; m. Delma Stuckey, June 30, 1946; 1 son, Mark Alan. BSME, Purdue U., 1946, MS in Engring., 1953; PhD, U. Ill., 1966. Instr. engring. U. Evansville, Ind., 1946-52, asst. prof., 1952-54, assoc. prof., 1954-63, head engring. dept., 1958-61, dir. Sch. Engring., 1961-68, prof. engring., 1963-85; Disting. prof. mech. engring., 1985-92; dean engring. U. Evansville, Ind., 1968-76, chmn. dept. mech. engring., 1977-85; Disting. prof. mech. engring. emeritus U. Evansville, 1992—; vice chmn. Evansville EPA, 1980—. Author: The Peltier Effect, 1958, Low Cycle Fatigue Strength Investigation of a High Strength Steel, 1966, Increased Productivity without Added Costs, 1989, Teamwork Enhances Productivity, 1990. Mem. exec. bd. Buffalo Trace coun. Boy Scouts Am., 1969—, chmn. svc. com., 1975-76; mem. Evansville Urban Transp. Adv., 1975—; pres. Tri-State Coun. Sci. and Engring., 1993—. With USAAF, 1942-43. Recipient Alumnus Cert. of Excellence, U. Evansville, 1972, Tech. Achievement award Tri-State Coun. for Sci. and Engring., 1979; Lilly Found. fellow, 1960, NSF fellow, 1961-62. Mem. ASME (life, faculty advisor student chpt. 1968-92, nat. com. divsn. solar energy com. on components 1975—, vice chmn. faculty advisors region VI 1975-76, chmn. faculty advisors region VI 1976-78, vice chmn. Evansville sect. 1980-81, chmn. Evansville sect. 1981-82, v.p. elect region VI 1982-83, v.p. region VI 1983-85, advisor to regional v.p. 1985-87, nat. bd. on issues mgmt. 1986-89, nat. bd. on profl. devel. 1988—, nat. nominating com. 1989-91, Centennial Svc. award 1980, Centennial medal 1980, Disting. Svc. award 1989, Faculty Advisor of Yr. region VI 1992, Nat. Agenda del. 1990-92, regional coll. rels. chmn. 1994—), ASTM, AAUP, AAAS, Am. Soc. Engring. Edn., ASHRAE (life, pres. Evansville chpt. 1966-67), Am. Soc. Metals, Phi Kappa Phi, Phi Beta Chi, Phi Tau Sigma. Methodist. Home: 1407 Green Meadow Rd Evansville IN 47715-6055

HARTSOCK, JANE MARIE, nurse, educator; b. Rock Island, Ill., Nov. 19, 1948; d. George Vincent and Patricia Anna (Holland) Woeber; m. Donald Lee Hartsock, Jan. 16, 1971; children: Cara Elizabeth, David Vincent. BS in Nursing, Marycrest Coll., 1977; MA, U. Iowa, 1982. Cert. oncology nurse. Head nurse U.S. Naval Hosp., Great Lakes, Ill., 1970-71; staff nurse Moline Pub. Hosp. (Ill.), 1971-72, instr. Sch. Nursing, 1977-87; nurse bone marrow transplant unit, U. Minn., 1987-92; instr. Mpls. C.C., 1988-92, Trinity Sch. Nursing, 1992-94; staff nurse oncology Trinity Med. Ctr., 1992—; assoc. prof. Trinity Coll. Nursing, 1994—. Contbr. chpt. in book. Song leader Blue Grass Ch., 1977-87. With USN 1970-72, capt. Nurse Corps USAR. Mem. AAUW, Am. Nurses Assn., Nurse Educators Assn. (pres. 1984-85), Oncology Nursing Soc, Internat. Platform Assn., Res. Officer Assn., Pioneer Club (Blue Grass, Iowa, sec. 1983-87), Sigma Theta Tau (pres.). Home: 2035 43rd St Rock Island IL 61201-4913

HARTWELL, JOHN MOWRY, marketing and sales consultant; b. Mpls., July 26, 1929; s. Arthur Mowry and Janet (Van Sickle) H.; m. Lucy Bell, Aug. 22, 1959; children: David, Jill Hartwell Geoffrion, Lucy Hartwell Heegaard, Charlie. BA, Yale U., 1951; MBA, Harvard U., 1953. Product mgr., mktg. mgr. Gen Mills, Mpls., 1956-69; pres. Land O Nod Co., Mpls., 1970-85; mktg., sales and new products cons., Wayzata, Minn., 1986—; cons. Mpls., 1991—. Trustee Northwestern Coll. Chiropractic, Mpls., 1973-88; bd. dirs. Project for Pride in Living, Mpls., 1990—, People Unltd., Mpls., 1991—, Minn. Internat. Ctr., Mpls., 1991—. Lt. (j.g.) USN, 1956. Recipient Torch of Honor award Found. for Chiropractic Edn. and Rsch., 1979. Mem. Mpls. Club, Woodhill Country Club. Home: 3350 Northome Rd Wayzata MN 55391-3016 Office: Bellcomb Techs 70 22nd Ave N Minneapolis MN 55411-2237

HARTWELL, MACK DAVID, financial consultant; b. Defiance, Ohio, Aug. 12, 1967. BA, Ohio State U., 1992. Fin. cons. Merrill Lynch, Dublin, Ohio, 1993—. Home: Apt C 1542 Northwest Blvd Columbus OH 43212-2545 Office: Merrill Lynch PO Box 657 555 Metro Pl N Dublin OH 43017

HARTZLER, ED, state legislator. State rep. Dist. 123 Mo. State Congress, 1993—. *

HARTZLER, GEOFFREY OLIVER, retired cardiologist; b. Goshen, Ind., Nov. 6, 1946; s. Robert Willis and Emma Irene (Blosser) H.; m. Lois Anne Kauffman, June 1967 (div. May 1983); children: Abigail, Christine, Amanda; m. Dorothy Eloise Arnn, July 1985. BA, Goshen Coll., 1968; MD with honors, Ind. U., 1972. Diplomate Am. Bd. Internal Medicine, Bd. in Cardiovascular Disease. Intern in medicine Mayo Grad. Sch. Medicine, Rochester, Minn., 1972-73; fellow in medicine Mayo Grad. Sch. Medicine, Rochester, 1973-74, fellow in cardiology, 1974-76; assoc. cons. in internal medicine and cardiovascular disease Mayo Clinic, Rochester, 1976-77; instr. in medicine Mayo Med. Sch. and Grad. Sch. Medicine, Rochester, 1976-79; cons. in cardiovascular disease and internal medicine Mayo Clinic and Mayo Found., Rochester, 1977-80; dir. invasive diagnostic electrophysiology Mayo Clinic, Rochester, Minn., 1979-80; cardiologist Cardiovascular Cons., Inc., Kansas City, Mo., 1980-93; clin. prof. medicine U. Mo., Kansas City, 1985-95; cons. cardiologist Mid-Am. Heart Inst., Kansas City, 1980-95; dir. advanced angioplasty fellowship program St. Luke's Hosp., Kansas City, 1985-92, med. dir. cardiovascular clin. rsch. ctr. Mid-Am. Heart Inst., 1993-95; cons. Advanced Cardiovascular Systems, Inc., Santa Clara, Calif., 1983-95; past mem. editl. or rev. bd. Am. Jour. Cardiology, Jour. Am. Coll. Cardiology, Cath. and CV Diagnosis, others; co-founder Ventritex, Inc., Sunnyvale, Calif., 1985-88, Triax Internat., Inc., Lenexa, Kans., 1989—; prin., bd. dirs. Kustom Signals, Inc., Lenexa, 1990—, LMP Steel & Wire Co., Maryville, Mo., 1992—, Lett Electronics, Inc., Topeka, 1995—. Contbr. numerous abstracts, articles to profl. jours., chpts. to books; made TV presentations to lay people on aspects of cardiology. Recipient KK Chen award, 1970, E.V. Allen scholarship, 1971, Osler award U. Miami, 1986, 1st Ann. Career Achievement award Cardiol. Rsch. Found., 1994. Fellow Am. Coll. Cardiology, Coun. on Clin. Cardiology of Am. Heart Assn., Soc. for Cardiac Angiography; mem. AMA, Mo. State Med. Assn., Kansas City Cardiovascular Roundtable, Jackson County Med. Assn., Am. Heart Assn. Office: 2600 Verona Rd Shawnee Mission KS 66208

HARTZLER, VICKY, state legislator. Mo. state rep. Dist. 124. Address: Rm 109-F 22804 E 299th St Harrisonville MO 64701

HARVEY, IRENE DELORES, real estate professional; b. Kansas City, Mo., Mar. 7, 1938; d. Verne Keith Covell and Louise Lena (Janeski) Covell Jackson; children: Todd Martin Hesher, Tedd Matthew Hesher; m. Wendell L. Harvey. BS, U. Fla., 1980; AA in Tech. Arts, Johnson County Coll., 1986. Cert. paralegal, Kans.; lic. securities, ins. dealer, Mo. and Kans. Legal sec. Lathrop, Koontz, Righter, Clagett, Parker and Norquist, Kansas City, 1972-75; fashion model Patricia Stevens Agy., Kansas City, 1975; with legal dept. U.S. Dept. Treasury, Kansas City, 1981-84; fin. planner, rep. IDS Am. Express, Overland Park, Kans., 1984-85; with real estate dept. Gage and Tucker, Kansas City, 1985-95; co-owner Harvey Homes, Inc., Joplin, Mo., 1995—. Mem. Kansas City Ballet Guild, 1970, Clay County Task Force for Juvenile Detention, Liberty, Mo., 1970; life mem. Nat. PTA, 1970—; sch. dist. lobbyist to Mo. Ho. Reps., Senate, Jefferson City, 1971; v.p. North Kansas City Dem. Club, 1976. Mem. Kansas City Assn. Legal Assts., Internat. Assn. Fin. Planners. Office: Century 21 Assoc Ltd 2203 East 32nd St PO Box 2100 Joplin MO 64803

HARVEY, JACK K., holding company executive; b. 1943. With Douglas County Bank & Trust Co., Omaha, 1960—; chmn. bd. State Bank Holding Co., Omaha. Office: Great Western Securities Inc 10834 Old Mill Rd Ste 1 Omaha NE 68154*

HARVEY, JAMES RAYMOND, electrical engineer; b. Cin., Sept. 6, 1945; s. Raymond James and Betty Ann (Schaefer) H.; m. Alvina May Owen, June 21, 1969; children: Janet Lynn, Erin Elisa. BSEE, U. Cin., 1969; profl. devel. in engring., U. Mich., 1976. Registered profl. engr., Ohio, Mich. Project engr. Detroit Edison, 1970-74; v.p. Moylan Engring., Dearborn, Mich., 1974-86; mgr. elec. engring. U. Mich. Hosps., Ann Arbor, 1986-96, U. Mich., Ann Arbor, 1996—. Moderator Detroit Metro Assn., United Ch. of Christ, 1994, past moderator, 1995; pres. St. Pauls United Ch. of Christ, Dearborn, 1980-96. With USNR, 1970-74. Mem. IEEE (sr., chmn. divsn. VII S.E. Mich. sect. 1984-94, chmn. design subcom. Industry Applications Soc. 1993—, facility chmn. Industry Applications Soc. conf. 1992), Nat. Fire Protection Assn., Illuminating Engring. Soc. N.Am., Assn. Energy Engrs. (cert. energy mgr., cert. lighting efficiency profl.). Home: 42215 Ladywood Dr Northville MI 48167-2019 Office: U Mich Facilities Planning and Design 236 E Hoover Ann Arbor MI 48109-1002

HARVEY, JOANNE H., genealogist; b. Cleve., July 24, 1932; d. Wilbur Joseph and Helen Ethel (McDougall) Snell; m. Kenneth James Harvey, June 12, 1954; children: Laura Harvey Peterson, Mary R. BA, Western Mich. U., 1954; MA in LS, U. Mich., 1956; AS in Bus., Lansing Community Coll., 1980. Cert. genealogist Bd. Cert. for Genealogists. Reference libr. Lansing (Mich.) Pub. Libr., 1955-60, Mich. State Libr., Lansing, 1967-69, Lansing Community Coll. Libr., 1970-78; genealogist Lansing, 1970—; legal asst. Office of Gov., State of Mich., Lansing, 1980-81. Author: From Glasgow to Fargo, The Living Record, Yesterday's Handwriting; contbr. articles to geneal. mags. Active Cen. United Meth. Ch., Lansing; docent Potter Park Zoo. Mem. AAUW, Assn. Profl. Genealogists, Mich. Geneal. Coun., Mid-Mich. Geneal. Soc., Nature Conservancy, Mich. Profl. Genealogists, Lansing Woman's Club. Home: 2420 Newport Dr Lansing MI 48906-3541

HARVEY, KATHERINE ABLER, civic worker; b. Chgo., May 17, 1946; d. Julius and Elizabeth (Engelman) Abler; student La Sorbonne, Paris, 1965-66; AAS, Bennett Coll., 1968; m. Julian Whitcomb Harvey, Sept. 7, 1974. Asst. libr. McDermott, Will & Emery, Chgo., 1969-70; librarian Chapman & Cutler, Chgo., 1970-73, Coudert Freres, Paris, 1973-74; adviser, organizer library Lincoln Park Zool. Soc. and Zoo, Chgo., 1977-79, mem. soc.'s women's bd., 1976—, chmn. libr. com., 1977-79, sec., 1979-81, mem. exec. com., 1977-81; mem. jr. bd. Alliance Francaise de Chgo., 1970-76, treas., mem. exec. com., 1971-73, 75-76, mem. women's bd., 1977-80, 95—; mem. Fred Harvey Fine Arts Found., 1976-78; hon. life mem. Chgo. Symphony Soc., 1975—; mem. Phillips Acad. Alumni Coun., Andover, Mass., 1977-81, mem. acad.'s bicentennial celebration com. class celebration leader, 1978, co-chmn. for Chgo. acad.'s bicentennial campaign, 1977-79, mem. student affairs and admissions com., 1980-81; mem. aux. bd. Art Inst. Chgo., 1978-88; mem. Know Your Chgo. com. U. Chgo. Extension, 1981-84; mem. guild Chgo. Hist. Soc., 1978—, bd. dirs., 1993—; mem. women's bd. Lyric Opera Chgo., 1979—, chmn. edn. com., 1980, mem. exec. com., 1980-84, 88—, treas. women's bd., 1983-84, 1st v.p. 1988-90; mem. women's bd. Northwestern Meml. Hosp., 1979—, treas., chmn. fin. com., 1981-84, 92-94, mem. exec. com., 1981-88, 92—, devel. com. 1995—, 2d v.p. 1996—, founding chair pres. com. 1993—; vis. com. Sch. Music Northwestern U., 1995—; bd. dirs. Found. Art Scholarships, 1982-83; bd. dirs. Glen Ellyn (Ill.) Children's Chorus, 1983-90 , founding chmn. pres.'s com., 1983—; mem. women's bd. Chgo. City Ballet, 1983-84; trustee Chgo. Acad. Scis., 1986-88; adv. coun. med. program for performing artists Northwestern Meml. Hosp., 1986-94, mem. exec. com., 1992—, bd. treas., 1992—; pres., bd. dirs. William Ferris Chorale, 1988-89; chmn. pres. com. Chgo. Children's Choir, 1991-93. Mem. Antiquarian Soc. of Art Inst. Chgo. (life); bd. dirs. Grant Park Concerts Soc., 1986-92, Guild of the Chgo. Historical Soc., 1994-96, Antiquarian Soc. Art Inst. Chgo., 1994—. Mem. Arts Club of Chgo. (dir. 1996—), Friday Club (corr. sec. 1981-83), Casino Club (gov. 1982-88, sec. 1984-85, 1987-88, 1st v.p. 1985-86, 2d v.p. 1986-87), Cliff Dwellers CLub. Home: 1209 N Astor St Chicago IL 60610-2300

HARVEY, ROBERT GENE, English language educator; b. Liberal, Mo., Jan. 6, 1942; s. Ernest and Ella (Hedges) H.; m. Barbara Kae Dobbins, Aug. 8, 1964; 1 child, Susan Kae Harvey Dunakey. BS in English Edn., Pittsburg (Kans.) State U., 1965, MS in English, 1969; DA in English, Ill. State U., 1983. English tchr. East Ctrl. Coll., Union, Mo., 1969—. Mem. Nat. Coun. Tchrs. of English, Am. Fedn. Tchrs., Mo. Assn. Cmty. and Jr. Colls., Phi Theta Kappa (hon.). Presbyterian. Office: East Ctrl Coll Dept English Union MO 63084

HARVEY, ROY JAMES, television producer; b. Houston, July 22, 1941; s. Harry J. and Renee Cecelia (Macon) H.; m. Karen Jane Engstrom, Aug. 13, 1963; children: Josh Emory, Jennifer Lara. BA, U. Wash., 1965; MFA, U. Iowa, 1967. With City of Chgo./Cable Office; founding assoc. Chgo. Books in Rev., assoc. editor, 1995—; host TV show Chgo. Books. Author: Life Histories from a Guerrilla War, 1974; co-author: Mediacracy: The Price of Freedom, 1995. Mem. Writers Bloc. Home: 919 N LaSalle Chicago IL 60610 Office: City of Chicago Cable Office 510 Peshtigo Ct Chicago IL 60610

HARVEY, TIM W., program manager, engineer; b. Kansas City, Mo., Apr. 28, 1959; s. Wayne Leroy and Beverly Joan (Stokes) H.; m. Tracy Jo Twenter, June 30, 1990. BA in Geology, U. Colo., 1984; postgrad., U. Mo., Rolla. Geologist Kodiak Petroleum, Denver, 1986-87; program mgr., engr. Eagle Picher Industries, Inc., Joplin, Mo., 1988—; cons. Everett Ritchie Pub. Mineral Mus., Joplin, 1989—. Contbr. articles to profl. jours. Roman Catholic. Home: 2525 E 25th Ct Joplin MO 64804-2443 Office: Eagle Picher Industries Inc 1215 W B St Joplin MO 64801-2869

HARVEY, WAYNE EVAN, secondary education educator, administrator; b. Dayton, Ohio, Nov. 15, 1952; s. Milton Earl and Florence (Heckert) H.; m. Pamela Sue Dean, Aug. 18, 1979; children: Austin B., Alison E. BS, Ohio State U., 1974; MEd, Ashland (Ohio) U., 1987. Cert. tchr., secondary adminstr. English tchr. Worthington (Ohio) City Schs., 1974—, dir. Linworth alternative program, 1991—; cons. Olentangy Schs. Curriculum Com., Delaware, Ohio, 1992; debate coach Worthington City Schs., 1974-77, theatre tech. asst., 1977-78, cross-country coach, 1978-83, golf coach, 1984-91. Vol. Olentangy Youth Athletic Assn., 1987—, Scioto Dog Club (4H), Delaware, 1992-94. Mem. ASCD, Nat. Coun. of Tchrs. of English, Nat. Soc. for Exptl. Edn., Phi Delta Kappa. Home: 1864 Africa Rd Galena OH 43021 Office: Linworth Alternative Prog 2075 W Dublin Granville Rd Worthington OH 43085-3304

HARVITT, ADRIANNE STANLEY, lawyer; b. Chgo., May 15, 1954; d. Stanley and Maryln (Loye) H.; m. Donald Martin Heinrich, Aug. 27, 1977; children: Patrick Loye, Christina Marie. AB, U. Chgo., 1975, MBA, 1976; JD with honors, Ill. Inst. Tech., 1980. Bar: Ill. 1980, U.S. Dist. Ct. (no. dist.) Ill. 1980, U.S. Ct. Appeals (7th cir.) 1985, (9th cir.) 1988, U.S. Supreme Ct. 1985, Wis. 1993. Fin. analyst Bell & Howell Co., Chgo., 1976-77; trial atty. U.S. Commodity Futures Trading Commn., Chgo., 1980-83; assoc. Hannafan & Handler, Chgo., 1983-85; ptnr. Harvitt & Gekas, Ltd.,

Chgo., 1985—. Mem. Law Rev. Chgo.-Kent Coll. Law, 1979-80. Mem. ABA, Ill. Bar Assn. (article hon. mention 1982), Chgo. Bar Assn., U. Chgo. Alumni Assn. (svc. citation 1995, bd. govs. 1996), U. Chgo. Women's Bus. Group (v.p. 1988-90), U. Chgo. Women's Bd., Art Inst. Chgo. Office: Harvitt & Gekas Ltd 135 S La Salle St Ste 2600 Chicago IL 60603-4501

HARWARD, GARY JOHN, retired utility company executive; b. Sioux City, Iowa, Dec. 2, 1941; s. John Morris and Edith Christine (Falk) H.; m. Linda Readout, Aug. 20, 1960; children: Kimberly Harward Ostler, Nancy Harward Anderson. BBA, Morningside Coll., 1964; MBA, U. S.D., 1982. Ops. officer Livestock Nat. Bank, Sioux City, 1964-68; in various mgmt. positions Iowa Pub. Service Co., Sioux City, 1968-71, asst. controller, 1971-74, controller, 1974-84; v.p., controller Midwest Energy Co., Sioux City, 1984-85, sr. v.p. fin., chief fin. officer, 1985-88, sr. v.p., chief fin. officer, 1988—; sr. v.p., chief fin. officer Iowa Pub. Svc. Co., Sioux City, 1991-94; bd. dirs. Firstar in Sioux City, Firstar Corp., Des Moines. Trustee Buena Vista Coll., Storm Lake, Iowa, 1987—; bd. dirs. Tax Research Conf., Sioux City, 1975—, chmn. bd., 1983-84; trustee Dakota Dunes Community Improvement Dist., North Sioux City, S.D., 1989—; bd. dirs. Family Svcs. Orgn., Sioux City, 1987—.

HARWOOD, JON CARL, minister; b. Detroit, Nov. 2, 1941; s. Ralph and Berth Lorene (Alday) H.; m. Cynthia Ann Corwin, June 6, 1964; children: Mary, Mark, Pamela, Joy, Craig, Jennifer, Martin, Sherrie, Frank. Student, Bapt. Bible Coll., Springfield, Mo., 1965; DDiv, Bapt. Theol. Sch. New England, Pascoag, R.I., 1993. Ordained to ministry, Bapt. Ch., 1969. Assoc. pastor Van Born Bapt. Ch., Dearborn Heights, Mich., 1968-69; pastor Calvary Bapt. Ch., Armada, Mich., 1969-82, Gaylord, Mich., 1982—; prin., tchr. Calvary Bapt. Acad., Armada, 1974-82, Calvary Bapt. Acad., 1983—. Author: Premarital Petting, 1981, Bad News and Good News, 1993, Forbidden, 1995. Campaign organizer Allen Lowe Campaign, Gaylord, 1992. With USMC, 1959-63. Mem. Am. Assn. Christian Schs., Mich. Assn. Christian Schs., Christian Law Assn. Office: Calvary Bapt Ch 225 S Wisconsin St Gaylord MI 49735

HARWOOD, VIRGINIA ANN, retired nursing educator; b. Lawrenceville, Ohio, Nov. 5, 1925; d. Warren Leslie and Ruth Ann (Wilson) H.; m. Kenneth Dale Juillerat, Dec. 21, 1946 (div. 1972); children: Rozanne Augsburger, Vicki Sue Terry, Carol Mann, Karen Juillerat. RN, City Hosp. Sch. Nursing, Springfield, Ohio, 1946; BSN, Ind. U., 1968; MS in Edn., Purdue U., 1973, PhD, 1982. Cert. psychiat./mental health nurse, ANA. Staff nurse various hosps., 1946-60; pub. health nursing supr. Whitley County Health Dept., Columbia City, Ind., 1960-65; nursing supr., coordinator staff devel. Ft. Wayne (Ind.) State Hosp., 1965-69; faculty sch. nursing Parkview Hosp., Ft. Wayne, 1969-74; faculty dept. nursing Ball State U., Muncie, Ind., 1974-77; dir. nursing program Thomas More Coll., Ft. Mitchell, Ky., 1977-79; faculty sch. nursing Purdue U., West Lafayette, Ind., 1979-80; dean sch. nursing Ashland (Ohio) Coll., 1980-83; retired, 1983-86; charge nurse admission psychiat. unit VA Med. Ctr., Marion, Ind., 1986-93, ret., 1994—. Active Rep. Nat. Com., 1978—, U.S. Senatorial Club, 1984—, Rep. Pres. Task Force, 1982—; mem. ch. coun. Grace Luth. Ch., Gas City, Ind., 1993—; bd. dirs. Luth. Ctr., Ball State U., Muncie, Ind. Mem. Am. Nurses Found., Mensa, Sigma Theta Tau. Home: 6611 Quail Ridge Ln Marion IN 46804

HASAN, SYED EQBAL, environmental geologist, educator; b. Patna, Bihar, India, Apr. 15, 1939; came to U.S. 1973; s. Syed Mohammad and Heyat (Imam) H.; m. Faruukh Hasan, Jan. 26, 1968; children: Danish, Zeenat, Zeba. BS, Patna U., 1960; MS, Roorkee U., India, 1963; PhD, Purdue U., 1978. Jr. geologist Geol. Survey of India, Lucknow, 1965-70, sr. geologist, 1971-73; vis. asst. prof. Mich. Tech. U., Houghton, 1978, U. Ariz., Tucson, 1978-79; asst. prof. geology U. Mo., Kansas City, 1979-84, assoc. prof., 1984—. Author: (textbook) Geology and Hazardous Waste Management, 1995. Fellow Geol. Soc. India (life), Geol. Soc. Am.; mem. Assn. Mo. Geologists, Assn. Engring. Geologists (chmn. Kansas City-Omaha sect. 1989-91), Internat. Assn. Engring. Geologists, Sigma Xi. Office: Univ of Mo Dept Geosciences Kansas City MO 64110-2499

HASARA, KAREN A., state legislator; b. Springfield, Ill., Oct. 17, 1940; m. Jerry Gott; 4 children. BA, Sangamon State U. Mem. dist. 50 Ill. State Ho. of Reps., 1986-91, 92-94; mem. appropriations I, elem. and sec. edn., counties and twps., agrl., children, aging, small bus., coal devel., mkt., fin. inst. and human svc. coms., now spokesman on mental health, now vicespokesman on state govt. adminstrn. Home: E-1 E Stratton Bldg Springfield IL 62706 Office: Ill State Senate State Capitol Springfield IL 62701-1725*

HASCHEK-HOCK, WANDA MARIA, veterinary pathologist, toxicologist, educator, researcher; b. London, Sept. 7, 1949; came to U.S., 1974; d. Karol A. Haschek and Maria U. Adamska; m. Vincent F. Hock, Jr., Aug. 7, 1976. BVSc, Sydney U., Australia, 1972; PhD, Cornell U., 1977. Diplomate Am. Coll. Vet. Pathologists, Am. Bd. Toxicology. Postdoctoral fellow Cornell U., Ithaca, N.Y., 1977; research assoc. Oak Ridge (Tenn.) Nat. Lab., 1981-82, research staff mem. I, 1981-82; assoc. prof. veterinary medicine U. Ill., Urbana, 1982-90; prof. U. Ill., 1990—; head Dept. of Vet. Pathobiology, 1994—, acting dir. Labs. of Vet. Diagnostic Labs., 1995-96; affiliate Inst. Environ. Studies, U. Ill., Urbana, 1983—; cons. Toxigenics, Inc., Decatur, Ill., 1982-83, Los Alamos (N.Mex.) Nat. Lab., 1986-87. Editor 1 book; contbr. chpts. to books, articles to profl. jours. Mem. AAAS, AVMA, Am. Coll. Vet. Pathologists (editl. bd. 1984-86, exam com. 1991-92), Soc. Toxicologic Pathologists (midwest region vice chair 1986-87, chair 1987-88, nat. program com. 1990-91, councillor 1992-96, chair exec. com. 1994-95, editl. bd. 1992-95), Soc. Toxicology (editl. bd. assoc. editor 1995—), Comparative Respiratory Soc. (bd. dirs. 1986-88), Phi Kappa Phi, Phi Zeta. Office: U Ill Dept Vet Pathobiology 2001 S Lincoln Ave Urbana IL 61801-6178

HASEK, JANE ELLEN, chancellor; b. Chgo., Feb. 23, 1940; d. Harold Chester and Margaret Lillian (Kennedy) Blecher; m. Wayne Earl HAsek, Aug. 7, 1960; children: Susan Randall, Mark. B of Liberal Studies, U. Okla., 1978; MS in Higher Edn., Drake U., 1982; D of Ednl. Adminstrn., U. No. Iowa, 1987. Instr. oper. rm. tech. St. Francis Hosp., Waterloo, Iowa, 1970-71; instr. emergency med. tech. Hawkeye Inst. Tech., Waterloo, Iowa, 1971-82; coord. cardiac rehab. program St. Francis Hosp., 1970-72, supr. spl. care units, 1970-74, dir. insvc., 1971-74; ednl. cons. Black Hawk Area Family Practice Residency Program, Waterloo, 1978-81; coord. adult health occupations Hawkeye Inst. Tech., 1974-80; v.p. edn. Allen Meml. Hosp., Waterloo, 1980-95; chancellor Allen Coll. Nursing, Waterloo, 1989—; mem. task force Iowa Bd. Nursing, Des Moines; cons. N.E. Iowa Family Practice Residency, Waterloo, 1977-83; mem. gov.'s task force Emergency Med. Svc., Des Moines, 1976-82. Newsletter editor: Tech. Edn. News, 1977, Iowa Bd. Nursing, 1989-90. Bd. dirs. Iowa State Dept. Health, Des Moines, 1989—; cmty. advisor Jr. League, Waterloo/Cedar Falls, Iowa, 1994-95; bd. dirs. Kiwanis, Waterloo, 1993-95; pres. sch. bd. Reinbeck (Iowa) Schs., 1981-90. Recipient Gov.'s award Outstanding Vol. Svc., Iowa, 1991; named Alumni of Yr., Lincoln Gen. Hosp. Sch. Nursing, 1989. Mem. ANA, Nat. League Nursing, Iowa Nurses Assn. (rsch. bd.), Iowa League Nursing (v.p. 1989-90), Phi Delta Kappa, Sigma Theta Tau. Independent. Methodist. Office: Allen Coll Nursing 1825 Logan Ave Waterloo IA 50703

HASELWOOD, JAMES EDWARD, automotive company executive; b. Elkhart, Ind., July 31, 1942; s. Willis Eads and Irma G. (Bockwitz) H.; m. Darlene Brosnan, Dec. 19, 1969 (div.); children: Barrett Devereaux, Devin Tyrell; m. Carolyn L. Haselwood, June 24, 1989. BS in Sci. Engring., U. Mich., 1965, BS in Engring. Math., 1965; MBA, Harvard U., 1969; MA in Econs., Wayne State U., 1983. Fin. analyst Chrysler Corp., Highland Park, Mich., 1969-72; plant comptroller Detroit Forge Plant Chrysler Corp., 1972-74; mgr. resource planning Parts div. Chrysler Corp., Center Line, Mich., 1974-78; mgr. ops. rsch. Chrysler Corp., Highland Park, 1978-80, mgr. fin. systems, 1980-82, mgr. white collar productivity, 1982-88; sales distbn. exec. Sales div. Chrysler Corp., Warren, Mich., 1988-90; mgr. applications support MIS Chrysler Corp., Center Line, 1990-91, process mgr. mgmt. control MIS, 1991-94, mgr. rapid application devel. IS, 1994-96, mgr. LAN & C/S Svcs. IS, 1996—. Lt. (s.g.) USNR, 1965-72. Mem. Crescent Sail Yacht Club, Doublehanded Sailing Assn. (commodore 1989), Detroit Area Econ. Forum (chmn. 1987), Stein Collectors Internat. (pres. 1995-96). Home: 29350 Jefferson Ave Saint Clair Shores MI 48081-2601 Office: Chrysler Corp 12000 Chrysler Center Dr Highland Park MI 48288

HASEMEIER, ERIC FRANCIS, osteopathic physician, educator; b. Mar. 1, 1954. BS in Indsl. Engring., Va. Polytech. Inst., 1976; MBA, U. S.C., 1979; DO, U. North Tex., 1991. Adminstr. Carolinas Hosp. and Health Svcs., Winnsboro, S.C., 1976-79, Shriners Hosp. for Crippled Children, Phila., 1979-82, Qualicare, Inc., Chalmette, La., 1982-84; exec. dir. NuMed Med., Inc., Groves, Tex., 1984-87; resident Riverside Osteo. Hosp., Detroit Hosp. Corp., 1991-92; owner Westernport (Md.) Family Clinic, 1992-94; assoc. dean Ohio U. Med. Sch., 1994-95; pres. On Call Med. Assocs., 1995—. Contbr. articles to regional newspapers. Mem. Md. Osteo. Assn. (past pres., Physician of Yr. award 1995), Psi Sigma Alpha, Alpha Pi Mu. Home: 9 Windsong Dr Athens OH 45701-8899 Office: On Call Med Assocs Athens OH 45701

HASENOHRL, DONALD W., state legislator; b. Marshfield, Wis., Nov. 25, 1935; m. Kathleen Hasenohrl; children: Dena, Charles, Donald. Former farmer; mem. from dist. 70 Wis. State Assembly, Madison, 1974—, mem. hwy. com., 1979—, mem. excise and fees com., 1983—, chmn. transp. com., 1983—, mem. transp. project coms., mem. energy and commerce com., 1991—. Chmn. Wood County Dem. Com., 1963-64; mem. Marshfield City Planning Com., 1966-67; bd. dirs. Ctrl. Wis. State Fair Assn. Named Outstanding Legislator of Yr., Wis. Mfr. Housing Assn., 1983. Mem. KC, Eagles, Bus. and Profl. Women's Club, Ctrl. Wis. Sportsmen's Club, Eau Pleine Boat Club. Home: 9516 Bluff Dr Pittsville WI 54466-9763*

HASEN-SINZ, SUSAN KATHERINE, state agency administrator, actress; b. LaGrange Park, Ill., Jan. 30, 1965; d. Hans and June Catherine (Huml) H. BA in Polit. Sci., Spanish, U. Ill., 1987; postgrad., Loyola U., Chgo. Actress Springfield (Ill.) Theatre Ctr., 1987—; mem. mgmt. staff Ill. Dept. Driver Svcs., Chgo., Gov.'s Office Ill. Dept. Pub. Aid; mgr. employee svcs., divsn. chief Gov.'s Office Ill. Toll Hwy. Authority, Downers Grove; speaker various youth groups, 1985—; dance instr. YMCA, Springfield, 1987, counselor Miss Ill./USA Pageant, Arlington Heights, Ill., 1987; fellow adminstrv. hearings under Sec. of State Jim Edgar, Springfield, 1987—. Lead actress A Day in Hollywood-A Night in the Ukraine, 1987 (Best of Springfield award), 42d St., Ill., 1991—, Oklahoma, Ill., The Dance Factory, Chgo., A...My Name Is Still Alice, Chgo.; actress Manny, nat. tour A Christmas Carol, 1989, Joseph and the Amazing Technicolor Dreamcoat, Ill.; supporting actress Singin' in the Rain, Ill.; backup singer Kenny Rogers Christmas Tour, Ill.; actress, singer, dancer Jesus Christ Superstar, 1992; singer Miss Ill./USA Pageant, 1987; understudy Puttin On the Ritz, Ill., West Side Story, Ill. Active in drama ministry Hope Ch., Springfield; soloist Christ Ch. of Oak Brook, Ill., 1983—, leader youth group Koinonia; student del. Internat. Strategic Affairs Conf., N.Y.C., 1987—; mem. campaign staff Jim Edgar for Gov. Ill., 1991; judge Miss Teen Ill./U.S.A. Pageant; staff asst. Congressman Harris Fawell's Office; rep. for 13th dist. Ill.; soloist Christ Ch. Oak Brook. Recipient Miss Amity award Miss. I.../U.S.A., 1986; scholarship winner Miss Illini contest. Mem. U. Ill. Alumni Assn. (named one of 100 top srs. at Champaign-Urbana campus 1986, named outstanding student 1986-87), Kappa Alpha Theta, Kappa Alpha Theta Alumni Assn. (chaplain, pres. standards com. 1986-87, songleader 1986-87). Home: 1447 Bannock Ct Bartlett IL 60103-2978 Office: One Authority Dr Downers Grove IL 60515-1703

HASKIN, J. MICHAEL, lawyer; b. Kansas City, Mo., Sept. 25, 1949; s. Harley V. and Geraldine E. (Porterfield) H. BA, Baker U., 1971; JD, U. Mo., 1976. Bar: Kans., Mo., U.S. Fed. Tax Ct., U.S. Supreme Ct. Ptnr., atty. Haskin, Hinkle, Slater & Snowbarger, Olathe, Kans., 1976-83, Dietrich, Davis, Dicus, Rowlands, Schmitt & Gorman, Kansas City, Mo., 1984-88; pres., atty. J. Michael Haskin, P.A., Olathe, 1989—; bd. dirs., exec. com., The Assn. K-10 Corridor Devel., Inc., Lawrence, 1993-95. City councilman-at-large City of Olathe, 1989-93, mayor, 1993-95; mem., vice chmn., chmn. Stormwater Mgmt. Adv. Coun., Johnson County, Kans., 1989-95; bd. dirs. Olathe Pub. Libr., 1989-90, 93-95; bd. dirs. Hidden Glen Arts Festival, vice chmn., chmn., 1990—); mem. Mid-Am. Regional Coun. Perimeter Transp. Com., 1995—. Recipient Boss of Yr. award Johnson County Legal Secs. Assn., 1991-92, Cmty. Leadership award Olathe Area C. of C., 1992. Mem. Kans. Bar Assn., Mo. Bar Assn., Olathe Rotary Club (bd. dirs., pres. 1981—, Paul Harris award 1992, Olathe Rotarian of Yr. 1995), Olathe Arts Alliance (pres. 1988), Kaw Valley Philological Soc. Republican. Methodist. Office: J Michael Haskin P A P O Box 413 100 E Park Ste 203 Olathe KS 66051

HASKINS, KRISTEN ELIZABETH, psychologist; b. Cleve., Mar. 22, 1944; d. Lester Ray Haskins and Helen Pauline (Maiden) Ecsy. BA, Antioch Coll., 1967; MA, U. Dayton, 1975; PsyD, Wright State U., 1981. Lic. psychologist, Ohio; diplomate Bd. Cert. Forensic Examiners. Dir. Operation Big Sister, Springfield, Ohio, 1967-68; rsch. asst. Fels Rsch. Inst., Yellow Springs, Ohio, 1968-69; probation counselor Montgomery County Juvenile Ct., Dayton, Ohio, 1969-73, psychol. asst., 1973-74; clin. coord. Buckeye Boys Ranch, Inc., Grove City, Ohio, 1974-77, clin. dir., 1977-79; intern psychology Dayton Mental Health Ctr., 1979-80, Wayne A. Oliver, Ph.D., Columbus, Ohio, 1980-81; psychologist, asst. dir. Netcare Forensic Psychiatry Ctr., Columbus, 1981-93, asst. dir., 1987-92, dir., 1992-93; pvt. practice Grove City, 1988—; psychology cons. Ohio Rehab. Svcs. Commn. Bur. Disability Determination, 1993—, Ctrl. Ohio Psychiat. Hosp. Timothy B. Moritz Forensic Unit, 1994—. Jr. Women's Club scholar, 1962. Mem. APA, Am. Coll. Forensic Examiners, Ohio Psychol. Assn., Ctrl. Ohio Psychol. Assn. Home: 2627 Dartmoor Rd Grove City OH 43123-3336

HASKINS, PERRY GLEN, insurance company executive; b. Idaville, Ind., Feb. 4, 1938; s. Homer G. and Dorothy H. (Adsit) H.; divorced; 1 child, Darla A.; m. Janet L. Cobble, May 25, 1962 (div. June 1987). Computer operator Hyster Co., Danville, Ill., 1960-62; agt. Farm Bur. Ins., Delphi, Ind., 1962-65; pres. The Haskins Co., Monticello, Ind., 1965—. Dist. extension chmn. Boy Scouts Am., Ind., 1974-75; pres. Community Recreation Inc., Monticello, 1975-76. With U.S. Army, 1956-62. Mem. AMVETS, CLU (pres. 1974-75), Life Underwriters Assn. (pres. 1970-71), Million Dollar Round Table, Estate Planning Coun., Rotary (pres. 1967-68, gov. 1974-75, citation for meritorious svc. 1974-75, disting. svc. award 1977-78), Moose. Republican. Baptist. Home and Office: The Haskins Co 919 N Main St Monticello IN 47960-1502

HASLER, ALEXANDER, advertising executive, consultant; b. Columbia, July 12, 1963; m. Sheila Hasler. Attended, U. Okla., 1983-86. Rep. candidate 1st dist. Mo. U.S. House of Reps., 1996. With USAF, 1982-87, Mo. Nat. Guard, 1987-90. Office: Hasler For Congress PO Box 16252 Saint Louis MO 63105*

HASLER DOGGETT, STACY LYNN, mental health counselor; b. Jefferson City, Mo., Aug. 23, 1966; d. William Edward and Linda Kay (Linsenbardt) Hasler; m. Michael Joseph Doggett, Sept. 18, 1993. BS in Psychology, Lincoln U. of Mo., 1988, MEd in Guidance Counseling, 1990. Lic. profl. counselor, Mo.; cert. nat. counselor. Title III program asst. Lincoln U. of Mo., Jefferson City, 1989-91; community support specialist Family Mental Health Ctr., Jefferson City, 1991-92; community support worker Ctr. for Psychiat. Rehab., Columbia, Mo., 1992-93, dir., 1993-95; counselor Profl. Counseling Assocs., Jefferson City, 1995—; mgr. Hasler's Stables, Jefferson City, 1992—; guest speaker TV program, Jefferson City, 1992; counselor Profl. Counseling Assocs., 1994—. Mem. Citizen Adv. Bd., Cole, Monteau and Osage Counties, 1992—; pres. Margaret cir., St. Paul's Evangelical Luth. Ch., 1994—, mem. choir, 1992—, mem. WELCA coun., 1994—. Mem. ACA, Mo. Counseling Assn. (state liaison to profl. bd. registration), Assn. Humanistic Edn. and Devel., Am. Assn. Marriage and Family Therapists, Assn. Play Therapy, Mo. Assn. Play Therapy, Am. Quarter Horse Assn. Office: Profl Counseling Assocs Doctors Park 1111 Madison St Jefferson City MO 65101

HASLEY, RONALD K., bishop; b. Butte, Mont., Oct. 25, 1935; m. Eleanore B. Hasley; children: Christine Marie Hasley Nakonechny, Russell Lee. BA, Pacific Luth. U., 1957; MDiv, Augustana Theol. Seminary, 1961; DD, Carthage Coll., Kenosha, Wis., 1990; LHD, Augustana Coll., 1991. Accredited chaplain, Coll. Chaplains, 1967. Pastor St. Mark's Luth. Ch., Winnipeg, Man., Can., 1961-66; chaplain res. Emanuel Hosp., Portland, Oreg., 1966-67; dir. pastoral care Luth. Hosp., Moine, Ill., 1967-87; bishop Evang. Luth. Ch. in Am., Rockford, Ill., 1987—; mem. exec. bd. Ill. Synod, 1982-88, human svcs. bd. Luth. Hosp., 1984-88; bd. dirs. Augustana Coll., Rock Island. Co-author: Befrienders, Teaching Lay People Caring. Mem. congregation Our Savior's Luth. Ch., Rockford, Ill.; bd. dirs. Am. Cancer Soc., Moline, 1980-86, Luth. Social Svcs. Ill. Fellow Coll. Chaplains Am. Protestant Health Assn. Home: 112 N Calvin Park Blvd Rockford IL 61107-4603 Office: Evang Luth Ch in Am No Ill Synod 103 W State St Rockford IL 61101-1105

HASSARD, HELENA, state legislator. Mem. S.D. Ho. of Reps., Pierre; mem. commerce, health and human svcs. coms. Republican.

HASSELBALCH, MARILYN JEAN, state official; b. Omaha, Jan. 2, 1930; d. Paul William and Helga Esther (Nodgaard) Campfield; m. Hal Burke Hasselbalch, June 13, 1954 (div. 1973); children: Kurt Campfield, Eric Burke, Peter Nels, Ane Catherine. BA with high distinction, U. Nebr., 1951. Cert. secondary tchr., Nebr. Pub. sch. tchr. Omaha and Long Beach, Calif., 1951-55; staff asst. U.S. Congressman Charles Thone, Lincoln, Nebr., 1973-78, Gov. of Nebr., Lincoln, 1978-82; exec. asst. Nebr. State Treas., Lincoln, 1983-86; sr. asst. Nebr. Gov. Kay A. Orr, Lincoln, 1987-91; exec. dir. Nebr. Appraiser Licensing Bd., Lincoln, 1991—. Mem. camp bd. dirs. YMCA, Nebr., 1969-70; mem. Nebr. Edn. Policies Commn., 1982; state conv. del. Rep. Party Nebr., 1986, 88; gov.'s rep. Nebr. State Hist. Soc., Lincoln, 1987-89; del. Edn. Commn. on States, Balt., 1988; participant strategic leadership for gubernatorial execs. Duke U., 1988; sec. Mission bd. Christ Luth. Ch., 1993—; treas. Danish Sisterhood # 90, 1995—. Named to Outstanding Young Women Am., 1961. Mem. Nat. Fedn. Rep. Women, Lancaster County Rep. Women (exec. bd. 1988), Am. Legion Aux., Assn. Appraiser Regulatory Ofcls. (bd. dirs. 1995—), Danish Sisterhood Am., Phi Beta Kappa, Theta Sigma Phi, Kappa Tau Alpha. Lutheran. Home: 4705 South St Lincoln NE 68506-1257 Office: Real Estate Appraiser Bd Nebr State Office Bldg Lincoln NE 68509

HASSELMO, NILS, university official, linguistics educator; b. Kola, Sweden, July 2, 1931; came to U.S., 1958; s. A. Wilner and Anna Helena (Backlund) H.; m. Patricia June Tillberg, Oct. 25, 1958; children: Nils Peter, Michael Erik, Anna Patricia. Fil. mag., Uppsala U., 1956, Fil. lic., 1962, Filosofie Doktor h.c., 1979; B.A., Augustana Coll., 1957; Ph.D., Harvard U., 1961. Asst. prof. Swedish Augustana Coll., Rock Island, Ill., 1958-59, 61-63; assoc. prof. Scandinavian langs. and lit. U. Minn., Mpls., 1965-70, prof., chmn. Scandinavian langs. and lit., 1970-73, dir. Ctr. for Northwest European Langs. and Area Studies, 1970-73, assoc. dean Coll. Liberal Arts, 1973-78, v.p. for adminstrn. and planning, 1980-83; sr. v.p. acad. affairs, provost U. Ariz., Tucson, 1983-88, prof. English and linguistics, 1983-88; pres. U. Minn., Mpls., 1988—; mem. vis. com. dept. Germanic langs. and lit. Harvard U., Cambridge, Mass., 1981-86; trustee Nat. Merit Scholarship Corp., 1992—. Author: Amerikasvenska, 1974, Swedish America: An Introduction, 1976; editor: Perspectives on Swedish Immigration, 1978. Bd. dirs. Swedish Council Am., 1978—, Walker Art Ctr., 1989-95; mem. Gov.'s Task Force on Technology and Improvement of Employment, Minn., 1982-83; mem. bd. overseers Mpls. Coll. Art & Design, 1982-83; trustee Am. Scandinavian Found., 1992—. Served to sgt. Royal Signal Corps, Swedish Army, 1951-54. Fulbright-Hays fellow, 1968; decorated Royal Order of North Star Sweden, 1973; recipient King Carl XVI Gustaf's Bicentennial medal in Gold Sweden, 1976, Swedish-Am. of Yr. award Swedish Govt. and Vasa Order Am., 1991, Ellis Island medal of honor, 1993. Mem. MLA, Soc. for Advancement Scandinavian Study (pres. 1971-73), Linguistic Soc. Am., Vetenskaps-Societeten, Royal Gustavus Adolphus Acad., Swedish-Am. Hist. Soc. (chmn. bd. 1984-86), Nat. Assn. State Univs. and Land Grant Colls. (exec. com. Acad. Affairs Coun. 1986-88, chmn. coun. pres. and chancellors 1992-93, chair bd. 1994-95), Univ. Rsch. Assn. (trustee 1993—).

HASSELQUIST, MAYNARD BURTON, lawyer; b. Amador, Minn., July 1, 1919; s. Harry and Anna F. (Froberg) H.; m. Lorraine Swenson, Nov. 20, 1948; children: Mark D., Peter L. BSL, U. Minn., 1941; JDL, U. Minn., 1947. Bar: Minn. 1948. Asst. mgr. taxation Gen. Mills Inc., Mpls., 1947-53; chmn. internat. dept. Dorsey & Whitney, Mpls., 1953-81, of counsel, 1981-91; retired, 1991; bd. dirs. McLaughlin Gormley King Co., Mpls. Bd. dirs. Gustavus Adolphus Coll., St. Peter, Minn., Swedish Council Am.; past chmn. Japan-Am. Soc. Minn.; bd. dirs., counsel James Ford Bell Library. Served with USN, 1941-46. Decorated knight Royal Order of North Star (Sweden). Mem. ABA, Minn. Bar Assn. Lutheran. Club: Mpls. Avocations: swimming, fishing, hiking, travel. Address (winter): 6834 Russet Sky Scottsdale AZ 85262 Office: Dorsey & Whitney 220 S 6th St Minneapolis MN 55402-4502

HASSERT, BRENT, state legislator. Owner Hassert Landscaping; mem. from 83d dist. Ill. Ho. of Reps. Formerly mem. Will County Bd. Commrs.; formerly chmn., exec. Pub. Works and Natural Resources Coms., Will County; formerly commr. Will County Forest Preserve; formerly mem. Ill. Task Force for Solid Waste Legislation. Home: RR 5 Lemont IL 60439-9805*

HASSETT, JACQUELYN ANN, retired nurse; b. La Crosse, Wis., Sept. 13, 1930; d. Frank Alois and Anne Helena (Milos) Spika; m. James John Hassett, Aug. 22, 1953; children: Barbara, Linda, Jean, Jane, Nancy, James David. Diploma in Nursing, St. Anthony de Padua Sch. Nursing, Chgo., 1951; BS, Barat Coll., 1977; MS, George Williams Coll., 1983. RN, Ill., Wis.; cert. coll. health nursing. Operating room nurse VA Hosp., North Chicago, Ill., 1951-54; part-time nursing positions St. Therese Hosp., Waukegan, Ill., 1954-58, Johnson Motors, Waukegan, 1958-64, VA Hosp., North Chicago, 1964-71; dir. health svcs. Coll. of Lake County, Grayslake, Ill., 1971-94; ret., 1994; co-chmn. Inst. Self-Study for Rehab. Act 1973, 1978. Mem. Project SUCCEED, No. Ill., 1980-81; com. mem. Health Systems Agy. Kane-Lake-McHenry Counties, 1978-80; vol. Lake County Cancer Soc., 1975—, Am. Heart Assn., 1975—; bd. dirs. Med. Svc. Adv. Com. Lake County Health Dept., 1980—. Recipient Appreciation cert. Lake County Bd. Commrs., 1978, Meritorious Svc. award Am. Heart Assn., 1979-82, Outstanding award No. Ill. Coun. on Alcoholism, 1982, Commendation for Svc. Lake County (Ill.) Health Dept., 1986. Mem. Am. Coll. Health Assn. (coun. of dels. 1978-80, 83—, program chmn. 1987-89, chmn. of sect. on nurse directed Coll. Health Svcs. 1989—, bd. dirs. region III rep. 1990—, Ruth E. Boynton award 1993, inducted into Fellows membership 1994), Mid-Am. Coll. Health Assn. (v.p. 1981-82, pres. 1983-84), No. Ill. Coll. Health Nurses Assn., Am. Legion Aux., Lake County Coun. Cath. Nurses. Roman Catholic. Home: 42749 Washington Ave Winthrop Harbor IL 60096-1033 Office: Coll of Lake County 19351 W Washington St Grayslake IL 60030-1148

HASSFURDER, LESLIE JEAN, principal; b. Bedford, Ind., June 26, 1943; d. Don Bernell and Rose E. (Bridwell) Armstrong; m. M. Duane Wilson, June 17, 1965 (dec. Aug. 1986); children: Douglas Troy, Marisa Lynn; m. Steven Wayne Hassfurder, Mar. 19, 1988; step-children: Holly Renee, Lorrie Leigh. BS, Ind. U., 1965, MS, 1971; EdS, Ind.-Purdue U., Indpls., 1984. Cert. tchr. and prin., Ind. Elem. tchr. Fontana, Calif., 1965-67, Churubusco, Ind., 1967-69; dir. presch., Goshen, Ind., 1977-80; prin. Pittsboro Elem. Sch. (Ind.), 1980—; dir. summer library. Co-author: Energy Play, 1982, operettas for local schs. Mem. Internat. Reading Assn., Mortar Bd., Enomone, Pleiades, Phi Delta Kappa, Alpha Delta Kappa. Republican. Mem. Christian Ch. (Disciples of Christ). Office: Pittsboro Elem Sch North Meridian Pittsboro IN 46167

HASSKAMP, KRIS, state legislator; b. Apr. 5, 1951. AA, Brainerd C.C.; BS, Bemidji State U. State rep. Dist. 12A, Minn., 1988—; mem. com. edn. judiciary & local govt. coms., vice chmn. energy com., com. & econ. devel.-tourism & small bus. divsn. com., mem. environ. & natural resources-fin. divsn. gen. legis., vet. affairs & elec. coms., Minn. Ho. of Reps. Home: 405 Superior Ave Crosby MN 56441-1264 Office: Minn State Senate State Capital Building Saint Paul MN 55155-1606*

HASSLER, DONALD MACKEY, II, English language educator, writer; b. Akron, Ohio, Jan. 3, 1937; s. Donald Mackey and Frances Elizabeth (Parsons) H.; m. Diana Cain, Oct. 8, 1960 (dec. Sept. 1976); children: Donald, David; m. Sue Smith, Sept. 13, 1977; children: Shelly, Heather. B.A. (Sloan fellow), Williams Coll., 1959; M.A. (Woodrow Wilson fellow), Columbia U., 1960, Ph.D., 1967. Instr. U. Montreal, 1961-65; instr. English Kent (Ohio) State U., 1965-67, asst. prof., 1967-71, assoc. prof., 1971-76, prof., 1977—, acting dean honors and exptl. coll., 1979-81, dir., 1973-83, coord. writing cert. program, 1986-91, chmn. undergrad. studies, 1987-91, dir. Wick Poetry Competition, 1987-91, coord. grad. studies, 1991—; sec. faculty senate Kent (Ohio State U., 1996—. Author: Erasmus Darwin, 1974, The Comedian as the Letter D: Erasmus Darwin's Comic Materialism, 1973, Asimov's Golden Age: The Ordering of an Art, 1977, Hal Clement, 1982, Comic Tones in Science Fiction, 1982, Patterns of the Fantastic, 1983, Patterns of the Fantastic II, 1984, Death and the Serpent, 1985, Isaac Asimov, 1991; mng. editor Jour. Extrapolation, 1986-87, co-editor, 1987-89, editor, 1990—; co-editor (with Sue Hassler) Letters of Arthur Machen and Montgomery Evans, 1923-1947, 1993, (with Clyde Wilcox) Political Science Fiction, 1996; adv. editl. bd. Hellas, 1988—; editl. bd. Paradoxa, 1994—. Co-chmn. Kent Am. Revolution Bicentennial Commn., 1974-77; deacon Presbyn. Ch., 1971-74, elder, 1974-77; sec. Kent State Faculty Senate, 1996—. Recipient J. Lloyd Eaton award Eaton Libr. Collection U. Calif., Riverside, 1993. Mem. Sci. Fiction Rsch. Assn. (treas. 1983-84, pres. 1985-86), Kiwanis (bd. dirs. 1974-76), Phi Beta Kappa (pres. 1983-84). Home: 1226 Woodhill Dr Kent OH 44240-2832

HASSLER, JON FRANCIS, novelist; b. Mpls., Mar. 30, 1933; s. Leo Blaise and Ellen Frances (Callinan) H.; children: Michael, Elizabeth, David. BA, St. John's U., 1955; MA, U. N.D., 1961; LLD (hon.), Assumption Coll., 1993, U. N.D., 1994, U. Notre Dame, 1996. Tchr. Melrose, Fosston, Park Rapids (Minn.) High Schs., 1955-65, Bemidji State U., Minn., 1965-68, Brainerd C.C., Minn., 1968-80; regents prof. St. John's U., Collegeville, Minn., 1981—. Author: Staggerford, 1977 (Friends of Am. Writers Novel of Yr. award 1978), Four Miles to Pinecone, 1977, Simon's Night, 1979, Jemmy, 1980, The Love Hunter, 1981, A Green Journey, 1985, Grand Opening, 1987 (Soc. of Midland Authors Best Work of Fiction award 1988), North of Hope, 1990, Dear James, 1993, Rookery Blues, 1995. Fellow Guggenheim 1980, Minn. State Arts Bd. 1979, 85. Roman Catholic. Office: St John's Univ Collegeville MN 56321

HASTERT, (J.) DENNIS, congressman; b. Aurora, Ill., Jan. 2, 1942; m. Jean Kahl, 1973; children: Joshua, Ethan. BA, Wheaton Coll., 1964; MS, No. Ill. U., 1967. Tchr., coach Yorkville (Ill.) High Sch.; mem. Ill. House Reps., Springfield, 1980-86, 100th-104th Congresses from 14th dist. Ill., 1987—; mem. commerce com. Lodge: Lions (Yorkville). Office: US Ho of Reps 2453 Rayburn HOB Washington DC 20515-1314*

HASTIE, RONALD LESLIE, sales executive; b. Perry, Iowa, July 29, 1941; s. Leslie Hope and Leona Nadine (Verchio) H.; m. Patricia Louise Agee, Apr. 29, 1961; children: Lori Lynn, Lisa Lynn, Jennifer Lynn. Grad. pub. schs., Rippy, Iowa. Salesman Standard Oil Co., Des Moines, 1960-70; sales mgr. Jewel Co., Perry, 1970-83; ter. mgr. sales, water treatment specialist State Chem. Co., Boone, Iowa, 1983—. Mem. NRA, Sportsman Club. Republican. Home: 221 Linn St Boone IA 50036-3733 Office: State Chem Co 3100 Hamilton Ave Cleveland OH 44114-3701

HASTING, SHARON RUTH, pediatric nurse; b. Rock City, Ill., Aug. 18, 1954; d. Howard Weede and Alta Mary (Tielkemeier) Kilpatrick; m. Robin Lee Hasting; children: William Howard, Joshua David. BS in Nursing, San Jose State U., 1983; MS in Nursing, U. Wis., 1991. Cert. pediat. nurse practitioner. Clin. nursing instr. Highland C.C., Freeport, Ill., 1983-84; staff nurse, cert. pediat. nurse practitioner Rockford (Ill.) Meml. Sys., 1984-96; cert. pediat. nurse practitioner Freeport Health Network, 1996—. Fellow Nat. Assn. Pediat. Nurse Practitioners & Assocs., Sigma Theta Tau. Lutheran. Home: 13216 E Krise Rd Stockton IL 61085 Office: Freeport Clinic 1036 W Stephenson St Freeport IL 61032

HASTINGS, WILLIAM CHARLES, retired state supreme court chief justice; b. Newman Grove, Nebr., Jan. 31, 1921; s. William C. and Margaret (Hansen) H.; m. Julie Ann Simonson, Dec. 29, 1946; children—Pamela, Charles, Steven. B.Sc., U. Nebr., 1942, J.D., 1948; LHD (hon.), Hastings Coll., 1991. Bar: Nebr. 1948. With FBI, 1942-43; mem. firm Chambers, Holland, Dudgeon & Hastings, Lincoln, 1948-65; judge 3d jud. dist. Nebr., Lincoln, 1965-79; judge Supreme Ct. Nebr., Lincoln, 1979-88, chief justice, 1988-95; ret., 1995; bd. dirs. Nat. Conf. Chief Justices, 1989-91. Pres. Child Guidance Ctr., Lincoln, 1962, 63; v.p. Lincoln Community Coun., 1968, 69; vice chmn. Antelope Valley coun. Boy Scouts Am., 1968, 69; pres. 1st Presbyn. Ch. Found., 1968—. Served with AUS, 1943-46. Mem. ABA, Nebr. Bar Assn. (George H. Turner award 1991, Pioneer award 1992), Lincoln Bar Assn., Nebr. Dist. Judges Assn. (past pres.), Nat. Conf. Chief Justices (past bd. dirs.), Phi Delta Phi. Republican. Presbyterian (deacon, elder, trustee). Club: East Hills Country (pres. 1959-60), Lincoln Univ., Nebr. Home: 1544 S 58th St Lincoln NE 68506-1407 Office: Nebr Supreme Ct 2413 State Capital Bldg Lincoln NE 68509

HATCH, EDWARD WILLIAM (TED HATCH), health care executive; b. Greenwich, Conn., Jan. 2, 1952; s. Denison Hurlbut and Louise (Bingham) H.; m. Jean Brummer, May 26, 1990. BA, Beloit Coll., 1974; MAHCA, George Washington U., 1978. Planning assoc. East Cen. Ill. Health Systems Agy., Champaign, 1978-81; mgr. planning & mktg. Evang. Health Systems, Oak Brook, Ill., 1981-82, coord. instl. planning & mktg., 1983-84; dir. mktg. Bethany Hosp., Chgo., 1985-86; v.p. planning Holy Family Hosp., Des Plaines, Ill., 1986-87; exec. dir. Behavioral Health Systems, Palos Heights, Ill., 1987-88, chief exec. officer, 1989-91; pres., CEO Behavioral Health Sys., Burr Ridge, Ill., 1991-94; phys. hosp. orgn. adminstr. Columbia Behavioral Health, Forest Park, Ill., 1996—. Contbr. articles to profl. jours. Mem. Am. Coll. Health Care Execs., Chgo. Health Execs. Forum (pres. 1989, sec. 1988, program chmn. 1987). Office: Behavioral Health Systems Ste 305 485 S Frontage Rd Burr Ridge IL 60521-7110

HATCHER, EDWARD LUVERNE, agriculturalist; b. Oskaloosa, Iowa, Sept. 10, 1946; s. Edward Luverne and Loretta Agnus (Armstrong) H.; m. Beverly Ann Arnaman, Nov. 29, 1968; children: Michael Aaron, Jason Edward. BS, Mo. State U., 1968, BS in Edn., 1968; MA, U. No. Iowa, 1972. Sci. tchr. Miles (Iowa) Community Schs., 1968-70; rsch. asst. U. No. Iowa, Cedar Falls, 1970-71, teaching asst., 1971-72; sci. tchr. Davenport (Iowa) Community Schs., 1972-79; adult edn. instr. Ea. Iowa Community Coll., Davenport, 1973-79; regional coord. Iowa Youth Conservation Corps, Des Moines, 1976-79; agriculturalist Grinnell, Iowa, 1979—; bd. dirs. Iowa Conservation Edn. Coun., Ames, 1979-80; environ. edn. cons. Iowa Youth Conservation Corps, 1976-80; asst. dist. commr. Iowa Dept. Soil Conservation, Malcom, 1981-84. Active Montezuma (Iowa) Cmty. Sch. Bd., 1984-93, pres., 1986-93; bd. dirs. Grinnel Regional Med. Ctr., 1991—, pres.-elect, 1996. Named Outstanding High Sch. Tchr. Iowa Iowa Conservation Edn. Coun., 1979, one of Outstanding Young Men Am., 1982; recipient Iowa Conservation award Des Moines Register, 1979. Fellow Iowa Acad. Sci.; mem. Iowa Sci. Tchrs. (pres. 1979-80), Beta Beta Beta, Iowa Youth Conservation Corps Assn. (Merit award 1980). Home and Office: 4633 70th St Grinnell IA 50112-8026

HATCHER, JAMES R., insurance executive; b. Muncie, Ind., May 14, 1942. BS in Edn., Ball State U., 1965, MEd, 1966; EdD, Ind. U., 1971. V.p. Albion (Mich.) Coll., 1979-85; pres. Ednl. and Instnl. Ins. Adminstrs., Chgo., 1985—, also bd. dirs.

HATCHER, MARIE THERESA, librarian; b. Evanston, Ill., Oct. 4; d. Lawrence William Sr. and Dorothy Agnes (Cullen) Lang; m. Bobby Dean Hatcher, June 14, 1975; children: Rosanne Marie, Robin Therese. BA, Coll. St. Francis, Joliet, Ill., 1970; MLS, Rosary Coll., 1971. Cert. libr. I, Wis. Libr. children E. St. Louis (Ill.) Pub. Libr., 1971-72; dir. Fox Lake (Ill.) Pub. Libr., 1972-76, Genoa City (Wis.) Pub. Libr., 1993—. Grantee State of Ill., 1970-71. Mem. ALA, Wis. Libr. Assn.

HATCHER, THOMAS FOUNTAIN, management consultant, publisher; b. Monroe, Mich., Dec. 26, 1931; s. Fountain H. and Cecilia E. (Boylan) H. m. Rosemary K. Downs, June 23, 1956; children: Mary Kathleen, Roberta Joan, Margaret Ann. BS, NYU, 1968. With Equitable Life Assurance Soc., N.Y.C., 1955-71, mgr. learning systems, 1968-71; owner Thomas Hatcher Assocs. Thomas Hatcher Assocs., Mpls., 1971-79; pres., owner Futures Unlimited, Inc., Mpls., 1979—; pres., CEO Profl. Publs., Mpls., 1988-90. Author: The Definitive Guide to Long Range Planning, 1981, 2d edit., 1988, Facilitator's Handbook for Planning, 1985. Mem. ASTD, Nat. Speakers Assn., Am. Soc. Profl. Cons. Roman Catholic. Home and Office: Futures Unlimited Inc 18525 Texas Ave Prior Lake MN 55372-3110

HATFIELD, JERRY LEE, plant physiologist, biometeorologist; b. Wamego, Kans., May 1, 1949; s. Virgil H. and Elsie L. (Fischer) H.; m. Patricia JoAnne Reigle, Sept. 1, 1968; children: Mark E., Andrew J. BS, Kans. State U., 1971; MS, U. Ky., 1972; PhD, Iowa State U., 1975. Biometeorologist U. Calif., Davis, 1975-83; plant physiologist USDA-Agrl. Rsch. Svc., Lubbock, Tex., 1983-89; lab. dir. Nat. Soil Tilth Lab., USDA-Agr. Rsch. Svc., Ames, Iowa, 1989—. Editor: Biometeorology and Integrated Pest management, 1982, Limitations to Plant Root Growth, vol. 19, Advances in Soil Science, 1992, Soil Biology: Impacts on Soil Quality, Advances in Soil Science, 1993, Crops Residue Management, Advances in Soil Science, 1994, Sustainable Agriculture Systems, 1994, Utilization of Manure as a Soil Resource, Advances in Soil Science, 1996; mem. editl. bd. Advances in Soil Sci.; contbr. over 220 articles to profl. jours. Fellow Soil Sci. Soc. Am., Am. Soc. Agronomy (editor jour. 1989-95), Crop Sci. Soc. Am.; mem. Am. Geophys. Union, Am. Meteorol. Soc. (chair agrl./forest com. 1980-81), Indian Agrometeorol. Soc. (hon.), Phi Kappa Phi. Republican. Office: USDA Agrl Rsch Svc Nat Soil Tilth Lab 2150 Pammel Dr Ames IA 50011-4420

HATFIELD, STUART A., stockbroker; b. Minot, N.D., June 13, 1964. Student, Franklin U., 1987-92. Lic. Nat. Assn. Securities Dealers. Stockbroker Corna Co. Investment, Columbus, Ohio, 1993—. Republican. Office: Corna Co Investments 5302 McKitrick Blvd Columbus OH 43235-7366

HATHAWAY, EDWARD WILLIAM, librarian; b. Mpls., July 14, 1961; s. Raymond Olmstead and Elaine Ormond (Bailey) H.; m. Pamela Mary Ann Haiden, Aug. 30, 1985; 1 child, Julia Mary Ann. BA, U. Minn., 1982; MLS, U. Wis., 1985. With Mpls. Pub. Libr. Mem. Soc. for Am. Baseball Rsch. (baseball online project dir. 1992—). Office: Mpls Pub Libr Sociology 300 Nicollet Mall Minneapolis MN 55401

HATHAWAY, RUTH ANN, chemist; b. Sidney, Ohio, Dec. 6, 1956; d. Earl Eugene and Mary Helen (Smith) Schmidt; m. Bruce Alan Hathaway, May 16, 1981. BS in Sci., Huntington Coll., 1979; postgrad., Purdue U., 1979-80. Instr. Harvey Mudd Coll., Claremont, Calif., 1981-82; head chemist So. Indsl. Products, Cape Girardeau, Mo., 1983-86; cons. Cape Girardeau, 1987-89; alterationist Patricks Cleaner, Cape Girardeau, 1988-89; lab. dir. Delta-Y Electric Co., Sedgewickville, Mo., 1989-91; quality control/quality assurance dir. Environ. Analysis South, Cape Girardeau, 1991-95; cons. Hathaway Cons., Cape Girardeau, 1995—. Editor: Safety Considerations in Microscale Lab, 1991; contbr. articles to profl. jours. Mem. exec. bd. dirs. NAACP, Cape Girardeau, 1986—; chmn. disaster com. ARC, Cape Girardeau, 1986-91; dir. S.E. Mo. Regional Sci. Fair, 1992—. Mem. Am. Chem. Soc. (divsn. environ. chem. health and safety 1989—, local sect. nat. chemistry week coord., 1988—), Am. Inst. Chemists, Internat. Assn. Water Quality, S.E. Mo. Local Emergency Planning Com. (chmn. 1989—). Republican. Home and Office: 1810 Georgia St Cape Girardeau MO 63701-3816

HATHEWAY, ALLEN WAYNE, geological engineer, educator; b. L.A., Sept. 30, 1937; s. Clarence Wilman and Marie Elizabeth (Sisto) H.; m. E. Anne Sellars, Apr. 4, 1959 (div. Jan. 1990); children: Shannon, Brian, Steven; m. Diane Rydell Anderson, July 15, 1994; stepchildren: James Anderson, Brendan Anderson. AB in Geology, UCLA, 1961; MS in Geol. Engring., U. Ariz., 1966, PhD in Geol. Engring., 1971, profl. degree in geol. engring., 1982. Registered profl. engr., Ariz., Calif., Mass., profl. geologist, Calif., Mo., Maine; cert. engr. geologist, Calif. Rsch. assoc. Lunar & Planetary Lab., Tucson, 1967-69; staff engr. Law Engring. Co., L.A., 1969-71; project mgr. geotech. br. U.S. Forest Svc., Arcadia, Calif., 1971-72; project mgr. Woodward-Clyde Cons., L.A., 1972-74; project geologist Shannon & Wilson Cons. Engrs., Burlingame, Calif., 1974-76; v.p., ch. geologist Haley & Aldrich Cons. Engrs., Cambridge, Mass., 1976-81; prof. geol. engring. U. Mo., Rolla, 1981—. Author: tech. manual) U.S. Army: Geotechnical Field Handbook, 1991; co-author: (textbook) Geology and Engineering, 3d edit., 1988, (tech. manual) Geophysical Methods for Hazardous Waste Site Characterization, 1992; editor, author: (tech. manual) AASHTO Manual of Subsurface Investment, 1988; editor jour. series Cities of the World, 1992—. Col. Corps. of Engrs. AUS, 1961-91, ret. Decorated U.S. Army Meritorious Svc. medal with 2 oak leaf clusters; recipient Cert. of Appreciation, Gov. of Mo., 1989. Fellow ASCE (Calif. Outstanding Young Civil Engr. 1973, Mead prize 1975), Geol. Soc. Am. (chmn. engring. geol. divsn. 1980, Burwell award 1981), Geol. Soc. London; mem. Assn. Engring. Geologists (pres. 1985, F.T. Johnston award 1994), Soc. Scabbard and Blade, Sigma Xi, Theta Xi, Sigma Gamma Epsilon. Home: 10256 Stoltz Dr Rolla MO 65401-7715 Office: U Mo Dept Geol Engring 129 Mcnutt Hall Rolla MO 65409-0230

HATHEWAY, JAY, history educator; b. L.A., Calif., Aug. 20, 1949; s. Joseph Gilbert and Joyce (Armstrong) H. BA, Claremont McKenna Coll., 1971; MA, Monterey Inst. Internat. Study, 1979; PhD, U. Wis., 1992. Publisher Among Friends Inc., Madison, Wis., 1982-87; adj. prof. history Cardinal Stritch Coll., Milw., 1987-91; assoc. dept. liberal studies U. Wis., Madison, 1989—; instr. history Edgewood Coll., Madison, Wis., 1991—; coord. human issues program Edgewood Coll., Madison, 1991-96; archivist of Edgewood Coll. Madison, 1996—. Contbr. articles to profl. jours. Active Gov. HIV Infection Adv. coun., Madison, 1989-90; bd. dirs. ACLU, Madison, 1991. 1st. lt. spl. forces U.S. Army 1971-76. Mem. Am. Historical Assn. Home: 217 W Washington Stoughton WI 53589 Office: Edgewood College Madison WI 53711

HATLEY, PATRICIA RUTH, school system administrator; b. Norborne, Mo., Sept. 8, 1945; d. William Bernard and Bessie (Evans) Henks; m. Richard V. Hatley, Aug. 17, 1985; children: Timothy Wilde, Kent Wilde; stepchildren: Christine, Angela. BS in Edn., Ctrl Mo. State U., 1966, MA, 1968; Ednl. Specialist, U. Mo., 1980, EdD, 1991. Cert. supt., prin., tchr., Mo. Tchr. English William Chrisman High Sch., Independence, Mo., 1968-80, asst. prin., 1980-87; asst. prin. for curriculum Blue Valley North High Sch., Overland Park, Kans., 1987-88; dir. secondary edn. Blue Springs (Mo.) R IV Schs., 1988—; chair lang. arts dept. Independence Pub. Schs., 1975-80; mem. adv. bd. Ea. Jackson County Alternative High Sch., Blue Springs, 1988-91, minority student summer program U. Mo., Columbia, 1991—. Active Planning and Zoning Commn., Blue Springs, 1976-80; mem. Mo. U. Alumni Bd., 1993-95. Recipient State Media award Mo. State Tchrs. Assn., 1988-89, 91, named Adminstr. of Yr., 1990. Mem. ASCD, Nat. Assn. Secondary Sch. Prins., Nat. Sch. Pub. Rels. Assn. (pres. Mo. chpt. 1995-96), Mo. Assn. Supervision and Curriculum Devel., Mo. Assn. Secondary Sch. Prins., Greater Kansas City Prins. Assn., Kansas City Network Women in Sch. Adminstrn. (pres. 1991-93), Mo. Network Women in Sch. Adminstrn. (chair exec. bd. 1995-96), Internat. Orgn. Women Edn., Internat. Reading Assn., C. of C., Phi Delta Kappa, Delta Kappa Gamma, Beta Sigma Phi (pres. 1979-80). Democrat. Roman Catholic. Office: Blue Springs R-IV Schs 1801 W Vesper St Blue Springs MO 64015-3219

HATLEY, RICHARD V(ON), education educator; b. Goodnight, Tex., Oct. 19, 1936; s. R.V. and Rula Belle (Evans) H.; m. Patricia Ruth Henks, Aug. 17, 1985; children: Christine L., Angela K.; stepchildren: Timothy A. Wilde, Kent C. Wilde. BA, Ea. N.Mex. U., 1959, MA, 1967, EdS, 1968; EdD, U. N.Mex., 1970. Cert. tchr., prin., sch. supt., Mo. Tchr. English Borger (Tex.) Ind. Sch. Dist., 1963-65, Amarillo (Tex.) Ind. Sch. Dist., 1965-67; adminstrv. intern Portales (N.Mex.) Mcpl. Schs., 1967-68; fin. cons. N.Mex. Dept. Edn., Santa Fe, 1968; grad. asst. U. N.Mex., Albuquerque, 1968-70; asst. prof., then assoc. prof. U. Kans., Lawrence, 1970-76; chair dept. ednl. adminstrn. U. Mo., Columbia, 1976-86, prof. ednl. leadership and policy analysis, 1976—; fin. cons. to Republic of Nicaragua, U.S. AID, Managua, 1971; salary cons. Platte County Schs., Platte City, Mo., 1980; reorgn. cons. St. Joseph (Mo.) Pub. Schs., 1982; referendum strategy cons. Jefferson City (Mo.) Pub. Schs., 1984, Ft. Osage (Mo.) Pub. Schs., 1991-92. Contbr. articles, revs. to profl. publs.; author reports, monographs. Active Blue Springs (Mo.) Schs. Citizens Adv. Com., 1988—. Grantee U.S. Office Edn., 1972, U.S. Dept. Edn., 1982-85. Mem. ASCD, Am. Ednl. Rsch. Assn. (program chair. 1983), Univ. Coun. Ednl. Adminstrn (exec. bd. 1983-89, pres. 1986-87), Masons, Phi Delta Kappa. Democrat. Office: U Mo Dept Ednl Leadership and Policy Analysis 211 Hill Hall Columbia MO 65211

HATLEY, WILLIAM PATRICK, investment executive; b. Mt. Glenn, Ill., June 17, 1941; m. Teresa S. Flamm, Nov. 24, 1960; children: Michael, Sabra, Shenee. Assoc., So. Ill. U., 1961. Engr. Luhr Bros. Cons., Columbia, Ill., 1961-70; owner Chrysler, Waterloo, Ill., 1970-83; investment exec. Stifel Nicolaus & Co., Belleville, Ill., 1983—, also bd. dirs., mem. pres.'s coun., 1993-95. Bd. dirs. Sch. Bd. Valmeyer, Ill., 1980-87. Mem. Red Bud Country Club. Office: Stifel Nicolaus & Co 1 Bronze Pt Belleville IL 62221-8190

HATTEBERG, DONALD G., electrical engineer; b. Storm Lake, Iowa, Oct. 16, 1958. BS in Elec. Engring., Iowa State U., 1981. Sr. elec. engr. ITT Corp., North St. Paul, Minn., 1990-92, FMCCorp., Mpls., 1985-90, 92—. Mem. IEEE. Home: 14203 Davenport St NE Ham Lake MN 55304-6826

HATTERVIG, ROBIN LYNN, dentist; b. Desmet, S.D., Apr. 4, 1958; s. Gene Willis and Harriet Ione (Larson) H.; m. Mirinda Marie Noonan, May 7, 1988; children: Erik Hunter, Auden Archer. BS, U. S.D., 1980; DDS, U. Nebr., 1984. Pvt. practice dentistry Howard, S.D., 1984—. Bd. dirs. East River Healthcare, 1991—, pres., 1992-94; trustee Bethany Luth. Ch., 1988-93, v.p., 1995—. Fellow Acad. Gen. Dentistry (pres. S.D. chpt. 1996—); mem. ADA, Am. Soc. Dentistry for Children, S.D. Dental Assn., S.D. Dental Found., Pierre Fauchard Acad., Howard Cmty. Club, Howard Svc. Club, Phi Beta Kappa, Omicron Kappa Upsilon. Republican. Lutheran. Home: 302 E Howard Ave Howard SD 57349-9021 Office: 112 N Main St Box W Howard SD 57349

HATTERY, ROBERT WILBER, political science educator; b. Chgo., Jan. 5, 1925; s. Wilber and Ruth (Adolphus) H.; m. Carolyn Potschke, Feb. 2, 1957 (dec. Feb. 1979); children: David Wilber, Lor Ruth, John Furer; m. Eleanor Lorraine Pumper, Dec. 28, 1984. PhB, U. Chgo., 1948, MA, 1954, PhD, 1961. From lectr. to asst. prof. U. Wis., Madison, 1955-62; from asst. to assoc. prof. Ind. U., Bloomington, 1962-87, assoc. prof. emeritus polit. sci. and continuing edn., 1987—; asst. dir. Salzburg Sem., Austria, 1960-61; adj. faculty, mem. adv. bd. Emeritus Coll., Coll. St. Scholastica, Duluth, Minn., 1994-95,. Reviewer books; contbr. articles to profl. jours. Bd. dirs. UN Assn., Duluth, 1991-94. Pfc. Inf., 1943-45. Decorated Purple Heart. Mem. AAAS, Am. Hist. Assn., Am. Polit. Sci. Assn., Internat. Studies Assn., Nat. U. Continuing Edn. Assn. 9bd. dirs. 1986-87), Ind. Acad. Social Scis. (life, sr. dir. studies 1980's), Nat. U. Continuing Edn. Assn. (bd. dirs. 1986-87, emeritus key holder 1987—). Home: HC 86 Box 575 Grand Marais MN 55604-9508

HATTON, CARY, counselor, mental health advocate/educator; b. June 20, 1949; d. Roy Elsworth Hatton and Loyce Elaine (Jarvis) Susco; m. Richard V. Gulley; children: Jessica E. Stone, Jessica A. Gulley, Elizabeth A. Gulley, Joshua C. Gulley. BA in English, Ohio U., 1970; MEd in Counseling, Wright State U., 1976; EdD in Counseling, U. Cin., 1984. Lic. profl. clin. counselor, Ohio. English tchr. Vandalia (Ohio) Butler Schs., 1971-75; counselor West Carrollton (Ohio) Schs., 1977-79; outpatient counselor South Cmty. Inc., Dayton, Ohio, 1980-83; dir. youth partial hospitalization program South Cmty. Inc., Dayton, 1983-87; dir. dist. II children's project Alcohol, Drug Abuse & Mental Health Svcs. Bd. Mont Co., Dayton, 1987-91; clin. dir. St. Joseph Children's Treatment Ctr., Dayton, 1991-93; svc. broker, adv. Alcohol, Drug Addiction & Mental Health Svcs. Sys. Mont Co., Dayton, 1993—; adv. bd. Millcreek Psychiat. Ctr. for Children, Cin., 1987-95; mem. children's case mgmt. task force Ohio Dept. Mental Health, Columbus, 1987-89; adj. prof. mental health Sinclair C.C., Dayton, 1993—; pvt. practice counselor Profl. Psychol. & Consultation, Dayton, 1993—. Contbr. chpt. to book. Office: South Cmty Children & Youth Svcs 349 W 1st Dayton OH 45402

HATZICHRONOGLOU, HELEN (LENA HATZICHRONOGLOU), Greek language and literature educator; b. Athens, Greece, Jan. 18, 1948; came to the U.S., 1974; U.S. citizen, 1994; d. Panayiotis and Zoe (Athanassiou) H. BA, U. Athens, 1971; MA, Cath. U. Am., 1977; PhD, Johns Hopkins U., 1985; postgrad., Am. Sch. Classical Studies, 1982, Dartmouth Coll., 1982. Tchr. high schs. Nafplion and Kiaton, Greece, 1972-74; instr. Internat. Ctr. for Lang. Studies, Washington, 1975-76; tchr. Greek Community Schs., Washington, Md. & Va., 1975-80; teaching asst. dept. classics Johns Hopkins U., Balt., 1979-80, instr. evening coll., 1982-83; vis. provisional asst. prof. classics and modern Greek U. Fla., Gainesville, 1983-85, asst. prof., 1985-90; modern Greek studies dir. Wayne State U., Detroit, 1990—; NEH reviewer, 1990—; reviewer Wayne State U. Press, 1993—; advisor text preparation of Nat. Greek Exam. Classical League, Amherst, Mass., 1991—; mem. grad. faculty of Fla., 1987, Wayne State U., 1991. Author: The Ideal of Arete and Its Treatment in Euripides, 1985; contbr. articles to profl. jours., chpts. to books. Grad. study fellow Cath. U. Am., 1975-76, Johns Hopkins U., 1977-83; D.M. Robinson traveling fellow, 1982; grantee Ourani Found. of Greek Acad., 1982, 92, 94, NEH summer seminar, 1985, 89; grantee U. Fla., 1986-87; Wayne State U. faculty summer rsch., 1992, 95; recipient Tchg. Excellence award U. Fla., 1986, 89. Mem. Am. Philol. Assn., Classical Assn. of Middle West and South, Mich. Classical Conf., Detroit Classical Assn.. Women's Classical Caucus, Modern Greek Studies Assn., Nat. Mus. of Women in Arts, Detroit Inst. Art, Soc. for Preservation of the Greek Heritage. Home: 3216 Country Club Dr Saint Clair Shores MI 48082-1087 Office: Wayne State U Dept Greek and Latin 431 Manoogian Hall Detroit MI 48202

HAUCK-FUGITT, CHRISTINE CLAIRE KRAUS, insurance executive; b. McKeesport, Pa., May 22, 1951; d. Lawrence Elmer and Anne Mae (Seinar) Kraus; m. David T. Hauck, Feb. 6, 1971 (div. Apr. 1986); chldren: Benjamin David, Christopher Thomas, Andrew Lawrence; m. Jonathan Fugitt, 1988. Student, Duquesne U., 1969-71, U. Pitts., 1972-78, U. Charleston, 1978-81; BA, Ohio State U., 1984. CPCU; cert. ins. counselor. Claims asst. John Hancock Ins., Pitts., 1971-73; underwriter Chubb Ins. Group, Pitts., 1973-76; account rep., ins. agt. Frank B. Hall, Columbus, Ohio, 1982-85; customer svc. rep., agt. Andrew Ins. Assoc., Columbus, 1986-88, sr. customer svc. rep., 1988-90; spl. accounts mgr., account exec. Willis Corroon Corp. Ohio, Inc., 1990-94; pres., sec. Positively Successful, Columbus, 1988—; comml. underwriter Acordia/McElroy Minister Co., Columbus, 1994—. Author poetry. Active Welcome Wagon, Upper Arlington, Ohio, 1981-84, Barrington Sch. Assn., Upper Arlington, 1982-87, Tremont Sch. Assn., Upper Arlington 1987-93, Upper Arlington Civic Assn., 1986-96; instr. St. Agatha Dept. Religious Edn., Upper Arlington, 1983-87; foster parent, 1975-95; active Jones Sch. Assn., 1988-96, Upper Arlington H.S. Assn., 1991-96; registered leader Boy Scouts Am., 1991-96, advancement chmn. troop 417, 1994—; mem. St. Agatha Folk Group, 1992—; mem. bd. Westminster-Thurber Cmty., 1995—. Recipient Bridgebuilder award Boy Scouts Am., 1992, Meritorious Svc. award Boy Scouts Am., 1995. Mem. NAFE, Steps to Greatness, Internat. Platform Assn., Phi Kappa Phi. Democrat. Roman Catholic. Home: 2121 Jervis Rd Columbus OH 43221-2727 Office: Positively Successful 2121 Jervis Rd Columbus OH 43221-2727

HAUGH, DAN ANTHONY, mechanical engineer; b. Lawrence, Kans., Feb. 16, 1953; s. Oscar Martin and Rita (Rosso) H.; m. Jay McLaughlin, Mar. 19, 1983; children: Alden Elizabeth, Emily Marston. BSME, U. Kans., 1978. Engr. R & D Boeing, Wichita, Kans., 1978-80, specialist engr. propulsion dept., 1980-83; midwest engring. mgr. PSI Bearings, Inc., Wichita, Kans., 1983-85; midwest sales mgr. Jamaica Bearings Co., Inc., Lawrence, 1983-91; dir. engring. Jamaica Bearings Co., Inc., New Hyde Park, N.Y., 1991—; bd. dirs. Aeros, Inc., Lawrence, 1986—. Bd. dirs. West Hills Home Assn., Lawrence, 1989-94. Mem. ASME, Internat. Gas Turbine Inst., Profl. Aviation Maintenance Assn., Robot Inst. Am., Sch. Engring. Soc., U. Kans. Alumni Assn., Exptl. Aircraft Assn., B-17 Hist. Soc. Home: 1512 University Dr Lawrence KS 66044-5148

HAUGH, JEFFREY L., electronic draftsman; b. Natrona Heights, Pa., Oct. 6, 1966; s. Frederick Carl and Loretta Ann (Scott) H. Drafting person Harco Inc., Medina, Ohio, 1985-86; electronic draftsman Chick Master Incubator Co., Medina, 1986—. Roman Catholic. Home: 405 W Friendship St Medina OH 44256 Office: Chick Master Incubator Co PO Box 704 Medina OH 44258-0704

HAUGH, JOYCE EILEEN GALLAGHER, education educator; b. Ironton, Ohio, Sept. 3, 1937; d. Lawrence James and Frances Irene (Wilson) Gallagher; m. Charles R. Haugh, July 29, 1978; children: Kevin Charles, Maria

Frances, Kateri Lynn. BS, Coll. St. Teresa, Winona, Minn., 1967; MEd, Ohio U., 1969; PhD, Loyola U. Chgo., 1975; ME/PD, U. Wis.-LaCrosse, 1984. Tchr. various schs., various locations, 1958-68; instr. psychology Coll. St. Teresa, Winona, Minn., 1969-72; v.p. student affairs, dean students Coll. St. Teresa, 1975-76; assoc. prof psychology St. Mary's Coll., Winona, 1976-82; assoc. prof. edn. St. Mary's Coll., 1982-86, prof. edn., 1986-95; prof. emeritus, 1995—, ind. beauty cons., edn. cons., 1995—; co-chmn. dept. edn. St. Mary's Coll., 1986-87, dir. grad. program in pastoral svc., 1986-87, dir. grad. program in pastoral svc., 1986-88, others; adj. prof. U. Wis.-LaCrosse, 1985, Winona State U., 1988; mem. Cath. Schs. Acreditation Visitation Team, 1988; NAEYC validator, 1988—. Franciscan cojourner, 1985—; chmn. continuing edn. com. Birthright, 1981, mem., 1980—; eucharistic min. Cathedral of the Sacred Heart, 1981—, others; bd. dirs. Winona Day Care, Inc., 1991-95. NDEA fellow, 1968-69. Mem. ACA, Nat. Assn. for Edn. Young Children, Nat. Early Childhood Tchr. Educators, Minn. Early Childhood Tchr. Educators (treas. 1989-91), Exch. Club Winona (treas. 1985-87, bd. dirs. 1985-90), Psi Chi, Phi Delta Kappa, Kappa Delta Pi (counselor 1989-95), Delta Epsilon Sigma (pres. 1993-95). Roman Catholic. Home: 1601 Clubview Rd Winona MN 55987-6220

HAUGLAND, BRYNHILD, retired state legislator, farmer; b. Ward County, N.D., July 28, 1905; d. Nels and Sigurda (Ringoen) H.; BA, Minot State Coll., 1956; LLD (hon.), N.D. State U., 1984. Mem. N.D. Ho. of Reps., 1938-90, chmn. com. social services and vets. affairs, mem. com. industry, bus. and labor. Mem. Def. Adv. Com. Women in Services, 1955-58. Vice chmn. N.D. Gov.'s State Health Planning Com., 1944-75; past mem. Ward County Zoning Commn., Minot City Planning Commn., N.D. Bicentennial Commn. Bd. dirs. Internat. Peace Garden, 1953—, Minot State Coll. Found., Minot Commn. on Aging; mem. N.D. Legislature, 1938-90; mem. adv. com. Women in Svcs. Nat. Defense, Washington, 1953-56; past mem. adv. coun. N.D. Employment Security Bur., Ward County Zonin Commn., Minot Planning Commn., N.D. Bicentennial Commn., 1976—. Named Outstanding Legislator, Nat. Assembly Govt. Employees, 1979; recipient Golden award for Outstanding Service, Minot State Coll. Alumni, 1968, Genie award Minot C. of C., 1973, award Nat. Coun. Advancement and Support Edn., 1988 ; Hon. Mem. Uniformed Fire Fighters N.D., 1976; recipient Milky Way award Dairy Industry N.D., 1977, Disting. Service award Western N.D. Health Systems Agy., 1977-78, N.D. Water Wheel N.D. Water Users Assn./N.D. Water Mgmt. Dists. Assn., 1981, Service to Mankind award Sertoma Clubs, 1983, Merit award Pub. Health Assn. N.D., 1983, Liberty Bell award State Bar Assn., 1983, Disting. Service award Mental Health Assn. N.D., 1983, award Minot Assn. Home Builders, 1984, Good Citizen Scouting award, 1984, Disting. Service award Am. Protestant Health Assn., 1985; recognized state conv. Rep. Party for Half Century of Dedicated Pub. Service, longest serving legislator in nation on date of retirement, elected 26 terms-52 yrs., Woman of Distinction award Minot YWCA, 1993, Theodore Roosevelt Rough Rider award, 1995; numerous others; inducted into Scandinavian Hall of Fame, 1984; com. rm. named for her N.D. State Capital Bldg., Bismarck, 1987; Paul Harris fellow Rotary, 1993. Mem. Bus. and Profl. Women's Club (named Woman of Yr. 1956, 71, 89), Am. Assn. Ret. Persons, Nat. Ret. Tchrs. Assn., Farmers Union and Farm Bur., Minot State Coll. Alumni Assn. (dir., award for 50 yrs. svc. bd. dirs. 1993), Eureka Homemakers Club, Quota Club, Delta Kappa Gamma. Lutheran. Home: RR 6, Box 362A Minot ND 58703-9265

HAUKOOS, MELVIN ROBERT, state representative; b. Walters, Minn., June 21, 1931; s. Russell and Emma Adaline (Hauskins) H.; m. Grace Louise McNeil, July 28, 1955; children: Miriam Ruth, Robert Ross. State rep. State of Minn., St. Paul, 1979-94; ret., 1994; field rep. for U.S. Rep. Gil Gutknecht, 1995-96. With USN, 1950-53, Korea. Recipient Herman Kleinman award Am. Lung Assn. Minn., 1993, Govt. Rels. award Am. Lung Assn. Minn., 1988, Disting. Svc. award U. Minn., 1985, Disting. Svc. award Ind. Bus. Assn., 1985, Champion Small Bus. award, 1988, Legis. Excellence award Legis. Evaluation Assembly. Mem. VFW, Sons of Norway, Am. Legion, Moose, Elks, Eagles. Republican. Baptist. Home: 111 Fairview Dr Albert Lea MN 56007-2219 Office: Minn Legislature 100 Constitution Ave Saint Paul MN 55155-1201

HAULMARK, GARY, state legislator; m. Karla Haulmark. Kans. state rep. Dist. 30, 1993—, sales assoc., cons., 1996—. Home: 8709 Gallery St Lenexa KS 66215-3225*

HAUPT, H. JAMES, mechanical design engineer; b. Palmerton, Pa., Jan. 3, 1940; s. Harry C. and Mary L. (Patrick) H.; m. Betty S. Niemi, Sept. 5, 1970; children: Nadine R., Heather J. AAS, Broome Tech. Coll., 1964; BS, Ill. Inst. Tech., Chgo., 1971. Lic. profl. engr. Mech. engr. Argonne (Ill.) Nat. Lab., 1964—. Co-contbr. articles to profl. publs. AEC scholar, Washington, 1969. Mem. Am. Nuclear Soc., Ill. Profl. Engrs., Phi Theta Kappa, Tau Beta Pi. Republican. Roman Catholic. Home: 3215 Saddle Dr Joliet IL 60435-1142 Office: Argonne Nat Lab 9700 Cass Ave Bldg 310 Argonne IL 60439-4803

HAURY, DAVID ARTHUR, historical administrator; b. Newton, Kans., Dec. 27, 1950; s. Robert Arthur and Ada Mae (Gressinger) H.; m. Rosemary Elaine Wiebe, Sept. 5, 1981; children: Emily Margaret, Benjamin Arthur. AB, Bethel Coll., Newton, Kans., 1973; AM, Harvard U., 1975, PhD, 1979; MLA, U. Ill., 1988. Cert. archivist. Archivist, dir. Mennonite Libr. and Archives, North Newton, Kans., 1979-89; asst. dir. Kans. State Hist. Soc., Topeka, 1989—; chair Gen. Conf. Hist. Commn., Newton, 1988-93, Kans. Records Adv. Bd., Topeka, 1989—, Kans. Preservation Coun., Topeka, 1992—. Author: Prairie People: A History of the Western District Conference, 1981, The Mennonite Congregation of Boston, 1979, A Guide to the Art Collection of the Mennonite Library and Archives, 1983, others; contbr. articles to profl. jours.; editor jour. series. Bd. dirs. Warkentin House, Newton, 1985-89; treas. Olive Branch, Topeka, 1994-95. Danforth fellow, 1973-79; Rotary Exch. fellow, 1973-74; NEH summer fellow, 1989. Mem. Midwest Archives Conf. (prodn. editor), Soc. Am. Archivists (publs. editor 1995—), Am. Assn. for State and Local History, Kans. Libr. Assn., Midwest Archives Conf. (newsletter editor 1986-90). Mennonite. Office: Kans State Hist Soc 6425 SW 6th St Topeka KS 66615-1099

HAUSAUER, ROY, state legislator; b. Ortonville, Minn., Apr. 12, 1920; m. Marion; four children. Grad., U. N.D., 1942. Former chmn. legis. coun., House Spkr.; N.D. State rep. Dist. 25, 1971—; former businessman; vice-chmn. appropriations com., mem. appropriations edn. and environ. divsn. com.; former nat. chmn. Coun. State Govt. Mem. VFW, Am. Legion. Home: PO Box 1295 Wahpeton ND 58074-1295*

HAUSER, ELLOYD, finance company executive. CEO United Check Clearing Corp. Office: United Check Clearing Corp 14276 23d Ave N Plymouth MN 55447*

HAUSMAN, ALICE, state legislator; b. July 31, 1942; M. Robert Hausman; 2 children. BS, Concordia Coll., 1963, MA, 1965. State rep. Minn. Ho. of Reps., Dist. 66B, Minn., 1989—; mem. Econ. Devel. Com., vice chmn. Environ. & Natural Resources com., Edn. Fin. Divsn. & Regulated Indsl. & Energy Coms., Minn. Ho. Reps. Home: 1447 Chelmsford St Saint Paul MN 55108-1404 Office: Minn Ho of Reps State Capital Building Saint Paul MN 55155-1606*

HAUSMAN, HERSHEL JUDAH, physicist, researcher; b. Pitts., Aug. 19, 1923; s. David and Sophie Hausman; m. Korene J. Brenner, May 29, 1944; children: Herbert, Sally, William. MS, Carnegie Mellon U., 1949; PhD, U. Pitts., 1952. Asst. prof. Ohio State U., Columbus, 1952-57, assoc. prof., 1957-63, prof., 1963-89, prof. emeritus, 1989—; cons. U.S.A.I.D., India, 1963-64. Contbr. articles to profl. jours. 1st lt. USAF, 1943-45, ETO. Rsch. grantee Nat. Sci. Found., 1963-89. Fellow Am. Phys. Soc. Home: 1290 Park Plaza Dr Columbus OH 43213 Office: Van de Graaff 1302 Kinnear Rd Columbus OH 43212-1156

HAUSMANN, JOHN EDMUND, real estate executive, mayor; b. N.Y.C., Dec. 12, 1944; s. Otto Joseph and Rita Marie (Hourigan) H.; m. Susan Ellen Dow, Jan. 30, 1971; children: Maia Elizabeth, Ketti Louise, John Edmund II. BA, Union Coll., 1966; MBA, U. Va., 1970. Pres. Hausmann Enterprises, Hinsdale, Ill., 1983—; bd. dirs. Capitol Fed. Bank for Savs., 1989-91, Uptown Fed. Savs., 1987-88, Sears Nat. Bank, Do-It-Right Industries. Trustee Village of LaGrange (Ill.), 1978-81, mayor, 1981-89; bd. dirs. Pace Suburban Bus. Divsn. Regional Transp. Authority, 1984-89, St. Coletta's of Ill. Exceptional Chldren, 1985-89. Roman Catholic. Home: 300 7th Ave La Grange IL 60525-6408 Office: Hausmann Enterprises 911 N Elm St Hinsdale IL 60521-3634

HAUSWIRTH, SANDRA FAY MARIE, newspaper editor; b. Lake Linden, Mich., Jan. 6, 1939; d. Joseph W. and Gabrielle (Levesque) Paquette; m. Paul L. Hauswirth Jr., Feb. 8, 1958; children: Fay Anttila, Robin Lynn. Grad., high sch., Lake Linden. Sec.-clk. Ontanagon (Mich.) Herald Co., 1967-69, asst. editor, 1970-77, 80—, advt. mgr., asst. editor, photographer, office mgr., 1980—. Election chmn. Ontonagon Elections Bd., 1960, 61; mem. Ontonagon Dem. Com., 1967—; bd. dirs. Citizens Ontonagon Meml. Hosp., chmn. polit. action com., chmn. fundraising com.; capt. Women's Softball Team, 1959-68, mem. volleyball, 1975-82, Women's Tuesday Bowling League, 1982—, Mixed Bowling League; v.p. bd. commrs. Ontonagon Twp. Park 1992—; chmn. polit. action com. Link to Health; mem. Citizens for Ontonagon Meml. Hosp., 1989—; active Holy Family Cath. Ch., 1958—. Mem. Nat. Newspaper Assn., Ontonagon C. of C. (sec. 1984-86, bd. dirs. 1986—), Ontonagon C. of C. (bd. dir. 1986—). Home: 410 Chippewa St Ontonagon MI 49953-1008 Office: Ontonagon Herald Co 326 River St PO Box 98 Ontonagon MI 39953

HAVELKA, THOMAS EDWARD, secondary education educator; b. Wheeling, W.Va., July 10, 1947; s. Alfred and Marilyn Eleanor (Hays) H.; m. Susan Kay Wilson, June 16, 1973; children: Trevor Hays, Havaleh Ann. BFA, Ohio U., 1969, MusM, 1975. Cert. tchr., Ohio; national registered music tchr. M.E.N.C. Music instr., chmn. fine arts dept. Bellaire (Ohio) Bd. Edn., 1969-74; choir dir., chmn. music dept. Coshocton (Ohio) City Bd. Edn., 1975—; founder Coshocton City Schs., Arts Festival, 1985—; state rep. All Am. Youth Honor Musicians, Miami, Fla., 1970-90; asst. condr. All Am. Youth Honor Choir, 1970, 77-78, condr., 1980-90; adjudicator Internat. Choir Fest., Mexico City, 1978, Dulcimer Festival, Roscoe Village, Ohio, 1986-88, Show Choir Festival, Portsmouth, Ohio, 1986, Lander Coll., S.C. Composer: Piece for String Quartet, 1974, (choral) Offertorium from Missae Requiem Brevis, 1974, Bless Ye the God of All, 1975. Mem. Big Bros./Big Sisters Assn., Columbus, 1970—; dist. exec., chmn. bd. Boy Scouts Am., Coshocton, 1979-80; sect. leader, asst. accompanist, asst. conductor Coshocton Community Choir, 1984—; active various theater groups, Coshocton and Wheeling, 1974—; singer St. Matthew's Episcopal Ch., Wheeling, W.Va., 1973-75; asst. organist Grace United Meth. Ch., Coshocton, 1986—; pres., bd. dirs. Ohio U. Sch. of Music Soc. of Alumni and Friends. Recipient awards from Mayors of Malaga, Spain, 1981, Agnani and Fuiggi, Italy, 1984 and Paris, 1985, Istra, USSR, 1989, award of Merit Coshocton City Schs., 1984. Mem. NEA, Ohio Edn. Assn., Ohio Music Edn. Assn. (asst. contest chmn., approved adjudicator in piano, voice, and choir, chmn. county membership com. 1977-78), Internat. Soc. for Music Edn., Internat. Fedn. for Choral Music, Am. Guild Organists, Am. Choral Dirs. Assn., Ohio Choral Dirs. Assn. (chmn. county membership com. 1978-79), Coshocton City Edn. Assn. (sec. 1984-85, 88-89), Music Educators Nat. Conf., Soc. Music Tchr. Edn., Kappa Kappa Psi, Phi Mu Alpha, Pi Kappa Lambda. Republican. Methodist. Home: 1628 Woodland Dr Coshocton OH 43812-3151 Office: Coshocton High Sch 1205 Cambridge Rd Coshocton OH 43812-2741

HAVENER, NEAL STEVEN, filmmaker, musician; b. Columbus, Ohio, June 20, 1961; s. William Henry and Phyllis Ann (Johnson) H.; m. Deborah Diane Pittenger, Oct. 28, 1994. Diploma in journalism, Ohio State U., 1993, diploma in econs., 1993, diploma in photography & cinema, 1993; diploma in theater, Bliss Coll., 1994; diploma in music, Capitol U., 1995. V.p. Herringbone Corp., Columbus, 1982-93; reporter Arab News, Jeddah, Suadi Arabia, 1993-94; prodn. supr. 2D Sys., Columbus, 1994—. Albums include This is Not a X-Mas Album, 1988, Time Doesn't Matter, 1992, Oceans & Deserts, 1994. Fellow Spank Monkey Gang (pres. 1990—); mem. Cryptic Warriors (pres. 1989—).

HAVENS, CHARNELL THOMAS, mamagement consultant; b. Dayton, Ohio, Mar. 14, 1938; s. Robert H. and Pauline (Buck) Thomas; m. Robert E. Havens, Mar. 2, 1961 (div. 1980, dec. 1989); children: Robin Havens Stoehr, Rene Havens Fitch, Amy Havens. BS, Ohio U., 1960. Systems engr. IBM, Columbus, Ohio, 1960-63; sr. systems analyst Sperry Univac, Washington, 1963-66; dir. strategic planning NCR Corp., Dayton, Ohio, 1968-84; sr. cons. Arthur D. Little, Inc., Cambridge, Mass., 1984-87; pres. Info. Frontiers, Inc., Eaton, Ohio, 1988-89; dir. channel strategies Unisys, Blue Bell, Pa., 1990-91; prin. cons. EDS, Southfield, Mich., 1991, EDS at Kearney, Dallas, 1995—; dir. Frameworks/Methods, Plano, Tex. Contbg. author: Technology 2001, 1991; co-contbr. articles to profl. jours. Editor Rep. Women's Club, Dayton, 1966-67; dir. YWCA bd., Dayton, 1980; trustee Preble County Libr. Bd., Eaton, Ohio, 1988-89. Mem. The Planning Forum (v.p. programs 1992-93), Eaton Country Club, Eldorado Country Club, Kappa Delta Alumnae. Methodist. Office: EDS 5400 Legacy Dr Plano TX 75024

HAVENS, KEITH CORNELL, artist; b. Mpls., Sept. 27, 1921; s. Lee Willard and Ruth Marguerite (Mallett) H.; m. Marian Gail Niggeler, Mar. 11, 1944; 1 child, Shelley Ross. Cert., Mpls. Sch. Art, 1949. Instr. drawing, painting and design Mpls. Sch. Art, 1949-58; assoc. prof. art Spl. Sch. Assoc. Arts, St. Paul, 1959-73; dir. studio classes Mpls. Sch. Art, 1949-58, instr. night sch. classes, 1949-58; co-founder, instr. Minnetonka Ctr. Art and Edn., Wayzata, Crystal Bay, Minn., 1950-70; dir. Twin Cities Theater Galleries, Mpls., St. Paul, 1952-72; architect's cons. Mpls. Sch. Art, 1956-58, designer spl. equipment, 1956-58; instr. watercolor painting St. Paul Sch. Art, 1958-59; judge Lutsen (Minn.) Art Fair, 1975, Mpls. Photo Club, 1975. Author: Fantanimals, 1980; paintings commd. by North Meml. Hosp., Robbinsdale, Minn., 1962, 63; exhibited in numerous one-man shows including Duluth Art Inst., 1994. Recipient 1st award Women's Club Art Show, 1952, 1st award-watercolor Minn. State Fair Art Exhibit, 1953.

HAVERHALS, JOHN S., mathematics educator; b. Ireton, Iowa, Sept. 27, 1937; s. Adrian J. and Jennie Marie (Kooi) H.; m. Bernice Anne Haekman, Aug. 9, 1963; children: Anne, Mary. BA in Mathematics, U. Iowa, Iowa City, 1960, MS in Mathematics, 1962. Tchg. asst. U. Iowa, Iowa City, 1960-63; faculty mem. Bradley U., Peoria, Ill., 1963—, prof. mathematics, 1963—, univ. ombudsman, 1995—; problem writer Am. Coll. Testing, Iowa City, 1985—; expert witness on pyramid schemes Peoria County, 1979, 82; reviewer various publs. mathematical textbooks, 1975—. elder First Reformed Ch., Peoria, 1964-95; v.p. Peoria Crusade of Voters, 1966-69; mem. bd. dirs. West Bluff Coun., Peoria, 1972—; pres. Moss-Bradley Revolving Fund, Peoria, 1987-90, 94-95, Moss Bradley Assn., Peoria, 1996-97. Mem. AAUP (chpt. pres. 1974-75, 81-82), Mathematical Assn. of Am. (Ill. sect. pres. 1981-82, Disting. Svc. award 1987), Gideons Internat. (local pres. 1995-96). Home: 1634 W Moss Peoria IL 61606 Office: Bradley U Bradley Hall Peoria IL 61625

HAVLIN, JOHN LEROY, soil scientist, educator; b. Chgo., May 8, 1950; s. Joseph Leroy and Dorothy Jean (Williams) H.; m. Saundra Joyce Crowley, July 7, 1979; 1 child, Jonathon Cary. MS, Colo. State U., 1980, PhD, 1983. Asst. prof. U. Nebr., Scottbluff, 1983-85; asst. prof. Kans. State U., Manhattan, 1985-90, assoc. prof. dept. agronomy, 1990—; sec. North Cen. Region Com. Sustainable Agr., 1991; mem. adv. bd. Farmland Industries, Kansas City, Mo., 1989—. Editor conf. proc. Great Plains Soil Fertility Conf., 1988, 90; author Soil Fertility at Fertilizers; contbr. articles to profl. publs., chpts. to book. Named Researcher of Yr. Nat. Fertilizer Solutions Assn., 1989; recipient Werner L. Nelson Rsch. award, 1991; Nat. Assn. Coll. Teachers of Agrl. Teacher Fellow, 1994. Mem. Am. Soc. Agronomy, Soil Sci. Soc. Am. (fellow 1995), Am. Woil and Water Conservation Soc., Sigma Xi, Phi Kappa Phi, Gamma Sigma Delta (Outstanding Tchr. award 1992). Republican. Presbyterian. Home: 3608 Brenda Ct Manhattan KS 66502-8132 Office: Kans State U Dept Agronomy Manhattan KS 66506

HAWES, JON MICHAEL, sales and marketing educator; b. Wheatland, Ind., Sept. 26, 1952; s. John P. and Lois Joy (Stephenson) H.; m. Lisa J. De Luca, May 16, 1986; children: Jennifer, Steven. BS, Ind. State U., 1973, MBA, 1975; PhD, U. Ark., 1981. Acct. mgr. NCR Corp., Grand Rapids, Mich., 1977-78; prof. mktg. U. Akron, Ohio, 1981—; dir. Fisher Inst. for Profl. Selling U. Akron, 1994—. Author: (book) Cases in Retail Management, 1989; contbr. articles to profl. jours.; assoc. editor Jour. of Personal Selling and Sales Management, 1995. Mem. Acad. of Mktg. Sci. (v. p. for programs 1990-92), Sales and Mktg. Execs. Internat. (cert. sales exec., award of excellence Akron chpt.). Office: Univ Akron Fisher Inst Profl Selling Akron OH 44325-4804

HAWK, CAROLE LYNN, insurance company executive; b. Springfield, Ill., June 17, 1947; d. Warren Wesley and Mary June (Moore) Weiser; m. Charles Edward Hawk, Aug. 2, 1963; 1 child, Cynthia Jean Hawk-Lindzy. Student, Lincoln Land C.C., Springfield, 1970-75, Ind. U., South Bend, 1982-83. Cert. data processor, computer programmer, systems profl., assoc. in customer svc. Systems analyst Office Ill. Sec. of State, Springfield, 1969-78; software specialist Clark Equipment Co., Buchanan, Mich., 1978-84; GC056 software analyst Contel Corp., Wentzville, Mo., 1984-87; tech. rsch. analyst The Horace Mann Cos., Springfield, 1988—. Fellow Life Mgmt. Assn.; mem. Data Processing Mgmt. Assn. (sec. Capital chpt. 1993-94, exec. pres. 1995, pres. 1996), Ctrl. Ill. Life Mgmt. Inst. (co. rep. 1995-96), Toastmasters (sec. Horace Mann chpt. 1992, pres. 1993, gov. area 1 1994-95, gov. dist. C 1995—).

HAWKINS, GERI SUE, interior designer, jewelry designer, realtor; b. Kansas City, Mo., Sept. 4, 1940; d. William S. McCune and Verla J. (Kempter) McCune Stoll; m. LeRay D. Long, Oct. 12, 1958 (div. Dec. 1961); 1 child, Lori Diane Long Seidl; m. Ray Eldon Hawkins, Oct. 9, 1964; children: Lynn M., John Ted; stepchildren: Celeste, Steve. Student Kansas City Bus. Coll., 1961-62, U. Mo., Kansas City, 1974-75; AA, Maple Woods Coll., 1974; student Wm. Jewel Coll. Interior designer Carpenter Bros. Inc., Kansas City, 1975-77; pres., designer Gerry Hawkins Interiors, Kansas City, 1977-81; interior designer R. D. Mann Inc., Kansas City, 1981-83; owner-designer Designs By Geri, Kansas City, 1983-89, 95-96, Interior Designs by Geri Inc., Parkville, Mo., 1989—, Greenstreet Interiors, 1993-94; realtor assoc. ERA Martin House, Platte City, Mo., 1984-85; interior designer Martin House Design, Platte City, 1984-85; sales rep. Ron Wood Real Estate, 1987-88; with J.D. Reece Realtors, 1988—. Local theatrical appearances, 1972-73. Leader Winding River council Girl Scouts U.S., 1966-71; mem. Grace Notes Singing Ensemble, Kansas City, 1980—; trustee Park Hill Bapt. Ch., Parkville, Mo., 1983-85. Mem. Platte County Bus. and Profl. Assn. (bd. dirs. 1980-81), Am. Soc. Interior Designers, Nat. Assn. Women Bus. Owners, Greater Kansas City C. of C., Platte County Women's Exch., Women in Bus., Gen. Fedn. Women's Clubs, Patrician Club, Lions (hon.). Republican. Baptist. Avocations: jewelry making, swimming, golf, theatre, gardening. Home: 9203 NW 76th Terr Weatherby Lake MO 64152

HAWKINS, JACQUELYN, elementary and secondary education educator; b. Russell Springs, Ky., Apr. 30, 1943; d. J.T. Hawkins and Maudie Bell Crew. BS, Andrews U., 1969; MEd, Xavier U., 1976. Cert. elem. tchr., Ohio, reading tchr. elem. and high sch., Ohio. Tchr. Cin. Pub. Schs., 1969—, Cummins Sch., Cin., 1971-81; tchr. Windsor Sch., Cin., 1982-83; tchr. Windsor Sch., 1983-89, acting contact tchr. chpt. 1 reading program, 1989-93; reading recovery tchr. Windsor Sch., Cin., 1993—; rep. Cin. Coun. Educators, 1986-89, 91-92, 92-93, mem. book com.; mem. sch. improvement program Windsor Sch., 1982-84; mem. Sch. Improvement Program Cin. Chairperson United Way at Windsor Sch. Cin., 1986-89, 90-92, United Negro Coll. Fund Cin., 1986-89, ARC, Windsor Sch., Cin., 1986-89, 90-92; rep. Fine Arts Fund Cin., 1986-88; co-leader 4-H Club, Cin., 1987-88; leader Girl Scouts U.S., Cin., 1988-93; tutor Tabernacle Bapt. Ch., 1989; co-chairperson Windsor ARC, 1991-92. Recipient Cert. Achievement Cummins Sch. Cin., 1978. Democrat.

HAWKINS, JOSEPH ELMER, JR., retired acoustic physiologist, educator; b. Waco, Tex., Mar. 4, 1914; s. Joseph Elmer and Maude Burke (Schlenker) H.; m. Jane Elizabeth Daddow, Aug. 24, 1939; children: Richard Spencer Daddow, Peter Douglas Huntington, James Marion Davis, William Alexander Parmley, Priscilla Ann (Mrs. Philip A. Leach). Student, Altes Realgymnasium, Munich, 1929-30; AB, Baylor U., 1933; postgrad., Brown U., 1933-34; BA in Physiology, U. Oxford, 1937, MA, 1966, DSc, 1979; PhD in Med. Sci., Harvard U., 1941. Tchg. fellow in physiology Harvard Med. Sch., 1937-41, instr., 1941-45; asst. investigator Nat. Def. Rsch. Com.-Office Sci. Rsch. & Devel., 1941-43; spl. rsch. assoc. Nat. Def. Rsch. Com./Office Sci. R & D, 1943-45; asst. prof. physiology Bowman Gray Sch. Medicine, Wake Forest Coll., 1945-46; rsch. assoc. neurophysiology Merck Inst. for Therapeutic Rsch., Rahway, N.J., 1946-56; assoc. prof. otolaryngology NYU Sch. Medicine, 1956-63; prof. physiol. acoustics U. Mich., Ann Arbor, 1963-84, prof. emeritus, 1984—; chmn. grad. program in physiol. acoustics U. Mich., 1969-81; assoc. dir. Kresge Hearing Rsch. Inst., 1979-82; disting. vis. prof. biology Baylor U., Waco, Tex., 1985-93; mem. NIH sensory diseases study sect., 1958-61, communicative disorders rsch. tng. com., 1965-69, communicative scis. study sect., 1975-79; mem. Nat. Libr. Medicine Communicative Disorders Task Force, 1977-79; lectr. Armed Forces Inst. Pathology, 1969-74; cons. various pharm. cos. Contbr. to: Ency. Brit, 15th edit., 1974: Editor: (with M. Lawrence and W.P. Work) Otophysiology, 1973, (with S.A. Lerner and G.T. Matz) Aminoglycoside Ototoxicity, 1981; contbr. sci. articles to profl. jours. Pres. Fleming Creek Neighborhood Assn., Washtenaw County, Mich., 1973-74; mem. Bd. Edn., Cranford, N.J., 1958-61. Rhodes scholar Tex. and Worcester Coll., U. Oxford, 1934-37; USPHS spl. fellow Öronkliniken, Sahlgrenska Sjukhuset U. Göteborg, Sweden, 1961-63; NAS exch. lectr. to Yugoslavia and Bulgaria, 1977; Chercheur étranger de l'INSERM, Lab. d'Audiologie Expérimentale, U. Bordeaux II, 1978; recipient Disting. Achievement award Baylor U., 1982, City of Pleven, Bulgaria medal, 1982, U. Bordeaux medal, 1983, Humboldt Rsch. award for sr. U.S. scientists U. Würzburg, 1991, Hon. Citizen award, Bordeaux, 1991, Disting. Alumnus award Baylor U., 1996. Fellow AAAS, Acoustical Soc. Am.; mem. Am. Physiol. Soc., Assn. for Rsch. in Otolaryngology (award of merit 1985), Collegium Oto-rhino-laryngologicum Amicitiae Sacrum, Bárány Soc., European Workshop for Inner Ear Biology, Am. Assn. for History of Medicine, History of Sci. Soc., Am. Otol. Soc. (assoc.), Prosper Menière Soc. (hon.), Pacific Coast Oto-ophthalmol. Soc. (hon.), Connétablie de Guyenne (Bordeaux, assoc.), Phi Beta Kappa, Sigma Xi. Anglican. Democrat. Home: 4004 E Joy Rd Ann Arbor MI 48105-9609 Office: U Mich Med Sch Kresge Hearing Rsch Inst Ann Arbor MI 48109-0506

HAWKINS, LAWRENCE CHARLES, management consultant, educator; b. Greenville County, S.C., Mar. 20, 1919; s. Wayman and Etta (Brockman) H.; m. Earline Thompson, Apr. 29, 1943; children: Lawrence Charles Jr., Wendell Earl. BA, U. Cin., 1941, BEd, 1942, MEd, 1951, EdD, 1970; AA (hon.), Wilmington Coll., 1979; LittD (hon.), Cin. Tech. Coll. Cert. sch. supt., Ohio. Elem./secondary tchr. Cin. Pub. Schs., 1945-52, sch. prin./dir., 1952-67, asst. supt., 1967-69; dean U. Cin., 1969-75, v.p., 1975-77, sr. v.p., 1977-83; vis. asst. prof. Eastern Mich. U., Ypsilanti, summers 1955-60; mem. Cincinnatus Assn., 1971-87; bd. dirs. Western and So. Life, 1990—; vice chair Student Loan Funding Corp., 1982—. Bd. dirs. Wilmington (Ohio) Coll., 1980-90, Bethesda Hosp., Cin., 1980-90; trustee Children's Home of Cin., 1978-90, Coll. Mt. St. Joseph, 1989-93; pres., CEO Omni-Man, Inc., 1981—; vice chmn. Greater Cin. TV Edn. Found., WCET-TV, 1983; co-chmn. Cin. area NCCJ 1980-87. Served to lt. USAAF, 1943-45. Recipient award of Merit, Cin. Area United Appeal, 1955, 73, cert. Pres.'s Council on Youth Opportunity, 1968, City Cin., 1968, Disting. Svc. citation Greater Cin. Nat. Conf. of Christians and Jews, 1988; named Great Living Cincinnatian Greater Cin. C. of C., 1989. Mem. NEA (life), Nat. Congress Parents and Tchrs. (hon. life; chmn. com.), Phi Delta Kappa, Kappa Delta Pi, Kappa Alpha Psi, Sigma Pi Phi.

HAWKINS, LORETTA ANN, secondary school educator, playwright; b. Winston-Salem, N.C., Jan. 1, 1942; d. John Henry and Laurine (Hines) Sanders; m. Joseph Hawkins, Dec. 10, 1962; children: Robin, Dionne, Sherri. BS in Edn., Chgo. State U., 1965; MA in Lit., Governor's State U., 1977, MA in African Cultures, 1978; postgrad. U. Chgo., 1994—. Cert. tchr., Ill. Tchr. Chgo. Bd. Edn., 1968—; lectr. Chgo. City Colls., 1987-89; tchr. English Gage Park H.S., 1988—; Mem. steering com. Mellon Seminar U. Chgo., 1990; tchr. adv. com. Goodman Theatre, Chgo., 1992, mem. cmty. adv. coun., 1996—. Author: (reading workbook) Contemporary Black Heroes, 1992, (plays) Of Quiet Birds, 1993 (James H. Wilson award 1993), Above the Line, 1994, Good Morning, Miss Alex; contbr. poetry, articles to profl. publs. Santa Fe Pacific Found. fellow, 1988, Lloyd Fry Found. fellow, 1989, Andrew W. Mellon Found. fellow, 1991, Ill. Arts Coun. fellow, 1993;

Cmty. Arts Assistance Program Award grantee Chgo. Dept. Cultural Affairs; recipient Feminist Writers 3d pl. award NOW, 1993, Zora Neale Hurston-Bessie Head Fiction award Black Writer's Conf., 1993, numerous others. Mem. AAUW, Nat. Coun. Tchrs. English, Am. Fedn. Tchrs., Women's Theatre Alliance, Dramatists Guild of Am., Internat. Women's Writing Guild. Home: 8928 S Oglesby Ave Chicago IL 60617 Office: Gage Park HS 5630 S Rockwell Chicago IL 60629

HAWKINS, PHELPS STOKES, broadcast news executive, consultant, journalist; b. Corpus Christi, Tex., May 29, 1948; s. Robert Bradshaw and Elizabeth Phelps (Stokes) H.; m. Sandra Lee Earley, Sept. 7, 1985; 1 child, Robert Graham Bradshaw. BA in History, Columbia U., 1975, MS in Journalism, 1979. News dir. Sta. KID-AM-FM-TV, Idaho Falls, Idaho, 1976-77, Guam Cable TV, Agana, 1977-78; reporter N.J. Nightly News, Trenton, 1978-81; asst. news dir. Sta. KMSP-TV, Mpls., 1981-82; mng. editor Sta. KARE-TV, Mpls., 1982-83; fgn. editor NBC News, N.Y.C., 1983-86; mgr. Asia ops. NBC News, Tokyo, 1986-90; dir. news and pub. affairs Sta. WTTW-TV, Chgo., 1990-91; sr. v.p., dir. news and info. Am. Pub. Radio, Mpls., 1991-94; cons. Marketplace, L.A., 1989-91. Trustee Phelps-Stokes Fund, N.Y.C., 1985. Petty officer USN, 1967-71, Vietnam. Recipient award for best newscast Nat. Cable TV Assn., Guam, 1978. Mem. Radio and TV News Dirs. Assn.

HAWKINS, TERRY D., chief engineer; b. Indpls., June 13, 1950. AS, Ind. U. Purdue U. Indpls., 1970. Co-owner Environ. Processing Systems Inc., Indpls., 1976-78; chief engr. Vibromatic Co., Inc., Noblesville, Ind., 1978—; bd. dirs. Vibromatic Co., Inc., Indpls., 1991—. Vol. local church. With USNR, 1970-72. Republican. Office: Vibromatic Co Inc 1301 S 6th St PO Box 1358 Noblesville IN 46060-3712

HAWKINS, WENDELL E., stockbroker, educator. BBA in Fin., Babson Coll., 1976. Stockbroker PaineWebber, Inc., Cin., 1977—; sec.-treas., fin. cons. Omni-Man, Inc., 1983—; chmn. bd. Beacon Fed. Savs., 1986-87; lectr. fin. U. Cin., 1988—; contbg. columnist Cin. Herald, 1978-83; frequent radio and TV appearances; frequent presenter and seminar and workshop leader on investments, econs. and fin. Trustee, chmn. membership com., v.p. resource devel. Cincinnatians Active To Support Edn., 1981-87; bd. dirs., chmn. econ. devel., v.p. Cin. chpt. NAACP, 1980-88; trustee Greater Cin. chpt. ARC, 1986-92, mem. fin. planning com., 1989; trustee Greater Cin. Literacy Task Force, 1987-89, Queen City Found., Cin., 1989-93, United Way Greater Cin., 1983-89; trustee United Home Care Greater Cin., 1980-90, mem. fin. com., 1980-84; trustee Seven Hills Neighborhood Houses, 1983-90, mem. fin. com., 1987-90; trustee St. Joseph Home, 1988-91, chmn. investment com., devel. com., 1989-91; trustee, mem. fin. com. MagnaCare Health Plan, 1989-91; trustee, mem. budget com. The Children's Home, 1990-92; bd. dirs. Owning the Realty, 1988-92, treas., chmn. fin. com., 1989-91, chmn., 1991-92; mem. jud. rating com. Cin. Bar Assn., 1983-93; mem. dean's adv. com. Coll. Design, Architecture, Art and Planning, U. Cin., 1983-93; mem. chmn. econ. devel. Cin. Cmty. Devel. Adv. Coun., 1981-87; mem. Cin. Loan Fund Task Force, 1983; bd. dirs. Cin. Devel. Fund; mem. Leadership Cin., 1983, mem. steering com., 1984-86. Recipient svc. and support award United Appeal, Cmty. Chest and Coun. of Greater Cin., proclamation of grateful appreciation for svc. City of Cin.; named One of 50 Leaders of Future, Ebony mag. Office: PaineWebber Inc 312 Walnut St Ste 3300 Cincinnati OH 45202-4061

HAWKINSON, CARL E., state legislator; b. Galesburg, Ill., Oct. 7, 1947; m. Karen Zeches; 3 chilren. BA, Park Coll.; JD, Harvard U. Law practice; mem. from 94th dist. Ill. Ho. of Reps., 1983-86; now mem. Ill. State Senate. Office: 4 Weinberg Arcade Galesburg IL 61401*

HAWKINSON, DON, financial consultant; b. Haven, S.D., Nov. 24, 1965. BS in Acctg. and Fin., No. State U., Aberdeen, S.D., 1988. Computer salesman Fireside Office Products, Bismarck, N.D., 1988-93; fin. cons. Smith Barney Inc., Bismarck, 1993—. Roman Catholic. Office: Smith Barney Inc 918 E Divide Ave Ste 305 Bismarck ND 58501-1959

HAWKINSON, THOMAS EDWIN, environmental and occupational health engineer; b. Worthington, Minn., Oct. 15, 1952; s. Robert Edwin and Vivian Julia (Foss) H.; m. Ann Elizabeth Koepsell, Aug. 14, 1977; children: Timothy, William, Elizabeth. BA in Chem., St. Olaf Coll., 1974; MS in Environ. Health, U. Minn., 1978. Cert. indsl. hygienist, cert. safety profl. Res. assoc. Indsl. Health Engr., Mpls., 1976-77; asst. teaching Univ. Minn., 1977-78; indsl. hygienist Medtronic, Inc., Mpls., 1978-86, corp. health environ. adminstr., 1986-93; safety and environ. engr. Gen. Mills, Inc., Mpls., 1993—; panel of advisors Minn. Safety Coun., 1986-89, bd. dirs., 1989-90. Mem. Am. Indsl. Hygiene Assn. (mem. upper Midwest local sect. 1988-89, chmn. local sects. coun. 1988-89, chmn. com. on tng. and edn. 1989-90), Am. Chem. Soc., Air and Waste Mgmt. Assn., Semiconductor Safety Assn. (dir. north ctrl. region 1989—). Home: 825 Pineview Ln N Plymouth MN 55441-5750 Office: Gen Mills Inc 1 General Mills Blvd Minneapolis MN 55426-1347

HAWKS, JAMES WADE, county highway superintendent, county surveyor; b. Lexington, Nebr., Mar. 20, 1957; s. Glenn Emmett and C. Jo Anne (Warren) H.; m. Janelle Sue Kloepping, May 14, 1977; children: James Matthew Hawks, Nathaniel Thomas Hawks. AA, Mid Plains C.C., North Platte, Nebr., 1992. Cert. govt. fin. mgr. Nebr. Safety Coun. Adv. Bd. Dawson county surveyors dept. Dawson County surveyor's/Engrs. Office, Lexington, 1980-87; engring. office mgr. Tagge Engring. Cons., North Platte, 1987-88; county surveyor, county hwy. supt. Lincoln county, North Platte, 1988—; adv. bd. Southeast Cmty. Coll., Milford. Chmn. Lincoln County Sheriff's Merit Commn., North Platte, 1990-91. Mem. Profl. Surveyors Assn. of Nebr. (chmn. exam workshop 1990—, bd. dirs. 1993—, v.p. 1995—), Nat. Assn. of County Engrs., Nebr. Assn. of County Engrs., Surveyors and Hwy. Supts. (sec.-treas. 1994, v.p. 1995, pres. 1996), North Platte Sunrise Rotary, Sigma Beta Delta, Phi Theta Kappa. Republican. Lutheran. Home: 1601 Sunset Dr North Platte NE 69101-6418 Office: Lincoln County Surveyor 2010 Rodeo Rd North Platte NE 69101-2603

HAWKS, JANE ESTHER HOKANSON, nursing educator; b. Sac City, Iowa, Apr. 8, 1955; d. Charles Wesley and Esther Pearl (Langbein) Hokanson; m. Edward Harold Hawks, May 24, 1980; 1 child, Jennifer Jane. BSN magna cum laude, St. Olaf Coll., 1977; postgrad., Iowa State U., 1978-79; MSN magna cum laude, U. Nebr., 1981; D in Nursing Sci. summa cum laude, Widener U., 1993. RN, Iowa, Nebr., Minn.; cert. med.-surg. nurse ANA. Nurse Rochester (Minn.) Meth. Hosp., 1976, 77-78; instr. Morningside Coll., Sioux City, Iowa, 1978-79, Jennie Edmundson Sch. Nursing, Council Bluffs, Iowa, 1979-81; instr., asst. prof. Coll. Nursing U. Nebr., Omaha, 1981-86; supr. pvt. duty nursing Family Home Care, Omaha, 1986; instr. Jennie Edmundson Sch. Nursing, Council Bluffs, 1986-88; instr. NCLEX rev. course Stanley H. Kaplan Ednl. Ctr., Omaha, 1986-89; asst. prof. nursing Clarkson Coll., Omaha, 1988-91, assoc. prof., 1991-92; asst. prof. nursing Midland Luth. Coll., Fremont, Nebr., 1992—; mem. Senator Harkin's Nursing Adv. Com., 1989—; mem. edn. com. Omaha Hospice Orgn., 1985-86; bd. dirs. Health Fair Midlands, 1988-95, vice chmn., 1992-94, chmn., 1994-95. Asst. editor Urologic Nursing, 1990—, mem. editorial com., 1988-90; co-author 2 books, several book chpts.; contbr. articles to profl. jours. Bd. dirs. Midwest ARC Regional Blood Svcs., 1992—, sec.-treas., 1995—, mem. nominations com. 1991-94, tissue donor, med. adv. exec. and fin. coms., 1993—; mem. Iowa Gov.'s Task Force on Long Term Care, 1984-85; bd. dirs. Pottawattamie County chpt. ARC, 1987-93, chmn., 1991-92, AIDS edn. speaker, 1988-93, mem. exec. com., 1991-93, mem. steering com., 1991-93, chmn. nursing and health com., 1988-93, facilitator bd. retreat, 1990. Recipient pub. awareness award Pottawattamie County chpt. ARC, 1988, Vol. of Yr. award Council Bluffs, 1989; scholar Evang. Luth. Ch. Am. div. Higher Edn., 1993, Am. Legion 40 and 8, 1991-92, Nurses Ednl. Funds, Inc., N.Y.C., 1991-92; nursing diagnosis rsch. grantee Midwest Nursing Diagnosis Task Force, 1989. Mem. AAUP, ANA, AACN, N. Am. Nursing Diagnosis Assn., Soc. Urologic Nurses and Assocs., Iowa Nurses Found. (bd.dirs., v.p. 1985-90, grant reviewer 1987-90), Iowa Nurses Assn. (state ethics com. 1985-86, state nursing edn. commn. 1989-93, chmn. state nursing rsch. com. 1994—, bd. dirs. dist. 9 1985-91, 9th Dist. Nurse of Yr. award 1983), Sigma Theta Tau (faculty counselor Theta Omega chpt., Leadership award 1996). Lutheran. Home: 514 North St Underwood IA 51576 Office: Midland Luth Coll 900 N Clarkson St Fremont NE 68025-4254

HAWLEY, ELLIS WAYNE, historian, educator; b. Cambridge, Kans., June 2, 1929; s. Pearl Washington and Gladys Laura (Logsdon) H.; m. Sofia Koltun, Nov. 3, 1953; children—Arnold Jay, Agnes Fay. B.A., U. Wichita, 1950; M.A., U. Kans., 1951; Ph.D. (research fellow), U. Wis., 1959. Instr. to prof. history North Tex. State U., 1957-68; prof. history Ohio State U., 1968-69; prof. history U. Iowa, 1969-94, prof. emeritus, 1994—, chmn. dept. history, 1986-89; hist. cons. Pub. Papers of the Presidents: Hoover, 1974-78. Author: The New Deal and the Problem of Monopoly, 1966, The Great War and the Search for a Modern Order, 1979, (with others) Herbert Hoover and the Crisis of American Capitalism, 1973, Herbert Hoover as Secretary of Commerce, 1981, Federal Social Policy, 1988, Herbert Hoover and the Historians, 1989; contbr. articles to profl. jours., essays to books. Investigator Project to Study Hist. in Iowa Pub. Schs., Iowa City, 1978-79; cons. Quad Cities hist. project Putnam Mus., Davenport, 1978-79. Served to 1st lt. inf. AUS, 1951-53. North Tex. State U. Faculty Devel. grantee, 1967-68, U. Iowa, 1975-76. Mem. Am. Hist. Assn., Orgn. Am. Historians, So. Hist. Assn., Soc. History Edn., AAUP (mem. exec. coun. Iowa chapt. 1982-84), Iowa Hist. Soc. Democrat. Home: 2524 E Washington St Iowa City IA 52245-3724 Office: U Iowa Dept History Iowa City IA 52242

HAWLEY, SANDRA SUE, electrical engineer; b. Spirit Lake, Iowa, May 7, 1948; d. Byrnard Leroy and Dorothy Virginia (Fischbeck) Smith; m. Michael John Hawley, June 7, 1970; 1 child, Alexander Tristin. BSEE, U. Dayton, 1981; BS in Math. and Stats., Iowa State U., 1970; MS in Stats., U. Del., 1975. Rsch. analyst State of Wis., Madison, 1970-71; rsch. asst. Del. State Coll., Dover, 1972-73; asst. prof. math. and statis. Wesley Coll., Dover, 1974-81, chmn. dept. math. and computer sci., 1978-80; elec. engr. Control Data Corp., Bloomington, Minn., 1982-85; sr. elec. engr. Custom Integrated Circuits, 1985-89; sr. lead engr. Cardiac Pacemakers, Inc., 1989-90; mgr. Tech. Rosemount Inc., 1990-94; prin. cons. Tri-Ess, Mpls., 1994—. Contbr. articles to profl. jours. Elder Presbyn. Ch. U.S.A., 1975—, mem. session Oak Grove Presbyn. Ch., Bloomington, 1985-88; moderator Presbyn. of Twin Cities Area, 1996—, chair Presbyn. Coun., 1994, chair Coun. United Action, 1989-92, adminstrv. comm., 1989-91, commr. to Synod of Lakes & Prairies, 1990, Gen. Assembly Coun., 1992—, com. on coun., 1992, commr. Gen. Assembly, 1991, chair Nat. Ministries divsn. Gen. Assembly, 1996—. NSF scholar U. Dayton, 1981. Mem. IEEE, Soc. Women Engrs. Office: Tri-Ess 7724 W 85th St Minneapolis MN 55438-1382

HAWLEY, WARREN JOHN, private school educator; b. Chgo., Apr. 13, 1947; s. Warren Fredrick and Margaret Elizabeth (Heh) H.; m. Mary Ellen Hawley, Feb. 8, 1974; children: Kate Meredith, Alexander Patrick. MS, Northeastern Ill. U., Chgo., 1979. Cert. tchr., Ill. Tchr. Marian Cath. H.S., Chicago Heights, Ill., 1970-78, Latin Sch. of Chgo., 1979—; mem. faculty DePaul U., Chgo., 1984—. Author: Foundations of Statistics, 1995. Mem. Nat. Coun. Tchrs. Math., Am. Math. Assn. Office: Latin Sch of Chgo 59 W North Blvd Chicago IL 60610

HAWORTH, DEBRA ELOISE DILL, physical therapist; b. Lafayette, Ind., July 5, 1951; d. William Granville and Daphne Eloise (Thurman) Dill; m. James Raymond Haworth, Sept. 12, 1968; children: James Raymond Jr., Mark Andrew, Mary Louise. BS, Tex. Women's U., 1982; M in health sci., U. Indpls., 1994. Lic. physical therapist, Ind. Dir. physical therapy Dill Medical Assocs., Atwood, Kans., 1982-83; dir., physical therapy Mesquite (Tex.) Cmty. Hosp., 1983-86; asst. dir. physical therapy Purdue U. Student Hosp., West Lafayette, Ind., 1986-87; staff therapist Arnett Clinic, Lafayette, Ind., 1987-91; dir. phys. therapy Rensselaer (Ind.) Care Ctr., 1991-93; adminstr. MedRehab Rehabilitation Ctr., West Lafayette, Ind., 1993-95, Sagamore Rehabilitation Ctr., West Lafayette, Ind., 1995—; bd. mem. Acad. Content Experts, Alexandria, Va., 1991-95. Mem. Am. Physical Therapy Assn., Am. Congress Rehabilitation Medicine, Am. Acad. Pain Mgmt. (clinical assoc.). Home: 307 S Bluff Monticello IN 47960 Office: Sagamore Rehabilitation Ctr 162-B Sagamore Pkwy W West Lafayette IN 47906

HAWORTH, STEVEN JOHN, software quality specialist; b. Chgo., Oct. 1, 1965; s. Henry Dillion and Jean Marie (Micale) H.; m. Joyce Eleanor Norton, Dec. 9, 1989; children: Timothy Henry, Jousha Clement. BS in Elec. Engring., Northwestern U., 1987. Applications programmer Semicondr. Lab., Northwestern U., Evanston, Ill., 1984-87; customer support assoc. Info. Data Mgmt., Rosemont, Ill., 1987-89; R&D assoc. Info. Data Mgmt., Lincolnwood, Ill., 1990-91, software engr., 1991-94; software quality specialist, resident lighting designer Stage Door Theatre Co., 1995—. Lighting designer How to Succeed in Business, 1992, A Christmas to Remember, 1992, Fake Ducks, 1993, Into the Woods, 1993, Madame Butterfly, 1994, Anything Goes, 1994, Wing Walkers, 1995, Smoke on the Mountain, 1996. Ill. State scholar, 1983, 84, 85, 86. Mem. IEEE (assoc.), USITT (assoc.). Evangelical Protestant. Office: Info Data Mgmt 9701 W Higgins Ste 500 Rosemont IL 60018-4703

HAWTHORNE, STEVEN C., design engineer; b. Little River, Kans., Aug. 1, 1955. Grad., high sch., 1973. Product design engr. Cross Mfg. Inc., Hays, Kans., 1976—.

HAXTON, LORI ANN, university administrator; b. Cedarburg, Wis., July 4, 1958; d. Roger Lee and Joan Elizabeth (Baumann) Butt; m. Jason Ross Haxton, Apr. 1, 1983; children: Ross, Laurel. BS, U. Wis., LaCrosse, 1980; MA, N.E. Mo. State U., 1983. Asst. hall dir. N.E. Mo. State U., Kirksville, 1981-83, residence hall dir., 1984-86, asst. dir. of residence life adminstn. and facilities, 1986-88; program coord. No. Ariz. U., Flagstaff, Mo., 1983-84; dir. admissions and enrollment svcs. Kirksville Coll. Osteo. Medicine, 1988—. Alderperson Greentop City Coun., 1993-95; vol. area hospice, 1993—; bd. dirs. Pk. Bd., Greentop, Mo., 1989—; sec. Still Nat. Osteo. Mus., kirksville, 1990—; advisor Adair County Advisor for Juveniles-2nd cir., Kirksville, 1990. Mem. Nat. Assn. Advisors for Health Professions, Ctrl. Assn. Advisors for Health Professions, Am. Assn. Collegiate Registrars and Admissions Officers, Am. Assn. of Colls. of Osteopathic Medicine Application Svc. (chairperson adv. com. 1990-92, chairperson diversity com. 1996—). Office: Kirksville Coll Osteo Medicine 800 W Jefferson St Kirksville MO 63501-1443

HAY, DONALD PETER, psychiatrist, educator; b. N.Y.C., Jan. 14, 1944; m. Linda Hay; 4 children. BA, Cornell U., 1966; MD, SUNY, Syracuse, 1970. Diplomate Nat. Bd. Examiners; lic. psychiatrist N.Y., Mont., Wis., Mo. Resident Upstate Med. Ctr., Syracuse, 1970-73; chief psychiatry svc. Holy Rosary Hosp., Miles City, Mont., 1973-78; svc. chief inpatient teaching ward Milw. County Mental Health Ctr., 1978-80; co-dir. geriatric psychiatry program Columbia Hosp., Milw., 1984-86, assoc. dir. electroconvulsive therapy treatment program, 1986-88, dir. geriatric psychiatry program, 1986-88; med. dir. geriatric psychiatry program Sinai-Samaritan Med. Ctr., Milw., 1988-91; dir. electroconvulsive therapy treatment program St. Mary's Hill Hosp., Milw., 1983-87, 91-93, dir. geriatric psychiatry program, 1991-93; dir. inpatient geriatric psychiatry program St. Louis U. Med. Sch., Mo., 1993—; assoc. prof. St. Louis U. Med. Sch., 1993—; asst. prof. dept. psychiatry and mental health scis. Med. Coll. Wis., Milw., 1978-80, asst. clin. prof., 1980-86, assoc. clin. prof., 1987-91, assoc. prof., 1991—, dir. div. geriatric psychiatry, 1991; assoc. clin. prof. U. Wis. Med. Sch., 1988-93; reviewer for various profl. jours. Contbr. numerous articles to profl. jours. Fellow Am. Psychiat. Assn. (corr. mem. coun. on aging 1989-96, long term care com. 1990), Am. Orthopsychiatry Assn.; mem. Wis. Psychiat. Assn. (pres. 1989-91), Assn. for Convulsive Therapy (exec. dir. 1989-95), Am. Geriat. Soc., Gerontol. Soc. Am., Boston Soc. for Gerontol. Psychiatry, Am. Assn. for Geriat. Psychiatry, Soc. Biologic Psychiatry, others. Office: St Louis U Med Sch 1221 S Grand Blvd Saint Louis MO 63104-1016

HAY, JOHN FRANKLIN, church administrator; b. Albany, Ky., Nov. 19, 1934; s. Martin M. and Lola (Avery) H.; m. Norma Janet Sheffield, Apr. 16, 1954; children: Debra Janita Retter, John Jr. AB, Trevecca Coll., 1958; DDiv (hon.), Olivet U., 1986. Ordained minister Ch. of the Nazarene, 1958. Pastor Ch. of the Nazarene, Albany, 1958-60, Charleston, W.Va., 1960-65, Parkersburg, W.Va., 1965-76; dist. supt. Indpls. Ch. of the Nazarene, 1976—. Author: Biography--Doug Slack, 1985, Promotional Ideas, 1982; contbr. articles to profl. jours. Trustee Mt. Vernon (Ohio) Nazarene Coll., 1972-76, Olivet Nazarene U., Kankakee, Ill., 1976—; capt. CAP, Indpls., 1986. Office: Indpls Ch of Nazarene 2799 Dan Jones Rd Plainfield IN 46168

HAY, RICK VANCE, nuclear medicine physician; b. Hailey, Idaho, July 14, 1949; s. Richard and Mary (Griffith) H.; m. Helayne Sherman, Sept. 18, 1988. AB, U. Chgo., 1971, PhD, 1977, MD, 1978. Diplomate Nat. Bd. Med. Examiners, Am. Bd. Nuclear Medicine. Resident anatomic pathology U. Chgo. Hosps. and Clinics, 1978-81; rsch. fellow Biocenter U. Basel, Switzerland, 1981-84; asst. prof. dept. pathology U. Chgo., 1984-91, assoc. prof., 1991-92; clin. fellow in nuclear medicine U. Mich., Ann Arbor, 1992-94; staff physician St. John Hosp. and Med. Ctr., Detroit, 1994—, med. dir. Dept. of Nuclear Med., 1995—; cons. Nat. Heart, Lung and Blood Inst., Bethesda, Md., 1987—. Contbr. articles to profl. jours. Recipient Sheard-Sanford award Am. Soc. Clin. Pathologists, 1979, Nat. Rsch. Svc. award NIH, 1982-84. Mem. Am. Heart Assn. (fellow coun. on arteriosclerosis, coun. on cardiovasc. radiology, Louis N. Katz rsch. prize 1976), Am. Soc. for Investigative Pathology, Am. Soc. Nuclear Cardiology, Soc. Cardiovasc. Pathology, Soc. Nuclear Medicine, Am. Coll. Nuclear Physicians, Ctrl. Soc. Clin. Rsch., Phi Beta Kappa, Alpha Omega Alpha. Office: St John Hosp and Med Ctr 22101 Moross Rd Detroit MI 48236

HAY, ROBERT PETTUS, history educator; b. Eagleville, Tenn., Oct. 23, 1941; s. Ira James and Alice Elizabeth (Pettus) H.; m. Carla Jean Humphrey, Dec. 31, 1966. BS with highest honors, Middle Tenn. State U., 1962; PhD, U. Ky., 1967. Instr. history Middle Tenn. State U., Murfreesboro, 1964; lectr. history U. Ky., 1966-67, instr. history Sch. Edn.'s Nat. Def. Edn. Act Inst., 1967; asst. prof. history Marquette U., Milw., 1967-71, assoc. prof., 1971—, asst. chmn. dept., 1975, chmn. dept., dir. grad. study, 1975-79. Assoc. history editor USA Today, 1980—; contbr. numerous articles and commentaries to hist., popular and profl. jours., book reviewer numerous publs.; author poetry and chpts. in books. Mem. Milw. County Zool. Soc., Milw. Art Mus., Friends of Milw. County Pub. Mus., Tenn. State Mus. Assn., Colonial Williamsburg Found., Friends of John F. Kennedy Libr. Found.; adv. coun. Bradley Inst. Dem. & Pub. Values, 1988-89; dir's. cir. Patrick & Beatrice Haggerty Mus. Art, Middle Tenn. State U. Found.; life mem. pres.'s coun. Marquette U.; life mem. U. Ky. Fellows; rsch. grantee Marquette U., 1968, grantee Bradley Inst. Democracy & Pub. Values, 1989; summer faculty fellow Marquette U., 1969, 73. Commd. Ky. Col. 1980, Woodrow Wilson fellow, 1962-63, 65-66, NDEA fellow, 1962-65, NEH fellow, 1969-70. Mem. AAUP, Orgn. Am. Historians (life), Am. Soc. for 18th Century Studies, So. Hist. Assn. (life), Soc. Historians Early Am. Rep. (life), Tenn. Hist. Soc. (life), Am. Cath. Hist. Assn. (life), Milw. County Hist. Soc. (life), Ky. Hist. Soc. (life), Filson Club (life), Am. Hist. Assn. (life), Milw. Met. Historians Assn., East. Tenn. Hist. Soc. (life), Nat. Trust Hist. Preservation, West Tenn. Hist. Soc. (life), Inst. Early Am. History and Culture, Ctr. for Study of Presidency, Wis. Assn. Promotion of History, Waukesha County Hist. Soc. (life), Wis. Club, Helfaer Recreation Ctr., Atlanta Track Club, Phi Alpha Theta, Pi Gamma Mu. Democrat. Roman Catholic. Avocations: running, gardening, poetry, weight-lifting, basketball. Home: 2146 Laura Ln Waukesha WI 53186-2858 Office: Marquette U PO Box 1881 Dept History Milwaukee WI 53201-1881

HAYASHI, ERIC, art association administrator. Exec. dir. Arts Commn., Topeka. Office: Arts Commn 700 Jackson St Ste 1004 Topeka KS 66612-1239*

HAYDOCK, WALTER JAMES, banker; b. Chgo., Dec. 14, 1947; s. Joseph Albert and Lillian V. (Adeszko) H.; student Harvard Bus. Coll., 1969-71, Daily Coll., 1971-73; BS in Acctg., DePaul U., 1976; m. Bonnie Jean Thompson, Aug. 22, 1970; children: Nicole Lynn, Matthew Michael. Computer operator, jr. programmer Pepper Constrn. Co., Chgo., 1972-73; input analyst Continental Bank, Chgo., 1973-76, data control supr., 1976-79, corporate fixed asset adminstr., 1979-83, properties systems analyst, 1983-87, props. sr. systems supr., 1987-91, unit chief conversions Fed. Deposit Ins. Corp., 1992-93, info. security specialist, 1993—; pres. Wal-Bon., Inc.; distbr. Lic. Disney Character Mdse. Mem. Southwest Suburban Bd. Realtors. Home: 14129 Somerset Ct Orland Park IL 60462-1142 Office: 500 W Monroe Chicago IL 60661

HAYEK, LINDA MARIE, mathematics educator; b. Lincoln, Nebr., Oct. 2, 1951; d. Marlin Glen and Dottie June (Henderson) DeBoer; m. Stan Lee Moore, Aug. 26, 1972 (div. 1985); children: Kristen Michelle, Erin Marie; m. David James Hayek Jr., Mar. 28, 1987. BS in Edn., U. Nebr., Omaha, 1972; MA in Computers in Edn., Lesley Coll., 1986; MA, U. Nebr., 1988. Cert. math. tchr. Tchr. math. Ralston (Nebr.) High Sch., 1973-77, 80—, Ralston Mid. Sch., 1978-80; mem. adj. faculty Coll. St. Mary, Omaha, 1990-91. Recipient NASA Edn. Workshop Math & Sci. Tchrs. award NSF, 1991, Cooper award Cooper Found., Nebr., 1992, Presdl. award for excellence in sci. and math. tchg., 1994, U. Nebr. at Omaha Disting. Alumni award, 1995; Ritonya Buscher Poehling grantee, Omaho, 1990, 91. Mem. NEA, ASCD, Nat. Coun. Tchrs. Math., Nebr. Assn. Tchrs. Math., Nebr. State Edn. Assn., Coun. Presdl. Awardees in Math., Phi Delta Kappa. Democrat. Presbyterian. Office: Ralston High Sch 8969 Park Dr Omaha NE 68127-3663

HAYES, BRENDA SUE NELSON, artist; b. Rockford, Ill., May 26, 1941; d. Reuben Hartvick and Mary Jane (Pinkston) Nelson; m. John Michael Hayes, Jan. 26, 1964; 1 child, Amy Anne. BFA in Graphic Design, U. Ill., 1964. Exec. officer JMH Corp., Indpls., 1971—. Exhibited at Art Source, Bethesda, Md., The Corp. Collection, Kansas City, Mo., The Hang Up Gallery, Sarasota, Fla., Susan Musleh-Art By Design, Inc., Indpls., Swan Coach House Gallery, Atlanta, Arnot Art Mus., Elmira, N.Y., Indpls. Mus. Art, Pindar Gallery, Soho, N.Y.; represented in permanent collections at Holy Family Hosp., Des Plaines, Ill., Lilly Endowment, Dow Venture Ctr. Internat. Hdqs., Wishard Hosp., Indpls., Deloitte Touche, Inc., Haskins & Sells, IBM, AT&T, U.S. Spring, NWS Corp., Chgo., Meth. Hosp., Indpls., Eli Corp. Offices, Hewlett-Packard, Trammell Crow, Dow Consumer Products, Melvin Simon & Assocs., Dow Elanco Corp. Hdqs., Copyrite Nat., Support Net, NBD Banking Processing Ctr. Lobby, Indpls., Cellular One Regional Offices, Nat. City Plaza, others. Bd. dirs. Contemporary Art Soc. for Indpls. Mus. Art, 1993—, sec., 1992-94; charter mem. Nat. Mus. Women in Arts. Lydia Bates scholar U. Ill., 1961-63, Ill. Found. of Study scholar, 1963-64, resident schoar, 1960-64; recipient Panhellenic award for Study U. Ill., 1963-64, Gallery Exhbn. awards. Mem. Nat. Mus. Women in the Arts (charter), Gamma Alpha Chi (Outstanding Woman in Journalism 1964). Home: 157 E 71st St Indianapolis IN 46220-1011 Studio: 921 E 66th St Indianapolis IN 46220-1137

HAYES, DEBRA TROXELL, family nurse practitioner; b. Highland, Ill., Oct. 11, 1952; d. Robert E. and Marilyn M. (Schwend) Troxell; m. Jay F. Hayes, May 31, 1985; children: Amy Myers, Eric Myers. Diploma, Graham Hosp. Sch. Nursing, 1973; BSN, Sangamon State U., Springfield, Ill., 1985; MS in Pub. Health Nursing, U. Ill., Chgo., 1995. RN, Ill.; cert. oncology nurse ONCC, cert. family practice nurse ANCC. Staff and relief charge nurse, head nurse Mason Dist. Hosp., Havana, Ill., 1973-77; staff and relief charge nurse, nursery charge nurse Graham Hosp., Canton, Ill., 1979-85; nurse coord. problem pregnancy program Cath. Social Svcs., Peoria, Ill., 1985-86; nurse clinician Oncology Hemtalogy Assocs., Peoria, 1986-95; FNP Coleman Clinic, Ltd., Canton, Ill., 1995—. McFarland scholar Mason Dist. Hosp., 1970, Illinois Farm Bur. Nurse Practitioner scholar, 1993-94. Mem. ANA, Ill. Nurses Assn., Ill. NP Coun., Ill. Rural Health Assn., Oncology Nursing Soc. Home: 9526 W Lake Lancelot Dr Mapleton IL 61547-9723

HAYES, ELIZABETH LAMB, biology educaotr; b. Portland, Oreg., Aug. 5, 1940; d. Clyde Chester and Helen (Penni) Lamb; m. Robert William Hayes; children: Andrew Chester, Margaret Elizabeth Anne, Jennifer Eleanor Carlotta. BA, Marylhurst Coll., Oswego, Oreg., 1962; postgrad., So. Ill. U., 1962-63, U. Wis., Milw., 1965, 66; MS, Marquette U., 1965. Rsch. assoc. Marquette U., Milw., 1966; mem. faculty Cardinal Stritch Coll., Milw., 1965-66, Milw. Area Tech. Coll., 1966-68; assoc. prof. biology U. Wis., Fond du Lac, 1968—. Contbr. articles to profl. jours. Pres. Fond du Lac Sch. Bd., 1988-91, bd. dirs., clk., 1986, 87, 92-95. Marquette Univ. fellow, grad. scholar, 1963-65. Mem. AAUW (pres. 1975-77, Postsecondary State Educator award), AAAS, Am. Inst. Biol. Scis., Soroptimist Internat., Round Table. Episcopalian. Home: N 7862 Sandy Beach Rd Fond Du Lac WI 54935 Office: U Wis Fond Du Lac 400 University Dr Fond Du Lac WI 54935

HAYES, HELEN, electronics company executive; b. Cin., Feb. 10, 1955. MBA (hon.). Mgr. Cin. Milacron, 1973—. Patentee in field. Office: Cin Milacron 4701 Marburg Ave Cincinnati OH 45209-1025

HAYES, JACQUELINE CREMENT, real estate broker and developer; b. Chgo., Aug. 12, 1941; d. John and Lottie (Czech) Crement; m. Larry G. Hayes, Mar. 4, 1972 (div. Dec. 1978). BA in Mgmt., DePaul U., 1977. Lic. real estate broker, Ill. Bldg. mgr. LaSalle Bank Bldg., Chgo., 1978-80; v.p., gen. mgr. The Hayman Co., Chgo., 1981-83; pres. Jacqueline Hayes & Assoc., Chgo., 1983—; ptnr. The Retail Group, Chgo., 1986-93; panelist retail planning seminar Dept. Planning, City of Chgo., 1988, steering com. River North urban design plan, 1987-89, pedestrian count, 1989, Streeterville urban design plan, 1990—, Downtown Framework Plan, 1990—; mem. mentorship program Woman of Destiny, 1992-93. Docent Chgo. Archtl. Found.; mem. Burnham Park Planning Bd., Chgo.; bd. dirs., mem. exec. com., v.p., chmn. planning, zoning and urban design Greater N. Michigan Ave. Assn., Chgo., 1986—; mem. adv. coun. Friends of Downtown, 1987-89; bd. dirs. Cactus Theatre, 1990-92; bd. dirs., chair nominating com. Lawson House YMCA, 1993—. Named Broker of Yr. Chgo. Sun-Times, 1986, one of Top Businesswomen Crain's Chgo. Bus., 1990-91, Woman of Destiny, 1990-92, one of 100 Women Who Make a Difference Today's Chgo. Woman, 1995. Mem. NAFE, Internat. Coun. Shopping Ctrs., Comml. Real Estate Orgn. (bd. dirs., v.p., chmn. membership 1986-89), Am. Biol. Inst. (rsch. bd. advisors, Disting. Leadership award), Chgo. Real Estate Exec. Women (bd. dirs., sec., mentorship program 1992), Chgo. Assn. Commerce and Industry, Urban Land Inst., River North Assn., Women in Planning and Devel., Women in Retail Leasing (founder 1993), Lambda Alpha (bd. dirs., sec., v.p. edn., v.p. programs, Mem. of Yr. 1995). Office: Jacqueline Hayes & Assocs Ste 700 400 E Randolph St Chicago IL 60601-7329

HAYES, JOHN MARION, civil engineer; b. Wingate, Ind., May 18, 1909; s. William Lucas and Margaret Eliza (Gallaher) H.; m. Coye Matilda Cunningham, June 22, 1935; children: Marian Sue Hayes Jernigan, Julia Kethleen Hayes Casey. BSCE, Purdue U., 1931; MS, U. Tenn., 1944, D in Civil Engring., 1946. Structural engr. TVA, Knoxville, Tenn. and Chattanooga, 1935-46; dist. bridge engr. U.S. Bur. Pub. Rds., Little Rock, 1946-48; assoc. prof. Purdue U., West Lafayette, Ind., 1948-58; prof. structural engr. Purdue U., West Lafayette, 1958-75, prof. emeritus, 1975—. Recipient Outstanding Engring. Alumnus award U. Tenn., 1975. Fellow ASCE (hon., dir. dist. 9 1964-66, v.p. zone III, 1969-70, Outstanding Civil Engr. Ind. sect. 1988), NSPE, Am. Concrete Inst., AAAS, Am. Welding Soc., ASTM, Am. Soc. Engring. Edn., Am. Inst. Steel Constrn. Inc. (Spl. Citation award 1971), Ind. Sci. Engring. Found. Inc., SAR (pres. Ind. Soc. 1990-92, nat. trustee 1992-94), Lions, Chi Epsilon Sigma Xi. Republican. Methodist. Home: 312 Highland Dr West Lafayette IN 47906-2406

HAYES, MARY JOANNE, special education educator; b. Bloomington, Ind., Feb. 3, 1944; d. John and Marie (Van Buskirk) Reeves; m. Jack Lee Hayes, June 25, 1983. BA, Olivet U., Kankakee, Ill., 1968; MA, Ind. U., 1972; postgrad., Ind. U., South Bend, 1987, Ind. State U., 1989. Lic. tchr., Ind. Tchr. 3rd grade Saulk View Sch., Steger, Ind., 1968-69; tchr. 1st grade Break-O-Day Sch., New Whiteland, Ind., 1969-83; tchr. emotionally handicapped David Turnham Edn. Ctr., Dale, Ind., 1987—. Mem. Coun. Exceptional Children, Coun. Behavorial Disorders, Ind. Reading Coun. Home: PO Box 191 Dale IN 47523-0191 Office: David Turnham Ednl Ctr Dale IN 47523

HAYES, MARY PHYLLIS, savings and loan association executive; b. New Castle, Ind., Apr. 30, 1921; d. Clarence Edward and Edna Gertrude (Burgess) Scott; m. John Clifford Hayes, Jan. 1, 1942 (div. Oct. 1952); 1 child, R. Scott. Student, Ball State U., 1957-64, Ind. U. East, Richmond, 1963; diploma, Inst. Fin. Edn., 1956, 72, 76. Teller Henry County Savs. and Loan, New Castle, 1939-41, loan officer, teller, 1950-62, asst. sec., treas., 1962-69, sec., treas., 1969-73, corp. sec., 1973-84; v.p., sec. Ameriana Savs. Bank (formerly Henry County Savs. and Loan), New Castle, 1984-91; exec. sec. Am. Nat. Bank, Nashville, 1943-44; corp. sec. Ameriana Fin. Svcs., 1984-91. Treas. Henry County Chpt. Am. Heart Assn., New Castle, 1965-67, 76-87, vol. Indpls. chpt. 1980—; membership sec. Henry County Hist. Soc., New Castle, 1975-90; sec. Henry County chpt. ARC, New Castle, 1976-91; elected mem. Found. Inst. Fin. Edn., 1991—; mem. Internat. Platform Assn., 1974—, Woman's Club 1992—; vol. Ind. Basketball Hall of Fame, 1993—. Mem. Inst. Fin. Edn. (sec.-treas. East Ctrl. Ind. chpt. 1973-91), Ind. League Savs. Insts. (25 Yrs. award 1975, 40 Yrs. Cert. award 1988), Internat. Platform Assn., Henry County Hist. Soc. (mem. sec.), Altrusa (past officer, bd. dirs. New Castle chpt.), PEO (past chaplain, sec., past pres. 1994-95), Woman's Club, New Castle Henry County C. of C., Guyer Opera House Guild, Art Ctr. of Henry County, Psi Iota Xi (past sec.-treas.). Mem. Christian Ch.

HAYES, PETER CHARLES, research chemist; b. Wellingborough, Eng., Jan. 7, 1953; came to U.S., 1980; s. Denis James and Joan Mary (Gostick) H.; m. Ivy Elizabeth Ellen Smith, Sept. 7, 1985. Postgrad., Royal Soc. Chemistry, Eng., 1970-75, 75-77; PhD, U. Keele, Staffordshire, Eng., 1980. Asst. chemist Scott-Bader Co., Ltd., Wollaston, Eng., 1970-77; teaching assoc. U. Keele, 1977-80; postdoctoral fellow Ohio State U., Columbus, 1980-82, U. Windsor, Ont., Can., 1983-84, U. Toronto, Can., 1984-86; sr. chemist ICI (Can.) Inc., Toronto, 1986-88; sr. rsch. chemist, process chemist BASF Can. Inc., Sarnia, 1988-91; polymerization coord., sr. rsch. chemist Gencorp. Specialty Polymers Divsn., Akron, Ohio, 1991-96; sr. rsch. assoc. BASF Corp., Charlotte, N.C., 1996—. Patentee vesiculated polymer granules, 1989, 90, polymer latex, 1994, low formaldehyde latex binder, 1994, 95; contbr. articles to profl. jours. Mem. Royal Soc. Chemistry (charter), Am. Chem. Soc., Internat. Churchill Soc. Home: 6601 Bevington Brook Ln Charlotte NC 28226 Office: BASF Corp Splty Polymers Div 11501 Steele Creek Rd Charleston NC 28273

HAYES, RANDY E., stockbroker; b. Elkhart, Ind., Aug. 4, 1953; s. Daniel E. and Mary K. (Branstetter) H.; m. Cecelia L. Holtz, Mar. 13, 1983; children: Dan, Nathan, Katie, Peter. BA, Ind. U., 1976. Salesman Coachman RV, Elkhart, 1983-85; stockbroker Painewebber, South Bend, Ind., 1985—, Roney & Co., Elkhart, 1988—. Mem. Elkhart Club. Republican. Roman Catholic. Office: Roney & Co 121 W Franklin # 303 PO Box 130 Elkhart IN 46515

HAYES, ROBERT E., state legislator; b. Battle Creek, Mich., Oct. 18, 1933; m. to Marilyn Hayes; children: Eric, Jennifer. BS, N.E. Mo. U.; JD, Ind. U. Pvt. practice law; state rep. Dist. 59 Ind. Ho. of Reps., 1974-80, 82—, asst. majority floor leader, mem. human affairs and edn. com., mem. judiciary com., cts. and criminal code com., mem. rules and legis. procedures com. Mem. Am. Legion, Kiwanis, Eagles, Phi Delta Phi. Home: 3221 Sherwood Pl Columbus IN 47203-2612*

HAYES, SAMUEL BANKS, III, banking company executive; b. Morristown, N.J., Nov. 30, 1936; m. Kathryn Hannam; 3 children. BA, Yale U., 1959; postgrad. in bus., Harvard U., 1970. Exec. tng. program Citibank, 1960-61, with nat. div., 1962, with petroleum dept., 1963-70, wholesale retail trade dept. head, 1970-73; area supr. 33 brs. Citibank, N.Y.C., 1973-74; div. mgr. 150 brs. Citibank, Bklyn., Queens, S.I., Nassau County and Suffolk County, N.Y., 1974-75; regional credit officer Citibank, Sidney, Australia, 1976-77; exec. v.p. Bank Okla., 1977-78, pres., chief operating officer, 1978-86; pres., chief exec. officer Boatmen's Nat. Bank St. Louis, 1986—, vice-chmn., 1989—; vice chmn. Boatmen's Bancshares Inc., 1989—; bd. dirs. Boatmen's Trust Co. Bd. dirs. Mcpl. Theatre; trustee St. Louis Art Mus.; bd. trustees Mo. Bot. Garden, St. Louis U.; bd. commrs. St. Louis Sci. Ctr.; chmn. Christmas in St. Louis, 1989; co-chmn. Zoofari St. Louis Sports Com., 1989. Served with U.S. Army, 1959, 61. Mem. Log Cabin Club, Old Warson Country Club, Mo. Athletic Club, Racquet Club, Saint Louis Club, Southern Hills Country Club. Clubs: So. Hills Country (bd. govs.); Golf Okla. (bd. govs.); Yale (pres.) (Tulsa). Office: Boatmen's Nat Bank 1 Boatmen's Plz 800 Market St Saint Louis MO 63101*

HAYES, STEPHEN KURTZ, author; b. Wilmington, Del., Sept. 9, 1949; s. Ira Maurice and Carolyn (Kurtz) H.; m. Rumiko Urata, Apr. 14, 1980; children: Reina Emily, Marissa Christine. BA, Miami U., Oxford, Ohio, 1971. Ordained Tendai sect Japanese Esoteric Buddhist priest, 1991. Author: The Ninja and Their Secret Fighting Art, 1981, Ninjutsu: Art of the Invisible Warrior, 1984, The Mystic Arts of the Ninja, 1985; Ninja: Spirit of the Shadow Warrior, Vol. I, 1980, Warrior Ways of Enlightment, Vol. II, 1981, Warrior Path of Togakure, Vol. III, 1983, Legacy of the Night Warrior, Vol. IV, 1984, Wisdom from the Ninja Village of the Cold Moon, 1984, Ninja Realms of Power, 1986, Tulku, 1985, Ancient Art of Ninja Warfare, 1988, Lore of the Shinobi Warrior, 1989, Action Meditation, 1992, Enlightened Self-Protection, 1992. Named to Black Belt Hall of Fame, Black Belt. mag., 1985. Mem. Tibetan Med. Inst. (life), Nine Gates Inst. (internat. dir. 1975—), Togakure Ryu Ninjutsu (10th degree black belt). Home: PO Box 326 Bellbrook OH 45305-0326 Office: Nine Gates Inst PO Box 291947 Dayton OH 45429-0947

HAYNES, DEBORAH GENE, physician; b. York, Neb., Feb. 18, 1954; d. Gene Eldridge and Margaret Lucille (Manchester) Haynes; m. Russell Larry Beamer, Mar. 3, 1979; children: Staci E. Beamer, Lindsay M. Beamer, Stephanie L. Beamer. BA in Biology cum laude, Wichita State U., 1976; MD, U. Kans., Wichita, 1979. Diplomate Am. Bd. Family Practice; cert. Added Qualifications-Geriatrics. Resident St. Joseph Hosp., Wichita, 1979-82; instr. dept. family and community medicine St. Joseph Family Practice Residency, U. Kans., Wichita, 1982-84, asst. prof. dept. family and community medicine, 1984-85; pvt. family practice Northeast Family Physicians, Wichita, 1985—; clin. asst. prof. U. Kans. Sch. Medicine, Witchita, 1985—; bd. govs. endowment assn. Wichita State U., 1995—; bd. dirs. Via Christi Regional Med. Ctr. Trustee Wichita Collegiate Sch., 1993—. Recipient P.G. Czarlinsky award for Disting. Clin. Svc., U. Kans., 1979, Wichita State U. Gore scholarship, 1992. Fellow Am. Acad. Family Physicians (del. 1991—, commn. on edn. 1991—, task force on procedures, Mead Johnson award 1990-91, chair COD credential com. 1994), Kans. Acad. Family Physicians (pres. elect 1988-89, pres. 1989-90), Kans. Med. Soc., Med. Soc. Sedgwick County (del. 1990-91, chair profl. investigation com. 1993-95), Alpha Omega Alpha. Presbyterian. Home: 1015 N Linden Cir Wichita KS 67206-4075 Office: 8100 E 22nd St N Bldg 2200 Wichita KS 67226-2301

HAYNES, GERALD WAYNE, aerospace manufacturing administrator; b. Canton, N.C., Dec. 9, 1942; s. Sidney P. and Anne M. (McCracken) H.; m. Judy Pressley, June 3; 1 child, Stephanie Leigh. AA, Mars Hill Coll., 1963; BSBA cum laude, Western Carolina U., 1966; MS in Logistics Mgmt., Air Force Inst. Tech., 1977; student def. systems, Mgmt. Coll., Ft. Belvoir, Va., 1982. Cert. profl. mgr. Process planner mfg. engring. dept. outdoor lighting GE, Hendersonville, N.C., 1966-67; commd. USAF, 1967, advanced through grades to lt. col.; officer in charge comm. ctrs. 2063 comm. group USAF, Lindsey Air Sta., Wiesbaden, Germany, 1968-71, long line circuit mgmt. staff officer hdqrs. European comm. area, 1971-72; commdr., ops. officer in charge recruiting detachment 301 USAF, Gunter AFB, Ala., 1972-76; contracts officer divsn. aero. systems USAF, Wright-Patterson AFB, Ohio, 1976-79; dep. mgr. programs integrated computer-aided mfg. materials lab., Wright-Patterson AFB, Ohio, 1979-82; asst. dir. aero. indsl. modernization office USAF, Wright-Patterson AFB, Ohio, 1984-85; chief mfg. divsn. plant rep. office at GE Co. USAF, Cin., 1982-84; dir. divsn. product assurance space systems USAF, L.A. AFB, 1985-88; ret. USAF, 1988; mgr. indsl. systems devel. Space Fligh Systems United Techs. Corp., Huntsville, Ala., 1988-90, program mgr. large aircraft robotic paints stripping program, 1991-93, product dir. aircraft systems, 1994; dep. program mgr. mfg. tech. spl. advanced studies Lawrence Assocs., Inc., Dayton, Ohio, 1994—. Contbr. tech. publs. to confs. Active parish coun. Gunter Chapel, Montgomery, Ala., 1973-76; active fund coun. Redstone Chapel, Huntsville, Ala.; area coord. Homeowners Assn., Dayton; team leader Neighborhood Protection and Improvement, Huntsville, 1989-94. Decorated USAF meritorious svc. medal with two oak leaf clusters. Mem. Soc. Mfg. Engrs. (sr.), Soc. Automotive Engrs., Nat. Mgmt. Assn., Nat. Contract Mgmt. Assn., Am. Soc. Materials, Air Force Assn., Ret. Officers Assn. Home: 6243 Pheasant Hill Rd Dayton OH 45424-4189 Office: Lawrence Assocs Inc 5100 Springfield St Dayton OH 45431-1261

HAYNES, MARCIA MARGARET, insurance agent; b. Bay City, Mich., June 28, 1931; d. Frederick O. and Margaret M. (Oakes) Rouse; m. N. Fred Haynes, July 20, 1957;children: Carol M. Krashen, David F. Haynes, Julie A. Haynes. BA, Denison U., Granville, Ohio, 1953. With advt.-sales dept. Birmingham (Mich.) Eccentric, 1953-55; tchr. Port Huron (Mich.) Area Schs., 1955-58; student tchr. coord. Mich. State U., Port Huron, Mich., 1967-70; insurance agent Northwestern Mut. Life Ins. Co., Port Huron, Mich., 1981—. Leader, Girl Scout U.S., Port Huron, 1956-57; treas. and bus. mgr., Port Huron Little Theater, Port Huron, 1959-161; sec., v.p., and pres., Mus. of Arts and History, 1968-69, 74-80; sec., v.p. bd. dirs., Port Huron Hosp. Aux., 1960-70; trustee, Hist. Soc. of Mich., Ann Arbor, 1975-81; coord. of preservation Round Island Lighthouse, Straits Mackinac, Mich., 1972-76; chmn. Horizons, Port Huron Bicentennial Com., Port Huron, 1976; active in Rep. State Bicentennial Com, Lansing, Mich. 1976; trustee, St. Clair County C.C., Port Huron, 1981-99, vice chmn., 1985-95; bd. dirs., Stuart House Mus., Mackinac Island, Mich., 1978, Internat. Symphony, Port Huron and Sarnia, Ont., Canada, 1983-86; sec., treas., and bd. dirs., Blue Water Area Tourism Bureau, Port Huron, 1985-87; adv. bd., Cmty. Found. of St. Clair County, Port Huron, 1986-91, 94—; vestry Grace Episcopal Ch., 1990-93; bd. dirs. Am. Heart Assn. St. Clair County, 1994—; v.p. fin. Blue Water Found. Boy Scouts Am., 1995—. Mem. Nat. Life Underwriters, Port Huron Life Underwriters, Port Huron Estate Planning Coun. (pres. 1985-86), Mich. Mus. Assn. (bd. dirs. 1984-86), Rotary, Port Huron Golf Club. Home: 813 Lakeview Ave Port Huron MI 48060-2103

HAYNES, MARILYN MAE, accountant, educator; b. Fond du Lac, Wis., Apr. 30, 1933; d. Clinton Charles and Addie May (Pavey) Ehrhardt; m. Ivan R. Haynes, Aug. 13, 1960. Jr. Acctg. diploma, Madison Bus. Coll., 1952; BE, Wis. State U., Whitewater, 1959; postgrad., U. Wis., 1975-77. Bookkeeper Gas Mags., Inc., Madison, Wis., 1952-55; various positions Wis., summers 1956-60; bus. edn. tchr. Sheboygan (Wis.) Sch. Vocat. and Adult Edn., 1959-60, Edgerton (Wis.) High Sch., 1960-61; acct. Graber Mfg. Co., Middleton, Wis., 1961-71; bookkeeper Alexander Grant and Co., Madison, 1971-79; night sch. bus. edn. instr. Stoughton (Wis.) Vocat.-Adult Ctr., 1961-82, Madison Area Tech. Coll., 1961—; acct. Dane County Housing Authority, Madison, 1979—. Chmn. ch. coun. United Meth. Ch., Stoughton, 1970-72, com. chmn., 1972-76, officer ch. cir., 1970-72, handbell ringer, choir mem., Monona, Wis., 1983—. Mem. Inst. Mgmt. Accts., Order of Ea. Star. Office: Dane County Housing Authority 2825 University Ave Madison WI 53705-3643

HAYS, J. JEFFERSON, state legislator; b. Archer City, Tex., Dec. 27, 1929; s. Joseph Collins and Vera (Pruett) H.; m. Mary Louise Hoffman, 1956; children: Lisa, Laura, Lynn, Christine, John. BS, U. Evansville, 1955. Purchasing agt. U. So. Ind.; state rep. Dist. 77 Ind. Ho. of Reps., 1970-72, 74—, mem. age and aging com., mem. com. on cities and towns, mem. com. on elec., mem. interstate coop. com., fin. insts. com., mem. pub. health com., chmn. com. and econ. devel. com., ranking minority mem., co-chmn. regulator flexibility com. Bd. dirs. Ind. Grocer's Found.; mem. Ind. Enterprise Zone Bd. With U.S. Army; Korea. Decorated Bronze Star medal. Mem. Pi Epsilon Phi. Home: 1705 S Green River Rd Evansville IN 47715-5743*

HAYS, NANCY, entertainment executive, entertainer; b. Urbana, Ill., May 15, 1958; d. Edward Parker and Mary Pearl (Johnson) H.; m. Sean Leahy Heffernan, Aug. 27, 1988; children: Mary Therese, Edward Sean, Matthew David. BS in Comm., U. Ill., 1980; MS in Advt., Northwestern U., Evanston, Ill., 1984. From acct. mgr. to sr. mgr. music and entertainment Jack Morton Prodns., Inc., Chgo., 1984-93; pres., CEO Nancy Hays Entertainment, Inc., Chgo., 1993—. Author, prodr., perfomer (videotape) Bring Back the Romance of Dance Instruction, 1995. Mem. Phi Kappa Phi. Mem. United Ch. of Christ. Home and Office: 6804 W Hurlbut Ave Chicago IL 60631

HAYS BUTLER, HOLLY LYNN, university youth extension educator; b. Newport News, Va., Nov. 21, 1962; d. Luther Marr and Joan (Anderson) Hays; m. Richard Michael Butler, Jr., Nov. 26, 1988. BS in Biol. Scis., Purdue U., 1985; MBA, Ind. Wesleyan U., 1991. Teller Union Fed. Savs. Bank, Indpls., 1987-88, asst. mgr., 1988-89, br. mgr., 1989-90, staffing coord./mgr. floating staff, 1990-91; youth educator coop. ext. svc. Purdue U., West Lafayette, Ind., 1991—. Judge crafts, pub. speaker 4-H; bd. dirs. Jr. Achievement-Boone County, 1991—, sec., 1993—. Mem. AAUW (rec. sec. 1989-92), Ind. Ext. Agts. Assn. (award youth sect. 1992, 93, 95, Bob Amicle award 1995), Nat. Assn. Ext. 4-H Agrs., Phi Beta Chi (nat. dir. properties 1988-89, nat. treas. 1989-93, nat. pres. 1993—, pres. Ctrl. Ind. alumnae chpt. 1990-91, publs. com. 1991-94). Home: 9752 N County Road 950 E Brownsburg IN 46112-9261

HAYZLETT, GARY K., state legislator; b. Lakin, Kans., Sept. 4, 1941; s. Lester Madison and Juanita (Coder) H.; m. Helen Yakel, 1961; children: Teresa Jane, Jennifer Jill, Wendy Marie. Student, Garden City C.C., 1960-61. County commr. Kearny County, Kans., 1974—; chmn. Kans. Legis. Policy Group; Kans. state rep. Dist. 122; owner, operator Gary's AG Grocery, Lakin, 1965-79, Dairy Queen/Brazier, 1979—. Mem. Kans. County Commrs. Assn., Masons (Emerald Lodge No. 289), Scottish Rite, Shriners. Home: PO Box 66 Lakin KS 67860-0066*

HAZEL, JAMES R. C., JR., small business owner, civic volunteer; b. Sturgis, Ky., Oct. 11, 1940; s. James R.C. Hazel Sr. and Lucille Vivian (Brumfield) Palmer; m. Donna Jean Wideman, July 8, 1960; children: Juliee Teresa Hazel Norman (dec.), James R.C. III. AA, Kellogg Community Coll., 1990; grad., E.K. Williams Profl. Mgmt. Sch. With family auto svc. sta., 1952-64, mgr., 1964; pres., owner Jim Hazel's Unocal 76 Svc. and Auto Parts Store, Battle Creek, Mich.; mem. adv. bd. Auto Wares, Inc.; bd. dirs. Battle Creek Community Found. Active S.W. Mich. coun. Boy Scouts Am., 1970—, vice chmn., 1987-93; chmn. Battle Creek Community Leadership Acad., 1985—; bd. dirs. Art Ctr. Battle Creek, 1985-88; chairperson small bus. div. fund drive United Arts Coun., 1987; mem. adv. bd. United Way; sponsor Youth to Sweden Hockey Tournament, 1979; charter mem. Y-Ctr., Binder Pk. Zoo; sponsor, patron various civic orgns.; mem. adv. com. youth initiaties program W.K. Kellogg Found., 1989. Named Dealer of Yr., Pure Oil Co., 1967, Super Citizen, City of Battle Creek, 1989; recipient Silver Beaver award Boy Scouts Am., 1983, George award Battle Creek Enquirer, 1988, Carnation Community Svc. award Battle Creek Vol. Bur., 1985, Sml. Bus. of Yr. award 1992, 1st Ann. Pride award Harper Creek Schs., 1992, Book of Golden Deeds award Exch. Club, 1994, Disting. Citzen award Calhoun Area Vocat. Ctr., 1989, Calhoun County Intermediate Sch., 1994. Mem. Mich. Svc. Sta. Dealers Assn. (bd. dirs. 1980-90, vice chairperson polit. action com.), Mich. Auto Parks Assn. (bd. dirs. 1989—), Battle Creek C. of C. (vice chmn. 1986-89, charter, chmn. Leadership Acad.), Ducks Unltd., Rotary (bd. dirs. Battle Creek chpt. 1992—), Optimists (life, sec., treas. Harper Creek Club 1979, Achievement in Edn. award 1989), Masons, Shriners. Home: 6695 E Drive N Battle Creek MI 49017-5223 Office: Jim Hazel's Unocal 76 Svc 14301 Beadle Lake Rd Battle Creek MI 49017-8213

HAZELTINE, JOYCE, state official; b. Pierre, S.D.; m. Dave Hazeltine; children: Derek, Tara, Kirk. Student, Huron (S.D.) Coll., No. State Coll., Aberdeen, S.D., Black Hills State Coll., Spearfish, S.D. Former asst. chief clk. S.D. Ho. of Reps.; former sec. S.D. State Senate; sec. of state State of S.D., Pierre, 1987—. Adminstrv. asst. Pres. Ford Campaign, S.D.; Rep. county chmn. Hughes County S.D. Mem. Nat. Assn. Secs. of State (exec. bd., pres.). Office: Sec of State's Office 500 E Capitol Ave Ste 204 Pierre SD 57501-5077

HAZLETT, PAUL EDWARD, realtor, information systems executive; b. Gallipolis, Ohio, Dec. 10, 1937; s. Vickers James and Wilma (Dickey) H.; m. Lynn Todd; 1 child, Esther. BBA, Cleve. State U., 1964. Freight sales N.Y. Cen., Cleve., 1964-66; with computer systems dept. Honeywell, Inc., Cleve., 1966-75; investment real estate Cleve., 1975-78; mgr. Fairview Gen. Hosp., Cleve., 1978-96; adj. faculty Cuyahoga Community Coll., Cleve.; cons. in field; real estate agt., Cleve. Bd. mgrs. West Side YMCA, 1987—. Home: 6987 Big Creek Pky Middleburg Heights OH 44130 Office: 13405 Smith Rd Middleburg Heights OH 44130

HE, LILI, electrical engineering educator, researcher. BS in Elec. Engring., Nanjing U., China, 1984; MS, Nanjing Electronic Inst., China, 1984; MA, SUNY, Buffalo, 1989, PhD, 1992. Rsch. engr. Nanjing Electronic Inst., 1984-87; tchg. asst. SUNY, Buffalo, 1987-89, rsch. asst., 1989-92; asst. prof. No. Ill. U., Dekalb, 1993—. Mem. IEEE, Am. Vacuum Soc., Material Rsch. Soc., Am. Soc. Engring. Edu. Office: No Ill U Dept Elec Engring De Kalb IL 60115

HEAD, MOSES M., municipal official; s. Moses and Beatrice (Peppers) H.; 1 child, Virgil. BS in Phys. Edn., Lincoln U., Jefferson City, Mo. Dir. street work program Inner City YMCA, St. Louis; job coach supr. Mayors Coun. on Youth, St. Louis; tchr., asst. prin. St. Louis Pub. Schs.; asst. dir. pub. works University City, Mo.; mem. human rels. com. University City Sch. Dist. Named Top City Official, University City Sch. Dist. Mem. Am. Pub. Works Assn., Am. Assn. Affirmative Action, Omega Psi Phi, Inst. Adminstrv. Mgmt. Democrat. Roman Catholic. Home: 7831 Trenton Ave University City MO 63130 Office: 6801 Delmar Blvd University City MO 63130-3104

HEADLEY, KATHRYN WILMA, secondary education educator; b. Grand Rapids, Mich., Mar. 10, 1940; d. William L. and Kathryn (Mekkes) H. BA, Hope Coll., 1967; MEd, Grand Valley Univ., 1981. Cert. tchr., Mich. Missionary, Reformed Ch. in Am., N.Y.C., summers, 1959-64; various ch. positions Ottawa Reformed Ch., West Olive, Mich., 1956—, Bible day camp dir., 1979-92; tchr. lang. arts/phys. edn. Jenison Pub. Schs. (Mich.), 1967—, head coach girls basketball, volleyball, 1967-78, head coach girls track, softball, 1967-73, head coach girls bowling, 1973-78, class advisor, 1983-90, numerous other sch. activities. coach girls soccer, basketball, Borculo Christian Sch., Mich., 1981-88. Bd. dirs. Ottawa County Tchrs. Credit Union, Grand Haven, Mich., 1978-90, 94—, v.p., 1984-88. Mem. Mich. Edn. Assn. (rep.), NEA, Jenison Edn. Assn. (rep.), Mich. High Sch. Athletic Assn. (ofcl.), Hope Coll. Alumni Assn., Mich. Christian Endeavor Bd., Delta Kappa Gamma. Mem. Reformed Ch. in Am. Home: 9111 96th Ave RR 1 Zeeland MI 49464 Office: Jenison Pub Schs 2140 Bauer Rd Jenison MI 49428-9539

HEADLEY, WILLIAM A., manufacturing company executive; b. Geneva, Ohio, Jan. 6, 1941. Machinist Parker Hannigan, Wickliff, Ohio, 1962-78, Fedco Systems, Odessa, Fla., 1978-83; pres. All Am. Machining Co., Inc., Madison, Ohio, 1983—. Home and Office: All Am Machining Co Inc 309 N Lake St Madison OH 44057-3119

HEADRICK, LINDA ANN, physician, educator; b. Rolla, Md., Nov. 28, 1955; d. Hubert Harold and Ethel Ruth (Capps) H.; m. David Ray Setzer, Aug. 13, 1977. BA, U. Mo., 1977; MD, Stanford U., 1981. Diplomate Am. Bd. Internal Medicine. Intern in medicine U. Md., Balt., 1981-82, resident in medicine, 1982-84, chief resident in medicine, 1984-85; asst. prof. medicine Sch. Medicine, Case Western Res. U., Cleve., 1985-93, assoc. prof., 1993—; staff physician, primary care clerkship dir. Met. Health Med. Ctr., Cleve., 1985-94. Author: Quality and Cost of Care, 5th edit., 1994, Clinical CQI: A Book of Readings, 1995. Mem. ACP, APHA, Soc. Gen. Internal Medicine, Physicians for Social Responsibility (nat. bd. dirs. 1990-95, pres. N.E. Ohio chpt. 1990-91), Physicians for Human Rights, Amnesty Internat. Home: 6435 Chagrin River Rd Chagrin Falls OH 44022-3540 Office: Met Health Med Ctr 2500 Metrohealth Dr Cleveland OH 44109-1900

HEADRICK, ROGER LEWIS, professional sports executive; b. West Orange, N.J., May 13, 1936; s. Lewis B. and Marian E. (Rogers) H.; m. C. Lynn Cowell, Sept. 29, 1962; children: Hilary R. H. Bell, Mark C., Christopher C., Heather R. AB, Williams Coll., 1958; MBA, Columbia U., 1960. Fin. analyst Standard Oil (N.J.), Esso Eastern, Inc., N.Y.C., 1960-65; treas. Standard Oil (N.J.), Esso Eastern, Inc., Tokyo, 1965-70; v.p. Standard Oil (N.J.), Esso Eastern, Inc., Manila, 1970-73; treas., mgr. fin. and planning Standard Oil (N.J.), Esso Eastern, Inc., Houston, 1973-78; dep. contr. Exxon Corp., N.Y.C., 1978-82; exec. v.p., chief fin. officer The Pillsbury Co., Mpls., 1982-89; now, pres., chief exec. officer Minn. Vikings, Eden Prairie, Minn.; bd. dirs. Rahr Malting Co., Crompton & Knowles Corp., Caremark Internat. Inc. Office: Minn Vikings 9520 Viking Dr Eden Prairie MN 55344-3825

HEADY, JUDITH EMILY, biology educator; b. Cedar Rapids, Iowa, Dec. 11, 1939; d. John Robert Miller and Rachel (Albright) Heneks; m. Stephen G. Heady, Feb. 8, 1958 (div. 1970); children: Elizabeth Annette, Kathleen Michelle. BA, Cornell Coll., 1962; MS, U. Iowa, 1963; PhD, U. Colo., 1970. Rsch. assoc. U. Colo. Med. Ctr., Denver, 1970-74; jr. investigator Marine

Biol. Lab., Woods Hole, Mass., summer 1974; asst. prof. biology U. Mich., Dearborn, 1974-79, assoc. prof., 1979—; independent investigator U. Wash., Friday Harbor, summer 1976; vis. asst. prof. biochemistry U. Colo. Med. Ctr., Denver, summer 1977; sabbatical leave U. Minn., St. Paul, 1980-81; vis. rsch. scientist Marine Biol. Lab., Woods Hole, 1987-88; vis. profl. biology U. Wis., 1995. Author 7 book chpts.; contbr. articles to profl. jours. Mem. Am. Assn. Higher Edn. (panel 1996), AAAS, NSTA, Soc. Coll. Sci. Tchr. (mem. girls and sci. panle 1993, editor. Home: 405 Evergreen Dr Ann Arbor MI 48103-2730 Office: U Mich Dept Natural Sci 4901 Evergreen Rd Dearborn MI 48128-1491

HEALEY, EDWARD HOPKINS, architect; b. Dubuque, Iowa, Jan. 3, 1925; s. George Beach and Marian (Hopkins) H.; m. Alice Letitia Dawson, Sept. 11, 1954; children: Susan Healey Toussaint, Carolyn Healey Olson, Ellen Hopkins Healey. BS in Architecture, U. Ill., 1950; cert., Ecoles D'Art Americaines, Fountainbleau, France, 1950. Registered architect, Iowa, Ill., Wis., Minn. Ptnr. Brown & Healey, Architects, Cedar Rapids, Iowa, 1953-60, Brown, Healey & Bock, Architects and Engrs., Cedar Rapids, 1960-81; pres. Brown, Healey & Bock, Architects, Planners, Interior Designers, Cedar Rapids, 1981-90, Brown, Healey, Stone & Sauer, Architects, Planners, Interior Designers, Cedar Rapids, 1990—. Del. The White House Conf. on Libraries and Info. Svcs., Washington, 1979, 91; pres. profl. adv. bd. dept. architecture Iowa State U., Ames, 1981-82; pres. East Cen. Regional Library Bd., Cedar Rapids, 1981-84; mem. Iowa Library Commn., Des Moines, 1987—, chmn., 1987-89; bd. dirs. Iowa Cultural Affairs Adv. Coun., Des Moines, 1987-89; trustee Linn County Hist. Mus., 1990—, Brucemore, 1983-89. Fellow AIA (pres. Iowa chpt. 1965-66); mem. ALA, Nat. Coun. Archtl. Registration Bds. (bd. dirs. 1975-77), Literary Club (sec. 1980-86, pres. 1987-88). Home: 2500 White Eagle Trl SE Cedar Rapids IA 52403-1548 Office: Brown Healey Stone & Sauer Architects PC 800 1st Ave NE Cedar Rapids IA 52402-5002

HEALEY, ROBERT WILLIAM, school system administrator; b. Charleston, Ill., Sept. 29, 1947; s. William Albert and Ruth M. (Wiedenhoeft) H.; m. Sharon Barbara Grande, Aug. 7, 1982; children: William Robert, Steven Anthony. BS in Elem. Edn., Ea. Ill. U., 1970, MS in Ednl. Adminstrn., 1972; EdD in Curriculum and Supervision, No. Ill. U., 1977. Cert. elem. teaching K-9, gen. adminstrv. K-12, Ill. Prin. Glidden Elem. Sch., De Kalb, Ill., 1972-74, Lincoln Elem. Sch., De Kalb, 1974-83, Littlejohn Elem. Sch., De Kalb, 1983-84, Littlejohn and Cortland Elem. Schs., De Kalb, 1984-85; prin., dist. coord. testing and evaluation Jefferson Elem. Sch., De Kalb, 1986-96; dir. personnel DeKalb Sch. Dist., 1996—; dir. Title I Elem. and Secondary Edn. Act., Pre-Sch. Base Line Program, 1972-74; dir. gifted edn. Bd. Edn. Negotiating Team, 1974-81, coordinator dist. testing and evaluation, 1981-84, coordinator spl. edn., 1984-86; mem. adv. bd. Evanston (Ill.) Educators Computer Software, 1983—; dir. testing DeKalb Sch. Dist. 428, 1986—; treas. No. Ill. Commn. for Gifted Edn., Oakbrook, 1980-82; mem. various elem. sch. planning and program councils, De Kalb, 1973—; coordinator numerous sch. programs, De Kalb, 1973—; leader numerous workshops DeKalb, 1976-85; sec. De Kalb Sch. Bd. Study com. on sch. lunch programs, 1976-77; cons. Scholastic Testing Service, 1980-83; chmn. dist. reading com., De Kalb, 1986—. Coordinator 10 yr. study of student achievement in DeKalb Schs., 1980-83; author numerous presentations, 1975-84; revisor DeKalb School District Parent Handbook, 1986; contbr. articles to profl. jours; inventor multi-purpose table and stage. Chmn. Task Force I DeKalb Sch. Dist., 1973-75; treas. No. Ill. Planning Commn., 1980-82; active Supts. Task Force on Spl. Edn., DeKalb, 1976-79, Mayor's Commn. DeKalb Planning Commn. for Yr. of Child, DeKalb, 1979, Dist. Computer Com., DeKalb, 1980-83, Dist. Revenue and Donations Com., 1980-83, Ill. PTA. Recipient Disting. Program award Nat. Assn. for Tchr. Educators, Chgo., 1978; named Citizen of Day, Sta. WLBK, De Kalb, 1983; Reading is Fundamental grantee Lincoln Sch., 1980-83, Ill. Ctr., 1980-83, Ill. Arts Coun., Littlejohn Sch., 1984, Jefferson Sch., 1986; named master, Ill. Adminstrs. Acad., 1995. Mem. NEA (life), ASCD, NAESP (Nat. Disting. Prin. award representing Ill. 1995), Ill. Prins. Assn. (Prin. of Yr. award 1995), Ill. Assn. for Supervsion and Curriculum Devel., Soc. Am. Inventors, Ill. Coun. Gifted Edn. Office: De Kalb Cmty Unit Sch Dist 901 S 4th De Kalb IL 60115-3275

HEALTON, BRUCE CARNEY, data processing executive; b. Montebello, Calif., Oct. 22, 1955; s. Donald Carney and Doris May (Kubler) H.; m. Deborah Louise Stevens, Nov. 26, 1977; children: Alexander Carney, Michaela Shawn. BA of Bus., Western Ill. Univ., 1977; Cert. Brokerage Ops., N.Y. Inst. of Fin., 1986. Programmer Westinghouse Learning Corp., Iowa City, 1977-78; contract programmer Cutler-Williams, Mpls., 1978-79; programmer/analyst Northwest Computer Svcs., Mpls., 1979-81; cons. Cytrol, Edina, Minn., 1981-90; cons./pres. Elegant Tech. Solutions, Brooklyn Park, Minn., 1990—; treas. Minn. Joint Computer Conf., Mpls., 1990-91, asst. treas., 1989-90. Mem. IEEE (cons. software com. 1989-90), Assn. for Computing Machinery, Twin Cities (sec. 1987-89, chair 1993—). Office: Elegant Tech Solutions 8480 Yates Ave N Minneapolis MN 55443-2186

HEALY, DAVID FRANK, history educator; b. River Falls, Wis., Oct. 21, 1926; s. Manley Burdette and Florence Louise (Moll) H.; m. Ann Karen Erickson, Oct. 17, 1959; children: Matthew David, Ellen Louise, Jonathan Joseph. BA in History, U. Wis., 1951, MA, 1957, PhD, 1960. Asst. prof. History Ill. Coll., Jacksonville, 1960-64; asst. prof. U. Del., Newark, 1964-66; assoc. prof. U. Wis., Milw., 1966-71, prof., 1971-93, prof. emeritus, 1993—. Author: The United States in Cuba 1898-1902, 1963, U.S. Expansionism, 1970, Gunboat Diplomacy in the Wilson Era, 1976, Drive to Hegemony, 1988. With USN, 1951-55. Mem. Am. Hist. Soc., Orgn. Am. Historians, Soc. for Historians of Am. Fgn. Rels. Home: Apt 1602 1626 N Prospect Ave Milwaukee WI 53202 Office: U Wis Milw PO Box 413 Milwaukee WI 53201-0413

HEALY, JOHN CHRISTOPHER, tax specialist; b. Monmouth, Ill., Feb. 16, 1950; s. Lambert J. and Catherine L. (Lehman) H.; m. Jacquelyn R. Hefel, Sept. 9, 1972; children: Jessica Lynn, James Russell. BS in Acctg., Marquette U., 1972; MS in Taxation, U. Wis., Milw., 1992. CPA, Wis. Gen. and tax acct. Manpower, Inc., Glendale, Wis., 1972-75; tax supr. GE Med., Waukesha, Wis., 1975-80; tax mgr. GE Med. Systems, Waukesha, Wis., 1980-88; state tax audit mgr. Miler Brewing Co., Milw., 1988—; adj. prof. Lakeland Coll., Milw., 1992—, U. Wis., Milw., 1996—; seminar leader U. Wis. Law Sch., Madison, 1992-95. Co-author: Multi State Corporate Tax Guide, 1992-94; contbr. articles to profl. jours. Pres. Waukesha Taxpayers League, 1994-95; campaign advisor econ. Hammersmith for Congress, Milw., 1992; campaign advisor Foley for Mayor, Waukesha, 1994; chmn. sch. choice com. Waukesha Cath. Sch. System, 1992-95. Arthur Melinger Found. scholar, 1971-72; recipient Cert. Appreciation Wis. State Legislature, 1991. Mem. AICPA, Wis. Inst. CPAs (chmn. taxation com. 1995, seminar leader 1995), Inst. Property Taxation (sales tax legis. com. 1993, Literary award 1991), Tax Execs. Inst. (chmn. state tax com. 1992), U. Wis./Milw. Tax Assn. (Manuscript award 1990).

HEALY, PATRICIA COLLEEN, social worker; b. Denver, Aug. 24, 1935; d. Cecil John and Gracia Maude (Walker) Schulte; m. John Patrick Healy III, Aug. 3, 1957 (div. Jan. 1972); 1 child, Sean Patrick. BA, Sacred Heart Coll., Wichita, 1957; MSW, U. Kans., 1983; postgrad., Wichita State U., 1974, 75, 89, Emporia (Kans.) State U., 1990. Lic. specialist clin. social worker, Kans.; cert. in spinal cord injury medicine. Proofreader Wichita Pub. Co., 1953; clk. typist Nat. Sales, Inc., Wichita, 1954-58, Dept. of Army, Ft. Leavenworth, Kans., 1958-60, Air Force, McConnell AFB, Kans., 1962-63; clk., typist VA Regional Office, Wichita, 1963-66; self-employed typist Wichita, 1966-70; ward clk., typist VA Regional Office and VA Med. Ctr., Wichita, 1970-73; vets. benefits counselor VARO, Wichita, 1973-83; social worker VA Med. Ctr., Wichita, 1983—. Author filmstrip, columns, book revs., feature stories and poetry. Former mem. Ctrl. Plains AAA Coun. on Aging; bd. dirs. Ind. Living Ctr. South Ctrl. Kans., 1990-96. Recipient Eddy L. Sutton award, Sunflower Subchapter, Paralyzed Vets. Am., 1992. Mem. Kans. Soc. Clin. Social Workers (mem. editl. bd. 1986-87), Paralyzed Vets. Am., Wichita Assn. Visually Impaired Handicapped (bd. dirs. 1989-92), Kans. Authors Club. Roman Catholic. Office: VA Med Ctr 5500 E Kellogg Dr Wichita KS 67218-1607

HEALY, STEVEN MICHAEL, accountant, city official; b. Chgo., July 20, 1949; s. Daniel Francis and Angelina (Massino) H. BA, U. Ill., Chgo., 1971; MBA, Rosary Coll., 1984. Br. mgr. Assocs. Capital Co., Chgo., 1971-74; credit analyst Motorola, Inc., Schaumburg, Ill., 1974-76; office mgr. Triple "S" Steel Corp., Franklin Park, Ill., 1976-79; accounts payable supr. Zenith Electronics, Chgo., 1979-84; supr. acctg. Village of Oak Park, Ill., 1984-86; bus. analyst Caleshion of Chgo., Oak Park, 1986-87; dir. fin. Village of Maywood, Ill., 1988-91; dir. fin., treas. City of DeKalb, Ill., 1991-93; dir. fin. Village of Cahokia, Ill., 1993—. Mem. Friends of Oak Park Libr., Friends of the Conservatory, Oak Park Village Players Group, Cahokia Econ. Devel. Commn.; bd. dirs. Oak Park Employees Credit Union; treas. Cahokia Assn. for the Tricentennial. Mem. Nat. Soc. Pub. Accts., Nat. Govt. Fin. Officers Assn., Ill. Govt. Fin. Officers Assn., U. Ill. Alumni Assn., Rosary Coll. MBA Alumni Assn. (founder, soc. com. 1984—), Oak Park Area Jaycees, Rotary Club of St. Clair Valley (chair, sec.), Cahokia C. of C., Cath. Alumni Club, Village Oak Park Chess Club (pres. 1984-86), Maywood Rosary, Kishwaukee Sunrise Rotary, Cahokia Kiwanis Club. Home: 2013 Oak Tree Ln Cahokia IL 62206-1408 Office: 103 Main St Cahokia IL 62206-1019

HEALY, WILLIAM JAMES, state legislator; b. Canton, Ohio, Mar. 4, 1939; s. Charles Wilson and Margaret (Higgins) H.; m. Barbara A. Clark, 1959; children: Joyce Renee, Jacqueline Ann, William James II. Student, Kent State U. Stark Br., 1960-63. Councilman Ward 6 and 12 Canton, 1969-74; state rep. Dist. 50 Ohio State Congress, 1975-92, state rep. Dist. 54, 1993—; mem. Stark County Dem. exec. and ctrl. coms., 1970—; chmn. econ. affairs, fed. rels. com. State Govt. Com.; with Corrigated Box Divsn. St. Regis Paper Co., Canton, 1960-73, Culligan Soft Water, Canton, 1974; adminstrv. dir. Goodwill Urban League Treatment Ctr., 1973-74. Recipient Outstanding Legis. Leadership award Stark County Sch. Supt., 1982, Award Ohio State Bar Assn., 1992, Franklin County Trial Lawyers, 1993; named Layman of Yr. Canton Profl. Edn. Assn., 1984. Mem. Stark County Talk About Potential Programs (co-founder), Jefferson Jackson Dem. Men's Club. *

HEANEY, WILLIAM MATTHEW, electric power industry executive; b. Duluth, Minn., June 8, 1949; s. Gerald William and Eleanor Rose (Schmitt) H.; divorced; children: Erin E., Mehgan R.; m. Marcia Ann Nelson, July 19, 1986; stepchildren: Peter S. Hansen, Eric C. Hansen. BS in Polit. Sci., U. Minn., Duluth, 1986. Right-of-way agt. Minn. Power & Light Co., Duluth, 1973-74, legistative asst., 1975-77, mgr. state legislative and regulatory affairs, 1978-80; mgr. state legislative affairs No. States Power Co., Mpls., 1980—; mgr. state legislative affairs No. States Power Co., Mpls., 1980—; mem. Minn. Gov.'s High Level Radioactive Waste Citizens' Coun., St. Paul, 1982-86; mem. Blue Ribbon Task Force of Minn. Water Quality Programs, 1995-96; antique dealer. Mem. Minn. Ethical Practices Bd., St. Paul, 1989-93. Mem. Minn. C. of C. (environ. com. 1984—), Midwest Labor Mgmt. Pub. Affairs Com. (steering com. and coord. 1982—). Home: 110 Cherry St W Stillwater MN 55082 Office: No States Power Co 414 Nicollet Mall Minneapolis MN 55401-1927

HEAP, JAMES CLARENCE, retired mechanical engineer; b. Trinidad, Colo.; s. James and Elsie Mae (Brobst) H.; m. Alma Mae Swartzendruber. Registered profl. engr., Wis. Sr. mech. engr. Cook Electric Research Lab, Morton Grove, Ill., 1955-56; assoc. mech. engr. Argonne (Ill.) Nat. Lab., 1956-66; sr. project engr. Union Tank Car Co., East Chicago, Ind., 1966-71; sr. engr. Thrall Car Mfg. Co., Chicago Heights, 1971-77; research design engr. Graver Energy Systems, Inc., East Chicago, Ind., 1977-79; mech. cons. design engr. Pollak & Skan, Inc., Chgo., 1979-83, ret., 1983; cons. mech. design and stress analysis, 1965-83. Author: Formulas for Circular Plates Subjected to Symmetrical Loads and Temperatures, 1966; contbr. tech. papers to profl. jour.; patentee in field. Served with USAF, 1946-47. Mem. ASME, Christian Businessmen's Com. U.S., The Gideon's Internat. Home: 1406 Ashton Ct Goshen IN 46526-4679

HEARN, JOHN PATRICK, biologist, educator; b. Limbdi, India, Feb. 24, 1943; s. Hugh Patrick and Cynthia Ellen (Nicholson) H.; m. Margaret Ruth McNair, Sept. 30, 1967; children: Shaun, Karina, Bruce, Adrian, Nicholas. BS, Univ. Coll., Dublin, Ireland, 1966, MSc, 1968; PhD, Australian Nat. U., Canberra, 1972. Lectr. in zoology Strathmore Coll., Nairobi, Kenya, 1967-69, head biology dept., dean sci., 1968-69; rsch. scholar zoology dept. Australian Nat. U., 1969-72; scientist med. rsch. coun. reproductive biology unit U. Edinburgh, Scotland, 1972-79; prof. in reproductive biology Univ. Coll., London, 1979-95; dir. Wellcome Labs. of Comparative Physiology, Inst. Zoology Zool. Soc. London, 1979-80, dir. sci., 1980-87; prof. dept. physiology Med. Sch. U. Wis., Madison, 1990—; dir. Wis. Regional Primate Rsch. Ctr., 1990—; cons. scientist WHO, Geneva, 1978-79; mem. coun. NIH Nat. Ctr. Rsch. Resources, 1995—, NAS Inst. for Lab. Animal Resources, 1991—; mem. tech. adv. com. Contraceptive Devel. Orgn., 1990—. Author, editor: Reproduction in New World Primates, 1983, Advances in Animal Conservation, 1985, Reproduction and Disease in Captive and Wild Animals, 1988, Conservation of Primates Studies in Biomedical Research, 1995. Recipient Bolliger award Australian Mammal Soc., 1972; fellow Inst. Biology, 1980. Fellow Zool. Soc. London (sci. medal 1983); mem. Am. Soc. Primatology, Soc. for Study of Reproduction, Soc. for Study of Fertility, Primate Soc. Gt. Britain (Osman-Hill medal 1986), Internat. Primatol. Soc. (pres. 1984-88). Office: U Wis Regional Primate Rsch Ctr 1220 Capitol Ct Madison WI 53715-1237

HEARNS, PATRICIA A., nurse practitioner; b. Paw Paw, Mich., Dec. 2, 1947; d. Dwayne Russell and Marion G. (Meyer) Guiter; m. Gregory J. Hagerman; children: William Arthur Hearns, Jennifer Lynn Hearns. Diploma, Butterworth Hosp., Grand Rapids, Mich., 1969; BS, Western Mich. U., 1982; MSN, Mich. State U., 1986. Cert. family nurse practitioner, ANCC, case mgr. Staff nurse Bronson Meth. Hosp., Kalamazoo, Mich., 1971-79, instr., 1979-81, supr., 1981-84, clin. nurse specialist, 1985-88; nurse practitioner Portage (Mich.) Med. Group, 1984-85, Cardiology Assocs., Kalamazoo, 1985; clin. nurse specialist Butterworth Hosp., Grand Rapids, 1988-91, Battle Creek (Mich.) Health System, 1992-93; mgr. CCU Borgess Med. ctr., Kalamazoo, 1993-95; FNP Otsego (Mich.) Family Physicians, 1995—; adj. faculty U. Mich., Ann Arbor, 1994—; adj. faculty Grand Valley State U., Allendale, Mich., 1987-93, 1995, Ferris State U., Big Rapids, Mich., 1988-89; cons. Genentech, Inc., South San Francisco, 1987—, Cardiology Assocs., Kalamazoo, 1991-93, Dimensions of Critical Care Nursing, Lakewood; rschr. Butterworth Hosp., Grand Rapids, 1988-91. Vol. March of Dimes, Vicksburg, Mich., 1991-92; alt. del. State Rep. Conv., Detroit, 1972. Grad. fellow Mich. State U., 1984, 85. Mem. ANA, AACN (hosp. liaison west Mich. chpt. 1990), Am. Heart Assn. (cert. BLS, ALS, sec. Kalamazoo chpt. 1987-88), Sigma Theta Tau (Alpha Psi chpt.). Republican. Methodist. Home: 312 S Michigan Ave Vicksburg MI 49097-1321 Office: Otsego Family Physicians 900 Dix Otsego MI 49078

HEASEL, JOHN FREDERICK, office automations specialist; b. Cin., Mar. 30, 1934; s. Harry Frederick and Louise Alma (Peppers) Heasel; m. Linda Hartman, Aug. 6, 1960. Student, U. Cin., 1952-54, 58-59, Tulane U., 1963-67, La. State U., 1967-69; BBA, LaSalle U., 1974. Cert. office automation profl. Engr. AVCO Corp., Cin. and Richmond, Ind., 1959-63, Space div. Chrysler Corp., New Orleans, 1963-69; corp./dealer identity Chrysler Corp., Highland Park, Mich., 1969-78; fleet/facility engr. Chrysler Transport Inc., Detroit, 1978-80; logistics engr. Gen. Dynamics, Warren, Mich., 1980-83; mgr. office automation Gen. Dynamics, Sterling Heights, Mich., 1983-93; founder, v.p. Motion Techs., Inc., 1989; instr. ethics tng. Gen. Dynamics, Troy, 1986; instr. microprocessors Apple Pub. Interest East, East Detroit, 1986. Contbr. articles to profl. jours. Active USCG Aux., Mich., 1975—; bd. dirs. Friends St. Clair Shores Libr., 1995—. With USN, 1954-58. Mem. Office Automation Soc. Internat., Nat. Mgmt. Assn., Auxop Assn. (founding pres. 1988-89), Internat. Naval Rsch. Orgn. (contbg.), Gt. Lakes Maritime Inst., U.S. Naval Inst., St. Clair Shores Hist. Soc., Greater Detroit Coast Guard Officers's Assn., Apple Core Club (v.p. 1983—), Apple P.I.E. Club (treas. 1986), Tailhook Assn., Jefferson Yacht Club (bd. dirs. 1990), Waterline Italia. Mem. Office Automation Soc. Internat., Nat. Mgmt. Assn., Auxop Assn. (Ofounding pres. 1988-89), Internat. Naval Rsch. Orgn. (contbg.), Gt. Lakes Maritime Inst., U.S. Naval Inst., Apple Core Club (v.p. 1983—), Apple P.I.E. Club (treas. 1986), Tailhook Assn., Jefferson Yacht Club (bd. dirs. 1990), Waterline Italia. Home: 22842 Avalon St Saint Clair Shores MI 48080-2461

HEATER, WILLIAM HENDERSON, psychology educator; b. Webster Groves, Mo., May 12, 1928; s. Elsor and Mary Eliza (Henderson) H.; m. Mary Ellen Fischbach, Jan. 22, 1955; children: John William, Susan Elizabeth Salinas, David Julius. BA, Denison U., 1950; MDiv, Union Theol. Sem., 1953; PhD, Mich. State U., 1967. Asst. min. Fort Street Presbyn. Ch., Detroit, 1953-56; min. First Bapt. Ch., Nitro, W.Va., 1956-59, Owosso, Mich., 1959-64; instr. Lansing (Mich.) Community Coll., 1966-69, chairperson, social sci. dept., 1969-86, prof., 1986-93; vis. scholar U. Mich., 1991. Mem. Lansing Bd. Edn., 1978-89, v.p., 1979, 80, 88, pres., 1981, 86, 87; bd. dirs. Habitat for Humanity, Lansing. Recipient Excellence in Teaching award United Ch. of Christ Gen. Synod, 1989, Vis. Scholar, U. Mich., 1991. Mem. Torch Club Internat. Democrat. Mem. United Church of Christ. Home: 2025 Cogswell Dr Lansing MI 48906-3610

HEATH, MARIWYN DWYER, writer, legislative issues consultant; b. Chgo., May 1, 1935; d. Thomas Leo and Winifred (Brennan) Dwyer; m. Eugene R. Heath, Sept. 3, 1956; children: Philip Clayton, Jeffrey Thomas. BJ, U. Mo., 1956. Mng. editor Chemung Valley Reporter, Horseheads, N.Y., 1956-57; self-employed freelance writer, platform speaker, editor Tech. Transls., Dayton, Ohio, 1966—; cons. Internat. Women's Commn., 1975-76; ERA coord. Nat. Fedn. Bus. and Profl. Women's Clubs, 1974-82; mem. polit. and mgmt. coms. ERAmerica, 1976-82, exec. dir., 1982-88; pres. Miami Valley Regional Transit Authority, 1986-88, bd. dirs. 1984-91; chair Regional Transit Coalition, 1991-94. Author: 75 Years and Beyond-BPW/USA, 1994. Mem. Gov. Ohio Task Force Credit for Women, 1973; mem. Midwest regional adv. com. SBA, 1976-82; mem. Ohio Women's Commn., 1990—, vice chair, 1993—; pres. Dayton Pres.'s Club, 1973-74; chmn. Ohio Coalition ERA Implementation, 1974-75; appt. joint civilian orientation conf., U.S. Dept. Def., 1988. Recipient Legion of Honor award Dayton Pres.'s Club, 1987, Keeper of Flame award Ohio Sec. of State, 1990; named One of 10 Outstanding Women of World Soroptimist Internat., 1982; named to Ohio Women's Hall of Fame. Mem. AAUW (dir. Dayton 1965-72, Woman of Year award Dayton 1974), Nat. Fedn. Bus. and Profl. Women's Clubs (pres. Dayton 1967-69, Ohio 1976-77, nat. polit. action com. 1985—, chmn. 1988—), Miami Valley Mil. Affairs Assn. (bd. dirs.), Ohio Women (v.p. 1983-86, bd. dirs. 1977-89), Assn. Women Execs., Women in Communications. Republican. Roman Catholic. Address: 10 Wisteria Dr Dayton OH 45419-3451

HEATHCOCK, JOHN EDWIN, clergyman; b. Detroit, Dec. 12, 1937; s. James Richard and Laurel Viola (Manwarren) H.; m. Kathryn Iva Trexler, Aug. 31, 1958 (div. 1978); children: Jean Marie, Jeffrey Daniel, Janet Iva; m. Elizabeth Ann Porter, Dec. 12, 1978. BS, Cen. Mich. U., 1966; M Div., Duke U., 1970, ThM, 1971; PhD, Internat. Coll., 1980. Ordained priest Episcopal Ch., 1984. Dir. pastoral care SW Texas Meth. Hosp., San Antonio, 1972-80, Amarillo (Tex.) Hosp. Dist., 1980-86; adminstr. St. Luke's Hosp., Chesterfield, Mo., 1986—; cons. Perkins Sch. Theology So. Meth. U., Dallas, 1973-76, Oblate Coll., San Antonio, 1973-76; faculty Episc. Theol. Sem., Austin, Tex., 1973-78; exec. dir. Found. for Pastoral Care, Amarillo, 1980-86; faculty asst. Tex. Tech. Med. Sch., Amarillo, 1981-83. Profl. advisor Child Growth and Devel. Complex, Amarillo, 1985. Served to 1st lt. USAR, 1957-72. Fellow Coll. Chaplains, Am. Protestant Hosp. Assn.; mem. Assn. for Clin. Pastoral Edn. (supr. clin. pastoral edn., treas. 1975-78, chmn. cert. com. 1983-86), Am. Assn. for Marriage and Family Therapy, Tex. Psychotherapy Assn. (bd. dirs. 1978). Lodge: Masons (master 1969). Office: St Luke's Hosp 232 S Woods Mill Rd Chesterfield MO 63017-3417

HEATON, CHARLES LLOYD, dermatologist, educator; b. Bryan, Tex., May 8, 1935; s. Homer Lloyd and Bessie Blanton (Sharp) H. BS, Tex. A&M U., 1957; MD, Baylor U., 1961; MA (hon.), U. Pa., 1973. Diplomate Am. Bd. Dermatology. Intern Jefferson Davis Hosp., Houston, 1961-62; resident Baylor U., 1962-65; sr. attending physician Phila. Gen. Hosp., 1965-69, chief of svc., 1970-77; mem. dept. dermatology U. Pa. Sch. Medicine, 1966-78; assoc. prof. dermatology U. Pa., 1973-78; assoc. prof. dermatology U. Cin., 1978-85, prof., 1985—. Author: Audiovisual Course in Venereal Disease, 1972, (with D.M. Pillsbury) Manual of Dermatology, 1980; contbr. 35 articles to profl. jours., 12 chpts. to books. Served to lt. comdr. USPHS, 1965-67. Fellow ACP, AAD, Coll. Physicians of Phila.; mem. AMA, Soc. Investigative Dermatology, Am. Venereal Disease Assn., Am. Dermatol. Assn., Royal Soc. Medicine (London), Cin. Dermatol. Soc., Alpha Omega Alpha. Home: 5534 E Galbraith Rd Apt 25 Cincinnati OH 45236-2840 Office: U Cin Coll Medicine Dept Dermatology 231 Bethesda Ave Cincinnati OH 45267-0523

HEBDA, LAWRENCE JOHN, data processing executive, consultant; b. East Chicago, Ind., Apr. 9, 1954; s. Walter Martin and Barbara (Matczynski) H.; m. Cynthia Ruta Aizkalns, June 17, 1978. BS, Purdue U., 1976; MBA, U. Iowa, 1983. Cert. data processor. Programmer Inland Steel Co., East Chicago, 1976-77; data analyst Deere & Co., Moline, Ill., 1977-82, systems analyst, 1982-83, project mgr., 1983-84, dealer systems cons., 1984-85, corp. planning analyst, 1985-87, systems edn. adminstr., 1987-88, telecommunications analyst, 1988; info. systems sr. cons. Hewitt Assocs., Lincolnshire, Ill., 1988-93, MIS bus. mgr., 1994—. Mem. Nat. Rep. Congl. Com., 1982-85; charter mem. Rep. Presdl. Task Force, 1980; chmn. pastoral coun. Roman Cath. Ch., 1994-95. Recipient Cert. Recognition, Nat. Rep. Congl. Com., 1982-85, Presdl. Achievement award Rep. Nat. Com., 1984. Mem. Data Processing Mgmt. Assn., Am. Legion, Internat. Platform Assn., DAV Comdr.'s Club, King's Men Religious Orgn. (v.p. 1985, pres. 1986-87), Toastmasters (assoc. area gov. 1983-84). Roman Catholic. Club: Toastmasters Internat. (assoc. area gov. 1983-84). Home: 306 Spring Ln Vernon Hills IL 60061-2123 Office: Hewitt Assocs 100 Half Day Rd Lincolnshire IL 60069-3258

HEBEL, DORIS A., astrologer; b. Chgo., Jan. 1, 1935; d. Erich and Anna Dorothea (Hircy) H.; m. Leon L. Bram, Apr. 29, 1961 (div. Dec. 1973); 2 children. Libr. Campbell-Mithun, Chgo., 1958-61, Kenyon & Eckhardt, Chgo., 1961-64; pres. Astro-Technic Forecasting, Chgo., 1965—. Author: Contemporary Lectures, 1975, Celestial Psychology, 1985; contbr. various articles in astrological jours. and magazines. Mem. Am. Fedn. Astrologers (life), Nat. Coun. for Geocosmic Rsch. (life, nat. bd. dirs. 1975-80), Nat. Astrol. Soc., Assn. for Astrol. Networking, Internat. Soc. for Astrol. Rsch. Home and Office: 151 N Michigan Ave Apt 1001 Chicago IL 60601-7543

HEBENSTREIT, JAMES BRYANT, agricultural products executive, bank and venture capital executive; b. Long Beach, Calif., Mar. 8, 1946; s. William Joseph and Jean (Stark) H.; m. Marilyn Bartlett, Aug. 23, 1986. AB, Harvard U., 1968, MBA, 1973. Pres. Terra-Light div. Butler Mfg. Co., Boston, 1980-82, Capital for Bus., Inc. (SB/C, venture capital affiliate Commerce Bancshares), St. Louis and Kansas City,, Mo., 1982-87; sr. v.p. fin., CFO Commerce Bancshares, Inc., Kansas City, 1985-87, bd. dirs., 1987—; pres. Bartlett and Co., Kansas City, 1992—. Lt. USNR, 1968-71. Home: 1016 W 58th St Kansas City MO 64113-1133 Office: Bartlett & Co 4800 Main St Kansas City MO 64112-2510

HEBERER, AMY SUE, farm office manager; b. Belleville, Ill., Oct. 30, 1960; d. Verlan Walter and Ima Jean (dec.) H.; m. Thomas A. Dutkanych, Mar. 17, 1984 (div. Feb. 1992); 1 child, Lauren Jean. AS in Arts and Sci., Bellveille (Ill.) Area Coll., 1980; BS in Foods in Bus., U. Ill., 1982, M in Extension Edn., 1991. WIC coord. Dept. Pub. Health, Champaign, Ill., 1982-84; home econs. advisor U. Ill. Coop. Ext. Svc., Belleville, 1984-86, Breese, 1986-89; farm mgr. Heberer Farms, Belleville, 1989—; adv. bd. Sec. Agr., Springfield, Ill., 1993—, Family Bus. Forum, Edwardsville, Ill., 1993—. Membership com. mem. Belleville (Ill.) Econ. Progress, 1992-95. Recipient Bellringer award Pork Prodrs. Assn., 1993. Mem. Am. Home Econ. Assn. (cert. home economist), Turkey Hill Grange, Freesurg C. fo C., St. Clair County Pork Prodrs., Family Bus. Forum. Republican.

HECHLER, ROBERT LEE, financial services company executive; b. Galesburg, Ill., Nov. 12, 1936; s. Wesley Paul and Mildred (Paden) H.; m. Beverly Lockwood, Mar. 31, 1990; 1 child, Marcie Lee. BS, U. Ill., 1958; MBA, U. Chgo., 1967. Mgr. sales acctg. R.H. Donnelley, Chgo., 1960-64; mgr. profit plan Interstate United Corp., Chgo., 1964-68; pres., CEO Waddell & Reed Inc., Kansas City, Mo., 1968—; pres. Waddell & Reed Svcs. Co.; bd. dirs. ICI Mut. Ins. Co. Mem. Fin. Execs. Inst., Investment Co. Inst. (bd. govs.). Office: Waddell & Reed Inc 6300 Lamar Ave Shawnee Mission KS 66202-4247

HECHT, HAROLD ARTHUR, orchidologist, chiropractor; b. St. Louis, Mo., Apr. 30, 1921; s. William Frederick and Myrtle Regina (Hugo) H.; m. Barbara Evelyne Ross, Nov. 19, 1942. D Chiropractic Medicine, Logan Coll. Sole practice St. Louis, 1942-95, orchidologist, 1950—; judge Orchid Digest Corp., 1959; internat. lectr., photographer in field. Contbr. articles to profl. jours. Mem. World Orchid Cong. (founding com. 1954), Mid-Am. Orchid Cong. (founder, pres. 1959, judge 1968), Am. Orchid Soc. (grand jurist, judge 1968), Mark Twain Orchid Soc. (pres. 1966, 90), Mo. Orchid Soc. (pres. 1959), European Orchid Congress (USA com. 1967). Republican.

HECK, DAVID ALAN, orthopaedic surgery educator, mechanical engineering educator; b. Syracuse, N.Y., Nov. 20, 1952; s. William C. and Shirley W. (Wolthausen) H.; m. Kimberly Kay North, Sept. 27, 1980; children: William Donald, Andrew David, Daniel Robert. BS in Elect. and Computer Engring. cum laude, Clarkson Coll. Tech., 1973; MD, SUNY, Syracuse, 1977. Cert. Am. Bd. Orthopaedic Surgery. Intern in gen. surgery U. Minn., Mpls., 1977-78; resident in orthpaedic surgery SUNY, Syracuse, 1978-82; resident in orthopaedic biomechanics Mayo Clinic, Rochester, Minn., 1982-83; asst. prof. Ind. U. Sch. Medicine, Indpls., 1983-87, assoc. prof., 1987—; attending physician Ind. U. Med. Ctr., Indpls., 1983—, VA Med. Ctr., Indpls., 1983—, Riley Hosp., 1983—, Wishard Meml. Hosp., 1983—; adj. asst. prof. Sch. Mech. Engring., Purdue U., West Lafayette, Ind., 1984-87, assoc. prof., 1987-96, prof., 1996—; chief orthopaedic surgery sect. VA Med. Ctr, 1993—, medipro advisor, 1986, bd. dirs. Indian Creek Hills, Inc., The Orthopaedic Rev. Course; lectr. various profl. orgns.; dir. Orthopaedic Biomechanics Lab., Ind. U. Med. Ctr., 1984—; mem. residency applicants rev. com. Ind. U., 1983—, orthopaedic chiefs of svcs. com., 1983—, search and screen com., 1984-86, adult ambulatory care com., 1986-90, orthopaedic basic sci. com., 1986-87, chmn. orthopaedic edn. com., 1987—, quality assurance com., 1988-91, med. admissions com., 1989-91, total quality mgmt. chmn., 1993-95. Editl. bd. Jour. Arthroplasty, Jour. Am. Acad. Orthopedic Surgeons; co-editor in chief Electronic Jour. Orthopedics; editl. reviewer Clin. Orthopaedics; contbr. numerous articles to profl. jours. Sports medicine advisor White River Park, 1984-86; bd. dirs. Hand Surgery Rsch. & Edn. Found. Mem. AMA, Am. Acad. Orthopedic Surgery (outcome com. 1990—, com. on comps. 1988-90), Knee Soc. (ex-officio, com. on evaluation, chmn. outcome com. 1991—, bd. dirs.), Am. Soc. Biomechanics, Ind. Med. Assn., Marion County Med. Soc., Orthopaedic Rsch. Soc., 7th Dist. Med. Soc., Eta Kappa Nu, Tau Beta Pi. Home: 11440 Valley Meadow Dr Zionsville IN 46077-9342

HECK, DEBRA UPCHURCH, information technology professional; b. Valparaiso, Fla., Nov. 4, 1956; d. Robert P. and Sallaine S. (Sledge) Upchurch; m. Robert J. Heck, May 31, 1980; children: Andrew W., Jennifer A. BS in Math., Purdue U., 1978, MS in Mgmt., 1980. Analyst mgmt. sci. Monsanto Corp. Mgmt. Sci., St. Louis, 1980-81; sys. analyst Monsanto Agr. Group, St. Louis, 1981-82, sr. sys. analyst, 1982-84; sr. analyst mgmt. sci. Monsanto Polymer Products Group, St. Louis, 1984-86; project mgr. Monsanto Chem. Co., St. Louis, 1986-88; group leader Monsanto Corp. MIS, St. Louis, 1988-92, sr. group leader, 1992-95; info. tech. dir. Monsanto Bus. Svcs.-Fin., St. Louis, 1995-96, Monsanto Bus. Svcs.-Fin. & Procurement, St. Louis, 1996—; total quality fundamentals instr. Monsanto Co., St. Louis, 1985-86. Trustee, chair fall gathering, doubles, social com. Ethical Soc., St. Louis, 1982—; mem. sci. adv. com., PTO bd. Parkway Sch. Dist., St. Louis, 1992—; vol. St. Louis Assn. for Retarded Citizens, 1978-85. Mem. Human Resource Sys. Profls., Leadership Am. Alumni (award 1994). Office: Monsanto Co 800 N Lindbergh Blvd Saint Louis MO 63167

HECK, RICHARD T., tree farmer; b. Madison, Ind., Sept. 16, 1924; s. Richard Charles and Virginia (Tevis) H.; m. Ruth Irwin Heck, June 27, 1948; children: Richard Gregory, Rebecca Jeanne. Student, Admiral Farragut Naval Acad., Pine Beach, N.J., 1942-43, Hanover Coll, 1947-48. Tree farmer Hanover, Ind., 1943—; vice chmn., bd. dirs. Madison Bank & Trust Co.; sec. Mite Fed. Savs. & Loan Assn., Madison; bd. dirs. Sagamore of the Wabash; pres., bd dirs. Southwestern Sch. Bldg. Corp., Rebel Sch. Bldg., Cmty. of Hanover Sch. Bldg. Corp. Mem. arson investigation team Jefferson County, Ind., 1983-90, Hanover Twp. Vol. Fire Co., 1956—; trustee Hanover Coll., 1991—. With USN, 1944-54. Named to Hon. Order of Ky. Cols., 1971; named Ind. Outstanding Tree Farmer, Ind. Tree Farm Commn., 1983, Nat. Outstanding Tree Farmer Am. Forest Coun., 1984, Good Steward award Nat. Arbor Day Found., 1984, North Cen. Region Outstandng Tree Farmer, 1984, Ind. Conservationist of Yr., Ind. Dept. Natural Resources, 1985, Forest Conservationist of the Yr. Ind. Wildlife Fedn., 1987. Mem. Soc. Am. Foresters (hon.), Ind. Foresty and Woodland Owners Assn. (bd. dirs. 1984—, Ind. state tree farm com. 1984—), NRA (life), Nat. Muzzle Loading Rifle Assn. (life), Nat. Eagle Scout Assn., Soc. Ind. Pioneers, Am. Legion, Wahpanipe Muzzle Loading Rifle Club, Connor Prairie Rifles Club, Masons, Elks. Republican. Presbyterian. Address: 163 Clemmons St Hanover IN 47243-9660

HECKEL, JOHN LOUIS (JACK HECKEL), aerospace company executive; b. Columbus, Ohio, July 12, 1931; s. Russel Criblez and Ruth Selma (Heid) H.; m. Jacqueline Ann Alexander, Nov. 21, 1959 (div. 1993); children: Heidi, Holly, John; m. Linda Holleran, Aug. 1, 1994. BS, U. Ill., 1954; PhD (hon.), U. San Diego, 1984. Div. mgr. Aerojet Divs., Azusa, Calif., 1956-70, Seattle and Washington, 1956-70; pres. Aerojet-Space Gen. Co., El Monte, Calif., 1970-72, Aerojet Liquid Rocket Co., Sacramento, 1972-77; group v.p. Aerojet Sacramento Cos., 1977-81; pres. Aerojet Gen., La Jolla, Calif., 1981-85; chmn., chief exec. officer Aerojet Gen., 1985-87; pres., chief operating officer GenCorp., Akron, 1987-94, also bd. dirs.; bd. dirs. WD-40 Corp., Advanced Tissue Sci., Inc., San Diego, Applied Power Inc., Milw. Bd. dirs. Applied Power Corp., Milw., San Diego Econ. Devel. Corp., 1983-86, Akron Regional Devel. Bd., Akron Gen. Hosp., Summit County United Way; pres. Summit Edn. Partnership Found., Akron. Recipient Disting. Alumni award U. Ill. Ann. Alumni Conv., 1979. Fellow AIAA (assoc.); mem. Aerospace Industries Assn. Am. (gov. 1981), Navy League U.S., Am. Def. Preparedness Assn., San Diego C. of C. (bd. dirs.).

HECKEMEYER, ANTHONY JOSEPH, circuit court judge; b. Cape Girardeau, Mo., Jan. 20, 1939; s. Paul Q. and Frances E. (Goetz) H.; m. Elizabeth Faye Littleton, Feb. 13, 1964; children: Anthony Joseph, Matthew Paul, Mary Elizabeth, Andrew William, Sarah Kathryn. BS, U. Mo., 1962, JD, 1972; grad., Nat. Judicial Coll., 1980, Juvenile Coll., 1984. Bar: Mo. Mem. Mo. Ho. Reps., Jefferson City, 1964-72; sole practice Sikeston, Mo., 1972-81; presiding cir. judge State of Mo., Scott and Mississippi Counties, 1981—; chmn. alcohol and substance abuse com. Nat. Council of Juvenile and Family Ct. Judges, Reno, 1987-88, presenter at U. Reno. Named Outstanding Conservation Legislator Sears, 1968, Found. Mo. Wildlife Fedn., 1968, Man of Yr., Sikeston C. of C., 1989. Office: Presiding Cir Judge PO Box 256 Benton MO 63736-0256

HECKENDORF, ALLEN HARVEY, insurance agency official; b. Bismarck, N.D., Apr. 3, 1941; s. William Harvey and Angela Veronica (Otto) H.; m. Susan Lynn Bylow, May 13, 1973; children: Joshua Allen, Jon William, Heidi Elizabeth. BS, U. Wis., Oshkosh, 1963. Lic. fraternal ins. counselor. Tchr. Milw. Pub. Schs., 1963-76, St. Paul's Evang. Luth. Ch., Cudahy, Wis., 1965-66; dist. rep. Aid Assn. for Luths., Appleton, Wis., 1976-89; mgmt. asst., tng. dir. The Prin. Fin. Group, Milw., 1989—. Art cons. Milw. Players Theater, 1968-88; sec. Wis. Luth. H.S. Endowment Fund, 1983—; treas. Wis. Luth. Child and Family Svc., 1986—; pres. Welsmen Ltd., 1984-90, 91-94; chmn. sch. bd. Calvary Luth. Ch., Thiensville, Wis., mem. ch. coun., 1989-96; 1st v.p. Wels Found., 1991—. Fellow Life Underwriter Tng. Coun., Mequon/Thiensville C. of C. Republican. Home: 314 Grand Ave Thiensville WI 53092-1306 Office: The Prin Fin Group 2323 N Mayfair Rd Ste 500 Milwaukee WI 53226-1507

HECKER, LAWRENCE HARRIS, industrial hygienist; b. Detroit, July 14, 1944; s. Joseph and Rose Vivian (Harris) H.; m. Phyllis Rosalind Cohen, June 29, 1966; children: Charles Aaron, David Aaron. BA in Geography and Chemistry, Wayne State U., 1965, MS in Indsl. Hygiene, 1967; MS in Air Pollution, U. Mich., 1969, PhD of Indsl. Health, 1972. Cert. indsl. hygienist Am. Bd. Indsl. Hygiene. Asst. prof. indsl. and environ. health U. Mich., Ann Arbor, 1972-78; mgr., dir. corp. indsl. hygiene Abbott Labs., North Chgo., Ill., 1978-94; dir. corp. health and safety regulatory affairs Abbott Labs., North Chgo., 1994—; cons. Ann Arbor, 1970-78; chief chemist, ind. hygienist Environ. Health Labs. Franklin, Mich., 1966-68; lab. technician Wayne State U., Detroit, 1964-66. Contbr. numerous articles to profl. jours. Mem. AAAS, APHA, ASTM, Am. Acad. Indsl. Hygiene, Am. Chem. Soc., Am. Conf. Govtl. Indsl. Hygienists, Am. Indsl. Hygiene Assn. (bd. dirs. 1983-86), Air Pollution Control Assn., Assn. for Advancement of Med. Instrumentation, Internat. Stds. Orgn. (U.S. del.), Chem. Mfrs. Assn. (occupl. safety and health com., OSHA legis. group), Ethylene Glycol Panel, Ethelyne Oxide Industry Coun. (vice chmn. of bd. and exec. com. 1982-95), Halogenated Solvents Industry Alliance, Health Industry Mfrs. Assn., Orgns. Resource Councillors (respirator com., risk assessment task force), Remote Sensing of Atmosphere ((NIST com.), Pharm. Mfrs. Assn., Pharm. Safety Group, Bus. Coun. on Indoor Air (bd. dirs.), Nat. Assn. Mfrs. (occupl. safety and health com., ergonomics com., chem. safety com. 1992—), Sigma Xi. Home: 3823 Russett Ct Northbrook IL 60062 Office: Abbott Labs 200 Abbott Pk Rd Bldg AP51 Abbott Park IL 60064-3537

HECKER, MEL JASON, publishing company executive; b. N.Y.C., July 2, 1946; s. Leo and Rose (Weber) H.; m. Monica Gerard-Sharp, June 23, 1976 (div. 1981); m. Diane Allan, June 23, 1990; children: Benjamin Allan, Raymond Grier. BA, Temple U., 1968; MA, U. R.I., 1972; Diploma, Oxford (Eng.) U., 1973; cert., Columbia U., 1986. Pub. rels. dir. Brown, Brown & Tutors, Yonkers, N.Y., 1976-77; acquisitions editor Oceana Publs., Dobbs Ferry, 1977-80; editor Funk & Wagnalls, N.Y.C., 1980-81; developmental editor Warren, Gorham & Lamont, N.Y.C., 1981-84; exec. editor McGraw-Hill, N.Y.C., 1984-88; editorial dir. Sci. Rsch. Assocs./Pergamon, St. Paul, 1988-89; v.p., pub. Paradigm Pub., Inc., St. Paul, 1989—. Author: The Greeks in America, 1978, Ethnic America, 1979; Contbr. articles to various jours. and revs. Served to sgt. NYARNG, 1968-74. Mem. ASTD, Soc. for Applied Learning Technology, Am. Assn. Pubs. (software com., steering com. 1987-88). Democrat. Office: Paradigm Pub Inc 300 York Ave Saint Paul MN 55101-3972

HECKERT, CHARLES EDWIN, industrial engineer; b. Dayton, Ohio, Apr. 21, 1941. B, U. Toledo, 1964. Corp. indsl. engr. Champion Speaking, Toledo, 1969-82, plant engr., 1982-84, mgr. indsl. mfg., 1984-89; mgr. indsl. engrs. Tecumseh Products Co., Salem, Ind., 1989—; adv. bd. Owens Tech. Coll., Toledo, 1982-89. Mem. civil svc. bd. Northwood Mcpl., 1980-89. Mem. Inst. Indsl. Engring. Republican. Office: Tecumseh Products Co RR 1 Box 178 Salem IN 47167-9779

HECKLER, TIMOTHY A., financial advisor; b. Toledo, Ohio, Apr. 9, 1969. BA, Alma (Mich.) Coll., 1992. Fin. advisor Robert W. Baird, Grand Rapids, Mich., 1992—. Office: Robert W Baird & Co Inc 333 Bridge St NW Ste 1000 Grand Rapids MI 49504-5356

HECKMAN, HENRY TREVENNEN SHICK, steel company executive; b. Reading, Pa., Mar. 27, 1918; s. H. Raymond and Charlotte E. Shick H.; AB, Lehigh U., 1939; m. Helen Clausen Wright, Nov. 28, 1946; children: Sharon Anita (dec.), Charlotte Marie. Advt. prodn. mgr. Republic Steel Corp., Cleve., 1940-42, editor Enduro Era, 1946-51, account exec., 1953-54, asst. dir. advt., 1957-65, dir. advt., 1965-82; partner Applegate & Heckman, Washington, 1955-56; advt. mgr. Harris Corp., 1956-57. Permanent chmn. Joint Com. for Audit Comparability, 1968-93; chmn. Media Comparability Coun., 1969-83; chmn. indsl. advertisers com. Greater Cleve. Growth Assn., 1973-76; chmn. publs. com. Lehigh U., 1971-76; pres.'s adv. coun. Ashland Coll., 1966-76; advt. adv. council Kent State U., 1976-81; exec. com. Cleve. chpt. ARC, 1968-74; mem. Republican Fin. Exec. Com., 1966-87; coord. adv. coun. pub. svcs. campaign Employer Support for Guard and Res., 1973-83, 90—. Comdr. USNR, 1942-46, 51-53; Korea. Named to Advt. Effectiveness Hall of Fame, 1967; named Advt. Man of Yr., 1969; recipient G.D. Crain, Jr. award, 1973; Disting. Alumnus award Lehigh U., 1979; elected to Cleve. Graphic Arts Council Hall of Distinction, 1981. Mem. Indsl. Marketers Cleve. (past pres., Golden Mousetrap award 1968), Bus. Profl. Advt. Assn. (pres. 1968-69, Best Seller award 1966, Hall of Fame, 1973), Assn. Nat. Advertisers (chmn. shows and exhibits com. 1966-74, dir. 1969-72), Am. Iron and Steel Inst. (com. chmn. 1961-69), Steel Service Center Inst. (advt. adv. com. 1965-77), SAR (pres. 1979), Mil. Order World Wars (comdr. 1980), Early Settlers, Cleve. Advt. Club (pres. 1961-62, Hall of Fame 1980), Center for Mktg. Communications (chmn. bd. 1965), Internat. Platform Assn. Clubs: Cheshire Cheese (pres. 1982), Cleve. Grays (trustee 1980-82), Cleve. Skating. Home: 375 Bentleyville Rd Chagrin Falls OH 44022-2413

HECK-RABI, LOUISE EVELYN, writer; b. Detroit; d. Andrew Martin and Mary (Varga) Heck; m. Gerald E. Naughton, Feb. 1, 1958 (div. 1965); m. Imre Rabi, Aug. 1, 1975 (dec. 1989). MA in Libr. Sci., U. Mich., 1960; MA, Wayne State U., 1971, PhD, 1976. With Wayne County Libr. Fedn., Detroit, 1954-62, Bacon Meml. Pub. Libr., Wyandotte, Mich., 1962-66, Soc. Mfg. Engrs., Dearborn, Mich., 1967-70; asst. prof. Wayne State U., Detroit, 1971-79; freelance writer Lincoln Park, Mich., 1980—. Author: (plays) Hier Ist Tobytown, 1971, The People Pound, 1980, (book) Women Filmmakers: A Critical Reception, 1984. Mem., various bd. positions Coop. Svcs., Inc., Oak Park, Mich., 1949—. Recipient Mich. Coun. of the Arts Creative Writing grant, Detroit, 1982. Mem. NOW (libr. Downriver br. 1979—, Woman Who Has Made History award 1992), ALA, AAUW, Mich. Women's Studies Assn., Poetry Soc. Mich., Detroit Women Writers, Dramatists Guild (assoc., N.Y.), Poets & Playwrights, Mich. Playwrights Group. Democrat. Home: 1459 Philomene Blvd Lincoln Park MI 48146-2396

HEDEGARD, JAMES MEREDITH, psychology educator, researcher; b. Chgo., Sept. 29, 1935; s. Jensen Meredith and Melinda (Lafoy) H.; divorced; 1 child, Philip Jensen; m. JS Hedegard, 1988. BS in Zoology, Ohio Wesleyan U., 1957; MS in Psychology, U. Mich., 1961, PhD in Psychology, 1967. Rsch. asst. prof. Miami U., Oxford, Ohio, 1964-67; asst. prof. Ea. Mich. U., Ypsilanti, 1963-64; rsch. psychologist Ctr. for Rsch. on Learning & Tng. U. Mich., Ann Arbor, 1967-70; assoc. prof. Meml. U. Nfld., St. John's, Can., 1970-74; rsch. social scientist Am. Bar Found., Chgo., 1974-79; assoc. prof. Roosevelt U., Chgo., 1979-84, prof., 1984—; cons. in field, Nfld. and Chgo., 1972—. Author: (book chpts.) Instruction: Contemporary Viewpoints, 1967, Black Students in White Schools, 1972; contbr. articles to profl. jours. Br. pres., bd. mem., sec. Lake View Citizens Coun., Chgo., 1975-79; mem. task force City of Chgo. Comty. Devel. Adv. Com., 1977-79; mem. local planning com. Met. Planning Coun., Chgo., 1978-82. Mem. Soc. for Psychol. Study Social Issues, Greater Chgo. Assn. Indsl. and Organizational Psychologists. Home: 2111 N Pinetree Dr Arlington Heights IL 60004 Office: Roosevelt U 430 S Michigan Ave Chicago IL 60605

HEDGCOTH, CHARLES, biochemistry educator, researcher; b. Graham, Tex., Jan. 29, 1936; s. Charlie and Edna Pearl (Pirkle) H.; m. Barbara Anne Graham, June 20, 1956; children: Kelli Michelle, Kimberly, Charles Michael. BS in Chemistry, U. Tex., 1961, PhD in Chemistry, 1965. Asst. prof. biochemistry Kans. State U., Manhattan, 1965-68, assoc. prof., 1968-76, prof., 1976—. Contbr. articles to scholarly and profl. jours. With USCG, 1954-58. Grantee NSF, NIH, USDA, Am. Cancer Soc.; NIH predoctoral fellow U. Tex., 1963-65; NATO/NSF sr. fellow U. B.C., 1975. Mem. AAAS, Am. Soc. Biochem. Molecular Biology, Am. Chem. Soc., Sigma Xi. Home: 1305 Waters St Manhattan KS 66503-2833 Office: Kans State U Dept Biochemistry Willard Hall Manhattan KS 66506-3702

HEDGES, JOHN KIM, actor, performing arts administrator, consultant; b. Alton, Ill., June 26, 1957; s. Joseph Taze and Lois Jane (Howle) H.; m. Marietta Christina Pucillo, Dec. 1, 1985. Student, Ind. State U., 1975-79; grad., Nat. Shakespeare Co. Conservatory, 1979; student, HB Studio, 1985; postgrad., U. Del. Mng. dir. Maine Stage Theatre Co., Springvale, Maine, 1984-86; gen. mgr. The Pearl Theatre Co., N.Y.C., 1986-87; rsch. coord. Theatre Communications Group, N.Y.C., 1987-88; bus. dir. Gloucester (Mass.) Stage Co., 1988-89; producing assoc. North Shore Music Theatre, Beverly, Mass., 1989-91; mng. dir. First Stage Milw., 1991-94; profl. actor Actors Equity Assn., 1994—; with Barter Theatre, Stage One, and Kentucky Shakespeare Festival; conf. panelist Am. Alliance for Theatre and Edn., 1993. Contbg. author Am. Theatre Mag., 1987-88. Bd. dirs. North of Boston Conv. and Vis. Bur., 1990-91, Stage Source, 1989-91. Recipient Theatre scholarship Ind. State U. Speech Communications, 1975-79, Scholarship award Lilith Baur Children's Theatre, 1976, scholarship Bradley U. Arts Inst., 1974; nominee Irene Ryan Acting award Am. Coll. Theatre Festival, 1978. Mem. Actors' Equity Assn. Home: 2434 Bradley Ave Louisville KY 40217

HEDGES, MARK STEPHEN, clinical psychologist; b. Chgo., Feb. 15, 1950; s. Norman T. and Doris Mae (Walters) H.; B.S., Purdue U., 1972; M.A., U. S.D., 1974, Ph.D., 1977; m. Janice Finnie, Aug. 16, 1975; children: Anna, Miriam. Psychology intern Western Mo. Mental Health Ctr., Kansas City, 1975-76; dir. children and adolescent svcs., psychologist Northeastern Mental Health Ctr., Aberdeen, S.D., 1977—; chmn. Northeastern Area Local Interagency Team. Mem. adv. bd. Luth. Social Svcs., 1978—, S.D. Mental Health Planning and Coord. Adv. Coun., S.D. Juvenile Justice Adv. Com. Mem. Am. Psychol. Assn., S.D. Assn. Sch. Psychologists, Phi Beta Kappa, Psi Chi, Phi Kappa Phi. Methodist. Office: Northeastern Mental Health Ctr 703 3rd Ave SE Aberdeen SD 57401-4508

HEDGES, NORMA ANN, retired secondary education educator; b. Depue, Ill., May 21, 1941; d. Memford Euing and Louise Gertrude (Krueger) H. BA, Knox Coll., 1963; MEd, U. Ill., 1973. Camp sec. Pilgrim Park Camps, Princeton, Ill., 1961-64; English tchr., counselor Malden (Ill.) H.S., 1963-78, Morris (Ill.) H.S., 1978-93. Author: History of Depue, Illinois, 1976. Vol. Morris Hosp. Gift Shop, 1993—. Mem. Bus. & Profl. Women (cmty. svc. chmn. 1994-96), Delta Kappa Gamma (scholarship chmn. 1992-96). Republican. Congregational.

HEDGES, RICHARD H., epidemiologist, lawyer; b. Louisville, July 16, 1952; s. Houston and Frances Ruth (Zemo) H.; m. Donna Jean Hough. BA, U. Ky., 1974; MA, Ea. Ky. U., 1975; PhD, U. Ky., 1986; MPA, Ea. Ky. U., 1983; JD, Capital U. Law, 1994. Bar: Ohio 1995. Rehab. specialist Commonwealth of Ky., Somerset, 1976-81; chief health planner Commonwealth of Ky., Frankfort, 1981-82; asst. prof. U. Ky., Lexington, 1985-87; rsch. assoc. dept. med. behavioral sci. U. Ky. Coll. Medicine, Lexington, 1982-85; program adminstr. Rollman Psychiat. Inst., Cin., 1987-88; asst. prof. Ohio U., 1988-92, assoc. prof., 1992—; dir. divsn. on aging Ohio U. Health Promotion and Rsch., 1990-92, MHA Grad Prog. Coord., 1995—. Contbr. articles to profl. jours. Fellow NIMH, 1984-86. Mem. ABA, ATLA, APHA, Ohio Acad. Trial Lawyers, Am. Soc. Law, Medicine and Ethics, Am. Coll. Health Care Execs., Nat. Health Lawyers Assn., Ohio State Bar Assn., Pi Sigma Alpha, Phi Delta Phi. Democrat. Episcopalian. Home: RR 2 Box 14 Mooreland Rd Belpre OH 45714 Office: Ohio U Health Sci 413 Peden Tower Athens OH 45701

HEDRICK, BASIL CALVIN, state agency administrator, ethnohistorian, educator, museum and multicultural institutions consultant; b. Lewistown, Mo., Mar. 17, 1932; s. Truman Bloice and M. LaVeta (Stice) H.; m. Anne Kehoe, Jan. 19, 1957 (div. 1979); 1 dau., Anne Lainer Hedrick Caraker; m. Susan Elizabeth Pickel, Oct. 2, 1980. A.B., Augustana Coll., Rock Island, Ill., 1956; MA, U. Fla., 1957; PhD, Inter-Am. U., Mex., 1965; cert., U. Vienna, Strobl, Austria, 1956. Asst. prof., assoc. prof., prof. So. Ill. U., Carbondale, 1967-74, asst. dir. Univ. Mus., 1967-70, dir. Univ. Mus. and Art Galleries, 1970-77, dean internat. edn., 1972-74; asst. dir. Ill. Div. Mus., Springfield, 1977-80; prof. history U. Alaska, Fairbanks, 1980-88, dir. U. Alaska Mus., 1980-88, dir. inter. affairs, 1985-87; founder, dir. Div. Mus., Archaeology and Publs. State of Mich., Lansing, 1988-91; multicultural cons., 1991—; dir. mktg. Rosalie Whyel Mus. Doll Art, Bellevue, Wash., 1991—; Fulbright sr. lectr., Brazil, 1972; mem. nat. register adv. panel, Ill., 1977-80; mem. Alaska Coun. on Arts, Anchorage, 1983-85; chmn. Fairbanks Hist. Preservation Commn., 1982-88; mem. Alaska Land Use Coun.; bd. dirs. Alaska Hist. Preservation Found., 1986-88; mem. Gov.'s Revitalization Task Force, Lansing, Mich., mem. ethnic coun., Mich., 1988-89; bd. dirs. East King County Visitors Bur., 1993—; officer, bd. dirs. Wash. Mus. Assn., 1993—. Author: (with others) A Bibliography of Nepal, 1973, (with Carroll L. Riley) The Journey of the Vaca Party, 1974, Documents Ancillary to the Vaca Journey, 1976, (with C.A. Letson) Once Was A Time, a Very Good Time: An Inquiry into the Folklore of the Bahamas, 1975, (with J.E. Stephens) In the Days of Yesterday and in the Days of Today: An Overview of Bahamian Folkmusic, 1976, It's A Natural Fact: Obeah in the Bahamas, 1977, Contemporary Practices in Obeah in the Bahamas, 1981; compilations and collections, 1959-69; editor: (with J. Charles Kelley and Riley) The Classic Southwest: Readings in Archaeology, Ethnohistory and Ethnography, 1973, (with J. Charles Kelley and Riley) The Mesoamerican Southwest: Readings in Archaelogy, Ethnohistory and Ethnology, 1974, (with Riley) Across the Chichimec Sea, 1978; (with others) New Frontiers in the Archaeology and Ethnohistory of the Greater Southwest, 1980; Trans. of Ill. Acad. Sci., 1979-81, (with Susan Pickel-Hedrick) Ethel Washington: The Life and Times of an Eskimo Dollmaker, The Role of the Steamboat in the Founding and Development of Fairbanks, Alaska, 1986, (with Susan Savage) Steamboats on the Chena, 1988; co-editor: Led Zeppelin live, 1993, 94; author and editor of various other publications; contbr. articles to profl. jours. Chmn. Goals for Carbondale, 1972; active various local state, nat. polit. campaigns. Mem. NMA (bd. dirs. 1989-91), Am. Assn. Mus. (leader accreditation teams 1977—, sr. examiner), Ill. Archaeol. Soc. (pres. 1973-74), Mus. Alaska, Assn. Sci. Mus. Dirs., Midwest Mus. Conf. (treas. 1977-80), Western Mus. Assn., Wash. Mus. Assn. (bd. dirs. 1994—, v.p. 1995—), BD Arts (bd. dirs. 1995-96), Phi Kappa Phi.

HEDRICK, GEARY DEAN, small business owner; b. Wytheville, Va., Feb. 9, 1940; s. James Luther and Alma June (Webb) H.; m. Priscilla Ann Moore, Dec. 27, 1958; children: Geary Dean Jr., Darla Ann, Darren Keith. BA in Econs., Wofford Coll., 1975. Enlisted U.S. Army, 1960, advanced through ranks to sgt. major, 1978, ret., 1982; pres. Hedrick Gen. Maintenance/ Contracting, Inc., Gurnee, Ill., 1982—. Del. Civic Ctr. Found. Libertyville, Inc., 1986—. Decorated Purple Heart, Bronze Star, DSM, Air medal; Cross of Gallantry with palm Rep. of Vietnam. Lodge: Lions (pres. 1987-88, various offices 1984—). Home and Office: 37055 Mulberry Ln Gurnee IL 60031-1057

HEDRICK, JAMES CHRIS, research and development specialist; b. Brookfield, Mo., Aug. 19, 1961; s. James William Hedrick and Maxine Margret Pancoast. Attended, U. Columbia Firefighter Rookie Sch., 1980, Allan Bradly, 1993, State Fair C.C., 1996. Fire fighter Marshall (Mo.) Fire Dept., 1978-85; rsch. and devel. specialist AMJO Infrared Sys. Inc., Marshall, 1985—. Patentee in field. Office: AMJO Infrared Dryers Inc 165 Court St Marshall MO 65340-2004

HEDRICK, LARRY WILLIS, airport executive; b. Newton, Kans., Dec. 23, 1939; s. A.C. and Goldie (Kerns) H.; m. Nancy Cashin, July 21, 1962; children: Christina, Kathleen, Thomas. BL, U. LaSalle, Chgo., 1973. Lic. airport mgr., Mass. Airport mgr., dir. civil def. Newton City-County Airport, 1966-73; airport mgr. Barnes Mcpl. Airport, Mass., 1973-77, Niagara Falls Internat. Airport, 1977-81, Greater Buffalo (N.Y.) Internat. Airport, 1981-87; appointed airport adminstr. Pt. Columbus Internat. Airport, Columbus, Ohio, 1987-91; appointed exec. dir. Columbus Airport Authority, 1991—; founding bd. mem. Airline Passengers of Am., 1987; guest speaker various univs. and airport confs. Bd. dirs. Greater Columbus Conv. and Visitors Bur., 1992; past squadron commdr. CAP Kans. Wing. With USN, 1958-62. Mem. Am. Assn. Airport Execs. (accredited 1973, nat. sec. 1982, treas. bd. dirs. 1983, 1st v.p. 1985, 2d v.p. 1984, nat. pres. 1986-87, Disting. Svc. award 1994), Nat. Fire Protection Assn. (airport industry's only rep.), Mass. Airport Mgmt. Assn. (pres. 1975-76). Office: Columbus Airport Authority 4600 Internat Gtwy Columbus OH 43219

HEDRICK, THOMAS RICHARD, SR., engineering executive; b. Norwalk, Ohio, Feb. 11, 1954. Toolmaker Kuhlman Corp., Norwalk, 1973-76; supt. tool rm. Sheller-Globe Corp., Norwalk, 1976-78; head engring. Sandusky (Ohio) Machine and Tool, 1978-92; pres., head engring. HBE Machine Inc., Monroeville, Ohio, 1985—; cons. Ehove Vocat.-Tech. Sch., Milan, Ohio, 1984—. Designer in field. Home: 259 Monroe St Monroeville OH 44847-9406

HEEBSH, SAUNDRA L., interior designer; b. New Albany, Miss., Apr. 15, 1946; d. Clyde H. and Carmel (Thomas) Wroten; m. Richard Dean Heebsh, Nov. 28, 1987; children: Jeffrey, Tammy, Michael. Student, Sheffield Sch. of Design. design participant Festival of Homes, Collierville, Tenn., 1993. Vol. United Way, Mt. Vernon, 1995; active First Bapt. Ch., Mt. Vernon, 1994-95. Mem. Mount Vernon/Knox County C. of C., Interior Design Soc. Baptist. Office: Heebsh Interiors 19157 Coshacton Rd Mount Vernon OH 43050

HEER, LAURIE ANN, physical therapist, educational consultant; b. Port Washington, Wis., Sept. 21, 1962; d. Bernard Michael and Myrtle Sara

(Godersky) Schreiner; m. Philip L. Heer, Sept. 1, 1990; 1 child, Benjamin Lee. BS in Phys. Therapy, Marquette U., 1985; MS in Adminstrv. Leadership, U. Wis., Milw., 1994, postgrad. in urban edn. Phys. therapist St. Francis Hosp., Milw., 1985-86, Rehab. Svc. of Wis., Milw., 1986-87; clin. coord. edn. West Allis (Wis.) Meml. Hosp., 1987-91; clin. coord., phys. therapist Novacare, Inc., Milw., 1991-94; phys. therapist, ednl. cons. MJ Care, Inc., 1994—. Mem. editl. bd. Gerinotes, 1994—; contbr. articles to prof. jours. CPR instr., St. Francis Cmty. Health, Milw., 1985—. Capt. USAR. Mem. Am. Phys. Therapy Assn. (geriat. liaison 1994—). Republican. Roman Catholic. Home: 2709 S Root River Pkwy West Allis WI 53227

HEETLAND, DAWN MICHELE, physical therapist; b. Blue Earth, Minn., May 17, 1965; d. Marvin Paul and Lynda Lou (Leach) Heidecker; m. Bruce Allen Heetland, Dec. 15, 1990; children: Shelby Dawn, Macy Maronna, MaKayla Lynn. BS, Iowa State U., 1988; MS in Phys. Therapy, Washington U., St. Louis, 1990. Lic. phys. therapist, Iowa; registered phys. therapist, Minn. Phys. therapist Fairmont (Minn.) Cmty. Hosp., 1991-93, United Hosp. Dist., Blue Earth, 1993—. Mem. Minn. Phys. Therapy Assn. (reimbursement com. 1993—), Occupational Health Phys. Therapy Group. Office: United Hosp Dist 515 S Moore Blue Earth MN 56013

HEFFERN, DEBBI MARIE, dietitian; b. Corona, Calif., May 5, 1956; d. William Anthony Sypniewski and Jacquelyn Agnes Allhoff Shumate; m. Patrick Allen Heffern, June 25, 1977; children: Kevin, Kathy, Michael. BS, Fontbonne Coll., St. Louis, 1978. Registered dietitian, Mo. Sales assoc. Saks Fifth Ave., St. Louis, 1973-77; kitchen supr. St. Mary's Health Ctr., St. Louis, 1977-78; dietetic intern VA Med. Ctr., St. Louis, 1978-79; cafeteria mgr. Our Lady of Lourdes Sch., St. Louis, 1979-80; community coord. LaLeche League Internat., Creve Coeur, Mo., 1983—; dist. advisor Cen. Mo. dist. LaLeche League Internat., 1985-90, dist. coord., 1987-89; state coord. Mo. LaLeche League Internat., 1992—; cons. Human Devel. Corp., St. Louis, 1988-91, Mo. Dept. Health, St. Louis, 1990—, Birthright, St. Louis, 1991—; lectr. in field. Author (booklet): Breast Feeding: What Nature Intended, 1990; contbr. articles to profl. jours. and popular mags. Leader Girl Scouts U.S., St. Louis, 1990-91; coord. Tiger Cub Scouts, St. Louis, 1990-91; contest coord. Creve Coeur Days Festival, 1989—. Mem. NAFE, St. Louis Dietetic Assn., Am. Dietetic Assn., LaLache League Internat., Internat. Lactation Cons. Assn., Lactation Cons. Metro. St. Louis. Home and Office: 11667 Chieftain Dr Saint Louis MO 63146-5463

HEFFERNAN, NATHAN STEWART, retired state supreme court chief justice; b. Frederic, Wis., Aug. 6, 1920; s. Jesse Eugene and Pearl Eva (Kaump) H.; m. Dorothy Hillemann, Apr. 27, 1946; children: Katie (Mrs. Howard Thomas), Michael, Thomas. BA, U. Wis., 1942, LLB, 1948; postgrad. in bus., Harvard U. Sch. Bus. Adminstrn., 1943-44; LLD, Lakeland Coll., 1995. Bar: Wis. 1948, U.S. Dist. Ct. (we. dist.) Wis. 1948, U.S. Dist. Ct. (ea. dist.) Wis. 1950, U.S. Ct. Appeals (7th cir.) 1960, U.S. Supreme Ct. 1960. Assoc. firm Schubring, Ryan, Peterson & Sutherland, Madison, Wis., 1948-49; practice in Sheboygan, Wis., 1949-59; partner firm Buchen & Heffernan, 1951-59; counsel Wis. League Municipalities, 1949; research asst. to gov. Wis., 1949; asst. dist. atty. Sheboygan County, 1951-53; city atty. City of Sheboygan, 1953-59; dep. atty. gen. State of Wis., 1959-62; U.S. atty. Western Dist. Wis., 1962-64; justice Wis. Supreme Ct., 1964—, chief justice, 1983-95; lectr. mcpl. corps., 1961-64, appellate procedure and practice U. Wis. Law Sch., 1971-83; faculty Appellate Judges Seminar, Inst. Jud. Adminstrn., NYU, 1972-87; former mem. Nat. Council State Ct. Reps., chmn., 1976-77; ex-officio dir. Nat. Ctr. State Cts., 1976-77, mem. adv. bd. appellate justice project; former mem. Wis. Jud. Planning Com.; chmn. Wis. Appellate Practice and Procedure Com., 1975-76; mem. exec. com. Wis. Jud. Conf., 1978—, chmn., 1983; pres. City Attys. Assn., 1958-59. Wis. chmn. NCCJ, 1966-67; past exec. bd. Four Lakes Coun., Boy Scouts Am.; gen. chmn. Wis. Dem. Conv., 1960, 61; mem. Wis. Found.; bd. dirs. Inst. Jud. Adminstrn.; visitors U. Wis. Law Sch., 1970-83, chmn., 1973-76; past mem. corp. bd. Meth. Hosp.; former curator Wis. Hist. Soc., curator emeritus, 1990; trustee Wis. Meml. Union, Wis. State Libr., William Freeman Vilas Trust Estate; v.p. U. Wis. Meml. Union Bldg. Assn.; former deacon Conglist. Ch. Lt. (s.g.) USNR, 1942-46, ETO, PTO. Recipient Disting. Svc. award NCCJ, 1968, Ann. Disting. Svc. award Wis. Mediation Assn., 1995, Lifetime Achievement award Milw. Bar Assn., 1995, Disting. Svc. award Dem. Party Sheboygan County, 1995; Disting. Jud. fellow Marquette U. Law Sch., 1996. Fellow Am. Bar Found. (life), Inst. for Jud. Adminstrn. (hon., bd. dirs., mem. faculty seminar); mem. ABA (past mem. spl. com. on adminstrn. criminal justice, mem. com. fed.-state delineation of jurisdiction, jud. adminstrn. com. on appellate ct., com. appellate time standards), Am. Law Inst. (life, adv. com. on complex litigation), Wis. Bar Assn. (Goldberg award for disting. svc.), Dane County Bar Assn., Sheboygan County Bar Assn., Am. Judicature Soc. (dir. 1977-80, chmn. program com. 1979-81), Wis. Law Alumni Assn. (bd. dirs., Disting. Alumni Svc. award 1989), Nat. Conf. Chief Justices (bd. dirs.), Nat. Assn. Ct. Mgmt., Order of Coif, Iron Cross, Phi Kappa Phi, Phi Delta Phi. Clubs: Madison Lit. (pres. 1979-80); Harvard (Milw.); Harvard Bus. Sch. (Wis.). Home: 17 Thorstein Veblen Pl Madison WI 53705

HEFFLEY, IRENE M., state legislator. Student, Contra Costa Coll., U. Calif., Berkeley. Real estate broker, appraiser, owner Brokers Exch.; mem. Ind. State Ho. of Reps. Dist. 97, rep. vice-precinct committeeman, mem. commerce and econ. devel. com., mem. pub. policy, ethics and vet. affairs coms., mem. roads and transp. com., vice-chmn. cts. and criminal code com. Mem. Nat. Assn. Realtors, Ind. Assn. Realtors.

HEFLER, WILLIAM LOUIS, elementary education educator; b. New Albany, Ind.; s. Louis C. and Elizabeth (Grimes) H.; divorced; children: Sarah Elizabeth, Matthew Joseph; m. Linda Gryszowka; children: Jason Michael Gryszowka, Justin Bradley Gryszowka. BS in Elem. Edn., Ind. U., 1980, MS in Elem. Edn., 1983. Tchr. 5th grade Washington Elem. Sch., Pekin, Ind., 1980-87; tchr. 6th grade Indpls. Pub. Sch., 1987-92; asst. prin. Indpls. Pub. Schs., 1992-94, M.S.D. of Wayne Twp., 1994—; chmn. various coms. Washington Elem. Sch., Pekin, Ind.; asst. prin. Indpls. Pub. Sch., 1992-94, Wayne Twp. (Ind.) sch. dist., 1994—; chmn. Indpls. Pub. Sch. sub-com. LEAP conf.; instr. Project Wild, Project Learning Tree, Ind. Deacon Cen. Christian Ch., 1984-86; coach 5th grade soccer, softball, track, E. Washington Elem. Sch., 1981-84, coach 7th grade basketball 1981-85; state reviewer textbooks in math., sci., health, 1984-86. Named one of Outstanding Men of Am., 1983, 85, 89, Outstanding History Tchr. in Washington County, DAR, 1984, Ky. Col., 1990; recipient C.L.A.S.S./I.P.L. Golden Apple award, 1992. Mem. NEA, Nat. Sci. Tchrs. Assn., Nat. Coun. Tchrs. English, Nat. Coun. Tchrs. Math., Nat. Coun. Social Studies, Ind. State Tchrs. Assn. (local pres. 1981-85, ins. trustee 1982-85, bd. dirs. 1986, chmn. various coms., del. various confs.), Ind. Coun. Tchrs. Math., Ind. Coun. Social Studies, Ind. Basketball Coaches Assn., Hoosier Assn. Sci. Tchrs., E. Washington Tchrs. Assn., Indpls. Edn. Assn., Indpls. Prins. Assn., Tau Kappa Epsilon, Phi Delta Kappa, Pi Lambda Theta, Kappa Delta Pi. Democrat. Home: 1549 Countryside Ln Indianapolis IN 46231-3312 Office: Stout Field Elem Sch 3820 W Bradbury Ave Indianapolis IN 46241

HEFLEY, JAMES CARL, publisher; b. Chillicothe, Ohio, June 2, 1930; s. Fred Joseph and Hester Hosanna (Foster) H.; m. Martha Lou Smedley, May 8, 1953; children: Cynthia, Cecilia, Cheryl. BA, Ouachita Bapt. U., 1950, LittD (hon.), 1981; MDiv, New Orleans Bapt. Sem., 1953; PhD, U. Tenn., 1982. Ordained to ministry, Bapt. Ch., 1948. Minister Chicot (Ark.) Bapt. Ch., 1952-53, Pontchartrain Bapt. Ch., New Orleans, 1953-58, Lakeside Bapt. Ch., Metairie, La., 1958-61; editor David C. Cook Pub. Co., Elgin, Ill., 1961-64; pub. Hannibal (Mo.) Books, 1989—; freelance writer Ill. and Tenn., 1964-84; writer-in-residence Hannibal-LaGrange Coll., Hannibal, 1984-93; pres. Hefley Communications, Hannibal, 1989—; comm. cons. Alaska Bapt. Conv., Anchorage, 1982, 1st Bapt. Ch., El Paso, Tex., 1983; dir. Mark Twain Writers Conf., Hannibal, 1984—; lectr. on mass media Staley Found., Boca Raton, Fla., 1982—. Author: Living Miracles, 1964 (White House Libr.), Lift-Off, 1970, Uncle Cam, 1970, Thinkables, 1970, The Cross and the Scalpel, 1971, Textbooks on Trial, 1976, Unique Evangelical Churches, 1977, The Church That Produced a President, 1977, Way Back in the Hills, 1985, The Truth in Crisis: The Controversy in the Southern Baptist Convention, 6 vols., 1986-91; co-author: (with M. Hefley) Intrigue in Santo Domingo, 1968, Dawn Over Amaznoia, 1972, The Church That Takes on Trouble, 1976, By Their Blood (Gold Medallion award), 1981 others. Mem. steering com. Citizens Opposed to Riverboat Gambling, Hannibal, 1992. scholar Bickel Found., 1980-82, Kappa Tau Alpha, 1982. Mem. Newton County Hist. Soc., Nat. Assn. Evangs., Christian Booksellers Assn. (assoc.). Home: 31 Holiday Dr Hannibal MO 63401-1913 Office: Hannibal Books 921 Center St Hannibal MO 63401-3446

HEFNER, PHILIP JAMES, theologian; b. Denver, Dec. 10, 1932; s. Theodore Godfred and Elizabeth Helen (Mittelstadt) H.; m. Neva Lamae White, May 25, 1956; children: Sarah Elizabeth, Martha White, Julia Margaret, Rebecca Mittelstadt. BA, Midland Luth. Coll., 1954, LHD, 1982; BD, Chgo. Luth. Theol. Sem., 1959; MA, U. Chgo., 1961, PhD, 1962; DD, Luther Coll., 1994. Ordained min., United Luth. Ch. in Am., 1962. Assoc. prof. systematic theology Hamma Div. Sch., Springfield, Ohio, 1962-64; prof. systematic theology Luth. Theol. Sem., Gettysburg, Pa., 1964-67; prof. systematic theology Luth. Sch. Theology, Chgo., 1967—, dir. grad. studies, 1979-88; dir. Chgo. Ctr. Religion and Sci., 1988—; vis. prof. Japan Luth. Theol. Coll. and Sem., Tokyo, 1982, 96, Inst. fuer Theologie, Technologie, Naturwissenschaft, Munich, Germany, 1994; rsch. lectr. Human Scis. Rsch. Coun., Republic of South Africa, 1988; disting. vis. scholar Okla. scholar leader enrichment program U. Okla., 1991; lectr. religion Chautauqua Instn., 1991; mem. Human Genome Core Group project NIH, 1991-94; Hein-Fry nat. lectr. Evang. Luth. Ch. in Am., 1996; lectr. Vatican Conf. on Evolution and Faith, Rome, 1996. Author: Faith and The Vitalities of History, 1966, Promise of Teilhard, 1970, The Human Factor: Evolution, Culture, Religion, 1993 (translated Japanese), Natur, Weltbild, Religion, 1995; co-author: Defining America, Christian Dogmatics; editor Zygon: Jour. of Religion and Sci., 1989—; dept. editor religion and sci. Religion in Geschichte und Gegenwart, 4th edit., 1993—; editorial assoc. Dialog: A Theol. Jour., 1982—; bd. cons. Jour. Religion, U. Chgo., 1995—; contbr. numerous articles to profl. jours. Mem. U.S.A. Luth.-Reformed Coordinating Com., 1992—. Fulbright scholar U. Tübingen, 1954-55; Rockefeller Found. Doctoral fellow, 1960-62, Russell fellow Ctr. for Theol. and Natural Scis., 1985; recipient Franklin Fry award for Scholarship, Luth. Brotherhood, 1977-78, Susan Colver Rosenberg award U. Chgo., 1963, Templeton Found. Book prize, 1995; Nobel lectr. Gustavus Adolphus Coll., 1987. Fellow Inst. on Religion in an Age of Sci. (pres. 1979-81, 84-87), Ctr. for Advanced Study in Religion and Sci. (grantee 1985), Soc. for Values in Higher Edn.; mem. AAAS (mem. judging panel, Sci. and Human Freedom award 1993-95), Am. Acad. Religion (chmn. cons. on theology and sci. group 1988-93), Internat. Luth./Reformed Dialogue, Soc. Midland Authors. Office: Luth Sch Theology 1100 E 55th St Chicago IL 60615-5112

HEFT, JAMES LEWIS, academic administrator, theology educator; b. Cleve., Feb. 20, 1943; s. Berl Ramsey and Hazel Mary (Miller) H. BA in Philosophy, U. Dayton, 1965, BS in Edn., 1966; MA in Theology, U. Toronto, 1971, PhD in Hist. Theology, 1977. Prof. theology U. Dayton, Ohio, chmn. religious studies dept., 1983-89, provost, 1989-94, lectr; bd. dirs. Inst. Edn1. Mgmt., Harvard U., 1989. Author: John XXII (1316-1334) and Papal Teaching Authority, 1986; contbr. numerous articles to profl. jours. Trustee U. Dayton, 1970-77; bd. dirs. Nat. Conf., 1990—. U. Toronto scholar, 1969-77; recipient Excellence in Tchg. award U. Dayton, 1983, 1st Pl. prize Cath. Press Assn., 1990. Mem. Nat. Cath. Edn. Assn. (bd. dirs. 1994-95), Coll. Theology Soc., Cath. Theol. Soc. Am., Assn. Cath. Colls. and Univs. (bd. dirs. 1993-95, vice chmn. 1996—), Mariological Soc. Am. Roman Cath., Collegium (bd. dirs. 1990-94). Avocation: theatre. Office: U Dayton 300 College Park Ave Dayton OH 45469-0001

HEFTER, GILBERT MORRIS, psychiatrist; b. Chgo., Aug. 7, 1932; s. Simon and Rebecca (Baskind) H. BA, UCLA, 1954; diploma, U. Paris, 1957; MD, U. Ill., Chgo., 1963. Diplomate Am. Bd. Psychiatry and Neurology. Pvt. practice Chgo., 1967—; dir. Mile Sq. Health Ctr. Mental Health Dept., Chgo., 1967-72; clin. dir. dept. psychiatry Northwestern Meml. Hosp., Chgo., 1972-84; dir. Northwestern Cmty. Mental Health Ctr., Chgo., 1972-84; assoc. prof. clin. psychiatry Northwestern U., Chgo., 1972—; cons. Redirections, Inc., Chgo., 1986—, Continental Bank, Chgo., 1986-94, Cook County Pub. Guardian, Chgo., 1982—, Replogle Counseling Ctr., Chgo., 1985-93, Blue Cross Blue Shield, 1995—. Contbr. articles to profl. jours. Bd. dirs. Travelers and Immigrant Aid Soc., Chgo. With U.S. Army, 1955-56. Fellow Am. Psychiat. Assn., Am. Orthopsychiat. Assn.; mem. AMA, Ill. Psychiat. Soc., Chgo. Med. Soc. Office: 540 N Michigan Ave # 308 Chicago IL 60611-3822

HEFTY, DUANE SEYMORE, management consultant; b. St. Johns, Mich., Dec. 4, 1923; s. Harley E. and Marian G. (Norton) H.; m. Shirley J. Kennedy, Aug. 30, 1947 (dec. June 1994); children: Diane, Paula, Andrea, Britton, Tracy; m. Louella Conly, Feb. 1996. BSME, U. Wis., 1946. Chief engr. Chamberlin Products, Detroit, 1946-50; plant mgr. Chamberlin Products, South Whitley, Ind., 1950-53, v.p. mfg., 1953-58, v.p., gen. mgr., 1958-61; dir. ops. Essex Wire Co., Detroit, 1961-73, United Tech., Detroit, 1973-74; v.p. automotive elec. products div. ITT, Detroit, 1974-80; mgmt. cons. pvt. practive Detroit, 1980-83, Traverse City, Mich., 1988—; pres. Fenwick/Woodstream, Westminster, Calif., 1983-88. Active Mizpah Temple, Ft. Wayne, Ind. Ensign USNR, 1943-46, PTO. Mem. Am. Legion, VFW, Valley Inn Country Club, Elk Rapids Golf Club, Masons. Home and Office: 13628 Rex Terrace Rd Rapid City MI 49676-9628

HEGARTY, MARY FRANCES, lawyer; b. Chgo., Dec. 19, 1950; d. James E. and Frances M. (King) H. BA, DePaul U., 1972, JD, 1975. Bar: Ill. 1975, U.S. Dist. Ct. (no. dist.) Ill. 1976, U.S. Supreme Ct. 1980. Ptnr. Lannon & Hegarty, Park Ridge, Ill., 1975-80; pvt. practice, Park Ridge, 1980—; dir. Legal Assistance Found. Chgo., 1983—. Mem. revenue study com. Chgo. City Coun. Fin. Com., 1983; mem. Sole Source Rev. Panel, City of Chgo., 1984; pres. Hist. Pullman Found., Inc., 1984-85; apptd. Park Ridge Zoning Bd., 1993-94. Mem. Ill. State Bar Assn. (real estate coun. 1980-84), Chgo. Bar Assn., Women's Bar Assn. Ill. (pres. 1983-84), NW Suburban Bar Assn., Park Ridge Women Entrepreneurs, Chgo. Athletic Assn. (pres. 1992-93). Democrat. Roman Catholic. Office: 301 W Touhy Ave Park Ridge IL 60068-4204

HEGEMAN, DANIEL JAY, state legislator; b. Cosby, Mo., Mar. 4, 1963; s. Donald Jay and Margaret Joan (Kowitz) H.; m. Francine Marie Walker, 1990; children: Hannah Marie, Joseph Daniel, Heidi Joan. BSA, U. Mo. Columbia. State rep. Dist. 6 Mo. State Rep., 1991-92, state rep. Dist. 5, 1992—; treas. Hegeman Farm, Inc., 1988—. Mem. NW Mo. Holstein Assn. (v.p. 1991-92, pres. 1993-94, bd. dirs. 1994-95), Mid-Am. Dairymen, Inc. Dist. 14 (v.p. 1991-92), Andrew County Ext. Coun. (pres. 1990), Andrew County Farm Bur., Buchanan & Andrew County Dairy Herd Improvement Assn. (treas.), Cosby Masonic Lodge 600 (Worshipful Master 1989-90); Alpha Zeta, Omicron Delta Kappa, Alpha Gamma Rho. *

HEGG, SCOTT W., executive manufacturing company; b. Hart, Mich., Sept. 22, 1969. AS, I.T.T., Grand Rapids, Mich., 1990; BS, I.T.T., Fort Wayne, Ind., 1991. Technician McJon Photo, Ft. Wayne, Ind., 1990-91, Witmark, Inc., Grand Rapids, Mich., 1991-92; gen. mgr. Cherry Techs., Shelby, Mich., 1992—. Vol. local ch. Office: Cherry Technologies Inc 3178 W Baseline Rd Shelby MI 49455-9633

HEIAR, KURT FRANCIS, health industry executive; b. Dubuque, Iowa; s. Merlin F. and Eileen B. (Savary) H.; m. Debra A. Lahr-Heiar, June 1993. BS, U. Iowa; postgrad., Pepperdine U. Pharm. sales Boehringer Pharms., Omaha, 1983-85; med. sales Baxter Healthcare Corp. Biotech Group, W. Des Moines, Iowa, 1986-88, product mgr. immunotherapy, 1988; global mktg. mgr. immunology Baxter Hyland Divsn.., Glendale, Calif., 1989-91; dir. Bus. Devel. and Planning, 1991-92; v.p. mktg. Baxter Biotech N.Am., Deerfield, Ill., 1993—. Recipient Nat. Healthcare award for Med. Advt., L.A., 1989. Mem. N.Y. Acad. Sci., U. Iowa Alumni Club, Health Industry Mfg. Assn., Am. Mktg. Assn., Acad. Health Scis., United Way (chairperson 1994-95). Office: 1625 Lakecook Rd LC IV Deerfield IL 60015

HEICK, LEON JOSEPH, data processing executive; b. New England, N.D., May 14, 1944; s. Joseph Philiph and Frances (Bosepflug) H.; m. Alicia Marie Finneman, July 13, 1968; children: Brent, Royce, Travis. BS in Bus. Adminstrn., U. Mary, Bismarck, N.D., 1991. Computer operator North Ctrl. Data Corp., Mandan, N.D., 1968-69, computer programmer, 1970-71, programming mgr., 1972-78, sys. mgr., 1979-83, asst. gen. mgr., 1984—; dir. Project Back Home Coop, Mandan, 1994-96, Rural Electric & Telephone Credit Union, Bismarck, N.D., 1993-96. Singer No. Lights Barbershop Chorus, Bismarck, 1991-93; active ch. choir. With U.S. Army, 1965-67, Vietnam. Mem. Am. Legion, KC, Elks, Amvets. Office: North Ctrl Data Corp Box 728 Mandan ND 58554

HEIDELBERG, HELEN SUSAN HATVANI, dentist; b. Greenville, Pa., July 30, 1957; d. Balazs Robert and Ilona Borbala (Nemeth) Hatvani; m. David Raymond Heidelberg, June 4, 1983; children: David William, Laura Shari, Lisa Nicole. AA, Cuyahoga Community Coll., 1977; BS in Biology magna cum laude, Cleve. State U., 1979; DDS, Case Western Reserve U., 1983. Resident in dentistry North Chicago (Ill.) VA Med. Hosp., 1983-84; assoc. dentist Steven D. Miller, DDS, Vernon Hills, Ill., 1984-85; gen. practice dentistry Norwalk, Ohio, 1986—. Mem. ADA, Ohio Dental Assn., N. Cen. Ohio Dental Soc., Great Lakes Dental Soc. (v.p. 1984), Norwalk C. of C. Home: 4 Victoria Cir Norwalk OH 44857-1656 Office: 30 Executive Dr Norwalk OH 44857

HEIDEMAN, DEAN GLEN, JR., electronic engineer; b. Waterloo, Iowa, Apr. 18, 1964; s. Dean Glen and Mildred Elizabeth (Clemons) H.; m. Vicky Sue Kzyer, May 20, 1994; 1 child, Mercedes; 1 child from previous marriage, Jason. Assoc. in Elec. Engring., Hawkeye Tech. Inst., Waterloo, 1985. Maintenance staff Douglas & Lomason, Red Oak, Iowa, 1989-92; electronic engr. Interwest Svcs. Ltd., Red Oak, 1992—. With USMC, 1987-88. Mem. Elks Club. Office: Interwest Svcs Ltd 103 S Broadway St Red Oak IA 51566-2601

HEIDEMAN, RENITA KAY, school district technology coordinator; b. Cin., July 26, 1952; d. Hal Heideman and A. Runell Judd. BS, Miami U., Oxford, Ohio, 1974, MEd, 1989. Cert. in phys. edn. and psychology, curriculum and supervision, Ohio. Tchr. Marion (Indian) Community Schs., 1974-76, N.W. Local Sch., Cin., 1976-77, 1977—, elem. computer cons., 1990-92, dist. chairperson phys. edn. dept., 1989—, dist. chairperson computer edn., 1992—; coach swimming, diving and volleyball Marion High sch., 1974-75, coach swimming and diving, 1975-76; volleyball coach N.W. High Sch., 1976-77, 79, 80, softball coach, 1976-81, basketball coach, 1977-78. Mem. Bevis PTA, Cin., 1980—; team capt. Am. Cancer Soc., Cin., 1987-89. Named Hamilton County Coach of Yr.-Softball, 1980. Home: 23 Doe Ct Fairfield OH 45014-4652 Office: NW Local Schs Curriculum Office 3240 Banning Rd Cincinnati OH 45239

HEIDEMANN, MARY ANN, community planner; b. Detroit, Feb. 17, 1950; d. O.K. and Mary Elizabeth (Berry) Rodewald; m. Karl Werner, June 19, 1982; children: Heather Lisa, Karl Kristoffer. BA in Archtl. History, Reed Coll., Portland, Oreg., 1970; postgrad., U. Pa., Phila., 1972-75; MA in Pub. Adminstrn., U. Wis., 1985, PhD in Land Resources, 1989. Profl. cmty. planner, Mich. Apprentice Paolo Soleri, Architect, Scottsdale, Ariz., 1970-71; staff planner Jack McCormick & Assocs., Devon, Pa., 1972-74; natural resource planner Brown County Planning Commn., Green Bay, Wis., 1976-78; planning cons. Champ, Parish, Raasch, De Pere, Wis., 1978-80; policy analyst U.S. EPA, Chgo., 1980-81; cmty. svc. specialist Wis. Dept. Natural Resources, Madison, 1981-85; chief environ. analysis Wis. Dept. Transp., Madison, 1985-86; project mgr. Wade-Trim/Impact, Taylor, Mich., 1987-88; owner, prin. planner Mary Ann Heidemann & Assocs., Rogers City, Mich., 1988—; lectr. U. Wis., Green Bay, 1977-78; asst. prof. Kans. State U., Manhattan, 1975-76; exec. dir. East Mich. Environ. Action, West Bloomfield, 1986-87; adj. prof. Lake Superior State U., Sault Ste. Marie, 1988—; mem. planner lic. bd. Gov. State Mich., Lansing, 1990-94. Founding mem. Bay Renaissance, Green Bay, 1979-80; mem. Orion Twp. Planning Commn., Mich., 1986-87; county commr. Presque Isle County Bd., Rogers City, Mich., 1992-93; bd. dirs. Presque Isle Harbor Assocs., 1993-96. Dean Webster Meml. scholar Reed Coll., Portland, Oreg., 1968-69; fellow NEH, San Diego, 1978. Mem. AAUW, Am. Inst. Cert. Planners (planning exam. com. 1992), Am. Planning Assn., Mich. Soc. Planning Ofcls. (tng. workshop instr.), Harmony Choraleers, Mich. Historic Preservation Network, Presque Isle Lighthouse Assn. Democrat. Presbyterian. Office: Mary Ann Heidemann & Assocs 150 S 3rd St Rogers City MI 49779-1710

HEIDLAGE, JEFFERY PAUL, manufacturing engineer; b. Batesville, Ind., Oct. 13, 1967; s. Robert C. and Carla R. Heidlage. Student, Cin. State Tech., 1988—. Sr. mfg. engr. Wood-Mizer Products, Greensburg, Ind., 1985—. Mem. Soc. Mfg. Engrs. Republican. Roman Catholic. Home: 28 Beechgrove Ave Batesville IN 47006-1413 Office: Wood-Mizer Products 8829 E State Rd 46 Greensburg IN 47240-7449

HEIDRICK, GARDNER WILSON, management consultant; b. Clarion, Pa., Oct. 7, 1911; s. R. Emmet and Helen (Wilson) H.; m. Marian Eileen Lindsay, Feb. 19, 1937; children: Gardner Wilson, Robert L. B.S. in Banking and Fin, U. Ill., 1935. Indsl. dist. sales mgr. Scott Paper Co., Phila., 1935-42; dir. pers. Farmland Industries, Kansas City, Mo., 1942-51; assoc. Booz, Allen & Hamilton, Chgo., 1951-53; co-founder partner, chmn. Heidrick & Struggles, Inc., Chgo., 1953-82; co-founder, chmn. Heidrick Ptnrs., Inc., Chgo., 1982—; mem. council Internat. Exec. Service Corp. Bd. dirs. U. Ill. Found. Served with USNR, 1945-46. Mem. U. Ill. Alumni Assn. (past pres., Achievement award 1989), Tower Club, Hinsdale Golf Club (past pres.), Little Club (Gulfstream, Fla.), Country Club Fla. (Delray Beach), Ocean Club (Delray Beach), DuPage Club (Oak Brook, Ill.), Phi Kappa Sigma. Office: Heidrick Ptnrs Inc 20 N Wacker Dr Ste 2850 Chicago IL 60606-2806

HEIKEN, JAY PAUL, physician; b. N.Y.C., Aug. 31, 1952; s. Martin and Sylvia (Fisher) H.; m. Barbara Ellen Rayburn, Dec. 11, 1976 (div. 1982); m. Francine J. Rosen, Apr. 29, 1990; 1 child, Lauren M. BA, Williams Coll., 1974; MD, Columbia U., 1978. Intern in internal medicine Emory U. Hosp., Atlanta, 1978-79; resident in radiology Columbia-Presbyn. Med. Ctr., N.Y.C., 1979-82; fellow abdominal radiology Mallinckrodt Inst. Radiology, St. Louis, 1982-83; asst. prof. sch. medicine Washington U., St. Louis, 1983-87, assoc. prof. sch. medicine, 1988-93; prof. sch. medicine, 1993—; dir. abdominal imaging Mallinckrodt Inst. Radiology, St. Louis; mem. cancer com. Barnes Hosp. Author, editor: Manual of Clinical Magnetic Resonance Imaging, 1986, 2d edit., 1991; editor: Computed Body Tomography with MRI Correlation, 3rd edit., 1996; contbr. articles to profl. jours. Mem. AMA, Radiol. Soc. N.Am., Am. Roentgen Ray Soc., Am. Coll. Radiology, Greater St. Louis Soc. Radiologists, Soc. Computed Body Tomography, Internat. Soc. Magnetic Resonance in Medicine, Soc. Gastrointestinal Radiologists, Assn. Univ. Radiologists. Home: 1801 Aston Way Chesterfield MO 63005-4579 Office: Mallinckrodt Inst Radiology 510 S Kingshighway Blvd Saint Louis MO 63110-1016

HEIKES, KEITH, science administrator; b. 1957. With Ralsten Purina, Chilicothe, Mo., 1978-81, Kabsu, Inc., Manhattan, Kans., 1981-90; with Noba Inc., Tiffin, Ohio, 1990—, now COO. Office: Noba Inc 752 E State Rte 18 Tiffin OH 44883*

HEILE, JOHN DAVID, stockbroker; b. Quebec City, Que., Can., Apr. 16, 1955; came to U.S., 1955; s. James E. and Elaine (Ibold) H. BA in History, U. Cin., 1982. Owner, mgr. Trinities, Mobile, Ala., 1975-80; investment broker Legg Mason, Cin., 1983-87; stockbroker Ross Sinclaire & Assocs. Inc., Cin., 1987—; bd. dirs. Murdock Inc., Cin., Caters of Tampa (Fla.) Inc. Contbr. articles to Cin. Bus. Courier. Fundraiser Explorers, Boy Scouts Am.; mem. Ohio Rep. Com. Mem. Univ. Club. Roman Catholic. Home: Riverwinds Condos 554 Davenport Ave Cincinnati OH 45204-1361 Office: Ross Sinclaire & Assocs Inc 36 E 7th St Ste 1550 Cincinnati OH 45202-4434

HEILICSER, BERNARD JAY, emergency physician; b. Bklyn., Jan. 19, 1947; s. Murray and Esther (Dubrow) H.; m. Marcia Cherry, June 2, 1976; children: Micah, Seth, Jacob. BA, SUNY, Binghamton, 1968; MS, Hahnemann Med. Coll., Phila., 1971; DO, Coll. Osteo. Medicine/Surgery, Des Moines, 1976. Diplomate Am. Bd. Emergency Medicine. Instr. anatomy and physiology U. Pa. and Hahnemann Med. Coll., Phila., 1971-73; staff physician Va. Inst. Tech., Blacksburg, 1977-78; asst. prof. emergency medicine Chgo. Coll. Osteo. Medicine, 1979; emergency physician St. Margaret Hosp., Hammond, Ind., 1979-83, Michael Reese Med. Ctr., Chgo., 1989-91, Ingalls Hosp., Harvey, Ill., 1983—; project med. dir. South Cook County Emergency Med. Svc., Harvey, 1984—; mem. faculty Chgo. Osteo.

Med. Ctr., 1987—; faculty trauma nurse specialist St. James Hosp., Chicago Heights, Ill., 1980—; preceptor nurse practitioners Purdue U., Hammond, 1981—; fellow MacLean Ctr. Clin. Med. Ethics, U. Chgo., 1993-94; chmn. ethics com., hosp. med. ethicist Ingalls Hosp., Harvey, Ill., 1994—; cons. The Nat. Bd. Osteo. Med. Examiners, Harvey, 1994—. Vol. fireman Flossmoor (Ill.) Fire Dept., 1985—, Matteson (Ill.) Fire Dept., 1980—. Fellow Am. Coll. Emergency Physicians; mem. Am. Osteo. Assn., Nat. Assn. Emergency Med. Svcs. Physicians, Nat. Assn. Emergency Med. Technicians, Prehosp. Care Providers Ill., Sigma Sigma Phi. Jewish. Office: Ingalls Hosp One Ingalls Dr Harvey IL 60426

HEILIGENSTEIN, CHRISTIAN E., lawyer; b. St. Louis, Dec. 7, 1929; s. Christian A. and Louisa M. (Dixon) H.; children: Christie; m. Liselotte Warbanoff, Feb. 6, 1981. BS in Law, U. Ill., 1953, JD, 1955. Bar: Ill. 1956, U.S. Dist. Ct. (so. dist.) Ill. 1956, U.S. Ct. Appeals (7th cir.) 1956, U.S. Dist. Ct. (cen. dist.) Ill. 1960, U.S. Supreme Ct. 1978. Assoc. Listeman & Bandy, East St. Louis, Ill., 1955-61; sole practice, Belleville, Ill., 1962-84; ptnr., pres. Heiligenstein & Badgley, Belleville, 1984—; bd. dirs. Magna Group, Inc., Magna Bank, N.A. Recipient Alumni of Month award U. Ill. Law Sch., 1982. Mem. Ill. State Bar Assn., Internat. Acad. Trial Lawyers (bd. dirs. 1991—), St. Clair County Bar Assn., St. Louis Bar Assn., Inner Circle Advs., Am. Bd. Trial Advs. (nat. bd. dirs. 1992, pres. St. Louis, So. Ill. region 1993), Am. Acad. Profl. Liability Attys. (Nat. bd. dirs.), ATLA (bd. govs. 1985-87), Ill. Trial Lawyers Assn. (bd. mgrs. 1975-88, pres. 1989), Mo. Athletic Club, Beach Club (bd. dirs. 1996), Magna Club. Democrat. Home: 5200 Turner Hall Rd Belleville IL 62220-5628 Office: Heiligenstein & Badgley 30 Public Sq Belleville IL 62220-1622

HEILMAN, CHRISTINE WEBER, language educator; b. Hamilton, Ohio, Aug. 9, 1952; d. Robert John and Delpha Elaine (Lotz) Weber; m. Rodney Paul Heilman, Aug. 11, 1984; 1 child, Katherine Marie. AB in English, Miami U. Ohio, 1974; MA in English, U. Cin., 1989. Adj. instr., asst. prof. U. Maine, Orono, 1989-91; instr. Cin. State Coll., 1992—. Bd. dirs. Cin. Waldorf Sch. Mem. Modern Lang. Assn., Nat. Coun. Tchrs. English, Soc. Tech. Comm. (author Procs. 1989, 92, 93), Women in Comm., Assn. Tchrs. Tech. Writing, Coun. Programs in Sci. and Tech. Comm. Democrat. Roman Catholic. Office: Cincinnati State Coll 3520 Central Pkwy Cincinnati OH 45223

HEILMAN, KATHRYN, nurse, consultant; b. Muskegon, Mich., Sept. 7, 1937; d. Francis Martin and Inez T. (Woodard) Mulready; m. Robert L. Heilman, June 14, 1958; children: Robert, Robin, Kelly, Sharon, Patricia, Kirk, Eric, Kathryn. ADN, Macomb County Community Coll., Mt. Clemens, Mich., 1970; BSN, Wayne State U., 1974, MS in Nursing, 1976, EdD in Instructional Tech., 1988. Cert. in nursing adminstrn., quality assurance/utilization rev. Unit dir. Havenwyck Hosp., Auburn Hills, Mich.; assoc. DON Macomb-Oakland Regional Ctr., State of Mich. Facility, Mt. Clemens; nurse cons. Mich. Dept. Pub. Health, Lansing; quality assurance/utilization rev. coord. Lafayette Clinic, Detroit. Mem. ANA, Mental Health Alliance, Am. Bd. Quality Assurance and Utilization Rev., Wayne State Nursing Alumni Assn. Home: 32415 Woody Rd Fraser MI 48026-2190

HEIM, JOSEPH PETER, political science educator; b. Milw., Jan. 26, 1942; s. Henry Francis and Vera Ann (Koltes) H.; m. Patricia Ellen Maslowski, Sept. 8, 1974. BA, Marquette U., 1964, MA, 1968; PhD, U. Wis., Milw., 1976. Asst prof. Wis. State U., La Crosse, 1968-71; grad. teaching asst. U. Wis., Milw., 1971-75; prof. polit. sci. U. Wis., La Crosse, 1975—; dir. pub. adminstrn. program U. Wis., La Crosse, 1975-80, chmn. dept. polit. sci., 1980-93; sr. polit. analyst WKBT-TV, La Crosse, 1991—; dir. La Crosse Survey with La Crosse Tribune, 1987—; cons. to local govts., 1980—. Contbr. articles to profl. jours.; pub. speaker to numerous orgns. in Wis. Dir. Select Coun. on Polit. Edn., La Crosse, 1983—; chmn. Study Commn. of Govtl. Reorgn., La Crosse, 1987; co-chmn. Coulee Region Collaboration Project, 1994—. Mem. Am. Polit. Sci. Assn. (exec. dir. Wis. Polit. Sci. Assn.), Midwest Polit. Sci. Assn., Am. Soc. Pub. Adminstrn. Home: W5866 Cedar Rd La Crosse WI 54601-8401 Office: Univ Wis La Crosse Dept Polit Sci La Crosse WI 54601

HEIM, KATHRYN MARIE, psychiatric nurse, author; b. Milw., Sept. 29, 1952; d. Lester Sheldon Wilcox and Laura Dora (Corpie) Wilcox Sears; m. Vincent Robert Gouthro, June 30, 1970 (div. 1976); 1 child, Robert Vincent; m. George John Heim, Sept. 17, 1977 (div. 1988). AS in Nursing, Milw. Area Tech. Coll., 1983; BS in Nursing, NYU, 1986; MS in Mgmt., Cardinal Stritch Coll., 1988; postgrad., Newport U., 1989—. Cert. psychiatric and mental health nurse, AMA. Staff geriatric nurse Clement Manor, Greenfield, Wis., 1983; nurse, health educator Milw. Boys Club, 1983-84; nurse mgr. Milw. County Mental Health Complex, Milw., 1984—, mem. gero-psychiat. inpatient adv. com., 1986-87; RN Psychiat. Acute Care Day Hosp., 1992—; mem. nursing rsch. com. Milwaukee County Mental Health Complex, 1986—; research on loneliness as it relates to mental health, 1989-92. Mem. wellness task force Milw. County Mental Health Complex, 1988-89, chairperson sensory deficit com. Geropsychiatry, 1989-90; active Boy Scouts Am., Milw., 1978-80. Mem. ANA (cert. gerontol. nurse), NAFE (network dir. Milw. chpt. 1982-92), Wis. Nurses Assn., NYU Alumni Assn., Cardinal Stritch Alumni Assn. (class rep. 1986-88), Milw. Area Tech. Coll. Alumni Assn. Home: 351 N 62d St Milwaukee WI 53213 Office: Milw County Mental Health 9455 W Watertown Plank Rd Milwaukee WI 53226-3559

HEIMAN, MARVIN STEWART, financial services company executive; b. Chgo., Sept. 16, 1945; s. Samuel J. and Mildred (Miller) H.; m. Adrienne Joy Nathan, Aug. 7, 1966; children: Scott, Michelle, Adam. Student, Roosevelt U., 1963-67. Pres. Curtom Record Co., Chgo., 1969-80, Gold Coast Entertainment, Chgo., 1980-82; ptnr. Profl. Real Estate Securities Co., Lincolnwood, Ill., 1982-86; pres., chmn. bd. Sussex Fin. Group, Inc., Skokie, Ill., 1986—; bd. dirs. Skokie Bank, Drovers Bank, Chgo.; ptnr. Cole Taylor Banks, Chgo., 1984—, bank examining com., 1986—, ptnr. Chgo. White Sox Am. League Baseball Club, 1981—, Gore/Bronson Bancorp, 1988, Sun Life of Can., 1993. Mem. Rep. Nat. Com., 1980—, Simon Wiesenthal Ctr., 1988. Recipient Men of Achievement award Cambridge, Eng., Nat. Quality award Nat. Assn. Life Underwriters, 1992. Mem. Internat. Assn. Fin. Planners, Chgo. Assn. Life Underwriters, Real Estate Securities Syndication Assn. Am., Nat. Assn. Securities Dealers (registered rep.), Am. Jewish Com. (Humanitarian award 1978), Internat. Platform Assn., Million Dollar Round Table, Pres.'s Club (Am. funds com. 1992). Office: Sussex Fin Group Inc 111 S Pfingsten Rd Ste 111 Deerfield IL 60015-4994

HEIMBURGER, ELIZABETH MORGAN, psychiatrist; b. Atlanta, Apr. 23, 1932; d. Henry Durand and Lillian Elizabeth (Palmour) Morgan; div.; children: Elizabeth Morgan Whitaker, Homer Aggie Whitaker III, Margaret Diane Heimburger, Richard Ames Heimburger Jr., Katherine Durand Heimburger. BS, Ga. State U., 1963; MD, Med. Coll. Ga., 1967. Diplomate Am. Bd. Psychiatry and Neurology. Intern in internal medicine Med. Coll. Ga., Augusta, 1967-68, resident in gen. psychiatry, 1968-70; fellow in child and adolescent psychiatry U. Tex., Galveston, 1970-72; asst. prof. dept. psychiatry U. Tex. Med. Br., Galveston, 1972-73, assoc. prof., dir. residency tng., 1980-87; asst. prof., assoc. prof., dir. psychosomatic svcs. U. Mo. Sch. Medicine, Columbia, 1973-80, clin. assoc. prof. dept. psychiatry, 1987—; pvt. practice specializing in adolescent psychiatry Columbia, 1987—; examiner Am. Bd. Psychiatry and Neurology, Chgo., 1977—; specialist, site visitor residency rev. Coun. Grad. Med. Edn., Washington, 1983—; exec. bd. Am. Assn. Dirs. Psychiat. Residency Tng., 1982-90; exec. coun. Tex. Psychiat. Soc., Austin, 1983-86; dir. confs., workshops on orgnl. and group dynamics. Editorial cons. bd. Am. Psychiat. Assn. Press., Inc., Washington,1 987-90; contbr. articles, scholarly papers to profl. publs. Bd. dirs. Mental Health Assn., Galveston, 1984-87, YMCA, Columbia, 1987-89. Grantee NIMH, 1978-80, 80-83. Fellow Am. Psychiat. Assn.; mem. Am. Soc. Adolescent Psychiatry, Am. Assn. Child and Adolescent Psychiatry (com.), A.K. Rice Inst. (bd. dirs. 1979-85, pres. Cen. States Ctr. 1979-88, bd. dirs. 1979-95), Am. Horticulture Soc. Episcopalian. Home and Office: 814 Hulen Dr Columbia MO 65203-1472

HEINDEL, LEE EDWARD, software marketing manager, consultant, researcher; b. Hanover, Pa., Aug. 8, 1944; s. Wilmer Henry and Myrtle Ruth (Wildasin) H.; m. Mary Belle Krecker, Dec. 19, 1965; children: Jason Andrew, Jennifer Elizabeth. BS in Math., Pa. State U., 1965; MS in Computer Scis., U. Wis., 1967, PhD in Computer Scis., 1970. Mem. tech. staff, specialist Bell Telephone Labs., Holmdel, 1970-74; dist. mgr. AT&T, Basking Ridge, N.J., 1974-82; dir. Bell Comms. Rsch., Piscataway, N.J., 1982-95; sr. cons. Howard Sys. Internat., Stamford, Conn., 1995—; adj. prof. math. Stevens Inst. Tech., Hoboken, N.J., 1972-73. Co-author: (with J.T. Roberto) Lang-Pak-An Interactive Language Design System, 1974; co-inventor (with V. Kasten) Enterprise Management Systems, 1994; contbr. over 35 articles to profl. jours. Mem. IEEE (sr.), PMI, Pi Mu Epsilon, Sigma Xi.

HEINECKE, BURNELL A., retired newspaper reporter; b. Mascoutah, Ill., June 11, 1927; s. Herman and Olivia Sophia (Emge) H. BA, McKendree Coll., Lebanon, Ill., 1950; postgrad., Harvard U., 1956-57. Reporter Belleville (Ill.) Daily Advocate, 1950-52; reporter, Capitol Bur. chief Chgo. Sun Times, Chgo. and Springfield, 1952-75; editor, operator, owner Heinecke News Svc., Springfield, 1975-78; adminstrv. asst. to Ill. state treas. Ill. State Treas.'s Office, Springfield, 1979-87; pub. info. officer Ill. Dept. Labor, Springfield, 1991-92; adj. prof. journalism Sangamon State U., Springfield, 1976-78; mem. Ill. Humanities Coun., Chgo., 1977-80. Bd. dirs. Western Ill. U. Found., Macomb, 1981—. Served with USN, 1945-46. Lucius W. Nieman fellow, 1956-57. Mem. McKendree Coll. Alumni Assn. (Peter Akers Alumni award 1969, Sesquicentennial Alumni citation 1979). Mem. United Ch. of Christ. Home: 1604 Lowell Ave Springfield IL 62704

HEINECKEN, MARTIN THEODORE (TED HEINECKEN), publishers sales representation company executive; b. Hebron, Nebr., Mar. 7, 1933; s. Martin John and Vera Louise (Fritschel) H.; m. Gisela Elizabeth Voehringer, June 6, 1959; children: Kai Stefan, Kim Kyrill. BA, Wartburg Coll., Waverly, Iowa, 1954; MA, U. Minn., 1957; postgrad., Luth. Theol. Sem., Phila., 1958-59. Book editor Muhlenberg Press, Phila., 1959-62, Ency. Brit. Press, Chgo., 1962-63; sales rep. Oxford U. Press, Chgo., 1963-68; v.p., ptnr. Heinecken-Ide Assocs., Inc., Chgo., 1968-77; pres. Heinecken & Assocs., Ltd., Chgo., 1978—. Editor: Encyclopedia of Biblical Animals, 1963. Mem. Nat. Assn. Ind. Pubs. Reps. (bd. dirs., pres. 1991-95), Midwest Book Travellers Assn. (pres. 1980-82). Democrat. Lutheran. Office: Heinecken & Assocs Ltd 1733 N Mohawk St Chicago IL 60614

HEINEMAN, DAVID, state official; b. Falls City, Nebr., May 12, 1948; s. Jean Trevers and Irene Larkin H.; m. Sally Ganem, 1977. BS, U.S. Mil. Acad., 1970. Sales rep. Procter & Gamble, 1976-77; campaign mgr. Daub for Congress, 1977-78; dep. dir. Policy Rsch. Office, Nebr., 1979; dir. Nebr. State Rep. Exec. Com., 1979-81; chief of staff to Congressman Daub, 1983-88, office mgr. for Congressman Berenter, 1990-94; city councilman City of Fremont, Nebr., 1990-94; state treas. State of Nebr., 1995—. Decorated Army Commendation medal; recipient Outstanding Rep. Vol. award Douglas County Rep. Party, 1976, Outstanding Young Am. award Jaycees, 1980. Office: Treasurer's Office PO Box 94788 Lincoln NE 68509*

HEINEMAN, WILLIAM RICHARD, chemistry educator; b. Lubbock, Tex., Oct. 15, 1942; s. Ellis Richard and Edna (Anderson) H.; m. Linda Margaret Harkins, Oct. 25, 1969; children: David William, John Richard. BS, Tex. Tech. U., 1964; PhD, U. N.C., 1968. Rsch. chemist Hercules, Inc., Wilmington, Del., 1968-70; rsch. assoc. Case Western Res. U., Cleve., 1970-71, The Ohio State U., Columbus, 1971-72; asst. prof. U. Cin., 1972-76, assoc. prof., 1976-80, prof., 1980-88, dist. rsch. prof., 1988--; mem. adv. bd. Analytical Chemistry, Washington, 1984-86, The Analyst, Eng., 1987—, Selective Electrode Revs., 1987-92, Fresenius Jour. Analytical Chemistry, 1991-94, Analytical Chimica Acta, 1991-93, Applied Biochemistry and Biotechnology, 1991—, Quimica Analitica, 1993—; U.S. editor Biosensors and Bioelectronics, Eng., 1987—; coun. Gordon Rsch. Confs. Author: Experiments in Instrumental Methods, 1984, Chemical Instrumentrumentation, 1989; editor: Laboratory Techniques in Electroanalytical Chemistry, 1984, Chemical Sensors and Microinstrumentation, 1989. Recipient Charles N. Reilley award in Electroanalytical Chemistry, 1995, Humboldt prize Humboldt Soc., 1989, Rieveschl award U. Cin., 1988, Japan Rsch. award, Japan, 1987; named Disting. Scientist Tech. Socs. Coun., 1984; fellow Japan Soc. for Promotion of Sci., 1981. Mem. Am. Chem. Soc. (treas. analytical chem. divsn. 1983-86, councilor 1984--, named Chemist of Yr. 1983), Soc. for Electroanalytical Chemistry (pres. 1984-85, bd. dirs. 1984-90). Office: U Cin Dept Chemistry PO Box 210172 Cincinnati OH 45221-0172

HEINEMANN, DAVID J., state legislator; b. West Point, Nebr., July 18, 1945; s. Lester Otto and Rita Charlotte (LaNoue) H.; m. Kristine Stroberg, 1972; children: Julie, Suzanne. BA cum laude, Augustana Coll., 1967; postgrad., U. Kans., 1967-68; JD, Washburn U., 1973. Rsch. asst. Govt. Rsch. Ctr. U. Kans., 1967-68; ptnr. Heinemann & Quint, 1973—; Kans. state rep. Dist. 123, 1968—, chmn. pension and investments, rules and jour., mem. juvenile matters com., vice-chmn. jud. com., mem. legis. post audit, assessment, mem. local govt., legis. and jud. reapportionment com., mem. social and rehab. svc. inst. spl. study com., mem. com. rev. plans for prison constrn., mem. joint com. handicapped accessibility, former chmn. energy and natural resources com., spkr. pro tem, 1985; bd. dirs. S.W. Devel. Svc. Inc.; author legis., 1977-82, Kans. Bar Assn. Jour., 1977-82. Contbr. articles to profl. publs. Pres. Garden City Cmty. Day Care Ctr., 1975—, bd. dirs., 1969-72; alt. del. Rep. Nat. Conv., 1972; dep. county atty. Finney County, 1975—; judge pro-tem Garden City Mcpl.; del. Kans. State Rep. Conv., 1972-78, 82; coord., primary and gen. campaigns for Sec. State Jakc Brier, 1978, 82; mem. Nat. Conf. State Legislators Pension Com., 1981-82, mem. Energy Com., 1983—; mem. Gov. Com. State Investment Practices. Named one of Outstanding Young Men of Am., 1982, Outstanding State Legis., Eagleton Inst. Polit., Rutgers U. Mem. Kans. Bar Assn., Garden City C. of C., Lions. Home: PO Box 1346 Garden City KS 67846-1346*

HEINEN, NEIL A., stockbroker; b. Mils., June 15, 1928. BA, Regis U., Denver, 1950. Stockbroker A.G. Edwards & Sons Inc. (formerly Brown Monroe), Milw., 1966—. Roman Catholic. Office: AG Edwards & Sons Inc 700 N Water St Ste 540 Milwaukee WI 53202-4206

HEINICKE, PETER HART, computer consultant; b. Madison, Wis., Mar. 26, 1956; s. Herbert Raymond and Janet Louise (Hart) H.; m. Karen Sue Michel, May 30, 1992; 1 child, Jeremiah Peter. BA in Physics, Washington U., St. Louis, 1977, MA in Math., 1977; MA in Physics, Princeton U., 1980; MS in Computer Sci., ITT, Chgo., 1985. Programmer, analyst Princeton (N.J.) Plasma Physics Lab, 1977-79; systems analyst Encoth, Princeton, 1978-79, Internat. Harvester, Melrose Park, Ill., 1980, Fermi Nat. Accelerator Lab., Batavia, Ill., 1981-89; pres. Precision Computer Methods, Inc., Geneva, Ill., 1979—; bd. dirs. CIM/DNC, Inc. McHenry, Ill.; cons. Rutgers U., New Brunswick, N.J., 1979, Dept. of Energy, Washington, 1979, Internat. Harvester, Melrose Park, 1981-83, Abbot Labs., Abbot Park, Ill., 1983, Digital Equipment Corp., Maynard, Mass., 1985, Avco Everett Rsch. Lab., Everett, Mass., 1986, Lawrence Livermore Lab., Livermore, Calif., 1987, Reuters Info. Tech., Inc., Oak Brook, 1991—, Design Tech., Westmont, Ill., 1987—, The Board Room, Inc., Tinley Park, Ill., 1992—, Environ. Waste Svcs., Elburn, Ill. Author: (software) Tinytach, 1990, EWSMS, 1995; contbr. articles to profl. jours. Treas. African Crusade Ministry, Inc. Warrenville, Ill., 1991-92, Faith Luth. Ch., Geneva,Ill., 1995—. Compton fellow Washington U., St. Louis, 1974-77, NSF Grad. fellow, Princeton, N.J., 1977-79; Nat. Merit scholar, St. Louis, 1974-77. Mem. IEEE, Am. Physical Soc., Digital Equipment Users Soc., Assn. Computing Machinery, Fellowship Cos. for Christ Internat., Am. Assn. Individual Investing. Republican. Lutheran.

HEINLEN, DANIEL LEE, alumni organization administrator; b. Columbus, Ohio, Nov. 16, 1937; s. Calvin Xenophon and Charlotte Elizabeth (Lanman) H.; m. Roberta Bishop, Mar. 20, 1966 (div. 1975); m. Gelene Vogel Kozlowski, June 17, 1978; children: Stephanie, Kate Kozlowski, Amy. BS in Social Work, Ohio State U., 1960. Youth program dir., extension dir. YMCA, Pitts., 1960-65; field dir. Alumni Assn., Ohio State U., Columbus, 1965-67, assoc. dir., 1967-73, dir. alumni affairs, 1973-92; pres., CEO Ohio State U. Alumni Assn., Inc., Columbus, 1992—; sec. Alumni Assn. Bd., Columbus, 1973—; pub. mag. Alumni Assn., Ohio State U., 1973—; ex-officio trustee Ohio State U. Found.; trustee Coun. for Advancement and Support of Higher Edn., Washington,1986-88, 90-94, chairperson, 1992-93; chmn. 75th anniversary Colloquium, Columbus, 1988, chmn. ann. assembly alumni track, 1988, chmn. ann. assembly, 1990; chmn. Mgmt. Inst. for Alumni Assn. Execs., Chgo., 1996; chmn. U. ProNet, Inc., Palo Alto, Calif., 1996—; chmn. alumni dirs. Big Ten, 1973, 84, 93; mem. Ohio State U. Pres.'s Coun. Author chpts. in books. Exec. com. NW Ordinance U.S. Constn. Bicentennial Commn., Ohio, 1986-88; bd. dir. Non-profit Mailers Fedn., Wash., 1985-88; mem. OSU Com. on Student Fin. Aids, Columbus, 1973—, Newcomen Soc. N.Am., 1975-90, 93—. Recipient Ohio State U. Coll. of Social Work Disting. Svc. award, 1996; named Hon. Trustee Easter Seal Rehab. Ctr. of Ctrl. Ohio, Columbus, 1988-92. Mem. Rotary (bd. dirs. Columbus Club 1986, v.p. 1987-89, pres. 1989-90), Univ. Club (bd. dirs., 2nd v.p. 1985-88, 94—, 1st v.p. 1996—), Faculty Club (mem. bd. control 1978-80), Kit Kat Club, Golden Key Nat. Honor Soc. (hon. mem.). Home: 2981 E Powell Rd Lewis Center OH 43035-9517 Office: Ohio State U Alumni Assn Alumni Assn 2400 Olentangy River Rd Columbus OH 43210-1061

HEINRICH, JAMES K., designer; b. St. Louis, Feb. 28, 1970. AAS, ITT Tech. Inst., St. Louis, 1990. Jr. designer Mittler Bros. Machine & Tool, Foristell, Mo., 1988—. Home: 7890 Highway N O'Fallon MO 63366-6703 Office: Mittler Bros Machine & Tool PO Box 110 Foristell MO 63348-0110

HEINTZ, CAROLINEA CABANISS, retired home economics educator; b. Roanoke, Va., Jan. 19, 1920; d. Luther Bertie and Emblyn Bird (Jennings) Cabaniss; m. Howard Elmer Smith, Dec. 19, 1942 (div. Aug. 1975); children: Emblyn Davis, Cynthia Shannon, Cheryl Peterson, Melyssa Sexton; m. Raymond Walter Heintz, May 21, 1977; 1 stepchild, James. BS in Home Econ. Edn., U. Ala., Tuscaloosa, 1941; vocat. home econ. degree, Montevallo Coll., 1941. Cert. vocat. home econs. tchr. Swimming instr. Camp Mudjekeewis, Centerlovel, Maine, summer 1940; home econs. tchr. Roanoke Pub. Schs., 1941-43; dietitian U. Va., Charlottesville, 1943; nutrition edn. specialist Liberty Health Ctr. Svcs., Liberty Center, Ohio, 1974-80; home economist Dayton Hudson Dept. Store, Toledo, 1980-84; splty . food instr., continuing edn. U. Toledo, 1984-85; pres., mem. Greater Toledo Nutrition Coun., 1966-92, 94-96; bd. dirs. Sunset House Aux., 1996. Spkr. United Way, Toledo, 1965-90; founder, pres. Mobile Meals Toledo, Inc., 1968-71, mem. adv. bd., 1988-95, bd. dirs., chmn. pub. rels., 1996—; affiliate mem. Arts Commn., Toledo, 1976-77; chmn. Sapphire Ball, Toledo Symphony Orch., Toledo Opera, 1978; adminstrv. coord. Feed Your Neighbor program Met. Chs. United, Toledo, 1979-86; deacon Collingwood Presbyn. Ch., 1969-71, elder, 1972-74, 77-79, trustee, 1984-86, elder, clk. of session, 1991-94, elder, stewardship chmn., 1996—, del. to Maumee Valley Presbytery, 1991-96; mem. steering com. Interfaith Hospitality Network, 1992-94, bd. dirs., 1993-94; alt. del. Gen. Assembly Presbyn. Ch. U.S.A., 1993, del.-commr., 1994. Recipient Woman of Toledo award St. Vincent Hosp. and Med. Ctr. Guild, 1967, 80, Outstanding Community Svc. award United Way, 1987. Mem. AAUW (bd. dirs. 1974-76, 94-96, chmn. mem. gourmet group 1972-80, 92-96, edn. found. chmn. 1994-96, book sale chmn.), Ohio Med. Aux. (1st v.p. 1973-74), Aux. Acad. Medicine (pres. 1967-68, chmn. med. gourmet group 1966, 92-94, 95-96, Health Care award 1974), Sigma Kappa (various alumni offices). Republican. Home: 3407 Bentley Blvd Toledo OH 43606-2860

HEINZ, JOHN WARREN, historian, artist, photographer; b. Chgo., Feb. 6, 1934; s. Harry Frederick and Lucile Mabel (Bryant) H.; m. Lisa Marie Travers, Oct. 31, 1987. BA, U. Ill., 1957; postgrad., U. Chgo., 1959-61, Northeastern Ill. U., Chgo., 1987-88; student, The Boat Sch., Hyannis, Mass., 1977-78. Reference libr. Art Inst. Chgo., 1961-70; head libr. Sch. of The Art Inst. of Chgo., 1971-77; cinema instr. Chgo. Acad. Fine Arts, 1971-72; yacht carpenter Grebe Shipyard, 1979-80; archtl. model builder Murphy/Jahn, Architects, 1980-86; libr. technician Northeastern Ill. U., Chgo., 1987-88; Gt. Lakes historian Aurora, Ill., 1988—; lectr. on Gt. Lakes history at local museums, 1984—. Author: Ships of the Great Lakes in Miniature, 1988; writer, photographer series on sea history in Model Ship Builder mag., 1978—; editor (newsletter) Quedah Merchant, 1980-83, 93-95, The Fife Rail, 1993—. Vol. Chgo. Maritime Soc., 1984-88; film chmn. Hyde Park Art Ctr., Chgo., 1964-66; tutor Vols. for Literacy, Aurora, 1988—; chmn. Aurora Writers and Artists, 1992-94. Recipient silver awards Manitowoc (Wis.) Maritime Mus., 1980-91. Mem. Nautical Rsch. Soc. Chgo., Nautical Rsch Guild, Assn. for Gt. Lakes Maritime History, Salt Creek Civil War Round Table. Democrat. Home and Office: 619 Glenview Ave Aurora IL 60505-1819

HEINZ, MICHAEL HAROLD, aerospace executive; b. Chgo., Jan. 19, 1944; s. Harold Michael and Grace Agnes (Sebald) H.; m. Margaret Clara Gass, June 28, 1969; children: Christine, Gregory. BA, U. Notre Dame, 1965, BS in Aerospace Engring., 1966; MS in Aerospace Engring., Stanford U., 1967; MBA, Washington U. St. Louis, 1988. Various positions including dir strategic bus. devel. McDonnell Douglas Missile Co., St. Louis, 1967-90; v.p. strategic bus. devel. MCDonnell Douglas Corp., St. Louis, 1990-92; v.p. mission planning MDA-East, St. Louis, 1992-93; v.p. gen. mgr. Harpoon/Slam Program McDonnell Douglas Aerospace, St. Louis, 1993-94, v.p. gen. mgr. Sys. Assessment and Planning, 1994—; mem. adv. com. Nat. Correlation Working Group, Washington, 1994-95; bd. govs. Cardinal Glennon Hosp. Mem. Navy League, Army Defense Preparedness Assn. Home: 12315 Ballas Ln Town and Country MO 63131 Office: McDonnell Douglas Aerospace PO Box 516 Saint Louis MO 63166

HEINZELMAN, EDWARD GEORGE, computer scientist; b. Waukesha, Wis., Aug. 11, 1950; s. Edward George and Alice Anne (Brandt) H.; m. Valerie Jean Christell, Sept. 21, 1952; 1 child, Edward Christell H. BFA, U. Wis., Milw., 1973; B in Mgmt. Sci., Milw. Sch. Engring., 1996. Owner On Broadway Plays, Milw., 1978-82; sales mgr. Ausman Nissan, Milw., 1982-84, Nichols Motors, Racine, Wis., 1984-85; gen. sales mgr. Westport Motors, Milw., 1985-86; fin. mgr. Jenkins Imports, Milw., 1986-90, parts mgr., 1991-93; sr. programmer, analyst Carson Pirie Scott & Co., Milw., 1993-95, project leader, 1995—. Bd. dirs. Milw. Mens Sr. Baseball, 1994—, Arts Guild U. Wis., Milw., 1993. Mem. IEEE Computer Soc., Tau Omega Mu. Home: 3115 S Superior St Milwaukee WI 53207

HEIPLE, JAMES DEE, state supreme court justice; b. Peoria, Ill., Sept. 13, 1933; s. Rae Crane and Harriet (Birkett) H.; B.S., Bradley U., 1955; J.D., U. Louisville, 1957; Certificate in Internat. Law, City of London Coll., 1967; grad. Nat. Jud. Coll., 1971; LLM U. Va., 1988; m. Virginia Kerswill, July 28, 1956 (dec. Apr. 16, 1995); children: Jeremy Hans, Jonathan James, Rachel Duffield. Bar: Ill. 1957, Ky. 1958, U.S. Supreme Ct. 1962; partner Heiple and Heiple, Pekin, Ill., 1957-70; circuit judge Ill., 10th Circuit 1970-80; justice Ill. Appellate Ct., 1980-90; justice Ill. Supreme Ct., 1990—. V.p., dir. Washington State Bank (Ill.), 1959-66; dir. Gridley State Bank (Ill.), 1958-59; village atty., Tremont, Ill., 1961-66, Mackinaw, Ill., 1961-66; asst. pub. defender Tazewell County, 1967-70., jud. clerk Ill. Appellate Ct., 1968-70. Chmn. Tazewell County Heart Fund, 1960. Pub. Adminstr. Tazewell County, Ill., 1959-61; sec. Tazewell County Republican Central Com. 1966-70; mem. Pekin Sch. Bd., 1970; mem. Ill. Supreme Ct. Com. on Profl. Responsibility, 1978-86. Recipient certificate Freedoms Found., 1975, George Washington honor medal, 1976. Fellow ABA (life), Ill. Bar Found. (life), Ky. Bar Found. (life); mem. Ky., Ill. (chmn. legal edn. com. 1972-74, chmn. jud. sect. 1976-77, chmn. Bench and Bar Council 1984-85), Tazewell County Bar Assn. (pres. 1967-68), Ill. Judges Assn. (pres. 1978-79), Ky., Ill., Pa. hist. socs., S.A.R., War of 1812, Sons of Union Vets., Delta Theta Phi, Sigma Nu, Pi Kappa Delta. Methodist. Clubs: Filson; Union League (Chgo.), Pekin Country, Country (Peoria). Lodge: Masons (33 degree). Office: PO Box 997 Pekin IL 61555-0997

HEIPLE, JONATHAN JAMES, lawyer; b. Peoria, Ill., June 24, 1964; s. James D. and Virginia Duffield (Kerswill) H. AB, Albion (Mich.) Coll., 1985; MBA, Ind. U., 1987; JD, U. Va., 1992. Bar: Ill. 1992, Mo. 1995, Ia. 1996; CPA. Acct. Coopers & Lybrand, Detroit, 1987-89; law clk. U.S. Dist. Ct. (ctrl. dist.) Ill., Springfield, 1992-94, Mo. Supreme Ct., Jefferson City, Mo., 1994-95; assoc. atty. Katz, McHard Law Firm, Rock Island, Ill., 1995—. Presdl. scholarship Albion Coll., 1982-85. Mem. Ill. State Bar Assn., Rock Island County Bar Assn., Masons, Shriners, S.A.R., VASA Order of Am. Scottish Rite, Phi Beta Kappa, Beta Gamma Sigma. Methodist. Home: 707 S 5th St Pekin IL 61554 Office: Katz McHard Law Firm 1705 Second Ave Rock Island IL 61201

HEISE, JESSE L., family practice physician; b. Hamlin, Kans., May 8, 1921; s. Edgar Christopher and Esther (Lenhert) H.; m. Fern Marie Hershey, June 15, 1951; children: Esther, Kenneth, Keith, Sue, Kurt. AB, Goshen Coll., 1948; MD, U. Cin., 1952. Diplomate Am. Bd. of Family Practice.

Intern Cin. Gen. Hosp., 1952-53; assoc. clin. prof. Family Practice Medicine, Wright State U. Sch. of Medicine, 1992—. Mem. Lions Internat. Mem. Brethren in Christ. Office: 702 N Main St Arcanum OH 45304-1425

HEISE, WENDY SUE PINNOW, veterinarian; b. Monroe, Wis., Oct. 27, 1956; d. Raymond Arthur and Eleanora Mae (Reigle) P.; m. Jonathan Robert Heise, May 30, 1981; children: Zachary, Joshua. BS, U. Wis., 1979; DVM, Purdue U., 1983. Assoc. vet. Pulaski (Wis.) Vet. Clinic, 1983-89, Janesville (Wis.) Vet. Clinic, 1989-93; relief vet. Pulaski (Wis.) Vet. Clinic, 1993-94; assoc. vet. Brodhead (Wis.) Vet. Svc., 1994—. Mem. AVMA, Am. Animal Hosp. Assn., Am. Assn. Small Ruminant Practitioners, Wis. Vet. Med. Assn., Rock Valley Vet. Med. Assn. (v.p. 1995, pres. 1996), Phi Zeta. Office: Brodhead Vet Svc W1175 Hwy 11-81 Brodhead WI 53520-1856

HEISLER, HAROLD REINHART, management consultant; b. Chgo.; s. Harold Reinhart and Beulah Mary (Schade) H.; B.M.E., U. Ill., 1954. Mgmt. cons. Ill. Power Co., Decatur, 1954—, mem. Nuclear Power Group, Inc., Argonne (Ill.) Nat. Lab., 1955-57; chmn. fossil fuel com., West Central region FPC, Chgo., 1966-68; chmn. evaluation com. Coal Gasification Group, Inc., 1971-75; chmn. Decatur Marine Inc., 1964-66; dir. Indsl. Water Supply Co., Robinson, Ill., 1975-77; pub. speaker in field; mem. Ill. Gov.'s Fuel and Energy Bd., 1970, Ill. Commerce Commn. Fuel and Energy Bd., 1971-75, Ill. Energy Resources Commn. Coal Study Panel, 1976-79, evaluation com. of kilngas process, 1976-80; mem. power plant productivity com. Ill. Commerce Commn., 1977-79; mem. com. on nuclear power plant constrn. Inst. Nuclear Power Ops. Mem. ASME, Nat., Ill. socs. profl. engrs., U. Ill. Alumni Assn., Sigma Phi Delta. Conceptual designer power plant sites and recreational lakes, Baldwin and Clinton, Ill. Home: 2350 W Main St Decatur IL 62522-1853 Office: Ill Power Co 500 S 27th St Decatur IL 62521-2200

HEIT, IVAN, packaging equipment company executive; b. Phila., Sept. 16, 1946; s. Julius and Sylvia (Kantor) H.; m. Joanne Bernard, Oct. 5, 1968; children: Brad Eric, Scott Harris, Mark Alan. BA in English, Pa. State U., 1968. Store mgr. Cameo Stores Inc., Phila., 1968-70; territory mgr. Lester Brooks Assocs., Pitts., 1970-73; dept. mgr. Garrett-Buchanan Co., Phila., 1973-76, div. mgr., 1980-83; pres. Flex-Packaging Systems Inc., Camden, N.J., 1976-80; regional mgr. Allied Automoation Inc., Dallas, 1983-85, mktg. mgr., 1985-87, mktg. dir., 1987-90; v.p. sales and mktg. Arpac Corp., Schiller Park, Ill., 1990—; guest lectr. St. Joseph's U., Phila., 1980-85. Mem. adv. bd. Spring Garden Coll., Phila., 1983-85; asst. dist. commr. Boy Scouts Am., Pitts., 1983; pres. Cherry Hill (N.J.) Eastern Little League, 1985; mgr. YMCA Athletic Program, Plano, Tex., 1986-87. Served with USCG, 1968. Mem. Inst. Packaging Profls. USA (profl. chmn. plastics in packaging tech. com. 1984-85, chmn. Greater Phila. chpt. 1981-84), Soc. Packaging and Handling Engrs. (profl.). Republican. Jewish.

HEITKAMP, HEIDI, state attorney general; b. Breckenridge, Minn.; m. Darwin Lange; children: Alethea Lange, Nathan Lange. BA, U. N.D., 1977; JD, Lewis and Clark Coll., 1980. Intern asst. Environ. Study Conf., Washington, 1976; legis. intern N.D. Legis. Coun., Bismarck, 1977; exec. dir. Northwestern Environ. Def. Ctr., Portland, 1978-79; rsch. asst. Nat. Resources Law Inst., Portland, 1979; atty. enforcement divsn. EPA, Washington, 1980-81; asst. atty. gen. Office of N.D. State Tax Commr., Bismarck, 1981-85, adminstrv. counsel, 1985-86, tax commr., 1986-92; atty. gen. State of N.D., Bismarck, 1993—; del. Am. Coun. Young Polit. Leaders, UK Internat. Def. Conf., 1988; trustee Fedn. Tax Adminstrs., 1991. N.D. State Crusade chmn. Am. Cancer Soc., 1988—. Recipient Young Achiever award Nat. Coun. Women, 1987; named One of 20 Young Lawyers Making a Difference, ABA Barrister mag., 1990; Toll fellow Coun. State Govts., 1986. Mem. Nat. Assn. Atty. Gens. Office: Attorney General State Capitol 600 E Boulevard Ave Bismarck ND 58505-0040

HEITKAMP, JOEL C., state legislator; m. Susan Heitkamp; 2 children. Student, U. N.D. Senator Dist. 27 N.D. State Senate, mem. fin., taxation and natural resources coms. Recipient Operator's award N.D. State Health Dept. Mem. Richland County Pheasants, Hankinson Dollars for Scholars, Mantador Fire Dept. and Cmty. Club. Home: 16543 94-1/2 St SE Hankinson ND 58041

HEITZLER, BECKY VIRGINIA, clinical psychologist; b. Sioux City, Nov. 29, 1959; d. Luther G. and C. Virginia (Wagner) Schember; m. Mark D. Kroeger, May 29, 1977 (div. Aug. 1983); children: Rachel V., Scott D.; m. Larry J. Heitzler, June 12, 1993. BA, U. So. Fla., 1980; MA, Southwestern U., 1983. Psychologist Bapt. Hosp., New Orleans, 1980-84; family therapist Burke & Assocs., Beverly Hills, Calif., 1984-93; clin. therapist family divsn. Sinnissippi Ctr., Inc., Dixon, Ill., 1993—; prof. U. So. Calif., L.A., 1985-86; advisor Calif. Profl. Ethics Bd., L.A., 1985-88. Author: Stepfamily Myths and Realities, 1994, Abuse Amongest Families, 1985. Vol. Cove Domestic Abuse Ctr., Sterling, Ill., 1990. Sgt. USMC, 1986-92. Mem. Internat. Profl. Soc. on Abused Children (bd. dirs. 1994—), Ill. Profl. Soc. on Abuse Children (bd. dirs. 1994—), Am. Psychol. Assn. Republican. Lutheran. Office: Sinnissippi Ctr Inc 325 IL Rt 2 Dixon IL 61021

HEITZMAN, LYNN NEEDHAM, labor relations consultant, educator; b. Cleve., Feb. 25, 1949; d. Raymond Henry and Lucille Helen (Szykowny) Needham; m. William Gary Heitzman, Aug. 14, 1971 (div. Sept. 1987); 1 child, Steven William. BS, Ohio State U., 1970; MEd, Cleve. State U., 1976. Cert. tchr., Ohio. Tchr. sci. Parma (Ohio) Bd. Edn., 1970-85; labor rels. cons. Ohio Edn. Assn., 1985—. V.p. Westlake (Ohio) Devel. Ctr., Parents, Tchrs., Cmty. United, 1991-93, pres., 1993-94, historian, 1994-96; chair bd. Sick Kids Need Involved People, Cleve., 1986-88. Mem. Pub. Sector Labor Rels. Assn. (exec. com. 1991-93), Profl. Staff Union (exec. com. 1988-93). Democrat. Roman Catholic.

HEITZ-PEEK, TAMERA, public relations executive; b. Belle Fourche, S.D., Sept. 16, 1970; d. Arthur Jr. and Maureen Katheryn (Schnell) H.; m. Harry Wesley Peek, June 6, 1991; 1 child, Alexis Lauren Peek. BS in Journalism, Evangel Coll., 1991; MA in Comms., Southwest Mo. State U., 1995; MS in Health Svcs. Adminstrn., Southwest Bapt. U., 1996. Pub. rels. asst. Evangel Coll., Springfield, Mo., 1989-91; pub. info. officer Southwest Bapt. U., Bolivar, Mo., 1991-94, assoc. dir. pub. rels., 1994—; membership chmn., Pub. Rels. of the Ozarks, Springfield, Mo., 1989—. Mem. Assemblies of God. Mem. Bapt. Pub. Rels. Assn. (resolutions com. mem. 1990), Soc. Profl. Journalists. Republican. Home: 1204 S Lillian Apt 31 Bolivar MO 65613 Office: Southwest Bapt U 1600 U Ave Bolivar MO 65613

HEJTMANEK, DANTON CHARLES, lawyer; b. Topeka, July 22, 1951; s. Robert Keith and Bernice Louise (Krause) H.; m. Julie Hejtmanek; 1 child, Brian J. BBA in Acctg., Washburn U., 1973, JD, 1975. Bar: Kans. 1976, U.S. Dist. Ct. Kans. 1976, U.S. Tax Ct. 1976. Ptnr. Schroer, Rice, Bryan & Lykins, P.A., Topeka, 1975-86, Bryan, Lykins & Hejtmanek, P.A., Topeka, 1986—. Mem. ABA (rep. young lawyers Kans. and Nebr.), ATLA, Kans. Bar Assn. (pres. young lawyers 1985), Kans. Trial Lawyers Assn., Sertoma (pres. 1983, internat. v.p. 1995-96). Republican. Presbyterian. Home: 2800 SW Burlingame Rd Topeka KS 66611-1316 Office: Bryan Lykins & Hejtmanek PA 222 W 7th St Topeka KS 66603

HEKMAN, JAMES L., stockbroker; b. Modesto, Calif., June 20, 1943. BA in Econs., Calvin Coll., 1966. Sales/mktg. exec. Mayflower Van Lines, Holland, Mich., 1976-93; stockbroker Robert W. Baird & Co. Inc., Holland, 1993—. Deacon, elder, v.p. Faith Christian Reformed Ch., 1966—. Mem. Rotary. Republican. Office: Robert W Baird & Co Inc 170 College Ave Ste 100 Holland MI 49423-2982

HELDEBRANDT, BETH MARIE, newspaper editor; b. Pana, Ill., July 1, 1968; d. Lawrence James and Rose Marie (Epley) Clavin; 1 child, Alexander Charles Heldebrandt. BS, So. Ill. U., 1989. Asst. night editor Mid. Ill. Newspapers, Mattoon, 1990-92, night editor, 1992-95, news editor, 1995—. Mem. Soc. Profl. Journalists. Office: Mid Ill Newspapers 100 Broadway Mattoon IL 61938

HELDENBRAND, LOIS ELAINE, academic administrator; b. Maryville, Mo., Sept. 4, 1950; d. Oren Eugene and Rosella (Mires) Trimble; m. Dennis Wayne Heldenbrand, June 3, 1972; children: Jason Bradley, Jennifer Anne. BS in Edn., Northwest Mo. State U., 1974, MS in Edn., 1989. Copywriter KSWO-TV, Lawton, Okla., 1972-74; instr. bus. Cameron (Mo.) R-II High Sch., 1975-81, Platt Coll., St. Joseph, Mo., 1984-85, Pattonsburg (Mo.) R-II High Sch., 1985-87; interim dir., counselor Northwest Mo. State U., Maryville, 1989, dir. student support svcs., 1989-95; dir. office excellence in customer svc. State of Mo., Jefferson City, 1995—; team leader Nat. Coun. Ednl. Opportunity Assns. policy sem., Washington, 1993, 94; examiner Bd. Examiners Mo. Quality Award, 1995, 96. Mem. AAUW, Am. Soc. Quality Control, Mid-Am. Coun. Ednl. Opportunity Program Personnel (sec. Mo.-Kans.-Nebr. chpt. 1991-92, pres.-elect 1992-93, pres. 1993-94). Methodist. Office: Office Excellence Customer Svc 301 W High Jefferson City MO 65102

HELDENBRAND, MARILYN LOUISE, township governmental official; b. Detroit, Jan. 4, 1939; d. Edwin Forest and Laura Evelyn (Helmer) Tompsett; m. Robert L. Heldenbrand, Apr. 11, 1938; children: Deborah, Robert. Student, Schoolcraft Coll., Livonia, Mich., 1973; cert. purchasing mgmt., Mich. State U., 1989, advanced acad. edn. cert., 1996. Cert. mcpl. clk., Mich. Parks commr. Redford (Mich.) Twp., 1976-78, trustee, 1978-88, twp. clk., 1988—; sales, svc. acct. rep. Clevite, Troy, Mich., 1966-88. Chmn. bd. dirs. Redford Cmty. Hosp., 1983-88; sec. Hazardous Toxic Waste Commn., Redford, 1984-87; sec.-treas. Wayne County chpt. Mich. Twp. Assn., 1989—; commr. Redford Zoning Bd. Appeals, 1978-80. Recipient Citizen of Yr. award Redford Rotary & Elks, 1988, Notable Women in Pub. Office award State of Mich., 1983. Mem. VFW, Redford Bus. and Profl. Women (pres. 1982, Woman of Yr. 1984), Am. Legion, Elks (Am. award 1987), Redford Suburban League, Kenwood Women's Club, Sister-City Orgn., LWV, Elkharts, Music Soc., Redford C. of C., Friends of Libr., Judges Commn. on Children Issues. Lutheran. Home: 19158 Lexington Redford MI 48240-2619

HELDER, BRUCE ALAN, metal products executive; b. Grand Rapids, Mich., July 1, 1953; s. Harry Martin and Margaret (Ditmar) H.; m. Arlene Faye Docter, May 29, 1975; children: Amanda Joy, David Ryan, Joel Brent, Jonathan Bruce, Brandon Michael. Student, Calvin Coll., 1972-73, Grand Valley State Coll., Allendale, Mich., 1974. Lic. realtor assoc.; cert. media specialist. Indsl. sales rep. Newman Communications, Inc., Grand Rapids, 1971-81; nat. sales mgr. Best Metal Products Co., Grand Rapids, 1981—; pres. Venture Property Mgmt. Co. Mem. Real Estate Bd. Grand Rapids. Republican. Mem. Christian Reformed Ch. Home: PO Box 88153 Grand Rapids MI 49518-0153 Office: Best Metal Products Co PO Box 888-440 3570 Raleigh Ave SE Grand Rapids MI 49512-2064

HELDER, JAN PLEASANT, JR., lawyer; b. Marysville, Calif., Jan. 18, 1963; s. Jan Pleasant Sr. and Roleane Phylis (Harrison) H.; m. Barbara Irene Loring, July 14, 1990; children: Russell Wright, Zachary Allen, David Grant. BA in Econs., Calif. State U., Sacramento, 1986; JD, Georgetown U., 1989. Bar: Mo. 1989, U.S. Dist. Ct. (we. dist.) Mo. 1989, Kans. 1990, U.S. Dist. Ct. Kans. 1990, U.S. Ct. Appeals (10th cir.) 1994, U.S. Tax Ct. 1994. Exec. asst. to pres. Sacramento Trade Exch., 1983-84; legis. asst. Calif. Postsecondary Edn. Commn., Sacramento, 1985-86; assoc. Spencer, Fane, Britt & Browne, Kansas City, Mo., 1989-94; assoc. Sonnenschein Nath & Rosenthal, Kansas City, Mo., 1994-96, ptnr., 1996—; bd. dirs. Edn., Inc., bd. sec., 1994-95; bd. dirs. Young Audiences, bd. sec., 1996—. Bd. editor Bus. Torts Reporter, 1996—. Chair Calif. State Student Assn., Sacramento and Long Beach, 1984-85; mem. Leadership Mo., Jefferson City, 1992; mem. Centurions Leadership Program, 1993-95, mem. steering com., 1994-95. Pursuit of Worthwhile Endeavors scholar Calif. State U., Sacramento, 1982. Mem. ABA (vice-chair bus. torts subcom., bus. and corp. litigation com., bus. sect. 1993-95, chair bus. torts subcom. 1995—), Nat. Inst. Trial Advocacy (western regional 1993), Mo. Bar Assn., Kans. Bar Assn., Kansas City Met. Bar Assn., Johnson County Bar Assn., Greater Kansas City C. of C. (chair subcom. on labor and jud. 1990-91, fed. affairs com. 1989—), Ross T. Roberts Inn Ct. (barrister 1991-92). Republican. Presbyterian. Home: 2216 W 63rd St Mission Hills KS 66208 Office: Sonnenschein Nath et al Twentieth Century Tower II 4520 Main St Ste 1100 Kansas City MO 64111

HELDRETH, LEONARD GUY, university administrator; b. Shinnston, W.Va., Apr. 8, 1939; s. Orie Guy and Grace Louise (Myers) H.; m. Lillian Ruth Marks, June 18, 1964; children: Randall Thomas, Terrence Lon. BS in Physics, W.Va. U., 1962, MA in English, 1964; PhD in English, U. Ill., 1973. Abstractor, editor Nat. Coun. Tchrs. of English Eric Clearing House, Urbana, 1968-70; instr. dept. English No. Mich. U., Marquette, 1970-73, asst. prof. dept. English, 1973-76, assoc. prof., 1976-81, prof., 1981—, head. dept. English, 1988-91, 92—, interim dean Coll. Art and Sci., 1991-92, assoc. dean, 1994—. Reviewer movies Sta. WNMU-FM Radio, Marquette, 1983-89; reviewer video cassettes Marquette Monthly newspaper, 1988—; contbr. articles to profl. jours. Pres. Urbana-Champaign Community Theatre, 1968-69. Recipient Distinguished Faculty award No. Mich. U., Marquette Mich., 1987, Research Grants No. MIch. U., Marquette Mich., 1983, 1984, 1987. Mem. Internat. Assn. for the Fantastic in the Arts (sec. 1990-95), Popular Culture Assn. (area chair fantasy and sci. fiction), Mich. Assn. Depts. English (treas., sec. 1989—), Sci. Fiction Rsch. Assn., Mich. Coun. Humanities (bd. dirs. 1989-93), Univ. Club No. Mich. U. Home: 367 E Hewitt Ave Marquette MI 49855-3711 Office: No Mich U English Dept Marquette MI 49855

HELDRICH, GERARD CHARLES, JR., lawyer; b. Perth Amboy, N.J., Mar. 20, 1933; s. Gerard Charles Sr. and Gertrude L. (Murphy) H.; m. Constance B. Heldrich, Nov. 26, 1955 (div. Nov. 1991); children: Gerard Charles III, Philip J., Michael G., Constance Ann; m. Jenny Lee Heldrich, Dec. 21, 1991; 1 child, Scott J. Czerniejewski. BA, Trinity Coll., Hartford, Conn., 1955; JD, IIT Chgo.-Kent Coll. Law, 1961. Bar: Ill. 1961. Asst. gen. counsel Combined Ins. Co. Am., Chgo., 1961-67; mem. faculty Chgo.-Kent Coll. Law, 1967-70; spl. asst. atty. gen. State of Ill., Chgo., 1970-74; ptnr. Rakowski, Heldrich & Gutman, Lincolnshire, Ill., 1970—, Heldrich Gutman & Assocs., Chgo., 1967—; bd. dirs. Lincoln Park Savs. Bank, Chgo.; bank counsel Richmond (Ill.) Sate Bank, Libertyville (Ill.) Bank. Author: Painting of Elmer, 1989. Sec. Northbrook (Ill.) Civic Found., 1980-82. Cpl. USMCR. Mem. ABA, ATLA, Ill. State Bar Assn., Chgo. Bar Assn. Baha'i' Faith. Office: Heldrich Gutman & Assocs 4018 N Lincoln Ave Chicago IL 60618 also: 430 N Milwaukee Ave Lincolnshire IL 60069

HELDRING, ERNST M., bank executive; b. Bryn Mawr, Pa., June 1, 1955; s. Frederick and Colette Marianne (Barr) H.; m. Margaret Anne Wilson, Oct. 13, 1991; children: Balthalan Wilson, Anna Colette. BS in fgn. svc., Georgetown U., 1977; MBA, U. Chgo., 1980. Asst. v.p. Harris Bank, Singapore, 1981-83; v.p. Harris Bank, Chgo., 1983-87; v.p., gen. mgr. Harris Bank Internat., N.Y.C., 1987-92; v.p., mgr. Bank Montreal, Seoul, Korea, 1992-94; mng. dir. Bank Montreal, Chgo., 1994—; vice chmn. Fgn. Bankers Assn., Seoul, 1992-94. Mem. Union League, Seoul Club (dir. 1992). Office: Bank Montreal 115 S LaSalle St Chicago IL 60690

HELDT, BRIAN PATRICK, systems engineer; b. Toledo, Dec. 26, 1963; s. William Roger and Barbara Ann (Krusner) H.; m. Jacqueline Sue Johnson, Sept. 24, 1988. BBA in Mktg., U. Toledo, 1986, MBA in Fin., 1993. Acct. mgr. Met Design, Toledo, 1986-89; systems engr. Dana Corp., Toledo, 1989—. Mem. Novell CNE. Republican. Office: Dana Corp 3130 Exec Pky Toledo OH 43606

HELFRICH, WAUNETA MEYNE, retired school social worker; b. Madison, Ind., Nov. 8, 1923; d. Harry Everett and Jessie Anderson (Copher) Wells; m. Robert Herman Meyne, June 19, 1943 (dec. Sept. 1972); children: Kathryn Meyne Johnson, Robert Wells; m. Howard Francis Helfrich, Aug. 6, 1977; 4 stepchildren. BS in Social Work, Ind. U., Bloomington, 1948; MS in Child Devel., Ind. State U., 1969; MSW in Psychiat. Social Work, Ind. U., Indpls., 1976. Lic. clin. social worker, Ill. Child welfare worker Hendaicks County Pub. Welfare Dept., Danville, Ind., 1948-49; instr. sociology Canterbury Coll., Danville, 1949-51; intake worker prenatal clinic Vis. Nurse Assn., Terre Haute, Ind., 1960-65; instr. family and child health, fellow Ind. State U., Terre Haute, 1967-69, instr. health dept., 1970-71; social worker Family Svc. Assn., Terre Haute, 1976-77; sch. social worker Lake Park H.S., Roselle, Ill., 1977-92; ret., 1992; social worker Planned Parenthood Assn., Terr Haute, 1962-64. Chmn. pers. com. YWCA, Terre Haute, 1959--76; disaster vol. Mid-Am. chpt. ARC, Chgo., 1990-91. Mem. NASW, Acad. Cert. Social Workers, Ill. Assn. Sch. Social Workers, DAR. Republican. Episcopalian.

HELGELAND, JOHN ALLEN, religion educator; b. Pueblo, Colo., Oct. 22, 1940; s. Sander N. and Annette (Rislov) H.; m. Mary Anita Anderson, Apr. 10, 1965 (div. June 1977); m. Susan Rae Lundberg, July 13, 1989; children Annalyssa, Elena. BA, Luther Coll., 1962; MDiv, Luther Sem., 1966; MA, U. Chgo., 1969, PhD, 1973. Instr. Luther Coll, Decorah, Iowa, 1972; asst. prof. St. John's U., Collegeville, Minn., 1972-77; prof. N.D. State U., Fargo, 1977—; bd. dirs. Charis, Moorhead, Minn., 1980—, media informant, 1985—. Author: Christians and the Military, 1985; contbr. articles to profl. jours. Remele rsch. fellow N.D. Humanities Coun., 1994-95. Mem. Am. Acad. Religion, Soc. Bib. Lit. (pres. 1984-85). Lutheran. Office: ND State U 402 Minard Hall Fargo ND 58105

HELGERSON, HENRY, state legislator; b. Jan. 12, 1952; m. Nickoli A. Flynn. Grad., Rockhurst U. Kans. state rep. Dist. 86, 1983—. Dir. Children's Mus. Home: 4009 Hammond Dr Wichita KS 67218-1221*

HELLER, FRANCIS H(OWARD), law and political science educator emeritus; b. Vienna, Austria, Aug. 24, 1917; came to U.S., 1938, naturalized, 1943; s. Charles A. and Lily (Grunwald) H.; m. Donna Munn, Sept. 3, 1949 (dec. Dec. 1990); 1 child, Denis Wayne. Student, U. Vienna, 1935-37; JD, U. Va., 1941, MA, 1941, PhD, 1948; DHL (hon.), Benedictine Coll., 1988. Asst. prof. govt. Coll. William and Mary, 1947; asst. prof. polit. sci. U. Kans., Lawrence, 1948-51; assoc. prof. U. Kans., 1951-56, prof., 1956-88, Roy A. Roberts prof. law and polit. sci., 1972-88, emeritus, 1988—, asso. dean Coll. Liberal Arts and Scis., 1957-66, asso. dean of faculties, 1966-67, dean, 1967-70, vice chancellor for acad. affairs, 1970-72; vis. prof. Inst. Advanced Studies, Vienna, 1965, U. Vienna Law Sch., 1985, Trinity U., Tex., 1992. Author: Introduction to American Constitutional Law, 1952, The Presidency: A Modern Perspective, 1960, The Korean War: A 25-Year Perspective, 1977, The Truman White House, 1980, Economics and the Truman Administration, 1982, USA: Verfassung und Politik, 1987, NATO: The Founding of the Alliance and the Integration of Europe, 1992, The Kansas State Constitution: A Reference Guide, 1992, The United States and the Integration of Europe, 1996. Mem. Kans. Commn. on Constl. Revision, 1957-61, Lawrence City Planning Commn., 1957-63, ednl. adv. commn. U.S. Army Command and Gen. Stagg Coll., 1969-72; bd. dirs. Harry S. Truman Libr. Inst., 1988-96, v.p., 1962-96; bd. dirs. Benedictine Coll., chmn., 1971-79; mem. nat. adv. coun. Ctr. for Study of Presidency, 1991—. 1st lt. arty. AUS, 1942-47, capt. 1951-52, maj. USAR, ret. Decorated Silver Star, Bronze Star with cluster; recipient Career Teaching award Chancellor's Club, 1986, Silver Angel award Kans. Cath. Conf., 1987. Mem. Am. Polit. Sci. Assn. (exec. council 1958-60), Order of Coif, Phi Beta Kappa, Pi Sigma Alpha (mem. nat. council 1958-60). Home: 3419 Seminole Dr Lawrence KS 66047-1622 Office: U Kans Sch Law Green Hall Lawrence KS 66045

HELLER, JOHN L., II, food products executive; b. Galesburg, Ill., Jan. 23, 1953; s. John L. and Wilma (Medows) H.; m. Brenda June Baxter, Nov. 17, 1972 (div. 1995); children: Holly Renee, Kelly Susanne. Sales rep. H&K Electric Supply, Inc., Chillicothe, Mo., 1971-73, Schwan Sales Enterprises, Inc., Chillicothe, 1973-79; sales mgr. Schwan Sales Enterprises, Inc., Aurora, Mo., 1979-81; nat. promotions mgr. Schwan Sales Enterprises, Inc., Marshall, Minn., 1981-86; pres. ABar Assocs., Inc., Marshall, 1986-89, ADCO Sales Advt. and Cons. Firm, Marshall, 1989-90; sales mgr. food svc. div. Cookies Food Products, Inc., Wall Lake, Iowa, 1989-90; regional sales mgr. Tony's Food Svc. divsn. Schwan's Sales Enterprises Inc., Blue Springs, Mo., 1990-93; regional dir. Zartic, Inc., Blue Springs, 1993-95, Redi-Foods, Inc., Blue Springs, Mo., 1995—. Mem. Nat. Premium Sales Exec., Blue Springs C. of C. Republican. Baptist. Home: 3603 SW Jackson St Blue Springs MO 64015-3386 Office: Redi Foods Inc PO Box 316 319 W Foxwood Raymore MO 64083

HELLER, RICHARD ELLIOT, retired surgeon, physician; b. Chgo., Aug. 20, 1907; s. Edward M. and Florence Heller; married; 1 child, Richard M. BS, U. Chgo., 1929, MD, 1934. Diplomate Am. Bd. Surgery. Intern Chgo. Meml. Hosp., 1933-34, preceptor, 1934-40; sr. attending surgeon emeritus Northwestern Meml. Hosp., Chgo., 1946-79; assoc. attending surgeon Cook County Hosp., Chgo., 1947-50; cons. surgeon Hines VA Hosp., 1950-53; lectr. Northwestern U. Med. Sch., Chgo., 1936—. Contbr. sci. articles to profl. jours.; artist, sculptor. Lt. col. M.C. U.S. Army, 1942-46. Fellow ACS; mem. AMA, Am. Assn. Surgery of Trauma, Am. Soc. Clin. Anatomists, Ill. Med. Soc., Chgo. Med. Soc., Chgo. Surg. Soc. Home: 860 N Dewitt Pl Chicago IL 60611-1759

HELLER, STANLEY J., lawyer, physician, educator; b. Phila., May 10, 1941; s. Albert Curtis and Blanche (Solton) H.; m. Martha Wright (div. 1975); children: Stephanie Gail, Michael Lawrence, Deborah Arlene; m. Brenda Anita West, Dec. 29, 1990. BA, Johns Hopkins U., 1962, MD, 1965; JD, Northwestern U., 1988. Diplomate Am. Bd. Internal Medicine, sub-bd. Cardiovascular Diseases; bar: Ill. 1988. Resident physician, medicine Rush-Presbyn. St. Lukes Hosp., Chgo., 1965-68; instr. U. Ill. Coll. Medicine, Chgo., 1968-70; asst. prof. Rush Med. Coll., Chgo., 1970-71; assoc. prof. Loyola Stritch Coll. Medicine, Chgo., 1971-79; clin. assoc. prof. Northwestern U. Medical Sch., Chgo., 1980—; dir. cardiac diagnostic lab. St. Joseph Hosp., Chgo., 1971-84; pres. Northside Cardiology Group, Ltd., Chgo., 1973-84; ptnr. Thomas R. Cirignani & Assocs., Chgo., 1988—; attending physician St. Joseph Hosp., Chgo., 1971-85, Grant Hosp., Chgo., 1972-85, Augustana Hosp., Chgo., 1973-86; cons. physician Columbus Hosp., Chgo., 1980-84. Cardiology fellow U.S. Pub. Health Svc., Chgo., 1968-70. Fellow Am. Coll. Physicians (Emeritus), Am. Coll. Cardiology (Emeritus), Am. Heart Assn. (Coun. Clin. Cardiology, Emeritus); mem. ABA, Ill. Bar Assn., Ill. Trial Lawyer Assn., Chgo. Bar Assn. Office: Thomas R Cirignani & Assocs 200 W Madison St Ste 3660 Chicago IL 60606-3417

HELLMANN, ROBERT F., lawyer, state legislator; b. Terre Haute, Ind., Jan. 16, 1947; m. Nancy Rains; 3 children. BA, Ind. State U., 1969; JD, St. Louis U., 1973. Atty. Hellmann, Cook and Alexander; asst. city atty.; rep. Dist. 43 Ind. Ho. of Reps., 1982-86; senator Dist. 38 Ind. State Senate, 1986—, asst. dem. leader, 1991—, minority floor leader, mem. edn. com., mem. judiciary, rules and legis. procedures coms., mem. pensions and labor coms. Mem. Ind. House, 1982-86, Ind. Senate, 1986—; Dem. candidate 7th dist. Mo. U.S. House of Reps., 1996. Served with Ind. Nat. Guard, 1968-92. Mem. Ind. State Bar Assn., Terre Haute Bar Assn., Shelby County Hosp. Assn., Travelers Protective Assn. Roman Catholic. Office: 22 N 5th St Ste 320 Terre Haute IN 47808*

HELLYER, TIMOTHY MICHAEL, protective services officer; b. Chgo., Nov. 30, 1954; s. William Al and Dotha Helen (Bucknum) H.; m. Nancy Ruth O'Donnell, Nov. 29, 1986; children: Jennifer Lynn, Allyson Jean. Student, So. Ill. U., 1985-86. Cert. firefighter III; cert. paramedic. Firefighter/paramedic Palatine (Ill.) Fire Dept., 1980—; instr. CPR, Chgo. Heart Assn., 1976—; pres. N.W. Assn. Provider Emergency Med. Svcs. Sys., 1989-92; mem. No. Ill. Critical Stress Debriefing Team. Deacon Palatine Presbyn. Ch., 1989-92. Named Firefighter of the Yr., Jaycees of Palatine, 1987. Mem. Prehosp. Care Providers Ill. (bd. dirs. 1990), St. Francis Hook and Ladder Soc., Ill. Profl. Firefighters Assn., Smithsonian Instn., Nat. Trust Historic Preservation, Nat. Geographic Soc., U.S. Naval Inst., Nat. Space Soc. Republican. Presbyterian. Home: 1600 Kensington Dr Algonquin IL 60102-5104 Office: Palatine Fire Dept 39 E Colfax St Palatine IL 60067-5207

HELMES, LESLIE SCOTT, architect; b. Fort Snelling, Minn., Oct. 27, 1945; s. Leslie Charles and Marilyn (Tomlinson) H.; m. Julie Williams, Sept. 15, 1967 (div. Dec. 4, 1974). BArch, U. Minn., 1968. Registered architect. Instr. U. Minn., Mpls., 1969-73; program coord. Mpls. Inst. Arts, 1970-74; dir. edn. programs Minn. Hist. Soc., St. Paul, 1974-77; dir. phys. planning Freerks Sperl Flynn Architects, St. Paul, 1977-80, Smiley Glotter Assocs., Mpls., 1980-82, Park Nicollet Med. Ctr., Mpls., 1982-85; sole proprietor Helmes Architects, Mpls., 1985-86; v.p. Skaaden Helmes Archs., Mpls., 1986-94; bd. dirs. Friends of Gillette Children's Hosp., St. Paul; bus. adv. coun. CAD/Mpls. Rehab. Ctr., 1990-92. Author: Metapoems, 1989, (poem) Kaldron, 1990; contbr. articles to profl. jours. Bd. dirs., founder Frosty Sch. for Mentally Retarded/Autistic/Down Syndrome, Mpls., 1973—; master coach Internat. Spl. Olympics, Washington, 1988-91, decorations commn., 1990-91. Recipient 1st Pl. award Gamut Mag., 1982. Mem. Am. Inst.

Architects, Inland Lake Yachting Assn., Minn. Soc. Am. Inst. Architects, Profl. Ski Instrs. Am. Home: 862 Tuscarora Ave Saint Paul MN 55102-3706 Office: Skaaden Helmes Architects 401 N 3rd St Ste 100 Minneapolis MN 55401-1300

HELMHOLZ, R(ICHARD) H(ENRY), law educator; b. Pasadena, Calif., July 1, 1940; s. Lindsay and Alice (Bean) H.; m. Marilyn P. Helmholz. AB, Princeton U., 1962; JD, Harvard U., 1965; PhD, U. Calif., Berkeley, 1970; LLD, Trinity Coll., Dublin, 1992. Bar: Mo. 1965. Prof. law and hist. Washington U., St. Louis, 1970-81; prof. law U. Chgo., 1981—; Maitland lectr. Cambridge U., 1987. Author: Marriage Litigation, 1975, Select Cases on Defamation, 1985, Canon Law and the Law of England, 1987, Roman Canon Law in Reformation England, 1990, Spirit of Classical Canon Law, 1996. Guggenheim fellow, 1986; recipient Von Humboldt rsch. prize, 1992. Fellow Am. Acad. Arts and Scis.; mem. ABA, Am. Soc. Legal History (prs. 1992-94), Selden Soc. (v.p. 1984-87), Univ. Club, Reform Club. Home: 5757 S Kimbark Ave Chicago IL 60637-1614 Office: U Chgo Law Sch 1111 E 60th St Chicago IL 60637-2702

HELMKE, (WALTER) PAUL, JR., mayor, lawyer; b. Bloomington, Ind., Nov. 24, 1948; s. Walter P. and Rowene Mary (Crabill) H.; m. Deborah Jane Andrews, Aug. 23, 1969; children: Laura Andrews, Kathryn Elizabeth. BA with highest honors, Ind. U., 1970; JD, Yale U., 1973. Bar: Ind. 1973, Fla. 1982. Lawyer Helmke Beams Boyer Wagner, Ft. Wayne, Ind., 1973-87; mayor City Ft. Wayne, 1988—; asst. county atty. Allen County, Ft. Wayne, 1974-87; pres. Nat. Rep. Mayors and Local Ofcls. Orgn., 1993; chair adv. bd. U.S. Conf. of Mayors, 1995—; bd. dirs. Nat. League of Cities, 1996—, chair pub. safety and crime prevention com., 1995. Chmn. Allen-Wells chpt. ARC, Ft. Wayne, 1985-87; candidate for Rep. nomination 4th U.S. Congl. Dist.-Ind., 1980. Recipient J.C. Gallagher prize Law Sch. Yale U., New Haven, Conn., 1972. Mem. Ind. Assn. Cities and Towns (1st v.p. 1995—), Phi Beta Kappa. Republican. Lutheran. Home: 1215 Korte Ln Fort Wayne IN 46807-2920 Office: Office of the Mayor City-County Bldg Rm 900 1 Main St Fort Wayne IN 46802-1804

HELMLE, RALPH PETER, computer systems developer, manager; b. Detroit, Sept. 12, 1962; s. Ronald and Ingeborg (Kalb) H. BSME, Lawrence Tech. U., 1987; MS in Systems Engring., Oakland U., Rochester, Mich., 1991. Registered profl. engr., Mich. Student designer Kent-Moore Stamping & Fabrication, Detroit, 1978-79; hardware tool and process engr. Fisher Body div. GM Corp., Warren, Mich., 1979-82; indsl. systems engr. Fisher Guide div. GM Corp., Troy, Mich., 1982-85; site personal computer adminstr. Delphi Interior and Lighting Systems, GMC, Troy, Mich., 1985—. Mem. Lambda Iota Tau. Home: 11584 Adams Dr Warren MI 48093-1137 Office: Delphi Interior and Lighting Systems GMC 1401 Crooks Rd Troy MI 48084

HELPPIE, CHARLES EVERETT, III, financial consultant; b. Highland Park, Mich., Feb. 1, 1952; s. Charles Everett and Patricia Elizabeth (Cote) H.; m. Vali Renée Terhune, July 29, 1972. Student, Ea. Mich. U., 1970-73. Sales rep., sales mgr. Mich. Autosonics, Inc., Ann Arbor, 1972-74; mgr. World Wide Movers, Inc., Ypsilanti, Mich., 1973; sales rep. Godfrey Moving & Storage Co., Ann Arbor, 1974-78; account exec. Merrill Lynch Pierce Fenner & Smith, Detroit, 1978-83, E. F. Hutton, Ann Arbor, 1983-87; asst. br. mgr. Shearson Lehman Hutton, Ann Arbor, 1987-90; fin. cons. Shearson Lehman Bros., Detroit, 1991-92; investment exec. Paine Webber, Inc., Farmington Hills, Mich., 1992—, branch office ins. coord., 1993—. Artist and engr. auto. models including MPC World Champion, 1977 (1st Pl. 1977). Campaign worker Dem. Com., Ypsilanti, 1965-71; organizer Anti-War Workshops, Ypsilanti, 1968-70; pres., organizer Fin. Svcs. Softball League, Detroit, 1979-83; mem. Colonial Leadership Coun., Boston. Mem. Am. Funds Group (All-Am. Team), Nameless Nat. Luminaries (founder, chartered), Detroit Tigers Fantasy Camp (chartered), Key and Kite Club, Aim Summit Club (chmns. coun. 1992—), Franklin Group of Funds, Paine Webber Premium Producers Guild. Republican. Office: Paine Webber Inc 32300 Northwestern Hwy Ste 150 Farmington Hills MI 48334-1570

HELTNE, PAUL GREGORY, museum executive; b. Lake Mills, Iowa, July 4, 1941; s. Palmer Tilford and Grace Katherine (Hanson) H.; children—Lisa, Christian. B.A., Luther Coll., Decorah, Iowa, 1962; Ph.D., U. Chgo., 1970. Asst. prof. Johns Hopkins U., Balt., 1970-82; dir. Chgo. Acad. Scis., 1982-91, pres., 1991—; cons. WHO, Am. Petroleum Inst. Author, editor: Neotropical Primates: Status and Conservation, 1976, Lion-Tailed Macaque, 1985, Science Learning in the Informal Setting, 1988, Understanding Chimpanzees, 1989, Chimpanzee Cultures, 1994. Trustee Balt. Zool. Soc., 1972-82. Mem. AAAS, Am. Assn. Mus. (edn. task force, accreditation site visitor), Assn. Sci. Mus. Dirs. (sec.-treas.), Am. Primatol. Soc., Internat. Primatology Soc., Am. Zool. Soc., Soc. for Study Evolution, Systematic Zoology Soc., Assn. Sci. and Tech. Ctrs. Office: Mus Chgo Acad Scis 2001 N Clark St Chicago IL 60614-4712

HELTON, WILLIAM STOKELY, JR., insurance executive; b. Middletown, Ohio, Aug. 25, 1943; s. William Stokely Sr. and Beulah (Pittman) H.; m. Caryn Klinedinst. Nov. 27, 1968 (div. Jan. 4, 1984); children: Christopher W., William S. III; m. Sally Heins, May 25, 1985; children: Elizabeth H., William Curry. BS, Fla. So. Coll., 1966; MEd, Xavier U., 1970. Assoc. Thomas E. Wood, Inc., Cin., 1975-87; pres. William S. Helton, Inc. (now Hammerlein Helton Ins. Agy., Inc.), Cin., 1987—; co-owner Fox Ins., Lawrenceburg, Ind.; bd. dirs. Mercantile Savings Bank. Bd. dirs. of Springer Ednl. Found., 1980-87, Friends of The Sch. for Creative and Performing Arts, 1984-85, pres. bd. trustees, 1984-85; chmn. bd. dirs., Clean Cin., Inc., 1982—, Cin. Regatta, 1981-87; pres. Cin. Br. of English-Speaking Union, 1981-83, bd. dirs. 1978-84; bd. dirs. Nat. Bd. of English Speaking Union, 1983-89, St. John's Social Service Ctr., Inc. 1984— (Franciscan award 1989), chmn., 1987-93, chmn., 1987-93; bd. dirs. The New Sch., 1984-90, Maple Knoll Village, 1985—, Miami Purchase Assn. for Hist. Preservation, 1984—, City CURE, 1992—, Prodigal Ministries, 1992—; chmn. Ch. of the Redeemer Found., 1982-86, The Episcopal Order of the Holy Cross Assocs., 1983—, Ohio campaign chmn., 1985-86; ins. com. of Episcopal Diocese of So. Ohio, 1984—, Com. to Save St. Bartholomew's, 1984; vice-chmn. ann. fund drive Coll. of Mt. St. Joseph, 1986, chmn. council, 1987—; mem. host com. conv. Nat. Assn. Ins. Comsnrs.' Conv., 1988-89; apptd. by gov. Keep Ohio Beautiful Comsn., 1989—; mem. area coun. trustees Franciscan Sisters of the Poor Found. at Cin., Inc., 1992—, adv. bd. Greater Cin. Flower and Garden Show Soc., 1991—. Mem. Cincinnatus Assn., The Cin. Country Club, U. Club Cin., Cin. Athletic Club, Miami Club, Travel Club Cin. Home: 1905 Wm H Taft Rd Cincinnati OH 45200 Office: Hammerlein Helton Ins Agy Inc 114 S Walnut St Cincinnati OH 45030-4373 also: Fox Ins 200 Eads Pkwy Lawrenceburg IN 47025

HEMENWAY, ROBERT E., university administrator, language educator; b. Sioux City, Iowa, Aug. 10, 1941; s. Myrle Emery and Katharine Leone (Cook) H.; m. Marilyn Wickstrom, June 16, 1962 (div. 1970); children: Gina, Jeremy; m. Mattie Fenter, May 12, 1972 (div. 1980); children: Robin, Karintha, Matthew, Langston; m. Leah Renee Hattemer, Dec. 19, 1981; children: Zachary, Arna. BA, U. Nebr., Omaha, 1963; PhD, Kent (Ohio) State U., 1966. Asst. prof. English U. Ky., Lexington, 1966-68; assoc. prof. Am. studies U. Wyo., Laramie, 1968-73; prof. U. Ky., Lexington, 1973-86; dean arts and scis. U. Okla., Norman, 1986-89; chancellor U. Ky., Lexington, 1989-95, U. Kans., Lawrence, 1995—; dean Gov.'s Scholar's Program, Ky., 1984-86. Author: Zora Neale Hurston, 1977 (Best Biography of 1977 award Soc. Midland Authors 1978, Rembert Patrick prize Fla. Hist. Soc. 1978). Mem. Gov.'s Task Force on Literacy, Okla., 1987-89; bd. dirs. Okla. High Sch. Sci. and Math., Oklahoma City, 1985-86, Coun. Colls. Arts and Scis., 1987-89. NEH fellow, 1974-75. Mem. MLA, Am. Studies Assn. (nat. coun.), South Atlantic Assn. Depts. English (pres. 1984-85). Lutheran. Office: Office of the Chancellor University Of Kansas KS 66045

HEMEYER, JOHN CLARK, protection services official; b. Jefferson City, Mo., May 8, 1949; m. Peggy Thoenen; children: Emily, William. B in Psychology, Lincoln U., 1973; M in Corrections, Ctrl. Mo. State U., 1976. Juvenile officer Cole County Juvenile Ctr., Jefferson City, Mo.; dep. sheriff Cole County Sheriff Office, Jefferson City, to 1986; sheriff Cole County, Jefferson City, Mo., 1986—. Bd. dirs. Rape and Abuse Crisis Svc., Jefferson City, Salvation Army, Jefferson City; bd. govs. Meml. Hosp., Jefferson City; bd. regents St. Mary's Health Ctr., Jefferson City. Mem. NRA (cert. firearms instr.), Mo. Sheriffs Assn. (adv. bd., pres. 1994), Ducks Unltd. Office: Cole County Sheriffs Office 301 E High St Jefferson City MO 65101

HEMLING, CALVIN L., stockbroker; b. Columbus, Wis., July 3, 1959; s. Bernie E. and Evelyn D. (Bork) H.; m. Diane E. Martin, July 18, 1986; 3 children. BA, U. Wis., 1981. Stockbroker Blunt Glis Lowi, Milw., 1981-87, A G Edwards & Sons Inc., Beaver Dam, Wis., 1987—; pres. coun. A G Edwards & Sons Inc., Beaver Dam, 1990—. Mem. ch. coun. Luth. Ch., Beaver Dam, 1991. Office: A G Edwards & Sons Inc 114 Monroe St Beaver Dam WI 53916-2437

HEMMING, BRUCE CLARK, microbiologist; b. Pocatello, Idaho; s. Parley Lynn and Vernetta (Clark) H.; m. Caroline McDaniel, May 20, 1973; children: Eric M., Heidi, Heather, Crystal Lynn, Keri Lynn. BS in Microbiology, Brigham Young U., Provo, Utah, 1974, MS in Biochemistry, 1977; PhD in Plant Pathology, Mont. State U., Bozeman, 1982. Staff rsch. assoc. dept. chemistry Brigham Young U., 1977-78; sr. rsch. biologist molecular biology Monsanto Co., St. Louis, 1982-84, rsch. specialist plant molecular biology, 1984-89, project leader biocontrol crop protection, 1989, sr. rsch. specialist crop protection, 1989-91; pres. Microbe Inotech Labs., Inc., 1991—; chmn. regional com. USDA, Washington, 1986-89, mem. tech. subcom. on biocontrol expt. sta. com. on policy, 1987-89; panel mem. Nat. Rsch. Coun. Briefing, Washington, 1987; disting. guest lectr. Coll. Sci. Utah State U., Logan, 1989. Author: Methods in Enzymology, 1979; co-editor: Iron Chelation in Plants and Soil Microorganisms, 1993; mem. editorial bd. Biology of Metals, Springer-Verlag, 1988-91. Troop committeeman Boy Scouts Am., Manchester, Mo., 1985. Mem. AAAS, Am. Phytopath. Soc., Am. Chem. Soc., Am. Soc. Microbiology, Nat. Registry of Environ. Profls. Office: Microbe Inotech Labs Inc 12133 Ridgeston Square Dr Hazelwood MO 63044

HEMMINGER, ALLEN EDWARD, retired insurance consultant; b. Oak Harbor, Ohio, Jan. 22, 1933; s. George Fredrick and Hulda Carolyn (Piehl) H.; m. Dora Jane Blanton, May 11, 1957; children: Gay Lynn, Teresa Ann. BSME, Ind. Inst. Tech., 1955. Cons. Indsl. Risk Insurers, Detroit, 1955-89. Mem. Unicycling Soc. Am. (bd. dirs. 1978-81), Internat. Unicycling Fedn. (sec.-treas. 1982-93), The Wheelmen, Internat. Jugglers Assn., The Mus. Box Soc. Internat. Home: 16152 Kinloch Redford MI 48240-2426

HEMZE, DAVID J., county official; b. Olivia, Minn., Apr. 26, 1965; s. Edward Joseph and Lorraine June (Anderson) H.; m. Julie Ann Meiners, Aug. 1, 1965; 1 child, Alexandra Lauren. BA in Pub. Adminstrn., St. Cloud State U., 1987; MA in Pub. Adminstrn., Hamline U., 1990. Rsch. analyst City of St. Cloud (Minn.), 1986-87; labor rels. asst. City of Mpls., Mpls., 1987-89, budget analyst, 1989; asst. to county adminstr. Stearns County, St. Cloud, 1989—. Mem. Internat. City/County Mgmt. Assn., Minn. Assn. of Urban Mgmt. Assts., Minn. City/County Mgmt. Assn., Nat. Assn. of County Adminstrs. Roman Catholic. Home: 6712 Timber Crest Dr Maple Grove MN 55311 Office: Stearns County Adminstrn Ctr Rm 121 705 Ct House Sq Saint Cloud MN 56303

HENDER, ERIC MARSHALL, securities company executive; b. Kalona, Iowa, Feb. 24, 1940. Degree in bus. and banking, Colo. Coll., 1962. Asst. v.p. Merchants Nat., Cedar Rapids, Iowa, 1963-70; pres. realty Life Investors, Cedar Rapids, 1970-75; pres. Securities Corp. Iowa, Cedar Rapids, 1975—; bd. dirs. Telecom USA Pub., Inc., 1993—, Ruffalo, Cody and Assocs., Inc., 1993—. Sgt. 1st class U.S. Army, 1960-67.

HENDERSON, BRODERICK, state legislator. Parking control officer; mem. fron dist. 35 Kans. State Ho. of Reps., Topeka. Address: 2710 N 8th St Kansas City KS 66101

HENDERSON, BRUCE WINGROVE, insurance executive; b. Balt., Feb. 20, 1946; s. Wilmer Paul and Margaret Virginia Henderson; m. Karen Todd, Sept. 14, 1968; 1 child, Katie Anne. BA in History, U. Balt., 1968. Sr. acct. exec. Conn. Gen. Life Ins. Co., Hartford, 1970-89; asst. v.p. Seabury & Smith, Indpls., 1989—. Author: (trademark for employee benefits plan design) Health Age/Actual Age Plan, 1994. Vol. Dayspring Ctr., Indpls., 1995. With USN, 1969-70. Mem. Soc. of Mary, Nat. Ind. Health Underwriters Assn., Ind. Astron. Soc., Am. Legion, Nat. History Honor Soc., U. Balt. (parliamentarian). Republican. Episcopalian. Home: 9009 Cloud Bay Ct Indianapolis IN 46236

HENDERSON, JAMES ALAN, engine company executive; b. South Bend, Ind., July 26, 1934; s. John William and Norma (Wilson) H.; m. Mary Evelyn Kriner, June 20, 1959; children: James Alan, John Stuart, Jeffrey Todd, Amy Brenton. AB, Princeton U., 1956; Baker scholar, Harvard U., 1961-63. With Scott Foresman & Co., Chgo., 1962; chmn., CEO Cummins Engine Co., Inc., Columbus, 1995; staff mem. Am. Rsch. & Devel. Corp., Boston, 1963; faculty Harvard Bus. Sch., 1963; asst. to chmn. Cummins Engine Co., Inc., Columbus, Ind., 1964-65; v.p. mgmt. devel. Cummins Engine Co., Inc., Columbus, 1965-69, v.p. personnel, 1969-70, v.p. ops., 1970-71, exec. v.p., 1971-75, exec. v.p., COO, 1975-77, pres., 1977-94, pres., CEO, 1994-95; chmn., CEO, 1995—; also bd. dirs. Cummins Engine Co., Inc., Columbus; bd. dirs. Cummins Engine Found., Inland Steel Ind., Chgo., Ameritech, Chgo., Rohm and Haas Co., Phila., Landmark Comm., Norfolk; mem. policy com. The Bus. Roundtable, Washington; mem. The Bus. Coun., Washington. Author: Creative Collective Bargaining, 1965. Chmn. exec. com., trustee Princeton U., 1986-92; pres. bd. trustees Culver Ednl. Found. Presbyterian. Home: 4228 N Riverside Dr Columbus IN 47203-1121 Office: Cummins Engine Co Inc Box 3005 MC 60912 Columbus IN 47202-3005

HENDERSON, JAMES HAROLD, entrepreneur, business executive, financial planner; b. Knoxville, Tenn., June 18, 1948; s. Harold Alpheus and Joanna Elizabeth (McCammon) H.; m. Jane Frances Dewey, Jan. 22, 1977; children: Jeanette Marie, Joanne Reneé, Joshua McCammon. BS in Mgmt. and Econs., U. North Ala., 1971; MS in Systems Mgmt., U. So. Calif., Los Angeles, 1981. Cert. fin. planner; registered investment advisor. Commd. U.S. Army, 1971, advanced through grades to capt., 1975, resigned, 1979; owner Worldwide Merchantile and Co., Clarksville, Tenn., Oscoda, Mich. and Cowley, Wyo., 1979—, Worlwide Merchantile and Co., Cowley, Wyo., 1979—; freelance fin. planner Clarksville, Tenn. and Oscoda, Mich., 1979-92; investment advisor James H. Henderson and Co., Oscoda, Mich., 1987-92; counselor Christian Fin. Concepts, Inc., 1985-89. Lt. col. USAR, 1971—; asst. attache to India, USAR, 1991—, def. and army attache to Nepal, 1994. Mem. Inst. Cert. Fin. Planners (cert.), Officer's Christian Fellowship (area coord. 1984-90), Nat. Eagle Scout Assn. Home and Office: PO Box 742 Cowley WY 82420-0742

HENDERSON, JOSEPH MARVIN, gastroenterologist; b. Milton, Fla., Nov. 7, 1959; s. Marvin and Ethel (Willis) H.; m. Lisa Marie Stevenson, Oct. 21, 1989. BA in Chemistry, U. South Fla., Tampa, 1982, MD, 1986. Diplomate Am. Bd. Internal Medicine with cert. in internal medicine and gastroenterology. Intern, resident internal medicine, fellow gastroenterology U. Ky. Med. Ctr., Lexington, 1986-91; asst. prof. medicine U. Ky. Coll. Medicine, Lexington, 1991-92; lectr. in medicine U. Mich. Med. Sch., Ann Arbor, 1992-94; staff gastroenterologist Cmty. Hosps. of Indpls., 1994—; pvt. practice, 1992—. Contbr. to book, articles to profl. jours. Fellow ACP; mem. Am. Coll. Gastroenterology, Am. Gastroent. Assn., Ind. State Med. Assn. Office: Gastroenterology Assocs Inc 1400 N Ritter Ave Ste 370 Indianapolis IN 46219-3049

HENDERSON, MICHAEL DEAN, electrical engineer; b. Richmond, Ind., June 29, 1961; s. Leo Vernon and Patricia Ann (Seely) H.; m. Ellen Priscilla Engelhardt, May 26, 1984. BSEE, Purdue U., 1984; AAS, St. Louis Community Coll., 1987. Quality engr. McDonnell Douglas, St. Louis, 1984-88, quality assurance engr., 1988-89, specialist procurement, 1989-92, sr. engr. quality, 1992—. Mem. IEEE, Am. Soc. Quality Control, John Purdue Club, Purdue Alumni Assn. Home: 16747 Deveronne Cir Chesterfield MO 63005-1618

HENDERSON, RUSS G., data processing consultant; b. Akron, Ohio, Sept. 20, 1959; s. Robert G. and Beverly G. (Donahue) H.; m. Diane Kuzmo, May 18, 1984 (div. May 1989). AS in Data Processing, Akron U., 1981. Programmer Summit Nat. Life Ins., Akron, 1981-85, Sedata System, Akron, 1985-86, Wright Tool, Barberton, Ohio, 1986-94, Ohio Lottery Commn., Cleve., 1994—. Mem. Aura Club (treas., sec.). Home: 2845 Kay Blvd Norton OH 44203

HENDERSON, STEPHEN JOHN, chemical company executive; b. Litchfield, Ill., Mar. 1, 1948; s. John Jr. and Darline Cora (Brakemeyer) H.; m. Diane Westphal, Aug. 4, 1977. BS in Chem. Engring., Washington U., St. Louis, 1970, MS in Chem. Engring., 1973. Registered profl. engr., Mo. Tech. svcs. engr. Krummrich Plant Monsanto Co., Sauget, Ill., 1970-73, environ. control engr., 1973-74, prodn. supr., 1974-79, mfg. oper. supt., 1979-83, 85-87, tech. oper. supt., 1983-85; mfg. mgr. hdqs. Monsanto Co., St. Louis, 1987-91; plant mgr. Everett (Mass.) plant Monsanto Co., 1991-92; plant mgr. Queeny Plant Monsanto Co., St. Louis, 1992—. Bd. dirs. South Side YMCA, St. Louis, 1992-94, St. Louis Boys Club, 1992—. Mem. AIChE. Office: Monsanto Co 1700 S 2nd St Saint Louis MO 63104-4610

HENDON, RICKY, state legislator. Formerly alderman City of Chgo.; now mem. from 5th dist. Ill. State Senate. Home: 3013 W Walnut St Chicago IL 60612-1835*

HENDRICH, THOMAS J., mechanical engineer; b. Toyoto, Japan, Sept. 27, 1967. BSME, U. Kans., Lawrence, 1993. Engr. H&S Products, Wichita, 1993—. Democrat. Home: 6701 Farmview St Wichita KS 67206-1010 Office: H&S Products Inc 2650 S Custer St Wichita KS 67217-1324

HENDRICHSEN, LARRY L., financial executive. BSBA, N.E. Mo. State U., 1969. Lic. series 7 Nat. Assn. Securities Dealers. Sole proprietor Hendrichsen & Assocs., Burlington, Iowa, 1983—. Office: Hendirchsen & Assocs 2528 Mount Pleasant St Burlington IA 52601-2118

HENDRICKS, STEPHEN E., mechanical engineer; b. Hawarden, Iowa, Dec. 15, 1953; s. Fay J. and Mildred (Millage) H.; m. Lisa M. Sogn, May 16, 1975; children: Stephanie, Andrea. BS in Mech. Engring., S.D. State U., 1976. Engr.-in-tng. Product engr. Dale Electronics, Inc., Columbus, Nebr., 1979—. Patentee in field. Repubican. Roman Catholic. Home: 6 Leland Dr Columbus NE 68601-8053 Office: Dale Electronics Inc PO Box 609 Columbus NE 68602-0609

HENDRICKSON, CARL H., state legislator. Mem. Mo. Ho. of Reps., Jefferson City. Republican.

HENDRICKSON, JOHN EDWARD, social services association executive; b. Chgo., Nov. 27, 1944; s. John Edward and Paula Marie (Knight) H.; m. Elizabeth Anne Evans, Dec. 16, 1978; children: Jennifer, Shannon, Kelsey. BS in Journalism, U. Md., 1967; MBA, Loyola U., Balt., 1982. Pub. affairs specialist S.E. area ARC, Atlanta, 1969-70; pub. affairs specialist S.E. Asia ARC, Saigon, Vietnam, 1970-71; asst. dir. pub. affairs ARC, Washington, 1971-73; dir. pub. affairs and fin. devel. ARC, Silver Spring, Md., 1973-76; asst. dir. pub. support ARC, Washington, 1976-79, exec. asst. to pres., 1979-83, nat. mktg. mgr. health and safety, 1983-89; dir. safety and health edn. svcs. ARC, Chgo., 1989—. Recipient Journalism Adminstrn. award Pi Delta Epsilon, 1966. Home: 408 Yorkshire Ct Grayslake IL 60030 Office: ARC Mid-America 43 E Ohio St Chicago IL 60611

HENDRIX, RONALD WAYNE, physician, radiologist; b. St. Louis, June 4, 1943; s. Arthur W. and Lida (Martin) H.; m. Miriam Jensen, June 14, 1969. AB, Wash. U., St. Louis, 1965, MD, 1969. Diplomate Am. Bd. Nuclear Medicine, Am. Bd. Radiology. Intern Wash. U., Barnes Hosp., St. Louis, 1969-70; resident U. Chgo., 1970-73, fellow in nuclear medicine, 1973-74; staff radiologist Symmes Hosp., Arlington, Mass., 1976-77; asst. prof. radiology Northwestern U. Med. Sch., Chgo., 1977-84, assoc. prof. radiology, 1984—; attending physician Northwestern Meml. Hosp., Chgo., 1977—, chief, musculoskeletal radiology, 1977—; dir. radiology Rehab. Inst. of Chgo., 1986—. Contbr. articles to profl. jours.; contbg. author to several books. Pres. LaSalle St. Ch., 1982-84, treas., 1984-86, chmn. fin. com., 1986-92. Lt. comdr. USN, 1974-76. Mem. Radiol. Soc. of N.Am., Am. Roentgen Ray Soc., Assn. of U. Radiologists, Am. Coll. Radiology, Internat. Skeletal Soc. Office: Northwestern Meml Hosp 710 N Fairbanks Ct Chicago IL 60611-3013

HENEBRY, MICHAEL STEVENS, toxicologist; b. Decatur, Ill., Jan. 19, 1946; s. Bernard Stevens and Lucille (Benard) H.; m. Virginia Godelsoson Azuela, Jan. 5, 1984; children: Jeffrey Adams, James Stevens. BA in Biology, Millikin U., Decatur, Ill., 1968; MS in Zoology, Ea. Ill. U., 1978; PhD in Aquatic Toxicology, Va. Poly. Inst. and State U., 1981. Teaching asst. zoology Ea. Ill. U., Charleston, 1974-76; teaching asst. biology U. Mich. Biol. Sta., Pellston, 1977-78; rsch. asst. zoology U. Mich. Biol. Sta., 1976-81; rsch. asst. biology Va. Poly. Inst. and State U., Blacksburg, 1967-80; teaching asst. biology Va. Poly. Inst. and State U., 1979-80; asst. prof. biology Ottawa U., Kans., 1981-82, Clarke Coll., Dubuque, Iowa, 1982-83; aquatic toxicologist/ecologist Ill. Natural History Survey, Champaign, Ill., 1983-88; acquatic toxicologist, lab. supr. ecotoxicology lab. Ill. EPA, Springfield, 1988—; cons. in field; lectr. in field; conductor seminars in field. Contbr. articles to profl. jours. Organizer Citizens Utility Bd., Chgo., 1976—, Am. Fedn. State, County and Mcpl. Workers, Springfield, 1983—. With USAF, 1969-73. Mem. ASTM, Soc. Protozoologists, Am. Microscopical Soc., Soc. Environ. Contamination and Toxicology, Ecol. Soc. Am., Midwest Pollution Control Biologists, Sigma Xi. Roman Catholic. Home: 3345 S 3rd St Springfield IL 62703-4612 Office: Ill Environ Protection Agy 2200 Churchill Rd Springfield IL 62702-3406

HENEGAR, DALE L., state legislator; three children. BS, S.D. State U., MS; postgrad., Pa. State U. N.D. State rep. Dist. 52, 1991-92, Dist. 30, 1993—; mem. human svcs. com. and natural resources com. Pres. N.D. Coun. Environ. Edn. Recipient N.D. Gov.'s award, 1983. Mem. Am. Legion, Elks (life), N.D. chpt. Wildlife soc., NRA, Muskies, Inc., Am. Zander Club. Home: 2421 E Avenue C Bismarck ND 58501-4849 Office: Game and Fish Dept 100 N Bismarck Expy Bismarck ND 58501-5086*

HENEGAR, KIT, state legislator; 1 child. Grad. high schs. Owner Capt. Kit's Marina, Lake Sakakawea, N.D.; rep. Dist. 49 N.D. Ho. of Reps., mem. human resources and natural resources coms. Home: PO Box 616 Riverdale ND 58565

HENEMAN, ROBERT LLOYD, management educator; b. Mpls., Jan. 17, 1955; s. Herbert G. Jr. and Jane R. Heneman; m. Renee Brausch, Sept. 9, 1989. BA, Lake Forest Coll., 1977; MA, U. Ill., 1979; PhD, Mich. State U., 1984. Personnel specialist Pacific Gas & Electric Co., San Francisco, 1979-80; assoc. prof. Mgmt. Ohio State U., Columbus, 1984—, dir. grad. programs in labor and human resources. Author: (books) Merit Pay, 1992, Staffing Organizations, 1994. Mem. ch. coun. Holy Trinity Luth. Ch., Columbus. Mem. Acad. of Mgmt. (exec. com. human rels. divsn. 1988-93, program chair 1992-93, divsn. chair 1994-95), Am. Compensation Assn. (rsch. com. 1992-93, edn. com. 1993-94), Phi Kappa Phi, Sigma Iota Epsilon, Psi Chi. Home: 4815 Lytfield Dr Dublin OH 43017-2174

HENG, STANLEY MARK, military officer; b. Nebraska City, Nebr., Nov. 4, 1937; s. Robert Joseph Sr. and Margaret Ann (Volkmer) H.; m. Sharon E. Barrett, Oct. 10, 1959; children: Mark, Nick, Lisa. Student, Command and Gen. Staff Coll., 1969, Nat. Def. U., 1979; BA, Doane Coll., 1987. Commd. adj. Nebr. N.G., 1966, advanced through grade to major gen., 1966-87; adj. Nebr. Mil. Dept., Lincoln, 1966-77, adminstrv. asst., 1978-86; adj. gen., civil def. dir. State of Nebr., Lincoln, 1987—. Mem. N.G. Assn. U.S., N.G. Assn. Nebr. (exec. sec. 1967-71, Svc. award 1970), Adj. Gens. Assn., Am. Legion. Democrat. Mem. United Ch. of Christ. Office: Mil Dept 1300 Military Rd Lincoln NE 68508-1090

HENINGER, KURT ALLEN, oil field service executive; b. Columbus, Ohio, Mar. 11, 1950; s. Robert Earl and Margaret Jorene (Sidle) H.; m. Beverly Anne Dunham, Mar. 23, 1974; children: Robert, Heather, Kurt Jr., Joseph. Student, State Tech. Inst. at Memphis, 1976-77. Jr. completion engr. Dresser Atlas, Gillette, Wyo., 1977-78; completion engr. Dresser Atlas, Williston, N.D., 1978-80, sr. completion engr., 1980-81; mgr., pres. Mo. Valley Perforating Inc., Williston, N.D., 1981—. Asst. scoutmaster Boy

Scouts of Am., Williston, 1987-92. With USAF, 1968-72. Recipient Eagle Scout honor Boy Scouts Am. Mem. Soc. Petroleum Engrs., Am. Legion, Kenmare Lions Club. Republican. Lutheran. Office: Valley Perforating Inc 4 Mile Industrial Pk Williston ND 58801

HENKE, JANICE CARINE, educational software developer and marketer; b. Hunter, N.D., Jan. 28, 1938; d. John Leonard and Adeline (Hagen) Hanson; children: Toni L., Tom L., Tracy L. BS, U. Minn., 1965; postgrad., misc. schs., 1969—. Cert. elem. tchr., Minn., Iowa. Tchr. dance, 1953-56; tchr. kindergarten Des Moines Pub. Schs., 1964-65; tchr. elem. Ind. Sch. Dist. 284, Wayzata, Minn., 1969-93; pvt. bus. history Wayzata, 1978—; marketer, promoter health enhancement Jeri Jacobus Cosmetics Aloe Pro, Am. Choice Nutrition, Multiway, KM Matol, Wayzata, 1978—; developer ednl. software, marketer of software Computer Aided Teaching Concepts, Excelsior, Minn., 1983—; authorized rep. Minn. Edn. Assn. with Midwest Benefit Advisers, Excelsior, Minn., 1993—; developer, author drug edn. curriculum, Wayzata, 1970-71; mem. programs com. Health and Wellness, Wayzata, 1988-93; chmn. Wayzata Edn. Assn. Ins. Com., 1991-93; mem. Staff Devel. Adv. Bd., Wayzata, 1988-93; coach Odyssey of the Mind, 1989-93. Author, developer computer software; contbr. articles to newspapers. Fundraiser Ind. Reps. Wayzata, 1976-79; mem. pub. rels. com. Lake Minnetonka (Minn.) Dist. Ind. Reps., 1979-81, fundraising chmn., 1981-82; chmn. Wayzata Ind. Reps., 1981-82; sec. PTO, Wayzata, 1981-82. Mem. NEA, Minn. Edn. Assn., Wayzata Edn. Assn. (bd. mem., ins. chairperson). Lutheran. Office: Computer Aided Teaching 20380 Excelsior Blvd Excelsior MN 55331-8733

HENKE, STEVEN JOHN, chemical company engineer; b. Beatrice, Nebr., July 11, 1948; s. Gaylord George and Hilda Marie H. BS, U. Nebr., 1970; MBA, Loyola U., Chgo., 1976; m. Janice Jo Barringer, Oct. 12, 1973. Rsch. engr. Amoco Chems., Naperville, Ill., 1970-76, rsch. supr., 1977-89, engring. mgr., 1989-94, devel. engr., 1994-96, account mgr., 1996—. Recipient William Heusel award U. Nebr., 1966. Mem. Soc. Plastics Engrs., Soc. Automotive Engrs., Ga. Football Ofcls. Assn. (cert.), Heritage Found., Phi Eta Sigma. Lutheran. Republican. Home: 3893 Highgreen Pl Marietta GA 30068-2577

HENLEY, JOSEPH OLIVER, manufacturing company executive; b. Sikeston, Mo., June 25, 1949; s. Fred Louis and Bernice (Chilton) H. m. Jane Ann Rhodes, Aug. 21, 1971. BSBA, U. Mo., 1972; MBA, Mich. State U., 1973. Ops. analyst Midland-Ross, Inc., Cleve., 1974, prodn. control mgr., 1974-75; engring. systems mgr. Cameron-Waldron div., Somerset, N.J., 1989-95, prodn. control mgr., 1976-77; prodn. planning and mfg. systems mgr. ICM div. Massey Ferguson, Inc., Akron, Ohio, 1977-78; sr. audit specialist mfg. United Techs. Corp., Hartford, Conn., 1978-82; mfg. control systems mgr. UT Diesel Systems div., Hartford, Conn., 1983-84, materials mgr., 1983-84, internal cons., 1984-86; inventory mgr. Pratt & Whitney Aircraft div., Hartford, Conn., 1986-89, mgr. sychronous mfg., 1989-95; dir. mfg. tech. Case Corp., Racine, Wis., 1996—. With Army N.G., 1970-72. Mem. Nat. Assn. Purchasing Mgmt., Am. Prodn. and Inventory Control Soc., Assn. for Mfg. Excellence (N.E. region bd. dirs.), Beta Gamma Sigma, Sigma Iota Epsilon, Omicron Delta Epsilon. Presbyterian. Home: 11 Sprucewood Ct Racine WI 53402 Office: Case Corporation 700 State St Racine WI 53404

HENLEY, ROBERT LEE, school system administrator; b. Aug. 7, 1934; m. Patricia J. Ellis; three children. BA, Washington U., St. Louis, 1957, MEd, 1958; EdD, U. Mo., 1967. Tchr., counselor, pers. office, bus. mgr., asst. supt. Mehlville Sch. Dist., St. Louis, 1958-75; supt. schs. Independence (Mo.) Pub. Schs., 1975-93; asst. prof. U. Mo., Kansas City, 1991—; cons. pub. & pvt. schs., fed. agys., 1970—, also various colls., univs., founds.; instr. various colls. & univs., St. Louis and Columbia, 1975—. Trustee Andrew Drumm Inst., Independence, 1980—; bd. dirs. Am. Cancer Soc., Independence, 1978—; mem. adv. com. Kansas City Arts Ptnrs. Program, 1990—. Recipient Community Leader award Comprehensive Mental health Svcs., Jackson County, Mo., 1983, Disting. Svc. award Mo. chpt. Am. Assn. on Mental Deficiency, 1983, Outstanding Educator award State of Mo., 1985, Innovation in Edn. award Nat. Ctr. for Ednl. Computing, 1985-86, Exec. Educator 100 award Exec. Educator Mag., 1987, Sch. Adminstr. award Kennedy Ctr./Alliance for Arts Edn., Washington, 1988, Disting. Svc. award Am. Assn. Sch. Adminstrs., 1993; named Mo. Supt. of Yr., 1992. Mem. Am. Assn. Sch. Adminstrs., Mo. Assn. Sch. Adminstrs. (exec. com. 1988—, Robert L. Pearce award 1991, Disting. Svc. award 1993), Jackson County Sch. Adminstrs. Assn. (pres. 1981), Mid-Am. Assn. Sch. Supts., Met. Sch. Study Group (pres. 1985-86), Independence C. of C. Office: Independence Sch Dist 1231 Windsor St Independence MO 64055-1151

HENN, JOHN I., civil engineer; b. Belmond, Iowa, Oct. 4, 1941. BS in Mech. Engring., Iowa State U., 1963. Design engr. John Deere, Dubuque, Iowa, 1966-92; civil engr. Buesing Ltd., Dubuque, 1992—. Patentee in field. 1st lt. C.E., U.S. Army, 1963. Mem. Soc. Automotive Engrs. Home: 2483 Knob Hill Dr Dubuque IA 52003-0247 Office: Buesing 1212 Locust St Dubuque IA 52001-4708

HENNESSY, FELICIA PLESIC, nuclear engineer; b. Balt., Feb. 1, 1956; d. Edward Rudolph and Margarette (Marcum) Plesic; m. William Joseph Hennessy, Sept. 29, 1984; children: Erin Cathleen, Meagan Elizabeth. B-SChemE, Columbia U., 1978; MS in Nuclear Engring., Iowa State U., 1984. System engr. Gen. Atomic Co., San Diego, 1978-82; nuclear engr. E.I. Dupont Savannah River Plant, Aiken, S.C., 1984-89; chemistry mgr. Wis. Electric Co., Two Creeks, 1989—, mgr. chemistry dept., 1992—. Bd. dirs. Manitowoc-Two Rivers Br. AAUW. Mem. Am. Nuclear Soc. (chair profl. women com.). Office: Wis Electric Co 6610 Nuclear Rd Two Rivers WI 54241-9516

HENNESSY, MARGARET BARRETT, health care executive; b. Oak Park, Ill., Apr. 16, 1952; d. Bernard Leo and Frances (Madigan) H. BA in Sociology and Psychology, St. Norbert Coll., DePere, Wis., 1974; MS, Rush U., Chgo. Communications specialist Ill. Cancer Coun., Chgo., 1983-84; adminstrv. asst. Rush-Presbyn./St. Luke's Med. Ctr., Chgo., 1984-85; adminstrv. intern Cook County Hosp., Chgo., 1985-86; fin. analyst Loyola U. Med. Ctr., Maywood, Ill., 1986-89; operating officer Howard Brown Meml. Clinic, Chgo., 1989-93; hematology-oncology adminstr. Loyola U. Med. Ctr., Maywood, Ill., 1993-96; assoc. dir. primary care svcs. Lake County Health Dept., Waukegan, Ill., 1996—; guest lectr. Loyola U. Law Sch., 1989-90. Contbr. articles to profl. jours. Tchr. English as a second lang. World Relief Orgn., Chgo., 1989; cons. United Charities Camps, Chgo., 1989. Recipient Foster G. McGaw scholar, Am. Coll. health Care Execs., 1985. Mem. Rush U. Alumni Assn. (pres.), Chgo. Health Execs. Forum, Am. Coll. Healthcare Execs., Assn. Ambulatory Care Adminstrs. Office: Lake County Pub Health Dept 2400 Belvedere Rd Waukegan IL 60085

HENNIES, THOMAS LEE, protective services official; b. Wagner, S.D., Aug. 11, 1939; s. Lewis and Mariellen (Bailey) H.; m. Ann Luedemann, June 16, 1963; children: Shannon, Shane. AA, U. S.D., 1975; BS, Black Hills State U., 1975; MS, U. S.D., 1978; grad., FBI Nat. Acad., 1977, FBI Law Enforcement Exec. Sch., 1985. Cert. police exec. S.D. Stds. and Tng. Commn. Officer Rapid City (S.D.) Policy Dept., 1965—, chief of police, 1984—; adj. prof. S.D. Sch. of Mines, Black Hills State U., U. S.D., 1978-92; mem., chmn. exec. bd. Mid-States Organized Crime Info. Ctr., Springfield, Mo., 1980—. Elder Zion Luth. Ch.; mem. Dakota Boy's Ranch, Minot and Fargo, N.D. and Datzow, Mo., 1992—; founder, vice chmn. Rapid City Cmty. Care Ctr., 1987—. With U.S. Army, 1958-60. Mem. S.D. Police Chiefs Assn. (past pres.), VFW, Rapid City C. of C. (diplomat). Republican. Office: Rapid City Police Dept 300 Kansas City St Rapid City SD 57701

HENRICKS, ROGER LEE, social services administrator; b. Wauseon, Ohio, May 16, 1943; s. Clifford Seldon and Annabelle Mae (Perkins) H.; m. Judith Ann Shimp, Aug. 28, 1966 (div. Mar. 1981); children: Wendy, Craig, Joel; m. Helen Elizabeth Dennis, June 6, 1986. BA, Adrian (Mich.) Coll., 1966. Welfare caseworker Dept. Social Svcs., Adrian, Mich., 1966-68, protective svcs. caseworker, 1968-78, supr. protective svcs., 1978-94; exec. dir. Family Awareness Ctr., Adrian, 1994—; instr. Ea. Mich. U., Ypsilanti, 1977-82, Siena Heights Coll., Adrian, 1987—, Parent Nurturing Program, Adrian, 1985—; co-founder Family Awareness Ctr., Adrian, 1982-84; presenter in field. Founder, pres. Child Abuse and Neglect Coun., Adrian, 1977—, Sexual Abuse Task Force, Adrian, 1988—; pres., bd. dirs. Call Someone Concerned, Adrian, 1972-86, hon. bd. dirs., 1986—. Recipient Nancy Nichols award Office Substance Abuse, 1983, Mich. Pub. Servant of Yr. award Govt. Adminstrs. Assn. Found, 1988, Ray Helfer award Mich. Commn. for Prevention Child Abuse, 1989. Office: Family Awareness Ctr 199 Broad St Adrian MI 49221

HENROID, CAROL LYNN, nursing educator; b. St. Louis, July 4, 1952; d. Allen J. and June M. (Brethold) H. AA in Nursing, St. Mary's Coll., O'Fallon, Mo., 1973; BS in Nursing, St. Louis U., 1977, MS in Nursing, 1986. Staff nurse Deaconess Hosp., St. Louis, 1977-79, asst. dir. nursing, 1979-85, asst. head nurse, 1985-86; nurse cons. Nursing Resources Inc., St. Peters, Mo., 1987-91; staff nurse, liaison CompreHealth, St. Louis, 1986-90; med.-surg. instr. Barnes Coll., St. Louis, 1989-92; per diem nursing supr. Barnes Hosp., St. Louis, 1989-90, per diem at GI lab staff nurse, 1990; med.-surg. instr. St. Louis Coll. of Health Careers, 1994, nurse Camp Hickory Hill for Diabetic Children, Columbia, Mo., summers, 1987, 88. Home: 3636 Watson Saint Louis MO 63109

HENRY, BARBARA A., publishing executive; b. Oshkosh, Wis., July 23, 1952; d. Robert Edward and Barbara Frances (Aylesworth) H. BJ, U. Nev. Reporter Reno Newspapers, 1974-78, city editor, 1978-80, mng. editor, 1980-82; asst. nat. editor USA Today, Washington, 1982-83; exec. editor Reno Gazette-Jour., 1981-86; former editor, dir. Gannett Rochester Newspapers, Rochester, N.Y.; pub. Great Falls (Mont.) Tribune(part of the Gannett group), 1992—. Mem. Soc. Profl. Journalists, Associated Press Mng. Editors, Am. Soc. Newspaper Editors, Calif.-Nev. Soc. Newspaper Editors (bd. dirs.). Office: The Des Moines Register 715 Locust Street Des Moines IA 50309-3724

HENRY, (MARY) CATHERINE, publications director; b. N.Y.C., Mar. 14, 1949; d. James Buchanan and Eleanor Clark (Nixon) H.; m. James Laury Yuenger, Oct. 5, 1985 (dec. Aug. 1995); 1 stepson, Jay Noel Yuenger. BA magna cum laude, Yale Coll., 1972; student, UCLA, 1973-74; MA, U. Chgo., 1979. Legal asst. Kaye Scholer, Fierman, Hays & Handler, N.Y.C., 1972-73, Arnold and Porter, Washington, 1975-77, FMC Corp., Chgo., 1977-78, Jenner & Block, Chgo., 1979; dir. coll. pubs. U. Chgo., 1980-84; account exec./supr. Hill and Knowlton Inc., Chgo., 1984-85; English editor Jazz Forum Mag., Warsaw, Poland, 1986-87; section adminstr. ABA, Chgo., 1988-90; dir. pubs. Northwestern U., Evanston, Ill., 1990—. Author: (essays) The International Dictionary of Films and Filmmakers, vol. 1, 1984, vol. 3, 1986. Office: Northwestern U 555 Clark St Evanston IL 60208-1230

HENRY, CECIL JAMES, JR., insurance sales broker; b. DeSoto, Mo., Nov. 20, 1937; s. Cecil J. and Gertrude M. (Waldron) H.; m. Jane A. Henry, May 2, 1959; children: Eric J., Jason C. AB, William Jewell Coll., 1959; postgrad., U. Kans., 1959-60; MS in Fin. Svcs., Am. Coll., 1982, MS in Mgmt., 1988. CLU. Asst. food dir. William Jewell Coll., Liberty, Mo., 1955-59; ops. mgr. Graybar Electric, Kansas City, Mo., 1961-65; with Alexander Proudfoot, Chgo., 1966; spl. agt. Prudential Ins. Co., Wichita, Kans., 1966-67; prin. Henry Ins. Ltd., Wichita, 1967—; bd. dirs. Kirkpatrick Sprazker & Co. CPAs; mem. adv. bd. Sta. KNSS Radio, 1991—. Contbr. articles to mag. Bur. mem. United Way Wichita, 1974—; bd. dirs. Presbyn. Family Support Svcs., 1988—, chair, 1992—. Mem. Kans. Assn. Life Underwriters (pres. 1982-83, cert. 1983), Wichita Assn. Life Underwriters (pres. 1974-75), Better Bus. Bur. (bd. dirs. 1974-75), Nat. Assn. Life Underwriters, Nat. Assn. Life Underwriters (pres. Wichita chpt. 1974-75), Am. Soc. of CLUs and Chartered Fin. Cons., Am. Risk and Ins., Knife and Fork Club, Downtown Lions. Republican. Baptist. Home: 1903 E Lockwood St Wichita KS 67216-3368 Office: Henry Ins Ltd 1224 E Harry PO Box 3728 Wichita KS 67201-3728

HENRY, DEBORAH JANE, construction executive; b. Lake Village, Ark., June 17, 1952; d. Jack Ladd Henry and Dorothy Geneva (Wyatt) Cate; m. Karl Joseph Kenkel, Aug. 21, 1971 (div. July, 1978); children: Lori Ann, Scott Joseph. BS in History and Polit. Sci., Washington U., St. Louis, 1993; postgrad., U. Mo., 1995—. Mgmt. asst. Linclay Corp., St. Louis, 1973-78; adminstrv. asst. Turco Devel. Corp., St. Louis, 1978-79; asst. contractor adminstr. Tarlton Corp., St. Louis, 1979-81; project engr. McCarthy Constr. Co., St. Louis, 1981-86; project mgr. Wefelmeyer Constr. Co., St. Louis, 1986-87; constr. mgr. Paragon Group, Inc., 1987-90; constrn. mgr. Tricorp Constrn. Inc., Bridgeton, Mo., 1991-92; tchg. asst. U. Mo., St. Louis, 1994—. Mem. Greater Mo. Focus on Leadership, 1993, Metro St. Louis Tradeswomen Commn., Pride Study Commn. Edn. Mem. LWV, Nat. Assn. Women in Constrn. Home: 636 Pearl Ave Saint Louis MO 63122-2722

HENRY, DELYSLE LEON, lawyer; b. Cumberland, Apr. 17, 1935; s. Clarence Philip and Lillian Pauline (Hartley) H.; m. Kaye Claire Grulke, June 23, 1960; children: Reginald DeLysle, Lisa Kay. BA, Ea. Nazarene Coll., 1956; MA, U. Pa., 1958; JD, U. Balt., 1966; postgrad., Mich. State U. Bar: Mich. 1971, U.S. Dist. Ct. (ea. dist.) Mich. 1978, U.S. Ct. Appeals (6th cir.) 1979. Instr. law and govt. Alpena (Mich.) Community Coll., 1959-61, 66-89; pvt. practice Alpena, 1971—. Commr. County of Alpena, 1974-76. Mem. ABA, Nat. Orgn. Social Security Claimants' Reps., State Bar Mich., Am. Judicature Soc., Am. Bus. Law Assn., Fed. Bar Assn. (Detroit chpt.), Masons. Presbyterian.

HENRY, EDWARD FRANK, computer accounting service executive; b. East Cleveland, Ohio, Mar. 18, 1923; s. Edward Emerson and Mildred Adella (Kulow) H.; m. Nicole Annette Peth, June 18, 1977. BBA, Dyke Coll., 1948; postgrad. Case Western Reserve U., 1949, Cleve. Inst. Music, 1972. Cert. Notary Public Ohio. Internal auditor E.F. Hauserman Co., 1948-51; sales and radio announcer Sta. WSRS, 1951; office mgr. Frank C. Grismer Co., 1951-52; Broadway Buick Co., 1952-55; sec., treas. Commerce Ford Sales Co., 1955-65; nat. mgr. Auto Acctg. div. United Data Processing Co., Cin., 1966-68; v.p. Auto Data Systems Co., Cleve., 1968-70; pres. Profl. Mgmt. Computer Sys., Inc., Cleve., 1970—, ComputerEASE, Small Bus. Computer Ctrs. divsn. Profl. Mgmt. Computer Sys., Inc., 1985—, VideoEASE CompuAIDE Computerized Video Rental Sys. divsn. Profl. Mgmt. Computer Systems, Inc., 1987-89, CompuPRINT divsn. Profl. Mgmt. Computer Sys., Inc., 1995—, TravelEASE divsn. Profl. Mgmt. Computer Sys., Inc., 1996—. Photography published in Travel Agents Internat. mag., 1990 (hon. mention 1990). Exec. artistic dir. NorthCoast Cultural Centre, 1989—. Drum major, musician Wurlitzer Marching Band, Cleve., 1939-42; with USAF Marching Band, Kearns, Utah, 1943; charter pres. No. Ohio Coun. Little Theatre, 1954-56; founder, artistic and mng. dir. Exptl. Theatre, Cleve., 1959-63; dramatic dir., actor Euclid Little Theatres, Jewish Cmty. Ctr., and various cmty. theatres including Jewish Cmty. Ctr.; actor Cleve. Playhouse, 1961-63; bd. dirs. Cleve. Philharmonic Orch., 1972-74, Cleve. Jazz Orch., 1991—; Cleve. Opera League. 1st lt. USAAF, 1943-46, PTO; capt. USAAF Res., 1946-57. Decorated Bronze Star (3). Mem. Am. Mgmt. Assn., Inst. Mgmt. Accts., Mil. Order World Wars, Air Force Assn. (life), Ky. Cols., Data Processing Mgmt. Assn., Nat. Assn. Profl. Cons., Am. Soc. Profl. Cons., Res. Officers Assn., Mil. Order World Wars (Cleve. chpt., bugler, commdr., 1994-95), Mayfield Area C. of C., Associated Photographers Internat., Internat. Platform Assn., Nat. Assn. Met. Mus. Art of N.Y., Cleve. Mus. Art, Art Inst. Chgo., Phi Kappa Gamma (charter pres. Gamma chpt., past nat. pres.), Am. Legion, VFW. Republican. Presbyterian. Clubs: Acacia Country, Hermit, Univ., Cleve. Grays, Deep Springs Trout, Nat. Sojourners (Nat. Pres.'s cert. 1977-78, pres. Cleve. chpt. #23 1978), Heroes of '76 (comdr. Cleve. 1977). Lodges: DeMolay (master Cleve. chpt., 1942, Legion of Honor 1970), Masons (hon. 33d degree St. Bernard lodge, Dodge City, 50 year hon., 1994), Cuyahoga County Meml. Lodge (worshipful master 1993-94) KT, Scottish Rite (dramatic dir. 1967—, thrice potent master 1982-84, class named in his hon. 1994), Grotto, Shriners (dramatic dir. 1968-88), Cleve. Ct. #14, Jesters (dir. 1981, impresario 1984—, dramatic dir. 1971—, producer, dir. Nat. Book of the Play Acapulco, Mexico, 1985; nat. prodr., dir. Nat. Book of the Play Reno, 1988—, Bally's Celebrity Rm., Las Vegas, 1989-96, Royal Dramatist, 1989—, nat. chmn. emeritus ritual com. 1990-96, nat. rep. emeritus to nat. ct., 1996), Kachina, SOBIB, Rotary. Home: 666 Echo Dr Gates Mills OH 44040-9606 Office: Profl Mgmt Computer Systems Inc 19701 S Miles Rd Cleveland OH 44128-4257

HENRY, GERALD T., state legislator; m. Linda M. Becker. Mem. from dist. 48 Kans. State Ho. of Reps., Topeka; exec. dir. Achievement Svc. Address: 215 N 5th PO Box 17 Atchison KS 66002

HENRY, GLORIA JEAN MULLINS, secondary education educator; b. Davenport, Iowa, Nov. 26, 1952; d. Luther Mannon and Eva Mae (Smith) Mullins; m. Jerry L. Henry, Aug. 19, 1972; children: Carie Suzanne Henry, Austin Luke Henry. BA, Okla. Bapt. U., 1975; MA, Baker U., 1992. Cert. secondary tchr. Tchr., coach Valley Center (Kans.) High Sch., 1976-78; speech tchr., debate coach Ruskin High Sch., Kansas City, Mo., 1979—; chair Consol. Sch. Dist. #1, Kansas City, 1989—. Mem. NEA, Nat. Forensic League (double-diamond coach 1990, steering com. for the nat. debate, 1983, com. for nat. debate, 1993, judges chair for dist. debate 1980—), Speech Comm. Assn., Speech-Theatre Assn. of Mo., Nat. Fedn. of High Sch. Activities, Mo. NEA, United Tchrs. of Hickman Mills. Home: 12601 Woodland Ave Kansas City MO 64146-1308 Office: Ruskin High Sch 7000 E 111th St Kansas City MO 64134-3310

HENRY, JOHN THOMAS, retired newspaper executive; b. St. Paul, May 30, 1933; s. Harlan A. and Roxane (Thomas) H.; m. Carla Joyce Lechthaler, Jan. 2, 1982; children: Alexandra, Elizabeth, J. Thomas, Catherine. B.B.A., U. Minn., 1955. With St. Paul Pioneer Press Dispatch, 1955—, asst. to publisher, then bus. mgr., 1971-76, gen. mgr., chmn., pub., 1985-92; ret., 1992. V.p. St. Paul Jr. C. of C., 1965-66; bd. dirs., chmn. St. Paul Jr. Achievement; bd. dirs. Better Bus. Bur. of Minn., Boy Scouts Am., Minn. Coop. Office, Minn. Mus. Art; chmn. St. Paul Chamber Orch.; bd. dirs. St. Paul Downtown Coun., United Hosps., Minn. Sci. Mus., St. Paul United Way. With USAF, 1956-59. Recipient Disting. Service award Classified Advt. Mgrs. Assn., 1971. Mem. St. Paul C. of C. (chmn. bd. dirs. 1987). Lodge: Rotary. Home: 4436 Oakmede Ln Saint Paul MN 55110-7603 Office: NW Publs Inc 345 Cedar St Saint Paul MN 55101-1014

HENRY, JOSEPH KING, university administrator; b. St. Louis, Aug. 2, 1948; s. King and Geraldine (O'Neal) H.; m. Diana Edwards, June 17, 1973. BS in Edn., Lincoln U., 1973; MA, Boston U., 1974; postgrad., U. Iowa, 1977-85. Cert. secondary edn. tchr., Mo. Tchr. Humboldt Elem. Sch., St. Louis, 1972-73; coord. Met. Coun. for Ednl. Opportunity, Inc., Boston, 1974-77; student teaching asst. U. Iowa, Iowa City, 1982, 85, student tutor in history, 1983, student rsch. asst., 1983-84, acad. counselor spl. support svcs., 1985-86, grad. outreach counselor, 1986-89, grad. outreach coord., 1989-92, asst. to dean grad. coll., 1992—; mem. exec. com. African-Am. coun. U. Iowa, 1990-91; instr. Cornell Coll., Mt. Vernon, Iowa, 1985; counselor Upward Bound program U. Iowa, 1980. Contbr. articles to profl. jours. Martin Luther King fellow Boston U., 1973; recipient Harvard Book award, recognition award for successful student recruiting So. U. in New Orleans, 1994. Mem. Orgn. Am. Historians, Nat. Coun. for Black Studies, Nat. Assn. Grad. Admissions Profls., NAACP, Phi Alpha Theta. Presbyterian. Office: U Iowa Grad Coll 204 Gilmore Hall Iowa City IA 52242-1320

HENRY, JOSEPH PATRICK, chemical company executive; b. Mansfield, Ohio, Mar. 3, 1925; s. Harold H. and Louise A. (Droxler) H.; student Bowling Green State U., 1943-44; B.S., Ohio State U., 1949; m. Jeanette E. Russell, Oct. 26, 1957; 1 dau., Jeanette Louise. Ohio sales mgr. NaChurs Plant Food Co., Marion, Ohio, 1949-55; organizer, pres. Growers Chem. Corp., Milan, 1955—, Sandusky Imported Motors, Inc. (Ohio), 1958-78; pres. Homestead Motors, Inc., 1978-83; co-owner Homestead Inn Restaurant, Homestead Farms; v.p. Homestead Inn, Inc. Motels, South Avery Corp. Motels; dir. Erie County Bank, Vermilion, Ohio., Soc. Bank of Firelands. Served with USMCR, 1943-46; PTO. Mem. Nat. Fedn. Ind. Bus. (nat. adv. council), AAAS, Ohio Farm Bur. Fedn., Milan C. of C., Aircraft Owners and Pilots Assn., Internat. Flying Farmers, Ohio Restaurant Assn., Ohio Motel-Hotel Assn., Ohio Licensed Beverage Assn., Am. Horse Show Assn., Nat. Trust for Historic Preservation, N.A.M., Internat. Platform Assn., Huron County Hist. Soc., Ohio Farm Bur., (pres.), Ohio, Internat. (dir. 1978-84) Arabian horse assns. Clubs: Antique Automobile Am., Sports Car Am., N. Am. Yacht Racing Union, Sandusky Yacht, Sandusky Sailing, Catawba Island. Developer (with V.A. Tiedjens) foliage fertilization and direct to seed fertilization of comml. field crops. Home: 128 Center St Milan OH 44846-1700 Office: Growers Chem Corp PO Box 1750 Milan OH 44846-1750 also: Homestead Farms RR 1 Milan OH 44846-1700

HENRY, MICHAEL L., stockbroker, lawyer; b. Ft. Wayne, Ind., Mar. 18, 1953. BA, Ind. U., 1975, JD, 1978. Bar: Ind. 1978. Pvt. practice, 1978-83; stockbroker PaineWebber Inc., Ft. Wayne, 1983-87, Robert Thomas Securities, Ft. Wayne, 1987—. Mem. Ft. Wayne Bar Assn. Office: Robert Thomas Securities 9025 Coldwater Rd Ste 500 Fort Wayne IN 46825-2074

HENRY, PHILLIP MICHAEL, physicist, development engineer; b. St. Louis, Nov. 17, 1953; s. Hubert Ellis and Mary Lucille (Forbus) H. BSc in Nuclear Engring., U. Mo., 1975, PhD in Physics, 1984. Rsch. asst. Los Alamos (N. Mex.) Nat. Labs., 1979, Monsanto Co., St. Louis, 1980; scientist McDonnel Douglas Microelectronics, St. Louis, 1984-90; staff specialist McDonnell Douglas Missiles Co., St. Louis, 1990-91; tech. specialist avionics and signature tech. McDonnell Aircraft Co., St. Louis, 1991—. Contbr. articles to Jour. Applied Physics, Applied Physics Letters. Baptist. Office: McDonnel Douglas PO Box 519 Saint Louis MO 63166-0519

HENRY, RICHARD W., mechanical engineer; b. Urbana, Ill., Oct. 13, 1966. BSME, U. Ill., 1990. Mech. engr. CI Wescom, Rantoul, Ill., 1993—. Baptist. Office: CI Wescom 201 Shellhouse Dr Rantoul IL 61866-9711

HENRY, ROY MONROE, financial planner; b. Oct. 27, 1939; s. Roy Monroe and Nancy Lowe (Morse) H.; m. Meredith Elaine Hjelmstad, Aug. 20, 1961; children: Robin E., Roy M. III. BBA, Kennedy-Western, 1990. Registered prin., rep.-NASD. Airman 1st class USAF, Turkey, 1957-61; estimator Con P. Curran Printing Co., St. Louis, 1961-64; sales mgr. Prudential Ins. Co., St. Louis, 1964-72; pres. Roy M. Henry & Assocs., Chesterfield, Mo., 1972-76, St. Louis Fin. Planners, Chesterfield, Mo., 1976-83, First Fin. Planners, Chesterfield, Mo., 1983—; guest spkr. Purdue U., Yale U. Appeared on (TV show) 20/20, 1991; contbr. articles to profl. jours. Named Fin. Planner of Yr., 1987. Mem. Internat. Assn. Fin. Planners (bd. dirs. 1984-86), Mo. Athletic Club, Internat. Assn. of Registered Fin. Cons. (pres.). Republican. Lutheran. Home: 2031 Kehrsboro Dr Chesterfield MO 63005-6512 Office: First Fin Planners Inc 15455 Conway Rd Chesterfield MO 63017-2022

HENRY, STUART DENNIS, criminology educator; b. London, Oct. 18, 1949; s. Lionel Victor and Dorothy (Knowles) H.; m. L. Lee Doric, Mar. 5, 1988. BA in Sociology, U. Kent, Canterbury, Eng., 1972, PhD in Sociology, 1976. Rsch. sociologist Inst. Psychiatry, U. London, 1975-78; rsch. fellow Middlesex U., Enfield, Eng., 1978-79; sr. lectr. Nottingham Trent U., Nottingham, Eng., 1979-84; asst. prof. Old Dominion U., Norfolk, Va., 1984-87; assoc. prof. Ea. Mich. U., Ypsilanti, 1987-92, prof., 1992—; rsch. fellow U. Mich., 1989. Author: The Hidden Economy, 1978, Private Justice, 1983; co-author: Self-Help and Health, 1977, Markets Distribution and Exchange after Societal Cataclysm, 1989, Making Markets, 1992, The Deviance Process, 1993, Criminological Theory, 1995, Constitutive Criminology, 1996; editor: Informal Institutions, 1981, Degrees of Deviance, 1990, Employee Dismissal, 1994, Inside Jobs, 1994, Social Control, 1994; co-editor: The Informal Economy, 1987, Work Beyond Employment, 1993; mem. editl. bd. Howard Jour. Criminal Justice, Theoretical Criminology; contbr. articles to profl. jours. Grantee Ea. Mich. U., 1989, 92, 93, 94; recipient State of Mich. Teaching Excellence award, 1990, Disting. Faculty rsch. award 1995; rsch. grantee NSF, 1990. Mem. Am. Soc. Criminology, Am. Acad. Criminal Justice Scis., Law and Soc. Assn., Indsl. Rels. Rsch. Assn. Office: Eastern Mich U Dept Sociology Ypsilanti MI 48197

HENRY, THOMAS W., physical therapist; b. Cedar Falls, Iowa, Aug. 18, 1958; s. Marshall Paul and Carolyn Marie (Stoltenberg) H. BA in Sci., U. No. Iowa, 1983; cert. phys. therapy, U. Iowa, 1986. Resident phys. therapy Kaiser Permanente, Hayward, Calif., 1990-91; phys. therapist Meml. Hosp., South Bend, Ind., 1986-94, Cmty. Hosp. E, Indpls., 1994—; grad. asst. U. Indpls., 1994—. Fellow Am. Acad. Orthopedic Manual Phys. Therapy; mem. Am. Phys. Therapy Assn. Home: 6190 Guilford Ave Indianapolis IN 46220

HENRY, WILLIAM ROBERT, architect, engineer; b. Elkhorn, Wis., July 30, 1957; s. Lester John and Betty Jane (Clapper) H.; m. Kelly Lynn

Hughson, Oct. 31, 1981; children: Elizabeth Ashton, Chad Andrew. AAS, Milw. Sch. Engring., BS, 1978. Registered architect Calif., Ill., Oreg., Wis.; registered profl. engr., Calif., Oreg. Wis. Architect/engr. Goebel-Balestrieri & Assocs., Elkhorn, Wis., 1977-83, Edward & Lee Assocs., Ltd., Sussex, Wis., 1983-84; prin.-in-charge, owner Wm. R. Henry Assoc., Arch. & Engring., Elkhorn, 1984—; cert. inspector Dept. Industry, Labor & Human Rels. Rental Weatherization, State of Wis., Madison, 1984—; lectr. Archtl. Engring. Dept., Milw. Sch. Engring., 1983. Mem. Gateway Tech. Coll. Strategic Planning Task Force, Elkhorn, 1985-87, tech. edn. adv. com., 1988—. Named Outstanding Alumnus Milw. Sch. Engring., 1988; recipient Golden Trowel award Internat. Masonry Inst., 1994. Mem. Nat. Coun. Archtl. Registration Bds., Nat. Coun. Examiners for Engring. and Surveying, Milw. Sch. Engring. Alumni Assn. (bd. dirs. 1985—), Lions (pres. 1992-93). Baptist. Office: Wm R Henry Assocs 3 W Walworth St # 207 Elkhorn WI 53121-1736

HENSCH, SHIRLEY ANNE, psychology educator; b. Edmonton, Alta., Can., Apr. 17, 1955; came to U.S., 1990; d. Ronald and Marjorie (Morris) Wiggins; m. Timothy Grant Hensch, Nov. 11, 1985. Tchg. asst., U. Alta., Edmonton, 1985, MSc in Psychology, 1987, PhD in Psychology, 1991. Teaching asst. U. Alta., 1985-87, lectr., 1987-89, asst. prof., 1990; asst. prof. psychology U. Wis., Marshfield, 1990-95; assoc. prof. U. Wis., 1996—. Contbr. articles to profl. jours. Vol. Ronald McDonald Children's Charities, Marshfield, 1991. Nat. Sci. and Engring. Rsch. Coun. scholar, Can., 1987, 88; faculty fellow U. Alta, 1987, 88, 89, Wis. Teaching fellow, 1993, 94. Mem. APA, Coun. Tchrs. of Undergrad. Psychology, ASA. Office: U Wis-Ctrs 2000 W 5th St Marshfield WI 54449-3310

HENSCHEL, JOHN PETER, import export company executive; b. Mpls., July 1, 1952. BSBA, Mankato State U., 1978. V.p. site and bus. devel. APTUS, Mpls., 1982-90; mgr. permitting and compliance Westinghouse Environ. Svcs., Mpls., 1982-90; v.p. Export Import Mgrs. Co., Mpls., 1990—. Office: Export Import Mgrs Co 3140 Harbor Ln N Ste 227 Minneapolis MN 55447-5108

HENSELMEIER, SANDRA NADINE, training and development consulting firm executive; b. Indpls., Nov. 20, 1937; d. Frederick Rost Henselmeier and Beatrice Nadine (Barnes) Henselmeier Enright; m. David Albert Funk, Oct. 2, 1976; children: William H. Stolz, Jr., Harry Phillip Stolz II, Sandra Ann Stolz. AB, Purdue U., 1971; MAT, Ind. U., 1975. Exec. sec. to dean Ind. U. Sch. Law, Indpls., 1977-78; adminstrv. asst. Ind. U.-Purdue U., Indpls., 1978-80, assoc. archivist, 1980-81; program and communication coordinator Midwest Alliance in Nursing, Indpls., 1981-82; tng. coordinator Coll./Univ. Cos., Indpls., 1982-83; pres. Better Bus. Communications, Indpls., 1983—; adj. lectr. Ind. U.-Purdue U. at Indpls., 1971—, U. Indpls. Center Continuing. Mgmt. Devel. and Edn., Indpls., 1984—. Author: Successful Customer Service Writing, Winning with Effective Business Grammar, Successful Telephone Communication and Etiquette, Management Writing; contbr. articles to profl. jours. Bus. adv. com. computer programmer tng. Crossroads Rehab. Ctr.; exec. adv. bd. Profl. Secs. Internat. 500 chpt.; Indpls. customer adv. bd. Ameritech Small Bus. Svcs. Mem. ASTD, Am. Soc. Indexers, Soc. Tech. Communications, Indpls. C. of C., Economic Club Indpls. Republican. Presbyterian. Avocations: traveling, walking, reading, learning new ideas. Office: Better Bus Communications PO Box 20309 Indianapolis IN 46220-0309

HENSHEL, DIANE S. W., neuroscientist, educator; b. N.Y.C., Mar. 28, 1955; d. Harry Bulova and Joy (Altman) H.; m. Harry M. W. Banek, June 4, 1982; children: Artemis Kaolin, Ariel Gaian. BA, Brown U., 1978, BS, 1978; PhD, Washington U., St. Louis, 1987. Rsch. assoc. U. Calif., San Francisco, 1978-79, Washington U., St. Louis, 1987; post doctoral fellow U. B.C., Vancouver, Can., 1988-89, sessional lectr., 1989, rsch. assoc., 1990-92; asst. prof. Ind. U., Bloomington, 1992—; pvt. practice cons., Vancouver, Bloomington, 1989—. Vol. scientist Sci. by Mail Boston Mus. Sci., 1990—. Mem. AAAS, ASTM (chair subcom. 47.09 1993—), N.Y. Acad. Sci., Soc. Neurosci., Soc. Environ. Toxicology and Chemistry (bd. dirs. Ohio Valley chpt. 1995—), Assn. Women in Sci. (chair Bloomington chpt. 1994-95, 96—, bd. dirs. 1993—), Soc. Toxicology, Sigma Xi. Office: Ind U Dept Neuroscience Bloomington IN 47405

HENSLEY, ALBERT LLOYD, JR., research chemist, technical consultant; b. Rutherfordton, N.C., July 5, 1928; s. Albert Lloyd and Alice Edith (Houser) H.; m. Wilma Dorothy, Feb. 10, 1951; children: Stephen Lloyd, Edith C., David A., Amelia D. BS in Chemistry, Ind. U., 1951; MS in Inorganic Chemistry, Northwestern U., 1959. Chemist Mallinckrodt Chem., St. Louis, 1951-53, Sherwin Williams Co., Chgo., 1953-54, Amoco Oil Co., Hammond, Ind., 1954-74; chemist, cons. Amoco Oil Co., Naperville, Ill., 1974-94; ret., 1994. Contbr. articles to profl. jours.; patentee in field. Mem. Am. Chem. Soc., N.Am. Catalyst Soc. Home: 1204 35th St Munster IN 46321-2502 Office: Amoco Oil Co Warrenville Rd Naperville IL 60566

HENSLEY, ANTHONY, state legislator; b. Topeka, Sept. 2, 1953; s. Harland Leroy and Georgina (Haydon) H.; m. Deborah Hensley; 1 child, Kathleen. BS, Washburn U., 1975; MS, Kans. State U., 1985. Kans. state rep. Dist. 58, 1977-92, Kans. state senator Dist. 19, 1992—, spl. edn. tchr., 1975—. Chmn. Washburn U. Young Dems., 1972-73, Shawnee County Dem. Ctrl. Com., 1981-86, 2d Dist. Dem. Com., 1991-93; committeeman 8th precinct 4th Ward Dem. Com., Topeka, 1976—; mem. Breakthrough House. Named one of Outstanding Young Men in Am., 1978, 82. Mem. Legal Aid Soc., Optimists. Home: 2226 SE Virginia Ave Topeka KS 66605-1357*

HENSLEY, JEFFREY ALLEN, nuclear security; b. Monroe, Mich., June 25, 1963; s. George W. and Opal Cleo (Cupp) H.; m. Dawn Carol Daisher Hensley, Mar. 21, 1986 (div. Oct. 5, 1990); m. Tammy M. Barronton Hensley, Nov. 24, 1990; children: Amanda Carol. Matthew Allen, Jeffrey Thomas, Heather Susan. AA in Police Adminstrn., Monroe C.C., Mich., 1983. Parking enforcement officer Burns Security, Newport, Mich., 1982-85; reserve police officer Monroe Police Dept., 1982-85; owner J&T Cleaning, Monroe; nuclear security Detroit Edison, Newport, 1985—; nuclear fire protection inspector, 1996—; sec., treas. Monroe Med. Authority, 1992—; sec.-treas. Monroe Corrections Adv., 1994—; com. mem. Comms. Detroit Edison, Newport. Bd. mem. City of Monroe Recycling, 1986-91, Arthur Lesow Commx. Ctr., Monroe, 1984—; candidate for City Coun., City of Monroe, 1991, 93; pres. bd. dirs. Arthur Lesow Comms. Ctr., Monroe, 1993—; co-chair United Way Detroit Edison, Newport, 1994, chair, United Way drive, 1995-96. Recipient Cert. of Merit, Monroe (Mich.) Comms. Found., 1992. Mem. Security Officers Assn. Democrat. Lutheran. Home: 1724 S Custer Rd Monroe MI 48161 Office: Detroit Edison 6400 N Dixie Hwy Newport MI

HENSLEY, JERRY ROBERT, manufacturing engineer; b. Trenton, N.J., Oct. 19, 1951. BS in Indsl. Design, S.W. Mo. State U., 1987. Project engr. S.W. Mobile Sys., West Plains, Mo., 1974-87; sr. mfg. engr. A. B. Chance, Centralia, Mo., 1988—. With USNG, 1972-78. Mem. Am. Welding Soc.

HENSLEY, LEO BASIL, foundation administrator; b. Cumberland, Iowa, Mar. 13, 1944; s. Cleo Basil and Florence Veronica (Cullen) J.; m. Judy Lea Reinig, Mar. 1, 1969; children: Ann Veronica, Laura Lea. BA, U. No. Iowa, 1966, MA, 1971. Tchr., coach Delwood Cmty. Sch., Elwood, Iowa, 1971-74, Turkey Valley Cmty. Sch., Jackson Junction, Iowa, 1974-84; asst. athletic dir. Emporia (Kans.) State U., 1984-88; assoc. athletic dir. No. Ill. U., De Kalb, 1988-90; found. exec. dir. St. Joseph Med. Ctr., Joliet, Ill., 1990—. Bd. dirs. United Way of Will County, 1991-95, Boy Scouts Am., 1991-95, Will-Grundy Med. Clin., Joliet, 1991-95. Cpl. USMC, 1966-69, Vietnam. Recipient Navy achievement medal USMC, 1968, Navy commendation medal, 1968. Mem. VFW, Assn. Healthcare Philanthropy (bd. dirs.), Nat. Assn. Athletic Fundraisers (bd. dirs.), U.S. Capitol Hist. Soc., Rotary Internat., Lions (pres.), Am. Legion. Home: 24800 River Tr Channatton IL 60410

HENSON, PAUL HARRY, transportation executive; b. Bennet, Nebr., July 22, 1925; s. Harry H. and Mae (Schoenthal) H.; m. Betty L. Roeder, Aug. 2, 1946; children: Susan Irene Flury, Lizbeth Henson Barelli. BSEE, U. Nebr., 1948, MS, 1950; hon. doctorates, U. Nebr., Ottawa U., Bethany Coll., U. Mo., U. Kans. Registered profl. engr., Nebr. Engr. Lincoln (Nebr.) Tel. & Tel. Co., 1941-42, 45-48, div. mgr., 1948-54, chief engr., 1954-59; v.p. Sprint Corp., Kansas City, Mo., 1959-60, exec. v.p., 1960-64, pres., 1964-73, chmn., 1966-90, also bd. dirs., 1959-95; chmn. bd. Kansas City So. Industries, Inc., 1990—; also bd. dirs.; bd. dirs. Armco, Duke Power, Hallmark Cards; pres. Kansas City Equity Ptnrs., L.P. Trustee Midwest Rsch. Inst., Tax Found., U. Nebr. Found., Childrens Mercy Hosp., Greater Kansas City Cmty. Found. With USAAF, 1942-45. Mem. NSPE, IEEE, U.S. Telephone Assn. (bd. dirs. 1960-76, pres. 1964-65) Kansas City Country Club, River Club, Kansas City Club, Eldorado Country Club, Old Baldy Club, Masons, Shriners, Sigma Xi, Eta Kappa Nu, Sigma Tau, Kappa Sigma (Man of Yr. 1987). Office: Kansas City So Industries Inc 4200 Somerset Shawnee Mission KS 66208

HENZLIK, RAYMOND EUGENE, zoophysiologist, educator; b. Casper, Wyo., Dec. 26, 1926; s. William H. Henzlik and Adeline Adele (Brown) Wolff; m. Wilma Louise Bartels, Oct. 1, 1950; children: Randall Eugene, Nancy Jo. BS, U. Nebr., 1948, MS, 1952, PhD, 1960; postgrad., Cornell U., 1961-62. Tchr. biology and chemistry York (Nebr.) High Sch., 1948-50; sci. edn. supr. Tchrs. Coll., U. Nebr., Lincoln, 1951-53; tchr. biology Omaha North High Sch., 1953-56; instr. biology Nebr. Wesleyan U., Lincoln, 1957-59; asst. prof. zoology and biology U. Nebr., Lincoln, 1959-61; asst. prof. biology Ball State U., Muncie, Ind., 1962-67, assoc. prof. physiology, 1967-69, prof. physiology, 1970—; adj. vis. prof. vet. physiology Tex. A&M U., College Station, 1984-85; anatomy cons. Nat. Prescription Footwear Applications Assn., Muncie, 1962—; lectr. Orthopedic Tech. Program, Muncie, 1977—; cons. ednl. affairs Argonne (Ill.) Nat. Lab., 1970-76; dir. ednl. program Am. Diabetes Assn., Muncie, 1979-83; vis. prof. health sci. USAF European Ctr., Ramstein and Rhein Main, Germany, 1977-78; lectr. Ind. Health Care Assn., 1985-91. Author: Human Physiology Lab Manual, 1976-92; contbr. articles to profl. jours. Pres. Muncie Tech. Soc., 1975-80; mem. bd. Am. Diabetes Assn. Delaware County, Muncie, 1979-85. Radiation biology fellow NSF/AEC, U. Mich., 1960, Radiobiology fellow AEC/NSF, Cornell U., 1961-62, Radiation Biology Rsch. fellow U.S. Radiobiology Lab N.C. State U., 1965, P.R. Nuclear Ctr., 1967. Mem. AAAS, Nutrition Today Soc., Ind. Acad. Sci., Muncie Tech. Soc., Mensa, Sigma Xi, Phi Delta Kappa. Home: 5009 N Somerset Dr Muncie IN 47304-6501 Office: Ball State U Physiology and Health Sci Dept 2000 W University Ave Muncie IN 47306-1022

HEPPER, CALVIN DEAN, stockbroker; b. McLaughlin, S.D., Nov. 29, 1951. BS in Agr., N.D. State U., 1978. Farmer, N.D., 1978-83; program dir. State of N.D., Bismarck, 1984-88; stockbroker Smith Barney Inc., Fargo, N.D., 1988—; instr. Standing Rock C.C., Selfridge, N.D., 1978-83; fin. cons. Nat. Futures Assn., Chgo., 1990—. Mem. Am. Funds President's Club. Republican. Baptist. Home: 1625 30th Ave S Fargo ND 58103-5930 Office: Smith Barney Inc 23 Broadway Fargo ND 58102-4923

HERALY, THOMAS P., electrical engineer; b. Green Bay, Wis., Apr. 15, 1964; s. Eldred John and Rita Marie (Urban) H. BSEE, Milw. Sch. Engring., 1985, MS in Engring., 1995. Engine drives engr. Miller Electric Mfg. Co., Appleton, Wis., 1986-90, static equipment engr., 1990-91, robot equipment lead engr., 1991-94, flexible automation product mgr., 1994—. Mem. IEEE, Am. Welding Soc. (membership chair 1992-93). Home: 1019 W Franklin St Appleton WI 54914

HERBEL, ALVIN, computer specialist; b. Scottsbluff, Nebr., Feb. 23, 1950; s. Raymond Herbel and Caroline (Meier) McCole; m. Lois Marie Bloomfield, Apr. 10, 1976; children: Carolee Elizabeth, Matthew David. AAS, Nebr. Western Coll., 1970; BA in Biology and Psychology, Chadron State Coll., 1974, BA in Bus. Adminstrn./Data Processing, 1984. Farmer Gering, Nebr., 1974-77; agr. technician U. Nebr., Scottsbluff, 1977-79; mem. bridge constrn. crew Scottsbluff County Rds. Dept., 1979-81; owner Herbel Landscaping Contracting Co., Gering, 1981-87; computer operator Lockwood Corp., Gering, 1981-84; computer programmer analyst Western Nebr. Community Coll., Scottsbluff, 1985-92, computer specialist, 1992—. Mem. Gering Organized Baseball, 1992-93; floats chmn. Oreg. Trail Days, Gering, 1992—; mem. Sugar Valley Ralley, Scottsbluff, 1989-93, fin. sec. Rejoice Luth. Ch., Gering, 1987-89; mem. Gering Trouism Com., 1989—. Coop. Ministries Coun., Scottsbluff, 1984-92; bd. dirs. Panhandle Cmty. Svcs., Scottsbluff, 1984-91; mem. North Platte Valley Mus., 1990—; bd. dirs. Scottsbluff County United Way, 1994—. Republican. Home: 1570 Yucca Dr Gering NE 69341-3235 Office: Western Nebr Community Coll 1601 E 27th St Scottsbluff NE 69361-1815

HERBEL, LEROY ALEC, JR., telecommunications engineer; b. Ft. Carson, Colo., July 24, 1954; s. LeRoy Alec and Mabel Bertha (Huffman) H. BS, S.W. Mo. State U., 1976; MEd, Ga. So. U., 1978; MS in Telecommunications, Golden Gate U., 1987, MBA, 1990; student, Southern U., 1996. Asst. mgr. toy dept. Dillard's Dept. Store, Springfield, Mo., 1971-76; material controller GTE of the South, Durham, N.C., 1979-80; asst. prof. mil. sci. Army ROTC, U. N.H., Durham, 1982-85; tech. instr. Northern Telecom Inc., Raleigh, N.C., 1988-91; sr. engr. No. Telecom Inc., Raleigh, N.C., 1991-93; field engr. mgr. Western Wireless Corp., Bellevue, Wash., 1994-95; switch supr. Palmer Wireless (CellularOne), Ft. Myers, Fla., 1995—; adj. prof. DeKalb (Ga.) C.C., 1978-79, N.C. Wesleyan Coll., Rocky Mount, 1991. Scoutmaster Troop 213 Boy Scouts Am., Cary, N.C., 1990-93, asst. dist. commr. Dan Beard dist., 1992—, mem. merit badge staff Nat. Jamboree, 1993. Capt. U.S. Army, 1980-88; maj., USAR, 1988—. Recipient Scoutmaster award of merit Boy Scouts Am., 1991, Disting. Leadership citation Boy Scouts Am., 1991, Scoutmaster Key award Boy Scouts Am., 1992, Dist. Order of Merit Boy Scouts Am., 1994, Boy Scout Commr. Key award, 1995. Mem. Telephone Pioneers of Am., Phi Delta Kappa. Office: Palmer Wireless Corp 7001 Chatham Ctr Dr Ste 400 Savannah GA 31405

HERBERT, EDWARD FRANKLIN, public relations executive; b. N.Y.C., Jan. 30, 1946; s. H. Robert and Florence (Bender) H.; m. Rhonda J. Scharf, Aug. 20, 1967; children: Jason Dean and Heather Ann (twins). B.S. in Comm., Syracuse U., 1967, M.S., 1969. Assoc. dir. pub. relations Am. Optometric Assn., Washington, 1971; community relations specialist Gen. Electric Co., Columbia, Md., 1971-73, pub. relations account supr., 1973-75; dir. pub. affairs Nat. Consumer Fin. Assn., Washington, 1975-78; regional dir. pub. relations Montgomery Ward Co., Balt., 1978-80, fin. info. services dir., Chgo., 1980-81, internal comm. dir., 1981-82, corp. comm. dir., 1982-83; regional dir. pub. relations MCI Comm. Corp., Chgo., 1983-84; dir. comm. MCI Midwest, MCI Telecom. Corp., 1985-93; prin. Edward F. Herbert & Assoc., 1993—; Bd. dirs. United Cerebral Palsy of Chgo., Better Bus. Bur. Served with U.S. Army, 1969-71. Mem. Pub. Relations Soc. Am., Execs. Club of Chgo., Info. Industry Council. Home and Office: 830 Timberhill Ln Highland Park IL 60035-5121

HERBISON, PRISCILLA JOAN, public policy and law educator, consultant; b. Mpls., Sept. 13, 1943; d. Charles W. and Vonda C. (Rogers) H. BA, Coll. St. Catherine, St. Paul, 1965; MSW, U. Ill.-Urbana, 1969; JD, U. Minn., 1982. Bar: Minn. 1983; cert. Acad. Cert. Social Workers. Social worker Catholic Social Service, St. Paul, 1965-67, Cath. Welfare Service, Mpls., 1969-71; prof. social work U. W.Va., 1971-74; prof., dir. social work program St. Cloud (Minn.) State U., 1974—, chmn. dept. sociology, anthropology and social work, 1985-87; prof., dir. human devel. and psychology St. Mary's U. Minn., 1987—; cons., researcher in law; staff aide to speaker of Ill. Ho. of Reps., 1968-69; founder, dir. early childhood ctrs. in rural Appalachia, 1971-72. Fairchild fellow, 1980; grad. advisor of the year 1995-96. Mem. ABA, Acad. Cert. Social Workers, Nat. Assn. Social Workers, Christian Legal Soc., Lawyers Guild of St. Thomas More, Conf. Social Work Edn., Delta Theta Phi. Roman Catholic. Home: 5905 Columbus Ave Minneapolis MN 55417-3107 Office: Saint Mary's U 2510 Park Ave Minneapolis MN 55404-4403

HERBRUCKS, MARILYN, food products executive; b. 1929; m. Harry W. Herbrucks Jr. With Herbruck Poultry Ranch Inc., Saranac, Mich. Office: Herbruck Poultry Ranch Inc 6425 Grand River Ave Saranac MI 48881*

HERBRUCKS, STEPHEN, food products executive; b. 1950; s. Harry Herbrucks. Pres. Herbruck Poultry Ranch Inc., Saranac, Mich.; with Poultry Mgmt. Systems, Saranac, Mich., 1980—. Office: Herbruck Poultry Ranch Inc 6425 Grand River Ave Saranac MI 48881*

HERBSTER, MARTY L., manufacturing company executive; b. Falls City, Nebr., Sept. 12, 1969. BS in Agrl. Tech. Mgmt., Kans. State U., 1992. Designer, draftsman Alanco Environ. Mfg. Inc., Falls City, Nebr., 1992—. Office: Alanco Environ Mfg Inc Hwy 73 S Falls City NE 68355-0455

HERBSTER, STEVEN L., stockbroker; b. Lakeville, Ind., July 30, 1957; m. Tammy C. Padgett, May 12, 1979; children: Carrie, Stephanie, Jessica, Emily, Adam. BA, Liberty U., Lynchburg, Va., 1979. Sales rep. Midwest Dental Supply, South Bend, Ind., 1982-88; stockbroker Edward D. Jones & Co., Elkhart, Ind., 1988—. Chmn. bd. dirs. Greenkrof Found., Elkhart, 1991—; bd. dirs. Dollars for Scholars, 1994—, River Oaks Cmty. Ch., Elkhart, 1991—; campaign chmn. Am. Lung Assn., Elkhart, 1993—; v.p. Jefferson Elem. Sch. PTO, 1992—. Mem. Kiwanis. Republican. Office: Edward D Jones & Co PO Box 982 Elkhart IN 46515-0982

HERBSTREITH, YVONNE MAE, primary education educator; b. Wayne County, Ill., Aug. 18, 1942; d. Daniel Kirby and Rizpah Esther (Harvey) Smith; m. Bobbie L. Cates, Oct. 18, 1964 (div. 1969); 1 child, Shawn L.; m. Jerry Carrol Herbstreith, Sept. 15, 1979. BS, So. Ill. U., 1964. Cert. elem. tchr., Ill. Kindergarten tchr. Beardstown (Ill.) Elem., 1964-65, Pekin (Ill.) Pub. Schs. # 108, 1966-94. V.p. Pekin Friends of 47, 1986-91, pres. 1991-93, pres. Rebecca-Sarah Cir. 1st United Meth. Ch., Pekin, 1988—; trustee Sta. WTVP-TV, Peoria, Ill., 1990-91; active PTA, 1965-94, treas. 1992-93. Recipient Louise Alloy award Sta. WTVP, 1995. Mem. NEA (life), AAUW, Ill. Edn. Assn., Pekin Edn. Assn., Pekin Friends of Libr., Tazewell County Ret. Tchrs., Alpha Delta Kappa, Alpha Theta (chpt. pres. 1986-88, state sgt. at arms 1990-92, state chaplain 1992-94, state pres. 1996—). Democrat. Methodist. Home: 1922 Quail Hollow Rd Pekin IL 61554-6351

HERCHE, MARVIN C., mechanical designer; b. Milw., July 4, 1962. Designer mech. carbon parts Helwig Carbon Products, Inc., Milw., 1984—. Author catalog: Self Lubricating Mechanical Components, 1992. Lutheran. Office: Helwig Carbon Products Inc 8900 W Tower Ave Milwaukee WI 53224-2849

HERDER, HARRY JOSEPH, JR., retired educator; b. Red Wing, Minn., Sept. 7, 1925; s. Harry Joseph Sr. and Pauline Gertrude (Heinen) H.; m. Ann Marie Holt, Oct. 22, 1955; children: Susan Elizabeth, Abigail Holt. BSEd, U. Minn., 1956; MEd, U. Ill., 1966. Tchr. jr. h.s. San Diego (Calif.) City Schs., 1956-57; tchr. chemistry, coach Shattuck Sch., Faribault, Minn., 1957-59; tchr. sci., coach Milw. Country Day, 1959-63; tchr. jr. h.s., coach Albuquerque Acad., 1966-72, 74-86; tchr. jr. h.s., coach Brunswick Sch., Greenwich, Conn., 1972-74, ret., 1986; instr. Earlham Coll., Richmond, Ind., summer 1961, West Va. Wesleyan Coll., summer 1962. With U.S. Army, then USN, 1950-52. Decorated Purple Heart, Silver star. Home: Rt 8 Box 8324 Hayward WI 59843

HEREMANS, JOSEPH PIERRE, physicist; b. Leuven, Belgium, Jan. 8, 1953; came to U.S., 1984; s. Joseph Felix and Marie Therese (Bracke) H.; m. Claire Pierre Mali, July 1, 1978; children: Hilde Anne, Joseph Paul. Elec. Engr., U. Louvain, Belgium, 1975, PhD in Applied Physics, 1978. Aspirant Belgium Nat. Sci. Found., Louvain, 1978-80, charge de recherche, 1980-83; rsch. scientist GM Rsch., Warren, Mich., 1984-85, group leader, 1985-87, sect. mgr., 1987--; invited prof. U. Louvain, 1989; vis. scientist U. Tokyo, 1982, MIT, Cambridge, 1980-81. Editor: Growth, Characterization and Properties of Ultrathin Magnetic Films and Multilayers, 1989; contbr. articles to profl. jours. Fellow Am. Phys. Soc.; mem. AAAS, Materials Rsch. Soc., Sigma Xi. Office: GM Rsch Physics Dept 30500 Mound Rd Warren MI 48090-9055

HERKNER, BERNADETTE KAY, occupational health nurse; b. East Liverpool, Ohio, Apr. 29, 1947; d. Charles R. and Anna G. (Parr) Geon. Diploma in nursing, East Liverpool City Hosp., 1973; BS in Applied Sci., Youngstown (Ohio) State U., 1976. RN, Ohio, Mich., Fla; cert. in audiometrics, spirometry, ICD-9-CM; cert. case mgr. Charge nurse emergency rm. East Liverpool City Hosp., 1976-78; sr. occupl. health nurse Dow Chem. N.Am., Midland, Mich., 1978—. Active Vol. Action Ctr. Midland County. Recipient Best Bedside Nurse, Centennial award for svc. to humanity, 1973, Ctrl. Mich. Outstanding Occupl. Health Nurse of Yr. award, 1993; named Miss Hope Columbiana County unit Am. Cancer Soc., 1977. Mem. ANA, Am. Assn. Occupl. Health Nurses (cert.), Mich. Assn. Occupl. Health Nurses (bd. dirs.), Emergency Nurses Assn., Mich. Nurses Assn., Ctrl. Mich. Assn. Occupl. Health Nurses (bd. dirs., corr. sec. 1986-90, rec. sec. 1990-91, pres. 1991-95, legis. chmn. 1995—), East Ctrl. Mich. Emergency Nurses, Ohio Emergency Nurses Assn. (membership sec.), Individual Case Mgrs. Assn.

HERMAN, CHLOE ANNA, real estate broker; b. Chgo., Dec. 8, 1937; d. Robert Marius and Hope Manolatos; m. Ben Howse Herman, Oct. 16, 1960; children: Holly, Benjamin Andrew, Robert. BA, Northwestern U., 1959. Broker-assoc. Kole Real Estate, DesPlaines, Ill., 1972-76; broker-mgr. Century 21 Northwest, DesPlaines, 1976-77; broker-assoc. Wm. L. Kunkel & Co., DesPlaines, 1978-88; broker-mgr. Re/Max Suburban, Inc., Arlington Heights, Ill., 1988-90; pres. AAUW N.W. Suburban br., 1984-86. Past pres. Three Hierarchs, St. John The Baptist Ch.; dir. Holy Family Planned Gift Adv. Coun., 1986, United Way, DesPlaines, 1990— (pres. 1996). Mem. Women's Coun. Realtors (pres.-elect 1989-90, pres. 1990-91, gov. Ill. chpt. 1992, 93), N.W. Suburban Assn. Realtors (bd. dirs. 1991—, pres.-elect 1992-93, pres. 1993-94), Cert. Residential Specialists (charter, sec. 1989-90, 92—), Rotary. Office: Re/Max Suburban Inc 330 E Northwest Hwy Mount Prospect IL 60056-3361

HERMAN, ROGER ELIOT, professional speaker, consultant, futurist, writer; b. San Francisco, Cal., Dec. 11, 1943; s. Carlton Martin and Estelle (Nadler) H.; m. Janet I. Meyer, June 22, 1969 (div. Feb. 1974); 1 child, Scott Philip; m. Sandra Jean Steckel, May 2, 1974; children: Bruce, Jeffrey, Jennifer. BA in Sociology, Hiram Coll., 1969; MA in Pub. Adminstrn., Ohio State U., 1977. Cert. mgmt. cons.; cert. speaking profl. Mgr. Rayco, Inc., Kent, Ohio, 1970-72; pvt. practice sales Stow, Ohio, 1972-76; pub. service dir. City Hilliard, Ohio, 1976-78; city mgr. City Rittman, Ohio, 1978-80; pres. Herman Assocs., Inc., Rittman, 1980—. Author: Disaster Planning for Local Government, 1982, Emergency Operations Plan, 1983, The Process of Excelling, 1988, Keeping Good People, 1990, Turbulence!, 1995; contbr. mag. columns, articles to profl. jours. Commr. Ohio Boy Scouts Am., 1970, scoutmaster Texas (Ohio) Boy Scouts Am., 1966-70. Served with U.S. Army, 1965-68. Named Most Interesting Person In Northeast Ohio, Cleve. mag., 1981, named one of Outstanding Young Men Am., 1976, 77, 78, 79; recipient Arrowhead award Boy Scouts Am., Ohio, 1969. Mem. ASTD (chmn. profl. devel. 1987-88, program chmn. 1985-86, newsletter editor N.E. Ohio chpt. 1985-86), Nat. Spkrs. Assn. (Ohio Spkrs. Forum ethics com. 1985-86, co-chmn. industry rels. com., cert. speaking profl.), Inst. Mgmt. Cons. (cert. mgmt. cons., pres. Ohio chpt. 1991-95, bd. dirs.), World Future Soc. (profl.), Ohio Jaycees (Hilliard pres. 1976-77, Blue Chip Disting. Svc. award 1977), Toastmasters (dist. lt. gov. Texas, Ohio 1965-80, Able Toastmaster award 1969). Republican. Jewish. Office: Herman Assocs Inc PO Box 5351 Akron OH 44334-0351

HERMAN, WAYNE DELTON, rodeo entertainer; b. Bismarck, N.D., Jan. 10, 1964; s. Delton Wilfred and Carol Ann (Misslin) H.; m. Connie Renee Weisenberger, July 11, 1981; children: Justin Wayne, Jake Wayne. Student, Dickinson State U., 1983, 84. Profl. rodeo cowboy Colorado Springs, Colo., 1984—; founder Ronald McDonald House, 1991—. Supporter, fund raiser Ronald McDonald House, Bismarck, 1991-92. Res. World Champion Bareback Bronc Rider, 1991, World Champion Bareback Bronc Rider, 1992; qualifier 9 times Nat. Finals Rodeo. Mem. Profl. Rodeo Cowboys Assn. Lutheran.

HERMAN, WILLIAM JOHN, banker; b. Milw., Apr. 30, 1966; s. William Alex and Barbara Pose (Turiak) H.; m. Sandra Roberta Heminger, Oct. 14, 1989; children: Justin Alexander, Erika Maria. BBA, U. Notre Dame, 1988. Asst. plant mgr. Skyline Corp., Elkhart, Ind., 1992-93; asst. v.p. Mishawaka (Ind.) Fed. Savs., 1993—. Lt. (j.g.) USN, 1988-92. Mem. Preservation of the Res. (fin. sec. 1994—). Roman Catholic. Office: Mishawaka Fed Savs 121 S Church St Mishawaka IN 46544

HERMANCE, LYLE HERBERT, college official; b. Lincoln, Nebr., Dec. 10, 1939; s. Milo Lee Sr. and Amelia Henrietta (Schoneman) H.; m. Dorothy Kay Stanislav, June 12, 1960 (div.); children: Lane Alan, Lori Ann, Russell Joel; m. Janette Kay Sims, Oct. 11, 1986. BS, U. Nebr., 1964, MS, 1970. Cert. agr. edn. tchr., Nebr. Tchr. vocat. agr. and indsl. arts Emerson (Nebr.)-Hubbard Pub. Schs., 1964; tchr. vocat. agr. Waverly (Nebr.) Pub. Schs., 1964-79, chmn. dept. vocat. edn., 1973-79; coord. adult agr. program area cmty. svcs. div. S.E. C.C., Lincoln, 1979—, dir. Adult Edn. Ctrs. area cmty. svcs. div., 1991—, interim dir. div., 1992-94, dir. div., 1994—; rep. Nebr. Turkey Coun., 1968-72, Nebr. Grassland and Forage Coun., 1969—; nat. coord. computers in agr. demonstration contest Future Farmers Am. 1990-93; mem. adult edn. task force Nat. Coun. for Agrl. Edn., 1991—; mem. adv. coun. agrl. edn. dept. U. Nebr., 1987—; mem. S.E. Rsch. and Ext. Ctr. adv. team Inst. Agr. and Natural Resources, 1992—; asst. supt. Future Farmers Am. div. sheep show Nebr. State Fair, 1988-90, supt., 1990—; pres. Nebr. Vocat. Agrl. Found., 1970-71, bd. dirs., 1991-92. Bd. dirs. Lancaster County Pub. Nursing Adv. Com., 1972-76; mem. Lancaster County Extension Bd., 1990-95, pres., 1992-95; mem. Nebr. affiliate task force Am. Heart Assn., 1992—; mem. spl. com. on agrl. edn. Nebr. Coun. Vocat. Edn., 1986-88; charter bd. dirs., advisor Nebr. Agrl. Leadership Coun., Inc., 1980-82; charter mem. Nebr. Coalition for Agrl. Fin. Mgmt. Edn., 1990—, state co-chmn., 1991—; bd. dirs. Nebr. Assn. Vocat. Indsl. Clubs Am., 1995—, state coord. leadership and skills contest, 1996. Recipient hon. degree Future Farmers Am., 1994, Nebr. Disting. Svc. award, 1994, Nebr. Lifetime Svc. award, 1996. Mem. NEA, Nebr. Edn. Assn., Waverly Edn. Assn. (pres. 1970-71, Lancaster County Agrl. Soc. (bd. dirs. 1991), Nebr. Vocat. Agrl. Assn. (state pres. 1968-69, dist. chmn. 1987-89, Outstanding Young Mem. award 1969, Outstanding Post Secondary Instr. award 1988), Nebr. Vocat. Assn. (bd. dirs. 1976-80, state pres. 1980-81), Nat. Farm Ranch Bus. Mgmt. Edn. Assn. (nat. pres. 1991-92), Nebr. Assn. for Adult Agrl. Educators (charter, pres. 1988-89), Am. Vocat. Assn., Nat. Vocat. Agrl. Tchrs. Assn. Home: RR 3 Lincoln NE 68517-9801

HERMANIUK, MAXIM, retired archbishop; b. Nowe Selo, Ukraine, Oct. 30, 1911; emigrated to Can., 1948, naturalized, 1954; s. Mykyta and Anna (Monczak) H. Student philosophy and theology, Louvain, Belgium, 1933-35, Beauplateau, Belgium, 1935-39; ThD, Oriental Philology and History, 1943; postgrad., Maitre Agrege Theol., 1947; DD (hon.), U. St. Michael's Coll., Toronto, Can., 1988. Joined Redemptorist Congregation, 1933, ordained priest, 1938; supr. vice provincial Can. and U.S., 1948-51; consecrated bishop, 1951; aux. bishop Winnipeg, Man., Can., 1951; apostolic adminstr., 1956, archbishop met., 1956-92, archbishop emeritus, 1992—; editor Logos, 1993—; first editor Logos, 1993—, Ukraine Theol. Rev., 1950-51; mem. Vatican II Coun., 1962-65, Secretariat for Promoting Christian Unity, Rome, 1963; prof. moral theology, sociology and Hebrew, Beauplateau, 1943-45; prof. moral theology and holy scripture Redemptor Sem. Waterford, Ont., Can., 1949-51; mem. Pontifical Commn. for Revision of Kodex of Oriental Canon Law, 1983; mem. Coun. Secretariat for The Synod of Bishops, Rome; elected for preparation of Ius Speciale As Tempus, 1993, Ukranian Cath. Ch. Author: La Parabole Evangelique, 1947, Our Duty, 1960. Co-founder, mem. Ukrainian Relief Com., Belgium, 1942-48; co-founder 1st pres. Ukrainian Cultural Soc., 1947, organizer Ukrainian univ. students orgn., Obnova, Belgium, 1946-48, Can., 1953; mem. joint working group Cath. Ch. and World Council Chs., 1969; mem. council to Secretariat Synod of Bishops, Rome, 1977, 83. Decorated Order of Can., 1982. Mem. World Congress Free Ukrainians, Taras Shevchenko Sci. Soc., Ukrainian Hist. Assn., KC. Address: 235 Scotia St, Winnipeg, MB Canada R2V 1V7

HERMES, MARJORY RUTH, machine embroidery and arts educator; b. Caldwell, Kans., June 28, 1931; d. Truman Homer and Olive Ruth (Ridings) Brown; m. Ogden S. Jones, Jr., Dec. 17, 1949 (div. Aug. 1956); m. Richard Lawrence Hermes, July 18, 1963; children: Penelope, Peter, Deborah, Patricia, Pamela, Kristin. Student, U. Kans., 1949-50, Arkansas City Jr. Coll., 1953-54. Sec. Maurer-Neuer Corp., Arkansas City, Kans., 1954-56, Lesh, Bradley & Barrand, Lawrence, Kans., 1959-60; exec. sec. Houston Corp., Wichita, Kans., 1956-57; mgr. Ind. Ins. Co., Landstuhl, Fed. Republic Germany, 1960-62; sec. U. Kans., Lawrence, 1962-63; photograph restorer Herb's Studio, Lawrence, 1977-78; ptnr., agt. Hayes-Richardson-Santee Inc., Lawrence, 1978-83; instr. sewing and machine embroidery Self & Bob's Bernina, Lawrence, 1985—; mem. Lawrence Ins. Bd., 1980-83. Bd. dirs. United Way, Lawrence, 1981-83; host Am. Indian Athletic Hall of Fame, 1980-82; treas. local polit. campaigns, 1984, 88; leader Therapeutic Horse Riding Instrn., Lawrence. Mem. Nat. Machine Embroidery Instrs. Assn. (bd. dirs. for N.D., S.D., Nebr., Iowa, Mo., Minn. and Kans. 1987-90), Am. Sewing Guild, Am. Bus. Women's Assn. (v.p. Lawrence 1980-81, pres. 1981-82, Inner Circle award 1982, Woman of Yr. award 1984), Lawrence C. of C. (envoy 1978-83). Republican. Home: 2513 W 24th Ter Lawrence KS 66047-2818

HERNANDEZ, GLORIA J., consulting company executive; b. Man, W. Va., June 5, 1942. A in Acctg., U. Cin. Pvt. practice Wee-Care, Cin., 1987-91; beautician Identity, Cin., 1991-93; owner, v.p. FTS Consulting, Inc., Cin., 1993—. Mem. Womens Entrepreneur, Beckett Country Club. Republican. Protestant. Office: FTS Consulting Inc 10700 McSwain Cincinnati OH 45241-3165 Home: 10 Warwick Cincinnati OH 45246

HERNANDEZ, RAMON ROBERT, clergyman, librarian; b. Chgo., Feb. 23, 1936; s. Eleazar Dario and Marie Helen (Stange) H.; m. Fern Ellen Muschinske, Aug. 11, 1962; children: Robert Frank, Maria Marta. BA, Elmhurst (Ill.) Coll., 1957; BD, Eden Theol. Sem., St. Louis, 1962; MA, U. Wis., 1970. Co-pastor St. Stephen United Ch. Christ, Merrill, Wis., 1960-64; dir. youth work Wis. Conf. United Ch. Christ, Madison, 1964-70; dir. T.B. Scott Free Library, Merrill, 1970-75, McMillan Meml. Library, Wisconsin Rapids, Wis., 1975-83, Ann Arbor (Mich.) Pub. Library, 1983-94; pastor Comty. Congl. Ch., Pinckney, Mich., 1994—; seminar leader on pub. libr. long-range planning, budgeting and handling problem patrons. Editl. com. mem. Songs of Many Nations Songbook, 1970; contbr. articles to profl. jours. Treas. Ann Arbor Homeless Coalition, 1985-88; bd. dirs., sec., v.p. Riverview Hosp. Assn., Wisconsin Rapids, 1977-83; bd. dirs. Hist. Soc. Mich., 1988-90. Mem. ALA, Wis. Libr. Assn. (Leadership award 1980, pres. 1980), Mich. Libr. Assn., Rotary (pres. Merrill chpt. 1974-75, Community Svc. award 1975, pres. Ann Arbor chpt. 1990-91, Paul Harris fellow 1994). Office: Cmty Congl Ch PO Box 585 125 E Unadilla Pinckney MI 48169

HERNANDEZ, WANDA GRACE, rehabilitation counselor, sales manager; b. Detroit, Apr. 23, 1942; d. Harry Lee and Lillian Delores (Williams) Williams; m. Ignacio Heriberto Hernandez, Nov. 25, 1969 (div. April 1979); 1 child, Heriberto Alejandro. BS, Wayne State U., 1973, MA, 1977; BS in Nutrition, Am. Holistic Coll. Nutrition, Birmingham, Ala., 1994; MS in Nutrition, Am. Holistic Coll. Nutrition, 1995. Substance abuse counselor Boniface Community Action Corp., Detroit, 1972-73; vocations rehab. counselor Mich. Rehab. Svcs., Detroit, 1974—. Named Disting. Rehab. Profl., Nat. Disting. Service Registry Library of Congress, 1987. Fellow Nat. Rehab. Assn.; mem. Smithsonian Assocs., Confedn. Chivalry, Rails-to-Trails Conservancy, Nat. Parks and Conservation Assn., Mus. Heritage Soc., Am. Assn. Retired Persons. Moslem. Home: 9056 Patton St Detroit MI 48228-1622 Office: Mich Rehab Svcs 30 E Canfield St Detroit MI 48201-1804 also: PO Box 205 New South Wales, Manly 2095, Australia

HERNDON, STEVEN G., design engineer; b. Forest City, Iowa, July 7, 1961. BS in Mech. Engring., Iowa State U., 1984; MBA, U. Iowa, 1994. Engr. Winnebago Industries, Forest City, 1984-87; sr. design engr. Amana (Iowa) Refrigeration Inc., 1987—. Mem. Assn. Home Appliance Mfrs. (mem. adv. bd.). Roman Catholic. Home: 1427 Cardinal Ct NE Cedar Rapids IA 52402-3708 Office: Amana Refrigeration Inc Main St Amana IA 52203

HEROLD, JEFFREY ROY MARTIN, library director; b. Chgo., Aug. 9, 1941; s. Roy George and Anne (Polacek) H.; m. Carol Ann Courtial, June 20, 1964; children: Kristin Ann, Timothy Scott. MEd, SUNY, Buffalo, 1966; PhD, Ohio State U., 1969; MLS, Kent State U., 1986. Teaching assoc. Ohio State U., Columbus, 1965-69; asst. prof. edn. SUNY, Cortland, 1969-74, Ind. U. Pa., 1974-75; lectr. in edn. Kelvin Grove Coll., Brisbane, Australia, 1976-78; assoc. dir. office continuing edn. Ohio State U., Columbus, 1979-84; extension libr. Columbus Pub. Libr., 1985-87; dir. Bucyrus (Ohio) Pub. Libr., 1987—; bd. dirs. North Ctrl. Libr. Cooperative, Mansfield, Ohio, 1991-93. Book reviewer: Libr. Jour., 1988—. Chair McGovern for Pres. Com., Cortland County, N.Y., 1972; founder and pres. SUNY Founds. of Edn. Assn., 1971-72. Grantee Timken Found., 1989, 96, Ohio Humanities Coun., 1994, 95. Mem. ACLU, ALA, Pub. Libr. Assn. (Univ. Press books for pub. librs. com. 1990-93), Ohio Libr. Coun. Office: Bucyrus Pub Libr 200 E Mansfield St Bucyrus OH 44820

HERON, TIMOTHY EDWARD, special education educator, consultant; b. Ridley Park, Pa., Sept. 20, 1948; s. Raymond Charles and Bernice Marie (Dougherty) H.; m. Marguerite Agnes Campiglia, Aug. 19, 1972; children: Kathleen Marie, Christine Noel. BA, Temple U., 1970, MEd, 1972, EdD, 1976. Devel. supr. United Cerebral Palsy Delaware County, Boothwyn, Pa., 1970-71; tchr. Delaware County Intermediate Unit, Media, Pa., 1971-73; teaching asoc. Temple U., Phila., 1973-76; asst. prof. Ohio State U., Columbus, 1976-81, assoc. prof., 1981-86, prof., 1986—; ednl. cons. Children's Hosp. Behavior and Learning Disability Clinic, Columbus, 1982—. Co-author: The Educational Consultant, 1993, Applied Behavior Analysis, 1987, Focus on Behavior Analysis in Education, 1984, rev. edit., 1994; contbr. articles to profl. jours. Mission pilot, capt. Ohio CAP, Columbus, 1988—; pilot Airlifeline, Sacramento, 1990—. Doctoral fellow U.S. Office Edn., Washington, 1974, 75. Mem. Coun. Learning Disabilities (leadership chairperson 1984-86), Assn. Behavior Analysis, Coun. Exceptional Children, Ohio Coalition for Edn. of Handicapped Children (chpt. pres. 1979-81). Republican. Roman Catholic. Office: Ohio State Univ 1945 N High St Columbus OH 43210-1120

HERR, LEONARD JAY, plant pathologist; b. Orrville, Ohio, Dec. 21, 1928; s. Roy Albert and Orpha (Shoup) H.; m. Lucille Alice Adelsberger, Sept. 15, 1954; children: Lynn Allen, Karen Marie, Melissa Ann. Student, Antioch Coll., 1946-47, 48-49; BSc, Ohio State U., 1952, MSc, 1953, PhD, 1956. Instr. Ohio State U./Ohio Agrl. R&D Ctr., Wooster, 1956, asst. prof., 1957-62, assoc. prof., 1962-76, prof., 1977-95, prof. emeritus, 1995—. Contbr. articles to profl. jours. Mem. AAAS, Am. Phytopathol. Soc. (assoc. editor 1990-94), Am. Inst. Biol. Scis., Ohio Acad. Sci., N.Y. Acad. Sci., Assn. Applied Biology, Sigma Xi. Roman Catholic. Office: Ohio State Univ Dept Plant Pathology 1680 Madison Ave Wooster OH 44691-4114

HERR, PETER HELMUT FRIEDERICH, sales executive; b. Hamburg, Germany, Apr. 23, 1951; came to U.S., 1978; s. Helmut and Ellen (Schmidt) H.; m. Kim Lovett, Sept. 29, 1984 (div. Nov. 1991); 1 child, Andrew; m. Monika Berns, Nov. 19, 1991; 1 child, Jan. BS in Mech. Engring., U. Braunschweig, 1974, MS in Aero. Engring., 1978. Aero. engr. R&D Beech Aircraft Corp., Wichita, Kans., 1978-81; regional mgr. Beech Aircraft Corp., Wichita, 1981-86, sr. regional mgr., 1987-92, dir. internat. market devel., 1992-93, regional dir. western Europe and Africa, 1993-94; v.p. internat sales Raytheon Aircraft, Wichita, 1994—; sec., treas. Euroflight, Inc., Wichita, 1985—. Cpl. German Air Force, 1970-72. Lutheran. Home: 15229 Zimmerly Ct Wichita KS 67230 Office: Raytheon Aircraft Co 10511 E Central Ave Wichita KS 67206-2507

HERRERA, ALBERTO, JR., librarian; b. Bogotá, Colombia, Feb. 24, 1947; s. Alberto Herrera Salazár and Ada Emma (Miller) H.; m. Susan Louise Poorman, Aug. 21, 1971 (div. Dec. 1979). BS in Polit. Sci., U. Wis., 1968, MA in LS, 1982; MA in History, U. Oreg., 1973, postgrad., 1974-79. Grad. teaching fellow in history U. Oreg., Eugene, 1970-71, 74-78; claims rep. Social Security Adminstrn., Santa Ana, Riverside, Eureka, Calif., 1971-73; freelance hist. rschr., Eugene, 1978; job svc. rep. Oreg. Employment Div., Eugene, 1979-81; intern Libr. of Congress, 1982-83; reference libr. Congl. Rsch. Svc. Libr. of Congress, Washington, 1983-84; Am. history specialist Libr. of Congress, Washington, 1984-87; history reference and outreach libr. Golda Meir Libr., U. Wis., Milw., 1987-93; head of ref., 1993—; adj. instr. Sch. Libr. and Info. U. Wis., Milw., 1990, 91. Mem. Hispanic Coun. U. Wis., 1988—. Scholar Nat. Hispanic Scholarship Fund, 1978; Lyman Copeland Draper fellow, 1981. Mem. ALA, Assn. of Coll. and Rsch. Librs., Wis. Libr. Assn., Wis. Assn. Acad. Librs., Orgn. Am. Historians (contbg. editor for microforms Jour. Am. History 1988—), Western History Assn., State Hist. Soc. Wis. Office: U Wis Golda Meir Libr PO Box 604 Milwaukee WI 53201-0604

HERRERIAS, CARLA TREVETTE, epidemiologist, manager; b. Chgo., Apr. 8, 1964; d. Ludvik Frank and Carlotta Trevette (Walker) Koci; m. Jesus Herrerias, Feb. 25, 1989; children: Elena Mikele, Coco Trevette. BS in Med.Tech., Ea. Mich. U., 1987; MPH in Molecular and Hosp. Epidemiology, U. Mich., 1991. Med. clk. hydramatic divsn. GM, Ypsilanti, Mich., 1983-86; researcher, staff dept. human genetics U. Mich., Ann Arbor, 1987-91; program mgr. Am. Acad. Pediatrics, Elk Grove Village, Ill., 1991—. Project mgr., contbr.: Clinical Practice Guideline: Otitis Media with Effusion in Young Children, 1994. Mem. APHA, Ill. Pub. Health Assn., Assn. for Health Svcs. Rsch., U. Mich. Alumni Soc., U. Mich. Club Chgo. Office: Am Acad Pediatrics 141 Northwest Point Blvd Elk Grove Village IL 60007

HERRICK, JAMES ALLEN, communications educator; b. Madera, Calif., Oct. 6, 1954; s. R.D. and Deloris J. Herrick; m. Janet P. Herrick, Aug. 11, 1979; children: Daniel, Stephen, Laura, Alicia. BA, Calif. State U., Fresno, 1976; MA, U. Calif., Davis, 1979; PhD, U. Wis., 1984. Asst. prof. Hope Coll., Holland, Mich., 1984-89, assoc. prof. comm., 1990—, chair dept. comm., 1992—. Author: Critical Thinking,1991, Argumentation, 1994, Introduction to Rhetoric, 1996, Rhetoric of English Deists, 1996. Wis. Alumni Rsch. Found. fellow, 1982, Knight Found. fellow, 1990; recipient Excellence in Teaching award U. Wis., Madison, 1982, Rsch. Stipend NEH, 1992. Mem. Speech Comm. Assn., Am. Soc. for Study Rhetoric. Office: Hope Coll Holland MI 49423

HERRICK, KENNETH GILBERT, manufacturing company executive; b. Jackson, Mich., Apr. 2, 1921; s. Ray Wesley and Hazel Marie (Forney) H.; m. Shirley J. Todd, Mar. 2, 1942; children: Todd Wesley, Toni Lynn. Student public and pvt. schs., Howe, Ind.; LHD (hon.), Siena Heights Coll., 1974; HHD (hon.), Adrian Coll., 1975, Detroit Inst. Tech., 1980; LLD, Judson Coll., 1975; D Engring. (hon.), Albion Coll., 1981. With Tecumseh Products Co., Mich., 1940-42, 45—; v.p. Tecumseh Products Co., 1961-66, vice chmn. bd., 1964-70, pres., 1966-70, chmn. bd., chief exec. officer, 1970-86, chmn. bd., 1986—. Bd. dirs. Howe Mil. Sch., 1970-81, from Herrick Found., 1970; mem. exec. adv. bd. St. Jude Children's Hosp., from 1978. Served with USAAC, 1942-45. Recipient Hon. Alumni award Mich. State U., 1975; Disting. Svc. award Albion Coll., 1975. Mem. Lenawee Country Club, Elks, Tecumseh Country Club, Masons. Presbyterian. Office: Tecumseh Products Co 100 E Patterson St Tecumseh MI 49286-2041*

HERRICK, NICHOLAS JAY, JR., electrical engineer; b. Highland Park, Ill., June 16, 1972. BS in Engring., Swarthmore (Pa.) Coll., 1994. Internship, feature engr. Ford Motor Co., Allen Park, Mich., 1993; elec. and controls engr. DCT Advanced Engring., Inc., Detroit, 1994—. Mem. IEEE, Soc. Profl. Engrs. Office: DCT Advanced Engring Inc 20501 Hoover St Detroit MI 48205-1031

HERRICK, TODD W., manufacturing company executive; b. Tecumseh, Mich., 1942. Grad., U. Notre Dame, 1967. Pres., chief exec. officer Tecumseh (Mich.) Products Co. Office: Tecumseh Products Co 100 E Patterson St Tecumseh MI 49286-2041

HERRIFORD, ROBERT LEVI, SR., army officer; b. Lewistown, Ill., May 4, 1931; s. John and Lola (Braden) H.; m. Muriel Jean Davis, July 10, 1949; children: Robert Levi, Thomas Merle, David William, Deborah S., Traci Ann. B.S., U. Ariz., 1966, M.B.A., 1968. Enlisted in U.S. Army, 1948, commd. 2d lt., 1952, advanced through grades to maj. gen., 1979; service in Vietnam, 1966-67; comdr. 269th Ordnance Group Ft. Bragg, N.C., 1969-71; chief spl. items mgmt. Tank Automotive Command Detroit, 1971-72; comdr. Korean Procurement Agy. Seoul, 1973-74; dir. procurement Armaments Command Rock Island, Ill., 1974-76; comdr. Def. Contracts Region N.Y., 1976-78; asst. dep. chief of staff logistics Pentagon, 1978-80; dir. procurement and prodn. Devel. and Readiness Command Alexandria, Va., 1980-83; assoc. chief ops. officer, dir. support services Argonne Nat. Lab., 1983—. Chmn. Minority Bus. Opportunity Council, N.Y.C., 1976-78. Decorated Legion of Merit, D.S.M., Def. Superior Service medal, Bronze Star, Airmedal, numerous others. Mem. Am. Def. Preparedness Assn., Assn. U.S. Army, Am. Legion, Nat. Contracts Mgmt. Assn. (chpt. pres. 1975-76). Office: Argonne Nat Lab 9700 Cass Ave Lemont IL 60439-4803

HERRIN, CHRISTY L., investment representative; b. Washington, Mo., Apr. 1, 1954. BSBA in Econs. and Fin., Mo. So. State U., 1982; MS, Coll. Fin. Planning, 1990. CFP. Prodn. specialist Empire Electric, Joplin, Mo., 1974-86; fin. planner Baird Kurtz & Dobson, Joplin, 1986-94; investment specialist Edward D. Jones, Joplin, 1994—; agt. IRS, 1992—. Bd. dirs. Family Self-Help, 1994—. Mem. S.W. Mo. State Planning Coun., Soroptomist Internat., Women's Club (bd. dirs. 1993—). Office: Edward D Jones PO Box 2487 Joplin MO 64803-2487

HERRIN, FRANCES SUDOMIER, retired volunteer social worker; b. Hamtramck, Mich., Dec. 1, 1914; d. Wesley Valentine and Anna Theresa (Langowski) Sudomier; widowed. Grad., high sch., 1933. Sec. Parke Davis & Co., Detroit, 1946-47; assembler Gen. Motors, Detroit, 1947, Chrysler Corp., Hamtramck, 1950-57; vol. social worker, mem. adv. com. Detroit Area Agy. on The Aging, Detroit, 1981-92; spkr. St. Theresa Guild, 1981-92, Golden Agers, 1981-92, Polish-Am. Sr. Citizens, 1981-90; precision-tool tested parts of B-29 bomber planes in World War II, Henry Ford Aircraft Bldg., River Rouge Plant. Active in Dem. and Rep. election campaigns; mem. St. Florian's Hist. Commn., Hamtramck, 1985—; sr. citizen activist several sr. orgns., Washington; mem. ret. sr. vol. program Cath. Social Svcs., Wayne County, 1986-87; mem. Presdl. Task Force for Pres. Reagan; patron Cath. orgns. where missionaries provide relief of food, clothing and edn. to children, especially orphaned children of devasted countries. Recipient Medal of Merit from Pres. Reagan. Mem. St. Theresa's Guild. Roman Catholic.

HERRING, RAYMOND MARK, strategic planning and organizational development; b. Nashville, Sept. 23, 1952; s. Raymond Benjamin and Alma Ruth (Murrell) H. BA, Baylor U., 1974, MA, 1976, EdD, 1983. Rsch. and evaluation specialist McLennan County Med. Edn. and Rsch. Found., Waco, Tex., 1979-82; dir. edn., pub. rels. Providence Hosp., Waco, 1982-85, dir. ctr. for health promotion, 1983-85; v.p. John Leifer, Ltd., Shawnee Mission, Kans., 1985-86; pres. Mark Herring Assocs., Inc., Overland Park, Kans., 1986—; mem. adv. bd. Upjohn Healthcare Svcs., Waco, 1984-85; mem. editorial bd. Healthcare Mgmt. Rev., Rockville, Md., 1986-90. Contbr. articles to profl. jours. Mem. HealthPlus, Overland Park; bd. dirs. Am. Diabetes Assn., Waco, 1984-85, Tex. Soc. Hosp. Educators, 1983-85. Office: Mark Herring Assocs Inc 11564 Caenen St Shawnee Mission KS 66210-2728

HERRITT, DAVID R., elementary education educator; b. Canton, Ohio, Oct. 17, 1942; s. Ralph H. and Freda A. (Baker) H; m. Jean A. Quinn. BS in Edn., Malone Coll., 1969; MEd, Ashland (Ohio) Coll., 1985. Cert. tchr., Ohio. Educator, intermediate level Canton (Ohio) City Schs. Active Boy Scouts Am. Mem. NEA, Ohio Edn. Assn., ECOEA, CPEA, NESA. Home: 5535 Veldon Cir NE Canton OH 44721-3445

HERRMANN, ARTHUR DOMINEY, banker; b. Louisville, Sept. 29, 1926; s. Arthur Chester and Mattie Belle (Dominey) H.; m. Lucy Kindred, Apr. 7, 1951; children: Lucy W. Herrman Porter, Anne D. Herrman Phillips, Martha Kindred. BA, Ohio State U., 1947, JD, 1949; postgrad., Rutgers U., 1950. Bar: Ohio 1950. Asst. trust officer Huntington Nat. Bank, Columbus, 1951-56, pres., CEO, 1972-75, also bd. dirs, chmn., 1980-81; pres., CEO Huntington Bancshares, Inc., 1975-81, also bd. dirs.; chmn., pres., CEO, dir. BancOhio Corp., 1981-84; chmn., dir. BancOhio Nat. Bank (mem. Nat. City Corp.), 1984—; with Nat. City Bank Columbus, 1981—; bd. dirs. Nat. City Corp, N.Am. Broadcasting Co. Trustee Columbus Mus. Fine Art, from 1974, v.p. 1979-82, pres. 1982-84; trustee Ohio Dominion Coll. 1978—, chmn. 1984—; trustee Children's Hosp. of Columbus, 1985—, Ohio Cancer Found. 1977—; chmn. United Negro Coll. Fund Dr., 1984-85; trustee Capitol South Com. Urban Redevel. Corp., 1982—. Mem. Ohio Bankers Assn., Columbus Bar Assn., Ohio C. of C. (exec. com., trreas. 1979—), Columbus Area C. of C. (bd. dirs., vice chmn. exec. com. from 1983), Assn. Bank Holding Cos., Assn. Reserve City Bankers, Newcomen Soc., Sigma Chi, Phi Delta Phi. Clubs: Pres.' of Ohio State U.; Phi Delta Phi Legal Frat.; Cols.; Rocky Fork Hunt and Country; Castalia, Review. Office: Nat City Bank Columbus 155 E Broad St Columbus OH 43215-3609*

HERRMANN, JANE MARIE, physical therapist; b. St. Louis, Aug. 13, 1961; d. Harold Jack and Elizabeth Joan (Hogan) H. BS in Phys. Therapy, St. Louis U., 1984; M. Health Sci., Washington U., St. Louis, 1991. Registered phys. therapist, Ill., Mo.; registered/cert. athletic trainer. Staff phys. therapist St. Anthony's Med. Ctr., St. Louis, 1985-87; profl. staff coord. Divsn. of Med. Rehab. Profl. Phys. Therapy, Inc., St. Louis, 1987-91; dir. of phys. therapy Hillsboro (Ill.) Area Hosp. Med. Rehab., Hillsboro, 1991-94; phys. therapy cons. Continental Med. Svcs., Hillsboro, 1992-95, Sundance Corp., Litchfield, Ill., 1994—; clin. dir. MedRehab, Inc., Hillsboro, 1994-96; dir. rehab. Hillsboro Area Hosp., 1996—. Mem. Am. Phys. Therapy Assn., Nat. Athletic Trainers Assn., Ill. Phys. Therapy Assn. Roman Catholic. Office: Hillsboro Area Hosp 1200 E Tremont Hillsboro IL 62049

HERRMANN, JOHN W., engineer; b. Manitowoc, Wis., July 23, 1950. AD, Acme Inst. Tech., 1971. Draftsman HMF, Inc., Manitowoc, Wis., 1971-80, designer, 1980-90, engring. mgr., 1990—. Coach Little League Softball and Basketball, 1988-93; vol. Francis Creek Fire Dept., 1988-94.

HERRON, NED TALBERT, marketing professional; b. Indpls., Aug. 17, 1947; s. Charles Edward and Esther Isabelle (Allen) H.; m. Ethel E. Cremeens, Dec. 15, 1965 (div. Oct. 1984); children: Tamara Liane, Trina Lorraine, Tricia Lynette, Tiffany lane, Shaun; m. Ramona Kay Chaffin, Jan. 25, 1985; 1 child, Amanda Jo Esther. Lic. mutual fund sales. Sales rep. Alliance Assocs., Richardson, Tex., 1993—; motivational spkr. The Herron Agy., Inc., Lucasville, Ohio, 1990—. With U.S. Army, 1967-69. Mem. Gideons Internat. Home and Office: 237 Ghost Hollow Rd Lucasville OH 45648

HERRON, ORLEY R., college president; b. Olive Hill, Ky., Nov. 16, 1933; s. Orley R. and Hyllie W. (Weaver) H.; m. Donna Jean Morgan, Aug. 24, 1956; children: Jill Donette, Morgan Niles, Mark Weaver. B.A., Wheaton Coll., 1955; M.A., Mich. State U., 1959, Ph.D., 1965; Litt. D. (hon.), Houghton Coll., 1972; L.H.D. (hon.), Leslie Coll., 1983. Dean of students Westmont Coll., Santa Barbara, Calif., 1961-67; dir. doctoral program/student pers. U. Miss., 1967-68; asst. to pres. Ind. State U., 1968-70; pres. Greenville (Ill.) Coll., 1970-77, Nat Louis U. (formerly Nat. Coll. Edn.), Evanston, Ill., 1977; mem. Ill. Commn. for Improvement Elem. and Secondary Edn., 1983-1985; chmn. bd. Harris Bank, Wilmette, Ill., 1991—, also bd. dirs.; bd. dirs. Corp. Community Schs. of Am. Author: Role of the Trustee, 1969, Input-Output, 1970, New Dimensions in Student Personnel Administration, 1970, A Christian Executive in a Secular World, 1979, Who Controls Your Child?, 1980; author: cassette tape Governing Higher Education in the 70's, 1970. Rep. of Pres. U.S. 25th Anniversary UNESCO, 1971; mem. adv. bd. Expt. on Internat. Living, Santa Barbara.; mem. Gov.'s Task Force on Encouraging Citizen Involvement in Edn., 1986—; bd. dirs. Ch. Centered Evangelism; mem. Chgo. Sun. Evening Club, 1987—. Recipient Crusader Christian Contbn. award Wheaton Coll., 1955, 74, Outstanding Citizen award Greenville Jaycees, 1971, Outstanding Educator award Religious Heritage of Am., 1987. Mem. Am. Assn. Higher Edn., AAUP, Council on Inter-Instnl. Cooperation (pres.), Council Advancement Small Colls. (sec.), Christian Coll. Consortium (exec. com.), Fedn. Ind. Ill. Colls. (exec. bd. 1971—), Nat. Assn. Evangelicals (exec. com. 1974—), Assn. Free Meth. Ednl. Instns. (pres. 1973-75). Club: Kiwanian (hon.). Office: Nat Louis U 2840 Sheridan Rd Evanston IL 60201-1730*

HERSCH, RUSSELL LEROY, secondary education educator; b. Waterloo, Iowa, May 17, 1916; s. John David and Ethel Grace (Owen) H.; m. Irma Lucille Selg, Nov. 30, 1940; children: Jon Craig, Geri Kay, Janene Joy, James Jay Russell. BA, U. No. Iowa, 1939; MA, U. Minn., 1949; postgrad., St. Cloud U., 1960-64, Columbia U., summer, 1962, U. Alaska. Cert. tchr., Minn. Tchr. Geneseo Consol. Schs., Buckingham, Iowa, 1939-42, Lindstrom-Center City (Minn.) Sch., 1942-43; math. tchr., asst. prin. Cambridge (Minn.) High Sch., 1946-57; secondary sch. prin. Osseo (Minn.) Sch. Dist., 1957-82, substitute tchr., 1983—. Bd. dirs. Metro Bd. for Aged, 1992-95;

treas., bd. dirs. Christian Reaching Out in Social Svc., 1979-85. With USAF, 1943-46, ETO. Republican. Baptist. Home: 617 3rd Ave NW Osseo MN 55369-1018

HERSCHER, SUSAN KAY, English language educator; b. Wisconsin Rapids, Wis., Nov. 11, 1949; d. Martin Joseph and Marian Margie (Hentz) Arnold; m. Walter Ray Herscher, June 12, 1976; children: Anne, Brian. BS in Edn., U. Wis., Stevens Point, 1971; MS in Reading Edn., U. Wis., Oshkosh, 1983. Elem. tchr. Wausaukee (Wis.) Pub. Schs., 1971-73; elem. tchr., unit leader Hortonville (Wis.) Pub. Schs., 1974-82; adult basic edn. instr. Fox Valley Tech. Coll., Appleton, Wis., 1983—; master tchr., facilitator for Wis. Adult Basic Edn./English as a Second Lang. Summer Inst., 1993; presenter in field. Recipient Quality Improvement award Fox Valley Tech. Coll., 1994. Mem. Tchrs. of English to Speakers of Other Langs., Wis. Tchrs. of English to Speakers of Other Langs., Wis. East Cen. Assn. for Vocat. Edn., Wis. Edn. Assn., NEA. Home: 1341 W Cloverdale Dr Appleton WI 54914-5815 Office: Fox Valley Tech Coll PO Box 2277 1825 N Bluemound Dr Appleton WI 54913-2277

HERSETH, RALPH LARS, state legislator; m. Joyce Herseth; 2 children. Grad., U. S.D. Mem. S.D. Ho. of Reps.; mem. S.D. State Senate, mem. judiciary, legis. procedure and state affairs coms.; farmer, rancher, businessman. Home: RR 1 Box 106 Houghton SD 57449-9608*

HERSH, DAVID B., engineer; b. Toledo, Ohio, Aug. 12, 1949. Assoc. Electronics Engring., U. Toledo, 1976, B. Engring. Tech., 1980. Piping/combustion engr. Surface Combustion, Inc., Maumee, Ohio, 1973—. With U.S. Army, 1969-70, Vietnam.

HERSH, WILLIAM, social services administrator; b. Chgo., Mar. 7, 1938; s. Harry and Betty H. (Abrams) H.; m. Mary Claire Epstein, Aug. 25, 1967. BS, Ill. Inst. of Technology, 1960; MBA, U. Chgo., 1974. Sr. systems engr. IBM Corp., Chgo., 1964-92; pres. Uptown Chgo. Commn., 1993-96, also bd. dirs. Treas. 5000 Marine Drive Corp., Chgo., 1988-94. With U.S. Army, 1961-62. Home: 5000 Marine Dr Chicago IL 60640 Office: Uptown Chgo Commn Ste 710 4753 N Broadway Chicago IL 60640

HERSHBERGER, DANIEL D., executive; b. Holms County, Ohio, Apr. 8, 1930. Mechanic Balco Machine Co., Baltic, Ohio, 1954-66, owner, 1966—. Mem. Amish Ch. Office: Balco Machine Co 2851 State Route 557 Baltic OH 43804-9672

HERSHBERGER, JERRY RICHARD, automotive executive; b. Lebanon, Pa., Jan. 10, 1951; s. Richard Arthur and Marion Yvonne (Meck) H.; m. Diana Jean Hanson, Apr. 8, 1973 (div. June 1991); 1 child, Jeffrey John; m. Janet A. Long; 1 stepchild, Charles Kammer. AS in Bus., Grossmont Coll., 1978; BS in Bus. Mgmt., San Diego State U., 1978; MBA, Golden Gate U., 1984. Cert. internal auditor. Assoc. mgmt. auditor Dept. Transp. State of Calif., Sacramento, 1979-84; supervisory reviewer Farm Credit Banks Ops., Sacramento, 1984-85; dist. parts mgr. no. Calif. parts div. Am. Honda Motor, Inc., Sacramento, 1985-89; zone parts mgr. cen. U.S. Acura div. Am. Honda Motor, Inc., Chgo., 1989-91; central Acura zone parts, accessories mgr. Am. Honda Motor Co., Inc., Chgo., 1991-94, zone parts and svc. mgr. (ops. tech.), 1995—; nat. Acura bus. mgmt. mgr. Acura Nat. Hdqs., Torrance, Calif.; cons. bus. dept. Harper Coll., Hoffman Estates, Ill., 1990-91. Author (manual) Mgmt. Operational Analysis, 1985. Res. dep. San Diego (Calif.) County Sheriff Dept., 1975-76. With USN, Vietnam. Decorated Bronze Star, 1972, Purple Heart, 1972. Mem. Profl. Mgrs. Assn. Republican. Presbyterian. Office: Am Honda Motor Co Inc Acura Divsn 1919 Torrance Blvd Torrance CA 90501

HERSHER, RICHARD DONALD, management consultant; b. Atlantic City, May 24, 1942; s. Mayo Lawrence and Adele (Dahlman) H.; m. Betsy R. Schnitz, Mar. 15, 1970 (div. June 1983); children: Erin, Laura; m. Roza Khazina, Sept. 4, 1993. BS, U. Cin., 1966; MBA, U. Chgo., 1973. Indsl. engr. U.S. Steel Corp., Chgo., 1966-68; mfg. engr. Westinghouse Electric Corp., Chgo., 1968-73; sr. indsl. engr. Abbott Labs., North Chicago, Ill., 1973-76; plant mgr. DeMert & Dougherty, Chgo., 1976-79; pres. Hersher Assocs., Deerfield, Ill., 1979-83; exec. cons. Inst. Mgmt. Resources, Westlake Village, Calif., 1983-87; v.p. ops. Rex Precision Products, Gardena, Calif., 1987; sr. cons. Morris Anderson & Assocs., Rosemont, Ill., 1987-92; pres. Hersher Cons., Deerfield, 1992—. Mem. Inst. Indsl. Engrs., Am. Prodn. Inventory Control Soc.

HERSHISER, OREL LEONARD, IV, professional baseball player; b. Buffalo, Sept. 16, 1958; s. Orel Leonard H. III and Millie H.; m. Jaimie (Byars) Hershiser, Feb. 7, 1981; 2 sons, Orel Leonard V, Jordan Douglass. Student, Bowling Green State U. Pitcher minor league teams Clinton, Ia., 1979, San Antonio, 1980-81, Albuquerque, 1982-83; with Los Angeles Dodgers, 1983-94, Cleve. Indians, 1995—; mem. Nat. League All-Star Team, 1987, 88. Named Nat. League Cy Young award winner, 1988, Most Valuable Player 1988 World Series. NL Gold Glove, 1988, Major League Player of Yr. Sporting News, 1988, Nat. League Pitcher of Yr. Sporting News, 1988, Sporting News Nat. League All-Star Team, 1988, Sporting News Silver Slugger Team, 1993, All-Star Games, 1987-89. Office: Cleve Indians 2401 Ontario St Cleveland OH 44115

HERSHKOVITZ, PHILIP, zoologist; b. Pitts., Oct. 12, 1909; s. Abe and Bertha (Halpern) H.; m. Anne Pierrette Dode, Sept. 15, 1945; children: Francine, Michal Dode, Mark Alan. BS, U. Mich., 1938, MS, 1940. Mem. zool. expdn. Ecuador, Upper Amazon region, 1933-37, Colombia, Columbia, 1941-43, 48-52; mem. zool. expdn. Suriname, 1961-62, Peru, 1980-81, Brazil, 1984, 86-89; asst. curator mammal divsn. Field Mus. Natural History, Chgo., 1947-54, assoc. curator, 1954-56, curator, 1956-61, rsch. curator, 1961-74, curator emeritus, 1974—. Contbr. articles to profl. jours. with U.S. Army, 1943-46. Walter Rathbone Bacon Travelling scholar Smithsonian Inst., 1941-43, 46-47. Mem. Am. Soc. Mammalogists (hon.), Am. Soc. Primatologists (disting. primatologist award 1991), Explorer's Club (corresponding). Office: Field Mus Natural Hist Roosevelt Rd And Lake Dr Chicago IL 60607

HERSMAN, FERD WILLIAM, retired engineer; b. Cin., Apr. 27, 1922; s. Fernando William and Eliza Ann (Garforth) H.; m. Jill Ann Becker, June 30, 1951; children: Michael S., John A., F. William, Christopher B., Jan (dec.). BSChemE, U. Cin., 1949. Registered profl. engr., Ohio. Process engr. Frigidaire div. Gen. Motors, Dayton, Ohio, 1949-51; project engr. Vulcan-Cin., 1951-57; R&D engr. U.S. Indsl. Chems. div., Cin., 1957-61; v.p. Fischer Indsl. Equipment, Inc., Cin., 1961-83, pres., owner, 1983-89, charter com., 1987-88. Mem. Mayor's Fin. Com., Greenhills, Ohio, 1983, Charter Commn., Greenhills, 1988-89; trustee Greenhills Community Presbyn. Ch., 1985-88; elder Blue Ash. Presbyn. Ch., 1996. Staff sgt. U.S. Army, 1942-45, PTO; lt. USNR, 1950-67. Decorated Bronze Star with one oak leaf cluster. Mem. AIChE (chmn. Ohio Valley chpt. 1966-67), Ret. Engrs. and Scientists Cin., SAR. Republican. Presbyterian. Home: 46 Carpenter's Ridge Rd Cincinnati OH 45241-3274

HERTEL, CURTIS, state legislator; b. Detroit, Mar. 7, 1953; s. John and Marie (Kaufmann) H.; m. Vickie; children: Curtis Jr., Matthew. BS, Wayne State U., 1977. Precinct del. Mich. Dem. Party, 1976-78; legis. svc. dir. Detroit Health Dept., 1977-80; state rep. Dist. 12 Mich. Ho. of Reps., 1981-94, state rep. Dist. 2, 1995%. Author: An Ethnic Profile, 1976. Address: 12083 Wayburn St Detroit MI 48224-1037*

HERTEL, JAY ALAN, physician; b. Salem, Ohio, Sept. 21, 1962; s. Wilbert Ray and Linda Louise (Morris) H.; m. Susan Marie Warner, May 25, 1985; children: Zachary, Joshua, Abby. BA in Chemistry, U. Akron, 1984; DO, Ohio U. Coll. Osteo. Medicine, 1989. Family practice physician New Middleton, Ohio; team physician Leetonia (Ohio) High Sch. Football, 1991—. Mem. St. Paul's Luth. Ch. Coun., Leetonia, 1991-93. Mem. Am. Coll. Gen. Practitioners, Am. Osteo. Assn., Ohio Osteo. Assn., Elks. Home: 120 N Elm St Columbiana OH 44408 Office: 10949 Main St New Middletown OH 44442

HERTER, JOYCE MAE, registered nurse; b. LaSalle, Ill., Jan. 20, 1926; d. Adolph Albert and Wilhelmina (Schuster) Rabausch; m. George Herter, May 30, 1959; children: Lois, Rudolph, Jennifer. AA, Augustana Hosp. Sch. Nursing, Chgo., 1948. Instr. clin. nursing Evanston, Ill., 1950-52; legis. chmn. Suburban Occpl. Health Nurses of Chicago. Aux. bd. dirs. Resurrection Hosp., Chgo., 1992—. Mem. Infant Welfare Soc., LWV (chmn. bd. health Cook County 1991—, pres. Morton Grove). Lutheran. Home: 1110 W Villa Dr Des Plaines IL 60016-6271

HERTZ, DAVID MICHAEL, literature educator; b. Bay Shore, N.Y., May 30, 1954; s. Joseph H. and Sarah (Lehman) H. BA, Ind. U., 1976, BS in Music, 1977, MA in Comp. Lit., 1979; PhD in Comp Lit., N.Y.U., 1983. Mellon postdoctoral fellow NYU, 1983-84, asst. prof., 1984-86; asst. prof. Ind. U., Bloomington, 1987-89, assoc. prof. comparative lit., 1989-94, prof. comparative lit., 1994—; dir. undergrad. studies Comparative Lit., 1990-93, dir. grad. studies Comparative Lit., 1993-96. Author: The Tuning of the Word, 1987, Angels of Reality, 1992, Frank Lloyd Wright: In Word and Form, 1995; composer, lyricist The Rose Garden Conspiracy, 1988, China Songs, 1995. Mem. Modern Lang. Assn., Internat. Comp. Lit. Assn., Am. Comp. Lit. Assn. Office: Indiana Univ Comparative Literature Ballantine Hall 9th Fl Bloomington IN 47405-6606

HERZFELD-KIMBROUGH, CIBY, mental health educator; b. Mobile, Ala., Oct. 10, 1941; d. Julius Sr. and Nettie (Fraizer) Herzfeld; m. Charles C. Kimbrough, Nov. 28, 1964; children: Carolos R., Choron F. BS, U. Mo., 1970; MA, Wash. U., 1980; MAT, AGC, Webster U., 1982. Cert. tchr., Mo. Coord. children-adolescent svcs. Metro Comprehensive Mental Health Ctr., St. Louis; cons. C. Kimbrough and Assocs.; instr. minority mental health Wash. U., St. Louis; founder, exec. dir. Creative Inovative and Behavioral Experences, CIBE; mng. dir. CKAN Ltd., Nigeria; project coord. Children's Devel. Ctr., Lagos, Nigeria; intervention specialist, counselor Ferguson Florissant Schs.; adj. instr. St. Louis U.; developer Children's Treatment Program; established Metroties Day Treatment Sch., 1987. Knoxville Coll. acad. scholarship, 1961; NIMH fellow, 1979; recipient Outstanding Leadership award Woman's Collaboration Conf., 1985, Exceptional Tchr. award INROADS Pre-Coll. Inst., 1986, Devel. award MTS, Lagos, Nigeria. Mem. Nat. Black Child Devel. Inst. (pres. St. Louis affiliate, Outstanding Svc. award), St. Louis Assn. of Black Psychologists (membership chair), St. Louis Mental Health Assn. (children's svcs. coun., membership chair), Mo. Psychol. Assn. (St. Louis network for women psychologists sec.), Nigerian Field Soc. (membership chair), Internat. Platform Soc., 100 Black Women, Nigerian Federated Women, Am. Woman's Club. Home: 11752 Russet Meadow Dr Saint Louis MO 63146-4231

HERZOG, ANN ELIZABETH, marketing and advertising consultant; b. New Prague, Minn., Oct. 17, 1960; d. Alphonse William and Mary Theresa (O'Brien) H.; m. Lance Norman Olson, July 7, 1984; children: Wesley Herzog, Luke Tenney. BA in Journalism, U. Minn., 1984. Advt. mgr., asst. mgr. sales Minn. Daily, Mpls., 1981-84; acct. exec. Colle & McVoy, Mpls., 1984-89, Campbell Mithun Esty, Mpls., 1989-90; acct. supr. Case Foley Sackett, Mpls., 1990; mktg. mgr. MLT Inc., Minnetonka, Minn., 1990-93; owner, mgr. Herzog Mktg. Comms. Cons., Minnetonka, 1994—. Vol. Pauly for State House of Reps., Minn., 1983, 84, Ramstad for Congress, Mpls., 1990, 92, 94, 96; mem. steering com. Child Care Ctr., 1992-95, All Sts. Luth., Minnetonka, 1992, Church Coun., 1995—. Mem. Advt. Fedn. Minn. (Minn. chpt. bd. dirs. 1988-92, exec. bd. 1990-92, sec. 1990-92). Republican. Home and Office: 4217 Christy Ln Minnetonka MN 55345-3001

HESLEP, GRANT DANIEL, ophthalmologist; b. LaCrosse, Wis., Feb. 7, 1962; s. George Herbert and Eileen Jean (Tweten) H.; m. Lori Tyler, Oct. 22, 1988; children: Kristin, Daniel. BS with high honors, U. Fla., 1984, MD, 1987. Intern La. State U., Shreveport, 1988, resident, 1988-91, chief resident, 1991; chief ophthalmology Owatanna (Minn.) Clinic, 1991—; clin. instr. U. Minn., Mpls., 1992—; cons. VA Hosp., Mpls., 1992—; pres. Owatonna Hosp., 1996, v.p. med. staff, 1995. Wentworth scholar, U. Liberal Arts U. Fla., 1981, 82. Fellow Am. Acad. Ophthalmology; mem. AMA (del. 1984), Am. Soc. Cataract and Refractive Surgery, Minn. Med. Assn. (del. 1993-96), Minn. Ophthalmologic Soc. (sec. 1994, 96), Steele County Med. Soc. (pres. 1992—), Contact Lens Assn. Ophthalmologists, Lions, Phi Beta Kappa. Office: Owatonna Clinic 134 SOuthview Owatonna MN 55060

HESS, BARTLETT LEONARD, clergyman; b. Spokane, Wash., Dec. 27, 1910; s. John Leonard and Jessie (Bartlett) H.; BA, Park Coll., 1931, MA (fellow in history 1931-34), U. Kan., 1932, PhD, 1934; B.D., McCormick Theol. Sem., 1936; m. Margaret Young Johnston, July 31, 1937; children: Daniel Bartlett, Deborah Margaret, John Howard and Janet Elizabeth (twins). Ordained to ministry Presbyn. Ch., 1936; pastor Effingham, Kan., 1932-34, Chgo., 1935-42, Cicero, Ill., 1942-56, Ward Meml. Presbyn. Ch., Detroit, 1956-68, Ward Presbyn. Ch., Livonia, Mich., 1968-92, pastor emeritus, Presbyn. Ch., 1980-92; organizing pastor, pastor emeritus Knox Presbyn. Ch., Ann Arbor, 1992—, Ward Presbyn. Ch., 1992—; Tchr. ch. history, bible Detroit Bible Coll., 1956-60, bd. dirs., 1956—; minister radio sta. WHFC, Chgo., 1942-50, WMUZ-FM, Detroit, 1958-68, 78—, WOMC-FM, 1971-72, WBFG-FM, 1972-92, WWCN-AM, 1992—; missioner to Philippines, United Presbyn. Ch. U.S.A., 1961; mem. Joint Com. on Presbyn. Union, 1980; adviser Mich. Synod coun. United Presbyn. Ch.; mem. com. Billy Graham Crusade for S.E. Mich., 1976; mem. adminstrv. com. Evang. Presbyn. Ch., 1980-85; mem. joint com. missions Evang. Presbyn. Ch. and the Presbyn. Ch. of Brazil. Mem., organizer Friendship and Svc. Com. for Refugees, Chgo., 1940. Bd. dirs. Beacon Neighborhood House, Chgo., 1945-52, Presbyns. United for Bibl. Concerns, 1975-80; pres. bd. dirs. Peniel Community Center, Chicago, 1945-52. Named Pastor of Year, Mid-Am. Sunday Sch. Assn., 1974; recipient Svc. to Youth award Detroit Met. Youth for Christ, 1979, Father of Evangelical Presbyn. Ch. award, 1991. Mem. Cicero Mins. Coun. (pres. 1951), Phi Beta Kappa, Phi Delta Kappa. Author: (with Margaret Johnston Hess) How To Have a Giving Church, 1974; (with M.J. Hess) The Power of a Loving Church, 1977, How Does Your Marriage Grow, 1982, Never Say Old, 1984; contbr. articles in field to profl. jours. Traveled in Europe, 1939, 52, 55, 68; also in Greece, Turkey, Lebanon, Syria, Egypt, Israel, Iraq; condr. tour of Middle East and Mediterranean countries, 1965, 67, 73, 74, 76, 78, 80, 84, 90, China and Far East, 1982; missioner, India, 1981, 89, Brazil, 85, 86, 87, 89, 95, Argentina, 87, 89, 91, 95. Home: 16845 Riverside St Livonia MI 48154-2428 Office: 1514 Eisenhower Pl Ann Arbor MI 48108-3284

HESS, G(EORGE) ALFRED, JR., non-profit educational association administrator; b. Trenton, N.J., Jan. 26, 1938; s. G. Alfred and Frances Hess; m. Judith MacMelville, Aug. 24, 1963 (div. Jan. 1978); 1 child, Randall William; m. Mary Conway, July 16, 1984; 1 child, Sarah Katherine. BA, Coll. Wooster, 1959; STB, Boston U., 1962; PhD, Northwestern U., 1980. Asst. pastor Wilmington (Mass.) Meth. Ch., 1961-63; pastor William Butler United Meth. Ch., Shelburne Falls, Mass., 1963-66; adult edn. tchr. Inst. Cultural Affairs, Chgo., 1966-80; dir. field studies Northwestern U., Evanston, Ill., 1980-83; exec. dir. Chgo. (Ill.) Panel on Sch. Policy, 1983—; nat. adv. panel mem. Appalachia Edn. Lab., Charleston, W.Va., 1991—; cons. Mayor's Edn. Summit, Chgo., 1986-87. Author: School Restructuring Chicago Style, 1991, Restructuring Urban Schools: A Chicago Perspective, 1995; editor: Empowering Teachers and Parents, 1992. Recipient Ben Hubbard award Ill. State U., Normal, 1991. Fellow Am. Anthropology Assn.; mem. Am. Edn. Fin. Assn. (bd. dirs. 1991-94), Am. Edn. Rsch. Assn., Coalition for Ednl. Rights (pres. 1991-94), Coun. Anthropology Edn. (pres. 1996—). Office: Chgo Panel on Sch Policy 200 N Michigan Ave Rm 501 Chicago IL 60601-5909

HESS, JONATHAN ROBERT, architect; b. Highland Park, Ill., Jan. 3, 1956; m. Jody Hindsley; children: Catherine, Claudia. BS in Archtl. Studies, U. Ill., 1979, MArch, 1982. Designer Archtl. Spectrum, Champaign, Ill., 1979-82; asst. project architect James Assocs., Indpsl., 1982-84; project mgr. Browning Day Mullins Dierdorf Inc., Indpls., 1984-89, prin., 1989-91, exec. v.p., 1991—. Bd. trustees Eiteljorg Mus., Indpls., 1990-92. Mem. AIA (bd. dirs. Indpls. chpt. 1991-93). Methodist. Office: Browning Day Mullins et al 334 N Senate Ave Indianapolis IN 46204-1708

HESS, LEONARD WAYNE, obstetrician gynecologist, perinatologist; b. Richlands, Va., Nov. 23, 1949; s. Ralph Eugene and Lucille Cindy (Kennedy) H.; m. Sarah Mahala Leedy, Nov. 27, 1969 (div. July 1988); children: Gregory Scott, Lauren Ashley; m. Darla Irma Bakersmith, July 20, 1988; 1 child, Ever Marie. BSChemE, Va. Poly. Inst., 1973; MD, Va. Commonwealth U., 1977. Diplomate Nat. Bd. Med. Examiners, Am. Bd. Ob-Gyn., also sub.-bd. Maternal-Fetal Medicine. Intern U.S. Naval Hosp., Portsmouth, Va., 1977-78; resident in ob-gyn. U.S. Naval Hosp., Portsmouth, 1978-81; fellow in maternal-fetal medicine Naval Med. Command, Walter Reed Army Med. Ctr., Washington and Bethesda, 1981-83; staff dept. ob-gyn. U. Health Scis., Bethesda, 1981-85; dept. ob-gyn. U.S. Naval Hosp., Portsmouth, 1985-87; comdr. USNR, 1987-88; asst. prof. dept. ob-gyn. U. Miss. Med. Ctr., Jackson, 1987-91; assoc. prof. ob-gyn. U. Mo. Med. Ctr., Columbia, 1991-96, head obstetrics and maternal-fetal medicine, 1991-96, prof., chmn. ob-gyn., 1996—; mem. med. Ethics Com., U.S. Naval Hosp., Portsmouth, 1985-87; mem. Patient Care Com., U. Miss. Med. Ctr., Jackson, 1988-91, Infection Control Com., 1988-91. Cons. editor Obstetrics and Gynecology, 1988—, Am. Jour. Obstetrics and Gynecology, 1988—, Am. Jour. Med. Genetics, 1989—; contbr. numerous articles to profl. jours. Mem. AMA, USP (ob-gyn. adv. panel 1995—), Am. Coll. Obstetricians and Gynecologists, Soc. Perinatal Obstetricians, Am. Inst. Ultrasound in Medicine, Assn. Profs. Gynecology and Obstetrics, Cen. Assn. Obstetricians and Gynecologists, Am. Soc. Human Genetics, So. Med. Assn., Winifred L. Wiser Soc., Miss. State Obstet. and Gynecol. Soc., Cen. Med. Soc., Gynecic Soc., Med. Soc. Va., Portsmouth Acad. Medicine, Med. and Surgical Soc. of Md., Miss. State Med. Assn., Assn. Mil. Surgeons, Miss. Perinatal Assn., So. Perinatal Assn. Republican. Episcopalian. Office: U Mo Med Ctr HSC N617 Columbia MO 65212

HESS, MARGARET JOHNSTON, religious writer, educator; b. Ames, Iowa, Feb. 22, 1915; d. Howard Wright and Jane Edith (Stevenson) Johnston; B.A., Coe Coll., 1937; m. Bartlett Leonard Hess, July 31, 1937; children—Daniel, Deborah, John, Janet. Bible tchr. Cmty. Bible Classes Ward Presbyn. Ch., Livonia, Mich., 1959-96, Christ Ch. Cranbrook (Episcopalian), Bloomfield Hills, Mich., 1980-93, Lutheran Ch. of the Redeemer, Birmingham, Mich., 1993—. Co-author: (with B.L. Hess) How to Have a Giving Church, 1974, The Power of a Loving Church, 1977, How Does Your Marriage Grow?, 1983, Never Say Old, 1984; author: Love Knows No Barriers, 1979; Esther: Courage in Crisis, 1980; Unconventional Women, 1981, The Triumph of Love, 1987; contbr. articles to religious jours. Home: 16845 Riverside Dr Livonia MI 48154-2428

HESSE, BRUCE EDWARD, family therapist, social worker; b. Glenwood, Minn., Aug. 25, 1934; s. Lester Christian and Myrtle Evelyn (Wilson) H.; m. Jane Barbro Rotegard, Jan., 12, 1957; children: Greta Anne, Peter John, Joseph Bruce, Michael Richard. BA, St. Olaf Coll., 1956; BTh (now MDiv), Luther Theol. Sem., 1960; MSW, U. Mich., 1977. Lic. ind. clin. social worker, Minn. Pastor Lutheran chs., Minn., Ill. and Mich., 1960-74; planner Operation Hope: Cmty. Mental Health, Detroit, 1974-77; adminstr. S.D. Dept. Social Svcs., Pierre, 1977-81; dir. adolescent svcs. The Chanhassen (Minn.) Ctr., 1981-84; unit dir. Anoka (Minn.)-Metro Regional Tng. Ctr., 1984-93; pvt. practice family therapy PsychCare, Mpls., 1993—; bd. dirs. Tri County Mental Health Ctr., Grand Rapids, Minn., 1960-63, Family Svcs. Agy, Joliet, Ill., 1963-68; cons. Lutheran Ch. Am., Harrisburg, Pa., 1983. Treas. The Satyr, 1967-68; mem. youth com. NAACP, Joliet, 1964-66, bd. dirs., 1966-68. Recipient Sol. Tribute, Mich. Legislature, 1975, Operation Hope, 1978. Mem. NASW (Minn. chpt.). Office: PsychCare 1516 W Lake St Ste 226 Minneapolis MN 55408-2554

HESSE, DAVID A., electrical engineer; b. Hamilton, Ohio, May 5, 1949. A in Elec. Engring., Cin. Tech. Coll., 1988. Technician, elec. engr. Hamilton (Ohio) Tool, 1989-90; elec. design engr. Valco Cin., Cin., 1990—; pres. Investco, Fairfield, Ohio, 1989-90, Hesse Investors, Cin., 1995. Republican. Office: Valco Cincinnati 411 Circle Fwy Dr Cincinnati OH 45246-1213

HESSELBERG, GERRI SUE (GITEL SARAH), sales executive; b. Chgo., Mar. 27, 1959; d. Sam and Goldye (Seff) H. AA with honors, Oakton Cmty. Coll., Des Plaines, Ill., 1994. Adminstr. Yeshiva Migdal Torah, Chgo., 1988-91, 94; sr. cons. Discovery Toys, Des Plaines, 1994—; assoc. mgr. Mem. Mensa, Phi Theta Kappa.

HESSELINK, I(RA) JOHN, JR., theology educator; b. Grand Rapids, Mich., Mar. 21, 1928; s. Ira John Sr. and Anna (Mulder) H.; m. Etta Marie Ter Louw, Aug. 29, 1951; children: John III, Ann, Judson, Nathan, Gregory. BA, Ctrl. Coll., Pella, Iowa, 1950; DD (hon.), Ctrl. Coll., 1981; MDiv, Western Sem., 1953; ThD, Basel (Switzerland) U., 1961; LHD (hon.), Hope Coll., 1973. Ordained to ministry Reformed Ch. in Am., 1953. Missionary United Ch. Christ, Fukuoka, Japan, 1953-58; prof. hist. theology Tokyo Union Theol. Sem., 1961-73; pres. Western Theol. Sem., Holland, Mich., 1973-85, A. Van Raalte prof. systematic theology, 1986—; adj. prof. theology Meiji Gakuin U., Tokyo, 1962-66, Calvin Theol. Sem., Grand Rapids, Mich., 1988-89, Fuller Theol. Sem., 1987—; v.p. Gen. Synod, Ref. Ch. in Am., 1994, pres., 1995-96; editl. cons. Center Jour., 1981—, Standige Mitarbeiter, Zeitschrift fuer Dialektische Theologie, 1985-95; vis. scholar Free U., Amsterdam, 1985, Oxford (Eng.) U., 1993. Author: On Being Reformed, 1983, rev. edit., 1988 (Japanese edit. 1995, Korean edit. 1996), Christ's Peace, 1987, Calvin's Concept of the Law, 1992; editor Japan Christian Quar., 1955-58; co-translator: Theology of the Pain of God (Kitamori), 1965. Named (with wife) Ctrl. Coll. Alumni Couple of Yr., 1975; postdoctoral scholar U. Chgo. Div. Sch., 1971-72. Mem. Sixteenth Century Studies Soc., Am. Soc. Reformation Rsch., Karl Barth Soc. N.Am. (v.p. 1976-78, acting pres. 1978-92), John Calvin Studies Soc. (exec. com. 1975-77, v.p. 1989-90, pres. 1991), Mich. Acad. Theologians, Am. Theol. Soc., Century Club (v.p. 1988-89, pres. 1989-90), Gen. Synod Reformed Ch. Am. (v.p. 1994-95, pres. 1995-96, bd. Nat. Coun. Christian Chs. 1995—). Home: 98 W 12th St Holland MI 49423-3213 Office: Western Theol Sem 101 E 13th St Holland MI 49423

HESSLER, SCOTT ASHER, retail executive; b. Phila., July 9, 1948; s. Silas Avram and Adele (Asher) H.; m. Sandra Fay Siegel, May 20, 1971 (dec. Dec. 1975); m. Sheryl L. Berkoff, July 16, 1978; children: David, Rebecca. BS, Boston U., 1970; MBA, Harvard U., 1974. Buyer John Wanamaker's, Phila., 1970-72; group v.p. Macy's, N.Y.C., 1974-82; sr. v.p., gen. mdse. mgr. May D&F, Denver, 1982-86, May Dept.-Kaufmann's, Pitts., 1982-86; sr. v.p., gen. mdse. mgr. Broadway Stores, L.A., 1986-89, exec. v.p. merchandising and planning, 1989-90, sr. v.p., gen. mdse. mgr., 1990-92; sr. v.p. merchandising/mktg. Wherehouse Entertainment, Inc., Torrance, Calif., 1992-94; pres. Frank's Nursery & Crafts, Inc., Detroit, 1994—. Republican. Office: Frank's Nursery & Crafts 6501 E Nevada Detroit MI 48234

HESSLER, WILLIAM GERHARD, tax consultant; b. Chgo., May 20, 1926; s. William Gerhard and Rosemary (Kalb) H.; m. Kazuko Yonetsu, June 2, 1956 (dec. Mar. 1, 1995); children: Martha, George, Kay, Emmy. BSEE, Purdue U., 1946; MBA, Northwestern U., 1956. Cert. data processor; cert. individual tax profl. Tech. intelligence investigator U.S. Army, Tokyo, 1947-50; electronics engr. signal corps. U.S. Army, Yokohama, Japan, 1952-54; mfg., devel. engr. Western Electric, Chgo., 1955-61; engring. specialist Goodyear Aerospace Corp., Akron, Ohio, 1961-65; computer applications programmer analyst Goodyear Tire & Rubber Co., Akron, 1965-83, computer operating systems programmer, 1983-87; cons. Cutler-Williams, Independence, Ohio, 1987; systems engineer Profl. Support, Inc., Brecksville, Ohio, 1989; tax cons. and return preparer H & R Block, Greater Akron, 1969-80, Akron Nat. Tax & Notary, 1981, Hammer Tax Svc., Akron, 1982—; cons. in field, 1982—; agt. enrolled to practice before the U.S. Dept. Treasury IRS, 1984—. Scoutmaster Boy Scouts Am., Silver Lake, Ohio, 1972-77. With U.S. Army, 1950-52, Japan. Mem. Nat. Soc. Tax Profls., Nat. Assn. Tax Practitioners. Roman Catholic. Home: 3046 Lake Rd Cuyahoga Falls OH 44224-3814

HESSLUND, BRADLEY HARRY, program manager; b. Mpls., June 27, 1958; s. Harry A. and Dorothy (Tishi) H.; m. Diane M. Mahoney, June 13, 1992. AA, Normandale Community Coll., 1978; BS, U. Wis., Menomonie, 1981; MBA, U. Pitts., 1984. Cert. sr. indsl. technologist. Indsl. engr. Thermo King Corp. subs. Westinghouse Electric Corp., Bloomington, Minn., 1981-82; project engr. Westinghouse Electric Corp., Beaver, Pa., 1983; cost engr. IBM Corp., East Fishkill, N.Y., 1984-85; mfg. engring. supr. Hoffman Engring. Co. subs. Pentair Inc., Anoka, Minn., 1985-88; sr. cost analyst Naval Systems div. FMC Corp., Fridley, Minn., 1988-90; project mgr. Deltak Corp., Plymouth, Minn., 1990-94; mgr. project engring. Despatch Industries, Mpls., 1994—. Republican. Lutheran. Home: 3220 Pineview Ln

N Plymouth MN 55441-2864 Office: Despatch Industries PO Box 1320 Minneapolis MN 55440-1320

HESTAD, BJORN MARK, metal distributing company executive; b. Evanston, Ill., May 31, 1926; s. Hilmar and Anna (Aagaard) H.; m. Florence Anne Ragusi, May 1, 1948; children: Marsha Anne, Patricia Lynn Krueger, Peter Mark. Student Ill. Inst. Tech., 1947. Sales corr., Shakeproof, Inc., Chgo., 1947-50; indsl. buyer Crescent Industries, Inc., Chgo., 1950-51; purchasing agt. Switchcraft, Inc., Chgo., 1951-73, materials mgr., 1973-74, dir. purchasing, 1974-77; pres. Tool King, Inc., Wheeling, Ill., 1977-95, CEO, chmn. bd. dirs., 1995—; pres. H & H Enterprises of Northfield. Mgr. youth orgns. Northfield Jr. Hockey Club, 1968-71, Winnfield Hockey Club, 1972-73; bus. mgr. West Hockey Club, 1973-74. Served as cpl. USAAF, 1944-46. Mem. Tooling and Mfg. Assn., Steel Svc. Ctr. Inst., Sons of Norway, Waukegan Yacht Club, Lions. Republican. Mem. United Ch. Christ. Home: 850 Happ Rd Northfield IL 60093-1005 Office: Tool King Inc 275 Larkin Dr Wheeling IL 60090-6457

HESTAD, MARSHA ANNE, educational administrator; b. Evanston, Ill., Apr. 25, 1950; d. Bjorn Mark and Florence Anne (Ragusi) H. BS, U. Ill., 1972; MEd, Nat. Coll. Edn., Evanston, Ill., 1978; postgrad., Purdue U., 1985; PhD, Loyola U., Chgo., 1991. Cert. in elem. edn., spl. reading, gifted edn., gen. adminstrn., Ill., Ind. Tchr. 5th grade Deerfield (Ill.) Sch. Dist. 109, 1972-78; head tchr. North Aegean Acad., Kavala, Greece, 1978-81; gifted resource tchr. Alief Ind. Sch. Dist., Houston, 1983-84, TeKoppel, Evansville, Ind., 1984-85; field supr. Purdue U., West Lafayette, Ind., 1987; gifted coord. MSD Mt. Vernon, Ind., 1985-88; gifted resource Libertyville (Ill.) Sch. Dist. 70, 1988-91; instr. Coll. Lake County, Grayslake, Ill., 1991; clin. prof. Loyola U., Chgo., 1991; prof. Ind. State U., Terre Haute, 1992-93; tchr. lang. arts/lit. 7th grade, co-dir./prin. summer sch. Libertyville (Ill.) Sch. Dist. 70, 1993-94; prin. Chippewa Sch., Bensenville (Ill.) Dist. 2, 1994-96, Rockland Sch., Libertyville Ill., 1996—; bd. dirs. Odyssey of the Mind, Ind. and Ill.; cons. in field. Exec. co-producer Countdown interactive cable program, 1995-96; contbr. articles to profl. jours. Mem. ASCD, Am. Ednl. Rsch. Assn., Nat. Coun. Staff Devel., Midwest Ednl. Rsch. Assn., Phi Delta Kappa. Home: 850 Happ Rd Northfield IL 60093-1005

HESTER, STEVEN S., mechanical engineer; b. Hamilton, Ohio, July 29, 1962. BS in Mech. Engring., Miami U., Oxford, Ohio, 1984. Design engr. The Hamilton Tool Co., 1980—; pres. Credit Union, Hamilton Tool Co. Office: Hamilton Tool Co Walnut at 9th St Hamilton OH 45011

HETH, DIANA SUE, therapist; b. Robinson, Ill., Sept. 25, 1948; d. Quentin Wilson and Marguerite (Byrd) Abraham; m. Kenneth Lewis Greider, Aug. 16, 1970 (div. Mar. 1985); children: Kathryn Elizabeth, Susan Nicole, Jonathan Abraham; m. Harold Eugene Heth; children: Joseph Brockwell, Kiley Joy, Mark Quentin. BSE, Eastern Ill. U., 1970; MSW, U. Ill., 1992. Lic. clin. social worker. Exec. dir. Nat. Assn. Downs Syndrome, Chgo., 1976-77, Heartland Hospice, Effingham, Ill., 1983-88; office adminstr. Am. Family Life Assurance, Effingham, Ill., 1988-90; sec. design engring. dept. Fedders N.Am., Effingham, Ill., 1990; co-owner H&S Vending, 1990—; therapist sexual abuse Heartland Human Svcs., Effingham, Ill., 1992-94; child welfare specialist II Ill. Dept. of Children and Family Svcs., Olney, 1994—; mem. Profl. Adv. Com. for Hospice Lincolnland. Author: One Gift to the Next, 1983, Sundance Lady, 1990. Vol. Belleville (Ill.) Hospice, 1981-83; co-chmn. svc. and rehab. com. Am. Cancer Soc.; mem. parent adv. bd. Ill. State U., 1996—. Mem. NASW, Ill. State Hospice Orgn. (bd. dirs. 1985-86), Ill. Pub. Health Assn., County Orgn. SVc. Providers, Newcomers Club (pres. 1984-85), Compassionate Friends Club (bd. dirs. 1985-86), Topnotcher's 4-H Club (leader), Ill. State U. Parents Assn. (mem. adv. bd. 1996—). Republican. Methodist. Home: RR 1 Box 63 Shumway IL 62461-9722 Office: Olney Field Office Ill Dept Child/Family Svcs 1102A S West St Olney IL 62450-1321

HETLAGE, ROBERT OWEN, lawyer; b. St. Louis, Jan. 9, 1931; s. George C. and Doris M. (Talbot) H.; m. Anne R. Willis, Sept. 24, 1960; children: Mary T., James C., Thomas K. AB, Washington U., St. Louis, 1952, LLB, 1954; LLM, George Washington U., 1957. Bar: Mo. 1954, U.S. Dist. Ct. (ea. dist.) Mo. 1954, U.S. Supreme Ct. 1957. Ptnr., Hetlage & Hetlage, 1958-65, Peper, Martin, Jensen, Maichel & Hetlage, St. Louis, 1966—, chmn., 1994—. Served to 1st lt. U.S. Army, 1954-58. Fellow Am. Bar Found. (life); mem. Bar Assn. Met. St. Louis (pres. 1967-68), Mo. Bar (pres. 1976-77), ABA (chmn. real property, probate and trust law sect. 1981-82), Am. Coll. Real Estate Lawyers (pres. 1985-86), Am. Bar Found. Am. Judicature Soc., Anglo-Am. Real Property Inst. (chmn. 1991). Office: Peper Martin Jensen & Hetlage 720 Olive St Saint Louis MO 63101-2338

HETRICK, GREG ANDREW, sales executive; b. Hammond, Ind., Aug. 22, 1960; s. Everett Newton and Betty Ann (Terzarial) H.; m. Christine A. Churilla, Oct. 30, 1993. BA in Pub. Rels. and Comm., Purdue U., Hammond, Ind., 1987. Salesman Torco Oil Co., Chgo., 1987-88; dist. sales mgr. U-Haul Internat., Schererville, Ind., 1988—. Mem. N.W. Ind. Bd. Realtors, Am. Tae Kwon Do Assn. (black belt). Office: U-Haul Internat 1861 US Rt 41 Schererville IN 46375

HETSKO, CYRIL MICHAEL, physician; b. Montclair, N.J., May 25, 1942; s. Cyril Francis and Josephine (Stein) H.; m. Theresa Hottenroth, Jan. 2, 1988; 1 child, Michael Dimitri; B.A., Amherst Coll., 1964; M.D., U. Rochester, 1968. Intern, U. Wis. Hosps., Madison, 1968-69, resident in internal medicine, 1969-72, clin. assoc. prof. medicine U. Wis., 1975-95, prof. 1995—; practice internal medicine, infectious diseases Dean Med. Ctr., Madison, 1975—, dir. Dean Care HMO, Inc., 1983-94; chmn. dept. medicine St. Mary's Hosp. Med. Ctr., Madison, 1985-87; dir. Physicians Ins. Co. Wis., Madison, 1990-93; trustee Internal Medicine Ctr. To Advance Rsch. and Edn., Washington, 1991—; mem. White House Health Profls. Outreach Group, Washington, 1993-94; dir. Nat. Commn. Office Lab. Accreditation, 1994—; pres. N. Ctrl. Med. Conf., 1995-96. Trustee Internat. Childrens Alliance, Washington, 1995—. Mem. Editorial Adv. Bd. Internal Medicine News, 1993—. Served to maj. M.C., AUS, 1972-75. Diplomate Nat. Bd. Med. Examiners, Am. Bd. Internal Medicine. Mem. AMA (alt. del. 1983-93, del. 1994—, mem. nat. coun. on med. svc. 1995—), Am. Soc. Internal Medicine (del. 1987-91, trustee 1991—), Am. Soc. Microbiology, Assn. Mil. Surgeons U.S., State Med. Soc. Wis. (Councillor 1979-81, dir. 1981-88, vice speaker Ho. of Dels. 1988-90, chmn. task force on AIDS 1987—, pres. 1991-92, Meritorious Svc. award 1988), Dane County Med. Soc. (chmn. com. on prepaid health plans 1977-82, trustee 1993—, Pres.'s award 1981), Wis. Soc. Internal Medicine (councillor 1981-87, pres. 1987-88, Outstanding Wis. Internist 1990), Orgn. State Med. Assn. Presidents, N.Y. Acad. Scis., New Eng. Soc. in City N.Y., Nat. Found. for Infectious Disease, Madison Acad. Medicine. Club: Madison. Home: 1114 Sherman Ave Madison WI 53703-1620 Office: Dean Med Ctr 1313 Fish Hatchery Rd Madison WI 53715-1911

HETTICH, PAUL JOSEPH, theatre designer, military officer; b. Fort Jackson, S.C., June 16, 1965; s. Paul Ignatius and Mary Ann (Kloida) H. BA, Barat Coll., 1987; MA, No. Ill. U., 1992; cert. mktg., Coll. Lake County, Grayslake, Ill., 1992. Grad. asst. No. Ill. U., Dekalb, 1989-92; set designer Ctr. State Prodns., Antioch, 1988-92; asst. tech. dir. Coll. of Lake County, Grayslake, Ill., 1989-89; tech. dir. Absolute Theatre Co., Chgo., 1988-90, Lake Forest (Ill.) Symphony, 1985-93, The Genessee Theatre, Waukegan, Ill., 1987-90; cons. Chgo. Theatre's, 1987-92; owner Frisco Boarding Kennels. Ranger police, Lake County Forest Preserve, Libertyville, Ill., 1988—; mem. 1982—, Boy Scouts Am., 1980. Capt. USAR, 1987—. Mem. USMG Assn. Republican. Roman Catholic. Home and Office: Ctr Stage Prodns 4000 State Rt 173 Zion IL 60099-5107

HETTRICK, RICHARD HARRY, community organizer; b. Evansville, Pa., Nov. 17, 1930; s. Harry Willard and Carolyn Naomi (Pehlert) H.; m. Patricia Ann Ross, June 16, 1951; children: Richard Ross, Dirk Harry, Scott Randall, Brett Arnold. AA, Graceland Jr. Coll., 1951; BS, Temple U., 1958, postgrad., 1958-64; postgrad., St. Paul's Sch. Theology, Kansas City, Mo., 1974-76. Dist. exec. Phila. Boy Scouts, 1954-59; field dir. Boy Scouts Am., Phila., 1959-64; dist. pres. Reorganized Ch., Nauvoo, Ill., 1964-67; asst. stake pres. Jesus Christ of Latter Day Sts., Independence, Mo., 1967-76; exec. coord. The Independence Plan for Neighborhood Couns., 1976-96. Columnist (newspaper) What Do I Say When I Feel Like This,?, 1976-81 (MNPA award 1989); editor (mag.) Neighbor's Mag., 1970-81. Office: Independence Plan Neigh Cns 201 W Maple Independence MO 64050

HETZLER, SUSAN ELIZABETH SAVAGE, educational administrator; b. Monticello, Iowa, Mar. 18, 1947; d. Robert Engelbert and Josephine May (Ricklefs) Savage; children: Stephanine, Michael. BS in Edn., Rockford (Ill.) Coll., 1971; 2MS in Edn., No. Ill. U., 1978, cert. advanced study, 1984; PhD, Walden U., Mpls., 1989. Cert. elem. tchr., adminstr., Ill., Iowa; supr., sociology tchr., Ill. Elem. tchr. Freeport (Ill.) Sch. Dist., 1971-86; prof. elem. edn. Iowa State U., Ames, 1986-90; dir. tchr. edn. and devel. Iowa Dept. Edn., Des Moines, 1990—; curriculum cons. Ames Sch. Dist., 1985-90, Des Moines Sch. Dist., 1985-90; mem. ISU adv. bd., Ames, 1991—. Author: Elementary Education Practicum Teaching, 1988, Learning Centers, 1989. Comsnr. Drug and Alcohol Prevention Project, Freeport, 1976-85; chairperson Stephenson County (Ill.) Cancer Soc., 1976-78, small bus. dvsn. United Way, Freeport, 1980-85; vol. BSA and GSA, Freeport, 1974-85. Recipient Excellence in Teaching award Iowa State U., 1989-90, Outstanding Elem. Tchrs. Am. Ill., 1974, 81. Mem. AAUP, ASCD, NEA, Iowa ASCD, Am. Assn. Colls. of Tchr. Edn., Iowa Assn. Colls. of Tchr. Edn., Iowa Ednl. Rsch. and Eval. Assn., Assn. Tchr. Educators, Delta Kappa Gamma, Phi Delta Kappa. Protestant. Home: 713 NE Brook Haven Dr Ankeny IA 50021-4528 Office: Iowa Dept Edn Grimes State Office Bldg Des Moines IA 50319-0146

HEUER, ARTHUR HAROLD, material science and engineering educator; b. N.Y.C., Apr. 29, 1936; s. William Jacob and Hannah (Kaye) H.; m. Roberta Feinstein, Dec. 22, 1956 (div. 1974); children: Howard, Michael, James; m. Joan McKnee Hulburt, May 8, 1976. BS, CCNY, 1956; PhD, U. Leeds, Eng., 1965, DSc, 1977. Rsch. chemist Ind. Gen. Corp., Keasbey, N.J., 1956-60; rsch. engr. Electron Tube Div. Bendix Co., Eatontown, N.J., 1960-61; staff scientist AVCO Space Systems Div., Lowell, Mass., 1965-67; asst. prof. ceramics div. metall. and materials Case Western Res. U., Cleve., 1967-70, assoc. prof., 1970-74, prof., 1974—, dir. materials rsch. lab. Case Inst. Tech., 1974-80, Kyocera Prof. Ceramics, 1985—; external sci. mem. Max-Planck Inst. fur Metallforschung, Germany, 1990—. Editor: Zirconia I, Zirconia II; contbr. over 340 articles to profl. jours. Recipient Alexander von Humboldt award Max-Planck Inst., 1983, Gold Medal award ASM. Fellow Am. Ceramic Soc. (chmn. basic sci. com., Sosman Meml. lectr. 1986, editor jour. 1988-90, John Jeppson award 1990, Orton lectr. 1991, Disting. Life mem. 1996), U.K. Inst. Physics; mem. AAAS, NAE, ASM (Gold medal). Home: 13705 Shaker Blvd Cleveland OH 44120-5604 Office: Case Western Res U Materials Sci and Engring 10900 Euclid Ave Cleveland OH 44106-7204

HEUER, GERALD ARTHUR, mathematician, educator; b. Bertha, Minn., Aug. 31, 1930; s. William C.F. and Selma C. (Rosenberg) H.; m. Jeanette Mary Knedel, Sept. 5, 1954; children—Paul, Karl, Ruth, Otto. BA, Concordia Coll., 1951; MA, U. Nebr., 1953; PhD, U. Minn., 1958. Math. instr. Hamline U., 1955-56; math. instr. Concordia Coll., 1956-57, asst. prof., 1957-58, assoc. prof., 1958-62, prof., 1962—, Sigurd and Pauline Prestegaard Mundhjeld prof., 1988-95, chmn. dept., 1963-70, research prof., 1970-71; mathematician Remington Rand Univac, summer 1958; vis. prof. U. Nebr., 1960-61; mathematician Control Data Corp., summers 1960-62, cons., 1960-63; vis. lectr. Math. Assn. Am., 1964-66; cons. NSF-AID, India, 1968-69; guest speaker Minn. sect. Math. Assn. Am., 1956, Neb. sect., 1961, No. Central sect., 1974; vis. prof. dept. pure and applied math. Wash. State U., Pullman, 1980-81; vis. prof./scholar Math. Inst., Cologne (Germany) U., 1973-74, Inst. Stats., Econs. and Ops. Research, Graz U., Austria, 1987-88, rsch. prof. fall semester 1990; dir. U.S. Math. Olympiad Tng. Session, leader U.S. team Internat. Math. Olympiad, 1988-90; vis. prof. Graz U., Austria, 1994; invited plenary spkr. Internat. Symposium Ops. Rsch., Passau, Germany, 1995. Co-author: (With Ulrike Leopold-Wildburger) Balanced Silverman Games on General Discrete Sets, 1991, Silverman's Game, 1995; reviewer Zentralblatt für Mathematik, Berlin, 1967—, Math. Revs., Ann Arbor, Mich., 1978—; contbr. articles to profl. jours. NSF Faculty fellow, 1966-67; NSF rsch. grantee, 1963, 64, 66; Bush Rsch. scholar Concordia Coll., 1983-84, Centennial Rsch. scholar, 1992, 93, 94, 95. Mem. Math. Assn. Am. (com. on Am. math. competitions 1988—, nat. bd. govs. 1971-73, com. on Putnam prize 1987-90, pres. Minn. sect. 1959-60, cert. meritorious svc. 1994), Am. Math. Soc., Nat. Geographic Soc., Ops. Rsch. Soc. Am., Deutsche Math.-Vereinigung E.V. (Berlin), Österreichische Math. Gesellschaft (Vienna), Sigma Xi. Lutheran. Home: 1216 Elm St S Moorhead MN 56560-4049 Office: Concordia Coll Dept Math Moorhead MN 56562

HEUER, MARVIN ARTHUR, research and industry consultant; b. Mankato, Minn., Mar. 11, 1947; s. Marvin Ernst and Elaine Olive (Melahn) H.; children: David Walter, Michael Arthur. BA, Mankato State U., 1969; BS, U. Minn., Mpls., 1973, MD, 1973. Intership, resident family practice St. John's Hosp., St. Paul, 1973-80; ptnr. Family Med. Group practice Park Rapids (Minn.)/Walker Clin. LTD, 1980-81; assoc. med. dir. Smith Kline & French Corp., Phila., 1981-82, group dir. clin. rsch., 1982-84, acting v.p. worldwide ops., 1984-87; v.p. med. affairs, v.p. clin. rsch. worldwide Am. Home Products, N.Y.C., 1987-89; v.p. R&D Wallace Labs., Cranbury, N.J., 1989-92; v.p., dir. clin. rsch. Worldwide Smithkline Beecham Corp., London, 1992—; CEO Heuer Assocs., North Oaks, Minn., 1992—; physician Westview Clinic, West Saint Paul, Minn., 1991—; dir. clin. rsch. Allina Corp., Mpls., 1993; clin. asst. prof. Robert Wood Johnson Med. Sch., Dept. of Family Medicine, New Brunswick, N.J., 1981-91; clin. assoc. prof. U. Minn. Med. Sch., Dept. of Family Practice, 1992—; mem. biotech. adv. bd. Mankato State U.; mem. drug utilization rev. panel Dept. Health, Minn., 1992—. Contbr. 12 articles on drugs to profl. jours., tng. manual, Med. Monitors Guide 1983. Dir. youth activities St. Matthews Luth. Ch., Moorestown, N.J., 1981-86, trustee 1983-92, coun. mem., 1984-87, alt. bd. mem. 1986; fin. com. Incarnation Luth. Ch., St. Paul, Minn., 1991—, property com., 1991—. Fellow Am. Bd. Family Practice; mem. AMA, ACP, Am. Assoc. Physician Execs., Am. Acad. Family Physicians, Minn. Med. Soc., Pharm. Mfrs. Assn., Minn. Acad. Family Practice, Am. Coll. Cardiology, Am. Rheumatol. Assn., Med. Alley Assn., Nat. Geog. Soc., Drug Info. Assn., Soc. Clin. Trials. Republican. Home: 855 Village Ctr Dr Ste 170 North Oaks MN 55127-6512 Office: Westview Clinic 156 Emerson Ave W Saint Paul MN 55118-2125

HEUPEL, CAROL COLLINS, community health and womens health nurse educator; b. Wilmington, Del., Apr. 10, 1935; d. Herbert Deakyne and Marian Elizabeth (Vance) Collins; m. Hermann Wilhelm Heupel, June 4, 1955; children: Ursula, Renata, Douglas, Emily, Michele. BSN, U. Minn., 1976, MPH, 1978, PhD, 1986. RN, Minn.; cert. pub. health nurse; cert. obgyn. nurse practitioner. Instr. obstetrics nursing Deaconess Sch. Nursing, 1978-80; asst. prof. med.-surg. nursing Mankato (Minn.) State U., 1980-86, assoc. prof. cmty. health nursing, 1986—; staff nurse in emergency dept. Fairview Southdale Hosp., 1971-72, in obstetrics, 1979-80. Contbr. articles to profl. jours.; presenter in field. Vol. Teenage Med. Ctr., 1977-78, Bloodmobile, ARC, 1986-91; mem. Ch. Coun., 1994—. Mem. AWHONN, Nat. Assn. Nurse Practitioners in Reproductive Health, Minn. Nurses Assn. (del. state conv. 1980, 88, 89), Minn. Politically Involved Nurses (vice chmn. bd. dirs. 1988-90), Midwest Nursing Rsch. Soc., Sigma Theta Tau (v.p. Mu Lambda chpt. 1990-91). Lutheran. Home: 516 9th St NE Waseca MN 56093-3623 Office: Mankato State U Sch Nursing PO Box 8400 Mankato MN 56002-8400

HEWAK, BENJAMIN, chief justice; b. Winnipeg, Man., Can., Nov. 12, 1935; s. Michael and Stephania (Kokowska) H.; children: Deborah, Donna, Darcia. BA, U. Man., 1956, LLB, 1960. Crown atty. Govt. of Man., Winnipeg, 1960-65; ptnr. Pollock, Nurgitz, Bromley, Myers and Hewak, Winnipeg, 1965-71; judge County Ct. Winnipeg, 1971-77; judge Ct. of Queen's Bench of Man., Winnipeg, 1977-85, chief justice, 1985—. Mem. Can. Bar Assn., Can. Judges Conf., Can. Jud. Council, Can. Inst. Adminstrn. Justice. Ukrainian Catholic. Home: 67 Musgrove St, Winnipeg, MB Canada R3R 2J2 Office: Ct of Queen's Bench, Upper Level Law Cts Complex, Broadway and Kennedy, Winnipeg, MB Canada R3C 0V8

HEWES, ROBERT CHARLES, radiologist; b. Balt., Feb. 14, 1953; s. Gordon Cecil and Gladys Dorothy (Barringham) H.; m. Judith Renee Lacy, Mar. 23, 1975; children: Christy, Amy, Jeremy. Student, Columbia Union Coll., 1973, Kettering Coll. of Med. Arts, 1971; BS, Loma Linda U., 1976, MD. Diplomate Am. Bd. Med. Examiners, Am. Bd. Radiology. Resident in radiology Loma Linda (Calif.) U., 1978-81, asst. prof. radiology, 1983-84; fellow in orthopedic radiology Hosp. for Spl. Surgery Cornell U. Med. Ctr., N.Y.C., 1981-82; fellow in interventional radiology Johns Hopkins U. Hosp., Balt., 1982-83; assoc. prof. Wright State U.; mem. staff Kettering (Ohio) Med. Ctr., vice chmn. dept. radiology, 1985-87, chmn., 1988-95; pres. Kettering Radiologists, Inc., 1987-95, med. dir., 1996—; pres. Patient First Imaging Network, 1994-95; bd. dirs. Spring Valley Acad. Contbr. articles on radiology to profl. jours. Recipient Cert. of merit Am. Roentgen Ray Soc., 1983, Disting. Alumnus award Kettering Coll. of Med. Arts, 1990. Mem. AMA, Radiol. Soc. N.Am., Soc. Cardiovascular and Interventional Radiology, Miami Valley Radiol. Soc. (pres. 1994), Alpha Omega Alpha (award). Republican. Adventist. Office: Kettering Med Ctr Dept Radiology 3535 Southern Blvd Dayton OH 45429-1221

HEWITT, JAMES WATT, lawyer; b. Hastings, Nebr., Dec. 25, 1932; s. Roscoe Stanley and Willa Manners (Watt) H.; student Hastings Coll., 1950-52; BS, U. Nebr., 1954, JD, 1956, MA 1994; m. Marjorie Ruth Barrett, Aug. 8, 1954; children: Mary Janet, William Edward, John Charles, Martha Ann. Bar: Nebr. 1956. Practice, Hastings, 1956-57, Lincoln, Nebr., 1960—; v.p., gen. counsel Nebco, Inc., Lincoln, 1961—; vis. lectr. U. Nebr. Coll. Law, 1970-71; community dir. Norwest Bank, Lincoln. Mem. state exec. com. Rep. Party, 1967-70, mem. state central com., 1967-70, legis. chmn., 1968-70. Bd. dirs. Lincoln Child Guidance Center, 1969-72, pres., 1972; bd. dirs. Lincoln Community Playhouse, 1967-73, pres., 1972-73; trustee Bryan Meml. Hosp., Lincoln, 1968-74, 76-82, chmn., 1972-74; bd. dirs. Lincoln Libr., 1990—; trustee U. Nebr. Found., 1979—; dir. Bryan Meml. Hosp. Found., Lincoln, 1994—; exec. v.p., dir. Nebr. State Hist. Soc. Found., Lincoln, 1994—; dir. Nebr. State Chpt. The Nature Conservancy, 1993—. Served to capt. USAF, 1957-60. Fellow Am. Bar Found. (Nebr. state chmn. 1988-92, chmn. 1994-95)); mem. ABA (Nebr. state del. 1972-80, bd. govs. 1981-83), Nebr. State Bar (chmn. ins. com. 1972-76, chmn. pub. rels. com. 1982-84, pres. 1985-86), Fed., Lincoln bar assns., Newcomen Soc. (Nebr. chair 1995—), Am., Nebr., Lincoln rose socs., Round Table, Beta Theta Pi, Phi Delta Phi. Congregationalist. Clubs: Nebr., Country of Lincoln (Lincoln). Home: 2990 Sheridan Blvd Lincoln NE 68502-4241 Office: PO Box 80268 1815 Y St Lincoln NE 68501

HEWITT, THOMAS EDWARD, financial executive; b. West Lafayette, Ind., Sept. 7, 1939; s. Ernest Edward and Katherine (Thelen) H.; BA, Dartmouth Coll., 1961, MBA, 1962; CPA, Ill.; m. Jeraldine Lee Spurgeon, June 16, 1962; children: Debora Lynn, Laura Jean, Gregory Spurgeon. Staff acct. Ernst & Young, Chgo., 1966-67, acct. in charge, 1967, sr. acct., 1967-69; contr. Thorne United Inc., Addison, Ill., 1969-70, sec.-treas., 1970; supr. Ernst & Young, Chgo., 1971-76; contr. Waterloo (Iowa) Industries, Inc., 1976-79, v.p. fin., 1979-90, exec. v.p., 1991-92; v.p., CFO, sec. and treas. Cupples Co. Mfrs., St. Louis, 1993—, bd. dirs., 1993—. Treas., Salvation Army, Waterloo, 1977-78, 80-82, Cedar Valley United Way, 1983-87, Covenant Med. Ctr., 1986-91, St. Francis Hosp., 1986-89, vice chmn. Covenant Med. Ctr., 1992, chmn., 1992-93; assoc. campaign chmn. United Way of Black Hawk County, 1981, 82; spl. project chmn. Chgo. Jaycees, 1969; trustee Westminster United Presbyterian Ch., 1984-86, vice-chmn., 1985; bd. dirs. Wheaton Franciscan Svcs., Inc., Iowa, 1992-93. Capt. USMC, 1962-66. NROTC regular scholar, 1957-62. Mem. AICPAs, Mo. Soc.CPAs, Inst. Mgmt. Accts., Sunnyside Country Club (treas. 1984, pres. 1985, trustee, 1986-88), Greenbriar Hills Country Club. Home: 126 Frontenac Frst Saint Louis MO 63131-3220 Office: Cupples Co Mfrs 9430 Page Ave Saint Louis MO 63132-1539

HEWITT (VER HOEF), LISA CAROL, elementary education educator; b. Rock Rapids, Iowa, Oct. 7, 1963; d. Floyd Raymond and Carol Ann (Hollander) Ver H.; m. Douglas Ray Hewitt, July 22, 1995. BA summa cum laude, Buena Vista Coll., Storm Lake, Iowa, 1986. Cert. in elem. edn. and Spanish. Bilingual tchr. 2d grade Twombly Elem. Sch., Ft. Lupton, Colo., 1986-88; elem. tchr., technology trainer Rolling Green Elem. Sch., Urbandale, Iowa, 1988—. Mem. NEA, Iowa Edn. Assn., Urbandale Edn. Assn., Iowa Jaycees (state dir. 1989-90, mgmt. v.p. 1990-91, pres. 1991-92, dist. dir. 1992-93), Iowa Jaycee (adminstrv. v.p. 1993-94, region 7 regional dir. 1994-95). Methodist. Home: 4609 Woodland Ave # 8 West Des Moines IA 50266-1777 Office: Rolling Green Elem Sch 8100 Airline Ave Urbandale IA 50322-2658

HEWSON, MARY MCDONALD, civic volunteer; b. Larned, Kans., Nov. 5, 1922; d. William Michael and Bernice Ulata (Gregory) McDonald; m. Kenneth Dean Hewson, June 21, 1946; children: Rebecca Hewson Lewis, Roberta Hewson Grogan, Margaret Hewson Smith. BS in Edn. cum laude, Kans. State U., 1948, BS in Psychology, 1948. Cert. secondary edn. tchr. Freshman counselor Kans. State U., 1948-49; substitute tchr. Larned Unified Sch. Dist., 1958—, tchr. gifted program, 1988; at home tutor, 1938—; spkr. Nat. Fraternity Blue Key Kans. State U., 1995—. Trustee Kans. State U. Found., Manhattan, 1980—; mem. Kans. Farmers Union, McPherson, 1982—, Help Eliminate Abuse Locally, Larned, 1982—, Mental Helath Assn., Larned, 1982—; spokesperson 8 counties Pawnee County Health Resource, Kans., 1992—, Ctrl. Kans. Environ. Resource Planning Group, 1992—; chmn. Swims for Kids; mem. Pawnee County Fair Growth Com., 1995; vol. gifted tchr. aide, 1996—. Recipient Medallion award Kans. State U., 1986, Nat. Vol. of Yr. award Coun. for Advancement and Support of Edn., 1983; named to Nat. Women's Hall of Fame, 1996. Mem. AAUW (charter), DAR (officer), Kans. Press Women (life mem., patron ednl. support 1988), YMCA (bd. dirs.), Philanthropic Ednl. Orng., Kans. State U. Alumni Assn. (strategic planning com., student rels. com.), Phi Alpha Mu. Home: PO Box 102 Larned KS 67550-0102

HEYDERMAN, ARTHUR JEROME, engineer, civilian military employee; b. Bklyn., N.Y., Jan. 1, 1946; s. Herbert Robert and Sally (Baron) H.; m. Renee Linda Pearlman, July 4, 1967; children: Brian Douglas, Deborah Ann, Cathy Ruth. BS in Applied Math., Poly. Inst. Bklyn., 1966, MS in Applied Math., 1973; postgrad., Stevens Inst. Tech., 1982, Brookings Inst., 1992, Wharton Sch. Bus., U. Pa., 1993. Nuclear weapons engr. U.S. Army Armaments R&D Ctr., Picatinny Arsenal, N.J., 1971-83; asst. tech. dir. U.S. Army Armaments R&D Ctr., Picatinny Arsenal, 1983-84, chief prodn. program planning, 1984, assoc. tech. dir., 1984-86; armaments rsch. and devel. prog. mgr. U.S. Army Armaments Munitions and Chem. Command, Rock Island, Ill., 1986-93, chief of rsch. devel., test and evaluation integration, 1993-94; chief improved armor engring. U.S. Army Armaments Rsch., Devel. and Engring. Ctr., Rock Island, 1994-96; chief armor engring. U.S. Army Rsch., Devel. & Engring. Ctr., Rock Island, Ill., 1996—; bd. dirs., sec./treas., pres. Iowa-Ill. chpt. Am. Def. Preparedness Assn., Rock Island; lt. col. nuclear weapons officer USAR, Ft. Sheridan, Ill., 1989-93; pres. OPICON, Bettendorf, Iowa, 1989—; nat. coun. Am. Def. Preparedness Assn.; coun. mem. Quad-Cities Engring. and Sci. Coun.; adj. faculty U.S. Army Command and Gen. Staff Coll., Ft. Leavenworth, Kans., 1981-89. Contbr. column to Rock Island Argus/Moline Dispatch; guest editor Quad Cities Times; contbr. tech. papers on weapons and weaponry assessment to profl. meetings. Pres., bd. dirs. Sussex County Jewish Ctr., Newton, N.J., 1979-86; fundraiser United Jewish Fedn., Davenport, Iowa, 1986—; mem. Rock Island Arsenal Com. for Disabled, 1987-93; dir. intake Quad City chpt. ACLU; mem. platform com. Scott County Dem. Ctrl. Com., 1994—; mem. 1st dist. Iowa Dem. Ctrl. Com., 1994—; mem. platform com. Iowa State Dem. Party; chmn. Quad Cities WWII Commemoration Com.; mem. Iowa Sesquecentennial Commemoration Com., Scott County, Ill. C. of C. Spkrs. Bur., 1996—; bd. dirs. Jewish Fedn. of Quad Cities, 1996—. Capt. U.S. Army, 1968-71, Vietnam. Decorated Bronze Star; Cross of Gallantry (Vietnam); named to Hon. Order St. Barbara, U.S. Army Field Arty. Assn. Mem. VFW, NAACP (bd. dirs. Quad Cities chpt. 1996—), U.S. Army Acquisitions Corps, U.S. Army Engr. Assn., Assn. U.S. Army (v.p. Ft. Armstrong chpt. 1993—, acting pres. chpt. 1996—), Soc. Am. Mil. Engrs. (scholar 1966), Soc. Am. Mil. Comptrs., Federally Employed Women, Planned Parenthood (mem. cmty. coun.), Nat. Soc. Scabbard and Blade (chpt. v.p. 1965-66), Res. Officers Assn., Poly. Alumni Assn. (pres. Quad City chpt. 1989—), Mensa, Intertel, Vietnam Vets. Jewish. Home: 1430 Grapler Ct Bettendorf IA 52722-1847

HEYDINGER, THEODORE S., design engineer; b. Galcon, Ohio, Oct. 10, 1969. BS in Mech. Engring., Ohio No. U., 1993. Design engr. Ohio Locomotive Crane Co., Inc., Bucyrus, 1993—. Asst. scout master Boy

Scouts, Galion, 1988—. Mem. ASME. Office: PO Box 511 Bucyrus OH 44820-0511

HIATT, MARJORIE MCCULLOUGH, service organization executive; b. Cin., July 12, 1923; d. Robert Stedman and Mildred (Rogers) McCullough; m. Homer E. Lunken, Apr. 15, 1944 (dec. 1970); children: Karen (dec. 1948), Kathryn Lunken Summers, Margo Lunken Yesner; m. William McLeod Ittmann, Mar. 17, 1972 (dec. 1982); m. Harold Hiatt, Apr. 14, 1984. Student, U. Cin., 1941-43. Active Girl Scouts U.S., 1962—, chmn. conv. com., 1972, del. world convs., 1969, 72, 75, 78, 81, 84, 87, 93, chmn. pub. relations com., 1963-66, mem. nat. exec. com., 1963-75, mem. nat. bd., 1962—, 4th v.p., 1966-69, 1st v.p., 1969-72, nat. pres., 1972-75, chmn. nat. adv. council, 1975-82, mem. birthplace adv. com., 1980—; vice chmn. world conf., Orleans, France, 1981; mem. world com. World Assn. Girl Guides and Girl Scouts, 1978-87, vice chmn., 1984-87. Regional dir. Assn. Jr. Leagues Am., 1958-60, nat. pres., 1960-62; mem. br. Jr. League Cin., 1944-58, Nat. Tng. Labs., 1963-66, Nat. Assembly for Social Policy and Devel., 1968-71; mem. exec. com. Council Nat. Orgns. for Children and Youth, 1960-62, 68-72; bd. dirs. United Way Am., 1962-67, sec., 1965-66, v.p., 1966-67, 1989—; mem. policy com. Center Vol. Soc., 1971-72; bd. dirs. Coll. Prep. Sch., Cin., 1962-69, pres., 1964-69; bd. dirs. Cin. Speech and Hearing Center, 1955-66, v.p., 1958-62, pres., 1963-66, trustee emeritus, 1966—; mem. bd. Children's Theatre, Cin., 1948-58, pres., 1948-50; bd. dirs. Community Health and Welfare Council Cin., 1957-63, Hamilton County (Ohio) Research Found., 1963-65, Cancer Family Care, Cin., 1971-72, Boys Clubs Greater Cin., Marjorie P. Lee Home for Aged, Music Hall Assn., Cin. Symphony Orch.; bd. dirs. Beechwood Home for Incurables, 1975-87; bd. dirs. St. Margaret Hall, 1991—, Cin. Civic Garden Ctr., 1992-95; mem. Ohio Citizens Coun., 1956-58; mem. bd. 7th Presbyterian Ch., 1967-74, 85—, ruling elder, 1976-78, 95—, chmn. bd. trustees, 1992-94; sr. warden St. Martin's in the Field, Biddeford Pool, Maine; bd. dirs. Greater Cin. Found., 1979-87; bd. dirs. U. Cin. Found., 1979—, pres. 1986-88, vice chmn. 1988—, trustee emeritus, 1993—; pres. Garden Club Cin., 1984-86, co-chmn. zone X meeting, 1989, zone X chmn. pub.; bd. dirs. Friends Cin. Parks, 1987—, corr. sec., 1989-92; trustee Cin. Assn. Performing Arts, Inc.; founding bd. dirs. Emery Soc. Children's Hosp; pres. protem Cin. Parks Found., 1995. Mem. Olave Baden-Powell Soc. (v.p. 1991-93, pres. 1993—), World Found. for Girl Guides and Girl Scouts (v.p. 1989—), Garden Club Am. (vice chmn. founder's fund 1991-92), Am. Psychiat. Assn. Aux. (bd. dirs., rec. sec. 1991-92). Home: 2353 Bedford Ave Cincinnati OH 45208-2656

HIBBARD, EUGENE JOSEPH, graphic illustrator, photographer; b. Chgo., Dec. 10, 1932; s. Eugene Melvil and Florence Myrtle (Simpson) H.; m. Janet Grace Shaw; children: Teri M., Cori R., Lindsay E. BFA, Wayne State U., 1962. Indsl. illustrator Ford Motor Co., Dearborn, Mich., 1960-72; graphic illustrator Traverse Bay News, Traverse City, Mich., 1972-74; graphic illustrator, cartoonist, photographer Traverse City (Mich.) City Record-Eagle, 1975—; speaker, instr. in field. Cartoonist for "Local Scene" cartoon panels, 1975—; cartoonist: (book) A Boy, A Bike & Buster, 1994. With USAF, 1952-56. Mem. Am. Assn. Editorial Cartoonists, Nat. Press Photographers Assn. Republican. Office: Traverse City Record-Eagle 120 W Front St Traverse City MI 49684

HIBBS, CLYDE W., retired environmental sciences educator, consultant; b. Independence, W.Va., July 19, 1922; s. Samuel Jacob and Regina Anna (Kincaid) H. BS, W.Va. U., 1944, MS, 1949; MA, U. Mich., 1955, PhD, 1957. Vocat. agriculture tchr. Ravenswood (W.Va.) High Sch., 1944-52; soil conservationist USDA, Ann Arbor, Mich., 1953-56; prof. conservation U. Wis., Stevens Point, 1956-60; coord. outdoor edn. N.J. colls. N.J. Dept. Edn., Branchville, 1960-61; sci. tchr. N. Plainfield High Sch., Plainfield, N.J., 1961-62; prof. conservation and earth sci. Glassboro (N.J.) State Coll., 1962-64; prof. natural resources Ball State U., Muncie, Ind., 1964-90; adj. prof. sanitary engring. Rutgers U., New Brunswick, N.J., 1964; founder dept. natural resources Ball State U., Muncie, 1965-79; rsch. com. chair Environ. Edn. Bibliography, 1975-77; vis. prof. environ. studies Alderson-Broaddus Coll., Philippi, W.Va., 1992-93; cons., advisor in field. Establishment coord. Juanita Hults Environ. Learning Ctr., Albany, Ind., 1987-90, chmn. adv. com., 1987-90; alternate supr. Delaware County Soil Conservation Dist., Muncie, 1987-89; program coord. E. Ctrl. Ind. Sci. Fair, Ball State U., Muncie, 1989-92. Recipient Creative Programming award Nat. Univ. Ext. Assn., 1971, Key Man award Conservation Edn. Assn., 1977. Fellow Soil Conservation Soc. Am. (chair environ. edn. divsn. 1975-76), Ind. Acad. Sci. (chair soils sect. 1970); mem. N.Am. Assn. Environ. Edn. (global studies com. 1992), Nat. Wildlife Fedn., Conservation Edn. Assn. (v.p. 1972-74), Natural Resource Def. Coun., Environ. Edn. Assn. Ind. (pres. 1967-71). Home: 1704 N Riley Rd Muncie IN 47304-2563 Office: Ball State Univ Dept Nat Res and Env Mgmt 2000 W University Ave Muncie IN 47306-1022

HIBNER, RAE A., insurance company official, nurse; b. Libertyville, Ill., Jan. 31, 1956; d. Richard Douglas and Raelene Ann (Warren) Lyons; m. John Paul Hibner, June 21, 1986; children: Kevin John, Thomas Ivan. Diploma, Luth. Gen. Hosp. Sch. Nursing, Park Ridge, Ill., 1979; BS in Nursing, U. Ill., Chgo., 1984; MS, No. Ill. U., 1987. RN. Staff nurse Cardiac Telemetry Luth. Gen. Hosp., 1979-81, staff nurse CCU, 1981-82; staff nurse coronary ICU U. Ill. Hosp., Chgo., 1982-83, asst. head nurse coronary ICU, 1983-86, head nurse coronary ICU, 1986-88, staff nurse coronary-med. ICU, 1988-90; coord. utilization rev. Parkside Health Mgmt. Corp., Chgo., 1989-91; asst. dir. utilization mgmt. U. Ill., Chgo., 1991-93; risk mgr. Rush-Presbyn.-St. Lukes Med. Ctr., Chgo., 1993-96; claims cons. CNA Ins. Cos., Chgo., 1996—. Mem. ASHRM, HCRMSC. Republican. Roman Catholic.

HICKEN, JEFFREY PRICE, lawyer; b. Macomb, Ill., Oct. 25, 1947; s. Victor and Mary Patricia (O'Connell) H.; m. Mary Sarah Schmidt, Aug. 23, 1969; children: Andrew, Molly, Elizabeth. BA, Cornell Coll., 1969; JD, U. Ill., 1972. Bar: Minn. 1972, U.S. Dist. Ct. Minn. 1980, U.S. Ct. Appeals (8th cir.). Assoc. Weaver, Talle & Herrick, Anoka, Minn., 1972-77; sr. ptnr. Jensen, Hicken & Scott P.A., Anoka, 1977—. Bd. dirs. Anoka Lyric Arts; precinct chair Dem.-Farmer-Labor Party, Anoka, 1976-84; treas. Nelson Vols. Com., Anoka, 1982-88, Rike Vol. Com., Anoka, 1990. Capt. U.S. Army, 1969-77. Recipient J. Franklin Little scholarship Cornell Coll., Mt. Vernon, Iowa, 1969. Fellow Am. Acad. Matrimonial Lawyers (cert. arbitrator, bd. mgrs.); mem. Minn. State Bar Assn., Anoka County Bar Assn. (pres. 1990-91), City of Anoka Charter Commn. (chmn. 1978-84). Democrat. Methodist. Home: 1700 West Ln Anoka MN 55303-1923 Office: Jensen Hicken Gedde and Scott 2150 3rd Ave Ste 300 Anoka MN 55303-2200

HICKEY, JEROME EDWARD, investment company executive; b. Chgo., June 25, 1937; s. Matthew Joseph and Naomi (Pope) H.; m. Denise Coakley, May 20, 1967; children: J. Graham, Matthew, Elizabeth, George, Peter. BS in Econs., Coll. of the Holy Cross, 1959; MA in Philosophy, Boston Coll., 1964. Instr. Cranwell Sch., Lenox, Mass., 1964-66; acct. exec. Paine Webber, N.Y.C., 1966-68; v.p. Hickey & Co., Chgo., 1968-72, Ralph W. Davis, Chgo., 1972-75, Weeden & Co., Chgo., 1975-78; founder, pres. Jerome Hickey Assocs., Chgo., 1979-84; pres. No. Trust Brokerage, Chgo., 1984-87; sr. v.p. Stein Roe & Farnham, Chgo., 1988-93; sr. v.p., mng. dir. SEI Corp., Chgo., 1993—. Dir. Western Golf Assn., Golf, Ill., 1979—, chmn. exec. com., 1991—; trustee St. Ignatius Coll. Prep., Chgo., 1988-93, chmn., 1990-93. Named Outstanding Young Man in Am., 1971. Mem. Knollwood Club (Lake Forest, Ill., dir. 1976-79), The Tavern Club (Chgo.), Bond Club Chgo. (dir. 1974-75), Econ. Club Chgo., Desert Forest Golf Club, The Boulders. Roman Catholic. Home: 1923 N Fremont St Chicago IL 60614-5016 Office: SEI Corp 181 W Madison St Chicago IL 60602-4510

HICKEY, JOHN JOSEPH, state legislator; b. St. Louis, Feb. 23, 1965; m. Angela Dalton, 1992. State rep. Dist. 80 Mo. State Congress, 1993-94, 95-96; journeyman pipefitter. Mem. Northwest Twp. Airport Twp. and North County Young Dems., Pipefitters Local 562, North County Labor Club, Woodson Terr. Lions Club Internat. *

HICKEY, THOMAS M., stockbroker; b. Joliet, Ill., July 26, 1954. BS, U. Ill., 1976; MS, Ga. Inst. Tech., 1977. Stockbroker Merrill Lynch, Chgo., 1978—. Mem. Union League Club Chgo. Home: 4140 Hampton Ave Western Springs IL 60558-1309 Office: Merrill Lynch 141 W Jackson Blvd Ste 290 Chicago IL 60604-2905

HICKINBOTHAM, LETHA BELLE, real estate broker, business owner; b. New Haven, Mo., Feb. 8, 1935; d. Clarence Virgil and Gladine Louise (Helling) Laubinger; m. Floyd E. Hickinbotham, May 3, 1953; children: Floyd, Marjean, Twila, Scott. Student, East Ctrl. Coll., Union, Mo., 1970, 77, 79 86. Grad. Realtors Inst., Mo. Assn. Realtors. With acctg. and billing dept. Fed. Res. Bank, St. Louis, 1952-53; restaurant hostess Snell's Family Restaurant, Sullivan, Mo., 1958-61; with acctg. and billing dept. Crawford Electric Co-op, Bourbon, Mo., 1961-63, Authorized Investor Group, Inc., St. Clair, Mo., 1966-76; dist. clk., sec. Anaconda Sch. Dist. 87, St. Clair, 1966-76; real estate broker Hickinbotham Real Estate, Inc., St. Clair, 1976—; developer, owner Budget Lodging, St. Clair, 1989—, Subway Sandwich and Salad Restaurant, St. Clair, 1992—; pres. Franklin County Women's Coun. Realtors, St. Clair, 1980. Contbr. articles to profl. jours. Mem. Internat. Real Estate Policy Com., 1986-87; mem. bldg. and grounds com. Mt. Zion Bapt. Ch., St. Clair, 1990; bd. dirs. Sullivan Bapt. Hosp. Coun.; bd. mem. Mo. Bapt. Hosp. Cmty. Coun.; pres. East Ctrl. Coll. Found., 1995—. Named to Honor Soc., Mo. Assn. Realtors, 1986, 87, 88, to Nat. Honor Soc., Nat. Assn. Realtors, 1987. Mem. Tri-County Bus. and Profl. Women's Club (pres. 1981-82, Women of Yr. 1982), Franklin County Bd. Realtors (pres. 1985, Realtor of Yr. 1983), Mo. Women's Coun. Realtors (pres. 1983, Mo. Woman of Yr. 1985), Mo. Indsl. Devel. Coun., St. Clair C. of C. (bd. dirs. 1985, chair 1990), St. Clair Rotary (sec. and guide for Rotary Internat. team annual), East Ctrl. Coll. Found. (pres. 1994—). Democrat. Baptist. Home: 2366 S I 44 Outer Rd Saint Clair MO 63077 Office: Hickinbothm Real Estate Inc 862 S I 44 Outer Rd W Saint Clair MO 63077

HICKMAN, JAMES CHARLES, business and statistics educator, business school dean; b. Indianola, Iowa, Aug. 27, 1927; s. James C. and Mabel L. (Fisher) H.; m. Margaret W. McKee, June 12, 1950; children—Charles Wallace, Donald Robert, Barbara Jean. B.A., Simpson Coll., 1950; M.S., U. Iowa, 1952, Ph.D., 1961. Actuarial asst. Bankers Life Co., Des Moines, 1952-57; asst. prof. dept. statistics U. Iowa, 1961-64, asso. prof., 1964-67, prof., 1967-72; prof. bus. and statistics U. Wis., Madison, 1972-93; dean Sch. Bus. U. Wis., 1985-90; emeritus prof. and dean U. Wis., Madison, 1993—; mem. panel of cons. on social security fin. Senate Fin. and House Ways and Means Com., 1975-76; mem. adv. com. to Joint Bd. for Enrollment of Actuaries, 1976-78; mem. Actuarial Standards Bd., 1985-92; dir. Century Investment Mgmt. Co. Mem. bd. dirs. Blue Cross and Blue Shield United of Wis.; bd. pensions Presbyn. Ch. in U.S.A., 1989-95. With USAAF, 1945-47. Recipient Alumni Achievement award Simpson Coll., 1979, David Halmstad award for actuarial rsch. Actuarial Ednl. Rsch. Fund, 1979, 81, Disting. Alumni Achievement award U. Iowa, 1993. Fellow Soc. Actuaries (v.p. 1975-77, bd. govs. 1971-74, 91-94); mem. Soc. Actuaries Found. (bd. dirs. 1994—), Casualty Actuarial Soc., Am. Acad. Actuaries, Am. Statis. Assn., Swiss Assn. Actuaries (corr. mem.), Beta Gamma Sigma (bd. govs. 1988-92). Presbyterian. Home: 4917 Woodburn Dr Madison WI 53711-1347 Office: U Wis Sch Bus 975 University Ave Madison WI 53706-1324

HICKORY, BETTY MAY, songwriter, writer; b. Pekin, Ill., Mar. 1, 1934; d. Raymond Bliss and Nellie May (Pinkerton) Holler; m. Walter Edward Hickory, Nov. 14, 1954 (dec. Aug. 1959); children: Mary Elizabeth, Walter William. Student, Drury Coll., Springfield, Mo., 1972. Charge nurse Nursing Home, Springfield, 1964-82; songwriter, free-lance writer, 1982—. Author articles. Recipient awards for outstanding civic projects. Mem. Ozarks Note Worthy Songwriters Assn. (cons., mem. adv. bd., pres. 1992-95, Song of Yr. award 1995), Broadcast Music Inc. Methodist. Office: Ozarks NoteWorthy Songwriters Assn Inc 2303 S Luster Springfield MO 65804

HICKROD, GEORGE ALAN KARNES WALLIS, educational administration educator; b. Fort Branch, Ind., May 16, 1930; s. Hershell Roy and Bernice Ethel (Karnes) H.; m. Ramona Dell Poole, 1952 (dec.); m. Lucy Jen Huang, 1964 (dec.); 1 stepson, Goren Wallis Liu. AB, Wabash Coll., 1954; MA, Harvard U., 1955; EdD, Harvard U., 1966. Asst. prof. ednl. and social scis. Lake Erie Coll., 1962-67; assoc. prof. ednl. adminstrn. Ill. State U., Normal, 1967-71, prof., 1971-83, disting. prof., 1983-95, emeritus disting. prof., 1995—, dir. Ctr. for Study Ednl. Fin., 1974-95; dir. McArthur/Spencer Ill. Sch. Fin., 1987-92, Joyce Found. Sch. Fin. Study, 1990-92; pres. Coalition for Ednl. Rights Under the Constn., 1989-91, mem. ednl. rights com., 1990—. With USMC, 1950-52, Korea. Recipient Chgo. Urban League award, 1994, Van Miller Disting. Scholar award U. Ill., 1994; State of Ill. and U.S. Govt. grantee. Mem. Am. Edn. Fin. Assn. (v.p. 1983-84, pres. 1984-85, Disting. Svc. award 1992), Scottish-Am. Soc. Cen. Ill. Club (past chief), Clan Wallace Internat. Royal Order of Scotland Masonic, Phi Beta Kappa, Commun Gaidhleach Am., Masons, Elks. Democrat. Unitarian. Avocations: history, genealogy, travel, cooking, Gaelic (Albanach) lang. Home: 2 Turner Rd Normal IL 61761-4218

HICKS, AMELIA MARIE, secondary educator, consultant; b. Chgo., Sept. 28, 1945; d. Antonio and Anna Maria (Orsucci) Micheli; m. William S. Hicks, Aug. 2, 1969; children: James, Karen, Kristina. BS in Edn., No. Ill. U., 1967; MA in Mgmt., Nat. Louis U., Evanston, Ill., 1989. Cert. adminstr., Ill. Tchr. Glenbard Sch. Dist. 87, Glen Ellyn, Ill., 1967-74, Coll. of DuPage, Glen Ellyn, 1971-81; tchr. bus. tech. Naperville (Ill.) Sch. Dist. 203, 1981—; cons. Mentoring Leadership and Resource Network, 1992—. Mentoring resource editor, writer newsletter Mentoring Resource, 1992—. Mem. Ill. Consumer Edn. Assn. (exec. bd., pres., v.p., sec.), Ins. Edn. Found. (adv. bd. 1995—). Home: 1186 Redfield Naperville IL 60563

HICKS, CADMUS METCALF, JR., financial analyst; b. Hagerstown, Md., Dec. 21, 1952; s. Cadmus Metcalf Sr. and Marie Elizabeth (Keefauver) H.; m. Elizabeth Ann Dressel, May 31, 1980; children: Liza, Alethea, Cadmus III. BA, Wheaton (Ill.) Coll., 1974; MA, U. Chgo., 1976; PhD, Northwestern U., Evanston, Ill., 1980. Chartered fin. analyst. Rsch. analyst John Nuveen & Co. Inc., Chgo., 1980-85, asst. v.p., 1985-90, v.p., 1990—, asst. mgr. rsch. dept., 1993—. Author: (with others) The Municipal Bond Handbook, 1983; contbr. articles to profl. jours. Mem. Nat. Fedn. of Mcpl. Analysts (bd. govs. 1991-93), Chgo. Mcpl. Analysts Soc. (pres. 1991-92), Investment Analysts Soc. of Chgo., Assn. for Investment Mgmt. and Rsch. Republican. Office: 333 W Wacker Dr Chicago IL 60606

HICKS, CHERYL LEE, executive; b. Cin., Ohio, Sept. 2, 1948. Student, U. Miami. Sales mgr. Fortune 500 Co., Dayton, Ohio, 1978-85; v.p., treas. Groves Internat. Corp., Cin., 1985—.

HICKS, DARRELL LEE, applied and computational mathematician, educator, consultant; b. Clovis, N. Mex., July 3, 1937; s. Jason and Jessie Winona (Pierce) H.; m. Joy L. Rotton, June 20, 1960 (div. July 1975); 1 child, April; m. Kathryn J. Chaney, Mar. 3, 1979 (div. Sept. 1984); 1 child, Jason; m. Lorie Marie Liebrock, Oct. 18, 1985. BS in Math. and Physics, U. N.Mex., 1961, PhD in Math., 1969. Math. researcher weapons labs. USAF, Albuquerque, 1962-69; mem. tech. staff Sandia Nat. Labs., Albuquerque, 1969-81; prof. U. Colo., Denver, 1981-83; prof. math. Mich. Technol. U., Houghton, 1983—; cons. Idaho Nat. Engring. Labs., Idaho Falls, 1982-87, KMS Fusion, Inc., Ann Arbor, Mich., 1983-88, Sandia Nat. Labs., Albuquerque, 1992—, summer faculty 1984-85; dir. Ctr. for Exptl. Computation Mich. Tech. U., 1987-88; vis. scholar computer sci. dept./Nat. Sci. Found. Sci. and Tech. Ctr. for Rsch. on Parallel Computation Rice U., Houston, 1989-90; judge sci. fairs, N.Mex., 1969-81. Assoc. editor Applied Math. and Computation, 1984—; reviewer Math. Revs., 1980—, Computing Revs., 1984—; contbr. articles to profl. jours. Mem. Am. Math. Soc., Am. Acad. Mechanics, Math Assn. Am. (citation Mich. section1988), Soc. for Indsl. and Applied Math., Am. Physical Soc., Am. Nuclear Soc. Office: Mich Technol U Dept Math Scis 1400 Townsend Dr Houghton MI 49931-1200

HICKS, JANET BROOKS, lawyer; b. Leaksville, N.C., Apr. 28, 1959; d. R. Russell Jr. and Annie (Hicks) Moton; m. Frederick J. Hicks, July 4, 1992; children: Jaison, Jeffrey. BA in Bus. Mgmt., BA in Econs., N.C. State U., 1982; JD, U. Mo., Columbia, 1990. Bar: Mo. 1991, Ill. 1991, Iowa 1994. Assoc. Thompson & Mitchell, Attys. at Law, St. Louis, 1991-93; asst. gen. counsel Norwest Fin., Inc., Des Moines, 1994—; spkr. in field. Mem. ABA, Nat. Bar Assn., Mo. Bar Assn., Polk County Bar Assn., Iowa Bar Assn., Polk County Women's Atty. Assn. Baptist. Office: Norwest Fin Inc 206 Eighth St Des Moines IA 50309

HICKS, JUDITH EILEEN, nursing administrator; b. Chgo., Jan. 1, 1947; d. John Patrick and Mary Ann (Clifford) Rohan; m. Laurence Joseph Hicks, Nov. 22, 1969; children—Colleen Driscoll, Patrick Kevin. B.S. in Nursing, St. Xavier Coll., Chgo., 1969; M.S. in Nursing, U. Ill.-Chgo., 1975. Staff nurse Mercy Hosp., Chgo., 1969-70, nursing supr., 1970-73; cons. continuing edn. Ill. Nurses Assn., Chgo., 1974-75; dir. obstetrics and gynecology nursing Northwestern Meml. Hosp., Chgo., 1975-81; v.p. nursing Children's Meml. Hosp., Chgo., 1981-86; pres. Children's Meml. Home Health, Inc., 1986—, Children's Meml. Nursing Services, 1986—; pres. Allied & Children's Home Health and Nursing Services, 1988, CM Healthcare Resources, Inc., 1988—, The Pediatric Place, Inc., 1994—; dir. Near North Health Corp., Chgo., 1982-85; pres. Pediatric Excellence Program Svc.; bd. dirs. Infant Welfare Soc. Chgo., bd. dir. Nat. Breast Cancer Assn., Mem. Ill. Hosp. Assn. (chmn. Council on Nursing 1982-83), Inst. Medicine, Am. Soc. Nursing Adminstrs., Women's Health Exec. Network (pres. 1984-85). Roman Catholic. Home: 2206 Beechwood Ave Wilmette IL 60091-1508 Office: CM Health Care Resources 1181 Lake Cook Rd Deerfield IL 60015-5210

HICKS, SHERMAN GREGORY, pastor; b. Bklyn., June 22, 1946; s. Charles Sr. and Sarah Mae (Rollins) H.; m. Anna Marie Peck, Sept. 12, 1970 (div.); children: Andrea, Geoffrey, Christopher. BA, Wittenberg U., 1968; MDiv, Hamma Sch. Theology, 1973; DD (hon.), Carthage Coll., 1988, Elmhurst Coll., 1989, Wittenberg U., 1990. Ordained to ministry Luth. Ch., 1973. Pastor Concordia Luth. Ch., Buffalo, 1973-77; co-pastor Holy Trinity Luth. Ch., East Orange, N.J., 1977-79; asst. to bishop Ill. Synod, Luth. Ch. Am., Chgo., 1979-87; bishop Met. Chgo. Synod, Evang. Luth. Ch. in Am., Chgo., 1988-95; sr. pastor First Trinity Luth. Ch., Washington, 1996—. Pres. Interfaith Coun. for Homeless, Chgo., 1988, AIDS Nat. Interfaith Network, 1991; trustee Carthage Coll., Kenosha, Wis., 1988; bd. dirs. Luth. Social Svcs. Ill., 1988-95; mem. Coun. Religious Leaders, Chgo., 1988-95; bd. dirs. Leadership Coun. for Met. Open Cmty. Named One of Outstanding Young Men in Am., Jaycees, 1974; recipient Alumni Citation, Wittenberg U., 1993. Office: First Trinity Luth Ch 309 E St NW Washington DC 20001

HICKS, TADD D., investment broker; b. Jefferson City, Mo., Dec. 20, 1962; s. Darryl L. and Shirley (Ruggles) H.; m. Caren G. Gerald, Oct. 24, 1991; 1 child, Maddison. BS, U. Mo., 1986. Mgr. Hunt Concrete, Warrenton, Mo., 1986-90; investment broker Painewebber, Chesterfield, Mo., 1991—. Mem. Elephant Club. Republican. Office: Painewebber 15450 S Outer 40 Rd # 100 Chesterfield MO 63017

HIEBERT, DONALD LEE, insurance company executive; b. Newton, Kans., July 13, 1943; s. Olin Richard and Lovana Lov (Friesen) H.; m. Karla Paulette Rhodes, Apr. 22, 1967; children: Shanel LaRae, Brandi Donelle. Student, Wichita State U., 1961 & 66, NW Mo. State U., 1974, Southwestern Coll., 1975-76. Fire control tech. USN, 1962-66; sheet metal mech. Boeing Aircraft Co., Wichita, Kans., 1966-68, TWA, Kansas City, Mo., 1968-70; with sales mgmt. Midwestern Cemetry Cons., Kansas City, 1970-73; ins. agt. Fed. Ins. Co., Kansas City, 1973-86, Fred S. James of Mo., 1986-87, Nationwide Ins. Co., Kansas City, 1987-89; ind. agt., 1989-91; agt. Millers Mutual Ins., Kansas City, 1991-95, Dodson Group, Kansas City, Mo., 1995—. With USN 1962-66. Mem. Optimist Club of Northland (Kansas City), Meadowbrook North Swim Club(Gladstone, Mo.). Republican. Home: 6518 N Montgall Ave Kansas City MO 64119-1533 Office: Dodson Group 9201 State Line Rd Kansas City MO 64114

HIEMCKE, CHRISTOPH, engineering educator; b. Heide, Germany, Apr. 27, 1962; came to U.S., 1981; s. Hermann and Anke Bertha (Ruehmann) H.; m. Audra Ann Breeher, May 13, 1994. BS in Aerospace Engring., Iowa State U., 1986, MS in Aerospace Engring., 1989, PhD in Aerospace Engring., 1994. Rsch. asst. Iowas State U., Ames, 1990-94; asst. prof. engring. Loras Coll., Dubuque, Iowa, 1994—. Treas. Habitat for Humanity, Ames, 1989-91; co-founder Affordable Housing Coalition, Ames, 1991-92; faculty mem. Amnesty Internat., Dubuque, 1994—. Mem. AIAA, Am. Soc. for Engring. Edn., Tau Beta Pi, Sigma Gamma Tau, Sigma Xi. Office: Loras Coll PO Box 178 Dubuque IA 52004-0178

HIETALA, ALLAN, advertising executive; b. 1932. With Northrup King Co., Mpls., 1964-69; with Colle & McAvoy, Inc., Mpls., 1969—, chmn., CEO. Office: Colle & McVoy Inc 8500 Mormandale Lake Blvd Minneapolis MN 55437*

HIGBEA, JEROLD CARL, electrical engineer; b. Defiance, Ohio, Dec. 27, 1969. BSEE, U. Toledo, 1992. Project engr. Koester Corp., Defiance, 1993—. Mem. IEEE. Republican. Lutheran. Home: 3796 Domersville Rd Defiance OH 43512-9117 Office: Koester Corp 945 Cleveland Ave Defiance OH 43512-3617

HIGGENS, WILLIAM JOHN, III, sales executive; b. Evanston, Ill., May 26, 1951; s. William John Jr. and Delores Mae (Fuller) H.; m. Melanie Ann Mayer (div.); children: Melissa Lee, Tracy Ann; m. Barbara Carrie Simcoe, July 8, 1989. BS in Mktg. Mgmt., Miami U., Oxford, Ohio, 1973. Sales rep. A.B. Dick Co., Chgo., 1973-76; dist. sales mgr. McGraw-Hill Pub. Co., Chgo., 1976-85, CMP Publ., Inc., Chgo., 1985-91, McGraw-Hill Pub. Co., Chgo., 1991—. Mem. Bus. Mktg. Assn. (bd. dirs. 1984—, cert. bus. communicator 1989). Republican. Lutheran. Home: 230 Weidner Rd Buffalo Grove IL 60089-1949 Office: McGraw-Hill Pub Co 180 N Stetson Ave Chicago IL 60601-6710

HIGGINBOTHAM, MARK L., financial consultant; b. South Bend, Ind., May 12, 1958; m. Teri A. Spier, Nov. 22, 1981; children: Ross A., Emily J. BS, Ind. U., 1986; MS, DePaul U., 1989. With Allied Signal Aerospace, South Bend, 1978-83; fin. cons. IDS Am. Express Fin. Planning, South Bend, 1986-87, Merrill Lynch, South Bend, 1989—; mem. accountancy adv. bd. Ind. Tech. Vocat. Coll., South Bend, 1990—. Mem. alumni bd. DePaul U., Chgo., 1991—; mem. DePaul U. Athletic Found., 1993—. Home: 51945 Old Mill Rd South Bend IN 46637-1351 Office: Merrill Lynch 404 Columbia St South Bend IN 46601-2355

HIGGINS, BARBARA LORENE, school psychologist; b. Dubuque, Iowa, Jan. 24, 1947; d. William H. and Lorene C. (Tunis) H.; divorced. BS in Psychology, U. Iowa, 1969, MA, 1974, PhD in Ednl. Psychology, Stats, and Measurement, 1979. Cert. sch. psychologist, Iowa. Psychol. examiner State Svcs. for Crippled Children, Iowa City, Iowa, 1973-75; psychol. examiner, dept. pediatrics U. Iowa, Iowa City, 1973-75; preschool coord. La Crosse (Wis.) Pub. Schs., 1975-76; tech. assistance team Iowa Dept. of Edn., Des Moines, 1989—; preschool psychologist Area Edn. Agy. 7, Cedar Falls, 1976—; adj. prof. U. No. Iowa, Cedar Falls, 1981—. Bd. dirs., sec. Cedar Arts Forum, Waterloo, 1985—; various coms. Jr. League, Waterloo, 1981-87; bd. dirs. Waterloo-Cedar Falls Symphony; mem. Sierra Club of Cedar Prairie. Mem. Am. Psychol. Assn., Iowa Psychol. Assn., Coun. for Exceptional Children (sec. 1990-92). Home: 501 Columbia Cir Waterloo IA 50701-3035 Office: 3706 Cedar Heights Dr Cedar Falls IA 50613-6207

HIGGINS, FRANCIS EDWARD, history educator; b. Chgo., Nov. 29, 1935; s. Frank Edward and and Mary Alyce (Fahey) H.; B.S., Loyola U., Chgo., 1959, M.A., 1964; postgrad. Exeter Coll., Oxford (Eng.) U., 1962, Am. U. Beirut, 1966, McGill U., Montreal, Que., Can., 1967; adminstrn. cert. St. Xavier Coll., 1971; Ed.D., U. Sarasota, 1977. Tchr., Washington Jr. High Sch., Chicago Heights, Ill., 1959; tchr. Chgo. Vocat. High Sch., 1960-68, dept. chmn., 1964; asst. prof. social sci. Moraine Valley C.C., 1968-69; tchr. history Hillcrest High Sch., Country Club Hills, Ill., 1969-93; instr. nursing continuing edn. St. Francis Coll., 1978—. Mem. pres.'s council St. Xavier Coll., 1978—; mem. St. Germaine Sch. Bd., 1972-73, St. Alexander Sch. Bd., 1978-84; active Chgo. council Boy Scouts Am., 1969-77, asst. dist. commr., 1971-75, mem. dist. scout com., 1976-77; co-historian Palos Heights Silver Jubilee Com., 1984. Recipient Disting. Service award Chgo. council Boy Scouts Am., 1974; Brit. Univ. scholar, 1962; Fulbright fellow, summer 1966; English Speaking Union fellow, 1967. Mem. Ill. Hist. Soc., Del. Hist. Soc., Am. Cath. Hist. Soc., Nat. Council Social Studies, Ill. Council Social Studies, Nat. Curriculum and Supervisory Assn., Ill. Supervisory Assn., Ill. Assn. Supervision and Curriculum Devel. (editorial rev. bd. Jour. 1984-86), Chgo. Hist. Soc., Nat. Hist. Soc., Brit. Hist. Assn., Brit. Hist. Assn., Nat. Soc. Study Edn., Phi Delta Kappa, Phi Gamma Mu. Republican. Roman Catholic. Contbr. revs. to Am. Cath. Hist. Jour., History Tchr. Jour. Home: 7660 W 131st St Palos Heights IL 60463-1910

HIGGINS, JACK, editorial cartoonist; b. Chgo., Aug. 19, 1954; s. Maurice James and Helen Marie (Egan) H. BA in Econs., Coll. Holy Cross, 1976. Editorial cartoonist The Daily Northwestern, Evanston, Ill., 1978-81; free-lance editorial cartoonist Chgo. Sun-Times, 1980-84, editorial cartoonist, 1984—. Vol. worker Jesuit Vol. Corps, Washington, 1977. Recipient Peter Lisagor award Chgo. Soc. Profl. Journalists, 1984, 87, 91, 94, 1st prize Internat. Salon Cartoons, Montreal, Que., Can., 1988, Pulitzer prize for editl. cartooning, 1989, Disting. Svc. award Sigma Delta Chi, 1988, media svc. award Chgo. Lung Assn., 1993, Herman Kogan media awards Chgo. Bar Assn., 1993, 95; named Alumnus of Yr., St. Ignatius Coll. Prep. Sch., Chgo., 1992, Ill. Journalist of Yr., 1996; finalist for Pulitzer prize, 1986, for Robert F. Kennedy journalism award, 1993, 94. Mem. Nat. Soc. of Profl. Journalists (Disting. Svc. award). Roman Catholic. Home: 9545 S Bell Ave Chicago IL 60643-1005 Office: Chgo Sun-Times 401 N Wabash Ave Chicago IL 60611-3532

HIGGINS, JAMES JOSEPH, environmental consultant; b. Massillon, Ohio, May 15, 1920; s. John P. and Stella M. (Warth) H.; m. Gloria L. Pepoon, Aug. 20, 1949; children: Bruce J., Keith W., Anita L., Suzanne M. B in Chem. Engring., Ohio State U., 1942; MS, Lawrence Coll., 1948, PhD, 1951. Registered profl. engr., Ohio. Chem. engr. Fox River Paper Co., Appleton, Wis., 1946, Union Bag & Paper Co., Savannah, Ga., 1947; chemist Morris Paper Mills, 1948; devel. chemist Ohio Boxboard Co., Rittman, 1950-54; paper mill supt. Packaging Corp. Am., Rittman, 1954-57, research group leader, research and devel. mgr., 1958-61, dir. tech. services and environ. control, Grand Rapids, Mich., 1961-85; pvt. practice environ. cons., Grand Rapids, 1985—. Contbr. articles to profl. jours.; patentee in field. Served to capt. C.E., U.S. Army, 1942-46. Fellow Am. Inst. Chemists; mem. AIChE, Sigma Xi. Home and Office: 2035 Wilshire Dr SE Grand Rapids MI 49506-4013

HIGGINS, JAMES SCOTT, investment officer; b. Moberly, Mo., May 26, 1966. BA in Fin. and Econs., U. Iowa, 1988. Investment officer Dain Bosworth Inc., Iowa City, 1988—. Mem. Sertoma Internat. (v.p. 1993-95). Methodist.

HIGGINS, ROBERT ARTHUR, electrical engineer, educator, consultant; b. Watertown, S.D., Sept. 5, 1924; s. Arthur C. and Nicoline (Huseth) H.; m. Barbara Jeanne Fagerlie, 1958; children—Patricia Suzanne, Daniel Alfred, Steven Robert. BEE with honors, U. Minn., 1948; MSEE, U. Wis., 1964; PhDEE, U. Mo., 1969. Registered profl. engr. Engr. Schlumberger Well Survey Corp., Tex., 1948-57; rsch. technologist Mobil Rsch. and Devel. Corp., Tex., 1958-61; rsch. engr. United Aircraft Rsch. Labs., Conn., 1965; staff specialist Remote Sensing Inst., S.D., 1969-71; asst. prof. elec. engring. S.D. State U., 1969-74, assoc. dir. Engring. Expt. Sta., 1973-77, prof. elec. engring., 1974-79; cons. Mankato State U., 1980; prin. engr. Sperry Univac, 1981-85; prof. elec. engring. St. Cloud (Minn.) State U., 1985-95, prof. emeritus, 1995—; cons. Control Data Corp., 1977-80, Lawrence Livermore Lab., 1971-73, USAF Office Sci. Rsch., Fla., 1976, NCR-Comten, 1988-90, FMC Corp., 1991-92, Ontrack Computer Sys., 1993-95; project dir., cons. NSF, 1973-80, 87-89. Contbr. articles to profl. jours. Bd. dirs. Eden Prairie Bd. Edn., Minn., 1982-85, Nat. Storage Industry Consortium, 1995—. With CE, AUS, 1943-46. NASA fellow, 1966-68; grantee NSF, 1966, 72, 74, 86, AEC, 1971-73, Office Water Resources Research, 1971-74. Mem. IEEE (sr., life), Am. Soc. Engring. Educators, Sigma Xi, Eta Kappa Nu. Lutheran. Home: 11260 Windrow Dr Eden Prairie MN 55344-4055

HIGGINS, RUTH ELLEN, theatre producer; b. Streator, Ill., Jan. 23, 1945; d. Thomas Francis and Mary Madeline (Ahearn) H.; m. Byron L. Schaffer, Oct. 17, 1975 (dec. May 1990); 1 child, Kareth Madeline Schaffer. BS in Edn. and Theater, No. Ill. U., 1967; MA in Theater Arts, U. Nebr., 1968; postgrad., No. Ill. U., 1970-74. Instr. Glenbrook North H.S., Northbrook, Ill., 1968-69; dir. theatre Highland C.C., Freeport, Ill., 1969-73; co-prodr. Dinglefest Theatre Co., Chgo., 1972-77; arts cons. Chgo. Cmty. Trust, 1973-74; exec. dir., founder Chgo. Alliance for the Performing Arts, 1974-79; prodr. New Tuners Theatre, Chgo., 1974—; exec. dir., co-founder Chgo. Coalition for Arts in Edn., 1979-83; gen. mgr. Theatre Bldg., Chgo., 1981—; cons. Office Cook County Assessor, Chgo., 1980, Donors Forum, Chgo., 1981, Paramount Fine Arts Ctr., Aurora, Ill., 1979-81, North Park Village, Chgo., 1982; mem. theatre adv. panel Ill. Arts Coun., 1992. Co-prodr. over 60 world premieres, plays and musicals, 1972—; host (TV program) Arts & The Community, NBC's Knowledge, 1978. Mem. Chgo. Coun. on Fine Arts, 1976-79; panel mem. Dance Adv. Panel/Ill. Arts Coun., Chgo., 1979; mem. Ill. Arts Coun. theatre adv. panel 1992; mem. Nat. Endowment for the Arts, Opera Musical Theatre New Am. Works Panel, 1993; bd. dirs. Community TV Network, Chgo., 1980-84, Performance Community, Chgo., 1974—; mem. adv. bd. Gospel Arts Workshop, Chgo., 1979-85. Recipient Svc. to Arts & Edn. award Ill. Alliance for Arts in Edn., Chgo., 1984, 1st place award for direction Readers Theatre Nat. Competition Jr. Colls. Office: New Tuners Theatre Theatre Bldg 1225 W Belmont Ave Chicago IL 60657-3205

HIGGINS, THOMAS JAMES, electrical and computer engineering educator; b. Charlottesville, Va., July 4, 1911; s. Charles Henry and Eleanor Marie (Higgins) H.; m. Eva Louise Logan, Apr. 7, 1942 (dec. 1963); children: Janet Eleanor, James Logan; m. Mary Ellen Roach, July 18, 1976. BSEE, Cornell U., 1928, MA, 1933; PhD, Purdue U., 1941. Registered profl. engr., Wis. Instr. in math. Auburn (N.Y.) Inst., 1933-34; design and plant engr. Agfa Ascoo Corp., Binghamton, N.Y., 1934-35; instr. in engring. Wyomissing (Pa.) Poly. Inst., 1935-37; instr. in elec. engring. Purdue U., West Lafayette, Ind., 1937-41; asst. prof. elec. engring. Tulane U., New Orleans, 1941-42; assoc. prof. elec. engring. Ill. Inst. Tech., Chgo., 1942-47; prof. elec. engring. U. Wis., Madison, 1947-48. Author: Advanced Basic Automatic Control Theory, 1954. Mem. Am. Soc. Engring. Edn. (George Westinghouse Tchg. award 1954), Instrument Soc. Am. (Eckman award 1964), Wis. Soc. Profl. Engrs. (Engr. of Yr. 1964), Rotary Club West. Roman Catholic. Home: 12 Pin Oak Trail Madison WI 53717 Office: U Wis Dept Elec and Computer Engring 1415 Engineering Dr Madison WI 53706

HIGH, RON L., treasurer manufacturing company; b. Elkhart, Ind., Feb. 21, 1945. AS, Allied Inst. Tech., 1964. Tool and die maker C.T.C., Elkhart, Ind., 1976-79; EDM operator, mold maker Royal Mold and Die, Elkhart, 1979-88; treas. Hyco Machine & Mold, Inc., Elkhart, 1988—. Coach, team rep. Penn Hocky Club. Mem. Masons. Lutheran. Office: Hyco Machine & Mold Inc 3210 Middlebury St Elkhart IN 46516-5544

HIGH, SUZANNE IRENE, lawyer; b. Chgo., June 10, 1946; d. Jack G. and Irene (Sinko) H. A.B. cum laude, Syracuse U., 1968; M.A., Northwestern U., 1973; postgrad. Rosary Coll., 1974-75; J.D., DePaul U., Chgo., 1979. Bar: Ill. 1979, Fla. 1979, U.S. Sup. Ct. 1982. Tchr., Peace Corps, Wolisso, Ethiopia, 1968-70; researcher Compton's Ency., Ency. Brit., Chgo., 1970-72; pres. Renn & High, Chartered, Lisle, Ill, 1979—. Bd. dirs. Lisle Savs. and Loan Assn., 1978-86, Little Friends, Inc., 1985-86, Family Shelter Svc., 1992-94, chair personnel, mem. exec. com. Mem. DuPage County Estate Planning Coun.; bd. dirs. Fox Valley Estate Planning Coun., 1993—, v.p. 94-95, pres. 95—. Mem. ABA, NOW, Nat. Acad. Elder Law Atty's., Fla. Bar Assn., Ill. Bar Assn., DuPage County Bar Assn. (estate planning and probate com. 1987—, speakers' bur. 1985—), Women's Bar Assn. Ill., Fla. Women's Bar Assn., DuPage Assn. Women Lawyers, Internat. Assn. Fin. Planners, Kane County Bar Assn., Lisle C. of C. Office: 5007 Lincoln Ave Ste 300 Lisle IL 60532-2192

HIGHAM, ROBIN, historian, editor, publisher; b. London, June 20, 1925; came to U.S., 1940, naturalized, 1954; s. David and Margaret Anne (Stewart) H.; m. Barbara Davies, Aug. 5, 1950; children: Susan Elizabeth (dec.), Martha Anne, Carol Lee. A.B. cum laude, Harvard U., 1950, Ph.D., 1957; M.A., Claremont Grad. Sch., 1953. Instr. Webb Sch. Calif., 1950-52; grad. asst. in oceanic history Harvard U., 1952-54; instr. U. Mass., 1954-57; asst. prof. U. N.C., Chapel Hill, 1957-63; assoc. prof. history Kans. State U., 1963-66, prof., 1966—; historian Brit. Overseas Airways Corp., 1960-66, 76-78; editor Mil. Affairs, 1968-88, emeritus, 1989—; editor Aerospace Historian, 1970-88, emeritus, 1989—; editor, co-pub. Jour. of the West, 1977—; adv. editor Tech. and Culture, 1967-85; founder, pres. Sunflower Univ. Press, 1977—; mil. adv. editor Univ. Press Ky., 1970-75; cons. Epic of Flight, Time/Life Books, 1980-82; lectr. in field; mem. publs. ocm. Conf. Brit. Studies, 1965-93; advisor Core Collection for Coll. Librs., 1971-72; pres., cons. com. Revue Internat. d'Histoire Militaire, 1976-85, mem. mil. archives com., 1991—; founder, organizer Conf. Historic Aviation Writers, 1982—. Author: Britain's Imperial Air Routes, 1918-39, 1960, The British Rigid Airship, 1908-31, 1961, Armed Forces in Peacetime: Britain 1918-39, 1963, The Military Intellectuals in Britain: 1918-1939, 1966, (with David H. Zook) A Short History of Warfare, 1966, Hebrew edit., 1970, Chinese edit., 1985, The Compleat Academic (Macmillan Book Club choice), 1975, Air Power: A Concise History (selection Mil. Book Soc., History Book Club, Flying Book Club), 1973, 2d enlarged edit., 1984, 3d enlarged edit., 1988, (with Mary Cisper & Guy Dresser) A Brief Guide to Scholarly Editing, 1982, Diary of a Disaster: British Aid to Greece, 1940-41, 1986; editor: Bayonets in the Streets, 1969, 89, Civil Wars in the Twentieth Century, 1972, A Guide to the Sources of British Military History, 1971, A Guide to the Sources of U.S. Military History, 1975, (with Donald J. Mrozek) supplement, 1981, 86, 93, (with Carol Brandt) The U.S. Army in Peacetime: Essays in Honor of the Bicentennial, 1975, Intervention or Abstention, 1975, (with Jacob W. Kipp) Soviet Aviation and Air Power, 1977, Flying Combat Aircraft, Garland Military History Bibliographic Series, 1978-92, (with A. T. Siddall) vol. 1, 1975, (with Carol Williams) vol. 2, 1978 and vol. 3, 1981; editor (with George E. Ham) The Rise of the Wheat State: a History of Kansas Agriculture, 1986, (with Thomos Veremis) The Metaxas Dictatorship: Aspects of Greece, 1936-40; sr. advisor on Ency. of U.S. Mil. History, Acad. Mil. Scis., Beijing, 1988—; advisory editor Ency. of USAF, 1988-92; mem. aviation editorial adv. bd. Smithsonian Instn. Press, 1989-92; adv. Greenwood Press, 1992—; mem. editorial bd. Defence Analysis, 1984—; cons., contbr.: Dictionary of Business Biography, 1980-86, Encyclopedia of the American Military, 1994; contbr. The New Dictionary of National Biography, 1994-95; contbr. articles to profl. jours, also papers at internat. confs. Trustee U.S. Comm. on Mil., 1993—; mem. Kans. State Aviation Adv. Com., 1986-95, sec., 1992-95. Pilot RAF, 1943-46. Named Disting. Grad., Faculty Kans. State U., 1971; recipient Victor Gondos award Am. Mil. Inst., 1983, Samuel Eliot Morison award for disting. scholarship Am. Mil. Inst., 1986; Social Sci. Rsch. Coun. nat. security policy rsch. fellow, 1960-61. Mem. AIAA (standing com. history 1973—), Soc. History Tech., Am. Aviation Hist. Soc., RAF Hist. Soc., Friends of RAF Mus. (life), Burma Star Assn. (life), Air Force Hist. Found. (trustee 1984—), Soc. Army Hist. Rsch. (corr. mem. coun. 1980—), Am. Mil. Inst., WWII Studies Assn. (dir. 1973-75, 79-82, 83—, archivist 1977—), AMI Soc. for Aviation Hist., U.S. Commn. on Mil. History, Riley County Hist. Soc. (past dir., chmn. long-range planning com.). Home: 2961 Nevada St Manhattan KS 66502-2355

HIGHLEN, LARRY WADE, music educator, piano rebuilder, tuner; b. Warren, Ind., Oct. 31, 1936; s. Lawrence Wade and Anna Belle (Dungan) H.; m. Camille Pence (div. 1975); children: Laurel, Wade, Jennifer. Student, Niles Bryant Coll., 1967, Ivy Tech. Coll., Kokomo, Ind., 1975-76, Ivy Tech. Coll., Ft. Wayne, Ind., 1983-84. Pvt. piano tchr. Kokomo, 1967-85; piano tchr. Barbara Martin Piano Svc., Indpls., 1985-88, 1990—, Van Wezel Performing Arts Hall, Sarasota, Fla., 1988-90. Author: Piano Abstract, 1981. Fellow Ancient and Mystical Order Rosae Crucis. Home and Office: 1912 W Deffenbaugh St Kokomo IN 46902-6032

HIGHTOWER, JEANNE JACKSON, nursing administrator; b. Saratoga Springs, N.Y., Feb. 27, 1949; d. Billy G. and Jeanne Lois (Sickles) Jackson; m. Paul Dudley Hightower, July 6, 1971; children: Bradley, Brandon. BA in English, Mass Comm., Western Ky. U., 1971, ADN, 1973. RN, Ind., Ky. DON Holly Hill Health Care Facility, Brazil, Ind., 1983, Sisters Providence, St. Mary-of-the-Woods, Ind., 1984; staff nurse open heart surgery Terre Haute (Ind.) Regional Hosp., 1985, head nurse surgery, 1988, dir. surg. svcs., 1988-90, asst. DON, 1990-91, DON skilled transitional care unit, 1991-92, dir. special svcs., 1991-94, dir. med.-surg. svcs., 1994-96, coord. centralized scheduling, 1996—. Active troop com. Boy Scouts Am., Terre Haute, 1993, 94, 95, 96. Mem. Ind. State Nurse's Assn., Sigma Theta Tau. Republican. Mormon. Office: Columbia Terre Haute Regional Hosp 3901 S 7th St Terre Haute IN 47802-5709

HIGNITE, MICHAEL ANTHONY, computer information systems educator, researcher, writer; b. Baxter Springs, Kans., Jan. 23, 1954; s. Denver and Goldie Beatrice (Farris) H.; m. Lisa Jo Barger, May 15, 1976; 1 child, Anna. B.S. in Bus. Adminstrn., Okla. State U., 1976, M.S. in Bus., 1979; PhD in Bus. Edn. U. Mo., 1990. Computer programmer Atlantic Richfield Co., Dallas, 1979-80, 85-86, programmer, analyst, Tulsa, 1980-82, systems analyst, Anchorage, Alaska, 1982-85, cons., 1987, 88; asst. prof. Southwest Mo. State U., Springfield, 1990-95, assoc. prof., 1995—; adj. prof. computer sci. Anchorage Community Coll., 1982-85. Mem. Internat Assn. Computer Info. Systems, Sierra Club, Delta Sigma Pi, Beta Gamma Sigma. Republican. Methodist. Avocations: reading, running, collecting antiques, biking, camping. Home: 4760 S Connor Ave Springfield MO 65804-7518 Office: Southwest Mo State U 901 S National Ave Springfield MO 65804-0027

HILBERT, VIRGINIA LOIS, computer consultant and training executive; b. Detroit, June 4, 1935; d. Howard G. and Lois (Garner) Swaggerty; m. James R. Hilbert, Nov. 24, 1958; children: James Jr., Jennifer, Douglas, Alexandra. BA with honors, U. Mich., 1957. Govt. analyst dept. pers. City of Detroit, 1957-60; owner, dir. Profl./Tech. Devel., Inc. dba Lansing (Mich.) Computer Assn. and Lansing Computer Inst., 1978—; participant, del. work group Gov.'s Small Bus. Conf. Contbr. articles to profl. jours. Mem. adv. com. Capital Area Sci. and Math. Challenge Grant; mem. tech. bd. Capital Region Cmty. Found., mem. accrediting comn. career schs. and Colls. of tech., Bus. Edn. Alliance for progress, adv. com.Capital Area Sci. & Math, Capital Area Health Alliance; sec. Tennis Patrons Bd., Lansing, 1984-89, Pro Symphony, 1984—; active Lansing Art Gallery, 1978-84. Mem. ASTD, ASCD, Nat. Fedn. Ind. Bus. (guardian), CEO Network, Women Bus. Owners Assn., Mich. Tech. Coun., Nat. Bus. Edn. Assn., Gov.'s Small Bus. Conf. (del. gov.'s work group), Mich. Opportunity Card, Accrediting Commn. of Career Schs. and Colls. of Tech., Bus. Edn. Alliance for Progress, Capital Area Sci. and Math. Challenge Grant Adv. Com., Lansing C. of C. (small bus. coun., co-chair info. and seminar S.B.E., CHSN-TAG com. Capital Area Health Alliance, del. White House Conf. on Small Bus. 1995, regional chmn. human capital 1995, chair human capital region V, chair implementation human capital 1996, mem. bd. physician health plan 1996), Rotary, Zonta, Alpha Phi (pres. heart equip. fund bd. 1975-96, alumnae pres.). Episcopalian. Home: 938 Wildwood Dr East Lansing MI 48823-3050 Office: Lansing Computer Inst 501 N Marshall St Lansing MI 48912-2306

HILBOLDT, JAMES SONNEMANN, lawyer, investment advisor; b. Dallas, July 21, 1929; s. Grover C. and Grace E. (Sonnemann) H.; m. Martha M. Christian, Sept. 5, 1953; children: James, Katherine Hilboldt Farrell, Susanna Jean, Thomas. AB in Econs., Harvard U., 1952; postgrad., U. Chgo., 1952-53; JD, U. Mich., 1956. With comml. and trust dept. No. Trust Co., Chgo., 1952-53; sole practice Kalamazoo, 1956—, pvt. practice as registered investment advisor, 1971—; bd. dirs. Lafourche Realty Co., Inc., Kalamazoo, pres., 1971—, Meijer, Inc., Grand Rapids, Mich., Old Kent Bank S.W. (formerly Am. Nat. Bank and Trust Co.), Mich., 1966-94. Bd. dirs. Kalamazoo Tennis Patrons, Inc., 1974-95, Downtown Devel. Authority, Kalamazoo, 1982-88, Downtown Tomorrow, Inc., Kalamazoo, 1985—, sec., treas., 1995, Downtown Kalamazoo Inc., 1988-91; treas., trustee The Power Found., 1967—, sec., 1967-94. Sgt. USMC, 1946-48. Mem. ABA, Mich. Bar Assn., Kalamazoo County Bar Assn., Harvard Club Western Mich. (pres. 1972-74), Kalamazoo Country Club, Park Club, Harvard Club N.Y.C. Home: 4126 Lakeside Dr Kalamazoo MI 49008-2814 Office: 136 E Michigan Ave Kalamazoo MI 49007

HILDEBRAND, CONNIE MARIE, social worker; b. Minot, N.D., Sept. 14, 1944; d. Arnold Marvin and Sophie Clarice (Mickelson) Sevalson; m. James William Hildebrand, Jan. 2, 1972; 1 child, Travis James. BSW cum laude, U. N.D., 1966; MSW, Columbia U., 1968. Coord. group work svcs. Grand Forks County (N.D.) Social Svcs., 1968-70; dir. social work dept. United Hosp., Grand Forks, 1970-81; social worker Burleigh County Social Svcs., Bismarck, N.D., 1982-83, Casey Family Program, Bismarck, N.D., 1983-92; Profl. Rehab. Mgmt., Olathe, Kan., 1992-94; mem. Gov.'s Coun. on Human Resources, Bismarck, 1985-93. Com. chair Vol. Svcs. Bd., Grand Forks, 1968-70; bd. dirs. Big Bros., Grand Forks, 1970-72; exec. bd. Home Delivered Meals, Grand Forks, 1971-81; pres. Rape Crisis Bd., Grand Forks, 1978-79. Mem. NASW (pres. N.D. chpt. 1987-89), N.D. Pub. Health Assn. (pres. 1983-84), N.D. Conf. Social Welfare (exec. bd. 1980-83), Mental Health Assn. N.D. (child and youth com.), AAUW (state legis. chair 1986-88), Alpha Lambda Delta, Phi Alpha. Home: 421 E Brandon Dr Bismarck ND 58501-0410

HILDEBRAND, DANIEL WALTER, lawyer; b. Oshkosh, Wis., May 1, 1940; s. Dan M. and Rose Marie (Baranowski) H.; m. Dawn E. Erickson; children: Daniel G., Douglas P., Elizabeth A., Rachel E. BS, U. Wis., 1962, LLB, 1964. Bar: Wis. 1964, U.S. Dist. Ct. (we. dist.) Wis. 1964, N.Y. 1965, U.S. Dist. Ct. (so. and ea. dists.) N.Y. 1967, U.S. Ct. Appeals (2d cir.) 1968, U.S. Dist. Ct. (ea. dist.) Wis. 1970, U.S. Ct. Appeals (7th cir.) 1970, U.S. Supreme Ct. 1970, U.S. Tax Ct. 1986, U.S. Ct. Appeals (8th cir.) 1988, U.S. Ct. Appeals (D.C. cir.) 1991. Assoc. Willkie, Farr & Gallagher, N.Y.C., 1964-68; from assoc. to ptnr. DeWitt Ross & Stevens S.C., Madison, Wis., 1968—; lectr. U. Wis. Law Sch., Madison, 1972—; mem. Joint Survey Com. on Tax Ememptions Wis. Editor: U. Wis. Law Rev., 1963-64. Fellow Am. Bar Found.; mem. ABA (mem. fed. cts. com. litigation sect. ho. of dels. 1992—), Wis. Bar Assn. (bd. govs. 1981-85, 93-96, mem. exec. com. 1987-93, chmn. 1988-89, pres. 1991-92), N.Y. State Bar Assn., Dane County Bar Assn. (pres. 1980-81), 7th Cir. Bar Assn. Roman Catholic. Office: DeWitt Ross & Stevens SC 2 E Mifflin St Ste 600 Madison WI 53703-2860

HILDEBRAND, ROGER HENRY, astrophysicist, physicist; b. Berkeley, Calif., May 1, 1922; s. Joel Henry and Emily (Alexander) H.; m. Jane Roby Beedle, May 28, 1944; children: Peter Henry, Alice Louise, Kathryn Jane, Daniel Milton. AB in Chemistry, U. Calif., Berkeley, 1947, PhD in Physics, 1951. Physicist, U. Calif., 1942-51; physicist Tenn. Eastman Corp., Oak Ridge Nat. Lab., 1945; asst. prof. dept. physics Enrico Fermi Inst., U. Chgo., 1952-55, asso. prof., 1955-60, prof., 1960—, prof. dept. astronomy and astrophysics, 1978—, Samuel K. Allison Disting. Service prof., 1985—, chmn. dept. astronomy and astrophysics, 1984-88; dir. Enrico Fermi Inst., 1965-68, dean coll., 1969-73; assoc. lab. dir. for high energy physics Argonne (Ill.) Nat. Lab., 1958-64; chmn. sci. policy com. Stanford (Calif.) Linear Accelerator Ctr., 1962-66; mem. physics adv. com. Nat. Accelerator Lab., 1967-69; mem. sci. and ednl. adv. com. Lawrence Berkeley Lab., 1972-80; chmn. com. to rev. U.S. medium energy sci. AEC and NSF, 1974; chmn. airborne obs. users group NASA, 1983-84; chmn. sci. cons. group Stratopheric Obs. for Infrared Astronomy (SOFIA), NASA, 1985-89, mem. sci. working group, 1995—; mem. space astronomy and astrophysics Space Sci. Bd., 1987-90; mem. coun. Columbus Project, 1987-88; mem. sci. and tech. adv. panel for the submillimeter array Harvard/Smithsonian Ctr. for Astrophysics, 1989-95; mem. astronomy and astrophysics survey com. NAS Panel for Infrared Astronomy, 1989-90; chmn. Dannie Helneman prize com. Am. Inst. Physics, 1990; mem. sci. and tech. adv. group Large Millimeter Telescope, 1995—; mem. obs. vis. com. Assn. Univs. for Rsch. in Astronomy, 1993-96, chmn., 1995-96. Guggenheim fellow, 1968-69, Alfred P. Sloan Found. fellow, 1975. Fellow Am. Phys. Soc., Am. Acad. Arts and Scis.; mem. Am. Astron. Soc., Internat. Astron. Union, Midwestern Univs. Rsch. Assn. (dir. 19956-58, 62-68), Phi beta Kappa, Sigma Xi. Office: U Chgo Enrico Fermi Inst 5640 S Ellis Ave Chicago IL 60637-1433

HILDEBRANDT, GREG ALAN, small business owner; b. Logansport, Ind., Apr. 17, 1950; s. John Joseph and Virginia Ruth (Palmer) H.; m. Lela Ann Donnelly, Apr. 20, 1975 (dec. 1975); m. Gail Lynn Lemke, Feb. 10, 1981; children: Lowell, Whitney. BFA, Art Inst. Chgo., 1972. With prodn. dept. Kewanna (Ind.) Screen Print, 1973-76; pres. Mandala Screen Print, Inc., Winamac, Ind., 1976—, Tech-Mark Inc., Winamac, 1988—. Inventor screen print frame. Democrat. Home and Office: RR 1 Box 387 Winamac IN 46996-9779

HILDEBRANDT, H(ENRY) M(ARK), pediatrician; b. Ann Arbor, Mich., Oct. 23, 1926; s. Theophil Henry and Dora (Ware) H.; m. Jennie Parker (div. 1974); children: Marian, Carl, Janet, Jonathan, Lisabeth; m. Linda Figen (div. 1984); 1 child, Ursula; m. Deborah Bush-Black, 1986. BA, U. Mich., 1948, MD, 1952. Diplomate Am. Bd. Pediatrics. Intern, resident in pediatrics City Hosps. Cleve. and Babies and Children's Hosp., 1952-55; from clin. assoc. prof. to clin. asst. prof. U. Mich., Ann Arbor, Mich., 1958-71, clin. assoc. prof., 1971—; estab. univ. hosp.; pvt. practice Ann Arbor, 1955-87, Ypsilanti, Mich., 1987—; clin. assoc. prof. U. Mich., Ann Arbor, 1969-78, mem. affiliate faculty, 1978—, mem. Suspected Child Abuse and Neglect (SCAN) team, 1971. Mem. Am. Acad. Pediatrics, Ambulatory Pediatric Assn. Episcopalian. Home: 1930 Cambridge Rd Ann Arbor MI 48104-3651 Office: 5333 McAuley Dr Ste R 6011 Ypsilanti MI 48197-1014

HILDRETH, PATRICIA YVONNE, accounting executive; b. Clinton, Ind., Mar. 15, 1934; d. Leonard Adam and Wilma Vivian (Scifres) Prulhiere; m. James A. Hildreth, Jan. 20, 1954; children: John Alan, Patti Virginia, David Michael, Brian Spencer. Student Jackson Community Coll., 1974-80, Eastern Mich. U., 1980-81. Sales clk. Yeager Co., Akron, Ohio, 1951-52; acctg. clk. B.F. Goodrich Co., Akron, 1952-54; owner bookkeeping firm P.Y. Hildreth, Akron, 1965-72; owner Jackson Small Bus. Service (Mich.), 1972—; cons. in field. Millage campaign chmn. Jackson Pub. Sch., 1977, mem. various coms., 1972-81; active Girl Scouts U.S.A., Akron and Jackson; pres. PTA, Akron, 1968-70; treas. Jackson Med. Ctr. Inc., 1980-82, Jackson Interfaith Shelter, 1985—. Mem. Ind. Accts. Assn. of Mich. (edn. com. 1983-84, chmn. chpt. V 1991—, 3d v.p. 1995-96, 2nd v.p. 1996—), mem. NSPA. Republican. Mem. Ch. of Christ. Lodge: Civitan (treas. Jackson club 1981-85, mem. various coms.). Office: Jackson Small Bus Svc 1602 W Washington Ave Jackson MI 49203-1437

HILDRETH, WILLIAM BARTLEY, public administration educator; b. Troy, Ala., Sept. 8, 1949; s. M. Paul and Annie Lester (Crawley) H.; m. Rhonda F. Newberry, July 21, 1979; 1 child, Amy. BA, U. Ala., 1971; M In Pub. Adminstrn., Auburn U., 1974; D in Pub. Adminstrn., U. Ga., 1979. Aide U.S. Senator John Sparkman, Washington, 1971; mgmt. advisor S. Cen. Ala. Devel. Commn., Montgomery, 1973-75; rsch. asst. U. Ga., Athens, 1975-79; asst. prof. Kent (Ohio) State U., 1979-84, assoc. prof., 1984-85; dir. fin. City of Akron, Ohio, 1984-85; assoc. prof. pub. adminstrn. La. State U., Baton Rouge, 1985-90, prof. pub. adminstrn., 1990-94; Regents disting. prof. pub. fin. Wichita (Kans.) State U., 1994—. Author: (with others) Public Budgeting Laboratory, 1983, 2d edit., 1996, State and Local Government Debt Issuance and Management, 1996; editor: La. Fin. Quar., 1985-90, Mcpl. Fin. Jour., 1989—; co-editor Handbook on Public Personnel Administration and Labor Relations, 1983, Handbook of Public Administration, 1989, Handbook of Strategic Management, 1989, Handbook of Public Sector Labor Relations, 1994, Handbook of Public Personnel Administration, 1995, Case Studies in Public Budgeting and Financial Management, 1994, Handbook of Public Sector Labor Relations, 1994, Handbook of Public Personnel Administration, 1995, Budgeting, 1996; editor book revs. Internat. Jour. Pub. Adminstrn., 1980—; contbr. articles to profl. jours. 1st lt. USAF, 1972-73. Loman fellow, Cert. Property and Casualty Underwriter Loman Found., 1981. Mem. Am. Soc. Pub. Adminstrs. (pres. Cleve. chpt. 1982-83, chair Assn. for Budgeting and Fin. Mgmt. 1993-94), Govt. Fin. Officers Assn.

HILE, DUANE L., small business owner; b. Findlay, Ohio, June 18, 1945. AB, Wabash Coll., Crawfordsville, Ind., 1967; MBA, U. Notre Dame, 1973. Mktg. rep. Amoco, Detroit, 1967-68, South Bend, Ind., 1968-69; mgr. sales/mktg. Jessup Door Co., Dowagiac, Mich., 1969-71; assoc. A.T. Kearney, Inc., Cleve., 1973-75; sr. assoc. A.T. Kearney, Inc., London, 1976; mgr. A.T. Kearney, Inc., Chgo., 1977-78; pres. Hile Mgmt. Cons., Cleve., 1978—, Image Wear, Inc., Cleve., 1990—. Contbr. articles to profl. jours. Office: Hile Mgmt Cons 2559 Fenwick Rd University Heights OH 44118-4426

HILFIGER, GARY WILLIAM, clergyman; b. Buffalo, Oct. 26, 1950; s. William Raymond and Arline Ida (Zimmerman) H.; m. Sharon Ann Hart, June 14, 1975; 1 child, Matthew. AA, Concordia Coll., Bronxville, N.Y., 1970; BA, Concordia Sr. Coll., Ft. Wayne, Ind., 1972; MDiv, Evang. Luth. Theol. Sem., Columbus, Ohio, 1977; MA, Miami U., Oxford, Ohio, 1988. Ordained minister Lutheran Ch., 1977. Pastor Holy Trinity Luth. Ch., New Lexington, Ohio, 1977-84; co-pastor Bethlehem Luth. Ch., Middletown, Ohio, 1984-90; pastor Faith Luth. Ch., Jackson, Ohio, 1992—; Ohio coord. Luth. Peace Fellowship, 1978-83; bd. dirs. Jackson Area Ministries, 1993—. Home: 30 S David Ave Jackson OH 45640

HILKER, MARCUS DUDLEY, JR., manufacturing executive; b. St. Paul, Oct. 13, 1947; s. Marcus Dudley and Lou Ann (Parkin) H.; m. Georgeanne Bergquist, July 3, 1975; children: Matthew, Taylor. BA in Geology, Windham Coll., 1970; postgrad., Oreg. State U., 1978; MBA, U. St. Thomas, 1992. Programmer, analyst Northwestern Nat. Life Ins. Co., Mpls., 1981-84; systems analyst CitiBank, Sioux Falls, S.D., 1984-86; cons. Capstone Profl. Svc., Mpls., 1987-89; dir. Harvey Vogel Mfg., Mpls., 1990—. Mem. Assn. System Mgrs., Data Processing Mgmt. Assn. Republican. Episcopalian. Office: Harvey Vogel Mfg 425 Weir Dr Woodbury MN 55125

HILL, BEVERLY ELLEN, health sciences educator; b. Albany, Calif., May 20, 1937; d. Bert E. and Catherine (Doyle) H. BA, Coll. Holy Names, 1960; MS in Edn., Dominican Coll., 1969; EdD, U. So. Calif., 1978. Producer, dir. Health Scis TV U. Calif., Davis, 1966-69, coordinator Health Scis. TV, 1969-73; asst. dir. IMS U. So. Calif., Los Angeles, 1973-76, asst. dir. continuing edn., 1976-80, dir. biocommunications, 1976-80; dir. Med. Ednl. Resources Program Ind. U. Sch. Medicine, Indpls., 1980—; acting asst. dean continuing med. edn. Ind. U. Sch. Medicine, 1991-95; Presenter Cath. U. Nijmegen, Netherlands, 1980, 81, European Symposium on Clin. Pharmacy, Brussels, 1982, Barcelona, Spain, 1983. Contbr. articles to profl. jours. Pres. Indpls. Shakespeare Festival, 1982-83; mem. subcom. Ind. Film Commn., Indpls., 1984—. Recipient first place in rehab. category 4th Biannual J. Muir Med. Film Fest., 1980. Mem. Assn. Biomed. Communications (bd. dirs. 1985—), Health Scis. Com. Assn. (bd. dirs. 1976-79, First Place Video Festival, 1979), Assn. for Edn. Communications and Tech. Home: 5249 W 59th St Indianapolis IN 46254-1109 Office: Med Ednl Resources Program BR 156 1226 W Michigan St Indianapolis IN 46223

HILL, CLARENCE E., auditor; b. Centralia, Ill., Jan. 14, 1925; s. Clarence E. and Ruby Lee (Dixon) H.; m. Terry Wilson, Mar. 13, 1954; 1 child, Hussein A. BA, Roosevelt U., Chgo., 1951; MA, USDA Grad. Sch., Washington, 1989. CPA, N.Y.; cert. fraud examiner; cert. revenue auditor. Sr. auditor STate of Ill., Chgo., 1952-63; sr. auditor U. S. Army, Ft. Sheridan, Ill., 1963-69, Joliet, Ill., 1969-70; auditor U. S. Army, Ft. Sheridan, 1984-86, chief of divsn., 1986-88; auditor-in-chg. Commodity Exch. Authority, Chgo., 1970-80; agt. IRS, Chgo., 1980; auditor-in-chg. Housing Dept., Chgo., 1980-84; sr. tax agt. State Taxes Ohio, Des Plaines, Ill., 1988—; owner Hill Profl./Hill Acctg., Chgo., 1946—; cons. Cadillac Pers., Chgo., 1979-80; tax auditor City of Chgo., 1981; adv. bd. Chgo. Pub. Schs., 1973. Author: State Taxes in U.S.A., 1963. Coord. Vol. Income Tax Assistance, Chgo., 1994-95. With U.S. Army, 1944-46, lt. col. USAR, 1985-88. Decorated Army Commendation medal. Mem. Am. Assn. Ret. People (local coord. 1985—, tax aide 1988-94), Assn. Cert. Fraud Examiners. Home and Office: 9720 S Emerald Ave Chicago IL 60628

HILL, DALE A., packaging manager; b. Ft. Dodge, Iowa, Aug. 19, 1950. Designer Hotsy Corp., Humboldt, Iowa, 1974-80; packaging mgr. Douglas & Lomason Co., Inc., Humboldt, 1980—. Inventor: holds patent in material handling field. With U.S. Navy, 1970-74. Mem. Humbolt Rifle & Pistol Assn. Methodist. Office: Douglas & Lomason Co Inc Hwy 3 East Dr E Humboldt IA 50548

HILL, DAVID WILLIAM, design company executive; b. Youngstown, Ohio, Mar. 1, 1949; s. Eugene David and Eleanore Ruth (Welsh) H.; m. Penny M. Simon, Dec. 31, 1983 (div. Sept. 1986); m. Linda S. Lowe, July 16, 1988 (div. Jan. 1991); m. Susan J. McAlister, Sept. 7, 1991 (div. Dec. 1996); m. Jane I. Rexroth, June 6, 1996. Cert., USAF Sch. Acctg. and Fin., 1969. Cert. credit and fin. analyst Dun and Bradstreet. Office mgr. Oxford (Ohio) Auto Parts, 1971-72; sec. Mobile Enterprises, Inc., Ft. Wayne, Ind., 1973-78; owner, pres. Hill Ins. Agy., Ft. Wayne, 1978-82; v.p. Royal Oak Fin. Services, Inc., Ft. Wayne, 1983-84; exec. v.p. Spirit of Am. Corp., Ft. Wayne, 1986—, also bd. dirs.; bd. dirs., exec. v.p. MidAm. Design Svc. divsn. Spirit of Am. Corp., Ft. Wayne, 1984—, Mid-Am. Temporaries, Creative Bldg. Products divsn. Spirit of Am. Corp., 1984—; v.p. Silhouetes divsn. Spirit of Am. Corp.; bd. dirs. Miltec Engring. and Mfg. Co. divsn. Spirit of Am. Corp., Ft. Wayne; v.p., bd. dirs. Typhoid Larry O'Leary's divsn. Spirit of Am. Corp., Ft. Wayne; ptnr. Brown & Hill, 1989—; v.p. Treasured Gems, 1993; spkr. in field. Author plays/scripts Millard Fillmore Prodn., 1984—; contbr. software articles for system 36, IBM. Dep. registrar Bd. Election, Ft. Wayne, 1973-76; Dem. precinct committeeman, Ft. Wayne, 1973-76, asst. precinct committeeman, Youngstown, 1963-70. Served with USAF, 1969-70. Mem. Ind. Assn. Convenience Stores (Pinnacle Hole-in-One award 1986), Golf Digest (field adv. network 1987—), Minot (N.D.) Mut. Investment Club (pres. 1969-70), Elks Country Club (bd. govs. Ft. Wayne 1981-85, 90-95, trustee chmn. 1994-95), Elks (exalted ruler 1984-85). Lutheran. Home: 4823 Coventry Pky Fort Wayne IN 46804-3248 Office: Spirit of Am Corp 4307 Arden Dr Fort Wayne IN 46804-4446

HILL, DUANE C., manufacturing engineer; b. Amherst, Ohio, Sept. 10, 1963. Assoc. Autmoation and C.C. Programming, Lorain County C.C., 1989. Elec. draftsman R. E. Warner & Assoc., Loraine, Ohio, 1981-84; mfg. engr. Nordson Corp., Amherst, 1984—. Mem. Soc. Mfg. Engrs. Republican. Methodist. Office: 1090 Nordson Dr Amherst OH 44001-2422

HILL, EDWIN LEE, librarian; b. Des Moines, July 15, 1936; s. Clarence Slocum and Mabel Adele (Stine) H.; m. Janice Vortman, 1968 (div. 1974); m. Nancy Catherine Fulkerson, Jan. 31, 1976. BA, No. Ariz. U., 1964; MLS, Rutgers U., 1966; MS, U. Wis., La Crosse, 1978. Asst. reference libr. Western Ill. U., Macomb, 1966-68; documents libr. U. Wis., La Crosse, 1968-69, spl. collections libr., 1969—, dept. chmn. Murphy Libr., 1982-91. Co-editor: LaCrosse in Light and Shadow, 1992; contbr. essays, short stories to lit. mags. Mem. La Crosse County Hist. Soc.; mem. Miss. Valley Archaeology Ctr., bd. dirs., 1982-86; mem. State Hist. Records Adv. Bd., 1991—; chmn. Preservation Alliance of La Crosse, 1976-79. With U.S. Army, 1958-62. Grantee Am. Revolution Bicentennial Commn., 1975, Wis. Humanities Com., 1986. Home: 425 19th St S La Crosse WI 54601-5068 Office: Univ Wis Murphy Libr 1631 Pine St La Crosse WI 54601-3748

HILL, EMITA BRADY, academic administrator; b. Balt., Jan. 31, 1936; d. Leo and Lucy McCormick (Jewett) Brady; children: Julie Beck, Christopher, Madeleine. BA, Cornell U., 1957; MA, Middlebury Coll., 1958; PhD, Harvard U., 1967. Instr. Harvard U., 1961-63; asst. prof. Western Reserve U., 1967-69; from asst. prof. to v.p. Lehman Coll. CUNY, Bronx, N.Y., 1970-91; chancellor, grad. faculty Ind. U., Kokomo, Ind., 1991—. Mem. Am. Assn. Higher Edn., Assn. Am. Coll., Am. Soc. for 18th Century Studies, Am. Assn. State Colls. and Univs., Internat. Assn. Univ. Pres., Internat. Soc. for 18th Century Studies, Phi Beta Kappa. Office: Ind U PO Box 9003 2300 S Washington St Kokomo IN 46902-9003

HILL, FAY GISH, librarian; b. Rensselaer, Ind., Sept. 19, 1944; d. Roy Charles and Vergie (Powell) Gish; m. John Christian Hill, May 20, 1967; 1 child, Christina Gish. BA, Purdue U., 1967; MLS, U. Tex., 1971. Asst. librarian basic reference dept. Tex. A&M U., College Station, 1972, assoc. librarian sci. ref. dept., 1972-74, acting head librarian sci. reference dept., 1975; reference librarian Cen. Iowa Regional Library, Des Moines, 1984—. Troop leader Girl Scouts U.S., Ames, Iowa, 1983-88; bd. dirs. Friends of Fgn. Wives, Ames, 1982-86. Mem. ALA, Iowa Libr. Assn., Iowa Libr. Assn. Found. (bd. dirs. 1990-95). Presbyterian. Home: 5604 Thunder Rd Ames IA 50014-9448 Office: Cen Iowa Regional Libr Reference 515 Douglas Ave Ames IA 50010-6215

HILL, GARY DEAN, journalist; b. Green Bay, Wis., Apr. 11, 1952; s. Doc Allen and Helen Bernice (Hunt) H.; m. Minda Joyce Gilbert, Aug. 7, 1976; 1 child, Nathan Gilbert. BA, U. Wis., 1974. Film/video editor Sta. KSTP-TV, Mpls., 1974-76, photographer, 1976-79, weekend assignment editor, 1978-80, assoc. prodr., 1979-82, assignment editor, 1982-85, mng. editor, 1985—. Mem. Minn. Joint Media Com., 1993—, v.p.-elect. Mem. Soc. Profl. Journalists (pres. 1991-92, Mark of Excellence winner for investigative reporting 1995), Investigative Reporters and Editors Assn. Office: Sta KSTP-TV 3415 University Ave SE Minneapolis MN 55414-3348

HILL, HOWARD DARNELL, fraternal organization executive, educator; b. Texarkana, Ark., May 4, 1942; s. Howard, Jr. and Della Mae (Williams) H.; m. Clemmie Faye Coulter, Dec. 24, 1963; children: Ray Darnell, Edith Renee. BA in Social Studies, Philander Smith Coll., 1964; MSE in Secondary Sch. Adminstrn., Ark. State U., 1968; PhD in Curriculum and Instrn., Kans. State U., 1973; postdoctoral work in ednl. adminstrn. U. S.C., 1983-85. Secondary tchr. Jonesboro Pub. Schs., Ark., 1964-66; supr. instrn. Marion Schs., Ark., 1966-69; asst. prin. West Memphis Schs., Ark., 1969-70; secondary tchr. Tunica Pub. Sch., Miss., 1970-71; asst. prof. edn. U. Houston, 1973-77; assoc. prof. Miss. Valley State U., Itta Bena, 1977-78; prof., chmn., program coord. dept. edn. S.C. State U., Orangeburg, 1978-87; dir. chpt. programs Phi Delta Kappa Hdqrs., Bloomington, Ind., 1987—; cons. Nat. Ednl. Svc., Bloomington. Contbr. articles to profl. jours. and books. Bd. dirs. Big Brothers/Big Sisters Bloomington. Named Tchr. of Yr., S.C. State U. Sch. Edn., 1983. Mem. ASCD, John Dewey Soc., Am. Assn. Colls. Tchr. Edn., Nat. Coun. Social Studies, Nat. Alliance Black Sch. Educators. Home: 915 Eminence Way Bloomington IN 47401

HILL, HOWARD GEORGE, product developer; b. Akron, Ohio, Dec. 20, 1964; s. Howard George and Deanna Sue (Catlett) H. BS, U. Akron, 1989. Computer programmer CPAid, Inc., Kent, Ohio, 1989-94; product developer Mgmt. Reports, Inc., Cleve., 1994—; cons. Best Programs, Reston, Va., 1994. Mem. IEEE, Engrs. Computer Soc. Home: 680 Garry Rd Akron OH 44305 Office: Mgmt Reports Inc 23945 Mercantile Cleveland OH 44122

HILL, JOANNE FRANCIS, elementary education educator; b. Holland, Mich., Jan. 12, 1937. BA in Elem. Edn., Western Mich. U., 1961; postgrad., Mich. State U., 1961-65, Oxford U., 1965. Cert. elem. tchr. Sec. Am. Bus. Woman, Holland, 1972-74; tchr. West Ottawa Mid. Sch., Holland. Former leader Camp Fire Girls, Inc., Holland; mem. Holland Cmty. Theatre, 1972-89; Sunday sch. tchr. Ref. Ch., 1970-81, mem. choir, 1972—, elder, 1981-94. Mem. ASCD, Nat. Coun. Tchrs., Nat. Coun. Tchrs. English, Mich. Edn. Assn. (pres. 1993-94, past pres. 1994-95), Area Bargaining Coun. (sec. 1992-95), Sch. Employees Coun. (sec. 1992-93), West Ottawa Edn. Assn. (sec. 1984-85, v.p. 1985-86, pres. 1986—). Republican. Home: 1008 Bluebell Dr Holland MI 49423-6861 Office: W Ottawa Mid Sch 3700 140th Ave Holland MI 49424-8417

HILL, JOHN WALLACE, special education educator. BA in Elem. Edn. cum laude, Am. U., 1970, MEd in Spl. Edn., 1971, PhD in Edn., 1974. Dir. Learning Disabilities Clinic Meyer Children's Rehab. Inst., U. Nebr. Med. Ctr., Omaha, 1974-87; prof. spl. edn. Coll. of Edn., U. Nebr., Omaha, 1974—, Regents prof., 1989-95; adj. prof. Coll. of Pharmacy, U. Nebr. Med. Ctr.; lectr. various univs., assns. and confs.; former mem., bd. dirs. Omaha Head Start Program, Child and Family Devel. Corp. Contbr. articles to profl. jours. Fellow Am. Acad. for Cerebral Palsy and Devel. Medicine; mem. Phi Delta Kappa, Sigma Xi. Office: Univ Nebr at Omaha Dept Spl Edn Omaha NE 68182

HILL, PAUL MARK, clergyman; b. Cin., Aug. 29, 1953; s. Paul Frederick and Helen Faith (Skeen) H.; m. Rebecca Sue Helm, Dec. 29, 1977; children: Aaron Israel Paul, Revkah Lauren Amara, Hadassah Sue Elizabeth. BA in Biology, Asbury Coll., 1975; DivM, Anderson Sch. Theology, 1981; postgrad., Covenant Theol. Sem. Ordained to ministry Meth. Ch., 1984. Sr. pastor United Meth. Ch., Marion, Ind., 1978—, camp dir., 1990—; speaker and lectr. in field. Dir. TV show Offer Them Christ, 1986; partial designer grandfather clock, 1989. Actor Civic Theater, Logansport, Ind., 1981-82, Peru Civic Theater, 1981-82; coach baseball, basketball, soccer, Marion, Ind., 1986-89; baseball coach, Lafayette, Ind., 1995; organizer, dir. Stockwell Youth Orch., 1990; coach basketball, Lafayette, Ind., 1993-95. Named to Outstanding Young Men of Am., 1988.

HILL, PAUL RICHARD, financial aid director, educator; b. Madison, Ind., Nov. 14, 1951; s. Paul and Mary Ruth (Jackson) H.; m. Janet Lee Coleman, Feb. 13, 1976; 1 child: Trina Celeste. BA in Sociology, Ind. U., New Albany, 1980; MS in Vocat.-Tech. Adminstrn., Ind. State U., 1991. Aide learning resource ctr. Ivy Tech. State Coll., Madison, Ind., 1976-77, acctg. clk., 1977-81, bookstore supr., 1981-85, instr. math., sci. and bus., 1981—, mgr. student fin. aid, 1985—; instr. bus. comm., acad. coord. Oakland City (Ind.) U., 1993—. Treas. Madison Jaycees, 1980-82; mem. Jefferson County Vets.' Svc. Coun., 1989—, Jefferson Proving Groud Restoration Adv. Bd., 1994—; newsletter editor Save the Valley, Inc., 1989—, pres., 1991—; bd. dirs. Hoosier Environ. Coun., 1996—. Recipient Svc. award Jefferson County Vets.' Svc. Coun., 1991. Mem. Nat. Assn. Fin. Aid Adminstrs., Midwestern Assn. Fin. Aid Adminstrs., Elks. Home: 3800 W H&H Rustic Ln Madison IN 47250 Office: Ivy Tech State Coll 590 Ivy Tech Dr Madison IN 47250

HILL, PHILIP, retired lawyer; b. East Saint Louis, Ill., Mar. 13, 1917; s. Nehemiah William and Lulu Myrtle (Johnson) H.; m. Betty Jean Stone, July 4, 1942; children: William Stone, Thomas Chapman, Nancy Layton, Mary Anne. AB in Chemistry, U. Ill., 1937; PhD in Chemistry, Ohio State U., 1941; JD, John Marshall Law Sch., Chgo., 1968. Bar: Ill. 1968, U.S. Patent Office 1969, U.S. Ct. Appeals (fed. cir.) 1982. With Standard Oil Co. Ind., 1941-78, patent atty., 1969-73, dir. petroleum and corp. patents and licensing, 1973-78; ptnr. Hill & Hill, Lansing, Ill., 1978-86, pvt. practice law Philip Hill, P.C., 1987-96; ret., 1996; cons. Univ. Patents, Inc., Norwalk, Conn., 1980-89; treas. Am. Waste Reduction Corp., 1992-96. Mem. ABA, AAAS, Ill. State Bar Assn., Am. Intellectual Property Law Assn., Chgo. Patent Law Assn., Am. Chem. Soc., Phi Beta Kappa, Sigma Xi, Phi Kappa Phi. Methodist. Clubs: Kiwanis (Lansing, pres. 1959, 84). Contbr. articles to profl. jours.; patentee in field. Home: 3241 N Schultz Dr Lansing IL 60438-3205 Office: PO Box 187 Lansing IL 60438-0187

HILL, RAYMOND JOSEPH, packaging company executive; b. Chanute, Kans., May 4, 1935; s. Raymond Joseph and Emma Leona (Arthurs) H.; Asso. in Engring., Coffeyville (Kans.) Coll., 1955; m. Bettie Anne Handshumaker, Mar. 2, 1957; children: David, Dianne, Todd, Scott, Jennifer. MBA, U. Denver, 1977. Field engr. Phillips Petroleum Co., Bartlesville, Okla., 1957-59; design engr. Thiokol Chem. Corp., Brigham City, Utah, 1959-60; tech. supr. Hercules Chem. Corp., Salt Lake City, 1960-68; project mgr. aerospace div. Ball Corp., Boulder, Colo., 1968-70, plant mgr. and v.p. mfg. metal container div., Findlay, Ohio and Denver, Colo., 1970-78, pres. agrl. systems div., Westminster, Colo., 1978-85; v.p. plastic ops., sr. v.p. mfg. tech., ex. v.p. food plastics Am. Nat. Can Corp., Chgo., 1985-90, sr. v.p. mfg. tech., 1990-93, exec. v.p. food plastics N.Am.; pres. Chesnee Assocs., Inc., Internat. Cons., 1993—; bd. dirs. Navaho Agrl. Products Industries, United Energy Devel., Packaging Adv. Coun., Flex Packing Assn., The Hallmark Group, Garnet Distbn. Co., Classic Signatures, Inc.; mem. policy adv. com. to Office of U.S. Trade Rep., 1980—. Mem. Am. Ordnance Assn., Nat. Food Processors Assn., Soc. Tool Engrs., Irrigation Assn., Rotary. Republican. Episcopalian. Home: 909 Watercress Dr Naperville IL 60540-7660 Office: Chesnee Assocs Inc 2010 E Algonquin Rd Ste 210 Schaumburg IL 60173-4168

HILL, RICHARD A., advertising executive; b. Detroit. Student, Mich. State U.; MS in Mktg., Wayne State U. With J. Walter Thompson, Young & Rubicam; media supr. Buick/GMC Truck divsn., assoc. media dir. McCann-Erickson, Troy, Mich., 1970-75; sr. account exec. Buick account McCann-Erickson, Troy, 1975-77; v.p. media, mktg. dir. McCann-Erickson, Detroit, 1977-79, account supr. multi-products group, 1979-81, account supr. Buick, 1981-86, sr. v.p., mgmt. rep., 1986-91, dep. mgr., chmn. mgmt. bd., 1991-93, exec. v.p., gen. mgr., 1993—. Office: McCann-Erickson 755 W Big Beaver Rd Ste 2500 Troy MI 48084

HILL, ROBERT JOHN, aviation executive; b. Unity, Ohio, June 29, 1932; s. Harry H. and Alice Jo (Blair) H.; m. Eve Marie Duke, Feb. 16, 1957; children: Kathleen, Randall, Scott. BBA, Youngstown State U., 1960; postgrad. in aviation tech., U. Miami, 1963; postgrad. in aviation, Flight Safety Inst., 1973-86. Cert. various instr. and transp. ratings, FAA. Pilot Beckett Aviation, Youngstown and Cleve., Ohio, 1967-77; ops. inspector FAA, Indpls., 1977-78; pilot Republic Steel, Cleve., 1979-82; pres. R.J. Hill, Inc., Strongsville, Ohio, 1983—; chief pilot Flight Ops., Inc., Cleve., 1984-89; capt. Corp. Wings, 1989—; cons. Savors Aviation, Negley, Ohio, 1968-71, Brunswick (Ohio) Aviation, 1985-86, Grafton-Ea. Aviation Group, 1988-90. Asst. leader Boy Scouts Am., North Lima, Ohio, 1968-71; advisor Youth Riding Club, Strongsville, 1974-76; co-leader Teen Aviation Group, Columbiana, Ohio, 1984. Served with USN, 1950-54, Korea. Mem. Nat. Bus. Aircraft Assn. (assoc.), Exptl. Aircraft Assn. (v.p. 1983—), Quiet Birdmen, DAV. Methodist. Home: 16554 Whitney Rd Cleveland OH 44136-2411 Office: Corporate Wings 355 Richmond Rd Cleveland OH 44143-1420

HILL, ROBYN LESLEY, artist, designer; b. Sydney, Australia, Apr. 28, 1942; d. Frank Bragg and Florence Margorie (Turnham) H. Grad., Nat. Art Sch., Sydney, 1962; studied with Edward Betts, Claude Croney, Fred Leach, Maxine Masterfield, 1969-85. Art mistress S.C.E.G.G.S., Sydney, 1963-66; apprentice artist Am. Greetings, Cleve., 1967, conventional and specialities planning stylist, profl. designer and artist, 1967-73, mkgt. dept. gift wrap coord., 1973-75, prof. stylist books and stationery dept., 1976-78, art dir. creative devel., 1978-81; program dir. Those Characters from Cleve., 1982-94. Creative, designer (TV program) The Special Magic of Herself the Elf (Can. Emmy award 1982); exhibited at Catherine Lorillard Wolfe Nat. Exhbn., N.Y., Massillon Mus. Invitational, Ohio, Adirondacks Nat. Show, N.Y., Artists Soc. Internat., San Francisco, Am. Watercolor Soc. show and traveling show, Rocky Mountain Watercolor Nat. Exhbn., Internat. Art Expo, Dallas, Blue Grass 5th Biennial, Ky. Mem. Nat. Watercolor Soc. (signature), Nat. Watercolor USA Hon. Soc. (award Springfield Art Mus. 1984, signature), Am. Watercolor Soc. (assoc.), Midwest Watercolor Soc. (assoc.), Ohio Watercolor Soc. (So. Ohio Bank award 1983, signature), Pa. Soc. Watercolor Painters, Ga. Watercolor Soc. (assoc.), North Coast Collage Soc. (signature), Ky. Watercolor Soc. (exhibiting mem.). Episcopalian. Home: 27004 Lake Shore Blvd Euclid OH 44132-1242

HILL, SANDRA J., state legislator; b. Nov. 12, 1936; m. Donald M. Hill; children: Daniel J., Debra K. Mawer, Sharon S. Flint Jr. Coll., Easter Mich. U. State rep. Dist. 47 Mich. Ho. of Reps., 1992—; vice chair Conservation, Environment & Great Lakes com. Mich. Ho. of Reps., mem. Agriculture & Forestry, Oversights & Ethics & Inc. coms. Mem., bd. dirs. Genesee County Farm Bur., 1973-79, 81-89, pres., 1984-89; mem. WWomen's State Com. Mich. Farm Bur., 1978-90, state policy com., 1988-89. Mem. Mich. Food Safety Coun., Women for Survival of Agriculture in Mich. Home: 10253 Farrand Rd Montrose MI 48457-9733*

HILL, THOMAS ALLEN, lawyer; b. Salem, Ohio, Mar. 29, 1958; s. Charles Spencer and Dorothy Jane (Allen) H. BA magna cum laude, Hiram Coll., 1980; JD, George Washington U., 1984. Bar: Ohio 1984, Pa. 1987, D.C. 1988, U.S. Supreme Ct. 1989, Tex. 1990, Okla. 1991. Legis. intern Office of Hon. John Conyers, Jr., Washington, 1979; asst. to dean campus Life for Housing, conf. dir. Hiram (Ohio) Coll., 1980-81; corp. counsel Capital Oil & Gas Inc., Austintown, Ohio, 1984-93; gen. counsel, sec. North Coast Energy, Inc., Bedford Heights, Ohio, 1987—, Trinity Oil & Gas, Inc. subs. North Coast Energy Inc., Warren, Ohio, 1990-93; mem. mini-task force on notices of violation Ohio Div. Oil and Gas, Columbus, 1988-90. Mem. ABA, Ohio Bar Assn., Mahoning County Bar Assn., Pa. Bar Assn., Okla. Bar Assn., D.C. Bar Assn., State Bar Tex., Trumbull County Bar Assn., Ohio Oil and Gas Assn., Christian Legal Soc., Ea. Mineral Law Found., Fed. Energy Bar Assn., Ohio Land Title Assn., Ohio Geneal. Soc., Mahoning Valley Hist. Soc., Austintown Hist. Soc., Gen. Soc., War of 1812, Sons Am. Revolution, Order of Arrow, Kappa Delta Pi, Pi Gamma Mu. Republican. Home: 4841 Westchester Dr Apt 102 Youngstown OH 44515-2548 Office: North Coast Energy Inc 3896 Oakwood Ave Youngstown OH 44515-3033

HILL, THOMAS CLARK, lawyer; b. Prestonsburg, Ky., July 17, 1946; s. Lon Clay and Corinne (Allen) H.; m. J. Barbarie Friedly, June 13, 1968; children: Jason L., Duncan L. BA, Case Western Reserve U., 1968; JD, U. Chgo., 1973. Bar: Ohio 1973, U.S. Supreme Ct. 1976. Assoc. atty. Taft, Stettinius & Hollister, Cin., 1973-81, ptnr., 1981—. Trustee, treas. Wilmington (Ohio) Coll., 1982-94; treas. Friends World Commn. for Consultation, Sect. of the Ams., 1990-95, presiding clk., 1995—; trustee Wilmington Yearly Meeting of Friends (Quakers), 1986—. Mem. ABA, Ohio State Bar Assn., Cin. Bar Assn., Friends Hist. Assn. (bd. dirs. 1994-95). Republican. Mem. Soc. of Friends. Office: 1800 Star Bank Ctr 1800 Star Bank Ctr Cincinnati OH 45202-3957

HILL, THOMAS CLARKE, IX, accountant, systems specialist; b. Chgo., July 5, 1969; s. Thomas Clarke VIII and Arlene Mae (Wertz) H. BA in Polit. Economy and Politics, Lake Forest Coll., 1992. Legis. asst. State Sen. William E. Peterson, Prairie View, Ill., 1989-92, State Rep. William E. Peterson, Prairie View, 1992-94; project mgr. Vernon Twp., Prairie View, 1992-94; cons. Resource Tech. Assocs., Des Plaines, Ill., 1994-95; acct., systems specialist Green Acres Country Club, Northbrook, Ill., 1996—. Precinct com. Lake County (Ill.) Rep. Ctrl. Com., 1990—; chmn. Lake County Young Reps., 1993; del. state conv. Rep. Ctrl. Com., Peoria, Ill., 1992; election judge Office of County Clk., Lake County, 1988-90. Frances Beidler scholar Lake Forest Coll., 1990-91, 91-92. Mem. Nat. Eagle Scout Assn., Shriners, Scottish Rite, Masons, Mensa, Phi Beta Kappa, Pi Sigma Alpha. Home: 64 Berkshire Ln Lincolnshire IL 60069 Office: Green Acres Country Club 916 Dundee Rd Northbrook IL 60062

HILL, THOMAS STEWART, electronics executive, consultant, engineer; b. Wilmington, Del., Jan. 6, 1936; s. Abraham Fleming and Mary Agnes (Stewart) H.; m. Elizabeth Ann Sitterson, July 8, 1961; children: Douglas A., Stephen M., Thomas F., Bethany J. Student, Clemson (S.C.) U., 1954-56; BS, USAF Acad., 1961; MBA, Syracuse (N.Y.) U., 1977. Sales engr. Pratt & Whitney Aircraft Co., E. Hartford, Conn., 1965-66; with Cutler-Hammer, Inc., divsn. of Eaton Corp., Hartford, Conn., 1966-74; sales mgr. Cutler-Hammer, Inc., Syracuse, N.Y., 1975-77; divsn. mktg. mgr. Cutler-Hammer, Inc., Bethlehem, Pa., 1977-79; v.p. mktg. and sales div., gen. mgr. Melting Systems div. Pillar Corp., Milw., 1979-81; gen. mgr. Mo. Rsch. Labs., Albuquerque, 1981-85; v.p. mktg. Durakool, Inc., Elkhart, Ind., 1985-87; v.p. mktg. div. A.E. C. subs. Durakool, Inc., Elkhart, 1987-88; pres. Burgess Switch Co. N. Am. Ops., Elkhart, 1988-89, SAIA Motors (Switzerland), No. Am. Ops., Switzerland, 1988-89, Burgess Switch Co. (Eng.), 1988-89; v.p. mktg. Am. Electronic Components, Elkhart, Ind., 1989-93; chmn., CEO Am. Assn. Profl. Sales Engrs., Elkhart, 1993—; adj. prof. St. Louis U., 1984-85, Grad. Sch. Bus., Ind. U., 1991—; cons. S.C. State Devel.Bd., Columbia, 1989—. Photographer in field. Vol. baseball coach Armijo High Sch., Fairfield, Calif., 1961-63; mem. Curriculum Study Com., Coventry, Conn., 1969-71; elected mem. Coventry Bd. of Edn., 1971-75; advisor Jr. Achievement, Hartford, Conn., 1966; counselor Ch. Youth Group, Fairfield, 1961-63. Capt. USAF, 1961-65, Vietnam. Mem. IEEE, Am. Mgmt. Assn., Am. Assn. Profl. Sales Engrs. (founder, exec. dir., chmn. 1983—), Am. Foundryman's Soc., Internat. Platform Assn., Masons. Methodist. Home and Office: 55969 Jayne Dr Elkhart IN 46514-1325

HILL, WARREN HERBERT, government official; b. Moline, Ill., Dec. 30, 1937; s. Stanley Eugene and Frances Eugenia (Mendenhall) H.; m. Mary Grace Atchison, Apr. 9, 1960 (div. Sept. 1985); children: Damon Michael, Tammy Michelle; m. Betty J. Drelicharz, July 24, 1993. BA in Geology, U. Colo., 1960. Park ranger Death Valley Nat. Monument, Calif., 1960-64; park naturalist Gt. Sand Dunes Nat. Monument, Alamosa, Colo., 1964-67; park mgr. Grand Canyon Nat. Park, Ariz., 1967-71; park supt. Roosevelt-Vanderbilt Nat. Hist. Site, Hyde Park, N.Y., 1971-79; assoc. regional dir. midwest region Nat. Park Svc., Omaha, 1979-91; park supt. Niobrara-Mo. Nat. Scenic Riverways, Nat. Park Svc., O'Neill, Nebr., 1991—; mem. com. global climate change Nat. Park Svc., 1989-92, team leader Poland cultural landscapes, 1990. Recipient Point Light award U.S. Sec. Interior, 1989. Mem. Rotary (pres. Hyde Park 1975, dist. gov. Nebr. and Iowa 1986-87, charter pres. O'Neill 1992-93, Paul Harris fellow 1985), Nebr. Rural Devel. Commn. Lutheran. Home: PO Box 602 O'Neill NE 68763-0602 Office: Nat Park Svc PO Box 591 O'Neill NE 68763-0591

HILLARD, CAROLE, state official; b. Deadwood, S.D., Aug. 14, 1936; m. John M. Hillard; children: David, Sue Ellen, Todd, Eddie, Lornell. BA in Edn., Univ. of Ariz., 1957; MA in Edn., S.D. State Univ., 1982; MA in Polit. Sci., Univ. of S.D., 1984. State rep. State of S.D., 34th dist., 1991-95; lt. gov. State of S.D., 1995—; dir. Mich. Nat. Bank., Black Hills Regional Eye Inst., YMCA; mem. exec. bd. Nat. Crime Prevention Coun. Active Rapid City Common Coun., Rapid City C. of C., S.D. Bd. of Charities and Corrections, McGruff Crime Prevention Coun. (exec. bd.), S.D. Corrections Commn., Cmty. Care Ctr., S.D. Children's Home Soc., S.D. Assurance Alliance, Nat. Child Protection Partnership, First United Methodist Ch. (exec. bd.), Rapid City Econ. Devel. Partnership, F.L.A.G.S. Found.; mem. exec. bd. Bog Bros./Big Sisters. Recipient Pub. Svc. award, 1987, Gov.'s Outstanding

Citizen award, 1988, George award Rapid City C. of C., 1994; named Outstanding Chirperson, United Way, 1986, S.D. Guardian Small Bus., 1994. Mem. LWV, Women's Network, Mt. Rushmore Soc., Indian-White Coun., Toastmasters, Ninety-niners, Rapid City Fine Arts Coun. Republican. Methodist. Office: Office of Lt Governor State Capitol 500 E Capitol Ave Ste 204 Pierre SD 57501-5070

HILLARD, PAULA JANINE, physician, educator; b. Oak Ridge, Tenn., Apr. 4, 1952; d. Raymond Kenneth and Helen Louise (O'Kane) Adams; m. J. Randolph Hillard, Nov. 22, 1972; m. M. Elena, Ian J.A., Nathaniel K. BS, U. N.C., 1973; MD, Stanford U., 1977. Diplomate Am. Bd. Obstetricians-Gynecologists. Intern/resident N.C. Meml. Hosp./U. N.C., Chapel Hill, 1977-81; asst. prof. dept. ob-gyn. U. Va., Charlottesville, 1981-84; asst. prof. dept. ob-gyn. U. Cin., 1984-90, assoc. prof., 1990—, dir. ambulatory gynecology, 1987-92; assoc. prof. Pediatrics, 1995—; cons. gynecology div. adcolescent medicine Children's Hosp., Cin., 1984—. Co-author: Pregnancy and Childbirth, 1986; assoc. editor: Novak's Gynecology, 1996; contbg. editor Pregnancy and Birth, Parents mag., 1982-89; contbr. sci. articles to profl. jours. Mem. nat. med. com. Planned Parenthood Fedn. Am., 1991-93. Recipient Mead Johnson Fellowship for Clin. Rsch., U. N.C., Chapel Hill, 1982. Fellow Am. Coll. Obstetricians and Gynecologists (chair patient edn. com. 1991-93, chair adolescent Health Commn., 1994-96); mem. AMA, Am. Med. Women's Assn., N.Am. Soc. Pediatric Adolsecent Gynecology (program chair 1992), Assoc. Profls. Gyn.-Ob. Democrat. Unitarian-Universalist. Office: U Cin Dept Ob-Gyn 231 Bethesda Ave # 526 Cincinnati OH 45229-2827

HILLEGAS, WILLIAM JOSEPH, materials scientist; b. Quakertown, Pa., Aug. 31, 1937; s. William Joseph Hillegas and Olga Suzanne (Kulik) Hillegas Frable; m. Carolyn Jeanne Geyer, Sept. 9, 1961 (dec. 1971); children: Lisa Lynn, Gregory Charles; m. Carolyn Radford Chubbuck, Sept. 8, 1973 (div. 1982); 1 child, William James; m. Kathleen Mary Branson, Dec. 26, 1982; children: Sara E. Hawley, Jennifer A. Hawley. BS, Drexel U., 1960; MS, Northwestern U., 1967, PhD, 1968. Student engr. Philco Corp., Lansdale, Pa., 1956-60, engr., 1960-63; grad. student Northwestern U., Evanston, Ill., 1963-68; scientist Xerox Corp., Rochester, N.Y., 1968-78; rsch. mgr. KMS Fusion Inc., Ann Arbor, Mich., 1978-84; v.p., founder SoloHills Engring. Inc.; v.p., chief tech. officer SoloHill Labs., Inc., Ann Arbor, Mich., 1984—; also bd. dirs. and sec. SoloHills Labs., Inc. and SoloHill Engring. Inc., Ann Arbor, Mich.; also bd. dirs. SoloHill Therapeutics, Inc., Pitts. Contbr. more than 25 articles to profl. jours. County committeeman Dem. Com. Monroe County, Rochester, N.Y., 1971-78. Grantee Am. Iron and Steel Inst., Chgo., 1964-68, Nat. Cancer Inst., Washington, 1984—, Mich. State Rsch. Fund, Lansing, 1988-90, USN, Washington, 1990. Mem. AAAS, N.Y. Acad. Sci., Soc. of InVitro Biology. Home: 4936 Ravine Ct Ann Arbor MI 48105-9442 Office: SoloHill Labs Inc 4220 Varsity Dr Ann Arbor MI 48108

HILLEGONDS, PAUL, state legislator; b. Holland, Mich., Mar. 4, 1949; s. William C. and Elizabeth (Romaine) H.; m. Nancy; 1 child, Sarah. BA, U. Mich., 1971; JD, Coolegy Law Sch., 1986. Legis. asst. U.S. Rep. Philip Ruppe, Mich., 1971-74; adminstrv. asst. U.S. Rep. Philip Ruppe, 1974-78; mgr. Ruppe's Congl. Campaign, 1974, 76; state rep. Dist. 54 Mich. Ho. of Reps., 1978-94, state rep. Dist. 88, 1995—; asst. minority leader, 1983-85, minority leader, 1986—; mem. Workers Compensation & Unemployment Ins. Subcoms., Mich. Ho. of Reps.; chmn. Rep. Campaign Com., leader Rep. Policy Com., Mich. Ho. of Reps. Recipient Disting. Svc. award Holland Jaycees, 198, Disting. Svc. award Assn. Ind. Colls., 1985—; named One of Ten Outstanding Legislators of Yr., Nat. Rep. Legislators Assn., 1988—. Mem. Ripon Soc., Assn. Pub. Justice, Holland Jaycees, Common Cause, Kiwanis. Address: A-6530 142nd Ave Holland MI 49423-9746*

HILLENBRAND, ANNA M., health care information manager. MA, U. Minn., 1976; BA, U. N.D., 1964. Supr. med. records depts. St. Mary's Hosp., Mpls., 1970-73, St. Michael's Hosp., Grand Forks, N.D., 1954-70; coord., instr. health care mgmt. and med. sec. programs Inver Hills C.C., Inver Grove Heights, Minn., 1973—; health info. cons., 1973—; adv. com. Good Samaritan Health Care, Inver Grove Heights, 1994—. Recipient Recognition for Tchg. award Lawyers Advocates and Wives of Minn., 1987. Mem. Minn. Bus. Educators, Minn. & Am. Health Info. Assns., Delta Pi Epsilon. Home: 1880 Randolph Ave Saint Paul MN 55105 Office: 1880 Randolph Ave St Paul MN 55105-1797

HILLER, JOAN VITEK, sociologist; b. Mpls., Apr. 4, 1960; d. Thomas Mark and Louanne (Howard) Vitek; m. James G. Hiller, Aug. 28, 1987; 1 child, Thomas Joseph. BA, Coll. St. Catherine, 1982; MS, Tex. A&M U., 1985; PhD, Northwestern U., 1996. Lic. independent social worker, Minn. Statistician Ctr. Health Studies and Policy Rsch./Northwestern U., Evanston, Ill., 1985-87; sr. program evaluation specialist Minn. Dept. Human Svcs., St. Paul, 1987-89; dir. nonprofit svcs. Willowbrooke Orgn. Devel., Burnsville, Minn., 1990—; adj. instr. U. St. Thomas, St. Paul, 1989—, Hamline U., St. Paul, 1988-91, Coll. St. Catherine, 1994-95; rep. Gov.'s Com. Drug-Free Schs., 1987-89; ex-officio Minn. Juvenile Justice Adv. Com., St. Paul, 1986-87. Bd. dirs. Open Your Heart to the Hungry and Homeless, St. Paul, 1989-94, v.p., 1991-93. Mem. NAFE, Am. Sociol. Assn. (cert. applied social rsch., mem. com. on pub. affairs 1992-93), Mensa (v.p. Minn. chpt. 1992-94, pres. chpt. 1994-96), Sociologists Minn. (bd. dirs. 1991-93). Roman Catholic. Home: 3206 Red Oak Cir N Burnsville MN 55337-3307

HILLERT, GLORIA BONNIN, anatomist, educator; b. Brownton, Minn., Jan. 25, 1930; d. Edward Henry and Lydia Magdalene (Luebker) Bonnin; m. Richard Hillert, Aug. 20, 1960; children: Kathryn, Virginia, Jonathan. BS, Valparaiso (Ind.) U., 1953; MA, U. Mich., 1958. Instr. Springfield (Ill.) Jr. Coll., 1953-57; teaching asst. U. Mich., Ann Arbor, 1957-58; instr., dept. head St. John's Coll., Winfield, Kans., 1958-59; asst. prof. Concordia Coll., River Forest, Ill., 1959-63; vis. instr. Wright Jr. Coll., Chgo., 1974-76, Ill. Benedictine Coll., Lisle, 1977-78, Rosary Coll., River Forest, 1976-81; prof. anatomy and physiology Triton Coll., River Grove, 1982-92, prof. emeritus, 1992—; vis. asst. prof. Concordia U., 1993—; vis. instr. Wheaton (Ill.) Coll., 1988; advisor Springfield Jr. Coll. Sci. Club, 1953-57, Concordia Coll. Cultural Group, 1959-62; program dir. Triton Coll. Sci. Lectr. Series, 1983-87; participant Internat. Educators Workshop in Amazonia, 1993. Dem. campaign asst., Maywood, Ill., 1972, 88; vol. Mental Health Orgn., Chgo., 1969-73, Earthwatch, St. Croix, 1987, Costa Rica, 1989, Internat. Med. Care Team, Guatemala, 1995. Mem. AAUW, Ill. Assn. Community Coll. Biol. Tchrs., Nat. Assn. Biol. Tchrs. Lutheran. Home: 1620 Clay Ct Melrose Park IL 60160-2419 Office: Triton Coll 2000 N 5th Ave River Grove IL 60171-1907

HILLESHEIM, MARK THOMAS, physical therapist; b. Palatine, Ill., July 7, 1965; s. Thomas Omar and Barbara Elizabeth (Marchiando) H.; m. Amy Gerard Mathys, Nov. 9, 1991. BS in Phys. Therapy, Marquette U., Milw., 1987; postgrad., Cardinal STritch Coll., Milw. Lic. phys. therapist, Wis. Staff phys. therapist Curative Rehab. Ctr., Milw., 1987; dir. phys. therapy LaSalle Clinic, Neenah, Wis., 1987-90, Medrehab, Mequon, Wis., 1990-92; phys. therapist Spine Therapy Ctr., Green Bay, Wis., 1992—. Mem. Am. Phys. Therapy Assn., Wis. Phys. Therapy Assn., Assn. Orthopedic Manipulative Therapists. Republican. Roman Catholic. Home: 1428 Circle Dr Menasha WI 54952 Office: Spine Therapy Ctr 211 N Broadway Green Bay WI 54302

HILLESTAD, DONNA DAWN, nurse; b. Merrill, Wis., May 13, 1938; d. Martin T. and Edna (Frederick) Dietrich; m. John Curtis Hillestad, July 18, 1959; children: Dori Jean, David Jeffrey. BSN, Mankato U., 1962. RN, Minn. Office nurse Fairmont (Minn.) Clinic, 1963-65, pvt. duty, pub. health nurse, 1965-67; charge nurse, supr. Lakeview Meth. Health Care Ctr., Fairmont, 1967—; nurse ins. phys. for numerous ins. cos., 1980—. Active Fairmont Community Concert Assn.; host fgn. exch. students, 1989, 90, 91, 92. Mem. AAUW (pub. rels. com. 1986-87, historian 1982-84, bull. editor 1985-86, chmn. hospitality 1987-88, mem. cultural interests com. 1980-81, Internat. Rels. award 1991), Bus. and Profl. Women (chmn. internat. rels. 1986, emblem chmn. 1982-83, pub. rels. com. 1984-85, found. com. .1990, historian 1976, nominating sunshine com. 1989-90, auditing com. 1986-87, sec. 1985-86, 88-89), Holiday Travel Club (founder), Friendship Force (So. Minn. chpt. sec. 1995—), Tourist Club, Cmty. Club, Garden Club. Lutheran. Home: 803 S Hampton St Fairmont MN 56031-4308

HILLIARD, DAVID CRAIG, lawyer; b. Framingham, Mass., May 22, 1937; s. Walter David and Dorothy (Shortiss) H.; m. Celia Schmid, Feb. 16, 1974. BS, Tufts U., 1959; JD, U. Chgo., 1962. Bar: Ill. 1962, U.S. Supreme Ct. 1966. Mng. ptnr. Pattishall, McAuliffe, Newbury, Hilliard & Geraldson, Chgo. and Washington, 1984—; adj. prof. law Northwestern U., 1971—, chmn. Symposium Intellectual Property Law and the Corp. Client, 1987—. Author: Unfair Competition and Unfair Trade Practices, 1985, Trademarks, 1987, Trademarks and Unfair Competition, 1994, 2d edit., 1996, Trademark and Unfair Competition Law Deskbook, 1995; editor-in-chief Chgo. Bar Record, 1978-81. Trustee Art Inst. Chgo., 1980—, chmn. sustaining fellow, 1981-85, chmn. adv. com. dept. architecture, 1981—, pres. aux. bd., 1977-79, chmn. exhbns. com., 1993—, exec. com., 1995—; trustee Newberry Libr., 1983—, exec. com., 1987—; pres. Lawyers Trust Fund Ill., 1985-88; mem. vis. com. DePaul U. Law Sch., U. Chgo. Sch. of Law, chmn., 1987-88, Northwestern U. Assocs., 1985—; mem. profl. adv. bd. Atty. Gen. Ill., 1982-84; mem. Ill. Commn. on Rights of Women, 1983-85; bd. dirs. Ill. Inst. Continuing Legal Edn., 1980-82; pres. Planned Parenthood Assn. Chgo., 1975-77. Lt. JAGC, USN, 1962-66. Recipient Maurice Weigle award, 1974, Chgo. Coun. Lawyers award for jud. reform, 1983. Fellow Am. Coll. Trial Lawyers (chmn. courageous adv. com. 1995—); mem. ABA (chmn. trademark divsn. 1986-87, mem. coun. 1991-95, intellectural property law sect.), Ill. Bar Assn., Chgo. Bar Assn. (pres. 1982-83, founding chmn. young lawyers sect. 1971-72), Internat. Trademark Assn. (bd. dirs. 1989-91, ADR panel of neutrals 1994—), Chgo. Club, Econ. Club, Law Club, Legal Club (pres. 1989-90), Univ. Club, Casino, Wayfarers (pres. 1994-95). Home: 1320 N State Pky Chicago IL 60610-2118 Office: Pattishall McAuliffe Newbury Hilliard & Geraldson 311 S Wacker Dr Ste 5000 Chicago IL 60606-6618

HILLIARD, KIRK LOVELAND, JR., osteopathic physician, educator; b. Phila., Mar. 9, 1941; s. Kirk Loveland and Lillian Adele (Hinkle) H.; m. Janet Louise Moyer, Aug. 29, 1970; children: Michael Spence, Stephen Matthew, Allison Day. AB, Haverford Coll., 1963; DO, Phila. Coll. Osteo. Medicine, 1967. Diplomate Am. Coll. Osteo. Internists, Internal Medicine and Med. Diseases of Chest. Intern Doctors' Hosp., Columbus, Ohio, 1967-68, resident, 1970-72, sr. attending, 1977—, dir. respiratory svcs., 1978—; fellow Hahnemann Hosp., Phila., 1972-74; pvt. practice Columbus, 1974-95, part time practice pulmonary medicine, 1996—; asst. prof. Ohio U., Athens, 1979-88, assoc. prof., 1988—; med. dir. CP Home care, Columbus, 1986—; acting dir. Med. Edn. Doctors Hosp., Columbus, Ohio, 1991-92; bd. trustees Doctors Hosp., 1995, program dir. internal medicine, 1994-95; v.p. med. edn. Doctors Hosp., 1995—. Capt. M.C., U.S. Army, 1968-70, Vietnam. Fellow Am. Coll. Osteo. Internists; mem. Am. Osteo. Assn., Assn. Osteo. Dirs. Med. Edn., Am. Lung Assn., Am. Legion, Masons, Shriners. Office: Doctors Hosp 1087 Dennison Ave Columbus OH 43201

HILLIER, CHARLES FREDERICK, elementary school educator; b. Homestead, Fla., Oct. 29, 1949; s. William Donald and Margaret Grace (Mann) H.; m. Sharon Rose Kota, Aug. 6, 1977; children: Sara R., Charles A. Assoc. in Gen. Edn., St. Clair County C.C., 1970; BS, Ctrl. Mich. U., 1972; MA, Mich. State U., 1974; Edn. Specialist, Wayne State U., 1984. Elem. tchr. East China (Mich.) Pub. Schs., 1972—. Democrat. Episcopalian. Office: East China Pub Sch 1585 Meisner Rd East China MI 48054

HILLIG, TERRY THOMAS, journalist; b. Alton, Ill., Oct. 8, 1945; s. Harold and Mary A. (Darr) H.; m. Cheryl Ann McMurdo, Apr. 7, 1972 (div. Aug. 1977) 1 child, Jack Alexander. BA in Govt., So. Ill. U., 1967. Reporter Edwardsville (Ill.) Intelligencer, 1970-76, news editor, 1976-79; reporter Alton (Ill.) Telegraph, 1979—; editor editl. page, 1996—. Home: 3427 Edwardsville Rd Edwardsville IL 62025-7243 Office: Alton Telegraph 111 E Broadway Alton IL 62002

HILLMAN, CAROL ELIZABETH, real estate broker; b. Monticello, Ark., July 29, 1947; d. Horace Lavon McManus and Leathel Jeanette (Higgins) Losh; m. William Carlton Hillman, Oct. 21, 1967; 1 child, Carol Lynn. Grad. high sch., Monticello, 1965. Lic. real estate broker. Exec. sec. Hamburg (Ark.) Shirt Co., 1965-67; office and payroll mgr. Glamorise Founds., Inc., Dermott, Ark., 1967-69; cashier, customer svc. rep. Main Dept. Store, Rolla, Mo., 1975-77; office mgr., chiropractic asst. Dr. J.W. Moffett Chiropractic, Bolivar, Mo., 1977-80; salesperson Sta. KYOO Radio, Bolivar, 1980-83, sales mgr., 1983-91, gen. mgr., 1991-93; real estate broker-salesperson Perkins Realtors, Bolivar, 1993-94; owner Carol E. Hillman Real Estate Co., Bolivar, 1994—; bd. dirs. bus. adv. bd. students S.W. Bapt. U., Bolivar, 1992-93. Co-chair entertainment Bolivar Country Days, 1992—. Recipient High Series awards Outreach League, 1991. Mem. Bolivar Bd. Realtors, Ozark Bd. Realtors, Bolivar Area C. of C. (Sta. KYOO rep. 1983-93). Home: 1301 E 420th Rd Bolivar MO 65613-9803 Office: Carol E Hillman Real Estate Co 1301 E 420th Rd Bolivar MO 65613

HILLMAN, DOUGLAS WOODRUFF, federal judge; b. Grand Rapids, Mich., Feb. 15, 1922; s. Lemuel Serrell and Dorothy (Woodruff) H.; m. Sally Jones, Sept. 13, 1944; children: Drusilla W., Clayton D. Student, Phillips Exeter Acad., 1941; A.B., U. Mich., 1946, LL.B., 1948. Bar: Mich. 1948, U.S. Supreme Ct. 1967. Assoc. Lilly, Luyendyk & Snyder, Grand Rapids, 1948-53; partner Luyendyk, Hainer, Hillman, Karr & Dutcher, Grand Rapids, 1953-65, Hillman, Baxter & Hammond, 1965-79; U.S. dist. judge Western Dist. Mich., Grand Rapids, 1979—; chief judge Western Dist. Mich., 1986-91, sr. judge, 1991—; instr. Nat. Inst. Trial Adv., Boulder, Colo; dir. Fed. Judges Assn.; mem. jud. conf. com. on Adminstrn. of Magistrate Judges Sys., 1993—; chair 6th Circuit Standing Com. on Jud. Conf. Planning; mem. exec. com. ABA jud. adminstrn. divsn. Nat. Conf. Fed. Trial Judges, 1995—. Contbr. articles to profl. jours. Chmn. Grand Rapids Human Relations Commn., 1963-66; chmn. bd. trustees Fountain St. Ch., 1970-72; pres. Family Service Assn., 1967. Served as pilot USAAF, 1943-45. Decorated DFC, Air medal; recipient Annual Civil Liberties award ACLU, 1970, Disting. Alumni award Ctrl. High Sch., 1986, Raymond Fox Advocacy award, 1989, Champion of Justice award State Bar Mich., 1990, Profl. & Cmty. Svc. award Young Lawyers Sect., 1996, Svc. to Profession award Fed. Bar Assn., 1991; named one of 25 Most Respected Judges Mich. Lawyers Weekly. Fellow Am. Bar Found.; mem. ABA, Mich. Bar Assn. (chmn. client security fund, Profl. Cmty. Svc. award 1996), Grand Rapids Bar Assn. (pres. 1963), Am. Coll. Trial Lawyers (Mich. chmn. 1979, com. on teaching trial and appellate adv.), 6th Circuit Jud. Conf. (life), Internat. Acad. Trial Lawyers, Fedn. Ins. Counsel, Internat. Assn. Ins. Counsel, Internat. Soc. Barristers (pres 1977-78, chair annual Hillman Trial Adv. Seminar 1982), M Club of U. Mich. (com. visitors U. Mich. Law Sch.), Univ. Club (Grand Rapids), Torch Club. Office: US Dist Ct 682 Fed Bldg 110 Michigan St NW Grand Rapids MI 49503-2313

HILLMAN, LIN (LINDA LOU HILLMAN), nursing administrator; b. Hillsboro, Wis., July 1, 1948; d. Laurence Jones and Carole Louise (Sonnenberg) Anderson; children: Chad Anthony, Liza Lin. ADN in Tech. Nursing, Western Wis. Tech. Coll., 1984; BSN, Viterbo Coll., 1990; postgrad., Eau Claire, Wis. RN, Wis. Staff nurse ob-gyn. Tomah (Wis.) Meml. Hosp., 1984-85; staff nurse respiratory care Vets. Affairs Med. Ctr., Tomah, 1985-90, head nurse, 1990, instr. nursing edn., 1990-93, assoc. chief nursing svc./edn., 1993-94, assoc. chief nursing, 1994—. Vol. instr. English lang. local refugee family, LaCrosse, Wis., 1989—. Mem. ARC, Wis. Nurses Assn., Am. Soc. for Healthcare Edn. and Tng., Nurses Orgn. of Vets. Affairs, Red Cross. Home: 317 River Rd Apt 5 Black River Falls WI 54615-9210 Office: Dept Vets Affairs 500 E Veterans St Tomah WI 54660-3105

HILLMAN, ROBERT KENT, sales representative; b. Indpls., Jan. 10, 1939; s. James Oliver and Mary Isabel (Johnston) H.; m. Frances Lee Atwood, June 20, 1964; children: Karen S., Aimee J. BS in Bus. with honors, Ind. U., 1969. Apprentice The Bramwood Press, Indpls., 1956-61; printer Crippen Printing, Indpls., 1964-69, adminstrv. asst., 1969-72; sales rep. The Studio Press, Indpls., 1972-79, The Hennegan Co., Cin., 1979—. Bd. mem. Bloomfield Hills (Mich.) Bapt. Ch., 1988—; com. mem. Grace Evang. Free Ch., Birmingham, Mich., 1981-88, Devington Bapt. Ch., Indpls., 1956-81. With U.S. Army, 1961-63. Mem. Adcraft Club of Detroit. Republican. Home: 2761 Renshaw Dr Troy MI 48098-3745 Office: The Hennegan Co 275 E Big Beaver Rd Ste 165 Troy MI 48083

HILLS, RANDOLPH ALLEN, contractor; b. Port Huron, Mich., Aug. 10, 1954; s. John C. Hills and Elizabeth Ann (Pickelhaupt) Landschoot; children: John C., Joel M., Jason R. Cert. universal technician refrigerant, Ferris State U.; mobile technician refrigerant, IMACA. Lic. builder, Mich., real estate agt., Mich. Sales rep. Frito-Lay Inc., Marysville, Mich., 1979-95; CEO, pres. Randhil Devel. Corp., Port Huron, Mich., 1995—; mem. Mich. Thumb Bd. of Realtors, Marlette; instr. St. Clair County C.C., 1994. Author: Our $45.00 House Payment-Apartment Houses, 1982. Mem. St. Edwards on the Lake Ch., Lakeport, Mich. Mem. Pheasants Forever, Nat. Wild Turkey Fedn., Bldg. Industry Assn. of Southeastern Mich., Mich. Assn. of Home Builders, Nat. Assn. of Home Builders. Office: Randhil Devel Corp PO Box 611364 Port Huron MI 48061-1364

HILLSTROM, THOMAS PETER, engineering executive; b. Lakewood, Ohio, Apr. 20, 1943; s. Harry Edward and Mary Pauline (Mauss) H.; m. Jean Elizabeth Greenfield; children: Edward, Mary. BS in Mech. Engring., Northwestern U., Evanston, 1966; MBA, Northwestern U., Chgo., 1977. Design engr. Internat. Harvester, Hinsdale, Ill., 1966-74, project engr., 1974-78, product safety engr., 1978-82; mgr. engring. Fire Apparatus Div., FMC, Tipton, Ind., 1982-85; mgr. contract engring. FMC Naval Systems Div., Mpls., 1985-87, program mgr., 1987-90, mgr. splty. engring., 1990-91; program mgr. United Def., L.P., Mpls., 1985—. Patentee in field. Mem. Soc. Automotive Engrs., Am. Soc. Agrl. Engrs., System Safety Soc., Boy Scouts Am. Order of the Arrow. Republican. Home: 1635 Ranier Cir Minneapolis MN 55447-2673 Office: United Def LP 4800 E River Rd Minneapolis MN 55421-1402

HILTIBRAN, ROBERT COMEGYS, biochemistry educator; b. Urbana, Ohio, Sept. 24, 1920; s. Isaac Lester and Sara Elizabeth (Comegys) H.; m. Lois Marie Armstrong, Nov. 22, 1945; children: Robert Glen, Cheryl Marie, Karen Kaye. BS, Denison U., 1948; MS, U. Kans., 1951, PhD, 1954. Rsch. biochemist VA Hosp., Hines, Ill., 1953-55; postdoctoral fellow Ohio State U., Columbus, 1955-57; assoc. biochemist Ill. Natural History Survey, Urbana, 1957-69, biochemist, 1969-81; assoc. prof dept. agronomy U. Ill., Urbana, 1969—. Contbr. articles to sci. jours. Sgt. USAAF, 1942-45, ETO, MTO, NATOUSA. Mem. Mid-West Aquatic Plant Control Soc. (hon.), North Cen. Weed Control Conf. (hon.). Republican. Methodist. Home: 608 E Washington St Urbana IL 61801-4323

HILTON, DAVID B., automotive design stylist; b. Lansing, Mich., Sept. 13, 1966; s. James P. and Patricia D. (Reasoner) H. BS in Design, U. Cin., 1991. Automotive designer stylist Ford Motor Co., Dearborn, Mich., 1991—; lectr. Univ. Cin., 1991-94, Ctr. Creative Studies, Detroit, 1992-93. Designer of Synthesis 2010 Show Vehicle, Ford Motor, 1992, Smith ski goggle (Indsl. Design Magazine Annual Rev. hon. mention 1993), 1991. Home: 412 E 3rd Royal Oak MI 48067 Office: Ford Motor Design Center 21175 Oakwood Blvd Dearborn MI 48124-4079

HILYARD, JANICE ELAINE, college administrator; b. Vallejo, Calif., Jan. 13, 1945; d. Harold Ira and Juanita Mae (Barham) Barger; m. Clarence Hilyard (div.); 1 child, Anna Elissa Hilyard. BSEd, U. Cen. Okla., 1970, MEd, 1974. Coord., vocat. sec. Garden City (Kans.) Sr. High, 1970-73; coord. clerical program Garden City (Kans.) C.C., 1973-75; corp. treas. Western Bit & Supply, Inc., Ponca City, Okla., 1975-84; sales assoc. Coldwell-Banker Real Estate, Wichita, Kans., 1985-89; coord., distance edn. Butler County C.C., El Dorado, Kans., 1991-93, dir., distance edn., 1993—. Columnist: KAECT Jour., 1994—. Ambassador chair C. of C., El Dorado, 1996; com. mem. BCCC Endowment Assn., El Dorado, 1994; rep. ladies bd., Crestview CC, Wichita, 1989-90; treas. Turnberry Assn., Wichita, 1990-91. Mem. Kans. Assn. Distance Edn. (founding sec. 1993-95), Kans. Assn. for Edn. Comms. and Tech., U.S. Distance Learning Assn., Am. Assn. Women in Comm. Colls., Kans. Assn. for Post-Secondary Edn. Technologies. Home: 1525 Country Club rd El Dorado KS 67042 Office: Butler County Comm Coll 901 S Haverhill Rd El Dorado KS 67042

HIMEBAUGH, ELEANOR SCHMEDEL, editor; b. Indpls., June 18, 1937; d. Roland Rollings and Mildred Evelyn (Foxworthy) Schmedel; m. William Robert Himebaugh, Feb. 21, 1960; children: W. Andrew, Susan Elizabeth. BS in Edn., Ind. U., 1959. Tchr. Wabash (Ind.) Pub. Schs., 1959-60, North Muskegon (Mich.) Schs., 1960-62, Wayne (Mich.) Cmty. Schs., 1962-63; owner, mgr. Himebaugh's Mens & Boys Wear, Orleans, Ind., 1970-81; reporter The Times-Mail, Bedford, Ind., 1981-86, editor, 1986—. Sec., publicity chmn. Orleans Dogwood Festival, 1970-81; exec. sec. Orleans C. of C., 1977-81; chmn. Orleans Bicentennial Commn., 1975-76. Named Best Lifestyle Sect. Hoosier State Press Assn., Ind., 1992. Mem. Bedford Panhellenic Assn. (pres. 1979-80), Bedford Area C. of C., Bedford Hiking Club, Kappa Kappa Kappa. Office: The Times-Mail 813 16th St Bedford IN 47421

HIMENS, MARY KATHRYN, psychotherapist, consultant; b. Antioch, Ill., Sept. 24, 1929; d. Michael and Lucy Josephine (Bolte) H. AB, Coll. St. Francis, Joliet, Ill., 1951; MEd, St. Louis U., 1960; EdS, Western State Coll., 1970. Lic. clin. profl. counselor, Ill.; nat. cert. counselor; diplomate Am. Assn. Pastoral Counselors; entered Servants of the Holy Heart of Mary, Roman Cath. Ch., Sept. 1952. Vice-prin., tchr. Holy Family Acad., Beaverville, Ill., 1951-59, prin., 1959-65; coord. Newman parish and dir. religious edn. St. Peter's Parish, Gunnison, Colo., 1965-70; coord. counseling svcs., asst. prof. edn. Western State Coll., Gunnison, 1970-75; chaplain counselor Georgetown U. and Law Ctr., Washington, 1975-90; psychotherapist in pvt. practice Servants Counseling Svc., Champaign/Urbana, Ill., 1990—; mgmt. cons. U.S. Govt., State Dept., Libr. of Congress, 1984-89, Southland Corp., 1983-89; cons., planner various religious congregations, 1980-95; bd. dirs. ServantCor, Kankakee, Ill., Covenant Med. Ctr. Chmn. bd. dirs. Matthew House 18, Inc., Champaign, 1990—. Mem. Nat. Assn. Women in Edn. (v.p. profl. devel. 1985-87), Assn. for Psychol. Type, Delta Kappa Gamma, Alpha Sigma Nu. Home: 301 N Wright St Champaign IL 61820 Office: Servants of Holy Heart Mary Servants Counseling Svc 1405 W Park Urbana IL 61801

HIMES, GEORGE ELLIOTT, pathologist; b. Huntington, W.Va., Jan. 5, 1922; s. Connell Bradley and Elizabeth (Skeans) H.; m. Rita T. Wasniewski (dec. July 1993); children: Rita Ann Brust, Susan Ruth Burger, George Elliott Jr., Brent Lee; m. Barbara A. Cunningham, Dec. 21, 1994. Student, U. Cin., 1939-42; DO, Chgo. Coll. Osteo. Medicine, 1942-45. Intern Lamb Mem. Hosp., Denver, 1945-46; resident pathology Chgo. Osteo Hosp., 1946-48; asst. prof. pathology Chgo. Coll. Osteo Med., 1948-56; asst. lab. dir. Chgo. Osteo Hosp., 1948-51; dir. of labs Flint (Mich.) Osteo Hosp., 1951-87, dir. of labs and nuclear med., 1957-80; assoc. prof. pathology Coll. Osteo Med., Des Moines, 1968-89; adj. prof. pathology Coll. Osteo. Medicine Mich. State U., East Lansing, Mich., 1974-84; dir. sch. med. tech. Flint (Mich.) Osteo Hosp., 1975-85; mem. radiation, chem. & biol. safety com. Mich. State U., 1978—; mem. Am. Osteo. Bd. Pathology, 1959-68, Am. Osteo. Bd. Nuclear Medicine, 1974-84. Bd. dirs. ARC, Flint, 1963-74, United Way, 1964-72; pres. Flint Civitan Club, 1954. Mem. AMA, AAAS, Am. Osteo. Coll. Pathologists (past pres. and sec.-treas. 1954-72), Am. Osteo. Assn., Am. Assn. Blood Banks, Mich. Assn. Osteo. Physicians and Surgeons, Coll. Am. Pathologists, Am. Soc. Clin. Pathologists, Soc. Nuclear Medicine, Mich. Soc. Pathologists, Genesee Country Osteo. Assn., Flint Golf Club. Home: 444 Luce Ave Flushing MI 48433-1411 Office: Flint Osteopathic Hosp 3921 Beecher Rd Flint MI 48532-3602

HIMMELBERG, CHARLES JOHN, III, mathematics educator, researcher; b. North Kansas City, Mo., Nov. 12, 1931; s. Charles John and Magdalene Caroline (Batliner) H.; m. Mary Patricia Hennessy, Jan. 27, 1962; children: Charles, Ann, Mary, Joseph, Patrick. BS, Rockhurst Coll., 1952; MS, U. Notre Dame, 1954, PhD, 1957. Assoc. analyst Midwest Rsch. Inst., Kansas City, Mo., 1957-59; asst. prof. math. U. Kans., Lawrence, 1959-65, assoc. prof., 1965-68, prof., 1968—, chmn. dept. math., 1978—. Mem. editorial bd. Rocky Mountain Jour. Math, 1972-88; contbr. articles to profl. jours. Mem. Am. Math. Soc., Math. Assn. Am. Roman Catholic. Office: U Kans Dept Math Lawrence KS 66045

HIMSTEDT, RONALD EUGENE, union official; b. Red Bud, Ill., Sept. 8, 1943; s. Hilbert Henry and Valeria Catherine (Mees) H.; m. Dorthy Jean Russell, Aug. 3, 1990. Grad. high sch., Marissa, Ill. Distbn. clk. U.S. Postal Svc., Springfield, Mo., 1975—; pres. local union Am. Postal Workers Union, AFL-CIO, Springfield, 1979—; adminstrv. v.p. Mo. Postal Workers Union, AFL-CIO, Springfield, 1984-94, pres., 1994—; trustee Greater

Springfield Labor Coun., AFL-CIO, 1986-92; sec. treas. Springfield Mo. Ctrl. Labor Coun. AFL-CIO, 1992—. Mem. allocation panel United Way, Springfield, 1988—; bd. dirs. Ozark Counseling Ctr., Springfield, 1992-95, Cmty. Blood Ctr., Springfield. With USN, 1962-64; staff sgt. U.S. Army, 1966-74, Vietnam. Decorated Bronze Star. Mem. VFW, Am. Legion. Democrat. Home: 2802 W Madison St Springfield MO 65802-5035 Office: Am Postal Workers Union 309 N Jefferson Ave Springfield MO 65806-1172

HINDLE, LARRY, manufacturing engineer; b. Ft. Wayne, Ind., Nov. 21, 1961. A, ITT Tech. Inst., Ft. Wayne, 1984, B in Automated Mfg., 1985. Controls engr. M.P.I. Furnace Co., Ft. Wayne, 1986-91; mgr. controls engring. States Engring., Ft. Wayne, 1991—. Office: States Engring 4419 Ardmore Ave Fort Wayne IN 46809-9722

HINDSON, HARRY BURDETTE, III, music educator; b. Lawrence, Kans., Apr. 16, 1948; s. Harry Burdette Jr. and Helen Celeste (Dondanville) H.; m. Jean Marie Pederson, Aug. 21, 1982; children: Ellen Marie, Abigail Christine. BA in Music Edn., Luther Coll., 1970; MusM in Saxophone Performance, U. Md., 1977; DMA, U. Wis., 1992. Saxophonist concert band U.S. Navy Band, Washington, 1970-77; music educator Waubonsee C.C., Sugar Grove, Ill., 1978-84, U. Wis., La Crosse, 1987—; woodwind player, conductor Wis. 132d Army N.G. band, 1987—; saxophone instr. Winona (Minn.) State U., 1989-91; woodwind instr. St. Mary's Coll., Winona, 1989-90; pvt. teaching studio, 1977—; saxophone soloist Naperville (Ill.) Mcpl. Band, 1980—; prin. clarinet La Crosse Concert Band, 1989—; bassoonist La Crosse Symphony, 1989—. Bd. dirs. La Crosse Concert Band, 1990—; mem. orch. com. La Crosse Symphony, 1992—. Mem. N.Am. Saxophone Alliance, Wis. N.G. Enlisted Assn., Am. Fedn. Musicians (trustee 1989-92). Episcopalian. Home: 1524 Ferry St La Crosse WI 54601 Office: U Wis La Crosse Dept Music Ctr for the Arts La Crosse WI 54601

HINES, BRIAN A., electrical engineer; b. Miller, S.D., June 6, 1961; s. LaVerne Mark and C. Elaine (Schmidt) Lingscheit; m. Michele K. Bennett, Aug. 25, 1995. BSEE, S.D. State U., 1995. Engr.-in-tng., Kans. Rancher Ree Heights, S.D., 1987-91; software design intern Daktronics, Inc., Brookings, S.D., 1994-95; elec. engr. Black & Veatch, Overland Park, Kans., 1995—. With USN, 1981-87. Ctr. for Power Sys. Studies scholar, 1994, 95. Mem. Tau Beta Pi, Phi Kappa Phi.

HINES, ERIC D.(RIC), environmental engineer, tennis professional; b. Omaha, Nebr., May 9, 1956; s. Dale O. and Della E. (Albers) H.; m. Jane F. Zukaitis, July 3, 1980; children: Melissa M., Eric M. BS in Civil Engring., U. Nebr., 1980, MS in geotechnical, envrion. engring., 1985. Registered profl. engr., Nebr. 1984; cert. tennis profl. 1977. Project engr. Wells Engring. Inc., Omaha, 1979-86; project mgr. U.S. Army Engrs. Dist. Omaha, 1986-89; with Mo. River Divsn., Hazardous, Toxic & Radioactive Water U.S. Army Corp Engrs., Omaha, 1989—; tennis profl., 1975—. Mem. U.S. Profl. Tennis Assn. (cert.). Democrat. Roman Catholic. Home: 510 S 157th Cir Omaha NE 68118-2123 Office: US Army Corps Engrs 12565 W Center Rd Omaha NE 68144-3869

HINES, TIMOTHY CHARLES, financial consultant; b. New London, Conn., May 27, 1957. BBA, U. Iowa, 1979; MBA with distinction, Wake Forest U., 1985. Lic. series 7, 63, 65, Ill., Ind. Prodn. planner Thomas & Betts, Iowa City, 1980, employee rels. mgr., 1980-83; fin. analyst BF Goodrich, Akron, Ohio, 1985-86; acct. mgr. BF Goodrich, Santa Fe Springs, Calif., 1986-88; bus. unit contr. BF Goodrich, Akron, 1988-91, mktg. mgr., 1991-93; fin. cons. Merrill Lynch, Bloomington, Ill., 1993—; bd. dirs., v.p. Hines Motors, New London. Mem. Easter Seals, N.E. Ind., 1993-94, Arthritis Found., Bloomington, 1994; coach Pony League, Bloomington. Scholar Conoco, 1984, Charles Babcock Found., 1984. Mem. Promise Keepers, Lambda Chi Alpha. Republican. Office: Merrill Lynch 2103 N Veterans Pky Bloomington IL 61704-0908

HINES, WILLIAM ELVIS, health facility executive, family physician; b. St. Louis, June 16, 1958; s. Bessie M. (Jackson) Hines. BA, Northwestern U., 1980; MD, U. Mo., 1984; MS, Ohio State U., 1988. Resident in family practice Detroit Med. Ctr.-Wayne State U., 1984-87; fellow, clin. instr. family practice Ohio State U., 1987-88; clin. asst. prof. Howard U., 1989-90; clin. asst. prof., dir. family practice Indiana U. N.W. Ctr., 1990-92; chmn., pres. Hines Family Care Ctr., Florissant, Mo., 1992—; bd. dirs. Champion Health Plan, St. Louis. Recipient New Faculty Orientation award Soc. of Tchrs. of Family Medicine, 1991; Dean's Office scholar U. Mo., 1980-84. Fellow Am. Acad. Family Physicians; mem. Nat. Med. Assn. (chmn.-elect family practice sect. 1995—, fellowship 1980, 81), Kappa Alpha Psi (life, Percy H. Lee award 1984, 96). Office: Hines Family Care Ctr, Inc. 13300 New Halls Ferry Rd Ste C Florissant MO 63033

HINKE, PATRICK T., mechanical engineer; b. Racine, Wis., July 5, 1959. BSME, U. Wis., Milw., 1982. Registered profl. engr., Wis. Assoc.engr. McDonnell Douglas, Long Beach, Calif., 1982-84; sr. devel.engr. Allied Signal Aerospace, Tempe, Ariz., 1984-93; engring. mgr. Applied Power, Butler, Wis., 1994—. Mem. Land Use Com., Rochester, Wis., 1995—. Office: Applied Power 13000 W Silver Spring Dr Butler WI 53007-1018

HINKLE, ANITA LOUISE, export-import specialist, educator; b. Paoli, Ind., Feb. 7, 1943; d. Don P. and Bernice Marie (Tague) H. AB in French and Italian, Ind. U., 1969, MA in Middle Eastern Lang. and Lit., 1973, MBA in Fin., 1978. Export-import asst., credit analyst Union Commerce Bank, Cleve., 1978-81, internat. banking officer, fgn. corr., 1981-82; internat. banking officer internat. svcs. Huntington Nat. Bank, Cleve., 1982-87, asst. v.p. internat. svcs., 1987-90; cons., 1990—; adj. instr. Bryant & Stratton Coll., Cleve., 1991—; mem. export adv. bd. Akron Regional Devel. Bd., 1985-88; mem. Cuyahoga County Commr. Export Adv. Bd., 1979-80. Contbr. articles to profl. jours. Layreader Hist. St. John's Episcopal Ch., Cleve., 1985—; mem. Cursillo, No. Ohio, 1990—. Mem. Akron Fgn. Credit Assn. (v.p. 1989-90). Office: PO Box 94172 Cleveland OH 44101-6172

HINKLE, JO ANN, English language educator; b. Alton, Ill., Feb. 7, 1961; d. Joe and Dorothy Louise (Stoneburner) Christen; m. Robert Eugene Hinkle, Aug. 19, 1989. BA, So. Ill. U., Edwardsville, 1984; MA, So. Ill. U., 1992. Instr. English, Lewis and Clark Coll., Godfrey, Ill., 1988—. Democrat. Unitarian. Home: 11 Maple RR 1 Dorsey IL 62021

HINKLEY, GERRY, newspaper editor. Now dep. mng. editor Milw. Jour. Sentinel, 1995—. Office: Milw Sentinel PO Box 661 333 W State St Milwaukee WI 53201-0661*

HINNRICHS-DAHMS, HOLLY BETH, middle school educator; b. Milw., Oct. 31, 1945; d. Helmut Ferdinand and Rae W. (Beebe) H.; m. Raymond H. Dahms, June 11, 1983 (dec. Oct. 2, 1983). Student U. Wis., Milw., 1963-64, 66, 79—, Chapman Coll., 1965, 67, Internat. Coll. Copenhagen, summer 1968, Temple U., summer 1970, BA, Alverno Coll., 1971; postgrad. Marylhurst Coll., 1972, Chapman Coll. World Campus Afloat, summers 1973, 74, Inst. Shipboard Edn., 1978, 79, 94. V.p. Hinnrichs Inc., Germantown, Wis., 1964-72; tchr. Germantown Recreation Dept., 1965; coach Milw. Recreation Dept., 1966-67; rep. for Wis., Chapman Coll., Orange, Calif., 1967; clk. Stein Drug Co., Menomonee Falls, Wis., 1967-72; tchr. Milw. area Cath. Schs., 1967-72, 83, 90-91, 1996—, maths 96-8), German Town Schs., St. Lawrence Sch., 1991-92; asst. mgr. Original Cookie Co. (Mother Hubbard's) Cookie Store, Northridge Mall, Milw., 1977-84, SAU-U Warehouse Deli, 1984-85, mgr. office, 1985-90; with Pilgrim Message Ctr., 1987—; substitute tchr. cath. schs. Milw. area, 1975-80, 83-89, 90, 92—, St. Rose Sch., 1989-90; tchr. Indian Community Sch., Milw., 1971-72, 88, 94—, Martin Luther King Sch., 1973-74, Crossroads Acad., Milw., 1974-75, Harambee Community Sch., 1980-83; tutor Brookfield (Wis.) Learning Ctr., 1986-87; Midwest rep. World Explorer Cruises, 1978-82. Mem. Wis. Math. Council, Nat. Council Tchrs. Math., Internat. Inst. Milw. Friends of Mus., Alpha Theta Epsilon. Christian Scientist. Lodges: Order Eastern Star, Golden Rule, Miniss Kitigan Drum (Milw. chpt.). Home: N88w15041 Cleveland Ave # 3 Menomonee Falls WI 53051-2239

HINSON, TAMMI MARIE, retail executive; b. Vancouver, Wash., Feb. 24, 1966; d. Paula Diane (Long) Casebolt. BS in Bus., Emporia (Kans.) State U., 1988; M in Sport Mgmt., U.S. Sports Acad., Daphne, Ala., 1989. Sales assoc. Dillard Inc., Wichita, Kans., 1989; group sales account exec. Wichita Wings, 1989-90; tutor Wichita State U. Athletic Dept., 1988-91; mgr. Foster Lanes Bowling Ctr., Morale, Wellness/Readiness div., McConnell AFB, Kans., 1990-91; mktg. and promotions specialist Morale, Wellness, Readiness and Svcs. Squadron, McConnell AFB, 1991-93; mgr. Bresler's Ice Cream and Yogurt, Wichita, 1993-94, Regency Shoes, Wichita, 1994-95; mgr. ladies' shoe dept. Dillard Inc., Wichita, 1995—. Vol. Ark Valley Muscular Dystrophy Assn., Wichita, 1981—, bd. dirs., 1995—; big sister Big Bros./Big Sisters of Sedgwick County, Wichita, 1990-95; neighborhood watch coord. Historic Midtown Citizens Assn., 1991-92, v.p. projects, 1992-94; gate/vol. coord. Kans. Spl. Olympics, Wichita, 1991-94; sec. Citizens Police Acad. Alumni Assn., Wichita, 1992-93. Mem. Citizen Police Acad. Alumni Assn., Inc. (treas. 1993-94, v.p. 1995—), Wichita Flying Lions (3d v.p. 1993-94), Wichita Greyhound G.A.T.E. Club. Home: 1240 N Saint Francis St Wichita KS 67214-2839

HINTHORN, ALETHA SUE, editor, writer; b. Troy, Mo., Apr. 18, 1943; d. Arthur Henry and Frances Kathryn (Schloeman) Wehrman; m. Daniel Robert Hinthorn, May 30, 1964; children: Gregg, Arla. AA, Independence Jr. Coll.; B of Edn, Pitts. State U., 1965. Tchr. music Kans. State Sch. for Blind, Kansas City, 1965-67, Kansas City Coll. & Bible Sch., 1974-75. Author: The Satisified Heart, 4 vols., 1995. Mem. Women Alive (founder, pres. 1984—, mag. editor 1984—). Home: 8912 Hadley Pl Overland Park KS 66212

HINTZ, MICHAEL K., engineer; b. Eau Claire, Wis., Aug. 8, 1965. BSME, Wisconsin Platteville, 1988. Cert. profl. engr., Wis. Product devel. engr. Eaton Corp., Milw., 1988—. Lutheran. Office: Eaton Corp 4265 N 30th St Milwaukee WI 53216-1821

HINZE, KLAUS-PETER WILHELM, language educator; b. Berlin, Sept. 6, 1936; s. Wilhelm Albert and Charlotte (Gebauer) H.; children: Bettina Elisabeth, Jonathan O. PhD, Washington U., St. Louis, 1969. Asst. prof. Case Western Reserve U., Cleve., 1967-71; prof. German and Comparative Literature Cleve. State U., 1971—; vis. prof. Coll. of Edn., Germany, 1985-86. Author: Goethe's Tales, 1972, Ernst Weiss Bibliography, 1974, Ernst Weiss, 1977 (A. Stifter Soc. award 1977); contbr. chpt. to book. Rsch. grantee German Acad. Exchange Svc., 1980, Austrian Govt. rsch. grantee, 1981; Fulbright scholar, 1964, Heerman's scholar Washington U., 1964. Mem. Am. Assn. of Tchrs. of German, Internat. Assn. for Exile Studies, Internat. Assn. Democrat. Lutheran. Office: Cleve. State U. East 23rd & Euclid Ave Cleveland OH 44115

HIRAI, DENITSU, surgeon; b. Yokkaichi, Mie, Japan, July 27, 1943; came to U.S. 1969; s. Denyomu and Shizuo (Tanaka) H.; m. Fumiko Hada, June 14, 1969; 1 child, R. Lisa. MD, U. Tokyo, 1968. Diplomate Am. Bd. Surgery, Am. Bd. Quality Assurance and Utilization Review Physicians, Am. Bd. Surg. Critical Care. Intern and residency Waterbury (Conn.) Hosp., 1969-74; fellow Mt. Sinai Hosp., 1974-75; asst. chief surgery VA Med. Ctr., Lincoln, Nebr., 1975-80; chief surgery VA Med. Ctr., Lincoln, 1981—; asst. clin. prof. surgery Creighton U., Omaha, 1982-84, asst. prof. surgery, 1984—; clin. instr. U. Nebr., Omaha, 1986-88, clin. asst. prof. surgery, 1988—. Author: Brain Ticklers (Japanese), 1983. Mem. AAAS, AMA, ACS, Am. Soc. Parenteral and Enteral Nutrition, Soc. Am. Gastrointestinal Endoscopic Surgeons, Southwestern Surg. Congress, Soc. Critical Care Medicine, Assn. VA Surgeons. Office: VA Med Ctr 600 S 70th St Lincoln NE 68510-2451

HIRN, ROBERT WILLIAM, data processing company executive; b. Albany, N.Y., Jan. 6, 1960. BA in Polit. Sci., Northwestern U., 1983. V.p. Nat. Health Delivery Systems, Chgo., 1978—; tech. dir. Moscow Ian Freed Cons., Inc., 1993—; adv. bd. dirs. Chgo. Home Health Svcs. Inc. Bd. dirs. UN Assn. of Chgo., 1986-90. Mem. Chgo. Yacht Club. Office: Nat Health Delivery Systems 801 S Wells St Apt 902 Chicago IL 60607-4545

HIRSCH, ARLENE SHARON, career counselor; b. Chgo., Mar. 18, 1951; d. Kurt S. and Irma Hirsch. BA, U. Iowa, 1973; MA, Northwestern U., 1983. Pvt. practice career counseling Chgo., 1983—; instr. DePaul U., Chgo., 1988—, Northwestern U., Evanston, Ill., 1996; columnist Chicagoland Job Source Shop Talk, 1985-90; instr. Latin Sch., Chgo., 1985—. Author: VGM's Careers Checklists, 1991, Wall Street Journal Premier Guide to Interviewing, 1993, rev. edit., 1996, Love Your Work and Success Will Follow, 1996; contbr. articles to profl. jours. including Wall St. Jour.'s Nat. Bus. Employment Weekly, Bus. Week Careers mag., Today's Chgo. Woman. Cons. Women Employed Svcs., Chgo. Mem. Internat. Assn. of Career Mgmt. Profls. Office: 850 N State St Chicago IL 60610-3352

HIRSCH, JUNE SCHAUT, chaplain; b. Green Bay, Wis., Sept. 30, 1925; d. Clifford Charles and Eleanor Josephine (Arts) Schaut; m. Marshall E. Gilette, Jan. 23, 1946 (div. 1974); children: Ronald Leigh, Patrick Allen, Vicki Jeanne Baumann; m. Hubert L. Hirsch, Nov. 7, 1975. Student, St. Mary's Sch. Nursing, Rochester, Minn., 1943-45, U. Wis., Sheboygan, 1974-75. Cert. med. asst., 1966. Med. asst. James W. Faulkner, M.D., Phoenix, 1953-56; med. office mgr. Edward E. Houfek, M.D., Sheboygan, Wis., 1956-75; med. office cons. Profl. Mgmt. Inc., Milw., 1975-77; office mgr., adminstrv. asst. Schroeder & Holt Architects Ltd., Milw., 1977-90; vol. chaplain St. Camillus Health Ctr., Milw., 1991—, Children's Hosp. and Froedent Meml. Hosp., Milw., 1991-95; staff chaplain Froedert Meml. Hosp., 1995—; instr. med. asst. program Lake Shore Tech., 1975-76. Mem. Am. Assn. Med. Assts. (nat. trustee 1963-66), Wis. Soc. Med. Assts. (life, exec. bd. 1975-89), Lake ShoreMed. Assts. (exec. bd. 1959-75), Nat. Assn. Cath. Chaplains (cert.). Republican. Roman Catholic. Home: 10200 W Bluemound Rd Apt 918 Milwaukee WI 53226-4372 Office: Froedtert Meml Luth Hosp 9200 W Wisconsin Ave Milwaukee WI 53221

HIRSCH, SYROLA RUTH, gerontology rehabilitation nurse; b. Tripp, S.D., Dec. 17, 1921; d. Theodore and Pauline (Heinrich) Schaefer. Diploma, Luth. Sch. Nursing, Sioux City, Iowa, 1942; B. of Philosophy, Northwestern U., 1961; BSN, DePaul U., 1978; MA in Gerontology, Roosevelt U., 1987. RNC, CRRN; cert. gerontol. nurse, RNC; cert. registered rehab. nurse. Courier nurse Santa Fe RR, Chgo. and L.A., 1946-47; pvt. duty nurse First Dist. Nursing, Chgo., 1948-69; gen. duty cardiac nursing U. Chgo. Clinics, 1969-74; staff nurse surg. Michael Reese Hosp., Chgo., 1974-79; sr. staff nurse med.-surg. Johnston Bowman Rehab. Ctr., Rush Presbyn. St. Lukes Med. Ctr., Chgo., 1979-96; ret. Rush Presbyn. St. Lukes Med. Ctr., Chgo., 1996; rep. unit adv. com. Johnston Bowman Rehab. Ctr., Rush Presbyn. St. Lukes Med. Ctr., Chgo., 1984-87; mem. Citizen Ambassador Program Chinese Nursing Assn., Beijing, lectr. Hon. citizen Boys Town. Mem. ANA, Assn. for Rehab. Nursing, Ill. State Nurses Assn., Nat. Gerontol. Nursing Assn., Am. Assn. Neurosci. Nurses, Internat. Clown Assn., Am. Assn. for Therapeutic Humor, Nat. Assn. Orthopedic Nursing, Profl. Nursing Assn., Am. Diabetes Assn., Holistic Nursing Assn., Med.-Surg. Nurse Assn., Sigma Theta Tau. Home: 4800 S Chicago Beach Dr Chicago IL 60615-2009

HIRSCHBERG, PAUL D., manufacturing executive; b. Patterson, N.J., Aug. 8, 1965; s. Edward B. and Barbara F. (Schermieyer) H.; m. Natalie Sue Isgut, May 3, 1966; 1 child, Robert. Student, U. Mich. V.p. sales and mktg. TFI Battery, Redford, Mich., 1988—. Office: TFI Battery Inc 11931 Dixie St Redford MI 48239

HIRSCHI, MICHAEL CARL, agricultural engineering educator; b. Mpls., Dec. 29, 1955; s. Charles F. and R. Lillian (Malm) H.; m. Debra M. Germundsen, Sept. 16, 1978. AS in Gen. Studies, Anoka-Ramsey C.C., 1976; B of Agrl. Engring., U. Minn., 1978, MS in Agrl. Engring., 1980; PhD, U. Ky., 1985. Rsch. specialist Agrl. Engring. Dept., U. Ky., Lexington, 1980-85; asst. prof. Agrl. Engring. Dept., U. Ill., Urbana, 1985-91, assoc. prof., 1991—; acting asst. dir. Cooperative Extension Svc., Urbana, 1991, interim assoc. dir., 1992; rsch. assoc. U.S. Corps. of Engrs., Champaign, Ill., 1990-94; water quality program coord. Cooperative Extension Svc., Urbana, 1992—. Author: 50 Ways Farmers Can Protect Their Groundwater, 1993; contbr. articles to profl. jours. Mem. Am. Soc. Agrl. Engring. (com. chair), Sigma Xi (chpt. pres.), Epsilon Sigma Phi (Early Career award 1992). Office: U Ill Agrl Engring Dept Univ Ill 1304 W Pennsylvania Ave Urbana IL 61801

HIRSCHL, RICHARD C., investment broker; b. Washington, Mo., June 19, 1929. Owner Corn Cob Pipes Co., Washington, 1950-77; investment broker A G Edwards & Sons, Washington, 1981-86, JJB Hilliard W L Lyons Inc., Washington, 1986—. Chmn. Tri-County Comty. Arts, Washington, 1994—; mayor City of Washington, 1968-78; mem. adv. bd. St. Johns Mercy Hosp., Washington, 1969-79; bd. dirs. St. Mo. Health Comty., Sch. Dist. Found. for Excellence; pres. ch. coun. St. Peter United Ch. of Christ. Corp. Counter-Intelligence Corps, 1951-53. Mem. Shriners, Scottish Rite, Mason. Republican. Home: PO Box 353 Washington MO 63090-0353 Office: JJB Hilliard W L Lyons Inc 1201 Jefferson St Washington MO 63090-4426

HIRSCHMAN, SHERMAN JOSEPH, lawyer, educator; b. Detroit, May 11, 1935; s. Samuel and Anna (Maxmen) H.; m. Audrey Hecker, 1959; children—Samuel, Shari. BS, Wayne State U., 1956, JD, 1959, LLM, 1968. Bar: Mich. 1959, Fla. 1983, Wis. 1984. CPA, Mich., Fla.; cert. tax lawyer, Fla. Pvt. practice, Mich., 1959—; instr. comml. law Detroit Coll. Bus., 1971—. With U.S. Army Res., 1959-62. Mem. Mich. Bar Assn., Fla. Bar Assn., Wis. Bar Assn., Am. Arbitration Assn., Am. Assn. CPA Attys. Address: 340 Woodlake Wynde Oldsmar FL 34677-2119

HIRSCHY, GORDON HAROLD, real estate agent, auctioneer; b. Sturgis, Mich., Jan. 28, 1942; s. Harold L. and Clara L. (Roy) H.; m. Alice Ann Grossman, Aug. 8, 1964 (dec. 1983); m. Sarah Lee Gerber, Nov. 20, 1994; children: Daniel, Benjamin, Matthew, Kurtt, Lori, Hannah. BS in Gen. Agriculture, Purdue U., 1964; degree in auctioneering sci. and mgmt., Am. Acad. Auctioneers, 1990. FIC, LUTCF. State nitrogen engr., constrn. supr. Smith-Douglass Fertilizer Co., Indpls., 1965-67; asst. mgr. LaGrange County (Ind.) Farm Bur. Corp., 1967-72; county office mgr., agt. LaGrange County Farm Bur. Ins., 1972-80; owner, operator Community Ins. Svcs., Inc., LaGrange, 1980-88; ins. agt. Ins. Market Place, Inc., LaGrange, 1988-89; dist. rep. Modern Woodmen of Am., Inc., Rock Island, Ill., 1989-91; auctioneer Century 21 Fairfield Real Estate, Fort Wayne, Ind., 1991—. Named one of Outstanding Young Men Am., 1972, Rookie of Yr. Mich. Football Ofcls. Assn., 1988. Mem. N.E. Ind. Assn. Life Underwriters (pres. 1983, Mem. of Yr. 1982), Ind. Life and Health Ins. Leaders Club (exec. dir., sec. 1978-91), Ind. Auctioneers Assn., Am. Soc. Farm Equipment Appraisers, Gideons Internat. (meml. Bible sec.), Ind./Mich. Football Ofcls. Athletic Assns. Republican. United Methodist. Office: 3501 Fairfield Ave Fort Wayne IN 46807-1805 also: 5929 S Webster Rd New Haven IN 46774-9344

HIRT, GLENN C., investment broker; b. Grand Rapids, Mich., Mar. 29, 1952. BS, Mich. State U., 1975. With Moseley Securities Gruntale, N.Y.C.; self-employed broker Hinsdale, Ill., 1986-93; investment broker A.G. Edwards & Sons Inc., Traverse City, Mich., 1993—. Contbr. articles to various publs. mem. ACE/SCORE, Traverse City, 1995—. Mem. IMCA (founder, bd. dirs., v.p. Traverse City, Outstanding Achievement award 1987). Home: 619 S Bayshore Dr Elk Rapids MI 49629-9732 Office: AG Edwards & Sons Inc Delta Ctr 415 Munson Ave Traverse City MI 49686-3059

HISH, DON R., stockbroker, financial planner; b. Joliet, Ill., Nov. 19, 1938. BS in Edn., Ill. State U., 1960; MS, U. Ill., 1963. CFP. Tchr. Piper City H.S., Piper, Ill., 1960-62; guidance dir. Argena Sch. Dist., 1963-64; stockbroker White & Co., Bloomington, Ill., 1964-69, Stifel Nicolaus, Bloomington, 1969-73, Loewi & Co., Bloomington, 1973-79, Kemper Securities Inc., Bloomington, 1979—; lectr. investment courses various schs. Mem. IAFP, IBCFP. Home: RR 4 Box 499 Bloomington IL 61704-9337 Office: Kemper Securities Inc PO Box 187 1408 E Empire St Bloomington IL 61702

HISRICH, ROBERT DALE, business educator. BA, DePual U., 1966; MBA, U. Cin., 1969, PhD, 1971; PhD (hon.), Chuvesh State U., Russia, 1995, Miskole U., Hungary, 1996. From asst. to assoc. prof. mktg. Boston Coll., 1969-84; prof., Bovard chair entrepreneurial studies U. Tulsa, 1985-93; prof., A. Malachi Mixon III chair The Weatherhead Sch. of Mgmt., Case Western Res. U., 1993—; vis. prof. U. Limerick, Ireland, 1984-85; Fulbright prof. Internat. Mgmt. Ctr., Hungary, 1989. Office: Weatherhead Sch Mgmt Enterprise Hall 599 10900 Euclid Ave Cleveland OH 44106-7235

HITCH, ROBERT LANDIS, insurance company executive; b. Cinn., Nov. 16, 1947; s. Robert Howard and Dorothy Maxine (Shepherd) H.; m. Judith Ann Ross, Dec. 27, 1969; children: Robert Bradley, Charles Ross, Sarah Allison. BS in Bus. and Econs., U. Ky., 1969; postgrad. Grad. Exec. Program, U. Cin., 1992. CPCU; assoc. in reins. Underwriter trainee Aetna Life and Casualty, Louisville, 1971-72, underwriter, 1972-73, sr. underwriter, 1973-74; reinsurance underwriter Great Am. Ins. Co., Cin., 1974-80, treaty underwriter, 1980-81, sec., 1981-83, underwriting mgr., 1983-86, asst. v.p., 1986-88, div. sr. v.p., Japanese div., 1988-93, pres. Japanese div., 1993—. Chmn. ins. sect. United Way of Cin., 1992. Fellow U. Ky. Mem. Soc. CPCUs (pres. Cin. chpt. 1994, rsch. chmn. 1988-89, econs. instr. 1988—, treas., chmn. fin. com., editor CPCU internat. sect. newsletter 1994, 95, internat. com. 1993—, chmn. scholarship com. 1995-96, nat. dir. 1995), U. Ky. Alumni Assn., Japan Am. Soc. Ky., Japan Am. Soc. Greater Cin. (trustee, pres.-elect 1996—), M-Club, Bankers Club, Harry J. Loman Found., Sigma Phi Epsilon. Republican. Home: 2482 Kremers Ln Covington KY 41017-1163 Office: Gt Am Ins Co 4th St Ste 800 Cincinnati OH 45215-4862

HITCHCOCK, KIM ANITA, education educator; b. Cin., July 14, 1956; d. Ernest and Delores H.; children: Delorsa, Jabreel, Kabrina. EdD, U. Cin. Inspector, educator Cin. Health Dept., 1980-92; asst. prof. U. Cin., 1992-93; assoc. prof. Ctrl. State U., Wilberforce, Ohio, 1992—; bd. dirs. Ctr. for Peace Edn.; cons. Ctr. Applied Rsch., Cin., 1991—. NIH grantee. Mem. NAACP. Office: Ctrl State U 1400 Brush Row Rd Wilberforce OH 45384

HITE, ELINOR KIRKLAND, oil company human resources manager; b. Abington, Pa., Sept. 28, 1942; d. Bryant Mays and Bernice Eleanor (Tanis) Kirkland; m. Anthony L. Hite, July 7, 1967 (div. 1974); 1 child, Juddson Kirkland. BA in English, Denison U., Granville, Ohio, 1964; MA in Counseling, Princeton Theol. Sem., 1966. Asst. dir. pers. Edwards Bros. Printing Co., Ann Arbor, Mich., 1973-74; asst. dir. career counseling/placement U. Ill., Chgo., 1975-81; human rels. assoc. Amoco Corp., Chgo., 1981-82, sr. human rels. rep., 1982-85, staff human rels. rep., 1985-87, human rels. cons., 1987—; vol. career employment lectr., Chgo., 1985—. Chair clin. mgmt. com. Lorene Replogle Counseling Ctr., Chgo., 1981—; trustee, officer 4th Presbyn. Ch., Chgo., 1985—, elder, officer, 1985-91, chair pers. com., 1989—; pres. 200 S. Home Condo Assn., Oak Park, Ill., 1982-91, 93—; bd. dirs. Frank Lloyd Wright Mus., 1994—; chair human resources policies com., bd. trustees McCormick Theol. Sem., 1996—. Presbyterian.

HITE, JUDSON CARY, retired pharmaceutical company executive; b. Canton, Ohio, Oct. 12, 1939; s. Everett Corbett and Dorothy Elizabeth (Caley) H.; m. Mary Kay Woodman, July 14, 1962 (div. Mar. 1970); children: Judson Cary III, Kenneth Woodman; m. Elsie Adeline Lilly, Oct. 1, 1977; 1 child, Julie Christina. BS, Ohio State U., 1962. Mgmt. trainee The Upjohn Co., Kalamazoo, Mich., 1962-64, programming analyst, 1964-67, profl. acct., 1967-70, adminstrv. mgr., 1970-74, gen. audit mgr., 1974-81, dir gen. audit, 1981-85, dir. med. affairs, 1985-89, dir. info. systems, 1989-91, dir. rsch. contracts, 1991-93, dir. office mgmt. svcs., 1993-95; ret., 1995. Mem. Nat. Assn. Accts. (dir., v.p., 1964-74), Inst. Internal Auditors (dir. 1974-85), Lic. Execs. Soc., Sigma Chi (v.p. 1960-61). Republican. Home: 5961 Scenic Way Dr Kalamazoo MI 49009-9112

HITZ, DUANE EVERETT, brokerage executive; b. St. Paul, Nov. 24, 1939; s. Bernard R. and Marcella M (Kruel) H.; m. Theresa A. Bieza, June 30, 1962; children: Amy, Michelle, Duane, Junior. BA, U. Minn., 1962. Asst. underwriter St. Paul Fire & Marine Ins. Co., 1957-63; exec. v.p. E.W. Blanch Co., Mpls., 1963-82; pres. G.L. Hodson & Son, Inc., St. Paul, 1982-85; exec. v.p. G.L. Hodson & Son, Inc., New Hyde Park, N.Y., 1985-87; pres. Hitz and Assocs., Inc., Mpls., 1988-89; sr. v.p. E.W. Blanch Co., Mpls., 1989-91. Capt. Minn. N.G., 1957-68. Mem. Soc. CPCU (cert., bd. dirs. Minn. chpt. 1980-83), Internat. Ins. Seminars.

HIX, HARVEY LEE, philosophy educator; b. Stillwater, Okla., Nov. 24, 1960; s. Harry L. Jr. and Carol E. (Helt) H.; m. Sheila Denise Pedigo, Aug. 20, 1983. BA, Belmont Coll., Nashville, 1982; MA, U. Tex., 1985, PhD, 1987. Assoc. prof. philosophy Kansas City (Mo.) Art Inst., 1987—. Author: Morte d'Author: An Autopsy, 1990, Spirits Hovering Over the Ashes: Legacies of Postmodern Theory, 1995, The Kindling Point, 1995, Perfect Hell, 1996. Recipient Mo. Writers Biennial award Mo. Arts Coun., 1992; NEA fellow in poetry, 1995. Mem. Am. Philos. Assn., Am. Soc. for Aesthetics. Home: 18 W 73rd Ter Kansas City MO 64114-5710 Office: Kansas City Art Inst 4415 Warwick Blvd Kansas City MO 64111-1820

HIXON, JAMES EDWARD, physiology educator; b. Ames, Iowa, July 5, 1938; s. Ralph Malcom and Stella Viola (Sadler) H.; m. Anna Elsbeth Ripken, Nov. 25, 1967; children: Jill Elizabeth, Ernest Rudolf. BS, U. Calif., Davis, 1961, PhD, 1968. Research fellow Harvard U. Med. Sch., Boston, 1968-69; postdoctoral fellow U. Western Ont., London, Can., 1969-71; research assoc. Cornell U., Ithaca, N.Y., 1971-77; asst. prof. physiology U. Ill., Urbana, 1977-81, assoc. prof., 1981-86, prof., 1986—, asst. dean of students Coll. Vet. Medicine, 1995—. Contbr. numerous articles to profl. jours. Fogarty Sr. Internat. fellow NIH, 1985; recognized as an Excellent Tchr. by students, 1982, 87-92. Mem. Am. Soc. Animal Sci., Endocrine Soc., Soc. for Study Reproduction. Office: U Ill 2001 S Lincoln Ave Urbana IL 61801-6178

HIZER, MARLENE BROWN, library director; b. Shattuck, Okla., Mar. 29, 1940; d. Marvin Ira and Geneva Marie (Wright) Brown; m. Ammon M. Hizer, Mar. 19, 1960; children: Lori Marie Hizer Hunt, Holly Dot Hizer Caldwell. BS in Edn., N.W. Mo. State U., 1962; MS in Edn. emphasizing Libr. Sci., Ctrl. Mo. State U., 1966. Cert. tchr. libr. sci. Stenographer Butler Mfg., Kansas City, 1958-59; tchr., libr. Eastgate Jr. High Sch., Kansas City, 1962-69; dir. Nevada (Mo.) Pub. Libr., 1985—; lit. tutor, Nevada, Mo., 1992—; del. Mo. Gov.'s Conf., Jefferson City, 1990. Editor (newspaper) NEWSMAT, 1962-69, Northwest Missourian, 1958-62. Core communicator Mo. Citizen's Coun., Nev., 1980—; edn. counselor LDS Relief Soc., Nev., 1973-77; Sunday sch. tchr. LDS Ch., 1990—, sem. tchr., 1975-78, pub. affairs dir., 1990—; mem. Friends of Nev. Pub. Libr. Recipient Albert B. Fuson Meml. award for Highest Contbns., 1958, Scholastic award AAUP, 1962, Star award Nat. Scholastic Press Assn., 1962; named one of Outstanding Young Women of Am., 1970; Curator scholar U. Mo., 1958, scholar Bus. and Profl. Women's Assn., 1959. Mem. AAUW (cultural interest com. 1990-91), DAR (vice regent 1991-93), ALA, Mo. Libr. Assn., Pub. Libr. Assn., Pub. Libr. Dirs., Mo. State Libr. Inst., Mo. Pub. Libr. Coun. (recorder 1991-93), Vernon County Hist. Soc., Soroptimist Internat. (chair Internat. Goodwill and Understanding). Democrat. Home: RR 2 Box 158 Nevada MO 64772-9674 Office: Nevada Pub Libr 225 W Austin Blvd Nevada MO 64772-3343

HLADKY, JOSEPH F., JR., newspaper publisher, broadcasting executive; b. Cedar Rapids, Iowa, Aug. 25, 1910; s. Joseph Frank and Laura (Krchmar) H.; m. Jane Miller, Sept. 15, 1935; children: John Miller, Joseph Frank. Student, Coe Coll., Cedar Rapids, 1928-29, U. Iowa, 1930-31. Engaged in vending machine bus., 1931-35, newspaper publ., 1935—, broadcasting, 1947—; chmn. bd. Gazette Co. (pubs. Cedars Rapids Gazette), Cedar Rapids TV Co.; past chmn. bd. govs. ABC-TV Affiliates; dir. Mchts. Nat. Bank, Cedar Rapids, Iowa Nat. Mut. Ins. Co. Chmn. Cedar Rapids Airport Commn., 1973-85, Cedar Rapids Hwy. Com., 1960-85; mem. Iowa Devel. Commn., 1964—, Cedar Rapids Civic Planning Com., 1962—; bd. dirs. St. Luke's Methodist Hosp., Cedar Rapids, 1961-86, Cedar Rapids Met. YMCA, 1969—; trustee Coe Coll., 1968—. Recipient Master Editor and Pub. award, 1970; Community Recognition award, 1981; named Boss of Year, 1964. Mem. Am. Soc. Newspaper Editors, Am. Newspaper Pubs. Assn., Inland Daily Press Assn., AP, Nat. Assn. Broadcasters, Iowa Daily Press Assn. (past pres.), Cedar Rapids C. of C. (past pres.), Sigma Delta Chi. Clubs: Nat. Press (Washington); Cedar Rapids Country, Elmcrest Country, Sombrero Golf and Country, Marathon Yacht, Marathon, St. Andrews Golf, Isles Yacht. Lodges: Shriners; Elks; Royal Order Jesters. Office: Cedar Rapids Gazette Co 500 3rd Ave SE Cedar Rapids IA 52401-1608

HLAVACEK, PAULA JEAN, educational administrator; b. Chgo., July 26, 1951; d. Paul and Dorothy (Radzevich) Petrauskas. BS in Edn., No. Ill. U., 1973, MS in Edn., 1980; EdD, Vanderbilt U., 1993. Cert. tchr., ednl. adminstr. Tchr. St. Raphael Sch., Naperville, Ill., 1974-76, Henry Puffer Sch., Downers Grove, Ill., 1976-94; prin. East Prairie Sch., Skokie, Ill., 1994—; cons. Inst. Ednl. Rsch., Wheaton, Ill., 1983-84. Mem. ASCD, AAUW, Ill. Prins. Assn., Ill. Women Adminstrs. (co-dir. 1991-96), Kappa Delta Pi. Home: 6047 Washington Downers Grove IL 60516

HO, DAVID KIM HONG, professional studies educator; b. Honolulu, Mar. 5, 1948; s. Raymond T.Y. and Ellen T.Y. (Fong) H.; m. Joan Yee, July 6, 1968 (div. Apr. 1982); 1 child, Michael J.; m. Patricia Ann McAndrews, June 25, 1983. BS in Indsl. Engring., U. So. Calif., 1970; MBA, Butler U., 1976; MS in Acctg., U. Wis., Whitewater, 1981. Cert. fellow in prodn. and inventory mgmt. Indsl. engr. FMC Corp., Los Angeles, 1970-73; mgr. prodn. planning and inventory control FMC Corp., Indpls., 1973-77; materials mgr. Butler Mfg. Co., Ft. Atkinson, Wis., 1977-81; systems mgr. Butler Mfg. Co., Kansas City, Mo., 1981-82; dir. materials and systems Behlen Mfg. Co., Columbus, Nebr., 1982-84, v.p. operations, bd. dirs., 1984-86; mgr. corp. materials Lozier Corp., Omaha, 1986-90, plant mgr., 1990-91; v.p. mfg. Heatilator Inc., Mt. Pleasant, Iowa, 1991-93; prof. profl. studies Bellevue (Nebr.) U., 1993—; instr. Met. C.C., Omaha, 1989—, Iowa Wesleyan Coll, Mt. Pleasant, 1991-92. Mem. Nat. Assn. Purchasing Mgmt. (acad.), Am. Prodn. and Inventory Control Soc. Home: 11729 Fisher House Rd Bellevue NE 68123-1112 Office: Met CC PO 3777-Soc 121 Omaha NE 68103-0777

HO, LEO CHI CHIEN, Chinese government official; b. Tai Hu, An-Wei, Republic of China, Sept. 2, 1940; came to U.S., 1964, naturalized, 1971; s. Yu Yuan and Hung (King) H.; m. Julie Yu-Ling Hou, May 11, 1967; children: Albert, Alexander. BA, Nat. Cheng Chi U., Taipei, Republic of China, 1964; MLS, Atlanta U., 1967; PhD, Wayne State U., 1975. Libr. Tex. Tech U., Lubbock, 1966-69; dir. China Sci. Pub., Taylor, Mich., 1969-77; bus. libr. Detroit Pub. Libr., 1970-75; libr. Washtenaw Community Coll., Ann Arbor, Mich., 1977—; pres. Fin. Brokers' Exch., Farmington Hills, Mich., 1978-87, Sylvan Learning Ctr. Mich., West Bloomfield, 1987—; mem. Nat. Assembly, China, 1996—; chmn. bd. Intellectual Svcs., Inc., 1987—; commr. Chinese Overseas Commn., China, 1989—. Mem. adv. coun. Guide to Ethnic Mus., Librs., and Archives in the U.S., 1984. Bd. govs. Internat. Inst. of Greater Met. Detroit, 1985—; v.p., commr. Mich. Gov.'s Adv. Com. on Asian Affairs, Lansing, 1986—; pres. Detroit Chinese Culture Svc. Ctr., 89—. Recipient Outstanding Svc. award Detroit Chinese Cultural Ctr., 1984, 88, Spirit of Detroit award City Coun. Detroit, 1990, 93, Pres.'s Citation award Madonna U. Livonia, Mich., 1993, Dedicated Svc. award Overseas China Commn.-Taiwan, 1995. Mem. Assn. Chinese-Ams. (v.p. 1985—, Dedicated Svc. award 1984, 88, 89), Chinese Acad. and Profl. Assn. in Mid-Am. (bd. dirs. 1987—, Outstanding Svc. award 1988), Rotary. Home: 3810 Manchester Ct Bloomfield Hills MI 48302-1239 Office: Sylvan Learning Ctr 5829 W Maple Rd # 127 West Bloomfield MI 48322-2294

HOAG, EDWIN, advocate for the disabled; b. St. Louis, Aug. 17, 1955. Student, Trinity Bible Inst., 1991-93. Libertarian candidate for Mo. House of Reps., 1993, 94, 96; chmn. Dallas County Libertarian Party, 1996—. With U.S. Army, 1975. Roman Catholic. Office: Rte 1 Box 180-A5 Elkland MO 65644*

HOAGLAND, PETER JACKSON, lawyer, former congressman; b. Omaha, Nov. 17, 1941; s. Laurance and Naomi (Carpenter) H.; m. Barbara Joan Erickson, Sept. 1, 1973; children: Elizabeth, Kate, Christopher and David (twins), Nick. AB with Great Distinction, Stanford U., 1963; LLB, Yale U., 1968. Bar: Nebr. 1968, D.C. 1968. Assoc. Wald, Harkrader & Ross, Washington, 1968-69; law clk. to Hon. Oliver Gasch U.S. Dist. Ct. D.C., Washington, 1969-70; trial atty. Pub. Defender Service, Washington, 1970-73; pvt. practice Omaha, 1974-89; senator State of Nebr., Lincoln, 1979-86, chmn. judiciary com. and rules com.; mem. 101st-103rd Congresses from 2d Nebr. Dist., 1989-95, mem. House Ways and Means Com.; ptnr. Arent Fox Kintner Plotkin & Kahn, Washington, 1995—; mem. House Ways and Means Com. Served to 1st lt. U.S. Army, 1963-65. Recipient Conservation Achievement award Mo. Valley chpt. Sierra Club, Sch. Bell award for leadership in edn. in passage of L.B. 994, Tchrs. Assn., 1987. Democrat. Episcopalian. Home: 4521 Drummond Ave Chevy Chase MD 20815-5434 Office: Arent Fox Kintner Plotkin & Kahn 1050 Connecticut Ave NW Washington DC 20036-5339

HOAGLUND, LEORA M., emergency nurse; b. Cadillac, Mich., June 13, 1950; d. Merle and Betty Mae (Hall) Fewless; m. Elmo V. Hoaglund, May 17, 1969; children: Shawanee, Cherokee, Cheyenna, Joshua. ADN, Ferris State U., 1986; cert. EMT-S, Muskegon Community Coll., 1983; BSN, Ferris State U., 1991. RN, Mich.; CEN; cert. EMT specialist. Nurses aide Lakeview Manor Nursing Home, Cadillac, 1977-78; respiratory therapist Reed City (Mich.) Hosp., 1983-86, float nurse, 1986-87; staff nurse ICU-SCU Mercy Hosp., 1987-88, staff nurse emergency room, 1988—, profl. practice com. mem., 1991-96; home health nurse In Home Help, Big Rapids, Mich., 1988—, Amicare, 1994; instr. CPR, 1990—. Vol. EMT-S, Osceola County Emergency Med. Svc., Reed City, 1982—; leader 4-H, Osceola County, 1980-88; vol. fire and rescue person Tustin (Mich.) Area Fire Dept., 1980—, sec., 1986-92; 1st lt. vol. fire and rescue svc., 1992-94, 2d capt., 1994—.

HOAGSTROM, CARL WILLIAM, biology educator; b. Holdrege, Nebr., Aug. 24, 1940; s. Elmer George and Leona May (Shafer) H.; m. Maureen Ann Goertzen, June 5, 1965; children: Rebecca Ann, Christopher William, Sherwin Carl. BS, Kearney State Coll. (name changed to U. Nebr. at Kearney 1991), 1966; MS, Purdue U., 1968; PhD, U. Ariz., 1978. Sci. tchr. Arcardia (Nebr.) High Sch., 1968-69, Grand Island (Nebr.) High Sch., 1969-71; from instr. to assoc. prof. biology Ohio No. U., Ada, 1975-88, prof., 1988—. Contbr. articles to The Nobel Prize Winners: Physiology and Medicine, Magill's Survey of Sci.: Life Sci., also Applied Ssci., Survey of the Social Scis.: Govt. and Politics, Gt. Events in History II: Ecology and the Environment, Ready Reference: Am. Indians, Magill's Med. Guide: Health and Illness, 20th Century Gt. Sci. Achievements. With USMC, 1958-62. Mem. AAAS, Am. Inst. Biol. Scis., Ecol. Soc. Am., Am. Soc. Mammalogists, Phi Beta Kappa. Home: 1053 County Rd 80 Alger OH 45812-9645 Office: Ohio No U Dept Biol Sci Ada OH 45810

HOBBS, CHARLES FLOYD, research chemist; b. Lebo, Kans., Jan. 17, 1935; s. Floyd Douglas and Bessie Ruth (Jones) H.; m. Viola Irene Barton, July 17, 1955; children: Douglas, Deborah. AB, Emporia (Kans.) State U., 1956; PhD, U. Kans., 1960. Rsch. specialist Cen. Rsch. Lab., Monsanto Co., St. Louis, 1960-79; sr. rsch. specialist Monsanto Chem. Intermediate Co., St. Louis, 1979-83; sr. rsch. leader Monsanto Agrl. Chem. Co., St. Louis, 1983-93; chem. cons. Process Devel., St. Louis, 1993—. Chmn. Planning and Zoning Commn., Des Peres, Mo., 1975-76; chmn. Bd. Adjustment, Des Peres, 1978-90. NSF fellow, 1958-60. Fellow Am. Inst. Chemists; mem. Am. Chem. Soc. (chmn. St. Louis sect. 1983, dir. St. Louis sect. 1984-88). Methodist. Home and Office: 1100 Trinket Ct Saint Louis MO 63131-4622

HOBBS, HORTON HOLCOMBE, III, biology educator; b. Gainesville, Fla., Dec. 17, 1944; s. Horton Holcombe Jr. and Georgia Cates (Blount) H.; m. Susan Claire Krantz, Oct. 12, 1967; children: Heather H. Killion, Horton Holcombe IV. BA, U. Richmond, 1967; MS, Miss. State U., 1969; PhD, Ind. U., 1973. Instr. Christopher Newport Coll., Newport News, Va., 1973-75; asst. prof. George Mason U., Fairfax, Va., 1975-76; prof. biology, chair dept. biology Wittenberg U., Springfield, Ohio, 1976—; mem. com. Nongame Wildlife Tech. Adv. Com., Columbus, Ohio, 1989-95; trustee Island Cave Rsch. Ctr., 1987—. Author: The Crayfishes and Shrimp of Wisconsin, 1988; life scis. editor: Nat. Speleological Soc. Bull., Huntsville, Ala., 1985—; contbr. to profl. publs. Campaign co-chair County Park Dist., Springfield, 1980. Fellow Nat. Speleological Soc. (bd. govs. 1985-88), The Explorers Club; mem. Crustacean Soc. (coun. mem. 1980-83), Biol. Soc. Wash. (exec. coun. 1976-77), Cave Conservancy of the Virginias (bd. dirs. 1988—). Office: Wittenberg U Dept Biol Springfield OH 45501

HOBBS, HOWARD CORY, geologist; b. Ravenna, Ohio, Feb. 1, 1946; s. Clinton Howard and Olive Eddy (Cory) H.; m. G. Ann Bjornson, Sept. 23, 1972; children: Cory B., David K., Disa M. BS, Kent State U., 1970; MS, PhD, U. N.D., 1975. Geologist N.D. Geol. Survey, Grand Forks, 1976-77, Minn. Geol. Survey, St. Paul, 1977—; lectr. Weber State Coll., Ogden, Utah, 1975-76; mem. geol. sensitivity work group Waters div. Dept. Natural Resources, St. Paul, 1990-91. Author numerous geologic maps of Minn. and N.D. With U.S. Army, 1965-68. Mem. AAAS, Minn. Assn. Profl. Soil Scientists (Soil Scientist of Yr. 1993). Office: Minn Geol Survey 2642 University Ave W Saint Paul MN 55114-1032

HOBBS, ROBERT S., executive; b. Muskegon, Mich., Jan. 31, 1946. Cert. fund raising exec. Dir. devel. events World Vision Internat., Monrovia, Calif., 1973-85; exec. v.p. The Timothy Group, Inc., Grand Rapids, Mich., 1990—; mem. faculty Christian Mgmt., Diamond Bar, Calif., Christian Stewardship Assn., Denver, 1990—, Evang. Devel. Ministries, Dallas, 1991—. Home: 7768 22nd Ave Jenison MI 49428 Office: The Timothy Group Inc 3680 44th St SE Ste 5E Grand Rapids MI 49512

HOBSON, DAVID LEE, congressman, lawyer; b. Cin., Oct. 17, 1936; m. Carolyn Alexander; children: Susan Marie, Lynn Martha, Douglas Lee. BA, Ohio Wesleyan U., 1958; JD, Ohio State Coll. Law, 1963; hon. degree Ctrl. State U., Wittenberg U. Former resident counsel Kissell Co., Springfield, Ohio; former atty. Union Central Life Ins. Co., Cin.; mem. Ohio Senate, 1982-90, majority whip, 1986-88, pres. pro tem, 1988-90; mem. 102nd-104th Congresses from 7th Ohio dist., Washington, D.C., 1991—; house coms. appropriations, budget, standards of ofcl. conduct. Former trustee Wilberforce U., Ohio, Urbana U.; trustee Ohio Wesleyan; bd. dirs. Ohio. Mem. ABA, AMVETS, Ky. Bar Assn., Ohio Bar Assn., Springfield Bd. Realtors, Springfield Area C. of C. (past bd. dirs.), Non-Commissioned Officers Assn., Masons (32 degrees), Am. Legion, VFW, Moose, Elks, Rotary, Shrine Club. Home: PO Box 2691 Springfield OH 45501-2691 Office: 1514 Longworth Washington DC 20515-3507

HOBUS, RUTH NOLD, nursing educator and administrator; b. Onaka, S.D., Aug. 6, 1936; d. Leo F. and Katherine (Trefz) Nold; m. Maurice E. Hobus, Aug. 17, 1956; children: Lauri, Julie. Diploma in nursing, Northwestern Hosp., Mpls., 1956; BSN, S.D. State U., 1984, MSN, 1991. RN, S.D., Minn., Nebr. Staff nurse, pvt. duty nurse Gettysburg (S.D.) Meml. Hosp., 1956-65, staff nurse, supr., wellness dir., abuse team rep., 1975-87; staff nurse, insvc. dir. Holy Infant Hosp., Hoven, S.D., 1966-69; clin. dir. Cheyenne-Lakota Nursing Program, Eagle Butte, S.D., 1988-90; clin. nurse instr. S.D. State U., Brookings, 1990-92; nurse adminstr. Winnebago (Nebr.) PHS Hosp., 1992—; adj. clin. instr. S.D. State U., 1992—; lectr. in lit. in healing. Author, co-producer, asst. dir. teaching film Healing the Heart: Literature in Hospice Care, 1991; contbr. to profl. publs. Mem. Pleasant View Sch. Bd., Potter County, S.D., 1960-72; sec. S.D. Farm Bur., Potter County, 1963-66; vice-chmn. Potter County Reps., Gettysburg, 1962-70; mem. Potter County Child Protection Team, Gettysburg, 1984-90. Grantee S.D. Com. on Humanities, 1987, 90-91. Mem. ANA, S.D. Nurses Assn., Sigma Theta Tau, Phi Kappa Phi, Kappa Delta Phi. Mennonite. Home: 1720 F St Apt B-4 South Sioux City NE 68776-2536 Office: Winnebago PHS Hosp Box HH Winnebago NE 68071

HOCH, JOHN S., chemicals executive, engineering executive; b. Grand Rapids, Mich., Feb. 7, 1943; s. John J. and Amy Louise (Porcupile) H.; m. Constance J. Lahmeyer, Dec. 30, 1967 (div. Apr. 1987); m. Cathy Walter, Aug. 27, 1994; children: Jennifer, Jeffrey. Grand Rapids Jr. Coll., Grand Rapids (Mich.) Jr. Coll., 1961-63; BS in Indsl. Engring., Western Mich. U., 1966, MBA, 1967. Plastics tech. svc. Dow Chem. Co., Freeport, Tex., 1967-72; plastics sales Dow Chem. Co., Kansas City, Mo., 1972-78; project mgr. Dow Chem. Co., Midland, Mich., 1978-80, govt. rels. mgr., 1988-89; dist. sales mgr. agr. products Dow Chem. Co., Phila., 1980-88; group product mgr. Dow Elanco, Indpls., 1989, govt. rels. and pub. affairs mgr., 1989—; instr. Bronzosport Jr. Coll., Freeport, 1970-72, vis. lectr. Cornell U., 1985-86; chmn. state affairs com. Am. Crop Protection Assn.; bd. dirs. Denton Consulting, 1991—. Recipient Workhorse award Am. Crop Protection Assn., 1994. Mem. Am. Mktg. Assn., Am. Legis. Coun. (chair task force 1991-93), Nat. Coun. State Legis., State Govt. Affairs Coun. Republican. Lutheran. Home: 9037 Clemson St Indianapolis IN 46268

HOCHHALTER, GORDON RAY, advertising executive; b. Jerome, Idaho, Oct. 3, 1946; s. Ralph R. and Evelyn (McClellan) H. BA, Brigham Young U., 1972. Asst. promotion supr. Armstrong World Industries, Lancaster, Pa., 1972-74, promotion supr., 1974-76, sr. promotion supr., 1976; asst. advt. mgr. R.R. Donnelley & Sons Co., Chgo., 1976-79, asst. mgr. advt., sales promotion, 1979-81, advt. mgr., 1981-84, group mgr. mktg. com., creative devel., 1984-86, dir. mktg. com., creative dir., 1986-91; v.p., gen. mgr., creative dir. Mobium Corp. Design & Communications, Chgo., 1991—; v.p., creative cons. Caviale Fashions, N.Y.C., 1987—. Contbr. to profl. jours. and Libr. of Congress. Recipient London Internat. Advt. awards, 1987, One Show, Type Dirs. Club, Clio awrds, Art Dirs. Club awards, Andy awards, Addy awards, Internat. Advt. Festival AIGA awards, ProCom awards, Ace awards, 1987-95, Chgo. Tower awards, Am. Bus. Press Objective and Results award, 1992, Cresta Internat. Advt. award, 1993, Sawyer award Bus. Mktg. Mag., 1993, High-Tech. Advt. award MARCOM, 1994, Pinnacle award MARCOM, 1994, Icon award Bus. Week Mag., 1994-95. Mem. Am. Ctr. for Design, Am. Advt. Fedn., Am. Inst. Graphic Arts, Chgo. Advt. Fedn., Bus. Mktg. Assn., N.Y. Art Dirs. Club. Office: Mobium Corp The Merchandise Mart 200 World Trade Ctr Ste 2000 Chicago IL 60654

HOCHHAUSER, SHEILA, state legislator; b. May 23, 1951; m. David C. Margolies; 1 child. BA, Antioch U., 1973; MPH, U. Memphis, 1976; JD, U. N.C., 1984. Kans. state rep. Dist. 66, atty. Mem. Kans. Bar Assn., Kans. Trial Lawyers Assn. Home: 1636 Leavenworth St Manhattan KS 66502-4157 Office: Kans State Senate State Capital Topeka KS 66612*

HOCHMUTH, EDWARD CHRISTIAN, retail executive, tax consultant; b. St. Paul, Feb. 14, 1924; s. Paul Fredrick and Onlie J. (Volz) H.; m. Jane Lorraine Sauer, June 15, 1946; children: Leonard Edward, Patricia Jane Hochmuth Parker. BSA, Walton Sch. Commerce, Chgo., 1953. CPA, Ill. Acctg. supr. Toni div. Gillette Co., Chgo., 1946-58; sys. analyst Abbott Labs., North Chicago, Ill., 1958-70; account exec. Shearson Haydon Stone, Chgo., 1970-72; pres. Leonard's Mens and Boys Ltd., Northbrook, Ill., 1972—; mem. Chgo. Bd. Trade, 1970-72. Treas. Northbrook Civic Assn., 1956-58; mem. Village of Northbrook Indsl. Devel.Commn., 1989-93. Mem. AICPA, Masons. Republican. Presbyterian. Home: 2595 Crabtree Ln Northbrook IL 60062 Office: Leonard's Mens and Boys Ltd 1929B Cherry Ln Northbrook IL 60062

HOCKADAY, IRVINE O., JR., greeting card company executive; b. Ludington, Mich., Aug. 12, 1936; s. Irvine Oty and Helen (McCune) H.; m. Mary Ellen Jurden, July 8, 1961; children: Wendy Helen, Laura DuVal. A.B., Princeton U., 1958; LL.B., U. Mich., 1961, J.D., 1961. Bar: Mo. 1961. Atty. firm Lathrop, Koontz, Righter, Clagett and Norquist, Kansas City, 1961-67; atty., asst. gen. counsel, asst. to pres., v.p. Kansas City So. Industries, Inc., 1968-71, pres., chief ops. officer, 1971-80, pres., chief exec. officer, 1981-83; exec. v.p. Hallmark Cards, Inc., 1983-85, pres., chief exec. officer, 1986—, also bd. dirs., 1978—; Bd. dirs. Ford Motor Co., Continental Corp., Dow Jones and Co.; trustee Hall Family Found., Aspen Inst.; past chmn. bd. dirs. 10th dist. Fed. Res. Bank; past chmn. Civic Coun. Kansas City, 1987-89, Midwest Rsch. Inst. Club: Kansas City Country. Office: Hallmark Cards Inc PO Box 419580 2501 McGee Trafficway Kansas City MO 64141-6580

HODAPP, LARRY FRANK, accountant; b. Dayton, Ohio, Feb. 13, 1956; s. Ruey Frank Jr. and Carol Rose (Coons) H.; m. Susan Ann Harris, July 1, 1978; children: Ryan Frank Harris, Lauren Elizabeth, Benjamin Andrew. BS in Acctg. with honors, Ind. U., 1978. CPA, Ohio. Staff acct. Deloitte Haskins & Sells, Dayton, Ohio, 1978-79, sr. asst. acct., 1979-81, sr. acct., 1981-84, mgr., 1984-89, sr. mgr., 1989-90; sr. mgr. Deloitte & Touche, Dayton, 1989-90; v.p. fin. Bush Leasing, Wilmington, Ohio, 1990—, mem. challenge 95 environ. com., 1991-93. Chmn. Miami Valley Regional Bicycle Com., Dayton, 1985-90; dir. safety Thunder Rd. Bike-A-Thon, Dayton, 1982-90. Mem. AICPA, League Am. Wheelmen/Bicycle USA (nat. dir., treas. Balt. 1986-92), Ohio Soc. CPAs, Toastmasters (pres. 1985-86), Rotary (Kettering club pres. 1990-91, dist. treas. 1993-94), Ind. U. Alumni Assn. (pres. Dayton chpt. 1992-95). Home: 4724 Bokay Dr Dayton OH 45440-2025 Office: Bush Leasing 1600 W Main St Wilmington OH 45177-1072

HODEL, MARY ANNE, library director; b. St. Louis, Aug. 12; d. William George and Florence Marie (Betz) H.; children: Courtney Hodel Denham, Christian Hodel Denham. BA, U. Wis., 1968; MLS, Catholic U., 1973. Project libr. TRACOR-JITCO, Rockville, Md., 1973-74; from project mgr. to database mgr. Nat. Resources Libr. U.S. Dept. of Interior, Washington, 1974-77; cataloger USAF Base Libr., Ramstein, Germany, 1977-79; from project libr. to automation libr. Law Libr. Georgetown U., Washington, 1984-85, automation libr. Law Libr., 1985-91; chief state libr. resource ctr. Enoch Pratt Free Libr., Balt., 1991-95; dir. Ann Arbor (Mich.) Dist. Libr., 1995—; mem. Network Coord. Coun. Md. Librs., 1991-95; mem. Sailor implementation group, 1992-95, grants and devel. task force liaison, 1993-95. Mem. ALA, Am. Assn. Law Librs. (chair innovative interfaces users com. 1988-89, editor innovative interfacers survey 1989, program coord. ann. meeting 1987), Pub. Libr. Assn. (sys. sect. v.p./pres.-elect 1994-95, pres. 1995—), Md. Assn. Profl. Libr. Adminstrs., Md. Libr. Assn. (del. to ALA legis. day 1992, co-chair tech. interest group 1994, conf. planning com. 1993, 94, program coord. 1994), Law Librs. Soc. Washington (program coord. 1989, 90, chair innovative interfaces users workshop 1989, pres. acad. spl. interest sect. 1988-89, rec. sec. 1989-91). Home: 3910 Kipling Dr Ann Arbor MI 48105 Office: 343 S 5th Ave Ann Arbor MI 48104

HODES, MARION EDWARD, genetics educator, physician; b. N.Y.C., Aug. 6, 1925; s. Louis and Esterre (Berman) H.; m. Halina Zora Markowicz, Nov. 23, 1949; children: Marquis Z., Zachary I., Jonathan E., Abigail J. Student, Cornell U., 1941-43, U. Rochester, 1943-44; M.D., U. Buffalo, 1947; Ph.D., Columbia, 1955. Diplomate Am. Bd. Med. Genetics; cert. Am. Bd. Clin. Chemistry. Intern Jewish Hosp., Bklyn., 1947-48; officer-in-charge dept. physiol. chemistry U.S. Naval Med. Sch., 1951-52; resident Goldwater Meml. Hosp., N.Y.C., 1955-56; faculty mem. sch. medicine Ind. U., Indpls., 1956—; prof. medicine and biochemistry Ind. U., 1966-72, prof. med. and molecular genetics and medicine, 1972-91, prof. med. and molecular genetics, medicine and pathology, 1991—; sr. Fogarty Internat. fellow, Lady Davis vis. prof. Hebrew U., 1977-78; cons. Eli Lily & Co., 1958-62; med. cons. City of Hope Med. Ctr.; mem. adv. screening com. for sr. Fulbright awards in life scis. Coun. Internat. Exch. of Scholars, 1981-84. Chmn. internat. sci. coun., Israel Cancer Rsch. Fund, 1988-94, chmn. sci. rev. panel, 1988—. Eleanor Roosevelt fellow, 1962-63; Guggenheim fellow, 1969-70; Leukemia Soc. scholar, 1961-66. Fellow Am. Coll. Med. Genetics (founder), Ind. Acad. Sci.; mem. AAAS, Am. Assn. Cancer Rsch., Am. Soc. Biochemistry and Molecular Biology, Am. Assn. Clin. Chemists, Am. Chem. Soc., Am. Soc. Microbiology, Cen. Soc. for Clin. Rsch., Am. Soc. Human Genetics, Am. Fedn. Clin. Rsch., Soc. for Neurosci., N.Y. Acad. Scis., Sigma Xi. Home: 648 Edgemere Dr Indianapolis IN 46260-4107 Office: Ind U Med Ctr Dept Med & Molec Genetics 975 W Walnut St Indianapolis IN 46202-5251

HODGE, DOUGLAS KERN, property appraiser, consultant; b. Marlette, Mich., Apr. 27, 1956; s. Richard E. and Donna B. (Kern) H.; m. June Marie Wilcox, July 15, 1978; children: Shaun Richard, Timothy Russell. AA, Delta Coll., University Ctr., Mich., 1977; BS in Fin., Ferris State U., 1983. Loan officer Farm Credit Svcs., Caro, Mich., 1983-84; appraiser Doane Farm Mgmt., DeKalb, Ill., 1984-85, pvt. practice, Kingston, Mich., 1985-89, Trerice/Tosto, Birmingham, Mich., 1989-91; prin. Hodge and Assocs., Lapeer, Mich., 1991—. Mem. Lapeer County Planning Commn., 1991, Lapeer Econ. Devel. Corp., 1992—. Mem. Am. Soc. Farm Mgrs. and Rural Appraisers, ARA desig., MAI desig., Appraisal Inst. Office: Hodge & Assocs Inc 173 Saratoga Tr Lapeer MI 48446-2263

HODGE, ERNEST VANCE, banker; b. San Francisco, July 10, 1945; s. Meredith Vance and Julia Charlene (Robinson) H.; m. Claire Anne Burghardt, Dec. 18, 1968; children: Deborah, Susan. BA, Westminster Coll., 1967; MBA, U. Kans., 1971; sect. leader, Grad. Sch. of Banking, U. Wis., 1972—. 2d v.p. Continental Ill. (Bank of Am.-Ill.), Chgo., 1971-82; v.p. Nat. Westminster Bank, Chgo., 1982-94; br. mgr. NatWest Markets, Chgo., 1995—, head of corp. lending svcs., 1995—. Treas. Walker Sch. PTA, Clarendon Hills, 1982-84; elder in ch. Served with USAF. Mem. Am. Bankers Assn., Oak Brook Polo Club, Bombay Club. Republican. Presbyterian. Home: 345 E 59th St Hinsdale IL 60521-5002

HODGES, KARLA VINEYARD, organization development consultant; b. Sherman, Tex., Apr. 13, 1953; d. Jack Douglas and Valeta Mae (Jernigan) Vineyard; m. Donald Harrison Hodges Jr., Apr. 22, 1978; children: Travis Austin, Tyler Benjamin. BA in Psychology, U. Tex., Arlington, 1976; MA in Ednl. Leadership, Western Mich. U., 1985. Program mgr. Tarrant County Mental Health, Ft. Worth, Tex., 1977-80, Lena Pope Home, Ft. Worth, 1980; pvt. practice as behavioral cons. Ft. Worth, 1980-81; human resource profl. Upjohn Co., Kalamazoo, 1987-90; performance cons. Tng. Strategies Inc., Kalamazoo, 1990-92; pvt. practice as human resource cons. Kalamazoo, 1985-92; pres. Karla V. Hodges Assocs., Kalamazoo, 1992—. Author: Needs Assessment and Evaluation Tool Kit, 1994. Mem. AAUW, ASTD, NAFE, Nat. Orgn. Devel. Network, Internat. Soc. Performance and Improvement. Office: Karla V Hodges & Assocs 1020 Wickford Dr Kalamazoo MI 49009-9300

HODGES, LYDIA ROSE, journalist, reporter; b. Gary, Ind., Oct. 3, 1970; d. Curtis and Frances Claudette Hodges. BA, Ind. U., 1992. Part-time reporter The Gary Crusader, 1992; reporter The Bay City (Mich.) Times, 1993-95, South Bend (Ind.) Tribune, 1995—. Mem. Nat. Assn. Black Journalists, Soc. Profl. Journalists. Democrat. Baptist. Office: South Bend Tribune 123 Lincoln Way W Mishawaka IN 46544

HODGES, NATHAN ELDON, JR., professional investor; b. Silvis, Ill., May 15, 1970; s. Nathan Eldon Hodges Sr. BA in English, Otterbein Coll., 1993. Mgr. Wizard of Comics, Columbus, Ohio, 1989-90; pres. Hermes Cellular FL-8, Westerville, Ohio, 1989-92; profl investor in pvt. practice Westerville, 1992—. Office: PO Box 685 Westerville OH 43086

HODGES, RICHARD, state legislator; b. Oct. 12, 1963. BA with honors, Oberlin Coll., 1986; MPA, U. Toledo, 1991. Ind. fin. cons., 1986-89; treas. Fulton County, Ohio, 1987-92; state rep. 82d Dist., Ohio, 1993—. Co-regional coord. Voinovich for Gov., 1990; mem. Ohio adv. com. Bush for Pres., 1988; mem. Fulton County Republican Ctrl. and Exec. coms., 1986-90; mgr. Tom Van Meter for State Senator, 1986. Mem. Fulton County Farm Bur., Fulton and Defiance County Township Trustees Assn., Defiance County Pheasants Forever, Rotary. Republican. Home: 2980 Us Rt 20 Swanton OH 43558 Office: Ohio House Reps Vern Riffe Ctr Govt Columbus OH 43215

HODGMAN, VICKI JEAN, retired school system administrator; b. Joliet, Ill., May 22, 1933; d. Joseph and Mary (Desman) Mikolic; divorced; children: Michael James, Tudy Magnuson, Kathy Lynn. BEd, Ill. State U., 1954, MEd, 1970; postgrad., U. Bridgeport, 1972, U. Hawaii, 1982, No. Ill. U., 1978, 79, 80, Nat. Coll., 1983, 86, U. Utah, 1984, U. Ill., 1988. Cert. tchr., Ill., Md. Tchr. Will County (Ill.) Pub. Schs., Joliet, Rockdale and Lockport, 1954-55, 58-68, Balt. County (Md.) Pub. Schs., Sparrow's Point, 1955-56, McLean County (Ill.) Pub. Schs., Heyworth, 1957; tchr. spl. edn. So. Will County Coop. for Spl. Edn., 1969-79, supr., coordinator, 1979-93; sec. Pulse-Chicagoland Spl. Edn. Suprs., 1983-85. Vol. Youth with a Mission, Gospel Outreach, 1985; treas. Women's Ch. Council, Rockdale, Ill., 1966-67, Band Parents Assn., Rockdale, 1966-67. Mem. Coun. Exceptional Children, Ill. Coun. Exceptional Children (bd. dirs. 1991-92), Ill. Coun. Children with Behavior Disorders (pres.-elect 1988, pres. 1989, bd. dirs. 1986-87), Will County Reading Assn., Will County Coun. for Exceptional Children, Coun. Behavior Disorders, Divsn. Learning Disabilities, Ill. Alliance for Exceptional Children and Adults, ASCD, Ill. Ret. Tchrs. Assn., others. Republican. Mem. Assembly of God Ch. Home: 310 S Reedwood Dr Joliet IL 60436-1461

HODGSON, ARTHUR CLAY, lawyer; b. Little River, Kans., Aug. 22, 1907; s. Edward Howard and Flora Cleveland (Perry) H.; m. Annie Letitia Green, Jan. 5, 1939; children: Richard, David, Edward, Alice Anne, James. AB, U. Kans., 1929; JD, George Washington U., 1937. Bar: Kans. 1936, D.C. 1936, U.S. Supreme Ct. 1950. Sole practice law, Washington, 1936-38; practice, Lyons, Kans., 1938—, ptnr. Hodgson & Kahler, 1969—. Pres. Lyons Jaycees; bd. dirs. Lyons C. of C. With USN, 1943-45. Recipient Disting. Svc. award Lyons C. of C. Mem. ABA (ho. of dels. 1976-82), Kans. Trial Lawyers Assn. (bd. govs. 1957-89, pres. 1972-73), ATLA (bd. govs. 1973-76), Rice County Bar, S.W. Kans. Bar, Kans. Bar Assn. (del., disting. service award 1985), City Attys. Assn. Kans. (pres. 1960-61), Kans. State Hist. Soc. (1st v.p. 1995-96), Rotary, Masons. Democrat. Congregationalist. Home: 1240 28th Rd Little River KS 67457 Office: Hodgson & Kahler 119 1/2 W Main St Lyons KS 67554-0666

HODGSON, THOMAS RICHARD, health care company executive; b. Lakewood, Ohio, Dec. 17, 1941; s. Thomas Julian and Dallas Louise (Livesay) H.; m. Susan Jane Cawrse, Aug. 10, 1963; children: Michael, Laura, Anne. BSChemE, Purdue U., 1963, DEng. (hon.), 1993; MSE, U. Mich., 1964; MBA, Harvard U., 1969. Devel. engr. E.I. Dupont, 1964; assoc. Booz-Allen & Hamilton, 1969-72; with Abbott Labs., North Chicago, Ill., 1972—, gen. mgr. Faultless div., 1976-78, v.p. gen. mgr. hosp. div., 1978-80, pres. hosp. div., 1980-83, group v.p., pres. Abbott Internat. Ltd., 1983-84; also bd. dirs. Abbott Internat. Ltd.; exec. v.p. parent co., pres. Abbott Internat. Inc. Abbott Labs., North Chicago, Ill., 1985-90; pres., chief oper. officer Abbott Labs., Abbott Park, 1990—; mem. nat. adv. com. engring. U. Mich., 1993—. Mem. Lake Forest (Ill.) Bd. Edn., 1986-90; trustee and mem. exec. com. Rush-Presbyn. St. Luke's Med. Ctr. Chgo., 1992—; overseer Harvard Bus. Sch. Club Chgo., 1993—. Baker scholar; NSF fellow; recipient Disting. Engring. Alumni award Purdue U., 1985. Mem. Chgo. Coun. Fgn. Rels., Econ. Club, Knollwood Club, Shoreacres Club, Chgo. Club, Phi Eta Sigma, Tau Beta Pi. Home: 1015 Ashley Rd Lake Forest IL 60045-3379 Office: Abbott Labs 100 Abbott Park Rd Abbott Park IL 60064-3502

HODJAT, YAHYA, metallurgist; b. Tehran, Iran, Aug. 8, 1950; came to U.S., 1977; s. Javad and Robabeh (Fayaz) H.; m. Patricia Anne Gray, Dec. 17, 1980. BS, Arya-Mehr U., Tehran, Iran, 1972; MS, Ohio State U., 1978, PhD, 1981. Engr. trainee August Thyssen Corp., Oberhausen, Fed. Republic Germany, 1974-75; project mgr. Pahlavi Steel Corp., Ahwaz, Iran, 1975-77; grad. rsch. assoc. Ohio State U., Columbus, 1977-81; dir. ops. Intercontinental Metals, Miami, Fla., 1981-82; rsch. scientist The Standard Oil Co., Cleve., 1982-83; mgr. ops. devel. Gates Corp., Farmington Hills, Mich., 1983—; cons. Intercontinental Metals Corp., Miami, 1978-80. Asst. inventor Pyro-Technique Silver Refining, 1980; inventor pulley Poly-V Belt, 1989. Served to lt. Iranian Imperial Army, 1972-74. Mem. AIME, Am. Soc. Metals, Am. Foundrymen's Soc., Alpha Sigma Mu. Home: 410 N Baldwin Rd Oxford MI 48371-3410 Office: Gates Corp 37684 Enterprise Ct Farmington Hills MI 48331-3440

HOEFEL, ROSEANNE LOUISE, English language educator; b. Akron, Apr. 8, 1962; d. Clarence Philip and Anne Margaret (Foti) H.; m. Philip Shalom Terman, July 2, 1989. BA in English, U. Akron, 1983, BA in French, 1983, MA in English, 1985; PhD in English, Ohio State U., 1990. Interdisciplinary Cert. of Linguistics. Adminstrv. asst. Ednl. Rsch. and Devel. Ctr., Akron, Ohio, 1981-83; substitute tchr. Summit County Pub. Schs., Akron, Ohio, 1983-84; high sch. tchr. Howard High Sch., Columbia, Md., 1984-85; part time instr. U. Akron Community and Tech. Coll., Akron, Ohio, 1985-86; jr. high sch. tchr. Akron Pub. Schs., 1986-87; grad. teaching asst. U. Akron, 1983-87; grad. teaching assoc. Ohio State U., Columbus, 1987-90; adjunct asst. prof. Iowa State U., Ames, 1990-91; asst. prof. Alma (Mich.) Coll., 1991—; advisor for English Club Hon. Soc.; mem. Womens Issues Adv. Bd.; co-chair Diversity Task Force; coord. Women's Studies, Alma (Mich.) Coll., 1991—. Contbr. articles to profl. jours. Vol. W. Bernards Soupkitchen, Akron, Ohio, 1985-87, Ames (Iowa) Sr. Ctr., 1990-91, Alma (Mich.) Battered Womens Shelter. Named Ohio Bd. of Regents Scholar Akron, 1980-83, Outstanding Faculty in Humanities, 1994; nominee for Helen Hoover Santmyer prize Ohio State U., Columbus, 1991; recipient Young Careerist award Mich. Women's Bus. of Profls., Student Cong. Faculty Appreciation awards, Alma, 1992, 93, Barlow award for faculty excellence, 1993, Fulbright Lecturing award U. W.I., Jamaica, 1995. Mem. NOW, AAUW, Modern Lang. Assn., Midwest Modern Lang. Assn., Coll. English Assn., Multi-Ethnic Lit. in the U.S. Assn., Nat. Womens Studies Assn. Office: Alma Coll Dept English Superior Alma MI 48801

HOEFT, DOUGLAS L., state legislator. BA, Denison U., 1964; MAT, Northwestern U., 1965; EdD, No. Ill. U., 1975. Tchr. Am. history Flower H.S., Chgo., 1964-65; tchr. social sci. Elgin (Ill.) H.S., 1965-75; instr. Grad. Sch. Nat. Lewis U., Lombard, Ill., 1985-87; asst. regional supt. schs. Kane County, Ill., 1975-87, supt., 1987-93; Mem. Ill. Ho. of Reps., 1993—. Contbr. articles to profl. jours. Mem. Gov.'s Task Force on Drugs and Alcohol, 1984; mem. adv. bd. Ill. Dept. Children and Family Svc., 1987-90. Home: 614 Center St Elgin IL 60120-3717*

HOEGLER, JEAN SANDBERG, artist, art educator, computer programmer, analyst; b. Chgo., July 14, 1929; d. Leonard Raymond and Dessa Katherine (Olson) Sandberg; m. Robert F. Gerstung, Sept. 9, 1951 (dec. 1957); children: Daniel Robert, Susan Barbara; m. Fred C. Hoegler, Dec. 26, 1959 (div.); children: Frederick Craig, Jeanette Lynn. BA, Wheaton Coll., 1951; MEd, Nat. Louis U., Wilmette, Ill., 1976; student in programming, Control Data, Chgo., 1982. Adminstrv. asst. Associated Aviation Underwriters, Chgo., 1979-81; programmer, analyst No. Ill. Gas, Aurora, 1982-93; ret., 1993; vis. lectr. art, Trinity Coll., Deerfield, Ill., 1971-79. Mem. Am. Soc. Portrait Artists. Home: 319 W School St Villa Park IL 60181-2548

HOEHN, KEITH E., mechanical engineer; b. Cin., Sept. 25, 1961. AD in Mech. Engring., Cin. State U., 1982. Project engr. AF Industries, Cin., 1986-90, Ransohoff, Cin., 1990—. Office: Ransohoff 4933 Provident Dr Cincinnati OH 45246-1020

HOEKEMA, DAVID ANDREW, philosophy educator, academic administrator; b. Paterson, N.J., June 10, 1950; s. Anthony Andrew and Ruth Alberta (Brink) H.; m. Susan Alice Bosma, Jan. 2, 1972; children: Janna Elizabeth, Nicolas John. Grad. Cambridge (Eng.) Grammar Sch. for Boys, 1966; AB in Philosophy Calvin Coll., 1972; PhD in Polit. Philosophy Princeton U., 1982. Free-lance photographer, 1967—; copy editor Eerdmans Publ. Co., 1969-72; asst. in instrn. Princeton (N.J.) U., 1973-74; produce buyer Beggars Banquet food coop., 1976-77; asst. prof. philosophy, tutor in Paracoll. St. Olaf Coll., Northfield, Minn., 1977-84, coord. Self-Respect and Sex Roles Conf., 1981, field supr. St. Olaf Term in Far East., 1981-82; assoc. prof. U. Del., Newark, 1984-92; acad. dean, dir. grad. studies Calvin Coll., Grand Rapids, Mich., 1992—; vis. fellow Calvin Ctr. for Christian Scholarship, 1982-83; fellow Coolidge Rsch. Colloquium, 1991; cons. NSF, Rsch. Librs. Group, Del. Humanities Forum, Nat. Fedn. State Humanities Couns. on philosophy rsch. needs, computers in humanities, priorities in higher edn., acad. employment prospects; project dir. NEH Translation Grant.; invited speaker confs. in Dubrovnik, Yugoslavia, 1985, Jerusalem, 1988, London, 1989, U.S. univs. and colls. Author: Rights and Wrongs: Coercion, Punishment and the State, 1986, Handbook for Administration of Learned Societies, 1990, In Place of In Loco Parentis:, Campus Rules and Moral Community, 1994; guest editor Teaching Philosophy; contbr. articles to Christian Century, Commonweal, other profl. publs.; amateur musician voice, autoharp, piano; composer 3 pub. hymns. Mem. vestry, sr. choir Trinity Episc. Ch., Swarthmore, Pa. Fellow Soc. for Values in Higher Edn. (bd. dirs.); mem. Am. Philos. Assn. (exec. dir. 1984-92), Soc. Christian Philosophers, Am. Soc. for Aesthetics, Internat. Soc. Polit. and Legal Philosophy, Concerned Philosophers for Peace. Avocations: high fidelity recs., cooking. Home: 601 Kent Hills Rd NE Grand Rapids MI 49505-5110 Office: Calvin College Grand Rapids MI 49546

HOEKSTRA, PETER, congressman, manufacturing executive; b. Groningen, The Netherlands, Oct. 30, 1953; m. Diane M. Johnson; children: Erin, Allison, Bryan. BA, Hope Coll., 1975; MBA, U. Mich., 1977. Furniture exec. Herman Miller, Inc., 1977-92, project mgr., product mgr., dir. product mgmt., dir. dealer mktg., v.p. dealer mktg., 1988-92, v.p. product mgmt., 1992-93; mem. 103rd Congress from 2d Mich. dist., 1993-95; mem. Budget Com; chmn. econ. and ednl. opportunity subcom. on oversight and investigations. Contbr. to project devel. Equa Chair, recognized as outstanding product of 1980s by Time Mag. Republican. Office: US Ho of Reps Office Of Ho Mems 1122 Longworth Washington DC 20515-2202*

HOELSCHER, DARREL G., engineering executive; b. Bushton, Kans., Apr. 4, 1958. A.Mech.Engring., Kans. Tech. Inst., Salina, 1978. From mfg. engr. to pres. Hoelscher, Inc., Bushton, 1978—. Patentee in field. Mem. Bushton City Coun., 1995—. Republican. Methodist. Office: Hoelscher Inc PO Box 195 Bushton KS 67427-0195

HOENDORF, RAYMOND, mechanical engineer; b. Cin., Jan. 2, 1961. BSME, Ohio State U., 1984. Registered profl. engr., Ohio. Mech. engr. Champion Internat., Hamilton, Ohio, 1984-94, Black Clawson, Middleton, Ohio, 1994—. Office: Black Clawson Co 605 Clark St Middletown OH 45042-2117

HOERNEMAN, CALVIN A., JR., economics educator; b. Youngstown, Ohio, Sept. 30, 1940; s. Calvin A. and Lucille A. (Leiss) H.; m. Cheryl L. Morand, Aug. 10, 1973; children: David, Jennifer, Christina. BA, Bethany Coll., 1962; MA, Mich. State U., 1964, postgrad., Cambridge U. Mem. faculty, Delta Coll., University Center, Mich., 1966—, prof. econs., 1976—; cons. Prentice-Hall, Acad. Press, Goodyear Pub., Random House Pub.; econ. expert witness; Author: Poverty, Wealth and Income Distribution, 1969; co-author: "Caper" Principles of Economics Software Study Guide; contbr. articles to various publs. Recipient Recognition award AAUP, 1972, Bergstein award Delta Coll. Grad. Class, 1972, Competition for Excellence award IBM and the League for Innovation, 1988. Mem. AAUP, Am. Econ. Assn., Midwest Econ. Assn., Nat. Assn. Forensic Economist. Home: 5712 Lamplighter Ln Midland MI 48642-3137 Office: Delta Coll Dept Econs University Center MI 48710

HOESSLE, CHARLES HERMAN, zoo director; b. St. Louis, Mar. 20, 1931; m. Marilyn Mueller, Jan. 5, 1952; children: Maureen, Kirk, Tracy, Bradley. AA, Harris Tchrs. Coll., 1951; student, Am. Assn. Zool. Parks and Aquariums Zoo Mgmt. Sch., 1976-77; LLD (hon.), Maryville Coll., 1986, St. Louis U., 1990, U. Mo., St. Louis, 1994. Reptile keeper St. Louis Zoo, 1963, asst. curator, 1964, curator reptiles and curator edn., 1968-69, gen. curator and dep. dir., 1969-82, dir., 1982—; adj. prof. dept. biology St. Louis U., 1973-74, 81-82, 83; owner, operator Exotic Pet Shop, St. Louis; host St. Louis Zoo Show, 1968-78. Chmn. Reptile Study Merit Badge counselors, St. Louis; state chmn. UN Day, 1982; mem. St. Louis County Counts. With U.S. Army, 1952-54. Recipient Disting. Alumnus award Harris-Stowe State Coll., 1987. Mem. Internat. Union Dirs. Zool. Gardens, Am. Assn. Zool. Parks and Aquariums (bd. dirs. 1977-79, 85-87, v.p. 1988, pres. 1990-91, past pres. 1991-92, rep. to species survival commn. Internat. Union for Conservation Nature and Natural Resources), St. Louis Naturalists Club, St. Louis Ctr. for Internat. Rels. (bd. dirs. 1993—), St. Louis Mus. Collaborative (pres. 1993), Animal Protective Assn. (bd. dirs.), Internat. Friendship Alliance St. Louis County (chmn. cultural com.), Explorers, St. Louis Herpetological Society, Hawthorne Soc., St. Louis Rotary Club, St. Louis Ambassadors Club (bd. dir.). Home: 10814 Forest Circle Dr Saint Louis MO 63128-2007 Office: St Louis Zool Pk Forest Park Saint Louis MO 63110

HOFER, LONNIE JOE, evangelist; b. Mitchell, S.D., July 1, 1955; s. Joe K. Jr. and Lorraine M. (Mendel) H.; m. Sharon Rose Hofer, Sept. 2, 1978; children: Cristy Marie, Kimberly Lanae. BA, Grace U., 1978; ThM, Dallas Theol. Seminary, 1984, DMin, 1995. Pastor Hutterthal Mennonite Ch., Freeman, S.D., 1978-80; evangelist Grace Coll. of Bible, Omaha, 1984-90, Living for Eternity Ministry, Omaha, 1990—. Republican. Home and Office: 12946 Lillian St Omaha NE 68138-6032

HOFER, ROY ELLIS, lawyer; b. Cin., Oct. 10, 1935; s. Eric Walter and Elsie Katherine (Ellis) H.; m. Suzanne Elizabeth Sturtz, June 6, 1956 (div. 1974); m. Cynthia Ann Corson, June 5, 1981; children: Kimberly, Tracy, Eric. BChemE, Purdue U., 1957; JD, Georgetown U., 1961. Patent examiner U.S. Patent & Trademark Office, Washington, 1957-59; patent agt. Exxon Corp., Washington, 1959-61; ptnr. Brinks Hofer Gilson & Lione, Chgo., 1961—, pres., 1995—; adv. com. No. Dist. Ill., 1991-95. Contbr. articles to profl. jours. Bd. dirs. Chgo. Lung Assn., 1982-83, Ctr. for Conflict Resolution, 1983-88, 90-91, pres., 1991—; bd. dirs. Union League Boys and Girls Club, Chgo., 1985-94, Ill. Inst. Continuing Legale Edn., Chgo., 1986-88; chmn. Citizens Com. on Juvenile Ct., 1994-95. Mem. ABA (dir. litigation sect. 1982-87), Fed. Cir. Bar Assn. (pres. 1993-94), Ill. State Bar Assn., Chgo. Bar Assn. (pres. 1988-89), Patent Law Assn. Chgo., Am. Intellectual Property Law Assn., Law Club Chgo., Phi Eta Sigma, Tau Beta Pi, Omega Chi Epsilon. Republican. Office: Brinks Hofer et al 455 N Cityfront Plaza Dr Chicago IL 60611-5503

HOFER, THOMAS W., landscape company executive. Office: Spring Green Lawn Care Corp 11927 Spaulding School Dr Plainfield IL 60544*

HOFF, JOHN SCOTT, lawyer; b. Des Moines, Jan. 2, 1946; s. John Richard and Valetta R. (Scott) H.; m. Susan Murial Felver, June 21, 1972 (div. 1975); m. Shirley Jo Ward, June 21, 1975; children: Jennifer Jo, John Baron. BSBA, Drake U., 1967; MBA, Calif. State U., Fullerton, 1971; postgrad., Oxford (Eng.) U., 1973; JD, Southwestern U., L.A., 1975; MA in Mil. History, Am. Mil. U., 1995. Bar: Iowa 1976, U.S. Ct. Claims 1976, U.S. Ct. Customs and Patent Appeals 1976, U.S. Ct. Mil. Appeals 1976, Ill. 1977, U.S. Dist. Ct. (no. dist.) Ill. 1977, U.S. Ct. Appeals (7th cir.) 1979, Calif. 1980, U.S. Supreme Ct. 1982, Nebr. 1983, D.C. 1983, Wis. 1984, U.S. Dist. Ct. (so. dist.) Iowa 1987, U.S. Ct. Appeals (9th and 10th cirs.) 1988, U.S. Dist. Ct. Ariz. 1990, U.S. Ct. Appeals (6th cir.) 1990, Mich. 1991, U.S. Ct. Appeals (8th cir.) 1991, N.Y. 1995, Minn. 1996, U.S. Dist. Ct. (cen. dist.) Ill. 1996; CPCU; chartered cost analyst. Staff atty. FAA Hdqrs., Washington, 1975-76; assoc. Lord, Bissell & Brook, Chgo., 1976-81; ptnr. Lapin, Hoff, Slaw & Laffey, Chgo., 1981-92, John Scott Hoff & Assocs., P.C., Chgo., 1992—; real estate broker Ill. Dept. Profl. Regulation, Springfield, 1980—;. Contbr. articles to profl. jours. Capt. USAF, 1967-75; col. USAFR, 1975—. Mem. Aviation Ins. Assn. (v.p. 1990-92, pres. 1992-94), Air Force Assn. (v.p., pres. 1980-93), Internat. Soc. Air Safety Investigation (v.p.), Aircraft Owners and Pilots Assn., Exptl. Aircraft Assn., Nat. Assn. Flight Instrs., Aero. Club Chgo. Republican. Presbyterian. Office: Ste #2210 20 S Clark St Chicago IL 60603-1805

HOFF, KATHRYN SUSAN, technology educator, consultant; b. Davenport, Iowa, Mar. 19, 1950; d. Buford Laurice and Mary Bess (Standley) Hamburg; m. Ricky A. Hoff, Aug. 31, 1968 (div. Mar. 1985); 1 child, Marianne. BA in Comms., Bowling Green State U., 1986, MEd in Career and Tech. Edn., 1988, PhD in Higher Edn., 1996. Human rels. mgr. Toledo Edison Co., 1978-84; mgr. Norrell Svcs., Dearborn, Mich., 1986-87; tech. and ednl. dir. Profl. Resource Ctrs., Leawod, Kans., 1989; human rels. adminstr. Whirlpool Corp., Clyde, Ohio, 1989-92; pres., cons. Concepts, Bowling Green, Ohio, 1992—; vis. assoc. prof. Mendeleyev U. Chem. Tech., Moscow, 1996; cons. U. Toledo, 1992, Bowling Green State U., 1984-95; mem. adv. bd. Ohio Coop. Edn. Assn., 1991-92. Bowling Green State U. Internat. Travel scholar, Moscow, 1996. Presbyterian.

HOFFA, MICHAEL D., electrical engineer; b. Des Moines, Aug. 11, 1955. BSEE, U. Houston, 1988. Design engr. R&D machine Lincoln Elec. Co., Cleve., 1989—. Patentee in field. Active United Meth., Euclid, Ohio, 1994. Mem. IEEE. Office: Lincoln Electric Co 22801 Saint Clair Ave Euclid OH 44117-2524

HOFFBECK, LOREN JOHN, research agronomist; b. Ortonville, Minn., Aug. 26, 1932; s. Roy Clifton and Myrtle P. (Chaussee) H.; m. Helen Maria Shea, June 18, 1960; children: Joan K. Hoffbeck Dubnicka, Mark D., Joseph P., Amy M. Hoffbeck Reynolds, Susan R. Hoffbeck Takacs. BS, S.D. State U., 1954; MS, U. Wis., 1959, PhD, 1962. Rsch. agronomist USDA, Greeneville, Tenn., 1961-66; corn breeder Pioneer Hi-Bred Internat., Tipton, Ind., 1966—, rsch. dir., 1984-89, rsch. fellow, 1990—. 1st lt. U.S. Army, 1954-57. Mem. Kiwanis. Roman Catholic. Office: Pioneer Hi-Bred Internat 1000 W Jefferson St Tipton IN 46072-9423

HOFFER, ALMA JEANNE, nursing educator; b. Dalhart, Tex., Sept. 15, 1932; d. James A. and Mildred M. (Zimlich) Koehler; m. John L. Hoffer, Oct. 7, 1954; children: John Jr., James, Joseph, Jerome. BS, Bradley U., 1970; MA, W.Va. Coll. Grad. U., 1975; EdD, Ball State U., 1981, MA, 1986; postgrad., Wayne State U., 1986-87. RN, Calif., Fla., Ind., Ohio, W.Va. Sch. nurse South Bend (Ind.) Sch. Corp., 1970-71; instr. Morris Harvey Coll., Charleston, W.Va., 1973-75; asst. prof. W.Va. Inst. Tech., Montgomery, 1975-76, Ball State U., Muncie, Ind., 1976-77, Purdue U., Ft. Wayne, Ind., 1977-81; from dean grad. edn. to prof. Akron (Ohio) U., 1981-93; prof., dir. grad. nursing edn. St. Francis Coll., Ft. Wayne, 1993—; bd. dirs., trustee No. Ind. Trust, Ft. Wayne, John L. Hoffer, Inc., Akron; bd. dirs. quality assessment St. Joseph Hosp., Ft. Wayne. Co-author: Family Health Promotion, 1989, 2d edit., 1995, Classification of Nursing Diagnosis, 1993. Vol. NEC Firestone World Series of Golf, Akron, 1991-95; advisor No. Ohio Med. Coll., Akron, 1986-90; active Gov. Celeste Ad Hoc Com. in Higher Edn., Columbus, Ohio, 1987-89. Rsch. grantee Ohio Rsch. Challenge, 1988. Mem. Nat. League for Nursing (com. mem. 1980, 95), Midwest Nursing Rsch. Soc. (com. mem. 1981—), Transcultural Nursing (membership com. 1986—), Ohio Nursing Assn. (com. mem., Cert. Appreciation 1991), Sigma Theta Tau (com. mem. 1994-95). Republican. Roman Catholic.

HOFFERT, FRANK, JR., secondary education educator; b. Cleve., June 10, 1937; s. Frank Sr. and Vida (Kuhar) H.; m. Geraldine Joyce Siat, June 11, 1960; children: Stephen, Susan, Paul. BA, Western Res. U., 1959, MA, 1964. Social studies tchr. Euclid (Ohio) High Sch., 1959-69, chmn. dept. social studies, 1969—. Recipient Charles R. Keller award John Hay Fellows, 1967, Outstanding Tchr. award U. Chgo., 1988; Jenning scholar, 1967-68. Mem. NEA, Ohio Edn. Assn., Euclid Tchrs. Assn. (Outstanding Educator 1990), Greater Cleve. Coun. for Social Studies (exec. v.p., pres. 1968-71), Nat. Coun. for Social Studies (ho. of dels. 1968-71), Common Cause. Roman Catholic. Office: Euclid High Sch 711 E 222nd St Euclid OH 44123-2033

HOFFHEIMER, DANIEL JOSEPH, lawyer; b. Cin., Dec. 28, 1950; s. Harry Max and Charlotte (O'Brien) H.; children: Rebecca, Rachel, Leah. Grad., Phillips Exeter Acad., 1969; AB cum laude, Harvard Coll., 1973; JD, U. Va., 1976. Bar: Ohio 1976, U.S. Dist. Ct. (so. dist.) Ohio 1976, U.S. Ct. Appeals (6th crct.) 1977, U.S. Ct. Appeals (D.C. and fed. crcts.) 1986, U.S. Ct. Internat. Trade 1986, U.S. Tax Ct. 1992, U.S. Supreme Ct. 1980, U.S. Tax Ct. 1992. Assoc. Taft, Stettinius & Hollister, Cin., 1976-84, ptnr., 1984—; lectr. law Coll. Law, U. Cin., 1981-83; trustee Judges Hogan & Porter Meml. Trust; mem. adv. bd. Ohio Dist. Ct. Rev. Editor-in-chief U. Va. Jour. Internat. Law, 1975-76; co-author: Practitioners' Handbook Ohio First District Court Appeals, 1984, 2d edit., 1991, Federal Practice Manual, U.S. 6th Circuit Court of Appeals, 1993, Manual on Labor Law, 1988; contbr. articles to profl. jours. Mem. Cin. Symphony Bus. Rels. Com., 1977-86, Cin. Composers Guild, 1988-93, Ohio Supreme Ct. Com. Racial Fairness, 1993—; mem. steering com. Underground R.R. Freedom Mus., 1994—; mem. adv. bd. for Consumer Protection, Cin., 1978-80, Hoxworth Blood Ctr. Univ. Cin. Hosp., 1994—; mem. bd. Hebrew Union Coll. Jewish Inst. Religion, 1994—, WGUC-FM Pub. Radio, 1988—, vice chmn., 1993-96, chmn., 1996—; trustee Cin. Chamber Orch., 1977-80, Seven Hills Sch., Cin., 1980-86, Internat. Visitors Ctr., Cin., 1980-84, Friends Coll. Conservatory of Music, Cin., 1985-86, Cin. Symphony Orch., 1988-94, 96—, Children's Psychiat. Ctr., Cin., 1986-89, treas., 1987-89; vice chmn. Jewish Hosp., Cin., 1989-92; Leadership Cin., 1989-90; sec., trustee Cin. Symphony Musicians Pension Fund, 1989—, Jewish Cmty. Rels. Coun., 1990—, vice chmn., 1996—; sec. Nat. Conf. Christians and Jews, 1992—; counsel Cin. AIDS Commn., 1991—, Cin. Inst. Fine Arts Govt. Affairs Com., 1993-94, B'nai B'rith Nat. Coun. Legacy Devel., 1996—. Named Outstanding Young Man, U.S. Jaycees, 1984. Fellow Am. Bar Found., Ohio Bar Found.; mem. ABA, Internat. Bar Assn., Internat. Trade Bar Assn., Internat. Arbitration Assn. (comml. arbitrator 1991-95), Fed. Bar Assn. (treas. 1984, sec. 1985, v.p. 1986-87, pres. 1987-88), Ohio State Bar Assn., Cin. Bar Assn. (trustee 1988-93, v.p. 1990-91, pres. 1992-93), Harvard Club of Cin. (bd. dirs. 1980-88, v.p. 1983-86, pres. 1986-87). Democrat. Home: 3672 Willowlea Ct # A Cincinnati OH 45208-1816 Office: 1800 Star Bank Ctr 425 Walnut St Cincinnati OH 45202-3904

HOFFLANDER, TIM G., stockbroker; b. Stanley, Wis., Feb. 11, 1962. BA, Olivette U., 1989. Stockbroker Credit Thrift, Kankakee, Ill., 1988-89, First of Mich. Corp., Adrian, Mich., 1990—. Author booklet; contbr. articles to newsletter. Mem. Lions (lion tamer 1990—). Office: First of Mich Corp 123 E Maumee St Adrian MI 49221-2703

HOFFMAN, ALAN CRAIG, lawyer, consultant; b. Chgo., Oct. 1, 1944; s. Morris Joseph and Marie E. H. BA, Carthage Coll., 1968; JD, John Marshall Law Sch., 1973. Bar: Fla. 1973, Ill. 1973, U.S. Dist. Ct. (no dist.) Ill. 1974, U.S. Dist. Ct. (mid. dist.) Fla. 1981, U.S. Ct. Appeals (7th cir.) 1974, U.S. Ct. Appeals (5th and 11th cirs.) 1981, U.S. Supreme Ct. 1977. Staff atty. Cook County Legal Assistance Found., Brookfield, 1973-74, Patient Legal Svcs., Chgo., 1974; pvt. practice law, Chgo., 1973—, River Grove, Ill., 1973-86, Oak Brook, Ill., 1980-87—, Hinsdale, Ill., 1987-93; with assocs., 1980—; spl. asst. atty. gen. Ill. Criminal Justice Div., Chgo., 1977-79, Ill. Condemnation Div., Chgo., 1980-87; pres. Almar, Ltd., 1986-91; v.p. Marach, Ltd., 1986-89, Hoffman Realty, 1978—; pres., dir. North Shore Greenview Bldg. Corp., 1978—; asst. prof. law Lewis U., 1974-79, vis. prof. Coll. Law Paraprofl. Center, 1974-76, adj. prof., 1979-80; assoc. prof. No. Ill. U., 1979-80; v.p. Adv. Adv. Service, Inc.; cons. med.-legal cases, 1982—. Mem. Oak Park Twp. (Ill.) Mental Health Bd., 1975-80, v.p. 1975, chmn. program com. 1975-77, pres. 1978; governing bd. WINGS, 1994, 95; bd. govs. Jewish Fedn. of Chgo., coun. for elderly, 1995—. Fellow Am. Coll. Legal Medicine (assoc. in law 1975, profl. devel. com. 1990—, student awards com. 1993—, moot court competition com. 1992—, co-chair com. violence and abuse in the family 1993, textbook update com. 1988, program com. 1988—, legal com. 1988—, editl. bd. med. and legal textbook com. 1987—); mem. ABA (civil procedure and evidence com. 1993—, commercial tort com. 1993—), Ill. State Bar Assn. (vice-chmn. standing com. on mentally disabled 1975-77, chmn. 77-78), Chgo. Bar Assn., DuPage Bar Assn., West Suburban Bar Assn., Chgo. Acad. Law and Medicine, Am. Soc. Law and Medicine, Mensa, Ill. Trial Lawyers Assn. (profl. negligence com. 1982), Fla. Bar Assn. (health law com. 1983-84, out-of-state practitioner com. 1988-91), Assn. Trial Lawyers Am., Phi Alpha Delta, Mensa. Author: (with F. Lane and D. Birnbaum) Lane's Medical Litigation Guide, 1981; contbr. articles to Med. Trial Technique Quar., numerous articles in field; speaker, lectr., presenter in field U.S., Europe, Israel, Africa; editorial bd. Jour. Legal Medicine, 1980—, Medical Malpractice Prevention, 1986—, Medical Malpractice Prevention Ob-Gyn, 1987—; contbg. author Legal Medicine: Legal Dynamics of Med. Encounters, 1988, 2d edit., 1991, supplement, 1990, 91, 92, 93, 94, 3rd. edit. 1995.

HOFFMAN, BARBARA JO, health and physical education educator, home economist; b. Dayton, Ohio, Aug. 10, 1952; d. Harold Lee and Virginia May (Dafler) H. BA, Otterbein Coll., 1974; MEd, Ashland Coll., 1987. Tchr. Harrison Hills City Schs., Hopedale, Ohio, 1974—; coach volleyball, track, and basketball Cadiz (Ohio) High Sch., 1974-85. Key advisor Ohio FHA/HERO, Columbus, 1990-96, mentor advisor, 1992. Recipient Golden Apple Achiever award Ashland Oil, Inc., 1989, Ohio Home Econs. Tchr. of Yr. award, 1991, Vocat. Home Econs. Program award, 1990, Pacesetter award, 1992, 93. Mem. NEA, AAHPERD, Am. Assn. Family and Consumer Scis., Ohio Assn. Vocat., Ohio Assn. Family and Consumer Scis., Family and Consumer Scis. Tchrs. Republican. Methodist. Home: 647 Kerr Ave Cadiz OH 43907-1022 Office: Cadiz High Sch 440 E Market St Cadiz OH 43907-1244

HOFFMAN, JAMES PAUL, lawyer, hypnotist; b. Waterloo, Iowa, Sept. 7, 1943; s. James A. and Luella M. (Prokosch) H.; m. Debra L. Malone, May 29, 1982; 1 dau., Tiffany K. B.A., U. No. Iowa, 1965, J.D. U. Iowa, 1967. Bar: Iowa 1967, U.S. Dist. Ct. (no. dist.) Iowa 1981, U.S. Dist. Ct. (so. dist.) Iowa 1968, U.S. Dist. Ct. (so. dist.) Ill, U.S. Tax Ct. 1971, U.S. Ct. Appeals (8th cir.) 1970, U.S. Supreme Ct. 1974. Sr. mem. James P. Hoffman, Law Offices, Keokuk, Iowa, 1967—; chmn. bd. Iowa Inst. Hypnosis. Fellow Am. Inst. Hypnosis; mem. ABA, Iowa Bar Assn., Lee County Bar Assn., Assn. Trial Lawyers Am., Ill. Trial Lawyers Assn., Iowa Trial Lawyers Assn. Democrat. Roman Catholic. Author: The Iowa Trial Lawyers and the Use of Hypnosis, 1980. Home and Office: PO Box 1087 Middle Rd Keokuk IA 52632-1087

HOFFMAN, JAY C., state legislator; b. Nov. 6, 1961; m. Laurie Hoffman; children: Emily, Katelyn. Grad., Ill. State U., 1983; JD, St. Louis U., 1986. Bar: Ill. 1986. Mem. from Dist. 112, Ill. Ho. of Reps., Dem. floor leader; mem. exec. fin. inst., jud. criminal com., welfare reform task force Ill. H. of Reps. Dem Cand. for U.S. House, 20th district, I.L., 1996. Named Outstanding Legislator of Yr., Ill. State Atty. Assn., 1994. Home: 7 Driftwood Collinsville IL 62234-1416*

HOFFMAN, JERRY IRWIN, dental educator; b. Chgo., Nov. 20, 1935; s. Irwin and Luba (Fox) H.; m. Sharon Lynn Seaman, Aug. 25, 1963; children: Steven Abram, Rachel Irene. Student, DePaul U., 1953-56; BS in Biology and Chemistry, Roosevelt U., 1956; DDS, Loyola U., Chgo., 1960; M of Health Care Adminstrn., Baylor U., 1972. Certificate, General Practice Residency, U.S. Army, 1978. Commd. officer U.S. Army, 1960 (served to 1962, returned 1964), advanced through grades to col., 1978; hdqrs. rep. local dental tng. confs. Europe U.S. Army, Garmisch, Fed. Republic Germany, 1965-67; cons. to Comdg. Gen. U.S. Army Med. Research and Devel. Command, Washington, 1972-76; cons. Office of Surgeon Gen. U.S. Army, Washington, 1972-76, liaison rep. to Nat. Adv. Council and Oral Biology and Medicine Study Sessions of the Nat. Inst. Dental Research and NIH, 1973-76; resident in Gen. Practice Residency U.S. Army, 1976-78; comdg. officer U.S. Army Dental Activity, Fort Monmouth, N.J., 1979-82; ret., 1982; pvt. practice dentistry Chgo., 1962-64; assoc. prof. operative dentistry Loyola U. Sch. Dentistry, Maywood, Ill., 1982-93, dir. gen. practice residency, 1982-85, coordinator extramural dental resources, 1983-85, assoc. dean for clin. affairs, 1985-93; dir. sci. programs Chgo. Dental Soc., 1993—; staff dentist Silas B. Hayes Army Hosp., Fort Ord, Calif., 1976-79, Patterson Army Hosp., Ft. Monmouth, 1979-82; lectr., presenter seminars in field. Contbr. articles, research papers to profl. jours. Decorated Legion of Merit, Meritorious Svc. Medal with oak leaf cluster. Fellow: Am. Coll. Dentists, Internat. Coll. Dentists; master: Acad. Gen. Dentistry; mem. ADA, Ill. Dental Soc., Chgo. Dental Soc., Am. Assn. Dental Schs., Am. Soc. Assn. Execs., Assn. Healthcare Execs., Profl. Conv. Mgmt. Assn., Omicron Kappa Upsilon.

HOFFMAN, JOAN BENTLEY, public relations consultant; b. Trenton, N.J., Dec. 7, 1946; d. Harold William and Harriet Maude (Stallings) Bentley; m. Michael Charles Hoffman, July 31, 1971 (separated 1994); children: Amy Elizabeth, Cara Christine, Jennifer Michelle. AB, Goucher Coll., 1969; M Arts in Edn., Yale U., 1971; postgrad., U. Chgo., 1989—. Traffic coord. Sta. WBAL (NBC) Radio, Balt., 1970-71; music tchr. Pleasant Plains Elem. Sch., Balt., 1972-75; accompanist, coach Wheaton (Ill.) Coll. Suzuki Program, 1980-85, music theory instr., 1985-90; cons. pub. rels., Wheaton, 1979-87. Music dir. (plays) St. Matthews Dramatic Soc., Balt., 1973, 74, Wheaton Drama, 1985, Village Theater Guild, Glen Ellyn, Ill., 1987. Dem. precinct capt., Wheaton, 1984—; treas. Glen Ellyn (Ill.) Jr. Woman's Club, 1984-85, v.p., 1985-86; sec. 5th Dist. Ill. Jr. Woman's Club, 1986-87; bd. dirs. DePage County Ulster Project, 1991-92; organist, choir dir. St. Luke Luth., Glen Ellyn, 1995—; accompanist One Voice Choir, Glen Ellyn, 1994—. Returning scholar U. Chgo., 1988-89. Mem. Goucher Coll. Club (pres. Chgo. chpt. 1982-95, Alumni bd. 1988—, head regional rep. 1991—), Wheaton Music Club (sec. 1989-91). Home: 470 22d St Apt 420 Glen Ellyn IL 60137

HOFFMAN, JOHN HARRY, lawyer, accountant; b. Chgo., June 18, 1913; s. Dave and Rose (Gewirtzman) H.; J.D., John Marshall Law Sch., 1938; m. Gwen Zollo, Dec. 30, 1949; children: Alana Sue Glickson, Edward Jay, Gayle Beth Hoffman Olsen. Bar: Ill. 1938, U.S. Tax Ct., U.S. Supreme Ct. 1956; registered investment adviser. Propr. John H. Hoffman & Co., 1952—, sr. prin. Friedman, Goldberg & Mintz, 1991—; pres. John H. Hoffman p.c., 1972, Hoffman Fin. Planning, Ltd., 1989. Sec. Security Exchg. Commn. Registered investment adviser, Ill., Fla.; CPA, Ill., Fla. Mem. ABA, Ill. Bar Assn., Chgo. Bar Assn., AICPA, Ill. Soc. CPAs, Inst. Cert. Fin. Planners (cert.), Decalogue Soc., Twin Orchard Country Club (Long Grove, Ill.), Boca Raton Country Club, Masons (32d degree), Shriners, B'nai B'rith. Office: 155 N Pfingsten Rd Ste 150 Deerfield IL 60015-4928

HOFFMAN, JOHN KORBUT, physical therapist, consultant; b. Kadena AFB, Okinawa, Oct. 2, 1955; (parents Am. citizens); s. George Edward and Frances Evangeline (Korbut) F.; 1 child, Leah Caroline. AAS, Penn Valley C.C., Kansas City, Mo., 1976; B in Health Sci. Phys. Therapy cum laude, U. Mo., 1981. Lic. phys. therapist, Mo.; cert. sports clin. specialist, Am. Phys. Therapy Assn. Dir. phys. therapy and sports medicine LifeWell Svcs. Inc.-Cass Med. Ctr., Harrisonville, Mo., 1981—. Inducted phys. therapist/sports medicine World Sportsmedicine Hall of Fame, 1993. Mem. Am. Sports Medicine Assn. (pres. Mo. chpt. 1994—), Harrisonville Kiwanis Club (pres. 1993-94). Home: 1113 Pleasant Raymore MO 64083 Office: LifeWell Svcs Inc Cass Med Ctr 1800 E Mechanic Harrisonville MO 64701

HOFFMAN, LAWRENCE WAYNE, software engineer, systems consultant; b. Massillon, Ohio, Apr. 18, 1945; s. Donferd Dale and Alice Louise (Helline) H.; m. Sue Ellen Stephan, Oct. 28, 1967. BS in Math., U. Dayton, 1967; postgrad., George Washington U., 1972; MS in Ops. Rsch., Ohio State U., 1976. Tchr. Immaculate Conception Sch., Dayton, Ohio, 1967-68; commd. 2d lt. U.S. Army, 1967, advanced through grades to lt. col., 1989; ordnance corps officer U.S. Army, various locations, 1968-78; resigned U.S. Army, 1978; product design engr. Ford Motor Co., Livonia, Mich., 1978-80; tech. cons. ADP Network Svcs., Dayton, Ohio, 1980-82; systems cons. Softech, Inc., Fairborn, Ohio, 1982-94; computer scientist Computer Scis. Corp., Dayton, 1994-96; sr. computer sys. analyst Boeing Info. Svcs., Inc., Beavercreek, Ohio, 1996—; cons. U.S. Army Material Command, Rock Island, Ill., 1979-92, Human Factors Soc., Anaheim, Calif., 1986-88. Mem. Assn. Computing Machinery, Alpha Pi Mu. Democrat. Roman Catholic. Home: 2174 Green Springs Dr Kettering OH 45440-1120 Office: Boeing Info Svcs Inc 4025 Executive Dr Beavercreek OH 45430

HOFFMAN, M. KATHY, graphic designer, packaging designer; b. Sidney, Nebr., Aug. 30, 1956; d. Norman and Irline (Dillon) Barnica; m. Jeffrey W. Hoffman, Apr. 16, 1988. BA, U. Nebr., Kearney, 1978, BFA, 1984, MA, 1987. Product quality assurance Baldwin Filters, Kearney, Nebr., 1978-88, product technician, 1988-90, product devel. technician, 1990-92, product identification coord., 1992—, packaging and graphics designer, 1993—. Mem. Inst. Packaging Profls., Assn. Corel Artists and Designers, Women in Packaging. Office: Baldwin Filters 4400 Highway 30 E Kearney NE 68847-9797

HOFFMAN, MICHAEL CHARLES, otolaryngologist; b. N.Y.C., Mar. 9, 1947; s. Arthur and Julia (Cherepanya) H.; m. Joan Bentley, July 31, 1971; children: Amy Elizabeth, Cara Christine, Jennifer Michelle. BA, Johns Hopkins U., 1969, postgrad., 1969-71; MD, U. Md., Balt., 1976. pres. med. staff Ctrl. DuPage Hosp., 1991-93. Resident in gen. surgery U. Md. Hosp., Balt., 1976-77, resident in otolaryngology, 1977-80; dir. hearing and speech ctr. Greater Balt. Med. Ctr., 1971-72; practice medicine specializing in otolaryngology Glen Ellyn (Ill.) Clinic, 1980—, pres., bd. dirs., 1987-91. Fellow Am. Acad. Otolaryngology; mem. AMA, Ill. State Med. Soc., Dupage County Med. Soc., Md. Surg. Soc. Office: Glen Ellyn Clinic SC 454 Pennsylvania Ave Glen Ellyn IL 60137-4402

HOFFMAN, PAUL ERNEST, utility executive; b. Yeadon, Pa., June 21, 1957; s. Ernest Louis Jr. and Janis (Cole) H.; m. Alison Perry, Nov. 24, 1989; children: Gregory Paul, Jonathan Carl. BS in Bus., Ea. Ill. U., Charleston, 1979; MBA, Ariz. State U., Tempe, 1980. Customer svc. supr. Ill. Power, Bloomington, 1981-83; recruiting specialist Ill. Power, Clinton, 1983-84, supr. nuclear pers., 1984-85; asst. area mgr. Ill. Power, Champaign, 1985-87; regional dir. labor rels. Ill. Power, Decatur, 1987-90; area mgr. Ill. Power, Wood River, 1990-91; dir. employment compensation and benefits Ill. Power, Decatur, 1991-96, mgr. energy delivery, 1996—. Planning and zoning commr. Village of Forsyth, Ill., 1994—. Mem. Ea. Ill. U. Alumni Assn. (pres. 1989-90, bd. dirs. 1985-91). Republican. Lutheran. Office: Ill Power 2409 Federal Dr Decatur IL 62526

HOFFMAN, PAUL JUIAN, mechanical engineer; b. Bklyn., June 11, 1958; s. Frank Julian and Thelma Genel (Cobb) H.; m. Anittra Michelle Alexander, Nov. 7, 1992. BSME, MIT, 1980; MSME, Stanford (Calif.) U., 1981. Design engr. Xerox Corp., Henrietta, N.Y., 1979, Fermi Nat. Acc. Lab., Batavia, Ill., 1980-81; thermal/hydraulics engr. Westinghouse Electric Corp., Madison, Pa., 1982-83; controls project engr. GE Co., Evendale, Ohio, 1984-91; controls systems engr. Cummins Engine Co., Columbus, Ind., 1991-96; sr. controls engr. Telodyne-Ryan Aeronaut., Toledo, 1996—. Mem. ASME (assoc.), Soc. of Automotive Engrs. Home: 26779 Lake Vue Dr Apt 5 Perrysburg OH 43551 Office: Telodyne-Ryan Aeronautical PO Box 6971 1330 Laskey Rd Toledo OH 43612

HOFFMAN, PHILIP EDWARD, state senator; b. Jackson, Mich., Nov. 10, 1951; s. Ralph Jacob Jr. and Nancy Joan (Vanantwerp) H.; m. Dennise Fitzgerald, Jan. 29, 1977; children: R. Jacob, Benjamin, Philip. BS, Ferris State U., 1974; postgrad. in edn., Mich. State U., 1975. Law enforcement officer Jackson County Sheriff's Dept., 1974-82; mem. Mich. Ho. of Reps., Lansing, 1982-93; mem. Mich. Senate, Lansing, 1993—, asst. pres. pro tem. Mem. Rep. Exec. Com.; pres. Great Saulk Trail coun. Boy Scouts Am., 1995-96. Named Outstanding Legis. Mem. of Yr., Am. Legis. Exch. Coun., 1992, Outstanding Legislator of Yr., Mich. Assn. Chiefs Police, 1993, Legis. Conservationist of Yr., Mich. United Conservation Clubs, 1994; Federalism Summit, 1995; Toll fellow, 1995; Fleming fellow, 1995. Mem. Am. Legis. Exch. Coun. (Outstanding Legis. Mem. of Yr. 1992), Jackson C.C. Alumni Assn. (Disting. Svc. award 1987), Ferris State U. Alumni Assn. (Disting. Alumnus 1990), Mich. Jaycees (1 of 10 Outstanding Young People in Mich. 1985), Eagles, Moose, Ducks Unltd., Pheasants Forever, Alpha Sigma Chi. Republican. Roman Catholic. Office: State Capitol Lansing MI 48913

HOFFMAN, RICHARD GEORGE, psychologist; b. Benton Harbor, Mich., Oct. 6, 1949; s. Robert Fredrick and Kathleen Elyce (Watts) H.; m. Julia Ann May, Dec. 18, 1970; children: Leslie Margaret, Michael Charles, Angela Lynn, Jennifer Elizabeth. BS with honors, Mich. State U., 1971; MA in Psychology, Long Island U., 1974, PhD in Clin. Psychology, 1980. Lic. con. psychologst. Instr. pediatrics U. Va., Charlottesville, 1977-80; asst. prof. pediatrics and family med. U. Kans., Wichita, 1980-84; asst. prof. behavioral sci. U. Minn., Duluth, 1984-90, assoc. prof. behavioral sci., 1990—, dir. neuropsychology lab., 1986—, co-dir. hypothermia and water safety lab., 1987—, co-dir. neurobehavioral toxicology lab., 1990—; vis. sr. fellow in human clin. neuropsychology U. Okla. Health Scis. Ctr., 1995-96; assoc. dir. Child Evaluation Ctr., Wichita, 1981-82; dir. adminstrn. Comprehensive Epilepsy Clinic, Wichita, 1983-84; cons. psychologist U. Assocs., P.A., Duluth, 1984—. contbr. articles to profl. jour. Pres. Home and Sch. Assn., St. Michael's Sch., Duluth, 1986. Rsch. grantee NIH, 1985, USCG, 1986, Sch. Medicine U. Kans., 1984, U. Minn., 1984, U.S. Army Med. Rsch. Command, 1988—, U.S. Naval Med. Rsch. Command, 1988, Gt. Lakes Protection Fund, 1991—, Agy. for Toxic Substances and Disease Registry, 1992-95, 95—. Fellow Am. Psychol. Soc., Am. Assn. Applied and Preventive Psychology; mem. APA, Nat. Acad. Neuropsychologists. Democrat. Roman Catholic. Home: 219 Occidental Blvd Duluth MN 55804-1365 Office: U Minn Dept Behavioral Scis Duluth MN 55812

HOFFMAN, SUE ELLEN, elementary education educator; b. Dayton, Ohio, Aug. 23, 1945; d. Cyril Vernon and Sarah Ellen (Sherer) Stephan; m. Lawrence Wayne Hoffman, Oct. 28, 1967. BS in Edn., U. Dayton, 1967; postgrad., Loyolla Coll., 1977, Ea. Mich. U., 1980; MEd, Wright State U., 1988. Cert. reading specialist and elem. tchr., Ohio. 5th grade tchr. St. Anthony Sch., Dayton, Ohio, 1967-68, West Huntsville (Ala.) Elem. Sch., 1968-71; 6th grade tchr. Ranchland Hills Pub. Sch., El Paso, Tex., 1973-74; 3rd grade tchr. Emerson Pub. Sch., Westerville, Ohio, 1976, St. Joan of Arc Sch., Aberdeen, Md., 1976-78, Our Lady of Good Counsel, Plymouth, Mich., 1979-80; 5th grade tchr. St. Helen Sch., Dayton, 1980—. Selected for membership Kappa Delta Pi, 1988. Mem. Internat. Reading Assn., Ohio Internat. Reading Assn., Dayton Area Internat. Reading Assn., Nat. Cath. Edn. Assn. Roman Catholic. Home: 2174 Green Springs Dr Kettering OH 45440-1120 Office: St Helen Sch 5086 Burkhardt Rd Dayton OH 45431-2043

HOFFMAN, VALERIE JON, religion educator; b. Rockville Centre, N.Y., Apr. 27, 1954; d. Robert Edward and Dolores Muriel (Ogren) H.; m. Steven James Ladd, May 26, 1984 (div. Mar. 21, 1995); children: Rachel, Michael, Deborah. BA in Anthropology, U. Pa., 1975; postgrad., Am. U., Cairo, Arab Republic of Egypt, 1975-76; MA in Islamic Studies, U. Chgo., 1979, PhD in Islamic Studies, 1986. Vis. lectr. U. Ill., Urbana, 1983-86, asst. prof., 1986-94, assoc. prof., 1994—. Mem. editl. bd. Jour. Am. Acad. Religion, 1994—; author: Sufism, Mystics and Saints in Modern Egypt, 1995. Recipient William and Flora Hewlett award 1996; appointed U. Ill. scholar 1996; NEH fellow, 1991-92, Fulbright rsch. fellow, Cairo, 1987-88, rsch. fellow Am. Rsch. Ctr. in Egypt, Cairo, 1980-81, NDEA Title VI fellow U. Chgo., 1976-79. Mem. Am. Acad. Religion (steering com. Study of Islam sect. 1989-93), Mid. East Studies Assn. (bd. dirs. 1995—), Assn. Mid. East Women's Studies, Am. Rsch. Ctr. in Egypt, Am. Inst. Maghrebi Studies. Office: U Ill Prog for Study of Rel 3014 FLB 707 S Mathews Ave Urbana IL 61801

HOFFMAN, WILLIAM KENNETH, retired obstetrician, gynecologist; b. Milw., Jan. 18, 1924; s. William Richard and Marian (Riegler) H.; student U. Wis., 1942-43; student U. Pa., 1943-44, postgrad, 1954-55; MD, Marquette U., 1947; m. Peggy Folsom, July 28, 1952; children: Janet Susan, Ann Elizabeth. Intern, Columbia Hosp., 1947-48, resident in obstetrics and gynecology, 1948-49, mem. staff, 1949-91; ret., 1991; preceptor R.E. McDonald, MD, Milw., 1949-50; resident in ob-gyn U. Chgo., 1950-51; practice medicine specializing in ob-gyn, Milw., 1955-74; mem. staff, Columbia Hosp.; dir. health service U. Wis.-Milw., 1974-91, cons. Sch. Nursing, 1976-77, clin. assoc. prof., 1979-91, vice chmn., mem. instl. rev. bd., 1976-91, mem. instl. safety and health com., 1981-91, chmn., 1984-88; ret., 1991. Bd. dirs. Wis. sect. Am. Cancer Soc., 1983-88. Mem. Am. Coll. Ob-Gyn, Am. Coll. Health Assn., Am. Coll. Sports Medicine, Royal Soc. Medicine, Am. Cancer Soc. (bd. dirs. Wis. div. 1983-88, public edn. com. Milw. div.). Home: 4629 N Murray Ave Milwaukee WI 53211-1259

HOFFMANN, GREGG J., journalist, author; b. Oak Park, Ill., Feb. 23, 1949; s. Robert and Jeanine (Casper) H.; m. Pauline Ehlen, July 20, 1974. BA in Journalism, U. Wis., 1973; MA in Comm., U. Wis., Milw., 1985. Assoc. editor Burlington (Wis.) Std. Press, 1973-76; owner, operator M & T Comm., Whitefish Bay, Wis., 1976—; sr. lectr. U. Wis., Milw., 1987—; Milw. corr. Kenosha News, USA Today, Baseball Weekly; sr. lectr. U. Wis., Milw., 1987—; bd. dirs. Internat. Soc. Gen. Semantics, Concord, Calif.; trustee Inst. Gen. Semantics, Englewood, N.J., 1991—; cons. in field. Author: The American Challenge, 1979, Media Maps and Myths, 1993, What You Can Do to Help the Hungry Feed Themselves, 1994; contbr. articles to profl. jours. Recipient Enterprise Reporting award Wis. Newspaper Assn., 1973-74, Freedom Found. Honor medal, 1980, Top Journalism award Am. Planning Assn., 1980; Sanford Berman fellow Internat. Soc. Gen. Semantics, 1989. Mem. Midwest Soc. Gen. Semantics (founder), Assn. Educators Mass Communication, Soc. Profl. Journalists, Milw. Press Club, Soc. Environ. Journalists, Pro Basketball Writers Assn. Home and Office: 4842 N Shoreland Ave Milwaukee WI 53217

HOFFMEISTER, ANN ELIZABETH, elementary education educator; b. Manitowoc, Wis., Mar. 27, 1957; d. William Anthony and Shirley Mary (Remiker) Gigure; m. Randal Thomas Hoffmeister, Apr. 3, 1982. BS in Spl. Edn., U. Wis., Eau Claire, 1979; MS in Curriculum and Instrn., U. Wis., Madison, 1986, MS in Ednl. Psychology, Gifted Edn., 1992. Cert. tchr., Wis.; lic. reading tchr., reading specialist. Tchr. Verona (Wis.) Area Schs., 1979—, computer coord., 1985-88, learning resource and reading coord., 1990—; whole lang. instr. U. Wis., Platteville, 1992-95; Action Rsch. instr. U. Wis., Plattville, 1996—; Action Rsch. site coord. Verona (Wis.) Area Schs., 1994; cons. Wis. Writing Project, Madison, 1983-90; grad. level cons. U. Wis., Oshkosh, 1993, 94, 96; elem. curriculum specialist fo rart of teaching with multicultural arts Duquesne U., 1996. Co-author: Building Self Esteem Through Writing, 1983, Fletcher's Fabulous Folks! An Integrated Imaginative Writing, Art, and Technology Project Using the Arts Propel Model. Mem. Verona Jaycees, 1987-92. Grantee Wis. Arts Bd., 1994. Mem. ASCD, Wis. Coun. for Gifted/Talented, Wis. State Reading Assn. (Pat Bricker Meml. Rsch. award 1992, 93, 94), Wis. Edn. Assn., So. Wis. Edn. Insvc. Orgn., Internat. Reading Assn., Verona Edn. Assn. (treas. 1983-86). Office: Sugar Creek Elem Sch 420 Church Ave Verona WI 53593-1803

HOFMAN, JOHN ERWIN, accountant; b. St. Louis, Mar. 6, 1960; s. James A. and Marian G. (Stevens) H.; m. Mary Shea, June 3, 1983. BBA, U. Mo., 1982. CPA, Mo. Staff acct. Price Waterhouse, St. Louis, 1984—. Treas. Citizens Against Annexations and Incorporating, St. Louis County, 1986. Named one of Outstanding Young Men of Am., U.S. Jaycees. Mem. Am. Inst. CPA's, Mo. Soc. CPA's. Roman Catholic.

HOFMAN, LEONARD JOHN, minister; b. Kent County, Mich., Jan. 31, 1928; s. Bert and Dora (Miedema) H.; m. H. Elaine (Ryskamp) H., Aug. 19, 1949; children: Laurie, Janice, Kathleen, Joel. BA, Calvin Coll., 1948; BTh, Calvin Sem., 1951, MDiv, 1981. Pastor Wright Christian Reformed Ch., Kanawha, Iowa, 1951-54, Kenosha Christian Reformed Ch., Kenosha, Wis., 1954-59, North St. Christian Reformed Ch., Zeeland, Mich., 1959-65, Ridgewood Christian Reformed Ch., Jenison, Mich., 1965-77, Bethany Christian Reformed Ch., Holland, Mich.; pres. bd. trustees Christian Reformed Ch., Grand Rapids, Mich., 1977-82; gen. sec. Christian Reformed Ch. in N.Am., Grand Rapids, 1982-94, chmn. bd. dirs., adminstrv. sec. for interchurch rels., 1995—. Sec. bd. trustees Calvin Coll., Grand Rapids, 1970-76. Recipient Outstanding Service award Calvin Alumni Assn., 1978. Mem. Nat. Assn. Evangelicals (mem. bd. adminstrn., exec. com., 1st v.p.). Home: 2237 Radcliff Cir SE Grand Rapids MI 49546-7725 Office: Christian Reformed Ch 2850 Kalamazoo Ave SE Grand Rapids MI 49508-1433

HOFMANN, PHILLIP J., business executive; b. Kansas City, Mo., June 16, 1961. MBA, U. Chgo., 1987. CFA. V.p. J.M. Lafferty & Assoc., Chgo., 1990—. Mem. Investment Analyst Soc. of Chgo. Office: JM Lafferty Assocs 100 S Wacker Dr Ste 1860 Chicago IL 60606-4006

HOFRICHTER, DAVID ALAN, management consultant; b. Lakewood, Ohio, July 10, 1948; s. David Christian and Virginia Amelia (Rickley) H.; m. Carol Ann Rybak, May 15, 1971; children—Kristin Ann, Matthew David. BA, Baldwin-Wallace Coll., 1970; MA, Duquesne U., 1972, PhD, 1976. Assoc., Hay Group, Inc., Pitts., 1977-78, prin., 1978-80, dir. orgn. and manpower svc., 1980-81, gen. mgr., Cin., 1981—, ptnr., gen. mgr., 1983-85, v.p., gen. mgr., Cin., 1985-86, sr. v.p., gen. mgr., Chgo., 1986-89, v.p., regional mgr., 1989-90, v.p., mng. dir., 1990-94, v.p., mng. dir. global account mgmt. and midwest ops., 1994—; mem. ptnrs. mgmt. com. Hay Group, Inc., 1990—; bd. dirs. Nat. Health Care Practice, Chgo., 1985—; lectr. Hay Compensation Confs.; spkr. Conf. Bd. Fortune Mag. Conf., 1996. Author: Executive Compensation in Health Care, 1986, Selecting People Who Can Implement Strategy, 1989, Reinforcing Organizational and Individual Competencies Through Compensation, 1992, Broad Banding: Fit or Fad, 1993, The Changing Nature of Work and Organization, 1993, People, Performance and Pay, 1996; Mem. Am. Psychol. Assn., Am. Soc. Cons. Mgmt. Engrs., Fin. Planning Assn. for City Chgo., Pa. Psychol. Assn., Nat. Register Health Svc. Providers in Psychology, Ruth Lake Country (Hinsdale, Ill.), Oak Brook (Ill.) Polo Club. Republican. Roman Catholic. Avocations: golf, swimming, flying, tennis, shooting. Home: 60 Derby Ct Oak Brook IL 60521-2650 Office: Hay Group 205 N Michigan Ave Chicago IL 60601-5925

HOFSOMMER, DONOVAN LOWELL, history educator; b. Ft. Dodge, Iowa, Apr. 10, 1938; s. Vernie George and Helma J. (Schager) H.; m. Sandra Louise Rusch, June 13, 1965; children: Kathryn Anne, Kristine Beret, Knute Lars. BA, U. Northern Iowa, 1960, MA, 1966; PhD, Okla. State U., 1973. Tchr. Fairfield (Iowa) High Sch., 1961-65; instr. U. Northern Iowa, Cedar Falls, 1965-66, Lea Coll., Albert Lea, Minn., 1966-70; teaching asst. Okla. State U., Stillwater, 1970-73; assoc. prof. and dept. head Wayland Coll., Plainview, Tex., 1973-81; corp. historian So. Pacific Co., San Francisco, 1981-85; hist. cons. Burlington No. Inc., Seattle, 1985-87; vis. prof. U. Mont., Missula, 1986-87; exec. dir. ctr. Western studies Augustana Coll., Sioux Falls, S.D., 1987-89; prof. history St. Cloud (Minn.) State U., 1989—; cons. Dyanelectron and Dynarail, Pueblo, Colo., 1979-81, Grand Trunk Corp., Detroit, 1988-95; mem. editl. bd. annals of Iowa, Iowa City, 1975-94, R.R. history, Akron, Ohio, 1975—. Author: Prairie Oasis, 1975, Katy Northwest, 1976, Southern Pacific 1901-1985, 1986; co-author: History of Great Northern Railway, 1988, Quanah Route, 1991, Grand Trunk Corp., 1995; editor: Lexington Group Transport History, 1975—; mem. editl. bd. Annals of Iowa, Iowa City, 1975-92, R.R. History, Akron, Ohio, 1975—. With U.S. Army, 1960-66. Mem. Okla. Hist. Soc. (Wright Heritage award 1979), Ry. and Locomotive Hist. Soc. (Book award 1988, Sr. Achievement award 1995), Western History Assn., Orgn. Am. Historians, State Hist. Soc. Iowa, Am. Assn. for State and Local History. Democrat. Presbyterian. Home: 1803 13th Ave SE Saint Cloud MN 56304-2231 Office: St Cloud State U Dept History Saint Cloud MN 56301

HOGAN, ANDREW J., controls engineer, educator; b. Innsbruck, Austria, Feb. 2, 1968; s. Sam P. and Larissa A. (Demczuk) H. BS in Elec. and Computer Engring., U. Wis., 1992. Design engr. Blue Feather Co., New Glarus, Wis., 1992; controls engr. CIM Software Corp., Mpls., 1992—. Mem. IEEE, Minn. Triangle Frat. Alumni Orgn. (pres. 1995—). Office: CIM Software Corp 5735 Lindsay St Minneapolis MN 55422

HOGAN, MICHAEL RAY, insurance company executive; b. Newark, Ohio, Apr. 21, 1953; s. Raymond Carl and Mary Adele (Whalen) H.; m. Martha Ann Gorman, July 24, 1976; children: Colleen Michael, Patrick Gorman, Mary Kate. BA, Loyola U., Chgo., 1978; M in Mgmt. with distinction, Northwestern U., 1980. Cert. FLMI, HIA. Assoc. McKinsey & Co., Inc., Chgo., 1980-81, engagement mgr., 1982-83; sr. v.p., treas. FBS Ins. Co., Mpls., 1984-85; group v.p., gen. mgr. Gen. Am. Life Ins. Co., St. Louis, 1986, v.p., 1987-89, exec. v.p., 1990-95; pres., CEO Cova Corp., St. Louis, 1995-96; corp. v.p., controller Monsanto Co., St. Louis, 1996—; cons. Swedish Trade Commn., Chgo., 1978; Lee Wards Creative Crafts Co., Elgin, Ill., 1979; chmn. Consultec, Inc., Atlanta, 1990-95, Cova Fin. Life Ins. Co., Oakbrook Terrace, 1995; chmn., CEO Genelco, Inc., St. Louis, St. Louis Reins Co., Genmark, St. Louis, 1990-95. Contb. articles to profl. jours. Active Experience St. Louis, 1986; mem. Leadership Ctr. of Greater St. Louis, 1987—, bd. dirs., 1988-95, v.p. comms., 1989-90, pres., 1991-92; bd. dirs. Combined Health Appeal of Greater St. Louis, 1992—, v.p. programs, 1992-94, pres., 1995—; bd. dirs. St. Louis Coll. Pharmacy, 1995—. Scholar F.C. Austin Found., 1978-80, Phi Gamma Nu, 1980. Mem. Confluence St. Louis, Beta Gamma Sigma. Roman Catholic. Club: Stadium. Home: 9368 Robyn Hills Dr Saint Louis MO 63127 Office: Monsanto Co 800 N Linbergh Blvd Saint Louis MO 63167-3146

HOGAN, ROBERT KEVIN, rehabilitation services professional; b. Springfield, Ill., Mar. 13, 1961; s. Robert Joseph and Carol Lee (Spears) H. AA, Springfield (Ill.) Coll., 1981; BA, Rosary Coll., River Forest, Ill., 1983; MPA, U. Ill., 1991. Rehab. counselor Ill. Dept. Rehab. Svcs., Chgo., 1984-92; rehab. svcs. supr. Ill. Dept. Rehab. Svcs., Champaign, 1992—. Pres. F.O.C.U.S. on Early Intervention, Danville, Ill., 1994—; co-chmn. Transition Planning Coun., Champaign, 1992—; mem. Ill. Job Placement and Devel. Divsn., 1994—, pres., 1994. Mem. Nat. Rehab. Assn., Ill. Rehab. Assn. (editor newsletter 1993—), U. Ill. Alumni Assn., Ill. Rehab. Counseling Assn. (pres. 1996). Roman Catholic. Home: 1827 Valley Rd Champaign IL 61820

HOHNSTEIN, DEAN HARLAN, mechanical engineer; b. Clay Center, Nebr., Dec. 27, 1937; s. George and Pauline H. BSME, U. Nebr., 1959. Engr. N.Am. Aviation, L.A., 1959, Allis Chalmers, West Allis, Wis., 1959-84, Siemens Allis, Bradenton, Fla., 1984-88, Siemens Energy, Cin., 1988—. Patentee (2) in field. Mem. Pi Tau Sigma, Pi Mu. Epsilon. Office: Siemens Energy and Auto 4620 Forest Ave Cincinnati OH 45212-3396

HOHULIN, MARK E., electronics specialist, drafting educator; b. Peoria, Ill., Jan. 30, 1960. AS, Purdue U., 1992. CAD cons. Xcell Computers, Mishawaka, Ind., 1984-87; CAD/CAM mgr. Wells Electronics, South Bend, Ind., 1987—; instr. drafting Purdue U. Office: Wells Electronics 1701 S Main St South Bend IN 46613-2211

HOHULIN, MARTIN, state legislator; b. Ft. Scott, Kans., May 1, 1964; m. Marilyn Hohulin; 1 child, William. State rep. Dist. 126 Mo. State Congress, 1991—; mem. agr.-bus. consumer protection com., ranking rep. appropriations and labor com.; farm owner and operator. Mem. Cattlemens Assn., Barton County Farm Bur., Lamar Metro Club. *

HOKE, EUGENA LOUISE, special education educator; b. Chgo., Feb. 26, 1949; d. Edward LaMar and Edna Lucille (Weikert) H. BS, Bowling Green State U., 1971; MEd, U. Maine, Orono, 1977. Cert. educator. Tchr. educable mentally retarded Marion Local Schs., Maria Stein, Ohio, 1971-73, Tri-Valley Local Sch., Dresden, Ohio, 1973-74; tchr. Edgewood Local Schs., Trenton, Ohio, 1974-78; learning disabilities tchr. Oak Hills Local Sch. Dist., Cin., 1978—; mem. prin.'s adv. com. C.O. Harrison Elem. Sch., Cin., 1987-88, 92-93, mem. tchr. asst. team, 1988-90. Mem. Vol. in Parks, Hamilton County, Ohio, 1981-88; vol. Cin. Symphony Assn., 1988—, Friends of Pops, 1991—, Mus. Ctr., 1991, Aronoff Ctr. for the Arts, 1995—. Mem. NEA, Ohio Edn. Assn., Oak Hill Edn. Assn., Cin. Arts. Assn. Methodist. Home: 5566 Biscayne Ave Cincinnati OH 45248-4225

HOKE, JAMES RICHARD, finance executive, management consultant; b. Dayton, Ohio, Mar. 16, 1946; s. Charles Richard and Leona Christine (Benanzer) H.; m. Mary Catherine Rodighero, June 7, 1969. BBA in Fin., U. Notre Dame, 1968; MBA in Fin. and Banking, Wright State U., 1975. Ops. rsch. analyst Winters Nat. Bank & Trust, Dayton, 1968-69; fin. analyst NCR Corp., Dayton, 1969-71, mgr. R & D Budgets, 1971-73; sr. acctg. supr. Monsanto Co.-Mound Labs., Miamisburg, Ohio, 1973-75; from supr. project acctg. to mgr. fixed assets acctg. Monsanto Co., St. Louis, 1975-88; dir. fin. and adminstrn. Kinetek Systems Inc., St. Louis, 1988-91; chief fin. officer Mo. Goodwill Industries, St. Louis, 1991-95; city clk. and assessor City of Olivette, Mo., 1992-94, councilman, 1994—; pres. QVS Golf, St. Louis, 1994—; cons systems devel. SSE, Inc., St. Louis, 1985-86; pres. chief exec. officer Datamatics, Inc., St. Louis, 1986-88; prof. Washington U., St. Louis, 1994—. Loaned exec. Urban League of St. Louis, 1981, ARC Bi-State chpt., St. Louis, 1984; mem. United Way Greater St. Louis Aid to Disabled Com., 1985-88, Spl. Needs Com., 1988-91, Priorities Com., 1991, Cert. Volunteerism, 1986-90. Mem. Mo. Venture Forum, Greenbriar Hills Country Club (chmn. long range planning 1987-88, sec. 1988). Roman Catholic. Home: 9227 Ladue Hills Dr Saint Louis MO 63132-4320 Office: QVS Golf 8962 Watson Rd Saint Louis MO 63119

HOKE, SUSAN CANDICE, law educator; b. Raleigh, N.C., 1955; d. H.R. and Getty Anne H.; m. George H. Taylor, 1989. BA, Hollins Coll., 1977; postgrad., U. Chgo., 1978-79; JD, Yale U., 1983. Law clk. to presiding justice U.S. Ct. Appeals 1st Cir., Boston and Concord, N.H., 1983-85; assoc. atty. Hill & Barlow, Boston, 1985-87; asst. prof. of law U. Pitts. Sch. of Law, 1987-93; vis. prof. law Case Western Res. U. Law Sch., Cleve., 1993—. Office: Case Western Res Law Sch 11075 East Blvd Cleveland OH 44106

HOKENSON, DAVID LEONARD, secondary school educator; b. Mpls., Nov. 9, 1950; s. Raymond Leonard and Barbara Jean (Hooker) H.; m. Cynthia Jane Luehmann, July 28, 1979. BA, St. Olaf Coll., 1972; postgrad., U. Minn., 1977, 78, 82. Lic. secondary sch. social studies and history tchr., Minn. Social studies tchr. Preston (Minn.)-Fountain Pub. Schs., 1972-93, Fillmore Cen. H.S., Harmony, Minn., 1993-95; Fillmore Cen. Mid. Sch., Preston, Minn., 1995—; mem. team evaluation State Dept. Edn., St. Paul, 1981, 83, 91. Precinct chair Dem.-Farmer-Labor Party, Preston, 1990—; treas. Preston-Fountain Edn. Assn., 1987-93, negotiator, 1993-94; treas. Fillmore Cen. Edn. Assn., 1994—; mem. evaluation team North Cen. Accreditation Assn., 1994; participant Project 120, 1995; mem. Nat. Trust for Hist. Preservation, Minn. Hist. Soc. Recipient scholarship Minn. Inst. for Advancement of Teaching, St. Paul, 1992. Mem. Nat. Geog. Soc., Am. Scandinavian Found., Am.-Swedish Inst. Office: Fillmore Cen Schs PO Box 50 Preston MN 55965

HOKIN, LOWELL EDWARD, biochemist, educator; b. Chgo., Sept. 20, 1924; s. Oscar E. and Helen (Manfield) H.; m. Mabel Neaverson, Dec. 1, 1952 (div. Dec. 1973); children: Linda Ann, Catherine Esther (dec.), Samuel Arthur; m. Barbara M. Gallagher, Mar. 23, 1978; 1 child, Ian Oscar. Student, U. Chgo., 1942-43, Dartmouth Coll., 1943-44, U. Louisville Sch. Medicine, 1944-46, U. Ill. Sch. Medicine, 1946-47; MD, U. Louisville, 1948; PhD, U. Sheffield, Eng., 1952. Postdoctoral fellow dept. biochemistry McGill U., 1952-54, faculty, 1954-57, asst. prof., 1955-57; mem. faculty U. Wis., Madison, 1957—, prof. physiol. chemistry, 1961-68, prof. pharmacology, 1968—, prof., chmn. pharmacology, 1968-93; chmn. pharmacology. Contbr. numerous articles to tech. jours., chpts. to numerous books on phosphoinositides, biol. transport, the pancreas, the brain and lithium in manic-depression. With USNR, 1943-45. Mem. AAAS, Am. Soc. Biochemistry and Molecular Biology, Biochem. Soc. (U.K.), Am. Soc. Pharmacology and Exptl. Therapeutics, N.Y. Acad. Scis. Home: 5 Nokomis Ct Madison WI 53711-2710 Office: U Wis Med Sch Dept Pharm 1300 University Ave Madison WI 53706

HOLABIRD, JOHN AUGUR, JR., retired architect; b. Chgo., May 9, 1920; s. John Augur and Dorothy (Hackett) H.; m. Donna Katharine Smith, Nov. 25, 1942 (div. 1969); children: Jean, Katharine, Polly, Lisa (dec.); m. Marcia Stefanie Fergestad, June 28, 1969 (dec. Mar. 1994); children: Ann, Lynn; m. Janet Nothhelfer Connor, May 7, 1996. BA, Harvard U., 1942, MArch, 1948. Archtl. designer Holabird & Root, Chgo., 1948-49, 55-64; assoc. firm Holabird & Root, 1964-70, ptnr., 1970-87; tchr. drama Francis Parker Sch., Chgo., 1949-55; stage designer NBC-TV, 1955. Major: archtl. works include Francis Parker Sch, Chgo., Ravinia Stage and Restaurant, Highland Park, Ill., 1970, Bell Telephone Labs, Naperville, Ill., 1975, Canal Bldg, Chgo., 1974. Pres. Park West Community Assn., 1962; dir. Lincoln Park Conservation Assn., 1960-64, Corlands, 1979-85; mem. Chgo. Commn. on Historic and Archtl. Landmarks, 1981-85; bd. dirs. Lincoln Park Community Conservation, 1964; trustee Francis Parker Sch., Ravinia Festival Assn., Ill. Inst. Tech., 1980-86. Served with U.S. Army, 1942-45. Decorated Silver Star, Bronze Star; Fourragère (Belgium); Order of William (The Netherlands). Fellow AIA (pres. Chgo. chpt. 1977-78); mem. Tavern Club, Harvard Club (dir. 1974-78), Phi Beta Kappa. Democrat. Home: 2715 N Pine Grove Ave Chicago IL 60614-6109 Office: Holabird & Root 300 W Adams St Chicago IL 60606-5101

HOLBROOK, DON ALLEN, economic development professional; b. Lexington, Ky., Apr. 14, 1960; s. M. Floyd and Sarah Elizabeth (Allen) Osman; m. Laurie Ann Lutz, Sept. 21, 1990; 1 child, Ian Connor. BA, Wright State U., 1982; MBA, Lasalle U., 1994, PhD, 1995. Cert. econ. devel. fin. profl. Nat. sales dir. Honeywell, Inc., Mpls., 1980-86; pres. Trinity Plastics, Inc., Dayton, Ohio, 1986-88; dir. mkgt. Kintec, Inc., L.A., 1988-89; dir. econ. devel. City of South St. Paul, 1990-92; exec. dir. Crookston (Minn.) Econ. Devel. Authority, 1992—; pres. Interactive Econ. Devel. Network, Crookston, 1994—; mem. adv. bd. Telecommuter Resources, Mpls., 1994—; expert, presenter and spkr. in field. Contbr. articles to profl. jours. V.p., bd. dirs. Mid-Am. Econ. Devel. Coun., Chgo., 1994—. 1st lt. U.S. Army 10th Spl. Forces, 1980-86. Mem. Nat. Coun. Urban Econ. Devel., Nat. Rural Econ Devel. Assn., Nat. Assn. Devel. Orgns., Nat. Congress Cmty. Econ. Devel., Econ. Devel. Assn. Minn. Roman Catholic. Office: Interactive Econ Devel Network PO Box 691 Crookston MN 56716

HOLBROOK, THOMAS, state legislator. Ill. state rep. Dist. 113, 1995—. Office: Ste 4 9200 W Main Belleville IL 62223

HOLDEN, BOB, state official; b. Kansas City, Mo.; m. Lori Hauser; children: Robert, John. BS in Polit. Sci., Southwest Mo. State; Degree Kennedy Sch. Govt. for Public Execs. and Flemming Fellow Leadership Inst., Harvard U. Former adminstrv. asst./liaison U.S. Congressman Richard Gephardt, St. Louis; mem. Mo. Ho. of Reps., 1983-89; now state treas. State of Mo., Jefferson City; chmn. gen. appropations com.; co-sponsor Excellence in Edn. Act; mem. Bd. Fund Commrs., Mo. State Employees Retirement System, Mo. Bus. Coun., Mo. Rural Opportunities Coun.; past chmn. Mo. Housing Devel. Commn. Dean Am. Legion Mo. Boy's State Legislative Sch.; mem. Holden Scholarship Fund, Leadership St. Louis; former mem. Confluence's Edn. Implementation, Tower Grove Hgts. Neighborhood Assn., Save the Children's Program; mem. Mo. Coun. Econ. Edn., Coun. State Govts.; vice-chair Mo. Cultural Trust. Mem. Nat. Assn. State Treas. (legis. chair). Office: St Treasurer PO Box 210 Jefferson City MO 65102-0210

HOLDEN, ROBERT WATSON, radiologist, educator, university dean; b. Brazil, Ind., Mar. 31, 1936; s. John William and Naomi Ellen (Watson) H.; m. Miriam Ann Bognanno, June 20, 1964; children: Anne, Robert II, Jennifer. BS in Pharmacy, Purdue U., 1958; MD, Ind. U., 1963. Diplomate Am. Bd. Radiology. Intern L.A. County Gen. Hosp., 1963-64; resident radiology Vanderbilt U., Nashville, 1970-73; asst. prof. Ind. U. Sch. Medicine, Indpls., 1973-77, assoc. prof., 1977-82, prof., 1982—, prof., chmn. dept. radiology, 1991—, dean, 1995—; chief vascular and interventional radiology Wishard Meml. Hosp., Indpls., 1973-79, chief radiology, 1977-91; counselor NIH, 1990-94. Contbr. over 100 articles to profl. jours. Chmn. bldg. com. 1st United Meth. Ch., Mooresville, 1988—. Capt. U.S. Army, 1964-66. Fellow Soc. Cardiovascular & Interventional Radiology, 1987; named Disting. Alumnus, Purdue U. Sch. Phharmacy, 1992. Mem. Am. Coll. Radiology (fellow 1988, counselor), Radiologic Soc. N.Am. (counselor), Ind. Roentgen Soc. (past pres.). Republican. Office: Ind U Sch Medicine 550 University Blvd Indianapolis IN 46202-5270

HOLDERNESS, SUSAN RUTHERFORD, religious organization administrator, at-risk educator; b. Cherokee, Iowa, Nov. 5, 1941; d. Parker William and Ruth Elvera (Peterson) Rutherford; m. Michael Aaron Holderness, Aug. 12, 1961; children: Lauren, Lisa, Jennifer, Joshua. BA in Edn., Wayne State U., Nebr., 1964; student, Iowa State U., 1960-61, Vocat. Cert., 1973. Tchr. various high schs. including Norwalk (Iowa) High Sch., 1968-78; tchr. South Alternative and East H.S., Des Moines, 1968-78; hist. site interpreter Salisbury House, Des Moines, 1971-78, 84-88, Minn. State Hist. Soc., St. Paul, 1978-84; cons. Profl. Match Cons., Des Moines, 1985-90; tour guide and conv. planner Des Moines Tour and Conv. Svcs., 1987-92; also dir. Christian edn. Douglas Ave. Presbyn. Ch., Des Moines; owner gourmet food shop, 1973. V.p. fundraising Des Moines Symphony Guild, 1990-92; bd. dirs., treas., sec. playground bldg. project Greenwood Sch. PTA, Des Moines, 1986-89; co-chmn. Civic Music Assn., Des Moines, 1987; pres., v.p., tour dir. St. Paul New Residents, 1980-83, others in past; bd. dirs. Ramsey County Friends of the Libr., 1981-83, Symphony Assn., mem., steering com. showhouse and ball, fundraising v.p. Mem. Iowa Victorian Soc., Compass Club (internat. pres. 1986-87), Internat. Platform Assn., Kappa Delta Pi, Gamma Phi Beta. Republican. Presbyterian. Office: Walnut Creek Campus 1101 5th St West Des Moines IA 50265

HOLDREN, RICHARD LYELL, engineering executive; b. Parkersburg, W.Va., Feb. 19, 1951. BS in Welding Engring., Ohio State U., 1973. Registered profl. engr., Ohio, Ind. Welding engr. Col-x Corp., Columbus, Ohio, 1975-79, sr. welding engr., 1980-81; welding quality engr. Jeffrey Mining Machinery, Columbus, 1979-80; v.p. Welding Cons. Inc., Columbus, 1981—. Contbr. articles to profl. jours. Fellow Am. Soc. Non-Destructive Testing; mem. Am. Welding Soc., Nat. Assn. Corrosion Engrs., ASM.

HOLDRIDGE, WILLIAM ERNEST, justice; b. Peoria, Ill., Mar. 30, 1948; s. Marvin Harms and Mary (Holzinger Galvin) H. BS in Edn., Ill. State U., 1970, MS, 1971; PhD, U. Ill., 1973; JD, So. Ill. U., 1984. Prof. San Jose (Calif.) State U., 1971-72, U. Ill., Urbana, 1972-73, Ill. State U., Normal, 1973-76, So. Ill. U., Carbondale, 1976-84; pvt. practice law Peoria, 1984-90; appellate ct. clk. State of Ill. 3d Dist., Ottawa, 1984-90; clk. State of Ill. Supreme Ct., Springfield, 1990; judge State of Ill. 9th Cir., Galesburg, Ill., 1990-94; justice State of Ill. Appellate Ct., Peoria, 1994—; mem. exec. bd. Ill. Jud. Conf., 993—; mem. Fed.-State Jud. Coun., 1994—; mem. com. Ill. Supreme Ct., Springfield, 1991—. Contbr. articles to profl. jours. City atty. City of Farmington, Ill., 1988-90; mem. capital devel. com. W.D. Boyce coun. Boy Scouts Am., Peoria, 1989-90; mem. stewardship appeal com. Peoria Diocese, 1989-90; mem. So. Ill. U. Alumni Bd., Carbondale, 1990—. Mem. Am. Judicature Soc., Am. Judges Assn., Ill. State Bar Assn., Ill. Judges Assn., Ill. Farm Bur., Rotary. Office: 207 Main St Ste 600 Peoria IL 61602

HOLIDAY, PATRICK JAMES See MANFRO, PATRICK JAMES

HOLLADAY, ERIC DAN, stockbroker; b. Kansas City, Kans., Mar. 21, 1960. BA, Ea. N.Mex. U., 1983. Stockbroker B.C. Christopher, Wichita, Kans., 1988-92, A. G. Edwards & Sons Inc., Wichita, 1992—. Mem. Optimist Club. Republican. Home: 5813 E 17th St N Wichita KS 67208-1705 Office: A G Edwards & Sons Inc 201 N Main St Ste 300 Wichita KS 67202-1500

HOLLAND, GARY V., investment broker; b. Evansville, Ind., Dec. 22, 1947. BS, So. Ill. U., 1974. Sales mgr. Miners Home Furnishings, Carmi, Ill., 1975-94; investment broker J.J.B. Hilliard W.L. Lyons Inc., Carmi, 1994—; bd. dirs. Ill. Oil and Gas Assn., Mt. Vernon, 1984—. Campaign mgr. for Congressman Simons, Carbondale, Ill., 1976. Sgt. USMC, 1970-73. Mem. VFW, Am. Legion, Elks. Baptist. Office: JJB Hilliard WL Lyons Inc PO Box 487 711 E Main St Carmi IL 62821

HOLLAND, GEORGE FRANK, II, investment company executive; b. N.Y.C., Jan. 19, 1931; m. Elizabeth R. Hardy, Aug. 31, 1957; children: Steven Todd, William Eric, Roger Hardy, Ellen. AB, Ind. U., 1953, MBA, 1957. Asst. v.p. Am. Fletcher Nat. Bank, Indpls., 1957-70; exec. v.p., dir., sec. Traub Co. Inc., Indpls., 1970—. Contbr. articles to profl. jours. Lt. col. USAFR, 1953-77. Mem. Indpls. Soc. Fin. Analysts (past pres.), Res. Officers Assn., Ret. Officers Assn., Ind. U. Alumni Assn., Carmel Breakfast Club Sertoma Club (past pres.), Indpls. Stock & Bond Club, Am. Legion, Sigma Chi Alumni Assn. Republican. Episcopalian. Home: 20 Wildwood Dr Carmel IN 46032-1416 Office: Traub Co Inc 320 N Meridian St Indianapolis IN 46204-1719

HOLLAND, JOY, health care facility executive; b. N.Y.C., Oct. 24, 1946; d. Harry Walson and Edna May (Simmons) H.; m. Chesley Roderick Richardson, Sept.21, 1985; children: Carl Allen Fields, Craig Anthony Fields. AA in Nursing, Olive-Harvey Coll., 1972; BS, St. Joseph Coll., Bklyn., 1976; M in Health Adminstrn., C.W. Post Coll., 1978. Staff nurse U. Chgo. Hosp. and Clinics, Chgo., 1972; head nurse N.Y. Hosp., N.Y.C., 1972; clinic adminstr. Morrisania-Montefiore Hosp., Bronx, N.Y., 1973; head nurse, supr. Pilgrim Psychiat. Hosp., Brentwood, N.Y., 1974, assoc. dir. staff devel., 1974-76, dir. nursing, 1976-78; surveyor, cons Joint Commn. on Accrediation of Hosps., Chgo., 1978-82; dir. Ypsilanti (Mich.) Regional Psychiat. Hosp., 1986-90, Clinton Valley Ctr., Pontiac, Mich., 1990-93, Huron Valley Ctr., Ypsilanti, Mich., 1993—; dep. commr. dept. mental health State of Ohio, 1980-82; cons. Joint Commn. Accreditation of Hosps.; adj. lectr. Sch. Nursing, U. Mich.; cons. specialist, bd. dirs. Holland-Richardson Assocs., Detroit. Contbr. author (book) Guide to J.C.A.H. Nursing Standards, 1985, 86 edits. Bd. dirs. Women in Crisis, Inc., N.Y.C., 1979-85, Washtenaw County (Mich.) ARC; bd. dirs. psychiatry dept. Chelsea (Mich.) Hosp., 1989-91. Mem. N.Y. Acad. Sci. (life), Bus. and Profl. Women, Inc., Masons, Order Ea. Star, Alpha Kappa Alpha, Sigma Theta Tau. Republican. Office: Huron Valley Center 3511 Bemis Rd Ypsilanti MI 48197-9307

HOLLAND, LOUIS EDWARD, II, virologist; b. Kansas City, Mo., Nov. 15, 1948; s. Louis Garratt and Evelyn (Plunkett) H.; m. Mary Lynn Lambert, Apr. 21, 1977; children: Michael, Jeffrey. BS, Baker U., 1970; PhD, U. Calif., Irvine, 1979. Postdoctoral fellow U. Mich., Ann Arbor, 1979-84; sr. molecular biologist So. Rsch. Inst., Birmingham, Ala., 1984-88; sr. virologist IIT Rsch. Inst., Chgo., 1988—. With U.S. Army, 1970-72. Mem. Am. Soc. Microbiology, Am. Soc. Virology, Internat. Soc. Antiviral Rsch., Internat. AIDS Soc. Office: IIT Rsch Inst 10 W 35th St Chicago IL 60616-3799

HOLLAND, PAUL V., stockbroker; b. Fargo, N.D., Feb. 20, 1965. BA in Econs., Concordia Coll., Morehead, Minn., 1987. Stockbroker A.G. Edwards & Sons Inc., Fargo, 1987—; mem. Coun. Advisors for Bus., Morehead, 1995—. Home: 2608 38th Ave S Fargo ND 58104-7016 Office: AG Edwards & Sons Inc 902 28th St S Fargo ND 58103-2322

HOLLAND, RICHARD MANSON, educational foundation executive; b. Shirley, Mass., Nov. 7, 1961; s. Peter Anderson and Marjorie (Lynn) H.; m. Alison Randall Welles, June 25, 1988; children: M. Tucker, Madison Randall. BA in English, Syracuse Univ., 1983. Leadership cons. Delta Upsilon Internat. Fraternity, Indpls., 1983-84, chpt. svcs. dir., 1984-85; admissions rep. Burdett Sch., Boston, 1985-86; sr. sports reporter Lincoln Jour., Acton, Mass., 1985-90; pers. cons. Franklin-Pierce, Assoc., Boston, 1986-90; dir. devel. Delta Upsilon Ednl. Found., Indpls., 1990-92, exec. dir., 1992—; mem. faculty Founds. Seminar, Indpls., 1994. Co-author: The Cornerstone, 1988; writer The Quar., 1990-95, editor, 1995. Mem. Nat. Interfraternity Conf., Nat. Soc. Fund Raising Execs., Fraternity Execs. Assn., Dikaia Found. (v.p.). Home: 2 Curtis Ln Medway MA 02053-2431 Office: Delta Upsilon Ednl Found 8705 Founders Rd Indianapolis IN 46268

HOLLANDER, ADRIAN WILLOUGHBY, accounting software company executive; b. Sumter, S.C., Oct. 12, 1941; s. Willard Fisher and Mildred Hanna (Willoughby) H.; m. Eleanor Busby Smith, May 26, 1963; children: Richard, David, Robert. BS, Iowa State U., 1963. CPA; cert. info. system auditor; cert. internal auditor; cert. bank auditor. Mem. audit and cons. staff Arthur Andersen and Co., Chgo., 1965-71; auditor Beverly Bancorporation, Chgo., 1971-73; v.p. Cullinane Corp., Chgo., 1973-78; auditor Cen. Nat. Bank in Chgo., 1978-79; pres. EDP Audit Assocs., Inc., Summit, Ill., 1980; pres. Complus, Inc., Hickory Hills, Ill., 1982-87, Chgo., 1987—; cons., owner EDP Audit Service, Chgo., 1979—. Contbr. articles to profl. jours. Trustee St. Paul's Union Ch., Chgo., 1973-75; bd. dirs. Beverly Improvement Assn., Chgo., 1972-88; council of dels. Beverly Area Planning Assn., Chgo., 1980-85; del. Chgo. Agenda for Pub. Edn., 1983-87. Served to 1st lt. U.S. Army, 1963-65. Mem. AICPA, Ill. CPA Soc. (sec. Chgo. South chpt. 1991-92, treas. 1992-93, v.p. 1993-94, sr. v.p. 1994-95, pres. 1995-96), Info. Systems Audit and Control Assn., Inst. Internal Auditors, Chgo. Beverly Ridge Lions Club (pres. 1992-93). Republican. Home: 9360 S Pleasant Ave Chicago IL 60620-5644 Office: Complus Inc 9500 S Vanderpoel Ave Chicago IL 60643-1228

HOLLANDER, DORIS ANN, psychologist, consultant, businesswoman, author; b. St. Louis, Oct. 13, 1941; d. Samuel and Rose (Heller) H.; m. Jerrold Blumoff, June 9, 1963 (div. July 1988); children: Sam, Rebecca. BA, Washington U., St. Louis, 1964; MA with distinction, DePaul U., 1972; PhD, Loyola U., Chgo., 1979. Caseworker Mo. Div. Welfare, St. Louis, 1964-65; research assoc. Inst. Juvenile Research, Chgo., 1967-68; instr. ednl. psychology Loyola U., Chgo., 1972-73; psychologist, program developer Women's Achievement Program, Hammond, Ind., 1976-78; pres. Whole Food & Grain Depot, Oak Park, Ill., 1972-78; asst. prof. psychology Webster U., St. Louis, 1979-83, co-chmn. psychology dept., 1982-83; pres. New Options, Inc., 1983—; sr. prin. Capital Consulting Group, 1991—; co-chmn. psychology, sociology and anthropology, dir. adult learner project, Webster U.; lectr. Washington U. Sch. Bus. Exec. v.p., program chmn. Oak Park Mental Health Bd., 1976-79. Author: The Doom-Loop System: A Step-by-Step Guide to Career Mastery, 1991, 101 Lies Men Tell Women and Why Women Believe Them, 1995; editor Mo. Psychologist. Mem. Assn. Community Mental Health Authorities Ill. (del.), Am. Psychol. Assn., Mo. Psychol. Assn. (sec. 1985-86, pres. 1987-88, chmn. women's issues com. 1983-84), St. Louis Network Women Psychologists (coordinator 1981-84, pres. 1982-84, bd. dirs. 1984-87, historian 1985-87), Soc. Psychologists Mgmt. (bd. dirs., pres. 1991-92), St. Louis Psychol. Assn. (program chmn. 1984-85, pres. 1985-86). Home: 665 S Skinker Blvd Saint Louis MO 63105-2300 Office: 1200 N Nash St Apt 823 Arlington VA 22209 also: 501 N Lindbergh Blvd Saint Louis MO 63141-7829

HOLLANDER, ELIZABETH RUSSELL, urban planner; b. Bryn Mawr, Pa., Dec. 1, 1939; d. Joseph Russell and Mildred (Akin) Lynes; m. Sidney Hollander, Sept. 8, 1963 (div. Jan. 1992); children: Daniel, Rachel. BA in Polit. Sci. with honors, Bryn Mawr Coll., 1961. Cert. planner. Program dir. Ill.-Ind. Bi-State Commn., Chgo., 1975-79; assoc. dir. Task Force Int. of Ill., Chgo., 1979-80; exec. dir. Metro Planning Coun., Chgo., 1980-83; commr. of planning City of Chgo., 1983-89; exec. dir. govt. assistance project The Chgo. Cmty. Trust, 1989-94; exec. dir. Monsignor John J. Egan Urban Ctr., DePaul U., Chgo., 1994—; freelance planning cons., Chog. Author articles. Treas. Woodstock Inst., 1986—; mem. bd. advisors Nat. Civic League, 1993—; mem. Chgo. bd. advisor Pub. Allies, 1992—; mem. Nat. Commn. on State and Local Pub. Svc., 1991—; trustee Ill. Inst. Tech., 1988—, Chgo. State U., 1996—. Fellow Nat. Acad. Pub. Adminstrn.; mem. Inst. Cert. Planners, Am. Planning Assn., The Chgo. Network, The Econs. Club, Lambda Alpha. Democrat. Jewish. Office: Egan Urban Ctr/DePaul U 243 S Wabash Ave Chicago IL 60604

HOLLANSKY, BERT VOYTA, stock brokerage executive; b. Prague, Czech Republic, May 9, 1944; came to U.S., 1954; BS, U. Ill., 1967; MBA, Am. Grad. Sch., Phoenix, 1969. Mgr. internat. devel. Cummins Engine Co., Columbus, Ind., 1969-81; v.p. Prudential Securities Inc., Columbus, 1981-89; v.p., stockbroker J.J.B. Hilliard W.L. Lyons Inc, Columbus, 1989—. Mem. Columbus C. of C.

HOLLE, REGINALD HENRY, retired bishop; b. Burton, Tex., Nov. 21, 1925; s. Alfred W. and Lena (Nolte) H.; m. Marla C. Christianson, June 16, 1949; children: Todd, Joan. BA, Capital U., 1946, DD (hon.), 1979; MDiv,

Trinity Luth. Sem., 1949; D. Ministry, Ohio Consortium Religious Stdy, 1977; DD (hon.), Wittenberg U., 1989. Ordained minister Evang. Luth. Ch. Am., then bishop. Assoc. pastor Zion Luth. Ch., Sandusky, Ohio, 1949-51; sr. pastor Salem Meml. Luth. Ch., Detroit, 1951-72, Parma Luth. Ch., Cleve., 1973-78; bishop Mich. dist. Am. Luth. Ch., Detroit, 1978-87; bishop NW Lower Mich. Synod Evang. Luth. Am., Lansing, 1988-95; chmn. bd. dirs. Inst. for Mission in U.S.A., Columbus, Ohio, 1982—; bd. dirs. Augsburg Fortress Pub. House, Wittenberg U. Author: Planning for Funerals, 1978; contbr. to Augsburg Sermon Series. Recipient Pub. Svc. citation Harper Woods City Coun., 1976, Recognition for Community Svc., Detroit Pub. Schs., 1974.

HOLLEB, DORIS B., urban planner, economist; b. N.Y.C., Oct. 26, 1922; m. Marshall M. Holleb, Oct. 15, 1944; children: Alan, Gordon, Paul. BA magna cum laude, Hunter Coll., 1942; MA, Harvard U., 1947; postgrad. U. Chgo., 1959-60, 65-66. Economist Fed. Res. Bd., Washington, 1943-44; freelance journalist, 1945-63; econ. cons. Chgo. Dept. City Planning, 1963-64; rsch. assoc. Ctr. Urban Studies, U. Chgo., 1966-78, sr. rsch. assoc., 1978-88, dir. Met. Inst., 1973-84, professorial lectr., 1979—; chmn., Francis W. Parker Sch. Ednl. Coun., 1963-80; cons., 1980-92; bd. dirs. Adlai E. Stevenson Inst., 1972-79; mem. adv. coun. Ctr. for the Study Democratic Inst., 1975-79; bd. dirs. Inter. Am. Found., 1980-84, Pacific Basin Inst., 1981—; mem. nat. adv. com. White House Conf. on Balanced Nat. Growth and Econ. Devel., 1978; mem. Northeastern Ill. Planning Commn., 1973-77; mem. Chgo. Met. Area Transp. Coun., 1980-84; mem. adv. coun. to Nat. Ctr. Rsch. on Vocat. Edn., Dept. Edn., 1979-82, Dept. State adv. com. internat. investment, tech. and devel., 1979-81; commr. Chgo. Plan Commn., 1986—; bd. dirs. Internat. Ctr. for Rsch. on Women, 1985-91. Author: Social and Economic Information for Urban Planning, 1968, Colleges and the Urban Poor, 1972; contbr. articles to profl. jours.; mem. editorial bd. Illinois Issues, 1977—, v.p. 1992—. Mem. Am. Inst. Cert. Planners, Am. Planning Assn., Am. Econ. Assn., Arts Club, Univ. Club, Quadrangle Club, Harvard Club N.Y.C., Phi Beta Kappa, Lambda Alpha.

HOLLEB, MARSHALL MAYNARD, lawyer; b. Chgo., Dec. 25, 1916; s. A. Paul and Sara (Zaretsky) H.; m. Doris Bernstein, Oct. 15, 1944; children—Alan R., Gordon P., Paul D. BA, U. Wis., 1937; MBA, Harvard U., 1939, IA, 1941, JD, 1942. Bar: Ill. 1947, U.S. Supreme Ct. 1960. Assoc. Levenson, Becker & Peebles, Chgo., 1947-51; ptnr. Yates & Holleb, Chgo., 1952-59, Holleb, Gerstein & Glass, Chgo., 1960-81; sr. ptnr. Holleb & Coff, Chgo., 1982—; dir. Acorn Fund; chmn. bd. dirs. Urban Assocs. Chgo., Inc. Life trustee Hull House Assn., pres., 1980-82; trustee Nat. Bldg. Mus., Chgo. Inst. Psychoanalysis; life trustee, gen. legal counsel Mus. Contemporary Art Chgo.; mem. adv. bd. Landmarks Preservation Coun., Fair Housing Ctr. Home Investments Fund, Citizens Sch. Com.; mem. vis. coms. Oriental Inst. and Visual Arts U. Chgo.; bd. dirs. Internat. Visitors Ctr., Mostly Music, Inc., Chgo. Fund on Aging and Disability; mem. Ill. Internat. Trade and Port Promotion Adv. Com., 1982, Chgo.'s Future Project Com. of Trust, Inc., 1982, Pacific Basin Inst.; mem. nat. adv. bd. on internat. edn. programs U.S. Dept. Edn., 1981, City Chgo. Local Cultural Devel. Commn.; pres. Chgo. Theater Preservation Group Ltd., sec., bd. dirs. Arts Club Chgo.; bd. dirs. Chgo. Maritime Soc.; mem. industry sector adv. com. on svcs. for trade policy matters U.S. Dept. Commerce, 1995—; mem. nat. adv. com. and del. White House Conf. on Aging 1971, 81; mem. Ill. Coun. on Aging, 1961-81, chmn., 1973-81; panel mem. Ill. Statewide Comprehensive Outdoor Recreation Plan; mem. weatherization adv. com. Ill. Dept. Bus. and Econ. Devel. 1975—; mem. Ill. appeal bd. SSS 1966-73; cons. Vt. research project HUD. 1st lt., U.S. Army 1943-46. Recipient Humanitarian of Yr. Henry Booth House award, Hull House Assn., 1979; Am. Heritage award Am. Jewish Com., 1986, Arts award Mostly Music Inc., 1986, City Brightener award Bright New City, Chgo., 1987. Mem. ABA, Ill. Bar Assn., Chgo. Bar Assn., Fed. Bar Assn., Am. Soc. Internat. Law, Am. Arbitration Assn. (nat. panel), Am. Inst. Planners, Nat. Assn. Housing and Redevel. Ofcls., Urban Land Inst., Lambda Alpha. Democrat. Clubs: Arts, Univ., Bryn Mawr Country, Execs. (Chgo.). Contbr. articles to profl. jours. Office: Holleb & Coff 55 E Monroe St Ste 4100 Chicago IL 60603-5702

HOLLENBECK, MARYNELL, municipal government official; b. Nashville, May 2, 1939; d. Lee B. and Beulah B. (Bradley) Reifel; children: Braeson, Danelle. BA, Iowa State U., 1976, MS, 1980; PhD, ABD, 1981. Cert. regulatory mgr. EPA, DOT, OSHA regulation. Dir. environ. svcs. Bd. Pub. Utilities, Kansas City, Kans.; prof. Southwest Mo. State U., Springfield, Mo.; instr. Iowa State U., Ames; profl. cons. to Springfield Newspapers, Inc., Victims of Domestic Violence, Springfield Health Dept., 1984-86, Southwest Ctr. for Ind. Living, 1986-88. Contbr. articles to profl. jours. Advisor Gamma Sigma Sigma, 1984-86; mem. Hazardous Materials Ctr. Rsch. Inst., Kansas City (Kans.) Hazardous Materials Adv. Bd.; mem. Greene County Ctrl. Dem. Com., 1981-86, Story County Ctrl. Dem. Com., 1977-81; v.p. bd. dirs. Battered Women's Program, 1985-86; bd. dirs., sec. Sherwood Ctr. for Exceptional Children. Recipient Bus. and Profl. Women award for Leadership and Service, 1976. Mem. Air & Waste Mgmt. Assn. (dir. midwest sect.), Am. Pub. Power Assn. (past chair environ. sect.), Nat. Assn. Hazardous Waste Generators, Gamma Sigma Delta, Phi Kappa Phi, Alpha Kappa Delta, Sigma Xi (E.A. Ross award for sci. rsch. 1977, Von Tungeln award for leadership, rsch. and svc. 1980). Unitarian. Office: 1211 N 8th St Kansas City KS 66101-2129

HOLLENBECK, SUE J., elementary education educator; b. Dubuque, Iowa, June 17, 1946; d. Irenaeus J. and Lois M. (Jorgensen) Timmerman; m. Michael D. Hollenbeck, July 23, 1966; children: Dean M., Dan T. 2 yr. teaching degree, Vernon County Tchrs. Coll., Viroqua, Wis., 1966; BS, U. Wis., Platteville, 1968; MS in Profl. Devel., U. Wis., La Crosse, 1988. Tchr. grades 1-7 Belmont (Wis.) Schs., 1966-67; tchr. art and music Shullsburg (Wis.) Schs., 1967-68; tchr. grade 1 Benton (Wis.) Pub. Schs., 1968-71; tchr. grades 1,2,3 DeSoto Schs., Ferryville, Wis., 1973-77; tchr. grade 1 DeSoto Schs., DeSoto, 1977-81; tchr. grade 6 DeSoto Schs., Stoddard, Wis., 1981-85, tchr. grade 4, 1985—; geography bee coord. DeSoto Sch. Dist., Stoddard, 1993-95; spelling bee coord., DeSoto Sch. Dist., 1981-91. Recipient Dist. Tchr. of Yr. award DeSoto Schs., 1981-82, Newspaper in Edn. award LaCrosse (Wis.) Tribune, 1983. Mem. NEA, ASCD, Wis. Edn. Assn., DeSoto Edn. Assn. (adv. bd. SIM 1983-95), Western Wis. Edn. Assn., Midwest Wis. Reading Coun. Home: RR 1 Stoddard WI 54658-9801

HOLLENSBE, RONDA LEE, accounting educator; b. Denison, Iowa, May 21, 1953; d. Walter Henry and Wiladene Marie Grell; m. Brant Wyatt Hollensbe, June 29, 1974; 1 child, Sonda. BS, Iowa State U., 1975; BSBA, U. N.D., 1979; MBA, Drake U., 1988. CPA; cert. mgmt. acct. Staff acct. Hogan & Hansen, Waterloo, Iowa, 1979-81, McGladrey & Pullen, Des Moines, 1985-86; trust officer Hawkeye Bank, Sibley, Iowa, 1981-82; instr. acctg. Iowa Lakes C.C., Estherville, 1982-84; prof. Acctg. Grand View Coll., Des Moines, 1986—. Sunday sch. tchr. Valley United Meth. Ch. Recipient Nat. 4-H Horse award, 1971; faculty scholar U. N.D., 1979. Mem. AICPA, Inst. Mgmt. Accts. (bd. dirs. 1990-91), Iowa Soc. CPAs (chairperson com. 1990-91, mem. com. 1987—). Democrat. Home: 512 36th St West Des Moines IA 50265-3915 Office: Grand View Coll 1200 Grandview Ave Des Moines IA 50316-1529

HOLLENSHEAD, ROBERT EARL, judge; b. St. Louis, July 24, 1940; s. Earl Finley and Marguerite Louise (Milburn) H.; m. Shirley Ann Kimmel, Dec. 28, 1974; children by previous marriage: Cynthia Estelle, David Hugh. B.A., U. Mich., 1963, JD, 1966. Bar: Mich. 1967, U.S. Dist. Ct. (ea. dist.) Mich. 1967, (we. dist.) Mich. 1972. Law clk., assoc. Langs, Molyneau & Armstrong, Detroit, 1966-67; assoc. firm Stommel Sharp Walsh O'Sullivan Beauchamp & Edson, Port Huron, Mich., 1971-72; adminstrv. law judge Mich. Pub. Service Commn., Lansing, 1972—; adj. prof. Cooley Law Sch., Lansing, 1977; faculty advisor Nat. Jud. Coll., 1982, 90. Served to capt. JAGC, U.S. Army, 1967-71. Mem. State Bar Mich. (coun. adminstrv. law sect. 1976-84, pub. utility law com., adminstrv. law judges com.), Mich. Assn. Adminstrv. Law Judges (v.p. 1975-76, pres.-elect 1991, pres. 1992-93), Nat. Assn. Regulatory Utility Commrs. (staff subcom. on adminstrv. law judges 1984-89), Phi Alpha Delta. Mem. Unity Ch. Home: 2415-11 Aurelius Rd Holt MI 48842 Office: Mich Pub Svc Commn PO Box 30221 6545 Mercantile Way Lansing MI 48909

HOLLI, MELVIN GEORGE, history educator; b. Ishpeming, Mich., Feb. 22, 1933; s. Walfred and Sylvia (Erickson) H.; m. Betsy Biggar, Aug. 12, 1961; children: Susan, Steven. BA, North Mich. U., 1957; MA, U. Mich., 1958, PhD, 1969. Curator manuscripts Bentley Libr., U. Mich., Ann Arbor, 1962-64; asst. prof., assoc. prof. history U. Ill., Chgo., 1965, prof., 1975—, chmn. dept., 1991-94; Fulbright prof. U. Finland, 1978, 89-90. Author: Reform in Detroit, 1969, Detroit, 1975, Ethnic Chicago, 1981, 3d edit., 1995 (nonfiction prize Soc. Midland Authors 1985, best book award Ill. Polit. Sci. Assn. 1985), Bashing Chicago Traditions, 1989, Restoration: Chicago Elects a New Daley, 1991, The Mayors: The Chicago Political Tradition, 1995; bd. editors: Urban Affairs Quar., 1992-95; editor: U. Ill. Press Ethnic History in Chicago book series. Mem. Am. Hist. Assn., Orgn. Am. Historians, Swedish Am. Hist. Soc. (mag. bd. 1990-93), Soc. Midland Authors (bd. dirs. 1989-93). Home: 1311 Ashland Ave River Forest IL 60305-1029 Office: Dept History U Ill Chicago IL 60680

HOLLIDAY, ROBERT JAMES, purchasing agent, county government official; b. Portsmouth, Va., Mar. 6, 1953; s. Kenneth William and Marilyn Louise (Jones) H.; m. Julie Anne Jurgens, Oct. 15, 1983; children: Thomas Michael, Allyson Aileen. AS, Black Hawk Coll., 1980. Mem. shipping/receiving sales promotion dept. John Deere Co., East Moline, Ill., 1975-81; timekeeper Bank Bldg. Corp., Bettendorf, Iowa, 1981-82; job corps recruiter Job Svc. Iowa, Davenport, 1982; purchasing specialist Scott County Courthouse, Davenport, 1982—; bus. mgr. Miss Iowa. Editor Nat. Chief Petty Officer's Assn. newspaper. Mem. com. camp steering subcom., adminstrn./fin. St. Paul Luth. Ch., Davenport. Mem. Am. Numismatic Assn. (com. pers. and awards coms.), Eastern Iowa Govtl. Purchasing Assn. (pres. 1991), Miss. Thespian Soc. (adminstrv. dir. 1994-95), Davenport Jaycees (pres. 1989-90), Iowa Jaycees (dist. dir. 1990-91, regional dir. 1991-92), Order of Demolay (chmn. adv. coun. Bettendorf chpt. 1994-95), Masons (past jr. warden Hamilton lodge), Scottish Rite (membership chmn. 100th anniversary 1995), Lions (3d v.p. 1995, pres. 1996), Shriners (Kaaba temple 1994—). Lutheran. Home: 2325 Elm St Davenport IA 52803 Office: Scott County Courthouse 416 W Fourth St Davenport IA 52801

HOLLINGSWORTH, GARY MAYES, Internet access provider company; b. Mexico, Mo., June 1, 1944; s. Allan Dee and Mabel Etta (Mayes) H.; m. Theresa Ann LaRoche, June 30, 1984; children: Lisa Marie, Allan Dee, Sarah Elizabeth. BS, N.E. Mo. State U., 1972; MA, Webster U., St. Louis, 1982. CPA, Mo. Staff announcer Sta. KXEO-KWWR-FM, Mexico, 1962-64, news dir., 1964-65, program dir., account exec., 1969-72; sr. acct. KPMG Peat, Marwick, St. Louis, 1972-75; audit mgr. T.G. Bancshares Co., St. Louis, 1975-76; group contr. Wetterau Inc., St. Louis, 1976-80; chief fin. officer Gen. Grocer Co., St. Louis, 1980-84; v.p., sec., bd. dirs. Dana Brown Pvt. Brands, Inc., St. Louis, 1984-92; exec. v.p., gen. mgr. Private Brands Coffee & Tea Co., St. Louis, 1992-93; nat. sales mgr. store brands Chock Full O' Nuts Corp., N.Y.C., 1993-96; exec. v.p. Inlink Comm., St. Louis, 1996—; mem. adj. faculty Maryville U., St. Louis, 1982-83, The Dive Shop of St. Louis, 1990—; bd. dirs. Phythe Group, Ltd., St. Louis. Mem. Zoning Bd. of Adjustment, Olivette, Mo.; mem. long-range planning commn. Univ. United Meth. Ch., University City, Mo., 1989-91; mem. bus. endowment fund, adv. coun. N.E. Mo. State U.; devel. bd. PARA QUAD, Inc., 1990—; pres. trustee Bon Aire Subdivsn., 1990. Capt. U.S. Army. Mem. AICPA, Mo. Soc. CPAs, Fin. Exec. Inst. (bd. dirs. St. Louis chpt. 1988—, pres. 1993—), Profl. Assn. Dive Instrs. (cert.), Clayton Jaycees (pres. 1979), M.C. Investment Club (pres. 1991-92), Masons. Methodist. Home: 14 Bon Aire Dr Saint Louis MO 63132-4301 Office: Inlink Comm Inc Ste 200 PO Box 410890 443 N New Ballas Rd Saint Louis MO 63141

HOLLIS, WILLIAM FREDERICK, information scientist; b. Cleve., May 25, 1954; s. Raymond Frederick and Elizabeth (Meyer) H.; m. Jo Anne Kohlenberg, June 25, 1977; children: George Anthony, Dawn Elizabeth. BS, Bowling Green State U., 1976; MLS, Kent State U., 1979, EdD, 1992. Cert. chemistry/physics educator Ohio. Info. specialist B.F. Goodrich Rsch. & Devel. Ctr., Breckville, Ohio, 1979-82; instr. libr. & info. sci. Coll. Wooster (Ohio), 1982-84; sr. info. specialist GenCorp Rsch., Akron, 1984, acting head tech. info., 1985, head tech. info ctr., 1986—; instr. sci. & tech. Stark Tech. Coll., Canton, Ohio, 1983-84. Elder United Ch. of Christ, Suffield, Ohio, 1986-89. Mem. Am. Chem. Soc., Am. Inst. Physics, Am. Soc. Info. Sci., Assn. Ednl. Communications & Tech. Home: 1547 Suffield Oaks Ln Mogadore OH 44260 Office: GenCorp Tech Ctr 2990 Gilchrist Rd Akron OH 44305-4418

HOLLIS-ALLBRITTON, CHERYL DAWN, retail paper supply store executive; b. Elgin, Ill., Feb. 15, 1959; d. L.T. and Florence (Elder) Saylors; stepparent Bobby D. Hollis; m. Thomas Allbritton, Aug. 10, 1985. BS in Phys. Edn., Brigham Young U., 1981; cosmetologist, 1981. Retail sales clk. Bee Discount, North Riverside, Ill., 1981-82, retail store mgr., Downers Grove, Ill., 1982, Oaklawn, Ill., 1982-83, St. Louis, 1983; retail tng. mgr. Arvey Paper & Office Products (divsn. Internat. Paper), Chgo., 1984, retail store mgr., Columbus, Ohio, 1984—. Republican. Mem. LDS Ch. Avocations: writing, reading, travel. Office: Arvey Paper & Office Products 431 E Livingston Ave Columbus OH 43215-5533

HOLLISTER, NANCY, state official. Lt. gov. State of Ohio, 1995—. Office: Office of Lt Governor Riffe Tower 77 S High St 30th Fl Columbus OH 43215-6108*

HOLLOWAY, DONALD PHILLIP, lawyer; b. Akron, Ohio, Feb. 18, 1928; s. Harold Shane and Dorothy Gayle (Ryder) H.; BS in Commerce, Ohio U., Athens, 1950; JD, U. Akron, 1955; MA, Kent State U., 1962. Bar: Ohio 1955. Title examiner Bankers Guarantee Title & Trust Co., Akron, 1950-54; acct. Robinson Clay Product Co., Akron, 1955-60; librarian Akron-Summit Pub. Library, 1962-69, head fine arts and music div., 1969-71, sr. librarian, 1972-82; pvt. practice law, Akron, 1982—. Payroll treas. Akron Symphony Orch., 1957-61; treas. Friends Library Akron and Summit County, 1970-72. Mem. Music Library Assn., ABA, Ohio Bar Assn., Akron Bar Assn., Ohio Library Assn., ALA, Nat. Trust for Hist. Preservation, Internat. Platform Assn., Soc. Archtl. Historians, Coll. Art Assn., Art Libraries North Am., Akron City Club, North Coast Soc. Republican. Episcopalian. Avocations: art and architecture, music, travel. Home: 601 Nome Ave Akron OH 44320-1682

HOLLOWAY, H(ARRY) REX, JR., osteopath; b. Kirksville, Mo., Jan. 22, 1930; s. H. Rex and Gertrud M. (Vogel) H.; m. Patricia Hammond, Jan. 27, 1951 (dec.); children: Susan, Steven, Margan, Elizabeth; m. Jacquelyne Ann Fletcher, June 28, 1984; children: John, Jacob. Student, Kalamazoo Coll., 1947-50; DO, Kirksville Coll. Osteo., 1954. Diplomate Am. Bd. Quality Assurance and Utilization Review Physicians. Intern Riverside Osteopathic Hosp., Trenton, Mich., 1954-55; pvt. gen. practice Profl. Ctr. Clinic, Taylor, Mich., 1955-89; physician advisor Seaway Hosp., Trenton, 1985—, Outer Dr. Hosp., Lincoln Park, Mich., 1986-89; dir. quality assurance/utilization rev. Riverside Osteopathic Hosp., Trenton, 1987—; physician advisor Heritage Hosp., Taylor, 1990-94; asst. med. dir. Health Plus of Mich., Bloomfield Hills, 1990-94; med. dir. Assoc. Physicians of Riverside Osteopathic Hosp., Trenton, 1987—; cons. Horizon Med. Assocs., Taylor, 1991-93; med. dir. employee health svc. Riverside Osteo. Hosp., 1994—. Fellow Am. Coll. Med. Quality; mem. Am. Osteopathic Assn., Mich. Assn. Osteopathic Physicians and Surgeons, Wayne County Osteopathic Assn., Grosse Ile Golf and Country Club, Grosse Ile Racquet Club. Office: Riverside Osteo Hosp 150 Truax St Trenton MI 48183-2151

HOLM, JOY ALICE, psychology educator, art educator, artist, goldsmith; b. Chgo., May 21, 1929; d. Alvin Herbert and Willette Eugenia (Miller) H. BFA, U. Ill., 1952; MS in Art Edn. Inst. Design, Ill. Inst. Tech., 1956; PhD in Edn., U. Minn., 1967. Tchr. art, Eng. West Chgo. H.S., 1952-54; instr., tchr. art J.S. Morton H.S. & Jr. Coll., Cicero, Ill., 1954-65; asst. prof. art & design Mankato (Minn.) State U., 1965-66; asst. prof. art Ill. State U., Normal, 1966-69; assoc. prof. art & design So. Ill. U., Edwardsville, 1969-71; assoc. prof. art, art edn. Winona (Minn.) State U., 1971-75; assoc. prof., chmn. dept. art St. Mary's Coll. of Notre Dame, Ind., 1975-76; assoc. prof. art & design, secondary, continuing edn. U. Wis., Eau Claire, 1976-78; assoc. prof. art & design Sch. Art & Design Kent (Ohio) State U., 1978-80; lectr. Jungian studies C.G. Jung Inst., Evanston, Ill., 1980-82; adj. assoc. prof. art edn. Sch. Art and Design, Sch. Edn. U. Ill., Chgo., 1981-82; lectr. U. Calif. Ext., Santa Cruz, 1983—; adj. prof. art edn., design San Jose (Calif.) State U., 1983-84; owner bus. designer-goldsmith Oak Park, Ill., 1980-82, Carmel, Calif., 1982-87; owner bus. designer-goldsmith Atelier XII, Winona, 1988—; curriculum cons. North Ctrl. Assn. Accreditation Team State of Ill., Edwardsville, 1970; regional cons. Supt. Pub. Instrn., Springfield, Ill., 1970; juror exhbns.; panelist, spkr., presenter confs., meetings. Contbr., cons. Alternative Medicine: A Definitive Guide, 1994; contbr. articles to profl. jours; one-woman shows: J. Sterling Morton H.S. & Jr. Coll., 1963, Russell Art Gallery, Bloomington, 1968, Owatonna (Minn.) Art Ctr., 1980, 86; exhbns. include La Grange (Ill.) Art League (Best of Show, 1st Place award prints), 1963, 64, Minn. Mus. Art, 1974, 75, Craft & Folk Art Mus., L.A., 1978, The Gallery Kent State U., 1978, 79, Saenger Nat. Small Sculpture and Jewelry Exhibit, 1978, Diamonds Internat., N.Y., 1978, Inst. Design Alumni, 1988, Internat. Biographical Ctr. Congress Exhbn., Edinburgh, Scotland, 1994, others. Fellow World Lit. Acad.; mem. AAUP, Nat. Art Edn. Assn. (rep. Wis. Women's Caucus Houston Conf. 1978, higher edn. divsn. 1961—), Am. Assn. Higher Edn., Coll. Art Assn., Soc. N.Am. Goldsmiths, Internat. Sculpture Ctr., Gemological Inst. Am., C.G. Jung Inst. (Chgo., San Francisco), Hon. Soc. Illustrators (hon.), Internat. Soc. Study of Subtle Energies and Energy Medicine, Assn. Transpersonal Psychology, Inst. Noetic Scis., Alpha Lambda Delta (hon.), Phi Kappa Phi (hon.). Methodist. Home: PO Box 183 Winona MN 55987-0183 Office: Atelier XII PO Box 183 Winona MN 55987-0183

HOLM, LEO JEROME, agricultural engineer, public speaker; b. Osceola, Wis., Feb. 11, 1945; s. Carl F. and Irene J. Holm; m. Aug. 8, 1965 (div.); children: Todd, Michelle, Jodi, Jason, Jill; m. Barbara L. Holm, May 12, 1995. B in Agrl. Engring., U. Minn., 1970. Registered agrl. engr., Minn., profl. engr. Agrl. engr. Minn. Dept. Hwys., St. Paul, 1970-74; asst. founds. engr. Minn. Dept. Transp., St. Paul, 1974-83, agrl. engr., prin., 1983-92, sect. dir. environ. svcs., 1992—; mem. rev. bd. State of Minn. Pesticide Licensing, 1989—; mem. grading com. Assoc. Gen. Contractors, 1988—; mem. integrated pest adv. bd., State of Minn., 1995—, mem. gov.'s wildflower task force, 1988-89, mem. gov.'s exec. task force on use of compost, 1983; spkr. numerous presentations and tng. workshops on erosion control, integrated vegetation mgmt., use of herbicides, 1983—. Co-author: Erosion Prevention Manual, 1970. Recipient Spl. Recognition award Fish and Wildlife Assn., 1991. Mem. Minn. Erosion Control Assn. (v.p. 1989-94, pres. 1994—). Home: 4350 Woodduck Cir Eagan MN 55122 Office: Minn Dept Transp 3485 Hadley Ave Oakdale MN 55128

HOLM, RUTH E., state legislator. Home: 620 1st St N Fargo ND 58102-4543 Office: ND Ho of Reps State Capitol Bismarck ND 58505*

HOLMAN, JAMES LEWIS, financial and management consultant; b. Chgo., Oct. 27, 1926; s. James Louis and Lillian Marie (Walton) H.; m. Elizabeth Ann Owens, June 18, 1948 (div. 1982); children: Craig Stewart, Tracy Lynn, Mark Andrew; m. Geraldine Ann Wilson, Dec. 26, 1982. BS in Econs. and Mgmt., U. Ill., Urbana, 1950, postgrad., 1950; postgrad. Northwestern U., 1954-55. Traveling auditor, then statistician, asst. controller parent buying dept. Sears, Roebuck & Co., Chgo., 1951-54; asst. to sec.-treas. Hanover Securities Co., Chgo., 1954-65; asst. to controller chem. ops. div. Montgomery Ward & Co. Inc., Chgo., 1966-68; controller Henrotin Hosp., Chgo., 1968; bus. mgr. Julian, Dye, Javid, Hunter & Najafi, Associated, Chgo., 1969-81, cons. 1981-84; vol. cons., adminstrv. asst. Fiji Sch. Medicine, Suva, 1984-86, cons., 1987-89; vol. bus. cons. U.S. Peace Corps, Honduras, 1989, cons., 1989—; cons., dir., sec.-treas. Comprehensive Resources Ltd., Glenview (Ill.), Wheaton (Ill.) and Walnut Creek, Calif., 1982; bd. dirs., sec.-treas. Medtran, Inc., 1980-83; sec. James C. Valenta, P.C., 1979-82; sponsored project adminstr. Northwestern U., Evanston, Ill., 1984. Sec., B.R. Ryall YMCA, Glen Ellyn, Ill., 1974-76, bd. dirs., 1968-78; trustee Gary Meml. United Meth. Ch., Wheaton, 1961-69, 74-77; bd. dirs. Goodwill Industries Chgo., 1978-79, DuPage (Ill.) Symphony, 1954-58, treas., 1955-58. Served with USN, 1944-46. Baha'i. Mem. Kiwanis (bd. dirs. Chgo. 1956-60, bd. dirs. youth found. 1957-60, pres. 1958-60). Home and Office: 1571 Burr Oak Ct # B Wheaton IL 60187-2709

HOLMAN, WILLIAM BAKER, surgeon, coroner; b. Norwalk, Ohio, Mar. 22, 1925; s. Merlin Earl and Rowena (Baker) H.; m. Jane Elizabeth Henderson, June 24, 1951; children: Craig W., Mark E., John S. BS, Capital U., 1946; MD, Jefferson Med. Coll., 1950. Intern, St. Luke's Hosp., Cleve., 1950-51, resident in gen. surgery, 1951-52, 55-57; practice medicine specializing in surgery, Norwalk, 1957-92; coroner Huron County, Norwalk, 1962-95, health commr., 1985-95; asst. clin. prof. surgery Med. Coll. Ohio at Toledo, 1984-92; Bd. dirs. REMSNO, Toledo, 1974-92, Norwalk Profl. Colony, 1983-92 ; mem. exec. com. Huron County Republican Com., Norwalk, 1980; bd. dirs. Fisher-Titus Med. Ctr., 1977-82, chmn., 1982; bd. dirs. Norwalk Area Health Svcs., Inc., 1987-92, 94—; mem. Norwalk City Sch. Bd. Edn., 1962-78, pres., 1964, 67-71, 78. Served to 1st lt. U.S. Army, 1952-54; Korea. Fellow ACS; mem. AMA, Ohio State Med. Assn., Huron County Med. Soc. (pres. 1978), Ohio State Coroners Assn., Nat. Assn. Med. Examiners. Lutheran. Avocations: boating; photography; stamp collecting; gun collecting. Home: 39 Warren Dr Norwalk OH 44857-2447 Office: Huron County Health Dept 180 Milan Ave Norwalk OH 44857-1168

HOLMBERG, RAYMON E., state legislator; b. Grand Fords, N.D., Dec. 10, 1943; s. Leslie Orwell and Nina Marchildon H.; children: Mariah Jay, Brady Jon. BS, U. N.D., 1965, MS, 1976. N.D. State sen. Dist. 17, 1977—; counselor, tchr. Grand Forks Pub. Sch.; mem. judiciary, polit. subdivns. and joint constrn. rev. coms.; formerly Rep. Caucus leader and mem. appropriations com. Mem. N.D. Centennial Commn., 1985-91; past bd. dirs., pres. Greater Grand Forks Comm. Theater. Named Champion of People's Right to Know, Legislator of Yr., NRA. Mem. Elks, Nat. and N.D. edn. assns. Office: 621 High Plains Ct Grand Forks ND 58201-7717*

HOLMEN, REYNOLD EMANUEL, chemist; b. Essex, Iowa, Oct. 23, 1916; s. John Algott and Clara Amelia (Christensen) H.; m. Betty Jane Heginbottom, June 20, 1942 (dec. 1990); children: Karen C. Maass, John R., Robert C.; m. Johnnie Mae Leak, Nov. 20, 1993. AB, Augustana Coll., Ill., 1936, MS, U. Mich., 1937, PhD, 1949. Rsch. chemist DuPont Co., Phila., also Flint, Mich., 1937-46; sr. rsch. chemist ctrl. rsch. dept. 3M Co., St. Paul, 1948-55, sect. mgr. tech. info. and patient liaison, 1955-57, sect. mgr. tech. info. and patent liaison, 1957-62, organic scouting mgr., 1959-62, mgr. R&D Lab., Reflective Product divsn., 1962-71, mgr. R&D spl. enterprises dept., 1971-82; v.p. R&D KEMSERCH, Inc., Onamia, Minn., 1984-96. Author: Kasimir Fajans: The Man and His Work, 1990. With med. corps. U.S. Army, 1941. Rackham scholar U. Mich., 1936-37. Mem. Am. Chem. Soc., AAAS, Phi Lambda Upsilon, Sigma Gamma Epsilon. Lutheran. Home: 2225 Lilac Ln White Bear Lake MN 55110

HOLMES, BARBARA DEVEAUX, college president; b. Miami, Fla., Nov. 26, 1947; d. Robert Eugene and Lula Mae (Stewart) Deveaux; m. Roosevelt Leon Holmes, June 19, 1970; children: Michael, Courtney. BA, Stetson U., 1969, MEd, 1972; PhD, U. Conn., 1974. Tchr. English, Seabreeze Sr. High Sch., Daytona Beach, Fla., 1969-72; dir. instnl. rsch. and planning Fayetteville (N.C.) State U., 1974-77, asst. to chancellor, 1977-79; dir. rsch. and planning Mo. Dept. Higher Edn., Jefferson City, 1979-81; v.p. adminstrv. svcs. Hillsborough Community Coll., Tampa, Fla., 1981-85; provost No. Va. Community Coll., Annandale, 1985-89; provost, v.p. acad. affairs Va. State U., Petersburg, 1989-90; pres. Milw. Area Tech. Coll., 1990—. Mem. Greater Milw. Com., Pvt. Industry Coun.; bd. dirs. Sinai Samaritan Med. Ctr. Fellow U. Conn. Grad. Sch., 1971-74. Mem. Am. Assn. Community and Jr. Colls., Nat. Coun. on Black Am. Affairs, Presidents Roundtable, Tempo, Rotary. Home: PO Box 10411 Conway AR 72033-2003

HOLMES, CARL DEAN, state representative, landowner; b. Dodge City, Kans., Oct. 19, 1940; s. Haskell Amos and Gertrude May (Swander) H.; m. Willynda Coley, Nov. 29, 1986; 1 child from previous marriage, Randall; 1 stepson, Bret Carpenter. Student, Kans. U., 1958-60; BBA, Colo. State U., Ft. Collins, 1962. Mgr. Holmes Motor Co., Plains, Kans., 1962-65; v.p. Holmes Chevrolet, Inc., Meade, Kans., 1962-78; owner Holmes Sales Co., Plains, 1965-80; land mgr. Holmes Farms, Plains, 1962—. Chmn. Greater S.W. Regional Planning Commn., Garden City, Kans., 1980-82; del. Rep. Dist. Conv., Great Bend, Kans., 1984, Rep. State Conf., Great Bend, Kans., 1984, Rep. State Conv., Topeka, 1984, Rep. Dist. Conv., Russell, Kans., 1988, Rep. State Conv., Topeka, 1988; City of Plains Councilman, 1977-82, Coun. pres., 1979-82, mayor, 1982-89; mem. 125 dist. Kans. Ho. Reps., Topeka, 1985—; precinct committeeman Meade County Reps., 1986-89; pres. Kans. Mayors Assn., 1984-85; pres. League Kans. Municipalities, 1987-

88; chmn. Kans. Ho. of Reps. Energy & Natural Resources com., 1993—, Kans. flood task force, 1993, Kans. Electric Utility Restructuring Task Force, 1996—; mem. energy standing com. Nat. Conf. State Legislatures State and Fed. Assembly, 1989-94; mem. environ standing com. NCSL-SFA, 1995—; mem. Am. Legis. Exch. Coun., Nat. Task Force on Energy, Environ. and Natural Resources. Mem. Liberal C. of C., Lions, Masons (past master), Scottish Rite, R.A.M., K.T., S.A.R. Methodist. Home and Office: PO Box 2288 Liberal KS 67905-2288

HOLMES, FREDERICK FRANKLIN, medical educator, physician, researcher; b. Tacoma, Wash., Oct. 16, 1932; s. Allan Russell and Margaret A. (Beistel) H.; m. Grace Elinor Foege, June 26, 1955; children: Heidi, Cynthia (dec.), Lisa, Theodore, Julia, Andrew. BA, Coll. Puget Sound, 1953; MD, U. Wash., 1957. Diplomate Am. Bd. Internal Medicine. Intern U. Kans. Med. Ctr., Kansas City, 1957-58, resident, 1963-65, fellow hematology, 1965-66; med. missionary Luth. Ch. Clinic, Menglembu, Malaysia, 1959-63; chief medicine Kilimanjaro Christian Med. Centre, Moshi, Tanzania, 1970-72; asst. prof. U. Kans. Med. Ctr., Kansas City, 1966-70, from assoc. prof. to prof., 1978-82, Edward Hashinger disting. prof., 1982—. Contbr. articles to profl. jours., chpts. to books. Vol. Am. Cancer Soc., Topeka, 1972—, nat. del., 1988. Recipient Humanitarian award U. Wash. Sch. Medicine, 1995; named Alumnus Cum Laude U. Puget Sound, 1985, Hon. Prof. Henan Med. U., 1989. Fellow ACP, Royal Soc. Medicine; mem. AAAS, AMA, Am. Fedn. for Aging Rsch., Am. Geriatrics Soc., Royal Soc. for Asian Affairs, Soc. for the Preservation and Encouragement of Barbershop Quartet Singing in Am. Lutheran. Office: U Kans Med Ctr 39th And Rainbow Kansas City KS 66160-7376

HOLMES, GARY S., real estate developer; b. Aug. 9, 1947. BA in Econs., U. Minn., 1970. Owner, pres. CSM Corp., St. Paul, 1976—; owner, dir. Century Bank, Norcraft Cos. Founder, bd. dirs. Mpls. Heart Inst.; active Abbott Northwestern Hosp., United Negro Coll. Fund, others. Mem. NAIOP, Nat. Apt. Assn., Minn. Multi-Housing Assn. Office: CSM Corp 2561 Territorial Rd Saint Paul MN 55114-1500

HOLMES, JACK EDWARD, political science educator; b. Wichita, May 16, 1941; s. Herbert Paul and Marguerite Elizabeth (Duerr) H. BA, Knox Coll., 1963; MA, U. Denver, 1967, PhD in Internat. Studies, 1972. Asst. prof. Hope Coll., Holland, Mich., 1969-72; dist. asst. Congressman Don Brotzman, Denver, 1973-75; asst. prof. Hope Coll., 1975-76, assoc. prof., 1976-87, prof., 1987—; chmn. polit. sci. dept. Hope Coll., 1988-95. Author: Mood/Interest Theory of American Foreign Policy, 1985; co-author: American Government Essentials and Perspectives, 1991, 94, 98. Campaign chmn. Ottawa County Reps., Holland, 1978, 82—. Capt. U.S. Army, 1967-69. Mem. Internat. Studies Assn., Am. Polit. Sci. Assn., Holy Cross Wilderness Def. Fund, Nat. Policy Forum (U.S. leadership in changing world policy coun.). Presbyterian. Home: 751 Riley St Holland MI 49424-1549 Office: Hope Coll 210 Lubbers Hall Holland MI 49422-9000

HOLMES, JEFFREY H., business executive; b. Milw., Jan. 30, 1950. V.p. Trend Cons. Inc., Menomonee Falls, Wis., 1988—. Office: Trend Cons Inc PO Box 850 Menomonee Falls WI 53052-0850

HOLMES, JOHN STEVEN, II, electrical engineer; b. Bloomington, Ind., Aug. 11, 1961; s. J. Steven and Anita L. (Ennis) H.; m. Julia M. Ritter, June 7, 1980; children: Julianna L., Jennifer K., Joshua W. AS, Purdue U., 1984, BS, 1986; MS in Electronics & Computer Tech., Ind. State U., 1995. Engr. in tng. Svc. technician Hess Duplicator, Inc., Indpls., 1981-83; asst. nat. svc. mgr. Standard Change Makers, Indpls., 1983-85, electronics engr., 1985-87; sr. design engr. Boehringer Mannheim Corp., Indpls., 1987—; adj. instr. Purdue U., Indpls., 1986—; cons. Autovend, Inc., Indpls., 1990-91, Loyal Mfg., Indpls., 1991, Utilitrack Corp., Columbus, Ind., 1994—. Mem. IEEE. Republican. Roman Catholic. Home: 6132 Ashway Ct Indianapolis IN 46224-2115 Office: Boehringer Mannheim PO Box 50457 9115 Hague Rd Indianapolis IN 46250-1045

HOLMES, KATHRYN LOUISE, medical technologist; b. Parsons, Kans., Nov. 20, 1937; d. Howard Morrison and Kathryn (Stallard) Frame; m. Lewis Dwayne Holmes; Mar. 4, 1956; children: Dee Wayne, Darin Wade, Melinda Kate Holmes Mitchell. AA, Parsons (Kans.) Jr. Coll., 1956; grad., St. John's Sch. Med. Tech., 1958; student, Pittsburg (Kans.) State U., 1959. CLT (HEW). Lab. supr. Mercy Hosp., Parsons, 1957-58, Howard Elliott, M.D., Pittsburg, 1958-62; med. technologist Kiowa County Hosp., Greensburg, Kans., 1966-68, Labette County Med. Ctr., Parsons, 1969-71; med. technologist and lab. supr. Fredonia (Kans.) Regional Hosp., 1971—. Vice-pres. Bd. Edn., Fredonia, 1989-92, pres. 1992-93; rep. Tri-County Spl. Edn. Co-Op, Independence, Kans., 1988-92, Kans. Sch. Bd. Assn. Govtl. Rels. Network, Fredonia, 1991-93. Named to Outstanding Women of Am., 1970. Mem. Fredonia Arts Coun., Fredonia C. of C., Wilson County Hist. Soc., Fredonia Geneaol. Soc., Gold Dust, Fredonia Regional Hosp. Aux., Sacred Heart Altar Soc., Fredonia Footlights, Am. Soc. Med. Technologists, Internat. Soc. Clin. Lab. Technologists. Roman Catholic.

HOLMES, RICHARD WINN, retired state supreme court justice, lawyer; b. Wichita, Kans., Feb. 23, 1923; s. Winn Earl and Sidney (Clapp) H.; m. Gwen Sand, Aug. 19, 1950; children—Robert W., David K. B.S., Kans. State U., 1950; J.D., Washburn U., 1953, LLD (hon.), 1991. Bar: Kans. 1953, U.S. Dist. Ct. 1953. Practice law Wichita, Kans., 1953-77; judge Wichita Mcpl. Ct., 1959-61; instr. bus. law Wichita State U., 1959-60; justice Kans. Supreme Ct., 1977-90, chief justice, 1990-95; ret., 1995; of counsel Goodell, Stratton, Edmonds & Palmer, Topeka, 1995—. Served with USNR, 1943-46. Mem. Kans., Topeka, Wichita bar assns., Am. Judges Assn. (founder, bd. govs. 1980-88). Home: 2535 SW Granthurst Ave Topeka KS 66611-1271

HOLMGREN, KIM JAMES, financial planner; b. Sheboygan, Wis., Jan. 5, 1951; m. Nancy S. Sullivan, June 19, 1981; children: Jennifer, Luke. BS, U. Wis., Milw., 1974, U. Wis., Stevens Point, 1976. CFP. Fin. planner AIG Investors Group, Mpls., 1987-89, Fin. Network, Crystal Lake, Ill., 1989—. Contbr. articles to newspapers. Mem. local sch. bd., Fox River Grove, Ill., 1993—. Mem. Chgo. Soc. CFPs (bd. dirs. 1993). Republican. Roman Catholic. Home: 514 Opatrny Dr Fox River Grove IL 60021-1119 Office: Fin Network Investment Corp # 2-A 44 N Virginia St Crystal Lake IL 60014-4106

HOLMGREN, MIKE, professional football coach; b. June 15, 1948; m. Kathy Holmgren; children: Gretchen, Emily, Jenny and Calla (twins). BS in Bus. Fin., U. So. Calif., 1970. Coach Lincoln High Sch., San Francisco, 1971-72, Sacred Heart High Sch., 1972-74, Oakgrove High Sch., 1975-80; quarterbacks coach, offensive coord. San Francisco State U., 1981-82; quarterbacks coach Brigham Young U., 1982-85; quarterbacks coach San Francisco 49ers, 1985-89, offensive coord., 1989-92; head coach Green Bay Packers, 1992—. Office: Green Bay Packers PO Box 10628 Green Bay WI 54307-0628

HOLMGREN, MYRON ROGER, social sciences educator; b. Willmar, Minn., Mar. 19, 1933; s. Alfred and Cleora Victora (Scott) H.; m. Ellen Mary Shaheen, June 9, 1957; children: Brian, Mary Jo Haas. BA, Mankato State U., 1958; MA, No. Colo. State U., 1959. Instr. Grinnell (Iowa) H.S., 1959-62, Joliet (Ill.) Jr. Coll., 1962-66; instr., fin. advisor Am. Express Fin. Advisors, Joliet, 1966-72; instr. Benedictine Coll., Atchison, Kans., 1973, Moraine Valley C.C., Palos Hills, Ill., 1974-75; instr. Minooka (Ill.) H.S., 1974—; dept. chmn. Minooka H.S., 1984-87, local dir. Xerox Award in Humanities, 1988-93, dir., coach Scholastic Bowl Team, 1976-93, chmn. philosophy & goals North Etrl. Accreditation, 1987-88. Author: Profitable Pricing Techniques, 1973; contbr. articles to profl. jours. Block chmn. March of Dimes, Am. Cancer Soc., 1989, 92-93; treas. bd. dirs. The Family Counseling Agy. of Will and Grundy Counties, 1996—. Asian Found. grantee, 1962. Mem. NEA, Ill. Edn. Assn., Ill. Assn. Econ. Tchrs., Ill. Consumer Edn. Assn., Internat. Platform Assn. Republican. Episcopal. Home: 1314 Douglas St Joliet IL 60435

HOLOWINSKI, JOHN JOSEPH, state executive; b. Chgo., June 4, 1956; s. Joseph John and Sophie Helen (Porzezinski) H.; m. Linda Jean LeRoy, Oct. 24, 1987. BA in Polit. Sci., DePaul U., 1979. Mgr. Substandard Specialists, Inc. Conn. Mutual Life Ins. Co., 1977-78; ins. agt. Sun Life Ins. Co. of Am., Lincolnwood, Ill., 1978-79; asst. dir. instnl. care Dept. of Health, Chgo., 1979-80, asst. planner, 1980-81, asst. to the budget dir., 1981-82; supr. Dept. of Econ. Devel., Chgo., 1982-88; fin. institutions examiner II Office of the Commr. of Savs. and Residential Fin., Chgo., 1988-92; program policy advisor Dept. of Fin. Instns., Chgo., 1992—. Active campaign mgr., field operative, ops. coord., press sec. various candidates. Democrat. Roman Catholic. Home: 5822 S Archer Ave Chicago IL 60638 Office: State of Ill Ste 15-700 100 W Randolph Chicago IL 60601

HOLSCHER, TODD TIMOTHY SCOTT, sales and marketing professional; b. Naperville, Ill., Oct. 28, 1965; s. Lee Carlos and Sandra Jo (Scott) H.; m. Jane Woodson Mullender, Nov. 3, 1993. BS in Journalism, U. Kans., 1989. Sales rep. Telecable Advt., Overland Park, Kans., 1989-90; account exec. More Than Media Mktg., Westport, Mo., 1990-91; rt. salesperson Frito-Lay, Inc., Lenexa, Kans., 1991-93, sales mgr., 1993-94; promotions decision group Frito-Lay, Inc., Topeka, 1993—, account sales mgr., 1994—. Mem. Phi Beta Kappa. Democrat. Episcopalian. Home: 3951 Vesper Ct Naperville IL 60564

HOLSCHUH, JOHN DAVID, federal judge; b. Ironton, Ohio, Oct. 12, 1926; s. Edward A. and Helen (Ebert) H.; m. Carol Eloise Stouder, May 25, 1952; 1 child, John David Jr. BA, Miami U., 1948; JD, U. Cin., 1951. Bar: Ohio 1951, U.S. Dist. Ct. (so. dist.) Ohio 1952, U.S. Ct. Appeals (6th cir.) 1953, U.S. Supreme Ct. 1956. Atty. McNamara & McNamara, Columbus, Ohio, 1951-52, 54; law clk. to Hon. Mell. G. Underwood U.S. Dist. Ct., Columbus, 1952-54; ptnr. Alexander, Ebinger, Holschuh, Fisher & McAlister, Columbus, Ohio, 1954-80; judge U.S. Dist. Ct. (so. dist.) Ohio, 1980—, chief judge, 1990—; adj. prof. law Ohio State U. Coll. Law, 1970; mem. com. on codes of conduct Jud. Conf. U.S., 1985-90. Pres. bd. dirs. Neighborhood House, Columbus, 1969-70; active United Way of Franklin County, Columbus. Fellow Am. Coll. Trial Lawyers; mem. Order of Coif, Phi Beta Kappa, Omicron Delta Kappa. Home: 2630 Charing Rd Columbus OH 43221-3628 Office: US Dist Ct 109 US Courthouse 85 Marconi Blvd Rm 109 Columbus OH 43215-2823

HOLSTEIN, JOHN CHARLES, state supreme court chief justice; b. Springfield, Mo., Jan. 10, 1945; s. Clyde E. Jr. and Wanda R. (Polson) H.; m. Mary Frances Brummell, Mar. 26, 1967; children: Robin Diane, Mary Katherine, Erin Elizabeth. BA, S.W. Mo. State Coll., 1967; JD, U. Mo., 1970; LLM, U. Va., 1995. Bar: Mo. 1970. Atty. Moore & Brill, West Plains, Mo., 1970-75; probate judge Howell County, West Plains, 1975-78, assoc. cir. judge, 1978-82; cir. judge 37th Jud. Cir., West Plains, 1982-87; judge so. dist. Mo. Ct. Appeals, Springfield, 1987-88, chief judge so. dist., 1988-89; judge Supreme Ct. Mo., Jefferson City, 1989—, chief justice, 1995-97; instr. bus. law S.W. Mo. State Coll., 1976-77. Lt. col. USAR, 1969-87. Mem. ABA. Office: Supreme Ct Mo PO Box 150 Jefferson City MO 65102-0150

HOLSTEN, MARK, state legislator; b. Sept. 5, 1965; m. Lisa; 1 child. BA, U. Minn. State rep. Minn. Ho. Reps., Dist. 56A, Minn., 1993—; tchr. U. St. Thomas. Home: 7790 Minar Ln N Stillwater MN 55082-9363*

HOLT, DOROTHY JEAN, critical care nurse; b. Granite City, Ill., Jan. 1, 1959; d. Eugene Marion and Evelyn Marie (DuBish) H. ADN, Belleville Area Coll., 1979; BSN cum laude, St. Louis U., 1983; postgrad., So. Ill. U. RN, Mo., Ill. Nurse orthopedics dept. St. Louis U. Med. Ctr., 1979-81, nurse coronary med. ICU, 1981-87, nutrition support nurse, dept. of surgery, 1987-88, clin. nurse specialist, div. cardiology, 1991-92, staff nurse coronary ICU, 1992-95; nurse cons./in-svc. coord. Profl. Med. Products, St. Louis Br., Greenwood, S.C., 1987; lectr. in field, 1987-88; rsch. nurse, 1991; study coord. NIH grant, 1988-91. Contbr. articles to profl. jours. Rsch. grantee NIH, 1988-90, 90-91. Mem. Sigma Theta Tau. Home: PO Box 309 Madison IL 62060-0309

HOLT, GLEN EDWARD, library administrator; b. Abilene, Kans., Sept. 14, 1939; s. John Wesley and Helen Laverne (Schrader) H.; m. Leslie Edmonds, Jan. 29, 1994; children from previous marriage: Kris, Karen, Gordon. BA, Baker U., 1960; MA, U. Chgo., 1965, PhD, 1975. From instr. to asst. prof. Wash. U., St. Louis, 1968-82; dir. honors div. Coll. Liberal Arts, U. Minn., 1982-87; exec. dir. St. Louis Pub. Libr., 1987—; cons. Chgo. Hist. Soc., 1976-79, Mo. Hist. Soc., St. Louis, 1979-87, NEH, Washington, 1980-82; mem. Online Computer Libr. Ctr. Pub. Libr. Adv. Com., 1991-95. Co-editor: St. Louis, 1975; co-author: Chicago, A Guide to the Neighborhoods, 1979. Bd. dirs. U. Mo. Sch. Libr. and Info. Sci., 1987—. Named Woodrow Wilson Found. fellow, 1963-64, Danforth fellow, 1963-68. Mem. Am. Libr. Assn., Pub. Libr. Assn., Spl. Librs. Assn. (St. Louis com. on fgn. rels.), Media Club. Home: 4954 Lindell Blvd Apt 4W Saint Louis MO 63108-1520 Office: St Louis Pub Libr 1301 Olive St Saint Louis MO 63103-2325

HOLT, JOHN MANLY, retired corporate lawyer; b. Chgo., July 15, 1925; s. Newton Ormand and Annie Marie (Hoover) H.; m. Barbara Lenfesty, Dec. 23, 1950; children: Mark B., Susan Holt Braun, Brent D. AB, DePauw U., 1950; JD, Ind. U., Indpls., 1956. Bar: Ind., D.C., U.S. Supreme Ct. Indsl. engr. Eli Lilly & Co., Indpls., 1952-54, pers. rep., 1954-55, supr., 1955-56, atty., 1956-64, asst. counsel, 1964-69, sr. counsel, 1969-77, sec., gen. counsel Pharm. divsn., 1977-87; ret., 1987; cons. Nat. Commn. on Marijuana & Drug Abuse, Washington, 1971-73; trustee Food and Drug Law Inst., Washington, 1976-87; chmn. adv. com. Ind. divsn. Addiction Svcs., 1976-82; mem. Ind. Prescription Abuse Study Commn., 1988. Mem. bd. visitors Ind. U. Sch. Law, Indpls., 1991-95; mem. Pepper Com., City/County Govt., Indpls., 1989, Tax Adjustment Bd. of Marion County, Indpls., 1989-94; bd. dirs. Indpls. Park Found., 1992-95. Served with U.S. Army, 1943-46, PTO, also 1950-52. Named Sagamore of the Wabash by Gov. of Ind., 1988; recipient Spirit of Philanthropy award Ind. U./Purdue U., 1991, Order of Constantine, Internat. Sigma Chi, 1989, Disting. Alumni Svc. award Ind. U. Sch. Law, Indpls., 1992. Mem. Ind. Bar Assn., Indpls. Bar Assn., D.C. Bar Assn., Svc. Club Indpls., columbia Club Indpls., Indpls. Alumni Assn. (dir. Ind. U. Sch. Law 1968-71, 92-95), Sigma Chi (pres. Indpls. chpt. 1964, chmn., 1985-95). Republican. Presbyterian. Home: 3421 Bay Road North Dr Indianapolis IN 46240-2970

HOLT, MARA DAWN, English educator; b. Weisbaden, Germany, May 24, 1951; came to U.S., 1951; d. William Joseph and Marguerite Angeline (Mangum) H.; m. Leon Anderson, June 3, 1986. BS in Psychology, U. Ala., 1973, MA in English, 1976; PhD in English, U. Tex., 1988. Instr. Ala. State U., Montgomery, 1977-80; asst. prof. Embry-Riddle Aero. U., Daytona Beach, Fla., 1980-83; from asst. to assoc. prof. Ohio U., Athens, 1983—; cons. reader Coll. Composition and Comm., 1993—, conf. proposal reviewer, 1993, 95, conf. nominating com., 1996. Mem. editl. bd. Jour. Tching. Writing, 1990-94; contbr. articles to profl. jours. Bklyn. Coll. Collaborative Learning Inst. fellow, 1980, 82; recipient Outstanding Tchg. award Coll. Arts and Scis./Ohio U., 1995; NEH grantee, 1990. Mem. NCTE, AAUP, Coun. Writing Program Adminstrs. Democrat. Presbyterian. Home: 15 Elizabeth Dr Athens OH 45701 Office: Ohio Univ English Dept Ellis 385 Athens OH 45701

HOLT, ROBERT ANTHONY, museum administrator; b. Leavenworth, Kans., Nov. 14, 1967; s. Robert Noah and Agnes Marie (Stein) H. BA in Sociology, St. Mary Coll., 1990. Day care dir. Leavenworth Cath. Sch., 1984-90; mus. exec. dir. Leavenworth County Hist. Soc., 1987—. Bd. dirs. Leavenworth Cath. Sch. Found., 1991—, Leavenworth Rural Water Dist., 1991—; chmn. Leavenworth Conv. and Vis. Bur., 1995—. Recipient Kans. Svc. award Kans. Dept. Tourism, 1989, 92, Key award Kans. 4-H, 1986. Mem. Am. Philatelic Soc., Kans. Hist. Soc., Kans. Mus. Assn., Leavenworth Stamp Club (pres. 1989-92), Eagles Club, Lions, KC (chancellor 1992-93, Grand Knight 1994—). Republican. Roman Catholic. Home: 30525 172nd St Leavenworth KS 66048-7538 Office: Leavenworth County Hist Soc 1128 5th Ave Leavenworth KS 66048-3213

HOLTER, ARLEN ROLF, cardiothoracic surgeon; b. Sullivan's Island, S.C., Feb. 1, 1946; s. Arne and Helen (Soderberg) H.; m. Elizabeth Anne Reid, Nov. 9, 1974; children: Matthew Arlen, Peter Reid, Andrew Douglas. BS, Stanford U., 1968; MS, U. Chgo., 1971, MD, 1973. Diplomate Am. Bd. Thoracic Surgery; Am. Bd. Surgery. Intern in surgery Mass. Gen. Hosp., Boston, 1973-74, resident in surgery, 1974-78; sr. registrar in cardiac surgery Southampton Chest Hosp., Eng., 1978; resident in cardiac surgery Yale U., New Haven, 1978-80; pvt. practice medicine specializing in cardiothoracic surgery Mpls., 1980—; instr. surgery Yale U., 1979-80. Contbr. articles to profl. jours. Recipient Franklin McLean rsch. award U. Chgo., 1973. Fellow ACS, Am. Coll. Cardiology, Am. Coll. Chest Physicians; mem. Soc. Thoracic Surgeons, Am. Heart Assn., Mpls. Acad. Medicine, Pan Pacific Sur. Soc. Lutheran. Office: Cardiac Surg Assocs 920 E 28th St Ste 420 Minneapolis MN 55407

HOLTHAUS, THOMAS ANTHONY, hospital administrator; b. Melrose, Minn., Feb. 20, 1941; s. Andrew Joseph and Leona (Hofmann) H.; m. Elizabeth Nelson, Oct. 20, 1970. BA, U. Minn., Morris, 1966. Trainee med. adminstrn. VA Hosp., Fargo, N.D., 1966-67; asst. chief med. adminstrn. svc. VA Hosp., Ft. Meade, S.D., 1967-69, Lexington, Ky., 1969-70; chief med. adminstrn. svc. VA Hosp., Saginaw, Mich., 1970-71, Tacoma, Wash., 1971-74; hosp. adminstr. specialist VA Cen. Office, Washington, 1974-76; trainee, asst. dir. VA Hosp., Castle Point, N.Y., 1976-77; assoc. dir. VA Hosp., Butler, Pa., 1977-79, Marion, Ind., 1979-81, Little Rock, 1981-84, San Juan, P.R., 1984-86; dir. VA Med. & Regional Office, Togus, Maine, 1986-90, VA Hosp., St. Cloud, Minn., 1990—; mem. faculty mgmt. coll. VA Region 2, Albany, N.Y., 1988-90. Mem. Am. Acad. Med. Adminstrs., Assn. Mil. Surgeons of U.S., Sr. Exec. Svc., Am. Legion, Kiwanis, Eagles, Elks. Served with U.S. Army, 1960-63. Roman Catholic. Home: 6625 Riverview Loop NW Sauk Rapids MN 56379-9323 Office: Vet Affairs Med Ctr 4801 8th St N Saint Cloud MN 56303-2015

HOLTKAMP, DORSEY EMIL, medical research scientist; b. New Knoxville, Ohio, May 28, 1919; s. Emil H. and Caroline E. (Meckstroth) H.; m. Marianne Church Johnson, Mar. 20, 1942 (dec. 1956); 1 son, Kurt Lee, 1 stepchild; m. Marie P. Bahm Roberts, Dec. 20, 1957 (dec. 1982); 2 stepchildren; m. Phyllis Laurence Bradfield, Sept. 1, 1984; 3 stepchildren. Student, Ohio State U., 1937-39; AB, U. Colo., 1945, MS, 1949, PhD, 1951, student Sch. Medicine, 1941-42, 46-49. Sr. rsch. scientist biochemistry sect. Smith, Kline & French Labs., Phila., 1951-57, endocrine-metabolic group leader, 1957-58; head endocrinology dept. Merrell-Nat. Labs. div. Richardson-Merrell, Inc., Cin., 1958-70, group dir. endocrine clin. rsch., med. rsch. dept., 1970-81; group dir. med. rsch. dept. Merrell Dow Pharms. subs. Dow Chem. Co., Cin., 1981-87; ind. cons. in med. rsch. Lebanon, Ohio, 1987—. Contbr. articles to profl. publs. U. Colo. Med. Sch. fellow, 1946, biochemistry rsch. fellow, 1948-51. Fellow AAAS; mem. AMA (affiliate), Am. Soc. Clin. Pharmacology and Therapeutics, Endocrine Soc., Am. Fertility Soc., Am. Chem. Soc., Am. Soc. Pharmacology and Exptl. Therapeutics, N.Y. Acad. Sci., Soc. Exptl. Biology and Medicine, Am. Assn. Lab Animal Scis., Internat. Soc. for Reproductive Medicine, Pacific Coast Fertility Soc., Reticuloendothelial Soc., Internat. Platform Assn., Sigma Xi, Nu Sigma Nu. Republican. Presbyterian. Home and Office: 130 S Liberty Keuter Rd Lebanon OH 45036-9333

HOLTZ, ALAN STEFFEN, SR., surgeon; b. Moline, Ill., Feb. 5, 1922; s. Gustav and Clara Helena (Steffen) H.; m. Janet Ellen Wright, Dec. 27, 1950 (dec. 1995); children: Alan S. Jr., Janet Ann. BA in Biology, U. Mo., 1947, BS in Medicine, 1949; D in Medicine, Washington U., St. Louis, 1951. Diplomate Am. Bd. Surgery. Intern, surg. resident St. Louis City Hosp., 1951-56, dir. emergency dept., 1957-66, fellow in surgery, 1962; chief resident surgeon U. N.C. Meml. Hosp., Chapel Hill, 1956-57; pvt. practice, staff surgeon St. Joseph Hosp., Kirkwood, Mo., 1957-84, v.p. med. affairs, 1984-87; field staff surveyor Am. Coll. Surgeons Commn. on Cancer, Chgo., 1988—; bd. dirs. Grace Hill Neighborhood Health Ctr., St. Louis, 1988—. Staff sgt. U.S. Army, 1942-46, ETO; col. USAR, 1979-82. Fellow ACS; mem. St. Louis Med. Soc., St. Louis Surg. Soc., Nathan A. Womack Surg. Soc. Democrat. Episcopalian. Home: 4525 Laclede Ave Saint Louis MO 63108-2152

HOLTZ, DANIEL ALEXANDER, financial consultant; b. Elkhart, Ind., Dec. 6, 1961; s. Donald J. and Carol (Bailey) H.; m. Rita Maria Yadevia, Nov. 26, 1994. BA, Ind. U., 1985; MS, London Sch. Econs., 1989; MBA, U. Chgo., 1990. Investment banker Merrill Lynch, N.Y.C., 1988, 90-91; fin. cons. Merrill Lynch, Clearwater, Fla., 1991-93, Roney & Co., Elkhart, Ind., 1993—. Adminstrv. asst. Ind. House Ways and Means Com., 1985-87; mem. St. Vincent Youth Group, 1994—; state del. Rep. Party, 1993—, precinct committeeman. Mem. Rotary. Republican. Roman Catholic. Home: 300 Stratford Pl Elkhart IN 46516-4393 Office: Roney & Co # 303 121 W Franklin St Elkhart IN 46516-3239

HOLTZ, GLENN EDWARD, band instrument manufacturing executive; b. Detroit, Jan. 15, 1938; s. Edward Christian and Evelyn Adele (Priehs) Foutz H.; m. Mary Eleanor Russell, Nov. 25, 1981; children by previous marriage: Robert, Kimberly, Rene, Letitia, Kimberly, Pamela. B. Mus. Edn., U. Mich., 1960, M. Mus. Edn., 1964; cons. motivation student Personnel Dynamics, Mpls., 1980. Mus. tchr. Middleville H.S. (Mich.), 1960-62; dist. mgr. Selmer Co., Elkhart, Ind., 1965-74, sales mgr., 1974-76; pres. Knapp Mus. Co., Grand Rapids, Mich., 1976-80; v.p. mktg. sales Gemeinhardt/CBS, Elkhart, 1981-83, gen. mgr., 1983—; v.p. CBS, 1985; pres., CEO Gemeinhardt Co., Inc.; pres., bd. dirs. Vandercook Coll. Mus., also trustee. Dist. gov. Lion's Internat., Jackson, Lansing, Battle Creek, Mich., 1970-71; pres. Middleville Bd. Edn., 1964-66; bd. dirs. Midwest Band and Orch.; mem. bd. music Ind. Coun. Recipient Disting. award Lion's Internat., Mich., 1971. Mem. Nat. Assn. Band Instrument Mfrs. (pres. 1986-88), Am. Music Conf. (bd. dirs. 1987—, past pres. nat. Fla. ind. coun.), Nat. Assn. Music Merchants (bd. dirs.). Republican. Office: Gemeinhardt PO Box 788 Elkhart IN 46515-0788

HOLTZ, LOUIS LEO, college football coach; b. Follansbee, W.Va., Jan. 6, 1937; m. Beth Barcus, July 22, 1961; children: Luanne, Skip, Kevin Richard, Elizabeth. BA, Kent State U., 1959; MA, U. Iowa, 1961. Asst. football coach U. Iowa, Iowa City, Coll. William and Mary, Williamsburg, Va., U. Conn., Storrs, U. S.C., Columbia, Ohio State U., Columbus; head football coach Coll. William and Mary, 1969-71, N.C. State U., Raleigh, 1972-75; coach N.Y. Jets, 1976; head football coach U. Ark., Fayetteville, 1977-83, U. Minn., Mpls., 1983-85, Notre Dame U., Ind., 1986—. Author: Kitchen Quarterback, Fighting Spirit. Named NCAA Dist. Coach of Yr., 1973, Nat. Coach of Yr. Football Writers, Sporting News, 1977; S.W. Conf. Coach of Yr. AP, UPI, 1979; team Nat. Champions, 1988, longest consecutive winning streak (23), 1988-89; named Nat. Coach of Yr., 1988. Roman Catholic. Office: U Notre Dame Athletic Dept Notre Dame IN 46556

HOLTZEE, JON B., program specialist; b. Arlington Heights, Ill., Oct. 10, 1962; s. Donald Peter and Sharon Lyn (Schultz) H.; m. Diana Carole Turowski, Nov. 30, 1991. BS in polit. sci., No. Ill. U., 1985. Customer svc. mgr. Amoco Motor Club, DeKalb, Ill., 1987-88; mktg. rep. KDK, DeKalb, 1989; program specialist Office of Speaker Ill. Ho. Reps., Springfield, 1989—; regional dir. Il. Ho. Dem. Majority, Springfield, 1992—; campaign cons.; Strauss for Alderman, DeKalb, Ill., 1993, Connes for Alderman, Rockford, Ill., 1993, Ill. Ho. Dem. Majority, Springfield, 1989-92. County bd. mem. DeKalb County Bd., Sycamore, Ill., 1984. Mem. Am. Ski Assn. Presbyterian. Home: 822 S MacArthur Blvd Springfield IL 62704 Office: Office Dem Leader 1114 Stratton Bldg Springfield IL 62706

HOLTZER, MARILYN EMERSON, physical chemist, educator; b. East St. Louis, Ill., July 22, 1938; d. Robert August and Ethel Ruth (Hodges) Emerson; m. Alfred Melvin Holtzer, June 24, 1969; children: Rachel, Dan. AB in Math., Washington U., St. Louis, 1960, AM in Chemistry, 1963, PhD in Chemistry, 1966. Instr. Washington U., 1972-80, rsch. asst. prof., 1990—; asst. prof. Webster U., Webster Groves, Mo., 1967-69; instr. John Burroughs Sch., St. Louis, 1969-70; vis. asst. prof. U. Mo., St. Louis, 1971-72; vis. prof. chemistry Chiba (Japan) U., 1992. Exhibited fiber art in various shows including St. Louis Artist's Guild; one-person show Fiber folding AAAS, Washington, 1993; contbr. articles to profl. jours. Shell fellow, 1964; recipient Du Pont Rsch. award, 1963. Mem. Biophys. Soc., St. Louis Weavers' Guild (past sec., treas., exhibit chmn.), St. Louis Artists' Guild (Arachne prize 1977, 79, Crawford prize 1980, 83), Handweaver's Guild Am., Midwest Weavers' Conf. Office: Washington U Dept Chemistry Campus Box 1134 One Brookings Dr Saint Louis MO 63130

HOLTZMAN, ROBERTA LEE, French and Spanish language educator; b. Detroit, Nov. 24, 1938; d. Paul John and Sophia (Marcus) H. AB cum laude, Wayne State U., 1959, MA, 1973; MA, U. Mich., 1961. Fgn. lang. tchr. Birmingham (Mich.) Sch. Dist., 1959-60, Cass Tech. High Sch., Detroit, 1961-64; from instr. to prof. of French and Spanish Schoolcraft Coll., Livonia, Mich., 1964-84; chair French and Spanish depts. Schoolcraft Coll., 1984—. Trustee Cranbrook Music Guild, Ednl. Community, Bloomfield Hills, Mich., 1976-78. Recipient Fulbright-Hays award, Fulbright Commn., Brazil, 1964. Mem. AAUW, NEA, MLA, Nat. Mus. Women in Arts (co-founder 1992), Am. Assn. Tchrs. of Spanish and Portuguese, Am. Assn. Tchrs. of French, Mich. Edn. Assn. Office: Schoolcraft Coll 18600 Haggerty Rd Livonia MI 48152-3932

HOLZBACH, RAYMOND THOMAS, gastroenterologist, author, educator; b. Salem, Ohio, Aug. 19, 1929; s. Raymond T. and Nelle A. (Conroy) H.; m. Lorraine E. Cozza, May 26, 1956; children—Ellen, Mark, James. BS, Georgetown U., 1951; MD, Case Western Res. U., 1955. Diplomate Nat. Bd. Med. Examiners, Am. Bd. Internal Medicine. Intern, asst. resident U. Ill. Research and Edn. Hosps., Chgo., 1955-56; sr. asst. resident medicine Cleve. Met. Gen. Hosp., 1959-60; asst. chief gastroenterology Case Western Res U., 1961-63; physician Gastroenterology Unit U. Hosps. of Cleve., 1961-63; instr. medicine Case Western Res. U. Sch. Medicine, Cleve., 1961-64; clin. instr. medicine Case Western Res. U. Sch. Medicine, 1964-71; head gastrointestinal research unit, assoc. physician div. medicine St. Luke's Hosp., Cleve., 1967-73; dir. div. gastroenterology St. Luke's Hosp., 1970-73; head gastrointestinal research unit dept. medicine Cleve. Clinic Found., 1973—; vis. prof. numerous instns. including Mayo Med. Sch., 1974, U. Calif., San Diego, 1977, U. Heidelberg, 1978, U. Pa., 1979, U. Zurich, 1980, U. Munich, 1982, U. Minn. Med. Ctr., 1985, med. ctrs., numerous Japanese univs., 1985, 92, Karolinska Inst., 1986, Royal Soc. London, 1987, Pa. State U. Sch. Med., U. Helsinki, RWTH-Aachen, Düsseldorf, Fed. Republic of Germany, U. Groningen, Utrecht, U. Amsterdam, The Netherlands, 1989, U. Perugia, Italy, Va. Commonwealth U.-Med. Coll. Va., Richmond, Christ Ch. Sch. Medicine, U. Otago, New Zealand, SUNY, Buffalo Sch. Medicine, 1990, Pontifical/Cath. U. Chile Sch. Medicine, 1991, Hiroshima U. Sch. Medicine, 1992, Kyoto U. Sch. Medicine, 1992, Sch. Medicine U. Jikei, Tokyo, 1992, Tel Aviv U., Israel Sch. Medicine, 1995, U. Leipzig, Germany, 1996, U. Heidelberg, Germany, 1995; lectr. in field. Mem. editl. bd. Gastroenterology jour., 1984-89; contbr. revs. and articles to med. jours. Served to capt. USAF, 1957-59. Recipient Alexander von Humboldt Found. Spl. Program award, 1978, 82. Fellow ACP; mem. ABA, Am. Gastroent. Assn. (rsch. com. 1976-79), Ctrl. Soc. Clin. Rsch., Am. Assn. for Study of Liver Diseases, AAAS, Am. Soc. Biol. Chemists, Am. Physiol. Assn., Biophys. Soc., Internat. Assn. Study of Liver, Am. Fedn. Clin. Rsch., Midwest Gut Club, Am. Soc. Clin. Nutrition, Ohio State Med. Assn., Sigma Xi. Unitarian. Home: 39251 Lander Rd Chagrin Falls OH 44022-2146 Office: Cleve Clin Found 9500 Euclid Ave Cleveland OH 44195-0001

HOLZER, EDWIN, advertising executive; b. June 22, 1933. MusB, Yale U., 1954, MusM, 1955; postgrad., Ind. U., 1956. Acct. exec. Benton & Bowles Inc., N.Y.C., 1959-62; account supr. William Esty Co., N.Y.C., 1962-66; account supr. Grey Advt. Inc., N.Y.C., 1966-68, mgmt. supr., 1968-70; exec. v.p. Grey-North Inc., Chgo., 1970-73, pres., CEO, COO, 1973-85; chmn., CEO, Grey Chgo. (name changed to LOIS/GGK 1988), 1988; chmn., pres., CEO LOIS/USA, Chgo., 1988—. Office: LOIS/USA 2300 Merchandise Mart Chicago IL 60654

HOM, THERESA MARIA, osteopathic physician; b. Detroit, Oct. 25, 1957; d. Richard Gay and Elizabeth Marie (Moye) H.; m. Rick L. Anderson, June 30, 1990 (dec. Dec., 1994). BS in Biology, U. Mich., 1979; DO, Mich. State U., 1984. Diplomate Am. Osteo. Bd. Gen. Practice. Intern Oakland Gen. Hosp., Madison, Mich., 1984-85; resident, gen. practice Doctors Hosp., Columbus, Ohio, 1985-86; family physician Madison Clinic, 1986-87, Community Family Health Ctr., Columbus, 1987—; clin. prof. Ohio U. Coll. Osteo. Medicine, Columbus, 1989—; apptd. osteo. mem. Ohio State Med. Bd., 1990-93, supervisory mem., 1993, v.p., 1993. Physician Columbus Free Clinic, 1990. Featured poet Larry's Poetry Forum, Columbus, 1991. Mem. Am. Osteo. Assn., Am. Med. Women's Assn., Ohio Osteo. Assn. (del. 1989, 93), Pax Christi Columbus (coord. program 1989-91), Am. Coll. Osteo. Gen. Practice, Am. Acad. Med. Acupuncturists. Roman Catholic. Office: The Doctor's Office 400 E Mound Columbus OH 43215

HOMAN, GARY REX, chemist; b. Hesperia, Mich., Aug. 30, 1951; s. Rex Jr. and Arlene Marie (Thompson) H.; m. Margene Eloise Place, July 22, 1972; children: Trisha, Tonya, Matthew. AAS in Chemistry, Ferris State U., 1973; BS in Chemistry, Saginaw Valley State U., 1979. Chem. technician Dow Corning Corp., Midland, Mich., 1973-79, devel. chemist, 1979-83, R&D group leader, 1983-86, fin. controller, 1986-88, global R&D mgr., 1988-93; gen. mgr. Pressure Sensitive Industries, 1993—. Author tech. publs. Participant Boys State of Am., Mich., 1967; chmn. loaned exec. United Way, Midland County, 1989. Mem. Am. Chem. Soc. Republican. Methodist. Home: 2801 Dawn Dr Midland MI 48642-4754

HOMAN, JAMES D., engineering systems administrator; b. Le Mars, Iowa, June 15, 1963. AS, Western Iowa Tech., Sioux City, 1989. Design engr. Gomaco Corp., Ida Grove, Iowa, 1989-91; project mgr. Gomaco Corp., Ida Grove, 1991-94, engring. systems administrator, 1994—. Vol. leader Boy Scouts Am., Ida Grove, 1992—. Office: Gomaco Corp Hwys 59 & 175 Ida Grove IA 51445

HOMBS, CHARLTON D., stockbroker; b. Booneville, Mo., June 2, 1970; s. Harold K. and Nancy L. (Green) H. BS, U. Mo., 1992. Stockbroker Edward D. Jones & Co., Fenton, Mo., 1992—. Active Devel. Assn., Fenton, 1994. Mem. C. of C. Baptist. Office: Edward D Jones & Co 52 Fenton Plz Fenton MO 63026-4110

HOMBURGER, THOMAS CHARLES, lawyer; b. Buffalo, Sept. 16, 1941; s. Adolf and Charlotte E. (Stern) H.; m. Louise Paula Shemin June 6, 1965; children: Jennifer Anne, Richard Ephraim, Kathryn Lee. BA, Columbia U., 1963, LLB, 1966. Bar: Ill. 1966, U.S. Dist. Ct. (no. dist.) Ill. 1966. Assoc. and ptnr. Sonnenschein, Carlin, Nath & Rosenthal, Chgo., 1966-86; ptnr., chmn. real estate dept. Bell, Boyd & Lloyd, Chgo., 1986—; adj. prof. law John Marshall Law Sch., Chgo., 1989—. Contbr. chpts. and articles to legal publs. Chmn. Chgo. regional bd. Anti-Defamation League, B'nai Brith, 1986-88; mem. nat. exec. com., nat. vice chmn. Anti-Defamation League, Glencoe Bd. Edn., Ill., 1984-89; bd. dirs., exec. com. Ill. Ambs. Mem. ABA (real property div., probate & trust law sect., fin. subcom.), Ill. Bar Assn. (real property sect.), Chgo. Bar Assn. (chmn. real property law com. 1984-85), Am. Coll. Real Estate Lawyers, Law. Club of Chgo., Chgo. Mortgage Attys. Assn. (pres. 1975-77), Lamda Alpha Internat., Standard Club, Metropolitan Club. Home: 123 Euclid Ave Glencoe IL 60022-2106 also: 880 N Lake Shore Dr Apt 12H Chicago IL 60611 Office: Bell Boyd & Lloyd 70 W Madison St Ste 3300 Chicago IL 60602-4207 also: 880 N Lake Shore Dr Apt 12H Chicago IL 60611

HOMEYER, AUGUST HENRY, former chemical company executive; b. Chgo., Apr. 21, 1908; s. Henry and Johanna Rebecca (Klipp) H.; m. Ruth Marianna Hemminghaus, Oct. 13, 1934; children: Bruce A., Charles F. BSChemE, Washington U., St. Louis, 1930; MS in Chemistry, Pa. State U., 1931, PhD in Chemistry, 1933. Chemist, engr. Mallinckrodt, Inc., St. Louis, 1933-49, assoc. dir. rsch., 1949-62, also bd. dirs., 1950-73, gen. mgr. internat. div., 1962-73, corp. v.p., 1969-73, cons., 1973-83, retired, 1983; mng. dir. Mallinckrodt Can., Inc., Pt. Claire, Que., Can., 1963-73, Lab. Rey Mol, S.A. de C.V., Mexico City, 1963-73, Byk-Mallinckrodt GmBH, Dietzenbach, Fed. Republic Germany, 1966-73, Daiichi Radioisotope Labs., Tokyo, 1968-73. Contbr. 12 articles to profl. jours.; 33 patents in field. Recipient Engring. Alumni Achievement award Washington U., 1981, Disting. Alumni award, 1995. Mem. AAAS, Am. Chem. Soc. (chmn. St. Louis sect.), Am. Inst. Chemists. Home: 9033 Greenridge Dr Saint Louis MO 63117-1005

HOMOLKA, C(ALVIN) DEAN, II, lawyer; b. Wichita, Kans., Nov. 9, 1950; s. Calvin Dean and Marjorie Nadine (Parmenter) H. BA in Econs., U. Kans., 1975, JD, 1979. Bar: Kans. 1979. Assoc. Render & Kamas, Wichita, 1981-82; pvt. practice Wichita, 1982-. Vol. fundraiser Goodwill, Easter Seals, 1987-90. Mem. Kans. Bar Assn., Wichita Bar Assn., Wichita Ind. Bus. Assn., Downtown Y's Men, U. Kans. Alumni Assn. Office: 200 E First St #542 Wichita KS 67202-2110

HONADLE, GEORGE HOLMES, social sciences educator; b. Trenton, N.J., July 25, 1944; s. Harold Eugene and Ruth (Holmes) H.; m. Beth Walter, July 30, 1977; 1 child, Forrest Jeffrey. AB, Dickinson Coll., 1966; postgrad. diploma, U. Edinburgh, Scotland, 1972; MPA, Syracuse U., 1973, PhD, 1978. Sr. staff mem. Devel. Alternatives, Inc., Washington, 1976-86; pvt. cons., 1986-95; assoc. dir., adj. prof., sr. rsch. assoc. Ctr. for Natural Resource Policy and Mgmt., U. Minn., St. Paul, 1991-95; advisor on sustainable devel. initiative Environ. Quality Bd., St. Paul, 1992-94; adv. bd. oversight Great Lakes Protection Fund, Chgo., 1993-95; adv. panel on natural resources Minn. State Demographer, St. Paul, 1994-95; mem. Minn. Roundtable Sustainable Devel., 1996—. Sr. author: Implementation for Sustainability, 1985; sr. editor: International Development Administration, 1979; contbr. chpts. to books and articles to profl. jours. Peace corps vol. Ministry of Agr., Malawi, 1967-70; citizen advisor Chisago County Comprehensive Water Plan, Center City, Minn., 1990-92. Rsch. grantee N.W. Area Found., St. Paul, 1991-92. Mem. ASPA (nat. chmn. sect. on internat. and comparative adminstrn. 1986-87), Izaak Walton League Am. (chpt. bd.), Soc. for Conservation Biology, Wildlife Mgmt. Inst., Internat. Assn. Camel Breeders (life mem.), Pi Alpha Alpha. Unitarian. Home: Hidden Creek Farm 39844 Poor Farm Rd North Branch MN 55056

HONERKAMP, FRANK W., university administrator; b. Manhasset, N.Y., June 10, 1969; s. Frank W. Jr. and Virginia C. (DeVoe) H.; m. Kelly Lynn Brooks, Feb. 26, 1994. BSBA, U. Richmond, 1991; MEd in Coll. Counseling, U. Del., 1993. Hall dir. U. Del., Newark, 1991-93; resident dir. Ohio U., Athens, 1993—. Author, editor: (daily planner) New Directions, 1995. Mem. Nat. Assn. Student Pers. Adminstrs., Am. Coll. Pers. Assn., Ohio Coll. Pers. Assn. (co-chair registration com. 1995). Home: PO Box 361 Athens OH 45701 Office: Residence Life S Green Office Athens OH 45701

HONEYWELL, LARRY GENE, retired publishing company executive, retired travel company executive; b. Clinton, Iowa, Jan. 4, 1935; s. Robert L. and Anna F. (Hansen) H.; m. Carol J. Skidmore, Aug. 22, 1957 (div.); children: Kenneth, Karen, Diane, Thomas, Stephen; m. Nancy H. Shultz, July 11, 1992. BS in Commerce, State U. Iowa, 1957. Credit reporter Dun & Bradstreet, N.Y.C., 1959-62, computer programmer, 1962-68, mgr. systems, 1968-69; dir. data processing Moody's Investor Svc., N.Y.C., 1969-71, v.p., 1971-72; sr. v.p. Official Airline Guides Inc., Oak Brook, Ill., 1972-86; v.p. fin. A.C. Nielsen, Northbrook, Ill., 1986-88; exec. v.p., chief operating officer Nielsen Clearing House, Clinton, 1989; pres. Thomas Cook Travel, Oak Brook, 1989, Official Airline Guides, Oak Brook, 1989-95. Pres. Coll. DuPage Found., Glen Ellyn, Ill., 1983-85. Lt. U.S. Army, 1957-59. Mem. Travel Industry Assn. (bd. dirs.).

HONG, PAUL CHONGKUN, management and accounting educator; b. Seoul, Korea, Feb. 15, 1952; came to U.S., 1977; s. Ki Chui and Bong Ju (Ku) H. m. Sarah Young Sook, June 13, 1975; children: Sarah Jihyun, Faith Sohyun, Augustine Paul, Albert Luther. BA in econs., Yonsei U., Seoul, 1975; MA in Econs., MBA in Acctg., Bowling Green State U., 1985; PhD in Mfg. Mgmt., U. Toledo, 1992—. Cert. mgmt. accountant. Staff accountant Korea Shipbuilding Corp., Seoul, 1974-75; dir. Univ. Bible Fellowship, Bowling Green, Ohio, 1979-85, Toledo, Ohio, 1990; instr. U. Toledo, 1987-91, asst. prof., 1992-94, assoc. prof., 1995—; senator Faculty Senate U. Toledo, 1991-93; cons., advisor Rad Co. Industries, Toledo, 1995—; referee articles, 1995. Author: Genesis, Samuel, Romans, 1994; contbr. articles to profl. jours. Mem. Rep. Party, Toledo, 1995, Internat. Hapkido Fedn., Toledo, 1995, judge, 1995. Grad. scholar Bowling Green State U., 1980-84. Mem. AAUP, Inst. Mgmt. Acct. Dirs., Am. Soc. Quality Control. Presbyterian. Office: U Toledo Dept Bus Techs Dept Econs Toledo OH 43606

HONG, PETER LEE, manufacturing executive; b. Wilmington, Del., Mar. 3, 1956; s. Van Yee She and Olive (Lee) H.; m. Annette Christine Kuenning, Aug. 12, 1978; children: David Allen, Kristina Lien. BSME, U. Ill., 1979. Registered profl. engr., Ill. Engr. Deere & Co., East Moline, Ill., 1975-90; v.p. engring. Positech Corp., Laurens, Iowa, 1990-91, pres., 1991—; bd. dirs. Laurens Indsl. Found., 1992—; chmn. ergonomics coun. Material Handling Inst. Pres. Quad City Chinese Assn., Moline, Ill., 1985; chmn. Pocahontas County Bd. Health, 1994; regional rep. Iowa Gov.'s Quality Coalition, 1992—. Mem. NSPE (pres. Black Hawk chpt. 1988-89), Soc. Mfg. Engrs., Des Moines Club. Office: Positech Corp 191 N Rush Lake Rd Laurens IA 50554-1250

HONIGMAN, DAVID, state legislator; b. Detroit, Dec. 10, 1955; m. Joann. BA, Yale U.; JD, U. Mich. Law Sch. State rep. Mich. Ho. of Reps.; state senator Dist. 17 Mich. State Senate, 1990-94, state senator Dist. 15, 1995—; mem. Oakland County Rep. Exec. Com., Leadership Com., House Campaign Com. Mich. Ho. of Reps.; chmn. Labor, Local Govt. & Urban Devel. Coms.; vice-chmn. Edn. com. Mich. State Senate. Mem. Mich. Bar Assn., LWV, Optimist's Club, Bloomfield C. of C., Anti-Defamation League of B'nai B'rith. *

HONOR, NOËL EVANS, social services supervisor; b. Indpls., Apr. 11, 1948; d. Fredrick Harris and Shirley (Richardson) Evans; m. Herbert Lincoln Martin, Aug. 18, 1972 (div. Aug. 19, 1982); 1 child, Lisa Rochelle Martin; m. Alan Thompson Honor, Sept. 14, 1990. BA in Psychology, Fisk U., 1970; MSW, Ind. U.-Purdue U., 1972. Cert. social worker; lic. social worker, Ind.; diplomate Am. Bd. Examiners in Social Work. Social worker Wis. Dept. Health & Social Svcs., Madison, 1972-75; ct. svcs. social worker Mental Health Ctr. of Dane County, Madison, 1976-85; field practicum supr. in social work U. Wis., Madison, 1983-84; lead group facilitator, social worker Multi Resource Ctr., Inc., Mpls., 1985-86; coord. teen incest program Parental Stress Ctr., Madison, 1986; psychiat. social work case mgr. Goodwill Industries, Madison, 1986-87; outreach therapist BOOST Program of Mental Health Ctr. of Dane County, Madison, 1987-88; outreach social worker St. Elizabeth's, Indpls., 1988-91, supr. social svcs., 1991—; psychiat. social worker, group therapist for incest victims Wishard Hosp. Midtown Mental Health, Indpls., 1988—; field placement instr. Ind. U., Indpls., 1992, 94—. Active Holy Angels Cath. Ch., Indpls., 1988—, ladies aux. Knights of St. Peter Claver, 1993—, Grand Lady, 1994-96, ret., 1996. Mem. Alpha Kappa Alpha. Democrat. Roman Catholic. Office: Saint Elizabeth's 2500 Churchman Ave Indianapolis IN 46203-4613

HOOD, EARL JAMES, lawyer, state legislator; b. Spearfish, S.D., Apr. 28, 1947; s. Earl Kenneth and Florence Lorraine (Castor) m. Judith G. Witzel, June 2, 1968 (div. Sept. 1974); children: Jason, Jared Jon; m. Kathleen Gay Donahue, Sept. 13, 1975; 1 child, Stewart Lee. BS, Black Hills State Coll., 1969; JD, U. S.D., 1972. Assoc. Richards Law Firm, Spearfish, 1972-74; ptnr. Richards and Hood, Spearfish, 1974-78, Richards, Hood and Brady, P.C., Spearfish, 1979-90, Richards, Hood, Brady & Nies, P.C., Spearfish, 1990-95; mem. S.D. Ho. of Reps., Pierre, 1983-92; speaker pro tem Pierre, 1989-90; speaker of the house S.D. Ho. of Reps., Pierre, 1991-92; officer, dir., shareholder Richards, Hood & Nies, P.C., 1995—; city atty. City of Spearfish, 1972-76, 87—. Chief Spearfish Vol. Fire Dept., 1982-83; pres. Black Hills State Coll. Found., Inc., Spearfish, 1986; mem. S.D. Pvt. Industry Coun., 1993-94; mem. S.D. Quality Govt. Commn., 1993-94; chair Kids Voting, Spearfish, 1993-95, bd. dirs., 1994-95; chair Workforce Devel. Coun. S.D., 1994-95. Recipient Vigil Honor Order of Arrow, BSA, 1965, Disting. Alumnus award Black Hills State U., 1990; named S.D. Firefighter of Yr. Keep S.D. Green Assn., 1984, Friend of Edn. S.D. Edn. Assn., 1990. Mem. S.D. Bar Assn., S.D. Trial Lawyers Assn., Lions, Masons (Spearfish Lodge #18), Order Eastern Star (Queen City chpt #89). Republican. Home: 101 S 5th St PO Box 611 Spearfish SD 57783-0611 Office: Richards Hood & Nies PO Box 759 Spearfish SD 57783-0759

HOOD, JAMES, internist, consultant; b. Leslie, Fife, Scotland, Sept. 5, 1930; came to U.S., 1966; s. James and Mary J. (Keith) H.; m. Margaret Ferguson Goodman, Aug. 21, 1953; children: James Derek, Margaret Lesley. M.B., Ch. B., U. of Edinburgh, Scotland, 1952. Diplomate Am. Bd. Internal Medicine, Am. Bd. of Nutrition. Registrar in medicine and chest diseases Newmarket Gen. Hosp., Suffolk, Eng., 1958-60; med. registrar, clin. tutor Edinburgh Ea. Gen. Hosp., 1960-62; sr. med. registrar Hampstead Gen. Hosp., Royal Free Hosps. Med. Sch., London, 1962-63; clin. researcher Med. and Biol. Rsch. div. Sandoz Inc., Basle, Switzerland, 1964-66; fellow in clin. nutrition, instr. in medicine U. Hosps., Iowa City, Iowa, 1966-70; staff internal medicine St. Luke's and Mercy Hosps., Cedar Rapids, Iowa, 1970-88, Mid Mich. Regional Med. Ctr., Midland, 1989—; assoc. Midland Internal Medicine Assocs., 1989-93; internist, consultant pvt. practice, Midland, Mich., 1993—; advisor drug evaluations AMA, Chgo., 1971. Author: (with others) Current Therapy, 1975; contbg. editor: Nutrition Revs., 1967-70; contbr. articles to New Eng. Jour. Medicine, Am. Jour. Clin. Nutrition, Jour. Clin. Investigation, Vitamins and Hormones, Am. Jour. Hosp. Pharm. Surgeon lt. Royal Naval Vol. Res., 1954-56. Fellow ACP, 1970, Royal Coll. of Physicians of Edinburgh, 1971, Am. Coll. Nutrition, 1988. Mem. Am. Soc. Internal Medicine, Fedn. of Am. Socs. for Exptl. Biology, Am. Soc. for Nutritional Scis., Am. Soc. Clin. Nutrition, Am. Fedn. Clin. Rsch., European Assn. Internal Medicine, Mich. Med. Soc., Midland County Med. Soc., Rotary. Presbyterian. Home: 5907 Harwood Dr Midland MI 48640-2742 Office: Ste B 4915 Hedgewood Dr Midland MI 48640

HOOD, MORRIS, state legislator; b. June 5, 1934. Wayne State U. State rep. Dist. 6 Mich. Ho. of Reps., 1970-94, state rep Dist. 11, 1995—; chmn. Higher Edn. & Regulatory Subcoms., mem. Appropriations Com. Mich. Ho. of Reps. Del. Dem. Nat. Conv., 1980; chmn. Mich. State Black Caucus. Mem. NAACP, Mich. Dem. Black Caucus, Econ. Club, Trade Union Leadership Coun., Urban Alliance, Detroit Urban League. Home: 8872 Cloverlawn St Detroit MI 48204-2729*

HOOD, RON, state legislator. BS, BA, Ohio State U. Mktg. cons. Canfield, Ohio; rep. dist. 57 Ohio Ho. of Reps., Columbus.

HOOD, RONALD LEE, electrical engineer; b. Toledo, Feb. 20, 1945; s. Douglas Crary and Pauline Edna (Thurston) H.; m. Beata Caroline Hetzel, June 8, 1968; children: Jason, Deanna, Krista, Molly. BSEE, U. Toledo, 1968, MSEE, 1976. Cert. profl. engr. Rsch. engr. SCI Inc., Huntsville, Ala., 1968-69; elec. engr. Owens Corning Fiberglas, Toledo, 1969-73; devel. engr. Reliance Electric-Haughton, Toledo, 1973-74; sr. engr. Owens Corning Fiberglas, Toledo, 1974, supr., 1974-91, mgr. CPG elec. controls engring., 1991—; CPG Div. Control Systems Gate Keeper Owens Corning Fiberglas, 1993; mgr. control systems tech. and engring. CPG Global, 1993; mgr. elec. control systems AVCA Engrs. and Architects, 1994—; cons. AVCA Engring., BEN Engring. and Lott Project, Toledo. Contbr. articles to profl. jours. Mem. IEEE (section bd. dirs.), Instrument Soc. of Am. (sr. Area Coun. on Technology), Phi Kappa Psi Frat., Am. Bible Soc. Republican. Methodist. Home: 98 Karyl Ct Waterville OH 43566-1041 Office: AVCA Engrs & Architects 1684 Woodlands Dr Maumee OH 43537-4057

HOOD, TERRY BRYANT, social worker, consultant; b. Lansing, Mich., Mar. 31, 1948; s. George Louis and Norma Caroline (Platt) H.; m. Paula Jane Clegg, Sept. 20, 1975; 1 child, Rachel. BS, Mich. State U., 1972; MA, Western Mich. U., 1983. Cert. social worker, Mich. Sr. educator/clinician Starr Commonwealth, Albion, Mich., 1975—; cons. child care facilities, 1983—. Trustee Bd. Edn., Concord, 1994—. Mem. Mich. Assn. Children's Alliances (cons. 1984—, Hugh Whipple award 1994), Child Welfare League, Black Child Devel. Inst. Home: 340 Wood Hills Dr Concord MI 49237 Office: Starr Commonwealth 13725 Starr Comm Rd Albion MI 49224

HOODJER, KIMBERLY KAY, state agency administrator; b. Hampton, Iowa, Aug. 17, 1959; d. Jay Francis and Sharon Kay (Pieters) Kurth; m. Jay Kevin Hoodjer, July 22, 1977 (div. Sept. 1990); children: Joshua, Tylor, Kathryn. AA, Ellsworth C.C., Iowa Falls, Iowa, 1990; BA, U. No. Iowa, Cedar Falls, 1993; postgrad., Iowa State U., 1993-94. Owner, mgr. Skay's Variety Store (merger Needleart Creations, 1986), Ackley, Iowa, 1983-88; mgr. Pronto Market, Ackley, 1989-90; intern art therapy Covenant Med. Ctr., Waterloo, Iowa, 1992-93; mgr. Pizza Hut, Ft. Dodge, Iowa, 1994; state coord. Nacel Cultural Exchs. (Iowa region), St. Paul, Minn., 1994—. Artist, creator electroplated container, Container I (hon. mention 1993). Bd. dirs. Ackley C. of C., 1985-87; mem. Ackley Hist. Soc. 1987-88; active local PTAs 1986—. Mem. Nat. Art Educators Assn., Iowa Art Educators Assn., Leonardo Art Club (sponsor), Phi Theta Kappa, Beta Sigma Phi. Roman Catholic. Home and Office: Nacel Cultural Exchs 503 Mitchell St Ackley IA 50601

HOOGWERF, BYRON JAMES, physician; b. Sioux Falls, S.D., Feb. 8, 1945; s. Henry (dec.) Hoogwerf and Nellie (Verbrugge) Hoogwerf-Christians; m. Judith Anne Barrett, Aug. 16, 1966 (div. 1985); children: Jennifer Anne, Byron James II; m. Heidi Ellen Gaenslen, Dec. 21, 1985; 1 child, Rebecca Alexandra. BA, Calvin Coll., 1967; MD, U. Minn., 1971. Cert. diabetes edn. Intern Hennepin County Med. Ctr., Mpls., 1971-72, resident internal medicine, 1976-78; fellow, endocrinology Univ. Minn., Mpls., 1978-81, asst. prof., 1981-85; staff physician Cleve. Clinic Found., 1985—, chmn., endocrinology, 1988-91. Contbr. chpts. to books and over 50 articles to profl. jours. Bd. dirs. Diabetes Assn. Greater Cleve., 1986-95, pres. bd. dirs., 1992-93; bd. dirs. Camp Ho Mito Koda, Cleve., 1986—. Recipient Tng. grant NIH, U. Minn., 1978-79, Nat. Rsch. Svc. award NIH, U. Minn., 1979-81, Spl. Emphasis Rsch. Career award NIH-Nat. Inst. Aging, U. Minn., 1982-85, NIH Post CABG Trial award, 1987-95. Fellow ACP; mem. AAAS, Am. Assn. Clin. Endocrinologists, Am. Diabetes Assn. (chmn. publs. com. coun. on nutritional scis. and metabolism 1988-91, 96—, profl. practice com. 1992—), Endocrine Soc., Soc. for Clin. Trials. Presbyterian. Home: 2237 Demington Dr Cleveland OH 44106-3320 Office: The Cleveland Clinic Found 9500 Euclid Ave Cleveland OH 44195-0001

HOOK, WILLIAM FRANKLIN, radiologist; b. Williston, N.D., May 26, 1935; s. Charles Ellis and Ann (Franklin) H.; m. Margo Joanne Booth, June 21, 1958 (div. Sept. 1968); children: William, Christopher, Paul; m. Merry Jean Schimke, Nov. 26, 1968 (div. 1987); 1 child, Kari Ann; m. Linda Marie Rohrich, Aug. 18, 1988. AB, Stanford U., 1957; MD, Jefferson Med. Coll., 1961. Diplomate Am. Bd. Radiology, Am. Bd. Nuclear Medicine. Staff radiologist O&R Clinic, Bismarck, N.D., 1969-74; dir. nuclear radiology O&R Clinic, Bismarck, 1983—; chmn. dept. radiology, 1990—; chief dept. radiology Bismarck Hosp., 1970-74; dir. dept. radiology Mandan (N.D.) Hosp., 1974-81; staff radiologist Meth. Hosps., Dallas, 1981-83, Med. Ctr. One, 1984—; co-dir. Regional MRI Ctr., Bismarck, 1987-92; asst. clinical prof. U. N.D., 1978—. Author: Common Sense and Modern First Aid, 1967; contbr. articles profl. jours. Lt. USNR, 1961-64, col. res.; comdr. USAR hosp., Persian Gulf, 1991-92. Mem. AMA (Physician's Recognition award 1983-86, 86-92), Am. Coll. Radiology, Soc. Nuclear Medicine, N.D. State Radiol. Soc., 6th Dist. Med. Soc. Lutheran. Home: RR 5 Box 145A Bismarck ND 58501-9805 Office: O&R Clinic 222 N 7th St Bismarck ND 58501-4436

HOOKER, JAMES TODD, manufacturing executive; b. Ashland, Ohio, Dec. 21, 1946; s. Melvin Todd and Harriett (Lutz) H.; m. Sallie Foulkrod Utz, Feb. 22, 1975; 1 child, Stephanie Rae. BSBA magna cum laude, Ashland U., 1973. Advt. mgr. The Gorman-Rupp Co., Mansfield, Ohio, 1974-76, mfg. engr., 1976-79; asst. service mgr. The Gorman-Rupp Co., Mansfield, 1979-80, gen. service mgr., 1980-86, asst. sales mgr., 1986-90; mgr. mfg. The Gorman-Rupp Co., Mansfield, Ohio, 1990-95, dir. mfg., 1995—. Solicitor United Way, Mansfield, 1982, 83, 87; moderator, bd. deacons Presbyn. Ch., 1988-89, elder, 1990-95; mem. Session, 1990-95; bd. Trustees Richland County Leadership Unltd.; mem. Heritage Found.; plank owner USN Meml. Found. With USN, 1965-71. Decorated Vietnamese Gallantry Cross. Mem. Omicron Delta Epsilon. Republican. Home: 1090 Trout Dr Mansfield OH 44903-9144 Office: The Gorman-Rupp Co 305 Bowman St Mansfield OH 44903-1689

HOOPER, KELLEY RAE, delivery service executive; b. Tulsa, Aug. 24, 1960; d. Kenneth Roe Sharp and Beverly Jane (Phillips) Jenkins; m. John Patrick Hooper, Apr. 30, 1988 (dec. Oct. 1990). BS, Okla. State U., 1982; postgrad., So. Nazarene U., 1991—. Ter. mgr. Am. Fidelity Ins. Co., Oklahoma City, 1982-87; account exec. United Parcel Svc., Inc., Oklahoma City, 1987-89, customer svc. office supr., 1991, next day air letter ctr. coord., 1990, dist. office mgr., 1991-92, dist. area mgr.; dist. sales mgr. ctrl. Ohio United Parcel Svc., Inc., Columbus, 1994—. Dist. region grant com. United Parcel Svc. Found., Oklahoma City, 1992; mem., donor Omniplex Sci. Mus., Oklahoma City, 1990—, Ballet Okla., Oklahoma City, 1992—, Oklahoma City Arts Mus., 1992—. Mem. NAFE, Nat. Trust for Historic Preservation, 1995; Art Inst. Chgo., Sierra, Okla. State U. Alumni Assn., Pi Sigma Alpha.

Democrat. Home: 948 S Remington Rd Bexley OH 43209-2459 Office: United Parcel Svc 5101 Trabue Rd Columbus OH 43228-9613

HOOPER, MARCIA SARITA, pediatric critical care nurse; b. Detroit, Dec. 31, 1954; d. Alphonso and Annie M. (Garland) H. BSN, Mercy Coll. Detroit, 1977. RN, Mich.; CCRN; cert. pediatric nurse practitioner, pediatric critical care nurse preceptor; cert. PALS instr., BCLS instr. Staff nurse Children's Hosp. of Mich., Detroit, 1977-91, preceptor, 1991—. Mem. AACN (cert. critical care nurse).

HOOT, MARVIN JAY, computer consultant; b. Garrett, Ind., June 2, 1948; s. Darrell William and Margaret Helen (Rogers) H.; m. Apryl Lee Shifler, Oct. 13, 1972; children: Joshua, Catherine, Jennie. BS in Math., Ind. Inst. Tech., Ft. Wayne, 1970; MS in Bus. Adminstrn., St. Francis Coll., Ft. Wayne, 1976. Programmer, analyst Advanced Computer Svc., Ft. Wayne, 1970-74, REA Magnet Wire, Ft. Wayne, 1974-77; lead programmer, analyst Lincoln Nat. Corp., Ft. Wayne, 1977-92; lead analyst Indpls. Life Ins. Co., 1992-93; v.p. ACTS, Inc., Woodburn, Ind., 1993—; part-time faculty Ind. Vocat. Tech. Coll., Ft. Wayne, 1982—. Ward chmn. Dem. Party, Allen County, Ind., 1982; pres. Christian Action Coun., Allen County, 1990; exec. dir. Rutherford Inst. Ind., Indpls., 1991-92; trustee, bd. dirs. East Allen County Schs., 1994. Evangelical Christian. Home: 4232 Ort Dr Woodburn IN 46797 Office: Applied Computer Tech Solutions 4232 Ort Dr Woodburn IN 46797

HOOVEN, MICHAEL DAWSON, medical products executive, engineer; b. Ann Arbor, Mich., Oct. 6, 1955; s. John Galloway Hooven and Betty Ann Corcoran; m. Susan Spies, Oct. 31, 1988; 1 child. BS in Physics, U. Mich., Ann Arbor, 1978, MSME, 1981. Rsch. assoc. U. Mich., Ann Arbor, 1978-81; mgr. neurosurgical engring. Cordis Corp., Miami, 1981-86; mgr. pacemaker divsn. Siemens/Pacesetter, Sylmar, Calif., 1986-88; dir. product devel. Ethicon Endosurgery, Cin., 1988-94; pres., CEO Enable Med. Corp., West Chester, Ohio, 1994—; chmn. bd. dirs. Enable Med. Corp., West Chester, 1994—. Inventor; numerous patents in field including endoscopic surg. sys. with sensing means, 1995, endoscopic instrument having torsioaclly stiff shaft, 1995, implantable blood oxygen sensor and method of use, 1989, three stage implantable flow control valve with improved valve closure member, 1988, three stage valve, 1988, intercranial pressure regulator valve, 1988, infusion pump, 1988, three stage intracranial pressure control valve, 1987, three stage valve with flexible valve seat, 1987, implantable servo valve having integral pressure sensor, 1987, plural valve three stage pressure relief system, 1987, adjustable implantable valve having non-invasive position indicator, 1987, three stage pressure regulator valve, 1987, three stage intracranial pressure relief valve having single piece valve stem, 1986, manufacture of tubing assembly for drainage catheter, 1986, portable instrument to test pressure-flow of ventricular shunt valves, 1986, self-calibrating defferential condition sensor, 1986, servo valve, 1985, non-invasively adjustable valve, 1985; contbr. numerous articles to profl. jours. Fellow ASME; mem. Edison Bio Technology Ctr. Office: Enable Med Corp 6345 Centre Park Dr West Chester OH 45069

HOOVER, DIANE E., business executive; b. Seattle, July 4, 1945. From mgr. to claims supr. N.W. region SSA, 1963-88; program analyst SSA, Seattle, 1988-90; v.p. Allsup Inc., Belleville, Ind., 1990-92; v.p. Benefit Team Svcs. Inc., Kansas City, Mo., 1992—; mgr. fed. womens program Seattle region SSA, 1978-81. Office: Benefit Team Svcs Inc PO Box 901-606 Kansas City MO 64190-1606

HOOYMAN, THOMAS GERAND, medical ethicist, consultant; b. Chgo., Dec. 23, 1955; s. Floyd Peter and Margaret Jane (McMahon) H.; m. Nancy Ann Wilcox, Mar. 23, 1981; children: Andrew, Christopher. BA in Biology, St. Louis U., 1979, MA in Religious Studies, 1981, PhD in Moral Theology, 1994. Ethicist St. John's Mercy Health Sys., St. Louis, 1990—; adj. prof. St. Louis U., 1989—; mem. adv. bd. St. Louis Times, 1994—; chmn. pub. policy com. Mo. Cath. Conf., Jefferson City, 1994—; chmn. Gateway Cath. Ethics Network, St. Louis, 1994—. Trustee Aquinas Inst. Theology, St. Louis, 1987-93. Mem. Cath. Theology Soc. Am., Soc. for Health and Human Values, Soc. for Bioethics Consultation, Am. Bioethics Assn. Office: St John's Mercy Health Sys 615 S New Ballas Rd Saint Louis MO 63141

HOPKINS, JACK WALKER, former university administrator, environmental educator; b. Fitzgerald, Ga., Feb. 16, 1930; s. Milton Newton and Hattie Lee (Walker) H.; m. Katherine Lee Arthur, Apr. 20, 1957; children—David Arthur, Mark Steven, Susan Kay. Student, North Ga. Coll., 1947-48; B.A., U. N.C., 1951; M.A., Emory U., 1962; Ph.D., U. Fla., 1966. Asst. prof. polit. sci. Ga. Inst. Tech., 1965-66, Ga. State Coll., Atlanta, 1966-67; assoc. prof. Emory U., Atlanta, 1967-71; prof., chmn. dept. Tex. Tech. U., Lubbock, 1971-75; prof. pub. and environ. affairs Ind. U., Bloomington, 1975—; provost Malaysia Program, Ind. U., Shah Alam, Malaysia, 1985-86; assoc. dir. Ind. Ctr. on Global Change and World Peace, 1992-94, dir., 1994-95; research cons. Inst. Pub. Adminstrn. (Peru), N.Y.C., 1964-65. Author: The Government Executive of Modern Peru, 1967, Latin America in World Affairs, 1976; editor: Latin America and Caribbean Contemporary Record, (4 times) 1982-86, Latin America: Perspectives on a Region, 1987, 2d edit., 1995, The Eradication of Smallpox, 1989, Policymaking for Conservation in Latin America, 1995. Dist. chmn. Dem. Ctrl. Com., DeKalb, Ga., 1970; del. Dem. Nat. Conv., 1976; mem. Bloomington Common Coun., 1991-95, pres., 1993. Fulbright lectr. to Argentina, 1968; NASPAA/ASPA pub. adminstrn. fellow, 1970-71; Rockefeller found. scholar, 1982. Mem. Am. Soc. Pub. Adminstrn., Latin Am. Studies Assn. Democrat. Home: 725 S Meadowbrook Dr Bloomington IN 47401-4230 Office: Ind U Sch Pub and Environ Affairs Bloomington IN 47405

HOPKINS, JILL D., anthropologist, educator; b. Cassville, Mo., Aug. 12, 1963; d. John Bruce and Geraldine Gladys (Millard) Davidson; m. Brett Allen Hopkins, Feb. 13, 1981; 1 child, Jared Jackson. BA with honors, U. Ark., 1985; MA, U. Mo., 1988, postgrad. Instr. anthropology Stephens Coll., Columbia, Mo., 1993—; rsch. asst. Mo. Chiwere Lang. Project Mo. U., Columbia, 1989-93, 95—. Recipient Chiwere Oral Traditions award Am. Philos. Soc., 1990. Mem. Am. Anthropol. Assn., Soc. Linguistic Anthropology, Soc. for Study of Indigenous Lang. Am., Mo. Folklore Soc., Phi Beta Kappa. Office: Stephens Coll Social Scis History Program Box 2073 Dudley Hall Columbia MO 65215

HOPKINS, LINDA KAY, intellectual property consultant; b. St. Paul, Minn., Nov. 3, 1948; d. Lyle E. and Emily Griesman Hopkins. BA, U. Minn., 1979; MA, U. N.Mex., 1987; grad. cert., U. St. Thomas; postgrad., William Mitchell Sch. Law, 1994—. Hearing asst. Social Security Adminstrn., Office of Appeals, Mpls., 1972-80; instr., spl. edn. dir. Albuquerque Pub. Schs., Meml. Hosp., 1987; contracting officer Vets. Med. Bldg., Bloomington, Minn., 1988-89; contract specialist Dept. of Def. Contract Adminstrn. Office, Bloomington, 1989-92; columnist Tech Access Jour., Novate, Calif., 1995—; chairperson working group on intellectual property Govt. Info. Access Coun., State of Minn., St. Paul, 1995-96; reporter upper midwest region The Russian Mag., San Diego, 1996—; policy adv. Whit Ho. Nat. Econ. Coun., SBA, Dept. of Justice, Washington; cons. , trainer Intelliware, St. Paul; adv. Bulgarian Patent Office, Sofia, Bulgaria; spkr. in field; adj. prof. Grad. Sch. Pub. Adminstrn. Hamline U., St. Paul; presenter workshops on govt.; moderator Electronic Nat. Conf. on Intellectual Property Law. Author: Licensing Law Handbook 1994, 1994; author newspaper editl. Minn. Women's Press, 1990. Mem. ABA, Minn. Bar Assn., Women's Bar Assn. Minn., Christian Law Students Minn., Biotech. Assn., Nat. Contract Mgmt. Assn. (2 scholarships 1990, 91). Home: 6836 Buckingham Ct Woodbury MN 55125

HOPKINS, ROBERT ELLIOTT, music educator; b. Greensboro, N.C., Oct. 2, 1931; s. Julian Setzer and Elizabeth Stewart (Daniel) H. MusB, U. Rochester, 1953, MusM, 1954, D Mus. Arts, 1959; postgrad., Acad. for Music, Vienna, Austria, 1959-60. Instr. Mars Hill Coll., 1954-57, 60-63; prof. music Youngstown (Ohio) State U., 1963-93; prof. emeritus, 1993—. Editor: Alexander Reinagle: The Philadelphia Sonatas, 1978; contbr. New Grove Dictionary of Music and Musicians, 1980, New Grove Dictionary of American Music, 1987, New Grove Dictionary of Opera, 1992. Music dir. various chs., N.C. and Ohio, 1954-81; chmn. Nat. Piano Concerto Competition, Youngstown Symphony Soc., 1986-90. Recipient Disting. Prof. award Youngstown State U., 1990; Fulbright-Hays grantee, 1959-60, rsch. grantee Youngstown State U., 1969-70, 83. Fellow Am. Guild. Organists (dean Youngstown chpt. 1968-69, 73-74, S. Lewis Elmer award 1962, 66); mem. Am. Musicological Soc., Am. Matthay Assn.

HOPP, DENNIS WILLIAM, physical therapist; b. Hardtner, Kans., Aug. 27, 1951; s. Ralph Lee and Joann May (Spano) H.; m. Suzanne Celeste Noon, Sept. 18, 1980; children: Gabrielle, Shannon, Timothy, Laura, Colleen. BS, U. Nebr. Med. Ctr., Omaha, 1986. Staff phys. therapist Immanuel Med. Ctr., Omaha, 1986-87; phys. therapy dir. Cogley Med. Ctr., Council Bluffs, Iowa, 1987—. Mem. Am. Phys. Therapy Assn. Democrat. Roman Catholic. Office: Cogley Physical Therapy 715 Harmony St Council Bluffs IA 51503

HOPP, NANCY SMITH, marketing executive; b. Aurora, Ill., Nov. 1, 1943; d. C. Dudley and Margaret (McWethy) Smith; m. Edward Thompson Reid, July 19, 1963 (div. Feb. 1966); 1 child, Edward Thompson Jr.; m. James C. Hopp, Feb. 4, 1978. Cert., Chgo. Sch. Interior Design, 1965; BA in Social Scis., Aurora U., 1968, MS in Bus. Mgmt., 1982. Dir. pub. rels. Sta. WLXT-TV, Aurora, 1969-70; bookstore mgr. Waubonsee Coll., Sugar Grove, Ill., 1970-79, dir. purchasing, 1979-85, dir. pub. rels., 1984-85; dir. devel. Assn. for Individual Devel., Aurora, 1985-87; dir. pub. rels. Mercy Ctr. Health Care Svc., Aurora, 1988-95; dir. mktg. Dreyer Med. Clinic, aurora, 1995—; mem. Ninety for the 90s Commn., Ill. Dept. Aging, 1989. Editor: Volunteers Make the Difference, 1982; author Pigeon Woods Cookbook; producer (film) Caring Counts; contbr. articles to profl. jours. Bd. dirs. Family Support Ctr., Aurora, 1984-90, Aurora Area United Way, 1990-96, Corridor Group, 1993-94; mem. adv. coun. Mercy Ctr. Health Care, Aurora, 1985-87; moderator New Eng. Congl. Ch., Aurora, 1983; charter mem. bd. dirs. Aurora Cmty. Coordinating Coun., 1985-86; mem. Block Grant Working Com., Aurora, 1987—, Kane County Health Com., 1994; bd. dirs., sec. Cities in Schs./Aurora 2000, Inc., 1993-94. Recipient citation U.S. Dept. HEW, 1969, Christian Svc. award, 1996; named Woman of the Day, Sta. WAIT-AM, Chgo., 1974, Optimist of Yr. for Cmty. Svc., 1987, Woman of Distinction, YWCA, 1990. Mem. Women in Mgmt. (bd. dirs., sec., treas., Nat. Charlotte Danstrom Woman of Achievement award 1984), Nat. Soc. Fund Raising Execs. (ethics com. Chgo. chpt. 1987), Ill. Assn. Coll. Stores (pres. 1976), Nat. Assn. Ednl. Buyers (com. 1984)), Exch. Club. Republican. Home: 175 S Western Ave Aurora IL 60506-4617 Office: Dreyer Med Clinic 1877 W Downer Pl Aurora IL 60506

HOPPE, JOHN LESLIE, business executive; b. Lincoln, Nebr., Oct. 25, 1917; s. William F. and Gertrude J. Hoppe; m. Claire L. Rudenbdall, Mar. 15, 1942; children: Elizabeth Ann, John L. Jr., Ward F. BS of Archl. Engring., U. Nebr., 1939. Pres. Hoppe Lumber and Supply Co., Nebraska City, 1946-55; v.p. W.F. Hoppe Lumber Co., Lincoln, 1955-66; pres. John L. Hoppe Lumber Co., Lincoln, 1966-86; chmn. Hoppe Inc., Lincoln, 1986—. Lt. comdr. USN, 1941-45. Mem. U. Nebr. Found. (trustee), Elks, Am. Legion, Sigma Alpha Epsilon. Republican. Presbyterian. Office: Hoppe Inc PO Box 6035 Lincoln NE 68506

HOPPE, THOMAS J., state legislator; b. Evanston, Ill., Mar. 21, 1957. BA, Benedictine Coll., 1979. State rep. Dist. 46 Mo. State Congress, 1991—; mem. edn., fees and salaries com., local govt. and related matters com., urban affairs com.; mktg. cons. Mem. KC, Grandview, Belton & Kansas City C. of C. *

HOPPER, GEORGE, lawyer; b. Hebburn-on-Tyne, U.K., Mar. 10, 1913; came to the U.S., 1924; s. Samuel Jackson and Margaret (Gibson) Hopper; m. Jessie Elizabeth Taylor, Feb. 18, 1939; children: George David Keith, Kevin James. AB magna cum laude, Wittenberg U., 1932; JD, U. Cin., 1935. Atty. Procter & Gamble Co., Cin., 1934-73; of counsel Kevin J. Hopper Co. LPA, Cin., 1973—. With USN, 1944-46, PTO. Mem. Cin. Bar Assn., Anderson Hills Swim and Tennis Club (treas. 1976-95), Wittenberg Alumni Assn. (pres. 1961), Phi Gamma Delta, Phi Delta Phi, Omicron Delta Kappa. Republican. Presbyterian. Home: 767 Dunwoodie Dr Cincinnati OH 45230 Office: Kevin J Hopper Co LPA 7420 Jager Ct Cincinnati OH 45230

HOPPER, PATRICK M., securities trader; b. Detroit, Apr. 9, 1970. BS in Fin., Hillsdale (Mich.) Coll., 1992; MBA in Fin., Wayne State U., 1995. Registered rep. East West Brokerage Firm, Harper Woods, Mich., 1993, 1st of Mich. Corp., Grosse Pointe Woods, Mich., 1993—. Mem. Grosse Pointe Crisis Club, 1994—; precinct del. Grosse Pointe Rep. Com., 1993—. Mem. Lions.

HOPPERT, GLORIA JEAN, food products executive; b. LaFollette, Tenn., Apr. 2, 1949; d. Fred and Mona Ruth Cawood; m. Herschel M. Hoppert, Aug. 22, 1970; children: Hadden, Freya. BSChemE, U. Mich., 1971; MBA, Xavier U., 1975. Registered profl. engr., Wis., Pa., Nev., Ill. Staff engr., supr. div. shortening and oil Procter & Gamble Co., Cin., 1972-75, product tech. engr. div. paper, 1975-77; sr. project engr. Joseph Schlitz Brewing Co., Milw., 1977-78; sr. project engr. M&M/Mars Inc., Elizabethtown, Pa., 1978-81, mgr. maintenance sect., 1982-84, mgr. ops. Kudos, 1984-87; plant mgr. Sheba Kal Kan, Inc., Columbus, Ohio, 1987-88; mgr. mfg. Ethel M Chocolates, Las Vegas, Nev., 1988-91; mgr. ops. M&M/Mars, Inc., Chgo., 1991—; keynote speaker U. Dayton, 1980; cons. Transition to Mgmt. Conf., 1983, Mid-Atlantic Change Workshop Conf., N.Y.C. Contbr. articles to profl. jours. Merit scholar Mich. Higher Edn., 1967-71, Coll. Engring. scholar U. Mich., 1971. Fellow Soc. Women Engrs. (bd. dirs. 1978-80, sec. 1979); mem. NSPE. Lutheran. Home: 343 N Elmwood Ln Palatine IL 60067-7711 Office: M&M/Mars Inc 2019 N Oak Park Ave Chicago IL 60635-3345

HORAN, JANET K., lawyer; b. Mason City, Iowa, Feb. 5, 1939; d. Kenneth N. and Wilma J. (Cheney) Millard; m. Stephen J. Horan, Aug. 22, 1970. BA, U. No. Iowa, Cedar Falls, 1961; MA, U. Colo., 1970; JD, Chgo.-Kent Coll. Law, 1979. Bar: Ill. 1979. Tchr. English and speech high sch., Chgo. suburban area, 1961-77; staff atty. Property Loss Rsch. Bur., Schaumburg, Ill., 1981-83; dir. govt. affairs Ill. Dept. Employment Security, Chgo., 1983-88; sr. legis. counsel AMA, Chgo., 1988-95; dir. clin. and profl. affairs Ill. Hosp. and Health Systems Assn., Naperville, 1995—. Mem. Nat. Health Lawyers Assn., Chgo. Bar Assn., Ill. Health Lawyers Assn. Office: Ill Hosp & Health Sys Assoc 1151 E Warrenville Rd Naperville IL 60566

HORINEK, CHARITY ANN, editor; b. Goodland, Kans., Oct. 8, 1967; d. Billy Dean and Wilma June (Armstrong) Whitney; m. Mark Douglas Horinek, May 23, 1992. BA in Journalism, Ft. Hays State U., 1990. Editor Syracuse (Kans.) Jour., 1990-93, Southwest Daily Times, Liberal, Kans., 1993-94, Haskell County Monitor, Sublette, Kans., 1994-96, Southwest Daily Times, Liberal, Kans., 1996—. Mem. Jaycees (mgmt. v.p. Sublette, Kans. 1995-96, Hamilton County 1993-94, individual devel. v.p. 1992-93, sec. 1991-92, State Jaycee of Month 1991). Democrat. Roman Catholic. Home: PO Box 597 Sublette KS 67877

HORISBERGER, DON HANS, conductor, musician; b. Millersburg, Ohio, Mar. 2, 1951; s. Hans and Jeanette (Grossniklaus) H. MusB, Capital U., 1973; MusM, Northwestern U., 1974, MusD, 1985. Dir. music 1st Presbyn. Ch., Waukegan, Ill., 1976-88; with Chgo. Symphony Chorus, 1977—, sect. leader, 1984-91, asst. condr., 1990—; dir. Waukegan Concert Chorus, 1979—; organist/choirmaster Ch. of the Holy Spirit, Lake Forest, Ill., 1988—; lectr. in music Capital U., Columbus, Ohio, 1974-75; asst. to lang. coach Chgo. Symphony Chorus, 1978—. Fulbright-Hayes grantee 1975. Mem. Am. Choral Dirs. Assn. (chair community choruses cen. div. spl. interest 1988-91), Mid-Am. Prodns. in N.Y.C. (nat. forum advisors), Assn. Profl. Vocal Ensembles (chorus Am.).

HORN, CHARLES F., state senator, lawyer, electrical engineer; b. Bellefontaine, Ohio, July 20, 1924; s. Huber H. and Mary C. (Steig) H.; m. Shirley E. Horn, Aug. 1, 1953; children: Holly E., Charles J., Heidi E. BSEE, Purdue U., 1949; LLB, Cleve. State U., 1954. Application engr. Westinghouse Electric, Cleve., 1949-51; engr. Hertner Electric Co., Cleve., 1951-53; owner, engr. Leare Equipment Engring., Cleve., 1953-61; owner, ptnr. IRBATCO, Cleve., 1953-61; atty. Dayton, Ohio, 1961—; city coun. mem. City of Kettering, Ohio, 1963-69, mayor, 1969-80; county commr. Montgomery County, Ohio, 1980-84; mem. Ohio State Senate, Columbus, 1985—; corp./minority owner, chmn. bd. Advanced Computer Suss., Dayton, 1971-89; adv. panel Office of Sci. and Tech.; chair Econ. Devel., Tech. and Aerospace Com.; senate rep. Thomas Edison Tech. Bd., Devel. Financing Policy Bd., Ohio Indsl. Tng. Program Bd.; chair Fed. Labs Consortium Adv. Bd., Wright-Patterson AFB, 1980-83; cons. NSF; participant U.S. Conf. Mayors. Organizer Miami Valley Coun. Govts., Montgomery County; turstee Nat. Aviation Hall of Fame, Cox Arboretum, Cmty. Devel. Corp.; past trustee Grandview Hosp., Kettering C. of C., Dayton Area Sr. Citizents, Kidney Soc., Leukemia Soc., Pub. Opinion Ctr.; founder, chmn. Camp for Kids Who Can't; past adv. bd. Kettering Meml. Hosp.; past chmn. mcpl. sect. United Way Campaign; promoter formation of Ohio Avanced Tech. Ctr.; serve Ohio's School-to-Work Task Force. Served with U.S. Army Air Corps, 1942-45, CBI Theatre. Recipient numerous awards including Michael A. DeNunzio award U.S. Conf. of Mayors, 1980, Citizen award Pub. Children Svc. Assn. Ohio, 1988, Legislator of Yr. award Nat. Assn. Social Workers, 1989, Tech. award Dayton Area Tech. Network, 1989, Disting. Legis. Svc. award Ohio Human Svcs. Dirs. Assn., 1989, Pub. Svc. award Quality Dayton, 1990, Tom Bradley Regional Leadership award Nat. Assn. Regional Coun., 1989, Vol. of Yr. award Camp Kern YWCA, Pub. Svc. award Ohio Computer Tech. Ctr., 1990. Republican. Office: Horn Coen & Rife 2323 W Schartz Kettering OH 45409 also: State Senate State Capital Columbus OH 43215

HORN, JOAN KELLY, political research and consulting firm executive; b. St. Louis, Oct. 18, 1936; M. E. Terrence Jones; 6 children from previous marriage. BA, U. Mo., St. Louis, 1973, MA, 1975. Pre-sch., elem. sch. Montessori tchr.; founder pre-schs. St. Louis and St. Joseph, Mo.; adj. faculty dept. polit. sci. U. Mo., St. Louis, 1982-86; with St. Louis County Office Community Devel., 1977-80, St. Louis Housing Authority, 1980-82; pres. Community Cons. Inc., 1975-90; elected to 102nd Congress from 2nd dist. Mo., 1990, mem., 1991-92. Author articles on pub. policy issues. Mem. Dem. State Com.; Dem. candidate for U.S. House, 1992, 96. Mem. U. Mo. Alumni Alliance, U. Mo.-St. Louis Alumni Assn. (bd. dirs.). Roman Catholic. Office: Joan Kelly Horn for Congress PO Box 1661 Ballwin MO 63011*

HORN, STANLEY DALE, automotive technology educator; b. Wyandot County, Ohio, May 13, 1941; s. Chester Alfred and Nora D. (Wolford) H.; m. Deanie Phyllis Spradling, Aug. 29, 1964; children: Susan, Dennis, Deanna. BS in Edn., Miami U., Oxford, Ohio, 1964. Cert. tchr., Ohio; cert. master auto technician, master truck technician, master engine machinist, body paint technician, advanced engine performance technician, alt. fuel technician. Auto-truck technician, 1960-73; indsl. arts tchr. Lockland (Ohio) Pub. Schs., 1964-73; auto diagnostic equipment sales and tng. Sun Electric Corp., Cin., 1973-83; fleet truck technician R.A. Miller Constrn., Hamilton, Ohio, 1983-86; automotive instr. Great Oaks Inst. Tech. and Career Devel., Sharonville, Ohio, 1986—; mem. auto adv. com. Great Oaks Inst. Tech. and Career Devel., 1973-83; mem. adv. com. Cin. Vocat. Sch., 1976-78; inspection team leader Nat. Auto Svc. Cert., Herndon, Va., 1987. Trustee First Ch. of God, Hamilton, 1981-83, missions com., 1990—; scout leader Boy Scouts of Am. Troop #969, Fairfield, 1977-83. Named to Automotive Hall of Fame Automotive Svc. Industry Assn., 1988. Mem. Am. Vocat. Assn., Ohio Vocat. Assn., Toastmasters (pres. Network Plus). Home: 851 Sando Dr Fairfield OH 45014-2733 Office: Great Oaks Inst Tech and Career Devel 3254 E Kemper Rd Sharonville OH 45241-1540

HORNBECK, HAROLD DOUGLAS, psychotherapist; b. Ashtabula, Ohio, Dec. 12, 1952; s. Harold Garnet and Garnet Jean (Osburn) H. BS, Ohio State U., 1977; MS in Social Adminstrn., Case Western Res. U., 1987. ACSW, LISW, QCSW; diplomate NASW; cert. Cleve. Ctr. for Cognitive Therapy. Child life worker Rainbow Babies and Children's Hosp., Cleve., 1977-85; psychotherapist Cmty. Counseling Ctr., Ashtabula, 1985-88, Riverview Psychiat. Assocs., Ashtabula, 1988—; adj. faculty Ursuline Coll., Pepperpike, Ohio, 1989; clin. dir. Critical Incident Stress Mgmt. Team, Ashtabula, 1993—; chmn. Ohio Children's Trust Fund LAB, Ashtabula, 1988—; v.p. bd. HIV/AIDS Task Force Ashtabula County, 1989—; bd. dirs. Homesafe Shelter for Battered Women, Ashtabula, 1988-92. Camp dir. Matthew Salem Camp for Cystic Fibrosis, Lakewood, Ohio, 1993—, bd. dirs., counselor, 1978—; bd. dirs. Early Childhood Intervention Project, Ashtabula, 1988-93; advisor Jr. Achievement, Ashtabula, 1992-94; group leader HIV/AIDS Support Group, Ashtabula County, Lake County, Geauga County, 1993—; mentor Ashtabula City Schs., 1993; facilitator I Can Cope Am. Cancer Soc., Ashtabula, 1988—, bd. dirs. We-Can-Week-End, Columbus, Ohio, 1990-94; bd. dirs. Ashtabula County Cmty. Housing Devel. Orgn., Inc., 1996—. Recipient Recognition of Excellence award Ashtabula County Med. Ctr., 1990, Vol. of Yr. award Ashtabula chpt. ARC, 1995. Mem. NASW, Acad. Cert. Social Workers, Assn. for Care Children's Health, Ohio Soc. for Clin. Social Work (v.p. bd. Cleve. chpt. 1995-96, pres. 1996—, state level sec. 1996—). Democrat. Methodist. Home: 1805 W 11th St Ashtabula OH 44004 Office: Riverview Psychiat Assocs 345 Rogers Pl Ashtabula OH 44004

HORNBY, ROBERT RAY, mechanical engineer; b. La Crosse, Wis., Dec. 2, 1958; s. William James and Nancy Kay Boettcher H.; m. Michal Rae Berrey, Aug. 2, 1980; children: Tabitha Kay, Maria Rae, Felicia Anne, Belinda Jo. BS in Mech. Engring., U. of Wis., Platteville, 1981. Registered profl. engr., Wis. Engring. cons. Geoscan Svcs. Co., Tulsa, Okla., 1983-84; sr. project engr. Howard Rotavator Co., Inc., Muscoda, Wis., 1984; mech. design engr. Rayovac, Portage, Wis., 1984-85; designer Gilman Engring. Co., Janesville, Wis., 1985-86; assoc. mech. design engr. Gilman Engring. Co., Janesville, 1986-87; sr. mech. design engr. Giddings Lewis, Janesville, 1989-92, project mgr., 1992-95; sr. engr. NIMCO Corp., Crystal Lake, Ill., 1995—. Edn. chmn. Good Shepherd Luth. Ch., Janesville, 1985-88, religious counselor, 1992—; com. chmn. Explorer Post 400 Boy Scouts Am., Janesville, 1985-91; scoutmaster Troop 516, Janesville, 1985-95. Recipient Scoutmaster award of merit Boy Scouts Am., 1990, Dist. Award of Merit, 1992; named Outstanding Leader Exploring Koshkonong Dist. Boy Scouts Am., Janesville, 1991, 93. Mem. ASME (assoc.), Nat. Soc. Profl. Engrs., Soc. Mfg. Engrs. Home: 844 Pleasant St Woodstock IL 60098-2245 Office: NIMCO Corp 4012A Rt 14 Crystal Lake IL 60039-0320

HORNELL, CHARLES A., financial consultant; b. Pitts., Oct. 23, 1931. BA, Rensselaer Poly. Inst., 1953; MA in Bus., Boston Coll., 1965. Sr. cons. Coachman Inc., Elkhart, Ind., 1981-84; fin. cons. McDonald & Co. Securities Inc., Elkhart, 1985—. Lt. comdr. USN, 1953-57. Mem. Nat. Assn. Bus. Economists, Rotary. Roman Catholic. Office: McDonald & Co Securities PO Box 1228 214 S Main St Elkhart IN 46515

HORNER, JAMES MICHAEL, pediatric endocrinologist; b. Fort Wayne, Ind., Mar. 13, 1947; s. Charles Edward and Helen (Griffin) H.; m. Christina Jean Kelsey, May 25, 1974 (dec. 1990); children: Elizabeth, Jennifer, Stephen; m. Deborah Lynn Romero, June 1, 1991; children: David, Joel. BA in Biology, Albion Coll., 1969; MD, U. Mich., 1973. Resident in pediatrics Columbus (Ohio) Children's Hosp., 1973-75, U. Calif., San Francisco, 1975-76; fellow in pediatric endocrinology Stanford (Calif.) U., 1976-79; from asst. to assoc. prof. pediatrics Med. Coll. Ohio, Toledo, 1979—; dir. Diabetes Connection, Toledo, 1989—; med. liaison Juvenile Diabetes Found., Toledo, 1989—. Patentee in field; contbr. articles to profl. jours. Mem. Assn. Profl. Ball Players Am., Am. Diabetes Assn., Juvenile Diabetes Assn., Lawson Wilkins Pediatric Endocrine Soc., Am. Acad. Pediatrics. Home: 4631 Country Walk Ln Sylvania OH 43560 Office: Med Coll Ohio 3000 Arlington Toledo OH 43699

HORNING, ALICE SILVERBERG, rhetoric and linguistics educator; b. Aug. 7, 1950. BA in English, Boston U., 1971; PhD in English, Mich. State U., 1977. Asst. prof. Wayne State U., Detroit, 1974-82; asst. prof. Oakland U., Rochester, Mich., 1982-86, assoc. prof., 1986-94, prof., 1994—; bibliographer Conf. on Coll. Composition and Comm., 1992—; cons. reader Jour. Advanced Composition, Tampa, Fla., 1990—, Interpersonal Computing and Tech., State College, Pa., 1992—, Nat. Acad. Advising Assn. Jour., 1992-95, Modern Lang. Jour., 1994—. Author: Readings in Contemporary Culture, 1979, Teaching Writing as a Second Language, 1987, The Psycholinguistics of Readable Writing, 1993; contbr. articles to profl. jours. Mem. Nat. Coun. Tchrs. English, Conf. on Coll. Composition and Comm., Nat. Acad. Adv. Assn., Am. Assn. for Applied Linguistics, Assn. for Psychol. Type, Mich. Linguistic Soc. Office: Oakland Univ Dept Rhetoric Rochester MI 48309

HORNING, ANDREW MICHAEL, technical writer and illustrator; b. Indpls., June 20, 1958; s. Donald Mitchell and Libby (Marshalek) H.; m. Karin Wendyl Warbasse; children: Phillip Andrew, Sean Michael, Erin Alexis, Joseph Hallowell. BA in English and Writing, Ind. U., 1990. R.D.C.S., Am. Registry of Diagnostic Med. Sonographers. Intern arbovirus surveillance Ind. State Bd. Health, Indpls., 1979; rsch. technician Krannert Inst. Cardiology, Indpls., 1980-82; instr. Ivy Tech. Coll., Indpls., 1990; echocardiographer, cardiology technician Meth. Hosp., Indpls., 1983-88, Northside Cardiology, Indpls., 1988-90, Midwest Heart Assocs., Indpls., 1989-91; tech. writer/clin. applications specialist Nova MicroSonics, Indpls. and Allendale, N.J., 1991—; art. dir. So. Ind. Sportsd Jour., Evansville, 1982. Co-author, artist: The Pocket Guide to Stress Echocardiography, 1995; author poems; editor: Bremen Enquirer/Plymouth Pilot News, 1979; contbr. articles to profl. jours. Libertarian candidate Ind. State Ho. of Reps., 1996—.

HORNUNG, GEORGE LEONARD, stockbroker; b. Marshalltown, Iowa, June 29, 1952. BS, Iowa State U., 1974. Broker Wilson Foods, Cedar Rapids, Iowa, 1974-77, Livestock Heinhold, Kouts, Ind., 1977-91; stockbroker A.G. Edwards, Mt. Vernon, Ill., 1991—. Mem. Elks. Republican. Methodist. Home: RR 2 Box 54 Fairfield IL 62837-9604 Office: AG Edwards & Sons Inc 3450 Broadway St # A Mount Vernon IL 62864-2270

HOROWITZ, FRED L., dentist, administrator, consultant; b. Chgo., June 10, 1954; s. Jacob and Celia (Morgenstern) H. BA, Washington U., St. Louis, 1976, DMD, 1979; cert. of residency, Sinai Hosp. Detroit, 1980. Gen. practice dentistry Chgo., 1981-92; chief dental cons. Charter Barclay Hosp., Chgo., 1985-89; mem. med. teaching staff Ravenswood Hosp., Chgo., 1983-92, Michael Reese Hosp., Chgo., 1984-90; mem. med. staff St. Francis Hosp., Evanston, 1987-91; pres., CEO, TDC, Chgo. and St. Louis; v.p. Employers Health Ins. Co., Green Bay, Wis.; cons. Humana HMO, 1992-94; trustee Coun. on Dental Benefit Processing Stds., 1992; CEO The Amherst Group, Ltd., 1993-94. Contbg. author: EDI Primer for the Dental Office, 1995; contbr. articles to Ravenswood Hosp. publs. Mem. ADA, Am. Assn. Hosp. Dentists, Health Ins. Assn. of Am. (dental rels com.), Acad. Gen. Dentistry, Chgo. Dental Soc., Nat. Assn. Prepaid Dental Plans (bd. dirs., treas. 1994, vice-chair 1995, chair pub. rels. commn. 1996), Ill. Ambs., Alpha Omega (Leadership award 1979). Office: TDC Ste 700 222 N La Salle St Chicago IL 60601-1103 Office: Dental Concern Ltd 555 N New Ballas Rd Creve Coeur MO 63141-6825

HORRALL, KENNETH BRUCE, geophysicist, geologist, researcher, consultant; b. Olney, Ill., Aug. 1, 1939; s. Robert Bruce and Pauline LaFern (Fisher) H.; m. Patricia Ann Froedge, Nov. 12, 1961 (div. Dec. 1972); 1 child, Meredith Jessica (dec.). BA, So. Ill. U., 1963; MS, No. Ill. U., 1966; PhD, U. Mo., Rolla, 1982. Cert. secondary tchr., Ill. Math. tchr. Roosevelt Sr. H.S., St. Louis, 1968; geophysicist U.S. Naval Oceanographic Office, Washington, 1974-75; petroleum geologist Phillips Petroleum Co., Denver, 1981-82; asst. prof. geology and physics Adrian (Mich.) Coll., 1986-88; cons. geologist, geophysicist Triple-C Oil Producers, Inc., Casey, Ill., 1988—, Eastern Am. Energy Corp., Charleston, W.V., 1988—, Petroleum Capital, Inc., Dallas, 1988—, Am. Trust Oil Co., Olney, Ill., 1988—. Contbr. articles to profl. pubs. including Economic Geology, also others. vol. cons. Concerned Citizens Against a Low Level Nuclear Waste Facility, Marshall and Fairfield, Ill., 1988—. Nat. Defense Ednl. Act fellow U. Mo., 1966, Vachel H. McNutt Mem. Found. fellow , 1980; Sahara Coal Co. forestry scholar So. Ill. U., 1957; various grad., rsch., tchg. assistantships, 1963-80. Mem. Soc. of Econ. Geologists, Knights of Columbus (3d degree), Sigma Xi, Sigma Gamma Epsilon. Roman Catholic. Home: 225 N Elliott St Olney IL 62450-2655

HORSFALL, BRUCE D., marking products manufacturer; b. Lakewood, Ohio, Feb. 6, 1933; s. J. David and Laura E. (Seifried) H.; m. Carolyn Lapp, Dec. 18, 1954 (div. 1984); children: Jennifer, Christie. BA in Indsl. Mgmt., Bowling Green State U., 1955. Dir. Excelsior Marking Products Co., Cleve., 1960—, v.p., 1965-75; pres., CEO Excelsior Marking Products Co., Stow, Ohio, 1975—; cons. Excelsior Sys., Stow, 1975—. Capt. USAF, 1955-60, Europe. Unitarian. Office: Excelsior Marking Products 4524 Hudson Dr Stow OH 44224

HORSLEY, DOC, meteorologist; b. Carbondale, Ill., Jan. 20, 1943; s. Alpha and Ruth Horsley; children: Andrea, Tim; m. Marilyn Horsley, Apr. 27, 1989. BS, So. Ill. U., 1963, MS, 1965, PhD, 1974; MS, Ind. State U., 1968. Prof., meterologist So. Ill. U., Carbondale, 1974—; meteorologist So. Ill. Meteorol. Svcs., Carbondale, 1979—; cons. univs. in China and Africa, 1985, 89, Haiti, 1992, Brazil, 1996, numerous broadcast outlets and legal firms. Pres. Little League, 1975-87. Home: PO Box 3335 Carbondale IL 62902 Office: So Ill U Faner Bldg 4520 Carbondale IL 62902

HORSLEY, JACK EVERETT, lawyer, author; b. Sioux City, Iowa, Dec. 12, 1915; s. Charles E. and Edith V. (Timms) H.; m. Sallie Kelley, June 12, 1939 (dec.); children: Pamela, Charles Edward; m. Bertha J. Newland, Feb. 24, 1950 (dec.); m. Mary Jane Moran, Jan. 20, 1973; 1 child, Sharon. AB, U. Ill., 1937, JD, 1939. Bar: Ill. 1939. Ptnr. Craig & Craig, Mattoon, Ill., 1939—, sr. counsel, 1983—; vice-chmn. bd. dirs. Ctrl. Nat. Bank, 1976-91, legal counsel to exec. com., 1993—, chmn. truste com., mem. exec. com., 1986-91, dir. emeritus, ex officio mem. and counsel to Trust Dept. 1991—; mem. Harlan Moore Heart Rsch. Found., 1968—; mem. lawyers adv. coun. U. Ill. Law Forum, 1960-63; lectr. Practising Law Inst., N.Y.C., 1967-73, U. Ill., Champaign, 1974, Ct. Practice Inst., Chgo., 1974—, Coll. Law Inst. Continuing Legal Edn. U. Mich., 1968, Bankers' Seminar, 1992; vis. lectr. Orange County (Fla.) Med. Soc., 1975, San Diego Med. Soc., 1970, U. S.C., 1976, Duquesne Coll., 1970, U. Ill. Law Forum, 1972, alumni adv. com., 1991—; lectr. med./legal seminars on tour Chgo., Cleve., Pa., Orlando, 1995; chmn. rev. bd. Ill. Supreme Ct. Disciplinary Commn., 1973-76; lectr. Cleve. Hosp., Shelby, N.C., 1976; legal cons. Cenbank Trust Co., 1992—. Narrator: Poetry Interludes, Sta. WLBH-FM, 1977-91; author: Trial Lawyer's Manual, 1967, Voir Dire Examinations and Opening Statements, 1968, Current Development in Products Liability Law, 1969, Illinois Civil Practice and Procedure, 1970, The Medical Expert Witness, 1973, The Doctor and the Law, 1975, The Doctor and Family Law, 1975, The Doctor and Business Law, 1976, The Doctor and Medical Law, 1977, Testifying in Court, 1973, 3s edit., 1993, 3d edit., 1988, 4th edit., 1991, supplement 4th edit., 1993, Anatomy of a Medical Malpractice Case, 1984, 2d edit., 1990, 3d edit., 1993, History of Craig & Craig, Attourneys, 1968-89, 1990, supplement, 1993, 2d edit., 1994, Municpals: G.O. of Revenue, 1992, Trial Techniques, 1995; monographs include Colateral Adequacy, 1993, Principles of Property Appraisal, 1993, Bank Trust Deptartment Law, 1994; minutes of meetings as chair Ctrl. Bank Trust Com.; author: World War II, D-Day, 1994; contbr. articles to profl. jours. including RN Mag. and Forensic Scis. (co-author all edits. 1975-92); editor, cons., contbr. Med. Econs., 1969—; leagal cons. Mast-Head, 1972; contbr. A.L.L. Life, Stafford, Va., 1988—. Alternate del. to Rep. Platform Com., 1992; active Senatorial Reelection Com., 1993; co-chair Ill. Phil Gramm for Pres., 1995; founding mem. U.S. Air Mus., Am. Air Mus.; pres. bd. edn. sch. dist. 100, 1946-48; bd. dirs. Harlan Moore Heart Rsch. Found., 1968-91, hon. dir., 1991—; vol. reader in rec. texts Am. Assn. for Blind, 1970-72; chmn. exec. com. U. Ill. Law Forum, 1990-91; pres. Res. Officers Assn. East Ctrl. Ill., 1988-89; founder Bertha Newland Horsley award St. John's Coll. Nursing, Springfield, Mary Jane Horsley award trophy Mattoon (Ill.) H.S. Lt. col. JAGD U.S. Army, 1942-46, ETO, USAR (hon., ret.). Decorated Purple Heart. Recipient Disting. Svc. award U. Ill., 1995. Fellow Am. Coll. Trial Lawyers; mem. ABA, Ill. Bar Assn. (exec. coun. ins. law 1961-63, com. chmn. banking law 1972, lectr. law course for attys. 1962, 64-65, sr. counsellor 1989—, Disting. Svc. award 1982-83), Coles-Cumberland Bar Assn. (v.p. 1968-69, pres. 1969-70, chmn. com. jud. inquiry 1976-80, chmn. membership com. 1981—, elected sr. counsellor 1989, co-author Forensic Scis. Jour. 1991), Am. Arbitration Assn. (nat. panel arbitrators), U. Ill. Law Alumni Assn. (life mem., pres. 1966-67, Alumni of Month Sept. 1974, exec. com. 1990-91), Ill. Appellate Lawyers Assn., Soc. Legal Scribes, Ill. Def. Counsel Assn. (pres. 1967-88), Soc. Trial Lawyers (chmn. profl. activities 1960-61, bd. dirs. 1966-67), U.S. Supreme Ct. Hist. Soc. (co-chair), Adelphic Debating Soc., Assn. Ins. Attys., Internat. Assn. Ins. Counsel, Am. Judicature Soc., Appellate Lawyers Assn., Res. Officers Assn. (pres. 1946-50, pres. emeri. Ill. Alumni Assn. (exec. com. 1990-91), Soc. Legal Scribes, Masons (Sr. Master award 1992), Scribes, Delta Phi (exec. com. alumni assn. 1960-61, 67-68), Sigma Delta. Lutheran. Home: 913 N 31st St Mattoon IL 61938-2271 Office: Craig & Craig 1807 Broadway PO Box 689 Mattoon IL 61938-0689 also: 227 1/2 S 9th St PO Box 1545 Mount Vernon IL 62864

HORSLEY, TERI LYNNE, advertising sales representative; b. Hamilton, Ohio, Nov. 23, 1961; d. James Murray and Margaret Jean (McDowell) Hoel; m. Michael Anthony Horsley, Aug. 11, 1984 (div. 1991). BA in Radio/TV/Film, No. Ky. U., 1984; postgrad., Wright State U., 1992—. With Vaughn Auctioneers, Hamilton, Ohio, 1982-85; news reporter/anchor D.J. Sta. WMOH Radio, Hamilton, Ohio, 1983-85; weather graphics asst. Sta. WKRC-TV, Cin., 1984-85; disc jockey Sta. WING Radio, Dayton, Ohio, 1985; news anchor/reporter Sta. WLW Radio, Cin., 1985-87; news stringer ABC News, 1985-87; pres., owner T.J.'s Dee-Jays - D.J. Svc., Fairfield, Ohio, 1987-89; intake interviewer Butler County Forensic Ctr., Hamilton, 1989-90; news dir., talk host Sta. WMOH Radio, Hamilton, 1989-95; news stringer Sta. WCKY News, 1989-94; stringer Sta. WSAI News, 1994-95; adv. sales rep. Thomson Newspapers/Directories, Middletown, Ohio, 1995—; instr. Conn. Sch. Broadcasting, Cin., 1990; radio news anchor Cinn. Newswatch, 1995—. Mem. panel Civitan Cmty. Disaster Team, Fairfield, 1990-91; judge Rotary Sci. Fair, Hamilton, 1991; bd. dirs. Greater Hamilton Safety Coun., 1989—, Family Svcs., 1991-94; lobbyist Arthritis Found., 1993; bd. dirs. Nat. Butler County Mental Health Ctr., 1993-95,local emergency planning com. bd., 1994-95. Mem. Soc. for Human Resources Mgmt., Lions (pres. Hamilton club 1992-93). Republican. Office: Thomson Newspapers/ Directories 52 S Broad St Middletown OH 45042-0490

HORSMAN, REGINALD, history educator; b. Leeds, Eng., Oct. 24, 1931; came to U.S., 1954, naturalized, 1965; s. Alfred William and Elizabeth (Thompson) H.; m. Lenore Lynde McNabb, Sept. 3, 1955; children: John, Janine, Mara. B.A., U. Birmingham, Eng., 1952, M.A., 1955; Ph.D., Ind. U., 1958. Mem. faculty U. Wis.-Milw., 1958—, prof. history, 1964-73, distinguished prof., 1973—, chmn. dept., 1970-72. Author: The Causes of the War of 1812, 1962, Matthew Elliott: British Indian Agent, 1964, Expansion and American Indian Policy, 1967, The War of 1812, 1969, The Frontier in the Formative Years, 1970, Napoleon's Europe: The New America, 1970, Race and Manifest Destiny: The Origins of American Racial Angl-Saxonism, 1981; The Diplomacy of the New Republic, 1776-1815, 1985, Josiah Nott of Mobile: Southerner, Physician and Racial Theorist, 1987, Frontier Doctor: William Beaumont, America's First Great Medical Scientist, 1996. Guggenheim fellow, 1965-66; recipient Kiekhofer teaching award U. Wis., 1961, U. Wis.-Mulw. Alumni Assn. award for Teaching Excellence, 1995. Mem. Am. Hist. Assn., Orgn. Am. Historians, Soc. for Historians Early Am. Republic, Soc. Am. Historians, Phi Beta Kappa (hon.), Phi Kappa Phi (hon.), Phi Eta Sigma (hon.), Phi Alpha Theta. Home: 3548 N Hackett Ave Milwaukee WI 53211-2637

HORST, BRUCE EVERETT, manufacturing company executive; b. Three Rivers, Mich., Feb. 17, 1921; s. Walter and Genevieve (Turner) H.; m. Patricia Kranish, Oct. 4, 1969; children: Michael, Diane, Mark. BS in Bus. and Engring. Adminstrn, Mass. Inst. Tech., 1943. With Barber-Colman Co., Rockford, Ill., 1946-76, pres., 1965-75, vice chmn. bd., 1975-76; pres. Mid-States Screw Corp., 1976—, Redin Corp., 1979—; sr. treas. P.J. Maxwell Co., 1987—. Bd. dirs. Rockford YMCA, 1964-75, pres., 1965-67. Served to 1st lt. USAAF, 1943-45. Decorated Air medal. Mem. Rotary, Univ. Club (Rockford), Forest Hills Country Club (Rockford) (past sec.), Moorings Country Club (Naples), Yacht Club at Lake Geneva (Wis.). Home: 2625 Harlem Blvd Rockford IL 61103-4117 Office: Mid-States Screw Corp 1817 18th Ave Rockford IL 61104-7317

HORST, DEENA LOUISE, state legislator; b. Sacramento, Feb. 14, 1944; s. Orlo John and Louise Helena (Schultz) Poovey; m. Gordon Lee Horst, 1966; children: Randall, Rebecca. BSE, Emporia State U., 1966, MA, 1972; postgrad., Kans. State U., 1993—. Elem. tchr. Peabody Sch., 1966-68; mid. sch. art tchr., dept. chmn. South Mid. Sch., Unified Sch. Dist. # 305, 1968—; mem. from dist. 69 Kans. State Ho. of Reps., 1995—. State and nat. ofcl. U.S. Jaycee Women, 1968-84; sec. Saline County Rep. Ctrl. Com., Kans., 1992-95. Named Outstanding State Pres., U.S. Jaycee Women, 1979-80. Mem. C. of C., Phi Alpha, Alpha Theta Rho, Phi Delta Kappa, Epsilon Sigma Alpha (Zone Outstanding Sister award 1990). Address: 920 S 9th Salina KS 67401

HORTON, BETTY JOAN, anesthesia nurse, organization administrator; b. Decatur, Ill., Aug. 10, 1936; d. Paul Revere and Nona Bernice (Sneller) Beggs; m. Earl Monroe Horton, Nov. 10, 1958; children: Diane, Steven, Wayne. Diploma, Decatur Macon County Hosp., 1958; cert. in anesthesia, Decatur Meml. Hosp., 1968; BS, Coll. St. Francis, Joliet, Ill., 1978; MA, Sangamon State U., 1980; MSN, Case Western Res. U., 1994. RN, Ill. Head nurse obs. Decatur Meml. Hosp., 1958-65, staff anesthetist, 1969-70, dir. nurse anesthetists, 1970-89; adj. asst. prof. Sangamon State U., Springfield, Ill., 1981-85; adj. prof. nursing Bradley U., 1988-89; clin. instr. nurse anesthesia Case-Western Res. U., Cleve., 1992; dir. accreditation Coun. on Accreditation, Park Ridge, Ill., 1990—; sec. Coun. on Postsecondary Specialized Accreditation, Washington, 1992-93; mem. adv. bd. Commn. on Edn. Grant, Park Ridge, 1992-94; presenter profl. confs. in field; assoc. project dir. U.S. Dept. Edn. FIPSE Grant, 1994—. Mem. editl. bd. Advanced Practice Nursing Jour.; contbr. articles to profl. publs. Bd. dirs. Peer Assistance Network for Nurses, 1991-94; den mother Decatur area Boy Scouts Am., 1970. Mem. ANA, Nat. League Nurses, Ill. Nurses Assn., Ill. Assn. Nurse Anesthetists (pres. 1987-88, past bd. dirs., chairperson edn. com.), Am. Assn. Nurse Anesthetists (cert. nurse anesthetist, dir. edn. 1996—), Sigma Theta Tau. Home: RR 2 Box 145 Tower Hill IL 62571-9653 Office: Coun on Accreditation 222 Prospect Ave Park Ridge IL 60068

HORTON, FRANK ELBA, university official, geography educator; b. Chgo., Aug. 19, 1939; s. Elba Earl and Mae Pauline (Prohaska) H.; m. Nancy Yocom, Aug. 26, 1960; children: Kimberly, Pamela, Amy, Kelly. BA, Western Ill. U., 1963; MS, Northwestern U., 1964, PhD, 1966. Faculty U. Iowa, Iowa City, 1966-75; prof. geography U. Iowa, 1966-75; dir. Inst. Urban and Regional Research, 1968-72, dean advanced studies, 1972-75; v.p. acad. affairs, research So. Ill. U., Carbondale, 1975-80; prof. geography and urban affairs, chancellor U. Wis., Milw., 1980-85; prof. geography, pres. U. Okla., Norman, 1985-88; prof. geography, higher edn. adminstrn., pres. U. Toledo, 1988—; mem. commn. on leadership devel. and acad. adminstrn. Am. Coun. on Edn., 1983-85; mem. presdl. adv. com. Assn. on Governing Bds., 1986—; dir. 1st Wis. Nat. Bank of Milw., 1980-85, Liberty Nat. Bank, Oklahoma City, 1986-89, Trustcorp. Bank, 1989-90; bd. dirs. Interstate Bakeries. Author, editor: (with B.J.L. Berry) Geographic Perspectives on Urban Systems - With Integrated Readings, 1970, Urban Environmental Management - Planning for Pollution Control, 1974; editor: (with B.J.L. Berry) Geographical Perspectives on Contemporary Urban Problems, 1973; editorial adv. bd.: (with B.J.L. Berry) Transportation, 1971-78. Co-chmn. Goals for Milw. 2000, 1981-85, Greater Milw. Com., 1980; mem. bus. devel. sub-com. Okla. Coun. Sci. and Tech., 1985-88; mem. Harry S. Truman Library Inst., 1985-88, William Rockhill Nelson Trust, 1985-88; bd. govs. Am. Heart Assn., Wis., 1980-85, Ohio Supercomputer Ctr., 1993—; mem. exec. com. Okla. Acad. State Goals, 1986-88; trustee Toledo Symphony Orch., 1989—, Toledo Hosp., 1989—, Pub. Broadcasting Found. Northwest Ohio, 1989-93, Soc. Bank & Trust, 1990—, Ohio Aerospace Inst., 1990—; chair Inter-Univ. Coun. Pres. of Ohio Public Univs., 1992-93; mem. exec. com. Com. of 100, Toledo, 1989-92. Served with AUS, 1957-60. Mem. AAAs (nat. coun. 1976-78), Assn. Governing Bds. (mem. presdl. adv. commn. 1986—), Assn. Am. Geographers, nat. Assn. State Univs. and Land Grant Colls. (chair urban affairs div. 1983-85, chmn. Coun. of Pres. 1987-88, exec. com. 1983-88), Nat. Hwy. Rsch. Soc., Okla. Coun. on Sci. and Tech., MidAm. State Univs. Assn. (pres. 1987-88), Ohio Supercomputer Ctr. (bd. govs. 1993), Ohio Aerospace Inst. (trustee 1990—), Okla. Acad. State Goals (pres. 1987-88), Okla. State C. of C. and Industry (v.p. 1987-88), Toledo Area C. of C. (vice chmn. bd. dirs. 1991-93). Home: 3883 W Bancroft St Toledo OH 43606-2532 Office: U Toledo 2801 W Bancroft St Toledo OH 43606-3328

HORTON, JACK, state legislator; b. Jan. 1, 1995; m. Fay; children: Janelle, Seth, Bethany. BA, Grand Rapids Bapt. Coll., 1977; postgrad., Grand Rapids Bapt. Sem., Calvin Coll. Precinct del., 1982-88; del. Rep. State Conv.; del. 5th Dist. rep. State Issues Com., 1989—; state rep. Dist 90 Mich. Ho. of Rep., 1990-94, state rep. Dist. 73, 1995%; nat. asst. dir. Bapts. for Life, 1988-90. Home: 1625 Parnell Ave N Lowell MI 49331-9793*

HORTON, WILLIAM DAVID, JR., survivability analyst; b. Memphis, Oct. 25, 1953; s. William David and Maynell (Holland) H.; m. Rebecca Jean Griffin, Oct. 11, 1975; children: Elizabeth Anne, Wendy Leigh, William Robert. BS in Physics, U. Miss., 1975; MS in Physics, MIT, 1979. Commd. 2d lt. U.S. Army, 1975, advanced through grades to lt. col., 1992; ret., 1995; rsch. coord. directed energy directorate U.S. Army, Redstone, Ala., 1983-85, asst. project mgr. remotely piloted vehicles, 1985-86; br. chief dir. combat devel. U.S. Army, Ft. Knox, Ky., 1987-90, divsn. chief dir. combat devel., 1990-91; asst. project mgr. PM survivability sys. U.S. Army, Warren, Mich., 1991-95; asst. project mgr. Orion Internat. Tech., 1995; countermeasure analyst Orion Internat. Techs., White Sands Missile Range, N.Mex., 1995-96; survivability analyst Opti Metrics, Inc., Ann Arbor, 1996—; invited spkr. courses on infrared countermeasures U. Mich., 1994, 95, invited spkr. on thread precision quided munitions and their susceptibilities. Author reports, manuals, requirements documents for Electronic Warfare Survivability Enhancements. Mem. Armor Assn. 2d Armored Cavalry Assn. (life), Armed Forces Comms. and Elec. Assn., Am. Legion, Old Crows. Home: 9331 Harbor Cove Cl Apt 331 Whitmore Lake MI 48189 Office: Opti Metrics Inc 3115 Professional Dr Ann Arbor MI 48104-5131

HORVATH, BROOKE KENTON, English language educator; b. Elyria, Ohio, Sept. 7, 1953; s. Eugene Rudolph and Nancy Jane (Dunkle) H.; m. Janet Lee Stone, Sept. 16, 1975; children: Susan, Jordan. BA, Kent State U., 1975; MA, SUNY, Binghamton, 1977; PhD, Purdue U., 1986. Teaching asst. SUNY, Binghamton, 1975-77; teaching asst. Purdue U., West Lafayette, Ind., 1979-86, vis. prof., 1986-88; asst. prof. English, lit. Kent State U., Canton, Ohio, 1988-93, assoc. prof., 1993—; presenter workshops, seminars, poetry readings; lectr. in field. Mng. editor Modern Fiction Studies, West Lafayette, 1984-87; assoc. editor Rev. Contemporary Fiction, Normal, Ill., 1989—; book rev. editor Aethlon: Jour. Sport Lit., Johnson City, Tenn., 1991-95; author: In A Neighborhood of Dying Light, 1995, Consolation at Ground Zero, 1995; co-editor: William Goyan and the Terrible Embrace of Art, 1997; contbr. chpts. to books, articles and revs. to scholarly publs., poetry to lit publs. Grantee Tippicanoe Arts Coun., 1988. Mem. MLA, Nat. Coun. Tchrs. English, Sport Lit. Assn., Associated Writing Programs, Nat. Book Critics Circle, Assn. of Literary Scholars and Critics. Home: 2642 Oak Park Blvd Cuyahoga Falls OH 44221-2916 Office: Kent State Univ Dept English 6000 Frank Ave NW Canton OH 44720-7548

HORVATH, JULIANA, special education educator; b. LaPorte, Ind., Feb. 8, 1948; d. Philip Andrew and Mary Louise (Wozniak) Nowatzke; m. Michael John, Aug. 1, 1970; children: Angela Danielle, Valerie Nicole. BS, Ind. U., 1971, MS, 1973, postgrad., 1974-75; postgrad., Fort Hays State U., 1985-86, Bradley U., 1994-95. Cert. tchr., Ind., Kans., Ill. Tchr. New Prairie United Sch. Corp., New Carlisle, Ind., 1971-74; learning disability cons. Cass County Intermediate Dist., Cassopolis, Mich., 1974-75; tchr. Tucson Unified Dist. # 1, 1975-78; lectr., supr. Marywood Coll., Scranton, Pa., 1978-80; grad. supr. Ind. U., South Bend, 1980-83; tchr. Lourdesmont Sch., Pa., 1982; instr., coord. Fort Hays (Kans.) State U., 1983-84; tchr. LaCrosse, Kans. Coop., McCracken, 1984-86; joint appointment tchr. United Dist., Hays, 1984-89; learning disability tchr. Peoria (Ill.) Pub. Schs., 1989-95. Co-author: (research paper), 1984. Chmn. St. Nicholas of Myra Parish, Hays, 1986-87, coord., 1987-88; treas. Ft. Hays State U. Faculty Wives, 1984, 87. Mem. NEA, Coun. for Exceptional Children, Phi Delta Kappa, Alpha Delta Kappa (pres. chpt. 1994-95). Democrat. Roman Catholic. Home: 620 W Jaccard Pl Joplin MO 64801-1019

HORVATH, RALPH STEVE, electrical engineering educator; b. Scranton, Pa., Feb. 9, 1936; s. Vincent and Mary (Ambrose) H.; m. Catherine Horvath, Nov. 9, 1957 (div. 1981); children: Elizabeth, Ruth; m. Constance Ruth Sherry, Sept. 4, 1982. BSEE, Mich. Tech. U., 1960; MSEE, NYU, 1962; PhD, Worcester (Mass.) Poly. Inst., 1968. Registered profl. engr., Mich. TV serviceman Houghton, Mich., 1956-60; mem. tech. staff Bell Telephone Labs., Holmdel, N.J., 1960-62; rsch. assoc. Worcester Found. for Exptl. Biology, Shrewsbury, Mass., 1967-68; lectr. U. Md./Europe, 1984-85; vis. prof. Darling Downs Inst. Adv. Edn., Toowoomba, Queensland, Australia, 1988; assoc. prof. elec. engring. Mich. Technol. U., Houghton, 1962—; lectr. Nat. Tech. U., Boulder, Colo., 1987—, Mich. Soc. Profl. Engrs., Gen. Motors; vis. assoc. prof. U. Auckland (N.Z.), 1993-94; fire investigator, 1970—. Author five books on microprocessors; inventor/patentee in field. With USMC, 1953-56. Named Disting. Faculty, Mich. Assn. Govt. Bds., 1983, Teetor award, SAE, 1981, others. Mem. IEEE (sr. mem.), Internat. Assn. Arson Investigators, Sigma Xi. Office: Mich Technol Univ Elec Engring College Ave Houghton MI 49931

HORWITZ, ALAN FREDRICK, cell and molecular biology educator and researcher; b. Mpls., Oct. 26, 1944; s. Burt and Helen (Bolnick) H.; m. Carole Joanne Rosen, Nov. 26, 1972; children: Jeremy J., Rachel T. BA in Chemistry with honors, U. Wis., 1966; PhD in Biophysics, Stanford U., 1969; MA (hon.), U. Pa., 1978. NIH postdoctoral fellow Lab. Chem. Biodynamics, U. Calif., Berkeley, 1970-72, chemist P-5, 1972-73; scientist Biozentrum der Universitat Basel, Switzerland, 1973-74; asst. prof. dept. biochemistry and biophysics Sch. Medicine, U. Pa., Phila., 1974-78, assoc. prof., 1978-84, prof., 1984—; prof., head dept. cell and structural biology U. Ill., Urbana, 1987-95, chmn. biophysics program, 1978-85, assoc. dir. med. scientist tng. program, 1986-87, dir. cell and molecular biology tng. program, 1988-92; mem. commn. on cell and membrane biophysics Internat. Union Pure and Applied Biophysics, 1975-82; mem. sci. adv. com. biochemistry and chem. carcinogens Am. Cancer Soc., 1977-81; mem. spl. study sects. Nat. Inst. Gen. Med. Scis. NIH, 1980—, mem. rev. com. cellular and molecular basis of disease Nat. Inst. Gen. Med. Sci., 1984-88; mem. spl. study sects. Nat. Inst. Aging, Nat. Cancer Inst. Nat Inst. Gen. Med. Sci., 1980—, mem. biotech. rev. panel, 1988, mem. adv. coun., 1994; mem. innovative aging rsch. com. VA, 1983; lectr. various nat. and internat. symposia; steering com. Howard Hughes Inst. Med. Rsch., U. Pa., adv. com. for H.M. Watts, Jr. Neuromuscular Disease Rsch. Inst., U. Pa., 1986. Mem. editl. bd. Jour. Cell Biology, 1989—, Jour. Cell Sci., 1990—, Cell Adhesion and Comm., 1992—, Trends in Cell Biology, 1994—, Current Opinion in Cell Biology, 1995—; assoc. editor: Devel. Biology, 1989-95; sect. editor Current Opinion in Cell Biology, 1994; contbr. articles to profl. jours. Recipient Dr. William Daniel Stroud Established Investigator award Am. Heart Assn., 1975-80, NIH Merit award, 1992; prin. investigator, grantee in field, 1974. Mem. Biophys. Soc., Am. Soc. Biol. Chemists, Am. Soc. Cell Biology (pub. policy com. 1986—, nominating com. 1988, program com. 1995), Am. Assn. Anat. Chmn. Home: 3410 S Persimmon Cir Urbana IL 61802-7128 Office: U Ill Dept Cell & Structural Biology Urbana IL 61801

HORWITZ, CLIFFORD WOLF, lawyer; b. Chgo., May 25, 1959; s. Andrew J. and Donna (Magida) H. Student, U. Colo.; BS, U. Fla., 1981; JD, Loyola U., Chgo., 1984; postdoctoral, Northwestern U. Ptnr. Horwitz, Horwitz & Assocs., Chgo., 1977—. Host (TV show) Lawtalk, Chgo. Mem. ABA, Fed. Bar Assn., Appellate Bar Assn., Chgo. Bar Assn., ATLA, Ill. Trial Lawyers Assn. (mem. polit. com.), Phi Kappa Phi. Home: 368 Washington Glencoe IL 60022 Office: Horwitz Horwitz & Assocs 180 N La Salle St Ste 1025 Chicago IL 60601-2506

HORWITZ, WILLIAM J., treasurer; b. St. Louis, Jan. 10, 1946; s. Harold S. and Henrietta H.; m. Abby Klein, Aug. 1, 1971; children: Harris Saul, Pallas Hannah Eleanor. AB, Harvard U., 1967; MPhil, Yale U., 1969, PhD, 1971. Assoc. prof. classics dept. U. Okla., Norman, 1971-79; treas. Bride's House, St. Louis, 1979—. Contbr. articles to profl. jours. Recipient Woodrow Wilson fellowship, 1967, John Harvard Hon. scholarship, 1964, 66. Mem. Harvard Club of St. Louis (v.p. 1988-90, chmn. various coms. 1986-88), Yale Club of St. Louis. Office: Bride's House 1010 Locust St Saint Louis MO 63101-1306

HOSKINS, W. LEE, banker; b. L.A., Feb. 7, 1941; s. E. W. and Mary E. (Taylor) H.; m. Gail Entrekin, Oct. 23, 1964. BA in Econs., UCLA, 1962, MA, 1964, PhD in Econs., 1969. With Fed. Res. Bank Phila., 1969-80, rsch. officer, economist, 1972-73, v.p., dir. econ. rsch., 1973-80; sr. v.p., chief economist PNC Fin. Corp. and Pitts. Nat. Bank, 1980-87; pres. Fed. Res. Bank, Cleve., 1987-91; pres., CEO Huntington Nat. Bank, Columbus, Ohio, 1991-93, chmn., CEO, 1993—; vice chmn. Huntington Bancshares Inc.,

1991—. Contbr. articles to profl. and bus. publs. Trustee Carnegie Mellon U., Children's Hosp., United Way Franklin County, Inc., mem. pres.' bus. adv. coun. Ohio State U. Mem. Assn. Res. City Bankers, Nat. Assn. Bus. Econs. (past pres.), Columbus C. of C. (bd. dirs.), Mont Pelerin Soc., Western Econ. Assn. Internat. (former mem. exec. com.). Office: Huntington Nat Bank Huntington Ctr Columbus OH 43287

HOSKINS, WILLIAM KELLER, pharmaceutical company executive, lawyer; b. Cin., Feb. 22, 1935; s. John Hobart and Gertrude Louise (Keller) H.; m. Elizabeth Ann Grimm, Aug. 5, 1961; children: Bruce, Andrew, John, Elizabeth, Allison. BA, Yale U., 1956; LLB, Harvard U., 1962. Bar: Ohio 1962, U.S. Dist. Ct. (so. dist.) Ohio 1963, U.S. Tax Ct. 1963, U.S. Ct. Appeals (6th cir.) 1964, N.Y. 1982, Mo. 1983. Assoc., Frost & Jacobs, Cin., 1962-68; gen. counsel Drackett Co., Cin., 1968-71, v.p., gen. counsel, 1971-81; assoc. gen. counsel Bristol Myers Co., N.Y.C., 1981, spl. counsel, 1982; v.p., gen. counsel, sec. Hoechst Marion Roussell (formerly Marion Merrell Dow Inc.), Kansas City, Mo., 1982—, also bd. dirs., 1989; chmn. household div. Soap and Detergent Assn., N.Y.C., 1978-79, chmn. Chem. Spltys. Mfg. Assn., Washington, 1982; bd. dirs. J.C. Nichols Co. Kansas City, Mo. Mem. Hamilton County Rep. Cen. Com., Ohio, 1970-81; sec.-treas. Marion Labs. Polit. Action Com., 1982-89; sec.-treas. polit. action com. Mid-Am. Com. Sound Govt., Lake Quivira, Kans., 1982-86; bd. dirs. Landmark Legal Found., Kansas City, Mo., 1995—. Lt. (j.g.) USN, 1956-59. Mem. ABA, Mo. Bar Assn., Ohio Bar Assn., Cin. Bar Assn., Lawyers Assn. of Kansas City, Harvard Law Sch. Alumni Assn. (bd. dirs.). Roman Catholic. Home: 1101A W 47th St Kansas City MO 64112-1216 Office: Hoechst Marion Roussel Inc PO Box 9627 JS M1540 10236 Marion Park Dr Kansas City MO 64137-1405

HOSMAN, SHARON, elementary education educator; b. Springfield, Mo., May 20, 1939; d. Charles E. and Jewell A. (Allgood) Beckerdite; m. Ralph W. Hosman, Jan. 1, 1980; children: Kevin Cook, Melissa Cook, Shawn Cook. BS, SW Mo. State U., 1964, MS, 1980. Tchr. music Pleasant Hope (Mo.) Sch., 1964-66; elem. tchr. Willard (Mo.) Pub. Schs., 1966-93. Mem. Morrisville/Aldrich United Methodist Chs., piano player. Mem. Internat. Reading Assn., Am. Fedn. Tchrs. Methodist. Home: HCR 80 Box 782 Camdenton MO 65020

HOSMER, CRAIG, state legislator; b. Springfield, Mo., Mar. 16, 1959. BA, U. Mo. Columbia, 1982; JD, George Washington U., 1986. State rep. Dist. 138 Mo. State Congress, 1991—; mem. appropriations com., correctional insts. com., judiciary com., labor com. *

HOSTETLER, JOHN D., systems engineer; b. Canton, Ohio, Apr. 11, 1964. BS in Indsl. and Sys. Engring., Ohio State U., 1987. Engr.-in-tng., Ohio. Draftsman Hostetler & Decker, Deck-TEC, Canton, 1983-87, sys. engr., 1987—. Contbr. articles to profl. jours. Office: Hostetler-Decker Deck-TEC 825 Navarre Rd SW Canton OH 44707-4058

HOSTETLER, JOHN JAY, systems consultant; b. Hutchinson, Kans., Nov. 20, 1957; s. Melvin C. and Bette Jane (Hall) H.; m. Kay Charisse Siemens Ward, June 20, 1981 (div. Mar. 1992); children: Holden, Jordan; m. Renny Ann Justice, Sept. 11, 1992; children: Nichole, Keith. BA in Clin. Psychology, Wichita (Kans.) State U., 1980; MA in Psychology, Clayton U., St. Louis, 1989. Computer programmer Boeing Computer Svcs., Wichita, 1983-85, program mgr., 1985-86; sr. systems analyst Pizza Hut, Inc., Wichita, 1986-89, mgr., 1989; systems cons. Boeing Comml. Airplane, Wichita, 1989—; coaching cons. Boeing Productivity Plus, Boeing Co., Wichita, 1992—, instr., tchr. Boeing Edn. & Tng., 1989—. Author, editor: Whispers From the Past, 1991, A Christmas Spirit, 1995, For Kid Sake, 1996. Recipient Alumni award Hutchinson C.C., 1992. Mem. Andover Cmty. Theater, Project Mgmt. Inst., Wichita State U. Alumni Assn., Phi Kappa Phi, Psi Chi (v.p. 1979-82). Republican. Presbyterian. Home: #1 Swallow Ln Wichita KS 67230 Office: Boeing Co 4200 Southeast Blvd Wichita KS 67210

HOSTETTER, JAMES WILLIAM, lawyer; b. Newark, Ohio, May 10, 1948; s. James O. and Joanne A. (Abel) H.; m. Lynn Susan Kudlack, June 19, 1971; children: Brad A., Eric A. BS, Wittenberg U., 1970; JD, Capital U., 1976. Bar: Ohio 1976, U.S. Dist. Ct. (so. dist.) Ohio 1977, U.S. Supreme Ct. 1979. Tchr. Berne Union Schs., Sugar Grove, Ohio, 1970-71, East Muskingum Schs., New Concord, Ohio, 1971-72; work-study coord. Licking County Schs., Newark, 1972-73; with legal div. Ohio Dept. Taxation, Columbus, 1973-76; ptnr. Schaller, Hostetter & Campbell, Newark, 1976—; asst. pros. atty. Licking County Prosecutor's Office, Newark, 1976-79, 84-92; dir. of law City of Newark (Ohio), 1992—; clk. Heath (Ohio) Civil Svc. Comn., 1981-83; real estate instr. Cen. Ohio Tech. Coll., Newark, 1978-83. Mem., pres. Lakewood Local Bd. Edn., Hebron, Ohio, 1980-84; mem. exec. com. Licking County Rep. party, Newark, 1982—; vol. Licking County United Way, Cancer Soc., Heart Fund, Newark. Mem. Ohio State Bar Assn., Licking County Bar Assn., Newark Lions Club, Newark Maennerchor, Moose. Republican. Office: Dir Law City of Newark 30 W Locust St Newark OH 43055-5526

HOSTETTLER, JOHN N., congressman; b. Evansville, Ind., July 19, 1961; s. Earl Eugene and Esther Aline (Hollingsworth) H.; m. Elizabeth Ann Hamman, Nov. 12, 1983; children: Matthew, Amanda, Jaclyn. BSME, Rose-Hulman Inst. Tech. Reg. profl. engr. Engr. So. Ind. Gas and Electric, Evansville, 1986-94; congressman U.S. Congress, Washington, 1995—. Deacon 12th Avenue Gen. Baptist, 1986—. Republican. Baptist. Office: 1404 Longworth House Office Bldg Washington DC 20515

HOTALING, ROBERT BACHMAN, community planner, educator; b. Syracuse, July 19, 1918; s. Elliot Danforth and Florence (Bachman) H.; m. M. Janet Kelley, Nov. 20, 1943 (dec.); children: Marilyn Kelley, Brock Elliot, William Austin, Richard Chapman; m. Jeanne Bryant, July 31, 1971. BS in Environ. Sci. and Forestry, Syracuse U., 1942; M of Urban and Regional Planning, Mich. State U., 1952. Staff dir. McFadzean, Everly Rose and Assocs., Chgo., 1946-49; dir. state and local planning R.I. Exec. Dept., Providence, 1952-55; tech. coord. for planning Interstate hwy. sytems through New England, R.I., Mass. and Conn., 1954-55; city planning dir., urban renewal planner Portland, Maine, 1955-57; acting dir., sec. Greater Portland Regional Planning Commn., 1956-57; prof. urban and regional planning Coll. Social Sci., Mich. State U., East Lansing, 1957-81; prof. lifelong edn. Inst. Community Devel., Mich. State U., East Lansing, 1957-81; prof. emeritus Mich. State U., 1981—; assoc. McKenna and Assocs., Farmington Hills, Mich., 1992—, Freeman, Smith & Assocs., Lansing, Mich., 1992—, Pub. Sector Cons., Lansing, 1992—; pres. Urban Cons., Inc., 1962-66; pres., owner Robert B. Hotaling and Assoc., 1949—; expert witness to law firms, state and fed. agys., philanthropic orgns.; cons., lectr., seminarian Mich. Twp. Assn., 1963-81, Mich. Mcpl. League, 1978—; mem. Mich. State Bd. of Registration for Profl. Community Planners, 1967-81, chmn., 1970-72, 76-79; cons. to state agys., polit. orgns. and corps. Author: Michigan Local Planning Commissioners Handbook (3 edits.), Michigan Township Planning and Zoning Handbook (2 edits.); chmn. editorial com. Mich. Laws Relating to Planning (3 edits.); contbr. articles to profl. jours. Mem. twp. planning commn. 1958-70, 87-94, chmn. 1969-70, Meridan Twp., Ingham County, Mich.; mem. Meridian Twp. charter com., chmn., 1970-73; mem. Meridian Twp. Zoning Bd. of Appeals, 1969-70, 87, chmn. 1969-70; mem. strategic planning com. for planning future of Meridan Twp., Gov.'s State Legis. Zoning Revision Com., 1977-79; bd. dirs. Mich. Parks Assn., 1960-68; charter mem. Am. Inst. Cert. Profl. Community Planners, 1954-81; mem. Mich. State Bd. Registration for Profl. Community Planners State Examination Com., 1969-71, Am. Inst. Planners Nat. Examination Com. for Profl. Planners, 1977-78. Capt. U.S. Army Corps. Engrs., 1942-46. Recipient Meritorious Svc. award Mich. Mcpl. League, 1994. Mem. Mich. Soc. Consulting Planners (bd. dirs. 1979—). Episcopalian. Home and Office: PO Box 304 Haslett MI 48840-0304

HOTCHKISS, EUGENE, III, college president emeritus; b. Berwyn, Ill., Apr. 1, 1928; s. Eugene and Jeanette (Kennan) H.; m. Suzanne Ellen Troxell, Nov. 17, 1962; 1 dau., Ellen Sinclair. A.B., Dartmouth Coll., 1950; Ph.D., Cornell U., 1960; LL.D. (hon.), Ill. Coll., 1976, Lake Forest Coll., 1993. Asst. to dean Dartmouth Coll., 1953-54, asst. dean, 1954-55, asso. dean, 1958-60; asst. dean Cornell U., Ithaca, N.Y., 1955-58; dean students, lectr. history Harvey Mudd Coll., Claremont, Calif., 1960-63; dean coll. Harvey Mudd Coll., 1962-68; exec. dean Chatham Coll., Pitts., 1968-70; pres. Lake Forest (Ill.) Coll., 1970-93, pres. emeritus, 1996—; sr. fellow Assn. of Governing Bds. Served to lt. (j.g.) USNR, 1950-53. Mem. Phi Beta Kappa, Phi Kappa Phi, Chi Phi. Office: Lake Forest Coll 555 N Sheridan Rd Lake Forest IL 60845

HOTELLING, HAROLD, law and economics educator; b. N.Y.C., Dec. 26, 1945; s. Harold and Susanna Porter (Edmondson) H.; m. Barbara M. Anthony, May 4, 1974; children: Harold, George, James, Claire, Charles. AB, Columbia U., 1966; JD, U. N.C., 1972; MA, Duke U., 1975, PhD, 1982. Bar: N.C. 1973. Legal advisor U. N.C., Chapel Hill, 1972-73; instr. bus. law U. Ky., Lexington, 1977-79, asst. prof., 1980-84; asst. prof. dept. econs. Oakland U., Rochester, Mich., 1984-89; assoc. prof. econs. Lawrence Technol. U., Southfield, Mich., 1989—; chmn. dept. humanities Lawrence Technol. U., Southfield, 1994—. Contbr. articles to profl. jours. Episcopalian. Home: 2112 Bretton Dr S Rochester Hls MI 48309-2952 Office: Lawrence Technol U Dept Humanities Southfield MI 48075

HOTRA, MIKE A., maintenance engineer; b. Detroit, Mar. 4, 1957. B, Lawrence Inst. Tech., 1981. Maintenance engr. Duramet Corp., Warren, Mich., 1981—. Coach Little League Baseball and Football, Warren, 1993—. Office: Duramet Corp 11350 Stephens Rd Warren MI 48089-1833

HOTTINGER, JAY, state legislator; m. Cheri Hottinger. BA, BS summa cum laude, Capital U., Columbus, Ohio. Mgr. Jay Co.; city councilman City of Newark, Ohio; pres. pro tem Newark City Coun.; rep. dist. 77 Ohio Ho. of Reps., Columbus. Bd. dirs. East Mound Comty. Devel. Corp., Am. Cancer Soc. (Newark). Named Outstanding Young Man of Licking County, 1992. Mem. Police Athletic League, Newark Area C. of C.

HOTTINGER, JOHN CREIGHTON, state legislator, lawyer; b. Mankato, Minn., Sept. 18, 1945; s. Raymond Creighton and Hilda (Baker) H.; m. Miriam Jean Willging, Oct. 31, 1971; children: Julie, Creighton, Janna. BS, Coll. St. Thomas, St. Paul, 1967; JD, Georgetown U., 1971. Bar: Minn. 1972, U.S. Dist. Ct. Minn. 1977, U.S. Dist. Ct. (no. dist.) Ohio 1981, U.S. Ct. Appeals (5th cir.) 1991, U.S. Supreme Ct. 1992. Legis. asst. Hon. Donald M. Fraser, Washington, 1968-69, Dem. Study Group, Washington, 1969-73; ptnr. Farrish, Johnson, Maschka & Hottinger, Mankato, 1973-85; sr. ptnr. Hottinger Law Offices, Mankato, 1985-91; ptnr. Gislason, Dosland, Hunter & Malecki, Mankato, 1991-95; sr. ptnr. Hottinger Law Office, Mankato, 1995—; mem. Minn. Senate, 1991—, asst. majority whip, 1993—; chair Bd. of Govt. Innovation and Cooperation, 1995. Dem. candidate for Minn. Senate, 1982, for U.S. Ho. of Reps., 1994. Mem. ABA, 5th Dist. Bar Assn., Minn. Bar Assn. Roman Catholic. Office: Hottinger Law Office Box 3183 Mankato MN 56002-3183

HOUCHINS, WILEY JACK, marketing professional; b. Moberly, Mo., Aug. 22, 1955; s. Oscar Tucker and Nancy May (Adams) H.; m. Cynthia Ann Lesak, Aug. 13, 1977; children: Thomas Wiley, Jacqueline Elizabeth. BS in Animal Sci., U. Mo., 1977; MBA, Govs. State U., University Park, Ill., 1991. Territory salesperson Wayne Feeds-Continental Grain Co., Chgo., 1977-78, dist. salesperson, 1978-81, asst. regional sales mgr., regional sales mgr., 1981-83, nat. mktg. mgr.-dairy, 1983-85, mgr. bus. devel., 1985-86, area distbn. mgr., 1986-90, dir. sales, 1990-94, dir. bus. devel., 1994—; mgr. market rsch. and strategic planning; cons. U.S. Feed Grain Coun., Washington, 1991. Mem. Nat. Agri Mktg. Assn., Am. Feed Industry Assn., Am. Mgmt. Assn., Kiwanis. Roman Catholic. Office: Continental Grain Co Ste 900 222 S Riverside Plz Chicago IL 60606

HOUCK, CAROLYN MARIE KUMPF, special education educator; b. Brazil, Ind., Aug. 20, 1945; d. Paul Melvin and Dorothy Evadean (Welch) Kumpf; m. Robert Mercer (div. 1970); children: Judith E., Cynthia D.; m. David Jome Houck, Aug. 1, 1977; 1 child, Andrew. BS, Ind. State U., 1968, MS, 1975, postgrad., 1978-79. Speech therapist Indpls. Pub. Schs., 1968-70, Child Adult Resources Svcs., Inc., Rockville, Ind., 1970-72; lang. specialist Porter County Spl. Edn. Coop., Valparaiso, Ind., 1972-73; speech and lang. specialist Child-Adult Resource Svcs., Inc., Rockville, Ind., 1973-78; tchr. learning disabilities Greencastle (Ind.) H.S., 1979—. Precinct committeewoman Dem. Party, Greencastle, 1992-95; mem. Cloverdale (Ind.) United Meth. Ch. Mem. NEA, PEO (sisterhood), Ind. State Tchrs. Assn., Delta Kappa Gamma (Epsilon chpt. Alpha Epsilon state orgn.). Home: 610 Highwood Ave Greencastle IN 46135-1339 Office: Greencastle High Sch Washington St Greencastle IN 46135

HOUGH, LESLIE SELDON, educational administrator; b. Springfield, Ohio, Oct. 2, 1946; s. Donald Woodrow and Stella Alta (Finney) H.; m. Sharon Ann Cornell, May 31, 1969; children: Amity Melinda, Amanda Michelle, Leslie Elizabeth. BA, Olivet Nazarene U., 1969; MA, U. Va., 1973, PhD, 1977. Cert. archivist. Co-dir. Ohio labor history project Ohio Hist. Soc., Columbus, 1975-77; dir. spl. collections Ga. State U., Atlanta, 1977-92; dir. archives labor urban affairs Walter P. Reuther Libr. Wayne State U., Detroit, 1992—; cons. Clayton County Water Authority, Riverdale, Ga., 1988-90, Equifax, Inc., Atlanta, 1990—. Mem. adv. bd. Mich. Hist. Records, Lansing, 1993; bd. dirs. Ga. Humanities Coun., Atlanta, 1988-92. With U.S. Army, 1970-71. Democrat. Mem. Soc. of Friends. Home: 28118 Golf Pointe Blvd Farmington MI 48331-2932 Office: Wayne State University Walter P. Reuther Library 5401 Cass Ave Detroit MI 48202-3613

HOUGH, WINSTON, artist; b. Hartford, Mich., July 12, 1928; s. Elbert Vere and Dorris Elizabeth H.; m. Joan Gimse, Oct. 23, 1954 (div. June 1985); m. Alice Christine Daly, Nov. 30, 1985; children: Elliott Vere, Geoffrey Winston, Elise Ingrid, Roderick Garret. BFA, Sch. of Art Inst., Chgo., 1953; MA, Northeastern Ill. U., 1970. Asst. prof. art Va. Commonwealth U., Richmond, 1956-62; lectr. art U. Ill., Chgo., 1964-65; tchr. City Colls. Chgo., 1969-90; tchr. art dept. Va. Commonwealth U., 1956-62; guest lectr. art dept. U. Ill., Chgo., State U. Ill., 1963-64. One person shows include South Bend Art Ctr., 1954, Morris Gallery, N.Y.C., 1957, Palmer House Galleries, 1959, I.F.A. Gallery, Washington, 1961, Paul Theobald Book Store Art Gallery, 1978, Winnetka Pub. Libr., 1986, Beverly Arts Ctr., Pillsbury Concourse Gallery, 1988, Art Reach Gallery, Columbus, Ohio, 1990; exhibited in group shows Exhbn. Momentum, 1953, Art Inst. Chgo., 1955-59, Valentine Mus., 1957-58, 60, Winston-Salem Gallery of Fine Arts, 1958-68, Roko Gallery, N.Y.C., 1964, I.F.A. Gallery, 1961-83, Evanston Art Ctr., 1973, Benjamin Galleries, 1975, Mclean County Art Ctr., Bloomington, 1987-95, 4th Presbyn. Ch., 1989; represented in pub. collections Midwest Stock Exch. Svc. Corp., Champion Fed. Savs. and Loan. Recipient Birmingham Ala. Watercolor Soc. award, 1958; Daniell Vandergrift scholar, 1952; Huntington Hartford Found. fellow, 1959. Mem. Chgo. Artists Coalition. Address: 937 Echo Ln Glenview IL 60025

HOUGHAM, NORMAN RUSSELL, controller; b. Correctionville, Iowa, Sept. 28, 1937; s. Russell Lowell and Geneva Marie (Lafferty) H.; m. Evelyn Joy Foley, Apr. 10, 1960; 1 child, Jill. Ed., Am. Inst. Banking, 1969; diploma, U. Wis., 1980. Clk. Earlham (Iowa) Savs. Bank, 1959-60; cashier Capital City State Bank, Des Moines, 1960-76; v.p. Brenton Nat. Bank, Des Moines, 1976-82; sr. v.p. Am. Fed. Savs. and Loan, Des Moines, 1982-90; mng. agt. Resolution Trust Corp., 1990-94; contr. Midwest Fin. Svcs. Ltd., 1995—. Bd. dirs. Earlham Swim Pool Devel. Corp., 1972; mem. bd. edn. Earlham Sch., 1986; bd. dirs., treas. Pioneer Pl. Retirement Homes, Earlham, 1996, Earlham Ch. of Christ, 1996; trustee Earlham Pub. Libr., 1990. Recipient Bd. Dirs. award Des Moines chpt. Am. Inst. Banking, 1972, Instr. Appreciation award Inst. for Fin. Edn., 1983, award of merit Earlham Bd. Edn., 1986, Spl. Achievement award FDIC, 1992, Cert. of Appreciation RTC, 1992. Mem. Kiwanis, Jaycees (pres. 1973-74), Masons. Republican. Home: 235 NE 3d St PO Box 344 Earlham IA 50072 Office: 210 N 10th St PO Box 267 Adel IA 50003-0267

HOULETTE, FORREST THOMAS, computer trainer, software consultant, writer; b. San Bernardino, Calif., Dec. 27, 1954; s. Walter John and Wilberta Ruth (Murray) H.; m. Sydna Lee Herren, Aug. 13, 1977(div. 1981); m. Judith Rogers Kasey, Oct. 9, 1982; 1 child, Alexandra Kasey. BA in English, Miami U., Ohio, 1977, MA in English, 1979; PhD in Linguistics and Rhetoric, U. Louisville (Ky.), 1982. Writing ctr. dir. U. Louisville, 1981-82; asst. prof. English U. Okla., Norman, 1982-83; asst. prof. English Ball State U., Muncie, 1983-89, assoc. prof., 1989-93, prof., 1990-93; instr. Learning Tree Internat., 1995—; adminstr. Ind. Writing Project, Muncie, 1987-89, dir., 1989-95; software developer, computer author Write Environ., Muncie, 1989—. Author: Nineteenth Century Rhetoric: An Enumerative Bibliography, 1989; author/co-author 18 computer books on Windows and Windows applications, 1992—; writer, product developer New Riders Pub., Carmel, Ind., 1992-93; contbr. articles to profl. publs. Vol. Old Washington St. Festival, Muncie, 1985—, publicity writer, 1987-88. Recipient Masters Of Innovation Competition 1st Place award Zenith Data Systems, Chgo., 1990, finalist Ellen Nold award Computer and Composition Jour., 1991, Grad. Sch. Disting. Svc. award Ball State U., Muncie, 1991; Ind. Writing Project grantee Ind. Dept. Edn., Indpls., 1985-92. Mem. IEEE Computer Soc., Assn. for Advancement of Computers in Edn., East Ctrl. Neighborhood Assn., Phi Beta Kappa, Phi Kappa Phi. Democrat.

HOULIHAN, JAMES WILLIAM, criminal justice educator; b. Chgo., Aug. 3, 1939; s. James William and Julia Dorothy (Nash) H.; m. Patricia Louise Halper, Apr. 11, 1964; 1 child, Erin Candice. BSBA in Fin. and Mgmt., Loyola U., Chgo., 1968; MBA in Econs. and Mgmt., DePaul U., Chgo., 1971; EdD, No. Ill. U., 1996. Spl. agt. Criminal Investigation divsn. U.S. Treasury Dept., Chgo., 1963-91, dir. tng., 1984-91, spl. staff asst. to chief, 1988-90; various positions U.S. Army/U.S. Army Res./N.G., various locations, 1962-69, USAF/USAFR, various locations, 1969-92; comdr. USAF Intelligence Command, Glenview, Ill., 1988-92; prin. E.C. Cons., St. Charles, Ill., 1991—; assoc. prof. Lewis U., Romeoville, Ill., 1990—; adj. mgmt. prof. Elgin (Ill.) C.C., 1977—, mem. adv. com., mgmt. program, 1982—; adj. mgmt. prof. Ctrl. Tex. Coll., 1988—, Vincennes U., 1991—; mem. adv. com. criminal justice program St. Xavier U., Chgo., 1973—; mem. adminstrv. rev. bd. Ill. Dept. of Corrections, 1995—. Mem. Inst. on Edn. and Athletics, U. Chgo., 1983-89; mem. Roosevelt Inst. on Pub. Policy Studies, U. Ill., Chgo., 1986-88; mem. Pres.'s Club, St. Ignatius Coll. Prep., Chgo., 1989—. Recipient George Washington Honor medal Freedoms Found. at Valley Forge, 1977, 80, 81, 86, 92, Albert Gallatin award Sec. of U.S. Treasury, 1991. Mem. Am. Legion (exec. com.), Res. Officers Assn., Air Force Assn., Air War Coll. Alumni Assn., Am. Assn. Adult and Continuing Edn. Roman Catholic. Office: Lewis U Rte 53 Box 1029 Romeoville IL 60446

HOULIHAN, STEVEN J., stockbroker; b. Peoria, Ill., Aug. 13, 1964. BS in Bus. Comm., Bradley U., 1987. With mktg. and sales depts. Dontech Pub., Peoria, 1988-92; stockbroker A.G. Edwards & Sons Inc., Peoria, 1992—. Monthly columnist on interbus. issues, 1994-95. Instr. Jr. Achievement, Peoria, 1987—. Mem. Nat. Assn. Securities Dealers, Kiwanis (pres. Peoria 1991-92, bd. dirs. 1992—). Republican. Roman Catholic. Home: 10022 Indian Ridge Ct Edwards IL 61528-9668 Office: AG Edwards & Sons 4900 N Glen Park Place Rd Peoria IL 61614-4655

HOUNSCHELL, JOHN CHARLES, software engineering manager and programmer; b. Neosho, Mo., June 17, 1955; s. John Charles and Mildred Loraine (Crabtree) H.; m. Susan Daugherty, Mar. 4, 1977 (div. July 1990); 1 child, Jeramiah Sky; m. Linda Susan Melaven, Aug. 2, 1991; 1 child, Erin. Student, Elecs. Inst., 1973-74. Test technician King Radio, Inc., Olatha, Kans., 1973-74; from programmer to mgr. systems software Harmon Elecs., Grain Valley, Mo., 1974—. Coord. World Bible Sch., East Independence Ch. of Christ, 1996—. Mem. Ch. of Christ. Home: 1400 SE 16th Pl Oak Grove MO 64075-9431 Office: Harmon Elecs Argo & Dillingham Rds Grain Valley MO 64029

HOUPIS, CONSTANTINE HARRY, electrical engineering educator; b. Lowell, Mass., June 16, 1922; s. Harry John and Metaxia (Gourokous) H.; student Wayne U., 1941-43; BS, U. Ill., 1947, MS, 1948; postgrad. Ohio State U., 1952-56; PhD, U. Wyo., 1971; m. Mary Stephens, Aug. 28, 1960; children: Harry C., Angella S. Spl. research asst. U. Ill., 1947-48; devel. elec. engr. Babcock & Wilcox Co., Alliance, Ohio, 1948-49; instr. elec. engring. Wayne State U., 1949-51; prin. elec. engr. Battelle Meml. Inst., Columbus, Ohio, 1951-52; prof. elec. engring. Air Force Inst. Tech., Wright-Patterson AFB, Ohio, 1952—; guest lectr. Nat. Tech. U. Athens, 1958, U. Patras, 1984, Weizmann Inst. Sci., 1984, U. Strathclyde, 1995, Binghampton U., 1996; sr. rsch. assoc. Air Force Flight Dynamics Directorate. Served with AUS, 1943-46. Recipient Outstanding Engr. award Dayton area Nat. Engrs. Week, 1962. Fellow. IEEE; mem. Am. Soc. Engring. Edn., Am. Hellenic Edn. Progressive Assn., Tau Beta Pi, Eta Kappa Nu. Mem. Greek Orthodox Ch. Author: (with J.J. D'Azzo) Feedback Control System Analysis and Synthesis, 1960, 2d edit., 1966; Principles of Electrical Engineering: Electric Circuits, Electronics, Energy Conversion, Control Systems Computers, 1968; Linear Control Systems Analysis and Design: Conventional and Modern, 1975, 4th edit., 1995; (with J. Lubelfeld) Outline of Pulse Circuits; (with G.B. Lamont) Digital Control Systems: Theory Software, Hardware, 1985, 2nd edit., 1992; also articles on automatic controls in profl. jours. U.S., Eng., Greece. Home: 1125 Brittany Hills Dr Dayton OH 45459-1415 Office: Air Force Inst Tech 2950 P St Bldg 642 Dayton OH 45433-7765

HOURIGAN, MAUREEN MARMION, English educator; b. Buffalo, N.Y., Sept. 28, 1942; d. John Malachy and Mary Irene (Ryan) Marmion; m. James Francis Hourigan, Sept. 19, 1964; children: Kevin V., Kristin Hourigan White, Karen O'B. AB, Le Moyne Coll., 1963; MA, SUNY, Buffalo, 1966; PhD, U. S. Fla., 1992. Instr. English Cardinal O'Hara H.S., Tonawanda, N.Y., 1964-66; grad. teaching fellow SUNY, Buffalo, 1964-65; instr. English Erie Cmty. Coll., Buffalo, 1971-75; lectr. English Gannon U., Erie, Pa., 1979-85; grad. teaching asst. U. S. Fla., Tampa, 1986-87; instr. English St. Petersburg (Fla.) Jr. Coll., 1986-91; dir. freshman composition U. Nev., Las Vegas, 1992-94; asst. prof. English Kent State U., Warren, Ohio, 1994—. Author: Literacy as Social Exchange, 1994. Mem. MLA, Conf. on Coll. Composition and Communication, Nat. Coun. Tchrs. English, Nat. Coun. Writing Program Adminstrs., Coll. English Assn., Assn. Tchrs. Advanced Composition. Home: 558 Plantation Ct Erie PA 16505 Office: Kent State U Trumbull Camp 4314 Mahoning Ave NW Warren OH 44483

HOUSE, TED, state legislator; b. Kansas City, Mo., Aug. 22, 1959; s. Keith and Ilene House; m. Mardi House. BA, Meth. Coll., 1981; JD, U. Mo. Kansas City, 1984. Intern legis. U.S. Congressman Ike Skelton, 1979; state rep. Mo. State Congress, 1980; atty. gen. State of Mo., 1982-84; state rep. Dist. 15 Mo. State Congress, 1988-94, state senator Dist. 2, 1995—; mem. appropriations com., edn. and pub. safety com., transp. com., labor and indsl. rels. com., conservation, parks and tourism com., econ. devel. com. Francis Howell Sch. Dist.; vice chmn. civil and criminal law com., ins. and housing com.; EMT Howard County Ambulance Svc.; legal investigator Trade Offense Divsn. Office Miss. Atty. Gen.; assoc. Heggs, Pryor & House. Mem. St. Charles C. of C. (govt. concerns com.), Salvation Army (bd. dirs.), Teen Parent Day Care Ctr., Phi Mu Alpha. *

HOUSEMAN, GERALD L., political science educator, writer; b. Marshalltown, Iowa, Apr. 12, 1939; s. Lawrence D. and Mary N. (Smith) H.; m. Penelope Lyon, Feb. 11, 1961 (dec. 1994); children: Christopher, Elisabeth, Victoria; m. Soendari, 1994. BA, Calif. State U., Hayward, 1965, MA, 1967; PhD, U. Ill., 1971. Asst. prof. polit. sci. Ind. U., Ft. Wayne, 1971-76, assoc. prof., 1976-82, prof., 1982—; vis. prof. Brock U., St. Catharines, Can., summer 1970, New Coll., Durham, Eng., 1975-76, Calif. State Polytech. U., San Luis Obispo, 1983-84, U. Calif., Irvine, 1984-85, St. Mary's Coll. Calif., 1985-86, Ind. U. Coop. Program in Malaysia, 1989-94, Fulbright Program, Indonesia, 1993-94. Mem. Transit Authority Bd., Ft. Wayne, 1973-75; city plan commr., 1982-83; active ACLU. Served with USMC, 1954-57. Grantee NSF, 1970, Ford Found., 1973, 74, NEH, 1977-78, 87; Ind. U. fellow, 1973, 74, 77. Mem. Am. Polit. Sci. Assn. (seminar grantee 1980, 81), Asian Studies Assn., Ind. Pplit. Sci. Assn. (pres. 1979-80). Author: (with H. Mark Roelofs) The American Political System, 1983; G. D. H. Cole, 1979; The Right of Mobility, 1979; City of the Right: Urban Applications of American Political Thought, 1982, State and Local Government: The New Battleground, 1986; (with Michael W. MaCann) Judging the Constitution, 1989, Questioning the Law in Corporate America: Agenda for Reform, 1993, America and the Pacific Rim: Coming to Terms with New Realities, 1995. Precinct committeeperson, 1973-75; Dem. candidate 4th dist. Mo. U.S. House of Reps., 1996.*

HOUSER, BETTY JO, mental health nurse; b. Rocky Ford, Colo., Mar. 13, 1940; d. Otis Willard and Mary Agnes (Hayden) Love; m. Wallace Dan Houser, July 29, 1963; children: Danny, Theresa, Tom. BSN, Loretto

Heights Coll., Denver, 1962; MS, U. Wis., 1991. RN, Wis., Colo., Kans. Staff nurse Fort Logan Mental Health Ctr., Denver, 1962, Menninger Clinic, Topeka, Kans., 1963; pvt. duty nurse USAFB Hosp., Tachikawa, Japan, 1964-65; ARC nurse Dep. Sch. Program and Dispensary, Johnson AFB, Japan, 1964-66; staff nurse St. Mary's Hosp. Med. Ctr., Madison, Wis., 1970-75; nurse clinician II Mendota Mental Health Inst., Madison, 1985-90, nurse clinician III, 1990-95, clin. specialist child adolescent adult mental healh nursing, 1993—; asst. prof. Mo. So. State Coll., Joplin, 1995—; faculty asst. U. Wis., Madison, 1991, affiliate clin. instr. Sch. Nursing, 1994. Mem. ANA (cert.), Am. Psychiat. Nurses Assn., Mo. Nurses Assn., Sigma Theta Tau Internat. Home: 705 W Briarbrook Lane Carl Junction MO 64834 Office: Mo So State Coll Sch Nursing Joplin MO 64834

HOUSER, CHARLES WILLIAM, automotive company executive; b. Richmond, Va., Dec. 9, 1946; s. Aubrey Alphin Jr. and Phyllis Kay (McIlhenny) H.; m. Maureen Davidica Mayes, Dec. 18, 1976; children: David Steven Mayes, Edwards Charles Mayes. BA, U. Va., 1973; MS in Engring., W.Va. U., 1985. Aerospace modelmaker Dynamic Engring., Newport News, Va., 1975-76; quality control supr. Ford Motor Co., Cleve., 1977-79, mfg. process engr., 1979-81; product planning analyst Ford Motor Co., Dearborn, Mich., 1985-88; vehicle devel. engr. Ford Motor Co., Dearborn, 1988-91; tchr. fin. W.Va. U., Morgantown, 1982-84; pres. Automotive Systems Analysis Corp., Farmington Hills, Mich., 1991—. Author: North American Vehicle Matrices, 1992-95; contbr. articles to profl. jours. Active various civic and social orgns. Sgt. U.S. Army, 1968-71. Mem. Soc. Mfg. Engrs., Soc. Auto Historians, Sports Car Club Am. Episcopalian. Office: Automotive Systems Analysis 28467 Wellington St Farmington Hills MI 48334-4275

HOUSEWORTH, LOUISE, administrator; b. Phoenix, Ariz., Feb. 22, 1956; d. Richard Court and Laura Louise (Jennings) H. BA, U. Redlands, 1978; M of Pub. Adminstrn., Syracuse U., 1979. Pub. mgmt. intern City of Kansas City, Mo., 1979-80, budget and sys. analyst, 1980-86; asst. city mgr. City of Wichita Falls, Tex., 1986-91; coord. planning and budget adminstrv. computer ctr. U. Md. at College Park, 1992-93; assoc. dir. bus. and fin. Iowa Bd. of Regents, Des Moines, 1993-94, dir. bus. and fin., 1994—. Mem. strategic planning Jr. League of Des Moines, 1994—; bd. dirs. Leadership Wichita Falls, 1987-92; campaign cabinet United Way of Greater Wichita Fallas, 1988-91; bd. dirs. YMCA of Wichita Falls, 1990-92. Named Young Leader in Action Women's Hall of Fame of North Tex., 1986. Mem. Phi Beta Kappa. Home: 300 Walnut #17 Des Moines IA 50309 Office: Iowa Bd Regents Old Historical Bldg Des Moines IA 50319

HOUSINGER, WARREN DONALD, retired secondary education educator; b. Chgo., Feb. 26, 1937; s. Alfred John and Hulda Johanna (Rost) H.; m. Margaret M. Urban, Aug. 20, 1994. BEd in Trade and Tech., Colo. State U., 1969; MS in Guidance, Purdue U., 1972. Cert. tchr., Ill. Automotive mechanic Ridgeway Chevrolet, Lansing, Ill., 1954-63; automotive instr. Chgo. Vocat. High Sch., 1963-65; regional tng. coord. Chrysler Corp., Centerline, Mich., 1965-66; automotive instr. Thornton Fractional High Sch., Calumet City, Ill., 1966-75, applied tech. instr., 1975-94, 95; auto instr. Thornton Community Coll., Harvey, Ill., 1968-72; dir. Met. Round Table # 5, 1973-74. Author: (with others) Drive Right, 1972. Sponsor U.S. Shooting Team. With U.S. Army, 1957-59. Mem. Am. Vocat. Assn., Ill. Vocat. Assn., Ill. Automotive Tchrs. Assn., Ill. Automotive and Aviation Tchrs. Assn. (v.p. 1967-69, pres. 1969-74, treas. 1974-76), NRA, Colo. State Alumni Assn., Iota Lambda Sigma.

HOUSLEY-ANTHONY, MARY PAT, community relations administrator; b. Manistique, Mich., Oct. 26, 1944; d. Victor Joseph and Mary (Kerrigan) Schuster; m. Donald Dean Housley, Aug. 21, 1964 (dec. Dec. 1975); children: Cynthia Machuta, Jennifer Housley; m. Charles Ellis Anthony, Nov. 6, 1988 (dec. June 11, 1995); stepchildren: Thomas Anthony, Mark Anthony, Terri Anthony Manz. Diploma, Borgess Sch. of Nursing, Kalamazoo, 1964; BA cum laude, Cen. Mich. U., 1987; postgrad., Mich. State U., 1994. Nutrition site dir. Isabella County Commn. on Aging., Mt. Pleasant, Mich., 1978-84; reporter, editor CM Life (Univ. newspaper), Mt. Pleasant, Mich., 1985-87; reporter Gratiot County Herald, Ithaca, Mich., 1987, Morning Sun, Mt. Pleasant, Mich., 1987-89; editor Isabella County Herald, Mt. Pleasant, Mich., 1989—; writer, publs. specialist Ctrl. Mich. U., Mt. Pleasant, 1993—; dir. cmty. rels., physician recruiter Ctrl. Mich. Cmty. Hosp., Mt. Pleasant, 1995—; media rep., chair Community Corrections Adv. Bd., Mt. Pleasant, Mich. Contbr. poems to lit. publs. Founder., mem. Hospice of Ctrl. Mich., 1982-87; mem. Bldg. Ties Com., Mt. Pleasant, 1988, President's Club, Benefactors' Soc., Ctrl. Mich. U., Mt. Pleasant, 1988—; bd. dirs. United Way, 1996—; vol. asst. dir. Mt. Pleasant Area Cmty. Found., 1992—; vol. Action for Our Kids Coalition, 1992—, Civil Legal Svcs. Mid. Mich. Bd., 1992—; mem. Art Reach of Mid Mich., 1988—. Recipient awards for media coverage Child Protection Coun., 1989-92, United Way, 1989-91. Mem. Soc. Profl. Journalists, Mt. Pleasant C. of C. (Citizen of Yr. com. 1992), Phi Kappa Phi. Home: 1003 Fairfield Mount Pleasant MI 48858-9590

HOUSTON, WILLIAM ROBERT MONTGOMERY, ophthalmic surgeon; b. Mansfield, Ohio, Nov. 13, 1922; s. William T. and Frances (Hursh) H.; B.A., Oberlin Coll., 1944; M.D., Western Res. U., 1948; m. Marguerite LaBau Browne, Apr. 25, 1968; children: William Erling Tenney, Marguerite Elisabeth LaBau, Selby Cabot Truitt Vanderbilt. Intern, Meth. Hosp. Bklyn., 1948-49, Ill. Eye and Ear Infirmary, Chgo., 1949-50; resident N.Y. Eye and Ear Infirmary, 1950-52; practice medicine specializing in ophthalmic surgery, Mansfield, 1952—; fellow retinal vascular disease NYU, 1968-69; mem. staffs Mansfield Gen. Hosp., Peoples Hosp., Mansfield, N.Y. U. Bellevue Med. Center, N.Y.C.; assoc. prof. clin. ophthalmology N.Y. U. Sch. Medicine. Pres. Mansfield Symphony Soc., 1965-68, Mansfield Civic Music Assn., 1965; mem. Mansfield City Sch. Bd., 1962-65, v.p., 1965. Served to capt. M.C. USAF, 1952-55. Diplomate Am. Bd. Ophthalmology. Recipient Honor award Acad. Ophthalmology. Fellow Internat. Coll. Surgeons; mem. SR (color guard 1961-71), Nat. Geneal. Soc. (award of Merit), Ohio Hist. Soc. (life), Western Res. Hist. Soc. (life fellow), N.Y. Geneal. and Biog. Soc. (life), Ohio Geneal. Soc. (trustee 1955—). Editor, Ohio Records and Pioneers Families, 1970—. Address: 456 Park Ave W Mansfield OH 44906-3118

HOUTZ, LYNNE ELAINE, education educator; b. Omaha, Feb. 18, 1949; d. Albert John and Lavina Marie (Schiferl) Goracke; m. Rodney Andrew Johnsen, Sept. 6, 1969 (div. Jan. 1977); children: Michelle Elaine, Jessica Lyn; m. Steven John Houtz, Aug. 21, 1987. BS in Edn., Kent State U., Omaha, 1971; MS, U. Nebr., Omaha, 1985; PhD, U. Nebr., 1992. Tchr. 4th grade learning disabled Field Local Sch. Dist., Brimfield, Ohio, 1971-72; tchr. 4th grade Sch. Dist. #70, Libertyville, Ill., 1972; substitute tchr. pub. schs., Ill. and Ohio, 1973-77; tchr. Jonathan Alder Schs., Plain City, Ohio, 1977-82; tchr. sci. Harrison Elementary Sch., Omaha, 1982-89, Omaha Pub. Schs., 1989-91, 92-93; instr., grad. asst. U. Nebr., Lincoln, 1991-92; tchr. sci. Omaha Pub. Schs., 1993-94; asst. prof. edn. Nebr. Wesleyan U., Lincoln, 1994—; presenter in field. Mem. Nat. Sci. Tchsr. Assn. (local leader), Nat. Assn. Rsch. in Sci. Teaching, NAt. Coun. Tchrs. Math., Nebr. Assn. Tchrs. Sci. (scholar), Coun. Elem. Sci. Internat., Assn. Edn. Tchrs. in Sci. Home: 1310 N 163d Cir Omaha NE 68118-2415 Office: Nebr Wesleyan U 5000 St Paul Ave Lincoln NE 68504-2796

HOVEN, TIM, state legislator; b. Dec. 22, 1963. BA, U. Wis., Oshkosh. Assemblyman Wis. State Dist. 60, 1994—; mem. Ozaukee County (Wis.) Bd., Port Washington (Wis.) Bd. Rev., Ozaukee County Econ. Devel. Corp. Mem. Ducks Unltd. Address: 111 N Milwaukee St Port Washington WI 53074

HOVERSTEN, ELLSWORTH GARY, insurance executive, producer; b. Minneota, Minn., Jan. 1, 1941; s. Emmanuel and Frieda Louise (Fligge) H.; m. Lillie Mae Jones, Oct. 29, 1965; children: Athena Marie, Dionne Shawn. LLB, LaSalle Ext. U., 1971. CPCU. Teller First. Nat. Bank, Ivanhoe, Minn., 1960-68; ins. mgr. First State Ins., Ivanhoe, 1968-87; ins. mng. v.p. Community Ins. Inc., Ivanhoe, 1987—; contact person Epilepsy Founds. Minn., Ivanhoe, 1980—. EMT Ivanhoe Ambulance, 1967-84; sec., treas. Ivanhoe Fireman and Relief Assn., 1969-84, Lions, 1968-83; CPR instr. Ivanhoe, 1980-83; treas. Mulder for State Rep., Ivanhoe, 1992, 94, 96; treas. Lincoln County Salvation Army; pres. Ivanhoe Housing Bd., 1993—, dir., 1980—. With USAF, 1962-66. Mem. Soc. CPCUs, Soc. Cert. Ins. Counselors (cert.), Am. Legion (adjutant 1988—), Rotary (pres. 1991-92), Lions (sec., treas. Ivanhoe 1968-83), Rotary Found. Office: Community Ins Inc 323 N Norman Box L Ivanhoe MN 56142-0150

HOW, PHILIP HARRISON, stockbroker; b. Phila., Mar. 3, 1935. BA, Ursinus Coll., Collegeville, Pa., 1956; MSW, U. Pa., 1960. Exec. dir. Infant Welfare Soc. Chgo., 1972-82; assoc. v.p. Dean Witter Reynolds, Riverwoods, Ill., 1982—. Democrat. Office: Dean Witter Reynolds 2500 Lake Cook Rd Deerfield IL 60015-3851

HOWARD, ALAN CHARLES, retired English language educator; b. Manistee, Mich., Aug. 27, 1944; s. Edmund Witherell and Esther Marie (Watrous) H.; m. Lois Marie Zimmer, June 20, 1965 (div. May 1990); children: Jennifer, Rebecca; m. Judy Kay Miller, May 29, 1992. AB in English, Cen. Mich. U., 1967; MA in English, U. Mich., 1968. Lectr. English Southgate Tech. Coll., London, 1975-76; asst. prof. English Bay de Noc Community Coll., Escanaba, Mich., 1968-75, 76-95. Pres. Bay Area Campus Ministry, Escanaba, 1985—; sec., v.p. PTO, Escanaba, 1983-85; chmn. Bay de Noc C.C. Global Awareness Com., 1989—; mem. Escanaba City Recreation Bd., 1989—. Fulbright grantee, 1975-76, 91; named one of Outstanding Young Men of Am. U.S. Jaycees, 1977. Mem. Nat. Council Tchrs. of English, Conf. Coll. Composition and Communication. Home: 1322 N 16th St Escanaba MI 49829-1713 Office: Bay de Noc Community Coll College Ave Escanaba MI 49829-9565

HOWARD, ALDA BEVERLY, medical surgical nurse; b. San Diego, Mar. 17, 1958; d. Paul Laverne and Alda Beverly (Rezentes) Sparks; m. Larry Vernon Howard, Oct. 7, 1978; children: Jason Matthew, Leigha Michelle. LPN, Kirksville Vo-Tech. Sch., 1988; ADN, Indian Hills C.C., 1992. RN, Mo. Charge nurse Kirksville (Mo.) Manor Care, 1988; medication nurse Grim Smith Hosp., Kirksville, 1988-92, charge nurse, 1992-94; medical care coord., 1994—; adv. bd. LPN program Kirksville Vo-Tech. Sch., 1989-92. Democrat. Roman Catholic. Home: PO Box 107 Brashear MO 63533-0107

HOWARD, ARLAN J., design engineer; b. Pineville, Ky., Mar. 13, 1959. AD in Mech. Engring., U. Cin., 1988. Design engr. Buschman Conveyor, Cin., 1987-92, Lelond Makino Co., Mason, Ohio, 1992—. Cpl. U.S. Army, 1980-85. Christian. Office: Leblond 7689 Innovation Way Mason OH 45040-9695

HOWARD, BRIAN ROBERT, buyer; b. Bedford, Ohio, Sept. 8, 1964; s. William R. and Joyce A. (Harvey) H.; m. Sandra I. Piasecki, May 21, 1988; 1 child, Kristi Lynn. BS in Indsl. Mgmt., U. Akron, 1988; postgrad., Kent State U., 1994—. Asst. retail mgr. Reiders Stop-n-Shop, Solon, Ohio, 1979-90; purchasing mgr. Martin Sheet Metal, Cleve., 1990-92; supr. finished goods purchasing Little Tikes Co., Hudson, Ohio, 1992—. Mem. Soc. Plastics Engrs. (affiliate), Am. Prodn. and Inventory Control Soc. (sec. Akron chpt. 1995-96, exec. v.p. 1996-97), Gold Key. Home: 1770 Sunview Dr Twinsburg OH 44087 Office: Little Tikes Co 2180 Barlow Rd Hudson OH 44236

HOWARD, CHARLES P., drilling company executive; b. Crizo Spring, Tex., July 26, 1941. Cert., U. Okla., 1982. V.p., co-owner C.H.P. Drilling Co., Traverse City, Mich., 1984—. Republican. Baptist. Home: 3909 Altaire Dr Traverse City MI 49686-9253 Office: 954 Business Park Dr Traverse City MI 49686-8683

HOWARD, DAVID A., marketing professional; b. Detroit, Apr. 13, 1959; s. Richard A. and Josephine Howard. BBA, Grove City Coll., 1981. Sales mgmt. trainee J&L Steel, Inc., Bettendorf, Iowa, 1981-82; sales rep. J&L Steel, Inc., Milw., 1982-84; sales rep LTV Steel, Inc., Milw., 1984-85, Chgo., 1985-88; regional mgr. WCI Steel, Inc., Chgo., 1988-90; mktg. mgr. WCI Steel, Inc., Warren, Ohio, 1990—; mem. constrn. market com. Am. Iron and Steel Inst., Washington, 1994. Mem. exec. com. March of Dimes, 1994—, co-chmn., 1994. Republican. Lutheran. Home: 109 Aspen Pl Cortland OH 44410 Office: WCI Steel Inc 1040 Pine Ave SE Warren OH 44483

HOWARD, GLENN L., state legislator; m. Florence Howard. Student, Ala. State U., U. Indpls. Mem. Ind. State Senate from 33d dist.; mem. Judiciary, Planning & Pub. Svc., Transp., Health & Environ. Affairs, Pub. Policy and Internat. Cooperation Coms. Ind. State Senate. Mem. Indpls. City County Coun.; active Cmty. Affairs & News Media Rels., pub. affairs Indpls. Power & Light Co., Ind. State Black Expo and Urban League; bd. dirs. Noble Ctrs.; mem. Father Kelly's Youth Club; bd. dirs. Meals on Wheels, Indpls. Housing Strategy, Indpls. Campaign for Healthy Babies. Democrat. Home: 1005 W 36th St Indianapolis IN 46208-4129*

HOWARD, JANET C., state legislator; m. Allen Howard; children: Shirle, Raymond, George. Student, Ea. Ky. U., U. Cin. Councilwoman City of Forest Park, Ohio; senator Ohio State Senate, Columbus. Mem. Nat. Fedn. Rep. Women; bd. dirs. Hamilton County Rep. Women's Club; mem. Beechwood PTA, Forest Park Commn. Forum, adv. coun. Winton Woods Sch., adv. bd. Hamilton County Human Svcs., task force Forest Park Quality of Life. Mem. Greenhills-Forest Park Kiwanis.

HOWARD, JERRY THOMAS, state legislator; b. Oak Ridge, Mo., Mar. 28, 1936; s. John Thomas and Sylvia Ann (Brecheisen) H.; m. Shirla Jean Rathjen McFaddin, 1976; children: Eliza Jane, John Trevor, Erin Penney, Michael Penney, Bill McFaddin. BS, Southeast Mo. U., 1960. State rep. Dist. 156 Mo. State Congress, 1973-77, 87-93, senator, 1993—; chmn. farm to market roads and bridges subcom., 1975-76; vice chmn. govt. rev. com., agr. com., agr. spl. com.; chmn. aging, families and mental health, com. wet lands and spl. com., NAFTA; farmer. Recipient Good Conduct medal. Mem. Elks 2439, Am. Legion, Lions Internat., AF&AM 532, Scottish Rite, Shriners. *

HOWARD, JOANNE FRANCES, marketing executive, funeral director, extended care coordinator, research analyst; b. St. Louis, Feb. 5, 1953; d. Frank Henry and Evelyn Julia (Haeckel) Spellazza; m. Claude Lorrain Howard, May 20, 1978; children: Amy Julia, Laura Ann. BA, U. Mo.-St. Louis, 1975; MS, Western Ill. U., 1976. Lic. funeral director. Analyst, Streett Industries, Inc., St. Louis, 1977-78; research analyst Gallup & Robinson Co., Princeton, N.J., 1978-80, Jack Eckerd Corp., Clearwater, Fla., 1980-82, sr. research analyst, 1982-88; mktg. cons. Howard Assocs., 1986—; cons. Anson Lee Rector Inc., Tarpon Springs, Fla., 1982-83, Med-Op Clinics, Tarpon Springs, Fla., 1983-88; funeral dir., extended care coord. Pugh Funeral Home, Golden City, Mo., 1992—; analyst, cons. H.L. Pugh Assocs. Consulting, Golden City, 1992—. Editor monthly newsletter Florida West Coast chpt. Am. Mktg. Assn., 1982-83. Mem. Pinebrook Homeowners Assn., Largo, Fla., 1983-84. Mem. Am. Mktg. Assn. (past sec.-treas.), Mo. Funeral Dirs. Assn., Nat. Funeral Dirs. Assn., Mo. Inst. Funeral Profls. Democrat. Home and Office: 708 SE 70th Ln Golden City MO 64748-8152

HOWARD, JOHN, state legislator; m. Beverly; two children. Past mem. Carrington City Coun.; N.D. State rep. Dist. 29, 1989—; svc. rep. Otter Tail Power Co.; mem. jud., polit. subdivsn. and ops. divsn. coms.; vice-chmn. appropriations-govt. Mem. Kiwanis, Am. Legion. Home: 295 Furst St N Carrington ND 58421*

HOWARD, JOHN HAZEL, JR., pastor, counselor; b. Burlington, N.J., Dec. 28, 1946; s. John Hazel and Mary Elizabeth H.; m. Lillie Pearl, Nov. 1, 1969; children: John H. III, Chevon D., Danielle S., Moses A. Student, Morgan State U., Balt., 1965-66, N.C. A&T, Greensboro, 1966-67, West L.A. City Coll., Culver City, 1982-84; MDiv, Fuller Theol. Sem., Pasadena, Calif., 1989. Sales person Sears Roebuck, L.A., 1971-74; records specialist So. Calif. Rapid Transit Dist., L.A., 1975-81; owner, mgr. Deli-Restaurant, Marina Del Ray, Calif., 1981-82; youth coord. Synod of So. Calif. and HI, L.A., 1982-83; christian edn. profl. Knox Presbyn. Ch., L.A., 1983-84; asst. to pastor First Presbyn. Ch., L.A., 1985-90; pastor Pine Ave. United Presbyn. Ch., Chgo., 1991—; cons. Oak Park and Austin Tutoral Bd., Chgo., 1992—. Author: I Am Somebody. 1982. Chairperson 1984 Olympics, L.A., 1984, Ecumenical-Religious Svc., planner for the 1984 Olympics; comty. organizer 10th Councilmatic Dist., L.A., 1991; workshop leader 37th Ward Expo 92, Chgo., 1992; mem. Westside Pastors Coalition for AIDS, 1995—, Westside Ch. Devel. Coun., 1995—; bd. dirs. Family Cir. Care Med. Ctr, Chgo., 1995—. Sgt. USMC, 1967-70, Vietnam. Mem. Oak Park and Austin Cluster of Ch. Democrat. Mem. Presbyterian Ch. Office: Pine Ave United Presbyn Ch 1015 N Pine Ave Chicago IL 60651-2704

HOWARD, JOHN SEBASTIAN, English educator; b. Pensacola, Fla., Sept. 24, 1963; s. Billy Ray and Mary Elizabeth (Mollica) H.; m. Becky Lynn Falcetti, Aug. 15, 1987; children: Margaret Elizabeth, Ian Richard. BA, Concordia U., Austin, Tex., 1985; MA, U. Tex., 1989; PhD, St. Louis U., 1996. Asst. instr., fellow rhetoric and composition U. Tex., Austin, 1988; tchg. fellow St. Louis U., 1989-92, lectr. of English, 1992-95; lectr. of English Meramec C.C., St. Louis, 1995—; adj. prof. philosophy Jefferson Coll., Hillsboro, Mo., 1995—; lectr., dir., panel chair, moderator various confs. in field. Contbr. articles to books and jour. in field. Rsch. fellow St. Louis U., 1994; recipient Walter J. Ong Soc. Jesuits award Libr. Assocs. of St. Louis U., 1995. Mem. MLA, Tchrs. for a Dem. Culture, Am. Conf. on Romanticism, Mo. Philological Assn., Am. Conf. on Romanticism. Democrat. Office: St Louis U Dept English 221 N Grand Blvd Saint Louis MO 63103

HOWARD, KAREN ANN, village official; b. Rockford, Ill., Oct. 29, 1952; d. John W. and Virginia Alberta (Herring) Patton; m. Donald Wayne Howard, Aug. 1, 1970; children: Donald Wayne, Kathrine Louise Howard-Wilkinson. Grad. high sch. Cert. EMT, CPR/medic instr. trainer. EMT, lt. Davis Junction Fire Dept., 1982—; CPR/medic first aid coord. Swedish Am. Hosp., Rockford, 1994—; village pres. Davis Junction, Ill. Mem. Stillman Valley Fire Dept., 1993—. Office: Swedish Am Health Mgmt 1358 4th Ave Rockford IL 61104

HOWARD, KATHLEEN, computer company executive; b. Norman, Okla., Nov. 3, 1947; d. Robert Adrian and Jane Elizabeth (Morgens) H.; m. Lawrence W. Osgood, Aug. 10, 1968 (div. Sept. 1970); m. Norman Edlo Gibat, Oct. 15, 1971. Student U. Okla., 1966-68. Typesetter, Selenby Press, Norman, 1968-72; owner, pres. Noguska Industries, Fostoria, Ohio, 1973—; co-founder Home Wine Mchts., Chgo., 1976; cons. Bechtel Corp., Ann Arbor, Mich. and Gaithersburg, Md., 1980—; chairperson Am. Software Project, 1985; ptnr. Popular Topics Pubs., 1993—. Author: All You Need to Know About MSDOS, 1993; co-author, illustrator: Lore of Still Building, 1972; co-author: Making Wine, Beer and Merry, 1973, Computer Comix Mag., 1986; pres. Popular Topics Press, Inc., also jours. and bus. mgmt. software. Treas. United Way of Fostoria, 1986-88, 2d v.p. 1988-90; bd. dirs. Pvt. Industry Coun., 1988-90. Recipient Founders award Home Wine and Beer Trade Assn. Chgo., 1976. Mem. Better Bus. Bur., Nat. Fedn. Ind. Bus., C. of C. (bd. dirs. 1986-92), Employer's Assn. Toledo, Altrusa Internat. Club (sec. Fostoria chpt. 1984-85, pres. 1986-88, editor dist. #5 1988-90). Avocations: painting, printing, travel, reading. Office: Noguska Industries 735-741 N Counryline Fostoria OH 44830-1004

HOWARD, MARK A., stockbroker; b. Cleve., July 31, 1952. BS, U. Toledo, 1975. Prin. Agora Toledo (Ohio) Inc., 1972-86; stockbroker Roney & Co., Ft. Wayne, 1986—. Mem. TPA of Am. (v.p. 1988—). Home: 8406 Talmage Ct Fort Wayne IN 46835-4470 Office: Roney & Co 202 W Berry St Ste 105 Fort Wayne IN 46802-2242

HOWARD, MICHAEL JOSEPH, communications executive, real estate developer; b. Detroit, Oct. 26, 1951; s. Thomas Angel and Margaret Jane (Uttenweiler) H.; divorced; children: Jennifer Paula, Daniel Joseph. Student, Schoolcraft Coll., 1971. Lic. real estate broker, Mich.; lic. residential builder, Mich. Mem. field svc. staff ITT, Southfield, Mich., 1971-81; pres. Howard Properties, Inc., Southfield, 1988—, Allied Alarm Systems, Inc., Southfield, 1988—, Allied Communications, Inc., Southfield, 1979—. Commr. Downtown Devel. Authority, Southfield, 1989—. Mem. Nat. Assn. Home Builders, Nat. Fedn. Ind. Bus., Mich. Assn. Home Builders, Mich. Pay Telephone Assn. (treas. 1986), Southfield C. of C., Optimist Club (charter). Republican. Roman Catholic. Office: Allied Communications Inc 21125 Northwestern Hwy Southfield MI 48075-5038

HOWARD, PHILIP MARTIN, insurance agent; b. Chgo., Dec. 16, 1939; s. Anthony Gerald and Mary Elizabeth (Smith) H.; m. Diane R. Miller, Sept. 12, 1964; children: Anne Marie, Philip Martin II, Kevin Vincent. Student Chgo. parochial schs. Laborer, tree trimmer Chgo. Bur. Forestry, 1963-66; sales rep. O.H. div. Bell & Howell, Chgo., 1966; Allstate Ins. Co., 1967—, agent 1967-72, acct. agent 1972-76, sr. acct. agent, 1976—. With USMCR, 1962-67. Republican. Roman Catholic. Home: 11324 S Lawndale Ave Chicago IL 60655-3424 Office: Allstate Ins Co 10200 S Cicero Ave Ste 203 Oak Lawn IL 60453-4000

HOWARD, STEPHEN RAYMOND, apartment project manager; b. Fort Wayne, Ind., Sept. 21, 1942; s. Earl Junion and Jean Constance (Macke) H.; m. Barbara Jean Parker, Oct. 13, 1962; children: Matthew, Stacie, Kurt (dec.), Brett. Mgr. Monroe Twp. Adv. Bd., Monroeville, Ind., 1986—. Author: Brown Paper Rams and Horse Marines, 1994. Sec. Monroeville Vol. Fire Dept., Monroeville, 1980-91. Mem. Sons of Union Vets. of the Civil War (chaplain 1995—). Democrat. Roman Catholic. Home: 307 Mulberry St Monroeville IN 46773

HOWARDS, LAWRENCE ALLEN, anesthesiologist; b. Antigo, Wis., Jan. 19, 1933; s. Charles Zachary and Ida (Smith) Horwitz; m. Joyzele Y., Aug. 28, 1955; children: Ianne Mae, Mari Lynn. BS, U. Wis., Madison, 1950-54, MD, 1954-58. Diplomate Am. Bd. Anesthesiology; MD - Wis., Calif. Intern Mount Sanai Hosp., Milw., 1958-59; resident in anesthesia VA Hosp., Wood, Wis., 1960-62; mem. staff Sinai Samaritan Med. Ctr., Milw., 1962—, chief anesthesiology, 1975-78, 1990-93; co-dir. Sinai Samaritan Pain Inst., Milw., 1994—. Recipient Westinghouse Sci. medal. Fellow Am. Coll. of Anesthesiology; mem. Phi Delta Epsilon. Home: 2305 W Woodbury Ln Milwaukee WI 53209-1857

HOWE, JOHN KINGMAN, manufacturing, sales and marketing executive; b. Everett, Wash., Nov. 7, 1945; s. John Cutler and Nancy Carpenter (Kingman) H.; m. Loretta Kerr, Aug. 27, 1966; children: Steven Cutler, Nancy Kingman. Student Ohio State U., 1963-65. Field technician Data Corp., Dayton, Ohio, 1965-66; letter carrier U.S. Post Office, Dayton, 1966; sales rep. E.S. Klosterman Co., Dayton, 1966-71, v.p. 1971-72; v.p. sales, dir. Springfield Binder Corp., Ohio, 1981-84, dir., pres., chief exec. officer, 1984-95; dir., pres. The John K. Howe Co., Inc., Dayton, Ohio, 1972-87, chmn., chief exec. officer, dir. 1987—; pres. Cutler-Kingman, Inc. div. Thump Properties, Cin., 1979-86, owner, 1986—; gen. ptnr. H&B Enterprises, Dayton, 1977-86, Design Investment Properties, Dayton, 1979-86, BMR Properties, Ltd., Dayton, 1979-82; adminstr. John K. Howe Co./Profit Sharing, Cin., 1973—, John K. Howe Co./Pension Plan, 1976—; owner Androscoggin Designs, Dayton, 1979-86. Pres. South Dixie Bus. Assn., Kettering, Ohio, 1978-82; mem. design review com. Lincoln Park Owner's Assn., 1989-91, chmn., 1992-94; pres. Woods of Lincoln Park Homeowner's Assn., 1992-94, mem. Fraze Pavilion fund raising com., 1991-92; mem. Confrerie de la Chaines de Rotisseurs Bailliage de Cin., 1993—. Mem. Cin. C. of C., Dayton C. of C. Republican. Presbyterian. Office: The John K Howe Co Inc Ste 6 400 Pike St Cincinnati OH 45202-4216 also: Springfield Binder Corp Ste 6 400 Pike St Cincinnati OH 45202-4216 also: John K Howe Co Inc Warehouse Fulfillment & Mailing Ops 310 Culvert St Cincinnati OH 45202-2229

HOWE, JOSEPH A., mechanical designer; b. Cleve., Apr. 29, 1949. A in Mech. Engring., Lakeland Cmty. Coll., Kirtland, Ohio, 1977. Sr. mech. designer Picker Xray, Highland Heights, Ohio, 1978-81, Allen-Bradley, Highland Heights, 1981-90, Telxon, Akron, Ohio, 1990—. Served with USN, 1968-71. Mem. Hudson (Ohio) Jaycees. Republican. Roman Catholic. Office: Telxon 3330 W Market St Akron OH 44333-3306

HOWE, STANLEY MERRILL, manufacturing company executive; b. Muscatine, Iowa, Feb. 5, 1924; s. Merrill Y. and Thelma F. (Corriel) H.; m. Helen Jensen, Mar. 29, 1953; children: Thomas, Janet, Steven, James. B.S., Iowa State U., 1946; M.B.A., Harvard U., 1948. Prodn. engr. HON Industries, Muscatine, Iowa, 1948-54, v.p. prodn., 1954-61, exec. v.p., 1961-64, pres., 1964-90, chmn., 1984—, chief exec. officer, 1979-91; chmn. bd. dirs. Holga, The Gunlocke Co., BPI Inc., Ring King Visibles, The Hon Co., XLM Co., Heatilator, Inc. Trustee Iowa Wesleyan Coll. Gerard Swope fellow Harvard U., 1948. Mem. NAM, Bus. Instl. Furniture Mfrs. Assn. Methodist. Clubs: Rotary, Elks, 33. Office: Hon Industries Inc 414 E 3d St PO Box 1109 Muscatine IA 52761

HOWE, WILLIAM HUGH, artist; b. Stockton, Calif., June 18, 1928; s. Edwin Walter and Eugenia (Mercante) H. AB, Ottawa (Kans.) U., 1951. Illustrator Western Auto Supply, Kansas City, Mo., 1952, Kansas City Mdse. Mart, 1953-56; comml. artist U.S. Army C.E., Kansas City, 1958-64, Howard Needles Tammen & Bergendoff Cons. Engrs., Kansas City, 1964-68, Urban & Regional Planning, 1968-70; freelance artist, 1970—. Exhibited paintings of butterflies Philbrook Art Ctr., Tulsa, Ft. Worth Children's Mus., Montserrat Gallery, N.Y.C., Witte Meml. Art Mus., San Antonio, Anthropology Mus., Chapultepec Park, Mexico City; represented in permanent collections: Smithsonian Instn., Washington, Franklin Mint (Pa.), Cranbook Inst., Bloomfield HIlls, Mich., U. Mich. Exhibits Mus., Ann Arbor, Oak Knoll Mus., Clayton, Mo., Am. Mus. Natural History, N.Y.C., Denver Mus. Natural History, Am. Baptist Assembly, Green Lake, Wis., Mowbray Union, Ottawa U., Kans., Cen. Mo. State Coll., Warrensburg, Mich. State U., East Lansing, U. Wyo. Art Mus., Laramie, San Diego Mus. Nat. History, Balboa Park, U. Ariz., Tuscon, Ill. State Mus. Art, Springfield, Mont. Hist. Soc., Helena, Wyo. State Art Mus., Cheyenne, Ariz. State U., Tempe, Milw. Pub. Mus., State Capitol Bldg., Denver, Denver Pub. Libr., Kansas City (Mo.) Mus. History Sci., Presdl. Palace, Tamazunchale, San Luis Potosi, Mexico, Ottawa (Kans.) Jr. H.S., others; Am. Heritage Wildlife cards Am. Butterflies, 1983, U. Kans., 1994, U. Calif. Berkeley, Allyn Mus. Entomology, Sarasota, U. Colo., Colo. State U., Calif. Acad. Scis., San Francisco, Oakland (Calif.) Mus., James Ford Bell Mus., U. Minn. (Mpls); Author-artist: Our Butterflies and Moths, 1964, the Butterflies of North America, 1975, Butterfly Chart of North America, 1979, Butterfly sect. Readers Digest North American Wildlife, 1980; co-author (with Carlos R. Beutelspacher Baights), U.N.A.M., Mexico City, 1984; one man show Caroline Kingcade Gallery, North Kansas City, Mo., 1988; TV show Hoy Mismo, 1986. Mem. Ottawa Community Arts Coun., Leavenworth Arts. Coun.; mem. Larry Hatteberg's "Kans. People" KAKE-TV, Wichita. Named Am. Artist Am. References, 1990. Mem. Jour. Lepidopterists Soc., Burroughs Nature Club, Audubon Soc. Mo., Central States Entomo. Soc., Los Angeles County Mus. Democrat. Episcopalian. Home and Studio: 822 E 11th St Ottawa KS 66067-3138

HOWELL, ANDREW, state legislator. Law enforcement officer Ft. Scott, Kans.; mem. from dist. 4 Kans. State Ho. of Reps., Topeka. Address: 728 S Holbrook Fort Scott KS 66701

HOWELL, CAMILLE FLY, university public relations administrator; b. Water Valley, Miss., Sept. 14, 1953; d. Earl Kirkman and Eunice Bell (Forbes) Fly; m. Michael Wayne Howell, Aug. 14, 1981. BA, U. Miss., 1975, PhD, 1983; MA, Vanderbilt U., 1978. Instr. art Northwest Miss. C.C., Senatobia, 1977-81; sec. Pub. Rels. Office Davidson (N.C.) Coll., 1981-82; lectr. art history U. N.C. Charlotte, 1983; art critic Charlotte Observer, 1982-83; art critic, staff writer Mpls. Star Tribune, 1983-84; dir. pub. rels. Coll. of Ozarks, Point Lookout, Mo., 1984—; art critic Springfield (Mo.) News Leader, 1987—; radio show host From the Point KCOZ FM Radio, Point Lookout, 1986—; lectr., art exhibit juror numerous art orgns, 1982—. Contbr. articles to profl. jours. and newspapers. Elder First Presbyn. Ch., chair pers. com., nominating com., mem. worship music com., 1995—. Mem. Branson/Hollister Rotary Club (internat. com.), Branson Arts Coun. Home: PO Box 422 Point Lookout MO 65726 Office: Pub Rels Dept College of Ozarks Point Lookout MO 65726

HOWELL, DONALD J., engineer; b. Ottawa, Kans., Mar. 11, 1937; s. Harley Roy and Velma Gladys (Van Meter) H.; m. Cleona Hurt, Sept. 7, 1958 (div.); 1 child, Stirling; m. Glenda Avis Roberts, Apr. 4, 1990. Tool designer United Airlines, San Francisco, 1962-66, Boeing Aircraft, Seattle, 1966-70; chief engr. Skyhook Corp. & Sponco Mfg., Ottawa, Kans., 1973—. Patentee in field. With USAF, 1958-62. Mem. NRA, Masonic Lodge (past master 1992, trustee), Shriners of Franklin County (past pres. 1993). Republican. Home: 1680 Louisiana Rd Princeton KS 66078-9115 Office: Skyhook Corp Sponco Mfg 1640 S Main St Ottawa KS 66067-3805

HOWELL, GAIL A., critical care nurse, educator; b. St. Charles, Ill., Feb. 25, 1954; d. George Austin and Genevieve Bertha (Zornow) H. AAS, Waubonsee Community Coll., Sugar Grove, Ill., 1978; BSN, Aurora (Ill.) U., 1985, MSN, 1990. RN, Ill.; CCRN; cert. ACLS provider, instr. Staff nurse med.-surg. Delnor Hosp., St. Charles, 1978-79, staff nurse ICU, 1979-81; staff nurse ICU Mercy Ctr. for Health Care, Aurora, Ill., 1982-84, head nurse ICA, 1984-88; staff nurse ICU/ICA Copley Meml. Hosp., Aurora, 1988-89, critical care nurse, educator, clinical specialist, 1989-90; instr. med.-surg. nursing Coll. of DuPage, Glen Ellyn, Ill., 1990-92, Aurora (Ill.) U., 1992-93; nursing educator Morton Coll., Cicero, Ill., 1993-94; capt. U.S. Army, Ft. Leonard Wood, Mo., 1994—; instr. Waubonsee Community Coll., Sugar Grove, Ill., fall, 1989, 90, spring 1992. Mem. AACN, ANA, Nat. League for Nursing, Sigma Theta Tau (past treas.), Lambda Upsilon (at-large).

HOWELL, GEORGE BEDELL, equity investing and managing executive; b. Schenectady, Sept. 19, 1919; s. Jesse M. and Grace (Gerhaeusser) H.; m. Mary Barbara Crohurst, July 10, 1944; children: Raymond Gary, Terry Barbara, Janice Patricia, Nancy Jo, George Bedell Jr. BS in Adminstrv. Engring., Cornell U., 1942. With GE, 1946-59; v.p. mfg. Leece Neville Co., Cleve., 1959-61, Royal Electric Co., Pawtucket, R.I., 1961-62; dir. ops. packaging equipment and product devel. Acme Steel Co. (merged with Interlake Steel Corp. 1965), 1962-64; v.p. adminstrv. svc. Interlake Steel Corp., Chgo., 1964-66; v.p. internat. divsn., v.p. Acme Products divsn. Interlake Steel Corp., 1966-70; CEO Golconda Corp., Chgo., 1970-72; v.p. devel. Internat. Minerals & Chems. Corp., 1972-73, sr. v.p., pres. industry group, 1974-77, exec. v.p., 1977-81; pres., CEO Wurlitzer Co., 1982-86, chmn., pres., CEO, 1986-87, vice chmn., 1988-89; prin. Mid West Ptnrs., Chgo., 1988-89; gen. ptnr. Pfingsten Ptnrs., Chgo., 1989-94, ptnr., 1994—; chmn. Hallcrest Holding Corp., 1992—; chmn. Hollcrest Holding Corp., 1993—. Chmn. bd. trustees Village of Oak Brook, Ill., 1965-73, pres., 1973-79; trustee Christ Ch., Oak Brook, vice chmn., 1992—. N.Y. State and Univ. scholar Cornell U., 1942. Mem. McGraw Wildlife Found., Chgo. Athletic Club, Medinah Country Club, Econ. Club (Chgo.), Ocean Reef Club (Fla.), DuPage Club. Home: 5 Brighton Ln Oak Brook IL 60521-2323 Office: 520 Lake Cook Rd Ste 375 Deerfield IL 60015-4926

HOWELL, MATTHEW D., pension manager; b. Pensacola, Fla.. BA, Mich. State U., 1983. Pension mgr. Pathway Investment, Grand Rapids, 1987—. Republican. Mem. Reformed Ch. Office: Pathway Investments 4301 Canal Ave SW Ste 101E Grandville MI 49418-2200

HOWELL, NORBERT ALLEN, architect; b. Hamilton, Ohio, Nov. 22, 1951; s. Kenneth Norbert and Juanita Jane (Baker) H.; m. Sherrie Lynn Schroeder, Dec. 16, 1972; children: James Michael, Theresa Marie. BS in Architecture, Ohio State U., 1978, MArch, 1980. Teaching asst. Ohio State U., Columbus, 1978-80; archtl. applications programmer Caudill Rowlett Scott (CRS), Houston, 1980-83; dir. computer ops., project mgr. Daniel Cline and Assocs., Columbus, 1983-91; owner Howell Architects & Assocs., Columbus, 1991-93; pres. AEC Cadcon, Inc., 1991—; guest lectr. Ohio State U., Columbus, 1983—; adj. prof. Columbus State C.C., 1992—. Active Boy Scouts Am. Mem. AIA, Cen. Ohio Intergraph Graphic Users Group (pres. 1984-86). Office: AEC Cadcon Inc Ste B 1051 Old Henerson Rd Columbus OH 43220

HOWELL, ORVIE LEON, geologist; b. Wichita, Kans., Sept. 4, 1931; s. Orville Clements and Hettie-Elizabeth (Brock) H.; m. Lillian marlene Mendioner, Apr. 15, 1995; children: Dale, Richard, Susan, Sally. B.S. in Geology, Wichita State U., 1954. Geologist, Lion Oil Co., Wichita, Kans., 1954-58; dist. geologist Lario Oil and Gas Co., Wichita, 1958-63, exploration mgr. Hinckle Oil Co., 1963-73, gen. mgr. Hinkle Oil Co., Wichita, 1973—; chmn. GEO adv. assn. Wichita State Univ., 1992-94. Mem. Am. Assn. Petroleum Geologists (speaker 1969-70, co-editor jour. 1969-70), Kans. Geol. Soc. (hon., pres. 1968-69, bd. advisor 1991), N.Mex. Geol. Soc., Am. Inst. Profl. Geologists (pres. 1995), Rocky Mountain Assn. Geologists, Kans. Geol. Found. (pres. 1994), Kans. Ind. Oil and Gas Assn. Republican. Methodist. Clubs: Tallgrass Country, Crestview Country, Petroleum (Wichita). Avocations: Flying, travel. Home: 9031 Lakepoint Dr Wichita KS 67226-2117 Office: Hinkle Oil Co 1016 Union Ctr Wichita KS 67202

HOWELL, RAYMOND GARY, financial executive; b. Lynn, Mass., Aug. 19, 1947; s. George and Barbara (Crohurst) H.; m. Marilyn Abazoris, July 10, 1971; children: Barret, Shannon. BA in Econs., Knox Coll., 1969; MBA, Washington U., 1971. CPA, Ill. Area credit mgr. Am. Hosp. Supply, McGaw Park, Ill., 1973-74, nat. credit mgr., 1974-75, zone contr., 1975-77; asst. div. contr. Am. Hosp. Supply, McGaw Park, 1977-79; dist. fin. mgr. Digital Equipment, Rolling Meadows, Ill., 1979-81; area contr. Motorola, Schaumburg, Ill., 1981-86; nat. svc. contr. Motorola, Schaumburg, 1986-88, corp. mgr. fin. mgmt. devel., 1988-92; dir. fin. Motorola New Enterprises, 1993-95; dir. ops. Motorola Software Enterprises, 1995—. Capt. U.S. Army, 1971-73. Mem. Ill. Soc. CPAs, Medinah Country Club, Seabrook Island Club, Max McGraw Wildlife Found. Republican. Home: 26680 Countryside Lake Dr Mundelein IL 60060-3316

HOWERTON, JIM, state legislator. Mem. Mo. Ho. of Reps., Jefferson City. Republican.

HOWES, BRIAN THOMAS, lawyer; b. Sioux Falls, S.D., July 23, 1957; s. Thomas A. and Joyce L. (McFarland) H.; m. Robin Kay Schoonover, June 2, 1979; children: Phillip, Adam, Jason. BSBA in Acctg., BA in Polit. Sci., Kans. State U., 1979; JD, U. Kans., 1982. Bar: Mo. 1982, U.S. Dist. Ct. (we. dist.) Mo. 1982, U.S. Supreme Ct. 1989. Assoc. Shughart, Thomson & Kilroy, Kansas City, Mo., 1982-85; exec. v.p., COO, gen. counsel Tenenbaum & Assocs., Inc., Kansas City, 1985-95; ptnr., nat. dir. property tax svcs. Ernst & Young LLP, Kansas City, Mo., 1995—. Contr. articles to profl. jours; writer, speaker in field. Contbg. mem. Dem. Nat. Com.; bd. dirs. Kansas City Wheelchair Athletic Commn., 1987-89, Vol. Atty. Project, 1984—. Mem. ABA, Assn. Trial Lawyers Am., Kansas City Met. Bar Assn., Lawyers Assn. Kansas City, Am. Corp. Counsel Assn., Inst. Property Taxation, Internat. Assn. of Assessing Officers. Episcopalian. Home: 4901 W 130th St Shawnee Mission KS 66209-1864 Office: Ernst & Young LLP One Kansas City Pl 1200 Main St Kansas City MO 64105

HOWETH, DIANE KATHRYN, mental health nurse; b. Spalding, Nebr., Sept. 22, 1956; d. Joseph J. and Ethel A. (Purdy) Happ; m. Thomas E. Howeth, Sept. 19, 1987; children: Bernadette A., Louis Thomas. ADN, U. Nebr., Omaha, 1977, postgrad., 1993—. Cert. instr. in therapeutic crisis mgmt. Charge nurse Luth. Gen. Hosp., Omaha, 1977-79; charge nurse psychiat. inpatient ICU Richard Young Hosp., Omaha, 1979-88, clin. supr. psychiat inpatient ICU, 1988-92, clin. supr. psychiat. gen. adult programs, 1992-93, staff nurse adult partial program, 1993—, also care coord., patient educator. Mem. Omaha Cath. Nurses Assn.

HOWIE, ALLEN D., marketing executive; b. Danville, Ill., Oct. 22, 1955. BS in Bus., Ea. Ill. U., 1985. Fin. svcs. officer Palmer Am. Nat. Bank, Danville, Ill., 1978-88; v.p. mktg. and bank svcs. Cozad Investment Svcs., Champaign, Ill., 1988-90; v.p. The Mktg. Co., New Albany, Ind., 1990—; mem. Bridgepointe Ctr., Clarksville, Ind., 1992—. Contbr. critic Louisville Courier Jour., 1992—. Grad. Leadership So. Ind., Jeffersonville, 1995; vol. United Way, Jeffersonville, 1978—. Recipient Aspen Design grant Nationwide Papers, 1993. Mem. Louisville Graphic Design Assn. (bd. dirs. 1994—), Advt. Club Louisville, Ind. Bank Mktg. Assn. Office: The Mktg Co 113 E Spring St # 216 New Albany IN 47150-3436

HOWLETT, PHYLLIS LOU, athletics conference administrator; b. Indianola, Iowa, Oct. 23, 1932; d. James Clarence and Mabel L. (Fisher) Hickman; m. Jerry H. Howlett, Jan. 2, 1955 (dec.); children: Timothy A., Jane A. Field; m. Ronlin Royer, Dec. 30, 1977. BA, Simpson Coll., 1954. Tchr. Oskaloosa (Iowa) High Sch., 1954-55; psychometrist Drake U., Des Moines, 1956-57, asst. to men's athletics dir., 1974-79; asst. dir. athletics U. Kans., Lawrence, 1979-82; asst. commr. Big Ten Conf., Park Ridge, Ill., 1982—; mem. football TV com. NCAA, 1980-87, chmn. NCAA com. on women's athletics, 1987-94, NCAA exec. com., 1990—, NCAA women's golf com., 1983-89, spl. com. NCAA women's basketball TV, 1989-90, chair NCAA com. for women's corp. mktg., 1990-94, NCAA Divsn. I championship com., 1990-95, chair NCAA task force on gender equity, 1992-94, NCAA exec. dir. search com., 1993, spl. NCAA com. divsn. I football playoff, NCAA adminstrv. com., 1995, NCAA joint policy bd., 1995—, NCAA sec., treas., 1995—. Chmn. Iowa Commn. Status of Women, 1976-79; pres. Vol. Bur. of Greater Des Moines, 1969-70; chair Arts and Recreation Coun. of Greater Des Moines, 1975; pres. Iowa Children's and Family Svcs., 1973; nat. pres. Assn. Vol. Burs., Inc., 1972-73, svc. award. Inducted into Simpson Coll. Hall of Fame. Mem. Nat. Assn. Dirs. of Collegiate Athletics (exec. com. 1986-90, NACDA award for adminstrv. excellence 1994), Nat. Assn. Women's Athletics Adminstrs., Simpson Coll. Alumni (Achievement award 1988). Republican. Office: 1500 Higgins Rd Park Ridge IL 60068-6500

HOY, GEORGE PHILIP, clergyman, food bank executive; b. Indpls., Feb. 5, 1937; s. Clarence Augustus Hoy and Margaret Louise (Etter) Wooley; m. Barbara J. Turpen, Aug. 11, 1957 (dec. Feb. 1987); children: Rene Hoy Riegle, Sherri Hoy Haas, Matthew Philip; 1 foster child, Richard H. Johnson; m. Margie S. Cissell (div.). BA, Ky. Wesleyan Coll., 1958; MDiv, So. Bapt. Theol. Sem., Louisville, 1962. Ordained to ministry United Ch. of Christ, 1962. Pastor Union United Ch. of Christ, Evansville, Ind., 1962-72, Faith United Ch. of Christ, Ft. Wayne, Ind., 1975-80, St. Matthew's United Ch. of Christ, Evansville, 1981-87; dir. Youth Svc. Bur., Evansville, 1972-75; pastor St. Peter's United Ch. of Christ, Evansville, 1988-94; mem. faculty Brescia Coll., Owensboro, Ky., 1970-72; chaplain Evansville State Hosp., 1966-72, Fraternal Order Police, Evansville, 1982-92; dir. Tri-State Food Bank, Evansville, 1987—; del. gen. synod Ind.-Ky. Conf., United Ch. of Christ, 1978-81. Religion columnist Evansville Press, 1983-93. Vol. Habitat for Humanity, Americus, Ga., 1980-81; mem. City-County Human Rels. Commn., Evansville, 1984-93; bd. dirs. Leadership Evansville, 1987-92, Outreach Ministries, Evansville, 1987-93; mem. regional bd. advisors Ch. World Svc., 1987—; mem. Ill. and Ind. Hunger Coalitions; mem. vol. outreach svcs. com., gifts-in-kind com. United Way; mem. Bread for the World, Amnesty Internat., Food Rsch. and Action, Police Athletic League; mem. Vanderburgh County Coun., 1992—, pres., 1994-95. Recipient ecumenical award Evansville Area Coun. of Chs., 1987, Native Am. award Coun. of Bear, Evansville, 1988. Mem. NAACP, ACLU, Southwestern Ind. Psychol. Assn., Tri-State Pastors Circle (pres. 1984-85), Northside Ministerial Assn., Evansville Tri-State Assn. (pres. 1972-75), Greenpeace. Republican. Home: 217 Cherry St Evansville IN 47713-1242

HOY, SUELLEN, historian; b. Chgo., Aug. 14, 1942; d. Christopher J. and Imelda E. Hoy; m. Walter Nugent, Nov. 1, 1986. BA, St. Mary's Coll., Notre Dame, Ind., 1965; MA, Ind. U., 1971, PhD, 1975. Asst. prof. SUNY, Plattsburgh, 1974-75; dir. Pub. Works Hist. Soc., Chgo., 1975-81; asst. dir. N.C. Div. Archives & History, Raleigh, 1981-87; adj. prof. U. Notre Dame, 1987-91; NEH fellow NEH, Granger, Ind., 1992-93; vis. prof. U. Coll. Dublin, Ireland, 1991-92; vis. assoc. prof. U. Notre Dame, 1995—. Author: Chasing Dirt: American Pursuit of Cleanliness, 1995; co-author: History of Public Works in The United States, 1976, Public Works History in The United States, 1982, From Dublin to New Orleans: The Journey of Nora and Alice, 1994. Bd. dirs. N.C. Humanities Com., Greensboro, 1984-87. Recipient Irish Am. Cultural Inst. award, Dublin, 1991-92; NEH fellow, 1986-87, 92-93. Mem. Orgn. Am. Historians (exec. bd. 1986-89), Am. Hist. Assn. (nominating com. 1987-89), Nat. Coun. Pub. History (bd. dirs.), Pub. Works Hist. Soc. (pres. 1986-87). Home: 1 Lupine Ln Chesterton IN 46304-1013

HOYT, MARGUERITE, city official; b. Amboy, Ill., Feb. 5, 1928; d. Patrick Henry and Mary Agnes (McGlynn) O'Hare; m. Frank W. Hoyt; children: Eileen Nehring, Patricia Smith, William P., Fran, Jeanne Ratfield. Dep. assessor Twp. of Dekalb, Ill.; city clk. City of Dekalb. Sec. DeKalb (Ill.) Credit Union, 1978-93; v.p. Safe Passage, 1988, also sec.; pres. Barb City Manor Inc., 1995; active Cath. Daus., 1989, Sycamore (Ill) Credit Union, 1993—. Mem. Mcpl. Clks. of Ill. (dist. chmn., treas., sec., newsletter editor), N.W. Mcpls. Clks. Assn. (pres.). Office: City of DeKalb 200 S 4th St De Kalb IL 60115

HRINKO, DANIEL DEAN, clinical counselor; b. Springfield, Ohio, Dec. 14, 1955; s. Peter and Jean Ayr (Wallace) H.; m. Lisa Marie Rykowski, Oct. 23, 1976; children: Peter Daniel, Matthew David. BA, Muskingum Coll., 1976; MA, Ball State U., 1977; doctor profl. psychology Wright State U. Cottage therapist Oesterlen Svcs. for Youth Ctr., Springfield, Ohio, 1978-79; dir. day treatment Dayton (Ohio) Youth Drug Program, 1980-82; pvt. practice adolescent and family counseling, Springfield, Ohio, 1982-84; dir. assessment Alcohol and Drug Council Clark County, 1984-86; therapist adolescent psychiat. unit, Dettmer Hosp., Troy, Ohio, 1986-87, unit coordinator adolescent psychiatric unit, Dettmer Hosp. Troy, 1987-89; pvt. practice Philip J. Gibeau & Assocs., 1994—; cons. agys. Vol. German Twp. Fire Dept., 1978-93; commr. Clark County Park Commission, 1992—; development bd. Mental Retardation Disabilities Board of Clark County, 1993—. Mem. Am. Psychol. Assn. Lutheran. Lodge: Masons (past master). Address: 3643 Troy Rd Springfield OH 45504-4463 Office: 2100 E High St Ste 112-114 Springfield OH 45505

HRUSKA, RONALD JOHN, JR., physical therapy and rehabilitation administrator; b. Seward, Nebr., May 2, 1955; s. Ronald John Sr. and Rita Jean (Rolenc) H.; m. Robin Irene Hansen, May 26, 1978; children: Renee, Rachelle, Ron III. BS in Life Sci., U. Nebr., Lincoln, 1978; BS in Phys. Therapy, U. Nebr., Omaha, 1980, MPA, 1985. Dir. phys. rehab. and handicapped program YMCA, Lincoln, 1976-78; staff phys. therapist Omaha VA Med. Ctr. Dept. Phys. Therapy Restorative Medicine Svcs., Omaha, 1980-83; asst. chief and clin. dir. Omaha VA Med. Ctr. Dept. Phys. Therapy Rehab. Medicine, Omaha, 1983-84; dir. phys. therapy St. Elizabeth Community Health Ctr., Lincoln, 1984-88, dir. phys. and occupational therapy depts., 1988-93, dir. phys. therapy and rehab. svcs., 1993—; chmn. phys. therapy bd. Nebr. Dept. Health Bur. of Examining Bds., Lincoln, 1990—; med. advisor Kinetics Inc., 1990—; mem. phys. therapy program adv. com. Creighton U., Omaha, 1989-93, clin. asst. prof. Creighton U., Omaha, 1995—; vol. faculty mem. U. Nebr. Med. Ctr., 1983—; lectr. in field. Contbr. articles to profl. jours. Active St. John's Parish, Lincoln, 1984—; organizer, dir. med. coverage Nebr. Cornhusker State Games, 1986-90; vol. med. coverage YMCA Games, 1984-90. Recipient NE-APTA M.E. Sackseder award, 1993; named Bus. Assoc. of Yr., Am. Bus. Women Assn., 1992. Mem. Nebr. Am. Phys. Therapy Assn. (pres. 1987-89, pres-elect 1985-87, chmn. student liason com.), Am. Phys. Therapy Assn. (ho. of delegates 1986, 87, 90—, chief delegate, del., mem. jud. com. 1990-95, chair 1995). Democrat. Roman Catholic. Home: 8831 E Avon Ln Lincoln NE 68505-7808

HRUSOVSKY, JOHN JOSEPH, II, systems consulting manager; b. Warren, Ohio, Apr. 24, 1963; s. John Joseph and Irene Josephine (Kicko) H.; m. Bobbi Jo. Feutz, Apr. 22, 1989; children; Nathaniel John, Jarad Robert. BSBA, Ohio State U., 1986. Systems cons. mgr. Andersen Cons., Columbus, Ohio, 1986—. Mem. Ohio State U. Stadium (treas. 1992-94), Scholarship Dormitory Alumni Soc. (bd. govs. 1994—), The Athletic Club Columbus, Human Resources Systems Profls. Roman Catholic. Home: 6155 Dustin Rd Galena OH 43021 Office: Andersen Cons 41 S High St Ste 2000 Columbus OH 43215

HSIEH, PHILIP PO-FANG, mathematics educator; b. Tainan, Taiwan, July 10, 1934; came to U.S. 1959; s. Chai-Seng and Tsai-Pin (Wang) H.; m. Emmy Hui Mei Su, July 8, 1961; children: Paul S., Timothy I. BSc, Nat. Taiwan U., 1957; MA, U. Minn., 1961, PhD, 1964. Asst. prof. math. Western Mich. U., Kalamazoo, 1964-67; assoc. prof. math. Western Mich. U., 1967-73, prof. math., 1973—; rsch. mathematician Naval Rsch. Lab., Washington, 1970-71. Editor: Analytic Theory of Differential Equations, 1971, Trends and Developments in Ordinary Differential Equations, 1994; contbr. articles to profl. jours. Naval Rsch. Pub. awardee Naval Rsch. Lab., 1972; Disting. Faculty Scholar awardee Western Mich. U., 1995. Mem. Am. math. Soc., Math. Soc. Am., Math. Soc. Japan, Soc. Indsl. and Applied Math. Office: Western Mich U Dept Math And Statisti Kalamazoo MI 49008

HSU, CHUNG YI, neurologist; b. Taipei, Taiwan, China, Oct. 14, 1944; s. Huo and Jane (Wu) H.; m. Amy Yang, Sept. 27, 1974; children: Alice L., Virginia, Charles Y. MD, Nat. Taiwan U., Taipei, 1970; PhD, U. Va., 1975. Diplomate Am. Bd. Psychiatry and Neurology. NIH fellow Diabetes Rsch. Ctr., U. Va., Charlottesville, 1975-77; fellow dept. pharmacology Med. U. S.C., Charleston, 1977, intern dept. medicine, 1977-78, resident dept. neurology, 1978-80, chief resident dept. neurology, 1980-81, fellow clin. neuropharmacology, 1981, dir. neuropharmacology dept. neurology, 1981-89; dir. neuropharmacology div. restorative neurology Baylor Coll. Medicine, Houston, 1989-93; head cerebrovascular disease sect., dept. neurology Washington U. Sch. Medicine, St. Louis, 1993—; mem. adv. panel on drug info. U.S. Pharmacopeial Conv., Rockville, Md., 1985-90; mem. CNS adv. panel Eastman-Kodak/Sterling, Malvern, Pa., 1988-94; mem. study sect. Nat. Inst. Neurol. Disease and Stroke, NIH, 1988—. Mem. editl. bd. Stroke, Jour. Cerebral Blood Flow and Metabolism, Jour. Neurotrauma; mem. guest editl. bd. Jour. Formosan Med. Assn.; editor 2 monographs; contbr. articles to profl. jours. Pres. Taiwanese Assn., Charleston, 1984-85. 2d lt. Taiwan Navy, 1970-71. Grad fellow U.Va. Sch. Medicine, Charlottesville, 1971-75; recipient Nat. Rsch. Svc. award USPHS, 1977, 81, NIH Tchr. Investigator Devel. award 1983-88, NIH Javits Neurosci. Investigator award, 1991—, Disting. Rschr. award Vivian L. Smith Found., 1993-94. Fellow Am. Acad. Neurology; mem. Am. Heart Assn. (fellow stroke coun.), Am. Neurol. Assn., Taiwan Stroke Soc., Taiwan Neurol. Soc., Internat. Soc. Cerebral Blood Flow and Metabolism, Neurotrauma Soc. (pres. 1992-93), N.Am. Taiwanese Prof. Assn. (pres.-elect 1994-95, pres. 1995-96, past pres. 1996—), Dana Alliance for Brain Initiatives. Home: 538 Conway Village Dr Saint Louis MO 63141-5807 Office: Washington U Sch Medicine Dept Neurology Box 8111 660 S Euclid Ave Saint Louis MO 63110

HSUI, ALBERT T., geophysicist, educator; m. Loretta Y. Lee, June 19, 1971; children: Emily F., Jennifer F. BS, U. Mass., Lowell, 1968; M in Engring., Cornell U., 1969, PhD, 1972. NRC rsch. assoc. NASA/Ames Rsch. Ctr., Moffett Field, Calif., 1972-73; mem. tech. staff Bell Labs., Allentown, Pa., 1973-76; rsch. assoc. MIT, Cambridge, Mass., 1976-79; prof. U. Ill., Urbana, 1980—, assoc. head, 1994—. Fgn. editor Newton mag., 1990—; assoc. editor Jour. Geophys. Rsch., 1993—, Jour. Computational Seismology, 1993-95. Mem. Am. Geophys. Union, Soc. Exploration Geophysicists. Office: U Ill Dept Geology 245 NHB, 1301 W Green St Urbana IL 61801

HUANG, CHARLES, software engineer; b. Taiwan, Jan. 22, 1959; came to the U.S., 1978; Student, U. Md., 1978-79; BSEE, U. Mich., 1982, BS in Computer Engring., 1985, M in Indsl. and Ops. Engring., 1992. Project engr. Syron, Ann Arbor, 1982-84; sr. software engr. Unisys Corp., Plymouth, Mich., 1985—. Home: 40300 Finley Dr Canton MI 48188-1583 Office: Unisys Corp 41100 Plymouth Rd Plymouth MI 48170-1856

HUANG, CHI-LUNG (DOMINIC), mechanical engineer, educator; b. Zang-Zhou, Fujian, China, Oct. 10, 1930; came to U.S., 1959; s. T.C. Huang and C. Chien; m. Li-Fang Claire, Aug. 20, 1960; children: Agnes S., Dennis F., Donald J., Thomas J. BS, Nat. Taiwan U., Rep. of China, 1954; MS, U. Ill., 1960; PhD, Yale U., 1964. Registered profl. engr., China. Engr. Taiwan Power Co., 1955-58, Ammann & Whitney, N.Y.C., 1960-61; rsch. asst. Yale U., New Haven, 1961-64; prof. Kans. State U., Manhattan, 1964—. Author: Heat Transfer in Porous Media, 1982; editor: Developments in Mechanics, 1979; contbr. over 200 articles to profl. jours. Vol. Riley County Police and Hosps., Manhattan, 1975—. Recipient Phi Kappa Phi Faculty Scholar award, 1991; named an Internat. Man of Yr. for Teaching and Rsch., Internat. Biog. Ctr. of Cambridge, Eng., 1994. Mem. ASME, AIAA, Am. Acad. Mech. Engrs., Soc. Engring. Sci., Kans. State C. of C. (bus. exch. 1987), Rotary Club (internat. youth exch., Manhattan, other coms. 1986—), Sigma Xi, Phi Tau Phi, Phi Kappa Phi. Home: 2925 Roma Ter Manhattan KS 66502-2035 Office: Kans State U Dept Mech Engring Durland Hall Manhattan KS 66506

HUANG, VICTOR TSANGMIN, food scientist, researcher; b. Republic of China, Dec. 12, 1951; came to U.S., 1975; s. Shen Tan and Yeh Gee (Lai) H.; m. Jean Fong Chen, June 9, 1978; children: Hank Su, Andrea Su. BS, Hsing-Hua U., Hsin-Chu, Republic of China, 1973; MS, U. Chgo., 1977; PhD, Ohio State U., 1981. Teaching asst. U. Chgo., 1975-77; rsch. assoc. Ohio State U.,

Columbus, 1977-81; food scientist Pillsbury Co., Mpls., 1981—; presenter dairy, baby and bakery product formulation field, 1977-94. Contbr. articles to profl. jours.; patentee frozen desserts and microwave food formulation fields in U.S. and Europe. Vice pres. Minn. Taiwanese Assn., Mpls., 1985. 2d lt. Taiwan Army, 1973-75. Mem. Am. Dairy Sci. Assn., Inst. Food Technologists, Am. Assn. Cereal Chemists, Am. Chem. Soc., Toastmasters (pres. Mpls. 1988). Office: Pillsbury Tech Ctr 330 University Ave SE Minneapolis MN 55414-1779

HUBACEK, JAMES T., developement engineer; b. Menaminee Falls, Wis., Jan. 24, 1970. BSME cum laude, Marquette U., 1993. Engring. coop. A & E Engring, Racine, Wis., 1991—; adv. Future Cities Competition, Milw., 1994-95. Roman Catholic. Home: W18773 Silver Spring Rd Menomonee Falls WI 53051

HUBBARD, DAVID FRED, real estate broker; b. Urbana, Ill., Dec. 7, 1914; s. Fred Clark and Martha Caroline (Koehn) H.; m. Frances Pauline Leonhardt, Apr. 16, 1937; children: Fred Leonhardt Hubbard, John David Hubbard, Kay Hubbard Duchemin, Carol Pauline Hubbard. BS in Agrl., U. Ill., 1937. Tchr. vocat. agrl. Cmty. H.S., Virden, Ill., 1937-41; farm investment mgr. Equitable Life Assurance Soc. U.S., Ill., Ind., 1941-77; real estate broker Urbana, Ill., 1952—; instr., farm appraisals Am. Soc. Farm Mgrs. and Rural Appraisers, Ill., 1951-65, U. Ill., 1951-65; expert witness Cir. Ct. Ill. Mem. Ill. Soc. of Profl. Farm Mgrs. and Rural Appraisers (pres. 1951, Hall of Fame 1989), Urbana Exch. Club (pres. 1956, So Proudly We Hail award 1989). Republican. Baptist. Home: 303 E George Huff Dr Urbana IL 61801

HUBBARD, DEAN LEON, university president; b. Nyssa, Oreg., June 17, 1939; s. Gaileon and Rhodene (Barton) H.; m. Aleta Ann Thornton, July 12, 1959; children: Melody Ann, Dean Paul John, Joy Marie. BA, Andrews U., 1961, MA, 1962; diploma in Korean Lang., Yunsei U., Seoul, Korea, 1968; PhD, Stanford U., 1979. Dir. English Lang. Schs., Seoul, 1966-71; asst. to pres. Loma Linda U., Calif., 1974-76; acad. dean Union Coll., Lincoln, Nebr., 1976-80, pres., 1980-84; pres. NW Mo. State U., Maryville, 1984—; chair Acad. Quality Consortium, 1993—; examiner Malcolm Baldridge Nat. Quality Award, 1993—; judges panel Mo. Quality Award, 1994-96. Bd. dirs. Alliance of Univs. for Democracy, 1993—. Office: NW Mo State U Office of President Maryville MO 64468-6001

HUBBARD, FRANCES PAULINE LEONHARDT, bowling executive; b. St. Louis, Oct. 21, 1918; d. Fred William and Pauline Frances (Juergens) Leonhardt; m. David Fred Hubbard, Apr. 16, 1937; children: Fred Leonhardt Hubbard, John David Hubbard, Kay Hubbard Duchemin, Carol P. Hubbard. BS with highest honors, U. Ill., 1939. Dir. Ill. Womens Bowling Assn., 1966—, pres., 1979-93; pres. Champaign-Urbana Womens Bowling Assn., 1962-78; pres. Young Am. Bowling Alliance, 1986-91; mem. Bowling Coun. of Ill., 1990-92. Pres. PTA, legis. chmn.; den mother Boy Scouts Am.; girl scout leader Girl Scouts Am.; leader 4-H; pres. Urbana H.S. Music Boosters; moderator Am. Bapts., 1st Bapt. Ch., 1982—, area III pres., guild leader Am. Bapt. Women Regional Bd. Conf., chmn., local ch. treas., pres. area III; chmn. christian edn. ABC of GRR. Elected to Ill. Women's Bowling Assn. Hall of Fame, Champaign-Urbana Women's Bowling Assn. Hall of Fame; recipient Exch. Club "So Proudly We Hail" award, 1992. Home: 303 E George Huff Dr Urbana IL 61801

HUBBARD, JOHN MORRIS, golf course executive; b. Beech Creek, Pa., Feb. 13, 1916; s. Morris R. and Ina May (Putman) H.; m. Virginia A. Nelson, June 4, 1938; children: Robert, Nancy. Student, Gen. Motors Engring. and Mgmt. Inst., 1938, U. Detroit, 1939. Sr. engr. Fisher Body, Warren, Mich., 1935-74; pres. Oxford Hills Golf and Country Club, Pontiac, Mich., 1974—; advisor Ferris State Coll., Big Rapids, Mich., 1960-74; instr. math. U. Indpls., summer 1991; designed and constructed Oxford Hills Golf Course, 1961. Mem. Soc. Engring. Illustrators (bd. dirs., Outstanding Achievement award 1981). Republican. Lodges: Rotary (bd. dirs. Oxford club 1981-82), Elks, Masons (master mason 1960-61). Home: 350 E Drahner Rd Oxford MI 48371-0233 Office: Oxford Hills Golf and Country Club 300 E Drahner Rd Oxford MI 48371-0233

HUBBARD, STANLEY STUB, broadcast executive; b. St. Paul, May 28, 1933; s. Stanley Eugene and Didrikke A. (Stub) H.; m. Karen Elizabeth Holmen, June 13, 1959; children: Kathryn Elizabeth Hubbard Rominski, Stanley Eugene II, Virginia Anne Hubbard Morris, Robert Winston, Julia Didrikke. BA, U. Minn., 1955; hon. doctorate, Hamline U., 1995. With Hubbard Broadcasting, St. Paul, 1950—, pres., 1967—, chmn., CEO, 1983—; chmn. U.S. Satellite Broadcasting Co., Inc.; bd. dirs. Fingerhut Corp., Minn. Bus. Partnership, U.S. Satellite Broadcasting Co., Inc.; mem. braodcast adv. com. to comm. subcom. Ho. of reps., 1977-79; mem. FCC Adv. Com. on Advanced TV, 1988-95; mem. U.S. Nat. Inf. Infrastructure Adv. Coun., 1994-96. Contbr. articles to profl. jours. Chmn. St. Croix Valley Youth Ctr., 1968—; trustee Hubbard Found.; bd. dirs. U. Minn. Found., Mpls., Am. Friends of Jamaica, Assn. Maximum Svc. TV, U. St. Thomas, Bapt. Hosp. Fund Sponsor Bd., Broadcast Pioneers Libr., Minn. Bus. Partnership; past advisor Gov.'s Crime Commn., Ramsey County Ice Arena Com.; past bd. dirs. The Guthrie Theater, The Psychoanalytic Found. of Minn., Sci. Mus. of Minn., Minn. Internat. Ctr.; mem. Hazelden Adv. Com.; mem. Met. Airports Pub. Found. Adv. Bd. Recipient Mitchell Charnley award Northwest Broadcast News Assn., 1991, Internat. Humanitarian award Am. Friends of Jamaica, 1989, Arthur C. Clarke award Satellite Broadcasting and Comm. Assn., 1994, DreamMaker award Children's Cancer Rsch. Fund, 1994, Disting. Svc. award Nat. Assn. Broadcasters, 1995, Spurgeon award Boy Scouts Am., 1985, Avatar award Broadcast Cable and Fin. Mgmt., 1995, Human Rights award Am. Jewish Com., 1995, Cmty. Leadership award Mpls./St. Paul chpt. Alzheimer's Assn., 1995, Most Innovative Product award Minn. High Tech. Coun., 1995, Journalism Innovator award U. Nebr., 1996, Minn. Family Bus. award U. St. Thomas, 1996, Disting. Alumnus award Breck Sch., 1996; inductee Broadcasting and Cable Hall of Fame, 1991, Soc. Satellite Profls. Internat. Space Hall of Fame, 1992. Mem. Broadcast Pioneers, Internat. Radio and TV Soc., Minn. Execs. Orgn., Royal TV Soc. of London, Soc. Profl. Journalists, Soc. Satellite Profls. Internat., World Bus. Coun. Office: Hubbard Broadcasting Inc 3415 University Ave W Saint Paul MN 55114-1019

HUBBARD, Z(ONIA) DIANNE, telephone company official; b. Ypsilanti, Mich., Nov. 26, 1950; d. George Lorenzo and Mattie Lorene (Burton) H. BA, Mich. State U., 1973. Svc. rep. Mich. Bell Tel. Co., Taylor, 1973-77, supr. collections, 1977-79; mgr. collections Mich. Bell Tel. Co., Livonia, 1979-81; mgr. orders Mich. Bell Tel. Co., Allen Park, 1981-84; staff mgr. svc. ctr. ops. Mich. Bell Tel. Co., Southfield, 1984-85; staff mgr. fin. Mich. Bell Telephone Co., Oak Park, 1985-88, staff mgr. comptr. ops., 1989-90, mgr. data ctr. ops., 1990-91; mgr. br. office adminstrn. Ameritech Svcs., Inc., 1991-92; mgr. data ctr. OPRNS Ameritech Network Svcs., 1993—; fashion cons. Bd. dirs. Friendship Manor Nursing Home, Detroit, 1986-93; mem. nominating com. Mich. Metro Girl Scout Coun., Detroit, 1988, chmn. vols. recognition com., mem. fund devel. com., mem. pers. com., bd. dirs., 1989-93; mem. women's com. United Negro Coll. Fund, Detroit, coord., 1988-89, sec. women's com. exec. coun., 1992-93, vice chair, 1993—; chair Ebony Fashion Fair, 1994; mem. Detroit Urban League; mem. Penn Ctr. (S.C.) Mich. Support Group; trustee Children's Mus. Detroit, 1995—. Mem. NAACP, Detroit Grand Prix Assn., Women's Econ. Club, Zonta (v.p. 1994—, bd. dirs., chair ways and means com., chair pub. rels. com., mem. long-range planning com., corr. sec., chair inter-city commn., sec. dist. XV bd. dirs., del. internat. conv. 1994, chair dist. XV fall conf. 1995, chair status of women com.). Democrat. Baptist. Home: 23877 Merrill Ave Southfield MI 48075-3496 Office: Ameritech A230 23500 Northwestern Hwy Southfield MI 48075-3301

HUBBARTT, MORRIS W., JR., retail executive; b. Shelbyville, Ill., Mar. 2, 1963; s. Morris William and Luella May (Vermillion) H.; m. Lisa Ann Bailey, Apr. 2,1983; children: Adam, Rachel. Grad. high school, Pana, Ill. Mgr. v.p. Roadrunner Lawn Ornaments Inc., Pana, 1984—. Baptist. Office: Roadrunner Lawn Ornaments Inc RR 2 Box 272 Pana IL 62557-9308

HUBBS, RONALD M., retired insurance company executive; b. Silverton, Oreg., Apr. 27, 1908; s. George W. and Ethel (Burch) H.; B.A., U. Oreg.; LL.D. (hon.), William Mitchell Coll. Law, Macalester Coll. H.L.D., (hon.), Carleton Coll., m. Margaret S. Jamie, Sept. 9, 1935; 1 son, George J. With St. Paul Fire & Marine Ins. Co., 1936-77, asst. to pres., 1948-52, v.p., 1952-59, exec. v.p., 1959-63; pres., chief exec., 1963-68, chmn., 1968-73; pres., chief exec. officer St. Paul Cos., Inc., 1968-73, chmn., 1973-77; past dir. Western Life Ins. Co., past chmn. Toro Credit Co.; past chmn. AFIA Worldwide Ins. Past bd. dirs. Minn. Coun. on Econ. Edn.; bd. dirs., founding trustee Twin Cities Pub. TV Corp., James H. Hill Reference Libr.; adv. bd. U. Minn. Sch. Mgmt.; task force U. Minn. Writing Standards, Lt. Gov. Minn. on Womens' History Ctr.; Gov.'s Adv. Com. on Literacy; bd. dirs. emeritus William Mitchell Coll. Law; trustee emeritus Coll. St. Thomas, Carleton Coll.; retired chmn. bd. trustees F.R. Bigelow Found.; past trustee, past chmn. Ins. Inst. Am.; mem., past chmn. pres.'s coun. St. Catherine's Coll.; gov. Internat. Inst. Seminars, Inc.; bd. dirs. Charles Lindbergh Fund, Cath. Digest; bd. overseers emeritus U. Minn. Sch. Mgmt.; bd. dirs. Inst. Philos. Rsch.; hon. trustee St. Paul Found., North Star Found.; bd. overseers Hill Monastic Manuscript Libr. and Univ. Without Walls; trustee Sci. Mus. Minn. elector Ins. Hall Fame. Served from 1st lt. to col. AUS, World War II, ret., 1989. Decorated Legion of Merit; recipient St. Thomas Aquinas medal Coll. St. Thomas; creative leadership in adult edn. award MACAE; Life-long learning award Met. State U.; Disting. Community Builder award Indianhead coun. Boy Scouts Am.; Great Living St. Paulite award St. Paul C. of C.; Pres. Coun. award Minn. Pvt. Colls.; King's medal Carl XVI Gustaf of Sweden; Disting. Svc. award Minn. Humanities Commn.; Humanitarian award St. Paul YWCA; Minn. Gov.'s Leadership award; John Myers award for community svc.; Heckman award Minn. Coun. Founds., U. Oreg. Disting. alumnus award, Svc. award Midwest China Ctr. Community, Disting. Svc. award Coll. St. Thomas; named Minnesotan of Yr. Minn. Territorial Pioneers. Mem. Am. Inst. Property and Liability Underwriters (past chmn., trustee), Orgn. Am. Historians, Minn. Hist. Soc. (past pres.), Co. Mil. Historians, Sherlock Holmes Soc. of London, Orchid Soc., Minn. Club (past pres., Alpha Tau Omega, Phi Delta Phi, Scabbard and Blade, Friars, Beta Gamma Sigma. Episcopalian (past trustee diocese Minn.). Home: 689 Wentworth Ave W # 102 Saint Paul MN 55118-2704 Office: 385 Washington St Saint Paul MN 55102-1309

HUBER, DON MORGAN, plant pathologist, educator; b. Mesa, Ariz., Mar. 19, 1935; s. Albert Elmo and Emma Lapreel (Davis) H.; m. Paula Elese Towery, Feb. 19, 1959; children: Brenda, Joyce, Aaron, Louise, Lynette, Sharon, Sarah, Elese, Natalie, Kevin, Derek. BS, U. Idaho, 1957, MS, 1959; PhD, Mich. State U., 1963. Cert. secondary tchr., Idaho. Asst. prof. U. Idaho, Moscow, 1963-67, assoc. prof., 1967-71; assoc. prof. plant pathology Purdue U., West Lafayette, Ind., 1971-81, prof., 1981—; assoc. dir. Armed Forces Med. Intelligence Ctr., Ft. Detrick, Md., 1984-89; owner DecaH Mfg., West Point, Ind., 1978—; cons. maj. agribus. cos., 1965—, U.S. Govt., 1980—, Office of Tech. Assessment, U.S. Congress, 1976-78. Co-author: Diseases of the Tropics/Subtropics, 1984; contbr. articles to profl. jours.; patentee in field. Sch. trustee Moscow Sch. Bd., 1968-71, Tippecanoe Sch. Corp., Lafayette, Ind., 1992—. Col. U.S. Army, 1953-89. Recipinet Outstanding Rsch. award Idaho-Oreg. Seed Assn., 1965, Pioneering Rsch. award Dow Chem. Co., 1980, Meritorious Svc. medal Dept. Def., 1989, CAP 1, 2, and 3 awards Ind. Sch. Bds. Assn., 1993-95. Mem. Am. Phytopathol. Soc. (com. chair), North Ctrl. Phytopathol. Soc. (pres. 1988), Internat. Soc. Plant Pathology, Lafayette C. of C. (3d house com. 1993—), Sigma Xi, Alpha Zeta. Office: Purdue U 1155 Lilly Bldg West Lafayette IN 47907

HUBER, GREGORY B., state legislator; b. Jan. 25, 1956. MD, U. Wis., 1981. Asst. dist. atty. Marathon County Dist. Atty.'s Office; mem. from dist. 85 Wis. State Assembly, Madison, 1985, 88—. Pres. Rib Mountain State Park. Mem. Wausau Jaycees (past bd. dirs.), Wis. Alumni Club (bd. dirs.). Office: 406 S 9th Wausau WI 54401*

HUBER, JAMES DAMIAN, rental real estate owner; b. St. Louis, Aug. 27, 1951; s. James Richard and Eugenia Elizabeth (Ruess) H.; m. Sharon Ann Blumstengel, Oct. 17, 1973; children: Kurt James, James Sylvester. Auto worker Chrysler Corp., Fenton, Mo., 1973-74; sales mgr. Sound Motor Co., Fenton, 1974-83; gen. mgr. A-1 Antenna, St. Louis, 1983-84; bookbinder Buxton Skinner Printing Co., St. Louis, 1984-90; landlord Huber Properties, Fenton, 1990—. Sustaining mem. Rep. Nat. Com., 1993—; mem. Nat. Rep. Senatorial Com., 1993—, Ho. Rep. Congl. Com., 1994—, Jefferson County (Mo.) Rep. Club, 1993—. With USN, 1970-73, Vietnam. Mem. NRA (benefactor), Gun Owners Am., USN Seabee Vets. (life).

HUBER, RITA NORMA, civic worker; b. Cin., July 16, 1931; d. Andrew Elwood and Mary Gertrude (Hille) Stewart; student Cin. Coll. Conservatory Music, 1949-50, Berlitz Sch., Cin., 1951-52; m. Justin G. Huber, July 17, 1954; children: Monica Ann, Sarah Marie, Rachel Miriam. Tchr. Russian lang. for officers' wives Ft. Sill, Okla., 1955-56; bd. dirs. United Community Svcs., Cedar Rapids, Iowa, 1969; founder, chairperson Linn County Consumers League, 1969-70; founder, pub. rels. dir. Cedar Rapids Rape Crisis Svcs., 1974—; owner/operator Huber Janitorial Svcs., 1982-84; chairperson Linn County Dem. Womens Club, 1966-67, Linn County Com., Eugene McCarthy for Pres., 1967-68; campaign mgr. Delores Cortez for Iowa Legislature, 1968, Jan V. Johnson for Iowa Legislature, 1970, Stanley Ginsberg for county supr. Linn County, 1974, E.L. Colton for Cedar Rapids pub. safety commr., 1977; chairperson Linn County Dem. Cen. Com., 1976-77, 88-90; state coord. Jerry Brown for Pres., 1976; chairperson Pat Kane for Linn County Recorder, 1982; chmn. Linn County Bd. Health, 1982-85; supr. Linn County, 1990-95; chairperson Linn County bd. Suprs., 1992; instr. parliamentary procedures Cedar Rapids Women's Community Leadership Inst., 1975-77; lectr. local colls. and svc. orgns.; tchr. conversational Russian, Pierce Elementary Sch., Cedar Rapids, 1976; instr. Russian, Community Edn. div. Kirkwood Community Coll.; mem. care rev. com. Pineview Care Ctr., Cedar Rapids, 1987-90. Named to Iowa Dem. Party DVP Hall of Fame, 1986; recipient Woman of Yr. award Women's Equality Day Cedar Rapids Iowa, 1993. Mem. Am. Inst. Parliamentarians. Roman Catholic (extraordinary minister of Eucharist). Composer: She is Risen, 1973. Home: 2050 Glass Rd NE Cedar Rapids IA 52402-3451

HUBERT, JEAN-LUC, chemicals executive; b. Metz, Moselle, France, Mar. 13, 1960; s. Andre and Franziska (Schmidt) H. Diplome Ingenieur, Ecole Centrale Paris, 1982, Diplome Detudes Approfondies, 1982; MS in Mech. and Nuclear Engring., Northwestern U., 1985; M in Project Mgmt. with distinction, Keller Grad. Sch., 1996. Simulation engr. Didier Werke, Wiesbaden, Fed. Republic Germany, 1981; engr. Iron and Steel Rsch. Inst., Metz, France, 1983; applications engr. L'Air Liquide, Paris, 1985-86; R&D mgr. cryogenic refrigeration processes Liquid Air Corp., Countryside, Ill., 1986-89, project mgr. new processes devel. group, 1989-93; multi project mgr., primary metals and combustion, mktg. and applications group Air Liquide America Corp, Countryside, Ill., 1993-95; applied tech. engring. dept. mgr. Air Liquide Am. Corp., Countryside, Ill., 1995—; new process devel. cons. Liquid Air Corp./Energy Systems, Lake Charles, La., 1987-90, BIG3/INS, Houston, 1990-91, exceptional ops. mgr., coord. subcontractors, regional svc. and sales coord. applications unit, 1992-93. Patentee cryogenic food freezing, cryogenic embrittlement processes, pipeline rehab. processes, multi-step combined mech./thermal stripping processes. 2d lt. French Navy, 1982-83. Tuition fellow Georges Lurcy Found., 1984, Henri Blanchenay fellow French Inst., 1984, Bieneck/Didier fellow, Fed. Rep. Ger., 1984, Northwestern U. Rsch. assistantship, 1984. Mem. ASME (assoc.), Inst. Food Technologists (profl.), Internat. Inst. Refrigeration, Iron & Steel Soc. Home: 253 Woodstock Ave Clarendon Hills IL 60514-2822 Office: Air Liquide Am Corp 5230 East Ave La Grange IL 60525-3133

HUBLER, MARY, state legislator; b. Milw., July 31, 1952. BS, U. Wis., Superior, 1973; JD, U. Wis., Madison, 1980. Former tchr., coach, atty.; mem. from dist. 75 Wis. State Assembly, Madison, 1984—, vice chairwoman tourism, recreation and forest product coms., 1985—, mem. joint fin. com. Mem. Wis. Bar Assn. Office: 1966 Hawthorne Ln Rice Lake WI 54868 Office: Wis State Assembly State Capitol Madison WI 53702*

HUCKABEE, COLLEEN J., school system administrator; b. Washington, Mar. 10, 1936. BA, Bates Coll., 1958; MAT cum laude, Harvard U., 1959. Cert. biology tchr., gifted edn. tchr., Ohio. Instr. Harvard-Newton (Mass.) Summer Inst., 1959-61; sci. instr. Peddie Sch., Hightstown, N.J., 1971-75; head sci. dept. Hayes High Sch., Delaware, Ohio, 1976-90; dir. enrichment Delaware City Schs., 1976—. Trustee People in Need, Delaware, 1989-92; past pres. Delaware/Omutnisk Sister City Project, Delaware, 1984—; pres. Delaware Unitarian-Universalist Fellowship, 1982—. Grantee Ohio Dept. Gifted Edn., 1990-92, 93-95. Mem. Ohio Assn. for Gifted Children, Nat. Assn. for Gifted Children, Gifted Commn. Sch. Study Coun. Ohio, Phi Beta Kappa. Democrat. Office: Delaware City Schs 248 N Washington St Delaware OH 43015-1649

HUCKSHOLD, WAYNE WILLIAM, elementary education educator; b. St. Louis, Mar. 5, 1952; s. Albert Clarence and Jane Martha (Stewart) H.; m. Paula Louise Ransin, June 14, 1977 (div. Apr. 1982); 1 child, Kristen Louise. BS in Edn., U. Mo., 1976, MS in Edn., 1977. Cert. elem. edn. K-8, phys. edn. K-9, health edn. K-12, sci. 7-9, Mo.; Nat. Coun. Accreditation of Tchr. Edn.; cert. personal trainer Am. Coun. Exercise. Tchr. grade 3 Camdenton (Mo.) R-III, 1977-81, coach football, track and cross country, 1978-81; fitness instr., athletic trainer Columbia (Mo.) Sports Medicine, 1981-84; student athletic trainer U. Mo., Columbia, 1983-84, grad. tchg. asst., 1984-85; elem. tchr. Francis Howell Sch. Dist., St. Charles, Mo., 1985-91, elem. tchr. phys. edn., 1991—, mem. supt.'s comm. coun., 1992-93; master's swim coach West County YMCA, Chesterfield, Mo., 1991—, personal trainer, 1992—. Named YMCA Endurance Athlete of Yr., YMCA, St. Louis, 1990; grantee Union Electric Co., St. Louis, 1989; fellow Tchrs. Acad. Class 1994, Network for Ednl. Devel., Danforth Found., 1993-94. Mem. NEA, Mo. Edn. Assn., Francis Howell Edn. Assn., Am. Alliance for Health, Phys. Edn., Recreation and Dance, Mo. Alliance for Health, Phys. Edn., Recreation and Dance, U.S. Phys. Edn. Assn., Nat. Assn. for Sport and Phys. Edn., Assn. for Advancement Health Edn. Home: 1549 Milbridge Dr Chesterfield MO 63017-4611 Office: John Weldon Elem 7370 Weldon Springs Rd Saint Charles MO 63304-8618

HUDDLESTON, KENNETH FRED, business education educator; b. Chgo., Jan. 17, 1944; s. Fred and Pauline H.; m. Evelyn Kay Huddleston, June 12, 1965; 1 child, Cheryl. BS, Ill. State U., 1965; MS, No. Ill. U., 1968; EdD, U. Ill., 1972. Bus./mktg. tchr. Dundee (Ill.) Sch. Dist., 1965-68; vocat. edn. coord. West Bend (Wis.) Sch. Dist., 1968-70, Coop. Svc. Agy., Waupun, Wis., 1972-75; bus. area coord. Fox Valley Tech. Coll., Appleton, Wis., 1975-86; prof. bus. mgmt. U. Wis. Ext., Madison, 1986—; nat. fellow Adv. Study Ctr., Ohio State U., Columbus, 1981-82; rschr. U. Wis. Ext., 1991-92. Contbr. articles to profl. jours.; author: Direct Mktg. Newsletter, 1990; co-author planning guide: Alternative Enterprises, 1988. Co-leader Ripon (Wis.) Young Life, 1983-92; sec., bd. dirs. Indsl. Commn., Ripon, 1989-91. Mem. Wis. Community Devel. Assn. (Rookie of the Yr. 1987), Wis. Ext. Assn., Am., Soc. Tng. and Devel. (com. dir. 1981-88), Assn. for Quality and Participation. Office: Univ of Wis Ext 500 E Sunnyview Rd Oshkosh WI 54971

HUDDLESTON, MICHAEL RAY, counseling administrator, consultant, educator; b. Joplin, Mo., Nov. 28, 1948; s. Virgil Lavern and Dorothy Fay (Fields) H. BA, Drury Coll., 1971; MS, S.W. Mo. State U., 1972; PhD, Fla. State U., 1985; MS, Pittsburg (Kans.) State U., 1996. Lifetime cert. (Mo.) sch. counselor grades 7-12, sch. psychol. examiner grades K-12, social studies instr. grades 7-12. Sch. counselor Lincoln H.S., Tallahassee, Fla., 1986-91; pres. Internat. Career Consultants, Pittsburg, Kans., 1991—; adj. prof. Edn. and Human Resource Devel. Pittsburg (Kansas) State U., 1993—; dir. counseling Liberal (Mo.) R-II Schs., 1993—; vis. prof. Chiangmai (Thailand) U., 1990. Author: The Worldwide Student Guide for Studying in America, 1995, The Worldwide Career Guide for Planning and Development. Recipient Outstanding Counselor Achievement award Fla. Sch. Counselors Assn., 1989. Mem. ACA, Nat. Career Devel. Assn., Acad. Human Resource Devel. Home: 222 E 39th St Joplin MO 64804 Office: Internat Career Consultants PO Box 507 Pittsburg KS 66762

HUDEC, PATRICK J., financial advisor; b. Cleve., Sept. 17, 1963. Student, John Carroll U., 1981-82; BS in Econs., Marquette U., 1985. Salesman CBS Computers, Independence, Ohio, 1985-86; fin. advisor Prudential Securities Inc., Cleve., 1986-88, Smith Barney Inc., Cleve., 1988-91, McDonald & Co. Securities Inc., Pepper Pike, Ohio, 1991—. Mem. Rotary (pres.-elect North Royalton, Ohio 1994-95). Roman Catholic. Office: McDonald & Co Securities Inc 30050 Chagrin Blvd Ste 150 Pepper Pike OH 44124-5704

HUDETZ, FRANK C(LARENCE), printing, packaging company executive; b. Chgo., Aug. 11, 1948; s. John Francis and Gwendolyn Marie (Palmer) H.; m. Carolyn E. Monaco, Aug. 2, 1970; children: E. Heather, Frank J. AD, Coll. DuPage, 1972; postgrad., North Ctrl. Coll. Reservationist Eastern Airlines, Oak Brook, Ill., 1969-70; acct. exec. Solar Press, Naperville, Ill., 1970-72; pres., CEO Solar Press, 1973-90, chmn., CEO, 1990—; bd. dirs. Direst Mktg. Assn's. Card Pack Coun., N.Y.C., 1982-91, Nat. Assn. Printers and Lithographers; chmn. internat. coun., inc. coun., Growing Cos., Chgo., 1991, state chmn. Ill. coun., 1992-93. Coach YMCA Youth Basketball, Naperville, 1982-83, pres. Boys Little League Baseball, Naperville, 1984-85, bd. dirs. St. Francis High Sch. Adv. Bd., 1990—. With USN, 1966-69. Recipient Mgmt. Gol. award, Nat. Assn. Printers Lithographers, 1989, 91; named Entrepreneur of Yr., Ernst & Young, Chgo., 1990, Entrepreneurial Sucess, U.S. Amall Bus. Adminstrn., 1990. Mem. Am. Mgmt. Assn. (bd. dirs. coun. growing cos. 1993—), European Direct Mktg. Assn., Chgo. Assn. Direct Mktg., Direct Mktg. Assn., 3rd Class Mail Assn., Stonebridge Country Club, Union League Club (Chgo.), Exec. Club (Chgo.), East-West Corp. Corridor Assn., Ill. State C. of C., Naperville C. of C., The Executive Club. Roman Catholic. Office: Solar Press Inc 1120 Frontenac Rd Naperville IL 60563-1749

HUDIK, MARTIN FRANCIS, hospital administrator, educator; b. Chgo., Mar. 27, 1949; s. Joseph and Rose (Ricker) H.; 1 child, Theresa Abraham. BS in Mech. and Aerospace Engring., Ill. Inst. Tech., 1971; BPA, Jackson State U., 1974; MBA, Loyola U., Chgo., 1975; postgrad. U. Sarasota, 1975-76. Cert. health care safety mgr., hazard control mgr., hazardous materials mgr., OSHA hazardous materials response instr., hazardous materials incident comdr., disaster coord., police instr., Ill., security certification instr., Ill. With Ill. Masonic Med. Ctr., Chgo., 1969—, dir. risk mgmt., 1974-79, asst. adminstr., 1979—; part-time sr. lt. tng. divsn. Cicero (Ill.) Police Dept., sr. lt. Tng. and Internal Affairs Divsn., 1971—; instr. Nat. Safety Coun. Safety Tng. Inst., Chgo., 1977-85; cons. mem. Coun. Tech. Users Consumer Products, Underwriters Labs., Chgo., 1977—; instr., lt. U.S. Def. Civil Preparedness Agy. Staff Coll., Battle Creek, Mich., 1977-85; liaison officer to Cook County, asst. dir. Emergency Svcs. and Disaster Agy., Town of Cicero, 1988—, asst. dir.; pres. bd. dirs. Cook County Emergency Mgmt. Coun., 1991-92; mem. bd. dirs. Cook County Emergency Mgmt. Agy., 1992—; bd. dirs. Northside Cmty. Fed. Credit Union, 1992-93; mem. U.S. Postal Svc. Postal Customer Adv. Coun., Cicero, Ill., 1996—. Pres. sch. bd. Mary Queen of Heaven Sch., Cicero, 1977-79, 84-86; pres. Mary Queen of Heaven Ch. Coun., 1979-81, 83-86; pres. I.M.M.C. Employee Club, 1983-86. Ill. State scholar, 1969-71; recipient Meritorious Svc. award Town of Cicero, 1990, Spl. Svc. award Underwriters Labs., 1992, Outstanding Svc. award Cook County Sheriffs Dept., 1993. Mem. Am. Coll. Healthcare Execs., Am. Soc. Hosp. Risk Mgmt., Nat. Fire Protection Assn., Am. Soc. Safety Engrs. (profl.), Am. Soc. Law and Medicine, Ill. Hosp. Security and Safety Assn. (co-founder 1976, founding pres. 1976-77, hon. dir. 1977-82), Cath. Alumni Club Chgo. (bd. dirs. 1983-84, 86), Mensa, Masons (Berwyn, Ill. chpt.), Pi Tau Sigma, Tau Beta Pi, Alpha Sigma Nu. Republican. Roman Catholic. Lodges: KC (Cardinal coun.), Masons. Home: 2116 S 51st Ct Cicero IL 60650-2345 Office: Ill Masonic Med Ctr 2116 S 51st Ct Chicago IL 60650-2345

HUDKINS, CAROL L., state legislator; b. North Platte, Nebr., Feb. 21, 1945; m. Larry Hudkins; children: Janet, Kathy. Mem. Nebr. Senate, 1992—; mem. agr. gen. affairs com.; mem. judiciary com. Republican. Methodist. Home: 8600 NW 112th St Malcolm NE 68402-9768

HUDNUT, WILLIAM HERBERT, III, senior resident fellow, political scientist; b. Cin., Oct. 17, 1932; s. William Herbert Jr. and Elizabeth (Kilborne) H.; m. Beverly Guidara; children: Michael Conger, Laura Anne, Timothy Norton, William Herbert IV, Theodore Beecher, Christopher Shew. BA magna cum laude, Princeton, 1954; MDiv summa cum laude, Union Theol. Sem., N.Y.C., 1957; DD (hon.), Hanover Coll., 1967, Wabash Coll., 1969; LLD (hon.), Butler U., 1980, Anderson Coll., 1982, Franklin Coll., 1983, Millikin U., 1987, Ind. U., 1994, Elmhurst Coll., 1996; LittD (hon.), U. Indpls., 1981; DPS (hon.), Blackburn Coll., 1987. Ordained to ministry Presbyn. Ch., 1957; asst. minister Westminster Ch., Buffalo, 1957-

60; pastor 1st Presbyn. Ch., Annapolis, Md., 1960-63; dir. Westminster Found., Annapolis, 1960-63; sr. minister 2d Presbyn. Ch., Indpls., 1963-72; mem. 93d Congress from Ind., 1973-74; dir. dept. community affairs Ind. Central U., Indpls., 1975; mayor City of Indpls., 1976-91; fellow Inst. Politics Harvard U., 1992; sr. fellow Hudson Inst., Indpls., 1992-94; pres. Civic Fedn., Chgo., 1994-96; sr. resident fellow The Urban Land Inst., Washington, 1996—; mem. Presdl. Adv. Com. on Federalism, 1981-84. Author: Minister/Mayor, 1987, The Hudnut Years in Indianapolis, 1976-1991, 1995;editor: Union Sem. Quar. Rev., 1956-57; contbr. sermons, articles to profl. publs. Mem. Bd. Pub. Safety, Indpls., 1970-71, Rep. Nat. Com., 1987; pres. Anne Arundel County Mental Health Assn., 1961-63; pres., bd. dirs. Marion County Mental Health Assn., 1966-68, Westminster Found., Purdue U., 1969-73; bd. dirs. Cmty. Svc. Coun. Met. Indpls., 1964-68, Weekday Religious Edn., Marion County, 1964-69, Family Svc. Assn., 1966-72, Ind. Mental Health Assn., 1968-69, Flanner House, 1968-72; pres. trustees Darrow Sch., New Lebanon, N.Y., 1968-75; mem. Intergovtl. Sci., Engring. and Tech. White House Adv. Panel, 1976-77; mem. New Coalition Welfare Reform Task Force, 1976-77, Task Force on Fed. Deficit, 1981; mem. Adv. Commn. on Intergovtl. Rels., 1984-90; bd. dirs. Indpls. Ctr. for Adv. Rsch., 1976-91, Humane Soc., 1983-91; trustee Roosevelt Ctr. Am. Policy Studies, Washington, 1984-87; environ. fin. bd. EPA, 1969-91, Pleasant Run Children's Home Found. bd., 1992-94, Children's Home & Aid Soc. Ill., 1994—; co-vice chmn. Alliance for Redesigning Govt., 1992—. Recipient William Booth award Salvation Army, 1984, Russell G. Lloyd disting. svc. award Ind. Assn. Cities and Towns, 1985, Rosa Parks award Am. Assn. for Affirmative Action, 1992, Woodrow Wilson award Princeton U., 1986, disting. urban mayor award Nat. Urban Coalition, 1987; named All-Pro City Mgmt. Team, City and State mag., 1986, 89, 92; fellow Nat. Acad. Pub. Adminstrn., 1994—. Fellow Nat. Acad. Pub. Adminstrn.; mem. Ind. Rep. Mayors Assn. (pres. 1980), Nat. Conf. Rep. Mayors and Mcpl. Elected Ofcls. (pres. 1987), Nat. Assn. Securities Dealers Regulatory Bd., Nat. League of Cities (pres. 1981), Ind. Assn. Cities and Towns (pres. 1979), U.S. Conf. Mayors (adv. bd. 1988-91), Nat. Alliance of Bus. (bd. dirs. 1985-91), Univ. Club. Chgo., Columbia Club Indpls., Kiwanis, Masons (33 deg.), Phi Beta Kappa. Office: The Urban Land Inst 1025 Thos Jefferson St NW Washington DC 20007-5201

HUDSON, ARTHUR CLEVE, electronics engineer; b. Columbus, Ind., Mar. 22, 1943; s. Mitchell Paul and Josie Fay Hudson; m. Judith Mae Hetzler, Nov. 26, 1977; 1 child, Kimberly Judith. Student, Ind. U., 1962-64; BSEE, Purdue U., 1972. Testing technician Arvin Industries, Columbus, 1968-69, electronics engr., 1972-73; electronics engr. Def. Electronics Supply Ctr., Dayton, Ohio, 1973—. Staff sgt. USAF, 1964-68. Mem. IEEE, Stds. Engring. Soc. (sec. 1995-96). Home: 1546 Mapledale Dr Dayton OH 45432

HUDSON, CELESTE NUTTING, education educator, reading clinic administrator, consultant; b. Nashville, Sept. 18; d. John Winthrop Chandler and Hilda Bass (Alexander) Nutting; m. Frank Alden Hudson III, Dec. 30, 1948 (dec.); children: Frank Alden IV (dec.), Jo Ann Hudson Algermissen, Celeste Jane Hudson Hayes Norman, John Winthrop Nutting; m. Robert Daniel Quartell, June 3, 1989. BS, Oreg. Coll. Edn., 1952; MS, So. Ill. U., 1963, PhD, 1973. Cert. tchr., Tenn., Oreg., Mo., Iowa. Tchr. pub. schs., Crossville, Tenn., 1949-51, Salem, Oreg., 1952-53, West Walnut Manor and Jennings, Mo., 1953-54, Normandy Sch. Dist., St. Louis County, Mo., 1954-66; reading coord. Sikeston (Mo.) Pub. Schs., 1966-71; traveling cons. Ednl. Devel. Labs., Huntington, N.Y., 1970-71; mem. clin. staff So. Ill. U. Reading Ctr., 1972; asst. prof. edn. St. Ambrose Coll., 1972-75, U. Tenn.-Chattanooga, 1975-76; project dir. Learning Skills Ctr., St. Ambrose Coll. (became St. Ambrose U., 1986), 1976-80, asst. prof. edn., 1976-78, assoc. prof., 1979-86 , dir. elem. edn., 1972-75, 76-94, chmn. dept. edn., 1980-84, div. chmn., 1984-87 prof. edn., 1986-94, prof. emeritus, 1995—, dir. Reading Clinic, 1976-94; faculty vice chair St. Ambrose U., 1989-90, faculty chair, 1990-91; cons. reading; pvt. practice. Mem. Kimberly Village Bd., Davenport, Iowa, 1979-83; chmn. worship comm., 1985-90, choir and bell choir Asbury Meth. Ch., 1985—. Mem. AAUP, ASCD, AAUW, DAR, Assn. Tchrs. Educators, Iowa Assn. Colls. Tchr. Edn. (exec. bd. 1989-92), Internat. Reading Assn. (Scott County council), Am. Assn. Colls. Tchr. Edn., Miss. Bend Coun., Assn. Tchr. Educators, New Eng. Women (pres.-elect 1994—), Original Music Students Club (corresponding sec. 1995—), Orgn. Tchr. Educators Reading, Internat. Platform Assn., Women in Ednl. Adminstrn., United Daus. Confederacy, Women of the Moose, Alpha Delta Kappa (past pres.), Kappa Delta Pi (sponsor), Phi Delta Kappa. Master gardener. Author: Handbook for Remedial Reading, 1967; Cognitive Listening and the Reading of Second Grade Children, 1973, The Effect of Visual Fatigue on Reading, 1990, Longitudinal Study of Children in Clinical Reading, 1994. Address: St Ambrose U Box E 140 518 W Locust Davenport IA 52806

HUDSON, DENNIS LEE, lawyer, retired government official, arbitrator, educator; b. St. Louis, Jan. 5, 1936; s. Lewis Jefferson and Helen Mabel (Buchanan) H.; m. Linda Kay Adamson; children: Karen Marie, Karla Sue, Mary Ashley. BA, U. Ill., 1958; JD, John Marshall Law Sch., 1972. Bar: Ill. 1972, U.S Dist. Ct. (so. dist.) Ill. 1972, U.S. Dist. Ct. (no. dist.) Ill. 1972. Insp., IRS, Chgo., 1962-72; spl. agt. GSA, Chgo., 1972-78, spl. agt.-in-charge, 1978-83, regional insp. gen., 1983-87; supervisory spl. agt., Dept Justice-GSA Task Force, Washington, 1978; arbitrator Cir. Ct. Cook County, Ill.; assoc. prof. of criminal justice Coll. Dupage. Bd. govs. Theatre Western Springs, Ill., 1978-81, 91-92; deacon Grace Lutheran Ch., LaGrange, Ill., 1977-81. Served with U.S. Army, 1959-61. John N. Jewett scholar, 1972. Mem. ABA, Ill. Bar Assn. Home: 109 51st Pl Western Springs IL 60558-2002 Office: Coll Dupage Bus & Svcs Div 22D St Lambert Rd Glen Ellyn IL 60137

HUDSON, HAROLD DON, veterinarian; b. Audrain County, Mo., Nov. 22, 1943; s. Harold F. and Greta Arlene (Boyd) H.; A.A., Hannibal (Mo.) La Grange Coll., 1963; B.S., U. Mo., 1967, D.V.M., 1970; m. Carole Jacqueline Spence, Aug. 30, 1964; children—Dale Brent, Kim Marie. Asso. Clarinda (Iowa) Vet. Clinic, 1970-71, Bethany (Mo.) Vet. Clinic, 1971-72, Vet. Clinic, Mexico, Mo., 1972—. Mem. AVMA, Mo. Vet. Med. Assn., Am. Assn. Bovine Practitioners, Am. Assn. Swine Practitioners. Baptist. Home: 933 Emmons St Mexico MO 65265-2138 Office: 1624 US Highway 54 E Mexico MO 65265-3536

HUDSON, MUTSUKO ENDO, Japanese language educator; b. Sapporo, Hokkaido, Japan, Aug. 30, 1949; came to U.S., 1973; d. Kotaro and Toshi (Yamada) Endo; m. Grover Milton Hudson, July 22, 1992. BA, Internat. Christian U., Tokyo, 1973; MA, U. Mich., 1977, PhD, 1989. Cert. Japanese oral proficiency tester. Lectr. U. Mich., Ann Arbor, 1974-87; instr. Middlebury (Vt.) Coll., 1987-89; asst. prof. Mich. State U., East Lansing, 1989-95, assoc. prof., 1995—; vis. lectr. DePauw U., Greencastle, Ind., 1973-74; vis. asst. prof. workshop for tchrs. of Japanese, Middlebury Coll., 1989, 90, vis. asst. prof. Inst. in Japanese Lang. Pedagogy, Columbia U., N.Y.C., 1991—; instr. Japanese Lang. Sch., Middlebury Coll., 1981-83, 87; interpreter for Gov. James J. Blanchard of Mich., 1984-86; keynote spkr. Va. Workshop Japanese Lang., Pedagogy, 1991, Princeton Japanese Pedogogy Workshop, 1995; cons. Mich. Japanese Lang. Improvement Project, Mich. Dept. Edn., 1993-95. Author: A Practical Guide for Teachers of Elementary Japanese, 1984, Supplementary Grammar Notes to an Introduction to Modern Japanese, part 1, 1986, part 2, 1987, English Grammar for Students of Japanese, 1994; co-author: Shuushoku, 1991; contbr. revs. and articles to profl. jours. Exch. Student scholar Am. Field Svc., 1967-68, Rackham Non-Traditional Student scholar U. Mich., 1983-84, Rackham Dissertation scholar U. Mich., 1989; teaching fellow U. Mich., 1975-76, 77-78, Lilly Endowment Teaching fellow Indpls., 1992-93; Material Devel. grantee Japan Found., 1987, Japanese-Lang. Teaching Materials Donation grantee Japan Found., 1990, 92, Rsch. grantee Japan Forum, 1990-93, Workshop grantee Assn. Asian Studies, Japanese Found., 1993, 95. Mem. Am. Coun. on Teaching Fgn. Langs., Assn. Asian Studies, Assn. Tchrs. of Japanese (bd. dirs. 1993—), Linguistic Soc. Am., Mich. Linguistics Soc. Office: Mich State U Dept Linguistics And L East Lansing MI 48824

HUDSON, RONALD MORGAN, aviation planner; b. Anniston, Ala., May 7, 1954; s. James Alphus and Mildred Christine (Morgan) H.; m. Marsha Carol Smith, Dec. 27, 1974 (div. Aug. 1989); children: Jereme Brandon, Sara Elizabeth; m. Connie M. Luckey, Nov. 13, 1993. BS in Aviation Mgmt., Auburn U., 1976. Aviation planner Wainwright Enging. Co., Montgomery, Ala., 1978-81, Ralph Burke Assocs., Park Ridge, Ill., 1981-85; sr. assoc. mgr. aviation Knight Architects, Engrs., Planners, Inc., Chgo., 1985-96; sr. assoc. and aviation mgr. Hanson Engrs. Inc., Oak Brook, Ill., 1996—. Mem. Am. Planning Assn., Am. Inst. Cert. Planners, Am. Assn. Airport Execs., Ill. Pub. Airports Assn. Home: 1710 E Oakton St Arlington Heights IL 60004-5000

HUEBSCH, MICHAEL D., state legislator; b. July 19, 1964. Grad., Oral Roberts U. Assemblyman Wis. State Dist. 94, 1994—; mem. LaCrosse County Bd., Wis., LaCrosse Area Devel. Corp. Mem. Rotary. Address: 401 16th Ave N Onalaska WI 54650

HUEG, WILLIAM FREDERICK, agronomy educator, dairy owner; b. N.Y.C., Jan. 12, 1924; s. William Frederick and Mary Lavinia (Lynch) H.; m. Alvina Louise Sauer, Feb. 5, 1949 (div. Mar. 1975); children: William III, Anne, Thomas, John, Paul, Mark, Michael; m. Hella Lindemyer Mears, Aug. 12, 1978. BS, Cornell U., 1948; MS, Mich. State U., 1954, PhD, 1959. Asst. county agt. SUNY, Herkimer, 1948-50; instr. farm crops SUNY, Alfred, 1950-55, Mich. State U., East Lansing, 1955-57; assoc. prof. agronomy U. Minn., St. Paul, 1957-62, asst. dir. agrl. expt. sta., 1962-66, dir. agrl. expt. sta., 1966-75, v.p. agr. for. home econs., 1974-83, prof. emeritus agronomy and plant genetics, 1983—; bd. dirs. NSF, Washington, 1976-82; pres., bd. dirs. Coun. Agrl. Sci. and Tech., Ames,. Iowa, 1977-84; owner, mgr. Bhella Holsteins, Hammond, Wis., 1984—; cons. Asian Devel. Bank, Manila, 1990—. Trustee United Bd. for Christian Higher Edn. in Asia, N.Y.C., 1991—, Nitrogen Fixing Tree Assn., Maui, Hawaii, 1992-95. Fellow AAAS, Crop Sci. Soc., Agronomy Soc.; mem. Phi Kappa Phi. Baptist. Home: 1170 Dodd Rd Saint Paul MN 55118-1823

HUEGEL, WILLIAM MORTIMER, retired civil engineer; b. Milw., July 3, 1928; s. Arthur John and Carol Marie (Mortimer) H.; m. Joan B. Bacon (dec.); children: Elizabeth G., Christopher A., William B., John P. Student, U.S. Naval Acad., 1949-50; BCE, U. Wis., 1956. Design engr. Wis. Gas. Co., Milw., 1956-94. Mem. Glandale-River Hills Sch. Bd., Wis., 1971, Nicolet H.S. Bd., Glendale, 1977-89; alderman City of Glendale, 1991—. Mem. ASCE (chair edn. com. 1975-80), Royal Order Scotland. Lutheran. Home: 6660 N River Rd Milwaukee WI 53217-4060

HUELSMAN, JOANNE B., state legislator; b. Mar. 21, 1938; married. JD, Marquette U., 1980. Attorney, realtor, businesswoman; former mem. Wis. Assembly from 31st dist.; mem. Wis. State Senate from 11th dist. Republican. Home: 235 W Broadway Ste 210 Waukesha WI 53186-2845 Office: Wis State Senate PO Box 7882 Madison WI 53707

HUESER, ROBERTA JEAN, city official; b. Dallas, Iowa, Oct. 3, 1932; d. Carl Robert and Lucille Julia (Logue) Wheeler; student Wayne (Nebr.) State Coll., Colo. State Coll., Greeley, Northwestern Coll., Orange City, Iowa; m. William Joseph Hueser, Jan. 9, 1956; children—Kyle Robert, Jon William. Sch. tchr. in Iowa, 1953-63; city clk. George (Iowa), 1977-94. Chmn. bd. George Bicentennial Mus., 1976-86; adv. bd. George Good Samaritan Ctr., 1978-91; chmn. George Centennial Celebration; treas. bd. dirs. Evergreen Lawn Cemetery. Mem. Lyon County Mcpl. League (sec.-treas. 1977-78, 84-85). Democrat. Mem. Ch. of Christ. Club: Facts and Fun (pres. 1978-80). Co-author: In and Around George 1872-1912. Home: 209 W Ohio Ave George IA 51237-1044 Office: City Hall 12012 Main George IA 51237

HUETHER, ROBERT, state legislator; m. Karen; four children. Student, N.D. State U. N.D. State rep. Dist. 27, 1989—; dir. Cass County Elec./ Minnkota Power; farmer; mem. state and fed. govt. appropriations/human resources divsn., edn. and transp. coms. Home: RR 1 Box 87 Lisbon ND 58054-9801*

HUFF, DAVID CHARLES, retired sales executive; b. Indpls., Sept. 13, 1936; S. Leonard Malecki and Gwendolyn Marie (Prange) H.; m. Patricia Ann Dain, June 16, 1956; children: David Charles Jr., Michael Leonard, Laura Lynn. Student, Oreg. State U., 1955-56. With sales dept. Colgate-Palmolive Co., N.Y.C., 1959-91. Active City Coun. City of Lenexa, Kans., 1993—, Kans. League of Cities, Topeka, Nat. League of Cities, Washington, Econ. Devel. Coun., Lenexa, 1995, Leadership Lenexa, 1993, Lenexa Hist. Soc. Mem. Optimists, Lenexa C. of C., Overland Park Athletic Club, Kans. City Racquet Club. Republican. Home: 10458 Caenen Lake Rd Lenexa KS 66215

HUFF, DAVID NEIL, engineering manager; b. Glens Falls, N.Y., Aug. 31, 1937. AS, RCA Inst., N.Y.C., 1959. Cons. Various Broadcasting Stations, 1979-88; engring. mgr. Lincoln (Mich.) Precision Carbide, 1988—. Trustee Lincoln United Meth. Ch., Lincoln, 1993—. With U.S. Army, 1955-65. Home: 106 S F 41 Harrisville MI 48740-9723 Office: Lincoln Precision Carbide PO Box 129 Lincoln MI 48742-0129

HUFF, DAVID RICHARD, funeral home executive; b. St. Joseph, Mo., Aug. 24, 1948; s. Harry Francis and Frances Emily (Knopinski) H.; m. Catherine Ann Chitwood, Aug. 7, 1976. BA, Rockhurst Coll., 1970; PA, U.S. Med. Ctr., 1975; postgrad., Fla. State U., 1975-76, Loyola U., New Orleans, 1989-90. Lic. funeral dir., Mo.; lic. educator, Mo.; lic. med. records specialist; lic. pharmacy specialist. Tchr. St. Francis Sch., St. Joseph, 1970; med. records clk. Fed. Prison Health Systems, Leavenworth, Kans., 1971; hosp. adminstrv. asst. Fed. Prison Health Systems, Leavenworth, 1971-73, physician asst., 1974-84; asst. hosp. adminstr. Fed. Prison Health Systems, El Reno, Okla., 1977-79; health systems adminstr. Fed. Prison Health Systems, Big Spring, Tex., 1979-84; bus. mgr. Heaton-Bowman-Smith Funeral Home, Inc., St. Joseph, Mo., 1984—; corp. treas. Heaton-Bowman-Smith FH Inc., St. Joseph, 1991—. Coord. comty. health screenings City of Big Spring, 1980-84; bd. suprs. Citizens Fed. Credit Union, Big Spring, Tex., 1981-84, sec., 1983-84; Roman Cath. Eucharistic Min., 1970— (Diocese Kansas City-St. Joseph, Mo., 1970-73, 84—, Springfield-Cape Girardeau, Mo., 1973-74, Pensacola-Tallahassee, Fla., 1974-77, Oklahoma City, 1977-79, San Angelo, Tex., 1979-84); lay min. Our Lady of Guadalupe Parish, St. Joseph, 1986—; vol. lay Cath. chaplain Mo. Dept. Corrections, 1995—; bd. dirs. Am. Heart Assn., Big Spring, 1982-83, Country Sq. Home Assn., St. Joseph, 1987-92, pres., chmn. bd. dirs., 1988-89, v.p., 1989-90; hon. bd. dirs. Rockhurst Coll., Kansas City, 1983-91, assoc. alumni recruiter team, 1988-91; Dem. committeeman Buchanan County, Mo., 1988-94, treas., 1990-92; vice-chair Mo. 28th Legis. Dist. (formerly 9th) Dem. Com., 1990-92, chmn., 1992-94; active League St. Maur, Maur Hill Sch., 1992-94; host/sponsor students EFL Internat., 1986-96. Mem. St. Joseph C. of C. (Diplomat's Club 1985-92), OLG 3-M (treas. 1989-92), KC (4th degree), Alpha Sigma Nu. Democrat. Roman Catholic. Home: 4211 Buckingham Ct Saint Joseph MO 64506-2427 Office: Heaton-Bowman-Smith Funeral Home 3609 Frederick Blvd Saint Joseph MO 64506-3033

HUFF, GAYLE COMPTON, advertising agency executive; b. Washington, Nov. 28, 1956; d. Walter Dale and Jeanne (Parker) C.; m. Lanny Ross Huff, May 22, 1982. B in Gen. Studies, U. Mich., 1978. Mgr. br. merchandising CBS Records, Chgo., 1978; local promotion, mktg. mgr. CBS Records, Indpls., Boston, N.Y.C., 1978-81; spl. projects supr. Pickwick Internat. Musicland Group, Mpls., 1981-82; account exec. Campbell-Mithun Advt., Mpls., 1982-85; mktg. mgr., communications Universal Foods Corp., Milw., 1985-86; nat. advt. mgr. Thorobred Advt. Agy. (Jockey Internat., Inc.), Wis., 1986-88; dir. consumer and trade advt. Thorobred Advt. Agy. (Jockey Internat., Inc.), 1988-89, v.p. advt., 1990-92; dir. mktg./advt. Allen-Edmonds Shoe Co., Port Washington, Wis., 1993-95; v.p., dir. Fin. Mktg. Plus Direct Mktg. Group, Libertyville, Ill., 1995—; v.p., sec. Java Masters, Inc., 1992—. Mem. Traffic Audit Bur. for Media Measurement (bd. dirs. 1988-93), Assn. Nat. Advertisers (print adv. com., out of home advt. com. 1989-92). Office: Fin Mktg Plus Direct Mktg 1019 W Park Ave Libertyville IL 60048

HUFF, JOHN DAVID, church administrator; b. Muskegon, Mich., Nov. 20, 1952; s. Lucius Barthol and Marian (Brainard) H.; m. Diane Lynn Church, May 17, 1975; children: Joshua, Jason, Jessica. B in Religious Edn., Reformed Bible Coll., 1977; MA in Sch. Adminstrn., Calvin Coll., 1983; postgrad., Western Mich. U. Cert. ch. educator. Dir. edn. 1st Christian Reformed Ch., Visalia, Calif., 1977-79, Bethany Reformed Ch., Grand Rapids, Mich., 1979-83; dir. edn. Haven Reformed Ch., Kalamazoo, 1983-90, exec. dir. ops., 1990-93; dir. Manitoqua Ministries, Frankfort, Ill., 1993—; cons. David C. Cook Pubs., 1988-90, Office Evangelism Reformed Ch. in Am., 1987-91; tchr. trainer, mem. renewal forum Synod of Mich. Reformed Ch. in Am., 1987-90; regional evangelism trainer Synod of Mid-Am., 1995—; bd. dirs. Chgo. Christian Counseling Ctr., bd. officer, 1996. Author: Effective Decision Making for Church Leaders, 1988, Leader's Guide for Out of the Saltshaker and into the World, 1988. Vice chmn. Youth Com. Bill Glass Crusade, Visalia, 1978, chmn. Cen. Valley Ch. Workers Conf., Visalia, 1978; mem. Youth Com. City-Wide Easter Svcs., Visalia, 1979; trustee Reformed Bible Coll., Grand Rapids, 1984-91, mem. exec. com., 1985-91, asst. sec. bd. dirs., 1986-87, sec. bd. dirs., 1987-90; chmn. S.W. Mich. Christian Discipleship Com., 1984-85. Recipient DeVos award Reformed Bible Coll., 1977; Mich. State scholar, 1970. Mem. Bibl. Archeol. Soc., Christian Educators-Reformed ch. Am., Inst. for Am. Ch. Growth (cons. 1986-93), Christian Mgmt. Assn. Cen. Valley Youth Ministers (sec. 1978-79), Alban Inst., Am. Camping Assn. (bd. dirs. Ill. chpt. 1995—), Christian Camping Internat., Delta Epsilon Chi. Republican. Home and Office: 8122 W Sauk Trl Frankfort IL 60423-9785

HUFF, MICHAEL ALLAN, electrical engineering educator; b. Washington; s. Roger Allan and Jane Patricia (Jackson) H.; m. Deanna Cosima Velasco, Jan. 28, 1993. BSEE, Ga. Inst. Tech., 1984; MSEE, MIT, 1988, MS in Material Sci., 1988, PhD in Elec. Engring., 1993. Rsch. asst. Microsystems Tech. Labs. MIT, Cambridge, 1985-93, tchg. asst., 1985, 1989; elec. engr. Raytheon Corp., Bedford, Mass., 1984-88; tech. fellow Baxter Healthcare, Round Lake, Ill., 1993-94; asst. prof. Case Western Res. U., Cleve., 1994—; cons. Baxter Healthcare, Round Lake, 1994—, Orbital Rsch., Cleve., 1994—, Cleve. Med. Devices, 1995—. Inventor in field; contbr. articles to profl. jours. Glennon fellow CWRU, Cleve., 1994, tech. fellow Baxter Healthcare, Deerfield, Ill., 1993; grantee Whitaker Found., Washington, 1995. Mem. IEEE, Assn. for Advancement of Med. Instrumentation, Electrochem. Soc., Sigma Xi. Home: 11477 Mayfield Rd 308 Cleveland OH 44106 Office: Case Western Res Univ Dept EEAP 10900 Euclid Ave Cleveland OH 44106

HUFF, RONALD GARLAND, mechanical engineer; b. Toledo, Ohio, Dec. 29, 1930; s. Blenn Chalmer and Helen Ester (Schling) H.; m. Nancy Carroll Warns, June 29, 1957; children: Dennis Lee, Deborah Lynn. BSME, U. Toledo, 1953. Aero. engr. Nat. Adv. Com. for Aeronautics, Cleve., 1955-58; aerospace tech. NASA, Cleve., 1958-87; cons./proprietor Ronald G. Huff & Assocs., Cleve., 1986—. Contbr. articles to profl. jours. Photographer North Olmsted Band Boosters, Ohio, 1974-80; active PTA, North Olmsted, 1969-72. 1st lt. U.S. Army, 1953-55. Mem. ASME (chmn. winter ann.meeting 1986), AIAA. Congregationalist. Home and Office: Huff & Assocs 3741 Cinnamon Way Westlake OH 44145-5717

HUFFINE, COY LEE, retired chemical engineer, consultant; b. Knoxville, Tenn., Apr. 2, 1924; s. Coy Mann and Inez Belle (Story) H.; m. Virginia Elizabeth Browne, Mar. 31, 1951; children: Jeremy Bennett, Lucinda Jane. B.S., U. Tenn., 1945, M.S., 1947; Ph.D., Columbia U., 1953. Prin. engr. Gen. Electric Co., Oak Ridge and Cin., 1951-59; research ceramist Gen. Electric Research Lab., Schenectady, 1959-60; project mgr. devel. and mfg., space systems div. Avco Corp., Lowell, Mass., 1960-67; with IBM, Rochester, Minn., 1968-87, mgr. component tech., info. systems div., 1980-87; cons. and lectr. in field. Served with USN, 1945-46. Mem. Am. Inst. Chem. Engrs., AIME, Nat. Inst. Ceramic Engrs., Am. Ceramic Soc., N.Y. Acad. Scis., Sigma Xi. Home: 2247 5th Ave NE Rochester MN 55906-4017

HUFFINGTON, ROSE, artist, consultant; b. Manhattan, Kans., Oct. 25, 1956; d. Pavel and Gražina Strolaka; m. Clifford Harrington, May 15, 1975 (div. 1977); life ptnr. Geraldine Clay. BFA, Rutgers U., 1977. Cons. Werik Studio, St. Louis, 1985-95; owner, cons., 1995—. One-woman shows include Narada Gallery, Topeka, 1980 (Haines award), 86, Wichita (Kans.) Mus. Art, 1985; group exhbns. include William O. Lehrer Gallery, Tucson, 1988; represented in permanent collections Bank Ariz., Melme, Inc. Democrat. Studio: Werik Studio 9641 Manchester Rd Saint Louis MO 63119-1333

HUFFMAN, JIM D., industrial engineer; b. Ft. Wayne, Ind., Mar. 19, 1955. Tool maker Indsl. Engring. Inc., Ft. Wayne, 1973-80, Wind-A-Matic Corp., Ft. Wayne, 1980-83; design supr. Inds. Engring. Inc., Ft. Wayne, 1983—. Office: Indsl Engring Inc 4430 Tielker Rd Fort Wayne IN 46809-1543

HUFFMAN, JOHN P., mechanical engineer; b. Kansas City, Mo., Jan. 18, 1962. BSME, U. Mo., 1984, MS in Engring., 1985. Registered profl. engr., Mo. R&D engr. McDonnell-Douglas, St. Louis, 1985-89; projects engr. Watlow Electric, St. Louis, 1989-90; engring. mgr. Marlo Coil, High Ridge, Mo., 1990—. Mem. ASME, ASHRAE, Am. Welding Soc. Office: Marlo Coil PO Box 171 High Ridge MO 63049-0171

HUFFMAN, PATRICIA ANN, sales executive; b. Winchester, Ind., Dec. 4, 1936; d. Robert Thomas and Beatrice Leola (Shively) Klinck; m. Herbert Basil Huffman, Oct. 22, 1955 (div. Oct. 1971); children: Susan Bea (dec.), Kevin Ray, Brian Scott. Grad., McKinley Sch., 1954. Clk. United Grain & Feed, Winchester, 1954, Sumwalt Jewelers, Winchester, 1956-57, Haines Rexall Drugs, Winchester, 1957-58; proofreader, society reporter News & Jour. Herald, Winchester, 1954-55; billing clk. Gen. Telephone, Winchester, 1955-56; cost acct. Ind. Bridge Co., Inc., Muncie, 1958-63; inside sales assoc. A. E. Boyce Co., Inc., Muncie, 1971-84, sales rep., 1984—. Mem. Am. Bus. Women Assn. (editor newsletter 1986-87), Moose (sr. regent 1991, chaplain 1975-76). Republican. Home: 4429 N Wheeling Ave Muncie IN 47304-1210 Office: A E Boyce Co Inc 501 W Riggin Rd Muncie IN 47303-6414

HUFFMAN, PHYLLIS V., administrative assistant; b. Lawton, Okla., Dec. 17, 1943; d. George Robert and Frances V. (Willoughby) Otto; m. George Huffman, June 4, 1966; children: Kimberly, Gary. BS, Ill. State U., 1964; postgrad., Govs. State U. Cert. tchr. K-8, 7-12, Ill. Tchr. grade 2-3 Spring Grove (Ill.) Schs., 1965-66; tchr. Calumet Park (Ill.) Schs., 1966-69; pre-sch. tchr. St. Pauls United Ch. of Christ, Monee, Ill., 1978-80; adminstrv. asst. Monee Twp., 1980—. Mem. Will County Bd. and Forest Preserve Bd., Joliet, Ill., 1988—; pres., bd. dirs. Ea. Will County Sr. Svcs., Monee, 1995-96, mem., 1990—; trustee Monee Village Bd., 1985-88; past 2d v.p., treas. Ea. Will County Rep. Women, Crete, Ill., 1991-95, mem., 1987—; mem. Will County Bd. Health, Joliet, 1989-93; commr. Will County Forest Preserve, Joliet, 1988—; bd. dirs. Monee Twp. C. of C., 1982-88; mem. access to care com. Will County Health Dept., Joliet, 1994—. Mem. Monee Women's Club. Republican. Congregational. Home: 26020 Briar Ln Monee IL 60449 Office: 26121 Egyptian Trail Monee IL 60449

HUFFMAN, ROBERT MERLE, insurance company executive; b. Libertyville, Iowa, Nov. 8, 1931; s. Hollis Hiram and Jessie Ila (Harrison) H.; m. Carolyn A. Stowell, Dec. 10, 1955; children: Cheryl E. Hawkins, John D., Debra L. Otte. Student, Drake U., 1967. Various positions Grinnell (Iowa) Mut. Reins. Co., 1955-71; sec.-treas., CEO Clark Mut. Ins. Co., Kahoka, Mo., 1971—. Treas., mgr. Kahoka Housing Corp. (retirement facility), 1973-82; pres. Kahoka C. of C., 1973-74. Mem. Nat. Assn. Mut. Ins. Cos. (bd. dirs. Merit Soc. 1990-93, Svc. award 1993), Mo. Assn. Mut. Ins. Cos. (chmn. bd. 1989-90, bd. dirs. 1983-86, past vice-chmn., past chmn.-elect, chmn. 1989-90, former mem. legis. com.), Kiwanis (v.p.). Baptist. Office: Clark Mut Ins Co 108 N Washington St Kahoka MO 63445-1458

HUFFMAN-HINE, RUTH CARSON, adult education administrator, educator; b. Spencer, Ind., Sept. 13, 1925; d. Joseph Charles Carson and Bess Ann Taylor; m. Joe Buren Hine; children: Paulette Walker, Larry K., Annette M. AA in Fine Arts, Ind. Cen. Coll., 1967; BS in Edn., Butler U., 1971; MS in Adult Edn., Ind. U., 1976; PhD in Ednl. Adminstrn., Greenwich U., 1995. Cert. elem. edn. Subs. tchr. Met. Sch. Dist. Wayne Twnshp., Indpls., 1956-60; tchr. of homebound Met. Sch. Dist. Decatur Twnshp., Indpls., 1964-66; adult edn. tchr. Met. Sch. Dist. Wayne Twnshp., Indpls., 1971-75, adminstr. adult edn., 1975—; cons. Ind. Adoption System, Indpls., 1985—; regional rep. Ind. Assn. Adult Adminstrs., 1984—; program rep. Ind. Literacy Coordinators, Indpls., 1985—; speaker, mem. literacy research and evaluation com. Ind. Adult Literacy Coalition, Indpls., 1980-86. Author: Driving Regulations and Courtesies; co-author Learning for Everyday Living, 1978, Table Approach to Education, 1984, Developing Educational Competencies for Individuals Determined to Excel, 6 vols., 1980 (ERIC System award 1980), (ERIC System award 1985), Collection, Evaluation, Dissemination of Special Research Projects, 1984, Automobile Driving

Rules and Regulations, 1988. Vice com. person Rep. Orgn., Indpls., 1968-72; charter mem., sec. Project READ, LITERACY, 1988. Recipient Extra Mile award Met. Sch. Dist. Wayne Twp., 1990. Mem. Internat. Reading Assn. (Celebrate Literacy award 1984), Ind. Assn. for Adult & Continuing Edn. (treas. 1984—, pres. 1990-93, Outstanding Adult Educator 1979), Beta Phi Delta (pres. 1986—), Beta Phi, Delta Kappa Gamma (v.p. 1985-86, fellowship chmn. 1982-84), Phi Delta Kappa. Republican. Mem. Christian Ch. Home: 138 Abner Creek Pky Danville IN 46122-9602 Office: Adult Basic Edn Ctr 5248 W Raymond St Indianapolis IN 46241-4700

HUGGINS, CHARLES BRENTON, surgical educator; b. Halifax, N.S., Can., Sept. 22, 1901; s. Charles Edward and Bessie (Spencer) H.; m. Margaret Wellman, July 29, 1927; children: Charles Edward, Emily Wellman Huggins Fine. BA, Acadia U., 1920, DSc (hon.), 1946; MD, Harvard U., 1924; MSc, Yale U., 1947; DSc (hon.), Washington U., St. Louis, 1950, Leeds U., 1953, Turin U., 1957, Trinity Coll., 1965, U. Wales, 1967, U. Mich., 1968, Med. Coll. Ohio, 1973, Gustavus Adolphus Coll., 1975, Wilmington (Ohio) Coll., 1980, U. Louisville, 1980; LLD (hon.), U. Aberdeen, 1966, York U., Toronto, 1968, U. Calif., Berkeley, 1968; D of Pub. Service (hon.), George Washington U., 1967; D of Pub. Service (hon.) sigillum magnum, Bologna U., 1964. Intern in surgery U. Mich., 1924-26, instr. surgery, 1926-27; with U. Chgo., 1927—, instr. surgery, 1927-29, asst. prof., 1929-33, assoc. prof., 1933-36, prof. surgery, 1936—, dir. Ben May Lab. for Cancer Research, 1951-69, William B. Ogden Disting. Service prof., 1962—; chancellor Acadia U., Wolfville, N.S., 1972-79; Macewen lectr. U. Glasgow, 1958, Ravdin lectr., 1974, Powell lectr., Lucy Wortham James lectr., 1975, Robert V. Day lectr., 1975, Cartwright lectr., 1975. Trustee Worcester Found. Exptl. Biology; bd. govs. Weizmann Inst. Sci., Rehovot, Israel, 1973—. Decorated Order Pour le Mérite Germany; Order of The Sun Peru; recipient Nobel prize for medicine, 1966, Am. Urol. Assn. award, 1948, Francis Amory award, 1948, AMA Gold medals, 1936, 40, Société Internationale d'Urologie award, 1948, Am. Cancer Soc. award, 1953, Bertner award M.D. Anderson Hosp., 1953, Am. Pharm. Mfrs. Assn. award, 1953, Gold medal Am. Assn. Genito-Urinary Surgeons, 1955, Borden award Assn. Am. Med. Colls., 1955, Comfort Crookshank award Middlesex Hosp., London, 1957, Cameron prize Edinburg U., 1958, Valentine prize N.Y. Acad. Medicine, 1962, Hunter award Am. Therapeutic Soc., 1962, Lasker award for med. research, 1963, Gold medal Virchow Soc., 1964, Laurea award Am. Urol. Assn., 1966, Gold medal Worshipful Soc. Apothecaries of London, 1966, Gairdner award Toronto, 1966, Chgo. Med. Soc. award, 1967, Centennial medal Acadia U., 1967, Hamilton award Ill. Med. Soc., 1967, Bigelow medal Boston Surg. Soc., 1967, Disting. Service award Am. Soc. Abdominal Surgeons, 1972, Sheen award AMA, 1970, Sesquicentennial Commemorative award Nat. Library of Medicine, 1986; Charles Mickle fellow, 1958. Fellow ACS (hon.), Royal Coll. Surgeons Can. (hon.), Royal Coll. Surgeons Scotland (hon.), Royal Coll. Surgeons England (hon.), Royal Soc. Edinburgh (hon.), La Academia Nacional de Medicina (Mexico, hon.); mem. NAS (Charles L. Meyer award for cancer research 1943), Am. Philos Soc. (Franklin medal 1985), Am. Assn. Cancer Rsch., Can. Med. Assn. (hon.), Alpha Omega Alpha. Home: 5807 S Dorchester Ave Chicago IL 60637-1729

HUGGINS, CHARLOTTE SUSAN HARRISON, secondary education educator, author, travel specialist; b. Rockford, Ill., May 13, 1933; d. Lyle Lux and Alta May (Bowers) H.; student Knox Coll., 1951-52; AB magna cum laude, Harvard U., 1958; MA, Northwestern U., 1960, postgrad., 1971-73; cert. in conversational French Berlitz Lang. Sch.; m. Rollin Charles Huggins, Apr. 26, 1952; children: Cynthia Charlotte Peters, Shirley Ann Cooper, John Charles. Asst. editor Hollister Publs., Inc., Wilmette, Ill., 1959-65; tchr. advanced placement English New Trier High Sch., Winnetka, Ill., 1965—; master tchr., 1979; leader tchr., 1988; Task Force Commn. on Grading, 1973-74; Sabbatical project 1 yr. world travel History-Lit. Prospectus; cons. Asian Studies New Trier, 1987-88; mem. New Trier Supts. Commn. on Censorship, 1991; instr. critiquing Northwestern U.; cons. McDougall-Littel's Young Writer's Manual, 1985-88; asst. sponsor Echoes, 1981, Trevia, 1982, 83; sponsor New Trier News, 1988—; pres. Harrison Farms, Inc., Lovington, Ill., 1976—; speaker North Suburban Geneal. Soc., 1990; presenter Asian lit. Ill. Humanities Coun., 1992, Nat. Scholastic Press Assn. Conv., 1993; speaker Ill. High Sch. Scholastic Press Assn., No. Ill. Sch. Press Assn., 1992, 93, 94; instr., travel expert New Trier Adult Edn. Keys to the World's Last Mysteries, 1986—. Author: A Sequential Course in Composition Grades 9-12, 1979, A History of New Trier High School, 1982, Passage to Anaheim: An Historical Biography of Pioneer Families, 1984, Cambodia: A Place in Time, 1987; (video tapes) The Glory That Was Greece, 1987, The World of Charles Dickens, 1987. Mem. women's bd. St. Leonard's House, Chgo., 1965-75; Central Sch. PTA Bd., Wilmette, 1960-64; mem. jr. bd. Northwestern U. Settlement, Chgo., 1965-75. Recipient DAR Citizenship award, 1953, Phi Beta Kappa award, 1957, Am. Legion award, 1959, cert. of merit Graphic Arts Competition Printing Industries of Am., 1983, Quill and Scroll George Gallup award, 1990, 1st pl. award Am. Scholastic Press Assn., 1990, cert. of merit Am. Newspaper Pubs. Assn., 1990. Mem. MLA, NEA, ASCD, Ill. Edn. Assn., New Trier Edn. Assn. (sec. 1992, pres.-elect 1994, pres. 1995—), Nat. Coun. Tchrs. English, Ill. Assn. Tchrs. English, Women Comm., Inc., Northwestern U. Alumni Assn., Jr. Aux. U. Chgo. Cancer Research Bd., Mary Crane League, Nat. Huguenot Soc., Ill. Huguenot Soc., Columbia Scholastic Press Assn. (del 1990, newspaper judge, medalist award), Ill. Journalism Edn. Assn. (awards chmn., bd. dirs. 1992—, sec. 1994-95), Quill and Scroll (George Gallup award 1990, bd. dirs. 1992-93), Nat. Scholastic Press Assn. (spring convention rep. 1991-92, 92-93, 93-94, 94-95, 95-96, newspaper judge, conv. del. 1991, All-Am. Newspaper award 1990-91, 91-92, Fall and Spring conv. presenter 1993-94, 94-95, 95-96), Women in Comm., Newberry Libr. (assoc.), Art Inst. Chgo. (life), Terra Mus. Chgo. (charter), Lyric Opera (assoc.), Women's Club Wilmette, Mich. Shores Club, Univ. Club Chgo., Knox Coll. Alumni Assn., Radcliffe Coll. Alumnae Assn., Harvard U. Alumni Assn., Pi Beta Phi (North Shore Chgo. alumnae bd., publicity chair). Home: 700 Greenwood Ave Wilmette IL 60091-1748 Office: 385 Winnetka Ave Winnetka IL 60093-4238

HUGGLER, TOM, freelance writer, photographer; b. Detroit, June 19, 1945; s. Eldon A. and Leona C. (Thompson) H.; children: Brian T., Jennifer; m. Laura A. Albrecht, July 15, 1989. BA, U. Mich., FLint, 1968; MA, U. Mich., Ann Arbor, 1972. Tchr. high sch. English Genesee (Mich.) Schs., 1968-82; freelance writer, photographer Lansing, Mich., 1982—. Author: Westwind Woods, 1978, Midwest Meanders, 1984, Hunt Michigan, 1984, Fish Michigan--Great Lakes, 1986, Cannon's Guide to Freshwater Fishing with Downriggers, 1987, Quail Hunting in America, 1987, Grouse of North America, 1990, Fish Michigan--100 Southern Michigan Lakes, 1992, Fish Michigan--100 Upper Peninsula Lakes, 1994, Fish Michigan--50 Rivers, 1995, Fish Michigan--50 More Rivers, 1996; prodr. (videotapes) Walleye Tactics, 1991 (Teddy award 1991), Grouse Hunting 1994 (Teddy and N.Am. Outdoor awards 1994), Pheasant Hunting, 1995. Recipient various photography and writing awards. Mem. Outdoor Writers Assn. Am. (bd. dirs. 1986-89, pres. 1992-93), Mich. Outdoor Writers Assn. (bd. dirs. 1985-88), Assn. Great Lakes Outdoor Writers (bd. dirs. 1986-89). Methodist. Office: Outdoor Images PO Box 250 Sunfield MI 48890-0250

HUGH, GREGORY JOSEPH, finance company executive; b. Chgo., Sept. 23, 1942; s. Dong Loy and Shee (Moy) H.; m. Linda Lim, Mar. 10, 1963; children: Dianne Elizabeth, Brian Gregory. BA, St. Ambrose U., Davenport, Iowa, 1964. Cert. Real Estate Brokerage Mgr., Grad. Realtor Inst. V.p. Lava-Simplex Internat., Chgo., 1967-69; advt./sales promotion mgr. Baker Rhodes Mktg. Corp., Bloomington, Minn., 1969-73; dir. advt. Mail Mktg. & Sys., Inc., Bloomington, 1973-74; mfrs. rep. Mutual Bus. Assocs., Hopkins, Minn., 1974-76; sales mgr. Realty World-Hessburg Realtors, Shorewood, Minn., 1976-79; reg. rep. Waddell & Reed, Inc., Bloomington, 1979-86; owner/broker Good Earth Realty, Inc., Minnetonka, Minn., 1979-86; br. mgr. Realty World - TCF Realty, Inc., Minnetonka, 1986-87; reg. mgr. TCF Fin., Inc., Excelsior, Minn., 1987-89; v.p. Cityside Fin., Minnetonka, Minn., 1989; account mgr. Mut. Bus. Assocs., Minnetonka, 1990—; pres. Hugh Enterprises, Inc., Minnetrista, Minn., 1995—; instr. Inst. Fin. Edn., Chgo., 1987-88. Author: Personal Financial Planning...The Sensible Approach to Investing, 1982; contbr. articles to fin. jours. Res. officer St. Bonificus-Minnetrista Dept. Pub. Safety, 1987-90. Mem. Greater Mpls. Area Bd. Realtors (awarded cert. real estate brokerage mgr. and GRI designations). Home: 6520 S Bay Dr Excelsior MN 55331-9684

HUGHES, ANN, state legislator; b. Ogdensburg, N.Y., Sept. 28, 1943. BA in Biology, Wells Coll., 1965; student, McHenry County C.C., 1982. m. Earl Hughes; 3 children. Sec.-treas. Hughes Seed Farms; mem. Ill. Ho. of Reps., 1993—; chmn. com. on counties and twps., mem. insurance com., mem. health care and human svcs. com., mem. environ. and energy com., mem. global climate task force. Home: 407 N Dimmel Rd Woodstock IL 60098-9264 Office: Ill Ho of Reps State Capitol Springfield IL 62706 also: 2114-N Stratton Bldg Springfield IL 62706 also: 5400 W Elm St Ste 212 Mc Henry IL 60050-4049*

HUGHES, BARBARA BRADFORD, nurse; b. Bragg City, Mo., Jan. 21, 1941; d. Lawrence Hurl Bradford and Opal Jewel (Prater) Puttin; m. Robert Howard Hughes, Dec. 9, 1961; children: Kimberly Ann Hayden, Robert Howard II. ASN, St. Louis Community Coll., 1978; student, Webster U., 1980. RN, Mo. Med. surg. nurse Alexian Bros. Hosp., St. Louis, 1979-80; staff nurse Midwest Allergy Cons., St. Louis, 1980; nurse high altitude Aviation Nurse, Ltd., St. Louis, 1980-81; cardiac telemetry staff nurse Jefferson Meml. Hosp., Crystal City, Mo., 1992-94; pvt. practice real estate mgmt., 1962—. Vol. Luth. Hosp., St. Louis, 1967-70; mem. Mo. Bot. Garden, St. Louis, 1976—, Mo. Hist. Soc., 1993—, St. Louis Zoo Friends Assn., 1986-87, Nat. Trust for Hist. Preservation, 1990—; Channel 9-Ednl. TV, St. Louis; vol. blood drive ARC, St. Louis, 1980; vol. health tchr. Spartan Aluminum Products, Sparta, Ill., 1984. U. Mo. scholar, 1959. Mem. Mo. Pilots Assn., Women in Aviation Internat. (charter), U.S. Pilots Assn., Tyospaye Club. Republican. Home: 736 Windsor Harbor Rd Imperial MO 63052-2503

HUGHES, JAMES, radio station official; b. Merrill, Mich., Dec. 29, 1919. Student Jackson (Mich.) Jr. Coll., 1940-41. Staff announcer Sta. WIBM, Jackson, 1938-47, Sta. WKNX, Saginaw, Mich., 1947-48, Sta. WGFG, Kalamazoo, 1948-49, Sta. WKLA, Ludington, Mich., 1949, Sta. WTAC, Flint, Mich., 1949-53, Stas. WKNX-AM-TV, Saginaw, 1953-61; news dir. Sta. WSWM-FM, Mid-State FM Network, East Lansing, Mich., 1961-64, Sta. WCEN-AM-FM, Mt. Pleasant, Mich., 1964-87, Stas. WMMI and WCZY-FM, Mt. Pleasant, 1989—. Victim witness adv. Isabella County Prosecutor's Office. With AUS, 1942-45, ETO. Recipient Mich. Minute Man award Greater Mich. Found., 1971, publicity award Mich. Assn. Farmer Coops., 1971, Goodwill Amb. Extraordinare award Duluth C. of C., 1968, Order of White Hat award, Ctrl. Mich. U., 1987, communicator award Isabella County Farm Bur., VFW, VFW Aux., Mt. Pleasant, cert. of recognition Isabella County United Way, 1986, resolution of appreciation Mt. Pleasant Commn., 1987, cert. of appreciation Isabella County Sheriff's Dept., Mt. Pleasant State Police Post, also others. Roman Catholic. Office: Stas WMMI-WCZY 4065 E Wing Rd Mount Pleasant MI 48858

HUGHES, JEROME MICHAEL, education foundation executive; b. St. Paul, Oct. 1, 1929; s. Michael Joseph and Mary (Malloy) H.; m. Audrey M. Lackner, Aug. 11, 1951; children—Bernadine, Timothy, Kathleen, Rosemarie, Margaret, John. BA, Coll. of St. Thomas, St. Paul, 1951; MA, U. Minn., 1958; EdD, Wayne State U., 1970; postdoctoral fellow, U. Minn., 1985. Tchr. Shakopee Sch. Dist., Minn., 1951-53; tchr. St. Paul Sch. Dist., 1953-61, counselor, 1963-66, rsch. asst., 1966-67, edn. cons., 1968-87; mem. Minn. Senate, St. Paul, 1966-93, chmn. edn. com., 1973-83, chmn. elections and ethics com., 1983-93, pres., 1983-93; mem. faculty U. Minn., 1986-95; pres. Minn. Edn. Found., Roseville, 1995—; mem. Edn. Commn. of States, Denver, 1973-93; mem. Nat. Cmty. Edn. Adv. Coun., Washington, 1980-83; mem. Nat. Conf. State Legislature State/Fed. Assembly, 1983-93; adj. faculty U. Minn., 1986-95. Chair Goodwill/Easter Seals, 1993-95; bd. dirs. Nat. Parenting Assn. Minn., 1994—, STate Legis. Leaders Found., 1985-93. Mott fellow, 1967-68, Ford Found. fellow George Washington U., 1974-75, Bush Summer fellow, U. Calif., 1975; Disting. Policy fellow George Washington U., 1977-78; postdoctoral fellow U. Minn., 1980-81; recipient Pennell award Minn. Fedn. Tchrs., 1974; Disting. Svc. award Minn. Elem. Sch. Prins. Assn., 1982; named Community Educator of Yr. Minn. Community Edn. Assn., recipient other awards. Mem. Phi Delta Kappa. Democrat. Office: Minn Edn Found PO Box 13643 Roseville MN 55113-9998

HUGHES, KAREN SUE, geriatrics nurse; b. Wooster, Ohio, Oct. 16, 1955; d. Alvin S. and Pauline Katheryn (Troyer) Yutzy; m. Christopher Charles Marek, Sept. 3, 1977 (div. 1993); m. Raymond H. Hughes, July 20, 1993. LPN, Wayne County Vocat. Sch., 1974; BSN, Akron U., 1994. LPN, RN, Ohio. LPN, GPN, nurse aide Wooster Community Hosp., 1974-76; LPN Apple Creek (Ohio) Devel. Ctr., 1976-77, Smithville Western Care Ctr., Wooster, 1977-78, 78-80; supervisory LPN Gruter Found., Wooster, 1980-87; light indsl. worker Victor Temporary Svcs., Mansfield, Ohio, 1988-89; plant mgr. asst. Detroit Detroit Inc., Wayne, Mich., 1988-89; LPN charge nurse West View Manor, Wooster, 1989, Doylestown (Ohio) Health Care Ctr., 1989-93; charge nurse Manor Care Barberton, Ohio, 1993-94; RN supr., asst. dir. nursing Manor Care of Barberton, Ohio, 1994-95; RN Healthaven Nursing Home, Akron, Ohio, 1995—. Home: 985 Saxon Ave Akron OH 44314-2648

HUGHES, KATHERINE DODSON, technical writer, editor, developmental scientist; b. Oakland, Calif., Sept. 30, 1960; d. Jerrold Homer and Janice Berlene (Gibson) Dodson; m. Charles Evan Hughes, May 24, 1986; 1 child, Jerrold Christopher. BA in Biology, Coe Coll., 1982; MS in Biology, U. S.C., 1984; postgrad., U. Pitts., 1984-86. Lab. technician Abbott Labs., North Chicago, Ill., 1979; teaching asst. dept. biol. scis. U. S.C., Columbia, 1982-84; grad. student rschr. Western Psychiat. Inst. and Clinic, U. Pitts., 1984-85, grad. teaching asst. dept. biol. scis., 1985-86; tech. analyst Environ. Policy Staff Monsanto, St. Louis, 1986-91; devel. editor Mosby Yr. Book, St. Louis, 1991—; rsch. technician Jewish Hosp. St. Louis, 1992-93; devel. scientist Abbott Labs., 1994—. Deacon 1st Presbyn. Ch., St. Louis, 1988-93, 1st Presbyn. Ch., Waukegan, 1995-96. Ivy R. McManus Meml. scholar U. Pitts., 1985. Mem. AAAS, Soc. for Tech. Communication, Mensa, Sigma Xi, Phi Eta Sigma, Alpha Lambda Delta. Home: 1426 Hickory St Waukegan IL 60085-1937

HUGHES, KENNETH G., elementary school educator; b. Colorado Springs, Colo., Feb. 12, 1952; s. George V. and Martha (Stark) H. BS in Elem. Edn., U. Pitts., 1983; MEd in Edn. Leadership, U. Ctrl. Fla., 1993. Cert tchr., Fla., Pa., Ohio; cert. Level 1 adminstrv., Fla. Head tchr. Learning Tree, Inc., Pitts., 1983-85; tchr. 1st grade, 3d grade, 4th grade Dr. Phillips Elem. Sch., Orlando, Fla., 1985-89; tchr. 1st grade, 4th grade McCoy Elem. Sch., Orlando, 1989-91; tchr. curriculum resource Dr. Phillips Elem. Sch., Orlando, 1991-95; adult edn. ESOL, Mid-Fla. Tech. Inst., Orlando, 1990-91. Recipient Innovative Classroom Practices award-Orange County, Walt Disney World, 1991,92. Mem. Phi Delta Kappa. Home: 28530 Willet Cir North Olmsted OH 44070

HUGHES, KEVIN E., state trooper, emergency medical technician; b. St. Paul, Aug. 4, 1957; s. Nick G. Sr. and Nancee J. (Hauser) H.; divorced, 1986. AA in Liberal Arts with honors, Sauk Valley Coll., Dixon, Ill., 1977; BA in History, No. Ill. U., 1982; cert. in criminal justice, Kennedy-Western U., Agoura Hills, Calif., 1990. Cert. EMT, instr. and trainer, Ill. Dept. Pub. Health. Dir. religious edn., youth min. St. Anne's Cath. Ch., Barrington, Ill., 1980-82; libr. clk. No. Ill. U. Founders Libr., DeKalb, 1982-84; state trooper Ill. State Police Dist. 2, Elgin, 1984-87; state trooper, EMT trainer, supr. Ill. State Police Acad., Springfield, 1989-93; state trooper, exec. security Ill. State Police, Springfield, 1993—. Bd. dirs. Am. Heart Assn., Springfield, 1990-93, Gov.'s HIV Adv. Bd., Springfield, 1990-93; com. chmn. March of Dimes, Springfield, 1994; asst. scoutmaster Boy Scouts Am., Sycamore, Ill., 1987-90. Recipient Lifesaving award Am. Heart Assn., 1988, letter of commendation Dept. Justice/FBI, 1991. Mem. NRA, Law Enforcement Alliance Am., Frat. Order of Police (lodge 41), Am. Motorcyclist Assn., Blue Knights Internat. (dir. 1993—). Republican. Office: Ill State Police Exec Security Governors Mansion Springfield IL 62701

HUGHES, MARK DOUGLAS, journalist, communications director; b. Farmington, Mo., Mar. 23, 1958; s. Billy Gene and Pauline Fern (Thomore) H.; m. Jacqueline Lee Parker; 1 child, Lauren Ashley. AA, Mineral Area Coll., 1983; B in Journalism, U. Mo., Columbia, 1987. Feature writer Mineral Area Press, Farmington, 1980-81; reporter, staff writer Farmington (Mo.) Press Advertiser, 1983-84, front page editor, 1984-85; comm. asst. Mo. Senate, Jefferson City, 1985; reporter Columbia (Mo.) Missourian, 1986-87; comm. officer Mo. Senate, Jefferson City, 1987-93, comm. dir., 1994—; dir., exec. prodr. Legis. Video Info. Svcs., Jefferson City, 1988-95; pres. Expressions Multimedia, Columbia, Mo., 1994-95; cons. Logistics Internat., Boulder, Colo., 1994-95, Lottery-Edn. Telesatellite Sys., Jefferson City, 1994-95. Dist. del. St. Francis County Dem. Com., Farmington, 1984; campaign mgr. Com. to Re-elect Senator Staples, Eminence, Mo., 1986; contbg. mem. Senatorial Dem. Com., Jefferson City, 1987-95. Mem. NRA, Nat. Conf. State Legislators, Internat. TV Assn., Phi Theta Kappa. Office: Mo Senate The Capitol Rm 424B Jefferson City MO 65101

HUGHES, MICHAEL JOSEPH, counselor, psychologist; b. Scranton, Pa., Jan. 20, 1951; s. Michael Robert and Mary Catherine (Race) H.; m. Patricia Staley, Sept. 26, 1987. BS, U. Scranton, 1972, MS, 1974; EdD, W.Va. U., 1977. Lic. counselor, psychologist W.Va., Ohio. Counselor Clarks-Summit (Pa.) State Hosp., 1974-75; counselor, instr. W.Va. U., Morgantown, 1975-77; dir. clin. svcs. Prestera Ctr., Huntington, W.Va., 1977-90; cons. VA Med. Ctr., Huntington, 1984-91; counselor Shawnee State U., Portsmouth, Ohio, 1990—; cons. Shawnee Mental Health Ctr., Portsmouth, 1990-95. Mem. APA, ACA, Am. Coll. Counseling Assn., Ohio Mental Health Counselors Assn., W.Va. Psychol. Assn., W.Va. Counseling Assn., W.Va. Mental Health Counselors Assn., Am. Mental Health Counselors Assn., Ohio Counseling Assn. Roman Catholic. Office: Shawnee State U 940 2nd St Portsmouth OH 45662-4347

HUGHES, MICHAEL SCOTT, physicist; b. St. Louis, Sept. 13, 1958; s. Robert Charles and Suzanne Marie (Dritsch) H.; m. Martha Minton, Dec. 18, 1987; children: Alexander, Alea. BA in Math./Physics cum laude, Washington U., 1980, MS in Physics, 1982, PhD in Physics, 1987. Teaching asst. Washington U., St. Louis, 1980-82, rsch. asst., 1982-85, NASA grad. rsch. fellow, 1985-87; physicist Ctr. for Non-Destructive Evaluation Iowa State U., Ames, 1988-92; sr. rsch. physicist Mallinckrodt Med., Inc., St. Louis, 1992-95, rsch. assoc., 1995—. Inventor technique for nonuniform poling of piezo transmission, 1990, an entropy based signal detector, 1990, thermodynamic signal analysis, 1990, entropy based signal, transmission reception and signal analysis method and appartus, 1995. Mem. IEEE. Office: Mallinckrodt Med Inc 675 Mcdonnell Blvd Saint Louis MO 63134

HUGHES, MICHELE EVALINDE, artist, design company executive; b. Graz, Austria, May 3, 1946; came to U.S., 1978; d. Anton Fritz and Josephine (Domany-Kramer) Blanche; children: Verena Corinna, Shelly Jo. BA in Costume Design/Dance, Vienna (Austria) U., 1963; M in History of Art and Design, Vienna State and Munich State, 1964; BA in Music, Liechtenfels Lyzeum, Graz, 1965; diploma in Austrian Doctrine Design, State Univs., Vienna, 1965; PhD in History of Art and Design, Vienna State U., 1966. Designer Vienna State Opera, 1966-68, Spanish Courtriding Sch., Vienna, 1969-73; CEO M.M. Designs, Munich, 1974-75; co-author G. Ball Pub., Munich, 1974-78; dir. mktg. devel. Yves Montand Co., Mt. View, Calif., 1979-80; staff designer L.A. Actors Theatre, 1981-85; costume designer Am. Film Inst., L.A., 1985-86, Fox TV, L.A., 1986-88; CEO Petite Belvedere Corp., Wellfleet, Nebr., 1988—; personal design cons. Joan Rivers, Martin Sheen, C.Ch. Pounder, L.A., 1986-88; lectr. philosophy and art Munich State U., 1975; restorator Count Arco Von Pallffy Estates, Austria and Germany, 1971-74; lectr. advanced design Austrian Designers Union Inst., Baaden-Vienna, 1965-70. Biographer, co-author: C. Jurgens, 1974, H. Ruehmann, 1975, G. Groebe, 1976; painter, sculptor (chapel mural) Good Shepherd Convent, 1966 (Hist. Soc. award 1967, 68, 69); designer stage prodns.; exhbited sculpture in Spokane Walsdorf Gallery, 1989-91. Designer, rschr. CBS "Samaritan", 1985; active vol. L.A. Mission, 1985-88; campaign devel. and rsch. Waldheim Kreisky for Austrian Senate, Vienna, 1969, 72; developer, exec. Green Kindergarden Housing, Vienna, 1968-69. Recipient Emmy nominee Acad. TV Arts and Scis., 1986, Best Drama-Comedy award La Opinion, Argentina, 1982, Critic's award Calif. Theatre, 1982. Mem. Sacred Art Soc. (pres. 1968— Disting. Achievement award 1976), Altar Soc. St. Williams (pres. 1993-94), Nat. Hist. Preservation Soc. (Honor award 1993), Nat. Wildflower Rsch., Pheasants Forever, Nat. Human Edn. Soc. (Honor award 1994), C. Designers Guild. Roman Catholic. Office: Petite Belvedere Corp Rt 1 Box 3 Wellfleet NE 69170

HUGHES, RUTH PIERCE, retired educator; b. Utica, N.Y., Sept. 2, 1919; d. Gilbert Davis and Elizabeth Bertha (Bennett) Pierce; m. Walter Emerson Hughes, Apr. 8, 1950 (div. 1968); children: Betty Ann, Carol Ellen; m. James Wallace Moyer, Jan. 23, 1993. BS, Cornell U., 1941, MS, 1949, PhD, 1969. Tchr. home econs. various schs., N.Y., 1941-44, 46-65; rsch. assoc., asst. Cornell U., Ithaca, N.Y., 1965-68; div. dir. W. Va. U., Morgantown, 1968-71; prof., dept. head Iowa State U., Ames, 1971-87, disting. prof., prof. emeritus, 1980—; cons. in field. Contbr. articles to profl. jours. Mem. adminstrv. bd. 1st United Meth. Ch., Ames, 1976—; bd. dirs., pres. Northcrest Retirement Ctr., Ames, 1990—, Ames Internat. Orch. Festival Assn. Guild, 1988—. Recipient Outstanding Svc. award Am. Vocat. Assn., Alexandria, Va., 1985, Career Excellence award Nat. Ctr. Rsch. in Vocat. Edn., Columbus, Ohio, 1985. Republican. Home: 1520 Stone Brooke Rd Ames IA 50010-4100

HUGHES, STEVEN JAY, lawyer; b. Fayetteville, Ark., Nov. 7, 1948; s. Howard and Jimmie Louise (Williams) H.; m. Leora Donna Halfhill, July 22, 1972; children: Christopher Blake, Clayton Brent. BS in Edn., U. Ark., Fayetteville, 1970; JD, U. Ark., Little Rock, 1978; LLM, DePaul U., 1993. Bar: Ark. 1978, U.S. Dist. Ct. (ea. dist.) Ark. 1978, U.S. Ct. Appeals (8th cir.) 1978, U.S. Supreme Ct. 1981, Mo. 1993. Sole practice Jacksonville, Ark., 1978-92; owner Hughes Legal Rsch., 1994—; bd. dirs. Tiara Condominium Property Owners Assn., chmn., 1994—. Alderman Jacksonville City Coun., 1979-81; commr. Jacksonville Planning Commn., 1982-85; mem. U. Ark. Razorback Letterman's Club, Little Rock, 1985, Ark. Sports Hall of Fame, 1985; bd. dirs. Jacksonville Boys Club, 1979-92, pres., 1982-83. Mem. Assn. Trial Lawyers Am., Ark. Bar Assn., Delta Theta Phi (life, dist. chancellor 1983-93). Baptist. Lodge: Kiwanis (pres. Jacksonville club 1983-84, Kiwanian of Yr. award 1979-80, Disting. Club Pres. award 1984). Home and Office: 6147 N Sheridan Rd # 26-c Chicago IL 60660-2881

HUGHES, TRICIA EMILY, nurse; b. St. Louis, July 27, 1962; d. Leonard and June (Klipstine) Burkard; m. Joseph M. Hughes, Oct. 18, 1985; children: Meagan, Michael, Stephanie. ADN, Maryville U., St. Louis, 1982, BS in Health Care Mgmt., 1991. RN, Mo.; cert. telemetry; CPR, ACLS. Charge nurse orthopedics fl. St. Louis U. Hosp., 1982-86; night charge nurse on telemetry St. Anthony's Hosp., St. Louis, 1986; staff, charge nurse St. Joseph's Hosp., Kirkwood, Mo., 1987-89; coord. adult medicine Group Health Plan, St. Louis, 1989-95, coord. ob-gyn., 1995—. Home: 2941 Melton Dr Arnold MO 63010-3706 Office: Group Health Plan 10822 Sunset Office Dr Saint Louis MO 63127-1009

HUGLEY, BETTY JEAN, retired insurance analyst, poet; b. Sherill, Ark., July 21, 1933; d. Johnny Parker and Sue Belle Owens; m. Oscar C. Davis, Dec. 1950 (div. 1957); children: John A., Michael L., Don F., Kenneth L., Glen E.; m. S.T. Hugley, Aug. 14, 1971 (div.). Student, Wayne County C.C., Detroit, 1970. Nursing attendant State of Mich., Northville, 1956-66, nursing svc. supr., 1966-69, community living worker, 1969-76, nursing svc. supr., 1976; claims examiner, unemployment ins. analyst State of Mich., Detroit, 1976-94. Author: (poetry book) Solace: Past and Present, 1993. Recipient Crystal award Miller High Alumni, Inc., Detroit, 1995. Mem. Optimist, Detroit Urban League, Emma V. Kelley Temple (vice-dau. ruler 1994-95). Democrat.

HUGOSON, GENE, state legislator, farmer; b. Sept. 1945; m. Patricia Hugoson; one child. BA, Augsburg Coll.; postgrad., Mankato State U. Farmer; Dist. 26A rep. Minn. Ho. of Reps., St. Paul, 1986—; former mem. econ. devel., internat. trade and redistricting coms., Minn. Ho. of Reps.; mem. Agr., rules and legis. adminstrn., transp. and transit, and taxes coms.; asst. minority leader. Home: RR 2 Box 218 Granada MN 56039-9530*

HUIBREGTSE, JAYNE LYNNOR, medical surgical nurse; b. Pipestone, Minn., Jan. 27, 1952; d. Vern Ray and Alvera Augusta (Wittfoth) H. Diploma, Sioux Valley Hosp. Sch. Nursing, 1973. RN, Minn., S.D. Psychiat. staff nurse McKennan Hosp., Sioux Falls, S.D.; dir. nursing svc. Palisade Manor Nursing Home, Garretson, S.D.; staff nurse operating rm. Sioux Valley Hosp., Sioux Falls; staff and charge nurse Pipestone County Med. Ctr. Mem. Minn. Nurses Assn.

HUISINGA, THEODORE, food products executive; b. 1924. Student, U. Minn., 1946-50. Chmn. bd., CEO Willmar (Minn.) Poultry Co. Inc., 1951—; with Farm Svc. Elevator Co., Willmar, 1954—, Willmar Poultry Farms, Inc., 1963—. With U.S. Army, 1943-46. Office: Willmar Poultry Co Inc 3735 County Rd 5 SW Willmar MN 56201*

HUISINGH, ROGER J., securities trader; b. Emmons County, S.D., May 1, 1944; m. Carol E. Scheppers, Dec. 21, 1965; children: Sharon, David, Wendy. BS, Western Mich. U., 1966. Securities trader H.B. Shane & Co., Grand Rapids, Mich., 1984-87, Prscott Ball Turbin, Grand Rapids, 1987-88, Kemper Securities Inc., Grand Rapids, 1988—. Republican. Home: 4115 Meadowfield Dr Hudsonville MI 49426-9342 Office: Kemper Securities Inc Campau Square Blvd 180 Monroe Ave NW Ste 1000 Grand Rapids MI 49503-2626

HUIZENGA, BERNARD ANDREW, orthopedic surgeon; b. Waupun, Wis., Mar. 23, 1939; s. William E. and Johanna (Tamminga) H.; m. Judith L. Wilson, June 9, 1962; children: Beth, Jill, Jane. BA, U. Wis., 1959, MD, 1962. Diplomate Am. Bd. Orthopedic Surgery. Intern with U.S. Army Wm. Beaumont Gen Hosp., El Paso, Tex., 1962-63; resident in gen. surgery Wood VA Hosp., Milw., 1965; resident in orthopedic surgery Columbia Hosp., Milw., 1966; mem. staff Orthopedic Assocs. Milw., S.C., 1969-94, Milw. children's Hosp., 1966-67, Milw. County Hosp., 1967-68, VA Hosp., Milw., 1968-69; assoc. clin. prof. Med. Coll. Wis., Milw., 1965-95. Capt. U.S. Army, 1962-65. Fellow Scoliosis Rsch. Soc., Am. Acad. Orthopedic Surgery; mem. Wis. State Orthopedic Soc., Milw. Orthopedic Soc. Office: Orthopedic Spine Cons SC 2350 W Villard Ave Ste 111 Milwaukee WI 53209-5081

HUKLE, JAMES R., stockbroker; b. Oklahoma City, Apr. 13, 1956. BJS, Wichita State U., 1990. Stockbroker PaineWebber, Wichita, Kans., 1979-87; stockbroker, instnl. salesman A.G. Edwards & Sons Inc., Wichita, 1987—. Mem. Wichita Country Club. Home: 102 N Terrace Dr Wichita KS 67208-3940 Office: AG Edwards & Sons Inc 201 N Main St Ste 300 Wichita KS 67202-1500

HULBERT, SAMUEL FOSTER, college president; b. Adams Center, N.Y., Apr. 12, 1936; s. Foster David and Wilma May (Speakman) H.; m. Joy Elinor Husband, Sept. 3, 1960; children: Gregory, Samantha, Jeffrey. B.S. in Ceramic Engring., Alfred U., 1958, Ph.D., 1964. Registered profl. engr., La, S.C. Asst. varsity and freshman football coach Alfred U. (N.Y.), 1959-61; lab. instr. N.Y. State Coll. Ceramics, Alfred, 1958-59; instr. math and physics Alfred U., 1960-64; asst. prof. ceramic and metall. engring. Clemson U. (S.C.), 1964-68, head div. interdisciplinary studies, assoc. prof. materials and bioengring., 1968-71; assoc. dean engring research and interdisciplinary studies, prof. materials engring. and bioengring., dir. materials engring. and bioengring., 1970-73; prof. bioengring., dean Sch. Engring. Tulane U., New Orleans, 1973-76; pres.-designate spl. asst. to pres. Rose-Hulman Inst. Tech., Terre Haute, Ind., 1976, pres., 1976—; bd. dirs. Carbon Implants, Inc., Innoventure, Inc., Ind. Bus. Modernization & Tech. Corp., Sofamor Danek Group, Inc., Citizens Bank of Western Ind. Mem. editorial bd. Annals of Biomed. Engring., 1974, Jour. Biomed. Materials Rsch., 1970—; contbr. articles in field of biomaterials and artificial organ design to profl. jours. Mem. exec. com. Wabash Valley chpt. Boy Scouts Am.; mem. Ind. Humanities Coun., 1991—. Recipient medal Italian Soc. Orthopaedics, 1973; recipient Delitala medal Instituto Ortopedico Rizzoli, 1973. Fellow Am. Inst. for Med. and Biol. Engring.; mem. Am. Soc. Artificial Internal Organs, Biomed. Engring. Soc., Soc. Biomaterials (dir. 1974—, pres. 1975-76), Am. Ceramic Soc., Nat. Inst. Ceramics Engrs., Am. Soc. Engring. Edn., Assn. Advancement Med. Instrumentation, Ind. Colls. and Univ. Assn., Ind. Colls. of Ind., Ind. Conf. Higher Edn., Assn. Ind. Tech. Univs. (sec., treas. 1977-78, pres. 1987-90), Presidents of Ind. Colls. and Univs., Vigo County Hist. Soc. (dir. 1979—), Keramos Blue Key, Ind. Acad., Internat. Acad. Ceramics, Rotary, Sigma Xi. Republican. Office: Rose Hulman Inst Tech Office of Pres 5500 Wabash Ave Terre Haute IN 47803-3920

HULETT, BARBARA JUNE, elementary and special education educator; b. Kansas City, Mo., Nov. 12, 1933; d. William August and Clema Cecil (Cannaday) Kiefer; m. Robert Prentiss Hulett, Aug. 31, 1956; children: Paul Robert, Linda Gayle. A in Commerce, Kansas City Jr. Coll., 1953; BEd, B in Spl. Edn., Avila Coll., 1973; MA in Spl. Edn., Learning Disabilities, U. Mo., Kansas City, 1980. Med. sec. Orthopedic Surgeons, Kansas City, 1953-56; pres./officer Women's Soc. Christian Svc., Kansas City, 1959-69; substitute tchr. Consol. Sch. Dist. # 1 Hickman Hills, Kansas City, 1969-70; sch. sec. Sch. Dist. 1 Hickman Mills, Kansas City, 1970-71; profl. educator #1 Sch. Dist. Hickmann Mills, Kansas City, 1973—; pres. pre-sch. PTA, Pinkerton Elem., 1963-64; elected mem. Profl. Devel. Com., 1991-95, Tercon Leadership Com., 1990—. Vol. poll worker Local/State Elections, Hickman Mills, Kansas City; lifetime mem. Women's Soc. Christian Svc. Mem. AAUW, Mo. Nat. Educators Assn. (elected rep. assembly 1989-91, 96—), Hickman Mills United Tchrs. Assn. (bd. officer), Alpha Delta Kappa (Alpha Gamma chpt. pres. 1982-84, Kans. State historian 1990-92). Republican. Methodist. Home: 11120 Walrond Ave Kansas City MO 64137-2225

HULL, CHARLES WILLIAM, special education educator; b. East St. Louis, Ill., Feb. 23, 1936; s. William Semple Hull and Jessie Marie (Brennan) Poole; m. Beverly Kay Julian, Aug. 19, 1967; 1 child, William Kenneth. BA in Econs., Cen. Meth. Coll., 1964; MEd, Olivet Nazarene Coll., 1974; AA (hon.), Joliet Jr. Coll., 1987. Tchr. elem. grades Taft Sch., Lockport, Ill., 1965-67; tchr. spl. edn. S.W. Cook County Coop. Assn. for Spl. Edn., Oak Forest, Ill., 1967—. Permanent exhibits include Tchr's Ret. Office Bldg., Springfield, Ill. Past bd. dirs., v.p., chmn. fund raising Easter Seals Will and Grundy Counties; dist. leader Am. Cancer Soc., 1984, residential campaign chmn., 1985; vol., mem. adv. bd. Big Bros.-Big Sisters Will County; Cub Scouts com. chmn. Boy Scouts Am., 1980-81, commr. Rainbow coun., bd. dirs. troop 6l; mem. choir, past trustee Faith United Meth. Ch.; Will County walkathon chmn. March of Dimes, 1979; chmn. Canal Days events Will County Hist. Soc., 1987; active numerous other orgns. Cpl. USMC, 1955-58. Recipient Congl. Medal of Merit, 1985, Frederick Bartleson Meml. award Will County Hist. Soc., 1985, Citizen of Week award Sta. WBBM, Chgo., 1985, Leadership award Am. Cancer Soc., 1985, Outstanding Svc. award Big Bros.-Big Sisters Will County, letter of commendation Pres. of U.S., 1986, 89, Disting. Svc. award Joliet Jr. Coll., 1987, Citizen of Month award Southtown Economist, plaque KC. Mem. 1st Marine Div. Assn., Coun. for Exceptional Children, Internat. Platform Assn., Will County Old-Timers Baseball Assn., Am. Legion, Masons (32 degree), Shriners (pres. Joliet club 1983, Shriner of Yr. 1989), KC, Moose, Medina Temple, Lions (pres. Manhattan club 1984, chmn. youth and fgn. exch. dist. 1986-87, bd. dirs. Lockport chpt.), Will County Hist. Soc. (pres. 1989), Royal Order Scotland, Masons, Phi Delta Kappa. Republican. Methodist. Home: 403 N Farrell Rd Lockport IL 60441-2363 Office: SW Cook County Coop Assn Spl Edn 6020 151st St Oak Forest IL 60452

HULL, CHRISTOPHER NEIL, state agency biologist; b. Flint, Mich., Feb. 25, 1953; s. Darwin Blain and Rosemary (Mobile) H. BS in Biology, U. Mich., Flint, 1976; MS in Natural Resources, U. Mich., Ann Arbor, 1980; postgrad., Mich. State U., Lansing (Mich.) C.C., 1984—. Cert. instr. Shodan, Tae Kwon Do, Internat. Tae Kwon Do Fedn.; cert. instr. Nidan, Aikado, Aikido Yishinki Assn. N. Am. Park ranger, parks divsn. Mich. Dept. Natural Resources, 1974-83; water quality specialist, acquatic biologist Mich. Depts. Natural Resources, Environ. Quality, Lansing, Mich., 1984—; tchr. martial arts, biology, ecology and natural history for numerous orgns., 1973—. Free lance rschr., writer in field biology, ecology, natural history, especially ornithology, and conservation, 1977—; author numerous articles in sci. jours. and popular publs.; mng. editor The Jackpine Warbler, 1987-90. Environ. organizer, lobbyist. Recipient Earth Angel award Sta WKAR-TV, 1990 and others. Mem. Numerous sci. rsch. and environ. orgns. including: Am. Wildlife Found., Am. Ornithol. Union, Cornell Lab. of Ornithology, Environ. Defense Fund, Fund for Animals, Mich. Humane Soc., Mich. Profl. Employees Soc., Nat. Wildlife Fedn., Ornithol. Socs. N. Am. and others. Office: Mich Dept Environ Quality PO Box 30273 Lansing MI 48909

HULL, DUANE G., financial planner; b. Cadillac, Mich., Aug. 31, 1930. BS, Mich. State U., 1953, MS, 1961. CLU. Asst. supt. of schs. Rochester (Mich.) Cmty. Schs., 1966-85; fin. planner Scripter & Assocs. Inc., Troy, Mich., 1985—. Active St. Phillips Episc. Ch., Rochester, 1983—, treas., 1989, Rochester Avon Youth Assistance, 1983—. 1st lt. U.S. Army, 1953-55. Mem. Internat. Assn. Fin. Planners. Office: Scripter & Assocs Inc 3155 W Big Beaver Rd Ste 103 Troy MI 48084-3006

HULL, ELIZABETH ANNE, English language educator; b. Upper Darby, Pa., Jan. 10, 1937; d. Frederick Bossart and Elizabeth (Schmik) H.; m. Dean Carlyle Beery, Feb. 5, 1955 (div. 1962); children: Catherine Doria Beery Pizarro, Barbara Phyllis Beery Wintczak; m. Frederik Pohl, July 1984. Student, Ill. State U., 1954-55; AA, Wilbur Wright Jr. Coll., Chgo., 1965; B in Philosophy, Northwestern U., 1968; MA, Loyola U., Chgo., 1970, PhD, 1975. Teaching asst. Loyola U., Chgo., 1968-71; prof. English, coord. honors program William Rainey Harper Coll., Palatine, Ill., 1971—; judge nat. writing competition Nat. Coun. Tchrs. of English, 1975—, John W. Campbell award, 1986—. Co-editor: (with F. Pohl) Tales from the Planet Earth; contbr. articles to profl. jours. Pres. Lexington Green Condominium Assn., Schaumburg, Ill., 1982-84; bd. dirs. Hunting Ridge Homeowner's Assn., Palatine, 1984-86, bd. dirs. Palatine LWV, 1992—;Candidate U.S. Rep. Ill. 8th Congrl. Dist., 1996. Recipient Northwestern U. Alumni award for Merit, 1995. Mem. MLA, Midwest MLA, Popular Culture Assn., Sci. Fiction Rsch. Assn. (editor 1981-84, sec. 1987-88, pres. 1989-90), Ill. Coll. English Assn. (pres. 1975-77), World Sci. Fiction Assn. (N.Am. sec. 1978—, pres. Honors coun. Ill. region 1992-93), Palatine Area LWV (bd. dirs. 1991—, v.p. 1995—), Am. Assn. for Women in C.C. (v.p. comm., bd. dirs. Harper Coll. chpt. 1993—). Democrat. Home: 855 Harvard Dr Palatine IL 60067-7026 Office: William Rainey Harper Coll 1200 W Algonquin Rd Palatine IL 60067-7373*

HULL, GRAFTON HAZARD, JR., social work educator; b. Great Bend, Kans., Nov. 24, 1943; s. Grafton H. and Mary Kathryn (Hagerty) H.; divorced; children: Michael, Patrick. BS, U. Wis., Madison, 1967; MSW, Fla. State U., 1969; EdD, U. S.D., 1979. Social worker Cen. State Hosp., Milledgeville, Ga., 1969; chief social work sect. Mental Hygiene Cons. Svc., Ft. Knox, Ky., 1969-71; social worker, then social work supr. Manitowoc County Dept. Social Svc., Manitowoc, Ky., 1971-74; asst. prof., chair dept. sociology Morningside Coll., Sioux City, Iowa, 1974-79; assoc. prof., chair dept. social welfare U. Wis., Whitewater, 1979-82, prof., chair dept., 1982-88; prof., chair dept. social work U. Wis., Eau Claire, 1988-93; dir. Sch. Social Work S.W. Mo. State U., Springfield, 1993-96; dir. divsn social work Ind. Univ. NW, Gary, 1996—; site visitor Coun. Social Work Edn., Washington, 1981—; cons. in field. Co-author: Understanding Generalist Practice, Building the Undergraduate Social Work Library, Case Studies in Generalist Practice; cons. editor Jour. Social Work Edn., 1989-95, Aretê, 1993—; contbr. articles to profl. jours. Chmn. Landmarks Commn., Whitewater, 1982-88; city councilman, mem. planning and architecture rev. commn. City of Whitewater, 1987-88. Capt. U.S. Army, 1969-71. Mem. NASW (chair west ctrl. Wis. br. 1989-91), Baccalaureate Program Dirs. Assn. (pres. 1991-93), Coun. Social Work Edn. (commn. on accreditation 1987-93, bd. dirs. 1993—), Wis. Coun. Social Work Edn. (pres. 1984-91), Inst. Advancement Social Work Rsch. (sec.-treas. 1993-95), Mo. Consortium of Social Work Edn. Programs (pres. 1995—). Democrat. Home: 912 W Elm Pl Griffith IN 46319 Office: Ind Univ NW Gary IN 46408

HULL, JOANNE PETERSEN, health facility administrator; b. Council BLuffs, Iowa, July 19, 1963; d. Kenneth Paul and Doris Lorraine (Nelsen) Petersen; m. Allan Paul Hull, June 24, 1989; children: Chelsea Louise, Samantha Rose. BA, U. Iowa, 1985. Program prodn. Bluffs Run, Council Bluffs, Iowa, 1986; media tech. Area Edn. Agy. 13, Treynor, Iowa, 1986-90; communications asst. Midlands Cmty. Hosp., Papillion, Nebr., 1990-93, communications specialist, 1993—. Mem. Soc. Profl. Journalists, Internat. Assn. Bus. Communicates, Phi Beta Kappa. Republican. Lutheran. Office: Midlands Cmty Hosp 11111 S 84th St Papillion NE 68046

HULL, ROBERT DALE, insurance agent, investment executive; b. Shenandoah, Iowa, Nov. 18, 1946; s. Dale Andrew and Evelyn Marie (Campbell) H.; m. Sue Ellen McCall, May 27, 1972; children: Patrick, Jonathan. BS, NW Mo. State U., 1968; grad. degree, So. Meth. U., 1985. Chartered fin. cons. Agrl. mgmt. specialist USDA/FMHA, Eldon, Mo., 1970-74; banking officer Bank of Osborn (Mo.), 1974-75; agrl. loan officer 1st Nat. Mercantile Bank, Montgomery City, Mo., 1975-78; sr. v.p. Citizens Bank, Grant City, Mo., 1978-83; spl. agt. Northwestern Mut. Life, Grant City, 1983-90, dist. agt., 1990-93, field dir., 1993—; investment officer Robert W. Baird & Co., Inc., St. Joseph, Mo., 1993-94; spl. agt., 1994—. Mem. CLU Assn., Midland Empire CLU Assn. (pres. 1993—), St. Joseph Life Underwriter Assn., Lions, Masons (sec. Grant City lodge 1988-90). Home: South Pleasant St Grant City MO 64456 Office: Northwestern Mut Life 308 S Main Grant City MO 64456

HULME, MARY ANN K., women's health nurse, administrator; b. Galion, Ohio, July 25, 1952; d. Walter Herman and Mary Elizabeth (Prim) Kumm; m. Roy Allan Hulme, Jan. 8, 1977; children: Eric A., Ann E. BSN, Capital U., 1974; MSN, Case Western Res. U., 1993. RN, Ohio; cert. in ob-gyn., neonatal nursing ANCC. Staff and charge nurse, labor and delivery St. Ann's Hosp., Columbus, Ohio, 1974-76, head nurse, dir. ob-gyn. outpatient clinic, 1976-77; clin. nurse, sr. clin. nurse, head nurse mgr. labor/delivery Univ. Hosps., Cleve., 1977-94; head nurse mgr. labor/delivery antepartum U. Hosps. Cleve., Cleve., 1994—; clin. instr. maternity and gynecology nursing Case Western Res. U., Cleve., 1986—. Contbr. articles to profl. jours. Recipient Silver medals U.S. Figure Skating Assn. Mem. ANA, Assn. Womens Health, Obstet. and Neonatal Nursing, Assn. Oper. Room Nurses, Ohio Nurses Assn., Lake Erie Coun. Nurse Execs., Cleve. Skating Club, Sigma Theta Tau. Lutheran. Home: 16070 S Park Blvd Cleveland OH 44120-1673

HULSE, DEXTER CURTIS, manufacturing executive; b. Woodland, Calif., Oct. 6, 1952; s. Dexter Curtis Hulse and Geraldine Ezabell (Ratliff) Curtis; m. Nancy Sue Culp., Aug. 14, 1971 (div. Jan. 14, 1995); children: Sandra Marie, Jennifer Lynn; m. Diane F. Schultz, Feb. 24, 1995. B.Indsl. Engring., Shawnee State U., Portsmouth, Ohio, 1973; Deg. in Computer Aided Design, Shawnee State U., 1992. Numerical control operator Lodge & Shippley, Cin., 1973-76; journeyman machinist Nat. Mine Svc. Co., Ashland, Ky., 1976-86; regional mgr. A.L. Williams Mktg., Minford, Ohio, 1982-87; pres. D & D Emergency, Wheelersburg, Ohio, 1987-88, Dexter Mfg., Wheelersburg, Ohio, 1988—; instr. Shawnee State Univ., 1988—; sr. inspector Piketon Uranium Enrichment Facility Lockheed Martin Utility Svc., 1995—; mem. computer-aided design adv. bd. Shawnee State U., 1990-92; cons. Scioto Bus. Cons., Wheelersburg, 1986—. Vol. fireman Porter Twp. Fire Dept., Wheelersburg, 1985. Mem. Ch. Nazarene. Office: 8088 Bell St Wheelersburg OH 45694-1613

HULSHOF, KENNY, public defender, prosecutor, state assistant attorney general; b. Sikeston, Mo., May 22, 1958; m. Renee Lynn Howell. BS, U. Mo., 1980; JD, U. Miss., 1983. Rep. candidate for Boone County Prosecutor, 1992, U.S. House, 1994, 96. Roman Catholic. Office: Hulshof for Congress PO Box 1621 Columbia MO 65205*

HULSMAN, ART J., aeronautical engineer; b. Berea, Ohio, Aug. 4, 1967. BS in Aero. and Astron. Engring., Ohio State U., 1989. Sr. project engr. BV Technologies, Cleve., 1991—; cons. BV Technologies, Cleve., 1993—. Mem. Jr. C. of C. (Cleve.) (bd. dirs. 1993—). Office: BV Technologies 5310 W 161st St Cleveland OH 44142-1610

HULTGREN, DENNIS EUGENE, farmer, management consultant; b. Union County, S.D., Mar. 19, 1929; s. John Alfred and Esther Marie (Johnson) H.; grad. high sch.; m. Nelda Ethelyn Olson, Aug. 3, 1957; children: Nancy Hultgren Klemme, Jean Hultgren Doty, Jahn Dennis, Ruth Dorothy Hultgren Henneman. Farmer, Union County, 1953—; commr., chmn. Union County Planning and Zoning Bd., 1972-83; mem. bd. bylaw revision Union County Electric Co., 1983-85. Pres. bd. Union Creek Cemetery, 1958—; pres. bd. mgrs. Union-Sayles Watershed Dist., 1965-70. Treas., Sioux Valley Twp., Union County, 1980—; treas., bd. dirs. W. Union Sch., 1957-67; chmn. Union County Sch. Bd., 1961-68; pres. Alcester (S.D.) Sch. Bd., 1970-77; chmn. Alcester PTA, 1967-68; mem. tech. bd. rev. Southeastern Council Govts., Sioux Falls, S.D., 1976-77; bd. dirs. Siouxland Interstate Met. Planning Council, Sioux City, Iowa, 1977-83, sec. council ofcls., 1978-83; bd. dirs. Old Opera House Community Theater, Akron, Iowa, Akron Area Action Assn., 1983-85, 1983-84, Akron Devel. Corp., 1985-90; Rep. precinct committeeman, 1970—, Union County Rep. Cen. Com., 1970—; chmn. S.D. State Bd. Equalization, 1987-95; mem. synod stewardship bd. Western Iowa Synod Luth. Ch., 1987-90, elected synod assembly bus. and coun. com., 1991-93; S.D. del. Rep. Nat. Conv., New Orleans, 1988. Served with AUS, 1951-53, Korea. Recipient outstanding dedication and service award Old Opera House Community Theatre, 1984, Sioux City Siouxland Disting. Citizen award Siouxland Interstate Met. Planning Council, 1983, Jefferson award Sta. KELO-TV, 1985, Outstanding Community Service award Lions Internat., 1985. Mem. Farm Bur., Farmers Union (exec. bd. Union County 1987-90), S.D. Livestock Feeders Assn., Nat. Cattlemen's Assn., Associated Sch. Bds. S.D. (Merit award 1976), Am. Legion (exec. bd. Akron 1978-92, comdr. Akron 1980-81, 85—, historian 1981—, trustee 1983-90, vice comdr. 9th dist. 1989, chaplain 9th dist. 1990, comdr. 9th dist. 1991, chmn. athletics and contest com., 1991-92, judge advocate 9th dist., Iowa, 1993—), VFW (Alcester, S.D. vice-comdr. 1995—). Lutheran (mem. bd. 1967-70, 82-84, 90-93, lay chmn. 1970, 82-93, chmn. centennial com. 1974). Address: Hulteboda Farm RR 1 Box 227 Akron IA 51001-9601

HULTSTRAND, DONALD MAYNARD, bishop; b. Parkers Prairie, Minn., Apr. 16, 1927; s. Aaron Emmanuel H. and Selma Avendla (Liljegren) H.; m. Marjorie Richter, June 11, 1948; children—Katherine Ann, Charles John. B.A. summa cum laude, Macalester Coll., 1950; B.D. summa cum laude, Kenyon Coll., 1953; M.Div. summa cum laude, Colgate-Rochester Theol. Sem., 1974; D.D. honoris causa, Nashotah Divinity Sch., 1986. Ordained priest Episcopal Ch., 1953, consecrated bishop, 1982. Vicar St. John's Episcopal Ch., Worthington, Minn., 1953-57; rector Grace Meml. Ch., Wabasha, Minn., 1957-62, St. Mark's Episcopal Ch., Canton, Ohio, 1962-68, St. Paul's Episcopal Ch., Duluth, Minn., 1969-75; assoc. rector St. Andrew's Episcopal Ch., Kansas City, Mo., 1968-69; exec. dir. Anglican Fellowship of Prayer, 1975-79; rector Trinity Episcopal Ch., Greeley, Colo., 1979-82; bishop Episcopal Diocese of Springfield, Ill., 1982-91; exec. bd. Episcopal Radio (TV Found.), Atlanta, 1982-87, Anglican Fellowship of Prayer, 1968-93; adv. bd. Episcopal Boys' Homes, Salinas, Kans., 1983-91; com. of execs. Ill. Conf. Chs., 1982-91; mem. House of Bishops, 1982—, Minn. Standing Com., 1970-73; chmn. Minn. Examining Chaplains, 1954-61; chaplain Pewsaction Fellowships U.S.A., 1983-92; pres. Living Ch. Found., 1992—; advisor Diocesan Youth of Minn., 1956-60. Author: The Praying Church, 1978, And God Shall Wipe Away All Tears, 1968, Intercessory Prayer, 1972, Upper Room Dialogues, 1980, Revelations of Effective Prayer, 1995; co-author: The Parish as a Center of Prayer, 1996. Bd. dirs. Sr. Citizens Housing, Duluth, 1972-75, St. Luke's Hosp., Duluth, 1969-75; pres. Low-Rent Housing Project, Greeley, 1979-82. Served with USNR, 1945-46. Recipient Disting. Service award Young Life Minn., 1974; named hon. canon Diocese of Ohio, Cleve., 1967. Mem. Pi Phi Epsilon. Address: 1701 S Lake Le Homme Dieu Dr NE Alexandria MN 56308

HUMBER, WILBUR JAMES, psychologist; b. Winnipeg, Man., Can., June 21, 1911; came to U.S., 1922; s. Arthur W. and Annie Humber; m. Jean Adriansen, May 25, 1945; children: Philip, Scott, Michael. BA, Macalester Coll., 1930; MA, U. Chgo., 1937; PhD, U. Minn., 1942. Diplomate clin. psychology. Dean Kalamazoo (Mich.) Coll., 1941-43; prof. Lawrence U., Appleton, Wis., 1943-46; psychologist Rohrer, Hibler & Replogle, Chgo., 1947-52; sr. ptnr. Humber, Mundie & McClary, Milw., 1952—; bd. dirs. Hopkins Savs. & Loan, Milw., Pope Sci. Corp., Menomonee Falls, Wis. Co-author: Development of Human Behavior, 1951, Introduction to Social Psychology, 1968; editl. bd. Jour. of Consultation. Bd. dirs. Lakeside Children Ctr., Milw., 1966-86; pres. Wis. Mental Health Assn., Milw., 1962-63. Fellow APA, N.Y. Acad. Sci., AAAS; mem. Wis. Psychol. Assn. (founder, 1st pres., Disting. Contbn. award 1984), Milw. Club, Milw. Country Club. Congregationalist. Home: 4012 W Canterbury Ct Mequon WI 53092 Office: Humber Mundie & McClary 111 E Wisconsin Ave Ste 1950 Milwaukee WI 53202-4809

HUMBERT, JAMES RONALD, pediatrician, educator; b. Geneva, Mar. 7, 1938; came to U.S., 1965; s. Roger Williams and Edmee (Germain) H.; m. Hiltrud Maria Hack (div. 1983); children: Christophe, Philippe, Gabriel; m. Linda Lea Heckman. BS, Coll. of Geneva, 1957; MD, U. Geneva, 1964; MS in Pediatrics, U. Colo., 1968; Privat Docent, U. Geneva, 1970. Diplomate Am. Bd. Pediatrics, Am. Bd. Pediatric Hematology-Oncology. Intern and resident in pediatrics U. Colo. Med. Ctr., Denver, 1965-68, rsch. fellow in hematology, 1968-70; chief clinic dept. pediatrics U. Geneva, 1970-72; asst. prof. pediatrics and genetics U. Colo. Health Sci. Ctr., Denver, 1972-76; dir. hematology Children's Hosp., Buffalo, 1976-87; assoc. prof. pediatrics SUNY, Buffalo, 1976-82, prof. pediatrics, 1982-87, prof. microbiology, 1984-87; prof. pediatrics, head hematology-oncology sect. Tulane U. Sch. Med., New Orleans, 1987-92; dir. Sickle Cell Ctr. So. La., New Orleans, 1987-92; dir. hematology-oncology dept. Children's Med. Ctr., Dayton, Ohio, 1992-95; prof. pediatrics Wright State U., Dayton, Ohio, 1992—; dir. Hemophilia Ctr. Western N.Y., dir. transfusion svc. and Sickle Cell Ctr., Children's Hosp., Buffalo, 1975-87; dir. Sickle Cell Program Children's Med. Ctr., Dayton, 1994—; vis. prof. dept. pediatrics U. Geneva Med. Sch., 1995—. Co-author books, contbr. articles in field to profl. jours. Bd. dirs. Ronald McDonald House, New Orleans, Hemophilia Found., Buffalo; bd. trustees Am. Leukemia Soc., New Orleans, S.W. Ohio Chpt. Hemophilia Found.; med. cons. Assn. Rsch. Childhood Cancer, Buffalo; mem. Niagara Frontier Assn. for Sickle Cell Disease, Buffalo. Fellow Am. Acad. Pediatrics; mem. AMA, Internat. Hemophilia Assn., Swiss Nat. Med. Soc., Coll. Immunology Buffalo. Democrat. Presbyterian.

HUMBLE, JIMMY LOGAN, engineer; b. Columbia, Ky., Dec. 6, 1944; s. William Rymon and Maxine (Brockman) H. B.S. in Elem. Edn., Western Ky. U., 1972. Field reporter Adair County, Columbia, 1963-66; surveyor Agr. Stabilization Com., Muskingum County Edn. Dept., Zanesville, Ohio, 1966-73; road engr. ARA/Smith's, Columbus, Ohio, 1974-88; trustee Teamster's Local 413, Columbus, 1983-85; mem. Colonial Williamsburg Found., Ohio Historical Soc., Nat. Trust for Historic Preservation, Athens Co. Hist. Soc., Meigs Co. Hist. Soc., People For Am. Way, Nat. Geog. Soc. Mem. Fraternal Order Police, Smithsonian Instn., Regenerative Agr. Assn., Internat. Platform Assn., Ohio Ctr. Sci. and Space Industry, Pub. Libr. Columbus and Franklin County (fellow), Ohio Auto Club, Centurian (Columbus) Club, 4-H (Columbia) Club, Future Farmers Am. Sentinel Club, WKU Club (life), Moose Lodge. Democrat. Methodist. Avocations: reading, travel, writing. Home: 351 Garden Heights Ave PO Box 28098 Columbus OH 43228-0098

HUME, DEAN BRADLEY, secondary education educator, writer; b. Akron, Ohio, June 9, 1958; s. Harold Earnest and Honora Devine (Smith) Hume. BSEd, Ohio U., 1981; MA in Journalism, Kent State U., 1992. Tchr. journalism, advisor publs. Lakota H.S., West Chester, Ohio, 1992—; mem. North Ctrl. accreditation com. Hamilton H.S., 1995-96; adj. prof. Sch. Journalism Kent State U., 1990-93. Author: textbook on sportswriting and interviewing, 1992; contbg. editor C:JET quar., 1995—; sports stringer Del. Gazette, 1982-90. Youth coach Delaware (Ohio) Parks and Recreation Baseball Assn., 1982-89; dir., 1986. Recipient awards; named Adviser of Yr. Dow Jones Newspaper Fund Dist., 1993. Mem. Soc. Profl. Journalists, Journalism Edn. Assn., Journalism Assn. Ohio Schs. (v.p. 1995, pres. 1996—). Home: 6834 Sampson Ln No 3 Cincinnati OH 45236 Office: Lakota HS 5050 Tylersville Rd West Chester OH 45069

HUME, DONALD E., state legislator; b. Winslow, Ind., June 13, 1926; m. Shirley; children: Denise, Roxanne, Darcee. Grad., Oakland City Coll.; AA, Ind. State U., BA, MA. Mem. dist. 63 Ind. State Ho. of Reps., 1974—; minority whip, 1981-82, mem. ethics com., fin. inst. and ways and means coms., co-chmn. taxation com., vice-chmn. aged and aging com., also tchr. Mem. PTA. Mem. NEA, VFW, Am. Legion, Ind. State Tchrs. Assn. Home: RR 2 Box 40 Winslow IN 47598-9609 Address: RR 1 Winslow IN 47598*

HUME, HORACE DELBERT, manufacturing company executive; b. Endeavor, Wis., Aug. 15, 1898; s. James Samuel and Lydia Alberta (Sawyer) H.; student pub. schs.; m. Minnie L. Harlan, June 2, 1926 (dec. May 1972); 1 child, James; m. Sarah D. Lyles Rood, Apr. 6, 1973 (dec. Jan. 1988); m. Dorothy L. Bohan Greenwood, Nov. 15, 1989 (dec. May 1994). Stockman and farmer, 1917-19; with automobile retail business, Garfield, Wash., 1920-21, ptnr. and asst. mgr., 1921-27; automobile and farm machine retailer, Garfield, ptnr., mgr., 1928-35, gen. mgr. Hume-Love Co., Garfield, 1931-35, pres., 1935-57; ptnr., gen. mgr. H.D. Hume Co., Mendota, Ill., 1944-52; pres. H.D. Hume Co., Inc., 1952—; ptnr. Hume and Hume, 1952-72; pres. Hume Products Corp., 1953-95; pres., dir. Hume-Fry Co., Garden City, Kans., 1955-73; dir. Granberry Products, Inc., Eagle River, Wis. Mayor, Garfield, Wash., 1938-40, Hart Carter Co., Mpls., 1965-71. Named to Sr. Illinoisians Hall of Fame, 1995. Bd. dirs. Mendota Hosp. Found., 1949-73, pres., 1949-54; bd. dirs. Mendota Swimming Pool Assn.; mem. City Planning Commn., 1953-72, chmn., 1953-69; mem. Regional Planning Commn., LaSalle County, Ill., 1965-73, chmn., 1965-71; active Schs. Central Com., 1953—, LaSalle County Zoning Commn., 1966—, LaSalle County Care and Treatment Bd., 1970-73; chmn. Mendota Watershed Com., 1967-73; pres. Hume Found., 1993, Mendota Mus. & Hist. Soc., 1993, 95. Recipient Key to City City of Mendota, 1988, Cert. of Appreciation City of Mendota, 1988, Wisdon of Honor award The Wisdom Soc., 1970, Friends of the Graves-Hume Libr. Philanthropic and Humanitarian Svcs. award, Am. Patriot award The Founders Soc., 1994, Cmty. Bldrs. award Mendota Lodge No176AF8AM, 1994; named Grand Marshall Sweet Corn Fesitval Parade by Mendota Ill. C. of C., 1993; recognized part of 100 Most Significant Contbr. to Mechanization of Agr. 1893-1993, by Equipment Mfrs. Inst.; Am. Soc. Agrl. Engring. Hist. Landmark named in honor, 1993. Mem. Am. Soc. Agrl. Engrs., Eagle River (Wis.) C. of C. (pres., dir. 1962-63), Mendota C. of C. (pres. 1948-49, dir. 1946-49, Cmty. Svc. award 1972, H.D. Hume Award named in his honor 1993, Ill. 1st Libr. Ptnrs. Carnegie award 1994). Republican. Presbyterian (elder). Clubs: Kiwanis (pres. 1953, dir. 1954, Paul Harris fellow, George F. Hixson award 1994, Legion of Honor-50Yrs.), Masons (named Master Mason), Shriners, Order Eastern Star, Elks. Patentee in various fields. Home: 702 Carolyn PO Box 677 Mendota IL 61342 Office: 1015 Main St Mendota IL 61342-1604

HUME, LINDEL O., state legislator; m. Judith Hume. BS, Oakland city Coll.; postgrad., U. Evansville. Mgr. internal auditing Potter & Brumfield; rep. Ind. Ho. of Reps., 1974-82; senator dist. 48 Ind. State Senate, 1982—, minority whip, mem. agr. and small bus. com., mem. ethics, interstate coop and transp. com., ranking mem. elec. com., mem. rules and legis. procedure com., ranking minority mem. govt. and regulatory affairs com. Mem. adv. bd. Gibson County Salvation Army. Mem. Inst. Internal Auditors (past pres.), Kiwanis (past pres.). Home: 1797 Concord Dr Princeton IN 47670-9762 Office: State Senate State Capitol Indianapolis IN 46204*

HUMERICKHOUSE, JOE D., state legislator; m. Thelma Humerickhouse. Ind. fee appraiser Osage City, Kans.; mem. from dist. 59 Kans. State Ho. of Reps., Topeka. Address: 912 S 5th Osage City KS 66523

HUMES, H(ARVEY) DAVID, nephrologist, educator; b. Honolulu, Nov. 20, 1947; s. William and Nancy Humes; m. Dolores Humes; 1 child, Michael David. BA, U. Calif., Berkeley, 1969; MD, U. Calif., San Francisco, 1973. Diplomate Am. Bd. Internal Medicine. Intern Moffit Hosp. and U. Calif. Hosps., San Francisco, Calif., 1973-74; resident U. Calif. Hosps., San Francisco, 1974-75; clin. fellow nephrology U. Pa. Hosp., Phila., 1975-76; rsch. fellow lab. kidney & electrolyte physiology Peter Bent Brigham Hosp., Boston, Mass., 1976-77; instr. Harvard U., Boston, Mass., 1977-78; asst. prof. medicine Harvard U., Boston, 1978-79; asst. prof. internal medicine U. Mich., Ann Arbor, 1979-82, assoc. prof. internal medicine, 1982-86, prof. internal medicine, 1986—; founder, gen. ptnr., mgr. EpiGenesis, LLC; founder, dir., pres. Nephros Therapeutics, Inc.; cons. Sandoz Pharm., Bristol-Myers-Squibb, Sterling-Winthrop, AmGen.; instr., asst. prof. Peter Bent Brigham Hosp., Boston, 1977-79; dir., chief Nephrology Rsch. Labs., U. Mich., Ann Arbor, 1980-81, chmn. dept. internal medicine, 1996—; chief med. svc. VA Med. Ctr., Ann Arbor, 1983-96. Contbr. articles to profl. jours. Grantee Nat. Kidney Found., 1981-83, 84-85, 87-88, PHS, 1982-93, 87—, VA, 1982-83, 83-87, 87-90, 90-93, 93—, Am. Heart Assn., 1982-87, 94-95. Fellow, ACP; mem. AAAS, Am. Physiol. Soc., Am. Soc. Biol. Chemists, Am. Soc. Renal Chemistry & Metabolism, Am. Soc. Clin. Investigation, Am. Heart Assn., Am. Soc. Nephrology, Am. Fedn. Clin. Rsch., Internat. Soc. Nephrology, Nat. Kidney Found., Nat. Kidney Found. Mich. (pres.'s award), Ctrl. Soc. Clin. Rsch., Alpha Omega Alpha, Phi Beta Kappa. Office: U Mich Med Ctr 3101 Taubman Box 0368 1500 E Medical Ctr Dr Ann Arbor MI 48109-0368

HUMKE, RAMON L., utility executive; b. Quincy, Ill., Nov. 19, 1932; s. E.G. and Florence K. (Koch) H.; m. Carolyn Jacobs Humke, Nov. 20, 1955; 1 child, Steven K. Ed., Quincy Coll., 1952-53, Springfield (Ill.) Coll., Ill., 1956-58, Carleton Coll., 1968; LLD, U. Indpls., 1988. Various mgmt. positions Ill. Bell Telephone Co., 1951-73; dir. forecasting and productivity AT&T, N.Y.C., 1974-75; v.p. pers. Ill. Bell Tel. Co., Chgo., 1978-82; v.p. corp. affairs Ameritech, Chgo., 1982-83; pres., CEO Ind. Bell Telephone Co. Inc., Indpls., 1983-89, Ameritech Svcs., 1989-90; pres., COO Indpls. Power & Light Co., 1990—; vice chmn. Ipalco Enterprises, Inc. Indpls., 1991—; chmn. bd. Meridian Ins. Group, Meridian Mut. Ins. Co.; bd. dirs. NBD Bank, N.A., LDI Mgmt., Indpls. Power and Light Co., Ipalco Ent., Inc. Chmn. Indpls. Symphony Found., 1990—, 500 Festival, 1991—, Infrastructure Commn., 1990, Indpls.; vice chmn. Indpls. C. of C., 1990—; bd. dirs. Cmty. Hosp., 1993—; trustee U. Indpls., 1987—. With U.S. Army, 1953-56, ETO. Named Ky. Col., 1983, Ark. Traveler, 1985, Sagamore of the Wabash, 1987, 89; recipient medal of merit U.S. Treasury Dept., 1984, 85, Charles Whistler award, 1989, Benjamin Harrison medallion award, 1990, Americanism award, 1991, Good Scout award Boy Scouts Am., 1993, Hoosier Heritage award, 1993. Mem. Columbia Club, Crooked Stick Golf Club, Indpls. Athletic Club, Meridian Hills Country Club, Skyline Club (bd. govs.), Twin Lakes Golf Club.

HUMMEL, JOHN WILLIAM, agricultural engineer; b. Grantsville, Md., Nov. 1, 1940; s. Harry Wilmer and Rhoda Ruth (Shumaker) H.; m. Judith Carol Minick, Aug. 1, 1964; children: John William Jr., Lisa Marie, Mark Devon, Lori René. BS Agrl. Engring., U. Md., 1964, MS, 1966; PhD, U. Ill., 1970. Registered profl. engr., Md. Asst. prof. agrl. engring. U. Md., College Park, 1969-73, assoc. prof. agrl. engring., 1973-76; agrl. engr. USDA-Agrl. Rsch. Svc., Urbana, Ill., 1976—; cons. Doxiadis Assoc. Internat., Athens, Greece, 1974-75. Contbr. over 80 articles to profl. jours. USDA-ARS grantee, 1985-86, 88-89. Mem. Am. Soc. Agrl. Engrs., Exchange (pres. Urbana club 1994-95). Home: 504 E Mumford Dr Urbana IL 61801-6216 Office: USDA-Agrl Rsch Svc 1304 W Pennsylvania Ave Urbana IL 61801-4726

HUMMER, TERRY G., stockbroker; b. Topeka, Jan. 16, 1951. BS in Archtl. Engring., Kans. U., 1974. Head designer Whelans Lumber Co., Topeka, 1972-75, ArmCo Steel, Topeka, 1975-77; v.p. Flynn Hills Devel., Topeka, 1977-80; owner RUH Inc., Topeka, 1980—; stockbroker Paine Webber, Topeka, 1986—. Coach various soccer clubs, 1978—. Mem. C. of C. Republican. Home: 4431 NW Green Hills Rd Topeka KS 66618-5812 Office: Paine Webber 634 S Kansas Ave Topeka KS 66603-3804

HUMMER, THOMAS MICHAEL, transportation executive; b. Toledo, Nov. 12, 1942; s. Lawrence Finton and Edity May (Bell) H.; m. Anne Marie Warnement, Apr., 16, 1966. BBA, U. Toledo, 1968. Office clk., mgr. Jones Transfer Co., Toledo, 1962-71; traffic mgr. Jones Transfer Co., Monroe, Mich., 1971-84, asst. sec., 1981-84, v.p., dir. traffic, 1984-87; v.p. mktg. support svcs. Customer First, Inc./City Transfer and Storage Co., Monroe, 1987; v.p. bus. analysis Trans Jones, Inc and subs., Monroe, 1988—, corp. sec., dep. dir. info. svcs. and tech., 1989; instr. transp. regulation U. Toledo, 1978-84, instr., transp. mgmt. program coord. Cmty. and Tech. Coll., 1993—; mem. adv. com. Henry Ford C.C., Dearborn, Mich., 1983-84, adv. com. Inst. Traffic and Transp., Cleve., 1985; chmn. communications project team Automotive Industry Action Group, Southfield, Mich., 1984-85. Bd. dirs. Canterbury Forest Lot Owners Assn., Lamberville, Mich., 1972-73; mem. 2025 regional transp. plan task force Toledo Met. Area Coun. Govts., 1995-96. Mem. Assn. Transp. Practitioners (chpt. pres. 1983-84, chpt. bd. dirs. 1984-88, nat. com. on edn. 1987-89, cert.), Am. Soc. Transp. Logistics, Inc., Coun. Logistics Mgmt. (v.p. edn. Toledo Roundtable 1995—), Delta Nu Alpha Transp., Theta Chi. Republican. Roman Catholic. Home: 5455 Brookshire St Monroe MI 48161-5001 Office: U Toledo Cmty & Tech Coll Scott Pk Campus Rm FA 136 Toledo OH 43606-3390

HUMPHREY, HUBERT HORATIO, III, state attorney general; b. Mpls., June 26, 1942; s. Hubert Horatio and Muriel (Buck) H.; m. Nancy Lee Humphrey, Aug. 14, 1963; children: Lorie, Pam, Hubert Horatio IV. B.A. in Polit. Sci., Am. U., Washington, 1965; J.D., U. Minn., 1969. Bar: Minn. Sole practice law, 1970-82; mem. Minn. State Senate, 1972-82; atty. gen. State of Minn., St. Paul, 1983—. Bd. mgmt. Northwest br. YMCA. Mem. ABA, Minn. Bar Assn., Hennepin County Bar Assn., Nat. Assn. Atty.'s Gen. (pres. 1993-94). Mem. Democratic-Farmer-Labor Party. Office: Office of Atty Gen State Capitol Rm 102 Saint Paul MN 55155

HUMPHREY, RONALD MURRAY, educator, publisher; b. San Jose, Calif., Sept. 4, 1941; s. Robert Murray and Roberta Marie (Spedding) H.; m. Joanne Fenton, Aug. 15, 1980; 1 child, Robert. BS, Cal Poly U., San Luis Obispo, 1962-65. Mgr. Harris, Inc., Cleve., 1966-68, Datilgrew Mfg. Co., San Francisco, 1968-70; vocat. print. tchr. Dos Pueblos H.S., Goleta, Calif., 1970-78; prof. Cuyahoga Cmty. Coll., Cleve., 1979—; cons., prof. graphic arts industry; pub. short vols. for local artists Windhammer Adventure Pub. Mem. Graphic Arts Tech. Found., Craftman's Club, Printing Industries of Am. Home: 289 S Franklin St Chagrin Falls OH 44022 Office: Cuyatioga Cmty Coll 11000 Pleasant Valley Rd Parma OH 44129

HUMPHREYS, DAVID LEROY, musician; b. Oak Park, Ill., Nov. 2, 1941; s. George Wilson and Mary Ann (Drennan) H. BA, N. Ctrl. Coll., 1965. Sr. systems engr. IBM, Oak Brook, Ill., 1965-91; musician, concert promoter Downers Grove, Ill., 1957—; bd. dirs. Plank Rd. Folk Music Soc., Brookfield, Ill., 1985—. Pres. DuPage County Bd. Health, Wheaton, Ill., 1977-84; trustee Downers Grove Pub. Libr., 1993—; commr. Comty. Events Commn., Downers Grove, 1987—; bd. dirs. Vis. Bur., Downers Grove, 1989—; dir. Two Way St. Coffee House, Downers Grove, 1970—. Mem. N.Am. Folk Music and Dance Alliance. Home and Office: 4221 Saratoga Ave Apt 315 Downers Grove IL 60515-1968

HUMPHRIES, ROGER LEE, postal service administrator; b. Lexington, Ky., Dec. 11, 1951; s. Walter Kenneth and Margaret Louise (Campbell) H.; m. Donna Kay Mraz, June 27, 1987; children: Christopher Alan, Jillian Louise. A in Criminal Justice, U. Nebr., Omaha, 1976, BS in Criminal Justice, 1977; A in Comml. Photography, Metro Tech. C.C., Omaha, 1985, A in Postal Mgmt., 1991. Youth svc. counselor Christian Home, 1977-78; letter carrier U.S. Postal Svc., Omaha, 1978-82, computerized forwarding supr., 1982, sta. ops. supt., 1982-92, customer rels. mgr., 1993—, mem. Omaha postal customer coun., 1993—, mem. Metro Omaha postal customer adv. coun., 1993—. Pres. Benson Neighborhood Assn., Omaha, 1994-95; bd. dirs. Omaha Neighborhood Courage, 1995—, Omaha Food Bank, 1995—. Named to Order of Ky. Cols., Order Nebr. Admirals. Mem. Nat. Assn. Postal Suprs. (legis. com), Pub. Rels. Soc. Am. (com. 1994-95), Omaha Press Club (com. 1994-95), Greater Omaha Commodore Computer Club (pres., sec., news editor 1982-95), Bryan Sta. Alumni Assn., U. Nebr. Omaha Alumni Assn. Democrat. Baptist. Home: 4971 Miami St Omaha NE 68104-4475 Office: US Postal Svc 1124 Pacific St Omaha NE 68108-9802

HUNEKE, WAYNE ROBERT, insurance company financial executive; b. Council Bluffs, Iowa, June 10, 1951; s. Fred and Virginia Mae (Hickox) H.; m. Marily Jean Huso, June 13, 1975; children: Thomas, Sara. B of Bus. Adminstrn., U. Iowa, 1973. CPA, Minn. Various positions Coopers & Lybrand, Mpls., 1973-86; various positions ReliaStar Fin. Corp., Mpls., 1986-94, CFO, 1994—. Mem. Bus. Econs. Edn. Found. (bd. dirs. 1995—).

HUNGATE, WILLIAM LEONARD, retired federal judge, former congressman; b. Benton, Ill., Dec. 14, 1922; s. Leonard Wathen and Maude Irene (Williams) H.; m. Dorothy N. Wilson, Apr. 13, 1944; children: William David, Margie Kay (Mrs. Branson L. Wood III). A.B., U. Mo., 1943; LL.B., Harvard U., 1948; LL.D. (hon.), Culver-Stockton Coll., Canton, Mo., 1968; J.D. (hon.), Central Meth. Coll., Fayette, Mo., 1975. Bar: Mo. 1948, Ill. 1949, U.S. Supreme Ct 1960, D.C. 1967. Practiced law Troy, Mo., 1948-68, St. Louis, 1977-79; sr. partner firm Hungate and Grewach, 1956-68; partner firm Thompson and Mitchell, St. Louis, 1977-79; judge U.S. Dist. Ct. Eastern Dist. Mo., 1979-92; pros. atty. Lincoln County, Mo., 1951-55; spl. asst. atty. gen. of Mo., 1958-64; rsch. adminstrn. criminal justice in U.S. Am. Bar Found., 1956; mem. 88th-94th congresses, 9th Dist. Mo.; mem. judiciary com., chmn. subcom. criminal justice, select com. on small bus., chmn. subcom. on activities of regulary agys.; vis. prof. polit. sci. U. Mo., St. Louis, 1977-79. Author: It Wasn't Funny at the Time, 1994. Chmn. small bus. adv. com. Treasury Dept., 1977; chmn. Mo. Gov.'s Commn. on Campaign Reform and Ofcl. Conduct, 1978-79; mem. Adv. Com. on Criminal Rules, 1977-86. Mem. ABA (nat. conf. of fed. trial judges exec. com. 1980-86, chmn. 1985-86), FBA, ASCAP, Ill. Bar Assn., Mo. Bar Assn., Harvard Law Sch. Assn. Mo. (pres. 1962-64, 83-84, coun. mem.), Mo. Squires, Jud. Conf. U.S. (com. on jud. br. 1987-90), 8th Cir. Dist. Judges Assn. (pres. 1984-86). Mem. Troy Christian Ch. (chmn. bd. 1964). Club: Kiwanian (Troy) (pres. 1951, lt. gov. 1959). Home: 26 Chapel Hill Est Saint Louis MO 63131-1315 Office: Hungate Rsch Consulting 180 S Weidman Rd Ste 123 Ballwin MO 63021-5724

HUNGIVILLE, MAURICE NEILL, educator; b. Bradford, Pa., July 10, 1936; s. Maurice Hungiville and June (Neill) Hulme. BA, St. Bonaventure, 1959; MA, Western Res. U., 1961; PhD, U. Tenn., 1965. Instr. Marshall U., Huntington, W.Va., 1962-64; prof. Mich. State U., East Lansing, 1966-95; cons. editor Mich. State U. Press, East Lansing, 1995—. Author: From a Single Window: A History of the Michigan State University Press, 1996; contbr. articles to profl. jours. Home: 4746 Ottawa Dr Okemos MI 48864 Office: Mich State Univ Press 1405 S Harrison Rd East Lansing MI 48824

HUNHOFF, BERNIE P., state legislator; b. Yankton, S.D., Sept. 5, 1951; s. Bernard P. Sr. and Margaret (Modde) H.; m. Myrna Mulloy, 1974; children: Katie, Chris. BA, Mt. Marty Coll., 1974. Legis. aide U.S. Rep. Frank Denholm, 1974; chmn. Yankton County Dem. Party, 1984-86; mem. S.D. Senate, 1993—, mem. appropriations com.; pub. rels. dir. U. S.D. Sch.Medicine, 1977-79; editor, pub. The Observer, Yankton, S.D., 1979-85, S.D. Mag., Yankton, 1985—. Co-author: Uniquely S.D., 1989—. Home: PO Box 175 Yankton SD 57078-0175*

HUNT, DAVID CLAUDE, sales and marketing executive; b. Chippewa Falls, Wis., June 16, 1957; s. Claude Martin and Lucille Johanna (Gehl) H.; m. Cheryl Elizabeth Martens, Mar. 21, 1980; children: Elizabeth Anne, Rebecca Jeanne. B in Music Edn., U. Wis., Eau Claire, 1980. Bookkeeper Claude Hunt Dry Wall Service, Chippewa Falls, 1971-79; band dir. Glenwood City (Wis.) Middle Sch., 1980; band dir., computer instr. Toulon-Lafayette (Ill.) Schs., 1980-84; band dir. Cathedral High Sch., St. Cloud, Minn., 1984-86; with computer sales dept. Team Electronics, St. Cloud, 1986; dir. edn. sales and mktg. Computers of St. Cloud, 1987-91, dir. support svcs., 1992; devel. dir. Ed Tech, St. Cloud, 1993; agent The Franklin Ins. Co., St. Cloud, 1993-94; pres. Hunt Enterprises, 1994—; mktg. comm. mgr. JDL Techs., Mpls., 1995—; instr. in computers Dist. 742 Schs. Community Edn., St. Cloud, 1985-90; cons. Computer Tutor Svcs., St. Cloud, 1985-88; presenter at profl. confs. Contbr. articles to profl. jours.; editor: (newsletter) Education Solutions, 1987-93. Mem. nat. adv. bd. Achievement Acad., 1984; founder, dir. Stark County Cmty. Band, 1981-83; mem. com. Ctrl. Luth. Ch., Chippewa Falls, 1979; mem. coun. Salem Luth. Ch., St. Cloud, 1989-91, Discovery Elem. Sch. Site Coun., 1993-96. Recipient Computing Family of Yr. 5th pl. award, 1986, Apple Computer Ednl. Newsletter award, 1988-89, Apple Edn. Visionary award, 1992. Mem. Nat. Assn. Desktop Pubs., Internat. Soc. for Tech. in Edn., Ctrl. Minn. Volkssport Assn. (co-founder, v.p. 1991, treas. 1993), Am. Volkssport Assn. (program devel. com. 1991-93, publicity com. 1993-95, recipient Meritorious Svc. award 1993), Minn. Volkssport Assn. (treas. 1989, pres. 1990-93), Phi Mu Alpha Sinfonia. Republican. Office: JDL Techs Inc 5555 W 78th St Edina MN 55439-2702

HUNT, DIXIE LOUISE, career counselor; b. Stuart, Iowa, May 30, 1937. Sales trainer Con-Stan Industries, Des Moines, 1968-78; sales assoc. Pitney Bowes, Des Moines, 1978-82; v.p. Pers. Inc., Des Moines, 1982-95; herbalist, reflexologist, iridologist, natural health advisor Stuart, Iowa, 1995—; facilitator Exec. Circle, Des Moines, 1983-94. Mem. T.G.I.F. Republican. Pentecostal. Office: 604 Locust St Ste 516 Des Moines IA 50309-3720

HUNT, DOUGLAS A., state legislator; b. May 31, 1945; m. Marlene Hunt. BA, U. Notre Dame, 1967. Indsl. developer; state rep. Dist. 10 Ind. State Senate, 1976—, mem. fin. com., ranking minority mem., mem. planning and pub. svc. com., mem. transp. interstate coop. com., mem. consumer affairs com. Home: 915 Weber Sq South Bend IN 46617-1850 also: State Senate State Capitol Indianapolis IN 46204*

HUNT, FERN ENSMINGER, retired home economics educator, researcher; b. Mount Perry, Ohio, May 11, 1926; d. Charles Henry and Mary Elpha (Koehler) Ensminger; m. David Simeon Hunt, June 13, 1953 (dec. Mar. 1990). BS, The Ohio State U., Columbus, 1948, MS, 1954, PhD, 1965. Home svc. rep. Ohio Edison Co., Akron, 1948-52; grad. tchg. asst. The Ohio State U., Columbus, 1952-54; instr. to prof. Ohio Agrl. Rsch. & Devel. Ctr. & Ohio State U., Columbus, 1954-88; prof. emeritus The Ohio State U., Columbus, 1988; trustee Underwriters Labs., Inc., Northbrook, Ill., 1979-88; reviewer Food Technology, Chgo., 1975-85, Family and Consumer Scis. Rsch. Jour., Arlington, Va., 1975—. Vol. statistician Internat. Vis. Coun., Inc., Columbus, 1990—. Recipient Disting. Svc. award Coll. of Home Econs. Ohio State U., 1988, Home Economist of the Yr. award Ohio Home Econs. Assn., 1989. Fellow AAAS; mem. Am. Assn. Family and Consumer Scis. (chmn. rsch. sect. 1948—, chmn. profl. sect.), Inst. Food Technologies, Phi Upsilon, Omicron Nu. Home: 4692 Scenic Dr Columbus OH 43214

HUNT, H. TY, stockbroker; b. Cleve., June 12, 1955. Stockbroker E. F. Hutton, Cleve., 1987-88, Prescott-Ball-Turbon, Cleve., 1988-92, McDonald & Co. Securities, Cleve., 1992—. Host radio show on investments. Active Boy Scouts Am. Republican. Roman Catholic. Office: McDonald & Co Securities 30050 Chagrin Blvd Ste 150 Cleveland OH 44124-5704

HUNT, JEFFREY BRIAN, lawyer; b. Huntington, W.Va., Sept. 23, 1958; s. Bernard Ray and Nadine Dora (Meadows) H.; m. Krista Moorman, May 14, 1983. BA magna cum laude, Marshall U., 1980; JD summa cum laude, U. Ky., 1983. Bar: Mo. 1983, Ill. 1984, U.S. Ct. Appeals (8th cir.) 1984. Assoc. Lewis & Rice, 1983-93; mem. Lewis, Rice & Fingersh, L.C., St. Louis, 1993—; adj. instr. Washington U., St. Louis, 1983-89, 96—. Mem. Bar Assn. Met. St. Louis, Order of Coif, Omicron Delta Kappa. Democrat. Methodist. Home: 2220 Stonegate Manor Ct Chesterfield MO 63017-7126 Office: Lewis Rice and Fingersh LC 500 N Broadway Ste 2000 Saint Louis MO 63102-2130

HUNT, JOHN STEPHEN, inference reader, spiritual counselor; b. Ann Arbor, Mich., Aug. 20, 1935; s. Robert Edgar and Katherine Rachel (McDonald) H. Student, George Washington U., 1954, U. Exeter, 1955, U. Calif., Berkeley, 1966-68, Harvard U., 1968. Cert. psychic counselor. Rights and permissions asst. New Am. Libr. Inc., N.Y.C., 1961-63; intake coord. Lake Bluff Homes for Children, Chgo., 1971-73; office mgr. Metro-Help/Nat. Runaway Switchboard, Chgo., 1974-75; lit. agt. pvt. practice, Chgo., 1978-80; acquisitions/outreach Lambda Resource Ctr. for Blind, Chgo., 1981-86; spiritual counselor The 1st Temple of Universal Law, Chgo., 1991—; inference reader pvt. practice, Chgo., 1986—. Author of poetry. Co-founder Lambda Resource Ctr. for Blind, 1979; mem. Horizons Community Svcs., Chgo., 1979. With U.S. Army, 1956-57. Mem. Am. Apitherapy Soc. Inc., Gay and Lesbian Press Assn., Nat. Lesbian and Gay Journalists Assn., Gerber-Hart Libr. Archives, Lesbian/Gay Studies Newsletter, Clippers Club. Democrat. Home and Office: 4727 N Malden St Ste 202 Chicago IL 60640-4807

HUNT, LAMAR, professional football team executive; b. 1932; s. H.L. and Lyda (Bunker) H.; m. Norma Hunt; children: Lamar, Sharron, Clark, Daniel. Grad., So. Meth. U. Founder, owner Kansas City Chiefs, NFL, 1959—, pres., 1959-76, chmn., 1977-78; founder, pres. AFL, 1959; (became Am. Football Conf.-NFL 1970); pres. Am. Football Conf., 1970—. Bd. dirs. Profl. Football Hall of Fame, Canton, Ohio. Named Salesman of Yr., Kansas City Advt. and Sales Execs. Club, 1963, Southwesterner of Yr., Tex. Sportswriters Assn., 1959. Office: Kans City Chiefs 1 Arrowhead Dr Kansas City MO 64129-1651

HUNT, LAWRENCE HALLEY, JR., lawyer; b. Chgo., July 15, 1943; s. Lawrence Halley Sr. and Mary Hamilton (Johnson) H.; children: Caroline Smith, Laura Hamilton, Darwin Halley. AB, Dartmouth Coll., 1965; Cert. l'Institut d'Etudes Politiques, Paris, 1966; JD, U. of Chgo., 1969. Bar: N.Y. 1970, Ill. 1971, U.S. Ct. Appeals (9th cir.) 1980, U.S. Ct. Appeals (2nd cir.) 1981, U.S. Supreme Ct. 1981. Assoc. Davis Polk & Wardwell, N.Y.C., 1969-70; assoc. Sidley & Austin, Chgo., 1970, ptnr., 1975—; chmn. commodities, futures and options subcom. Internat. Bar Assn., 1993-95. Advisor securities adv. com. Ill. Sec. of State, Springfield, 1977-87; prof. IIT Chgo.-Kent Coll. Law Grad. Program Fin. Svcs. Law, 1987—. James B. Reynolds scholar Dartmouth Coll., 1965-66. Mem. ABA (com. on commodity regulation, past chmn. subcom. on futures commn. merchants, mem. exec. coun.). Republican. Clubs: Mid-Day, Chgo., Indian Hill (Winnetka, Ill.). Office: Sidley & Austin One First Nat Plz Chicago IL 60603

HUNT, LUKE LELAND, secondary education educator; b. Gillet, Wis., Dec. 24, 1940; s. Adolph A. and Natalie (Barthuly) H.; m. Darlene E. Goeringer, June 30, 1962; children: Laurel Ann, Kristin Kay, Stephen Luke. Student, Grace Bible Coll., Grand Rapids, Mich., 1961; BS in Biol. Sci., Manchester Coll., North Manchester, Ind., 1965; MS in Sci. Edn., St. Francis Coll., Ft. Wayne, Ind., 1972. Cert. in biol. sci. edn. Tchr. biology and physics Caribbean Grace Acad., Ponce, P.R., 1965-68; tchr. vocat. taxidermy Upper Wabash Vocat. Sch., Wabash, Ind., 1968-70; tchr. biology, applied sci., environ. sci. Whitko H.S., South Whitley, Ind., 1970—. Editor newsletter; author articles and procs. Explorer advisor Boy Scouts Am., South Whitley, 1988-95. Recipient Alumni Svc. award Manchester Coll., 1993; Lilly Endowment fellow, 1989; Eisenhower grantee, 1991; Miami Indian Tribe sci.-math. fellow, 1994. Mem. NEA, Ind. State Tchr. Assn., Nat. Sci. Tchr. Assn., United Teaching Profession (pres. of local), Hoosier Assn. Sci. Tchrs., Ind. Assn. Biology Tchrs. (pres. 1993), Ducks Unltd. (chair Manchester chpt. 1991-92), Phi Delta Kappa. Home: 1502 Briarwood Dr North Manchester IN 46962

HUNT, MARY REILLY, organization executive; b. N.Y., Apr. 17, 1921; d. Philip R. and Mary C. (Harten) Reilly; m. Robert R. Hunt, Apr. 10, 1943,; children: Marianne Schram, Philip R., Robert R., Elise Paul. Student, CCNY, 1939. Tax investigator Ind. Dept. Revenue, 1970-80; pres. Ind. Right to Life, 1973-77; treas. Nat. Right to Life Com., Washington, 1974, 77, 78, mem. exec. com., 1974, 76-81, vice chmn., 1976, exec. dir., 1978, dir. devel., 1979-94, v.p. devel., 1994—, hon. bd. mem., 1983—; pres. Mary Reilly Hunt & Assoc., Inc., South Bend, Ind., 1985—. Bd. dirs., v.p. YWCA, 1968-73, bd. dirs. Mental Health Assn. St. Joseph Co., 1972-78; candidate for state legis., 1988; mem. St. Joseph County Rep. precinct com., South Bend, 1964-79, alt. del. to Nat. Rep. Conv., 1976, 84, 88, 92. Mem. NAFE, Women Bus. Owners, South Bend Symphony Women's Assn. Republican. Roman Catholic. Office: Nat Right to Life Com 1102 N Lafayette Blvd South Bend IN 46616-1136

HUNT, MICHAEL O'LEARY, wood science and engineering educator; b. Louisville, Dec. 9, 1935; s. George Henry and Tressie (Truax) H.; children: Elizabeth H. Schwartz, Lynne T. Lattimer, Michael O. Jr. BS, U. Ky., 1957; M.Forestry, Duke U., 1958; PhD, N.C. State U., 1970. Product engr. Wood Products div. Singer Co., Pickens, S.C., 1959-60; asst. prof. wood sci. Purdue U., West Lafayette, Ind., 1960-70, assoc. prof., 1970-79, prof. and dir. Wood Rsch. Lab., 1979—. Contbr. articles to over 60 scientific and technical publs. V.p. Wabash Valley Trust for Historic Preservation, Lafayette, 1991-96. Recipient Servaas Meml. award Hist. Landmarks Found. of Ind., 1994. Mem. ASTM, Forest Products Soc. (pres. 1990-91, Fred Gottschalk Meml. award 1984), Soc. of Wood Sci. and Tech., Rotary. Office: Purdue Univ Wood Rsch Lab West Lafayette IN 47907

HUNT, ROBERT G., film critic, educator; b. St. Louis, June 18, 1957; s. Bobby Hunt and Rose (Trovillion) King; m. Lynn Yarrington, Sept. 18, 1977; children: Jonathon, Blake, Samuel. Film reviewer The Riverfront Times, St. Louis, 1981-83, St. Louis Weekly, 1983-85; host, announcer KSLH-FM, St. Louis, 1985-86; film reviewer KWMU-FM, St. Louis, 1986; theatre mgr. Tivoli Theatre, St. Louis, 1986-89; prof. film studies St. Louis Community Coll., 1987—, Webster U., St. Louis, 1991—; film/video columnist The Riverfront Times, St. Louis, 1989—; artistic dir. St. Louis Film Festival, 1992, 93; guest lectr. St. Louis Art mus., Webster U., Mo.

Hist. Soc., St. Louis. Named Best Film Critic St. Louis Mag., 1983, 91. Home: 6529 Clayton Ave Saint Louis MO 63139-3368

HUNT, ROGER, state legislator; m. Sharon Hunt; 3 children. Student, Augustana Coll., U. S.D., George Washington U. Mem. S.D. Ho. of Reps., 1993—, mem. judiciary and edn. coms.; atty., tchr. Home: RR 1 Box 875 Brandon SD 57005-9747*

HUNTER, DAVID W., stockbroker; b. Portsmouth, Va., May 28, 1946. Mktg. rep. Olga Co., Calif., 1973-80; stockbroker Merrill Lynch, St. Louis, 1981-82; br. mgr. A.G. Edwards & Sons Inc., Alton, Ill., 1982—. Sgt. U.S. Army, 1966-71. Presbyterian. Office: AG Edwards & Sons Inc PO Box 338 215 E Center Dr Alton IL 62002

HUNTER, HENRY BIRDSALL, municipal official; b. Hartford, Conn., July 23, 1949; s. Gilbert Thurston and Harriet (Calkins) H.; m. Kathleen Margaret Sampson, July 1, 1972; 1 child, Jennifer. BA, Miami U., Oxford, Ohio, 1971; M in Urban and Regional Planning, U. Pitts., 1974. Cert. planner. Exec. dir. Churchill (Pa.) Area Coun. Govts., 1973-74; cmty. planner Washington (Pa.) County Planning Commn., 1974-77; urban planner City of Fairborn, Ohio, 1977-87; cmty. devel. dir. City of Fairborn, 1987—. Chair Old Osborn Christmas Festival, Fairborn, 1990—. With USNR, 1971-72. Mem. Am. Planning Assn. (cert.), Ohio Conf. Planning, Ohio Devel. Assn., Ohio Conf. Cmty. Devel. (ann. conf. chair 1994), Fairborn C. of C. (econ. devel. coun.), I70/I75 Devel. Assn. (v.p. 1993-95), Fairborn Rotary Club (environ. chair 1992-93), Dayton Cycling Club (area touring coord. 1988-89). Methodist. Office: City of Fairborn 44 W Hebble Ave Fairborn OH 45324

HUNTER, JAMES JEROME, library director; b. Akron, Ohio, Dec. 12, 1946; s. Robert V. and Mary W. (Goodall) H.; m. Janet Ellen Novak, June 16, 1973; children: Allison, Anne. BA in Polit. Sci., Kent State U., 1969, MLS, 1973. Libr. dir. Columbus (Ohio) Dispatch, 1974—. Capt. U.S. Army, 1969-72. Episcopalian. Home: 4473 Sussex Dr Columbus OH 43220 Office: Columbus Dispatch 34 S 3d St Columbus OH 43216

HUNTER, LINDA MASON, author; b. San Juan, P.R., Nov. 23, 1946; d. Ronald Eugene and Alice Marie (Kenworthy) Mason; m. Eldon C. Johnson, Oct. 28, 1965 (div. 1972); children: Kimberlyn Hammond, Scott Adam; m. Robert Chappell Hunter, May 28, 1977; stepchildren: John Randall, Jocelyn MacDonald Grotenhuis. BS, Iowa State U., 1969; MA, Drake U., 1980; Cert. of Proficiency, Forester Instituto Internat., San Jose, Costa Rica, 1992. TV editor Register & Tribune, Des Moines, 1970-72; publicist Meredith Corp., Des Moines, 1972-74; asst. dir. pub. rels. Drake U., Des Moines, 1974-77; editor Meredith Corp., Des Moines, 1982-85; mng. editor Rodale Press, Emmaus, Pa., 1986, renovation editor, 1987; freelance writer Hunter Ink, Des Moines, 1985—; cons. Practical Homeowner Mag., Rodale Press, Ammaus, 1986-89; judge Better Home and Gardens Remodeling Contest, Des Moines, 1985-86; owner Healthy Home Designs. Author: The Healthy Home: An Attic-To-Basement Guide to Toxin-Free Living, 1989, 1,001 Do-It-Yourself Tips, 1995, Kitchens: Your Guide to Planning and Remodeling, 1996, Baths: Your Guide to Planning and Remodeling, 1996. Speaker in field. Recipient 1st Pl. Publicity Campaign, Ark. Addy Awards, 1980, 1st Pl. Poetry, Iowa State Fair, 1980, 1st Pl., Iowa Addy Awards, 1976, 1st Pl., Coun. for Advance and Support of Edn., 1976. Mem. AIA, Soc. Profl. Journalists, Authors Guild. Democrat. Mem. Soc. of Friends. Home: 4423 Kingman Blvd Des Moines IA 50311-3419 Office: Hunter Ink 4423 Kingman Blvd Des Moines IA 50311-3419

HUNTER, MICHAEL P., information systems professional; b. Clarksville, Tenn., Feb. 10, 1962. BS in Art, Art Acad., 1986; MFA, Pratt Inst., 1991. Multimedia developer The Human Element, Blue Ash, Ohio; pres. Interactive Technologies Inc., Blue Ash, 1994—. Office: Interactive Technologies In 11316 Williamson Rd Cincinnati OH 45241-2233

HUNTER, SALLY IRENE, interior designer; b. East Liverpool, Ohio, Oct. 8, 1936; Charles E. and Thelma E. (Rice) H. BA, Kalamazoo Coll., 1958. Certified Am. Soc. Interior Designers. Interior designer The Higbee Co., Cleve., 1958-70; interior designer, v.p., dir. of design Harrisons Fine Furniture and Interiors, Lakewood, Ohio, 1970—. Mem. Nat. Trust Hist. Preservation. Mem. Am. Soc. Interior Designers (profl.), Cleve. Mus. Art, Cleve. Zool. Soc. Home: 22535 Detroit Rd Cleveland OH 44116-2056 Office: Harrisons Fine Furniture & Interiors 14518 Detroit Ave Cleveland OH 44107-4317

HUNTINGTON, MARK KENNETH, physician, microbiologist; b. Mpls., Sept. 11, 1965; s. Archie V. and Lina A. H.; m. Charlene Stayer; children: Linda (dec.), M. Kenneth II, Seth, Samuel. BSc, Grace Coll., 1988; MD, Mich. State U., 1995, PhD, 1996. Lab tech. asst. Grace Coll., Winona Lake, Ind., 1984-88; orderly Mason Health Care Facility, Warsaw, Ind., 1988; teaching and rsch. asst. Mich. State U., East Lansing, 1988-95; resident in family medicine U. Cinn. Dept. Family Medicine, 1995-96; adj. faculty Mich. State U.; cons. SciTech Dental, Bellevue, Washington, Wearh Chem., East Lansing, Mich., Bio-Serve, Boca Raton, Fla. Mem. editorial bd. Doctor/Doctor, 1991-92; contbr. articles to profl. jours., abstracts and presentations at various confs. Active in Children's Ministries at local church, Mich. State Med. Soc. Com. Bioethics, 1988-89; vol. Mich. State U. Immunization Clinic, 1988-90, Migrant Workers' Health Clinic, 1989-92. Scholar Grand Rapids Clinic Health Professions, 1984-85, Alpha Chi Region V, 1987, Itasca Meml. Hosp. Aux., 1987-88, Alworth Meml. scholar, 1984-92, Park Nicollet Med. Ctr. Med. Student scholar, 1992, Bernard H. Smookler scholar, 1992; Summer Undergraduate Rsch. fellow Baylor U. Dept. Chemistry, 1986, Summer Undergraduate Rsch. fellow Ohio U. Coll. Osteo. Medicine, 1987. Mem. AMA, Am. Acad. Family Physicians, Am. Soc. Tropical Medicine and Hygiene, Am. Soc. Parasitologists, Christian Med. and Dental Soc., Mich. State Med. Soc., N.Y. Acad. Sci. Office: Mich State U Lab for Environ Pathobiology B307 Clin Ctr East Lansing MI 48824 also: Providence Hosp U Cin 2446 Kipling Ave Cincinnati OH 45239

HUNTLEY, KENNES CALVIN, insurance educator; b. Toeterville, Iowa, Apr. 9, 1932; s. Kennes Fred and Leona Minnie (Brandt) H.; m. Mary Ione Hesla, Aug. 11, 1962; children: Kendrea Sue Bibbs, Calden Scott. BS, Mankato (Minn.) State U., 1960, MS, 1962; PhD, U. Iowa, 1967. CLU, CPCU. Instr. bus. Carpenter (Iowa) H.S., 1960-61; dir. ednl. svc. Am. Coll. Life Underwriters, Bryn Mawr, Pa., 1968-70; assoc. prof. bus. adminstrn. Mankato State U., 1967-68, prof. ins., 1970—, chair dept. fin., ins. and real estate, 1995—. Contbr. articles to profl. jours. Bd. dirs., treas. Lake Washington Improvement Assn., 1991-93. Staff sgt. USAF, 1951-55. Mem. Am. Risk and Ins. Assn., So. Risk and Ins. Assn., Western Risk and Ins. Assn., Risk and Ins. Mgmt. Soc., Minn. Chpt. CPCU. Lutheran. Home: 6312 Killarney Ct Madison Lake MN 56063

HUNTLEY, THOMAS, state legislator, science educator; b. Feb. 1938; m. Gail Huntley; two children. BS, U. Minn.; PhD in Biochemistry, Iowa State U. Assoc. prof.; Dist. 6B rep. Minn. Ho. of Reps., St. Paul, 1993—. Home: 1924 Wallace Ave Duluth MN 55803-2461*

HUNTRESS, BETTY ANN, former music store proprietor, educator; b. Poughkeepsie, N.Y., Apr. 29, 1932; d. Emmett Slater and Catherine V. (Kihlmire) Brundage; m. Arnold Ray Huntress, June 26, 1954; children: Catherine, Michael, Carol, Alan. BA, Cornell U., 1954. Tchr. high sch., Bordentown, N.J., 1954-55; part-time asst. to prof. Delta Coll., Northwood Inst., Midland, Mich., 1958-71; part-time tchr. Midland Pub. Schs., 1968-79, 83—; owner, mgr. The Music Stand, Midland, 1979-82. Bd. dirs. Midland Center for Arts, 1978-86 ; v.p. MCFTA (Arts Center), 1980-84 ; mem. charter bd. mgrs. Matrix Midland Ann. Arts and Sci. Festival, 1977-80; cons. Girl Scouts U.S., 1964-76; mem. Mich. Internat. Council, 1975-76; bd. dirs. Literary Council Midland County, 1986-94, sec., 1987-91. Named Midland Musician of Yr., 1977. Mem. Music Soc. Midland Center for Arts (dir. 1971-86, chmn. 1976-79), AAUW (dir. 1962-73, pres. 1971-73, mem. Mich. state div. bd. 1973-75, 1st v.p. Mich. state div. 1983-85 , bd. dirs. 1993-95, outstanding woman as agt. of change award 1977, fellowship grant named in her honor 1976), Midland Symphony League Soc. (2d v.p.), LWV (bd. dirs. 1986-90, com. charter schs. 1995—), Community Concert Soc., Women's Study Club of Midland (pres. 1995—), Friends of Libr.,Kappa Delta Epsilon, Pi Lambda Theta, Alpha Xi Delta. Presbyterian. Home: 5316 Sunset Dr Midland MI 48640-2536

HUNTZICKER, WILLIAM EDWARD, journalism educator; b. St. Paul, Aug. 18, 1946; s. Kenneth Verndale and Edith Hale (Bennion) H.; m. Linda DeLaurenti, 1974; children: James William, Rachel Lyn. BA in History, Mont. State U., 1968; MA in Am. Studies, U. Minn., 1973, PhD, 1978, cert. social studies, 1989. Ranch hand various family ranches, Miles City, Mont., 1964; electronic tech. Teledyne, Inc., Miles City, 1965; reporter, photographer Miles City Daily Star, 1966-67; reporter, editor Associated Press, Mpls., 1968-69; writer U. Minn. News Svc., Mpls., 1970-79; asst. prof. journalism U. Wis., River Falls, 1979-86; media writer Minn. Ho. of Reps., St. Paul, 1987; lectr. sch. of journalism and mass communication U. Minn., Mpls., 1988—; freelance Wis. corr. St. Paul Pioneer Press, 1984-86. Contbr. articles to profl. jours. Chair parks com. Marcy Holmes Neighborhood Assn., Mpls., 1977-86, pres., 1981-82, sec., 1982-83; co-pres. S.E. Mpls. Planning and Coord. Com., 1982-83, sec., 1978-79. Congregationalist. Home: 415 8th St SE Minneapolis MN 55414-1223

HURAS, WILLIAM DAVID, bishop; b. Kitchener, Ont., Can., Sept. 22, 1932; s. William Adam and Frieda Dorothea (Rose) H.; m. Barbara Elizabeth Lotz, Oct. 5, 1957; children—David, Matthew, Andrea. BA, Waterloo Coll., Ont., 1954; BD, Waterloo Sem., Ont., 1963; MTh, Knox Coll., Toronto, Ont., 1968; MDiv, Waterloo Luth. U., 1973; DD (hon.), Wilfred Laurier U., Waterloo, 1980, Huron Coll., London, Ont., 1989. Ordained to ministry Luth. Ch. in Am., 1957. Pastor St. James Luth. Ch., Refrew, Ont., 1957-62, Advent Luth. Ch., North York, 1962-78; bishop Eastern Can. Synod Luth. Ch. in Am., Kitchener, 1978-85, Eastern Synod Evangel. Luth. Ch. in Can., 1986—; mem. exec. com. Can. sect. of Luth. Ch. in Am., 1969-79; mem. exec. com. Luth. Merger Commn., Can., 1978-85; pres. Luth. Council Can., 1985-88. Bd. govs. Waterloo Luth. U., 1966-75, Waterloo Luth. Sem., 1973-75, 78—. Mem. Order of St. Lazarus of Jerusalem (Ecclesiastical Grand cross 1985). Office: Eastern Synod Evang Luth Ch in Can, 50 Queen St N 3d Fl, Kitchener, ON Canada N2H 6P4

HURD, BYRON THOMAS, newspaper executive, retired; b. Roseville, Mich., 1933; s. Clark Frank and Evelyn (Sybelden) H.; m. Barbara Jean Ekeroth; children: Thomas E., Roger A., J. Douglas, James B. BSBA in Advt. and Mktg., Wayne State U., 1954. Sales mgr. Detroit Free Press, 1954-55, Milne & Jones, Royal Oak, Mich., 1955-56, Detroit Times, 1956-59; account mgr. Milne Circulation Sales, Inc., Bloomfield Hills, Mich., 1959-65; agt. Bankers Life Co., Des Moines, Iowa, 1965-66; promotion mgr. Chgo. Today, Chgo. Tribune, 1966-74; owner, cons. Circulation Specialists, Homewood, Ill., 1974-77; exec. dir. circulation The Star Newspapers, Chicago Heights, Ill., 1977-95; ret., 1995; panelist, discussion leader, session master, com. mem. No. Ill. Newspapers Assn., DeKalb. Contbr. Publishers handbook, 1988. Elder, pres. governing bd. Flossmoor (Ill.) Community Ch., 1988. Mem. Cen. States Circulation Mgrs. Assn., Suburban Newspapers Am. (conf., sem. com. mem.), Audit Bur. Circulation (voting rep.), Circulation Mgmt. Ill., Rotary (dir. community svc. 1978-79, dir. internat. svc. 1979-80, sec. 1981-82, v.p. 1982-83, pres. 1983-84, dist. dir. pub. rels. 1984-86, dist. govs. aide 1986-87, dist. dir. vocat. svc. 1987-88, host Soviet Emerging Leaders 1988, Finnish 1989, dist. dir. group study exchange with India 1990, dist. conf. com. master ceremonies 1987-88, dist. conf. com. chmn. 1989-90), Flossmoor Country Club (sports and pastimes com. mem. 1988).

HURD, G. DAVID, insurance company executive; b. Chgo., Dec. 14, 1929; s. Gerald Walton and Hilldur Ingabore (Hallgren) H.; m. Patricia Ann Lamb, Feb. 12, 1955; children—Janet Susan, Sally Jane, Michael David. B.A., Mich. State U., 1951. With The Prin. Fin. Group (formerly Bankers Life Co.), Des Moines, 1954—, officer, 1960-71, v.p., 1971-83, sr. v.p., 1983-85, exec. v.p., 1985-87; pres. The Prin. Fin. Group, 1987-88, pres., chief exec. officer, 1989; now chmn. Prin. Mut. Life Ins. Co., Des Moines; bd. dirs. Prin. Mut. Life Ins. Co., Des Moines ; mem. Pension Research Council, U. Pa. Wharton Sch. Bus., 1979-85. Mem. Adv. Council on Employee Welfare and Pension Benefit Plans, Dept. Labor, Washington, 1977-80; bd. dirs. Drake U., 1986—, Nature Conservancy; chmn. Group Assurance Internat. Network, 1987-89; mem. steering com. Bus. for Peace. Served to 2d lt. C.E., U.S. Army, 1951-53, Korea. Mem. Employee Benefit Research Inst. (bd. dirs. 1979-86), Assn. Pvt. Pension and Welfare Plans (chmn. bd. 1985-87), Des Moines C. of C. (bd. dirs. 1985—). Clubs: Prairie, Des Moines. Home: 3930 Grand Ave Apt 406 Des Moines IA 50312-3523 Office: Prin Fin Group 711 High St Des Moines IA 50392-0001*

HURLEY, JOHN G., foundation executive; b. Carbondale, Ill., Dec. 18, 1938; s. Hubert G. and Helen G. (Needham) H.; m. Rita A. Franzone, Feb. 8, 1964 (div. 1990); children: Mark L., Laura M., David A. BA, DePauw U., 1960; MA, Va. Poly. Inst. and State U., 1975. Vol. Peace Corps, Malaysia, 1962-64, assoc. dir., 1964-66; Malaysia ops. officer Peace Corps, Washington, 1966-67; dir. Peace Corps, Fiji, 1967-69; dir. evaluation Peace Corps, Washington, 1969-70; profl. assoc. bd. on sci. and tech. for internat. devel. NAS, Washington, 1970-82, dir. bd., 1982-91; assoc. v.p. John D. and Catherine T. MacArthur Found., Chgo., 1991—; mem. com. on sci. and tech. for developing countries Internat. Coun. Sci. Unions, Paris, 1986-90; pres. NAS Fed. Credit Union, 1977. Contbg. author: Energy and the Developing Nations, 1981, Earth and the Human Future, 1986; also articles. Bd. dirs., sec. Malaysia-Am. Soc., Washington, 1987-91; bd. visitors DePauw U., 1992-95. Mem. AAAS, Chgo. Coun. on Fgn. Rels. (Chgo. com. 1992—), Univ. Club of Chgo. Office: MacArthur Found 140 S Dearborn St Ste 1100 Chicago IL 60603-5202

HURLIN, KRISTIN J., illustrator; b. Detroit, Oct. 21, 1954; d. Kenneth Peter and Shirley F. (Reno) H.; m. Paul May, May 2, 1981; children: Liana, Keenan. Oakland C.C., 1974, U. Idaho, 1975-77, U. Mich., 1978. Freelance illustrator Glen Arbor, Mich., 1986—. Illustrator T-shirt art, 1980—, mags. including Organic Gardening, Farmers Almanac, Highlights for Children, 1981— (Hidden Picture of Yr. award 1990), book covers for Bantam Books, 1994-95, American Spoon Foods catalogue, 1986—. Home: 5964 S Ray St Glen Arbor MI 49636

HURNI, JERRY A., stockbroker; b. Jackson, Mich., Dec. 19, 1969. BA in Fin., Mich. State U., 1992. Br. mgr. Olde Discount Corp., Glenview, Ill., 1992—. Republican. Presbyterian. Office: Olde Discount Corp 1701 E Lake Ave Ste 100 Glenview IL 60025-2085

HURT, JEANETTE CLARICE, city reporter, educator; b. Maywood, Ill., Aug. 27, 1971; d.Tom and Mary (Rudnik) H. BA, Marquette U., 1993. Reporter McKay Publs., Lombard, Ill, 1988-93, City News Bur., Chgo., 1993-94, Milw. Sentinel, 1994-95, Milw. Jour. Sentinel, 1995—; instr. Marquette U., Milw., 1995—. Editor lit. mag. Porcupine, 1995. Mem. Soc. Profl. Journalists (bd. dirs. Milw. chpt. 1996), Assn. Women Journalists. Home: W66-N482 Madison Ave Cedarburg WI 53012 Office: Milw Jour Sentinel 66 N 200 Commerce St Cedarburg WI 53012

HUSAR, JOHN PAUL, newspaper columnist; b. Chgo., Jan. 29, 1937; s. John Z. and Kathryn (Kanupke) H.; AA, Dodge City Coll., 1958; BS in Journalism, U. Kans., 1962; m. Louise Kay Lewis, Dec. 28, 1963; children: Kathryn Coyle, Laura. Reporter, Clovis (N.Mex.) News-Jour., 1960; night wire editor Okinawa Morning Star, 1961; city editor Pasadena (Tex.) Daily Citizen, 1962; bus. editor Topeka Capital-Jour., 1963; regional news editor Wichita (Kans.) Beacon, 1963-65; sports columnist and writer Chgo. Tribune, 1966—; panelist ESPN-TV. Chmn., Village of Willow Springs (Ill.) Zoning Commn., 1975-77; mem. Ill. Forestry Adv. Com., 1981-82; mem. adv. com. Ill.-Mich. Canal Nat. Heritage Corridor, 1982; profl.-in-residence U. Kans. Sch. Journalism, 1985. Served with U.S. Army, 1960-62. Recipient 1st pl. award in sportswriting Ill. UPI, 1977, Ill. AP, 1984, 1st pl. award in feature writing Bowling mag., 1979, environ. reporting award Chgo. Audubon Soc., 1979, Disting. Alumnus award Dodge City Coll., 1983, 2d pl. award for pub. svc. reporting Ill. AP, 1980, 2d pl. award for sports column writing, 1981, spl. writing award Chgo. Tribune, 1980, Jacob A. Riis award Friends of Parks, 1981, Peter Lisagor award Chgo. chpt. Sigma Delta Chi, 1985, DuPont Stren Edit. Excellence award, 1986, Founders award Ill.-Mich. Canal Nat. Heritage Corridor Civic Ctr. Authority, 1987, Ryobi Am. Conservation Writing award 1987, Stren-Plano-Remington Lifetime Conservation Achievement award, 1996. Mem. Round Table Profl. Daily Newspaper Outdoor Writers (nat. chmn. 1990-92), Assn. of Great Lakes Outdoor Writers (past dir.), Golf Writers Assn. Am. (past dir.), Baseball Writers Assn. Am., Outdoor Writers Assn. Am., Green River Sportsmen's Club (bd. dirs.), Phi Kappa Theta. Office: Chgo Tribune Co 435 N Michigan Ave PO Box 25340 Chicago IL 60625-0340

HUSARIK, ERNEST ALFRED, educational administrator; b. Gary, Ind., July 2, 1941; married, 2 children. BA in History, Olivet Nazarene U., Kankakee, Ill., 1963; MS in Ednl. Adminstrn., No. Ill. U., DeKalb, 1966; PhD in Ednl. Adminstrn. and Curriculum Devel., Ohio State U., Columbus, 1973; m. Elizabeth Ann Bonnette; children: Jennifer, Amy. Supt., Ontario (Ohio) Pub. Schs., 1973-75; supt. Euclid (Ohio) Pub. Schs., 1975-86, Westerville (Ohio) Pub. Schs., 1986—. Past pres. Sch. Study Coun. Ohio; bd. govs. Westerville Fund; mem. adv. and distbn. com. Martha Holden Jennings Found. Named one of top 100 Edn. Adminstrs. North Am., Exec. Educator, 1993; Ohio Supr. of the Year, 1994, Exec. Educator, 1993. past chair, Franklin County Ednl. Coun. Mem. Am. Assn. Sch. Adminstrs., Buckeye Assn. Sch. Adminstrs. (dir., pres.), Ohio State U. Edliners (pres.), Nat. ASCD, Ohio Assn. Supervision and Curriculum Devel., Franklin County Area Supt's. Assn. (exec. com.), Westerville Area C. of C. (bd. dirs.), Olivet Nazarene U. Alumni Assn. (past mem. alumni bd. dirs.), Rotary (pres. Westerville, Rotarian of Yr.), Phi Delta Kappa (past chpt. pres.), Sigma Tau Delta. Contbr. articles in field to profl. jours. Home: 1029 Wood Glen Rd Westerville OH 43081-3240 Office: 336 S Otterbein Ave Westerville OH 43081-2396

HUSBAND, WILLIAM SWIRE, computer industry executive; b. Hinsdale, Ill., Dec. 18, 1939; s. William Thompson and Arlene Martha (Frey) H.; m. Janet Goatley, Nov. 26, 1965; children: Scott, Andrea. BS, Iowa State U., 1962. Mktg. rep. IBM, San Francisco, 1966-70; dist. mktg. mgr. DPF, Des Plaines, Ill., 1971-78; v.p. Celtic Computer Investment Co., Palatine, Ill., 1978; pres. 20th Century Systems, Inc., Palatine, 1978-96; dir. tech. AT&T Capital, Bloomfield Hills, Mich., 1996—; presenter symposium for U. Calif.-Berkeley Systems Technology Inst., Milan, 1987, 88, 89; speaker World Congress of Computing, Chgo., 1988. Author, pub.: Computer Acquisition and Disposition Planning, 7th edit., 1987; editor COMPUTALK mag., 1987—. IBM Technology and Product Strategies in the 80's, 1986; contbg. editor Computer Econs. mag., 1986—. Active Buehler YMCA, Palatine Boys' Baseball, 1978-85. Served to lt. (j.g.) USN, 1962-66. Republican. Presbyterian. Office: 20th Century Systems 6235 Mission Dr West Bloomfield MI 48324-1396

HUSBY, ANITA KAY, educational administrator; b. Rice Lake, Wis., Apr. 20, 1950; d. Robert Matthew and Louise Eileen (Knutson) Anderson; m. James Ernest Husby, Nov. 16, 1969 (div. 1990); 1 child, Jeffrey. BA magna cum laude, U. Wis., Eau Claire, 1973; MS, U. Wis., Menomonie, 1977, EdS, 1986. Cert. music and speech tchr., K-12 sch. counselor, K-8 prin., Wis. Elem. tchr. music Flambeau Schs., Tony, Wis., 1973-76; grad. asst. U. Wis.-Stout, Menomonie, 1976-77; elem. counselor, cons. Fall Creek (Wis.) Sch. Dist., 1977-90; elem. prin., cons., speaker Beloit (Wis.) Turner Schs., 1990-96; dir. of instrn. Greenfield Sch. Dist., 1996—; pvt. tchr. piano and music, Eau Claire, Wis., 1969-90; presenter in field. Author curriculum guides. Mem. Mental Health Assn., Eau Claire, 1983-90, Beloit Recycling Com., 1990—. Found. scholar Barron County Campus, 1970; ESEA Title IV grantee Wis. Dept. Pub. Instrn., 1980. Mem. NAESP, ASCD, Assn. Wis. Sch. Adminstrs., Madison Area Quality Improvement Network, Zonta, Phi Delta Kappa. Lutheran. Office: Sch Dist Beloit Turner 620 Hillside Ave Beloit WI 53511-1770

HUSBY, JEAN ANN, marketing educator, consultant; b. Superior, Wis., Jan. 16, 1960; d. Walter Joseph and Irene Kay (Kubalak) Urbaniak; m. Bradley David Husby, Dec. 28, 1985. AAS, We. Wis. Tech. Coll., LaCrosse, 1982; BS, U. Wis.-Stout, 1987, MS, 1993. Cert. mktg. educator. Customer svc. rep. Consumers Coop. Assn., Menomonie, Wis., 1983-84; advt. mgr. Dunn County News and Shopper, Menomonie, 1984-87; mktg. educator U. Wis.-Stout, Menomonie, 1987-90; mktg. instr. Chippewa Valley Tech. Coll., Eau Claire, Wis., 1990—; advisor Wis. Mktg. and Mgmt. Assn., Eau Claire, 1990—. Mem. NEA, Mktg. Edn. Assn., Am. Vocat. Assn., Wis. Vocat. Assn., Wis. Mktg. Edn. Assn., Wis. Edn. Assn. Coun., Distributive Edn. Clubs Am. (pres. 1977-78), Delta Epsilon Chi (pres. 1981-82). Roman Catholic. Home: E2508 470th Ave Menomonie WI 54751-6100 Office: Chippewa Valley Tech Coll 620 W Clairemont Ave Eau Claire WI 54701-6120

HUSE, EUGENE FRANKLIN, newspaper publisher; b. Norfolk, Nebr., Jan. 17, 1927; s. Eugene Franklin and Lucy (Neubold) H.; m. Karla Amelia Schnurr, Dec. 30, 1957; children: Mary Elizabeth Huse Olsen, William Harris. BA, U. Minn., 1950. Asst. pub. Norfolk Daily News, 1950-56, pub., 1956—, pres., 1961—; pres. Bellevue (Nebr.) Leader Co., 1984—, WJAG, Inc., 1961—. Pres. Greater Norfolk Corp. With USNR, 1945-46. Mem. Nebr. Press Assn. (bd. dirs. 1984-93, pres. 1991-92). Republican. Episcopalian. Office: Norfolk Daily News PO Box 977 Norfolk NE 68702-0977

HUSEBOE, ARTHUR ROBERT, American literature educator; b. Sioux Falls, S.D., Oct. 6, 1931; s. Carl and Lillian Ruth (Auby) H.; m. Doris Louise Eggers, May 27, 1953. BA, Augustana Coll., 1953; MA, U. S.D., 1956; PhD, Ind. U., 1963; LHD (hon.), Dana Coll., 1984. Teaching assoc. Ind. U., Bloomington, 1959-60; instr. U. S.D., Vermillion, 1960-61; prof. Augustana Coll., Sioux Falls, S.D., 1961—; pres. S.D. Humanities Found., Sioux Falls, 1994-96, Fedn. of State Humanities Couns., Washington, 1988-91; exec. dir. Nordland Heritage Found., Sioux Falls, 1980—, Ctr. Western Studies, Augustana, 1989—. Author: An Illustrated History of the Arts in South Dakota, 1989, Sir George Etherege, 1987, Herbert Krause, 1985, Sir John Vanbrugh, 1976. Bd. dirs. S.D. Symphony, Sioux Falls, 1966—; mem. Nordland Fest Assn., Sioux Falls, 1975—. With U.S. Army, 1953-55. Grantee NEH, 1975-77, 79-83, 92-94; recipient Gov.'s award in the Arts State of S.D., 1989. Mem. Modern Lang. Assn., We. Lit. Assn. (pres. 1971-72), Norwegian-Am. Hist. Assn. (bd. dirs.), S.D. Hist. Soc. Lutheran. Home: 813 E 38th St Sioux Falls SD 57105-5939 Office: Ctr for Western Studies Box 727 Augustana Coll Sioux Falls SD 57197

HUSEBOE, DORIS LOUISE, educator, arts consultant; b. Sioux Falls, S.D., Mar. 10, 1933; d. Delbert W. and Erna (Schneider) Eggers; m. Arthur Robert Huseboe, May 27, 1953. BS, Ind. U., 1959, MS, 1961; EdD, U. S.D., 1985. Cert. tchr., S.D. Tchr. Vermillion (S.D.) Jr. High Sch., 1960-61, Patrick Henry Jr. High Sch., Sioux Falls, 1960-66; dir. student activities Augustana Coll., Sioux Falls, 1966-86, dean summer sch., 1986-87, dean pub. events, 1987-90, assoc. v.p. devel., dean of spl. events, 1990-93; dir. devel. S.D. Symphony, 1994—; dir. Minn. Pub. Radio, St. Paul, 1987-93, Guthrie Theater Bd., Mpls., 1976-82; com. mem. Scandinavia Today, Mpls., 1982-83. Co-chair Met. Opera com., Sioux Falls, 1976-86; mem. 1st Luth. Ch. Media Ministry Bd., Sioux Falls, 1987—, Community Playhouse Bd., Sioux Falls, 1979-85, Nordland Fest Assn., Sioux Falls, 1974—, Nordland Heritage Found. Bd., 1993—; devel. dir. S.D. Symphony; active Jr. Svc. League. Grad. scholar Delta Kappa Gamma-U. S.D., 1979-80; recipient Leader award YWCA, 1978; named Outstanding Young Women of Yr. 1968. Mem. AAUW, Delta Kappa Gamma. Office: 300 N Dakota Ave Sioux Falls SD 57102-0321

HUSK, DONALD ESTEL, retired state official; b. Oakland City, Ind., Dec. 10, 1925; s. George Raymond and Hazel Rita (Ashley) H.; grad. high sch.; m. Velma Cunningham, June 7, 1946; children: Robert, Mark. With Hoosier Cardinal, Inc., Evansville, Ind., 1946; asst. cashier English State Bank (Ind.), 1949; with Ind. Dept. Financial Instns., 1953-93, sr. examiner, 1958-70, supr. div. banks and trust cos., Indpls., 1970-86; dep. dir. depository instns., 1986-91, chief dep. dir., 1991-93, ret., 1993. Served with USNR, 1943-46. Certified fin. examiner. Mem. Hist. Record Assn., Soc. Fin. Examiners. Clubs: Masons, Plainfield Optimists. Home: 424 Wayside Dr Plainfield IN 46168-2062 Office: Wo66 W Washington St Indianapolis IN 46204

HUSLIG, BILL, engineer; b. Fowler, Kans., Feb. 14, 1950. BA in Math., St.Mary's Plains, Dodge City, Kans., 1975. Draftsman Crust Buster, Spearville, Kans., 1975-78; project engr. Lely-Clark, Independence, Mo., 1978-83, Midwest Conveyor, Kansas City, Kans., 1984—. Mem. Am. Prodn. and Inventory Control Soc. Office: Midwest Conveyor 2601 Mid West Dr Kansas City KS 66112-0950

HUSS, DAVID L., mechanical engineer; b. Fremont, Ohio, Oct. 9, 1953. A in Mech. Engring., Terra Tech. Coll., Fremont, Ohio, 1972. Detailer Neilson Elect, Fremont, Ohio, 1969-70; mech. design engr. Continentle, Fremont, Ohio, 1970-85; engr. Echo Waters, Middletown, Ohio, 1985-91, Dupps Co., Germantown, Ohio, 1991—. Mem. Eagles. Office: Dupps Co PO Box 189 Germantown OH 45327

HUSS, PHILIP F., electrical engineer; b. Tiffin, Ohio, Sept. 18, 1965. BS in Elec. Engring., U. Toledo, 1988. Elec. engr. Nat. Machinery Co., Tiffin, 1989—. Office: Nat Machinery Co PO Box 747 Tiffin OH 44883-0747

HUSS, WILLIAM LEE, accountant; b. Freedom, Wis., May 18, 1956; s. Donald John and Elaine Mary (Vandenberg) H.; m. Beth Ellen Braun, Oct. 4, 1980 (div. Sept. 1984); m. Carol Ann Lindemann, Dec. 26, 1987. BBA, U. Wis., Oshkosh, 1978. CPA, Wis. Staff acct. Clifton, Gunderson & Co., Neenah, Wis., 1979-80; contr., sec.-treas. Chief Equiptment, Inc., Oshkosh, 1980-83; tax and systems mgr. Exptl. Aircraft Assn., Oshkosh, 1983-89; acctg. prof. Marian Coll., Fond du Lac, Wis., 1986-89; v.p. fin., sec., treas. Weaver's Bus. Interiors, Inc., Milw., 1989-92; acctg. mgr. The Tribute Cos., Inc., Delafield, Wis., 1993—; acctg. instr. Fox Valley Tech. Inst., Oshkosh, 1980-92. Adv. editor book revs. McGraw Hill Book Co., 1983. Vol. Big Brother, 1976-89; pres., bd. dirs. Big Bros. of Oshkosh, 1985-88. Fellow Wis. Inst. CPA's; mem. Am. Inst. CPA's. Roman Catholic. Home: 496 Park Hill Dr Pewaukee WI 53072-2456 Office: The Tribute Cos Inc 383 Williamstowne Delafield WI 53018-2332

HUSSAINI, AKBAR SYED, mechanical engineer; b. Hyderabad, India, Mar. 6, 1966; came to the U.S., 1990, naturalized; BS in Mech. Engring., Osmanik U., Hyderabad, 1987; postgrad., Case Western Res. U., 1994—. Sales engr. Ingersoll Rand, Hyderabad, 1988-90, Spirax Sarzo, N.Y.C., 1990-91; project engr. Gorman Rupp Inc., Bellville, Ohio, 1991—. Mem. ASME, The Entrepreneur's Assn. Moslem. Home: 1809 Sawtooth Pl Mansfield OH 44904-1880

HUSTAD, THOMAS PEGG, marketing educator; b. Mpls., June 15, 1945; s. Thomas Earl Pegg and John Charles and Dorothy Helen (Anderson) H.; m. Sherry Ann Thomas, Jan. 30, 1971; children: Kathleen, John. BS in Elec. Engring., Purdue U., 1967, MS in Indsl. Mgmt., 1969, PhD in Mktg., 1973. Vis. asst. prof. Purdue U., West Lafayette, Ind., 1971-72; asst. prof. Faculty of Adminstrv. Studies, York U., Toronto, 1972-74, assoc. prof., 1974-76, assoc. prof., mktg. area coord., 1976-77; assoc. prof. mktg. Sch. Bus., Ind. U., Bloomington-Indpls., 1977-82, prof., 1982—; chmn. MBA program, 1983-85, program chmn. Ind. U. Ann. Bus. Conf., 1983, 84, co-founder Exec. Forum; adj. prof. philanthropic studies, 1992-96; exec. dir. Ind. U. Internat. Bus. Forum, 1981-85; cons. N. Am. corps., Can. Govt.; condr. seminars for U.S., Singapore, Can., European, Asian and Venezuelan industry. Fulbright fellow, 1987; recipient Eli Lilly MBA Teaching Excellence award, 1990. Fellow Ind. Univ. Ctr. for Entrepreneurship and Innovation, John and Marilyn Kosin Faculty fellow, 1993—; Crawford fellow of Product Innovation 1993; recipient Elsevier Sci. Pub. Co. Editorship award 1993. mem. Am. Mktg. Assn. (award 1973), Product Devel. and Mgmt. Assn. (program chmn. 3d ann. conf., v.p. confs. 1979, pres. elect 1980, pres. 1981, dir. 1982-83, chmn. publ. com. 1982-84, sec./treas. 1984-96, bd. dirs. 1984—, Presdl. award 1987), Ancient and Hon. Arty. Co. Mass., Internat. Assn. Jazz Record Collectors, Brown U. alumni Assn. (Associated Alumni award 1963), Phi Eta Sigma, Tau Beta Pi, Beta Gamma Sigma. Author: Approaches to the Teaching of Product Development and Management, 1977; editor in chief: International Competition: The American Challenge, 1986, Managing the Product Development Process, 1989, Product Development: Prospering in a Rapidly Changing World, 1990; founder, editor-in-chief Jour. Product Innovation Mgmt., 1986—; contbr. articles to books and profl. jours. Home: 3101 Daniel St Bloomington IN 47401 Office: Ind U Sch Bus 10th and Fee Ln Bloomington IN 47405

HUSTIG, CHARLES HAROLD, scientific administrator; b. Milw., Sept. 16, 1945; s. Harold H. and Lula Mae H.; divorced; children: Ricarda Ann, Dawn Marie, Christopher Charles. BS, U. Wis., 1968, MS, 1969. Sr. engr. 3M Corp., St. Paul, Minn., 1972-80; tech. dir. Applied Spectrum Techs., Mpls., 1980-88; chief scientist Wadia Digital, River Falls, Wis., 1988—. Patentee in field. Pres. Hudson Jaycees, 1980. 1st Lt. U.S. Army, 1969-70. Recipient Disting. Grad. award U.S. Army Signal Sch. Office: Wadia Digital 624 Troy St River Falls WI 54022-1572

HUSTOLES, PAUL JOHN, theater educator; b. Chgo., Mar. 4, 1952; s. Edward J. and Mary Catherine (Syoen) H.; m. Mary Jo Henderson, June 23, 1973; children: Elizabeth A., Brian E. BFA, Wayne State U., 1973; MA, U. Mich., 1974; PhD, Tex. Tech U., 1984. Teaching asst. U. Mich., Ann Arbor, 1974-77; artistic dir. MM Prodns., Ann Arbor, 1976-77; dir. theatre, assoc. prof. Tarkio (Mo.)Coll., 1977-83; artistic dir. The Mule Barn Theatre, Tarkio, 1977-83; instr. Tex. Tech U., Lubbock, 1983-84; assoc. prof., mng. dir. dept. theatre U. Miss., Oxford, 1984-85; producer Highland Summer Theatre, Mankato, Minn., 1985—; chmn., prof. dept. theatre arts Mankato State U., 1985—; acting v.p. for univ. advancement Mankato State U., 1993-94. Prodr. more than 250 theatrical prodns.; artistic dir. over 120 theatrical prodns. Mem. Kennedy Ctr./Am. Coll. Theatre Festival (vice chmn. region V 1992-94, chmn. region V 1994—), Mid-Am. Theatre Conf., Assn. Theatre in Higher Edn., Minn. Citizens for Arts, Minn. Alliance for Arts in Edn., Assn. for Comm. Adminstrs., Nat. Assn. Schs. Theatre. Office: Mankato State U Dept Theatre Arts Mankato MN 56002

HUSTON, JEFFREY CHARLES, mechanical engineer, educator; b. Johnstown, Pa., Jan. 30, 1951; s. Charles Virgil and Pauline (Brubaker) H.; m. Patricia Ann Lemmon, June 1, 1974; children: Tiffany, Roger. BS, Ill. Inst. Tech., 1972; MS, W.Va. U., 1973, PhD, 1975. Registered profl. engr., Iowa. Mech. engr. Morgantown (W.Va.) Energy Rsch. Ctr., 1975-76; asst. prof. W.Va. U., Morgantown, 1975-76; asst. prof. Iowa State U., Ames, 1976-80, assoc. prof., 1980-87, prof. aerospace engring., engring. mechs., biomed. engring., 1987—; cons. in field. Contbr. articles to profl. jours.; inventor hip pad protective clothing, 1990. Witness testimony pub. hearing on safety of ATVs U.S. Consumer Product Safety Commn., Milw., 1985. Fellow W.Va. Found., 1972-75. Mem. ASME, NSPE, Am. Soc. Engring Edn. (awards chair 1987-89, Mickol award 1984), Iowa Profl. Engring. Soc. (Order of Engr. 1987), Soc. Automotive Engrs. (recreational vehicle com. 1980—, Ralph Teetor award 1980), Sigma Xi. Democrat. Methodist. Home: 535 Valley West Ct West Des Moines IA 50265-4047 Office: Iowa State U AE & EM 3022 Black Engineering Ames IA 50011

HUSTON, KATHLEEN MARIE, library administrator; b. Sparta, Wis., Jan. 7, 1944. BA, Edgewood Coll., 1966; MLS, U. Wis., Madison, 1969. Libr. Milw. Pub. Libr., 1969-90; city libr. Milw. Pub. Libr. System, 1991—. Office: Milwaukee Pub Libr 814 W Wisconsin Ave Milwaukee WI 53233-2309

HUSTON, KENT ALLEN, rheumatologist; b. Wichita, Kans., May 14, 1944; s. George W. and Elizabeth (Nordyke) H.; m. Janet Kay Heims, June 12, 1968 (div. 1985); children: Kent K., Heather J., Elizabeth K.; m. Susan Jolene Held, Dec. 2, 1990; 1 child, Boris H. BA, U. Kans, lawrence, 1966; MD, U. Kans, Kansas City, 1970. Diplomate Am. Bd. Internal Medicine and Rheumatology. Intern Wesley Med. Ctr., Wichita, 1970-71; resident in internal medicine Mayo Clinic, Rochester, Minn., 1971-75, fellow in rheumatology, 1975-77; pres. Mid-Am. Med. Cons., Kansas City, Mo., 1977-91, Ctr. Rheumatic Disease, Kansas City, 1991—; preceptor U. Kans. Sch. Medicine, 1978—; clin. assoc. prof. U. Mo.-Kansas City Med. Sch., 1982—; mem. organizing com. Mid-Am. Rehab. Hosp.; dir. Mo. State Regional Arthritis Ctr., 1988—. Contbr. to profl. publs. Bd. dirs. Western Mo. chpt. Arthritis Found., 1980-90, chmn. med. and sci. com., 1984-87; mem. Mo. Arthritis Adv. Bd., Jefferson City, 1984—. Capt. USAF, 1971-73. Fellow ACP; mem. AMA, Am. Soc. Internal Medicine, Am. Coll. Rheumatology, Southwest Clin. Soc., Kansas City Met. Med. Soc., Kansas City Rheumatism Soc. (pres. 1991—). Office: Ctr Rheumatic Disease 4330 Wornall Rd Kansas City MO 64111-3201

HUTCHINGS, S. DOUGLAS, financial development professional; b. Marshfield, Wis., Apr. 16, 1959; s. William Ray and Betty Lou (Orrell) H.; m. Patricia Ellen Ostrenga, May 26, 1984. BS, U. Wis., Oshkosh, 1981; postgrad., Marquette U., Milw., 1986, U. Dubuque, Iowa, 1984-85. Mgr. ops. and promotions NWCTV, Inc., Suring, Wis., 1981-83; univ. devel. officer, dir. alumni U. Dubuque, Iowa, 1983-85; dir. devel. Arthritis Found.-Wis. chpt., Milw., 1985-87, Edgewood Coll., Madison, 1987-90; dir. planned and major gifts Children's Hosp. Found., Inc., Milw., 1990—. Author, editor Children's Benefactor, 1990—, Children's Gift Planner, 1992—; editor Children's Gift Advisor, 1992—, The Art of Giving: Edgewood Coll., 1987-90. Mem. exec. bd. Boy Scouts Am.-Four Lakes coun., Madison, 1986-87, mem. adv. devel. com. Milw. County coun., 1990-91. Recipient Meritorious award Coun. for Advancement and Support Edn., Washington, 1986. Mem. Nat. Soc. Fundraising Execs., Nat. Com. Planned Giving, Chgo. Coun. on Planned Giving (dir. 1995—), Assn. Healthcare Philanthropy, Rotary Club of Wauwatosa-Mayfair (dir. 1994-95, 96—). Office: Childrens Hosp Found PO Box 1997 MS 3030 Milwaukee WI 53201-1997

HUTCHINS, BECKY J., state legislator; m. Joel R. Hutchins. Mem. from dist. 50 Kans. State Ho. of Reps., Topeka. Address: 700 Wyoming Holton KS 66436

HUTCHINS, ROBERT AYER, architectural consultant; b. N.Y.C., Oct. 19, 1940; s. Robert Senger and Evelyn Reed (Brooks) H.; m. Saran Niel Morgan, Jan. 4, 1964; children: Amey, Elisabeth, Margaret. BA, Harvard U., 1962, March., 1965; MDiv, McCormick Theol. Sem., 1992. Registered architect. Skidmore, Owings & Merrill, Chgo., 1966-89, ptnr., 1980-89. Pres., Chgo. Architecture Found., 1983-86, v.p., 1986-89; v.p., bd. dirs. Lincoln Park Zool. Soc., Chgo., 1976-91; bd. govs. Met. Planning Coun., Chgo., 1977—; bd. trustees McCormick Theological Sem., 1990-91. Mem. AIA (corp.), Chgo. Cultural Affairs Adv. Bd. (vice chmn. 1984-90), Chgo. Presbytery Svc. Corps.

HUTCHINSON, ELEANOR LOUISE, nursing administrator; b. Mpls., Nov. 9, 1928; d. Paul Carl Theodore and Amanda Marie (Doell) Ewert; R.N., Swedish Hosp., Mpls., 1951; B.S. in Nursing Edn., U. Minn., 1956; m. Richard Westervelt Hutchinson, Mar. 6, 1965; children—David Henry, Susan Elizabeth. Instr., clin. supr. pediatrics Hennepin County Gen. Hosp., Mpls., 1956-60; supr. pediatric and young adult unit Fairview Hosps., Mpls., 1961-67; dir. nursing, staff devel. coordinator Indianola (Iowa) Long-Term Care Facility, 1973-80; DON Madison County Meml. Hosp., Winterset, Iowa, 1980-92; DON The Village, 1992—. Mem. Nat. Nurses Assn., Nat. League Nursing, AAUW, U. Minn. Alumni Assn., Koinonia Group. Presbyterian. Club: Order Eastern Star. Home: PO Box 397 Indianola IA 50125-0397 Office: 1203 N E St Indianola IA 50125-1196

HUTCHINSON, JAMES A., engineer; b. Racine, Wis., July 5, 1966. BSME, U. West Milw., 1989. Project application engr. Phoenix divsn. Harnischfeger Corp., Milw., 1990—. Treas. Zion Evang. Lutheran Ch., Bristol, Wis., 1989. Republican. Lutheran. Office: Phoenix Divsn Harnischfeger 2969 S Chase Ave Milwaukee WI 53207

HUTCHINSON-GROSS, DOROTHY A., non-profit organization administrator; b. Lebanon, Mo., July 31, 1963; d. Bob Dean and Jocelyn Marie (Parker) Hutchinson; m. Jason Jeffrey Gross, Sept. 23, 1989; 1 child, Rachel Alexandra. BA in Bus. Adminstrn. and Econs., Ill. Coll., Jacksonville, 1985; MS in Mktg. Comms., Roosevelt U., 1988. Adminstrv. asst., aide State Senator Dawn Clark Netsch, Springfield, Ill., 1985-86; mktg. assoc. Fed. Sign, Chgo., 1986-88; dir. pub. rels. and mktg. I.A.C.M.H.A., Springfield, 1988-91; pub. rels. mgr. media Girl Scout Coun. Greater St. Louis, 1991-94; exec. dir. Pride, Inc., Alton, Ill., 1994—. Mem. River Bend Growth Assn. Democrat. Office: Pride Inc Alden Hall 5800 Godfrey Rd Godfrey IL 62035

HUTCHISON, CHARLOTTE PANCOAST (SHERRY HUTCHISON), civic worker; b. Phila., Jan. 13, 1919; d. Charles Snowden and Minnie Loretta (Percell) P.; m. Lawrence O. Hutchison, May 18, 1945 (dec. Mar. 1988); children: Perry, Lawrence. AB, Bryn Mawr Coll., 1940. mem. pers. com. Friends Com. on Nat. Legislation. Contbr. poetry to Saturday Evening Post, 1943-45. Newsletter editor, chair racism com. Women's Internat. League for Peace and Freedom, Des Moines, 1981-89; mem. Iowa com. Am. Friends Svc. Com., 1977-93; mem. joint oversight com. Iowa Peace Network, Des Moines, 1976—; newsletter editor Des Moines Valley Friends Meeting, 1971—; mem. Discipline Rev. Com. Iowa Yearly Meeting of Friends, 1989—; mem. platform com. Polk County and Dist. Dem. Party, 1972-88. Recipient Woman of Yr. award Greater Des Moines YWCA, 1990. Mem. Amnesty Internat. (case coord. 1986-94), LWV, Nat. Soc. Colonial Dames (v.p. Des Moines Borough 1991-92). Mem. Soc. of Friends. Home: 1328 Birch Ln Des Moines IA 50315-3020

HUTCHISON, DAVE, state legislator; b. July 26, 1943. BA, St. Norbert Coll. Assemblyman Wis. State Dist. 1. Producer Touring All Canada Touring Show. Mem. Rotary, YMCA, Luxemburg C. of C. Address: N8915 State Rd 57 Luxemburg WI 54217

HUTCHISON, KEVIN DON, librarian, writer; b. Detroit, May 9, 1954; s. Joseph Donald and Lola Mae (Smith) H. BS, No. Mich. U., 1976; MSLS, Wayne State U., 1988. Cert. profl. libr., Mich. Libr. Wayne County Libr., Detroit, 1988—. Author: World War II in the North Pacific, 1994, Operation Desert Shield/Desert Storm, 1995; contbr. articles to profl. publs. Lectr. Boy Scouts Am., S.E. Mich., 1993—. With USN, 1983-84. Mem. ALA, Mich. Libr. Assn., Assn. Ancient Historians, U.S. Naval Inst. Office: Greenwood Pub Co PO Box 5007 88 Post Rd W Westport CT 06881-5007

HUTMACHER, JAMES K., state senator, water drilling contractor. Water drilling contractor, Chamberlain, S.D.; mem. S.D. Senate, Pierre, mem. agr., natural resources, edn. and taxation coms. Democrat.

HUTNICK, VICTOR, engineering consultant; b. Cleve., June 3, 1956. B, Case Western Reserve U., 1978; M, Cleve. State U., 1984. Chief engr. Autron Mfg., Cleve., 1980—. Chmn. bd. appeals Copley Twp. (Ohio), 1988—. Mem. Soc. Automotive Engrs.

HUTSON, JEFFREY WOODWARD, lawyer; b. New London, Conn., July 19, 1941; s. John Jenkins and Kathryn Barbara (Himberg) H.; m. Susan Office, Nov. 25, 1967; children: Elizabeth Kathryn, Anne Louise. AB, U. Mich., 1963, LLB, 1966. Bar: Ohio 1966, Hawaii 1970. Assoc. Lane, Alton & Horst, Columbus, Ohio, 1966-74, ptnr., 1974—. Trustee, vice-chmn. Six Pence Sch., 1983-88; mem. com. creeds and professionalism Ohio Supreme Ct., 1989-90; chair, bd. dirs. Northwest Counseling Svcs., 1990-92; regional v.p. Def. Rsch. Inst, 1991-93. Lt. comdr. USNR, 1967-71. Fellow Am. Coll. Trial Lawyers; mem. ABA, Ohio Bar Assn. (past chmn. litigation sect.), Ohio Assn. Civil Trial Attys. (past pres.), Columbus Bar Assn., Internat. Assn. Def. Counsel, Fed. Counsel, Faculty Def. Coun. Trial Acad., Univ. Club, Scioto Country Club, Athletic Club. Avocations: cycling, reading, music. Office: Lane Alton & Horst 175 S 3rd St Columbus OH 43215-5134

HUTTAR BAILEY, JULIA RUTH, music director, educator; b. Beverly, Mass., May 3, 1961; d. Charles Adolph and Joy Anne (Culbertson) Huttar; m. Richard Weld Bailey, July 7, 1990. BA, Hope Coll., 1983; MusM, U. Mich., 1987. Dir. choir Grace Episcopal Ch., Holland, Mich., 1979-83; dir. music Trinity Episcopal Ch., Belleville, Mich., 1983-84, St. Clare's Episcopal Ch., Ann Arbor, Mich., 1984—; pres. Youth Commn. Diocese of Western Mich., 1978-79; chair Diocese of Mich. Commn. on Liturgy and Ch. Music, 1988; tchr. piano Ann Arbor, 1983—. Music dir. Vocal Arts Ensemble, Ann Arbor, 1994-95; bd. dirs. Ann Arbor Cantata Singers, 1987-90, pres., 1990. Mem. Assn. Diocesan Liturgy and Ch. Music Commns., Am. Guild Organists (bd. dirs. Ann Arbor chpt. 1994—). Home: 1609 Cambridge Rd Ann Arbor MI 48104 Office: St Clare's Episcopal Ch 2309 Packard Rd Ann Arbor MI 48104

HUVAERE, RICHARD FLOYD, auto dealer; b. Detroit, Dec. 2, 1944; s. Jerome and Kathryn Huvaere; m. Joan F. Nimmo, May 23, 1970 (div. 1989); children: Jason J.D., Sara E.L.; m. Stephanie Marie Roscia, May 27, 1995; stepchildren: Ronald, Ryan. A in Auto Mktg., Northwood U., Midland, Mich., 1966, BA in Bus., 1968. Pres., CEO Richmond (Mich.) Chrysler-Plymouth Dodge, 1968—; vice chmn. Mich. Auto Dealers Self-Insured Fund, Ypsilanti, 1990-93. Chmn. Centennial Bldg. Fund, Richmond, 1990—; mem. St. Clair County Airport Adv. Bd., Port Huron, Mich., 1988—. Recipient Outstanding Alumni award Northwood U., 1989. Mem. Nat. Auto Dealers Assn., Mich. Auto Dealers Assn. (bd. dirs.), Detroit Auto Dealers Assn., Greater Detroit Chrysler-Plymouth Dealers Assn., Greater Detroit Dodge Dealers Assn., Richmond C. of C., Rotary, Grosse Pointe Power Squadron, Detroit Yacht Club, The Old Club. Republican. Lutheran.

HYDE, DEAN ARNOLD, civil engineer; b. Wagner, S.D., Sept. 26, 1936; s. Henry Harold and Anne (Hamminga) H.; m. Evelyn Louise Deuter, July 1, 1961; children: Brenda Kay, James Arnold, Lisa Ann, Mark Edward. BS, U. S.D., 1958. Registered profl. engr., S.D. Bridge design engr. S.D. Dept. Transp., Pierre, 1958-89, office engr. plannning and programming, 1989—; mem. gov.'s pers. adv. bd. State of S.D., Pierre, 1992-95. With USAF, 1959. Mem. NSPE, S.D. Engring. Soc. (Engr. of Yr. 1989, chpt. pres.), Toastmasters (club pres.), S.D. State Employee's Org. (state bd. treas.). Republican. Methodist. Home: 703 N Madison Pierre SD 57501 Office: SD Dept Transp 700 E Broadway Pierre SD 57501

HYDE, HENRY JOHN, congressman; b. Chicago, Ill., Apr. 18, 1924; s. Henry Clay and Monica (Kelly) H.; m. Jeanne Simpson, Nov. 8, 1947; children: Henry J., Robert, Laura, Anthony. Student, Duke U., Durham, 1943-44; B.S., Georgetown U., Washington, 1946; J.D., Loyola U., Chicago, 1949. Bar: Ill. 1950. Mem. Ill. Gen. Assembly, 1967-74, 94th-103rd Congresses from 6th Ill. dist., 1975—; mem. internat. rels. com., chmn. jud. com. Served with USN, 1944-46. Mem. Chgo. Bar Assn. Republican. Roman Catholic. Office: House of Representatives Washington DC 20565*

HYDE, LAWRENCE LAYTON (FRED HYDE), ophthalmologist; b. Chgo., Feb. 4, 1930; s. Lawrence Victor and Beatrice (Mattox) H.; divorced; children: Cynthia, Carla, Mark, Michelle; m. Dolores Endt Gardella, July 1993. BS, U. Neb., 1950; MD, U. Nebr., 1954. Intern St. Luke's Hosp., Denver; resident U. Kans. Med. Ctr., 1957-60; private practive Kans. City, 1960-71; clin. prof. U. Kans. Med. Ctr., 1991—; founder Kans. City Eye Inst., 1986—. Researcher, patentee in field. With USAF, 1957-60. Mem. MENSA, ACS, AMA, S.E.E. Internat., Mo. Med. Soc., Am. Acad. Ophthal. (course instr. 1976—), Mo. Ophthal. Soc., Kansas City Soc. Ophthal./Otolaryn. (past pres.), Flying Physicians Assn. (past v.p., bd. dirs.), Castroviejo Soc. Home: Apt 2203 San Francisco Twr 2510 Grand Blvd Kansas City MO 64108-2678 Office: Kansas City Eye Inst 3101 Broadway St Ste 990 Kansas City MO 64111-2416

HYDE, ROBERT T., investment banker; b. Medina, Ohio, Apr. 27, 1932. Student, Kent State U., 1950-52; B of Fin., Akron U., 1957. Owner Hugert, Medina, 1955-76; divsn. pres. Standex Internat., Salem, N.H., 1976-85; investment broker A. G. Edwards & Sons Inc., Medina, 1985—. With USCG, 1952-55. Mem. Elks. Republican. Methodist. Office: A G Edwards & Sons Inc 5041 Victor Dr Medina OH 44256-9624

HYDE, RODERICK MICHAEL, medical technician; b. Pierre, S.D., Apr. 11, 1954; s. Richard Moorehead and Ruth Marie (Curry) H.; m. Margaret McLean Lacey, July 12, 1990; children: Raj, Robert. BA in Psychology, Bethany Nazarene Coll., 1979; BS in Medicine, U. Okla., 1983; MPH, Okla. Coll. Pub. Health, 1993. Cert. physician asst. Nat. Comm. Cert. Physician Assts., 1983. Physician asst. Harmon Meml. Hosp., Hollis, Okla., 1983-86, Children's Hosp., Oklahoma City, 1986-91, VA Hosp., Oklahoma City, 1991-93, Med. Assocs. Clinic, Pierre, S.D., 1993—; bd. dirs. Okla. Acad. Physician Assts., Oklahoma City, 1989-93; clin. assoc. prof. family medicine U. Okla., Oklahoma City, 1988-91. Fellow Am. Acad. Physician Assts.; mem. S.D. Acad. Physician Assts. (treas. 1993—), Mensa Soc. Republican. Methodist.

HYLAND, STEVEN E., business administrator; b. St. Louis, Feb. 11, 1953. AS, So. Plains C.C., Levelland, Tex., 1974; MS in Engring. Mgmt., U. Mo., Rolla, 1980; BTMT, Washington U., St. Louis, 1988, M of Engring. Mgmt., 1992. Cert. quality engr., quality auditor. Quality engr. Westinghouse Electric Corp., St. Louis, 1981-90; mgr. quality sys. Hussmann Corp., Bridgeton, Mo., 1990-92; mgr. vendor quality Nordyne, St. Louis, 1992—. Coach, trustee sub-div. Little League, St. Louis. Served with USAF, 1973-76. Mem. Am. Soc. Quality Control, Alpha Phi Omega. Office: Nordyne 1801 Park 270 Dr Saint Louis MO 63146-4020

HYNES, JOHN THOMAS, food scientist; b. Bklyn., Sept. 6, 1933; s. Patrick Joseph and Mary Ann (Greaney) H.; m. Elaine Marie Biers, Aug. 31, 1957; children: Karen, David, Teresa, Sean, Patricia, Christopher, Margaret. BS, Manhattan Coll., 1956. Scientist I Nat. Dairy Products Corp., Oakdale, N.Y., 1956-60, scientist II, 1960-65; rsch. scientist Kraft Gen. Foods, Glenview, Ill., 1965-70, group leader, 1970-74, sr. scientist I, 1974-79, sr. scientist II, 1979-84, sect. mgr., 1984-89, rsch. prin., 1989—; ret., 1993, dairy rsch. and industry cons., 193—. Mem. Inst. Food Technologists, Am. Chem. Soc.

HYSLOP, DAVID JOHNSON, arts administrator; b. Schenectady, June 27, 1942; s. Moses McDickens Hyslop; m. Sally Fefercorn; 1 child, Alexander. BS in Music Edn., Ithaca Coll., 1965. Elem. sch. vocal music supr. Elmira Heights, N.Y., 1965-66; mgr. Elmira Symphony Choral Soc., 1966; asst. mng. dir. Minn. Orch., Mpls., 1966-72; gen. mgr. Oreg. Symphony Orch., Portland, 1972-78; exec. dir. St. Louis Symphony Soc., 1978-89, pres., 1989-91; pres. Minn. Orch., 1991—. Bd. dirs. Am. Symphony Orch. League, 1988-96, chmn., 1994, mem. exec. and nominating coms., 1990-93; bd. dirs. Bach Soc. St. Louis, 1991—, Minn. Citizens for Arts, Mpls. Downtown Coun., 1992—, Mpls. Visitors and Conf. Bur., 1996—; mem., co-chmn. arts edn. task forceMo. Arts Coun., 1989-90; mem. rec. panel Nat Endowment for Arts, 1986-88, mem. challenge grant panel, 1987-88, mem. music overview panel, 1987-88; chmn. music and performing arts com. Regional Commerce and Growth Assn., St. Louis, 1987-89; mem. St. Louis Ctr. Martha Baird Rockefeller grantee, 1966. Mem. Am. Symphony Orch. League (chmn. major mgrs. and policy com. 1985-87, orch. mgmt. fellowship program 1979-88, orch. assessment program 1988), Regional Orch. Mgrs. Assn. (founder), Minn. Orchestral Assn., Mpls. Club, Arena Club. Home: 2019 Irving Ave Minneapolis MN 55405 Office: Minn Orch 1111 Nicollet Ave Minneapolis MN 55403-2406

HYZER, JAMES BANDT, forensic engineer, consultant; b. Janesville, Wis., Dec. 1, 1957; s. William Gordon and Mary Ann (Bandt) H. BS in Engring. Mechanics, U. Wis., 1981, MS, 1985; PhD in Mech. Engring., Strathclyde U., 1991. Rsch. asst. U. Wis., Madison, 1983-84; rsch. fellow U. Strathclyde, Glasgow, Scotland, 1985-88; cons. Janesville, 1989—; litigation cons. and expert witness, 1990—. Contbr. articles to profl. jours. Apptd. to Historic Commn., Janesville, 1992-93. Fellow Am. Acad. Forensic Scis.; mem. Am. Bd. Forensic Examiners, Soc. for Exptl. Mechanics, Illuminating Engrs. Soc. N. Am. Office: 1018 Oakland Ave Janesville WI 53545

IACOBELLI, MARK ANTHONY, dentist; b. Cleve., Aug. 27, 1957; s. Anthony Peter and Irene Margaret (Pordash) I.; m. Theresa Louise West, Aug. 8, 1991. BS, Case Western Res., 1979, DDS, 1982. Dentist, co-owner Iacobelli & Iffland, Canton, Ohio, 1982-85; gen. practice dentistry North Royalton, Ohio, 1985—; co-lectr. Jamison Cons. and Midwest Implant Inst. Named one of Outstanding Young Men Am., 1982. Fellow Acad. Gen. Dentistry; mem. ADA, Ohio Dental Assn., Cleve. Dental Assn., Am. Assn. Functional Orthodontics (Achievement award 1982), Padua Franciscan Alumni Assn. (chmn. devel. drive 1986, chmn. 1989, 90). Republican. Roman Catholic. Home: 4480 Oak Ridge Dr North Royalton OH 44133-2069 Office: 8030 Corporate Cir North Royalton OH 44133-1245

IANNI, LAWRENCE ALBERT, university administrator, English language educator; b. New Kensington, Pa., Apr. 19, 1930; s. Paul and Mary (Principe) I.; m. Mary Ellen Weeks, Apr. 26, 1952; children—Laura, Beth. BS in English Edn., Clarion U., 1952; MA in English, Case Western Res. U., 1956, PhD in English, 1962. Tchr. English Conneaut Valley High Sch., Conneautville, Pa., 1952-54, Mentor High Sch., Ohio, 1954-59; assoc. prof., prof. English Indiana U. of Pa., 1960-75; dean faculty San Francisco State U., 1975-78, provost, acad. v.p., 1978-87; chancellor U. Minn., Duluth, 1987—; mem. admissions adv. com. Calif. State U. Systems, Long Beach, 1981—; mem. math. and sci. tng. council San Francisco Consortium, 1982—. Contbr. articles to profl. jours. Solicitor trainer United Way, Indiana

County, Pa., 1963-69; trustee Pacific Grad. Ctr., Menlo Park, Calif., 1985-87. Recipient Alumnus of Yr. award Clarion U. Pa., 1984. Mem. Linguistic Soc. Am. Methodist. Home: 1025 E Skyline Pky Duluth MN 55805-1542*

IAQUINTA, LEONARD PHILLIP, university development and alumni official; b. Kenosha, Wis., Aug. 1, 1944; s. Anthony Sam and Mary Natalie (Gallo) I. BJ, Northwestern U., 1966; M in Journalism, Columbia U., 1967. Dir., cons. World Studies Data Bank Acad. for Ednl. Devel., N.Y.C., 1969-76; dir. field svcs. Alumni Rels. Northwestern U., Evanston, Ill., 1977-81; dir. Nat. Alumni Program Columbia U., N.Y.C., 1981-82; devel. officer, alumni dir. CUNY, 1982-86; dir. devel. and alumni affairs Indiana-Purdue Univs. at Fort Wayne, 1986-95; dir. devel. Northea. Ill. U., Chgo., 1995—. Assoc. editor: Notes on Negotiating, 1974; contbr. articles to profl. jours.; author various devel. manuals. Exec. dir. Kenosha United Way, 1976-77. Recipient 3 nat. alumni programming and fundraising awards Council for Advancement and Support of Edn., 1981, 84, 88, 15 Who Care award Vol. Connection of Switchboard of Ft. Wayne, 1990. Mem. Nat. Soc. Fund Raising Execs., Coun. for Advancement and Support of Edn., Chgo. Planned Giving Coun., Rotary, Sigma Delta Chi. Mem. Congregational Ch. Home: 6033 N Sheridan Rd # 31-G Chicago IL 60660-3022 Office: Northea Ill Univ Office of Dir Devel 5500 N Saint Louis Ave Chicago IL 60625-4699

IBAROLE, WAYNE R., stockbroker; b. San Francisco, Oct. 22, 1955. BA in Biology, Wayne State Coll., 1978. Dist. sales mgr. Ralston Purina, Columbus, Nebr., 1978-81; stockbroker First Mid. Am./Paine Webber, Lincoln, Nebr., 1981-84; stockbroker Edward D. Jones & Co., Charles City, Iowa, 1984-90, St. Louis, 1990-94, Yankton, S.D., 1994—; mem. tng. team bd. Edward Jones & Co., St. Louis, 1992-94. Mem. endowment fund bd. Cath. ch., St. Louis/Yankton; mem. Comty. Concert Bd., Yankton, 1994—; vol. Homeless Shelter, St. Louis; coach youth basketball Ch. Youth Programs, 1991-93. Mem. Rotary Club (past pres. 1985-92), Optimist Club, Elks, KC, Hillcrest Country Club. Republican. Office: Edward D Jones & Co 221 W 3rd St Yankton SD 57078-4322

ICE, ORVA LEE, JR., history educator; b. Elkhart, Ind., Mar. 10, 1920; s. Orva Lee Sr. and Frances Marian (Grimes) I.; m. Jean Ellen Ice, July 31, 1944. AB, U. Pitts., 1942; MA, U. Chgo., 1948; EdM, Wayne State U., 1959; PhD, Mich. State U., 1970. Cert. social worker, Mich. Export mgr. J.C. Jensen Co., Chgo., 1949-52; counselor Gary (Ind.)-Lake County Schs.; tchr. East Detroit (Mich.) Pub. Schs.; registrar Macomb Community Coll., Warren, Mich., 1961-68, prof. history, 1971—, prof. spl. studies in Asia and Latin Am., 1984—. With U.S. Army, 1942-46. Fulbright fellow. Mem. ASCD, Latin Am. Studies Assn., Asian Studies Assn, Phi Delta Kappa. Home: 11926 15 Mile Rd Sterling Heights MI 48312-5108

IGLAUER, BRUCE, record company executive. Educated, Lawrence U. Shipping clerk Delmark Records, 1970; founder Alligator Records, 1971. Produced recording of Hound Dog Taylor and the Houserockers, 1971; producer for artists including Big Walter Horton, Son Seals and Fenton Robinson. Office: Alligator Records PO Box 60234 Chicago IL 60660-0234

IHDE, AARON JOHN, history of science educator emeritus; b. Neenah, Wis., Dec. 31, 1909; s. John Lewis and Ella (Haase) I.; m. Olive Jane Tipler, June 14, 1933 (dec. Mar. 28, 1988); children: Gretchen (Mrs. Hendrick Serrie), John. BS, U. Wis., 1931, MS, 1939, PhD, 1941. Chemist Blue Valley Creamery Co., Chgo., 1931-38; instr. chemistry Butler U., Indpls., 1941-42; mem. faculty U. Wis.-Madison, 1942—, prof. chemistry, integrated liberal studies and history of sci., 1958-80, emeritus prof., 1980—, chmn. dept. integrated liberal studies, 1963-70; Carnegie intern in gen. edn. Harvard, 1951-52; Mem. Wis. Food Standards Adv. Com., 1955-68, chmn., 1964-65. Author: The Physical Universe, 1963, Development of Modern Chemistry, 1964, 2d edit., 1984, Selected Readings in the History of Chemistry, 1965, (with others) Joseph Priestley, Scientist, Theologian, and Metaphysician, 1980, Chemistry: As Viewed from Bascom's Hill, 1990. Recipient Dexter award history of chemistry divsn. Am. Chem. Soc., 1968, U. Wis. Chancellors award for disting. teaching, 1978. Mem. AAAS, History of Sci. Soc., Am. Chem. Soc. (Dexter award history of chemistry div. 1968), Soc. History of Tech., Wis. Acad. Scis., Arts and Letters (pres. 1963-64), Sigma Xi, Phi Lambda Upsilon. Unitarian. Home: 2606 Marshall Pky Madison WI 53713-1028

IHDE, CRAIG ALLEN, aerial specialists executive; b. Milw., June 26, 1952; s. Glenn Kenneth and Shirley Jane (Roeder) I.; m. Susan Beth Beitzel, Oct. 16, 1976; children: Brett David, Dale Adam. Student, U. Wis. Regional svc. mgr. Badgerland Equipment, Bettendorff, Iowa, 1974-76, Mi-Jack Products, Wolcott, Iowa, 1976-80; regional salesman Aerial Platform Equipment, Milw., 1980-83; head tech. support Simon Aerials-USA, Milw., 1985-87; pres., dir. Aerial Specialists Inc.-USA, Racine, Wis., 1983—. Active Racine Assemblies of God. Mem. Soc. of Automotive Engrs. (affiliate), Internat. Powered Access Fedn. U.K., U.S. C. of C. (bus. mem.). Office: Aerial Specialists Inc PO Box 85114 Racine WI 53408

IKEDA, SHIGEMASA, anesthesiologist; b. Okayama, Japan, Aug. 7, 1937; came to U.S., 1969; s. Tamakichi and Kimika (Hatano) I.; m. Kazuko Yamana, Aug. 16, 1968; children: Megumi, Ken Kiyoshi, Hiroshi Daniel. MD, Okayama U., 1965, PhD, 1972. Diplomate Am. Bd. Anesthesiology. Clin. rsch. assoc. U. Vt., Burlington, 1969-72; instr. Okayama U., 1972-73; asst. instr. SUNY, Syracuse, 1973-75; asst. prof. St. Louis U., 1975-85, assoc. prof., 1985-91, prof. anesthesiology, 1991—; mem. U.S.-Japan Coop. Sci. Program NSF, 1971; chief anesthesiology svc. St. Louis VA Med. Ctr. Fellow Am. Coll. Anesthesiologists. Office: St Louis U Dept Anesthesia 915 N Grand Blvd Saint Louis MO 63109

IKENBERRY, STANLEY OLIVER, education educator, former university president; b. Lamar, Colo., Mar. 3, 1935; s. Oliver Samuel and Margaret (Moulton) I.; m. Judith Ellen Life, Aug. 24, 1958; children: David Lawrence, Steven Oliver, John Paul. BA, Shepherd Coll., 1956; MA, Mich. State U., 1957, PhD, 1960, LHD (hon.); LLD (hon.), Millikin U.; LHD (hon.), Ill. Coll.; LLD (hon.), Rush U., W.Va. U. Instr. office Mich. State U., 1958-60, instr. instl. rsch. office, 1960-62; asst. to provost for instl. rsch., asst. prof. edn. W.Va. U., 1962-65, dean coll. human resources and edn., assoc. prof. edn., 1965-69; prof., assoc. dir. ctr. study higher edn. Pa. State U., 1969-71, sr. v.p., 1971-79; pres. U. Ill., Urbana, 1979-95, pres. emeritus, Regent prof., 1995—; bd. dirs. Harris Bankcorp, Chgo., Pfizer, Inc., N.Y.C., UtiliCorp United Inc., Kansas City. Contbr. articles to profl. jours. Chmn. Carnegie Found. for Advancement Tchg.; bd. dirs. Nat. Mus. Natural History. Named hon. alumnus Pa. State U. Mem. Am. Coun. Edn. (past chmn., pres. 1996—), Assn. Am. Univs. (past chmn.), Inst. for Ill. (bd. dirs.), Nat. Soc. Study Edn., Comml. Club Chgo., Mid-Am. Club, Tavern Club (Chgo.). Office: U Ill 1007 W Nevada Urbana IL 61801

ILIADIS, NICK, mechanical engineer; b. Athens, Greece, Nov. 23, 1951; came to U.S., 1956; s. Nickolas Iliadis and Agatha Colesnicenco; m. Susan Linda Fidler, June 28, 1975; children: Michelle Brooke, Jamie Lynn. BME, U. Ill., Chgo., 1974; A in Physics, U. London, 1978. Registered profl. mfg. engr., Ill. Mfg. engr. Alphatype Corp., Niles, Ill., 1974-76, EMI MEd. Inc., Northbrook, Ill., 1976-81; mech. engr. Williams Electronics, Chgo., 1981-84; project engr. Safety-Kleen Corp., Elgin, Ill., 1984-85, mgr. quality assurance, 1985—. Children's soccer coach. Mem. ASME, Soc. Mfg. Engrs. (sr., instr. engring. systems 1983—), Soc. Bio-med. Engrs. Office: Safety-Kleen Corp 1000 N Randall Rd Elgin IL 60123-7857

ILITCH, MARIAN, professional hockey team executive; m. Michael Ilitch; children: Denise Ilitch Lites, Ron, Mike Jr., Lisa Ilitch Murray, Atanas, Christopher, Carole. Owner, sec.-treas. Detroit Red Wings; owner, sec.-treas. Detroit Tigers Baseball Team, 1993—, also bd. dirs.; sec.-treas. Little Caesar Internat., Olympia Arenas, Inc., Fox Theatre. Recipient Pacesetter award, 1988, Michiganian of Yr. award, 1988, Nat. Preservation award Nat. Trust Hist. Preservation, 1990. Office: Detroit Red Wings 600 Civic Center Dr Detroit MI 48226-4408 also: Detroit Tigers Tiger Stadium Detroit MI 48216*

IMSANDE, JOHN DAVID, geneticist, researcher, educator; b. Grass Range, Mont., June 14, 1931; s. Louis H. and Freda M. (Dengel) I.; m. Elizabeth Blanchard, June 2, 1956 (div.); children: Carol Imsande Batastini, Louis D.; m. Marica F. Doerschug, Aug. 13, 1976. BA in Math. and Edn., U. Mont., 1953; MS in Chemistry, Mont. State U., 1956; PhD in Biochemistry, Duke U., 1960. Postdoctoral fellow U. Calif. Berkeley, 1960-61; lectr., postdoctoral fellow Princeton (N.J.) U., 1961-62; asst. prof. Case Western Res. U., Cleve., 1962-64, assoc. prof. dept. biology, 1964-69; assoc. prof. genetics and biochemistry Iowa State U., Ames, 1969-73, prof. genetics, 1973-86, prof. agronomy and genetics, 1990—; vis. scientist U. Edinburgh, Scotland, 1968-69; vis. prof. U. Calif., San Diego, 1976-77; vis. prof. dept. agriculture U. Queensland, Brisbane, Australia, 1986-87, 90-91. Author: (chpt.) The ENZYMES-Pyrophosphorylases, Methods in Enzymology, 1961, Biology of the Rhizobiaceae, 1981; contbr. over 50 articles to profl. jours. Cpl. U.S. Army, 1953-55. NIH fellow USPHS, 1957-60, 60-62; grantee NIH, USDA. Mem. Crop Sci. Soc. Am. Democrat. Home: 204 Arrasmith Trl Ames IA 50010-9720 Office: Iowa State U Dept Of Agronomy Ames IA 50011

INBODY, DALE DEWAYNE, farmer; b. New Paris, Ind., Dec. 27, 1925; s. John Paul and Laura (Haberstich) I.; m. Doris Ilene Burkey, Mar. 23, 1957; children: Randal, Thomas, Carla. Pres. Elkhart Co. Farm Bur. Coop., Goshen, Ind. 1st lt. Elkhart County Fire Dept., Goshen, 1951-71; v.p. Elkhart County Planning Commn.; pres. Elkhart County Bd. Zoning Appeals. Sgt. U.S. Army, 1954-56. Mem. Gideons Internat. Ind. Farm Bur. Co-op. Assn. (bd. dirs. 1983-91, pres. Gideons-Elkhart South Camp), Countrymark Co-op (bd. dirs. 1991-92). Democrat. Methodist.

INCROPERA, FRANK PAUL, mechanical engineering educator; b. Lawrence, Mass., May 12, 1939; s. James Frank and Ann Laura (Leone) I.; m. Andrea Jeanne Eastman, Sept. 2, 1960; children: Terri Ann, Donna Renee, Shaunna Jeanne. BSME, MIT, 1961; MS, Stanford U., 1962, PhD, 1966. Jr. engr. Barry Controls Corp., Watertown, Mass., 1959; thermodynamics engr. Aerojet Gen. Corp., Azusa, Calif., 1961; heat transfer specialist Lockheed Missiles and Space Co., Sunnyvale, Calif., 1962-64; mem. faculty Purdue U., 1966—, prof. mech. engring., 1973—, head dept., 1989—; cons. in field. Author: Introduction to Molecular Structure and Thermodynamics, 1974, Fundamentals of Heat Transfer, 1985, 90, 96; Fundamentals of Heat and Mass Transfer, 1981, 85, 90, 96; also articles. Recipient Solberg Teaching award Purdue U., 1973, 77, 86, Potter Teaching award, 1973, Von Humboldt sr. scientist award Fed. Republic Germany.$Dorchester Reed Warner medal Am. Soc. of Mechanical Engineers, 1995. Fellow ASME (Melville medal 1988, Heat Transfer Meml. award 1988, Worcester Reed Warner award 1995); mem. Am. Soc. Engring. Edn. (Ralph C. Roe award 1982, George Westinghouse award 1983), Nat. Acad. Engring. Office: Sch Mech Engring Purdue U West Lafayette IN 47907

INDERMARK, ELLEN ANN, therapist; b. Blue Mound, Ill., Apr. 27, 1933; d. Russel Dole and Julia (Hayden) Meachum; m. Roger Indermark, Nov. 27, 1952; children: Christine Indermark Diamond, Sheila Indermark Boehner, John, George. BA, Sangamon State U., 1986, MA, 1988. Mgmt. positions Ill. Bell Telephone Co., Springfield, Ill., 1958-85; therapist, cons. Lutheran child and family /DCFS Gateway Found., Springfield, Ill., 1985-89; owner, therapist Stillmeadow Counseling Ctr., Springfield, Ill., 1989—. Mem. ACA, Am. Assn. Marraige and Family Therapy, Ill. Alcohol and Drug abuse Profl. Cert. Assn., Inc., Chi Sigma Iota. Home: RR 7 Stillmeadow Springfield IL 62707 Office: Stillmeadow Counseling Ctr 833 S 4th St Springfield IL 62703-2220

INFUSINO, ACHILLE FRANCIS, construction company executive; b. Kenosha, Wis., Feb. 8, 1953; s. Frank and Irene (Rende) I.; m. Joyce Marie, Nov. 22, 1975; children: Daniel, Nicholas, Jaclyn, Timothy. BA, Carthage Coll., 1982; MBA, Marquette U., 1987. Pres. Infusino Constrn. Co., Inc., Kenosha, 1987—, Cellular City Communications, Kenosha, 1987—, Hunter's Ridge Realty Corp., Kenosha, 1988—; mng. ptnr. C.S.I. Land Devel., Kenosha, 1988—; sec. Al & Lou's Gas & Groceries, Wis., 1991—; mng. ptnr. Southport Energy Ptnrs., Kenosha, Wis., 1991—; founder, sr. project mgr. Project Mgmt. Cons., Kenosha, 1994—; bd. dirs. Family Med. Ctr., Kenosha; instr. Carthage Coll., 1990; sec. Al & Lou's Convenience Stores. Bd. dirs. Kenosha Area Devel. Corp., 1981-87, Salvation Army Adv. Bd., Kenosha, 1983-85; pres. St. Joseph's Interparish Jr. High Sch., Kenosha, 1986-91; chmn. Bd. Building Appeals, City of Kenosha, 1986-88. Mem. Italian Am. Soc., MBA Execs., Assn. Constrn. Insps., Environ. Assessment Assn. Office: Project Mgmt Cons 2315 30th Ave Kenosha WI 53144-1411

INGEMAN, JERRY ANDREW, artist; b. Hallock, Minn., Nov. 3, 1950; s. Lavern Norman and Helaine Ann (Carlson) I.; m. Karen Kay Koll, June 25, 1983; 1 child, Maja Chalong. AA with distinction, Willmar (Minn.) State Jr. Coll., 1971; BA magna cum laude, St. Cloud State U., Minn., 1988. Purchasing agt. Nat. Bushing and Parts, St. Cloud, 1971-79; graphic artist St. Cloud State U., 1979-80; supr. Perkins Restaurant, St. Cloud, 1980-82; owner Jaiman Arts, 1985—; editl. asst. Payne Studios, Mpls., 1996—; cons. artifact restoration Evelyn Payne Hatcher Mus. of Anthropology, St. Cloud, 1984—. Exhibited in group shows throughout U.S.; contbr. booklets to profl. jours. Winner Best of Show Celebration of the Arts, Cedar Rapids, Marion, Iowa, award of Excelence Art in the Park, Appleton, Wis., Founder's award Arts in the Park, Brainerd, Minn., 1st prize craft competition Art Horizon, N.Y.C., Best in Jewelry Oconomowoc Festival of Arts. Mem. Am. Craft Coun., Am. Soc. for Aesthetics, Internat. Sculpture Ctr., Soc. N.Am. Goldsmiths. Office: Jaiman Arts PO Box 236 Monticello MN 55362-0236

INGERSOLL, DONALD PAUL, management consultant; b. Peekskill, N.Y., Apr. 15, 1944; s. James Richard and Ann (Ilovichny) I.; m. Jacqueline Jarvis, Feb. 3, 1967; children: Kimberly, Brian. BSBA, Mich. Tech. U., 1967; MBA, Wayne State U., 1974. Cert. govt. fin. mgr. Mgr. GAO, Detroit, 1967-95; sr. ptnr., owner Bardon Kruman Assocs., Northville, Mich., 1995—; exec. dir. Midwest/Intergovt. Audit Forum, Great Lake states, 1981-84, tech. advisor, 1989-91. Treas. Avondale Bd. Edn., Auburn Hills, Mich., 1987-95; v.p. Avondale Little League, Troy, Mich., 1985-88; mem. Avondale Curriculum Adv. Com., Auburn Hills, 1984-85; conv. del. Episcopal Diocese of Mich., 1987-93. Lt. USNR, 1967-69, Vietnam. Mem. Assn. Govt. Accts. (nat. exec. com. 1995—, nat. bd. dirs. 1987-88, 92-93, 95—, edn. dir. Detroit chpt. 1986, chpt. pres. 1987-88, chmn. exec. com. 1988-91, regional v.p. 1992-93), Mich. Assn. Sch. Bds., Oakland County (Mich.) Sch. Bd. Assn. Home: 6839 Dublin Fair Rd Troy MI 48098-2118 Office: Bardon Kruman Assocs Ste 202 42000 W 6 Mile Northville MI 48167

INGERSOLL, GAIL LAURA, nursing administrator, nursing educator, nursing researcher; b. Utica, N.Y., Apr. 25, 1949; d. Robert James and Elnora Catherine (Bracken) I. AAS in Nursing, Alfred State Coll., 1971; BSN, Alfred U., 1980; MSN, U. Rochester (N.Y.), 1983, EdD in Adminstr., 1986. RN, N.Y., Ind. Asst. clinician surg. ICU U. Rochester Med. Ctr., 1974-77, surg. ICU staff nurse, 1971-74, 77-79, clinician I surg. outpatient dept., 1979-82, assoc. dir. office clin. practice evaluation, 1988-89, dir. rsch. clin. nursing practices, 1988-89; clin. nurse specialist/instr. critical care U. Rochester Sch. Nursing, 1985-86, clin. nurse specialist/instr. trauma/spinal cord injury, 1985-86, asst. prof., 1986-92, interim chmn. div. health restoration, 1988-89; chmn. div. health restoration U. Rochester (N.Y.) Sch. Nursing, 1989-91; assoc. prof., chmn. dept. nursing adminstrn. and tchr. edn. Ind. U. Sch. Nursing, Indpls., 1992-95; prof., 1995—; asst. dir. nursing for adminstrn. Ind. U. Hosps., Indpls., 1992—; prof., chmn. dept. nursing adminstrn. and tchr. edn. Ind. U. Sch. Nursing, Indpls., 1995—; lectr. and cons. in field; manuscript reviewer Critical Care Nurse, 1986-89, Image, The Jour. Nursing Scholarship, 1989—, Nursing Outlook, 1992—. Contbr. articles to Western Jour. Nursing Rsch., 1991—. Robert Wood Johnson Clin. Nurse scholar, U. Pa., postdoctoral fellow, 1988. Fellow Am. Acad. Nurses; mem. ANA, Nat. League for Nursing, Coun. Nurse Researchers, Midwest Nursing Rsch. Soc., Assn. Health Svcs. Rsch., Sigma Theta Tau (Leadershpi award Delta Sigma chpt.), Kappa Delta Pi, Sigma Xi. Office: Ind U Sch Nursing 1111 Middle Dr Indianapolis IN 46202-5243

INGHAM, NORMAN WILLIAM, Russian literature educator, genealogist; b. Holyoke, Mass., Dec. 31, 1934; s. Earl Morris and Gladys May (Rust) I. AB, Middlebury Coll. in German and Russian cum laude, 1957; postgrad. Slavic philology, Free U. Berlin, 1957-58; MA in Russian lang. and lit., U. Mich., 1959; postgrad. in Russian lang. and lit., Leningrad (USSR) State U., 1961-62; PhD in Slavic langs. and lit., Harvard U., 1963. Cert. genealogist. Postdoctoral researcher Czechoslovak Acad. Scis., Prague, Czechoslovakia, 1963-64; asst. prof. dept Slavic langs. and lits. Ind. U., Bloomington, 1964-65; asst. prof. Harvard U., Cambridge, Mass., 1965-70, lectr., 1970-71; assoc. prof. U. Chgo., 1971-82, prof., 1982—, chmn. dept., 1977-83, dir. Eastern Europe and USSR lang. and area ctr., 1978-91; mem. Am. Com. Slavists, 1977-83; mem. com. Slavic and Ea. European studies U. Chgo., 1979-91, chmn., 1982-91, also other coms.; dir. Ctr. for East European and Russian/Eurasian Studies, 1991—; rep. internat. Rsch. and Exch. Bd.; cert. genealogist, 1994—. Author: E.T.A. Hoffman's Reception in Russia, 1974; editor: Church and Culture in Old Russia, 1991; co-editor: (with Joachim T. Baer) Mnemozina: Studia litteraria russica in honorem Vsevolod Setchkarev; mem. editorial bd. Slavic and East European Jour., 1978-87, adv. bd., 1987-89; assoc. editor Byzantine Studies, 1973-81; contbg. editor The Am. Genealogist, 1995—; contbr. and translator articles and book revs. Fulbright fellow, 1957-58, fellow Dumbarton Oaks Ctr. for Byzantine Studies, 1972-73. Mem. Am. Assn. Advancement Slavic Studies (rep. coun. on mem. instns. 1985—, area rep. nat. adv. com. for Ea. European lang. programs 1985—), Am. Asns. Tchrs. Slavic and East European Langs., Early Slavic Studies Assn. (v.p. 1993-95, pres. 1995—), Chgo. Consortium for Slavic and East European Studies (v.p. 1982-84, pres. 1984-86, exec. coun. 1992—), Phi Beta Kappa. Office: U Chgo Slavic Dept 1130 E 59th St Chicago IL 60637-1543

INGLESIAS, BYRON F., investment officer; b. South Bend, Ind., Oct. 26, 1962; s. Antonio and Rosetta (Theobald) I. BA, Mich. State U., 1985. Fin. planner Am. Express, Mpls., 1986-93; investment officer Norwest Investment, Ft. Wayne, Ind., 1993—. Republican. Roman Catholic. Home: 1913 Bayview Dr Fort Wayne IN 46815-4212 Office: Norwest Investment Svcs Inc 800 Northcrest Shopping Ctr Fort Wayne IN 46805-1224

INGRAM, TERRENCE NEALE, insurance agent; b. Shullsburg, Wis., Nov. 21, 1939; s. Forrest R. and Ida D. (Fiedler) I.; m. Nancy June Fleming Laun, May 30, 1981. BS, U. Wis.-Platteville, 1961. Instr. physics and math. U. Wis., Platteville, 1961-64; Bald Eagle rschr., 1964-65; bird instr. Wis. Audubon Camp, 1964-65; tchr. high sch., Mauston, Wis., 1965-66, Cuba City, Wis., 1966-67; instr. physics U. Wis., Platteville, 1967-68; tchr. high sch., Harvard, Ill., 1968-70; field underwriter N.Y. Life Ins. Co., 1970-84; ind. agent, 1984—; founder, pres., exec. dir. Eagle Valley Environmentalists, 1972-84, The Eagle Found., 1984-88; instr. physics Highland C.C., Freeport, Ill., 1989—. Editor: Inland Bird Banding Assn., 1961-65. Mem. sch. bd. Cmty. Unit Dist 205, 1987-91; bd. dirs. North Central Audubon Council, 1966-70, Ill. Audubon Soc., 1963-70, v.p., 1970; pres., exec. dir. Eagle Nature Found., Ltd., 1995—; mem. adv. bd. Savanna Army Depot Restoration, 1995—; pres. Jo Daviess County Agrl. Soc., 1990-91. Recipient Honor Roll award Izaak Walton League Am., 1976; Sol Feinstone Environ. award SUNY-Syracuse, 1979; Protector of Environment award Chgo. Audubon Soc., 1981. Mem. Assn. Life Underwriters, Wis. Acad. Sci., Northwest Ill. Guernsey Assn. (pres. 1982—, Southwestern Wis. Guernsey Assn. (bd. dirs. 1989-93), Inland Bird Banding Assn. (pres. 1983-85). Republican. Editor: Inland Bird Banding News, 1961-65; editor, pub. Small Beekeepers Jour., 1990—, Bald Eagle News, 1990—. Coordinator: No. Am. Bird Bander, 1984-90. Home: 8384 N Broadway Rd Apple River IL 61001-9401 Office: 300 Hickory St Apple River IL 61001

INMAN, DAVID RICHARD, municipal official; b. Chgo., Dec. 22, 1957; s. Richard James Inman and Lorraine (Bubacz) Inman Meehan; m. Emily Wolfson, Sept. 19, 1987; children: Richard David, Peter James. BS in Chemistry, U. Ill., 1979; MBA, U. Chgo., 1989. Asst. coach U. Ill. Hockey Team, Champaign, 1979-81; chemist IEPA, Champaign, 1979-81; asst. rschr. CPC-Moffett Tech. Ctr., Bedford Park, Ill., 1981-85; shift mgr. Corn Products Refinery, Bedford Park, 1985-88; prodn. supr. Helene Curtis, Inc., Chgo., 1988-90; asst. commr. Chgo. Dept. Environment, 1990—; mem. adv. bd. Wright Coll. Environ. Tech. Program, Chgo., 1994—; chair Chgo. Emissions Reduction Credit Com., 1995—. Mem. adv. staff environ. affairs Fifth Congl. Dist., Chgo. area, 1981-83. Mem. Air and Waste Mgmt. Assn. (dir. Lake Mich. States sect. 1994—), Chgo. Coun. on Fgn. Rels. Democrat. Roman Catholic. Office: Chgo Dept Environment 30 N LaSalle St Ste 2500 Chicago IL 60602

INMAN, MARIANNE ELIZABETH, college administrator; b. Berwyn, Ill., Jan. 9, 1943; d. Miles V. and Bessee M. (Hejtmanek), Pizak; m. David P. Inman; Aug 1, 1964. BA, Purdue U., 1964; AM, Ind. U., 1967; PhD, U. Tex., 1978. Dir. Comml. Div. Worl Instruction and Translation, Inc., Arlington, Va., 1969-71; program staff mem. Ctr. for Applied Linguistics, Arlington, 1972-73; lectr. in French No. Va. Community Coll., Bailey's Crossroads, 1973; faculty mem., linguistic researcher Tehran (Iran) U., 1973-75; intern mgmt. edn. rsch. & devel. S.W Ednl. Devel. Lab., Austin, Tex., 1977-78; asst. prof., program dir. Southwestern U., Georgetown, Tex., 1978; dir. English lang. inst. Alaska Pacific U., Anchorage, 1980-87, chairperson all-U. requirements, 1984-88, assoc. dean acad. affairs, 1988-90; v.p. dean of coll. Northland Coll., Ashland, Wis., 1990-95; pres. Ctrl. Meth. Coll., Fayette, Mo., 1995—; contbr. Pres. Commn. Foreign Lang. and Internat. Studies, Washington, 1978-79; manuscript evaluator The Modern Lang. Jour., Columbus, Ohio, 1979-84; cons. Anchorage Sch. Dist., 1984-90; cons., evaluator N. Cen. Assn. Colls. and Schs., Chgo., 1990—; mem. dean's task force Coun. on Ind. Colls., 1993—. Co-author: English for Medical Students, 1976; co-author and editor: English for Science and Engineering Students, 1977; contbr. articles to profl. jours. Treas. Alaska Humanities Forum, Anchorage, 1982-87; mem. Anchorage Matanuska-Susitna Borough Pvt. Industry Coun., 1983-86; treas. Sister Cities Commn., Anchorage, 1984-90; mem. Multicultural Edn. Adv. Bd., Anchorage, 1987-90; active speakers bur. Wis. Humanities Com., 1992-95, Mcpl. Libr. Bd., 1993-95. Named Fellow of Grad. Sch., U. Tex. Austin, 1977-78, Nat. Teaching Fellow, Alaska Pacific U., Anchorage, 1980-81; recipient Pub. Svc. award Sister Cities Commn., Anchorage, 1987, Kellogg Found. Nat. fellowship, Battle Creek, Mich., 1988-91. Mem. League of Women Voters, Nat. Assn. Women in Edn., Am. Assn. for Higher Edn., Am. Coun on Teaching of Foreign Langs., Tchrs. of English to Speakers of Other Langs., Nat. Coun. Tchrs. of English, Sigma Kappa. Office: Ctrl Meth Coll 411 CMC Sq Fayette MO 65248-1198

INNIGER, DEAN LEE, structural engineer; b. Ft. Wayne, Ind., Mar. 7, 1967. BS in Mech. Engr. Tech., Purdue U., Ft. Wayne, 1991. Design engr. PHD, Inc., Ft. Wayne, 1992—. Mem. Soc. Automotive Engrs.

IQBAL, ZAFAR MOHD, cancer researcher, biochemist, pharmacologist, toxicologist, consultant; b. Hyderabad, India, Dec. 12, 1938; came to U.S., 1965, naturalized, 1973; s. M.A. and Haleemunissa (Begum) Rahim. BSc, Osmania U., 1958, MSc, 1962; PhD, U. Md., 1970. Diplomate Am. Bd. Toxicology; diplomate, bd. cert. forensic medicine and forensic exxaminer. Asst. prof. pharmacology Case Western Res. U., Cleve., 1974-76; assoc. dir. ERC programs in occupational toxicology U. Ill. Med. Ctr., Chgo., 1980-81, assoc. prof. microbiology, 1977-80, assoc. prof. occupational medicine and environ. health, 1976-93, assoc. prof. preventive medicine, 1982-93; dir. Carcinogenesis Labs. Carcinogenesis Labs. in U. Ill. Grad. Coll., Chgo., 1983-93, U. Ill. Grad. Coll., Chgo., 1977-93; chair HIV hazards in rsch. com., 1990-93; dir. Toxicology-Cancer Cons., Inc., Chgo., 1987—; affiliate Lurie Cancer Ctr., Northwestern U., 1996—; cons. in field to OSHA, 1980-81, Clements Assocs., 1976-79, Expert Resources, 1982—, Ill. Cancer Coun., 1989; lectr continuing edn.; grant reviewer study sects.NIH; merit grant reviewer VA, 1981-82; mem. tech. bd. panel Gt. Lakes Protection Fund, 1989—; participant profl. confs.; NSF-Coun. Sci. and Indsl. Rsch. exch. scientist, 1981; sponsor, trainer India-U.S. exch. scientists NSF, 1985-86; peer reviewer for sci. books and films Cancer Rsch., Jour. Biochem., Toxicology, Carcinogenesis and others; spl. advisor RRL (India) Dirs., 1980—; mem. U.S. AID's-Asia Environ. Partnership and Environ Tech. Network Asia, 1994—, Environ. and Tech. Network Asia-Latin Am. Program, 1996—. Editor: Molecular Mechanisms of Toxic Response; Pancreatic Carcinogenesis Mechanisms; editor Jour. Molecular Toxicology and Carcinogenesis; mem. editorial bd. Forensic Examiner, 1995—; contbr. more than 50 articles to profl. jours. NSF-CSIR exch. scientist, 1981; sponsor, trainer India-U.S. Exch. Scientists, NSF, 1985-86; spl. advisor RRL (India) Dirs., 1980—; pres. Rahim Meml. Fedn., 1995—. Fellow Coun. Sci. and Indsl. Rsch., India, 1963-65; Fogarty Internat. fellow Nat. Cancer Inst., NIH, 1970-71, staff fellow, 1971-74, grantee 1974-93; grantee Nat. Inst. Occupational Safety and Health, EPA, State of Ill., 1974-93. Fellow Am. Coll.

Forensic Examiners (life, diplomate, bd. cert. forensic medicine); mem. AAAS, Am. Assn. Cancer Rsch., Am. Pancreatic Assn., N.Y. Acad. Scis., Am. Chem. Soc., Soc. Toxicology, Am. Coll. Toxicology, Nat. Registry of Forensic Examiners, B.E.S.T. N.Am., Registry Global World Leaders, Soc. Toxicology (molecular biology, carcinogenesis and mechanics splty. sects.), Sigma Xi. Office: Toxicology-Cancer Inc PO Box 60267 Chicago IL 60660-0267

IRBY, KENNETH LEE, poet, English language educator; b. Bowie, Tex., Nov. 18, 1936; s. Addison Craft and Dora Elizabeth (East) I. BA, U. Kans., 1958; AM, Harvard U., 1960, postgrad., 1962-63; MLS, U. Calif., 1968. Grad. teaching asst. dept. Far Ea. lang. Harvard U., Cambridge, Mass., 1963; lectr. dept. English Tufts U., Medford, Mass., 1971-72, asst. prof., 1972-73, 74-75; vis. lectr. English Inst., U. Copenhagen, 1973-74; lectr. U. Kans., Lawrence, 1985—; mem. faculty Milton Avery Grad. Sch. Arts, Bard Coll., Annandale-on-Hudson, N.Y., 1990-92, summer writing program Naropa Inst., Boulder, Colo., 1996. Author: Relation, 1970, Catalpa, 1977, Orexis, 1981, A Set, 1984, Call Steps, 1992, Antiphonal and Fall to Fall, 1994. With U.S. Army, 1960-62. Mem. Masons, Phi Beta Kappa. Home: N-311 N Regency Pl Lawrence KS 66049 Office: U Kans Dept English Wescoe Hall Lawrence KS 66045

IREDELL, ROBERT, IV, advertising executive; b. 1941. Grad., Kenyon Coll., 1963, Harvard Sch. Bus. Sr. Mgmt. for Advt. Agy. Execs., 1982. With Sta. KVIZ-TV, Cleve., 1963-70, Hesselbart & Mitten, Akron, Ohio, 1970-75; with Meldrum Fewsmith Yellow Pages, Cleve., 1975—, v.p., 1978-81, sr. v.p., 1981, now bd. dirs.; exec. v.p., gen. mgr. Cleve. ops. Meldrum Fewsmith Yellow Pages, 1986-88, pres., 1988—. Office: Meldrum & Fewsmith Inc 1350 Euclid Ave Cleveland OH 44115*

IRELAND, DELORES W. (DOLLY IRELAND), post-anesthesia nurse; b. Mt. Clemens, Mich., Apr. 18, 1949; d. Earl Louis and Wilma Lucille (Landerschier) Kraft; children: Heather, Shannon, Jason. Diploma, Hurley Med. Ctr., 1970; student, U. Detroit-Mercy. Cert. ambulatory post anesthesia nurse. Clin. nurse William Beaumont Hosp., Royal Oak, Mich., 1970-77, Troy, Mich., 1977-87; clin. nurse II William Beaumont Hosp., Troy, 1989—; nursing coord. Gen. Dynamics Overseas Clinic, Heliopolis, Cairo, Egypt, 1988-89; founding dir. Am. Bd. of Post Anesthesia Nursing Cert., Richmond, Va., 1984-87, certs. of publ., 1986, 87, 91; speaker in field. Contbr. articles to profl. jours. Leader Girl Scouts of Am., Romeo, Mich., 1979-83; pres. Dynamic Women, Heliopolis, Cairo, Egypt, 1988-89; fellowship lay minister Our Redeemer Luth. Ch., Washington, Mich., 1989—. Mem. Am. Soc. Post Anesthesia Nurses (dir. Mich. chpt. 1990-93, mem. exec. com. 1991-92, pres.-elect 1992-93, pres. 1993-94), Mich. Assn. Post Anesthesia Nurses (sec. 1982-83, v.p. 1983-84, pres. 1984-85). Republican. Home: 66800 Busch Ct Washington MI 48095-1920 Office: William Beaumont Hosp 44201 Dequindre Rd Troy MI 48098-1117

IRELAND, LANCE W., mechanical engineer; b. Washington, Oct. 8, 1958. BSME, Purdue U., 1981. Project engr. Marley Goalingtower, Louisville, 1983-86; engring. support mgr. Coldjet, Loveland, Ohio, 1986-87; application engr. Valco Cin., Cin., 1987—. Office: Valco Cincinnati 411 Circle Fwy Dr Cincinnati OH 45246-1213

IRSAY, JAMES STEVEN, professional football team executive; b. Lincolnwood, Ill., June 13, 1959; s. Robert Irsay and Harriet Pogerzelski; m. Margaret Mary Coyle, Aug. 2, 1980; children: Carlie Margaret, Casey Coyle, Kalen. B in Broadcast Journalism, So. Meth. U., 1982. With Balt. Colts., from early 1970's; now v.p., gen. mgr. Indpls. Colts; corp. mem. Indiana Sports Corp., Indpls., 1985-87. Composer, performer single Hoosier Heartland, 1985, single and video Go Colts, 1985, Colors, 1990. Bd. dirs. Noble Ctrs. Retarded Children, Indpls., 1985-87, Motorcycle Drill Team, Indpls. Police Dept., 1985-87. Office: Indpls Colts PO Box 535000 Indianapolis IN 46253-5000

IRVINE, PHYLLIS ELEANOR KUHNLE, nursing educator, administrator; b. Germantown, Ohio, July 14, 1940; d. Carl Franklin and Mildred Viola (Erisman) Kuhnle; m. Richard James Irvine, Feb. 15, 1964; children: Mark, Rick. BSN, Ohio State U., 1962, MSN, 1979, PhD, 1981; MS, Miami U., Oxford, Ohio, 1966. Staff nurse VA Ctr., Dayton, Ohio, 1962-66; mem. nursing faculty Miami Valley Hosp. Sch. Nursing, Dayton, 1968-78; teaching asst., lectr. Ohio State U., Columbus, 1979-82; assoc. prof. Ohio U., Athens, 1982-83; prof., dir. N.E. La. U., Monroe, 1984-88; prof., dir. sch. nursing Ball State U., Muncie, Ind., 1988—. Reviewer Health Edn. Jour., Reston, Va., 1987; contbr. articles to profl. jours. Mem. Mayor's Commn. on Needs of Women, La., 1984-88; 1st v.p., bd. dirs. United Way of Ouachita, La., 1986-88. Mem. ANA, Ind. Nurses Assn., Ind. Coun. Deans & Dirs. of Nursing Edn. (pres. 1992-96), Internat. Coun. Women's Health Issues (bd. dirs. 1986-92), Assn. for the Advancement Health Edn., Sigma Theta Tau. Office: Ball State U Cn418 Nursing Muncie IN 47306

IRVINE, ROBERT KEITH, librarian; b. Kansas City, Mo., Aug. 11, 1955; s. Robert Joseph and Ruby Berniece (Dehner) I. AA, Maplewoods C.C., 1976; B of Music Edn., U. Mo., 1979, MEd, 1987, Edn. Specialist, 1989. Cert. tchr., Mo. (lifetime). Substitute tchr. Pub. Sch. Dist., North Kansas City, Mo., 1975-80; libr. asst. U. Mo., Kansas City, Mo., 1980-89, U.S. Cts., Kansas City, Mo., 1984-89; educator High Sch., Kansas City, Mo., 1989-94, Maplewoods Coll., Kansas City, Mo., 1992-94, Kansas City (Mo.) Pub. Schs., 1994—; curriculum writer free lance, 1992-95; travel counselor E.F. Educational Tours, 1994-95. Composer: (opera) Thespis, 1980, (song cycle) The Road Goes Ever On, 1985; author: (play) A Christmas Carol, 1990, Cinderella, 1994. Founder Cmty. Theatre, Kansas City North, 1984; higher edn. dir. Avondale United Meth. Ch. Coun. on Ministries, Kansas City, 1993—. Recipient Prodn. grant Victor Herbert Found., 1985-90, Edn. Achievement award U. Mo., 1987. Mem. Nat. Coun. Tchrs. of English, Libr. of Congress, Nat. Geog. Soc., Smithsonian Instn., Sir Arthur Sullivan Soc., Pi Lamba Theta, Phi Kappa Phi. Democrat. Methodist. Home: 2608 Waples Kansas City MO 64117 Office: Kansas City Mo Pub Schs 1211 McGee Kansas City MO 64111

IRVINE, WILLIAM KENNEDY, marketing consultant; b. Glen Ridge, N.J., Oct. 26, 1938; s. Hugh Laurance and Muriel (Hills) I.; m. Mary Ann Shira, Mar. 4, 1961; children: Nancy Catherine, William Douglas, Andrew McCallum. BSBA, Miami U., Oxford, Ohio, 1960, MBA, 1961. Cert. substance abuse tchr. Sr. account exec. Mkt. Rsch. Corp. Am. (now MRCA Info. Svcs.), Chgo., 1964-68; mng. dir. Opinion Rsch. Corp., Chgo., 1969-70; pres. Consumer Insights, Inc., Chgo., 1971-76; mktg. rsch. dir. Beatric Cos., Chgo., 1976-81; group supr. Nat Panel Diary (now NPD Group), Rosemont, Ill., 1981-84; mktg. mgr. R.R. Donnelley & Sons, Inc., Chgo., 1984-85; pres. Irvine Cons., Park Ridge, Ill., 1985—. Author: (with others) History of The Department of Marketing, 1992; contbr. articles to profl. jours. Bd. dirs. Econ. Devel. Corp. Park Ridge, Ill., 1991—, Ednl. Learning Found., Park Ridge, 1994—; mem. Long Range Planning Com. Dist. 64, Park Ridge, 1992-93; chmn. Ednl. Adv. Coun. Ill. 55th Dist., Des Plaines, 1995-96. Mem. Am. Mktg. Assn., Ill. Assn. Sch. Bus. Offls., Jaycees (bd. dirs. Park Ridge club 1966-72). Republican. Home and Office: 17 Gillick St Park Ridge IL 60068

IRWIN, DOUGLAS ALEXANDER, economics educator; b. East Lansing, Mich., Oct. 31, 1962; s. Manley R. and Doris J. (Bunn) I. BA, U. N.H., 1984; MA, Columbia U., 1985, PhD, 1988. Staff economist Coun. Econ. Advisors, Exec. Office of Pres., Washington, 1986-87; economist, bd. govs. FRS, Washington, 1988-91; assoc. prof. Grad. Sch. Bus. U. Chgo., 1991—. Author: Against the Tide: An Intellectual History of Free Trade, 1996; contbr. articles to profl. jours. Mem. Am. Econ. Assn., Royal Econ. Soc. Office: U Chgo Grad Sch Bus 1101 E 58th St Chicago IL 60637-1511

IRWIN, STANLEY ROY, music educator, singer, conductor; b. Henderson, Tex., Jan. 23, 1941; s. Forrest Herbert and Hazel Marie (Gray) Irwin; m. Jane Parker, June 14, 1969; 1 child, Mark Alexander. BA, Baylor U., 1963; B Ch. Music, Southwestern Bapt. Theol. Sem., 1966; MusM, Southern Meth. U., 1969; MusD, Ind. U., 1988; diploma, Internat. Opera Ctr., 1974. Instr. music, choir dir. Simpson Coll., Indianola, Iowa, 1971-73; profl. singer Zurich Opera, Switzerland, 1973-75; prof. voice, dir. choirs Sch. Music DePauw U., Greencastle, Ind., 1975—. Profl. singer Indpls. Symphony Orch., 1978, 79, 83, 85, Manhattan Philharmonic, N.Y., 1988, Philharmonia of London, 1988, Martinuu Philharmonic, 1995, Indpls. Chamber Orch., 1996, PBS, 1982, 91, NPR 1983, 85, Ill. Pub. Radio, 1982, 87, 91, WQXR, N.Y., 1988, Carnegie Hall, 1987, 96, Avery Fisher Hall, Lincoln Ctr., 1988, Barbican Hall, London, 1988, Dvorak Hall, Prague, 1995, Konzerthaus, Vienna, 1995, Indpls. Festival Orch., 1993, rec. (CD Gothic), 1993; condr. various concerts Kennedy Ctr., 1979, Lincoln Ctr., 1984, Music Ctr., L.A., 1986, Carnegie Hall, 1990, 94, White House, 1990; contbr. articles to profl. jours. Bd. dirs. DePauw Choir, Greencastle, 1977—. Grantee DePauw U., 1983, 1987, John W. and Janice B. Fisher Fund, 1990. Mem. Nat. Assn. Tchrs. Singing, Am. Choral Dirs. Assn., AAUP, Pi Kappa Lambda (pres. Omicron chpt. 1986—). Home: 522 E Washington St Greencastle IN 46135-1723 Office: DePauw Univ Sch Music Performing Arts Ctr 121E Greencastle IN 46135

ISAAC, BINA SUSAN, data processing executive; b. Nainital, India, Jan. 9, 1958; came to U.S. 1980; d. Rajan Kurian and Susan (Thomas) George; m. Mathew Isaac, July 14, 1980; children: Sonya Susan, Shawn George. BA, Sarah Tucker Coll., Tirunelvelli, India, 1978; MA, Madurai U., India, 1980; MEd, U. Toledo, 1981, MBA, 1984. Coord. computer svcs. and computer ctr. Lourdes Coll., Sylvania, Ohio, 1984-85; dir. computer svcs. and computer ctr. Lourdes Coll., Sylvania, 1985-95, dir. info. tech. dept. svcs., 1995—, dir. info. tech. dept./svcs., 1995—; instr. Continuing Edn. Dept., Sylvania, 1985—; dir. Instnl. Info. Tech., 1995—. Mem. Assn. Systems Mgmt., Ohio Assn. Ind. Rsch., SIG 3X Inc. (spl. interest group). Home: 7328 Gibley Park Rd Toledo OH 43617-2252 Office: Lourdes Coll 6832 Convent Blvd Sylvania OH 43560-2853

ISAAC, STANLEY EUGENE, accountant; b. Indpls., May 18, 1942; s. E. Edward and S. Garnette (Davis) I.; m. Marsha M. Shelton, Aug. 26, 1965; children: Berkley, Derek. BBA, U. Cin., 1965; MBA, Ind. U., 1987. CPA, Ind. Supr. Ernst & Young, Indpls., 1965-77, exec. v.p. Whipple & Co., 1977-86; v.p. Fitzgerald/Isaac p.c., Indpls., 1986—. 1st lt. U.S. Army, 1966-69. Mem. AICPA (com. mem. 1970-95), Estate Planning Coun. (past pres. 1977-95), Ind. CPA Soc. (com. chair 1970-95, instr.), Masons, Scottish Rite. Office: Fitzgerald/Isaac pc 9245 N Meridian #302 Indianapolis IN 46260

ISAACS, KENNETH S(IDNEY), psychoanalyst, educator; b. Mpls., Apr. 7, 1920; s. Mark William and Sophia (Rai) I.; m. Ruth Elizabeth Johnson, Feb. 21, 1951 (dec. 1967); m. Adele Rella Bodroghy, May 17, 1969; children: Jonathan, James; stepchildren: John, Curtis, Peter and Edward Meissner. BA, U. Minn., 1944; PhD, U. Chgo., 1956; postgrad., Inst. Psychoanalysis, 1957-63. Intern Worcester State Hosp., Mass., 1947-48; trainee VA Mental Hygiene Clinic, Chgo., 1948-50; chief psychologist outpatient clinic system Ill. Dept. Pub. Welfare, 1949-56; research assoc., assoc. prof. U. Ill. Med. Sch., Chgo., 1956-63; practice psychoanalysis Evanston, Ill., 1960—; supr. psychiat. residency program Evanston Hosp., Northwestern U., 1972-81, Northwestern Meml. Hosp.; pres. Chgo. Ctr. Psychoanalytic Psychology, 1984-87; cons. to schs., hosps., clinics, pvt. practitioners and industry; sr. cons. Beta Consulting Ltd.; pres. Kenisa Drilling Co., Kenisa Securities Co., Kenisa Oil Co. Author: (book) Again with Feeling, 1989, (syndicated newspaper column) A Psychologist's Notebook; contbr. articles to profl. publs. Served with AUS, 1943-45, ETO. Mem. AAAS, APA (bd. dirs. divsn. pschoanalysis), Chgo. Psychoanalytic Soc., Am. Bd. Psychoanalysis (chair bd. dirs.), Am. Bd. Profl. Psychology (bd. trustees 1994—), N.Y. Acad. Sci., Sigma Xi.

ISAACS, S. TED, engineering executive; b. Louisville, July 13, 1914; s. Max and Rose (Kaplan) I.; m. Ann Fabe, June 7, 1939; children: Marjorie McKelvey Isaacs, Susan Freund Isaacs. ChE, U. Cin., 1936, AA, 1944. Registered profl. engr. , Ohio; cert. sr. grade fluid power tech. Instrument engr. Standard Oil Co. Ohio, Latonia, Ky., 1936-41; instrumentation mgr. Wright Aero. Corp., Lockland, Ohio, 1941-45; sr. process engr. Drackett Co., Cin., 1945-48; pres. The Isaacs Co., Cin., 1948-86; mng. gen ptnr. AFTI Systems, Cin., 1986—; v.p. sales, pres. Indsl. Engring. Corp., Louisville, 1951-55. Contbr. articles to profl. jours. Energy commn. chmn. City Environ. Task Force, Cin., 1970-72; personal reader Cin. Radio Reading Svc. Mem. Nat. Assn. R.R. Passengers, Ohio Assn. R.R. Passengers, Instrument Soc. Am. (sr., life, local bd. dirs. 1946-47), Assn. Engrs. and Archs. in Israel, Engring. Soc. Cin. (life, pres. jr. chpt. 1947-48), Fluid Power Soc., Metric Assn. (v.p. 1962-65), Cephalo-Caudad Investment Club (pres. 1992-93), Cin. Hatikva Investment Club (pres. 1991-93, v.p. rsch. 1994—), Sierra Club. Democrat. Jewish. Home: 8080 Springvalley Dr Cincinnati OH 45236-1352 Office: AFTI Systems 1840 Amberlawn Ave Cincinnati OH 45237-3297

ISAAK, ALAN CHARLES, political science educator; b. Cleve., Jan. 21, 1940; s. A.C. and Rose E. (Gibbons) I.; m. Elizabeth T. Koester; children: Eric, Greta Baker, Josh. BA, Western Res. U., 1962; MA, Ind. U., 1965, PhD, 1966. Asst. prof. polit. sci. Western Mich. U., Kalamazoo, 1966-69, assoc. prof., 1969-81, prof., 1981—. Author: Scope and Methods of Political Science, 1985, An Introduction to Politics, 1987. Mem. Phi Beta Kappa. Office: Western Mich U Dept Polit Sci Kalamazoo MI 49008

ISABEL, ROBERT STEPHEN, interior designer; b. Painesville, Ohio, May 30, 1925; s. Albert Stephen and Isabel Katherine (Sanborn) I.; m. Patricia Ann Bosley, Dec. 23, 1946 (div.); 1 child, Pamela; m. Jean Zink, Dec. 27, 1952. Student, Hiram (Ohio) Coll., 1945-47. Prin. Curiosity Shop Interiors, Hudson, Ohio, 1952—. Pres. Repeal State Income Tax, Hudson, 1979. With USAF, 1943-45. Recipient Best Comml. Bldg. award Ohio State Builders Assn., 1994. Mem. Walden Country Club. Office: Curiosity Shop Interiors 2341 Danbury Ln Hudson OH 44236

ISABELL, DAVID THOMAS, retired city administrator; b. Kansas City, Kans., July 31, 1943; s. James David and Mary (Ruzick) I.; m. Patricia Kay Blankenship, June 12, 1965; 1 child, Sean Thomas. BA in Bus. Adminstrn./Fin., Rockhurst Coll., Kansas City, Mo., 1973; MA in Pub. Adminstrn. (hon.), U. Kans., 1993. Planning tech. City of Kansas City, 1967-73, dep. city clk., 1973-78, cityclk., 1978-85, interim city adminstrn., 1983, fin. dir., 1983-90, city adminstr./fin. dir., 1985-90, city adminstr., 1985-95. Red Feather mem. United Way of Wyandotte County, Kansas City; mem. Ctrl. Ave. Betterment Assn., Kansas City, Total Quality Mgmt. Coun.; mem. Gov.'s Study Commn. on KPERS. Mem. Internat. City Mgrs. Assn., Govt. Fin. Officers Assn., Optimists.

ISABELLA, JOSEPH NOEL, lawyer; b. Cleve., Dec. 23, 1953; s. Joseph Paschal and Angela Maria (Costanzo) I.; m. Maria Tijanich, May 6, 1978; children: Nina A., Damien J., Julia M., Monica A., Andrea N. BBA, Cleve. State U., 1977, M in Acctg. and Fin. Info. Systems, 1983, JD, 1989. Bar: Ohio, 1993; lic. realtor, cert. real estate salesman, constr. supt., student pilot. Supt., forman Schirmer Constrn. Co., Cleve., 1977-82; grad. asst. Cleve. State U., 1982-83; computer auditor Bancsystems, Cleve., 1983-84; sr. fin. analyst Broadview Savs. and Loan, Cleve., 1984-85; dir. investments VSV Co., Cleve., 1985-88; prin. JBS, Procyon, J. Noel, Inc., Cleve., 1988-93; assoc. in constrn. and real estate law Warrell & Isabella, Cleve., 1993-95, ptnr. in constrn. and real estate law, 1995—. Vol. Dem. Orgn., 1992; coach boy's basketball team; referee H.S. basketball team; active Father's Club, St. Ignatius H.S. and Magnificat H.S. Mem. ABA, Greater Cleve. Growth Assn., Cleve. Area Bd. Realtors, Coun. Smaller Enterprises, Builders Exch., Holy Name Soc., Caruso Endowment Fund. (treas. 1990-92), Cleve.-Marshall Coll. Law Alumni Assn., Cathedral Latin Alumni Assn., Ohio State Bar, Cuyahoga County Bar Assn. Roman Catholic. Home: 15834 Edgecliff Ave Cleveland OH 44111-1911 Office: Warrell & Isabella Lakewood Ctr West 14650 Detroit Ave Ste 118 Lakewood OH 44107

ISALY, EDWIN ROBERT, principal, curator; b. Youngstown, Ohio, Jan. 30, 1938; s. Edwin Eugene and Alice Roberta (Eckert) I.; m. Margaret Jean Simerlink, Dec. 28, 1968; 1 child, Anna Bernice. BA in Elem. Edn., Youngstown State U., 1959; postgrad., Westminster Coll., 1959-60; MA in Elem. Adminstrn., Kent State U., 1962; postgrad., U. Dayton (Ohio), 1970. Cert. elem. tchr., elem. adminstrn., Ohio. Tchr. Cleveland Elem. Sch., Youngstown, Ohio, 1959-62, Jackson Elem. Sch., Youngstown, Ohio, 1962-67;.tchr. corps adminstr. U.S. Office to Developing Countries, Sierra Leone, West Africa, 1966; prin. Mapleridge Elem. Sch., Mahoning County, Ohio, 1967-68, Roosevelt Elem. Sch., Lakewood, Ohio, 1968-87, Horace Mann Mid. Sch., Lakewood, 1981-87; acting coord. art Lakewood City Schs., 1976-77, coord. special programs, 1987-90, cons., 1990—; curator Lake Erie Islands Hist. Soc., Put-in-Bay, Ohio, 1989-95; coord. Colligial Decision Making Techniques, Greater Cleveland (Ohio) Devel. Ctr., 1983-85; exchange adminstr., cons. Collegio Americano, Quito, Ecuador, 1985; part time staff Special Edn. Svc. Ctr., Kent State U., Cuyahoga County, 1985-91; supr. student tchrs. Bowling Green State U., 1992-95; presenter in field. Co-chmn. 178th Anniversary Celebration of the Battle of Lake Erie and the Return of the Flagship Niagara; bd. dirs., charter mem., past treas. Friends of Perry's Victory & Internat. Peace Meml.; trustee Lakewood Hist. Soc.; charter mem., past sec., past treas. Lake Erie Islands Hist. Soc., charter mem. Ottawa County Heritage Coalition. Mem. NEA (life), Ohio Edn. Assn. (life, past mem. of Profl. Rights & Responsibilities Commn.), Ohio Retired Tchrs. Assn. (life), Youngstown Edn. Assn. (past pres.), Youngstown Coll. Student Edn. Assn. (past pres.), Youngstown State U. Alumni Assn., Lakewood Adminstrs. Assn. (charter mem., past pres.), hon. mem. Biology Fraternity Youngstown State U., Pi Mu. Methodist. Home: 2000 King James Pkwy #118 Westlake OH 44145 Office: Lake Erie Islands Hist Soc PO Box 25 Put In Bay OH 43456

ISBERG, LARRY ALGER, software professional; b. Jackson, Mich., Mar. 23, 1948; s. Paul Walter and O. Lila (Streeter) I.; m. Jacqueline Rae Cripps, Apr. 19, 1970; 1 child, Michael Paul. BS, Western Mich. U., 1970. Store mgr. Independence (Mo.) Regional Health Ctr., 1970-71; dir. purchasing Children's Mercy Hosp., Kansas City, Mo., 1971-76; surgical instrument specialist Hawley Surg. Instruments, Lenexa, Kans., 1976-77, Aesculap Instruments, Burlingame, Calif., 1977-83, Sur-Med Instruments, St. Louis, 1983-84; sales rep. L'AMY, Inc., Milford, Conn., 1984-85; software implementation specialist Continental Healthcare Systems, Overland Park, Kans., 1985-90; supr. software implementation Continental Healthcare Systems, Overland Park, 1990—. Co-author: Surgical Instruments, 1980; contbr. articles to profl. publs. Mem. Alpha Phi Omega. Home: 328 NW Blue Beech Pt Lees Summit MO 64064-1812 Office: Continental Healthcare Sys 7300 W 110th St Shawnee Mission KS 66210-2330

ISHII, THOMAS KORYU, electrical engineering educator; b. Tokyo, Mar. 18, 1927; came to U.S., 1956; s. Yoshitada and Taka (Furukawa) I.; m. Eiko Bernadette Ishida, Nov. 29, 1958; children: Mutsumi Michael, Naomi Bernadette, Megumi Margaret, Mayumi Mary. BS, Nihon U., Tokyo, 1950, Dr.Engring., 1961; MS, U. Wis., 1957, PhD, 1959. Registered profl. engr., Wis. Instr. in elec. engring. Nihon U., Tokyo, 1950-56; rsch. asst. U. Wis., Madison, 1956-59; asst. prof. elec. engring. Marquette U., Milw., 1959-60, assoc. prof. elec. engring., 1960-64, prof. elec. engring., 1964—. Author: Microwave Engineering, 1966, 2d edit., 1989, Maser and Laser Engineering, 1980, Practical Microwave Electron Devices, 1990; contbg. author: Microwave Power Engineering, 1968, Handbook of Filters and Circuits, 1995; editor: Handbook of Microwave Technology, Vols. 1 and 2, 1995. Mem. IEEE, AAUP, Am. Soc. Engring. Edn., Nat. Soc. Profl. Engrs., Sigma Xi, Tau Beta Pi, Eta Kappa Nu, Alpha Sigma Nu. Roman Catholic. Home: 1525 West Manor Ln River Hills WI 53217 Office: Marquette U 1515 W Wisconsin Ave Milwaukee WI 53233-2222

ISON, JOHN D., investment representative; b. Pitts., Aug. 31, 1960. BS, Pitts. State U., 1981. Investment rep. Edward D. Jones & Co., Pitts., 1981—. Advisor Cal Sch. Bus. Bd., 1989—, Mt. Carmel Hosp. Found., 1995—, St. Mary Cogorn Booster Bd., 1989—; bd. dirs. St. Pious Neman, 1988—; fin. bd. Lady of Lourdes, 1989—. Paul Harris scholar, 1988. Mem. Rotary (past pres. 1987). Roman Catholic. Home: 612 W Quincy St Pittsburg KS 66762-5533 Office: Edward D Jones & Co 109 E 9th St Pittsburg KS 66762-3912

ISRAELITE, AARON, marketing professional; b. Evanston, Ill., Jan. 13, 1970. BBA, U. Mo., 1991; postgrad., Rockhurst Coll., Kansas City, Mo., 1995—. Lic. series 7 Nat. Assn. Securities Dealers. Fin. planner Phoenix/Home Life, Overland Park, Kans., 1992; sales mgr. Home Base Realty, Chgo., 1992-93; sr. mktg. rep. BMA Fin. Svcs., Westwood, Kans., 1993—; pub. FS Flyer, monthly newsletter, 1994—. Mem. Kansas City Securities Assn. Republican. Roman Catholic. Office: BMA Fin Svcs 1901 W 47th Pl Ste 210 Westwood KS 66205-1834

ISRANI, KIM, civil engineer; b. Dadu, Pakistan, Dec. 24, 1930; s. Watumal and Vani I.; m. Yashi Israni, May 26, 1964; children: Vijay, Mamta, Sanjay. BS in Engring., Poona U., 1960; MS in Engring., Memphis State U., 1972. Asst. dir. Cen. Water and Power Commn., New Delhi, Ind., 1960-70; civil engr. Pollard Cons., Memphis, 1971-73; design engr. Talbot & Assoc., Orlando, Fla., 1974-75; facilities engr. Dept. Nat. Resources, Des Moines, 1976-91; environ. specialist Dept. Agr., Des Moines, 1992—. Author: India: A Superpower, 1989; contbr. articles to profl. jours. Chmn. Indian sect. Internat. Food Fair, Des Moines, 1977—; dir. Indian dance group Iowa State Fair, Des Moines, 1982—. Mem. Iowa Assn. Profl., Managerial and Sci. State Employees (bd. dirs. 1986—), Iowa Engring. Soc., Toastmasters Internat. Republican. Hindu. Home: 4024 83rd St Des Moines IA 50322-2307 Office: Dept Agr Wallace Bldg Des Moines IA 50319

ISSELHARD, DONALD EDWARD, dentist; b. Belleville, Ill., Apr. 11, 1941; s. Bertram Joseph and Margaret Eda (Dobbins) I.; m. Annette Scanaliato, Mar. 1, 1980; children: Kerstin, Nissa, Michele, Tara. Student, St. Louis U., 1959-62; BS in Dentistry, U. Ill., Chgo., 1970, DDS, 1966; MBA, Maryville U., 1994. Gen. practice dentistry Clayton, Mo., 1967-70, Creve Coeur, Mo., 1970—; assoc. instr. Forest Park C.C., St. Louis, 1973-77; asst. prof. Washington U., St. Louis, 1975-77; lectr. Continuing Edn. Ctrs. Am., 1977-79; pres. Tempo Condo. Investment Corp., 1994—, Strategic Empowerment Inc., 1994. Author: (with others) Anatomy of Orofacial Structures, 1977, 5th edit., 1994; contbg. author Comprehensive Rev. of Dental Hygiene, 1986. Fellow Acad. Gen. Dentistry Dentistry Internat., Masters Acad. Gen. Dentistry; mem. ADA, Mo. Acad. Gen. Dentistry (v.p. 1996—), Greater St. Louis Dental Assn., Gateway Practice Devel. Assn. (pres. 1986-90). Home: 17726 Drummer Ln Chesterfield MO 63005-4223 Office: 12401 Olive Blvd Saint Louis MO 63141-6408

ISTOCK, VERNE GEORGE, banker; b. Sept. 20, 1940. BA in Econs., U. Mich., 1962, MBA in Fin., 1963. Credit analyst trainee NBD Bancorp, Inc., Detroit, 1963-71, group head, 1971-77, head U.S. divsn., 1977-82, sr. v.p., 1979-82, exec. v.p., 1982-85, vice chmn., dir., 1985-93, chmn., CEO, 1994-95, also bd. dirs.; chmn. NBD Bank; pres., CEO First Chgo. NBD Corp., Detroit, 1995—, chmn., 1996—; bd. dirs. Kelly Svcs. Inc.; dir. Internat. Monetary Conf. Dir., treas. United Way Cmty. Svcs. of Southeastern Mich.; bd. trustees Citizens Rsch. Coun.; mem. U. Mich. Corp. Adv. Coun.; dir. Chgo. Coun. on Fgn. Rels. Mem. U. Mich. Alumni Assn. (past pres., lifetime dir.), Bankers Roundtable (dir.), Mich. State C. of C. (bd. dirs.), Greater Detroit C. of C. (mem. bd. expansion coun.), Econ. Club Detroit, Greater Detroit and Windsor Japan-Am. Soc., Comml. Club Chgo., Econ. Club Chgo. Office: First Chicago NBD Corp One First National Plz Chicago IL 60670

IVANCIC, CHRIS, insurance executive; b. Gloversville, N.Y., June 17, 1950. V.p. Advanced Ins. Mgmt., Fort Wayne, Ind., 1987—. Mem. Elks. Republican. Roman Catholic. Office: Advanced Ins Mgmt 6642 Saint Joe Rd Fort Wayne IN 46835-1933

IVERS, DREW RUSSELL, geneticist, plant breeder; b. Vincennes, Ind., Aug. 12, 1946; s. Odell Perry and Gilda Mayola (Shipley) I.; m. Dottie Sue Awman, Aug. 10, 1968; children: Andrew Awman, Audelee Sue, Ashley Russell. AS, Vincennes U., 1966; BS, Purdue U., 1968; PhD, Iowa State U., 1974. Rsch. assoc. Iowa State U., Ames, 1972-74; rsch. mgr. Cargill, Inc., Aurora, Ill., 1974-76; rsch. geneticist Land O' Lakes, Inc., Ft. Dodge, Iowa, 1977-85, dir. corn and soy rsch., 1985-88, dir. plant rsch., 1988—; appointed to Nat. Plant Genetic Resources Bd. sec. USDA, Washington, 1982-88. Nat. del. Nat. Rep. Party Conv., Detroit, New Orleans, Houston, and San Diego, 1980, 88, 92, 96; mem. state com. Rep. Party of Iowa, Des Moines, 1984-88; state chmn. Robertson for Pres. campaign, Iowa, 1988, Buchanan for Pres. campaign, Iowa, 1996. With U.S. Army, 1968-70, Vietnam. Decorated Purple Heart; recipient Faculty Alumni citation Vincennes U., 1982. Mem. Am. Seed Trade Assn. (chmn. basic soy rsch. com., 1987-89), Nat. Coun. Comml. Plant Breeders, Crop Sci. Soc. Am. (mem. rsch. award com., 1968—). Baptist. Office: Land O' Lakes Rsch Farm 1025 190th St Webster City IA 50595-9802

IVERSON, ROBERT LOUIS, JR., internist, physician, intensive care administrator, medical educator; b. Borden, Ind., Sept. 3, 1944; s. Robert L. and Agnes Maxine (Knight) I.; m. Elsa Maschmeyer, Sept. 3, 1967 (div. 1982); children: Nathan, Kirsten; m. Deborah A. Budd, June 16, 1984; children: Richard, Colin. Student, Wabash Coll., 1962-64; BA, Ind. U., 1970, MD, 1974, Intern, 1974-75. Diplomate Am. Bd. Internal Med., diplomate in critical care medicine, Am. Bd. Internal Med. Resident (internal med.) Methodist Hosp., Indpls, 1975-77; fellow in critical care med. U. So. Calif. Shock Rsch. Unit, Ctr. for Critically Ill, L.A., 1977; visiting lectr. U. So. Calif., L.A., 1977; co-dir. critical care, teaching staff, Dept. of Med. Methodist Hosp., Indpls, 1977-84; asst. prof. Med. Wayne State U., Detroit, 1984—; vice chief med. staff Hutzel Hosp., 1995—, dir. med. affairs, 1996—; mem. bd. Rudgate Neighborhood Assocs., Bloomfield Hills, Mich. 1996—, assoc. dir. Intensive Care, Harper Hosp., Detroit, 1984-86; dir. Intensive Care Unit Hutzel Hosp, Detroit, 1986—, chief Dept. Critical Care Med., 1988—; participant Ind. Malpractice Review Panels, 1981-85. Author: (with others) Respiratory Care of the Neurosurgical Patient, 1983, Septic Shock in Critical Care Clinics, 1988; established adminstrv. core curriculum for intensivists Critical Care Clinics, 1993; contbr. abstracts and articles to profl. jours. Med. advisor to Ind. Coun. Emergency Response Teams, 1980-85, mem. (singing) Ind. Symphonic Choir, 1970-84, trustee, 1983-84; hon. dep. sheriff Marion County Sheriff's Dept., 1982-84; bd. dirs. City of Bloomfield Hills, Mich., Rudgate Neighborhood Assn., 1996—. With U.S. Army, 1964-67, Vietnam. Fellow Am. Coll. Physicians, Am. Coll. Chest Physicians; mem. AMA, Soc. Critical Care Med., Soc. for Parenteral and Enteral Nutrition, Mich. Area Radio Enthusiasts, Wayne County Med. Soc. (elected del. 1990-91), Phi Beta Kappa. Home: 165 Harlan Dr Bloomfield Hills MI 48304-3316 Office: Hutzel Hosp Dept Critical Care Med 4707 Saint Antoine St Detroit MI 48201-1427

IVES, H. WILLIAM, retired pest control company executive; b. Chgo., Mar. 31, 1930; s. Harlem Benjamin and Carrie (Hollatz) I.; m. Mary Louise Reed, Aug. 17, 1951; children: H. Russell, Catherine, James R., Carolyn. BA, Kalamazoo Coll., 1951; MS, U. Wis., 1952. Pub. rels. mgr. Rose Exterminator Co., Troy, Mich., 1952-57, v.p., 1958-67, pres., 1968-79, chmn., 1979—. Bd. dirs. YMCA Met. Detroit, 1975-83, Detroit Osteo. Hosp., Highland Park, Mich., 1972-77; trustee Detroit Sci. Ctr., 1988-92. Mem. Nat. Pest Control Assn. (pres. 1977-78), Detroit Rotary Club (pres. 1968-69, Disting. Svc. award 1974), Rotary Internat. (dir. 1983-85), The Rotary Found. of Rotary Internat. (trustee 1977-79). Methodist. Office: Bio-Serv Corp 1130 Livernois Rd Troy MI 48083-2711

IVY, CONWAY GAYLE, paint company executive; b. Houston, July 8, 1941; s. John Smith and Caro (Gayle) I.; m. Diane Ellen Cole, May 25, 1973; children: Brice McPherson, Elizabeth Cole. Student U. Chgo., 1959-62; BS in Natural Scis., Shimer Coll., 1964; postgrad. U. Tex., 1964-65; MBA, U. Chgo., 1968, MA in Econs., 1972, postgrad. 1972-74. Geol. asst. John S. Ivy, Houston, 1965-72; securities analyst Halsey Stuart & Co. and successor Bache & Co., Chgo., 1973-74, Winmill Securities Inc., Chgo., 1974; econ. and fin. cons., Chgo., 1974-75; dir. corp. planning Gould Inc., Rolling Meadows, Ill., 1975-79; v.p. corp. planning and devel. Sherwin-Williams Co., Cleve., 1979-88, v.p., treas., 1989-92, v.p. corp. planning and devel., 1992—; pres. Ivy Minerals Inc., Boise, Idaho, 1978—. Trustee Michelson-Morley Centennial Celebration, 1987, Cleve Inst. Music, 1983-94, treas., 1987-90, vice chmn., 1990-94. Mem. Am. Econs. Assn., Soc. Mining Metallurgy and Exploration, Am. Inst. Mining Engrs., Houston Club, Phi Gamma Delta. Republican. Author of numerous analytical reports for brokerage industry. Office: 101 W Prospect Ave Cleveland OH 44115-1027

IWANSKI, MARY, parochial school educator; b. Sacramento, Feb. 12, 1947; d. John Joseph Iwanski and Philomena Astorino Iwanski Glassy. BS, Ill. Benedictine Coll., Lisle, 1969; MS, U. Wis., Milw., 1973; postgrad., Corcordia U., River Forest, Ill., 1992-93, U. Calif., 1980-82, 91. Cert. high sch. tchr., Ill.; joined Inst. Blessed Virgin Mary, 1964. Tchr. high sch. physics and math. Loretto Cath. Ctrl. High Sch., Sault Sainte Marie, Mich., 1969-71; tchr. high sch. algebra and phys. sci. Sault Area Pub. High Sch., Sault Sainte Marie, 1971; tchr. high sch. geometry and physics St. Francis High Sch., Wheaton, Ill., 1971-72; tchr. math., physics, physical sci. Unity Cath. High Sch., Chgo., 1972-76; jr. high sch. tchr. math. and sci., cons. Our Lady of the Assumption, Carmichael, Calif., 1976-82; 8th grade tchr. math. and sci. St. John of the Cross Sch., Western Springs, Ill., 1982-88; high sch. math. tchr. Mother McAuley Liberal Arts High Sch., Chgo., 1989—; sci. cons. St. John of the Cross Sch., 1982-88, math. coach/cons., 1983-88; mem. faculty/staff coun. Mother McAuley Liberal Arts H.S., Chgo., 1990-93, Math Macs team coach, 1994—. Recipient Photography award Joliet (Ill.) Park Dist., 1977; Heart of the Sch. award, 1995-96. Mem. Assn. Women Math., Nat. Coun. Tchrs. Math., Nat. Cath. Ednl. Assn., Sigma Pi Sigma. Office: Mother McAuley Libl Arts HS 3737 W 99th St Chicago IL 60655

IZATT, JOSEPH ADAM, biomedical engineering researcher; b. Las Cruces, N.Mex., Apr. 24, 1962; s. Jerald RAy and MaryAnn Louise I.; m. Susan Diane Izatt. BS, MIT, 1986, MS, 1988, PhD, 1991. Postdoctoral assoc. MIT, Cambridge, 1991-94; asst. prof., medicine and biomed. engring. Case Western Res. U., Cleve., 1994—; dir. endoscopy rsch. lab. U. Hosps. of Cleve., 1994—; lectr. in field. Contbr. articles to profl. jours. Fellow Am. Soc. for Laser Medicine and Surgery; mem. Am. Phys. Soc., Optical Soc. of Am., IEEE Engring. in Medicine and Biology Soc. Office: U Hosps of Cleve 11100 Euclid Ave Cleveland OH 44106-5066

JABERG, EUGENE CARL, theology educator, administrator; b. Linton, Ind., Mar. 27, 1927; s. Elmer Charles and Hilda Carolyn (Stuckmann) J.; m. Miriam Marie Priebe; children: Scott Christian, Beth Amy, David Edward. BA, Lakeland Coll., 1948; BD, Mission House Theol. Sem., 1954; MA, U. Wis., 1959, PhD, 1968. Ordained to ministry, United Ch. of Christ, 1959. Staff announcer WKOW-TV, Madison, Wis., 1955-58, 67-68; minister Pilgrim Congl. Ch., Madison, 1956-57; assoc. prof. speech Mission House Theol. Sem., Plymouth, Wis., 1958-62; asst. prof. communications United Theol. Sem., New Brighton, Minn., 1962-76; prof. communications United Theol. Sem., New Brighton, 1976-91, dir. admissions, 1984-87, dir. MDiv program, 1988-90, prof. emeritus, 1991—; bus. ptnr. Dimension 3 Media Svcs., Mpls., 1988-90; coord. spl. projects CTV North Suburbs Cable Access, 1992—; vis. scholar Cambridge U., England. Author, editor: A History of Lakeland-Mission House, 1962; author: The Video Pencil, 1980; contbr. articles, revs. to various publs.; producer films, videotapes. Artistic dir. Interfaith Players, Mpls., 1965-73; TV producer, moderator Town Meeting of Twin Cities, Mpls., 1967-70; producer, writer, host various radio and TV series, Mpls., 1970—; mem. Ctr. Urban Encounter, Mpls., 1972-74, New Brighton Human Rights Commn., 1975-77; bd. mem. office communications United Ch. Christ, N.Y.C., 1975-81; mem. North Suburban System Cable Access Commn., 1986-91. Corr. U.S. Army, 1949-50. Kaltenborn Radio scholar, 1957; grantee Assn. Theol. Sems., 1983; recipient Minn. Community TV award, 1993. Mem. Religious Speech Communication Assn. (co-chmn. 1972-74), World Assn. Christian Communication. Democrat. Home: 1601 Innsbruck Dr Minneapolis MN 55432-6046 Office: United Theol Sem 3000 5th St NW Saint Paul MN 55112-2507

JACHE, ALBERT WILLIAM, retired chemistry educator, scientist; b. Manchester, N.H., Nov. 5, 1924; s. William Frederick and Esther (Ruemely) J.; m. Lucy Ellen Hauslein, June 14, 1948; children: Ann Gail, Ellen Ruth, Philip William, Heidi Verena. BS, U. N.H., 1948, MS, 1950; PhD, U. Wash., 1952. Sr. chemist Air Reduction Co., Murray Hill, N.J., 1952-53; rsch. assoc. dept. physics Duke U., 1953-55; asst. prof. dept. chemistry Tex. A&M U., College Station, 1955-58, assoc. prof., 1958-61; cons. Ozark Mahoning Co., Tulsa, 1960-61, assoc. rsch. dir., 1961-64; sr. rsch. assoc. Olin Mathieson Chem. Corp. (now Olin Corp.), New Haven, 1964-67, sect. mgr., 1965-67, cons., 1967-75; prof. chemistry Marquette U., Milw., 1967-90, prof. emeritus, 1990—, chmn. chem. dept., 1967-72, dean Grad. Sch., 1972-77, assoc. acad. v.p. for health scis., 1974-77, assoc. v.p.-acad. affairs, 1977-85; scientist-in-residence Argonne (Ill.) Nat. Lab., 1985-86, scientist, 1991—, temporary appointment, 1991—; program coordination com. Med. Center S.E. Wis.; lectr. U. Tulsa, 1963-64, New Haven Coll., 1967; cons. Allied Chem. Corp., 1977-78. Trustee Milw. Sci. Ednl. Found.; pres. Milw. Sci. Ednl. Trust, 1973—; trustee Argonne Univs. Assn., 1977-80; chmn. Assn. Grad. Schs. in Cath. Univs., 1973-75; mem. AUA nuclear engring. edn. com. U. Chgo, 1977-89, chmn., 1984, sec., 1989. With AUS, 1943-46. Fellow AAAS, Am. Inst. Chemists; mem. Am. Chem. Soc. (chmn.-elect, program chmn. div. fluorine chemistry 1981, chmn. div. fluorine chemistry 1982), Sigma Xi, Omicron Kappa Upsilon. Home: 301 Ohio St Marietta OH 45750-3139 Office: Marquette U Dept Chemistry Milwaukee WI 53233

JACK, DONALD M., JR., broker; b. Hornell, N.Y., May 4, 1930. Broker Hanover Bank, N.Y.C., 1956-59, Eastman Dillman Securities, Chgo., 1959-63; broker instnl. McDonald & Co. Securities, Cleve., 1963—. Lt. USN, 1953-56. Mem. Country Club, Cleve. Athletic Club, Princeton Club. Republican. Episcopalian. Home: 22225 Parnell Rd Shaker Hts OH 44122-2728 Office: McDonald & Co Securities 800 Superior Ave E Cleveland OH 44114-2601

JACKLIN, WILLIAM THOMAS, county official, educator; b. Chgo., Dec. 26, 1940; s. Robert Theodore and Florence Carrie (Dombrow) J.; m. Bonnie Joy Winquist; 1 child, Laura Carrie. BS, Roosevelt U., 1967; MS in Bus., Ind. U., 1968. Cert. fraud examiner, govt. fin. mgr. Assoc. instr. Ind. U., 1967-69; V.p. DuPage Corp., Lombard, Ill., 1970-73; inst. bus. Coll. DuPage, Glen Ellyn, Ill., 1969—; chief dep. auditor DuPage County, 1973, county auditor, 1973—; v.p. DuPage County Employees Credit Union, 1978-79, pres., 1979-80; fiscal officer DuPage Met. Enforcement Group, 1987-94; exec. bd. Midwestern Intergovtl. Audit Forum; bd. dirs. Franciscan Ministries, Inc. Announcer CRIS Radio for the Blind. Member Ill. Prairie Path, DuPage County Rep. Cen. Com.; sec. York Twp. Rep. Orgn., 1978-80; treas. Highland Hills Assn., 1975-78; chmn. DuPage County com. Gerald R. Ford presdl. campaign, 1976; alt. del. 1992 Rep. Nat. Conv.; mem. fin. mgmt. project com. Ill. Dept. Commerce and Community Affairs, 1980-82, bd. dirs. Lombard Hist. Soc., v.p., 1983-87, pres., 1987-91. Mem. Assn. Cert. Fraud Examiners, Nat. Assn. Local Govt. Auditors, Inst. Internal Auditors (govt. and pub. affairs com. 1976-82), Ill. Assn. County Auditors (sec.-treas. 1976-78, v.p. 1978-80, pres. 1980-84), Assn. Govt. Accts., Ind. Soc. of Chgo., Phi Delta Kappa. Christian Scientist. Lodge: Masons (sec. 1979-80). Home: 411 E 17th St Lombard IL 60148-4907 Office: DuPage Ctr 421 N County Farm Rd Wheaton IL 60187-3978

JACKSON, A(ASE) OSA LITTRUP, physical therapy educator; b. Copenhagen, Jan. 3, 1950; d. Gunnar and Gerda (Petersen) Littrup; 1 child, Marius. BS, U. Mich., 1972, MA in Ednl. Adminstrn., 1973, PhD, 1979; student, Hartford Family Inst., 1980, Feldenkrais Practioner Tng. Program, 1981-84. Dir. rehab. Roseville (Mich.) Nursing Home, 1973-74, St. Joseph Nursing Home, Hamtramck, Mich., 1972-75; asst. clin. prof. NYU, N.Y.C., 1975-77; dir. rehab. Hartford Hosp., 1977-79; ptnr. Glastonbury (Conn.) Health Assocs., 1980; founder, pres. Geriatric Inst, Inc., Glastonbury, 1980-81; vis. prof. dept physiotherapy U. Queensland, Brisbane, Australia, 1983-85; assoc. prof., chmn. div. kinesiological scis. Oakland U., Rochester, Mich., 1986-89, assoc. prof. phys. therapy, 1989—; adj. faculty dept. phys. therapy U. Conn., Stoors, 1978-79; asst. prof. dept. phys. therapy U. Md., 1980; lectr. dept. family medicine U. Conn., Farmington, 1981, Diakonissehusets Nursing Sch., Oslo, 1982-85, Oslo Sch. Physiotherapy, 1983-85, Andrew U., Berrien Springs, Mich., 1987—; adj. asst. prof. dept. phys. therapy U. Pitts., 1984—; cons. in field; asst. trainer Feldenkrais, 1989. Author: Physical Therapy of the Geriatric Patient, 1983, Therapeutic Considerations for the Elderly, 1987, Natural Ease For Work-Can You Move To Get The Job Done?, 1994; co-editor Jour. of Geriatric Phys. and Occupational Therapy, 1980-81; mem. editorial bd. Jour. Gerontology and Geriatric Edn., 1980-83, Internat. Phys. Therapy, 1984—; contbr. articles to profl. jours. Mem. Am. Gerontol. Soc., Am. Geriatric Soc., Norwegian Phys. Therapy Assn. (faculty 1983-85, program devel. 1985—), AAUP, Am. Phys. Therapy Assn. (del. 1978-80, pres. Conn. chpt. 1981, chmn. sect. on geriatrics 1982, Joan Mills award 1987, Clin. Excellence award 1995), Am. Heart Assn. (chmn. cardiac rehab.). Home: 1800 Campus Ct Rochester Hls MI 48309-2158 Office: Oakland U Sch Health Scis Rochester MI 48309

JACKSON, ALEX MAURICE, protective services official, comedian; b. Quincy, Ill., Dec. 7, 1957; s. William and Jill (Johnson) J.; m. Kimberly Marie Mullen, July 30, 1977; children: Mareo Lee, Maurice Deon. Diploma, Brooklyn Center Sr. H.S. Firefighter Mpls. Fire Dept., 1980—; comedian Mpls., 1985—. Mem. Mpls. African Am. Fire Fighters Assn. (pres. 1992—). Home: 4263 Queen Ave N Minneapolis MN 55412

JACKSON, BETTY L. DEASON, real estate developer; b. Wichita, Kans., Mar. 31, 1927; d. Orville John and Ida Mabel (Wolfe) Deason; m. James L. Jackson, July 2, 1966 (dec. Feb. 1983); children: Rebecca Lou, Jennifer Mae. AA, SW Baptist U., Bolivar, Mo., 1946; BA, Cen. Mo. State U., 1963; MA, U. Mo., 1964. Salesperson Sears, Kansas City, Mo., 1943-44; bookkeeping clk. Hallmark Cards, Kansas City, Mo., 1945-46; civil service Camp Pendleton, Oceanside, Calif., 1947; sec. Ford Motor Co., Kansas City, Mo., Jim Taylor Olds Co., Independence, Mo., 1952-54; tchr. Consol. Sch. Dist. #2, Mo., 1954-55; tchr. adminstr. Consol. Sch. Dist. #2, Raytown, Mo., 1963-78; owner mgr. B.J.'s Florist Car Wash Laundramat, Stockton, Mo., 1979-82; owner, ptnr. J and S Realty, Stockton, Mo., 1983—; officer J-S Corp., Stockton, 1986-94. Mem. Nat. Assn. Realtors, 5-County Bd. Realtors, Mo. Bd. Realtors, Mo. C. of C., AARP. Democrat. Baptist. Home: Lakeview Cir Owl Haven Estates Stockton MO 65785 Office: J-S Realty Sotckton Lake Pla PO Box 159 S Hwy 39 Ste 101 Stockton MO 65785

JACKSON, BILL D., newspaper editor; b. Mulberry, Ark., Apr. 23, 1937; s. Ernest W. and Mattie (Murray) J.; m. Alice Ann Morgan, Sept. 5, 1959; children—Kimberly, Kerry, Rod, Ryan; m. Jill Kremer, June 22, 1991. Student, Fort Smith Jr. Coll., Ark., 1955-56, U. Tulsa, Okla., 1956-59, Ind. State U., Evansville, 1972-73, 78. Mng. editor Jacksonville Daily Progress, Tex., 1960-61; news editor, mng. editor Paris News, Tex., 1961-63; city editor, mng. editor, editor Evansville Courier, Ind., 1963-86; editor Evansville Press, 1986—, pres., 1991—; instr. U. Evansville, Ind., 1970-71. Bd. dirs. Vision 2000, Albion Fellows Bacon Shelter for Battered Families, United Way S.W. Ind., 1978-83; pres. Leadership Evansville, 1982-83; pres. Southwestern Ind. Easter Seals Soc., 1986; pres. Albion Fellows Bacon Ctr., 1994. Mem. Am. Soc. Newspaper Editors. Ind. Associated Press Mng. Editors (pres. 1985-86), Met. Evansville C. of C. (dir. 1978-87), Sigma Delta Chi (pres. Cardinal states chpt.). Home: 917 Plaza Dr Evansville IN 47715-4411 Office: The Evansville Press 300 E Walnut St Evansville IN 47713-1938

JACKSON, BO (VINCENT EDWARD JACKSON), professional baseball, former football player; b. Bessemer, Ala., Nov. 30, 1962; m. Linda Jackson. Student, Auburn U. Baseball player Kansas City Royals, 1986-91; football player L.A. Raiders, 1987-90; baseball player Chicago White Sox, 1991-93, California Angels, 1994-95. Recipient Heisman Trophy, 1985, All-Star Game MVP, 1989; mem. NFL Pro Bowl Team, 1990; mem. A.L. All-StarTeam, 1989, named Comeback Player of Yr., Sporting News, 1993. Address: C/O Susan Mckee 1765 Old Shell Rd Mobile AL 36604*

JACKSON, CURTIS MAITLAND, metallurgical engineer; b. N.Y.C., Apr. 20, 1933; s. Maitland Shaw and Janet Haughs (Dunbar) J.; m. Cordelia Ann Shupe, July 6, 1957 (div. 1985); children: Carol Jackson Adams, David Curtis. B.S. in Metall. Engring., NYU, 1954; M.S., Ohio State U., Columbus, 1959, Ph.D. (Battelle staff fellow), 1966. Registered profl. engr., Ohio. Prin. metall. engr. Columbus div. Battelle Meml. Inst., 1954-61, project leader, 1961-67, asso. chief specialty alloys, 1967-77, asso. mgr. phys. and applied metallurgy, 1977—; researcher in metall. tech. Chmn. bd.: Wire Jour, 1976-77; dir., 1973-78; Contbr. tech. articles profl. jours. Mem. troop com. Boy Scouts Am., 1975-83 , asst. scoutmaster, 1978-83 ; advisor Order of DeMolay, 1954-57, 78-86; mem. ofcl. bd. Methodist Ch., 1957-66. Recipient IR-100 award Indsl. Research Mag., 1976; recipient certificate of appreciation Soc. Mfg. Engrs., 1977, awards Order of DeMolay, 1955, 1978, 83. Mem. Wire Found. (dir. 1974-86), Wire Assn. Internat. (v.p. 1973-76, pres. 1976-77, dir. 1970-78, Mordica Meml. award 1977, J. Edward Donnellan award 1978, Meritorious Tech. Paper award 1981), N.Y. U. Metall. Alumni Assn. (pres. 1966-68), Am. Inst. Mining, Metall. and Petroleum Engrs. (chmn. Ohio Valley sect. 1964-66, chmn. North Central U.S. region 1965-66), Am. Soc. Metals, Am. Vacuum Soc., NYU, Ohio State U. alumni assns., Sigma Xi, Alpha Sigma Mu, Phi Lambda Upsilon. Club: NYU. Home: 5088 Dalmeny Ct Columbus OH 43220-2693 Office: 505 King Ave Columbus OH 43201-2696

JACKSON, DAVID A., retired newspaper editor; b. Litchfield, Ill., Oct. 7, 1924; s. David Winchester and Maude Abbot (McEwen) J.; m. Mina Jean Miller, Feb. 18, 1950; children: Anne, David M., Jennifer E., Jeffrey A. Student, Tex. A&M U., 1943, Pasadena Jr. Coll., 1943; BA, Ill. Coll., 1949. Apprentice printer Litchfield News-Herald, 1946, mgr. classified advt., 1949-58, advt. mgr., 1958-74, editor, 1974-89; columnist Break Time, 1979—. Mem. Montgomery County Bd., 1994—, Litchfield Postal Adv. Com.; trustee Litchfield Carnegie Pub. Libr., 1957-95, pres. 1959-92, 93-95; v.p., sec. Lewis and Clark Libr. Sys., Edwardsville, Ill., 1965-71, 77-83, 86; chmn. Litchfield Fire and Police Commn., 1985-95; bd. dirs. Bottomley-Ruffing-Schalk Baseball Mus. Recipient Dedicated Leadership plaque Ill. Coll., 1984, Disting. Citizen award, 1986, County Master Citizen award Montgomery County Fair Bd., 1987, Spl. Mayoral award City of Litchfield, 1987, Civic Activities award Litchfield Rotary Club, 1987, Statesman of the Yr., Litchfield C. of C., 1990, 91; So. Ill. U. Journalism Hall of Fame, 1996. Mem. Ill. Hist. Soc., Montgomery County Geneal. Soc. (pres. 1990-91, 92-95), Ill. Coll. Alumni Assn. (sec. 1977-83, nat. pres. 1984), Ill. Geneal. Soc., Macoupin County Geneal. Soc., Iredell County Geneal. Soc., VFW, Moose, Am. Legion. Republican. Lutheran. Home: 17 Northcrest Dr Litchfield IL 62056-1372

JACKSON, DAVID LEE, real estate executive; b. Youngstown, Ohio, Dec. 3, 1946; s. Harold Truman and Helene Irene (DeVoe) J.; m. Lauren Janine Hite, May 27, 1977. BA, Malone Coll., 1968; MA, Kent State U., 1975. Br. mgr. Boebinger Realtors, Alliance, Ohio, 1975-80; real estate broker, pres. D.L. Jackson Agy., Inc., Alliance and Canton, Ohio, 1980—. Mem. Alliance Area Bd. Realtors (pres. 1982), Canton-Massillon Bd. Realtors, Rotary. Republican. Home and Office: 5337 Cherokee Ave NW Canton OH 44720-6841

JACKSON, DENNIS R., auctioneer; b. Cin., Sept. 27, 1946; s. Ellis and Ruth (Vito) J.; m. Sheila Kay Smart, June 21, 1969; children: Bryan, Michele. BA, Anderson U., 1968; MA, Ball State U., 1973. Cert. tchr., Ind; cert. auctioneer of real estate. Tchr. Little Miami High Sch., Morrow, Ohio, 1968-70; middle sch. tchr. Anderson (Ind.) Community Schs., 1970-79; auctioneer Anderson, 1971—, realtor, 1974; owner Jackson's Auction Gallery, Inc., Anderson, 1978—; sr. auctioneer of fine arts Jackson & Wickliff Auctioneers, Inc.; bd. govs. Auction Mktg. Inst, 1993-94. Bd. trustees Christian Counseling Ctr., Anderson, 1987-92, Anderson Cmty. Schs., 1988-93, pres., 1991-92, sec., 1992-93. Mem. Nat. Auctioneers Assn. (CAI award 1985, mem. antiques and personal property coun. 1988-92), Nat. Auctioneers Assn. (Advt. award 1985), Ind. Auctioneers Assn. (bd. dirs. 1987-93, pres. 1991-92, Advt. award 1975, Hoosier Bid Calling champion 1988), Am. Bd. Realtors, Amici Club (Anderson U., pres. 1967-68). Office: Jackson's Auction Gallery Inc 5330 Pendleton Ave Anderson IN 46013-9718

JACKSON, DONALD ERNEST, health facility administrator; b. Minden, Nebr., May 15, 1947; s. Roy Lavern and Violet Ann (Louden) J.; 1 child, Jennifer Ann; m. Judith Rochelle Landry Gazaway, Aug. 15, 1984; 1 child, Stephen Wesley Gazaway. AA, McCook Coll., 1967; BA, Hastings Coll., 1970; cert. in phys. therapy, Northwestern U., 1971; MS, DePaul U., 1981. Phys. therapist Cook County Hosp., Chgo., 1971-74; mgr. phys. therapy Westlake Community Hosp., Melrose Park, Ill., 1974-75; chief rehab. svcs. Suburban Home Health, Inc., Des Plaines, Ill., 1975-76; pres., dir. Rehab. Systems Ill., Ltd., Oak Park, Ill., 1976—; dir. Commn. on Accreditation Rehab. Facilities, Tucson, 1991-93. Exec. v.p., chief operating officer Nat. Easter Seal Soc., Chgo., 1991—; treas. Suburban Adult Day Care, Oak Park, 1979-86, pres., 1987. Mem. Am. Phys. Therapy Assn. (treas. 1990-93, sec. 1983-89), Ill. Phys. Therapy Assn. (pres. 1979-82, treas. 1977-78). Office: Nat Easter Seal Soc 230 W Monroe St Chicago IL 60606-4703

JACKSON, FIELDS LEE, JR., healthcare manufacturing executive; b. Orange, N.J., Sept. 6, 1957; s. Fields Lee and Audrey (Brown) J.; m. Cheryl Charvis, May 3, 1986; children: Chelsea Rae, Fields Lee III. BA, Allegheny Coll., 1980. Adminstrv. mgr. Marine Bank, Erie, Pa., 1980-82; sales rep. Am. Sterilizer, Hartford, Conn., 1982-84; product mgr. Am. Sterilizer, Erie, 1984-88; mktg. mgr. AMSCO Internat., Erie, 1988-89; gen. mgr. AMSCO Internat., Detroit, 1989-91, Chgo., 1991—. Bd. dirs. Big Bros. and Big Sisters, Erie, 1981, treas., 1982; bd. dirs. Family Svcs., Inc., Erie, 1981. Named Outstanding Vol., Big Bros. and Big Sisters, 1982. Democrat. Roman Catholic.

JACKSON, GARNET NELSON, elementary education educator, writer; b. New Orleans, May 27, 1944; d. Israel George Nelson and Carrie (Brent) Sherman; m. Anthony M. Jackson, Dec. 30, 1970 (div. Mar. 1978); 1 child, Damon M. Jackson. BA, Dillard U., New Orleans, 1968. Tchr. Flint Cmty. Schs., 1968—; columnist The Flint (Mich.) Jour., 1990-95; author Paramount Pub., Modern Curriculum Press, Parsippany, N.J., 1993-95; freelance writer The Flint (Mich.) Jour., Harcourt Brace Pub., San Antonio, 1996. Author: (children's books) I Am An African American Child, 1990, The Little African King, 1990, Benjamin Banneker Scientist, 1992, Frederick Douglas Freedom Fighter, 1993, Elijah McCoy Inventor, 1993, Garret Morgan Inventor, 1993, Rosa Parks Hero of Our Times, 1993, Phyllis Wheatley Poet, 1993, Selma Burke Artist, 1994, Shirley Chisholm Congresswoman, 1994, Charles Drew Surgeon, 1994, Mae Jemison Astronaut, 1994, Thurgood Marshall Supreme Court Justice, 1994, Maggie Walker Businesswoman, 1994, Toni Morrison Author, 1995. Mem. NAACP, Flint, 1985—, The Urban League, Flint, 1990—, The Greater Flint Optimist Club, 1991—. Recipient Hon. Mention for Outstanding Poetry award R. Poetry Club, 1987, Harambee medal NAACP, 1991, Educator of the Yr. award, 1991, Spl. Tribute award State Rep. Floyd Clack, State of Mich., Flint, 1992, Mayor's Proclamation of Garnet Jackson Day City of Flint Mayor Stanley, 1992, Proclamation of Outstanding Citizenship House of Reps. Congressman Dale Kildee, 1992, Finer Womanhood Hall of Fame award Zeta Phi Beta Sorority, 1993. Mem. Mich. Reading Assn., Broome's Book Club, Internat. Reading Assn. Democrat. Baptist. Office: PO Box 190471 Burton MI 48519

JACKSON, GAYLE PENDLETON WHITE, venture capitalist, international energy specialist; b. Orange, N.J., June 22, 1946; d. Harold Dee and Marion Marvin (Harris) W.; m. Lothrop Brewster Jackson II, June 8, 1968 (div. 1986); m. Frederick T. Kraus, June 11, 1995; stepchildren: Grant, Madeleine, Caroline. BA cum laude, Smith Coll., 1967; MA in Polit. Sci., Washington U., 1969, PhD in Polit. Sci., 1972. Asst. prof. polit. sci. Washington U., St. Louis, 1972-73; market analyst Ralston Purina Co., St. Louis, 1973-74, adminstr. corp. energy dept., 1974-76; regional rep. to Sec. of Commerce U.S. Dept. of Commerce, Kansas City, Mo., 1976-78; dir. corp. planning Peabody Coal Co., St. Louis, 1978-81; v.p. bus. devel. Gateway Terminals, Peabody Holding Co., St. Louis, 1981-82; v.p. Premier Coal Sales Co., Peabody Holding Co., St. Louis, 1982-85; prs. Gayle P.W. Jackson, Inc., St. Louis, 1985—; chief of staff coal industry adv. bd. Internat. Energy Agy., Paris, 1985—. Chmn., pres. St. Louis County Local Devel. Co., 1979-84; bd. dirs. Webster U., St. Louis, 1983—, Ctr. for Internat. Pvt. Enterprise, 1993—, St. Louis Health Care Network, 1995—; bd. adjustment City of Clayton, St. Louis, 1985-91; st. councillor Atlantic Coun., 1993. Recipient Spl. Leadership award St. Louis YWCA, 1984; fellow Woodrow Wilson, 1971-72, Fulbright-Hays, 1971-72. Mem. Mo. Women's Forum (pres. 1992), Internat. Women's Forum (bd. dirs. 1986-94, treas. 1991-93, v.p. 1993-95, leadership found. 1993—). Office: Gayle P W Jackson Inc 6445 Cecil Ave Saint Louis MO 63105-2224

JACKSON, GREGORY STUART, information systems specialist; b. Canton, Ohio, Oct. 22, 1961. BS in MIS, Bowling Green (Ohio) State U., 1985; MBA, Ashland U., 1995. Sys. analyst The Hoover Co., N. Canton, 1985-88; sr. sys. analyst Kaiser Permanente, Cleve., 1988-89; project mgr., 1989-90, Oakland, Calif., 1990-92; dir. MIS Ohio Dept. Taxation, Colubus, 1992—; conf. on Innovative Orgns., Duke U., Durham, N.C., 1994, Strategic Leadership for State Execs., Duke U., Durham, N.C., 1993. Home: 5455 Coachman Rd #M Columbus OH 43220 Office: Ohio Dept Taxation 800 Freeway Dr North Columbus OH 43229

JACKSON, GREGORY WAYNE, orthodontist; b. Chgo., Sept. 4, 1950; s. Wayne Eldon and Marilyn Frances (Anderson) J.; m. Nora Ann Echtner, Mar. 17, 1973; children: Eric, David. Student, U. Ill., 1968-70; DDS with honors, U. Ill., Chgo., 1974; MSD, U. Wash., 1978. Practice dentistry specializing in orthodontics Chgo., 1978—; instr. orthodontic dept. U. Ill. Coll. Dentistry, Chgo., 1978-81. Coach Little League Baseball, Oak Brook, Ill., 1986-89. Served to lt. USN, 1974-76. Mem. ADA, Ill. State Dental Soc., Chgo. Dental Soc., Am. Assn. Orthodontists, Midwestern Soc.

Orthodontists, Ill. Soc. Orthodontists, Omicron Kappa Upsilon. Evangelical. Office: 6435 S Pulaski Rd Chicago IL 60629-5148

JACKSON, ISAIAH, conductor; b. Richmond, Va., Jan. 22, 1945; s. Isaiah Allen and Alma Alverta (Norris) J.; m. Helen Tuntland, Aug. 6, 1977; children: Benjamin, Katharine, Caroline. BA cum laude, Harvard U., 1966; MA, Stanford U., 1967; MS, Juilliard Sch. Music, 1969, DMA, 1973. Founder, condr. Juilliard String Ensemble, N.Y.C., 1970-71; asst. condr. Am. Symphony Orch., N.Y.C., 1970-71, Balt. Symphony Orch., 1971-73; assoc. condr. Rochester (N.Y.) Philharmonic Orch., 1973-87; music dir. Dayton (Ohio) Philharm. Orch., 1987-95, 1987-95; prin. condr. Royal Ballet, Covent Garden, London, 1986, music dir., 1987-90; prin. guest condr. Queensland (Australia) Symphony Orch., 1993—; music dir. Youngstown (Ohio) Symphony, 1996—; guest condr. N.Y. Philharm. Orch., 1978, Boston Pops Orch., 1983, 90-94, Detroit Symphony Orch., 1983, 85, San Francisco Symphony, 1984, Toronto Symphony, 1984, 90, Orch. de la Suisse Romande, 1985, 88, BBC Concert Orch., 1987, Berlin Symp hony, 1989-95, Dallas Symphony, 1993, Royal Liverpool Philharm., 1995, Houston Symphony, 1995; numerous recordings for Koch, Australian Broadcasting Corp. Recipient First Gov.'s award for arts in Va., Commonwealth Va., 1979, Signet Soc. medal for the arts Harvard U., 1991. Office: care United Arts 3906 Sunbeam Dr Los Angeles CA 90065-3551

JACKSON, JAMES SIDNEY, psychology educator; b. Detroit, July 30, 1944; s. Pete James and Johnnie Mae (Wilson) J. B.S., Mich. State U., 1966; M.A., U. Toledo, 1970; Ph.D., Wayne State U., 1972. Probation counselor Lucas County Juvenile Ct., Toledo, Ohio, 1967-68; teaching and research asst. Wayne State U., Detroit, 1968-71; from asst. prof. to prof. psychology U. Mich., Ann Arbor, 1971—, faculty assoc. Research Ctr.for Group Dynamics, Inst. for Social Research, 1971—, research scientist, 1986—, faculty assoc. Inst. Gerontology, 1976—, faculty assoc. Ctr. Afro-Am. and African Studies, 1982—, assoc. dean Rackham Sch. Grad. Studies, 1987-92, prof. pub. health, 1990—, dir. program for rsch. on Black Ams., 1976—, Daniel Katz Disting. Univ. Prof. Psychology, 1995—; Daniel Katz Collegiate prof., 1994-95; Hill Disting. vis. prof. U. Minn., 1995; chair sociol psychology tng. program U. Mich., 1980-86, 93—; cons. Emergency Sch. Aid Project, 1973-74, Commn. on Equal Opportunity in Psychology, 1970, Project to Provide Psychol. Svcs. to Head Start Programs, 1973-74, European Econ. Commn. Project on Racism, Xenophobia and Immigration, 1989—; mem. com. on aging and com. on status of Black Ams., NAS; mem. com. on African Am. Population Year 2000 U.S. Census bur.; rschr. invite Ecole des Hautes Etudes en Sciences Sociales, Paris, 1992—; acting dir. Rsch. Ctr. Group Dynamics, Inst. Social Rsch., 1991-92; disting. lectr. gerontology UCLA, 1992; dir. Rsch. Ctr. for Group Dynamics, Inst. for Social Rsch., 1996—. Author: The Black American Elderly: Research on Physical and Psychosocial Health, 1988, (with Gurin P., Hatchett S.) Hope and Independence: Blacks Response to Electoral and Party Politics, 1989, Life in Black America, 1991, (with Chatters L., Taylor R.) Aging in Black America, 1993, (with H. Neighbors) Mental Health in Black America, 1996; editl. cons. Jour. Behavioral and Social Scientists; editl. bd. Jour. Gerontology, Applied Social Psychology Ann., Psychol. Bulletin, Jour. Social Issues; cons. editor Psychology and Aging; contbr. articles to profl. jours. Bd. dirs. Pub. Commn. on Mental Health; mem. rev. panel Nat. Inst. Aging, 1982-86, chmn., 1985-86. Recipient Disting. Faculty Svc. award U. Mich., 1976; Urban Studies fellow Wayne State U., 1969-70; NSF fellow, 1969; Sr. Postdoctoral fellow Groupe d'Études et de Recherches sur la Science, École des Hautes Études en Sciences Sociales, 1986-87; Sr. Ford Found. Minority Postdoctoral fellow, 1986-87; Fogarty Sr. Internat. fellow, 1993-94; Robert W. Kleemeier award for research, Geroontological Soci. of Am. Fellow Am. Psychol. Assn. (divs. 9-20, policy and planning bd., fin. com. 1984-86, award for early contbns. 1983), Am. Psychol. Soc., Gerontol. Soc. Am. (task force on minority issues in gerontology, chmn. 1988-92, ann. sci. conv. program com.); mem. Assn. Advancement of Psychology (trustee 1973-89, chmn. 1978-80), Black Students Psychol. Assn. (nat. chmn. 1970-71), Assn. Black Psychologists (nat. chmn. 1972-73), Soc. Psychol. Study of Social Issues, World Future Soc., Assn. Behavioral and Social Scientists, Internat. Platform Assn., NIMH (nat. mental health coun., panel on equal access com. on instl. cooperation 1989-92), Psi Chi, Alpha Phi Alpha. Home: 517 Fairview Cir Ypsilanti MI 48197-2112 Office: U Mich 5110 Inst Social Rsch 426 Thompson St Ann Arbor MI 48104-2321

JACKSON, JAMES T., operations manager; b. St. Joseph, Mo., Apr. 16, 1957. B in Journalism, U. Mo., 1988. Ops. mgr. Jackson Galleries, St. Joseph, 1988-93; advt. staff Cablevision Advt., St. Joseph, 1993; ops. mgr. Dyna Mag Inc., St. Joseph, 1993—. Republican. Office: Dyna Mag INc RR 1 Saint Joseph MO 64507-9801

JACKSON, JENNIFER CLAIRE, marine underwriter; b. Cleve., Mar. 6, 1970; d. James Coleman and Patricia (Ivory) J. Diploma, U. Strasbourg, France, 1991; BA in Internat. Politics, Pa. State U., 1993, BA in French Lang. and Culture, 1993. Assoc. marine underwriter Marine Office of Am. Corp., N.Y.C., 1993-96; mgr. No. Imports Inc., Columbus, Ohio, 1996—. Mem. NAFE.

JACKSON, JESSE, JR., lawyer; b. Greenville, S.C., Mar. 11, 1965; m. Sandra Jackson. BS, N.C A&T U., 1987; MA, Chgo. Theol. Sem.; JD, U. Ill., 1993. Mem. U.S. House of Reps., 2nd Dist., Ill., 1995—. Baptist. Office: 312 Cannon House Office Bldg Washington DC 20515*

JACKSON, JOHN CHARLES, retired secondary education educator, writer; b. Columbus, Ohio, Mar. 12, 1939; s. John Franklin and Mari Jane (Lusch) J.; m. Carol Nancy Tiggelbeck, June 24, 1990. Tchr. social studies Buckeye Local Sch., West Mansfield, Ohio, 1961-62, Grandview Heights (Ohio) City Schs., 1962-91; ret., 1991. Cooperating tchr. Project Bus. program Jr. Achievement, Grandview, 1984-91. Recipient Career Tchr. award Ohio State U. Coll. Edn. Alumni Soc., 1995; Martha Holden Jennings Found. scholar, 1968-69. Mem. Ohio Ret. Tchrs. Assn. (life.), Franklin County Ret. Tchrs. Assn. (life), Ohio State U. Alumni Assn. (life), Am. Mensa Ltd. Republican. Methodist. Home: 5741 Aspendale Dr Columbus OH 43235-7506

JACKSON, M. DOROTHY, medical surgical nurse, researcher; b. Ohsweken, Ont., Can., July 12, 1945; d. Charles E. and Effie Irene (Montour) Hill; m. Richard A. Jackson, July 29, 1972; 1 child, Helki Orenda. Diploma in nursing, Greater Niagara Gen. Hosp., Niagara Falls, Ont., 1968; student, Wayne State U., Washtenaw Community Coll., Ann Arbor, Mich. RN, Can., Mich.; cert. med.-surg. nurse ANA. Staff nurse Fed. Govt. Can., Ottawa, Ont.; nurse clinician III gynecol. and med.-surg. units U. Mich., Ann Arbor, 1992-93; med.-surg. home health care nurse, 1994—. Mem., chmn. resource com. Women of Colour Task Force, 1987-89, 93—. Mem. ANA (cert. med.-surg. nurse ANCC), Mich. Nurses Assn., Livingston-Washtenaw-Monroe Counties Nurses Assn.

JACKSON, MARTIN A., industrial designer; b. Mansfield, Ohio, Mar. 10, 1963. Student, Ctrl. Ohio Tech. Coll., 1985-89. Mech. draftsman Atiel Corp., Mt. Vernon, Ohio, 1981-86; rsch. technician Halophane, Newark, Ohio, 1986-90; design machine mgr. Allied Machine and Engring. Co., Dover, Ohio, 1990—. Mem., coach Perry Heights Baseball Assn., Canton, Ohio, 1993—. Republican. Office: Allied Machine & Engring Co 485 W 3rd St Dover OH 44622-3103

JACKSON, NATHANIEL RICHARD, investment broker; b. Anoka, Minn., Jan. 21, 1963. BA in English, BA in Bus., Concordia Coll., 1985. Investment broker Edward D. Jones & Co., River Falls, Wis., 1986—; bd. dirs. U. Wis. Bus. Directorship, River Falls, Wis.; bd. dirs. grass roots task force Edward D. Jones & Co., River Falls; bd. dirs. round table quality circle. Past chair Ch. Coun., River Falls, 1990—. Mem. Lions Club (past pres. 1987—), River Falls C. of C. Republican. Home: 1870 Golf View Dr River Falls WI 54022-2500

JACKSON, NICOLE RENÉE, mechanical engineer; b. Cleve., July 15; d. Eddie and Juliette Jackson. BS in Mech. Engring., N.C. State U., Raleigh, 1988; MS in Materials Engring. Follow up svcs. engr. Underwriters Labs., Research Triangle Park, 1989-90; sr. mfg. engr., Advanced Mfg. Tech. Delphi Chassis, Dayton, Ohio, 1990—. Contbr. articles to profl. jours. Mem. membership com. Nat. Bus. League, Dayton, 1992-93; tutor Edn. Partnership with Patterson H.S., Dayton, 1993-95. Gem fellow, 1996. Mem. Nat. Soc. Black Engrs. (membership chair 1992-93). Address: 6591 Brigham Sq Centerville OH 45459

JACKSON, PATRICIA ANNE, environmental executive; b. Chgo., Jan. 20, 1945; d. Grant Edward Jackson and Anna Louise (Eison) Thompson; m. Leslie David Sparks, Apr. 1972; 1 child, Nyia Mercedes. BA, Columbia Coll., 1979; cert., John Marshall Law Sch., 1989. Mgr. Addie's & Bill's Beauty Salon, Chgo., 1980-85; property inspector Chase Investigations, Chgo., 1985-87; adminstrv. asst. The Resource Ctr., Chgo., 1989-93; environ. policy coord. People for Cmty. Recovery, Chgo., 1993—; founder, exec. dir. Mothers for an Environmentally Safe Habitat; cons. Great Lakes Auto Pollution Prevention Alliance, Chgo., 1994—; stakeholder U.S. EPA's Common Sense Initiative, Washington, 1994—; rep. Chgo. Brownfield Redevelopment Forum, 1994—; started asthma support group and hold workshops Atgeld Gardens U.S. EPA and Am. Lung Assn. Met. Chgo.; co-authored environ. justice ordinance Ctr. Neighborhood Tech. Chgo. Legal Clinic and Citizens for a Better Environment. Co-founder, editor (newsletter) Fighting A Toxic Environment, 1992. Trainee environ. edn. Argonne Nat. Lab., Chgo., 1993; vol. Cancer Prevention Coalition, Chgo., 1994—. Grantee Joyce Found., 1994-95, 95-96, EPA, 1995-96. Office: People for Cmty Recovery 13116 S Ellis Ave Chicago IL 60627 also: Mothers for an Environmentally Safe Habitat 1438 E 52nd St Chicago IL 60615

JACKSON, REGINALD SHERMAN, JR., lawyer; b. Toledo, Ohio, Oct. 8, 1946; s. Reginald Sherman and Frances (Holland) J.; m. Joanne Marie Warren, Aug. 31, 1968; children: Reginald Sherman III, Michael W., Adam H. BA, Ohio State U., 1968, JD, 1971. Bar: Ohio 1971, U.S. Supreme Ct. 1976. Mem. Fuller, Henry, Hodge & Snyder, Toledo, 1971-76; asst. U.S. atty. no. dist. Ohio, U.S. Dept. Justice, 1976-78; ptnr. Connelly, Soutar & Jackson, 1978—; adj. prof. trial practice U. Toledo Coll. Law, 1976-89. Trustee Toledo Boy's Club, 1981—; mem. Maumee Ohio Civil Svc. Commn., 1990—, chair, 1994—. Fellow Ohio State Bar Found., Toledo Bar Found. (pres. 1994—); mem. ABA (ho. of dels. 1996—, litigation sect.), Ohio Bar Assn. (coun. dels. 1990—, bd. govs. 1996—), Toledo Bar Assn. (pres. 1989-90), Toledo Country Club (trustee 1981-91, pres. 1991-93), Rotary (trustee 1994-96, 1st v.p.). Home: 2907 River Rd Maumee OH 43537-3740 Office: Connelly Soutar & Jackson 405 Madison Ave Ste 1600 Toledo OH 43604-1207

JACKSON, ROBERT LORING, science and mathematics educator, academic administrator; b. Mitchell, S.D., June 8, 1926; s. Olin DeBuhr and Edna Anna (Hanson) J.; m. Elizabeth Denise Koteski; children: Charles Olin, Catherine Lynne, Cynthia Helen. BS, Hamline U., 1950; MA, U. Minn., 1959; PhD, 1965. Tchr. math. and sci., pub. schs., Heron Lake, Minn., 1950-52; tchr. math. Lakewood (Colo.) Sr. High Sch., 1952-53, Nouassuer Air Force Sch. Casablanca, Morocco, 1953-54, Baumholder (Germany) Elem. Sch., 1954-55, U. Minn. Univ. Lab. Sch., Mpls., 1955-60; asst. prof. sci. and math. edn. U. Minn., Mpls., 1965-66, assoc. prof., 1966-70, prof., 1970-94; emeritus prof. 1994—, head sci. and math. edn., 1980-84, assoc. chmn., dir. undergrad. studies, curriculum and instrn., 1984-88, assoc. chmn., 1989-92; vis. prof. Hamline U., St. Paul, 1958, Mont. State U., Bozeman, 1981, Bethel Coll., St. Paul, 1981, No. Mich. U., Marquette, 1983-84; cons. math. Minn. Dept. Edn., St. Paul, 1960-62. Bd. dirs. Oratorio Soc. Minn., Minn. Chorale, Mpls., 1973-88, pres., 1978-80. With U.S. Army, 1944-46. Decorated Purple Heart; recipient First Alumni award 1988, Disting. Teaching award Coll. Edn., U. Minn., 1984. Mem. Minn. Coun. Tchrs. Math., Nat. Coun. Tchrs. Math., Math. Assn. Am., Internat. Platform Assn. Methodist. Co-author: (book/man series) Laboratory Mathematics, 1975-76. Home: 810 Purple Sage Ter Henderson NV 89015-5692

JACKSON, TRICIA A., financial planner; b. Connersville, Ind., Feb. 26, 1970; d. Gilbert E. and Cheryl K. (Jones) J. BAS, Miami U., Oxford, Ohio, 1992. Fin. planner Alles Fin., Dublin, Ohio, 1993—. Office: Alles Fin 4248 Tuller Rd Dublin OH 43017-5025

JACKSON, VICKI RAE, adult nurse pracititioner; b. Ft. Leavenworth, Kans., Nov. 18, 1954; d. William Sarge and Virgie Evelyn (Hicks) J. LPN, State Fair C.C., Sedalia, Mo., 1976, ADN, 1978; BSN, Webster U., 1992; MSN, U. Mo., Kansas City, 1995. RN, Mo.; cert. adult nurse practitioner. Staff nurse Bothwell Regional Health Care Ctr., Sedalia, 1975-83; clin. supr., dir. profl. svcs. Upjohn Healthcare Svcs., Kansas City, 1983-84; nurse mgr. surg. svcs. Lakeside Hosp., Kansas City, 1984-87; clin. coord. emergency svcs. Rsch. Med. Ctr., Kansas City, 1988-94, mem. triage task force, 1988-91, mentor Coll. of Nursing, 1990-94, preceptor EMT/paramedic students, 1989-94; triage nurse Humana Health Care Plans, Kansas City, 1994-95; adult nurse practitioner Humana Health Care Plans, 1995—; adj. nursing instr. State Fair Community Coll., Sedalia, 1977-78; women's health advocate. CPR instr. ARC, Kansas City, 1983-84, breast self-exam. facilitator, 1986-87; sustaining mem. Planned Parenthood Fedn. Am., Kansas City, 1990-92; vol. Teen Connection Hotline for Greater Kansas City, 1992. Mem. ANA, Am. Acad. Nurse Practitioners, Sigma Theta Tau. Baptist. Home: 4309 NE Arbor Rd Kansas City MO 64117-1616

JACKSON, WILLIAM COLE, manufacturing executive; b. Glasgow, Scotland, Nov. 11, 1939; came to the U.S., 1966; s. William and Mary Violet (Coles) J.; m. Linda L. Hanson, Oct. 19, 1990 (div. 1995); children: Stewart C., Tracey J. Marut, Shaaron C. Kanute. BS in Mech. Engring., Stow Coll. Engring., 1956, Strathclyde U., 1960. Apprentice marine engr. Fairfield Shipbldg. Co., Glasgow, 1955-60; quality control mgr. Mine Safety Appliances, Glasgow, 1960-64; cons. engr. Peter Stobie and Co., Thornlee Bank, Scotland, 1964-66; asst. quality control mgr. Burgess Norton Mfg., Geneva, Ill., 1966-68; asst. sales mgr. Functional Products Divsn., Geneva, 1968-71; pres. Carbo-Bond Abrasive Co., St. Charles, Ill., 1971-82; pres., CEO AVK Carbo-Bond Inc., La Fox, Ill., 1982—. Fellow ASME; mem. Am. Soc. Quality Control. Republican. Office: AVK Carbo-Bond Inc 1N046 Linlar Dr La Fox IL 60147

JACKSON, WILLIAM GENE, computer company executive; b. Opelika, Ala., Nov. 22, 1946; s. John Willis and Lucy (Jackson) J.; m. Rosalyn Miller-Bennett, June 17, 1989; children: Verzelia Yvett, Gena Nichole, William Gene, Alisa Claire Bennett. BS in Mgmt. and Mktg., Syracuse U., 1979, AAS in Mgmt., 1976; postgrad. Pace U. With IBM, 1966—, customer engr. Huntsville, Ala., 1966-72, sr. customer engr., Atlanta, 1972-73, field mgr., Miami, Fla., 1973-75, eastern region ops. analyst Harrison, N.Y., 1975-76, br. mgr., N.Y.C., 1976, region ops. mgr. region 3, Montvale, N.J., 1977-78, employee rels. program mgr. pers., office products divsn. hdqrs., Franklin Lakes, N.J., 1979, adminstrv. asst. to dir. ops. west, office products divsn. hdqrs., Franklin Lakes, 1980, IBM corp. svc. staff, Armonk, N.Y., 1981-82, adminstrv. asst. to pres. customer svc. divsn., Franklin Lakes, 1983, region mgr. customer svc. divsn., region 7, Southfield, Mich., 1983-84, dir. svc. support Nat. Svc. divsn. Area 4, 1984-87, regional mgr., 1987-92, dir. quality U.S. Gt. Lakes area 4, 1992-95, corp. dir. teleops., 1995—. Bd. dirs. spl. affairs Jaycees, Wanaque, N.J., 1978-79; mem. Black exec. exch. program Nat. Urban League. Mem. Am. Mgmt. Assn., Am. Exec. Mgmt. Excellence, Am. Execs. for Mgmt. Excellence, Am. Soc. for Quality Control. Home: 30552 Sunderland Dr Farmington MI 48331-5909 Office: IBM Corp 18000 Nine Mile Rd Southfield MI 48086

JACKSON, YVONNE DENISE, physical therapist; b. Detroit, May 22, 1967; d. George and Mary Lee (Houston) Williams; m. Anthony Barry Jackson, July 3, 1993; children: Taylour Denise, Anthony Barry II. BS in Phys. Therapy, Wayne State U., 1990, MA in Sports Adminstrn., 1993; cert. myomassologist, Irene's Myomassology Inst. Mich., 1996. Registered phys. therapist; lic. phys. therapist, Mich.; cert. coach, CPR instr. Phys. therapist Rehab. Inst., Detroit, 1991-94, Bd. Edn. City of Detroit, 1994—; exec. dir. Aerosport Acad., Detroit, 1994—; med. cons. Rehab East, Warren, Mich., 1993; gymnastics tchr. Spirit of Detroit Aerosports, 1993; student trainer Wayne State U., Detroit, 1992-93; cons. Bishop Burgess High Sch., Detroit, 1995. Christian edn. tchr. Tried Stone Bapt. Ch., 1991—. Mem. NAFE, IMF, AMMI, NASE, Delta Sigma Theta. Democrat. Home and Office: 11307 Lansdowne Detroit MI 48224

JACOB, ELIZABETH ANN, elementary education educator; b. Highland Park, Mich., May 14, 1950; d. Theodore George and Helen Mae (Kressbach) J. BS, Ea. Mich. U., 1972; MA, Cen. Mich. U., 1976. Tchr. Tawas City (Mich.) Elem. Sch., 1972—; dir. region II MCTM, 1995. Sunday sch. tchr. Zion Luth. Ch., Tawas City, 1976-89, mem. bd. edn., 1990, mem. bd. fin., 1995-96; instr. water safety Oscoda-Iosco County chpt. ARC, 1979—; treas. Animal Humanitarians Iosco, 1995-96. Office: Tawas City Elem Sch 825 2nd St Tawas City MI 48763-9102

JACOB, HERBERT, political science educator; b. Augsburg, Germany, Feb. 10, 1933; came to U.S., 1940, naturalized, 1946; s. Ernest I. and Annette (Loewenberg) J.; m. Lynn Susan Carp, Aug. 19, 1968; children: Joel Benjamin, David Samuel, Jenny Ellen, Michael Max. AB, Harvard U., 1954; MA, Yale U., 1955, PhD, 1960. Mem. faculty Tulane U., 1960-62; mem. faculty U. Wis.-Madison, 1962-69, prof., 1967-69; prof. polit. sci. Northwestern U., Evanston, Ill., 1969-84, 85—, chmn. dept., 1974-77; Hawkins disting. prof. polit. sci. U. Wis., Madison, 1984-85; vis. prof. Johns Hopkins U., 1972; prin. investigator Govtl. Responses to Crime Project, 1978-81; vis. fellow Center for Sociolegal Research, Oxford U., 1981. Author: Law and Politics in the U.S., 2d edit., 1995, Law, Court, and Politics in Comparative Perspective, 1996; editor: Law and Politics Book Review, 1991—. Mem. Human Rels. Commn. Evanston, 1971-73. With AUS, 1955-57. Recipient Emil H. Steiger award U. Wis., 1964; NSF faculty fellow, 1967-68; fellow Ctr. for Advanced Studies in Behavioral Scis., 1973-74, Ctr. for Socio-legal Research, Oxford U., 1981. Mem. Law and Society Assn. (pres. 1981-83). Home: 2234 Asbury Ave Evanston IL 60201-2653

JACOB, KEN, state legislator; b. St. Louis, Jan. 23, 1949. BS, U. Mo. Columbia. State rep. Dist. 25 Mo. State Congress, 1983—; social worker. *

JACOB, ROBERT EDWARD, small business and non-profit tax consultant; b. Detroit, June 14, 1954; s. John Joseph and Eleanore Alice (Grates) J.; m. Mary Louise Teran, July 8, 1983; children: Matthew, Autumn, Jason. BA, Mich. State U., 1977; MBA, Wayne State U., 1987. Cert. tax profl., cert. mgmt. acct., cert. practitioner of taxation; enrolled agt. Gen. ledger acct. Weltronic, Southfield, Mich., 1978-79; acctg. mgr. R.L. Polk, Detroit, 1979-81; chief acct. Family and Neighborhood Svcs., Inkster, Mich., 1981, contr., 1981-82, v.p. fiscal, 1982-84, sr. v.p., 1984-90; exec. v.p. for operations, chief fin. officer, 1990-93; fin. dir. Warren/Conner Devel. Coalition, Detroit, 1993-95; pres. R.E. J.'s Acctg. and Tax Svc. Inc., Southgate 1977—; treas. Tamson Ctr. Inc., Taylor 1983-84. Cons. Acctg. Aid Soc., Detroit, 1981—. Mem. Inst. Mgmt. Accts. (Stuart Cameron Soc., nat. dir. 1989-94, pres. Mich. coun. 1988-89, 90-91, pres. Detroit chpt. 1988-89, 90-91, v.p. 1987-88, Jaycee of Month 1979), Nat. Assn. Enrolled Agts., Inst. Cert. Mgmt. Accts., Inst. Cert. Practitioners, Mich. State Alumni Assn., Wayne State Alumni Assn. (treas. 1993—), Aquinas Men's Club, KC. Roman Catholic. Home: 15436 Richmond St Southgate MI 48195-2613 Office: REJ's Acctg and Tax Svc Inc 12985 Northline Rd Ste 105 Southgate MI 48195-1111 Office: REJ's Acctg and Tax Svc Inc 11141 Harper Ave Detroit MI 48213

JACOBI, FREDRICK THOMAS, newspaper publisher; b. Neenah, Wis., July 10, 1953; s. H. Paul and Patricia Mary (Steele) J.; m. Kim Lee Muenchow, Aug. 23, 1980; children: James Paul, Steven Thomas. AA in Bus., U. South Fla., 1973; BBA in Fin., Mktg., U. Wis., 1976; MBA in Mktg., U. Wis., Whitewater, 1980. Cert. newspaper circulation. City dist. mgr. Madison (Wis.) Newspapers Inc., 1977-79, city circulation mgr., 1979-80, circulation mgr., 1980-81, mktg. mgr., 1981-82, circulation dir., 1982-85; circulation dir. Gannett Co., Inc., Reno, Nev., 1985-88; regional circulation dir. Gannett Co., Inc., Arlington, Va., 1988-90; pub., pres. Wausau (Wis.) Daily Herald, Gannett Co., Inc., 1990-92, Springfield (Mo.) News-Leader, 1993-96; v.p. Midwest region Gannett Co., Inc., 1993-96; pub., pres. Ft. Myers (Fla.) News-Press, 1996—; com. chmn. Sales and Mktg. Exec., Madison, 1985. Editor Circulation-Central States, 1985. Program chmn. Jr. Achievement of Nev., Reno, 1987-88; pres. Springfield Bus. and Devel. Corp., 1996; bd. dirs. Ozarks Press Assn., Make A Wish Mo. Mem. Internat. Circulation Mgr. Assn., Rotary. Republican. Roman Catholic. Home: 2442 Martin Luther King Blvd Springfield MO 65809-2234 Office: Springfield News-Leader 651 N Boonville Ave Springfield MO 65806-1005

JACOBI, JAN DE GREEFF, school administrator; b. N.Y.C., Oct. 26, 1944; s. Edwin George Jacobi and Marjorie (de Greeff) Litchfield; m. Virginia Powell Newton, July 26, 1986; children: Edwin, Marjorie, Peter. BA, Stanford U., 1967; MA, Columbia U., 1976. Asst. headmaster, English tchr. The Harvey Sch., Katonah, N.Y., 1973-82; head lower sch. St. Louis Country Day Sch., 1982-93; head mid. sch. Mary Inst. and St. Louis Country Day Sch., 1993—. Home: 86 Aberdeen Pl Saint Louis MO 63105-2273 Office: Mary Inst and St Louis Country Day School 101 N Warson Rd Saint Louis MO 63124-1326

JACOBI, PETER PAUL, journalism educator, author; b. Berlin, Mar. 15, 1930; came to U.S., 1938, naturalized, 1944; s. Paul A. and Liesbeth (Kron) J.; m. Harriet Ackley, Dec. 8, 1956 (div. 1979); children: Keith Peter, John Wyn. BS in Journalism, Northwestern U., 1952, MS, 1953. Mem. journalism faculty Northwestern U., Evanston, Ill., 1955-81, profl. lectr., 1955-63, asst. prof., 1963-66, assoc. prof., 1966-69, prof. journalism, 1969-81, assoc. dean, 1966-74; communications cons. N.Y.C., 1980-84, Bloomington, Ind., 1985—; prof. journalism Ind. U., Bloomington, 1985—; news assignment editor, newscaster, theatre and music reporter NBC, Chgo., 1955-61; news editor ABC, Chgo., 1951-53; radio commentator on music and opera, 1958-65; theatre and film critic Sta. WTTW, Chgo., 1964-74, arts critic, 1975-77; theatre and film critic Hollister Newspapers Suburban Chgo., 1963-70; music columnist Chicagoan mag., 1973-74; script cons. Goodman Theater, Chgo., 1973-75; syndicated commentator on arts and media N.Am. Radio Alliance, 1978-80; arts corr. Christian Sci. Monitor, 1956-81; music critic, columnist Bloomington (Ind.) Herald-Times, 1985—; columnist Arts Indiana, 1987—, Editors Only, 1994—, Editor's Workshop, 1995—. Author: Writing with Style, The News Story and the Feature, 1982, The Messiah Book-The Life and Times of G.F. Handel's Greatest Hit, 1982, (with Jack Hilton) Straight Talk about Videoconferencing, 1986, The Magazine Article: How to Think It, Plan It, Write It, 1991; contbg. essayist Lyric Opera Companion, 1991; editor Chgo. Lyric Opera News, 1958-61, Music Mag./Musical Courier, Chgo., 1961-62; contbr. articles on writing to Folio, Ragan Report, other mags., articles on arts to Sat. Rev., Chgo. Daily News, N.Y. Times, Highlights for Children, World Book, others. Mem. AAUP, NATAS, Assn. Edn. in Journalism, Ind. Arts Commn. (chmn. 1990-93), Arts Midwest, Soc. Profl. Journalists. Home: 3003 N Browncliff Ln Bloomington IN 47408-1317 Office: Ind U Sch Journalism Bloomington IN 47405

JACOBOWITZ, RUTH SCHERR, writer, public relations consultant, lecturer; b. Pitts., Apr. 12, 1933; d. Irving and Claire (Chernoff) Scherr; m. B. Paul Jacobowitz, Jan. 19, 1952; children: Jan, Jody, Julie. Student, U. Pitts., 1951-53, Cuyahoga Community Coll., 1960-63, Ursuline Coll., Cleve., 1978. Free-lance writer Cleve. Plain Dealer, 1965-67, book reviewer, 1978-82; pub. rels. dir. Mt. Sinai Med. Ctr., Cleve., 1967-73, v.p. pub. affairs, 1973-84; pres. Ruth Jacobowitz Assocs., Cleve., 1984—; mem. pub. relations com. Univ. Circle, Cleve., 1976-84; regional chmn. Am. Assn. Med. Colls., Washington, 1978-79; mem. pub. affairs com. Ctr. for Health Affairs, Cleve., 1983-85; bd. dirs. Cleve. Breast Cancer Coalition, 1994—. Author: 150 Most Asked Questions About Menopause: What Women Really Want To Know, 1993, 150 Most Asked Questions About Osteoporosis, 1993, 150 Most Asked Questions About Midlife Sex, Love and Intimacy, 1995; co-author: Managing Your Menopause, 1990; columnist Eternelle, Your Health, Chagrin Valley Times, Women's Health Exch. Mem. Nat. Coun. on Women's Health. Mem. NOW, Pub. Rels. Soc. Am., Internat. Assn. Bus. Communicators (editor quar. mag. Caring, 1974-85), Authors Guild, Am. Assn. of Sex Educators, Therapists and Counselors, Am. Soc. Journalists and Authors, Sex Info. and Edn. Coun. U.S., Greater Cleve. Hosp. Assn. (chmn. pub. rels. com. 1980-82), Womenspace, N.Am. Menopause Soc. (founding mem.), Internat. Menopause Soc., Jacobs Inst. For Women's Health, Press Club.

JACOBS, ANDREW, JR., congressman; b. Indpls., Feb. 24, 1932; s. Andrew and Joyce Taylor (Wellborn) J.; m. Kim Hood; children: H.B. James Andrew, B.N. Steven Michael. B.S., Ind. U., 1955, LL.B., 1958. Bar: Ind. Practiced in Indpls., 1958-65, 73-74; mem. 89th-92d congresses from 11th Dist., 1965-73, 94th-97th congresses from 11th Dist. Ind., 1975-83, 98th-

103rd Congresses from 10th Dist. Ind., 1983—; Mem. Ind. Ho. of Reps., 1958-60; ranking minority mem. ways & means subcom. on social security. Served with USMC, 1950-52. Mem. Indpls. Bar Assn., Am. Legion. Democrat. Roman Catholic. Office: US Ho of Reps 2313 Rayburn Washington DC 20515-1410*

JACOBS, BURLEIGH EDMUND, foundry executive; b. Milw., Feb. 3, 1920; s. Burleigh Edmund and Ora (Harmon) J.; m. Janet Eloise Grede, Nov. 1, 1942; children: Mary (Mrs. Merrill York), Bruce, Scott, William. B.A., U. Wis., 1942. Joined Grede Foundries, Inc., Milw., 1945; successively works mgr. Iron Mountain Foundry, 1947-49; works mgr. Milw. Steel Foundry, 1950-51, asst. sales mgr., 1952-57, asst. v.p., 1957-60, pres., 1960-73, chmn., chief exec. officer, 1973—; bd. dirs. Marshall & Ilsley Corp., Milw. Pres. bd. Met. Milw. YMCA, 1968-70; mem. Greater Milw. Com., 1969—; bd. dirs. Jr. Achievement, 1968-71, Better Bus. Bur. Served with USNR, 1942-45. Recipient Frederick A. Lorenz Meml. Gold medal Steel Founders' Soc. Am., 1970, Disting. Svc. Engr. award, U. Wis., Madison, 1980, Disting. Bus. Alumnus award Sch. Bus., U. Wis., Madison, 1990; named Mktg. Man of Yr., Sales and Mktg. Execs. Milw., 1980. Mem. Steel Founders' Soc. Am. (pres. 1966-69), Am. Foundrymen's Soc. (v.p. 1971-72, pres. 1972-73, Peter L. Simpson gold medal 1983), Cast Metals Fedn. (pres. 1974), Gray and Ductile Iron Founders' Soc. (Gold medal 1973). Congregationalist. Club: Bluemound Country (Wauwatosa, Wis.). Home: 1020 Madera Cir Elm Grove WI 53122-2126 Office: Grede Foundries Inc 9898 W Bluemound Rd Milwaukee WI 53226-4319

JACOBS, CARL EUGENE, printing company official; b. Ft. Wayne, Ind., Nov. 28, 1942; s. Earl Oscar and Marguerite Louise (Unger) J.; m. Linda Maureen Peralta, Sept. 6, 1974; children: Brett, Kim, Kris. BS in Edn., Ball State U., 1965, MA in Speech, 1970. Tchr. Ft. Wayne Community Schs., 1965-70; instr. Ft. Hays (Kans.) State U., 1970-73; dir. pubs. Nat. Collegiate Athletic Assn., Mission, Kans., 1973-77; v.p. sales, mktg. The Lowell Press, Kansas City, Mo., 1977-94; dir. internat. sales Constable-Hodgins Printing Co., Kansas City, Kans., 1994—. Trustee Kansas City Conservatory of Music, 1983-94; bd. dirs. Genesis Sch., Kansas City, 1987; ruling elder, mem. session Southridge Presbyn. Ch., Roeland Park, Kans., 1985-87, 89-91. Mem. Internat. Assn. Bus. Communicators (hon. life chpt. and dist., chpt. pres. 1978, internat. v.p., bd. dirs. 1981, trustee rsch. found. 1990-93), Kiwanis (bd. dirs., v.p. Downtown Kansas City Mo. club 1988-90, pres. 1991-92, Kiwanian of Yr. award 1994). Republican. Home: 5720 Willow Pl Parkville MO 64152-6131

JACOBS, CINDEE ANN, service executive; b. South Bend, Ind., Aug. 21, 1956; d. Billie George and Joyce Ann (Beatty) Bowser; m. Michael E. Jacobs, Oct. 14, 1977; children: Heather L., Jason M., Nicholas A. A in Acctg. and Bus. Adminstrn., Ind. U., 1977. Audit clk., receivable supr. Allied Signal, South Bend, Ind., 1983-87; mgr. regional sales Contempo Fashions, Kansas City, Kans., 1988-92; account exec. LDDS Comm., South Bend, 1992-94; CFO, cons. Jake's Janitorial Svcs. Inc., New Carlisle, Ind., 1994—; cons. Advanced Inventory Specialists, South Bend, 1980—. Bd. dirs. New Carlisle Hist. Soc.; instr. Jr. Achievement, South Bend, 1993-94; advisor St. Joseph 4-H Club, South Bend, 1993—. Mem. South Gateway Rotary (bd. dirs.), South Bend Tipps, Elkhart Tipps. Home and Office: 130 E Chestnut St PO Box 11 New Carlisle IN 46552-0011

JACOBS, DENNY, state legislator; b. Moline, Ill., Nov. 8, 1937; s. Oral G. and Caroline Harroun (Pinkerton) J.; m. Mary Ellen Duffy, 1955; 6 children. BA, Augustana Coll., 1959. Co-owner J & J Music, 1966-82; mktg. dir. Group W Cable, 1985-86; mayor East Moline, Ill., 1973—; mem. Ill. State Senate, 1986—; vice chmn. transp. com., mem. agr., conservation, energy and environment com., chmn. citizens coun. econ. devel., chmn. intergovt. com. Ill. State Senate. Mem. Moose, Elks (Disting. Citizen award 1986), Eagles, KC. Home: 3511 8th St East Moline IL 61244-3521*

JACOBS, DONALD P., banking and finance educator; b. Chgo., June 22, 1927; s. David and Bertha (Nevod) J.; children: Elizabeth, Ann, David; m. Dinah Nemeroff, May 28, 1978. B.A., Roosevelt Coll., 1949; M.A., Columbia U., 1951, Ph.D., 1956. Mem. research staff Nat. Bur. Econ. Research, 1952-57; instr. Coll. City N.Y., 1955-57; mem. faculty to Morrison prof. fin. Northwestern U. Grad. Sch. Mgmt., 1970-78, chmn. dept., 1969-75, dean, 1975—, Gaylord Freeman Disting. prof. banking, 1978—; participant Inst. Internat. Mgmt., Burgenstock, Switzerland, 1965—; dir. Commonwealth Edison, Hartmarx Corp., Union Oil Co., 1st Chgo., Whitman Corp., Conf. Savs. and Residential Financing; co-dir. fin. studies Presdl. Commn. Fin. Structure and Regulation, 1970-71; sr. economist banking and currency com. U.S. Ho. of Reps., 1963-64. Editor proc.: Conf. Savs. and Residential Financing, 1967, 68, 69; contbr. articles to profl. jours. Served with USNR, 1945-46. Ford Found. fellow, 1959-60, 63-64. Mem. Am. Econ. Assn., Am. Statis. Assn., Am. Fin. Assn., Econometrics Soc., Inst. Mgmt. Sci. Home: 617 Milburn St Evanston IL 60201-2407 Office: Northwestern Univ J L Kellogg Grad Sch Mgmt 2001 Sheridan Rd Evanston IL 60208-0814

JACOBS, DONALD PHILLIP, telecommunications technician; b. Escanaba, Mich., Nov. 18, 1924; s. Phillip Louis and Irene Mary (Cotnoir) J.; m. Naomi Jean Johnston, Feb. 7, 1953; children: Constance Jean, Dyan Marie, Patricia Lynn. Grad. high sch., Escanaba. Telecommunications technician Mich. Bell Telephone Co., Escanaba, 1948-83; founder, owner, mgr. Don Jacobs and His N.Am. Lumberjacks, The French Renegade, Escanaba, 1964—, Renegade Telecommunications Systems, Escanaba, 1983—; coach Internat. Log Rolling Competition, 1965-88. Organizer, coach, promoter County Wide Log Rolling and Lumberjack Sports Program, Escanaba, 1963-88; mem. Escanaba City Recreation Bd., 1970-76. With USMCR, 1942-46, PTO. Recipient 9 Sr. Div. World Championship Titles in Log Rolling. Mem. Internat. Log Rolling Assn. (v.p. 1965-83, Russ Ellison Meml. award 1987). Roman Catholic. Home and Office: 1600 12th Ave S Escanaba MI 49829-2919

JACOBS, ERNEST CHRISTOPHER, physician; b. Rochester, N.Y., July 16, 1957; s. Robert Michael and Maria (Kulbieda) J.; m. Elisabeth de Guinald Farre, Aug. 9, 1980; children: Christopher, Michael, Katrina. BS in Chemistry, Carnegie-Mellon U., 1979; MD, U. Pitts., 1982. Resident in pediatrics Mercy Hosp. of Pitts., 1982-83; pvt. practice computer cons. Pitts., 1983-84; med. staff fellow NIH, Bethesda, Md., 1984-86, sr. staff fellow div. computer rsch. and tech., 1986; clin. assoc. Cleve. Clinic Found., 1986-89, asst. staff, 1989-93, assoc. staff, 1993—. Co-author: (chpts.) Surgery of Epilepsy, 1991, Progress in Standardization in Health Care Informatics, 1993; contbr. articles to Cleve. Clinic Jour. of Medicine, Jour. Clin. Monitoring, IEEE Computer and IEEE Transactions in Biomed. Engring. Mem. IEEE, AMA, ASTM (subcom. chmn. 31.16), Am. Med. Informatics Assn., HL7 Tau Beta Pi. Democrat. Roman Catholic. Office: Cleve Clinic Found Dept Neurology S51 9500 Euclid Ave Cleveland OH 44195-5221

JACOBS, HARVEY COLLINS, newspaper editor, writer; b. Trafalgar, Ind., Sept. 6, 1915; s. Ralph L. and Ruth Marie (Ragsdale) J.; m. Florence Giddings, Apr. 5, 1942 (div. 1979); children: Phillip, Kenneth; m. Charlene Clark, Aug. 7, 1980. A.B., Franklin (Ind.) Coll., 1938, Litt.D., 1974; M.A., Ind. U., 1949; Litt.D., Sussex Coll. Tech., Eng., 1973. Reporter, editorial writer and columnist Franklin Evening Star, 1937-44; dir. pub. relations Franklin Coll., 1941-49, head dept. journalism, 1949-55; asst. editor Rotarian mag., Evanston, Ill., 1955-56; head program div. Rotary Internat., 1956-58, undersec., 1958-63; founder, chmn. dept. journalism and mass communications N.Mex. State U., Las Cruces, 1963-74; dir. Center Broadcasting and Internat. Communications, 1970-74; editor Indpls. News, 1974-92; adj. prof. journalism, disting. editor in residence, Franklin (Ind.) Coll. Author: Rotary: 50 Years of Service, 1955, Seven Paths to Peace, 1959, Adventure in Service, 1961, We Came Rejoicing, 1968, Hugging the Heartland, 1989; co-writer: This Great Land, 1983. Bd. dirs. Ind. Acad. Recipient Disting. Alumnus Citation Franklin Coll., 1957, Nat. Headliner award U. Okla., 1970, Disting. Svc. award N.Mex. Broadcasters Assn., 1971, Carl Towley award Journalism Edn. Assn., 1974, Golden Crown award Columbia U., 1975, Community Svc. award Hoosier Press Assn., 1976, Best Columnist award, 1975, 76, 80, 82, 87, 88, 90, First Elmer Davis award Franklin Coll., 1990; inducted to Ind. Journalism Hall of Fame, 1991. Fellow Pub. Rels. Soc. Am.; mem. Assn. Edn. Journalism, Am. Soc. Newspaper Editors, Authors Guild, Ind. Hist. Soc., Indpls. Press Club, Athletic Club, Rotary (past dist. gov.), Sigma Delta Chi. Home: 524 Leisure Ln Greenwood IN 46142-8315 Office: Franklin Coll 216 State St Franklin IN 46131-2506

JACOBS, HENRIETTA MARIE, early childhood educator, consultant; b. Polk, Nebr., Dec. 13, 1920; d. Wilbur Arnold and Henrietta Martha (Whitacre) Refshauge; m. Vernon Frederick Jacobs, July 11, 1943; children: Randall Alan, Jonathan Frederick, Martin Karl. BS in Edn., U. Nebr. Kearney, 1943; postgrad., Tulsa U., 1965, 67, Pepperdine Coll., 1970, UCLA, 1971, U. Mo. St. Louis, 1978, 79. Instr. vocat. home econs. Minden (Nebr.) H.S., 1944-45; instr. Tulsa Pub. Schs., 1963-67; tchr. Downey (Calif.) Ind. Sch. Dist., 1968-71; dir. social svcs. Tabitha Home, Lincoln, Nebr., 1971-75; instr., dir. early childhood edn. Kansas City (Mo.) Pub. Schs., 1976-80; dir. First Luth. Ch. Pre-Sch., Omaha, 1981-84; cons. Omaha, 1984—. Mem. Women of Evang. Luth. Ch. Am. (Syndocial Constn. com. 1986-87, instr., bd. dirs.), Midland Women, P.E.O. (pres. Nebr. chpt. DY 1995-97). Home: 11429 Sahler St Omaha NE 68164

JACOBS, HYDE SPENCER, soil chemistry educator; b. Declo, Idaho, May 15, 1926; s. Rex Haynes and Clare Julia (McHale) J.; m. Gareldene Marchant, Aug. 4, 1950; children: Stanalee, Ruth, Julia Jacobs Spresser, Merrie Jacobs Houser, Marcia. MS, U. Idaho, 1954; PhD, Mich. State U., 1957. Cert. profl. agronomist; cert. profl. soil scientist. Prof. soils Kans. State U., Manhattan, 1967-95, asst. dir. ext., 1981-86, asst. to dean of agr., 1986-95, dir. Evapotranspiration Lab., 1964-80; dir. Kans. Water Resources Rsch. Inst., Manhattan, 1964-74, 88-95; dir. Evapotranspiration Lab. Kans. State U., Manhattan, 1964-74, 88-95; liaison rep. Gt. Plains Agrl. Coun., Ft. Collins, Colo., 1987-92; sec. Kans. Food and Agrl. Coun., Manhattan, 1984-92; legis. liaison Agrl. Expt. Sta., Manhattan, 1986-93, Coop. Ext. Svc., 1986-93. Contbr. articles to profl. jours. Fellow Am. Soc. Agronomy, Soil Sci. Soc. Am., Soil and Water Conservation Soc.; mem. Kans. Crop Improvement Assn. (hon. mem.). Mem. LDS Ch.

JACOBS, JEFFREY LYNDON, food products executive; b. Circleville, Ohio, Jan. 8, 1961; s. Robert Ray and Carol Lynne (Kern) J.; m. Beth Ann Bullock, June 30, 1984 (div. Feb. 1990); children: Lauren Elizabeth, Kristen Nicole. Student, Franklin U., 1982. Health care asst. Berger Hosp., Circleville, 1976-79; sales mgr. Health Care Logistics, Inc., Circleville, 1980-82; ops. dir. McNeill Enterprises, Inc., Chillicothe, Ohio, 1982-87; cons. Domino's Pizza, Inc., Worthington, Ohio, 1987-88, dist. supr., 1988-91; franchise cons. Domino's Pizza, Inc., Ann Arbor, Mich., 1992—. Mem. 4-H Club, Circleville, Trinity Luth. Ch. Mem. Nat. Safety Coun. (trainer 1986—), Luther League (pres. 1973-79).

JACOBS, JERRY L., investment advisor; b. Bluffton, Ind., Sept. 7, 1945. BA, Ball State U., Muncie, Ind., 1967. CFP; CFS. Investment advisor Merrill Lynch, Ft. Wayne, Ind., 1970-77, PaineWebber Inc., Ft. Wayne, 1977-91, Robert Thomas Securities (formerly Atlas Capital Investment), Ft. Wayne, 1991—. Office: Robert Thomas Securities 9025 Coldwater Rd Ste 500 Fort Wayne IN 46825-2074

JACOBS, JO ELLEN, philosophy educator; b. Flora, Ill., Nov. 21, 1952; d. Gene Stanley and Patricia Ann (Staser) Workman; m. Gary William Jacobs, June 7, 1975; children: Megan Elizabeth, Emily Christine. Student, LaTrobe U., Melbourne, Australia, 1973; BA, Ea. Ill. U., 1973; MA, Boston Coll., 1975; PhD, Washington U., St. Louis, 1977. Asst. prof. Ea. Ill. U., Charleston, 1977-78, asst. to v.p. acad. affairs, 1980-81; asst. prof. Millikin U., Charleston, 1981-87, assoc. prof., 1987-93, prof., 1993—, Griswold disting. prof. philosophy, 1990-92, 95—, chair philosophy dept, 1995—. Contbr. articles to profl. jours. Bd. dirs. Coalition Against Domestic Violence, Charleston, 1982-96. Grantee Decatur Area Arts Coun., 1989, Ill. Humanities Coun., 1989, faculty devel. grantee Millikin U., 1990; philosophy del. to China for Citizen Ambassador Program, 1993. Mem. AAUW (corp. rep.), LWV, Am. Soc. Aesthetics, Soc. Advancement Am. Philosophy, Am. Philos. Assn., Phi Kappa Phi. Home: 2339 Ellington Pl Charleston IL 61920-3824 Office: Millikin Univ 1184 W Main St Decatur IL 62522-2039

JACOBS, JOEL, state legislator, business educator; m. Carol Jacobs; six children. BS, Moorhead State U.; postgrad., St. Cloud State U. Bus. instr.; Dist. 49B rep. Minn. Ho. of Reps., St. Paul, 1972—; chmn. regulated industries and energy com., vice chmn. ways and means com., mem. rules and legis. adminstrn. and taxes coms., Minn. Ho. of Reps. *

JACOBS, LEONARD J., state legislator; m. Carol Jacobs; five children. Farmer and rancher, county commr., 1991—; rep. N.D. State Ho. Reps. Dist. 35, 1993—, mem. indsl., bus. and labor coms.; treas. S.W. Water Authority. Mem. Assn. Counties, N.D. Water Users, Adams County Social Svc., Lions, K.C. Home: HC 2 Box 2 Reeder ND 58649-9409*

JACOBS, LINDA ROTROFF, elementary school educator; b. Peebles, Ohio, June 10, 1942; d. Joseph Harold Rotroff and Mary Lucille (Peterson) Nixon; m. Donald Eugene Jacobs, Nov. 29, 1968; 1 child, Donald Brett. BS in Edn., Ohio State U., 1963; MA in Edn., U. Cin., 1968; postgrad., U. Cin., Miami U., Xavier U., 1968—, Coll. Mt. St. Joseph, 1968—. Cert. tchr., Ohio. Tchr. kindergarten Forest Hills Bd. Edn., Cin., 1963-74, 77—, Chillicothe (Ohio) Bd. Edn., 1974-77; tchr. reading adult edn. Cin., 1975; tchr. kindergarten Mercer Elem. Forest Hills, Cin., 1977—; cooperating tchr. student tchrs. Ohio U., U. Cin., No. Ky. U., 1965—; tchr. summer sch. 4th, 5th, and 6th grades math./lang. arts, Cin., 1964-68, kindergarten and 1st grade Forest Hills, Cin., 1978-82; tchr. rep. Head Start, Chillicothe, 1975-77; kindergarten coord. Forest Hills and Hamilton County, Cin., 1965-70, 83-85; mem. supt.'s coun. Forest Hills, Cin., 1979, 82, 88; tchr. rep. PTA, Cin., 1967, 73, 82, 89; facilitator Forest Hills Summer Sch., 1993-96; master tchr./advisor entry tchrs. Forest Hills, 1993—; career mentor Ashford-McCarthy Resources, Inc., 1993-94; coord. early entrance screening Hamilton County, 1994, 95, faculty mem. Intervention Based Multifactored Evaluation Com., 1994, 95, mem. Collaboration Team for Inclusion of Spl. Children, 1994, 95; mem. responsive classroom team, 1996. Author: Getting Ready for Kindergarten, 1978, Parenting Tips, 1982, Intervention Assistance Team Handbook, 1992;. Cons. Women Helping Women, Cin., 1989. Recipient Ohio State U. Scarlet and Gray award, 1995; named Hamilton County Tchr. of Yr., 1965. Mem. NEA, Nat. PTA (rep.) Tchrs. Applying Whole Lang., Ohio Edn. Assn. (del. 1965), Southwestern Ohio Edn. Assn., Forest Hills Educators Assn. (sec. 1964-68, Martha Holden Jennings scholar 1976-77), DAR, Ohio State U. Alumni Club of Clermont County (sec. 1995-96), Alpha Kappa Delta (sec. 1975—). Mem. Ch. of Christ.

JACOBS, MERLE EMMOR, zoology educator, researcher; b. Nov. 30, 1918; s. Paul Anthony and Trello Elizabeth (Risch) J.; m. Elizabeth Beyeler, June 6, 1959. BA, Goshen Coll., 1948; PhD, Ind. U., 1953. Assoc. prof. Duke U., Durham, N.C., 1953-57; prof. Bethany (W.Va.) Coll., 1957-61, Ea. Mennonite Coll., Harrisonburg, Va., 1961-64; rsch. prof. Goshen (Ind.) Coll., 1964-86. Contbr. articles to profl. jours. Recipient Eigenmann award Ind. U., 1950. Home: 2214 S Main Goshen IN 46526 Office: Goshen Coll 1700 S Main Goshen IN 46526

JACOBS, PETER JAMES, electrical engineer; b. Stevens Point, Wis., July 1, 1950; s. James Peter and Marjorie Ann (Hester) J.; m. Kim Ellen Slavik, Jan. 10. 1978 (div.); children: Nathan, Adam; m. Virigina Jane Hughes, Jan. 1, 1996. Registered profl. engr., Wis. Electronic technician Hammersmith TV, Sister Bay, Wis., 1972-75, U. Wis., Madison, 1975-76, Peterson Builders, Inc., Sturgeon Bay, Wis., 1976-79; broadcast engr. WISC-TV, Madison, 1975; electronic engr. Supr. of Shipbuilding, USN, Sturgeon Bay, 1979-88; elec. engr. O,S,M, & Assocs., Inc., Mpls., 1988-90; staff engr. Peterson Builders, Inc., Sturgeon Bay, 1990-93; chief engr. PdM Engrs., Baileys Harbor, Wis., 1993—; electrical engr. Performa, Inc., DePere, Wis., 1995—. Mem. IEEE, Soc. Amateur Radio Astronomers, Penninsula Animal Lovers Soc. (bd. dirs. 1991-94, pres. 1994, charter mem.), Friends of Rock Island (charter dir., treas. 1994—). Home: 3581 County Rd E Baileys Harbor WI 54202-9019 Office: PdM Engrs Baileys Harbor WI 54202-9019 also: Performa Inc 421 Lawrence Dr DePere WI 54115-7429

JACOBS, RICHARD DEARBORN, consulting engineering firm executive; b. Detroit, July 6, 1920; s. Richard Dearborn and Mattie Phoebe (Cobleigh) J.; divorced; children: Richard, Margaret, Paul, Linden, Susan. BS, U. Mich., 1944. Engr., Detroit Diesel Engine div. Gen. Motors, 1946-51; mgr. indsl. and marine engine div. Reo Motors, Inc., Lansing, Mich., 1951-54; chief engr. Kennedy Marine Engine Co., Biloxi, Miss., 1955-59; marine sales mgr. Nordberg Mfg. Co., Milw., 1959-69; marine sales mgr. Fairbanks Morse Engine div. Colt Industries, Beloit, Wis., 1969-81; pres. R.D. Jacobs & Assocs., cons. engrs., naval architects and marine engrs., Roscoe, Ill., 1981—. Served with AUS, 1944-46. Registered profl. engr., Ill., Mich., Wis., Miss. Mem. ASTM, Soc. Naval Architects and Marine Engrs. (chmn. sect. 1979-80), Soc. Automotive Engrs., Am. Soc. Naval Engrs., Soc. Am. Mil. Engrs., Navy League U.S., Propeller Club U.S., Nat. Forensic Ctr., Rockford Polo Club, Masons. Unitarian. Office: 11405 Main St Roscoe IL 61073-9569

JACOBS, VERNON KENNETH, publisher; b. Chgo., June 25, 1936; s. Jerome and Marguerite (Brown) J.; m. Marcia Lynn Mountain, July 2, 1960; children: Deanne Lynn Letourneau, Laura R. Fields. BBA in Acctg., Wichita State U., 1962. CPA, Kans.; CLU. Auditor Deloitte, Haskins & Sells, CPAs, Kansas City, Mo., 1962-66; acctg. mgr. Old Am. Ins. Co., Kansas City, Mo., 1966-72, v.p., controller, 1972-79; editor Tax Angles Kephart Communications, Inc., Alexandria, Va., 1977-84; pres. Syntax Corp., Prairie Village, Kans., 1978-89; ptnr., dir. tax svcs. Heartland Mgmt. Co., Overland Park, Kans., 1992-93; author/cons. Vernon K. Jacobs, CPA, Prairie Village, 1979—; pres. Rsch. Press, Inc., Prairie Village, 1981—; seminar instr. Coll. of Fin. Planning, Denver, 1980-81, Hallmark Cards, Inc., Kansas City, Mo., 1979; instr. MBA tax course Rockhurst Coll., Kansas City, 1979; instr. acctg., pers. mgmt. Johnson County Community Coll., Lenexa, Kans., 1969-75. Author: Taxpayers' Counterattack, 1979, The New Taxpayers' Counterattack, 1980, The Taxpayers' Audit Survival Manual, 1980, Taxwise Investing, 1984, Tax Factors in Selecting a Form of Business, 1989, The Zero Tax Portfolio Manual, 1990, 3d edit., 1993, How to Legally Beat the Pension Estate Tax, 1992, How to Protect Yourself from Clinton's New Taxes, 1993, Vern Jacobs' Guide to Retirement Tax Savings, 1994; author software: Shortax Plus, 1979, 80, 81, 82, 84, 86, The Penplan System, 1988, 89, 90, 92; tax columnist Pvt. Practice Mag., Oklahoma City, 1979-92; cons. editor Jour. Acctg. and EDP, 1988-91; editor Asset Protection Strategies, 1993—, Fin. Solutions On-Line, 1995—. With USN, 1954-58. Mem. AICPAs, Am. Soc. CLUs (Kansas City chpt. bd. dirs. 1992-93), Mid-Am. Planned Giving Coun., Ea. Kans. Estate Planning Coun. Republican. Congregationalist. Home: 4500 W 72nd Ter Prairie Village KS 66208 Office: Rsch Press Inc PO Box 8137 Prairie Village KS 66208

JACOBS, WILLIAM RUSSELL, II, lawyer; b. Chgo., Oct. 26, 1927; s. William Russell and Doris B. (Desmond) J.; m. Shirley M. Spiegler, Mar. 21, 1950; children: William R. III, Richard W., Bruce Allen. BS, Northwestern U., 1950, JD, 1953. Bar: Ill. 1953, U.S. Dist. Ct. (no. dist.) Ill. 1958, U.S. Ct. Appeals (7th cir.) 1958, U.S. Supreme Ct., 1962. Atty. Continental Casualty Co., Chgo., 1955-58; assoc. Horwitz and Anesi, Chgo., 1958-62; prin. William R. Jacobs and Assocs., Chgo., 1962—; adj. prof. Lewis Coll. Law, Glen Ellyn, Ill., 1975-76; dir., tchr. Ct. Practice Inst., Chgo., 1974—; lectr. Ill. Inst. Continuing Legal Edn., Chgo., 1967—. Elected alderman Des Plaines (Ill.) City Coun., 1953-54; mem. Ill. Bar Assembly, 1973—. 1st lt. inf. U.S. Army, 1946-48. Mem. Ill. State Bar Assn., Am. Acad. Matrimonial Lawyers. Congregationalist. Office: William R Jacobs & Assocs 601 Lee St Des Plaines IL 60016-4616

JACOBS-CIRANNI, MARY LAURALEE, elementary education educator; b. Ft. Meade, Md., July 1, 1962; d. Ronald Matthew and Leona Rosemary (Gagnon) J. BA in Edn. and German, Coll. of St. Catherine, St. Paul, 1984. Cert. elem. edn. tchr., Md. Tchr. 2d grade Holy Cross Elem. Sch., Garrett Park, Md., 1984-86, dir. after care program, 1985-90, tchr. kindergarten, 1986-90; tchr. kindergarten thru 2d grade Buechel Elem. Sch., Kennfus, Fed. Republic of Germany, 1990-93. Dir. summer camp Holy Cross Elem., summer 1985, 86, 87, 88, 89. Roman Catholic.

JACOBSEN, THOMAS H(ERBERT), banker; b. Chgo., Oct. 15, 1939; s. Herbert Rogde and Catharine (Ball) J.; m. Diane Leisa DeMell. BS, Lake Forest (Ill.) Coll., 1963; LLD, Lake Forest (Ill.) U., 1995; MBA, U. Chgo., 1968; grad., Advanced Mgmt. Program, Harvard U., 1979. From asst. cashier to v.p. First Nat. Bank Chgo., 1963-76; from v.p. to vice chmn., dir. Barnett Banks, Inc., Jacksonville, Fla., 1976-89; chmn., pres., chief exec. officer Mercantile Bancorp. Inc., St. Louis, 1989—; bd. dirs. Union Electric Co., St. Louis, TWA, St. Louis, Student Loan Mktg. Assn., Washington; 8th dist. rep. Fed. Res. Adv. Coun. Life trustee, past chmn. bd. trustees St. Louis Symphony Soc.; trustee Washington U., St. Louis; chmn. St. Louis area coun. Boy Scouts Am.; bd. dirs. Nat. Boy Scouts Am.; past chmn. United Way of Greater St. Louis, Inc.; treas. Civic Progress. Mem. Bankers Round Table, Bob O'Link Golf Club (Highland, Ill.), Bogey Club, St. Louis Country Club. Office: Mercantile Bancorp Inc Mercantile Tower Tram 14.0 PO Box 524 Saint Louis MO 63166

JACOBSON, ANNA SUE, finance company executive; b. Ft. Smith, Ark., Aug. 13, 1940; d. Ray Bradley and Joy Anna (Person) McAlister, (stepfather) Cleve J. McDonald, Sr.; m. Lyle Norman Jacobson, Nov. 23, 1958; children: Lyle Michael, Daniel Ray, Julie Anne, Eric Joseph. Cert. in Fin. Planning, Coll. for Fin. Planning, 1984. Certified fin. paraplanner. Office mgr. Twin Cities Lithographic Inst., St. Paul, 1963-66; sec., St. Paul, Mpls., 1971-78; asst. to pres., office mgr. Planners Fin. Svcs., Mpls., 1978-85, asst. corp. treas., 1987-88; fin. paraplanner McAlmont Investment Co., Mpls., 1985-96, office mgr., 1988-96; registered rep. USR Fin. Svc. Inc., 1996—; ind. fin. cons.; bd. dir. Planners Fin. Svcs.; mem. bd. advisors Coll. for Fin. Planning, Denver, 1982—; v.p., CFO J&J Specialty Co., 1993—; sr. v.p. AdPro Internat., Inc., Wayzata, Minn., 1996—; speaker various orgns. Co-creator Paraplanning Profession Advisor; mem. firm Fin. Alternatives of Mpls., Wayzata, Minn., 1996—, Mpls., 1985—. Del. Dem. Farmer Labor Com., St. Paul, 1980; campaign chmn. mayoral election, Roseville, Minn., 1983, county commr., city coun. election, Roseville, 1980, 84; local chmn. for passage of ERA, Minn.; mem. Am. Lung Assn., St. Paul, Ramsey Found. of Minn., Como conservatory Hist. Soc.; past. pres. PTA, Minn.; mem. exec. coun. Boy Scouts Am., 1977-81; mem. adv. bd. Sch. Dist. 623, Roseville, Minn., 1978-81; fund raising com. mem. Twin Cities Pub. TV Sta., 1975—; mem. ch. coun. deacons St. Michael's Luth. Ch., St. Paul, 1996—. Recipient Volunteerism award State of Minn., 1981, Cert. of Appreciation Minn. Bicentennial Com., 1976; named 1st Fin. Paraplanner in history of industry. Mem. Internat. Assn. Fin. Planning, Twin Cities Assn. Fin. Planners, Internat. Assn. Bus. and Profl. Women (bd. dirs. 1977-86, pres. 1980-82, Woman of Yr. 1982), Minn. Women's Consortium, Como Conservatory Hist. Soc., Concordia Acad. Booster Club, Beta Sigma Phi Nu Phi Mu Chpt. Democrat. Lutheran. Avocations: tennis, riding, reading, piano, harp. Home: 2171 Dellwood Ave Saint Paul MN 55113-4329 Office: Fin Alternatives of Mpls 1550 Twelve Oaks Ctr Wayzata MN 55391

JACOBSON, DANIEL CHRISTOPHER, music educator; b. Glendale, Calif., July 24, 1955; s. Levi Lloyd and Anne Leora (Flanagan) J.; m. Grace Eugenia Mannion, Dec. 20, 1986; children: Megan Elizabeth, William Le. AA in Voice, Santa Ana Coll., 1976; BA in Voice, Westminster Coll., 1979; MA im Music History, Calif. State U., Long Beach, 1981; PhD in Musicology, U. Calif., Santa Barbara, 1986. Instr. Santa Ana (Calif.) Coll., 1981-86; lectr. music U. Calif., Santa Barbara, 1986-89; assoc. prof. music U. N.D., Grand Forks, 1989—; sec. Music Theory Midwest, 1994-95; dir. N.D. dist. Met. Opera Assn., Grand Forks, 1991-94. Author: Listener's Introduction to Music, 1995; contbr. articles to profl. jours. NEH fellow, 1991. Mem. Am. Musicological Soc., Internat. Schubert Soc., Coll. Music Soc., Soc. Music Theory, Assn. Tech. in Music Instruction. Home: 12 Vail Cir Grand Forks ND 58201 Office: U ND Box 7125 Dept Music Grand Forks ND 58202

JACOBSON, ELLIOTT ROY, political and public relations consultant, film production advisor, writer, actor; b. Balt., June 6, 1942; s. Sidney and Mildred (Hoffman) J. BA in Soviet and Russian History, L.I. U., 1971; postgrad. in internat. rels., Claremont Grad. Sch., 1981-83. Home office rep. Columbia Pictures Corp., N.Y.C., 1963-68; aide to mayor N.Y.C., 1972-73; dir. of advance various polit. campaigns, N.Y.C., 1974; exec. asst. to mayor City of Syracuse, N.Y., 1975-77; polit. cons. Carter/Mondale Reelection and Presdl. Com., 1979; asst. to sec. U.S. Dept. Transp., Washington, 1980-81; campaigning mgr. George Brown Reelection Com., San Bernadino, Calif., 1982; state dir. John Glenn Pres. Com., Chgo., 1983-84; downstate dir. Mondale/Ferraro Presdl. Com., Springfield, Ill., 1984; exec. asst. for press rels. and govtl. affairs Ill. State Comptroller, Chgo., 1985-87; prin. E-J Enterprises, Chgo., 1987—; state dir. Simon for Pres. Com., Southfield, Mich., 1988. Appeared in films including The Music Box, The Package, Opportunity Knocks, Only the Lonely, Gladiator, A League of Their Own, Hero, The Fugitive, (TV series) The Untouchables; prodr. films of The Velvet Revolution and collapse of Berlin Wall in Czechoslovakia and East Germany, 1989; interviewee, debator numerous TV shows. State dir. Kerry for Pres. Ill. campaign; bd. dirs. Hispanic Inst. of Law Enforcement; mem. Chgo. Coun. on Fgn. Rels., 1990—, The Carter Ctr., Atlanta, 1989, Vols. for Israel, N.Y.C., 1991—, Channel 11 Ptnrs., Chgo., 1990—; writer numerous campaign publs. and speeches. With U.S. Army, 1964. Mem. Am. Assn. Polit. Cons., Carter/Mondale Alumni Assn., Nat. Geographic Soc., Facets Cinematheque, East Bank Club, Phi Alpha Theta. Democrat. Jewish.

JACOBSON, EUGENE E., industrial professional; b. Wolbach, Nebr., Sept. 13, 1924; s. George Ray and Alice Minnie (Pedersen) J.; m. Wilma Ilene Rauert, Feb. 24, 1952; children: Connie, Diane, Janet. Pres. Jacobsons Inc., Wolbach, Nebr., 1940—. Mem. Eagles, Am. Legion. Methodist. Office: Jacobsons Inc 101 Kendall Wolbach NE 68882

JACOBSON, HAROLD KARAN, political science educator, researcher; b. Detroit, June 28, 1929; s. Harold Kenneth and Maxine Anna (Miller) J.; m. Merelyn Jean Lindbloom, Aug. 25, 1951; children: Harold Knute, Eric Alfred, Kristoffer Olaf, Nils Karl. AB, U. Mich., 1950; MA, Yale U., 1952, PhD, 1955. Asst. prof. U. Houston, 1955-57; mem. faculty U. Mich., Ann Arbor, 1957—; assoc. prof. U. Mich., 1961-65, prof., 1965—, Jesse Siddal Reeves prof. polit. sci., 1984—, research scientist, 1977—, chmn. dept., 1972-77, acting chmn., 1981, dir. Ctr. for Polit. Studies, 1986-96; interim assoc. v.p. for internat. acad. affairs U. Mich., Ann Arbor, 1990-92; acting dir. Inst. for Social Rsch., Ann Arbor, Mich., 1992-93, 94-95; vis. prof. Grad. Inst. Internat. Studies, U. Geneva, 1965-66, 70-71, 77-78; World Affairs Center fellow, 1959-60; vis. research scholar European Center Carnegie Endowment for Internat. Peace, Geneva, 1970-71. Author: The USSR and the UN's Economic and Social Activities, 1963, Networks of Interdependence, 1979, 84, (with Eric Stein) Diplomats, Scientists, and Politicians, 1966 (with R.W. Cox and others) The Anatomy of Influence, 1973, (with Dusan Sidjanski and others) The Emerging International Order, 1982, (with David A. Kay and others) Environmental Protection: The International Dimension, 1983, The Shaping of Foreign Policy, 1969, (with William Zimmerman) Behavior, Culture and Conflict in World Politics, 1994, (with Peter B. Evans and Robert D. Putnam) Double-Edged Diplomacy: International Bargaining and Domestic Politics, 1993; edtl. bd. Internat. Orgn., 1968-76, 78-90, Am. Jour. Internat. Law, 1979-91, 95—, Internat. Studies Quar., 1980-85, Jour. Conflict Resolution, 1961-72, Am. Polit. Sci. Rev., 1985-88.IMF, The World Bank, GATT, 1993. Mem. U.S. Nat. Commn. for UNESCO, 1980-85. Woodrow Wilson fellow, 1984, Ctr. for Advanced Studies in Behavioral Scis. fellow, 1988-89, Ctr. for Internat. Climate and Environ. Rsch. fellow, Oslo, 1996; recipient award for Internat. Sci. Cooperation AAAS, 1994. Fellow Am. Acad. Arts and Scis.; mem. AAAS (AAAS Award for Internat. Sci. Cooperation 1995), AAUP, UN Assn. U.S. (bd. dirs. 1980-93), Internat. Social Sci. Coun. (chmn. human dimensions of global environ. change program 1990-94), Internat. Studies Assn. (pres. Midwest div. 1969-70, pres. 1982-83), Internat. Polit. Sci. Assn. (program chmn. 1985-88, v.p. 1988-91), Coun. Fgn. Rels., Detroit Com. Fgn. Rels. (chmn. 1984-86), Am. Polit. Sci. Assn., Midwest Polit. Sci. Assn., Internat. Inst. Strategic Studies (London), Cosmos Club (Washington), Yale Club (N.Y.C.), Club de la Fondation Universitaire (Brussels), Phi Beta Kappa, Phi Kappa Phi. Home: 2174 Delaware Dr Ann Arbor MI 48103-6017 Office: U Mich Inst for Social Rsch PO Box 1248 Ann Arbor MI 48104-2321

JACOBSON, JEFF, state legislator. BA, Yale U., 1983; JD summa cum laude, Dayton Law Sch., 1988. State rep. Dist. 40 Ohio State Congress; precinct capt. Montgomery County Reps., chmn.; exec. v.p. Ohioans for Fair Representation; lawyer. Mem. Antioch Temple Shrine, Mason (32d degree). *

JACOBSON, JOHN HOWARD, JR., college president; b. Evanston, Ill., Nov. 6, 1933; s. John Howard and Grace Katharine (Whitney) J.; m. Jeanne G. McKee, Aug. 15, 1954; children: John Edward, Jean Katharine, Jennie Grace, James George. BA with high honors, Swarthmore Coll., 1954; MA, Yale U., 1956, PhD, 1957; LHD (hon.), Empire State Coll. Asst. prof. philosophy Hamilton Coll., Clinton, N.Y., 1957-63; assoc. prof. Fla. Presbyn. Coll., St. Petersburg, 1963-67, dean, 1967-72; dean Rochester Ctr. Empire State Coll., N.Y., 1972-74; v.p. acad. affairs Empire State Coll., Saratoga Springs, 1974-87, provost, 1980-87; pres. Hope Coll., Holland, Mich., 1987—; bd. dirs. Old Kent Bank of Holland. Author: (with others) Logic: A Programmed Text, 1963. Mem. exec. com. Assn. Ind. Colls. and Univs. of Mich. Mem. Am. Philos. Assn., Gt. Lakes Colls. Assn. (bd. dirs., chmn. bd. 1996—, exec. com.), Mich. Intercollegiate Athletic Assn., West Mich. Colls. Consortium, Holland Area C. of C. (bd. dirs. 1994—), Yale Club, Century Club, Holland Country Club. Mem. Reformed Ch. in America. Home: 92 E 10th St Holland MI 49423-3516 Office: Hope Coll PO Box 9000 141 E 12th St Holland MI 49422-9000

JACOBSON, LLOYD ELDRED, retired dentist; b. Madison, Minn., Mar. 9, 1923; s. Jacob Elton and Hilda Emily (Larson) J.; m. Ruth Solveig Skinsnes, Jan. 26, 1945; children: Rolf, Kathryn, Heidi. Student, St. Olaf Coll., 1943-44, 46-47, U. Chgo., 1945-46; DDS, U. Minn., 1951. Gen. practice dentistry Kenyon, Minn., 1951-91; ret., 1991. Chmn. Am. Luth. Ch. Coun., Mpls., 1972-74; vol. World Brotherhood Exch., Bumbuli, Tanzania, 1965; treas. Kenyon Sch. Bd., 1958-60, Kenyon Devel. Corp., 1955-60. 1st lt. 14th Aif Force (Flying Tigers), USAAF, 1943-45, CBI. Recipient Outstanding Alumni award St. Olaf Coll., 1972, Disting. Alumni award U. Minn. Sch. Dentistry, 1987. Mem. Minn. Dental Assn. (treas. 1980-86), S.E. Dist. Dental Soc. (pres. 1979-80, sec.-treas. 1976-79), Rice County Dental Soc. (pres. 1969). Republican. Lodge: Lions (pres. Kenyon club 1952-54, dist. sec.-treas. 1974, Citizen of Yr. award 1986). Home: 521 Spring St Kenyon MN 55946-1519

JACOBSON, PHIL D., investment advisor; b. Chicago City, Minn., Oct. 9, 1964. BS, U. Minn., 1988. Investment advisor Dain Bosworth, Inc., Rockford, Ill., 1988—. Republican. Lutheran. Office: Dain Bosworth Inc 6277 E Riverside Blvd Rockford IL 61114-4417

JACOBSON, PHYLLIS MAE, development resource director; b. Roscoe, S.D., June 2, 1941; d. Harold C. and Winnifred (Haar) Ehresmann; m. Thoams O. Jacobson, June 26, 1965; children: Dawn, Troy. BS, Augustana Coll., 1963. Instr. phys. edn., math. Grand Meadow (Minn.) Pub. H.S., 1963-65, Glenville (Minn.) Pub. H.S., 1967-68; instr. phys. edn., health DeLavan (Minn.) Pub. Elem. and H.S., 1968-69; coach sr. h.s. tennis and basketball Wells Pub. Schs., 1970-78; deve. dir. Luth. Bible Camp, Spicer, Minn., 1983—; cons. part-time Spicer, 1987—. Sunday sch. tchr. Faith Luth. Ch., Spicer, 1985—; mem. vision 2000 com. New London (Minn.) Spicer Schs., 1988-90; sec. Women of the ELCA conf. bd., 1994—. Mem. Assn. Luth. Devel. Execs. (bd. dirs. 1992-94), Little Crow Life Underwriters. Home: 354 Kevin Dr Spicer MN 56288 Office: Green Lake Luth Ministries 9916 Lake Ave S Spicer MN 56288

JACOBUCCI, NICOLA JOSEPH, family physician, educator; b. Cleve., Dec. 8, 1954; s. Alphonse Joseph and Concetta (Sciarra) J.; m. Susan Ann Gallick, June 20, 1980; children: Mia Elizabeth, Vincent Alphonse. BA in Biology, Case Western Reserve U., 1976; MD, Med. Coll. of Ohio, 1980. Diplomate Am. Bd. Family Practice. Assoc. physician Field Med. Group, Chgo., 1983; pvt. practice family medicine Hillendale Health Ctr., Clinton, Pa., 1984-86; assoc. physician Mt. Sinai Family Practice, Cleve. Heights, Ohio, 1986-89; med. dir. O'Mitchell's Immediate Care Ctr., Middleburg Heights, Ohio, 1989-90; sr. clin. instr., family physician HMO Health Ohio, Cleve., 1990-92; asst. clin. prof. family medicine Fairview Gen. Hosp., Cleve., 1993—; Author: (with others) Medical Practice, 1994. Mem. Am. Acad. Family Physicians, Soc. for Tchrs. of Family Medicine. Home: 19787 S. Sagmore Rd Fairview Park OH 44126 Office: Hassler Ctr Family Medicine 18200 Lorain Ave Cleveland OH 44111

JACOVER, JEROLD ALAN, lawyer; b. Chgo., Mar. 20, 1945; s. David Louis and Beverly (Funk) J.; m. Judith Lee Greenwald, June 28, 1970; children: Aric Seth, Evan Michael, Brian Ethan. BSEE, U. Wis., 1967; JD, Georgetown U., 1972. Bar: Ohio 1972, Ill. 1973, U.S. Ct. Appeals (7th cir.) 1974, U.S. Ct. Appeals (Fed. cir.) 1983. Atty. Ralph Nader, Columbus, Ohio, 1972-73, Willian Brinks Hofer, Gilson and Lione, Chgo., 1973—. Mem. Evanston (Ill.) Environ. Control Bd., 1983-86; bd. dirs. Evanston Youth Baseball Assn., 1991-93. Mem. Am. Intellectual Property Law Assn. (com. chmn. 1980-86, bd. dirs. 1994—, co-editor jour. 1980-81), ABA, Decalogue Soc. Lawyers, Intellectual Property Law Assn. Chgo. (treas. 1983-84, bd. dirs. 1993-94), Intellectual Property Law Assn. of Chgo. Ednl. Found. (pres. 1990-93), Am. Techion Soc. (v.p. 1985-91, treas. 1988-91, bd. dirs. 1985—, pres. 1994—), Nippersink Community Club (bd. dirs. 1978-86, pres. 1987-88). Jewish. Home: 1409 Lincoln St Evanston IL 60201-2336 Office: Willian Brinks Hofer Gilson & Lione 455 N Cityfront Plaza Dr Chicago IL 60611-5503

JACOX, JOHN WILLIAM, mechanical engineer and consulting company executive; b. Pitts., Dec. 12, 1938; s. John Sherman and Grace Edna (Herbster) J.; 1 child, Brian Erik; m. Roma Jankauskaite, Sept. 3, 1993. BSME in Indsl. Mgmt., Carnegie Mellon U., 1962, BS in Indsl. Mgmt, 1962. Mfg. engr. Nuclear Fuel div. Westinghouse Elec. Co., Pitts., 1962-64; rsch. engr. Continental Can Co. Metal R&D Ctr., Pitts., 1964-65; data processing sales engr. IBM, Pitts., 1965-66; mktg. mgr. nuclear products MSA Internat., Pitts., 1966-72; v.p. Nuclear Cons. Svcs., Inc., Columbus, Ohio, 1973-84; v.p. NUCON Internat., 1981-84; bd. dirs. NUCON Europe Ltd., London, 1981—; pres. Jacox Assocs., Inc., 1984—; cons., lectr. Nat. Ctr. for Rsch. in Vocat. Edn., 1978-84 ; author, presenter, session chmn. DOE/Harvard U. Nuclear Air Cleaning Confs., 1974—; lectr. Harvard U. Sch. Pub. Health Air Cleaning Lab., 1986—; co-chmn. program subcom. Tech. Alliance Cen. Ohio, 1984-85, vice-chmn., chmn.-elect dir. subcom., 1986-87, chmn. bd. trustees, 1986; tech. transfer com. Dayton Area Tech. Network; program com. World Trade Devel. Club; mem. legis. svcs. com. coop. edn. adv. com. Otterbein Coll., 1978-82; industry advisor Franklin U. Grad. Sch. Bus., 1994—. Mem. NRA (patron), ASHRAE (standards com. 3.2 and 9.4), ASTM (chmn. F-21), ASME (code com. nuclear air and gas treatment, main exec. com., chmn. subcom. field test procedures), Am. Nuclear Soc. (pub. info. com.), N.Y. Acad. Scis. (life), Ohio Acad. Sci. (life), Am. Nat. Stds. Inst., Internat. Soc. Nuc. Air Treatment Techs. (co-founder, officer), Columbus Area C. of C. (tech. roundtable 1983), Air Force Assn. (life), Mensa, Sun Bunch (pres. 1980-81), Dayton Area Tech. Network (subcom. on tech. transfer), Tech. Transfer Soc. Home: 5874 Northern Pine Pl Columbus OH 43231-2331 Office: PO Box 29720 Columbus OH 43229

JACQUEZ, GEOFFREY MARK, biomedical software company executive; b. N.Y.C., May 6, 1955. BS in Biology, U. Mich., 1977, MS in Natural Resource Policy and Law, 1983; PhD in Ecology and Evolution, SUNY, Stony Brook, 1989. Field biologist zoology dept. Ariz. State U., Tempe, 1979-80; computer programmer U. Mich. Sch. Natural Resources, Ann Arbor, 1981-82; investigator Nepal Alpine Zone Rsch. Project, 1983; teaching asst. dept. ecology and evolution SUNY, 1983, rsch. asst., 1984-87; prin. investigator Applied Biomath., Setauket, N.Y., 1987-93; pres. BioMedware Inc., Ann Arbor, Mich., 1990—; presenter in field, 1984—. Contbr. articles and revs. to sci. jours. Recipient Disting. Software award for Ramas/a EDUCOM, 1987; gen. univ. scholar U. Mich., 1977, 83; grantee Dept. Energy, 1989, NIH, 1990, 91-93, Electric Power Rsch. Inst., 1990-94, Nat. Cancer Inst., 1993-96, John Wiley and Sons, 1993-94. Mem. Explorers Club, Sigma Xi (assoc.). Home: 1707 Broadway St Ann Arbor MI 48105-1813 Office: BioMedware Inc BioMedware Bldg 516 N State St Ann Arbor MI 48104

JACQUINOT, TERRY J., stockbroker; b. Girard, Kans., Jan. 28, 1947; m. Joanna Jacquinot, Oct. 31, 1970; children: Amy, Justin. BS in Bus., Pittsburg (Kans.) State U., 1970. Sales rep. Quaker Oats Co., Wichita, Kans., 1971-72; stockbroker PaineWebber, Topeka, 1972—. With USAR, 1966-72. Republican. Roman Catholic. Home: 3415 SE Pueblo Pl Topeka KS 66605-9002 Office: PaineWebber 634 S Kansas Ave Topeka KS 66603-3804

JAEGER, ALVIN A. (AL JAEGER), secretary of state; b. Beulah, N.D., 1943; m. Naomi Berg, 1969 (dec. 1979), m. Kathy Grangaard Anderson, 1986; children: Todd, Stacy, Heidi. Grad., Bismarck State Coll., Dickinson State U.; student, U. N.D., Montana State U. Tchr. Killdeer High Sch., Kenmare High Sch.; with Mobil Oil Corp.; real estate broker; sec. of state N.D., 1993—. Mem. adv. com. mktg. edn. With N.D. Army N.G. Named Realtor of Yr. Mem. Fargo-Moorhead Area Assn. Realtors (mem. coms. edn., profl. stds., bylaws, multiple listing svc.), N.D. Assn. Realtors (past chairperson state bylaws), Bismarck Kiwanis Club, Charity Luth. Ch. Office: 600 E Boulevard Ave Bismarck ND 58505-0500

JAFFE-NOTIER, PETER ANDREW, secondary education educator; b. Holland, Mich., Apr. 9, 1947; s. M. Robert and Ann Jean (Jackson) Notier; m. Vicki Janet Westbrook, Aug. 11, 1971 (div. 1982); children: Andrew Wright Notier, Matthew Westbrook Notier, Timothy Jackson Notier; m. Tamara Jane Jaffe, July 11, 1986; children: Zachary Hayden, Claire Emanuelle. AB cum laude, Dartmouth Coll., 1969; MA, Harvard U., 1972. Cert. secondary tchr. English tchr. Lyons Twp. High Sch., La Grange, Ill., 1973—; English instr. U. Ill., Urbana-Champaign, Ill., 1983-84; sponsor LION sch. newspaper, LaGrange, Ill., 1986—, Menagerie sch. mag., LaGrange, 1986-95; coord. Discovery Ctr., 1991-94. Tchr. Peace Corps, Kingdom of Tonga, 1969-71; mem. chair Lyons Twp. Youth Commn., LaGrange, 1975-81; mem., pres. Irving Park Community Food Pantry, Chgo., 1985-88; bd. dirs. Irving Park Homeless Shelter, Chgo., 1986—; mem. Chgo. Sanctuary Alliance, Chgo., 1984-88; mem. Oak Park Farmer's Market Commn., 1990-94. Named Outstanding Young Man in Am. Jaycees, 1971, Outstanding Secondary Tchr. U. Chgo., 1980-82, 86; recipient Community Svc. award Chgo. Fedn. Community Coms., 1975, Gold Crown award Columbia Scholastic Press Assn., 1987-95. Mem. NEA, Nat. Coun. Tchrs. of English, Assn. for Supervision and Curriculum Devel. Mem. Reformed Ch. in Am. Office: Lyons Twp High Sch 100 S Brainard Ave La Grange IL 60525-2101

JAGIELLA, DIANA MARY, lawyer; b. Chgo., Sept. 16, 1959; d. John James and Mildred Helen (Lapinskas) J.; m. Charles John Thorbjornsen, June 9, 1984; children: Kenneth James, Rachael Frances, Lauren Kellie. BA, Purdue U., 1983; JD, DePaul U., 1987; postgrad., U. Chgo., 1989—. Bar: Ill. 1987, U.S. Dist. Ct. (cen. dist.) Ill. 1987, U.S. Ct. Appeals (7th cir.) 1989. Assoc. Hinshaw & Culbertson, Chgo., 1987-88, Howard & Howard, Attys., P.C., Peoria, Ill., 1991—; atty. CilCorp, Inc., Peoria, 1988-91. Contbr. articles to legal jours. Chmn. Police and Fire Commn., Peoria, 1990—; mem. allocation panel United Way, Peoria, 1991—; mem. spl. com. Peoria C. of C., 1989-90; pres., bd. dirs. Abuse Shelter, Peoria, 1991-92; mem. Rotary North Peoria Sch. Bd., 1989—. Sheridan scholar, 1986; recipient Recognition award Women's Law Caucus, 1986. Mem. ABA (environ. sect.), Ill. Bar Assn. (environ. sect.), Peoria Bar Assn. (chmn. law day 1990-91, pres. women lawyers sect. 1988-90). Republican. Roman Catholic. Office: Howard & Howard Attys PC 321 Liberty St Peoria IL 61602-1403

JAGNER, RONALD PAUL, financial administrator, consultant; b. Highland Park, Mich., May 11, 1942; s. Walter Alex and Mary Ann (Stasys) J. BS, U. Detroit, 1965; MBA, Cen. Mich U., 1967. Comml. teller Nat. Bank Detroit, 1962-64; acct. Electronic Bookkeeping, Detroit, 1964-66; asst. div. mgr. Sears Roebuck & Co., Lincoln Park, Mich., 1966; instr. bus. Southwestern Mich. Coll., Dowagiac, 1967-69; mgr. bus. adminstrv. offices Lakeview Sch. Dist., Battle Creek, Mich., 1969-74; bus. mgr. Lakeview Sch. Dist., Battle Creek, 1974—; adj. instr. econs., acctg., investments Kellogg C.C., Battle Creek, 1970—; fin. chair, trustee Calhoun Mental Health, Battle Creek, 1983-91; asst. treas. Sch. Employees Credit Union, Battle Creek, 1981-90; bd. dirs., treas. Lakeview Bus. Assocs., 1977-83, v.p., 1993—. EPA accredited asbestos insp., mgmt. planner U. Ill., 1988. Mem. Assn. Sch. Bus. Ofcl. Mich. Sch. Bus. Ofcls., Southwestern Mich. Sch. Bus. Ofcls. (pres. 1977-79), Kiwanis (bd. dirs., treas. Lakeview chpt. 1977-83). Democrat. Roman Catholic. Home: 98 Brookfield Ct Battle Creek MI 49015-4757 Office: Lakeview Sch Dist 15 Arbor St Battle Creek MI 49015-2903

JAGODZINSKI, RONALD EDWARD, mechanical engineer, consultant; b. La Salle, Ill., May 4, 1957; s. Edward Walter and Adele Marie (Soberalski) J.; m. Barbara Jane Stoetzel, Oct. 13, 1979; children: Megan, Melissa, Matthew. AS, Illinois Valley C.C., Oglesby, Ill., 1987; BSME, Bradley U., 1989. Registered profl. engr., Ill.; cert. indoor air quality profl. Elec. technician Complete Indsl. Enterprises, La Salle, Peru, Ill., 1980-87; project engr. Natkin Svc. Co., Peoria, Ill., 1987-89; plant engr. Precision Coatings Inc., Spring Valley, Ill., 1989-91; mech. engr. Crawford, Murphy & Tilly, Inc., Springfield, Ill., 1991—. With USN, 1975-80. Named Jaycee of Yr., La Salle-Peru Jaycees, 1982. Mem. ASHRAE, ASME, Assn. Energy Engrs., KC. Roman Catholic. Home: 6 Carl St Riverton IL 62561-9642 Office: Crawford Murphy & Tilly Inc 2750 W Washington St Springfield IL 62702-3465

JAHN, GARY ROBERT, foreign language educator; b. Mpls., Sept. 29, 1943; s. Robert Gerhardt and Katherine Joann (Johnson) J.; m. Kathryn Justine Raynoha, Aug. 26, 1968 (div. Dec. 1982); children: Thomas, Phillip, Helen; m. Sandra Anne Martin, Mar. 10, 1984; children: Katherine, Nathaniel. BA cum laude, U. Minn., 1965; MA, U. Wis., 1968, PhD, 1971. Asst. prof. St. Olaf Coll., Northfield, Minn., 1971-72; asst. prof. SUNY, Buffalo, 1972-77; asst. prof. U. Minn., Mpls., 1977-81, assoc. prof., 1982—; editor Slavic and East European Jour., 1988-93. Author: Russian Conjugation and Declension, 1990, The Death of Ivan Ilich: An Interpretation, 1993; contbr. articles on Russian lit. to various publs. Mem. Am. Assn. for the Advancement of Slavic Studies, Am. Assn. Tchrs. of Slavic and East European Langs. (exec. coun. 1988-93). Office: U Minn Inst Linguistics Dept Asian and Slavic Langs 192 Klaeber Ct Minneapolis MN 55455

JAHN, HELMUT, architect; b. Nurnberg, Germany, Jan. 4, 1940; came to U.S., 1966; s. Wilhelm Anton and Karolina (Wirth) J.; m. Deborah Ann Lampe, Dec. 31, 1970; 1 child, Evan. Dipl. Ing.-Architect, Technische Hochschule, Munich, 1965; postgrad., Ill. Inst. Tech., 1966-67; D.F.A. (hon.), St. Mary's Coll., Notre Dame, Ind., 1980. Registered architect, Ill., Calif., Colo., Fla., Ind., Minn., N.Y., Tex., Va., Nat. Coun. Archtl. Registration Bds. Germany. With P.C. von Seidlein, Munich, 1965-66; with C.F. Murphy Assocs., Chgo., 1967-81, asst. to Gene Summers, 1967-73, exec. v.p., dir. planning and design, 1973-81; prin. Murphy/Jahn, Chgo., 1981—, pres., 1982—, chief exec. officer, 1983—; mem. design studio faculty U. Ill., Chgo., 1981; Elliot Noyes prof. archtl. design Harvard U., Cambridge, Mass., 1981; Davenport vis. prof. archtl. design Yale U., New Haven, 1983; thesis prof. IIT, Chgo., 1989-92. Prin. works include Kemper Arena, Kansas City, Mo., 1974 (Nat. AIA honor award, Am. Inst. Steel Constrn. award), Auraria Library, Denver, 1975, John Marshall Cts. Bldg., Richmond, Va. 1976, H. Roe Bartle Exhbn. Hall, Kansas City, Mo., 1976, Fourth Dist. Cts. Bldg., Maywood, Ill., 1976, Monroe Garage, Chgo., 1977, Michigan City (Ind.) Library, 1977 (AIA Ill. Council honor award, AIA-ALA First honor award, Am. Inst., Steel Constrn. award), St. Mary's Coll. Athletic Facility, South Bend, Ind., 1977 (AIA Ill. Council Honor award, AIA Nat. honor award, Am. Inst. Steel Constrn. award), Springfield Garage, Ill., 1977, Glenbrook Profl. Bldg., Northbrook, Ill., 1978, Rust-Oleum Corp. Hdqrs., Vernon Hills, Ill., 1978 (Am. Steel Constrn. award), La Lumiere Gymnasium, La Porte, Ind., 1978, Prairie Capital Convention Ctr.-Parking Garage, Springfield, Ill., 1979, W.W. Grainger Corp. Hdqrs., Skokie, Ill., 1979, Xerox Centre, Chgo., 1980, De La Garza Career Ctr., East Chicago, Ind., 1981 (ASHRAE Energy award), Area 2 Police Hdqrs., Chgo., 1981, Oak Brook (Ill.) Post Office, 1981, Commonwealth Edison Dist. Hdqrs., Downers Grove, Ill., 1981 (ASHRAE Energy award), First Source Ctr., South Bend, Ind., 1982, Argonne (Ill.) Program Support Facility, 1982 (Owens-Corning Fiberglass Energy Conservation award), One South Wacker Office Bldg., Chgo., 1982, Addition to Chgo. Bd. of Trade, 1982 (Reliance Devel. Group Inc. award for Disting. Arch., Am. Inst. Steel Constrn. award, Structural Engrng. Assn. Ill. award), Mercy Hosp. Addition, Chgo., 1983, 11 Diagonal St., Johannesburg, Republic of South Africa, 1983, U. Ill. Agrl. Engrng. Sci. Bldg., Champaign, 1984, Learning Resources Ctr., Coll. of DuPage, Glen Ellyn, Ill., 1984, Plaza East, Milw., 1984 (Disting. Architect award Milw. Art Commn.), Shand Morahan Corp. Hdqrs., Evanston, Ill., 1984, 701 Fourth Ave. S., Mpls., 1984, O'Hare Rapid Transit Sta., Chgo., 1984 (Nat. Honor award), State of Ill. Ctr., Chgo., 1985 (Structural Engrng. Assn. Ill. award, AIA Chgo. chpt. award 1986), Parktown Stands, Johannesburg, 1986, Two Energy Ctr., Naperville, Ill., 1986, Hawthorne Ctr. Office Bldg., Vernon Hills, Ill., 1986, Park Ave. Tower, N.Y.C., 1986, 300 E. 85th St. Apts., N.Y.C., Northwestern Terminal, Chgo., 1987 (Structural Engrng. Assn. of Ill. award 1987), United Airlines Terminal, 1987 (Structural Engrng. Assn. of Ill. award, Nat. AIA Honor award, R.J. Reynolds Meml. award, 1988, AIA Chgo. chpt. award), One Liberty Place, Phila., 1987, Oakbrook (Ill.) Terr. Tower, 1987, O'Hare Internat. Airport, 1988 (AIA Chgo. chpt. award), Merchandise Mart Bridge, Chgo., 1988, Wilshire/ Westwood Office Bldg., L.A., 1988, 425 Lexington Ave, N.Y.C., 1989, 750 Lexington Ave., 1989, Cityspire, N.Y.C., 1989, Messe Frankfurt Convention Ctr., Germany, 1989, Barnett Ctr., Jacksonville, Fla., 1990, Messe Frankfurt Tower, Germany, 1991 (AIA Chgo. chpt. award 1992), Livingston Plaza, Bklyn. Hgts., N.Y., 1991, Two Liberty Place, Phila., 1991 (AIA Chgo. chpt. award 1992), 120 N LaSalle, Chgo., 1992 (AIA Chgo. chpt. award 1992), One Am. Plz., Trolley Sta., San Diego, 1992 (AIA Chgo. chpt. award 1992), Mannheim (Germany) Ins. Bldg., 1992 (AIA Chgo. chpt. award 1992), Hyatt Roisy, Paris, 1992, Munich (Germany) Order Ctr., 1993, Hitachi Tower, Singapore, 1993, Caltex House, Singapore, 1993, Kempinski Hotel, Munich, 1994, Pallas, Stuttgart, Germany, 1994; contbr. to numerous group and solo exhbns. of archtl. drawings and design. Recipient citation Progressive Architecture, 1977, award for Chgo. cen. area plan, 1985, Dean of Architecture award Chgo. design awards, 1991; Arnold W. Brunner meml. prize in architecture, 1982; Chgo. chpt. award AIA, 1975-79, 81-83, 86-88, nat. honor award, 1979, 87, N.Y. State award, 1986; lst honor award ALA, 1978, energy award ASHRAE, 1981, Presdl. Desirn award Nat. Endowment Arts, 1988, R.S. Reynolds Meml. award, 1988; numerous others. Fellow AIA, Architecture Soc./Art Inst. Chgo., Chgo. Archtl. Club; mem. AIA (numerous Chgo. chpt. awards 1975—). Roman Catholic. Clubs: Comml. of Chgo., Economic of Chgo., Saddle & Cycle. Office: Murphy/Jahn 35 E Wacker Dr Chicago IL 60601

JAHNKE, PAMELLA EMRICK, emergency nurse; b. Indpls., May 2, 1956; d. Harold Benjamin and Betty Mae (Cunningham) Emrick; m. Lawrence Everett Jahnke, Aug. 16, 1975; children: Leslie Ann, Kimberly Diane. ADN, U. Indpls., 1976; BS in Health Arts, Coll. St. Francis, 1984; BSN, Ball State U., 1990. RN, Ind.; CEN; cert. instr. BLS and ACLS, Am. Heart Assn. and TNCCI, ENPC. Charge nurse cardiopulmonary unit Midwest Med. Ctr., Indpls., 1984; staff and charge nurse ICU Cmty. Hosp. East, Indpls., 1976-84; staff and charge nurse level II emergency dept. Cmty Hosp. East, Indpls., 1984-91, emergency level III staff nurse, 1992-96; emergency dept. clin. facilitator for practice Cmty. Hosp. East, Indpls., 1996—; coord. patient care emergency/admitting, level III RN Ind. U. Med. Ctr., U. Hosp., Indpls., 1991-92; nurse examiner Sexual Assault Response Team. Jr. troop leader Girl Scouts U.S., Indpls., 1991-92; mem. Children's Mus., Indpls., 1987—, Indpls. Zoo, 1987—, Hoosier Environ. Coun., Indpls., 1991—; lectr. Marion County Emergency Nurses Cancel Alcohol Related Emergencies. Mem. ANA, Emergency Nurses Assn. (cert.; trauma nurse provider/instr. nursing practice com., pres. Ind. state chpt. 1995), Ind. State Nurses Assn., Emergency Med. Svc. Coun. Marion County, (sec. 1994—), Consortium Ind. Nursing Orgns. (chmn. 1995—), Sigma Theta Tau. Baptist. Home: 6250 Woburn Dr Indianapolis IN 46250-2740 Office: Cmty Hosp East 1500 N Ritter Ave Indianapolis IN 46219-3027

JAIN, NEMI CHAND, chemist, coating scientist, educator; b. Kota, Rajasthan, India, Oct. 15, 1951; came to U.S., 1983, naturalized, 1993; s. Chand Mal and Raj Devi (Nopra) J.; m. Shashi Bala Jain, Jan. 29, 1981; children: Nimisha, Seema. BSc, U. Rajasthan, 1971, MSc, 1973, PhD, 1978; postgrad., N.D. State U., 1990. Lectr. chemistry Nat. Coun. of Edn. Rsch. Tng., Ajmer, India, 1976-77; asst. prof. U. Delhi, 1977-83; postdoctoral rsch. assoc. U. Va., Charlottesville, 1983-85; rsch. assoc./asst. lab. dir. Colo. State U., Ft. Collins, 1985-89; rsch. scientist/team leader Sherwin-Williams Co., Chgo., 1989—; cons. and lectr. in field. Developer waterborne coatings; developer coating test course Sherwin-William U., 1995; contbr. numerous articles to profl. jours. Judge Chgo. Sci. Fair, 1992, 95, 1st Responder/ Indsl. Med. Tech., 1995—, U. No. Colo, 1989. CSIR fellow, 1973-76, Sardar Patel U. fellow, 1972, Lucknow U. tchr. fellow, 1979; recipient Disting. Nat. award for study abroad Govt. of India, 1983-85, State Govt. Rajasthan merit scholar, 1967-73. Fellow Am. Inst. Chemists; mem. ASTM, Am. Chem. Soc., Internat. Union Pure and Applied Chemistry, Sigma Xi. Jain. Home: 10603 S Vicky Ln Palos Hills IL 60465-1925 Office: Sherwin Williams Co 10909 S Cottage Grove Ave Chicago IL 60628-3812

JAIN, RAJ, educator; b. Satna, India, Aug. 17, 1951; came to U.S., 1974; s. Shanti Lal and Svlochana Devi Jain; m. Neelu Hathishah; children: Sameer, Amit. B of Engring., A.P.S. Univ., Rewa, India, 1972; M of Engring., Indian Inst. of Sci., 1974; PhD, Harvard U., 1978. Sr. engr. Digital Equipment Corp., Maynard, Mass., 1978-80; prin. engr. Digital Equipment Corp., Hudian, Mass., 1980-82; cons. engr. Digital Equipment Corp., Littleton, Mass., 1983-90, sr. cons. engr., 1991-94; prof. Ohio State U., Columbus, 1994—; faculty MIT, 1984, 85, 87; spkr. at confs. Author: Control Theoretic Formulation of Operating Systems Resource Management, 1979, The Art of Computer Systems Performance Analysis, 1991 (award 1992), FDDI Handbook: High-Speed Networking with Fiber and Other Media, 1994; patentee in field. Sec. Jain Ctr. of Greater Boston, Wellesley, Mass., 1978-84. Fellow IEEE, Assn. Computing Machinery; mem. Internet Soc. Home: 4591 Lanercast Way Columbus OH 43220 Office: Ohio State Univ Dept Computer and Info Sci Columbus OH 43210-1277

JAIN, RAKESH, division manager of electrical product company; b. New Delhi, India, Nov. 10, 1951; came to U.S., 1989; BS, India Sch., India, 1973. Divsn. mgr. Hupp Elec., Cedar Rapids, Iowa, 1989—. Mem. IEEE, Iowa Soc. Engrs. Office: Hupp Electric 275 33rd Ave SW Cedar Rapids IA 52404-4605

JAKALA, CHESTER, business executive; b. Chgo., Sept. 5, 1950. MBA, U. Chgo., 1972. Pres. Jakala Group Inc., Chgo., 1976—. Home: 1255 N Sandburg Ter Chicago IL 60610

JAKUBAUSKAS, EDWARD BENEDICT, college president; b. Waterbury, Conn., Apr. 14, 1930; s. Constantine and Barbara (Narstis) J.; m. Ruth Friz, Aug. 29, 1959; children—Carol, Marilyn, Mark, Eric. B.A., U. Conn., 1952, M.A., 1954; Ph.D., U. Wis., 1961. Economist FPC, 1956, Dept. Labor, 1956-58; instr. U. Wis., 1961-62, asst. prof. econs., 1962-63; asst. prof. Iowa State U., 1963-65, assoc. prof., 1965-66, prof., 1966-71; dean U. Wyo., 1971-76, prof. econs., 1971-79, v.p. acad. affairs, 1976-79; pres. SUNY, Geneseo, 1979-88, Cen. Mich. U., Mt. Pleasant, 1988-92; cons. in higher edn., 1992—. Author: Manpower Economics, 1971. Served with U.S. Army, 1954-56. Mem. Am. Assn. State Univs. and Colls. Mem. United Chs. of Christ.

JAMES, ALLEN DEWAYNE, designer; b. Anniston, Ala., July 25, 1950; s. Lewis A. and Annie Vernell (Otwell) J.; m. Kathie Sue Lloyd, Feb. 3, 1979; children: Sarah, Amanda, Melinda. Student, Jr. Coll., Ft. Worth, 1971. V.p., engring. mgr. Rich Color Sys., Wylee, Tex., 1976-85; sr. designer King Concept Corp., Mpls., 1985-90, FSI Internat., Chaska, Minn., 1991—; adv. com. mem. CAM Impletation, 1994—. Coach Girls Basketball & Softball, Bloomington, Minn., 1992. Republican. Baptist. Home: 11010 Washburn Ave S Bloomington MN 55431-3830 Office: FSI Internat 322 Lake Hazeltine Dr Chaska MN 55318-1034

JAMES, BETTY L. See JEHN, BETTY L.

JAMES, CLAUDIA ANN, business educator and trainer, motivational speaker; b. Kansas City, Mo., July 23, 1948; d. Claude Jr. and Edna Mae (Henderson) Hinton; m. Wavy L. James, Oct. 21, 1967 (dec. Apr. 1991); children: Edward Allan, Sheryl Evonne. AA, Maple Woods C.C., Kansas City, Mo., 1987; BSE cum laude, Mo. Western State Coll., St. Joseph, 1989. Fin. sec. EBC, Kansas City, Mo., 1977-87; instr. Capital City Bus. Coll., Kansas City, Mo., 1989-90, Career Point Bus. Sch., Kansas City, Mo., 1990-91; owner James Ednl. Mtgs./Seminars (JEMS), Kansas City, Mo., 1992—; instr. Am. Mgmt. Assn., 1993—, Mo. Western State Coll., St. Joseph, 1993—, Independence (Mo.) Sch. Dist., Park Hill Sch. Dist., Kansas City, Mo., North Kansas City Sch. Dist., 1993—, Maple Woods C.C., Kansas City, 1990—, Johnson County C.C., Overland Park, Kans., 1994—; guest spkr. on radio and TV. Mentor WNET-SBA, Kansas City, 1992—. Higgs Art scholar, 1987. Mem. Home Bus. Connection (v.p. 1994), Mo. Home BAsed Bus. Assn. (pres. 1994—), Clay County Women's Exch. (nteworking chair 1993—), Kansas City C. of C., Nat. Assn. Women Bus. Owners, Mo. We. State Coll. Alumni Assn., Kappa Delta Phi. Democrat. Baptist. Office: James Ednl Meetings/Seminar 1001 NE 86th St Kansas City MO 64155-2667

JAMES, ERNEST WILBUR, lawyer; b. N.Y.C., July 21, 1931; s. Ernest Leaman and Lola Marguerita (Clancy) J.; m. Jane Gallagher; children: Ernest Jude, Sean Patrick, Patrick Logan, Sharon Ann; 1 stepchild, Susan Bartsch. BS, U.S. Naval Acad., 1956; MS in Aero. Engring., U.S. Naval Postgrad. Sch., 1964; JD, St. Louis U., 1979. Bar: Mo. 1979. Title examiner Queens County Registrar's Office, N.Y.C., 1949-51; commd. ensign USN, 1956, advanced through grades to comdr., 1971, designated naval aviator, 1958, aviation maintenance mgr., 1956-69, maintenance mgmt. planning engr., 1969-76, ret., 1976; atty., dir. risk mgmt. Bi-State Devel. Agy., St. Louis, 1979-84; assoc. Haley, Fredrickson and Walsh, 1984-86, ptnr., 1986-88; ptnr. Trakas and James, St. Louis, 1985-88, Stuart, Maue, Mitchell and James, 1988—; adj. prof. safety Cen. Mo. State U. Active Maryville Homecoming Assn. Decorated D.F.C., Air medal (3), Navy Commendation medal. UMTA grantee, 1978. Mem. ABA, Mo. Bar Assn., Met. St. Louis Bar Assn., Met. St. Louis Safety Council, Naval Acad. Alumni Assn., U.S. Naval Inst., Am. Def. Preparedness Assn., Met. St. Louis Bar Assn., VFW. Home: 7416 Foley Dr Belleville IL 62223-2301

JAMES, JEFFERSON ANN, performing company executive, dancer, choreographer, educator; b. Washington, July 12, 1943; d. Robert Mitchell and Dorothea Jefferson (Lewis) Miller; m. Martin Edward James, June 16, 1964; 1 child, Rachel Eleanor. Student Juilliard Sch. Music, N.Y.C., 1961-63, Columbia U., 1963-64; BFA, Coll. Conservatory Music, U. Cin., 1970. Vis. prof. Western Coll., Oxford, Ohio, 1970-72; artistic dir. Dance '70, Cin., 1970, Contemporary Dance, Theater, Cin., 1972—; bd. dirs. Cin. Commn. on Arts. 1981-87, OhioDance, Assn., Cleve., 1984-92. Choreographer: Corbett Awards Finalist, 1975, artist category, 1995; dir. Corbett Awards (Arts Orgn. 1982, finalist 1990, 95). Mem. presenting/touring panel Ohio Arts Coun., 1993—; active Cin. Arts Allocation Com., 1994—; cmty. arts coord. for grand opening celebration Aronoff Ctr. for Arts, 1995. NEA fellow, 1978; Individual Artist fellow OAC, 1978-79; Contemporary Dance Theater chosen to present dance Nat. Performance Network NEA; recognition OAC, NEA, Cin. Fine Arts Fund, Greater Cin. Found. Mem. Cin. Bicentennial Com., Dance Cin. (mem. adv. bd. 1983-86), Ohio Dance (trustee 1983-91), Dance Action Cin. Avocations: tennis, gardening, sewing, knitting and travel. Office: Contemporary Dance Theater Inc PO Box 19220 Cincinnati OH 45219-0220

JAMES, MARIE MOODY, clergywoman, musician, vocal music educator; b. Chgo., Jan. 23, 1928; d. Frank and Mary (Portis) Moody; m. Johnnie James, May 25, 1968. B Music Edn., Chgo. Music Coll., 1949; postgrad., U. Ill., Champaign-Urbana, 1952, 72, Moody Bible Inst., Chgo., 1963-64; MusM, Roosevelt U., 1969, MA, 1976; DD, Internat. Bible Inst. and Sem., Plymouth, Fla., 1985; postgrad., Trinity Evang. Div. Sch., Deerfield, Ill., 1995; DRE, Logos Grad. Sch., 1995. exec. dir. House of Love DayCare, 1983, 89; Mary P. Moody Christian Acad., 1989, supt., 1989, founder, 1989; bd. dirs. Van Moody Sch. Music, Chgo.; dir. Handbell Choir for Srs. Maple Park United Meth. Ch., 1988-92. Key punch operator Dept. Treasury, Chgo., 1950-52; tchr. Posen-Robbins Bd. Edn., Robbins, Ill., 1952-59; tchr. vocal music Englewood High Sch., Chgo., 1964-84; music counselor Head Start, Chgo., 1965-66; exec. dir. House of Love DayCare, 1983, 88, Mary P. Moody Christian Acad., 1989, supt., 1989; dir. Handbell Choir for Srs. Maple Park United Meth. Ch., 1988-92. Composer, arranger choral music: Hide Me, 1963, Christmas Time, 1980, Come With Us, Our God Will Do Thee Good, 1986, The Indiana House, 1987, Behold, I Will Do a New Thing, 1989, Mary P. Moody Christian Academy School Song 1989, Glory and Honor, 1992. Organist Allen Temple A.M.E. Ch., 1941-45; asst. organist Choppin A.M.E. Ch., 1945-49; organist-dir. Progressive Ch. of God in Christ, Maywood, Ill., 1950-60; missionary Child Evangelism Fellowship, Chgo., 1955-63; unit leader YWCA, New Buffalo, Mich., 1956-58; min. of music God's House of All Nations, Chgo., 1960-80; pastor God's House of Love, Prayer and Deliverance, Robbins, 1982—; chmn. Frank and Mary Moody Scholarship Com., 1984—; dir. music Christian Women's Outreach Ministry, 1984-88; mem. Robbins Community Coun., 1987-88; camp counselor Abraham Lincoln Ctr., 1951-53. Coppin A.M.E. Ch. scholar, 1946; recipient Humanitarian award God's House of Love, Prayer and Deliverance, 1992, Disting. Leadership award Am. Biog. Inst., 1995. Mem. Music Educators Nat. Conf., Good News Club (tchr. 1987-90, Robbins, Ill.). Home: 8154 S Indiana Ave Chicago IL 60619-4712

JAMES, MARILYN SHAW, secondary education educator, social service worker; b. Chgo., Apr. 6, 1926; d. Harry and Louise A. (Milkey) Shaw; m. Eugene Nelson James, June 17, 1950; children: Jim, Mark, Katherine, Caroline. BS, Carthage Coll., 1947; MA, U. Iowa, 1954. Tchr. home econs. Highland Park (Ill.) High Sch., 1947-50, Hampshire (Ill.) High Sch., 1950-51; instr. home econs. No. Ill. U., DeKalb, 1963-65; tchr. Winkie Bear, Sycamore, Ill., 1970-71; sub. tchr. DeKalb and Sycamore Sch. Dists., 1969—, Hinckley-Big Rock, Ill., 1973-80; homemaker coord. Family Svc. Agy., DeKalb, 1980-88. Stage mgr. Stage Coach Players, DeKalb, 1954—; moderator First Congl. Ch., DeKalb, 1983-84; v.p. Kishwaukee Symphony Assocs., 1988-90, pres., 1990, mem. adv. com. on elder concerns, 1991—; bd. dirs. Family Svc. Agy., DeKalb, 1971-79. Named Stage Coacher of Yr., Stage Coach Players, 1990. Mem. AAUW (v.p. scholar 1980, 90, 93, 94, 95, 96), LWV (legis. chair 1983), DeKalb County Home Economists, DeKalb Drama Club (pres. 1986-87), Univ. Women's Club (pres. 1991), Family Svc. Aux. (v.p.), DeKalb Women's Club (bd. dirs.), Thursday Arts Lit. Club, 1995—. Democrat. Home: 212 Tilton Park Dr DeKalb IL 60115-1942 Office: Family Svc Agy 3131 Sycamore Rd De Kalb IL 60115

JAMES, NICHOLAS, corporate executive; b. Nov. 19, 1951. Address: 1284 Corporate Center Dr Saint Paul MN 55121-1246

JAMES, PHILIP B., physicist, educator; b. Kansas City, Mo., Mar. 18, 1940; s. Benjamin and Catharine (Bagley) J.; m. Sharon Lynn Check, Aug. 28, 1965; children: Eric B., Kevin P., Kirsten L. BS, Carnegie Mellon U., 1961; PhD, U. Wis., 1966. Rsch. assoc. U. Ill., Urbana, 1966-69; prof. dept. physics U. Mo., St. Louis, 1969-90; chmn. dept. physics and astronomy U. Toledo, 1990—; NRC sr. assoc. Jet Propulsion Lab., Pasadena, Calif., 1977-78; prin. investigator Hubble Space Telescope, Balt., 1990—; co-investigator MARCI Camera for 1998 Mars Orbiter, San Diego, 1996—. Editor, asst. editor Am. Jour. Physics, 1979-89; contbr. articles to profl. jours., chpts. to books. NASA grantee, 1979—. Fellow Am. Phys. Soc.; mem. Am. Astron. Soc., Am. Geophys. Union. Office: U Toledo Dept Physics and Astronomy Toledo OH 43606

JAMES, THOMAS BARRY, lawyer; b. San Luis Obispo, Calif., Sept. 11, 1956; s. Arthur Franklin and Jean Marie (Bell) J.; m. Jacqui Lee Holt, Aug. 4, 1979 (div. Feb. 1984); m. Susan Jean Porth, July 29, 1991. BA in Philosophy, U. Calif., Berkeley, 1979; JD, Southwestern U. Sch. of Law, L.A., 1984. Bar: Minn. 1986, Fed. Ct. 1995. Lawyer Cokato, Minn., 1987—; ct. dep. Hennepin County, Minnetonka, Minn., 1990-95; tchr. Fathers Resource Ctr., Mpls., 1994—; vol. atty. Vol. Lawyers Program, Mpls., 1994—, Ctrl. Minn. Legal Svcs., 1995—. Editor, author ManPower, 1994. Co-founder Lawyers Assistance Program, Mpls., 1994. Recipient Outstanding Legal Achievement award Am. Jurisprudence, 1984, Outstanding Achievement award Hennepin County Dist. Ct., 1993. Mem. Hennepin County Bar Assn., Minn. State Bar Assn. (laweyrs assistance program co-founder 1994—), Alliance for the Mentally Ill, Calif. Alumni Assn., Men's ACtion Coun. (dir. 1994-95). Libertarian. Quaker. Home and Office: 440 N Broadway Ave Cokato MN 55321

JAMES, TROY LEE, state legislator; b. Texarkana, Tex.; s. Samuel and Anniebell James; m. Betty Jean Winslow; 1 child, Laura. Student, Bethany Coll., Case We. Res. U., Fenton Coll. State rep. Dist. 12 Ohio State Congress, 1967-92, state rep. Dist. 10, 1993—; chmn. environ. and natural resources com., econ. devel. and small bus. com.; mem. rules, aging and housing com., labor, hwys. and pub. safety com., select com. on Deinstitutionalization, select com. to investigate problems of maintaining basic utility rates; precinct committeeman Ward 11 Dem. Orgn., pres. Mem. Black Elected Dems. Ohio exec. com. Nat. Conf. State Legislatures, Common Fed. Taxation, Trade and Econ. Devel.; self-employed businessman; with Ohio Crankshaft; bd. dirs. Fedn. Cmty. Planning; mem. Consumer Progection Agy., Cleve. Recipient Nat. award Nat. Soc. State Legislators, 1974, ENA award Nat. Assn. Career Women, 1978; named Legislator of Yr. Communicative Disorders Commn., 1988. Mem. NAACP, Nat. Soc. Social Workers, Ohio Soc. State Legislators, Boy Scouts Am., 40th and 43d St. Neighborhood Block Club, 11th Ward Dem. Club. *

JAMES, WILLIAM W., banker; b. Springfield, Mo., Oct. 12, 1931; s. Will and Clyde (Cowdrey) J.; AB, Harvard U., 1953; m. Carol Ann Muenter, June 17, 1967; children: Sarah James Banks, David William. Cert. trust and fin. advisor. Asst. to dir. overseas div. Becton Dickinson & Co., Rutherford, N.J., 1956-59; stockbroker Merrill Lynch, Pierce, Fenner & Smith, Inc., St. Louis, 1959-62; with trust div. Boatmen's Nat. Bank of St. Louis, 1962-90, v.p. in charge estate planning, 1972-90, sr. v.p., 1984-90; sr. v.p. Boatmen's Trust Co., 1989—; bd. dirs. Heer-Andres Investment Co., Springfield. Mem. gift and bequest coun. Barnes Hosp., St. Louis, 1963-67, St. Louis U., 1972-78; dir. Mark Twain Summer Inst., St. Louis, 1987-92. Served with U.S. Army, 1953-55. Mem. Estate Planning Council St. Louis, Mo. Bankers Assn., Am. Inst. Banking, Harvard Alumni Assn. (bd. dirs. 1987-90), Harvard Club of St. Louis (pres. 1972-73), Harvard Faculty Club (Cambridge, Mass.), Mo. Athletic Club, Noonday Club (St. Louis). Republican. Office: Boatmen's Trust Co PO Box 14737 Saint Louis MO 63178-4737

JAMESON, JOHN ROBERT, historian, researcher, educator; b. Annapolis, Md., May 30, 1945; s. Robert Olen and Martha Marie (Stinson) J.; m. Marie Wakefield Dickinson, June 22, 1968; children: John Jr., Andrew. BA, Austin Coll., 1967; MA, East Tex. State U., 1970; PhD, U. Toledo (Ohio), 1974. Hist. site adminstr. Tex. Hist. Commn., Bonham, 1974-78; asst. assoc. prof. history Wash. State U., Pullman, 1979-88; assoc. prof. Kent (Ohio) State U., 1988—. Author: Big Bend: Formative Years, 1980, Big Bend: Biography of a National Park, 1987, The Story of Big Bend National Park, 1996. Sr. warden, mem. vestry Holy Trinity Episc. Ch., Bonham, 1975-78; jr. warden vestry St. James Episc. Ch., Pullman, 1983-86; mem. vestry St. Timothy's Episc. Ch., Macedonia, Ohio, 1994—. With USMCR, 1967-69. Planning grantee Nat. Endowment for the Humanities, 1978. Episcopalian. Office: Kent State U Dept History Kent OH 44242

JAMESON, PATRICIA MADOLINE, science librarian; b. Rhinelander, Wis., Mar. 17, 1939; d. Errol Donald and Mary Maxine (Shields) J. BS, Carroll Coll., 1961; PhD, Ind. U., 1965; MLIS, U. Wis., Milw., 1988. Microbiologist U.S. Dept. Def., Frederick, Md., 1965-69; instr. Med. Coll. Wis., Milw., 1969-70, asst. prof., 1970-80, assoc. prof., 1980-88; asst. prof. Eastern Ill. U., Charleston, 1989-91; reference librarian U. Wis., Milw., 1991—; cons. P-L Biochems., Milw., 1969, Wadley Inst. Medicine, Dallas, 1978, World Book-Childcraft Internat., Chgo., 1979. Contbr. articles to profl. jours. Mem. AAAS, ALA, Wis. Libr. Assn., Wis. Assn. Acad. Librs. (bd. dirs. 1994-95), Spl. Libr. Assn. (bd. dirs sci-tech. sect. 1994-96), Am. Guild Organists, Am. Theatre Organ Soc., Photog. Soc. Am., Kimball Theatre Organ Soc. (bd. dirs.), Order of Eastern Star (Wauwatosa chpt., office 1995-96, trustee 1995—), Order of Amaranth (Milw. chpt., officer 1996—), Order of True Kindred (officer Aloha Conclave), Daus. of the Nile (officer Shelomoth Temple 1993-94). Office: U Wis Milw Golda Meir Libr PO Box 604 Milwaukee WI 53201

JAMES-STRAND, NANCY KAY LEABHARD, advertising executive; b. Oak Park, Ill., July 30, 1943; d. Arthur Ferdinand and Virginia Stella (Albertelli) Leabhard; m. Jack William Strand, July 1, 1971. Student, U. Madrid, 1963-64; BA in Teaching Spanish, U. Ill., 1965. With advt. sales Chgo. Tribune, 1968-69; asst. mgr. Nationwide Advt., Chgo., 1969-78, regional mgr., 1978—. Home: 140 S Grove Ave Oak Park IL 60302-2806 Office: Nationwide Advt 35 E Wacker Dr Chicago IL 60601

JAMIAN, JOHN, state legislator; b. Detroit, Nov. 7, 1954; m. Cynthia; children: Michelle, Sean. BSS, Oakland U., Rochestery, Minn. Pres. Americare/Ameristaff, 1986—; state rep. Dist. 40 Mich. Ho. of Reps., 1990—; chmn. Pub. Health Com.; mem. Ins. Econ. Devel., Tourism & Recreations Coms. Mich. Ho. of Reps. Mem. Glencoe Estates Homeowners Assn. (pres.), Birmingham Youth Assistance Com. (bd. dirs.), Steamship His. Soc. N.Am., Internat. Shipmasters Assn., Birmingham Family Br. YMCA of Met. Detroit (bd. dirs.). Home: 3965 Quarton Rd Bloomfield Hills MI 48302-4060*

JAMISON, FRANK RAYMOND, communications educator; b. Independence, Mo., Mar. 25, 1938; s. Eldon Verl and Pauline Francis (Mericle) J.; m. Paula Ann Wissing; children: Diana Cherie, Thomas Marshall, Noel Avery. BA, U. Mo., Kansas City, 1960; MS, Syracuse U., 1962; Edn. Specialist, U. No. Colo., 1967. Continuity dir. Sta. WEAR, Syracuse, N.Y., 1961; sales svc. dir. Sta. KCMO-TV, Kansas City, Mo., 1961-62; found., gen. mgr. KUNC-FM-U. No. Colo., Greeley, 1966-67; dir. radio and TV U. No. Colo., 1962-67; mgr. TV svcs. Western Mich. U., Kalamazoo, 1967-84, prof. instnl. media, 1977—, head media svcs., 1984-91; founder, gen. mgr. Edu-CABLE, Kalamazoo, 1991—; mgr. video distbn. Western Mich. U., Kalamazoo, 1991—; bd. dirs. Alliance for Cmty. Media, Washington, 1984-87, sec., 1986; mem. internat. adv. senate Amity Bus. Sch., New Delhi, India, 1995—; mem. nat. convention com. Assn. for Ednl. Comms. and Tech., Washington, 1992. Exec. prodr. TV series Every Child a Wanted Child, 1983 (Cable Ace award 1984); prodr. TV series Poets in Their Time, 1977-79 (Ohio State award 1980); assoc. prodr. radio program Where Are We?, 1969 (Armstrong award 1970); TV prodr. 12th World Scout Jamboree, 1967 (Silver Anvil award). Faculty advisor Students for a Free Tibet, 1995—; founding chair U.S. Postal Svc. Customer Adv. Coun., S.W. Mich. Coun. Boy Scouts Am., 1967-70, 92-95; pres. Buddhist Assn. S.W. Mich., 1990—. Sgt. USAR, 1956-62. Recipient Philo T. Farnsworth award Nat. Found. Local Cable Progamming, 1984, Hometown U.S.A. award Nat. Found. Local Cable Programming, 1985, Network Founder award Scola TV Network, 1990; various grants for acad. projects. Mem. AAUP (various coms.), West Mich. Men's Coun. (sec. bd. dirs. 1994—), Buddhadharma Soc. (faculty advisor 1991—), Am. Philatelic Soc. (25 Yr. award 1991), Arabian Philatelic Assn. Home: 2906 Memory Ln Kalamazoo MI 49006-5535 Office: Western Mich U 1490 Dunbar Kalamazoo MI 49008-5001

JAMISON, ROGER W., pianist, piano educator; b. Marion, Ohio, June 18, 1937; s. Harold Theodore and Martha Louise (Haas) J.; m. Caroline R. Hansley, Jan. 26, 1957; children: Lisa Renee, Eric Karl. BS, Ohio State U., 1959, MA (scholar), 1961; postgrad. Oberlin Conservatory, Oakland U.; student George Haddad, Columbus, Ohio, Mischa Kottler, Detroit. Piano faculty mem. Detroit Conservatory of Music, 1964-68, Cranbrook Schs., Bloomfield Hills, Mich., 1981-84; performer in one-man mus. presentation Spirits of Great Composers, 1979—; dir. music Birmingham Temple, Farmington Hills, Mich., 1984-95; soloist Brunch with Bach series Detroit Inst. Arts., Detroit Symphony Orch.'s Internat. Brahms Festival; regular soloist Christ Ch., Cranbrook, 1982-95; concert tour of Eng., 1991; cons. Royal Oak Arts Council; adjudicator Am. Coll. Musicians. Mem. Nat. Guild of Piano Tchrs. (past pres. Oakland-Macomb chpt.) Address: 173 W Heffner St Delaware OH 43015-1258

JAN, GEORGE POKUNG, political science educator; b. Peking, Jan. 6, 1925; came to U.S., 1955; s. Yunan and Tehchieh (Lee) J.; m. Norma Yingchiang Wen, Sept. 28, 1946; children: Gregory, David, Daniel. BA, Nat. Chengchi U., Nanking, China, 1949; MA, So. Ill. U., 1956; PhD, NYU, 1960. Various positions including editor newspaper/mag., tchr., writer, dean, 1949-55; instr. Chinese NYU, N.Y.C., 1959-60; asst. prof. polit. sci. No. Ill. U., DeKalb, 1961; asst. to full prof. of govt. U. S.D., Vermillion, 1961-68, dir. Summer Inst. for Asian Studies, 1964-66; prof. polit. sci. U. Toledo, 1968-93, prof. emeritus, 1993—, chmn. Asian studies program, 1970-93, dir. Inst. for Asian Studies, 1990-93; pres. Am. Inst. Tech., Toledo, 1993—; vis. prof. polit. sci. Beijing U., China, 1988; sr. rsch. fellow Rsch. Ctr. for Contemporary China, Beijing U., 1988—; pres. Am. Inst. Tech., 1993—. Author: The Chinese Commune Experiment, 1964, A Practical English Grammar for Junior Middle Schools, 1953, A Study of English Words, 1955, How to Do Business with China, 1994, others; editor: Government of Communist China, 1966, The International Politics of Asia, 1969; bd. editors Asian Profile Jour., 1983-86, Jour. Econs. and Internat. Rels., 1986—, The New World of Politics, 1991—; contbr. articles to profl. jours., ency. and books. Pres. Chinese Assn. Greater Toledo, 1983-84; bd. dirs. Toledo Coun. on World Affairs, 1969-76; chmn. keynote session, Symposium on Chinese Ams. in the 1990s, Detroit, 1987. Recipient Outstanding Svc. award The Internat. Inst. of Greater Toledo, 1983, teaching grants Asia Found., Japan Soc., 1964, 65, 66, rsch. grants U. Toledo, U. S.D., U. Mich., U. Chgo. numerous years, Significant Contribution award Pacific Cultural Found., Republic of China, 1988; named Hon. Rsch. Fellow, Rsch. Ctr. for Contemporary China, Beijing U., 1988, others. Mem. AAUP, Am. Polit. Sci. Assn., Midwest Polit. Sci. Assn., Assn. Asian Studies, Ohio Chinese Acad. and Profl. Assn. (bd. dirs. 1991—, pres. 1994-95), Mich. Chinese Acad. and Profl. Assn. (outstanding leadership award 1992), Am. Assn. Chinese Studies, Internat. Studies Assn., Ohio Internat. Edn. Assn. (chmn. planning and program com. 1976-77), Chinese Acad. and Profl. Assn. of Mid-Am. (bd. dirs. 1986-89), Internat. Biographical Ctr. (hon. adv. coun.), Phi Beta Kappa, Pi Sigma Alpha, Phi Kappa Phi, Pi Gamma Mu, Phi Beta Delta. Home: 3041 Valley View Dr Toledo OH 43615-2237 Office: U Toledo 2801 W Bancroft St Toledo OH 43606-3328

JANARDAN, KONANUR GUNDAPPASETTY, mathematics and statistics educator; U.S. citizen; m. Aru Janardan; 3 children. BSc in Stats. and Math., U. Mysore, 1956, MSc in Indsl. Stats., 1957; MA in Maths., Pa. State U., 1968, PhD in Math. Stats., 1970. Instr. in stats. Pa. State U., University Park, 1969-70; asst. prof. Montclaire State Coll., Upper Montclaire, N.J., 1970-71; assoc. prof. math. systems Sangamon State U., Springfield, Ill., 1971-80, dir. statis. lab. and tech. svcs., 1973-77, chmn. dept. math. systems, 1977-80, prof. math. systems, 1980-83; prof. stats., dir. math. scis. cons. div. math. scis. N.D. State U., 1983-86, dir., prof. stats., 1985-86; prof. stats. dept. maths. Ea. Mich. U., Ypsilanti, 1986—; vis. prof. stats. dept. maths. and stats. U. Pitts., 1980-81; vis. prof. to Dr. Sir. M. Visvesvaraya, chair U Mysore, India, 1993-94, cons. Div. Water Pollution Control, Ill. EPA, Springfield, 1972-83, Div. Air Pollution Control, 1973; rsch. for Ill. Econ. and Fiscal Commn., 1973; statis. cons. So. Ill. U., 1974; cons. Ill. Dept. Pub. Aid, 1975, Ill. Inst. Natural Resources, Chgo., 1978, Lockheed Engring. & Mgmt. Svcs. Co., Las Vegas, Nev., 1982, Northern Great Plains Rsch. Ctr., Mandan, N.D., 1983-86, Red River Valley Potato Rsch. Lab., East Grand Forks, 1983-88, Metabolism and Radiation Rsch. Lab. USDA Agr. Svc., Fargo, N.D., 1983-86, U.S. Constrn. Engring. and Rsch. Lab. Dept. Army, Champaign, Ill., 1985-86, EPRI of Detroit Edison, 1989-92, cons. to BBK-Financial, turnaround & crisis mngmnt., 1994. Assoc. editor, Communications in Statistics, 1995—, Reviewer Am. Statistician, Jour. Am. Statis. Assn., Sankhya, Can. Jour. Stats., Communications in Stats., BioSci., Statis. Distbns. in Sci. Work, Jour. Statis. Planning and Inference, Statis. and Probability Letters; reviewer stats. WEST Pub. Co., McMillan Pub. Co., PWS-Kent Pub. Co.; contbr. numerous articles to profl. jours. Maharaja's Coll. scholar, Mysore, 1956, U. Mysore scholar, 1957. Fellow Inst. Combinatorics and Applications; mem. Biometric Soc., Am. Statis. Assn. (founding sec., v.p. cen. Ill. chpt. 1977-78, sec. elect 1978-79, 81-82, pres. elect 1979-81, com. minorities in statis. 1984-87), Am. Water Works Assn. (nat. standards com., 1984-87). Home: 3056 Cedarbrook Rd Ann Arbor MI 48105-3403 Office: Ea Mich U 504 Pray Harrold Hall # D Ypsilanti MI 48197-2210

JANAVARAS, BASIL JOHN, university business educator, consultant; b. Corinth, Corinth, Greece, Nov. 1, 1943; came to U.S., 1962; s. John Basil and Loukia Demetra (Tzakona) J.; m. Linda Mae Larson, Aug. 19, 1972; children: Loukia Linda, John Basil (dec.). BA, Minot State U., 1967; MS, U. N.D., 1969; EdD, No. Ill. U., 1974. Bus. instr. Mankato (Minn.) State U., 1969-72, asst. prof., 1974-76, assoc. prof., 1977-80, prof., 1980-85; dir. Internat. Bus. Inst., Mankato, 1986-89, chairperson, dir., 1990-91; dir. internat. bus. studies U. St. Thomas, St. Paul, 1992-94; pres. Odyssey Gift Shops, Mankato, 1978-94; dir. Internat. Bus. Exec. Program, St. Paul, 1988-95, Minn. State U. Sys., Vienna, Austria, 1990-92; pres., CEO Janavaras & Assocs. Internat. Inc., Mankato, 1990—. Author: Student Guide to International Business, 1988, Student Resource Manual, 1992; contbr. articles to profl. jours. Grantee Mankato State U., 1988-89, U.S. Dept. Edn., 1988-90, So. Minn. Initiative Fund, 1988-90. Mem. Nat. Assn. Small Bus. Internat. Trade Educators (bd. dirs. 1988—), Acad. Internat. Bus., Acad. Mgmt., Minn. World Trade Week (bd. dirs. 1983-90, pres. 1989), Minn. Dist. Export Coun., Minn. World Trade Assn. Home: 27 Capri Dr Mankato MN 56001-4119 Office: Mankato State U Dept Mktg Box 14 Mankato MN 56002-8400

JANDES, KENNETH MICHAEL, superintendent; b. Berwyn, Ill., Aug. 6, 1943; s. George Jerry Jandejska and Dorothea Frieda (Grabow) Clara; m. RoseMary Patricia Klingebiel, June 18, 1966; children: Michael Jon, Kenneth Mark. BS in Edn., Ill. State U., 1966; MEd, Loyola U., Chgo., 1972; EdD, No. Ill. U., 1984. Cert. tchr., chief sch. bus. official, gen. adminstrv., supt., Ill. Math. tchr. Brook Park Sch., LaGrange Park, Ill., 1966-69, sci. tchr., 1969-74, acting prin., 1972-74; prin. Waterman Sch., South Holland, Ill., 1974-79, Berger-Vandenberg Sch., Dolton, Ill., 1979-95; supt. Lincoln Sch. Dist. # 156, Calumet City, Ill., 1995—; chmn. dept. applied saxophone Am. Conservatory Music, Chgo., 1968-78 ; owner, operator Midwest Music Mart, Riverside, Ill., 1968-73; primary sci. cons. Instructor Mag., Dansville, N.Y., 1969-73; adj. prof. Govs. StateU., University Park, Ill., 1985-93; performing saxophonist Andy Tecson Jazz Ensemble. Composer of numerous choral, band, and orchestral works, 1961—; contbr. articles to profl. jours. Bd. dirs. Community Family Svc. and Mental Health Ctr. La Grange, 1968-74, Echo Spl. Edn. Cooperative, Thornton Fractional Ednl. Cooperative; mem. com., treas. Boy Scouts Am., Woodridge, 1985—; baseball coach Woodridges Athletic Assn., 1980-89; active com. on youth traffic safety Ill. Sec. of State, 1987-91, chancel choir St. Luke Presbyn. Ch., 1976—, bd. elders, 1980-86, 92—. Named one of Outstanding Young Men Am. Jaycees, 1970. Mem. Am. Assn. Sch. Adminstrs. (Nat. award 1986), Ill. Assn. Sch. Adminstrs., Ill. Assn. Sch. Bus. Ofcls., Ill. Congress Parents and Tchrs. (hon. life), Kappa Delta Pi, Phi Mu Alpha Sinfonia, Phi Delta Kappa. Home: 6671 Wheatfield St Woodridge IL 60517 Office: Lincoln Sch Dist 156 410 W 157th St Calumet City IL 60409

JANDIK, LINDA JEAN, studio executive; b. Cedar Rapids, Iowa, Mar. 28, 1946; d. Robert Earl and Jean Alta (Weis) Elliott; m. Stanley George Accola, June 5, 1965 (dec. June 1973); 1 child, Robinette Lynn Accola-Shaver; m. David Richard Jandik, Apr. 5, 1975; stepchildren: Kathryn Kay Jandik, Kenneth Allen Jandik. AAS, Kirkwood Coll., 1975. Adminstrv. asst. Hoover Health Coun., Cedar Rapids, 1975-76; acct. Dee, Gosling & Co., CPAs, Cedar Rapids, 1976-79; office mgr. Mitchell & Benson Photography, Cedar Rapids, 1979-88; pvt. practice accounting Cedar Rapids, 1988—; pres., chief exec. officer DLJ Studio Prodns., Inc., Cedar Rapids, 1990—. Staff parish com. Salem United Meth. Ch. Mem. Nat. Assn. Women Bus. Owners (treas. Cedar Rapids chpt.), Phi Theta Kappa, Alpha Beta Gamma. Methodist. Office: DLJ Studio Prodns Inc 137 30th Street Dr SE Cedar Rapids IA 52403-1402

JANELLO, DAVID A., music composer, computer scientist; b. Bridgeport, Conn., May 16, 1960; s. Kenneth A. Janello and Sylvia DeMatteo Surdoval; m. Rei Hotoda, May 25, 1991. BA, Yale U., 1982; M Music, U. So. Calif., 1984, PhD in Music Theory, 1994. Sr. software engr. Allstate Ins./Investment Sys., Northbrook, Ill., 1995—; composer-in-residence Long Beach (Calif.) Chorale, 1995—, Long Beach Chamber Orch., 1995—; adj. faculty U. So. Calif., L.A., 1990-95. Author: In the Realm of Timbre and Orchestration, 1994; composer: (choral symphony) The Gospel of Thomas, 1995, (orch. symphony) At the Sea of Clouds, 1990; patentee in field. Bd. dirs. Euterpe Opera Theatre, L.A., 1992-95. Pierre Boulez fellow L.A. Philharmonic, 1984; grantee MIT Coun. Arts, 1990; laureate Concert Artists Guild, Lincoln Ctr., N.Y., 1994. Mem. ASCAP. Episcopalian. Office: Allstate Investment Sys 3075 Sanders Rd Northbrook IL 60062

JANEZICH, JERRY R., state legislator, small business owner; b. Mar. 16, 1950; m. Patricia Janezich; three children. BS, St. Cloud State U. Small bus. owner; Dist. 5B rep. Minn. Ho. of Reps., St. Paul, 1992—; vice chmn. judiciary, local govt. and met. affairs com., mem. commerce, regulated industries and taxes coms., Minn. Ho. of Reps. Home: 518 8th St NE Chisholm MN 55719-1338*

JANKLOW, WILLIAM JOHN, governor; b. Chgo., Sept. 13, 1939; s. Arthur W. and LouElla Bernice (Gulbranson) J.; m. Mary Dean Thom, Sept. 3, 1960; children—Russell, Pam, Shonna. B.S.B.A., U. S.D., 1964, J.D., 1966. Bar: S.D. bar 1966, U.S. Supreme Ct. bar 1970. Staff atty. S.D. Legal Services, 1966-67, directing atty., chief officer, 1967-72; chief trial atty. S.D. Atty. Gen.'s Office, Pierre, 1973-74; atty. gen. S.D. Atty. Gen.'s. Office, 1975-78; gov. S.D., 1979-87, 1995—; lectr. in field. Bd. dirs. Nat. Legal Services Corp. Served with USMC, 1956-59. Recipient Nat. award for legal excellence and skill Nat. Legal Aid and Defenders Assn., 1968. Mem. Nat. Assn. Attys. Gen., Am., S.D. trial lawyers assns., Am. Judicature Soc. Republican. Lutheran. Office: Office of the Governor 500 E Capitol Ave Pierre SD 57501

JANNING, JOHN LOUIS, research scientist, consultant; b. Dayton, Ohio, Mar. 30, 1928; s. Eugene Alois and Frieda Marie (Kessen) J.; m. Dolores Mary Nartker, Nov. 29, 1952; children: Kathleen, Janet, Theresa, Lawrence, Thomas, Richard, Jacqueline. Electronic technician U. Dayton, 1956-58; cons. engr. NCR Corp., Dayton, 1958-88; liquid crystal display cons. JLJ, Inc., Dayton, 1988—. Contbr. articles to profl. jours.; numerous patents in high tech. field including implantable med. devices; inventor thermal printing wafer, plasma displays and LCDs. With inf. U.S. Army, 1950-52. Recipient Outstanding Profl. Achievement award Affiliate Socs. Coun. Engring. and Sci. Found. Dayton, 1982. Mem. IEEE, Soc. for Info. Display, Inventors Coun. Dayton. Roman Catholic. Home and Office: 332 Vindale Dr Dayton OH 45440-3364 also: Lab at 4656 Wilmington Pike Dayton OH 45440

JANOVER, ROBERT H., lawyer; b. N.Y.C., Aug. 17, 1930; s. Cyrus J. and Lillian D. (Horwitz) J.; B.A., Princeton U., 1952; J.D., Harvard U., 1957; m. Mary Elizabeth McMahon, Oct. 23, 1966; 1 child: Laura Lockwood. Admitted to N.Y. State bar, 1957, U.S. Supreme Ct. bar, 1961, D.C. bar, 1966, Mich. bar, 1973; practice law, N.Y.C., 1957-65; cons. Office of Edn. HEW, 1965, legis. atty. Office of Gen. Counsel, HEW, 1965-66; asst. gen. atty. Mgmt. Assistance Inc., N.Y.C., 1966-71; atty. Ford Motor Credit Co., Dearborn, Mich., 1971-74; mem. firm Freud, Markus, Slavin, Toohey & Galgan, Troy, Mich., 1974-79; sole practice law, Detroit, 1979—, Bloomfield Hills, Mich., 1982—. Bd. dirs. Oakland Citizens League, 1976-96, v.p., 1976-79, pres., 1979—; bd. dirs. Civic Searchlight, 1979-96. Served to 1st lt. U.S. Army, 1952-54. Mem. ABA, Mich. State Bar, N.Y. State Bar, Detroit Bar Assn., Bar Assn. D.C., Assn. Bar of City of N.Y., Princeton Club (pres., Mich. 1991-92). Home: 685 Ardmoor Dr Bloomfield Hills MI 48301-2415 Office: 100 W Long Lake Rd Ste 200 Bloomfield Hills MI 48304-2774

JANSKY, LARRY RICHARD, communication specialist; b. Omaha, May 25, 1952; s. Frank and Sidonia (Bodlak) J.; m. Janice Marie Dejnozka, Sep. 8, 1979; 1 child, Amanda May. BS in Broadcasting, U. Nebr., Omaha, 1975. First Class Radio-Telephone lic., Minn. FM operator, interim coord. Sta. KEFM-FM, Sta. KOIL, Omaha, 1974-76, FM coord., 1976-77; med. dispatcher U. Nebr. Med. Ctr., 1977-83, med. comm. supr., 1983-86, med. comm. coord., 1986—; weekend announcer Sta. KRCB, Council Bluffs, Iowa, 1977, Sta. KESY-FM, Omaha, 1979, Sta. KOMJ-FM, Omaha, 1988-90; studio videographer, Sta. WOWT-TV, Omaha, 1979-82.

JANSSEN, DANIEL JOE, roofing manufacturer field advisor, consultant; b. Cedar Falls, Iowa, Oct. 5, 1966. BA, Ea. Ill. U., 1988. Advt. salesman State Jour. Register, Springfield, Ill., 1988-91; salesman Isringhausen (Car) Imports, Springfield, Ill., 1991-92; copier sales mgr. IBM/Lanier, Springfield, Ill., 1992-94; sales rep./field cons. TREMCO/B.F. Goodrich, Cleve., 1994—. Recipient Ring of Truth award Copley Press, 1990. Mem. Am. Inst. Plant Engrs. (affiliate), Constrn. Specifiers Inst. (pres. elect 1996). Home and Office: 4423 Foxbury Ln Springfield IL 62707

JANSSEN, LARRY LEONARD, economics educator, researcher; b. Nebraska City, Feb. 21, 1949; s. Harry William and Veletta M. (Windhorst) J.; m. Marcia Kay Parsons, June 30, 1973; children: Matthew Kane, Lara Lindsay, Tiffany Dawn. BS in Agrl. Econs., U. Nebr., 1971; MS, Okla. State U., 1974; PhD, U. Nebr., 1978. NDEA fellow, grad. student Okla. State U., Stillwater, 1971-73; credit analyst-trainee Farm Credit Banks of Omaha, 1973-74; rsch. asst. U. Nebr., Lincoln, 1974-78; asst., assoc. prof. S.D. State U., Brookings, 1978-89; prof. Econ., 1989—; instr. profl. workshops, PRO-ED, Sioux Falls, S.D., 1993-95. Contbg. author: Changing Size and Structure of American Farms, 1993, Research in Rural Sociology and Development, 1993; contbr. articles to profl. jours. Pres. First Luth. Ch. Volga, S.D., 1994-95. Recipient Outstanding Young Man of Am., 1986, Outstanding Tchr., 1993, Outstanding Rsch., 1992, S.D. State U. Gamma Sigma Delta. Mem. Am. Agrl. Econ. Assn., Western Agrl. Econ. Assn., Rotary, Sigma Xi, Gamma Sigma Delta. Lutheran. Home: 113 Adams Ave Volga SD 57071 Office: South Dakota State Univ 103 Scobey Hall Brookings SD 57007

JANSSEN, RAMON E., state legislator; b. Hooper, Nebr., July 5, 1937; m. Nancy Janssen; children: Nick, Michael, Nola. Owner City Meat Market, Hooper, Nebr., Nickerson Meat Market; mem. from dist. 15 Nebr. State Senate, Lincoln, 1992—, mem. bldg. maintenance, edn., mem. govt., mil., and vet. affairs coms.; bd. dirs. Farmer's Home Ins. Co. Mem. Hooper Comml. Club, Elkhorn Valley Golf Club (past pres.), Lions Club. Office: Nebr State Senate State Capitol Rm 1522 Lincoln NE 68509*

JANSSON, JOHN FREDRICK, journalist; b. Beloit, Wis., July 24, 1936; s. Oscar Fredrick and Bertha Marie (Hanson) J.; m. Margaret Jean Johnson Jansson, June 25, 1960 (div. July 3, 1979); children: Kirsten Margaret Jansson Gibbs, Ingrid Marie Jansson, Thomas Christian, Fredrick Jansson; m. Carol Eileen Steenbock Jansson, July 10, 1982; 1 child, Paul Steenbock Jansson. AA, North Park Coll., Chgo., 1956; BA, U. Iowa, Iowa City, 1958; MA in Journalism, Northwestern U., Evanston, Ill., 1959. Reporter, copy editor Chicago Tribune, 1959-65; makeup editor, 1965-75, editor technology, 1975-85, edotpr Info. Sys., 2985—; mgr. Chicago Tribune Info. Ctr., 1985—; wire standards task force Am. Newspaper Pub. Assn., Reston, Va., 1975-83; co-chair Tribune Co. Archiving Task Force, Chgo., 1983-85; mem. Tribune Co. Photo Archiving Task Force, Chgo., 1990—; co-chair, tech. Spl. Libr. Assn. News Divsn., Washington, 1991-93. Mem. Soc. profl. Journalists, Spl. Libr. Assn., James Chorale. Home: 199 Church Rd Winnetka IL 60093 Office: Chicago Tribune 435 N Michigan Ave Chicago IL 60611

JANTZE, R. DALE, retired educator; b. Milford, Nebr., Apr. 5, 1926; s. Ralph and Esther (Reil) J.; m. Margaret Lorraine Pederson, June 5, 1962. BA, Goshen Coll., 1951; MEd, U. Nebr., 1953, EdD, 1961. Cert. tchr., adminstr., Nebr. Supt. Staplehurst (Nebr.) pub. schs., 1951-54; instr. biology and physics Exeter (Nebr.) pub. schs., 1954-56; supt. Diller (Nebr.) pub. schs., 1956-60; prof., chmn. tchr. edn. Friends U., Wichita, Kans., 1961-78; adminstr. N.W. Wichita Child Devel. Ctr., 1978-94; cons. Mid-Continent Regional Edn. Lab., Kans. City, Mo., 1966-70, in interaction analysis Emporia State U.; pres. Kans. Assn. Edn. Comm. and Tech., 1968-69, Kans. Assn. Colls. Tchr. Edn., 1972-74; chmn. Kans. Profl. Tchg. Standards Bd., Topeka, 1972-78. Active Mennonite Econ. Devel. Assocs., 1988-95. Mem. Optimist Internat. (life), Kans. Optimist Dist. (lt. gov. 1975-76), Wichita-W. Optimist Club (pres. 1974-75), Phi Delta Kappa (25 year pin). Home: 2301 Westport Wichita KS 67203

JANTZEN, GORDON JOHN, human resources specialist; b. Marion, Ind., Dec. 1, 1960; s. John Benjamin and Anna (Dick) J.; m. Roxanne Irene Bergman, Jan. 8, 1983; children: Jessica Nannette, Andrew Gordon, Natalie Kathleen. BA, Westmont Coll., Santa Barbara, Calif., 1983. Cert. in employee rels. law; cert. instr. situational leadership. Budget/relocation analyst Carter Hawley Hale, Inc., L.A., 1987, tng. and devel. specialist, 1987-90, mgr. edn. and devel., 1990-91; mgmt. devel. specialist Payless Cashways, Inc., Kansas City, Mo., 1991-93; regional tng. mgr. Payless Cashways, Inc., Overland Park, Kans., 1993; regional human resource mgr. Payless Cashways, Inc., Cin., 1993—. Mem. Nat. Soc. Performance and Instrn., Human Resource Mgmt. Assn. Home: 6292 Arrowpoint Dr Loveland OH 45140 Office: Furrow Bldg Materials 27 Triangle Park Dr Cincinnati OH 45246

JANZEN, NORINE MADELYN QUINLAN, medical technologist; b. Fond du Lac, Wis., Feb. 9, 1943; d. Joseph Wesley and Norma Edith (Gustin) Quinlan. BS, Marian Coll., 1965; med. technologist St. Agnes Sch. Med. Tech., Fond du Lac, 1966; MA, Cen. Mich. U., 1980; m. Douglas Mac Arthur Janzen, July 18, 1970; 1 son, Justin James. Med. technologist Mayfair Med. Lab., Wauwatosa, Wis., 1966-69; supr. med. technologist Dr.'s Mason, Chamberlain, Franke, Klink & Kamper, Milw., 1969-76, Hartford-Parkview Clinic, Ltd., 1976-94, patient svc. ctrs. supr. Med. Sci. Labs., Wauwatosa, Wis., 1994—; coord. health in bus. Hartford Parkview Clinic, 1990-91, drug program coord., 1991-94; co-chair joint mtg. Clin. Lab. Mgrs. Assn. and Wis. Assn. for Clin. Lab. Scientists, 1993-94. Substitute poll worker Fond du Lac Dem. Com., 1964-65; mem. Dem. Nat. Com., 1973—. Mem. Am. Soc. for Clin. Lab. Scientists (people to people clin. lab. scientist del. to People's Republic of China 1989), Nat. Soc. Clin. Lab. Scientists (awards com. chair 1984-87, 88-91, chmn. 1986-88, nominations com. 1989-92), Wis. Assn. Clin. Lab. Scientists (exec. sec. 1991—, chmn. awards com. 1976-77, 84-85, 86-87, treas. 1977-81, pres.-elect 1981-82, pres. 1982-83, dir. 1977-84, 85-87, Mem. of Yr. award 1982, 95, numerous svc. awards, chair ann. meeting 1987-88), Clin. Lab. Mgmt. Assn. (co-chair joint meeting 1993-94), Milw. Soc. Clin. Lab. Scientists (pres. 1971-72, bd. dir. 1972-73), Communications of Wis. (originator, chmn. 1977-79), Southeastern Suprs. Group (co-chmn. 1976-77), LWV, Alpha Delta Theta (nat. dist. chmn. 1967-69, nat. alumnae dir. 1969-71), Alpha Mu Tau. Methodist. Home: N98w17298 Dotty Way Germantown WI 53022-4618 Office: Med Scis Labs 11020 W Plank Ct Ste 100 Wauwatosa WI 53226

JAPP, NYLA F., infection control services administrator; b. Sterling, Colo., Jan. 8, 1948; d. Leonard W. and Eleanor M. (Barnts) J. Assoc. in Nursing, Garden City Community Coll., 1980; diploma, Pikes Peak Inst. Med. Tech., 1970; BS in Human Resources Mgmt., Friends U., 1992. RN, Kans. With surg. unit St. Catherine Hosp., Garden City, Kans.; sanitarian Finney County Commrs., Garden City; mgr. sterile processing St. Catherine Hosp., Garden City, Kans., mgr. infection control. Mem. Am. Soc. Hosp. Ctrl. Svc. Pers. (regional bd. dirs., chmn. recognition com., mem. tech. cert. com., APIC liaison, AORN liaison, JCAHO liaison, educator of yr., Tom Samuels rsch. award), Great Plains Soc. Hosp. Ctrl. Svc. Pers. (chmn. program com., mem. newsletter com., chmn. nominating com., rsch. com., pres., bd. dirs.), Nat. Inst. for Cert. Healthcare Sterile Processing and Distbn. Pers. (bd. dirs.), Internat. Assn. Hosp. Ctrl. Svc. Mgmt., Assn. Practitioners in Infection Control. Home: 1712 E Fair St Garden City KS 67846-3558

JARABEK, DENNIS JOSEPH, brokerage executive; b. Mitchell, S.D., May 31, 1945; s. Joseph and Lorenne D. (Lucken) J.; m. Janelle E. Jarabek, Aug. 12, 1972; children: Christine N., Gretchen A., Bradley J. BS, U. S.D. CLU, ChFC. Staff acct. John Morrell & Co., Sioux Falls, S.D., 1970-72; plant mgr. Sioux Land Packing Co., Sioux Falls, 1972-73; agt. N.Y. Life Ins., Sioux Falls, 1973-79, tng. supr., 1979-86; agy. mgr. Woodmen Accident and Life, Sioux Falls, 1986-95; brokerage agy. mgr. Prin. Mutual Life, Sioux Falls, 1996—. Bd. trustees Our Saviors Luth. Ch., Sioux Falls, 1981-84, bd. dirs. found., 1984-87, lobbyist Nat. Assn. Life Underwriters, Washington, 1993; lobbyist, legis. chmn. S.D. Life Underwriters, Pierre, 1993—; basketball coach YMCA, Sioux City, 1985-95; bus. ptnrs. with high sch. C. of C., Sioux Falls, 1991-92. Mem. Sioux Falls Dist. Life Underwriters Assn. (pres. 1984, Life Underwriter of Yr. 1995), S.D. Assn. of Life Underwriters (pres. 1988, Ed Downs Meml. Life Underwriter of Yr. award 1992), Ea. S.D. CLU Soc. (v.p. 1986-89), Gen. Agts. and Mgrs. Assn. (treas. 1990-92, Career Devel. award 1989-94). Lutheran. Home: 2321 Mockingbird Cir Sioux Falls SD 57103

JARAMILLO, CARLOS ALBERTO, civil engineer; b. Medellin, Colombia, Dec. 5, 1952; came to the U.S., 1986; s. Alberto and Maria (Restrepo) J.; children: Daniel J., Nicolas. BCE, U. Nacional, Medellin, 1978; MS, U. Minn., 1980. Registered profl. engr., Wis., Colombia. Engr. Integral S.A., Medellin, 1977-79, sr. design engr., 1980-86; rsch. asst. St. Anthony Falls Lab., Mpls., 1979-80; civil engr. Mead & Hunt Inc., Madison, Wis., 1986-89; sr. geotech. engr. Harza Engring. Co., Chgo., 1989—; prof. Escuela de Ingenieria de Antioquia, Medellin, 1981-86; designer numerous dams & underground structures. Contbr. articles to profl. jours. Mem. ASCE (rock mechanics com.), U.S. Com. Large Dams, U.S. Nat. Soc. Soil Mechanics and Found. Engring. Internat. Assn. Hydraulic Rsch., Phi Kappa Phi. Office: Harza Engring Co Sears Tower 233 S Wacker Dr Chicago IL 60606-6392

JARMER, GARY EDWARD, dean; b. Garden City, Kans., July 7, 1941; s. Cyril Leslie and Elizabeth Emma (Baldwin) J.; m. Sharon Kay Christesen, July 30, 1966; children: Mark, Travis. BS, Kans. State U., 1964, MS, 1968, PhD, 1974. Vocat. ag. tchr. Lyndon (Kans.) High Sch., 1964-66, Winfield (Kans.) High Sch., 1966-68; tchr. prod. ag. NCK Area Vo-Tech Sch., Beloit, Kans., 1968-70; dir. Unified Schs. Assn. Vocat. Edn., Hill City, Kans., 1970-72; instr. Kans. State U., Manhattan, 1972-74; prog. designer N.W. Kans. Edn. Svc. Ctr., Colby, Kans., 1974-77; with Jarmer Inc., Garden City, Kans., 1977-85; reg. sales mgr. Finn Distbg. Co., Wichita, Kans., 1985-88; dean tech. edn. Garden City (Kans.) Community Coll., 1988—; cons. in field; mem. commn. workforce skills in found. firms., Modernization Forum. Dir. Housing Authority, Garden City, 1975-77; chmn. bd. trustees Garden City Community Coll., 1983-88. Kans. State Dept. Edn. grantee, 1970-94, Kans. Tech. Ent. Corp. grantee, 1989. Mem. Kans. Vocat. Assn., Am. Vocat. Assn., Nat. Coun. for Occupational Edn., Southwind Country Club, K.C., Kiwanis (pres. 1980, lt. gov. 1983). Republican. Roman Catholic. Home: 702 Fleming St Garden City KS 67846-6219 Office: Garden City Community Coll 801 Campus Dr Garden City KS 67846-6333

JAROS, MIKE, state legislator, administrative assistant; b. Apr. 12, 1944; m. Annette Nordine; three children. BA, U. Minn., Duluth; Dist. 7B rep. Minn. Ho. of Reps., St. Paul, 1973-80, 85—; former chmn. higher edn. divsn. edn. com., Minn. Ho. of Reps., former mem. labor-mgmt. rels. com.; chmn. commerce and econ. devel.-internat. trade, technology and econ. devel. divsn. coms., mem. taxes com. Recipient Nat. Scholastic Press award, Nat. Latin Testing award. Office: 559 State Office Bldg Saint Paul MN 55155-1201*

JARRETT, ALEXIS, insurance professional; b. Independence, Kans., July 2, 1948; d. Robert Patterson and Betty June (Johnson) J.; m. Victor K. O'Yek, Apr. 12, 1987. BS, U. Minn., Duluth, 1970; postgrad., U. Mo.; student, John Marshall Law Sch., 1996—. Lic. in Property and Casualty Ins., Ind., Life and Health Ins., Ind., Life Underwriting Tng. Coun. fellow; cert. coach, Minn. Tchr. Esko (Minn.) Pub. Schs.; pvt. practice Schererville, Ind.; asst. dir. athletics, head coach basketball, softball and track, U. Mo., Columbia; women's basketball and softball color analyst, Regional Radio Sports, N.W. Ind. Contbr. articles on sports to newspapers. Sponsor Lake County (Ind.) H.S. Girls Basketball Banquet; mem. adv. bd. indsl. rsch. liason program Ind. U., Bloomington; bd. dirs. Samaritan Counseling Ctr. N.W. Ind., pres. 1994; bd. dirs. VNA Found., sec.-treas., 1994; mem. mktg. and promotional subcom. Ind. U. N.W. Scholarship Fundraiser Com.; celebrity Am. Heart Assn. Celebrity Dinner; v.p. S.W. Lake divsn. Am. Heart Assn., 1992, 93, 94. Mem. Nat. Life Underwriters (bd. dirs. N.W. Ind. chpt. 1995), Lake County Med. Soc. Alliance (pres.), Am. Bus. Women's Assn. (pres. New Image chpt. 1983, Woman of Yr. 1993), Ind. State Med. Assn. Alliance (chair media rels. 1990-91, 93-94, treas. 1992-93). Address: 2330 Wicker Blvd Schererville IN 46375-2810

JARRETT, GRACIE MAE, junior high school guidance counselor; b. Kansas City, Kans., Feb. 8, 1944; d. Hosea George Washington and Sylvia Ann (McCluney) Canady; m. Gennie Jarrett, Jr., July 11, 1987; children: Tony Jarrett, André D. Oden, Dale Marie Jarrett. AA, Coffeyville (Kans.) JUCO, 1964; BS, Kans. State Coll., 1968; MS, Troy (Ala.) State U., 1975. Cert. tchr.; cert. guidance counselor. Nurse aide, cashier Kansas City U. Med. Ctr., 1962-67; phys. edn. tchr. Kansas City Mo. Dist., 1968-73; sch. social worker Okaloosa County Schs., Ft. Walton Beach, Fla., 1973-76; spl. agt. tng. FBI, Quantico, Va., 1976; substitute tchr. Berryessa Sch. Dist., San Jose, Calif., 1976; personal lines underwriter Reliance Ins. Co., Shawnee Mission, Kans., 1977-81; vocat. edn. counselor Operation P.U.S.H., Kansas City, Mo., 1981; casemanager Kansas Youth Trust, Kansas City, Kans., 1982-83; guidance counselor Sch. Dist. #204, Bonner Springs, Kans., 1983—; trainer, spkr. U. Mo., Kansas City, 1989—; trainer Adult Illiteracy Program, Kansas City, 1993-94; del. Minority Leadership Tng., Bonner Spring, 1995. Co-sponsor, chaperone Spl. Olympics of Fla., Fort Walton Beach, 1973-75; vol. Community Action Program, Kansas City, 1978-82, Hotline, Kansas City, 1978-80; mem. Kansas Polit. Action, Bonner Springs, 1994—; nominating com. Senator Al Ramirez, Bonner Springs, 1991-93. Scholarship Delta Sigma Theta, 1964; named Kappa Sweetheart Kappa Alpha Psi. Mem. NEA, ACA, NAACP (bd. dirs. 1977—), Kans. Nat. Edn. Assn. (HCR commr. chair 1994-95, pres. 1990), Bonner Springs Edn. Assn. (pres., rep., del. 1982—), Delta Kappa Gamma. Baptist. Home: 1746 S 98th St Kansas City KS 66111-3528 Office: Robert E Clark Jr High 420 N Bluegrass St Bonner Springs KS 66012-1608

JARVI, NEEME, conductor; b. Tallinn, Estonia, June 7, 1937; came to U.S., 1980; s. August and Elss Jarvi; m. Lilia Jarvi, Sept. 2, 1961; children: Paavo, Kristjan, Maarika. Diploma in Music and Conducting, St. Petersburg (USSR) State Conservatorium, 1960; hon. doctorate, U. Aberdeen, Scotland, Music Conservatory of Talinn, Estonia, Gothenberg (Sweden) U. Condr. Estonian Radio Symphony Orch., 1960-63, chief condr., 1963-76; chief condr. Estonian State Opera, 1963-76, Estonian State Symphony, 1976-80, Gothenburg (Sweden) Symphony Orch., 1982—; prin. condr., music dir., condr. laureate Royal Scottish Orch., Glasgow, 1984-88; music dir. Detroit Symphony Orch., 1990—; prin. guest condr. Birmingham (Eng.) Symphony Orch., 1980-83; guest condr. N.Y. Philharm Orch., Boston Symphony Orch., Phila. Orch., Chgo. Symphony, Royal Concertgebow Amsterdam, The Philharmonia London, London Symphony, all Scandinavian Orchs., several operas at Met. Opera House, N.Y.C.; exclusive rec. contract with Chandos Records of Gt. Britain. Recs. include music of Ellington, Barber, Beach and Ives with DSO; complete symphonies of Sibelius, Stenhammar, Berwald, Dvorak, Gade, Svendsen, Brahms, R. Strauss, Glasounov, Eduard Tubin Schostakovitch, Prokoffiev, Rimski-Korsakov, Part, many others. Decorated knight comdr. North Star Order (Sweden); recipient 1st prize in conducting Accademia Nazionale di Santa Cecilia, 1971. Office: Detroit Symphony Orch Hall 3711 Woodward Ave Detroit MI 48201-2005*

JARVIS, RON, manufacturing engineer; b. Torrance, Calif., July 26, 1964. BS in Mfg. Engring., Brigham Young U., Provo, Utah, 1990. Engr. Winding Technol., Springfield, Utah, 1990; mfg. engr. Cessna Aircraft, Wichita, Kans., 1990-93; product engr. Vornado Air Circulation Sys., Inc., Wichita, 1993—. Mem. Soc. Mfg. Engrs., Soc. Plastics Engrs. LDS. Office: Vornado Air Circ Sys Inc 550 N 159th St E Wichita KS 67230-7517

JASHEL, LARRY STEVEN (L. STEVEN ROSE), entrepreneur, consultant; b. Dayton, Ohio, Jan. 21, 1950; s. Joseph John and Ruth Margarete (Race) J. Studetn, Harper Coll., Palatine, Ill., 1968-70. Pub.'s asst. Pub.'s Devel. Corp., Chgo., 1971-73; pub. rels. dir. Ill. Entertainer/Chgo. Star/Bankers' Guide, Chgo., 1973-76; v.p. Internat. Media Prodns., Inc., Chgo., 1976-78, Microdynamics Corp., Chgo., 1978-80; exec. v.p. Calif. Aqua Tech, Inc., L.A., 1980-82; pres., CEO Ra-Tel Comms. Corp., Chgo., 1982-88; founder Steven Rose Prodns. and L.S. Jashel Assocs., Chgo., 1988—; TV producer, dir., writer Ind. Broadcasting, Chgo., 1982—; radio producer, on-air personality Nat. Pub. Radio, Chgo. and Washington, 1982—; music producer for ind. rec. artists, Chgo., 1982—; cons. Corp. for Pub. Broadcasting, 1982—; speaker at librs. and seminars. Musician, singer, composer 173 copyrighted songs; author: Song of a New Age, 1990, A Bakers Dozen, 1995, (book and TV script) Lovestar--The Exciting Adventures, 1994, 95; author, producer, director Spuppets (puppets in space), 1996; published in The National Library of Poetry's Morning Song, 1996. Recipient Order of the Arrow, Boy Scouts Am., 1964, Blue Ribbon Athlete award, Midwest Sports Assn., 1968, Film Festival award 1984, Am. Svc. award Am. Svc. Corp., 1988; named delegation rep. to Presidential Inauguration Ball, Washington, 1980. Mem. Nat. Assn. Rec. Arts and Scis. (Grammy awards 1982, 87), Nat. Assn. Pvt. Enterprise, Smithsonian Instn. (nat. assoc.), Nat. Cable TV Assn., Internat. Assn. Bus., Eckankar. Office: Steven Rose Prodns 8285 Archer Rd Ste 1 Willow Springs IL 60480

JASIORKOWSKI, ROBERT LEE, real estate broker, computer consultant; b. Milw., Nov. 17, 1954; s. Thomas Joseph and Alice Rosemary (Lee) J. BA, U. Wis., Milw., 1987. Real estate broker, info. sys. mgr., property mgr. Nat. Realty Mgmt., Inc., Milw., 1990—; real estate broker ERA Worth Realty, Inc., Glendale, Wis., 1991-94; computer cons. Hometrak Realty, Milw., 1986-90. Mem. Nat. Assn. Realtors, Nat. Assn. Real Estate Appraisers (cert.), U. Wis.-Milw. Alumni Assn. (life). Republican. Home: 3561 S Honey Creek Dr Milwaukee WI 53220-1246 Office: Nat Realty Mgmt Inc 9800 W Bluemound Rd Wauwatosa WI 53226-4353

JASPER, DORIS J. BERRY, nurse; b. Banner, Miss., Sept. 12, 1933; d. William Richard and Lena Martha (Gambill) Berry; m. Lyman W. Jasper, Jan. 8, 1949; children: Richard L., Lynn William. Student, Blytheville (Ark.) Sch. Nursing, 1949, Purdue U., Westville, Ind., 1979-80, Lake Mich. Coll., Benton Harbor, 1977-80. Staff nurse St. Anthony's Hosp., Michigan City, Ind., 1951-66; pvt. duty nurse Michigan City, 1962-68; emergency rm. nurse St. Anthony's Hosp., 1968-74; charge nurse, emergency rm. nurse Meml. Hosp., Michigan City, 1974-75; pvt. duty nurse Three Oaks, Mich., 1972-84, Michigan City, 1981-88; staff nurse Alpha Christiansan Registry,

New Buffalo, Mich., 1988—; pvt. practice Three Oaks, 1989-90; owner, practitioner Jaspers Health Care, Three Oaks, 1991—; owner, mgr. D.J.'s Frolick Kennel; pvt. practice No. Ind., So. Mich.; co-owner, mgr. grain farm. Mem. Bus. and Profl. Women's Club, Inc. (legis. chair dist. 2 1987-88, rec. sec. dist. 2, exec. bd. mem.), Mich. Fedn. Bus. Profl. Women USA (legis. chair dist. 9), New Buffalo Area Bus. Profl. Women (legis. chair), Tenn. Walking Horse Assn., Smithsonian Inst. Republican. Baptist. Home and Office: 101 Jasper Dr Three Oaks MI 49128

JASSIN, LAWRENCE EVAN, sales professional; b. Rochester, N.Y., Nov. 28, 1960; s. Samuel and Jane (Owerbach) J.; m. Lisa Kay Thoburn, Mar. 18, 1989; children: Benjamin David, Elizabeth Ashley. BS in Chem. Engring., U. Wis., 1983. Mgr. tech. sales Ill. Water Treatment, Rockford, Ill., 1984-87; regional mgr. Pall Corp., Chgo., 1987-93; product mgr. Eichrom Industries, Inc., Darien, Ill., 1993—. Mem. U. Wis. Alumni Assn., Alpha Chi Sigma. Home: 1405 Abourndale Ct Wheeling IL 60090-5300

JASSO, PAUL J., manufacturing company executive; b. St. Louis, Apr. 28, 1934. Student, Washington U., St. Lois, 1950s. Pres. Empire Machine & Mfg. Co., St. Louis, 1973—. Served with U.S. Army, 1956-57. Roman Catholic. Office: Empire Machine & Mfg Co 10420 Trenton Ave Saint Louis MO 63132-1223

JASSO, WILLIAM GATTIS, public relations executive; b. Akron, Ohio, Mar. 2, 1953; s. Joseph and Jean E. (Gattis) J.; m. Jeanne Marie Taylor, Aug. 20, 1977; 1 child, Megan Elizabeth. BA in Communications, U. Akron; student Crisis Mgmt. Sch. and Advanced Pub. Affairs Sch., Fed. Emergency Mgmt. Agy.; student, Mich. State Sch. Bus., 1993. News dir. Sta. WHLO, Akron, 1972-81; news anchor, editor Sta. WNEO-TV, Northeast Ohio, 1978-81; govt. affairs mgr. Warner Cable Communications, Dublin, Ohio, 1981-83, corp. dir. pub. rels., 1983-85; v.p. communications Nat. Golf. Found., Jupiter, Fla., 1985-88; asst. to mayor City of Akron, 1988-94; dir. govt. affairs and media rels. Time Warner Cable of N.E. Ohio, Akron, 1994-95; dir. pub. affairs Time Warner Cable N.E. Ohio, 1995-96; v.p. pub. affairs, 1996—; guest lectr. U. Akron, Kent State U., 1988—; pub. rels. chmn. Ohio Sports Fest, 1988-90; motivator Youth Motivation Task Force, Akron, 1989—; City of Akron liaison NEC World Series of Golf, 1988-94; nat. selection panel mem. Golf Digest 100 Best Golf Courses in U.S., 1987—; organizer 1st Golf Summit, Westchester C. of C., N.Y., 1986. Editor: Golf Curriculum Kit, 1987, Golf Driving Range Manual, 1987, (mag.) GolfMarket Today, 1986-88, The Spirit of Akron, 1989; producer, reporter (documentary) John Lennon--Beatle Without A Country, 1975. Committeeman Great Trail Coun. Boys Scouts Am., 1989-91; bd. trustees All-Am. Soap Box Derby; mem. 1993-94 class Leadership Akron; bd. dirs. Akron Child Guidance Ctr., 1995—; mem. Akron Regional Devel. Bd. pub. affairs com. Recipient 6 awards AP, 1975-81, 8 awards Akron Press Club, 1974-81. Mem. Pub. Rels. Soc. Am. (accredited pres. Akron chpt. 1990-91, Presdl. Citation award 1993), Cable TV Pub. Affairs Assn. Office: Time Warner Cable NE Ohio Office of Mayor 1655 Brittain Rd Akron OH 44310-2700

JAUCH, ROBERT, state legislator; b. Wheaton, Ill., Nov. 22, 1945; married; 2 children. Student, U. Wis., Eau Claire, 1968-71, U. Wis., Superior, 1973. Mem. staff U.S. Rep. David Obey, Wausau, Wis., field rep.; mem. from dist. 73 Wis. State Assembly, Madison, 1982-86; mem. from dist. 25 Wis. State Senate, Madison, 1986—, mem. joint fin. com. Mem. VFW, Am. Legion. Office: Wis State Senate Box 635 5271 S Maple Dr Poplar WI 54864*

JAUQUET-KALINOSKI, BARBARA, library director; b. Crystal Falls, Mich., Mar. 12, 1948; d. Herbert Francis and Lenore Mary (Roell) Jauquet; m. Gregory Clem Kalinoski, Nov. 12, 1983; children: Stacia Amee, Sara Amee, Michael Thomas and Thomas Michael (twins.). BS, No. Mich. U., 1970; MLS, Western Mich. U., 1974. Adminstrv. asst. Mid-Peninsula Libr. System, Iron Mountain, Mich., 1970-74, asst. dir., 1975-79; periodical libr. U. Wis., Superior, 1980; dir. N.W. Regional Libr., Thief River Falls, Minn., 1981—; vice chmn. libr. devel. and svcs. adv. com. Minn. Dept. Edn., chmn. Clime com, LDS; chmn. planning, evaluation and reporting curriculum com. for sch. dist. Treas. St. Bernard's Home and Sch. Assn.; mem. Thief River Falls Acad. Boosters Club. Named Woman of Honor, AAUW, 1990. Mem. ALA, Minn. Libr. Assn. (pres.-elect, mem. of continuing edn. com.), Thief River Falls C. of C., Rotary (past pres.). Roman Catholic. Office: NW Regional Libr 101 1st St E Thief River Falls MN 56701-2041

JAW, ANDREW CHUNG-SHIANG, software analyst; b. Tainan, Taiwan, Feb. 10, 1953; came to U.S., 1978; s. Ping-Tsen and Pey-Yuh Jaw; m. Amy Chi, July 30, 1979; children: Andrew, Anfin, Audrey. BS in Mech. Engring., Tatung Inst. Tech., Taipei, Taiwan, 1974; MS in Metallurgical Engring., Poly. Inst. N.Y., 1981; MSEE, Syracuse U., 1987. Engr. Tatung Co., Taipei, 1976-78; sr. assoc. engr. IBM Corp., Endicott, N.Y., 1980-89, Rochester, Minn., 1990-91; software cons. A BOC Health Care Co., Madison, Wis., 1991-92; sr. software engr. A Rockwell Internat. Co., Milw., 1992-94; staff software analyst ARDIS Co., Lincolnshire, Ill., 1994—. Patentee in field. Recipient Cert. of Merit, Assembly of the State of N.Y., 1985; rsch. fellow Poly. Inst. N.Y., 1979. Mem. IEEE.

JAWOR, JOHN DAVID, stockbroker; b. Chgo., Apr. 24, 1955. BA, U. Mont., 1977. Sales rep. RR Donnelly, Chgo., 1977-89; nat. account salesperson Chgo. Press Corp., 1990-91; salesperson A.B. Dick, Chgo., 1991; stockbroker Dean Witter Reynolds, Riverwoods, Ill., 1992—. Mem. St. Barnabas Men's Club. Home: 9952 S Winchester Ave Chicago IL 60643-1808 Office: Dean Witter Reynolds PO Box 765 2500 Lake Cood Rd Riverwoods IL 60015

JAYE, DAVE, state legislator; b. Feb. 2, 1958. BA with hons., U. Mich., 1981, MA with hons., 1982. State rep. Dist. 26 Mich. Ho. of Reps., 1988-94, state rep. Dist. 32, 1995—; real estate broker, 1996—; mem. Liquor Control, Corps. & Fins. Coms. Mich. Ho. of Reps. Named Man of Yr., State Young Reps., 1985. Mem. Macomb County Taxpayers, Kiwanis, KC. Home: 53859 Luann Dr Shelby Township MI 48316-1950*

JEANSON, JOHN BOUDUIN, clothing designer; b. Rotterdam, The Netherlands, Dec. 26, 1927; came to U.S., 1961; s. Nicholaas Jacobus and Huberta Maria (Messelaar) J.; m. Jean Elizabeth Lavington, Dec. 25, 1957; children: Hans A., Frank G., Michael A., Sharon E., Thomas A., Judith A. Student in fashion and textile design, Govt. Acad., Utrecht, Holland, 1947; student, Charles Montaigne Acad., Paris, 1953. Designer N. V. Rocobé Mfg. Co., Utrecht, 1950-55, Textile Specialties Mfg. Co., Windsor, Ont., Can., 1955-61, Sacony Apparel Mfg. Co., Cheraw, S.C., 1961-63, Weatherbee Coats Inc., Youngstown, Ohio, 1963-71; mgr. design dept. Stahl Urban div. Kellwood, Brookhaven, Wis., 1971-83; dir. design dept. Oshkosh (Wis.) B'Gosh, Inc., 1983—. Mem. Internat. Designers Assn., K.C. (Grand Knight). Republican. Roman Catholic. Home & Office: Fox Hunt Tailors 450 McEntire Rd Tryon NC 28782

JECKELL, WILLIAM WILSON, retired financial executive and journalist; b. Youngstown, Ohio, Nov. 7, 1912; s. Charles and Grace Bell (Patterson) J.; m. Betty Virginia Smith, July 1, 1935; children: Judy, Jeana. BS in Journalism, Ohio State U., 1934. Adjuster Comml. Credit Co., Youngstown, 1934-36; unit mgr., office mgr. Comml. Credit Co., Pitts., 1936-44; office mgr. Comml. Credit Co., Columbus, Ohio, 1946-55; asst. divsn. mgr. Comml. Credit Co., Cin., 1955-57, divsn. v.p., 1957-73; pres., bd. dirs. Greenhills (Ohio) Jour., 1973-93; ret., 1993. Columnist, reporter Greenhills Jour., 1959—. Precinct exec. Rep. Party, Greenhills. Lt. USN, 1944-46. Mem. Am. Legion, Athletic Committeemen Ohio State, Elks, Chi Phi (nat. pres. 1969-73), Sigma Delta Chi. Episcopalian. Home: 417 Ingram Rd Cincinnati OH 45218-1137

JECKLIN, LOIS UNDERWOOD, art corporation executive, consultant; b. Manning, Iowa, Oct. 5, 1934; d. J.R. and Ruth O. (Austin) Underwood; m. Dirk C. Jecklin, June 24, 1955; children: Jennifer Anne, Ivan Peter. BA, State U. Iowa, 1992. Residency coord. Quad City Arts Coun., Rock Island, Ill., 1973-78; field rep. Affiliate Artists, Inc., N.Y.C., 1975-77; mgr., artist in residence Deere & Co., Moline, Ill., 1977-80; dir. Vis. Artist Series, Davenport, Iowa, 1978-81; pres. Vis. Artists, Inc., Davenport, 1981-88; pres., owner Jecklin Assocs., 1988—. asst. to exec. dir. Walter W. Naumburg Found., N.Y.C., 1990—; cons. writer's program St. Ambrose Coll., Davenport, 1981, 83, 85; mem. com. Iowa Arts Coun., Des Moines, 1983-84; panelist Chamber Music Am., N.Y.C., 1984, Pub. Art Conf., Cedar Rapids, Iowa, 1984; panelist, mem. com. Lt. Gov.'s Conf. on Iowa's Future, Des Moines, 1984; trustee Davenport Mus. Art, 1975—, Nature Conservancy Iowa, 1987-88; mem. steering com. Iowa Citizens for Arts, Des Moines, 1970-71; bd. dirs. Tri-City Symphony Orchestra Assn., Davenport, 1968-83; founding mem. Urban Design Council, HOME, City of Davenport Beautification Com., all Davenport, 1970-72; bd. gov. Am. Craft Mus., N.Y.C., 1995—. Recipient numerous awards Izaak Walton League, Davenport Art Gallery, Assn. for Retarded Citizens, Am. Heart Assn., Ill. Bur. Corrections, many others; LaVernes Noyes scholar, 1953-55. Mem. Nat. Assn. Performing Art's Mgrs. and Agents, Am. Symphony Orch. League, Crow Valley Golf Club, Outing Club, Rotary. Republican. Episcopalian. Home and Office: 2717 Nichols Ln Davenport IA 52803-3620

JEFFERIES, GREGORY SCOTT, professional baseball player; b. Burlingame, Calif., Aug. 1, 1967. With N.Y. Mets, 1985-91, Kansas City Royals, 1991-93, St. Louis Cardinals, 1993-94, Phila. Phillies, 1994—; mem. Nat. League All-Star Team, 1993-94; Appalachian League Player of Yr., 1985;named Carolina League MVP, 1986, Tex. League MVP, 1987. Office: Phila Phillies PO Box 7575 Philadelphia PA 19101*

JEFFERS, THOMAS LEE, accountant; b. Chgo., Oct. 18, 1956; s. Bruce R. and Georgia C. (Flagg) J.; m. Treva Marie Shipley, June 2, 1979 (div. 1992); children: Thomas L. II, Troy W. AS in Acctg., Ind. Vocat. Tech. Coll., 1985; BSBA, Thomas A. Edison State Coll., 1989. CPA, Ind. Mdse mgr. Volume Shoe Corp., Topeka, 1976-84; staff acct. J.L. Barr & Assocs., Terre Haute, Ind., 1985-86; founder, pres. Jeffers, Inc., Terre Haute, 1986—, Taxmasters, Inc., Terre Haute, 1992, Hoosier Tax Accts., Inc., 1994—. Mem. AICPA, Ind. CPA Soc., Nat. Assn. Tax Profls., Alpha Lambda Delta. Republican. Mormon. Office: Hoosier Tax Accts Inc 561 North 13th St Terre Haute IN 47807

JEFFERSON, DANIEL, manufacturing executive; b. Bismarck, N.D., Oct. 28, 1960; s. Bert and Irma (Long) K.; m. Jan Munn, Oct. 2, 1993. BA, U. N.D., 1982, postgrad., 1989—. Salesman Werik Pl., Bismarck, 1982-87, sales mgr., 1987-91, v.p. sales, 1991-96; sr. v.p. sales 1996—. Vol. St. Mary's Hosp., Bismarck Hist. Soc. Mem. NRA, Lions (sec./treas. 1992—), Phi Beta Kappa. Republican. Lutheran. Office: Werik Pl 2910 E Broadway Ave Bismarck ND 58501-5186

JEFFERSON, RICHARD H., state legislator; b. Jan. 31; m. Mary Louise Jefferson; five children. BS, Xavier U., New Orleans. Chemist (ret.) U.S. Bur. Mines; Dist. 58B rep. Minn. Ho. of Reps., St. Paul, 1986—; former mem. health and human svcs., housing, local govt., and redistricting coms., Minn. Ho. of Reps.; vice chmn. govt. op. and gaming-state govt. fin. divsn. com., mem. capital investment, and transp. and transit coms. Address: 577 State Off Bldg Saint Paul MN 55155*

JEFFRES, LEO WAYNE, communication educator; b. Bridgeport, NE, Oct. 3, 1944; s. Laurence Joseph and Edna Roberta (McCracken) J. BA in Journalism, U. Idaho, 1967; MA in Comm., U. Wash., 1968; PhD in Mass Comm., U. Minn., 1976. Asst. prof. Cleve. State U., 1976-80, assoc. prof., 1980-92, chmn. dept. comm., 1986-92, prof. comm., 1992—. Author: Mass Media Processes, 1994, Mass Media Processes and Effects, 1986; edi-tor: numerous articles, Journalists' Handbook, 1988. Fulbright scholar, Philippines, 1983-84. Mem. Midwest Assn. Pub. Opinion Rsch. (pres. 1987-88), Neighborhood Cmty. Press Assn. (founder), Soc. Profl. Jour-nalists (pres. Cleve. chpt. 1986-87). Democrat. Lutheran. Home: 5015 Bridge Ave Cleveland OH 44102-3341 Office: Cleve State U Dept Comm Cleveland OH 44115

JEFFREY-SMITH, LILLI ANN, biofeedback specialist, educator, administrator; b. Bedford, Ind., 1944; d. Charles Constantine and Adelai (Malon) Jeffrey-Smith. Grad. Ind. Bus. Coll., 1963; B.S., Ind. U., 1973; grad. Psychosomatic Medicine Clinic, Berkeley, Calif. (accredited by Albert Einstein Coll. Medicine); PhD in Behavioral Sci., Kennedy-Western U., 1988. Cert. biofeedback specialist. Project assoc., stress mgmt. clinician City of Indpls., 1973-79; cons. Airport Med. Clinic, Indpls., 1981; outreach coord. Abbot-Northwestern Hosp., Mpls., 1981; dir. biofeedback dept. Sister Kenney Inst., Mpls., 1979-81, Noran Neurol. Clinic, Mpls., 1981-83; instr., dir. Biofeedback Tng. and Treatment Ctr., Edina, Minn., 1979—; pres. Biofeedback Rsch. and Devel. Co. Ltd., Edina, 1983—; cons. to biofeedback depts. St. Joseph Hosp., Mankato, Minn., 1984—, Lakeview Clinic, Waconia, Minn., 1983, Psychiat. Clinic of Mankato, 1983—, Fairview Ridges Hosp., Burnsville, Minn., 1987—. Author, narrator health and wellness tape series. Mem. Republican Presdl. Task Force, 1984—, NSC, 1985; co-chmn. Mayor's Handicapped Task Force, Indpls., 1975; founder, pres. Miss Wheel Chair of Ind., Inc. Named Hon. Lt. Gov., State of Ind., 1978; given Key to the City of Indpls., 1973, Flag of the City of Indpls., 1975. Mem. Am. Inst. Stress, N.Y. Acad. Sci., NAFE, AAAS, AAUW, Edina C. of C., Minn. Women's Network, Biofeedback Soc. Am., Biofeedback Soc. Minn., Am. Assn. Control Tension, Am. Assn. Behavioral Therapists, Am. Assn. Biofeedback Clinicians, Nat. Assn. Women Bus. Owners, Soc. Open Focus and Tng. Rsch., Am. Assoc. of U. Woman, Nat. Assoc. of Female Execs., Assn. Trainers in Clin. Hypnosis, Internat. Stress and Tension Control Assn., Minn. Assn. Rehab. Providers, Nat. Assn. Exec. Women, Internat. Platform Assn. Avocations: music, stamp collecting, shooting, poetry. Office: Biofeedback Tng & Treatment Ctr 7300 France Ave S Ste 200 Minneapolis MN 55435-4542

JEFFRIES, THOMAS WILLIAM, microbiologist; b. New Orleans, Oct. 31, 1947; s. Charles William J. and Dorothy Ruth (Hibbs) Modlish; m. Giovanna Miceli, June 1, 1974; children: Angelica R., Carla Dorothy, Francesca Maria. BS, Calif. State U., Long Beach, 1969, MS, 1972; PhD, Rutgers U., 1975. Rsch. intern Rutgers U., New Brunswick, N.J., 1973-75; staff scientist Lawrence Livermore (Calif.) Lab., 1975-77; rsch. assoc. Columbia U., N.Y.C., 1977-79; microbiologist Forest Products Lab., Madison, Wis., 1979-84, rsch. microbiologist, 1984-86, supervisory microbiologist, 1986—; assoc. prof. U. Wis., Madison, 1991—. Fellow Internat. Acad. Wood Sci.; mem. AAAS, Am. Soc. for Microbiology (editorial bd. 1993-95), Am. Chem. Soc., Soc. for Indsl. Microbiology (editorial bd. 1992-95). Office: Forest Products Lab 1 Gifford Pinchot Dr Madison WI 53705-2366

JEFFRIES ASHFORD, ALECIA, accounting analyst; b. Chapel Hill, N.C., June 28, 1964; d. James William and Esther Jerlene (Hayes) J.; m. Jerry L. Ashford, Oct. 8, 1994. BS in Acctg., Elon Coll., 1987; postgrad., Lindenwood Coll., 1991—. With accounts receivable dept. Roche Biomed. Labs., Burlington, N.C., 1984-86; asst. mgr. Ashby's Ltd., Durham, N.C., 1987-88; placement dir. Rutledge Coll., Durham, 1988-89; cash mgmt. analyst DNS/MEMC Electronic Materials (formerly Monsanto Electronic, St. Peters, Mo., 1989, cost analyst, 1989-90; corp. property acct. DNS/MEMC Electronic Materials (formerly Monsanto Electronic Materials), St. Peters, Mo., 1990—; cost analyst Smiths Industries, Grand Rapids, Mich., 1992-94; fin. analyst United Techs. Automotive, Dearborn, Mich., 1994—. Bd. dirs. Grand Rapids Urban League, 1993; active Big Brother/Big Sister, Grand Rapids, 1993—; bd. dirs. fin. Grand Rapids Urban League, 1993—; cons. Grand Rapids Jr. Achievement, 1992—. Mem. NOW, NAFE, Nat. Assn. Accts., Inst. Mgmt. Accts., Profl. Women's Alliance. Home: 12970 E Outer Dr Detroit MI 48224-2731 Office: United Techs Automotive 5200 Auto Club Dr Dearborn MI 48126-4212

JEHN, BETTY L. (BETTY L. JAMES), retired computer science educator; b. Leesville, Ohio, Aug. 30, 1921; d. Earl James and Mary Caroline (Dolt) James; m. Lawrence A. Jehn, May 27, 1944; children: David, Judith, James, Paul, Joseph, Ann, Chris, Theresa, John. BA in History, U. Dayton, 1943, MS in History, 1970. Asst. libr. Dayton (Ohio) Pub. Libr., 1939-44, Providence Athenaeum, 1944-45; tchr. Centerville (Ohio) High Sch., 1971-82; adj. prof. computer sci. U. Dayton, 1982-88; ret., 1988; vice-chair Nat. Ednl. Computing Conf., 1984; chair nat. symposium Spl. Interest group Computer Sci. Edn., Atlanta, 1988. Co-author computer technology cards. Mem. Assn. Computing Machinery. Home: 6014 Aqua Pl Dayton OH 45459-2902 Office: U Dayton Computer Sci Dept Dayton OH 45469

JEHN, LAWRENCE ANDREW, computer science educator; b. Dayton, Ohio, Aug. 7, 1921; s. Arthur Francis and Alice Elizabeth (Gallagher) J.; m. Betty Lou James, May 27, 1944; children: David, Judith, James, Joseph, Paul, Ann, Theresa, Chris, John. BME, U. Dayton, 1943; postgrad., Brown U., 1944-45; MS, U. Mich., 1949, postgrad., 1949-50. Registered profl. engr., Ohio, Colo. Test engr. United Aircraft Products, Inc., Dayton, 1943-44; design engr. Am. Aircraft, Dayton, 1944, 45-46; math. instr. U. Dayton, 1946-47, asst. prof. math., 1950-56, assoc. prof. math., 1957-62, rsch. mathematician, 1962-67, prof. computer sci., 1967-89; chair computer sci., 1982-86; prof. emeritus U. Dayton, 1989—; rsch. mathematician U. Mich., Ann Arbor, 1956-57; chair computers in edn. div. Am. Soc. Engring. Edn., 1970-72, computer sci. conf., 1979, 86. Mem. Assn. Computing Machinery (chair computer sci. conf. steering com. 1987-89, chair computer sci. conf. 1979, 86). Home: 6014 Aqua Pl Dayton OH 45459-2902 Office: U Dayton Dept Computer Sci Dayton OH 45469-2160

JEKEL, JOSEPH FRANK, government official; b. Kansas City, Mo., Jan. 31, 1958; s. Herbert and Gertrud Ruth (Leiter) J. BA in Polit. Sci., Rockhurst Coll., 1980. Tax examiner IRS, Kansas City, Mo., 1982-82; benefit authorizer Social Security Adminstrn., Kansas City, Mo., 1982—. Mem. Greater Kansas City Mo. Young Reps. (program dir. 1989-90, 93-94, membership dir. 1988-89, sgt. at arms 1990-92), Johnson County Kans. Young Reps. (sec. 1994-95, treas. 1995—), Greater Kansas City Mo. Jr. C. of C. (sec. 1988-89, mgmt. devel. v.p. 1989-90, state dir. 1990-91), Kansas City JC Toastmasters. Republican. Jewish. Home: 9258 Reeder Dr Overland Park KS 66214-2130

JELINEK, RICHARD CARL, hospital management consultant company executive, educator; b. Czechoslovakia, Apr. 3, 1937; came to U.S., 1959; s. Jindrich Henry and Jarmila Jana (Ziska) J.; children: Valerie, Rick, Hope, Jan. BS in Indsl. Engring., U. Mich., 1961, MBA, 1962, PhD in Indsl. Engring., 1964. Project engr. U. Mich. Med. Ctr., Ann Arbor, 1959-63; asst. prof. indsl. engring. and hosp. adminstrn. U. Mich., Ann Arbor, 1964-67, assoc. prof., 1968-70; project engr. St. Joseph's Hosp., Ann Arbor, 1959-63, Ypsilanti (Mich.) State Hosp., 1961-62; co-founder, v.p. The Medicus Corp., Chgo., 1970-72; pres. Medicus Systems Corp., Evanston, Ill., 1972-74; pres., chief exec. officer The Medicus Corp., Evanston, 1974-77, Medicus Affiliates, Inc., Evanston, 1977-81; chmn., chief exec. officer Whittaker Medicus, Inc., Evanston, 1981-83, Mediflex Systems Corp., Medicus Systems Corp., Evanston, 1983-85, Jelinek, Inc., Medicus Systems Corp., Evanston, 1985—; mem. adv. coun. Health Program Systems Ctr. and div. Indian health USPHS, 1967-74; mem. research adv. com. Am. Nursing Found., 1969-72; prof. Coll. Nursing and Allied Health, Rush U., Chgo., 1973-75, prof. dept. health systems mgmt., 1975-88; complemental faculty mem. dept. health systems mgmt., 1988—, Pres.'s Pvt. Sector Survey on Cost Control, Automated Data Processing and Office Automation Task Force, 1982; adv. mem. Nat. Invitational Conf. on Nursing Productivity, Georgetown U., Washington, 1986; cons. and lectr. in field. Contbr. articles to profl. jours. Fellow U. Mich., 1959-61, W.K. Kellogg Bur. Hosp. Adminstrn., U. Mich., 1962-64; grantee HEW, 1965-68, 72-76, W.K. Kellogg Found., 1967-70. Mem. Am. Hosp. Assn., Am. Pub. Health Assn., Health Mgmt. Edn. Assn., Hosp. Mgmt. Systems Soc., Health Issues Study Soc., Am. Inst. Indsl. Engrs., Young Pres.'s Orgn., Chgo. Pres.' Orgn., World Bus. Council, Alpha Pi Mu, Beta Gamma Sigma, Phi Kappa Phi. Office: Medicus Systems Corp One Rotary Ctr Suite 400 Evanston IL 60201-4802

JELKEN, JAMES FRANKLIN, computer programmer; b. Akron, Iowa, Apr. 28, 1960; s. Dickie V. and Marjorie R. (Morehead) J.; m. Paula A. Van Wyhe, Dec. 7, 1991. BS, Oral Roberts U., 1982. CPCU. Sr. project coord. Berkley Info. Svcs., Luverne, Minn., 1982—. Bd. dirs. Green Earth Players, Luverne, Rock County Cmty. Libr., Luverne, 1993—. Mem. Data Processing Mgmt. Assn., Rotary Internat., Sioux Empire CPCU (chpt. pres. 1995-96). Home: 813 Blue Mound Luverne MN 56156 Office: Berkley Info Svcs PO Box 657 Luverne MN 56156

JELLEMA, JON, state legislator; b. Bloomington, Ind., Dec. 7, 1943; s. William Harry and Frances (Peters) J.; m. Betsy Zevalkink; children: Frances, Kate, Jon R., Elizabeth. BA, Calvin Coll., 1966; MA and ABD, Mich. State U., 1972. Prof. Grand Valley State U., Allendale, Mich., 1972-94; asst. dean William James Coll., Grand Valley State U., Allendale, 1986-87; dir. liberal studies program Grand Valley State U., Allendale, 1988-89, chmn. English dept., 1989-91, prof. English dept., 1991-94; mem. Mich. Ho. of Reps., Lansing, 1994—; mem. appropriations com., chmn. subcom. on transp., vice chair pub. health subcom. Pres. Grand Haven (Mich.) Pub. Sch. Bd., 1972-84; founder North Ottawa Cmty. Coalition. Mem. Assn. for Values in Higher Edn., Modern Lang. Assn., Mich. Assn. Sch. Bds., Phi Kappa Phi. Home: 510 Park Ave Grand Haven MI 49417-2107 Office: 711 Olds Plaza Bldg Lansing MI 48909

JELLICO, NANCY ROSE, painter, sculptor; b. LaGrange, Ga., Sept. 22, 1939; d. James Davis and Mary Myrtle (Capley) Norris; m. John Anthony Jellico, Dec. 22, 1960 (div. 1981); children: Janice Lee, Carol Anne, Kenneth Alan; m. Glenn Howard Hildebrandt, May 2, 1987 (div. 1992). Diploma, Colo. Inst. Art, 1960. registrar Colo. Inst. Art., Denver, 1961-64, instr., 1964-65. Group exhibits include Gene Autry Western Heritage Mus., L.A., 1994-95, Wyo. Meml. Pioneer Mus., Douglas, 1992-95, Tucson Mus. Art, 1991-94, Murisaki Gallery, Tokyo, 1992, numerous others; commd. works include The Upjohn Co., Kalamazoo, 1983-90, St. Thomas Theol. Sem., Denver, 1985, 88, 90, Pro Rodeo Hall Fame & Mus. Am. Cowboy, Colorado Springs, 1983; illustrator featured articles numerous publs. including Art of the West mag., 1990, Equine Images mag., 1989, Cowboy Internat. mag., 1987, Southwest Art mag., 1986, Wild West mag., 1995. Mem. Pastel Soc. Am. (assoc.), Nat. Soc. Painters in Casein and Acrylic (assoc.), Pastel Soc. S.W., Knickerbocker Artists (assoc.). Office: Jellico Studio Western Art HC 86 Box 49A Amelia NE 68711-9711

JELLISON, JAMES LOGAN, II, retired banker; b. Chgo., June 3, 1922; s. James Logan and Ethel (Reynolds) J.; Ph.B., DePaul U., Chgo., 1943; B.M.E., Northwestern U., 1948; M.B.A., U. Louisville, 1959; m. Charlotte Jean Scott, Oct. 20, 1951; children—James Logan, Jeanene Lynn, Jennifer Lee. Mgr. mktg. research Gen. Electric Co., Holland, Mich., 1961-85; fin. svcs. rep. D&N Savs. Bank, 1985-90; ret., 1990—. State and County Conv. del. Republican Party; bd. dirs. Ottawa County ARC; chmn. bd. govs. Fountain St. Ch., Grand Rapids, Mich. Served to 1st lt. AUS, 1943-46, ETO. Decorated Bronze Star, Purple Heart; registered profl. engr. Mem. Am. Mktg. Assn., Am. Legion, Elfun Soc., Kappa Sigma. Republican. Home: 729 Lugers Rd Holland MI 49423-6845

JENEFSKY, JACK, wholesale company executive; b. Dayton, Ohio, Oct. 27, 1919; s. David and Anna (Saeks) J.; m. Beverly J. Mueller, Feb. 23, 1962; 1 child, Anna Elizabeth; 1 stepchild, Cathryn Jean Mueller. BSBA, Ohio State U., 1941; postgrad. Harvard Bus. Sch., 1943; MA in Econs., U. Dayton, 1948. Surplus broker, Dayton, 1946-48; sales rep. Remington Rand-Univac, Dayton, 1949-56, mgr. AF account, 1957-59, br. mgr. Dayton, 1960-61, regional mktg. cons. Midwest region, Dayton, 1962-63; pres. Bowman Supply Co., Dayton, 1963—. Selection adv. bd. Air Force Acad., 3d congl. dist., chmn., 1974-82; chmn. 3d. dist. screening bds. Mil. Acad., 1976-82; coord. Great Lakes region, res. assistance program CAP, 1970-73. Served from pvt. to capt. USAAF, 1942-46; CBI, maj. USAF, 1951-53; col Res. Mem. Air Force Assn. (comdr. Ohio wing 1957-58, 58-59), Res. Officers Assn. (pres. Ohio dept. 1956-57, nat. council 1957-58, chmn. research and devel. com. 1961-62), Dayton Area C. of C. (chmn. spl. events com. 1970-72, chmn. rsch. com. on mil. affairs 1983-87), Miami Valley Mil. Affairs Assn. (trustee 1985—, pres. bd. trustees 1987-88), Ohio State U. Alumni Assn. (pres. Montgomery County, Ohio, 1959-60), Nat. Sojourners (pres. Dayton 1961-62). Jewish. Club: Harvard Bus. Sch. Dayton (pres. 1961-62, chmn, selection com., Fed. Govt. Employee of Yr 1991, 92). Lodge: Lions. Home: 136 Briar Heath Cir Dayton OH 45415-2601 Office: Bowman Supply Co PO Box 1404 Dayton OH 45401-1404

JENG, TZYY-WEN, biochemist; b. Taichung, Taiwan, Nov. 2, 1947; came to U.S., 1974; s. Ching-Po and Yu-Ju (Wong) J.; m. Kwan-Yee Sum; children: Howard L., Way A. BS, Nat. Taiwan U., Taipei, 1970; PhD, U. Calif., Berkeley, 1978. Rsch. assoc. U. Ariz., Tucson, 1979-84, rsch. asst. prof., 1984-86, rsch. specialist and rsch. asst. prof., 1986-88; sr. rsch. biochemist Abbott Labs., Abbott Park, Ill., 1988-90, rsch. investigator, 1991-92, assoc.

rsch. fellow, 1992—. Author: Natural Toxins, 1980; contbr. articles to Jour. Molecular Biology. Wilhelm Bernard Fund grantee Internat. Congress on Electron Microscopy, 1982. Mem. N.Y. Acad. Scis. Office: Abbott Labs Apt 20 100 Abbott Park Rd Abbott Park IL 60064-3500

JENKINS, ANTHONY CURTIS, sales executive; b. Kirkwood, Mo., Apr. 16, 1958; s. Allen C. and Phyllis K. (Kley) J.; m. Angela K. Roberts, Sept. 17, 1983. BS, Maryville U., 1982, MS, 1985. Merchandising mgr. CMC Corp., St. Louis, 1980-87; v.p. Cellular Hotline, St. Louis, 1988-89; v.p. sales GPX, Inc., St. Louis, 1990—; officer exec. com., Hagemeyer Consumer Electronics, Inc. Roman Catholic.

JENKINS, BRIEN LEE, manufacturing supervisor; b. St. Joseph, Mich., Feb. 3, 1955. AS, Lake Mich. Coll., Benton Harbor, Mich., 1988. Maintenance technician Gast Mfg., Benton Harbor, Mich., 1974-82; electrician Weldun Internat., Bridgman, Mich., 1982-84; supervisor Weldun Internat., Bridgman, 1984—; mem. tech. bd. Lake Mich. Coll. Leader Youth Group, local ch.; tchr. 11th grade. Recipient Achievement awards Dale Carnegie Inst. Mem. Berrien County Sportsman Club. Republican. Office: Weldun Internat 9850 Red Arrow Hwy Bridgman MI 49106-9710

JENKINS, FRED WILLIAM, librarian; b. Cin., Apr. 13, 1957; s. Frederick Edwin and Ethel Mae Jenkins; m. Nancy Diane Courtney, Oct. 31, 1992. BA in Classics, U. Cin., 1979; AM in Classics, U. Ill., 1981, PhD in Classical Philology, 1985, MS in Libr. and Info. Sci., 1986. Historical collections cataloger Coll. of Physicians of Phila., 1986-87; catalog/rare book libr. U. Dayton, Ohio, 1987-96, coord. and head of collection mgmt., 1996—. Author: Classical Studies: A Guide to the Reference Literature, 1996; contbr. articles to profl. jours. Mem. Am. Philol. Assn., Am. Soc. Papyrologists, Acad. Libr. Assn. Ohio (mem. program com. 1991-93, Rsch. award 1993), Assn. Coll. and Rsch. Librs. (WESS classical, medieval and renaissance discussion group 1994), Phi Beta Kappa. Home: 209 James St Dayton OH 45410 Office: U Dayton 300 College Park Dayton OH 45469-1360

JENKINS, GEORGE HENRY, photographer, educator, writer; b. Shanghai, China, Oct. 24, 1929 (parents Am. citizens); s. Clarence O. and Efransinia M. (Pomorenkoff) J.; m. Madge Marie Vickroy, Aug. 19, 1967 (div. 1991); children: George, Alan, Deborah, Douglas; m. Patricia Pietras, Aug. 5, 1992. Grad. N.Y. Inst. Photography, 1952; student Purdue U., 1952-55; student Ind. U., 1955-58, BBA, Ind. No. U., 1972; MEd, Wayne State U., 1976, PhD, 1985; PhD, Columbia Pacific U., 1984. Cert. data processor, data educator, sys. profl. Photographer, Ft. Wayne (Ind.) Jour.-Gazette, 1952-55; computer programer GE Co., Ft. Wayne, 1955-61; data processing mgr. Columbia Record Club subs. CBS, Terre Haute, Ind., 1961-63; adminstrv. coord. Capital Record Club, Scranton, Pa. and Toronto, Ont., Can., 1963-64; mktg. sys. analyst Xerox Corp., Detroit, 1964-66; dir. sys. and data processing Nicholson File Co., Anderson, Ind., 1966-69; hosp. adminstr. Wayne County Gen. Hosp., Eloise, Mich., 1969-78; asst. prof. bus. Western Washington U., Bellingham, 1978-80; asst. prof. Lima (Ohio) Tech. Coll., 1980-83; prof. U. Findlay (Ohio), 1983-96; freelance photographer, 1969—, writer/prodr., 1984—. Author: The Principals of Wedding Photography, 1977, Training Needs Assessment of the Business Systems Analysis Profession, 1986, Data Processing Policy and Procedure Manual, 1991, Information Systems Policy and Procedure Manual, 1996. Chmn. supervisory bd. Eloise Credit Union, 1972-76. Served with USAF, 1948-52. Mem. Photog. Soc. Gt. Britain, Photog. Soc. Am., Am. Inst. Indsl. Engrs., Data Processing Mgmt. Assn. of Lima (pres. 1984-85), 8-16 Film and Video Movie Makers Club, Detroit Yacht Club. Home: 4526 W Central Ave Toledo OH 43615-1676 also: 404 Fedhaven Rd Fedhaven FL 33854-9075

JENKINS, JAMES WILLIAM, osteopath; b. Columbus, Ohio, May 15, 1953; s. William Harvey and Irene Barbara (Kacsor) J.; m. Deborah Susan Dorrance, June 16, 1987. BA in Biology, Calif. State U., Fullerton, 1976; DO, Coll. Osteopathic Med. Pacific, 1984; diploma in emergency medicine, Ohio State U., 1988. Intern Warren (Ohio) Gen. Hosp., 1984-85; resident in emergency medicine Meml. Osteopathic Hosp., York, Pa., 1985-87; rsch. fellow, clin. instr. Coll. Medicine, Ohio State U., Columbus, 1987-88; clin. emergency physician, med. edn. coord. emergency dept. Dr.'s Hosp., Columbus, 1988-89; med. dir. emergency dept. Greenfield (Ohio) Area Med. Ctr., 1989-93, clin. emergency/trauma physician, 1991-93; med. dir. Chillocothe (Ohio) Correctional Inst., 1993—; emergency med. svc. med. advisor Franklin Twp. Fire Dept., Columbus, 1988-89; clin. asst. prof. Coll. Osteo. Medicine Pacific, Pomona, Calif., 1989. Contbr. articles to profl. publs., chpt. to book. Mem. CPR com. ARC, Santa Ana, Calif., 1978-81; instr. trainer Am. Heart Assn., Santa Ana, 1972-80; instr., course coord. basic trauma life support Am. Coll. Emergency Physicians, Columbus, 1988—. Rsch. grantee Emergency Medicine Found., 1988, Kellogg Found., 1979-80; recipient rsch. fellow award Emergency Medicine Residents Ohio, 1988, Armstrong Lit. award, 1980. Mem. Am. Coll. Emergency Physicians, Am. Osteo. Assn., Beta Beta Beta.

JENKINS, MARILYN ELIZABETH, pediatric burn nurse, administrator; b. Cin., Dec. 21, 1942; d. C. William and Rosemary H. (Moorman) Barkalow; m. John F. Jenkins, Apr. 8, 1967 (div. 1983). Diploma, Good Samaritan Hosp., Cin., 1963; BA in Psychology with honors, Calif. State U., Sacramento, 1981; MBA, U. Cin., 1989; postgrad., Bellarmine Coll., Louisville, 1991—. RN, Ohio, Calif.; cert. nursing adminstr.; cert. BLS, ACLS, ATLS, ABLS, PALS. Team leader surg. unit St. Mary's Hosp., Cin., 1962-64, Johns Hopkins Hosp., Balt., 1964; hosp. supr. Cin. Gen. Hosp., 1965-67, 70; nurse respiratory ICU Tucson Med. Ctr., 1967-68; team leader, charge nurse Santa Clara Valley Med. Ctr., San Jose, Calif., 1968-69, 74-77; clin. rsch. nurse Shriners Burns Inst., Cin., 1982-88, dir. inpatient nursing, 1988-92, assoc. dir. clin. rsch., 1991, dir. nursing, 1992—; mem. clin. faculty U. Cin. Coll. Nursing and Health, 1994—; presenter in field. Contbr. chpts. to books, articles to profl. jours. Mem. adv. com. Mt. St. Joseph Coll. Nursing, 1994—. Recipient numerous grants. Mem. AACN, Am. Burn Assn. (mem. com. for burn ctr. verification), Am. Soc. Parenteral and Enteral Nutrition (Nursing Discipline award for rsch. 1989, 91), Am. Assn. Respiratory Care, Internat. Soc. for Burn Injuries, Nat. Flight Nurses Assn., Assn. for Care of Children's Health, Ohio Soc. for Parenteral and Enteral Nutrition, Phi Kappa Phi, Sigma Theta Tau. Home: 3059 Queen City Ave Cincinnati OH 45238-2432

JENKINS, SPEIGHT, opera company executive, writer; b. Dallas, Jan. 31, 1937; s. Speight and Sara (Baird) J.; m. Linda Ann Sands, Sept. 6, 1966; children: Linda Leonie, Speight. B.A., U. Tex.-Austin, 1957; LL.B., Columbia U., 1961; DMus (hon.), U. Puget Sound, 1992; HHD, Seattle U., 1992. News and reports editor Opera News, N.Y.C., 1967-73; music critic N.Y. Post, N.Y.C., 1973-81; TV host Live from the Met, Met. Opera, N.Y.C., 1981-83; gen. dir. Seattle Opera, 1983—; classical music editor Record World, N.Y.C., 1973-81; contbg. editor Ovation Mag., N.Y.C., 1980—, Opera Quar., Los Angeles, 1982—. Served to capt. U.S. Army, 1961-66. Recipient Emmy award for Met. Opera telecast La Boheme TV Acad. Arts and Scis., 1982. Mem. Phi Beta Kappa Assocs. Presbyterian. Home: 903 Harvard Ave E Seattle WA 98102-4561 Office: Seattle Opera Assn PO Box 9248 Seattle WA 98109-0248

JENKINS, WALTER DONALD, real estate executive; b. Lockport, N.Y.; s. Walter Kimball and Mary Elizabeth (Erler) J.; m. Teda Anne Yelton, May 21, 1977; children: Benjamin Donald, Andrew Kimball, Natalie Anne. BA, U. Ill., 1976. Draftsman Skidmore, Owings & Merrill, Chgo., 1976; constrn. sales Ramm Brick and Material, La Grange, 1976-77; supt., project mgr. U.S. Home Corp., Hanover Park, 1977-78; asst. project mgr. Morse Diesel Inc., Chgo., 1979-81; project mgr. La Salle Ptnrs. Inc., Chgo., 1981-86, Inland Constrn. Co., Chgo., 1986-89; M.W. region constrn. mgr. Embrey Investment Inc., 1989-91; sr. v.p. Equis Project Mgmt., Chgo., 1991—. Deacon 1st Congregational Ch., LaGrange, Ill. Mem. The Phoenix Soc., La Grange Hist. Soc. Republican. Office: Equis Project Mgmt 321 N Clark St Ste 1000 Chicago IL 60610-4715

JENNER, BILL EDWIN, computer engineer; b. Freeport, Ill., Dec. 23, 1943. B, No. Ill. U., 1974. Mgr. engring. adminstrn. Ingersoll Milling Machine, Rockford, Ill., 1963-85; mgr. computer ops. Mattison Techs., Inc., Rockford, Ill., 1985—. Bd. dirs. Rockford Jr. Coll., 1990—, Rockford Little League, 1992—. Republican. Baptist.

JENNER, WILLIAM ALEXANDER, meteorologist, educator; b. Indianola, Iowa, Nov. 10, 1915; s. Edwin Alexander and Elizabeth May (Brown) J., m. Jean Norden, Sept. 1, 1946; children: Carol Beth, Paul William, Susan Lynn. AB, Cen. Meth. Coll., Mo., 1938; certificate meteorology U. Chgo., 1943; MEd, U. Mo., 1947; postgrad. Am. U., 1951-58. Instr. U. Mo., 1946-47; rsch. meteorologist U.S. Weather Bur., Chgo., 1947-49; staff Hdqrs. Air Weather Svc., Andrews AFB, Md., 1949-58, Scott AFB, Ill., 1958-84, dir. tng., 1960-84. Mem. O'Fallon (Ill.) Twp. High Sch. Bd. Edn., 1962—, sec., 1964-71, pres., 1971-83, 1985-87, 93—, v.p., 1990-93; pres. St. Clair County Regional Vocat. System Bd., 1986-89, active, 1986—; vice chmn. southwestern div. Ill. Assn. Sch. Bds., 1987-89, chmn., 1989-95, dir., 1994—; comdr. 507th Fighter Group Assn. Inc., 1987-89; mem. O'Fallon Planning Commn., 1973-84, sec., 1979-81, sub-div. chmn., 1978-84; alderman City of O'Fallon, 1984-93; elected mem. gov. bd. Belleville Area Spl. Svcs. Coop., 1996. With AUS, 1942-46. Recipient Disting. Svc. award O'Fallon PTA, 1968, Disting. Svc. award City of O'Fallon, 1985, Community Svc. award O'Fallon Toastmasters Club, 1991, Master Bd. Mem. award Ill. Assn. Sch. Bds., 1991, award of Excellence O'Fallon C. of C., 1991. Merit cert. St. Clair County, 1987, Exceptional Civilian Svc. award Dept. Air Force, 1984, Jenmer Award established by Air Weather Svc., 1984. Fellow Am. Meteorol. Soc.; mem. APA, Am. Psychol. Soc., Wilson Ornithol. Soc., Am. Philatelic Soc., Am. Philatelic Congress, Am. Meteorol. Soc., AAAS, Nat. Soc. Study Edn., Ill. Assn. Sch. Bds. (bd. dirs. 1994—), Nat. Audubon Soc., Nat. Arbor Day Found., Tree City USA, Nat. Parks and Conservation Assn., Nat. Wildlife Fedn., Nat. Resources Defense Coun., Nature Conservancy, Vt. Inst. Natural Sci., Leadership St. Louis., The World Wildlife Fund, N.Y. Acad. Scis., Internat. Platform Assn., Am. Legion, The Wilderness Soc., The Wildlife Conservation Soc., Rails to Trails Conservancy, Phi Delta Kappa, Psi Chi. Club: O'Fallon Sportsmen's. Lodges: Masons, Shriners, Sierra. Home: 307 Alma St O'Fallon IL 62269

JENNETTEN, JOHN PETER, higher education executive; b. Belleville, Ill., Sept. 21, 1943; s. Peter Nicholas and Marie Ann (Wienstroer) J.; m. Judi Delores Grasher, June 22, 1968; children: Paul, Patrick. BA, Quincy (Ill.) U., 1965; PhD in Higher Edn., So. Ill. U., 1974. Tchr. Mater Dei H.S., Breese, Ill., 1965-69, Ferguson-Florissant (Mo.) Schs., 1969-70; dir. fin. aid officer So. Ill. U., Edwardsville, 1972-91; chief program officer Ill. Student Assistance Commn., Deerfield, Ill., 1991—; cons. Dept. of Edn., Washington, 1976-80. Mem. Ill. Assn. of Student Fin. Aid Adminstrs. (pres. 1990-91, v.p.), Midwest Assn. of Student Fin. Aid Adminstrn. Roman Catholic. Home: 1106 Pine Tree Ln Libertyville IL 60048 Office: Ill Student Assistance Commn 1755 Lake Cook Rd Deerfield IL 60015

JENNINGS, JOSEPH N., stockbroker; b. Independence, Kans., Aug. 9, 1943. Student, Nichols Coll., 1961-64; BS, Detroit Inst. Tech., 1967; post-grad., Wayne Coll., 1969. Lic. N.Y. Stock Exch. Mgr. Detroit Bank & Trust, 1967; computer salesperson NCR, Detroit, 1969-71; stockbroker Watling Lurchin, Detroit, 1971-79, Dean Witter Reynolds, Detroit, 1979—. Councilman Grosse Pointe (Mich.) City Coun., 1993—. Sgt. U.S. Army, 1967-69, Vietnam. Mem. Am. Legion. Republican. Episcopalian. Home: 16910 Village Ln Grosse Pointe MI 48230-1550 Office: Dean Witter Reynolds 333 W Fort St Detroit MI 48226-3134

JENNINGS, LOREN G., state legislator, business owner; b. June 1951; m. Bonnie Jennings. Student, Vocat.-Tech. Sch. Bus. owner; Dist. 18B rep. Minn. Ho. of Reps., St. Paul, 1984—; former vice chmn. appropriations com., Minn. Ho. of Reps., former mem. environ. and natural resources, housing and regulated industries coms.; vice chmn. health and human svcs.-human svcs. fin. divsn., mem. fin. instns. and ins. and regulated industries and energy coms. Office: PO Box 27 Rush City MN 55069-0027*

JENNINGS, MARY ELLEN, journalist; b. St. Louis, Feb. 12, 1957; d. John Joseph and Marcella Mary (Ebers) Schwarz; m. Marc Emery Jennings, Aug. 26, 1978; children: Katherine Anne, Glen Emery. B in Comms., U. Louisville, 1984. Copywriter Reston Publishing, Fort Lee, N.J., 1981-83; reporter, editor Courier-Journal, Louisville, Ky., 1983-92; reporter courts Cin. Enquirer, Cin., 1992-96; freelance writer, 1996—. Rschr., interviewer: (play) Digging In, 1987. Com. mem. Mt. Washington Elem. Sch., Cin., 1993-95. Mem. Soc. Profl. Journalists (Best in Bus. Reporting award 1992). Democrat.

JENNINGS, NANCY ANN, retired elementary education educator; b. Bristow, Okla., July 11, 1932; d. John Linard and Charlie Estelle (Hooper) Stucker; m. Jerald Leon Jennings, June 4, 1951; children: Jan, Catherine Jennings Hackman, Elizabeth Jennings Pineda. BS, U. Okla., 1956; MS, Washburn U., Topeka, Kans., 1974. Cert. elem. tchr., Kans. Tchr. Whitson Grade Sch. Dist. 501, Topeka, 1970-75, Delia Grade Sch Dist. 321, St. Marys, Kans., 1978-79, Silver Lake (Kans.) Grade Sch. Dist. 372, 1979-85, ret., 1985. Mem. Kans. Hist. Soc. Mem. NEA (life), AAUW (bd. dirs.), DAR (regent Topeka chpt. 1989-91, sec.-treas. N.E. dist. Kans. 1992-95, chmn. pres.-gen.'s project state com. 1992-95), Topeka Area Ret. Tchrs. Assn. (v.p. 1992-93), Internat. Reading Assn. (sec. 1983-84), Topeka Aux. Kans. Engring. Soc. (pres. 1987-88), Woman's Club (2d v.p. 1989-91), PEO Kans. (corr. sec. 1993—, guard 1994—, pres. 1995-97), Alpha Delta Kappa (pres. 1989-91), Kappa Delta Pi, Alpha Phi (2d v.p. 1989-90). Presbyterian. Home: 11340 NW 13th St Topeka KS 66615-9620

JENNINGS, STEPHEN GRANT, academic administrator; b. Indpls., Dec. 6, 1946; s. Grant Orville and Helen Zura (MacDonald) J.; m. Sarah Ferguson, Apr. 26, 1969; children: Amy Christina, Meredith Zoe. BA, Trinity U., 1968; MS, Miami U., Oxford, Ohio, 1970; PhD, U. Ga., 1976; diploma, Harvard U., 1982. Asst. dean for resident life So. Meth. U., Dallas, 1970-73; asst. dir. housing U. Ga., Athens, 1973-76; assoc. dean students Tulane U., New Orleans, 1976-80; v.p. student svcs. Furman U., Greenville, S.C., 1980-83; pres. Coll. of Ozarks, Point Lookout, Mo., 1983-87, Simpson Coll., Indianola, Iowa, 1987—; instnl. cons. Am. Coll. in London, 1995; bd. dirs. Centerre Bank, Branson, Mo., Homeland Bank, Indianola. Bd. dirs. United Way of Cen. Iowa, Iowa Sci. Ctr. Mem. Coun. Ind. Colls., Nat. Assn. Schs., Colls. and Univs. (bd. dirs. 1993—), Nat. Assn. Intercollegiate Athletics (coun. of pres. 1983-87), So. Assn. Colls. and Schs. (vis. teams 1982—), North Cen. Assn. Colls. and Schs. (vis. teams 1989—), So. Assn. Coll. Student Pers. (pres. 1983), Harvard U. Alumni Assn. (class rep.), Rotary (treas. Branson club 1986-87, Indianola club 1987—), Sigma Alpha Epsilon. Office: Simpson Coll Office of the Pres 701 N C St Indianola IA 50125-1202

JENNISON, ROBIN L., state legislator; s. Denise Jennison. Grad., Fort Hayes State U. Kans. state rep. Dist. 117, 1990—, farmer, stockman. Mem. Kans. Farm Bur., Kans. Livestock Assn., Kans. Wheat Growers Assn. Home: RR 1 Box 132 Healy KS 67850-9509*

JENS, ELIZABETH LEE SHAFER (MRS. ARTHUR M. JENS, JR.), civic worker; b. Monroe, Mich., Jan. 25, 1915; d. Frank Lee and Mary (Bogard) Shafer; m. Arthur M. Jens, Jr., Aug. 14, 1937; children: Timothy V., Christopher E., Jeffrey A. Student, Kalamazoo Coll., 1932-34, U. Wis., 1935, Northwestern U., 1934-36, BS, 1936; postgrad. Wheaton Coll., 1965; Lic. Practical Nurse, Triton Coll., 1968-69; Gray lady, Hines, (Ill.) Hosp., 1948-49, 51-53; vol. Elgin (Ill.) State Hosp., 1958-72; writer Newsletter Vol. Planning Coun., 1960-62; mem. Family Svc. Assn. Du Page County; vol. coord., chmn. bd. dirs., treas. Thursday Evening Club, social club for recovering mental patients Du Page County, 1966—; vol. FISH orgn., 1973-84. Bd. dirs. Du Page County Mental Health Soc., 1962-68, sec., 1963-64, 65-68, chmn. forgotten patient com., 1963-68, chmn. new projects, 1965-68; co-chmn. Glen Ellyn unit Cen. Du Page Hosp. Assn. Women's Aux., 1959-60; bd. dirs. chmn. com. on pesticides, Ill. Audubon Soc., 1963-73; mem. Ill. Pesticide Control Com., 1963-73, Citizens Com. Dutch Elm Disease, Glen Ellyn, 1960; bd. dirs. Natural Resources Coun. Ill., 1961-67, sec., 1961-64; bd. dirs. Du Page Art League, 1958-68, chmn. bd., 1961-63, Paint-out chairperson, 1968-84, 91—, chmn. new bldg. com., 1968-75, Best in Show award 1991; bd. dirs. mem. planning com., publicity chmn. Du Page Fine Arts Assn., 1965-67; bd. dirs. Friends Libr. Glen Ellyn, 1967-68; mem. adv. bd. Rachel Carson Trust for Living Environment 1971-74; bd. dirs. Mental Health Assn. of Du Page, 1973—, sec., 1973-75, pres., 1980-81, chmn. community liaison, 1981—, chmn. action group, 1976—; mem. Du Page Subarea adv. coun. Suburban Cook County-Du Page County Health Systems Agy., 1977-83; bd. dirs. Du Page County Comprehensive Health Planning Agy., 1976, DuPage County Bd. of Health, 1987-95; mem. DuPage County Mental Health Adv. Bd., 1977—; mem. com. on midlife and older women Ill. Commn. on Status of Women, 1978-85; bd. dirs., publicity chmn., DuPage County Coun. Vol. Coords., 1977-78; bd. dirs., membership chmn. Homemakers Equal Rights Assn. in DuPage County, 1979-84; publicity chmn., v.p. Homemakers Coalition for Equal Rights, 1984—, pres. 1986—; mem. ERA Ill. Bd., 1987—, v.p. 1994—; mem. DuPage County Health Planning Coun., 1984-94, chairperson task force on residences for mentally ill, 1990-93; mem. Community Care Coalition of DuPage County, 1988-93, NAACP; mem. pub. rels. com. Bethlehem Ctr. Food Bank of DuPage County, 1987-89; tour guide Stacy's Tavern-Glen Ellyn Hist. Mus., 1986—; chmn. Grass Roots Com. to Pass Ill. Marital Property Act, 1982—; mem. adv. bd. Older Adult Inst. Coll. DuPage, 1989-94; del. for Mental Health Assn. Du Page to DuPage County Consortium, 1989—, DuPage Consortium, Prevention and Intergenerational Task Force, 1991—; vol. Hospice of DuPage, 1990—; bd. dirs. Willowbrook Wildlife Found., 1992—, v.p., 1992-94; bd. dirs. Dupage area Older Women's League, chairperson publicity, 1992— (recipient Wonderful Older Woman ann. award. 1990); with clown ministry Fox Valley unity Ch., 1991—. Recipient Pathfinders award, 1965; hon. mention in Nat. Sonnet contest, 1967; Vol. of Yr. Ill. Mental Health Assn., 1975; Svc. award Ill. Rehab. Assn., 1980; named DuPage County Outstanding Woman Leader in Arts and Culture W. Suburban YWCA, 1984, Friend of the Mentally Ill, Alliance for the Mentally Ill of Dupage County Ann. award, 1988, Adade Wheeler award Coll. of DuPage, 1994, Mental Health Person of the Yr. Mental Health Assn. of Ill., 1995, Pub. Svc. award Ill. State Med. Soc., 1996. Mem. Mental Health Assn. DuPage, Wilderness Soc., Humane Soc. U.S., Nat. Trust for Hist. Preservation, Du Page County Hist. Soc. (life), Glen Ellyn Hist. Soc. (life), Nat. Audubon Soc., Nat. Writers Club (monthly meeting chmn. Midwest chpt. 1973-74, 4th award Ann. Mag. Con. test 1978), DuPage Art League (hon. life, Best of Show award 1991), Defenders of Wildlife, Theosophical Soc. Am. (Quest Study Group 1992—), Nature Conservancy Ill. (hon.), Chgo. Art Issn. Mental Health (dir. 1966-68), Amnesty Internat., Pi Beta Phi. Writer column Mental Health and You for Press Publs., 1969-90, Life Newspapers, 1982-93, Pioneer Newspapers, 1984, Herald Newspapers, 1986-94; author: The Jewelled Flower: The True Account of a Courageous Young Man's Life and Death By His Own Hand, 1987. Home: 22W 210 Stanton Rd Glen Ellyn IL 60137-7111

JENSEN, BILL H., production manager; b. Iowa City, Oct. 26, 1962. Grad. high sch., Iowa Falls, Iowa. Prodn. mgr. CAm Spray, Iowa Falls, Iowa, 1982—. Office: Cam Spray 520 Brooks Rd Iowa Falls IA 50126

JENSEN, GWENDOLYNN MARIE, special education educator; b. Duluth, Minn., Feb. 14, 1944; d. Glenn Willard and Helen Marie Moen; divorced; 1 child, Halden Brys (dec.). BS in Elem. Edn. and French, U. Minn., Duluth, 1967; cert. spl. learning disabilities, Moorhead State U., 1972; MS in Edn., U. Wis., Superior, 1991. Life lic. elem. edn. and French, Minn.; lic. spl. edn. K-12, counseling for h.s., Minn. Tchr. elem. sch. Duluth Pub. Schs., 1967-69; tchr. spl. learning problems Moorhead (Minn.) Pub. Schs., 1970-74; tchr. spl. learning disabilities Willow River (Minn.) Pub. Schs., 1977-78; asst. tchr. Headstart Willow River and Askov (Minn.) Pub. Schs., 1980, lead tchr. Headstart, 1981; tchr. spl. learning dept. Moose Lake (Minn.) Ind. Sch. Dist. 97, 1981—; chair Continuing Edn. Com., Moose Lake, 1986-91; mem. transition curriculum com. Cloquet (Minn.) Spl. Edn. Co-op, 1992—; co-founder grantwriting Women in Need Depending on Other Women, Sandstone, Minn., 1984-87. Staff writer: (coll. weekly publ.) Statesman, 1962-64. Chmn. swimming com. ARC, Willow River, 1979-81; rep. Willow River Comty. Edn., 1981-91; sec. twp. planning and zoning commn. Kettle River Twp., Minn., 1984-91; co-chmn. Pine County Polit. Party, 1991. Recipient Arrowhead award Boy Scouts Am., 1982. Mem. Minn. Assn. Vocat. Spl. Needs Pers., Artists of Minn., Carlton County Geneol. Soc., Arrowhead Art Club, Mensa (proctor 1994), Women of the Moose (sr. regent 1996-97). Home: 4908 County Rd 12 Moose Lake MN 55767 Office: Moose Lake H S 413 Birch Ave Box 489 Moose Lake MN 55767

JENSEN, JIM, state legislator; b. Omaha, Jan. 17, 1934; m. Joan Vecera, 1959; children: Jon, Jeff, Jill, Jay, Joel. Student, Omaha U. Contractor pvt. practice, Omaha, 1959—; state senator State of Nebr., Lincoln, 1994—. Chmn. Omaha Zoning Bd. Appeals, 1987—; vice chmn. Papio/Mo. River Natural Resources Bd., 1990—. Mem. Pride Omaha (bd. dirs. 1989—), Met. Omaha Builders Assn. (bd. dirs. 1960—), Rotary Club.

JENSEN, JOHN GORDON, JR., police officer; b. Madison, Wis., May 31, 1949; s. John Gordon Jensen and Patricia Jean (Searl) Chapman; m. Elizabeth Ann Miller, May 6, 1972 (div.); 1 child, Amy Jean. AS in Bus. Adminstrn., Davenport Coll., Grand Rapids, Mich., 1969; AS in Criminal Justice, Lansing Community Coll., 1977. Dep. sheriff Grand Traverse Sheriff's Dept., Traverse City, Mich., 1976-81, detective, 1981-85, sgt., 1985-86; dep. sheriff Grand Traverse Sheriff's Dept., 1987—; police officer San Angelo (Tex.) Police Dept., 1986-87; hostage negotiator Grand Traverse Sheriff's Dept., 1982—, search/recovery diver, 1979—, def. tactics instr., 1979—, field tng. officer, 1992—, arson investigator, 1983—, criminal interogation and behavioral analysis instr., 1982—, weapons retention instr., 1989—. Author: Women's Self-Defense, 1983, Use of Force - Police Tools, 1985. Named Police Officer of the Yr. Optimists Internat., 1979, others. Mem. Police Officers Assn. Mich., Dep. Sheriff's Assn. Am., Du/Tu/Ruffeo Grouse Soc., N.Am. Hunt Club (life), Nat. Rifle Assn., Elks. Republican. Episcopalian. Home: 10406 S West Bay Shore Dr Traverse City MI 49684-5228 Office: Grand Traverse Sheriffs Dep 320 Washington St Traverse City MI 49684-2548

JENSEN, KATHRYN PATRICIA, public broadcaster; b. Fairbanks, AK, June 20, 1950; d. Edward Leroy and Doris Patricia (Fee) Bigelow; m. Timothy Lyle Jensen, May 19, 1973; 1 child, Alexander Morgan. BA, U. Alaska, 1974. Sta. mgr., program dir. Sta. KUAC-FM U. Alaska, Fairbanks, 1976-82; acting gen. mgr. Sta. KUAC-FM-TV U. Alaska, Fairbanks, 1981-82, gen. mgr., 1982-87; gen. mgr. Sta. WCPN-FM, Cleve., 1987—; vis. com. Coll. Edn., Cleve. State U., 1990-95; founding mem. Alaska Pub. Radio Network, 1978-85; mem. adv. com. on arts mgmt. Case Western Res. U., 1991—. Trustee Mid-Town Corridor, Cleve., 1988-89, Libr. Found., Fairbanks, 1985-88; bd. dirs. Make-A-Wish Found. Northwest Ohio, 1992-95; mem. Cleve. Bicentennial Commn. Adv. Bd., 1993; mem. coun. Cleve. Opera, 1991; mem. Leadership Cleve., 1991-92. Recipient Elaine B. Mitchell award Alaska Pub. Radio Network, 1988, Oebie award, 1992, 95, award WVXU-WCPN 1991 Challenge, William H. Kling Innovation and Entrepreneurship award Pub. Radio Internat., 1995. Episcopalian. Office: Sta WCPN-FM The Cleve Centre 3100 Chester Ave Cleveland OH 44114-4604

JENSEN, MICHAEL J., food service administrator; b. Racine, Wis., Dec. 6, 1947; s. Clarence Sidney and Virginia Margaret (Vance) J.; m. Carol Ann Goltz, Aug. 18, 1973; 1 child, Christopher Andrew. BA in Bus., Mich. State U., 1974. Unit mgr. Howard Johnson's, Lansing, Mich., 1974-75, Bonanza Restaurants, Lansing, 1975-76; foodsvc. dir. Riverside Correctional Faculty, Ionia, Mich., 1976—; mem. Mich. State Purchasing Adv. Com., Lansing, 1985—. Mem. Bd. Edn., Belding (Mich.) Area Schs., 1981—. With USAF, 1966-69, Thailand and Japan. Mem. Am. Correctional Food Svc. Assn., Belding Lions Club (sec. 1992—). Congregationalist. Home: 121 W Washington St Belding MI 48809 Office: Riverside Correctl Facility 777 W Riverside Dr Ionia MI 48846

JENSEN, SCOTT R., state legislator; b. Aug. 24, 1960. BA, Drake U.; MA, Harvard U. Pub. rels. exec.; aide Gov. Tommy Thompson, Madison, Wis.; mem. from dist. 23 Wis. State Assembly, Madison. Dir. assembly Rep. Caucus. Address: 850 S Springdale Waukesha WI 53186*

JENSON, KATHY LAVON, marketing director; b. Bismarck, N.D., Oct. 24, 1943; d. Edward Michael and Clara Catherine (Ficker) Degen; m. Roy Kenneth Jenson, Oct. 22, 1977; children: Patricia, Elizabeth. BS in Math., N.D. State U., 1965; MBA in Mktg., U. St. Thomas, 1980. Sys. mgr. Control Data Corp., Bloomington, Minn., 1965-74, mgr. strategic planning, 1980-87; major account mgr. Digital Equipment Corp., Mpls., 1974-80; area applications sales mgr. Wang Labs., Mpls., 1987-89; nat. sales mgr. Faxbank Inc., St. Paul, 1990-91; dir. mktg. & sales Solutronix Corp., Eden Prairie,

Minn., 1991-92; mktg. dir. NCS, Edina, Minn., 1992—; Baldridge quality examiner, 1996; guest spkr. in field. Vol. Bel Canto Voices, Mpls., 1990—, Regional Dance Competitions, Mpls., 1987—; pres. Edina H.S. Thespian Boosters. Mem. Soc. Consumer Affairs Profls., Am. Mktg. Assn., Sales and Mktg. Execs., Am. Soc. Quality Control, Minn. Quality Award Com. (Minn. Quality Award examiner 1994, sr. Minn. Quality Award examiner 1995).

JENTZ, JEFF J., multicultural educator; b. Wahpeton, N.D., May 15, 1949; s. Arnold Louis and Norma Anne (Sellner) J.; m. Karen Rambo, Feb. 17, 1979; children: Coral Shirin, Gretchen Layli, Heidi Ruha. BA in English, U. N.D., 1977, MA in English Lit., 1982; MFA in Creative Writing, U. Ark., 1985. Tchr. English Crow Creek Sioux Reservation H.S., Stephan, S.D., 1978-79; sr. lectr. dept. English U. N.D., Grand Forks, 1985-86, 90—; asst. prof. dept. English U. Ark., Fayetteville, 1985-86; poet in schs. S.D. Arts Coun., Sioux Falls, 1986-87; instr. basic English Sinte Gleska Coll., Rosebud, S.D., 1987-89; developer Flowering Tree Writing Approach to Multicultural Literacy, 1992—; performance poet, storyteller, Minn., N.D., S.D., Mich., 1990—; vis. poet Bemidji (Minn.) State U., fall 1993. Contbr. poetry to anthologies and mags. Initiator, organizer 1st Sobriety Walk, Rosebud Lakota Reservation, 1988; co-organizer Bemidji Baha'i Comty. Race Unity Walks, 1990-91; co-founder Cir. of Many Cultures, Bemidji, 1991-92. Recipient 5 lit. awards including Robert Hayden Poetry fellowship Louhelen Baha'i Sch., 1992. Mem. The Linguistics Cir., Bahai Coll. Club U. N.D. (faculty advisor 1994—). Baha'i. Home: RR 1 Box 18 Shevlin MN 56676 Office: U N D English Dept Merrifield 100 Grand Forks ND 58202

JERMIASON, JOHN LYNN, elementary school educator, farmer, rancher; b. Rochester, Minn., Jan. 9, 1958; s. Orlyn and Evelyn S. (O'Grady) J.; m. Ann M. Gebhardt, July 30, 1990. BA in Music, Psychology, St. Olaf Coll., 1981; AS in Agr., N.D. State U., 1982; BS in Edn., Minot State U., 1990. Sales rep. Century 21 Real Estate, Minot, N.D., 1989; ind. farmer, rancher Minot, 1982—; substitute elem. tchr. Minot Pub. Schs., 1993—. Prin. violist Minot Symphony Orch., 1983—; mem. ch. coun. Augustana Luth. Ch., Minot, 1989-91. Mem. Elks, Gideons Internat., Phi Mu Alpha, Kappa Delta Pi. Home: RR 3 Box 222A Minot ND 58701-9541

JERNIGAN, ALVIN, JR., automobile sales executive; b. Marshall, Tex., Sept. 4, 1933; s. Alvin Jernigan Sr. and Katherine Whitfield; m. Dorothy Jernigan, June 15, 1981 (div. May 1990); children: Darnell J., Delbert W., Dori Ann. Student, Bay City Jr. Coll., 1953-54; AA in bus. and mktg., Delta Coll., 1979. Food svc. supr. VA Hosp., Downey, Ill., 1959-62; TWA comms. West Side VA, Downey, 1962-64; with prodn. dept. Gen. Motors, Flint, Mich., 1964-65; with sales dept. Garber Pontiac Cadillac, Saginaw, Mich., 1966-80; ins. agent Allstate Ins. Co., Saginaw, 1980-85; auto sales exec. Labadie Old Cadillac GMC, Bay City, Mich., 1986—. Sch. bd. mem. Buena Vista Sch. Dist., 1988—; mem. Buena Vista Recreation Com., Saginaw, 1985—, IOC Adv. Bd. Fundraising Group, Saginaw, 1991-93, Buena Vista Cmty. Coun., 1988-91; vol. United Negro Coll. Fund, Saginaw, 1991-93. Mem. Cadillac Cres Club (with distinction), Frontiers Club (pres. 1982-83, Man of Yr. 1980), Saginaw Bay Fish Masters (v.p. 1993-94), Optimist Club. Democrat. Baptist. Home: 3010 Welland Dr Saginaw MI 48601

JEROSKI, ANTHONY JOSEPH, JR., artist, designer; b. Logansport, Ind., Jan. 16, 1948; s. Anthony Joseph and Elizabeth Anne (Burrous) J. BS, Ball State U., 1971, MFA, 1982. Art instr. Brownstown (Ind.) Community Sch., 1971-72; advt. coord. Muncie (Ind.) Power Products, Inc., 1973—; prin. A.J. Designs, Inc., 1985—. Group exhibitions: Objects and Crafts , 1971 Indpls Mus. of Art (Grand Prize), Alumni Invitational Show, Ball State U., 1978, Annual Drawing and Small Sculpture Show, Ball State U., 1979, Art 500 Exhibit, Indpls. Art League; one man shows: Ball State Art Gallery, 1979, Presentation in Ceramics and Metal Design, Minnetrista Ctr., Muncie, Ind., 1980; Largest work: architectural sculpture, "BotanicalPanorama" temporarily installed at Emens Auditorium, Muncie, Ind., 1988-90; mixed media sculptures, pvt. commns. through midwest galleries, design firms. Recipient Grand Prize Ind. Ceramics Exhibit, DePauw U., 1979. Mem. Internat. Sculpture Soc., Hist. Soc., Hist. Alliance. Home: PO Box 576 Muncie IN 47308-0576 Office: AJ Designs Inc PO Box 576 Muncie IN 47308-0576

JERVIS, DAVID THOMPSON, political science educator; b. Bryn Mawr, Pa., Mar. 16, 1954; s. Walter T. and Mary Charlotte (Abernethy) J. BA, Eastern Coll., St. Davids, Pa., 1976; MA, Villanova U., 1978; PhD, Temple U., 1985. Asst. prof. Washburn U., Topeka, 1985-92, assoc. prof. polit. sci., 1992-96, prof., 1996—, asst. dir. Internat. Ctr., 1991—; vis. prof. U. Orebro, Sweden, 1995, U. Witwatersrand, South Africa, 1995. Contbr. articles to profl. jours. Bd. dirs. Internat. Ctr. Topeka, 1988—. Mem. Internat. Studies Assn., Nat. Com. Internat. Studies and Program Adminstrs., Acad. Polit. Sci., Pi Sigma Alpha, Phi Alpha Theta, Phi Kappa Phi, Phi Beta Delta. Office: Washburn U Dept Polit Sci Topeka KS 66621

JETT, CHARLES CRANSTON, management consultant; b. Bowman, N.D., July 26, 1941; s. Wood Kaylor Jett and Helen (Cranston) Peterson; m. Marcia Holden, Oct. 23, 1971; children: Charles Holly, Christopher Holden. BS, U.S. Naval Acad., 1964; MBA, Harvard U., 1972. Staff officer 1st Chgo., 1972-74; assoc. Booz Allen & Hamilton, Chgo., 1974-79; v.p. Spencer Stuart, Chgo., 1979-82; exec. dir. Russell Reynolds, Chgo., 1982-86; ptnr. McFeely Wackerle Jett, Chgo., 1986-90; prin. Charles C. Jett, Ltd., Wheaton, Ill., 1987—; ptnr. Ward Howell Internat., 1992-94. Author: Community Service 2000, Coop 2000, Field Studies 2000, Critical Skills and the CEO, Whatever Happened to Corporate Loyalty, The Doom Loop; patentee in field. Bd. dirs. Glen Ellyn (Ill.) Children's Chorus, 1988-94, DuPage Health Sys., Inc., 1995—; pres. The Critical Skills Found., 1991—. Mem. Econ. Club Chgo., Glen Oak Country Club (Glen Ellyn). Home & Office: Charles C Jett Ltd 1113 Irving St Wheaton IL 60187-3842

JETT, FRANK HUBERT, broadcast executive; b. Terre Haute, Ind., Sept. 11, 1939; s. John Rabb and Dorothy Mae (Tuttle) J. BS, Rose Poly. Inst., 1958; BS in Radio-TV, Ind. State U., 1961; postgrad. in behavioral psychology, U. Miami, 1962. Disc jockey WBOW-AM; booth announcer, dir. children's and pub. affairs programs WTHI-TV; mgr. WPIX-TV, N.Y.C., WKID-TV, Ft. Lauderdale, Fla., KTTV-TV, L.A.; dir. implementation Golden West Subscription Television, L.A., 1979-81; dir. program opers. The Premiere Network, L.A., 1981-82; mgr. long-rangeplanning and facilities bus. affairs Hughes Aircraft Company Space and Comms. Group, L.A., 1982-90; exec. v.p., exec. in charge of prodn. Nostalgia Network, Inc., L.A., 1990-93; pres., CEO Nostalgia Network, Inc., 1993—; also chmn. bd. dirs., retired, 1994; COO, chmn. bd., full ptnr. BackSeat Entertainment, Inc., Calif.; pres. Entertainment Resource Assocs., Wis., 1994—; co-owner Green Lantern Antiques; pres., chmn. bd. Black Elk Enterprises, Inc., Mineral Point, Wis. Bd. dirs. Mineral Point Main St. Program; involved in other civic and charitable activities. Mem. Nat. Assn. TV Program Execs., Nat. Assn. Broadcasters, Nat. Cable TV Assn., Acad. TV Arts and Scis., Wis. Antique Dealers Assn., Mineral Point Hist. Soc., Alpha Tau Omega, Theta Alpha Phi. Office: Entertainment Resources Assocs P O Box 342 Mineral Point WI 53565

JETTER, ARTHUR CARL, JR., insurance company executive; b. Omaha, Oct. 9, 1947; s. Arthur Carl and Virginia Ann (Turner) J.; m. Jennifer Ann Jochim, Mar. 30, 1974; children: Arthur Carl III, Sarah Ann. BBA, Dana Coll., 1974. Registered health underwriter; CFP, CLU; registered employee benefits cons.; FLMI. Sales rep. life ins. Guarantee Mut., Omaha, 1974-81; pres. Art Jetter & Co., Omaha, 1981—, Employers Mut. Acceptance Co., Omaha, 1981—. Capt. inf. U.S. Army, 1968-72, Vietnam. Fellow Life Mgmt. Inst.; mem. CLU (cert., edn. chmn. Omaha chpt. 1984-91), Nat. Assn. Health Underwriters (pres. 1991-92, Gordon Meml. award 1995, Health Ins. Industry person of yr. 1995). Republican. Lutheran. Home: 13624 Parker Cir Omaha NE 68154-3829 Office: Art Jetter and Co 11305 Chicago Cir Omaha NE 68154-2676

JETTKE, HARRY JEROME, retired government official; b. Detroit, Jan. 2, 1925; s. Harry H. and Eugenia M. (Dziatkiewicz) J.; B.A., Wayne State U., 1961; m. Josefina Suarez-Garcia, Oct. 22, 1948; 1 child, Joan Lillian Clark. Owner, operator Farmacia Virreyes/Farmacia Regina, Toluca, Mex., 1948-55; intern pharmacist Cunningham Drug Stores, Detroit, 1955-63; drug specialist, product safety specialist FDA, Detroit, 1963-73; acting dir. Cleve., U.S. Consumer Product Safety Commn., 1973-75, compliance officer, 1975-78, supr., investigations, 1978-82, regional compliance officer, 1982-83, sr. resident, 1983-90; ret., 1990. Served with Fin. Dept., U.S. Army, 1942-43. Drug specialist FDA. Mem. Am. Soc. for Quality Control (sr., chmn. Cleve. sect. 1977-78, cert. quality technician, cert. quality engr.), Asociación Nacional Mexicana de Estadistica y Control de Calidad, Ohio Gun Collectors Assn., Cleve. Fed. Exec. Bd. (policy com.), 1985. Roman Catholic. Home: 25715 Yeoman Dr Cleveland OH 44145-4745

JEWEL, JULIE STEPHANIE, clergy member, minister; b. Jackson, Miss., Apr. 16, 1953; d. Jack R. and Evelyn M. (Abbey) J.;. B in Mgmt. of Human Resources, Spring Arbor (Mich.) Coll., 1985; MDiv, Garrett Evang. Theol. Sem., 1996. cert. profl. sec. Exec. sec. Nat. Bank of Jackson, 1973-74; office mgr. Citizens Probation Authority, Jackson, 1975; deputy clerk Jackson County 12th Dist. Ct., 1975-76; reg. asst. A.G. Edwards, 1976-92; assoc. pastor Epworth & Salem United Meth. Chs., Valley City, N.D., 1994-95; Chaplain Sheyenne Care Ctr., Valley City, 1995. Mem. Profl. Secs. Internat. (treas. 1985-87, Sec. of the Year 1986), Bus. and Profl. Women (dist. dir., 1989-91, Woman of the Year 1983). United Methodist.

JIBBEN, JEFFREY JOHN, minister; b. Lawrenceburg, Ind., May 19, 1966; s. John Jacob and Luanna Marie (Powers) J.; m. Michelle René Wallner, Sept. 5, 1987; children: Zechariah Joel, Josiah John. BA in Biology/Chemistry, Gustavus Adolphus Coll., St. Peter, Minn., 1988; MDiv, Assemblies God Theol. Seminary, Springfield, Mo., 1991, MA, 1995; postgrad., Bethel Theol. Seminary, St. Paul, 1995—. Ordained minister Assemblies of God, 1993. Itinerate preacher Assemblies of God, various states, 1992-93; mem. faculty part-time North Ctrl. Bible Coll., Mpls., 1994—; sr. pastor Elysian (Minn.) Assembly of God, 1993—; ctrl. buyer retail dept. Gen. Coun. of Assemblies of God, Springfield, 1991-93. Contbr. articles to profl. jours. Rep. del. Ind. Reps., Lesueur County, Minn., 1993—; planning commr. City of Elysian, 1994—. Mem. Evang. Theol. Soc., Soc. Pentecostal Studies, Am. Assn. Christian Counselors, Singing Hills Trail Assn. (com. mem.). Home and Office: PO Box 180 Elysian MN 56028

JIBBEN, LAURA ANN, state agency administrator; b. Peoria, Ill., Oct. 1, 1949; d. Charles Otto and Dorothy Lee (Skaggs) Becker; m. Michael Eugene Hagan, July 7, 1967 (div. Apr. 1972); m. Louis C. Jibben, July 14, 1972. BA in Criminal Justice, Sangamon State U., 1984; MBA, Northwestern U., 1990. Asst. to chief of adminstrn. Ill. Dept. Corrections, Springfield, 1974-77, exec. asst. to dir., 1977-80, dep. dir., 1980-81; mgr. toll services Ill. Tollway Dept., Oak Brook, 1981-86; chief adminstrv. officer Regional Transp. Authority, Chgo., 1986-90, fund mgr. loss financing plan, 1987-90, also, chmn. pension trust; exec. dir. Regional Transp. Authority, 1990-96; v.p., gen. mgr. MTA, Inc., Chgo., 1996—; cons. labor studies Sangamon State U., Springfield, 1981; bd. dirs. Chgo. Found. for Women. Apptd. mem. transp. adv. bd. City of Naperville, 1988-90; bd. dirs. Family Shelter Svcs., 1990-91. Recipient Appreciation award VFW, Chgo., 1983, award Ill. State Toll Hwy. Authority, 1986; named Woman of Yr., Nat. Women's Transp. Seminar, 1991, AAUW, 1991. Mem. NAFE, Women's Transp. Seminar (Woman of Yr. award Chgo. chpt. 1991, Nat. Woman of Yr. 1991), Beta Sigma Phi (treas., v.p., corr. sec. Naperville and Easton, Ill. chpts.), Lambda Alpha. Office: MTA Inc Ste 915 111 N Canal St Chicago IL 60602

JILHEWAR, ASHOK, gastroenterologist; b. Nanded, Maharashtra, India, Jan. 30, 1947; came to U.S., 1977; naturalized 1987; BS, Marathwada U., Aurangabad, India, 1970; MB, Marathwada U., 1970; MD, Govt. Med. Coll., Aurangabad, 1970. Diplomate Am. Bd. Internal Medicine, Am. Bd. Gastroenterology, Am. Bd. Geriatric Medicine, Am. Bd. Quality Assurance and Utilization Rev. Physicians. Rotatory intern Med. Coll. Hosp., Aurangabad, India, 1968-70; resident St. Luke's Hosp. and Royal infirmary, Huddersfeild, Bolton, Eng., 1970-72; med. registrar internal medicine Gen. Hosp., Sligo, Ireland, 1973-77; chief resident PG1 and internal medicine U. Health Scis.-Chgo. Med. Sch. and VA Hosp., 1977-79; clin. instr. U. Heath Scis.-Chgo. Med. Sch., 1978-79; fellow in gastroenterology Michael Reese Hosp., Chgo., 1980-81; mem. exec. com. Meth. Hosp., Chgo, 1985-90, chmn. dept. med., 1988-90; mem. staff dept. medicine Grant Hosp., Chgo., 1986—; lectr. preventive and social medicine Med. Coll., Aurangabad, 1970; mem. exec. com. Meth. Hosp. Chgo., 1985-90, v.p. med. staff, 1987-88, treas., sec. 1985-87, chmn. dept. medicine, 1988-90; med. dir. approved homr for intermediace care nursing home, 1986-95; med. advisor Office Hearings and Appeals, HHS, 1985—; med. reviewer Ill. Med. Rev. Orgn., 1993—, Crescent Cmty. Found. for Med. Care, 1994—. Fellow Royal Coll. Physicians Can., Am. Coll. Internat. Physicians; mem. AMA, ACP, Am. Gastroenterol. Assn., Royal Coll. Physicians U.K., Royal Coll. Physicians Ireland, Ill. State Med. Assn., Chgo. Med. Soc. (PRO study com., fee mediation subcom. 1992). Office: North Park Stomach Clinic 5393 N Milwaukee Ave Chicago IL 60630-1251

JIMENEZ, BETTIE EILEEN, retired small business owner; b. LaCygne, Kans., June 8, 1932; d. William Albert and Ruby Faye (Cline) Montee; m. William R. Bradley, Aug. 21, 1947 (div. Sept. 1950); 1 child, Shirley; m. J.P. Jimenez, Feb. 20, 1951 (div. Nov. 1978); children: Pamela, Joe Jr., Robin Michelle. Student, Ft. Scott Jr. Coll., Paola, Kans., 1979-81. Reporter LaCygne Jour., 1943-45; union recorder I.L.G.W.U., Paola, 1956-57; mgr. Estes Metalcraft, Osawatomie, Kans., 1977-82; owner El Rey Tavern, Osawatomie, 1980-95; ret., 1995. Home: 516 Walnut Ave Osawatomie KS 66064-1254

JINKS-WEIDNER, JANIE, editor; b. Greenfield, Ohio, Feb. 11, 1948; d. Roy Earl and Imagene (Patton) Jinks; m. JAcob M. Greenlee, Feb. 24, 1966 (div.); children: James Lee, Jason Kirk; m. Leonard D. Weidner, Feb. 28, 1971; 1 child, Jennifer Lynn. Student, Ohio State U., 1978-81. Co-owner Indian River Industries, Westerville, Ohio, 1972—, Indian River Artifacts, Westerville, Ohio, 1980—; owner Weidner Publishing, Sunbury, Ohio, 1981—; editor, owner Prehistoric Antiquities Quarterly, Sunbury, Ohio, 1981-91; editor Artifacts, Whitehall, Ohio, 1983-84, Who's Who in Indian Relics, Westerville, 1987—; owner Carriage House Antiques, Sunbury, 1991—. Editor: Who's Who in Indian Relics, 1987-92. Named to Hon. Order Ky. Cols. Mem. Ctrl. States Archaeology Soc., Ohio Archaeological Soc., Genuine Indian Relic Soc. (sec. 1989). Republican. Presbyterian. Home: 13706 Robins Rd Westerville OH 43082-9702 Office: Carriage House Antiques 31 E Granville St Sunbury OH 43074

JIRKANS, MARIBETH JOIE, school counselor; b. Cleve., May 3, 1945; d. Raymond Wenceslaus and Elsie Koryta J.; children: Annemarie Gurchik, Keith Robert Gurchik. Student, U. Vienna, Austria, 1965; BS in Edn., Coll. Mt. St. Joseph, 1967; MEd, Cleve. State U., 1984; postgrad., U. Akron, 1986-88, Kent State U., 1989—. Cert. elem., spl. edn. and adult edn. tchr., counselor. Tchr. North Olmstead (Ohio) City Schs., 1967-76; tchr. adult edn. Polaris Vocat. Sch., Middleburg Heights, Ohio, 1978; tchr. adult edn., ESL Lakewood (Ohio) City Schs., 1978-79; tchr. 2d grade Saint Rose Sch., Cleve., 1979-80; tchr. learning disabilities Cleve. Pub. Schs., 1980-85; tutor handicapped Cleve. Christian Home, 1982-84; elem. sch. counselor Cleve. Pub. Schs., 1985—; counselor West Side Community Mental Health Ctr., Cleve., 1983-84; sales mgr. Field Enterprises Inc., Cleve., 1977-82. Contbr. articles to newspapers. Vol. Fairview Gen. Hosp., Cleve., 1959-63, Cerebral Palsy Camp, 1959-63, Allen Halfway House for Children, Cin., 1963-67; cofounder Westshore Separated, Divorced and Remarried Caths., Cleve., 1975-85; chairwoman North Olmsted Jr. Women's Club; mem. parish coun. St. Brendan Ch., North Olmstead, 1975-87; mem. com. Cleve. Symphony, Cleve. Art Mus. Recipient Speaker's United Torch award United Way, Cleve., 1st Pl. prize in clothing design Stretch & Sew, 1975, 1st Pl. prize in needlepoint Framemakers Art, 1983. Mem. AACD, N.E. Ohio Counselor Assn., Coun. for Exceptional Children, Am. Sch. Counselor Assn., Internat. Assn. Marriage and Family Counselors, NOW, ASCD, Gestalt Inst., Audubon Soc., Eagle Valley Athletic Club, Greenpeace, Sierra Club, Cleve. Natural History Mus., North Coast Sailing Club, Holden Arboretum, Pi Lambda Theta. Democrat. Home: 727 Tollis Pky Cleveland OH 44147-1813

JIROVEC, RONALD LOUIS, social work educator; b. Cleve., June 19, 1946; s. Joseph J. and Louise (Lisy) J.; m. Mary M. Marmoll, Aug. 7, 1971; children: Lisa M., Jason. BA, U. Ill., Chgo., 1968; PhD, Brandeis U., 1978. Cert. Acad. Cert. Social Workers. Social worker Mayor's Officer Sr. Citizens, Chgo., 1970-72, Miriam Hosp., Providence, 1975-76; prof. social work U. Wyo., Laramie, 1976-80, Wayne State U., Detroit, 1980—; exec. dir. Common Cause, Cheyenne, Wyo., 1979-80; grant adminstr. Aging Tng., U. Wyo., 1977-78. Contbr. articles to jours. Bd. dirs. Community Svcs. of Oakland Madison Heights, Mich., 1983—. Recipient Faculty Rsch. award Wayne State U., 1987, rsch. stimulation grantee, 1989; Adminstrn. on Aging fellow Brandeis U., 1972-75. Mem. NASW, AAUP (contract implementation officer Wayne State U. 1989—, chmn. polit. action com. 1988—), Am. Soc. on Aging, Gerontol. Soc. Am., Nat. Citizens Coalition for Nursing Home Reform, Alzheimers and Related Diseases Assn., Mich. League for Human Svcs. Office: Sch Social Work Wayne State U Detroit MI 48202

JISCHKE, MARTIN C., academic administrator; b. Chgo., Aug. 7, 1941; m. Patricia Fowler; children: Charles, Marian. BS in Physics with honors, Ill. Inst. Tech., 1963; MS in Aeronautics and Astronautics, MIT, 1964, PhD in Aeronautics and Astronautics, 1968. Engr. Rand Corp., Santa Monica, Calif., 1965; research engr. Battelle N.W. Lab., Richland, Washington, 1970; research fellow Donald W. Douglas Lab., Richland, 1971, Nat. Aeronautics and Space Adminstrn., Moffett Field, Calif., 1973; from asst. prof. to prof. aerospace, mech. and nuclear engring. U. Okla., 1968-75, prof., dir. Sch. Aerospace, Mech. and Nuclear Engring., 1977-81, interim pres., 1985, dean Coll. Engring., 1981-86, mem. various coms., 1985; White House fellow, spl. asst. to sec. of transp. U.S. Dept. Transp., Washington, 1975-76; chancellor U. Mo., Rolla, 1986-91; pres. Iowa State U., Ames, 1991—; bd. dirs. Kerr McGee Corp., Mo. Alliance for Sci., The Keystone Found., Mo. Corp. for Sci. and Tech., vice-chmn., 1990-91; participant Japanese Econ. Found. Vis. Leaders Program, 1983; mem. Gov.'s Coun. on Sci. and Tech. State of Okla., 1983-84, Gordon Rsch. Conf. on Geophysics; mem. planning com. for 80's Okla. State Regents for Higher Edn.; mem. organizing com. 14th Midwestern Mechanics Conf.; mem. adv. com. for engring. sci. NSF Engring. Directorate, 1985-88; mem. com. on statewide postsecondary telecomm. policy Mo. Coordinating Bd. for Higher Edn., 1987-91; chmn. Congrl. Aero. Adv. Com., 1987-89; sci. adviser to Gov. of Mo., 1990-91; mem. Am. Coun. on Edn. Com. on Math. and Sci., 1990-91. Contbr. articles and reports to profl. publs. Civilian aide Sec. of Army, State of Mo. East, 1987-91; bd. dirs. Bankers Trust, 1991, Iowa Spl. Olympics. Recipient Ralph Teetor award Soc. Automotive Engrs., 1971, Brandon H. Griffith award U. Okla., U. Okla. Regents award for superior teaching, 1975, IIT Prof. Achievement award, 1992, Delta Tau Delta Achievement award, 1992, Engrs. Club St. Louis Achievement award, 1991, Dept. Army Outstanding Civilian Svc. medal, 1991; NASA fellow, 1966; NSF fellow, 1965; AEC/NORCUS summer faculty fellow, 1970-71, NASA/ASEE fellow, 1973. Fellow AAAS, AIAA (assoc., sec.-treas. Okla. chpt., vice chmn., chmn.); mem. ASME, AAUP (v.p., pres. Okla. chpt.), NSPE, Am. Phys. Soc., Am. Soc. Engring. Edn. (Centennial Medallion 1993), Nat. Assn. State Univs. and Land Grant Colls. (bd. dirs.), Assn. Big Twelve Univs. (pres. 1994—), Mo. Soc. Profl. Engrs., Rotary, Phi Beta Kappa, Tau Beta Pi, Sigma Xi, Pi Tau Sigma, Sigma Gamma Tau, Sigma Pi Sigma, Phi Eta Sigma. Home: The Knoll Iowa State U Ames IA 50014 Office: Iowa State U Office of Pres Ames IA 50011-2035

JOACHIM, JAMES MICHAEL, computer information systems educator; b. Owatonna, Minn., Dec. 13, 1953; s. Joseph Anthony and Abbie Mildred (Wanous) J.; m. JoAnn Faye Lyle, July 31, 1982; children: Michael, Nicole, Matthew. Student, Albert Lea (Minn.) Tech. Coll., 1990. Designer, draftsman Hydo Ax Blount Inc., Owatonna, 1990—; mem. adv. bd. Albert Lea Tech. Coll., 1991—. Cub Scout den leader Boy Scouts Am., Owatonna, 1991—. Mem. KC (outside guard 1992-93). Roman Catholic. Home: 630 18th St NE Owatonna MN 55060-1402 Office: Hydro Ax Blount Inc PO Box 568 Owatonna MN 55060-0568

JOBE, MURIEL IDA, medical technologist, educator; b. St. Louis, Apr. 17, 1931; d. Ernest William and Mable Mary (Hefflinger) Meissner; m. James Joseph Jobe, Sr., May 17, 1952 (dec. 1984); children: James J. Jr., Timothy D. (dec. 1976), Jonathan J., Daniel D. BS, Wash. U., St. Louis, 1971; med. technologist tng., Mo. Bapt. Hosp., St. Louis, 1973-74; postgrad., Webster U., St. Louis, 1981-83. Cytogenetic tech. St. Luke's Hosp., St. Louis, 1963-65; med. technologist Mo. Bapt. Hosp., St. Louis, 1974-76, 82-84, sr. instr., 1976-82, lead technologist, 1985; mgr., clin. instr. St. Louis U. Hosp., 1985-96; retired, 1996; mem. student selection com. Mo. Bapt. Hosp. Med. Technologists, St. Louis, 1975-78; observer Nat. Com. Clin. Lab. Standards, Villanova, Pa., 1989-90, advisor, 1991-92, 93—. Co-author: Clinical Hematology: Principles, Procedures, Correlations, 1991, 2d edit., 1996, 8th Revision PER Handbook, A Review Manual for Clinical Laboratory Exams., 1992. Counselor La Leche League; participant Ecology Day; community rels. chmn. The Life Seekers, St. Louis. Mem. Am. Soc. Clin. Pathologists (staff asst. 1984, 86, 88, 89, 94, 95, dir. workshops 1990, 91, bd. dirs. 1990-92, state advisor 1992—, chmn. regional adv. com., adminstrv. bd. assoc. mem. sect., regional assoc. mem. award 1994), Am. Assn. Clin. Chemists, Am. Soc. Med. Tech. (dir. workshop 1984), Mo. Soc. Med. Tech. (pres. 1985-86), Clin. Lab. Mgrs. Assn. (chmn. devel. St. Louis chpt.). Mem. United Ch. of Christ. Office: St Louis U Hosp Hematology Lab 4 FDT 3635 Vista Ave Saint Louis MO 63110-2539

JOBES-PLATT, PATRICIA A., stockbroker; b. Greenville, Ohio, May 30, 1946. Stockbroker Corna Co. Securities, Columbus, Ohio, 1990-93, First Montauk Securities Corp., Powell, Ohio, 1993—; officer WPS Investments, Powell, Ohio, 1994. Home: 430 Olde Mill Dr Westerville OH 43082-1028 Office: First Montauk Securities 240 N Liberty St PO Box 250 Powell OH 43065

JOBIN, KENNETH JOSEPH, robotic applications designer; b. Chgo., Dec. 16, 1965; s. William Auther and Therese Francis (Wazny) J. Student, Elkhart Area Career Ctr., 1985, Purdue U., 1986, Ivy Tech, Indpls., 1990. Recreational vehicle pattern maker Leisure Design, Elkhart, Ind., 1983-85; draftsman Daman Products Inc., Mishawaka, Ind., 1986-87; recreational vehicle and boat seating designer/prototype Innovative Designs, Elkhart, 1987; designer, draftsman Universal Coops., Goshen, Ind., 1987-89; designer The Kent Co., Elkhart, 1990—; co-creator Creative Cards, Elkhart, 1990—; pres. K. J. Designs, Elkhart, 1991—. Creator, artist computer generated pictures/artwork, 1986—. Mem. Michiana Autocad Club, Autocad Cons., Michiana Lions.

JOHANN, CHRIS JOSEPH, electronics engineer; b. Springfield, Ill., Jan. 18, 1971. BSEE, U. Mo., 1993; postgrad., Washington U., St. Louis, 1995—. Summer intern Sporlan Value Co., Washington, Mo., 1994; sr. engr. electronics McDonnell Douglas Corp., Hazelwood, Mo., 1994—. Mem. IEEE. Lutheran. Office: McDonnell Douglas Corp F-15 AIS 325 McDonnell Blvd Hazelwood MO 63042

JOHANSEN, BRUCE ELLIOTT, communication and Native American studies educator; b. San Diego, Jan. 30, 1950; s. Julian Elliott and Hazel Elizabeth (Rees) J.; m. Patricia Ellen Keiffer, Nov. 12, 1988; 1 stepchild, Shannon James Keiffer. BA with honors, U. Wash., 1972, PhD, 1979; MA, U. Minn., 1975. Staff writer Seattle Times, 1972-76; dir. grants devel. El Centro de la Raza, Seattle, 1980-81; prof. communication and Native Am. studies U. Nebr., Omaha, 1982—; curriculum reviewer N.Y. State Dept. Edn., 1988-92; manuscript reviewer Nat. Geographic, Washington, 1987, Wadsworth Pubs., Belmont, Calif., 1991. Author: Wasichu, 1979, Forgotten Founders, 1982, 89, El Pueblo, 1983, Exemplar of Liberty, 1991, Life and Death in Mohawk Country, 1993, Ecocide of Native America, 1995, Debating Democracy, 1996, Native American Political Systems and the Evolution of Democracy: An Annotated Bibliography, 1996. Recipient Tchg. Freedom of Expression 3d prize Assn. for Edn. in Journalism and Mass Comm., 1992; Univ. Com. on Rsch. summer fellow, 1983; Robert T. Reilly professorship, 1996—. Office: U Nebr at Omaha Dept Communication Omaha NE 68182

JOHANSEN, HERMAN JOHN, financial consultant; b. Springfield, Mo., Nov. 29, 1957; s. Marvin John and Rosemary (Graf) J.; m. Catherine Louise Netzer, Oct. 7, 1978; children: Cassandra L., Nathan J. BFA in Theatre, Southwest Mo. State U., 1980. Sales rep. Mut. of Omaha, Springfield, Mo., 1980-85; sales rep. Mut. of N.Y., Springfield, Mo., 1985—; owner, planner The Johansen Group, Springfield, Mo.; dir. Greene County Estate Planning Coun., Springfield, 1991-93; class moderator Life Underwriters Tng. Coun., Washington, 1984-88. Contbr. articles to profl. jours. Charter pres. Puppetry Arts League Springfield, 1988-92; fundraiser, event coord. Area 6 Spl. Olympics, Springfield, 1992, 93; fundraising event chmn. A Sporting Chance,

1994, 95, 96. Recipient Vol. of Yr. award Springfield Little Theatre, 1989, 91, 95. Mem. Nat. Assn. Life Underwriters, Am. Soc. CLUs and ChFCs, Springfield Area C. of C. (social com. 1991-96), Greene County Estate Planning Coun., Gen. Agts. and Mgrs. Assn. (dir. 1989-93, past pres.), Elks, Tower Club. Mem. Christian Ch. Office: 5337-C S Campbell Springfield MO 65810

JOHGART, STEVE R., index editor; b. Ann Arbor, Mich., Apr. 15, 1952; s. Herbert M. and Sarah (Riggs) Taggart; m. Nancy L. Johnson, Aug. 18, 1981; children: Sean M., Abra W. BA, Mich. State U., 1975. Proofreader State of Mich. Legis. Svc. Bur., Lansing, 1980; proofer, editor UMI, Ann Arbor, 1981-84, reproof editor, 1984-89, CDI index editor, 1989—; membership sec. MacTechnics, Ann Arbor, 1990-93, BBS operator, bd. dirs., 1993—. Editor two issues All Ways Free, 1986. Mem. Am. Soc. Indexers, Great Lakes Rainbow (focalizer).

JOHN, ERWIN ERNEST, editor; b. Mankato, Minn., May 23, 1917; s. Emil Otto and Gertrud (Gieschen) J.; m. Sherrill Marguerite Schlatter, Aug. 1, 1942; children: Linda, Spencer Paul. BE, Tchrs. Coll., Mankato, Minn., 1938. High sch. tchr. New London, Minn., 1938-39, St. Clair, Minn., 1939-41; meteorologist Northwest Airlines, Mpls., 1946-47, U.S. Weather Bur., Mpls., 1947-73; book store supr. Augsburg Pub. House, Mpls., 1973-82; ch. libr. Mt. Olivet Luth. Ch., Mpls., 1950-65. Author: Key to a Successful Church Library, 1958; editor Luth. Librs., 1958-83; contbr. articles on ch. librs. to profl. jours. With USAF, 1941-45. Recipient award for significant contbns. to ch. librs. Ch. and Synagogue Libr. Assn., St. Paul, 1971. Mem. Luth. Ch. Libr. Assn. (founder).

JOHN, GERALD WARREN, hospital pharmacist; b. Salem, Ohio, Feb. 16, 1947; s. Harold Elba and Ruth Springer (Pike) J.; m. Jean Ann Marie Orris, Nov. 5, 1977; children—Patrick Warren, Jeanette Lynn. B.S.Ph., Ohio No. U., 1970; M.S., U. Md., 1974. Registered pharmacist, Ohio, Md. Staff pharmacist North Columbiana County Community Hosp., Salem, 1970-72; asst. resident in hosp. pharmacy U. Md. Hosp., Balt., 1972-73, sr. resident, 1973-74, chmn. patient care pharmacies, 1974-76; dir. pharmacy Ohio Valley Hosp., Steubenville, Ohio, 1976—; preceptor profl. externship program Ohio No. U. Sch. Pharmacy, 1977—; adj. clin. instr. practical experience program Duquesne U. Sch. Pharmacy, 1976—. Columnist Weirton Daily Times, 1990-94. Trustee, v.p. Valley Hospice Inc., 1985—. Named Hosp. Pharmacist of Yr., Md. Soc. Hosp. Pharmacists, 1976, Outstanding Young Man of Am., U.S. Jaycees, 1977. Fellow Am. Soc. Cons. Pharmacists; mem. Am. Soc. Hosp. Pharmacists, Ohio Soc. Hosp. Pharmacists, Jefferson County Acad. Pharmacy, Southeastern Ohio Soc. Hosp. Pharmacists (pres. 1985-87), Rho Chi, Phi Eta Sigma. Methodist. Mem. adv. bd. Contemporary Pharmacy Practice, 1977-83.

JOHN, HUGO HERMAN, natural resources educator; b. Natoma, Kans., Feb. 13, 1929; s. Lorenz Louis and Clara Marie (Doehrmann) J.; m. Prudence Patricia Shuck, Sept. 9, 1950; children: Patrick, Peter, Sarah. BS, U. Minn., 1959, MS, 1961, PhD, 1964. From asst. prof. to assoc. prof. Coll. Forestry U. Minn., St. Paul, 1964-69, prof., 1969-72; prof. Coll. Forestry, Wildlife and Range Scis., assoc. dean U. Idaho, Moscow, 1972-74; dean, prof. Sch. Natural Resources U. Vt., Burlington, 1974-83; dean Coll. Agriculture and Natural Resources, dir. Agrl. Expt. Sta. and Coop. Extension U. Conn., Storrs, 1983-87, prof. natural resources, 1987-94, prof. emeritus, 1994—; forestry expert UN Food and Agr. Orgn., Puerto Cabezas, Nicaragua, 1965-66, Nat. Univ. Medellin, Colombia, 1969-71; cons. Taconic Found., N.Y.C., Internat. Paper Co., N.Y.C., 1981-84; sr. cons. UN Devel. Programme, Humane Soc. of U.S., 1993—; devel./planning cons. Internat. Exec. Svcs. Corps., Zimbabwe, 1996. Contbr. articles to profl. jours. Mem., treas. bd. dirs. Smokey House Project, Danby, Vt., 1976—; bd. dirs. Merck Forest Found., Rupert, Vt., 1980-83, Ea. States Expn., West Springfield, Mass, 1989—, mem. Conn. trustees, 1984—, chmn., 1989—. With U.S. Army, 1950-52. Mem. Soc. Am. Foresters (chmn. accreditation com. 1981-84), Am. Forestry Assn. Home: Box 732 501 4th Ave SE Mapleton MN 56065

JOHN, K. K. (JOHN KURUVILLA KAIYALETHE), minister; b. Erath, India, May 24, 1936; came to U.S., 1962; s. Kuruvilla Korula and Rachel (Yohannan) K.; m. Tamara Fogel, Sept. 3, 1963; children: Nava, David, Mihal. Diploma in Theology, Zion Bible Coll. and Sem., Mulakuzha, India, 1957; ThD, Kingsway Coll. and Sem., 1986; DD (hon.), Jameson Christian Coll. Nat. dir. Christian edn. and youth Ch. of God, India, 1957-61; sr. pastor Ch. of God, Bombay, 1960-61; free-lance journalist Jerusalem, 1961-62; pres. Internat. Student Fellowship, 1966-71; founder-dir., dir. Assemblies of God Campus Ministries, 1967-74, min., conf. speaker, ch. growth cons., 1974—; min., conf. speaker; nat. dir. edn. and Sunday schs. India; v.p. U. Minn. Council Religious Advisors. Mem. U.S. Presdl. adv. com. Commn. Campus Unrest; mem. Parent Adv. Commn., Mpls. Pub. Schs., 1986—; nat. bd. dirs. Reaching Across Divisions-Presbyn. Chs. Am.; mem. anti-racism initiative steering group Minn. Coun. Chs.; mem. inter-religious com. Temple Israel; active pioneered adult edn., active participant in interfaith movements.

JOHN, MERTIS, JR., record company executive; b. Detroit, May 22, 1932; s. Mertis and Lillie G. (Robinson) J.; m. Essie M. Wincher, June 16, 1957; 1 child, Darryl E. AA, Wayne Coll., 1978. Songwriter for King Records, Cin. and N.Y.C., 1955-67; founder Mertis Music Co., Detroit, 1962—; founder, pres. Meda Records, 1961—; co-producer Inside Music, 1977; also musician, songwriter; author (poem) A World of Freedom, 1989 (book) Speaking from the Heart, 1996. With U.S. Army, 1952-54, Korea. Recipient Golden Poet award World of Poetry, 1989, 90. Mem. Broadcast Music Inc., Detroit Soc. Musicians and Entertainers (chmn. bd. dirs. 1984—), Nat. Acad. Rec. Arts and Scis., Am. Fedn. Musicians, Broadcast Music Inc. (corr.), Masons (32nd degree). Baptist. Composer over 300 songs.

JOHN, RICHARD C., integrated petroleum company executive; b. Milw., Mar. 17, 1950; s. Richard C. and Mary W. (Widrig) J.; m. Carolyn H. Finn, June 2, 1973; children: Catherine M., Meredith C. BBA, U. Wis., 1972; MBA, Northwestern U., 1982. CPA. Supr. sr. acct. Price Waterhouse, N.Y.C., 1972-78; various positions Amoco Corp., Chgo., 1978-83; supr. fin. contr. Amoco Prodn. Co. Internat., Chgo., 1983-84; mgr. acctg. Amoco Oil Co., Chgo., 1984-85; staff dir. budgets Amoco Corp., Chgo., 1985-87; mgr. fin. & adminstrn. Amoco Chem. Co., Houston, 1987-89; contr. Amoco Performance Products, Atlanta, 1989-93; mgr. Amoco Corp., Chgo., 1993-96; v.p. fin. and adminstrn., CFO Opportunity Internat., Elmhurst, Ill., 1996—. Bd. dirs. Flagstaff Mission to the Navajos, 1996—; deacon 4th Presbyn. Ch., 1979-87; elder, treas. Clear Lake Presbyn. Ch., 1988-89; officer, mem. choir Johnson Ferry Bapt. Ch., 1990-93; mem. missions com. Wheaton Bible Ch., 1994—. Mem. AICPA, Fin. Execs. Inst., Inst. Mgmt. Accts. Office: Opportunity Internat 360 W Butterfield Rd Elmhurst IL 60126

JOHNS, ALEXANDER B., company executive; b. 1961. BA in Philosophy, U. Chgo., 1983, MBA, 1987. Sr. cons. Frank Lynn and Assoc., Chgo., 1988-91; prin. Quality Directions, Inc., Chgo., 1991—. Mem. Am. Soc. for Quality Control, The Planning Forum. Office: Quality Directions Inc 150 S Wack Dr Ste 470 Chicago IL 60606-4101

JOHNS, BEVERLY ANNE HOLDEN, special education administrator. BS, Catherine Spalding Coll., 1968; MS, So. Ill. U., 1970; postgrad., numerous univs., 1970—. Cert. elem. tchr., early childhood spl. edn., gen. adminstrv., spl. type 10 K-12 tchg. and supervising learning disabilities and social and emotional disorders. Sch. administr., program supr. Four Rivers Spl. Edn. Dist., Jacksonville, Ill., 1972—; adj. instr., demontration tchr. So. Ill. U., Carbondale, Ill. Dept. of Mental Health, 1970-72; part-time instr. MacMurray Coll., Jacksonville, 1977-79, 90—; adminstrv. intern Ill. State Bd. of Edn., Springfield, 1981. Author: Techniques for Managing Verbally and Physically Aggressive Students, 1995, Reduction of School Violence: Alternatives to Suspension, 1995. Bd. dirs. Jacksonville Area Assn. for Retarded Citizens, Spl. Olympics. Fellowship So. Ill. U., 1968; recipient Cert. of Recognition Ill. Atty. Gen.; named Jacksonville Woman of Yr. Bus. and Profl. Women's Club. Mem. Internat. Coun. Exceptional Children, Internat. Coun. for Children with Behavioral Disorders (v.p. 1995), Internat. Divsn. Learning Disabilities (sec. 1994—), Ill. Coun. Exceptional Childrem (pres., Lifetime Achievement award 1989, Presdl. award 1983), Coun. Exceptional Children (pres. chpt. 99), Ill. Alliance Exceptional Children and Adults (v.p. 1982—), Ill. Coun. for Children with Behavioral Disorders (founder, past pres. Ill. divsn. for learning disabilities), Lambda State, Delta Kappa Gamma, Phi Delta Kappa. Home: PO Box 340 Jacksonville IL 62651

JOHNS, MICHAEL DOUGLAS, public policy analyst, consultant, writer; b. Allentown, Pa., Sept. 8, 1964; s. Glenn Franklyn and Nancy Louise (Hummel) J.; m. Nicole Denise Miles, Sept. 30, 1995. Student, Cambridge (Eng.) U., 1984; BBA in Econs., U. Miami, 1986. Editl. intern Nat. Journalism Ctr., Washington, 1983; Lyndon Baines Johnson intern Congressman Don Ritter, Washington, 1984; asst. editor Policy Rev. Mag., Washington, 1986-88; fgn. policy analyst The Heritage Found., Washington, 1988-91; spl. asst. to pres. Drew U., Madison, N.J., 1991-92; speechwriter to Pres. of U.S. The White House, Washington, 1992; speechwriter to U.S. Sec. Commerce U.S. Dept. Commerce, Washington, 1992-93; dir. rsch. Internat. Rep. Inst., Washington, 1993-94; mgr. corp. comm., sr. writer Eli Lilly and Co., Indpls., 1994-95; pub. policy analyst, cons., writer Fairfax, Va., 1995—; adj. fellow Alexis de Tocqueville Instn., Arlington, 1994—; fgn. policy group advisor Dole for Pres., Inc., 1996—; authored speeches and ofcl. statements for former pres. George Bush, including July 4th nat. TV address to the nation, departure statement with Japanese Prime Minister, speeches to Office of Nat. Drug Control Policy, Nat. Inst. for Responsible Fatherhood and Family Devel., Am. Legion/Boys Nation and others; sr. advisor to devel. projects Internat. Rep. Inst., Kuwait, Turkey, and other nations, 1993-94; directed and contributed to nat. and internat. mktg. and comms. strategies for cancer, cardiovascular, ctrl. nervous system, endocrine, and infectious disease pharm. products. Eli Lilly and Co., 1994-95; guest polit and pub. policy analyst for numerous TV and radio programs including MacNeil/Lehrer News Hour, C-SPAN, CNBC, Fox Morning News, Voice of Am., BBC, others; guest lectr. UN, Vassar Coll., U. N.C., Chapel Hill, others; U.S. adv. coun. Mozambique Inst., London. Author: U.S. and Africa Statistical Handbook, 1990, 2d edit., 1991; contbg. author: Freedom in the World: The Annual Survey of Political Rights and Civil Liberties, 1993, Strengthening Central European Policy Institutes, 1995; contbg. editor USSR Monitor newsletter, The Heritage Found., 1989-91, Window & Door Fabricator Mat., Nat. Glass Assn., McLean, Va., 1996—; peer reviewer The Harvard Internat. Jour. of Press/Politics Harvard U.; alumni bd. advisors Campus mag. Intercollegiate Studies Inst., Wilmington, Del.; contbr. numerous articles to profl. jours, periodicals and newspapers, including Wall St. Jour., Christian Sci. Monitor, others; author numerous acad. and pub. policy rsch. studies; reported from Africa, Asia, L.Am., Middle East, Persian Gulf and former Soviet Union for numerous publs. Key club mem. United Way; active Luth. Ch. of the Holy Spirit, Emmaus, Pa.; mem. The Coca-Cola Civic Action Network. Recipient Shell Oil Co.'s Century III Leadership award, 1981, Svc. award Kiwanis, 1982, cert. appreciation Spl. Olympics, 1983, award of appreciation Lao Vets Am., 1995, numerous citations in Congl. Record, U.S. Congress; named to Lambda Chi Alpha internat. Hall of Fame, 1996. Mem. Nat. Journalism Ctr. Alumni Coun., Iron Arrow Honor Soc. U. Miami, Assn. on Third World Affairs, Reagan Alumni Assn., Bush/Quayle Alumni Assn., Puente de Jovenes Profls. Cubanos, The Coca-Cola Co. Civic Action Network, Pub. Rels. Soc. Am., Washington Ind. Writers, Lambda Chi Alpha (Hall of Fame 1996). Republican. Lutheran. Home: 4150 Zinnia Ln Fairfax VA 22030

JOHNS, WILLIAM HOWARD, psychiatrist, neurologist; b. Hamilton, Ohio, Apr. 18, 1941; s. Howard William and Martha (Sleigh) J.; m. Catherine Marie O'Keefe, May 30, 1982; children: Howard William II, Stephanie Marie. AB, Princeton U., 1963; MS in Anatomy, U. Cin., 1968; DO, Kirksville (Mo.) Coll. Osteo. Medicine, 1973; ed. spl. student program, Topeka Inst. for Psychoanalysis, 1984-90. Instr. anatomy Kirksville Coll. Osteo. Medicine, 1967-73; intern Grandview Hosp., Dayton, 1973-74; resident in neurology Cleve. Clinic Hosp., 1974-77; asst. prof. neurology Ohio U. Coll. Osteo. Medicine, Athens, 1977-78; pvt. practice neurology Dayton, Ohio, 1978-82; resident psychiatry The Menninger Found., Topeka, Kans., 1982-85, psychiatrist, staff psyciatrist, 1985—, asst. team leader, 1985-89; team leader The Menninger Found., 1989—, comprehensive out-patient evaluations, 1985-89; faculty mem. Karl Menninger Sch. Psychiatry, Topeka, 1990-95; pvt. practice psychiatry, 1995—, pvt. practice neurology, 1996—; dir. Psychotic Disorders Study Program, 1993-95, neuropsychiatry consultations, 1992-95; pvt. practice psychiatry, 1996—; clin. asst. prof. neurology Wright State U. Sch. Medicine, Dayton, 1979-82, Ohio U. Coll. Osteo. Medicine, Athens, 1979-82, W.Va. Sch. Osteo. Medicine, Lewisburg, 1979-82. Recipient Outstanding Clin. Faculty award Dayton region Ohio U. Coll. Osteo. Medicine, 1982, Sydney M. Kanev Meml. award Am. Coll. Neuropsychiatrists, 1985, Outstanding Clun. Faculty award Dayton region Ohio Coll. Osteo. Medicine. Mem. Am. Acad. Neurology, Am. Neuropsychiatric Assn. Home: 517 SW Danbury Ln Topeka KS 66606-2229 Office: The Menninger Found PO Box 829 Topeka KS 66601-0829

JOHNS, WILLIAMS DAVIS, JR., geologist, educator; b. Waynesburg, Pa., Nov. 2, 1925; s. William Davis and Beatrice (VanKirk) J.; m. Mariana Paull, Aug. 28, 1948 (dec. Apr. 1993); children: Sydney Ann, Susan Helen, David William, Amy Matilda. BA, Coll. Wooster, 1947; MA, U. Ill., 1951, PhD, 1952. Spl. rsch. asst. petrology Engring. Expt. Sta., U. Ill., 1949-52; rsch. asst., then asst. prof. geology U. Ill., 1952-55; mem. faculty Washington U., St. Louis, 1955-69, prof. earth scis., 1964-69, chmn. dept., 1962-69; now with dept. geology U. Mo., Columbia; vis. prof. U. Pitts., 1990-91, U. Vienna, 1994. Recipient U.S.-German Scientist award U. Goettingen, 1976-77; Fulbright fellow U. Goettingen, 1959-60, U. Heidelberg, 1968-69, U. Vienna, 1983-84. Fellow Geol. Soc. Am., Mineral. Soc. Am.; mem. Mineral. Soc. Great Britain and Ireland, Mineral. Soc. Can., Deutsches Mineralogisches Gesellschaft, Geochem. Soc., Phi Beta Kappa. Presbyterian (elder). Home: 2200 Yuma Dr Columbia MO 65203-1452

JOHNSON, ALAN E., financial consultant; b. Muskegon, Mich., Aug. 5, 1965. BS, Ctrl. Mich. U., Mt. Pleasant, 1987. Fin. analyst Dunn & Bradstreet, Chgo., 1987-91; fin. cons. Smith Barney Inc., Grand Rapids, Mich., 1991—. Republican. Office: Smith Barney Inc 99 Monroe Ave NW Ste 200 Grand Rapids MI 49503-2639

JOHNSON, ALICE M., state legislator; b. Apr. 1, 1941; four children. AA, Mpls. Cmty. Coll., 1986; BA, Concordia Coll., St. Paul, 1993. Dist. 48B rep. Minn. Ho. of Reps., St. Paul, 1986—; chair K-13 education fin. divsn.; mem. labor mgmt. rels., Internat. Trade Com. Minn. Ho. Reps. Home: 801 Ballantyne Ln NE Minneapolis MN 55432-2054 Office: Minn Ho of Reps State Capital Bldg Saint Paul MN 55155-1606*

JOHNSON, ANDREW P., financial consultant; b. St. Louis, Dec. 7, 1969. BS, S.E. Mo. State U., Kaygerado, 1991. Fin. cons. Cutter & Co., Chesterfield, Mo., 1992—. Baptist. Office: Cutter & Co 15510 Olive Blvd Ste 204 Chesterfield MO 63017-0710

JOHNSON, ANDREW PAUL, veterinarian; b. Worthington, Minn., Mar. 7, 1951; s. Cecil Paul and Georgie Lorraine (McGuigan) J.; m. Monica Ruth Eshleman, Aug. 19, 1972; children: Nathan, Megan, Zachary. BS, U. Minn., 1974, DVM, 1976. Dairy veterinarian Valley Vet. Clinic, Seymour, Wis., 1976-90, Total Herd Mgmt. Svcs., Seymour, 1986-95; dairy advisor Monsanto Co., 1992-95, Diamond Animal Health, 1994-95, Smith Kline Beccham, 1994. Author: Professional Approach to Quality Milk, 1995. Pres. bd. Crystal Springs Golf Club, Seymour, 1981-85. Mem. AMVA, Am. Assn. Bovine Practioners (Excellence award in Dairy 1989), Wis. Vet. Med. Assn. (pres. 1992-93, bd. dirs., Veterinarian of Yr. 1994). Home and Office: 824 Woodside Dr Seymour WI 54165

JOHNSON, ANTHONY COLBERT, assistant dean, educator; b. L.A., Mar. 28, 1947; s. Matthew L. Johnson and Mary Ellen (Greene) Staples; m. Karen Marie Williams, Aug. 10, 1974; 1 child, Anissa Camille. BS in Agr., U. Wis., 1975, MS in Counseling, 1982. Nat. cert. counselor Nat. Bd. Cert. Counselors. Mechanical designer Collins Radio Co., Cedar Rapids, Iowa, 1966-69; specification analyst Ohio Med. Products, Madison, Wis., 1969-77; admissions counselor U. Wis., Madison, 1977-79, counselor/advisor to students, 1979-87, sr. advisor, 1987-89, student svcs. coord., 1989-93, asst. dean, 1993—; pres., owner Johnson Resource Svcs., Madison, 1990—. V.p. Equal Opportunity Commn., Madison, 1993; pres. Madison Acad. Staff Assn., 1992; bd. dirs. Madison Westside Track Club, 1993; mem. Acad. Staff Exec. Com., nominating com., 1991-94. Recipient Mentor for Youth award Met. Sch. Dist., 1995, Outstanding Parents award, 1988; scholar Wis. Realtors Assn., 1991. Mem. Wis. Assn. Ednl. Opportunity (chair conf. 1978-80, cert. 1985), Capitol City Lodge # 2 Prince Hall Affiliate (sec. 1975-80), Order Ea. Star (Worthy Patron Friendship chpt. # 2 1989-93). Roman Catholic. Office: U Wis-Madison 1300 Linden Dr Madison WI 53706

JOHNSON, ARNOLD WILLIAM, mortgage company executive; b. Axtell, Kans., June 5, 1916; s. William and Hilda Elizabeth (Hedstrom) J.; m. Bertha Mildred Scott, Oct. 9, 1940; 1 child, Jill Lynn. BSBA, Kans. U., 1940. Pres., prin. Arnold W. Johnson Ins. Agy., Topeka, 1940—, also chmn.; pres., prin. C.R. Scott Mortgage Co. Inc., Topeka, 1956—, chmn.; bd. dirs. Preferred Fire Ins. Co., Topeka, 1950-75, Capitol Abstract and Title Co., Topeka, 1965-75, Pioneer Nat. Life Ins. Co., Topeka, 1967-83, treas., Kans. Mut. Ins. Co., Topeka, 1979—, dir. Fidelity State Bank and Trust Co., Topeka. Active adv. bd. Topeka Capitol City Ctrl. Bus. Dist. Redevel., 1984-90, Kans. Watertower Place Redevel., 1984-90; trustee, deacon, treas. First Congl. Ch. With USN, 1942-45. Recipient Silver Found. award YMCA, 1989, Outstanding Svc. award Kans. Mut. Ins. Co., 1987. Mem. Topeka Bd. Realtors, Kans. Bd. Realtors, Nat. Bd. Realtors, Profl. Ins. assn., Topeka C. of C., Downtown Topeka Inc., Topeka Retail Credit Bur. and Better Bus. Bur., Knife and Fork Club Internat., Cosmopolitan Club Internat., Moose, Elks, Masons, Shriners, Royal Order Jesters, VFW, Am. Legion, Alpha Kappa Psi. Republican. Home: 1531 SW Lakeside Dr Topeka KS 66604-2529 Office: CR Scott Mortgage Co Inc 420 Bank Iv Tower Topeka KS 66603-3426 also: 534 S Kansas Ave Ste 420 Topeka KS 66603-3426

JOHNSON, AUDREY ANN, options trader, stockbroker; b. Chgo., June 7, 1954; d. Elmer and Diane Ann (Vassiv) J. Student, North Ctrl. Coll., 1972-75, U. Ill. Registered stockbroker, real estate salesperson, Ill. Real estate salesperson Century 21 Cahill Bros., Chgo., 1975-80; stockbroker Charles Schwab, Chgo., 1980-87; Chgo. Bd. Options Exch. floor trader Drexel Burnham, Chgo., 1987-90; pvt. practice specializing in futures, options, indexes and equities Chgo., 1990—; options broker, stockbroker Profl. Trader's Inst. Securities, Chgo., 1990—; real estate salesperson Coldwell Banker, Palos Heights, Ill., 1995; arbitrator Chgo. Bd. Options Exch., 1989-92; guest spkr. Chgo. TV Channel 26, 1993-94; participant in NAFTA. Mem. Nat. Assn. Securities Dealers, Ind. Floor Members Assn., Chgo. Bd. Options Exch., Palos Hills Horseman's Assn. Democrat. Roman Catholic. Home: 9174 South Rd Palos Hills IL 60465-2135

JOHNSON, BADRI NAHVI, sociology educator, real estate business owner; b. Tehran, Iran, Dec. 1, 1934; came to U.S., 1957; d. Ali Akbar and Monir (Khazraii) Nahvi; m. Floyd Milton Johnson, July 2, 1960; children: Robert, Rebecca, Nancy, Shahla. BS, U. Minn., 1967, MA, 1969; postgrad., 1994—. Stenographer Curtis 1000, Inc., St. Paul, 1958-62; lab. instr. U. Minn., Mpls., 1966-69, teaching asst., 1969-72; chief exec. officer Real Estate Investment and Mgmt. Enterprise, St. Paul, 1969—; instr. sociology Anoka-Ramsey Community Coll., Coon Rapids, Minn., 1973—; pub. speaker, bd. dirs., sponsor pub. radio KFAI, Mpls., 1989-93; established an endowed scholarship for women Anoka Ramsey C.C., 1991. Radio talk show host KCW, Brookline Parks, Minn., 1993. Organizer Iranian earthquake disaster relief, 1990. Recipient Earthquake Relief Orgn. citation Iranian Royal Household, 1968. Mem. NEA, Minn. Edn. Assn., Sociologists of Minn., U. Minn. Alumni Assn., Minn. Club. Home: 1726 Iowa Ave E Saint Paul MN 55106-1334 Office: Anoka-Ramsey Community Coll 11200 Mississippi Blvd NW Minneapolis MN 55433-3470

JOHNSON, BENJAMIN LEIBOLD, former education training and management analyst; b. Norborne, Mo., Nov. 23, 1950; s. Murrell Faxton and Chlora Pauline (Naylor) J. BA, Central Mo. State U., 1971, BS, 1974, MS, 1976; MPA, U. Okla., 1988. Tchr., Raytown and Independence (Mo.) Public Schs., 1974-76; with Wayne Regan, Inc., Realtors, Shawnee, Kans., 1976; tchr., chmn. dept. social studies, English, French, Breckenridge (Mo.) Pub. Schs., 1979-80; career intern edn. specialist Ft. Sill, Okla., 1980-82, tng. analyst/edn. specialist, 1982-85; edn. specialist/instr. U.S. Army Engrs. Sch., Fort Belvoir, Va., 1985-88; mgmt. analyst, directorate of resources manpower and orgn. divsn. USAF Office Spl. Investigations, Bolling AFB, D.C., 1988-94. dept. chmn. social studies, English and French, also edn. specialist. Served with USNR, 1976-79. Mem. Assn. Am. Geographers, Nat. Soc. for Performance and Instruction, Am. Acad. Polit. and Social Scis., Am. Soc. for Pub. Adminstrn., Project Mgmt. Inst., Naval Enlisted Res. Assn., Starfleet Internat. Star Trek Fan Club (various offices), Masons, Order DeMolay. Home: 1503 Eisner Ave Apt F2 Sheboygan WI 53083-2963

JOHNSON, BETH ANN, pediatric nurse, gerontology nurse; b. Rochester, Minn., June 15, 1960; d. Robert D. and Mary Ann (Postier) Senjem; children: Sara Johnson, Kristen Johnson. ADN, Rochester Community Coll., 1989. RN, Minn. Charge nurse Bethany Samaritan Heights, Rochester; home health aide Joseph Postier, Byron, Minn.; pediatric nurse Shamrock Nursing Svc., Dodge Center, Minn.; staff nurse Hiawatha Homes, Rochester, 1993, asst. health svcs. dir., 1994, health svcs. dir., 1995-96; clin. nurs. Fed. Med. Ctr., Rochester, 1996—.

JOHNSON, BETTY LOU, secondary education educator; b. Stockwell, Ind., Apr. 4, 1927; d. Paul Stanley Jones and Ethel Leona (Royer) J.; m. Kenneth Odell Johnson, Aug. 5, 1950; children: Cynthia Jo (Mrs. James P. Greaton), Gregory Alan. BS in Home Econs., Purdue U., 1948; postgrad., Northwood Inst. Culinary Arts, 1981, 83. Cert. home economist. Tchr. LaCrosse (Ind.) Jr.-Sr. High Sch., 1948-49, Wendell L. Willkie High Sch., Elwood, Ind., 1949-51, Thomas Carr Howe High Sch., Indpls., 1951-57; substitute tchr. Gt. Oaks Joint Vocat. Sch. Dist., Cin. Mem. AAUW, Am. Home Econs. Assn. (life), Ohio Home Econs. Assn. (life), John Purdue Club, Purdue U. Alumni Assn. (life), Gamma Sigma Delta. Home: Indian Hill Village 8360 Arapaho Ln Cincinnati OH 45243-2718

JOHNSON, BOB, state legislator, social worker; b. 1945; one child. BA, Bemidji State U. Social worker, spl. edn. educator; Dist. 4A rep. Minn. Ho. of Reps., St. Paul, 1986—; former vice chmn. environ. and natural resources com., Minn. Ho. of Reps.; vice chmn. govt. op. and gaming com., mem. state govt. fin. divsn., commerce and econ. devel.-tourism, small bus. divsn. gen. legis., vet. affairs, and election coms.; asst. majority leader. Home: RR 2 Box 145 Bemidji MN 56601-8205*

JOHNSON, BRENDA KAY, biology educator; b. Fayetteville, N.C., Nov. 8, 1946; d. William Craft and Dorothy Mae (Kiger) Moore; m. Thomas C. Johnson, Sept. 2, 1977; children: Ivy Christina, Elisa Anne. BS in Biology, Meth. Coll., Fayetteville, 1968; MS in Secondary Edn., Tex. A&I U., 1972; EdD in Elem. Edn., U. S.D., 1977. Cert. curriculum specialist, S.D. Tchr. biology Ben Bolt (Tex.) Sch. Dist., 1968-69, Kingsville (Tex.) Sch. Dist., 1969-72; adj. asst. prof. U. S.D., Vermillion, 1977-79, 86; asst. prof. sci. edn. Sioux Falls (S.D.) Coll., 1987-89; asst. prof. biol. scis. Western Mich. U., Kalamazoo, 1989-91; adj. asst. prof. Dakota State U., Madison, 1992-94. Editor: K-3 Science Activities, 1978; contbr. articles to profl. jours. Vol. ch. and comty. Grantee NSF, 1978, S.D. Bd. Regents, 1988, 89. Mem. AAAS, AAUW, Nature Conservancy. Democrat. Lutheran.

JOHNSON, BRUCE, state legislator; m. Kelley Johnson; children: Shane, Meagan, Connor, Morgan. BS, BA, Bowling Green State U.; JD, Capital U. Bar: Ohio. City prosecutor Columbus; senator Ohio State Senate, Columbus, chmn. judiciary com. Recipient Watchdog of the Treasury award United Conservatives of Ohio, 1996. Mem. Ohio State Bar Assn., Columbus Bar Assn.

JOHNSON, CALVIN STEWART, tax accountant; b. Brainerd, Minn., Mar. 31, 1959; s. Jay Jerome and Lucycle (Daniels) J.; m. Tammy Lynn Greenhill. BS, Crown Coll., 1981; MS, Wheaton (Ill.) Grad. Sch., 1986. Trust officer The No. Trust Co., Chgo., 1986—. Home: Unit 8 4131 N Pheasant Trail Ct Arlington Heights IL 60004-7995

JOHNSON, CARL RANDOLPH, chemist, educator; b. Charlottesville, Va., Apr. 28, 1937. BS, Med. Coll. Va., 1958; PhD in Chemistry, U. Ill., 1962. NSF rsch. fellow chemistry Harvard U., 1962; from asst. to prof. chemistry Wayne State U., Detroit, 1962-90, Disting. prof., 1990—; Humboldt sr. scientist, 1991; bd. dirs. Organic Syntheses, Inc. Mem. adv.

bd. Jour. Organic Chemistry, 1976-81. Alfred P. Sloan fellow, 1965-68. Mem. Am. Chem. Soc. (assoc. editor jour. 1984-89, Harry and Carol Mosher award 1992), Royal Soc. Chemistry. Office: Wayne State Univ Dept Chemistry Detroit MI 48202

JOHNSON, CHARLES RICHARD, publisher; b. Boonville, Ind., Apr. 3, 1912; s. Charles Hunter and Emma Helen (Laswell) J.; m. Verna Louise Miles, July 11, 1940. AB, Ind. U., 1935. Editor Boonville Standard, 1935-44, pub., 1944-60; pub., owner Warrick Newspapers, Boonville, 1960-83; cons., 1983—; dir. Peoples Trust and Savs. Bank. Sustaining mem. Rep. Nat. Com.; elder and fin. sec. Hemenway Meml. Presbyn. Ch.; commr. Presbytery Ohio Valley; mem. adv. coun. Ind. U. Sch. Medicine, 1972. Lt. USNR, 1944-46, PTO. Named hon. sec. state State of Ind., 1985. Mem. Am. Fedn. Musicians (profl. musician), Nat. Newspaper Assn., Ky. Press Assn., Ind. Rep. Editorial Assn. (pres. 1971-72, Editor of Yr. award 1972), Hoosier Press Assn. (pres. 1957-58), Warrick C. of C. (Disting. Svc. award 1985), Order of Ky. Cols., Coun. Sagamores of Wabash, Columbia Club (Indpls.), Ind. Soc. Chgo., Petroleum Club (Evansville, Ind.), Soc. Profl. Journalists (pres.'s club), Kennel Club (Evansville), Rolling Hills Country Club (Newburgh, Ind.), Masons, Shriners, Jesters, Sigma Delta Chi, Phi Gamma Delta (trustee Beechwood Ednl. Found. Inc.). Republican. Presbyterian. Home: 10 Lakeshore Dr Boonville IN 47601-2287 Office: Warrick Pub Co Inc 204 W Locust St Boonville IN 47601-1522

JOHNSON, CHRISTINE ANN, nurse; b. Omaha, Nebr., Aug. 23, 1951; d. Ralph James and Marlene (Marlenee) Matney; m. Timothy Carl Johnson, Aug. 1, 1970; children: Erik Carl, Christine Nicole. Cert. practical nurse, Met. Tech. Community Coll., 1973; BA cum laude, Creighton U., 1989. LPN, Nebr.; cert. pregnancy exercise instr.; cert. lactation cons. EKG technician Bishop Clarkson Meml. Hosp., Omaha, 1971-74, lic. practical nurse, 1978—, instr. pregnancy exercise, 1984-86, instr. sibling preparation, 1985-86, instr. breastfeeding, 1985-95; LPN Cons. in Cardiology, P.C., Omaha, 1974-78; tchr. asst. Creighton U. Dept. Psychology, Omaha, 1987-88; lactation cons. Bergan Mercy Med. Ctr., Omaha, 1994—; teaching asst. dept. psychology, child psychology, adolescent psychology, devel. psychology Creighton U., 1987-88. Assoc. editor (cons.' corner) Jour. Human Lactation, 1994—. Sec. United Meth. Women First United Meth. Ch., 1984-85, chmn. 1985-86; vol. Radio Talking Book, 1985; mem. Omaha Pub. Schs. Superintendent's Task Force on Human Growth and Devel., 1986. Mem. Internat. Lactation Cons. Assn., Psi Chi. Methodist. Home: 4618 N 129th Ave Omaha NE 68164-1708 Office: Bergan Mercy Med Ctr 7500 Mercy Rd Omaha NE 68124

JOHNSON, CINDY COBLE, councilwoman, marketing executive; b. El Paso, Tex., Aug. 20, 1956; d. Walter Mylen and Dewyria Shirley (Hendrix) Coble; m. David Johnson, Feb. 8, 1974; children: David, Luke, Phillip. G-rad. high sch., Plattsmouth, Nebr. OB technician Clarkson Hosp., Omaha, 1975-76; pers. asst. Target, Lincoln, Nebr., 1985-86; loan adminstr. 1st Nat. Bank, Lincoln, 1987-91; past chair Lincoln City Coun., 1995-96, chair, 1995-96; pers. cons. Talent +, Lincoln, 1994-96; mktg. mgr. Sings Now, Inc., Lincoln, 1996—; mem. Joint Budget Com., Lincoln, 1993-94, Highlands Tech. Park Com., Lincoln, 1993-95. Pres. MADD, Lancaster County, 1985-91; past chair Traffic Safety Com., Lincoln, 1989-94; trustee Lighthouse-At Risk Youth, Lincoln, 1993-94; past bd. dirs. People's City Mission, Lincoln,, 1993-96; active MAD DADS; sec. Houses of Hope. Recipient Bradley Cuda Meml. award Lincoln Bd. Realtors, 1990, Svc. to Mankind award Sertoma, 1991, Pub. Svc. award U.S. Dept. Transp., 1991, Ptnrs. in Prevention award Lincoln Coun. on Alcoholism and Drugs, 1994, Free enterprise award LIBA, 1996. Mem. Lincoln Ind. Bus. Assn. (Free Enterprise award 1996), C. of C. Office: Signs Now Inc 525 N 48th St Lincoln NE 68504

JOHNSON, CURTIS SCOTT, engineer; b. Faribault, Minn., Aug. 15, 1954; s. Robert Alfred and Alice Lucille (Backstrom) J.; m. Elaine Marlys Fitzner, Dec. 4, 1976; children: Erik, Scott. BSEE, Iowa State U., 1976. Registered profl. engr., Iowa. Engr. in tng. Iowa So. Utilities, Centerville, Iowa, 1976-78; distbn. engr. Cedar Falls (Iowa) Utilites, 1978-81, asst. mgr. engring., 1981-89, mgr. dept. engring., 1989—. Asst. cubmaster Cub Scout Pack 179, Cedar Falls, 1990-92, cubmaster, 1992-94, chmn., 1994-96; bd. govs. Iowa Maths. Coalition, Des Moines, 1991-95. Mem. NSPE (v.p. Iowa chpt. 1989-95, pres. 1995-96, John Dunlap-Sherman Woodward award 1987), IEEE, Cedar Falls C. of C. (bd. dirs. 1995-98). Republican. Lutheran. Home: 1210 Clay St Cedar Falls IA 50613-4106 Office: Cedar Falls Utilities 612 E 12th St PO Box 769 Cedar Falls IA 50613

JOHNSON, DARLENE ANN, nurse; b. Pine Ridge, S.D., Aug. 2, 1949; d. Homer Francis and Opal Leona (Whipple) Johnson; m. Mervin Duane Sr. (div.); children: Minnie, Francis, Arlene. BS in Nursing, Sacramento State Coll., 1971; MA in Health Adminstrn., Chadron State Coll., 1984. Head nurse med. unit VA Med. Ctr., Topeka, Kans., 1976-79; relief supr. VA Med. Ctr., Hot Springs, S.D., 1979-80, head nurse med. unit, 1982-85; staff nurse West Nebr. Gen. Hosp., Scottsbluff, 1980-82; dir. of nursing Pub. Health Svc. Indian Hosp., Pine Ridge, S.D., 1985-87; MCH program cons. Aberdeen (S.D.) Area Ind. Health Svc., 1987-91; dir. nursing Pub. Health Svc. Indian Hosp., Rosebud, S.D., 1991-95; quality assurance dir. Carl T. Curtis Health Edn. Ctr., Nacy, Nebr., 1995—. Mem., sec. Title IV Parent Com. Hot Springs, 1985-87, Johnson O'Malley Parent Com., Rapid City, 1987-88. Capt. U.S. Army, 1969-76; comdr. USPHS, 1985-90. capt. 1991—. Recipient Achievement medal USPHS, Rockville, M.D., 1986. Mem. AACN, ANA (cabinet on nursing practice 1989-90, congress of nursing practice 1990-94), S.D. Nurses Assn. (dist. pres. 1986, bd. dirs. 1988-90), Am. Indian/ Alaskan Native Nurses Assn., Nat. League Nursing. Am. Legion (adjutant 1991-94). Democrat. Home: PO Box 448 Nacy NE 68039 Office: Carl Curtis Health Edn Ctr Quality Assurance Dept Nacy NE 68039

JOHNSON, DAVEY (DAVID ALLEN JOHNSON), baseball team manager; b. Orlando, Fla., Jan. 30, 1943; children: Dave Jr., Dawn, Andrea. Student, Johns Hopkins U.; B.S., Trinity U. Baseball player Balt. Orioles, 1965-72; baseball player Atlanta Braves, 1973-75, Phila. Phillies, 1977-78, Chgo. Cubs, 1978; mgr. Inter-Am. League, Miami, 1979, Jackson League, Tex., 1981, Tidewater, Internat. League, 1983, N.Y. Mets, N.Y.C., 1984-90, Cin. Reds, 1993-96, Balt. Orioles, 1996—. Recipient Am. Gold Glove, 1969-71; mem. Am. League All-Star Team, 1968, 70, Nat. League All-Star Team, 1973; mgr. Nat. League All-Star Team, 1986, World Series championship team, 1986. Office: Balt Orioles 333 W Camden St Baltimore MD 21201*

JOHNSON, DAVID ALLEN, singer, songwriter, investor, minister; b. Indpls., Dec. 15, 1954; s. Eugene Robert and Vivian Claire (Moon) J. BA in English, Ind. U., 1977; cert., Columbia Sch. of Broadcasting, 1985. Ordained to ministry United Ch. of Christ, 1996. Founder, pres. Worldwide Assn. Disabled Entrepreneurs, Indpls., 1993—; treas. TechnoBillz Internat. Corp.; midwestern U.S coord. Network Tool, Inc.; trustee Network Tool Share Found. Singer, songwriter gospel and love songs; contbr. poems and articles to various publs.; concert promoter in field. Mem. Am. Creativity Assn. (bd. dirs.). Republican. Home and Office: 6008 Laurel Hall Dr Apt 4 Indianapolis IN 46226-2455

JOHNSON, DAVID CHESTER, university chancellor, sociology educator, academic administrator; b. Jan. 21, 1933; s. Chester Laven and Olga Henriett (Resnick) J.; m. Jean Ann Lunnis, Sept. 10, 1955; children: Stephen, Andrew, Jennifer. BA, Gustavus Adolphus Coll., 1954; MA, U. Iowa, 1956, PhD, 1959, LLD, Luther Coll., 1993. Instr. to prof. sociology Luther Coll., Decorah, Iowa, 1957-69; dean arts and scis. East Stroudsburg (Pa.) U., 1969-76; v.p. acad. affairs St. Cloud State U., Minn., 1976-83; dean Gustavus Adolphus Coll., St. Peter, Minn., 1983-90; chancellor U. Minn., Morris, 1990—. Cons. evaluator Norh Ctrl. Assn. Coll., 1993; mem. steering com. Kellogg Found. Vision for Change Project; mem. membership com. Collaboration for Tchg. and Learning. NSF sci. faculty fellow Inst. Social Research, Oslo, 1965-66; Adminstrv. fellow Am. Council Edn., Luther Coll., 1968-69, Summer Leadership fellow Bush Found., Inst. Edn. Mgmt., Harvard U., 1981; grantee Kennedy Swedish Fund, Sweden, 1976. Mem. S.W. Minn. Higher Edn. Orgn. for Telecomm., Kiwanis (chair). Democrat. Lutheran. Home: RR 1 Box 24 Morris MN 56267-9704 Office: U Minn Office of Chancellor Morris MN 56267

JOHNSON, DAVID GRANT, emergency physician; b. Gallipolis, Ohio, June 30, 1949; s. Lester Grant and Ruth Marie (Board) J.; m. Sharon E. Carr, Mar. 14, 1978. BS in Physics, Mich. State U., 1971; MD, W.Va. U., 1975. Diplomate Am. Bd. Emergency Medicine. Commd. ensign USN, 1972, advanced through grades to lt. comdr., 1979; intern USN, Portsmouth, Va., 1975-76; gen. med. officer USN, Okinawa, Japan, 1976-77, Norfolk, Va., 1977-78, Kittery, Maine, 1978-80; resigned USN, 1980; resident W.Va. Univ. Hosp., Morgantown, 1980-82, emergency physician, 1982-85; emergency physician St. Joseph's Hosp., Parkersburg, W.Va., 1985-93, Camden Clark Meml. Hosp., Parkersburg, W. Va., 1994-95, Marietta (Ohio) Meml. Hosp., 1995—. Fellow Am. Coll. Emergency Physicians. Roman Catholic.

JOHNSON, DAVID LEE, management educator; b. Beulah, Mich., Nov. 12, 1930; s. Andrew and Garnet Chicora (Daily) J.; m. Audrey Eileen Forrester, Mar. 1, 1953; children: Eric L., Timothy L., Susan L. BA, Mich. State U., 1955, MA, 1956, PhD, 1976. Tchr., counselor Warren (Mich.) Consolidated Sch., 1956-62, asst. prin., 1962-66, dir. cmty. edn., 1966-68, deputy supt., 1968-75; supt. Howell (Mich.) Pub. Schs., 1975-88; edn. cons. U. Mich., Ann Arbor, 1987-89; chair dept. mgmt., mktg. Davenport Coll., Lansing, Mich., 1989—; pres. bd. dirs. Met. Detroit Bur. Sch. Studies, 1982-88; chmn. bd. dirs. Mich. Assn. Sch. Adminstrs., Lansing, 1985-88. With USAF, 1949-52. Mem. Am. Soc. Quality Control, Howell C. of C. (bd. dirs. 1984-87), Rotary (pres. bd. dirs. 1985-88). Home: 151 Lakeview Ln Brighton MI 48116 Office: Davenport Coll 220 E Kalamazoo Lansing MI 48933

JOHNSON, DEAN ELTON, state legislator, Lutheran pastor; b. June 24, 1947; m. Avonelle Johnson. BA, Luther Coll.; MDiv, Luther Theol. Sem. Lutheran pastor; state rep. Minn. Ho. of Reps., St. Paul, 1977-82; Dist. 15 senator Minn. State Senate, St. Paul, 1982—; mem. elections and ethics, fin., gen. legis. and pub. gaming, transp., rules and adminstrn. and gaming regulation coms., Minn. State Senate; minority leader. Address: 910 11th St SW Willmar MN 56201-3029*

JOHNSON, DEBORAH K., investment advisor; b. Rice Lake, Wis., Jan. 28, 1955. BS in Speech Pathology, U. Wis., 1977. Speech clinician Osseo (Minn.) Sch. Dist., 1977-80, Univ. Tutoring Svcs., Seattle, 1981-84; investment advisor PaineWebber Inc., Cedar Rapids, Iowa, 1985-89, A.G. Edwards & Sons Inc., Cedar Rapids, 1989—. Republican. Office: AG Edwards & Sons Inc PO Box 75010 425 2d St SE Cedar Rapids IA 52407

JOHNSON, DENNIS E., state legislator; m. Donna Johnson; three children. Student, Wahpeton State Sch. Sci. Trucker, farmer and custom harvester; rep. N.D. State Ho. Reps. Dist. 12, 1993—, mem. edn. and agr. coms. Mem. Am. Legion. Home: PO Box 333 Minnewaukan ND 58351-0333*

JOHNSON, DOROTHY PHYLLIS, counselor, art therapist; b. Kansas City, Mo., Sept. 13, 1925; d. Chris C. and Mabel T. (Gillum) Green; BA in Art, Ft. Hays. State U., 1975, MS in Guidance and Counseling, 1976, MA in Art, 1979; m. Herbert E. Johnson, May 11, 1945; children: Michael E., Gregory K. Art therapist High Plains Comprehensive Mental Health Assn., Hays, Kans., 1975-76; art therapist, mental health counselor Sunflower Mental Health Assn., Concordia, Kans., 1976-78, Pawnee Mental Health Svcs., 1978-91, co-dir. Project Togetherness, 1976-77, coord. partial hospitalization, 1978-82, out-patient therapist, 1982-91; pvt. practice, 1991—; dir. Swedish Am. State Bank, Courtland, Kans., 1960—, sec., 1973-77. Mem. Kans., Am. art therapy assns., Am. Mental Health Counselors Assn., Am. Counseling Assn., Kans. Counseling Assn., Assn. for Humanistic Psychologists, Assn. Transpersonal Psychologists, Assn. Specialists in Group Work, Phi Delta Kappa, Phi Kappa Phi. Contbr. articles to profl. jours. Home: PO Box 200 Courtland KS 66939-0200 Office: 520 Washington St # B Concordia KS 66901-2117

JOHNSON, DOUGLAS EUGENE, manufacturing executive; b. Marshalltown, Iowa, Nov. 30, 1949. BS, Iowa State U., 1976. Plant mgr. Webco Mfg. Co., Olatha, Kans., 1986-89; v.p. tech. ops. Beam Industries, Webster City, Iowa, 1989—. Co-inventor Muffler Ctrl. Vacuum Systems. (pat. pending). Scoutmaster Troop 511 Boy Scouts Am., Webster City, 1991—. Mem. ASTM (com. mem.), Am. Welding Soc., Soc. Mfg. Engrs., Epsilon Pi Tau. Office: Beam Industries PO Box 788 Webster City IA 50595-0788

JOHNSON, DOUGLAS J., state legislator, secondary education counselor; b. Aug. 17, 1942. AA, Va. Jr. Coll.; BS, U. Minn., Duluth; MEd, Wis. State U. H.s. counselor; state rep. Minn. Ho. of Reps., St. Paul, 1970-74; Dist. 6 senator Minn. State Senate, St. Paul, 1976—; chmn. tax laws and taxes com., Minn. State Senate, mem. elections and ethics, pub. utilities and energy, redistricting, rules and adminstrn., jobs, energy and cmty. devel. coms. Office: PO Box 395 Cook MN 55723-0395 also: State Senate State Capitol Building Saint Paul MN 55155-1606*

JOHNSON, ELIZABETH, probation officer; b. Mpls., July 1, 1966; d. Herbert R. and Brydies (Reid) J. BS in Bus. Mgmt., Jackson State U., 1988; BA in Criminal Justice, Met. State U., 1993. Case mgr. intern Hennepin County Bur. Corrections, 1992-93; 911 telecommunicator St. Paul Police, 1988-94; employment guidance counselor Ramsey County Cmty. Human Svcs., St. Paul, 1994-96; juvenile probation officer Ramsey County Corrections, St. Paul, 1996—; cons. Jr. Achievement, Edina, Minn., 1990—, Edison H.S., Mpls., 1989—. Vol. Big Sisters, Mpls., 1989-91. Me. Jackson State U. Twin Cities Alumni Assn. (pres. 1993—, Outstanding Mem. award 1991). Democrat.

JOHNSON, ERIC CARL, software company executive; b. St. Louis, Nov. 21, 1951; s. Charles Leo and Esther Agnes (Rutledge) J.; m. Constance Maria Bearden, Mar. 7, 1981; children: Nicholas Karl, Ryan Patrick. BBA, U. Mo., 1974. Account mktg. rep. IBM, St. Louis, 1974-82; mktg. rep. Gen. Software Systems, Inc., St. Louis, 1983-85, v.p./owner, 1985-89, pres., owner, 1989—; sr. mktg. cons. R.A. Kottmeier & Assocs., St. Louis, 1990-94; area mgr. REAL - Industry Solutions Group, Inc., 1994—; cons. St. Louis Med., 1983—; br. sales mgr. REAL-ISG, St. Louis, 1996—; cons. to distbn. industry. Bd. dirs. Great Forest Park Balloon Race, St. Louis, 1975—. Mem. Am. Mgmt. Assn., Associated Gen. Contractors, U. Mo. Alumni Assn. Roman Catholic. Home: 15330 Schoettler Estates Dr Chesterfield MO 63017-5461 Office: 10411 Clayton Rd Ste 308 Saint Louis MO 63131-2913

JOHNSON, EUGENE WALTER, mathematics editor; b. El Paso, Tex., May 25, 1939; s. Walter Albert and Lillian Ann (Martinets) J.; m. Sandra Sue Gilbert, Oct. 16, 1959; 1 dau., Catherine Mary. Student, Riverside City Coll., 1958-60; BA, U. Calif., Riverside, 1963, MA, 1964, PhD, 1966. Asst. prof. Eastern N.Mex. State U., 1966; asst. prof. math. U. Iowa, Iowa City, 1966-70; asso. prof. U. Iowa, 1970-75, prof., 1975—, chmn. dept., 1976-79. Author: Linear Algebra with Maple, 1993, Linear Algegra with Mathematics, 1995; co-author: Maple Flight Manual, 1992; contbr. articles to profl. jours. Mem. Am. Math. Soc., Math. Assn. Am. Democrat. Home: 4320 Oakridge Trail Iowa City IA 52240 Office: Univ Iowa Dept Math Iowa City IA 52242

JOHNSON, GARY KEITH, pediatrician; b. Chgo., Aug. 26, 1951; s. John Edward and Dorothy Lucille (Rudder) J. AB, Dartmouth Coll., 1973; MD, U. Ill., Chgo., 1979, MPH, 1985. Diplomate Am. Bd. Med. Examiners, Am. Bd. Pediatrics. Intern Columbus Hosp., Chgo., 1980, resident in pediatrics, 1980-83; fellow in ambulatory pediatrics Cook County Hosp., Chgo., 1983-85; dir. ambulatory pediatrics Hurley Med. Ctr., Flint, Mich., 1986-92; clin. pediatrician McCree North Health Ctr., Flint, 1992-95; participant scholars program Mich. Pub. Health Leadership Inst., Flint, 1995-96; med. dir. Genesee County Health Dept., 1995—; asst. prof. pediatrics Mich. State U., East Lansing, 1986—, tchr. med. ednl. program Coll. Human Medicine and U. Affiliated Hosp. of Flint (Mich.), Inc., 1986—; participant Mich. Public Health Leadership Inst. scholars program, Okemos, Mich., 1995-96; presenter in field. Contbr. numerous articles to profl. jours. and cmty. newspapers. Chairperson Early On program Genesee County, 1993-94. Primary Care Faculty Devel. fellow Mich. State U., 1988-89. Fellow Am. Acad. Pediatrics (Mich. chpt. exec. com. cmty. access to child health, state facilitator 1990—); mem. AMA, Chgo. Pediatric Soc., Genessee County Med. Soc., Mich. State Med. Soc., Ambulatory Pediatric Assn., Am. Pub. Health Assn. Democrat. Presbyterian. Home: 5443 Waters Edge Way Grand Blanc MI 48439-9720 Office: Genesee County Health Dept 630 S Saginaw St Flint MI 48502

JOHNSON, GARY ROBERT, political scientist, editor; b. Shenandoah, Iowa, June 30, 1949; s. Glen Robert and Norma Jean (Otte) J.; m. Margaret Delaina Maddox, Aug. 30, 1975; children: Samuel Maddox, Katherine Elizabeth. BA, Augustana Coll., Rock Island, Ill., 1972; MA, U. Cin., 1975, PhD, 1979. Teaching asst., rsch. asst. U. Cin., 1972-78; rsch. cons. Frost & Jacobs, Attys.at Law, Cin., 1976; instr., then asst. prof. polit. sci. Lake Superior State U., Sault Ste. Marie, Mich., 1978-84, assoc. prof. polit. sci., 1984-90, head dept. social scis., 1981-89, prof. polit. sci., 1990—; vis. lectr. Drake U., Des Moines, 1986-87; manuscript referee various jours., pubs., 1986—; mem. faculty workgroup on undergrad. instrnl. quality Gov.'s Commn. on Future of Higher Edn. in Mich., 1984. Bibliography co-editor Politics and the Life Scis. jour., 1986-91, editor, 1991—; contbr. articles, book revs. to profl. jours., edited books. Grantee State of Mich., 1987. Mem. AAAS, Am. Polit. Sci. Assn. (panel discussant, chair 1989—, sect. program chair 1990-91), Assn. Politics and Life Sci. (exec. dir. 1996—), Internat. Soc. Polit. Psychology, Midwest Polit. Sci. Assn., Internat. Soc. Human Ethology, Am. Anthrop. Assn., Assn. Polit. Legal Anthropology, Human Behavior and Evolution Soc. Home: 924 Johnston St Sault Sainte Marie MI 49783-3324 Office: Lake Superior State U Dept Polit Sci 1000 College Dr Sault Sainte Marie MI 49783-1699

JOHNSON, GEORGE ROBERT, retired government official; b. Grand Forks, N.D., Sept. 30, 1927; s. Sam A. and Olga (Bjorge) J.; m. Marjorie F. Dorsher, Nov. 24, 1948; children: Sam, Margie, Peter, Kari, Robert. PhB, U. N.D., 1949, postgrad., 1963; postgrad., N.D. State U., 1949, George Williams Coll., 1950, Oreg. State U., 1950-52, U. So. Calif., 1952-53, George Washington U., 1972. With YMCA, 1941-52; gen. sec. YMCA, Kelso, Wash., 1950-52; rsch. dir. John Danz Found., Seattle, 1952; intern, placement dir. sch. pub. adminstrn. U. So. Calif., L.A., 1952-53; mem. staff fed. pers. programs various orgns., 1953-85. Founder Down Syndrome News; co-founder Down Syndrome Papers and Abstracts for Profls.; editor People with Spl. Needs/Down Syndrome Report. Promoter of study, treatment and communication throughout the world in relation to Down Syndrome; active PVA, DVA, VFW. With U.S. Army, 1946-47, assigned to Far East War Crimes Tribunal. George R. Johnson scholarship founded at U. N.D. in his honor. Mem. Classification and Compensation Soc. (founder, pres. 1969-70, Svc. award 1970), Aberdeen Pers. Assn. (pres. 1989-91), Down Syndrome Congress (founder, Svc. award 1978), Am. Assn. Mental Retardation, Assn. Retarded Citizens. Home: 1409 N 1st St Aberdeen SD 57401-1915

JOHNSON, GEORGE TAYLOR, training and manufacturing executive; b. Kansas City, Mo., Jan. 12, 1930; s. George Dewey and Geneva (Van Leu) J.; BA, Columbia Coll., 1977; m. Pamela Kay Cole, Aug. 30, 1981; children: Van L., Victoria Johnson-Beineke, Wendell O., Marcella Johnson-Stewart, Julia I. Enlisted in U.S. Army, 1947, served to 1967; chief instr. rotary wing sect. U.S. Army Transp. Sch., Ft. Eustis, Va., 1965-67; ret., 1967; group leader aerospace publs. Beech Aircraft Corp., Wichita, Kans., 1968-79, adminstr. aerospace logistics programs, 1979-87; staff asst. program mgmt., 1987-88, staff adminstr. program mgmt., 1988-92; ret., 1992; pres., CEO Diversified Ednl. Tng. and Mfg. Co., 1992—. Founder U.S. Army Black Pilots Reunions, U.S. Army Black Aviators Assn. (pres.); mem. Cmty. Action Agy., Wichita, 1973-75, State of Kansas Aviation Adv. Com., 1991—, Pvt. Industry Coun., Wichita, 1994—; Kans. del. White House Conf. on Small Bus., Washington, 1995. Decorated D.F.C., Air medal with V and four oak leaf clusters. Mem. Negro Airmen Internat. (state dir.), Nat. Bus. League (regional v.p.), NAACP, Army Aviation Assn. Am., Assn. U.S. Army, Soc. Logistics Engrs., VFW, 9th and 10th Cav. Assn., Wichita C. of C. (bd. dirs. 1996—), Wichita Ind. Bus. Assn. (bd. dirs. 1996—), Optimist. Baptist. Home: 202 S Miles Ave Valley Center KS 67147-2039 Office: 2102 E 21st St N Wichita KS 67214

JOHNSON, GEORGE WILLIAM, resource manager; b. Elkhorn, Wis., Feb. 22, 1949; s. Roy Ernest and Bea (Marcellia) J.; m. Margaret Kay Gregg, Sept. 22, 1979 (div. Sept. 1985). BS, BE, U. Wis., Whitewater, Wis., 1974, postgrad., 1980—. Cert. soil tester, lake mgr., secondary sch. sci. educator. Ptnr. Biol. Svcs., Lake Geneva, Wis., 1967-73; lakefront mgr. Village of Williams Bay, Wis., 1973-77; resource mgr. Geneva Lake Environ. Agy., Fontana, Wis., 1979—; cons. Biol. Svcs., Lake Geneva, 1973-76. Contbr. planning reports to profl. publs. Alderman Village of Williams Bay, 1986-90, 93-94; chmn. Geneva Lake Access Com., 1990-91, Geneva Lake Citizen Adv. Com., Lake Geneva, 1986-87; sec. Fontana Blue Ribbon Com., 1986-88. Recipient Audubon Conservation award Lakeland Audubon, 1989, Tech. Excellence award North Am. Lake Mgmt. Soc., 1986; named Outstanding Jaycee, 1984. Mem. N.Am. Lake Mgmt. Soc., Natural Areas Assn., Soc. Ecol. Restoration, Am. Water Resources Assn., Wis. Assn. Lakes, Geneva Lake Land Conservancy, Geneva Lake Found. (dir. 1990-96). Office: Geneva Lake Environ Agy PO Box 190 Fontana WI 53125-0190

JOHNSON, GREGORY R., design engineer; b. Mpls., Aug. 5, 1952. A, Anoka Ramsey Coll., Coon Rapids, Minn., 1972. Engring. mgr. Gen. Fabrication Corp., Forest Lake, Minn., 1974-85; pres. East Range Techs., New Brighton, Minn., 1985-90; chief design engr. Zercom, Merrifield, Minn., 1990—. Patentee in field. Leader, Boy Scouts Am. Mem. ASTE, North Long Lake Assn. (pres.). Office: Zercom PO Box 84 Zercom Dr Merrifield MN 56465-0084

JOHNSON, GUY CHARLES, music educator, musician; b. Marinette, Wis., Nov. 8, 1933; s. Everton Ellsworth and Anna Mae (Brazier) J. BFA, U. Wis., Milw., 1955; MusM, Ind. U., 1956. Asst. prof. piano Drury Coll., Springfield, Mo., 1956-57, Luther Coll., Decorah, Iowa, 1959-68; assoc. prof. music Friends U., Wichita, Kans., 1968-96; impresario Lewis and Selma Miller Recital series, Wichita, 1976-86. Recital debut Athenaeum Hall, Milw., 1955; appearances with numerous symphonies including Rochester (Minn.) Symphony, Milw. Symphony, Santa Barbara (Calif.) Symphony; accomapnist for various operas, ballet cos. Mem. Wichita-Sedgwick County Hist. Mus. Mem. Wichita Area Piano Tchrs. League (pres. 1969, 90—), Kans. Music Tchrs. Assn., Nat. Guild Piano Tchrs., Wichita Art Assn. Home: 640 N Rock Rd Wichita KS 67206-1703

JOHNSON, HERMAN, secondary education educator; b. Chgo., Feb. 25, 1940; s. William and Beatrice (Beamon) J.; m. Elaine Glenn, Dec. 10, 1960; children: Pamela, Herman II, Joseph, Tessa, Verna, Ivan. BS in Edn., Chgo. State U., 1971; MA, Northeastern Ill., 1974; MEd, DePaul U., 1982. Cert. tchr. elem. 3-8, secondary 9-12, Ill. Data files clk. VA, Chgo., 1962-63; clk., carrier U.S. Post Office, Chgo., 1963-69; tchr. Chgo. Bd. Edn., 1972-95, ret., 1995; bd. dirs. Chgo. Tchr. Ctr., 1980-85, Ill. State Tchr. Ctr., Springfield, 1982-83. Bd. dirs. Friends of Oak Park Libr., 1975; commr. Community Rels. Commn., Oak Park, 1976, N.E. Ill. Planning Commn., Chgo., 1977. With USAF, 1959-62, Korea. Recipient Outstanding Svc. award, Ill. State Bd. Edn., Springfield, 1983, Meritorious Svc. award, Chgo. Police Dept. Mem. Am. Fedn. Tchrs. (del.), Ill. Fedn. Tchrs. (del.), Chgo. Tchrs. Union (del., dist. supt. 1972—), Nat. Coun. Social Studies, Am. Legion, Alpha Phi Alpha, Phi Beta Kappa. Home: 325 Rowan Ct Naperville IL 60540-7822

JOHNSON, HOWARD MICHAEL, professional baseball player; b. Clearwater, Fla., Nov. 29, 1960. Student, St. Petersburg Jr. Coll. With Detroit Tigers, 1979-84, N.Y. Mets, 1984-93, Colo. Rockies, 1993-95, Chgo. Cubs, 1995—. Named to All-Star team, 1989, 91, Sporting News Nat. League All-Star Team, 1989; recipient Silver Slugger award, 1989, 91; holds Nat. League single season rec. for most home runs by a switch-hitter. Office: Chgo Cubs 1060 W Addison St Chicago IL 60613-4397

JOHNSON, IAN BRUCE, minister, legal assistant; b. Wichita, July 26, 1955; s. Robert Bruce Johnson and Mary Lynn (Culbert) Schweiter; m. JaNella Mari Power, Feb. 25, 1978; children: Elnathan, Titus, Benjamin, Daniel. BS in Chemistry, Wichita State U., 1976, BA in Linguistics, 1976; MS in Biochemistry, Iowa State U., 1982; JD, U. Iowa, 1982, MA in History, 1984; postgrad., U. Kans., 1984-85. Cert. legal asst. Grad. asst., teaching asst. Iowa State U. Dept. Biochemistry, Ames, 1976-80; rsch. asst. U. Iowa Coll. Law, Iowa City, 1982-84; grad. teaching asst. U. Kans. History Dept., Lawrence, 1984-85; chemist Challenger Products Corp., Topeka, 1986-88; chemist, physicist, theoretician Kanza, Inc./Martin Tractor Co., Topeka, 1989-90; legal asst. Weathers & Riley, Topeka, 1991—; asst. minister Randel Ministries, Inc., Topeka, 1994—; bd. sec. Randel Ministries, Inc., 1993—. Precinct committeeman Shawnee County Rep. Party, Topeka, 1988—; mem. ctrl. com. 2d Congrl. Dist. Rep. Party, Kansas, 1994—. Mem. Am. Chem. Soc., Kans. Found. Coop. Econ. Devel., Internat. Union Pure & Applied Chemistry, Prison Fellowship. Home: 1601 SE Maryland Ave Topeka KS 66607 Office: Weathers & Riley 4848 SW 21st Ste 202 Topeka KS 66604

JOHNSON, JAMES I., stockbroker; b. Mt. Vernon, Ill., Sept. 18, 1947. BA, So. Ill. U., 1975. Stockbroker R. Rowland, St. Louis, 1977-88, A.G. Edwards & Sons Inc., Mt. Vernon, Ill., 1988—. Staff sgt. U.S. Army, 1966-69. Mem. VFW, Am. Legion.

JOHNSON, JANET HELEN, Egyptology educator; b. Everett, Wash., Dec. 24, 1944; d. Robert A. and Jane N. (Osborn) J.; m. Donald S. Whitcomb, Sept. 2, 1978; children: J.J., Felicia. BA, U. Chgo., 1967, PhD, 1972. Instr. Egyptology U. Chgo., 1971-72, asst. prof., 1972-79, assoc. prof., 1979-81, prof., 1981—; dir. Oriental Inst., 1983-89; research assoc. dept. anthropology Field Mus. of Natural History, 1980-84, 94—. Author: Demotic Verbal System, 1977, Thus Wrote Onchsheshonqy, 1986, 2d revised edit., 1991, (with Donald Whitcomb) Quseir al-Qadim, 1978, 80; editor: (with E.F. Wente) Studies in Honor of G.R. Hughes, 1977, Life in a Multi-Cultural Society, 1992. Smithsonian Instn. grantee, 1977-83; NEH grantee, 1978-81, 81-85; Nat. Geog. Soc. grantee, 1978, 80, 82. Mem. Am. Rsch. Ctr. in Egypt (bd. govs. 1979—, exec. com. 1984-87, 90—, v.p. 1990-93, pres. 1993-96). Office: U Chgo Oriental Inst 1155 E 58th St Chicago IL 60637-1540

JOHNSON, JEANNETTE SELBY, vocational education educator; b. Warren, Ohio, July 20, 1950; d. William Edward and Agnes (Newell) Selby; m. Dan Frederick Johnson, Mar. 16, 1974; children: Shelley, Robyn, Kimberly. BS in Home Econs., Ohio State U., 1972, MA in Edn., 1974. Cert. tchr., Ohio. Student pers. asst. Ohio State U., Columbus, 1972-74; home economist Children's Hosp., Columbus, 1976-80; instr. Sch. Home Econs. Ohio U., Athens, 1987-89, vis. prof. Sch. Theater, 1989; substitute tchr. Athens City Schs., 1989; adult instr. family life edn. Tri-County Vocat. Sch., Nelsonville, Ohio, 1989-92; adult instr. displaced homemakers Tri-County Vocat. Sch., Nelsonville, 1993-94; tchr. home econs. Trimble Mid. Sch., Glouster, Ohio, 1992-93; adult instr. On My Own Tri-County Vocat. Sch., Nelsonville, Ohio, 1994—; dir. day camp Girl Scouts U.S., Athens, 1990-91; instr. aerobics YWCA, Columbus, 1978-80; mem. Ohio Studen Aid Commn. S.E. adv. com., 1995. Leader 4-H Clubs Am., Columbus, 1978-79; v.p. Dennison Pl. Community Orgn., Columbus, 1978-84; co-chair Residents for Community Revitalization, Columbus, 1983; tchr. Sunday sch. 1st Presbyn. Ch., Athens, 1989-94. Recipient award of recognition Pres.'s Com. on Employment of Handicapped, 1972, Outstanding Leader award Girl Scouts U.S., 1990. Mem. Ohio State U. Alumni Assn. Home: 23 Greenbrier Dr Athens OH 45701-3202

JOHNSON, JEFF D., research and development engineer; b. Omaha, Aug. 14, 1967; s. David K. and Kay B. (Stevens) J.; m. Dawn M. Westendorf, May 23, 1990. BS in Mech. Engring., Iowa State U., 1990. R&D engr. GOMACO, Ida Grove, Iowa, 1992—. Lutheran. Office: GOMACO Hwy 59 & 175 Ida Grove IA 51445

JOHNSON, JEFFREY D., state legislator. BA, Kent State U., 1980; postgrad., Cornell U.; MA, Case We. Res. U., 1984, JD, 1984. City councilman Ward B Cleve., 1984-90; state senator, asst. minority whip Ohio State Congress, 1990—; mem. rules, health and human svc., edn., retirement and aging and judiciary coms., task force on health care, correctional inst. inspection com., state criminal sentencing com., joint legis. com. on Medicaid oversight. Mem. Fedn. Cmty. Planning Legal and Legis. Com., Ohio Dems. Exec. com., Cuyahoga County Dem. com. Recipient Leaders of Future award Ebony Mag., 1985, 87. Mem. NAACP, Ohio Bar Assn., Urban League Greater Cleve. Office: 9024 Parkgate Ave Cleveland OH 44108*

JOHNSON, JEFFREY, deputy state librarian; b. Toledo, Dec. 4, 1944; s. Donald Parker and Catherine Jeannette (Fournier) J.; m. Deborah King Harris, Apr. 24, 1982. BA with honors, U. Toledo, 1966; MLS, U. Mich., 1971. Ref. libr. Toledo Lucas County Pub. Libr., 1970-72; army libr. U.S. Army Europe, Germany, 1972-80; dir. Woodlands Libr. Coop., Albion, Mich., 1980-85; dep. state libr. Libr. of Mich., Lansing, 1985—; trustee Mich. Libr. Consortium, Lansing, 1990—; mem. U. Mich. Sch. Info. and Libr. Sci. Adv. Com., 1985-90; 2d v.p. Mich. Libr. Assn. Bd., Lansing, 1984-85. Trustee Mich. Libr. Assn. Ednl. Found. Bd., Lansing, 1983-84; mem. Mich. Libr. Assn. Legis. Com., Lansing, 1981-84. Mem. ALA, Mich. Libr. Assn., Mich. Assn. Media in Edn. Office: Libr of Michigan PO Box 30007 717 W Allegan Lansing MI 48909

JOHNSON, JEFFREY FERRELL, pastor; b. Madison, Wis., Sept. 17, 1951; s. Carl Samuel and Marjorie Ann (Ferrell) J. BA, St. Olaf Coll., 1973; MDiv, Luther Seminary, St. Paul, 1983. Ordained Lutheran minister. Chaplain-in-residence St. Joseph's Hosp., St. Paul, 1979, N.C. Meml. Hosp., Chapel Hill, 1979-80; pastoral intern St. Thomas Lutheran Ch., Bloomington, Ind., 1981-82; pastor St. Paul's/Our Savior's Lutheran Parish, Curtiss, Wis., 1983-86, Grace Lutheran Ch., Thiensville, Wis., 1986-87; chaplain DePaul Hosp., Milw., 1987, St. Mary's Hosp., Milw., 1988; interim pastor Adoration & St. Thomas Lutheran Ch., Milw., 1988-89; pastor Zion Lutheran Ch., Ashippun, Wis., 1989-96; nominating com. N. Wis. dist. Am. Lutheran Ch., 1985; quality control com. Lutheran Homes of Oconomowoc, Wis., 1990-96. Dir. Beaver Dam (Wis.) Cmty. Theatre, 1972, Northfield (Minn.) Arts Guild, 1972; lighting designer Abbotsford (Wis.) Cmty. Theatre, 1985. Mem. Assn. Clin. Pastoral Edn.

JOHNSON, JOE CARL, small business owner; b. Ishpeming, Mich., June 30, 1965; s. Terry James and Susan Mary (Solka) J.; m. Christine Diana La Forest, June 11, 1988; 1 child, Lyndsey. Master cert. mechanics, Mich. Mechanic Metro Toyota, Kalamazoo, 1985-87, Choice Toyota, Marquette, Mich., 1987-92; owner J&J Automotive, Ishpeming, 1992—. Mem. Nat. Mobile Air Conditioning Assn. Democrat. Roman Catholic. Office: J&J Automotive 301 N Main St Ishpeming MI 49849-1907

JOHNSON, JOHN ANDREW, construction executive; b. Grand Rapids, Mich., Apr. 10, 1942; s. Arnold L. and Ione A. (Christenson) J.; m. Peggy J. Ruckman, June 12, 1971; children: Perry T., John C-G. Assoc. in Engring., Mich. State U., E. Lansing, 1964; diploma, U.S.A. Signal Sch., Ft. Monmouth, 1966, Detroit Diesel Allison, Indpls., 1972. Tech. writer Massey-Ferguson, Inc., Indpls., 1965-66, 1969-70; svc. rep. Massey-Ferguson, Inc., Akron, Ohio, 1970-73; regional svc. mgr. Massey-Ferguson, Inc., Detroit, 1973-78; regional sales mgr. Massey-Ferguson, Inc., Columbus, Ohio, 1978-84; pres. Johnson and Assocs., Ind., 1984-86; svc. mgr. Hanomag Baumaschinen GmbH, Hannover, Fed. Republic Germany, 1986-90, Samsung Constrn. Equipment, Seoul, Republic of Korea, 1990—. With U.S. Army, 1966-69. Mem. Soc. Automotive Engrs., Profl. Photographers Assn., Pierceton C. of C., Am. Legion. Republican. Lutheran. Home: 7406 E Shoop Rd Pierceton IN 46562-9149 Office: Samsung Constrn Equipment 5521 Meadowbrook Ct Rolling Meadows IL 60008-3852

JOHNSON, JOHN EDWIN, orthodontist; b. Waverly, Ky., Aug. 9, 1931; s. Richard Spalding and Margaret (Vize) J.; m. Margaret Josephine Smith, Dec. 29, 1956; children: Catherine Margaret, Michael John. DDS, St. Louis U., 1956. Diplomate Am. Bd. Orthodontics. Pres. John E. Johnson, DDS, DP Corp., New Albany, Ind., 1956—; bd. dirs., sec. DePaul Sch. for Dyslexia, Louisville, 1974-78. Contbr. articles to profl. publs. Capt. U.S. Army, 1956-58. Mem. ADA, Am. Assn. Orthodontists, European Orthodontic Soc., So. Orthodontic Assn., South Ctrl. Dental Soc., Ind. Dental Soc. (pres. south ctrl. component 1968-69), Rotary (pres. New Albany, Ind. club 1992-93), Big Springs County Club. Roman Catholic. Office: 215 E Spring St New Albany IN 47150-3422

JOHNSON, JOHN H., publisher, consumer products executive, chairman; b. Arkansas City, Ark., Jan. 19, 1918; m. Eunice Johnson; children: John Harold (dec.), Linda Johnson Rice. Student, U. Chgo., Northwestern U., Howard U.; LL.D., Central State Coll., Shaw U., N.C. Coll., Benedict Coll., Carnegie-Mellon Inst., Morehouse Coll., N.C. A. and T. State U., Syracuse U., Eastern Mich. U., Hamilton Coll., Lincoln U., Malcolm X Coll., Upper Iowa Coll., Wayne State U., Pratt Inst., Chgo. State U., Northeastern U. Pub., chmn. chief exec. officer Johnson Pub. Co., Inc., Chgo. N.Y.C., L.A., Washington, 1942—; pub., editor Ebony, Jet, EM-Ebony Man (mags.); pres. Sta. WJPC-AM-FM, Chgo., Sta. WLOU, Louisville, Fashion Fair Cosmetics, Chgo., Eboné Cosmetics, Supreme Beauty Products; chmn., chief exec. officer Supreme Life Ins. Co., Chgo.; bd. dirs. Greyhound Corp., Dillard Dept. Stores, Inc. Author: Succeeding Against the Odds, 1989. Trustee Art Inst., Chgo. Named Outstanding Young Man U.S. Jaycees, 1951, Communicator of Yr. U. Chgo. Alumni Assn., 1974, Chicagoan of Yr., Chgo. Boys Club, 1983; recipient Horatio Alger award, 1966; John Russwurm award Nat. Newspaper Pubs. Assn., 1966, Spingarn medal NAACP, 1966, Henry Johnson Fisher award Mag. Pubs. Assn., 1971,Columbia Journalism award, 1974, Honors Disting. Accomplishment United Negro Coll. Fund, 1983, Robie award Jackie Robinson Found., 1985, Disting. Contbrn. to Journalism award Nat. Press Found., 1986; named to Acad. Disting. Entrepreneurs Babson Coll., 1979; Chgo. Bus. Hall of Fame, 1983; named to Entrepreneur of Decade Black Enterprise Mag., 1987; inducted into Black Press Hall of Fame, 1987, Pub. Hall of Fame Folio Ednl. Trust Inc., 1987, Ill. Bus. Hall of Fame, 1989, Nat. Sales Hall of Fame, 1989, Chgo. Journalism Hall of Fame, 1990; recipient Harold H. Hines Jr. Benefactors' award United Negro Coll. Fund, 1988, Excel award Internat. Assn. Bus. communicators, Founders award NCCJ, 1989, Disting. Svc. award Harvard U. Grad. Sch. Bus. Adminstrn., 1991, Salute to the Media award Impact Publs., Africa's Future award UNICEF, 1992, Booker T. Washington Speaker's award Booker T. Washington Bus. Assn., Heritage award Exec. Leadership Coun., 1992, Dow Jones Entrepreneurial Excellence award Dow Jones and the Wall Street Jour., 1993. Fellow Sigma Delta Chi; mem. U.S. C. of C. (dir.), Mag. Pubs. Assn. Also: 1270 Avenue of the Americas New York NY 10020-1700 Also: 1750 Pennsylvania Ave NW Washington DC 20006-4502

JOHNSON, JOHN JAY, automotive company administrator; b. Toledo, Aug. 9, 1954; s. Charles W. and Eloise F. (Cousino) J.; m. Sue L. Postlewait, Sept. 13, 1975; children: Jerame S., Chad A. BBA, U. Toledo, 1981; M of Sci. Adminstrn., Ctrl. Mich. U., 1991. Purchasing mgr. Am. Motors Corp., Detroit, 1985-87; purchasing specialist Chrysler Corp., Hamtramck, Mich., 1988-89; Can. integration mgr. Chrysler Corp., Centerline, Mich., 1989-90, catalog mgr., 1990-91, part set-up and catalog mgr., 1991-94, spl. order svcs. mgr., 1994—; chair Chrysler Recognition Com., 1991—. Deacon, vice chair, elder First Christian Ch., Sylvania, Ohio, 1992—, chmn. membership com., 1992—, advisor Jr. Logos, 1991-93; advisor Jr. Achievement of Southeastern Mich., Lincoln Park, 1991-93, CYO H.S. Ch. Youth Group, 1994—. Recipient Cert. of Appreciation, Jr. Achievement, 1992, Product of Yr. award, 1993. Mem. Chrysler Mgmt. Club, Sigma Iota Epsilon. Home: 11625 Belleterre St Erie MI 48133-9702 Office: Chrysler Corp 26311 Lawrence Ave Center Line MI 48015-1241

JOHNSON, JOHN LEE, retired civil servant, writer; b. Altheimer, Ark., June 10, 1945. AAS, Florissant Valley Coll., 1978; BS, St. Louis U., 1980; DD, New World Theol. Seminary, 1993. Clerk, carrier, supervisor U.S. Post Office, 1970-92. Author: The Black Biblical Heritage, 1975-94, God's Kinship with Dark Colors, 1996. Corp. USMC, 1966-69. Recipient Nat. Citation Medal, USMC, 1967-68, Vietnam Campaign Medal for Combat Action; honored with Key to city of El Paso, Tex. NAACP, 1994. Home: 8312 Pepperidge Dr Berkeley MO 63134

JOHNSON, JOYCE MARIE, school system administrator; b. Des Moines, Oct. 23, 1952; d. John F. and Betty R. (Dale) Erquist; m. Jack R. Johnson, Mar. 15, 1974; 1 child, Mary D. BA, Buena Vista Coll., 1991. Sec. sch. bd. Adair-Casey (Iowa) Cmty. Sch. Dist., 1984—; adult edn. instr. Adair-Casey Cmty. Sch. Dist., 1991—. Contbr. articles to profl. jours. Mem. Iowa Assn. Sch. Bus. Ofcls., Assn. Sch. Bus. Ofcls. Internat. Office: Adair-Casey Cmty Sch Dist 3384 Indigo Ave Adair IA 50002

JOHNSON, JUDY M., artist, writer; b. Marquette, Mich., Aug. 11, 1946; d. Lowell Kenneth and Helen C. (Heath) Johnson; children: Jenny R. Taliadoros, Kenneth R. Taylor. Student, Mich. State U., 1964-66. Artist B. Shackman Pub., N.Y.C., 1984-90, Dover Publs., N.Y.C., 1986-94; writer miscellaneous nat. publs., 1984—; artist/writer Magnattraction, Concord, Mass., 1995—; owner Judy's Place, Mich., 1978—; writer of verse Marion Heath Greeting Cards, Wareham, Mass., 1994-95; chmn. Art on the Rocks, Marquette, 1994-96; mng. editor Original Paper Doll Artists Guild "OPDAG News", Kingfield, Mass., 1984—. Author, artist paper dolls; author, editor 2 Twp. Centennial History Books, 1992, 95, pictorial archives; author, pub. herb books, humor books; pub. Lake Superior Art Assn. newsletter KIOSK. Cmty. activist in ecology and art, Mich., 1960—; lay spkr. United Meth. Ch., Alma and ctrl. Mich., 1983-88. Mem. Lake Superior Art Assn. (chair arts show 1994—). Home: PO Box 176 Skandia MI 49885 Office: Judy's Place PO Box 176 Skandia MI 49885

JOHNSON, JULIE MARIE, lawyer/lobbyist; b. Aberdeen, S.D., Aug. 7, 1953; d. Howard B. and Jerauldine (Dilly) J.; m. Bryan L. Hisel. BA in Polit. Sci., Communication, U. S.D., 1974, MA in Polit. Sci., 1976, JD, 1976. Bar: S.D. 1977, U.S. Dist. Ct. S.D. 1977. Assoc. Siegel, Barnett Law Firm, Aberdeen, 1977; law clk. Fifth Judicial Circuit Ct., Aberdeen, 1977-78; ptnr. Maloney, Kolker, Fritz, Hogan & Johnson, Aberdeen, 1978-84; dep. sec. S.D. Dept. Labor, Aberdeen, Pierre, 1983-84, 1985-87; pres. Industry and Commerce Assn. of S.D., Pierre, 1987-95; sep. sec. S.D. Dept. Revenue, Pierre, 1995; exec. dir. S.D. Rural Devel. Coun., Pierre, 1995—. Treas. S.D. Cmty. Found., Pierres, 1987-95; mem. Pvt. Industry Coun., 1985-87, S.D. Coun. on Vocat. Edn., 1985-87; bd. dirs. Mo. Shores Women's Resource Ctr., Pierre, 1988-89; chmn. S.D. Main St. Adv. Coun., 1987-91; bd. dirs. United Way, 1988—, chmn., 1991; mem. Shortgrass Arts Coun., 1987—, South Dakotans for the Arts, 1981—, Solid Waste Mgmt. Plan Task Force, 1990, S.D. Citizens Adv. Coun. on Hazardous Waste, 1991-92; bd. dirs. Hist. S.D. Found., 1996—; founding mem., legal counsel Outdoor Women of S.D., Inc., 1995—; bd. trustees USD Found., 1992—, Dakota Wesleyan U., 1996—; founding mem., treas. S.D. Discovery Ctr. and Aquarium, Inc., bd. dirs., 1988-92; mem. S.D. Water Congress, 1990—, bd. dirs., 1987-95. RJR Nabisco fellow Women Execs. in State Govt., Harvard, 1986; named Outstanding Young Citizen Jaycees, Aberdeen, 1982, S.D. Jaycees, 1983. Mem. S.D. Bar Assn., Industry and Commerce Assn. S.D. (bd. dirs. 1985-87), U. S.D. Alumni Assn. (exec. com. 1987—, pres. 1990-92), AAUW, Bus. and Profl. Women U.S.A. (nat. legis. chmn. 1987-88, 92-94, nat. chmn. issues mgmt. 1991-93, pres. S.D. 1984-85, Woman of Yr. award Aberdeen chpt. 1982), Women Execs. in State Govvt. (bd. didrs. 1985-87), Coun. State Mfrs. Assn., S.D. Mining Assn. (bd. dirs. 1991-95), Nat. Indsl. Coun., Coun. State C.'s of C., Ducks Unltd., Rotary, Zonta. Republican. Lutheran. Home: B-5 174 Skerrols Dr Fort Pierre SD 57532 Office: SD Rural Devel Coun 174 Skerrols St B-5 Fort Pierre SD 57532

JOHNSON, KARLA J., counselor; b. Chgo., Feb. 16, 1971; d. Robert C. and Norma J. (Mangum) J. BS in Psychology, Ill. State U., 1992, MEd, 1994. Counselor Rosemoor Assessment, Chgo., 1995, Healthcare Alternatives, Chgo., 1995—. Mem. Alpha Kappa Alpha. Democrat. Baptist. Office: Healthcare Alternative Sys 2755 W Armitage Chicago IL 60647

JOHNSON, KATHLEEN CARLTON, librarian; b. Laurium, Mich., Feb. 14, 1948; d. Robert F. and Margaret M. (Taylor) Carlton; m. Robert E. Johnson, Aug. 16, 1980; children: Robert E. Jr., Joseph F., Margaret Jean, Regina Francis. BA, Coll. William and Mary, 1970; MA, Villanova U., 1973, MLS, 1974. Tchr. art Isle of Wright County, Va.; sch. librarian Sch. Dist. 63, Ill.; sch. and public libr. Lake Linden-Hubbell Pub. Libr. Author: Tales of a Keweenaw Mom; author of poems. Mem. ALA, REMC (pres. 1990-91). Office: Lake Linden Hubbell Pub Lib 601 Calumet St Lake Linden MI 49945-1002

JOHNSON, KAY DURBAHN, real estate manager, consultant; b. Crookston, Minn., Apr. 4, 1937; d. Wilbert John and Frieda (Johnson) Durbahn; m. Ray Arvin Johnson, May 14, 1960; children: Sherry Kay Johnson Johnston, Diane Rosalind Johnson Peterson, Laura Faye Johnson. BA, U. Minn., 1959. Reference analyst Indsl. Rels. Ctr. U. Minn., Mpls., 1959-61; real estate mgr. Minnetonka, Minn., 1976—; ptnr. Broadmoor Plantation Investors, Fargo, N.D., 1976—; v.p. D&T Property, Inc., Minnetonka, 1990—, also bd. dirs.; tax reduction cons. R.A. Johnson & Assocs., Minnetonka, 1985—. City of Minnetonka Planning Commn., 1972-74, vice chair, 1973-74; mem. Land Use Task Force, 1972-74; liaison Ridgedale Devel., 1972-74; chair Evangelism Bd. Minnetonka Luth. Ch., 1974-76, 85-87, chair Stewardship Bd., 1992-94, mem. choir; mem. GMC Motorcoach Assn. Mem. Mpls. Inst. Arts. Republican.

JOHNSON, K(ENNETH) O(DELL), aerospace engineer; b. Harville, Mo., Aug. 31, 1922; s. Kenneth D. and Polly Louise (Wilson) J.; B.S. in Aero. Engring., Purdue U., 1950; m. Betty Lou Jones, Aug. 5, 1950; children—Cynthia Jo, Gregory Alan. Engr., design, quality and production mgmt. Gen. Lamp Co., Elwood, Ind., 1950-51; mem. staff aircraft gas turbine engine design Allison div. Gen. Motors Corp., Speedway, Ind., 1951-66; mem. turbofan aircraft engines plus marine, indsl. gas turbine engine design mgmt. staff Gen. Electric Co., 1966-86, cons. aerospace engring. Belcan Corp., Cin., 1986—. Served to capt. USAF, 1942-45. Assoc. fellow AIAA. Republican. Methodist. Holder over 20 patents in field. Recipient UDF Pioneer & Extraordinary Service award for unducted fan invention and patent, Gen. Electric Co., 1985, cert. recognition NASA, 1987; named to Gen. Electric Aircraft Engines Propulsion Hall of Fame, 1987. Home: 8360 Arapaho Ln Cincinnati OH 45243-2718 Office: Belcan Corp Dept Engring 10200 Anderson Way Cincinnati OH 45242-4700

JOHNSON, KENNETH STUART, publisher, printer; b. Chgo., Aug. 22, 1928; s. William Moss and Lucille (Carsellio) J.; student Wright Jr. Coll., 1949-50, U. Ill., 1951-52; m. Joanne Barbaria Johnson; children: Cynthia Diane, Randall, Andrew, Peter. Dir., chmn. Free Press, Inc., Carpentersville, Ill., 1965-92; pres. Johnson Enterprises Inc. Served with U.S. Army, 1946-47. Named Man and Boy of Year, 1963. Mem. Cook County Pubs. Assn. (pres. 1963, dir.), Profl. Journalistic Soc., Sigma Delta Chi. Home: 44 Park Ln Park Ridge IL 60068-2830

JOHNSON, KIRK, financial consultant; b. Ft. Wayne, Ind., Oct. 26, 1960. BBA, Ind. U., 1984, MS in Orgnl. Devel., 1990. Lic. N.Y. Stock Exch., Nat. Assn. Securities Dealers. Fin. cons. Paine Webber, 1985-90; devel. dir. St. Frances Coll., Ft. Wayne, 1990-94; fin. cons. Merrill Lynch, Ft. Wayne, 1994—. Bd. dirs. St. Frances Coll., Ft. Wayne, 1993—; mem. Big Bros./Big Sisters, Ft. Wayne, 1983—. Mem. Am. Fedn. for Horticulturists, U.S. Triathlon Fedn., Ind. Order Odd Fellows, Lions, Kappa Lambda Theta, Kappa Delta Pi. Office: Merrill Lynch PO Box 130 Fort Wayne IN 46801-0130

JOHNSON, L. NEIL, school system administrator; b. Anjean, W.Va., Sept. 4, 1940; s. Charles M. and Lillian Bea (Wright) J.; m. Joyce Ann Waybright, June 23, 1962; children: Michael Neil, Bryan Lewis. Student, Glenville (W.Va.) State Coll., 1961-62; BA, Miami U., Oxford, Ohio, 1966, MA, 1968; EdD, Ball State U., 1973. Tchr. Butler Twp. Schs., Arcanum, Ohio, 1964-65, Milton-Union Schs., West Milton, Ohio, 1966-67; asst. prin. Wayne Twp. Schs., Dayton, Ohio, 1967-71; asst. supt. Mad River Twp. Schs., Dayton, 1972-74; supt. Celina (Ohio) City Schs., 1974-77, Groveport (Ohio)-Madison Local Schs., 1977-81; CEO Phoenix Bookshops, Columbus, Ohio, 1981-84; supt. Gallia County Local Schs., Gallipolis, Ohio, 1984-90, Brecksville (Ohio)-Broadview Hts. City Schs., 1990—; cons. Midland (Mich.) Intermediate Schs., 1991; chair exec. com. S.E. Ohio Edn. Coop., Athens, 1984-86; mem. Ohio State Supt Adv. Com. on Spl. Edn., Columbus, 1986-88; presenter on student sexual abuse. Co-author: Interactive Television: Progress and Potential, 1989; autor, narrator videotape Technology in Education: Implications for Teaching, 1989; contbr. articles to profl. jours. Mayor of West Milton, Ohio, 1969-73. With USN, 1958-61. Named Outstanding Young Educator Milton-Union Jaycees, 1967. Mem. Am. Assn. Sch. Adminstrs. (del. 1981), Buckeye Assn. Sch. Adminstrs. (exec. com. 1978-81), Greater Cleve. Sch. Supts. Assn. (exec. com. 1991-92, 94-95, pres. elect, pres. 1995-96), Greater Cleve. Sch. Coun. (exec. com. 1994—, chmn. 1995-96), Alliance for Adequate Sch. Funding (exec. com. 1991—, chair exec. com. 1992—), North Ohio Tech. Assn. (chmn. 1995—), Brecksville and Broadview Heights C. of C., City Club of Cleve., Kiwanis, Masons. Republican. Methodist. Home: 1271 Emerald Creek Dr Broadview Hts OH 44147-2577 Office: Brecksville-Broadview Hts Schs 6638 Mill Rd Brecksville OH 44141-1512

JOHNSON, LARRY M., mechanical designer; b. Freedom, Okla., Apr. 13, 1944. Student, Ctrl. Bus. Coll., Wichita, 1967. Elec.-mech. designer Beach Aircraft, Wichita, 1967-68, Tex. Instruments, Dallas, 1969-73, NCR, Wichita, 1974-91, ATT/GIS Symbios, Wichita, 1992—. Mem. steering com. Augusta (Kans.) Theatre, 1995. Sgt. USAF, 1962-66. Office: Symbios Logic Group 3718 N Rock Rd Wichita KS 67226-1308

JOHNSON, LARRY ROBERT, education educator; b. Nome, N.D., Dec. 9, 1943; s. Samuel Harold and Myrtle Evelyn (Fjeld) J.; m. Mae Marie Wolf, June 12, 1965; children: Tanya Ann, Cameron Mark, Angela Marie, Sara Elizabeth. BS, Valley City State U., 1965; BD, Inter-Luth. Theol. Sem., 1969; postgrad., U. N.D., 1968-69; MA, Ind. U., 1977; ThM, Fuller Theol. Sem., 1992. Elem. tchr. Anchorage Borough Sch. Dist., Alaska, 1965-66; instr. Inter-Lutheran Theol. Sem., Plymouth, Minn., 1969-71; missionary, linguist Luth. Bible Translators, Aurora, Ill., 1971—; instr. U. Liberia, Monrovia, 1974-75; lang. project adminstr. The Inst. for Liberian Langs., Monrovia, 1978-80, translation cons., 1985—; hon. translation advisor United Bible Soc., 1987—; teaching asst. Fuller Theol. Sem., 1990-93. Translator: St. Mark in Kisi, 1982, St. Matthew in Kisi, 1986, Luke and Acts in Kisi, 1987, Six Booklets Scripture Selections in Kisi, 1987, 88, New Testament in Kisi, 1989. Recipient Grad. award Luth. Brotherhood Ins. Co., 1971, Nat. Def. Edn. Act Title VI award Ind. U., 1976, Bible Translation award Fuller Theol. Sem., 1992. Mem. Kappa Delta Pi. Lutheran. Home: PO Box B Nome ND 58062-0089 Office: Luth Bible Translators, PO Box 10-0513, 1000 Monrovia 10, Liberia also: Luth Bible Translators Box 2050 Aurora IL 60507-2050

JOHNSON, LARRY W., newspaper editor, educator; b. Ottumwa, Iowa, Sept. 17, 1952; m. Sue Ann Ferguson, Aug. 3, 1974; children: Nathaniel, Anne, Laura, Emily. BA, U. Iowa, 1974, MA, 1991. Editor Corydon (Iowa) Times-Rep., 1977; reporter The Ledger, Fairfield, Iowa, 1977-78, mng. editor, 1978-85; editor The Ledger, Fairfield, 1985-88, The Messenger, Fort Dodge, Iowa, 1988—; instr. Iowa Ctrl. C.C., Fort Dodge, 1991—; freelance writer. Mediator, com. mem. Iowa Employee Support/Guard and Reserve, Des Moines, 1990-95; English lang. tutor Iowa Ctrl. C.C., Fort Dodge, 1993-94; bd. dirs. Fort Dodge YMCA, 1988-91. Recipient 1st Place Feature Writing award Nat. Newspaper Assn., 1987, Nat. Clarion award Women in Comm., 1992. Mem. Iowa Newspaper Assn. (news adv. com. 1982-92, Disting. Svc. award 1992), Iowa AP Mng. Editors, Rotary. Methodist. Home: 2531 16th Ave N Fort Dodge IA 50501 Office: The Messenger 713 Central Ave Fort Dodge IA 50501

JOHNSON, LEIF O., political activist; b. N.Y.C., Nov. 12, 1940; m. Susan Parmacek. BS, Queens Coll.; postgrad., U. Washington. Candidate for N.Y. Contr., 1973, Chgo. Bd. Aldermen, 1987; Dem. candidate for U.S. House, 1990, 92, 96. Office: 604 Clairvoix Webster Groves MO 63119*

JOHNSON, LENNART INGEMAR, materials engineering consultant; b. Mpls., Dec. 23, 1924; s. Sixten Richard Wilhem and Marie Augusta (Johansson) J.; m. Muriel Grant, Oct. 7, 1961; 1 child, Sandra Lee. BS in Chem. Engring., U. Minn., 1948. Petroleum engr. Northwestern Refining Co., New Brighton, Minn., 1948-49; sr. engr. Ordnance Div. Honeywell, Hopkins, Minn., 1949-67, prin. materials engr. Def. Sys. Div., 1967-69, supr. engring. Def. Sys. Div., 1969-87; staff engr. Armament Sys. Div. Honeywell Inc., Hopkins, Minn., 1987-88; cons. Soc. Automotive Engring., Warrandale, Pa., 1989—; cons. Ecubed Assocs., Inc., 1993—; forum leader and presenter, U. Wis. Engring. Inst., Madison, 1965. Contbr. articles to profl. jours. Mem. credentials com. Hennepin County Rep. Conv., Minn., 1972, alt. del., 1974. Recipient Prize Paper award, Inst. Elec. Engrs. Fellow Am. Inst. Chemists; mem. Soc. Automotive Engrs. (sec. composites com. 1986-87, chmn. 1987-88), Am. Inst. Chem. Engrs. Home and Office: 14109 Mount Ter Minnetonka MN 55345-3826

JOHNSON, LINDA ARLENE, petroleum transporter; b. Sparta, Wis., Mar. 6, 1946; d. Clarence Julius and Arlene Mae (Yahnke) Jessie; children: Darrick, Larissa. With Union Nat. Bank & Trust Co., Sparta, 1964-69, Hill, Christensen & Co., CPA's, Tomah, Wis., 1969-75; owner Johnson of Wis. Oil Co., Inc., Tomah, 1969-95; with Larry's Express, Inc., Tomah, 1975-78; owner Johnson Rentals, 1979—, Johnson of Wis. Transport Co., Inc., Tomah, 1982—. Mem. St. Paul's Luth. Ch., Tomah. Mem. Petroleum Marketers Assn. Am., Nat. Assn. Convenience Stores, Nat. Fedn. Ind. Bus., Am. Trucking Assn., Wis. Assn. Convenience Stores, Petroleum Marketers Assn. Wis., Wis. Ind. Businessmen, Inc., Tomah Area C. of C., Tomah Area Credit Union (bd. dirs. 1993—, sec. 1993-94), Rotary Club Tomah. Home and Office: RR 1 Box 428 Tomah WI 54660-9602

JOHNSON, LLOYD PETER, retired banker; b. Mpls., May 1, 1930; s. Lloyd Percy and Edna (Schlampp) J.; m. Rosalind Gesner, July 3, 1954; children: Marcia, Russell, Paul. B.A., Carleton Coll., Northfield, Minn., 1952; M.B.A., Stanford U., 1954. With Security Trust & Savs. Bank, San Diego, 1954-57; vice chmn. Security Nat. Bank, L.A., 1957-84; chmn., chief exec. officer Norwest Corp., Mpls., 1985-92, chmn. bd. dirs., 1993-95; ret., 1995; mem. faculty Pacific Coast Banking Sch., 1969-72, chmn., 1979-80; bd. dirs. Valmont Industries Inc., Cargill Inc., Musicland Stores Corp.; trustee Minn. Mut. Life Ins. Co. Vice chmn. Carleton Coll., Mpls. Inst. Arts; mem. adv. com. Minnegasco; mem. bd. overseers U. Minn. Mem. Calif. Bankers Assn. (pres. 1977-78).

JOHNSON, LOWELL C., state commissioner; b. Dodge County, Nebr., June 12, 1920; B.S. in Mech. Engring., U. Nebr., 1942; m. Ruth Marion Sloss, June 21, 1943; children: Mark C., Kent R., James S., Nancy L. Farm and property mgmt. exec.; pres. Johnson-Sloss Land Co., North Bend, Nebr.; mem. Nebr. Legislature, 1980-93, vice-chmn. legis. appropriations com., mem. com. on coms.; commr. Nebr. Pub. Svc. Commn., 1995—; former bd. dirs. Equitable Fed. Savs. Bank, Fremont, Nebr.; former trustee Meml. Hosp. Dodge County; former mem. adv. council Nebr. Dept. Labor; mem. behavioral scis. adv. com. Immanuel Hosp., Omaha; former mem. County Sch. Reorgn. Com.; former field rep. Congressman Charles Thone; former pres. bd. dirs. North Bend Sr. Citizens Home. Mem. Am. Legion, Fremont and North Bend C. of C. Clubs: Masons, Shriners, Rotary. Office: PO Box 370 North Bend NE 68649-0370

JOHNSON, MARGARET DOUGLAS, retail executive; b. Indpls., Feb. 17, 1951; d. Lawrence and Doris (Tacke) O'Keefe; m. Terry Scott Douglas, July 3, 1971 (div. Jan. 1980), m. Lyman Tyler Johnson, May 18, 1980. AA, Marymount Coll., 1971. Store mgr. Courys Resort Apparel Inc., Coronado, Calif., 1972-77, The Shop for Pappagallo, Carmel, Calif., 1977-79, Colette, San Francisco, 1979-80; dept. mgr. Blocks, Indpls., 1980-83, human resources dir., 1983-87; store mgr. Pappagallo Inc., Indpls., 1987-93; mktg. dir. The Fashion Mall Keystone at the Crossing, Indpls, 1993—. Bd. dirs. Blocks Credit Union, Indpls., 1983-87. Democrat. Roman Catholic. Home: 6102 Crittenden Ave Indianapolis IN 46220-2306 Office: The Fashion Mall Office 8701 Keystone Crossing Indianapolis IN 46240

JOHNSON, MARGARET H, welding company executive, author; b. Chgo., June 3, 1933; d. Harold W. and Clara J. (Pape) Glavin; m. Odean Jack Johnson, Nov. 18, 1950; children: Karen Ann, Dean Harold. Student Moody Bible Inst., 1976-78. V.p., sec. Seamline Welding, Inc., Grayslake, 1956—, dir.; trustee SWCEPS, Grayslake, 1963—. Author: Living Faith, 1973, 80, Lord's Ladder of Love, 1976, God's Rainbow, 1982; contbr. articles to religion mags. Life mem. Rep. Presdl. Task Force, 1982—, trustee, 1986-88; charter founder Ronald Reagan Rep. Ctr., 1987; mem. Lake View Neighborhood Group, Chgo., Small Group Ch. Community; active Mary, Seat of Wisdom Cath. Women's Club, 1970-90, renew facilitator 1986-88, co-chairperson 1986-88; Sunday sch. tchr., 1985; mem. St. Gilbert's Parish, 1990—. Mem. ASCAP, Fedn. Ind. Small Bus., Internat. Platform Assn., Women's Aglow Fellowship Internat., Grayslake C. of C.. Exch. Club Grayslake, Grayslake Devel. Corp. Home: 20 Hawley Ct Grayslake IL 60030-1517

JOHNSON, MARK ALAN, psychologist; b. Duluth, Minn., Sept. 7, 1950; s. Einard G. and Mary Vey (DeVries) J.; m. Nancy Rae Puttonen, Mar. 4, 1972; children: Ryan T., Joel Erik, Aaron C., Matthew G. BS, U. Minn., Duluth, 1972; MS, U. Wis., Superior, 1981; PhD, The Fielding Inst., Santa Barbara, Calif., 1991. Lic. psychologist, Minn. Tchr. art Gary (Ind.) Pub. Schs., 1973, Ind. Sch. Dist. #710, Virginia, Minn., 1974-77, Jamestown (N.D.) Pub. Schs., 1978-80; psychotherapist Harbour North Clinic, Duluth, 1980-88; psychologist St. Luke's Hosp., Duluth, 1987-88, Arrowhead Psychol. Clinic, Duluth, 1988-94, Spectra Inc., Duluth, 1985—, Dakota Clinic, Park Rapids/Walker, Minn., 1994—; adj. faculty Minn. Sch. Profl. Psychology, Duluth, 1994—. Bd. dirs. Learning Disabilities of N.E. Minn., Duluth, 1993-94, Together for Twin Ports Youth Gay-Lesbian, Duluth, 1993-94; mem. sch. bd. Ind. Sch. Dist. 709, Duluth, 1991-93. Recipient Therapist Appreciation award Profl. Assn. Treatment Homes, 1991. Mem. Minn. Psychol. Assn. Lutheran. Home: 3825 Crescent View Ave Duluth MN 55804-1713 Office: The Dakota Clinic Park Rapids 120 N Main Park Rapids MN 56870

JOHNSON, MARLENE M., furniture company executive; b. Braham, Minn., Jan. 11, 1946; d. Beauford and Helen (Nelson) J.; m. Peter Frankel. BA, Macalester Coll., 1968. Founder, pres. Split Infinitive, Inc., St. Paul, 1970-82; pres., bd. dirs. Face to Face Health and Counseling Clinic, 1977-78; with Working Opportunities for Women, 1977-82; lt. gov. State of Minn., St. Paul, 1983-91; sr. fellow Family Support Project, Ctr. for Policy Alternative, 1991-93; assoc. adminstr. for adminstrn. GSA, Washington, 1994-95; v.p. for people and strategy Rowe Furniture Corp., McLean, Va., 1995—; founder, past chmn. Nat. Leadership Conf. Women Execs. in State Govt.; mem. exec. com., midwestern chair Nat. Conf. Lt. Govs.; bd. dirs. AFS-USA, Inc.; mem. adv. bd. Ctr. for Children in Poverty, Columbus U. Chmn. Minn. Women's Polit. Caucus, 1973-76, Dem.-Farmer-Labor Small Bus. Task Force, 1978, Child Care Task Force, 1987; dir. membership sect. Nat. Women's Polit. Caucus, 1975-77; vice chmn. Minn. Del. to White House Conf. on Small Bus., 1980; co-founder Minn. Women's Campaign Fund, 1982; bd. dirs. Nat. Child Care Action Campaign; chair Children's 2000 Commn., 1990; candidate for Mayor St. Paul, 1993. Recipient Outstanding Achievement award St. Paul YWCA, 1980, Disting. Svc. award St. Paul Jaycees, 1980, Disting. Citizen citation Macalester Coll., 1982, Disting. Contbns. to Families award Minn. Coun. on Family Rels., 1986, Minn. Sportfishing Congress award, 1986, Royal Order of Polar Star Govt. Sweden, 1988, Children's Champion award Def. Fund, 1989, Jane Preston award Minn. State Coun. on Vocat. Tech. Edn., 1989, Legis. Leadership award Am. Fedn. Tchrs., 1991; named One of Ten Outstanding Young Minnesotans, Minn. Jaycees, 1980; Swedish Bicentennial Commn. grantee, 1987. Mem. Nat. Assn. Women Bus. Owners (past pres.).

JOHNSON, MARVIN MELROSE, industrial engineer, consultant; b. Neligh, Nebr., Apr. 21, 1925; s. Harold Nighram and Melissa (Bare) J.; m. Anne Stuart Campbell, Nov. 10, 1951; children: Douglas Blaikie, Harold James, Phyllis Anne, Nighram Marvin, Melissa Joan. B.S., Purdue U., 1949; postgrad., Ill. Inst. Tech., 1953; M.S. in Indsl. Engring, U. Iowa, 1966, Ph.D., 1968. Registered profl. engr., Iowa, Mo., Nebr. Quality control supr., indsl. engr. Houdaille Hershey, Chgo., 1949-52; indsl. engr. Bell & Howell, Chgo., 1952-54; with Bendix Aviation Corp., Pioneer Ctrl. Divsn., Davenport, Iowa, 1954-64, successively chief indsl. engr., staff asst., supr. procedures and systems, reliability engr. Pioneer Cen. div., 1954-64; indsl. engring. cons., Bendix Aviation Corp. (Pioneer Central div.), Alcoa, Brunswick, Rapid City, S.D., 1964—; lectr. indsl. engring. State U. Iowa, 1963-64; instr. U. Iowa, 1965-66; assoc. prof. U. Nebr., 1968-73, prof., 1973-88, emeritus prof., 1988—; vis. prof. S.D. Sch. Mines and Tech., 1989-91, Ervin Pietz prof., 1991; U.S. AID adviser mgmt. engring. and food processing, Kabul, Afghanistan, 1975-76; vis. prof. indsl. engring. U. P.R., Mayaguez, 1982-83. Editor The Johnson Reporter, 1980-88. Served with AUS, 1943-46, ETO. Fellow Inst. Indsl. Engrs.; mem. ASME (life), Ops. Rsch. Soc., Sigma Xi, Tau Beta Pi, Pi Tau Sigma, Alpha Pi Mu. Presbyterian. Home: 119 N 19th St Saint Joseph MO 64501-2436

JOHNSON, MARY LOU, lay worker; b. Moline, Ill., July 15, 1923; d. Percy and Hope (Aulgur) Sipes; m. Blaine Eugene Johnson, May 30, 1941; children: Vivian A. Johnson Sweedy, Michael D. (dec.), Amelia Johnson Harms Thomas, James Michael (dec.). Grad. high sch., Moline. Chmn. Christian edn. 1st Christian Ch., Moline, 1971-73, 77-79, 84-86, elder, 1973-76, 77-80, chmn. official bd., 1979-81, dir. Christian edn., 1988-93, ret., 1993; Sunday sch. tchr. 1st Christian Ch, Moline, 1958-84; cluster del. Christian Chs. Ill. and Wisc., Moline, 1988-89. Author: (poem) What Is A Mother?, 1965. Officer various positions PTA, Moline, 1972-75, hon. life mem. State of Ill., 1972; leader, dist. dir. Girl Scouts U.S., Moline, 1955-65; skywatcher USAF Ground Observer Corps, Moline, 1955-57; vol. telethon coord. Muscular Dystrophy Assn., Moline, 1971-94; del. lt. gov.'s Commn. on Aging, Springfield, Ill., 1990. Recipient numerous appreciation awards Muscular Dystrophy Assn., 1964-94. Republican. Home: 2014 9th St Moline IL 61265-4779

JOHNSON, MARY LUCILLE, nurse; b. Harper, Kans., July 15, 1954; d. Arthur Harold and Geneva Mary (Schmitz) Drouhard; m. William Edward Johnson. Diploma, St. Joseph Sch. Nursing, 1975; BSN, St. Mary of the Plains Coll., 1982; MSN, Wichita State U., 1992. RN, Kans; cert. ACLS, advanced registered nurse practitioner. Nurse asst. St. Luke's Hosp., Wellington, Kans., 1972-75, St. Joseph Med. Ctr., Wichita, Kans., 1973-75; RN Swedish Med. Ctr., Seattle, 1975-78, St. Joseph Med. Ctr., Wichita, 1978—; mem. nursing com. recruitment, retention St. Joseph Med. Ctr., 1987-91, hosp. wide recruitment, retention com., 1991-93. Bd. dirs. Am. Heart Assn., Wichita, 1982-89; mem. profl. edn. com., Sedgwick County Div., 1986—; CPR instr. ARC, Sedgwick, 1983—; mem. Blessed Sacrament Choir, Wichita, Kans.; active Kans. Lupus Found., Arthritis Found. Mem. AACN, St. Joseph Federated Alumni Club, Sigma Theta Tau (treas. Iota Chi chpt. 1989-91). Republican. Roman Catholic. Home: 1450 S Webb Rd Apt 213 Wichita KS 67207-4256 Office: via Christi Regional Med Ctr St Joseph Campus 3600 E Harry St Wichita KS 67218-3713

JOHNSON, MARY THERESA, marketing professional. Asst. mgr. Sirloin Stockade, Marshfield, Wis., 1990-91; co-owner, v.p. Computerized, Dairy Svc. Inc., Marshfield, 1990—; conversion analyst Donnelley Mktg., Marshfield, 1995—. Vol. Christ Luth., Marshfield, 1990—. Democrat.

JOHNSON, MELVIN HENRY, JR., physician; b. Grand Rapids, Mich., Dec. 14, 1935; s. Melvin H. and Margaret J.; m. Barbara Ann Shilling, June 22, 1957; children: Michael W., Matthew S., Douglas H. MD, U. Mich., 1960. Diplomate Am. Bd. Radiology. Radiologist Battle Creek (Mich.) Health Sys., 1966—, chmn. dept. radiology, 1975-94, chief of staff, 1980-82, mem. gov. bd., 1982-89; pres. Radiology Consultants, P.C., 1975-94. Capt. USAR, 1964-66. Mem. Am. Coll. Radiology, Mich. State Med. Soc., Radiol. Soc. N.Am. Home: 148 Smithfield Rd Battle Creek MI 49015 Office: Radiology Consultants PC 3 Heritage Oak Ln Battle Creek MI 49015

JOHNSON, MICHAEL RANDY, insurance company executive; b. York, Nebr., Jan. 29, 1946; s. Sheldon Albert and Mary Lynn (Barbur) J.; m. Virginia L. Allgood, Apr. 5, 1975; children: Cory Michael, Scott Alan, Adam Todd. Student, Doane Coll., 1964-66, U. Nebr., 1966-68. Farmer Geneva, Nebr., 1968-84; field reporter Agrl. Stabilization and Construction Svc., Geneva, 1973-80; adjuster Fed. Crop Ins. Corp., Kansas City, Kans., 1979-81, North Ctrl. Crop Ins., Eau Claire, Wis., 1981-84, Acceptance-Redland Ins. Co./Am. Agrisurance-Agrijusters, Council Bluffs, Iowa, 1984-86; field supr. Acceptance-Redland Ins. Co./Am. Agrisurance-Agrijusters, Council Bluffs, 1986-88, tng. supr., 1988-90, regional claims supr., 1990-92, v.p., asst. claims mgr., 1993-94, claims mgr., sr. v.p., 1994—; cons. Segura La Comml., Monterey, Mex., 1988-92, Segures Am., Mexico City, 1988-92; contbg. bd. mem. Code of Ethics Bd. Nat. Crop Ins. Svc., Overland Park, Kans., 1992—; speaker in field. Author: (reference handbook) Grop Growth Patterns and Loss Adjustment, Mexico, 1991; editor: Crop Adjusting Manual, 1990, '91, '92. Mem. Masons. Methodist. Home: PO Box 7 810 E Elm Missouri Valley IA 51555 Office: Acceptance-Redland Ins Co/ Am Agrisurance-Agrijusters 535 W Broadway Council Bluffs IA 51503-0812 Also: PO Box 7 Missouri Valley IA 51555-0007

JOHNSON, MONICA LYNN, elementary education educator; b. Dubuque, Iowa, Mar. 8, 1962; d. Hugo and Arlene Isabel (Netzer) Fritz; children: Justus, Kyle. BS, No. Ill. U., 1985. Cert. Gare ceramics tchr., 1995. Elem. art educator Saratoga Elem. Sch., Morris, Ill., 1987-92, 94—, Immaculate Conception Sch., Morris, Ill., 1991-92, Troy Shorewood-Dist. 30C, Joliet, Ill., 1992-94; with Saratoga Elem. Sch., Morris, Ill., 1994—; muralist Saratoga Sch., Morris, 1990, 95, Immaculate Conception Sch., Morris, 1991, 92, Mary Crest Sch., Joliet, 1991, Troy Shorewood Sch., Joliet, 1993; owner Monicom, Personalized Children's Books, Morris. Mem. Nat. Art Edn. Assn., Ill. Art Edn. Assn. (cert. Duncan ceramics tchr. 1994).

JOHNSON, NIEL MELVIN, archivist, historian; b. Galesburg, Ill., July 28, 1931; s. Clarence Herman and Frances Albertina (Nelson) J.; m. Verna Gail Applegate, May 1, 1952; children: Kristin, David. BA, Augustana Coll., 1953; MA, State U. Iowa, 1965, PhD, 1971. Tchr. Unit #115, Biggsville, Ill., 1954-57; asst. historian U.S. Army Weapons Command, Rock Island, Ill., 1957-60, chief historian, 1960-63; instr. Augustana Coll., Rock Island, Ill., 1967-69; asst. prof. Dana Coll., Blair, Nebr., 1969-74; vis. asst. prof. U. Nebr., Omaha, 1975-76; archivist, historian Harry S. Truman Libr., Independence, Mo., 1977-92; pres. Portal to the Plains, Inc., Blair, Nebr., 1973-77, Am. Friends of Emigrant Inst. Sweden, East Moline, Ill., 1984-89. Author: George S. Viereck: German-American Propagandist, 1972, Portal to the Plains, 1974; co-author: Rockford Swedes: American Stories, 1993; contbr. articles in field to profl. jours., newspapers. coord. New Sweden '88 com. of Greater Kansas City, Mo.; chmn. Historic Trails City Com., Independence, 1988-93. Recipient Commendation, Concordia Hist. Inst., St. Louis, 1977. Mem. Orgn. Am. Historians, Oral History Assn., Midwestern Archives Conf., Jackson County Hist. Soc., Scandinavian Club (pres. 1987-89). Democrat. Lutheran. Home: 15804 Kiger Cir Independence MO 64055-3750

JOHNSON, PAUL OWEN, lawyer; b. Ft. Wayne, Ind., Jan. 26, 1919; s. Paul Ephriam and Pauline May (Ebersole) J.; m. Arlyn Marie Munson, Aug. 3, 1945; m. Louise Marie Skoglund, Feb. 11, 1972; children: Roxanne Marie, Dianne Marie. BSL, U. Minn., 1941, LLB, 1943, JD, 1967. Bar: Minn. 1943, U.S. Dist. Ct. Minn. 1948. V.p., counsel United Capital Life Ins., Mpls., 1965-70; assoc. editor Am. Trial Lawyers Jour., 1970-75; ptnr. Johnson & Ildstad, Edina, Minn., 1975—; bd. dirs. Interchange Investors, Mpls.; corp. counsel Thunderbird Hotel and Conv. Ctr. Corp.; mem. alt. dispute resolution com. Minn. Supreme Ct. Contbr. articles to Minn. Trial Lawyer Jour. Mem. Mayo Found. Served to lt. comdr. USN, 1941-46, PTO. Mem. ABA, Am. Arbitration Assn. (lectr.), Am. Judicature Soc., Minn. Bar Assn., Am. Trial Lawyers Assn., Minn. Trial Lawyers Assn. (pres. 1957, bd. dirs.), U.S. Naval Inst., Am. Legion (comdr., judge adv. 1980—), Minn. Alumni Assn. (life), U.S. Navy League (nat. dir. 1995), Submarine Vets. U.S. (life, submarine chaser), VFW, Fireside Investors Club, Masons, Shriners, Gamma Eta Gamma. Congregationalist. Home: 109 Meadow Ln S Minneapolis MN 55416-3404

JOHNSON, PAULINE BENGE, nurse, anesthetist; b. London, Ky., May 10, 1932; d. Chester G. and Bertha M. (Hale) Benge; m. Scottie W. Johnson, Apr. 29, 1950 (dec. 1976); children: Rita Johnson, Nita Johnson Yaw, Gina Johnson Carlson. AA, U. Ky., 1968; diploma, U. Cin. Sch. Nurse Anesthesia, 1971; BS summa cum laude, U. Cin., 1974, M., 1977, D., 1981. RN, Ohio, Ky., Tenn., Ind., W.Va., Fla., Tex.; cert. lic. RN anesthetist; cert. RN anesthetist. Staff anesthetist Jewish Hosp., Cin., 1971-72, Mercy North Hosp., Hamilton, Ohio, 1972-86, Ft. Hamilton Hosp., Hamilton, 1972-86, McCullough-Hyde Hosp., Oxford, Ohio, 1986-88; freelance anesthetist multiple hosps. Ohio, Ky., 1982-88; staff anesthetist, ind. contractor Shriner Burn Inst., Cin., 1989; pres., staff anesthetist, ind. contractor multiple hosps. Pauline B. Johnson Co., Inc., Ohio, Ky., Tenn., Ind., W. Va., Fla., Tex., 1989—; provider hosp. anethesia relief svcs. to under-serviced rural hosp. oper. rms., 1990—. Ch. clk. Lindenwald Bapt. Ch., Hamilton, 1955-72, mem. 1955-85, instr., 1955-76; mem. 1st Bapt. Ch., Hamilton, 1985—, NOW, 1978—, nominating com. major polit. party, Hamilton, 1986-89; mem., med. com. Planned Parenthood, Hamilton, 1987—; vol. various rural hosps., 1990—. Scholar U. Cin., 1969-71, 77-81; recipient Spl. Recognition Higher Edn., Laurel County Homecoming, London, Ky., 1988. Mem. Am. Assn. Nurse Anesthetists (speaker nat. conv. 1982, speaker rsch. forum nat. meeting 1989, mem. nominating com. 1978), Ohio State Assn. Nurse Anesthetists (state bd. dirs. 1989-92, 88-90, 79-80, chair bylaws com. 1991-92, 92-93, nominating com. 1993-94, chair edn. com. 1990-91, pres. 1982-84, state editor Highlights 1974-82, co-chair state meeting 1982, pres. dist. 5 Cin. 1978, govt. rels. chpt. Greater Cin. chpt. 1976-87, speaker meetings), Kappa Delta Pi. Home: 128 S F St Hamilton OH 45013-4710

JOHNSON, PORTER WEAR, physics educator; b. Chattanooga, Sept. 4, 1942; s. Samuel Wear and Lila Watkins (Kirkman) J.; m. Aura Frances Mabry, June 22, 1963; children: Erik B., Deborah M. BS, Case Inst. Tech., Cleve., 1963; PhD, Princeton U., 1967. Postdoctoral Case Western Res. U., Cleve., 1967-69; from asst. prof. to prof. physics Ill. Inst. Tech., Chgo., 1969—; sr. rsch. assoc. State U. Groningen, Netherlands, 1975-76, 81-82, Argonne (Ill.) Nat. Lab., 1974, 82. Contbr. over 70 articles to sci. jours. Alfred P. Sloan scholar, N.Y.C., 1959-63; NSF fellow, Washington, 1963-66. Mem. Am. Phys. Soc., Am. Assn. Physics Tchrs., Tau Beta Pi. Home: 406 N Elmwood Ave Oak Park IL 60302-2226 Office: Ill Inst Tech Physics Dept Chicago IL 60616

JOHNSON, RAY O., research scientist; b. Kansas City, Mo., May 25, 1955; s. Orville Raymond and Rita Jean (Terry) J.; m. Joan Irene Vance, Oct. 11, 1991; children: Michael Steven, Alexander Benjamin. BSEE, Okla. State U., 1984; MSEE, Air Force Inst. Tech., 1987, PhD of Elec. Engring., 1993. Electronics technician USAF, 1975-81; engr. digital telecomm. Fgn. Tech. divsn. USAF, Dayton, Ohio, 1984-86; engr. low observables Strategic Air Command USAF, Omaha, 1987-90; maj., sr. rsch. scientist Wright Lab., Dayton, 1993-95, tech. dir., 1995—; sensor adv. panel mem. Advanced Rsch. Projects Agy., Arlington, Va., 1995-96; sensor tech. panel mem. SPECTRA, Washington, 1995. Active St. George's Episc. Ch., Dayton, 1990—. Mem. IEEE, Internat. Soc. Optical Engring., Tau Beta Pi, Eta Kappa Nu, Phi Kappa Phi. Republican.

JOHNSON, REDGE, electrical engineer, company executive; b. Lincoln, Nebr., Nov. 11, 1951. Cert. photog. engr. Pres. Wireless Cord Co., Lincoln, 1968-74, Images II, Lincoln, 1974—; profl. magician, Lincoln, 1965—. Patentee on lasers, optics and elec. engring. Recipient svc. award Advt. Fedn. Lincoln, merit award USMC. Mem. Soc. Am. Magicians, Magic Cir. Presbyterian. Office: Images II 1700 O St Lincoln NE 68508-1735

JOHNSON, REGINALD AMIN, writer; b. Ecorse, Mich., May 9, 1948; s. William and Mattie Bell (White) J.; m. Joan Thompson, May 10, 1980. Student, Grand Valley State Coll., 1973-75, Wayne State U., 1978-79; BA, Spring Arbor Coll., 1988. Editor Megaphone, Muskegon, Mich., 1986-89; writer Temporary Times, Ionia, Mich., 1989-91; copy editor Ryan Rev., Detroit, 1991-94; freelance writer Detroit, 1994—. Mem. NAACP (Male Mentors), Internat. Black Writers (bd. dirs. 1990-94). Office: Muslim Brotherhood #115613 17600 Ryan Rd Detroit MI 48212

JOHNSON, RICHARD DEAN, pharmaceutical consultant, educator; b. De Kalb, Ill., July 8, 1936; s. Arthur Dean and Evelyn Alice (Telford) J.; BS, U. Calif., Berkeley, 1960; PharmD, U. Calif., San Francisco, 1961, MS, 1962, PhD, 1965; MBA, Rockhurst Coll., Kansas City, Mo., 1984; m. Paula Marcellus Jennings, Nov. 3, 1942; children: Janet Telford, Julie Tess, Richard Dean, Jennings Brodie. Sect. head R & D Allergan Pharms., Irvine, Calif., 1965-67; dir. regulatory affairs Syntex Labs., Inc., Palo Alto, Calif., 1967-73; mng. dir. licensing Marion Labs., Inc., Kansas City, Mo., 1973-79, v.p. licensing, 1980-82, v.p. corp. devel., 1983-87, v.p. bus. alliances, 1987-89; corp. v.p. Marion Merrell Dow Inc., Kansas City, Mo., 1989-91, ret., chmn., CEO KC Pharma, Mo., 1991—; adj. prof. Sch. Pharmacy U. Mo., Kansas City, 1991-95, rsch. coun., 1993—, adj. grad. prof., 1995—; bd. dirs. Dey Labs. Inc., Concord, Calif., Tanabe-Marion Labs., Kans. City, U.S. Biosci. Inc., Blue Bell, Pa., ImmunoPharmaceutics, Inc., San Diego, Lovelace Med. Found., Albuquerque, San Diego, Micrologix Inc., Vancouver, B.C.; guest lectr. U. S.C. Coll. Bus. Adminstrn., Columbia, 1975-79. Presdl. exchange exec. U.S. Dept. Commerce, Washington, 1970-71, U.S. Pharmacopeia Com. of Rev., 1990-94, 95—; trustee U. Mo., Kansas City Pharmacy Found., 1993—, v.p., 1994-95, pres. 1995—, chmn. devel. com., 1994—, dean's adv. bd., 1995—; trustee Kansas City Cmty. Found., 1993—; mem. dean's adv. bd. Sch. Pharmacy U. Calif., San Francisco, 1994—, Sch. Pharmacy U. Mo., Kansas City, 1995—; active De La Salle Sch. Devel. Com., 1993—, St. Lukes Hosp. Stroke Com., 1993—, USP Drug Nom. Com., 1990-94, 95—, ARC, Kirkwood Soc. Recipient Grad. award Borden Co., 1962; Am. Found. for Pharm. Edn. fellow, 1962-64; Sir Henry S. Wellcome Meml. fellow, 1962-63; Am. Inst. Chemists fellow, 1965-70. Mem. AAAS, ACS, ARC Kirkwood Soc., Am. Assn. Pharm. Scis., Am. Pharm. Assn., Am. Assn. Pharm. Scis., Acad. Pharm. Sci., N.Y. Acad. Sci., Pharm. Mfrs. Assn., Fedn. Internat. Pharmacy, Licensing Exec. Soc., Sigma Xi, Rho Chi, Phi Lambda Sigma. Republican. Clubs: Balboa Bay (Newport Beach, Calif.), Carriage (Kansas City, Mo.), Hallbrook Country Club. Contbr. articles to pharm. jours. Home: 5330 Ward Pky Kansas City MO 64112-2369 Office: KC Pharma LLC 222 W Gregory Blvd Kansas City MO 64114-1110

JOHNSON, RICHARD JEROME, computer company executive; b. Kenyon, Minn., Oct. 30, 1932; s. Joseph Alexander and Marie Sylvina (Dale) J.; m. Laura Ann Sparstad, June 27, 1953; children: Dawn, James, Mark, Karen. BA in Bus., Augsburg Coll., 1954; MS in Computer Systems, Am. U., Washington, 1972. Commd. 2d lt. USMC, 1954, advanced through grades to col., 1978, ret., 1980; sr. staff. cons. Sperry Corp., St. Paul, 1981-82, dir. advanced tech., 1983-84; dir. strategic planning Unisys Corp., St. Paul, 1985-87; dir. navy systems Unysis Corp., St. Paul, 1988-89, mgr. internat. program, 1990-93; ret., 1993; industry rep. U. Minn., Mpls., 1984-88, Mankato (Minn.) State U., 1988-89. Twp. planner Cannon Falls, Minn., 1989-92; vice chmn. County Parks and Recreation Bd., 1995—. Decorated Legion of Merit, Purple Heart, Bronze Star. Mem. VFW, DAV, Am. Legion, Mil. Order Purple Heart, Marine Corps League, Lions Internat. (pres. 1987-88, vice dist. gov. 1994-95, dist. gov. 1995-96, coun. chmn. 1996—). Republican. Lutheran.

JOHNSON, RICHARD NED, mechanical engineer, research executive; b. Perry, Iowa, Jan. 4, 1942; s. Harding Richard and Dorothy Margret (Nelson) J.; m. Lila Lee Herron, June 24, 1978 (dec. Oct. 1984); children: Jana, David, Rachel; m. Karen L. Friedman, May 18, 1986. BS in Applied Math., U. Wis., 1964; MS in Engring. Mechanics, Case Inst., Cleve., 1968; PhD in Engring. Mechanics, U. Wis., 1972; MBA with honors, Roosevelt U., Chgo., 1980. Project mgr. Lewis Research div. NASA, Cleve., 1964-70; teaching asst. U. Wis., Madison, 1970-71; dept. mgr. Gen. Am. Research Div./GATX Corp., Niles, Ill., 1971-82; sect. mgr. Borg-Warner Research, Des Plaines, Ill., 1982-87; dept. mgr. Borg Warner Automotive Rsch., Des Plaines, Ill., 1987-88, Packer Engring., Naperville, Ill., 1989; program mgr., assoc. dir. Indsl. Rsch. Lab./Northwestern U., Evanston, Ill., 1991—, assoc. dir., 1991—; cons. Gen Dyn, Psych Systems, Axionixx, legal firms. Author: Handbook of Manufacturing High Technology, 1986; co-inventor tire degradation monitor, rubber bond inspection. NASA research grantee, 1970. Mem. Soc. Mfg. Engrs. (sr.), Inst. Indsl. Engrs. Home: 15w755 Shepard Ln Burr Ridge IL 60521-6849 Office: Indsl Rsch Lab 1801 Maple Ave Evanston IL 60201-3135

JOHNSON, RICHARD WALTER, investment executive; b. Mpls., Oct. 2, 1928; s. Walter Benjamin and Evelyn (Peterson) J.; m. Marlys Jean Tiller, Feb. 21, 1988; children: Richard Walter, William Charles, Nancy Ann, Thomas Gregory, Michael Richard. B.B.A. with distinction, U. Minn., 1949. C.P.A., Nebr., Ill. With Arthur Andersen & Co. (C.P.A.'s), 1949-74; mng. partner Arthur Andersen & Co. (C.P.A.'s), Omaha, 1960-74; chmn. bd., chief exec. officer Western Securities Co. of Del., Omaha, 1975—; pres. Modern Equipment Co., Omaha, 1975—. Bd. dirs., exec. com. Jr. Achievement Omaha, 1962—, pres., 1966-67; gen. campaign chmn. Heart of the Midlands United Way, 1972, chmn. pacemaker sect. fund raising campaign, 1964, chmn. corporate standards com., 1966, assoc. gen. chmn., 1968, treas., mem. exec. com., 1969; bd. dirs. Fontenelle Forest Nature Ctr. Assn. Mid-Am. council Boy Scouts of Am., Omaha Symphony Assn., Omaha Big Bros. Assn., Omaha Playhouse Assn.; Trustee Creighton U. Pres.'s Council. Recipient One of Outstanding Young Men in Am. award, 1965. Mem. AICPA, Nebr. Soc. CPAs, Newcomen Soc. N.Am., Omaha C. of C. (chmn. membership rels. com. 1962—, bd. dirs. 1965—, mem. exec. com., v.p. 1968), Omaha Club, Omaha Country Club, Garden of the Gods Club (Colorado Springs), Masons, Shriners, Rotary Internat., Beta Gamma Sigma, Beta Alpha Psi. Home: 1323 N 98th Ct Omaha NE 68114-2112 Office: 2000 Cuming St Omaha NE 68102-4324

JOHNSON, ROBERT DALE, information systems consultant; b. Greensburg, Ind., May 25, 1965; s. Lester Wilburn and Mildred Louise (Ray) J. Assoc. in Elec. Engring., ITT Tech. Inst., 1985, BS in Automation, 1986; BSBA, Ind. Wesleyan U., 1989. GTE Midwestern Tel. Ops. GTE Midwestern Telephone Ops., Westfield, Ind., 1984-87; computer network specialist Midwestern Tel. Ops./GTE North, Carmel, Ind., 1987-89; mktg. adminstr. GTE Telecom, Indpls., 1988-89; tech. svcs. coord. GTE North/GTE Data Svcs., Westfield, Ind., 1989; data products salesman GTE Telecom, Muskegon, Mich., 1989-90; products divsn. mgr. Genzink Steel Corp., Holland, Mich., 1992-95; pres. Trinity Cons. for Sys. and Svcs. Inc., Spring Lake, Mich., 1990—; instr. Ind. U.-Purdue U. at Indpls., 1989. Mem. Soc. Mfg. Engring. (past chmn.), U.S. Space Found., Bass Anglers Sportsman Soc. Republican. Wesleyan. Home: 17664 148th Ave Spring Lake MI 49456-9517 Office: PO Box 393 Spring Lake MI 49456

JOHNSON, ROBERT EDWARD, theology educator; b. Farmville, Va., Nov. 5, 1950; s. Clyde Thompson and Margaret Ann (Denton) J.; m. Celia Claycomb, June 4, 1976; children: Rebekah Ann, Robert William. BA in Religion, U. Richmond, 1973; MDiv, Southwestern Bapt. Theol. Sem., Ft. Worth, 1977, PhD in Ch. History, 1984. Ordained to ministry So. Bapt. Conv., 1970. Pastor Chestnut Grove Bapt. Ch., Appomattox, Va., 1970-73; prof. ch. history Faculdade Teológica Batista, São Paulo, Brazil, 1980-91, dean grad. studies, 1988-89; prof. ch. history Baptistische Theologische Hochschule Rüschlikon, Zurich, Switzerland, 1991-92; assoc. prof. ch. history Midwestern Bapt. Theol. Sem., Kansas City, Mo., 1992—; missionary Fgn. Mission Bd., So. Bapt. Conv., São Paulo, 1979-91; guest prof. Southwestern Bapt. Theol. Sem., Ft. Worth, 1989-90. Author: Uma Breve História da Reforma Protestante, 1989; contbr.: O Enciclopédia Evangélica de Teologia; also articles. Bd. dirs. Inst. Bapt.-Anabaptist Studies, Rüschlikon. Mem. Am. Soc. Ch. History, Sixteenth Century Soc., Conf. on Faith and History, So. Bapt. Hist. Soc., Associação Batista de Institutos Bíblicos e Teológicos. Home: 3017 NE 73rd St Kansas City MO 64119-1420 Office: Midwestern Bapt Theol Sem 5001 N Oak Trafficway Kansas City MO 64118-4620

JOHNSON, RONALD HENRY, engineer, consultant; b. Chgo., Oct. 17, 1936; s. Halvard Osiana and Violet (Bohse) J.; m. Beverly Bade, June 13, 1959; children: Cynthia, Kimberly, Patricia, Pamela. BEE, Valparaiso U., 1960. Registered profl. engr., Ill., Tex., Ind. With Hays Corp., 1960-69; assoc. Sargent & Lundy, Chgo., 1969—. Mem. Instrument Soc. Am. (chmn. SP77). Lutheran. Office: Sargent & Lundy 55 E Monroe St Chicago IL 60603-5702

JOHNSON, SAMUEL CURTIS, wax company executive; b. Racine, Wis., Mar. 2, 1928; s. Herbert Fisk and Gertrude (Brauner) J.; m. Imogene Powers, May 8, 1954; children: Samuel Curtis III, Helen Johnson-Leipold, Herbert Fisk III, Winifred Johnson Marquart. BA, Cornell U., 1950; MBA, Harvard U., 1952; LLD (hon.), Carthage Coll., 1974, Northland Coll., 1974, Ripon Coll., 1980, Carroll Coll., 1981, U. Surrey, 1985, Marquette U., 1986, Nijenrode U., 1992. With S.C. Johnson & Son, Inc., Racine, 1954—, internat. v.p., 1962-63, exec. v.p., 1963-66, pres., 1966-67, chmn., pres., chief exec. officer, 1967-72, chmn., chief exec. officer, 1972-88, chmn., 1988—; bd. dirs. Johnson Wax Cos., Eng., Switzerland, Deere & Co., Moline, Ill., H.J. Heinz Co., Phila., Mobil Corp., N.Y.C., Graco Children's Products Inc., Elverson, Pa.; chmn. bd. dirs. Johnson Worldwide Assocs., Inc., Johnson Internat. Inc. Trustee Am. Mus. Natural History, N.Y.C.; trustee emeritus The Mayo Found., Cornell U., presdl. councillor; chm Johnson's Wax Fund, Inc., Johnson Found., Inc.; founding chmn. emeritus Prairie Sch., Racine; chmn. adv. coun. Cornell U. Grad. Sch. Mgmt.; regent emeritus Smithsonian Instn.; mem. Bus. Coun.; mem. nat. bd. govs. The Nature Conservancy. Mem. Chi Psi. Clubs: Cornell (N.Y.C., Milw.); Univ. (Milw.); Racine Country; Am. (London). Home: 4815 Lighthouse Dr Racine WI 53402-2666 Office: S C Johnson & Son Inc 1525 Howe St Racine WI 53403-5011

JOHNSON, SANDRA KAY, marketing professional; b. Montrose, Colo., July 6, 1939; d. Conrad Per Muhr and Lorrena (Boruff) Muhr Roland; m. Duane L. Johnson, Apr. 2, 1955 (div. June 1982); children: Randall D., Terry Johnson Erickson, Kurt L. BA in Human Rels., N.Mex. State U., 1982. Buyer Gen. Cable Corp., Hot Springs, Ark., 1970-72; office mgr. Muncrief Wheeler Printing, Hot Springs, 1972-76; loan officer, customer svc. CitiCorp-Person-to-Person, Riverton, Wyo., 1978-79; adminstrv. asst. Gulf Oil Co.-Real Estate Divsn., Grants, N.Mex., 1981-82; office mgr. Wind River Dental, Salt Lake City, 1982-83; search specialist Mgmt. Recruiters, Salt Lake City, 1983-84; advt./mktg. mgr. Pyke Mfg. Co., Salt Lake City, 1984-88; dir. mktg. Security By Design, Concord, Calif., 1988-95; family svc. counselor PreNeed Sys., Des Moines and Garland, Tex., 1996—; adv. bd. Indian Gaming Mag., Rockeville, Md., Bellvue, Wash., 1991-93; co-chmn. vendor adv. com. Nat. Indian Gaming Assn., Washington, 1992-93. Bd. dirs., sec.-treas. United Way of Cibola County, Grants, 1980-82; women's bd. Westminster Coll., Salt Lake City, 1984-88; allocations com. mem. United Way Quad Cities, Rock Island, Ill., 1995-96. Mem. Soc. Mktg. Profl. Svcs. (cert. mktg. profl., accommodations chair San Francisco chpt. 1991-92, treas. 1993-94), Am. Soc. Indsl. Security (Quad-Cities chpt. co-chairperson, pres. 1996). Democrat. Presbyterian. Home: 1416 W 15th St Davenport IA 52804 Office: Halligan McCabe Funeral Home 614 Main St Davenport IA 52803

JOHNSON, SHARON DENISE, office administrator, treasurer; b. Kans. City, Mo., Nov. 18, 1947; d. Leland Earl and Leona (Gover) Dailey; m. Herbert Johnson, Oct. 27, 1973. AA in Studio Art, Met. C.C., Kans. City, Mo., 1967; BA in Studio Art, U. Mo., Kans. City, 1969, MPA, 1976. Draftsman, stat. analysis JBM & Assoc., Kans. City, 1969-73; office mgr., adminstr. Felix Camera & Video, Overland Park, Kans., 1976-93; contr., treas. Hedlund & Assoc., Mission, Kans., 1993—. Chair fin. com. Luth. Ch. of Resurrection, Prairie Village, Kans., 1992-95, chair computer com., 1993—, mem. coun., 1991-95. Mem. Inst. Mgmt. Accts., William Jewell Fine Arts Guild, Phi Kappa Phi. Republican. Home: 8404 Meadow Ln Leawood KS 66206-1422 Office: Hedlund & Assoc 5909 Martway St Mission KS 66202-3338

JOHNSON, SHIRLEY, state legislator; b. Dec. 14, 1937; m. Cliff 1957; two children. Oakland C.C., Wayne State U. Dir. Oakland County Rep. Club; chairwoman Oakland County Cmty. Devel. Adv. Coun., 1977-80; charter mem. Oakland County Chpt. Mich. Rep. Womens Task Force; precinct del., 1996—; mem. Oakland County Rep. Exec. Com., 1996—; rep. city dir. for Royal Oak, 1996—; state rep. Dist. 68 Mich. Ho. of Reps., 1980-94; state rep. Dist. 41, 1995—; mem. Appropriations com. Mich. Ho. of Reps., 1982—. Del. Mich. State Rep. Conv., 1973—; mem. Royal Oak Rep. Women's Club (former pres.). Named Legislator of Yr. Mich. Judges Assn., 1986—,; recipient Legis. Leadership award Mich. Area Gy. on Aging, 1988, Steering Wheel award Mich. Automobile Club, 1988, Legis. Recognition award Oakland County Sch. Bd. Assn., 1990. Mem. PTA, LWV, Royal Oak Boys & Girls Club (bd. dirs.), Royal Oak Concerned Citizens for Better Schs., Optimist Club. Home: 4222 Sheridan Dr Royal Oak MI 48073-6230 Office: Mich State Senate State Capitol Lansing MI 48909*

JOHNSON, SHIRLEY ELAINE, management consultant; b. Terre Haute, Ind., Sept. 15, 1946; d. Mervil Ray and Sarah Kathryn (Tucker) W.; children: Richard Alan, Gary Michael. BA, DePaul U., 1991. Sec. to v.p. fin. Cenco Inc., Oak Brook, Ill., 1972-74, exec. asst. to group pres., 1974-75, asst. to chmn., 1975-77, corp. personnel/office mgr., 1977-80; corp. sec. Acadia Petroleum Corp., Denver, 1980-82; mgr. office Chapman, Klein & Weinberg, PC, Denver, 1982-84; asst. to chmn. The Heidrick Ptnrs., Inc., Chgo., 1984-92, v.p., 1992—. Mem. NAFE, Am. Mgmt. Assn., Exec. Women Internat., The River Club, Rsch. Roundtable. Home: 820 McKenzie Sta Dr Lisle IL 60532 Office: The Heidrick Ptnrs Inc 20 N Wacker Dr Ste 2850 Chicago IL 60606-3101

JOHNSON, SIDNEY, state legislator. State senator Dist. 34 Mo. State Congress. *

JOHNSON, SONDRA LEA, accountant; b. Kansas City, Mo., May 11, 1952; d. Albert John Oscar and Dorothy Mae (Hudgens) J. AA, Longview Coll., 1972; BSBA cum laude in Acctg., Cen. Mo. State U., 1974, MBA, 1980. CPA, Mo. Acct. Farmland Industries, Kansas City, 1974-76; acct., auditor Ernst & Whinney, Kansas City, 1976-79, Laventhol & Horwath, Kansas City, 1980-81; corp. acct., mgr. Butler Mfg. Co., Kansas City, 1981-84; audit supr. Grant Thornton Internat., Kansas City, 1984-89; sr. fin. analyst Hoechst Marion Roussel, Kansas City, 1989-95; with fin. reporting dept. UtiliCorp United, Inc., Kansas City, 1996—; specialized instr. nat. continuing edn. tng. program, Grant Thornton Internat., various locations U.S.A.; acctg. instr. Cen. Mo. State U., Warrensburg, 1979-80, Rockhurst Coll., Kansas City, 1981-82, Avila Coll., Kansas City, 1989-90. Mem. AICPAs, Inst. Mgmt. Accts., Mo. Soc. CPAs, Women's C. of C. of Kansas City, Phi Kappa Phi. Democrat. Lutheran. Office: UtiliCorp United Inc 10700 E 350 Hwy Raytown MO 64138

JOHNSON, STEPHEN MICHAEL, ophthalmologist; b. Indpls., Jan. 17, 1950; s. Frank Samuel and Jean Ann (Gaston) J.; m. Candy Mae Young, July 21, 1954; children: Benjamin, Stuart, Jean. BA in Biol. Scis., Ind. U., 1972; MD, Ind. U., Indpls., 1976. Resident ophthalmology Ind. Univ., Indpls., 1980; chief ophthalmology Vets. Hosp., Indpls., 1981-82; fellow cornea and external diseases Baylor U., Houston, 1982; sect. head cornea and external diseases Midwest Eye Inst., Indpls., 1982—; med. dir. Cryobiology Inst., Indpls., 1983—. Fellow Am. Acad. Ophthalmology, Ind. Acad. Ophthalmology; mem. Paton Soc., Alpha Omega Alpha. Office: Midwest Eye Inst 201 Pennsylvania Pkwy Indianapolis IN 46280

JOHNSON, STEVEN CRAIG, financial company executive; b. Salina, Kans., Nov. 29, 1965; s. Eldon Bernard and Ramona Rosalie (Berndt) J. BS in Agrl. Econs., Kans. State U., 1988; MBA, U. Chgo., 1993. Intern Senate Office Bob Dole, Washington, 1986, WIBW Radio & TV (CBS), Topeka, 1987-88; fin. planner IDS Fin. Svcs. (Am. Express), Charlottesville, Va., 1988-90; grad. mgmt. devel. IDS Fin. Svcs. (Am. Express), Chgo., 1990-91; compensation analyst IDS Fin. Svcs. (Am. Express), Mpls., 1991-92; mgr. asset allocation Am. Express Fin. Advisors, Mpls., 1992—; speaker in field. Co-author/editor: Basics of Asset Allocation, 1995. State speaking leadership judge 4-H, Minn., 1993—; ski instr. deaf children Minn. Ski Coun., Eden Prarie, 1995—. Mem. Kans. State U. Pres. Club. Republican. Lutheran. Home: 210 W Grant #709 Minneapolis MN 55403 Office: Am Express Fin Advisors IDS Tower 10 T22/271 Minneapolis MN 55440

JOHNSON, STEVEN FREDERICK, computer software developer, internet service; b. Chgo., Aug. 5, 1956; s. John Frederick and Mary Alice (Rammer) J.; m. Carol Woodling Schmidt, July 12, 1980; children: Gregory R., Marianna B. BS in Physics, Math. with highest honors, DePaul U., 1977; MS in Computer, Info. Sci., Ohio State U., 1979. Mem. tech. staff Bell Tel. Labs., Columbus, Ohio, 1979-80; computer specialist Ohio State U. Hosps. Coll. Med., Columbus, Ohio, 1980-83; software project leader Scientific Columbus div. of Esterline Corp., 1983-85; software mgr. Affinitec Inc., St. Louis, Mo., 1985-87; software project mgr. Siemens Ultrasound, Inc., San Ramon, Calif., 1987-91, Automotive Diagnostics div. of SPX Corp. (formerly Allen), Kalamazoo, Mich., 1991—; co-owner NetLink Sys., L.L.C., Kalamazoo, Mich., 1995—. Patentee mng. dynamic vehicle data. Pres. Birchwood Hills Neighborhood Assn., Inc., Kalamazoo, Mich. 1993-95; longhouse mem. YMCA Indian Guides program, Kalamazoo, 1993-94; instr. Project Charlie (Chem. Abuse Reduction Lies In Edn.), Portage Pub. Schs., 1993-94; mem. Publicity Com. The Kalamazoo Singers., 1994—. Mem. IEEE, Kalamazoo C. of C. Home: 5390 Glen Harbor Dr Kalamazoo MI 49009

JOHNSON, STEVEN HAROLD, engineer; b. Baldwin, Wis., Oct. 17, 1956; s. Harold Edward and Ruth Marilyn J; children: Christina Mae, Nicholas Steven. B, Milw. Sch. Engring., 1979; postgrad., Northwestern U. Mgr. prodcut devel. John Deere Comml. Products, 1979—. Patentee in field. Vol. Jr. Achievement, 1982-86. Mem. FPS, SAW. Lutheran. Office: John Deere Horicon Works 203 E Lake St Horicon WI 53032-1260

JOHNSON, STEVEN R., state legislator; m. Shannon Johnson. BS, Ind. U., MBA. Supr. chem. lab. Ind. U., Kokomo; owner Tuess Inc., pres.; rep. Ind. Ho. of Reps., 1980-82, 84-86; senator Dist. 21 State Legis., 1986—, mem. legis. appointment and elec. com., ranking mem. ethics com., mem. corrections, crime and civil procedures com., chmn. planning and pub. svc. com. Chmn. Howard County Reps., 1988-91; mem. Cmty. Assistance Found. Mem. Kokomo c. of C., Christian Businessman's Com., Elks, Rotary. Home: 2515 Greentree Ln Kokomo IN 46902-6402 Office: State Senate State Capitol Indianapolis IN 46204*

JOHNSON, THERESE MARIE BROWNE, admissions counselor; b. Chgo., Apr. 24, 1966; d. Thomas Edward and Kathleen Louise (Carroll) B. BA, U. Houston, 1988, MEd in Guidance and Counseling, 1991. Counselor in ednl. svcs. and programs No. Ill. U., DeKalb, 1991-94; admissions counselor Ill. Math. and Sci. Acad., Aurora, 1994—. Mem. Am. Counseling Assn., Ill. Counseling Assn. (co-presneter St. Charles, Ill. conf. 1992), No. Ill. U. Counseling Assn., Ill. Assn. Coll. Admissions Counselors. Roman Catholic. Home: 9533 S Longwood Ave Chicago IL 60643 Office: Ill Math and Sci Acad 1500 W Sullivan Rd Aurora IL 60506

JOHNSON, THOMAS FLOYD, college president, educator; b. Detroit, June 1, 1943; s. Edward Eugene and Adella Madeline (Norton) J.; m. Michele Elizabeth Myers, Mar. 26, 1965; children: Jason, Amy, Sarah. BPh, Wayne State U., 1965; BD, Fuller Theol. Sem., 1968; ThM, Princeton Sem., 1969; PhD, Duke U., 1979. Pastor Presbyn. Ch. U.S.A., Pa., Mich., 1969-76; asst. prof. U. Sioux Falls, S.D., 1978-83; acad. dean Sioux Falls (S.D.) Coll., 1981-83, pres., 1988—; prof. N.Am. Baptist Sem., Sioux Falls, 1983-88. Contbr. 9 articles to Internat. Standard Bible Ency., 1988; author: 1, 2, and 3 John New International Biblical Commentary, 1993. Bd. dirs. Children's Home Soc. S.D., Sioux Falls, 1980-86, S.D. Symphony Orch., 1988-92, Carroll Inst., 1989-93, Coalition Christian Colls. and Univs., 1992—. Mem. Am. Bapt. Assn. Colls. and Univs. (pres. 1992-94), Soc. Bibl. Lit., Sioux Falls C. of C. (bd. dirs. 1992-95), Rotary (bd. dirs. Downtown Club 1991-95, pres. 1993-94). Office: Univ Sioux Falls 1101 W 22nd St Sioux Falls SD 57105-1699

JOHNSON, THOMAS LEE, state legislator; b. Oakland, Calif., Apr. 30, 1945; s. WallaceJ.; m. Virginia Van Der Molen, 1968; children: Sorne, Derek, Kirk. BA, U. Mich., 1970; JD, DePaul U., 1974. Investigator State Atty.'s Office, DuPage County, Ill., 1970-74; assoc. Laraia, Solano, Berns & Kilander, Ltd., Wheaton, Ill., 1976-77; atty. Johnson, Westra, Broecker, Whittaker & Newitt, PC, Carol Stream, Ill., 1977—; mem. Ill. Ho. of Reps., 1993—, chmn. judiciary, criminal law, pub. utilities coms., also health care, human svcs., appropriations coms.; owner Buterfird Hardware Store, Wheaton, 1977—. Past chmn. Winfield Twp. (Ill.) Rep. com.; past precinct committeeman Winfield Twp.; candidate U.S. Congress, 1984; del. Dole, 1988; campaign advisor Citizens to Elect Jim Ryan, 1990; mem. Sci. Tech. Mus., Wheaton Youth Outreach, Family Inst., Christian Legal Soc. Mem. ABA, Ill. Bar Assn., DuPage County Bar Assn., Am. Legion. Office: Ill State Rep J Stratton Bldg Springfield IL 62706*

JOHNSON, THOMAS STUART, lawyer; b. Rockford, Ill., May 21, 1942; s. Frederick C. and Pauline (Ross) J. BA, Rockford Coll. 1964, LLD, 1989; JD, Harvard U., 1967. Bar: Ill. 1967. Pres.Williams & McCarthy, Rockford, 1967—; bd. dirs. John S. Barnes Corp., Rockford, Odin Corp., Rockford; lectr. in field. Contbr. numerous articles to profl. jours. Chmn. bd. trustees Rockford Coll., 1986-89; trustee Eastern Ill. U., 1996—; chmn. bd. dirs. Ill. Inst. Continuing Legal Edn., Chgo., 1984-86; trustee Emanuel Med. Ctr., Turlock, Cal., 1984-86, trustee Swedish Covenant Hosp., Chgo., 1984-86; treas. Lawyers Trust Fund of Ill., Chgo., 1984-86; mem. bd. govs., 1985-90, Regent's Coll., London, 1985-89; bd. dir. benevolence bd. Covenant Ch. Am., Chgo., 1984-86; chmn. Regent's Found. for Internat. Edn., London. With U.S. Army, 1965-67. Fellow Am. Bar Found., Am. Coll. Trust and Estate Counsel; mem. ABA (ho. dels. 1982-89, chmm. commn. on advt. 1984-88), Ill. Bar Assn. (bd. govs. 1976-82, sec. 1981-82), Winnebago County Bar Assn. (pres. 1990), Am. Judicature Soc. (bd. dirs. 1986-90), Rockford Country Club, Rotary (pres. Rockford 1992-93). Republican. Home: 913 N Main St Rockford IL 61103

JOHNSON, TIMOTHY PATRICK, health researcher; b. Batavia, N.Y., July 14, 1954; s. Elmore Thomas and Sara (McKinsey) J.; m. LuEllen Doty, June 20, 1988; children: Sara Elizabeth, Elliott William. BA, Western Ky. U., 1977; MA, U. Wis., Milw., 1978; PhD, U. Ky., 1988. Sr. rsch. analyst dept. human resources State of Ky., Frankfort, 1979-80; rsch. analyst dept. medicine U. Ky., Lexington, 1980-82, rsch. coord. survey rsch. ctr., 1982-88; staff assoc. for psychometrics Am. Bd. Family Practice, Lexington, 1988-89; asst. rsch. prof. epidemiology and biometry sch. pub. health U. Ill., Chgo., 1991—, project coord. survey rsch. lab., 1989-91, asst. dir. survey rsch. lab., 1991-93, assoc. dir., 1993-96; interim dir., 1996—. Contbr. articles to profl. jours. Mem. APHA, Am. Sociol. Assn., Am. Assn. Pub. Opinion Rsch. Roman Catholic. Office: U Ill Survey Rsch Lab 910 W Van Buren St Ste 500 Chicago IL 60607

JOHNSON, TIMOTHY PETER, congressman; b. Canton, S.D., Dec. 28, 1946; s. Vandal Charles and Ruth Jorinda (Ljostveit) J.; m. Barbara Brooks, June 6, 1969; children—Brooks Dwight, Brendan Vandal, Kelsey Marie. B.A., U. S.D., 1969, M.A., 1970, J.D., 1975; postgrad., Mich. State U., 1970-71. Bar: S.D. 1975, U.S. Dist. Ct. S.D. 1976. Fiscal analyst Legis. Fiscal Agy., Lansing, Mich., 1971-72; sole practice Vermillion, S.D., 1975-86; mem. S.D. Ho. of Reps., 1978-82, S.D. Senate, 1982-86, 101st-103rd Congresses from S.D., Washington, D.C., 1987—; adj. inst. U. S.D., Vermillion, 1974-83; mem. S.D. Code Commn., Pierre, 1982-86. Mem. Vermillion City Planning Commn., 1977-78; treas. Clay County Dem. Com., Vermillion, 1978; del. Dem. Nat. Conv., 1988, 92. NSF grantee, 1969-70. Mem. S.D. Bar Assn., Clay County Bar Assn., Phi Beta Kappa, Omicron Delta Kappa. Democrat. Lutheran. Office: US Ho of Reps 2438 Rayburn Ofc Bldg Washington DC 20515

JOHNSON, TIMOTHY VINCENT, state legislator. Home: 129 W Main St Urbana IL 61801-2714*

JOHNSON, TOM, state legislator; b. Zanesville, Ohio, Apr. 14, 1949; m. Joyce Johnson; children: Julie, Kristi. BA, Muskingum Coll. Asst. U.S. Senator Bob Dole; state rep. Dist. 96 Ohio State Congress, 1977—; mem. fin.-appropriations com., energy and environ. com., rules com., joint legis. budget com., unreclaimed strip mined lands bd. Mem. Twp. Trustees and Clks. Assn., Farm Bur., League Ohio Sportsmen. *

JOHNSON, VERNA MAE, accounting educator; b. Salina, Kans., June 29, 1930; d. Dave and Hulda Christine (Olson) J. BA, Kans. Wesleyan U., 1952; MA, Kans. State U., 1986. Tchr. bus. subjects Circleville (Kans.) High Sch., 1952-53, Glen Elder (Kans.) High Sch., 1953-54, Roxbury (Kans.) High Sch., 1954-57, Kensington (Kans.) High Sch., 1957-60; instr. acctg. Brown Mackie Coll., Salina, 1960—. Mem. AAUW (Salina chpt., pres. 1983-85, treas. 1986-90, rec. sec. 1990-91, fellowship 1985, Outstanding Br. mem. 1991, program v.p. 1992-96, treas. 1996—), Delta Kappa Gamma Mu (Salina chpt., v.p. 1976-78, 88-90, pres. 1978-82, 90-92). Home: 524 W Wilson St Salina KS 67401-4828 Office: Brown Mackie Coll 126 S Santa Fe Ave Salina KS 67401-2810

JOHNSON, VIRGIL JOEL, state legislator, farmer; b. Caledonia, Minn., Apr. 23, 1932; s. John Emannuel and Ethel Ann (Mitchell) J.; m. Mary Ann Muenkel, 1966. Farmer Houston County, Minn., 1950—; Dist. 32B rep. Minn. Ho. of Reps., St. Paul, 1982—; mem. Houston County (Minn.) Planning Commn., 1965—, past chmn. Welfare Bd., 1965—, past chmn. Bd. Commrs., 1965—; former mem. appropriations com., Minn. Ho. of Reps.; mem. environ. and natural resources, environ. and natural resources fin., local govt. and met. affairs and transp. and transit coms. Mem. Minn. Rep. State Task Force com. on govt. ops., 1969-70, Rep. State Ctrl. Com., 1969-70, chmn. Houston County Rep. Com., 1969-70. Mem. VFW, Assn. Minn. Counties (bd. dirs. 1972-77, pres. 77-78, mem. com. on planning, recreation and natural resources, 1965—), Minn. Welfare Assn., Minn. Assn. Retarded Children, Caledonia (Minn.) C. of C., Caledonia Rod & Gun Club. Home: RR 2 Box 88 Caledonia MN 55921-9620*

JOHNSON, W. LLOYD, baseball historian, consultant; b. Oklahoma City, Jan. 23, 1951; s. Walter Forest and Mary Louise (Brown) J.; m. Brenda J. Ward, Aug. 22, 1980 (div. Aug. 1996). BA in History, Okla. State U., 1973; MA in History, U. Tulsa, 1980. Sr. rsch. assoc. Nat. Baseball Hall Fame, Cooperstown, N.Y., 1985; exec. dir. Soc. for Am. Baseball Rsch., Cooperstown, Kansas City, Mo., 1985-89; dir. Negro Leagues Baseball Mus., Kansas City, 1990-92; instr. baseball history U. Mo., Kansas City, 1987—; cons. ABC-TV, L.A., 1985, Johnson County Hist. Mus., Shawnee, Kans., 1989, Kansas City Parks and Recreation Dept., 1988, 90-92; bd. dirs. Negro Leagues Baseball Mus. Author: Baseball's Dream Teams, 1990, Minor League Encyclopedia, 1993, Baseball Timeline, 1991, Who's Who in Baseball History, Baseball: A Pictorial Tribute; editor, contbr. numerous books including Whole Baseball Catalog; editor newsletter Here's the Pitch, 1989-91; contbr. articles to profl. jours. Coach Cub Scout Baseball Team, 1990. Named Hon. Lt. Gov. State of Okla., 1968, Okla. Amb., 1989—. Mem. Soc for Am. Baseball Rsch. (editor bull. 1985-89, pres. 1991-93), N.Am. Soc. Sport History. Home and Office: 205 W 66th Ter Kansas City MO 64113-1854

JOHNSON, WATTS CAREY, lawyer; b. Chgo., June 21, 1925; s. Carey R. and Leone (VanMechelen) J.; m. Claire Hayes Johnson, June 4, 1950; children: Gregory, Philip, Carolyn, Brian, Barbara. BA, Western Mich. U., 1947; JD, Northwestern U., 1950. Bar: Ill. 1950, U.S. Supreme Ct. 1967. Justice of the peace Princeton Twp., Bureau County, Ill., 1952-56; asst. state's atty. State's Atty. Office, Bureau County, 1957-64; ptnr. Johnson, Martin & Russell, Princeton, Ill., 1969-88; ptnr. Johnson, Martin, Russell, English, Scoma & Beneke, Princeton, Ill., 1988-95, ret., of counsel, 1995—; mem. rules commn. Ill. Supreme Ct., 1977-95; commr. State of Ill. Ct. of Claims, 1989—; mem. Atty. Registration and Disciplinary Commn. State of Ill., 1973-92, inquiry divsn., 1973-76, hearing divsn., 1976-78, rev. bd., 1979-90, commr., 1991-95. Pres. Bureau County chpt. ARC, 1959-62; pres. Princeton Jaycees, 1954; chmn. Bureau County Merit Commn., 1985-88. Fellow Am. Coll. Trust and Probate Counsel; mem. Ill. Cts. Commn., Ill. Appellate Lawyers Assn., Ill. Def. Counsel, Internat. Assn. Def. Counsel. Republican. Baptist. Office: Johnson Martin Russell English Scoma & Beneke 10 Park Ave W Princeton IL 61356-2019

JOHNSON, WILLIAM ARTHUR, gallery representative, historian; b. Kansas City, Mo., Aug. 29, 1950; s. Samuel Arthur and Nellie Lee J. BA in History, U. Mo., Kansas City, 1972, MA in History, 1976, BA in Edn., 1993. Maintainer of supplies Commerce Bank of Blue Hills, Kansas City, 1972, 79-82; mil. pay clk. USMC, Kansas City, 1978-79; archival aide Fed. Archives, Kansas City, 1979; records and supply coord. Laurel Am. Bank, Kansas City, 1982-85; return items blotter clk. United Mo. Bank of Kansas City, 1985-87; gallery rep. The Nelson Atkins Mus. Art, Kansas City, 1987—. Author, editor polit. history data Kansas City Votes, 1853-1979, 1981. Sustaining sponsor Ronald Reagan Presdl. Found., Calif., 1989. Mem. NRA, U. Mo. Kansas City Alumni Assn. (life). Home: 1115 E 83rd Ter Kansas City MO 64131-2538 Office: The Nelson Atkins Mus Art 4525 Oak St Kansas City MO 64111-1818

JOHNSON, WILLIAM BRUCE, university dean; b. Denver, Feb. 13, 1948; s. William Bruce and Evelyn Alice (Jones) J.; m. Candy Jean Cameron, Mar. 21, 1970 (div. July 1979); 1 child, Cory Elizabeth; m. Diane Helen Ramsey, Nov. 28, 1981. BA, U. Oreg., 1970; MA, Ohio State U., 1973, PhD, 1975. Asst. prof. U. Wis., Madison, 1975-80, Northwestern U., Evanston, Ill., 1980-87; assoc. prof. U. Iowa, Iowa City, 1987-92, prof., 1993—; vis. asst. prof. U. Chgo., 1986-87, J.L. Kellogg Grad. Sch. mgmt., Northwestern U., 1980-81; dir. McGladrey Inst. for Acctg. Rsch., U. Iowa, 1988-90; presenter in field. Editorial bd.: Acctg Rev., 1979-82; contbr. articles to profl. jours., books; referee numerous jours. in field. Named Phillips Outstanding Prof., U. Iowa, 1988, Arthur Andersen Prof., 1992, others; recipient Standard Oil scholarship, 1969-70. Mem. Am. Acctg. Assn., Am. Inst. for Decision Scis. (nat. mtg. program chmn. acctg. 1983), Beta Gamma Sigma, Beta Alpha Psi. Office: U Iowa Sch Mgmt 121 Phillips Hall Iowa City IA 52242-1323

JOHNSON, WILLIAM J., state legislator; m. Elma Johnson; 4 children. Grad. high sch., Harding County, S.D. Mem. S.D. State Senate, 1993—, chmn. local govt. com., mem. appropriations, govt. oper. and audit coms.; tchr. Home: PO Box 185 Buffalo SD 57720-0185*

JOHNSON, WILLIAM K., sales executive; b. Oak Park, Ill., May 9, 1940. BA, Carleton Coll., Northfield, Minn., 1962. V.p. sales CS First Boston, Chgo., 1967-89; salesperson William Blair & Co., Chgo., 1989—.

Vice pres. New Trier H.S. Bd., Winnetka, Ill., 1991—; mem. Winnetka Pub. Libr. Bd., 1984-85. Lt. USN, 1962-65. Mem. Bond Club of Chgo., Univ. Club of Chgo. Home: 241 Essex Rd Winnetka IL 60093 Office: William Blair & Co 222 W Adams St Chicago IL 60606

JOHNSON, WILLIAM LLOYD, training specialist, retired; b. Chgo., Mar. 28, 1925; s. William and Fannie Helen (Booth) J.; m. Lucille Althea Fulton, Mar. 8, 1959; 1 child, Melrose. BS, Chgo. State U., 1985, MS, 1986. Photographer Chgo., 1945-50; photostat operator U.S. Arsenal, Joliet, Ill., 1950-51; postal worker U.S. Postal Svc., Chgo., 1951-79; shift mgr. Salvation Army T.C., Chgo., 1986-89; tng. specialist City Coll. Chgo., 1989-92. With U.S. Army, 1943-45, ETO. Mem. Acad. Criminal Justice Scis., Midwest Criminal Justice Assn., Nat. Geneal. Soc., Afro-Am. Geneal. and Hist. Soc. Chgo., Alpha Phi Sigma. Democrat. Home: 2801 S King Dr Apt # 118 Chicago IL 60616

JOHNSON, WILLIAM M., manucfaturing engineer; b. Kansas City, Kans., Dec. 12, 1945. B, Finley Engring. Coll., Kansas City, Mo., 1971. Design and mfg. engr. Jim Walters Windows, Sioux Falls, S.D., 1976-84; indsl. engr. Litton Industries, Sioux Falls, S.D., 1984-91; sr. engr. Berkley, Spirit Lake, Iowa, 1991-94; mgr. mfg. engring. Arts-Way, Armstrong, Iowa, 1994—. Patentee in field. Vol. local ch. With USN, 1964-68. Mem. Soc. Mfg. Engrs. Home: 1511 Falcon Dr Apt 202 Fairmont MN 56031-4553 Office: Arts-Way PO Box 288 Armstrong IA 50514-0288

JOHNSON, YVONNE AMALIA, elementary education educator, science consultant; b. DeKalb, Ill., July 1, 1930; d. Albert O. and Virginia O. (Nelson) J. BS in Edn., No. Ill. State Tchrs. Coll., 1951; MS in Edn., No. Ill. U., 1960. Tchr. Love Rural Sch., DeKalb, 1951-53, West Elem. Sch., Sycamore, Ill., 1953—; Bd. dirs. Sycamore Pub. Libr., 1974-84, pres. bd. dirs., 1984—, major donor chmn. capitol fund drive for addition to existing bldg. Contbr. articles to profl. publs. Bd. dirs. Sycamore Pub. Libr., 1974-84, pres. bd. dirs., 1984—, chmn. maj. fund drive for addition to libr., 1994—. Named DeKalb County Conservation Tchr., 1971, Gov.'s Master Tchr., State of Ill., 1984, Outstanding Agrl. Tchr. in the Classroom Dekalb County Farm Bur., 1993; grantee NSF, 1961, 62, 85, 86, 87; Sci. Lit. grantee State of Ill., 1992-94. Mem. NEA, ASCD, NSTA (cert. in elem. sci.), Ill. Sci. Tchrs. Assn., Ill. Edn. Assn., Sycamore Edn. Assn., Coun. for Elem. Sci. Internat. Office: West Elem Sch 240 Fair St Sycamore IL 60178-1641

JOHNSON-LEESON, CHARLEEN ANN, former elementary school educator, insurance agent, insurance consultant; b. Battle Creek, Mich., June 10, 1949; d. Kenneth Andrews Leeson and Ila Mae (Weed/Lesson) McCutcheon; m. Lynn Boyd Johnson, Aug. 8, 1970; children: Eric Andrew, Andrea Marie. BA, Spring Arbor Coll., 1971; MS, Reading Specialist, Western Ill. U., 1990. Cert. elem. and secondary tchr., Mich., elem. tchr., Ill., reading K-9, Ill. Tchr. Hanover (Mich.) Horton Schs., 1972-73, Virden (Ill.) Elem. Sch., 1984-90; ins. agt. State Farm Ins., Virden, Ill., 1990—; collegiate and jr. high sch. cheerleading advisor in field; course leader Agt. Schs. 1, 2, and 3. Music dir., pianist Zion Luth. Ch., Farmersville, Ill., 1979-88, organist, pianist Olvie St. Friends, Battle Creek, 1961-67. Recipient Honor the Educator award World Book, 1988, 89, Soaring Eagle award, 1991; Wilson Stone scholar, 1990, Mich. State scholar, 1967. Mem. AUA, Internat. Reading Assn., Ill. Assn. Life Underwriters, Sangamon Valley Estate Planners, Wise Buys Investment Club, Millionaire Club (v.p. 1992), Multi Illini Club, Alpha Upsilon Alpha. Home: 2512 W Lake Dr Springfield IL 62707 Office: State Farm Agy Field Office 3001 Spring Mill Dr Springfield IL 62704

JOHNSON-MCKENZIE, JANIS, state legislator; b. Hastings, Nebr., Feb. 28, 1955; m. John Dee McKenzie; 1 child, Nathan. BS with distinction, U. Nebr.; ME, U. Conn. Adminstrn. coord. U. Nebr.; curriculum specialist, enrichment coord., elem. tchr.; mem. from 34th dist. Nebr. State Seante, 1993—, mem. edn. and natural resources coms., 1993—; adj. prof. Pacific U., Oreg., U. Conn., U. Nebr., Kearney. Mem. adv. com. for gifted, edn. exec. com. Nebr. State Bd. Edn. Mem. Nebr. Edn. Assn., Sutton Edn. Assn., Sandy Creek Edn. Assn. (treas.), Harvard Edn. Assn. (v.p.), Nebr. Assn. for Gifted (pres. 1988-90, exec. com. 1987—, conf. chair 1987-88, legis. chair 1990-92), Phi Delta Kappa, Omicron Nu, Phi Upsilon Omicron. Office: Nebr State Senate State Capitol Rm 1021 Lincoln NE 68509*

JOHNSRUD, DUWAYNE, state legislator; b. Boscobel, Wis., Sept. 4, 1943; s. Gordon and Louise Johnsrud; m. Jacqueline Johnsrud, 1965; children: Jennifer, Jaret, Zachary. BS, U. Wis., La Crosse, 1970. Farmer Eastman, Wis.; mem. from dist. 96 Wis. State Assembly, Madison, 1984—. Mem. Eastman Sch. Bd., 1982; mem. Crawford County Bd., 1982—; mem. Crawford County Farm Bur. Mem. Am. Legion, Prairie du Chien Lions Club, Eagles, Delta Sigma Pi. Office: Rt 1 Box 91A Eastman WI 54626*

JOHNSTON, ALLAN JAMES, English language educator; b. San Diego, Oct. 25, 1949; s. Robert Bethel and Nancy (Cameron) J.; m. Guillemette Claude Chaumont, Nov. 28, 1980. BA, Calif. State U., 1973; MA, U. Calif., Davis, 1981, PhD, 1988. Editor Great Books Found., Chgo., 1989-91; lectr. in English Oakton C.C., Chgo., 1994—. Author: (poetry collection) Tasks of Survival, 1996; contbr. articles, poems to profl. jours. Mem. MLA.

JOHNSTON, CAROLYN M., gynecologist, oncologist; b. Prince George County, Md.; d. Donald Earl and Mary Ann (Janik) J. BA, Wesleyan U., 1980; MD, Yale U., 1984. Intern, resident, then chief resident U. Chgo. Hosp., 1984-88; house officer on call Little County Mary Hosp., Evergreen Pk., Ill., 1987-88, Alexion Brother's Hosp., Elk Grove Village, Ill., 1988; fellow in gynecologic oncology Mt. Sinai Hosp., N.Y.C., 1988-90; rsch. technician, Endocrine/Physiology lab. Wesleyan U., Middletown, Conn., 1988-90; instr. U. Mich., Ann Arbor, Mich., 1990-92, asst. prof. gynecologic oncology, 1992—; dir. women's svcs. Veterans Adminstrn., Ann Arbor, Mich., 1994—; cons. Oakwood Hosp., Dearborn, Mich. 1990—; staff gynecologist Outpatient Resident Colposcopy Clinic, Oakwood Hosp., 1990-94; mem. Multidisciplinary Sarcoma Clinic, Gynecologic Oncology rep., Oakwood Hosp., 1993—; staff Breast Care Ctr., U. Mich. Med. Ctr., Ann Arbor, 1992; instr. to med. students 1988-90, 92—; rschr., lectr., presenter in field. Contbr. numerous articles, abstracts to profl. pubs., chpts. to books. Grantee NSF, 1979, Yale U., 1981, NIH, Organon, Inc., Parke-Davis Pharmaceutical Rsch. Divsn., Smith-Kline Beecham, and numerous others. Fellow Am. Coll. Obstetricians and Gynecologists; mem. U. Mich. Medical Ctr. Cancer Ctr. Office: Univ Mich Med Ctr D2241 Med Profl Bldg 1500 E Med Ctr Dr Ann Arbor MI 48109-0718

JOHNSTON, CHARLES BRUCE, computerized certification/license testing company executive; b. Park Rapids, Minn., Jan. 12, 1951. BA summa cum laude, St. Olaf Coll., 1973; PhD, U. Minn., 1986. Instr. U. Minn., Mpls., 1973-79; instrnl. designer courseware ops. Control Data, Mpls., 1979-84, tech. cons. tng. and edn., 1984-87, mgr. advanced tech. tng. and edn., 1987-90; v.p. tech. Drake Prometric, Mpls., 1990-95; v.p. client svcs. Sylvan Prometric, Mpls., 1995—. Mem. Phi Beta Kappa.

JOHNSTON, GARY, consulting company executive; b. St. Louis, Nov. 30, 1948; s. Charles Willard and Thelma Marie (Jackson) H.; m. Stacy Johnston, June 30, 1979; 1 child, Ryan. BA in English, U. Mo., St. Louis, 1971. Copywriter Christian Bd. Publ., St. Louis, 1972-75; sr. copywriter Concordia Pub. House, St. Louis, 1975-79; pvt. practice writing, cons. St. Louis, 1979-81; asst. mgr. communications Wausau Ins. Co., St. Louis, 1981-85; creative account exec. Advt. Assocs., Inc., St. Louis, 1985-86; mgr. advt., sales promotion Nat. Casualty Co./Hickey Mitchell Co., St. Louis, 1986-93; v.p. Nat. Assn. Cons., Inc., St. Louis, 1993—. Mem. Advt. Club Greater St. Louis, Dir. Mktg. Club St. Louis. Home: 4506 Meadowford Dr Saint Louis MO 63129-2516 Office: Nat Assn Cons 1819 Clarkson Rd Chesterfield MO 63017-5071

JOHNSTON, GLADYS STYLES, university official; b. St. Petersburg, Fla., Dec. 23, 1942; d. John Edward and Rosa (Moses) Styles; m. Hubert Seward Johnston, July 30, 1966. BS in Social Sci., Cheney U., 1963; MEd in Ednl. Adminstrn., Temple U., 1969; PhD in Ednl. Adminstrn.-Orgnl. Theory, Cornell U., 1974. Tchr. Chester (Pa.) Sch. Dist., 1963-66; tchr. West Chester (Pa.) Sch. Dist., 1966-67, asst. prin., elem. prin., dir. Summer Sch., 1968-71; dir. Head Start Chester County Bd. Edn.,, West Chester, 1967-69; teaching asst., rsch. asst. Cornell U., Ithaca, N.Y., 1971-74; asst. prof. ednl. adminstr. and supervision Rutgers U., New Brunswick, N.J., 1974-79, assoc. prof., chmn. dept. Grad. Sch. Edn., 1979-83, chmn. dept. mgmt. Sch. Bus., 1983-85; dean, prof. Coll. Edn., Ariz. State U., Tempe, 1985-91; provost, v.p. for acad. affairs DePaul U., Chgo., 1991—; disting. Commonwealth vis. prof. Coll. William and Mary Sch. Edn., Williamsburg, Va., 1982-83; manuscript reviewer Jour. Higher Edn., Jour. Ednl. Leadership, Prentice Hall Pub. Co., Englewood Cliffs, N.J.; speaker and conf. presenter in field; cons. AT&T, Ednl. Testing Svc., Prentice-Hall Pub. Co.; cons. to coordinating bd. Tex. Coll. and Univ. System. Author: Research and Thought in Administration Theory, 1986; mem. editorial bd. Ednl. Evaluation and Policy Analysis, Ednl. Adminstrn. Quar., Ednl. and Psychol. Rsch. Jour.; contbr. articles and book revs. to profl. jours., chpts. to books. Bd. dirs. Edn. Law Ctr., 1979-86, Sta. KAET-TV, Phoenix, 1987—, Found. for Sr. Living, 1990-91; mem. adv. coun. to bd. trustees Cornell U., 1981-86; trustee Middlesex Gen. Univ. Hosp., 1983-86. Recipient Outstanding Alumni award Temple U.; Andrew D. White fellow Cornell U. Mem. ASCD, Am. Assn. Colls. for Tchr. Edn., Nat. Conf. Profs. Ednl. Adminstrn., Am. Ednl. Rsch. Assn. (proposal reviewer 1979—, chmn. task force for participation and membership 1981—, chmn. E.F. Linquist award com. 1985, mem. govt. rels. com. 1986—, publ. com. 1986—), Phi Kappa Phi, Phi Delta Kappa, Alpha Phi Sigma. Office: U of Nebraska at Kearney 25th St & Ninth Ave. Kearney NE 68849-0001*

JOHNSTON, HOLLY WATKINS, medical surgical nurse; b. Cleve., Aug. 8, 1954; d. Roger Harold and Mary Mildred (Nickerson) Watkins; m. Jay Jerome Johnston, Mar. 3, 1984. BA in Nursing, Gustavus Adolphus Coll., 1976. Cert. in med.-surg. nursing; cert. ENT nurse. Staff nurse St. Luke's Hosp., Milw., 1976-79; clin. educator Hennepin County Med. Ctr., Mpls., 1979-94, sr. staff nurse, 1994—; mem. profl. practice com. Hennepin County Med. Ctr., trauma edn. developer; instr.-trainer CPR. Mem. profl. practice editorial bd. Hennepin County Med. Ctr.. Mem. Soc. Otolaryngology/Head and Neck Nurses (pres. Minn. chpt.), Acad. Med.-Surg. Nurses, Soc. Urologic Nurses ans Assocs., Inc. Home: PO Box 122 Forest Lake MN 55025-0122 Office: Hennepin County Med Ctr 701 Park Ave S Minneapolis MN 55415

JOHNSTON, JOHN WAYNE, educational administrator; b. McAlester, Okla., Oct. 8, 1943; s. Cecil Wayne and Hazel Elena (Robinson) J.; m. Lynda Faith Gee, Feb. 4, 1971 (div.); 1 son, Ian Sean. Student Graceland Coll., 1961-62, William Jewell Coll., 1962-63; BS in Journalism, Kans. U., 1964; MA in Edn. and Sociology, U. Mo.-Kansas City, 1966; MA in Polit. Sci., History and Econs., Goddard Coll., 1972; EdD in Ednl. Adminstrn., Internat. U., 1974; PhD (hon.), Calif. Western U., 1975, Alvescot Coll., 1972; PhD in Social Psychology, Internat. U., 1975; PhD in Ch. Hist. Internat. Bible Coll. & Sem., 1980; PhD in Health Sci., Honolulu U., 1993. Instr. Central Mo. State U., Independence, 1969-72; founder, chancellor The Internat. U., Independence, 1973—; Editor: T.I.U. Press, 1973—. Bd. dirs. Good Govt. League, Independence, Com. for County Progress, Jackson County, Mo.; varsity soccer coach Ft. Osage H.S., 1983-88, New Hope Bapt. H.S., 1990-92; Internat. Bible Coll., 1993—. mem. Church of Jesus Christ (ordained minister). Author: Divided for Plunder, 1984; Turmoil in the North, 1984, Crisis in Northern Ireland, 1985, The University of the Future, 1985, Higher Education for the 21st Century, 1990, The Continuing Collapse of Public Education, 1991.

JOHNSTON, KERRY ALAN, oil and gas company executive; b. St. Paul, Jan. 11, 1954. BA in Geol. Engring., U. Minn., 1977; MBA, U. St. Thomas, 1984. Staff geologist Dames & Moore, Chgo., 1977-80; v.p. Kerns Oil & Gas Inc., Mpls., 1989—. Active St. Odilias Cath. Ch., Shoreview, Minn., 1989—. Office: Kerns Oil & Gas Inc 2600 Fernbrook Ln N Ste 138 Minneapolis MN 55447-4752

JOHNSTON, ROBERT MORRIS, religious studies educator; b. Palo Alto, Calif., May 8, 1930; s. Arthur Martin and Mary Elizabeth (Butler) J.; m. Madeline Steele, July 29, 1956; children: Paul Martin, Robert Thomas, Elizabeth Ann, Margaret Kathryn. Student, Stanford U., 1948-49; BA, Pacific Union Coll., Angwin, Calif., 1954; BD, Andrews U., Berrien Springs, Mich., 1966; PhD, Hartford (Conn.) Seminary, 1977. Secondary tchr. Fresno (Calif.) Union Acad., 1956-58; prof. theology Korean Union Coll., Seoul, 1958-69, Philippine Union Coll., Manila, 1969-70, Seventh-day Adventist Theol. Seminary, Berrien Springs, 1974-84; prof. New Testament Seventh Day Adventist Theol. Seminary, Berrien Springs, 1984—; chmn. New Testament dept. New Testament Seventh Day Adventist Theol. Seminary, Berrier Springs, 1988—; pres. Andrews Soc. for Religious Studies, 1981; del. Gen. Conf. Seventh Day Adventists, 1990. Author: Peter and Jude, 1995; contbr. Seventh-day Adventist Bible Dictionary, 1979, Sabbath in Scripture and History, 1982; co-author: They Also Taught in Parables, 1990; contbr. articles to profl. jours. Recipient Moses Bailey prize Hartford Seminary, 1971. Mem. Soc. Bibl. Lit., Chgo. Soc. for Bibl. Rsch., Am. Acad. Religion. Home: 8742-1 N Ridge Ave Berrien Springs MI 49103 Office: Andrews U Dept of Theology Seminary Berrien Springs MI 49104-1500

JOHNSTON, SHERWOOD A., engineering executive; b. St. Croix, Wis., June 17. Mgr. R&D Nor Lake Corp., Hudson, Wis., 1988-89; engring. mgr. Axia Corp., Mpls., 1989-93; mgr. regulations compliance Laser Machining Inc., Somerset, Wis., 1993—; mem. ansi B-11/21 com. Am. Nat. Standards Inst. With U.S. Army, 1959-61. Mem. ASSE. Office: Laser Machining Inc 500 Laser Dr Somerset WI 54025-9774

JOHNSTON, SHERYL L., communications executive; b. Portland, Oreg., Feb. 18, 1944; d. Frank F. and Edith A. (Vallereux) Neels; m. Robert K. Johnston, Feb. 14, 1973; 1 child, James Patrick. Student, Portland State U., 1962-65, 67-68, Sch. of the Art Inst., Chgo., 1972-74, Northwestern U., 1975; BA, Columbia Coll., Chgo., 1993. Adminstrv. asst. Art Inst. Chgo., 1971-75; asst. editorial dir. Sta. WLS-TV, Chgo., 1975-76; dir. pub. rels. Prime Time Sch. TV, Chgo., 1976-77; v.p. J. Walter Thompson Co., Chgo., 1977-82; pres. Sheryl Johnston Communications, Chgo., 1982—; tchr. Columbia Coll., 1991, 95, 96. Mem. Country Music Assn. (pub. rels. com. 1981, 82, 85). Democrat. Episcopalian. Office: 623 W Oakdale Chicago IL 60657-5309

JOHNSTON, TERRY D., state legislator, insurance agent; b. May 27, 1947; m. Don Johnston; three children. Student, U. N.D. Ins. agent; Dist. 35 senator Minn. State Senate, St. Paul, 1990—; mem. edn., met. affairs, transp., vet. and gen. legis., commerce and consumer protection, fin. and state govt. divsn. transp. and pub. transit coms., Minn. State Senate. Home: 3960 140th St NW Prior Lake MN 55372-3206*

JOHNSTON, THOMAS PATRICK, pharmaceutics educator; b. Chgo., Oct. 16, 1956; s. James Michael and Claire Ann (Fowler) J.; m. Jocelyn Elaine Stanwell, Nov. 28, 1986; 1 child, Gillian Claire. BS, U. Minn., 1980, PhD, 1987. Postdoctoral fellow pediatric cardiology and pharmaceutics U. Mich. Med. Sch., 1987-88; asst. prof. pharmaceutics U. Ill. Coll. Pharmacy, Chgo., 1988-95; assoc. prof. pharmaceutics U. Mo., Kansas City, 1995—; lectr. and presenter in field. Reviewer Jour. Pharm. Sci. and Tech., 1989—; contbr. Internat. Jour. Pharmacy, Jour. Pharm. Sci. and Tech., Jour. Pharm. Sci., Jour. Applied Polymer Sci., Jour. Controlled Release, others. Recipient Rho Chi Rsch. award U. Minn., 1980; Am. Soc. for Artificial Internal Organs Travel fellow, 1988, Theodore J. Rowell fellow, U. Minn., 1983-84. Mem. Am. Assn. Pharm. Sci., Am. Pharm. Assn., Am. Assn. Coll. Pharm., Controlled Release Soc., Parenteral Drug Assn., Minn. State Pharm. Assn., N.Y. Acad. Scis., Rho Chi. Office: U Mo-Kansas City Katz Pharmacy Bldg 5100 Rockhill Rd Kansas City MO 64110-2499

JOHNSTON, TIMOTHY SIDNEY, computer engineer; b. Royal Oak, Mich., Nov. 30, 1966; s. Sidney Charles and Kathleen Ann (Backer) J. BS with high honors, Rochester Inst. Tech., 1991. Data processing clk. City of Madison Hts., Mich., 1987; maint. programmer Compuware Corp., Farmington Hills, Mich., 1988; tech. assoc. AT&T Bell Labs., Naperville, Ill., 1989; archtl. verification software team mem. Semiconductor Engring. Group, DEC, Hudson, Mass., 1991; project engr. Applied Computer Engring., Inc., Warren, Mich., 1992-94; software engr. Brendan Sci. Corp., Oak Park, Mich., 1994—; part-time tchr. Am. Sign Lang., 1992—. Staff mem. Deaf Teen Club Youth Leadership Tng. Program, Pontiac, Mich., 1991—; staff writer The Deaf Nation Newspaper, Waterford, 1992—; Bible study group leader Our Savior Luth. Ch. of the Deaf, Royal Oak; dir. Miss. Deaf Mich. Pageant. Mem. Mich. Deaf Assn., Phi Beta Kappa, Alpha Sigma Lambda, Phi Kappa Phi, Tau Alpha Pi, Kappa Phi Theta. Office: Brendan Sci Corp 29500 Greenfield Rd Oak Park MI 48237

JOHNSTON, WILLIAM ARNOLD, playwright; b. Cambuslang, Scotland, May 31, 1942; came to U.S., 1951; s. James Reid and Eliza (Arnold) J.; m. June Eve Lavalley, June 27, 1963 (div. Sept. 1969); m. Kristin Lucille Tyrrell, Sept. 16, 1972 (div. Dec. 1992); m. Deborah Ann Percy, Feb. 27, 1993. PhB, Wayne State U., 1963; MA, Del. U., 1965, PhD, 1969. Prof. English Western Mich. U., 1966—; pres. New Vic Theatricals, Inc., Kalamazoo, Mich., 1976-80, 85-87; rev. panelist Mich. Coun. for the Arts, Detroit, 1979-90; writer in residence Creative Writers in the Schs., Midland, Mich., 1970-92; rev. panelist Arts Fund of Kalamazoo, 1988-94; guest artist Saugatuck (Mich.) Red Barn Theatre, 1974; Western Mich. U. Theatre Dept., Kalamazoo, 1986, 90. Playwright: The Witching Voice, 1972, Scrimshaw, 1974, The Edge of Running Water, 1981, Suitors, 1986, (with Deborah Percy) The Zamboni Situation, 1990, Automatic Telling, 1991; writer, editor radio drama series Voices From Michigan's Past, 1976; writer, translator mus. revue Closer to Brel, 1990, Frauentanz, 1990. Grantee Mich. Coun. for the Arts, 1981, 82, Kalamazoo Found./NEA, 1988, 90; recipient Community Arts medal Arts Coun. of Greater Kalamazoo, 1986, Disting. Svc. award New Vic Theatre, 1988, Alumni Teaching Excellence award Western Mich. U., 1990; winner Dogwood Nat. One-Act Play contest (with Deborah Percy), 1990, Market House Theatre One-Act Competition (Deborah Percy), 1991. Mem. AAUP, Am. Theatre Assn., Mich. Theatre Assn., Associated Writing Programs, Arts Coun. of Greater Kalamazoo, Poets & Writers Inc. Office: Western Mich U English Dept Kalamazoo MI 49008

JOHNSTON, WILLIAM DAVID, health care company executive; b. Chgo., Nov. 5, 1944; s. Samuel David and Jeanne (Williams) J.; m. Susan Diane Ward, Aug. 19, 1966; children: Kimberly Dawn Sites, Kirk David, Tiffany Dee Hansen, Kyle Donald, Ryan Daryl. BS in Chemistry, Brigham Young U., 1969, PhD in Organic Chemistry, 1974. V.p. Parish Chem. Co., 1973-75; mgr. materials control Travenol Labs., Inc., 1975-80, group mgr., polymer rsch. and material control, 1980-84, dir. Material and Membrane Tech. Ctr., 1984-86, v.p. applied scis., 1987-93; v.p., gen. mgr. gene therapy div. Baxter Healthcare Corp., Round Lake, Ill., 1993—; mem. adv. bd. Ill. Jr. Acad. Sci., Springfield, 1984-86; bd. dirs. Ill. Hi-Tech. Assn., 1990-92; mem. adv. bd. Coll. Engring., U. ill., Chgo., 1988-92, dept. chem. engring. Northwestern U., Evanston, Ill., 1989—. Contbr. articles to profl. jours.; patentee in field. Coun. stake pres. LDS Ch., Schaumburg, Ill., 1982-88, stake pres., Buffalo Grove, Ill., 1988—; exec. coun. N.E. Ill. coun. Boy Scouts Am., 1989—; chmn. bd. LDS Social Svcs., Naperville, Ill., 1990—; bd. dirs. Neocrin Co., 1992-96. Brigham Young U. scholarship. Mem. AAAS, Am. Chem. Soc., Internat. Soc. for Artificial Organs, Internat. Soc. Blood Purification (exec. bd. 1991—), Soc. for Biomaterials, Internat. Soc. of Cell Transplantation, Sigma Xi. Home: 20851 W Yorkshire Dr Kildeer IL 60047-7951 Office: Baxter Healthcare Corp Baxter Technology Park Round Lake IL 60073

JOINER, LARRY J., retired police chief; b. Macon County, Mo., Oct. 18, 1939; s. Clay and Leota Mae (Harrison) J.; m. Dorothy Jean Swallow, May 31, 1959; children: Georgia Mae, Larry Christopher, Deborah Ann. BS, Cen. Mo. State U., 1970, MA, 1974. Class c patrolman Kansas City Police Dept., Mo., 1960-61, class b patrolman, 1961-62, class a patrolman, 1962-65, corp., 1965-67, sgt., 1967-70, capt., 1970-76, major, 1976-81, lt. col., 1981-84, chief of police, 1984-90; U.S. marshall Western Dist. Mo., Kansas City, 1991-94; dir. mktg. Ameritel Connection Svcs., Lee's Summit, Mo., 1994—. Cabinet mem. United Way. Served with U.S. Army, 1957-60. Recipient Meritorious Service award Kansas City Police Dept., 1981. Mem. Internat. Assn. Chiefs of Police, Mo. Police Chiefs Assn. Office: 611 SW 3d St Lees Summit MO 64063

JOLLY, DANIEL EHS, dental educator; b. St. Louis, Aug. 25, 1952; s. Melvin Joseph and Betty Ehs (Koehler) J.; m. Paula Kay Haas, 1972 (div.); 1 child, Farrell Elisabeth Ehs; m. Barbara Lee Lindahl, 1988 (div.). BA in Biology and Chemistry, U. Mo., Kansas City, 1974, DDS, 1977. Resident in hosp. dentistry VA Med. Ctr., Leavenworth, Kans., 1977-78; pvt. practice Newcastle, Wyo., 1978-79; asst. prof. U. Mo., Kansas City, 1979-87; chief restorative dentistry Truman Med. Ctr., Kansas City, 1979-87; dir. dental oncology Trinity Luth. Hosp., 1982-87; assoc. prof., dir. gen. practice residency program Ohio State U., Columbus, 1987—; prof., dir. gen. practice residency program, 1993—; dir. Honduras Clinic Project, 1992—; bd. dirs. Rinehart Found., U. Mo. Dental Sch., Kansas City, 1985-87; cons. Lee's Summit (Mo.) Care Ctr., 1984-87, Longview Nursing Ctr., Grandview, Mo., 1986-87; sec. Combined Hosp. Dental Staff, Columbus, 1989-90, v.p., 1990-91, pres., 1991-92. Author: (manual) Hospital Dental Hygiene, 1984, Hospital Dentistry, 1985, OSU Manual of Hospital Dentistry, 1989-96, (booklet) Nursing Home Dentistry, 1986, Dental Oncology, 1986. Mem. regional coun. Easter Seal Soc., Kansas City, 1985-87, mem. profl. adv. coun. Nat. Easter Seal Soc., 1986-92; sec. bd. dirs. Easter Seal Rehab. Ctr., Columbus, 1990-93. Recipient Alumni Achievement award in dentistry U. Mo., Kansas City, 1995. Fellow Acad. Dentistry Internat., Am. Soc. Dentistry for Children, Am. Assn. Hosp. Dentists (regional v.p. 1993—), Acad. Gen. Dentistry, Am. Soc. Geriatric Dentistry, Acad. Dentistry for Handicapped (pres. 1992), Am. Coll. Dentistry, Pierre Fauchard Acad.; mem. ADA, Internat. Assn. Dentistry for Handicapped (pres. 1994—), Mo. Dental Assn., Internat. Assn. Dental. Handicap, Greater Kansas City Dental Soc., Fedn. Spl. Care Orgns. in Dentistry (chmn. 1992-93), Southwest Oncology Group, Internat. Soc. for Oral Oncology, Ohio Dental Assn. Club: Magna Charta Barons. Home: 5322 Bay Meadows Ct Columbus OH 43221-5703 Office: Ohio State U Coll Dentistry 305 W 12th Ave Columbus OH 43210-1249

JONAS, JIRI, chemistry educator; b. Prague, Czechoslovakia, Apr. 1, 1932; s. Frantisek and Jirina (Vondrak) J.; m. Ana M. Masiulis, June 1, 1968. BSc, Tech. U. Prague, 1956; PhD, Czechoslovak Acad Sci., 1960. Research assoc. Inst. Organic Chemistry, Czechoslovak Acad. Sci., Prague, 1960-63; vis. scientist, dept. chemistry U. Ill., Urbana, 1963-65, from asst. to assoc. prof., 1966-72, prof., 1972—, dir. sch. chem. scis., 1983-93; dir. Beckman Inst. Advanced Sci. and Tech., 1993—; sr. staff mem. Materials Research Lab. U. Ill., Urbana, 1970—, prof. Ctr. for Advanced Study, 1996—. Mem. editl. bd. Jour. Magnetic Resonance, 1975—, Jour. Chem., 1980-83, Jour. Chem. Physics, 1986-89, , Ann. Rev. Phys. Chemistry, 1991-95, Accts. of Chem. Rsch., 1990-93; assoc. editor Jour. of Am. Chem. Soc.; contbr. 270 articles in field of chem. phys. to profl. publs. J.S. Guggenheim fellow, 1972-73, Alfred P. Sloan fellow, 1967-69; Univ. Sr. scholar U. Ill., 1985-88; recipient U.S. Sr. Scientist award Alexander von Humboldt Found., 1988. Fellow Am. Acad. Arts and Scis., AAAS, Am. Phys. Soc.; mem. Nat. Acad. Scis., Am. Chem. Soc. (Joel Henry Hildebrand award 1983), Materials Research Soc. Roman Catholic. Clubs: U. Ill. Tennis; NBTC (Naples, Fla.). Office: Univ of Ill Beckman Inst 405 N Mathews Ave Urbana IL 61801-2325

JONES, ALAN PORTER, JR., food manufacturing executive; b. Milw., Feb. 27, 1925; s. Alan Porter and Eleanor Pratt (Bright) J.; m. Jean Drummond, Sept. 12, 1953; children: Richard, Susan, Cynthia, Alexandra. BA, Harvard U., 1948, MBA, 1950. With Jones Dairy Farm, Ft. Atkinson, Wis., 1950—, asst. treas., 1953-61, treas., 1961-74, v.p., treas., 1974-93, also bd. dirs.; pres. Uncle Josh Bait Co., 1978—; bd. dirs. Bank Ft. Atkinson, 1966—, PDQ Corp., 1967-94. Dir. Dwight Foster Pub. Libr., 1952-87, Wis. Livestock and Meat Coun., 1981—, Ft. Atkinson C. of C., 1985-88; mem. Ft. Atkinson Sch. Bd., 1968-69, Wis. Gov.'s Adv. Com. on Internat. Trade, 1981—, Wis. Citizens Environ. Coun., 1980-84, Wis. Radioactive Waste Policy Coun., 1984-87; trustee Ripon Coll., Wis., 1974-77, Wis. Nature Conservancy, 1992-95. With Inf. U.S. Army, 1943-45. Decorated Bronze Star, Combat Inf. Badge. Mem. Nat. Audubon Soc., Sierra Club. Republican. Home: 433 Adams St Fort Atkinson WI 53538-1401 Office: Jones Dairy Farm PO Box 808 Fort Atkinson WI 53538

JONES, BENNIE RAY, sociologist, draftsman; b. Monroe, La., Nov. 20, 1948; s. Louis and Marilyn (Campbell) J. BA, Roosevelt U., Chgo., 1993; AS, Southeastern Ill. U., Harrisburg, 1994. With Bethlehem Steel Corp., Chgo., 1973-76; security officer Read Zone Ctr. of Ill., Chgo., 1976-79; seaman U.S. Navy, Sand Point, Wash., 1979-90; with Jones' Prison Rights Group, Vienna, Ill., 1990—; dir. Homeless and Aging Rescue, Chgo., 1993-95, Adult Literacy, Vienna, 1995. Author: Society Without Law, 1993.

Polit. advisor Prison Rights Group, Vienna, 1995. Mem. Rosecrucian Lodge (treas. 1994). Republican. Mem. Ch. of God. Home: 12 S Kennedy St PO Box 4 Colp IL 62921 Office: Jones' Prison Rights Group PO Box 400 Hwy 146 E Vienna IL 62995

JONES, BETTY JEANNE, school superintendent; b. Decatur, Ill., Aug. 8, 1946; d. Theodore F. and Grace Helen (Stich) Hoewing; m. Derrold Dean Jones, June 11, 1966; children: Frederick R., Daniel K. BS in Edn., Greenville Coll., 1972; MS in Edn., Eastern Ill. U., 1986, EdS, 1993. Tchr. Vandalia (Ill.) Community Schs., 1972-73, 78-86; prin. Brownstown (Ill.) Comty. Unit Schs., 1986-95, supt., 1995—; bd. dirs. Ednl. Svc. Ctr. #15, Charleston, Ill., 1985-95, sec. Curriculum Coop. Mem. strategic planning com. Greenville Coll., 1994. Mem. ASCD, Ill. Assn. Sch. Adminstrs., Friends of the Old Capitol (sec. 1995—), Optimist, Phi Delta Kappa. Methodist. Office: Brownstown Cmty Unit Sch Dist # 201 421 S College Ave Brownstown IL 62418-1129

JONES, BRIAN MATTHEW, private investigator, small business owner; b. Kansas City, Kans., Jan. 19, 1959; s. George Raymond and Caryl Jean (Stephens) J.; m. Martha Jean Lonegran, Oct. 12, 1980 (div. June, 1981); m. Patrica Ann Hixon, Sept. 4, 1982; 1 child, Brandie Michelle. AA, Johnson County C.C., Overland Park, Kans., 1989; student, Emporia State U., 1990—. Lic. private investigator, Kans. Pres. Olathe, Olatha, Kans., 1984-86, Eagle Investigations, Spring Hill, Kans., 1986—; speaker Johnson County C.C. Seminar, Overland Park, 1986; tchr. Citizen Ambassador Program, Russia, 1993. Mem. Nat. Assn. of Investigative Specialists, Spring Hill C. of C. Democrat.

JONES, C. LEE, librarian, consultant; b. Anderson, Ind., Sept. 22, 1936; s. Claud Clymer and Mary Isabelle (Stookey) J.; m. Patricia Ann Turner, Jan. 21, 1964 (div. Oct. 1970); children: Robin Dayle McMahan, George Cleveland; m. Eileen Usovicz, May 10, 1991; 1 child, Vannis Eileen. BA, Carleton Coll., Northfield, Minn., 1959; MLS, U. Tex., 1965. Dir. tech. svcs. Trinity U., San Antonio, 1965-67; libr. dir. U. Tex. Med. Br., Galveston, 1967-73; dir. health scis. libr. Columbia U., N.Y.C., 1973-79; program officer Coun. on Libr. Resources, Washington, 1979-84; pres., program cons. CBR Cons. Svcs., Kansas City, Mo., 1984—; pres. The MicrogrAphic Preservation Svc., Bethlehem, Pa., 1986-93, Linda Hall Libr., 1993—; isnt. rep. group on med. edn. Assn. Am. Med. Colls. Columbia U., 1974-78; chair com. on alternate patterns of svc. and funding Med. Libr. Ctr., N.Y., 1975-76; adv. com. N.Y., N.J. Reg. Med. Libr., 1974-78; preservation adv. com. Pa. State Libr., 1987-88; bibliographic svc. devel. program Coun. Libr. Resources, 1978-85, Linked Sys. Project, 1981-85; bd. dirs. Image Permanence Inst., 1988-93. Contbr. over 30 articles to profl. publs., publs. in field; mem. editl. bd. Tex. Reports on Biology and Medicien, 1968-73; mem. libr. adv. bd. John Wiley, 1996—. Adv. bd. Excerpta Medica, 1979-83; bd. dirs. William Temple Found., Galveston, 1969-70, United Way San Antonio, 1966-67, United Way Galveston, 1971-73 (also chair health group 1971-72, chair budget com. 1972-73), United Way Bethlehem, Pa., 1989-93; men's spl. gifts com. Am. Cancer Soc., N.Y.C., 1977-78. Served to sgt. U.S. Army, 1959-62, served in U.S.M.C., 1955-56. Grantee Nat. Libr. Medicine, 1967-75, Moody Found., 1969, Regional Med. Program of Tex., 1968-72, Mellon Found., 1974-75, 89-90, Upjohn Co. 1976, Exxon Edn. Found., 1986-89, NEH, 1989-93. Mem. Am. Libr. Assn. (ACRL 1968—, LITA 1982—, LAMA 1991—, RTSD 1989-91, RTSD stds. com. 1988-91, RTSD ad hoc com. on distbn. microforms 1988-89), Med. Libr. Assn. (contbg. editor Handbook Med. Libr. Practice 1977-83, coun. devel. med. librs. 1968-76, chair 1969-70, chair orgn. com. TALON regional group 1972, editl. adv. com. 1972-73, editl. adv. com. Bull. of the Med. Libr. Assn., 1972-75, chair 1974-75, bd. cons. editors 1974-77, MLA publs. com. 1974-75, com. on MLA continuing publs. 1974. Presbyn. Home: 7321 Terrace St Kansas City MO 64114-1256

JONES, CYNTHIA L., investment broker; b. Salem, Ill., Sept. 12, 1959; d. Charles W. and Mary L. (Feather) J.; m. Richard Bryan. BS, Eastern Ill. U., Charleston, 1981. Br. liaison City Bank, Chgo., 1977-89; investment broker A. G. Edwards & Sons Inc., Mt. Vernon, Ill., 1989—. Home: 4225 Sassafras Ln Mount Vernon IL 62864-2109 Office: AG Edwards & Sons Inc 3450 Broadway St # A Mount Vernon IL 62864-2270

JONES, DANNY CLYDE, healthcare products executive; b. Dayton, Ohio, Aug. 18, 1945; s. John Frank and Hazel Irene (Apple) J.; m. Karen Sue Goff, Sept. 15, 1981 (div. June 1984). BS, Ohio State U., 1971; MA, Ctrl. Mich. U., 1975. Profl. svc. rep. Allergan, Irvine, Calif., 1971-76; v.p. internat. sales Artromick Internat., Inc., Columbus, 1976—. Troupe mem. The Dance Connection, Columbus, Ohio, 1994-95. With USN, 1964-67. Recipient Adminstrs. award for excellence U.S. Small Bus. Adminstrn., 1994. Mem. VFW. Republican. Home: 1247 W 6th Ave Columbus OH 43212 Office: Artromick Internat Inc 4800 Hilton Corporate Dr Columbus OH 43232

JONES, DAVID RICHARD, die designer, purchasing administrator; b. Rush City, Minn., July 27, 1953; s. Wesley and Viola Jones. Student, Anoka (Minn.) Tech. Sch., 1971-72. Toolmaker Real Precision Mfg., Vadnais Heights, Minn., 1972-84; design engr. Dahlmans Inc., Braham, Minn., 1984-85; engr. Stepp Mfg., Sunrise, Minn., 1985, L & G Products, Rock Creek, Minn., 1985-86; die designer Branch Mfg., North Branch, Minn., 1986—. Mem. bd. elders Clover Cmty. Ch., Hinckley, Minn., 1989-95, deacon, 1995—. Republican. Office: Branch Mfg 702 Pine St North Branch MN 55056-5115

JONES, DOUG E., healthcare researcher, real estate broker, oil company owner; b. Parsons, Kans., Apr. 1, 1946; divorced; 2 children. BS, Southwest Mo. State U., 1969. Dem. candidate U.S. Senate, 1994, 96. Office: PO Box 3085 Springfield MO 65808*

JONES, EMIL, JR., state senator; b. Chgo., Oct. 18, 1935; s. Emil Sr. and Marilla (Mims) J.; m. Patricia Sterling, Dec. 14, 1974; children: Debra, Renee, John, Emil III. A in Bus. Adminstrn., City Coll. Chgo., 1970. Mem. Ill. Ho. Reps., Springfield, 1972-82, Ill. Senate, Springfield, 1982—; Senate Dem. leader Ill. Senate, mem. exec. com.; chmn. ins. pensions and lic. activities com. Ill. Senate, Springfield, vice chmn. local govt. com., co-chmn. joint com. adminstrv. rules, minority leader, mem. exec. com. Active Task Force on Long Term Care, Morgan Pk. Civic League, Chgo. Recipient Beautiful People award Chgo. Urban League, 1981, Friend of Edn. award Ill. State Bd. Edn., 1983, Legis. Leadership award Ill. Dept. Human Rights, 1984, Leadership award Nat. Bar Assn., 1985,. Mem. Nat. Black Caucus State Legislators, Nat. Conf. State Legislators, Knights of St. Peter Claver, Shriners. Democrat. Roman Catholic. Home: 11357 S Lowe Ave Chicago IL 60628-4714 Office: 507 W 111th St Chicago IL 60628-4019 also: James R Thompson Ctr 100 W Randolph St Ste 16 600 Chicago IL 60601-3220*

JONES, EUGENE GORDON, pharmaceutical company executive; b. Lookout, W.Va., June 26, 1929; s. Alphus Raymond and Mona Blanche (Bobbitt) J.; m. Nancy Lee Hall, Aug. 19, 1951; children: Gene Douglas, Michael Gordon, Rebecca Lee, Jody Lynn. BS, Va. Tech. U., 1951. Med. rep. The Upjohn Co., Charlottesville, Va., 1956-60; profl. svcs. mgr. The Upjohn Co., Washington, 1960-63; sr. med. rep. The Upjohn Co., Roanoke, Va., 1963-68; hosp. med. rep. The Upjohn Co., Richmond, Va., 1968-70; dist. sales mgr. The Upjohn Co., Va., 1970-73; tng. specialist The Upjohn Co., Kalamazoo, Mich., 1973-76, tng. mgr., 1976-87, nat. tng. dir., 1987-90; pres. Global Meeting Planners, 1991—; dir. Kalamazoo Speciality Plants, 1991—. Author: (self instrn. course) Managed Health Care, 1985, Arthritis Primer, 1976. Pres. Am. Diabetes Assn., Roanoke chpt., 1967, Richmond chpt., 1971, state del., 1970; bd. dirs. United Way, Kalamazoo, 1990, 91, Mich. Diabetes Assn., Detroit, 1979; deacon River Rd. Presbyn. Ch.; mem. Rep. Presdl. Task Force. Lt. U.S. Army, 1951-53, Korea, capt. USAR, 1953-60. Mem. Nat. Soc. Pharm. Sales Trainers (hon., pres. Western chpt. 1980-81, pres. nat. orgn. 1987-88, dir. 1985-90, founder newsletter 1987), Meeting Planners Internat., Internat. Meeting Planners, Mil. Order World Wars (treas. 1964-68), Kalamazoo Air History Mus., Charles Garfield Group (hon.), Korean War Vets. Assn. Home: 2828 Kalarama Rd Kalamazoo MI 49002-2321

JONES, GEORGE HUMPHREY, retired healthcare executive, hospital facilities and communications consultant; b. Kansas City, Mo., July 10, 1923; s. George Humphrey and Mary R. (Marrs) J.; m. Peggy Jean Thompson, Nov. 23, 1943; children: Kenneth L., Daniel D., Kathleen Jones Carrigan, Carol R. Jones Johnson, Janet S. Jones Fitts. Student, U. Mo., Kansas City, 1940-43, Wis. State Coll., 1943. Police officer Kansas City (Mo.) Police Dept., 1947-51; elec. contr. Paramount Elec. Svc., Kansas City, 1947-50; electrician Automatic Temp. Control Co., Kansas City, 1951-57; pres., chief ops. George H. Jones Co., Kansas City, 1957-65; sales mgr. Nycon Inc., Lee's Summit, Mo., 1965; design engr. Midland Wright Corp., Kansas City, 1966; dist. sales mgr. Communications Electronics, Kansas City, 1967; plant ops. supr. Research Med. Ctr., Kansas City, 1968-77; dir. plant ops. and communications Research Med. Ctr., 1977-90; hosp. facilities and communications cons. Overland Park, Kans., 1990—; guest lectr. Nat. U., San Diego, 1987. Mem. Met. Emergency Preparedness Coun.; bd. dirs. Camellot Fine arts Acad., 1974-76, v.p. bd. dirs., 1975, 76; vol. program devel. Mid-Am. chpt. Multiple Sclerosis Soc.; vol. emergency svcs. Salvation Army; vol. emergency ops. and comms. Kansas City Area Hosp. Assn.; mem. Confederate Air Force. With USAAF, 1942-46, U.S. Army, 1950-51. Fellow Am. Soc. Hosp. Engring., Healthcare Info. and Mgmt. Systems Soc.; mem. Kansas City Area Hosp. Engrs. (pres. 1985, bd. dirs. 1985-89), Am. Legion, Alpha Phi Omega. Presbyterian. Home and Office: 6022 W 86th St Shawnee Mission KS 66207-1521

JONES, GORDON KEMPTON, dentist; b. Rochester, N.Y., July 22, 1946; s. Joseph Kempton and Eunice (Patten)J.; m. Kathleen Anne FitzSimmons, July 24, 1971; children: Bryan Kempton, Brendan Austin, Graeme Meghan, Michael Cameron, Meredith Hunter, Mallory Sterling. BA in chemistry, U. N. C., 1968; DDS, U. N.C., 1976; MS in Restorative Dentistry, U. Mich., 1984. Lic. dentist, Ill., N.C. Commd. lt. USN, 1976, advanced through ranks to capt., 1993; resident Naval Regional Medical Ctr., Camp Pendleton, Calif., 1977; dentist U.S.S. Holland USN, Holy Loch, Scotland, 1977-80; dentist regional med. ctr. USN, Great Lakes, Ill., 1980-82; head dept. operative dentistry Naval Dental Clinic, Great Lakes, Ill., 1984-90, 93—; head dept. operative dentistry Naval Dental Ctr., Norfolk, Va., 1990-93, dir. managed care, 1993—; cons. operative dentistry Naval Dental Clinic, Great Lakes, Ill., 1984-90, 93-96; dir. managed care Naval Dental Ctr., Great Lakes, Ill., 1993—; dir. branch dental clinic Naval Dental Ctr., 1996—; clinic dir. Naval Dental Ctr., Great Lakes, Ill., 1996—; cons. operative dentistry Naval Dental Ctr., Norfolk, 1990-93; featured spkr. Memphis Dental Soc., 1990, Coastal Carolina Dental Soc., 1992; cons. Naval Hosp. Great Lakes, 1984-86, 93—; asst. clin. prof. Northwestern U. Dental Sch., Chgo., 1985-90, 95—; quality assurance coord., head advanced clin. program in gen. dentistry, Norfolk, 1990-93. Contbr. articles to profl. jours.; speaker in field. Course dir. ARC, Great Lakes, 1984-90. Mem. ADA (USN Operative Dentistry (com. chmn. 1987—, pres. 1996—, exec. coun. 1996—), Acad. Operative Dentistry (mem. jour. editl. bd. 1993-95, 96), Internat. Assn. Dental Rsch., Acad. Gen. Dentistry, Am. Assn. Dental Schs., Am. Legion, Omicron Kappa Upsilon, Alpha Phi Omega, Delta Sigma Delta. Home: 1541 N McKinley Rd Lake Forest IL 60045-1377

JONES, GRAHAM ALFRED, mathematics educator; b. Brisbane, Queensland, Australia, Oct. 29, 1937; came to U.S., 1991; s. Charles Henry and Doris Beatrice (Powell) J.; m. Marion Rose Rudge, Dec. 15, 1962; children: Timothy Charles, Cameron Philip. BSc, U. Queensland, 1960, BEd with 1st honors, 1964; MA, San Diego State U., 1968; PhD, Ind. U., 1974. Tchr. Cavendish Rd. High Sch., Brisbane, 1961-66; Fulbright Exch. tchr. John Francis Poly., L.A., 1966-67; head dept. math. Kelvin Grove Tchrs. Coll., Brisbane, 1968-71; head dept. math. Kelvin Grove Coll. Advanced Edn., Brisbane, 1974-76, dean of sci., 1976-82; campus prin. Brisbane Coll. Advanced Edn., Carseldine campus, Brisbane, 1982-85; pro-vice chancellor, prof., dir. Gold Coast (Australia) Univ. Coll., Griffith U., 1985-91; prof. math. Ill. State U., Normal, 1991—; mem. Bd. Tchr. Edn., Brisbane, 1982-86; chair Math. Adv. Com. of Queensland, Brisbane, 1968-71, 74-76. Author monographs, reports and rsch. articles. NSF scholar, 1967-68. Fellow Australian Inst. Mgmt., Australian Coll. Edn.; mem. Math. Edn. Rsch. Group of Australasia (life, founding pres. 1980-84), Am. Ednl. Rsch. Assn., Nat. Coun. Tchrs. Math. (reviewer for jours. 1991—). Presbyterian. Home: 705 Kathleen Dr Normal IL 61761-4031 Office: Ill State U Dept Math Stevenson Bldg Normal IL 61790-4520

JONES, H. W. KASEY, financial planning executive, author, lecturer; b. Burlington, Iowa, Feb. 11, 1942; s. Herbert Warren and Mary Kathryn (Gardner) J.; m. Ellen E. Toon, Mar. 11, 1961 (div. Dec. 1969); children: Kari Lynne, Kevin C., Anthony W.; m. Janice C. Freyre, Jan. 9, 1994. Student, Bradley U., 1960-61, Coll. Fin. Planning, 1988. Cert. fin. planner. Gen. mgr. sales Wickstrom Chevrolet, Roselle, Ill., 1967-80; v.p. mktg. Re-Direct Svcs., Villa Park, Ill., 1980-81, pres., chief exec. officer, 1982-91; chmn. bd. dirs. Re-Direct Svcs., Villa Park, 1983-91; registered rep. and prin. Long Grove Trading, Inc., Itasca, Ill., 1990—; midwest regional dir. Coll. Bound Student Athletes, Cedarburg, Wis., 1991-94; pres. Linchpin Fin. Group Ltd., McHenry, Ill., 1992—; founding sponsor, mem. speakers' bur. Nat. Ctr. for Fin. Edn., San Francisco, 1984—. Mem. AARP, Internat. Assn. Fin. Planners, Inst. Cert. Fin. Planners, Nat. Spkrs. Assn., Grand Geneva Resort and Spa (Lake Geneva, Wis.), Kiwanis, McHenry (Ill.) Country Club, McHenry C. of C. Home: 1202 S Green St Mc Henry IL 60050-8186

JONES, JAMES E., state legislator; b. Ashby, Nebr., Nov. 19, 1931; m. Patricia Ann McConnell, 1953; children: Gordon, Steven, Vernon, Gregg. Farmer, rancher Nebr.; mem. Nebr. State Senate, Lincoln, 1992—, mem. banking, comml. and ins., natural resources coms. Office: Nebr State Senate State Capitol Rm 1117 Lincoln NE 68509*

JONES, JAMES HENRY, utility company executive; b. Dover, Ohio, Jan. 4, 1941; s. Henry Elias Jones and Frances Lucille (Barkley) Shoemaker; m. Sandra Lee Page, July 12, 1969; children: Stephanie Larissa, Tyler James. BEE, Ohio State U., 1965. Registered profl. engr., Ohio. Relay engr. Ohio Power Co., Canton, 1965-70, sr. relay engr., 1970-76; adminstrv. asst. to divsn. mgr. Ohio Power Co., Steubenville, 1976-77, divsn. transmission and distbn. supt., 1977-83; sta mgr. Ohio Power Co., Canton, 1983-90, distbn. mgr., 1990-92, acting transmission & distbn. dir., 1992-93; protection and measurement engring. and ops. mgr. Combined Columbus (Ohio) So. and Ohio Power Cos., 1993-95; protection and control engring. mgr. Am. Electric Power, Columbus, 1996—; chmn. Stark Tech. Coll.-Pres.'s Adv. Com., Canton, 1974-76; mem. Jefferson Tech. Coll. Electronics Adv. Com., Steubenville, 1977-82. Treas., sec. Lion's Club, Steubenville, 1976-83; troop com. boy Scouts of Am., North Canton, 1985-95; mem. Rotary Club, Plain Twp., North Canton, 1991-93. Recipient Young Engr.'s award Canton Regional Soc. Profl. Engrs., 1976. Mem. IEEE (sr.; sect. chmn. 1973-75, winter meeting Power Engring. Soc. student activities chair 1993). Republican. Methodist. Office: American Electric Power 1 Riverside Plz Columbus OH 43215-2373

JONES, JOHN O., state legislator. Ill. state rep. Dist. 107, 1995—. Office: PO Drawer 1787 1116 Main Mount Vernon IL 62864

JONES, KRISTI LYNNE, business consultant; b. Dallas, Mar. 24, 1969. BA, U. Ctrl. Okla., 1993. V.p. ops. Rome and Assocs. Ltd., Chgo., 1993—. Vol. Chgo. Cares, 1993—, Infant Crisis Svcs., Oklahoma City, 1992-93; team coord. Discovery Program, Chgo., 1994-95. Democrat. Methodist.

JONES, LAWRENCE WILLIAM, educator, physicist; b. Evanston, Ill., Nov. 16, 1925; s. Charles Herbert and Fern (Storm) J.; m. Ruth Reavley Drummond, June 24, 1950; children: Douglas Warren, Carol Anne, Ellen Louise. B.S., Northwestern U., 1948, M.S., 1949; Ph.D., U. Calif. at Berkeley, 1952. Research asst. U. Calif. Radiation Lab., Berkeley, 1950-52; mem. faculty U. Mich., Ann Arbor, 1952—; prof. physics U. Mich., 1963—, chmn. dept. physics, 1982-87; vis. physicist Lawrence Radiation Lab., Berkeley, 1959—, cons., 1964-66; vis. scientist CERN, Geneva, Switzerland, 1961-62, 65, 85—, assoc., 1988—; vis. physicist Brookhaven Nat. Lab., Upton, N.Y., 1963—; vis. physicist Fermi Nat. Accelerator Lab., Batavia, Ill., 1971—; vis. prof. Tata Inst. Fundamental Rsch., Bombay, India, 1979, U. Sydney Australia, 1991; mem. elem. particle physics panel of physics survey com. NRC; cons. ctrl. design group Superconducting Super Collider Nat. Lab., 1985-87, vis. physicist, 1991-94; trustee Univs. Rsch. Assn., 1982-87; disting. vis. scholar U. Adelaide, 1991; vis. scientist U. Auckland, 1991. Mem. adv. panel for Cosmic Rays Jour. of Physics G., 1991-95. Named Disting. prof., U. of Adelaide, 1991; Guggenheim fellow, 1965; Sci. Rsch. Coun. fellow, 1977. Fellow Am. Phys. Soc. Home: 2666 Parkridge Dr Ann Arbor MI 48103-1731 Office: U Mich Dept Physics Ann Arbor MI 48109-1120

JONES, LEANDER CORBIN, educator, media specialist; b. Vincent, Ark., July 16, 1934; s. Lander Corbin and Una Bell (Lewis) J.; A.B., U. Ark., Pine Bluff, 1956; M.S., U. Ill., 1968; Ph.D., Union Grad. Inst., 1973; m. Lethonee Angela Hendricks, June 30, 1962; children: Angela Lynne, Leander Corbin. Tchr. English pub. high schs., Chgo. Bd. Edn., 1956-68; vol. English-as-fgn. lang. tchr. Peace Corps, Mogadiscio, Somalia, 1964-66; TV producer City Colls. of Chgo., 1968-73; communications media specialist Meharry Med. Coll., 1973-75; assoc. prof. Black Americana studies Western Mich., U., 1975-89, prof., 1989—, chmn. African studies program, 1980-81, co-chmn. Black caucus, 1983-84; pres. Corbin 22 Ltd., 1986—; dir. 7 art workshop Am. Negro Emancipation Centennial Authority, Chgo., 1960-63. Mem. Mich. Commn. on Crime and Delinquency, 1981-83; mem. exec. com. DuSable Mus. African Am. History, 1970—; mem. Prisoners Progress Assn., 1977-82, South African Solidarity Orgn., 1978—, Dennis Brutus Def. Com., 1980-83; chmn. Kalamazoo Community Relations Bd., 1977-79; bd. dirs. Kalamazoo Civic Players, 1981-83; pres. Black Theater of Kalamazoo, 1978-85; dir., dramaturg Mich. Black Repertory Theatre, 1987-90; exec. prodr. Ransom Street Playhouse, Kalamazoo, 1993—. Served with U.S. Army, 1956-58. Faculty Enrichment grantee Govt. Can., 1992. Mem. Assn. Study African-Am. History , NAACP (exec. com. Kalamazoo br. 1978-82), Theatre Arts and Broadcasting Skills Ctr. (pres. 1972—), AAUP, Mich. Orgn. African Studies, Nat. Council Black Studies, Popular Culture Assn., 100 Men's Club, Kappa Alpha Psi. Dir. South Side Ctr. of Performing Arts, Chgo., 1968-69, Progressive Theatre Unltd., Nashville, 1974-75, Mich. Black Repertory Theatre, 1987-90; chmn. Tenn. Region N.AM. Zone of 2d World Festival Black and Artican Arts and Culture, 1975, Nat. Black Media Consortium, 1985; writer, producer, dir. TV drama: Roof Over my Head, Nashville 1975; designer program in theatre and TV for hard-to-educate; developer edn. programs in Ill. State Penitentiary, Pontiac, and Cook County Jail, Chgo., 1971-73. Writer, dir. 10 Score!, 1976, Super Summer, 1978; dir. Trouble in Mind, 1979, Day of Absence, 1981, 85, Happy Ending, 1981, Who's Got His Own, 1983, Take A Giant Step, 1985; producer For Colored Girls Who Have Considered Suicide When the Rainbow is Enuf, 1984; featured at Civic Theater, Kalamazoo, in Great White Hope, 1979, Dutchman, 1980, Moon On a Rainbow Shawl, 1980, Five on the Black Hand Side, 1982, Who's Got His Own, Guys and Dolls, Black Girl, Tambourines to Glory, 1983, Day of Absence, Take a Giant Step, 1985, Soldier's Play, 1986, Beef, No Chicken, 1989, Black Eagles, 1994; author: Roof Over My Head, 1975, Africa is for Reel, 1983, Journal of Black Studies, 1985; exec. producer and host TV series Fade to Black, 1986—. Home: PO Box 2404 Portage MI 49008 Office: Western Mich U 3721 S Westnedge Ave Ste 222 Kalamazoo MI 49008-2979

JONES, LEE A., school system administrator, consultant, small business owner; b. Seneca, Ill., Mar. 23, 1948; s. Chester N. and Ruth A. (Laymon) J.; m. Adrian Farris Jones, Mar. 9, 1969; children: Laura A., Trent L. BS, U. Ill., 1972, MEd, 1973; MS, Ea. Ill. U., 1987; PhD, Ind. State U., 1988. Tchr. Wheaton (Ill.) Sch. Dist. 200, 1977-83, Hutsonville (Ill.) Sch. Dist. 2, 1983-87; prin. Gibault Sch., Terre Haute, Ind., 1987—; owner Country Woods Cabinets, Ill., 1973-88. Mem. Acad. & Athletic Booster Club, Casey, 1985-90; leader Boy Scouts Am., Casey, 1989-90. With USMC, 1966-70. Office: Seneca Sch Dist #160 307 E Scott Box 20 Seneca IL 61360

JONES, LOVANA S., state legislator; b. Mansfield, Ohio, Mar. 28, 1935; 2 chilren. BA, Ohio State U. Mem. from 5th dist. Ill. Ho. of Reps., formerly asst. majority leader; mem. children and family law com., edn. fin. elections com., pub. safety and infrastructure appropriationcoms., chmn. reapportionment com., mem. state govt. com. Supr. anti-gang program Chgo. Intervention Network. Office: Ill State Senate State Capitol Springfield IL 62706*

JONES, MARGARET L., finance company executive; b. Chgo., Ill., Sept. 10, 1947. BS in Polit. Sci., Loyola U., 1979. Administrv. asst. to chmn. Metropolitan Structures, Chgo., 1986-90; v.p. Primerica Fin. Svcs., Westchester, Ill., 1989—. Author: Eddie-Book 2, 1978. Vol. Greer's Residential Ctr., Chgo, 1992—. Democrat. Baptist. Office: Primerica Fin Svcs 9909 W Roosevelt Rd Westchester IL 60154-2773

JONES, MARLENE WISEMAN, elementary education educator, reading specialist; b. Zanesville, Ohio, Oct. 8, 1939; d. Mark Andrew Wiseman and Elizabeth Wiseman (Wilkins) Doughty; m. Herbert Pearce Jones, Sept. 2, 1961. BS in Edn., Muskingum Coll., New Concord, Ohio, 1962; MEd, Ohio U., Zanesville, 1984. Elem. tchr. Zanesville City Schs., 1962-65, reading specialist, 1967—; reading instr. Ohio Univ., Zanesville, 1984, Muskingum Area Tech. Coll., Zanesville, 1991-94. Co-author book Diagnosis for Reading, 1975; creator Games for Reading, 1973. Recipient Outstanding Elem. Tchr. award, 1973. Mem. NEA, Ohio Edn. Assn., Zanesville Edn. Assn., Heisey Collectors of Am., Zanesville Art Ctr., Order Ea. Star. Democrat. Lutheran. Home: 2219 Hazel Ave Zanesville OH 43701-2022 Office: Zanesville City Schs 160 N 4th St Zanesville OH 43701-3518

JONES, MATTHEW LEON, sales and acquisition specialist; b. Wichita, Kans., July 30, 1948; s. Frank Waldon and Phyllis Norine (Atkins) J. AA, Haskell Indian Jr. Coll., 1973; B of Gen. Studies, Wichita State U., 1984. Minority TV producer Sta. KAKE-TV, Wichita, 1979-84; job tng. dir. Otoe-Missouria Tribe of Okla., Red Rock, Okla., 1985-86; program and project coord. Nat. Am. Pub. Broadcasting, Lincoln, Nebr., 1986-90, sales and acquisition specialist, 1990—; chairperson Multi Cultural Edn. Com., Lincoln, 1994—; advisor Lincoln Pub. Sch. Sys., Lincoln, 1988-92. Co-producer (documentary) In the White Man's Image, 1992. Cmmdr. Am. Legion Post 7722, Lincoln, 1994; programmer Mayor's Internat. Friendship com. 1989—. With U.S. Army, 1968-70. Recipient Gabriel award Cath. Film Soc., 1992, Achievement of Merit award, Ohio State U., 1993, Erik Barnouw award Orgn. of Am. Historians, 1993. Fellow Ctr. for Great Plains Studies; mem. Nat. Indian Edn. Assn., Am. Indian Libr. Assn. (v.p. 1994—), Capital City Kiwanis (bd. dirs. 1988—). Office: Native Am Pub Telecomm Inc Consortium 1800 N 33rd St Lincoln NE 68583

JONES, MICHAEL ALLEN, mechanical engineering supervisor; b. Covington, Ky., Nov. 7, 1951. BSME, U. Cin., 1981. Project engr. DuBois Chem., Cin., 1977-91; design engr. Ferno-Washington, Wilmington, Ohio, 1991-93; project supr. Cin. Indsl. Mach, 1994—. With USAF, 1971-75. Republican. Church of Christ. Office: Cincinnati Indsl Mach PO Box 62027 Cincinnati OH 45262

JONES, NORMA LOUISE, librarian, educator; b. Poplar, Wis.; d. George Elmer and Hilma June (Wiberg) J. BE, U. Wis.; MA, U. Minn., 1952; postgrad, U. Ill., 1957; PhD, U. Mich., 1965; postgrad., NARS, 1978, 79, 80, Nova U., 1983-96. Librarian Grand Rapids (Mich.) Public Schs., 1947-62; with Grand Rapids Public Library, 1948-49; instr. Central Mich. U., Mt. Pleasant, 1954, 55; lectr. U. Mich., Ann Arbor, 1954, 55, 61, 63-65, asst. prof., 1966-68; librarian Benton Harbor (Mich.) Public Schs., 1962-63; asst. prof. library sci. U. Wis., Oshkosh, 1968-70; assoc. prof. U. Wis., 1970-75, prof., 1975—, chmn. dept. library sci., 1980-84, exec. dir. librs. and learning resources, 1987-93; dir. Adult Ctr., 1993-95. Recipient Disting. Teaching award U. Wis.-Oshkosh, 1977. Mem. ALA (chmn. reference cons. 1975), Wis. Libr. Assn., Assn. Libr. and Info. Sci. Educators, Spl. Libr. Assn., Wis. Spl. Libr. Assn., Soc. Am. Archivists, Wis. Assn. Acad. Librs., Phi Beta Kappa, Phi Kappa Phi, Pi Lambda Theta, Beta Phi Mu, Sigma Pi Epsilon. Home: 1220 Maricopa Dr Oshkosh WI 54904-8121

JONES, NORMAN M., finance executive; b. Fargo, N.D., Aug. 28, 1930; s. Maurice H. Jones and Minnie (Dustrud) Bohlig; m. Eunice Skurdahl, Dec. 20, 1950; children: Janet, Marrietta, Mark, Steven Jones. Student, Concordia Coll., 1949-50. With Met. Fed. Bank, Fargo, 1952-83; chmn., pres., chief exec. officer Met. Fin. Corp., Mpls., 1983-94; bd. dirs. First Bank Sys., Mpls.; past vice chair Fed. Home Loan Bank Bd., Des Moines; bd. dirs. First Bank System; chmn. First Bank Savs.; bd. trustees, exec. com. S&L Computer Trust, Des Moines. Mem. thrift adv. council Fed. Reserve; bd. trustees Lutheran Hosps. and Homes, Fargo; past pres. First Luth. Ch., Fargo; past chmn. Am. Lutheran Ch. Ea. N.D. Dist. Council; nat. steering com. Commitment to Mission Am. Luth. Ch.; past. bd. dirs., v.p., Fargo Jr. C. of C.; founding mem. Fargo Housing Authority; bd. dirs. Red River Valley Council Boy Scouts Am.; bd. regents Concordia Coll., Moorhead, Minn. Served with U.S. Army, 1949-51. Recipient Pres.'s award Concordia Coll., Moorhead, Minn., 1973, 74, Regent's award, 1977, Sole Dio Gloria award, 1977, Martin Luther award, 1989; named Outstanding Bus. Leader N.D. Bus. Found., 1978. Mem. Frago C. of C. (past bd. dirs.), Fargo Country Club, Minikahda Club. Republican. Office: First Bank System 601 Seeona Ave S Minneapolis MN 55402

JONES, PATRICIA LOUISE, elementary counselor; b. Moorhead, Minn., Aug. 20, 1942; d. Harry Wilfred and Myrtle Louise Rosenfeldt; m. Edward L. Marks (div.); m. Curtis C. Jones, July 16, 1973; children: Michon, Andrea, Nathan, Kirsten, Leah. BS, Moorhead State U., 1965; MS, Mankato State U., 1990. Cert. K-12 sch. counselor, Minn. Tchr. Anoka (Minn.) Hennepin Schs., 1966-68; pvt. practice Youth Ctr., Truman, Minn., 1969-72; bookkeeper Fairmont (Minn.) Glass & Sign, 1973, Truman Farmers Elevator, 1973-87; libr. Martin County Libr., Truman, 1988-89; sch. counselor St. James (Minn.) Schs., 1989—; coord. Internat. Fun Fest, St. James, 1992, 96; originator, advisor Armstrong After Sch. Hispanic Club, St. James, 1991—. Coord. Truman Days Parade, 1991, 92, 94, 95, 96; mem. adv. bd. Watonwan County Big Buddy Program, 1993—. Mem. Am. Counseling Assn., Am. Sch. Counselors Assn., Minn. Sch. Counselors Assn., S.W. Minn. Counselors Assn. (Elem. Counselor of Yr. 1993). Office: Saint James Sch Dist 1273 10th Ave N Saint James MN 56081-2029

JONES, PHILIP ALAN, broadcasting executive; b. Cairo, Ill., June 27, 1944; s. Charles E. and Doris E. (Hogendobler) J.; m. Lynnsay Williams, Sept. 6, 1967; children: Whitney, Spencer. B.J., U. Mo., Columbia, 1966; postgrad., Harvard U., 1976. Salesman KCMO-FM, Kansas City, Mo., 1966-67, KMBR Radio, Kansas City, 1967-68; local salesman WDAF-TV, Kansas City, Mo., 1968-70; local sales mgr. WDAF-TV, 1970-74; gen. sales mgr. WTAF-TV, Phila., 1974-76; gen. mgr. WGR-TV, Buffalo, 1976-79; v.p., gen. mgr. Sta. KCTV, Kansas City, Mo., 1979-89; exec. v.p. Meredith Corp. Broadcasting, Des Moines, 1989, pres., 1989—; past chmn. bd. CBS-TV Affiliates, chair long range planning com. CBS Affiliate. Bd. dirs. March of Dimes, 1980-81, Conv. Bur. Greater Kansas City, 1980-84, Greater Kansas City YMCA, Learning Exchange; bd. dirs., exec. com. Starlight Theatre, 1980—; mem. communications com. United Way, 1979-85; mem. Nelson Gallery Soc. Fellows, 1980—; bd. govs. Mayor's Task Force on Neighborhood Crime, 1981. Mem. Nat. Assn. Broadcasters, TV Bur. Advt., Assn. Maximum Service Telecasters, United Minority Media Assn. (mem. adv. bd.), Am. Women in Radio and TV, Kans. Broadcasters Assn., Mo. Broadcasters Assn. (program com.), C. of C. Greater Kansas City, Carriage Club (Kansas City, Mo.), Mission Hills Country Club, Ducks Unlimited Club, Confrerie de la Chaine des Rotisseurs Club, Alpha Delta Sigma, Phi Delta Theta. Methodist. Home: 2730 Verona Ter Shawnee Mission KS 66208-1275 Office: KCTV Box 5555 4500 Shawnee Mission Pky Fairway KS 66205-2563*

JONES, POLLY S., investment company executive; b. Belleville, Ill., Jan. 30, 1947. BA, Ea. Ill. U., Charleston, 1969; MA, So. Ill. U., Edwardsville, 1975. CFP. Mem. faculty So. Ill. U. Sch. Bus., 1975-82; v.p. investments A.G. Edwards & Sons Inc., Belleville, 1982—. Bd. dirs. Metro East Women's Crisis Ctr., St. Louis, 1988—, Earthway House, St. Louis, 1994—; pro bono fin. advisor various orgns., 1985—. Mem. Delta Phi Epsilon.

JONES, RADFORD WEDGEWOOD, security manager; b. Balt., Sept. 30, 1939; s. Don A. and Violet Mabel (Weedon) J.; m. Nancy Edwina Heiss, July 13, 1963; children: Todd E., Elizabeth W., Kimberly E. BS, Mich. State U., 1962; postgrad., Am. Univ., 1972. Police officer Mich. State U. Dept. Pub. Safety, E. Lansing, Mich., 1962-63; spl. agent U.S. Secret Svc., Washington, 1963-69, asst. spl. agent, 1969-77, spl. agent in charge, 1977-83; fire and security mgr. Ford Motor Co., Dearborn, Mich., 1983-89; mgr. security and fire protection Ford Motor Co., Dearborn, 1989—; legis. chmn. Downtown Detroit Security Exec. Coun., 1984-90; chmn. Dearborn Security Network, 1993; cons. U.S. State Dept. Overseas Security Adv. Coun., Washington, 1987—; internat. lectr. on phys. and exec. security procedures. Coach Am. Softball Assn., Rochester, Mich., 1988; mem. adv. bd. Sch. Criminal Justice, Mich. State U., 1989—; com. mem. Mich. Gov.'s Adv. Coun. on Substance Abuse, Nat. Access Control Adv. Bd., Leadership and Mgmt. Program in Security Adv. Bd., Mich. State U., 1992—. Recipient Spl. Achievement awards U.S. Treasury Dept., 1966, 73, Plaque of Appreciation Royal Canadian Mounted Police, 1977, 1979, Disting. Pub. Svc. award Restaurant Assn. Wash., 1979, Award of Merit Washington State Patrol, 1979. Mem. Internat. Assn. Chiefs Police, Mich. Assn. Police Chiefs, Am. Soc. Indsl. Security, Greater Detroit C. of C. (safe street alliance), Mich. State U. Criminal Justice Alumni Assn. (bd. dirs. East Lansing 1980, coord. Dearborn 1988), Nat. Model R.R. Assn., Optimists. Home: 2644 Long Winter Ln Oakland MI 48363 Office: Ford Motor Co The American Rd Rm 418 Dearborn MI 48126-2798

JONES, RANDY S., engineering executive; b. Lincoln, Kans., Mar. 6, 1958. BSME, Kans. State U., 1980. Product engr. Richson Mfg., Canker City, Kans., 1981-84; engring. mgr. Great Plains Mfg., Inc., Assaria, Kans., 1985—. Office: Great Plains Mfg 108 W 2nd St Assaria KS 67416

JONES, REGINALD LORRIN, clinical psychologist, consultant; b. St. Petersburg, Fla., Dec. 12, 1951; s. Daniel George Jones and Susie Beatrice (Lewis) W.; m. Helen Elizbeth Lightfoot, Aug. 18, 1984; children: Tammy LeVette McKay, Myla Carmel, Regina Yvonne, Deneale Elizabeth Hand. BA, Clark Coll., 1973; MA, U. Cin., 1977, PhD, 1980. Lic. psychologist, Ohio. Statistician Atlanta Pub. Schs., 1973-74; psychology trainee U. Cin., 1974-80; team leader, supr. Social Skills Program, Cin., 1980-81; psychologist, unit dir. Day-Mont West, C.M.H.C., Dayton, Ohio, 1981-83; field psychologist advisor Ohio Indsl. Commn., Dayton, 1983-87; pvt. practice psychology, Dayton, 1983—; clin. asst. prof. Wright State U., Dayton, 1981—; cons. Adapt Inc., Springfield, Ohio, 1986-94; cons. Sickle Cell Awarness Group, Cin., 1986-90, v.p., 1981. Mem. adv. bd. Drew Sickle Cell Ctr., 1989-92; trustee Family Svc. Assn. Dayton, 1989-92. Named One of Outstanding Young Men of Am., 1984. Mem. APA, Nat. Assn. Black Psychologists, Ohio Psychol. Assn., Dayton Area Psychol. Assn., Am. Soc. Clin. Hypnosis, Dayton Assn. Black Psychologists (prs. 1983-84, Svc. award 1986), Nat. Register Health Svc. Providers in Psychology, Prescribing Psychologist Register. Democrat. Home: 180 Folsom Dr Dayton OH 45405-1108

JONES, RICHARD A., stock broker; b. Columbus, Ind., Mar. 23, 1945. BSChemE, Rose Hulman Inst. Tech., 1967. Chem. engr. Comml. Solvents, Terre Haute, Ind., 1967-72; stock broker Dupont, Terre Haute, 1972-74, AG Edwards and Sons, Terre Haute, 1974—. Patentee chem. processing. Republican. Presbyterian. Office: AG Edwards and Sons 9325 South Point LaSalle Rd Bloomington IN 47401

JONES, ROBERT E., company executive; m. Mary Jane Jones; 1 child, Tom. Student Washington U. With The Jones Co., St. Louis, 1953—, pres., 1961—, chmn. bd.; dir. St. John's Bank and Trust Co. Chmn. labor com. Home Builders Assn. Greater St. Louis; tech. advt. com. St. Louis County Planning Commn.; chmn. bd. Met. St. Louis Sewer Dist. Mem. Nat. Assn. Home Builders (life dir.). Address: JE Jones Construction Company Inc 13100 Manchester Rd Saint Louis MO 63131-1703

JONES, ROBERT LYLE, emergency medical services leader, educator; b. Washington, Feb. 6, 1959; s. Herman Aven and Dorothy Edith (Fisher) J.; m. Cynthia Celia Bogdanowicz, May 15, 1996. B in Gen. Sci., U. Kans., 1982; MA in Adult and Continuing Edn., U. Mo., 1990. Registered paramedic, Kans., Kans. cert. Emergency Med. Svcs. Tng. Officer, 1992—. Paramedic team leader Johnson County (Kans.) Med. Action, 1983-89, dist. supr., 1989-92, edn. supr., 1992—; BCLS instr., 1979-87, affiliate faculty, 1987—, ACLS instr., 1985-88, affiliate faculty, 1988—, PALS instr., 1993—. Served to Capt. USAR, 1979-94. Mem. Nat. Assn. EMTs (prehosp. trauma life support instr. 1986—), Nat. Soc. EMS Adminstrs., Nat. Soc. EMT Paramedics, Assn. Profls. in Infection Control and Epidemiology. Home: 7137 Lowell Dr Shawnee Mission KS 66204-1837 Office: Johnson County Med Action 111 S Cherry St Ste 300 Olathe KS 66061-3441

JONES, RONALD VANCE, health science association administrator; b. Springfield, Ill., Oct. 7, 1946; s. Dallas Vance and Bertha Henrietta (Bentley) J.; m. Patricia Ann O'Neill, Feb. 1, 1969; children: Devon Vance, Zachary Brice. BS, U. Ill., 1969, MEd, 1972. Tchr. English lang. Ottawa (Ill.) Twp. H.S., 1969-70; rsch. assoc. U. Ill., Urbana, 1970-73; dir. cmty. programs Ga. Dept. Youth Svcs., Atlanta, 1973-79; dir. planning Ga. Dept. Mental Health, Atlanta; capital project planner Ill. Dept. Mental Health, Springfield, 1979-85; bus. adminstr. Chester (Ill.) Mental Health Ctr., 1985-92; asst. supt. Malcolm Bliss Mental Health Ctr., St. Louis, 1992-96; chief operating officer Met. St. Louis Psychiatric Ctr., 1996—. Editor: tchr. guidebooks for elem. schs., 1971-73. Vice-chmn., bd. dirs. Lullwater Sch. Atlanta; vol. St. Louis Easter Seal Soc., 1987-88. Mem. Ill. Health Facilities Planning Bd., Ill. Hosp. Licensing Bd., Ill. Long Term Care Facilities Bd., Gov's. State Bldgs. Energy Cons. Bd., Kappa Delta Pi, Phi Delta Kappa. Home: 12 Zinnia Dr Belleville IL 62221-4341 Office: Malcolm Bliss Psychiatric Ctr Dept of Mental Health Saint Louis MO 63112

JONES, RONALD WOODBRIDGE, human resources specialist, small business owner; b. Boston, Oct. 7, 1932; s. James Robert and Whilma Alythia (Isaacs) J.; m. Alice Eugenia Henderson, Feb. 24, 1957; children Alice Eugenia Jones Ward, Sharon Marie. BA in Am. History, St. Benedict's Coll., 1969; MA in Am. History, St. Louis U., 1974. Enlisted U.S. Army, 1954, commd. 2nd lt., 1955, advanced through grades to major, 1967, ret., 1974; sr. assoc. Grant Cooper & Assocs., Saint Louis, 1974-85, vp., dir., 1985-89; pres., owner Woodbridge Assocs., Saint Louis, 1989—. dir. SPROG, Inc., Kirkwood, 1978-84; bd. dirs. Murphy Blair Resident Housing Corp., 1980-88, 90-94, Grace Hill Settlement House, St. Louis, 1979-88, pres., 1983-87; curriculum com. Kirkwood H.S., 1981, citizen's adv. fin. com. City of Kirkwood, 1983-89, chmn. 1986-89; standing com. Episcopal Diocese Mo., 1975-78, 84-88, pres. 1987-88; vestryman Grace Episcopal Ch., Kirkwood, 1972-75, 78-82, sr. warden, 1979-82. Decorated with Bronze Star with Cluster, U.S. Army. Mem. Boston Latin Sch. Alumni Assn., Harvard Club St. Louis, Notre Dame Club St. Louis, Media Club, St. Louis Symphony Soc., Kirkwood Meml. Post # 156, Am. Legion (post comdr. 1990—), Gateway Voiture # 448, Forty & Eight, St. Louis Vets.' Home Com. (life mem.), Phi Alpha Theta. Episcopalian. Home: 327 Oakley Ln Kirkwood MO 63122-2816 Office: Woodbridge Assocs 12025 Manchester Rd Ste 70G Saint Louis MO 63131-4420

JONES, ROSEMARY, education director; b. Washington, Pa., Aug. 15, 1951; d. Roy F. and Grace Vivian (Beton) J. BA in Sociology, Ohio State U., 1974, MA in Pub. Adminstrn., 1977. Mgmt. analyst office planning studies Ohio State U., Columbus, 1974-76; staff assoc., edn. rev. com. Ohio Gen. Assembly, Columbus, 1977-78; from adminstr. to asst. dir. info. systems and rsch. Ohio Bd. Regents, Columbus, 1978-90; from project dir. instl. rsch. to dir. rsch. planning Lakeland C.C., Mentor, Ohio, 1990-93; dist. dir. instl. planning evaluation Cuyahoga C.C., Cleve., 1994—; mem. com. on info. sys. design Ohio Bd. Regents, 1995—, subsidy cons. com., 1996; mem. com. on student outcomes measures Nat. Post Secondary Edn. Coop., 1996; mem. NPECSS planning com. Dept. Edn., 1994-96, NPEC student outcomes data working group, 1996, NCES coop. sys. fellows program, 1996; mem. com. on revising info. sys. for higher edn. Ohio Bd. Regents, Columbus, 1994-96, mem. subsidy consultation com., 1996, cons., 1990-91. Consumr adv. bd. United Health Plan, Columbus, 1978-82, chair, 1980-82; vol. Ronald McDonald House, Columbus, 1989, operating bd. mem., 1989; bd. dirs. Netcare Found., Columbus, 1988; state and regional conf. chair ASPA, Columbus, 1981, 83-84; steering com. Ctrl. Ohio Salute to Pub. Employees, Columbus, 1983. Mem. Assn. Instl. Rsch., Ohio Conf. for Coll. and Univ. Planning, Ohio Assn. Instl. Rsch. (two-yr. campus coun. rep. 1994-96), Cleve. Planning Forum, Soc. for Coll. and Univ. Planning, Cleve. Commn. on Higher Edn. Strategic Planning Com. (temp. chair 1991). Office: Cuyahoga CC 700 Carnegie Ave Cleveland OH 44115-2833

JONES, RUSSELL TED, financial consultant; b. Macomb, Ill., Dec. 27, 1944. BS in Phys. Edn., Bradley U., 1967; MS in Fin. Svcs., Am. Coll., 1986. CLU, ChFC. Salesperson J C Penney, Pekin, Ill., 1960-63, Bell Clothing, Peoria, Ill., 1963-67; life ins. profl. various cos., 1968-85; fin. cons. Smith Barney Inc., Peoria, 1985—. Author CLU study guide, 1980-81. With USN, 1967-68, Vietnam. Mem. Am. Soc. CLU, Peoria Life Ins. Underwriters. Methodist. Office: Smith Barney 401 Main St Peoria IL 61602-1241

JONES, SANDRA, electronics executive; b. Frankfurt, Fed. Republic Germany, Oct. 5, 1946; came to U.S., 1949; d. Irving and Lena (Koonigstein) Zak; m. Charles E. Jones, Dec. 18, 1973; stepchildren: Katherine Jones Mearns, Terry Jones, Cynthia E. Jones. Grad. sch. grad. Mgr. ops. J&L Builders, Cleve., 1968-71; v.p. Sabin Machine Co., Cleve., 1971-75; pres. Security Products Col, Cleve., 1975—, also bd. dirs., 1975-90; pres. Sandra Jones & Co., Chardon, Ohio, 1990—; spokesperson Electronic Security Industry; participant Consumer Products Safety Commn.; industry rep. Ad Hoc Window Falls Com. Bd. dirs. Nat. Burglar and Fire Alarm Assn., Security Industry Assn. (bd. dirs. 1985—, v.p. 1986-88, pres. elect 1988—, exec. dir.), Nat. Assn. Wholesalers (trustee 1986—, bd. dels.). Jewish. Office: 10100 Sherman Rd Chardon OH 44024-9443

JONES, SHIRLEY M., state legislator; b. Chgo., Nov. 9, 1939; 2 children. Ed., George Williams Coll. Mem. from Dist. 6, Ill. Ho. of Reps., 1987—, vice chmn. aging com.; also mem. higher edn., housing, human svc. appropriations, pub. utilities, revenue and state adminstrn. coms. Home: Ste 2306 541 W Roosevelt Rd Chicago IL 60607-4915 Office: Ill State Senate State Capitol Springfield IL 62706*

JONES, STANLEY CONROY, communications company executive; b. Shelby, Miss., Sept. 12, 1964; s. Samuel and Annell (Thompson) J. BS, Tougaloo Coll., 1987; MS, Howard U., 1989. Mem. tech. staff AT&T Bell Labs., Naperville, Ill., 1987-93; chmn. AT&T Synergy in Action Conf., 1990. Chmn. AT&T co. fund dr. United Negro Coll. Fund, Naperville, 1990, mem. steering com., Chgo., 1990—; tutor Cabrini Green Tutoring Program, Chgo., 1989—; trustee Heritage Club Found., Wheaton, Ill., 1990—. Recipient meritorious svc. award United Negro Coll. Fund, 1990-92. Mem. Nat. Tech. Assn., Alpha Phi Alpha Fraternity, Inc., Alpha Kappa Mu, Alpha Lambda Delta. Home: 92 Olesen Dr Apt 300E Naperville IL 60540-5856

JONES, TREVOR OWEN, automobile supply company executive, management consultant; b. Maidstone, Kent, Eng., Nov. 3, 1930; came to U.S., 1957, naturalized, 1971; s. Richard Owen and Ruby Edith (Martin) J.; m. Jennie Lou Singleton, Sept. 12, 1959; children: Pembroke Robinson, Bronwyn Elizabeth. Higher Nat. Cert. in Elec. Engring., Aston Tech. Coll., Birmingham, Eng., 1952; Ordinary Nat. Cert. in Mech. Engring., Liverpool (Eng.) Tech. Coll., 1957. Registered profl. engr., Wis.; chartered engr., U.K. Student engr., elec. machine design engr. Brit. Gen. Electric Co., 1950-57; project engr., project mgr. Nuclear Ship Savannah, Allis-Chalmers Mfg. Co., 1957-59; with Gen. Motors Corp., 1959-78, staff engr. in charge Apollo computers, 1967, dir. electronic control systems, 1970-72, dir. advanced product engring., 1972-74; dir. Gen. Motors Proving Grounds, 1974-78; v.p. engring., automotive worldwide TRW Inc., Cleve., 1978-80, v.p. transp. electronics group, 1980-87; chmn. bd. Libbey-Owens-Ford Inc., 1987-94; chmn., CEO Internat. Devel. Corp., 1987—; vice chmn. Echlin Inc., 1995—; vice chmn. Motor Vehicle Safety Adv. Council, 1971; chmn. Nat. Hwy. Safety Adv. Com., 1976. Author, patentee automotive safety and electronics. Trustee Lawrence Inst. Tech., 1973-76; mem. exec. bd. Clinton Valley council Boy Scouts Am., 1975; bd. govs. Cranbrook Inst. Sci., 1977. Served as officer Brit. Army, 1955-57. Recipient Safety award for engring. excellence U.S. Dept. Transp., 1978. Fellow Brit. Instn. Elec. Engrs. (Hooper Mem. prize 1950), IEEE (exec. com. vehicle tech. soc. 1977-81), Soc. Automotive Engrs. (Arch T. Colwell paper award 1974, 75, Vincent Bendix Automotive Electronics award 1976, Edward N. Cole award 1988); mem. NAE, Engring. Soc. Detroit and Cleve., Union Club, Kirtland Country Club, Bloomfield Hills Country Club. Republican. Epsicopalian. Home: Two Bratenahl Pl Bratenahl OH 44108

JONES, VEDA RAE BOYD, author; b. Sulphur Springs, Ark., Nov. 30, 1948; d. Raymond Eugene and Dorothy Lucille (Brown) Boyd; m. Jimmie L. Jones, Nov. 15, 1975; children: Landon Boyd, Morgan Perry, Marshall Adam. AA, Crowder Coll., Neosho, Mo., 1968; BA, Pittsburg State U., Kans., 1970; MA, U. Ark., 1974. Instr. creative writing Crowder Coll., 1993—; lectr. in field; instr. for Inst. Children's Lit. Author: April's Autumn, 1991, Gentle Persuasion, 1993, Under a Texas Sky, 1993, The Governor's Daughter, 1993, A Sign of Love, 1994, Callie's Mountain, 1995, Callie's Challenge, 1995, A Question of Balance, 1996; writer for children's mags. including: Highlights, Cricket, Wee Wisdom, Humpty Dumpty, Pockets, Hopscotch, Wonder Time, The Friend; contbr. articles to ref. books including Ency. Am. Humorists, Guide to Am. Hist. Biography, Guide to European Hist. Biography, Popular World History, Guide to Lit. for Young Adults; articles in adult mags.; The Writer, Harris' Farmer's Almanac, Evangel, Country Am., Instr., New Writer's Mag., Writer's Digest, Tchg. K-8, Learning. Head tour guide Joplin (Mo.) Pub. Libr., 1991—. Mem. AAUW (pres. Joplin br. 1987-89), Mo. Writers Guild, Ozark Writers League, Joplin Writers Guild. Home: 505 W 34th St Joplin MO 64804-3613

JONES, WALTER DEAN, community program director; b. Rockport, Ind., May 14, 1938; s. Kenneth Walter and Marjorie Lucille (Leonard) J.; m. Alice Dorothy Boger, May 21, 1966; 1 child, Julie Dean. BS in Agr., Purdue U., 1961; MS in Community Devel., U. Louisville, 1970. Farmer Jones Feed Svc., Grandview, Ind., 1955-65; exec. dir. Lincoln Hills Devel. Corp., Tell City, 1965-73; county extension dir. Purdue U., LaGrange, 1973-76, Vincennes, 1976-80; area community devel. agt. Purdue U., Ft. Wayne, 1980-83; county extension dir. Purdue U., Lake County, Ind., 1983—; treas. Lake County Econ. Devel. Authority, Highland, 1984-92; pres. Lake County Parks and Recreation Bd., Crown Point, 1990-91; coord. Lake County Community Devel., Crown Point, 1983—. Editorial adv. com.: The Times (Hammond, Ind.); contbr. articles to profl. jours. Mem. Lake County Libr. Found., Merrillville, 1986, pres., 1988, 89; pres. Lake County Planning Commn., 1992; bd. dirs. Leadership Northwest Ind., sec. 1992, treas., 1996; mem. Borman Beautification Task Force. With U.S. Army, 1961-63. Recipient Achievement award Nat. Assn. County Agrl. Agts., 1981. Mem. Ind. Extension Agts. Assn. (pres. 1989), Ind. Agrl. and CD Agts. (pres. 1988), Ind. Community Devel. Soc., Crown Point Rotary Club (pres. 1995-96), Epsilon Sigma Phi, Gamma Sigma Delta. Office: Lake County Coop Ext 2293 N Main St Crown Point IN 46307-1854

JONES, WILLIAM AUGUSTUS, JR., retired bishop; b. Memphis, Jan. 24, 1927; s. William Augustus and Martha (Jones) J.; m. Margaret Loaring-Clark, Aug. 26, 1949; 4 children. B.A., Southwestern at Memphis, 1948; B.D., Yale U., 1951. Ordained priest Episcopal Ch., 1952; priest in charge Messiah Ch., Pulaski, Tenn., 1952-57; curate Christ Ch., Nashville, 1957-58; rector St. Mark Ch., LaGrange, Ga., 1958-65; asso. rector St. Luke Ch., Mountainbrook, Ala., 1965-66; dir. research So. region Assn. Christian Tng. and Service, Memphis, 1966-67; exec. dir. Assn. Christian Tng. and Service, 1968-72; rector St. John's, Johnson City, Tenn., 1972-75; bishop of Mo. St. Louis, 1975-93.

JONES, WILLIAM ERNEST, chemistry educator; b. Sackville, N.B., Can., Aug. 7, 1936; s. Frederick W. and Jennie E. (Tuttle) J.; m. Norma Florence McKinney Reid, Aug. 9, 1958; children: Mary Ellen E., Jennifer A.J., Sarah A.L., K. Martha M. B.Sc., Mt. Allison U., 1958, M.Sc., 1959; Ph.D., McGill U., 1963. Asst. prof. Dalhousie U., Halifax, N.S., 1962-68, assoc. prof., 1968-73; prof. chemistry Dalhousie U., Halifax, 1973-91, chmn. dept. chemistry, 1974-83; chmn. univ. senate Dalhousie U., Halifax, N.S., Can., 1983-89; prof. chemistry, dean of sci. Saint Mary's U., Halifax, N.S., Can., 1989-91; prof. chemistry, v.p. acad. affairs U. Windsor, Ont., Can., 1991—, prof. chemistry, 1991—. Contbr. articles to profl. jours. Fellow Chem. Inst. Can.; mem. Can. Assn. Physicists, Spectroscopy Soc. Can., Sigma Xi. Home: 2555 St Patrick's Ave, Windsor, ON Canada N9E 3G5 Office: U Windsor, 401 Sunset Ave, Windsor, ON Canada N9B 3P4

JONES-GROOMS, REBECCA S., deaf education educator, consultant; b. Springfield, Ill., Nov. 21, 1955; d. James Luther and Clara Jean (Stewart) J.; m. David L. Grooms, Nov. 21, 1987; 1 child Rachel Faith Jones-Grooms. BS in Deaf Edn., MacMurray Coll., Jacksonville, Ill., 1977; MS in Ednl. Adminstrn., Ill. State U., Normal, 1986. Cert. tchr. type 75 K-12 gen. adminstrv., type 10 K-12 deaf and hard of hearing. Tchr. Williamson County Spec. Edn., Marion, Ill., 1978-81; total commn. cons. U. Ill., Springfield, 1984-85; study skills specialist Lincoln Land C.C., Springfield, 1981-85; interpreter So. Ill. U., Carbondale, 1986-87; tchr. Williamson County Spl. Edn., Marion, Ill., 1986-88; adult edn. instr. John A. Logan Coll., Carterville, Ill., 1988-92; asst. prof. deaf studies MacMurray Coll., Jacksonville, Ill., 1994—; cons.-sign lang. U. Ill., Springfield, 1984-85; supervisor student tchrs. MacMurray Coll., Jacksonville, 1994—. Co-author: (curriculum base) Study Skills Success, 1984. Mem. Am. Assn. Univ. Profs., Ill. Tchrs. of Hearing Impaired, Internat. Vineyard Christian Fellowship. Office: MacMurray Coll Box 1079 447 E College Jacksonville IL 62650

JONSSON, SKULI, construction company executive; b. 1949. With The Law Co. Inc., Wichita, Kans., 1970-74; v.p. Midwest Drywall Co., Inc., Wichita, Kans., 1974—. Office: Midwest Drywall Co Inc 1351 S Reca St Wichita KS 67209*

JOODI, PIROOZ, engineer; b. Tehran, Iran, Apr. 4, 1951; came to U.S., 1975; s. Mahmood and Shokoofeh (Pourmehdian) J.; m. Ellen Woke, Sept. 9, 1955; children: Christopher, Joanthan, Benjamin and Nicholas (twins.). BS, Pahlavi U., 1972; MS, Fairleigh Dickinson U., 1978; postdoctoral, Columbia U., 1983. Registered profl. engr. Ohio. Engr. Curtiss Wright, Passaic, N.J., 1978, Burns & Roe, Inc., ORadell, N.J., 1978-79; engr. Gibbs & Hill, Inc., N.Y.C., 1979-82, sr. engr., 1982-85; sr. engr. Am. Elec. Power, Columbus, Ohio, 1985-93; prin. info. engr. Boeing Info. Svcs., Inc., Columbus, Ohio, 1993-94, mgr., 1994—. Mem. IEEE, Air Force Communications Engring. Assn. (membership chair 1994—), Data Warehouse Inst., Columbia U. Alumni Assn. Office: Boeing Info Svcs Inc 77 Outer Belt St Columbus OH 43213

JORDAN, JIM, state legislator; m. Polly Jordan; children: Rachel, Benjamin, Jessie, Isaac. BS, U. Wis., 1986; MA, Ohio State U., 1991. Asst. wrestling coach Ohio State U., Columbus; rep. dist. 85 Ohio Ho. of Reps., Columbus. Mem. Champaign County Rep. Exec. Com., Mad River Valley Young Rep. Club, Citizens Against Govt. Waste, Right to Life Orgns. Big Ten and NCAA wrestling champion, 1985, 86.

JORDAN, MARK A., agricultural engineer; b. Rensselaer, Ind., Jan. 18, 1970. BS in Agrl. Engring., Purdue U., West Lafayette, Ind., 1992. Design engr. John Deere, Ottumwa, Iowa, 1993—. Mem. Am. Soc. Agrl. Engrs. Roman Catholic. Office: John Deere Co Ottumwa Wks 928 E Vine St Ottumwa IA 52501-4352

JORDAN, MARK D., school administrator; b. Chgo., Oct. 22, 1953; s. Herbert and Lavina Eliza (Holgate) J.; m. Verna Zemorra Harris, Aug. 1, 1981; 1 child, Jeremy Ajani. BA in Edn., Chgo. State U., 1976; MEd, Nat. Louis U., 1993. Cert. tchr., Ill. Tchr. Chgo. Pub. Schs., 1976—; asst. prin. Gompers Fine Arts Sch., Chgo., 1989—; bd. dirs. Suzuki Music Acad. Chgo., 1978-87; adviser leadership conf. Ill. State Bd. Edn., Springfield, 1990—; child expert panelist McDonalds Corp., Chgo., 1990; facilitator Nat. Bd. Profl. Teaching Standards, Chgo., 1991; oresebter address Presdl. Commn. on Music Edn., Chgo. and Washington, 1990. Organist Greater Instnl. Meth. Ch., Chgo., 1983—; accompanist Chgo. All-City Youth Chorus, 1984—. Named Disting. Educator Ill. State Bd. Edn.-Milken Family Found., 1989, Maremont Dedicated Tchr. Chgo. Region PTA, 1989; recipient Nat. Excellence in Edn. award Burger King/Nat. Assn. Secondary Sch. Prins., 1990, Cert. Appreciation Ednl. Svc. Region Cook County, Ill., 1993, Mayoral Proclamation of Ednl. Excellence from Hon. Mayor Richard M. Daley, Chgo., 1993, Thanks to Tchrs. award Sta WBBM-TV, Bennigan's Corp., Chgo. State U., 1993; grantee Chgo. Found. Edn., 1991. Mem. Assn. Supervision and Curriculum Instrn., Music Educators Nat. Conf., Ill. Music Educators Assn., Am. Choral Dirs. Assn., Ill. Alliance Arts Edn., Nat. Dropout Prevention Assn. Home: 8156 S Rhodes Ave Chicago IL 60619-5024 Office: Gompers Fine Arts Sch 12302 S State St Chicago IL 60628-6811

JORDAN, MARY LEE, retired elementary education educator; b. Cin., Oct. 22, 1931; m. T. Paul Jordan, July 29, 1975 (dec. 1988); children: Aaron, Marc, Carrie. BS in Edn., U. Cin., 1965, AA, 1984. First grade tchr. St. Louis County, Mo., 1963-65; first grade, kindergarten tchr. Cin., 1965-80;

sec. personnel dept. Longview State Hosp., 1983; word processor Nat. Inst. Occupational Safety & Health, 1984; bookkeeper L. Levine & Co., Inc., 1985-88; Bd. dirs., membership chmn., newsletter co-producer Cin. Alliance for the Mentally Ill, 1983-86; park ranger U.S. Nat. Park Svc., Cin., 1993—. Author: History of Camp Dennison, Ohio, 1956. Pres. Cin. chpt. Zero Population Growth, 1976. Mem. AAUW (v.p. Cin. br. 1994—, bd. dirs. 1970-71), LWV (pres. N.C. br. 1994—, program coord. 1970-71), Am. Horse Show Assn., Ohioana Libr. Assn., DAR (vice-regent, mus. trustee Mariemont, Ohio chpt. 1988-89, regent 1990-91). Home: 27 Sherry Rd Cincinnati OH 45215-4225

JORDAN, MICHAEL JEFFERY, professional basketball player, retired baseball player; b. Bklyn., Feb. 17, 1963; s. James and Deloris J.; m. Juanita Vanoy, Sept., 1989; 2 sons: Jeffery Michael, Marcus James; 1 daughter: Jasmine. Student, U. N.C., 1981-84. Basketball player Chicago Bulls, 1984-93, 95—; baseball player Chicago White Sox AA Team, 1994-95; mem. NCAA Championship Team, 1982, U.S. Olympic Team (received Gold Medal), 1984, 92; holder record for most points in an NBA playoff game with 63. Author: RareAir: Michael on Michael, 1993. Recipient Naismith award, 1984, Wooden award, 1984, Rookie of Yr. award, NBA, 1985, IBM award, 1985, 89, Schick Pivotal Player award, 1985, 89; named Seagram's NBA Player of Yr., 1987, Slam-Dunk Championship winner, 1987, 88; named to Sporting News All-Am. first team, 1983-84, NBA All-Star team, 1985-93, 96, All NBA First Team, 1987-93, 96, NBA All-Def. Team, 1988-93, 96, NBA All-Star Game Most Valuable Player, 1988, 96, NBA Def. Player of Yr., 1988, NBA Most Valuable Player, 1988, 91, 92, 96, NBA Finals MVP 1991, 92, 93, 96; mem. NBA championship team, 1991, 92, 93, 96. Office: Chgo Bulls 1901 W Madison St Chicago IL 60612

JORDAN, SHARIE CECILIA, industrial artist; b. Grand Rapids, Mich., Sept. 12, 1961; d. Erwin Francis and Ardis Jean (Gilbert) Schmuker; m. Thomas William Jordan, Dec. 4, 1982. Registered well drilling contractor, Mich., 1996. Fashion cons. Mullberry Bush, Houghton Lake, Mich., 1982-84; freelance artist Houghton Lake, Mich., 1984-90; owner Jordan Illustration and Design, Houghton Lake, Mich., 1991—; co-owner Jordan Well Drilling, Houghton Lake, Mich., 1994—; cons. Buyers Guide Weekly, Houghton, 1988-90. Founding chmn. Annual Meml. Day Parade, Houghton Lake, 1992—. Recipient Emily Hilton-Janice Reeney Art award, 1979. Mem. Eagle Aux. (chaplain 1991-92, activity chmn. 1991-92, trustee 1992-94, v.p. 1992-94, Mrs. Eagle award 1991-92, Outstanding Vol. Work and Svc. award 1991-92).

JORGENSEN, ANN, farmer; b. Cedar Rapids, Iowa, Sept. 16, 1940; d. Kenneth Edward and Velma Ann (Baumhoefener) Fry; m. Marlyn L. Jorgensen, Feb. 27, 1961; children: Christopher, Peter, Timothy, Jennifer. BA, U. Iowa, 1962. Lic. commodity broker. Tax acct. Bill Burrell Tax Svc., Urbana, Iowa, 1968-70, Hansen Acctg., Vinton, Iowa, 1970-75; commodity broker First Mid. Am., Cedar Rapids, 1975-85; owner Lakeview Enterprises, Osage Beach, Mo., 1975-85; v.p., treas. Timberlane Hogs, Ltd., Garrison, Iowa, 1971—; mng. ptnr., owner Jorg-Anna Farms, Garrison, 1963—; pres., founder Farm Home Offices, Vinton, 1981—; bd. dirs. Farm Bur. Mut. Funds, Des Moines; commr. Interstate Agrl. Grain Commn. Midwest Compact, 1986-88; mem. Agriculture Products Adv. Bd., Des Moines, 1990—, bd. dirs.; spkr. in field; mem. environ. com. Nat. Pork Producers Coun., 1996—; chair info. tech. com. Am. Farm Bur. Fedn., 1996—. Author: Put PaperWork in its Place, 1982; contbr. articles to profl. jours. Mem., chair Iowa Arts Coun., 1973-79; regent Iowa Bd. Regents, 1979-85; dir., pres. Iowa Alcoholic Beverages Commr., Des Moines, 1985-88; nat. chair Tauke for U.S. Senate, Iowa, 1987-88; bd. dirs. Iowa Dept. Econ. Devel., 1988—; chair bd. Iowa Rural Devel. Coun., 1991-95; mem. Iowa Supreme Ct. Study Com., 1995-96. Named to Iowa Vol. Hall of Fame, 1989. Mem. AACC (bd. dirs. 1995—), Vinton Am. Assn. U. Women (various offices 1980—), Iowa Pub. TV Found. (sec. 1987-95). Home: 1965 64th St Garrison IA 52229-9647 Office: Farm Home Offices PO Box 840 Vinton IA 52349-0840

JORGENSEN, DANIEL FRED, academic director; b. May 3, 1947; m. Susan Jorgensen, June 20, 1969; children: Kari, Becky. BA in Journalism, S.D. State U., 1969, MS in Journalism, 1974; postgrad., Colo. State U.; grad. with honors, U.S. Army's Def. Info. Sch., 1970. Writer news and sports Sioux Falls (S.D.) Argus-Leader, 1969-70; asst. editor news and sports, part-time instr. S.D. State U. Comm. Office, 1972-74; from publ. editor to asst. dir. Colo. State U., 1974-78; editor news and sports Hot Springs (S.D.) Star, 1978-81; exec. dir. Black Hills (S.D.) Girl Scout Coun., 1981-83; dir. devel. and pub. rels. St. Martin's Acad., Rapid City, S.D., 1983-84; dir. news svc. St. Olaf Coll., Northfield, Minn., 1984-88, dir. pub. rels., 1988—; weekly humor columnist "Jargon" appears in 11 weekly and daily newspapers, Minn. and S.D.; bd. dirs. Norwest Bank Northfield. Author: Killer Blizzard, 1976, Sky Hook, 1985, Dawn's Diamond Defense, 1988, Andrea's Best Shot, 1988, Kelli's Choice, 1991; Jargon--The Book, 1995; co-author: (with R. Brandt) Family Hiking Trails in South Dakota, 1981; contbg. author: Tapestry, 1985; contbr. articles to popular mags. Bd. dirs. Northfield Hosp., 1990—, United Way, 1989-91, vice-chair, 1989-90, chair 1990-91, Northfield Rotary Club, 1987-92, v.p., 1990-91, pres. 1991-92, Northfield Hist. Soc., 1989-90, Northfield Community Edn. and Recreation, 1987-90, chair 1988-90, Northfield Arts Guild, 1985-86; mem. coun. St. John's Luth. Ch., 1989-90, chair edn. bd.; parents adv. coun. Greenvale/Longfellow Elem. Sch., 1985-88, chair, 1987-88; chair Community Edn. Youth Adv. Com., 1986. 1st lt. U.S. Army, 1970-72. Named to first class Leadership Rapid City, 1982-83; honored for community svc. City of Northfield, 1992; recipient Rice County Vol. award, 1992. Mem. Coun. for the Advancement and Support of Edn. (nat. coms. mem. 1991—), Nat. Assn. Sci. Writers, Minn. Press Assn., Kappa Tau Alpha, Sigma Delta Chi. Home: 505 Wilson Ct Northfield MN 55057-1374 Office: St Olaf Coll Pub Rels Ofc Northfield MN 55057

JORGENSEN, KAY SUSAN, state legislator; b. Winner, S.D., Mar. 25, 1951; d. Arnold and Twyla (Richter) J.; m. Michael R. Pangburn, 1975; children: Merideth Kay, Christopher Joe. Grad., Ft. Smith Auction Sch., 1967; student, Chapman Coll., 1971; BS, Black Hills State Coll., 1974. Mem. S.D. Ho. of Reps., 1979-84, 93—, mem. retirement laws, state affairs and taxation coms.; auctioneer, 1967—; substitute tchr. Highmore, S.D., 1975-76; page adv. S.D. Legislature, 1975-78; mgr., owner Bell Boy Drive-In, Spearfish, S.D., 1976-77, Food Concession Black Hills Passion Play, 1977-80, 84—; pvt. bus.; mem. exec. bd. Legis. Rsch. Coun., 1983; v.p. S.D. Bd. Regents, 1986-89; mem. S.D. Centennial Com., 1986-90, pres. 1986-88; bd. regents Midcontinental Regional Edn. Lab., 1989—, pres. bd. regents, 1987-88. Bd. dirs. High Plains Heritage Ctr., 1979-80, 88. Named Outstanding Alumnus Black Hill State Coll., 1981, Centennial Alumnus, 1989. Mem. AAUW, Queen City Bus. and Profl. Women, High Plains Heritage Soc. (exec. dir. 1979-82), Black Hills Coll. Alumni Assn. (past pres., bd. dirs. 1976-79, 89—). Home: 1909 Stagebarn Cir Spearfish SD 57783-2945*

JORGENSEN, PAUL C., computer scientist, educator; b. Oak Park, Ill., May 27, 1942; s. George T. and Alice L. (Carlson) J.; m. Carol Ann Griggs, July 1, 1978; children: Kirsten, Katia. BA, North Ctrl. Coll., Naperville, Ill., 1964; MA, U. Ill., 1965; PhD, Ariz. State U., 1985. Tech. staff GTE, Phoenix, 1965-86; asst. prof. Ariz. State U., Tempe, 1986-88; assoc. prof. Grand Valley State U., Allendale, Mich., 1988—. Author: Software Testing: A Craftsman's Approach, 1995; co-author: Structural Methods, 1993, Mathematics for Data Processing, 1970. Mem. IEEE, Assn. Computing Machinery, Sigma Xi. Home: 6967 Camino Del Rey Rockford MI 49341 Office: Grand Valley State U Dept of Computer Science Allendale MI 49401

JORGENSEN, ROBERT WILLIAM, manufacturing engineer; b. Allegan, Mich., Jan. 8, 1946. BS in Aerospace Engring., U. Mich., 1969; AS, Radio Electronics Tech. Sch., South Bend, Ind., 1971. Engr. Kawneer Corp., Niles, Mich., 1970-80; tech. dir. Raco, Inc., South Bend, Ind., 1980—; mem. adv. coun. Underwriter's Assn. Inventor: holds 22 patents on elec. boxes and fittings. Mem. Underwriters Labs., Nat. Elec. Mfrs. Assn., Nat. Fire Protection Assn., Internat. Assn. Elec. Insps. Home: 1353 Thompson Rd Niles MI 49120-9332 Office: Raco Inc PO Box 4002 South Bend IN 46634

JORSTAD, ROBERT BERNARD, geologist, educator; b. Bemidji, Minn., May 15, 1946; s. Robert E. and Bernadette (Given) J.; m. Mary E. Abrahamson, Dec. 21, 1969; children: Connie M., Robert J. BS in Edn., Bemidji State U., 1969, MS in Edn., 1972; PhD, U. Idaho, 1983. Sci. tchr. Isle (Minn.) High Sch., 1968-69, East Grand Forks (Minn.) Jr. High Sch., 1972-75; teaching asst. U. Idaho, Moscow, 1980-81; geologist, educator Eastern Ill. U., Charleston, 1982—. Contbg. editor: Gen. Environ. Econ. Geology Stratigraphy East-Ctrl. Ill., 1991. The Status and Future of Field Geology, 1993; author geology lab. exercises, computer programs. With U.S. Army, 1969-71, Vietnam. Mem. Nat. Assn. Geology Tchrs. (v.p. ctrl. sect. 1993, pres. ctrl. sect. 1993-94), Geol. Soc. Am., Am. Assn. Stratigraphic Palynologists, Soc. Econ. Paleontologists and Mineralologists, Computer Oriented Geol. Soc. Office: Eastern Ill U Geology Geography Dept Charleston IL 61920

JOSCELYN, KENT BUCKLEY, lawyer, research scientist; b. Binghamton, N.Y., Dec. 18, 1936; s. Raymond Miles and Gwen Buckley (Smith) J.; children: Kathryn Anne, Jennifer Sheldon. BS, Union Coll., 1957; JD, Albany Law Sch., 1960. Bar: N.Y. 1961, U.S. Ct. Mil. Appeals 1962, D.C. 1967, Mich. 1979. Atty., adviser Hdqrs. USAF, Washington, 1965-67; asso. prof. forensic studies Coll. Arts and Scis., Ind. U., Bloomington, 1967-76, dir. Inst. Rsch. in Pub. Safety, 1970-75; head policy analysis div. Hwy. Safety Rsch. Inst., U. Mich., 1976-81, dir. transp. planning and policy, Urban Tech., Environ. Planning Program, 1981-84; prin. firm Joscelyn and Treat, P.C., 1981-93; prin. Joscelyn, McNair and Jeffrey, P.C., 1993—; cons. Law Enforcement Assistance Adminstrn., U.S. Dept. Justice, 1969-72; Gov.'s appointee as regional dir. Ind. Criminal Justice Planning Agy., also vice chmn. Ind. Organized Crime Prevention Council, 1969-72; commr. pub. safety City of Bloomington, 1974-76. Served to capt. USAF, 1961-64. Mem. NAS, ABA, D.C. Bar Assn., Mich. Bar Assn., N.Y. State Bar Assn., Internat. Bar Assn., NRC, Transp. Research Bd. (chmn. motor vehicle and traffic law com. 1979-82), Am. Soc. Criminology (life), Assn. for the Advancement Automotive Medicine (life), Soc. Automotive Engrs., Acad. Criminal Justice Scis. (life), Assn. Chiefs Police (assoc.), Nat. Safety Council, Assn. Former Intelligence Officers (life), Product Liability Adv. Coun., Sigma Xi, Theta Delta Chi. Editor Internat. Jour. Criminal Justice. Office: Joscelyn McNair and Jeffrey PC 110 Miller Ave Ste 100 PO Box 130589 Ann Arbor MI 48113-0589

JOSE, VICTOR RUDOLPH, publishing executive, editor; b. Indpls., Mar. 13, 1922; s. Victor Rudolph and Amy (Elliott) J.; m. Faye Stewart, June 3, 1944; children: Cynthia, V. Stewart, James, David. BA with honors, Swarthmore Coll., 1944; MA in Journalism, Northwestern U., 1947. Editor, publisher The Graphic Newspaper, Richmond, Ind., 1953-90; owner Graphic Partners, Richmond, Ind., 1990—; dir. First Bank of Richmond, Ind., 1971-94; founder Ind. Free Papers of Am., 1980. Author: Thailand Revisited, 1975. Bd. dirs. Salvation Army, Richmond, Ind., 1976—; pres. Wayne County (Ind.) Found., 1987-92. Lt. (j.g.) U.S.N., 1943-46. Mem. Richmond Area C. of C. (pres. 1971-72, Citizen of Yr. award 1986), Nat. Assn. Advtsing. Publishers, Kiwanis Club (pres. 1963, Citizen of Yr. award 1983), Elks (Citizen of Yr. award 1971). Presbyterian. Home: 15 N W 10th St Richmond IN 47374

JOSEPH, CHARLES HOMER, III, emergency services director; b. Cleve., Nov. 6, 1948; s. Charles Jr. and Virginia (Sloss) J.; 1 child, Kristin. MS, Case Western Res. U., 1992. Lic. ind. social worker. Counselor Cleve. Drug Abuse Program, 1973-74; drug edn. coord. Free Clinic, Cleve., 1974-76; warehouseman Clark Oil and Chem., Cleve., 1978-82; planner Am. Greetings Corp., Cleve., 1983-84; foreman Anderson Door Co., Cleve., 1984-86; social worker Sr. Achievement Ctr., Lorain, Ohio, 1986-87; dir. Cath. Comm., Lorain, 1987-90; dir. emergency svcs. Cath. Charities, Cleve., 1990—; vol. Peace Corps, Sorokdo, South Korea, 1976-78; bd. dirs. N.E. Ohio Coaliton for Homeless, Cleve., 1992. Bd. dirs. WCPN Pub. Radio, Cleve., 1990-92. Mem. NASW. Office: Cath Charities 1111 Superior Ave Cleveland OH 44114-2507

JOSEPH, DONALD LOUIS, management consultant; b. Chgo., Dec. 29, 1942; s. Herbert H. and Florence (Gaertner) J.; BS in Engring. Sci., Washington U., St. Louis, 1964; MBA, Harvard U., 1966; m. Joyce H. Brand, Dec. 20, 1981; children: Richard A., Michael B. Cert. mgmt. cons. Systems Engr. Teletype Corp., Skokie, Ill., 1966-68; sr. assoc. Brandon Applied Systems, Inc., Chgo., 1968-71; sr. cons. Daniel D. Howard Assoc., Inc., Chgo., 1971-72; dir. mgmt. systems Opelika Mfg. Corp., Chgo., 1972-77; dep. exec. dir. Am. Soc. Clin. Pathologists, Chgo., 1978-80, v.p. fin. and adminstrn., 1980-81; pres. DLJ Assos., Chgo., 1981—; sr. project cons. Stone Mgmt. Corp., 1982-84; bd. dirs. Inst. Mgmt. Cons., Chgo. chpt., mgmt. adv. svcs. Shepard, Schwartz & Harris, C.P.A.s, Chgo., 1985-87 ; dir. Office Automation Systems, Hise, Donahue & Assocs., Inc., 1983-84; controller Meystel, Inc., 1987-92, v.p., 1993-94; v.p., asst. sec. Russell-Field Paper Co., Inc., 1994—; mem. faculty Elmhurst Mgmt. Program Elmhurst Coll., 1982-89. Bd. dirs. Horizon House, Chgo., pres., 1981-82, 89-90; nominating com. Glencoe Sch. Bd., 1994—, vice chmn., 1996—. Mem. Harvard U. Bus. Sch. Assn. Chgo., Am. Soc. Assn. Execs., Inst. Mgmt. Cons. (dir., v.p. membership Midwest chpt.), Tau Beta Pi, Omicron Delta Kappa. Home: 1125 Hohlfelder Rd Glencoe IL 60022-1018

JOSEPH, JEFF, investment advisor; b. Chgo., Sept. 4, 1957. Cert. funds specialist, Inst. Cert. Funds Specialists, 1993. lectr. on investments. Investment advisor Joseph Trading, Chgo., 1983-92; pres. Natomas Capital Mgmt., Glenview, Ill., 1992—; participant Profl. Fund Advisor, no-load mut. fund cons. svc. Past pres. Assn. for Ret. Citizens Advantage. Mem. Midwest Soc. Profl. Cons. Office: Natomas Capital Mgmt 1245 Waukegan Rd Glenview IL 60025-3068

JOSEPH, MARTIN F., chemical engineer; b. Oct. 14, 1968. BSChemE, U. Cin., 1992. Chem. engring. co-op USEPA Haz Wastewater Treatment, Cin., 1988, G.E. Aircraft Engines ACSC, Cin., 1989, Westinghouse Material Co. of Ohio, Cin., 1990; specialist II Ohio EPA Divsn. of Air Pollution Control, Columbus, Ohio, 1993—. Home: 2450 Onyx Ct Grove City OH 43123 Office: Ohio EPA DAPC 1600 WaterMark Dr Columbus OH 43215-1034

JOSEPH, RENÉ MICHELE, artist, painter; b. St. Paul, Feb. 19, 1958; s. Earl and Alma Joseph. BES, U. Minn., 1979; studied with, Mary Abbott. Math. and poetry tchr. for learning disabled James J. Hill Sch., St. Paul, 1976-77; art intern Minn. Mus. Art, St. Paul, 1978; conf. speaker Mpls. Coll. Art and Design, 1979; teaching asst. U. Minn., 1977-80; buyer art supplies N.C. Gen. Store, 1983-85; art tchr. Anderson Elem., 1984; art resident Mpls. Park Bd., 1989, 94; fundraiser Art Paper, 1989-91; designer shaped painting for archtl. site Mr. & Mrs. Drew Simonson, Mpls., 1988; program developer, fundraiser lecture series U. Minn., Mpls., 1978-79. Contbg. author: Best of Art Calendar, V. 1, 1992, 95. Neighborhood rep. Mpls. Art Commn., 1991-92. Recipient awards Mpls. Arts Commn., 1988, Met. Arts Coun., St. Paul, 1989, NYU, 1990, Arts Midwest, 1992. Studio: 328 3d Ave NE Minneapolis MN 55413

JOSEPHSON, JOHN RICHARD, computer scientist; b. Cleve., Nov. 2, 1944; s. Robert Heidler and Ruth (Shiffman) J.; m. Susan Victoria Goodman, Sept. 13, 1966; children: Jason Ananda, Seth Joshu. BS in Math., Ohio State U., 1968, MS, 1970, PhD in Philosophy, 1982. Teaching assoc. in philosophy Ohio State U., Columbus, 1973-79, teaching assoc., lectr. in math., 1979-83, lectr. dept. computer and info. sci., 1983, postdoctoral rsch. assoc. artificial intelligence group, 1983-85, asst. dir. lab. for artificial intelligence rsch. (LAIR), 1985-88, assoc. dir. LAIR dept. computer and info. sci., 1988—, rsch. scientist dept. computer and info. sci., 1989—; chair workshop on abductive inference AAAI-91 Nat. Conf. on Artificial Intelligence, 1991; mem. tech. adv. bd. Pilot's Assoc. Program, 1987-91; mem. organizing com. Workshop on Plan Recognition Internat. Joint Conf. on Artificial Intelligence, 1989. Co-editor: Abductive Inference, 1994; contbr. articles to profl. jours. Home: 93 E Riverglen Dr Worthington OH 43085-3665 Office: Ohio State U LAIR CIS Dept 2015 Neil Ave 395 Dreese Lab Columbus OH 43210

JOSLYN, WALLACE DANFORTH, psychologist; b. Cape Girardeau, Mo., Apr. 13, 1939; s. Lewis Danforth and Margaret Bernice (Gallup) J.; m. Annette Andre, Aug. 27, 1966 (div. Feb. 1969); m. Moreen V. Drescher, May 26, 1979; children: Jonathan David, Sarah Analisa Malathi. BA, U. Va., 1961; MS, U. Wis., 1965, PhD, 1967. Lic. psychologist, Iowa. Rsch. assoc. Oreg. Regional Primate Rsch. Ctr., Beaverton, 1967-71; clin. psychologist Dept. Vets. Affairs Med. Ctr., Knoxville, Iowa, 1972—; adj. asst. prof. U. Oreg. Health Scis. U., 1970; diplomate Viktor Frankl Inst. Logotherapy. Contbr. articles to profl. jours. Mem. Nat. Register for Health Care Providers in Psychology. Fellow NIMH. Home: 802 E Competine Knoxville IA 50138-1955 Office: VA Med Ctr Knoxville IA 50138

JOST, LEE FRED, employee benefits consultant; b. Milw., June 21, 1928; s. Gustav and Emily Jost; m. Mary Ellen Scalissi; 1 child, David; stepchildren: Jo Ellen, Scott, Jennifer. BS, Marquette U., 1952, MA, 1954. Tchr. Marquette U., Milw., 1952-56; physician liaison Wis. Med. Soc., Madison, 1956-60; benefit plan adminstr., employee benefits cons. Russell M. Tolley & Assocs., Milw., 1960-81; pres. Benefit Plan Adminstrn. Wis./Lee Jost & Assoc., Inc., Brookfield, Wis., 1981—; adminstrv. mgr. Bldg. Trades United Pension Trust Fund, Milw. area, 1960—. Co-author: Guide to Professional Benefit Plan Administration, 1980; co-editor: Benefit Plan Administration, 1988. Staff sgt. U.S. Army, 1946-48, Korea. Mem. Internat. Found. Employee Benefit Plans (bd. dirs., mem. com.), Soc. Profl. Benefit Adminstrs. (sec.-treas. 1989, pres. 1991), Am. Legion, Alpha Sigma Nu, Delta Sigma Rho.

JOY, MARILYN D., nurse; b. Rockford, Ill., Nov. 29, 1956. BSN, Viterbo Coll., 1978. RN, Ill.; cert. ACLS. Med.-surg., ICU nurse Rockford (Ill.) Meml. Hosp., 1978-80, 86-87; nurse, mgr. Willows Health Ctr., Rockford, 1980-86; cardiac ICU nurse St. Anthony Med. Ctr., Rockford, 1987-90; Medicare/home health nurse St. Therese Med. Ctr., Waukegan, Ill., 1991-95; ICU nurse Centegra No. Ill. Med. Ctr., McHenry, 1995—; resource nurse local ch., Rockford, 1984-86. Author poetry. Fellow Am. Biog. Inst. (award), Internat. Biog. Ctr. (award); mem. NAFE. Home: 4411 Sheffield Ct Gurnee IL 60031

JOYCE, CHRISTIE LYNNE, medical surgical nurse; b. Iola, Kans., Nov. 3, 1960; d. Altis Gordon and Peggy Ann (Dixon) Ferree; 1 child, Ryan A. LPN, Neosho County Coll., Chanute, Kans., 1979; RN, Newman Sch. Nursing, Emporia, Kans., 1982. LPN Allen County Hosp., Iola, 1979-82; RN St. John's Regional Med. Ctr., Joplin, Mo., 1982-87, RN, neuro coord. operating room, 1987—, RN, case cart coord., 1988—, RN, inventory control coord., 1989—, RN, computer coord., 1990—, operational budget/materials mgr. surgery ctr., 1994—. Active local chs. and orgns. for missionary work. Mem. Assn. Operating Room Nurses, Am. Assn. Neurosci. Nurses. Republican. Office: Saint Johns Med Ctr 2727 Mc Clelland Blvd Joplin MO 64804-1626

JOYCE, EMMETT MICHAEL, radio broadcaster; b. Durham, N.C., June 27, 1944; s. Emmett Robert and Alice Durham (Fowler) J.; m. Demetra Lattos, Jan. 2, 1967; children: Jamie Michelle, Michael Durham. PhB in Comms., Northwestern U., 1977, MA in Speech, 1979. Writer suburban features Chgo. Tribune, 1982-83; broadcaster Voice of Am., Chgo., 1985—; freelance writer Chgo., 1978—. Co-author: Shoot to Miss, 1980. Home: 440 Lake St Crystal Lake IL 60014 Office: Voice of Am 230 S Dearborn St Chicago IL

JOYCE, MICHAEL DANIEL, personal resource management therapist and consultant, neurolearning therapist; b. St. Cloud, Minn., June 8, 1948; s. Francis Daniel and Bernadette (Ferkinhoff) J.; m. Patricia Mary Boom, July 7, 1969. BA in Psychology and Sociology, St. Cloud State U., 1973, postgrad., 1977; postgrad., Moorhead State U., 1993, Atwood Inst., 1993, Biofeedback Tng. and Treatment Ctr., 1994. Cert. behavior analyst, Minn.; cert. rsch. analyst, Minn.; cert. master practitioner of neuro-linguistic programming, Colo.; cert. hypnotherapist, neurolearning therapist. Resident mgr. Dan J. Brutger, Inc., St. Cloud, 1969-71; rsch. analyst Faribault (Minn.) State Hosp., 1974-75, behavior analyst, 1975-76; therapist/behavior analyst Ctrl. Minn. Mental Health Ctr., St. Cloud, 1977-78; emotional/behavior disabled facilitator, chpt. 1 tutor Perham (Minn.) Dent Schs., 1978-92; tech. cons. Inclusive Edn. Tech. Assistance Team, Region IV, State of Minn., Perham, 1991-93, Personal Resource Strategies, Vergas, Minn., 1994—. Co-author: Life-Threatening Behavior: Analysis and Intervention, 1982. Coord. Youth Assn. for Retarded Citizens, St. Cloud, 1977-78; respite care provider Ctrl. Minn. Mental Health Ctr., St. Cloud and Perham, 1977-78, 79-86; vol. Perham Schs., 1978—, Spl. Olympics - Winter Games, Duluth, Minn., 1980, 81. Named Mem. of Yr. Minn. Sch. Employees Assn., 1989. Mem. Neuro-Linguistic Programming (cert. master level), Internat. Med. and Dental Hypnotherapy Assn. (cert. neurolearning therapist). Home: RR 1 Box 311A Vergas MN 56587-9760

JOYCE, MICHAEL STEWART, foundation executive, political science educator; b. Cleve., July 5, 1942; s. William Michael and Anna Mae (Stewart) J.; m. Mary Jo Olsen, June 2, 1989; children from previous marriage: Mary Therese, Martin Michael. B.A., Cleve. State U., 1967; Ph.D., Walden U., 1974. Intake clk. Cuyahoga County Welfare Dept., Cleve., 1961-64, unit supr., 1964-65; tchr., athletic dir. St. Adelbert Sch., Berea, Ohio, 1965-67; tchr., coach St. Edward High Sch., Lakewood, Ohio, 1965-67; social sci. research assoc. Ednl. Research Council Am., Cleve., 1970-73, asst. dir. social scis., 1973-74, asst. to pres., 1974-75; instr. polit. sci. Baldwin-Wallace Coll., 1972-73; exec. dir. Morris Goldseker Found., Balt., 1975-78, Inst. for Ednl. Affairs, N.Y.C., 1978-79, John M. Olin Found., N.Y.C., 1979-85; pres. Lynde and Harry Bradley Found., Milw., 1985—, also bd. dirs.; trustee John M. Olin Found., N.Y.C., 1982-85, Pinkerton Found., N.Y.C., 1984—, Found. for Cultural Rev., N.Y.C., 1983—, Md. Acad. Scis., Balt., 1976-78, Md. Hist. Soc., Balt., 1977-78; sec. Inst. for Ednl. Affairs, Washington, 1983—; panelist NEH grant rev., Washington, 1983, 84; chmn. Philanthropy Roundtable, 1987—; mem. selection com. Clare Booth Luce Fund, 1988—. Author: (textbook) Youth and the Law, 1973; contbg. editor: (8 vols. textbook series) The Human Adventure, 1971, (2 vols. textbook series) The American Adventure, 1975; contbr. articles to profl. jours. and chpts. to books. Mem. Cardinal's Com. on Laity Archdiocese N.Y., 1983—; mem. commn. Catholic Social Teaching and U.S. Economy, 1984-85; nat. co-chmn. Scholars for Reagan-Bush, 1984; mem. exec. com. Pres.'s Pvt. Sector Study Cost Control the Grace Commn., 1983—; exec. com. Caths. for Bush, 1988; mem. adv. bd. USIA for Internat. Ednl. Exchange, 1982—; mem. Eastern Regional Selection Panel on White House Fellowships, 1983—; asst. to chmn. Nat. Productivity Adv. Com., 1982; mem. Presdl. task force on Pvt. Sector Initiatives, 1981; mem. Presdl. transition team, 1980-81; trustee N.Y. Foundling Hosp., 1982-86, Orch. Piccola, Balt., 1976-78. Mem. Mt. Pelerin Soc., Sovereign Mil. Order Malta, Union League Club (N.Y.C.), Milw. Club., University Club. (Milw.). Republican. Roman Catholic. Home: Cedarburg WI 53012 Office: Lynde and Harry Bradley Found 777 E Wisconsin Ave Milwaukee WI 53202-5302

JUAREZ, MARTIN, priest; b. Kansas City, Kans., Mar. 23, 1946; s. Martin Huerta and Hermelinda (Rocha) J. AS, Colby Community Coll., 1971; BA in sociology, U. Mo., Kansas City, 1974; MDiv, St. Thomas Sem., Denver, 1985; cert. in Hispanic ministry, Oblate Sch. of Theology, San Antonio, 1991, Mexican-Am. Cultural Ctr., 1991. Priest Archdiocese of Kansas City, Kans., 1981—. Bd. dirs. Pioneer Village, Topeka, 1983-88; co-dir. El Centro, Topeka, 1989. Mem. Kans. Registered Animal Hosp. Techs. Assn., N.Am. Veterinary Tech. Assn., U. Mo. Alumni Assn., KC. Office: PO Box 410695 Kansas City MO 64141-0695

JUDD, LAURENCE CECIL, sociology and Asian studies educator, consultant; b. Houston, Aug. 27, 1920; s. Nathan Banks and Laura Cecilia (Lehmann) J.; m. Virginia Agnes (Moffat); children: Jonathan Bruce, Patrick Arthur, Kathryn Ann, David Alan, Steven Moffat. BA, Rice U., 1942; BD, Yale U., 1946; MS, Cornell U., 1954, PhD, 1961. Sec. youth work New Haven (Conn.) Conf. Chs., 1942-44; pastor Foxon Congl. Ch., East Haven, Conn., 1944-46; asst. min. Chinese Presbyn. Ch., San Francisco, 1946-47; missionary United Presbyn. Ch., China and Thailand, 1948-70; tchr. Bangkok Christian Coll., Thailand, 1948-51; acting mgr. Padung Rashdr Sch., Pitsanuloke, Thailand, 1951-53; dir. Nan Rural Project, Thailand, 1954-59; assoc. dir. rural life dept. Ch. Christ in Thailand, 1961-70; prof. sociology, dir. Asian studies program Ill. Coll., 1970-86; exec. sec. Christian Rural Fellowship Thailand, 1966-70, pres. Coun. Thai Studies, 1974-76; dir. Ill. Coll. S.E. Asia Study Tours, 1976, 80, 83, 86, rsch. assoc. Payap U., Chiang Mai, Thailand, 1986—. Author: Chao Rai Thai: Dry Rice Farmers in North Thailand, 1977, A Vision to Some, 1987, Chao Rai Thai 1987 Update, In Perspective: Trends in Rural Development Policy and Programs in Thailand 1947-87, 1989; editor: Rural Leaders Handbook (in Thai), 1968, JAX PAX News, 1986—; contbr. articles to jours. in field. Bd. dirs. Morgan County Inter Agy. Coun., 1971-79, chmn., 1973-74; bd. dirs.

Jacksonville Symphony Soc., 1971-81, Gt. Rivers Presbytery, 1970—; chmn. adv. coun. Health Edn. Ctr. West Cen. Ill., 1979-80, Prairie Coun. on Aging, 1991—, Project Life Area Agy. on Aging, 1992—; program chair Jacksonville Peace Coalition, 1986—. Comparative Edn. fellow Ford Found., 1960-61, Med. Humanities fellow So. Ill. U. Sch. Medicine, 1978; summer rsch. grantee U. Chgo., 1979. Mem. NAACP, Jacksonville Rotary, Rotary in Thailand, LWV, Assn. Asian Studies, Union Concerned Scientists, Physicians for Soc. Responsibility, Phi Kappa Phi. Democrat. Home and Office: 900 W Chambers Jacksonville IL 62650

JUDGE, BERNARD MARTIN, law bulletin editor, publisher; b. Chgo., Jan. 6, 1940; s. Bernard A. and Catherine Elizabeth (Halloran) J.; m. Kimberly A. Wehrli, July 9, 1966; children: Kelly, Bernard R., Jessica. Student, John Carroll U., 1957-61. Reporter City News Bur., Chgo., 1965-66; reporter Chgo. Tribune, 1966-72, city editor, 1974-79, asst. mng. editor met. news, 1979-83; editor, gen. mgr. City News Bur. Chgo., 1983-84; assoc. editor Chgo. Sun-Times, 1984-88; editor Chgo. Daily Law Bull., 1988—; pub. Chgo. Lawyer, 1989—; v.p. Law Bull. Pub. Co., Chgo., 1988—. Bd. dirs. Constnl. Rights Found., Chgo., 1992—, chmn. bd. dirs., 1995—; mem. bd. trustees Fenwick Cath. Prep. H.S., Oak Park, Ill., 1989—. Mem. Sigma Delta Chi. Home: 1141 N Euclid Ave Oak Park IL 60302-1218 Office: Law Bull Pub Co 415 N State St Chicago IL 60610-4607

JUDGE, JOHN EMMET, manufacturing company marketing executive; b. Grafton, N.D., May 5, 1912; s. Charles and Lillian (Johnson) J.; m. Clarita Garcia, Apr. 18, 1940; children: Carolyn Judge Stanley, John Emmet, Maureen Judge Barron, Eileen Judge Horowitz, Susan Judge Lloyd. B.S. in Elec. Engring., U. N.D., 1935. Asst. to adminstr. Rural Electrification Adminstrn., 1937-39, Fed. Works Agy., Washington, 1939-42; staff specialist Exec. Office Pres., Washington, 1942; staff Wallace Clark & Co. (mgmt. cons.), N.Y.C., 1943-46; v.p. Morgan Furniture Co., Asheville, N.C., 1946-48; mgr. financial analysis Lincoln-Mercury div. Ford Motor Co., 1949-53, asst. gen. purchasing agt., 1953-55, mgr. mdse. and product planning, 1955-58, marketing mgr., 1958-60; product planning mgr. Lincoln-Mercury div. Ford Motor Co., Dearborn, Mich., 1960-62; v.p. mktg. services Westinghouse Elec. Corp., Pitts., 1963-67; v.p. mktg. Indian Head, Inc., 1967-68; mktg. cons., 1969—; dir. Capital Corp. of Am. (investments), Intertek Industries, Kratos, Inc., Cashiers Plastics Corp., Cambridge Instruments, Inc.; Mem. adv. com. to U.S. sec. of commerce. Chmn. Birmingham Library Com., 1957; mem. bd. Boysville of Mich., 1957—. Named to Order of the Holy Sepulchre of Jerusalem. Mem. Am. Ordnance Assn., Soc. Advancement Mgmt., AAAS, N.A.M. (chmn. marketing com.), Am. Soc. M.E., Engring. Soc. Detroit, Nat. Assn. Accountants, Soc. Automotive Engrs., U. N.D. Alumni Assn. (pres.), KC, Sigma Tau, Alpha Tau Omega. Roman Catholic. Clubs: Detroit Athletic, Economic; Orchard Lake (Mich.). Address: S Lake Shore Dr Harbor Springs MI 49740

JUE, RICHARD, food service executive; b. Needles, Calif., June 14, 1956; s. Hoy Ngok and Jean (Chan) J.; m. Marlene Yee, Sept. 9, 1978; children; Alexander Richard, Jacqueline Elizabeth. BS in Bus., Ohio State U., 1978. Account mgr. Quaker Oats, Chgo., 1978-79; owner Golden Dragon, Cleve., 1979—; sales mgr. Seven Seas Trading, Cleve., 1986—; property mgr. RJW Co., Cleve., 1992—. Mem. Fraternal Order of Police Assn. Home: 16770 Lucky Bell Ln Chagrin Falls OH 44023-5161

JUENEMANN, JULIE ANN, psychologist, educator; b. Grosse Pointe, Mich., July 29, 1956; d. Joseph Guy Jr. and Betty Marjorie (Bourg) J.; m. Kurt Edward Stanley, June 21, 1980. BS with honors, Mich. State U., 1978; MA, U. Pa., 1980; PhD, Mich. State U., 1985. Lic. psychologist, Mich. Clin. child psychology intern dept. psychiatry Sch. of Medicine, U. N.C., Chapel Hill, 1983-84, vis. clin. instr. dept. psychiatry, 1985, vis. clin. asst. prof. psychiatry, 1985-86; psychologist, ind. contractor Evergreen Counseling Ctrs.-Ednl. Resources, St. Clair Shores, Mich., 1986-91; sch. psychologist Livonia (Mich.) Pub. Schs., 1989-91, student assistance and family edn. specialist, 1991—; psychologist, ind. contractor Adult-Youth Devel. Svcs., P.C., Farmington, Mich., 1991-93. Member PTA. Fellow NIMH, 1981-83; recipient Martin S. Wallach award U. N.C., 1984. Mem. APA, NASP, Mich. Assn. Sch. Psychologists, Mich. Psychol. Assn., Phi Kappa Phi, Alpha Lambda Delta. Home: 16340 Houghton Dr Livonia MI 48154-1234 Office: Livonia Pub Schs Kennedy Elem Sch 14201 Hubbard St Livonia MI 48154-4133

JUGEL, RICHARD DENNIS, corporate executive, management consultant; b. Winside, Nebr., July 25, 1942; s. Donald Jerome and Ilene Mae (Christensen) J.; m. Marlene Ann Meyer, Jan. 15, 1966; children: Lisa Ann, Lynn Marie. Student, Valparaiso U., 1960-61, Wayne State Coll., 1963. Mgr., dir. Info. Mgmt. Tech., Fargo, N.D., 1968-70; system engr., sales Electronic Data Systems, Dallas, 1970-75; data processing officer Mut. of Omaha, 1975-83; exec. v.p. NewAm. Tech., Inc., Omaha, 1983-85; pres. Richard D. Jugel & Co., Omaha, 1985-95; v.p. R&D Cydata, Inc., Omaha, 1995—; bd. dirs. New Age Systems, Inc., Omaha; cons. Distributed Info. Systems Corp., Dallas, 1984—, Dennison S. Doyle and Assocs., Washington, 1992—; v.p. dir. Paradigm Cons. Corp., 1990-91; sec., dir. Hamilton Color Lab., Inc., 1990—. Emergency coordinator USMC Affiliated Radio Service, Omaha. 1978-82; active disaster communications ARC, Omaha, 1980—. Mem. Data Processing Mgmt. Assn., Am. Guild Patient Account Mgrs., Nebr. Amateur Radio Emergency Svcs., Am. Radio Relay League (life), Amateur Trapshooting Assn. (life), AK-SAR-BEN Amateur Radio Club (life, pres. 1980). Republican. Lutheran. Home: 5005 S 181st Plz Omaha NE 68135-1917 Office: 111 S 108th Ave Omaha NE 68154-2621

JUHL, DANIEL LEO, manufacturing and marketing firm executive; b. Sioux City, Iowa, Aug. 18, 1935; s. Burnett Andrew and Margret Anne (Osinger) J.; m. Colleen Ann Eagan, Dec. 20, 1958; children: Gregory, Michael, Jennifer. Student, U. S.D., 1956; BSME, UCLA, 1959; postgrad., Harvard U., 1976. Design engr. Edler Industries, Newport Beach, Calif., 1959-61; v.p. mfg. Raybestos-Manhattan Corp. (now Rayteck Corp.), Trumbull, Conn., Can. and Europe, 1961-80; v.p. ops. Easco/KD Tools, Lancaster, Pa., 1980-83; mgr. ops. S.K. Wellman Corp., Bedford Heights, Ohio, 1983-86; gen. mgr. N.Am. Systems, Bedford Heights, 1986; indsl. mgmt. cons., 1987; pres., chief exec. officer Stanhope Products Co., Brookville, Ohio, 1987—, Nat. Extrusions Co., Bellefontaine, Ohio, 1987—, Nathan Hale Furniture Co., 1987—. Contbr. numerous articles to trade jours.; patentee high temperature lightweight plastic insulation, molecular sieve used in auto air conditioning. Fund raiser United Way, 1980—. Recipient Disting. Alumni award UCLA, 1991. Mem. Soc. Automotive Engrs. (chmn. com. 1987), Soc. Plastics Industry, Elks. Office: Stanhope Products Co 379 Albert Rd Brookville OH 45309-9247 also: Nat Extrusion and Mfg Co Orchard at Elm Bellefontaine OH 43311-0464 also: Nathan Hale Furniture Co 244 N Franklin St Red Lion PA 17356-1503

JUISTER, BARBARA JOYCE, retired mathematics educator; b. Ottawa, Ill., Sept. 4, 1939; d. Ralph Edward and Imogene (Wilson) Weber; m. Robert Milton Gibson, Sept. 9, 1959 (dec. May 1961); 1 child, Robert Milton Jr.; m. Charles Harry Juister, Apr. 2, 1966 (div. Dec. 30, 1991); children: Charles Edward, Leslie Elizabeth. BS in Math. Edn., Ill. State U., 1961; MA in Math. Teaching, Purdue U., 1965. Tchr. math. Lew Wallace High Sch., Gary, Ind., 1961-63, Paxton (Ill.) High Sch., 1963-64; prof. math. Elgin (Ill.) C.C., 1964-95; ret., 1995; reviewer textbooks for numerous pubs., 1977—; article reviewer Math. Tchr. mag., 1983—; reviewer modules Univ. Math. Applications Project, 1978—. Author: (book) The Development of the Illinois Mathematics Association of Community Colleges Through 1994. Treas. Sybaquay coun. Girl Scouts U.S.A., 1985-92; del. Nat. Coun. Girl Scouts, 1993-96: elder 1st Presbyn. Ch., Elgin, 1986-92. Recipient Faculty Mem. of Yr. award Ill. C.C. Trustees Assn., 1992, Ctrl. region Outstanding Faculty Mem. award Assn. C.C. Trustees, 1993, Excellence in Tng. award Nat. Inst. Staff and Organizational Devel., 1993, Leader award for Edn. Elgin YWCA, 1994. Mem. Math. Assn. Am. (vis. lectr. 1981-92, bd. dirs. Ill. sect. 1985-94, chmn. 1992-93, Ill. Sect. Disting. Svc. award 1995), Am. Math. Assn. 2-yr. Colls. (libr. subcom. edn. com. 1990-91, Ill. del. to Del. Assembly 1992-96), Ill. Math. Assn. C.C. (sec. 1978-83, pres. 1984-85, Disting. Svc. award 1992), Nat. Coun. Tchrs. Math. (speaker nat. meeting 1988), Ill. Coun. Tchrs. Math. (program com. 1988-89, spkr.), No. Ill. Assn. Tchrs. Math. (bd. dirs. 1994-96), Consortium for Math. and Its Applications, Altrusa Internat. Svc. Club (treas. Elgin chpt. 1995—). Presbyterian.

JULIAN, THOMAS MICHAEL, medical educator, gynecologic surgeon; b. Mpls., June 30, 1949; s. Earl Eugene and Pearl Louise (Passi) J.; m. Kathryn Ann Chalupsky, June 12, 1971; children: Christine, Andrew, Matthew. BA, St. Cloud (Minn.) State Coll., 1971; MD, U. Minn., 1978. Diplomate Am. Bd. Ob-Gyn. Intern U. Minn., Mpls., 1978-79, resident, 1979-82, assoc. prof., program dir. dept. ob-gyn., 1982-88; prof., program dir. dept. ob-gyn. U. Wis., Madison, 1988—; invited instr. Internat. Vaginal Surgery Conf., St. Louis, 1994, 95. Author: Review of Obstetrics and Gynecology, 1994, Manual of Colposcopy, 1996; mem. editorial bd. The Colposcopist, 1994-95; contbr. numerous articles to profl. jours. Recipient Outstanding Med. Writing award Minn. State Med. Soc., 1985, Teaching award Assn. Profs. Ob-Gyn., 1995. Mem. AAUP, Am. Soc. Colposcopy and Cervical Pathology (bd. dirs. 1992-95), Soc. Gynecologic Surgeons, Minn. Ob-Gyn. Soc. (sec.-treas. 1984-88, pres.-elect 1988). Roman Catholic. Home: 4892 Foxfire Trail Middleton WI 53562 Office: U Wis 600 Highland Ave Madison WI 53792

JULIFS, SANDRA JEAN, community action agency executive; b. Jersey City, July 12, 1939; d. Roy Howard and Irma Margrete (Barkhausen) Walters; m. Harold William Julifs, July 22, 1961; children: David Howard, Steven William. BA, U. Va., 1961; postgrad., U. Minn., 1962-63, Mankato State Coll., 1963. Cert. comty. action profl. Tchr. St. James (Minn.) Pub. Schs., 1961-62; substitute tchr. Sleepy Eye (Minn.) Pub. Schs., 1963-67, home bound tutor, 1967; lay reader, rater U. Wis., Stevens Point, 1968; co-founder Family Planning Service Portage County, Stevens Point, 1970-72; family planning dir. Tri-County Opportunities Coun., Rock Falls, Ill., 1971-77; energy programs coord. Tri-County Opportunities Coun., Rock Falls, 1977-78, planner, EEO officer, 1978-83, pres., chief exec. officer, 1983—; sec. Ill. Ventures for Comty. Action Springfield, 1983-91, bd. dirs. 1991-94, 96—. Mem. Nat. Cmty. Action Found., Washington, 1987—; bd. dirs. Twin Cities Homeless Coalition, 1989—; mem. adv. coun. Sauk Valley Coll. Human Svcs., 1990—; mem. Whiteside County Overall Econ. Devel. Coun., 1990—; mem. adv. coun. Inst. for Social and Econ. Devel., 1992-95; cons. com. No. Ill. Synod Evang. Luth. Ch. Am., 1993—, churchwide assembly del., 1995. Recipient Appreciation award Western Ill. Agy. on Aging, 1980, 81, Spl. Recognition award Ill. Head Start and Day Care Assn., Recognition award Ill. Community Action Fund, 1984, Recognition award Ill. Ventures for Cmty. Action, 1996. Mem. AAUW, NAFE, Am. Soc. Pub. Adminstrn., Whiteside County Welfare Assn., Lee County Welfare Assn. (sec.-treas. 1983-84), Nat. Cmty. Action Assn., Ill. Cmty. Action Assn. (com. chair 1985-88, dir. exec. com. 1986-95, treas. 1988, 89, sec. 1989, 90, v.p. 1991-93, pres. 1993-95, Recognition award 1985-95). Lutheran. Office: Tri-County Opportunities Coun 405 Emmons Ave PO Box 610 Rock Falls IL 61071

JULIUS, NORMAN B., lawyer; b. Chgo., Feb. 1, 1956; s. Emanuel and Esther Julius. BS in Acctg. with highest honors, U. Ill., 1977; JD, U. Chgo., 1980. Bar: Ill. 1981, U.S. Dist. Ct. (no. dist.) Ill. 1981, U.S. Ct. Appeals (7th cir.) 1988. Ptnr. Vedder, Price, Kaufman & Kammholz, Chgo., 1980—. Mem. subcom. allocations United Way, Chgo., 1986-88; treas. Lamb's Farm Associate Bd., Libertyville, Ill., 1989-91, pres., 1991-92. Mem. ABA, AICPA, Ill. State Bar Assn., Chgo. Bar Assn. (vice chmn. profl. fee com. 1992-93, chmn., 1993-94), Union League Club, Beta Alpha Psi (pres. 1976-77).. Office: Vedder Price Kaufman et al 222 N La Salle St Chicago IL 60601-1003

JULIUSSON, MARGUERITE, sales executive; b. Bklyn., Nov. 2, 1956; d. John Joseph and Margaret (Murphy) Lobiak; m. Steven Victor, Apr. 25, 1981 (div. Mar. 1990); m. Thomas J. Clark, June 20, 1993. BA in English, Le Moyne Coll., Syracuse, N.Y., 1978. Art producer Nat. Lampoon Mag., N.Y.C., 1979-81; assoc. producer Wyse Advt., N.Y.C., 1981-82; sales rep. Glenn Films, Chgo., 1983-84; sr. sales rep. The Artists Co., Chgo., 1984-90; sales rep. Petermann/Moss Films, Chgo., 1990—; ind. rep. Marguerite Juliusson & Cos., 1993—. Home and Office: 1658 N Orchard St Chicago IL 60614-5114

JULSTROM, BRYANT ARTHUR, computer science educator; b. Macomb, Ill., Feb. 26, 1950; s. Clifford Arthur and Rosa Streng (Drake) J.; m. Anne Catherine Nolan, May 28, 1994. BA summa cum laude, Augustana Coll., 1972; MS, U. Iowa, 1973, 82, PhD, 1987. Instr. Western Ill. U., Macomb, 1977-79; vis. asst. prof. U. Minn., Duluth, 1987-88; asst. prof. Coe Coll., Cedar Rapids, Iowa, 1988-89; assoc. prof. computer sci. St. Cloud (Minn.) State U., 1989-93, prof., 1993—. Del. Dem. Nat. Conv., 1984. Mem. Am. Assn. for Artificial Intelligence, Internat. Neural Network Soc., Assn. for Computing Machinery. Office: St Cloud State U 720 4th Ave S Saint Cloud MN 56301-4442

JUMP, LINDA GAIL, personnel executive; b. Searcy, Ark., Aug. 31, 1949; d. Melton Howard and Ila Mae (Sewell) Henderson; m. Charles Thomas Morgan, Apr. 21, 1967 (div. 1972); children: Amy Catherine, James Lawrence; m. Michael James Jump, Feb. 28, 1976; 1 child, Chad Michael. High sch. grad., Grandview (Mo.) High Sch., 1967. Sec. to div. mgr. Torotel, Grandview, Mo., 1972; with Kelly Svcs. Inc., various locations, 1972-74, 76-90; account rep. Kelly Svcs. Inc., Little Rock, 1981-82; br. mgr. Kelly Svcs. Inc., Huntington, W.Va., 1983, Shreveport, La., 1983-85; resident br. mgr. Kelly Svcs. Inc., Grandview, Mo., 1985-89, Kansas City, Mo., 1989-90; pers. sec. Marley Co., Olathe, Kans., 1974-76; import sec. House of Lloyd, Grandview, 1978; account exec. Bus. Pers. Svcs., Kansas City, Mo., 1990-92; br. mgr. Interim Pers. (formerly Pers. Pool Temporary Svcs.), Kansas City, Mo., 1992-93; adminstrv. asst. Electronic Data Sys., Overland Park, Kans., 1993—. Active in past in various charitable orgns. Fellow S. Kansas City C. of C., Grandview C. of C. (bd. dir.), Profl. Women's Network, Am. Bus. Women's Assn. (Bus. Assoc. of Yr. 1989), Goodwill Industries (adv. bd.). Democrat. Baptist. Office: EDS 10975 Benson # 400 Overland Park KS 66210

JUMPER, ROY EULLISS, political science educator; b. Springfield, S.C.; s. James Franklin and Lucile Narcissus (Odom) J.; m. Mary Ruth Linville, Nov. 2, 1957; children: Davis Linville, Mary Ashley Gallagher. BA, MA, U. S.C., 1949; PhD, Duke U., 1954. Postdoctoral fellow Ford Found., Saigon, Vietnam, 1954-56; prof. polit. sci. Wake Forest U., Winston-Salem, N.C., 1956-59, 60-62; fellow in East Asian studies Harvard U., Cambridge, Mass., 1959-60; program dir. Middle East Ford Found., Beirut, Lebanon, 1962-72; prof. pub. affairs Ind. U., Bloomington, 1972-86; provost Ind. U.-Malaysia, Shah Alam, 1986-91; prof. emeritus Ind. U., 1991—; CEO Linville Family Trust, Winston-Salem, 1991—; cons. Pew Family Trust, Warsaw, Poland, 1992, U.S. AID, Cairo, Egypt, 1981-86, U.S. Info. Svc., Francophone, Africa, 1979-81. Contbr. articles to profl. jours.; author (monograph) Government and Politics of Viet Nam, 1972. Pres. Midwest Univ. Internship Consortium, 1978-82. Staff sgt. U.S. Army, 1944-46. Fulbright scholar U. Paris, 1953-54. Fellow Am. Coun. Learned Socs., 1958; mem. Am. Polit. Sci. Assn., Sultans Club Shah Alam. Methodist. Home: 1214 E 1st St Bloomington IN 47401-5008

JUNEAU, SHARYN S., healthcare administrator; b. Madison, Wis., Aug. 5, 1947; d. Earl and Helme (Nelmark) Steinke; m. Terry Ninneman, Nov. 14, 1964 (div. June 1979); children: Kristine Martiny, Michelle Ninneman, Garrett Ninneman; m. Patrick James Juneau, Apr. 20, 1991. BSN, U. Wis., 1974; MS in Health Svc. Adminstrn., Joliet, Ill., 1987. RN, Wis.; cert. in nursing adminstrn.-advanced. Staff nurse VA Hosp., Madison, Wis., 1974-75; critical care nurse Madison Gen. Hosp., 1975-77; pub. health/home health nurse Dane County Pub. Health Dept., Madison, 1977-79; cons. in nursing State of Wis. Div. of Health, Madison, 1979-85; profl. svcs. cons. Hillhaven Corp., Menasha, Wis., 1985-87; dir., adminstr. St. Joseph's Hosp. Home Health Agy., Marshfield, Wis., 1987-93; home care supr. Joint Commn. on Accreditation of Health Care Orgns., Oakbrook Terrace, Ill., 1994—; CEO, pres. InterWeave, Inc., Marshfield, 1993—; health care cons. Marshfield, Wis., 1993—; cons. TN Mag., Marshfield, 1988-93; chair rehab. com. Am. Cancer Soc., Marshfield, 1987-89; subject matter specialist Cancer Info. Project, Marshfield, 1991-93. Chair Profl. Adv. Bd., Marshfield, 1987-93; mem. Am. Heart Assn., Milw., 1991-92. Mem. ANA, Wis. Nurses Assn., Wis. Home Care Orgn. (quality assurance com. 1988-93, pub. rels. com. 1987-89), Nat. Assn. Home Care. Office: JCAHO 1 Renaissance Blvd Oakbrook Terrace IL 60181 also: InterWeave Inc 401 S Schmidt Ave Marshfield WI 54449

JUNG, CHRISTOPHER HAROLD, otolaryngologist; b. Glenridge, N.J., July 3, 1943; s. Frederick William and Irene Elizabeth (Schoeneweis) J.; m. Myra S. Brady Nov. 13, 1993; children and stepchildren: Janet Ann Williams, Christopher Harold Jr., Daniel Frederick, Michelle Lynn Volkerding, Richard Estel Volkerding. AB, U. Mo., 1966, MD, 1969. Diplomate Am. Acad. Otolaryngology. Rotating intern Menorah Med. Ctr., Kansas City, Mo., 1969-70, resident gen. surgery, 1970-71; resident otolaryngology U. Mo. Med. Ctr., Columbia, 1971-74; attending physician, pvt. practice St. Francis Med. Ctr., S.E. Mo. Hosp., Doctors Park Surgery, Cape Girardeau, Mo., 1974—; pres. Doctors Park Surgery, Cape Girardeau, 1984-85; dir. Mo. State Med. Found., Jefferson City, 1986-92; dir. Intermed Ins. Co. (The Penere Group). Committeeman Rep. party Brown Owl Twp., 1986; state bd. dirs. Mo. Easter Seals, St. Louis, 1985-89. Maj. USANG, 1970-92. Recipient Intern of Yr. award Menorah Med. Ctr., 1970, Civic award Municipality of Jolo, Philippines, 1988, Great Golden Spectrum award Westport Free Health Clinic, Kansas City, Mo., 1970; Pres. award Honduras La Ceiba, 1985. Fellow AMA, Christian Med. Soc. (del. 1991-93), Pan Am. Soc. Bronchoesophagology, Mo. State Med. Assn., Cape Girardeau County Area Med. Soc. Home: 133 Wellington Ln Cape Girardeau MO 63701-9502 Office: SE Mo ENT Cons Ltd 1 Doctors Park Cape Girardeau MO 63703-4927

JUNGEBERG, THOMAS DONALD, lawyer; b. Berea, Ohio, June 12, 1950; s. Wilbert Donald and Carolyn Francis (Gaube) J.; m. Kathleen Ann Killmer, Oct. 5, 1973; children: Kimberlee Ann, Allison Lynn, Zebulun Thomas, Nathan Aaron. BA, Kent State U., 1972; JD, Cleve. State U., 1976. Bar: Ohio 1976, U.S. Dist. Ct. (no. dist.) Ohio 1977, U.S. Tax Ct. 1980, U.S. Supreme Ct. 1980. Tchr., Berea City Schs., Ohio, 1972-75; staff atty. Palmquist & Palmquist, Medina, Ohio, 1977-80, Gibbs & Craze, Parma Heights, Ohio, 1980-81; sole practice, Medina, 1981-87; v.p., gen. counsel, corp. sec. Shelby (Ohio) Ins. Co., 1987-95; prin. Lexington (Ohio) Ins. Cons., 1995-96; sole practice, Lexington, 1995-96; v.p. legal Reliance Nat., Cleve., 1996—. Tchr., First Baptist Christian Sch., Medina, 1981-84; elder, sec. First Bapt. Ch. of Medina, 1979-86, chmn. First Bapt. Christian Sch., Medina, 1984; bd. govs. Ohio Med. Profl. Liability Underwriting Assn., 1993-95; dir. Ins. Inst. Ind., 1994-95. Mem. Ohio State Bar Assn., Am. Corp. Counsel Assn. Republican. Avocations: piano; golf; archery. Home: 20236 Foxwood Dr North Royalton OH 44133

JUNGK, THOMAS RICHARD, civil engineer; b. Dubuque, Iowa, Oct. 28, 1943; s. Arthur Francis and Mabel Emma (Hark) J.; divorced; children: Lara, Sherre. BS in Liberal Arts, Loras Coll., 1968; BSCE, U. Iowa, 1968. Constrn. insp. Ill. Dept. Transp., Dixon, 1968-69, resident engr., 1971-79, design engr., 1979-81, bridge and hydraulics engr., 1981—. Co-author: Illinois Drainage Manual, 1989. Mem. planning & zoning bd., Whiteside County, Ill, 1995. With U.S. Army, 1969-71, Vietnam. Roman Catholic. Office: Ill Dept Transp 819 Depot Ave Dixon IL 61021

JUNKEL, ERIC FRANZ, engineering executive; b. Oak Park, Ill., Mar. 2, 1959. BSME, MIT, 1981, MSME, 1984; MBA, U. Chgo., 1988. Engr. IBM, San Jose, Calif., 1982-86; corp. devel. analyst Amoco Tech. Co., Naperville, Ill., 1988-90; ops. mgr. Nanophase Techs., Darien, Ill., 1990-91; pres. Tylwyth, Inc., Mt. Prospect, Ill., 1991—. Mem. ASME, IEEE. Home: 2001 Webster Ln Des Plaines IL 60018 Office: Tylwyth Inc PO Box 439 Mount Prospect IL 60056-0439

JUNKER, DAVID A., financial advisor; b. Frankfurt, Germany, Sept. 25, 1969. BA, Purdue U., 1992. Sales rep. EBRA Food Products, Huntly, Ill., 1992-93; fin. advisor Prudential Securities, South Bend, Ind., 1993—. Mem. South Bend C. of C., Kiwanis. Republican. Home: 516 River Ave South Bend IN 46601-3236 Office: Prudential Securities Inc 431 E Colfax # 100 PO Box 1957 South Bend IN 46634

JURGENS, LEONARD JOHN, retired range conservationist; b. Pickrell, Nebr., May 2, 1933; s. Wilke J. and Freda C. (Wolken); married; children: Glenn S., Mark A., Yvonne L. BS in Agronomy, U. Nebr., 1959. Range conservationist USDA Soil Conservation Svc., Burwell, Nebr., 1959-64, Franklin, Nebr., 1964-66; area range conservationist USDA Soil Conservation Svc., Emporia, Kans., 1966-81; state range conservationist USDA Soil Conservation Svc., Bismarck, N.D., 1981-85, Lakewood, Colo., 1985-94; pvt. practice cons. Emporia, 1994; adj. prof. U. Emporia, 1970-81. With U.S. Army, 1953-55. Mem. Soc. Range Mgmt., SRM (pres. 1976 K-O sect., Colo. sect.). Home and Office: 2617 W Ridge Dr Emporia KS 66801-6627

JURKIEWICZ, MARGARET JOY GOMMEL, secondary education educator; b. Indpls., Sept. 5, 1920; d. Dewey Ezra and Joy Agnes (Edie) Gommel; m. Walter Stephen Jurkiewicz, Jan. 1, 1942; children: Mary Margaret, Dewey John, Walter Stephen Jr., Hugh Louis. BS, Ind. U., 1941; postgrad., U. Minn., 1942-43, Butler U., 1950-51, U. Cin., 1958-60, Ind. U., 1971-72, Ball State U., 1974-75. Cert. secondary tchr., Ind., Ohio. Tchr. home econs. Plymouth (Ind.) H.S., 1941-42, Indpls. Pub. Schs., 1949-57, Mt. Confort-Hancock Co. Schs., Mt. Comfort, Ind., 1957-58, Cin. Pub. schs., 1958-61; tchr. 6th grade Plymouth (Ind.) Sch. corp., 1961-63; tchr. home econs. and art Argos (Ind.) Cmty. Schs., 1963-67; thcr. home econs. Penn-Harris-Madison Schs., Mishawaka, Ind., 1967-83; tchr. chapt. I South Bend (Ind.) Sch. Corp., 1983-85; vol. teacher art various schs., Ind., 1985—, Mich., 1985-96, Ill., 1985-96. Author newsletter and booklet Polish Cultural Soc., 1979—, Ind. Home Econ. Assn., 1975—; editor newsletter Marshall County Chpt. Am. Assn. Ret. Persons, Plymouth, Ind., 1993—. Bd. dirs. Area Agy. on Aging Coun., Plymouth, Ind., 1987-94, Garden Cts. Sr. Housing, Plymouth, 1989-96. Mem. AAUW (pres., chair various coms.), Am. Home Econs. Assn., Am. Assn. Ret. Persons, Ind. Home Econ. Assn., Ind. Polish Cultural Soc. (v.p., chair various coms.), Marshall County Ret. Tchrs. (pres. 1993-95), Plymouth Pub. Libr. Friends (pres., chair various coms.), Tippecanoe Audubon Soc., PEO Sisterhood. United Methodist. Home: 11570 W 9th A Rd Plymouth IN 46563

JURRUS, KATHLEEN SUE, post-anesthesia care nurse; b. Toledo, July 30, 1949; d. Earl Martin and Rae Grace (Koch) J. Diploma in nursing, Flower Hosp. Sch. Nursing, Toledo, 1970; Assoc. in Respiratory Therapy Health Tech., U. Toledo, 1976; BSN, Toledo/Med. Coll. of Ohio, 1994. RN, Ohio; cert. post anesthesia nurse, ACLS, respiratory therapy technician. Staff nurse ICU/CCU St. Luke's Hosp., Maumee, Ohio, 1970-74, staff therapist respiratory therapy, 1974-76, asst. dir. respiratory therapy, 1976-78, staff nurse PACU, 1991—; staff nurse Post Anesthesia Care Unit Flower Hosp., Sylvania, Ohio, 1978-84, 86-94, staff nurse Post Anesthesia Care Unit, Outpatient Surgery, 1986-94; head nurse Post Anesthesia Care Unit Toledo Clinic Outpatient Surgery Ctr., 1984-86; mem. Am. Bd. PeriAnesthesia Nursing Certification, 1988-94, treas., 1989-93. Mem. AACN, Am. Soc. Post Anesthesia Nurses (charter mem., bd. dirs. 1995—), Ohio PeriAnesthesia Nurses Assn. (pres. 1983-84, bd. dirs. 1978—), N.W. Ohio Post Anesthesia Nurses Assn. (pres. 1983-84, bd. dirs. 1986—), Mich. Assn. Post Anesthesia Nurses, Sigma Theta Tau. Lutheran. Office: St Lukes Hosp Post Anesthesia Care Unit 5901 Monclova Rd Maumee OH 43537-1855

JURS, ADDIE POOLE, marketing professional, publishing executive; b. Phila., Aug. 26, 1941; d. Harry Ralston and Adelaide Amanda (Lash) Poole; m. Jerry M. Jurs, Aug. 6, 1963; children: Michael, Stuart, Douglas. BS in Edn., Northwestern U., Evanston, Ill., 1963. Tchr. Avoca Sch. Dist., Wilmette, Ill., 1963-67; pres. AJ Mktg., Inc., Clarendon Hills, Ill., 1989—, Clarendon Hills Publ., 1993—. Author: TV-Becoming Unglued: A Guide to Help Children Develop Positive TV Habits, 1992. Pres. Christ Ch. Women, Oak Brook, Ill., 1984, head deaconess, 1990.

JUSTICE, BRADY RICHMOND, JR., medical services executive; b. Albertville, Ala., Dec. 26, 1930; s. Brady R. and Kate (McEachern) J.; m. Sandra Gearner, Dec. 29, 1956; children: David, Michael, Lori Blankenship, Kathryn Baker. BBA, Baylor U., 1953. CPA, Ind. Ptnr. Arthur Andersen & Co., Dallas, 1953-64, Indpls., 1964-72; exec. v.p. Basic Am. Industries, Inc., Indpls., 1972-83; pres. Basic Am. Med., Inc., Indpls., 1983-92; sr. v.p. Columbia Hosp. Corp., 1992-93; chmn. Heritage Capital Corp., Indpls., 1993—. Mem. Columbia Club, Lions (pres. Indpls. chpt.). Republican. Baptist. Home: 5435 Hedgerow Dr Indianapolis IN 46226-1625 Office: Heritage Capital Corp 6900 Gray Rd Indianapolis IN 46237-3227

JUSTICE, PHILLIP HOWARD, securities broker; b. Pikeville, Ky., Aug. 29, 1948; s. Howard and Opal Fanny (Hatfield) J.; m. Janice Y. McCollum; children: Phillip Wayne, Benjamin Howard. Student, Pikeville Coll., 1966, 67, Free Will Bapt. Coll., 1972; DD (hon.), Welcome Bapt. Inst., 1987. Minister Nat. Assn. Free Will Bapts., Springfield, Ohio, 1969-78; sales rep. Reynolds and Reynolds, Evansville, Ind., 1978-81; account exec. Merrill Lynch, Evansville, 1981-83, E.F. Hutton, Evansville, 1983-88; assoc. v.p. investments Dean Witter Reynolds, Inc., Evansville, 1988-91, Prudential Securities, Evansville, 1991-95, Citizen's Nat. Bank, Evansville, 1995—. Bd. dirs. Evansville unit Am. Heart Assn., 1990, 91. Mem. Rockport Area C. of C. (v.p. 1990, pres. 1991), Lions, Optimists, Rotary Club (bd. dris. 1995—). Republican. Office: Primerica Fin Svcs 6106 E Oak St Evansville IN 47715

JUSTICE, PHYLLIS C., newspaper editor; b. Milbank, S.D., Dec. 16, 1915; d. William Sylvester and Christine Anne (Olson) Dolan; m. Clarence Wayne Justice, Oct. 22, 1955. BA in Journalism, Minn. U., 1938. With advt. sales dept. Mankato (Minn.) Free Press, 1939; reporter Mpls. Star, Jour. and Tribune, 1939-44; asst. dir. USO Club, Renton, Wash., 1944-45; pub. rels. dir. Nat. Cath. Community Svc., 1946; editor Grant County Rev., Milbank, 1957—. Active Grant County Dems., Milbank; 1st woman pres. S.D. Newspaper Assn., 1982-83; mem. St. Lawrence Cath. Ch. Fin. Coun.; bd. dirs. St. Bernard Valley Hospice. Recipient McKinney award Nat. Newspaper Assn., 1985. Mem. Nat. Newspaper Assn., S.D. Newspaper Assn. (Hall of Fame 1989), Milbank C. of C., Cath. Daus., Grant County Hist. Soc.

KABAT, LINDA GEORGETTE, civic leader; b. Cleve., Nov. 26, 1951; d. Michael G. and Georgette (deVos) Paul; m. John Edward Kabat Jr., Apr. 23, 1977; 1 child, Susan Marie. Student, Cleve. Inst. Music, 1969-72. With sales dept. Higbee Co., Fairview Park, Ohio, 1972; customer svc. rep. Ashland Chem. Co., Cleve., 1972-74, Celanese Corp., Lakewood, Ohio, 1974-76; with sales dept. May Co., North Olmsted, Ohio, 1979; customer service rep. Diamond Shamrock Corp., Cleve., 1979-82; in sales May Co., North Olmsted, 1989—. Chpt. pres. Cath. War Vets. Aux., Cleve., 1973-75, pres. Ohio, 1975-77, nat. sec., 1977-79, state sec., 1991-92. Mem. Mu Phi Epsilon (pres. 1971-72, historian 1970-71). Republican.

KACHIROUBAS, CHRISTOPHER, assessor, real estate appraiser; b. Berwyn, Ill., Sept. 7, 1955; s. Louis and Doris Rose (McCloudry) K.; m. Laura Lee Anderson, Apr. 25, 1992; children: Alexander, Chandler. BA, Monmouth Coll., 1977. Cert. residential appraiser, Ill. Deputy assessor Addison (Ill.) Twp., 1977-81, chief deputy assessor, 1981-84; pers. dir., mgr. Ill. State Toll Hwy. Authority, Oakbrook, Ill., 1984-86; appraiser M. Ward Fleming & Assocs., Addison, 1986-88; chief deputy assessor Addison Twp., 1988-91, assessor, 1991—. Treas. Addison Twp. Rep. Party, 1982—, precinct committeeman, 1977—. Fellow Coll. Registered Pub. Appraiser; mem. Am. Cancer Soc. (chmn. Addison Twp. unit), Northern Ill. Twp. Assessors' Assn. (pres. 1993), Assessor Assn. DuPage County (v.p. 1991-92), Am. Inst. Real Estate Appraiser, Internat. Assn. Assessing Officers, Cert Ill. Assessing Officers, Am. Soc. Appraisers, Moose Lodge, Americans Italian Descent. Roman Catholic. Office: Addison Twp 401 N Addison Rd Addison IL 60101-2701

KACMARYNSKI, NANCY C., librarian, nurse; b. Ft. Dodge, Iowa, May 24, 1954; d. Leon H. and Caroline E. (Sandvig) Ralph; m. Michael L. Bergstrom,. June 24, 1972 (div. Nov. 1982); children: Martin, Jessica; m. James E. Kacmarynski, Jan. 22, 1983; children: Kristen, Stephanie. Grad., Iowa Lakes C.C., Emmetsburg, Iowa, 1980. LPN, Iowa. Nurse Iowa Bd. Nursing, 1980-95; libr. Mallard (Iowa) Pub. Libr., 1995—. Roman Catholic. Home: 709 Wilson PO Box 24 Mallard IA 50562-0024 Office: Mallard Pub Libr 609 Inman Mallard IA 50562-0248

KACZMAREK, KURT ALAN, scientist; b. Arlington Heights, Ill., Aug. 5, 1960; s. Eugene Peter and Evelyn Elaine (Goy) K.; m. Nancy Ann Hoffman, Apr. 20, 1991; children: Daniel Peter, Marie Helene. AS, Willian Rainy Harper Coll., 1980; BS, U. Ill., 1982; MS, U. Wis., 1984, PhD in Elec. Engring., 1991. Sr. engr. Baxter Labs., Round Lake, Ill., 1984-86; scientist U. Wis., Madison, 1992—. Contbr. chpts. to books. Mem. IEEE. Roman Catholic. Home: 4308 S Owen Dr Madison WI 53711 Office: U Wis 1300 Univ Ave Madison WI 53706

KADAKIA, PRATISH, mechanical engineer; b. India, Apr. 10, 1956. BSME, India, 1979. Project engr. Litton, Memphis, 1987-89, Fisher Price, Buffalo, 1989-90, Frigidaire Co., Webster City, Iowa, 1990—. Patentee in field. Office: Frigidaire 400 Des Moines St Webster City IA 50595

KADLEC, JOHN WOODROW, chemical industry manager; b. Eustis, Fla., Aug. 15, 1951; s. John Woodrow and Eva Clare (Doar) K.; m. Gayle Leslie Wirth, Oct. 8, 1977; children: Jessica Leigh, Kathryn Lane. B Engring., Stevens Inst. Tech., Hoboken, N.J., 1973; MBA, U. West Fla., 1982. Process engr. Rohm & Haas Co., Bristol, Pa., 1973-77; process engr., prodn. supt., quality assurance mgr. Air Products and Chems., Inc., Pensacola, Fla., 1977-88; prodn. mgr. GE Silicones, Waterford, N.Y., 1988-91; site mgr. PQ Corp., Kansas City, Kans., 1992-94; dir. ops. Avery Dennison, Schererville, Ind., 1994—. City councilman, Pensacola, Fla., 1987-88. Home: 1905 Emmett Ct Valparaiso IN 46383 Office: Avery Dennison 650 W 67th Ave Schererville IN 46375

KADUK, JAMES ALBERT, crystallographer; b. Cleve., June 21, 1952; s. Edward Eugene and Patricia Ann (Getts) K.; m. Catherine Ann Goodnetter, Aug. 27, 1978; children: Anne Elizabeth, Benjamin James. BS, U. Notre Dame, 1973; MS, Northwestern U., 1975, PhD, 1977. Rsch. chemist Amoco Chem. Co., Naperville, Ill., 1977-81, staff rsch. chemist, 1981-85; staff rsch. chemist Amoco Corp., Naperville, 1985-88, sr. rsch. scientist, 1988-91, assoc. rsch. scientist, 1991—. Patentee synthesis of the zeolite ferrierite using chelating templates, process for the preparation of an alkali metal/silica gel catalyst having a uniform metal dispersion; contbr. articles to profl. jours. Pres. Naperville Cmty. Chorus, 1989-91; bd. dirs. DuPage Symphony, 1991-94, v.p., 1992-93. 1st. lt. USAF, 1979. Mem. U.S. Nat. Com. for Crystallography, Internat. Ctr. for Diffraction Data (chmn. sales and mktg. subcom. 1992-96, new product R&D 1992-94, PDF database 1990-92, 94-96, rep. to U.S. Nat. Com. for Crystallography 1992-94, rep. to Internat. Union Crystallography Commn. on crystallographic data 1994—, rep. to Internat. Union Crystallography calendar com. 1994-96, mem.-at-large bd. dirs. 1990-94, 96—), Am. Crystallographic Assn. (chmn. svc. crystallographic spl. interest group 1990-92, chmn.-elect materials sci. spl. interest group 1996—, apparatus and stds. com. 1994-96). Office: Amoco Rsch Ctr PO Box 3011 150 W Warrenville Rd Naperville IL 60563-8473

KADZBAN, DOUGLAS WALTER, civil engineer; b. Manistee, Mich., Mar. 30, 1957; s. Aloise A. and Marvine J. (Bowers) K.; m. Nancy J. Van Klompenberg, Aug. 16, 1980; children: Douglas W. Jr., Rebekah J. AAS in Civil Engring., Mich. Tech. U., 1978. Land surveyor Moore & Bruggink, Grand Rapids, Mich., 1978-80, J.D. Duncan, Broken Arrow, Okla., 1982-83; engring. svcs. supr. City of East Grand Rapids, Mich., 1984—. Mem. Mich. Soc. Profl. Surveyors, S.W. Mich. Pub. Works Assn. (v.p. 1995—), Am. Water Works Assn., Wis. Soc. Land Surveyors, N.D. Soc. Profl. Land Surveyors, Am. Pub. Works Assn. Roman Catholic. Office: City of East Grand Rapids 750 Lakeside Dr SE Grand Rapids MI 49506

KAHANOVSKY, LUIS, physical therapist; b. Buenos Aires, Argentina, Apr. 17, 1934; came to U.S., 1972; s. Naum and Vera (Sacsagansky) K.; m. Elizabeth Ann Bogdan, Jan. 24, 1974. Diploma in physical therapy, U. Buenos Aires, 1965. Staff physical therapist U. Hosp., Buenos Aires, 1965-67; dir. orthopedic rehab. Pirovano Hosp., Buenos Aires, 1967-71; staff physical therapist Henry Ford Hosp., Detroit, 1972-77; pres., dir. Farmington Physical Therapy, Farmington Hills, Mich., 1977—. Treas. Phys. Therapy Network, Inc., 1989-92; ; dir. Phys. Therapy Provider Network, Inc., 1993—. Mem. Am. Physical Therapy Assn., Physical Therapists in Pvt. Practice Inc. (exec. dir., treas. 1982-85), United Soc. Physiotherapists N.Y. (past v.p., past pres., Devotion to Profl. Standards award 1984), Physical Therapy Provider Network, Inc. (dir. 1992). Republican. Jewish.

KAHLE, GLENN J., design engineer; b. Lima, Ohio, July 28, 1961. A of Arts and Scis., Ohio State U., 1982, BSISE, 1984. Design engr. Liqui-Box, Columbus, 1984-89, Gelzer Syss. Co., Westerville, Ohio, 1989-90, A.T.S. Ohio, Westerville, 1990—. Achievements include patent for transistor feeder, 1994. Office: A T S Ohio 425 Enterprise Dr Westerville OH 43081

KAHLOR, ROBERT A(RNOLD), communications company executive. Chmn., CEO Jour. Communications, Inc., Milw. Office: Jour Comm Inc PO Box 661 Milwaukee WI 53201-0661

KAHN, GENE, stockbroker; b. Cairo, Ill., June 17, 1935. BA in Bus., So. Ill. U., 1957. Stockbroker Dempsey, Tegler, St. Louis, 1960-70, Edward D. Jones & Co., St. Louis, 1970—. Office: Edward D Jones & Co 201 Progress Pky Maryland Heights MO 63043-3003

KAHN, JAMES STEVEN, museum director; b. N.Y.C., Oct. 14, 1931; 3 children. BS in Geology, CCNY, 1952; MS in Minerology, Pa. State U., 1954; PhD in Geol. Sci., U. Chgo., 1956. Instr. U. R.I., Kingston, 1957, asst. prof., 1958-60, research assoc. Narragansett Marine Lab., 1957-60; group leader U. Calif., Livermore, 1960-70; dept. head Physics Internat. Co., San Leandro, Calif., 1970-71; div. head geophysics U. Calif., Livermore, 1971-75; dep. assoc. dir. human resources U. Calif., 1975-78, assoc. dir. nuclear testing, 1978-80, dep. dir. lab., 1980-87; pres., chief exec. officer, dir. Mus. Sci. and Industry, Chgo., 1987—; trustee Mus. Sci. and Industry; strategic planning com. Econ. Devel. Commn. of City of Chgo., 1988-91; mem. math. scis. edn. bd. NAS; chmn. sci. adv. com. Gov. Ill.; mem. rev. com. dept. geol. scis. Northwestern U., 1996; mem. vis. com. divsn. phys. scis. U. Chgo., 1996—. Co-author: Statistical Analysis in Geological Sciences, 1962, Microstructure, 1968; contbr. articles to scientific jours. Bd. dirs. Franklin and Eleanor Roosevelt Inst.; rector sci. and medicine Lincoln Acad. of Ill. Centennial fellow Pa. State U. Coll. Earth and Mineral Scis., 1996. Fellow Geol. Soc. Am.; mem. Quadrangle Club, Econs. Club, Chgo. Club, Sigma Xi. Office: Mus Sci & Industry 57th St & Lake Shore Dr Chicago IL 60637

KAHN, JAN EDWARD, manufacturing company executive; b. Dayton, Ohio, Aug. 29, 1948; s. Sigmond Lawrence and Betty Jane K.; m. Deborah Ann Deckinga, Nov. 28, 1975; children: Jason Edward, Justin Allen, Julie Ann. BS in Metall. Engring., U. Cin., 1971. Mgmt. trainee U.S. Steel Corp., Gary, Ind., 1971-72; plant metallurgist Regal Tube Co., Chgo., 1972-74, gen. foreman, 1974-76, supt., 1976-77, mgr. tech. svc., 1978-80, materials mgr., 1980-81; mgr. quality control Std. Tube Co., Detroit, 1977-78; dir. ops. Boye Needle Co., Chgo., 1981-82, v.p. ops., 1982-83, v.p., gen. mgr., 1984-85, pres., 1985-88; v.p. sales and mktg. Caron Internat., Rochelle, Il., 1988—. Mem. Am. Soc. Metals, AIME, ASTM, Ravenswood Indsl. Coun. (bd. dirs. 1983-84, pres. 1985), Hand Knitting Assn. (chmn. 1986-88), Triangle Club. Republican. Mem. Christian Reformed Ch. Home: 13909 Teakwood Dr Lockport IL 60441-8697 Office: Caron Internat 200 Gurler Rd Ste 1 De Kalb IL 60115

KAHN, MARK LEO, arbitrator, educator; b. N.Y.C., Dec. 16, 1921; s. Augustus and Manya (Fertig) K.; BA, Columbia U., 1942; MA, Harvard U., 1948, PhD in Econs., 1950; m. Ruth Elizabeth Wecker, Dec. 21, 1947 (div. Jan. 1972); children: Ann Mariam, Peter David, James Allan, Jean Sarah; m. Elaine Johnson Morris, Feb. 12, 1988. Asst. economist U.S. OSS, Washington, 1942-43; teaching fellow Harvard U., 1947-49; dir. case analysis U.S. WSB, Region 6-B Mich., 1952-53; mem. faculty Wayne State U., Detroit, 1949-85, prof. econs., 1960-85, prof. emeritus, 1985—, dept. chmn., 1961-68, dir. indsl. rels. M.A. Program, 1978-85; arbitrator union-mgmt. disputes. Editorial bd.: Employee Responsibilities and Rights Journal, 1988—. Bd. govs. Jewish Welfare Fedn. Detroit, 1976-82; bd. dirs. Jewish Home for Aged, Detroit, 1978-93, Lyric Chamber Ensemble, Southfield, Mich., 1995—; bd. dirs. Detroit Empowerment Zone Devel. Corp., 1996—. Served to capt. AUS, 1943-46. Decorated Bronze Star; recipient Disting. Svc. award U.S. Nat. Mediation Bd., 1987, Am. Arbitration Assn., 1992. Mem. Indsl. Rels. Rsch. Assn. (pres. Detroit chpt. 1956, exec. sec. 1979-89, nat. exec. bd. 1986-88), AAUP (past chpt. pres.), Nat. Acad. Arbitrators (bd. govs. 1960-62, v.p. 1976-78, chmn. membership com. 1979-82, pres. 1983-84, chmn. nominating com., 1995-96), Soc. Profls. in Dispute Resolution (v.p. 1982-83, pres. 1986-87). Co-author: Collective Bargaining and Technological Change in American Transportation, 1971; contbr. articles to profl. jours. Home and Office: 4140 2nd Ave Detroit MI 48201-1704

KAHN, PHYLLIS, state legislator; b. Mar. 23, 1937; m. Don Kahn; two children. BA, Cornell U.; PhD in Biophysics, Yale U.; MPA, Harvard U. Dist. 59B rep. Minn. Ho. of Reps., St. Paul, 1972—; former chmn. state dept. divsn. appropriations com., Minn. Ho. of Reps., former mem. econ. devel., agr., environ. and natural resources coms.; chmn. govt. op. and gaming com., mem. ways and means, state govt. fin. divsn. and edn.-higher edn. fin. divsn. coms. Home: 369 State Office Bldg Saint Paul MN 55155 Office: Minn State Senate State Capital Building Saint Paul MN 55155-1606*

KAHN, SANDRA S., psychotherapist; b. Chgo., June 24, 1942; d. Chester and Ruth Sutker; m. Jack Murry Kahn, June 1, 1965; children: Erick, Jennifer. BA, U. Miami, 1964; MA, Roosevelt U., 1976. Tchr. Chgo. Pub. Schs., 1965-67; pvt. practice psychotherapy, Northbrook, Ill., 1976—. Host Shared Feelings, Sta. WEEF-AM, Highland Park, Ill., 1983—; author: The Kahn Report on Sexual Preferences, 1981, The Ex Wife Syndrome Cutting The Cord and Breaking Free After The Marriage Is Over, 1990; columnist Single Again mag. Mem. Ill. Psychol. Assn., Chgo. Psychol. Assn. (past pres. 1990). Jewish. Office: 2970 Maria Dr Northbrook IL 60062-2017

KAINZ, HOWARD PAUL, philosophy educator; b. Inglewood, Calif., June 9, 1933; s. Howard Paul and Cecelia Gertrude (Gallas) K.; m. Cathryn Louise Drozdik, Feb. 28, 1970; children: Alexander, Monica, Erika. BA, Loyola Marymount Coll., L.A., 1957; MA, St. Louis U., 1964; PhD, Duquesne U., 1968. Asst. prof. philosophy Duquesne U., Pitts., 1966-67; asst. prof. philosophy Marquette U., Milw., 1968-74, assoc. prof., 1974-80, prof., 1980—. Author: Paradox, Dialectic and System, 1988 (Choice Disting. Scholarly Book award), Democracy and the Kingdom of God, 1993, An Introduction to Hegel, 1995; translator: Hegel's Phenomenology Selections, 1994; editor: Philosophical Perspectives on Peace, 1987. Mem. Internationale Hegel Gesellschaft, Hegel Soc. Am., Am. Philos. Assn. Roman Catholic. Office: Marquette U Dept Philosophy Milwaukee WI 53233

KAISER, DAVID GILBERT, chemist; b. Detroit, Aug. 25, 1928; s. Jerome William and Elsie Bertha (Waldow) K.; m. Nancy Gay Sackett, Apr. 8, 1961; children: Catherine M., David W. BS, Detroit Inst. Tech., 1952; MS, Purdue U., 1954, PhD, 1959. Registered pharmacist, Mich. With Upjohn Co., Kalamazoo, 1959—, disting. scientist, 1991-96; ret., 1996. Contbr. articles to profl. jours. Fellow AAAS, Acad. Pharm. Scis.; mem. Am. Chem. Soc. Home and Office: 6605 Robinswood St Kalamazoo MI 49002-3138

KAISER, FRAN ELIZABETH, endocrinologist, gerontologist; b. N.Y.C., Dec. 6, 1949; d. Philip Francis and Bronia (Weiss) K.; m. T.B. Levine, June 1, 1975 (div. 1987). BS, CCNY, 1970; MD, N.Y. Med. Coll., N.Y.C., 1974. Diplomate Am. Bd. Internal Medicine, Am. Bd. Geriatrics. Intern Beth Israel Med. Ctr., N.Y.C., 1974-75, resident to chief resident, 1975-78; fellow in endocrinology and metabolism U. Minn., Mpls., 1978-81, instr. dept. medicine, 1980-81, asst. prof., 1981-86; asst. prof. in residence UCLA Sch. medicine, 1986-89; assoc. prof. medicine St. Louis U., 1989-94, prof., 1994—, assoc. dir. divsn. geriatric medicine, 1989-94; chief sect. endocrinology and metabolism Dept. Internal Medicine, St. Paul Ramsey Med. Ctr./U. Minn. Hosps., St. Paul, 1981-86; John A. Hartford Geriatric Faculty Devel. award scholar Hartford Found., N.Y.C./UCLA Sch. Medicine, 1986-87; chief geriatric medicine Olive View Med. Ctr./UCLA San Fernando Valley Program, Sylmar, Calif., 1987-89; med. dir. Hosp. Based Home Care, VA Med. Ctr., Sepulveda, 1987-89. Ad hoc reviewer Jour. Clin. Endocrinology and Metabolism, Endocrinology, Jour. AMA, Jour. Am. Geriatrics Soc.; mem. editl. bd. Am. Geriatric Soc., Internat. Medicine Bull.; contbr. articles to profl. jours. Grantee NIH, 1980-81, Genetech, 1987-89, Syntex Corp. 1990-92, Hoechst-Roussel, 1992-94, Bur. Health Professions, 1991-97, VIVUS, 1993—, Merck, 1994—, Upjohn, 1995—. Mem. AAAS, Am. Diabetes Assn.,Endocrine Soc., Am. Fedn. Clin. Rsch., N.Y. Acad. Sci., Women's Caucus of the Endocrine Soc., Gerontol. Soc. Am., Am. Geriatrics Soc. (mem. editl. bd. Internal Medicine Bull., Jour. Am. Geriatrics Soc., Jour. Geriatric Nephrology & Urology). Office: St Louis U Med Sch 1402 S Grand Blvd # 238M Saint Louis MO 63104-1004

KAISER, MARTIN, newspaper editor. Mng. editor Milw. Jour.- Sentinel. Office: Milwaukee Journal PO Box 661 333 W State St Milwaukee WI 53201-0661*

KAISER, TIM MICHAEL, mechanical engineer; b. St. Cloud, Minn., Aug. 15, 1956. A, St. Cloud Vocat. Tech., 1976. Design engr. Komo Machine Inc., Sauk Rapids, Minn, 1987-90, plant mgr., 1990-92, project mgr., 1992—. Patentee in field. Mem. ASME, NRA, Minn. Waterfall. Office: Komo Machine Inc 11 Industrial Blvd Sauk Rapids MN 56379-8709

KAISERMAN, DAVID NORMAN, music educator; b. Cleve., July 15, 1937; m. Sonia Uvezian, Jan. 12, 1962. BS, The Juilliard Sch., N.Y.C., 1959, MS, 1960; DMA, U. Iowa, 1977. Asst. prof. Iowa State U., Ames, 1963-68; assoc. prof. U. Puget Sound, Tacoma, Wash., 1968-75, prof., 1975-77; prof. U. Okla., Norman, 1977-80; prof. U. Louisville, 1980-85, chmn. piano dept., 1983-85; prof. Northwestern U., Evanston, Ill., 1985—, chmn. piano dept., 1985-91. Performer concerts, recitals, adjudications, master classes and radio/TV programs worldwide, 1958—; contbr. articles to profl. jours. Finalist in various piano competitions, N.Y.C., Chgo., 1958-65; recipient various awards and scholarships The Juilliard Sch., 1954-60, Josephine Fry Bi-Annual award Piano Tchrs. Congress of N.Y., 1963, Nat. Arts Club Auditions, N.Y.C., 1958, N.Y. Madrigal Soc. Town Hall award, 1963; winner audtions, Hour of Music, N.Y.C., 1963, others. Mem. Nat. Guild Piano Tchrs. (Grand prize, tchr. div. 1973, 83), Music Tchrs. Nat. Assn. (master tchr. cert. 1983), Coll. Music Soc., Soc. Am. Musicians, AAUP, Am. Liszt Soc., Pi Kappa Lambda. Office: Northwestern U Sch of Music 711 Elgin Rd Evanston IL 60208-1200

KAIYALETHE, JOHN KURUVILLA See JOHN, K. K.

KAKABAKER, KENNETH GRAHAM, mechanical engineer; b. Kalamazoo, Mar. 31, 1944; s. Erw Hartman and Colleen Lou (Patterson) K.; m. Nancy Ellen Foster, Oct. 22, 1966; children: Kristine Marie, Karen Lynn. BS in Mech. Engring., Tri-State Coll., 1966. Registered profl. engr., Mich. Mgr. rsch. Durametallic Corp., Kalamazoo, 1979—. Patentee for fluid sealing devices. Office: Durametallic Corp 2100 Factory St Kalamazoo MI 49001

KAKUTANI, AKIKO, Japanese language and linguistics educator; b. Tokyo; m. Mitsuo Kakutani, Dec. 21, 1968; children: Kota, Taho. BA, Internat. Christian U., 1965; MA, McGill U., 1978; student, U. Md., 1980. Asst. prof. Japanese Earlham Coll., Richmond, Ind., 1980-86, assoc. prof., 1986-88, prof., 1988—; dir. Learning and Teaching About Japan project, lang. programs, Ind., 1987—. Author: (textbook) Nihongo I, II, 1990, rev. 1992, III, 1992. Mem. Assn. Asian Studies, Am. Coun. Teaching Fgn. Langs., Assn. Tchrs. Japanese. Office: Earlham Coll National Rd W Richmond IN 47374-4095

KALATA, RICHARD NEIL (RICK), design engineer; b. Chgo., Sept. 14, 1971; s. Richard E. and Geraldine (Vroom) M.; m. Cheryl A. Curtiss, Sept. 17, 1994. AA in Mech. Design, Morraine Valley C.C., Palos Hills, Ill., 1989-92; cert. in CAD, 1993. Project engr. Belden Tools Inc., Broadview, Ill., 1992—. Mem. Mustang Club Am., Late Model Mustang Owners Assn., SVT Cobra Owners Assn.

KALCEVIC, TIMOTHY FRANCIS, airline pilot, educator; b. Glenwood Springs, Colo., May 11, 1950; s. Victor and Marjorie Ann (Golden) K.; m. Dora L. Sterling, Jan. 15, 1994; stepchildren: Lisa Koehn, Ericka Koehn. BA in Acctg., Mich. State U., 1972; MBA cum laude, Roosevelt U., 1982; MA in Econs., U. Ill., Chgo., 1986; postgrad, U. Ill. CPA, Ill.; lic. airline transport pilot. Officer, pilot USN, various, 1972-79; pilot Am. Airlines, Chgo., 1979-81, 1984—; acct. Morton Mfg., Libertyville, Ill., 1981-82; acctg. mgr. Dexter Corp., Midland div., Waukegan, Ill., 1982-84; instr. McHenry County (Ill.) Coll., 1983; ind. cons. acctg. Waukegan, 1984-85. Lt. USN, 1972-79. Mem. Am. Econ. Assn., Allied Pilots Assn. (chmn. scheduling com. Chgo. chpt. 1989-91, chmn. chgo. chpt. 1991-93), Am. Ind. Cockpit Alliance (chmn. fin. 1994). Office: Pilot-Am Airlines O'Hare Internat Airport PO Box 66065 AMF Ohare IL 60666-0065

KALDOR, LEE, state legislator; m. Cynthia Kaldor; two children. BS, Maryville State U. Farmer, tax practitioner, real estate appraiser; rep. N.D. State Ho. Reps. Dist. 20, asst. minority leader, former mem. judiciary, transp. and joint constn. rev. coms., mem. appropriations, edn. and environ. divsn. com.; former dir. Farmers Union Oil and Hillsboro Day Care. Dir. N.D. Assn. Rural Elec. Coop., Midwest Elec. Consumers Assn., Hillsboro Pub. Sch. Mem. Hist. Soc., Jaycees. Home: PO Box 215 Mayville ND 58257-0215*

KALEBA, RICHARD JOSEPH, healthcare consultant; b. Chgo., Mar. 29, 1949; s. Joseph John and Josephine (Rogoszewski) K.; m. Kathleen Ann McCormick, June 13, 1970; children: Matthew, John, Daniel, Nicholas, David. BS in Biology, DePaul U., 1971, MBA in Systems Mgmt., 1974. Diplomate Am. Coll. Healthcare Execs. Support svcs. supr. Augustana Hosp., Chgo., 1973; dir. materials mgmt. Westlake Cmty. Hosp., Melrose Park, Ill., 1974-76, adminstrv. asst. planning, 1977-86; v.p. planning and ancillary svcs. Mercy Hosp., Davenport, Iowa, 1977-86; COO Manatee Meml. Hosp., Bradenton, Fla., 1986-89; CEO Rome (N.Y.) Hosp., 1989-94; sr. mgr. bus. devel. Gilbane Bldg. Co., Chgo., 1994-95; sr. cons. PRISM Healthcare Consulting, Glen Ellyn, Ill., 1995—; cons. in field, Rome, 1992-94. Co-author: Returning the ER to Financial Viability, 1991. Bd. dirs. Leadership Manatee County, Bradenton, 1987-89, Diocese of Venice (Fla.) Sch. Bd., 1987-90. Mem. Chgo. Health Exec. Forum, Am. Soc. Healthcare Engrs. Office: PRISM Healthcare Consulting Bldg 4 Ste 317 799 Roosevelt Rd Glen Ellyn IL 60137

KALINA, CHRISTINE MARIE, occupational health nurse; children: Clarissa, Cathleen. Diploma, St. Francis Hosp. Sch. Nursing, Evanston, Ill., 1968; BS, Coll. St. Francis, Joliet, Ill., 1991, MS in Health Svcs. Adminstrn., 1992; postgrad., Coll. St. Francis. RN, Ind., Ill., Tex.; cert. occupl. health nurse. Supr. emergency rm. St. Margaret Hosp., Hammond, Ind., 1968-73; staff nurse emergency rm. Meth. Hosp., Gary, Ind., 1974-76, St. Catherine Hosp., East Chicago, Ind., 1976-79, 81-85; sr. occupational health nurse Amoco Oil Corp., Whiting, Ind., 1973-96; mgr. med. case mgmt. Amoco Corp., Chgo., 1996—; mem. safety com., disaster com., employee assistance com. Amoco Oil Corp., Whiting, 1990—; hon. co-faculty dept. nursing Purdue U.-Hammond, Ind. U. N.W.; instr. EMT; presenter in field. Contbr. articles to profl. jours. Bd. dirs. N.W. Ind. Heart Assn., 1993, 94, 95. Recipient Disting. Svc. award Am. Heart Assn., 1981, 86, 91. Mem. ANA, Am. Assn. Occupl. Health Nurses (cert.; state and regional bd. dirs.), N.W. Ind. Assn. Occupl. Health Nurses (bd. dirs., v.p.), Emergency Dept. Nurses Assn., N.W. Ind. Coaches Assn., Sigma Theta Tau. Office: Amoco Oil Corp 2815 Indianapolis Blvd Whiting IN 46394-2197

KALIS, HENRY J., state legislator, farmer; b. Mar. 2, 1937; m. Violet Kalis; four children. Farmer; Dist. 26B rep. Minn. Ho. of Reps., St. Paul, 1974—; former chmn. transp. com., Minn. Ho. of Reps., former mem. agr., appropriations, health and human svcs. coms., former ex officio environ. and natural resources fin., health and housing, higher edn. human svcs., judiciary and state govt. divsn. coms.; chmn. capital investment com., mem. econ. devel., infrastructure and regulation fin., and ways and means coms. Home: RR 1 Box 55 Walters MN 56092-9722*

KALLEN, DAVID JOHNSON, clinical sociologist, educator; b. Danbury, Conn., July 21, 1929; s. Horace Meier and Rachel (Oatman) K.; m. Suzanne Libby, Feb. 1, 1952 (div. July 1985); children: Hugh Anthony, Benjamin Thomas, Nina Elizabeth; m. Sandra Ames Greenwood, Apr. 25, 1992. BA, Cornell U., 1951; MA, U. Mich., 1953, PhD, 1958. Rsch. asst. U. Mich., Ann Arbor, 1951-54, rsch. assoc., 1954-57; rsch. dir. Health & Welfare Coun. Balt. Area, Balt., 1957-62; health sci. adminstr. NIH, Bethesda, Md., 1962-70; assoc. prof. Mich. State U., East Lansing, 1970-74, prof., 1974—; v.p. SKF Assocs., Lansing, Mich., 1990—; bd. dirs. Sci. Analysis Corp., San

Francisco. Editor: (jour.) Clin. Sociology Rev., 1985-91. Mem. APA, Sociol. Practice Assn. (cert. clin. sociologist, Award of Merit 1986, pres. 1993-96), Am. Sociol. Assn. (com. chair 1990-93, Lifetime Achievement award Sociol. Practice sect. 1992), Soc. for Study of Social Problems (com. chair). Democrat. Jewish. Home: 13375 Forest Hill Rd Grand Ledge MI 48837 Office: Mich State U Dept Pediats Human Devel C202 E Fee Hall East Lansing MI 48824

KALLNER, NORMAN GUST, management information systems manager; b. Rockford, Ill., Apr. 28, 1950; s. Gust and Vera May (Brinkmeyer) K.; m. Mary Ann Wikoff, July 30, 1976; 1 child, Stephanie Ann. Student, U. Ill., 1968-70, No. Ill. U., 1975-79; BS in Bus. Adminstrn./Computer Info. Sys. summa cum laude, Culver-Stockton Coll., 1994. Programmer Woodward Gov. Co., Rockford, 1970-73, Rock Valley Coll., Rockford, 1973-74; programmer/analyst Kysor of Byron (Ill.), 1974-76; systems programmer Rockford Bd. Edn., 1976-80; systems programmer Harris Corp., Quincy, Ill., 1980-84, mgmt. info. systems tech. support mgr., 1984-86, prin. software, data base analyst, 1986-92, prin. sys. analyst, 1992—; cons. Outboard Marine Corp., Beloit, Wis., 1979-80. Treas. Our Redeemer Luth Ch., Quincy, 1986-87, vice chmn., 1992-93, pres. 1995-96; asst. leader Girl Scouts Am., Quincy, 1986—, trainer scout leaders, 1989—. Home: 1520 S 28th St Quincy IL 62301-6302 Office: Harris Corp PO Box 4290 Quincy IL 62305-4290

KALLSTROM, CHARLES CLARK, dentist; b. Chgo., Jan. 15, 1943; s. Charles Edward and Margaret Jane (Clark) K.; m. Roberta Lou Easterday, June 19, 1965; children: Cynthia Ann, Heidi Lynn, Karen Kristine. BS in Chem. Engring., Purdue U., 1965; DDS, Northwestern U., Chgo., 1971. Project engr. Chgo. Bridge & Iron Co., Oakbrook, Ill., 1965-67; pvt. practice dentistry Geneva, Ill., 1973—; mem. dental staff Cmty. Hosp., Geneva, 1974—, chmn., 1980-81; chmn. Elgin C.C. Dental Assisting Adv. Bd., 1994—. Author, editor: Dental Assisting for the Red Cross Aide, 1971. Bd. dirs. Tri City Family Svcs., Geneva, 1983-90, v.p., 1985-87, pres., 1988-90, chmn. capitol gifts campaign, 1992-93; bd. dirs. Men's Found. Delnor Cmty. Hosp., Geneva, 1979—; pres. Geneva chpt. Am. Cancer Soc., 1986-88. Lt. USN, 1971-73. Fellow Am. Coll. Dentists, Internat. Coll. Dentists; mem. ADA, Acad. Gen. Dentistry, Ill. State Dental Soc. (dental edn. com.1989-92, bd. trustees 1992—, access to care com. 1992-93, fin. and planning com. 1992-95, chmn. annual planning com. 1993-94, dental benefits com. 1994-95, ins. com. 1995—), Fox River Valley Dental Soc. (sec. 1986, treas. 1987, v.p. 1988, bd. dirs. 1988-91, pres. 1989), Ill. Acad. Dental Practice Adminstrn., Geneva Golf Club (sec. 1988, bd. dirs. 1986-88, 92-95, v.p. 1995). Republican. Presbyterian. Home: 615 Carriage Dr Batavia IL 60510-1159 Office: PO Box 488 302 Randall Rd Ste 105 Geneva IL 60134-4203

KALSOW, KATHRYN ELLEN, library clerk; b. Stevens Point, Wis., Dec. 31, 1938; d. Wilbert Otto and Vivian Frances (Peterson) K. BA, Luther Coll., 1961. Libr. clk. Luther Coll. Libr., Decorah, Iowa, 1961—. Del. county conv. Rep. com., Decorah, Iowa, 1970-84, state conv., Des Moines, 1970-84; del. Nat. Fedn. Rep. Women, Washington, 1971. Mem. AAUW (treas. 1966-68, 79-81, internat. rels. area rep. 1975-77, 85-87, 90-92, named Gift Honoree, 1982), UN Assn. of USA, Iowa Libr. Assn. Lutheran. Home: Luther Coll Instrnl Media 700 College Dr Decorah IA 52101

KALTER, ALAN, advertising agency executive; m. Chris Lezotte. With W.B. Doner & Co., Southfield, Mich., 1967—, exec. v.p., dir. retail divsn., 1990, vice chmn. account mgmt., 1990-92, pres., COO, 1992-95, CEO, 1995—; CEO W. B. Doner & Co., Southfield, Mich., 1995—. Office: W B Doner & Co 25900 Northwestern Hwy Southfield MI 48075-1067

KAMBACK, MARVIN CARL, psychologist; b. Yankton, S.D., July 15, 1939; s. Carl Melvin and Pauline Elizabeth (Albrecht) K.; children: Elizabeth, Christopher. BA in English, U. S.D., 1961, MA in Psychology, 1962; PhD, Vanderbilt U., 1965. Diplomate Am. Coll. Forensic Examiners, Am. Bd. Profl. Disability Conss.; cert. psychologist, Md. Lic. psychologist, Wyo., Calif. Instr. U. S.D., 1962, asst. prof. dept. psychology, physiology, 1967-71; fellow neuro-psychology Stanford (Calif.) U. Med. Sch., 1966-67; psychol. intern Balt. City Hosps., 1971-74, family therapy intern, 1974-78; asst. prof. John Hopkins U. Med. Sch., Balt., 1971-74; assoc. prof. U. Md. Med. Sch., Balt., 1974-78; dir. Washakie County Mental Health Services, Worland, Wyo., 1978-79; dir. psychol. services Raleigh Hills (Calif.) Hosps., 1979-84; clin. psychologist Behavior Therapy & Research Inst., Newport Beach, Calif., 1979-84; pvt. practice neuropsychology, rehab., chronic pain, hypnotherapy, and behavioral medicine; dir. psychol. services Alcoholism Program, Advanced Health Services, Newport Beach, 1979-84. NIMH fellow. Mem. APA, AAAS, Nat. Register Health Service Providers in Psychology, Soc. for Gen. Systems Research. Contbr. chpts. to books and articles to profl. jours. Home: 613 Douglas Ave Yankton SD 57078-3528 Office: Yankton Med Clinic 1104 W 8th St Yankton SD 57078-3306

KAMESAR, ADAM, literature educator; b. Milw., Mar. 7, 1956; s. Armon Ellie and Barbara Lee (Blacker) K.; m. Laura Banon, Jan. 10, 1981; children: Micah, Victor. BA, Hebrew U., Jerusalem, 1980; DLett, Cath. U. of the Sacred Heart, Milan, 1983; DPhil, U. Oxford, Eng., 1987. From asst. prof. to prof. Judaeo-Hellenistic lit. Hebrew Union Coll., Cin., 1987—. Author: Jerome, Greek Scholarship and the Hebrew Bible, 1993; assoc. editor Hebrew Union Coll. Ann., 1996—; contbr. articles to profl. jours. Mem. Am. Philological Assn., Soc. Bibl. Lit. Office: Hebrew Union Coll 3101 Clifton Ave Cincinnati OH 45220-2404

KAMIN, KAY HODES, financial planner, lawyer, historian, educator; b. Chgo., July 3, 1940; d. Barnet and Eleanor (Cramer) Hodes; m. Malcolm S. Kamin, June 12, 1963; children: Kim Alison, Kyle Barret. BA, Vassar Coll., 1961, MA, U. Chgo., 1962, PhD, 1970, CFP, 1992; JD cum laude, Northwestern U., 1981. Bars: Ill. 1981, U.S. Dist. Ct. (no. dist.) Ill. 1981. Registered investment adviser, Ill. History tchr. Lincoln Park High Sch., Chgo., 1963-67; social studies coord. U. Chgo., 1968-69; assoc. prof. edn. Rosary Coll., River Forest, Ill., 1970-76; jud. law clk. Ill. Appellate Ct., Chgo., 1981-83; assoc. Mayer, Brown & Platt, Chgo., 1983-85; v.p., gen. counsel Glencorp Inc., 1985-93, also bd. dirs.; pres. Sutton Place Fin., Inc., Chgo., 1993—. Co-author: Contract Law, 1983; fin. editor, columnist Today's Chgo. Woman, 1996—; contbr. articles to profl. jours. Pres. Chgo. Coun. for Social Studies, 1967-69; bd. govs., life mem. Chgo. Art Inst., 1974—; pres. Soc. for Contemporary Art, 1974-76; pres. Sedoh Found., 1986—; bd. dirs. Women's Bd. Northwestern U.; fellow U. Chgo. Grad. Sch., 1967-70; exec. com. collectors forum Chgo. Mus. Contemporary Art. Mem. ABA, Chgo. Bar Assn. (vice chair fin. svcs. com. 1995—). Club: Arts, John Evans (Northwestern U.), Chgo. Capital (founder 1995). Avocations: golf, jogging, skiing, art collecting. Office: Sutton Place Financial Inc 1305 N Sutton Pl Chicago IL 60610-2007

KAMINSKI, EDWARD JOZEF, pathologist, toxicologist educator; b. Torun, Poland, Mar. 24, 1926; came to U.S., 1956; m. Krystyna Karpinski, Sept. 15, 1951; children: Norbert E., Yvonne K. PhB, Northwestern U., Evanston, Ill., 1960, PhD, 1964. Diplomate Am. Bd. Toxicology. Rsch. technologist U. Edinburg, Scotland, 1946-51, Royal Cancer Hosp./U. London, 1951-53; med. technologist Mt. Sinai Hosp., Toronto, Can., 1953-56; rsch. technologist Northwestern U., Chgo., 1956-60, lectr. in chemistry, 1963-67, prof. pathology, 1964-95, prof. emeritus, 1996—; cons. in toxicology Indsl./Bio-Test Labs, Northbrook, Ill., 1964-79, various legal cases, 1980—. Editorial bd. BioMaterial Med. Devices Internat. Jour., 1973-89; contbr. 80 articles to profl. jours./abstracts. Bd. mem. Niles Twp. High Sch. Dist., Skokie, Ill., 1974-78. Mem. AAAS, Soc. Toxicology (pres. midwest regional chpt. 1982-83), Polish Inst. Arts and Scis. Am., Am. Chem. Soc., Omicron Kappa Upsilon, Sigma Xi. Home: 5813 Capri Ln Morton Grove IL 60053-1573 Office: Medical Dent Path Dept Northwestern Univ 311 E Chicago Ave Chicago IL 60611-3008

KAMINSKI, JEROME MICHAEL, instructional technologist; b. Highland Park, Mich., June 9, 1958; s. Jerome Phillip and Lorraine Lucille (Loneski) K.; m. Mary Jo Tompkins, May 20, 1989; children: Bradley Justin, Jessica Michele. AA, SUNY, Albany, 1984; BS, So. Ill. U., 1984; MEd, Wayne State U., 1989. From computer sys. tech. to sr. devel. supervisor U.S. Navy, Virginia Beach, 1976-85; edn. design specialist EDS Corp., Southfield, Mich., 1985-91; from instrnl. tech. project mgr. to dir. merchandise project KMart Corp., Troy, Mich., 1991-95; sr. instrnl. designer Gen. Physics Corp., Troy, 1995—; adj. faculty Oakland C.C., Bloomfield Hills, Mich., 1993—, Macomb C.C., Fraser, Mich., 1991—; pres. Kaminski & Assocs., Pleasant Ridge, Mich., 1991—. Mem. Nat. Soc. for Performance & Instrn., Distance Edn. & Tng. Network, Detroit Area Trainers Assn., Macomb County Speakers Bur. Republican. Roman Catholic. Home: 17 Fairwood Blvd Pleasant Ridge MI 48069 Office: Gen Physics Corp 580 Kirts Blvd Troy MI 48084

KAMISAR, YALE, lawyer, educator; b. N.Y.C., Aug. 29, 1929; s. Samuel and Mollie (Levine) K.; m. Esther Englander, Sept. 7, 1953 (div. Oct. 1973); children: David Graham, Gordon, Jonathan; m. Christine Keller, May 10, 1974. AB, NYU, 1950; LLB, Columbia U., 1954; LLD, CUNY, 1978. Bar: D.C. 1955. Rsch. assoc. Am. Law Inst., N.Y.C., 1953; assoc. Covington & Burling, Washington, 1955-57; assoc. prof., then prof. law U. Minn., Mpls., 1957-64; prof. law U. Mich., Ann Arbor, 1965-92, Clarence Darrow disting. univ. prof., 1992—; vis. prof. law Harvard U., 1964-65; disting. vis. prof. law Coll. William and Mary, 1988; cons. Nat. Adv. Commn. Civil Disorders, 1967-68, Nat. Commn. Causes and Prevention Violence, 1968-69; mem. adv. com. model code pre-arraignment procedure Am. Law Inst., 1965-75. Reporter-draftsman: Uniform Rules of Criminal Procedure, 1971-73; author: (with W.B. Lockhart, J.H. Cooper and S. Shiffrin), Constitutional Law: Cases, Comments and Questions, 8th edit., 1996; (with W. LaFave and J. Israel) Modern Criminal Procedure: Cases and Commentaries, 8th edit., 1994, Criminal Proedure and the Constitution: Leading Cases and Introductory Text, 1988; (with F. Inbau and T. Arnold) Criminal Justice in Our Time, 1965; (with J. Grano and J. Haddad) Sum and Substance of Criminal Procedure, 1977, Police Interrogation and Confessions: Essays in Law and Policy, 1980; contbr. articles to profl. jours. Served to 1st lt. AUS, 1951-52. Recipient Am. Bar Found. Rsch. award, 1996. Home: 2910 Daleview Dr Ann Arbor MI 48105-9684 Office: U Mich Law Sch 625 S State St Ann Arbor MI 48109-1215

KAMM, CHRISTIAN PHILIP, manufacturing company executive; b. Lakewood, Ohio, Oct. 30, 1967; s. Jacob and Judith (Steinbrenner) K. BA cum laude, Ohio Wesleyan U., 1990; MBA, Baldwin Wallace Coll., 1992. Chief fin. analyst, asst. treas. Electric Furnace Co., Salem, Ohio, 1992-93; v.p., treas. Wilkinson Co., Inc., Stow, Ohio, 1993-94; pres. Ostalden Corp., Cleve., 1994—; pres., COO Wilkinson Co., Inc., Stow, Ohio, 1994—; bd. dirs., exec. com. Electric Furnance Co., Inc., Salem; bd. dirs. Wilkinson Co., Inc., Stow, Canefco, Ltd., Toronto, Can., Turner Machine Co. Inventor recycle bin system, home recycle chute system. Mem. Cleve. Athletic Club, Akron City Club. Office: Wilkinson Co Inc 1530 Commerce Dr Stow OH 44224

KAMMERDIENER, RANDALL ROBERT, political operative; b. Springfield, Mo., Oct. 3, 1964; s. Ronald T. Kammerdiener and Mona Gale (Andrews) Werges. B of Journalism, U. Mo., 1988, MPA, 1996. Computer programmer Mo. Dept. of Revenue, Jefferson City, Mo., 1985-90, publs. specialist, 1990-91; polit. dir. Mo. Repoublican Party, Jefferson City, Mo., 1991-94, dep. exec. dir. for polit. affairs, 1994-95; campaign mgr. Kelly for Gov., Jefferson City, 1996—. Author, pub.: more than 200 separate campaign brochures. V.p. Capital Area Young Reps., Jefferson City, 1991; del. Rep. Nat. com. Campaign Mgmt. Coll., L.A., 1991; mem. City Coun., Jefferson City, 1995—. Named Man of the Yr., Mo. State Young Reps., 1991; winning campaign mgr. in 7 out of 7 spl. elections for state rep. Mo. Rep. Party, 1993-94. Mem. Capital Area Young Reps., Cole County Rep. Club. Republican. Baptist. Home: 1704 Hayselton Dr Jefferson City MO 65109 Office: Mo Rep Party PO Box 73 Jefferson City MO 65102

KAMPMEIER, CURTIS NEIL, management consultant; b. Evanston, Ill., Aug. 15, 1941; s. Carlos Otto and Neva Lou (Brown) K.; m. Susan Brooks, Dec. 30, 1961; children: Rand, Elizabeth, Paul, John. BA with honors, Coll. of Wooster (Ohio), 1964; cert. bus. program, Alexander Hamilton Inst., N.Y.C., 1967. Sales rep. Westminster Press, Phila., 1964-67, Random House, Inc., N.Y.C., 1967-73; owner, cert. mgmt. cons. The Kampmeier Group, Columbus, Ohio, 1973—; lectr. in field. Author numerous articles and The Bus. Skills Inventory, 1993; book rev. editor Jour. Mgmt. Cons. Trustee Ohio Presbyn. Retirement Svcs., Columbus, 1984-87, Westminster Thurber Community, Columbus, 1984-87; commencement speaker Shawnee State Coll., Portsmouth, Ohio. Mem. Inst. Mgmr. Cons., Columbus C. of C.

KAMSLER, MILTON A., JR., internist; b. Phila., July 12, 1923; s. Milton A. and Mercia Marie Etta (Trenner) K.; m. Ruth M. Harris, Sept. 3, 1946; children: Scott, Susan, Kirk. BA, Amherst Coll., 1945; MD, U. Pa., 1947, postgrad. student, 1950-51. Diplomate Am. Bd. Internal Medicine. Intern Good Samaritan Hosp., Portland, Oreg., 1947-48; gen. practice Salem, Oreg., 1948-50; fellowship in internal medicine Cleve. Clinic, 1951-53; assoc. staff Henry Ford Hosp., Detroit, 1955-56; pvt. practice internal medicine Burlingame, Calif., 1956-83; staff internist VA Med. Ctr., Poplar Bluff, Mo., 1985-90; retired Brookfield, Wis., 1990—. Candidate for Rep. Congressional Nomination, Burlingame, Calif., 1978. Capt. U.S. Army Med. Corps, 1953-55. Mem. AMA, Am. Coll. Physicians. Home: 4520 Compton Ct Brookfield WI 53045-8164

KANE, CAROLYN, language professional, writer; b. Hereford, Tex., July 25, 1944; d. John Ewing and Katherine Edna (Miller) K. BA, Hendrix Coll., 1966; PhD, U. Ark., 1973. Writing cons. Hendrix Coll., Conway, Ark., 1972-74; asst. prof. English Henderson State U., Arkadelphia, Ark., 1974-75, King Coll., Bristol, Tenn., 1975-76; prof. English Culver-Stockton Coll., Canton, Mo., 1977—. Author: The Bored Wizard, 1985, The Witch Who Wasn't Sensible, 1987, Creative Writing, 1995, The Fabulous Royal Junque, 1995, The Mystery of the Lost Letter, 1995, Gramma and Composition, 1996; contbr. articles to profl. jours. Adminstrv. v.p. River Rd. Toastmasters, Canton, Mo., 1989-91; mem. exec. coun. Mo. conf. AAUP, 1991-95. Recipient Best Novel Manuscript award Children's Book Writers Midwest Conf., 1987. Mem. Nathaniel Hawthorne Soc. (adv. bd. 1985-87), Soc. Children's Book Writers and Illustrators, Nat. Coun. Tchrs. of English. Office: Culver-Stockton College Canton MO 63435

KANE, MICHAEL J., dean; b. Phila., Feb. 26, 1953; s. Harry James Jr. and Nancy Louise K.; m. Alisa G. Edwards, June 18, 1976; children: Bethany A., Michael J., Robert E. BS, Central Miss. State U., Warrensburg, 1975; ThM, Dallas Theol. Sem., Dallas, 1983; PhD, U. North Texas, Denton, 1990. Biochemist Gulf Oil Chem. Co., Merriam, Kans., 1976-78; owner/mgr. Texas Green Lawn Hydromulchers, 1979-82; asst. registrar Dallas Theol. Sem., Dallas, 1981-86, dir. ch. data svc., 1985-86, instr. Christian edn., 1985-86; assoc. prof. edn. Providence Coll., Otterburne, 1986-93; dean, edn. svcs. Moody Bible Inst., Chicago, 1993—; cons. Scripture Press; interim pastor Grunthal EMB 1989-90, Springfield Cmty. Ch. 1990-92, Mission Bapt. Ch., 1992-93. Contbr. articles to profl. jours. Mem. Am. Assn. for Higher Edn. Office: Moody Bible Institute 820 N LaSalle Blvd Chicago IL 60610

KANE, ROBERT B., mathematics educator, academic dean; b. Oak Park, Ill., July 27, 1928; married; 5 children. BS in Math., U. Ill., 1950, MS in Math. Edn., 1958, PhD in Math. Edn., 1960. Secondary sch. math. tchr., 1950-51; math. analyst Armed Forces Security Agy., 1951-53; with mktg. dept. Standard Oil Co., 1953-57; exec. sec. Ill. Citizens' Edn. Com., 1957-58; rsch. assoc. U. Ill., Champaign, 1958-60; asst. prof. edn. & math. Purdue U., West Lafayette, Ind., 1960-63, assoc. prof., 1963-68, prof. edn. & math., 1968-93, chmn. math. & sci. edn., 1970-75, head dept. edn., dir. tchr. edn., 1975-88; dean sch. edn. Purdue U., West Lafayette, 1988-91; vis. rsch. prof. edn. U. Canterbury, Christchurch, New Zealand, 1969-70, dean edn. and prof. emeritus math. edn., 1993; cons. Depts. Pub. Instrn., Ind., N.Y., N.C., Pa., Tex., N.J., also sch. dists. in 20 states and Washington, D.C.; cons. New Zealand Ministry Edn.; condr. 120 workshops for tchrs., suprs., sch. adminstrs.; math. cons. New Standard Encyclopedia; proposal evaluator NSF; mem. Edn. Senates Purdue U. Schs. Humanities, Social Sci.; mem., chair area com. for social scis. & edn. Purdue U. Grad. Coun.; mem. select joint com. on minimal competency testing Ind. State Legislature; instl. rep., mem. steering com. Midwest region Holmes Group; mem., vice-chair curriculum standards com. Ind. Curriculum Adv. Coun.; editorial advisor jours. Arithmetic Tchr., Jour. Rsch. in Math. Edn., Math. Tchr. Co-author: The Modern Mathematics Series (108 total vols.), 1963-64, Operating with Mathematics, 1969, New Goals in Mathematics, 1969, Action Masters for Mathematics in Action (6 total vols.), 1969, Activity Books for Mathematics in Action (12 total vols.), 1970, Target: Meeting Mathematics (78 total vols.), 1973-74, Trigonometry, 1973, College Algebra and Trigonometry, 1974, Helping Children Read Mathematics, 1974, Algebra and Trigonometry, Structure and Method, 1977, 86, General Mathematics, 1977, Fundamentals of Mathematics, 1982, Pre-Algebra, 1985, 35 other math. texts, tchr's. edits.; contbr. over 50 articles to profl. jours. Recipient 18 grants USOE, NSF, Purdue Rsch. Found., Phi Delta Kappa, U.S. Dept. Edn., U.S. Info. Agy., 1959-90. Fellow AAAS; mem. Am. Ednl. Rsch. Assn., Ind. Coun. Tchrs. Math. (bd. dirs. 1967-70, editor Ind. Math. Newsletter 1963-65), Nat. Coun. Tchrs. Math. (speakers' core 1967-71), Math. Assn. Am., Ind. Assn. Colls. for Tchr. Edn. (exec. com. 1977, v.p. 1979-80, pres. 1980-82), Am. Assn. Colls. for Tchr. Edn. (chief instl. rep. 1975-91), Big Ten/Big Eight Dean's Network, Phi Delta Kappa. Office: Purdue U Main Campus Dept Curriculum and Instrn Sch Edn West Lafayette IN 47907

KANET, ROGER EDWARD, political science educator, university administrator; b. Cin., Sept. 1, 1936; s. Robert George and Edith Mary (Weaver) K.; m. Joan Alice Edwards, Feb. 16, 1963; children: Suzanne Elise, Laurie Alice. PhB, Berchmanskolleg, Pullach-bei-Muenchen, Ger., 1960; AB, Xavier U., Cin., 1961; MA, Lehigh U., 1963; AM, Princeton U., 1965, PhD, 1966. Asst. prof. polit. sci. U. Kans., Lawrence, 1966-69, assoc. prof., 1969-74; joint sr. fellow Russian Inst. and Rsch. Inst. Communist Affairs, Columbia U., N.Y.C., 1972-73; vis. assoc. prof. U. Ill., Champaign, 1973-74; assoc. prof. U. Ill., Urbana-Champaign, 1974-78; prof. polit. sci. U. Ill., Urbana, 1978—, head dept. polit. sci., 1984-87, assoc. vice chancellor for acad. affairs, dir. internat. progs. and studies, 1989—; partipant exch. with Hungary and Poland, Internat. Rsch. and Exchs. Bd., 1976; cons. Inst. Pub. Policy Devel., Washington, 1977-79; assoc. Ctr. Advanced Study, U. Ill., 1981-82; mem. Coun. on Fgn. Rels., N.Y., 1991—; mem. Chgo. com. Chgo. Coun. on Fgn. Rels.; chair internat. edn. panel Com. Instl. Coop. (Big 10 & Chgo.); co-founder Ill. Consortium for Internat. Edn. Editor: The Behavioral Revolution and Communist Studies, 1971, On the Road to Communism, 1972, The Soviet Union and the Developing Countries, 1974, Soviet and East European Policy, 1974, Soviet Economic and Political Relations with the Developing World, 1975, Background to Crisis: Policy and Politics in Gierek's Poland, 1981, Soviet Foreign Policy and East-West Relations, 1982, Soviet Foreign Policy in the 1980s, 1982, The Soviet Union, Eastern Europe and the Third World, 1987, Asia in Soviet Global Strategy, 1987, The Limits of Soviet Power in the Developing World: Thermidor in the Revolutionary Struggle, 1989, The Cold War as Cooperation: Superpower Cooperation in Regional Conflict Management, 1991, Soviet Foreign Policy in Transition, 1992, Regional Conflicts and Conflict Resolution, 1995, Coping with Conflict After the Cold War, 1996; contbr. numerous articles to scholarly jours. and books. Co-founder, pres. Kans. Parents Assn. Hearing-Handicapped Children, 1968-70. Recipient U.S. Dept. State Rsch. award, 1976, Excellence in Undergrad. Teaching award U. Ill., 1981, 84, Faculty Achievement award Burlington No. Found., 1989,U.S. Inst. Peace award, 1991; fellow NDEA, 1963-66, NATO, 1976, Internat. fellow Fed. Inst. for East European and Internat. Studies, Cologne, Fed. Republic of Germany, 1988; Am. Coun. Learned Socs. grantee, 1972-73, 78. Mem. Am. Assn. Advancement of Slavic Studies, Am. Polit. Sci. Assn., Assn. Internat. Edn. Adminstrs. (bd. dirs.), Internat. Polit. Sci. Assn., Internat. Studies Assn. (chairperson Am.-Soviet rels. sect. 1990-92), Midwest Slavic Conf. (program chmn. 1980-81), Internat. Coun. for Ctrl. and Ea. European Studies (program chmn. 1st World Congress 1974), Ctrl. Slavic Conf. (pres., program chmn. 1966-67), Midwest Polit. Sci. Assn., Assn. Internat. Edn. Adminstrs., Midwest Univ. Consortium Internat. Activities (bd. dirs. 1989—), Nat. Assn. State Univ. and Land Grant Colls. (internat. commn. 1992—), Ill. Consortium for Internat. Edn. (co-founder 1993, chair com. for instrnl. coop. internat. program officers 1993—). Roman Catholic. Home: 3805 Farhills Dr Champaign IL 61821-9304 Office: U Ill 303 Internat Studies Bldg 910 S 5th St Champaign IL 61820-6216

KANFER, JULIAN NORMAN, biochemist, educator; b. Bklyn., May 23, 1930; s. Benjamin N. and Clara (Lichtenberger) K.; m. Beverly Kanfer; children—Brian, Rachel. B.Sc., Bklyn. Coll., 1954; M.Sc., George Washington U., 1958, Ph.D., 1961. Biochemist Mass. Gen. Hosp., Boston, 1969-75; dir. biochem. research E.K. Shriver Center, Waltham, Mass.; also dir. research W.E. Fernald State Sch., Waltham, 1969-75; adj. asso. prof. biochemistry Brandeis U., Waltham, 1969-75; asso. prof. neuropathology Harvard, 1969-75, prin. research assoc., 1974-75; prof. U. Man., Winnipeg, Can., 1975—; head dept. biochemistry U. Man., 1975—; cons. Health Scis. Centre, Winnipeg, 1976—; mem. med. adv. bd. Nat. Tay-Sachs Found., N.Y.C., 1970—; mem. study sect. on pathobiol. chemistry NIH, 1974—; postdoctoral fellowship com. NRC, 1983—; mem. Grant Commn. Nutrition and Metabolism Med. Rsch. Coun., Can., 1992—; vis. prof. dept. psychiatry U. Pitts. Med. Ctr., 1993-94. Contbr. articles to profl. jours. Bd. dirs. Winnipeg chpt. Multiple Sclerosis Soc. Can., 1976. Fellow Inst. de la Sante et de la Recherche Medicale (France); mem. Am. Soc. Biol. Chemistry, Am., Internat. neurochemistry socs., Am. Chem. Soc., AAAS, Soc. for Complex Carbohydrates, Fedn. Am. Socs. for Exptl. Biology, Can. Fedn. Biol. Socs., Canadian Biochem. Soc. Office: 770 Bannatyne St, Winnipeg, MB Canada R3E 0W3

KANG, JUAN, pathologist; b. Chang-Young, Kyung-Nam, Republic of Korea, Aug. 10, 1935; came to U.S., 1965; s. Bugon and Umchun (Chung) K.; children: Angie, Alex, Erik. PreMed, Kyung-Pook U., Taegu, Republic of Korea, 1955; MD, Kyung-Pook U., 1959. Diplomate Am. Bd. Pathology, Am. Bd. Radioisotopic Pathology, Am. Bd. Hematology, Am. Bd. Dermatopathology. Capt. Med. Corps Republic of Korea Army, 1959-65; intern Watts Hosp., Durham, N.C., 1965-66; resident St. Louis U. Hosp., 1968-70; pathologist Allen Pathology Group, St. Louis, 1971—; clin. asst. prof. St. Louis U. Med. Sch., 1979--. Mem. AMA, Am. Soc. Clin. Pathologists, Coll. Am. Pathologists, Internat. Acad. of Pathologists, Am. Soc. Dermatopathology, Soc. for Hematopathology. Home: 12939 Banyan Town Dr Saint Louis MO 63146-4300 Office: Christian Hosp NE 11133 Dunn Rd Saint Louis MO 63136-6119

KANNE, MICHAEL STEPHEN, federal judge; b. Rensselaer, Ind., Dec. 21, 1938; s. Allen Raymond and Jane (Robinson) K.; m. Judith Ann Stevens, June 22, 1963; children: Anne, Katherine. Student, St. Joseph's Coll., Rensselaer, 1957-58; BS, Ind. U., 1962, JD, 1968; postgrad., Boston U., 1963, U. Birmingham, Eng., 1975. Bar: Ind. 1968. Assoc. Nesbitt and Fisher, Rensselaer, 1968-71; sole practice Rensselaer, 1971-72; atty. City of Rensselaer, 1972; judge 30th Jud. Cir. of Ind., 1972-82, U.S. Dist. Ct. (no. dist.) Ind., Hammond, 1982-87, U.S. Ct. Appeals, Chgo., 1987—; chmn. U.S. Cts. Design Guide, 1988-95; lectr. law St. Joseph's Coll., 1975-89, St. Frances Coll., 1990-91; faculty Nat. Inst. for Trial Advocacy, South Bend, Ind., 1978-88. Bd. visitors Ind. U. Sch. Law, 1987—, Ind. U. Sch. Pub. and Environ. Affairs, 1991—; trustee St. Joseph's Coll., 1984—. Served to 1st lt. USAF, 1962-65. Recipient Disting. Service award St. Joseph's Coll., 1973, Disting. Grad. award Nat Cath. Ednl. Assn.; named Outstanding Alumnus Today's Catholic Teacher, 1991. Mem. Fed. Bar Assn., Ind. State Bar Assn. (bd. dirs. 1977-79, Presdl. citation 1979), Jasper County Bar Assn. (pres. 1972-76), Tippecanoe County Bar Assn., Law Alumni Assn. Ind. U. (pres. 1980). Roman Catholic. Home: PO Box 1340 Lafayette IN 47902 Office: US Ct Appeals 219 S Dearborn St Chicago IL 60604-1702

KANNENBERG, KENNETH KARL, media center administrator; b. Goldfield, Iowa, Jan. 2, 1937; s. Carl Ernest and Ruth Margaret (Dean) K.; m. Patricia Rae Hillary, Sept. 14, 1958; children: Kristi Ann, Kenneth Kyle, Kenda Rae. BA, Buena Vista U., Storm Lake, Iowa, 1958; MA in Div., Garrett Bibl. Inst., Evanston, Ill., 1961; MA in L.S., U. No. Iowa, Cedar Falls, 1974. Ordained to ministry Methodist Ch., 1961. Min. United Meth. Ch., Calamus, Iowa, 1961-63; tchr. English and speech West Bend (Iowa) Cmty. Schs., 1963-69, Spirit Lake (Iowa) Cmty. Schs., 1969-75; dir. Media Ctr. Spirit Lake (Iowa) Cmty. Schs., 1973—. Mem. NEA, Iowa State Edn. Assn., Spirit Lake Edn. Assn. (pres. 1972, membership chair 1993), Iowa Ednl. Media Assn., Ducks Unltd., Pheasants Forever. Office: Spirit Lake HS 900 20th St Spirit Lake IA 51360

KANNING, EUGENE H., food service company executive; b. Bessemer, Mich., Jan. 30, 1939. BSCE, Valparaiso (Ind.) U., 1961. Indsl. sales engr. Peoples Energy Co. of Chgo., 1961-70; engr., sales coord. F.W. Boelter, Milw., 1970-78; v.p. Food Syss., Inc., Wauwatosa, Wis., 1978-86; pres. E.H. Kanning, Wauwatosa, 1986—; cons. Milw. Co. Minority Food Svc. Vendor,

1980-90. Contrb. articles to profl. jours. Constrn. coord. St. Paul Lutheran Ch., Chgo., 1970, Hope Lutheran Ch., Milw., 1984; leader Boy Scouts Am., Wauwatosa, Wis., 1988-90. Blue Ribbon award Foof Mgmt. Mag., 1994. Mem. Am. Soc. Food Svc. Cons. Republican. Lutheran. Office: E H Kanning & Assocs 11611 W North Ave Milwaukee WI 53226-2100

KANOUSE, ANDREW ROBERT, government official; b. Elgin, May 8, 1954; s. Robert and Gertrude (Bala) K. BA, No. Ill. U., 1978. Contbr. articles and photographs to Inscape and Visual Art. Interviewer Cook County Legal Assistance Found., Inc., Arlington Heights, Ill., 1983-85; supporter Campaign for Oxford, U. Oxford. Mem. Am. Polit. Sci. Assn., Am. Hist. Assn., Am. Assn. for the Advancement of Slavic Studies, Friends of Taliesin (Frank Lloyd Wright Found.'s support group), Royal Photographic Soc. Gt. Britain, Internat. Ctr. Photography, N.Y.C., Friends of Creative Monochrome, Eng. Home: 215 N Brighton Pl Arlington Heights IL 60004-6345

KANOUSE, DONALD LEE, wastewater treatment executive; b. Kankakee, Ill., Mar. 11, 1935; s. Rueben Thomas and Ethel Lee (Small) K.; m. Delourese Mae Welch, May 9, 1967; children: Roseanna, Michael, Karen, Kristine. Student, LaSalle U., 1970, Mich. U., 1991. Gen. foreman Kroehler Furniture Mfg., Kankakee, 1963-80; ops. supr. Met. Wastewater Utility, Kankakee, 1980—. Mem., environ. del. to China, People to People Citizen Amb. Program divsn. Internat. Amb. Programs, Inc., 1994. With USN, 1951-52, U.S. Army, 1954-57, 60-63, USAR, 1957-60. Named Parent of Yr. Eureka Coll., 1989-90. Mem. Nat. Platform Assn., Ill. Assn. Wastewater Opers., Water Environ. Fedn., Am. Legion (post 85). Home: 988 S Nelson Ave Kankakee IL 60901-5639 Office: Kankakee Met Wastewater Utility PO Box 588 1600 W Brookmont Blvd Kankakee IL 60901-2023

KANSTEINER, BEAU KENT, municipal official; b. St. Charles, Mo., Mar. 15, 1934; s. Herbert Henry and Coramery (Wallenbrock) K. BS in Mech. Engring., U. Kans., 1957. Engr. The Boeing Co., Seattle, New Orleans and Wichita, Kans., 1961-68, 69, 71, Beech Aircraft Corp., Wichita, 1970; mgr. prodn. distbn. Leavenworth (Kans.) Water Works Bd., 1971—. Lt. comdr. USN, 1957-61, USN Res. ret. Mem. NRA, Am. Water Works Assn. (chmn. Kans. sect. 1984-85, dir. 1991-94), Naval Res. Assn., U. Kans. Alumni ASsn. Office: Leavenworth Water Dept 601 Cherokee St Leavenworth KS 66048-2627

KANTER, BURTON WALLACE, lawyer; b. Jersey City, Aug. 12, 1930; s. Morris and Beatrice (Wilsker) K.; m. Naomi R. Krakow, June 17, 1927; children: Joel, Janis, Joshua. BA, U. Chgo., 1951, JD, 1952. Bar: Ill. 1952. Cons. U.S. Treasury Dept., 1959-61; atty.-advisor Tax Ct. U.S., 1954-56; mem. Law Offices of David Altman, Chgo., 1956-60; ptnr. Altman, Levenfeld & Kanter, Chgo., 1961-64, Levenfeld & Kanter, Chgo. and San Francisco, 1964-80, Kanter & Eisenberg, Chgo., 1980-87, of counsel Neal, Gerber, Eisenberg, 1987—; bd. dirs. Sci. Measurement Systems, Inc., Logic Devices, Inc., HealthCare COMPARE Corp., Power-Cell, Inc., Channel Am. LPTV, Inc.; chmn. Walnut Fin. Svcs. Inc.; faculty U. Chgo. Law Sch. Mem. adv. bd. Wharton Real Estate Ctr. U. Pa.; bd. dirs. Chgo. Internat. Film Festival, Midwest Film Ctr. of Sch. Art Inst.; mem. U. Chgo. Tax Policy Council; trustee Mus. Contemporary Art. Mem. ABA, Ill. Bar Assn., Chgo. Bar Assn., Urban Land Inst. Editor Jour. Taxation; contbr. articles to profl. jours. Office: 22nd Fl 2 N La Salle St Chicago IL 60602-3702

KANTER, JEROME JACOB, insurance company executive; b. Detroit, May 30, 1957; s. Austin A. and Harriet (Egrin) K.; m. Sherry Lynn Grossinger, Aug. 9, 1980; children: Jason Aaron, Joshua Samuel. BA, U. Mich., 1979; JD, Wayne State U., 1982. Agent Nat. Life of Vt., Detroit, 1980—, middle mgr., 1985-89, asst. gen. agent, 1990—; gen. agent, 1991—; chief oper. officer Kanter & Assocs., ABG, Detroit, 1989-91; gen. agt. Nat. Life of Vt., Detroit, 1991—. Mem. liaison bd. Jewish Welfare Fedn. Mem. Nat. Assn. Life Underwriters, Greater Detroit Assn. Life Underwriters, Gen. Agts. and Mrs. Assn., Southeast Mich. Agts. and Mgrs. Assn. (bd. dirs. 1991, pres.-elect).

KANZEG, DAVID GEORGE, radio programming director; b. Cleve., Apr. 9, 1948; s. George and Ida Marie Ada (Hienz) K. BA, Coll. Wooster (Ohio), 1970; MS, Syracuse (N.Y.) U., 1971; postgrad., SUNY, 1972. Cert. ESL lang. instr. Instr. English Meyer Lang. Ctr., Bogota, Colombia, 1969; grad. teaching asst. Syracuse U., 1971; instr. speech State U. Coll. at Buffalo, N.Y., 1971-73; exec. producer Sta. WCMU-FM Cen. Mich. U., Mt. Pleasant, 1973-76; radio program mgr. Sta. WLRH/Madison County Pub. Libr., Huntsville, Ala., 1976-77; radio program dir. Sta. WOUB-AM-FM Ohio U. Telecommunications, Athens, 1977-83; mgr. programming Sta. WNYC/N.Y. Pub. Radio, N.Y.C., 1983-86; sta. advisor Corp. for Pub. Broadcasting, Cleve., 1978-87; dir. programming Sta. WCPN/Cleve. Pub. Radio, 1987—; cons. Corp. for Pub. Broadcasting Mgmt. Consulting Svc., 1993—; participant seminars on future pub. radio, San Francisco and Washington, 1984-85; panel mem. Airlie IV Seminar on Art of Radio, N.Y.C., 1983; radio organizer Nat. Assn. Ednl. Broadcasters, Washington, 1976-78; exec. producer Future Forward Nat. Radio Series, 1985. Author: Transit Revisions, 1988, Ever Young: Douglas Moore and the Persistence of Legend, 1993; contbr. articles to pubs. Mem. Isabella County sub-com. on transp., Mt. Pleasant, Mich., 1975; incorporator Mid-Mich. Opera Assn., Mt. Pleasant, 1975, Tenn. Valley Opera Assn., Hunstville, 1976; mem. media panel Ohio Arts Coun., Columbus, Ohio, 1979-80; active Airlie II Seminar on Art of Radio, 1979. Recipient Tech. Prodn. award Ohio Ednl. Broadcasting, 1980, Ohio State award, 1986. Mem. Ohio Pub. Radio Programming (group chmn. 1978-80), Assn. Inds. in Radio, No. Ohio Bibliophilic Soc., Sigma Delta Pi. Home: 16253 Shurmer Rd Cleveland OH 44136-6115 Office: Sta WCPN/Cleve Pub Radio 3100 Chester Ave Cleveland OH 44114-4604

KAO, LESLIE M., developement engineer; b. Tai Pei, Taiwan, May 5, 1966. BSME, U. Wash., 1991; ME, Cornell U., 1992. Devel. engr. Allen-Bradley Co., Milw., 1993—. Christian. Office: Allen-Bradley Co 1201 S 2nd St Milwaukee WI 53204

KAO, WILLIAM CHISHON, dentist; b. Santiago, Chile, July 10, 1952; s. John S. and Mary Kao; m. Susie M. Moy, June 3, 1978; children: Jonathan, Kristen. BS with high honors, U. Ill., Chgo., 1974, BS in Dentistry with honors, 1976, DDS with honors, 1978. Comprehensive inst. U. Ill. Coll. Dentistry, Chgo., 1978-80; dentist, assoc. Dental Bldg., Oak Lawn, Ill., 1978-83; pvt. practice Carol Stream, Ill., 1978-82; dentist Preventive Dental Group, Glendale Heights, Ill., 1982-86; pvt. practice Roselle, Ill., 1986—. Mem. ADA (presiding chmn. ltd. attendance clinic at midwinter conv. 1980), Am. Acad. Implant Dentistry, U.S. Dental Inst., Ill. State Dental Soc., Chgo. Dental Soc., Ill. Dental Soc., Roselle C. of C., Bloomingdale Study Club, Lake Park Hockey Club (sec.). Office: 1150 Lake St Roselle IL 60172-3365

KAPETANSKY, GLENN, insurance company executive; b. Columbus, Ohio, Sept. 25, 1959; s. Frederick Maurice and Audrey (Rosin) K.; m. Esther Eva Rubin, June 16, 1987; children: Dena Devorah, Netanya Reva, Ezra Levi. BS in Computer Sci., Math cum laude, Rose-Hulman Inst. Tech., Terre Haute, Ind., 1981; MS in Computer Sci., U. Ill., 1984. System engr. Chem. Abstracts Svc., Columbus, 1980-81; mem. tech. staff AT&T Bell Labs., Naperville, Ill., 1983-96; dir. Internet techs. CNA Ins. Cos., Chgo., 1996—. Mem. IEEE, Computer Profls. for Social Responsibility, Computer Profls. and Tech. Pers. (co-chmn. 1988-96). Office: CNA Ins Cos CNA Plz Chicago IL 60685

KAPITAN, MARY L., retired nursing administrator, educator; b. Lawrence, Mass., July 9, 1920; d. Vincent and Concetta (Tomaselli) Zazzo; m. John A. Kapitan, Sept. 6, 1947. Diploma, Somerville (Mass.) Hosp., 1944; BS in Nursing Edn., DePaul U., Chgo., 1960, MS in Nursing Adminstrn., 1962. RN; lic. health facility adminstr., Ind. Occupational health nurse E. I. duPont de Nemours & Co., Lincolnwood, Ill., Senco Corp., Newtown, Ohio; asst. prof. psychiat. and med. nursing No. Ky. U., Highland Heights; nursing coord. VA Hosp., Butler, Pa.; instr. psychiat. nursing Ohio Valley Community Hosp., McKees Rocks, Pa.; dir. nursing svc. Presbyn. Home, Evanston, Ill., Edgewater Hosp., Chgo., Franklin Blvd Hosp., Chgo. 1st lt. U.S. Army Nurse Corps, 1944-47. Mem. ANA, Am. Assn. Occupational Health Nurses, Am. Coll. Health Facility Adminstrs., Ohio Nurses Assn., Ill. Nurses Assn., Ind. Nurses Assn., Mass. Nurses Assn., Southwestern Ohio Assn. Occupational Health Nurses (chmn. legislation and edn. com.), Women in Mil. Svc. for Am., Women's Meml. Found.

KAPLAN, BERNICE ANTOVILLE, anthropologist, educator; b. N.Y.C., Apr. 21, 1923; d. Meyer and Marie (Antoville) K.; m. Gabriel Ward Lasker, July 31, 1949; children: Robert Alexander, Edward Meyer, Anne Titania. B.A., Hunter Coll., N.Y.C., 1943; M.A. (Univ. fellow 1944-45, Univ. and Field Mus. fellow 1945-46), U. Chgo., 1947, Ph.D., 1953. Asso. in anthropology Am. Mus. Natural History, 1941-44, Field Mus. Natural History, 1947-48; instr. anthropology and sociology U. Wis., 1946-47, Hobart and William Smith Colls., 1948-49; instr. to asso. prof. anthropology Wayne State U., Detroit, 1949-67; asso. prof. Wayne State U., 1967-79, prof., 1979—; lectr. U. Mich., Ann Arbor and Grand Rapids, summers 1955, 59, U. Calif., Berkeley, 1960-61; field work, Michoacán, Mex., 1948, 52, 53, 59, 61, 65, and Province of Lambayeque, Peru, 1957-58, London, 1977. Contbr. articles to profl. jours. Rep., Birmingham (Mich.) PTA Council to Birmingham Bd. Edn., 1971-76; bd. dirs. Southfield Jr. Symphony, 1972-75. Fulbright scholar, 1957-58; fellow-commonorship Churchill Coll., Cambridge U. (Eng.), 1983-84; named to Hunter Coll. Hall of Fame, 1988. Fellow Am. Anthrop. Assn., AAAS (chmn. sect. H 1973-74), Am. Assn. Phys. Anthropologists, Soc. for Applied Anthropology (mem. exec. bd. 1976-79); mem. Am. Ethnological Soc. (sec. 1978-82), Central State Anthrop. Soc. (pres. 1972-73, co-editor Central Issues in Anthropology 1978-89), Sigma Xi. Home: 31339 Pierce St Birmingham MI 48025-5513 Office: Wayne State U Dept Anthropology Manoogian Hall Detroit MI 48202

KAPLAN, JARED, lawyer; b. Chgo., Dec. 28, 1938; s. Jerome and Phyllis Enid (Rieber) K.; m. Rosellen Engstrom, Dec. 28, 1964 (div. 1978); children: Brian F., Philip B.; m. Maridee Quanbeck, June 2, 1990. AB, UCLA, 1960; LLB, Harvard, 1963. Bar: Ill. 1963, U.S. Dist. Ct. (no. dist.) Ill. 1969, U.S. Tax Ct. 1978. Assoc. Ross & Hardies, Chgo., 1963-69, ptnr., 1970; ptnr. Roan & Grossman, Chgo., 1970-83, Keck, Mahin & Cate, Chgo., 1983-94, McDermott, Will & Emery, Chgo., 1994—; bd. dirs. ESOP (Employee Stock Ownership Plan) Assn., Washington, 1987-90, Chicagoland Enterprise Ctr., Chgo., 1987-89; adv. coun. Ill. Employee-Owned Enterprise, Chgo., 1984—; chmn. Ill. Adv. Task Force on Ownership Succession and Employee Ownership, 1994-95. Editor in chief: Callaghan's Fed. Tax Guide, 1988; author: Employee Stock Ownership Plans, 1991. Nat. pres. Ripon Soc., Washington, 1975-76; adv. council mem. Rep. Nat. Com., Washington, 1978-80; alt. delegate Rep. Nat. Conv., Detroit, 1980. Fellow Ill. Bar Found.; mem. ABA (chmn. section of taxation, administrv. practice com. 1978-80), City Club, Chgo. (bd. govs. 1982-92), Univ. Club. Republican. Jewish. Home: 105 W Delaware Pl Chicago IL 60610-3200 Office: McDermott Will & Emery 227 W Monroe St Fl 44 Chicago IL 60606-5096

KAPLAN, MITCHELL PHILIP, consulting engineer, marketing executive; b. Chgo., Jan. 8, 1942; s. Fred Aaron and Geraldine (Aprill) K.; m. Susan Lois Schecter, Aug. 7, 1966; children: Jennifer, Barry. BS in Metall. Engring., U. Ill., 1965; MS in Materials Sci., U. So. Calif., L.A., 1969. Registered profl. engr., Ill. Mfg. engr. McDonnell-Douglas Aircraft, Santa Monica, Calif., 1965-66; rsch. scientist Lockheed Aircraft Corp., Burbank, Calif., 1966-71; mem. tech. staff Rockwell Internat., El Segundo, Calif., 1971-72; br. scientist fracture Aero. Systems div. USAF, Dayton, Ohio, 1972-79; engring. specialist FAA, Chgo., 1979-81; sr. scientist Triodyne Inc., Niles, Ill., 1981-84; v.p. Willis & Kaplan, Inc., Buffalo Grove, Ill., 1984—; pres. Larry McGee Co., Chgo., 1991—; designated engring. rep. on structures, engines and powerplant FAA, 1991—; cons. on safety and design, failure analysis Ins. & Mfg. co., 1981—; dir. new product design Larry McGee Co., 1991—. Contbr. articles to profl. jours. and handbooks; referee tech. articles various profl. orgns.; mem. engr.'s coun. Design News Mag. NSF grantee, 1969. Mem. ASTM, SAE, ASM Internat., Am. Welding Soc. Office: Willis & Kaplan Inc 720 Armstrong Dr Buffalo Grove IL 60089-1884

KAPLAN, PAUL ELIAS, physiatrist, educator; b. N.Y.C., Oct. 26, 1940; m. Candia Starling Post, June 18, 1966; children: Steven Post Hitchcock, Heather, Danielle Richards. BA cum laude, Amherst Coll., 1962; MD, UCLA, 1966. Diplomate Am. Bd. Phys. Medicine and Rehab., Am. Bd. Electrodiagnostic Medicine. Intern in internal medicine Ohio State U. Hosp., Columbus, 1966-67; resident in internal medicine Cedars-Sinai Med. Ctr., L.A., 1969-70, UCLA Med. Ctr., 1970-71; NIH fellow, resident in phys. medicine & rehab. U. So. Calif. Med. Ctr., L.A., 1971-73; pvt. practice Beverly Hills, Calif., 1973-74; prof. medicine and internal medicine Inst. of Chgo./Northwestern U., 1974-86; prof., dept. chmn., med. dir. Rusk Rehab. Ctr. U. Mo., Columbia, 1986-89; Bert C. Wiley prof., chair phys. medicine and rehab. Ohio State U., Columbus, 1989—, chmn. dept., 1989-94, dir. residency program, 1992-94. Author several textbooks on phys. medicine and rehab.; editor-in-chief jour. Yearbook of Rehab., 1984-89; alt. editor Archives of Phys. Medicine and Rehab., 1988—; cons. editor Advance and Rehab Management, 1995—; contbr. more than 100 articles to profl. jours. Fellow ACP, Am. Acad. Phys. Medicine and Rehab.; mem. Assn. Acad. Psychiatrists (pres. 1987-89, pres. coun. of chairpersons), Am. Spinal Injury Assn. Office: Ohio State U Dodd Hall Rehab Ctr 480 W 9th Ave Columbus OH 43210-1245

KAPLAN, RANDY KAYE, podiatrist; b. Detroit, Sept. 18, 1954; s. Earl Gene and Renee Joy (Sheftel) K. D of Podiatric Medicine, Ohio Coll., Cleve., 1979. Diplomate Am. Bd. Podiatric Surgery. Resident Kern Hosp., Warren, Mich., 1979-80; pvt. practice specializing in podiatric medicine, surgery Detroit, 1980—; clin. instr., mem. staff Kern Hosp., Warren, 1980—; adj. prof. Ohio Coll. Podiatric Medicine, 1986—, Pa. Coll. Podiatric Medicine, 1986—; mem. staff Providence Hosp., 1995; lectr. in field. Contbr. articles to profl. jours. Co-founder The Great Lakes Conf., 1989. Recipient Earl G. Kaplan award for polit. action excellence, 1994; Inspector Gen's. Integrity award U.S. HHS, 1995. Fellow Am. Coll. Foot Surgeons; mem. Am. Diabetes Assn., Am. Podiatric Med. Assn. (mem. continuing edn. com. 1988—, mem. labor rels. com. 1990—), Mich. Podiatric Med. Assn. (bd. dirs. 1985—, 2nd v.p. 1988-90, pres. 1990-91, 92-93, Podiatrist of Yr. Southeastern divsn. 1987-88, Shining Star award for excellence 1992), Kern Hosp. Resident Alumni Assn., Mich. Pub. Health Assn., Phi Alpha Pi (Man of Yr. 1979). Jewish. Office: 20511 Dequindre St Detroit MI 48234-1259

KAPLAN, THOMAS ABRAHAM, physics educator; b. Phila., Feb. 24, 1926; s. Michael Jay and Nellie (Cohan) K.; m. Patricia Ruth Roe, Nov. 24, 1956; children: Melissa Ann, Andrea Jean, Laurie Michelle. BSME, U. Pa., 1948, PhD in Physics, 1954. Rsch. assoc. Engring. Rsch. Inst., U. Mich., Willow Run, 1954-56; rsch. assoc. Brookhaven Nat. Lab., Upton, N.Y., 1956-58; staff mem. Lincoln Lab., MIT, Lexington, Mass., 1959-70; prof. physics Mich. State U., East Lansing, 1970-95, prof. emeritus, 1995—; cons. Naval Rsch. Lab., Washington, summer 1979-80; vis. scientist Max-Planck Inst. für Festkörperforschung, Stuttgart, Fed. Republic Germany, 1981-82, 88-89, summer 1983-84, Inst. für Festkörperforschung der Nuclear Physics Rsch. Inst. Jülich, Fed. Republic Germany, 1982; disting. vis. prof. U. Tsukuba, Ibaraki, Japan, 1989. Contbr. numerous articles on theoretical condensed matter physics to profl. jours. Petty officer 2nd class USNR, 1944-46. Recipient sr. scientist award Alexander von Humboldt Stiftung, 1981. Fellow Am. Phys. Soc.; mem. Sigma Xi. Democrat. Jewish. Office: Mich State U Dept Physics Astronomy East Lansing MI 48824

KAPLAN, YAKOV, mechanical design engineer; b. Gomiel, USSR, Feb. 21, 1959; came to U.S., 1990; M Mech. Engring., Mech. Inst., Gomel, 1985. Design engr., project Advanced Indsl. Mfg., Inc., Columbus, Ohio, 1990-91, Panasonic, Troy, Ohio, 1991-94; with ATE divsn. Schlumburger, Westerville, 1994—. Patentee for assembly line equipment, geoscience, umbrella, USSR; contbr. articles to profl. jours. Office: Schlumberger Techs 8377 Green Meadows Dr N Westerville OH 43081-9443

KAPPES, KEN J., stockbroker; b. Mpls., Dec. 27, 2940. BS in Mktg., St. Cloud (Minn.) State U., 1965. Claims adjuster Crawford & Co., Atlanta and Kalamazoo, 1965-66, St. Paul Ins. Co., St. Cloud, 1966-70; claims mgr. Millbank Mut., Fargo, N.D., 1970-79; stockbroker Dain Bosworth, Inc., Fargo, 1979—. With USN, 1958-61. Mem. KC. Republican. Roman Catholic. Office: Dain Bosworth Inc 74 Broadway Fargo ND 58102-4934

KAPPES, PHILIP SPANGLER, lawyer; b. Detroit, Dec. 24, 1925; s. Philip Alexander and Wilma Fern (Spangler) K.; m. Glendora Galena Miles, Nov. 27, 1948; children: Susan Lea, Philip Miles, Mark William. BA cum laude, Butler U., 1945; JD, U. Mich., 1948. Bar: Ind. 1948, U.S. Supreme Ct. 1970; ct. cert. mediator, Ind. Pvt. practice Indpls., 1948; assoc. Armstrong and Gause, 1948-49, C. B. Dutton, 1950-51; ptnr. Dutton, Kappes & Overman, 1952-85, of counsel, 1983-85; ptnr. Lewis Kappes Fuller & Eads, Indpls., 1985-89, Lewis & Kappes, Indpls., 1989-92, Lewis & Kappes PC, Indpls., 1993—, Labeco Properties, Creston Group, Indpls.; pres., dir. K&K Realty, Inc., Indpls.; sec., dir., mem. exec. com. Lab. Equipment Corp., Mooresville, Ind., sec., dir. Labthermics Tech. Inc.; instr. bus. law Butler U., 1948-49, chmn. bd. govs., 1965-66, bd. trustees, 1987-90; chmn. Ovid Butler Soc., 1982-83. Life bd. dirs. Crossroads Am. coun. Boy Scouts Am., 1965—, v.p. fin., mem. exec. com., pres., 1977-79, chmn. trustees endowment fund, 1987-92, trustee, 1987—; bd. dirs. Fairbanks Hosp., Indpls., 1986-94, chmn. bd., 1988-91, exec. com., 1987-94, mem. audit and fin. com., 1992-94, life dir. emeritus, 1994—, chmn. nominating com., 1991; trustee Butler U., 1987-90, Children's Mus., Indpls., 1969-88, pres. bd. trustees, 1984-85, bd. disting. advisors, 1990—; mem. First Meridian Heights Presbyn. Ch., 1933—, chmn. bd. trustees, 1958-61, ruling elder, deacon, 1950-58. Recipient Paul H. Buchanan award of excellence Indpls. Bar Found. Mem. ABA (ho. of dels. 1970-71), Ind. State Bar Assn. (ho. dels. 1959—, chmn. pub. rels. exec. com. 1966-69, sec. 1973-74, bd. mgrs. 1975-77, chmn. law practice mgmt. com. 1991-92), Indpls. Bar Assn. (treas., 1st v.p. 1965, pres. 1970, bd. mgrs. 1968-71, 75-77, chmn. law day com. 1991-92, settlement week com. 1989—, co-chair Family Law Study Commn., co-chair ct. liaison com. 1992-93, family law implementation com. 1993—, mem. exec. com. bd. mgrs. 1994—, counsel bd. mgrs. 1994), Am. Judicature Soc., Indpls. Legal Aid Soc., Indpls. Jr. C. of C. (past 1st v.p., dir.), ct. unification implementation com. (chmn. 1995—) Butler U. Alumni Assn. (past pres.), Mich. Alumni Assn, Masons (33 degree, most wise master Indpls. chpt. Rose Croix 1982-84), Shriners, Meridian Hills Country Club, Lawyers Club, Gyro Club (pres. 1966), Mystic Tie Lodge (worshipful master 1975), Phi Delta Theta (chpt. advisor 1950-82), Tau Kappa Alpha. Republican. Presbyterian. Home: 624 Somerset Dr W Indianapolis IN 46260-2924 Office: 1210 One American Sq Indianapolis IN 46282-0003

KAPTUR, MARCIA CAROLYN, congresswoman; b. Toledo, Ohio, June 17, 1946. B.A., U. Wis., 1968; M. Urban Planning, U. Mich., 1974; postgrad., U. Manchester, (Eng.), 1974, MIT; LLD (hon.), U. Toledo. Urban planner; asst. dir. urban affairs domestic policy staff White House, 1977-79; mem. 98th-103rd Congresses from 9th Ohio dist., Washington, D.C., 1983—; mem. Appropriations com., subcom. Agrl., D.C., Veterans, HUD, indep. agys. Bd. dirs. Nat. Ctr. Urban Ethnic Affairs; adv. com. Gund Found.; exec. com. Lucas County Democratic Com.; mem. Dem. Women's Campaign Assn. Mem. Am. Planning Assn., Am. Inst. Cert. Planners, NAACP, Urban League, Polish Mus., U. Mich. Urban Planning Alumni Assn. (bd. dirs.), Polish Am. Hist. Assn. Roman Catholic. Clubs: Lucas County Dem. Bus. and Profl. Women's, Fulton County Dem. Women's. Office: US House of Reps 2104 Rayburn Bldg Washington DC 20515-0005

KARA, PAUL MARK, lawyer; b. Valparaiso, Ind., Mar. 7, 1954; s. Charles J. and June F. (Williams) K.; m. Elizabeth Louise Smith, Aug. 18, 1979; children: Adeline M., Emily L., Charles J., Phillip H. BA, Ind. U., 1977, JD, 1980. Bar: Mich. 1980, U.S. Dist. Ct. (we. dist.) Mich. 1980, U.S. Ct. Appeals (6th cir.) 1985. Assoc. Landman, Luyendyk, Latimer Clink & Robb, Muskegon, Mich., 1980-84, ptnr., 1984-86; ptnr. Varnum, Riddering, Schmidt & Howlett, Grand Rapids, Mich., 1986—. Pres., bd. dirs. Sr. Services of Muskegon, Inc., 1985—, Cath. Social Services of Muskegon, 1985—. Glenn Peters fellow, Ind. U., 1977-79, Louden Meml. fellow Ind. U., 1977-79. Mem. ABA (labor law sect., litig. sect., com. on devels. under NLRA), Mich. Bar Assn. (labor rels. law sect. coun. 1985-87, chairperson 1995—), Muskegon County Bar Assn. (pres. 1985-86), Grand Rapids Bar Assn., Univ. Club Chgo. Republican. Home: 3905 Norton Hills Rd Muskegon MI 49441-4456 Office: Varnum Riddering Schmidt & Howlett Bridgewater Place PO Box 352 Grand Rapids MI 49504

KARABASZ, FELIX FRANCOIS, engineering and manufacturing company executive; b. Phila., June 3, 1939; s. Victor Stanislaus and Mary Audry (Pie) K.; m. Norma Christine Goss, June 8, 1963; children: Michael J., Douglas N. BS in Naval Sci., U.S. Naval Acad., 1963. Commd. ensign USN, 1963, advanced through grades to lt. comdr., 1971, resigned, 1967; lt. comdr. USNR, 1972—; with Container Corp. Am., Phila., 1967-72, Masonite Corp., 1972-80; plant mgr. Sun Electric Corp., Crystal Lake, Ill., 1981; v.p., dir. mfg. Hart & Cooley, Holland, Mich., 1982-86; sr. v.p. ops. Lau div. Philips Industries, Dayton, Ohio, 1986; v.p., gen. mgr. Indsl. Air div. Philips Industries, Amelia, Ohio, 1987-91; gen. mgr. Quickdraft div. C.A. Litzler Co., Inc., Canton, Ohio, 1992—. Home: 5536 Armistice Ave NW Canton OH 44718-1300 Office: Quickdraft PO Box 80659 1525 Perry Dr NW Canton OH 44708-1829

KARG, THELMA AILEEN, writer, retired educator; b. Crawfordsville, Ind., June 30, 1918; d. Fred and Orpha Fern (Stewart) Crow; m. Henry Herbert Karg, Aug. 18, 1944 (dec. June 1982); children: Susan Marie Chrysler, Karen Ann Weiss. BS, Taylor U., 1952; MS, Ind. State U., 1968. With Harry N. Fine Atty. at Law, Crawfordsville, Ind., 1936-37; office control clerk R.R. Donnellys & Sons Co., 1937-42, Allisons Gen. Motors, Indpls., 1942-43; accts. receivable Mid States Steel and Wire, 1943-46; tchr. Ind. State Tchrs. Assn.-Nat. Edn. Assn., Milw., Oreg., 1952-55, ISTA-NEA, Crawfordsville, Ind., 1955-62; tchr. Evang. United Brethren Ch., Terre Haute, Ind., 1962-65, Harrison, Ohio, 1968-70; tchr. Perrysville Highland Elem. Sch., Perrysville, Ind., 1970-74, various schs., Danville, Ill., 1975-76; tchr. Shelbyville, Ind., 1976-82, Waldron, Ind., 1983-95. Contbr. article to profl. jours. and newspapers. Mem. Nat. Rep. Congrl. Com., 1993—, senatorial com.; spkr. ladirs groups United Meth.; nurse's aid ARC. Recipient Editor's Choice award Nat. Soc. Poets, 1992-95. Mem. Christian Writers' (leader 1983-95), Ind. State Tchrs. United Methodist. Home: 1004 Cottage Ave Crawfordsville IN 47933-1506

KARIM, MUHAMMAD BAZLUL, international studies educator; b. Mymensingh, Bangladesh, Dec. 26, 1949; arrived in U.S., 1975; s. Abdul and Akika Khatoon Bari; m. Jean Ellickson, July 26, 1975. BA with honors, Dhaka (Bangladesh) U., 1972, MA in Geography, 1973; MA in Geography, Western Ill. U., 1978; cert. in computer programming, Strayer Coll., Washington, 1981; MA in Internat. Studies, U. Denver, 1984, cert. in devel. studies, 1985, PhD in Internat. Studies, 1991. Asst. dir. Integrated Rural Devel. Program, Dhaka, 1973-74; rsch. asst. Rajshahi (Bangladesh), 1974-75; rsch. assoc. Ethikos Rsch., Inc., Silver Spring, Md., 1980-81; rsch. asst. Internat. Food Policy Rsch. Inst., Washington, 1981; owner, pres. MBK Software Products, Macomb, Ill., 1993-95; instr. Spoon River Coll., Macomb, 1991-95; asst. prof. Western Ill. U., Macomb, 1994—; presenter in field. Author: A Farmer's Market in America, 1981, The Green Revolution: An International Bibliography, 1986, Structural Constraints to Participatory Development: An Examination of Social Stratification System in Rural Bangladesh, 1992, Participation, Development and Social Structure: An Empirical Study in a Developing Country, 1994; contbr. articles and rsch. reports to profl. jours. Vol. flood victims, Kampsville, Ill., 1993; election judge primary and gen. election Macomb City Precinct #7, McDonough County, Ill., 1990. Rsch. fellow Shell Cos. Found., 1987; grad. rsch. assistantship U. Denver, 1984-85, stipend and tuition scholar, 1983-84. Fellow Internat. Biog. Assn.; mem. ASCD, Internat. Studies Assn. (environ. studies sect.), Am. Polit. Sci. Assn., Assn. Asian Studies, Assn. Am. Geographers (population specialty group, rural devel. specialty group), Assn. 3d World Studies, Inc. Home: 155 Doe Run Macomb IL 61455

KARKUT, RICHARD THEODORE, clinical psychologist; b. Derby, Conn., Apr. 28, 1948; s. Harry Chester and Mary (Katz) K. AB, William Jewell Coll., 1971; MA, U. Mo., Kansas City, 1976; D Psychology, Forest Inst. Profl. Psychology, 1988. Lic. psychologist, Ohio, Ind.; cert. in biofeedback. Psychology intern Burrell Mental Health Ctr., Springfield, Mo., 1987-88; clin. psychologist Wabash Valley Hosp., Lafayette, Ind., 1989-91, Quinco Cons., North Vernon, Ind., 1991-93; CEO Adkar Assocs., Inc., Bloomington, Ind., 1993—; cons. Div. Family Svcs., Lafayette, 1989-90. Guest editor jour. Ind. Psychologist; contbr. articles to profl. jours. Mem. Am. Psychol. Assn., Soc. Behavioral Medicine, Assn. Applied Psychophysiology and Biofeedback, Am. Pain Soc., Am. Soc. Clin. Hypnosis, Am. Orthopsychiat. Assn., Am. Assn. Counseling and Devel., Am. Mental Health

Counselor's Assn., Ind. Psychol. Assn., Ill. Psychol. Assn., Ind. Biofeedback Soc. Anglican. Home: PO Box 1396 Bloomington IN 47402-1396

KARL, RANDALL GREGORY, electrical engineer; b. Peru, Ill., Dec. 13, 1954; s. Russell George and Ella Evelyn (Frew) K.; m. Debra Lefkowitz, Mar. 28, 1987; children: Emily, Michael. BS in Elec. Engring. Tech., So. Ill. U., 1977, BA in Computer Sci., 1981; MS in Computer Sci., U. Mo., Rolla-St. Louis, 1992. Elec. engr. Westclox div. Talley Industries, LaSalle, Ill., 1977-79; teaching asst., programming cons. So. Ill. U., Carbondale, 1979-81; elec. engr., software engr. Electronics & Space Corp., St. Louis, 1981—. Author procs. Mem. IEEE, ESCO Engrs. Club, St. Louis Unix Users Group. Home: 1747 Wishingwell Saint Louis MO 63146

KARLEN, DOUGLAS LAWRENCE, soil scientist; b. Monroe, Wis., Aug. 28, 1951; s. Lawrence Herman and Marian Bertha (Trumpy) K.; m. Linda Sue Bender, June 9, 1973; children: Sarah Jean, Steven Douglas, Holly Lin. BS, U. Wis., 1973; MS, Mich. State U., 1975; PhD, Kans. State U., 1978. Rsch. soil scientist Coastal Plains Soil, Water Conservation Rsch. Ctr., USDA-ARS, Florence, S.C., 1978-88, Nat. Soil Tilth Lab. USDA-ARS, Ames, Iowa, 1988—; team leader Leopold Ctr. for Sustainable Agr., Ames, 1989-94. Asst. scoutmaster, com. chmn. Boy Scouts Am., Ankeny, Iowa, 1991—. Fellow Am. Soc. Agronomy, Crop Sci. Soc. Am. (assoc. editor 1988-93, tech. editor 1994—), Soil Sci. Soc. Am. (chmn. divsn. S6 1993); mem. Coun. Agrl. Sci. and Tech., Soil and Water Conservation Soc. Am. Episcopalian. Office: USDA-ARS-MWA-NSTL 2150 Pammel Dr Ames IA 50010

KARLIN, GARY LEE, insurance executive; b. Chgo., Jan. 18, 1934; s. Jack and Pearl (Malin) K.; children: David, Paige; m. Cheryl Daneman. Student U. Ill., 1951-52, Roosevelt U., 1952. With Mut. of N.Y., 1956-62, sales mgr., Chgo., 1958-62, regional trainer, 1962-63; pres. Exec. Motivation, Inc., Chgo., 1964—; fin. planner, 1980—; chmn. field underwriters benefits/contracts com. MONY, 1974-85; v.p. Exec. Planning Svcs. div. Alexander & Alexander, Inc.; dir. Vasocor, Inc., Miami, Fla., 1990—, Perception, Inc., Miami, 1993—; v.p., treas. Exec. Fin. Group divsn. F.P.I.S., Inc., 1993—; cons. in field; speaker numerous ins. seminars. Contbg. editor Profl. Mgmt. mag., 1965-67; subject (poem) There are No Hero's Anymore; contbr. articles to profl. jours; subject of ins. film Impressions of Life (award). Mem. Internat. Assn. Fin. Planners, Chgo. Assn. Life Underwriters (past. bd. dirs.), Nat. Assn. Life Underwriters (life), Million Dollar Round Table (Top of Table), Ill. Leaders Round Table (past pres.). Home: 839 N Dearborn St Chicago IL 60610-3373

KARLIN, JAMES EDWARD, accountant, tax specialist; b. Kansas City, Mo., Feb. 1, 1950; s. Alphonse Joseph and Emma Elizabeth (Bleier) K.; m. Linda Susan Pickett, June 9, 1973; children: Brian James, Lisa Dyane. BS in Acctg., Kans. State U., 1972. CPA, Kans. Sr. auditor Peat Marwick Mitchell & Co., Kansas City, Mo., 1972-75; cons. Larsen Barth & Assocs., Kansas City, 1975-76; sr. analyst Butler Mfg. Co., Kansas City, 1976-79, internal audit mgr., 1979-83, asst. contr., 1983-90, dir. tax, 1990-93; dir. tax. GS Techs. Corp., 1994-95; dir. tax UtiliCorp United, Inc., Kansas City, Mo., 1995—. V.p., treas. Ozanam Home for Boys, Kansas City, 1986-93; treas. troop 265 Boy Scouts Am., Overland Park, 1991-93, com. chmn., 1994-95; vol. Big Bros., Kansas City, 1974-76. Mem. AICPA, Tax Execs. Inst. (pres. 1989-90), Alvamar Country Club. Republican. Roman Catholic. Home: 10328 Cody St Overland Park KS 66214-2690 Office: UtiliCorp United Inc 10700 E 350 Hwy PO Box 11739 Kansas City MO 64138

KARLL, JO ANN, state agency administrator, lawyer; b. St. Louis, Nov. 16, 1948; d. Joseph H. and Dorothy Olga (Pyle) K.; m. William Austin Hernlund, Sept. 9, 1990. Bar: Mo. 1993. Ins. claims adjuster, 1967-88; state rep. Mo. Gen. Assembly dist. 104, 1991-92; mem. from dist. 105 Mo. Gen. Assembly, 1992-93; dir. Mo. State Divsn. Worker's Compensation, Jefferson City, 1993—. Mem. exec. bd. Jefferson County Dem. Club, 1988-92; committeewoman Jefferson County Ctrl. Dem. Com., Rock Twp., 1988-91; bd. dirs. Mid-East Area Agy. on Aging, 1991-93. Mem. NOW, Nat. Women's Polit. Caucus, Bus. and Profl. Women's Clubs (treas. 1987-89). Office: Mo St Divsn Worker's Compensation 3515 W Truman Blvd Jefferson City MO 65109-5715

KARLOWSKI, RICHARD MARTIN, reliability engineer; b. Highland Park, Mich., Apr. 9, 1958. BS, Mich. Tech. U., 1980; MS, U. Mich., 1982. Quality assurance specialist Gen. Dynamics Land Systems, Sterling Heights, Mich., 1983-93; sr. reliability engr. Saturn Cor./GM, Madison Heights, Mich., 1993—. Planning com. Greenfield Village Colonial Mus., Dearborn, Mich., 1993. Mem. Am. Soc. Quality Control (cert. quality and reliability engr.), Soc. Reliability Engr. Home: 2031 N Lovington # 102 Troy MI 48083 Office: Saturn Corp P O Box 7025 Troy MI 48007-7025

KARNATH, JOAN EDNA, editor; b. St. Paul, July 14, 1947; d. Charles Omar and Marie Edna (Gorg) League; m. Richard John, July 24, 1971 (div. Mar. 1981). BS in Elem. Edn., Winona State U., 1970, MS in Elem. Edn., 1978. Tchr. Ind. Sch. Dist. 234, Rushford, Minn., 1971-82; beauty cons. Mary Kay Cosmetics, Dallas, 1982-84; hostess Ramada Hotel, Inc., St. Paul, 1983-84; coord., computer ctr. 3M Co., St. Paul; lead editor Unisys Corp., St. Paul, 1984—; mem, sec. Rushford Edn. Assn., 1971-82. Editorial advisor Info. DesigNews, 1990—. Precinct Chairwoman Ind. Reps., Winona, 1980-81; Sec. Eden Home Assn., Eagan, 1987-92. Recipient award of merit Soc. Tech. Commn., 1989, 94, 95, award of distinction, 1993, 94, 95, achievement award Soc. Tech. Commn., 1995. Mem. AAUW, NEA, TESOL, Minn. Edn. Assn., U. Minn. Global Edn. Com., Profl. Editors Network, Unisys Profl. Women's Forum, Toastmasters Internat. Republican. Roman Catholic. Home: 4423B Clover Ln Saint Paul MN 55122-2437 Office: Unisys Corp 2276 Highcrest Rd Saint Paul MN 55113-2510

KARNES, EVAN BURTON, II, lawyer; b. Chgo.; s. Evan Burton and Mary Alice (Brosnahan) K.; m. Bridget Anne Clerkin, Oct. 9, 1976 (dec. June 1994); children: Kathleen Anne, Evan Burton III, Molly Aileen, Lauren Jean. AB, Loyola U., Chgo., 1975; JD, DePaul U., 1978; grad. civil trial advocacy program, U. Calif. Hastings Coll. Law, 1979. Bar: Ill. 1978, U.S. Dist. Ct. (no. dist.) Ill. 1978, U.S. Ct. Appeals (7th cir.) 1978, U.S. Dist. Ct. (no. dist.) Ind., 1995, U.S. Supreme Ct. 1983. Trial atty. Chgo. Milw. St. Paul & Pacific R.R., Chgo., 1978-81; litigation dept. Baker & McKenzie, Chgo., 1981-87; sr. litigation counsel, Levin & Ginsburg Ltd., Chgo., 1987-89; of counsel Oppenheimer, Wolff & Donnelly, 1989-91; prin. Law Offices of Evan B. Karnes II & Assocs.; bd. dirs. Triad Communications Inc, Albuquerque, chmn. bd., 1988. Mem. fin. com. Village of Northfield, Ill., mem. planning and zoning commn., 1990—, vice-chmn. 1994—. Mem. ABA, ATLA, Ill. Bar Assn., Fed. Bar Assn. (bd. mem. Chgo. chpt.), Chgo. Bar Assn., Def. Rsch. Inst., Nat. Assn. R.R. Trial Counsel (chmn. sci. evidence com. 1995—), Ill. Trial Lawyers Assn., Union League Club, Blue Key (sec. Loyola U. chpt. 1974-75), Pi Sigma Alpha, Phi Alpha Delta. Office: Xerox Centre 55 W Monroe St 32d Fl Chicago IL 60603

KARNES, JAN ARLA, marketing executive; b. Kalamazoo, Mich., May 31, 1960; d. John Arlon and Joyce Elizabeth (Fountain) Zielinski; m. Joseph Allen Karnes, Aug. 25, 1990. BA in Econs., U. Mich., 1982, MBA, 1984. Brand asst. The Procter and Gamble Co., Cin., 1984-85, asst. brand mgr., 1985-88; mktg. mgr. level 1 Campbell Soup Co., Camden, N.J., 1988-89; mktg. mgr. level 2 Campbell Soup Co., Camden, 1989-90; dir. mktg. level 1 Hills div. Colgate-Palmolive, Topeka, 1990-93; dir. mktg. level 2 Hills div. Colgate-Palmolive, 1993—. Big sister Big Bros./Big Sister, Cin., 1987-88. Recipient Bronze Echo award Direct Mktg. Assn., 1991, POPAI Gold award, 1994. Office: Colgate-Palmolive Hills Div 400 SW 8th Ave Topeka KS 66603-3925

KARNIOTIS, STEVEN PAUL, computer scientist; b. Detroit, July 27, 1963; s. Christ Emmanuel and Mary (Zangkas) K. BA in Computer Sci., Wayne State U., 1985, MBA in Mgmt. Info. Systems, 1994. Cert. Oracle database adminstr., cert. Oracle 7 database adminstr. Computer lab. mgr. Wayne State U., Detroit, 1982-85; programmer, analyst A.J. Foland & Co., Dearborn and Livonia, Mich., 1984-85; ednl. cons. CompuWare Corp., Farmington Hills, Mich., 1985-88; programmer, analyst Compuware Copr., Farmington Hills, Mich., 1989-92, oracle database adminstr., 1990—, mgr. oracle tech., 1993—; v.p. Detroit Oracle Users Group, 1994—; tech. advisor Oracle VMS Spl. Interest Group, 1991—, Midwest Oracle User Group, 1992—; v.p., advisor Oracle for MVS Spl. Interest Group, Redwood Shores, California, 1990-93; tech. judge Ednl. Testing Svc., Princeton, N.J., 1995. Contbr. articles to jours. and newsletters. Treas., bd. dirs. Greek Orthodox Young Adult League Detroit Diocese, 1991—. Recipient Peer Recognition award Ford Motor Co. Powertrain Ops., 1994. Mem. Alpha Kappa Psi (life, pres. Wayne State U. chpt. 1984-85). Office: Compuware Corp 31440 Norhtwestern Hwy Farmington Hills MI 48334

KARNS, MARGARET PADELFORD, political science educator; b. Winchester, Mass., Oct. 14, 1943; d. Norman J. and Helen (Proctor) Padelford; m. David Alan Karns, Apr. 29, 1967 (div. Sept. 1984); 1 child, Paul Alan. BA, Denison U., 1965; MA, U. Mich., 1966, PhD, 1975. Rsch. asst. Brookings Instn., Washington, 1969-70; instr. SUNY, Cortland, 1970-71; asst. to dean Cornell U., Ithaca, N.Y., 1971-72; asst. prof. Wells Coll., Aurora, N.Y., 1972-73; asst. prof. polit. sci. U. Dayton, Ohio, 1976-83, assoc. prof., 1983-90, prof., 1990—, dir. Ctr. for Internat. Studies, 1983—; rsch. fellow Roosevelt Ctr. for Am. Policy Studies, Washington, 1982-83; vis. prof. Hopkins-Nanjing (China) Ctr. for Chinese and Am. Studies, Nanjing, 1995-96; fellow Am. Coun. on Edn., Washington, 1988-89; assoc. Mershon Ctr., Ohio State U., Columbus, 1986—; Fulbright lectr., Brazil, 1992. Co-author, co-editor: The United States and Multilateral Institutions, 1990; co-author: The United Nations in the Post-Cold War Era, 1995; also numerous articles. Pres. bd. dirs. Dayton Coun. on World Affairs, 1984-85. Mem. Am. Polit. Sci. Assn. (coun. 1985-87), Internat. Studies Assn. (v.p. 1991-92), Internat. Polit. Sci. Assn., Acad. Coun. on UN System (coun. 1988-91), Rotary. Office: Univ Dayton Ctr for Internat Programs Dayton OH 45469-1481

KAROLIN, STELLA HELENE, psychiatrist; b. Estonia, July 3, 1922; came to U.S., 1950; d. Arnold Mihkel and Johanna Helene (Wiedebaum) Pohla; m. Arno Karolin, Dec. 17, 1949; children: Jaak, Mari-Ann, Andres. Student, Tartu U., Estonia, 1942-44; MD, Georg August U., Göttingen, Germany, 1950. Diplomate Am. Bd. Psychiatry and Neurology. Intern Meml. Hosp., Albany, N.Y., 1954-56, mem. housestaff, 1957-58; resident in psychiatry Ohio State U. Hosp., Columbus, 1962-65; unit chief, physician advisor, dir. tng.-edn. and residency Cen. Ohio Psychiat. Hosp., Columbus, 1965-77, staff privileges, 1965-88; staff psychiatrist S.W. Community Mental Health Ctr., Inc., Columbus, 1977-80, dir. psychiat. svcs., 1980-86; med. dir. acute care unit, then med. dir. Netcare, Inc., Columbus, 1986-88; ret., 1988; part-time pvt. practice, Worthington, Ohio, 1989—; bd. dirs. Mary Haven, Inc., 1968-70, cons. psychiatrist, 1970-77; staff psychiatrist Concord Mental Health Ctr., Westerville, Ohio, 1989-92; cons. psychiatrist Cath. Social Svcs., Columbus, 1989—; courtesy staff Mt. Carmel Med. Ctr., Columbus. Recipient Leadership award Franklin County Mental Health Assn., 1988; named to Franklin County Mental Health Bd. Hall of Fame, 1988. Mem. Am. Psychiat. Assn., Internat. Soc. for Study of Dissossiations, Ohio Psychiat. Assn., Ctrl. Ohio Psychiat. Assn. Office: 951 High St Lower Level Worthington OH 43085

KARON, BERTRAM PAUL, psychologist, educator; b. Taunton, Mass., Apr. 29, 1930; s. Harold Banny and Celia (Silverman) K.; m. Mary Kathryn Mossop, Oct. 17, 1957; 1 son, Jonathan Alexander. A.B., Harvard, 1952; M.A., Princeton, 1954, Ph.D. (USPHS fellow), 1957; grad., Council fellow; grad. Social Sci. Research Council Inst. Maths. for Social Scientists, Dartmouth, summer 1953. Research fellow psychometrics Ednl. Testing Service and Princeton, 1952-55; intern in direct analysis John N. Rosen, M.D., Gardenville, Pa., 1955-56; sr. clin. psychologist Annandale (N.J.) Reformatory, 1958; psychologist, dir. research Akron (Ohio) Psychol. Cons. Center, 1958-59; research psychologist Phila. Psychiat. Hosp., 1959, USPHS fellow, 1959-61; practice clin. psychology Phila., 1961-62; asst. prof. psychology Mich. State U., 1962-63, asso. prof., 1963-68, prof., 1968—; vis. lectr. Calif. Sch. Profl. Psychology, Los Angeles; vis. scholar Wright Inst., Los Angeles, 1979; Research cons. U.S. Naval Hosp., Phila., 1962, U. Pa., 1962; lectr. psychiatry Ypsilanti (Mich.) State Hosp., 1964-65; cons. VA Hosp., Allen Park, Mich., 1966-75, Ann Arbor, Mich., 1971-72. Author: The Negro Personality: A Rigorous Investigation of the Effects of Culture, 1958, rev. edit., Black Scars, 1975, (with others) Psychotherapy of Schizofrenia: The Treatment of Choice, 1981; contbg. author: Projective Techniques in Personality Assessment, 1968, Techniques for Behavior Change, 1971, The Schizophrenic SyndromeL An Annual Review, 1971, The Construction of Madness, 1976, Assessment with Projective Techniques: A Concise Introduction, 1981; editor: Affects, Imagery, and Consciousness (Silvan S. Tomkins), vols. 1 and 2, 1962, 63; contbr. numerous articles on schizophrenia and psychoanalysis to profl. jours. NIMH grantee, 1966-71. Fellow Am. Psychol. Assn. (divsn. psychotherapy, clin. phsychology, divsn. psychoanalysis); mem. Soc. Psychothreapy Rsch., Am. Statis. Assn., Psychologists Interested in Study Psychoanalysis, Mich. Psychoanalytic Coun. (pres. 1993-95). Home: 420 John R St East Lansing MI 48823-3710

KARP, DANIEL JOSEPH, manufacturing executive; b. N.Y.C., Dec. 26, 1928; s. Aaron and Margaret (Melman) K.; m. Shaney K. Karp, June 6, 1954 (dec. May 1987); m. Rosemary O. Karp, Feb. 20, 1995; children: Philip, Susan, Amie. BA, George Washington U., Washington, 1966. V.p. adminstrn. Heuristic Concepts, N.J., 1968-69; dir. distbn. Gallo Wine of N.Y., Bklyn., 1969-71; dir. ops. Keene Lighting, Union, N.J., 1972-81; sr. group dir. materials mgmt. Revlon, Edison, N.J., 1981-85; dir. planning Caswell Massey, N.Y.C., 1985-88; exec. v.p., dir. ops. Devine Design, North Kansas City, Mo., 1988-94. Mem. editl. rev. bd. Production and Inventory Management Jour., 1995. Pres. Greater PTA of Anchorage, 1961-62. Lt. col. USAF, 1948-68, Korea, Vietnam. Mem. Am. Prodn. and Inventory Control Soc. (pres. N.J. chpt. 1980, chmn. pres. coun. 1983). Office: Devine Design 1 Design Dr North Kansas City MO 64116-3096

KARPINSKI, DONALD G., stockbroker; b. Grand Rapids, Mich., Sept. 24, 1934. BA, Mich. U., 1956. CPA. Acct. Alexander Grant, Grand Rapids, Mich., 1969-81; stockbroker Peninsular Securities Co., Grand Rapids, 1981—. Contbr. articles to profl. jours. With U.S. Army, 1957-59. Mem. Exch. Club (past pres.). Roman Catholic. Office: Peninsular Securities Co 161 Ottawa Ave NW Ste 100-a Grand Rapids MI 49503-2701

KARR, GERALD LEE, agricultural economist, state senator; b. Emporia, Kans., Oct. 15, 1936; s. Orren L. and Kathleen M. (Keller) K.; B.S., Kans. State U., 1959; M.S. in Agrl. Econs., So. Ill. U., 1962, Ph.D. in Econs., 1966; m. Sharon Kay Studer, Oct. 18, 1959; children: Kevin Lee, Kelly Jolleen. Livestock mgr. Eckert Orchards Inc., Belleville, Ill., 1959-64; grad. asst. So. Ill. U., Carbondale, 1960-64; asst. prof. econs. Central Mo. State U., Warrensburg, 1964-67; asst. prof. agrl. econs., head dept. Njala U., Sierra Leone, West Africa, 1967-70; asst. prof. agrl. econs. U. Ill., Urbana, 1970-72; asso. prof. agrl. econs., chmn. dept., mgr. coll. farms Wilmington (Ohio) Coll., 1972-76; farmer, Emporia, Kans., 1976—; mem. Kans. Senate, 1981—, elected minority leader, 1991; rsch. advisor Bank of Sierra Leone, Freetown, summer 1967; agrl. sector cons. Econ. Mission to Sierra Leone, IBRD, 1973. Mem. Am. Agrl. Econs. Assn., Lyon County Farmer Union, Lyon County Livestock Assn., Omicron Delta Epsilon, Farm House. Contbr. articles to profl. jours. Democrat. Methodist. Club: Kiwanis. Office: State Senate State Capitol Topeka KS 66612

KARR, JAMES BARRY, financial programmer; b. Elmhurst, Ill., May 30, 1945; s. John Melvin and Katherine Karr; m. Laurel Ann Spruth, May 3, 1966; children: Lisa A., Alison L., Jamie R., Samuel J. BBA, Elmhurst (Ill.) Coll., 1973; MBA in Prodn. Mgmt., Fla. Inst. Tech., 1977. Commd. 2d lt. U.S. Army, 1967, advanced through grades to lt. col., 1967-86; registered rep. and dist. agt. USPA & IRA, Ft. Worth, 1986—, dist. mgr., 1989—. Bd. dirs. Kansans for a Strong Ft. Riley, 1992-96. Decorated Bronze Star. Mem. Nat. Assn. Def. Preparedness, Manhattan (Kans.) C. of C. (mil. rels. com. 1986-96), Assn. of U.S. Army (bd. govs. 1995-96). Republican. Mem. Christian Ch. Clubs: Ducks Unltd., N.Am. Versatile Hunting Dog Assn. Home: 13315 Military Trail Rd Saint George KS 66535 Office: USPA & IRA 424 Delaware St Ste C-2 Leavenworth KS 66048

KARR, KENNETH JOHN, insurance broker executive; b. Evergreen Park, Ill., Nov. 23, 1962; s. Joseph Peter and Marilyn Elizabeth (Calder) K. A. in Biology, Moraine Valley C.C., Palos Hills, Ill., 1983; BA, St. Xavier U., Chgo., 1989. Lic. ins. salesperson, Ill. Co-founder Oak Profl. Maintenance, Oak Lawn, Ill., 1977-90; agro-forestry trainee Peace Corps, Guatamala, 1990; salesperson State Farm Ins., Chgo., 1991-95; owner/pres. Karr Ins. Svcs., Chgo., 1996—. Fundraiser Care, Inc., Chgo., 1993; vol. Habitat for Humanity Internat., 1993-95. Mem. K.C. Roman Catholic. Home: 10624 S Kildare Ave Oak Lawn IL 60453 Office: 4008 W 57th Pl Chicago IL 60629

KARRAKER, LOUIS RENDLEMAN, retired corporate executive; b. Jonesboro, Ill., Aug. 2, 1927; s. Ira Oliver and Helen Elsie (Rendleman) K.; m. Patricia Grace Stahlheber, June 20, 1952; children: Alan Louis, Sharon Elaine Cohen. BA, So. Ill. U., 1949, MA, 1952; postgrad., U. Wis., 1951-52, Washington U., St. Louis, 1954-56. V.p. personnel Am. Appraisal Assocs., Inc., Milw., 1969-73, v.p. adminstrn., 1973-74, group v.p., dir., 1974-77, exec. v.p., dir., 1977-79, pres., dir., 1979-82; bus. mgr. Concordia Coll., Ann Arbor, Mich., 1986-91; cons. in field, 1982-86; asst. to chmn. Parker Pen Co., Janesville, Wis., 1967-69, personnel mgr., 1964-67; asst. to pres. Augustana Coll., Sioux Falls, S.D., 1962-64, acting chmn., dept. social scis., 1960-61, asst. prof. history, 1956-60. Columnist The Jour. Times, Racine, Wis., 1993—; speaker Rep. and civic groups, Wis., 1993—. Trustee Better Bus. Bur., Milw., 1979-82, Citizens Govtl. Rsch. Bur., Milw., 1979-82; speaker, canvasser Rep. Party, S.D., 1956-60. With USNR, 1952-53, Korea. Mem. The Heritage Found., Hoover Presdl. Libr. Assn., Am. Legion. Lutheran. Home: 217 South 7th St Condo 11 Waterford WI 53185

KARS, RICHARD Y., stockbroker; b. Grand Rapids, Mich., Dec. 14, 1968. BA in Fin., Mich. State U., 1980. Sales rep. Equitable, Grand Rapids, 1990-94; stockbroker Stifel Nicolaus & Co., Grand Rapids, 1994—. Republican. Lutheran. Home: 5111 Fighter Rd Freeport MI 49325-9704 Office: Stifel Nicolaus & Co Ste # 301 2100 Raybrook St SE Grand Rapids MI 49546-5783

KARST, GREGORY MARK, physical therapist, educator; b. Great Bend, Kans., Aug. 14, 1954; s. Ralph Lawrence and Esther Marie (Dietz) K.; m. Melanie Jo Fron, Sept. 25, 1993. BS in Phys. Therapy cum laude, Wichita State U., 1976; MS in Animal Physiology, U. Ariz., 1984, PhD in Physiology, 1989. Cert. phys. therapist, Ariz., Nebr. Phys. therapist St. Mary's Hosp., Tucson, 1976-78, Tucson Gen. Hosp., 1978-79; phys. therapist in pvt. practice Tucson, 1979-84; rsch. asst. NASA-Ames Rsch. Ctr., Moffett Field, Calif., 1983-84; grad. teaching asst. U. Ariz., Tucson, 1984-89; asst. prof. U. Wis., Madison, 1989-92; assoc. prof. U. Nebr. Med. Ctr., Omaha, 1992—; instr. Pima C.C., Tucson, 1987-88. Contbr. chpt. to book, articles to profl. jours. Mem. Am. Phys. Therapy Assn., Am. Physiol. Soc., Soc. for Neurosci. Office: U Nebr Med Ctr 600 S 42d St Omaha NE 68198-4420

KARSTEN, BRIAN S., investment broker; b. Grand Rapids, Mich., Feb. 21, 1955. Owner, mgr. pub. co., Grand Rapids, 1979-80; office mgr. Bldg. Repair Grand Rapids, 1980-83; investment broker Kent King Securities, Fremont, Mich., 1983—. Mem. found. bd. Kellogg Phil Christian Sch., Kentwood, Mich., 1985—. Mem. Fremont C. of C. (bd. dirs. 1993—), Rotary. Republican. Mem. Christian Reformed Ch. Office: Kent King Securities PO Box 238 25 W Main St Fremont MI 49412

KARTSIMAS, JAMES M., investment broker, veterinarian; b. Traverse City, Mich., Feb. 18, 1953; m. Tisha C. Hovas, Aug. 13, 1983; children: Katherine, Juliana. BS, Ohio State U., 1975, DVM, 1979. Owner, veterinarian South Coast Equine, Santa Barbara, Calif., 1979-92; investment broker A.G. Edwards & Sons Inc., Traverse City, 1993—. Chmn. Walk Am., March of Dimes, Traverse City, 1994—; treas. Congl. Ch. Mem. Humane Soc., Kiwanis. Republican. Home: 4220 Deerfield Ln Traverse City MI 49684-8146 Office: AG Edwards & Sons Inc Delta Ctr 415 Munson Ave Traverse City MI 49686-3059

KARU, GILDA M(ALL), lawyer, government official; b. Oceanport, N.J., Dec. 1, 1951; d. Harold and Ilvy (Meriloo) K.; m. Frederick F. Foy, May 23, 1981. AB, Vassar Coll., 1974; JD, Ill. Inst. Tech., 1987. Bar: Ill. 1987, U.S. Dist. Ct. (no. dist.) Ill. 1987. Quality control reviewer Food and Nutrition Svc. USDA, Robbinsville, N.J., 1974-77, team leader, 1977-78, supr., 1978-81; sect. chief Food and Consumer Svc. USDA, Chgo., 1991—; employer adviser Ctr. for Rehab. and Tng. Disabled Persons, Chgo., 1986-93; chief mgmt. negotiator for collective bargaining agreement Nat. Treasury Employees Union, 1990. Bd. dirs., legal counsel, regional dir. North Ctrl. Estonian Am. Nat. Coun., N.Y.C.; v.p. 1st Estonian Evang. Luth. Ch., Chgo., treas., 1994—; mem. Chgo. Vol. Legal Svcs., Friends of Arlington Heights Meml. Libr.; vol. dep. voter registration officer Cook County, Ill.; pres. Arlington Heights-Mt. Prospect-Buffalo Grove area LWV. Recipient cert. of recognition William A. Jump Meml. Found., 1987, Arthur S. Flemming award Washington Downtown Jaycees, 1987, Ill. Dem. Ethnic Heritage award, 1989, cert. of appreciation Assn. for Persons with Disabilities in Agr., 1992, Group Honor award for work on 1993 Miss. River Flood Disaster Relief, Sec. of USDA, 1994. Mem. ABA, NAFE, LWV (bd. dirs. 1992—), Ill. Bar Assn., Chgo. Bar Assn., Baltic Bar Assn., United Coun. on Welfare Fraud, Internat. Platform Assn., Nat. Audubon Soc., Mensa, Vassar Club (chpt. treas. 1988-90, v.p. 1990-91, coord. pub. rels. 1991—). Office: USDA Food and Consumer Svc 20th Fl 77 W Jackson Blvd Fl 20 Chicago IL 60604-3504

KASCHAK, LAWRENCE MICHAEL, lawyer; b. Streator, Ill., July 29, 1966; s. Lawrence John and Mardella Ann (Fischer) K. BS in Polit. Sci., Northern Ill. U., 1988; JD, John Marshall Law Sch., 1991. Staff atty. State Appellate Prosecutor, Ottawa, Ill., 1992—. Mem. Ill. State Bar Assn. Roman Catholic. Home: 705 W First St Streator IL 61364 Office: State Appellate Prosecutor 628 Columbus St Ottawa IL 61350

KASICH, JOHN R., congressman; b. McKees Rocks, Pa., May 13, 1952. B.A., Ohio State U., 1974. Administrv. asst. Ohio State Senate, 1975-77; mem. Ohio Legislature, 1979-82, 98th-104th Congressse from 12th Ohio dist., Washington, D.C., 1983—; mem. nat. security com. 98th-104th Congressse from 12th Ohio dist., Washington, mem. house budget com., chmn. Office: House of Reps 1131 Longworth Washington DC 20515-0004*

KASIK, JOHN EDWARD, medical educator; b. Chgo., Aug. 9, 1927; s. Joe and Anna (Gilbertson) K.; m. Sherle Jones; children: Robert L., James E., Alan J., John W., Peter G., Susan Ann. BS, Roosevelt U., 1949; MS, U. Chgo., 1953, MD, 1954, PhD, 1960. Diplomate Am. Bd. Internal Medicine; lic. Ill., Iowa. Asst. prof., assoc. prof. U. Chgo., 1959-70; assoc. prof., prof. U. Iowa, Iowa City, 1970-80, assoc. dean, 1980—; cons. Velsicol Chem., Chgo., 1967-80, 1st Am. Corp., Salt Lake, 1980—. Contbr. numerous articles to profl. jours. Fellow Am. Thoracic Soc., Am. Phys. Soc. (Laureate award Iowa chpt. 1994). Office: VA Med Ctr Iowa City IA 52240

KASIMOS, JOHN NICHOLAS, pathologist; b. Chgo., Jan. 26, 1955; s. Nicholas John and Mia (Panos) K.; m. Helen Papadakis, July 10, 1994. BS in Biology, Loyola U., Chgo., 1978; MS in Biology, Ill. Inst. Tech., 1980; DO, Chgo. Coll. Osteopathic Med., 1984. Diplomate Nat. Bd. Examiners for Osteo. Physicians and Surgeons, Am. Osteo. Bd. Pathologists, Anatomic Pathology and Lab. Medicine. Intern Chgo. Osteo. Health Systems, 1984-85, resident pathology, 1985-89, pathologist, 1989—; asst. prof. pathology Chgo. Coll. Osteo. Medicine, 1989-93; assoc. prof. pathology Midwestern U., 1993—; acad. mentor, advisor Chgo. Coll. Osteo. Medicine, 1989—, dir. residence tng. dept. pathology, dir. deptl. edn./rsch., vice chmn. dept. pathology, 1993—. Fellow Coll. Am. Pathologists, Am. Soc. Clin. Pathologists; mem. Am. Osteo. Assn., Am. Osteo. Coll. Pathologists, U.S. and Can. Acad. Pathologists, Ill. Assn. Osteo. Physicans and Surgeons, Ill. Pathology Soc., Chgo. Pathology Soc. Greek Orthodox. Office: Olympia Fields Osteo Hosp & Med Ctr Dept Pathology 20201 Crawford Ave Olympia Fields IL 60461-1010

KASISCHKE, LOUIS WALTER, lawyer; b. Bay City, Mich., July 18, 1942; s. Emil Ernst and Gladys Ann (Stuady) K.; m. Sandra Ann Colosimo, Sept. 30, 1967; children: Douglas, Gregg. BA, Mich. State U., 1964; JD, Detroit Coll. Law, 1967; LLM, Wayne State U., 1971. Bar: Mich. 1968, U.S. Dist. Ct. (southeastern dist.) Mich. 1968; CPA. Acct. Touche Ross & Co., Detroit, 1967-71; atty. Dykema Gossett, Detroit, 1971—; pres. Pella Window and Door Co., West Bloomfield, Mich., 1990—; bd. dirs. Barton Malow Co., Southfield. Author: Michigan Closely Held Corporations, 1986; contbr. articles to profl. jours. Mem. ABA, AICPA, State Bar Mich. (editor column Mich. Bar Jour. 1971-83), Mich. Assn. CPAs, Am. Coll. Tax Counsel.

Republican. Lutheran. Home: 810 Hidden Pine Rd Bloomfield Hills MI 48304-2409 Office: Dykema Gossett 1577 N Woodward Ave Ste 300 Bloomfield Hills MI 48304-2820

KASKUBAR, BRUCE EDWARD, foundation executive; b. Racine, Wis., Jan. 12, 1954; s. Edward Joseph and Lucille Marie Kaskubar; m. Jessica Ariane Grosset, May 23, 1986; children: Andrew, Erin, Daniel, Mallorie. BS, Northwestern U., 1976. Analyst Modine Mfg., Racine, 1976-80, Mayo Found., Rochester, Minn., 1980—. Pres. Children's Rights Coun. of Minn., Rochester, 1993—; co-chair Olmsted County Reps., Rochester, 1995—. Home: 5905 Chateau Rd NW Rochester MN 55901

KASPUTIS, EDWARD, state legislator; b. Ashtabula, Ohio, Apr. 21, 1961; s. Edward and Vivian Kasputis; m. Lee Ferguson, children: Megan, Jay. BA, Case We. Res. U., 1983; JD, Cleve. State, 1984, MBA, 1987. State rep. Dist. 16 Ohio State Congress; owner ice cream bus.; assoc. lawyer Edward F. Kasputis & Assocs. Recipient Leadership award Freedom Forum, 1994, Watchdog of Treasury award United Conservatives, 1994. Mem. Nat. Lawyers Assn., Rocky River C. of C. (founder, pres.), Empowerment Found., Lions Club. *

KASS, LINDA S., writer, communications consultant, child advocate; b. Columbus, Ohio, Dec. 31, 1953; d. Ernest and Aurelia (Rosenminer) Stern; m. Michael Rubin (div.); 1 child, Matthew Stern Rubin; m. Franklin Eiferman Kass, June 8, 1987; children: Jessica Antonina (dec. 1990), Alexandra Jessica. BS, U. Pa., 1975; MA, Ohio State U., 1978. Freelance writer various publs., Columbus and Detroit, 1976-80; instr. dept. journalism Wayne State U., Detroit, 1978-80; dir. press rels. Warner Amex Cable Comm., Inc., N.Y.C., 1980-84; dir. corp. comm. Westinghouse Broadcasting Co., N.Y.C., 1984-87; cmty. vol. Columbus, 1989—; bd. trustees Mt. Carmel Health Found., Columbus, 1991—; found mem. Quality Childhood Collaborative of Franklin County, Columbus, 1993-94; bd. dirs. Columbus Ctr. for Media Edn. Co-author: The Real Life Nutrition Book, 1992. Bd. trustees Columbus Symphony Orch., 1994—; v.p. bd. edn. Bexley (Ohio) City Schs., 1994—, mem. Bexley Edn. Found., 1994—; pres. sustaining bd. Columbus Montessori Edn. Ctr., Columbus, 1993—, pres. bd. trustees, 1990-92. Recipient Hon. Mention in Nat. Clarion Award competition Women in Comm., 1979, "George" award for outstanding svc. and commitment to children Columbus Montessori Edn. Ctr., 1993. Mem. Ohio Sch. Bds. Assn. Home: 267 N Parkview Ave Columbus OH 43209

KASSEBAUM, NANCY LANDON, senator; b. Topeka, July 29, 1932; d. Alfred M. and Theo Landon; children: John Philip, Linda Josephine, Richard Landon, William Alfred. BA in Polit. Sci, U. Kans., 1954; MA in Diplomatic History, U. Mich., 1956. Mem. Maize (Kans.) Sch. Bd., 1972-75; mem. Washington staff Sen. James B. Pearson of Kans., 1975-76; mem. U.S. Senate from Kans., 1979—, mem. fgn. relations com., labor and human resources com., Indian Affairs com.; mem. com. fgn. rels., subcom. African affairs, 1980—, mem. subcom. arts, edn. Arts & Humanities, mem. com. banking, housing & urban affairs, subcom. internat. fin. & monetary policy. Mem. Kans. Press Women's Assn., Women's Assn. Instnl. Logopedics. Republican. Episcopalian. Office: US Senate 302 Russell Senate Bldg Washington DC 20510*

KASSON, SHIRLEY A., library administrator; b. Wahoo, Nebr., June 21, 1934; d. John Henry Vybiral and Mildred Lucille Croshaw; m. Charles Willis Kasson, May 31, 1955; children: Charles Jr., Anne, Daniel, Laura, Steven, Judith. BA in Edn., Western Mich. U., Kalamazoo, 1975, MLS in Librarianship, 1977; MLA Leadership (Hon.), MLA Leadership Acad., Lansing, Mich., 1990. Cert. librarian, Mich. Library asst. Comstock (Mich.) Twp. Library, 1973-75; asst. librarian children's dept. Comstock Twp. Library, 1975-77, library dir., 1977—; reference librarian Kalamazoo Valley C.C., 1989—; pres. Southwest Mich. Library Co-op, Paw Paw, 1981-82, mem. exec. bd., 1982-83, mem. budget and finance com., 1992-96, mem. personnel com., 1993-94, mem. evaluation com., 1995-96. Mem. Mich. Library Assn. (annual presenter 1992), Kappa Delta Pi, Beta Phi Mu. Office: Comstock Twp Library 6130 King Hwy Comstock MI 49041

KASTANTIN, JOSEPH THOMAS, accounting educator; b. Ottumwa, Iowa, Aug. 30, 1947; s. Brony Frank and Virginia Mae (Smith) K.; m. Jane A. Mondanaro, Sept. 16, 1966 (div. Jan. 1971); children: Anthony Joseph, Leilani Michelle; m. Linda Krause, Sept. 21, 1974 (div. Dec. 1994); 1 child, Andrew Thomas. AA, El Paso Community Coll., 1974; BS, Marian Coll., 1976; MBA, Butler u., 1979; faculty devel. in internat. bus. & fin., U. S.C., 1992. CPA, cert. mgmt. acct. Enlisted U.S. Army, 1966, advanced through grades to sgt. 1st class, 1975, resigned, 1978; controller Top Value Fabrics, Carmel, Ind., 1978-79; bus. mgr. Ray Hutson Chevrolet, La Crosse, Wis., 1979-80; mgr. Frank Uhler Assocs. CPAs, La Crosse, 1980-82; pres. Horizon Designs, Inc., Kearney, Nebr., 1982-83; asst. prof. acctg. U. Wis., La Crosse, 1983—; cons. Small Bus. Devel. Ctr., La Crosse, 1984—; tchr. internat. acctg. and internat. bus., Dalkeith, Scotland, 1991, Caen, France, 1993, 94. Author: Professional Accounting Practice Management, 1988, (novel) God Gave Teeth; co-author: The Management Accountants Guide to Fraud Discovery and Control, 1991; contbr. articles to profl. jours. Pres., bd. dirs. Vis. Nurses Assn., 1988-89; pres. Western Wis. Regional Arts, La Crosse, 1986-87. Decorated Bronze Star, 1972; recipient Lybrand Cert. Merit for Literary Excellence, 1986; named Disting. Alumnus Marian Coll., 1988; Fulbright Fgn. scholar Slovak Republic, Mates Bel U., Banska Bystrica, Slovak Republic, 1995-96. Mem. Vietnam Vet. Assn., AICPA, Wis. Inst. CPAs (treas. West Ctrl. chpt. 1989-90), Nat. Assn. Accts. (pres. LaCrosse/Winona chpt. 1990-91). Republican. Congregationalist. Home: 2502 King St La Crosse WI 54601-4330 Office: U Wis 1725 State St La Crosse WI 54601-3742

KASTELIC, JOSEPH ERNEST, pediatrician; b. Maple Heights, Ohio, Jan. 26, 1928; s. Louis Loysius and Antonia (Jordan) K.; m. Joanne King Storks, June 18, 1960 (div. 1981); children: Katherine, Kevin, Joseph, Susan, Timothy, John, Jeffrey. BS, John Carroll U., 1950; MD, St. Louis U., 1959. Tchr. math. Benedictine H.S., Cleve., 1950-55; intern St. Vincent Charity Hosp., Cleve., 1959-60; resident in pediatrics L.A. Children's Hosp., 1960-61, U. Mich. Hosp., Ann Arbor, 1961-62; pediatrician Kaiser Med. Group, Panorama City, Calif., 1962-63; fellow hematology and oncology U. Mich., Ann Arbor, 1963-66; pediatrician Cmty. Health Found., Cleve., 1966-67; dir. pediatric edn. St. Luke's Hosp., Cleve., 1967-72; assoc. hematologist and oncologist Children's Hosp. Med. Ctr., Akron, Ohio, 1972—; assoc. prof. pediatrics Northeaster Ohio Univs. Coll. of Medicine, 1985—. Roman Catholic. Home: 318 Mull Ave Akron OH 44313 Office: Children's Hosp Med Ctr One Perkins Sq Akron OH 44308

KASTEN, MARY ALICE C., state legislator; b. Matthews, Mo., June 6, 1928; d. Clarence Alvin and Ruth (Hill) Critchlow; m. Melvin C. Kasten, 1949; children: Mark, Michael, Margaret. BS, Southeast Mo. State U., 1949; postgrad., U. Pitts. State rep. Mo. State Congress; del. Nat. Conf. Edn. and Citizenship; mem. Cape Girardeau Sch. Bd., Nat. Joint Com. Representing Sch. Bd. Assn., Mo. State Bd. Edn., State Adv. Com. on Vocat. Edn. Bd. Regents mem. Southeast Mo. State U. Mem. Nat. Sch. Bd. Assn., Mo. Sch. Bd. Assn. Office: Mo Ho of Reps State Capitol Building Jefferson City MO 65101-1556*

KASTENS, BEVERLY ANN, special and elementary education educator; b. Wichita, Kans., June 22, 1941; d. Ray Francis and Ava Marie (Lambert) Poole; children: Kelly, Cyndi; m. Gary Michael Kastens, Apr. 22, 1978. BA in Elem. Edn. magna cum laude, Wichita State U., 1973; MS in Edn., Kans. State U., 1980. Cert. tchr., Kans. Math. lab. instr. Goddard (Kans.) Sch. Dist., Unified Sch. Dist. #265, 1973-74, reading lab. instr., 1975-76, 8th grade remedial reading tchr., 1976, 6th grade tchr., 1977-78, 5th grade tchr., 1979-91, tchr. gifted grades K-9, 1992—; faculty advisor Intermediate Learning Ctr., Goddard, 1979, 81, 83, gifted screening com., 1980-83, dept. head, 1984-91; curriculum com. Unified Sch. Dist. #265, Goddard, 1987-88. Author: (teaching curriculum) Christmas Traditions, 1979, (poetry) Memoirs of Grandma, 1979, Memoirs of Student, 1982. Facilitator Wichita (Kans.) Park Bd., 1988-89; cast Voices of Ctrl. Community, Wichita, 1990—, Majesty of Christmas-Easter, Wichita, 1990—. Named Master Tchr., Intermediate Learning Ctr., Goddard, 1985, 87, 89; recipient grant in literature Kans. State Dept. Edn., Topeka, 1987. Mem. Nat. Assn. for Gifted Children, Nat. Rsch. Ctr. on the Gifted and Talented, Kans. Nat. Edn. Assn. (negotiator 1973-91, faculty rep.-negotiation team NEA, Goddard 1985-88). Republican. Mem. Church of God. Home: 547 Pamela St Wichita KS 67212-3733 Office: Clark Davidson Sch 333 S Walnut Goddard KS 67052

KASTER, ROBERT ANDREW, classics educator; b. N.Y.C., Feb. 6, 1948; s. A. Russell and Gloria Kaster; m. Laura Alyx Blumenson, June 22, 1969; children: Paul Adam, Anna Claire. BA summa cum laude, Dartmouth Coll., 1969; MA, Harvard U., 1971, PhD, 1975. Instr. classics Colby Coll., Waterville, Maine, 1973-74; asst. prof. classics U. Chgo., 1975-82, assoc. prof., 1982-89, prof., 1989—, chmn. dept., 1994—. Author: Guardians of Language, 1988 (Goodwin award of merit Am. Philol. Assn. 1991), Transmission of the Text of Vergil's Aeneid, 1990, Studies on the Text of Suetonius, 1992, Suetonius: De Grammaticis et Rhetoribus, 1995; editor Classical Philology, 1981-90; contbr. numerous articles and revs. to scholarly jours. Fellow NEH, 1980-81, Guggenheim fellow, 1991-92. Mem. Am. Philol. Assn. (pres. 1996), Assn. Ancient Historians, Vergilian Soc. Am. Office: U Chgo Dept Classics 1050 E 59th St Chicago IL 60637-1512

KASTNER, CHRISTINE KRIHA, newspaper correspondent; b. Cleve., Aug. 27, 1951; d. Joseph Calvin and Grace (Weber) Kriha; m. Donald William Kastner, June 30, 1979; 1 child, Paul Donald. Assoc., Lakeland C.C., 1976; BA in Comms., Cleve. State U., 1983. Asst. editor, comms. specialist TRW, Inc., Cleve., 1978-85; editor Kaiser Permanente, Cleve., 1985-87; dir. pub. rels. Northeastern Ohio chpt. Arthritis Found., Cleve., 1991-92; newspaper corr. The Plain Dealer, Cleve., 1992—. Contbg. author: Encyclopedia of Cleveland History, 1988. Recipient Gold Addy award Am. Advt. Fedn., 1986, Award of Excellence Women in Comms., Inc., 1987, Bronze Quill award Internat. Assn. Bus. Communicators, 1987. Mem. Soc. Profl. Journalists. Roman Catholic. Home: 1383 Gordon Rd Lyndhurst OH 44124-1349

KASZAK, NANCY, state legislator, lawyer; b. July 21, 1950; m. Tom Heaney; 1 child, Krysta. BA, Elmhurst Coll.; MA, Roosevelt U.; JD, Northern Ill. U. Instr. Ill. Benedictine Coll.; gen. atty. Chgo. Park Dist.; commr. City Landmarks Commn., Chgo.; legis. analyst Ill. Ho. Reps. Dem. staff; Dist. 34 rep. Ill. Ho. Reps., Springfield. Mem. Lake View Citizens Coun.; former pres. Landmarks Preservation Coun. Named one of two Top Citizens of Yr., Lerner-Booster Newspaper, 1985. Home: 3838 N Greenview Ave Chicago IL 60613-2706*

KATH, RANDY JAMES, management information services; b. Pardeeville, Wis., Sept. 6, 1954; s. Clifford William and Francis Beatrice K.; m. Valerie Lynn. AS, U. Wis., Baraboo, 1974; BS, U. Wis., Madison, 1978; MS, U. Wis., Milw., 1995. Mgr. area sales Forage King Industries, Ridgeland, Wis., 1978-80; mgr. mgmt. info. svcs. Square D Co., Milw., 1980-91; dir. mgmt. info. svcs. Dawes Transport Inc., Milw., 1991—. Chmn. worship & music Lord of Life Luth. Ch., Oconomoowoc, Wis., 1981-82; mem. bd. elders Hales Croners (Wis.) Luth. Ch., 1992-93. Holme: 10440 W Vera Ave Milwaukee WI 53224 Office: Dawes Transport Inc 9160 N 107th St Milwaukee WI 53224

KATH, RUTH ROBERT, foreign language educator; b. New Britain, Conn., Apr. 17, 1948; d. Randolph B. and Ruth (Carlisle) Robert; children: Eleanor, Jessica. BA, Syracuse U., 1970; MA, U. Conn., 1974; PhD, U. Iowa, 1982. Instr. Luther Coll., Decorah, Iowa, 1979-82; asst. prof. Luther Coll., Decorah, 1982-87, assoc. prof., 1987-93, prof., 1993—, dept. head modern langs., 1987-92, 95; charter mem. Gov. Commn. on Fgn. Langs., State of Iowa, 1988-91. Author: Bertolt Brecht's Children's Poetry, 1982, The Correspondence of Gerhard Marcks and Marguerite Wildenhain 1970-81, 1991; contbr. articles to profl. jours. Recipient Deutscher Akademischer Austauschdienst Exch. award German Edn. Exch., Emmendingen, Germany, 1972, Sr. award Germany Summer Sem., Fulbright Commn., Bonn, Germany, 1985; Travel to Collections grantee NEH, Frankfurt, Germany, 1985, Visitors grantee Smithsonian Instn., Washington, 1987. Mem. Am. Assn. Tchrs. German (pres. Iowa chpt. 1984-85), Am. Literary Translators Assn., Iowa Fgn. Lang. Assn. Home: 409 High St Decorah IA 52101-1051 Office: Luther College 700 College Dr Decorah IA 52101-1045

KATHREIN, MICHAEL LEE, leasing company executive, real estate company executive; b. Chgo., Nov. 26, 1953; s. Joseph A. and Mildred M. Kathrein; m. Paula Kathrein, 1981; children: Jane Emily, Joseph Andrew, Theodore Michael, Elizabeth Grace. BS in Acctg., U. Nebr., 1978; M in Mgmt., Northwestern U., 1985. CPA, Ill.; lic. real estate broker, pilot. Tax mgr. Touche Ross & Co., Chgo., 1978-84; corp. contr., v.p. Lettuce Entertain You Enterprises, Chgo., 1984-86; pres., CEO Kathrein Leasing Co., Chgo., 1983—; also bd. dirs.; pres., chief exec. officer Empire Real Estate Investment Co., Chgo., 1986—; bd. dirs., speaker Nat. Speakers Bur., N.Y.C., 1985-94; cons. Fla. Investor, Inc., Cocoa, 1986—. Author: (how-to book) Real Estate Comparative Analysis, 1986. Bd. dirs. Revenue Crusade of Mercy, United Way, Chgo., 1980. Mem. AICPA, Cert. Mgmt. Accts. Assn. (cert.), Cert. Internal Auditors Assn. (cert.), Nat. Assn. Realtors, Young Pres.'s Orgn., Northwestern U. Alumni Assn., Mensa. Home: Ste 335 1555 Sherman Ave Evanston IL 60201-4421

KATSIANIS, JOHN NICK, financial executive; b. Chgo., Oct. 27, 1960; s. John Nick and Rosalie A. (Kitzberger) K. BS in Acctg. and Fin., U. Ill., Chgo., 1982. CPA, Ill. Staff acct. gen. acctg. Svc. Master Industries, Inc., Downers Grove, Ill., 1983-84, staff acct. spl. projects, 1984-85; staff acct. Svc. Master Home Health Care Svcs., Downers Grove, 1985, controller, 1985-89; dir. fin., asst. treas. Rush-Presbyn.-St. Luke's Med. Ctr., Chgo., 1989-93; sr. v.p., CFO NYL Care Health Plans of the Midwest, Oak Brook, Ill., 1993—; regional pres. Avanti Health Sys. Ill., Inc., 1995-96. Vice pres. Countryside (Ill.) Police Pension Bd., 1987—. Mem. AICPA, Ill. CPA Soc., Healthcare Fin. Mgmt. Assn., Chgo. Healthcare Exec. Forum. Baptist. Home: 860 Tam Oshanter Bolingbrook IL 60440

KATSNELSON, ESFIR Z., physicist; b. Mogilev, USSR, June 28, 1933; came to U.S., 1989; d. Zalman and Dveyra (Berman) K. MS, Byelorussian State U., USSR, 1955; PhD, Inst. Solid State and Semiconductor Physics, Minsk, USSR, 1970. Asst. physicist Inst. Solid State and Semiconductor Physics Byelorussian Acad. Scis., Minsk, 1958-76, rsch. physicist, 1977-88; vis. scholar dept. physics and astronomy Northwestern U., Evanston, Ill., 1990—. Contbr. articles to Jour. Applied Physics, Physica Status Solidi A and B; contbr. over 33 articles to profl. jours. Mem. Am. Physical Soc., Materials Rsch. Soc. Office: Northwestern U Dept Physics 2145 Sheridan Rd Evanston IL 60208-0834

KATTAS, PAULA LOUISE, purchasing agent; b. Lorain, Ohio, July 7, 1959; d. Emil George Kattas and Irene Pearl (Thompson) Barton. B of Mus. Arts cum laude with honors, Bowling Green State U., 1981; MBA, Baldwin-Wallace Coll., 1987. Cert. purchasing mgr. Substitute tchr. various schs., Elyria, Lorain, Ohio, 1981-82; traffic clk. Lorain Products/Reliance Electric, 1983-87, buyer, 1987-94; tchr. self employed Lorain, 1981-95; sr. group buyer Allied Signal, Elyria, 1994-96, commodity specialist, 1996—. Composer ensemble pieces including The Loch Ness Sea, (solo piano piece) Juxtaposition, (vocal song) Lorain, The International Town. Mem. Lorain City Schs. Curriculum Adv. Com. for IMPACT Home Econs., 1993-94; advisor Jr. Achievement, 1991; 2d v.p. Cleve. Philharm. Orch., 1990-92. Recipient Women of Achievement Merit award YWCA, 1987. Mem. Nat. Assn. Purchasing Mgmt. (Cleve. chpt., instr. CPM rev. classes 1993-95), Phi Kappa Phi. Office: Allied Signal Truck Brake Systems Co 901 Cleveland St Elyria OH 44035-4109

KATZ, AMY BETH, editor, magazine; b. Bklyn., Feb. 16, 1970; d. Donald Lester and Amy Beth Katz. B in Journalism, U. Mo., 1992. Asst. editor Tex. Alcade Mag., Austin, 1992-94, Tex. Banking Mag., Austin, 1994; assoc. editor S&VC, Austin, 1995—.

KATZ, AVRUM SIDNEY, lawyer; b. Melrose Park, Ill., Oct. 10, 1939; s. Joseph George and Bessie Goldie (Ancel) K.; m. Sheela Cara Cooperman, Sept. 1, 1963; children: Julie Anne, Aaron Richard, Michele Sharon. BS in Elec. Engring., Ill. Inst. Tech., 1962; JD, George Washington U., 1966. Bar: Ill. 1966, U.S. Dist. Ct. (no. dist.) Ill. 1967, U.S. Patent Office 1967, U.S. Supreme Ct. 1977, U.S. Ct. Appeals (7th cir.) 1978, D.C. 1991; examiner U.S. Patent Office. Assoc. Leonard G. Nierman, Chgo., 1966-67; assoc. Fitch, Even, Tabin, Flannery & Welsh, and predecessor firms, Chgo., 1967-70, ptnr., 1971-82; ptnr. Welsh & Katz, Chgo., 1983—. Author (with others) Effective Litigation Against Knockoffs, 1984, Chip, Mask and Program Protection, 1985, Electronics and Computer Patent and Copyright Practice, 1988, 2d edit., 1990. Mem. ad hoc com. Lake Forest (Ill.) City Council, 1970. Recipient award of distinction Patent Resources Group, 1983. Mem. ABA, Ill. Bar Assn., Chgo. Bar Assn., Patent Law Assn. Chgo., IEEE, Delta Theta Phi, Tau Beta Pi, Eta Kappa Nu, Sigma Iota Epsilon. Home: 475 Turicum Rd Lake Forest IL 60045-3363 Office: Welsh & Katz Ltd 120 S Riverside Plz 22nd Flr Chicago IL 60606

KATZ, RICHARD, architect, lawyer; b. Chgo., Dec. 19, 1948; s. Jules and Esther (Zuckerstein) K.; m. Susan Rae Ehrlich, Aug. 28, 1977; children: Rachel Elaine, Julian Nathan. BArch in Design, U. Ill., Chgo., 1974; JD with honors, Chgo.-Kent Coll Law, 1995. Bar: Ill.; registered architect Ill., Wis. Prin. R. Katz and Assocs., Oak Park, Ill., 1980—; cons. various law firms, 1980—; faculty mem. Triton Coll., River Grove, Ill., 1986. Prin. works include The Holmes Sch. Playground for All Children, Restoration of Historic Ed Brooke Brownstone, The Master Residence. Recipient cert. appreciation State of Ill., 1989. Jewish. Office: 711 Clarence Ave Oak Park IL 60304-1305

KATZ, ROBERT STEPHEN, rheumatologist, educator; b. Balt., July 31, 1944; s. Irving Gilbert and Shirley Ann (Feldman) K.; m. Carlen Jo Levin, Dec. 12, 1972; children: Jeremy, Alexandra, Gena. BA, Columbia U., 1966; MD, U. Md., 1970. Diplomate Am. Bd. Internal Medicine. Fellow in rheumatology Johns Hopkins Hosp., Balt., 1974-76; assoc. prof. medicine Rush-Presbyn. St. Luke's Med. Ctr., Chgo., 1976—; intern Jewish Hosp. St. Louis/Washington U. Med. Ctr., 1970-71, resident in internal medicine, 1971-72; mem., chmn. med. adv. bd. Lupus Found. Ill.; chmn. med. sci. com. No. Ill. chpt. Arthritis Found., 1985-87. Med. editor WBBM-TV, 1991-92, med. editor Fox TV WFLD, 1993—; chmn. Med. Adv. Bd. Chicago Sun-Times Medlife sect.; contbr. articles to profl. jours. Lt. USN, 1970-72. Mem. AMA, Cen. Rheumatism Soc., Am. Coll. Rheumatology, Chgo. Med. Soc. Office: Dept Internal Medicine Rush Presbyn St Luke Med Ctr 1725 W Harrison St Ste 1039 Chicago IL 60612-3828

KATZEL, JEANINE ALMA, journalist; b. Chgo., Feb. 20, 1948, d. LeRoy Paul and Lia Mary (Arcuri) Katzel; B.A. in Journalism, U. Wis., 1970; M.S. in Journalism, Northwestern U., 1974. Publs. editor U. Wis. Sea Grant Program, Madison, 1969-72; editor research div. agrl. sch. U. Wis., Madison, 1972; research editor Prism mag. AMA, Chgo., 1972-73; free lance writer, 1974-75; lit. editor Plant Engring. mag. Tech. Pub. Co., Barrington, Ill., 1975-76, news editor, 1976-77, asso. editor, 1977-79, sr. editor, 1979—; sr. editor Plant Engring mag Cahners Pub., Des Plaines, Ill., 1987—. Judge assoc. ann. competition Engring. Coll. Mag., 1978-83, 85—. Recipient Elsie Bullard Morrison prize in Journalism, U. Wis., 1969; Peter Lisagor award in bus. journalism, 1983. Mem. Women in Communications, Am. Soc. Bus. Press Editors (pres. Chgo. chpt. 1977-78), Soc. Profl. Journalists, Soc. Fire Protection Engrs., Am. Inst. Plant Engrs., Am. Inst. Chem. Engrs., Am. Chem. Soc., Nat. Audubon Soc., Nat. Fire Protection Assn., Am. Soc. Safety Engrs., Internat. Soc. Fire Service Instrs., Phi Kappa Phi. Home: 708 Cimarron Dr Cary IL 60013-3354 Office: 1350 E Touhy Ave PO Box 5080 Des Plaines IL 60018

KAUFERT, DEAN R., state legislator; b. Neenah, Wis., May 23, 1957. Grad., Neenah H.S. Owner trophy and engraving shop Neenah; mem. from dist. 55 Wis. State Assembly, Madison, 1990—. Bd. dirs. Neenah-Menasha Bowling Assn., Youth Go Bd. Mem. Optimists. *

KAUFFMAN, CHARLES WILLIAM, aerospace engineer; b. Waynesboro, Pa., Dec. 6, 1939; s. Charles Edgar and Florence Evelyn (Neibert) K.; m. Carol Ann Dussinger, Sept. 12, 1964. MS, Pa. State U., 1963; PhD, U. Mich., 1971. Engr. Martin Aircraft Co., Balt., 1961-62; physicist HRB-Singer Inc., State College, Pa., 1963-65; asst. prof. U. Cin., 1971-75, assoc. prof., 1975-77; rsch. scientist U. Mich., Ann Arbor, 1977-85, assoc. prof., 1986-95, prof., 1995—; pres. Explosion Rsch., Whitmore Lake, MIch., 1981—; sci. advisor Utah-Russia Inst.; cons. OSHA, Washington, 1979—. Contbr. articles to profl. jours. Recipient Smolenski medal Polish Acad. of Sci., 1988. Mem. ASME, AIAA, Combustion Inst. (pres. ctrl. state sect. 1991-95), Soc. Automotive Engrs. Episcopalian. Home: 9669 Hermitage Way Whitmore Lake MI 48189-9624 Office: U Mich Dept Aerospace Engring Ann Arbor MI 48109-2118

KAUFFMAN, SANDRA DALEY, state legislator; b. Osceola, Nebr., Jan. 26, 1933; d. James Richard and Erma Grace (Heald) Daley; m. Larry Allen Kauffman, Sept. 4, 1955; children: Claudia Kauffman Boosman, Matthew Allen. BA, U. Nebr., 1954; postgrad., U. Kansas City, summer 1957. Tchr. Falls City (Nebr.) High Sch., 1954-55, Westport High Sch., Kansas City, Mo., 1955-59; sales rep. Manson Industries, Topeka, Kans., 1974-75; dir. pub. affairs Bishop Hogan High Sch., Kansas City, 1985-86; mem. Mo. Ho. of Reps., Jefferson City, 1987—. Mem. Kansas City Citizens Assn., 1981—, Kansas City Consensus, 1985—; mem. women's coun. U. Mo., Kansas City, 1986—; mem. rsch. mental health bd., bd. govs. Carondelet Aging Svcs., 1992—. Recipient Fried of Edn. award Ctr. Edn. Assn., 1986, Disting. Legislator award Mo. C.C. Assn.; named Mem. of Yr., Mo. Congress Parents and Tchrs., 1979. Mem. Am. Legis. Exch. Coun., Nat. Conf. State Legislatures, Network Bd., Nat. PTA (hon. life), Nat. Order Women Legislators, Mo. PTA (hon. life), South Kansas City C. of C., Grandview C. of C., Women C. of C., Mo. Women's Coun., Women Legislators Mo. (pres.). Republican. Methodist. Home: 620 E 90th Ter Kansas City MO 64131-2918 Office: Mo Ho of Reps State Capitol Building Jefferson City MO 65101-1556

KAUFHOLD, LAUREN WARD, health facility administrator, physical therapist; b. Summit, N.J., Nov. 24, 1956; d. Joseph Donald and Sally Ann (Davenport) McMillan; m. Dennis Wade Griffith, July 16, 1977 (div. Apr. 1989); children: Caleb Joel, Ashley Danielle; m. James Norman Kaufhold, Oct. 10, 1992. BS in Phys. Therapy, St. Louis U., 1978; postgrad., Maryville U., 1990—. Lic. phys. therapist, Mo. Staff phys. therapist DePaul Health Ctr., Bridgeton, Mo., 1978-82, Gateway Rehab., St. Louis, 1982-84, Assoc. Rehab., St. Peters, Mo., 1984-87, Midwest Orthopedic Phys. Therapy, Bridgeton, 1987-89; asst. dir. St. Luke's Hosp., Chesterfield, Mo., 1989-93, Therapy Finders, Inc., St. Louis, 1993—; ctr. coord. clin. edn. St. Louis U., 1989-92, Wash. U., St. Louis, 1989-92, Maryville U., St. Louis, 1989-92, St. Louis C.C., 1989-92. Mem. Am. Phys. Therapy Assn., Mo. Phys. Therapy Assn. (peer rev. com. 1993—), St. Louis Phys. Therapy Dir.'s Forum (chairperson 1992-94). Home: 311 Oakmont Farm Dr Ballwin MO 63021 Office: Therapy Finders Inc 135 W Adams Ste 305 Saint Louis MO 63122

KAUFMAN, BARTON LOWELL, financial services company executive; b. Shelbyville, Ind., Mar. 28, 1941; s. Nathan and Hortense (Schwartz) K.; m. Judy Dorman, June 17, 1962; children: Grant, Wendy Kaufman Siegel, Emily, Hannah. BS, Ind. U., 1962, JD, 1965. Bar: Ind. 1965. Agt. Kaufman Multi-Million Dollar Agy., Indpls., 1965-70; pres., CEO Kaufman Fin. Corp., Indpls., 1970—; pres. Twenty-Five Million Dollar Internat. Forum, Chgo., 1989. Republican. Jewish. Office: Kaufman Fin Corp 201 W 103rd St Indianapolis IN 46290-1094

KAUFMAN, DONALD WAYNE, research ecologist; b. Abilene, Tex., June 7, 1943; s. Leo Fred and Marcella Genevieve (Hobbie) K.; m. Glennis Ann Schroeder, Aug. 5, 1967; 1 child, Dawn. BS, Ft. Hays Kans. State Coll., 1965, MS, 1967; PhD, U. Ga., 1972. Postdoctoral fellow U. Tex., Austin, 1971-73; asst. prof. U. Ark., Fayetteville, 1974-75, SUNY, Binghamton, 1975-77; assoc. program dir. Population Biology, NSF, Washington, 1977-80; asst. prof. biology Kans. State U., Manhattan, 1980-84, assoc. prof. biology, 1984-91, prof. biology, 1991—; vis. scientist Savannah River Ecology Lab., Aiken, S.C., 1973-74; acting dir. Konza Prairie Rsch. Natural Area, 1986-87, coord., 1990-91; dir. Konza Prairie Long-Term Ecol. Rsch. Program, 1985-90; grant rev. panelist EPA, 1981-85, USDA, 1995-96; cons. NSF, 1984. Contbr. articles to profl. jours. NDEA fellow, 1967-69; NSF grantee, 1981—. Mem. AAAS, Am. Soc. Mammalogists (award 1972, bd. dirs. 1989-92), Ecol. Soc. Am., Am. Inst. Biol. Scis., Soc. for the Study Evolution. Office: Kans State U Div Biology Ackert Hall Manhattan KS 66506

KAUFMAN, ETHAN ALLEN, retired business owner; b. Warsaw, Ind., Sept. 9, 1913; s. Horatio Seymour and Fanny Louise (Trachsel) K.; m. Georgia Kathryn Loveday, Feb. 27, 1937; children: Kathryn Allyn, Betty Louise. Grad. high sch., Upland, Ind. With Warsaw Park Bd., 1948-52, Kosciusko County (Ind.) Bd. Tax Rev., 1959-61, Ind. Office Bldg. Comsn., 1961-65; pres. Warsaw Community Sch. Bd., 1959-67; ret., 1972. With U.S. Coast Guard, 1942-45, World War II. Mem. DAV (life), Nat. Chief Petty Officers Assn. (life), U.S. Coast Guard Chief Petty Officers Assn. (life), Am. Legion, Coun. of Sagamores of Wabash, Elks, Tippecanoe Lake Country Club. Democrat. Presbyterian. Home: 1610 E Center St Warsaw IN 46580-3651

KAUFMAN, GLENNIS ANN, research ecologist, biologist, educator; b. Deshler, Nebr., Nov. 13, 1947; d. Norman August and Marie Amanda (Renken) Schroeder; m. Donald Wayne Kaufman, Aug. 5, 1967; 1 child, Dawn Michelle. BS, Kans. State U., 1984, PhD, 1990. Rsch. asst. Savannah River Ecology Lab., Aiken, S.C., 1968-71, 73-74, Dept. Zoology, U. Tex., Austin, 1971-73; rsch. asst. Dept. Biology, Kans. State U., Manhattan, 1981-84, grad. asst., 1984-90, asst. scientist, 1991-95; rsch. asst. prof. Kans. State U., Manhattan, 1996—. Contbr. more than 55 articles to profl. jours. Leader Girl Scouts U.S.A., 1978-80. Recipient Coll. Arts and Scis. Disting. Grad. Teaching award, Kans. State U., 1990, Michael Scott Watkins Meml. Award for Excellence in Teaching, 1989; Mid-Am. State U. Assn. traveling scholar, 1986; grantee, Am. Soc. Mammalogists, 1985, Sigma Xi, 1985. Mem. Am. Soc. Mammalogists (A. Brazier Howell award 1989, assoc. editor 1994-96), Animal Behavior Soc., Ecol. Soc. Am., Soc. for Study of Evolution. Office: Kans State Univ Div Biology Ackert Hall Manhattan KS 66506

KAUFMAN, IRA GLADSTONE, judge; b. N.Y.C., Dec. 13, 1909; s. Joseph and Esther K.; m. Margaret Kaufman, Sept, 1988; children: Harvey David, Sylvia Kaufman Delin. BS, NYU, 1933, JD, 1936; DSc in Bus. Adminstrn. (hon.), Cleary Coll., Ypsilanti, Mich., 1976. Bar: Mich. 1939. Pvt. practice law, Detroit, 1939-59; judge of probate Wayne County Probate Ct., Detroit, 1958-84, presiding judge, 1962-63, 66-67, 72-73, 77-85; chief judge pro tem Wayne County Probate and Juvenile Ct., 1981-85; Moot Ct. judge U. Detroit, 1966-72; lectr. Trustee Children's Hosp. of Detroit, chmn. devel., 1980-83, hon. chmn. ann. concert 1983, chmn. ad hoc com. alcoholism Detroit United Cmtys. Svcs., 1967-68; chmn. Detroit Com. Fgn. Rels., 1974-76; trustee Mich. Cancer Found., 1973, hon. life trustee emeritus, 1985; trustee Detroit Inst. Tech., 1962-72, Park Cmty. Hosp., 1962-73; pres. Inter-Agy. Council on Alcoholism, 1967; pres., chmn. bd. Met. Soc. for Blind, 1966-70, bd. dirs., 1960—; mem. Gov.'s Com. Mental Health Statute Rev. Commn., 1970-72, Mich. Soc. Mental Health, 1960—; hon. life mem. Children's Charter Mich., 1965-75; exec. bd. League Handicapped-Goodwill 1949-60; bd. overseers Dropsie Coll., 1973-75; bd. dirs. Hebrew Free Loan Soc. Detroit, 1979-84, Jewish Nat. Fund Bd.; v.p. United Hebrew Schs. Detroit, 1947-58; founding sec. Midrasha Coll. Hebrew Studies, 1948-58; pres. Adat Shalom Synagogue, 1945-51, founder cemetary, 1948, hon. life pres. 1953; founding chmn. Einstein Luncheon Forum, 1986—. Fellow Mich. State Bar Found. (life mem.); mem. ABA, Mich. Probate and Juvenile Ct. Assn. (exec. bd. 1969-72, pres. 1970-71), Mich. Bar Assn., Detroit Bar Assn., Supreme Ct. Hist. Soc., Mental Health Assn. Mich. (Advocacy award 1989), U.S. Air Force Assn. (ann. installing officer 1983-84), B'nai B'rith (hon. pres. Tikvah Lodge 1974), Knollwood Country Club, Savoyard Club, Valley of Detroit, Masons (33 degree, sovereign prince), Shriners, Jesters. Contbr. biog. sketches of Mich. judges to Jewish Hist. Soc. publ., 1983-84. Home: 4224 Wabeek Lake Dr S Bloomfield Hills MI 48302-1663

KAUFMAN, JEFFREY ALLEN, publisher; b. Mpls., May 28, 1952; s. Theodore and Jean Louise (Tiegs) K. Student, Mankato State U., 1970-71, Ariz. State U., 1971-72; BA, U. Minn., 1975. Pres. Creative Resources, Inc., Mpls., 1976-80; sr. v.p. Literary Resources, Inc., Phoenix, 1980-81; pres. Multi-Media, Phoenix, 1981-83, Where To Go, Inc., Excelsior, Minn., 1983-86; v.p. The Old Utica Co., Mpls., 1986-88; chmn. Actif, Inc., Wayzata, Minn., 1988-89; ptnr. S&K Group, Mpls., 1989-90; editor in chief Spl. Events Pub., Inc., Mpls., 1990-92; founder Electronic Claims Processing, Inc., Edina, Minn., 1992—; cons. Control Data Corp. Mpls., 1978-81; dir. Nexus Inc. Mpls., 1978-81; founder ECP Inc., 1992. Author: (books) Where To Go in Minneapolis and Saint Paul, 1984, Where To Go in Los Angeles, 1985, (screenplay) Born To Be Chief, 1985. Home: PO Box 204 Excelsior MN 55331-0204

KAUFMAN, JEROME BENZION, neurosurgeon; b. Waterloo, Iowa, July 22, 1934; s. Louis and Dorothy (Rosenbloom) K.; m. Judith Ellen Lasker, June 29, 1967; children: David, Jonathan, Jefferey. BA, Wayne State U., 1955, MD, 1961; postgrad., U. Madrid. Diplomate Am. Bd. Neurol. Surgery, 1975. Rotating intern Michael Reese Hosp. and Med. Ctr., Chgo., 1961-62; resident in internal med. Michael Reese Hosp. and Med. Ctr., Chgo., 1962-63; resident in gen. surgery VA Hosp., Bronx, 1965-66, resident in neurology, 1966, resident in neurosurgery, 1967, from sr. to chief resident neurosurgery, 1969-70; resident neurosurgery Neurol. Inst. N.Y., Columbia Presbyn. Hosp., 1968; resident neuropathology Mt. Sinai Hosp. and Med. Sch., N.Y.C., 1968; chief resident neurosurgery City Hosp., Elmhurst, N.Y., 1969; chmn. dept. neurosurgery Carle Clinic Assn. and Found. Hosp., Urbana, Ill., 1972—; cons. neurosurgery McKinley Hosp., Urbana, Covenant Hosp., Urbana; asst. instr. internal medicine Chgo. Med. Sch., 1963; clin. assoc. prof. neurosurgery U. Ill. Coll. Medicine, Urbana, 1982—. Contbr. articles to profl. jours. Served to capt. USAF, 1963-65. Fellow ACS, Am. Assn. Neurol. Surgeons (Continuing Edn. award in neurosurgery 1980, 83, 85, 87, 89, 93, 96), Internat. Coll. Surgeons (vice regent) N.Y. Acad. Scis.; mem. AMA (Physicians Recognition award 1980, 82, 85, 89, 93), Ill. Med. Soc., Champaign County Med. Soc., Congress Neurol. Surgeons, Ctrl. Neurosurg. Soc., Assn. Mil. Surgeons U.S., Chgo. Neurol. Soc. Home: 2104 Zuppke Dr Urbana IL 61801-6706 Office: 602 W University Ave Carle Clinic Assn Urbana IL 61801

KAUMEYER, GREGORY WALTER, physical therapist, athletic trainer; b. Lancaster, Ohio, June 28, 1951; s. Walter Frederick and Gloria Rachel (Graupner) K.; m. Pamela Sue Baltzer, July 27, 1974; children: Jason, Nicholas. BS in Phys. Edn., Ohio State U., 1974; MS in Health Scis. Edn., Case Western Res. U., 1976; MS in Phys. Therapy, Duke U., 1978. Lic. phys. therapist, Ill.; cert. athletic trainer, Ill. Dir. phys. therapy Life Scis., New Haven, Conn., 1978-80, Newsome Phys. Therapy & Sports Medicine Ctr., Joliet, Ill., 1980-85; co-owner Phys. Therapy & Sports Injury Rehab., Hazel Crest, Ill., 1985—; cons. Promatek, Joliet, 1985-93; mem. adv. bd. Rehab. Svcs. Network, Chgo., 1993-94. Author: (with others) Orthopaedic & Sports Physical Therapy, 1985. Bd. dirs. Our Savior Luth. Ch., Joliet, 1982-86, 90-94. Mem. Am. Phys. Therapy Assn. (pvt. practice sect., nominating com. sports phys. sect. 1980-82, sec. 1982-83), Nat. Athletic Tng. Assn. Home: 1102 Geneva St Shorewood IL 60436 Office: Phys Therapy & Sports Injury Rehab 1816 W 170th St Hazel Crest IL 60429

KAUN, THOMAS DAVID, electrochemical engineer, inventor; b. West Bend, Wis., Mar. 5, 1951; s. Willard H. and Elaine L. K.; m. Wendy L. Batker, Aug. 14, 1976; children: Benjamin, Stephen. BS in Chem. Engring., U. Wis., 1973, MS in Chem. Engring., 1975. Electrochem. engr. Argonne (Ill.) Nat. Lab., 1974—; pres. Inventek Corp., New Lenox, Ill., 1989—. Patentee in field. Ill. Tech. Challenge grantee Ill. Dept. Commerce and Cmty. Affairs, 1990-92; recipient Bipolar Li/FeS2 Battery and Sulfide Cermaic Materials R&D 100 awards Rsch. and Devel. mag., 1991, 93, Rechargeable Thermal Battery Army STTR, 1996. Lutheran. Home: 320 Willow St New Lenox IL 60451-1047 Office: Argonne Nat Lab CMT 9700 Cass Ave Argonne IL 60439-4803

KAUSEK, ALBERT JOSEPH, quality consultant, educator, former naval officer; b. Orlando, Fla., Mar. 28, 1957; s. Albert Joseph and Joan Camille (Friar) K.; m. Melinda Eileen Batisto, July 30, 1977; children: Brian Lee, Sarah Lynn, Rachel Lauren. BS in Human Resources Mgmt., New Sch. for Social Rsch., N.Y.C., 1984; Internat. MBA, Point Pk. Coll., 1994. Enlisted USN, 1975, commd. ensign, 1985, crewmember USS Phila., 1977-80, instr. S7G prototype, 1980-84, crewmember USS Providence, 1984-85, engring. staff asst. Pitts. Naval Reactors, 1985-89, project officer Pitts. Naval Reactors, 1989-92, dir. vendor quality assurance Pitts. Naval Reactors, 1992-95; ret., Mgmt. Resources Internat., Saline, Mich., 1995, quality cons., 1995—; mem. faculty Ea. Mich. U., 1995—; mem. bd. examiners Pa. Quality Leadership Awards, 1994; ISO 9000 lead assessor Registration Accreditation Bd., 1994. Mem. IEEE, Am. Soc. for Quality Control (cert. quality auditor, quality engr.), Am. Welding Soc., Am. Mgmt. Assn., Am. Nuclear Soc., Alpha Sigma Lambda. Republican. Home: 6470 Ann Arbor-Saline Rd Saline MI 48176 Office: Mgmt Resources Internat 6485 Hollowtree Ct Saline MI 48176

KAUTZ, RICHARD CARL, chemical and feed company executive; b. Muscatine, Iowa, Aug. 1, 1916; s. Carl and Leah (Amlong) K.; m. Mary Elda Stein, Dec. 24, 1939; children: Linda Kautz Osterkamp, Judith, John Terry, Thomas R., Susan E. Kautz, Sarah J. Kautz Aavang, Mary Catherine Kautz Huff. Student, U. Ariz., 1936-37; BS with high distinction, U. Iowa, 1939; DHL, George Williams Coll., 1973. Supr. in fin. dept. Gen. Electric Co., 1939-43; with Grain Processing Corp. and Kent Feeds, Inc., Muscatine, 1943-88, chmn. bd. dirs., mem. exec. com., 1966-88; with Varied Investments, Inc., 1988—; chmn., dir., mem. exec. com., chmn. fin. com., 1988—; mem. adv. com. Export-Import Bank U.S., 1984—. Mem. citizens com. Rock Island dist. U.S. Army Engrs.; bd. trustees, mem. Herbert Hoover Presdl. Library Assn., 1976—; chmn. nat. bd. dirs. YMCA, 1970-73, mem. exec. com. and bd. dirs.; mem. exec. com. World Alliance YMCA's, 1973—, mem. pres.'s com., exec. com.; mem. Bd. Trustees YMCA's; trustee YMCA Retirement Fund, Ctr. for Study of Presidency, 1977—; bd. dirs., mem. exec. com., chmn. Bus.-Industry Polit. Action Com., 1977—. Named to Iowa Bus. Hall of Fame, 1987. Mem. NAM (bd. dirs., chmn. exec. com. 1977, chmn. fin. com. 1978, vice chmn. 1975, chmn. 1976), Iowa Mfrs. Assn. (bd. dirs.), Muscatine C. of C., DeMolay Legion of Honor, Beta Gamma Sigma (dirs. table), Sigma Chi (named Significant Sig.). Presbyterian. Clubs: Union League (Chgo.); Met., Capitol Hill (Washington); Marco Polo, Met., Canadian (N.Y.C.); U. Iowa Pres.'s, Univ. Athletic (Iowa City); Des Moines, Lincoln (Des Moines). Lodges: Masons, Shriners, Elks, Rotary. Home: 2355 200th St Muscatine IA 52761-8441 Office: Varied Investments Inc 1600 Oregon St Muscatine IA 52761-1404

KAVALOSKI, VINCENT, philosophy educator; b. St. Paul, Jan. 15, 1946; s. Carl and Elvene (Phillips) K.; m. Jeanne Schaefer, Oct. 14, 1967 (div. 1972); children: Joshua, Alainya; m. Jane Hammatt, June 4, 1978. BA, St. Thomas U., St. Paul, 1968; MA, U. Chgo., 1970, PhD, 1974. Lectr. U. Chgo., 1970-71, U. Pitts., 1974-75; postdoctoral fellow Pa. State U., State College, 1975-76; faculty mem. Shimer Coll., Waukegan, Ill., 1976-81; lectr. in philosophy U. Wis., Richland County, 1981-90, Platteville, 1987-90; co-dir. Ecumenical Partnership, Madison, Wis., 1984-95; prof. philosophy Edgewood Coll., Madison, 1990-95, prof. philosophy, dept. chmn., 1995—; dir. High Sch. World Peace Study Program, Wis., 1986—; tchr. UNESCO, Poland, 1983, 85; summer faculty mem. Internat. People's Coll., Helsinger, Denmark, 1987-89; bd. dirs. AFSC, Phila., 1989-90; speaker in field. Author: Dreaming the World Awake, 1993; co-editor, writer jour. Metanoia, 1984-94; contbr. articles to profl. publs. Mem. Fellowship of Reconciliation (speaker 1990, 92). Mem. Soc. of Friends. Home: 3817 Evans Quarry Rd Dodgeville WI 53533-9786

KAWA, NANCY ANN, accountant; b. Cleve., June 21, 1967; d. Frank David and Peggy Marie (Hoenigman) K. BSBA, John Carroll U., 1989. Customer svc. banker Soc. Nat. Bank, Mayfield Heights, Ohio, 1987-89; data processor Ohio Savs. Bank, Euclid, 1989; asst. acct. Cleveland Heights (Ohio) Pub. Libr. Bus. Office, 1989-90; staff acct., cash mgr. Kline Bros. Co., Cleve., 1990-93; cash acct. Oglebay Norton Co., Cleve., 1993-96; with R.S.I. Co., 1996. South Euclid PTA scholar, 1985, Pres.'s Honor Award scholar, 1985-89, M. J. Pacelli scholar, 1988, Mark C. Treuhaft Am. Values scholar, 1988. Mem. Beta Gamma Sigma, Alpha Sigma Nu. Republican. Roman Catholic. Home: 4298 Tamalga Dr Cleveland OH 44121-3520

KAWAHARA, FRED KATSUMI, research chemist; b. Penngrove, Calif., Feb. 26, 1921; s. Kentaro and Kiku (Seo) K.; m. Sumiko Hayami, May 5, 1952; children: Robert Katsumi, Kiku Seo, Richard Hojo; m. Andrea L. Eary, June 29, 1991. BS with honors, U. Tex., 1944; PhD, U. Wis., 1948. Assoc. chemist USDA, Peoria, Ill., 1948-51; postdoctoral fellow U. Chgo., 1951-53; sr. rsch. scientist Amoco Corp. (formerly Standard Oil of Ind.), Whiting, 1953-65; rsch. chemist EPA, Cin., 1965—; cons., expert witness U.S. Dept. Def., U.S. Dept. Air Force, U.S. Dept. Justice, State of Pa., State of N.J.; mentor EPA, others, 1965—; lectr. in field. Co-author: Fossil Energy Extraction, 1983, Innovative Side Remediation Technology, Chemical Treatment, vol. 2, 1994; contbr. 6 chpts. to books, more than 60 articles to profl. jours. Recipient Five Hundred Gold Medal, Superior Svc. award Bur. Indsl. and Agrl. Chemistry. Fellow Am. Inst. Chemists. Home: 1632 Cumberland St Covington KY 41011-3716 Office: US EPA 26 Martin Luther King Dr W Cincinnati OH 45220-2242

KAWER, DINA ROCHELLE, artist; b. Detroit, Feb. 26, 1957; d. Benjamin and Esther (Horowitz) K.; children: Shay Daniel, Shanna Lynn. BFA, Wayne State U., 1979. Med. photographer Children's Hosp. Mich., Detroit, 1980-81; profl. artist Huntington Woods, Mich., 1975—; artist-in-residence Burton Elem. Sch., Huntington Woods, 1991-92; vis. artist Miami (Fla.)-Dade Pub. Schs., 1993. One-woman shows include Southfield (Mich.) Cultural Arts Ctr., 1982, Pierce St. Gallery, Birmingham, Mich., 1990, 93; exhibited in group shows at Clarence Kennedy Gallery, Cambridge, Mass., 1980, Halsted 831 Gallery, Birmingham, 1982, Linda Hayman Gallery, Boca Raton, Fla., 1991, Detroit Inst. Arts, 1991, 93 (grand winner Arts and Flowers 1991), Delta Coll., Saginaw, Mich., 1992, Scarab Club, Detroit, 1992, Profl. Photographers Expo '93, L.A., Bacardi Art Gallery, Miami, Fla., 1993, Very Spl. Arts Gallery, Washington, 1993, Paine Webber Art Gallery, N.Y.C., 1993, Detroit Inst. Arts, 1993, Bayfront Gallery, San Francisco, 1994, Moss Rehab., Phila., 1994; exhibited in Creative Will, Multiple Sclerosis Soc., 1993-94, Fed. Res. Bank, Phila. Moss Rehab. Invitational, 1994, Govt. Ctr., Stamford, Conn., 1995; represented in permanent collections Detroit Inst. Arts, Polaroid Collection, Cambridge, Mass., Paper Art Mus., Tokyo, Pierce St. Gallery, Calif. Mus. Photography, Riverside, Southfield Cultural Arts Commn.; featured in The Creative Will, 1993, 1996 calendar, arts mags., local newspapers. Mem. adv. com. on creative will Nat. Multiple Sclerosis Soc., N.Y.C. Recipient Spl. Distinction award Mich. Coun. Arts, 1987-88, 1993/94 Arts Midwest/Nat. Endowment for the Arts Regional Visual Artist Fellowship award. Mem. Friends of Photography (San Francisco). Jewish.

KAY, ALAN EDWARD, editor; b. Chgo., Dec. 19, 1965; s. Dennis Matthew and Judy Ray (Kalinsky) K. BA in News Editorial Journalism, Marquette U., Milw., 1988. Sports writer Baraboo (Wis.) News-Republic, 1988-89, Marshfield (Wis.) News-Herald, 1989-91; mng. editor The Courier, Waterloo, Wis., 1991-96, The Ind., Cottage Grove, Wis., 1996—. sports writer Chgo. Bear Report, 1989-91, Hockey Ink!, 1995—. Recipient Hon. Mention, Nat. Newspaper Assn., 1995. Mem. Wis. Newspaper Assn. (1st pl. spl. sect. editl. 1996, 2nd pl. editl. page, 1996, 1st pl. editl. page 1993, 2d pl. sports feature story 1993, 3d place sports photo 1992, 1993, 1st pl. front page 1992), Soc. Profl. Journalists. Roman Catholic. Home: 314 Shane Ct # 1 Sun Prairie WI 53590

KAY, ALBERT JOSEPH, textile executive; b. Cleve., June 3, 1920; s. Simon and Eszther (Rosenzweig) K.; m. Irene Pramisloff, June 11, 1944; children: Leslie Andrejewski, Stephen, Adrienne Gallagher. Student, Cuyahoga Community Coll., 1961. Sales rep. The Carnegie Textile Co., Cleve., 1938-68, v.p., gen. mgr., 1968-94, pres., 1994—; mem. citizens adv. com. Cleve. Electric Illuminating Co., 1991—; adv. bd. ARC, 1988-93. Pres. Mayfield H.S. PTA, 1968-69; former pres. Mayfield Boys Baseball League; past. sect. chmn. United Way; founder Mayfield Heights Bicentennial Com., Mayfield Area Recreation Coun.; mem. Citizens Com. for Edn., 1968; chmn. Citizens for Honest Govt., 1965; past pres. Friends of Hillcrest Libr.; coun. mem. City Mayfield Heights, 1969—, coun. pres., 1981-85, 1996-97; campaign co-chmn. Aveni for State Rep., Ohio, 1975; chmn. levy renewal com. Cuyahoga County Pub. Libr., 1989; past. mem. exec. com. Hillcrest Dem. Caucus, Acad. Booster's Club; former chmn. planning and zoning commn. City Mayfield Heights; trustee Schnurmann House, 1970—, Assn. Retarded Citizens, 1992-94; cmty. coord. Clinton-Gore campaign, 1992; mem., founder Edn.-Bus. Cmty. Alliance, Mayfield City Schs., 1994—. With U.S. Army, 1943. Recipient Cmty. Svc. award Nat. Exch. Club, 1984, Outstanding Svc. award Mayfield Heights C. of C., 1979, Citizenship award VFW, 1976, Disting. Svc. award Assn. for Retarded Citizens, 1991, Citizen of Yr. award (with wife) Mayfield City Schs., 1995. Mem. Internat. Assn. Wiping Cloth Mfrs. (bd.dirs. 1981-85, 89-93, Outstanding and Dedicated Svc. award 1985), Am. Assn. Ret. Persons (bd. dirs. East Suburban Cuyahoga County chpt. 371 1993—), Secondary/Materials and Recycled Textiles, Jewish Vets Cleve. (comdr. 1946-48), Masons. Democrat. Jewish. Home: 1835 Beham Dr Cleveland OH 44124-3121 Office: The Carnegie Textile Co 1734 Ivanhoe Rd Cleveland OH 44112-1623

KAY, DENNIS MATTHEW, publishing company official; b. Chgo., Sept. 20, 1936; s. Edward Francis and Rose Anne (Koziel) Kolodzinski; m. Judy R. Kalinsky, Jan. 9, 1965; 1 child, Alan Edward. BBA, Loyola U., 1976. Customer svc. agt. Am. Airlines, Chgo., 1959-69; expeditor Time Inc., Chgo., 1969-73, traffic mgr. People mag., 1973-75, Time mag. traffic mgr., 1975-78, ops. mgr., 1978-81, electronic data mgr., 1981-83; plant mgr. Time Inc., Waterloo, Wis., 1983-88, field ops. mgr., 1988-95, nat. prodn. analyst, 1995—. With U.S. Army, 1959-61. Recipient MM&D Excellence award Time Inc., 1989, Prodn. Excellence awards, 1993, 94, Pres. award, 1993. Mem. Moose Lodge River Grove 378 (gov. 1982-83). Roman Catholic. Home: 1028 S Birchwood Rd Wisconsin Dells WI 53965 Office: Time Inc 187 Jackson St Waterloo WI 53594-1311

KAY, IRENE PRAMISLOFF, school system administrator; b. Cleve., Mar. 26, 1920; d. Benjamin and Anna Esther (Kahan) Pramisloff; m. Albert Joseph Kay, June 11, 1944; children: Leslie Kay Andrzejewski, Stephen W., Adrienne Kay Gallagher. AA in Bus., Cuyahoga C.C., 1971. Sec. Cleve. Job Corps Ctr., 1970-88, Soc. for Prevention Violence, Auctor Assoc., Inc., Cleveland Heights, Ohio, 1988-95; mem., past v.p., past pres. Mayfield (Ohio) City Sch. Bd., 1965-91, mem. emeritus, 1992—; mem. All N.E. Region Sch. Bd., 1975, 83, All Ohio Sch. Bd., 1983; past adv. com. mem. Star Bank, Mayfield Heights, Ohio; past legis. com., mem. Cuyahoga County Auditor Citizens Adv. Bd.; past mem. health care/human svcs. com.; custody rev. bd. mem. Cuyahoga County Juvenile Ct., 1981-83. Trustee Schnurmann House, Mayfield Heights, Friends of Mayfield Regional Libr., past pres., chmn. levy replacment campaign, 1984, 89; chmn. book fair Cuyahoga County Libr. Sys., 1993; founder, past pres., past treas. Mayfield Area Recreation Coun.; appointee Ohio Lottery Commn., 1983-92, chmn., 1986-92; mem. Cuyahoga County Dem. Exec. Com.; Mayfield Heights precinct committeeperson; past mem. maypr's adv. com. City Mayfield Heights; former bd. trustees, cmty. rep. WomenSpace; Mayfield Heights coord. Clinton-Gore-Glenn campaign, 1992; mem. Cuyahoga County Adv. Coun. for Sr. and Adult Svcs., 1993—, Mayfield Heights Commn. in Aging, 1993—, Cuyahoga County Office on Aging Com., 1995—; former mem. Cuyahoga County Urban County Cmty. Devel. Block Grant Com.; coord 2 campaigns Mayfield Heights Richard Celeste for Gov.; mem. exec. bd. Mayfield Heights Bicentennial Com., 1974-76; former adv. com. East Shore divsn. ARC; mem. cmty.-wide svcs. panel United Way, 1983-86; mem. edn. com. Cleve. Bicentennial Commn., 1993—; active State Sen. Sheerer's adv. com.; cmty. capt. Mayfield Heights City Schs. Bond/Levy campaign, 1994. Honored in resolutions Ohio Senate, Ohio Ho. Reps., govs. spl. recognition; recipient commendation U.S. Congress, 1990, Cuyahoga County Auditor, 1992, Cert. Recognition Ohio Atty. Gen., 1992, Spl. Friend award Cuyahoga East Vocat. Edn. Consortium, 1992; named (with Albert Kay) Citizen of Yr. Mayfield City Schs., 1995; nominated Keeper of Flame award Ohio Sec. State, 1990, Resolution, Mayfield Bd. Edn., 1990, City Mayfield Heights, 1990, Ohio Women's Hall Fame, 1986, 92, CitiSun of Yr. Sun Newspapers, 1992. Mem. LWV (v.p. Cuyahoga County unit bd. dirs., past pres., bd. dirs. Hillcrest Area unit), Am. Assn. Retired Persons (legis. com., past pres. chpt. 371, Outstanding Svcs. award 1994, program chmn. 1991-94, bd. dirs. 1995—). Home: 1835 Beham Dr Cleveland OH 44124

KAY, JERALD, child psychiatry educator, researcher; b. Washington, Mar. 26, 1945; s. Max and Miriam (Schwartz) K.; m. Rena Lynn Victor, Aug. 17, 1968; children: Sarah Jennifer, Rachel Hannah, Jonathan Emile. BA, Washington U., 1967; MD, U. Md., 1971; diploma, Cin. Psychoanalytic Inst., 1984. Diplomate Am. Bd. Psychiatry and Neurology. Resident in psychiatry Cin. Gen. Hosp., 1971-73, fellow in child psychiatry, 1973-75; instr. child psychiatry U. Cin. Coll. Medicine, 1971-77, asst. prof. child psychiatry, 1977-82, assoc. prof. child psychiatry, 1982-89, prof. child psychiatry, 1989-90; prof., chair dept. psychiatry Wright State U. Sch. Medicine, Dayton, Ohio, 1990—; dir. med. student edn. U. Cin. Dept. Psychiatry, 1975-82, dir. residency tng., 1982—, dir. med. student edn.; mem. psychiatry com. Nat. Bd. Med. Examiners, 1988-90; specialist site visitor Accreditation Coun. Grad. Med. Edn., 1986—. Editor Jour. Psychotherapy Practice and Rsch., 1990—; mem. editorial cons. bd. Am. Psychiat. Press, Inc., 1987, mem. editorial bd. Acad. Psychiatry; contbr. articles on child and adult psychiatry, psychoanalysis, psychotherapy, ethics, psychiat. and cardiac transplantation edn. to profl. jours. Recipient Golden Apple Teaching award U. Cin. Coll. Medicine, 1979; named Exemplary Psychiatrist Nat. Alliance for the Mentally Ill, 1994, Educator of Yr. Assn. Acad. Psychiatry, 1996. Fellow Am. Psychiat. Assn. (chmn. med. studies edn. com. 1982-86, coun. med. edn. 1989, career devel. 1986—, chmn. 1989, mem. com. on psychotherapy, program com.); mem. Am. Coll. Psychiatrists, Am. Psychoanalytic Assn., Am. Acad. Child and Adolescent Psychiatry, Am. Assn. Chmn. Depts. of Psychiatry (chmn. edn. com.), Acad. Psychosomatic Medicine, Alpha Omega Alpha. Home: 4192 Rose Hill Ave Cincinnati OH 45229-1421 Office: Wright State U Sch Medicine PO Box 927 Dayton OH 45401-0927

KAY, LESLIE, public relations consultant, journalist; b. Cleve., Dec. 25, 1946; d. Albert Joseph and Irene (Pramisloff) K.; m. Thomas Stanley Andrzejewski, Sept. 9, 1973; 1 child, David Aaron. BA in Journalism, Pa. State U., 1967. Asst. travel editor The Plain Dealer, Cleve., 1968-69, reporter, 1969-85, asst. state editor, 1985-87, asst. metro editor, 1987-90; propr. bus. providing editorial svcs. Cleve., 1990—; v.p. Oppidan Group Inc., Cleve., 1992—. Chief contbr./editor: A Citizen's Guide to Cleveland, 1992. Recipient Silver Gavel award ABA, 1979, Spl. Media award Nat. Assn. Criminal Def. Lawyers, 1979, 1st Pl. award in investigative reporting Ohio AP, 1982, Press Club/Sigma Delta Chi, 1981, others. Office: The Oppidan Group Inc 75 Public Sq 1230 Cleveland OH 44113

KAY, PATRICIA KREMER, business owner; b. Arlington, Va., July 10, 1957; d. George Andrew and Eileen Lois (Ludwig) Kremer; m. Jimmy Lamar Kay, Dec. 4, 1989; children: Sabrina Lea, Kelly Marie. Dir. admissions Sawyer Coll., Dayton, Ohio, 1985-89; mgr. shipping/receiving Stolle R & D, Cin., 1989-90; materials mgmt. customer svc. rep. Medisorb Techs. Internat. L.P. a Stolle/Dupont Co., Cin., 1990-91; customer svc. adminstr. Medisorb Techs., Cin., 1991-93; adminstr. shipping/receiving Medisorb Techs., Wilmington, Ohio, 1993-94, purchasing agt., 1994—; svc., mktg. purchasing mgr. Medison Technologies Internat. Republican. Baptist. Office: 265 Olinger Cir Middletown OH 45044

KAY, PETER STEVEN, business consultant; b. Milw., Sept. 24, 1937; s. Otto J. and Edith W. Kay. BA, Cornell U., 1959; PhD, Purdue U., 1966. Various sci. positions, 1959-73; dist. sales mgr. photo products dept. E.I. du Pont de Nemours & Co., Inc., Wilmington, Del., 1973-75, product mgr., 1975-76; nat. sales mgr. photo products dept. E.I. du Pont de Nemours & Co. Inc., Wilmington, Del., 1976-77, mgr. thermal analysis photo products dept., 1977-79, mgr. liquid chrom. photo products dept., 1979-80, nat. sales mgr. elec. materials photo products dept., 1980-82; dir. mktg. Harshaw Chem. Co. (Gulf Oil), Cleve., 1982-84; gen. mgr. Picker Internat., X-Ray Products, Cleve., 1984-86; prin. Strategic Mgmt. Adv. Group, Cin., 1986—. Contbr. articles to JACS. Bd. dirs. Greater Cin. Sports & Events Commn., 1989—; dean's adv. bd. Sch. of Sci., Purdue U., 1995—; mem. steering com. Leadership Cin., 1995-96. Fellow Am. Inst. Chemists; mem. Am. Chem. Soc., AAAS, Greater Cin. C. of C. (chmn. sports coun. 1987—, mem. 3 coms. 1986—), Purdue U. Crew Fund, Phi Lambda Upsilon, Sigma Xi. Home: 6 Mariners Cv Cincinnati OH 45249-1791

KAY, RICHARD M., physician assistant; b. Oct. 19, 1958. Diploma, Chgo. Urban Skill Ctr., 1984; AAS with honors, Kennedy King Coll., 1988; Physician Assistant, Cook County Hosp., Chgo. CPR instr.; lic. clergyman; nat. certified physician asst. Epidemiologist Dept. Health, Chgo., 1980-81; asst. supr. Cermak Hosp. Cook County Dept. Corrections, Chgo., 1981-85; nurse Hyde Park Community Hosp., Chgo., 1989, Michael Reese In House Registry, Chgo., 1989—; paramedic officer Chgo. Fire Dept., 1985—; asst. supr. EMT's; adj. faculty Kennedy King/Chgo. City Wide Colls., 1987—; mem. physician asst. program MXC/Cook County Hosp., 1995. Named to Dean's List; recipient Superior Achievement in Anatomy and Physiology/

Obstetrical Nursing award, Unit Performance award, Paramedic of Valor award. Home: 8858 S Crandon Chicago IL 60617-1222

KAYE, CHRISTOPHER JAMES, project engineer; b. Wilkes-Barre, Pa., June 18, 1957; s. Peter Paul and Donna Nora (Noblit) K. BS in Indsl. and Systems Engring., U. Dayton, 1979, MS in Engring. Mgmt., 1988; postgrad., Wright State U., 1995—. Quality control engr. Monsanto Rsch. Corp., Miamisburg, Ohio, 1979-81, product engr., 1981-87, sr. product engr., 1987-88; sr. product engr. EG & G Mound Applied Tech., Miamisburg, Ohio, 1988-90, sr. mfg. engr., 1990-91, mfg. engring. specialist, 1991-92; project engr. Master Inds., Piqua, Ohio, 1992-96; molding devel. supr. Plastic Trim Inc., Dayton, 1996—; plastics cons., Dayton, Ohio, 1992—. Contbr. articles to profl. jours. Scientist-in-residence partnership U. Dayton, 1994. Recipient DOE Quality Improvement award, Dept. Energy, Albuquerque, 1989, DOE Weapons Recognition of Excellence award, Washington, 1988. Mem. Soc. Mfg. Engrs. (sr.), Soc. Plastics Engrs. Roman Catholic. Home: 3432 Diamondback Dr Dayton OH 45414 Office: Plastic Trim Inc 3909 Research Blvd Dayton OH 45430

KAYE, GERARD W., association executive; b. N.Y.C., Sept. 18, 1944; s. Nathan and Sandra (Kohn) K.; m. Paula Langfeld, Jan. 28, 1967; children: Michelle Sari Silverman, Leora Rachel. BA, DePaul U., 1968; MA, Roosevelt U., 1972; cert. med. psychotherapy, Chgo. Med. Sch./U. Health Sci. Dir. Olin-Sane-Ruby Union Inst., Chgo., 1970—; cons. Strategies for the Year 2000, Wilmette, Ill., 1994—; tng. coord. UAHC Task Force on Substance Abuse and Youth Suicide Prevention, N.Y.C., 1990—. Recipient Alexander M. Dushkin Disting. Educator award Bd. of Jewish Edn., 1990, Guardian of Hope award Keshet, 1989. Fellow Am. Orthopsychiat. Assn.; mem. Nat. Assn. Temple Educators (reform Jewish educator), Pi Kappa Delta (degree of spl. distinction). Jewish. Home: 517 Park Ave Wilmette IL 60091 Office: Olin-Sane-Ruby Union Inst 600 Lacha Belle Dr Oconomowoc WI 53066

KAYE, JENNIFER LYNN, healthcare executive; b. Vallejo, Calif., Oct. 15, 1964; d. Edward Humphrey and Susan Kathy (Album) Bogart. BA in Psychology, U. Va., 1987. Programmer analyst U. Va. Med. Ctr., Charlottesville, 1987-88; personal computer cons. Northwestern U., Chgo., 1988-90; rsch. analyst Blue Cross Blue Shield Minn., St. Paul, 1990-93; mgr. nat. sales Pharmacy Gold, Inc., St. Paul, 1993-94; sr. dir. mktg. and ops. Group Health Cooperative of Eau Claire, Altoona, Wis., 1994—; instr. Grad. Mgmt. Admissions Test preparatory course, Bar Bri, Mpls., 1990-92. Vol. adult self-sufficiency program Project for Pride in Living, Mpls., 1991; vol. mission control officer 1st flight launch action group (1st flag) Minn. Air N.G. Mus., Mpls., 1994-95. Mem. Am. Coll. Healthcare Execs.

KAYE, RICHARD WILLIAM, utility company executive; b. Chgo., May 14, 1939; s. Albert Louis and Helen (Beckman) K.; m. Betty Ann Terry, Aug. 7, 1964; children: Ronald, William, Richard, Timothy. AB, Cornell U., 1960; MBA, Columbia U., 1962. Various fin. positions Inland Steel Co., Chgo., 1964-81; dir. info. svcs. No. Ind. Pub. Svc. Co., Hammond, 1981-86, dir. econ. analysis, 1986-88; vis. dir. Purdue U., 1988; cons., ct. appointed receiver, 1989—; mgmt./fin. cons., 1990—. Advisor Calumet Coll., Whiting, Ind., 1985—; active Village Planning Commn. Lt. (j.g.) USNR. Mem. Am. Mgmt. Assn., Cornell U. Alumni Assn., Columbia U. Alumni Assn., Rotary. Home: 2801 Cherrywood Ln Hazel Crest IL 60429-2126 Office: No Ind Pub Svc Co 401 S State St Chicago IL 60605

KAYNE, JON BARRY, industrial psychologist; b. Sioux City, Iowa, Oct. 20, 1943; s. Harry Aaron and Barbara Valentine (Daniel) K.; m. Bunee Ellen Price, July 25, 1965; children: Nika Jenine, Abraham; m. Sandra Kay Fossbender, Jan. 5, 1985; 1 child, Shay-Marie Kathryn. BA, U. Colo., 1973; MSW, U. Denver, 1975; PhD, U. No. Colo., 1978. With spl. svcs. Weld County Sch. Dist. 6, Greeley, Colo., 1975-77; forensic diagnostician Jefferson County (Colo.) Diagnostic Unit, 1977-78; assoc., dir. mktg. 1 Dow Ctr., assoc. prof. psychology Hillsdale (Mich.) Coll., 1978-87; pres. Jon B. Kayne, P.C., Hillsdale, 1980-87; pres. bd. dirs. Lang. Learners in Partnership of Omaha, 1989-93; chmn. bd. dirs., CEO Am. Internat. Mgmt. Assocs., Ltd., Denver, 1984-87; prof. bus. adminstrn. and psychology Bellevue (Neb.) U., 1987—, v.p. profl. and continuing edn. studies, 1987-93, v.p. acad. affairs, 1993—. Chmn. bd. dirs. Domestic Harmony, 1979-82; bd. dir. religious sch., Greeley, 1975-77; candidate for sheriff of Boulder County, 1974. With USAR, 1962. Mem. Am. Psychol. Assn., Am. Soc. Clin. Hypnosis, Am. Statis. Assn., Internat. Neuropsychol. Soc., Mich. Soc. Investigative and Forensic Hypnosis (chmn. bd., pres. 1982), N.Y. Acad. Scis., Phi Delta Kappa, Psi Chi, Alpha Gamma Sigma. Office: Bellevue U 1000 Galvin Rd S Bellevue NE 68005-3058

KAZA, GREG JOHN, state representative, economist; b. Wyandotte, Mich., Nov. 11, 1960; s. John J. and Mary A. (Lazurek) K. BA in Econ., U. Detroit, 1989. Staff A.T. Kearney & Co., Alexandria, Va., 1982-83; journalist Washington and Mich., 1983-89; v.p. policy rsch. The Mackinac Ctr., Midland, Mich., 1989-91; adj. prof. Northwood Inst., Troy, Mich., 1991-93; state rep. State of Mich., 1993—. Author: Michigan: An Agenda for the 90's, 1990, Liberty In the House, 1995. Named Nat. Legislator of Yr., Rep. Liberty Caucus, 1994, one of Outstanding Young Men of Am., 1992. Fellow Nat. Journalism Ctr.; mem. Highpointers Mountaineering Club. Republican. Roman Catholic. Home: 284 Woodside Ct Rochester Hls MI 48307-4159 Office: Ho of Reps State Capitol Lansing MI 48909

KAZAN, ROBERT PETER, neurosurgeon; b. Chgo., Mar. 29, 1947; s. Peter Joseph and Genevieve (Pauga) K.; m. Janet Rae Hoiland, June 21, 1975. BS, Loyola U., Chgo., 1969, MD, 1973. Diplomate Am. Bd. Neurol. Surgeons; lic. physician Ill., Minn. Intern in surgery Mayo Clinic, Rochester, Minn., 1973-74, resident in neurosurgery, 1974-78; neurosurg. cons. West Suburban Neurosurg. Assocs., Hinsdale, Ill., 1978-92; med. dir. neurosci. dept. Hinsdale Hosp., 1992; clin. asst. prof. neurosurgery U. Ill., Chgo., 1983—; various teaching appointments West Suburban Hosp. Dept. Surgery, Chgo. Med. Soc. Midwest Conf., Northwestern U.; staff neurosurgeon Hinsdale Hosp., vice chmn. surgery, 1988-90, chmn. dept. surgery, 1990—, med. dir. neurosci., 1992. Contbr. articles to profl. jours. Fellow ACS; mem. AMA, DuPage County Med. Soc., Ill. Med. Soc., Mayo Clin. Neurosurg. Soc., Congress Neurosurg. Surgeons, Am. Assn. Neurol. Surgeons, Cen. Neurosurg. Soc., Soc. Med. Cons. Armed Forces U.S., Am. Assn. Neurol. Surgeons (joint sec. trauma and disorders of spine and peripheal nerves), Congress Neurol. Surgeons (joint sect. trauma and disorders of spine and peripheal nerves), Internat. Skullbase Soc., Ill. State Neurosurg. Soc. (membership chmn. 1995). Republican. Roman Catholic. Home: 120 Lakewood Cir Hinsdale IL 60521-6339 Office: West Suburban Neurosurg Assocs 20 E Ogden Ave Hinsdale IL 60521-3543

KAZIK, JOHN STANLEY, newspaper executive; b. Chgo., May 31, 1942; s. John B. and Rose A. (Antolak) Kazikiewicz; m. Beverly A. Adams, Nov. 28, 1964 (div. Aug. 1975); children: Kimberly A., John S. Jr. BSME, Ill. Inst. Tech., 1964, MBA, 1968. Design engr., devel. engr. Allis-Chalmers Co., Harvey, Ill., 1964-68; prodn. engr. Chgo. Tribune, 1968-72, prodn. planning mgr., 1973, plant mgr., 1974-76, project mgr., 1977-81, v.p., info. systems, 1981-88; v.p., info. systems Tribune Co., Chgo., 1989-92, sr. v.p., 1993—; bd. dirs. bus. adv. bd. U. Ill. at Chgo., The Ctr. for Info. Tech. Mgmt.; chmn., gov. bd. Info. Tech. Resource Ctr., 1986—. Mem. Soc. for Info. Mgmt., Newspaper Systems Group, Info. Tech. Resource Ctr. (governing bd. dirs. 1986—). Home: 19 Eastings Way South Barrington IL 60010-5318 Office: Tribune Co 435 N Michigan Ave Chicago IL 60611-4001

KAZIMIERCZUK, MARIAN KAZIMIERZ, electrical engineer, educator; b. Smolugi, Poland, Mar. 3, 1948; came to U.S., 1984; s. Stanislaw and Stanislawa (Tomaszewska) K.; m. Alicja Nowowiejska, July 5, 1973; children: Andrzej, Anna. MS, Tech. U. of Warsaw, Poland, 1971, PhD, 1978, DSc, 1984. Instr. elec. engring. Tech. U. of Warsaw, Poland, 1972-78, assoc. prof., 1978-84; project engr. Design Automation, Inc., Lexington, Mass., 1984; vis. prof. Va. Poly. Inst., Blacksburg, 1984-85, Wright State U., Dayton, Ohio, 1985—. Author: Resonant Power Converters, 1995; contbr. numerous articles to profl. jours. Recipient Univ. Edn. and Tech. award Polish Ministry of Sci. award, 1981, 84, 85, Polish Acad. Sci. award, 1983. Mem. IEEE (Harrel V. Noble award 1990), Assn. Polish Engrs., Polish Soc. Theoretical and Applied Elec. Scis. Roman Catholic. Home: 3620 Cypress Ct Dayton OH 45440-4515 Office: Wright State U Dept Elec Engring Dayton OH 45435

KEACH, MARGARET SALLY, writer, lecturer; b. Rolla, Mo., Apr. 16, 1903; d. John A. and Laura (Freeman) Sally; m. A.V. Eulich, May 1, 1922 (dec. 1937); children: Eric V., John F.; m. John Russell Keach, Apr. 1944. Student, Springfield Tchrs. Coll., 1921, Mo. Sch. Mines, 1924, Kansas City U., 1930. Columnist Johnson County Herald, Mission, Kans.; chmn. bd. Hospitalized Vets. Writing Project, Mission, 1952-91; founder, publ Vets. Voices mag., Mission, 1952-91; lectr. in field; bd. dirs. Menninger Found., Topeka, Kans., Univ. Mo. Kansas City. Author: White Mother in Africa, 1939, A New African Song, 1962; contbr. feature articles to various publs. Founding mem. women's div. Kansas City Mus., 1945-90; Kans. adviser March of Dimes, 1955-66; trustee William Allen White Found., 1963-91; bd. dirs. Kans. Mental Health Ctr., 1965-66; co-founder Soroptimist Club of Shawnee Mission, Kans. Named Patriot of Yr. Kansas City chpt. SAR, 1973; recipient Headline award Washington, 1988. Fellow Internat. Inst. Arts and Letters; mem. Women in Communications (nat. v.p. 1953-56, past area pres.), Woman's City Club. Office: Hospitalized Vets Writing Project 5920 Nall Ave Ste 102 Shawnee Mission KS 66202-3456 Address: 2911 Turtle Creek Blvd Ste 450 Dallas TX 75219-6244

KEANE, STEPHEN E., securities company official; b. Milw., May 13, 1943; s. Steven E. and Geraldine E. (Cox) K.; m. Kathleen Maloney, Aug. 2, 1969; children: Steven W., Peter D. BA, Coll. of St. Thomas, St. Paul, 1965. Mgr. rsch. Robert W. Baird & Co. Inc., Milw., 1965—, also bd. dirs. Bd. dirs. St. Mary's Hosp., Milw., 1991—, Milw. Better Bus. Bur., 1995—, Sacred Heart Hosp., Milw., 1995—. Staff sgt. USAR, 1966-72. Mem. Assn. Investment Mgmt., Soc. CFA's, Milw. Investment Analysts Soc. (pres. 1984-85), Ozakee Country Club. Republican. Roman Catholic.

KEANE, STEVEN EDWARD, lawyer; b. Aberdeen, S.D., Oct. 25, 1915; s. Stephen Edward and Freda (Host) K.; m. Geraldine Ellen Cox, Jan. 17, 1942; children: Stephen Edward, John Patrick, Kevin Gerard, Mary Elizabeth. Student No. State Tchrs. Coll., Aberdeen, S.D., 1932-34; LLB, Marquette U., 1937. Bar: Wis. 1937, U.S. Dist. Ct. (ea. and we. dists.) Wis. 1937, U.S. Ct. Appeals (7th cir.) 1956, U.S. Supreme Ct. 1956. Assoc. Foley & Lardner and predecessors, Milw., 1937-47, ptnr., 1947—. Bd. dirs. emeritus St. Mary's Hosp., Milw., 1962—, Chmn., 1965-67; bd. dirs. Better Bus. Bur., Milw., 1968—, Seton Health Care Found., Milw., 1983—, chmn. bd., 1988—; trustee emeritus Marquette U., Milw., 1969—, chmn. bd. trustees and exec. com., 1971-73; co-chmn. Wis. region NCCJ, 1971—; bd. dirs. Sacred Heart Sch. Theology, Milw., 1982—. Served to lt. j.g. USNR, 1943-46. Recipient Brotherhood award NCCJ, 1968; named Alumnus of Yr., Marquette U., 1970. Fellow Am. Coll. Trial Lawyers (elected 1959, chmn. Wis. Fellows 1972-73), Am. Bar Found.; mem. Milw. Bar Assn. (pres. 1968), State Bar Wis. (Charles L. Goldberg Disting. Svc. award 1988), ABA (chmn. Sherman Act com. and mem. council Antitrust Sect. 1965-69, mem. standing com. on fed. judiciary 1979-84, resource devel. council 1983—, ho. of dels. 1970-80), Bar Assn. Seventh Fed. Cir., Am. Law Inst. (life), Am. Judicature Soc., Am. Arbitration Assn., U.S. Supreme Ct. Hist. Soc. (chmn. Membership Com. Wis.), Marquette U. Alumni Assn. (dir. 1963-69), Marquette U. Law Alumni Assn. (dir., chmn. 1957-58). Republican. Roman Catholic. Clubs: Univ., Ozaukee Country. Home: 929 N Astor St Unit 2408 Milwaukee WI 53202-3490 Office: Foley & Lardner 1st Wisconsin Ctr #3800 777 E Wisconsin Ave Milwaukee WI 53202-5302

KEANEY, WILLIAM REGIS, engineering and construction services executive, consultant; b. Pitts., Nov. 2, 1937; s. William Regis Sr. and Emily Elizabeth (Campi) K.; m. Sharon Lee Robinson, Feb. 23, 1956; children: William R., James A., Robert E., Susan Elizabeth. BBA in Mktg. and Internat. Mktg., Ohio State U., 1961. Sales engr. Burdett Oxygen Co., Cleve., 1961-64, A.O. Smith Co., Milw., 1964-66; pres. W.R. Keaney & Co., Columbus, Ohio, 1966-71, Power Equipment Service Corp., Columbus, 1971-80, Gen. Assocs. Corp., Worthington, Ohio, 1980—; cons. Mannesmann, Houston, 1984-85, TVA, Knoxville, 1984-86, Power Authority of N.Y., White Plains, 1985-86, Utility Power Corp., Atlanta, 1985-86; mem. various task forces in the field. Vol. Cen. Ohio Lung Assn., Columbus, 1984-86. Mem. ASME (subgroups on nonferrous alloys, strenght/nonferrous alloys), ASTM (B2 com.), Am. Welding Soc., Welding Rsch. Coun., Worthington C. of C. (leadership program 1991-92), Mil. Vehicle Collectors Club, Masons. Democrat. Methodist. Home: 1314 Oakview Dr Columbus OH 43235-1135 Office: Keaney & Co PO Box 762 Columbus OH 43085-0762

KEARNEY, MICHAEL JOHN, banker; b. Clinton, Iowa, Jan. 2, 1940; s. Vincent Joseph and Evelyn Lorraine (Lynch) K.; m. Lisa von Kaenel, Sept. 8, 1973; children: Bridget, Andrew, Patrick. BSEE, Washington U., St. Louis, 1962; MBA, U. Pa., 1964. Tech. draftsman Alfred E. Teves K.G., Frankfurt, Fed. Republic of Germany, 1966-67, Hussmann Refrigerator Co., Mexico City, Mex., 1967-68; gen. mgr. Hussmann Refrigerator Co., Guatamala City, Guatamala, 1968-71; internat. sales mgr. Hussmann Refrigerator Co., Buenos Ares, Argentina, 1971-72; loan officer 1st Nat. Bank Chgo., Mexico City, 1972-76; asst. v.p. 1st Nat. Bank Chgo., Chgo., 1976-79; v.p. 1st Nat. Bank Chgo., 1979-86, Phila. Nat. Bank, Chgo., 1986-88; regional mgr. Valuation Rsch. Corp., Milw., 1988-90, v.p. internat. ops., 1990-94; v.p., group head credit Deutsche Genossenschaftsbank, N.Y.C., 1995—. Author: Midwest Families, 1979. Pres. St. Stephen's Green Property Owners, Northbrook, Ill., 1982-90, treas., 1980-82; mem. Northbrook Caucus, 1986-87, pres., 1987-89. 1st lt. U.S. Army, 1964-66. Mem. Japan Am. Soc. Chgo., Assn. Corp. Growth, U. Club Chgo., Beta Theta Pi (dist. chief 1982-90, Dist. Chief of Yr. 1987, asst. gen. treas. 1995—), Omicron Delta Kappa (pres. 1961-62). Republican. Roman Catholic. Home: 187 Weaver St Greenwich CT 06831-4304 Office: DG Bank Bldg 609 5th Ave New York NY 10017-1021

KEARNS, MERLE GRACE, state senator; b. Bellefonte, Pa., May 19, 1938; d. Robert John and Mary Catharine (Fitzgerald) Grace; m. Thomas Raymond Kearns, June 27, 1959; children: Thomas, Michael, Timothy, Matthew. B.S., Ohio State U., 1960. Tchr. St. Raphael Elem. Sch., Springfield, Ohio, 1960-62; substitute tchr. Mad River Green dist., Springfield, 1972-78; instr. Clark Tech. Coll., Springfield, 1978-80; commr. Clark County, Ohio, 1981-91; mem. Ohio State Senate from 10th dist., 1991—; chair Senate human svcs. and aging com.; mem. edn. com., health com.; vice chair Senate agrl. com.; co-chair Supreme Ct. domestic violence com.; mem. Joint Com. Agy. Rule Review; pres. bd. county commrs., 1982, 83, 86, 87, 90, v.p., 1985, 88, 89. Bd. dirs. Springfield Symphony, 1980-86, Arts Council, 1980-85, County Commrs. Assn. of Ohio, sec., 1988, 2d v.p., 1989-90, 1st v.p., 1990; mem. exec. com. Springfield Republicans, 1984—; bd. pres. Ohio Children's Trust Fund, 1995-96. Ohio State U., scholar, 1957-59; named Woman of Yr. Springfield Pilot Club, 1981, Wittenberg Woman of Accomplishment, 1991, Watchdog of Treasury, 1991. Mem. LWV (bd. dirs. 1964-78, pres. 1975-78), Ohio Nurses Assn. (Legislator of the Yr. 1995). Rotary, Omicron Nu. Roman Catholic. Avocations: reading, golf. Office: Ohio Senate Senate Bldg Rm 041 Columbus OH 43215

KEATHLEY, GEORGE, performing arts executive. dir. daytime dramas including, One Life to Live (recipient Emmy award), The Doctors, Another World, All My Children, stage productions include Sweet Bird of Youth, The Heiress, Square Root of Wonderful, The Glass Menagerie, M. Butterfly, A Midsummer's Night Dream, Death of a Salesman, Rough Crossing, Romeo and Juliet, Broadway Bound, Lady Day at Emerson's Bar & Grill, Hing Lear, King Richard III, Our Town, Of Mice and Men, Born Yesterday, Jekyll!, The Road To Mecca, The Emperor Jones, The Great Sebastians, The Curious Adventures of Alice, and All My Sons. Office: Mo Repertory Theatre 4949 Cherry St Kansas City MO 64110-2229*

KEATING, DANIEL BERNARD, field service engineer; b. Dayton, Ohio, June 24, 1954; s. Tristan Jack and Helen (Condron) K. Repair technician M-R Electric, Dayton, 1974-77; field svc. engr. Nat. Waterlift Co., Kalamazoo, 1977-81, Cadillac Gage Textron, Warren, Mich., 1984—; lab. technician Sinclair C.C., Dayton, 1981-84. Mem. Toledo Zool. Soc., Rep. Nat. Com. Mem. NRA (life), Am. Def. Preparedness Assn. (life), Rep. Presdl. Task (life, Legion of Merit award), N.Am. Hunting Club (life), Elks, KC. Home: 4165 Odema Dr Lima OH 45806-1252 Office: Cadillac Gage Textron 25760 Groesbeck Hwy Warren MI 48089-1544

KEATING, PAMELA JOAN, nurse anesthetist; b. Chgo., Mar. 30, 1950; d. Harry Atkinson and Margaret Pruit (Keith) Ruyter; m. Kevin Thomas Keating, June 27, 1976. BS in Psychology, Loyola U., Chgo., 1972; diploma in nursing with honors, Luth. Gen. and Deaconess Hosp., Park Ridge, Ill., 1976; diploma in nurse anesthesia, Ravenswood Hosp., Chgo., 1981; MS in Nursing with distinction, DePaul U., 1992; postgrad., Loyola U., Chgo., 1994—. RN, Ill. Lab. technician Bio-Labs, Inc., Northbrook, Ill., 1973; staff nurse surg. unit, then alcoholism treatment unit Luth. Gen. Hosp., Park Ridge, 1973-76; nurse anesthetist, instr. Ravenswood Hosp. Med. Ctr., Chgo., 1981—, asst. program dir. Sch. of Anesthesia, 1992—. Mem. Am. Assn. Nurse Anesthetists (cert.), Ill. Assn. Nurse Anesthetists. Home: 1115 S Seminary Ave Park Ridge IL 60068-4369 Office: Ravenswood Hosp Med Ctr 4550 N Winchester Ave Chicago IL 60640-5205

KEATS, GLENN ARTHUR, manufacturing company executive; b. Chgo., July 1, 1920; s. Herbert J. and Agnes H. (Streich) K.; m. Olga Maria Loor Hurtado, Feb. 13, 1946; children: Maria Susana Keats Eggemeyer, Allwyn Dolores Keats Gustafson. BS in Commerce, Northwestern U., 1941. Sales exec. Keats-Lorenz Spring Co., Chgo., 1947-56; controller, auditor Plantaciones Ecuatorianas, S.A., Guayaquil, Ecuador, 1956-58; co-founder Keats Mfg. Co., Wheeling, Ill., 1958—. Sec. Hispanic Soc. Chgo., 1965—. Lt. comdr. USN, 1941-47. Mem. Spring Mfrs. Inst., Northwestern U. Alumni Assn., Sigma Nu. Republican. Lutheran. Club: Evanston Golf, Amelia Island (Fla.). Home: 368 Woodland Rd Highland Park IL 60035-5055 Office: 350 Holbrook Dr Wheeling IL 60090-5812

KECK, DAVID MICHAEL, school administrator; b. Toledo, Nov. 17, 1947; s. Marvin Wendell and Eleanor Lucille (Elwing) K.; children: Christian David, Stephen Patrick. Student, U. Toledo, 1967; BS in Edn., Ohio U., 1969, MEd, 1971; postgrad., Ohio State U., 1981—. Cert. tchr., prin., Ohio. Tchr. social studies Athens High Sch., The Plains, Ohio, 1969-73, Westerville (Ohio) South High Sch., 1973-86; tchr. social studies Dublin (Ohio) High Sch., 1986-92, adminstrv. asst., 1992—, summer sch. adminstr., 1987-95; pres. Ohio Capital Conf. Acad. League, 1995-96; pres. Ctrl. Ohio H.S. Soccer league, Columbus, 1975-77; vrsity soccer coach Westerville South H.S., 1974-85, Watterson H.S., 1985-86, Dublin H.S., 1986-88. Editor: Crew Chief, 1991; contbr. articles to profl. jours. Chmn. high sch. youth edn. com. Columbus Coun. World Affairs, 1990-91; issues adviser, staff mem. Linda Reidelbach for U.S. Congress, Columbus, 1992. Recipient Citizen Achievement award Westerville Parks and Recreation Dept., 1979; named Coach of Yr. Ohio Capital Conf., Franklin County, 1982. Mem. ASCD, Nat. Coun. Social Studies, John Dewey Soc., Ohio Assn. Secondary Sch. Adminstrs., Theodore Roosevelt Assn., Licking County Soccer Ofcls. Assn., Ohio U. Coll. Edn. Soc. Alumni and Friends (bd. dirs.), Ohio Scholastic Soccer Coaches Assn. (pres. 1982-85), Ohio Geneal. Soc. (v.p. 1988-89, trustee 1988-92), Maumee Valley Hist. Soc., Phi Delta Kappa. Republican. Lutheran. Home: 3503 Hunting Brook Dr Apt 203 Columbus OH 43231-4937 Office: Dublin Scioto High Sch 4000 Hard Rd Dublin OH 43016

KECK, JOE D., stockbroker; b. Knoxville, Tenn., May 11, 1951. BS in Fin., Ind. U., 1977. Stockbroker City Securities, Indpls., 1977-90; owner Prince Investments, Lafayette, Ind., 1990-92; stockbroker W.L. Lyons Inc., Lafayette, 1992—; founder Lafayette Bus. to Bus., 1989; mem. Ind. Coun. Econ. Edn., Lafayette, 1985; instr. fin. Purdue U., 1979-83. Capt. USAR, 1969-90. Republican. Baptist. Office: JJB Hilliard PO Box 5588 25 Executive Dr Lafayette IN 47905

KEECH, ELOWYN ANN, interior designer; b. Berrien County, Mich., Oct. 5, 1937; d. Earl Docker and Elizabeth Hall (Paullin) Stephenson; 1 child, Robert Earl Stephenson. Cert. contract interior designer. Print designer, copywriter newspaper accounts, dept. stores, resorts, svc. orgns., industry, 1957-75; freelance interior designer, photoset and video set designer, St. Joseph, Mich., 1975—; owner Fog Horn Records & Tapes. Bd. dirs. Blossomland United Way, 1981-86; bd. dirs., mem. steering and long-range planning coms. United Way Mich., 1980-87. Designer interiors 1st Fed. Savs. & Loan Assn., Three Oaks, Mich., 1975, Holland (Mich.) Cen. Trade Credit Union, 1978, 1st. Fed. Savs. & Loan Assn., Holland, 1978, Yonker Realty, Co., Holland, 1979, People's Bank of Holland, 1979, exec. offices Whirlpool Corp., 1980—, human resources St. Joe div., 1985, Claeys Residence, 1984, Calley Dental Office, 1985, Sarett Nature Ctr., 1985, Imperial Printing, 1986, Miller Residence, 1986, Schraders Super Market, 1986, Dave's Garage, 1987, Merritt Residence, 1987-88, Smith Residence, 1988, Emergency Shelter Svcs. 1991, Butzbach Residence, 1992, Merritt Residence, Del Mar, Calif., 1993-94, Fister Better Homes & Gardens Conf. Room, 1994, Vanderboegh Residence, 1994-96, S.W. Mich. Regional Airport, 1994—, Berrien Hills Country Club, 1994-96, Butzbach Offices, 1995, Molhoek Residence, 1996, Merritt Residence, Houston, 1996, Mich. Maritime Mus., 1996, other contract and residential projects. Trustee Mich. Martime Mus., 1994—. Mem. AIA (profl. affiliate S.W. Mich. chpt.), Nature Conservancy, Nat. Trust Hist. Preservation Forum, Assn. Great Lakes Maritime History, Econ. Club of S.W. Mich., Am. Rottweiler Club, Internat. Interior Design Assn., Rotary. Home and Office: 375 Ridgeway St Saint Joseph MI 49085-1062

KEEHN, SILAS, retired bank executive; b. New Rochelle, N.Y., June 30, 1930; s. Grant and Marjorie (Burchard) K.; m. Marcia June Lindquist, Mar. 26, 1955; children: Elisabeth Keehn Lewis, Britta Keehn-Scott, Peter. A.B. in Econs, Hamilton Coll., Clinton, N.Y., 1952; M.B.A. in Fin, Harvard U., 1957. With Mellon Bank N.A., Pitts., 1957-80; v.p., then sr. v.p. Mellon Bank N.A., 1967-78, exec. v.p., 1978-79, vice chmn., 1980; v.p. Mellon Nat. Corp., 1979-80, vice chmn., 1980; chmn. bd. Pullman, Inc., Chgo., 1980; pres. Fed. Res. Bank Chgo., 1981-94; ret., 1994; Bd. dirs. ABN Amro Bank, N.V., Amsterdam, ABN Amro Holding, N.V., Amsterdam. Trustee Rush-Presbyn.-St. Luke's Med. Ctr., Hamilton Coll., Clinton, N.Y.; mem. Northwestern U. Assocs. With USNR, 1953-56. Mem. Chgo. Club, Comml. Club Chgo. (treas.), Econ. Club Chgo., Fox Chapel Golf Club, U. Club, Links Club (N.Y.C.), Rolling Rock Club (Ligonier, Pa.), Indian Hill Club, Nat. Futures Assn., Chgo. Bd. Options Exch., Inc. Office: 707 Skokie Blvd Ste 600 Northbrook IL 60062

KEELER, JOHN S., state legislator; b. Indpls., July 11, 1949; s. Ohoi Jr. and Janet Keeler; m. Shari Keeler, 1971. BS, U. Ariz.; JD, Ind U., Indpls. Atty. Freihofer, Minton, Keeler & McClamroch; asst. majority counsel Ind. State Senate, 1979-80; rep. Dist. 86 Ind. Ho. of Rep., 1982—, ranking mem. judiciary com., chmn. pub. safety com., ranking mem. rules and legis. procedure com. Mem. NRA, Am. Legion, Indpls. Athletic Club, White River Yacht Club, Masons. Broad Ripple Lodge, Sigma Chi. Home: 1620 E 75th St Indianapolis IN 46240-3181*

KEENER, POLLY LEONARD, illustrator; b. Akron, Ohio, July 14, 1946; d. George Holman and Alice June (Bolinger) Leonard; m. Robert Lee Keener, Dec. 29, 1967; children: Robert Edward Alan, June Whitney. Student, Kent State U., 1967, Princeton U., 1968, 73; BA, Conn. Coll., 1968. Cert. tchr., Ohio. Illustrator Akron, 1969—; instr. cartooning Northeastern Ohio Univs. Coll. Medicine, 1992-94; instr. cartooning U. Akron, 1979—, instr. soft sculpture, 1979-84; cartoon text writer Prentice Hall Pubs., Englewood Cliffs, N.J., 1985—; pres. Keener Corp., Akron, 1977—; judge arts and crafts competition, Akron, 1982—. Author: Cartooning, 1992; illustrator: Eat Dessert First, 1987, It's Our Serve, 1989, 80+ Great Ideas For Making Money At Home, 1992; contbr. articles to profl. jours. Trustee Stan Hywet Hall Found., Akron, 1972—; trustee and v.p. Women's History Project, Akron, 1993-96; v.p. Jr. League, Akron, 1988-89, Western Res. Acad. Women's Bd., Hudson, Ohio, 1987-88; active Women's Bd. Blossom Music Ctr., Penninsula, Ohio, 1969—. Named Woman of Yr. Women's History Project Ohio, 1989; recipient Unsung Hero award Jr. League Akron, 1988. Mem. AAUP, DAR (trustee, vice-regent Cuyahoga-Portage chpt. 1992—), Nat. Cartoonists Soc. (chmn. Ohio/Mich. chpt. 1996—), Soc. Illustrators, Coll. Art Assn., Portage Country Club. Episcopalian. Home: 37 Elmdale Ave Akron OH 44313-7645

KEENEY, DENNIS RAYMOND, soil science educator; b. Osceola, Iowa, July 2, 1937; s. Paul N. and Evelyn L. (Beck) K.; m. Betty Ann Goodhue, June 20, 1959; children: Marcia, Susan. BS, Iowa State U., 1959; MS, U. Wis., 1961; PhD, Iowa State U., 1965. Postdoctoral research assoc. Iowa State U., Ames, 1965-66; prof. U. Wis., 1966-88, Romnes research prof., 1975—; chmn. dept. soil sci. U. Wis., Madison, 1978-83; chmn. land resources program Inst. Environ. Studies, Madison, 1985-88; prof. dept. agronomy Iowa State U., Ames, 1988—, dir. Leopold Ctr. for Sustainable Agr., 1988—; dir. Iowa State Water Resources Inst., 1991—; sr. research scientist grasslands Dept. Sci. and Indsl. Research, Palmerston North, N.Z., 1975-76. Fellow Am. Soc. Agronomy (rsch. grantee 1986, pres. 1992-93), Soil Sci. Soc. Am. (pres. 1987-88, rsch. grantee 1981, Profl. Svc. award 1994). Office: Iowa State U 209 Curtiss Hall Ames IA 50011-1050

KEENEY, WILLIAM ECHARD, educator, minister; b. Fayette County, Pa., July 17, 1922; s. William Leroy and Kathryn Olive (Echard) K.; m. Willadene Hartzler, Oct. 12, 1947; children: Lois Ruth Keeney Palmer, Carol Louise, William Leroy, Richard Lowell. AB, Bluffton Coll., 1948; BD, Bethany & Mennonite Bibl. Sem., 1953; STM, Hartford Theol. Sem., 1957, PhD, 1959. Ordained to ministry gen. conf. Mennonite Ch., 1953. Cmty. assoc. and acting dir. edn. divsn. Nat. Mental Health Found., Phila., 1946-47; relief worker in Germany Mennonite Ctrl. Com., 1948-49, dir. Netherlands program, 1949-50, rep. Netherlands, chair European Peace com., 1961-63, peace sect. study sec. Inst. Mennonite Studies fellow, 1973-74; asst. to pres., instr. Bible Bluffton (Ohio) Coll., 1953-56, asst. prof. Bible, 1958-59, assoc. prof. Bible, 1959-65, dir. publicity, 1958-61, 63-65, prof. Bible, 1965-68; acad. dean Bethel Coll., 1968-72, prof. Bible and religion, 1968-80, prof. peace studies, 1974-80, provost, 1972-73, dir. Mennonite Hist. Libr. and Archives, 1972-73, dir. experiential learning, 1974-78, dir. continuing edn., 1975-80, exec. dir. consortium on peace rsch., edn., and devel., 1978-84; vis. asst. prof. integrative change Kent (Ohio) State U., 1980-86, asst. prof. peace and conflict studies, 1987-90, acting dir. Ctr. for Peaceful Change, 1987-89; asst. pastor Woodlawn Mennonite Ch., Chgo., 1952-53, Nepaug (Conn.) Congl. Ch., 1956-57, Trinity Mennonite Ch., Hillsboro, Kans., 1976, First Mennonite Ch., Hillsboro, 1976-77, Mcpherson, Kans., 1977-78, Wadsworth, Ohio, 1983-84, Summit Mennonite Ch., Barberton, Ohio, 1984-86, among others. Author: The Development of Dutch Anabaptist Thought & Practice from 1539-1564, 1968, Lordship as Servanthood: The Biblical Basis of Peace, 1975; co-author, translator: The Writings of Dirk Philips, 1992, Preaching the Parables: Series II, Cycle A, 1995, Preaching the Parables: Series II, Cycle B, 1996; cons. editor Mennonite Quar. Rev.; assoc. editor Fides et Historia, 1976-77. Chairperson Harvey County Edn. Action Coun., 1976-80; mem. adv. coun. self-directed profl. devel. program Prairie View Mental Health Ctr., 1976-80; mem. Delegation in Dialogue for Reconciliation to Teheran, 1980; co-chairperson Kent Ecumenical Peace Group, 1983-88, mem., 1988-91; mem. Gov.'s Commn. on Peace and Conflict Mgmt., 1988-89, co-chair task force on pub. edn., 1988-89; incorporator, bd. dirs. Franklin Mills Mediation Svc., Kent, 1988-90, sec., treas. bd. dirs., 1988-90; chairperson Peace and Change Exec. Com., 1985-87; mem. Et Cetera (Self Help and Thrift) Shop, 1991—, chair, 1991—; mem., chair Ctrl. Dist. Conf. Hist. Com., 1992—; bd. dirs. Chgo. Mennonite Learning Ctr., 1992—; bd. missions, peace and svc., First Mennonite Ch., Bluffton, 1992-95, vice-chair, 1992-95, moderator, 1995—. Named Outstanding Alumni Bluffton Coll., 1988. Mem. Lions (bd. dirs. 1991-93). Home: 140 N Lawn Ave Bluffton OH 45817-1275

KEETS, JOHN DAVID, JR., insurance company executive; b. Atlantic City, N.J., Apr. 1, 1948; s. John D. and Doris F. (Fleiss) Keets; m. Julianne Zellers, Nov. 3, 1973; children: J. David, Brian. BA, High Point Coll., 1970. CLU., cert. fin. planner, chartered fin. cons. Account exec. Mgmt. Recruiters, Phila., 1972-75; sales mgr. Cigna Fin. Svc., Miami (Fla.), Balt., 1975-82; agy. mgr. Fidelty Mut., Balt., 1983-85, Provident Mut. Ins. Co., Phila., 1985-88; regional v.p. Equitable Ins. Co., Mpls., 1988-90; prin. Keets & Assocs., Mpls., 1991-93; mgr. Prudential Ins. Co., Mpls., 1993-94; v.p. bus. devel. Carlson Mktg. Group, Mpls., 1994—. With U.S. Army, 1970-72, Germany. Mem. Mpls. Assn. Life Underwriter, Gen. Agts. & Mgrs. Assn, Internat. Assn. Fin. Planners, Am. Soc. CLU, Chartered Fin. Cons. Home: 2420 Comstock Ln N Minneapolis MN 55447-2303

KEEVEN, RON, state legislator. Mem. Mo. Ho. of Reps., Jefferson City. Republican.

KEHEW, WILLIAM JAMES, environmental, quality assurance engineering manager; b. Newport, R.I., June 29, 1937; s. William Francis and Dorothy Catherine (Sheehan) K.; m. Barbara Ann Boudreau, Oct. 29, 1966; children: Katherine, Meghan, Eileen. BS, Nat. U., San Diego, 1974; MBA, Nat. U., 1976. Registered profl. engr., Calif.; cert. quality engr. Constrn. engr. Martin Marietta Corp., Denver, 1960-65; mgmt. systems analyst North Am. Aviation, Tulsa, 1965-67; staff engr. to dir. Quality Assurance Honeywell Info. Systems, San Diego, 1967-73; quality assurance auditor Gen. Atomic Corp., San Diego, 1973-75; sr. engr. Westinghouse Corp., Monroeville, Pa., 1975-76; dir. quality assurance U.S. Doe, Idaho Falls, Idaho, 1976-85; mgr. quality assurance U.S. Doe, Chgo., 1985-92; acting dir. quality assurance U.S. Doe, Fernald, Ohio, 1992—; acting dir., Office of Civilian Radioactive Waste Mgmt., Washington, 1988; liaison mem. NAS, Washington, 1989-90. Contbr. articles to profl. jours. Mem. Soc. Mech. Engrs. (vice chmn. 1980-92), Am. Soc. for Quality Control (vice chmn. 1972-73, Energy Divsn. Exec. Com. for Auditing 1983-84). Home: 2231 Kyle Ln Hebron KY 41048-9522 Office: DOE Fernald Field Office PO Box 398704 Cincinnati OH 45239-8704

KEIM, BARBARA HOWELL, university administrator, biology educator, association administrator; b. Detroit, Mar. 9, 1946; m. James Albert Keim, Jan. 4, 1975. BA, U. N.C., 1967; MS, Rutgers U., 1969; PhD, U. Va., 1976; MBA, Bradley U., 1988. Instr. Wheaton Coll., Norton, Mass., 1975-76; asst. prof., adj. prof. Bradley U., Peoria, Ill., 1976-80, dir. exec. and profl. devel., 1991—; assoc. prof. Eureka (Ill.) Coll., 1980-87; dir. of vols. ARC, Peoria, 1989-90, dir. fin. devel., 1990-91. Bd. dirs. Coll. Nursing, St. Francis Med. Ctr., Peoria, 1986-95, Peoria Woman's Civic Fedn., 1989-91. Mem. Phi Kappa Phi, Phi Sigma, Beta Beta Beta. Home: 516 W Stratford Dr Peoria IL 61614-7250 Office: Bradley U Baker Hall Peoria IL 61625

KEIM, WILLIAM ALAN, retired educator; b. Pitts., Nov. 25, 1923; s. William Joseph and Sara Mae (Klarner) K.; m. Alva Lee Rylee, Jan. 26, 1946 (dec. Sept. 1978); children: Carolyn, John, Curtis; m. Marybelle Chase, June 15, 1979. BA, Whittier (Calif.) Coll., 1949, MEd, 1954; EdD, U. So. Calif., 1969. Tchr., adminstr. Whittier H.S., 1950-60; dir. learning resource Cerritos Coll., Norwalk, Calif., 1961-65, asst. supt., 1965-70; assoc. prof. Va. Tech., Blacksburg, 1971-75; founding pres. Pioneer Coll., Kansas City, Mo., 1975-78; pres. Maple Woods Coll., Kansas City, 1978-79; dist. dir. mktg. Metro Cmty. Coll., Kansas City, 1979-86; v.p., gen. mgr. Metro Bus. Arch, L.A., 1986-87; vis. prof. So. Ill. U., Carbondale, 1987-94; cons. various colls., 1966-89; mem. Congrl. Affairs Com., Clay County, Mo., 1983-84. Contbr. chpts. to books and articles to profl. jours. Mem. bd. Boys Club, Kansas City, 1976-77. With U.S. Army, 1942-46. Named Man of Yr. Nat. Coun., 1973, Person, of Yr., 1978. Fellow Acad. of Higher Edn.

KEISER, GEORGE J., state legislator; m. Kathy Keiser; four children. Owner Quality Printing Svc.; former commr. Bismarck City, N.D.; rep. N.D. State Ho. of Reps. Dist. 47, 1993—, vice chmn. indsl., bus. and labor com., mem. transp. com. Home: 2959 Domino Dr Bismarck ND 58501-0146*

KEITH, ALEXANDER MACDONALD, state supreme court chief justice; b. Rochester, Minn., Nov. 22, 1928; s. Norman and Edna (Alexander) K.; m. Marion Sanford, April 29, 1955; children: Peter Sanford (dec.), Ian Alexander, Douglas Scott. BA, Amherst Coll., 1950; JD, Yale U., 1953. Assoc. counsel, mem. Mayo Clinic, Rochester, 1955-60; state sen. Olmstead County, St. Paul, 1959-63; lt. gov. State of Minn., St. Paul, 1963-67; pvt. practice law Rochester, 1960-73; ptnr. Dunlap Keith Finseth Berndt and Sandberg, Rochester, 1973-89; assoc. justice Minn. Supreme Ct., St. Paul, 1989-90, chief justice, 1990—. Sen. del. White House Conf. on Aging, Washington, 1960; U.S. del. UN Delegation for Funding Developing Countries, Geneva, 1966; bd. dirs. Rochester Grad. Edn. Adv. Com., 1988-89, Ability Bldg. Ctr. Inc. 1st lt. USMC, 1953-55, Korea. Named Outstanding Freshman Minn. State Sen., St. Paul. Office: Minn Supreme Ct 25 Constitution Ave Saint Paul MN 55155-1500

KEITH, DALE MARTIN, utilities management consultant; b. Kansas City, Mo., Oct. 22, 1940; s. Floyd LeRoy and Pauline Constance (Brown) K.; m. Judith Ann Reynolds, May 8, 1964; children: Stephanie Deanna, Kirsten Michelle. BSBA in Indsl. Mgmt., U. Mo., 1965. Cert. mgmt. cons. Staff analyst Black & Veatch, Kansas City, Mo., 1965-68, asst. project mgr., 1968-75, adminstrv. coord., 1975-77, project mgr., 1977-88, mktg. dir., 1988-90, project dir., 1990-92; pres. Cert. Mgt. Cons., 1992—, Keith and Assocs., Ltd., Kansas City, 1993—; internat. speaker, trainer, advisor Coun. of Econ. Regulation, Washington, 1988—. Mem. Eggs & Issues Forum, Kansas City, 1988—. Mem. Am. Mgmt. Assn., Assn. Energy Engrs., Inst. Mgmt. Cons. (mem. Coll. Firm Prins., bd. dirs., past chmn., pres. Kansas City chpt., founding bd. mem. LAW Spl. Interest Group, IMC Comms. Com. chmn., 1996 IMC Nat. Conv. chpt. leadership and mgmt. com.), Assn. Mgmt. Cons., Nat. Trust for Scotland, St. Andrews Soc., Menninger, Kansas City C. of C. (quality com. 1988—), U.S. Energy Assn. (tech. collaboration com.), Inst. of Ams., Internat. Platform Assn., Internet Soc., Optimists Internat. (bd. dirs., pres.-elect Blue Valley chpt., Optimist Youth Homes). Republican. Presbyterian. Home: 17101 Canterbury Dr Stilwell KS 66085-9035

KEITH, THOMAS WARREN, JR., marketing executive; b. Evanston, Ill., Sept. 27, 1951; s. Thomas and Patricia (Ogden) K.; m. Anita Slomski, Oct. 6, 1990. BA, Colgate U., Hamilton, NY, 1973; MBA, Columbia U., N.Y.C., 1975. Acct. exec. Leo Burnett Co., Chgo, 1975-80, Needham Harper & Steers, Chgo, 1980-81; acct. supr. Tatham-Laird & Kudner, Chgo, 1981-85; mktg. dir. Dean Foods Co., Franklin Park, IL, 1986-90; pres. Thomas Keith & Assoc., Mktg. Svcs., Evanston, Ill.; dir. Dairy Nutrition Coun., Ill., 1989-90; dir. Dairy Coun. of Wis., Ill., 1987-90. Home and Office: 1016 Mulford St Evanston IL 60202-3317

KEJR, JOSEPH, state legislator; m. Geena Kejr. Kans. state rep. Dist. 67, farmer. Home: 10143 W Stimmel Rd Brookville KS 67425-9719*

KELCH, ROBERT PAUL, pediatric endocrinologist; b. Detroit, Dec. 3, 1942; s. Paul and Iona Bertha (Schmitt) K.; m. Jeri Anne Parker, Aug. 17, 1963; children: Randall Paul, Julie Marie. PhB, Wayne State U., Detroit, 1964; MD, U. Mich., Ann Arbor, 1967. Intern then Wyeth pediatric residency fellow U. Mich. Med. Center, 1967-70, research fellow, 1969-70, mem. faculty, 1972-94, prof. pediatrics, 1977-94, acting chmn. dept., 1979-80, chmn. dept., 1981-94; physician-in-chief C.S. Mott Children's Hosp. U. Mich., 1983-94; chief clin. affairs U. Mich. Hosps., 1989-92; NIH trainee pediatric endocrinology U. Calif. Med. Center, San Francisco, 1970-72; prof. pediatrics, dean U. Iowa Coll. Medicine, Iowa City, 1994—. Co-author: A Practical Approach to Pediatric Endocrinology, 1975; contbr. articles med. jours. Served with USNR. Fellow Am. Acad. Pediatrics; mem. Soc. Pediatrics Rsch. (pres. 1988), Am. Bd. Pediatrics (sec.-treas. 1992, chmn. elect 1994, chmn. 1995), Endocrine Soc., Am. Fedn. Clin. Rsch., Am. Soc. Clin. Investigators, Assn. Med. Sch. Pediatric Dept. Chmn. (pres. 1989), Ctrl. Soc. Clin. Rsch., Lawson Wilkns Pediatric Endocrine Soc., Midwest Soc. Pediatric Rsch. (pres. 1983-84). Methodist. Home: 620 Larch Ln Iowa City IA 52245-3435 Office: U Iowa Coll Medicine 212 CMAB Iowa City IA 52242-1101

KELLER, DENNIS JAMES, management educator, business executive; b. Chgo., July 6, 1941; s. Ralph and Dorothy (Barckman) K.; m. Constance Bassett Templeton, May 28, 1966; children: Jeffrey Breckenridge, David McDaniel, John Templeton. A.B., Princeton U., 1963; M.B.A., U. Chgo., 1968. Account exec. Motorola Communications, Chgo., 1964-67; v.p. fin. Bell & Howell Comm., Waltham, Mass., 1968-70; v.p. mktg. Bell & Howell Schs., Chgo., 1970-73; pres. Keller Grad. Sch. Mgmt., Chgo., 1973-81, chmn., chief exec. officer, 1981—; chmn. bd., chief exec. officer DeVry Inc., 1987—; cons., evaluator North Central Assn., Chgo., 1979—; chmn. bd. Precision Plastics, Inc., Columbia City, Ind., 1981—; bd. dirs. Templeton Kenly & Co., Broadview, Ill., Nicor Inc. Trustee Glenwood Sch. for Boys, Ill., 1980—, Chgo. Zool. Soc., Brookfield, Ill., 1979—, Princeton (N.J) U., 1994—, Lake Forest Acad.-Ferry Hall, Ill., 1980-87, George M. Pullman Found., Chgo., 1987—; bd. dirs. Great Books Found., Chgo., 1986—; chmn. U. Chgo. Grad. Sch. Bus. Coun., 1994—, Princeton (N.J.) U. Sch. Engring. and Applied Scis. Leadership Coun., 1992—; commr. North Cen. Assn.-Commn. on Instns. of Higher Edn., 1985-88. Nat. Merit scholar, 1959-63; U. Chgo. Grad. Sch. Bus. fellow, 1967-68. Republican. Mem. United Ch. of Christ. Mem. Hinsdale Golf Club, Econ. Club, Comml. Club Chgo., Chgo. Club. Office: DeVry Inc 1 Tower Ln Fl 10 Oakbrook Terrace IL 60181-4671

KELLER, DIANE MARIE, English language educator, school media specialist; b. Michigan City, Ind., Aug. 13, 1950; d. Norman Martin and Dolores Mae (Waite) Foldenauer; 1 child, Jeffrey James. BA in English, Purdue North Cen., Westville, Ind., 1972; MA in English, Purdue Calumet, Hammond, Ind., 1979; MLS, U. Ind., 1995. Cert. tchr. English, Ind., Mich.; cert. media specialist, Ind., Mich. Tchr. English Concord Jr. High Sch., Elkhart, Ind., 1981-89, Heritage Mid. Sch., Middlebury, Ind., 1989-93, Purdue U. North Ctrl., Westville, Ind., 1993-94; sch. media specialist St. Joseph (Mich.) H.S., 1995—. Contbr. articles to profl. jours. Coach Concord H.S. and Northridge H.S., Concord & Middlebury Jr. High Schs., 1981-93. Mem. Am. Lib. Assn., Nat. Edn. Assn., Mich. Assn. Media Edn., Nat. Coun. Tchrs. English. Democrat. Roman Catholic. Home: 128 1/2 Indiana Ave Mishawaka IN 46544-2535 Office: St Joseph H S 2521 Stadium Dr Saint Joseph MI 49085

KELLER, ELIOT AARON, broadcasting executive; b. Davenport, Iowa, June 11, 1947; s. Norman Edward and Millie (Morris) K.; m. Sandra Kay McGrew, July 3, 1970; 1 child, Nicole. BA, U. Iowa, 1970; MS, San Diego State U., 1976. Corr. Sta. WHO-AM-FM-TV, Des Moines, 1969-70; newsman Sta. WSUI, Iowa City, Iowa, 1968-70; newsman, corr. Sta. WHBF-AM-FM-TV, Rock Island, Ill., 1969; newsman Sta. WOC-AM-FM-TV, Davenport, 1970; freelance newsman and photographer Iowa City, 1969-77; pres., dir. KRNA, Inc., Iowa City, 1971—, mem. exec. com., 1982—; gen. mgr. Sta. KRNA, 1974—, Sta. KQCR, Cedar Rapids, Iowa, 1994-95, Sta. KXMX, Cedar Rapids, Iowa, 1995—; adj. instr. dept. comm. studies U. Iowa, Iowa City, 1983, 84. Mem. Mid-Continent Ry. Hist. Soc., R.R. Passenger Car Alliance, Iowa Assn. RR Passengers (excursion chair). Jewish. Home: 1244 Devon Dr NE Iowa City IA 52240-9628 Office: Sta KRNA 2105 Act Cir Iowa City IA 52245-9636

KELLER, HAROLD WILLIAM, chemical company executive; b. Grand Forks, N.D., Aug. 24, 1922; s. Charles Earl and Margaret Ann (Carlson) K.; student U. N.D., 1940-42, 46-48; m. S. Betty Larsen, Oct. 31, 1947; children—Charles William, Kenneth Earl. Asst. dir. research Ill. Water Treatment Co., Rockford, 1952-68, service mgr., 1968-69, mgr. market devel., 1969-72; v.p. Techni-Chem, Inc., Cherry Valley, Ill., 1972-77, pres., 1977-92, also owner, corp. exec., dir. Served with USAAF, 1942-46. Mem. Am. Chem. Soc., Am. Oil Chemists Soc., Am. Inst. Chem. Engrs., Am. Soc. Sugar Beet Tech., Lambda Chi Alpha. Home: 7633 Lucky Ln Rockford IL 61108-2630 Office: 6853 Indy Dr Belvidere IL 61008-8769

KELLER, HARRY ALLAN, electronics technician; b. Columbus, Nebr., Dec. 19, 1943; s. Guy and Charlotte (Cameron) K. Degree in electronic technology, Radio Engring. Inst., Omaha, 1965; cert. of tng., Sears Ext. Inst., Dallas, 1969. Lead electronic technician Dale Electronics, Columbus, 1965-70; electronic mech. technician Sears & Roebuck, Columbus, 1969-70; electronic technician Ed's TV, North Bend, Nebr., 1970-73, P&K Electronics, Columbus, 1973-77; electronic mechanic Wards, Columbus, 1977-79; electronic mech. technician Becton Dickinson, Columbus, 1979—. Active State of Nebr. R.A.C.E.S., Civil Def. Nebr. Races Network, Colfax County, 1992. Recipient Speech Craft Cert. Toastmasters Internat., 1970. Mem. Inst. Electronics Engrs. Inc., Am. Radio Relay League (v.p. local club 1976-79). Republican. Methodist. Home: RR5 Box 231 Rogers NE 68659 Office: Becton-Dickinson PO box 987 Columbus NE 68602

KELLER, JAMI ANN, special education educator; b. Hastings, Nebr., Jan. 4, 1961; d. Donald Lee and Gail Angela (England) Stilley; m. Mark Lee Keller, June 19, 1982; children: William England, Robert John Thomas, Alexander James Stilley. BS with distinction, U. Nebr., 1984. Tchr. spl. edn. Grand Island (Nebr.) Pub. Schs., 1985-92, Papillon (Nebr.)/La Vista Pub. Schs., 1992-93. PTA scholar Nebr. PTA, 1983, Beach-Byer scholar, 1983. Mem. NEA, Nebr. Edn. Assn., Pi Lambda Theta, Mu Epsilon Nu.

KELLER, JOHN FRANCIS, II, industrial engineer; b. York, Pa., June 16, 1947; s. John F. and Marie C. K.; m. Jacqueline Schroder, Apr. 20, 1974; children: Bethany J., Heather M., John F. III. BS, MS in Indsl. Engring., Pa. State U., 1969. Registered profl. engr., Ohio. Indsl. engr. Procter & Gamble, Cin., 1969—. Child advocate Oak Hills Sch. Dist., Cin., 1991-95. Roman Catholic. Home: 1239 Hickorylake Dr Cincinnati OH 45233 Office: Procter & Gamble PO Box 104 11511 Reed Hartman Hwy Blue Ash OH 45241

KELLER, JOSEPH C., physician; b. Cin., Sept. 25, 1956; divorced; 3 children. BA, Harvard U., 1977; MD, U. Nebr., 1980. Dem. candidate for U.S. House 3rd Dist., Mo., 1996. Episcopalian. Office: Keller for Congress PO Box 6291 Chesterfield MO 63006*

KELLER, KENNETH CHRISTEN, advertising executive; b. Toledo, Feb. 17, 1939; s. Theodore G. and Edna L. (Christen) K.; m. Mary Carolyn Folsom, Sept. 10, 1960; children: Kathryn Elizabeth Keller Oulevey, David Folsom Keller. Student Ohio State U., 1957-59. Part-time staff announcer Sta. WMNI, Columbus, Ohio, 1958-59, Sta. WTVN, Columbus, 1959, Sta. WBNS-TV, Columbus, 1959; staff announcer Sta. WRFD, Worthington, Ohio, 1959-61; staff announcer, news supr., program dir. Sta. WOSU, Columbus, 1961-65; on-air talent Sta. WBNS, Columbus, 1962-65; copywriter Joe Hill & Assocs., Columbus, 1965-66; creative dir. Myers, Ault & Assocs., Columbus, 1966-70; co-owner, account exec. Angeletti, Wise & Keller, Columbus, 1970-72; co-owner TRIAD, Columbus, 1972-86, owner, 1986—, v.p., dir. creative services, 1972-85, pres., 1985—. Bd. dirs. Friends of WOSU, 1981-88, pres., 1985-87; apptd. by Franklin County Commrs. to bd. dirs. Cen. Ohio Mktg. Council, 1986-89. Lyricist, co-composer Best Radio Comml. award Internat. Assn. Fairs and Expns., Ohio State Fair, 1978, 81. Mem. AFTRA (chpt. pres. 1978). Home: 270 Park Blvd Columbus OH 43085-3660 Office: TRIAD 6525 Busch Blvd Columbus OH 43229-1789

KELLER, PETER JOSEPH, investment banker; b. Berwyn, Ill., Sept. 25, 1947. BA, Trinity Coll., Hartford, Conn., 1969. V.p., dir. A.S. Hansen Inc., Lake Bluff, Ill., 1975-87; prin. William M. Mercer, Chgo., 1987-90; ptnr. Ernst & Young, Chgo., 1990-92; cons. Alexander & Alexander, Chgo., 1992-94; investment banker United Capital Group, Chgo., 1994—; cons. Midwest Ctr. for Citizen Initiatives, Oak Park, Ill., 1994—; officer, pres., dir. Pegasus, Lake Zurich, Ill., 1992—. With U.S. Army Res., 1971-77. With U.S. Army Res., 1971-77. Mem. Univ. Club Chgo. Republican. Presbyterian. Home: 520 Butler Dr Lake Forest IL 60045-3016 Office: United Capital Group 175 W Jackson Blvd Ste 1003 Chicago IL 60604-2701

KELLEY, CHARLES AARON, dean; b. Waxahachie, Tex., Oct. 14, 1947; s. Charles Wesley and Margaret Louise (Fuller) K.; m. Shelly Wynee Heath, June 8, 1991. BA, U. Md., 1973; MBA, U. Utah, 1976; PhD, U. North Tex., 1979. Dir. bus. affairs Troy State U., Wiesbaden, Germany, 1975-76; asst. prof. mgmt. East Tex. State U., Commerce, 1978-80; asst. prof. U. Colo., Denver, Boulder, 1980-81; asst. assoc. prof. U. Louisville, Ky., 1981-88, dept. chair, assoc. dean, 1988-93; dean Ohio U., Athens, 1993—; vis. sr. lectr., Chinese U. Hong Kong, 1987; cons. in strategic mgmt., Kelley Associates, Inc., Louisville, Ky., 1977-90; computer opers., USAF, Wiesbaden, Germany, 1971-74. Contbr. articles to profl. jours. Bd. dirs. Ky. Jr. Achievement, Louisville, 1990-92, Innovations Ctr. and Rsch. Park, Athens, Ohio, 1993—. Internat. Bus. Coun. grantee, US Dept. Edn., 1990; recipient Bronze Achievement award Kentuckian Jr. Achievement, 1990. Mem. Acad. Mgmt., Southwest Acad. Mgmt., Soc. Advancement of Mgmt., Athens C. of C., Louisville Spkrs. Forum, Louisville C. of C., Phi Kappa Phi, Delta Sigma Pi. Republican. Roman Catholic. Office: Ohio U Coll Bus Copeland Hall Athens OH 45701

KELLEY, FRANK JOSEPH, state attorney general; b. Detroit, Dec. 31, 1924; s. Frank Edward and Grace Margaret (Spears) K.; m. Nancy Courtier; children: Karen Ann, Frank Edward II, Jane Francis. Pre-law cert., U. Detroit, 1948, JD, 1951. Bar: Mich. 1952. Pvt. practice law Detroit, 1952-54, Alpena, 1954-61; atty. gen. State of Mich., Lansing, 1962—; instr. econs. Alpena Community Coll., 1955-56; instr. pub. adminstrn., Alpena County, 1956; atty. city real estate law U. Mich. Extension, 1957-61. Mem. Alpena County Bd. Suprs., 1958-61; pres. Alpena Community Svcs. Coun., 1956; chmn. Gt. Lakes Commn., 1971; Founding dir., 1st sec. Alpena United Fund, 1955; founding dir., 1st pres. Northeastern Mich. Child Guidance Clinic, 1958; pres., bd. dirs. Northeastern Mich. Cath. Family Svc., 1959. Mem. ABA, 26th Jud. Cir. Bar Assn. (pres. 1956), State Bar Mich., Nat. Assn. Attys. Gen. (pres. 1967), Internat. Movement Atlantic Union, Alpha Kappa Psi, KC (4 deg., past legal adv.). Office: Office of Atty Gen PO Box 30212 Lansing MI 48909-7712

KELLEY, JOSEPH R., financial consultant; b. Phila., Dec. 25, 1962; s. Richard D. and Florence M. (Sweeney) K.; m. Dana Malley Kelley, Aug. 24, 1991; children: Megan K., Claire M. BS, Purdue U., 1986. Stockbroker K J Brown, Indpls., 1987-88; fin. cons. Smith Barney, Indpls., 1988—. Mem. Athletic Club (sports com.). Republican. Roman Catholic. Office: Smith Barney Inc 111 Monument Cir Ste 3100 Indianapolis IN 46204-5131

KELLEY, MICHAEL JOHN, newspaper editor; b. Kansas City, Mo., July 5, 1942; s. Robert Francis and Grace Lauretta (Schofield) K.; 1 child, Anne Schofield. BA, Rockhurst Coll., 1964. Reporter, polit. writer Kansas City Star & Times, 1960-69; asst. Sen. Thomas F. Eagleton, Washington, 1969-76; pres. Swensen's Midwest, Inc., Kansas City, 1976-80; exec. asst. Cen. States Pension Fund, Chgo., 1981-83, 85-87; asst. mng. editor Kansas City Times, 1984; editor The Daily Southtown, Chgo., 1987—. Office: The Daily Southtown 5959 S Harlem Ave Chicago IL 60638-3103

KELLEY, PATRICK MICHAEL, minister, state legislator; b. Maryville, Mo., Oct. 27, 1948; s. Gilbert B. and Wilma M. K.; m. Nancy E. Schroeder, July 30, 1976; children: Ryan, Shane, Kristen. BS, William Jewell, 1970; MDiv, St. Paul, 1985. V.p. Kelley-Rickman Construction Col, 1970-72, pres., 1972-75; salesman Sequoia Supply Co., North Kansas City, Mo., 1975-77; owner, pres. Energy Expositions, North Kansas City, 1977-83; pastor United Meth. Chs., Bates County, Mo., 1983-87, Aldersgate United Meth. Ch., Lee's Summit, Mo., 1987-90, Glenwood Park United Meth. Ch., Independence, Mo., 1990—; Rep. caucus chmn. Mo. State Ho. Reps., 1991, 92, minority floor leader, 1993, 94. Chmn. Lee's Summit D.A.R.E. task force; adv. bd. Community Mental Health Svcs., Lee's Summit; bd. dirs. Community Svcs. League, Lee's Summit. Mem. Lee's Summit Rep. Club (treas., pres.). Home: 3924 SW Windsong Dr Lees Summit MO 64082-4051 Office: Mo Ho Reps Capitol Bldg Jefferson City MO 65101

KELLEY, STEVE, state legislator, lawyer; b. 1953; m. Sophie Kelley; two children. BA, Williams Coll.; JD, Columbia U. Lawyer; Dist. 44A rep. Minn. Ho. of Reps., St. Paul, 1993—. Home: 121 Blake Rd S Hopkins MN 55343-2020*

KELLIS, RANDAL ANTHONY, sales executive; b. Columbus, Ohio, Oct. 15, 1960; s. Floyd Charles and Betty Jane (Meyer) K.; m. Stephanie Lynn Webb, Oct. 15, 1988. BSBA, U. Mo., 1985. Sales rep. Bristol-Myers, Cape Girardeau, Mo., 1985-86; regional adminstrv. asst. Bristol-Myers, Chgo., 1986; dist. supr. Bristol-Myers, Cleve., 1986-87; sales adminstrv. asst. Bristol-Myers, N.Y.C., 1987-88; dist. mgr. Chesebrough-Ponds, Cleve., 1988-89; regional food broker mgr. Chesebrough-Ponds, St. Louis, 1989-92; sales planning mgr. Ralston Foods, St. Louis, 1992-93, nat. account mgr., 1993—. Mem. Am. Mktg. Assn., K.C. Roman Catholic. Home: 16656 Chesterfield Manor Dr Chesterfield MO 63005-1641

KELLISON, DONNA LOUISE GEORGE, accountant, educator; b. Hugoton, Kans., Oct. 16, 1950; d. Donald Richard and Zepha Louise (Lowry) George. BA in Elem. Edn. with honors, Anderson (Ind.) U., 1972; MS in Elem. Edn., Ind. U., 1981. CPA, Ind.; lic. tchr., Ind. Tchr. elem. Maconaquah Sch. Corp., Bunker Hill, Ind., 1972-73; office mgr. Eskew & Gresham, CPA's, Louisville, Ky., 1973-78; para-profl. Blue & Co., Indpls., 1979-83, tax compliance specialist, 1983-84, tax sr., 1984-86, tax supr., 1986-87, tax mgr., 1987-90, tax prin., 1990-92, tax sr. mgr., 1992-94, dir., 1995—. Vol. Children's Clinic, Indpls., 1985—; chairperson Most Wanted campaign Am. Cancer Soc., 1995; bd. dirs. Indpls. Estate Planning Coun., 1995-96, sec., 1996—. Mem. AICPA, Ind. CPA Soc. (tax inst. com. 1989-93, chairperson 1993-94, govt. rels. com. 1994—), Toastmasters (sec. Indpls. 1986). Presbyterian. Home: 9318 Embers Way Indianapolis IN 46250-3419 Office: Blue & Co PO Box 80069 Indianapolis IN 46280-0069

KELLOGG, DENNIS LEE, history educator, consultant; b. Des Moines, June 23, 1947; s. H.M. and Bertha Juliet (Mars) K.; m. Deborah Ann Ruebke, May 20, 1978. B of Gen. Studies magna cum laude, S.E. Mo. State U., 1979, MA with distinction, 1981; cert. specialization, Des Moines Area C.C., 1989. Hist. cons. Bootheel Regional Planning Commn., Malden, Mo., 1981-83; program dir. Sci. Ctr. of Iowa, Des Moines, 1983-87; paralegal rschr. Hawkins & Norris Law FIrm, Des Moines, 1988-89, Morain & Burlingame Law Firm, West Des Moines, Iowa, 1989-90; history cons. Des Moines, 1986—; instr. history Des Moines Area C.C., Ankenny, Iowa, 1991—, Grand View Coll., Des Moines, 1995—; adj. instr. history Upper Iowa U., Des Moines, 1991—; mus. cons. Goldstar Mil. Mus., Camp Dodge, Iowa, 1991—; hist. cons. Valley Junction, West Des Moines, 1992—. Author: Wilson's Creek, 1982, Post War Histerias, 1984; editor: Old Sainte Genevieve, 1982. Chmn. Des Moines Area Network of Community Agys., 1985-86. With USAF, 1971-75. Recipient award of professionalism Inst. Mus. Svcs., 1985, Govs. Vol. award, 1994. Mem. Am. Hist. Assn., Kans. Hist. Soc. (life), State Hist. Soc. Mo. (life), Des Moines Civil War Roundtable (speakers bur. 1984), Nat. Audubon Soc., Nature Conservancy, Trout Unltd., Ducks Unltd. Republican.

KELLOM, GAR E., university official; b. Beaver Dam, Wis., Feb. 26, 1947; s. Emerson Edwin and Verna Rose (Glaesman) K.; m. Kolleen Renee Egan; children: Meagna, Guthrie, Tocher. BA, Lawrence U., 1969; MA, MDiv, Pacific U. Religion, Berkeley, Calif., 1973; profl. cert. studies in India, U. Calif., Berkeley, 1976; PhD, U. Calif.-Grad. Theol. Union, Berkeley, 1983. Coord. student activities, asst. to v.p. student affairs Grand Valley State Coll., Allendale, Mich.; adminstrv. asst. to vice chancellor U. Calif., 1977-78; dean students St. Mary's Coll., Winona, Minn., 1978-84; v.p. student devel., dean students Carroll Coll., Waukesha, Wis., 1984-92; v.p. for student affairs St. John's U., Collegeville, Minn., 1992—; cons. on acad. advising and assessment Am. Coll. Testing, Iowa, 1988-90; cons. Alcohol Edn. Tri-state Consortium, Winona, 1980-84; cons. on alcohol and drug edn. Coop. Coll. Rsch. Project; presenter in field. Bd. dird. Winona Treatment Ctr., 1982-84, Mental Health Clinic, Waukesha, 1990-92; mem. diaconate bd. 1st Congl. Ch., Waukesha, 1998-92; soccer coach Waukesha Park and Recreation Bd., 1988-90. Recipient President's award Carroll Coll., 1987, Multicultural award, 1990; tri-coll. spl. svc. grantee St. Mary's Coll., 1980. Mem. ACA, Am. Coll. Pers. Assn. (chmn. commn. X internat. dimensions of student devel. 1990-92, chmn. 5-yr. linkage com. 1992—, Disting. Svc. award 1992), Assn. Coll. Jud. Affairs (founding), Nat. Assn. Student Pers. Adminstrs., AAHE, NAFSA, NASPA, NAACP, Theta Alpha Kappa. Home: 2201 33d St S Saint Cloud MN 56301 Office: St John's U Office Student Affairs Collegeville MN 56321

KELL-SUTTON, JENIFER ANN, public relations executive; b. Moline, Ill., Oct. 16, 1959; d. Murle J. and Annabelle (Blackman) K.; 1 child from previous marriage, Nathaniel Glen Kell Hardy; m. Edward S. Sutton, Oct. 18, 1991. Student, Monmouth Coll., 1977-78, Carl Sandburg Jr. Coll., 1978-79; cert. in landscape design cons., Lifetime Career Sch., 1982. Farmer Carthage, Ill., 1978-88; staff writer, photographer Hancock County Jour. Pilot, Carthage, 1978-79; bookkeeper, receptionist Hancock Svc. Co., Carthage, 1979; spl. programs dir. WCAZ Radio, Carthage, 1981-82; legis. asst. Ill. State Rep. Kent Slater, 1987-88; pub. rels. dir. Meml. Hosp. and Hancock County Nursing Home, Carthage, 1988-91; mktg. mgr., govt. rels. specialist, co-owner Sutton & Sons Refuse Disposal Svc., Inc., St. Louis, 1991—; speaker in field. Editor, writer newsletter STAT. Cem. Nat. Women's Polit. Caucus, 1983—; campaign coord. Kent Slater for State Rep., Hancock County, 1983-88; mem. Hancock County Rep. Women, 1984—; bd. dirs. Quad City Coalition Against Domestic Violence, 1985-88, v.p. 1987-88, co-chair fundraising 1986-87; mem. home econs. program coun. Hancock County Coop. Extension Svc. 1984-88, sec., 1985-86, chair, 1986-88, sec.-treas. exec. coun., 1985-86, chair, 1986-88; sec. young farmer com. Hancock County Farm Bur., 1985-88. Recipient award Young Farmers Dist. award Ill. Farm Bur., 1987. Mem. Ill. Healthcare Pub. Rels. Soc., Am. Soc. for Hosp. Mktg. and Pub. Rels., Am. Hosp. Assn. (mem. spl. pub. rels. subcom. task force 1988-89), Carthage Bus. and Profl. Women (fin. com. 1985, legis. com. 1986-91, mem. young careerist com. 1988-89), Future Farmers Am. Alumni (life), Hancock County Econ. Devel. Assn. (sec. 1988-89, 1st v.p. 1990-91, chair healthcare subcom. 1989-91, mem. transp. com. 1988-89). Republican. Office: Sutton & Sons Ref Dis Svc 8870 Frost Saint Louis MO 63134

KELLY, ANN TERESE, elementary education educator; b. St. Louis, Jan. 29, 1954; d. Robert Victor and Mary Magdalen (Debrecht) K. BS in Elem. Edn., U. Mo., St. Louis, 1977, postgrad., 1978-79, 86-88; postgrad., U. Mo., St. Louis, 1995, Webster U., St. Louis, 1990, U. Mo., Columbia, 1990-92; SUNY, Brockport, 1994. Tchr. 4th grade St. Paul (Mo.) Sch., 1974-75, Assumption Sch., O'Fallon, Mo., 1977-79; tchr. grades 6 to 8 St. Raphael, St. Louis, 1979-86; tchr. grade 7 Our Lady of Sorrows, St. Louis, 1986-88, tchr. grade 5, 1988—; tchr. trainer Sci. Olympiad, St. Louis, 1987—; presenter weather workshops, 1991—; trainer Gr. 5 Developmental Approaches in Sci. and Health, 1993, Archdiocese of St. Louis, 1994—; Am. Meteorol. Soc./Nat. Oceanic and Atmospheric Adminstrn. workshop presenter Maury Project oceanographic studies, 1994—. Mem. Nat. Sci. Tchrs. Assn., Sci. Tchrs. Mo., Cath. Educators Network. Roman Catholic. Home: 10126C Puttington Dr Saint Louis MO 63123-5258 Office: Our Lady of Sorrows 5831 S Kingshighway Blvd Saint Louis MO 63109-3571

KELLY, ARTHUR LLOYD, management and investment company executive; b. Chgo., Nov. 15, 1937; s. Thomas Lloyd and Mildred (Wetten) K.; m. Diane Rex Cain, Nov. 25, 1978; children: Mary Lucinda, Thomas Lloyd, Alison Williams. BS with honors, Yale U., 1959; MBA, U. Chgo., 1964. With A.T. Kearney, Inc., 1959-75, mng. dir., Dusseldorf, Federal Republic Germany, 1964-70, v.p. for Europe, Brussels, 1970-73, internat. v.p., London, 1974-75, ptnr., dir., 1969-75, mem. exec. com., 1972-75; pres., COO, dir. LaSalle Steel Co., Chgo., 1975-81; pres., CEO, dir. Dalta Corp., Chgo., 1982—; mng. ptnr. KEL Enterprises L.P., Chgo., 1983—; chmn., bd. dirs. ARCH Devel. Corp., Chgo.; dir. BMW A.G., Munich, Federal Republic Germany, Cimlinc, Inc., Itasca, Ill., DataCard Corp., Minnetonka, Minn., Deere & Co., Moline, Ill., Internet Systems Corp., Chgo., Nalco Chemical Co., Naperville, Ill., Northern Trust Corp., Chgo., Snap-On, Inc., Kenosha, Wisc., Tejas Gas Corp., Houston, Thyssen Industrie A.G., Essen, Germany, Bankhaus Trinkaus & Burkhardt KGaA, Dusseldorf, Fed. Republic of Germany, Waccamaw Corp., Myrtle Beach, S.C. Trustee U. Chgo., mem. exec. com., chmn. vis. com. div. phys. scis.; mem. adv. coun. Ditchley Found., Oxford, Eng.; bd. dirs. Ill. Humanities Coun., Chgo. Coun. Fgn. Rels., Am. Coun. on Germany, N.Y.C. Mem. World Pres.' Orgn., Econ. Club, Comml. Club, Racquet Club, Casino Club, Brook Club, Yale Club, Beta Gamma Sigma. Office: 135 S La Salle St Chicago IL 60603-4105

KELLY, DANIEL JOHN, physician; b. Binghamton, N.Y., June 23, 1940; s. William James and Mary Elizabeth (Schmitt) K.; m. Lois Ann Lanshe, Aug. 21, 1965; children: Britton James, Jeffrey Daniel, Reid William, Piper Ann. AB in History, Yale U., 1962; MD, Jefferson Med. Coll., 1966. Diplomate in Pathology, Nuclear Medicine, Dermatopathology. Intern Naval Hosp., Boston, 1966-67; resident Naval Hosp., Oakland, Calif., 1966-71; asst. chief lab. Naval Hosp., Great Lakes, Ill., 1971-73, chief lab. svcs., 1973-75; co-dir. lab. Highland Park (Ill.) Hosp., 1992—, dir. lab., 1980-89; co-dir. lab. Lake Forest (Ill.) Hosp., 1992—, dir. lab., 1989-91; with Dean, Hoffman & Clark Pathologists S.C., Lake Forest, 1975—; chief of staff elect Highland Park (Ill.) Hosp., 1992-94, chief of staff, 1994-96, also bd. dirs.; mem. med. exec. com. Highland Park Hosp., 1992—, Lake Forest Hosp., 1989-91. Bd. dirs. Lake Forest Hist. Preservation Soc., 1979-80; mem. bldg. rev. bd. City Govt., Lake Forest, 1989-93; mem. clin. lab. and blood bank adv. bd. Ill. Dept. Pub. Health, 1990-95; mem. Am. Pathology Found. Comdr. USNR, 1966-75. Fellow Coll. Am. Pathology, Am. Soc. Clin. Pathology, Internat. Acad. Pathologists, Am. Assn. Clin. Scientists; mem. AMA, Am. Soc. Nuclear Medicine, Ill. Soc. Pathologists, Am. Soc. Microbiology, Am. Soc. Dermatopathology, Internat. Soc. Dermatopathology, Am. Acad. Dermatology, Assn. Military Surgeons. Roman Catholic. Home: 499 E Illinois Rd Lake Forest IL 60045-2364 Office: Pathology and Nuclear Medicine Assocs 101 Waukegan Rd Ste 1250 Lake Bluff IL 60044-1687

KELLY, DONALD PHILIP, entrepreneur; b. Chgo., Feb. 24, 1922; s. Thomas Nicholas and Ethel M. (Healy) K.; m. Byrd M. Sullivan, Oct. 25, 1952; children: Patrick, Laura, Thomas. Student, Loyola U., Chgo., 1953-54, De Paul U., 1954-55, Harvard U., 1965. Mgr. tabulating United Ins. Co. Am., 1946-51; mgr. data processing A.B. Wrisley Co., 1951-53; mgr. data processing Swift & Co., 1953-65, asst. controller, 1965-67, controller, 1967-68, v.p. corporate devel., controller, 1968-70, fin. v.p., dir., 1970-73; fin. v.p., dir. Esmark, Inc., Chgo., 1973, pres., COO, 1973-77, pres., CEO, 1977-82, chmn., pres., CEO, 1982-84; pres. Kelly, Briggs & Assocs., Inc., Chgo., 1984-86; chmn. Beatrice Co., Chgo., 1986-88; chmn., CEO E-II Holdings Inc., Chgo., 1987-88; pres., CEO D.P. Kelly & Assocs., L.P., Oak Brook, 1988—;, 1989-96. With USNR, 1942-46. Mem. Chgo. Club, Comml. Club Chgo., Econ. Club Chgo. Office: DP Kelly and Assocs LP Ste 1990 701 Harger Rd Oak Brook IL 60521-1490

KELLY, ERIC DAMIAN, lawyer, educator; b. Pueblo, Colo., Mar. 16, 1947; s. William Bret and Patricia Ruth (Ducy) K.; children: Damian Charles, Eliza Jane, Valissitie Christina Heeren, Douglas Ray Heeren. BA, Williams Coll., 1969; JD, U. Pa., 1975, M of City Planning, 1975; PhD, Union Inst., 1992. Bar: Colo. 1975, U.S. Dist. Ct. 1976, U.S. Tax Ct. 1976, U.S. Ct. Appeals (10th cir.) 1986. Chief citizens' participation unit Region III EPA, Phila., 1971-72; project planner Beckett New Town, N.J., 1972-73; v.p., project mgr. Rahenkamp Sachs Wells & Assocs., Inc., Denver and Phila., 1973-76; sole practice Pueblo, 1976-83; pres. Kelly & Potter, P.C., Pueblo, Albuquerque and Santa Fe, 1983-90; adj. prof. U. Colo. Coll. Architecture and Planning, 1976-90; chmn., prof. Dept. cmty. and regional planning Iowa State U., 1990-95; adj. asst. prof. grad. sch. bus. U. So. Colo., 1986-90; dean coll. architecture and planning Ball State U., 1995—; mem. city devel. bd. State of Iowa, 1991-95. Gen. editor Zoning and Land Use Controls, 1995—; author: Enforcing Zoning and Land Use Codes, 1988, Managing Community Growth: Policies, Techniques and Impacts, 1993, Selecting and Retaining Consultants, 1993, Planning, Growth and Public Facilities: A Primer for Public Officials, 1994; editor, prin. author: The Roadtripper, 1969; contbr. articles to profl. planning and legal jours. Mem. adv. bd. Mcpl. Legal Studies Ctr., S.W. Legal Found., 1989—; mem. nat. adv. bd. Rocky Mountain Land Use Inst. Coll. Law U. Denver, 1992—; bd. dirs. Broadway Theatre League, Pueblo, 1976-77, Pueblo Beautiful Assn., 1978-82, Better Bus. Bur., 1988-89; trustee Sangre de Cristo Arts and Conf. Ctr., 1981-87, chmn. 1986; trustee Christ Congl. Ch., 1982-83. With U.S. Army, 1969-71. Named Outstanding Student, Am. Inst. Planners, 1976; recipient Outstanding Faculty award Order of Omega, 1992. Mem. ABA, Am. Inst. Cert. Planners (charter), Am. Planning Assn. (pres. Iowa chpt. 1994-95, Excellence award 1989, nat. bd. dirs. 1996—, pres. elect 1996—, chair planning & law divsn. 1996—, amicus curiae com. 1988-94, 95—), Williams Coll. Alumni Assn. (class sec. 1969-74, regional sec. 1980-82, class agt. 1985-89), Rotary (local dir. 1988-90, dir., pres. Pueblo Rotary Found. 1988-89, v.p. 1988-89, pres. 1989-90, area rep. for dist. gov. 1991-92), Phi Kappa Phi. Democrat. Office: Ball State U Coll Architecture/Planning Muncie IN 47306

KELLY, EUGENE, engineer; b. Lexington, Mo., Jan. 16, 1961; s. Eugene and Thelma Lee (Guthrie) m. Deborah Lee Snyder, July 13, 1984. BS in Elec. Engr., U. Mo., 1983; MBA, U. Mo., Kansas City, 1988. Assoc. engr. Allied-Signal Aerospace Co., Kansas City, 1983-84, engr., 1984-88, sr. engr., 1988-92; staff engr., 1992-93; program mgr. Allied-Signal Aerospace Co., 1993-95; quality engrng. mgr. Allied-Signal Aerospace Co., Kansas City, 1995—. V.p. Big Bros. and Sisters, Kansas City, 1988, participant Kansas City Tomorrow-Community Program; mem. United Way Citizen Rev. Com., Cen. High Sch. Task Force, bd. dirs. Kansas City Tomorrow alumni assn. Recipient Alumni Recognition award Nat. Action Coun. for Minorities in Engrng., 1986, Black Achievers in Industry award Kansas City chpt. So. Christian Leadership Conf., 1993. Mem. U. Mo. Alumni Assn. (legis. liaison). Democrat. Roman Catholic. Office: Allied-Signal Aerospace Co 2000 E 95th St Kansas City MO 64131-3025

KELLY, GAY ANNE, social worker, educator; b. Peoria, Ill., Nov. 13, 1951; d. Walter Reuel and Ada Frances (Dixon) Wright; children: James, N. Jason, Justin; m. Kevin J. Kelly, May 14, 1994. AA, Lincoln Land C.C., 1975; BA in Child Family Comty. Svc., U. Ill. Sangamon campus, 1978; MEd, U. Ill., 1990. Cert. child protective investigator, child devel. specialist II, Ill. Case coord. Jacksonville (Ill.) Area Assn. Retarded Citizens, 1975-76; surrogate parent/ednl. advocate Ill. State Bd. Edn., Vermillion County, 1977-79; child care specialist Parents Anonymous, Champaign, Ill., 1990-91, parent facilitator, 1991-93; child devel. specialist Devel. Svcs. Ctr., Champaign, 1990-94; child protective investigator Ill. Dept. Children and Family Svcs., Urbana, 1994—; parent group facilitator, sponsor Parents Anonymous, Champaign, Ill., 1990-92; vol. EMT Midleford Vol. Ambulance, Potomac, Ill., 1986-89; surrogate parent/ednl. advocate Ill. State Bd. Edn., Vermillion County, 1986-89; grad. rsch. asst. dept. spl. edn. U. Ill., Champaign, 1987-90; v.p., rep. dept. spl. edn. Coun. Grad. Students in Edn., U. Ill., Champaign, 1987-90. Sec. Middlefork Twp. Vol. Ambulance, Potomac, Ill., 1987-89. Grantee Kappa Delta Pi, U. Ill., Champaign, 1990; Hilton-Perkins scholar, 1993. Mem. Coun. Exceptional Children (div. phys. handicaps, div. mental retardation, div. early childhood), Ill. Div. Early Childhood, Kappa Delta Pi. Republican. Mem. LDS Ch. Home: 1706 Nancy Beth Champaign IL 61821 Office: Ill Dept Children and Fam Svcs 508 S Race Champaign IL 61821-2099

KELLY, GLENDA MARIE, former mayor; b. San Diego, June 3, 1944; d. Glenn Adrian and Donna Louise (Embrey) Molsberry; m. Ronald Worth Campbell, June 3, 1962 (div. 1969); children: Gina Marie, Chad Loren; m. Dennis Patrick Kelly, Sept. 18, 1970. BS in Sociology cum laude, Mo. Western State Coll., 1989. Legal sec. Stanley S. Kalender, St. Joseph, Mo., 1960-88; dep. mayor City of St. Joseph, 1986-89, mayor, 1989-94; mem. Mo. Ho. Reps. 27th Dist., Mo., 1995—. Mem. Buchanan County Social Welfare Bd., 1979-85; mem. steering com. YWCA Women's Abuse Shelter, 1980; vice chair, chair budget com. Citizen's Adv. Commn., 1980-81; mem. task force Mo-Kan Regional Food Bank, 1981-83, City St. Joseph Fair Housing, 1984, Pony Express Region Tourist Info. Ctr., 1982, bd. dirs., 1983; bd. dirs. Pony Express Hist. Assn., 1983-84, Econ. Opportunity Corp., 1984-85, YWCA, 1985-86, Mo. Mcpl. League, 1990-94, St. Joseph Hist. Soc., 1979-80, sec., 1979-80; mem. St. Joseph City Coun., 1986, Governance Coun. Cmty. Based Health Care for Children, 1994—. Recipient Outstanding Community Vol. award United Way, Civic Recognition award City St. Joseph, Vol. award VFW Aux., 1980, Recognition award St. Joseph's br. NAACP, 1990, James C. Kirkpatrick Good Govt. award Northwest Mo. Press Assn., Historic Preservation award for Leadership in Historic Preservation Issues St. Joseph Landmark Commn., 1993; named Woman of Month by YWCA, 7/93, Outstanding Woman of Yr. YWCA, 1993. Mem. LWV (bd. dirs. St. Joseph area, co-chair local govt. com. 1978-79, chair budget com. 1979-80, 1st v.p. 1981, chair drug awareness com. 1981, pres. 1985-86), St. Joseph Area C. of C. (urban action com. 1985, econ. devel. coun. 1988—, bd. dirs. 1994—). Democrat. Roman Catholic. Home: 3415 N 3rd St Saint Joseph MO 64505-3046

KELLY, JAMES JOSEPH, printing company executive; b. Steubenville, Ohio, Feb. 26, 1941; s. James Geary and Mary Catherine (Maley) K.; m. Judith Ann Miller, June 29, 1963; children: James M., Heather, Sean. BS in Econs., Xavier U., 1963. Acct. exec. Western Pub. Co., Racine, Wis., 1969-79; sales rep. Alden Press, Inc., Chgo., 1979—. 1st lt. U.S. Army, 1963-65. Mem. Direct Mktg. Assn., Mid. Ohi Direct Mktg. Club, St. Louis Direct Mktg., Xavier U. Alumnae Assn. (v.p., then pres. St. Louis chpt.). Republican. Roman Catholic. Home: 216 Greenburn Dr Saint Charles MO 63304-9999 Office: Alden Press Inc 3379 N Us Highway 67 Ste A Florissant MO 63033-1604

KELLY, JAMES PATRICK, cardiothoracic surgeon; b. Peoria, Ill., Nov. 28, 1946; s. James Lavelle and Mary Magdelan (McGrath) K.; m. Christine Marie McLean, July 12, 1975; children: Brian, Kevin, Elizabeth, Patrick. BS in Chemistry summa cum laude, St. Louis U., 1969; MD, Northwestern U., 1973. Diplomate Am. Bd. of Thoracic Surgeons. Asst. prof. surgery Tulane U., New Orleans, 1982-94; assoc. prof. surgery Tulane U., 1984-86; attending Cardiothoracic Surgery of South Bend, Ind., 1986—. Mem. AMA, Am. Bd. Thoracic Surgery, Am. Coll. Cardiology, Am. Coll. Chest Physicians, Soc. Thoracic Surgery, So. Thoracic Surgery Soc, Phi Beta Kappa. Home: 17022 Shandwick Ln South Bend IN 46530 Office: Ste 501 707 N Michigan South Bend IN 46601

KELLY, JAMES STEWART, associate professor, associate director; b. Oswego, N.Y., Apr. 27, 1947; s. Daniel Patrick and Elizabeth Belle (Pitsley) K.; m. Sarah McHugh, May 20, 1989; 1 child, Nora McHugh Kelly. BA, SUNY, Oswego, 1971; MA, Ohio State U., Columbus, 1979, PhD, 1983. Visiting asst. prof. Miami U., Oxford, Ohio, 1983-87; asst. prof. Elmhurst Coll., Elmhurst, Ill., 1987-89; asst. prof. Miami U., Oxford, 1989-92, assoc. prof., 1993—, assoc. dir. honors program, 1994—; cons.-evaluator North Ctrl. Assoc. Coll., Chicago, 1995—. Contbr. articles to profl. jours. Nat. Endowment for Humanities fellow Indiana U., 1984, Univ. N. C., 1989. Mem. Am. Philos. Assn., Assn. for Integrative Studies, Internat. Soc. for Value Inquiry, So. Soc. for Philosophy/Psychology, Am. Assoc. of Philosophy Tchrs. Office: Miami U Dept of Philosophy Oxford OH 45056

KELLY, JAY THOMAS See KELLY, TOM

KELLY, JERRY BOB, social services administrator; b. Chgo., Feb. 6, 1942; s. Robert Lee and Mildred Florence (Griffin) K.; m. Diane Joyce Wilburn, Nov. 29, 1969; children: Jerold Robert, Joycelyn Reneé. B.S. in Acctg., Roosevelt U., 1968. Lic. real estate salesman and life ins. prodr., Ill. Acct. Weather Bloc Mfg. Co., Chgo., 1967-68; programmer Morton Salt Co., Chgo., 1968-69; br. mgr. Chgo. Econ. Devel. Corp., 1970-77; ptnr. Smith Distbrs., 1977-79; mgr. fin. and adminstrn. Suburban Cook County Area Agy. on Aging, Chgo., 1979-85; exec. dir. Lawndale Bus. and Local Devel. Corp., Chgo., 1985-88; dir. fin. No. Cook County Pvt. Industry Coun., Chgo., 1988-89; contr. Howard Area Cmty. Ctr., Chgo., 1989—; bd. dirs. Northside Cmty. Fed. Credit Union. Treas. Day Care Crisis Coun. Met. Chgo., 1973-76, appreciation award; 1st v.p. West Side Health Planning Orgn., 1974-76, appreciation award; treas. Met. Chgo. chpt. Nat. Caucus and Ctr. on Black Aged, 1992-94; bd. dirs. St. Leonard's House; Cook County State's atty. African-Am. Adv. Coun., 1995—; vol. Ill. CPA. Soc. Served with AUS, 1964-67. Recipient appreciation award Chgo. Black Caucus, Am. Fedn. Tchrs., Chgo. Bd. Election Commrs., Comprehensive Health Planning Orgn. Chgo. Mem. Assoc. Photographers Internat. Baptist. Club: Elks (2d v.p. Ill.-Wis., past grand exalted ruler). Research on redevel. plans for East Garfield. Home: 1415 N Mayfield Ave Chicago IL 60651-1015 Office: Howard Area Community Ctr 7648 N Paulina St Chicago IL 60626-1018

KELLY, JOE F., publisher, editor; b. Teaneck, N.J., Nov. 15, 1954; s. Joseph Francis and Eleanor Mary (Barnes) K.; m. Nancy E. Gruver, Nov. 12, 1953; children: Mavis B., Antonia B. Grad. high sch. Actor/technician Omaha (Nebr.) Playhouse, 1977-80; domestic violence counselor The Shelter, Omaha, 1980-81; juvenile delinquent counselor YMCA, Mpls., 1981-83; dispatcher Roto-Rooter, Inc., Mpls., 1983-85; news dir. KMHL Radio, Marshall, Minn., 1985-88; reporter/prodr. Minn. Pub. Radio, Duluth, 1988-92, news dir., 1992-93; pub., mng. editor New Moon Mag. for Girls, Duluth, 1993—. Dir. Whole Foods Coop, Duluth, 1992-95. Recipient Disting. Achievement award Ednl. Press Assn. Am., 1994, Alternative Press award Utne Reader, Mpls., 1994, Gold award Parents' Choice Found., 1995; named Feminist of the Yr., Feminist Majority Found., 1993. Office: New Moon Publishing PO Box 3620 Duluth MN 55803

KELLY, JOHN LEO, finance company executive; b. Peoria, Ill., Dec. 5, 1949. Student, U. Notre Dame, 1967-69, U. Ill., 1973. Corr. Comml. Nat. Bank, Peoria, 1973-76; broker Hornblower & Weeks, Peoria, 1976-94; v.p. Smith Barney (formerly Hornblower & Weeks), Peoria, 1994—; mem. Smith Barney Chmn.'s Coun. Sr. Alchemist Soc. Mem. Downtown Redevel., Peoria; troop com. chmn. Boy Scouts Am., Peoria, 1989—. Sgt. U.S. Army, 1969-72, ETO. Republican. Roman Catholic. Office: Smith Barney # 1000 401 Main St Peoria IL 61602-1241

KELLY, JOSEPH BENJAMIN, ceramic engineer; b. Ellicottville, N.Y., July 6, 1937; s. Bernard M. and Katherine (Hart) K.; m. Francine A. Hart, Sept. 5, 1964; children: Kathleen, Sean, Aileen. BS in Ceramic Engring., Alfred (N.Y.) U., 1959; postgrad., Pa. State U., 1967. Ceramic engr. PPG Industries Inc., Harmarville, Pa., 1959-65, devel. engr., 1966-68; sr. devel. engr. PPG Industries Inc., Crestline, Ohio, 1969-70, sr. process engr., 1970-89, sr. engring. assoc., 1989—. Contbr. over 3 articles to profl. jours. Bd. dirs. Crestline Area United Appeal, 1971-78, pres. bd. dirs., 1972, 73; mem. State Health Systems Agy., Wooster, Ohio, 1978-84. With C.E., U.S. Army, 1960-61. Mem. Kiwanis (pres. 1976, 95). Republican. Roman Catholic. Home: 1029 Clink Blvd Crestline OH 44827-1005 Office: PPG Industries Inc Crestline OH 44827-0269

KELLY, JOSEPHINE KAYE, social worker; b. Grand Rapids, Mich., May 30, 1944; d. Clark Everet Peterson and Dorothy Jane (Mudd) Schaefer; m. Raymond Luke Kelly, July 19, 1969; children: William Lawrence, Kenneth James. BA with honors, Grand Valley State Coll., 1967; MA, Western Mich. U., 1993. Registered social worker. Exec. dir. Voluntary Action Ctr., Grand Rapids, 1970-77; project coord. Area Agy. on Aging, Grand Rapids, 1977-79; program coord. Aquinas Coll., Grand Rapids, 1979-80; psychiat. social worker Kent Oaks Psychiat. Unit, Grand Rapids, 1980-87; continued care social worker St. Mary's Hosp., Grand Rapids, 1987-88; co-owner Hidden Lake Farm, Conklin, 1969—; med. social worker Alpine Manor Inc., Grand Rapids, 1988-91; coord. Alzheimer's Living Ctr., Birchwood Care Ctr., Horizon Healthcare Corp., Marne, 1994-96; dir. Good Shepherd Home, Resthaven Care Ctr., Resthaven Patrons, Inc., Holland, 1996—. Coord. Alzheimer's Living Ctr., Birchwood Care Ctr., Horizon Healthcare Corp., Marne, 1993—; bd. pres. North West Ambulance, 1993—; bd. dirs. Ottawa County Cmty. Mental Health, 1993—; trustee Chester Twp., 1984-96, mem. canteen svcs. unit, 1984-94; mem. planning bd. St. Mary's Hosp., Grand Rapids, 1981-82; mem. lay adv. bd. Cath. Info. Ctr., Grand Rapids, 1983-85, pres., 1984-85; pres. Coun. on Aging of Kent County, Grand Rapids, 1979-80, mem., 1977—; mem. transp. adv. commn. Coopersville (Mich.) Area Pub. Schs., 1977-81; sec. Conklin Food Coop., 1977-80; bd. dirs. Women's Resource Ctr., Grand Rapids, 1977-79, steering com., 1972-73; mem. Alzheimer's Profl. Devel. Network, 1995—, Interhcange-Orgn. West Mich. Comm. Profls., 1994—. Mem. AAUW, Am. Legion (aux.), Mich. Beefalo Breeders Assn. (sec.-treas. 1982-84, v.p. 1993-95, pres. 1995—), Am. Beefalo World Registry, Vol. Mgmt. Assn. Western Mich. (founder, 1st pres. 1975-76), Conklin Brotherhood Assn., Internat. Beefalo Found. (bd. dirs.). Republican. Roman Catholic. Home: 3616 Coolidge St Conklin MI 49403-9509

KELLY, MARGARET BLAKE, accountant, state official; b. Crystal City, Mo., Sept. 17, 1935; d. Emory and Florine (Stovesand) Blake; m. William Clark Kelly; children: Kevin, Tom, John. BSBA, U. Mo., 1957; MBA, S.W. Mo. State U., 1975; D in Bus. Administrn. (hon.), S.W. Bapt. U., 1986. CPA, Mo.; cert. govt. fin. mgr. Acct. Williams-Keepers, Columbia and Jefferson City, Mo., McNabb, Westermann, Mitchell & Branstetter, Springfield, Mo., Fox & Co., Springfield; county auditor Cole County, Mo., 1982-84; state auditor State of Mo., Jefferson City, 1984—. Rep. nom. for lt. gov., 1992; Rep. candidate for U.S. House Governor Mo., 1996. Recipient Faculty-Alumni Gold Medal award U. Mo., 1985. Mem. AICPA, Assn. Govt. Accts., Nat. State Auditors Assn. (past pres.), Nat. Assn. State Auditors, Comptrs., and Treas. (first v.p.), Am. Soc. Women Accts., Am. Women Soc. CPAs, Mo. Soc. Cert. Pub. Accts., Women Execs. in State Govt., Govt. Fin. Officers Assn., Delta Gamma. Republican. Baptist. Office: Friends of Margaret Kelly PO Box 104613 Jefferson City MO 65110*

KELLY, MARTIN JOSEPH, state official; b. Columbus, Ohio, Aug. 15, 1940. Student, Ohio Wesleyan U., 1958-59, Franklin U., 1960-61; BA in Econs., Ohio State U., 1968, postgrad. real estate, 1969. Timekeeper, prodn. planner, inventory control clk. Dennison div. Abex Corp., Delaware, Ohio, 1960-68; urban planner C.V. Hill and Assocs., Columbus, Ohio, 1968-70; devel. specialist community devel. div. Ohio Dept. Devel., Columbus, 1970-83, financing specialist, 1983—, program mgr. div. econ. devel. financing. Home: 5ll Bowtown Rd Delaware OH 43015 Office: Ohio Dept Devel 77 S High St Columbus OH 43215

KELLY, NORMA RUTH, nursing educator, medical surgical nurse; b. Avon, Ill., July 30, 1938; d. Harry Harper and Helen Edna (Ridle) Spangler; m. A.J. Gatzemeyer, Aug. 15, 1987; children: Kevin Kelly, Kara Kelly, Kathleen Kaphaem, Lee Gatzemeyer, Brian Gatzemeyer, Michelle Penn. Diploma, St. Francis Hosp. Sch. Nursing, Peoria, Ill., 1959; MS in Nursing, U. Ill., Chgo., 1968; BSN, Avila Coll., Kansas City, Mo., 1972; PhD, Ill. State U., 1989. RN, Ill., Mo. Staff nurse St. Francis Hosp., mem.

faculty Sch. Nursing; staff nurse Menorah Hosp., Kansas City; faculty, level coord. St. Francis Med. Ctr. Coll. Nursing, Peoria; clin. asst. prof. U. Ill., Chgo., regional dir. Peoria programs. Mem. ANA, Nat. League for Nursing, Sigma Theta Tau (grantee Epsilon Epsilon chpt.), Kappa Delta Pi. Home: 33 Pennsylvania Ct Morton IL 61550-1795

KELLY, PATRICK S., accountant; b. L.A., Sept. 18, 1958; s. Joseph Edward and Bertha Rebala (Eyler) K.; m. Julie Lynn Bogkmann; children: Jeffrey Ryan, Katelyn Nicole. BS in Acctg., U. Idaho, 1980. CPA, Tex. Acct. Shell Oil Co., Houston, 1980-81; acct. to asst. contr. Elf Aquitaine, Houston, 1981-90; fin. dir. LUMH Groupe, N.Y.C., 1990-91; gen. mgr. Supermarket Systems, Inc., Chgo., 1991—. Office: Supermarket Systems Inc 648 W Randolph Chicago IL 60661

KELLY, RANDY C., state legislator; b. Aug. 2, 1950; m. Kathy Kelly; two children. BA, U. Minn. Dist. 67 rep. Minn. Ho. of Reps., St. Paul, 1974-90; Dist. 67 senator Minn. State Senate, St. Paul, 1990—; vice chmn. fin. com., mem. crime prevention, fin. divsn. family svc., fin. state govt. divsn., and jobs, energy and cmty. devel. coms., Minn. State Senate. Home: 1630 David St Saint Paul MN 55119-3007*

KELLY, RAYMOND CASE, anthropology educator; b. Bridgeport, Conn., Feb. 16, 1942; s. Rowland Leigh and Helen Janet (Varkala) K.; m. Mary Pfender, Aug. 28, 1966 (div. 1979); 1 child, Kathryn Elizabeth; m. Sherry Beth Ortner, Oct. 4, 1979 (div. 1991); 1 child, Gwendolyn Ida. BA in Anthropology, U. Chgo., 1965; MA in Anthropology, U. Mich., 1966, PhD in Anthropology, 1974. Lectr. dept. anthropology U. Mich., Ann Arbor, 1971-73, asst. prof. dept. anthropology, 1974-77, assoc. prof. dept. anthropology, 1977-86, full prof. dept. anthropology, 1986—; Rackham divisional bd. social sci. U. Mich. Horace H. Rackham Grad. Sch., Ann Arbor, 1983-84, assoc. chair, mem. exec. com. dept. anthropology, 1984-85, 89-93, acting chair 1993-94; exec. com. U. Mich. Press, 1987-90. Author: Etoro Social Structure, 1977, The Nuer Conquest, 1985, Constructing Inequality, 1993; contbr. numerous articles to profl. jours. NEH fellow, 1979-80, Guggenheim Found. fellow, 1982-83, Ctr. for Advanced Study in Behavioral Scis. fellow, 1982-83. Office: U Mich Dept Anthropology 1054 Lsa Bldg Ann Arbor MI 48109

KELLY, ROBERT VINCENT, JR., metal company executive; b. Phila., Sept. 29, 1938; s. Robert Vincent and Catherine Mary (Hanley) K.; m. Margaret Cecilia Taylor, Feb. 11, 1961; children: Robert V. III, Christopher T., Michael J., Tasha Marie. BS in Indsl. Mgmt., St. Joseph's U., Phila., 1960; postgrad., Roosevelt U., 1965-66. Gen. foreman prodn. Republic Steel Corp., Chgo., 1963-68; supt. prodn. Phoenix Steel Corp., Phoenixville, Pa., 1969-73; gen. supt. ops. Continental Steel Corp., Kokomo, Ind., 1973-77; gen. mgr. Mac Steel div. Quanex Corp., Jackson, Mich., 1977-81; corp. v.p. Quanex Corp., Houston, 1979—; pres. steel and bar group Quanex Corp., Jackson, 1982—; pres. La Salle Steel Co., Hammond, Ind., 1985-87, Arbuckle Corp., Jackson, 1984-88. Leader, com. mem. Boy Scouts Am., Jackson. Lt. USN, 1960-63. Mem. Am. Mgmt. Assn. (pres.), Inst. Indsl. Engrs., Assn. Iron and Steel Engrs., Am. Soc. for Metals, USN Inst., Jackson C. of C. Clubs: Jackson Country. Home: 1734 Metzmont Dr Jackson MI 49203-5379 Office: Quanex Corp 1 Jackson Sq Jackson MI 49201-1446

KELLY, ROBERTO CONRADO (BOBBY KELLY), professional baseball player; b. Panama City, Panama, Oct. 1, 1964. Student, Jose Dolores Moscote Coll., Panama. With N.Y. Yankees, 1982-92, Cin. Reds, 1992-94, Atlanta Braves, 1994, Montreal Expos, 1994-95, L.A. Dodgers, 1995—; mem. Am. League All-Star Team, 1992, Nat. League All-Star Team, 1993. Office: LA Dodgers 1000 Elysian Park Ave Los Angeles CA 90012*

KELLY, THOMAS, state legislator. BS, Fordham U.; MS, L.I. U. Mem. from dist. 17 Mich. State Ho. of Reps., Lansing, 1995—, mem. edn., transp., house oversight and ethics coms., 1995—. City councilman City of Wayne, Mich. Address: PO Box 30014 Lansing MI 48909-7514

KELLY, TOM (JAY THOMAS KELLY), major league baseball club manager; b. Graceville, Minn., Aug. 15, 1950; s. Joseph Thomas and Anna Grace (Heisenbottle) K.; children: Sharon Clare, Thomas John. Student, Mesa (Ariz.) Jr. Coll., 1968-69. Profl. baseball player Minn. Twins, Mpls., 1968-77, coach, 1982-86, mgr., 1987—; mgr. minor league team Minn. Twins, Toledo, Ohio, 1978-82. Managed Minn. Twins team to World Series Championship, 1987, 91; named Am. League Mgr. of Yr. Sporting News, 1991. Mem. Assn. Profl. Baseball Players, U.S. Trotting Assn., Nat. Greyhound Assn. Office: Minn Twins Hubert H Humphrey Metrodome 501 Chicago Ave Minneapolis MN 55415-1517

KELLY, TONY S., publisher; b. Davenport, Iowa, Dec. 31, 1929; s. James Anthony and Angela (Searle) K.; m. Margaret Mirfield (div.); children: Michael, Clare, Max. Reporter Davenport (Iowa) Times Newspaper, 1957-60, photographer, 1960-62; freelance photographer, 1962-92; co-editor Evanston (Ill.) Clarion Newspaper, 1992-93, publisher, 1993—; adj. lectr. Northwestern U., Evanston, 1988-95; dir. midwest chpt. Am. Soc. Mag. Photographers, 1979-81; cons. in field. With U.S. Army, 1948-49. Mem. Soc. Prof. Journalism, Soc. Newspaper Design (conf. coord. 1991-94), N.Y. Photography Admisntrs. Home and office: 1311 Main Evanston IL 60202

KELM, BONNIE G., art museum director, educator; b. Bklyn., Mar. 29, 1947; d. Julius and Anita (Baron) Steiman; m. William G. Malis; 1 child, Michael Darren. BS in Art Edn., Buffalo State U., 1968; MA in Art History, Bowling Green (Ohio) State U., 1975; PhD in Arts Adminstrn., Ohio State U., 1987. Art tchr. Toledo Pub. Schs., 1968-71; ednl. cons. Columbus (Ohio) Mus. Art, 1976-81; prof. art Franklin U., Columbus, 1976-88; legis. coord. Ohio House of Reps., Columbus, 1977; pres. bd. trustees Columbus Inst. for Contemporary Art, 1977-81; tech. asst. cons. Ohio Arts Coun., Columbus, 1984-88; dir. Bunte Gallery Franklin U., Columbus, 1978-88; dir. art mus. Miami U., Oxford, Ohio, 1988-96; assoc. prof. Miami U., 1988-96; dir. Muscarelle Mus. of Art Coll. of WIlliam & Mary, 1996—, assoc. prof. art & art history, 1996—; grant panelist Ohio Arts Coun., Columbus, 1985-87, 91—; art book reviewer William C. Brown Pub., Madison, Wis., 1985-92; mem. acquisitions adv. bd. Martin Luther King Ctr., Columbus, 1987-88; field reviewer Inst. Mus. Svcs., Washington, 1990—; chairperson grant panel Art in Pub. Places, 1992-95; trustee Ohio Mus. Assn., 1993—; state apptd. mem. adv. com. Ohio Percent for Art, 1994—. Author, editor (mus. catalogues) Connections, 1985, Into the Mainstream: Contemporary Folk Art, 1991, Testimony of Images: PreColumbian Art, 1992, Collecting by Design: The Allen Collection, 1994, Photographs by Barbara Hershey: A Retrospective, 1995; contbr. chpt. to book, articles to profl. jours. Founding mem., mem. adv. coun. Columbus Cultural Arts Ctr., 1977-81; coord., curator Cultural Exch. Program, Honolulu-Columbus, 1980; mem. acad. women achievers YWCA, 1991; guest speaker 1991 Scholastic Arts Award, Cin., 1991; keynote speaker Ohio Mus. Assn., ann. meeting, 1992; speaker Internat. Coun. Mus. Triennial Conf., Quebec City, 1992; session chair Midwest Mus. Assn. ann. meeting, St. Louis, 1993. Recipient Marantz Disting. Scholar award Ohio State U., 1995, Gelpe award YWCA, 1987, Cultural Advancement of City of Columbus award, The Columbus Dispatch, 1984, Disting. Svc. award, Columbus Art League, 1984, Critic's Choice award Found. for Cmty. of Artists, N.Y., 1981; Fulbright scholar USIA, 1988 (The Netherlands); NEH fellow East-West Ctr., Honolulu, 1991. Mem. Am. Assn. Mus. (advocacy task force), Assn. of Coll. and Univ. Mus. and Galleries, Midwest Mus. Assn., Fulbright Assn., Coll. Arts Assn., Internat. Coun. Mus., Ohio Mus. Assn. (bd. dirs. 1993—). Office: Muscarelle Mus of Art Coll William & Mary PO Box 8795 Williamsburg VA 23187-8795

KELMAN, DONALD BRIAN, neurosurgeon; b. Brandon, Man., Can., Apr. 3, 1942; came to U.S., 1979; s. Alexander and May Marguerite (Ronayne) K.; m. Joan Ann Thompson, July 10, 1966 (div. Sept. 1985); children: Carl Michael, Melanie Catherine, Leslie Jane, Brian Andrew; m. Cynthia Marie Esser, Mar. 21, 1986; 1 child, Craig Richard. BA in Biology, U. Sask., 1964, MD, 1968. Diplomate Am. Bd. Neurol. Surgery. Jr. rotating intern St. Joseph's Hosp., Victoria, B.C., Can., 1968-69; pvt. practice Victoria, 1969-70; resident in neurosurgery Mayo Grad. Sch. of Medicine, Rochester, Minn., 1970-76; pvt. practice Prince George, B.C., Can., 1976-79; neurosurgeon Marshfield (Wis.) Clinic/St. Joseph's Hosp., 1979—; chmn. neurosurgery dept. Marshfield Clinic, 1984—. Wis. rep. Joint Coun. of State Neurol. Socs., 1990, 91, 92, 93, 94, 95, 96. Mem. AMA, Am. Assn. Neurol. Surgeons, Wis. Med. Soc., Wis. Neurosurg. Soc. (sec., treas. 1987, pres. 1989). Home: 1403 N Broadway Ave Marshfield WI 54449-1321 Office: Marshfield Clinic 1000 N Oak Ave Marshfield WI 54449-5703

KELPE, PAUL ROBERT, engineer, consultant; b. St. Louis, July 6, 1948; s. Robert Frederick and Doris Jean (Wood) K.; m. Janice Pauline Frey, Apr. 10, 1971; children: Brian Paul, Mark Robert. BA, Ottawa U., 1970; MS, U. Nebr., 1973; diploma in energy mgmt., Va. Poly. Inst., 1985. Cert. tchr., Nebr. Stationery engr. King Louie Corp., Overland Park, Kans., 1967-70; head tchr. sci. dept. Westside Community Schs., Omaha, 1970-81, energy dir., 1981-92; apptd. mem. Nebr. Energy Coun., 1991-92; sci. instr. Westside Middle Sch. Contbr. articles to profl. jours. Troop com. chmn. Boy Scouts Am., Omaha, 1987-92; bd. trustees Sanitary and Improvement Dist., 1980-84; candidate Sub-Dist. 7 PNRD, Omaha, 1988-89; mem. Gov.'s Energy Policy Coun., 1991-92. Recipient Energy award State of Nebr., 1987; grantee Nebr. Energy Office, 1982-92. Mem. ASHRAE (award 1988), Nebr. Acad. Scis., Nat. Sci. Tchrs. Assn., Nebr. State Tchr. Assn., NEA, Phi Delta Kappa. Republican. Lutheran. Office: Westside Community Schs 909 S 76th St Omaha NE 68114-4519

KELSCH, RAEANN, state legislator; m. Thomas D. Kelsch; 3 children. BBA, U. N.D. Mem. N.D. Ho. of Reps.; vice chmn. judiciary com., mem. govt. and vets. affairs com. Bd. dirs. United Way; active AID, Inc. Republican. Home: 611 Craig Dr Mandan ND 58554-2353 Office: ND Ho of Reps State Capitol Bismarck ND 58505

KELSH, JEROME, state legislator; b. Fullerton, N.D., Oct. 25, 1940; s. George L. and Freda (Nelson) K.; m. Romona Keller; children: Scott, Jock, Steven. BS, U. N.D., 1962. Mem. N.D. Senate, 1985—, chmn. agr. com., mem. edn. com., mem. transp. com.; agribusinessman. Mem. adv. bd. Ellenda Hosp.; past chmn. Fullerton Centennial Com.; past mem. Fullerton Sch. Bd.; mem. Fullerton Betterment Bd. Office: Rte 1 Box 27 Fullerton ND 58441 also: State Senate State Capitol Bismarck ND 58505*

KELSO, BECKY, state legislator; b. 1948; m. Michael Kelso; 2 children. BA in Comm., U. Minn. Mem. Minn. Ho. of Reps., 1986—; mem. capital investment com., mem. edn. com., mem. regulated industries and energy com., mem. transp. and transit com. Home: 60 S Shannon Dr Shakopee MN 55379-8025 Office: Minn State Senate State Capital Building Saint Paul MN 55155-1606 also: 415 State Office Bldg Saint Paul MN 55155

KELSO, CAROL, state legislator; b. May 26, 1945. BA, Iowa State U. Assemblywoman Wis. State Dist. 88; pres. Brown County Planning Commn.; mem. Brown County Harbor Commn., 2020 Hwy. Coalition. Address: 416 E LeCapitaine Cir Green Bay WI 54302

KEMMER, FRANK NELSON, consulting water chemist and engineer; b. Badin, N.C., Dec. 7, 1917; s. Frank Raymond and Annie Margaret (Nelson) K.; m. Carol Elizabeth Pancost, May 9, 1942; children: Susan J. Kemmer Keating, Gretchen, Molly P. Kemmer Box, Carolyn Kemmer DeOliver. BSChemE, Lehigh U., 1939. Registered profl. engr., Pa. Sales engr. Cochrane Corp., Phila., 1939-48, dir. rsch. and devel., 1948-52; nat. accts. mgr., mgr. of cons. Nalco Chem. Co., Chgo., 1952-64, mktg. mgr. pollution control dept., 1969-74, tng. specialist, 1974-79; ret.; cons., Clarendon Hills, Ill., 1979—. Author: Water, The Universal Solvent, 1977; editor: The Nalco Water Handbook, 1979; also articles. Former v.p. Gt. Lakes Found., Ann Arbor, Mich.; chmn. legal redress com. NAACP, La Grange, Ill., 1968-69. Recipient Medgar Evers award La Grange br. NAACP. Fellow Am. Inst. Chemists; mem. TAPPI (chmn. water quality com. 1967-69), Am. Chem. Soc. (past membership chmn. environ. chemistry div.), Tau Beta Pi. Democrat. Episcopalian. Home: 50 Waverly Ave Clarendon Hills IL 60514-1237

KEMNITZ, WILLIAM F., retired electrical engineer; b. Varna, Ill., Jan. 8, 1927; s. Frederick William and Elfrieda Louise (Junker) K.; m. Mary Ann Lundberg, Aug. 13, 1949; children: Michael, Debra. BS in Edn., Ill. State Normal U., 1949; BS in TV Engring., Am. TV Inst., 1954. TV cameraman Chgo. Ednl. TV Assn., 1956-59; instr., mgr. RCA Svc. Co., Cherry Hill, N.J., 1959-63, Collins Radio Co., Dallas, 1963-78; instr. Digital Equipment Corp., Maynard, Mass., 1978-89. Author: Down by the Junction, 1995. Bd. dirs. Marshall County Hist. Soc., sec., 1989—. With USN, 1944-46. Republican. Lutheran.

KEMP, PATRICIA ANN, principal; b. Wawatosa, Wis., Dec. 24, 1932; d. Lloyd Wolfe and Lydia (Henry) Worden; children: Becky Ann, Barrett George. AB, Albion (Mich.) Coll., 1954; MEd, Wright State U., Dayton, 1979; MRC, Wright State U., 1985. Tchr. St. Marys (Ohio) City Schs., 1961-86; instr. counseling Wright State U., Celina, Ohio, 1985-87; counselor Kinross Correctional Facility, Kinross, Mich., 1985; pvt. counselor Office of Dr. Douglas W. Johnson, PhD, St. Marys, 1985-87; tchr., dir. De Tour Village (Mich.) Day Care, 1987-89; tchr. De Tour (Mich.) Village Pub. Schs., 1989-91, elem. prin., 1991—. Mem. AAUW, Mich. Elem. and Mid. Sch. Prins. Assn., Am. Rehab. Cousneling Assn., Ohio Assn. Counseling and Devel., Ohio Rehab. Counseling Assn., Delta Kappa Gamma, Kappa Delta. Home: HC 54 Box 493 De Tour Village MI 49725-9718 Office: De Tour Area Schs PO Box 68 De Tour Village MI 49725

KEMP, WILLIAM BRADLEY MACLAREN, marketing and development director; b. Kansas City, Mo., July 6, 1961; s. Walter Horace and Marilyn Jean (Hanback) K. BArch, Kans. State U., 1985; postgrad., U. Ariz., 1986-87; MS, U. Kans., 1991. Publicity coord. U. Kans. Office of Univ. Rels., Lawrence, 1987-92; mktg. and devel. dir. U. Kans. Natural History Mus., Lawrence, 1992—; ind. publs. cons., Lawrence, 1989—. Mem. Am. Assn. Museums, Mid-Continent Consortium of Natural History Museums, Kans. Museums Assn. Home: 1846 Barker St Lawrence KS 66044 Office: Kans U Natural History Mus Dyche Hall Lawrence KS 66045

KEMPENICH, KEITH, state legislator; m. Melinda. Mem. N.D. Ho. of Reps., vice chmn. transp. com., mem. indsl., bus. and labor com.; rancher; crop adjuster. Mem. Lions, Farm Bur., Farmers Union, Aircraft Owners and Pilots Assn. Home: HC 4 Box 6 Bowman ND 58623-8808*

KEMPF, JANE ELMIRA, marketing executive; b. Phila., Sept. 28, 1927; d. Albert Thomas and Alice (Gaston) Mullen; m. Peter Kempf, Sept. 4, 1948 (dec. Mar. 1985); children: Peter Albert, Jan Michael, Richard Allen, Jeffery Val. Grad. high sch., Yeadon, Pa. News dir. Sta. WIFF, Auburn, Ind., 1968-69; city editor The Evening Star, Auburn, 1969-76, columnist, 1969—; paralegal Warren Sunday Atty., Auburn, 1977-85; mktg. mgr. City Nat. Bank, Auburn, 1986-89; with communications mktg. Lincoln Fin. Corp., Ft. Wayne, Ind., 1989-90; prin. JK Communications Bus. Svcs., Auburn, Ind., 1990—; bd. dirs. Tri-County Power Wash, Inc. Contbr. articles to profl. jours. Mem. Auburn Network Enterprising Women, Ladies Literary Club, PEO Sisterhood (past pres.), Auburn C. of C. (past sec., bd. dirs.). Presbyterian. Home: 1117 Packard Pl Auburn IN 46706-1340 Office: JK Communicatons Bus Svcs PO Box 430 Auburn IN 46706-0430

KEMPINERS, WILLIAM LEE, professional association executive; b. Oak Park, Ill., Jan. 26, 1942; s. Wilbur H. and Margaret E. (Hardesty) K.; m. July 5, 1978 (div. 1989); children: J.J., Jeffrey T. BA, Augustana Coll., Rock Island, Ill., 1964. Lic. ins. broker, Ill. Legis. asst. to dir. govt. rels. Ill. State Med. Soc., Chgo., 1970-71; mem. Ill. Ho. of Reps., 39th Dist., 1973-79; dir. Ill. Dept. Pub. Health, Springfield, Ill., 1979-84; exec. dir. Coop. Health Plan, Oak Brook, Ill., 1984-86; health care cons. Geneva, Ill., 1986-89; exec. dir. Ill. Health Care Assn., Springfield, 1989—; advisory com. health econ., mgmt. and planning program U. Ill., 1993—. Mem. ctrl. Ill. adv. bd. Ill. Lung Assn.; mem. fin. com. U.S. Rep. J. Dennis Hastert, Batavia, Ill.; chmn. health sci. acad. adv. coun. Sch. Dist. # 186; mem. Nat. Com. on Vital and Health Stats., Washington, 1983-86; bd. dirs. Augustana Coll., Rock Island, 1975-86. With U.S. Army, 1966-68. Named one of 10 Best Ill. Legislators Chgo. Sun Times, 1979; recipient Spl. Award of Recognition Ill. Pub. Health Assn., 1985, Disting. Svc. award Ill. Dept. Pub. Health, 1989. Mem. Ill. Soc. Assn. Execs., Am. Coll. Health Care Adminstrs., Assn. of State Health Care Assn. Execs. Republican. Lutheran. Home: 140 Joan Dr Divernon IL 62530-9744 Office: Ill Health Care Assn 1029 S 4th St Springfield IL 62703-2224

KEMPSKI, RALPH ALOISIUS, bishop; b. Milw., July 16, 1934; s. Sigmund Joseph and Cecilia Josephine (Chojnacki) K.; m. Mary Jane Roth, July 30, 1955; children—Richard, Joan, John. B.A., Augsburg Coll., 1960; M.Div., Northwestern Luth. Theol. Sem., 1963; D.Div., Wittenberg U., Springfield, Ohio, 1980. Pastor Epiphany Luth. Ch., Mpls., 1963-68, St. Stephen Luth. Ch., Louisville, Ky., 1968-71, Our Saviour Luth. Ch., West Lafayette, Ind., 1971-79; bishop Ind.-Ky. Synod Luth. Ch. Am., Indpls., 1979-87, Ind.-Ky. Synod Evang. Luth. Ch. Am., 1987—; bd. dirs. Ind. Coun. Chs., 1979-96, v.p., 1991-94, pres., 1994-96 ; bd. dirs. Ky. Coun. Chs., 1979—, Luth. Sch. Theology, Chgo., 1979-87, Luth. Sch., Columbia, S.C., 1987-96, Trinity Luth. Sem., 1996, Wittenberg U., Springfield, Ohio, 1979—; governing bd. Nat. Coun. Chs. Christ U.S.A., N.Y.C., 1981-88, Luth. Theol. So. Sem., 1988—. Office: Ind-Ky Synod Evang Luth Ch Ste 200 911 E 86th St Indianapolis IN 46240

KENAT, THOMAS ARTHUR, chemical engineer, consultant; b. Cleve., Aug. 6, 1942; s. Arthur Brian and Frances Lillian (Kuenzli) K.; m. Wynne Irene Kalvesmaki, June 13, 1964; children: Steven Thomas, Lisa Marie. BSChemE, Carnegie Inst. Tech., 1964, MSChemE, 1965; PhD in Chem. Engring., Carnegie-Mellon U., 1968. Registered profl. engr., Ohio. Rsch. engr. Chemstrand Rsch. Ctr., Durham, N.C., 1968-69; rsch. engr. B. F. Goodrich Co., Brecksville, Ohio, 1969-74, sr. rsch. engr., 1974-80, sr. engring. scientist, 1981-83, sr. R & D assoc., 1983-88; sr. R & D assoc. Camet Co., Hiram, Ohio, 1988-89; sr. project mgr. Quantum Techs., Inc., Twinsburg, Ohio, 1989-92; ind. cons. KenaTech Process Engring., Medina, Ohio, 1992—. Contbr. articles to profl. jours. Elder Prince of Peace Luth. Ch., Medina, Ohio, 1975-90; mem. Medina Community Band, 1983—. Mem. NSPE, AIChE, Am. Chem. Soc., Am. Guild Organists, Nat. Assn. Corrosion Engrs., Kiwanis. Republican. Lutheran. Office: KenaTech Process Engring PO Box 1842 Medina OH 44258-1842

KENDALL, EARNEST JAMES, mental health nurse; b. Kalamazoo, Mar. 4, 1948; s. Earnest Glenn and Mary Eileen (Holcomb) K.; children: Earnest David, Julie Erin. ADN, Penn Valley Community Coll., Kansas City, Mo., 1973; BA in Psychology, U. Mo., Kansas City, 1977, BSN, 1990, MA in Counseling and Guidance, 1981, MSN, 1994. Cert. psychiat./mental health nurse. Staff nurse, head nurse St. Mary's Hosp., Kansas City, Mo., 1973-81; staff nurse St. Luke's Hosp., Kansas City, Mo., 1981-82, Menorah Med. Ctr., Kansas City, Mo., 1982-95, Trinity Lutheran Hosp., Kansas City, Mo., 1995—. With U.S. Army, 1967-70; capt. USAFR. Mem. Sigma Theta Tau, Phi Kappa Phi, Phi Theta Kappa. Home: 6025 Brookside Blvd Kansas City MO 64113-1427

KENDALL, JAMES WILLIAM, manufacturing company executive; b. Ashland, Ky., June 9, 1932; s. J. William and Mary Lee (Wright) K.; m. Mary Ann Smith, June 26, 1955; children—Susan Lupton, Thomas Fairchild, James William, Sally Ann. B.A., DePauw U., Greencastle, Ind., 1954. Bus. mgr. Rev. Pub. Co., Indpls., 1960-62; sales mgr. Elec. Metals Corp., Indpls., 1962-63; asst. advt. mgr. Am. United Life Ins. Co., Indpls., 1963-66; spl. accounts mgr. Arvinyl Div., Arvin Industries, Columbus, Ind., 1966-74, v.p. market devel., 1974-77, v.p., personnel, Metals, 1977-85, v.p. community relations, 1986-95, ret., 1996. Bd. dirs. Arvin Found., Columbus, 1978—; vice chmn. S. Central Pvt. Industry Council, 1984-85, chmn. 1986-87; chmn. Columbus Enterprise Devel. Corp.; sec.-treas. Jr. Achievement Bartholomew dir. Columbus Regional Hosp. Fedn., 1993-95; pres., bd. dirs. Columbus Disting. Visitors Series, Columbus, 1978-79, Bartholomew Consol. Sch. Found., Columbus, 1978-79, United Way Bartholomew County, Columbus, 1979-80; pres., bd. dirs. Columbus Found. Youth, 1986, trustee The Nature Conservancy (ind. chpt.); chmn. Ind. Coun. Econ. Edn.. Served to 1st lt. USAF, 1955-57. Mem. Rotary Club. Republican. Methodist. Avocations: tennis, sailing, civic activities, reading. Home: 4566 Carya Sq Columbus IN 47201-8933 Office: Arvin Fedn Inc 1 Noblitt Plaza Columbus IN 47201-6073

KENDALL, KAY LYNN, interior designer; b. Cadillac, Mich., Aug. 20, 1950; d. Robert Llewellyn and Betty Louise (Powers) K.; 1 child, Anna Renee Easter. BFA, U. Mich., 1973. Draftsman, interior designer store planning dept. Jacobson Stores, Inc., Jackson, Mich., 1974-79; sr. interior designer store planning dept. Jacobson Stores, Inc., Jackson, 1981—; prin. Kay Kendall Designs, Jackson, 1979—; cons. in field. Mem. Am. Soc. Interior Designers (profl. mem., assoc. Cen. Mich. chpt.). Home: 701 Church St Grass Lake MI 49240 Office: Jacobson Stores Inc 3333 Sargent Rd Jackson MI 49201-8847

KENDALL, LAUREL ANN, geotechnical engineer; b. Detroit, Dec. 4, 1956; d. James McNair and Dorothy Mildred (Frost) K. BSE in Environ. Sci., U. Mich., 1979, MSCE, 1983. Registered profl. engr., Mich., Ill., Ohio. Geotech. egnr. Bechtel Assocs., Ann Arbor, Mich., 1979-84; with Bechtel Assocs. P.C., 1979-84; instr. Lawrence Inst. Tech., Southfield, Mich., 1985-91, Wayne State U., 1991-95. Mem. ASCE (past pres. southeastern br., officer Mich. sect. 1990—), Mich. Soc. Profl. Engrs. (officer 1990—), Engring. Soc. Detroit. Congregationalist. Office: Wayne Disposal-Canton Inc 5011 S Lilley Canton MI 48188

KENDALL, ROBERT E., investment executive; b. Grand Rapids, Mich., June 22, 1934. BS, Mich. State U., 1957. Salesman Donald Carol Medals, Chgo., 1957-59; investment executive Painewebber, Muskegon, Mich., 1959—. Mem. Am. Bus. Club (past pres. 1960). Office: Painewebber 945 W Norton Ave Muskegon MI 49441-4105

KENDALL, ROBERT STANTON, newspaper editor, journalist; b. Greensburg, Ind., July 30, 1921; s. Wilber Lawrence and Marguerite (Groenier) K.; m. Dorothy Jane Rumbold, Oct. 2, 1943; children: Mark Curtis, Lee Rachel, Amy Robin Kendall Uhls. BA, Coll. of Wooster, 1946. Asst. pub. Martinsville (Ind.) Daily Reporter, 1946-49, editor, 1949—; chmn. Reporter-Times Inc., Martinsville, 1983—, Adkins Inc., Martinsville. 2d lt. USAAF, 1943-45, ETO. Decorated Air medal; recipient Meritorious Svc. award Am. Legion, Martinsville, 1973, citation Coun. for Def. of Freedom, 1978, Honor medal DAR, 1987. Mem. Am. Soc. Newspaper Editors, Kiwanis, Phi Beta Kappa, Phi Alpha Theta. Republican. Lutheran. Home: 460 Park Pl Martinsville IN 46151-1237 Office: Reporter-Times Inc 60 S Jefferson St Martinsville IN 46151-1968

KENDALL, SUSAN HAINES, library director; b. Greenville, Ohio, Nov. 5, 1952; d. Kenneth Edward and Zelda Lucille (Delk) Haines; m. John Leroy Sweigart, May 25, 1974 (div. 1986); m. Patrick William Kendall, Nov. 28, 1986. BS in Edn., Wright State U., 1977; MLS, Ball State U., 1981. Cert. tchr., Ohio; cert. libr., Ohio. Libr. clk. Greenville (Ohio) Pub. Libr., 1971-77; libr. asst. Flesh Pub. Libr., Piqua, Ohio, 1977-78, Amos Meml. Pub. Libr., Sidney, Ohio, 1978-81; libr. dir. Preble County Dist. Libr., Eaton, Ohio, 1981—; mem. tech. task force Ohio Pub. Libr. Info. Network, Columbus, 1993-95, bd. dirs. 1995—. Editor Preble's Pride quar., 1986—. Mem. ALA, Ohio Libr. Assn. (mem. S.W. chpt. mem. coun. 1984-86, asst. coord. 1986-87, coord. 1988-89), Commodore-Preble DAR, Preble County Genealogy Soc., Eaton Area C. of C. Republican. Methodist. Office: Preble County Dist Libr 450 S Barron St Eaton OH 45320

KENDRICK, WILLIAM MONROE, insurance company executive; b. Chgo., June 20, 1941; s. Walter and Cordelia (Rogers) K.; m. Julie Oehlsen (div. Jan. 1990); children: Todd, Kevin; m. Jeanne Pierce, Feb. 26, 1994. BA, Ill. Wesleyan, 1964; MS in Fin. Svcs., Am. Coll., 1990. CLU; cert. employee benefits specialist. Claim adjuster Continental Casualty, Chgo., 1964-68; brokerage mgr. Continental Ins., Chgo., 1968-70; employee benefit cons. Can. Am., Chgo., 1970-71; regional dir. Aetna Life, Chgo., 1971-77, Crown Life, Chgo., 1977-82; sr. regional pension mgr. Minn. Mut., Itasca, Ill., 1982-85; sr. account exec. CIGNA, Chgo., 1985-86; regional sales mgr. New Eng. Retirement Svcs., Chgo., 1986—. columnist Ill. Broker, 1991—. Vol. coord. Luth. Gen. Hosp., Mundelein, Ill., 1983-86. Mem. CLUs (dir. Chgo. chpt. 1990-92, v.p. 1992-95, pres. 1995-96), Working Employees Benefits, Cons. Roundtable, Mensa, Cert. Employee Benefit Specialists. Office: NERS 120 S Riverside Plz Ste 2100 Chicago IL 60606

KENDZIOR, ROBERT JOSEPH, marketing executive; b. Chgo., Mar. 24, 1952; s. Joseph W. and Josephine R. Kendzior. BArch, Ill. Inst. Tech., 1975. Account supr. Burger King Corp., Rogers Merchandising, Inc., Chgo., 1975-77; account exec. Walgreen Corp., Eisaman, Johns & Laws Advt., Inc., Chgo., 1977-78; v.p./mktg. Dunkin Donuts Am., Inc., Randolph, Mass., 1978-95; v.p., chief mktg. officer Factory Card Outlet Am., Inc., Chgo., 1995—. Recipient Most Valuable Promotion award PepsiCo, 1984. Mem. Triangle Fraternity, Chgo. Advt. Club.

KENEKLIS, THEODORE PETER, research scientist, trainer; b. New Bedford, Mass., May 15, 1944; s. Peter Theodore and Erickety (Righellis) K.; m. Judith Ellen Bonnoyer, June 18, 1967; children: Christopher Eric, Jason Daniel. BA, Drake U., 1966; MS, L.I. U., 1970; PhD, U. Lausanne, 1975. Rschr. Swiss Inst. Exptl. Cancer Rsch., Lausanne, Switzerland, 1970-76; postdoctoral fellow Uniformed Svcs. Univ., Bethesda, Md., 1977-78; sr. rschr. Raven Systems and Rsch., Washington, 1978-79; sr. scientist Dynamac Corp., Rockville, Md., 1979-83; nuclear trainer Wis. Pub. Svc. Corp, Green Bay, Wis., 1983—. N.Y. State scholar incentive, Bklyn., 1966-67; fellow L.I. Univ., Bklyn., 1967-68; predoctoral fellow Swiss Sci. Rev. Found., Bern, Switzerland, 1972-74, postdoctoral fellow, 1975-76, Nat. Cancer Inst., Bethesda, 1977. Mem. ASTD (pres. N.E. Wis. chpt. 1994), Masons, Shriners. Republican. Greek Orthodox. Home: 3310 Cameo Ct Green Bay WI 54301-1546 Office: Wis Pub Svc Corp 490N Hwy 42 Kewaunee WI 54216

KENISON, RAYMOND ROBERT, fraternal organization administrator, director; b. Mo., Sept. 23, 1932; s. Raymond Roy and Emma Oleta (Holder) K.; m. Marjorie White, Feb. 1, 1955; children: Debra Kenison Brown, Peggy Kenison Crim, Raymond Roger, Robert B. AA, Hannibal LaGrange Coll., 1953; BA, U. Mo., 1961; postgrad., Cen. Bapt. Sem., Kansas City, 1957, Midwestern Bapt. Sem., Kansas City, 1965; cert. fin. planner, Coll. Fin. Planning, Denver; DivD, Hannibal LaGrange Coll., 1994. Cert. instr. Pastor First Bapt.Ch., Bates City, Mo., 1954-56, Friendship Bapt. Ch., Mexico, Mo., 1956-62, Immanuel Bapt. Ch., Hannibal, Mo., 1962-77; dir. devel. Mo. Bapt. Children's Home, Bridgeton, 1977-80, exec. dir., 1980—; pres., 1992—; pres. bd. trustees Hannibal-LaGrange Coll. Mem. Child Welfare League of Am. Inc.; Nat. Soc. of Fund Raising Execs.; pres. Hannibal Coun. Alcohol & Drug Abuse, bd. dirs. Hannibal Community Chest, 1974-79, pres. Hannibal Ministerial Alliance. Kenison Complex named in his honor. Mem. Nat. Foster Parents Assn., So. Bapt. Child Care Execs. (pres.), Nat. Assn. of Homes for Children (sec.), Mo. Child Care Assn. (bd. dirs., pres. 1994—), S.W. Assn. of Child Care Execs., Inst. CFPs, Hannibal Investment Club (pres. 1976-78, 82-83). Home: 193 Lake Apollo Dr Hannibal MO 63401-6218 Office: Mo Bapt Children's Home 11300 Saint Charles Rock Rd Bridgeton MO 63044-2721

KENLEY, HOWARD, state legislator; b. Ft. Stockton, Tex., Mar. 28, 1945; s. Howard A. Jr. and elvira (Hayten) K.; m. Sally Kenley; children: John, Bill, Betsy. AB, Miami U., Oxford, Ohio, 1967; JD, Harvard U., 1972. Atty. Cadick, Burns, Duck & Neighbours, Indpls., 1972-73; pres., owner Kenley's Supermarkets, Noblesville, Ind., 1974-93; judge Noblesville City Ct., 1974-89; senator Dist. 20 Ind. State Senate, 1992—, ranking mem. correctons, criminal and civil procedures coms., mem. fin. com., judiciary com., planning/pub. svc. com.; bd. dirs. Society Bank of Ind. Grand marshall homecoming Noblesville H.S., 1989—, Christmas Parade, City of Noblesville, 1992—; chmn. allocations com. Greater Indpls. United way, 1992—; bd. dirs. Boys and Girls Club of Noblesville. with U.S. Army; Vietnam. Deocrated Army Commendation medal; named Bd. Mem. of Yr. Noblesville Boys and Girls Club, 1984-85. Mem. Ind. State Bar Assn., Hamilton County Bar Assn., 50 Club of Hamilton County, Elks, Beta theta Pi. Home: 102 Harbour Trees Ln Noblesville IN 46060-9079*

KENNARD, LAWRENCE PAUL, financial planner; b. Cleve., Nov. 16, 1946. BSBA, John Carroll U., 1968. CFP. Tchr. Padua Franciscan Sch., Parma, Ohio, 1968-72; owner, mgr. Kennard Valente Assocs., Cleve., 1974-80; fin. planner Kennard Fin. Svcs., Cleve., 1981—; br. mgr. WRP Investments, Garfield, Ohio, 1979—. Mem. Inst. CFP's, Internat. Assn. for Fin. Planning (bd. dirs. N.E. Ohio 1993—), John Carroll U. Alumni Assn. Roman Catholic. Office: Kennard Fin Svcs Ste 100 5250 Transportation Blvd Cleveland OH 44125

KENNEDY, ARTHUR J., II, stockbroker; b. Kansas City, Mo., Apr. 29, 1962; m. Tonyia Kennedy. BSBA in Fin., U. Mo., 1986. CFA. Stockbroker B.C. Christopher Securities, Kansas City, Mo., 1987-91, Piper Jaffray Inc., Kansas City, Mo., 1991—. Roman Catholic. Home: 5521 W 61st Ter Mission KS 66202-3508 Office: Piper Jaffray Ste 1200 4600 Madison Ave Kansas City MO 64112

KENNEDY, CHARLES ALLEN, lawyer; b. Maysville, Ky., Dec. 11, 1940; s. Elmer Earl and Mary Frances Kennedy; m. Patricia Ann Louderback, Dec. 9, 1961; 1 child, Mimi Mignon. AB, Morehead State Coll., 1965, MA in Edn., 1968; JD, U. Akron, 1969; LLM, George Washington U., 1974. Bar: Ohio 1969. Asst. cashier Citizens Bank, Felicity, Ohio, 1961-63; tchr. Triway Local Sch. Dist., Wooster, Ohio, 1965-67; with office of gen. counsel Fgn. Agr. and Spl. Programs Div., U.S. Dept. Agr., Washington, 1969-71; ptnr. Kauffman, Eberhart, Cicconetti & Kennedy Co., Wooster, 1972-86, Kennedy, Cicconetti & Rickett, Wooster, 1986—. Mem. ABA, Fed. Bar Assn., Assn. Trial Lawyers Am., Ohio State Bar Assn., Ohio Acad. Trial Lawyers, Ohio Assn. Criminal Def. Lawyers, Wayne County Bar Assn., Phi Alpha Delta, Phi Delta Kappa. Republican. Club: Exchange (Wooster). Lodges: Lions, Elks. Home: 1770 Burbank Rd Wooster OH 44691-2240 Office: Kennedy Cicconetti & Rickett 558 N Market St Wooster OH 44691-3406

KENNEDY, CHERYL LYNN, museum director; b. Pekin, Ill., Nov. 25, 1946; d. Paul Louis and Ann Marie (Bingham) Wieburg; children: Kurt Alan, Kimberly Ann. Grad. high sch., Pekin, Ill. Prin., and profl. quilter Mahomet, Ill., 1976-81; program coord. Early Am. Mus., Mahomet, 1981-85; dir. Early Am. Mus. Champaign County Forest Preserve, Mahomet, 1986—; chmn. Ill. quilt documentation project Early Am. Mus. and Land of Lincoln Quilt Assn., 1986—. Historian Meth. Local History Com., Mahomet, 1984-86; chair The Attractions Coun., Champaign-Urbana Conv. and Visitors Bur. Mem. Midwest Mus. Coun., Am. Assn. Mus., Am. Assn. State and Local History Mus., Ill. Assn. Mus. (past pres., Heritage Awareness chair), Ill. Heritage Assn., Ill. State Hist. Soc., Champaign County Hist. Soc., Nat. Quilt Assn., Am. Quilt Soc., Antique Quilt Study Group, Quilt Conservancy, Nat. Soc. Fundraising Execs., Rural Ptnrs. (bd. dirs.). Home: 219A S Lake Of The Woods Rd Mahomet IL 61853-9201 Office: Early Am Mus PO Box 1040 Mahomet IL 61853-1040

KENNEDY, ELIZABETH, health facility administrator; b. Binghamton, N.Y., Mar. 19, 1944; d. Robert D. and Doris Beverly (Bryde) Courtright; m. Leon C. Kennedy, Aug. 29, 1964; children: Andrew, Tracey, Brian, Kristie. AAS, Ind.-Purdue U., 1986; BSN, Ind. Wesleyan U., 1996. RN, Ind.; lifetime ARC nurse. DON Summit House, Ft. Wayne, Ind., 1986-87; staff nurse Mark Souder, M.D., Auburn, Ind., 1988; DON Kendallville (Ind.) Nursing Home, 1988-89, Lifecare Ctr., Lagrange, Ind., 1989-91; owner Profl. Nursing Svcs., 1989—; asst. Don Arbors at Ft. Wayne, Ind., 1991-92; nursing supr. Allen Home, Health Care & Hospice, 1993-95; DON Courtland Health and Rehab. Ctr., Ft. Wayne, 1996—; instr. ARC. Recipient Scottish Rite Nursing scholarship. Home: 5135-6 Stone Hedge Rd Fort Wayne IN 46835

KENNEDY, FREDERICK MORGAN, secondary education educator; b. Oklahoma City, May 5, 1943; s. Fredrick Theodor and Ruthy Marie Kennedy; m. Claudette Alberta Carter, Aug. 14, 1966; children: Kimberly Michelle, Cheryl Ann. BS, Langston U., 1965; MA, Kent State U., 1979. Cert. tchr., Ohio. Tchr. math., occupational work adjustment Cleve. City Schs., 1965—; mem. curriculum writing com. Cleve. City Schs., 1987, 89, 92. Treas. Quinn Chapel AME Ch., Cleve., 1985, ch. adminstr., 1989. Mem. Ohio Vocat. Assn. (life), Indsl. Arts Club (membership com. 1992), Occupational Work Adjustment (instrs. div.). Democrat. Home: 17201 Dynes Ave Cleveland OH 44128-3320 Office: Harry L Eastman Sch 996 Hines Hill Rd Hudson OH 44236-1620

KENNEDY, GARY L., agricultural organization administrator; b. Harrisburg, Ill., Mar. 5, 1956; s. Jack Dale and Mildred JoAnn (Miskelly) K.; m. Cheryl Ann Thomas, Jan. 4, 1980; children: Nicole, Hailey, Ashley. AS, Southea. Ill. Coll., 1976; BS, So. Ill. U., 1978. Cert. mgr., Ill. Farm Bur. Clk. TSC Stores, Harrisburg, 1973-78; instr. vocat. agriculture Hamilton County Schs., McLeansboro, Ill., 1978-80; mgr. trainee Ill. Farm Bur., Bloomington, 1980; mgr. Wabash County Farm Bur., Mt. Carmel, Ill., 1980-84, Clinton County Farm Bur., Breese, Ill., 1984—; mem. adv. bd. Kaskaskia C.C., Centralia, Ill., 1989-95, Ctrl. H.S., Breese, 1993-95. Bd. dirs. Clinton County Fair Assn., 1992-95; bd. dirs., deacon Carlyle (Ill.) Christian Ch., 1993-95. Office: Clinton County Farm Bur 1165 N 4th St Breese IL 62230

KENNEDY, MERI BETH, women's health nurse; b. Decatur, Ill., Mar. 29, 1956; d. Joe D. and Goldie L. (Owens) K.; m. Donald Fluker, Oct. 28, 1978; children: Ryan, Meryn. Student, U. Ill., 1974-75; BSN, U. Iowa, 1978; MS, U. Mich., 1989. RN, Mich. Rsch. asst., project mgr. U. Mich. Sch. Nursing, Ann Arbor, 1987; nurse practitioner Planned Parenthood Mid-Mich., Ann Arbor, 1988; lectr., student counselor U. Mich. Sch. Nursing, Ann Arbor, 1989; nurse practitioner U. Mich. Health Ctrs., Brighton and Ann Arbor, 1990—; adj. faculty U. Mich. Sch. Nursing, 1993—, bd. dirs. North Campus Nursing Ctr., 1994—. Hartwell C. Howard scholar, LuAnn Gerlach scholar; Rackham Minority fellow. Mem. ANA, Mich. Nurses Assn., Mich. Assn. Nurse Practitioners Reproductive Health, Sigma Theta Tau. Office: 2200 Green Rd Ann Arbor MI 48105-2948

KENNEDY, SANDRA ANNE, physical therapist; b. Chgo., Nov. 30, 1965; d. Ronald John and Ruby Jeannette (Woods) K. BS in Phys. Therapy, Marquette U., 1987. Lic. phys. therapist, Ill. Phys. therapist Alexian Bros. Med. Ctr., Elk Grove Village, Ill., 1987-89, New Medico of Wis., Waterford, 1989, Rehab. Achievement Ctr., Wheeling, Ill., 1989-93, Edgewater Rehab. Assocs., Northbrook, Ill., 1993—; inpatient coord. phys. medicine and rehab. N.W. Cmty. Hosp., Arlington Heights, Ill., 1995, home care phys. therapist, 1996—. Vol. area coord. Compassion Internat., Colorado Springs, 1991—. Mem. Am. Phys. Therapy Assn., Ill. Phys. Therapy Assn., Nat. Assn. Christian Phys. Therapists. Office: NW Cmty Hosp 800 W Central Rd Arlington Heights IL 60005-2392

KENNEDY-REED, CHERYL LYNN, nurse, family case manager; b. Minden, Nebr., July 28, 1957; d. Marlin Wayne and Shirley Ann (Pitts) Kennedy; m. Doyle Marc Reed, Nov. 28, 1981. BSN, U. Nebr., Kearney, 1980, MEd, 1987; MSN, Creighton U., 1994. RN, Nebr.; cert. clin. nurse specialist. Clin. nurse Family Med. Ctr., Holdrege, Nebr., 1981-85; stress mgmt. coord. Richard Young Hosp., Kearney, 1985-89, employee health nurse, 1988-89; case mgr. Kearney Orthopedic Fracture Clinic, 1992—; program chair Phelps County unit Am. Heart Assn., 1982-83, pres., 1983-84, CPR instr., 1982-84; parenting instr. ARC, Holdrege, 1983-84; co-chair Candystriper program, founder infant-child restraint loan program Phelps Meml. Svc. League, Holdrege, 1983-84. Bd. dirs. Christian Sojourn to Haiti, Holdrege, 1984—; group co-leader U. Nebr. Adult Children of Alcoholics, Kearney, 1989-90; 1st call for help vol. Kearney United Way, 1990—. Recipient Outstanding Vol. award Am. Heart Assn., 1982-83, Outstanding Nebr. Unit award, 1983-84; named Young Career Woman Holdrege Bus. and Profl. Women's Club, 1983. Mem. Nebr. Nurses Assn., Sigma Theta Tau, Omicron Delta Kappa. Home: RR 3 Box 124 Holdrege NE 68949-9473

KENNER, HOWARD A., state legislator; b. Chgo., Dec. 26, 1957; s. Tyrone and Emma (Payne) K. BS, U. Ill., 1980. CPA. Ill. state rep. Dist. 24; mem. Appropriations Gen. Svc., Elem. and Secondary Edn. and Revenue Coms.; acct. Kenner and Assocs., 1980—. Office: 130 E Garfield Blvd Chicago IL 60615

KENNER, MARILYN SFERRA, civil engineer; b. Youngstown, Ohio, Oct. 16, 1959; d. Joseph James and Mary (Conti) Sferra; m. Walter Sherden Kenner, July 7, 1984. B in Engring., Youngstown State U., 1982. Registered profl. engr., Ohio. Design and constrn. engr. Mahoning County Engr.'s Office, Youngstown, 1982-89, chief dep. engr., 1989—; mem. engring. dean search com. Youngstown State U. Mem. Mahoning Valley Soc. Profl. Engrs. (pres., v.p. 1990-93, treas. 1987-90). Democrat. Roman Catholic. Home: 6941 Lockwood Blvd Youngstown OH 44512 Office: Mahoning County Engr Office 940 Bears Den Rd Youngstown OH 44511-1218

KENNEY, SUSAN C., stockbroker; b. Milw., Oct. 22, 1948. BA, U. Wis., 1971; MA, NYU. Stockbroker Chitter Peabody, Milw., 1983-87, A.G. Edwards & Sons Inc., Milw., 1987—. Office: AG Edwards & Sons Inc 700 N Water St Ste 540 Milwaukee WI 53202-4206

KENNEY, T. MICHAEL, financial consultant; b. Dayton, Ohio, Oct. 30, 1960. BS in Polit. Sci., Wright State U., 1983. Lic. series 7. Mgr. Bob Evans Restaurant, Dayton, 1983-84; gen. mgr. Foster Med., Columbus, Ohio, 1984-89; salesperson Anacomp Inc., Columbus, 1989-92; stockbroker Ohio Co., Columbus, 1992—; lectr. investment seminars. Mem. Masons. Roman Catholic.

KENNEY, WILLIAM PATRICK, state legislator; b. San Francisco, Jan. 20, 1955; s. Charles Frances and Barbara Clare Kenney; m. Sandra Louise Ehrlich, Dec. 29, 1979; children: Kristin Allison, William Charles, Carlton Patrick, Elizabeth Alexandria. AA, Saddleback Jr. Coll., 1976; BA, U. No. Colo., 1978. Player Kansas City Chiefs, 1978-89, Washington Redskins, 1989; broker, officer Bill Kenney and Assocs., Lee's Summit, Mo., 1992—; broker assoc. J.D. Reece Realtors, Lee's Summit, 1994—; mem. dist. 8 Mo. Ho. of Reps., Lee's Summit, 1995—, Mo. Senate, Lee's Summit, 1995—. Named Most Valuable Player Kansas City Chiefs, 1983; named to Pro Bowl Am. Football Conf. NFL, 1983. Office: 2410 SW Hook Rd Lees Summit MO 64082

KENNON, ROZMOND HERRON, physical therapist; b. Birmingham, Ala., Dec. 12, 1935; m. Gloria Oliver; children: Shawn, Rozmond Jr. BA, Talldega Coll., 1956; cert., U. Colo., 1957. Asst. chief phys. therapist St. John's Hosp., St. Paul, 1957-58, Creigthon Meml. St. Joseph's Hosp., Omaha, 1958-61; asst. chief, phys. therapist Sister Kenny Inst., Mpls., 1962, chief phys. therapy, 1962-64; cons. in phys. therapy Mt. Sinai Hosp., Mpls., 1963-70; pvt. practice, 1964. Contbr. articles to profl. jours. Bd. dirs. Southdale YMCA, Edina Human Rights, Southside Med. Ctr. Mem. Am. Phys. Therapy Assn., Am. Registry Phys. Therapists, Minn. Phys. Therapy Assn. (mem. social-econ. com., past chmn. profl. practice com., bd. dirs., past sec.). Home: 6135 N Forestview Ln Plymouth MN 65442 Office: 1518 E Lake St # 206 Minneapolis MN 55407

KENNY, RAYMOND PATRICK, greeting card company executive; b. Chgo., Dec. 16, 1933; s. Robert Emmett and Lauretta (Carmody) K.; m. Barbara Mae Clark, Sept. 23, 1955; children: Raymond, Kathleen, Kevin, Nancy, Tim, Sharon, Janellen. BSEE, Fournier Inst., Lemont, Ill., 1955; MBA, U. Chgo., 1958. Engr. Motorola, Chgo., 1955-56, Stewart Warner, Chgo., 1956-58; supr. Hughes Aircraft Co., Fullerton, Calif., 1958-65; mgr. Hallmark Cards, Kansas City, Mo., 1965-73; pres. Kenny Assocs., Overland Park, Kans., 1973-78; v.p. Am. Greetings Corp., Cleve., 1978—; bd. dirs. Celsat Am. Inc., Celsat, Inc. Mem. strategic planning com. ARC, Cleve. Mem. Inst. Mgmt. Sci., Strategic Leadership Forum. Office: Am Greetings Corp One American Rd Cleveland OH 44144-2398

KENT, JEFFREY C., electrical engineer; b. Bucyrus, Ohio, July 29, 1968. BSEE, Ohio State U., 1992. Design engr. Buckeye Machine Fabricators, Forest, Ohio, 1993—. Recipient Steinmetz award Gen. Electric, 1986. Mem. NSPE.

KENYON, THEO JEAN, reporter; b. Peoria, Ill., Sept. 5, 1922. BA cum laude, Northwestern U., 1944. Reporter Peoria Jour. Star; charter mem., pres. Peoria Newspaper Guild, 1958—. Author: History of the First National Bank of Peoria, 1963, 88. Mem. Phi Beta Kappa. Universalist Unitarian. Office: Peoria Jour Star 1 News Plz Peoria IL 61611

KEOGH, LAURENCE D., educator, gerontology consultant; b. N.Y.C., Feb. 6, 1937; s. John James and Margaret Mary (Stokes) K.; m. Janice Marie Powers, Nov. 17, 1971; children: Stephen, Christopher, David. BA in History, Marist Coll., 1958; MA in History, CUNY/Hunter Coll., 1963; MS in Sociology, Ill. Inst. Tech., 1969; MA in Psychology, Adler Sch. of Prof. Psychology, 1993; PhD, U. Mich., 1980. Sci. tchr. Mt. St. Michael H.S., N.Y.C., 1958-60, Bishop Dubois H.S., N.Y.C., 1960-63; hist. dept. chair St. Agnes, N.Y.C., 1963-66, St. Joe's, Trumbull, Conn., 1966-67, Marist H.S., Chgo., 1969-71; prof. Moraine Valley Coll., Palos Hills, Ill., 1969-95; dir. gerontology Adler Sch., Chgo., 1990-94; adj. faculty Govs. State U., Univ. Park, Ill., 1994-95, Trinity Christian Coll., Palos Hills, Ill., 1995; gerontology cons. Sisters of Mercy, Chgo., 1975-76, Little Bros., Chgo., 1986-87. Sch. bd. mem. Lockport (Ill.) H.S., 1989—; pres. home owners assn. Forest Hills, Lockport, Ill., 1990—. Recipient NSF award U.S. Govt., 1968-69, vol. award City of Chgo., 1980. Mem. Mid-Am. Congress on Aging, Am. Soc. on Aging. Office: Moraine Valley Coll 10900 S 88th Ave Palos Hills IL 60465

KEOUGH, JAMES GILLMAN, JR., minister; b. Reading, Pa., June 2, 1947; s. James Gillman Sr. and Nora (Deturck) K.; m. Dawn Eileen Wiest, Sept. 17, 1976; children: Cynthia Ann, James Michael, Wendy Sue, Danielle Lynn, Erin Mae, Bevin Leigh. BA in History Edn., Messiah Coll., Grantham, Pa., 1970; MDiv, Lancaster (Pa.) Theol. Sem., 1973; D of Ministry, Ashland (Ohio) Theol. Sem., 1980. Ordained to ministry United Ch. Christ, 1973. Minister St. Luke's United Ch. Christ, Kenhorst, Pa., 1972-75, Congl. Ch., Winchester, Va., 1975-78, 1st Congl. Ch., Newton Falls, Ohio, 1978-82, Cen. Congl. Ch., Middleboro, Mass., 1982-85; sr. minister 1st Congl. Ch., Pontiac, Mich., 1985—. Author: Teaching Prayer in the Local Parish, 1980. Bd. dirs. Clinton Valley coun. Boy Scouts Am.; bd. dirs. Boys Clubs Am., Pontiac; pres. Somebodycares, Pontiac, 1983—; active Dem. Century Club. Mem. Nat. Assn. Congl. Christian Chs., S.E. Mich. Congl. Ministerium, Independence Twp. Pastors Assn., Kiwanis. Home: 3062 St Jude Dr Waterford MI 48329-4359 Office: 1st Congl Church Clarkston Rd at Pine Knob Rd PO Box 221 Clarkston MI 48347-0221

KEOUGH, TY, soccer coach; b. St. Louis, Dec. 19, 1956; s. Harry Joseph and Alma (Flores) K.; m. Abigail Moore, Sept. 25, 1982; children: Meredith Rose, Madeleine Louise. BA in Spanish, St. Louis U., 1979, cert. in bus. adminstrn., 1979. Lic. soccer coach. Profl. soccer player Cin. Kids, 1978-79, San Diego (Calif.) Sockers, 1979-82, St. Louis Steamers, 1979-85, Kansas City (Mo.) Comets, 1985-86; men's soccer coach Wash. U., St. Louis, 1987—; sports broadcaster various sports channels, St. Louis, 1987—; dir. Wash. U. Soccer Camp, 1988—; staff coach Olympic Devel. Program, St. Louis, 1991—, USSF Nat. Coaching Schs., St. Louis, 1992—; mem. U.S. Olympic Team, 1980, U.S. World Cup Team, 1980; World Cup analyst ABC, ESPN, 1994; sportscaster Major League Soccer ESPN, 1995; head coach North Men's Soccer Squad Olympic Sports Festival, Colo., 1995. Coord. Soccer Start for Inner City, St. Louis, 1990-94; com. mem. Puma Cup, St. Louis, 1995. Named to Sports Fall of Fame St. Louis U., 1994. Mem. Nat. Soccer Coaches Assn., U.S. Coaches, Profl. Soccer Reporters Assn., U.S. Soccer Fedn. (nat. bd. dirs. 1988-91). Office: Washington Univ Campus Box 1067 One Brookings Dr Saint Louis MO 63130

KEPLER, JAMES ALAN, communications executive; b. Dayton, Ohio, Apr. 22, 1936; s. Joseph Paul and Ora Eugenia (Rice) K.; m. Ann Linda Overtree, Aug. 28, 1965; 1 child, Thomas Alan. BA, Ohio State U., 1964. Communications instr. State of Ohio, Columbus, 1964-68; advt. mgr. Bennett Mfg. Co., Westerville, Ohio, 1968-70; salesman Optimum Book Mktg. Inc., N.Y., 1970-72, Harper & Row Pubs., N.Y., 1972-77; writer, lectr. and cons. Kepler Assocs., Chgo., Ill., 1977—; ptnr. Kepler-Ranshaw Assocs., 1991—; cons. editor Lyle Steel Lit. Agy., 1990—. Co-author: (with William Blair) Fire Prevention and Survival, 1983, (with Jerold Kellman) The First 100 Years, 1984, (with Ann Kepler) The After-50 Pharmacy, 1986 (Beth Fonda Award Excellence 1987), (with Ann Kepler) Children's Medicine, 1985, (with Richard L. Clarke) Careers in Healthcare Financial Management, 1991; editor Midwest Engr. mag., 1991—. Bd. dirs. Dem. Ctrl. Com., Evanston, Ill., 1980; exec. dir. Evanston Ecumenical Action Coun., 1982-83; pres. Unitarian Ch., 1982-84; chmn. Cmty. Partnership, 1984; bd. dirs. ctrl. midwest dist. Unitarian Universalist Assn., 1990-94, pres., 1994-98; v.p. Unitarian Universalist Dist. Pres. Assn., 1994-95, pres., 1996-97; mem. Evanston Housing Commn., 1991-94. Mem. Ind. Writers Chgo. (pres. 1986), Nat. Coun. Writers Orgns. (exec. v.p. 1988), Midwest Soc. Profl. Cons., Assn. Profl. Writing Cons. Democrat. Home: 1322 W Sherwin Ave Chicago IL 60626-2020 Office: Kepler Assocs 1322 W Sherwin Ave Chicago IL 60626-2020

KEPPELER, ALEXIS ERIC, senior benefits consultant; b. Detroit, June 20, 1944; s. Richard Albert and Betty Virginia (Barr) K.; m. Barbara Zacharkow, June 1, 1975 (div. July 1995); children: Nicholas A., Catherine A. BS with hons., Mich. State U., 1966; MDiv, Episcopal Theol. Sch., Cambridge, Mass., 1969. Asst. rector St. Luke Episcopal Ch., Allen Park, Mich., 1969-71; vicar, priest-in-charge Ch. of the Mediator, Lakeside, Mich., 1971-74; software engr. Computer Hardware, Inc., Jackson, Mich., 1975-78; programmer, analyst Consumers Power Co., —, 1978-81, EDP internal auditor, 1981-84, systems analyst, 1984-87, retirement plans adminstr., 1987-95; sr. benefits cons., 1995—; rector St. Demetrius Orthodox Ch., —, 1976-94; auditor Orthodox Ch. in Am., Syosset, N.Y., 1986-89. Mem. Met. Cmty. Ch., Ypsilanti, Mich. Office: Consumers Power Co 212 W Michigan Ave Jackson MI 49201-2236

KEPPNER, LARRY E., stockbroker; b. Quincy, Ill., Mar. 25, 1943. BA, Quincy Coll., 1968. Self-employed, Quincy, 1970-83; broker rep. Edward D. Jones, Collinsville, Ill., 1983-89, LPL Fin., Collinsville, 1989—. Mem. Elks. Republican. Office: LPL Fin 526 Saint Louis Rd Collinsville IL 62234-2442

KERBIS, GERTRUDE LEMPP, architect; m. Walter Peterhans (dec.); m. Donald Kerbis (div. 1972); children: Julian, Lisa, Kim. BS, U. Ill.; MA, Ill. Inst. Tech.; postgrad., Grad. Sch. Design, Harvard U., 1949-50. Archtl. designer Skidmore, Owings & Merrill, Chgo., 1954-59, C.F. Murphy Assocs., Chgo., 1959-62, 65-67; pvt. practice architecture Lempp Kerbis Assocs., Chgo., 1967—; lectr. U. Ill., 1969; prof. William Rainey Harper Coll., 1970—, Washington U., St. Louis, 1977, 82, Ill. Inst. Tech., 1989-91; archtl. cons. Dept. Urban Renewal, City of Chgo.; mem. Northeastern Ill. Planning Commn., Open Land Project, Mid-North Community Orgn., Chgo. Met. Housing and Planning Council, Chgo. Mayor's Commn. for Preservation Chgo.'s Hist. Architecture; bd. dirs. Chgo. Sch. Architecture Found., 1972-76; trustee Chgo. Archtl. Assistance Ctr., Glessner House Found., Inland Architect Mag.; lectr. Art Inst. Chgo., U. N.Mex., Ill. Inst. Tech., Washington U., St. Louis, Ball State U., Muncie, Ind., U. Utah, Salt Lake City. Prin. archtl. works include U.S. Air Force Acad. dining hall, Colo., 1957, Skokie (Ill.) Pub. Library, 1959, Meadows Club, Lake Meadows, Chgo., 1959, O'Hare Internat. Airport 7 Continents Bldg, 1963; prin. developer and architect: Tennis Club, Highland Park, Ill., 1968, Watervliet, Mich. Tennis Ranch, 1970, Greenhouse Condominium, Chgo., 1976, Webster-Clark Townhouses, Chgo., 1986, Chappell Sch., 1993; exhibited at Chgo. Hist. Soc., 1984, Chgo. Mus. Sci. and Industry, 1985, Paris Exhbn. Chgo. Architects, 1985, Spertus Mus.; represented in permanent archtl. drawings collection Art Inst. Chgo. Active Art Inst. Chgo.. Recipient award for outstanding achievement in professions YWCA Met. Chgo., 1984. Fellow AIA (bd. dirs. Chgo. chpt. 1971-75, chpt. pres. 1980, nat. com. architecture, arts and recreation 1972-75, com. on design 1975-80, head subcom. inst. honors nomination); mem. Chgo. Women in Architecture (founder), Chgo. Network, Internat. Women's Forum, Arts Club Chgo., Cliff Dwellers (bd. dirs. 1987-88, pres. 1988, 89), Lambda Alpha. Office: Lempp Kerbis Assocs 172 W Burton Pl Chicago IL 60610-1310

KERICH, JAMES PATRICK, manufacturing company executive; b. Wichita, Kans., May 25, 1938; s. Bernard William and Helen Marie (Hendrickson) K.; m. Julia Jean Grosjean, June 28, 1958; children: Marie Suzanne, Julie Ann, Wendy Kathryn. Student Kans. U. Dir. ops. Skyline Corp., Elkhart, Ind., 1974-79, v.p., officer, 1982-89; chief exec. officer, chmn. bd. Mallard Coach Co., 1989-92; CEO, majority owner, Midwest Vans Inc., 1992—; ptnr. gas and oil ops. Okla. Farming, 1981—; pres. ON TV, Detroit, 1979-81; sports negotiator, cons., investor Pay TV, Chgo., Detroit and Dallas, 1981-82; cons. Buford TV, Chgo., 1981, Golden West Broadcasting, L.A., 1981. Recipient Fin. World's Chief Exec. Officer of Yr. award, 1991. Mem. Italian-Am. Club, Elks. Republican. Roman Catholic. Home: 1525 Greenleaf Blvd Elkhart IN 46514-3722

KERN, FRANKLIN LORENZ, auditor; b. Frankenmuth, Mich., Aug. 22, 1932; s. Ruben William and Regina (Bernthal) K.; m. Loretta L. Gehrke, Apr. 22, 1962; children: Andrew James, Sara Beth. B.A., Mich. State U., 1954; diploma, Bank Adminstrn. Inst. and Northwestern U., 1963, Bank Adminstrn. Inst. and U. Wis., 1971. Cert. fraud examiner. Asst. to controller Second Nat. Bank, Saginaw, Mich., 1963-65, v.p., auditor, 1965-96; forensic audit mgr. Citizen's Bank (formerly Second Nat. Bank), Saginaw, 1996—; regional audit mgr. fin. Citizens Banking Corp., Saginaw, 1989-91, v.p., forensic audit mgr., 1992—; seminar speaker Mich. Bankers Assn. and I.I.A. chpt. 1992; instr. Mich. Bankers Assn. Auditors Sch., 1994—. Sec.-treas. Frankenmuth Cmty. Band, 1967-72; chmn. Student Aid Fund St. Lorenz Luth. Congregation, 1964-74, elder, 1974-80; sec. 125th anniversary com. Frankenmuth, Mich., 1969; bd. dirs., treas. Saginaw Civic Symphony Assn., 1971-73, Luth. Homes of Mich., Inc., 1983-87, The Luth. Home-Frankenmuth, 1983-87, pres., 1985-87; mem. Sesquicentennial Music Com. St. Lorenz, 1989-95; chmn. Sesquicentennial Festival Concert, 1994-95. Mem. Bank Adminstrn. Inst. (pres. ea. Mich. chpt. 1968-69), Mich. State U. Alumni Assn., Frankenmuth H.S. Alumni Assn. (past sec., treas.), Tri-County Econs. Club of Mich., Inst. Internal Auditors (bd. govs. mid-Mich. chpt. 1994-96). Office: Citizens Bank 101 N Washington Ave Saginaw MI 48607-1206

KERN, GARY L., golf course architect; b. Kendallville, Ind., Dec. 27, 1937; s. Ralph Maynard and Edith Mae (Ford) K.; m. Frances Geraldine Tipp, June 9, 1957 (div. Aug. 1981); 1 child, Ronald. Student, Tex. A&M U., 1957-58, Purdue U., 1958-59. V.p. Weihe Engrs. Inc., Carmel, Ind., 1960-70; pvt. practice golf course architecture Carmel, 1970-83, St. Louis, 1983—. Mem. Am. Soc. Golf Course Architects, Fox Run Golf Club, Lake Forest Golf and Country Club, Wolf Run Golf Club. Republican. Lutheran. Home: 2440 Clayborn Dr Chesterfield MO 63017-7874 Office: 15444 Clayton Rd Ste 324 Ballwin MO 63011-3166

KERN, GILBERT RICHARD, history educator; b. Detroit, Dec. 5, 1932; s. Gilbert Richard K. and Gertrude O. (Dykstra) Smith; m. Marilyn Ruth Rayle, June 26, 1955 (div. Aug. 1981); children: Christopher, Kathleen, Kevin, Carolyn; m. Sharon Jo Hershey, Dec. 23, 1982. AB, Findlay (Ohio) Coll., 1954; BD, Winebrenner Theol. Sem., Findlay, 1958; MA, U. Chgo., 1960, PhD, 1968. Prof. Winebrenner Theol. Sem., Findlay, 1960-70, pres., 1963-70; prof. religion Findlay Coll., 1970-75, prof history, 1975—. Author: John Winebrenner-19th Century Reformer, 1974, Findlay College: The First Hundred Years, 1984 (award 1986); editor: A View From the Back Bench, 1986; author, editor: A History of the Ohio Conference, 1986. Bd. mem. Ohio Humanities Coun., Columbus, 1985-91, Hancock County Mus. Assn., Findlay, 1988—. Recipient Disting. Alumnus awards Winebrenner Theol. Sem., Findlay, 1981, Findlay Coll., 1989. Mem. Findlay Symposium (pres. 1988-89), Beacon Club of Findlay (pres. 1990—), Rotary (Findlay sec. 1990-92), Am. Ethical Union (leader). Home: 315 W Lincoln St Findlay OH 45840-3139 Office: U Findlay 1000 N Main St Findlay OH 45840-3653

KERN, PATRICIA JOAN, media specialist; b. Ft. Wayne, Ind., Dec. 1, 1933; d. Wesley Emery and Ruth Mae (Adams) Pritchett; m. Kenneth Charles Kern, Mar. 9, 1951; children: Ralph, Theresa, Catherine Holman, Norman. BFA, Ft. Wayne Art Inst., 1976; BA, Indiana U., Ft. Wayne, 1977; MS Ed., St. Francis Coll., Ft. Wayne, 1981, Indiana U., Ft. Wayne, 1983. Art instr. Ft. Wayne Art Inst., 1975-77; art tchr. South Side High Sch., Ft. Wayne, 1978-81; art history instr. Ind. U., Ft. Wayne, 1979-83; art tchr. k-6 Shambaugh Elem., Ft. Wayne, 1981-82; media tchr. Jefferson Mid. Sch., Ft. Wayne, 1982—; assoc. faculty Fine Arts and Women's Studies Indiana U., 1988—. Painter and sculptor Portrait of Lora, 1973 (Best of Show award 1973), Figure Study, 1973 (1st Tri-Kappa 1973), Mandala, 1975 (1st Tri-Kappa 1975), Portrait of Monica, 1979; work included in computer art exhbn., Ind. U., 1992. Active Ft. Wayne Women's Bur., 1977—. Named Beatty scholar Delta Kappa Gamma, Indpls., 1988. Mem. NEA, Ind. State Tchrs. Assn., Assn. Ind. Media Educators, Ft. Wayne Edn. Assn., Delta Kappa Gamma (2nd v.p. 1988-92). Office: Jefferson Mid Sch 5303 Wheelock Rd Fort Wayne IN 46835-9706

KERN, RON LEE, golf course architect, photographer; b. Kendalville, Ind., Mar. 2, 1958; s. Gary Lee and Frances Geraldine (Tipp) K.; m. Julie Marie Satchwill, July 12, 1980. BSCE, Purdue U., 1980. Hydraulics engr. Ind. Dept. Hwys., Indpls., 1980-86; golf course arch. Gary Kern, Golf Course Arch., Carmel, Ind., 1986-93; golf course arch., owner Ron Kern, Golf Course Arch., Carmel, Ind., 1993—; founder, dir. Invision Alliance of Photog. Artists, 1994—. Mem. Am. Soc. Golf Course Archs., John Purdue Club, Fox Run Golf Club, Twin Lakes Golf Club. Republican.

KERN, STEPHEN ROGER, history educator; b. L.A., Jan. 28, 1943; s. Seymour and Jessie (Kraus) K.; m. Mary Kay Damer, Jan. 3, 1983; children: Justin, Simone. BA, U. Calif., Berkeley, 1964; MA, Columbia U., 1965, PhD, 1970. Asst. prof. history No. Ill. U., DeKalb, 1970-77, assoc. prof., 1977-84, prof., 1984-88, disting. rsch. prof., 1988—; hon. rsch. fellow Harvard U., Cambridge, Mass., 1977-78. Author: Anatomy and Destiny: A Cultural History of the Human Body, 1975, The Culture of Time and Space 1880-1918, 1983, The Culture of Love: Victorians to Moderns, 1992, Eyes of Love: The Gaze in English and French Culture 1840-1900, 1996. Home: 39w793 Reindeer Trl Saint Charles IL 60175-6982 Office: No Ill U Dept History De Kalb IL 60115

KERNER, JOSEPH FRANK, JR., management consultant, educator; b. Cleve., Dec. 29, 1938; s. Joseph Frank Sr. and Magarat Ann (Majoris) K.; m. Marilyn Joy Long, June 14, 1964; children: Joseph, Mark, Michael, Erin. BA, Miami U., Oxford, Ohio, 1961; postgrad., Case Western Res. U., 1963-68. Dir. bus. tech. Marion (Ohio) Tech. Coll., 1969-75; mgr. benefits Cen. Net Bank, Cleve., 1975-78; mgr. compensation L.B. Foster, Pitts., 1978-80; mgr. compensation and benefits Rubbermaid, Wooster, Ohio, 1980-82; dir. compensation and benefits ChemLawn, Columbus, Ohio, 1982-84; v.p. First Nat. Bank of Commerce, New Orleans, 1984-85; instr. Bliss Coll., Columbus, 1985-88; regional v.p. Primerica Fin. Svcs., Columbus, 1985-95; pres. JFK Consultancy & Kerner Connection, Columbus, 1988—; mktg. dir. WMA Securities, 1995—; v.p. mktg., environ. energy Alt. Fuel, 1995—; mktg. advisor TAASI, 1995—; adj. instr. Coll. Fin. Planning, 1988-89; bd. dirs. Environ. Energy, Inc. Author: National Underwriter: Agent Exposes Himself, 1987, Pension Actuary: My Vision, 1994. Bd. dirs. Environ. Energy, Inc. Mem. Am. Soc. Pension Actuaries (bd. dirs. 1966-69, edn. coord. 1990—, joint bd. enrolled actuary exam. rev. com., editor Pension Actuary 1994, govtl. affairs com. 1993—), Kiwanis (pres.), Data Processing Mgmt. Assn. (faculty student chpt. of yr. 1970), Worthington C. of C. (mem. small bus. assistance com.). Republican. Lutheran. Home: 247 Windmere Pl Westerville OH 43082

KERNS, STEVE, geneticist. Pres. Universal Pig Genes, Eldora, Iowa. Office: Universal Pig Genes 30355 260th St Eldora IA 50627*

KERPPOLA, TOM KLAUS WILLIAM, research scientist, educator; b. Helsinki, Finland, Oct. 21, 1962; came to U.S., 1981; s. Klaus William Mikael Kerppola and Mariitta Anna Aulikki (Meurman) Tuomala; m. Raili Emilia Kulmala, Sept. 19, 1982; 1 child, Marianna Eeva Aulikki. BS in Biochemistry and Biophysics, Wash. State U., 1985, BS in Biology, 1985, MS in Biochemistry and Biophysics, 1985; PhD of Biochemistry, U. Calif., Berkeley, 1989. Undergrad. rsch. asst., grad. rsch. asst. Wash. State U., Pullman, 1982-85; grad. rsch. asst., postdoctoral fellow U. Calif., Berkeley, 1985-90; postdoctoral fellow Roche Inst. Molecular Biology, Nutley, N.J., 1990-92; rsch. fellow Roche Inst. Molecular Biology, Nutley, 1992-94; asst. investigator Howard Hughes Med. Inst., 1994—; asst. prof. dept. biol. chemistry U. Mich., 1994—. Contbr. articles to profl. jours. Deacon First Congl. Ch., Montclair, N.J., 1991-94. Mem. Phi Beta Kappa, Phi Kappa Phi. Lutheran. Office: Howard Hughes Med Inst U Mich Med Sch 4570 MSRB II 1150 W Med Ctr Dr Ann Arbor MI 48109

KERR, DAVID MILLS, state legislator; b. Pratt, Kans., May 4, 1945; s. Fred H. and Eleanor Mills (Barrett) K.; m. Mary Patricia O'Rourke, Aug. 24, 1979; children: Ryan, Daniel. BA, Kans. State U., 1968; MBA, U. Kans., 1970. Auditor Trans World Airlines, Kansas City, Mo., 1970-72, mgr. fin., 1972-76; pres. Agronomics Internat., Hutchinson, Kans., 1976-84; mem. Kans. State Senate, Topeka, 1984—, chmn. edn. com., 1992, chmn. ways and means com., 1995; bd. dirs. Kans. Tech. Enterprises Corp.; chmn. Senate econ. devel. com., 1988, edn. com., 1993, Senate ways and means com., 1995; chmn. com. on econ. devel. Nat. Conf. State Legislatures; mem. Gov.'s Criminal Justice Coordinating Coun., 1988. Mem. Advanced Tech. Commn., Topeka, 1985; chmn. Task Force on Capitol Markets and Tax, Topeka, 1986; bd. dirs. Hutchinson Hosp. Corp., 1993. Named Kans. Exporter of Yr., Internat. Trade Inst., 1981. Mem. Kans. C. of C. (bd. dirs. 1983-86). Republican. Presbyterian. Home: 72 Willowbrook St Hutchinson KS 67502-8948 Office: PO Box 2620 Hutchinson KS 67504-2620 Office: State Senate State Capital Topeka KS 66612

KERR, DIANNE LYNNE, health educator; b. Canonsburg, Pa., June 3, 1955; d. James Robert Jr. and Victoria Kathleen (Falconi) Berglund. BS, Slippery Rock (Pa.) State Coll, 1976; MEd, Bowling Green (Ohio) State U., 1981; MA, Ohio State U., 1987, PhD, 1992. Cert. health edn. specialist. Tchr. Villa Maria Acad., Erie, Pa., 1977-79; teaching asst. Bowling Green State U., 1980-81; instr., asst. prof. Notre Dame Coll. Ohio, S. Euclid, 1981-85; teaching asst. Ohio State U., Columbus, 1985-87; dir. AIDS edn. project Am. Sch. Health Assn., Kent, Ohio, 1987-90; asst. prof. health edn. Kent State U., 1990—; cons. Aspen Sys. Corp., Rockville, Md., 1991—. Author: (with others) School-Based HIV Prevention, 1991; contbr. articles to profl. jours. Expert Rev. panelist Ctrs. for Disease Control, Atlanta, 1988, 90, U.S. Dept. of Edn., Washington, 1990; co-chair gen. pub. edn. HIV Cmty. Planning Group, Akron, Ohio, 1994—. Recipient Ohio AIDS Svc. award Ohio Dept. Health, 1992; grantee Met Life Found., 1990, U.S. Dept. of Edn., 1990. Mem. Am. found. AIDS Rsch. (edn. adv. com. 1990—, grantee 1989), Am. Sch. Health Assn., Am. Coll. Pers. Assn., Sex Info. and Edn. Coun. U.S., Assn. Advancement Health Edn. Home: 186 Pinehurst Rd Munroe Falls OH 44262 Office: Kent State U PO Box 5190 316 White Hall Kent OH 44242

KERR, GARY ENRICO, lawyer, educator; b. Kewanee, Ill., Feb. 8, 1948; s. Roy Harrison and Marietta (Dani) K.; m. Eileen Elizabeth Straeter, Aug. 18, 1978; 1 child, Victoria Elizabeth. BA, No. Ill. U., 1970; JD, Northwestern U., Chgo., 1973. Bar: Ill. 1974, U.S. Dist. Ct. (cen. dist.) Ill. 1982, U.S. Ct. Appeals (7th cir.) 1983, U.S. Supreme Ct. 1983. Adminstrv. asst. Office Supt. Pub. Instrn. State Ill., Chgo., Springfield, 1971-74; asst. legal advisor Ill. State Bd. Edn., Springfield, 1974-78; spl. counsel Ill. State Comptroller, Springfield, 1978-79; pvt. practice Springfield, 1979—; adj. faculty Sangamon State U., Springfield, Ill., 1994; pres., dir. counsel Kerr Products, INc., Kewanee, Ill., 1980—; instr. paralegal program Robert Morris Coll., Springfield, 1992. atty. South County Democrats, Sangamon County, Ill. Fellow Ednl. Policy program Inst. Ednl. Leadership, George Washington U., 1976-77. Mem. ABA, Ill. State Bar Assn. (chmn. sch. law sect. coun. 1983-84), Sangamon County Bar Assn. Office: Gary Kerr Ltd 1020 S 7th St Springfield IL 62703-2417

KERR, WAYNE NELSON, data processing professional; b. Bristol, Pa., Nov. 20, 1961; s. Robert Fleming and Doris (Frailey) K.; m. Catherine N. Hack, Oct. 20, 1990. AAS in Computer Programming, Purdue U., 1983, BS in Info. Systems/Programming, 1985. Computer programmer, analyst Automated Concepts, Inc., Chgo., 1985-88, Computer Aid, Inc., Chgo., 1988-89; database adminstr. Brandenburg Indsl. Svc. Co., Chgo., 1989-91; cons. Kerr Cons., Chgo., 1991, 93—; sr. cons. Sybase, Inc., Chgo., 1992-93; pres. Kerr Profl. Svcs., Inc., Chgo., 1993—. Home and Office: 1312 Prestwick Ln Itasca IL 60143-1974

KERREY, BOB (J. ROBERT KERREY), senator; b. Lincoln, Nebr., Aug. 27, 1943; s. James and Elinor K.; children: Benjamin, Lindsey. B.S. in Pharmacy, U. Nebr., 1965. Owner, founder, developer outlets in Omaha and Lincoln Grandmother's Restaurants, Omaha, 1972-75; owner, founder fitness enterprises Prairie Life Ctr., Lincoln and Omaha, Nebr.; gov. State of Nebr., Lincoln, 1983-87; ptnr. Printon, Kane & Co., Lincoln, 1987-89; U.S. Senator from Nebraska, 1989—; mem. Agrl., Nutrition & Forestry Com.; ranking minority mem. Appropriations subcom. on Treasury, Postal Svc. & Gen. Govt., select com. on Intelligence. Bd. dirs. Lincoln Ctr. Assn.; bd. dirs. Nebr. Easter Seal Soc. Served USN, 1966-69, Vietnam. Decorated medal of Honor; decorated Bronze Star, Purple Heart. Mem. Am. Legion, VFW, DAV, Lincoln C. of C.; mem Phi Gamma Delta. Congregationalist. Lodges: Sertoma; Lions. Office: US Senate 303 Senate Hart Bldg Washington DC 20510*

KERRIGAN, JOHN E., academic administrator. Chancellor U. Wis., Oshkosh. Office: U Wis Office of Chancellor 800 Algoma Blvd Oshkosh WI 54901-3551

KERRIGAN, WALTER W., II, financial planner; b. Pitts., May 6, 1953; s. Walter W. and Doris E. (Ward) K.; m. Susan F. Jagniszak, Apr. 8, 1978; children: Kelly F., Taylor M. BA, U. Pitts., 1978. Cert. fin. planner. Chief exec. officer Inst. Fin. Planning, Novi, Mich., 1981—. Mem. Internat. Assn. Fin. Planners (bd. dirs. S.E. Mich. chpt. 1984-86, co-founder, pres., chmn. bd. dirs. Metro Detroit Soc. chpt. 1985-86), Nat. Assn. Personal Fin. Advisors, Inst. Cert. Fin. Planners. Republican. Presbyterian. Office: Inst Fin Planning Inc 39570 Westminster Circle Novi MI 48375-3719

KERSKA, STEVE J., mechanical engineer; b. La Crosse, Wis., Aug. 19, 1953. AD in Mech. Engring., Western Tech. Inst., La Crosse, 1977. Design draftsman FMC, Cedar Rapids, Iowa, 1977-82; project engr. Iowa Precision Industries, Cedar Rapids, 1984—. Lutheran. Home: 410 Rockvalley Ln NW Cedar Rapids IA 52405-3162 Office: Iowa Precision Industries Cedar Rapids IA 52404-4814

KERWIN, KENNETH HILLS, II, technology and management consultant, electronic systems and electro-optics specialist; b. San Francisco, Apr. 11, 1939; s. Kenneth H. and Helen E. (Schraubstädter) K.; m. Norma Larsen, Nov. 3, 1974. B in Physics, Pomona Coll., 1961; postgrad., Stanford U., 1968-70. Process engr. Data Disc, Inc., Palo Alto, Calif., 1964-67; rsch. engr. Stanford Rsch. Inst., Menlo Park, Calif., 1967-75; dir. Electronics Facility U. Calif., Santa Cruz, 1975-78, lectr. in physics, 1976-78; mgr. of engring. Balzers Corp., Hudson, N.H., 1978-81; v.p. tech. Ferrofluidics Corp., Nashua, N.H., 1981-86; engring. mgr. Thermal Tech., Inc., Concord, N.H., Santa Rosa, Calif., 1987-89; propr. Kerwin & Assocs., Chesterland, Ohio, 1961—; sr. technologist Cleve. Crystals, Inc., Cleve., 1994—; co-founder Data Disc, Inc., 1959-60, 64-67; founding dir. Diskos Electronics Corp., Mountain View, Calif., 1968-72, Quantum Electro-Optical Devel. Corp., San Jose, Calif., 1989-91, Modular Process Tech. Corp., Santa Clara, Calif., 1991-92. Inventor TV instant replay, thin-film memory disc, fully-automated growth of semicondr. and optical crystals, (with others) instruments for vision rsch./med. practice, specialties in single-crystal and thin-film materials processing and electronic/electro-optical systems. 1st lt. S.C., U.S. Army 1961-64. Republican. Christian. Office: Cleve Crystals Inc 676 Alpha Dr Cleveland OH 44143-2123

KERZMAN, JAMES A., state legislator; m. Jill; 10 children. Student, Dickinson State U., N.D. State Sch. Sci. Committeeman Agr. Stabilization and Conservation Svc.; mem. N.D. Ho. of Reps., 1991—, mem. human svc. com.; mem. agr. com.; farmer, rancher; mem. Rural Electric Coop. Recipient Children's Caucus award, Soil Conservation award. Mem. KC. Home: RR 3 Box 36 Mott ND 58646-9167*

KESSEL, LLOYD R., acute care nursing director, educator; b. Dickinson, N.D., Oct. 24, 1952; s. Wendell Kasper and Tomasita (Martinez) Kessel; m. Kathleen Kessel, Nov. 24, 1988; children: Taylor Steven, Danielle Rose. BSN, Mary Coll., Bismarck, N.D., 1975; MSN, U. of Mary, Bismarck, 1989. Dir. nursing svcs. Richardton (N.D.) Community Hosp.; sr. staff nurse oper. rm. Whittaker Life Scis., Khamis Mushayt, Saudi Arabia; health care officer S.W. Milti-County Correction Ctr., Dickinson, N.D.; nursing instr. Dickinson State U.; oper. rm. nurse mgr. St. Joseph's Hosp. Poet; contbr. articles to profl. jours. Mem. ANA, Assn. Operating Room Nurses, N.D. Psychiatric Nursing Edn. Coun., S.W. Mental Health Assn., N.D. Nursing Assn. (ethics com., psychiatric/mental health nursing coun.), Sigma Theta Tau. Home: 1041 Dell Ave Dickinson ND 58601-4135

KESTENBAUM, LAWRENCE, political science educator; b. Chgo., Sept. 13, 1955; s. Justin Louis and Maryhelen (Dietrich) K.; m. M. Janice Gutfreund, Nov. 17, 1990. BA in Econs., Mich. State U., 1979; JD, Wayne State U., 1982; postgrad., Cornell U., 1988-90. Bar: Mich. Atty., cons. East Lansing, Mich., 1983-88, Ithaca, N.Y., 1988-90, Ann Arbor, Mich., 1990—; commrs. Ingham County, Mason, Mich., 1983-88; program assoc. Mich. Citizen's Lobby, Lansing, 1983-85; computer lab. dir. Mich. State U., East Lansing, 1992-95, acad. specialist polit. sci. dept., 1995—; adj. faculty Ea. Mich. U., Ypsilanti, 1991—. Contbg. author: At the Campus Gate, 1976; contbr. articles to profl. jours. Mem. planning commn. City of E. Lansing, 1977-79; replacement del. Dem. Nat. Mid-term Conv., 1978; county commr. Ingham County, Mason, Mich., 1983-88; mem. hist. dist. commn., City of Ann Arbor, 1992—; bd. dirs. Mich. State U. Student Housing Corp., East Lansing, 1978-79, Ann Arbor Hist. Found., 1992—, Arbornet, Inc., Ann Arbor, 1993-95; mem. univ. planning com., Wayne State U., Detroit, 1980-82; vice-chmn. Ann Arbor Dem. Party, 1994—; mem. Temple Beth Emeth. Recipient Arthur F. Lederle scholarship Wayne State U. Law Sch., Detroit, 1979. Mem. State Bar of Mich., Nat. Trust for Historic Preservation. Democrat. Jewish. Home: 108 Kenwood Ave Ann Arbor MI 48103 Office: Mich State U Polit Sci Dept 303 S Kedzie Hall East Lansing MI 48824

KETCHUM, IRENE FRANCES, library trustee; b. Hammond, Ind., Jan. 19, 1914; d. Peter H. and Theresa C. (Weis) Young; m. Alden W. Ketchum, Sept. 17, 1936 (dec. 1973); 1 child, William H. Grad. high sch., Hammond, 1932. Cert. mcpl. clk. Mng. editor Herald Newspapers, Gary, Ind., 1950-55; clk.-treas. Town of Highland, Ind., 1956-79; trustee, bd. sec. Lake County Pub. Libr., Merrillville, Ind., 1980-95; past trustee, 1995—, pres., 1995. kActive Ind. State Libr. Adv. Coun., Indpls., 1988-90; treas. Highland Cmty. Events Coun., 1975—; pres. Highland Women's Dem. Club, 1978; auditor Highland Dem. Club, 1980—; mem. Friends of Ind. Librs., Friends of Lake County Pub. Libr., Lake County Pub. Libr. Found. Mem. Internat. Inst. Mcpl. Clks., Ind. League Mcpl. Clks. and Treas. (assoc., treas., sec., v.p., pres. 1967-68), Altrusa Internat. of Calumet Area, Inc., Girl Scouts USA (life). Roman Catholic.

KETCHUM, SALLY DEBOLT, writer; b. Detroit, June 19, 1937; d. G. Frederick and Esther B. (Rahn) DeBolt; m. Thaddeus K. Kethum, June 27, 1959; children: Karl Richard, Blake Elizabeth, David Alexander. BA, U. Mich., 1959; postgrad., Wayne State U., 1958-70, Mich. State U., 1980, Ctrl. Mich. U., 1980. Tchr. Fraser (Mich.) H.S., 1950-60, Albion (Mich.) Coll., 1960-64, Yeshivah Beth Yehudah, Oak Park, Mich., 1978; tchr., instr. Elk Rapids (Mich.) H.S., 1979-94; founder, dir., Acad. Festival, 1980-94. Author: Kid Lit!, Moon Wants, Super Student/Happy Kid, 1995; and artlcles. Nominated Nat. Tchr. of Yr., Dow Jones News Group, 1980, Deaf Woman of Yr., Quota Club, 1995. Mem. AAUW (book chmn.), Alpha Xi Delta. Lutheran. Home: 9740 Pine Needle Ln Williamsburg MI 49690

KETNER, JOSEPH DALE, museum director, art historian; b. Anderson, Ind., Oct. 30, 1955; m. Patricia Ketner; 2 children. BA, Ind. U., 1977, MA, 1980. Curator, registrar Ft. Wayne (Ind.) Mus. Art, 1979-82; curator Washington U. Gallery of Art, St. Louis, 1982-89, acting dir., 1984-86, 88-89, dir., 1989—, adj. lectr. in art history, 1995—. Author: Robert S. Duncanson (1921-1972), 1993, A Gallery of Modern Art, 1994; author, curator (exbhn. catalogs) The Beautiful, The Sublime and the Picturesque, 1984, Carl F. Wimar, 1991. Chmn. Mayor's Visual Arts Com., Ft. Wayne, 1982. Office: Washington U Gallery Art 1 Brookings Dr Saint Louis MO 63130-4862

KETT, KATHLEEN MARIE, nurse midwife, maternal nurse, consultant; b. Wisconsin Rapids, Wis., Mar. 29, 1951; d. Alex Frank and Dorothy Lucille (Gaulke) Macha; m. Jeffrey Allen Kett, Oct. 2, 1971; children: Andrew, JoAnne. BSN, U. Wis., Milw., 1972, MSN, 1988; postgrad., Marquette U., 1994-95. Cert. nurse midwife. Staff nurse Sheboygan (Wis.) Meml. Hosp., 1972-74, Columbia Hosp., Milw., 1974-76, St. Mary's Hosp., Milw., 1976-78; staff nurse Columbia Hosp., Milw., 1978-81, head nurse mgr., 1981-84; prenatal support nurse Wis. Ind. Physician Assn., Milw., 1988-89; physiologic diagnostic svcs. nurse adminstr. TOKOS Med. Corp., Milw., 1989-92, account rep., insvc. educator, 1991-92; sales specialist, insvc. educator Healthdyne Perinatal Svcs., Milw., 1992-93, rsch. cons., educator, 1993-95; prenatal care coordination home vis. nurse Sinai Samaritan Med. Ctr., 1993-95; pvt. practice as nurse midwife; nurse midwife pvt. practice, Milw., 1995—; cons. Milw. Based Home Care Agy., 1984-88. Recipient State Nurse traineeship State of Wis., Milw., 1986, Sigma Theta Tau Eta Nu Scholarship, 1994. Mem. NAACOG, Wis. Assn. for Perinatal Care (treas. 1988-92), U. Wis.-Milw. Alumni Assn. (pres., bd. dirs. 1990-92). Lutheran. Home: 1951 W Rochelle Ave Milwaukee WI 53209-2854

KETTENSTOCK, RICHARD EDWARD, computer software and consulting company owner; b. Pontiac, Mich., Feb. 4, 1967; s. Edward Joseph and Judith Jane (Porter) K. BS in Computer Sci., U. Mich., 1990. Cons. Ernst & Young, Cleve., 1990-92; programmer MEDSTAT, Ann Arbor, Mich., 1993; sr. programmer, cons. Kettenstock Computer Contract Cons., Ann Arbor, 1993—. Adult leader Cub Scout Pack 245, Walled Lake, Mich., 1993—. Mem. IEEE. Office: Kettenstock Computer Contract Cons 5890 Plum Hollow #10 Ypsilanti MI 48197-8802

KETTER, JAMES PATRICK, accountant; b. St. Joseph, Mo., May 20, 1956; s. Melvin P. and Mildred (Gawatz) K.; m. Sharon E. Krautmann, Dec. 31, 1982; children: Patrick Jerome, Daniel Marcel, Benjamin Francis. BSBA in Finance & Acctg. magna cum laude, Marquette U., 1978. CPA, Mo., Kans. Acct., audit mgr. Melvin Ketter, P.C., St. Joseph, 1976-84, tax specialist controlled foreign corps., 1979-84, mcpl. contract arbitrator, 1982-84; audit mgr. Coopers & Lybrand, Kansas City, Mo., 1985-86; mgr. accting. and auditing Mayer, Hoffman & McCann, Kansas City, Mo., 1986-89; mgr. Thomas King & Co., Kansas City, 1989-92; CEO JK Consulting Group, Prairie Village, Kans., 1992—; shareholder, ptnr. in charge of acctg. and auditing Douglas C. Miller & Co., Westwood, Kans., 1994—. Mem. friends of Art, Kansas City, 1986, Friends of Symphony, Kansas City, 1986; account exec. United Way, 1985-87; specialist not-for-profit orgns., 1988—; mem. Friends of the Zoo, 1987, ad hoc com. on recycling City of Prairie Village, 1989—; bd dirs., sec. Corinth Hills Homes Assn., 1989-92; mem. strategic planning subcom. for city svcs., 1991—; cantor Curé of Ars Parish, 1989—, coord. of eucharistic mins., cub master Cureé of Ars Cub Scout Pack; chair fin. mgmt. Vol. Leadership Coun. of the Ctr. for Mgmt. Assist., 1993—, cons., instr.; dir., fin. com. chmn. Children's Mercy Cancer Ctr., 1991—, treas. 1993—; adv. coun. St. Joseph Health Ctr., 1992—. Mem. Am. Inst. CPA's, Mo. Soc. CPA's (tax com. Kansas City chptr.), Kansas Soc. CPA's, Inst. Bus. Appraisers, Beta Gamma Sigma, Alpha Sigma Nu. Roman Catholic. Lodge KC. Home: 5400 W 80th Shawnee Mission KS 66208-4911 Office: Ste 204 1901 W 47th Pl Westwood KS 66205

KETTER, KIM A., investment company executive; b. Carbondale, Ill., Mar. 5, 1954. BA, Oklahoma City U., 1985. V.p. A.G. Edwards & Sons Inc., Carbondale, 1981—. Mem. Rotary. Republican. Baptist. Office: AG Edwards & Sons Inc PO Box 2407 206 W College Carbondale IL 62901

KETTLE, SALLY ANNE, consulting company executive, educator; b. Omaha, Feb. 2, 1938; d. Elaine Josephine (Winston) Smiley; m. William Frederick Kettle, July 20, 1968 (div. 1973); children: Christopher, Winston. BEd, U. Nebr., 1960, postgrad. Cert. tchr., S.C., Nebr. Tchr. Omaha Pub. Schs., Omaha, 1966-72; owner, mgr. The Rick Rack, Ltd., Lakewood, Colo., 1974-75; coord. merchandising communications 3M, St. Paul, 1978-80, sr. coord. internat. corp. comm., 1981-83; corp. dir. communications Intran Corp., St. Paul, 1984; pres. Sally Kettle & Co., Bloomington, Minn., 1985—; mem. cmty. faculty Met. State U., Mpls., 1983-90, St. Olaf Coll., Northfield, Minn., 1992—; mem. adj. faculty U. Minn. Sch. Journalism and Mass Comm., Mpls., St. Thomas U., 1994-95. TV hostess City of Bloomington Cable TV, 1984-86. Co-founder Women's Resource Ctr., bd. dirs., mem. adv. bd., 1978-88; chair 13th Precinct, Bloomington, 1978-83; bd. dirs. 41st Sen. Dist., Bloomington, 1982-83; cable TV commr. Bloomington City Coun., 1984-85; pub. rels. com. U.S. Olympic Festival, 1989-90; bd. dirs. Minn. Prayer Breakfast Bd., 1984—; mem. Better Bus. Bur.; founder Ad Rev. Coun.; v.p. Christian Mgmt. Assn., Minn.; internat. com. bd. Carlson Grad. Sch. Mgmt., U. Minn.; mem. state ctrl. com. and platform commn. DFL, 1988-90; bd. dirs. Fellowship of Christian Athletes, 1988-89; pub. rels. com. '96 Billy Graham Minn. Crusade, 1996; bd. commrs. Shoreland Zoning Commn. Dakota County, Minn., 1996—. Named one of Outstanding Young Women of Am., 1965. Mem. Am. Advt. Fedn. (conf. com. 1985-87, pub. svc. com. 1986-88), Pub. Rels. Soc. Am., Advt. Fedn. Minn. (bd. dirs. 1982-86), Women's Econ. Roundtable, Internat. Platform Assn., Nat. Grad.

Women's Honor Soc., Minn. Press Club (co-chair newsmaker com., bd. dirs. 1989-92), Phi Delta Gamma, Kappa Alpha Theta. Home: 13390 Gunflint Path Apple Valley MN 55124-7376

KETTLER, DANIEL JAMES, manufacturing engineer; b. Clinton, Iowa, Sept. 26, 1967. BS in Mfg. Engr., Bradley U., 1990. Engr. John Deere, Horicon, Wis., 1990—. Patentee in field. Mem. Old Hickory Country Club. Office: John Deere Horicon Works PE2E 400 N Vine St Horicon WI 53032-1062

KETTLESON, DAVID NOEL, retired orthopaedic surgeon, timber manager; b. St. Paul, Dec. 20, 1938; s. John Benton and Dorothy S. (Elkins) K.; m. Karen Nordstrom, Aug. 25, 1961; children: Maria, Daniel, Laura. BA, U. Minn., 1960, BS, MD, 1964. Diplomate Am. Bd. Orthopaedic Surgery. Intern St. Mary's Hosp., Duluth, Minn., 1964-65; resident in othopaedic surgery U. Minn. Hosp., Mpls., 1965-69; v.p., sec., treas. Orthopaedic Surgery, Inc., Omaha, 1971-92; pres. Nebr. Spine Surgeons, Omaha, 1992-94; ret., 1994; owner Eagleview Farms, Crosslake, Minn., 1994—; chmn. dept. orthopaedics Immanuel Med. Ctr., Omaha, 1978-82. Served to maj. USAF, 1969-71. Fellow N.Am. Spine Soc.; mem. AMA, Mid Cen. States Orthopaedic Soc. (sec. 1974-85), Scoliosis Rsch. Soc. Republican. Office: Eagleview Farms PO Box 40 Crosslake MN 56442-0040

KEUER, JEAN ELEANORE, physical therapist; b. Owen, Wis., Feb. 22, 1946; d. Kenneth Lee and Dorothy Elizabeth (Usack) Truax; m. Brian Stuner, July 1, 1967 (div. Jan 1981); m. James Robert Keuer, June 5, 1982; 1 child, Sarah Beth. BS, U. Wis., 1968. Cert. in phys. therapy. Phys. therapist Waukesha (Wis.) Meml. Hosp., 1968-69, Elmbrook Meml. Hosp., Brookfield, Wis., 1969-71, Westmoreland Manor, Waukesha, Wis., 1971-72; phys. therapist, supr. Meml. Hosp. of Taylor Co., Medford, Wis., 1973-81; phys. therapist Northwoods Rehab. Assn., Woodruff, Wis., 1981-82; phys. therapist, supr. Sacred Heart-St. Mary's Hosp., Rhinelander, Wis., 1982-85; phys. therapist, owner Phys. Therapy Ctr. of Rhinelander, 1985—. Mem. Am. Phys. Therapy Assn. Methodist. Home: 8422 Pinemere Ln Minocqua WI 54548 Office: Phys Therapy Ctr of Rhinelander 1831 N Stevens Rhinelander WI 54501

KEWNEY, RHONDA KATHRYN, mental health service professional; b. Pittsburg, Calif., Dec. 9, 1948; d. Bob Farrell and Joan Gerada (Fischer) Chandler; m. Robert Kewney, Apr. 26, 1975; children: Adrianne, Nicle, Alex. BA in Psychology, Quincy Coll., 1971; MSW, U. Mo., 1990. Lic. clin. social worker, Ill. Rehab. supr., day program supr., coord. quality assurance Adams County Mental Health Ctr., Quincy, Ill., 1971-90; pvt. therapist Quincy, 1990-94; coord. clin. svcs. Adams County Mental Health Ctr., Quincy, 1994—; clin. instr. behavioral medicine So. Ill. Sch. Medicine, 1990—. Mem. Soc. Tchrs. of Family Medicine. Democrat. Roman Catholic. Home: 20 Westview Dr Quincy IL 62301 Office: Transitions 4409 Maine St Quincy IL 62301

KEY, MARCELLA ANN, computer information specialist; b. St. Louis, Nov. 26, 1947; d. Wallace Albert and Dorothy (Croskery) F.; m. Philip Odell, Nov. 18, 1967; children: Heather Colleen, Philip Sean. BA in English magna cum laude, U. Mo., St. Louis, 1969. Info. operator Southwestern Bell Tel., St. Louis, 1965-69; army procurement intern U.S. Army Mobility Equipment Command, St. Louis, 1969-70; army contract price analyst U.S. Army Weapons Command, Rock Island, Ill., 1970-72; army data processing intern U.S. Army Mgmt. Engring. Tng. Activity, Rock Island; computer programmer U.S. Army Logistics Mgmt. System Activity, St. Louis, 1973-77; computer specialist USRCPAC, 1977, U.S. Army Logistics Mgmt. System Activity, St. Louis, 1977-80; computer specialist, cons., instr. U.S. Army Mgmt. Engring. Coll., Rock Island, 1980-88; data base adminstr. U.S. Army Aviation Troop Command, St. Louis, 1988-91; project mgr. U.S. Army Aviation Systems Command, St. Louis, 1991—; pres., v.p., sec., Army Data Base Users' Group, Rock Island, 1982-85. Co-Author: Orgn. Study of the Automation, 1983, An Info. Mgmt. Evaluation, 1987. Guardian Treas. Jobs Daughters Bethel #5, 1986-88; dir. Epochs Bethel #2, Hazelwood, Mo., 1989-93, guardian sec., 1993—; Troop com. mem. Boy Scouts Am., St. Charles, 1992—. Mem. Army Materiel Command Data Base Users Group. Ind. Dutch Reformed. Home: 4251 Greensboro Dr Saint Charles MO 63304-1612 Office: US Aviation Troop Command 4300 Goodfellow Blvd Saint Louis MO 63120-1703

KEYE, WILLIAM RICHARD, JR., physician, educator; b. Mineola, N.Y., Oct. 31, 1943; s. William Richard and Jane Elizabeth (Snell) K.; m. Suzanne Marie Edstrom, Aug. 13, 1965; children: Deborah Sue, Jeffrey Scott. BA, U. Minn., 1965, BS, 1969, MD, 1969. Diplomate Am. Bd. Ob-Gyn, Bd. Reproductive Endocrinology. Intern, U. Minn. Mpls., 1969-70, resident, 1970-72; resident U. Mich., 1972-73, U. Calif., San Francisco, 1973-77; physician Caylor-Nickel Clinic, Bluffton, Ind., 1977-78; asst. prof. U. Utah, Salt Lake City, 1979-84, assoc. prof., 1984-90; dir. divsn. reproductive endocrinology & infertility William Beaumont Hosp., Royal Oak, Mich., 1990—; clin. assoc. prof. U. Mich., 1992—. Editor: Laser Surgery in Obstetrics and Gynceology, 1984, 2nd edit., 1990, PMS, 1988, Infertility: Diagnosis and Treatment, 1995. Contbr. articles to profl. jours. Med. advisor Resolve of Utah, Salt Lake City, 1979-90. Maj. USAF, 1974-76. Fellow Am. Coll. Ob-Gyn, Am. Soc. Reproductive Medicine (dir. 1994—), Soc. Reproductive Endocrinology; mem. Gynecol. Laser Soc., Soc. Reproductive Surgeons (treas. 1990-91, sec. 1991-92, v.p. 1992-93, pres. 1993-94).

KEYES, JAMES HENRY, manufacturing company executive; b. LaCrosse, Wis., Sept. 2, 1940; s. Donald M. and Mary M. (Nodolf) K.; m. Judith Ann Carney, Nov. 21, 1964; children: James Patrick, Kevin, Timothy. BS, Marquette U., 1962; MBA, Northwestern U., 1963. Instr. Marquette U., Milw., 1963-65; CPA Peat. Marwick & Mitchell, Milw., 1965-66; with Johnson Controls, Inc., Milw., 1967—, mgr. systems dept., 1967-71, div. controller, 1971-73, corp. controller, treas., 1973-77, v.p., chief fin. officer, 1977-85, exec. v.p., 1985-86, pres., 1986—, chief operating officer, 1986-88, chief exec. officer, 1988—, also chmn.; bd. dirs. Baird Capital Devel. Fund. 1st Wis. Trust Co., LSI Logic, Inc., Universal Foods Corp. Active Milw. Symphony Orch., 1980—. Mem. Fin. Execs. Inst., Am. Inst. CPA's, Wis. Inst. CPA's., Machinery and Allied Products Inst. Office: Johnson Controls Inc PO Box 591 5757 N Green Bay Ave Milwaukee WI 53209-4408*

KEYES, JAMES LYMAN, JR., diesel engines distributor company owner; b. Peru, Ind., Apr. 27, 1928; s. James Lyman and Mary Edith (Weigle) K. AB, Wabash Coll., 1950; MBA, Harvard U., 1952; LLD (hon.), Wabash Coll., 1987. Mgr. Cummins Diesel Sales Corp., Columbus, Ind., 1959-61; dir. mktg. svcs. Cummins Engine Co., Inc., Columbus, 1962-65; gen. sales mgr. Cummins Engine Co., Inc., 1966-67, v.p. OEM sales, 1968-70, v.p. nat. accounts, 1971-73, v.p. indsl. mktg., 1974-76; chmn., CEO, owner Cummins Ohio, Inc., Columbus, Ohio, 1976-94, 1994—; bd. dirs. Ohio Trucking Assn., 1980—. Mem. Newcomen Soc., Columbus, Ohio, 1984—, Coun. for Ethics in Econs., Columbus, Ohio, 1987—, Rotary Internat., Columbus, Ohio, 1983; chmn. Mayor's Econ. Devel. Coun., Columbus, Ohio, 1982-84; pres. Columbus (Ohio) Landmarks Found., 1976-77; bd. dirs. Columbus (Ohio) Coun. on World Affairs, 1982—; bd. trustees Wabash Coll., Crawfordsville, Ind., 1980—, v.p., 1990—, chmn. exec. com., 1987-89; elder Presbyn. Ch., 1979-82; mem. commn. Columbus Met. Airport and Aviation, 1989-91. 1st lt. USAF, 1952-54. Recipient Christopher Columbus Achievement award City of Columbus (Ohio), 1987. Mem. Nat. Assn. Wabash Coll. Men (pres. 1974-76), Ind. Assn. for Retarded Children (pres. 1965-68), Nat. Assn. for Retarded Children (v.p. 1968-72), Univ. Club (Columbus, Ohio), Masons, Shriners, Kappa Sigma. Republican. Office: Cummins Ohio Inc 4000 Lyman Dr Hilliard OH 43026-1212

KEYES, LEA RAE, healthcare and case management consultant; b. Sleepy Eye, Minn.; d. Lawrence Raymond and Lois May (Wandersee) K.; m. Charles Kenneth Lucas. BSN, Mankato (Minn.) State U., 1974. Cert. pub. health nurse, ins. rehab. specialist, case mgr.; qualified rehab. cons. Pub. health nurse Anoka County, Minn., 1975-82; account rep. IMARC, Mpls., 1982-83; program mgr. Cromer Mgmt., Mpls., 1983-84; reg. case mgmt. coord. INTRACORP, Mpls., 1984-85; mktg. mgr. Assoc. Rehab. Cons., Mpls., 1985-88; branch mgr. Kimberly Quality Care, St. Paul, Minn., 1988-89; cons., educator Keyes & Assocs., Ltd., Anoka, Minn., 1989—; dir., case mgr. Advanced Case Mgmt., Inc., Mpls., 1992—; qualified rehab. cons. and disability case mgr. Med-Voc Assoc. Inc., Mpls., 1989—. Speaker in field. Mem. Am. Assn. Legal Nurse Cons. (pres. Minn. chpt.), Ind. Case Mgrs. Assn., Minn. Case Mgrs. Network (pres.). Office: Advanced Case Mgmt Inc 1200 Osborne Rd NE Minneapolis MN 55432-2838

KEYS, PAUL ROSS, university dean; b. St. Louis, Mar. 21, 1940; s. Charles and Josie (Jones) K. BS, St. Louis U., 1963, MSW, 1971; PhD, U. Wis., Milw., 1983. Exec. dir. Champaign (Ill.) Urban League, 1969; dep. dir. Concentrated Employment Program, St. Louis, 1971; asst. dir. legis. NASW, Washington, 1971-74; exec. dir. Community Svcs. Coun. Columbia, Mo., 1974-76; dir. Broward County (Fla.) Dept. of Human Svcs., 1976-78; deputy adminstr. Community Svcs. Div. State of Wis., 1978-81; prof. Hunter Coll., CUNY, 1983-94; faculty doctoral program CUNY, 1987-94; dean Coll. Health and Human Svcs., S.E. Mo. State U., Cape Girardeau, 1994—; fellow Ctr. Social Adminstrn., Hunter Coll., 1985-94. Author: New Management in Human Services, 1988, 2d edit., 1995; founding editor Jour. Multicultural Social Work, 1989—; contbr. articles to profl. jours. Sec. Nat. Network for Social Work Mgrs., Washington, 1989. Cpt. USAF, 1963-69. Recipient Martin Luther King/Woodrow Wilson fellowship, 1970, Commendation Resolution, Mo. Gen. Assembly, 1976, GARIOA/Fulbright Rsch. fellowship, Tokyo, 1990-91. Mem. Am. Pub. Welfare Assn. (exec. com. 1988), ASPA (exec. com. 1988—), Omega Psi Phi (Cmty. Svc. award 1977). Office: Coll Health and Human Svcs Southeast Mo State U Cape Girardeau MO 63701-4799

KEYSER, E. GLEN, nutritional biochemist; b. Bellaine, Ohio, Dec. 24, 1929; s. James Wesley and Mary Helen (Greenlee) K; m. Nancy Louise Kessler Keyser, Dec. 31, 1954; children: Gregory Alan, Laurel Susan Graham, Diane Louise, Christopher Jon, Kevin Glen, Karen Elizabeth Quinn. BS in Agrl. Bus., The Ohio State U., Columbus, 1956; MS in Extension Edn., Mich. State U., E. Lansing, 1959; MS in Poultry Nutrition, U. Ark., Fayetteville, 1968; PhD in Nutritional Biochemistry, The Ohio State U., Columbus, 1971. Cert. profl. Agronomist, crop scientist, soil scientist Am. Soc. Agronomy, Madison, Wis., 1984—; cert. profl. microbiologist Am. Soc. Microbiology, Washington, 1984—; dir. rsch. and mktg. A.O. Smith Herostore Products, Co., Arlington Heights, Ill., 1972-77; dir. rsch. Agrl. Labs. Inc., Columbus, Ohio, 1977-85; rsch. chmn. bd. Bio-One Internat., Grove City, Ohio, 1986—. Inventor in field. Sch. bd. Southwestern City Sch., Grove City, Ohio, 1969-79; exec. com. Opera Columbus, 1982—. Sgt. USAF, 1947-51, Washington. Fellow Urania Lodge # 311. Lutheran. Home: 6261 White Sulphir Ct Grove City OH 43123-9501

KEYSER, GEOGRE J., industrial engineer; b. Warren, Ohio, June 14, 1955. A in Drafting and Design, Youngstown State U., 1983; student, Kent State U. Project mgr. Transworld Fabricating, Niles, Ohio, 1978-79; draftsperson Valley Mold & Iron, Hubbard, Ohio, 1979-80; indsl. engr. Peerless Winsmith Inc., Warren, 1980—. Active St. Roberts Ch., Courtland, Ohio, 1991—. Sgt. USAF, 1973-77. Mem. N.E. Ohio Numerical Control User Soc. Roman Catholic. Office: Peerless Winsmith Inc 1401 W Market St Warren OH 44485-2785

KHAIRALLAH, FARID, engineering manager; b. Phamdoun, Lebanon, Jan. 2, 1959; came to U.S., 1978; BS, W. Va. Univ. Tech., 1982; MS, Notre Dame U., 1984. Project engr. Bendix Aerospace, South Bend, Ind., 1984-92; engring. mgr. TRW, Farmington, Mich., 1992—. Mem. ESD, Am. Mgmt. Assn. Office: TRW 24175 Research Dr Farmington Hills MI 48335-2634

KHALIMSKY, EFIM, mathematics and computer science educator; b. Odessa, USSR, June 23, 1938; came to U.S., 1978; s. David Khalimsky and Olga Weizman; m. Elena Merems, May 19, 1962; 1 child, Olga. MS in Math. with honors, Pedagogical Inst., Odessa, 1960; PhD in Math., Pedagogical Inst., Moscow, 1969. Tchr. high sch. Odessa, 1960-66; assoc. prof. Pedagogical Inst., Magnitogorsk, USSR, 1969-72; sr. research scientist Research and Prodn. Inst. for Food Industry, Odessa, 1972-73, Econs. Inst. Acad. Sciences, Odessa, 1973-77; asst. prof. Manhattan Coll., Riverdale, N.Y., 1980-85; assoc. prof. CUNY, 1979-80, Coll. of Staten Island (N.Y.), 1985-89; prof. Cen. State U., Wilberforce, Ohio, 1989—. Author: Ordered Topological Spaces, 1977, (with others) The Planning of Economic and Ecological Research at Sea Basins, 1976, (with others) Economical and Ecological Management of Water Resources, 1976, (with others) Methodological Foundations on Developing MIS System for Water Resources, 1976; area editor Jour. Applied Math. and Simulation, 1987—; contbr. numerous articles to profl. jours. Named Best Scientist USSR Acad. Sciences, 1986. Mem. IEEE, Am. Math. Soc., Assn. Computing Machinery, Soc. Indsl. and Applied Math., Ops. Research Soc. Am. Home: 1260 Brentwood Dr Dayton OH 45406-5713

KHO, EUSEBIO, surgeon; b. Philippines, Dec. 16, 1933; s. Joaquin and Francisca (Chua) K.: came to U.S., 1964; AA, Silliman U., Philippines, 1955; MD, State U. Philippines, 1960; fellow in surgery, Johns Hopkins, 1965-67; m. Grace Casas Lim, May 24, 1964: children: Michelle Mae, April Tiffany, Bradley Jude, Jaclyn Ashley, Matthew Ryan. Rotating intern Philippine Gen. Hosp., U. Philippines, 1959-60; resident gen. practice Silliman U. Med. Ctr., 1960-63; virology researcher Van Howelling Lab. Silliman U., 1963-64; intern in surgery Francis Scott Key Med. Ctr., 1964-65, resident in gen. surgery, 1965-67; rsch. assoc. pediatric surgery U. Chgo. Hosps., 1967-68; resident in gen. surgery, then chief resident U. Tex. Hosp., San Antonio, 1968-70; hosp. surgeon St. Anthony Hosp., Louisville, 1970-72; practice medicine specializing in surgery, Scottsburg, Ind., 1972—; chmn. dept. surgery Scott County Meml. Hosp., 1973—; cons. surgeon Washington County Meml. Hosp., Salem, Ind., also Clark County Meml. Hosp., Jeffersonville, Ind., 1973—; courtesy surgeon Suburban Hosp., Louisville, 1973—; gen. surgeon 5010 U.S. Army Hosp., Louisville, 1980—. Bd. dirs. Make-A-Wish Found. Ind., 1992—. Served to col. M.C., USAR, 1980—, Operation Desert Storm, 1990-91, Operation Eastern Castle, Amman, Jordan, 1994, Exercise Yama Sakura XXVII, Japan, 1995, U.S. Army Task Force Fuertes Caminos, El Salvador, 1996. Named to Hon. Order Ky. Cols., 1991. Diplomate Am. Bd. Surgery. Fellow A.C.S., Am. Soc. Abdominal Surgeons, Am. Coll. Emergency Physicians; mem. Am. Coll. Internat. Physicians (founding mem., trustee 1974—), AMA (Physician's Recognition award 1969, 72), Ind. State Med. Assn., Ky. Med. Assn., Philippines Med. Assn. of Ind. and Ky., Internat. Coll. Surgeons, Soc. Philippine Surgeons in Am. (life), Assn. Philippine Practicing Physicians in Am. (life), Assn. Mil. Surgeons of U.S. (life), Res. Officers Assn. of U.S. (life), Mark Ravitch Surg. Assn., Bradley Aust Surg. Soc., N.Y. Acad. Scis. Presbyterian. Clubs: Optimists, Masons. Home: 14 Carla Ln Scottsburg IN 47170-9707 Office: 137 E McClain Ave Scottsburg IN 47170-1846

KHODOR, LEONID, mechanical engineer; b. Kiev, USSR, July 20, 1948; came to U.S., 1990.; ME, Leningrad, 1977. Project engr. Aero Internat., Cleve., 1991-92, BELCAN, Cleve., 1992—. Patentee in field. Recipient medal Show of New Machinery, USSR. Jewish.

KHOURY, GEORGE GILBERT, printing company executive, baseball association executive; b. St. Louis, July 30, 1923; s. George Michael and Dorothy (Smith) K.; m. Colleen E. Khoury Czerny, Apr. 3, 1948; children—Colleen Ann, George Gilbert. Grad. St. Louis U., 1946. Vice pres. Khoury Bros. Printing, St. Louis, 1946—; exec. dir. George Khoury Assn. Baseball Leagues, Inc., St. Louis, 1967—. Served with U.S. Army, 1943-45, NATOUSA, MTO. Decorated Purple Heart with oak leaf cluster. Roman Catholic. Office: George Khoury Assn Baseball Leagues 5400 Meramec Bottom Rd Saint Louis MO 63128-4624

KIBBEY, HAL STEPHEN, science writer; b. West Point, N.Y., Oct. 29, 1943; s. Donald Eugene and Mary Elizabeth (Lichliter) K.; m. Martha Ann Harsanyi, Dec. 12, 1970; children: Carolyn Ann, Laura Ann. BA, Cornell U., 1965; MA, Ind. U., 1969. Rsch. asst., rsch. assoc. Ind. U., Bloomington, 1970-75, publ. editor, 1975-79, sci. writer, 1979—; free lance writer and editor, Bloomington, 1985—. Editor: Science Development: The Building of Science in Less Developed Countries, 1975. Pres. Rogers-Binford Elem. Sch. PTO, 1991-93; bd. dirs. Monroe County Civic Theater, 1995-96. Mem. ACLU, Nat. Assn. Sci. Writers, U.S. Chess Fedn. (life). Democrat. Methodist. Home: 1109 E Hunter Ave Bloomington IN 47401-5035 Office: Ind U Office Comm & Mktg 400 E 7th St Bloomington IN 47405-3801

KIBBY, ARTHUR STEPHEN, video and film producer, director of photography; b. Perry, Iowa, Oct. 30, 1937; s. Elvin LaVerne and Edna Louise (Karrer) K.; m. Joyce I. Johnson, Aug. 27, 1960; children: Pamela, Steven, Kristen. BA, U. Iowa, 1961; cert. in energy mgmt., U. Cin., 1985. Dir. cinematography Sta. WHAS-TV, Louisville, 1964-67; dir. photography Grant Film Prodn., Jeffersonville, Ind., 1967-71; ptnr. Spectrum Films, Louisville, 1971-73; owner Art Kibby-Filmmaker, Louisville, 1973-74; gen. mgr. Film Prodn. Cin., Cin., 1974-77; co-owner Kibby Raynor Prodn., Ltd., Cin., 1977—. Capt. U.S. Army, 1961-64, Germany. Mem. Internat. TV and Video Assn. Democrat. Home: 7714 Forest Rd Cincinnati OH 45255 Office: Kibby Raynor Prodn Ltd 24 Whitney Dr Ste D Milford OH 45150

KIBLER, LOUIS, Romance languages educator; b. Clifton Forge, Va., July 23, 1939; s. Arland Edward and Gladys Gordon (Clark) K.;m. Ruth Ann Dupont, Apr. 14, 1960; children: Marc Louis, Lisa Michelle, Katrina Elizabeth. BA, Ind. U., 1960, PhD, 1965; postgrad., Yale U., 1961-62. Asst. prof. Ind. U., Bloomington, 1965-72; assoc. prof. Sweet Briar (Va.) Coll., 1972-74; assoc. prof. Wayne State U., Detroit, 1974—, chair Romance langs., 1994—; manuscript cons. Macmillan Pub., N.Y.C., Holt, Rinehart, Winston, N.Y.C., Houghton Mifflin, Boston. Author: Giorno per giorno, 1972; translator: Ezio D'Enrico's Theater of the Absurd, 1992. Woodrow Wilson fellow, 1961, Carnegie Mellon grantee, 1973. Mem. MLA, Am. Assn. Tchrs. Italian (exec. coun. 1982-87, 89-92, sec.-treas. 1988-92), Am. Assn. Italian Studies, Dante Alighieri Soc. Mich. Democrat. Office: Wayne State U Dept Romance Lang Detroit MI 48202

KIDD, DEBRA JEAN, communications executive; b. Chgo., May 13, 1956; d. Fred A. and Jean (Pezzopane) Winchar; m. Kim Joseph Kidd, July 22, 1978; children: Jennifer Marie, Michele Jean. AA in Bus. with high honors, Wright Jr. Coll., 1977. Legal sec. Sidley & Austin, Chgo., 1977-80; investment adminstr. Golder, Thoma & Co., Chgo., 1980-81, exec. asst., 1981-84; sales rep. Dataspeed, Inc., Chgo., 1984, midwestern regional mgr. Dataspeed, Inc., Chgo., 1985; comm. cons. Chgo. Comm., Inc., Chgo., 1986-88; owner, founder Captain Kidd's Video, Niles, 1981-84. Vol. Am. Lung Assn., Chgo., 1979; vol. tchr. religious edn. Our Lady Mother of Ch., Norridge, Ill., 1981-83, St. Raymonds, Mt. Prospect, 1993-94; vol. Parents Who Care, 1988-94, pres., 1991-93; vol. PTA Lion's Park Sch., 1993-95, bd. dirs., 1993-94; editor Lion's Roar, 1993-95; founder Young Journalist Club, 1994-95; leader Girl Scouts, 1992—, cons., 1994-95. Mem. NAFE, Nat. Assn. Bus. Women, Nat. Assn. Profl. Saleswomen, Phi Theta Kappa. Roman Catholic. Avocations: camping, skiing, snorkeling, sailing, reading, needlepoint.

KIEFER, GARY, newspaper editor. Now mng. editor Columbus (Ohio) Dispatch. Office: Columbus Dispatch 34 S 3rd St Columbus OH 43215-4201

KIEFER, JACQUELINE LORRAINE, special education educator, consultant; b. Dayton, Ohio, Nov. 6, 1947; d. Elmer Louis Kiefer and Lorraine (Siefert) K. BS in Educ., U. of Dayton, 1969; MED in Curr and Super., Wright STate U., 1978; MED, Wright State U., 1987. Sp. edn. tchr. Milton Union Village Sch., West Milton, Ohio, 1969-88; spl. edn. cons. Medina (Ohio) County Bd. Edn., 1988—; supr. part-time Amateur Trap Shooting Assn., Vandalia, Ohio, 1969-93. Author: Packets of Activities - Kids N Summer, math Box of Activities, Math Box. chairperson Disaster Services, Am. Nat. Red Cross, Dayton, Ohio, Fund raiser, Cancer Soc., Heart Assn., Dayton; mem. Women in Ednl. Leadership; vol. Miami Valley Hosp., Ohio Pub. Images, Miami Valley Spl. Edn. Regional Resource Ct. Recipient Disting. Service award, Spl. Olympics, Ohio, Cert. of Merit, Milton Union Sch., Council of Exceptional Children. Mem. Ohio Assn. Supr., N.E. Ohio Suprs. Assn., Coun. Exceptional Children, Assn. Curriculum Supervision, Lizotte Reading Coun., Assn. Curiculum Devel., Dayton Ski Club, Kappa Delta Pi, Phi Delta Kappa. Home: 10 W Sherry Dr Trotwood OH 45426-3522 Office: Medina Bd Edn 144 N Broadway St Medina OH 44256-1902

KIEFER, RICHARD LAWRENCE, sales representative; b. N.Y.C., Oct. 5, 1950; s. Henry and Mildred Helen (Barnstorf) K.; m. Cheryl Ann DeVoss, May 1, 1976; children: Jacqueline Denise, Stephanie Lynn, Beth Ann. Student, Waynesburg Coll., 1968-69, Ohio State U., 1971-73. Sales estimator Columbus (Ohio) Vicon Co., Inc., 1977-79, Steel Door, Inc., Columbus, 1979-81, Tri-State Builders Hardware, Columbus, 1981-85; regional sales mgr. DORMA Door Controls, Reamstown, Pa., 1985-86; sales rep. Barnaby Assocs., Worthington, Ohio, 1986—. Pres. AWHA Homeowners Assn., Westerville, Ohio, 1992. Mem. Door & Hardware Inst. (exec. com. Buckeye chpt., sec. 1994-95, cert. archtl. cons. 1983, cert. door cons. 1993). Home: 690 Autumn Tree Pl Westerville OH 43081 Office: Barnaby Assocs 7792 Olentangy River Rd Worthington OH 43235

KIEFFER, ROBERT PAUL, financial planner; b. St. Louis, June 1, 1944; m. Mary Jane Ajmacher, June 17, 1972; children: Melanie, Todd, Paul, Megan, Jordan. BA, St. Louis U., 1966, MBA, 1973. Owner, salesman St. Louis Fin. Planners, Chesterfield, Mo., 1976—. Chmn. Vietnam Vets. Leadership Program, St. Louis, 1976—, pres., 1980—; pres. Mo. Vets. Devel. Corp., St. Louiis, 1995—. Capt. U.S. Army, 1966-69, Vietnam. Roman Catholic. Office: St Louis Fin Planners 1415 Elbridge Payne Rd Ste 140 Chesterfield MO 63017-8522

KIEFFER, THOMAS A., financial executive; b. St. Louis, Sept. 20, 1940. BS, St. Louis U., 1962. Advisor MONY, St. Louis, 1964-74; pres., sr. acct. St. Louis Fin. Planner, Chesterfield, Mo., 1974—. Sgt. U.S. NG, 1962-68. Republican. Roman Catholic. Office: St Louis Fin Planner # 140 1415 Elbridge Payne Rd Chesterfield MO 63017-8522

KIEFT, GERALD NELSON, mechanical engineer; b. Chgo., Dec. 29, 1946 s. Ralph and Alice (Nelson) K.; m. Linda Louise Fank, Oct. 28, 1967 children: Gerald Nelson II, Dawn Michelle. BSME, Midwest Coll. Engring., Lombard, Ill., 1971. Sr. designer Clark Equipment Co., Aurora, Ill. 1971-73; project engr. Elgin (Ill.) Sweeper Co., 1974-86, GPI Industries, W Chgo., Ill., 1986—. Inventor in field. Company chmn. United Wa Campaign, Elgin, 1977. Presbyterian. Home: 42w192 Silver Glen Rd Sain Charles IL 60175-8339 Office: GPI Industries 1400 Powis Ct West Chicag IL 60185

KIEKHAEFER, RUTH HEINS, healthcare executive; b. Lincoln, Nebr. Feb. 3, 1938; d. John Henry and Helen Anna (Kastner) Heins; m. Theodor Charles Kiekhaefer, Sept. 13, 1959; children: Kristin Dunn, Phillip, Ann Kiekhaefer Sackett, Michael. Student, Concordia Coll., 1955-56; BSN Nebr. U., 1959; postgrad., U. Ariz., 1963-64; M in Nursing, Kans. U., 1987. RN, Mo.; cert. pediatric nurse practitioner; cert. devel. specialist. Staff nurs Univ. Hosp., Omaha, 1959-60; pediatric instr. Children's Hosp., Omaha 1960-62; staff nurse Tuscon Med. Ctr., 1963-64; tchr. Happy Time Nurser Sch., Superior, Nebr., 1970; dir. nursing svc. and edn. Good Samaritan Ctr Superior, Nebr., 1971-73; dir. health Industry Resources, Inc., St. Joseph Mo., 1981-83; cons. Progressive Evaluation and Rehab. Cons., Shawne Mission, Kans., 1985; pres. Healthwise, Inc., St. Joseph, 1986—; cons. Mec Clinic St. Joseph, 1986—; instr. Mo. Western State Coll., 1992—; assoc. clir faculty U. Mo. at Kansas City, 1995. Mem. exec. bd. Family Guidance Ctr 1992-94. Fellow Nat. Assn. Pediatric Nurse Assocs. & Practitioners (cer 1994); mem. ANA, Nat. Assn. Pediat. Nurses, Clin. Nurse Specialist Coun Mo. Nurses Assn. (bd. dirs. dist. 1 1988-90), Buchanan County Med. Au (pres. 1990), Mo. State Med. Assn. Aux. (v.p., state health chair 1992-93 N.W. Mo. Wellness Coun. (chair 1992), Sigma Theta Tau, Delta Delta Delt (Alumni pres. 1989-91). Republican. Lutheran. Home: 18939 Evergreen D Saint Joseph MO 64505-4058 Office: Pediat and Adolescent Medicine 395 Sherman Ave Saint Joseph MO 64506-3649

KIENOL, MARK STEVEN, accountant; b. Hampton, Iowa, Aug. 28, 195 s. Glenn Herman and Eileen Joan (Vietor) K. Student, Hamilton Coll 1974-76, Grand View Coll., 1982-85, St. Louis U., 1986. Acct. Garst Co Coon Rapids, Iowa, 1976, Kessler Distbg. Co., Inc., Fairfield, Iowa, 197 78; staff acct., acctg. supr. Younkers, Inc., Des Moines, 1978-81; staff acct divisional acct. supr. Mid Continent Bottlers, Inc., Des Moines, 1981-85; fi analyst 7 Up Bottling Co. St. Louis, Hazelwood, Mo., 1985-89; pvt. practi St. Peters, Mo., 1989-92, 95—; acct. supr. Innsbrook Corp., Clayton, M 1992-95. Mem. RIMS, Jaycees (v.p. St. Charles chpt. 1988-89, state 1986-87, pres. Clive, Iowa chpt. 1981-82, v.p. 1980-81, state dir. Fairf chpt. 1978-79, v.p. Iowa Jaycees 1985-86, Outstanding State Treas. 1

Outstanding Young Man. Am. 1980, 84, 86, 87, 89), Kiwanis (bd. dirs. Coon Rapids chpt. 1976). Democrat. Lutheran.

KIENZLE, WILLIAM XAVIER, author; b. Detroit, Sept. 11, 1928; s. Alphonso and Mary Louise (Boyle) K.; m. Javan Herman Andrews, Nov. 29, 1974. BA, Sacred Heart Sem., Detroit, 1950; postgrad., U. Detroit, 1960-63. Ordained priest Roman Cath. Ch., 1954. Priest Archdiocese of Detroit, 1954-74; editor-in-chief Mpls. Mag., 1974-77; assoc. dir. Ctr. for Contemplative Studies, Kalamazoo, 1977-78; dir. Ctr. for Contemplative Studies, Irving, Tex., 1978-79; instr. writing course St. Mary's Coll., Orchard Lake, Mich. Author: The Rosary Murders, 1979, Death Wears a Red Hat, 1980, Mind Over Murder, 1981, Assault with Intent, 1982, Shadow of Death, 1983, Kill and Tell, 1984, Sudden Death, 1985, Deathbed, 1986, Deadline for a Critic, 1987, Marked for Murder, 1988, Eminence, 1989, Maquerade, 1990, Chameleon, 1991, Body Count, 1992, Dead Wrong, 1993, Bishop As Pawn, 1994, Call No Man Father, 1995, Requiem for Moses, 1996; contbr. to Sound of a Sermon; editor-in-chief The Mich. Cath., 1962-74. Home and Office: PO Box 645 Keego Harbor MI 48320-0645

KIERNOZEK, TED. J., marketing professional; b. Cleve., Aug. 8, 1970. Student, Cleve. State U., 1991-93. Mktg. and sales mgr. APS Internat., Cleve., 1993—. Roman Catholic. Office: APS Internat 4848 W 130th St Cleveland OH 44135-5163

KIERSCHT, CHARLES M., financial company executive; b. Des Moines, Iowa, 1939. Grad., U. Iowa. Pres., chief operating officer, dir. Kemper Fin. Services, Inc., Chgo.; pres., dir. Kemper Growth Fund, Chgo., Kemper Income and Capital Preservation, Chgo., Kemper Investors Life Ins. Co., Chgo., Kemper Money Market Fund, Chgo., Kemper Mcpl. Bond Fund, Chgo., Kemper Summit Fund, Chgo., Kemper Total Return Fund, Chgo. Office: Kemper Fin Svcs Inc 120 S La Salle St Fl 21 Chicago IL 60603-3402

KIESEL, WILLIAM R., financial consultant; b. Dec. 14, 1938; m. Sharon Kiesel; children: Lori Ann Wolfe, William Scott. BSBA, Ind. Cen. Coll., 1963; postgrad., Butler U. Grad. Sch.; grad. cert. in comml. banking, Am. Inst. Banking; LHD (hon.), U. Indpls., 1989. V.p., prin., mgr. fixed income dept. Traub & Co., Indpls., 1971-81; v.p., fin. cons. Merrill Lynch Pierce Fenner & Smith, Indpls., 1981-90, Smith Barney Shearson, Inc., Indpls., 1990—. Vice chmn., bd. trustees U. Indpls., mem. exec. com., fin. com., chmn. faculty affairs com., chmn. athletics com., chmn. presdl. search com., chmn. strategic long range planning com., alumni bd. dirs., chmn. ann. fund dr.; mem. bd. trustees, investment com., fin. com. Eden Theol. Sem.; past mem. bd. trustees, past mem. investment com., past mem. fin. com. United Theol. Sem.; chmn. Ind.-Ky. conf. United Ch. of Christ, chmn. exec. coun., 1987-89, ex officio mem. Ind.-Ky. conf. bd. dirs., mem. exec. coun., 1983-89, chmn. fin. & budget com. denomination, 1985-87, chmn. search com. for CEO of Ind.-Ky. conf., chmn. asset mgmt. com. Ind.-Ky. conf., pres. local ch. bd., elder Immanuel United Ch. of Christ; chmn. Soc. Stephan, Altenheim Comty., chmn. Altenheim Adv. Bd., chmn. Altehnheim Comty. Support Group; bd. dirs. Tri County Mental Health Found., strategic planning com., sec. to bd. dirs., chmn. leadership gifts capital campaign; past mem., bd. mgrs. YMCA; past dir., treas. PTAI Perry Twp. Athletics, Inc.; past mem. Mayor's Greater Progress Com. Recipient Ben Herber award for support for aging Altenheim Comty., 1990. Mem. U. Indpls. Pres. Club, U. Indpls. Greyhound Club, Indpls. Bond Club, Indpls. Security Traders, 500 Festival Assocs., Sertoma Found., Sertoma Club of Downtown Indpls. (past pres., past bd. dirs.), Skyline Club.

KIESER, RANDALL JOHN, family practice, addiction medicine and emergency medicine physician; b. Milw., Aug. 24, 1958; s. Jan Russell and Odean Janet (Kramer) K.; m. Mara Alane McElwee, Aug. 31, 1985; children: Jessica, Jeremy. BS, U. Wis., 1980, MD, 1984. Diplomate Am. Bd. Family Practice, Am. Soc. Addiction Medicine. Intern St. Michael Hosp., Milw., 1984-85, resident, 1985-87; Staff physician Gundersen-Farrell Clinic, Prairie du Chien, Wis., 1987-91; staff physician PDC Mem. Hosp., Prairie du Chien, 1987-91; acad. fellow U. Wis., Madison, 1992; staff physician Meriter Hosp., Madison, 1993-95; emergency medicine physician Richland Hosp., Richland Center, Wis., 1995—, Southwest Health Ctr., Platteville, Wis., 1995—. Team physician Prairie du Chien High Sch. football team, 1987-91. Mem. AMA, State Med. Soc. Wis. (med. manpower 1988-89, bd. rep. task force 1989-90, Physician's Alliance Commn. 1989-90, commn. on addictive diseases 1991—), Am. Acad. Family Physicians, Am. Soc. Addiction Medicine. Republican. Roman Catholic. Home and Office: 820 Maple Rd Verona WI 53593-1636

KIESLER, CHARLES ADOLPHUS, psychologist, academic administrator; b. St. Louis, Aug. 14, 1934; m. Teru Morton, Feb. 28, 1987; 1 child, Hugo; children from previous marriage: Tina, Thomas, Eric, Kevin. B.A., Mich. State U., 1958, M.A., 1960; Ph.D. (NIMH fellow), Stanford U., 1963; D (hon.), Lucian Blaga U., Romania, 1995. Asst. prof. psychology Ohio State U., Columbus, 1963-64, Yale U., New Haven, 1964-66; assoc. prof. Yale U., 1966-70; prof., chmn. psychology U. Kans., Lawrence, 1970-75; exec. officer Am. Psychol. Assn., Washington, 1975-79; Walter Van Dyke Bingham prof. psychology Carnegie Mellon U., Pitts., 1979-85; head psychology Carnegie Mellon U., 1980-83, acting dean, 1981-82, dean Coll. Humanities and Social Scis., 1983-85; provost Vanderbilt U., 1985-92; chancellor U. Mo., Columbia, 1992—. Author: (with B.E. Collins and N. Miller) Attitude Change: A Critical Analysis of Theoretical Approaches, 1969, (with S.B. Kiesler) Conformity, 1969, The Psychology of Commitment: Experiments Linking Behavior to Belief, 1971, (with N. Cummings and G. VandenBos) Psychology and National Health Insurance: A Sourcebook, 1979, (with A.E. Sibulkin) Mental Hospitalization: Myths and Facts About a National Crisis, 1987, (with C. Simpkins) The Unnoticed Majority: Psychiatric inpatient care in general hospitals, 1993. Served with Security Service USAF, 1952-56. Recipient Disting. Alumnus award Mich. State U., 1987, Gunnar Myrdal award for Evaluation Practice Am. Evaluation Assn., 1989. Fellow AAAS, Am. Psychol. Assn. (Distng. Contbr. to Rsch. in Pub. Policy award 1989), Am. Psychol. Soc. (founding past pres. 1988-90); mem. AAUP, Inst. of Medicine of Nat. Acad. Scis., Sigma Xi, Psi Chi, Phi Kappa Phi. Office: Univ Mo-Columbia Chancellors Office 105 Jesse Hall Columbia MO 65211

KIESSLING, RONALD FREDERICK, retired federal government executive; b. Cleve., Jan. 13, 1934; s. E. Oscar and Carolina Martha (Goetz) K.; m. Lois L. Nimrichter, Sept. 10, 1955 (dec. 1981); children: Elizabeth, Christopher, David; m. Jeanette Metzger, Apr. 5, 1984. Diploma, John Marshall High Sch., Cleve., 1954-90; ret., NASA Lewis Rsch. Ctr., Cleve., 1990. With NASA Lewis Rsch. Ctr., 1954—, head advanced systems/spacecraft testing sect., 1974-80, chief communications, energy and flight hardware br., 1980-82, chief materials and engine components br., 1982-85, dep. chief space tech. ops., 1985-86, dep. chief logistics mgmt. div., 1986-89. Mem. Retired and Sr. Vol. Program, adv. com. electronic tech., Akron U., 1973-89. Sgt. USMC, 1951-54. Recipient Presdl. citation, 1971. Mem. AQP, Marine Corps. League (state and local officer), NASA Suprs. Club (pres. 1976), K.P. (chancellor command 1978, grand chancellor Ohio 1993), Am. Legion Post 421. Lutheran. Home: 19 Schuberts Aly Olmsted Falls OH 44138-3027

KIEWEL, HAROLD DEAN, architect; b. Belle Fourche, S.D., Sept. 30, 1951; s. Robert Burton and Barbara Anne (Shaykett) K.; m. Patricia Anne Patrick, Dec. 28, 1974; children: Claire Elise, Celeste Marie. BA, U. Minn., 1973, MArch, 1987. Registered architect, Minn. Cons. City of Mpls., 1975-76; planner State of Minn., St. Paul, 1976-79, housing officer, 1979-82; cons. St. Paul, 1982-86; architect TKDA & Assocs., St. Paul, 1986-92; cons. Universal Designers & Cons., Inc., St. Paul, 1992-93; pvt. practice architect Accessible Bldg. Cons., White Bear Lake, 1994—. Co-editor: Accessible Architecture, 1977; contbr. articles to profl. jours. Bd. dirs. Handicap Housing Svc., Inc., St. Paul, 1976-79. Recipient Rose & Jay Phillips award Courage Ctr., 1990. Mem. AIA (bd. dirs., pres. St. Paul chpt. 1994, nat. diversity com. 1995-96), Constrn. Specifications Inst., Toltzmasters' Toastmasters (pres. 1988, 89).

KIGIN, THOMAS JOHN, lawyer, broadcast executive; b. St. Cloud, Minn., Sept. 29, 1948; s. Jerome Joseph and Marjorie Marie (Bellig) K.; m. Donna Louise Avery, Sept. 6, 1980; children: Mackenzie Louise, Elizabeth Hannah. BA cum laude, St. John's U., 1970; JD cum laude, U. Minn., 1977. Bar: Minn. 1977. V.p., gen. counsel Minn. Pub. Radio, St. Paul, 1977—; mem. distbn. interconnection com. Nat. Pub. Radio, Washington, 1986-92; treas., bd. dirs. Fitzgerald Theater Co.; exec. v.p., sec., treas., gen. counsel Greenspring Co., Minn. Monthly Publs., Inc., The MNN Radio Networks, Inc., Rivertown Trading Co., St. Paul, 1987—; bd. dirs. Continental Cablevision of St. Paul; mem. exec. com. Shoreview FM Group, 1995—. Bd. dirs. Children's Heartlink, 1995—, Face to Face, 1996—. Served to 1st lt. USMC, 1970-73. Mem. ABA, Univ. Club. Office: Minn Pub Radio 45 7th St E Saint Paul MN 55101-2202

KILBOURNE, BARBARA JEAN, health and human services consultant; b. Milw., Mar. 21, 1941; d. Burton Conwell and Marjorie Janet (Tufts) K.; m. Kenneth Keith Kauffman, Feb. 10, 1962 (div. 1983). BA, U. Minn., 1972; MBA, Coll. St. Thomas, St. Paul, 1980. Adminstr. Ebenezer Soc., Mpls., 1974-85; v.p., dir. housing Walker Residence and Health Svcs., Inc., Mpls., 1985-88; exec. v.p. Oblate Ministries Health and Aging, West St. Paul, Minn., 1988-94; cons., 1995—; bd. dirs. Westminster Resident Svcs. Corp., St. Paul, chmn., 1996—, River Region Health Svcs., Red Wing, Minn., chmn. seminary plaza, 1995—, St. Olaf Residence; mem. commn. on aging Cath. Charities USA, Washington, 1989—; presenter, cons. and spkr. in field. Author: Family Councils in Nursing Homes, 1981. Chmn. bd. dirs. Dakota Inc., Eagan, Minn., 1985-96, Minn. Assn. Homes for Aging, 1991-92, Sem. Plz., Red Wing, 1995; project chair Dialog 2000, Dakota County, Minn., 1988-91. Episcopalian. Home: 1021 Sibley Memorial Hwy Lilydale MN 55118-6100

KILDE, SANDRA JEAN, nurse anesthetist, educator, consultant; b. Eau Claire, Wis., June 25, 1938; d. Harry Meylan and Beverly June (Johnson) K. Diploma Luther Hosp. Sch. Nursing, Eau Claire, 1959; grad. anesthesia course Mpls. Sch. Anesthesia, 1967; BA, Met. State U., St. Paul, 1976; MA, U. St. Thomas, 1981; EdD, Nova Southeastern U., 1987. RN, Wis., Minn. Operating room nurse Luther Hosp., Eau Claire, 1959-61, head nurse operating room, 1961-63; supr. operating room Midway Hosp., St. Paul, 1963-66; staff anesthetist North Meml. Med. Ctr., Robbinsdale, Minn., 1967-68, St. Joseph's Hosp., St. Paul, 1992—; program dir. Mpls. Sch. Anesthesia, St. Louis Park, Minn., 1968-96; adj. assoc. prof. St. Mary's U., Winona, Minn., 1982-96, adj. prof., 1996—, program dir. Masters Degree Program, 1984-96, nurse anesthesia cons., 1996—; ednl. cons. accreditation visitor Coun. on Accreditation of Nurse Anesthesia Ednl. Programs, Park Ridge, Ill., 1983-92, elected to coun., 1992—, vice chmn., 1994—; presentations in field. Recipient Good Neighbor award Sta. WCCO, Mpls., 1980, Disting. Alumni Achievement award Nova Southeastern U., 1993. Mem. Am. Assn. Nurse Anesthetists (pres. 1981-82, pres. and bd. dirs. Edn. and Rsch. Found. 1981-83, cert. profl. excellence 1976, Program Dir. of Yr. award 1992), Minn. Assn. Nurse Anesthetists (pres. 1975-76). Lutheran. Avocations: gardening, fishing, photography, choir directing, playing guitar and piano. Home: PO Box 80 Palisade MN 56469-0080

KILDEE, DALE EDWARD, congressman; b. Flint, Mich., Sept. 16, 1929; s. Timothy Leo and Norma Alicia (Ullmer) K.; m. Gayle Heyn, Feb. 27, 1965; children: David, Laura, Paul. BA, Sacred Heart Sem., 1952; tchr.'s cert., U. Detroit, 1954; MA, U. Mich., 1961; postgrad. (Rotary Found. fellow), U. Peshawar, Pakistan, 1958-59. Tchr. U. Detroit High Sch., 1954-56; Tchr. Flint Central High Sch., 1956-64; mem. Mich. Ho. of Reps., 1964-74, Mich. Senate, 1975-76, 95th-103rd Congresses from 7th (now 9th) Mich. Dist., 1977—; ranking minority mem. econ. & ednl. opportunity subcom. on early childhood, youth, & families, mem. resources com., mem. congl. auto caucus. Mem. NAACP (life), Am. Fedn. Tchrs., Urban League, Phi Delta Kappa. Lodges: K.C; Optimists. Home: 516 Kensington Flint MI 48503 Office: US Ho of Reps 2187 Rayburn House Bldg Washington DC 20515 also: 432 N Saginaw Ste 410 Flint MI 48502

KILDSIG, NANCY EVALINE, consultant pharmacist; b. International Falls, Minn., July 7, 1936; d. Oscar Carl Lundgren and Alta Maude Wetmore Brown; m. Dane Olin Kildsig, Feb. 2, 1958; children: Dane Olin, Douglas Gustav. BS, U. Wis., 1958; MS, Purdue U., 1972. Registered pharmacist. Pharmacist Meth. Hosp., Madison, Wis., 1958-61, Hogan's Pharmacy, Madison, Wis., 1962-64, Bill Long Pharmacy, West Lafayette, Ind., 1974-81; cons. pharmacist Healthcare Prescription Svcs., Indpls., 1982-95; dir. ops. TeamCare, Indpls., 1995—; presenter healthcare seminars, Indpls., 1983—; workshop presenter and facilitator. Vice-chair Salute to Women Banquet, Tippecanoe County, Ind., 1991, chair, 1992. Fellow Am. Soc. Cons. Pharmacists; mem. AAUW (br. pres. 1977-79, 90-92, state pres. 1979-81, dir. Great Leakes region 1989-91, Ind. dir. pub. policy 1991-93), Ind. Pharmacists Assn. (ednl. affairs coun.), Ind. Soc. Cons. Pharmacists (sec.-treas.). Home: 2526 Shagbark Ln West Lafayette IN 47906-4531 Office: Team Care Pharm Svcs 5644 W 74th St Indianapolis IN 46278

KILGORE, RANDALL FREEMAN, healthcare administrator; b. Birmingham, Ala., June 10, 1955; s. Isaac D.L. and Daisy Jewell (Bray) K. BS, U. Ala., 1978; M in Religious Edn., Midwestern Bapt. Theol. Sem., Kansas City, Mo., 1991. Registered record adminstr, Am. Health Info. Mgmt. Assn. Asst. dir. med. record svc. Baptist Med. Ctr., Montgomery, Ala., 1978-80; asst. health info. mgmt. Stephen's Coll., Columbia, Mo., 1980-82; dir. quality/risk mgmt. svcs. Boone Hosp. Ctr., Columbia, 1982-87; coord. risk mgmt. svcs. U. Mo. Hosp. Clinics, Columbia, 1987-90; dir. health info. svcs. Charter Behavioral Health Sys., Columbia, 1991—; interim dir. Christian edn. First Bapt. Ch., Columbia, 1990-91; long term care cons., Montgomery, 1978-80. Com. Boone Cunty Commn. Scenic Rds., 1995, Boone County Hist. Soc., 1995. Mem. Soc. Med. Records Conf. (sec. 1980-81), Am. Health Info. Mgmt. Assn., Ala. Med. Record Assn. (sec. 1979-80, historian 1979-80, editor newsletter 1978-80, chmn. legis. com.), Montgomery Regional Med. Record Assn. (pres. 1979-80), Mo. Med. Record Assn. (nominating com., ad-hoc scholarship com., dir. exec. com. 1983-84, pres.-elect 1984-85), Mid-Mo. Med. Record Assn. (sec. 1982-83). Methodist. Home: 201 N Roby Farm Rd Rocheport MO 65279 Office: Charter Hosp of Columbia 200 Portland St Columbia MO 65201

KILLINGSWORTH, MARK M., investment broker; b. Walla Walla, Wash., May 6, 1958; s. Clyde and Jacquelyn (Malley) K.; m. Lisa A. Peters, June 12, 1982; children: Benjamin, Laura. BS in Agr., U. Wis., 1982. Investment broker Kemper Securities, Beaver Dam, Wis., 1986-92, A.G. Edwards & Sons, Beaver Dam, 1992—. Bd. dirs. YMCA, Beaver Dam, 1993—. Mem. Lions (past pres. Beaver Dam). Office: AG Edwards & Sons Inc PO Box 397 114 Monroe Beaver Dam WI 53916

KILLIUS, RICHARD W., stockbroker; b. Cleve., Sept. 23, 1932. BS, U. Colo., 1954. Stockbroker Hayden Miller, Cleve., 1960-63, J.M. Russell, Cleve., 1963-78, McDonald & Co. Securities, Cleve., 1978—. 1st lt. USAF, 1954-59. Republican. Presbyterian. Office: McDonald & Co Securities 800 Superior Ave E Ste 2100 Cleveland OH 44114-2601

KILPATRICK, CAROLYN CHEEKS, state legislator, educator; b. Detroit, June 25, 1945; d. Marvell and Willa Mae (Henry) Cheeks; divorced; children: Kwame, Ayanna. AS, Ferris State Coll., Big Rapids, Mich., 1965; BS, Western Mich. U., 1972; MS in Edn., U. Mich., 1977. Tchr. Murray Wright High Sch., Detroit, 1972-78; mem. Mich. Ho. of Reps., Lansing, 1978—; Dem. whip, mem. appropriations com.; del. Dem. Convs., 1980, 84, 88. Rep. Detroit Substance Abuse Adv. Coun.; participant Mich. African Trade Mission, 1984, UN Internat. Women's Conf., 1986; del. participant Mich. Dept. Agr. to Nairobi (Kenya) Internat. Agr. Show, 1986. Recipient Anthony Wayne award Wayne State U., Disting. Legislator award U. Mich., Disting. Alumni award Ferris State U., Woman of Yr. award Gentlemen of Wall St., Inc., Burton-Abercrombie award 15th Dem. Congrl. dist. Mem. Nat. Orgn. 100 Black Women, Nat. Black Caucus of State Legislators (chairperson Mich. legis. session 1983-84), Nat. Order Women Legislators, Nat. Orgn. Black Elected Legis. Women (treas.). Mem. Pan African Orthodox Christian Ch. Office: House Reps State Capitol Lansing MI 48909

KILPATRICK, JEAN ANN, elementary education educator; b. Clinton, Iowa, July 25, 1957; d. James Irwin and Barbara Elizabeth (Gillespie) K. BS in Edn., Western Ill. U., 1979. Cert. elem. tchr., Ill. Tchr. Galesburg (Ill.) City Unified Sch. Dist. 205, 1979—. Deacon 1st United Presbyn. Ch., Galesburg, 1989-91; mem. state steering com. Ill. Network Accelerated Schs., 1990-92; lay leader Chrysalis, Galesburg, 1992; supt. Bethel Bapt. Asst. Sunday Sch., 1993. Recipient Thomas B. Herring Cmty. Svc. award Galesburg C. of C., 1991, Ill. State Bd. Edn. Award of Excellence, 1991. Mem. Galesburg Community Chorus (pres. 1990-92), Altrusa Club (Galesburg). Republican. Baptist. Office: 1480 W Main St Galesburg IL 61401-3318

KIM, H. J. (SHAUN KIM), engineering company executive; b. Seoul, Korea, Apr. 20, 1943; s. Derk Joe and Sue K. (Lee) K.; m. Bernadette Elaine; children: Mary Lisa, Michelle A. BSME, U. Md., 1965; MS in Engrng., George Washington U., 1970; MBA, U. Chgo., 1982. Registered profl. engr., N.J. From engr. to project mgr. Lever Bros. Co., Balt. and N.Y.C., 1965-78; dir. engrng., plant mgr. Nabisco Brands Inc., Chgo. and Clinton, Iowa, 1978-83; sr. dir. engrng., v.p. engrng. William Wrigley Jr. Co., Chgo., 1983—. Office: William Wrigley Jr Co 3535 S Ashland Ave Chicago IL 60609-1318

KIM, YOON BERM, immunologist, educator; b. Pyongnam, Korea, Apr. 25, 1929; came to U.S., 1959, naturalized, 1975; s. Sang Sun and Yang Rang (Lee) K.; m. Soon Cha Kim, Feb. 23, 1959; children: John, Jean, Paul. M.D., Seoul Nat. U., 1958; Ph.D., U. Minn., 1965. Intern Univ. Hosp. Seoul Nat. U., 1958-59; mem. faculty U. Minn., Mpls., 1960-73; assoc. prof. microbiology U. Minn., 1970-73; mem., head lab. ontogeny of immune system Sloan Kettering Inst. Cancer Research, Rye, N.Y., 1973-83; prof. immunology Cornell U. Grad. Sch. Med. Scis., N.Y.C., 1973-83; chmn. immunology unit Cornell U. Grad. Sch. Med. Scis., 1980-82; prof. microbiology, immumology and medicine, chmn. dept. micorbiology and immunology Finch U. Health Scis., Chgo. Med. Sch., 1983—, acting dean Sch. Grad. and Postdoctoral Studies, 1994-95; mem. Lobund adv. bd. U. Notre Dame, 1977-88. Contbr. numerous articles on immunology to profl. jours. Recipient rsch. career devel. award USPHS, 1968-73, Morris Parker Rsch. award U. Health Scis., Chgo. Med. Sch., 1984. Fellow Am. Acad. Microbiology; mem. AAAS, Assn. Gnotobiotics (pres.), Internat. Assn. for Gnotobiology (founding), Am. Assn. Immunologists, Am. Soc. Microbiology, Am. Assn. Pathologists, Korean Med. Assn., N.Y. Acad. Scis., Soc. for Leucocyte Biology, Internat. Soc. Devel. Comparative Immunology, Harvey Soc., Internat. Soc. Interferon and Cytokine Rsch., Chgo. Assn. Immunologists (pres.), Assn. Med. Sch. Microbiology and Immunology Chairs, Internat. Endotoxin Soc. (charter), Soc. Natural Immunity (charter), Sigma Xi, Alpha Omega Alpha. Home: 313 Weatherford Ct Lake Bluff IL 60044-1905 Office: Finch U Health Scis Chgo Med Sch 3333 Green Bay Rd North Chicago IL 60064-3037

KIMBALL, DONALD ROBERT, food company executive; b. Anderson, Ind., Mar. 4, 1938; s. Robert Martin and Mary Lucille (Gibson) K.; m. Mari-Anne Talbot, Apr. 6, 1985; children: Randy, Rick, Sharon-Lee, Douglas, David. BS in Agr., Purdue U., 1960. Registered profl. sanitarian, Ind. Pub. health sanitarian Div. Dairy Products, Ind. Bd. Health, LaPorte, 1962-66; milk sanitation rating officer Div. Dairy Products, Ind. Bd. Health, Indpls., 1966-75; chief milk sanitation rating officer Div. Dairy Products, Ind. Bd. Health, 1973-75, dir., 1975-87; dir. regulatory affairs Dean Foods Co., Rockford, Ill., 1987—, dir. farm rels., 1990—. Contbr. articles to profl. jours. Capt. U.S. Army, 1960-68. Recipient Disting. Svc. award, Midwest Dairy Products Assn., 1988. Mem. Internat. Assn. Milk, Food, Environ. Sanitarians, Nat. Conf. Interstate Milk Shipments (MMSR com., coun. III), Assn. Food and Drug Ofcls., Dairy Practices Coun., Midwest Dairy Foods Assn. (bd. dirs.). Methodist. Office: Dean Foods Co Technical Ctr 555 Colman Center Dr Rockford IL 61125-7005

KIMBALL, EDWARD MARTIN, data processing consultant; b. Cin., Aug. 22, 1946; s. H. Lawrence and Ruth Florence (Teper) K.; m. Dorothy Jean Sweeney, Aug. 31, 1969; children: Ronald, Amy. BA, Yale U., 1968; MA, U. Mich., 1971. Mathematician USAF, 1968-70; mgr. Comshare, Inc., Ann Arbor, Mich., 1972-76; v.p. E.J. Gainer and Assocs., Inc., Ann Arbor, 1977-80; dir. consulting Nat. Data Corp., Ann Arbor, 1980-83; corp. scientist Vector Rsch., Inc., Ann Arbor, 1983-95; prin. cons. Prince Waterhouse LLP, Chgo., 1995—. Mem. IEEE Computer Soc., Assn. Computing Machinery (sec.-treas. Ann Arbor chpt. 1980-82), Data Adminstrn. Mgmt. Assn. Office: 200 E Randolph Dr Chicago IL 60601

KIMBERLING, PAUL LEROY, brokerage executive; b. Marshalltown, Iowa, Nov. 21, 1953; s. Paul O. and Morna G. (Wineman) K.; m. Denise K. Bass, Aug. 16, 1975 (div. 1983); 1 child, Bobbie Jean; m. Mary Helen Hass, Nov. 29, 1986 (div. 1994). BS in Sociology, Coll. of the Ozarks, 1980. Dept. mgr. Sears Roebuck & Co., Columbia, Mo., 1976-78, Jefferson City, Mo., 1978-79; stockbroker Edward D. Jones & Co., West Plains, Mo., 1980—, ltd. ptnr, 1983—, mem. hiring team, 1986—, mem. tng. team, 1990—. Dir. ch. camp, Cliff Springs, Mo., 1989-94. Republican. Methodist. Home: Rt BB West Plains MO 65775-1967 Office: Edward D Jones & Co 210 W Main St West Plains MO 65775

KIMBLE, AL E., engineering executive; b. Akron, Ohio, Jan. 16, 1958. BS, Akron U., 1981. Registered profl. engr., Ohio. Cons. Massey Ferguson, Akron, 1978-83; mgr. engrng. JRB Co., Inc., Akron, 1983—. Mem. SAE. Democrat. Roman Catholic. Office: JRB Co Inc 2444 Gilchrist Rd Akron OH 44305-4408

KIMBLE, JAMES A., management consultant, accountant; b. Owosso, Mich., June 16, 1937; s. Gaylord Browning and Iva I. (Ansted) K.; children from previous marriage: Kim, Katherine, Kerri, Charles; m. Anne Park, June 13, 1970; 1 child, Jeffrey. BBA, U. Toledo, 1959. With The PM Group Toledo Inc., 1961—, v.p., 1964-90, pres., 1990—; mem. Accreditation Coun. Accountancy, 1975, Accreditation Coun. Taxation, 1984; bd. dirs. Black and Skaggs Assocs., chmn. bd., 1994; bd. dirs. Nat. Assn. Health Care Cons., Inc., 1992-95. Pres. Citizens for Metroparks, Toledo, 1976-77; v.p., commr. Met. Park Dist., 1977-86; pres. Metroparks, Toledo, 1986-94; chmn. July spl. events Toledo Sesquicentennial, 1987. Recipient Treasury Card IRS, 1976. Mem. Soc. Profl. Bus. Cons. (bd. dirs. 1977-80, cert.), Inst. Cert. Profl. Bus. Cons., Black & Skaggs Assocs. Republican. Office: The PM Group Toledo Inc 3150 N Republic Blvd Toledo OH 43615-1514

KIMBROUGH, BARBARA E., investment consultant; b. Leroy, Kans., Dec. 31, 1934. BBA, Washburn U., 1959. CSP. Clk., hosp. adminstr. USAF, Topeka, 1951-60; fin. mgr. Richards AFB, Mo., 1960-73; housing mgr. HUD, Topeka, 1973-79; investment cons. B.C. Christopher Securities, Topeka, 1979—. Sec.-treas. Mulvane Women's Bd., 1983-93; bd. dirs. Peppertree Park, 1991-94. Mem. Topeka Dental Assn. Aux. (pres. 1978-79). Republican. Office: BC Christopher Securities 534 S Kansas Ave Topeka KS 66603-3406

KIMBROUGH, WILLIAM WALTER, III, psychiatrist; b. Cleve., Sept. 26, 1928; s. William Walter and Wilhelmina Grace (Champion) K.; student Cornell U., 1945-46; BS, U. Mich., 1948, MD, 1952; m. Jo Ann Greiner, July 6, 1953; children: Elizabeth, Douglas. Intern, Ohio State U. Health Ctr., Columbus, 1952-53; resident U. Chgo. Clinics, 1955-56, Ypsilanti (Mich.) State Hosp., 1956-59; assoc. psychiatrist U. Mich. Health Ctr., Ann Arbor, 1959-61; practice medicine specializing in psychoanalytic psychiatry, Ann Arbor, 1961—; cons. atty. gen. U.S., 1974—, Ctr. for Forensic Psychiatry, 1958—, Brighton Found. for Alcoholism, 1961—, Washtenaw County (Mich.) Community Mental Health Svcs., 1978—, Mich. Dept. Social Svcs., 1978—, Mich Dept. Mental Health, 1989—; reviewer Mich. Peer Rev. Orgn.; clin. dir. Livingston County (Mich.) Community Mental Health Svcs., 1983-85, Mich. Dept. Corrections, 1985-88; exec. com. Northville Regional Psychiatric Hosp.; pres. Northville (Mich.) Psychiat. Assn., 1991-93; pres. Physicians for Mercy, 1995—. Capt. USPHSR, 1953-94. Recipient Physicians Recognition awards AMA, 1972-94. Fellow Am. Acad. Psychiatry and Law, Am. Soc. Psychoanalytic Physicians; mem. AAAS, Am. Acad. Psychotherapists, Am. Psychiat. Assn. (life), Ann Arbor Psychiat. Assn., Northville Psychiat. Assn. (pres. 1991-93), Am. Acad. Psychiatrists in Alcoholism and Addiction (founding mem.), Mich. Psychiat. Soc. (com. on legislation and govt. affairs), pres. Physicians for Mercy, N.Y. Acad. Sci., Hon. Order Ky. Cols., Sigma Alpha Epsilon, Phi Rho Sigma. Clubs: Ann Arbor Town, Ann Arbor Racquet, Univ., Travis Pointe Country (Ann Arbor); Little Harbor (Harbor Springs, Mich.), Round Table (Plymouth, Mich.). Home: 1903 Boulder Dr Ann Arbor MI 48104-4165 Office: 400 Maynard St Ann Arbor MI 48104-2440

KIMM, ROBERT GEORGE, animal science educator; b. Marengo, Iowa, Sept. 15, 1943; s. Albert Ernest and Irene Maxine (Smith) K.; m. Barbara

Ann Stripe, Dec. 28, 1966; children: Theodore Robert, Florence Marie. BS in Animal Sci., Iowa State U., 1965, MS in Agrl. Edn., 1969. Dist. sales rep. Ralston Purina, St. Louis, 1965-67; instr., coord. animal sci. Hawkeye C.C., Waterloo, Iowa, 1969—; internationally recognized sheep judge, 1975—; beef and sheep cons. Hawkeye C.C., 1969—; organizer Iowa Jr. Suffolk Sheep Assn., 1984, advisor 1984-89, coord. 1992. Chair Nat. Lamb and Wool Show, 1978-82, coord., 1992. With USAR, 1966-71. Recipient Disting. Svc. award Iowa Assn. Future Farmers, 1981, Iowa Vocat. Agr. Tchrs. Assn., 1995, Beresford-Quaife award Iowa State U. Extension, 1982, Pres.'s award for Outstanding Svc. to Hawkeye C.C., 1986, Nat. Teaching Excellence award U. Tex., 1988. Mem. Cedar Valley Lamb and Wool Assn. (Hall of Fame 1991), Nat. Suffolk Sheep Assn. (chair wether sire com. 1991-93), Iowa Suffolk Sheep Assn. (pres. 1982-84), Iowa Sheep Industry Assn. (pres. 1984-85, master lamb prodr. 1980), Am. Sheep Industry Assn. (chair ssedstock com. 1989-92), Iowa Cattlemen's Assn. (vice chair rsch. and edn. 1995-96). Methodist. Office: Hawkeye CC 1501 E Orange Rd Waterloo IA 50701-9014

KIMMEL, JOHN E., state legislator; m. Nancy Kimmel. Student, Ind. State U., Ivy Tech. Coll. Owner, pres. East 40 Sports, Inc.; mem. Ind. State Ho. of Reps. Dist. 43, mem. ways and means com., vice chmn. judiciary com. Active Seelyville Vol. Fire Dept., United Cerebral Palsy. Mem. C. of C., Masonic Lodge, Scottish Rite, Breakfast Optimist Club.

KIMMER, BRIAN K., engineering buyer; b. Readwood Falls, Minn., July 11, 1959; s. Darrell G. and Marlene H. (Lamb) K. A in Indsl. Electronics, Area Vocat. Tech. Sch., Granite Falls, Minn., 1979. Engrng. technician King Radio, Olathe, Kans., 1979-83; customer svc. mgr. Polaris Electronics, Olathe, 1983-86; engrng. buyer Engineered Specialty Products, Olathe, 1986—; pres. AB Products, Osawatomie, Kans., 1993—. Office: Engineered Specialty Products 1200 S Payne St Ste F Olathe KS 66061-5262

KINDER, DAVID C., small business owner; b. Ft. Worth, Tex., Jan. 7, 1959. Lead operator AB Chance, Centralia, Mo., 1977-81; owner Kinder Machine, Moberly, Mo., 1981—. Office: Kinder Machine 100 E Carpenter St Moberly MO 65270-2110

KINDER, PETER, state legislator; s. James A. and Mary Frances (Hunter) K. JD, St. Mary U., 1979; postgrad., U. Mo. Columbia, SE Mo. State U. Spl. asst. Rep. Bill Emerson, 1981-82; state senator Dist. 27 Mo. State Congress; staff counsel, real estate rep., 1983-87; assoc. publ., 1987—; campaign mgr., 1980, 82. Mem. Mo. Bar Assn., Am. Cancer Soc., Mo. Farm Bur., Area Wide United Way, Lions Club. *

KING, ADELE COCKSHOOT, French language educator; b. Omaha, July 28, 1932; d. Ralph Waldo and Thera Cecil (Brown) Cockshoot; m. Bruce Alvin King, Dec. 28, 1955; 1 child, Nicole Michelle. BA, U. Iowa, 1954; MA, U. Leeds, England, 1960; Doctorate in French Lit., U. Paris, 1970. Lectr. in French U. Ibadan, Nigeria, 1963-65, U. Lagos, Nigeria, 1967-70; reader in French Ahmadu Bello U., Zaria, Nigeria, 1973-76; prof. French Ball State U., Muncie, Ind., 1986—, chmn. dept. fgn. langs., 1991-94; vis. assoc. prof. U. Mo., Columbia, 1976-77. Author: (critical studies) Camus, 1964, 3d edit., 1968, Proust, 1968, Paul Nizan: écrivain, 1976, The Writings of Camara Laye, 1980, French Women Novelists: Defining a Female Style, 1989; (study guides) L'Enfant Noir, L'Etranger, Farewell to Arms, The Power and the Glory, Ghosts, 1980-82; editor: Camus's L'Etranger Fifty Years On, 1992; co-editor Modern Dramatists, 1982—, Women Writers, 1987—; contbr. articles to profl. jours. Summer Rsch. grantee Ball State U., 1987, 90, 95; postdoctoral fellow AAUW, 1977-78. Mem. MLA, Assn. Drs. of Univs. of France (v.p. 1991—), Am. Comparative Lit. Assn., Soc. des Etudes Camusiennes, Am. Assn. Tchrs. French, Marguerite Yourcenar Soc., Women in French (sec. 1988-92, v.p. 1996—, editor Women in French Studies 1996—). Office: Ball State Univ Dept Modern Langs Muncie IN 47306

KING, ALICE MAE, occupational health nurse; b. Ft. Wayne, Ind., Mar. 4, 1954; d. Henry Edward and Dorothy E. (Dressler) Franke; m. Jeffery Alan King, May 5, 1990; step children: Robert, Timothy, Thomas, Nicole, Jeffery Jr. Cert., Ft. Wayne Community Sch. Practical Nursing, 1976; student, Ind. U.-Purdue U, 1977-78; diploma, Parkview Sch. Nursing, Ft. Wayne, 1987; BSN, Ball State U., 1995. Files clk. Lincoln Nat. Life Ins. Co., Ft. Wayne, 1972-74; mail clk. K-Mart Distbn. Ctr., Ft. Wayne, 1974-75; practical nurse Parkview Meml. Hosp., Ft. Wayne, 1976-87, nurse, 1987-92; nurse Med-One, Ft. Wayne, 1992-93; nurse, case mgr. Summit Med. Staffing Inc., Ft. Wayne, 1993-94; nurse mgr. Am. Nursing, Ft. Wayne, 1994; clin. mgr. ResCare, Ft. Wayne, 1994-95; with Food Mktg., Ft. Wayne, 1995—. Ind. Regional Vocat. Rehab. scholar, 1975-76. Lutheran. Home: 7308 Baylor Dr Fort Wayne IN 46819-1618 Office: Food Mktg 4815 Executive Blvd Fort Wayne IN 46808

KING, CARL WILLIAM, electrical engineer; b. Evansville, Ind., June 1, 1956; s. John D. and Patricia R. (Ramsey) K.; m. Sheila R. Polk, Aug. 20, 1976; children: Kristopher W., Jedidiah C. BSEE, U. Evansville, 1993. Cert. eng.-in-tng., Inc. Master electrician Peabody Coal Co., Lynnville, Ind., 1978-90; elec. engr. PSI Energy, Owensville, Ind., 1992—. Pres. Boonville (Ind.) Swim Team, 1990-92, 94. Mem. IEEE. Home: 3844 Folsomville Rd Boonville IN 47601 Office: PSI Energy Gibson Sta RR 1 Box 300 Owensville IN 47665

KING, CAROL A., business executive; b. Des Moines, June 14, 1957. V.p. E.L. King & Assoc., Inc., Des Moines, 1985—. Editor (newsletter) Indoor Environmental News, 1991—, Comfort Zone, 1991; contbr. articles to profl. jours. Treas. Eastside Co-op, Des Moines, 1983—. Republican.

KING, CHARLES HOMER, manufacturing executive; b. Chgo., July 30, 1938; s. Merle Marine and (Serge) K.; m. Kathie Theiss, May 5, 1984; children: Dennis, Denise, Patricia, Justin. BS in Mgmt. and Mktg., Louisville U., 1967; MA in Computer Data Mgmt., Webster U., Jeffersonville, Ind., 1983. Product forecasting and product distbg. control Navistar Internat. Corp., Louisville, 1973-76; material requirements planning mgr. Navistar Internat. Corp., Springfield, Ohio, 1984-90; specialist in integrated factory mgmt., shop floor control and MRP II. Mem. bus. adv. bd. Clark State Coll. Fellow Am. Prodn. and Inventory Control Soc. (cert. in prodn. and inventory mgmt., cert. in resource mgmt., v.p., bd. dirs. region III), Fraternal Order of Eagles, Springfield Model Airplain Club. Republican. Home: 4904 Snyder Domer Rd Springfield OH 45502-9012

KING, CHARLES ROSS, physician; b. Nevada, Iowa, Aug. 22, 1925; s. Carl Russell and Dorothy Sarah (Mills) K.; m. Frances Pamela Carter, Jan. 8, 1949; children—Deborah Diane, Carter Ross, Charles Conrad, Corbin Kent. Student, Butler U., 1943; B.S. in Bus., Ind. U., 1948, M.D., 1964. Diplomate Am. Bd. Family Practice. Dep. dir. Ind. Pub. Works and Supply, 1949-52; salesman Knox Coal Corp., 1952-59; rotating intern Marion County Gen. Hosp., Indpls., 1964-65; family practice medicine Anderson, Ind., 1965—; sec.-treas. staff Cmty. Hosp., 1969-72, pres.-elect, dir., chief medicine, 1973—, bd. dirs., 1973-75; sec.-treas. St. John's Hosp., 1968-69, chief medicine, 1972-73, chief pediatrics, 1977—; bd. dirs. Rolling Hills Convalescnet Ctr., 1968-73; pres. Profl. Ctr. Lab., 1965—; vice chmn. Madison County Bd. Health, 1966-69, chmn., 1986—; chmn. bd. dirs. Star Fin. Bank, Anderson. Bd. dirs. Family Svc. Madison County, 1968-69, Madison County Assn. Mentally Retarded, 1972-76; chmn. bd. dirs. Anderson Downtown Devel. Corp., 1980—; mem. Paramont Restoration Steering Com., 1994—; trustee, sec.-tread. St. John's Med. Ctr., 1989—; mem. exec. com. Madison United Way Fund, vice-chmn., 1995, chmn., 1996; mem. exec. com. Stop Teen Pregnancy Program, 1995—; exec. commr. Health Search Madison County, 1995—. With U.S. Army, 1944-46. Recipient Dr. James Macholtz award Spl. Olympics, 1986—. Fellow Royal Soc. Health, Am. Acad. Family Practice (charter); mem. AMA (numerous Physicians Recognition awards), Ind. Med. Assn., Pan Am. Med. Assn., Am. Acad. Gen. Practice, Madison County Med. Soc. (pres. 1970), 9th Dist. Med. Soc. (sec.-treas. 1968), Anderson C. of C. (bd. dirs. 1979-82), Indpls. Mus. Art (corp. mem.), Anderson Country Club (bd. dirs. 1976-79), Phi Delta Theta (pres. Alumni Assn. 1952), Phi Chi. Methodist. Club: Anderson Country (bd. dirs. 1976-79). Home: 920 N Madison Ave Anderson IN 46011-1208 Office: 1933 Chase St Anderson IN 46016-4238

KING, DOROTHY JACKSON, psychologist, marriage-family counselor, therapist; b. Dundee, Miss., Dec. 13, 1955; d. Allan Jackson and Cliftee (Miller) Davis; m. Savoid Lester King, Jan. 27, 1979; children: Darren, Ranando. MDiv, Emmanuel Sch. Religion, Johnson City, Tenn., 1989; M Counseling, Evangel Sch. Religion, Monroe, La., 1990; PhD in Philosophy, Friends Christian U., Merced, Calif., 1992. Ordained, 1985. Assoc. pastor St. Andrew's Meth. Ch., Memphis; pastor Limestone and Jonesborough Chs., Johnson City, Tenn.; physician asst. Drs Motley and Medlock, Memphis; family advocacy rep. USN and Hawaii Family Ct., Honolulu; mem. child abuse adv. bd. Makalapa Abuse Com., Honolulu. Author: Psychological Development in Minorities, 1993; contbr. articles to various publs. Lt. USN. Fellow ACA; mem. Am. Mental Health Assn., Assn. Marriage and Family Counselors, Multicultural Assn., Am. Assn. Profl. Hypnotherapists, Assn. Clin. Pastoral Edn.

KING, GEORGE RALEIGH, manufacturing company executive; b. Benton Harbor, Mich., May 13, 1931; s. Maurice Peter and Opal Ruth (Hart) King; m. Phyllis Stratton, Apr. 10, 1950; children: Paula King Zang, Angela King Young, Philip. Student Adrian Coll., 1950-51. Cert. purchasing profl. exec. status. With Kirsch Co., Sturgis, Mich., 1951—, data processing trainee, 1951-53, data processing mgr., 1953-59, asst. purchasing agt., 1959-62, purchasing agt., 1962-68, asst. dir. purchasing, 1968-71, dir. purchasing, 1971—. Author: Rods & Rings, 1972. Elder, 1st Presbyterian Ch., Sturgis, 1970; pres. Sturgis Civic Players, 1972. Recipient citation Boy Scouts Am., 1966, Jr. Achievement, 1967; nominated candidate for adminstr. Fed. Procurement Policy, Reagan Adminstrn., Washington, 1980. Mem. Am. Purchasing Soc. (pres. 1979-81), Nat. Assn. Purchasing Mgmt., Southwestern Purchasing Assn. Clubs: Klinger Lake Country, Exchange (pres. Sturgis 1959, dist. gov. dist and nat. clubs 1961). Masons, Elks. Home: 1804 Lakeshore Dr Apt 16 Saint Joseph MI 49085-1616

KING, GUADALUPE VASQUEZ, psychology and social work educator; b. Evans, Colo., Sept. 20, 1947; d. Marcos and Louise (Arzate) Vasquez; m. Daniel Patrick King, Dec. 11, 1971. BA, Sam Houston State U., Huntsville, Tex., 1970; MSW, U. Wis., Milw., 1973, PhD in Edn., 1996; cert. bus. mgmt., Marquette U., 1990. Social worker Wis. Dept. Health and Social Svcs., Milw., 1970-74; instr. U. Wis., 1974-77; prof. social work & psychology Milw. Area Tech. Coll., 1976—; dir. social svc. Coun. for Spanish Speaking, Milw, 1976; dir. LaGuadalupana, Inc., Milw., 1977-79. Bd. dirs. DePaul Hosp., Milw., 1976-91, NCCJ, Milw., 1976—, Epilepsy Assn., Milw., 1989. Recipient Change Maker award Wis. Fedn. Women's Clubs, 1978, Outstanding Dedicated Svc. award LaGuadalupana, Inc., 1979, Outstanding Contbn. award Milw. Commn. on Community Rels., 1980, cert. of appreciation Office of Wis. Gov., 1980, Office County Exec., 1980. Mem. NASW, NAt. Hispanic Women's ORgn., Hispanic Profl. Orgn. Soc. (founding), Zonta, Phi Delta Kappa, Pi Lambda Theta, Alpha Kappa Delta. Republican. Baptist. Home: 5125 N Cumberland Blvd Milwaukee WI 53217-5747 Office: Milw Area Tech Coll 700 W State St Milwaukee WI 53233-1419

KING, HEATHER ANN, freelance journalist; b. Waukegan, Ill., Oct. 27, 1939; d. Marion Vincent and Elaine Ann (Ramage) Warton; m. Peter Austin Randall, Feb. 29, 1964 (div. July 1982); children: Holly Elizabeth, Melissa Leigh; m. Richard Harding King, Aug. 11, 1984. BA, Macalester Coll., St. Paul, 1960; student, Cordon Bleu Sch. Cooking, 1964-65. Mgmt. trainee Dayton Co., Mpls., 1960-61; indsl. editor, pub. rels. Luth. Brotherhood Ins. Soc., Mpls., 1961-64; asst. regional adminstr. Jefferson County ARC, Lakewood, Colo., 1965-67; freelance writer, editor Mpls., 1970-80; feature writer Mpls. Star, 1980-82; freelance copywriter, editl. cons., pub. rels., mktg. Mpls., 1982—; bd. dirs. ARC. Editor/copywriter: The Global Gourmet, Ten Thousand Tastes of Minnesota, Savor the Flavor, The Best of Byerly's Vol. I & II; awarded U.S. Patent for gift/gourmet bag in Oct. 1994. Bd. dirs. AAUW, Minn. Orch., Friends of the Mpls. Inst. Arts, Edina Art Ctr., Edina Newcomers, Jr. League Mpls.; adv. bd. Concordia Lang. Villages; past pres. Edina Federated Women's Club; house com., bulletin, Art Godfrey House, scholarship co-chair, food chair Bus. Women's Forum, Woman's Club of Mpls.; fundraising Twin Cities Pub. TV; comm., outreach, stewardship Westminster Presbyn. Ch.; group facilitator Metro Drug Awareness Program; mem. LWV, Blake Sch. Parents Assn. Recipient Nat. Book awards, Tabasco Cmty. Cookbook award McIlhenny Co., 1993. Mem. Nat. Assn. Female Execs., Macalester Coll. Alumni Assn. (fundraising, reunion com.), Mpls. Club, Interlachen Country Club, 1006 Summit Ave. Soc. Republican. Home: 5218 Green Farms Rd Edina MN 55436 Office: Copy à la King 4445 W 77th St Edina MN 55435

KING, JAMES MICHAEL, process engineer; b. Cleve., May 3, 1957. Student, Cuyahoga C.C., Parma, Ohio, 1976, Cleve. State U., 1979. Quality control mgr. Philway Products, Inc., Lodi, Ohio, 1980-87; gen. mgr. Nat. Printed Cirs., Norwalk, Ohio, 1987-88; gen. foreman Fero Corp., Cleve., 1988-90; gen. mgr. Philway Products Inc., Lodi, 1990-93; process engr. Philway Products Inc., Ashland, Ohio, 1993—. Republican. Roman Catholic. Home: 10168 Crawford Rd Homerville OH 44235-9753 Office: Philway Products Inc 701 Virginia Ave Ashland OH 44805-1945

KING, JERRY WAYNE, research chemist; b. Indpls., Feb. 19, 1942; s. Ernest E. and Miriam (Sanders) K.; m. Bettie Maria Dunbar, Aug. 8, 1965; children: Ronald Sean, Valerie Raquel, Diana Lynn. BS, Butler U., 1965; PhD, Northeastern U., 1973; fellow, Georgetown U., 1973-74. Research chemist Union Carbide Corp., Bound Brook, N.J., 1968-70; asst. prof. dept. chemistry Va. Commonwealth U., Richmond, 1974-76; research scientist Arthur D. Little, Inc., Cambridge, Mass., 1976-77; research assoc. Am. Can Co., Barrington, Ill., 1977-79; research scientist CPC Internat., Summit-Argo, Ill., 1979-86; lead scientist NCAUR-ARS div. USDA, Peoria, Ill., 1986—; guest lectr. various sci. groups, meetings, 1964—; v.p. Supercritical Confs. Mem. editl. bd. Italian Jour. Food Sci., Jour. Supercritical Fluids, Supercritical Fluid Sci. and Tech. Series, Seminars in Food Sci.; contbr. articles to profl. jours. Recipient Scientist of Yr. award Nat. Ctr. Agrl. Utilization Rsch., Agrl. Rsch. Svc., USDA, 1993, Chgo. Chromatography Discussion Group Merit award, 1995; named v.p. Supercritical Confs. Mem. Assn. Ofcl. Analytical Chemists (Harvey W. Wiley award 1992), Inst. Food Technologists, Am. Oil Chemists Soc., Am. Chem. Soc., Acad. Georgofili (Italy) (corr.). Home: 1820 W Sunnyview Dr Peoria IL 61614-4662 Office: USDA Nat Ctr Agrl Utilization Rsch ARS 1815 N University St Peoria IL 61604-3902

KING, JOHN (JACK), human services administrator; b. Chgo., Nov. 9, 1930; s. John Joseph and Catherine (Clifford) K.; m. Betty Jane King, Mar. 29, 1957; children: Katherine, Kelly, John, Patricia, Maureen, Colleen, Jeremiah, Eileen. Grad., Betty Ford Ctr. Profls., Plam Springs, Calif. Lic. recovery house Ill. Dept. Alchoholism and Substance abuse; cert. counselor. Supr., rte. salesman Honey Crust Corp., Chgo., 1953-59; fire fighter City fo Chgo. Fired Dept., 1959-90; house mgr. Wayback Inn Halfway House, Maywood, Ill., 1982-83; founder, exec. dir. Guildhaus, Blue Island, Ill., 1985—, also past pres. bd.; lectr. in field. With USAF, 1949-53, Korea. Recipient First Annual Cmty. Svc. award South Suburban Coun. Alchoholism and Subastance Abuse, 1993, City of Chgo. award Mayro Richard M. Daly and Commr. Raymond E. Orozco, Sertoma award, 1995. Mem. Ill. Addictions Counselors Assn., Ill. Alchoholism and Drug Dependent Assn., Ill. Assn. Residential Extended Care Facilites (v.p. 1992-94), Blue Island Cmty. Coun. (pres. 1991-93), Assn. Halfway House Alchoholism Programs, Internat. Assn. Fire Fighters (employee assistance program), Lions Internat., Am. Legion, Amvets, VFW. Roman Catholic. Home: 2413 Canal St Blue Island IL 60406 Office: Guildhaus 2413 Canal St Blue Island IL 60406

KING, JOHN JOSEPH, manufacturing company executive; b. Toledo, Jan. 12, 1924; s. Walter and Frances (Gwozd) Kawecka; m. Joy G. Mohler, Jan. 28, 1950; children: Catherine M., Carolyn S., David J., Michael R., Mark A.R. BSME magna cum laude, U. Toledo, 1957, MS in Indsl. Engring., 1961. Registered profl. engr., Ohio. Draftsman, Tecumseh Products Co., 1941-42; die designer Bingham Stamping Co., 1942-46; tool designer Spicer Mfg. Co., 1946-47; product designer Am. Floor Surfacing Co., 1947-50; founder, mgr. engr. Kent Industries, 1950-52; mech. engr. Owens Ill. Inc., Toledo, 1953-63; mgr. rsch. and devel. Permaglass Inc., Genoa, Ohio, 1963-69; founder, pres. Ashur Inc., Rossford, Ohio, 1969—, also chmn. bd. dirs. Patentee in field. Mem. Am. Ceramic Soc., Soc. Mfg. Engrs., Phi Kappa Phi, Tau Beta Pi. Republican. Roman Catholic. Clubs: Devils Lake Yacht. Lodges: KC, Eagles. Home: 1111 W Elm Tree Rd Rossford OH 43460-1338 Office: Ashur Inc 28663 Glenwood Rd Perrysburg OH 43551-3011

KING, JOHN NORMAN, English language educator, researcher; b. N.Y.C., Feb. 2, 1945; s. Luther Waddington and Alba (Iregui) K.; m. Pauline Marie Laure Grondin, Jan. 18, 1986; 1 child, Jonathan Paul. BA cum laude, Randolph-Macon Coll., 1965; MA cum laude, U. Chgo., 1966, PhD, 1973. Lectr. Abdullahi Bayero U., Kano, Nigeria, 1967-69; from asst. prof. to prof. Bates Coll., Lewiston, Maine, 1971-89; prof. English, Ohio State U., Columbus, 1989—, dir. NEH summer seminar for coll. tchrs., 1990; vis. lectr. Oxford (Eng.) U., 1978-79. Author: English Reformation Literature: The Tudor Origins of the Protestant Tradition, 1982, Tudor Royal Iconography: Literature and Art in an Age of Religious Crisis, 1989, Spenser's Poetry and the Reformation Tradition, 1990; editor: The Vocation of John Bale (1553), 1990, Anne Askew's Examinations (1546-47), 1997; editor Lit. and History, 1989—; literature editor Reformation, 1995—; asst. editor Brit. Studies Monitor, 1979-82. Bd. govs. Manchester Coll., Oxford, Eng., 1978—. Residential fellow NEH, Brown U., 1981-82, sr. resident fellow Folger Shakespeare Libr., 1986-87, sr. fellow Huntington Libr., 1984, Andrew Mellon Found. rsch. fellow Huntington Libr., 1992, NEH fellow for univ. profs., 1994-95. Mem. MLA, Am. Milton Soc., Renaissance English Text Soc. (editl. bd. 1990—), Renaissance Soc. Am., Spenser Soc., John Foxe Soc., Tyndale Soc., Coun. Editors Learned Jours., Phi Beta Kappa. Office: Ohio State U Dept English 164 W 17th Ave Columbus OH 43210-1326

KING, KAY SUE, investment company executive; b. Indpls., Sept. 14, 1948; d. George W. and Nadine M. K.; 1 child, Christopher G. Student, U. Ariz., 1966-70; BS in Edn., Ind. U., 1971; MA in Speech Communication, U. Hawaii, 1974. Tchr. Indpls. High Schs., 1971-1973; sec., treas. G. W. King Co., Indpls., 1974—; domestic sales mgr. Regal Travel, Indpls., 1975-90; pres., bd. dirs. K.S. King, Inc., Indpls., 1977—; mng. ptnr. K.S. King Co., Indpls., 1982—. Mem. pub. rels. com. Indpls. Zoolog. Xoc., 1976-85; vol. Indpls Humane Soc., 1966—, Indpls. Aid to Zoo Horse Show, 1974-78, Save the Ducks campaign, Indpls., 1978, Pan Am. Games Olympic Sports Com., Indpls., 1981-82; tchr. Sunday sch. Meridian St. Methodist Ch., Indpls., 1988-90. Elected Festival Princess 500 Festival Assn., Indpls., 1968. Mem. Internat. Assn. Bus. Communicators, Internat. Wildlife Fedn., Indpls. Zool. Soc. (charter), Indpls. Pub. Libr., Indpls. Children's Mus., Indpls. Ski Club, U. Ariz. Alumni Assn., Ind. Univ. Alumni Assn., Channel 20, Riviera Club, Lilly Pool, Meridian Hills Country Club, Delta Delta Delta. Home: 702 Holliday Ln Indianapolis IN 46260-3589 Office: King Co 5665 N Meridian St Indianapolis IN 46208-1502

KING, KENNETH PAUL, secondary education educator; b. Omaha, Oct. 28, 1960; s. Richard Carlyle King and Karen (Cushman) Cheyney; m. Tina Anne, July 6, 1990. BS, Iowa State U., 1986; MS in Edn., No. Ill. U., 1991, postgrad., 1991—. Cert. secondary edn., Iowa, adminstrv., Ill. Writer, editor Quaransan Group, Northbrook, Ill., 1991; tchr. physics Sch. Dist. #46, Elgin, Ill., 1986-95; grad. asst. No. Ill. U., DeKalb, 1995—, instr. sci. teacing methods, 1996—. Camp dir. Boys Scouts of Am., St. Charles, Ill., 1992, sect. dir. nat. camping sch., Kansas City, Mo., 1983-92. Recipient U. Chgo. Teaching Commendation award, 1993. Mem. ASCD, Assn. for Rsch. in Edn., Ill. Assn. for Supervision and Curriculum Devel. Home: 1010 Blackhawk De Kalb IL 60116 Office: No Ill U Gabel Hall De Kalb IL 60115

KING, KENNETH R., state legislator; m. Ruth King. Kans. state rep. Dist. 77, farmer, stockman. Home: RR 1 Leon KS 67074-9803*

KING, LAUREN ALFRED, English language educator; b. Avilla, Ind., Apr. 17, 1904; s. Alfred Hiram and Alberta (Bodenhafer) K.; m. Helen Chrystal Stahl, June 3, 1927; children: Miriam Helen, David Lauren. AB, Asbury Coll., 1927; PhD, Ohio State U., 1930. Instr. English Asbury Coll., Wilmore, Ky., 1927-28, prof. English, 1932-35; prof. English Houghton (N.Y.) Coll., 1930-31, 46-47, dean of coll., 1947-50; prof. English State Coll., Peru, Nebr., 1931-32; assoc. and prof. English Wheaton (Ill.) Coll., 1935-46; chmn. Dept. English Muskingum Coll., New Concord, Ohio, 1950-66; v.p. academic devel. Malone Coll., Canton, Ohio, 1966-69, prof. English, 1969-74; emeritus prof. English Malone Coll., Canton, 1974—. Author: Building Better Sentences, 1941, The Way You Believe, 1991, Verses for Helen, 1992; contbr. articles to ednl. and religious jours. Mem. Soc. of Friends. Home and Office: 10635 Belle Dr Norwich OH 43767-9759

KING, LEE ANN, ballet instructor, choreographer; b. Ann Arbor, Mich., Jan. 19, 1953; d. Jay B. and Wanda Mae (Hicks) K.; m. Chris Shankland, Jan. 20, 1973 (div. 1981); 1 child, Ryan. Grad. high sch., Ann Arbor. Class demonstrator Sylvia Studio Dance, Ann Arbor, 1967-71, asst. instr., 1975-77, instr., 1977-81, dir., instr., 1981—; dancer, asst. dir. Ann Arbor Civic Ballet, 1975-82, dir., choreographer, 1982—. Choreographer, dir. (ballets) Windbourne, 1979, Vienese Fantasy, 1980, Haunted Castle, 1982, L'Etude Classique, 1983, Serenade in the Park, 1985, La Boutique Fantastique, 1991, Rag-Time Cards, 1992, 12 varieties Mall, Peter and the Wolf, 1996. Fellow Cecchetti Coun. Am. (gen. bd. mem. 1977-83, nat. exec. bd. 1984—, gen. bd. chmn. 1988-89, nat. bd. examiners 1988—, gen. bd. scholarship 1980, nat. pres. 1994-95, nat. tchr. prin. and past pres. 1996-97). Home: 210 N Union St PO Box 74 Manchester MI 48158-9586 Office: Sylvia Studio Dance 525 E Liberty St Ann Arbor MI 48104-2209

KING, MARGARET ANN, communications educator; b. Marion, Ind., Feb. 27, 1936; d. Paul Milton and Janet Mary (Broderick) Burke; m. Charles Claude King, Aug. 25, 1956; children: C. Kevin, Elizabeth Ann, Paul S., Margaret C. Student, Ohio Dominican, 1953-56, U. Kans., 1980-81; BA in Communication, Purdue U., 1986, MA in Pub. Communication, 1990. Regional rep. Indpls. Juv. Justice Task Force, 1984-85; vis. instr. dept. communication Purdue U., West Lafayette, Ind., 1992; lectr. dept. communication, 1992—; bd. mem. Vis. Nurse Home Health Svcs. Grad. mem. Leadership Lafayette, 1983. Purdue U. fellow, 1986-87. Mem. AAUW, Speech Comm. Assn. Am., Ctrl. States Comm. Assn. (conf. presenter 1989), Golden Key, Phi Kappa Phi. Republican. Roman Catholic. Home: 1613 Redwood Ln Lafayette IN 47905-3939 Office: Purdue U Dept Communication West Lafayette IN 47907

KING, MICHAEL HOWARD, lawyer; b. Chgo., Mar. 10, 1943; s. Warren and Betty (Fine) K.; m. Candice M. King, Aug. 18, 1968; children—Andrew, Julie. B.S. Washington U., St. Louis 1967, J.D. 1970. Bar: Ill. 1970, U.S. Dist. Ct. (no. dist.) Ill. 1970, U.S. Dist. Ct. (ea. dist.) Wis. 1972, U.S. Ct. Appeals (7th cir.) 1974, U.S. Ct. Appeals (5th cir.) 1979, U.S. Supreme Ct. 1975, U.S. Ct. Appeals (3d cir.) 1983, U.S. Tax Ct. 1987, U.S. Ct. Appeals (10th cir.) 1987, U.S. Dist. Ct. (no. dist.) Calif. 1987, U.S. Dist. Ct. Nebr. 1988, U.S. Dist. Ct. (ctrl. dist.) Ill. 1992, U.S. Dist. Ct. (no. dist.) N.Y. 1992, U.S. Ct. Appeals (2nd cir.) 1994. Spl. atty. organized crime, racketeering sect. U.S. Dept. Justice, Washington, 1970-73; asst. U.S. atty. No. Dist. Ill., Chgo., 1973-75; assoc. Antonow & Fink, Chgo., 1976, ptnr., 1977-79; ptnr. Ross & Hardies, Chgo., 1979-95; chmn. Bd. Commr. Office of State Appellate Defender. Co-author Model Jury Instructions in Criminal Antitrust Cases, 1982, Handbook on Antitrust Grand Jury Investigations, 1988. Bd. dirs. Chgo. Youth Ctrs., 1977-82; trustee Cove Sch., 1984-88, the Goodman Theatre, 1993—. Mem. ABA (litigation sect., antitrust sect., criminal practice procedure com.), Ill. Bar Assn., Chgo. Bar Assn. (judiciary com., antitrust com.), Am. Judicature Soc., Fed. Bar Assn., Assn. Trial Lawyers Am., Mid-Am. Club (bd. govs.), Econ. Club, Phi Delta Phi, Alpha Epsilon Pi. Home: 2025 Windy Hill Ln Highland Park IL 60035-4233 Office: Ross & Hardies 150 N Michigan Ave Ste 2500 Chicago IL 60601-7525

KING, MICHAEL LAYTON, agricultural products executive; b. Decatur, Ill., Mar. 26, 1959; s. Robert and Maribeth (Ward) K.; m. Joyce Ann Geissert, June 13, 1981 (div. Jan. 1987); 1 child, Justin; m. Wendy K. Walker, Feb. 27, 1988; children: Jordan, Shelby, Celina. Lab technician Archer Daniels Midland, Decatur, Ill., 1981-83; bus. mgr., corp. pres. Mari-Mann Herb Co., Inc., Decatur, 1983—; corp. pres. King Dry Fragrance Co., Decatur, 1992—, Mari-Mann Herb Fest, Decatur, 1994, The Solid Scents Co., Decatur, 1995. Inventor in field. Recipient Outstanding Young Farmer award Decatur Jaycees and WDZQ-FM, 1986-87, Leadership award Ill. Dept. Rehab. Svcs., 1994; named Employer of Yr. Epilepsy Assn. Lincoln Land, 1990. Mem. Ill. Herb Assn. (charter), Tau Kappa Epsilon, Alpha

Epsilon Delta, Sigma Zeta. Republican. Office: Mari-Mann Herb Co Inc 1 Mari-Mann Ln Decatur IL 62521

KING, ROGER EDWARD, manufacturing engineer; b. Columbus, Ohio, Feb. 27, 1943; s. Roger and Nova K.; m. Twila, May 3, 1965; children: David, Roger Jr., Susanne. AAS in Design Engring., Ohio U., 1980. Draftsman McBee Systems, Athens, Ohio, 1965-67; designer Lancaster (Ohio) Glass Corp., 1967-74; plant engr. McAuley Mfg., Bremen, Ohio, 1974—. With U.S. Army, 1961-64. Mem. Am. Legion. Office: McAuley Mfg 211 Broad St PO Box 106 Bremen OH 43107-1003

KING, S(ANFORD) MACCALLUM, business owner, consultant; b. St. Catherines, Ont., Can., May 21, 1926; came to U.S., 1948; s. Sanford Walter and Mary Agnes (McCallum) K.; m. Virginia Jackson, Dec. 29, 1950 (div. June 1983); children: Marilyn, Nancy, Gordon, Laura; m. Iris Krueger, June 16, 1984. BS in Agr., U. Toronto, Ont., Can., 1948; MS, Purdue U., 1950; PhD, U. Wis., 1956; MBA, Keller Grad. Sch. Mgmt., Chgo., 1981. Soil scientist Std. Fruit & Steamship Co., LaCeiba, Honduras, 1951-53; rsch. asst. prof., sta. supt. Mich. State U., Chatham, 1956-61; agronomist, supr., mgr. product devel., tech. svcs., R&D Internat. Minerals & Chem. Corp., Skokie and Libertyville, Ill., 1962-70; dir. agr. Devel. & Resources Corp., Sacramento, 1971-73; v.p. Taralan Corp., Geneva, Ill., 1973-87; sr. v.p. Competitive Edge, Inc., Glencoe, Ont., Can., 1988-90; pres. King Internat., Lake Zurich, Ill., 1970—; sr. advisor Pro-Crop Inc., Mundelein, Ill., 1992-94; cons. Devel. Planning & Rsch. Assocs., Manhattan, Kans., 1973, 75, 77, FMC Internat., San Jose, Calif., 1974, Potash Corp. Sask., Saskatoon, Can., 1980-82, Devres, Inc., Bethesda, Md., 1990—, IMC Global, Inc., Mundelein, Ill., 1994—; instr. mktg. No. Ill. U., DeKalb, 1990-91, 93—. Contbr. articles to profl. and popular jours. Pres. PTA, Glenview, Ill., 1966. Mem. Am. Soc. Agronomy (chair com. 1966-73), Soil Sci. Soc. Am. Republican. Presbyterian.

KING, SHERYL JAYNE, secondary education educator, counselor; b. East Grand Rapids, Mich., Oct. 29, 1945; d. Thomas Benton III and Bettyann Louise (Mains) K. BS in Family Living, Sociology, Secondary Edn., Cen. Mich. U., 1968, M in Counseling, 1971. Educator Newaygo (Mich.) Pub. Schs., 1968-72; interior decorator Sue King Interiors, Grand Rapids, Mich., 1972-73; dir. girl's unit Dillon Family and Youth Svcs., Tulsa, 1973-74; mgr. Fellowship Press, Grand Rapids, Minn., 1974-76; educator, counselor Itasca Community Coll., Grand Rapids, 1977-81; dept. head Dist. 318, Grand Rapids, 1977-81, 85-87; bd. dirs., chairperson program com. Marriage and Family Devel. Ctr., Grand Rapids, 1985-89. Treas. Cove Whole Foods Coop., 1978-80; chmn. bd. Christian Community Sch., 1977-78; jr. high softball coach, 1983-86; mem. issues com. No. Minn. Citizens League, Grand Rapids, 1984—, Blandin Found. Study, 1985-86; chairperson Itasca County Women's Consortium, Grand Rapids, 1983-87; Women's Day Conf., Grand Rapids, 1983-87; bd. dir. audio tech. Fellowship of Believers, Grand Rapids, 1974-87, 90—, deaconess, 1974—; bd. dir. audio tech Camp Dominion, Cass Lake, Minn., 1976-80; mem. fitness com., chmn. aquatic com., YMCA, Grand Rapids, 1974-87. Recipient 6 Outstanding Svc. awards Fellowship of Believers, 1974-79. Mem. Alpha Delta Kappa. Republican. Home: 1914 McKinney Lake Rd Grand Rapids MN 55744-4330

KING, TERRY LEE, statistician, mathematician; b. Akron, Iowa, Feb. 24, 1945; s. Stanley W. and Hazel M. (Peck) K.; m. Carol Elizabeth Glass, June 12, 1971; children: Kevin, Shawn, Heather. B.A. cum laude, Westmar Coll., 1967; M.S., U. Iowa, 1969; Ph.D., Pa. State U., 1980. Instr., Thiel Coll., Greenville, Pa., 1969-71; statistician Desmatics, Inc., State College, Pa., 1975-79; instr. Frostburg State Coll., Md., 1979-81; assoc. prof. math./stats., 1981-89, chmn. dept. math./stats. N.W. Mo. State U., Maryville, 1988-93, prof. mathematics and statistics, 1989—. Editorial collaborator Current Index to Statistics, 1980-89. Deacon, active in music program First Bapt. Ch.; asst. scout master Boy Scouts of Am. Mem. Am. Statis. Assn. (membership com. 1982-84, mem. com. on stats. and disability 1995—), Math. Assn. Am. (vice-chair Mo. sect. 1990-91, chmn., 1991-92, past chair 1992-93), Biometric Soc., Rotary Internat. (Maryville chpt., program chair 1995-96, sec. 1996—), Phi Kappa Phi, Kappa Mu Epsilon, Pi Mu Epsilon. Office: NW Mo State U 800 University Dr Maryville MO 64468-6015

KING, THOMAS ELLWOOD, accountant, educator; b. Balt., May 12, 1942; s. Ellwood John and Dolores Katherine (Lentz) K.; m. Robin Marie Schroeder, Sept. 9, 1983; 1 child, Thomas Bradley. BS, Calif. State U., Northridge, 1965; MBA, UCLA, 1966, PhD, 1973. CPA, Ill. Acct. Braveco Express Co., L.A., 1965-68; ind. cons. L.A., 1968-69; teaching assoc. UCLA, 1969-70; asst. prof. U. Iowa, Iowa City, 1972-77; assoc. prof. So. Ill. U., Edwardsville, 1977-82, prof. acctg., 1982—. Co-author: Advanced Financial Accounting, 1988, 2d edit., 1993, 3d edit., 1996; contbr. to profl. publs. Mem. AICPA (Elijiah Watt Sells award 1984), Ill. Soc. CPAs (Gold medal 1984), Fin. Execs. Inst., Inst. Internal Auditors (gov. 1991—), Inst. Mgmt. Accts., Am. Acctg. Assn. Office: So Ill U Campus Box 1104 Edwardsville IL 62026

KING, (JACK) WELDON, photographer; b. Springfield, Mo., Jan. 19, 1911; s. Clyde Nelson and Mary Blanche (Murphy) K.; B.A., Drury Coll., 1934, Mus.B., 1934. Chief still photographer African expdns. including Gatti-Hallicrafters Expdn., 1947-48, 12th Gatti Expdn., 1952, Wyman Carroll Congo Expdn., 1955, 13th Gatti Expdn., 1956, 14th Gatti Expdn., 1957; also freelance photog. expdns., Africa, 1960, 66, 76-77; trips for GAF Corp. to S.Am., 1962, 63, 77-78, Australia and N.Z., 1972-73; Alaska, 1982, Europe, 1983; one-man shows include Faces and Places at Springfield (Mo.) Art Mus., 1989, also numerous assignments throughout U.S. Served as photographer with Coast Arty. Corps, U.S. Army, 1941-42; PTO; Japanese prisoner of war, 1942-45. Mem. Internat. Ctr. Photography. Contbr. photographs to numerous art books, mags., encys., textbooks. Address: 1234 E Grand St Springfield MO 65804-0004

KING, WILLIAM STEWART, II, public relations executive; b. Neptune, N.J., Nov. 8, 1954; s. William Stewart and Helen Irene (Moysiuk) K.; m. Shelley Ann Bundy, July 17, 1983; children: Bentley, Hallie. BA, Morris Harvey Coll., 1976. Sports info. dir. Morris Harvey Coll., Charleston, W.Va., 1974-76; asst. promotions dir. Tulane U., New Orleans, 1977; pub. relations dir. Milw. Bucks NBA, 1977—; mem. NBA Pub. Rels. Adv. Bd. Editor Milw. Bucks Media Guide, 1977-96, HOOP game program, 1977-96. Active in charitable orgns. including Midwest Athletes Against Childhood Cancer Fund; bd. dirs. Make-A-Wish Found. of Wis. Home: 39214 Lakeview Ln Oconomowoc WI 53066-1960 Office: Milw Bucks 1001 N 4th St Milwaukee WI 53203-1314

KINGDON, JOHN WELLS, political science educator; b. Wisconsin Rapids, Wis., Oct. 28, 1940; s. Robert Wells and Catherine (McCune) K.; m. Kirsten Berg, June 16, 1965; children: James, Tor. B.A., Oberlin Coll., 1962; M.A., U. Wis., 1963, Ph.D., 1965. Asst. prof. polit. sci. U. Mich., Ann Arbor, 1965-70, assoc. prof., 1970-75, prof., 1975—; chmn. dept. polit. sci. U. Mich., 1982-87. Author: Candidates for Office, 1968, Congressmen's Voting Decisions, 1973, 3d rev. edit., 1989, Agendas, Alternatives and Public Policies, 1984, 2d edit., 1995. NSF grantee, 1978-82, Soc. Sci. Research Council grantee, 1969-70; Guggenheim fellow, 1979-80, Ctr. for Advanced Study in Behavioral Scis. fellow, 1987-88. Fellow Am. Acad. Arts and Scis.; mem. Midwest Polit. Sci. Assn. (pres. 1987-88). Office: U Mich Polit Sci Dept Ann Arbor MI 48109

KINGSBURY, JAMES D., stockbroker; b. Denver, May 12, 1952. BS, Colo. State U., 1975. Resident mgr. Merrill Lynch, Chesterfield, Mo., 1975—. Mem. Chesterfield C. of C., Rotary. Office: Merrill Lynch 16100 N Outer 40 Dr Chesterfield MO 63006

KINGSLEY, JAMES GORDON, healthcare executive; b. Houston, Nov. 22, 1933; s. James Gordon and Blanche Sybil (Payne) K.; m. Martha Elizabeth Sasser, Aug. 24, 1956 (div. 1992); children: Gordon Alan, Craig Emerson; m. Suzanne H. Patterson, Oct. 30, 1993; 1 child, Aaron T. AB, Miss. Coll., 1955; MA, U. Mo., 1956; BD, ThD, New Orleans Bapt. Theol. Sem., 1960, 65; HHD (hon.), Mercer U., 1980; LittD (hon.), Seinan Gakuin U., Japan, 1989; postgrad., U. Louisville, 1968-69, Nat. U. Ireland, 1970, Harvard U., 1976. Asst. prof. Miss. Coll., 1956-58; instr. Tulane U., 1958-60; asst. prof. William Jewell Coll., Liberty, Mo., 1960-62; assoc. prof. Ky. So. Coll., Louisville, 1964-67, prof., 1967-69; prof. lit. and religion William Jewell Coll., 1969-93, dean, 1976-80, pres., 1980-93; v.p. Health Midwest, Kansas City, Mo., 1994-95, 96—; dep. dir. Nelson-Atkins Mus. of Art, 1995-96; assoc. prof. Ky. So. Coll., Louisville, 1964-67, prof., 1967-69; vis. fellow Cambridge (Eng.) U., 1988. Author: A Time for Openness, 1973, Frontiers, 1983, Conversations with Leaders for a New Millenium, 1991, A Place Called Grace, 1993; contbr. articles to profl. jours. LaRue fellow, 1976. Mem. English Speaking Union, Burren Conservancy, Friends of the Bog, Cambridge Soc. Episcopalian. Home: Lakewood 402 NE Point Dr Lees Summit MO 64064-1561 Office: Health Midwest 2310 E Meyer Blvd B-15 Kansas City MO 64132

KINI, RANJAN BAILUR, management information systems educator; b. Mangalore, Karnataka, India, Dec. 17, 1954; came to U.S., 1978; s. Mohandas Achuth and Sumanabai (Pai) K.; m. Nivedita R. Kini, Aug. 15, 1987. BSME, Karnataka Regional Engring. U., 1976; MBA, No. Ill. U., 1981; PhD, Tex. Tech U., 1985. Mech. engr. Teletube Electronics (Pvt) Inc., Ghaziabad, India, 1976-77; prodn. engr. Engring. Projects (India) Ltd., Kuwait City, Kuwait, 1977-78; grad. asst. No. Ill. U., DeKalb, 1978-81, instr., 1981-82; part-time instr. Tex. Tech U., Lubbock, 1982-85; asst. prof. dept. info. systems U. N.C., Greensboro, 1985-90; assoc. prof. divsn. bus. and econs. Ind. U.-N.W., Gary, 1990—; dir. LakeNet, Electronic Cmty. Net., Lake County, Ind. Contbr. articles to profl. jours. Mem. Am. Prodn. and Inventory Control Soc. (dir. textile/apparel specific interest group 1989—), Decision Scis. Inst., Rotary (bd. dirs. Schererville club). Hindu. Home: 1032 Spruce Dr Schererville IN 46375-1124 Office: Ind Univ NW Divsn Bus and Econs 3400 Broadway Gary IN 46408-1101

KINKEAD, VERDA CHRISTINE, non-profit organization executive, consultant; b. Plant City, Fla., Feb. 12, 1931; d. Ernest Glenn and Mina Lee (Alexander) K. Diploma, Bronson Meth. Hosp. Sch. Nursing, Kalamazoo, 1952; BA in Humanities, Adrian Coll., 1963; MA Guidance-Counseling, Mich. State U., 1964. RN, Mich. Nurse Bronson Meth. Hosp., 1952-54; 2d sr. surg. nurse West Side Med. Group, Kalamazoo, 1954-60; mentor, resident asst. Adrian (Mich.) Coll., 1962-63; head resident Alma Coll., 1964-65, asst. dean student affairs, dean women, 1965-69; co-founder, co-dir. Handicappers Info. Coun. and Patient Equipment Locker, Inc., Alma, 1981-87, pres., CEO, co-chmn. bd. dirs., 1987-95, pres., CEO emeritus, founding co-chair, 1995—; ednl. asst. East Main Meth. Ch., Kalamazoo, 1959-60. Former editor Saginaw Valley Dynamo; editor Challenger newsletter, 1986—; contbr. poetry to various publs. Bd. dirs. Saginaw Valley br. Nat. Multiple Sclerosis Soc.; past treas.; sec. bd. dirs., fair sec. Gratiot Agrl. Soc., Ithaca, Mich., 1977-83; vol. counselor Gratiot County Mental Health Ctr., Alma, 1983—; chmn. Gratiot County Early Intervention Coun., 1989-90; organizer group facilitator Ptnrs. in Renewal, Alma, 1989—; lay speaker United Meth. Ch.; mem. Go Grow Gratiot, 1989—, co-chair awards com. 1989-90, chairperson, 1990-91. Recipient Outstanding Svc. award Mich. Coll. Pers. Assn., 1972, Saginaw Valley br. Multiple Sclerosis Soc., 1986, First Lady award Mich. Women's Commn., 1987, vol. leadership award Greater Mich. Found., 1988, Outstanding Alumni award Adrian Coll., 1988, Order of the Tartan Alma C. of C. Outstanding Citizen award, 1993, State Mich. Helping Handicapped award, 1995, Gratiot County Bd. Commrs., 1995; Paul Harris fellow Rotary Internat., 1994. Mem. AAUW (sec. Alma br. 1965), Order Eastern Star (chaplain 1988-89, assoc. conductress 1989-91, conductress 1991-93, assoc. matron 1993-94, starpoint Ruth 1994—), Alma Woman's Club (v.p. 1990, pres. 1991-92, 92-93), Rotary (handicapper com. 1991—, world community svc. com. 1992—, project SEVA com. co-chair 1991—, sgt. at arms 1993-94), Phi Delta Kappa. Republican. Home: 3060 N Union Rd Alma MI 48801-9740 Office: Handicappers Info Coun 1022 Michigan Ave Alma MI 48801-1330

KINKEL, ANTHONY G., state legislator, educator; b. Nov. 1960. BA, U. Minn., Duluth. Educator; Dist. 4B rep. Minn. Ho. of Reps., St. Paul, 1986—; former mem. gen. legis., vet. affairs, and gaming coms., Minn. Ho. of Reps.; vice chmn. commerce and econ. devel. com., mem. edn.-higher edn. fin. divsn., and tourism and small bus. divsn. coms. Home: PO Box 568 Park Rapids MN 56470-0568*

KINNAIRD, ANGUS G., machinist; b. Waukegan, Ill., Nov. 28, 1935; s. Felix Grant and Ruby (Dark) K. Inspector Monarch Machine, Springfield, Mo., 1965-68; owner, machinist AK Machine and Welding, Springfield, 1975—. With USAF, 1954-59. Episcopalian. Office: AK Machine & Welding 4151 W Church St Springfield MO 65802-1078

KINNAMAN, THEODORE DWIGHT, music educator; b. Evanston, Ill., Nov. 19, 1928; s. Theodore James and Mamie Carolyn (Robinson) K.; m. Janice Marilyn Herrington, Aug. 7, 1953; children: Jacqueline Ann, Kathleen Joyce, Theodore James. B Music Edn., Northwestern U., 1950, MusM, 1957; postgrad., U. Iowa, 1962, 65-66, 69. Tchr. instrumental vocal music pub. schs., Manlius, Ill., 1950-51, Lanark, Ill., 1951-54, Galena, Ill., 1954-66; prof. music U. Wis. Center Rock County, Janesville, 1966-94; prof. emeritus, 1994—; concert reviewer Janesville Gazette, 1966—. Chmn. Wis. New Dem. Coalition, 1969; founding mem. Rock Prairie Arts Coun., Janesville-Beloit, 1974-75, pres., 1976; 1st dist. rep. adminstrv. com. Wis. Dem. Com., 1980-88; bd. dirs. Madison (Wis.) Inst., 1984—; sch. bd. commr. Janesville Pub. Schs., 1994—. Fellow NEH, 1975. Mem. Am. Musicological Soc., Am. Soc. for Aesthetics, Pi Kappa Lambda. Home: 1213 Columbus Cir Janesville WI 53545-2528 Office: U Wis Center Rock County 2909 Kellogg Ave Janesville WI 53546-5606

KINNEY, RICHARD GORDON, lawyer, educator; b. Chgo., May 8, 1939; s. Michael James, Sr., and Blanche Marie (Gill) K.; m. Katherine Choffen, Dec. 26, 1969; 1 son, Richard Greg. BSEE, U. Ill., 1961; JD, U. Chgo., 1964. Bar: Ill. 1964, U.S. Dist. Ct. (no. dist.) Ill. 1964, Ind. 1981, U.S. Ct. Customs and Patent Appeals, 1975, U.S. Ct. Appeals (7th cir.) 1976, U.S. Ct. Appeals (3d cir.) 1981, U.S. Ct. Appeals (9th cir.) 1979, U.S. Ct. Appeals (D.C. cir.) 1976, U.S. Supreme Ct. 1970, U.S. Ct. Appeals (fed. cir.) 1982, U.S. Dist. Ct. (no. dist.) Ind. 1983. With patent dept. Zenith Radio Corp., Chgo., 1963-64; with patent dept. Borg-Warner Corp., Chgo., 1968-73; div. patent counsel Baxter Travenol Labs., Inc., Deerfield, Ill., 1973-76; prin. Richard G. Kinney & Assocs., Chgo. and Merrillville, Ind., 1976-95; pres. Richard G. Kinney, P.C., 1995—. Rep. candidate Ill. State Senate, 1976; chmn. 6th Congl. Dist. Citizens for Goldwater-Miller, 1964. Mem. Am. Patent Law Assn., Ind. Bar Assn., Patent Law Assn. Chgo. Roman Catholic. Club: Union League (Chgo.). Lodge: Lions. Home: 12 Shore Dr Ogden Dunes IN 46368 Office: Richard G Kinney PC PO Box 11119 Merrillville IN 46411-1119

KINNISON, WILLIAM ANDREW, retired university president; b. Springfield, Ohio, Feb. 10, 1932; s. Errett Lowell and Audrey Muriel (Smith) K.; m. Lenore Belle Morris, June 11, 1960; children—William Errett, Linda Elise, Amy Elisabeth. A.B., Wittenberg U., 1954, B.S. in Edn., 1955; M.A., U. Wis., 1963; Ph.D. (1st Flesher fellow), Ohio State U., 1967; postgrad., Harvard U. Inst. Ednl. Mgmt., 1970; LL.D., Calif. Luth. Coll., 1983; Th.D., John Carroll U., 1983; LLD, Lenoir-Rhyne Coll., 1987; LHD, Capital U., 1995. Asst. dean admissions Wittenberg U., Springfield, 1958-65; asst. to pres. Wittenberg U., 1967-70, v.p. for univ. affairs, 1970-73, v.p. adminstrn., 1973, pres., 1974-95, pres. emeritus, 1995—. Author: Samuel Shellabarger: Lawyer, Jurist, Legislator, 1969, Building Sullivant's Pyramid: An Administrative History of the Ohio State University, 1970, Concise History of Wittenberg University, 1976, An American Seminary, 1980, Springfield and Clark County: an Illustrated History, 1985, also articles. Asst. to dir. Sch. Edn. Ohio State U., Columbus, 1965-67; past chmn. Assn. Ind. Colls. and Univs. Ohio; trustee Ohio Found. Ind. Colls., 1974-95, vice chair bd. trustees, 1995; chmn. standing com. Luth. World Ministries, 1976-82; mem. exec. coun. Luth. Ch. in Am., 1978-86; mem., chmn. Commn. for a New Luth. Ch., 1982-86; bd. dirs. Am. Assn. Colls., 1982-84. With U.S. Army, 1956-58. Mem. Clark County Hist. Soc. (trustee 1963—), Orgn. Am. Historians, Blue Key, Phi Beta Kappa, Phi Delta Kappa, Kappa Phi Kappa, Pi Sigma Alpha, Tau Kappa Alpha, Delta Sigma Phi, Omicron Delta Kappa. Clubs: Cosmos, Rotary. Home: 1820 Timberline Dr Springfield OH 45504

KINNOIN, MEYER D., state legislator; m. Diane; 4 children. Mem. N.D. Senate, 1989—; vice chmn. state and fed. govt. com.; past mem. agr. com., fin. and tax. com. N.D. Senate; former mem. Mountrail County Park Commn., Housing Commn., U.S. Dept. Agr.; farmer. Recipient Disting. Svc. Award Jaycees. Home: HC 1 Box 88A Palermo ND 58769-9631*

KINSER, DOUGLAS M., state legislator; b. New Castle, Ind., May 6, 1947; m. Jennifer Kinser; children: Michelle, Beth. BS, Ind. U., 1971; MA, Ball State U., 1978. Health care cons.; rep. Dist. 54 Ind. Ho. of Reps., 1988—, chmn. judiciary com., mem. fin. insts. com., urban affairs com, pub. health com. Councilman New Castle City Coun., 1976-88; dir. Henry County Econ. Devel. Corp.; active United Way. Mem. Hagertown and Henry County C. of C., New Castle Rotary. Home: 1405 Woodbrooke Dr New Castle IN 47362-1757*

KINTNER, HALLIE JOANNE, demographer; b. Seattle, Mar. 14, 1952; d. Robert Montgomery and Frances Hallie (Castleman) K. BA magna cum laude in Sociology, U. Wash., 1974; MA in Sociology, U. Mich., 1976, MS in Biostats., PhD in Sociology, 1982. Rsch. investigator U. Mich. Med. Sch., Ann Arbor, 1983-84; rsch. scientist GM Rsch. Labs., Warren, Mich., 1984—; rsch. affiliate population studies ctr. U. Mich., Ann Arbor, 1990—; mem. census adv. com. of profl. assns. U.S. Census Bur., 1989—, rep. of bus. roundtable adv. com. on yr. 2000 census, 1991—. Co-editor: Demographics: A Casebook for Business and Government, 1994; contbr. articles to profl. jours. Mem. rsch. adv. com. Kenny Mich. Rehab. Found., 1988-91. NSF grad. fellow, 1975-78, German Acad. Exch. Svc. fellow, 1979-80, NIH rsch. grantee, 1989-92; recipient McCuen award GM Rsch. Labs, 1995. Mem. Population Assn. Am. (chair com. on applied demography 1993—), Internat. Union for the Sci. Study of Population, Am. Statis. Assn., Am. Sociol. Assn., Social Sci. History Assn. Office: GM Rsch Labs 30500 Mound Rd Warren MI 48090

KINZELBERG, HARVEY, leasing company executive; b. Chgo., Mar. 4, 1945; s. Harry and Elaine (Feigenbaum) K.; BS in Ops. Rsch., Cornell U., 1967; MS (Ford fellow) in Econ. Planning, Stanford U., 1968; m. Linda Sue Gerber, June 18, 1969; children: John David, Scott Michael. Mktg., nat. account mgr. IBM, Chgo., 1968-73; exec. v.p., dir. Triarco, Inc., Wheeling, Ill., 1973-76; leasing specialist Itel Corp., Chg., 1976-79; pres., chmn., dir. Meridian Leasing Corp., Deerfield, Ill., 1979-92; pres., CEO Sequel Capital Corp., 1992—; chmn., CEO Entrepeneurial Inst. Am., 1993—, Sequel Security Sys., Inc., 1993—. Asst. treas. Lakeland Health Care Svcs.; trustee Highland Park Hosp., Cornell U., 1992-94; mem. Cornell U. Coun., mem. adv. bd. Cornell U. Ctr. for Environment, mem. exec. com. Cornell U. Entrepreneurship and Personal Enterprise Program, mem. investment com., vice chmn. bldgs. & grounds com.; trustee Cornell U., 1993—. Named Entrepreneur of Yr., Ernst & Young/Merrill Lynch, Inc., mag., 1991, U. Ill., Arthur Andersen, Cornell U. Entrepreneur of Yr., 1992, U. Ill. at Chgo. Entrepreneur Hall of Fame, 1993. Mem. Northmore Country Club (Highland Park, Ill.), Cornell U. Tower Club, Tau Beta Pi. Jewish. Office: Sequel Capital Corp 570 Lake Cook Rd Ste 405 Deerfield IL 60015-4955

KINZIE, RAYMOND WYANT, banker, lawyer; b. Chgo., Oct. 20, 1930; s. Raymond Allen and Florence (Wyant) K.; m. Dorothy Cherry Beek, Sept. 17, 1955; children: Diana K. Wieczorek, Dorothy K. Tedeschi, Raymond Wyant Jr., Susan Hawthorne (dec.). BA, Carleton Coll., 1952; LLB, Yale U., 1955, JD, 1964. Bar: Ill. 1956, U.S. Dist. Ct. (no. dist.) Ill. 1959, U.S. Ct. Appeals (7th cir.) 1961, U.S. Supreme Ct. 1964. Assoc. McBride and Baker, Chgo., 1955-56; atty. Continental Ill. Nat. Bank & Trust Co. (now Bank Am. Chgo.), Chgo., 1956-59; trust officer Lake View Trust and Savs. Bank, Chgo., 1959-65, asst. v.p. loans and credit, 1965-71, v.p., trust officer, 1971-82, sr. v.p., sr. trust officer, 1982-88; sr. v.p., sr. trust officer LaSalle Bank Lake View subs. Algemene Bank Nederland (now known as ABN-AMRO Bank), Chgo., 1988-90; sr. v.p. trust svcs. ABN-AMRO Bank subs. LaSalle Nat. Trust, N.A., 1990-92; sr. v.p. wealth mgmt. group LaSalle Nat. Trust, N.A., 1993—; bd. dirs. Land Trust Coun. of Ill., Chgo.; adv. bd. Nat. Coll. Edn. (Lewis U.), Evanston, Ill., 1975—; radio editl. rebuttals Sta. WBBM; talk shows commentator WLS. Contbr. to Time, Newsweek, Chgo. Tribune, Chgo. Sun Times, Crain's Chgo. Bus., other profl. publs. Bd. dirs., sec.-treas. Ravenswood Hosp. Med. ctr., Chgo., 1975-85; bd. dirs., sec. Ravenswood Health Care Found., 1975-80. Mem. Am. Mgmt. Assn., Ill. State Bar Assn., Chgo. Bar Assn., Chgo. Estate Planning Coun., Land Trust Coun. Ill. Home: 1027 N Marion St Oak Park IL 60302-1374 Office: LaSalle Nat Trust NA 3201 N Ashland Ave Chicago IL 60657-2107

KINZLER, STEPHEN BOYD, software engineer; b. Jamestown, N.D., Sept. 28, 1964; s. Norbert and Carol Ann (Spilloway) K.; m. Rosa Maria Angulo, July 27, 1991. BA in Math. and Computer Sci., Jamestown Coll., 1986; MS in Computer Sci., Ind. U., 1987. System programmer Jamestown Coll., 1985; assoc. instr. Ind. U., Bloomington, 1986-87, rsch. asst., 1986-87, software engr., 1988—; sr. computer engr. Olympic Tng. Ctr., Barcelona, 1992; instr. Ind. U., 1996—. Mem. Am. Assn. for Artificial Intelligence, Assn. for Computing Machinery, Electronic Frontier Found., League for Programming Freedom, Usenix, Alpha Chi (chpt. pres. 1985-86), Gamma Sigma. Office: Ind U Computer Sci Lindley Hall 430E Bloomington IN 47405

KIONKA, EDWARD JAMES, lawyer; b. Oak Park, Ill., Feb. 18, 1939; s. Edward Frederick and Antoinette (Marcus) K.; m. Sandra Sellers, Aug. 17, 1958 (div. Apr. 1974); children: Thomas Edward, Meredith Ann, David James; m. Debra Ann Kosydor, Dec. 31, 1981 (div. Apr., 1996); children: James Bradley, John Conner, Caroline Reid. BS, U. Ill., 1960, JD, 1962; LLM, Columbia U., 1974. Bar: Ill. 1962, U.S. Ct. Appeals (7th cir.) 1970, U.S. Supreme Ct. 1971, U.S. Dist. Ct. (so. dist.) Ill. 1978). Assoc. Leibman, Williams, Bennett & Baird (now Sidley & Austin), Chgo., 1962-64; instr. U. Mich. Law Sch., 1964-65; exec. dir. Ill. Inst. Continuing Legal Edn., Springfield, 1965-67; asst. dean, asst. prof. law U. Ill. Coll. Law, 1967-71; cons. atty. Ill., 1971-72, 74-75; part-time, 1973—; assoc. prof. law So. Ill. U., Carbondale, 1973-75, 76-77, prof., 1977—, assoc. dean, 1984-85, acting dean, 1985; spl. counsel gen. govt. com. 6th Ill. Constl. Conv., 1970; cons. to lawyers on civil trials, appeals; mem. com. rules of evidence Ill. Supreme Ct., 1976-79, reporter com. jury instructions in civil cases, 1979-95; bd. dirs. Ill. Inst. Continuing Legal Edn., 1967-72, 73-85, mem. exec. com., chmn. curriculum com., 1967-71, treas., 1980-82, vice-chmn., 1982-83, chmn., 1983-84. Author: Torts in a Nutshell, 1977, 2d edit., 1992, Handbook for Appeals to the Illinois Supreme and Appellate Courts, 1978, 2d edit., 1980, 3d edit., 1993, Torts Black Letter, 1989, 2d edit., 1993; co-author: Materials for the Study of Evidence, 1983, 3d edit., 1991; assoc. editor in chief U. Ill. Law Forum, 1961-62; editor: Illinois Civil Practice After Trial, 1970. Krulewitch fellow Columbia U., 1974. Fellow Am. Acad. Appellate Lawyers (bd. dirs. 1992—); mem. ABA, Ill. Bar Assn. (mem. publs. com. 1979-85, sec. 1981-82, vice-chmn., 1982-84, chmn. 1984-85, mem. assembly 1990-92), Appellate Lawyers Assn. (treas. 1974-75, sec. 1975-76, v.p. 1976-77, pres. 1977-78), Am. Judicature Soc., Order of Coif, Scribes (bd. dirs. 1989-94, treas. 1993-94), Phi Delta Phi. Home: PO Box 10 Carbondale IL 62903 Office: So Ill U Law Sch Lesar Law Bldg Carbondale IL 62901-6804

KIPPER, BARBARA LEVY, corporate executive; b. Chgo., July 16, 1942; d. Charles and Ruth (Doctoroff) Levy; m. David A. Kipper, Sept. 9, 1974; children: Talia Rose, Tamar Judith. BA, U. Mich., 1964. Reporter Chgo. Sun-Times, 1964-67; photo editor Cosmopolitan Mag., N.Y.C., 1969-71; vice chmn. Chas Levy Co., Chgo., 1984-86, chmn., 1986—; pres. Charles and Ruth Levy Found.; life dir. The Joffrey Ballet of Chgo. Mem. exec. com. Spertus Inst. Jewish Studies, Golden Apple Found.; life dir. The Joffrey Ballet of Chgo.; trustee Chgo. Hist. Soc. Recipient Deborah award Com. Women's Equality, Am. Jewish Congress, 1992, Shap Shapiro Human Rels. award The Anti-Defamation League of B'nai B'rith, 1993, WSFRE's Chgo. chpt. Disting. Philanthropist award, 1995. Mem. Nat. Found. Fund Raising Execs. (disting. philanthropist 1995), Com. of 200, Coun. on Founds., Chgo. Women in Philanthropy, Econ. Club of Chgo., Chgo. Found. for Women, Chgo. Network, Women's Issues Network, The Standard Club. Jewish. Office: Chas Levy Co 1200 N North Branch St Chicago IL 60622-2410

KIPPERMAN, MARK, English language educator; b. Bklyn., Apr. 4, 1952; s. Boris and Renee (Garfinkel) K. BA, SUNY, Binghamton, 1974; PhD, U. Pa., 1981. Asst. prof. Princeton (N.J.) U., 1980-86; assoc. prof. No. Ill. U., Dekalb, 1986—. Author: Beyond Enchantment: German Idealism and English Romantic Poetry, 1986; contbr. articles to profl. jours. Fellow Am. Coun. Learned Socs., 1982-83, Nat. Endowment for the Humanities, 1992.

Mem. MLA, Keats-Shelley Assn. Am. Office: No Ill U Dept English De Kalb IL 60115

KIPPERT, ROBERT JOHN, JR., lawyer; b. Detroit, Aug. 29, 1952; s. Robert John Sr. and Jeanne Marcella (DeYonker) K.; m. Dorothy Marie Cunningham, Oct. 28, 1978 (div. June 1988); 1 child, Cristie; m. Kim Denise Katherine Greenman, Feb. 10, 1990. BBA, U. Mich., 1974; JD, Wayne State U., 1977, LLM in Taxation, 1994. Bar: Mich. 1979; CPA. Tax staff acct. Arthur Young & Co., Bloomfield Hills, Mich., 1977-78; tax staff sr., mgr. McEndarffer, Hoke & Bernhard, P.C., Bloomfield Hills, 1978-84; tax supr. Cen. Transport, Inc., Sterling Heights, Mich., 1984-85; tax atty. Chrysler Fin. Corp., Southfield, Mich., 1985-89, mgr. non-income taxes and licensing, 1989-95, staff counsel, 1995—. Charter pres. Sterling Heights Jaycees. Mem. AICPA, ABA, Mich. Bar Assn., Mich. Assn. CPA's, Am. Arbitration Assn. (panel mem.). Republican. Roman Catholic. Home: 201 N Squirrel Rd Apt 1013 Auburn Hills MI 48326-4025 Office: Chrysler Fin Corp 27777 Franklin Rd Southfield MI 48034

KIRBY, DOROTHY MANVILLE, social worker; b. Burke, S.D., Oct. 23, 1917; d. Charles Vietz and Gail Lorena (Coonen) Manville; m. Sigmund Kirby, July 11, 1941 (div. 1969); children: Paul Howard, Robert Charles. BA, Wayne State U., 1970, MSW, 1972. Cert. social worker, Mich.; lic. marriage and family therapist, Mich. Pvt. practice social work Allen Park, Mich., 1973—; conduct seminars on stress, personal effectiveness and communication for various orgns., hosps. and bus. Pres. Allen Park Symphony Orch., 1990-92. Mem. AAUW, Am. Group Psychotherapy Assn., Nat. Assn. Social Workers (clin.), Nat. Assn. Marriage and Family Counseling, Mich. Assn. Marriage and Family Counseling (sec. 1982), LWV (pres. Allen Park 1965-66). Presbyterian. Lodge: Soroptimists. Home and Office: 15720 Wick Rd Allen Park MI 48101-1535

KIRBY, FRANK EUGENE, musicology educator, author, editor; b. N.Y.C., Apr. 6, 1928; s. Russell Thorp and Dorothy (Clement) K.; m. Emily Baruch, Aug. 17, 1952; children: Russell, Nicholas, Paula, Nathaniel. BA, Colo. Coll., 1950; PhD, Yale U., 1957. Music catalogue Peabody Inst. Libr., Balt., 1956-57; Ford Found. teaching intern Williams Coll., 1957-58; vis. asst. prof. U. Va., 1958-59; guest asst. prof. U. Tex., Austin, 1959-60; asst. prof. W.Va. U., 1961-63; asst. prof. music Lake Forest (Ill.) Coll., 1963-66, assoc. prof., 1967-76, prof., 1977—; cons. in field. Author: A Short History of Keyboard Music, 1966, An Introduction to Western Music, 1970, Music in the Classic Period, 1979, Music in the Romantic Period, 1986, Music for Piano, A Short History, 1995; contbr. numerous articles to profl. jours. Grantee W.Va., 1962, Lake Forest Coll., 1965-66, 68, Alexander von Humboldt-Stiftung grantee, 1966, 79, 87. Mem. AAUP, Am. Musicological Soc., Internat. Musicological Soc., Deutsche Gesellschaft fuer Musikforschung, Coll. Music Soc., Am. Soc. for 18th Century Studies. Office: Lake Forest Coll Sheridan And Coll Rd Lake Forest IL 60045

KIRCHER, JOHN JOSEPH, law educator; b. Milw., July 26, 1938; s. Joseph John and Martha Marie (Jach) K.; m. Marcia Susan Adamkiewicz, Aug. 26, 1961; children: Joseph John, Mary Kathryn. BA, Marquette U., 1960, JD, 1963. Bar: Wis. 1963, U.S. Dist. Ct. (ea. dist.) Wis. 1963, U.S. Ct. Appeals (7th cir.) 1992. Sole practice, Port Washington, Wis., 1963-66; with Def. Research Inst., Milw., 1966-80, research dir., 1972-80; with Marquette U., 1970—, prof. law, 1980—, assoc. dean acad. affairs, 1992-93; chmn. Wis. Jud. Council, 1981-83. Author: (with J.D. Ghiardi) Punitive Damages: Law and Practice, 1981; editor: Federation of Insurance and Corporate Counsel Quarterly; mem. editorial bd. Def. Law Jour.; contbr. articles to profl. jours. Recipient Teaching Excellence award Marquette U., 1986, Disting. Service award Def. Research Inst., 1980, Marquette Law Rev. Editors' award, 1988. Mem. ABA (Robert B. McKay Professor award 1993), Am. Law Inst., Wis. Bar Assn., Wis. Supreme Ct. Bd. of Bar Examiners (vice-chair 1989-91, chair 1992), Am. Judicature Soc., Nat. Sports Law Inst. (adv. com. 1989—), Assn. Internationale de Droit des Assurances, Scribes. Roman Catholic. Office: PO Box 1881 Milwaukee WI 53201-1881

KIRCHHOFF, MICHAEL KENT, economic development executive; b. Effingham, Ill., Apr. 3, 1963; s. Robert D. and Violet M. (Baumann) K; m. Lynn Reilly, May 27, 1989. BA in Econ., East Ill. U., 1986, BS in Bus., 1986; postgrad., Econ. Devel. Inst., U. Okla., 1995. Cert. Ill. Assessing Officer. Owner, mgmt. cons. Spectrum Cons., Springfield, 1985-90; intern govs. office Ill. Dept. Revenue, Springfield, 1986-87, property tax analyst, 1987-89; econ. devel. prof. Dept. Commerce and Community Affairs, Springfield, 1989-92; data analyst Ill. Dept. Pub. Aid, Springfield, 1992; mkt. devel. researcher Ill. Power Co., Decatur, 1992-95; joint purchasing coord. State of Ill., Springfield, 1995—; owner Phoenix Assocs., Springfield, 1995-96; exec. dir. Tuscola (Ill.) Area Improvement Assn., 1996—. Asst. scoutmaster, scoutmaster Big Bros./Big Sisters, I-Search for Children, Project Safeplace; v.p. Sangamon County Reps., Operation Snowball; treas., bd. dirs. Ctrl. Ill. Youth Svc. Bur. Recipient Charles Carter Meml. award Inter-Fraternity Coun., 1984. Mem. Am. Soc. Pub. Adminstrn., Acad. Polit. Sci., Mid Am. InterFraternity Coun. Assn. (Outstanding State Coord. 1984, Outstanding Area V.P. 1985), Nat. Trust for Hist. Preservation, Springfield Jaycees, Order of Omega, Omicron Delta Epsilon, Beta Sigma Psi. Republican. Lutheran. Home: 310 Douglas Dr Tuscola IL 61953 Office: Tuscola Are Improvment Assn PO Box 11 Tuscola IL 61953

KIRCHHOFF, W. JAMES, school district administrator; b. Indpls., Dec. 29, 1935; s. William J. and Agnes E. (Kettler) K.; m. Loretta H. Kirchhoff, June 19, 1960; children: Karen, John, Lisa. BS, Concordia Tchrs. Coll., River Forest, Ill., 1957; AM, U. Chgo., 1965; EdD, No. Ill. U., 1976. Tchr., musician Christ English Luth. Ch., Chgo., 1957-59; tchr., prin., musician Hope Luth. Ch., Park Forest, Ill., 1959-69; prin., musician Bethany Luth. Ch., Naperville, Ill., 1969-79; supr. schs. No. Ill. Dist./Luth. Ch.-Mo. Synod, Hillside, 1979—; mem. pres.'s commn. on higher edn. Luth. Ch.-Mo. Synod, St. Louis, 1983-86; vis. prof. Concordia U., 1976, 79. Contbr. articles to Luth. Edn., Interaction, No. Light. Dir. cmty. chorus Naperville Sesquicentennial, 1981; chmn. Commn. on Ministerial Growth, 1992-95; chmn. Ill. Adv. Commn. on Non-Pub. Schs., 1987-89, 93-96. Mem. ASCD, Luth. Edn. Assn. (pres. 1980-82), Am. Assn. Sch. Adminstrs., Ill. H.S. Assn. (cert. ofcl. 1969-96). Office: Luth Ch-Mo Synod No Ill Dist 2301 S Wolf Rd Hillside IL 60162

KIRCHNER, JAMES WILLIAM, retired electrical engineer; b. Cleve., Oct. 17, 1920; s. William Sebastian and Marcella Louise (Stuart) K.; m. Eda Christene Landfear, June 11, 1950 (dec. May 1977); children: Kathleen Ann Kirchner Duda, Susan Lynn Kirchner Buonpane. BS in Elec. Engring., Ohio U., 1950, MS, 1951. Registered profl. engr., Ohio. Instr. elec. engring. Ohio U., Athens, 1950-52; mgr. liaison engring. Lear Siegler Inc., Maple Heights, Ohio, 1952-64; coordinator engring. services Case Western Res. U., Cleve., 1964-72, gen. mgr. Med. Ctr. Co. (CWRU), 1972-91; ret., 1991; sec. of corp. Thermagon, Inc., Cleve., 1992. Mem. Portage County Republican Exec. Com., 1961-62; treas. PTA, Aurora, Ohio, 1963-65, v.p., 1965-66; mem. The Ch. in Aurora, 1956—. Served with USAAF, 1942-45, PTO. Mem. NSPE (life), IEEE (life), Ohio Soc. Profl. Engrs. (life), Cleve. Engring. Soc. (chmn. environ. com. 1976), Am. Soc. Engring. Edn. (life). Home: Unit 1 668 2d St Unit 1 Fairport Harbor OH 44077

KIRCHNER, L.R. (LARRY), writer, publishing executive; b. Kansas City, Dec. 9, 1944; s. Louis Leo and Alice Marie (Collins) K.; m. Janet Rose, July 4, 1981; stepchildren: Colin, Cameron, Clayton Pinkman. Student, Wentworth Milit. Jr. Coll., 1963-65, Northwest Mo. State, 1965-66, Mo. We., 1970-75; Kansas U., 1976-77, Mo. U., 1978-79. Undercover drug agent Fed. Narcotics Task Force, Dallas, 1970-76; owner Home Remodelers, Kansas City, 1970-76, Channel One Video Prodns., Kansas City, 1978-81, Kirchner Advtsg. & Photgraphy, Kansas City, 1981-93, Janlar Books, Kansas City, 1993—. Author, publisher: Triple Cross Fire! J. Edgar Hoover and the Kansas City Union Station Massacre, 1995. Newspaper editor, 49/63 Coalition, Kansas City, 1981-82; eagle scout, BSA, 1961. Mem. Kiwanis Internat. Republican. Office: Janlar Books P O Box 7255 Kansas City MO 64113

KIRCHNER, RICHARD JAY, retired physical education educator; b. Schenectady, Feb. 17, 1930; s. Richard Jacob and Leah (Williams) K.; BS, U. Wis., 1952, MS, 1955, postgrad., 1956; EdD, Mich. State U, 1962; m. Barbara Ann Crane, Feb. 2, 1952; children: Richard Alec, Barbara Jayne, Carolyn Diane, Robert Jay, Kathleen Kay. Instr. wrestling and track coach St. Cloud (Minn.) Tchrs. Coll., 1955-56; asst. prof., coaching staff Central Mich. U., Mt. Pleasant, 1956-62, prof. recreation, chmn. dept., 1962-87, with Office of Dean sch. edn., health and human svcs., 1987-88, sr. prof., 1988-92; retired 1992. chmn. pres.'s adv. com.; camp program dir., camp dir. Elkton-Pigeon-Bayport Sch. Camp, Caseville, Mich., 1962; mcpl. recreation dir. Petoskey (Mich.), 1963, cons., 1964-74; vice chmn. citizens adv. com. Recreation Svcs. div. Mich. Dept. Conservation, 1966-67. Pres. Mt. Pleasant Intermediate Sch. PTA, 1968-69; chmn. tech. planning com. Mt. Pleasant Recreation Commn. Served to capt. USMCR, 1952-54. Mem. AAHPER (v.p. Mich. 1966-67, v.p. Midwest dist. 1973-74), Nat Recreation and Parks Assn., Am. Assn. Leisure and Recreation (nat. pres. 1976-77, nat. accreditation council 1978-83, vice chmn. 1979-81, chmn. 1981-83), Am. Camp Assn., Mich. Soc. Arts, Sci. and Letters, Mich. Soc. Gerontology, Outdoor Edn. and Camping Council (charter), Mich. Recreation and Parks Assn. (v.p. 1968-70), Phi Eta Sigma, Phi Epsilon Kappa, Phi Delta Kappa. Home: 6953 Riverside Dr Mount Pleasant MI 48858-7930

KIRICK, DANIEL JOHN, agronomist; b. Port Jervis, N.Y., Nov. 8, 1953; s. Daniel and Mary Theresa Kirick; m. Jean Marie Guse, Sept. 27, 1986; children: Nicholas, John. BA in Biology, History, U. Minn., Duluth, 1976; BS in Agronomy, U. Minn., St. Paul, 1977. Cert. profl. agronomist. Agronomist Delft (Minn.) Farm Chems., 1978, Skelly Fertilizer, Trimont, Minn., 1978-80, Mower County Svc. Co., Sargeant, Minn., 1980-86, Cenex Supply, Ellis, S.D., 1986-88, Rice (Minn.) Farm Supply, 1988-91, Kirick Agronomy Svcs., St. Cloud, Minn., 1992—. Mem. Comty. Edn. Devel. Adv. Coun., Sauk Rapids, Minn., 1990-94, Youth Devel. Bd., Sauk Rapids, 1990, Benton County Ext. Com., 1993—, Cen. Minn. Forage Coun., 1994—. Mem. AAAS, Weed Sci. Soc. Am., Soil Sci. Soc. Am., Crop Sci. Soc. Am., Am. Soc. Agronomy. Roman Catholic. Home: PO Box 206 Rice MN 56367-0206 Office: Kirick Agronomy Svcs 3105 2nd St SE Saint Cloud MN 56304-9400

KIRILA, CAROL ELIZABETH, osteopathic physician; b. Mount Clemens, Mich., Oct. 28, 1952; d. Andrew William and Mary Margaret (Schmeltz) K. Diploma, Rsch. Med. Ctr. Sch. Nursing, Kansas City, Mo., 1974; BS in Biology, U. Mo., Kansas City, 1987; DO, U. Health Scis.-Coll. Osteo., 1991. RN, Mo. With Lakeside Hosp., Kansas City, 1969-74, 76-87, part time staff nurse, relief supr., 1988—; staff nurse Children's Mercy Hosp., Kansas City, 1974, U. Health Scis. Hosp., Kansas City, 1974-76, Rsch. Med. Ctr., Kansas City, 1976; part time staff nurse Kendallwood Pvt. Duty, 1988-91; intern Still Regional Med. Ctr., Jefferson City, Mo., 1991-92; resident internal medicine U. of Mo. Kansas City Sch. of Medicine, 1992—; insvc. instr. Lakeside Hosp., 1976-87. Catechumenate sponsor St. James Ch., Kansas City, 1982; mem. Manheim Park Neighborhood Assn., Kansas City, 1982-91. Recipient cert. of recognition U. Health Scis. Coll. Osteo. Medicine, 1988-89, Outstanding Svc. and Achievement award U. Mo.-Kansas City, 1986. Mem. Am. Osteo. Assn., AMA, ACP, Am. Coll. Internists, Sports Medicine Orgn. Democrat. Roman Catholic. Home: 2804 N 39th Ter Saint Joseph MO 64506

KIRK, COURTLANDT BLAINE, bond trader; b. Columbus, Ohio, June 29, 1965; s. Ballard Harry Thurston and Vera Elizabeth (Kitchener) K. Student Ohio State U., 1990, N.Y. Inst. Fin., 1994. Registered investment advisor. Advisor Investors Diversified Svcs.-Am. Express, Columbus, Ohio, 1989-92; fin. cons. Household Bank Internat., Chgo., 1992-94; fixed income trader Banc One Investment Advisors, Columbus, 1994—; spkr. Columbus (Ohio) Jewish League, 1993, Urbana Ohio Downtown Bus. Assn., 1994. Mem. Ohio State U. Alumni Assn. (life mem.). Republican. Home: 2459 Tremont Rd Columbus OH 43221

KIRK, FLORA KAY STUDE, artist, accountant, insurance company official; b. San Diego, Feb. 16, 1944; d. Lawrence Wilbur Stude and Lois Eileen (Johnson) Plunkett; m. Bobby Gene Kirkpatrick, Feb. 16, 1960 (div. 1974); children: Jeffery Lane, Ladina B.J. Kirkpatrick Wingfield; m. Charles Robert Kirk, June 11, 1977 (div.); 1 child, Robert Marcel. Student, Western Tex. Coll., 1973-74, Ft. Hays (Kans.) State Coll., 1974-75, U. Nebr., Kearney, 1988; AA, Mid-Plains C.C., North Platate, Nebr., 1987. Decorator, Snyder, Tex., 1960-73; bookkeeper, office mgr. Tri-State Constrn., Snyder, 1973-75; acct. Aid Feed Yard, Syracuse, Kans., 1975-77; agt., broker Woodmen Accident & Life Ins. Co., Lincoln, Nebr., 1977—; owner, mgr., artist Kirk's Pottery and Painting Studio, North Platte, 1984—; acct., corp. sec.-treas. Profl. Ag Products, Inc., North Platte, 1988-93; chmn. bd. Artists Coop. Art & Gift Gallery, North Platte, 1987—; ceramics & painting instr. Mid Plains C.C., 1992—; mem. artist Artists in Embassies Program, Washington, 1991, 92; artist Carolyn Nelson Galleries, Pasadena, Calif., 1992, Robert Henri Mus., Conad, Nebr., 1996. One-woman show Art & Gift Gallery, 1987-96, Morin-Miller Galleries, N.Y.C., 1989, Gt. Plains Regional Med. Ctr., 1989-96, Bismark State Coll., Arroyo Theatre Gallery, L.A., 1993, 94, Pen & Brush Club, 1995, Broom St. Gallery, N.Y.C., 1995, U.S. Senate, 1995, Vanderbilt Mus., 1995, Noyes Gallery, Lincoln, Nebr., 1995-96, Robert Henri Mus., Crozad, Nebr., 1996; exhibited in group shows Fiske Planetarium, Boulder (recipient 1st place award 1992-94, 1st pl. in 1993-94), Nat. Arts Club, N.Y.C., 1987, ARiel Gallery, N.Y.C., 1988, Univ. Place Gallery, Lincoln, 1990-93, Gallery 525, Loveland, Colo., 1990, 91, C.W. Post Coll., L.I. U., 1990, U. Colo., 1990, Jacob Javits Fed. Bldg. Gallery, N.Y.C., 1991-92, U.S. Ho. Reps., Washington, 1992, 94, 95, Antiquarium Gallery, Omaha, Artel Gallery, White Crane Gallery, Omaha, 1993, Cork Gallery, Lincoln Ctr. Performing Arts, N.Y.C., Arroyo Theatre Gallery, L.A., 1993, 94; represented in permanent collections Mus. Cultural Exch., Cairo, Prarie Peace Park, Lincoln, Bismark State Coll. Chmn. North Platte Arts and Humanities Coun., 1991-92; vol. Kerry for Pres. Campaign, North Platte, 1992. Mem. Soc. Exptl. Artists, Nat. Soc. Painters in Casein and Acrylic (assoc.), Nat. Watercolor Soc. (assoc.), Visual Individual United (1st place award 1992), The Artel (merit award 1991), North Platte Art Guild, Platter Painters Art Club (pres. 1987-88, 1st place award 1987-91), Assn. Nebr. Art Clubs, Phi Theta Kappa. Democrat. Home: 1021 W 4th St North Platte NE 69101-3715

KIRK, NANCY A., state legislator, nursing home administrator; m. Henry Kirk. Nursing home adminstr.; mem. from dist. 56 Kans. State Ho. of Reps., Topeka. Address: 932 Frazier Topeka KS 66606

KIRKHAM, JAMES ALVIN, manufacturing executive; b. Sumner County, Tenn., June 18, 1935; s. Shirley Barnes and Ouida Redempta (Bursby) K.; m. Shirley Ann Clouse, Sept. 3, 1954; children: Denise Anne, James Alvin II, Hughe Allan. Welder, Ind. Wire Co., 1952-54; truck driver Arthur Lowe Cigar & Candy Co., 1954-56; time study Insley Mfg. Co., 1957; salesman Am. Chicle Co., 1958-59; mgr. Ace Battery, Inc., Indpls., 1967—, v.p. L P Industries, Inc., Indpls., 1977—; pres. Rubber Recycling Corp., 1989—; ptnr. TKT Leasing, Indpls., 1978—, LDJ Leasing, Indpls., 1979—, Vets. Interstate Plan, Inc. Sec. Johnson County Pk. Bd.; bd. dirs. English Ave. Boys Club, State 4-H Horse and Pony Orgn.; pres. bd. dirs. Ind. Horse Coun. Found., Inc.; pres. PTO, Clark Twp. Sch. Dist.; v.p. Johnson County 4-H Fairboard; active Boy Scouts Am.; chmn. fund raising equestrian events 10th Pan Am. Games. Recipient Golden Boy award Indpls. Boys Club Alumni Assn., 1970; named Outstanding Show Mgr., Ind. State Fair, 1971. Mem. U.S. C. of C., Ind. Motor Truck Assn., Indpls. Motor Truck Assn., Indpls. C. of C. Clubs: Ind. Pony Exhibitors, Ind. Pony of Am., Ind. Shetland Pony Breeders, Ind. Saddle Horse Assn., Am. Hackney, Am. Horse Show Assn. Lodges: Masons, Shriners, Moose. Home: 1213 N Matthews Rd Greenwood IN 46143-8343 Office: 2166 Bluff Rd Indianapolis IN 46225-1983

KIRKLAND, ALFRED YOUNGES, SR., federal judge; b. Elgin, Ill., 1917; s. Alfred and Elizabeth (Younges) K.; m. Gwendolyn E. Muntz, June 14, 1941; children: Pamela E. Kirkland Jensen, Alfred Younges, James Muntz. BA, U. Ill., 1941, JD, 1943. Bar: Ill. 1943. Assoc. Mayer, Meyer, Austrian & Platt, Chgo., 1943; sr. ptnr. Kirkland, Brady, McQueen, Martin & Callahan and predecessor firms, Elgin, 1951-73; spl. asst. atty. gen. State of Ill., 1969-73; judge 16th Cir. Ct. Ill., 1973-74; judge U.S. Dist. Ct. (no. dist.) Ill., 1974-79, sr. judge, 1979—; mem. Coun. Practicing Lawyers U. Ill. Law Forum, 1969—, mem. adv. bd., 1972-73, mem. adv. coun. continuing legal edn., 1959-62; chmn. Ill. Def. Rsch. Inst., 1965-66. Outdoor editor: Elgin Daily Courier-News, Kewanee Star-Courier; fishing editor: Midwest Outdoors Mag. Pres. Elgin YMCA, 1963, chmn. bd. trustees, 1995—. 2d lt. inf. AUS, 1943-46. Fellow Am. Coll. Trial Lawyers, Am. Bar Found.; mem. ABA (ho. of dels. 1967-70), Ill. State Bar Assn. (pres. 1968-69), Chgo. Bar Assn., Kane County Bar Assn. (pres. 1961-62), Elgin Bar Assn. (pres. 1951-52), Am. Judicature Soc. (bd. dirs. 1967—), Ill. Bar Found. (bd. dirs. 1961-69), Ill. Def. Counsel (bd. dirs. 1966-69), Soc. Trial Lawyers, Legal Club Chgo., Law Club Chgo., Internat. Assn. Ins. Counsel, Fed. Ins. Counsel, Assn. Ins. Counsel, Outdoor Writers Assn. Am. (gen. counsel), Assn. Gt. Lakes Outdoor Writers (v.p., bd. dirs.), Ill. C. of C. (bd. dirs. 1969-70), Phi Delta Phi, Sigma Nu. Republican. Congregationalist. Clubs: Elgin Country (pres. 1956), Cosmopolitan. Lodges: Elks, Moose. Home: 2421 Tall Oaks Dr Elgin IL 60123-4844

KIRKLAND, GERRY PAUL, sales executive; b. Muscatine, Iowa, June 22, 1943; s. Paul L. and Mary (Shelter) K.; m. Carol Godske; children: Steffanie, Kevin, Kara, Peter. Student, Rockhurst Coll., 1961-64. Prodn. supr. Deere & Co., East Moline, Ill., 1964-71; loan officer Security State Bank, Bettendorf, Iowa, 1971-73; worldwide prodn. mgr. J.I. Case, Racine, Wis., 1973-86; v.p. mktg. and sales The Prime Mover Co., Muscatine, 1986-90; gen. mgr. Nissan Indsl. Equip. Co., Schaumburg, Ill., 1990-93; with Pettibone Corp., Schaumburg, Ill., 1993—; v.p. internat. ops. Pettibone Corp., Lisle, Ill., 1993—; pres. CTR Mfg., Inc., Union Grove, N.C.; bd. dirs. Backwaters Gamblers Ski Club, Rock Island, Ill., 1987-90; mem. pres.'s coun. Purdue U. Bd. dirs. Crime Stoppers, Muscatine, 1987-90; Rep. county and state del., Muscatine, 1988; active opns. edn. Muscatine Sch. Dist.; bd. dirs. Muscatine High Sch. Boosters; pres. Northwestern U. Parents Coun., 1983-87; mem. Purdue U. Parents Adv. Coun.; chmn. Sleepy Hollow Plan Commn., 1993—. Mem. Indsl. Truck Assn. (bd. dirs.), Am. Barefoot Water Ski Assn. (bd. dirs.), Rotary. Republican. Home: 222 Darien Ln Sleepy Hollow IL 60118-1861 Office: Pettibone Corp 4225 Naperville Rd Lisle IL 60532-3656 also: CTR Mfg Inc 774 Zeb Rd Union Grove NC 28689

KIRKLAND, GWENDOLYN VICKYE, investment broker, financial planner; b. Chgo., Apr. 24, 1961; d. Warren and Gwendolyn (Smith) K. BS, Bradley U., Peoria, Ill., 1972; MEd in Adminstrn. and Supervision, DePaul U., Chgo., 1976. Cert. fin. planner. Tchr. Chgo. Bd. Edn., 1972-80; sales rep. A.J. Nystrom, Chgo., 1980-82; assoc. v.p. Dean Witter Reynolds, Matteson, Ill., 1983-90; br. mgr. The Chapman Co., Chgo., 1990-94, Am. Investment Svcs., Matteson, 1994—. Bd. dirs. South Suburban Family Shelter, 1988-90; pres. Village West Growhomes, Hazel Crest, Ill., 1987-90. Recipient Black Achievers award Harlem YMCA, 1986. Mem. Nat. Assn. Securities Profls. (v.p. 1990-91), Delta Sigma Theta (chaplain, scholarship chair). Democrat. Office: Am Investment Svcs 600 Holiday Plz Dr # 236 Matteson IL 60443

KIRKMAN, WILLIAM H., air force officer; b. Honolulu, May 19, 1948; s. William Allen and Annie Henrietta (Restall) K.; m. Michele A. Layman, June 4, 1970 (div. July 1985); 1 child, Heather; m. Pamela Howard, July 3, 1987; 1 child, Alec. BSEE, USAF Acad., 1970; MS in Human Resource Mgmt., Pepperdine U., 1977; student, Air Command and Staff Coll., 1984-85. Commd. 2d lt. USAF, 1966, advanced through grades to col., 1992; wing tactics officer 509 Bomb (Med) Squadron, Pease AFB, N.H., 1978-81; dep. dir. enhanced Joint tactical info. distbn. sys. Electronic Sys. Divsn., Hanscom AFB, Mass., 1981-84; chief quality assurance Upper Heyford Royal AFB, Bicester, U.K., 1985-87; chief advanced tech. divsn. Hdqs. Air Force Sys. Command, Andrews AFB, Md., 1987-89; chief stealth and counter stealth Office of Sec. of Def., Washington, 1989-93; dir. aircraft product support office Aeronautical Sys. Ctr./SD, Wright Patterson AFB, Ohio, 1994—; dir. aerospace control and strike mission arm group Aeronautical Sys. Ctr./SD, Wright Patterson AFB, 1994—; sr. panel alt. mem. air force standing acquisition panel USAF, Washington, 1995—; mem. steering group aerial refueling sys. adv. group, Dayton, Ohio, 1995—. Bd. dirs., sec. Franconia Forrest Homeowners Assn., Alexandria, Va., 1990-93. Decorated D.F.C., Def. Superior Svc. medal, Def. Meritorious Svc. medal. Mem. Internat. Elec. Electronic Engr. Assn., Air Force Assn. (life), U.S. Air Force Acad. Assn. Grads. (life), Porsche Club Am. Home: 524 Metzger Dr Wright Patterson AFB OH 45434 Office: Aeronautical Sys Ctr/SD Wright Patterson AFB OH 45433

KIRKPATRICK, ANNE SAUNDERS, systems analyst; b. Birmingham, Mich., July 4, 1938; d. Stanley Rathbun and Esther (Casteel) Saunders; children: Elizabeth, Martha, Robert, Sarah. Student, Wellesley Coll., 1956-57, Laval U., Quebec City, Can., 1958, U. Ariz., 1958-59; BA in Philosophy, U. Mich., 1961. Systems engr. IBM, Chgo., 1962-64; sr. analyst Commonwealth Edison Co., Chgo., 1981—. Treas. Taproot Reps., DuPage County, Ill., 1977-80; pres. Hinsdale (Ill.) Women's Rep. Club, 1978-81. Club: Wellesley of Chgo. (bd. dirs. 1972-73). Home: 222 E Chestnut St #8B Chicago IL 60611 Office: Commonwealth Edison Co 72 W Adams St Ste 1450 Chicago IL 60603-5108

KIRKPATRICK, HOLLY JEAN, elementary education educator, special education educator; b. Santa Cruz, S.Am., Mar. 21, 1953; d. John Meridith and Alice Louise (Mitchell) K. BA, Earlham Coll., 1975; MA, U. Evansville, 1979. Cert. tchr., Ind. Tchr. Richmond (Ind.) Community Schs., 1975-76; substitute tchr. Indpls. Pub. Schs., 1976-77, North Gibson Schs., Princeton, Ind., 1977-79; tchr. Kokomo (Ind.) Ctr. Schs., 1979—. Bd. dirs. Kokomo unit Am. Heart Assn., 1990—; mem. communications coun. United Way, Kokomo, 1990—; mem. Mayor's Substance Abuse Adv. Coun., Kokomo, 1990—, Howard County Child Abuse Coun., Kokomo, 1990—. Named Master Tchr. for Ind. Migrant Edn. Coun., 1986, Outstanding Young Hoosier, Kokomo Jaycees, 1986, 92. Mem. NEA, ASCD, Internat. Reading Assn. (Honor Coun. 1992), Ind. State Reading Assn. (Honor Coun. 1992), Kokomo Area Reading Coun. (v.p. 1990-91, pres. 1991-92, Honor Coun. 1990-92), Ind. State Tchrs. Assn., Kokomo Tchrs. Assn. (pres. 1987—), Phi Delta Kappa, Delta Kappa Gamma. Methodist. Home: 1206 Gleneagles Dr Kokomo IN 46902-3184 Office: Roosevelt Sch 2200 N Washington St Kokomo IN 46901-5840

KIRKPATRICK, ROBERT HUGH, communications executive; b. Kingston, N.Y., Mar. 3, 1954; s. Oscar Hugh and Ann (Page) K.; m. Debra Cook, Oct. 25, 1986; 1 child, Page. BA in Polit. Sci. with high honors, SUNY, Oneonta, 1977; M in Pub. and Pvt. Mgmt., Yale U., 1979. Policy analyst edn. com. N.Y. State Assembly, 1977; mgr. mktg. Cummins Engine Co., Columbus, Ind., 1980-81, mgr. mktg. ops., 1982-83, dir. electronics mktg., 1984-86, dir. bus. devel. Svc. Products Co. subs., 1987-89; pres. Intelesis Inc., Columbus, 1989—; cons. in field, New Haven, 1978-79. Contbr. articles to bus. jours. Trustee SUNY, Albany, 1975-76; pres. Columbus Arts Guild, 1981-82; treas. San Souci, Inc., Columbus, 1983-85; mem. allocations com. United Way, 1990-92; mem. City Transp. Commn., Oneonta, N.Y., 1973-74; bd. dirs. Leadership Bartholomew County Alumni Assn., 1991-92; bd. dirs. Young Mothers' Ednl. Devel., Inc., 1994—. Mem. Assn. Telemessaging Svcs. Internat. (bd. dirs. 1993—, v.p., sec. 1994—), CADCOM Egt. Owners Assn. (bd. dirs. 1994—), Telocator Mobile Comm. Industry Assn., Yale Club Ind. (treas. 1981-85), Ind. Vocat. Tech. Coll. Found. (Columbus bd. dirs. 1991-93), Rotary (pres. 1996-97, bd. dirs. 1994—). Methodist. Home: 3973 W Wood Lake Ln Columbus IN 47201-8235 Office: Intelesis Inc PO Box 622 Columbus IN 47202-0622

KIRKSEY, ROBERT FREDERICK, company executive; b. Blytheville, Ark., Feb. 16, 1959; s. Roy Lee and Olive Esther (Wahl) K.; m. Pamela Kay Rector, June 6, 1981; children: Brittany Elizabeth, Robert Frederick II. BA, U. Ark., 1981; MS of Adminstn., Cen. Mich. U., 1986. Commd. USAF, 1981, advanced through grades to capt.; from dep. missile combat crew comdr. to missile combat crew comdr. USAF, Minot AFB, N.D., 1982-86, missile procedures trainer operator, 1986-87, protocol officer, 1982, security mgr. 91 SMW/DOT, 1986-87, chief DOTM tng., 1987, chief DOTM quality control, 1987, command post contr., 1988-90; chief airfield ops. USAF, Kunsan AFB, Korea, 1990-91; warning systems controller SAC hdqrs. Offutt AFB, NE, 1992, resigned, 1992; fleet mgr. J.B. Hunt, Hueytown, Ala., 1992-94; svc. mgr. Roadway Global Air, Indpls., 1994—. Mem. Air Force Assn., Arnold Air Soc. (outstanding sr. 1981). Home: 7614 Dartmouth Rd Indianapolis IN 46260 Office: 9200 Keystone Xing Indianapolis IN 46240-2121

KIRNER, PAUL TIMOTHY, lawyer; b. Cleve., July 1, 1947; s. Paul F. and Anna M. (Christy) K.; m. Deborah J. Horvat, July 25, 1970; children: Paul James, Peter S. BS, Marquette U., 1969; JD cum laude, Cleve. State U.,

1972. Bar: Ohio 1972, U.S. Supreme Ct. 1976. Assoc. Buckingham & Doolittle, Akron, Ohio, 1972-73, Quandt & Giffels, Cleve., 1973-74, Leary & Schifko, Parma, Ohio, 1974-89, Kirner & Boldt, North Royalton, Ohio, 1989—; spl. counsel to atty. gen. State of Ohio, 1982-96. Mem. Cuyahoga County Cen. Com., Ohio, 1977—; councilman City of Parma, 1987—; pres. pro tem Parma City Council, 1988—; chmn. Parma Fair Housing Com., 1983-88; pres. St. Anthony's Parish Council, 1981-84, Athletic Assn. St. Anthony, 1986-93; bd. dirs. St. Ignatius Fathers Club, Cleve., 1987-88. Served to 1st lt. C.E., U.S. Army, 1969-73. Mem. ABA, ATLA, Ohio Trial Lawyers Assn., Ohio State Bar Assn., Cuyahoga County Bar Assn., Cleve. Bar Assn., Parma Bar Assn. (pres. 1979-80, trustee 1980-83), Cleve. State U. Coll. Law Alumni (trustee 1969-70). Lodges: Elks, Lions (treas. Parma 1982-84). Democrat. Roman Catholic. Avocation: photography. Office: 8025 Corporate Cir Cleveland OH 44133-1257

KIRSCH, JEFFREY SCOTT, securities executive; b. Chgo., Nov. 11, 1947; s. Norton M. and Estelle (Kaufman) K.; m. Jodi Lynn Spak, May 20, 1985; children: Alexandra J., Jonathan Peter. BSBA, Babson Coll., 1970. V.p. Auto Gard Inc., Chgo., 1970-90; securities dealer Chgo. Bd. Option Exchange, 1973—, mem. arbitration com., 1978-79, mem. system and facilities com., 1980-81; pres. Kirsch Inc., Chgo., 1981—; pres. one-hr. photo systems Fromex, Chgo., 1981—. Bd. dirs. Young Men's Jewish Council, Chgo., 1978. Mem. Automotive Parts and Accessories Assn., Babson Coll. Alumni Com. Club: Standard (Chgo.). Home: 442 W Wellington Ave Chicago IL 60657-5804 Office: First Option Chgo 440 S La Salle St Chicago IL 60605-1028 also: Fromex Inc 188 W Washington St Chicago IL 60602-2306 also: 40 W Lake St Leo Burnett Bldg Chicago IL 60601

KIRSCHENMANN, FREDERICK LUDWIG, farmer; b. Medina, N.D., Feb. 4, 1935; s. Theodore and Pauline Kirschenmann; m. Edith Maria Hults, June 20, 1951 (div. 1968); m. Carolyn E. Raffensperger, Oct. 6, 1995; children: Ann Marie, Damon Frederick. BA, Yankton Coll., 1957; BD, Hartford Sem., 1960; MA, U. Chgo., 1962, PhD, 1964. Dept. chair Yankton (S.D.) Coll., 1962-68; dir. Consortium for Higher Edn. Religious Studies, Dayton, Ohio, 1968-73; acad. dean Curry Coll., Milton, Mass., 1973-77; mgr. Kirschenmann Family Farms, Windsor, N.D., 1977—; pres. Farm Verified Organic, Medina, 1988—, Organic Foods Prodn. Assn. N.Am., Greenfield, Mass., 1990-93. Contbr. articles to profl. jours. Pres. No. Plains Sustainable Agrl. Soc., Madia, N.D., 1983-88. Named Thompson fellow Hartford Sem., 1960-62, Rockefeller fellow U. Chgo., 1963-64, Safe Food Trailblazer, Ctr. for Sci. in the Pub. Interest, 1990. Home: RR 1 Box 73 Windsor ND 58424-9801 Office: PO Box 40A Medina ND 58467-0040

KIRSCHNER, RUTH BRIN, elementary education educator; b. Mpls., Mar. 12, 1924; d. Sigman and Leah (Chazankin) Brin; m. Norman Bernard Kirschner, June 19, 1949; children: Sally Jo Kirschner Minsberg, William Arthur. BS cum laude, U. Minn., 1946. Primary tchr. Robert Fulton Sch., Mpls., 1946-52; elem. tchr. St. Louis Park (Minn.) Schs., 1962—; tchr. religious sch. Adath Jeshurun Synagogue, Mpls., 1946-83, Bnai Emet Synagoguе, St. Louis Park, 1989—; primary tchr. Latch Key, Mpls., 1986-88; nursery sch. tchr. Westwood Luth. Ch., St. Louis Park, 1989—; customer svc. rep. Am. Automobile Assn., St. Louis Park, 1985—. Sec. 4th Dist. Dem. Com., St. Louis Park, 1986-90; state del. St. Louis Park Dem. Com., 1986, 88, 90; mem. Cmty. Rels. coun. St. Louis Park, 1986-88; mem. St. Louis Park Charter Commn., 1993—; pres. Friends of St. Louis Park Libr., 1987-88, sec., 1990—; pres. St. Louis Park Friends, 1991-92, 93-94; del. to 44th Dist. Dem. Farmer Labor Exec. Bd.; alt. to 5th Dist. Dem. Farmer Labor ctrl. com.; apptd. mem. charter commn. St. Louis Park, 1993—; mem. Visions, 1994; bd. dirs. Suburban Alliance, 1994. Mem. AAUW (sec.-treas. 1970-72, parliamentarian 1974-76), Lioness (pres. Lyn-Lake 1995—, v.p. 1993-95), Alpha Delta Kappa (state scholarship chmn. 1988-90, sec. Gamma chpt. 1990—). Jewish. Home: 3135 Colorado Ave S Minneapolis MN 55416-2050

KIRSHBAUM, JON ALAN, educational administrator; b. L.A., Nov. 5, 1942; s. George Alexander and Mary Elizabeth (Ball) K.; m. Anne Nofrey, Aug. 11, 1961 (div.); 1 child, Warren Ashley (dec.); m. Linda Louise Carl, Dec. 15, 1976; stepchildren: Gary Nicholas, Grant Adam. BS in Comprehensive Mktg., No. Ill. U., 1965, MBA in Fin., 1971, postgrad., 1988-93; MDiv, McCormick Theol. Seminary, Chgo., 1980. Cert. chief sch. bus. ofcl. IRD sales/DPD Br. Office adminstr. IBM Corp., Chgo., 1965-67; systems analyst/sr. assoc. planner IBM Corp., Endicott, N.Y., 1967-71; seminary asst. Lincoln Park Presbyn. Ch., Chgo., 1972-73; team/project leader Chgo. Pub. Schs., 1974-89, data base adminstr., 1989-92, supr. desktop pub., 1992-94, core team mem., Time re-engring. project, 1994-95; project leader Info. Technologies, Chgo., 1995—. Mng. editor: Today's Traveler Mag., Chgo., 1991-92, exec. editor/v.p. mktg., 1992—. Mem. DuPage County (Ill.) Geneal. Soc. (bd. dirs. 1986-89, pres. 1989-90), Soc. Profl. Journalists, Chgo. Headline Club, N.Am. Travel Journalists Assn. (regional v.p. 1993-94), Ill. Assn. Sch. Bus. Ofcls., Assn. Sch. Bus. Ofcls., Ill. Govt. Fin. Officers' Assn. Presbyterian. Office: Chicago Pub Schs Chicago IL

KIRSTEIN, JOE WALTER, design engineer; b. Pekin, Ill., Apr. 20, 1971; s. Ronald Wayne and Donna Ann (Farris) K. BS, No. Ill. U., 1994. Office systems coop. RR Donnelley & Sons, Chgo., 1992-94; design engr. Zenith Controls, Inc., Chgo., 1994—. Mem. IEEE. Home: 240 Woodstock St Crystal Lake IL 60014 Office: Zenith Controls Inc 830 W 40th St Chicago IL 60609

KIRTLEY, DAVID E., lawyer; b. Indpls., July 12, 1966; s. James Lee and Mary Patricia (Harmer) K.: m. Shari Rose Sparks, July 16, 1988. AB summa cum laude, Wabash COll., 1988; JD, Vanderbilt Law Sch., 1991. Bar: Mich., Ind. Assoc. Warner, Norcross & Judd, Grand Rapids, Mich., 1991-93, Barnes & Thornburg, Indpls., 1993-95; atty. Eli Lilly & Co., Indpls., 1995—. Mem. Ind. Bar Assn., Order of Coif, Phi Beta Kappa. Republican. Roman Catholic. Office: Eli Lilly & Co Lilly Corp Ctr Indianapolis IN 46285

KISABETH, TIM CHARLES, obstetrician, gynecologist; b. Forstoria, Ohio, Oct. 29, 1957; s. Donald C. and Doris J. (Smith) K. BA in Chemistry, Capital U., 1979; MD, Ohio State U., 1982. Diplomate Nat. Bd. Med. Examiners, Am. Bd. Obstetrics and Gynecology. Resident in ob-gyn Oakwood Hosp., Dearborn, Mich., 1982-86; chief resident Oakwood Hosp., Dearborn, 1985-86; pvt. practice Alton, Ill., 1986—; lab. dir. Alton Multispecialists, 1995—; also bd. dirs.; chmn. ob-gyn. dept. Alton (Ill.) Meml. Hosp., 1991-93, 95—. Mem. Greater Alton-Twin River Growth Assn., 1987—; bd. dirs. Pride, Inc., 1992—, chmn. Alton Lake com., 1993-95. Fellow Am. Coll. Ob-Gyn.; mem. AMA (del. resident sect. 1984-86, del. yhoung physicians sect. 1990-92), Ill. Med. Soc. (ho. of dels. 1987—, young physicians com. 1987-92, com. on pub. rels. and membership 1992—), Madison County Med. Soc. (pres. 1994-95), Am. Fertility Soc., Masons DeMolay (Legion of Honor award 1988), Alton Waterski Club. Lutheran. Home: 3312 Rosenberg Ln Godfrey IL 62035-1172 Office: Alton Multispecialists Ltd 2 St Anthony s Way Ste 111 Alton IL 62002-4569

KISCADEN, SHEILA M., state legislator; b. St. Paul, Apr. 21, 1946; d. Harvey Richard and Bea Mae (Conway) Martineau; m. Richard Craig Kiscaden, Sept. 12, 1970; children: Michael, Karen. BS in Edn., U. Minn., 1969; MS in Pub. Adminstrn., U. So. Calif., L.A., 1986. Tchr. So. St. Paul Secondary Schs., Minn., 1969-70, Jobs 70, Rochester, Minn., 1970-71; regional coord. Planned Parenthood, Rochester, Minn., 1971-76; vol. svc. coord. Olmsted County, Rochester, Minn., 1977-80, human svc. planner, 1980-82, legis. liaison, 1982-85; prin. Cons. Collaborator, Rochester, Minn., 1987—; senator Minn. State Senate, St. Paul, 1992—. Bd. dirs. Ability Bldg. Ctr. Found. Bd., Rochester, Minn., 1989-94, Dyslexia Inst. Minn., Rochester, Minn., 1989-94; team leader Global Vols., 1989—. Fulbright scholar, 1970. Mem. Phi Beta Kappa. Republican. Home: 724 11th St SW Rochester MN 55902-6339 Office: Minn State Senate State Office Bldg 143 Saint Paul MN 55155-1201

KISER, KAREN MAUREEN, medical technologist, educator; b. St. Louis, Sept. 28, 1951; d. Arthur John and Elizabeth M. (Boyer) Meier; m. Winston Kiser, July 21, 1973; children: Cynthia Kay, Jessica Lea. BS in Med. Tech., S.E. Mo. State U., 1973; MA in Health Care Edn., Cen. Mich. U., 1984. Part-time lab. asst. Luth. Med. Ctr., St. Louis, 1970-71; part-time lab. technician Jewish Hosp., St. Louis, 1972-73, med. technologist, 1973-77; assoc. prof., edn. coord. St. Louis C.C. at Forest Park, 1977—; on-site surveyor Nat. Accrediting Agy. for Clin. Lab. Sci., Chgo., 1986, 94; self-study reviewer, 1994, 95; reviewer F.A. Davis, 1995, W.B. Saunders Co., Phila., 1986-91; spkr. in field. Leader Girl Scouts U.S., 1986-90, 91-92, co-leader, 1990—; assoc. advisor Explorer Scouts, 1978-81; capt. United Way, St. Louis, 1989, 90, 93. Recipient Emerson Electric award for Teaching Excellence, 1993, Gov.'s award for Excellence in Teaching, 1993. Mem. NEA, Am. Soc. for Clin. Lab. Sci., Mo. Soc. for Clin. Lab. Sci., Am. Soc. for Microbiology, Mo. Edn. Assn., Mo. Assn. Cmty. and Jr. Colls., Am. Soc. Clin. Pathologists. Office: Saint Louis CC 5600 Oakland Ave Saint Louis MO 63110-1316

KISON, CAROL, nursing educator, critical care nurse; b. Milw.. Diploma, Sacred Heart; AAS, Milw. Area Tech. Coll.; BSN, Alverno Coll.; MSN, Clayton U., 1986; MSM, Cardinal Stritch, 1987; MSN, U. Wis., Milw., 1990; PhD in Health Svcs., Walden U., Minn. RN, Wis. adj. asst. prof. nursing Marian Coll., Fond du Lac, Wis.; DON long term care, scholarship com. U. Wis.-Milw. Mem. ANA, AACCN, Nat. League for Nursing, WND, GMAC, Wis. Nurses Assn., Doctorate Assn. N.Y. Educators, Sigma Theta Tau.

KISOR, HENRY DU BOIS, newspaper editor, critic, columnist; b. Ridgewood, N.J., Aug. 17, 1940; s. Manown and Judith (Du Bois) K.; m. Deborah L. Abbott, June 24, 1967; children: Colin, Conan. BA, Trinity Coll., 1962, LittD (hon.), 1991; MS in Journalism, Northwestern U., 1964. Copy editor Wilmington News-Jour. (Del.), 1964-65; copy editor Chgo. Daily News, 1965-73, book editor, 1973-78; book editor Chgo. Sun-Times, 1978—; adj. prof. Medill Sch. Journalism Northwestern U., Evanston, Ill., 1979-82. Author: What's That Pig Outdoors?: A Memoir of Deafness, 1990, Zephyr: Tracking a Dream Across America, 1994. Bd. dirs. Chgo. Hearing Soc., 1975-76. Recipient Stick-O-Type award Chgo. Newspaper Guild, 1981, 85, Outstanding Achievement award Ill. UPI, 1983, 85, 1st pl. award Ill. UPI columns divsn., 1985, James Friend Meml. Critic award Friends of Lit., 1988, Best Non-fiction award, 1991; finalist Pulitzer Prize nomination in criticism Columbia U., 1981; NEH seminar fellow, 1978. Office: Chgo Sun-Times 401 N Wabash Ave Chicago IL 60611-3532

KISS, ISTVAN L., manufacturing executive; b. Celldomolk II, Hungary, May 29, 1936; came to U.S., 1957; AD, Trade Sch. Pres. G.A. Machine Co., Detroit, 1975—. Vol. ARC. Mem. Hungarian Culture Soc. Office: GA Machine Co 8851 Mark Twain St Detroit MI 48228-2310

KISS, STEPHEN P., investment broker; b. Douglas, Mich., Feb. 28, 1962; m. Peggy Alexander, Mar. 27, 1982; children: Marne, Hillary. BA, Hope Coll., 1984. Investment broker First of Mich., Holland, Mich., 1986-89, Raffensberger Hughes, Holland, 1989-91, JJB Hilliard W L Lyons Inc., Holland, 1992—. Pres. Fennville (Mich.) Area Youth Svcs., 1993—. Mem. Fennville Area Lions Club (past pres.). Republican. Office: JJB Hilliard W L Lyons Inc 36 W 8th St Holland MI 49423-3153

KISSANE, SHARON FLORENCE, writer, consultant; b. Chgo., July 2, 1940; d. Bruno William and Agnes Evelyn (Payne) Mrotek; m. James Quin Kissane, July 2, 1966 (dec. June 1989); children: Laura Janine Ehrke, Elaine Marie Kissane. BA, De Paul U., 1962; MA, Northwestern U., 1963; PhD, Loyola U., 1970. Cert. tchr., Ill. Tchr. Notre Dame H.S., Chgo., 1959-61, Our Lady of Solace Sch., Chgo., 1961-62; tech. writer, editor Commerce Clearing House, Chgo., 1962-63; tchr. U. Ill., Chgo., 1963-66; mgr. Amalgamated Ins. Co., Chgo., 1966-68; editor Herald Newspapers, Des Plaines, Ill., 1968-69; assoc. dir. Montag Coll. Psycho-Ednl. Clinic, Chgo., 1970-72; dir. Learning Ctr., libr. Stevenson Elem. Sch., Des Plaines, 1972-73; dir. Park Ridge (Ill.) Reading Ctr., 1973-78; pres. Kissane Comms. Ltd., Barrington, Ill., 1979—. Author: What is Child Abuse?, 1993, Gang Awareness, 1995; co-author: Polish Biographical Dictionary, 1992, Career Success for Those With Physical Disabilities, 1996; contbr. articles to profl. jours. Bd. dirs. Barrington (Ill.) Children's Choir, 1984-85, LA FEP Student Exch. Program, Barrington, 1983-84, Barrington United Way; mem. task force Dist. # 220, Barrington, 1983-86; founding mem. Barrington Area Arts Coun., 1980, Park Ridge Hist. Soc., 1972; mem. curriculum com. Barrington H.S., 1981-84; elections judge South Barrington Precinct, 1989—. Recipient Dale Carnegie Speech scholarship Jr. Achievement, 1958; named Hon. Citizen of Korea, 1965. Mem. Nat. Assn. Women Bus. Owners (bd. dirs. 1982-83), Internat. Platform Assn., MIT Forum, Barrington Profl. Women, Midwest Soc. Profl. Cons., Phi Delta Kappa, Kappa Gamma Pi. Republican. Office: Kissane Comms Ltd 15 Turning Shores South Barrington IL 60010

KISSELL, DON R., state legislator. Mem. dist. 17 Mo. Ho. of Reps. Office: 408 Sutters Mill Rm 317-B Saint Peters MO 63376

KISSLING, RICHARD EUGENE, II, accountant; b. Grand Rapids, Mich., Sept. 26, 1947; s. Richard E. and Helen K. (Hedges) K.; m. Melody A. Sweet, June 28, 1970; children: Richard E. III, Mary A. BA, U. Indpls., 1970; MPA, Ind. U., 1981. Auditor Mut. Hosp. Svcs., Indpls., 1970-77; from asst. to assoc. dir. acctg. dept. Ind. U. Hosps., Indpls., 1977-87; acct., controller Corinthian Pharm. Systems, Indpls., 1988-89; pres., CEO Kissling Bookkeeping and Tax Svc., Indpls., 1989—. Mem. Nat. Soc. Pub. Accts. (assoc.), Nat. Assn. Tax Practitioners. Methodist. Office: 7212 N Shadeland Ave Ste 100 Indianapolis IN 46250-2030

KITA, TERRY J., mechanical engineer; b. Sturgeon Bay, Wis., Feb. 5, 1944. BS in Mech. Engring., U. Wis., 1967, postgrad., 1971. Tchg. cert. math.; registered profl. engr., Minn. Constrn. engr. ECOLAB, St. Paul, 1976-84; mech. engr. Fed. Cartridge Co., Anoka, Minn., 1984—; tchr. English UNESCO, Poland, 1994. Mem. Dem. Party, Mpls., 1989—. Mem. Am. Inst. Plant Engrs., EOS-ESD. Democrat. Office: Fed Cartridge Co 900 Ehlen Dr Anoka MN 55303-1778

KITT, WALTER, psychiatrist; b. N.Y.C., Dec. 18, 1925; s. Elias and Mary (Opiela) K.; m. Terry Escorcia, May 15, 1955 (dec. 1974); 1 child, Gregory; m. Sally Anderson Chappell, June 22, 1977. Student, CCNY, 1942-44; AB magna cum laude, Syracuse (N.Y.) U., 1948; MD, Chgo. Med. Sch., 1952. Diplomate Am. Bd. Psychiatry and Neurology. Resident Neuropsychiat. Inst., Chgo., 1953-56; practice medicine specializing in psychiatry Chgo., 1956-64, Munster, Ind., 1963-80; psychiatrist Lakeside VA Med. Ctr., Chgo., 1981-92; practice medicine specializing in psychiatry Park Ridge, Ill., 1992—; acting chief psychiat. services Lakeside VA Med. Ctr., Chgo., 1986-87; asst. prof. clin. psychiatry U. Ill. Med. Ctr., Chgo., 1958-64, Northwestern U., Chgo., 1974-96; chmn. divsn. psychiatry Our Lady of Mercy Hosp., Dyer, Ind., 1970-72. Mem. Am. Psychiat. Assn. Home: 3750 N Lake Shore Dr Chicago IL 60613-4238 Office: 1460 Renaissance Dr # 209 Park Ridge IL 60068

KITTELSEN, RODNEY OLIN, lawyer; b. Albany, Wis., Mar. 11, 1917; s. Olen B. and Nellie Winifred (Atkinson) K.; m. Pearle M. Haldiman, Oct. 12, 1940; children: Gregory S., James E., Bradley J. PhB, U. Wis., 1939, LLB, 1940. Spl. agt. FBI, Washington, 1940-46; ptnr. Kittelsen, Barry, Ross, Wellington & Thompson, Monroe, Wis., 1946—; dist. atty. Green County, Monroe, 1947-53; pres. State Bar Wis., Madison, 1976-77, 83-85; dir. Wis. Law Found., Madison, 1992—. Pres. Monroe Police and Fire Commn., 1947—; legal counsel X-FBI Inc., Quantico, Va., 1986—; mem. Am. Coll. Trust and Estate Coun., Chgo., 1983—. Recipient Outstanding Citizen award Monroe Jaycees, 1977, Outstanding Svc. award Albany FFA, 1991, Disting. Svc. award U. Wis. Law Sch., 1995. Fellow Am. Bar Found., Wis. Bar Found. (pres. 1976-77, 83-85, Goldberg award 1990). Home: 708 26th Ave Monroe WI 53566-1620 Office: 916 17th Ave Monroe WI 53566-2003

KITTLE, PAUL EDWIN, pediatric dentist; b. Meriden, Conn., Mar. 6, 1948; s. Paul Edwin and Mary Lee (Conway) K.; m. Linda Susan Holthaus, Mar. 2, 1973; children: Christopher Paul, Zachary Joseph. BA in Biology, U. Conn., 1970; DDS, Creighton U., 1975; Cert. in Pedodontics, U. Texas, 1981. Diplomate Am. Bd. Pediatric Dentistry. Commd. capt. U.S. Army, Ft. Riley, Kans., 1975; advanced through grades to col. U.S. Army, 1992; intern U.S. Army, Ft. Riley, Kans., 1976; gen. dental officer U.S. Army, Butzbach, Fed. Republic Germany, 1976-79; pediatric dental resident U.S. Army, San Antonio, 1979-81; chief pediatric dentist U.S. Army, Baumholder, Fed. Republic Germany, 1981-85, Ft. Leavenworth, 1985-89; asst. dir. pediatric dental residency program U.S. Army, Ft. Lewis, Wash., 1989-91, dir. pediatric dental residency program, 1991-93; pvt. practice pediatric dentistry Leavenworth, 1994—; clin. assoc. prof. Kans. U. Med. Ctr., Kansas City, 1994—. Mem. Am. Acad. Pediatric Dentistry (trustee-at-large 1994-96). Republican. Unitarian. Office: 309 S 2nd St Leavenworth KS 66048-2803

KITTO, JOHN BUCK, JR., mechanical engineer; b. Evanston, Ill., Dec. 22, 1952; s. John Buck and Marie (Comstock) K.; m. Cecilia Higgins, Aug. 17, 1974; children: Christopher Daniel, Andrew Comstock. BSME, Lehigh U., 1975; MBA, U. Akron, 1980. Reg. profl. engr., Ohio, Pa. Sr. engr. Babcock & Wilcox Co., Alliance, Ohio, 1975-80, research engr., 1980-81, program mgr., 1981-94, bus. devel. specialist, 1995—. Editor: Heat Exchangers for Two Phase Flow, 1983, Two-Phase Heat Exchanger, 1985, Maldistribution of Flow, 1987, Steam: Its Generation and Use, 1992; author and patentee in field. Fellow ASME (chmn. chpt. 1983-84, chmn. exec. com. of heat transfer divsn. 1992-93, v.p. region V 1992-95, officer bd. comms. 1991-95, sr. v.p. 1995—, Prime Movers award 1992, Dedicated Svc. award 1992, George Westinghouse Silver medal 1991); mem. NSPE (Young Engr. of Yr. award 1986), AIChE, Air Waste Mgmt. Assn., Tau Beta Pi, Pi Tau Sigma, Beta Gamma Sigma, Sigma Iota Epsilon. Republican. Home: 1150 7th St NE Canton OH 44720-2172 Office: Babcock & Wilcox Co Rsch and Devel Div 1562 Beeson St NE Alliance OH 44601-2165

KITTREDGE, MARIE, non-profit housing development manager; b. Cin., June 26, 1958; d. John Gholson and Cornelia (Nyce) Kittredge; m.Clark Douglas Broida, Aug. 1, 1987; children: Katharine, Michael, Samuel, Jacob. BA, Simon's Rock Coll., 1979; MCP, U. Cin., 1986; doctoral studies, MIT, 1986-89. Asst. mgr. Ctrl. Trust Bank, Cin., 1979-89, City of Cin., 1985-86, Boston Redevel. Authority, Boston, 1986-88; housing devel. mgr. Broadway Area Housing Coalition, Cleve., 1989—. V.p. Cleve. Sch. Bd., 1993—; mem. Cleve. Substance Abuse Initiative, 1994-95; peace and justice commn. mem. Diocese of Ohio, 1995. Democrat. Episcopalian. Office: 1380 E 6th St Cleveland OH 44114-1606

KITZMAN, SCOTT ALAN, retail lumber company executive; b. Janesville, Wis., Nov. 4, 1969; s. Richard Alan and Elizabeth Rose (Opensky) K. BA in Polit. Sci., Columbia Coll., 1992. V.p. Kitzman's Ltd., Rockford, Ill., 1992—. Moderator Comty. Awareness Program, Rockford, Ill., 1994-95; vol. United Way, Rockford, 1994-95. Mem. Rockford Area C. of C. (bd. dirs. 1996-99, Svc. award 1995), Univ. Club of Rockford, Alumni Columbia Coll. (rep. com.). Republican. Lutheran. Home: 867 Easton Pkwy Rockford IL 61108 Office: Kitzman's Ltd 6935 11th St Rockford IL 61109

KITZMILLER, GREG LOUIS, marketing educator, strategic consultant, conference speaker; b. Indpls., June 25, 1950. BS, Ball State U., 1972; MBA, Ind. U., 1981. Entrpreneur Ice Service, 1968-75; salesman Provident Mut. Ins., Indpls., 1972-73; dist. rep. Am. Cancer Soc., Indpls., 1973-74, exec. dir., 1974-76; product mgr. Gatorade, Stokely-Van Camp, Inc., Indpls., 1976-81; mkgt. mgr. Bayer AG, Leverkusen, Germany, 1986-87; sr. product mgr. Miles Inc., Elkhart, Ind., 1981-85, group product mgr., 1987-91, dir. sales support, 1991-94; mktng. dir. Business Development, 1994-95; guest lectr. U. Notre Dame, Ind., 1989-95, adj. lectr. Ind. U 1994-95, vis. adj. prof. mktng. Ind. U Sch. Business 1995—, speaker, Functional Foods for Health Annual Conference. U Ill. 1995, Nutracon-Natl. Nutritional Conference, Las Vegas 1995, Amer. Chemical Soc. Annual Conf., New Orleans 1995, council for Responsibl Nutrition, Lake Tahoe, 1995, co-chair Nutracon-Natl. Nutritional Conference, Nashville 1996. outstanding mktng. student award 1972, pres. BSU mktng. club 1972. Mem. Am. Mktg. Assn. (local bd. dirs. 1991—, Speaker's award 1992, state commitee: Profl. Development 1995—), Greater Elkhart C. of C., Gideons Internat. (v.p. Elkhart County 1991-92), council for Responsible Nutrition, Washington 1994, Amer. Cancer Soc. (local bd. 1994-95, state committee-Prevention 1995—). Office: Ind U Sch Business 10th & Fee Ln Bloomington IN 47405 office: Kitzmiller Consulting PO Box 7691 Bloomington IN 47407

KITZMILLER, KARL WILLIAM, dermatologist; b. Cin., Sept. 23, 1931; m. Alice Ann Meehan, Jan. 29, 1955; children: Sue, John, Dan, Sarah, Brian. BS, U. Cin., 1953, MD, 1960. Diplomate, Am. Bd. Dermatology. Intern Cin. Gen. Hosp., 1960-61; fellow in dermatology Mayo Clinic, Rochester, Minn., 1961-64, asst. clin. prof. for family medicine, assoc. clin. prof. for dermatology; pvt. practice Cin., 1964—; asst. clin. prof. Dept. of Family Medicine U. of Cin. Med. Ctr., assoc. clin. prof. Dept. of Surgery Div. of Plastic Reconstructive and Hand Surgery, clin. prof. Dept. Dermatology; attending staff, chief dermatology Good Samaritan Hosp., Deaconess Hosp.; cons. Wright Patterson AFB, Dayton, Ohio; courtesy staff Our Lady of Mercy Hosp., Holmes Hosp., Margaret Mary Community Hosp., Batesville, Ind.; staff Children's Hosp., Bethesda Hosp.; attending physician Univ. Hosp., 1966—, Jewish Hosp., 1966—, dir. dept. dermatology, 1977—; attending staff Christ Hosp., 1976—, sec. dept. dermatology, 1977—; mem. Choice Care Physician Leadership and Mgmt. Edn. program Xaiver U., 1990-91. Contbr. articles to med. jours. Lt. USAF, 1954-56. Recipient Neil McElroy award, United Way, 1991. Fellow ACP; mem. AMA (alt. del., recognition award 1969-89, 90), Soc. Dermatol. Surgery, Am. Acad. Dermatology (CME award 1990), Ohio State Med. Assn. (sec. dermatology sect. 1974—, del., 1st dist. councilor 1991—, recognition award 1990), Acad. Medicine Cin. (pres. 1987-89), Chgo. Dermatol. Soc., Cin. Dermatol. Soc. (pres. 1973-74, 89-90), Noah Worcester Dermatol. Soc. (sec.-treas. 1985-90, pres. elect 1990-91, pres. 1992-93), The Cincinnatus Assn., Leadership Cin. (Class XII), Assn. Ohio Commodores, Kidney Found., Cin. C. of C., Cin. Tennis Club, Rotary, Cin. Country Club. Roman Catholic. Office: Ste B-100 9403 Kenwood Rd Cincinnati OH 45242 Office: 9403 Kenwood Rd Ste B-100 Cincinnati OH 45242

KIVISTO, PETER JOHN, sociologist; b. Ishpeming, Mich., Nov. 17, 1948; s. John Rudolph and Emily (Nicholas) K.; m. Susan Hoy Langewisch, June 12, 1973' children: Sarah, Aaron. BA, U. Mich., 1970; MDiv, Yale U., 1973; MA, New Sch. Social Rsch., 1977, PhD, 1982. Projects dir. New Haven (Conn.) Housing Authority, 1976-80; rsch. sociologist Dept. Housing and Urban Devel., Washington, 1980-82; spl. lectr. George Mason U., Fairfax, Va., 1980-82; from. asst. to assoc. prof. Augustana Coll., Rock Island, Ill., 1982—; adj. prof. U. New Haven, 1977-80. Author: Immigrant Socialist in the United States, 1984, American All, 1995; co-author: Max Weber, 1989, For Democracy, 1993; editor: The Ethnic Enigma, 1988; co-editor: American Immigrants and Their Generations, 1990, The Rapture of Politics, 1995. Vice chmn. cmty. svcs. panel United Way, Rock Island, 1989—; v.p. Vis. Nurses Assn., Moline, Ill., 1987-90; bd. dirs. Ill. Luth. Coalition, 1987-91, 95—. Ctr. Advanced Study fellow, U. Iowa, 1991; Fulbright grantee, 1984. Mem. Am. Sociol. Assn., Midwest Sociol. Soc. (pub. com., nominating com.), Internat. Sociol. Assn., Assn. Sociology of Religion, Immigration History Soc., Soc. Study Social Problems (adv. planning com. 1984—), Social Sci. History Assn. Democrat. Lutheran. Office: Augustana Coll Sociology Dept Rock Island IL 61201

KLAGES, JOHN WILLIAM, automotive parts company executive; b. Columbus, Ohio, July 11, 1922; s. Reynold E. and Corinne M. (Krag) Klages; m. Helen Virginia Booze, Feb. 14, 1948 (dec. 1993); children: Ellen J., Mary K., Sarah M. AB, Harvard U.; MBA, Capital U. Mgmt. trainee The Columbus (Ohio) Auto Parts Co., 1948-53, asst. plant supt., 1953-62, exec. v.p., 1962-71, pres., CEO, 1971-87, ret., 1987. Author: History of Zanesfield Rod and Gun Club, 1989. Bd. dirs., treas. United Way of Franklin Co., Columbus, 1976-82, Vols. of Am., Inc., New Orleans, 1984—; bd. dirs., chmn. Vols. of Am. So. Ohio, 1958—; bd. dirs. Crittenton Family Svcs., Columbus, 1965-72, 84—. With U.S. Army, 1942-45. Named Boss of Yr. Worthington Jaycees, 1973, Exec. of Yr. Nat. Secs. Assn., 1977; recipient Award for Vol. Svcs. Mayor's Office, 1978, George Meany award AFL-CIO, 1986. Mem. Columbus Country Club, Zanesfield Rod and Gun Club (treas., pres., trustee). Home: 2630 Sherwood Rd Columbus OH 43209

KLAHR, MARGARET CAROL DECLUE, nursing administrator, nurse; b. Crystal City, Mo., June 10, 1937; d. Stephen Edward and Corinne Margaret (Jokerst) Declue; m. Saulo Klahr, Dec. 29, 1965; children: James Herman, Robert David. BSN, St. Louis U., 1960; MSN, Washington U., St. Louis, 1965. RN, Mo. Dir. clin. care Advanced Nursing Svcs. of St. Louis; clin. instr. in nursing St. Louis Community Coll.; med. oncology coord., rsch. assoc. Washington U./Jewish Hosp., St. Louis; dir. nursing Sch. of Medicine U. Miami, Fla. USPHS fellow. Mem. NAFE, AAUW, Mo. Alliance for

Home Care, Nat. Assn. Women Bus. Owners. Home: 11544 Ladue Rd Saint Louis MO 63141-8341

KLARICH, DAVID JOHN, lawyer, state senator; b. Hamilton, Ohio, July 17, 1963; s. Victor Martin and Janet Dawn (Carlson) K.; m. Cheryl Ruth O'Donnell, June 18, 1988. BA in Biology and Chemistry, U. Mo., 1985; MA in Pub. Policy, Regent U., 1990, JD, 1990. Bar: Mo. 1990. State rep. 92nd dist. Mo. Ho. of Reps., Jefferson City, 1990—; 26th dist. State Senate, Mo., 1994—; with Riezman and Blitz, PC, Clayton, Mo., 1995—. Active Queeny Twp. Rep. Orgn., Meramec Twp. Rep. Club, Meramec Twp. Citizens for Good Govt., St. Louis Young Reps., Coll. Reps., Pachyderms. Recipient Adminstrn. of Justice award Jud. Conf. Mo., 1991, Mo. Bar award, 1993, Mo. Hosp. Assn. award, 1995. Mem. Bar Assn. Met. St. Louis, Young Lawyers Assn., Vol. Lawyers Assn., St. Louis Lawyers Assn., Mo. Assn. Trial Attys., ABA, Federalist Soc., St. Louis Bus. Assn., St. Louis Eagle Scout Assn., Nat. Eagle Scout Assn., Jaycees, Lions, Mo. C. of C., Theta Xi. Mem. Assembly of God Ch. Home: 34 Roland Ave Ballwin MO 63021-5260 Office: Riezman and Blitz PC 120 S Central Clayton MO 63105

KLASSEK, CHRISTINE PAULETTE, behavioral scientist; b. Chgo., Dec. 28, 1947; d. Walter and Pauline (Bogolin) Strom; m. Alexander George Klassek, June 14, 1969; 1 child, Margaret Mary. BA in Applied Behavioral Sci., Nat. Louis U., 1989, cert. in leadership, 1993. Asst. juvenile libr. Bolingbrook (Ill.) Fountaindale Libr., 1974-79; behavior modification counselor J.P. Kennedy Sch. for Exceptional Children, Palos Park, Ill., 1982-86; tchr. spl. edn. Little Friends Orgn., Downers Grove, Ill., 1986-89; program dir. Carmelite Carefree Village, Darien, Ill., 1989—; bd. mem. Benedictine Univ. Adv. Bd. for Sr. Programs and Issues, 1996. Treas. Young Democrats Will County, 1972; chmn., pres. bd. dirs. Dem. Women's Com. DuPage Twp., Ill., 1973-76; leader Campfire Girls Assn.; mem. adv. coun. case mgmt. Little Friends Assn., 1988; cert. pastoral min. care St. Charles Borromeo Pastoral Ctr.; vol. Pub. Action to Deliver Svc., Helping Hands Rehab. Ctr., Ray Graham; active Cath. Coun. Women; bd. dirs., mem. human rels. com. J.P. Kennedy Sch. Exceptional Children, 1985-86. Recipient Cert. of Appreciation, Am. Cancer Soc., 1991, Achievement award Life Svcs. Network Ill., 1995, DuPage County Consortium Intergenerational Task Force, 1996. Mem. LWV, Assn. Sr. Svc. Providers, Ill. Activity Profl. Assn., Surburban Activity Therapists Assn., Jaycees. Roman Catholic. Home: 240 Davis Ln Bolingbrook IL 60440-2369 Office: Carmelite Carefree Village 8419 Bailey Rd Darien IL 60561-5361

KLATT, JOHN HAROLD, auditor; b. Mason City, Iowa, Jan. 14, 1956; s. Harold Albert and Elaine Marie (Kluss) K. AA, North Iowa C.C., Mason City, 1976; BA, Buena Vista Coll., Storm Lake, Iowa, 1978. Cert. fraud examiner. Acct. Anderson & Co., CPAs, Emmetsburg, Iowa, 1978-79; auditor health and human svcs. Office of Inspector Gen. for Audit Svcs., Des Moines, 1979-91; sr. audit specialist Resolution Trust Co.-Office of Inspector Gen. for Audit, Elk Grove Village, Ill., 1991—. Mem. Assn. Govt. Accts. Office: Resolution Trust Co Office Inspector Gen 4900 Main St Ste 700 Kansas City MO 64112-2644

KLATT, MELVIN JOHN, library consultant; b. Milw., May 19, 1929; s. John Edward and Marie Barbara (Palkowski) K.; m. Shirley Ann Ryan, Aug. 31, 1957; children: Mary, John, Peter. BS in History and Econ., U. Wis., 1956; MA in Libr. Sci., U. Denver, 1958; postgrad., Ind. U., 1969-72. Circulation asst. Wis. State Hist. Soc., Madison, 1955; head br. librs. Milw. Pub. Libr., 1958-62; head acquisitions dept. U. Ill., Chgo., 1962-65; head tech. svcs. U. Denver, 1965-67, dir. librs., 1967-69; asst. dean Rosary Coll. Grad. Sch. Libr. Sch., River Forest, Ill., 1972-74; head Libr. Elmhurst (Ill.) Coll., 1974-94; chair Suburbia and the Am. Dream Conf., Elmhurst, 1977; cons. St. Xaviers Coll., Chgo., 1982. Author-contbr.: Dictionary of Wisconsin Biography, 1960; book compiler Directory of Human Resources, 1979; co-editor Colo. Acad. Librs., 1968. Chairperson S.W. Denver Human Rels., Denver, 1968-69, v.p. mem. polit. action com., 1968-70; judge, mem. visual arts com. Ill Arts Coun., Chgo., 1979-81. With U.S. Army, 1951-53, Korea. City of Milw. scholar, 1957, Ill. Acad. Libr. of the Yr. award, 1994, LIBRAS (Ill. Consortium) Libr. of the Yr., 1995, Mel George award; Nat. Def. Edn. Act fellow, 1969, 70, 71. Mem. ALA, LIBRAS Consortium (pres. 1979-81), AAUP (exec. com. 1964-65), North Cen. Accreditation Assn. (chair resources com. 1979), Ill. Libr. Assn., Pvt. Acad. Librs. Ill. (pres. 1979-81), Chgo. Libr. Club (v.p. 1979-80, pres. elect 1983-85), Beta Phi Mu, Omicron Delta Kappa. Democrat. Roman Catholic.

KLAUS, ARLEEN ELIZABETH, rehabilitation nurse; b. Reserve, La., Dec. 16, 1944; d. Francois Edward and Denise Elizabeth (Songy) Cambre; m. Arthur Stephen Klaus, Oct. 3, 1970; 1 child, Stephen Joseph. Diploma in nursing, Mercy Hosp., New Orleans, 1965. Staff nurse Mercy Hosp., New Orleans, 1965-66, 97th Gen. Hosp., Frankfurt, Germany, 1966-68, Oschner Found. Hosp., New Orleans, 1968-69, Incarnate Word Hosp., St. Louis, 1969-76; staff nurse St. John's Regional Med. Ctr., Joplin, Mo., 1976-91, patient care mgr. rehab. unit, 1991—; coord. Head and Spinal Cord Injury Prevention Program, Joplin, 1991—; speaker Take the Safety Plunge, St. John's Hosp. Program, 1991—, Mo. Hwy. Dept. Safety, Nevada and Joplin, 1992. Pres. local stroke support group. Named Outstanding Clin. Nurse, Dept. Army, 1968, Employee of Month in Rehab., St. John's Regional Med. Ctr., 1990. Mem. Assn. Rehab. Nurses (cert. rehab. RN). Roman Catholic. Home: 4030 College View Dr Joplin MO 64801-1505

KLAUS, JOAN MCADAMS, association administrator; b. Chgo., June 26, 1943; d. Frank J. and Irene (Geary) McA.; m. Robert J. Klaus, June 4, 1966; children: Christian, Elizabeth, Conor. BA, Loyola U., Chgo., 1966. Tchr. Iowa City Community Sch. Dist., 1967-74; adminstrv. asst. Dept. Commerce & Community Affairs, Chgo., 1983-84; office mgr. Dept. Commerce & Community Affairs, 1984-87; exec. dir. U. Village Assn., Chgo., 1987—; bd. dirs. Cando, Chgo., Cable Access Corp., Chgo. Bd. dirs. Ill. Amb., Chgo., 1984-86, Holy Family Preservation Soc., Chgo., 1988—. Office: U Village Assn 925 S Loomis St Chicago IL 60607-4011

KLAUS, SUZANNE LYNNE, horticulturist, production specialist; b. Kansas City, Mo., May 2, 1956; d. John Wallace and Shirley Jane (Hoffman) K.; m. William D. Luebbert, Nov. 4, 1989. BS in Agr., U. Mo., 1978, MS in Horticulture, 1980. Prodn. mgr. John Klaus & Sons Greenhouses, Greenwood, Mo., 1972—; tchr. horticulture Longview C. of C., Lee's Summit, Mo., 1979-81; guest spkr., panel mem. Mo. State Florists Convs., 1981, 92, 86, 89; guest spkr. St. Louis Growers Assn., 1985, Ohio Florists' Conf., 1986, Ball's Grow Show, 1987, Kans. State Growers Conf., 1988. Floriculture judge for nat. conv. Future Farmers Am., 1984—. Mem. Mo. State Florists' Assn. (bd. dirs. 1980-89, res. 1987-88), Floral Acad. Mo. (bd. dirs. 1986-87, pres.-elect 1988-89), Nat. Assn. Women in Horticulture (pres. 1989-90), Ohio Florists' Assn., Pointsettia Growers Assn., Nemokan Floral Assn. (bd. dirs. 1987-89). Republican. Roman Catholic. Home: PO Box 376 Greenwood MO 64034-0376

KLAVITER, HELEN LOTHROP, magazine editor; b. Lima, Ohio, Mar. 5, 1944; d. Eugene H. and Jean (Walters) Lothrop; m. Douglas B. Klaviter, June 7, 1969 (div. 1982); 1 child, Elizabeth. B.A., Cornell Coll., Mt. Vernon, Iowa, 1966. Communication specialist Coop. Extension Service, Urbana, Ill., 1969-71; mng. editor Poetry Mag., Chgo., 1973—; editorial cons. Harper & Row, N.Y.C., 1983-87. Bd. dirs. Ill. Theatre Ctr., 1989-95, St. Clement's Open Pantry, 1990—, Episc. Diocese of Chgo. Hunger Commn., 1992—, Comms. Commn., 1993—. Episcopalian. Home: 395 Dogwood St Park Forest IL 60466-1863 Office: Poetry Mag Modern Poetry Assn 60 W Walton St Chicago IL 60610-3305

KLAWITTER, ROBERT LOUIS, environmentalist; b. Duluth, Minn., Oct. 31, 1938; s. Louis Edward and Louise Cecelia (St. Mary) K.; m. Sonja Elise Johnson, 1973 (div.); children: Jennifer, Margaret, Benjamin; m. Kathleen Ann Long; 1 child, Samuel. AB with highest distinction, Ind. U., 1960; PhD, Yale U., 1965. Asst. prof. Ind. U., Bloomington, 1964-72; subsistence farmer, 1973-86; dir. rsch. Protect Our Woods, Paoli, Ind., 1986-87, v.p., 1988-91, pres., 1991-93, exec. dir., 1992-96; pres. The Environ. Fund Ind., 1992—; external adv. coun. Pudue U. Dept. Forestry, 1996—. Editor Protect Our Woods, 1986-91; contbr. articles to profl. jours. Mem. Ind. Forest Resources Coord. Com., 1991—; mem. midwest tech. com. info. and edn. Ptnrs. in Flight, 1992—; mem. Ind. Working Group, 1993—; bd. dirs. Hoosier Environ. Coun., 1988-94, v.p., 1991-93; mem. panel on wood industry Ind. Econ. Devel. Coun., 1992. Woodrow Wilson fellow, 1960-61, Woodrow Wilson Dissertation Yr. fellow, 1963-64, Yale Sterling fellow, 1963-64; recipient Environmentalist of Yr. award Hoosier Environ. Coun., 1994; featured in Eternal Vigilance, Steve Higgs, 1995. Home: 11663 E 475N Dubois IN 47527-9664

KLEBBA, RAYMOND ALLEN, property manager; b. Chgo., Apr. 16, 1934; s. Raymond Aloysius and Marie Cecelia (Tobin) K.; m. Barbara Ann Gurbal, Oct. 7, 1961; children: Anne, Daniel, Mary, Theresa. Student, Loyola U., Chgo., 1954-56; cert. property mgr., Inst. Real Estate Mgmt., 1970. Corr., rep. Western R.R. Assn., Chgo., 1956-61; pres. Midland Warehouse, Chgo., 1961-68; v.p., gen. mgr. Strobeck, Reiss Sch. Mgmt. Co., Chgo., 1968-70, real estate mgr. and broker, 1970-83; v.p. Mid-Am. Nat. Bank, Chgo., 1983-90; br. mgr. Bank of Highwood/Deerfield, Ill., 1990-94; v.p. sales First Colonial Mortgage Corp., Chgo., 1994-95; bus. mgr. St. Matthias Parish, Chgo., 1995—. Mem. Bank Mktg. Assn., Chgo. Bd. Realtors (vice chmn. comml. and indsl. leasing property mgmt. coun.), Inst. Real Estate Mgmt. (chmn. chpt. of yr. com. 1975-76), Rotary, Moose. Home: 4933 N Leavitt St Chicago IL 60625-1308 Office: St Matthias Parish Chicago IL 60625

KLEE, ANDREW MARTIN, library assistant; b. Orrville, Ohio, Nov. 12, 1962; s. Hans H. and Maryann (Lana) K.; m. Ruth Victoria Heldman, Sep. 2, 1989. BA in Sociology, Coll. of Wooster, 1985. Porter Schweizerhof Hotel, Grindelwald, Switzerland, 1985-86; libr. tech. asst. Columbus (Ohio) Met. Libr., 1987-90, libr. asst., 1990-92, 1994—; travel lectr. Ohio State U. and various civic groups, 1994—. Author, pub.: Christmas in Syria, 1993; contbr. weekly travel column Columbus Times, 1995—; contbr. articles Mish-Mash Quarterly, 1992—. Home: 1042 Harrison Ave Columbus OH 43201 Office: Columbus Met Libr Hilltop 2955 W Broad St Columbus OH 43204

KLEEN, VERNON MELVIN, avian ecologist; b. North Platte, Nebr., Apr. 22, 1942; s. Melvin Henry and Lois Marjorie (Bartels) K.; m. Betty Jean Reuschel, July 28, 1973. BS, U. Md., 1965; MA, So. Ill. U., 1973. Cert. wildlife biologist. Rsch. biologist U. Md., College Park, 1965; field asst. Fla. State U., Western Panama, 1967; rsch. biologist Smithsonian Instn., Honolulu, 1968-69; rsch. asst. So. Ill. U., Carbondale, 1970-71; nongame biologist Ill. Dept. Conservation, Springfield, 1972-80, avian ecologist, 1980—; project coord. Ill. Breeding Bird Atlas, 1986—; chairperson Adams Wildlife Sanctuary, Springfield, 1983—. Regional editor Am. Birds, 1971-81, Ill. Audubon Bull., 1974-85, Ill. Audubon, 1985-89, Ill. Birds and Birding, 1985-91. With U.S. Army, 1965-67. Mem. The Wildlife Soc., Am. Ornithologists' Union (life), Wilson Ornithol. Soc. (life), Am. Birding Assn. (charter), Inland Bird Banding Assn. (v.p. 1972-79, pres. 1979-81), Ill. Audubon Soc. (dir. 1972—, chairperson several coms.), Ill. Ornithol. Records Com. Lutheran. Home: RR 2 Box 481 Athens IL 62613-9208 Office: Ill Dept Nat Resources 524 S 2nd St Springfield IL 62701-1787

KLEGERMAN, MELVIN EARL, microbiologist, educator; b. Chgo., Aug. 30, 1945; s. Hyman Joseph and Esther Elizabeth (Tartas) K.; m. Marjorie Sherwood Amsbary, Dec. 19, 1968 (div. 1973); children: Robin Howard Allen, Joshua Sherwood Allen; m. Wanda Ann Budzynski, Sept. 13, 1973; children: Melanie Esther, Jessica Ann. BA, U. Ill., Chgo., 1967; PhD, Loyola U., Chgo., 1984. Asst. editor Ency. Britannica, Chgo., 1970-73; rsch. assoc. Loyola U. Med. Ctr., Maywood, 1973-78, Evanston (Ill.) Hosp., 1979; rsch. investigator Michael Reese Hosp. and Med. Ctr., Chgo., 1980-86; rsch. assoc. Rush-Presbyn. St. Luke's Med. Ctr., Chgo., 1986-87; assoc. dir. Inst. Tuberculosis Rsch. U. Ill., Chgo., 1987—, asst. prof. pharms., 1988-95, adj. asst. prof. pharms., 1995—. Editor: Pharmaceutical Biotechnology: Fundamentals and Essentials, 1992; contbr. articles to Jour. Lab. Clin. Medicine, Jour. Infectious Disease, Cancer Letters, others. Grantee Organon Teknika, 1988, 93, WHO, 1989. Mem. AAAS, Am. Soc. Microbiology, Am. Assn. Pharm. Scientists, N.Y. Acad. Scis. Home: 1211 W Elmdale Ave Chicago IL 60660-2525 Office: Inst for Tuberculosis Rsch M/C 964 950 S Halsted St Chicago IL 60607

KLEIMAN, BERENICE ELKIN, company executive; b. N.Y.C., Oct. 22, 1937. BS in Edn., Syracuse U., 1959; MA in History, Ohio State U., 1977. V.p. Durborow & Assoc., Columbus, Ohio, 1976-79, Watt, Roop and Co., Cleve., 1981-87; exec. v.p. Kleiman Assoc., Inc., Cleve., 1987—. Bd. trustees Templum, Cleve., 1991—. Mem. Pub. Rels. Soc. Am. (cert., Cleve. pres. 1991), Syracuse U. Alumni Club Cleve. (v.p. 1993-94), Playwriters Club Cleve. Office: Kleiman Assocs Inc 21975 Westchester Rd Cleveland OH 44122-2962

KLEIN, CHARLES HENLE, lithographing company executive; b. Cin., Oct. 5, 1908; s. Benjamin Franklin and Flora (Henle) K.; student Purdue U., 1926-27, U. Cin., 1927-28; m. Ruth Becker, Sept. 23, 1938; children—Betsy (Mrs. Marvin H. Schwartz), Charles H., Carla (Mrs. George Fee III). Pres., Progress Lithographing Co., Cin., 1934-59, Novelart Mfg. Co., Cin., 1960—; dir. R.A. Taylor Corp. Founding mem. Chief Execs. Orgn., Losantiville Country Club, Queen City Club, Bankers Club. Home: Amberley Village 6754 Fair Oaks Dr Cincinnati OH 45237-3606 Office: Amberley Village 2121 Section Rd Cincinnati OH 45237-3509

KLEIN, FRANK, mechanical engineer; b. Cin., Apr. 2, 1961. BSME, Ohio U., 1986. Mech. engr. Ellis Wayereil, Troy, Mich., 1986, Stanley Widmar, Cin., 1987-90, Litton Industries, Hebron, Ky., 1990, Rykarrt, Hamilton, Ohio, 1991—.

KLEIN, FRED A., stockbroker; b. N.Y.C., Oct. 31, 1943. BA, CCNY, N.Y.C., 1965; MA, U. N.C., 1968; PhD, U. Wis., Milw., 1975. Mayor's aid City of Milw., 1975-81; stockbroker Smith Barney Inc., Milw., 1981—. Office: Smith Barney Inc 411 E Wisconsin Ave PO Box 2065 Milwaukee WI 53201

KLEIN, GABRIELLA SONJA, communications executive; b. Chgo., Apr. 11, 1938; d. Frank E. Vosicky and Sonja (Kosner) Becvar; m. Donald J. Klein. BA in Comm. and Bus. Mgmt., Alverno Coll., 1983. Editor, owner Fox Lake (Wis.) Rep., 1962-65, McFarland (Wis.) Community Life and Monona Community Herald, 1966-69; bur. reporter Waukesha (Wis.) Daily Freeman, 1969-71; community rels. staff Waukesha County Tech. Coll., Pewaukee, Wis., 1971-73; pub. rels. specialist JI Case Co., Racine, Wis., 1973-75, corp. publs. editor, 1975-80; v.p., bd. dirs. publs. Image Mgmt., Valley View Ctr., Milw., 1980-82; pres. Communication Concepts, Unltd., Racine, 1983—; mem. cmty. com. Racine Unified Sch. Bd. Past pres. Big Bros./Big Sisters Racine County; v.p. devel. Girl Scouts Racine County; bd. dirs. Racine Cmty. Found.; mem. steering com. Racine Cmty. Coalition for Youth; strategic issues co-chair Racine Area Mfrs. and Commerce Edn. Com. Recipient awards Wis. Press Assn., Nat. Fedn. Press Women; named Wis. Woman Entrepreneur of Yr., 1985, Vol. of the Yr. Racine Area United Way, 1995, Woman of Distinction Bus. Racine YWCA, 1995. Mem. Internat. Assn. Bus. Communicators (accredited mem.; bd. dirs. 1982-85, various awards), Ad Club of Racine. Home: 3045 Chatham St Racine WI 53402-4001 Office: 927 S Main St Racine WI 53403-1524

KLEIN, JOSEPH VINCENT, computer systems analyst; b. St. Louis, Aug. 13, 1940; s. Vincent Joseph and Dorothy Lillian (Bersett) K.; m. Susan Katherine Murphy, June 27, 1981; 1 child, Vincent John. BS in Sociology and Bus. Adminstrn., St. Louis U., 1963; MBA, Webster U., 1976. Computer programmer/analyst Sigma Chem. Co., St. Louis, 1963-70; computer programmer/analyst USAAMC SIMA, St. Louis, 1970-90, sr. computer systems analyst, 1991—. Pres. Oakville Jr. H.S. PTO, 1994-95; pres. People with Disabilities, St. Louis, 1988-91. Mem. K.C., Elks. Democrat. Roman Catholic. Home: 3043 Blue Mountain Dr Saint Louis MO 63129-5254 Office: USA AMC SIMA 1222 Spruce St Saint Louis MO 63103-2534

KLEIN, MARJORIE HANSON, psychiatry educator; b. Milw., Sept. 13, 1933; d. Norman Richard and Anna (Emery) Hanson; m. William A. Klein, June 26, 1956 (div. 1968); children: Jennifer K. Thompson, Susan E. Burns; m. Norman S. Greenfield, May 17, 1969; 1 stepchild, Ellen G. Simmons. BA in Psychology, Wellesley Coll., 1955, MA in Psychology, 1957; PhD in Psychology, Harvard U., 1964. Lic. psychologist, Wis. Lab. asst. Wellesley (Mass.) Coll., 1955-57; rsch. asst. sect. on personality NIMH, Bethesda, Md., 1957-59; project asst. psychotherapy rsch. group Wis. Psychiat. Rsch. Inst., U. Wis., Madison, 1962-64, postdoctoral rsch. fellow, 1964-65, rsch. assoc., 1965-66, 67-72; postdoctoral rsch. fellow NIMH, Bethesda, 1966-67; asst. prof. psychiatry U. Wis., Madison, 1972-75, assoc. prof. psychiatry, assoc. prof. women's studies prog., 1975-80, prof. psychiatry, prof. women's studies program, 1980—; mem. spl. rev. com. Psychotherapy of Depression Collaborative Program, NIMH, 1979-80, 83, mem. treatment devel. and assessment rsch. rev. com., 1979-81, 84-86, chmn., 1986-88, mem. Panel of Res. Reviewers, 1988—, mem. treatment devel. and assessment rsch. rev. com., clin. rsch. ctrs. subcom., 1989-96, chair, 1990-96, mem. sci. adv. bd. depression awareness, recognition and treatment, 1989—, mem. psychosocial rsch. adv. com., 1991; mem. spl. rev. com. Nat. Inst. Alcohol Abuse and Alcoholism, 1989. Editor: (with others) Personality and Depression: A Current View, 1992, Research in Mental Health Computer Applications: Directions for the Future, 1987; author: (with others) Research in Mental Health Computing: The Next Five Years, Computers in Human Services, 1987; contbr. articles to profl. jours.; editorial bd. Psychiatry, 1978—, Jour. Marital and Family Therapy, 1978-90, Clin. Psychology Rev., 1978-93, Computers in Human Behavior, 1984-94, Jour. Psychotherapy Practice and Rsch., 1989—, Current Opinion in Psychiatry, 1995—, Jour. Personality Disorders, 1992—. Grantee Nat. Libr. Medicine, 1980-85, NIMH, 1980—. MacArthur Found., 1991—, Upjohn Pharms., 1990-91, Nat. Inst. Aging, 1985-86, 91—, others. Mem. APA (editorial bd. div. 29 1976-79), Soc. Psychotherapy Rsch., Phi Beta Kappa, Sigma Xi. Office: U Wis 6001 Research Pk Blvd Madison WI 53719

KLEIN, MATTHEW M., state legislator; m. Isabell; 6 children. Student, Ellendale Coll., Amarillo Jr. Coll., U. So. Calif., UCLA; BS, N.D. State U. Mem. N.D. Ho. of Reps., 1993—, mem. judiciary com., mem. govt. and vet. affairs com.; cons. in English. Recipient Worldwide Constrn. Mgr. of Yr. award. Mem. Am. Legion. *

KLEIN, RICHARD TEMPLE, JR., hand tool manufacturing executive; b. Evanston, Ill., May 17, 1956; s. Richard Temple and Donna Grace (Hoyt) K.; m. Risa L., June 18, 1978; children: Richard Temple III, Jason Lewit, Jonathan Hoyt. BBA, U. Miami, Fla., 1978. dir. Mr. Tool Mfg., Roselle, Ill., Klein Tools Inc., Midwest Grinding, Inc., Skokie, Ill. Contbr. articles to profl. jours. Active Civil Air Patrol. Mem. Soc. Mfg. Engrs. Office: Klein Tools Inc 7200 N Mccormick Blvd Chicago IL 60645-2713

KLEIN, ROBERT EDWARD, publishing company executive; b. Cin., Dec. 27, 1926; s. Albert and Elisabeth (Muschnau) K.; m. Nancy Minter, May 28, 1958; children: Robert Schuyler, Elisabeth Susan. AB, Kenyon Coll., 1950; MBA, Cornell U., 1952; AM, U. Chgo., 1969, PhD, 1983. CEO Market Power, Inc., Chgo., 1966-69; dist. mgr. McGraw Hill Co., Chgo., 1969-88; v.p. sales Plastics Today, 1988-90; pres. Klein Assocs., 1990—; dist. mgr. Injection Molding Mag., 1993—; cons. U.S. Dept. Justice, 1967-71, Time/Life Books, 1980, Time Life History of WWII; lectr. in Soviet history Barat Coll., 1970-72; assoc. dept. history Northwestern U., Evanston, Ill., 1986—; lectr. European, German and bus. history Loyola U., Chgo., 1988—. Author: J.F.C. Fuller and The Tank, 1983. With U.S. Army, 1944-46. Grolier scholar, 1952. Mem. VFW, Am. Legion, Beta Theta Pi. Episcopalian. Lodge: Masons. Avocations: teaching, lecturing. Home: 1030 Greenleaf Ave Wilmette IL 60091-2707

KLEIN, ROBERT EMIL, electrical engineer; b. St. Marys, Ohio, May 1, 1955; s. Johann and Mary F. (Brueggeman) K.; m. Brenda K. Yeater Huff, Feb. 14, 1991; 1 child, Megan L.; 1 child from previous marriage, Benjamin R.; stepchildren: D. Joseph, Kevin R. ASEE, Elec. Tech. Inst., 1975. Elec. designer Stamco div. Monarch Machine, New Bremen, Ohio, 1975-76; elec. designer Crown Controls Corp., New Bremen, 1976-82, elec. project engr., 1982-85; elec. systems engr. Minster (Ohio) Machine Co., 1985-86, systems project mgr., 1986-89, sr. elec. designer, 1989—. Pres. Jaycees, New Bremen, 1981, Bremenfest, Inc., New Bremen, 1982-83, Village Coun., New Bremen, 1986-96; village mayor, New Bremen, 1996—. Home: 225 E Front St PO Box 92 New Bremen OH 45869-0092 Office: Minster Machine Co 240 W 5th St Minster OH 45865-0120

KLEIN, WOLFGANG, art educator; b. Berlin, Germany, Nov. 17, 1906; came to U.S., 1954; s. Jean Jaques and Sara Rose (Weissman) K.; m. Henriette Kutscha, Sept. 30, 1932; children: Peter, Evelyn, Gerd, Frank. Student, Ernst Lidwig Kirchner, Davos, Switzerland, 1920-22, State Art Sch., Frankfurt, Germany, 1924-26, City Art Sch., Darmstadt, Germany, 1926-29. Instr. Hochschule fur bildende Vunste, Berlin, 1945-49, Y.W.C.A., Milw., 1961-65, Alverno Coll., Milw., 1970-73, Marquette U., Milw., 1964-83; ret., 1983. One man shows include Charles Allis Art Libr., Alverno Coll., Milw., Kenosha (Wis.) Pub. Mus., and others; author: Basics in the Visual Arts, 1980, Perspective Projection from Observation, 1993. Home: 7004 W Kinnickinic Riv Pkwy Milwaukee WI 53219

KLEINBAUER, W. EUGENE, art history educator; b. L.A., June 15, 1937; s. Walter Eugene and Bernice (Barnett) K.; children: Christopher, Mark. BA, U. Calif., Berkeley, 1959, MA, 1962; MFA, Princeton U., 1964, PhD, 1967. Asst. prof. UCLA, L.A., 1965-72; chair dept. fine arts Ind. U., Bloomington, 1973-76, prof., 1977—, assoc. dir. Sch. Fine Arts, 1988-92, chair dept. art history, 1992-95; Morgan vis. prof. U. Louisville, 1996; Zacks vis. prof. Hebrew U., Jerusalem, 1978; pres. Internat. Ctr. Medieval Art, N.Y.C., 1987-90. Author, editor: Modern Perspectives in Western Art History, 1971, reprinted, 1989; editor: Art Byzantium and Medieval West, 1976, Gesta, 1980-83; co-author: Research Guide to Art History in America, 1983; author: Early Christian Byzantine Architecture, 1992. Recipient Ind. fellowship Nat. Endowment Humanities, Greece, 1976-77. Home: 412 S High St Bloomington IN 47401-5326 Office: Ind Univ Dept Art History Bloomington IN 47405

KLEINE, DAVID MATTHEW, investment advisor; b. Madison, Wis., Oct. 7, 1954; s. Richard A. and Barbara E. (Olson) K. BS, U. Calif., Santa Barbara, 1978. Sales mgr., product mktg. mgr. UNR-ROHN, Peoria, Ill., 1978-84; fin. cons. Merrill Lynch, Edina, Minn., 1985-93; investment advisor Dain Bosworth Inc., Edina, 1993-95; pres. NRG/Network Resource Group, 1996—. Vol. various civic orgns. Republican. Lutheran. Home: 4124 Abbott Ave S Minneapolis MN 55410

KLEINMAN, BURTON HOWARD, real estate investor; b. Chgo., Nov. 19, 1923; s. Eli I. and Pearl (Cohan) K.; m. Shirley A. Freyer, Sept. 6, 1950 (div. Oct. 1969); children: Kim, Lauri. BS in Engring., U.S. Naval Acad., 1948. Commd. ensign USN, 1948, resigned, 1949; v.p. C.F. Corp., Chgo., 1958-80, pres., 1980-85; owner B.H. Kleinman Co., Northfield, Ill., 1955—; ptnr. Middlefork Enterprises, Northfield, 1968—. Bd. dirs. United Way Northfield, 1970-72, North Shore Mental Health Assn., 1978-82. Mem. Northfield C. of C. (bd. dirs. 1976-81), Kenosha Pilots Assn. Republican. Unitarian. Clubs: Deerfield Singles (pres. 1974-75), Winnetka Tennis Assn., Ridge & Valley Tennis. Home: 570 Happ Rd Northfield IL 60093-1112 Office: BH Kleinman Co 456 W Frontage Rd Northfield IL 60093-3038

KLEINMAN, SUSAN PHYLLIS, travel writer, photographer, insurance salesperson; b. N.Y.C., Aug. 30, 1947; d. Sol and Hermina (Marder) K. BS, SUNY, Cortland, 1968; MS, U. Ill., Champaign-Urbana, 1973; PhD, U. Ill., 1978. CLU, chartered fin. cons., registered health underwriter. Tchr. phys. edn. John H. Glenn High Sch., Elwood, N.Y., 1968-71; substitute tchr. Chgo. Pub. Schs., 1973-74; instr. Oakton Community Coll., Morton Grove, Ill., 1974-77, U. Ill. Circle Campus, Chgo., 1974-76; vis. instr. U. Ill., Champaign-Urbana, 1977-78; asst. prof. health edn. U. Ill. Med. Ctr., Sch. Pub. Health, Chgo., 1978-81; sales rep. Paul Revere Cos., Arlington Heights, Ill., 1981-86; underwriter Sun Fin. Group, Rosemont, Ill., 1986-91; prin. Banks & Kleinman Enterprises, Around and About, Evanston, 1991—; head start cons. Kirschner Assocs., Chgo., 1975-77, Roy Littlejohn Assocs., Chgo., 1976-77; cons. health edn. Native Am. Edn. Service, Chgo., 1976-77. Contbr. articles to profl. jours. Chmn. Chgo.-City com. U.S. Com. for UNICER, 1996—. Mem. Nat. Assn. Life Underwriters (cert.), Nat. Assn. Health Underwriters (registered), Chgo. Assn. Life Underwriters, Eta Sigma Gamma. Jewish. Home: 736 Ridge Ave Evanston IL 60202-2683 Office: Images PO Box 6077 Evanston IL 60204-6077 also: Around & About Travel Image 736 Ridge Evanston IL 60202

KLEINSCHMIDT, RANDY FRED, investment broker; b. Mt. Carmel, Ill., Mar. 21, 1952; s. Adolf F. and Mary Jane (Gray) K.; m. Deborah A. Marlow, Sept. 23, 1972; children: Aaron, Andrew,. Assoc. Acctg., Lockyear Bus. Coll., Evansville, Ind., 1973. Agt. Prudential Ins. Co., Grayville, Ill., 1974-81; owner Grayville Ins., 1981-86; investment broker JJB Hilliard & W.L. Lyons, Carmi, Ill., 1987—. Mem. Grayville Athletic Assn., Grayville Cmty. Arts Assn., Carmi Kiwanis (sec. 1990—), Sheba Masons (lodge #200 sec. 1982), Moose. Office: JJB Hilliard WL Lyons Inc 1015 W Main St PO Box 487 Carmi IL 62821

KLEIS, DAVID, state legislator. Senator Dist. 16 State of Minn., St. Paul, 1995—. Office: Minnesota State Senate 151 State Office Bldg Saint Paul MN 55155-1298

KLEM, LYNNE ELLEN, developmental disabilities consultant, educator; b. South Bend, Ind., Dec. 1, 1957; d. Darwin Dale and Annie Olline (Michel) Listenberger; m. William Bruce Klem, Dec. 17, 1983 (div.); children: Matthew William, Alea Rose, Mikala Sage. BS in Edn., Ind. U., South Bend, 1976-81, MS, 1984. Cert. tchr. mentally retarded, physically handicapped, emotionally disturbed, behavior disordered, Ind. Spl. edn. tchr. Elkhart (Ind.) Joint Schs., 1981-84, Lewis Cass Intermediate Sch. Dist., Cassopolis, Mich., 1984-87; program dir. Corvilla, Inc., South Bend, 1987-89; ind. cons. Loka/Integrated Cons. Svcs., Granger, Ind., 1989—; mem. human rights com. Corvilla, Inc., 1989-95, Holy Cross Living Ctr., Mishawaka, Ind., 1990-95; presenter in field. Author, pub. Loka-Comprehensive Functional Assessment, 1994. Mem. Am. Assn. Mental Retardation, Nat. Assn. for Dual Diagnosis. Office: Loka PO Box 501 Granger IN 46530

KLEMM, RICHARD O., state legislator; b. Chgo., May 5; s. Oren E. and Edythe (Neilsen) K.; m. Nancy Klemm; 7 children. BS, Purdue U., 1954. Pres., mem. Crystal Lake Dist. 46 Bd. Edn., 1964-71; trustee Nunda Twp., 1964-72; chmn., mem. McHenry County Bd., 1972-80; Ill. state rep. Dist. 63, 1981-92, Ill. state sen., 1993—; vice-spokesman Exec. Com.; mem. Labor and Commerce Com.; former minority spokesman, mem. Constnl. Officers Com., Vets. Affairs Com.; former mem. Environ. and Energy Com. Ill. Ho. of Reps.; pres., bd. chmn. Food Warming Equipment Co., Inc., Crystal Lake, 1972—. Recipient numerous comty. svc. awards. Mem. Sigma Nu. Office: 3 W Crystal Lake Ave Crystal Lake IL 60014

KLEPPER, ROBERT RUSH, plant physiologist; b. Sculthorpe AFB, Norfolk, Wales, Nov. 8, 1957; came to U.S., 1958; s. Norman Eugene and Rosalind Violet (Rush) K.; m. Laurene Kay Wycoff, June 25, 1991; children: April Kaylynn, Candace Rose. AS, Iowa Lakes C.C., Estherville, Iowa, 1987; BS, Buena Vista Coll., Storm Lake, Iowa, 1990; MS, Iowa State U., 1992; PhD, Columbia Pacific U., San Rafael, Calif., 1994. Mgr. Milford (Iowa) Nursery, 1985-89; rsch. assoc. Iowa State U., Ames, 1989-90; adj. prof. Iowa Ctrl. C.C., Storm Lake, 1992—; dir. R&D TransAgra Internat., Storm Lake, 1990—; ind. cons., Linn Grove, Iowa, 1991—; sci. advisor Mus. Sci., Boston, 1994—; sci. day advisor Buena Vista Coll., Storm Lake, 1990—; adj. prof. Iowa Lakes C.C., Spencer, 1994—. Mem. Plant Growth Regulator Soc. Am., Am. Soc. Plant Physiologists, Coun. Agrl. Sci. and Tech., Am. Soc. Agronomy. Home: 4476 100th Ave Linn Grove IA 51033 Office: TransAgra Internat Inc 101 Hansen Rd Storm Lake IA 50588

KLESCHICK, WILLIAM ANTHONY, III, research chemist; b. New Bern, N.C., Jan. 12, 1950; s. William Anthony Jr. and Margaret Delores (Carey) K.; m. Leslie Anne Bjelk, Nov. 24, 1990; children: Andrew William, Daniel Joseph. BS in Chemistry, N.C. State U., 1972; PhD in Organic Chemistry, U. Calif., Berkeley, 1977. Postdoctoral fellow dept. chemistry Ga. Inst. Tech., Atlanta, 1977-78; rsch. fellow Calif. Inst. Tech., Pasadena, 1978-79; from sr. rsch. chemist to assoc. scientist Dow Chem. U.S.A., Walnut Creek, Calif., 1979-90; advisor to sr. advisor DowElanco, Indpls., 1990—; guest lectr. in indsl. chemistry U. Calif., L.A., 1982, Davis, 1989. Contbr. articles to Jour. of Heterocyclic Chemisty, Jour. Organic Chemistry. Mem. AAAS, Am. Chem. Soc., Internat. Soc. Heterocyclic Chemistry. Office: DowElanco PO Box 68955 Indianapolis IN 46268-0955

KLETZIEN, WILLIAM MARTIN, investment company executive; b. Neeneh, Wis., Apr. 25, 1952; s. William O. and Barbara (Below) K.; m. Sally Mortonson, May 24, 1975; children: Billy, Heidi. BS, U. Wis., 1975. With Harken VanGuard Marine, Milw., 1980-83; asst. mgr. Robert W. Baird & Co., Manitowoc, Wis., 1983—. Pres. Manitowoc County Inc. Ctr., 1993—. Mem. U. Wis. Alumni Club (dir. 1984—, Spark Plug award 1991), Rotary. Republican. Presbyterian. Office: Robert W Baird & Co Inc 980 Maritime Dr PO Box 40 Manitowoc WI 54221

KLEVEN, JEFFREY A., research and development manager; b. Allen Park, Mich., July 1, 1957. BS, Western Mich. U., 1980; MS, Ind. U., South Bend, 1988. Plant metal engr. Ex-Cell-O Corp., Topeka, Ind., 1980-86; metal and R&D engr. Micromatic Textron, Holland, Mich., 1986-93; R&D mgr. Indsl. Metal Products, Lansing, Mich., 1993—. Mem. Soc. Mfg. Engrs. Office: Indsl Metal Products 3417 W Saint Joseph St Lansing MI 48917-3707

KLEVEN, MARGUERITE, state senator. Mem. S.D. Senate, Pierre, 1995—, mem. appropriations and retirements laws coms. Republican.

KLINE, BRUCE EDWARD, clinical psychologist; b. Woodstock, Ill., Aug. 23, 1944; s. Bruce Leffingwell and Kneldrith Eileen (Harden) K.; m. Linda Sue Wallis, Aug. 20, 1964 (div. Aug. 1969); Leora Kathleen Martin, Dec. 27, 1970; children: April A., Jonathan D. AA, Cen. Coll., McPherson, Kans., 1964; BS, Greenville (Ill.) Coll., 1968; MS, Wichita (Kans.) State U., 1977; D in Psychology, Wright State U., 1982. Diplomate Am. Bd. Med. Psychotherapists. Licensed St. Bd. Psychology, 1983, Diplomate Am. Assn. Pain Mngmt. Intern Green Meml. Hosp., Green Hall, Ohio, 1980, Clark County (Ohio) Community Mental Health Ctr., 1981-82; resident in psychology Sch. Profl. Psychology Consortium, Wright State U., 1983; high sch. tchr. Unified Dist. 418, McPherson, Kans., 1968-75; prof. Sterling Coll., Kans., 1976-80; clin. dir. Mingenback Family Life Ctr., McPherson, 1977-80; dir. psychology Millcreek Psychiat. Hosp., Cin., 1983-86; pvt. practice Kline and Assocs., Dayton, Ohio, 1983—; dir. Ctr. Exceptional Children and Adults, Dayton, 1985—; owner, chmn. bd. Access Svcs. Inc., Wichita, Kans., 1979—; research assoc. Menninger Found. Hosp., Topeka, 1977-83. Co-author: Awareness and Change, 1981; exec. and prodn. producer of TeenTalk (prime time TV show), 1993-94; contbg. editor: The Roeper Rev., 1987-90; contbr. articles to profl. jours. Mem. Am. Psychol. Assn., Am. Assn. Pain Mgmt. (cert.), Ohio Psychol. Assn., World Coun. Gifted Children, Nat. Assn. Gifted Children, Ohio Assn. Gifted Children, Nat. Register of Health Care Providers, Prescribing Psychologists Register (charter). Methodist. Home: 4601 Carlyle Cir Dayton OH 45429-1803 Office: 529 E Stroop Rd Dayton OH 45429-3224

KLINE, FAITH ELIZABETH, college administrator; b. Lake Charles, La., Dec. 22, 1937; d. Walter Raymond and Erma Ruth (Gilbert) McClung; m. George Ellis Kline, Nov. 26, 1959; children: Alexandra M., George E. IV, Elizabeth A. BA, So. Nazarene U., 1960. Owner, ptnr. Country Peddler Gift Shop, Jackson, Mich., 1972-75; asst. dir. admissions Spring Arbor (Mich.) Coll., 1976-80; exec. sec. to pres. Camp Internat., Inc., Jackson, Mich., 1980-85; registered rep. IDS/Am. Express, Jackson, 1985-86; investment broker A. G. Edwards & Sons, Inc., Jackson, 1986-89; dir., trust and investment svcs., corp. asst. sec. The Free Meth. Found., Spring Arbor, 1989-92; adminstr. trusts and investments Hillsdale (Mich.) Coll., 1992—; mem. Jackson County (Mich.) Hosp. Fin. Authority, 1987-92; pres. Hearthstone Enterprises, Inc., 1996—. Author: The Klines of Evanston: 1848 to 1968, 1970. Trustee Concord (Mich.) Bd. Edn., 1979-95, v.p., 1991-93, pres., 1993-94; sec. Jackson County (Mich.) County Reps., 1984-85, mem. exec. com., 1993—; mem. Spring Arbor Twp. Hist. Com., Jackson Area Estate Planning Coun. Mem. LWV, Rotary Internat. Methodist. Home: 9023 Hammond Rd Concord MI 49237-9781 Office: Hillsdale Coll 33 E College St Hillsdale MI 49242-1205

KLINE, KENNETH ALAN, mechanical engineering educator; b. Chgo., July 11, 1939; s. George Lester and Beverly Gretchen (Hanson) K.; m. Nancy Ann Bixler, June 25, 1960; children: Lisa Suzanne, John Kenneth, Jeffery Eastbury, Gretchen Mary. BS, U. Minn., 1961, PhD, 1965. Rsch. asst. U. Minn., Mpls., 1961-62, rsch. fellow, 1962-65; sr. rsch. engr. Esso Prodn. Rsch. Co., Houston, 1965-66; assoc. prof. Wayne State U., Detroit, 1966-73, prof. mech. engring., 1973—, interim chair dept. mech. engring., 1986-87, chair, 1987-95, interim dean of engring., 1996—; cons. Ford Motor Co., Detroit, 1976—, vis. scientist, 1984-85; vis. prof. U. Munich, 1972-73. Editor Proc. 6th Internat. Conf. Vehicle Structures, 1986; contbr. articles to profl. jours. Patentee ops. in submarine wells, layng pipes in water. Rep. precinct del., Grosse Pointe Park, Mich., 1982-84; vol. Grosee Pointe Neighborhood Club, 1973-82. A.P. Sloan Found. nat. scholar, 1959-61; NSF fellow 1961-64, NASA fellow 1964-65; recipient Sr. U.S. Sci. award Alexander von Humboldt-Stiftung, Fed. Republic Germany, 1972; prin. investigator NSF Rsch. Experiences for Undergrad. Sites, 1995—. Fellow ASME (chair 1974-75, 89-91, program chair winter ann. meeting 1993, gen. chair internat. mech. engring. congress & expo. 1994), AIAA, Soc. Automotive Engrs. (chair 1984-86, Forest R. McFarland award 1993), Soc. Rheology, Engring. Soc. (vice chair Detroit 1988—). Office: Wayne State U Engring Rm 2105 Detroit MI 48202

KLINE, MABLE CORNELIA PAGE, retired secondary school educator; b. Memphis, Aug. 20, 1928; d. George M. and Lillie (Davidson) Brown; 1 dau., Gail Angela Page. Student LeMoyne Coll.; BSEd, Wayne State U., 1948, postgrad. Tchr., Flint, Mich., 1950-51, Pontiac, Mich., 1953-62; tchr. 12th grade English, Cass Tech H.S., Detroit, 1962-95, coord. Study Skills Program; ret., 1995; mem. English Book Selection com., 1986—. Life mem. YWCA, NAACP. Detroit Pub. Edn. Fund grantee, 1989. Mem. NEA (life), ASCD, Am. Fedn. Tchrs., Nat. Council Tchrs. English, Wayne State U. Alumni Assn., Delta Sigma Theta. Episcopalian. Home: 555 Brush St Apt 1512 Detroit MI 48226-4332 Office: Cass Tech High Sch English Dept 2421 2nd Ave Detroit MI 48201-2601

KLINE, PAUL EDWARD, financial consultant; b. Chgo., June 7, 1933; s. Dominic Alexander and Anna (Retlee) K.; m. Susan Reevers, Nov. 23, 1979; 5 children. BA in Math., Lawrence U., Appleton, Ill, 1955; MBA, U. Chgo., 1982. Data processor CNA Ins., Chgo., 1962-73; owner Paul Kline Real Estate, Flossmore, Ill., 1973-81, Homewood, Ill., 1973-81; fin. cons. Merrill Lynch, Merrillville, Ind., 1981—. 1st lt. USAF, 1956-58. Republican. Home: 6 Clark Dr La Porte IN 46350-1925 Office: Merrill Lynch 8585 Broadway # 590 Merrillville IN 46410-7064

KLINE, PHILLIP D., state legislator, lawyer; b. Kansas City, Kans., Dec. 31, 1959; s. James R. and Janet S. (Shirley) K.; m. Deborah Suzanne Shattuck, July 22, 1989; 1 child, Jacqueline Hillary. BS in Pub. Rels. and Polit. Sci., Cen. Mo. State U., 1982; JD, U. Kans., 1987. Bar: Kans. 1987, U.S. Ct. Appeals (10th cir.), U.S. Dist. Ct. Kans. News reporter WHB Radio, Kansas City, Mo., 1981-82; pub. rels. rep. Mid-America, Inc., Kansas City, Mo., 1982-84; assoc. Blackwell, Sanders, Matheny, Weary & Lombardi, Overland Park, Kans., 1987—. Nominee Kans. 2d Congl. Dist., 1986; mem. Kans. State Ho. of Reps. from 18th Dist., 1993—; chmn. taxation com., 1995—; fin. chmn. Johnson County Reps., 1990-91; chmn. Shawnee Reps., 1991-92; chmn., co-chmn. Corp. Woods Charity Jazz Festival, Overland Park, 1991-95; bd. dirs. Shawnee Mission Edn. Found., 1994-95, Rep. Ho. Campaign Com. Mem. Johnson County Bar Assn., Kans. Bar Assn., Rotary (bd. dirs., v.p. 1991-93, pres. 1994-95, Disting. Svc. award 1991). Methodist. Home: 10624 W 61st St Shawnee KS 66203-3016 Office: Blackwell Sanders Matheny Weary & Lombardi 9401 Indian Creek Pky Ste 1200 Overland Park KS 66210-2007*

KLINE, VICKI ANN, investment consultant; b. Monterey, Tenn., Oct. 26, 1948; d. William John and Betty (Coleman) Harden; children: David, John, Lori, Lisa, Daniel. BS in Acctg., Nova U., 1983; MBA, Kent State U., 1994. CPA, Ohio. Internal auditor Roadway Svc., Akron, Ohio, 1984-85; acctg. mgr. A. Schulman Inc., Fairlawn, Ohio, 1985-93; investment cons. Butler Wick & Co., Inc., Kent, Ohio, 1993—. Mem. AICPA, Ohio Soc. CPAs, Inst. Mgmt. Accts., Women's Network. Home: 1282 Congress Lake Rd Mogadore OH 44260-9690 Office: Butler Wick & Co Inc 149 N Water St Kent OH 44240-2418

KLINETOB, CARSON WAYNE, physical therapist; b. Berwick, Pa., Feb. 8, 1922; s. Dalbys Bryan and Margaret Jeannette (Hampton) K.; m. Edna Mae Ginader; children: Sandra Lynne, Diane Beth. BS, East Stroudsburg U., 1946; cert. phys. therapy, U. Pa., 1948; postgrad., NYU, Kingston, Pa., 1949. Lic. phys. therapist Pa., Ill., Wis., Ala. Staff phys. therapis VA Hosp., Wilkes-Barre, Pa., 1948, chief phys. therapist, 1949; chief phys. therapist Downey (Ill.) VA Hosp., 1953; owner Phys. Rehab. Ctr., Waukegan, Ill., 1955-60; co-owner, bd. dirs. Tri W-G Inc., Valley City, N.D., 1968-86; phys. therapist Wausau (Wis.) Med. Ctr., 1969—. Contbr. articles to profl. jours. With U.S. Army, 1943-45, ETO. Mem. Am. Phys. Therapy Assn., Wis. Phys. Therapy Assn., Am. Legion, DAV (life), Masons, Shriners, Acacia.

KLING, JOHN ROBERT, mechanical engineer; b. Winfield, Kans., Nov. 8, 1946; s. Harold Henry and Almira Anne (Miller) K.; m. Jean Marcel Haines, Jan. 2, 1971; children: Jason Harold, Jeffrey Adam. BSME, Kans. State U., 1969; MBA, Rockhurst Coll., 1982. Lic. profl. engr., Kans. Engr. The Boeing Co., Renton, Wash., 1969-70, Black & Veatch, Kansas City, Mo., 1970-71; engr., project engr. Black & Veatch, Overland Park, Kans., 1976—. Asst. scoutmaster troop 683 Boy Scouts Am. With USN, 1971-76, USNR, 76—. Mem. ISA (pres. Kansas City chpt. 1992-93), Toastmaster Club (pres. 1994). Republican. Methodist. Office: Black & Veatch 11401 Lamar Overland Park KS 66211

KLING, SUSAN SCHAEFER, librarian; b. Lincoln, Nebr., May 25, 1948; d. Victor Frederick and Rosa Florence (Klein) Shaefer; m. William Albert Kling, May 29, 1970; children: Kenneth William, Thomas Schaefer. BS in Elem. Edn., U. Nebr., 1970; MLS, Emporia State U., 1977. Interlibrary loans libr. Nebr. Libr. Commn., Lincoln, 1970-72, abstractor, indexer Nebr. state publ. checklist, 1973-74, supr. N.E. publs. clearinghouse, 1974-78, divsn. chief reference/interloan divsn., 1978-84, dir. libr. operation, 1984-86; dir. Marion (Iowa) Pub. Libr., 1987—. Pres. Nebr. Libr. Assn., 1985-86. Recipient Exemplary Mem. award Cornhusker chpg. Nat. Micrographics Assn., 1981. Mem. ALA (mem. GODORT election com. 1975-76), Iowa Libr. Assn. (exec. bd. 1992-94, conf. exhibits coord. 1989—), Mountain Plains Libr. Assn. (state libr. sect. 1974-85, chair 1974-75, chair JMRT 1976-77), Beta Phi Mu. Office: Marion Pub Libr 1095 6th Ave Marion IA 52302

KLING, WILLIAM HUGH, broadcasting executive; b. St. Paul, Apr. 29, 1942; s. William Conrad and Helen A. (Leonard) K.; m. Sarah Margaret Baldwin, Sept. 25, 1976. B.A. in Economics, St. John's U., 1964; postgrad., Boston U., 1964-66. Pres. Minn. Pub. Radio, Inc., St. Paul, 1966—, Greenspring Co., 1986—; founding dir. Nat. Pub. Radio, 1968-70, dir., 1977-80; founding pres. Public Radio Internat., 1982-86; vice chmn. Pub. Radio Internat., 1986-93; bd. dirs. St. Paul Cos., Wenger Corp., Irwin Fin., Inland Mortgage Co., Continental Cablevision St. Paul, Capital Group Cos.; mem. adv. bd. Investment Co. Am., 1984—; trustee New Economy Fund, 1987—, New Perspective Fund, 1987—, Euro Pacific Growth Fund, 1987—, Small Cap World Fund, 1990—. Bd. dirs. Minn. Orch., 1987-93; trustee J.L. Found., 1988—; bd. dirs., chmn. Fitzgerald Theater Corp., 1983—; mem. The James Madison Coun. of Libr. of Congress, 1992-94. Recipient Edward R. Murrow award, 1981, award for Excellence Business Mag., 1987; named Twin Citian of Yr., Twin Citian mag., 1987, Disting. Minnesotan, 1995. Mem. Mpls. Club, Minn. Club. Office: Minn Pub Radio Inc 45 7th St E Saint Paul MN 55101-2202

KLINGEL, PATTI JEAN, health facility administrator; b. Marion, Ohio, Dec. 28, 1955; d. Elmer N. and Reba J. (Freeman) Noe; m. Jeffrey J. Klingel, Aug. 16, 1974; children: Shane, Seth, Bethann. Lic. practical nurse, Marion Gen. Hosp. Sch. Nursing, 1975; student, Ohio State U., 1984-85; AD in Bus. Adminstrn. magna cum laude, Marion Tech. Coll., 1993; grad. summa cum laude Sch. Bus., Spring Arbor Coll., 1996. Assembler Whirlpool Corp., Marion, 1974; nurse Marion Gen. Hosp., 1975-79; childbirth educator, 1977-92; nurse Community Med. Ctr., Marion, 1981-83; instr., cons. Tri-Rivers Joint Vocat. Sch., Marion, 1996; office mgr., adminstrv. asst. J.T. Spare M.D., Inc., Marion, 1986-94; quality improvement coord. MedCtr. Hosp., Marion, 1994—; cons. Marion Tech. Coll., 1991. Spokesperson Nurse Hope-Am. Cancer Soc., Marion, 1982; advisor 4-H, Marion, 1986-93; bus. adminstr. United Way, Marion, 1989. Recipient scholarship Ohio State U., Columbus, 1985, Marion (Ohio) Tech. Coll., 1991, Walters scholarship, 1992-93, Wall St. Jour. award. Mem. NAFE, Nat. Assn. for Healthcare Quality, Ohio Assn. Healthcare Quality, Parents Assn. Childbirth Edn. (pres., instr. rep. 1976-92, top instr. 1989), Internat. Childbirth Edn. Assn., Am. Assn. Office Nurses, Lic. Practical Nurses Assn. (sec. 1975-76), Marion County Jr. Fair Bd. (advisor 1987-92). Mem. Assembly of God Church. Home: 3966 Cardington Rd Marion OH 43302 Office: 1050 Delaware Ave Marion OH 43302-6416

KLINGLER, GWENDOLYN WALBOLT, lawyer, alderman; b. Toledo, May 28, 1944; d. L. Byron and Elizabeth (Brown) Walbolt; m. Walter Gerald Klingler, June 11, 1966; children: Kelly Michelle, Lance. BA, Ohio Wesleyan U., 1966; MA, U. Mich., 1969; JD, George Washington U., 1981. Bar: Ill. Rsch. assoc. U. Mich., Ann Arbor, 1966-71; abstractor Year Book Med. Pub., Chgo., 1972-75; law clk. FDA, Rockville, Md., 1980; atty. Atty. Gen.'s Office State of Ill., Springfield, 1981-84, appellate prosecutor, 1984-92; ptnr. Boyle, Klingler & McClain, Springfield, 1992-95. Mem. Springfield Bd. of Edn., 1987-91, pres., 1988; alderman Springfield City Coun., 1991-95; Rep. Ill. Ho. of Reps., 100th Dist., 1995—. Recipient Woman of Achievement award in Govt., Women-in-Mgmt., 1994, Disting. Alumni award Leadership Springfield, 1996. Mem. AAUW, Cen. Ill. Women's Bar Assn. (chair membership com.), Sangamon County Bar Assn., Greater Springfield C. of C., Women-in-Mgmt. Republican. Presbyterian (elder). Home: 1600 Ruth Pl Springfield IL 62704-3362

KLINISKE, AMY N., state legislator. BA, U. N.D. Rep. Dist. 42 N.D. Ho. of Reps., mem. judiciary, govt. and vet. affairs coms. Cmty. vol. Grand Forks Mission, Am. Diabetes Assn., Prairie Harvest Found., Sch. for Blind, Good Samaritan Nursing Home. Mem. Mortar Bd., Kappa Alpha Theta (pres.). Home: PO Box 12982 Grand Forks ND 58208-2982

KLINKER, SHEILA ANN J., middle school educator, state legislator; m. Victor Klinker; children: Kerri, Kevin, Kelly. BS in Edn., Purdue U., MS in Elem. Edn., MS in Adminstrn. and Supervision. Tchr. Tecumseh Mid. Sch., 1982—; state rep. Ind. Ho. of Reps., Indpls., 1982—. Mem. St. Mary's Cathedral Parish; 1st woman appointee Tippecanoe Area Plan Commn.; bd. dirs. Lafayette Symphony, Opera de Lafayette, Tippecanoe County Chid Care, Purdue Musical Orgn.; past chairwoman pub. svc. divsn. United Way. Recipient Outstanding Svc. award Ind. Advocates for Children, Legis. award Assn. of RAAUW's Outstanding Woman in Politics, Woman of Distinction award Sycamore Girl Scout Coun., Salute to Women in Politics award, Outstanding Svc. for Pub. Interest award Ind. Optometric Assn., Pres.'s Spl. Svc. award Ind. Soc. Profl. Land Surveyors, Spl. Recognition award Ind. Chpt. NASW, Legis. Efforts Recognition award Ind. Residential Facilities Assn., Ind. Assn. for Counseling and Devel. Mem. Bus. and Profl. Women's Assn., Lafayette C. of C. (edn. com.), Delta Kappa Gamma, Phi Delta Kappa, Kappa Alpha Theta (mem. adv. bd.). Democrat. Home: 633 Kossuth St Lafayette IN 47905-1444 Office: Ind Ho of Reps State House Third fl Indianapolis IN 46204

KLOC, EMILY ALVINA, retired elementary school principal; b. Chgo., Apr. 8, 1933; d. Francis Joseph and Emily Mary (Gucwa) K. BMus, Mundelein Coll., Chgo., 1954; MEd, Loyola U., Chgo., 1960. Grade 2 tchr. Our Lady Help of Christians, Chgo., 1954-58; grades 5, 6, 7, 8 tchr. St. Mary of the Angels, Chgo., 1958-87, prin., 1987-95; ret., 1995. Mem. Near N.W. Orgn., Chgo., 1988—. Summer grantee U. Ill. NDEA Inst., Chgo., 1968; recipient Excellence in Mgmt. award Office Cath. Edn., Chgo., 1991, Tchr. Achievement award St. Mary of Angels Sch., Big Shoulders Fund, Chgo., 1992. Mem. ASCD, Nat. Cath. Educators Assn., Archdiocesan Prins. Assn. (chmn. coun. III-5A 1991—). Roman Catholic. Home: 1721 N Wood St Chicago IL 60622-1357 Office: St Mary of the Angels 1810 N Hermitage Ave Chicago IL 60622-1101

KLOCK, STEVEN WAYNE, engineering executive; b. Deadwood, S.D., Apr. 16, 1954; s. Earl Leroy and Irma Helena (Neamy) K.; m. Robin Ann Barney, June 25, 1982; children: Tana, Renee, Thomas, Stephanie. Cert., Denver Inst. Tech., 1974; BS, S.D. Sch. Mines and Tech., 1992. Test tech. Magnetic Peripherals Inc., Rapid City, S.D., 1974-76, group leader, 1976-81, test engring. tech., 1981-87; process engring. technician SCI Systems, Rapid City, 1987-92, quotes adminstr., 1992—. Mem. S.D. Emergency Med. Technician Assn. Democrat. Office: SCI Systems 222 Disk Dr Rapid City SD 57701-7805

KLODT, GERALD JOSEPH, office products executive; b. Ottumwa, Iowa, Feb. 6, 1949; s. Edward William and Isabelle Margaret (Herrmann) K.; m. Menzi Louise Behrnd, May 26, 1979. BFA, U. Iowa, 1971, MA, 1972; MFA, U. Ill., 1974, U. Wis., 1979. Designer Tevcin, Inc., Perry, Iowa, 1972-75; assoc. designer William Stumpf & Assocs., Middleton, Wis., 1975-77; prof. design U. Wis., Madison, 1977-84; pres., chief exec. officer Klodt & Assocs., Madison, 1977—; engr. Fel-Pro Energy Inc., Lake Geneva, Wis., 1982-83; v.p. research and devel., product engring., product design, product packaging, product quality W.T. Rogers Co., div. Newell, Madison, 1984-91; pvt. practice Klodt & Assocs., Madison, 1991—; dir. for product and graphic design Nordic Design Ltd. subs. of Nordic Group of Cos. Corp., Baraboo, Wis., 1994—; bd. dirs. Nordic Design Ltd.; cons. engr. Linton Assocs., Chesieres, Switzerland, 1984; project dir., engr. U.S. Dept. Energy, Madison, 1980-83; bd. dirs. Anatec Inc., 1989-91. Author: Earth Sheltered Housing, 1985; mech. and design patentee for office products, creator The Klodt Collection. Bd. dirs. Energy Idea Exchange, Madison, 1978-80; mem. Wis. State Resources Advisory Panel, 1978-80; leader, educator Am. Youth Found., Camp Miniwanca, Mich., 1977. Named Tchr Yr. dept. enging. and applied sci. U. Wis., 1982. Mem. Kappa Sigma. Home: 7422 Long Meadow Rd Madison WI 53717 Office: Klodt & Assocs 7422 Long Meadow Rd Madison WI 53717

KLOEHN, RALPH ANTHONY, plastic surgeon; b. Milw., Dec. 18, 1932; s. Ralph Charles and Virginia Mary (Kosak) K.; m. Mary Theresa Landers, Nov. 4, 1961; Children: Colleen, Gregory, Kristine, Patricia, Timothy, Philip, Michelle. BS, Marquette U., 1954, MD, 1958. Diplomate Am. Bd. Plastic Surgery. Rotating intern Charity Hosp. La., New Orleans, 1958-59; gen. surgery resident Marquette U. Hosps., Milw., 1961-65; resident in plastic and maxillofacial surgery U. Tex. Med. Br., Galveston, 1965-68; fellowship in plastic and reconstructive surgery African Med. Rsch. Found., Nairobi, Kenya, 1968-69; pvt. practice medicine specializing in plastic surgery Milw., 1969—; med. cons. Mentor/Sonique Surg. Sys., Santa Barbara, Calif. Contbr. articles to profl. jours. Lt. USNR, 1959-61. Fellow ACS, Internat. Coll. Surgeons; mem. AMA, Am. Soc. Aesthetic Plastic Surgery, Am. Soc. Plastic and Reconstructive Surgery, Singleton Surgical Soc., Am. Soc. Maxillofacial Surgeons, Can. Soc. Aesthetic for (Cosmetic) Plastic Surgery. Republican. Roman Catholic. Home: N14 W 30082 High Ridge Rd # 5 Pewaukee WI 53072 Office: Affiliated Cosmetic and Plastic Surgeons 2323 N Mayfair Rd Ste 503 Milwaukee WI 53226-1507

KLOS, JOHN WALTER, fire protection services financial officer; b. St. Louis, Oct. 12, 1951; s. Walter J. and Antoinette (Nowak) K.; m. Karen Lee Stuetzer, May 16, 1981; children: Michael S., Julie D. BSBA, U. Mo., St. Louis, 1974; MA in Mgmt., Webster U., 1982; MBA, Lindenwood Coll., 1984. Lead auditor U.S. Army Audit Agy., St. Louis, 1974-79; auditor in charge Def. Contract Audit Agy., St. Louis, 1979-80; sect. mgr. fiscal McDonnell Douglas Automation Co., St. Louis, 1980-87; dir. bus. affairs Maplewood-Richmond Heights Schs., St. Louis, 1987-93; ops. mgr., asst. v.p. Magnum Mortgage Co., St. Louis, 1993-94; dist. adminstr. Chesterfield (Mo.) Fire Protection Dist., 1994—. Sgt. 1st class USAR, 1970-77. Mem. Assn. Internal Auditors, Assn. Govt. Accts., Assn. Sch. Bus. Ofcls., Govt. Fin. Officers and Treas. Assn.

KLOSE, PATSY MAE ELLEN, nursing educator; b. Sebeka, Minn., Dec. 15, 1941; d. George and Iva Louise (McFarlane) Pendergrast; m. Lemoine Harry Klose, Apr. 20, 1963; children: Stephan Craig, Allen James. Diploma, Sister's of St. Joseph Sch., 1962; BS, Moorhead State U., 1978; MS, U. Minn., 1989. Cert. in psychiat. mental health nursing. Oper. rm. and emergency rm. nurse Trinity Hosp., Jamestown, N.D., 1962-63; clinic nurse Jamestown Clinic, Ltd., 1963; oper. rm., emergency rm. and pediatric nurse Trinity Hosp., Jamestown, 1964-65; clin. instr. N.D. State Hosp., Jamestown, 1965-87; behavioral outreach nurse Hennepin County Med. Ctr., Mpls., 1988; assoc. prof. Statewide Psychiat. Nursing Edn.

Program, Jamestown, 1989—, acting dir., 1992-93, 94-95; group therapist N.D. State Hosp., Jamestown, 1989—; 1992-93, 94-95; pre-admission screener Bock Assocs., St. Paul, 1990; cons. Progress Enterprises, Jamestown, 1991. Jamestown area coord. Dakota Radio Info. Svc., Bismarck, N.D., 1989-92; pub. speaker on self-esteem in chronic illness and self-esteem and women. Mem. ANA (psychiat. mental health coun. 1989-94), AAUW, Am. Psychiat. Nurses Assn. (state membership rep. 1992—, regional membership rep. 1994—, legis. rep. 1995—), N.D. Nurses Assn. (com. on continuing edn. 1990-96, chair 1993-94, mem.-at-large psychiat. mental health coun. 1990—, congress on edn. and profl. nursing practice 1991—, chair task force on 3d party reimbursement 1989-92), Sigma Theta Tau. Office: Statewide Psychiat Nursing PO Box 3000 Jamestown ND 58402-3000

KLOSINSKI, DEANNA DUPREE, medical laboratory sciences educator; b. Goshen, Ind., Dec. 28, 1941; d. George C. and Gertrude (Todd) Dupree (dec.); m. Michael A. Klosinski, Jan. 30, 1965; children: Elizabeth, John, Robert, Lara. BS, Ind. State U., 1964; MS, Purdue U., 1972; PhD, Wayne State U., 1990. Diplomate in lab. mgmt. Am. Soc. Clin. Pathologists; cert. med. technologist. Med. technologist South Bend (Ind.) Med. Found., 1959-68; lab. specialist Home Hosp., Lafayette, Ind., 1968-74; program dir. Ind. Vocat. Tech. Coll., Lafayette, 1968-75; clin. asst. prof. Oakland U., Rochester, Mich., 1985—; adj. asst. prof. Wayne State U., Detroit, 1991, Mich. State U., Lansing, 1991—, chair adv. com. Schs. Pub. Health, 1996—; chair adv. com. Schs. Allied Health; program dir., asst. adminstr. William Beaumont Hosp., Royal Oak, Mich., 1979—. Author: (videotape, monograph) Blood Collection: The Difficult Draw, 1992; co-author: (videotape, monograph) Blood Collection: The Routine Venipuncture, 1989 (chpt.) Molecular Biology and Pathology, 1993. Mem. pastoral coun. St. Hugo Cath. Ch., Bloomfield, Mich., 1991-94. Named Outstanding Bus. Person Mich. Coun. on Vocat., 1992, Mich. Clin. Lab. Scientist, 1993; rsch. grantee William Beaumont Hosp., 1989-90. Mem. Am. Soc. Clin. Pathologists (chmn. Tech. Sample 1984-93, mem. editl. bd. Lab. Medicine, editor Profl. Perspectives 1993-95, Technologist of Yr. 1994), Am. Assn. for Clin. Chemistry (mem. continuing edn. com. 1995-97), Am. Soc. for Clin. Lab. Sci. (mem. edn. sci. assembly, co-chairperson clin. lab. edn. conf. 1991, bd. dirs. edn. and rsch. fund 1996—), Assn. Women in Sci., Mich. Soc. for Clin. Lab. Sci. (treas. 1984-86, 88-92, pres. 1995-96), Sigma Xi (sec. Oakland U. chpt. 1994-96), Alpha Mu Tau (Scholarship award 1985, 87, 90), Delta Gamma Alumnae (treas. 1978-81, v.p. 1991-93, pres. 1993-95). Home: 90 Devon Rd Bloomfield Hills MI 48302-1119 Office: William Beaumont Hosp 3601 W Thirteen Mile Rd Royal Oak MI 48073-6769

KLOSKA, RONALD FRANK, manufacturing company executive; b. Grand Rapids, Mich., Oct. 24, 1933; s. Frank B. and Catherine (Hilaski) K.; m. Mary F. Minick, Sept. 7, 1957; children: Kathleen Ann, Elizabeth Marie, Ronald Francis, Mary Josephine, Carolyn Louise. Student, St. Joseph Sem., Grand Rapids, Mich., 1947-53; PhB, U. Montreal, Que., Can., 1955; MBA, U. Mich., 1957. Staff acct. Coopers & Lybrand, Niles, Mich., 1957, staff to sr. acct., 1960-63; treas. Skyline Corp., Elkhart, Ind., 1963, v.p., treas., 1964-67, exec. v.p. fin., 1967-74, pres., 1974-85, pres., chief ops. officer, 1985-91, vice chmn., chief adminstrn. officer, 1991-95, vice chmn., dep. CEO, chief adminstrn. officer, 1995—. With U.S. Army, 1957-60. Mem. Mich. Soc. CPAs, Ind. Soc. CPAs, South Bend Country Club. Roman Catholic. Home: 1329 E Woodside St South Bend IN 46614-1455 Office: Skyline Corp 2520 Bypass Rd Elkhart IN 46514-1518

KLOSTERBUER, JAMES ALBERT, environmental specialist; b. Luverne, Minn., May 14, 1944; s. Onno and Mildred Klosterbuer; m. Dorothy Schleiden; 1 child, David. BS in Physics, S.D. State U., 1966; MS in Physics, U. Ill., 1972; MBA, U. Iowa, 1988. Rsch. physicist U.S. Air Force Weapons Lab., Albuquerque, N. Mex., 1968-72; nuclear power engr. U.S. Dept. Energy Naval Reactors, Arlington, Va., 1974-79; mech., nuclear engr. Arlington, Va., 1979-80, licensing adminstr., 1980-82, group leader, 1982-83, supervising engr., 1983-87, prodn. svcs. specialist, 1987-88, environ. program mgr., 1988-92; prin. environ. specialist IES Utilities, Inc., Cedar Rapids, Iowa, 1992—. Capt. USAF, 1968-72. Office: IES Utilities Inc PO Box 351 Cedar Rapids IA 52406

KLOTH, RACHELL DARDEN, herbalist; b. Kinston, N.C., May 7, 1939; d. Johnnie White and Susan Winnifred (Stroud) Spychalla; m. N. Rollie Kloth; children: Jonathan, Janine. D. of Reflexology, Bernadean U., 1982; M. Herbalist, Emerson Coll., Canada, 1984. Cert. reflexologist, iripologist, nutritional cons. cons. in field. Home and Office: Kloth Health House 2210 S 57th St Milwaukee WI 53219-2205 Office: Kloth's Root Cellar 400 S Linwood Ave Appleton WI 54914

KLOTZ, IRVING MYRON, chemist, educator; b. Chgo., Jan. 22, 1916; s. Frank and Mollie (Nasatir) K.; m. Mary Sue Hanlon, Aug. 7, 1966; children: Edward, Audie Jeanne, David. B.S., U. Chgo., 1937, Ph.D., 1940. Rsch. assoc. in chemistry Northwestern U., 1940-42, instr., 1942- 46, asst. prof., 1946-47, assoc. prof., 1947-50, prof., 1950-63, Morrison prof. chemistry, 1963-86, prof. emeritus, 1986—; Lalor fellow Marine Biol. Lab., Woods Hole, Mass., 1947-48, corp. mem., 1947—, trustee, 1957-65. Author: Chemical Thermodynamics, 4th rev. edit., 1986, 5th rev. edit., 1994, Energies in Biochemical Reactions, rev. edit., 1967, Introduction to Biomolecular Energetics, 1986, Diamond Dealers, Feather Merchants, 1986; contbr. articles to sci. jours. Recipient Army-Navy cert. of appreciation for wartime research, 1948, William C. Rose award biochem. Am. Soc. Biochem. and Molecular Biology, 1993. Fellow Royal Soc. Medicine, Am. Acad. Arts and Scis., AAAS; mem. Nat. Acad. Scis., Am. Soc. Biol. Chemists, Am. Chem. Soc. (Eli Lilly award 1949, Midwest award 1970), Phi Beta Kappa, Sigma Xi, Phi Lambda Upsilon, Alpha Chi Sigma. Home: 2515 Pioneer Rd Evanston IL 60201-2203

KLOUCEK, FRANK JOHN, state legislator; b. Yankton, S.D., Sept. 27, 1956; s. Robert R. and Rose M. (Stekly) K.; m. Joan Marie Novak, 1980; children: Jennifer, Michelle, Kimberlee. BS, S.D. State U., 1978. Mem. S.D. Ho. of Reps., 1991-93; mem. S.D. Senate, vice chair senate agrl. com., 1993, 94, mem. health and human svcs., local govt. coms.; farmer; equipment mgr. Little Internat. Committeeman Bon Homme County Dem. Com., 1986-88, pres. 1989—; mem. St. Georges Cath. Ch., Scotland. Recipient Disting. Svc. award S.D. Pharm. Assn., 1995. Mem. S.D. Farmers Union (county pres. 1986, Action Officer award 1989, 90), S.D.Soybean Growers Assn. (state sec. 1987, recognition plaque 1987), Lions (Bon Homme), K.C., Block and Bridle, Animal Agriculture Orgn., Alpha Zeta, Alpha Epsilon. Roman Catholic. Home: RR 1 Box 56 Scotland SD 57059-9730*

KLOVER, JOHN MORGAN, mechanical engineer, consultant; b. Rantoul, Ill., Nov. 20, 1922. BSME, U. Cin., 1948; postgrad. in bus. mgmt., UCLA, 1972. Registered profl. engr., Ohio. Mgr. enrichment uranium Sys. Allied Signal, L.A., 1956-80, 86-87; mgr. enrichment Sys. Applied Signal, Sandusky, Ohio, 1980-85; mech. engr. Seifert Engring., Massillon, Ohio, 1990-93; cons. mech. engr. Hamrick Mfg. & Svc., Inc., Mogadore, Ohio, 1994—. Contbr. articles to profl. jours. 1st lt. U.S. Army, 1942-46, USAR, 1953. Home: 4608 Lindenwood Ave NE Canton OH 44714-1168 Office: PO Box 7033 Canton OH 44705

KLOWAK, MARVIN B., mechanical engineer; b. Marathon, Ont., Can., June 7, 1961. BSME, U. Wis., 1983. Registered profl. engr., Wis. Project engring. mgr. large engine divsn. Briggs & Stratton, Milw., 1983—. Mem. Soc. Automotive Engrs. (publicity chmn. 1989, lecture series chmn. 1990). Home: W166n10232 Calico Ln Germantown WI 53022-4740

KLUG, SCOTT LEO, congressman; b. Milwaukee, Wis., Jan. 16, 1953; s. Ralph William Klug and Josephine (Farrell) Weber; m. Tess Summers, Mar. 4, 1978; children: Keefe, Brett, Collin Phillip. BA, Lawrence U., 1975; MS in Journalism, Northwestern U., 1976; MBA, U. Wis., 1990. Reporter TV sta. Wausau, Wis., 1976-78; reporter Sta. KING-TV, Seattle, 1978-81; investigative reporter Sta. WJLA-TV, Washington, 1981-88; anchor, reporter Sta. WKOW-TV, Madison, Wis., 1988-90; v.p. pub. fin. dept. Blunt, Ellis & Loewi, Madison, 1990; mem. 102nd-104th U.S. Congress from 2d Wis. dist., Washington, D.C., 1991—. Reporter, producer documentaries (Emmy awards 1989, 90). Named Nat. Humanitarian of Yr., Humane Soc., 1986; John McCloy fellow Columbia U. Sch. Journalism, 1987. Republican. Office: 16 N Carroll St Rm 600 Madison WI 53703-2716 also: US Ho of Reps 1113 Longworth Bldg Ofc Washington DC 20515-0004

KLUGE, LEN H., director, actor, theater educator; b. Lakeview, Mich., Oct. 28, 1945; s. Leonhard H. and Edna Alvena (Paris) K. Diploma, Am. Acad. Dramatic Arts, 1967; student, Actors Studio, N.Y.C., 1968-69; BFA, Cen. Mich. U., 1977, MA in Counseling, 1978. Actor various mediums, N.Y., Calif., 1967-75; therapist Ionia County Mental Health Dept., Mich., 1978-79; exec. dir. Nat. Coun. on Alcoholism, Lansing, Mich., 1979-81; artistic dir. Spotlight Theatre, Grand Ledge, Mich., 1982—; prof. theater Spring Arbor Coll., 1983—; dir. The Actors Workshop, Lansing, 1986—. Appeared in: (soap opera) Another World, 1968-69, (off-Broadway play) Man with the Flower in His Mouth, 1969, (film) Rennaisance Man, 1994. Mem. Ctr. for the Arts, Lansing; bd. dirs. Child Abuse Prevention Svcs., 1993—. Recipient Obie award, 1969, Thespie X award Lansing State Jour., 1982, 84, 96-90, Decade of Excellence award for body of work, 1993, Barney award Okemos Barn Theatre, Lansing, 1984, 91, 95, 96, Star X award Spotlight Theatre, 1984-92. Lutheran. Home: 1937 Byrnes Rd Lansing MI 48906-3402

KLUGMAN, STEPHAN CRAIG, newspaper editor; b. Fargo, N.D., May 11, 1945; s. Ted and Charlotte (Olson) K.; m. Julie Sue Terpening, Sept. 18, 1971; children: Josh, Carrie. BA in Journalism, Ind. U., 1967. Copy editor Chgo. Sun-Times, 1967-68, asst. telegraph editor, 1968-72, telegraph editor, 1972-74, city editor, 1974-76, asst. mng. editor features, 1976-78; asst. prof. Medill Sch. Journalism, Northwestern U., Evanston, Ill., 1978-79, dir. undergrad. studies, 1979-82; editor Jour.-Gazette, Ft. Wayne, Ind., 1982--. Mem. Am. Soc. Newspaper Editors. Office: Jour-Gazette 600 W Main St Fort Wayne IN 46802-1408

KLUMB, JASON O., state legislator. State rep. Dist. 125 Mo. State Congress. *

KLUMPP, STEPHEN PAUL, architect; b. Rochester, N.Y., Nov. 4, 1952; s. Oscar Edward and Mary Elizabeth (Ladue) K.; m. Cheryl Anne Miller, May 17, 1986; 1 child, Andrew Ozcy. BArch, Ill. Inst. Tech., 1975. Registered architect, Ill., N.Y.; cert. Nat. Coun. Archtl. Registration Bds. Designer Communica Internat., LaGrange, Ill., 1975-76; ptnr. Schiller & Frank Architects, Wheeling, Ill., 1976-85; project architect Archiplan Internat., Rolling Meadows, Ill., 1985-91; pres., owner Ar-K-Teks Unltd., Ltd., Wheeling, 1981—. Pres. East-Fowler Adv. Coun., Chgo., 1973-75. Mem. AIA, Bldg Ofcls. and Code Adminstrs. Internat., Wheeling C. of C. Home: 300 11th St Wheeling IL 60090-2716 Office: Ar-K-Teks Unltd Ltd 300 11th St Wheeling IL 60090-2716

KLUNZINGER, THOMAS EDWARD, writer, actor, director, reapportionment specialist; b. Ann Arbor, Mich., Sept. 11, 1944; s. Willard Reuben and Katherine Eileen (McCurdy) K.; BA cum laude in Advt., Mich. State U., 1966. Copywriter Campbell-Ewald Advt. Co., Detroit, 1966-70; travel cons. Moorman's Travel Service, Detroit, 1973-74; media dir. Taylor for Congress campaign, East Lansing, Mich., 1974; communications specialist House Republican Staff, Lansing, Mich., 1975-80; trustee Meridian Twp., Ingham County, Mich., 1980-84; vice chmn. Econ. Devel. Corp., 1982-84; compliance officer The Eyde Co., Lansing, 1985-88; legis. aide Mich. Ho. of Reps., Lansing, 1988-90; comm. officer Mich. Capital Healthcare. Mem. Ingham County Rep. Com., 1976—, sec., 1986-88, 91-92, 96, Mich. Rep. State Com., 1981-85, 6th Dist. Rep. Com. sec., 1989-93; mem. Ingham County Bd. Canvassers, 1993—. Author: Chester!, 1981; Heavy Lady, 1983; Double Standards, 1985; A Villa in Unadilla, 1985, Losing It, 1987, The Wizards of Kyshtym/Deine Kleine Beine, 1988, Lounge Lizards/Managing Gran, 1989, Like A Brother, 1989, Loose Dogs Will Bite, 1990, Beloved Friend, 1990, To Be Announced, 1991, Okemos Passing, 1992, Song of the Whale, 1993, Mimsy Borogroves and the Tooth Fairy, 1993, What About the Hungarian?, 1995, The Last Days of Richard II, 1996. Mem. Dramatists Guild; pres. Riverwalk Theatre, 1990-92, sec. 1993-95. Mem. Am. Numismatic Assn., Mich. Numismatic Soc. (sec. 1991—, editor 1993—). Address: PO Box 16231 Lansing MI 48901-6231

KLUSMAN, JUDITH, state legislator; b. Neenah, Wis., Dec. 14, 1956; m. Timothy A. Klusman; children: Charles, James. Student, Concordia Coll. Mem. from dist. 56 Wis. State Assembly, Madison, 1988—, asst. majority leader, co-chair joint survey com. retirement svc.; mem. ways and means, assembly rules and orgn. coms. Wis. State Assembly; mem. com. on agr. and internat. trade Nat. Conf. State Legislators; mem. task force on agr. and environ; mem. Legis. Coun. Spl. Com. on Child Custody, Support and Visitation Laws; mem. Legic. Coun. Spl. Com. on Remediation of Environ. Contamination. Mem. Outagamie County Local Emergency Planning Com.; mem. Wis. Rural Leadership Program; mem. World Dairy Ctr. Authority Bd. Recipient Key award 4-H, 1975, Outstanding Young Farm Couple award Winnebago County Farm Bur., 1983, Friend of Edn. award Neenah chpt. Wis. Edn. Assn., 1986-87, Friend of Agr. award Wis. Farm Bur. Fedn., 1990, 92, 94, Outstanding Alumni Winnebago County 4-H, 1992, Buardian of Small Bus. award Fedn. of Ind. Bus., 1992. Mem. Rotary Internat., Wis. Rural Leadership Alumni. Address: 7544 Green Meadow Rd Oshkosh WI 54904*

KMENTA, JAN, economics educator; b. Prague, Czechoslovakia, Jan. 3, 1928; came to U.S., 1963; m. Joan Helen Gaffney, Aug. 9, 1959; children—David, Steven. B.Econs. with 1st class honors, Sydney U., 1955; M.A., Stanford U., 1959, Ph.D., 1964, hon. doctorate, U. Saarland, Germany, 1989. Lectr., U. N.S.W., Sydney, 1957-61; sr. lectr. Sydney U., 1961-63; asst. prof. U. Wis.-Madison, 1963-65; prof. Mich. State U., East Lansing, 1965-73; prof. U. Mich., Ann Arbor, 1973—; vis. prof. U. Bonn, Germany, 1971-72, 1979-80, U. Saarland, Saarbrucken, Germany, 1984, 85, 86. Author: Elements of Econometrics, 2d edit., 1986; editor: (with others) Evaluation of Econometric Models, 1980, Large-Scale Macro-Econometric Models, 1981; contbr. articles to profl. jours. Recipient U.S. Sr. Scientist Prize, Humboldt Found., Bonn, 1979; Fulbright scholar, 1957-59. Fellow Am. Statis. Assn., Econometric Soc.; mem. Am. Econ. Assn., Czechoslovak Soc. Arts and Scis. in Am. Home: 2511 Londonderry Rd Ann Arbor MI 48104-4017 Office: Dept Econs U Mich Ann Arbor MI 48109

KNAPP, GARY LEE, quality engineer; b. Rockford, Ill., Feb. 8, 1953; s. Karl Frederick and Alberta Delores (Pritchett) K.; m. Patricia Ann Jennings (div. 1990); children: Eric Jennings, Michael Christopher. BS in Polit. Sci. and Econs., U. Md., 1979. Cert. machinist, Md.; engring. specialist, Md. Machinist Naval Ship R & D Ctr., Annapolis, Md., 1974-80; engring. specialist Nat. Security Agy., Ft. George G. Meade, Md., 1980-90; tech. staff Phoenix Rsch. Group, Inc., Arlington, Va., 1991-92; statistician pvt. industry. Contbr. articles to profl. jours. Active Children, Inc., 1972-74, 1989-90, Plan Internat., 1989-90, Children Internat., 1989-90; coach Ft. George G. Meade Youth Soccer Program, 1981-84, Severna Pk. Soccer Program, 1985-87, Greater Glen Burnie Soccer Program, 1988. With USN, 1971-74, with Md. N.G., 1978, with USAR, 1979-81, with USAFR, 1981-87. Recipient cert. of appreciation, Def. Intelligence Coll., 1986. Mem. Am. Soc. Quality Control.

KNAUS, THOMAS JAMES, investments executive; b. Chgo., July 27, 1938. BS, Lewis U., 1960. Designer Vulcan (Wis.) Ski Hill, 1972-76; mgr. IDI Corp., Green Bay, Wis., 1976-83; asst. v.p. Everen Securities, Green Bay, 1983—. Author: Smokey, The Hobo. Active cerebral palsy telethons; vol. Nat. Railroad Mus. With USAF, 1960-64. Mem. Clowns Are Us, Green Bay Sailing Club, Curling Club. Roman Catholic.

KNEEBONE, BEVERLY, tax preparer; b. Madison, Wis., June 6, 1935; d. Martin J. and Lucille (Finn) Virnig; m. Ronald Kneebone, Sept. 25, 1954 (div. Nov. 1988); 1 child, Steven A. BS in Edn., U. Wis., 1979. tax preparer H&R Block, Madison, 1965—, office supr., 1980-90, speaker, 1981-88. Vol. chair Madison Art Ctr., 1993-94. Home: 1505 Stemp Terrace Madison WI 53711

KNEISER, RICHARD JOHN, accountant; b. Milw., Nov. 20, 1938; s. Frank Edward and Esther (Sobek) K.; m. Caroline Irene Stahl, Aug. 22, 1959; children: Richard J. Jr., Ronald V., Robert C. BS in Acctg., Marquette U., 1960. CPA. Staff mem. Arthur Andersen & Co., Milw., 1960-65, audit mgr., 1965-73, ptnr., 1973-94; mem. exec. bd. Wis. Pub. Utility Inst., Madison, 1982-94; advisor acctg. practices com. U.S. Cath. Conf., 1989—; mem. adv. bd. Biltmore Investors Bank, 1995—, N.Am. Clutch Corp., 1995—. Dir. Skylight Opera Theatre, Milw., 1987-95; active Marquette U. Pres. Exec. Senate, Milw. 1987-94; trustee Village of Oconomowoc Lake, Wis., 1991-95, mem. planning commn., 1989-93, chmn. fin. com. 1991-93. Mem. AICPA, Am. Prodn. and Inventory Control Soc., Wis. Inst. CPA's, Univ. Club Milw., Oconomowoc Lake Club (bd. dirs. 1988—, officer, 1989-95, commodore 1994-95), Beta Gamma Sigma, Beta Alpha Psi. Home: 35920 Pabst Rd Oconomowoc WI 53066-4519

KNEPP, VIRGINIA LEE HAHN, legal assistant; b. South Bend, Ind., Nov. 1, 1946; d. Charles William and Mary Louise (Hunter) Hahn; m. James Patrick Knepp, Apr. 20, 1968; children: Meredith Leigh, Melanie Leigh. BS in Bus., Ind. U., 1971. Legal asst. Hahn, Walz, Knepp & Dvorak, South Bend, Ind., 1983—; mem. Ind. allocation com. for Social Svc. Block Grants. Founder YWCA Women's Shelter, South Bend, 1978; founder, facilitator Women's Support Group, South Bend, 1979-90; vol. coord. Olympic Town Internat./Spl. Olympics, 1984-87, Kids Kingdom, South Bend, 1991, Children's Dispensary, South Bend, 1981-93, adv. coun., 1994, St. Joseph County Scholarship Found., 1990, Am. Cancer Soc., St. Joseph County, 1988-89; bd. dirs. Corvilla Inc., South Bend, 1989—; treas. Dvorak for State Rep., 1986—, Very Spl. Arts Ind., 1980—, pres., 1995-97, South Bend Heritage Found., 19990-95; active Gov. Bayh Commn., 1991—; chmn. Domestic Violence Prevention and Treatment Coun., Michiana Arts and Sci. Coun.'s Carnival for the Arts; bd. dirs. South Bend Heritage Found., 1991-95. Mem. AAUW, Hoosier Art Patrons, Thalia Sorority (pres. 1988), Ind. Lawyers Aux. Home: 17725 Juday Lake Dr South Bend IN 46635-1758 Office: Hahn Walz Knepp & Dvorak 509 W Washington St South Bend IN 46601-1527

KNEPPER, EUGENE ARTHUR, realtor; b. Sioux Falls, S.D., Oct. 8, 1926; s. Arlie John and May (Crone) K.; B.S.C. in Acctg., Drake U., Des Moines, 1951; m. LaNel Strong, May 7, 1948; children—Kenton Todd, Kristin Rene. Acct., G.L. Yager, pub. acct., Estherville, Iowa, 1951-52; auditor R.L. Meriwether, C.P.A., Des Moines, 1952-53; acct. govt. renegotiation dept. Collins Radio Co., Cedar Rapids, Iowa, 1953-54; head acctg. dept. Hawkeye Rubber Mfg. Co., Cedar Rapids, 1954-56; asst. controller United Fire & Casualty Ins. Co., Cedar Rapids, 1956-58; sales assoc. Equitable Life Assurance Soc. U.S., Cedar Rapids, 1958-59; controller Gaddis Enterprises, Inc., Cedar Rapids, 1959-61; owner Estherville Laundry Co., 1959-64; sales assoc., comml. investment div. mgr. Tommy Tucker Realty Co., Cedar Rapids, 1961-74; owner Real Estate Investment Planning Assocs., Cedar Rapids, 1974—; treas. Investment Properties Inc., 1994—; controlling ptnr. numerous real estate syndicates; cons. in field, fin. speaker; guest lectr. Kirkwood Community Coll., Cedar Rapids, Mt. Mercy Coll., Cedar Rapids, Cornell Coll., Mt. Vernon; creative financing instr. Iowa Real Estate Commn.-Iowa Assn. Realtors. Patron Cedar Rapids Symphony, 1983-86, treas., mem. exec. com., bd. dirs.; bd. dirs. Oak Hill-Jackson Outreach Fund, 1970-83, pres., 1973-74; bd. dirs. Consumer Credit Counseling Service Cedar Rapids-Marion Area, 1974-80, pres., 1974-80; mem. pub. rels. com. Cedar Valley Habitat for Humanity, contbr. newsletter, 1991—, mental health adv. vol., 1991—. Served with USNR, 1945-46. Recipient Storm Manuscript award, 1976. Mem. Nat. Assn. Realtors (state mcpl. legis. com., subcom. on multi-family housing), Iowa Assn. Realtors (pres. comml. investment div. 1973, 80, named life mem.; state legis. com., savs. and loan formation feasibility com., mcpl. and county legis. com.), Nat. Assn. Accountants, Nat. Inst. Real Estate Brokers (membership chmn. Iowa 1972-73), Real Estate Securities and Syndication Inst. (small group investment council, steering com. 1985, vice chmn. regional officers and state officers devel. com., gov. Iowa div., regional v.p.), Cedar Rapids Bd. Realtors, Internat. Platform Assn., Internat. Inst. Valuers. Methodist. Clubs: Cedar Rapids Optimist (past chmn. boys work com.); Eastern Iowa Execs. (dir., pres. 1981-82). Contbr. articles to profl. jours. Home: 283 Tomahawk Trl SE Cedar Rapids IA 52403-2037

KNEZOVICH, JEFFREY PAUL, professional association executive; b. Peoria, Ill., Jan. 21, 1957; s. John George and Rosemary (Bevis) K.; m. Kimberly Ann Miller, Sept. 13, 1986; children: Amanda Bevis, Ross Miller. BA in Polit. Sci., Ea. Ill. U., 1979. Acting exec. dir. Sigma Pi Fraternity Internat., Vincennes, Ind., 1979-81; br. coord. and specialty soc. adminstr. Chgo. Med. Soc., 1982-84; chpt. svcs. mgr. Am. Coll. Surgeons, Chgo., 1984-92; account exec. Smith, Bucklin and Assocs., Chgo., 1992—; exec. dir. Am. Acad. Cosmetic Surgeons, Chgo., 1992—, So. Thoracic Surg. Assn., 1993—; trustee, sec./treas. Sigma Pi Fraternity Ednl. Found., Vincennes, 1990—; bd. dirs. Ea. Ill. U. Found., Charleston, 1992—. Chair Lisle (Ill.) Twp. Regional Dem. Orgn., 1992-94, treas. 1994—; mem. Ea. Ill. U. Presdl. Search Commn., Charleston, 1992. Mem. Am. Soc. Assn. Execs., Chgo. Soc. Assn. Execs., Am. Assn. Med. Soc. Execs., Chgo. Assn. Healthcare Execs. (pres. 1991-92), Ea. Ill. U. Alumni Assn. (pres. 1991-92, bd. dirs. 1984-96). Roman Catholic. Home: 380 Prairie Knoll Dr Naperville IL 60565-4150 Office: Smith Bucklin & Assocs 401 N Michigan Ave Chicago IL 60611-4212

KNIESNER, JOHN THOMAS, librarian; b. Berea, Ohio, Dec. 19, 1949; s. Albert Henry and Elizabeth (Leonard) K.; m. Patti-Jo Samo, Sept. 8, 1979; children: Janet Deborah, Joseph David. BA, Kent State U., 1971; MLS, U. Mich., 1972. Profl. libr. I Columbus (Ohio) Met. Libr., 1972-76, profl. libr. II, 1977-78, profl. libr. III, 1979-85; dir. Bellaire (Ohio) Pub. Libr., 1986—; computer cons. Toledo-Lucas County Pub. Libr., Ohio, 1979, Richardson-Smith Indsl. Design, Columbus, 1984; libr. Ctrl. Ohio Transit Authority, Columbus, 1981-84. Film reviewer The News, 1985-86; contbr. articles to periodicals. Mem. steering com. Always a River, 1991; mem. adv. com. Ohio Humanities Coun., Columbus, 1993-94; water safety instr. ARC, Columbus and Bellaire, 1984—. Recipient Civitan award PTA, Bellaire, 1992, plaque for saving lives, Am. Red Cross, Wheeling, W.Va., 1987, commendation Columbus Area Shared Use Automated Resources, 1976. Mem. Ohio Libr. Coun. (facilitator 1981-82, 92), S.E. Ohio Libr. Assn. (pres. 1988-89), No. Ohio Valley Astronomy Educators (pub. rels. officer 1994-96), Ednl. Film Libr. Assn. (film judge 1980-83). Republican. Roman Catholic. Office: Bellaire Pub Libr 330 32d St Bellaire OH 43906

KNIFFEL, LEONARD JOHN, editor, librarian; b. Mt. Clemens, Mich., Aug. 25, 1947; s. John and Lucia Helen (Brodacki) K.; m. Judith Worthen, Aug. 22, 1969 (div. Apr. 1977). Ba, Oakland U., 1970; MA, Wayne State U., 1972, MLS, 1975. Libr. Detroit Pub. Libr., 1971-88; editor Am. Librs. Mag. Am. Libr. Assn., Chgo., 1988—; co-founder, bd. dirs. Poetry Resource Ctr. Mich., 1980-85; photographer, freelance writer. Publisher Fallen Angel Press, 1975-82; editor PRC Newsletter, 1980-85. Mem. Acad. Am. Poets, Gerber/Hart Libr. Archives (bd. dirs. 1994—), Polish Inst. Arts & Scis. Democrat. Roman Catholic. Home: 2743 N Greenview Chicago IL 60614 Office: Am Libr Assn 50 E Huron St Chicago IL 60611

KNIGHT, BOB, college basketball coach; b. Massilon, Ohio, Oct. 25, 1940; s. Carroll and Hazel (Henthorne) K.; m. Nancy Lou Knight, Apr. 17, 1963 (div.); m. Karen Edgar, 1988. BS, Ohio State U., 1962. Asst. coach Cuyahoga Falls (Ohio) High Sch., 1962-63; freshman coach U.S. Mil. Acad., West Point, N.Y., 1963-65; head basketball coach U.S. Mil. Acad., 1965-71, Ind. U., Bloomington, 1971—; speaker clinics in field; condr. tng. clinics for coaches and players. Trustee Naismith Meml. Basketball Hall of Fame. Served with U.S. Army. Recipient Big Ten Coach-of-Year award, 1973, 75, 76, 81, 89; named unanimously Nat. Coach of Year, 1975, 89, Nat. Coach of Yr. AP and Basketball Weekly, 1976; recipient appreciation plaque from team, 1979. Mem. Nat. Assn. Basketball Coaches (bd. dirs.). Methodist. Office: Indiana Univ Basketball Office Assembly Hall Bloomington IN 47405

KNIGHT, BRENDA LEE, quality engineer; b. Oil City, Pa., Aug. 22, 1958; d. Clarence Benjamin and Donna Jean (Grosteffon) K. BS in Indsl. and Ops. Engring., U. Mich., 1980; MBA, So. Ill. U., 1992. Cert. quality engr.; cert. quality auditor. Quality engr. Continental Gen. Tire, Inc., Mt. Vernon, Ill., 1981—. Mem. Am. Soc. for Quality Control, Am. Inst. Indsl. Engrs., Am. Mgmt. Assn., Beta Gamma Sigma. Home: 4411 Woodglen Ln Mount Vernon IL 62864-2171 Office: Continental Gen Tire Inc PO Box 1029 Mount Vernon IL 62864-1029

KNIGHT, CATHERINE O'CONNOR, developer, fundraiser; b. Ann Arbor, Mich., June 19, 1955; d. Gerald Anthony and Margaret Rose (Tilly) O'Connor; m. Daniel James Zelisko, July 1978 (div. May 1985); m. Robert James Knight, July 1991. Student in telecomm., Mich. State U., 1974-77, 87; student in comm., U. Ariz., 1977-78. Co-owner Evening Star Prodns., Inc., Scottsdale, Ariz., 1978-86; real estate sales assoc., mktg. dir. Oppenheimer Group, Inc., Ann Arbor, 1987-88; real estate sales assoc. Charles

Reinhardt Co., Ann Arbor, Mich., 1988-90; devel. dir. Wolverine Human Services, Inc., Detroit, 1990—; spl. event cons. Mich. Festival, Lansing, Mich., 1987, Spectrum Human Svcs., Inc., Livonia, Mich., Ark. and Washtenaw Assn. Citizens for Advocacy, Ann Arbor, Projects West, San Jose, Calif., McCain for Senate Campaign, Mesa, Ariz., Entertainment Group Phoenix, Inc., Mesa, Mill Ave. Merchants Assn., Tempe, 1980—; coord. numerous pvt. and corp. functions, restaurants, resort and nightclub promotions, 1980—. Mem. Nat. Assoc. of Fund Raising Execs., Greater Detroit Pub. Rels. Soc., Ann Arbor Advt. Club, Non-Profit Pub. Rels. Network. Office: Wolverine Human Svcs Inc 15100 Mack Ave Detroit MI 48224

KNIGHT, CHARLES FIELD, electrical equipment manufacturing company executive; b. Lake Forest, Ill., Jan. 20, 1936; s. Lester Benjamin and Elizabeth Anne (Field) K.; m. Joanne Parrish, June 22, 1957; children: Lester Benjamin III, Anne Field Knight Davidson, Steven P., Jennifer Lee. B.S. in Mech. Engring., Cornell U., 1958, M.B.A., 1959. Mgmt. trainee Goetzewerke A.G., Burscheid, W. Ger., 1959-61; pres. Lester B. Knight Internat. Corp., 1961-63; exec. v.p. Lester B. Knight & Assocs., Inc., Chgo., 1963-67; pres. Lester B. Knight & Assocs., Inc., 1967-69, pres., chief exec. officer, 1969-73; vice chmn. bd. Emerson Electric Co., St. Louis, 1973, sr. vice chmn. bd., corp. exec. officer, 1973, chmn. bd., 1974—, chief exec. officer, 1973—; bd. dirs. Southwestern Bell Corp., Caterpillar Inc., Baxter Internat. Inc., Anheuser Busch Cos., Inc., The Brit. Petroleum Co. p.l.c. Mem. Civic Progress, 1973; bd. dirs. Arts and Edn. Coun.; bd. dirs., trustee Washington U., St. Louis, Olin Found. Mem. St. Louis Country Club, Log Cabin Club (St. Louis), Cristal Downs Club (Traverse City, Mich.), Glen View Golf Club (Ill.), Chicago Club, Sigma Phi. Office: Emerson Electric Co 8000 W Florissant Ave Saint Louis MO 63136*

KNIGHT, DEBRA ANN MIZER, mental health services professional; b. Ft. Riley, Kans., June 8, 1960; d. Thomas Andrew and Winifred (Horn) Mizer; m. Jeffery Mark Knight, Sept. 19, 1981; children: Whitney, Katherine, Morgan, Allison. BS in Pub. Svc., West Liberty (W.Va.) State Coll., 1981; MEd, Ohio U., St. Clairsville, 1992. Spl. needs aide Harcatus Head Start, Dennison, Ohio, 1981-82; social worker Children's Svcs. unit Harrison County Dept. Human Svcs., Cadiz, Ohio, 1982-85; family planning worker Jefferson County Family Planning, Steubenville, Ohio, 1986-87; intake and referral coord. Harrison County Collaborative Group, Cadiz, 1989-90; social program specialist Tuscarawas County Bd. Mental Retardation/Devel. Disabilities, New Philadelphia, Ohio, 1990-94; supported living coord. Tuscarawas County Bd. Mental Retardation and Developmental Disabilities, New Philadelphia, Ohio, 1994-95, case mgmt. supr., 1995—; mem. policy coun. Harcatus Head Start, 1982-85; cluster coord. Tuscarawas and Carroll County (Ohio) Clusters, 1990-94. Office: Tuscarawas County Bd Mental Retardation 223 Fair Ave NW New Philadelphia OH 44663-3728

KNIGHT, JEANNE ELLEN, judge; b. Spokane, Wash., Sept. 15, 1949; s. Thomas Clyde and Adeline Christine (Sather) K. BA, Lawrence U., 1971; JD, 1976. Bar: Minn. 1976. Atty. Edward A. Kutcher & Assocs., Mpls., 1977-78, David K. Wendell & Assocs., Mpls., 1979-81; workers compensation judge State of Minn. Office Adminstrv. Hearings, Mpls., 1981—. Office: Office of Adminstrv Hearings 100 Washington Sq Ste 1700 Minneapolis MN 55401-2138

KNIGHT, KEVIN, state legislator; b. Sept. 1957; m. Bonnie Knight; 3 children. BA, U. Ariz. Small bus. owner; rep. Dist. 40B Minn. Ho. of Reps., 1994—. Home: 131 Maplewood Dr Bloomington MN 55420

KNIGHT, LOUISE WILBY, writer; b. Evanston, Ill., May 2, 1949; d. Augustus, Jr. and Frances (Berna) K.; BA, Wesleyan U., Middletown, Conn., 1972, MA in Tchg., 1972. Rsch. asst. Learning Mag., Palo Alto, Calif., 1973; mktg. editor Addison-Wesley Co., Menlo Park, Calif., 1973-74; editor, ann. report Fund for the Improvement of Postsecondary Edn., Washington, 1974-75; editor Edn. Funding Rsch. Coun., Washington, 1975-78; coord. Office of Rsch. Support Duke U., Durham, N.C., 1978-86; dir. Found. and Corp. Relations Wheaton Coll., Norton, Mass., 1986-91; dir. devel. United South End Settlements, Boston, 1991-92; trainer, cons. The Grantsmanship Ctr., L.A., 1993-96;, 1993-96; workshop leader, Coun. for Advancement and Aupport of Edn., Washington, 1989-91; cons. for nonprofits, 1992—; adj. faculty Spertus Coll., 1994—; resch. assoc. Five Coll. Women's Studies Ctr. Mt. Holyoke Coll., 1996. Author essays; contbr. articles to profl. jours., publs. Co-founder Durham Dispute Settlement, 1981-85; bd. dirs. Wesleyan U., Middletown, 1979-82, Boston Women's Fund, Boston, 1988-89; rsch. assoc. Five Coll. Women's Studies Rsch. Ctr., Mt. Holyoke Coll., 1996. Grantee Ind. U. Ctr. on Phil., 1993, NEH, 1992, Ludwig Vogelstein Found., 1989, Spencer Found., 1996. Office: PO Box 7038 Evanston IL 60201

KNIGHT, MARGARET L., librarian, educator; b. Rochelle, Ill., Feb. 13, 1920; d. Burton Eugene and Viola Amelia (Harter) K. BS in Edn., No. Ill. U., 1943; MLS, U. Ill., 1956. Rural sch. tchr. Ogle County, Rochelle, 1939-42; tchr. 6th grade, librarian Lee County, Dixon, Ill., 1943-56; librarian jr. high sch. Cook County, Park Ridge, Ill., 1956-57, dist. supr. libr.-media ctrs., 1957-75; librarian elem. sch. Ogle County, Lindenwood, Ill., 1994—, piano, organ tchr., 1976—. Mem. bd. dirs., treas. League of Women Voters, Rochelle, Ill., 1977—, mem. bd. dirs., sec.-treas. Lindenwood Water Assn., 1977—. Mem. No. Ill. Botanical Soc. (librarian 1990—), Ogle County Hist. Soc. (bd. dirs., sec., pres. 1977—), Ogle County Genealogical Soc., Prairie Preservation Soc. of Ogle County (treas. 1980—), Des Plaines Valley Geological Soc. (librarian 1994-96), Flagg Twp. Hist. Soc. (bd. 1990—).

KNIGHT, ROBERT EDWARD, banker; b. Alliance, Nebr., Nov. 27, 1941; s. Edward McKean and Ruth (McDuffee) K.; m. Eva Sophia Youngstom, Aug. 12, 1966. BA, Yale U., 1963; MA, Harvard U., 1965, PhD, 1968. Asst. prof. U.S. Naval Acad., Annapolis, Md., 1966-68; lectr. U. Md., 1967-68; fin. economist Fed. Res. Bank of Kansas City (Mo.), 1968-70, research officer, economist, 1971-76, asst. v.p., sec., 1977, v.p., sec., 1978-79; pres. Alliance (Nebr.) Nat. Bank, 1979-94, also chmn., 1983-94; pres. Robert Knight Assocs., banking and econ. cons., Cheyenne, 1979—; vis. prof., chair banking and fin. E. Tenn. State U., Johnson City, 1988; mem. faculty Stonier Grad. Sch. Banking, 1972—, Colo. Grad. Sch. Banking, 1975-82, Am. Inst. Banking, U. Mo., Kansas City, 1971-79, Prochnow Grad. Sch. Banking, U. Wis.; mem. extended learning faculty Park Coll., 1996—; mem. Coun. for Excellence for Bur. Bus. Rsch. U. Nebr., Lincoln, 1991-94, mem. Grad. Sch. Arts & Scis Coun., Harvard, 1994—; chmn. Taxable Mcpl. Bondholders Protective Com., 1991-94. Trustee, 1984-85, Knox Presbyn. Ch., Overland Park, Kans., 1965-69; bd. regents Nat. Comml. Lending Sch., 1980-83; mem. Downtown Improvement Com., Alliance, 1981-94; trustee U. Nebr. Found.; bd. dirs. Stonier Grad. Sch. Banking, Box Butte County Devel. Commn., Nebr. Com. for Humanities, 1986-90; mem. fin. com. United Meth. Ch., Alliance, 1982-85, trustee, 1990-93; Box Butte County Indsl. Devel. Bd., 1987-94; mem. Nebr. Com. for the Humanities, 1986-90; amb. Nebr. Diplomats. Woodrow Wilson fellow, 1963-64. Mem. Am. Econ. Assn., Am. Fin. Assn., So. Econ. Assn., Nebr. Bankers Assn. (com. state legis. 1980-81, com. comml. loans and investments 1986-87), Am. Inst. Banking (state com. for Nebr. 1980-83), Am. Bankers Assn. (econ. adv. com. 1980-83, cmty. bank leadership coun.), Western Econ. Assn., Econometric Soc., Rotary, Masons. Contbr. articles to profl. jours. Home: 429 W 5th Ave Cheyenne WY 82001-1249 Office: 429 W Fifth Ave Cheyenne WY 82001-1249

KNIGHT, ROBERT MILTON, journalist, educator; b. Tacoma, Dec. 2, 1940; s. Lawrence Leslie Knight and Marian Delphine (Humphrey) Gordy, (stepmother) Margaret Irene (Michael) K.; m. Susan Jan Guthrie, July 3, 1965; children: Kelly Leslie, Leigh April. BS in Journalism, U. Colo., 1967; MA in Integrated Studies, De Paul U., 1996. Statehouse reporter The New Mexican, Santa Fe, 1968-70; gen. newsman Sta. KOB-TV and Radio, Albuquerque, 1970-71; statehouse corr. Sta. KOAT-TV, Albuquerque, 1971-73; freelance journalism Chgo., 1973-74; product mgr. Deltak, Inc., Schiller Park, Ill., 1974-76; mgr. corp. comm. Advanced Sys., Inc., Elk Grove Village, Ill., 1976-79; account exec. Hill & Knowlton, Inc., Chgo., 1979-81; freelance writer Knight, Writer, Chgo., 1981-94; sr. editor City News Bur. of Chgo., 1994—; mem. adv. bd. PC/Expo Chgo., 1989-90; lectr. Northwestern U., 1984—. Contbr. articles to newspapers and mags. With USN, 1959-61. Mem. Soc. Profl. Journalists (bd. dirs. Chgo. Headline Club chpt. 1992—, regional conf. chairperson 1993, chpt. pres. 1994-95), Ind. Writers Chgo. (bd. dirs. 1983-85, program chairperson 1991-93). Home: 706 Clarence Ave Oak Park IL 60304-1306

KNIGHT, ROBERT VERNON, state agency administrator; b. Sioux City, Iowa, July 10, 1935; s. Gerald Asa and Robinette Ester (La Gue) K. BA, U. No. Iowa, 1977; MPA, Iowa State U., 1987. Commd. U.S. Army, 1955, advanced through grades to chief warrant officer, 1972, ret., 1976; employment counselor Midtown Mgmt., Waterloo, Iowa, 1977-78; gen. mgr. The Computer Ctr., Waterloo, 1979-80; personnel dir. City of Marshalltown, Iowa, 1980-86; dir. cen. adminstrn. Iowa Dept. Pub. Health, Des Moines, 1987-91; mgr. Landmark South Complex, Des Moines, 1992—. Mem. Internat. Personnel Mgmt. Assn., Am. Mgmt. Assn., Nat. Pub. Employers Labor Relations Assn., Iowa Pub. Employers Labor Relations Assn., Iowa Pub. Health Assn. Home: 220 Dickman Rd Apt 346 Des Moines IA 50315-6236 Office: Landmark South Complex 200 Dickman Rd Des Moines IA 50315-6262

KNIGHT, WILLARD, manufacturing executive; b. Shadyside, Ohio, Apr. 3, 1915. BA, Linsley Coll., 1942. Pres. Knight Mfg., Inc., Shadyside, Ohio, 1951—. Office: Knight Mfg Inc E 40th St PO Box 27 Shadyside OH 43947-0027

KNIPPING, RONALD L., financial advisor; b. Hackensack, N.J., Jan. 3, 1965. BS, West Point, 1987. Fin. advisor Prudential Securities, Grand Rapids, Mich., 1994—. Advisor Big Bro., Grand Rapids, 1994—. Capt. U.S. Army, 1983-93. Republican. Office: Prudential Securities Inc 99 Monroe Ave NW Ste 101 Grand Rapids MI 49503-2639

KNISELY BONK, HELEN, corporate customs broker; b. Cleve., Apr. 12, 1950; d. Angelo and Laura (Kelepouris) Pappis; m. Robert B. Knisely Sr., July 5, 1969 (div. Dec. 1986); children: Robert Jr., Laura; divorced; 1 child, Alexandra. Degree in computer, AG Computer Tng., Cleve., 1984-93; student, Columbia Pacific U., 1989; B in Internat. Bus./Law, World Trade Inst., 1991; cert. NAFTA specialist, U.S. Customs, 1994; cert. customs audits and investigations specialist, World Trade Inst., 1995. Lic. customs broker; cert. internat. law. Corp. customs broker Am. Greetings, others cos., worldwide locations, 1983—; pres., instr., seminar leader, cons. Internat. Trade Cons., Cleve., 1989—; fgn. buyer Am. Greetings Corp., Cleve., 1990—. Author: (trade book) Foreign Trade Zones and Subzones, 1993; contbr. articles to profl. jours. Named Woman of Yr., Orgn. Women in Internat. Trade, 1992-93. Mem. NAFE, Internat. Freight Assn. (hon.), Women in Internat. Trade, C. of C. (student sponsor 1993—). Republican. Greek Orthodox. Home: 3209 Bay Landing Dr Westlake OH 44145-4437 Office: Am Greetings Corp One American Rd Cleveland OH 44144

KNITTEL, DIANE LYNNE, insurance marketing executive; b. Warsaw, N.Y., Feb. 24, 1961; d. George Willard and Betty Jean (Wheeler) Sonricker; m. Philip James Knittel, June 3, 1989. BS in Microbiology, Pa. State U., 1983; Assoc. in Risk Mgmt., Ins. Inst. Am., 1993. Cert. profl. ins. woman. Agt. State Farm, Olean, N.Y., 1985; comml. marketer The Bowersox Ins. Agy., St. Louis, 1986-92, account exec., 1994—; comml. mktg. mgr. The Warren Group, Chesterfield, Mo., 1992-94; tchr. Met. St. Louis (Mo.) Ins. Assn., 1992—. Mem. Met. St. Louis Ins. Assn. (bd. dirs. 1993—, v.p. 1994-95, pres.-elect 1995, pres. 1996), Nat. Assn. Ins. Women.

KNITTER, GENE H., financial consultant; b. St. Joseph, Mich., Aug. 13, 1937; m. Elizabeth J. Johnston, Dec. 14, 1967; children: Stephen, Donald, Amy. BA, Mich. State U., 1967. Mktg. rep. IBM, 1967-92; fin. cons. Smith Barney Inc., Barrington, Ill., 1992—. Office: Smith Barney # 105 101 Lions Dr Barrington IL 60010-3147

KNOBLACH, JAMES MICHAEL, entrepreneur; b. Saint Cloud, Minn., Nov. 5, 1957; s. Marcellus Peter and Vivian Joyce (Lundgren) K.; m. Janet Helene Hughes, Sept. 3, 1988. BS in BA, St. John's U., Collegeville, Minn., 1979; MBA, Harvard U., 1981; MA in Am. Govt., Georgetown U., 1987. Lic. real estate broker, Minn. Exec. v.p. Mark's Realty/Better Homes & Gardens, St. Cloud, 1981-82; pres. Coldwell Banker, Crown Realtors, Alexandria, Minn., 1983—; div. mgr. Chem-Waste Control, subsidiary of Genetics Internat., Inc., Mpls., 1983-84; pres. Chem-Waste Control, Mpls., 1984-85; staff aide Subcom. on Intergovtl. Rels., U.S. Senate, Washington, 1986-87; dir. ops. Found. for Future Choices, Washington, 1986-87; pres. People's Mail Corp., Impact Mailing and subs., Mpls., 1987—; lectr. in field. Inventor in field. Pres. Riverview Tower Homeowners Assn., Mpls., 1987-89. Mem. Minn. Soc. CPA's, Nat. Bd. Realtors, Minn. Bd. Realtors. Republican. Mem. Christian Ch.

KNOBLOCH, IRVING WILLIAM, author, retired biology educator; b. Buffalo, Mar. 1, 1907; s. Johann Philipp and Henrietta Georgia (Linke) K.; m. Natalie Agatha Mueller, Dec. 28, 1934; children: Karen Gail, Keith Rickard, Craig Geoffrey. BA, SUNY, Buffalo, 1930, MA, 1932; PhD, Iowa State U., 1942. Wildlife specialist U.S. Dept. Interior, Red House, N.Y., 1933-37; asst. prof. biology SUNY, Buffalo, 1942-45; from asst. prof. to prof. Mich. State U., East Lansing, 1945-76; freelance writer East Lansing, 1976—. Author: Ferns etc. Chihuahua, Mexico, 1962, Prelim List Plant Coll. Mexico, 1983, Livable Planets Hard to Find, 1995; editor: Readings in Biological Science, 3 edits., 1948-75; author more than 125 articles. Grantee NSF, 1964-67, Ford Found., 1967-71, Mich. State U., 1967-69, Sigma Xi. Mem. AAUP (v.p. and pres. local), Am. Fern Soc. (nat. v.p. and pres. 1968-70), Bot. Soc. Am. (chmn. teaching sect. 1968-69), Hardy Fern Found., Nature Conservancy, Mich. Nature Assn., Am. Inst. Biol. Sci., Nat. Wildlife Fedn., Sierra Club, Mich. Bot. Club, Planned Parenthood, Zero Population Growth, Greenpeace, World Wildlife Fund, others. Republican. Home: 6104 Brookhaven Ln East Lansing MI 48823

KNODELL, ROBERT JAMES, manufacturing company executive; b. Chgo., May 28, 1932; s. Homer Edward and Mildred Jenette (Miller) K.; student Morton Jr. Coll., 1962-65; m. Jean Marie Klean, Jan. 29, 1955; children—James, Sandra, Richard. Lab. tech. Indsl. Bio-Test Labs., Northbrook, Ill., 1962-70; service sta. dealer Standard Oil of Ind., Brookfield, Ill., 1971-77; service tech. Hobart Corp., Broadview, Ill., 1977—; also freelance writer. Bd. dirs. Library Bd., Brookfield, 1977-81; Dem. precinct capt., 1965—; precinct coord., 1982-88. Mem. Chgo. Coun. on Fgn. Rels., Democrat. Presbyterian. Club: Kiwanis (past pres. Brookfield chpt.). Home: 9317 Jackson Ave Brookfield IL 60513-1225 Office: 1300 G Michael Dr Wood Dale IL 60191

KNOEPFLE, JOHN, writer; b. Cin., 1923; m. Margaret Sower, 1956; children: John, Molly, David, Christopher, James (dec.). PhB, Xavier U., 1947, MA, 1949; PhD, St. Louis U., 1967; LHD (hon.), Maryville U., 1996. Prodr., dir. Sta. WCET-TV, Cin., 1953-55; lectr. Fine Arts Divsn. Coll. of Music, Cin., 1954-55; asst. instr. Ohio State U., 1956-57; instr. East St. Louis Residence Ctr. So. Ill. U., 1957-61; honors instr. St. Louis (Mo.) H.S., 1961-62; instr. Mark Twain Summer Inst., Clayton, Mo., 1962, 63, 64; prof. Univ. Coll. Wash. U., 1963-66; asst. prof. Maryville Coll., St. Louis County, 1962-66, St. Louis U., 1966-70; asst. prof. modern lit. SUNY, Buffalo, 1969; assoc. prof. St. Louis U., 1970-72; prof. English Sangamon State U., Springfield, 1972-91, ret., 1991; cons. Ednl. Assocs. for OEO Project Upward Bound, 1966-70. Author: Rivers into Islands, 1965, Songs for Gail Guidry's Guitar, 1969, An Affair of Culture and Other Poems, 1969, After Gray Days and Other Poems, 1969, The Intricate Land, 1969, The Ten-Fifteen Community Poems, 1971, Dogs and Cats and Things Like That, 1971, Whestone: A Book of Poems, 1972, Our Street Feels Good, 1972, Deep Winter Poems, 1975, Thinking of Offerings, 1975, A Gathering of Voices, 1978, A Box of Sandalwood: Love Poems, 1979, Poems for the Hours, 1979, Selected Poems, 1985, Poems from the Sangamon, 1985, Dim Tales, 1989, Begging an Amnesty, 1994, The Chinkapin Oak; Poems 1993-95, 1995; works included in collections including Twenty Poems of Cesar Vallejo, 1961, Heartland: Poets of the Middle West, 1967, Voyages to the Inland Sea, I, 1971, Late Harvest: Poets of the Plains and Prairies, 1977, Five Missouri Poets, 1979, T'ang Dynasty Poems, 1985, Song Dynasty Poems, 1985, T'ang-Song Dynasty Poems, 1989, Illinois Fields in Summer, 1993, Inheriting the Land: Contemporary Voices from the Midwest, 1993; contbr. to profl. jours. With USN, 1943-46. Fellow Rockfeller Found., 1967, Nat. Endowment of the Arts, 1980, Ill. Arts Coun., 1986; recipient Mark Twain award for Disting. Contbns. to Midwestern Lit., Mich. State U., 1986, Ill. Author of Yr. award Ill. Assn. Tchrs. English, 1986, Springfield Areas Arts Coun., 1995, Literary Heritage award Ill. Ctr. for the Book, 1995.

KNOEPFLE, MARGARET SOWER, community organizer, educator, writer; b. Denver, Oct. 30, 1934; d. James Edmund and Agnes Howland (Close) Sower; m. John I. Knoepfle, Dec. 26, 1956; children: John M., Molly C., David E., Christopher B. BS in English, Washington U., St. Louis, 1972; MA in Comm., Sangamon State U., 1975. Assoc. editor Ill. Issues Sangamon State U., Springfield, Ill., 1975-92; part-time instr. Lincoln Land C.C., Springfield, 1984-86, Springfield Coll., 1993—. Author: (chap book of poems) Sparks from Our Hoofs, 1976; editor: After Alinsky: Community Organizing in Illinois, 1991, At the Edges of Our Comfort, 1993. Store mgr., bd. dirs. Heartland Peace Ctr., Springfield, 1993—; steward, butterfly monitor Ill. Nature Conservancy, Revis Prairie, Ill., 1993—; prodr.: (pub. access TV) Works in Progress, Springfield, 1989—. Recipient Cmty. TV award Access 4, 1995. Office: Heartland Peace Ctr YMCA 421 E Jackson Springfield IL 62701

KNOLL, ROBERT R., lawyer, county government official; b. Milw., Aug. 19, 1940; s. Edwin E. and Adeline (Barloga) K.; m. Naomi R. Bruss, Dec. 23, 1967; 1 child, Melinda J. BS, U. Wis., Milw., 1964; JD, Marquette U., 1968. Pvt. practice Milw., 1968-71; dep. register in probate County of Milw., 1971-74, register in probate, 1974—. Sec. Fire and Police Commn., Franklin, Wis., 1988-94. Mem. Wis. Bar Assn., Wis. Registers in Probate Assn. (v.p. 1989-91, chmn. legis. com. 1982—). Lutheran. Home: 8610 W Hawthorne Ln Franklin WI 53132-2508 Office: Milw County Courthouse Rm 207 901 N 9th St Milwaukee WI 53233-1425

KNOLLENBERG, JOSEPH (JOE KNOLLENBERG), congressman; b. Ill., 1934; m. Sandie Knollenberg; children: Martin, Stephen. Student, Eastern Ill. U. CLU. Agent, owner ins. co., 1960-93; mem. 103d-104th Congresses from 11th Mich. Dist., 1993—; mem. appropriations com., mem. econ. and ednl. opportunity com. Past chmn., Birmingham Cable TV Community Adv. Bd., 18th Dist. Rep. Com., Rep. Com. Oakland County, 1978-86; past pres. St. Bede's Parish Coun., Evergreen Sch. PTA (Birmingham Sch. Dist.), Bloomfield Glens Homeowner's Assn., Cranbrook Homeowner's Assn.; past coord. Southfield Ad Hoc Park and Recreation Devel. Com.; past mem. Southfield Mayor's Wage and Salary Com.; chmn. Candidate Assistance Com./State Com., Oakland County Campaign, 1978; former regional/vice chair 17th Dist. Com., 1975-77; mem. Rep. State Com; exec. com. mem. and fin. com. Rep. Com. Oakland County; founder, mem. Rep. Leadership Com. Oakland County, 1984—; mem. Allstate Ins. Co's P.A.C.; del. Rep. Nat. Conv., 1980; del. to every state convention since 1974. Named chmn. of one of the top twenty-five counties in the country by Rep. Nat. Com. Mem. Am. Soc. Chartered Life Underwriters, Detroit Assn. Life Underwriters, Oakland County Lincoln Rep. Club, Troy C. of C. (current vice chmn.). Office: US Ho Reps 1221 Longsworth House Washington DC 20515*

KNOOP, PAUL EUGENE, JR., naturalist, educator; b. Dayton, Ohio, May 28, 1934; s. Paul Eugene and Julia R. (Robinson) K.; m. Nancy Lou Wilson, May 9, 1955 (div.); children: Gregory, Jeffrey, Andrea; m. Catherine McConnell, Apr. 2, 1988. BS in Dairy Tech. and Biology, Ohio State U., 1956. Mus. naturalist Dayton (Ohio) Mus. Natural History, 1957-58; bacteriologist Beatrice Foods Co., Dayton, 1958-59; interpretive naturalist Nat. Audubon Soc., Dayton, 1959-64; dir. NAS-Aullwood Audubon Ctr., Dayton, 1964-78, edn. coord., 1978-94; environ. educator, natural areas cons., naturalist West Milton, Ohio, 1994—; cons. Indpls. Children's Mus., 1995—; leader African ecology trips Nat. Audubon Soc., N.Y.C., 1971, 75. Contbr. articles to profl. jours.; author ednl. guides; contbr. articles to newspapers and profl. jours. Treas. Environ. Edn. Inc., Dayton, 1985-95; bd. dirs., planning com. ODNR-Natural Areas and Scenic Rivers, Columbus, Ohio, 1970. Recipient Edn. award Ohio Forestry Assn., 1968, Conservation award Girl Scouts Am., 1983, Land Preservation award Nature Conservancy, 1990, Daisy Sticksel award Ohio Assn. Garden Clubs, 1991. Mem. Stillwater River Assn. (pres. 1993-95), Environ. Edn. Coun. Ohio (bd. dirs. 1975-95), Dayton Audubon Soc., Beaver Creek Wetlands Assn. (bd. dirs. 1990-95). Home and Office: 19772 Keifel Rd Laurelville OH 43135-9248

KNOP, PHILIP HENRY, finance executive; b. Detroit, Sept. 21, 1964; s. William and Irene Mary (Enderline) K. BSBA, Ctrl. Mich. U., 1986; MBA, Grand Valley State U., 1992. CPA, Mich. Auditor trainee Def. Contract Audit Agy., Grand Rapids, Mich., 1987-88, auditor, 1988-89, intermediate auditor, 1989-90, lead auditor in-charge, 1990-93; mgr. govtl. svcs. and compliance Lake Shore, Inc., Iron Mountain, Mich., 1993, mgr. finance svcs., 1993—; mem. supervisory com. Grand Rapids Credit Union, 1991-93. Mem. Am. Assn. CPAs, Mich. Assn. CPAs (treas. Upper Peninsula chpt. 1996—), Jaycees. Republican. Lutheran. Home: 800 E B St Iron Mountain MI 49801 Office: Lake Shore Inc 900 W Breitung Ave Iron Mountain MI 49801

KNORR, JOHN CHRISTIAN, entertainment agency executive, bandleader, producer; b. Crissey, Ohio, May 24, 1921; s. Reinhold Alfred and Mary (Rieth) K.; m. Jane Lucy Hammer, Aug. 10, 1922; children: Gerald William, Janice Grace Knorr Wilcox. Student Ohio No. U., 1940-41. Violin soloist with Helen O'Connell, 1934-35; reed sideman Jimmy Dorsey, Les Brown and Sonny Dunham orchs., 1939-48; mem. theater pit orchs. and club shows, Ohio, 1949-57; leader Johnny Knorr Orch, Toledo, 1958—; mgr. Centennial Terr.; owner Johnny Knorr Entertainment Agy.; bandleader, show producer; mem. Royal Ct. of Jesters #21, 1987. Recordings: Live at Franklin Park Mall, 1973, Let's Go Dancing, 1979, Encore, 1984, (TV spl.) An Era of Swing, 1973, Live at Centennial Terrace, 1986, Let's Dance, 1989. Trustee Presbyn. Ch. Served to cpl. AUS, 1944-45. Recipient outstanding dance band citations, Chgo., 1966, Des Moines, 1968, Las Vegas, 1969, Nat. Ballroom Operators Assn., Omaha, 1970, Entertainment Operators Assn., 1973; named Grand Duke of Toledo, King of the Hoboes, 1975; named to First Libbey H.S. Hall of Fame, 1994. Mem. Am. Fedn. Musicians, Am. Legion., Exch. Club, Circus Fans Am., Masons, Shriners, Ind. Order Foresters. Home and Office: 1751 Fallbrook Rd Toledo OH 43614-3251

KNOT, ALVAN PAUL, lawyer; b. Kalamazoo, Nov. 24, 1949; s. Bert and Adeline (Ruster) K.; m. Francesca E. Robles; children: Jonathan, Jason, Danielle, Andrea, Alli. BA with high distinction, U. Mich., 1973; JD cum laude, Thomas M. Cooley Law Sch., 1976. Bar: Mich. 1976, U.S. Dist. Ct. (we. dist.) Mich. 1976, U.S. Ct. Appeals (6th cir.) 1985, U.S. Supreme Ct. 1988. Assoc. Allen, Worth & Hatch, Marshall, Mich., 1977-79; asst. city atty. Lansing (Mich.) City Atty.'s Office, 1979-84, chief asst. city atty., 1984-87, city atty., 1987-93; ptnr., shareholder Alvan P. Knot, P.C., 1993—; adj. prof. law Thomas M. Cooley Law Sch., Lansing, 1979-83. Chair Mich. Controlled Substance Adv. Commn., 1990-92; mem. Jud. Evaluation Com. Ingham County, 1991—. Mem. Fed. Bar Assn., Ingham County Bar Assn. (com. chmn. 1988), Mich. Mcpl. Lawyers Assn. (mem. uniform traffic com. 1988, mcpl. liability com. 1992—), State Bar Mich. (pub. corp. coun. 1991—, charter revision commn., 1992—).

KNOWLTON, RICHARD L., food and meat processing company executive; b. 1932; m. Nancy Van Derbur. BA, U. Colo., 1954. With George A. Hormel & Co., Austin, MInn., 1948—; mgr. meat products div. and route car sales George A. Hormel & Co., Austin, Minn., 1967-69; asst. mgr. Austin plant George A. Hormel & Co., 1969; gen. mgr. George A. Hormel & Co., Austin, 1974, v.p. ops., 1974, group v.p. ops., 1975-79, pres., chief oper. officer, 1979, pres., 1981-92, CEO, 1981-95, chmn., 1981-95; also dir. Hormel Foods Corp.; chmn. bd. Hormel Found.; bd. dirs. ReliaStar Fin., Supervalu, First Bank Sys. Bd. dirs. Mayo Found. Mem. Horatio Alger Soc. (bd. dirs.). Office: Hormel Foods Corp 1 Hormel Pl Austin MN 55912

KNOX, ARTHUR LLOYD, investor; b. Perkins, Okla., May 12, 1932; s. Myrl Frank and Margaret (Grant) K.; BS, Okla. State U., 1955; m. Earlene Lois Luff, Feb. 19, 1955; children: Arthur Earl, Angela Marie (Mrs. Steve McCoy). With Lincoln (Nebr.) Steel Corp., 1957-84, exec. v.p., chief oper. officer, 1979-81, pres., 1981-84; sr. v.p. Commerce Capital Inc., 1984-90; ptnr. Reinox Devel., 1984-87; chmn. RF Investment Advisors, Inc., 1991-93; ptnr. 2LK Horse & Cattle Co., Knox Assocs., 1992; bd. dirs. Cornhusker Bank, Lincoln; adv. bd. Nebr. Dept. Econ. Devel., 1979-83; del. White House Conf. Small Bus., 1974—. Chmn., Lancaster County Young Reps., 1966-67, Nebr. Fedn. Young Reps., 1967-68, Lancaster County Rep. Com., 1972-76; asst. chmn. Nebr. Rep. Party, 1979-80; mem. Rep. Nat. Com.,

1980-84; co-chmn. Gov. Charles Thone Campaign, 1978, Gov. Kay Orr Campaign, 1986-90; mem. adv. com. Nebr. Small Bus. Adminstrn., 1986; mem. adv. com. Nebr. Econ. Devel. Commn., 1987, chmn., 1988; bd. dirs. Lower Platte South Natural Resources Dist., 1974—, chmn., 1988-89; presdl. elector for Nebr., 1976—; del. Rep. Nat. Conv., 1988; mem. Nebr. Diplomats, 1987—. With AUS, 1955-57. Recipient various Rep., Jaycee awards. Mem. Nebr. C. of C. and Industry, Lincoln C. of C. (dir. 1981-84), Rotary (bd. dirs., pres. 1993-94), Farmhouse. Presbyterian. Home: 920 Pine Tree Ln Lincoln NE 68521-4071 Office: 846 NBC Ctr Lincoln NE 68508

KNOX, CHARLES MILTON, purchasing agent, consultant; b. Tuscola, Ill., Mar. 1, 1937; s. Paul F. and Fern E. (Ewing) K.; m. Caryl A. Lossman, June 26, 1960; children: Ann E. Kendzior, Jeffrey C. BS, Ill. Wesleyan U., 1959; grad., CMI Mgmt. Inst. Cert. Purchasing Mgr. Exec. trainee Carson Pirie Scott & Co., Peoria, Ill., 1959-62; owner Knox True Value Hardware, Villa Grove, Ill., 1962-85; contract adminstr. Ill. Sec. of State, Springfield, 1985-87; sr. buyer U. Ill., Urbana, 1987—; pres. Profl. Purchasing Cons., Villa Grove, 1991—; guest lectr. Parkland C.C., 1993. Editor: University of Illinois Contract Procedures Manual, 1994; co-editor: History of Villa Grove, 1987, History of Douglas County, 1984, Illinois Secretary of State Contract Procedures, 1986; city, ch. and county hist. publs. Rep. area campaign coord. Sec. of State, 1986, state rep., 1992; committeeman Rep. Ctrl. Com., 1992, 94, 96; county chmn. Douglas County Rep. Ctrl. Com., 1994, 96; county coord. Congrl. Campaign, 1994, 96; pres. Libr. Dist., 1980-89, v.p., 1989—; bd. dirs. County Mus. With USNR, 1955-63. Recipient Outstanding Buyer of Yr. award U. Ill., 1989, 90, 92. Mem. Ill. Assn. Pub. Purchasing Ofcls. (Mgr. of Yr. 1994), Ill. Rep. County Chmns. Assn., Ill. State Hist. Soc., Douglas County Geneal. Soc. (v.p. 1984), Masons, Rotary (pres. 1963, dir. 1964, 65, 66), Alpha Kappa Psi, Tau Kappa Epsilon. Republican. Methodist. Home: 100 Hickory Dr Villa Grove IL 61956 Office: U Ill Purchasing Divsn 1321 S Oak St Champaign IL 61820-6903

KNOX, ELISABETH ANN, nurse, educator; b. Princeton, Ind., Dec. 31, 1936; d. Harry Dorsey and Mary Duncan (Fitzsimmons) Keneipp; B.S.N., Ind. U., 1958, M.S. Health Ed., 1968; M.S.N., U. Evansville, 1982; m. Lawrence J. Knox, Feb. 21, 1976; children—David L. Furr (dec.), Byron D. Furr (dec.). Staff nurse Riley Hosp., Indpls., 1958-59, VA Hosp., Indpls., 1959, Deaconess Hosp., Evansville, Ind., 1961; sch. nurse North Gibson Sch. Corp., Princeton, 1962-68; dir. assoc. degree program Olney (Ill.) Central Coll., 1968-72, assoc. dean allied health, 1985-86; project dir. nursing grant SHHS at Olney Cen. Coll., 1989-92; dir. assoc. degree nursing program U. Evansville, 1972-76, vis. asst. prof., 1982-85. Author: Ill. edit. Nursing Spectrum Disadvantaged Students and Nursing Education. Bd. dirs. Richland Meml. Hosp. Aux., 1977-79, Olney Cen. Coll. Found., 1977-81; mem. coun., bd. dirs. ministries 1st United Meth. Ch., 1978-89. Fellow Am. Sch. Health Assn.; mem. Community Adv. com. Grad. Nursing Studies Ind. State U., History Research Group So. Ill. U., Am. Nurses Assn., Ill. Nurses Assn. (awards com.), Dist. 12 Nurses Assn. (pres. 1978-80, 82, dir. 1976-78, 80-88), Nat. League Nursing (visitor for assoc. degree nursing programs 1973-76), Phi Kappa Phi, Sigma Theta Tau. Club: Richland Country. Address: 4347 E Lake Shore Cir Olney IL 62450-8932

KNOX, JAMES MARSHALL, lawyer; b. Chgo., Jan. 12, 1944; s. Edwin John and Shirley Lucille (Collett) K.; m. Janine Foster, July 18, 1964; children: Erik M., Christian S. BA, U. Ill., 1968; MA in Libr. Sci., Rosary Coll., 1973; JD, DePaul Coll. of Law, 1979. Bar: Ill. 1979, U.S. Dist. Ct. (no. dist.) Ill. 1979, U.S. Ct. Appeals (7th cir.) 1980. Head reference Northbrook (Ill.) Pub. Libr., 1973-76; asst. dir. hdqrs. Jackson (Miss.) Met. Libr. Sys., 1976-77; assoc., Fishman & Fishman, Ltd., Chgo., 1979-91; prin. Law Office James M. Knox, 1991—; gen. counsel Deerfield (Ill.) Pub. Libr., 1994—. Commr. Evanston Preservation Commn., 1991—. Mem. ABA, Ill. State Bar Assn., Ill. Trial Lawyer's Assn., Chgo. Bar Assn., U. Ill. Alumni Assn. (dir. 1986-91). Republican. Home: 1305 Lincoln St Evanston IL 60201-2334 Office: Law Offices 4000 Three 1st National Plz Chicago IL 60602

KNOX, SUSAN MARIE, paralegal; b. Crystal Lake, Ill., Oct. 7, 1941; d. Vernon J. and Hazel A. (Heimer) K. BA, Loretto Heights Coll., 1961; cert. paralegal, Roosevelt U., 1984. Legal sec. Wildman Harrold Allen & Dixon, Chgo., 1979-82; legal asst. Bishop, Callas & Wagner, Crystal Lake, 1982-84; legal sec., paralegal Karon, Morrison & Savikas, Chgo., 1984-86; legal asst. Wildman Harrold Allen & Dixon, Chgo., 1986-87; pres., owner Consider A Concierge, Crystal Lake, 1988—, Paralegal/Courier Svcs. of No. Ill., Crystal Lake, 1990—. Mem. Ill. State Bar Assn. Democrat. Roman Catholic. Home: 520 Devonshire Ln Crystal Lake IL 60014 Office: Paralegal/Courier Svc No Ill PO Box 1696 Crystal Lake IL 60039-1696

KNUCKLES, BARBARA MILLER, academic administrator; b. Hinsdale, Ill., Jan. 11, 1948; d. John Gillis and Anne Agatha (Albert) K.; m. Jeffry J. Knuckles, June 7, 1969; 1 child, James Albert. BA, U. Ill., 1970, MS, 1971. Editor ctr. for advanced computation U. Ill., Urbana, 1972-73; v.p., dir. rsch. Marsteller Inc., Chgo., 1973-78; corp. v.p. mktg. rsch. Beatrice, Chgo., 1978-86; v.p., gen. mgr. The Wirthlin Group, Chgo., 1986-88; pres. NNI, Inc., Naperville, Ill., 1988-95; dir. corp. and external rels. North Ctrl. Coll., Naperville, 1992—; bd. dirs. J.R. Short Milling Co., Chgo., Harris Bank, Naperville, Dollar Gen. Corp.; owner Naperville Nannies, Inc., 1985-95. Trustee Edward Hosp., Naperville, 1986—; elder Knox Presbyn. Ch., Naperville, 1995—; vol. Avery Coonley Sch., Downers Grove, Ill., 1988—. Named outstanding alumni U. Ill., 1986, outstanding vol. Second Harvest Food Bank, Chgo., 1986, Ill. 4-H Found., Urbana, 1988. Mem. Econ. Club Chgo., Woman's Athletic Club Chgo. (bd. dirs., com. chair), Rotary Club (Naperville). Presbyn. Office: North Cen Coll 30 N Brainard Naperville IL 60540

KNUDSON, RUTHANN, environmental consultant; b. Milw., Oct. 24, 1941; d. Sidney Olaus and Clara Ruth (Tappe) K. BA magna cum laude, U. Minn., 1963; MA, 1966; PhD, Wash. State U., 1973. Seasonal ranger Nat. Park Service, Bandelier Nat. Monument, N.Mex., 1963; instr. U. No. Colo., Greeley, 1966-68; vis. asst. prof. Wright State U., Dayton, Ohio, 1974; asst. prof. U. Idaho, Moscow, 1974-79, assoc. research prof., 1979-81; dir. cultural resource services Woodward Clyde Cons., San Francisco, 1981-86, sr. cons., v.p., 1986-88; prin. Knudson Assoc. (formerly Paleo-Designs), 1974—; cons. Am. Folklife Ctr., Washington, 1981-83, NRC, Washington, 1982, 83; resource cons. Calif. Heritage Task Force, 1983-84, Office Tech. Assessment, Washington, 1986. Author: Organizational Variability in Late Paleo-Indian Assemblages, 1983, Contemporary Cultural Resource Management, 1986; co-editor: The Public Trust and the First Americans, 1995. Bd. dirs. Preservation Action, Washington, 1980-85, 88—, Californians for Preservation Action, 1981-82; sec.-treas. Idaho NOW, 1977-78. Recipient Preservation award Nat. Conf. State Historic Preservation Officers, 1981, Conservation award Am. Soc. Conservation Archaeology, 1981; Woodward Lectr., 1985. Mem. Soc. Applied Anthropology, Am. Anthropol. Assn. (Margaret Mead award 1983), Soc. for Am. Archaeology (exec. bd. 1979-81), Soc. Am. Archaeology (exec. com. 1983-85, legis. coordinator 1979-82, chmn. com. pub. archeology 1980-82, 84-85), Women's Coun. Energy & Environ. (bd. dirs. 1994-96), Soc. Vert. Paleology, Phi Beta Kappa. Home: 347 River Rd Harrison NE 69346 Office: Agate Fossil Beds Nat Monument 301 River Rd Harrison NE 69346-2734

KNUE, PAUL FREDERICK, newspaper editor; b. Lawrenceburg, Ind., July 11, 1947; s. Paul F. and Neil (Beadel) K.; m. Elizabeth Wegner, Sept. 6, 1969; children: Amy, Katherine. BS in Journalism and English, Murray State U., 1969. Mng. editor Evansville Press, Ind., 1975-79; editor Ky. Post, Covington, 1979-83, Cin. Post., 1983—. Trustee Scripps Howard Found. Mem. Am. Soc. Newspaper Editors, AP Mng. Editors Assn., AP Soc. Ohio (trustee). Home: PO Box 30067 Cincinnati OH 45230 Office: E W Scripps Co 125 E Court St Cincinnati OH 45202-1211

KNULL, ERHARD, minister; b. Radomsko, Poland, June 25, 1929; came to U.S., 1952.; s. Richard and Martha (Kamchen) K.; m. Lydia Penno, July 21, 1956; children: Carmen Ruth Knull Bloomster, Ralph Erhard Carl. BA, Sioux Falls Coll., 1960; BD, No. Am. Bapt. Seminary, 1961; post grad., U. Tuebingen, Fed. Republic Germany, 1961-62; MA, Kent state U., 1973; MDiv, North Am. Bapt. Seminary, 1984; postgrad., Chaplain Tng. Sch., St. Louis, 1974, Samaritan Counseling Ctr., Lakewood, Ohio, 1982-83. Ordained to ministry Bapt. Ch, 1963; cert. VA chaplain, Washington. Min. Rosenfeld Bapt. Ch., Drake, N.D., 1962-65, Missionary Bapt. Ch., Parma, Ohio, 1965-69; lectr. Kent (Ohio) State U., 1965-69; staff chaplain dept. vets. affairs Cleve. Med. Ctr., Brecksville, 1970—; chaplain, counselor VA Community Outreach program, Cleve., 1978—. Contbr. articles to profl. jours. Active Parma Heights Bapt. Ch., also tchr., advisor men's fellowship. Mem. North Am. Bapt. Conf. (endorsed chaplain), North Am. Bapt. Sem. Alumni Assn. Baptist. Office: Cleve Med Ctr Dept Vets Affairs 10000 Brecksville Rd Cleveland OH 44141-3204

KNULL, RALPH ERHARD CARL, lawyer; b. Cleve., June 22, 1965; s. Erhard and Lydia (Penno) K.; m. Elizabeth Joy Klaehn, Oct. 15, 1994. BA magna cum laude, Baldwin-Wallace Coll., Berea, Ohio, 1987; MBA, Cleve. State U., 1989; JD, Ohio State U., 1991. Bar: Ohio 1992. Legal intern Greater Cleve. Regional Transit Authority, 1992; assoc. J. W. Hickey & Assocs., Inc., Columbus, Ohio, 1993; corp. counsel, human resource mgr. Ed Mullinax Ford, Inc., Amherst, Ohio, 1993—. Mem. ABA, Ohio State Bar Assn., Beta Gamma Sigma, Delta Mu Delta, Pi Sigma Alpha. Home: 5807 Charles Ave Parma OH 44129 Office: Ed Mullinax Ford Inc 8000 Leavitt Rd Amherst OH 44001

KNUTESON, MILES GENE, advertising executive; b. Wisconsin Rapids, Wis., Aug. 18, 1952; s. Kenneth Thomas and Myrtle Lucille (Knoll) K.; m. Christine Marie Coleman, Aug. 18, 1979; children: Katherine Marie, Emily Melissa. BS, U. Wis., Stevens Point, 1974. News reporter Sta. WHBY, Appleton, Wis., 1974-77; account exec. Sta. WHBY, Appleton, 1977-79; gen. sales mgr. Sta. WAPL, Appleton, 1979-80, Stas. WHBY, WAPL-FM, Appleton, 1980-81, Sta. WGEE, Green Bay, Wis., 1981-83; v.p., gen. mgr. Stas. KIOA/KDWZ-FM, Des Moines, 1983-88; v.p. sales, mktg. Midwest Communications, Inc., Des Moines, 1988-89; gen. sales mgr. Sta. WMEE/WQHK, Ft. Wayne, Ind., 1988-89, Stas. WTTS/WGCL, Bloomington, Ind., 1989-90; v.p., gen. mgr. Stas. WFHR/WGLX, Wisconsin Rapids, Wis., 1990—. Bd. dirs. United Way, Wisconsin Rapids, 1991-92, campaign chairperson, 1992, pres., 1994; chmn. adv. bd. Salvation Army, Appleton, 1981-83, mem. adv. bd., Bloomington; chmn. Distributive Edn. Adv. Bd., 1980, chmn. pub. rels. com., Des Moines, 1987. Recipient Pub. Affairs award N.W. Broadcast News Assn., 1976, Sch. Bell award Wis. Edn. Assn. Coun., 1976. Mem. Des.Moines Radio Broadcasters Assn. (v.p., sec., chmn.), Fox Cities C. of C. (amb.), Wisconsin Rapids Area C. of C. (bd. dirs. 1994—, chmn. 1996), Rotary (bd. dirs. Wisconsin Rapids chpt. 1995—). Lutheran. Home: 5411 Barberry Dr Wisconsin Rapids WI 54494-1524

KNUTSON, DAVID LEE, lawyer, state senator; b. Mpls., Nov. 24, 1959; s. Howard Arthur and Jerroldine Margo (Sundby) K.; m. Laurie Sjoquist, June 25, 1983; children: Ann Marie, Timothy David. BA, St. Olaf Coll., 1982; JD, William Mitchell Coll. Law, 1986. Bar: Minn. 1986, U.S. Dist. Ct. Minn. 1986, U.S. Ct. Appeals (8th cir.) 1987, U.S. Tax Ct. 1989. Ptnr. Knutson, Sheridan & Burns, P.L.L.P., Burnsville, Minn., 1986—; mem. Minn. Senate, 1993—. Bd. dirs. Our Saviour's Shelter for Homeless, Mpls., 1988-90, City Task Force on Arts, Burnsville, 1988, Legal Assistance Dakota County, Ltd., 1994—, Tech. Coll. Found., 1994—; bd. dirs. Minn. Valley YMCA, 1988—, chmn., 1991-93. Named one of Ten Outstanding Young Minnesotans, 1993. Mem. ABA, Minn. Bar Assn., Dakota County Bar Assn., Burnsville Jaycees (bd. dirs. 1988-90), Burnsville C. of C. (bd. dirs. 1990-92), Burnsville Rotary. Republican. Office: Knutson Sheridan & Burns 120 Midway Bank Bldg 14300 Nicollet Ct Burnsville MN 55306-4501

KNUTSON, ROGER CRAIG, marketing and sales professional, inventor; b. Omaha, Mar. 5, 1952; s. Roy Victor and Charlotte Ann (Rosa) K. B of Physics, BS in Math., U. Minn., 1975. Mgr., founder Ecumenical Coffeehouse, Omaha, 1967-69; instr. SCUBA, coach swim team City of Mpls., City of Omaha, 1969-75; qualifications test dir. aerospace divsn. Control Data Corp., Bloomington, Minn., 1974-77; regional product specialist GenRad Inc., Schaumburg, Ill., 1977-80; dist. mgr. Computervision, Indpls., 1980-91; owner, founder Computer Aided Tools and Svc., Indpls., 1991-94; sr. sales rep. MacNeal Schwendler Corp., Indpls., 1994—; chief technologist, founder Magitech Inc., Indpls., 1995, also bd. dirs. Patentee in field of environ. conservation and edn. Commr. Boy Scouts Am. Recipient Commendation for Heroism City of Mpls., 1974. Mem. MENSA, Intertel Soc. Home: 6444 Dover Rd Indianapolis IN 46220

KOBAK, ALFRED JULIAN, JR., obstetrician, gynecologist; b. Chgo., Feb. 10, 1935; s. Alfred J., and Rose B. (Baron) K.; m. Sue B. Stein, May 3, 1959; children—William, Steven, Jane, Deborah. B.S., U. Ill., 1957, M.D., 1959. Diplomate Am. Bd. Ob-Gyn. Intern Michael Reese Hosp., Chgo., 1959-60; resident Cook County Hosp., 1960-62, 64-65; practice medicine specializing in ob-gyn., Valparaiso, Ind., 1965—; mem. med. staff Porter Meml. Hosp., Valparaiso, 1965—, pres., 1981-82; asst. clin. prof. ob-gyn Ind. U.; clin. instr. ob-gyn Rush Med. Sch., Chgo.; pres. Ob-Gyn Assocs., Valparaiso, 1970—. Bd. dirs. Northwest Ind. Jewish Fedn., 1970-84, Porter County Bd. Health, 1991—. Served to capt. USAF, 1962-64. Fellow ACS, Internat. Coll. Surgeons, Am. Coll. Ob-Gyn.; mem. AMA, Am. Fertility Soc., Ind. Med. Assn., Cen. Assn. Obstetricians and Gynecologists, Porter County Med. Soc. (pres. 1979, 86), Chgo. Gynelogical Soc., Physicians Med. Alliance Ind. (bd. dirs.), Valparaiso Country Club. Republican. Contbr. articles to med. jours. Office: 1101 Glendale Blvd Valparaiso IN 46383-3724

KOBEK, KENNETH A., stockbroker; b. Chgo., Mar. 9, 1949. Stockbroker IDS Fin. Svcs., South Bend, Ind., 1978-79, Bache Holsee Stewart Shields, South Bend, 1979-85, E. F. Hutton, South Bend, 1985-91, A.G. Edwards & Sons Inc., South Bend, 1991—. Roman Catholic. Home: 1526 Sunnymede Ave South Bend IN 46615-1326 Office: AG Edwards & Sons Inc 205 W Jefferson Blvd South Bend IN 46601-1828

KOBER, ARLETTA REFSHAUGE (MRS. KAY L. KOBER), educational administrator; b. Cedar Falls, Iowa, Oct. 31, 1919; d. Edward and Mary (Jensen) Refshauge; BA, State Coll. Iowa, 1940; MA, U. No. Iowa; m. Kay Leonard Kober, Feb. 14, 1944; children: Kay Mary, Karilyn Eve. Tchr. high schs., Soldier, Iowa, 1940-41, Montezuma, Iowa, 1941-43, Waterloo, Iowa, 1943-50, 65-67, co-ordinator Office Edn. Waterloo Cmty. Schs., Waterloo, Iowa, 1967-84; head dept. co-op. career edn. West H.S., Waterloo, 1974-84. Mem. Waterloo Sch. Health Council; nominating com. YWCA, Waterloo; Black Hawk County chmn. Tb Christmas Seals; ward chmn. ARC, Waterloo; co-chmn. Citizen's Com. for Sch. Bond Issue; pres. Waterloo PTA Council, Waterloo Vis. Nursing Assn., 1956-62, 82—; pres. Kingsley Sch. PTA, 1959-60; v.p. Waterloo Women's Club, 1962-63, pres., 1963-64, trustee bd. clubhouse dirs., 1957-58; mem. Gen. Fedn. Women's Clubs, Nat. Congress Parents and Tchrs.; Presbyterial world svc. chmn. Presbyn. Women's Assn.; deacon Presbyn. Ch., 1995—; bd. dirs. Black Hawk County Republican Women, 1952-53, United Svcs. Black Hawk County, Broadway Theatre League, St. Francis Hosp. Found.; deacon Westminister Presbyn. Ch., 1995—. Mem. AAUW (v.p. Cedar Falls 1946-47), NEA, Internat. Platform Assn., LWV (dir. Waterloo 1951-52), Black Hawk County Hist. Soc. (charter), Delta Pi Epsilon (v.p. 1966-67), Delta Kappa Gamma. Club: Town (dir.) (Waterloo), P.E.O. Home: 3436 Augusta Cir Waterloo IA 50701-4608 Office: 503 W 4th St Waterloo IA 50701-1554

KOBLENTZ, ROBERT ALAN, lawyer; b. Columbus, Ohio, Aug. 20, 1946; s. Maurice Charles and Martha (Levelle) K.; m. Kathryn Anderson, Oct. 20, 1973; children: Maureen, Robert. BA, Ohio State U., 1967, JD, 1970. Bar: Ohio 1970, U.S. Dist. Ct. (so. dist.) Ohio 1971, U.S. Supreme Ct. 1992. Legal rsch. Bancroft-Whitney Co., San Francisco, 1970-71; atty. Tracy, DeLibera, Lyons & Collins, Columbus, 1971-78, DeLibera, Lyons, Koblentz & Scott, Columbus, 1978-80, Scott, Koblentz & Binau, Columbus, 1980-86; pvt. practice Columbus, 1986—. Bd. dirs. Friends of WOSU, Columbus, 1982-88, Opera Columbus, 1984-87, Upper Arlington Civic Assn., Columbus, 1988-90. Mem. ABA, Ohio State Bar Assn. (del. family law section 1979—), Ohio Acad. Trial Lawyers (chmn. family law sect. 1983), Columbus Bar Assn. (chmn. family law com. 1976-78), Franklin County Trial Lawyers (pres. 1985-86). Office: 35 E Livingston Ave Columbus OH 43215-5768

KOBUS, JOSEPH M., mechanical engineer; b. Lansing, Mich., Sept. 13, 1969. A in Drafting, Lansing C.C., 1989; BA in Mech. Engring., Farris State U., 1991. Project engr. Troy (Mich.) Design, 1991-92; design engr. Delco Electronics, Kokomo, Ind., 1992—. Mem. KC. Republican. Roman Catholic. Office: Delco Electronics 1800 E Lincoln Kokomo IN 46902

KOCH, ALBERT ACHESON, management consultant; b. Atlanta, May 16, 1942; s. Albert H. and Harriet M. (Acheson) K.; m. Bonnie Royce, June 6, 1964; children: Bradford Allen, David Albert, Robert Acheson, Donald Leonard. BS cum laude, Elizabethtown Coll., 1964. With Ernst & Young, 1964-88, nat. dir. client svcs. nat. office, Cleve., 1977-81, mng. ptnr. Detroit office, 1981-88; mng. dir. Equity Ptnrs. Am., Troy, Mich., 1988-94; mng. prin. Jay Alix and Assocs., Southfield, Mich., 1995—; bd. dirs. Numatics, Inc., Highland, Mich., Wittock Supply Co., Kingsford, Mich., 1992-94; mem. adv. com. on replacement cost implementation SEC, 1976. Bd. dirs. Detroit Med. Ctr., 1990-94, Harper-Grace Hosps., 1982-91, DMC Health Care Ctrs., 1984-94, New Detroit, 1986-87, Elizabethtown Coll., 1981-93, Met. Detroit YMCA, 1982-94, Mich. Colls. Found., 1981-96, Detroit Symphony Orch., 1983-88, Detroit Receiving Hosp. Univ. Clinic, 1988-94, Grace Hosp., 1991-92; trustee Bloomfield Hills Bd. Edn, 1992—. 1st lt. Fin. Corps, USAR, 1966-72. Recipient Educate for Svc. award Elizabethtown Coll., 1966. Fellow Life Mgmt. Inst.; mem. AICPA (Elijah Watt Sells Gold medal award 1965), Mich. Assn. CPAs. Clubs: Bloomfield Hills Country, Orchard Lake Country. Co-author: SEC Replacement Cost Requirements and Implementation Manual, 1976. Office: Jay Alix & Assocs 4000 Southfield Town Ctr Ste 500 Southfield MI 48075

KOCH, CAROLE JACKSON, human resources executive; b. Evergreen Park, Ill., Feb. 25, 1951; d. Robert Lawrence Capman and Norma Gene (Benson) C.; m. Donald Charles Jackson, Sept. 24, 1976 (dec. Mar. 1984); m. Curtis Gerard Koch, Aug. 28, 1987. BA with honors, U. Ill., Chgo., 1972. Job analyst U. Ill., Chgo., 1973-76, personnel coordinator, 1976-80, assoc. personnel dir., 1980-83; dir. human resources U. Ill. Hosp. and Clinics, Chgo., 1983—. Mem. human resources coun. Met. Chgo. Healthcare Coun., 1987—. Mem. Am. Soc. Healthcare Human Resources Adminstrn., Soc. Human Resource Mgmt. Office: U Ill Hosp 1740 W Taylor St Rm 1400 Chicago IL 60612-7232

KOCH, CHARLES DE GANAHL, oil industry executive; b. Wichita, Kans., Nov. 1, 1935; s. Fred Chase and Mary Clementine (Robinson) K. B.S. in Gen. Engring, MIT, 1957, M.S. in Mech. Engring., 1958, M.S. in Chem. Engring., 1959. Engr. Arthur D. Little, Inc., Cambridge, Mass., 1959-61; v.p. Koch Engring. Co., Inc., Wichita, 1961-63, pres., 63-71, chmn., 1967-78; pres. Koch Industries, Inc., Wichita, 1966-74, chmn., 1967—; bd. dirs. Intrust Fin. Corp. Chmn. Inst. for Humane Studies George Mason U. and Ctr. for Market Processes. Mem. Nat. Petroleum Coun., Mt. Pelerin Soc. Clubs: Wichita Country, N.Y. Athletic. Office: Koch Industries PO Box 2256 4111 E 37th St N Wichita KS 67220-2256

KOCH, CHARLES JOSEPH, banker; b. Cleve., Oct. 29, 1919; s. Charles Frank and Mary (Cunat) K.; m. Elizabeth Rusch, May 7, 1945; children: Charles John, John David. B.S., Case Inst. Tech., 1941. Dir. space div. Martin Marietta Corp., Balt., 1941-67; mgr. advanced program McDonnell Douglas Corp., St. Louis, 1967-68; chmn. bd., chief exec. officer Charter One Bank, Fed. Savs. Bank, Cleve., 1980-87; chmn. bd. dirs. Charter One Bank, FSB, Cleve., 1988-95, chmn. emeritus, 1995—; instr. Johns Hopkins U., U. Md., 1943-47; Mem. adv. com. NASA, 1956-67. Adv. bd. St. Alexis Hosp.; bd. dirs. Am. Cancer Soc. Mem. Northeastern Ohio Savs. and Loan League (Treas., past pres.); Mem. Nat. Council Savs. Instns., Ohio Savs. and Loan League (past chmn., bd. dirs.), Am. Mgmt. Assn., Greater Cleve. Growth Assn., Sigma Xi, Phi Kappa Theta, Tau Beta Pi. Clubs: Rotarian. (Cleve.), Union (Cleve.), Clevelander (Cleve.), Cleve. Athletic (Cleve.), Shaker Heights Country (Cleve.). Office: Charter One Bank 1215 Superior Ave E Cleveland OH 44114-3249

KOCH, CORY LEE, chiropractor; b. Withita, Kans., Jan. 20, 1965; s. Rick and Barbara (Church) K.; m. Gia Margaret, Mar. 17, 1990; 1 child, Chandler Dedrick. BS in Chemistry, Wichita State U., 1989; D of Chiropractic, Cleve. Chiropractic Coll., 1992. Chiropractor, owner Koch Chiropractic, Olathe, Kans., 1992—. Mem. Am. Chiropractic Assn., Kans. Chiropractic Assn. Office: Koch Chiropractic 2139 E 151st St Olathe KS 66062

KOCH, WILLIAM JOSEPH, public relations executive; b. Celina, Ohio, June 6, 1949; s. George Albert and Helen Marie (McKovich) K.; m. Susan Margaret Griffith, June 14, 1969; children: Brian William, Dana Marie. BA, U. Akron, 1974. Draftsman, Summit County Engr.'s Office, Akron, Ohio, 1968-72; pub. info. officer Ohio Dept. Transp., Ravenna, 1972-75; asst. dir. mktg. and pub. rels. Metro Regional Transit Authority, Akron, 1975-78; sr. account exec. Meeker-Mayer Agy., Akron, 1978-83; v.p. Meeker-Mayer Pub. Rels., 1983-84; exec. v.p., chief oper. officer, David A. Meeker & Assocs., Inc./Pub. Rels., 1984-87, mgr. pub. affairs Tricil, Inc., Akron, 1987-90; dir. corp. comm. Laidlaw Inc., Akron, 1990-94; dir. comm./pub. rels. Laidlaw Passenger Svcs. Group, Fairlawn, Ohio, 1994—. Co-author: No Surprises: The Crisis Comm. Management System, 1988. Mem. pub. rels. adv. com. Kent State U.; mem. pres. adv. bd. pub. rels. Carnegie Mellon U., Pitts.; comm. advisory com. Summit County Emergency Mgmt. Agy. Fellow Pub. Rels. Soc. Am.; mem. Nat. Sch. Pub. Rels. Assn., Jaycees (senator, Disting. Svc. award 1983), Akron Press Club. Democrat. Roman Catholic. Home: 3325 Bancroft Rd Akron OH 44333-3037 Office: 3250 W Market St Ste 307 Fairlawn OH 44333-3321

KOCHAN, ROBERT JOSEPH, advertising executive; b. Alton, Ill., Sept. 21, 1950; s. Joseph G. and Emma (Buttle) K.; 1 child, Emily Anne. BS in Mass Comm., So. Ill. U., 1972. Audience promotion intern Sta. KMOX-TV, St. Louis, 1971; entertainer Six Flags Over Mid-Am., Eureka, Mo., 1971, mgr. show ops., 1972-75, mgr. pub. rels. and publicity, 1975-77, mgr. pub. rels. and advt., 1977-79, mgr. advt. and promotion, 1979-84; dir. mktg. and entertainment S.S. Admiral, St. Louis, 1984-87; pres. Kochan & Co. Advt., Inc., St. Louis, 1987—. Co-chmn. VP Fair Pub. Rels., St. Louis, 1987; mem. riverfront devel. com. Downtown St. Louis, Inc., 1985-87, mktg. co-chmn., 1987; mem. riverfront devel. com. Downtown St. Louis, Inc., 1985-87, mktg. co-chmn., 1987; chmn. spl. events United Way of Greater St. Louis, 1981; bd. dirs. Found. of St. Louis Pub. Libr. Mem. St. Louis Radio Assn. (v.p. 1992, pres. 1986), The Ad Club Greater St. Louis (bd. govs. 1993—, Addy award 1989), Am. Assn. of Advt. Agencies (Mo. coun. bd.). Office: Kochan & Co Advt 800 Geyer Ave Saint Louis MO 63104-4048

KOCHER, JUANITA FAY, retired auditor; b. Falmouth, Ky., Aug. 9, 1933; d. William Birgest and Lula (Gillespie) Vickroy; m. Donald Edward Kocher, Nov. 18, 1953. Grad. high sch., Bright, Ind. Cert. internal auditor and compliance officer. Bookkeeper Mchts. Bank and Trust Co., West Harrison, Ind., 1952-56, teller, asst. cashier, 1962-87, br. mgr., 1979-87, internal auditor, 1987-96, ret., 1996; bookkeeper Progressive Bank, New Orleans, 1956-58; with proof dept. 1st Nat. Bank, Cin., Ohio, 1958-59; teller 1st Nat. Bank, Harrison, Ohio, 1959-62; bookkeeper Donald E. Kocher Constrn., Harrison, 1981—. Mem. Am. Bankers Assn., Ind. Bankers Assn. Home: 11277 Biddinger Rd Harrison OH 45030

KOCHER, KEN A., stockbroker; b. Chgo., Jan. 11, 1954. BBA, U. Iowa, 1976. Registered rep. Investors Diversified, Cedar Rapids, Iowa, 1976-77; mgr. MorAm., Cedar Rapids, 1977-84; with fin. and ins. dept. Dalle Ballstead Ford, Mt. Vernon, Iowa, 1984-85; with fin., ins. and leasing depts. 1st Avenue Chrysler-Plymouth, Cedar Rapids, 1985-87; registered rep. Berthel Fisher & Co., Cedar Rapids, 1987—. Past pres. Des Moines Jaycees. Office: Berthel Fisher & Co 5020 Council St NE Cedar Rapids IA 52402-2405

KOCO, LINDA GALE, writer; b. Chgo., Ohio, Sept. 3, 1945; d. Peter Robert and Laura Sylvia (Albert) Young; m. Gary Paul Kocolowski, Dec. 20, 1968 (div. 1987); 1 child, Charles Adam. BA with honors, Lake Forest (Ill.) Coll., 1967. Cert. secondary sch. educator, Ill. English and writing tchr. Lake Forest High Sch., 1967-68; writer, copywriter Allstate Ins. Co., Northbrook, Ill., 1969-70; staff writer Nat. Underwriter Co., Cin., 1970-73, asst. editor, 1974-78; assoc. editor Nat. Underwriter Co., Lakewood, Ohio, 1988-92, sr. editor, 1992—; pvt. practice Lakewood, 1970—; founder, coleader Cin. Poets' Workshop, 1973-78; founder, moderator Lakewood Poets Workshop, 1979-83; speaker numerous writing and bus. orgns., 1980—. Contbr. articles to numerous publs. Active Lakewood Congrl. Ch., 1984-92, chair diaconate, 1988-91; active Pilgrim Congrl. Ch., 1992—; learning ctr.

vol. Madison Sch., Lakewood, 1984-88; parent mem. young author's com. Lakewood Bd. Edn., 1987-93. Mem. Poets League Greater Cleve., NAFE, Habitat for Humanity, Phi Beta Kappa. Office: PO Box 771037 Lakewood OH 44107-0045

KODNER, MARTIN, art dealer, consultant; b. St. Louis, Nov. 25, 1934; s. Charles and Sofia K.; m. Penny Ann Worth, Oct. 6, 1957; children: Mark Charles, Jonathan Worth, David Oliver. BS, St. Louis Coll. Pharmacy, 1956. Pres., dir. Kodner Gallery of the Masters, St. Louis, 1974—; bd. dirs. Centerre Bank Ladue, St. Louis; mem. adv. bd. Boatmans Bank; expert cons. on Am. artists Oscar E. Berninghaus, Charles (Carl) Wimar. Contbr. articles to profl. jours. Mem. Jefferson Soc., Mo. Hist. Soc., St. Louis City Art Mus., Appraiser's Assn. Am., St. Louis Club, Lotos Club (N.Y.). Office: Kodner Gallery of Masters 9918 Clayton Rd Saint Louis MO 63124-1102

KOEHL, CAMILLE JOAN, accountant; b. Chgo., Nov. 9, 1943; d. Alfonse James and Genevieve V. (Riche) Daurio; children: David A., Laura L., Robert M., Karen M. BS in Acctg., De Paul U., 1976; postgrad., Roosevelt U., 1987—. CPA, Ill.; cert. fin. planner. Treas. Meritex Corp., Carpentersville, Ill., 1966-68; controller Di Com Corp., Glenview, Ill., 1968-73; v.p., treas. Ridge Road Co., Northbrook, Ill., 1982-87, Decker Gardens, Inc., Northbrook, 1979-87, S&L Engring. Co., Northbrook, 1973-87; ptnr. HJS Constrn. Co., Barrington Hills, Ill., 1979—; pres. Lé Tan Ltd., Palatine, Ill., 1984—, CJIC Enterprises Ltd., Barrington Hills, 1985—; owner Camille J. Koehl & Assoc., Barrington Hills, 1978—; pres. Koehl Constrn. and Devel. Corp., Barrington Hills, 1990—, Pressing Matters Ltd., East Dundee, Ill., 1990—. Mem. Internat. Bd. Cert. Fin. Planners, Ill. CPAs. Home and Office: 7 Bow Ln Barrington IL 60010-9618

KOEHLER, DONALD R., stockbroker; b. Cleve., Jan. 18, 1938. BSS, John Carroll U., 1960. Stockbroker, v.p. J. N. Russell, Cleve., 1960-75; 1st v.p., stockbroker McDonald & Co. Securities, Pepper Pike, Ohio, 1975—. Mem. Cleve. Jaycees, 1987-95. Corp. N.G., 1960-65. Republican. Roman Catholic. Home: 14461 E Carroll Blvd University Ht OH 44118-4666 Office: McDonald & Co Securities # 150 30050 Chagrin Blvd Pepper Pike OH 44124-5704

KOEHN, E. BRIAN, systems engineer; b. Belem, Brazil, Oct. 16, 1963. BS in Math. and Philosophy, Wheaton Coll., 1985. Systems engr. Design Resource Group, Dallas, 1986-87, Electronic Data Systems, Detroit, 1987-94; v.p. Benchmark Resources Inc., Troy, Mich., 1994—; cons. Bailey Controls, Detroit, 1994-95. Founder Kensington Cmty. Ch., Troy, 1990—. Republican. Office: Benchmark Resources Inc 888 W Big Beaver Rd Ste 610 Troy MI 48084-4737

KOEHN, WILLIAM JAMES, lawyer; b. Winterset, Iowa, Mar. 24, 1936; s. Cyril Otto and Ilene L. (Doop) K.; m. Francia C. Leeper, Sept. 6, 1958; children: Cynthia Rae, William Fredric, James Anthony. BA, U. Iowa, 1958, JD cum laude, 1963. Bar: Iowa 1963, U.S. Ct. Appeals (8th cir.) 1971, U.S. Ct. Appeals (10th cir.) 1972, U.S. Ct. Appeals (2d cir.) 1972, U.S. Ct. Appeals (5th cir.) 1977, U.S. Supreme Ct. 1971. Mem. Davis, Brown, Koehn, Shors & Roberts, P.C. (formerly Davis, Hockenberg, Wine, Brown, Koehn and Shors, P.C.), Des Moines, 1963—; prof., lectr. in U.S., Can., Europe. Bd. editors Iowa Law Rev., 1961-63; contbr. articles to profl. jours. Co-founder Big Bros.-Sisters of Greater Des Moines, 1969, pres., 1976-77; chmn. Des Moines Friendship Commn., 1970-71; bd. dirs. Greater Des Moines YMCA, 1983-90; co-chmn. Des Moines Bicentennial Commn., 1975-76; chmn. Environ. and Pub. Works Commn., Gov. Affairs Task Force, 1988-90; mem. Des Moines Chamber IMPACt com., 1990—; mem. adv. com. civil justice reform act, 1990; chmn. worldwide dispute resolution com. Lex Mundi, 1989-94, bd. dirs., 1992—. Lt. USNR, 1958-61. Mem. ABA (environ. litigation sub-com., construction com., internat. lit. environ. commn.), Iowa State Bar Assn. (environ. coun. 1989-92, litigation coun. 1992-95, proflism. com. 1994—), Polk County Bar Assn., Iowa Trial Lawyers Assn., Blackstone Inns of Ct., Order of Coif. Republican. Home: 9 Meadow Ln Cumming IA 50061-1015 Office: 666 Walnut St Ste 2500 Des Moines IA 50309

KOELLER, ROBERT MARION, lawyer; b. Quincy, Ill., Apr. 8, 1940; s. Marion Alfred and Ruth (Main) K.; m. Marlene Meyer, June 1962; children—Kristin, Katherine, Robert. A.B., MacMurray Coll., 1962; LL.B., Vanderbilt U., 1965. Bar: Ind. 1968. Asst. gen. csl. Nat. Homes Acceptance Corp., Lafayette, Ind., 1967-70; gen. csl., sec. Herff Jones Co., Indpls., 1970-74; ptnr. Warren, Snider, Koeller & Warren, Indpls., 1974-76; sole practice, Indpls., 1976—; mem. Coons, Maddox & Koeller, Indpls., 1993-96, Maddox, Koeller & Hargett, 1996—; dir. various cos. Mem. ABA, Ind. Bar Assn., Indpls. Bar Assn. Republican. Methodist. Home: 6858 Balfour Ct Indianapolis IN 46220-4305 Office: 7351 N Shadeland Sta Ste 190 Indianapolis IN 46256

KOENIG, JACK L., chemist, educator; b. Cody, Nebr., Feb. 12, 1933; s. John and Lucille (Ewart) K.; m. Jeanus Brosz, July 5, 1953; children: John, Robert, Stan, Lori. BS, Yankton Coll., 1955; MS, U. Nebr., 1957, PhD, 1959. Chemist E. I. DuPont, Wilmington, Del., 1959-63; prof. Case Western Res. U., Cleve., 1963—; program officer NSF, Washington, 1972-74. Author: Chemical Microstructure of Polymer Chains, 1982, Spectroscopy of Polymers, 1992; co-author: Physical Chemistry of Polymers, 1985, Theory of Vibrational Spectroscopy of Polymers, 1987. With U.S. Army, 1953-55. Recipient Disting. Lectr. award BASF, 1990, Internat. Rsch. award Soc. Plastics Engrs., 1991, Disting. Svc. award Cleve. Tech. Socs. Coun., 1991, Pioneer in Polymer Sci. award Polymer New Mag., 1991. Fellow Am. Physics Soc.; mem. Am. Chem. Soc., Soc. Applied Spectroscopy. Office: Case Western Res U 10900 Euclid Ave # 7202 Cleveland OH 44106-1712

KOENIG, WILLIAM JOSEPH, reporter; b. Bloomington, Ind., June 1, 1958; s. Arthur E. and Sharon R. (McCoy) K.; m. Jeanne Torbit, May 10, 1980; 1 child, Sarah E. BA, Ind. U., 1980. Reporter The Gleaner, Henderson, Ky., 1980, Daily News, Bowling Green, Ky., 1980-81, Birmingham (Ala.) Post-Herald, 1982-84, The Indpls. Star, 1984—. Recipient 1st place fo bus. writing Ind./Ill. UPI, 1989, best news story, 1985. Mem. Soc. Profl. Journalists (1st place bus. reporting, Ind., 1986), Newspaper Guild Local 70 (pres. 1992-94). Home: 7736 Gordon Way Indianapolis IN 46237 Office: The Indianapolis Star PO Box 145 Indianapolis IN 46206

KOENIGS, DEO ALOYSIUS, state representative; b. Meyer, Iowa, Jan. 30, 1935; s. Paul and Marie L. (Bissen) K.; m. Joan M. Niess, Apr. 11, 1956; children: Mark, James, Harold, Gregory, Paul, Lisa. State rep. Iowa Gen. Assembly, 1983—; farmer Mitchell County, Iowa, 1958—. With USMC, 1953-55. Democrat. Roman Catholic. Home: 39901 Foothill Ave Saint Ansgar IA 50472-9802

KOENIGSBERG, JUDITH Z. NULMAN, clinical psychologist; b. Bklyn., Apr. 21, 1951; d. Macy and Sarah (Rosenberg) Nulman; m. David I. Koenigsberg, June 18, 1972; children: Benjamin, Rachel. Grad. summa cum laude, Yeshiva U. Tchrs. Inst., New York City, 1971; BA with honors, Bklyn. Coll., 1972; MA, Northeastern Ill. U., 1980; postgrad., U. Chgo., 1980-82; MEd, Loyola U., Chgo., 1985; PhD in Psychology, Northwestern U., 1990. Lic. and reg. clin. psychologist, Ill.; Nat. Register of Health Service Providers in Psychology. Clin. specialist Charter Barclay Hosp., Chgo., 1985-86; psychology extern Luth. Gen. Hosp., Park Ridge, Ill., 1987-88; psychol. testing extern Evanston (Ill.) Hosp., 1988-89, psychology intern, 1989-90; psychology postdoctoral resident Loyola U. Chgo., 1991-92; clin. psychologist U. Chgo., 1993-94; cons. Tutors Unltd., Inc., 1995—; co-investigator rsch. project U. Chgo., 1995—. Contbr. articles to profl. jours. Recipient Outstanding Achievement award Nat. Culture Coun., 1972; scholarship award dept. modern langs. Bklyn. Coll., 1972, Kappa Delta Pi, 1972. Fellow Prescribing Psychologists' Register (cand.); mem. APA, Ill. Psychol. Assn., Chgo. Soc. for Psychotherapy Rsch., Northwestern U. Alumni Assn. Sch. Edn. and Social Policy (dir. bd. 1993-94), Early Career Preventionists Network (steering com. 1995). Office: 708 Church St Ste 243 Evanston IL 60201 also: 166 E Superior St Ste 311 Chicago IL 60611-2920 also: Tutors Unltd Inc 7366 N Lincoln Ave Ste 404 Lincolnwood IL 60646

KOENIGSMARK, JOYCE ELYN SLADEK, women's health nurse; b. Chgo., Sept. 29, 1938; d. John E. and Elsie (Volman) Sladek; m. Jerry Koenigsmark, Sept. 12, 1959; children: Jeffrey, Joy, Jocelyn, Joletta, Janine. Diploma in nursing, Presbyn. Sch Nursing, Chgo., 1959. RN, Ill.; cert. low risk nursery nurse. Co-owner Hawthorne Pharmacy and Gift Shop, Wheaton, Ill., 1967-78; staff nurse Parkway Terrace Nursing Home, Wheaton, Ill., 1977-78; staff nurse med./surg. Cen. DuPage Hosp., Winfield, Ill., 1978-80, staff and charge nurse well baby nursery, 1980-85; staff and charge nurse, advanced clinician well baby nursery, mother-baby care, spl. care nursery Edward Hosp., Naperville, Ill., 1985-94; prin. Joyce Koenigsmark, Document Examiner, 1978-84; staff nurse Alpha Christian Registry, 1995-96; prin. Joyce Koenigsmark, Master Graphoanalyst, 1978-86; staff nurse Alpha Christian Registry, Glen Ellyn, 1995-96, (Wheaton) Franciscan Sisters, Our Lady of Angels Convent, 1996—. Mem. AWHONN, Internat. Graphoanalysis Soc. (life, sec. Ill. chpt. 1980, v.p. 1981, pres. 1982, cert. Graphoanalyst 1978, Master Graphoanalyst 1983, Ill. Graphoanalyst of Yr. 1983, Pres.'s citation of merit 1983). Home: 1510 Center Ave Wheaton IL 60187-6102

KOEPKE, DONALD HERBERT, retired mechanical engineer and real estate professional; b. Milw., Sept. 19, 1923; s. Herbert Hugo and Lillie (Kirchen) K.; B.A. in Bus., Valparaiso U., 1949; B.S. in Mech. Engring., Purdue U., 1951; m. Helena Koepke; children: Debora, Andrew, Thomas. Vice pres. dealer relations Valeer Industries, Inc., Mundelein, Ill., 1974-76; dir. engring. Respiratory Care, Inc., Arlington Heights, Ill., 1976-80; pres. Sorbets, Inc., Hampshire, Ill., 1980-83; pres. Liquorland Enterprises, Inc., Elgin, Ill., 1962-84, also dir.; chief engr. Rinn, Inc., Elgin, 1984-86; with real estate sales dept. Windsor Realty, Elgin, 1988-90. Active Elgin Choral Union. Served with U.S. Army, 1943-46. Cert. mfg. engr. Mem. Soc. Automotive Engrs., Soc. Mfg. Engrs., Anvil Club, Elgin Country Club, Lions. Republican. Lutheran. Contbr. articles to profl. jours.; patentee in field. Home: 532 N Melrose Ave Elgin IL 60123-3336

KOEPKE, LONNIE DEAN, agricultural studies educator; b. Norfolk, Nebr., Apr. 25, 1956; s. Herman Otto Karl and Dorthy Ione (Knouse) K.; m. Suellen Kingsbury Sundell, June 25, 1983; children: Miranda Ellen, Marisalynn, Deann. BS, U. Nebr., 1978, MS, 1985. Vocat. agrl. instr. Norfolk Pub. Schs., 1978-80, Pierce (Nebr.) Pub. Schs., 1981-87; agrl. edn. instr. Filley (Nebr.) Consolidated Schs., 1987-89, Broken Bow (Nebr.) Pub. Schs., 1989—; adult welding instr. Mid Plains C.C., North Platte, Nebr., 1990—, S.E. C.C., Beatrice, Nebr., 1987-89. Treas. Our Savior Luth. Ch., Broken Bow, 1992. Recipient Crystal Apple C. of C., 1991. Mem. Nebr. Vocat. Assn. (pres. 1992-93), Nebr. Vocat. Agrl. Assn. (dist. v.p. 1992-93, dist. pres. 1993-95, pres.-elect 1995-96, pres. 1996—, Outstanding Young Mem. 1984), Nat. Vocat. Agrl. Tchrs. Assn., Nebr. State Ednl. Assn. (pres. of Filley 1988-89), Jaycees. Home: HC 74 Box 33D Broken Bow NE 68822-9405 Office: Broken Bow Pub Schs 323 N 7th Ave Broken Bow NE 68822-1718

KOEPPE, EUGENE CHARLES, JR., electrical engineer; b. Chgo., Sept. 15, 1955; s. Eugene Charles and Lucille (Luczak) K. BSEE, Ill. Inst. Tech., 1977, MSEE, 1984. Registered profl. engr.-in-tng., Ill. R & D engr. Teletype Corp., Skokie, Ill., 1977-85; mem. tech. staff AT&T Bell Labs., Skokie, 1985-90; mem. tech. staff AT&T Bell Labs., Naperville, Ill., 1990-96, feature engr. svc. cir. system, 1993-94; mem. tech. staff Lucent Techs. (formerly Bell Labs.), Naperville, 1996—; cert. TEMPEST engr., 1986-88. Mem. IEEE, NSPE, Am. Radio Relay League, Mensa, Tau Beta Pi. Office: Lucent Techs PO Box 3033 2000 N Naperville Rd Naperville IL 60566-7033

KOEPPEN, RAYMOND BRADLEY, lawyer; b. Valparaiso, Ind., July 9, 1954; s. Raymond Carl August and Thelma Gleda (Moore) K.; m. Debra Gail Ray, Dec. 21, 1985. BS, Ball State U., 1976; MA, Kent (Ohio) State U., 1983; JD, Valparaiso U., 1983. Bar: Ind. 1984, Fla. 1984. Assoc. Sachs & Hess, P.C., Hammond, Ind., 1984-85, Lucas Holcomb Medrea, Merrillville, Ind., 1985; city atty. City of Valparaiso, 1985-88; ptnr. Clifford, Clauden, Alexa & Koeppen, Valparaiso, 1988-90, Douglas, Alexa, Koeppen and Hurley, Valparaiso, 1991—. Mem. com. Valparaiso Popcorn Festival, 1985—; mem. Valparaiso Econ. Devel. Corp., 1986, 87; mem. Valparaiso C. of C.; bd. dirs. Boys and Girls Club of Porter County, 1986—, chmn. bd. dirs., 1995-97. Greek Ministry of Culture and Sci. scholar, 1975; Fulbright scholar U.S. Ednl. Found., 1976. Mem. ABA, Ind. State Bar Assn., Nat. Inst. Mcpl. Lawyers, Ind. Mcpl. Lawyers Assn., Porter County Bar Assn., Fla. Bar Assn., Phi Alpha Theta, Pi Gamma Mu, Beta Theta Pi. Presbyterian. Home: 2005 Beulah Vista Blvd Valparaiso IN 46383-2950 Office: Douglas Alexa et al PO Box 209 14 Indiana Ave Valparaiso IN 46383-5634

KOEPSELL, PAMELA ANN, neonatal nurse; b. Brookings, S.D., Nov. 9, 1959; d. Paul Loel and Delores Lillian (Johnson) K. Diploma, Sioux Valley Hosp., Sioux Falls, S.D., 1981; BSN, S.D. State U., 1989. Nursing case mgr. Midwestern Home Health Care Sioux Valley Hosp., Sioux Falls, 1988-91, charge nurse, 1982-87, neonatal flight nurse, 1982-93, primary nurse, 1986-93; clin. care coord., 1987—. Mem. Nat. Assn. Neonatal Nurses, S.D. Perinatal Assn., Sioux Valley Hosp. Nurses Alumni Assn. (2d v.p. 1985-86, 1st v.p. 1990-91), Sigma Theta Tau. Presbyterian. Home: 909 S Lowell Ave Sioux Falls SD 57103-2347 Office: Sioux Valley Hosp 1100 S Euclid Ave Sioux Falls SD 57105-0411

KOERTNER, CAMILLE KAY, dental hygienist; b. Agaña, Guam, Feb. 15, 1952; d. Harry Robert and Ruby (Benjamin) Ziegler; m. William Arthur Koertner, Oct. 6, 1973; children: Clark William, Alia Kristina. Degree in Dental Hygiene, Northwestern U., Chgo., 1973; BA with honors, U. Ill., Springfield, 1978. Registered dental hygienist, Ill. Pvt. practice Springfield, 1974-81; faculty Lincoln Land C.C., Springfield, 1981-82; pvt. practice Rochester, Ill., 1982—; mem. Sino-Am. Dental Exch. to People's Republic of China, 1983. Mem. Bd. of Edn., Ball-Chatham Sch. Dist. #5, Chatham, Ill., 1993—; bd. dirs. Old Capitol Art Fair, Springfield, 1994—; bd. dirs. Jr. League of Springfield, 1987-88, 91-92, exec. com., 1991-92; mem. Springfield Art Assn. Found. Recipient C.V. Mosby award Northwestern U., 1973. Mem. Springfield Area Dental Hygienists Assn. (sec.-treas. 1975-76, pres. 1977), The Book Rev. Club, Island Bay Yacht Club, PEO (chpt. treas. 1984-86, sec. 1989-90). Home: 236 Maple Grove Springfield IL 62707

KOESTER, JEFFREY ALLEN, physical therapist; b. Omaha, Sept. 28, 1960; s. Robert Allen and Marjorie Kathryn (Hertel) K.; m. Coleen Elizabeth Kelley, Oct. 6, 1990. BA in Biology, Luther Coll., Decorah, Iowa, 1982; student, U. Iowa, 1985. Cert. and lic. in phys. therapy, Iowa. Staff phys. therapist Carle Found. Hosp., Urbana, Ill., 1985-92, Lincolnland Phys. Therapy, Springfield, Ill., 1992—; guest lectr. phys. therapy program Bradley U., Peoria, Ill., 1993—. Illustrator: (anatomical drawing) Kinesiology, 1986. Named Therapist of Yr. Am. Bus. Clubs, Champaign-Urbana, 1988. Mem. Am. Phys. Therapy Assn. Republican. Office: Lincolnland Phys Therapy 911 W Jefferson Springfield IL 62702

KOESTERING, ERNEST JOHN, JR., semi-retired engineering and marketing consultant; b. Memphis, Jan. 19, 1928; s. Ernest John and Elizabeth (Zschokke) K.; m. Dolores Alberta Dinga, May 16, 1952; children: Hollis Dee, Shawn Marie. BS, Purdue U., 1947. Registered profl. engr., Mo. Safety engr. Libert Mut. Ins. Co., Chgo., 1947-50; sales engr. Gates Rubber of Denver, St. Louis, 1950-54, Granco Steel, Granite City, Ill., 1954-56; mktg. & engring. cons. St. Louis, 1956-93, arbitrator, expert witness, 1993—. Patentee in field. Chmn. human rights com. City of Kirkwood, Mo., 1968-71; dir. Lutheran Family & Childrens Svcs., St. Louis, 1970-76; bd. dirs. Concordia House, St. Louis, 1972-76; del. Nat. Conf. Christians & Jews, St. Louis, 1984. Mem. Prestressed Precast Concrete Inst. (Chgo. com. mem. 1978-85), Alpha Kappa Lambda. Republican. Methodist. Home: 1703 Marshall Rd Kirkwood MO 63122-6815

KOETTER, LEILA LYNETTE, college administrator; b. McCook, Nebr., June 12, 1963; d. Larry Wayne and Leanna Lois (Leibrandt) Hoyt; m. Darin Koetter, May 29, 1993; children: Michaela Nichole, Logan Walter. BS in Elem. Edn., U. Nebr., 1985, BS in Early Childhood, 1985; postgrad. in early childhood, U. Nebr. Lincoln at Kearney, 1987—. Asst. volleyball coach McCook (Nebr.) Community Coll., 1985-88; dir. nature camp YMCA, McCook, 1985-89; dir. nature camp child devel. ctr. McCook Community Coll., 1985-94, master tchr. child devel. ctr., 1985-90, faculty, instr., 1985—, adminstr. child devel. ctr., 1985—; adv. bd. head child devel. ctr. McCook Community Coll., 1985—; advisor, instr. Coun. for Early Childhood Profl. Recognition, Washington, 1990—; founder, coord. Cmty. Children's Fair (instr. Cmty. Discovery Week for Elementary Sch. children 1995—) 1995—. Coord. Week of Young Child, McCook; youth coach YMCA, McCook, 1987—; program coord. Sidewalk Culture Fair and Children's Fair, 1996. Mem. ASCD, Nat. Assn. Edn. Young Children, Nat. Coalition for Campus Childcare, Neb. Assn. Edn. Young Children, Nebr. Edn. Assn. Home: 306 W D St Mc Cook NE 69001-3639 Office: McCook Community Coll 1205 E 3rd St Mc Cook NE 69001-2631

KOFMEHL, KENNETH THEODORE, political science educator; b. Spokane, Wash., Jan. 31, 1920; s. Theodore August and Gladys (MacKenzie) K.; m. Jerrie Lorraine McGhee, May 22, 1985. BA in Polit. Sci., U. Idaho, 1941; MA in Polit. Sci., Columbia U., 1949, PhD in Polit. Sci., 1956. Vis. instr. U. Kans., Lawrence, 1955-56, vis. asst. prof., 1956-57; asst. prof. Purdue U., Lafayette, Ind., 1957-62; assoc. prof. Purdue U., Lafayette, 1962-67, prof. Polit. Sci., 1967-90, prof. emeritus, 1990—; cons. subcom. on Constitution, U.S. Senate Judiciary com., Washington, 1966-80, com. on Sci. and Pub. Policy, NAS, Washington, 1964, select com. on Coms., U.S. House Reps., Washington, 1973. Author: Professional Staffs of Congress, 1962, 2d rev. edit., 1969, 3rd rev. edit., 1977; contbr. articles to profl. jours. Panelist congl. debate Tippecanoe County Sta. WASK-AM, Lafayette, 1976; moderator LWV and Ind. Commn. on Humanities discussion group on Mondale-Dole debate, West Lafayette, 1976. Capt. U.S. Army, 1942-46, PTO. Named Outstanding Alumnus U. Idaho, 1991. Mem. Phi Eta Sigma, Phi Beta Kappa, Blue Key, Omicron Delta Kappa, Pi Sigma Alpha, Phi Gamma Delta. Democrat. Presbyterian.

KOFORD, STUART KEITH, electronics executive; b. North Hollywood, Calif., Oct. 25, 1953; s. Kenneth Harold and Theresa (Sutton) K.; m. Gail Anne Joerger, Dec. 28, 1985; 1 child, Michael Anne. BSME, Mich. Tech. U., 1976. Engr. Motorola, Schaumburg, Ill., 1976-77, sr. engr., 1977-79; engring. project mgr. Amphenol, Cicero, Ill., 1979-80, mgr. rsch. and devel., 1980-82; mgr. engring. Amphenol, Broadview, Ill., 1982—; pres. Koford Engring., Addison, Ill., 1982. Contbr. articles to profl. jours. Mem. IEEE (program com. Electronic Components Conf. 1979-91), Soc. Plastic Engrs., ASME, Electronic Connector Study Group (program chmn. 1982-84). Republican. Home: 1239 Cheshire Naperville IL 60540 Office: Koford Engring 445 Windy Point Dr Glendale Heights IL 60139-2196

KOGUT, KENNETH JOSEPH, consulting engineer; b. Chgo., Dec. 3, 1947; s. Joseph Henry and Estelle Theresa (Swiercz) K.; student Lewis Coll., 1966-68; BME, U. Detroit, 1971, ME, 1972, postgrad, 1972—; m. Darlene Agnes Jedlicka, June 15, 1974. Mech. engr. Fluor Pioneer Inc., Chgo., 1972-73, cons. engr., 1973-75; project mgr. Engring. Corp. Am., Chgo., 1976-77; sr. cons. pub. utilities DeLoitte, Haskins & Sells, Chgo., 1977-79; individual practice as energy and mgmt. cons., 1979—. Registered profl. engr., Ill.; cert. energy mgr. Sloan fellow, 1971-73; recipient award Pres.'s Program for Energy Efficiency, Corporate Energy Mgmt. award, 1981, Regional Energy Profl. Devel. award, 1984, Regional Energy Engr. of Yr. award, 1987, Ill. Energy award, 1988, Illiana Energy Mgmt. Exec. of Yr. award Assn. Energy Engrs. 1992, Excellence in Engring. award Am. Soc. Heating Refrigeration & Air-Conditioning Engrs. Ill. chpt., 1994. Mem. Am. Nuclear Soc., Nat., Ill. socs. profl. engrs., Assn. Energy Engrs. (pres Chgo. chpt. 1985, pres. Ill. chpt. 1990-93, regional v.p. 1993-95, dir. chpt. devel.), Environ. Engrs. and Mgrs. Inst., Demand-Side Mgmt. Soc., Exec. Hosp. Engrs. Soc. Ill., Blue Key, Tau Beta Pi, Pi Tau Sigma, Polish Nat. Alliance. Author: Energy Management for the Community Bank. Address: 5232 170th Pl Oak Forest IL 60452-4450

KOHL, DANIEL HOWARD, plant biologist; b. Cleve., July 30, 1928; s. Benjamin H. and Rose (Baskind) K.; m. Seena Ruth Bernstein, Jan. 30, 1950; children: George, Benjamin, Paul, Martha. BA, U. Calif., Berkeley, 1960; PhD, Washington U., St. Louis, 1965. From asst. to assoc. prof. plant biology Washington U., St. Louis, 1965-79, prof., 1979—. Home: 742 Trinity Ave Saint Louis MO 63130-3142 Office: Washington Univ Dept Biology Saint Louis MO 63130

KOHL, HERBERT, senator, professional sports team owner; b. Milw., Feb. 7, 1935. BA, U. Wis., 1956; MBA, Harvard U., 1956. Owner Milw. Bucks (NBA), part owner Milw. Brewers; U.S. senator from Wis., 1989—; pres. Herbert Kohl Investments; state chmn. Dem. Party, Wis., 1975-77; mem. com. on aging, Appropriations Com., Senate Dem. Steering & Coordination Com.; ranking minority mem. Jud. subcom. on Terrorism, Tech. & Govt. Info. With USAR, 1958-64. Office: US Senate 330 Hart Senate Office Bldg Washington DC 20510-4903 also: Milw Bucks Bradley Ctr 1001 N 4th St Milwaukee WI 53203-1314*

KOHL, JACQUELYN MARIE, lawyer; b. Bloomington, Ind., Nov. 29, 1950; d. George Henry and Betty Louise (Bach) K.; m. Jeffrey James Fisher, Feb. 23, 1973 (div. Apr. 1976). BA in Math., Ind. U., 1972; JD, Thomas M. Cooley Law Sch., 1981. Bar: Ind. 1981, Ill. 1981, U.S. Dist. Ct. (so. dist.) Ind. 1981, U.S. Dist. (no. dist.) Ind. 1982. Assoc. atty. Raskosky & Kohl, Hammond, Ind., 1981-85; ptnr. Raskosky & Kohl, Hammond, 1985—; hearing officer/dir. Unsafe Bldg. Program, Hammond, 1983; dep. prosecutor 31st Jud. Cir., Lake County, Hammond, 1984. Mem. Ind. State Bar Assn., Lake County Bar Assn. Democrat. Office: Raskosky & Kohl 5252 Hohman Ave Hammond IN 46320-1711

KOHLER, RUTH DEYOUNG, arts center executive; b. Chgo., Oct. 24, 1941; d. Herbert Vollrath and Ruth Miriam (DeYoung) Kohler; ed. Smith Coll., U. Hamburg (Ger.), Kunsthochschule, Hamburg, U. Wis. Instr. in fine arts U. Alta. (Can.), Calgary, 1964-66; asst. dir. John Michael Kohler Arts Center, Sheboygan, Wis., 1968-71, dir., 1972—; chmn. Wis. Arts Bd., 1974-77; mem. mus. adv. panel, crafts panel Nat. Endowment for Arts; dir., mem. Kohler Found., Inc.; mem. Wis. Am. Revolution Bicentennial Commn.; mem. Nat. Crafts Planning Bd., adv. bd. Spaces, L.A., 1990; hon. mem. coun. Nat. Coun. Edn. for Ceramic Arts; hon. mem. bd. James Renwick Alliance, Smithsonian Institution, Washington; hon. mem. Coll. Fellows of Am. Crafts Coun.; trustee, fellow Beloit Coll.; trustee Lake Forest Acad.; juror, speaker and cons. in field. Office: John Michael Kohler Arts Ctr PO Box 489 Sheboygan WI 53082-0489

KOHLMEIER, STEVEN BRUCE, insurance company professional; b. Eureka, Calif., Nov. 27, 1950; s. Waldemar Herman and Joan Carol (Kelly) K.; m. Paulette Marie Jezik, May 21, 1976; children: Stephanie Marie, Nicholas Andrew, David Christian. Student, St. Paul's Coll., 1969-71, Concordia Sr. Coll., 1971-74. Claim processor Worker Benefit Plans, St. Louis, 1974-76, benefit processor, 1976-78, benefit supr., 1978-81, benefit mgr., 1982—; dir. of music Trinity Luth. Ch., Bridgeton, Mo., 1974—. Profl. singer St. Louis Chamber Chorus, 1990—. Mem. Am. Guild Organists. Lutheran. Home: 10342 Janson Dr Dellwood MO 63136 Office: Luth Ch Mo Synod 1333 S Kirkwood Rd Saint Louis MO 63122

KOHN, KAREN JOSEPHINE, graphic and exhibition designer; b. Muskegon, Mich., Jan. 8, 1951; d. Herbert George and Catherine Elizabeth (Johnson) K.; m. Robert Joseph Duffy Jr. , July 10, 1982; children: Megan Kathleen, Sarah Evelyn. BFA, cum laude, U. Mich., 1973; MFA, Sch. Art Inst. Chgo., 1975. Free-lance designer, Chgo., 1976-77; designer Stevens Exhibits, Chgo., 1977-78; artist-in-residence Chgo. Council on Fine Arts, 1978-79; designer Chgo. Hist. Soc., 1979-81, dir. design, 81-84; prin. Karen Kohn & Assocs. Ltd., Chgo., 1985—. Work appeared in Mus. News, Kraft Gen. Foods hdqrs. Recipient Superior Achievement award for temporary exhbn. Congress of Ill. Hist. Socs. and Mus., 1985, Superior Achievement award for permanent exhbn., 1989, Cert. Excellence Strathmore Graphics Gallery, 1990, award of Merit Ill. Assn. Bus. Comm., 1993, Motorola Pinnacle award, 1994. Mem. Am. Assn. Mus. (Distinctive Merit awards 1982, 84, 85, Highest Honor awards 1982, 83, 84, 92), Nat. Assn. Mus. Exhibitors (Midwest regional rep. 1983-84), Am. Assn. Mus., Am. Ctr. Design, Am. Inst. Graphic Artists, Chgo. Women in Pub. (Individual Excellence in Design First prize 1995).

KOHN, MARY LOUISE BEATRICE, nurse; b. Yellow Springs, Ohio, Jan. 13, 1920; d. Theophilus John and Mary Katharine (Schmitkons) Gaehr; m. Howard D. Kohn, 1944; children: Marcia R., Marcia K. Epstein. AB, Coll.

Wooster, 1940; M.Nursing, Case Western Res. U., 1943. Nurse, 1943-44, Atlantic City Hosp., 1944, Thomas M. England Gen. Hosp., U.S. Army, Atlantic City, 1945-46, Peter Bent Brigham Hosp., Boston, 1947, Univ. Hosps., Cleve., 1946-48; mem. faculty Frances Payne Bolton Sch. Nursing Case Western Res. U., 1948-52; vol. nurse Blood Svc., ARC, 1952-55; office nurse, Cleve., part time 1955-94; free-lance writer. Author: (with Atkinson) Berry and Kohn's Operating Room Technique, 5th edit., 1978, 6th edit., 1986, 7th edit., 1992; asst. editor Cleve Physician Acad. Medicine, 1966-71. Bd. dirs. Aux. Acad. Medicine Cleve., 1970-72, officer, 1976; mem. Cleve. Health Mus. Aux., Am. Cancer Soc. vol.; mem. women's com. Cleve. Orch., 1970; mem. women's coun. WVIZ-TV. Mem. ANA, Ohio, Greater Cleve. Nurses Assn., alumni assns. Wooster Coll., Frances P. Bolton Sch. Nursing (pres. 1974-75), Assn. Oper. Rm. Nurses, Assn. Oper. Rm. Nurses of Greater Cleve., Antique Automobile Assn. Am., Western Res. Hist. Soc., Am. Heart Assn., Cleve. Playhouse Aux., Internat. Fund for Animal Welfare, Cleve. Animal Protective League, U.S. Humane Soc., Friends of Cleve. Ballet, Smithsonian Instn., Council World Affairs, Orange Cmty. Arts Coun., Cleve. Art Mus., Cleve. Children's Mus., Cleve. Zool. Soc., Cleve. Racquet Club, Women's City Club (Jewel award 1992). Home: 28099 Belcourt Rd Cleveland OH 44124-5615

KOHN, WALTER SAMUEL GERST, political scientist, educator; b. Lichtenfels, Germany, May 16, 1923; came to U.S., 1947; m. Rita Tevelowitz, 1955; 3 children. BS in Econs., U. London, 1947; MA in Polit. Sci., New Sch. Social Rsch., 1949, PhD of Polit. Sci., 1953. Lectr. econs., govt. Lawrence Coll., Appleton, Wis., 1952-54; asst. prof. social studies SUNY, Buffalo, 1954-56; from asst. prof. to prof. Ill. State U., Normal, 1956-86, prof. emeritus, 1986—; bd. dirs. Town of Normal Libr. Bd. Author: Governments and Politics of the German-speaking Countries, 1980, Women in National Legislatures, 1980; contbr. articles to profl. jours.

KOHNEN, NANCY STONE, museum director; b. Cin., Sept. 19, 1938; d. William Allen and Lillian Marie (Kenney) Stone; children: Allen Stone, Ralph William, Nan Marie Cahall, Daniel Hillenbrand. BS, U. Cin., 1960, Xavier U., 1982; A in Horticulture/Landscaping, Cin. Tech. Coll., 1987. Designer, salesperson Earthscapes Landscaping, Inc., Cin., 1987-89, Jones the Florist, Cin., 1989-90; dir. Cin. Fire Mus., 1990—; developer The Hogg Foundation, U. Tex.; instr. Xavier U., Coll. of Mt. St. Joseph, The Natural History Mus.; mgmt. cons. Mem. bus. migration and recruitment Hamilton County Task Force; mem. adv. bd. Vets. Meml. Hall; v.p., sec., exec. fin. com. Cath. Social Svc. of S.W. Ohio; mem. citizens adv. task force Cin. Bd. Edn., campaign chmn. United Sch. Slate; Hamilton County chmn. Title XX Task Force; vol. steering com. Project VIE; mem. future planning task force U. Cin., mem. adv. coun. for coll. cmty. svcs.; pres., cmty. affairs v.p., bd. trustees, mem. exec. com. Jr. League of Cin.; chmn., vice chmn. Zoo Arts Festival; area chmn. spl. com. The Fine Arts Fund; publicity chmn. The Charity Ball; trustee Cin. Preservation, 1994—; active The Walnut Hills Neighborhood Coun., Project Snap, The Action Squad. Mem. Nat. Assn. Jr. Leagues (pub. affairs dir.), Miami Purchase Assn. (mem. womens com.), Summit Country Day Sch. Alumni Assn. (pres.), Tri Delta Alumni Assn. (mem. house com., scholarship chmn.), Bus. and Profl. Womens Club (bd. trustees), Women's City Club (city-county rels. com.). Home: 2408 Maryland Ave Cincinnati OH 45204 Office: Cin Fire Mus 315 W Court St Cincinnati OH 45202

KOHR, ROLAND ELLSWORTH, retired hospital administrator; b. Middletown, Ohio, Dec. 22, 1931; s. Roland Meredith and Mildred (Brandeberry) K.; m. Hilda Scherz, Sept. 6, 1952; children: Linda Kohr Harper, Roland Meredith, Jeffrey Stuart. BS, U. Cin., 1954; MS in Health Adminstrn., Northwestern U., 1959. Resident and adminstrv. asst. Bethesda Hosp., Cin., 1958-60; adminstr. William S. Major Hosp., Shelbyville, Ind., 1961-66; pres. Bloomington (Ind.) Hosp., 1966-95; past chmn. bd. dirs. So. Ind. Med. Group, Inc., Bloomington Convalescent Ctr., Inc.; asst. prof., vis. lectr. Sch. Pub. and Environ. Affairs, Ind. U.; bd. dirs. Precision Healthcare, Inc., Bank One, Bloomington, VHA-Tri-State Inc., Indpls. Contbr. hosp. adminstrn. articles to profl. jours.; mem. editl. bd. Trustee mag. Past pres. United Way of Bloomington and Monroe County; mem. bd. dirs. Bloomingotn Cmty. Found., Inc. Named for disting. svc. Shelbyville C. of C., 1966, Ind. Hosp. Assn., 1987, Sagamore of the Wabash, Gov. of State of Ind.; Paul Harris fellow Rotary Internat.; hon. Ky. col. Fellow Am. Coll. Healthcare Execs.; mem. Bloomington and Monroe County C. of C. (bd. dirs.), Rotary (Bloomington chpt. pres. 1987-88, bd. dirs. Bloomington Rotary Found. 1988—), Ind. Hosp. Assn. (past chmn. bd. dirs.), Masons, Am. Hosp. Assn. (coun. on governance). Home: 2989 N Bankers Dr Bloomington IN 47408-1021 Office: Bloomington Hosp PO Box 1149 625 W 2d St Bloomington IN 47402

KOIVISTO, DON, state legislator; married. BS, Ctrl. Mich. U., 1971. State rep. Dist. 110 Mich. Ho. of Reps., 1980-86; chmn. Agrl. & Forestry Com. Mich. Ho. of Reps.; mem. Conservation, Tourism, Econ. Devel. Mich. Ho. of Reps., Mil. & Vets. Affairs Com., Mich. Ho. Reps.; senator Dist. 38 Mich. State Senate, 1990—; mem. Agriculture and Forestry, Health Policy, Joint Adminstrv. Rules & Natural Resources & Environ. coms. Mich. State Senate. Home: 735 Van Buskirk Rd Ironwood MI 49938-3140*

KOLAKOWSKI, DIANA JEAN, county commissioner; b. Detroit, Aug. 28, 1943; d. Leo and Genevieve (Bosh) Zyskowski; m. William Francis Kolakowski, Jr., Oct. 22, 1966; children: Wiliam Francis III, John. BS, U. Detroit, 1965. Lab. asst. chemistry dept. U. Detroit, 1961-65; rsch. chemist Detroit Inst. Cancer Rsch., Mich. Cancer Found., 1965-70; substitute tchr. Warren (Mich.) Consol. Schs., 1979-81; mem. Macomb County Bd. Commrs., Mt. Clemens, Mich., 1983—; vice chmn. Macomb County Bd. Commrs., Mt. Clemens, 1993-95, chmn., 1995—; dir. S.E. Mich. Transp. Authority, Detroit, 1983-85; trustee Macomb County Ret. System, Mt. Clemens, 1988-91, 92—; chmn. Macomb County Planning Commn., 1991—; del. S.E. Mich. Coun. Govts., Detroit, 1987—, vice chmn., 1995—. Contbr. articles to sci. jours. Trustee Myasthenia Gravis Found., Southfield, Mich., 1964-71; dir. Otsikita coun. Girl Scouts Am., 1995-96; mem., sec. Sterling Heights (Mich.) Bd. Zoning Appeals, 1978-83; mem. Macomb County Dem. Exec. Com., Eastpointe, 1982—, 10th and 12th Dem. Confl. Dist. Exec. Com., Warren, 1982—. GM scholar U. Detroit, 1961-65. Mem. Nat. Assn. Counties, Mich. Assn. Counties, Mich. Assn. Planning Ofcls., Am. Polish Cultural Ctr., Polish Am. Congress, Alpha Sigma Nu. Roman Catholic. Home: 33488 Breckenridge Dr Sterling Heights MI 48310-6082 Office: Office Bd Commrs Macomb Count Court Bldg 40 N Main Ave 2nd fl Mount Clemens MI 48043-5661

KOLANKO, JOHN RAYMOND, priest; b. Milw., Apr. 8, 1913; s. John and Victoria (Dentkosz) K. BA, St. Francis Sem. Ordained priest, 1940. Priest St. Joseph Ch., West Allis, SS Cyril & Methodius Ch., Milw., Blessed Sacrament Ch., Milw., Holy Family & St. Columbkille, Reeseville, St. James Ch., Franklin, Wis., 1959-80, Our Lady of Good Hope Ch., Milw., 1980—. Home: 7164 N 42d St Milwaukee WI 53209

KOLDA, THOMAS JOSEPH, non-profit organization executive; b. Chgo., Dec. 1, 1939; s. Amos Joseph and Cecilia Marie (Baxa) K.; BA, Coe Coll., 1961; MA, 1984, Ph.D. in Adminstrn. and Fin. Mgmt., Columbia Pacific U., 1986; m. Gail Judith Kettler, June 30, 1962; children: Brian Joseph, Jeffrey Thomas. Dir devel./pub. relations Mt. Mercy Coll., Cedar Rapids, Iowa, 1965-69; v.p. devel. St. Mary's Coll., Orchard Lake, Mich., 1969-71; dir. devel. Roman Catholic Diocese, Tucson, 1971-74; dir. devel./pub. relations The Pontifical Coll. Josephinum, Columbus, Ohio, 1975-77; dir. trusts and estates Ohio State U. Devel. Fund, Columbus, 1977-85; v.p. devel. Coe Coll., Cedar Rapids, Iowa, 1985-87; dir. trusts and estates Marquette U., Milw., 1987-92; pvt. practice cons. fin. and charitable gift planning 1992-95; v.p. for advancement Lambda Chi Alpha Internat. Fraternity, 1995—. Cert. fund raising exec. Mem. Nat. Soc. Fund Raising Execs. (past pres. Central Ohio chpt.), Internat. Assn. Fin. Planning (bd. dirs. 1991-95), Coun. Advancement and Support Edn., Nat. Assn. Estate Planners, Nat. Com. on Planned Giving. Office: 8741 Founders Rd Indianapolis IN 46268

KOLESON, DONALD RALPH, retired college dean, educator; b. Eldon, Mo., June 30, 1935; s. Ralph A. and Fern M. (Beanland) K.; children—Anne, David, Janet. B.S. in Edn., Central Mo. State U., 1959; M.Ed., So. Ill. U., 1973. Mem. faculty So. Ill. U., Carbondale, 1968-73; dean tech. edn. Belleville (Ill.) Area Coll., 1982-93; ret. 1993. Mem. Am. Vocat. Edn. Assn., Am. Welding Assn., Nat. Assn. Two-Year Schs. of Constrn. (pres. 1984-85). Clubs: Masons; Shriners, Jesters.

KOLICH, CYNTHIA LOUISE, emergency nurse; b. Kansas City, Mo., July 4, 1949; d. Roy Arnold and Vivian Louise (Boettcher) Stroup; m. Michael James Kolich, Jan. 15, 1977; children: Sean Michael, Aaron Russell. Diploma in nursing, Trinity Luth. Hosp Sch Nursing, Kansas City, 1972; BS, Kans. State U., 1974; BSN, Avila Coll., 1983; MSN, U Mo., Kansas City, 1992. Staff nurse ICU, Sacred Heart Hosp., Eugene, Oreg., 1972-74; staff nurse cardiothoracic ICU, U. Kans. Med. Ctr., Kansas City, 1974-76; from staff nurse to asst. head nurse surg. ICU, St. Luke's Hosp., Kansas City, Mo., 1976-77; physician asst.to cardiothoracic surgeon Kansas City, Kans., 1977-78; charge nurse office practice Old Westport Ear, Nose and Throat Group, Kansas City, Mo., 1978-80; instr. edn. dept. Olathe (Kans.) Med. Ctr., 1980-81, staff nurse ICU, 1981-85, staff nurse emergency rm., 1985-91, mgr. patient care emergency room and gastrointestinal lab., 1991—. HHS Profl. Nurse Traineeship grantee U. Mo. Kansas City Sch. Nursing, 1991-92. Mem. Emergency Nurse's Assn., Sigma Theta Tau. Republican. Methodist. Home: 15840 W 144th St Olathe KS 66062-4805

KOLKA, JULIE ANN, public relations executive; b. Appleton, Wis., Mar. 22, 1966; d. James Franklin and Patricia Kay (Stea) K. BS, Bradley U., 1988; MA, U. Wis., 1991. Sales mgr. Days Inn-Gateway, Savannah, Ga., 1988; media coord. Savannah Coll. Art and Design, 1989; acting/asst. dir. membership Wis. Union, Madison, 1990-92; pub. rels. coord. Directions Inc., Neenah, Wis., 1992—. Vol. Fox Cities Children's Mus., Appleton, 1992—; mem. Ring Dance sculpture com., 1995—. Mem. Pub. Rels. Soc. Am., Am. Assn. Mus. Home: 228 E Harris St # 1 Appleton WI 54911

KOLKEY, ERIC SAMUEL, screenwriter; b. Chgo., Sept. 30, 1960; s. Eugene Louis and Gilda P. (Cowan) K. Student, Columbia Coll., 1979-82. Booking agt. C.O.D. Club, Chgo., 1979-83; mgr. Video Plus, Chgo., 1984-90; freelance screenwriter, 1991—; lectr. Northwestern U., Evanston, Ill., 1982. Contbr. articles to film jours. Active Presdl. Trust, Washington, 1992, Nat. Rep. Senatorial Com., Washington, 1992, Rep. Party Platform Planning Com., Washington, 1992. Recipient Cert. of Recognition Rep. Nat. Com., 1991, Cert. of Award Rep. Presdl. Adv. Com., 1992. Home: 1100 N Lake Shore Dr Apt 21B Chicago IL 60611-1027

KOLKEY, GILDA P., artist; b. Chgo.; d. David and Evelyn (Jacobson) Cowan; widowed; children: Daniel, Sandor, Eric. BA in Painting, U. Ill., Champaign; postgrad., Art Inst. Chgo., 1978-79. art tchr. Highland Park (Ill.) Recreational Ctr., 1976. Group exhbns. include Art Inst., Chgo., 1949, 50, 56; contbr. paintings to Rainbow House for Battered Women, Traveler's Aid, Art Resources in Tchg., Art Encounter. Recipient award of Excellence, North Shore Art League, 1965-66, painting awards New Horizons in Painting, 1959, Scan Members Show, 1992, hon. mention Women's Club of Evanston, 1972. Mem. Arts Club Chgo., Mid.-Am. Club, Chgo. Soc. Artists. Republican. Home: 1100 N Lake Shore Dr Apt 21B Chicago IL 60611-1027

KOLLAR, KAREN L., university administrator; b. Glassport, Pa., Feb. 4, 1964; d. Milton G. and Nancy L. (Hanley) T. BA in Math. and Econs., Denison U., 1986; MBA, Pa. State U., 1988; MS in Exercise Physiology, U. Pitts., 1991. Aerobic coord., instr. Jewish Cmty. Ctr., Pitts., 1988-91; fitness intern Gen. Dynamics, San Diego, 1991-92; coord. fitness devel. Va. Tech., Blacksburg, Va., 1992-93; exercise physiologist Covenant Med. Ctr., Urbana, Ill., 1994—; asst. dir. fitness U. Ill., Champaign, 1993—; nat. collegiate alcohol awareness com. U. Ill., Champaign, 1993—, eating disorder awareness com., 1993—, first yr. impact program, 1995—. Author: Free Weights: A Reference Manual, 1991. Mem. Am. Coll. of Sports Medicine, Am. Coun. on Exercise (cert.), Aquatic Exercise Assn., Nat. Strength and Conditioning Assn., Internat. Assn. of Fitness Profls., Nat. Intramural Recreation Sport Assn. Home: 1601 DI Valley Rd Champaign IL 61820 Office: Univ Ill 170 IMPE Bldg 201 Peabody Dr Champaign IL 61820

KOLLARS, JAMES ROBERT, electronics technician; b. Madison, Nebr., Dec. 4, 1950. A in Tool and Die Design, Nebr. Vocat. Tech. Coll., Milford, 1970, A in Plastic Injection, 1974. Cert. electronics technician. Tool and die maker Air Force Weapons Lab., Albuquerque, 1986-88; electronics technician Capitol Bus. systems, Lincoln, Nebr., 1988; mgr. tool rm. Indls. Machine Specialty, Lincoln, Nebr., 1988—. Bd. elders Local Ch. Messiah Luth., 1993—. With USAF, 1970-74. Office: Indsl Machine Specialty 603 L St Lincoln NE 68508-2432

KOLLATH, DAVID MICHAEL, corporate traffic rate specialist; b. Green Bay, Wis., May 27, 1951; s. Ervin Oscar and Mathilda Ann (Boeder) K. Student, Concordia Tchrs. Coll., River Forest, Ill., 1969-71; AD in Transp., N.E. Wis. Tech. Coll., Green Bay, 1975. Supr. County Bd., Winnebago County, Wis., 1986—; pres. Advocap, Fond du Lac, Wis., 1988—, Elisha Smith Pub. Libr., Menasha, Wis., 1990—. Democrat. Lutheran. Home: 243 Edgewater Dr Menasha WI 54952

KOLLER, DON, state legislator; b. Granite City, Ill., Dec. 3, 1942. Mo. state rep. Dist. 153, 1985—; owner grocery store. Home: PO Box 135 Summersville MO 65571-0135*

KOLLER, KAREN KATHRYN, social services administrator; b. Lorain, Ohio, June 23, 1949; d. Harry Charles and Lavonne Rita (Ball) K. BA, Adrian (Mich.) Coll., 1971; MBA, Baldwin Wallace Coll., Berea, Ohio, 1977. Mgr. Harry C. Koller, Acct., Lorain, Ohio, 1974-79; sec.-treas. Credit Bur. of Lorain, Inc., 1971-79, Haytotter, Inc., 1979-80; ops. mgr. Lorain br. Credit Bur. Toledo, 1979-83; owner Karen Koller Bookkeeping, Lorain, 1979-95; ptnr. Crackabee Shelties, Lorain, 1980-95, K & K Co., Lorain, 1979-88; comptroller Neighborhood House Assn. of Lorain County, Inc., 1985-94; acct. Amethyst Inc., Columbus, 1995—. Treas. Erie Shores council Girl Scouts U.S., Lorain, 1987-93, bd. dirs., 1982-93; chmn. City of Lorain Adv. Bd. for Disabled, 1988; campaign chmn. Mem. Lorain Bus. and Profl. Women (treas. 1979-80), AAUW, Quota, Delta Mu Delta.

KOLLER, MARITA ANN, accountant; b. Chgo., June 6, 1955; d. Frank J. and Jean J. Koller. BA, Western Ill. U., 1976; MPA, Am. U., 1980; AAS, Oakton Coll., 1989. Acct. UOP, Des Plaines, Ill., 1986—; computer specialist Baxter Labs., Deerfield, Ill., 1985-86; actuarial asst. Towers, Perrin, Foster and Crosby, Chgo., 1981-85; instr. computer tech. Oakton Coll., Des Plaines, 1985—. U. Ill. scholar. Mem. Am. Mgmt. Assn., Am. Soc. Profl. and Women Execs., Nat. Soc. Pub. Accts. Home: 934 E Forest Ave Des Plaines IL 60018-1476

KOLODZIEJ, BERT KASIMIR, mechanical engineer; b. Chgo., Jan. 8, 1955. BSME, U. Ill., 1979. Registered profl. engr., Ill. Project engr. Union Spl., Huntley, Ill., 1980-84, ITW, Glenview, Ill., 1984-90, Reichel & Drews Inc., Itasca, Ill., 1990—. Mem. ASME. Republican. Roman Catholic. Home: 910 N Knight Ave Park Ridge IL 60068-2520 Office: Reichel & Drews Inc 1025 W Thorndale Ave Itasca IL 60143-1336

KOLPAK, DOUGLAS EDWARD, inventory planning supervisor; b. Chgo., Nov. 20, 1956; s. Edward Frank and Betty Lou (Funk) K.; m. Carrie Lynn Tilley, Oct. 4, 1980; children: Kyle Aaron, Kelley Marie. BA, Luther Coll., Decorah, Iowa, 1979; MS, Aurora U., 1984. Supr. quality control TRI Inc., Cary, Ill., 1979-80; supr. converter repair United Cable TV No. Ill., Carpentersville, 1980-84; inventory control planner AM Multigraphics, Mt. Prospect, Ill., 1984-86, prodn. control specialist, 1986-88, master scheduler, 1988-90, sr. buyer, 1991, supr. purchasing, 1991-92, mgr. purchasing, 1992-93, supr. inventory planning, 1993—. Trustee 1st United Meth. Ch., West Dundee, Ill., 1988-90; tenor 1st United Meth. Ch. Choir, West Dundee, Ill., 1990—; mem. planning commn. Village of East Dundee, Ill., 1993—; chmn. Greater Elgin Area Mobile Intensive Care Quality Assurance Com., 1994-95; mem. Sherman Hosp. Liason Com., 1994-95. Mem. Am. Prodn. and Inn Control Soc. (cert.). Republican. Home: 115 Barrington Ave East Dundee IL 60118 Office: AM Multigraphics 1800 W Central Rd Mount Prospect IL 60056

KOLZ, BEVERLY ANNE, publishing executive; b. Newark, Ohio, Dec. 25, 1946; d. Willard Joseph and Lydia Marie (Gaze) K. BA, Ohio Dominican Coll., 1968; MBA, U. Iowa, 1991. Prodn. editor Merrill Pub., Columbus, Ohio, 1968-69; series editor Merrill Pub., Columbus, 1969-75, media buyer, 1975-76, prodn. buyer, 1976-78, mng. editor, 1978-80, adminstrv. editor, 1980-85, exec. editor, 1985-86; v.p., dir. of ops. and prodn. William C. Brown Pub. Co., Dubuque, Iowa, 1986-91; corp. v.p. ops. William C. Brown Comm., Inc., Dubuque, 1991-92; exec. v.p., gen. mgr. William C. Brown Pubs., Dubuque, 1992-94, CEO, pres., 1995—. V.p. Altrusa, Columbus, 1985-86. Mem. Am. Ednl. Rsch. Assn., Women in Comm. (pres. 1979-80, 92-93), Chgo. Women in Pub. (Pub. Woman of Yr. 1993), Am. Assn. Pubs. (exec. coun. higher edn. divsn. 1992—), Nat. Assn. Coll. Stores (bd. trustees 1994-95), Dubuque Area C. of C. Office: William C Brown Pub Co 2460 Kerper Blvd Dubuque IA 52001-2224

KOMAR, JERRY J., management consulting executive; b. Nowy Sacz, Poland, Mar. 7, 1948; s. Joseph V. and Cecylia Komar. BA in Sociology, Alliance Coll., 1970; MEd, Edinboro U., 1974; postgrad., Calif. Coast U. Dean students Alliance Coll., Camb Springs, Pa.; program mgr. Temple U., Phila.; area exec. dir. Voca Corp., Dayton, Ohio; exec. dir. Cmty. Sys. Inc., Newark, Residential Horizons, Girard, Ohio; pres. TQM Cons., Boardman, Ohio; trustee N.E. Ohio Tng. Network, Girard, Ohio Pvt. Residential Assn., Girard. Author: 7 Steps to TQM, 1994, Total Quality Training Systems, 1994; pub., editor (newsletter) Total Quality News, 1995. Mem. Assn. for Retarded Citizens, Girard, 1987-88, Am. Assn. Mentally Retarded, Girard, 1987-94. Airman USAF, 1970-72. Mem. Internat. Exec. Svc. Corps, Internat. Freelance Photographers Orgn., Pi Gamma Mu, Lamda Alpha. Home and Office: 7059 W Blvd #237 Boardman OH 44512

KOMEN, LEONARD, lawyer; b. St. Louis, May 31, 1943; s. Meyer and Yetta (Ellman) K.; m. Sandra Gail Cytron, June 8, 1969; children: Douglas Steven, Matthew Todd. BA, U. Mo., 1965, JD, 1970. Bar: Mo. 1970, U.S. Dist. Ct. (ea. dist.) Mo. 1971, U.S. Supreme Ct. 1973, U.S. Dist. Ct. (we. dist.) Mo. 1980, U.S. Ct. Appeals (8th cir.), 1985, U.S. Claims Ct. 1992, U.S. Ct. Appeals (3d cir.) 1995. Assoc. Susman, Willer & Rimmel, St. Louis, 1970-74; assoc. Susman Schermer Rimmel & Parker, St. Louis, 1974-77, ptnr., 1977-80; prin., v.p. Selner, Glaser, Komen, Berger & Galganski, P.C., St. Louis, 1980—; ct.-apptd. trustee, examiner, receiver U.S. Bankruptcy Ct., 1988—. bd. dirs. Zeta Beta Tau Frat. Inc., 1984—, nat. sec., 1989-90, nat. v.p., 1990-92, nat. pres., 1992-94; mem. supervisory bd. Nat. Interfraternity Coun. Legal Advocacy Fund, 1993—. Pres. Creve Coeur Hockey Club Inc., St. Louis, 1987-88, bd. dirs., 1989-93; coord. Parkway North Hockey Club, 1989-91; pres., bd. dirs. Roswell Messing Ednl. Found., 1989—; bd. dirs. Zeta Beta Tau Centennial Found. 1990—. Recipient Merit citation Zeta Beta Tau Frat., Inc., 1977, 91, 92. Mem. ATLA, Comml. Law League Am., Met. St. Louis Bar Assn., Lawyers Assn. Jewish. Home: 14385 Stablestone Ct Chesterfield MO 63017-2502 Office: Selner Glaser Komen Berger & Galganski PC 700 Bonhomme Ave Ste 700 Saint Louis MO 63105-1924

KOMINEK, LEO ALOYSIUS, retired microbiologist, psychologist; b. Chgo., Apr. 11, 1937; s. Leo Anton and Sylvia Helen (Klarkowski) K.; m. Anita Joan Mars, Sept. 5, 1959; children: Stephen, Laura, Mary, Leo. BS, St. Joseph's Coll., 1959; PhD, U. Ill., 1964; MA, Western Mich. U., 1995. Rsch. scientist Upjohn, Kalamazoo, Mich., 1964-70, sr. rsch. scientist, 1970-73, sr. scientist, 1973-78, 79-96, ret., 1996; psychologist Borgess Behavioral Medicine, Kalamazoo, Mich., 1996—. Contbr. articles to profl. jours., including Antimicrobial Agents and Chemotherapy, Biochem. Biophys. Acta, Ann. N.Y. Acad. Sci. Fellow Am. Acad. Microbiology, Sigma Xi; mem. Am. Soc. Microbiology, N.Y. Acad. Scis., Am. Chem. Soc. Roman Catholic. Home: 2209 Hickory Point Dr Kalamazoo MI 49024 Office: Borgess Behavioral Medicine Delano Outpatient Clinic 1722 Shaffer St Kalamazoo MI 49001-1643

KOMMEDAHL, THOR, plant pathology educator; b. Mpls., Apr. 1, 1920; s. Thorbjorn and Martha (Blegen) K.; m. Faye Lillian Jensen, June 2, 1924; children: Kris Alan, Siri Lynn, Lori Anne. B.S., U. Minn., 1945, M.S., 1947, Ph.D., 1951. Instr. U. Minn., St. Paul, 1946-51, asst. prof. plant pathology, 1953-57, assoc. prof., 1957-63, prof., 1963-90, prof. emeritus, 1990—; asst. prof. plant pathology Ohio Agrl. Research and Devel. Ctr., Wooster, 1951-53, Ohio State U., Columbus, 1951-53; prof. continuing edn. and extension U. Minn., St. Paul, 1990—; cons. botanist and taxonomist Minn. Dept. Agr., 1954-60, Sci. Mus. Minn., 1990—; 7th A.W. Dimock lectr. Cornell U., 1979. Author: Pesky Plants, 1989; co-author: Scientific Style and Format, 1994; editor Minn. Fulbright newsletter, 1993—, Procs. IX Internat. Congress Plant Protection, 2 vols., 1981, Corn Disease newsletter, 1970-76; assoc. editor The Boghopper, 1996—; cons. editor McGraw Hill Ency. Sci. and Tech., 1972-78; editor-in-chief Phytopathology, 1964-67; sr. editor: Challenging Problems in Plant Health, 1982, Plant Disease Reporter, 1979; contbr. articles to profl. jours. Recipient Elvin Charles Stakman award, 1990, Award of Merit, Gamma Sigma Delta, 1994; Guggenheim fellow, 1961, Fulbright scholar, 1968. Fellow AAAS, Am. Phytopathol. Soc. (councilor 1958-60, pres. 1971, publs. coord. 1978-84, Disting. Svc. award 1984, 93, sci. adv. 1984—, mem. adv. bd. office internat. programs 1987-93); mem. Am. Inst. Biol. Scis., Bot. Soc. Am., Coun. Biology Editors, Internat. Soc. Plant Pathology (councilor 1971-78, sec.-gen. and treas. 1983-88, treas. 1988-93, editor newsletter 1983-93), Mycol. Soc. Am., Minn. Acad. Sci., N.Y. Acad. Scis., Weed Sci. Soc. Am. (award of excellence 1968), Fulbright Assn. (Minn. chpt., editor newsletter 1995—). Baptist. Home: 1666 Coffman St Apt 322 Saint Paul MN 55108-1340 Office: U Minn 496 Borlaug Hall 1991 Upper Buford Cir Saint Paul MN 55108-6030

KONA, MARTHA MISTINA, librarian, freelance information consultant; b. Banovce, Slovakia; came to U.S., 1950; d. Albert and Anna (Kubrican) Mistina; m. William Kona, Aug. 6, 1955 (dec. Dec. 1989); children: Olivia, Lindy Anne; m. William P. Mihalovic, Apr. 30, 1992. Student, U. Salzburg, 1950; BA, Rosary Coll., 1953, MA, 1958; postgrad., Roosevelt U., 1980. Libr. instr., prof. Univ. Ill., Chgo., 1958-63; rsch. libr. Cen. Soya Chemurgy, Chgo., 1965-73; asst. dir. Rush Univ. Libr., Chgo., 1973-78; pvt. practice cons., info. specialist Wilmette, Ill., 1980; pvt. practice author and lectr. Wilmette, 1985—; cons., liaison Matica Slovenska, Slovak Nat. Libr. and Archives, Martin, Slovak Republic, 1990—. Author: Soybean Proteins, 1969, Multi Media Catalog, 1975, Health Science Librarians of Illinois, 1977, Slovak Americans and Canadians, 1985; co-author, editor: Archbishop Dr. Karol Kmetko, 1989, PhD Dissertations in Slovakiana in the Western World: Bibliography, 1996; contbr. articles to profl. jours. Bd. dirs. Slovak Am. Found. Edn. and Sci., Inc., 1994. Mem. AAUW, AAUP (chair bylaws com. 1975-77), Health Sci. Librs. Ill. (co-founder, archivist 1970-77), Slovak World Congress (chair heritage commn. 1990—), First Slovek League of Am., Slovak Cath. Falcon, Ill. Audio Visual Assn. (pres. 1975-77), Slovak Inst. (Rome), Sovereign and Mil. Order of Temple Jerusalem (bd. dirs. 1974—), Imperial Order of Constantine the Great and St. Helen (bd. dirs. 1977—), Dames of the Order in the U.S.A. (Lady Comdr.), Order St. John Jerusalem, Woman's Club Wilmette Philanthropy (chair 1991-93), Pi Gamma Mu. Home: 600 Third St Wilmette IL 60091-1921

KONDAS, SHAWN JAMES, design engineer; b. Hicksville, Ohio, Aug. 23, 1961. Student, Four County Joint Vo-Tech. Sch, 1980-81. Assoc. design engr. Pent Assemblies, Kendallville, Ind., 1983—. Contbr. articles to profl. jours.; patentee in field. Pentecostal. Office: Pent Assemblies PO Box 246 Kendallville IN 46755-0246

KONIECZNY, SHARON LOUISE, insurance company executive; b. Madison, Minn., July 2, 1952; d. Frank H. and Elenore A. (Mikkelson) K. Student, Dakota Wesleyan U., 1970-71, U. Minn., 1971-72. CLU. Sales rep. Advance Schs., Bloomington, Minn., 1972; sales agt. ITT Life Ins., Mpls., 1973-75, mktg. auditor, 1975-76, supr. new bus., 1976-79, mgr. UND Issue, 1979-81, asst. v.p. new bus., 1981-83, asst. v.p.sales support, 1983-87, v.p., sales mktg., 1987-94; nat. dir. new bus. devel. UND Issue, 1994-95; v.p. mktg. Minn. Chamber Bus. Svcs., St. Paul, 1995—. Mem. United Way, Mpls. (vice chmn. 1984-85, chmn. 1985). Mem. Nat. Assn. Life Underwriters (gen. agt. mgmt. conf.), Nat. Assn. Health Underwriters, Am. Mktg. Assn., Nat. Assn. Ins. Women, Soc. Ins. Trainers and Educators, Internat. Assn. Fin. Planners. Democrat. Lutheran. Home: 12610 50th Ave N Minneapolis MN 55442-2060

KONIG, KENNETH WILLIAM, insurance agent; b. Milw., Jan. 11, 1969; s. Russell Elmer and Judith Frances (Gleisner) K. BA in Fin., Marquette

U., 1991. CLU, charterd fin. cons., fraternal ins. counselor. Newspaper carrier, night mgr. The Milw. Sentinel, 1982-91; ins. agt. Aid Assn. for Lutherans, Waukesha, Wis., 1991—, ins. mgr., 1994—; mem. adv. bd. AAL-Cy Pick Agy., Elm Grove, Wis., 1993. Mem. Fraternal Ins. Counselors, Am. Soc. CLU, Nat. Assn. Life Underwriters, Wis. Fedn. Life Underwriters, Gen. Agts. and Mgrs. ASsn. Republican. Lutheran. Office: 1510 David Ct # 2 Waukesha WI 53186

KONO, JEAN E., nursing educator; b. Marshalltown, Iowa, Oct. 20, 1941; d. Harold and Helen I. (Melton) Bailey; m. Frederick L. Kono, June 8, 1963; children: Matthew D., Kristine H. Diploma, Mercy Hosp., 1962; BSN, Mary Crest Coll., 1977; postgrad., U. Iowa, Coll. nursing. Head nurse, mental health St.Luke's Hosp., Cedar Rapids, Iowa; child therapist Vera French Mental Health Ctr., Davenport, Iowa; nurse mgr., mental health Mercy Hosp., Davenport, Iowa; clin. instr. Eastern Iowa Coll., Bettendorf, Iowa. Mem. APNA, Iowa Nurses Assn. (bd. dirs., dist. 6 pres.).

KONSIS, KENNETH FRANK, forester, educator; b. Danville, Ill., Dec. 3, 1952; s. Frank John and Regina Ann (Stefaniak) K.; m. Lorna Jean Wiesemann, May 6, 1978. AS, Danville Area Community Coll., 1972; BS in Forestry, So. Ill. U., 1974. Park ranger Vermilion County Conservation Dist., Danville, 1974-84, dist. forester, 1984-87, rsch. forester, instr. in outdoor edn., 1987-91, dep. dir., 1991-92, exec. dir., 1992—; state del. Ill. Conservation Congress, 1993, 94, 97, mem. tech. adv. com., 1994. Mem. Little Vermillion Drainage Dist., Georgetown, Ill., 1990—; chmn. VOTEC Agr. and Horticulture Adv. Com.; mem. citizen's adv. com. Dept. Natural Resources and Environ. Scis., U. Ill., 1993. Mem. Ill. Native Plant Soc. (pres. 1986-93, exec. com. 1986—), Nat. Walnut Coun. Ill. Woodland Owners and Users Assn., Ill. Lake Mgmt. Assn. (charter), Am. Chestnut Soc., Soc. Am. Foresters (edn. com. 1989—), Ill. Walnut Coun. (v.p. 1991-92, pres. 1992-93, regional bd. dirs. 1989-92, treas. 1994-96), Ill. Tree Farm Com., Shitake Growers' Assn. Wis., Am. Forestry Assn., Interstate 74 Corridor Planning Com., Ill. Assn. Conservation Dists. (v.p. 1995-96, 96-97). Roman Catholic. Home: 234 S Walnut St Westville IL 61883-1664 Office: Vermilion Co Conserv Dist Conservation Dist 22296-A Henning Rd Danville IL 61834

KONTOS-ROBERTS, NITA RAE, finance specialist; b. Bismarck, N.D., Feb. 13, 1939; d. Sam John and Adele (Volk) Kontos; divorced; 1 child. Restaurant mgr. Dutch Mill Family, Minot, N.D., 1958-75; office mgr. C. of C., Minot, 1958-68; real estate sec. Ask Inc., Minot, 1978-80; fin. mgr. Fisher Mtrs., Minot, 1982—. Creator: Adopt a Nun program, 1993, Glorious Grape Getaway, 1995. Bd. dirs. Sacred Heart Monastery, Richardton, N.D., N.D. Diabetes Assn., Minot. Mem. Rotary. Roman Catholic. Home: 1301 11 1/2 Ave SW Minot ND 58701 Office: Fisher Mtrs Minot ND 58701

KOOISTRA, WILLIAM HENRY, clinical psychologist; b. Grand Rapids, Mich., May 20, 1936; s. Henry P. and Marguerite (Brinks) K.; m. Jean Heynen, Aug. 24, 1957 (div. Dec. 1984); children: Kimberly Lynn, William Peter, Kristin Jean, Allison Carol; m. Carol Sue Smitter, Mar. 9, 1985. BA, Calvin Coll., 1957; PhD, Wayne (Mich.) State U., 1963. Diplomate Am. Bd. Profl. Psychology. Intern psychology Lafayette Clinic, Detroit, 1961-62; chief psychologist Pine Rest Christian Hosp., Grand Rapids, Mich., 1964-67; clin. psychologist Kooistra, Jansma, Elders, Teitsma & DiNallo, Grand Rapids, 1967—; instr. Wayne State U., 1959-63, Hope Coll., Holland, Mich., 1964, Calvin Coll., Grand Rapids, 1964-81, Grand Valley State U., 1987-92. Founder Project Rehab., Grand Rapids, 1968, bd. dirs., 1969—, pres., 1972-74; mem. Kent County Dem. Exec. Com., 1969-73, 79-82, 86—, mem. governing bd. Fountain Street Ch., 1989-95, pres. 1994; rep. 3d dist. Presl. Electoral Coll., 1992. Mem. Am. Psychol. Assn. (council rep. 1982-85), Am. Soc. Psychologists in Pvt. Practice (sec. 1973-75), Mich. Psychol. Assn.(pres. 1979), Mich. Soc. Forensic Psychology, Grand Rapids Area Psychol. Assn (pres. 1968). Home: 2946 Cascade Rd SE Grand Rapids MI 49506-1965 Office: 3330 Claystone St SE Grand Rapids MI 49546-7716

KOONS, SHIRLEY ANN, dietitian; b. Ft. LeonardWood, Mo., Nov. 19, 1950; d. Hulin Ellis and Pauline Laverne (Prickett) Kelly; m. Lawrence Wayne Coy, Dec. 29, 1971 (div. Feb., 1990); children: Michael, James, Jason Wayne; m. David Mark Koons, Apr. 27, 1991. BS in voc. home econ. edn., Okla. State U., 1973; MS in nutrition & food mgmt., Cen. State U., 1985. Voc. home econ. tchr. Mid-Del Sch. System, Midwest City, Okla., 1973-74, sub. tchr., 1974-80; admitting clerk Midwest City Hosp., Midwest City, Okla., 1980-86; diet technician Presbyn. Hosp., Oklahoma City, Okla., 1986-88; dietitian Bone & Joint Hosp., Oklahoma City, Okla., 1988-90; dietary svc. mgr. Camellia Care Ctr., Aurora, Colo., 1990-91; dietitian cons. Beverly Enterprise, Seattle, 1991-94; food production mgr. Beverly Enterprise, Omaha, Neb., 1994—; cons. dietitian in healthcare practice group. Den leader, cubmaster Boy Scouts Am., 1983-95. Mem. Am. Dietetic Assn., Nebr. Dietetic Assn. Democrat. Home: 9627 Walnut St Omaha NE 68124-1157 Office: 300 W Meigs Valley NE 68064

KOONS, SUSAN ANN, school guidance counselor; b. Des Moines, Apr. 4, 1949; d. George Edward and Hazel Olive (Boswell) K.; m. Norman Lee Halverson, Sept. 17, 1988; 1 child, Gabriel Lee Halverson. BA, U. Iowa, 1971, MA, 1972; MEd, Drake U., 1984. Cert. permanent profl. tchr., Iowa. Asst. cataloguer law libr. Drake U., Des Moines, 1972-74; media specialist Heartland Area Edn. Agy., Ankeny, Iowa, 1974-75, Hillside Jr. High Sch., West Des Moines, Iowa, 1975-77, Stillwell Jr. High Sch., West Des Moines, 1977-84; guidance counselor Watrous Elem. Sch., Des Moines, 1984-88, Park Ave. Elem. Sch., Des Moines, 1984-88, Merrill Mid. Sch., Des Moines, 1988—; cons. stress mgmt., ind. and family counseling Holdsworth, Inc., Des Moines, 1991—. Mem. Beyond War, Des Moines, 1984-86. Mem. NEA, Iowa State Edn. Assn., Iowa Counseling Assn., Des Moines Edn. Assn., Sierra Club (bd. dirs. Des Moines chpt. 1985-87). Democrat. Methodist. Home: 15 SW 42nd St Des Moines IA 50312-3043 Office: Merrill Mid Sch 5301 Grand Ave Des Moines IA 50312-2123

KOONTZ, EVA ISABELLE, medical technologist; b. Jetmore, Kans., Feb. 3, 1935; d. Vernon Ward and Lillian Mae (Bell) K. BS in Natural Scis., Sterling (Kans.) Coll., 1957; cert. in med. tech., U. Kans. Med. Ctr., 1958. Office technologist Group Practice, Mission, Kans., 1958-60; chemistry supr. Bethany Hosp., Kansas City, Kans., 1960-64; rsch. asst. pediatric hematology and metabolic rsch. U. Kans. Med. Ctr., Kansas City, Kans., 1964-72, R&D Tech., Providence-St. Margaret's Health Care Ctr., Kansas City, Kans., 1972-74; staff technologist St. Lukes Hosp., Kansas City, Mo., 1974-79; clin. lab. mgr. and supr. Quincy Rsch. Ctr., Kansas City, Mo., 1979-80; staff technologist Lakeside Hosp., Kansas City, Mo., 1980-82; med. technologist supr. Midwest Rsch. Inst., Kansas City, Mo., 1982-88; cert. toxicology scientist Clin. Reference Labs., Inc., Lenexa, Kans., 1988—. Mem. Am. Soc. for Med. Tech., Am. Assn. for Clin. Chemistry, Mo. Soc. Med. Technologists. Republican. Presbyterian. Home: 10251 Cedarbrooke Ln Kansas City MO 64131-4209 Office: Clin Reference Labs Inc 8433 Quivira Rd Lenexa KS 66215

KOOTSEY, JOSEPH MAILEN, physiology and computer science educator, administrator; b. Houston, Tex., Sept. 3, 1939; s. Joseph Steven and Esther Irene (Johnson) K.; m. Lynne Diane Wiles, Aug. 20, 1961; children: Brenden Lamont, Sean Alexander. BA in Physics, Pacific Union Coll., 1960; ScM in Physics, Brown U., 1964, PhD in Physics, 1966. Instr. Loma Linda (Calif.) U., 1965-67, asst. prof., 1967-69; postdoctoral fellow Duke U., Durham, N.C., 1969-71, asst. prof., 1971-76, research assoc. prof., 1979-84, assoc. prof., 1984-91; prof. Andrews U., Berrien Springs, Mich., 1976-79, 91—, dean arts and scis., 1991-94, v.p. acad. adminstrn., 1994—; cons. Albert L. Chaney Med. Lab., Glendale, Calif., 1966-69, Jones Med. Instrument Co., Oak Brook, Ill., 1967-71, Am. Edwards Labs., Santa Ana, Calif., 1980-83; dir. Nat. Biomed. Simulation Resource, Durham, 1983-91; pres. Simulation Resources Inc., Berrien Springs. Assoc. editor: Simulation Jour., 1985—; reviewer 9 sci. jours.; contbr. chpts. to books and articles to profl. jours.; achievements include development of general purpose software for simulation of biomedical systems; research in advances in the theory of ion transport and regulation in heart muscle cells. Postdoctoral fellow Bank Am., 1965-67; NIH grantee, 1980-90. Mem. AAAS, IEEE, Am. Assn. Higher Edn., Am. Assn. Physics Tchrs., Am. Phys. Soc., Assn. for Computing Machinery, Biophys. Soc., Cardiac Muscle Soc., Engring. in Medicine and Biology Soc., N.Y. Acad. Scis., Soc. Computer Simulation (v.p. SE region 1986-88, 91-92), Soc. Math. Biology, Sigma Xi. Democrat. Adventist. Home: 500 Laurel Dr Niles MI 49120-2914 Office: Andrews U Academic Administration Berrien Springs MI 49104 also: Simulation Resources Inc 300 S Bluff St Berrien Springs MI 49103-1202

KOPF, GEORGE MICHAEL, ophthalmologist; b. Chilton, Wis., Oct. 20, 1935; s. George and Mary (Schmid) K.; m. Sandra Mary Nolte, Dec. 29, 1962; children: Karen, Jennifer, Nancy. B.S., U. Wis.-Madison, 1958, M.D., 1961. Diplomate Am. Bd. Ophthalmology. Intern Luther Hosp., Eau Claire, Wis., 1961-62; resident in surgery Milw. County Hosp., 1962-63; resident in ophthalmology Detroit Gen. Hosp., 1965-68; practice medicine specializing in ophthalmology, Zanesville, Ohio, 1968—; mem. med. staff Bethesda Hosp., Zanesville; mem. med. Staff Good Samaritan Med. Ctr., Zanesville, pres., 1978, sec. bd. dirs., 1986—. Served to capt. USAF, 1963-65. Fellow Am. Acad. Ophthalmology, ACS; mem. Ohio Ophthal. Soc. (pres. 1976-77), Muskingum County Acad. Medicine (pres. 1983), Ohio State Med. Assn., AMA. Republican. Roman Catholic. Lodges: Elks, Rotary. Avocations: tennis, swimming, hiking, reading, traveling. Home: 2950 Ash Meadows Blvd Zanesville OH 43701-9081 Office: Ophthalmologists Inc 2315 Maple Ave Zanesville OH 43701-2028

KOPF, RICHARD G., federal judge; b. 1946. BA, U. Nebr., Kearney, 1969; JD, U. Nebr., Lincoln, 1972. Law clk. to Hon. Donald R. Ross U.S. Ct. Appeals (8th cir.), 1972-74; ptnr. Cook, Kopf & Doyle, Lexington, Neb., 1974-87; U.S. magistrate judge, 1987-92; fed. judge U.S. Dist. Ct. (Nebr. dist.), 1992—. Mem. ABA, Nebr. State Bar, Nebr. State Bar Found., Dawson County Bar Assn. Office: US Dist Ct 586 US Courthouse 100 Centennial Mall N Lincoln NE 68508-3803

KOPIS, F. JAN, real estate broker; b. Chgo., Dec. 21, 1942; s. Frank John and Marie Melvina (Herrmann) K.; m. Carol Ann Brune, June 1, 1965 (div. May, 1976); children: Kelly Sue, Casey Marie; m. Lois Jean Whermann, June, 1978. BA, U. Dayton, 1964. Lic. real estate broker; cert. residential specialist, Grad. Realtor Inst. Exec. tng. Marshall Field & Co., Oak Brook, Ill., 1964-67; mgr., owner The Music Shop, Downers Grove, Ill., 1967-78; real estate broker Re/Max Enterprises, Downers Grove, 1978—. Commr., pres. dist. of Downers Grove Park, Ill., 1975-85; councilman Village of Downers Grove, 1985-93. Recipient Gold medal Nat. Sports Found., 1984; named Citizen of the Yr., Village of Downers Grove, 1993. Mem. C. o C. Ambs. (past chmn.), Argonne Nat. Lab. Regional Consortium (village liaison 1986-92), Lions (past pres.).

KOPLIN, MARK A., urban planner, architect; b. Milw., Apr. 30, 1955; s. Alfred E. and Catherine M. (Keller) K.; m. Anne M. Wollensak, July 2, 1983; children: Kathryn, Patricia. BArch, U. Notre Dame, 1978; M of Urban Planning, U. Wis., Milw., 1983. Facilities architect Mercury Marine, Fond du Lac, Wis., 1978-80; supr., project engr. Harley-Davidson, Milw., 1980-81; planner South Fla. Regional Planning Coun., Hollywood, 1984-85; sr. planner City of Miami Beach, Fla., 1985-87; planner City of Ft. Lauderdale, Fla., 1985-87; prin. planner DuPage County, Wheaton, Ill., 1988-89; EDA project mgr. Village of Hoffman Estates, Ill., 1989—. Mem. Am. Planning Assn., Inst. Traffic Engrs. Home: 4913 Center Ave Lisle IL 60532 Office: Village of Hoffman Estates 1900 Hassell Rd Hoffman Estates IL 60195

KOPP, JOHN J., engineer; b. Marshfield, Wis., Mar. 3, 1954. A in Electronic Engring., DeVry, Chgo., Ill., 1974; BSEE, Marquette U., 1977. Product devel. engr. Vilter Mfg. Co., Milw., 1978. Achievements include 2 patents for refrigeration controls, 1983. Republican. Lutheran.

KOPPENDRAYER, LEROY J., state legislator, farmer; b. May 22, 1941; m. Carolyn Koppendrayer; four children. Student, Vermillion Cmty. Coll., Ely, Minn., Dunwoody Inst., Anoka (Minn.) Tech. Inst. Farmer, agrl. cons.; Dist. 17A rep. Minn. Ho. of Reps., St. Paul, 1990—; former mem. commerce, govt. structures divsn. coms., Minn. Ho. of Reps.; mem. agr., housing and edn.-K-12 edn. fin. divsn. coms. *

KOPRIVICA, DOROTHY MARY, management consultant, real estate and insurance broker; b. St. Louis, May 27, 1921; d. Mitar and Fema (Guzina) K. B.S., Washington U., St. Louis, 1962; cert. in def. inventory mgmt. Dept. Def., 1968. Mgmt. analyst Transp. Supply and Maintenance Command, St. Louis, 1954-57, Dept. Army Transp. Materiel Command, St. Louis, 1957-62; program analyst Dept. Army Aviation System Command, St. Louis, 1962-74, spl. asst. to comdr., 1974-78; ins. broker D. Koprivica, Ins., St. Louis, 1978—; real estate broker, St. Louis, 1978—. Mem. Bus. and Profl. Women (pres. 1974-75). Eastern Orthodox. Lodge: Order Eastern Star.

KOPSA, GREGORY JOE, school psychologist; b. Belleville, Kans., Feb. 15, 1948; s. LaVern Joe and Wilda Margaret (Morrison) K.; m. Connie Louise Fowler, June 7, 1970; children: Kyle, Kristi. BS in Edn., Kans. State Tchrs. Coll., 1970; MS, Emporia State U., 1973. Lic. sch. psychologist, Kans. Instr. Duane Hetlinger Sheltered Workshop, Emporia, Kans., 1969-70; instr. spl. edn. Osage City (Kans.) Sch., 1970-73; sch. psychologist Unified Sch. Dist. 273, Beloit, Kans., 1973—; cons. sch. psychologist Kans. Youth Ctr. in Beloit, 1990; sec. profl. devel. com., Beloit, 1990. Pres. Mitchell County Assn. Retarded Citizens, Beloit Young Men's Orgn.; bd. dirs. Salvation Army, Beloit; com. mem. Kans. 8-Man All Star Football Game, Beloit; deacon 1st Christian Ch., Beloit, 1980. Mem. Beloit Rotary Club (pres.), Kans. Assn. Sch. Psychologists (regional dir. 1975-76, ethics chmn. 1976-77). Republican. Office: Unified Sch Dist 273 1201 N Bell St Beloit KS 67420-1229

KOPSKY, MATT E., investment advisor; b. St. Louis, Dec. 21, 1966. BS, BA, Creighton U., 1989. Asst. v.p. Mark Twain Bank, St. Louis, 1989-93; investment advisor Paine Webber, Chester, Mo., 1993—. Office: Paine Webber Ste 100 15450 S Outer 40 Rd Chesterfield MO 63017

KORBITZ, BERNARD CARL, retired oncologist, hematologist, educator, consultant; b. Lewistown, Mont., Feb. 18, 1935; s. Fredrick William and Rose Eleanore (Ackmann) K.; m. Constance Kay Bolz, June 22, 1957; children: Paul Bernard, Guy Karl. B.S. in Med. Sci., U. Wis.-Madison, 1957, M.D., 1960, M.S. in Oncology, 1962; LL.B., LaSalle U., 1972. Asst. prof. medicine and clin. oncology, U. Wis. Med. Sch., Madison, 1967-71; dir. medicine Presbyn. Med. Ctr., Denver, 1971-73; practice medicine specializing in oncology, hematology, Madison, 1973-76; med. oncologist, hematologist Radiologic Ctr. Meth. Hosp., Omaha, 1976-82; practice medicine specializing in oncology, hematology, Omaha, 1982-95, ret., 1995; sci. advisor Citizen's Environ. Com., Denver, 1972-73; mem. Meth. Hosp., Omaha, 1977—; dir. Bernard C. Korbitz, P.C., Omaha, 1983—; bd. dirs., pres. B.C. Korbitz P.C., ret., 1996. Contbr. articles to profl. jours. Webelos leader Denver area Council, Mid. Am. Council of Nebr. Boy Scouts Am.; bd. elders King of Kings Luth. Ch., Omaha, 1979-80; bd. elders St. Mark Luth. Ch., Omaha, 1993—; mem. People to People Del. Cancer Update to People's Republic China, 1986, Eastern Europe and USSR, 1987; mem. U.S. Senatorial Club, 1984, Republican Presdl. Task Force, 1984. Served to capt. USAF, 1962-64. Fellow ACP, Royal Soc. Health; mem. Am. Soc. Clin. Oncology, Am. Coll. Legal-Medicine, Am. Soc. Internal Medicine, AMA, Nebr. Med. Assn., Omaha Med. Society, Omaha Clin. Soc., Phi Eta Sigma, Phi Beta Kappa, Phi Kappa Phi, Alpha Omega Alpha. Avocations: photography, fishing, travel. Home: 9024 Leavenworth St Omaha NE 68114-5150

KOREN, JEROME QUENTIN, publishing executive; b. Cleve., Aug. 4, 1947; s. Joseph Thomas and Monica Fran (Groh) K. BA in History, U. Western Ontario, Can., 1970. Mgr. Book Fairs Ltd., Oakville, Ontario, Can., 1970-72; buyer T. Eaton & Co., Toronto, Ontario, Can., 1972-76; owner Book Gallery Ltd., Toronto, Ontario, Can., 1976-78; dir. Prometheus Books, Buffalo, 1978-82; dir. mktg. Loyola U. Press, Chgo., 1982-85; co-founder Campion Books, Chgo., 1982-85; pres. Madison Ave. Inc., Chgo., 1985—; dir. edn. Chgo. Book Clinic, 1984-85. Office: Madison Ave Inc Ste A 431 N Northwest Hwy Park Ridge IL 60068-3254

KORINKE, JAMES LEVINE, JR., actor; b. Charles City, Iowa, July 24, 1946; s. James Levine and Edith Louise (Smith) K.; m. Elaine Karen Skaling, July 10, 1971 (div, Feb. 1983); m. Karen Lee Raftery, June 22, 1991. BS in Edn., Northwest No. State U., 1974, BA in Theatre, 1974, MA in Theatre, 1976. Actor, 1976—. Appeared in one man shows including Harrys S. Truman, 1991, Charlie Chaplin, 1993, Frank Sinatra, 1993; plays include Whose Life Is It Anyway, The Tempest, Lend Me A Tenor, Wife Begins at 40, Barefoot in the Park, Shear Madness, Babylon Gardens, Alone Together, Social Security, Extremities, California Suite, Fool For Love, Fallen Angels, On Golden Pond, The Rainmaker, Romantic Comedy, See How They Run, Loot; musicals include Guys and Dolls, Forbidden Broadway '93, 1940's Radio Hour, Geech the Moosical, Personals, Little Shop of Horrors, Best Little Whorehouse in Texas, The Wonder Years, Brigadoon, Baby; films The Spirit of the Season, Deathwish, The Student Body, Super Van; television movies include A Matter of Justice, People Do the Carziest Things, Mary White, Crime; also TV commercials. With USN, 1966-70. Mem. Am. Fedn. Television and Radio Artists, Screen Actor's Guild, Actor's Equity Assn., Wycliff Homes Assn. (bd. dirs. 1994—), Boorkridge Country Club (adv. com. 1994—). Independent. Roman Catholic.

KORN, CANDY LEE, legislative staff member; b. Cleve., Feb. 8, 1942; d. Milan and Vilma (Zevchik) Laska; m. Richard A. Korn (div. 1974); 1 child, Penelope Suzanne. Student, Baldwin Wallace U., 1960-62. Bookkeeper Jay F. Zook, Inc., Cleve., 1962-66; receptionist Metzenbaum, Gaines, etal, Cleve., 1966-76; office mgr. U.S. senator Howard Metzenbaum, Cleve., 1977-95; staff asst. U.S. Senator John Glenn, 1995—. Active Fedn. Cmty. Planning Coun. on Older Persons, 1979-95; auctioneer ann. auction Sta. WVIZ-TV, Cleve., 1984—; entertainment chmn. SOHIO Riverfest, Cleve., 1985-86; chmn. Broadview Heights Festival Parade, 1994. Enshrined in Broadcasters Hall of Fame, Akron, Ohio, 1991. Mem. Broadview Heights C. of C. (v.p.). Democrat. Office: 1240 E 9th St Ste 2957 Cleveland OH 44199-2001

KORN, IRENE ELIZABETH, elementary education educator, consultant; b. Wellston, Mo., May 28, 1937; d. Nicholas Anthony and Myrtle Marie (Knowles) Kuntz; m. Dale Stanley Korn, Sept. 12, 1959; children: Kurt Lawrence, Kenneth Dale, Nancy Ann. BS in Edn., U. Mo., St. Louis, 1969, MS in Edn., 1972, MS in Spl. Edn., 1985. Cert. K-12 reading, social studies tchr., learning disabilities, behavior disorders, Mo. Elem. tchr. N.W. R-1 Sch. Dist., House Springs, Mo., 1969—; tchr. cons. geography program adv. coun. U. Mo., 1989—, Advanced Summer Inst., summer 1990; writer test items Mo. Mastery Achievement Test, fall 1990; mem. social studies work group to write state stds. edn. Mo. Dept. Elem. and Sec. Edn., 1994-95; mem. task force to restructure cert. stds. for U. Mo., Coll. of Edn., 1994. Named Woman of Yr., George Khoury Baseball Leagues, St. Louis, 1987. Mem. ASCD, Nat. Coun. Social Studies, Nat. Coun. for Geographic Edn., Am. Geographical Soc., Mo. State Tchrs. Assn. (professorial rights and responsibilities com. 1987-91, pres. N.W. 1984-86), Nat. Coun. Social Studies, Jefferson County Dist. Edn. Assn. (pres.-elect 1988-89, 91-92), Mo. Geog. Alliance (steering com. 1991—, chmn. elem. curriculum materials 1991-92, tchr. cons. Columbia 1988—, Advanced Inst. P.R. 1992), Phi Delta Kappa. Home: 37 Black Oak Ln Fenton MO 63026-3409

KORNBREKKE, RALPH ERIK, colloid chemist; b. Bklyn., Nov. 22, 1951; s. Henning Norman and Esther (Pedersen) K.; m. Annette Elizabeth Kingman, Aug. 17, 1974. BS, Rensselaer Poly. Inst., 1974, PhD, 1981. Chemist Petroleum Action Inc., Rensselaer, N.Y., 1974-75, Rensselaer Rsch. Corp. Internat., Latham, N.Y., 1975-76; sr. rsch. chemist The 3M Corp., St. Paul, 1980-84; project leader Std. Oil of Ohio, Warrensville Hts., 1984-87; rsch. chemist IV The Lubrizol Corp., Wickliffe, Ohio, 1987-90, sr. rsch. chemist, 1990-91, rsch. scientist, 1991—; session chmn. Am. Chem. Soc. Nat. Meeting Colloid Div., N.Y.C., 1986; chmn. the Interface Sci. chpt. of 3M Tech. Forum, St. Paul, 1982-84; staff mem. NBS Molton Salts Data Ctr., Troy, 1975-76. Contbr. articles to profl. jours.; patentee in field. Pres. Oakwood Lustre Townhome Assn., Oakdale, Minn., 1981-84; judge Reg. Sci. Fair, Mpls., Cleve., 1981—; team capt. Cleve. Orch. Campaign Fund Raising, 1988-90. N.Y. State Regents scholar 1970; named J. Willard Gibbs Rsch. fellow, 1979-80. Fellow Am. Inst. Chemists; mem. AAAS, Internat. Assn. Colloid and Interface Scientists, Am. Chem. Soc., Soc. Automotive Engrs., Soc. Tribologists and Lubrication Engrs., Sigma Xi, Phi Lambda Epsilon. Home: 8340 Tulip Ln Chagrin Falls OH 44023-4675 Office: The Lubrizol Corp 29400 Lakeland Blvd Wickliffe OH 44092-2201

KORNEL, LUDWIG, medical educator, physician, scientist; b. Jaslo, Poland, Feb. 27, 1923; came to U.S., 1958, naturalized, 1970; s. Ezriel Edward and Ernestine (Karpf) K.; m. Esther Muller, May 27, 1952; children: Ezriel Edward, Amiel Mark. Student, U. Kazan Med. Inst., USSR, 1943-45; M.D., Wroclaw (Poland) Med. Acad., 1950; Ph.D., U. Birmingham, Eng., 1958. Intern Univ. Hosp., Wroclaw, 1949-50, Hadassah-Hebrew U. Hosp., Jerusalem, 1950-51; resident medicine Hadassah-Hebrew U. Hosp., 1952-55; Brit. Council scholar, Univ. research fellow endocrinology U. Birmingham, 1955-57, lectr. medicine, 1956-57; fellow endocrinology U. Ala. Med. Ctr., 1958-59, successively asst. prof., assoc. prof., prof. medicine, 1961-67; dir. steroid sect. U. Ala. Med. Center, 1962-67, assoc. prof. biochemistry, 1965-67; postdoctoral trainee in steroid biochemistry U. Utah, 1959-61; prof. medicine U. Ill. Coll. Medicine, Chgo., 1967-71; dir. steroid unit Presbyn.-St. Lukes Hosp., Chgo., 1967-93; assoc. biochemist Presbyn.-St. Lukes Hosp., 1967-70, sr. biochemist on sci. staff, 1970-71, attending physician, 1967-71; prof. medicine and biochemistry Rush Med. Coll., 1970-93, prof. emeritus of internal medicine and biochemistry, 1993—; sr. attending physician, sr. scientist Rush-Presbyn.-St. Lukes Med. Ctr., 1971—, dir. steroid hypertension rsch. lab., 1971—; hon. guest lectr. Polish Acad. Sci., Warsaw, 1965; vis. prof. Kanazawa (Japan) U., 1973, 82, 88, 93. Mem. editl. bd. Clin. Physiol. Biochemistry, 1975-94, Endocrinology, 1994—; co-editor: Yearbook of Endocrinology, 1986-90; co-author: Ency. of Human Biology, 1991, 96; contbr. articles on endocrinology and steroid biochemistry to profl.jours.; contbr. chpts to textbooks. Recipient Physicians Recognition award AMA, 1969, 73, 76, 81, 86, Outstanding New Citizen award Citizenship Council Met. Chgo., 1970. Fellow Am. Coll. Clin. Pharmacology and Chemotherapy, Nat. Acad. Clin. Biochemistry (bd. dirs. 1982-86), Royal Soc. health; mem. AMA, AAAS, AAUP, Endocrine Soc., Am. Fedn. Clin. Rsch., N.Y. Acad. Scis., Am. Physiol. Soc., Cen. Soc. Clin. Rsch., Israel Soc. for Biochemistry and Molecular Biology, Am. Acad. Polit. and Social Scis., Fedn. Am. Socs. for Exptl. Biology (nat. corr. 1975—), Fedn. Israel Socs. for Exptl. Biology, Sigma Xi. Home: 3950 N Lake Shore Dr Chicago IL 60613-3434 Office: Rush Presbyn St Lukes M C 1653 W Congress Pky Chicago IL 60612-3833

KORNOKOVICH, RON J., marketing research company executive; b. Cleve., Jan. 2, 1946; s. Ferdinand and Marie (Miketo) K.; m. Judith M. Linden, July 2, 1972; children: Carrie, Bryan. MBA, Cleve. State U., 1969. Acct. Ward Foods, Cleve., 1968-70; pres. Osban Mktg., Cleve., 1966-79, Consumer Pulse Corp., Cleve., 1979-95; pres, Opinionation, Cleve., 1996—; adj. instr. Garfield Sr. Coll., Cleve., 1970. Mem. Fariview Park (Ohio) Planning Commn., 1975; chmn. bicentennial City of Fairview Park, 1976; founder Merchants for Progress. Recipient Community Leader award, 1976. Mem. Am. Mgmt. Assn. (numerous coms.), Am. Mktg. Assn. (bd. dirs. chpt. v.p. 1990-92), Mktg. Rsch. Assn. (bd. dirs. treas. 1976-77, 93-94, Soc. of Quill award 1974, 78, Pres. award 1980).

KOROTKIN, FRED, writer, philatelist; b. Duluth, Minn., Oct. 25, 1917; s. Morris and Ethel (Billert) K. B.A., U. Minn., 1949. Writer-instr. Palmer Writers Sch., Mpls., 1961-66; editor Finance & Commerce, and Daily Market Record, Mpls., 1966-67; stamp editor Mpls. Star, 1970-74, White Bear Press, 1976, Minn. Suburban Newspapers, Inc., 1983-85, The Enterpri$e, 1988-89, Post Publs. Weekend, 1989-91; Mem. philatelic adv. panel Am. Revolution Bicentennial Commn., 1971-74, Am. Revolution Bicentennial Adminstrn., 1974, philatelic advisor, 1974-76; regional rep. Interphil '76, 1974-76, USO, AARP, So. Poverty Law Ctr./Klanwatch Project. Contbr. revs., articles to popular mags., newspapers. Pres. North High Alumni Assn., Mpls., 1946-47; mem. nat. adv. bd. The Generation After; assoc. Simon Wiesenthal Ctr. for Holocaust Studies; mem. St. Louis Park Centennial Commn., 1985-86, Am. Inst. Cancer Rsch.; charter mem. U.S. Holocaust Meml. Mus. With U.S. Maritime Svc., 1942-43, with Air Transport Command, U.S. Army, 1943-46. Recipient Disting. Topical Philatelist Hall of Fame award and invited to sign Disting. Topical Philatelist scroll of honor, 1962, Silver medal for Keeping Posted column in Mpls. Star Am. Philatelic Soc.-Chgo. Philatelic Soc. Conv., 1974, Silver award for Keeping Posted column in Post Publs. Weekend, sponsored by Coun. Philatelic Orgns., 1989. Mem. Am. Topical Assn. (founding pres. chpt. 1957-61, nat. pres. 1968-70, 70-72, dir., nat. adv. com.), Internat. Philatelic Press Club (gov.), Internat. Assn. Philatelic Journalists, Am. Philatelic Soc. (speakers' bur. 1977—, writers unit),

New Zealand Stamp Collector's Club Inc. (hon., anonymously donated annual Fred Korotkin Cup for best thematic entry 1966—), Christchurch Philatelic Soc., Inc., Royal Philatelic Soc. New Zealand, Collectors Club N.Y., Manuscript Soc., Statue of Liberty-Ellis Island Found. Inc. (charter), Nat. Com. To Preserve Social Security, Am. United for Separation of Ch. and State, Holocaust Survivors Assn. USA (nat. adv. bd.), Keren Or, Inc., Jerusalem Instn. for the Blind, Internat. Platform Assn., People for the Am. Way, DAV (life; comdr. Mpls. chpt. No 1, 1986). Home: Apt 512 4925 Minnetonka Blvd Minneapolis MN 55416-2271 also: Box 11053 Minneapolis MN 55411-0053

KORSCHOT, BENJAMIN CALVIN, investment executive; b. LaFayette, Ind., Mar. 22, 1921; s. Benjamin G. and Myrtle P. (Goodman) K.; m. Marian Marie Schelle, Oct. 31, 1941; children: Barbara E. Korschot Haehlen, Lynne D. Korschot Gooding, John Calvin. BS, Purdue U., 1942; MBA, U. Chgo., 1947. V.p. No. Trust Co., Chgo., 1947-64; sr. v.p. St. Louis Union Trust Co., 1964-73; exec. v.p. Waddell and Reed Co., Kansas City, Mo., 1973-74, pres., 1974-79, vice-chmn. bd., 1979-85; pres. Waddell & Reed Investment Mgmt. Co., 1985-86; chmn. bd. Waddell & Reed Asset Mgmt. Co., 1973-86; pres. United Group of Mut. Funds, Inc., Kansas City, Mo., 1974-85, chmn., 1985-86; vice-chmn. Roosevelt Fin. Group, St. Louis, 1968-91, chmn. adv. bd., 1991-92; treas. Helping Hand of Goodwill Industries, 1993-95, chmn. investment com., 1995—; bd. dirs., investment com. Mo. United Meth. Found., 1995—; chmn. bd. govs. Investment Co. Inst., 1980-82; chmn. bd. Fin. Analyst Fedn., 1978-79;. Contbr. articles on investment fin. to profl. publs. Mem. Civic Coun. Greater Kansas City, Mo., 1974-85; chmn. fin. com. ARC Retirement Sys., 1986-87. With USN, 1942-45, 50-52. Mem. Inst. CFAs, Fin. Execs. Inst., Kansas City Soc. Fin. Analysts, Kansas City Club, Indian Hills Country Club. Republican. Home: 101 NW Hackberry St Lees Summit MO 64064-1477

KORST, HELMUT HANS, mechanical engineer, educator; b. Vienna, Jan. 4, 1916; came to U.S., 1948; married, 1942; 4 children. Diploma in Engring., Vienna Tech. U., 1941, Dr. Tech. Sci., 1947. Rsch. engr. Maschinenfabrik Augsburg-Nurnberg AG, Germany, 1941-45; asst. prof. mech. engring. Vienna Tech. U., 1945-48, vis. lectr. gas dynamics, 1948-49; from assoc. prof. to prof. mech. engring. U. Ill., Urbana, 1949-84, head dept. mech. and indsl. engring., 1962-74, prof. emeritus, 1984—; chair naval air power engring. USN Postgrad. Sch., Monterey, Calif., 1979; Ebaugh Chair Mech. Engring. U. Fla., Gainesville, 1984; pvt. practice cons. Urbana, 1956—; vis. prof. Kans. State U., Manhattan, 1950, Va. Poly. Inst. and State U., Blacksburg, 1954; design specialist Gen. Dynamics Convair, Ft. Worth, 1955; propulsion specialist Rocketdyne div. N.Am. Aviation, 1960, 65-68; cons. GE, 1959, Adv. Group Aeronautical R & D NATO, 1964, U.S. Missile Command, 1971—. Sr. postdoctoral fellow NSF, 1957; recipient ASEE Centennial medal 1993, Daniel Guggenheim medal in aviation, 1994. Fellow ASME, AIAA; mem. Am. Soc. Engring. Edn., Sigma Xi. Address: 3 Eton Ct Champaign IL 61820-7602

KORTEBEIN, STUART ROWLAND, orthopedic surgeon; b. Evanston, Ill., Apr. 17, 1930; s. Rowland J. and Grace K.; m. Alice C. Johnson, July 10, 1954; children: William, David. AA, North Park Coll., 1950; BS, Wheaton Coll., 1952; postgrad., North Park Theol. Sem., 1952-53; MD, Loyola U., 1957; JD, Jefferson Coll. Law, 1983. Diplomate Nat. Bd. Med. Examiners, Am. Bd. Orthopaedic Surgery. Intern Akron (Ohio) Gen. Hosp., 1957-58, resident, 1961-64; resident Hines (Ill.) VA Hosp., 1960, Northwestern U., Chgo., 1964; pvt. practice medicine specializing in orthopedic surgery Arlington Heights, Ill., 1965-88; mem. orthopaedic surgeon staff U.S. Naval Regional Med. Ctr., Memphis, 1986—; pvt. practice medicine specializing in orthopedic surgery Milw., 1988—; chief dept. orthopedic surgery U.S. Naval Hosp., Great Lakes, Ill., 1987; mem. orthopaedic surgeon staff Sinai-Samaritan Med. Ctr., Milw., 1988—; attending surgeon N.W. Cmty. Hosp., Arlington Heights, 1965-90, chief orthopedics, 1976; v.p. Magnetrans Rsch. and Devel. Corp., 1972-84, Window Well Protectors, Inc., McHenry, Ill., 1983-86; coord. med. cons. Compusoft Corp., Darien, Ill., 1984—, Pomsoft Corp., Willowbrook, Ill.; instr. emergency medicine technician course Haper Coll., 1973-84; vis. instr. police self-def. tactics Oakton Cmty. Coll., 1984-88. Water safety instr. ARC, 1949-54; aux. police officer City of Rolling Meadows, Ill., 1984-89; bd. dirs. Chicagoland Drug Prevention Program, 1971-84; choir dir. First Bapt Ch., Twenty Nine Palms, Calif., 1959-60, tech. advisor Jubo-Kai Internat., 1977—. Lt. M.C., USNR, 1958-60. Mem. Am. Acad. Orthopaedic Surgeons, Physicians Martial Arts Assn., Soc. Black Belts Am., Christian Med. Soc., Wis. Orthopaedic Soc., Milw. Orthopaedic Soc., Hakko-Ryu Jitsu Fed., Jiu Jitsu Black Belt Fedn. Am. (pres. Ill., rep. 1971-74), Oikiru-Ryu Jitsu (Sandan instr. 1977-85), U.S. Judo Assn. (Sho Dan life mem.). Office: 500 N 19th St Milwaukee WI 53233-2123

KORTHAS, KEVIN JOHN, industrial engineer; b. Schenectady, N.Y., Mar. 19, 1964; s. Robert Hubert and Violet Jeanette (LaBier) K.; m. Sandra Lynn Jicha, Oct. 8, 1988. BSIE, SUNY, Buffalo, 1987, BA in Econs., 1987. Mem. mfg. mgmt. program Gen. Electric Co., Pittsfield, Mass., Milw., 1989-91; quality engr. Med. Systems div. Gen. Electric Co., Milw., 1991-92, group leader, 1992-93; program mgr., 1993—. Mem. IEEE, Inst. Indsl. Engrs., Soc. Mfg. Engrs. Home: 2535 N 69th St Wauwatosa WI 53213-1315 Office: GE Co W641 3000 N Grandview Blvd Waukesha WI 53188

KORVER, GERRY R(OZEBOOM), purchasing executive; b. Orange City, Iowa, June 17, 1952. BA, Northwestern Coll., 1977. Gen. mgr. purchasing K-Products, Inc., Orange City, 1978—. Mem. Nat. Assn. Purchasing Mgmt. (cert.). Home: 1602 Albany Ave NE Orange City IA 51041-2039 Office: K-Products Inc Industrial Air Park Orange City IA 51041

KOSCHMANN, TIMOTHY DURANT, educational researcher; b. Milw., Sept. 12, 1950; s. Martin Luther and Gloria (Smith) K.; m. Barbara Lenore Gross, Dec. 27, 1975; children: Nathaniel, Carl, Frederick. BA in Philosophy, U. Mo., Kansas City, 1972; postgrad., U. Wis., Madison, 1976; MS in Psychology, U. Wis., Milw., 1980; PhD in Computer Sci., Ill. Inst. Tech., 1987. Sr. sci. analyst Abbott Labs., North Chicago, Ill., 1978-83; chief computer scientist Chgo. Med. Sch., North Chicago, 1983-85; sr. mem. engring. staff Xerox Corp., Des Plaines, Ill., 1985-88; assoc. prof. med. edn. So. Ill. U. Sch. Medicine, Springfield, 1988—; adj. assoc. prof. U. Wis.-Parkside, Kenosha, 1981-82. Author: Common Lisp Companion, 1990; editor: CSCL: Theory and Practice of an Emerging Paradigm, 1996. Mem. IEEE Computer Soc., Am. Ednl. Rsch. Assn., Cognitive Sci. Soc., Assn. for Computing Machinery, Assn. for Advancement Computing in Edn., Am. Assn. Artificial Intelligence. Office: So Ill U Sch Medicine PO Box 19230 MS 1217 Springfield IL 62794-9230

KOSHAL, RAJINDAR KUMAR, economics educator; b. Ahmedgarh, Punjab, India, Jan. 15, 1934; came to U.S., 1961; s. Jiwa Ram and Shakuntla (Malhotra) K.; m. Manjulika Badhwar, Aug. 12, 1966; children: Vinita, Vipin. BS, U. Delhi, India, 1954; MS, Gauhati U., India, 1957; MA, U. Rochester, 1964, PhD, 1968. Econ. investigator Indian Planning Commn., 1957-61; asst. prof. econs. Ohio U., Athens, 1965-71, assoc. prof., 1971-74, prof., 1974-78, chmn. dept. econs., 1980-83. Contbr. articles to profl. jours. Chmn. Friends of India Endowment, Athens, 1983—90. Mem. Am. Econ. Assn., Atlantic Econ. Assn., Ea. Econ. Assn., Indian Stats. Inst. (vis. fellow 1971-72), Operational Rsch. Soc. Am., Midwest Bus. Econs. Assn. (pres. 1992-93). Office: Ohio Univ Haning Hall Athens OH 45701-3708

KOSINSKI, RICHARD ANDREW, public relations executive; b. Chgo., Aug. 12, 1951; s. Andrew Ignatius and Olga Sophia (Janusz) K.; m. Susan M. Mark, Oct. 13, 1974 (div. June 1985). BS, Loyola U. Chgo., 1974; MPA, Roosevelt U., 1979. From dir. parents assocs. to dir. dental devel. Loyola U. Chgo., 1976-79; assoc. dir. devel. Am. Fund for Dental Health, Chgo., 1979-80; dir. devel. & pub. rels. Niles Twp. Sheltered Workshop, Skokie, Ill., 1985-88; assoc. exec. dir. Leukemia Soc. Am., Chgo., 1988-93; mgr. major gifts Prevent Blindness Am., Schaumburg, Ill., 1993—. Mem. svc. and rehab. com. Am. Cancer Soc., 1986-88. Recipient Tribute U.S. Ho. of Reps., 1986. Roman Catholic. Home: 838 McIntosh Ct Unit 208 Prospect Heights IL 60070 Office: Prevent Blindness Am 500 E Remington Rd Schaumburg IL 60173

KOSINSKY, BARBARA TIMM, librarian; b. St. Louis, July 4, 1942; d. Paul E. and Virginia L. (Borcherding) T.; m. John P. Kosinsky, July 25, 1964; children: James Alan, Bethany Anne. BS in Edn., Concordia Coll., River Forest, Ill., 1964; BA in Computer Sci., North Cen. Coll., Naperville, Ill., 1986; MLS, SUNY, Buffalo, 1972. Cert. tchr., Ill., N.Y. Tchr. St. Paul Luth. Sch., North Tonawanda, N.Y., 1964-67; libr. Trinity Luth. Sch., West Seneca, N.Y., 1971-80, North Cen. Coll., Naperville, 1981-89; regional mktg. rep. Online Computer Libr. Ctr., Dublin, Ohio, 1990—; free-lance writer West Seneca and Naperville, 1978—. Contbr. articles to religious mags. and general interest publs. Mem. ALA, Am. Soc. Info. Sci., Nat. Writers Club, Wis. Libr. Assn. Home: 225 Carlin Ct Hartland WI 53029-1805 Office: PO Box 138 Hartland WI 53029-0138

KOSKAN, JOHN M., state legislator; b. Winner, S.D., Sept. 27, 1955; s. Milo Harlan and Juanita Mae (Mitchell) K.; m. Verna Gale Heying, 1973; children: Fawn Michelle, Tracy Michael, Joel Mathew, Joni Melissa. BS, S.D. Sch. Mines & Tech., 1977. Mem. Sch. Bd., Wood, S.D., 1984-90; mem. S.D. Ho. of Reps., 1991—, mem. taxation and transp. coms.; design engr. Boeing Aircraft, Wichita, Kans., 1977-79, Cessna Aircraft Co., Wichita, 1979-80; design cons.,mfr. Piper Advanced Technologies, Wichita, 1980-81; farmer, rancher Wood, S.D., 1981—. Home: PO Box 17A Wood SD 57585*

KOSLOW, ALAN R., cardiovascular surgeon; b. N.Y.C., Feb. 17, 1953; m. Margie Hill; children: Christina, Scott, Elizabeth. BS magna cum laude, SUNY, Buffalo, 1974, MD, 1978. Rsch. asst. dept. surgery Hosp. & Med. Ctr., Bronx, N.Y., 1967-68; rsch. asst. dept. surgery Montefiore Hosp. & Med Ctr., Bronx, N.Y., 1968-69, rsch. asst. Inst. Surg. Rsch., 1970-71; rsch. asst. dept. physiology SUNY, Buffalo, 1973; preceptor vascular surgery Englewood (N.J.) Hosp., 1975-76; rsch. asst. Meadox Med. Labs., N.J., 1976; preceptor vascular surgery St. Mary's Hosp./ U. London, 1977; intern, resident gen. surgery Stanford (Calif.) Univ. Med. Ctr., 1978-81; emergency physician Washington County Hosp., Hagerstown, Md., 1981-84, Shady Grove Hosp., Gaithersburg, Md., 1981-84, Holy Cross Hosp., Silver Springs, Md., 1981-84; rsch. fellow ARC Blood Rsch. Lab., Bethesda, Md., 1981-84; resident, chief resident surgery Univ. Medicine & Dentistry N.J., Newark, 1984-87; fellow, instr. vascular surgery U. Rochester (N.Y.) Med. Ctr., 1987-89; asst. prof. surgery, vascular surgery Albany (N.Y.) Med. Coll., 1989-91, Albany VA Med. Ctr., 1989-91, Loma Linda (Calif.) U. Med. Ctr., 1991-93; emergency rm. cons. Corona Regional Med. Ctr., 1993; cons. clin. issues Markley Group, 1993-95; physician Iowa Health Ctrs., Des Moines, 1995—, Mercy Hosp. Med. Ctr., Des Moines, 1995—, Broadlawns Med. Ctr., Des Moines, 1995—, Des Moines Gen. Hosp., 1995—. Contbr. articles to profl. jours. Recipient Dr. Heinrich Leonardt Excellence in Surgery prize, 1978, Citizen's Honor medal Balt. County Fire & Rescue, 1984; grantee Soc. Clin. Vascular Surgery, 1988. Mem. AMA, ACS, AAUP, Am. Heart Assn. (coun. cardiovascular surgery), Am. Fedn. Clin. Rsch., Iowa Med. Soc., N.Y. Acad. Sci., European Soc. Vascular Surgery, Polk County Med. Soc., Assn. Surg. Edn., Acad. Surg. Rsch., Peripheral Vascular Surgery Soc., Assn. Acad. Surgeons, Phi Lambda Kappa. Office: Iowa Heart Ctr 411 Laurel Ste 2250 Des Moines IA 50314

KOSO, MIC D., computer programmer, mechanical engineer; b. Falls City, Nebr., Dec. 22, 1956. BS in Indsl. Tech., Peru State Coll., 1985. Tchr. Tecumseh (Nebr.) H.S., 1981-82; deputy sheriff Richardson County, Falls City, Nebr., 1982-90; programmer Alanco Environmental, Falls City, Nebr., 1990—. Mem. Falls City Ambulance Squad, 1985-95. Mem. Elks Lodge. Republican. Mem. United Ch. Christ. Home: 2503 Schoenheight Falls City NE 68355 Office: Alanco Environmental Mfg PO Box 398 Falls City NE 68355-0398

KOSOBUCKI, JOHN EDMUND, career officer; b. Milw., July 25, 1949; s. Edmund Anthony and Rose Anne (Weltrowski) K. BA in History, Marquette U., 1971, JD, 1977; MA in Mgmt., Webster U., 1993. Commd. 2d lt. U.S. Army, 1971, advanced through grades to lt. col., 1987—. Dir., v.p. Messmer High Sch., Milw., 1979-82. Mem. Am. Soc. Mil. Comptrollers, State Bar of Wis., Reserve Officers Assn., Adjutant Gen.'s Corps Regimental Assn. (founder), Am. Legion. Roman Catholic. Home: 1131 Sunnyslope Dr Unit 6 Racine WI 53406-5620

KOST, MALINDA LENZ, home health nurse; b. New Albany, Ind., Nov. 9, 1948; d. Robert Lee and Ruth Day (Kist) Lenz; children: Alison, Leah, Shawn. ADN, Ind. U., 1970. Staff nurse Bartholomeuw County Hosp., Columbus, Ind., 1970-71, Floyd Meml. Hosp., New Albany, Ind., 1975-77; shift supr. Green Valley Convalescent Ctr., New Albany, 1978-80; office nurse Dr. Stephen W. Nale, M.D., New Albany, 1987-89; staff nurse Hoosier Hills Home Health, New Albany, 1987-89, DON, 1989-90, pres., 1990—. Mem. Wesley Chapel Meth. Ch., New Albany, Bus. and Profl. Women, New Albany, Bus. Women's Coun., New Albany; chairperson LPN Task Force, Indpls. Named Woman of Achievement, Bus. Women's Coun., 1994. Mem. Ind. Assn. Home Health Agys. (bd. dirs., chmn. pub. relations com.), Order Ea. Star, Internat. Order Job's Daus. (past Honored Queen New Albany chpt.), New Albany C. of C. Methodist. Home: 2211 E Arrowhead Dr New Albany IN 47150-6001 Office: Hoosier Hills Home Health 1919 State St Ste 108 New Albany IN 47150-6802

KOSTECKA, DAVE J., manufacturing engineer; b. Glencoe, Minn., June 10, 1945. Sales person Scott Equipment Co., New Prague, Minn., 1979-82, engr., 1982-87, mgr. engring., 1987—. With U.S. Army, 1966-69. Office: Scott Equipment Co 605 4th Ave NW New Prague MN 56071-1121

KOSTECKI, MARY ANN, financial tax consultant, small business consultant; b. St. Louis, Jan. 6, 1941; 4 children. Student, Forest Park Jr. Coll., 1969-72, Washington U., 1973-77. Dem. candidate for U.S House 2nd Dist., Mo., 1996. Office: 7446 Sieloff Hazelwood MO 63042*

KOSTELIC, THOMAS PATRICK, manufacturing executive; b. Youngstown, Ohio, May 6, 1954; s. John Thomas and Beatrice (Furlong) K.; m. Pamela Jean Gibboney, Oct. 26, 1973; children: Thomas Patrick, Matthew John. AAS, Youngstown State U., 1980, BS in Applied Sci., 1982. Registered profl. engr., Pa. Prodn. foreman Youngstown Sheet & Tube Co., 1979-80; designer, detailer, product engr. Republic Steel, Youngstown, 1980-81; chief draftsman, engr. Conn Fabricating & Engring., New Castle, Pa., 1981-85, ops. mgr., plant mgr., 1985-88; v.p. Ohio Structures, Inc., Canfield, 1988—. Bd. dirs. Canfield Swim Club, 1988—, Canfield Youth Soccer Club, 1986, Canfield High Sch. Swim Team, 1991. Mem. Assn. Bridge Constrn. and Design, Am. Inst. Steel Constrn., Am. Welding Soc., Ohio Contractors Assn. (specifications com. 1991). Home: 300 Shadydale Dr Canfield OH 44406-1030

KOSTEN, DONALD L., investment broker; b. Grand Rapids, Mich., Aug. 13, 1931; m. June L. Dyer, May 3, 1955. Br. mgr. Dempsey Tagler, Grand Rapids, 1957-69; ptnr. Edward D. Jones & Co., Grand Rapids, 1969—; mem. adv. bd. Edward D. Jones & Co., St. Louis. Bd. chmn. Pension Bd., Grand Rapids; bd. dirs. Zoning Bd. Appeals, Grand Rapids; pres. Metro Garden Coun., Grand Rapids, Living Message Fellowship, Grand Rapids; vice-chmn. Hosp. Bd., Grand Rapids. Named Master Gardener, Metro Garden Coun. Republican. Office: Edward D Jones & Co 161 Ottawa Ave NW Ste 605-c Grand Rapids MI 49503-2701

KOSTERE, KIM MARTIN, psychologist; b. Detroit, Jan. 22, 1954; d. Walter Thomas and Shirley Marian (Goebel) K. BA, Mercy Coll., 1977; MA, Ctr. Humanistic Studies, Detroit, 1983; PsyS, Ctr. Humanistic Studies, 1986; PhD, Union Inst., Cin., 1989. Therapist Metro T.A.G., Livonia, Mich., 1978-81, Highland Waterford Ctr., Waterford, Mich., 1981-83; psychologist, v.p. substance abuse svcs. Square Lake Counseling Ctr., Bloomfield Hills, Mich., 1983-90; psychologist, co-dir. Counseling Ctr., P. C., Bloomfield Hills, Mich., 1991—; co-founder, dir. Ont. (Can.) NLP Inst., 1979-80. Author: A Brief Account of the Center for Humanistic Studies, 1987; co-author: Get the Results You Want, 1987, Maps, Models and the Structure of Reality, 1989, Utilizing the Metaphor: An Ericksonian/NLP Approach, 1992. Democrat. Roman Catholic.

KOSTER-PETERSON, LOIS MAE, educational administrator; b. Carroll, Iowa, Aug. 31, 1957; d. Doyle John and Bernice Clare (Broich) Koster; m. Kent Roger Peterson, Sept. 3, 1988. AA, Iowa Ctrl. C.C., 1977; BA, Buena Vista Coll., 1979; MS, Iowa State U., 1984; EdD, No. Ariz. U., 1993; Ednl. Specialist, Piont Loma Coll., 1993. Cert. secondary tchr. and adminstr., Iowa, Kans, Wis., Calif. Tchr., coach Colo (Iowa) Community Sch., 1979-82; dean students, basketball coach Wahlert High Sch., Dubuque, Iowa, 1982-83; rsch. asst. Iowa State U., Ames, 1983; prin., activities dir. North Winneshiek Community Sch., Decorah, Iowa, 1985-88; asst. prin. jr. high Unified Sch. Dist. 443, Dodge City, Kans., 1988-89; prin. sr. high Wintereset (Iowa) Community Sch., 1989-90; interim prin. mid. sch. Ramona (Calif.) Unified Sch. Dist., 1992; assoc. prin. Shawnee Mission (Kans.) North High Sch., 1993—; exec. sec. Upper Miss. Valley Conf., Garnavillo, Iowa, 1986-87; mem. planning com. Teens in Distress Conf., Decorah, 1986-87. Lector, cathecism instr., sr. citizen asst. St. Mary's Ch., Colo, 1979-82; interview judge Iowa Academic Decathlon, Denison, 1990; mem. selection com. Chuck Burdick Scholarship, Des Moines, 1987. Recipient Thespian Kans. Adminstr. of Yr. award, 1995; inductee Buena Vista Athletic Hall of Fame, 1996. Mem. ASCD, Calif. Sch. Adminstrs. Assn., Ariz. Rsch. Assn., Sch. Adminstrs. Iowa (panel for Iowa selection of fine program 1989-90), Nat. Assn. Secondary Sch. Prins., Optimists, Phi Delta Kappa (v.p. Greater Kansas City chpt.). Roman Catholic. Home: 9107 W 73rd St # 203 Shawnee Mission KS 66204-1625

KOSTKA, JANICE ELLEN, automotive wholesale company administator; b. Chgo., Aug. 25, 1940; d. Nicholas Jr. and Sylvia Helen (Lissy) Smicklas; m. Roger Denis Kostka, Aug. 15, 1959; children: Joseph Nicholas, Laura Ann. Grad. high sch., 1958. Staff asst. sec. Sears, Roebuck & Co., Chgo., 1958-62; staff sec. IBM, River Forest, Ill., 1962-64; sec., statis. typist Rights Temps, Elmhurst, Ill., 1979-84; sec., tech. typist Secs., Inc., Oak Brook, Ill., 1979-84; realtor, sales assoc. Long Realty, Westmont, Ill., 1981-82, 89-90; owner, office mgr., sec. Kostka Bros., Inc., Chgo., 1964-89; hazardous materials and safety regulations coord. Kostka, Inc., Chgo., 1990—. Author: (manual) Do-It-Yourself Credit Repair, 1993. Bd. dirs. Oak Brook Civic Assn., 1978-79; mem. State of Ill. Gov.'s Small Bus. Environ. Task Force, Springfield, 1994. Mem. Automotive Wholesalers of Ill. (Appreciation award 1995).

KOSTKA, RONALD WAYNE, marketing consultant; b. Chgo., Sept. 13, 1931; s. James V. and Marie (Zvolanek) K.; m. Madonna Lou Miller, June 8, 1957 (div. Dec. 1980); children: Paul, Daniel, Jane; m. Irene Mary Harnett, Sept. 14, 1991. BS in journalism, U. Ill., Urbana, 1957. Reporter Champaign News Gazette, Champaign, Ill., 1956-57; copy editor Mpls. Tribune, Mpls., 1957-58; pub. rels. mgr. 3M Co., St. Paul, Minn., 1958-92; cons. mktg. Pub. Rel., Minnetonka, Minn., 1992—. Contbr. articles to profl. jours. Firearms safety instr. State of Minn., Minnetonka, 1967-77; docent Planes of Fame Air Museum, Eden Prairie, Minn., 1994—. Staff Sgt. USAF, 1951-55, Korea. Decorated Air medal (4 OLC), Purple Heart, Hwarang (Republic of Korea). Mem. DAV, Nat. Muzzle Loading Rifle Assn., NRA, Soc. of Profl. Jours. (cert 1957), Nat. Wildlife Fed., Minnetonka Game & Fish Club. Home: 1004 Sunset Dr Minnetonka MN 55305

KOSTUCH, DOROTHY ANN, art history educator; b. Detroit, June 13, 1935; d. Philip Albert and Cecilia Hedwig (Budnik) K. BA, Columbia U., 1971, MA, 1973, MPhil, 1978, PhD, 1985. Cloistered nun Sisters of Mary Reparatrix, Detroit, N.Y.C., Rome, 1954-67; resident asst. Barnard Coll., Columbia U., N.Y.C., 1967-73; sec. Mus. Hispanic Soc. Am., N.Y.C., 1973-77, asst. curator decorative arts, 1978-79; instr., adj. prof. Marymount Manhattan Coll., N.Y.C., 1980-83; assoc. prof. art history Ctr. Creative Studies Creative Studies Coll. Art and Design, Detroit, 1984—, pres. faculty assembly, 1992-93, acting chief acad. studies dept., 1994-95, self-study coord., 1995-96, chair liberal arts, 1996—. Dir. drawings and photographs: A Threatened Legacy: Detroit's Historic Churches, 1992; exhibited in group shows The Freer House, A Legacy to Treasure, 1991. Bd. dirs. Preservation Wayne, Detroit, 1989-91; mem. coordinating com. Detroit Cath. Pastoral Alliance, 1990—; mem. art com. Hist. Trinity Luth. Ch., Detroit, 1989—. Smithsonian Instn. grantee, 1976-78; Tannahill grantee Alliance Ind. Colls. for Art, 1980, 87; Andrew W. Mellon fellow Met. Mus. Art, 1983-84; Roothbert Fund scholar, 1980-81; Detroit Coun. Arts grantee, 1993. Mem. AAUW (nat. panelist 1991—, Elizabeth Avery Coulton fellow 1981-82), Coll. Art Assn. Am., Internat. Ctr. Medieval Art, Nat. Trust for Hist. Preservation, Am. Soc. Hispanic Art History Studies, Midwest Art History Soc., Soc. Archtl. Historians, Founders Soc.-Detroit Inst. Art. Democrat. Office: Coll Art & Design Ctr for Creative Studies 201 E Kirby St Detroit MI 48202-4048

KOSZEWSKI, BOHDAN JULIUS, internist, medical educator; b. Warsaw, Poland, Dec. 17, 1918; Came to U.S., 1952; s. Mikolaj and Helen (Lubienski) K.; children Mikolaj, Joseph, Wanda Marie, Andrzej Bohdan. MD, U. Zurich, Switzerland, 1946; MS, Creighton U., 1956. Resident in pathology U. Zurich, 1944-46, resident in internal medicine, 1946-50, assoc. in medicine, 1950-52; intern St. Mary's Hosp., Hoboken, N.J., 1953; practice medicine specializing in internal medicine Omaha, 1956-90; mem. staff St. Joseph's Hosp., Mercy and Meth. Hosps.; instr. internal medicine Creighton U., 1956-57, asst. prof., 1957-65, assoc. prof. internal medicine, 1965-90; cons. hematology Omaha VA Hosp., 1957-90. Author: Prognosis in Diabetic Coma, 1952; contbr. numerous articles to profl. jours. Served with Polish Army, 1940-45. Fellow ACP, Am. Coll. Angiology; mem. AAAS, Am. Fedn. Clin. Research, Internat. Soc. Hematology, Polish-Am. Congress Nebr. (pres. 1960-68, 82-92). Home: 2901 Park Place Dr Lincoln NE 68506-2818 Office: Lincoln Ctr Bldg Lincoln NE 68542

KOTALIK, GEORGE, marketing executive; m. Rebecca Kotalik; 1 child, Graham. Asst. v.p., creative dir. Aid Assn. for Luths., Appleton, Wis.; v.p., creative dir. Mktg. Assocs., Green Bay, Wis., 1993—; creative strategist J. Walter Thompson, Tathum/Laird/Kudner, D'arcy, Mac Manus, Masius, other nat. and internat. agys.; founder Toy Ties Inc. Office: Mktg Assocs PO Box 1925 1585 Allouez Ave Green Bay WI 54305-1925

KOTLARZ, JOSEPH S., state legislator, lawyer; b. Oct. 29, 1956; m. Heather Kotlarz, 1994. BA, DePaul U.; JD, John Marshall Law Sch. Alderman City of Chgo.; Dist. 20 rep. Ill. Ho. Reps., Springfield, 1993—; attorney, pvt. practice; chmn. claims & liabilities and licenses coms., mem. aging & disabled, housing, human rights, consumer protection, land acquisition, disposition and lease, spl. events and cultural affairs coms., City of Chgo., 1983-91. Home: 3659 N Avers Ave Chicago IL 60618-4017*

KOTTKE, JOHN WILLIAM, meteorologist; b. Adrian, Mich., Sept. 20, 1946; s. Carl Holtz and Lillian (Pearson) K.; m. Frances Anne Harsh, May 20, 1967; children: Sean C. Cavazos-Kottke, Aaron D. BS, Tex. A&M U., 1970. Copy clk. Austin (Tex.) Am.-Statesman, 1973; weathercaster KVUE-TV, Austin, 1974; meteorol. technician U.S. Dept. Commerce Nat. Weather Svc., Marquette, Mich., 1974-77; agr. meteorologist Nat. Weather Svc., Grand Rapids, Mich., 1977-81, West Lafayette, Ind., 1981-89; meteorologist in charge Nat. Weather Svc., Lansing, Mich., 1989-94; warning coord. meteorologist Nat. Weather Svc., Detroit, 1994-95, Grand Rapids. 2d lt. USAF, 1966-72. Office: Nat Weather Svc 4899 S Complex Dr SE Grand Rapids MI 49512

KOTULAK, RONALD, newspaper science writer; b. Detroit, July 31, 1935; s. John and Mary (Roman) K.; m. Jean Bond, May 6, 1961 (dec. July 1974); chidren: Jeffrey, Kerry, Christopher; m. Donna Clausonthue, July 19, 1980; stepchildren: Paul, Lisa. Student, Wayne State U., 1953-54; BJ, U. Mich., 1959. Mem. staff Chgo. Tribune, 1959—, sch. bd. reporter, 1961-63, sci. editor, 1965—. Recipient 1st pl. sci. writing award ADA, 1966, 1st pl. med. writing award AMA, 1968, 1st pl. Howard Blakeslee sci. writing award Am. Heart Assn., 1968, 1st prize Russell L. Cecil award Arthritis Found., 1969, 1st pl. Claude Bernard Sci. Journalism award Nat. Soc. Med. Rsch., 1971, James T. Brady award Am. Chem. Soc., 1974, Lifeline award Am. Health Found., 1976, Edward Scott Beck award Chgo. Tribune, 1965, 76, 91, 93, Outstanding Achievement award U. Mich., 1978, Robert T. Morse Writers award Am. Psychiat. Assn., 1982, 89, Helen Carringer Nat. Mental Health Journalism award Nat. Mental Health Assn., 1988, Excellence in Journalism award Am. Aging Assn., 1992, Pulitzer Prize for explanatory journalism, 1994, others. Mem. Nat. Assn. Sci. Writers (pres. 1972-73). Home: 737 N Oak Park Ave Oak Park IL 60302-1536 Office: The Chicago Tribune 435 N Michigan Ave Chicago IL 60611-4001

KOTYNEK, GEORGE ROY, mechanical engineer, educator, marketing executive; b. Lake Forest, Ill., Apr. 18, 1938; s. Anton Joseph and Zdenka K.; m. Virginia Jean Hyde, Sept. 4, 1965 (div. 1973); children: John Anton, Joseph George. BSME, Ill. Inst. Tech., 1960. Registered profl. engr., Ill.

Efficiency engr. Commonwealth Edison Co., Chgo., 1959-63; instr. physics Glenbard East High Sch., Lombard, Ill., 1963-67; systems engr. Sargent and Lundy, Chgo., 1967-77; prin. engr. Fluor Corp., Chgo., 1977-85; mgr. fossil tech. Stearns Catalytic World Corp., Oak Brook, Ill., 1985-86; mgr. mktg. Volund USA Ltd., New Providence, N.J., 1986-94; tech. cons. VECTRA Techs., Inc., Lincolnshire, Ill., 1994—; mem. hazardous materials adv. com. Waubonsee C.C., Sugar Grove, Ill., 1992—. Contbr. articles to profl. publs. Mem. People to People Internat. Conventional and Nuclear Power Engring. Delegation to People's Republic of China, 1987. Mem. ASME (newsletter editor 1980-82, vice chmn. membership 1982-83, vice chmn. programs 1983-84). Office: VECTRA Techs Inc Ste 400 300 Tri State Internat Lincolnshire IL 60069-4421

KOTZ, GEORGE J., industrial designer; b. Dubuque, Iowa, Sept. 13, 1944. Student, Lorau Coll., U. Wis., Platteville. Advance designer John Deere Dubuque (Iowa) Works, 1965—; mem. adv. bd. SAE Group Hydraulic Tube and Fittings, Warrendale, Pa., 1973. Inventor in field. Mgr. John Deere Crawler Softball Team, Dubuque, 1978; pres. The Lectors-Holy Ghost Cath., 1978-95. With USMC, 1962-65.

KOUFIS, JOHN THEODORE, accountant; b. East Lansing, Mich., June 28, 1965; s. Theodore John and Helen Constantinos (Athanasopoulos) K. BS in Acctg., DePaul U., 1987. CPA, Ill. Audit assoc. Coopers & Lybrand, Chgo., 1987-89, audit sr. assoc., 1989-93; asst. contr. NCH Promotional Svcs. divsn. Dun & Bradstreet, Lincolnshire, Ill., 1993-95, contr., 1995—. Mem. AICPAs, Ill. CPA Soc. Home: 1722 W Lonnquist Blvd Mount Prospect IL 60056-3513 Office: NCH Promotional Svcs Ste 400 75 Tri-State Internat Lincolnshire IL 60069

KOUMOULIDES, JOHN (THOMAS) ANASTASIOS, historian, educator; b. Greece, Aug. 23, 1938; came to U.S., 1956, naturalized, 1969; s. Anastasios Lazaros and Sophia (Theodosiadou) K. A.B., Montclair State Coll. (N.J.), 1960, A.M., 1961; Ph.D., U. Md., 1968; postgrad., Fitzwilliam Coll., Cambridge (Eng.) U., 1965-67; postgrad. vis. fellow, 1971-72. Grad. asst. U. Md., 1961-63; asst. prof. history Austin Peay State U., Clarksville, Tenn., 1963-65, Vanderbilt U., summer 1968; mem. faculty Ball State U., Muncie, Ind., 1968—; prof. history Ball State U., 1975—; vis. tutor Campion Hall, Oxford U., 1980-81. Author: Cyprus and the Greek War of Independence, 1821-1829, 2d edit., 1974, Byzantine and Post-Byzantine Monuments at Aghia in Thessaly, Greece: The Art and Architecture of the Monastery of Saint Panteleimon, 1975; co-author: Churches of Agia in Larissa, Greece, The Monastery of Tatarna: History and Treasures, 1991; also monographs, articles and revs.; editor: Greece in Transition: Essays in the History of Modern Greece, 1821-1974, 1977, Greece: Past and Present, 1979, Hellenic Perspectives: Essays in the History of Greece, 1980, Greece and Cyprus in History, 1960-85, 1986, Cyprus in Transition 1960-85, 1986, Greek Connections: Essays on Culture and Diplomacy, 1987, The Good Idea: Democracy in Ancient Greece, 1995; co-editor: Byzantine Perspectives: Essays in Byzantine History and Culture, 1986. Recipient Archon Chartophylax of the Ecumenical Patriarchate of Constantinople, 1979, Acad. of Athens prize, 1985; research grantee Ball State U., (7 awards) 1969-90, research grantee Am. Philos. Soc., 1973, 79, 90, research grantee Am. Council Learned Socs., 1969, 71, Fulbright-Hays research awardee Greece, 1977-78, 1987-88, Dumbarton Oaks research grantee, 1982-86; vis. fellow Wolfson Coll., Oxford U., 1983-84; guest scholar Woodrow Wilson Internat. Ctr. for Scholars, 1982; vis. fellow Fitzwilliam Coll., Cambridge U., 1989-90, The Golden Cross award of the Mitropolis of Dimitriados, 1991. Mem. The Soc. for Promotion of Hellenice Studies (hon.), Cambridge Philol. Assn., Cambridge U. Soc., Acad. Athens (corr.), Oxford U. Soc., Byzantine Soc. Greek Orthodox. Offices: Ball State U Dept of History Muncie IN 47306

KOUTSTAAL, CORNELIS W., university administrator; b. Rotterdam, The Netherlands, May 10, 1935; came to U.S., 1961; s. Arie and Martina (Leentvaar) K.; m. Murilyn E. Graves, June 21, 1961; children: Robbart Willem, Stanley Wellington. Diploma, Inst. Gehrels, The Hague, The Netherlands, 1957, Logopedic Acad., The Hague, The Netherlands, 1960, Acad. Pedagogy, The Hague, The Netherlands, 1958, Clarke Sch. Deaf, 1963; MS, Springfield Coll., 1963; PhD, Western Res. U., 1966. Lic. speech pathologist, audiologist. Tchr. Effatha Sch. Deaf, Voorburg, The Netherlands, 1958-61, Clarke Sch. Deaf, Northhampton, Mass., 1961-63; fellow Western Res. U., Cleve., 1963-66; prof. Bowling Green (Ohio) State U., 1966-74; chmn., prof. CUNY, Bklyn., 1974-79; dean, prof. Ithaca (N.Y.) Coll., 1979-87; exec. dir. Delano Med. Mgmt. Corp., Pacific Palisades, Calif., 1987-91; prof. head divsn. human potential and performance Truman State U., Kirksville, 1991—; lectr. U. Louvain, U. Groningen, 1969. Author: Back to Basics, 1987; editorial cons. Williams and Wilkins Pub., Phila., 1975-80; editor-in-chief Spine Print Newsletter, Delano, 1987-90; contbr. 42 articles to profl. jours., also 2 films. Bd. dirs. Boy Scouts Am., Rye, N.Y., 1975, N.E.M.O. Health Coun., Chariton Valley Assn. for Handicapped Citizens; cons. Med. Edn. Coney Island Hosp., Bklyn., 1974-78. Grantee NSF, 1967, NIH, 1979-81, U.S. Office Edn., 1970, 74-76, pvt. founds., 1979-86, corps., 1979—. Mem. APA, Am. Speech and Hearing Assn., Acoustical Soc. Am., Am. Assn. Phonetic Scis. (charter), Kirksville C. of C., Phi Kappa Phi, Sigma Xi Rsch. Soc. Am. Home: Lake Wood Estates #4 Kirksville MO 63501-9761

KOVACH, JOSEPH WILLIAM, management consultant, psychologist, educator; b. Hammond, Ind., Oct. 4, 1946; s. William Charles and Florence (Miotke) K. BA in Speech, St. Joseph Coll., Whiting, Ind., 1969; MA in Psychology, Roosevelt U., 1974; PhD, Ill. Inst. Tech., 1981; PhD in Clin. Psychology, Chgo. Sch. Profl. Psychology, 1986. Lic. sch. psychologist, Ill., Ind., Mo.; cert. marriage & family therapist, Ind. Asst. corp. merchandising mgr. Kroch's & Brentano's, Chgo., 1965-70; regional ops. mgr. Interstate Dept. Stores, Inc., Highland, Ind., 1971-73; chmn. divsn. social and behavioral scis. Calumet Coll. St. Joseph, Whiting, Ind., 1984—; dir. Ednl. Rsch. Exch., Calumet City, Ill., 1988—; pres. Joseph W. Kovach and Assocs., Ltd., Calumet City, 1969—; dir. Buzan Centre Ltd. of Chgo., 1992—; sr. cons. Calumet City Youth Svc. Bur., 1973-75; supr. Loyola U. Med. Ctr., Maywood, Ill., 1980-83, Northwestern Meml. Hosp., 1973-83, rsch. assoc., 1979-81; pre-doctoral intern Chgo. Read Mental Health Ctr., 1983-84, asst. program dir., 1988-89; sch. psychologist intern Sch. Dist. 163, Park Forest, Ill., 1986; grad. asst. Roosevelt U., Chgo., 1970-71; rsch. assoc. Northwestern U. Med. Sch., 1974-76, Loyola U. Med. Ctr., Maywood, 1976-78; adj. mem. faculty Thornton C.C. (name now South Suburban Coll.), South Holland, Ill., 1976, Purdue U. Calumet, Hammond, Ind., 1976-89; cons. in field. Bd. dirs. Milton H. Erickson Inst. No. Ill.; co-founder, bd. dirs. Internat. Acad. for Study of Virtual Reality; trustee Calumet Coll. St. Joseph. Mem. APA, Midwest Psychol. Assn., Ill. Sch. Psychologists Assn. Office: PO Box 113 Calumet City IL 60409-0113

KOVACIK, NEAL STEPHEN, hotel and restaurant executive; b. Toledo, Mar. 2, 1952; s. Albert Joseph and Phyllis (Lesinski) K.; m. Denise Reichert, Apr. 20, 1974 (div. June 1976). Student, Bowling Green State U., 1971-72, U. Toledo, 1973-74, Owens Tech. Coll., 1975. Dir. food and beverages Motor Inn of Perrysburg, Ohio, 1976-78; v.p. food and beverage ops. Bennett Enterprises, Perrysburg, 1978-82, v.p. hotel and restaurant ops., 1982—. Bd. dirs. Greater Toledo Office of Tourism and Convs., 1994—. Recipient Food and Beverage Dir. of Yr. award Holiday Inns. Inc. and Internat. Assn. Holiday Inns, 1976. Mem. Northwestern Ohio Restaurant Assn. (bd. dirs. 1980-84), Toledo Hotel and Motel Assn. Democrat. Roman Catholic. Home: 9640 Monclova Rd Monclova OH 43542-9709 Office: Bennett Enterprises Corp 27476 Holiday Ln Perrysburg OH 43551-3345

KOVACS, DIANE KAYE, internet training consultant; b. Denver, Oct. 3, 1962; d. Robert Joseph and Jean Ann (Finch) Engelbrecht; m. Michael J. Kovacs, June 23, 1984. BA in Anthropology, U. Ill., 1985, MS in Libr. and Info. Sci., 1989; MEd, 1993. Social scis. reference libr. Bucknell U., Lewisburg, Pa., 1989-90; assoc. prof., reference libr. Kent (Ohio) State U., 1990-95; internet tng. cons. Kovacs Consulting, Brunswick, Ohio, 1993—. Author: The Internet Trainers Guide, 1995; editor: Directory of Scholarly Electronic Conferences, 1991—; contbr. articles to profl. jours. Mem. SLA. Office: Kovacs Consulting 1117 Meadowbrook Blvd Brunswick OH 44212

KOVACS, JOSEPH ANTON, III, utility contract specialist; b. Angola, Ind., Dec. 12, 1950; s. Joseph Anton and Beatrice Gertrude (Gradl) K. Jr.; m. Linda Lee Walsh, July 22, 1953; children: Amy Lynn, Anne Marie. BS in Indsl. Mgmt., Purdue U., 1974. Cert. purchasing mgr. Buyer Simmons Co., Munster, Ind., 1973-75, Carson Pirie Scott Co., Chgo., 1975-77; purchasing agt. Bimba Mfg. Co., Monee, Ind., 1977-79; buyer Wis. Steel Co., Chgo., 1979-80; contract specialist No. Ins. Pub. Svc. Co., Hammond, Ind., 1980—. Mem. NAPM, Northwest Ind. Roman Catholic. Home: 9443 Olcott Ave Saint John IN 46373-9578 Office: No Ind Pub Svc Co 5265 Hohman Ave Hammond IN 46320-1722

KOVACS, ROSEMARY, newpaper editor. BS in Journalism, Bowling Green State U., 1968. Mng. editor prodn. The Plain Dealer, Cleve. Named to Bowling Green State U. Journalism Hall of Fame, 1988. Mem. Press Club of Cleve. (pres.). Office: Plain Dealer Pub Co 1801 Superior Ave E Cleveland OH 44114-2107

KOVALSKI, RAY J., chemical engineer, consultant; b. Mt. Pleasant, Ohio, July 30, 1946; s. Joseph A.; m. Mary Ann Laskowski Kovalski, June 14, 1969; children: Theresa M., Katherine A., William R. BS in Chem. Engring., Ohio U., 1969; MBA, Canisius Coll., Buffalo, N.Y., 1986. Engring. and plant supr. Allied Signal Corp., Moundsville, W.Va., 1968-76, area ops. supr., 1976-78; mgr. maintenance and engring. Buffalo Color Corp., 1978-80, mgr. engring. and constrn., 1980-86; mgr. ops. chem. products Gen. Electric Corp., Cleve., 1986-88, mgr. components mktg. and sales, 1988-90, divsn. mgr. inventory and prodn. planning, 1990-92; pres. Tubular divsn. HealthMor Industries Inc., Cleve., 1992—; pres., CEO RJK Analysis and Cons., Chagrin Falls, Ohio, 1991—. Co-chmn. St. Mary's Annual Picnic, Buffalo, N.Y., 1984-86; co-chair Sweethearts Ball, Moundsville, W.Va., 1973-76. Mem. AIChE, AIAA, Soc. Mfg. Engrs., Beta Gamma Sigma. Republican. Roman Catholic. Home: 542 Falls Rd Chagrin Falls OH 44022

KOVELESKI, KATHRYN DELANE, retired special education educator; b. Detroit, Aug. 12, 1925; d. Edward Albert Vogt and Delane (Bender) Vogt; BA, Olivet (Mich.) Coll., 1947; MA, Wayne State U., Detroit, 1955; m. Casper Koveleski, July 18, 1952; children: Martha, Ann. Tchr. schs. in Mich., 1947-88; tchr. Garden City Schs., 1955-56, 59-88, resource and learning disabilities tchr., 1970-88, ret. 1988. Sec. bd. Christian edn. Congl. Ch., 1988-89, chmn., 1988-90, mem. Mem. BPW (Woman of Yr. 1985-86 Garden City), Mich. Assn. Ret. Sch. Pers. , Wayne Hist. Soc., Wayne Garden Club, Wayne Lit. Club (past pres., treas. 1988-89), Sch. Masters Bowling League (v.p. 1984-88), Odd Couples Bowling League (pres. 82-83, treas. 1995-96), Wayne Garden Club, Wayne Hist. Soc.

KOVNAT, KAREL DEBRA, psychologist; b. Phila., Oct. 30, 1955; d. Arthur Samuel and Lorraine (Mostovoy) K.; m. Lee Paul Adler, Dec. 9, 1984. BA, Muhlenberg Coll., Allentown, Pa., 1977; MS, U. Pa., 1981, PhD, 1987. Lic. psychologist, Ohio, Pa.; diplomate Am. Bd. Profl. Psychology. Trainee Children's Aid Soc. of Pa., Phila., 1978-79; counselor Transitional Residence Ind. Svc., Camden, N.J., 1981-83; counselor/practicum coord. Resources for Human Devel., Ardmore, Pa., 1983; psychology intern Temple U. Hosp., Phila., 1986-87; postdoctoral fellow Case Western Res. U., Cleve., 1987-88; psychology dir. Westside Pain Relief Svc., Cleve., 1988-89; asst. prof. dept. psychology Case Western Res. U., 1991—; sr. clin. instr. Sch. Medicine Case Western Res. U., Cleve., 1991—; cons. Guardian Ad Litem Project, Cleve., 1991-95, Temple Tiferith-Israel, Cleve., 1988—. Contbr. articles to profl. jours. Trustee Nat. Multiple Sclerosis Soc., Cleve., 1991—. Recipient Cert. in Social Work, Children's Aid Soc. Pa., 1979, Cert. Clin. Supervision, U. Pa., 1986, grant Cleve. Elec. Illuminating Co., 1993, 94, 95. Mem. APA, Pa. Psychol. Assn., Ohio Psychol. Assn., Cleve. Psychol. Assn. (trustee 1992-95), Pa. Alumni Club of Cleve. Office: Heights Med Bldg 2460 Fairmount Blvd Ste 315 Cleveland OH 44106-3125

KOWALSKI, DAVID W., manufacturing executive; b. Łódź, Poland, Oct. 28, 1960; came to U.S., 1976; s. Stan and Irma Stepnoski. BA, U. Wis., 1982. Salesman Werik Assocs., Milw., 1982-87, sales mgr., 1987-91, v.p. sales, 1991-95; sr. v.p. mktg., 1995—. Vol. St. Mary's Hosp., Bayside Hist. Soc. Mem. NRA. Democrat. Roman Catholic. Office: Werik Assocs 8511 N Pelham Pky Milwaukee WI 53217-2444

KOWALSKI, KATHLEEN PATRICIA, reporter, publishing executive; b. Detroit; d. Arthur Aloysius and Theresa Joyce (Pathe) K. BA in English Lang. and Lit., U. Mich., 1987. Sales, divsn. trainer, mktg. mgr. Encyclopaedia Britannica, Southfield, Mich., 1981-86; computer graphics, comm. and systems coord. Kelly/Kelly Tech. Svcs., Troy, Mich., 1987-95; intern WJBK-TV, Southfield, 1990-91; host on air talent Cable TV Sta. WTRY, Troy, Mich., 1993-94; pres. Kowality Writing, West Bloomfield, Mich., 1993—. Author: Blossoming Rose, 1995. Mem. U. Mich. Alumnae Group, Ice Skating Inst. Am. Roman Catholic. Home: 2332 Woodrow Wilson Blvd #4 West Bloomfield MI 48324

KOWALSKI, KENNETH LAWRENCE, physicist, educator; b. Chgo., July 24, 1932; s. Florian Lawrence and Emily Helen (Sinoga) K.; m. Audrey Bellin; children—Eric Clifford, Claudia Gail. B.S., Ill. Inst. Tech., 1954; Ph.D. (Universal Match Found. fellow), Brown U., 1963. Aero. research scientist Lewis Research Center, NACA, 1954-57; research asso. in physics Brown U., summer 1962, Case Inst. Tech., Cleve., 1962-63; asst. prof. physics Case Inst. Tech., 1963-67, asso. prof., 1967-73; asso. prof. Case Western Res. U., 1967-73, prof., 1973—, exec. officer dept. physics, 1970-71, chmn. dept. physics, 1971-76; vis. prof. Inst. Theoretical Physics U. Louvain, Belgium, 1968-69; scientist-in-residence Argonne Nat. Lab., 1986-87. Author: (with S.K. Adhikari) Dynamical Collision Theory and It's Applications, 1991; editor: (with W.J. Fickinger) Modern Physics in America, 1988; contbr. articles to profl. jours. NSF grantee, 1972—. Mem. Am. Phys. Soc. Home: 2275 S Overlook Rd Cleveland OH 44106-3141 Office: Case Western Res U Dept Physics 10900 Euclid Ave Cleveland OH 44106-1712

KOWALSKI, LUCY ANN, retired nurse, educator; b. Sparta, Wis., June 11, 1936; d. Walter and Victoria (Kot) K. Diploma, St. Joseph's Hosp. Sch Nursing, Chgo., 1959; BSN, Viterbo Coll., 1989. RN, Wis. Staff nurse, relief head nurse, rehab. nurse VA Med. Ctr., Tomah, Wis., 1959-65, 67-68; staff nurse VA Med. Ctr., Wood, Wis., 1966; staff nurse kidney dialysis unit Mayo Clinic, Rochester, Minn., 1966; instr. nursing edn. insvc. and orientation programs. VA Med. Ctr., Tomah, 1968-92; presenter workshops orientation and insvc. programs. Officer Nurse Corps USAR, 1963-65. Mem. Am. Soc. Healthcare Edn. and Tng., LaCrosse Dist. Nurses' Assn. (nurse practice com.).

KOZAK, JOHN W., lawyer; b. Chgo., July 25, 1943; s. Walter and Stella (Palka) K.; m. Elizabeth Mathias, Feb. 3, 1968; children: Jennifer, Mary Margaret, Suzanne. BSEE, U. Notre Dame, 1965; JD, Georgetown U., 1968. Bar: Ill. 1968, D.C. 1968. Patent advisor Office of Naval Research, Corona, Calif., 1968-69; assoc. Leydig, Voit & Mayer, Ltd. (and predecessor firms), Chgo., 1969-74, ptnr., 1974—, chmn. mgmt. com., 1982-91; mem. United Charities Legal Aid Soc., 1989—. Mem. ABA, Am. Intellectual Property Assn., Licensing Execs. Soc., Chgo. Intellectual Property Law Assn., University Club (Chgo.), Law Club (Chgo.), Winter Club, (Lake Forest, Ill.). Office: Leydig Voit & Mayer 2 Prudential Pla Ste 4900 2 Prudential Pla Ste 4900 Chicago IL 60601

KOZANECKI, ROBERT FRANCIS, business executive, educator; b. Chgo., Apr. 30, 1932; s. Frank S. and Stella A. (Stawarz) K.; m. Lucille B. Lipinski, Aug. 7, 1954; children: Gary, Alice, Nancy. Attended, U. Ill., Chgo., 1950-53; BS in Health & Phys. Edn., George William Coll., 1959; AA in Real Estate, Loop Coll., 1970-71; postgrad., U.S. Space Acad., 1991. Personnel adminstr., supervisor U.S. Army, Alaska, 1955-56; tchr. Ursa Major Sch., Fort Richardson, Alaska, 1956-57; ins. adjuster Bankers Life, Chgo., 1957-68; tchr. Cook County Jail, Chgo., 1969-73, City Colls. of Chgo., 1973-83, Reed Zone Mental Hosp., Chgo., 1974; computer coord. Philo Carpenter Sch., 1959-95. Swimming coach Jr. Olympics, 1983-85, Prairie State Games, Ill., 1984l judge Non-Pub. Sci. Expo., Chgo., 1984-96, Ill. State Science Fair, Champaign, 1984-94; co-chair Ill. State Science Fair, Champaign, 1995-96; coord. Cosmic Challenge, 1994; solicitor Crusade of Mercy, Chgo., 1960-95. Recipient Tex. Inst. Calculator Comp. award, Appreciation award Crusade of Mercy, 1991-95. Mem. Chgo. Citizens Sch. Com., Tchrs. as Leaders Network, Tchrs. Task Force, CHgo. Found. for Edn., Chgo. Tchrs. Math Club. Home and Office: 8613 N Oleander Ave Niles IL 60714

KOZBERG, STEVEN FREED, psychologist; b. Mpls., Apr. 30, 1953; s. Martin L. and Lois (Bix) K. BA, Macalester Coll., 1975; MA, U. Minn.-Duluth, 1978; PhD, U. Wis.-Madison, 1981. Lic. psychologist, Minn. Research asst. dept. counseling and guidance U. Wis.-Madison, 1978-79, teaching asst., 1980-81, research asst. Guidance Inst. for Talented Students, 1979-80; counseling psychologist, asst. prof. psychology Carleton Coll., Northfield, Minn., 1981-88, counseling psychologist, lectr. psychology, 1988-92, counseling psychologist, sr. lectr. psychology, 1992-95, sr. lectr. psychology, 1995—, pvt. practice, Mpls., 1995—. Mem. APA, Minn. Psychol. Assn., Soc. Rsch. on Adolescence, Midwestern Psychol. Assn., Assn. Advancement of Psychology, Phi Kappa Phi. Home: 5121 Tifton Dr Minneapolis MN 55439-1464 Office: Lake Pointe Corporate Ctr 3100 West Lake St Ste 465 Minneapolis MN 55416

KOZBIAL, RICHARD JAMES, elementary education educator; b. Toledo, Nov. 11, 1933; s. Phillip and Bernice Bronislawa (Durka) K.; m. Jane Ardys Verny, July 8, 1961 (dec. Nov. 1983); children: Ardys Jane, Beth Lynne. EdB, U. Toledo, 1957, EdM, 1976. Tchr. Toledo Pub. Schs., 1956-58, 1962-84, Van Dyke Sch. Dist., Warren, Mich., 1958-62; intern tchr. cons. Toledo Pub. Schs., 1984-87, cons., 1987—; part-time faculty, supr. student tchrs., course facilitator U. Toledo, 1987—; ESL tchr. Szeged, Hungary, 1993—; textbook selection coms. Toledo Pub. Schs.; instr. student tchr. tng. programs Toledo U., 1962-84; instr. student tchr. tng. Bowling Green State U., 1962-84, Mich. State U., 1958-59; organizer Multi-Cultural Awareness Workshop Toledo Elem. Tchrs. Internat. Inst., 1986—; organizer Outdoor Edn. Program; participant Multi Unit Edn. Plan. Author Spelling Curriculum Guide Toledo Pub. Schs., 1968; prodr. (TV programs) WGTE Famous Ams. Born in Feb., Israel. Up with People Host Family, Ohio Arab Affairs Coun., 1989—, YCMA, ISS, USIA Host Family, 1986—; mem. Planned Parenthood N.W. Ohio, Toledo Mus. Modern Art, Nat. Trust Historic Preservation, 1988—; vestry mem. Trinity Episc. Ch., 1984-87, sesquicentennial com., chmn. music; baritone soloist Canterbury Choir; bereavement vol. Hospice N.W. Ohio, Nat. Hospice Assn.; exec. bd. Toledo/Poznan Alliance; mem. Bedford Polish Culture Club, 1989—; sponsor, coord. host families Zulu Choir, Durham, South Africa, Poznan (Poland) Nightengales. Named Outstanding Your Educator, Toledo C. of C., 1965-66; Jennings Founder scholar, 1979-80; recipient Miss Peach award Toledo Blade, 1963, Award of Excellence, 1983, Internat. Inst. Hall of Fame Disting. Svc. award, 1994, Letter of Commendation, Gov. Ohio. Mem. Am. Fedn. Tchrs., Ohio Fedn. Tchrs., Toledo Fedn. Tchrs. (life), Internat. Inst. Inc. (life, chmn. edn. com., bd. dirs. 1985—, pres. 1988—), Assn. Two Toledos (bd. dirs., 1st v.p. 1990-91), U. Toledo Alumni Assn. (life), U. Mich. Alumni Assn., Am. Assn. Ret. Persons, Lucas County Ret. Tchrs. (life), Mid. East Affairs Coun. (bd. dirs.), Ellis Island Found., Smithsonian Assocs., Nat. Coun. Sr. Citizens, Toledo Sister Cities Internat. (bd. dirs. 1995—, chmn. entertainment Masked Bash 1996, mem com. English lang. camp for students from Poland 1995, 96, chmn. host families), Greenpeace, Phi Delta Kappa, Kappa Delta Pi (Point of Excellence award 1992). Democrat. Home: 3823 Grantley Rd Toledo OH 43613-4218

KOZELKA, EDWARD WILLIAM, seed and feed company executive; b. Monona, Iowa, July 19, 1912; s. William Frank and Elizabeth (Tayek) K.; student Loras Coll., 1929-31; m. Beulah Annette Gunderson, Feb. 24, 1941; 1 dau., Gail Kathleen. Gen. mgr. Hall Roberts' Son, Postville, Iowa, 1932-46, v.p., gen. mgr., 1946-75, treas., 1975—; salesman Schiedel Real Estate, Postville, 1984—; dir. Postville State Bank, Postville Telephone Co. Mem. Postville City Coun., 1960-61; pres. Postville Hist. Soc., 1975-78; treas. Upper Explorerland Resource, Conservation and Devel. Com., 1969-87; chmn. Upper Explorerland Regional Planning Commn., 1971-80; chmn. N.E. Iowa River Basin Com., 1976-79; mem. Iowa Policy Adv. Coun. on Water Quality, 1976-82; mem. citizens adv. coun. Dept. Transp., 1977-87; mem. NE Iowa Water Resource Bd., 1986-87, Allamakee County Econ. Devel. Com., 1988—, Allamakee County E-911 Bd., 1990-92, planning and fin. com. Postville Hosp., 1959-60; chmn. bldg. com. Postville Hosp., 1960-61; co-chmn. fund raising com. Postville Good Samaritan Center, 1968; bd. dirs. Big 4 Fair, 1946-74; mem. adv. council Area Aging Com., 1983-92. Recipient Disting. Service award Jaycees, 1966; hon. future farmer FFA. Mem. Iowa Seed Dealers Assn. (pres. 1972), Iowa Grain and Feed Assn., Western Seed Dealers Assn. Republican. Roman Catholic. Clubs: Kiwanis, Postville Comml. Home: 205 E Williams St Postville IA 52162-9756 Office: PO Box 396 Postville IA 52162-0396

KOZIURA, JOSEPH F., state legislator; b. Aug. 21, 1946; m. Kitti Koziura; 1 child, Mary. Grad., Lorian County C.C.; BA, Dyke Coll. Chief dep. auditor Lorain, Ohio, 1971-76; city auditor Lorain, 1976-83; state rep. Dist. 55 Ohio State Congress, 1985-92, state rep. Dist. 61, 1993—; precinct committeeman Lorain Dems.; exec. com. mem. Loraine County Dems.; fin. cons. J.F. Koziura & Assocs. Mem. VFW, PLAY, Amvets, Vietnam Vets. Am., Elks, Moose. *

KOZLOWSKI, JAMES MICHAEL, urology and surgery educator; b. Chgo., Dec. 26, 1949; s. Leonard and Ruth (Brizzolara) K.; m. Mary Catherine Samples, Mar. 28, 1980. BS magna cum laude with honors, Loyola U., Chgo., 1971; MD with distinction, Northwestern U., Chgo., 1975. Diplomate Am. Bd. Surgery, Am. Bd. Urology. Intern Northwestern U. Med. Sch., Chgo., 1975-76, intern in surgery, resident in gen. surgery, 1976-77, 78-79, 81-82, resident in urology, 1977-78, 79-80, 80-81, instr. urology and surgery, 1980-82, assoc. in urology and surgery, 1982-83, asst. prof., 1984-90, assoc. prof., 1990—; mem. sect. urol. oncology Cancer Ctr., 1984—, dir. genitourinary oncology program, 1988—; vice chmn. dept. urology Northwestern U. Med. Sch., Chgo., 1992—; asst. attending surgeon Northwestern Meml. Hosp., Chgo., 1984-86, assoc. attending surgeon, 1986—; cons. in urology and surgery VA Lakeside Med. Ctr., Chgo., 1984—; editorial cons. Jour. Urology, 1984—, Jour. AMA, 1986—, Cancer Rsch., 1989—, Prostate, 1989—, Urology, 1989—; bd. dirs., mem. med. adv. bd. Nat. Kidney Cancer Assn., Chgo., 1990—; mem. prostate cancer task force Ill. div. Am. Cancer Soc., 1987; ad hoc mem. 2 workshops Nat. Cancer Inst., 1987, ad hoc mem. site visit team, 1987, spl. NIH study team, 1993. Contbg. author: Adult and Pediatric Urology, 1991, 95, Mastery of Surgery: Urology, 1992; contbr. articles to med. jours. Leander Riba rsch. fellow Northwestern U. Med. Sch., 1982-84, jr. faculty clin. fellow Am. Cancer Soc., 1984-86. Fellow ACS; mem. Soc. Univ. Urologists, Am. Urol. Assn., Soc. Clin. Urologists, Am. Assn. Cancer Rsch., Soc. Urologic Oncology, Am. Soc. Clin. Oncology, Soc. Surg. Oncology, Alpha Omega Alpha. Home: 4712 Northcott Ave Downers Grove IL 60515-3417 Office: Northwestern U Med Sch Tarry 11-715 303 E Chicago Ave Chicago IL 60611-3008

KRABILL, ROBERT ELMER, osteopathic physician; b. Wayland, Iowa, June 4, 1934; s. Robert H. and Amanda (Wyse) K.; m. Ellen Savage, Sept. 1, 1963; children: Keith Andrew, Angela Kay, Valerie Ann, Kelly Dawn. BS, Iowa Wesleyan Coll., 1961; DO, Kirkville (Mo.) Coll. Osteo. Medicine, 1966. Diplomate Am. Bd. Family Practice. Intern Cuyahoga Falls (Ohio) Gen. Hosp., 1966-67, mem. staff, 1967—; gen. practice osteo. medicine Uniontown, Ohio, 1967—; sec., treas. gen. practice dept. Cuyahoga Falls Gen. Hosp., 1985-86. Named one of Outstanding Young Men of Am., U.S. Jaycees, 1969. Mem. Am. Osteo. Assn., Ohio Osteo. Assn., Am. Coll. Gen. Practitioners Osteo. Medicine and Surgery. Mennonite. Home: 3733 N Vista St NW Uniontown OH 44685-8496 Office: 13017 Cleveland Ave NW Box 399 Uniontown OH 44685

KRAFT, JOHN A., lawyer; b. New Albany, Ind., Sept. 29, 1954; s. Robert M. and Patricia L. (Salmon) K.; m. Andrea G. Fultz, July 20, 1979; children: Alexis R., Charlanne K. BS, Ball State U., 1976; JD, U. Louisville, 1983. Lawyer Young Lind Endres Kraft, Lanesville, Ind. Mem. Kiwanis of Hist. New Albany (past officer/dir.). Office: 126 W Spring St New Albany IN 47150

KRAFT, LORENA, investment executive; b. Clay Center, Kans., Nov. 6, 1936. Cert. advanced broker devel. Investment profl. Chevrolet, Kansas City, Mo., 1950-70; mut. funds profl. Waddell & Reed, Kansas City, Mo.; broker Drexel Burnam, Kansas City, Mo., Piper Jaffray Inc., Kansas City, Mo., 1989—; lectr. seminars. Mem. Friends of Zoo, Kansas City, Mo.; participant Multiple Sclerosis Walk, Kansas City. Mem. Kansas City C. of C. Republican. Home: 9161 W 102nd Ter Overland Park KS 66212-4210

Office: Piper Jaffray Inc PO Box 26508 1100 Main St Kansas City MO 64196

KRAFVE, ALLEN HORTON, management consultant; b. Superior, Wis., Jan. 26, 1937; s. Richard Ernest and Frances Virginia (Horton) K.; m. Lois Anne Reed, Aug. 15, 1959; children—Bruce Allen, Anne Marie, Carol Elizabeth. B.S. in Mech. Engring., U. Mich., 1958, M.B.A., 1960, M.S. in Mech. Engring., 1961. Asst. prof. mech. engring. San Jose State U. (Calif.), 1961-65; various positions including quality control mgr. Ford Motor Co., Dearborn, Mich., 1965-77; engring. mgr. Kysor/Cadillac, Cadillac, Mich., 1977-82; mgmt. cons., Lake City, Mich., 1982—; bd. dirs. NOC Industries, Cadillac; pres. Lark Homes, Inc., 1979—; area mktg. dir. Lindal Cedar Homes, 1985-94. Co-author: Reliability Considerations in Design, 1962, internat. conf. paper, 1961. Bd. dirs. Crooked Tree coun. Girl Scouts U.S., Traverse City, Mich., 1983. Mem. ASME, Soc. Automotive Engrs., Am. Soc. Engring. Edn. Republican. Methodist. Home: 1725 S Duck Point Rd Lake City MI 49651-9082 Office: Allen H Krafve Cons 2604 Sunnyside Dr Cadillac MI 49601-9383

KRAINIK, ARDIS, opera company executive; b. Manitowoc, Wis., Mar. 8, 1929; d. Arthur Stephen and Clara (Bracken) K. BS cum laude, Northwestern U., 1951, postgrad., 1953-54, DFA (hon.), 1984; LHD (hon.), DePaul U., 1985, Loyola U., 1986, U. Wis., 1986; DFA (hon.), St. Xavier Coll., 1986, Knox Coll., 1987, Columbia Coll., Chgo., 1988, Lake Forest Coll., 1989, Roosevelt U., 1989; LLD (hon.), Albion Coll., 1990; D Mus. Arts (hon.), U. Ill., Chgo., 1990; LHD (hon.), No. Ill. U., 1990; HHD (hon.), Lewis U., 1991; MusD (hon.), Ind. U. N.W., 1992, Barat Coll., 1993; LHD honoris causa, Lawrence U., 1993; DFA (hon.), St. Mary's Coll., 1994. Tchr. drama, pub. speaking Horlick High Sch., Racine, Wis., 1951-53; exec. sec., office mgr. Lyric Opera, Chgo., 1954-59; asst. mgr. Lyric Opera, 1960-75, artistic adminstr., 1975-80, awd. mgr., 1981—, gen. dir., 1987—; bd. dirs. No. Trust Co. Trustee Northwestern U., mem. women's bd., mem. adv. coun. Kellogg Sch. Mgmt.; mem. governing bd. Ill. Arts Alliance; bd. dirs. Opera Am.;. Recipient commendator Italian Order Merit, 1983, Ill. Order Lincoln, 1985, Appdt. Rector, 1993, Grand Decoration of Honor in Silver, Republic of Austria, 1994, Alumni Merit award Northwestern U., 1986, award of Achievement Girl Scouts U.S., 1987, Dushkin Svc. award Music Ctr. of North Shore, 1987, Thomas de Gaetani award U.S. Inst. for Theatre Tech., 1990, Bravo award Rosary Coll., 1991, Career Svc. award Arts Mgmt. News Svc., 1992, Edward Moss Martin award Union League Club, 1993, Crystal award Chgo. Drama League, 1994, Exemplary Woman award Women in Charge, 1994, Sara Lee Frontrunner award 1994, Friendship award European Union, 1994, award Abraham Lincoln Ctr., 1995, Women of Achievement award Antidefamation League, 1995, Govt. of France/officier des L'ordre de Arts et Lettres, 1996; named to Crain's Chgo. Bus./Top 100 Business Women in Chgo., 1996, Exec. of Yr., 1990, Tribute to Chgo. Women Honoree Midwest Women's Ctr., 1986, one of Chicagoans of Yr. Boys and Girls Club, 1987. Mem. Ill. Arts Alliance (governing bd.), Internat. Assn. Opera Dirs., Opera Am. (bd. dirs.), Chgo. Hist. Soc. Guild, Northwestern U. Women's Bd., Northwestern U. Assocs., Northwestern U. Kellogg Sch. Mgmt. (adv. coun.), Mortar Bd., Econ. Club (bd. dirs.), Comml. Club (past pres.), Lake Geneva Country Club, Pi Kappa Lambda. Christian Scientist. Office: Lyric Opera of Chgo 20 N Wacker Dr Ste 860 Chicago IL 60606-2805

KRAKOWSKI, RICHARD JOHN, lawyer, public relations executive; b. Meppen, W.Ger., Apr. 3, 1946; came to U.S., 1951, naturalized, 1962; s. Feliks and Maria (Chilinski) K. M.B.A., DePaul U., 1979; J.D., John Marshall Law Sch., 1983. Bar: Ill. 1984. Personnel dir. Andy Frain, Inc., Chgo., 1973-78; pub. relations dir. Chgo. Health Systems Agy., 1978-84; assoc. firm Mangum, Smietanka & Johnson, Chgo., 1984-87; asst. atty. gen. Ill. Atty. Gen.'s Ofc., 1987-96; lectr. in field. Fundraising and pub. relations dir. Cabrini-Green Sandlot Tennis program, Chgo., 1979-83; sustaining mem. Republican Nat. Com., 1981—. Served to capt. U.S. Army, 1969-72. Mem. ABA, Nat. Advocates Soc., Ill. Bar Assn., Chgo. Bar Assn., Chgo. Council Fgn. Relations, Lyric Opera Guild, Art Inst. Chgo., Chgo. Soc. Polish Nat. Alliance. Roman Catholic. Club: Publicity (Chgo.). Co-author: Health Care Financing and Policy Making in Chicago and Illinois, 1982. Home: 1350 N Lake Shore Dr Apt 1215 Chicago IL 60610-2104 Office: 39 W Washington S 1420 Chicago IL 60602

KRALICK, RICHARD LOUIS, lawyer; b. Youngstown, Ohio, Dec. 7, 1933; s. Joseph Martin and Dorothy Louise (Canada) K.; m. Roselle A. Richmond, Sept. 10, 1955; children: Kris Ann, Richard II, Kolleen, Kathleen, Michael. BA, Mich. State U., 1955; JD, U. Mich., 1959. Assoc. Baker, Hammond and Baker, Adrian, Mich., 1960-62; ptnr. Hammond Baker and Kralick, Adrian, 1963—. Chmn. Mich. Girls Tng. Sch., Adrian, 1966-67; bd. dirs. Lenawee County Human Svcs. Coun., 1991-95, Lenawee United Way, 1991—; pres. Lenawee Family Coun. and Children's Svcs., Adrian, 1970-71; bd. dirs. Adrian YMCA, 1969-72, Lenawee Ams. with Disabilities Act Coun., 1993-95; v.p. Goodwill Industries, Adrian, 1972-73; bd. dirs. (LEAH) Lenawee Emergency Affordable Housing. Named Mich. Vol. of Yr. Mich. Family Coun. and Children's Svcs., 1971; recipient Good Willie award Goodwill Industries, Adrian, 1972, Disting. Svc. award Lenawee Cancer Soc., 1973, Crisis Hot Line, Adrian, 1992. Mem. ABA, Lenawee County Bar Assn. (pres. 1968-69), Mich. Trial Lawyers Assn., Mich. Def. Trial Lawyers, Mich. Bar Assn. Home: 5140 Wildwood Dr Manitou Beach MI 49253-9628 Office: Hammond Baker and Kralick Key Bank Bldg PO Box 278 Adrian MI 49221-0278

KRAM, GUENTHER REINHARD, manufacturing executive; b. Chgo., May 25, 1957; s. Siegmund and Emmy (Hedeker) K.; m. Deborah Ann Farrington, Nov. 5, 1988. BS in Acctg., DePaul U., 1979, MBA in Fin., 1985. CPA, Ill. Internal auditor Waste Mgmt., Oakbrook, Ill., 1979-80; divisional controller Waste Mgmt.-City Waste, Skokie, Ill., 1980-84, Waste Mgmt. - City Waste and Garden City, Bensenville, Ill., 1984-85; divisional controller Ill. Tool Works -Devcon Consumer, Wood Dale, Ill., 1985-87, ops. mgr., 1987-92; brand merchandising ops. mgr. Ill. Tool Works, Wood Dale, 1992—. Deacon Willow Creek Community Ch., South Barrington, Ill., 1987. Mem. Ill. CPA Soc., Beta Gamma Sigma. Republican. Office: Ill Tool Works Brand Merchandising 226 Gerry Dr Wood Dale IL 60191-1139

KRAMER, ALEX JOHN, dentist; b. Aurora, Ill., Dec. 21, 1939; s. Roy Edward and Frances (Astromskis) K.; m. Phyllis Rose Gonsky, July 15, 1967 (div. Sept. 1978); m. Brenda Jean Schillinger, Sept. 12, 1981; children: Ian Alexander, Elizabeth Katherine. Student, Marquette U., 1957-60; DDS, U. Ill., Chgo., 1964. Gen. practice dentistry Montgomery, Ill., 1966-88, Ashland, Wis., 1988-91; priv. practice craniofacial pain Duluth, Minn., 1991-94; gen. dental practice Duluth, 1994—. Mem. exec. bd. Two Rivers Boy Scouts Am., St. Charles, Ill., 1969-79. Lt. Dental Corps USNR, 1964-66. Master Internat. Coll. Craniomandibular Orthopedics; mem. ADA, Am. Assn. Maxillofacial Orthopedics, Ill. State Dental Assn., Chgo. Dental Soc., Wis. State Dental Assn., No. Wis. Dental Assn., Am. Acad. Gnathological Orthopedics, Am. Soc. Gen. Dentistry, Dentafacial Orthopedics Study Club Mo., Am. Assn. Functional Orthodontics, Internat. Acad. Orthomolecular and Preventive Medicine, Am. Acad. Pain Mgmt. (diplomate), Minn. State Dental Assn., U. Ill. Alumni Assn. (life), Pershing Rifles Hon. Mil. Frat., Psi Omega. Republican. Methodist. Club: Aurora (Ill.) Country. Lodge: Optimists. Home: 54 E Kent Rd Duluth MN 55812-1420 Office: 1601 Woodland Ave Duluth MN 55803-2629

KRAMER, BENJAMIN ROBERT, sheriff's deputy; b. Middletown, Ohio, Feb. 21, 1962; s. Benjamin Rudyard and Bonita Sue (McClanahan) K.; m. Donna May Kramer, May 15, 1995; 1 child, Joshua Sprinkles. Student, U. Md., Vincenza, Italy, 1984-86; AS in Paralegal Sci., Nat. Inst. Paralegal Arts/Scis, 1996. Cert. Ohio Peace Officer Tng. Coun., Advanced Traffic Investigation. Police officer Carlisle (Ohio) Police Dept., 1989-93; dep. sheriff Butler County Sheriff's Office, Hamilton, Ohio, 1994—. Author Vincenza Community Security Plan, 1986. Active Rep. Nat. Com., Washington, 1993, Ohio Rep. Party. Served with U.S. Army, 1980-88, Italy. Decorated Army Commendation medal (2). Mem. Buckeye State Sheriff's Assn. (assoc.), Fraternal Order of Police, Am. Legion, Masons, Scottish Rite, Eagles. Pentecostal. Office: Butler County Sheriff's Ofc 123 Court St Hamilton OH 45011

KRAMER, CARL EDWARD, historian, urban planner; b. New Albany, Ind., May 22, 1946; s. Douglas Manuel Kramer and Jane Anastasia (Markert) Kramer Pitman; m. Mary Elizabeth Kagin, June 16, 1990. BA, Anderson (Ind.) U., 1968; MA, Roosevelt U., Chgo., 1970; MS, U. Louisville, 1972; PhD, U. Toledo, 1980. Population analyst U.S. Bur. Census, Jeffersonville, Ind., 1970-71; rsch. planner Louisville-Jefferson County Planning Commn., 1971-72; adj. lectr. U. Louisville Sch. Urban Policy, 1976-91; pres. Kentuckiana Hist. Svcs., Jeffersonville, 1981—; exec. dir. Clark County Planning, Zoning and Bldg. Commn., Jeffersonville, 1991—; archtl. historian Louisville Hist. Landmarks & Preservation Dists. Commn., 1977-79; adj. lectr. history U. Louisville, 1982—; chmn. Regional Coordination Planning Com., Louisville, 1992-93; mem. edn. com. Hist. So. Ind., Inc., Evansville, 1991-93; mem. adv. com. Falls of Ohio Interpretive Ctr., 1991-94; mem. transp. tech. coord. com. Kentuckiana Regional Planning and Devel. Agy., 1992—, chmn., 1994-96. Author: Drovers, Dealers and Dreamers, 1984, Capital on the Kentucky, 1986, Sellersburg: A Century of Change, 1990; co-editor: Louisville's Olmstedian Legacy, 1988; contbr. articles to profl. jours. Mem. exec. bd. George Rogers Clark coun. Boy Scouts Am., 1976-92; coun. adv. bd. Lincoln Heritage Coun., 1993—, asst. coun. commr., 1993-94; sec. Clark County Emergency Shelter, 1985-95, Meth. Evang. Hosp. Found., Louisville, 1987-94; bd. dirs. Plymouth Community Renewal Ctr., Louisville, 1988-94; bd. dirs. Clark County chpt. ARC, 1991—, vice chmn., 1992-94, chmn. 1994—; mem. Ind State Svc. Coun., ARC, 1992-94; pres. Kentuckiana Assn., United Ch. of Christ, 1985-86; bd. dirs. Leadership So. Ind. Found., 1984-88, sec., 1987-88; bd. dirs. Clark County Youth Shelter, 1984-88, program chmn., 1986-88; del. Ind. Gov.'s Conf. on Small Bus., Indpls., 1984. Recipient Nat. Disting. Svc. award, Order of Arrow, Boy Scouts Am., 1973, dist. award of merit, 1976, Silver Beaver award, 1981; cert. for excellence in writing Internat. Assn. Bus. Communicators, 1985; named Ky. col. State of Ky., 1978. Mem. Am. Hist. Assn., Orgn. Am. Historians (publicity com. 1991), Nat. Coun. on Pub. History, Urban History Assn., Am. Soc. Ch. History, Ind. Hist. Soc., Ind. Assn. Historians, Ky. Hist. Soc., Am. Planning Assn., Ind. Planning Assn. (historian 1996—), Soc. Am. City & Regional Planning History, Filson Club (publ. adv. bd. 1990-93), Toastmasters (pres. 1990), Rotary (bd. dirs. 1995—, pres.-elect 1996-97), Phi Alpha Theta, Phi Kappa Phi, Alpha Chi, Gamma Nu, Alpha Phi Gamma, Phi Eta Sigma, Alpha Phi Omega. Democrat. Home: 38 Forest Dr Jeffersonville IN 47130-6867 Office: Clark County Planning Zoning and Bldg Commn City County Building Rm 300 Jeffersonville IN 47130

KRAMER, CAROL GERTRUDE, marriage and family counselor; b. Grand Rapids, Mich., Jan. 14, 1939; d. Wilson John and Katherine Joanne (Wasdyke) Rottschafer; m. Peter William Kramer, July 1, 1960; children: Connie R. Kramer Sattler, Paul Wilson Kramer. AB, Calvin Coll., 1960; MA, U. Mich., 1969; PhD, Holy Cross Coll., 1973; MSW, Grand Valley State U., 1985. Diplomate Internat. Acad. Behavioral Medicine, Counseling and Psychotherapy; cert. addictions/substance abuse counselor, Mich.; cert. hypnotist/psychotherapist. Elem. tchr. Jenison (Mich.) Pub. Sch., 1960-64; sch. social worker Grand Rapids Pub. Sch., 1964-81; pvt. practice marriage and family counselor Grand Rapids, 1973—; v.p. Human Resource Assocs., Grand Rapids, 1983-88; guest lectr. Calvin Coll., Mich. State U., Grand Valley State U., 1975-85. Co-author: Stop Sexual Abuse for Everyone program. Ruling elder 1st Presbyn. Ch., Grand Rapids, 1975-78; mem. Gerald R. Ford Rep. Women, Grand Rapids, 1980-87; mem. Mich. Bd. of Licensing Marriage Counselors, 1985-88, co-chair pastoral rels. com. Gun Lake Community Ch., 1989-91, v.p. consistory, 1991-93. Named one of Outstanding Young Women in Am., 1974; recipient Meritorious Svc. award Kent County Family Life Coun., 1983. Fellow Am. Assn. Marriage and Family Therapists; mem. NASW, Mich. Assn. Marriage Counselors (awards com. 1988, chmn. 1991, nominations com. 1992—), Kent County Family Life Coun. (pres. 1975), Voters Against Sexual Abuse (pres., bd. dirs. 1992—). Home: 12622 Park Dr Wayland MI 49348-9322 Office: Psychology Ctr 2059 Lake Michigan Dr NW Grand Rapids MI 49504-4742

KRAMER, DALE VERNON, English language educator; b. Mitchell, S.D., July 13, 1936; s. Dwight Lyman and Frances Elizabeth (Corbin) K.; m. Cheris Gamble Kramarae, Dec. 21, 1960; children: Brinlee, Jana. B.S., S.D. State U., 1958; M.A., Case Western Res. U., 1960, Ph.D., 1963. Instr. English Ohio U., Athens, 1962-63, asst. prof., 1963-65; asst. prof. U. Ill., Urbana, 1965-67, assoc. prof., 1967-71, prof. English, 1971—, acting head English dept., 1982, 86-87, assoc. dean Coll. of Arts & Scis., 1992-95; chmn. bd. editors Jour. English and Germanic Philology, 1972-95; assoc. vice provost, prof. English, U. Oreg., 1990. Author: Charles Robert Maturin, 1973, Thomas Hardy: The Forms of Tragedy, 1975, Thomas Hardy: Tess of the d'Urbervilles, 1991; editor: Critical Approaches to the Fiction of Thomas Hardy, 1979, Thomas Hardy, The Woodlanders, 1981, 85, Thomas Hardy, The Mayor of Casterbridge, 1987, Critical Essays on Thomas Hardy: The Novels, 1990. Served to capt. U.S. Army, 1958-66. Mem. Center for Advanced Study, 1971; Am. Philos. Soc. grantee, 1969, 86, NEH grantee, 1986. Mem. MLA, AAUP, RSVP, M/MLA, Soc. for Textual Scholarship, Victorian Periodicals Soc., Assn. for Documentary Editing. Congregationalist.

KRAMER, DON, state legislator. Senator State of Minn., 1994—. Office: Minnesota State Senate State Office Bldg 100 Constitution Ave Saint Paul MN 55155-1298

KRAMER, JOEL ROY, journalist, newspaper executive; b. Bklyn., May 21, 1948; s. Archie and Rae (Abramowitz) K.; m. Laurie Maloff, 1969; children—Matthew, Elias, Adam. B.A., Harvard U., Cambridge, 1969. Editor-in-chief Harvard Crimson; reporter Sci. Mag., Washington, 1969-70; free lance writer Washington, 1970-72; from copy editor to news editor, exec. news editor, asst. mng. editor Newsday, L.I., N.Y., 1972-80; exec. editor Buffalo Courier-Express, 1981-82; exec. editor Star Tribune, Mpls., St. Paul, 1983-91, pub., pres., 1992—; bd. dirs. Harvard Crimson Inc., 1969—, World Press Inst. Bd. chair Mpls. Children's Theatre Co. Co-recipient Pulitzer prize for Pub. Service, Newsday (The Heroin Trail), 1973; Best Legal Writing on Large Daily award N.Y. Bar Assn., 1974. Mem. Am. Soc. Newspaper Editors, Newspaper Assn. Am. Office: Star Tribune 425 Portland Ave Minneapolis MN 55488-0001*

KRAMER, JOHN ROBERT, JR., cardiologist, researcher; b. Cleve., July 29, 1942; s. John Robert and Janice Marion (Dye) K.; m. Joanne Soderquist, Dec. 28, 1966 (div. Apr. 1976); children: William Pearson, Charles Guy; m. Christine Elizabeth Wilber, Sept. 3, 1976; children: Mark Alan, Katherine Lindsey. BA in Biology with honors, Oberlin Coll., 1964; MD, U. Va., 1969. Med. intern Cleve. Clinic Found., 1969-70, resident, 1970-71, fellow in cardiology, 1971-73, staff invasive cardiologist, 1975—; vis. scientist MIT, Cambridge, 1983—, core investigator Laser Biomed. Rsch. Ctr., 1989—, Am. Internat. Health Alliance Cleve.-Ashgabat Ptnrs.; lectr. in Japan, The Netherlands, Fed. Republic Germany, Chile, Argentina, Turkey, Morocco, Egypt, Eng., France, Brazil, Can., Norway, Russia, Switzerland, Austria, Turkmenistan; referee Am. Heart Jour., Circulation, Cleve. Clinic Jour. Medicine, Jour. Am. Coll. Cardiology, Archives Internal Medicine, Catheterization and Cardiovascular Diagnosis. Contbr. 81 articles to sci. jours., chpts. to books. Maj. M.C., USAF, 1973-75. Fellow Am. Coll. Cardiology, Soc. for Cardiac Angiography and Interventions, Am. Coll. Angiology; mem. Chilean Soc. Cardiology and Cardiovascular Surgery (corr.), IEEE Lasers and Electro-optics Soc. Republican. Home: 530 Riverview Rd Gates Mills OH 44040-9649 Office: Cleve Clinic Found 9500 Euclid Ave Cleveland OH 44195-5066

KRAMER, LAURA JANE, journalist, touring company executive; b. Chgo., Oct. 3, 1968; d. Loren Bernard and Vivian June (Zlatnik) K. BA in Medieval and Renaissance Studies, U. Mich., 1990. Mktg. dir. Tainer Assocs., Chgo., 1990-91; pres., founder Custom Tours in Tuscany, Highland Park, Ill., 1991—; journalist La Repubblica, Vista, Neo, 1991—; cons. to PBS on documentary film, 1995. Dancer in film Portrait of a Lady, 1996. Mem. Women's Network of Florence, Italy (founding), Phi Beta Kappa. Office: Custom Tours in Tuscany 206 Ivy Ln Highland Park IL 60035 also: Via di Piazza Calda 1/A, 50125 Firenze Italy

KRAMER, LESLIE, dermatologist; b. Bklyn., Mar. 5, 1953; d. Joseph and Doris Kramer.; m. Miles Weinberger, Aug. 22, 1992. BS, Bklyn. Coll., 1976; MS, L.I. U., 1979; D of Osteopathy, U. Osteopathic Medicine and Health Scis., 1990. Tchr. N.Y.C. Bd. Edn., Bklyn., 1976-79; physician asst. HIP, USN, N.Y.C. Dept. Health, 1981-86; physician UMDNJ/Union (N.J.) Hosp., 1990-91; resident dermatology Kirksville (Mo.) Coll. Osteo. Medicine, 1994; dermatologist pvt. practice, Cedar Rapids, Iowa, 1995—. Recipient Fisons Resident award Fisons Pharm., 1994-95. Mem. Am. Osteo. Assn., Am. Osteo. Coll. Dermatology (trustee 1992), Am. Soc. Dermatology, Iowa Med. Soc., Soc. Pediatric Dermatology, Women's Dermatological Soc. Office: Cedar Rapids Dermatology 411 10th St SE Cedar Rapids IA 52403

KRAMER, MARILYN KOLL, technical writer, small business owner; b. Louisville, KY, Oct. 7, 1924; d. Raymond S. and Elsa G. (Geewe) Koll; m. Walter E. Kramer, Feb. 6, 1949; children: Steven, Barbara. BS in Sci., Purdue U., 1946, MS in Chemistry, 1949; teaching cert., Northeastern Ill. U., 1961. Cert. tchr., Chgo. Bd. Edn. Chemist Chgo. Dairy and Food Lab., 1946-47; tech. writer La Pine Sci. Co., Chgo., 1950-51; asst. editor New Standard Encyclopedia, Chgo., 1952-53; substitute tchr. Niles Twp. Schs., Niles, Skokie, Ill., 1962-75; tech. writer Sargent Welch Sci. Co., Skokie, Ill., 1975-90; cons. Sargent Welch Sci. Co., Skokie, 1991-93; co-owner Kramer & Kramer, Niles, 1991—. Pres. Niles (Ill.) Elem. Schs. PTA, 1973-74, Womens' Club of Niles, 1974-76. Recipient 2d pl. Better Investing Mag. Nat. Contest, 1987. Mem. LWV (past co-pres. Niles chpt.), Phoenix Investment Club (pres. 1992—), Iota Sigma Pi. Home and Office: Kramer & Kramer 7102 Seward St Niles IL 60714-3052

KRAMER, MARY ELIZABETH, health services executive, state legislator; b. Burlington, Iowa, June 14, 1935; d. Ross L. and Geneva M. (McElhinney) Barnett; m. Kay Frederick Kramer, June 13, 1958; children: Kent, Krista. BA, U. Iowa, 1957, MA, 1971. Cert. tchr., Iowa. Tchr. Newton (Iowa) Pub. Schs., 1957-61; tchr. Iowa City Pub. Schs., 1961-67, tchr., asst. supt., 1971-75; dir. pers. Younkers, Inc., Des Moines, 1975-81; v.p. human resources IASD Health Svcs Inc., Des Moines, 1981—; mem., asst. minority leader Iowa State Senate, Des Moines, 1990—. Bd. dirs. Polk County Child Care Rsch. Ctr., Des Moines, 1986—, YWCA, Des Moines, 1989-94; mem. Olympic adv. com. Blue Cross and Blue Shield Assn., Chgo., 1988-92. Named Mgr. of Yr. Iowa Mgmt. Assocs., 1985, Woman of Achievement YWCA, 1986, Woman of Vision Young Women's Resource Ctr., 1989. Mem. Soc. Human Resource Mgmt. (Profl. of Yr. 1996), Iowa Mgmt. Assn. (pres. 1988), Greater Des Moines C. of C. (bd. dirs. 1986—), Nexus, Rotary Internat. Republican. Presbyterian. Home: 1209 Ashworth Rd West Des Moines IA 50265-3546 Office: IASD Health Svcs Corp 636 Grand Ave Des Moines IA 50309-2502 also: Iowa State Senate State Capitol Des Moines IA 50319

KRAMER, PAUL A., manufacturing executive; b. Milw., June 12, 1952. AD, Northern Wis. Tech. Coll., 1980. Machinist Kearney & Trucker, Milw., 1973-78, Amplas, Inc., Green Bay, Wis., 1978-91; v.p. Ansys, Inc., De Pere, Wis., 1991—. Coach Little League Spftball; mem. dv. com. Boy Scouts Am. Mem. Optimists, KC. Republican. Roman Catholic.

KRAMER, ROBERTA M., antiques dealer; b. N.Y.C., Jan. 29, 1962; d. Martin Joseph and Mendelle T. (Noble) Milston; m. Samuel Gideon Kramer, Oct. 28, 1990. BA, Oberlin Coll., 1986; MA, Univ. Coll., London, 1988. Curator Ben Uri Art Soc., London, 1986-88; mgr. Rita Bucheit, Ltd., Chgo., 1988-89; dir. J. Rosenthal, F.A., Chgo., 1989-91; account exec. Leslie Hindman, Inc., Chgo., 1991-93; pres. Chgo. Antiques, Inc., 1993-94, Roberta Kramer, Ltd., Chgo., 1994—; auctioneer Susanins, Inc., Chgo., 1993-95; cons. appraiser Bernacki & Los, Inc., Chgo., 1994—. Auctioneer, fundraiser Arts & Bus. Coun., Chgo., 1995; auctioneer Celebrity Chair Auction, Chgo., 1994, 95. Mem. River North Antique Dealers Assn. (pres. 1994-95). Democrat. Jewish. Office: Roberta Kramer Ltd 220 W Kinzie St Chicago IL 60610

KRAMER, WILLARD GEORGE, JR., retired accountant; b. Pitts., Oct. 2, 1929; s. Willard George Sr. and Olive Francis (McVey) K.; m. Nora Mae Martin, June 26, 1951; children: Bradley, Patricia. BS in Commerce, Grove City Coll., 1952. CPA, Pa. Mich. Staff acct. Price Waterhouse, Pitts., 1952-56, audit sr., 1956-59, audit mgr., 1959-65; audit ptnr. Price Waterhouse, Detroit, 1965-76, mng. ptnr., 1976-88, group mng. ptnr., 1988-90. Chmn. Bon Secours of Mich. Healthcare, Grosse Pointe, 1982-90, Civic, Inc., 1982-95, St. Paul Evang. Luth. Ch., Grosse Pointe Farms, Mich., 1969-75. Sgt. Security Agy. U.S. Army, 1947-48. Mem. AICPA, Pa. Inst. CPA's, Mich. Assn. CPA's., Detroit Athletic Club, Lochmoor Club (pres., treas. Grosse Pointe Woods, Mich. 1971-79). Republican. Office: Price Waterhouse 200 Renaissance Ctr Ste 3900 Detroit MI 48243-1203

KRANZ, KENNETH LOUIS, JR., human resources company executive, entrepreneur; b. Evanston, Ill., July 7, 1946; s. Kenneth Louis Sr. and Florence A. (Knapton) K.; m. Susan Emilie Mueller, Apr. 3, 1976. BA, Tarkio Coll., 1969. Cert. compensation profl.; lic. IRS enrolled agt., adminstrv. svc. mgr., life and health agt. Cost acct. Fluid Power, Wheeling, Ill., 1969-71; cost acct. Wells Lamont Corp., Chgo., 1971-74, sr. cost acct., 1974-76, asst. mgr. cost, audit, 1977-80, asst. mgr. taxes, employee benefits, 1980-81, mgr. taxes, employee benefits, 1981-84; benefits mgr. Keeler Brass Co., Grand Rapids, Mich., 1984-86, employee benefits and compenstion mgr., 1986-90; human resources mgr. GRM Industries, Grand Rapids, 1990-92; co-owner Profl. Benefits Svcs., Inc., Grand Rapids, 1992-95; pres. Magnacare Group Inc., Grand Rapids, 1995—. Mem. Home Health Svcs. (treas. 1986-90), Internat. Soc. Pre-Retirement Planners, West Mich. Compensation Assn., Am. Compensation Assn., Human Resource Mgmt. Assn., Life Underwriters Assn. Republican. Lutheran. Office: Magnacare Group Inc Ste 120 6475 28th St SE Grand Rapids MI 49546

KRASEAN, THOMAS KARL, historian; b. South Bend, Ind., Feb. 21, 1940; s. William Henry and Rose Ercelia (Mariottini) K.; m. Arleen Ruth Llewellyn, June 19, 1965 (div. Oct. 1970); children: Thomas Karl, David William, Elizabeth Rose; m. Liliane Siahou, Nov. 4, 1972. AA, Kellogg Community Coll., 1960; student, U. Ala., 1960-61; BA, East Mich. U., 1963; MA, Western Mich. U., 1965. Field rep. Ind. State Libr., Indpls., 1965-69, state archivist, 1969-70; dir. Byron Lewis Libr., Vincennes (Ind.) U., 1970-77; field rep. Ind. Hist. Soc., Indpls., 1977-82, dir. field svcs. divsn., 1982-92; dir. community rels. divsn., 1992—; rep. Ind. Am. Revolution Bicentennial Commn., 1971-77; mem. Adv. Com. Historic Preservation, 1972-73, Adv. Com. Ind. Hist. Bur., 1980—; chmn. George Rogers Clark Trail Found., 1972-74; founder, pres. Old N.W. Corp., 1973-77; bd. dirs. Ind. Adv. Com. Nat. Hist. Publs. and Records Commn., 1979—. Mem. White River Park Task Force, Indpls., 1981-83. Mem. Am. Assn. State and Local History (state chmn. awards com. 1981-92, regional chmn. awards com. 1988-92, nominating com. 1992-95), Soc. Am. Archivists, Midwest Archives Conf. (charter), Ind. Hist. Soc. (adv. coun. Ind. Jr. Hist. Soc. 1971—), Ind. Oral History Roundtable (charter), Soc. Ind. Archivists (founder, sec., treas. 1972-92), Civil War Roundtable (pres. 1970-71, 79-80, 93-94), Indpls. Lit. Club (pres. 1989, treas. 1991—), Sagamore of the Wabash. Republican. Roman Catholic. Home: 6038 Castlebar Cir Indianapolis IN 46220-4107 Office: Ind Hist Soc 315 W Ohio St Indianapolis IN 46202-3210

KRAUS, ALBERT ANDREW, JR., retired medical supply company executive; b. Louisville, Ky., Mar. 3, 1948; s. Albert Andrew Sr. and Norma Agnes (Sinkhorn) K. Student, U. Louisville; grad., U. Ky., 1973. RN. Product mgr. Haemonetics Corp., Braintree, Mass., 1987-90, mgr. clin. svcs. life support systems, 1990-92; clin. marketing specialist EP Techologies, Inc., Sunnyvale, Calif., 1992-93; field clin. engr. Telectronics Pacing Systems, Englewood, Colo., 1994. Freelance writer and photographer, contbr. articles to mag. Bd. dirs. Leather Archives and Mus., Inc.; pres. WCBC, Inc., 1987-91, emeritus 1992, NLA Internat. Inc., co-chair 1993—. Recipient Vigil Honor Boy Scouts of Am. New Brunswick N.J. 1968, Special Achievement/Heroism VA St. Louis 1978; named to Hon. Order Ky. Cols., 1971, Capt. Jefferson County Ky. 1976. Mem. AORN, Dachshund Club Am., Dandie Dinmot Club Am. Roman Catholic. Home: 919 S Highland Ave Oak Park IL 60304-1530

KRAUS, HENRY, retired physician, educator; b. Akron, Ohio, Apr. 12, 1923; s. Charles Morton and Gertrude (Gibans) K.; m. Esther Elizabeth Mackey, July 7, 1946; children: Charles Thomas, Thomas Henry, Anne Elizabeth, James Douglas. Cert., Harvard U., 1943; MD, Case Western Res. U., 1947. Diplomate Am. Bd. Internal Medicine. Intern in medicine Univ. Hosps. Cleve., 1947-48, asst. resident in medicine, 1948-49; fellow in cardiology Thorndike lab. Boston City Hosp., 1949-50; sr. resident in medicine

West Roxbury Vets. Hosp., Boston, 1950-51; sr. attending physician Akron Gen. Med. Ctr., 1956-91, chief of medicine, 1958-62; assoc. clin. prof. medicine Northeastern Ohio U. Coll. of Medicine, Rootstown, 1980-91; ret., 1991; bd. of trustees Akron Gen. Med. Ctr., 1972—, mem. exec. com., 1972-88; bd. dirs. PIE Ins. Co., Cleve. Bd. dirs. Pioneer Western Life Ins. Co., 1959-76. 1st lt. USMC, 1953. Mem. ACP, Mayflower Club (Akron), Alpha Omega Alpha. Republican. Home: 395 Delaware Ave Akron OH 44303-1233

KRAUS, MICHAEL JOHN, English language and literature educator; b. Milw., Dec. 8, 1955; s. Martin Ewald and Jane (Ditter) K.; m. Linda Louise Flanigan, July 20, 1991. BA, Marian Coll., 1985; MA, U. Wis., Milw., 1988, postgrad., 1989—. Writing and rsch. lab. dir. Marian Coll., Fond du Lac, Wis., 1986-88, asst. prof., 1988—, chair human rels., 1989-92, co-chair English dept., 1990—, mem. values task force, 1991—; cons. in field. Mem. Fond Du Lac Human Rels. Coun., 1990-93. Recipient Wis. Libr. Honorarium, 1989, Underkofler Teaching Excellence award Wis. Power & Light. Mem. ACLU, MLA, Wis. Humanities Com., Nat. Coun. Tchrs. English, Amnesty Internat., Greenpeace, Delta Epsilon Sigma. Roman Catholic. Office: Marian Coll 45 S National Ave Fond Du Lac WI 54935-4621

KRAUS, RON, state legislator; b. May 13, 1956; m. Kathy Kraus; 2 children. Student, U. Minn., Duluth, St. Mary's Coll., Winona, Mankato State U. Minn. state rep. Dist. 27A, 1994—; bus. owner. Address: 2922 Campus Dr Albert Lea MN 56007

KRAUSE, CAROLYN H., state legislator, lawyer; m. David Krause. BA, U. Wis.; JD, IIT. Assoc. Foss, Schuman & Drake, Chgo., 1966-73; lawyer, solo practice Mt. Prospect, Ill., 1973-76; pvt. practice Krause & Krause, Mt. Prospect, Ill., 1976—; mayor Mt. Prospect, 1973-76; Dist. 56 rep. Ill. Ho. Reps., Springfield, 1993—; spokesman appropriations, gen. svcs., cities and villages, fin. instns., healthcare, and human svcs. coms., Ill. Ho. Reps. Apptd. by Gov. James Thompson (Ill.) to local govt. fin. study commn., 1980, criminal justice info. authority, 1985-87; past dir. Clearbrook Ctr.; chair Mcpl. Conf.; dir. Pub. Action to Deliver Shelter of Northwest Cook County. Mem. Ill. and Chgo. Bar Assns. Home: 204 S George St Mount Prospect IL 60056-3430 Office: Ill Ho of Reps State Capitol Springfield IL 62706*

KRAUSE, CHESTER LEE, publishing company executive; b. Iola, Wis., Dec. 16, 1923; s. Carl and Cora E. (Neil) K. Grad. high sch., Iola. Ind. contractor, 1946-52; chmn. bd. Krause Publs., Inc., Iola, 1952—. Co-editor: Standard Catalog of World Coins. Chmn. bldg. fund drive Iola Hosp., 1975-80; active Village Bd., 1963-72, Assay Commn., 1961, Marshfield Clinic Nat. Adv. Coun., 1992-96. With AUS, 1943-46. Named Wis. Small Businessman of Yr. Wis. Small Bus. Adminstrn. Adv. Coun., 1990; Melvin Jones fellow, 1989; recipient Meguiar award, 1995, Friend of Automotive History award Soc. Automotive Historians, 1995. Mem. Soc. of Automobile Historians (Friends of Automobile Historians 1995), Am. Numis. Assn. (medal of merit, Farren Zerbe award, Hall of Fame, Lifetime Achievement award), Can. Numis. Assn. Home: 290 E Iola St Iola WI 54945-9620 Office: 700 E State St Iola WI 54945-9642

KRAUSE, HEATHER DAWN, data processing executive; b. Kansas City, Kans., May 6, 1956; d. Jack E. Firth and Bonnie Jo (Reeves) Cupps; m. Kerry Murray Krause, May 23, 1981. Cert., Kansas City Skill Ctr., 1980. Cert. drafting tchr.; cert. in bus. supervision; cert. in Novell Netware system adminstrn. Assoc. drafter Black & Veatch, Kansas City, Mo., 1980; technician mech. design Wilcox Electric, Kansas City, 1980; coord. CAD design systems Smith & Loveless, Inc., Lenexa, Kans., 1980—; owner Digital Design Technologies, Kansas City, Mo., 1989—; tech. editor Que Books Macmillan Computer Pub., 1994—; instr. Longview C.C., Lee's Summit, Mo., 1987-93. Mem. NAFE, Kansas City Area AutoCAD Users Group, Heartland Windows User Group, Phi Theta Kappa. Democrat. Home: PO Box 11319 Kansas City MO 64112-0319

KRAUSE, JERRY (JEROME RICHARD KRAUSE), professional basketball team executive; b. Chgo., Apr. 6, 1939; s. Paul and Gertrude (Sherman) K.; m. Sharon Bergofsky, Oct. 16, 1969 (div. 1971); m. Thelma Frankel, July 1, 1979; children: Stacy, David. Student, Bradley U., 1957-61. Dir. scouting Balt. Bullets Basketball Club, 1962-65, 67-69; dir. scouting Chgo. Bulls Basketball Club, 1969-72, v.p. basketball ops., 1985—; dir. scouting Phoenix Suns Basketball Club, 1972-75; gen. mgr. Portland Baseball Club, Pacific Coast League, 1966; scout Cleve. Indians Baseball Club, 1967-72, Oakland (Calif.) Athletics Baseball Club, 1973-75; dir. scouting Los Angeles Lakers Basketball Club, 1977-79; supr. Midwestern scouting Seattle Mariners Baseball Club, 1977-79; spl. assignment scout Chgo. White Sox Baseball Club, 1979-85. Contbr. articles to profl. jours. Named Exec. of Yr. NBA, 1988, named to Bradley U. Athletic Hall of Fame, 1992. Mem. Nat. Basketball Assn. (competition com., Exec. of Yr. 1988). Office: Chgo Bulls 1901 W Madison St Chicago IL 60612

KRAUSEN, ANTHONY SHARNIK, surgeon; b. Phila., Feb. 22, 1944; s. B.M. and Kay S. (Sharnik) K.; m. Susan Elizabeth Park, Sept. 6, 1970; children: Nicole, Allison. Student Germantown Acad., 1949-61; B.A., Princeton U., 1965; M.D., U. Mich., 1969. Intern, Presbyn. Med. Center, Denver, 1969-70; resident St. Joseph Hosp., Denver, 1970-71, Barnes Hosp., St. Louis, 1972-76; with Milw. Med. Clinic, 1976—, head dept. facial plastic surgery, 1984—; mem. staffs Columbia, St. Michael, Children's, St. Mary Hosp., Oankee. Pres. Contemporary Art Soc., Milw. Art Mus., 1983, bd. dirs. Friends of Art. Served with U.S. Army Nat. Guard, 1970-76. Fellow ACS, Am. Acad. Cosmetic Surgery, Am. Acad. Facial Plastic and Reconstructive Surgery, Am. Acad. Otolaryngology; mem. Nat. Neurofibromatosis Soc. (med. advisor Wis. chpt. 1985-92), Wis. Otolaryngological Soc. Clubs: Ivy (Princeton, N.J.), Town Club (Milw.). Office: 3003 W Good Hope Rd Milwaukee WI 53209-2042

KRAUSHAAR, WILLIAM LESTER, physicist, educator; b. Newark, Apr. 1, 1920; s. Lester A. and Helen (Osterhoudt) K.; m. Margaret Freidinger, Feb. 27, 1943 (div. 1980); children—Mark Jourdan, Susan, Andrew Woolman; m. Elizabeth D. Rodgers, Aug. 9, 1980. B.S., Lafayette Coll., 1942; Ph.D., Cornell U., 1949. Physicist Nat. Bur. Standards, Washington, 1942-45; assoc. prof. physics MIT, 1956-62, prof., 1962-65; prof. physics U. Wis.-Madison, 1965-80, Max Mason prof. of physics, 1980—. Author: (with Uno Ingard) Introduction to Mechanics, Matter and Waves, 1960. Recipient Senior award Alexander von Humboldt Found., 1983; Guggenheim fellow, 1963, 73. Fellow Am. Phys. Soc., Am. Astron. Soc., Internat. Astron. Union, Am. Acad. Arts and Scis., Nat. Acad. Sci. Office: U Wis Dept Physics Madison WI 53706

KRAUSS, JOHN LANDERS, public policy and urban affairs consultant; b. Orange, N.J., Oct. 20, 1948; s. George Howard Jr. and Shirley (Landers) K.; m. Elizabeth M. Wood, May 23, 1976 (div. Sept. 1988); m. Eleanor C. Werbe, June 29, 1991. BA with honors in Polit. Sci., Colo. Coll., 1971; JD, Ind. U., Indpls., 1976. Bar: Ind. 1976, U.S. Dist. Ct. (so. dist.) Ind. 1976, U.S. Ct. Appeals (7th cir.) 1979, U.S. Supreme Ct. 1986. Spl. asst. to gov. Office of Gov. of Ind., Indpls., 1971-72; dep. dir. Greater Indpls. Progress Com. Inc., Indpls., 1972-73, exec. dir., 1973-81; dir. dept. met. devel. City of Indpls., 1981-82, dep. mayor, 1982-91; sr. fellow Ind. U. Ctr. for Urban Policy and Environment, Indpls., 1991—; mediator Ind. Edn. Employment Rels. Bd., 1991—; exec. dir. Ind. Adv. Commn. on Intergovtl. Rels., 1995—; mem. state adv. bd. Ind. Small Bus. Devel. Ctrs.; co-chmn. Charles L. Whistler Award Com.; bd. dirs. Nyhart Co., Inc. Trustee Indpls. Mus. Art, Ptnrs. for Livable Comtys., Washington; v.p. Ind. Sports Corp.; bd. dirs. Indpls. Project, Inc., Ind. Swiss Found.; past mem. exec. com., bd. dirs. Eiteljorg Mus. Am. Indian and Western Art; past mem. exec. com. Pan Am. Games Organizing Com., 1987; past vice chmn. Greater Indpls. Progress Com., Inc.; past mem. exec. com. Indpls. Econ. Devel. Corp., Commn. for Downtown, Inc. Ford Found. Venture grantee for ind. rsch. Mem. AIA (past bd. dirs. Indpls. chpt.), Soc. Individuals in Dispute Resolution, Am. Soc. Pub. Adminstrn. (pres. Ind. chpt. 1992-94, bd. dirs. Ind. chpt.), Ind. Comty. Devel. Soc. (bd. dirs.), Pi Gamma Mu. Office: Ind U Ctr Urban Policy/Envn 342 N Senate Ave Indianapolis IN 46204

KRAUTER, AARON JOSEPH, farmer, state senator; b. Dickinson, N.D., July 21, 1956; s. Adam Robert and Ann Christine (Grundhauser) K.; m. Cynthia Marie Nordquist, June 28, 1986; children: Emily Christine, Mitchell Aaron. BSEd., U. Mary, Bismarck, 1978, BSBA, 1981. Music instr. Cooperstown (N.D.) High Sch., 1978-79; store mgr. Best Product, Inc., Bismarck, 1979-85; ops. mgr. Best Product, Inc., Richmond, Va., 1985-87; farmer Regent, N.D., 1987—; mem. N.D. Senate, 1990—. Mem. N.D. Gov.'s Coun. on Children and Youth, Bismarck, 1989-94, N.D. Gov.'s Coun. on Phys. Fitness and Health, 1992-94; mem. agronomy seed adv. bd. N.D. State U., 1991—, mem. ext. adv. coun., 1991—; chair N.D. Senate Dem. Caucus, 1993—. Recipient Know Your State award N.D. Bar Assn., 1974, Excellence in Govt. award Assn. Counties, 1993, Flemming Fellow Leadership award. Mem. KC, Elks. Democrat. Roman Catholic. Home and Office: HC 1 Box 27 Regent ND 58650-9721

KRAUTKREMER, JAMES J., information scientist; b. Jordan, Minn., Apr. 18, 1934; s. James E. and Sophia M. (Hennes) K.; m. Shirley A. Bond, June 1, 1957; children: Julie, Dan, Paul, David. B in Edn., U. Nebr. Omaha, 1963. Cert. data processer. Computer programmer, analyst Mutual of Omaha, 1953-64; mgr. data processing Sister Kenney Found., Mpls., 1964-66; dir. mgmt. info sys. Midland Coops., Inc., Mpls., 1966-82; mgr. new technologies Land O'Lakes, Mpls., 1982-84; pres. Packaged Computer Sys., Mpls., 1984-87; cons. Krautkremer Cons., Mpls., 1987-89; exec. dir. State of Minn., St. Paul, 1989—. With U.S. Army, 1954-56. Mem. Rotary Internat. (Paul Harris fellow), Am. Legion, Citizens League. Democrat. Roman Catholic. Home: 3224 Highlands Rd Brooklyn Park MN 55443

KRAUTSCHUN, HARVEY C., state legislator; m. Joy Krautschun; 2 children. Sudent, Black Hills State Coll. Mem. S.D. Ho. Reps., vice chmn. appropriations com., mem. agr. and natural resources com., mem. judiciary and legis. procedure coms.; ins. agt. Address: PO Box 157 Spearfish SD 57783-0157*

KRAWETZ, ARTHUR ALTSHULER, chemist, science administrator; b. Chgo., Oct. 30, 1932; s. John and Grace (Altshuler) K. BS in Chemistry, Northwestern U., 1952; MS in Phys. Chemistry, U. Chgo., 1953, PhD in Phys. Chemistry, 1955. V.p. Phoenix Chem. Lab., Inc., Chgo., 1950-73, tech. dir., 1958—, pres., 1974—. Contbr. articles to profl. jours. Mem. Nat. Safety Coun. 1st Lt. USAF, 1956-58, capt. Res. Fellow Am. Inst. Chemists (life), Royal Soc. Chemistry (chartered chemist); mem. ASTM (chmn. sub-com. XI engrng. scis., sub-com. N-VI fire resistance 1974-84, sub-com. IX-D oxidation 1974-81, task force on precautionary statements for hazardous material and lab. ops. 1976-84, com. mem.), Am. Indsl. Hygiene Assn., Am. Chem. Soc. (divsn. phys. chemistry, analytical chemistry, petroleum chemistry, indsl. chemistry), Instrument Soc. Am., Air & Waste Mgmt. Assn., Soc. for Applied Spectroscopy, Soc. Automotive Engrs., Soc. Tribologists and Lubrication Engrs., Nat. Lubricating Grease Inst., The Coblentz Soc., Nat. Fire Protection Assn. (com. on classification and properties of hazardous chemical data), Chgo. Gas Chromatography Discussion Group, Internat. Assn. Stability and Handling Liquid Fuels (hon.), Phi Beta Kappa, Sigma Xi, Phi Lambda Upsilon, Pi Mu Epsilon. Office: Phoenix Chem Lab Inc 3953 W Shakespeare Ave Chicago IL 60647-3497

KRAWETZ, STEPHEN ANDREW, molecular biology and genetics educator; b. Fort Frances, Ont., Can., Sept. 17, 1955; s. Stephen and Michaelene (Medynski) K.; m. Lorraine Ruth St. John, Aug. 19, 1977; children: Rochelle Tairaesa, Alexandra Renée. BS, U. Toronto, Ont., 1977, PhD, 1983. Tchr. Scarborough Bd. Edn., Ont., 1976-77; Alberta Heritage Found. Med. Rsch. postdoc. fellow U. Calgary, Alta., Can., 1983-89; asst. prof. rsch. Ctr. for Molecular Biology Wayne State U., Detroit, 1989, asst. prof. molecular biology and genetics, 1989-92, asst. prof. obstetrics and gynecology and molecular biology and genetics, 1992-94, assoc. prof. ob/gyn. and molecular medicine and genetics, 1994—; biotech. cons., Calgary, 1985-89, Grosse Pointe Woods, Mich., 1989—; co-founder Genetic Imaging, Inc., 1988; mem. fetal therapy group Hutzel Hosp., Detroit, 1994—. Mem. editl. bd. BioTechniques, Ag Biotech News and Info., Gene-Combis; contbr. numerous articles to scholarly jours. Recipient B.C. Childrens Hosp. Rsch. award, Vancouver, 1984, Computer Applications in Molecular Biology award, IntelliGenetics Inc., Mountain View, Calif., 1988; Alta. Heritage Found. Med. Rsch. fellow, 1985-88. Mem. Can. Biochem. Soc., Am. Soc. Human Genetics, N.Y. Acad. Scis., AAAS. Home: 805 Canterbury Rd Grosse Pointe MI 48236-1285 Office: Dept Ob-Gyn Ctr Molecular Med Genetics CS Mott Ctr Detroit MI 48201

KRAY, ELAINE LOUISE, auditor; b. Pitts., Oct. 31, 1943; d. Richard Lewis and Elizabeth Barbara (Carrola) Reese; m. Roger W. Kray, May 8, 1965 (dec. 1983); children: Arlene Erickson, Jason Reese. AS, Pitts. Bus. Acad., 1962. Info. systems/staff mem. Allegheny Power Svcs., Greensburg, Pa., 1966-74; asst. to the pres. O.S.I. Inc., Pitts, 1987-89; auditor Aqua Marine Resort and Country Club, Avon Lake, Ohio, 1989-92, Holiday Inn, Westlake, Ohio, 1993—; owner Well Pleased Co., Avon Lake, Ohio, 1992—; cons. rooms divsn. Heaven on Earth Inn, Avon Lake, Ohio, 1993-94; hotel/restaurant evaluator OSI Inc., 1987—. Creator coupon filing system "Clipper Sheet", 1992. Found. Young Widowed Parents, Pitts., 1984-89; cert. grief counselor South Hills Health Sys., Pitts., 1986-89; cert. bereavement counselor New Life Hospice of Greater Lorain County, Elyria, Ohio, 1994—; coach Odyssey of the Mind, Avon Lake, 1992; vol. Lorain County Blood Bank, Avon Lake, 1991—. Mem. Am. Inst. of Wine and Food, Wine Tasters Guild, Intertel, Soc. for Creative Anachronism, DAR, Mensa (gifted children coord. 1986-88). Republican. Home: 32682 Carriage Ln Avon Lake OH 44012-1637

KRAYBILL, WILLIAM GRESS, JR., oncologist, educator; b. Omaha, Nebr., Feb. 15, 1943; s. William Gress Sr. and Betty (Dunsmore) K.; m. Judith Adams, Feb. 18, 1974; children: Anna, Lindsay, Jacob. BS, Earlham Coll., Richmond, Ind., 1965; MD, U. Cin., 1969. Intern Santa Clara VAlley Med. Ctr., 1969-70; resident U. Oreg. Health Scis. Ctr., Portland, 1972-76, surg. oncology fellow, 1975-76, chief resident, 1976-77, surg. oncology fellow in rsch. tumor immunology, 1977-78; surg. oncology fellow Meml. Sloan-Kettering Cancer Ctr., N.Y.C., 1978-80; assoc. dir. of surgery Ellis Fischel State Cancer Ctr., Columbia, Mo., 1980-85, acting dir. of surgery, 1980-85, mem. instl. rev. bd., 1980-88, chmn. infection control com., 1981-82, acting dir. of anesthesiology, 1982-86, chmn. edn. com., 1982-86, chmn. joint rsch. com., 1982-83, vice chief of staff, 1982-84, med. dir. of surg. ICU, 1982-88, med. cons. to rehab. svc., 1982-88, chmn. residency rev. com., 1983-84, chmn. surg. ICU com., 1983-88, dir. of surgery, 1985-88, chmn. cancer registry com., 1986-88, sec., med. staff, 1987-88, cons. staff mem., 1988—; courtesy staff Columbia Regional Hosp., 1981-88; asst. surgeon gen. surgery svc. Barnes Hosp., St. Louis, 1988—; assoc. staff mem. Jewish Hosp., St. Louis, 1988—; cons. staff mem. Children's Hosp., St. Louis, 1988—; attending staff mem. St. Louis Regional Med. Ctr., 1988—; assoc. sci. in surgery Cancer Rsch. Ctr., Columbia, 1980-88; asst. prof. Dept. of Surgery U. Mo. Health Scis. Ctr., Columbia, 1980-86; prin. investigator Nat. Surg. Adjuvant Breast Project, Pitts., 1980-88; participant Cancer and Leukemia Group B, 1986-88; assoc. clin. prof. of surgery Washington U. Sch. of Medicine, St. Louis, 1987-88, asst. prof. of surgery, 1988—. Contbr. articles to profl. jours.; contbr. chpts. to books. Capt. USAF, 1970-72, Vietnam. Fellow ACS (chmn. Field Liason Program Mo. Commn. on Cancer 1985—, rep. of Fellowship of Commn. on Cancer 1987—, mem. Cancer Liason Com. Commn. on Cancer 1987—, mem. Patient Care and Rsch. Com. Commn. on Cancer 1987—, mem. Task Force on Staging 1989—, mem. PCF subcom. 1989—); mem. AAAS, Am. Soc. of Clinical Oncology, Mo. State Med. Assn., Mo. State Surg. Soc., St. Louis Metro. Med. Soc., St. Louis Surg. Soc., Soc. of Am. Gastrointestinal Endoscopic Surgeons, Soc. of Critical Care Medicine, Soc. of Head and Neck Surgeons, Soc. of Surg. Oncology, The N.Y. Acad. of Sci., Am. Cancer Soc. (rsch. fellow 1975-78, 1978-80, Jr. Faculty Clin. fellow 1977-78).

KREAGER, EILEEN DAVIS, administrative consultant; b. Caldwell, Ohio, Mar. 2, 1924; d. Fred Raymond and Esther (Farson) Davis. BBA, Ohio State U., 1945. With accounts receivable dept. M & R Dietetic, Columbus, Ohio, 1945-50; complete charge bookkeeper Magic Seal Paper Products, Columbus, 1950-53, A. Walt Runglin Co., L.A., 1953-54; office mgr. Roy C. Haddox and Son, Columbus, 1954-60; bursar Meth. Theol. Sch. Ohio, Delaware, 1961-86; adminstrv. cons. Fin. Ltd., 1986—; ptnr. Coll. Administrv. Sci., Ohio State U., 1975-80; seminar participant Paperwork Systems and Computer Sci., 1965, Computer Systems, 1964, Griffith Found. Seminar Working Women, 1975; pres. Altrusa Club of Delaware, Ohio, 1972-73. Del. Altrusa Internat., Montreal, 1972, Altrusa Regional, Greenbrier, 1973. Mem. AAUW, Assoc. Am. Inst. Mgmt. (exec. council of Inst., 1979); Am. Soc. Profl. Cons., Internat. Platform Assn., Ohio State U. Alumna Assn., Columbus Computer Soc., Innovation Alliance, Toastmasters Internat., Ohio State U. Faculty Club, Univ. Club of Columbus, Delaware Country Club, Columbus Met. Club, Friends Hist. Costume & Textile Collection Ohio State U., Kappa Delta. Methodist. Home: PO Box 214 Columbus OH 43085-0214

KREBILL, LORRIE LEABO, secondary education educator; b. Davenport, Iowa; d. Dorwin Norman and Maxine Deloris (Jacobs) Leabo; m. Douglas Dwight Krebill (dec. 1996); children: Kelli Ann, Darin Douglas. BS, Iowa State U., 1970; MS in Edn., U. Wis., Platteville, 1992; postgrad., U. Wis., Stevens Point, White Water and LaCrosse, Carroll Coll., Viterbo Coll., La Cross, Wis. Cert. tchr., Wis.; lic. real estate salesperson, Wis. Bilingual personnel asst. Precision Twist Drill, Crystal Lake, Ill., 1979-80; reading, writing, and spelling tchr. Quail Valley Jr. High, Missouri City, Tex., 1982; Spanish tchr. Reedsburg (Wis.) Sch. Dist., 1984—; paralegal LaRowe & Gerlach, S.C., Reedsburg, 1989-90; mem. Power of Positive Students Com., Reedsburg, 1991-92. Alderperson City of Reedsburg, 1985—, pres. city coun., 1996, chmn., mem. parks and bldg. com., mem. wellhead protection com., 1996; v.p., commr. Reedsburg Utility Commn., 1989—; mem. Reedsburg Plan Commn., 1990—, sch. to work com. Sch. Dist. of Reedsburg, 1992—; fin. com. mem. Cmty. Devel. Auth.; mem. Indls. Devel. Commn. Mem. NEA, Wis. Edn. Assn., Reedsburg Edn. Assn.

KREBS, CAROL MARIE, architect, psychiatric therapist; b. St. Louis, May 6, 1958; d. Festus John and Virginia (Klohr) K. B in Environ. Design, U. Kans., 1982; MA in Edn. Counseling, St. Louis U., 1995. Archtl. intern GSA, Kansas City, Mo., 1980-81, Old Post Office Renovation, St. Louis, 1980-81; free-lance archtl. designer St. Louis, 1981-84; archtl. designer Interior Space, St. Louis, 1984, Gina Ward and Assoc., St. Louis, 1984-85, Michael Fox and Assoc., St. Louis, 1985-86; mgr. facility design and constrn. Southwestern Bell Telephone, St. Louis, 1986-88; mgr. int. arch. and design exec. facilities Southwestern Bell Corp. Asset Mgmt., St. Louis, 1989-94; psychiat. therapist DePaul Health Ctr., St. Louis, 1994—, St. Mary's Health Ctr., Comtrea, Inc.; therapist St. Mary's Health Ctr., Comtrea, Inc. Big sister Big Bros./Big Sisters of Greater St. Louis, 1986—; mem. Operation Food Search. Mem. AIA. Home: 965 Cleveland Ave Saint Louis MO 63122-2606

KREBS, EUGENE KEHM, II, state legislator; b. Hamilton, Ohio, Aug. 4, 1953; s. Eugene Kehm and Martha Logan (Magaw) K.; m. Janet Lynn Krepp, Dec. 27, 1975; children: Kindra, Alaina. BS, Bowling Green State U., 1975. Farmer Camden, Ohio, 1971—; mem. Ohio Ho. of Reps., Columbus, 1993—. Contbr. article to Wall St. Jour. Mem. Sch. Bd., Eaton (Ohio) City Schs., 1990-92. Republican. Methodist. Home: 12173 State Route 732 Camden OH 45311-9642 Office: Ohio Ho of Reps 77 S High St Columbus OH 43215-6108

KREDIT, KENNETH E., state legislator, automobile dealership executive. Mem. S.D. Ho. of Reps., Pierre, mem. appropriations com. Republican.

KREEGAR, PHILLIP KEITH, educational administrator; b. Anderson, Ind., Aug. 3, 1937; s. James Forrest and Uva Maxine (Johnson) K.; m. Martha Ann Kreegar, Aug. 10, 1958; children: Gregory, Pamela, Deborah. BS, Purdue U., 1959. Asst. prin., tchr. Harrison Twp. Sch. Corp., Kitchel, Ind., 1959-60; gen. fieldman Madison County Farm Bur. Coop., Anderson, Ind., 1962-65; pub. rels. asst. Ind. Farm Bur. Coop., Indpls., 1965-77, communications specialist, 1977-79, asst. mgr. edn., 1979-83, mgr. mem. rels., 1983-89, edn. specialist, 1989-91, edn. mgr., 1991—; rep. Ind. Youthpower Com., 1983-94; bd. dirs. Ind. FFA Found., Trafalgar; chmn. Ind. Coop. Edn. Com., Indpls., 1983—; mem. com. Nat. Coun. Farmer Coops., Washington, 1987—; mem. edn. com. Ohio Coun. Coops., Columbus, 1992—. Photographer, contbr. Coop. Ofcl. jour., 1967, Agrafacts mag., 1978; editor: Farm News newspaper, 1967. Chmn. advancement com. Bethany Boy Scouts of Am., Anderson, Ind., 1964; mem. activities com. Orchard Park Sch. PTO, Carmel, Inc., 1968; chmn. publicity com. Carmel Dad's Club, 1970. Capt. U.S. Army, 1960-62. Named Hon. Ind. Young Farmer, Ind. Young Farmers Assn., 1986, Disting. Svc. award, 1991, Hon. Commr. Agr. State of Ind., 1980; recipient Hon. Hoosier Farmer Degree, 1984, Hon. Am. FFA Degree, Nat. FFA Assn., 1989, Ohio Coop. Edn. award, 1995. Mem. Assn. Coop. Educators, Purdue Agr. Alumni Assn., Purdue Alumni Assn. Office: Countrymark Coop Inc 950 N Meridian St Indianapolis IN 46204

KREER, IRENE OVERMAN, association and meeting management executive; b. McGrawsville, Ind., Nov. 11, 1926; d. Ralph and Laura Edith (Sharp) Overman; m. Henry Blackstone Kreer, Dec. 22, 1946; children: Laurene (dec.), Linda Kreer Witt. BS in Speech Pathology, Northwestern U., 1948. Speech pathologist Chgo. pub. schs., 1947-49; staff asst., lectr. Art Inst. Chgo., 1962—; pres. Irene Overman Kreer & Assocs., Inc., Chgo., 1962—; frequent lectr. on art, arch., Chgo. area; TV appearances representing Art Inst. edn. programs. Past bd. dirs. Glenview (Ill.) Pub. Libr.; mem. The Art Inst. Chgo., Glenview Cmty. Ch., Field Mus., Chgo. Architecture Found., Smithsonian Assocs. Mem. Nat. Trust Hist. Preservation, Assn. Alumnae Northwestern U. (bd. dirs. 1975—), Delta Delta Delta. Republican.

KREEVOY, MAURICE MORDECAI, retired chemistry educator; b. Boston, Aug. 28, 1928; s. Edward Philip Kreevoy and Jennie (Gildesheim) Swerdlow; m. Raye Gladys Schwartz, Mar. 21, 1953 (dec. Mar. 1990); children: Edith Pamela Pang, William Seth. BS, UCLA, 1950; PhD, MIT, 1954. Postdoctoral fellow U. Utah, Salt Lake City, 1955-56; from asst. prof. chemistry to prof. chemistry emeritus U. Minn., Mpls., 1956—; cons. Gen. Mills., Ventron Corp., Medtronic Inc., others in field. Patentee in field. NSF fellow, Sloane Found. fellow; grantee NSF. Mem. Am. Chem. Soc., Croation Chem. Soc., Sigma Xi. Home: 15 S First St Apt 1619-A Minneapolis MN 55401 Office: U Minnesota Dept Chemistry 207 Pleasant St SE Minneapolis MN 55455

KREH BEIL, JULIE E., investment broker; b. Springfield, Ill., Apr. 15, 1964. BA, Ill. State U., 1986; MA, U. Ill., 1987. Agt. Lincoln Land Oil, Springfield, Ill., 1987-89; investment broker Marine Investment Mgmt., Springfield, Ill., 1989—, A.G. Edwards & Sons Inc., Springfield, 1991—. Mem. bd. Ill. State U., Springfield, 1993—; mem. Women Symphony Guild, 1994—. Mem. AAUW, Women in Mgmt. Home: 2301 Burgess Dr Springfield IL 62707 Office: AG Edwards & Sons Inc # 100 1 W Old State Capitol Plz Springfield IL 62701-1217

KREHBIEL, ROBERT, state legislator; m. Janice Krehbiel. Grad., Kans. U. Kans. state rep. Dist. 101, atty. Mem. Kans. Bar Assn., Reno County Bar Assn., Wichita Petroleum Landsman Assn. Home: PO Box 7 Pretty Prairie KS 67570-0007*

KREIBICH, ROBIN G., state legislator; b. June 4, 1959. BA, U. Minn.; postgrad., Brown Inst. Broadcasting. Former TV anchorman; former media specialist U. Wis., Eau Claire; mem. from dist. 93 Wis. State Assembly, Madison, 1992—. Address: 3437 Nimitz St Dr Eau Claire WI 54701-7200*

KREIDER, JIM, state legislator, farmer; b. Nurnburg, Germany, June 24, 1955; (parents Am. citizens); m. Debbie Kreider; children: Lacey, Neeley. Student, S.W. Mo. State U. Farmer Nixa, Mo.; mem. Mo. Ho. of Reps., Jefferson City; mem. agr.-bus. com., agr. com., edn. com., energy environ. com. Mem. com. Am. Soil Conservation Svc. Named Farm Family of Yr., 1992. Mem. Christian County Farm Bur. (v.p., legis. chmn.). Democrat. Home: RR 2 Box 182 Nixa MO 65714-9752*

KREIDER, LEONARD EMIL, economics educator; b. Newton, Kans., Feb. 25, 1938; s. Leonard C. and Rachel (Weaver) K.; m. Louise Ann Pankratz, June 10, 1963; children: Brent Emil, Todd Alan, Ryan Eric. Student, Bluffton Coll., 1956-58; BA, Bethel Coll., 1960; student, Princeton U., 1960-61; MA, Ohio State U., 1962, PhD, 1968. Economist So.

Ill. U., Carbondale, 1965-70; asst. prof. Beloit (Wis.) Coll., 1970—, prof., 1978, chmn. dept. econs. and mgmt., 1984-89, acting v.p. acad. affairs, 1987-88, Allen Bradley prof. econs., 1991—; chief of party Devel. Assocs., Asuncion, Paraguay, 1970; economist Deere and Co., 1973, Castle and Cooke, San Francisco, 1975-76, AmCore, Rockford, Ill., 1984, Rockford Meml. Hosp., 1990-91; cons. corps. and attys. Author: Development and Utilization of Managerial Talent, 1968; contbr. numerous articles, reports to profl. jours. Mem. Nat. Assn. Bus. Economists, Am. Econs. Assn., Am. Assn. Higher Edn., Soc. Internat. Devel. (pres. So. Ill. chpt. 1969), Indsl. Relations Research Assn. (elections com. 1974). Presbyterian. Home: 820 Milwaukee Rd Beloit WI 53511-5636 Office: Beloit Coll Dept Econ Mgmt Beloit WI 53511

KREININ, MORDECHAI ELIAHU, economics educator; b. Tel Aviv, Jan. 20, 1930; came to U.S., 1951, naturalized, 1960; m. Marlene Miller, Aug. 29, 1956; children: Tamara, Elana, Miriam. B.A., U. Tel Aviv, 1951; M.A., U. Mich., 1952, Ph.D., 1954. Asst. prof. econs. Mich. State U., East Lansing, 1957-59, assoc. prof., 1959-61, prof., 1961-90, univ. disting. prof. econs., 1990—; vis. prof. econs. UCLA, 1969, UN, Geneva, 1971-73, NYU, 1975, 93, 96, U. Toronto, 1978, others; vis. scholar Inst. Internat. Econs. Studies, U. Stockholm, 1978-80, U. B.C., summer, 1983, Monash U., Melbourne, Australia, 1987-94, NYU, 1993, Copenhagen Bus. Sch., Denmark, 1994-95; adj. rsch. assoc. East-West Ctr., Honolulu, 1990—; world lectr. tours on behalf of U.S. Info. Svc., 1974-96; cons. to U.S. Dept. Commerce, 1964-66, U.S. Dept. State, 1972-74, UN Coun. Fgn. Rels, N.Y.C., 1965-67, Brockings Instn., 1972-75, C. Am. Common Market, 1972-75, IMF, 1976, East-West Ctr., Honolulu, 1987—; mem. internat. econs. rev. bd. NSF, 1981, 85; bd. mem. Internat. Trade & Fin. Assn., 1990—, pres. 1993. Author: Israel and Africa: A Study in Technical Cooperation, 1964, Alternative Commercial Policies—Their Effects on the American Economy, 1967, International Economics—A Policy Approach, 7th edit., 1995, Trade Relations of the EEC—An Empirical Investigation, 1974, International Commercial Policy: Issues for the 1990's, 1993, Contemporary Issues in Trade Policy, 1995, (with L. Officer) The Monetary Approach to the Balance of Payments: A Survey, 1978, Economics, 1983, 2d edit., 1990; editor: Can Australia Adjust?, 1988, International Commercial Policy: Issues for the 90's, 1993, Contemporary Issues in Trade Policy, 1995; contbr. articles to profl. jours. NSF fellow, 1964-73, Ford Found. fellow, 1960-61; recipient Disting. Faculty award Mich. State U., 1968, State of Mich. Collegiate award, 1984, Whitefield Faculty award, 1994. Mem. AAUP, Am. Econ. Assn., Midwest Econ. Assn., Western Econ. Assn., Royal Econ. Assn., Internat. Trade and Fin. Assn. (bd. dirs. 1991-94). Jewish. Home: 1431 Sherwood Ave East Lansing MI 48823-1851 Office: Mich State U Dept Econs East Lansing MI 48824

KREISER, FRANK DAVID, real estate executive; b. Mpls., Sept. 20, 1928; s. Harry D. and Olive W. (Quist) K.; student U. Minn., 1950-51; m. Patricia Williams, Aug. 23, 1973; children: Sally, Frank David, Susan, Paul, Mark, Patti, Richard. Cert. real estate appraiser. Founder, owner Frank Kreiser Real Estate, Inc., Mpls., 1966-89, pres., 1979—; br. mgr. Merrill Lynch Realty, 1989-90, br. mgr., v.p. Burnet Realty, 1990—; ptnr., founder B & K Properties Co., Mpls., 1976—; chmn. bd., founder Transfer Location Corp., Atlanta, 1979-84 . Served with U.S. Army, 1948-50, Korea. Certified resdl. specialist and resdl. broker. Mem. Nat. Assn. Realtors, Mpls. Bd. Realtors (dir. 1972), St. Paul Bd. Realtors, Dakota County Bd. Realtors, Minn. Assn. Realtors, Realtors Nat. Mktg. Inst. Lutheran. Club: Decathlon Athletic. Address: 5036 France Ave S Minneapolis MN 55410-2033

KREJCSI, CYNTHIA ANN, textbook editor; b. Chgo., Dec. 28, 1948; d. Charles and Dorothea Bertha (Hahn) K.; m. Daniel Neil Ehlebracht, May 16, 1986 (div. Nov. 1988). BA, North Park Coll., 1970; postgrad. Nat. Coll. Edn., 1989—. Prodn. editor Ency. Brit., Chgo., 1970-71, style editor, 1971-72; asst. editor Scott, Foresman & Co., Glenview, Ill., 1972-77, assoc. editor, 1977, editor, 1978-84, sr. editor, 1984-95; sr. editor Benefic Press, Westchester, Ill., 1977-78; editl. mgr. Ligature, Chgo., 1995-96, Contemporary Books., Chgo., 1996—;. Mem. ASCD, Nat. Council of Tchrs. of English, Internat. Reading Assn. (program com., suburban coun.), Nat. Reading Conf., Assn. Ill. Mid. Schs. Home: 1425 Partridge Ln Arlington Heights IL 60004-7988 Office: Contemporary Pub Co 2 Prudential Plz Ste 1200 Chicago IL 60601

KREMER, MICHAEL JOHN, nurse anesthetist; b. Evanston, Ill., Aug. 17, 1953; s. Louis Martin Jr. and Eleanor Jane (Moretti) K. BA in Psychology, No. Ill. U., 1975, BSN, 1978; BS in Nurse Anesthesia, Sangamon State U., 1981; MSN in Nursing Leadership, Seattle Pacific U., 1991; postgrad., Rush U., Chgo., 1994—. Staff RN MICU Rush-Presbyn. St. Luke's Med. Ctr., Chgo., 1978-79; staff RN emergency rm./trauma St. John's Hosp., Springfield, Ill., 1979-81; staff anesthetist Swedish Hosp. Med. Ctr., Seattle, 1981-83; teaching assoc. dept. anesthesiology U. Wash., Seattle, 1983-92; chief nurse anesthetist U. Wash. Med. Ctr., 1992-93; staff nurse anesthetist Rush-Presbyn. St. Luke's Med. Ctr., Chgo., 1993—; tchg. asst. nurse anesthesia program Coll. of Nursing, Rush U., Chgo.; guest lectr. Sch. Health Scis., Seattle Pacific U., 1992; vis. lectr. Vet.'s Gen. Hosp., Taipei, Republic of China, summer 1990; treas. CRNA-PAC, 1994-95; mem. rsch. com., investigator closed claims staff Am. Assn. Nurse Anesthetists Found. Coauthor two textbook chpts.; contbr. articles to profl. jours. Mem. grad. adv. bd. Sch. Health Scis., Seattle Pacific U., 1991. Recipient Internship award Burroughs-Wellcome/Am. Assn. Nurse Anesthetists, 1991; fellow Burrough-Wellcome/Am. Assn. Nurse Anesthetists, 1991; nurse anesthesia faculty devel. grantee HHS, 1994-96. Mem. Wash. Assn. Nurse Anesthetists (bd. dirs. 1992), Wash. State Nurses Assn., Am. Assn. Nurse Anesthetists (CRNA, editl. adv. bd. AANA Jour. 1992—, Rsch. in Action award 1992), Ill. Assn. Nurse Anesthetists (bd. dirs. 1994—, chair pub. rels. com., mem. PAC com.), Sigma Theta Tau (at-large Psi chpt., corr. sec. Gamma Phi chpt.). Office: Rush U Coll Nursing SSH 301 1743 W Harrison St Chicago IL 60612-3823

KREML, FRANKLIN MARTIN, educational administrator, association executive; b. Chgo., Jan. 11, 1907; s. Frank Joseph and Sophia Valeria (Dvorak) K.; m. Margaret Charlotte Parker, July 11, 1927 (div. 1979); children: Franklin Parker, William Parker; m. Barbara Irene Bloom, 1980. Student, U. Wis., 1923-24, Northwestern U., 1925-29; JD, John Marshall Law Sch., Chgo., 1932. Agt. U.S. Bur. Rds., 1924-25; mem. Evanston Police Dept.; advanced through grades to lt. Evanston (Ill.) Police Dept., 1926, divsn. comdr., 1932-35, dir. Accident Prevention Bur., 1929-35; sec. City Council Commn. Traffic and Safety, Chgo., 1932; pub. safety specialist Purdue U., 1935-36; dir. Traffic Officers Tng. Sch. (Traffic Inst. 1936), Northwestern U., 1932-55, Transp. Center, 1955-62; v.p. univ. Northwestern U., 1962-71, lectr., 1954-71, 75—; assoc. dir. Northwestern U. Transp. Center, 1975-79; pres., CEO Motor Vehicle Mfrs. Assn. U.S., Detroit and Washington, 1971-75; pres. Consortium of Govtl. Counselors Inc., Evanston, 1981—; planning and devel. dir. for First Plan for the 70's Northwestern U. Campus, 1966-71; sr. U.S. motor vehicle industry rep., 1971-75, Bur. Permanente Automobiles Constructures Internat., Paris. Author, co-author several texts and manuals, numerous articles on transp., traffic and traffic safety. Pres. Chgo. Police Bd., 1960-72; chmn. Pres.'s Task Force on Hwy Safety, 1970; past v.p., vice chmn. Nat. Safety Coun. Lt. col. AUS, WWII, 1942-46, brig. gen. 1961-67. Decorated U.S. Legion of Merit, Bronze Star, Italian Bronze Star, Italian Cross; named Hon. Officer Order of Brit. Empire; elected disting. mem. regiment U.S. Army Transp. Corp., 1989; inducted into Safety and Health Hall of Fame Internat., 1994; recipient various civic awards, including Northwestern U. merit and svc. awards. Mem. Internat. Assn. Chiefs of Police (life, dir. traffic divsn. 1936-56), Am. Soc. Criminology, Econ. Club, Mil. Order of World Wars (life), Tavern Club, Westmoreland Country Club (Wilmette, Ill.), Met. Club (Washington), Theta Delta Phi, Delta Upsilon. Congregationalist. Home: 2327 W Greenleaf Ave Chicago IL 60645-3419 Office: Consortium Govtl Counselors 1625 Hinman Ave Evanston IL 60201

KRENTZ, EUGENE LEO, university president, educator, minister; b. Edmonton, Alta., Can., June 16, 1932; came to U.S., 1958; s. Emil and Natalie (Martin) K.; m. Joyce Ann Triolet, Feb. 1, 1958; children—Paul, Cynthia, Tamara. B.Th., Concordia Theol. Sem., Springfield, Ill., 1958, B.D., 1971, M.Div., 1973; M.A., Eastern Mich. U., 1973; Ph.D., U. Mich., 1980; LHD (hon.), Rosary Coll., River Forest, Ill., 1995. Ordained to ministry Lutheran Ch. 1958. Pastor St. Paul Luth. Ch., Susanville, Calif., 1958-61; pastor Trinity Luth. Ch., St. Joseph, Mich., 1961-65; prof. Concordia Coll., Ann Arbor, Mich., 1965-83; pres. Concordia U., River Forest, Ill., 1983-95. Contbg. author: Concordia Pulpit, 1974, 78, 80, 83, 85; contbg. editor: Luth. Edn., 1983-95. Chmn. coll. divsn. United Way, Ann Arbor; mem. troop com. Boy Scouts Am., Ann Arbor; peer reviewer U.S. Dept. Edn.; bd. dirs. Fedn. Ind. Ill. Colls. and Univs.; mem., past pres. Luth. Edn. Conf. N.Am. Recipient Servus Ecclaesiae Christi, Concordia Theol. Sem., Ft. Wayne, Ind., 1978, Servant of Christ award Condordia Coll., Bronxville, N.Y., 1995. Mem. Luth. Edn. Assn., Phi Delta Kappa. Home: 36395 N Tara Ct Ingleside IL 60041-9660

KRENTZ, JANE, state legislator, elementary education educator; b. Mpls., Dec. 24, 1952; children: Leah, Sarah, Jeremy. BA, Hamline U., 1971; MEd, U. Minn., 1996. Elem. sch. tchr.; Dist. 51 senator Minn. State Senate, St. Paul, 1993—. Mem. C. of C. Stillwater, Forest Lake, Anoka County (all Minn.). Home: PO Box 60 Marine Saint Crx MN 55047-0060 Office: Minn State Senate State Capital Building Saint Paul MN 55155-1606*

KRENZ, JAMES T., product designer; b. Milw., Apr. 19, 1944. Assoc. Diesen Mechanics, Milw. Area Tech. Coll., 1965, Assoc. Supervisory Mgmt., 1991, postgrad. Diesen technician Waukasha (Wis.) Motor Co., 1965-67; product designer Eaton Corp. Cutler Hammer, Milw., 1967—. Elder Benediction Luth. Ch., Milw., 1985—. Staff sgt. U.S. Army, 1962-67. Office: Eaton Corp Cutler Hammer 4265 N 30th St Milwaukee WI 53216-1821

KRETSCHMAR, WILLIAM EDWARD, state legislator, lawyer; b. St. Paul, Aug. 21, 1933; s. William Emanuel and Frances Jane (Peterson) K. BS, Coll. St. Thomas, 1954; LLB, U. Minn., 1961. Bar: N.D. 1961, U.S. Dist. Ct. N.D. 1961. Ptnr. Kretschmar & Kretschmar, Ashley, N.D., 1962—; mem. N.D. Ho. of Reps., Bismarck, 1972—, speaker, 1988-90, N.D. Comsn. Uniform State Laws, 1987—; bd. dirs. N.W. G.F. Mut. Ins. Co., Eureka, S.D.; del. N.D. Constl. Conv., Bismarck, 1971-72. Mem. ABA, State Bar Assn. N.D., Lions (pres. local club 1972-73, 93-94), Jaycees (pres. local club 1967-68), Elks. Republican. Roman Catholic. Avocations: hunting, swimming, hiking, bicycling, skiing. Home: PO Box A Venturia ND 58489-0114 Office: Kretschmar & Kretschmar 117 1st Ave NW Ashley ND 58413-7037 also: ND Ho of Reps State Capitol Bismarck ND 58505

KRETZER, DONALD E., manufacturing engineer; b. Ashland, Ky., June 10, 1963. B, Morehead (Ky.) State U., 1985, MS in Vocat. Edn., 1986. Indsl. engr. Irvin Industries, Richmond, Ky., 1988-89, Enro Mfg., Louisville, Ky., 1989; mgr. mfg. engring. Airguard Industries, Inc., New Albany, Ind., 1989—. Chmn. Exec. Steering Com., New Albany, 1994—. Home: 8211 Aspen Ave Louisville KY 40258-2150 Office: Airguard Industries Inc 2234 E Market St New Albany IN 47150-1508

KREUSER, JAMES E., state legislator; b. Kenosha, Wis., May 20, 1961; s. Harold Floyd and LaVerne Kreuser; m. Jane, 1990; children: Justin, James Jr. BA, U. Wis.-Parkside, 1983, MPA, 1986. Adminstrv. asst. Kenosha County Exec. Bd., Wis.; assemblyman Wis. State Dist. 64, 1993—; elections & constnl. law com. Wis. State Assembly, hwy. & transp. com., mandates com., spl. com. on electronic benefit transfer sys., legal council com. on Indian affairs. Past exec. bd. ARC. Mem. Kenosha Area Devel. Corp., Sr. Action Coun., Rotary, Masons, Danish Brotherhood, Kenosha Sport Fishing and Conservation Assn. Address: 3313 24th Ave Kenosha WI 53140

KRICHOFF, BENJAMIN JEFFERY, investment broker; b. Belleville, Ill., May 31, 1968. BS, Regis Coll., 1991. Investment broker Kemper Securities, Inc., Belleville, 1991—; assoc. v.p. investments Everen Securities, Inc. (formerly Kemper Securities), Belleville; bd. dirs. Four Cities Coal, Clayton, Mo, Forsyth. Republican. Methodist. Office: Everen Securities Inc 23 Public Sq # 404 Belleville IL 62220-1627

KRIEG, LAURENCE JOHN, computer educator; b. Caracas, Venezuela, Dec. 11, 1945; s. William Laurence and Laura Philinda (Campbell) K.; m. Martha Lenore Fessler, June 1, 1968; children: Katherine, Marjorie, Ian. BA in English, Coll. of Wooster, 1968; MA in Linguistics, U. Mich., 1974, PhD in Linguistics, 1980. Programmer analyst Computer Scis. Corp., Ann Arbor, Mich., 1980-81, Mfg. Data System, Ann Arbor, 1981-82; profl. faculty, CIS Washtenaw C.C., Ann Arbor, 1983—. Elder St. Luke Luth. Ch., 1989-95. Lutheran. Office: Washtenaw Comm Coll 4800 E Huron River Dr Ann Arbor MI 48104

KRIEG, MARTHA FESSLER, software engineer; b. Canton, Ohio, May 31, 1948; d. Herbert Thoburn and Suzanne Marie (Smith) Fessler; m. Laurence John Krieg, June 1, 1968; children: Katherine Joy, Marjorie Elissa, Ian William Herbert. BA, Coll. of Wooster, 1970; MA in Romance Langs., MLS, U. Mich., 1971, 72, PhD in Romance Linguistics, 1976, MS in Computer Sci., 1989. Lectr. in Spanish Macomb County Community Coll., Warren, Mich., 1977; rsch. asst. Middle English Dictionary U. Mich., Ann Arbor, 1975-81; instr. Washtenaw Community Coll., Ann Arbor, 1985, 87; sr. user cons. Univ. Computing Ea. Mich. U., Ypsilanti, 1988-89, vis. lectr. dept. computer sci., 1985-90, lectr. dept. computer sci., 1990-93; lead analyst IntelliSys Automotive, 1995; sr. software engr. T and B Computing, 1995—. Co-author: Getting Started with dBase III+, 1991; author: Microsoft Works for IBM-PC, 1990, Microsoft Works for Macintosh, 1990, Paradox Database Management System, 1990, Manuals for Dress Shop 2.0, 1994; contbr. articles and revs. to profl. publs.; author help pages for various systems. Troop leader Huron Valley coun. Girl Scouts U.S., 1986-93, coun. del., 1987-88, 90-92; fin. sec. St. Luke Luth. Ch., Ann Arbor, 1989-92; host family Youth for Understanding, 1994—. Named Leader of Yr. Huron Valley coun. Girl Scouts U.S., 1991. Mem. Assn. Computing Machinery, Mich. Acad. Scis., Arts and Letters (chair medieval studies 1980-83, chair computers 1987-90), Women's Rsch. Club U. Mich., Gt. Lakes Lace Group, Mensa, Phi Beta Kappa, Sigma Delta Pi, Beta Phi Mu. Office: Tand B Computing Inc PO Box 302 24 Frank Lloyd Wright Dr Ann Arbor MI 48106-0302

KRIEGER, LINDA ANNETTE, intensive care nurse; b. Detroit; d. George Frank and Christine Krieger. BSN, Madonna U., 1990, postgrad. Sch. Bus., 1992—. RN, Mich. Staff nurse Providence Hosp., Southfield, Mich., 1991—. Editor newsletter Stetho Scoop, 1989-90. Active Clowns of Am., Alley 76/Roamers, 1991—, treas., 1994—; vol. Phon-A-Thon and bingo Madonna U., 1986-90. Elected Clown of Yr., Clowns of Am., Alley 76/Roamers, 1994. Mem. AACN, Delta Mu Delta. Home: 44920 Byrne Dr Northville MI 48167-2107 Office: Providence Hosp PO Box 2043 16001 W 9 Mile Rd Southfield MI 48037

KRIEGER, ROBERT HENRY, JR., remote sensing specialist; b. Emporia, Kans., Apr. 7, 1956; s. Robert H. Krieger and Maxine M. (Miller) Loe; m. Sherry A. Jaster, Jan. 15, 1975; 1 child, Robert Aaron. BA in Environ. Studies, U. Kans., 1981. Rsch. asst. Kans. Applied Remote Sensing, Lawrence, 1980-81; cartographer Def. Mapping Agy., St. Louis, 1981-87; mil. analyst (terrain) Combined Arms Combat Devel. Activity, Ft. Leavenworth, Kans., 1987-88; mil. analyst (space systems) Army Space Inst., Ft. Leavenworth, 1988-90; phys. scientist Army Space Command, Colorado Springs, 1990-92, chief, remote sensing br., 1992-93, sr. tech. advisor, ops., 1993-94; account mgr. mil. sys. dept. ERDAS, Inc., Alexandria, Va., 1996; sr. systems analyst Geodynamics Corp., Colorado Springs, 1994, mgr. comml. dept., 1995, mgr. Kans. field office, Leavenworth, 1995. Contbr. articles to profl. jours. Sgt. U.S. Army, 1975-81, 86-88. Decorated Desert Storm medal U.S. Army. Mem. Am. Soc. Photogrammerty and Remote Sensing (chpt. pres. 1980-95, 86-87), Am. Congress on Surveying and Mapping (chpt. pres. 1984-87, 86-87). Office: ERDAS Inc Ste 206 22312 Shawnee Rd Alexandria VA 22312

KRINER, RICHARD WELLINGTON, civil engineer; b. Battle Creek, Mich., Oct. 7, 1931; s. Donald A. and Ethel E. (Kemmerling) K.; m. Nancy A. Williams, Mar. 27, 1955 (div. July 1993); children: Richard W. Jr., Steven J. BSCE, Mich. State U., 1955. Mgr. tech. svcs. and product devel. Lehigh Portland Cement Co., Allentown, Pa., 1955-95; pres. CEMCON Cons. Inc., South Haven, Mich., 1995—; mem. Civil Engring. Rsch. Found., Hwy. Innovative Tech. Evaluation Coun. Contbr. articles to profl. jours. Mem. camping com. YMCA, Allentown, 1968. Fellow ASTM (hon. mem. C-9 1993, vice chmn. C-9 1990-95, mem. exec. com.), Am. Concrete Inst. (bd. dirs. 1989-92, mem. long range planning com.); mem. ASCE (sr.; mem. materials engring. divsn. Lehigh Valley sect.), Portland Cement Assn. (mem. and past chmn. ten. tech. com. adv. com.), Expanded Shale Clay and Slate Inst. (bd. dirs.). Republican. Office: CEMCON Cons Inc 1155 Edgewater Terr South Haven MI 49090

KRINGEN, DALE ELDON, state legislator, trasportation executive; b. Chester, S.D., May 8, 1935; s. Palmer and Madeline (Amundson) K.; children from previous marriage: Brian, Brad, Kevin, Kane; m. Katherine T. Krinter, Aug. 27, 1990; 1 child, Anne. BS, S.D. State U., 1967, MEd, 1960. Tchr., coach Ruthton, Minn., prin.; supt. schs. Alexandria, S.D.; rep. Scott, Foresman Pub. Co., Glenview, Ill.; dir. S.D. Job Svc., Pierre, S.D.; owner Allied Transp. Svcs., Inc., Continental Transp. Svcs., Inc., Truck Bonding, USA, Truck Process Agents Am., Inc., Assist, Inc. Home: 1009 Twin Oaks Dr Madison SD 57042

KRINGSTAD, EDROY, state legislator; m. Faye Kringstad; 3 children. BS, Valley City State U.; MS, U. N.D. Senator Dist. 49 N.D. State Senate, mem. natural resources com., vice chmn. fin. and taxation com. Named to Hall of Fame, Valley City State U., Nat. Wrestling Hall of Fame; named Nat. Coach of Yr. Nat. Jr. Coll. Athletic Assn., Athletic Dir. and Dance Tchr. of Yr. N.D. Health, Phys. Edn. Recreation and Dance. Mem. Amvets, Am. Legion, Nat. Coaches Assn. (past pres.), Am. Fedn. Tchrs., Elks, Eagles. Home: 1807 N Seventh St Bismarck ND 58501

KRINKER, RONALD SCOTT, stockbroker; b. Vincennes, Ind., June 17, 1955. Comms. pers. Griffin Alexander, Ft. Walton Beach, Fla., 1983-87; stockbroker Dean Witter Reynolds, Riverwoods, Ill., 1987—. Vol. Rainbow Days, Chgo., 1994—. Home: PO Box 73663 Buffalo Grove IL 60089 Office: Dean Witter Reynolds PO Box 765 2500 Lake Cook Rd Riverwoods IL 60015

KRINKIE, PHILIP B., state legislator, business executive; b. St. Paul, Feb. 3, 1950; s. Frederic W. and Helen (Trieglaff) K.; m. Mary Ramsey, 1984. BA, Coe Coll., Cedar Rapids, Iowa, 1975. Pres. Shelling Co., 1981—; Dist. 53A rep. Minn. Ho. of Reps., St. Paul, 1991—; mem. govt. op. and gaming-state govt. fin. divsn., local govt. and met. affairs, and transp. and transit coms., Minn. Ho. of Reps. Chmn. 4th Congrl. Dist. Rep. Com., 1983-84. Recipient spl. achievement award, Army Corps of Engrs., 1976. Mem. Sigma Nu. Home: 337 State Office Building Bldg Saint Paul MN 55155-1201*

KRISE, PATRICIA LOVE, automotive industry executive; b. Indpls., July 28, 1959; d. John Bernard and Ann (Emmons) Love; m. Thomas Warren Krise, Sept. 5, 1987. BA magna cum laude, Hanover Coll., Ind., 1981; MBA with hons., Miami U., Oxford, Ohio, 1982. Substitute tchr. Henry County Sch. Dist., Knightstown, Ind., 1982-83; project mgr. Servaas Labs., Inc., Indpls., 1983-84; sales analyst Ford Motor Co., Mpls., 1984, outstate field mgr., 1984-86, met. field mgr., 1986-87, truck merchandising mgr., 1987-88, merchandising mgr., 1988-89; met. field dir. Denver dist. Ford Motor Co., 1989, market representation specialist Denver dist., 1990-91; regional market rep. mgr. Infiniti divsn. Nissan Motor Corp., Naperville, Ill., 1991-92, regional merchandising mgr., 1992-93, dealer ops. cons., 1993—, dealer ops. mgr., 1995—; advisor/presenter Ford Dealer Advt. Fund, Mpls., 1987-88. Tutor adult literacy. Recipient Outstanding Mktg. award Ctrl. Region Ford Motor Co., 1987, Wall St. Jour. award, 1982; named Internat. Woman of Yr., 1992. Mem. Twin Cities Sales Mgrs. Club, Hanover Coll. Alumni Assn., Women's Athletic Assn. (treas. 1979-80), Pre-Law Club (pres. 1980-81), Nat. Assn. Female Execs., Alpha Delta Pi. Republican. Roman Catholic.

KRISHER, ALBERT SHERMAN, chemical engineer; b. Oklahoma City, Aug. 28, 1929; s. Sherman and Gladys (Patterson) K.; m. Hilda Margaret Boyle, Nov. 25, 1954; children: Anita Lynn, Gregory Sherman. BS in Chem. Engring., Okla. State U., 1951. Registered profl. engr., Tex. Fellow Monsanto Co., St. Louis, 1970-80; sr. fellow Monsanto Co., 1980-85; tech. dir. Matls. Tech. Inst., St. Louis, 1985-88; exec. dir. Matls. Tech. Inst., 1988—; cons. ASK Assocs., St. Louis, 1985—. Contbr. articles to profl. jours. Mem. Nat. Assn. Corrosion Engrs., Am. Inst. Chem. Engrs., ASTM, ASM. Office: Materials Tech Inst 1215 Fern Ridge Pky Ste 116 Saint Louis MO 63141-4405

KRISHNAMACHARI, SADAGOPA IYENGAR, mechanical engineer, consultant; b. Chidambaram, Tamil Nadu, India, Sept. 14, 1944; came to U.S., 1982; s. Renga Iyengar and Alamelu Sadagopan; m. Lalitha Ramanujam, June 2, 1969; children: Sriram, Parashar. BS in Math., U. Madras, India, 1963, BSME, 1966; MS in Mechanics, Ill. Inst. Tech., 1984. Engr. Bharat Heavy Elecs. Ltd., Tiruchi, Tamil Nadu, 1967-73, sr. engr., 1973-77, mgr. nuclear engring., 1977-82; mgr. product design and devel. L.J. Broutman & Assocs., Chgo., 1984-91, mgr. computational svcs., 1991—; industry rep. Indian Boiler Regulatory Bd., 1976-77; mem. vis. faculty dept. mech. engring. Ill. Inst. Tech., Chgo., 1985—. Author: Applied Stress Analysis of Plastics--A Mechanical Engineering Approach, 1992. Founder classical music sch. for children, Tiruchi, 1978. Mem. ASME, Soc. Plastics Engrs., Soc. Exptl. Mechanics. Hindu. Office: LJ Broutman & Assocs 3424 S State St Chicago IL 60616-3834

KRISHNAMOORTHI, VISWANATHAN, materials engineer; b. Ayyampet, India, Apr. 9, 1941; came to U.S., 1973; s. K. Viswanathan and V. Pattammal (Iyer) Iyer; m. Chitra Sharma, Feb. 9, 1969; children: Arjun, Nandini. BS in Metall. Engring., Banaras Hindu U., 1966; MS in Metall. Engring., Ohio State U., 1977; MBA, Rensselaer Polytech. Inst., 1983. Metall. engr. Indian Link Chain Mfrs. Ltd., Bombay, 1966-73; metall. Nixdorff Chain Co., St. Louis, 1973-75; asst. foreman St. Louis Steel Castings, 1975; sr. metall. engr. Lucas Aerospace Power Transmission Corp., Utica, N.Y., 1977-89; metall. Superior Industries Internat., Inc., Pittsburg, Kans., 1990-92; sr. materials engr., supr. of materials sci. lab. Hutchinston (Minn.) Tech., Inc., 1993—. Mem. ASM Internat. (chpt. chmn. 1986-87, award 1987, vice chmn. 1985-86, treas. 1983-85, exec. com. 1981-88). Hindu. Home: 110 Orchard Ave SE Hutchinson MN 55350 Office: Hutchinson Tech Inc 40 W Highland Park Dr Hutchinson MN 55350

KRISTENSEN, DOUGLAS ALLAN, state legislator; b. Kearney, Nebr., Jan. 4, 1955; s. Donald M. and Mary Lou (Martin) K.; m. Teri S. Harder; 1 child. BA, U. Nebr., 1977; JD, Drake U., 1980. Ptnr. Lieske & Kristensen; mem. from dist. 37 Nebr. State Seante, Lincoln, 1988—, chmn. transp. com., 1991—, mem. intergovtl. coop. and revenue coms., mem. exec. bd., chair transp. com.; bd. dirs. young lawyers ssect. Nebr. Bar, 1984-88, Nebr. CLE Inc., 1986-90. Henry Toll fellow, 1991; recipient Pres.' award Nebr. Assn. County Ofcls., 1987. Mem. Nebr. Bar Assn., Iowa Bar Assn., Nebr. County Atty.'s Assn. (bd. dirs. 1985—), Rotary Internat., Optimists Club. Office: Nebr State Senate State Capitol Rm 1115 Lincoln NE 68509*

KRITSELIS, WILLIAM NICHOLAS, lawyer; b. Sault Sainte Marie, Mich., Apr. 5, 1931; s. Nicholas William and Theodora G. (Gianacopoulos) K.; m. Elaine John Jennings, Sept. 1, 1963; 1 child, Nicholas William. BA, Mich. State U., 1959; JD, Ohio No. U., 1962. Bar: Mich. 1962, U.S. Dist. Ct. (we. dist.) Mich. 1963, U.S. Supreme Ct. 1966, U.S. Dist. Ct. (ea. dist.) Mich. 1968. Asst. prosecutor Ingham County, Lansing, Mich., 1963-64, chief criminal div., 1964-65; sole practice Lansing, 1965—. Pres. Holy Trinity Greek Orthodox Ch., Lansing, 1977; lifetime mem. NAACP, Lansing. Served with USN, 1951-55. Recipient Outstanding Atty. of Yr. award Ingham County Bar Assn., 1992. Fellow State Bar Mich. Found.; mem. ABA, Fed. Bar Assn., Mich. Bar Assn. (med.-legal com. 1978-81, negligence com. 1982-85), Assn. Trial Lawyers Am. (lectr. product liability), Mich. Trial Lawyers Assn. (lectr. on construction, R.R. and product liabilty, bd. govs. 1978—), Lansing Trial Lawyers Assn. (pres. 1966-70), Am. Judicature Soc., Lawyers for Pub. Justice, Am. Arbitration Assn., Mich. State Alumni Assn., Mich. State U. Pres. Club. (East Lansing). Office: Church Kritselis & Wyble 3939 Capitol City Blvd Lansing MI 48906-2148

KRIVANEK, LOUIS, electrical engineer; b. N.Y.C., July 6, 1924. A in Elec. Engring., SUNY, Troy, 1951; Assn. Engring. Asst., TCLA Tech. GE, Schenectady, N.Y., 1955. Project engr. GE, Shelbyville, Ind., 1951-64; product mgr. Taylor Winfield, Warren, Ohio, 1964-85, Ajax Magnathesnic, Warren, Ohio, 1985-87; engring. cons. Omega Induction Svcs., Warren, Ohio, 1987—. Patent in Vacuum Arc Melting Furnaces, Wire Enameling

Oven Design, Vacuum Arc Metaling Controls. With USN, 1942-45. Mem. Am. Soc. Metals. Roman Catholic. Home: 5137 Copeland Ave NW Warren OH 44483 Office: Omega Induction Svcs 333 S Park Ave Warren OH 44483-5727

KRIVCHENIA, MEGAN LILLER, clinical counselor; b. Clarksburg, W.Va., Aug. 22, 1933; d. William Porter and Gwladys (Bodycombe) Liller; m. Gregory Bernard Krivchenia, June 5, 1953; children: Gregory Bernard II, Alexander Thomas, Mark Porter, Eric Liller, Megan. Student, Case Western Res. U., 1951-54; BA, Marietta (Ohio) Coll., 1969; MEd, Ohio U., 1980. Lic. prof. clin. counselor, Ohio. Therapist Horizons: The Counseling Ctr., Marietta, 1971-88, Counseling and Psychiat. Svcs., Marietta, 1988—; pres. Washington County Bd. Mental Retardation and Devel. Disabilities, Marietta, 1984-90; pres. Ohio Assocs. of County Bd. of Mental Retardation/Devel. Disabilities, Columbus; sec. Family and Child Enrichment Svcs., Marietta, 1993—. Mem. Ohio County Bd. Edn., Wheeling, W.Va., 1964-67; v.p. Marietta City Bd. Edn., 1990—; pres. Washington County Joint Vocat. Sch., 1990—; bd. dirs. Washington County Alcohol, Drug Addiction & Mental Health Svcs., 1995—. Named to Outstanding Young Women of Am., 1967. Mem. ACA, Am. Assn. Mental Health Counseling, Acad. Family Mediators, Ohio Assn. Mental Health Counseling, Phi Kappa Phi. Home: 500 Pine Alley Marietta OH 45750 Office: Counseling and Psychiat Svc 115 2d St Marietta OH 45750

KRIZAN, KELLY JOE, physician, leather craftsman; b. Winner, S.D., Jan. 16, 1951; s. Miles Woodrow and Sadie Mae (DeSmet) K.; m. Susan Barker, Aug. 21, 1971 (div. Aug. 1983); children: Jennifer Rebecca, Nicholas Miles; m. Cynthia Lydia Obras, Aug. 6, 1983. BS, S.D. State U., 1973; BS in Medicine, U. S.D., 1976; MD, Tufts U., 1978. Diplomate Am. Bd. Family Practice. Commd., Am. Bd. Radiology. (first active duty capt. U.S. Air Force, 1978, advanced through grades to lt. col., 1984. Intern USAF Med. Ctr., Scott AFB, Ill., 1978-79, resident, 1979-81; staff physcain USAF Hosp., Hill AFB, Utah, 1981-83; chief emergency svcs., chief family practice USAF Hosp., Hill AFB, Utah, Incirlik AB, Turkey, 1983-84, chmn. dept. family practice, 1985-86; resident radiology U. Wash., 1986-90, clin. asst. prof., 1990—; chmn. dept. radiology 13th AF Med. Ctr., Clark AB, Philippines, 1990-91, St. Mary's Health Care Ctr., Pierre, S.D., 1993—. Artist leather goods, winner various awards. U. S.D. Presdl. scholar, 1969. Fellow Am. Acad. Family Physicians; mem. Am. Coll. Radiology, Am. Roentgen Ray Soc., Radiological Soc. N.Am., Phi Kappa Phi. Roman Catholic.

KROCKOVER, GERALD HOWARD, science educator; b. Sioux City, Iowa, Nov. 12, 1942; s. Marvin H. and Rose (Holdowsky) K.; m. Sharon D. Shulkin, Jan. 30, 1965; children: Mark A., Chad B. BA, U. Iowa, 1964, MA, 1966, PhD, 1970. Cert. sci. tchr., Iowa, 1968. Mid. sch. sci. tchr. Bettendorf (Iowa) Community Sch. Dist., 1964-67; chemistry tchr. Univ. High Sch., Iowa City, 1967-70; asst. prof., assoc. prof. Purdue U., West Lafayette, Ind., 1970-80; prof. Purdue U., West Lafayette, 1980—; bd. dirs. Coun. for Elem. Sci. Internat., Washington, 1990-93; vis. scholar U. Tex., Austin, 1976. Author: Creative Sciencing: A Practical Approach, 1980, Activities Handbook for Energy Education, 1981, Creative Museum Methods and Educational Techniques, 1982, Creative Sciencing: Ideas and Activities for Teachers and Children, 1991, Creative Teaching: A Practical Approach, 1993. Grants com. mem. Pub. Sch. Found., Lafayette, Ind., 1986—; mem. Golden Apple awards com., Lafayette, 1988—, Tchr. Tng. and Licensing Adv. com., Indpls., 1991-92. Grants to improve insvc. sci. tchr. edn. 1971—. Fellow AAAS; mem. NSTA (bd. dirs. 1994—), Sch. Sci. and Math. (jour. reviewer), Nat. Assn. Rsch. in Sci. Teaching (jour. reviewer), Kappa Delta Pi, Phi Delta Kappa. Office: Purdue U 1442 Liberal Arts Edn Bldg West Lafayette IN 47907-1442

KROEBER, JOE, state legislator; m. Bonnie; 3 children. BS, Valley City State; MS, N.D. State U. Mem. N.D. Ho. of Reps., 1991—, mem. appropriations, govt. oper. divsn. coms.; tchr.; atheletic trainer. Mem. CPR Working Group. Eagles, Stutsman County Wildlife, Am. Heart Assn., Quarterback Club, Elks. Home: 1210 7th Ave SE Jamestown ND 58401-5618*

KROENING, CARL W., state legislator, public school principal; b. Apr. 19, 1928; m. Ruth Kroening; six children. BA, U. Minn., MA. Asst. prin. Mpls. pub. sch.; state rep. Minn. Ho. of Reps., St. Paul, 1974-80; Dist. 58 senator Minn. State Senate, St. Paul, 1980—; chmn. jobs, energy and cmty. devel. com., mem. commerce and consumer protection, and fin. state govt. divsn. coms., Minn. State Senate. also: 4329 Webber Pky Minneapolis MN 55412-1350*

KROENING, NATHAN G., investment officer; b. Madison, Wis., Nov. 19, 1969. BBA, U. Wis., Whitewater, 1992. Investment officer Robert Baird & Co. Inc., Manitowoc, Wis., 1993—. Mem. Elks Club. Republican. Roman Catholic. Office: Robert W Baird & Co Inc 980 Maritime Dr PO Box 40 Manitowoc WI 54221

KROHN, JONATHAN STUART, anesthesiologist; b. Bklyn., Oct. 8, 1963; s. Donald and Frances K. BS, Pa. State U., 1983; MD, Jefferson Med. Coll., 1985. Diplomate Am. Bd. Anesthesiology. Intern in internal medicine Mercy Cath. Med. Ctr., Darby, Pa., 1985-86; resident Mercy Hosp., Pitts., 1986-88; resident Mayo Clinic, Rochester, Minn., 1988-89, clin. instr., 1989; staff anesthesiologist Luth. Gen. Hosp., Park Ridge, Ill., 1990—; treas., dir. Park Ridge Anesthesiology Assocs., 1994-95. Contbr. articles to profl. jours. Patron Chgo. Coun. Fgn. Rels., 1993—. Mem. Am. Soc. Anesthesiologists, Alpha Omega Alpha. Office: 1775 Dempster St Park Ridge IL 60025

KROHN, MARTIN L., manufacturing engineer; b. Fremont, Nebr., Aug. 11, 1950. B, U. Nebr., 1973. Chief engr. Automatic Equipment, Pender, Nebr., 1979-90; farmer Herman, Nebr., 1990-92; engr. Tyler Ltd. Partnership, Benson, Minn., 1992—. Bd. dirs., tchr. bible study local ch. Mem. ASAE (com.). Mem. Assembly of God Ch. Home: 4030 Chip Swift St NE De Graff MN 56233-9101 Office: Tyler Ltd Partnership PO Box 249 Benson MN 56215-0249

KROKAR, JAMES PAUL, history educator; b. Chgo., July 17, 1948; s. Louis Joseph and Mary Theresa (O'Connell) K.; m. Christine Larsen, Sept. 4, 1982; 1 child, Andrew. BA, DePaul U., Chgo., 1969; MA, Ind. U., 1971, PhD, 1980. Edit. asst. Am. Hist. Rev., Bloomington, Ind., 1977-80; archives assoc. Ind. U., Bloomington, Ind., 1980-81; asst. prof. history dept. DePaul U., Chgo., 1981-89, assoc. prof., 1989—, dept. chair, 1991-93. Gen. editor Rhetoric and Civilization 2 vols.; contbr. articles to profl. jours. Served as sgt. U.S. Army, 1970-72, Germany. Woodrow Wilson Found. fellow, 1969, IREX fellow, 1974; research council grantee DePaul U., Chgo., 1985, 92. Mem. Am. Hist. Assn., Am. Assn. Advancement Slavic Studies, Southeast European Studies Assn., Ill. Assn. for Advancement History. Office: DePaul U Dept History Chicago IL 60614

KROLL, DENNIS EDWARDS, industrial engineering educator; b. Chgo., June 7, 1947; s. Witold Charles and Lillian Mary (Zwic) K.; m. Susan Ann Michalski, May 26, 1973 (div. Dec. 1979); children: Steven Edward, Brian Christopher; m. Karen Elizabeth Wood, Jan. 13, 1990 (div. Sept. 1994). BS in Indsl. Engring., Bradley U., 1970; MS in Indsl. Engring., U. Wis., 1973; PhD, U. Ill., 1989. Devel. engr. Western Electric Co., Chgo., 1970-74; plant mgr. Junis Mfg. Co., Franklin Park, Ill., 1974-75; sr. indsl. engr. Sunbeam Appliance Co., Chgo., 1975-76; sr. mfg. engr. Victor Comptometer, Chgo., 1976; indsl. engr. Methode Mfg., Rolling Meadows, Ill., 1976-77; planning engr. Western Electric div. AT&T Tech., Lisle, Ill., 1977-81; assoc. prof. indsl. engring. Bradley U., Peoria, Ill., 1981—. Founding editor Jour. Indsl. Engring. Design, 1995—; contbr. articles to profl. jours., chpt. to book. Precinct committeeman Peoria Rep. Com., 1981-82; mem. bd. West Peoria (Ill.) Street Light Dist., 1991-95; alderman City of West Peoria, 1993—. Recipient lab. devel. award Soc. Mfg. Engrs., 1990. Mem. Inst. Indsl. Engrs. (sr.; cert. sys. integrator, chpt. pres. 1982-83, 94-95), Am. Prodn. and Inventory Control Soc. (chpt. treas. 1990-92, chpt. v.p. 1992-94), Ops. Rsch. Soc. Am. (assoc.), Am. Legion, INFORMS, Planetary Soc. Roman Catholic. Office: Bradley U IMET Morgan 110 1501 W Bradley Ave Peoria IL 61625-0001

KROLL, JEFFREY JOSEPH, lawyer; b. Chgo., Feb. 24, 1964; s. Lawrence Stanley and Bernadine Joanne (Jurek) K. BSc in Fin./Econs., DePaul U., 1987, JD, 1990. Bar: Ill., U.S. Dist. Ct. (no. dist.) Ill. Assoc. Robert A. Clifford & Assocs., Chgo., 1990—; adj. prof. law DePaul U., Chgo., 1992—; lectr. in field; participant symposium of the future civil jury system in the U.S., Charlottesville, Va., 1992; mem. Ill. Supreme Ct. subcom. on selection and adminstrn. on juries, 1993; mem. host com. 9th Ann. meeting, Am. Inns of Ct., 1993. Mem. Chgo. Inn of Ct., 1989—, Ravenswood Community Coun., Chgo., 1990. Mem. ABA (long range planning group on civil justice system improvements, 1993, litigation sect., tort and ins. policy sect., co-program dir. sect. litigation ann. meeting 1995, mem. pub. rels. com. sect. tort and ins. practice 1993—), ATLA (mem. exec. com. product liability sect. 1994), Ill. State Bar Assn. (chair admiralty and maritime sect. 1995—), Ill. Trial Lawyers Assn. (med. malpractice com. 1992-93, pub. com. 1992-93, bd. advocates, 1993-94, amicus curiae com. 1993—), Chgo. Bar Assn. (lectr. 1992, pub. affairs com. 1993—, mem. core group CBA/YLS health and hosp. law com. 1995—), DePaul Law Devel. Com., Southwest Bar Assn. Chgo. Office: Clifford Law Offices PC 140 S Dearborn St Ste 700 Chicago IL 60603

KROLL, STEPHANIE J., stockbroker; b. Barrington, Ill., Nov. 17, 1970. BA, Albion Coll., 1992. Program mgr. Glenn Kirk, Mundelein, Ill., 1991-94; stockbroker asst. Smith Barney Inc., Barrington, 1994—; instr. figure skating. Alpha Xi Delta. Republican. Lutheran. Home: 233202 N Kelsey Ave Barrington IL 60016 Office: Smith Barney Inc 101 Lions Dr Ste 105 Barrington IL 60010-3147

KROMKOWSKI, THOMAS S., state legislator; b. South Bend, Ind., Sept. 2, 1942; m. Janeen Kromkowski, 1963; 2 children. With A M Gen. Corp.; rep. Dist. 7 Ind. Ho. of Reps., 1980—, chmn. elec. and apportionment com., ranking minority mem., mem. labor and employment com., mem. pub. health, aged and aging com. Mem. Westside Dem. and Civic Club, South Bend; vice chmn. United Auto Workers; mem. St. Joseph County Coun. Mem. VFW, Polish Falcons Am. Club. Home: 2508 Lincoln Way W South Bend IN 46628-1951*

KRONEGGER, MARIA ELISABETH, French and comparative literature educator; b. Graz, Austria, Sept. 23, 1932; came to U.S., 1962, naturalized, 1968; d. Karl and Josefine (Sparovitz) K. Grad., Karl-Franzens U., Austria, 1960; postgrad., U. Sorbonne, Paris, 1953-55; MA in English and Am. Lit., Kans. U., 1958; PhD in French and Humanities, Fla. State U., 1960. Instr. French, German and humanities Fla. State U., 1958-60; mem. faculty Internat. Coll., St. Gallen, Switzerland, 1961-62; asst. prof. Hollins Coll., Va., 1962-64; asst. prof. French and comparative lit. Mich. State U., East Lansing, 1964-67, assoc. prof., 1967-70, prof., 1970—. Author: James Joyce and Associate Image Makers, 1968, Impressionist Literature, 1973, The Life Significance of French Baroque Poetry, 1988; editor: Phénoménologie et Littérature: L'origine de l'oeuvre d'art, Hommages à A.-T. Tmieniecka, 1986, Phenomenology and Aesthetics: Approaches to Comparative Literature and the Other Arts, 1990, Dordrecht (Kluwer) vol. XXXIII of book series Analecta Husserliana, 1990; co-editor: Esthétique Baroque et Imagination Créatrice, 1992, Allegory Old and New in Literature, the Fine Arts, Music and Theatre, and its Continuity in Culture, 1994; co-editor: Life, The Human Quest for an Ideal, 1996; contbr. numerous articles on 17th and 20th century French and English lit., lit. and the other arts, lit. and phenomenology to scholarly publs. Bd. dirs. World Inst. Phenomenology, 1980—; pres. Internat. Soc. Phenomenology and Lit., Internat. Soc. Phenomenology, Fine Arts and Aesthetics; exec. v.p. World Inst. for Advanced Phenomenological Rsch. and Learning. Fulbright scholar, 1957-60; Ford Found. grantee, 1965-66. Mem. MLA, AAUP, Am. Soc. Aesthetics, Am. Comparative Lit. Assn., Semiotic Soc. Am., Chinese Comparative Lit. Assn., Internat. Soc. for Phenomenology and Lit. (pres. 1985—), Internat. Comparative Lit. Assn., Internat. Soc. Civilization, Internat. Semiotic Soc., South Atlantic MLA, Société Paul Claudel, Am. Assn. Tchrs. French, Fédération Internationale de Langues et Littératures Modernes, Gold Key Soc. (hon., Rsch. award). Roman Catholic. Home: 1324 Chartwell Carriage N Stonelake East Lansing MI 48823 Office: Mich State U Old Horticulture East Lansing MI 48824

KRONFOL, ZIAD ANIS, psychiatrist, educator; b. Beirut, Mar. 29, 1949; came to U.S., 1974; s. Anis and Inam (Ardati) K.; m. Rima Naja, Mar. 26, 1983; children: Zeina, Sara. BS, Am. U. Beirut, 1970, MD, 1974. Diplomate Am. Bd. Psychiatry and Neurology. Intern Am. U. Beirut, 1973-74, instr. psychiatry, 1977-79; resident in psychiatry U. Iowa, Iowa City, 1974-77, asst. prof., 1982-85; rsch. fellow U. Mich., Ann Arbor, 1979-82, assoc. prof. psychiatry, dir. psychoimmunology, 1986—; staff psychiatrist, rsch. dir. adult inpatient psychiatry U. Mich. Med. Ctr., Ann Arbor, 1986—; chief consultation/liaison psychiatry VA Med. Ctr., Iowa City, 1984-85; cons. intensive psychiat. cmty. care VA Med. Ctr., Ann Arbor, 1995—; presenter at profl. confs. Contbr. to profl. publs. Grantee NIMH, 1987-90, NIAAA, 1988. Mem. AAAS, Am. Psychiat. Assn., Soc. Biol. Psychiatry, N.Y. Acad. Scis., Am. Psychosomatic Soc., Soc. Neurosci., Internat. Soc. Neuroimmunomodulation (charter). Home: 1220 Severn Ct Ann Arbor MI 48105-2863 Office: Univ Mich Med Ctr 1500 E Medical Center Dr Ann Arbor MI 48109-0118

KROPCHUK, THOMAS A., electrical engineer; b. Toledo, Ohio, Nov. 17, 1952. Assoc. Electronics, U. Toledo, 1991, BET, 1991. Engr. Thermal Engring. Co., Toledo, Ohio, 1968—. Republican. Office: Thermal Engring Co 2022 Adams St Toledo OH 43624-1432

KROPP, NANCY ANN, public health nurse; b. Quincy, Ill., Nov. 2, 1949; d. Julius H. Wegs and Lucille Eleanor (Drew) Fagan; m. Michael Keith Kropp, Dec. 12, 1969; children: Leslie Renee, Kelley Michelle. ADN, Southeastern C.C., Keokuk, Iowa, 1987; BSN summ cum laude, Quincy Coll., 1992. RN, Ill.; cert. cmty. health nurse; cert. CPR instr., Am. Heart Assn., Ill. Critical care staff nurse Blessing Hosp., Quincy, Ill., 1987-90; staff nurse Blessing Home Care, Quincy, 1990-91, Brown County Pub. Health Dept., Mt. Sterling, Ill., 1991—. Mem. Am. Legion Aux., Mt. Sterling, 1974. Home: 115 E Union St Mount Sterling IL 62353-1535 Office: Brown County Pub Health 111 W Washington St Mount Sterling IL 62353-1212

KROTH, JEANNIE MAE, pediatrics nurse; b. Waverly, Ohio, May 3, 1944; d. Reginald Henry and Marjorie Ellen (Stephens) K.; 1 child, Regina Ellen. LPN, Shawnee State C.C., Portsmouth, Ohio, 1980; student, Ohio U. RN, Ohio, Ky. Staff nurse Mercy Hosp., Portsmouth, Ross County Med. Ctr., Chillicothe, Ohio, Am. Nursing Care Children's Hosp., Columbus, Ohio; staff nurse, supr. Pike Cmty. Hosp., Waverly, Western Med. Svcs., Columbus, Tri State Infusion, Portsmouth, Ohio. Mem. Phi Theta Kappa. Home: 98 Fish Game Rd Waverly OH 45690

KRSUL, JOHN ALOYSIUS, JR., lawyer; b. Highland Park, Mich., Mar. 24, 1938; s. John A. and Ann M. (Sepich) K.; m. Justine Oliver, Sept. 12, 1958; children: Ann Lisa, Mary Justine. BA, Albion Coll., 1959; JD, U. Mich., 1963. Bar: Mich. 1963. Assoc. Dickinson, Wright, Moon, Van Dusen & Freeman, Detroit, 1963-71; ptnr. Dickinson, Wright, Moon, Van Dusen & Freeman, 1971—. Asst. editor: U. Mich. Law Rev, 1962-63. Recipient Disting. Alumnus award Albion Coll., 1984; Sloan scholar, 1958-59; Fulbright scholar, 1959-60; Ford. Found. grantee, 1964. Fellow Am. Bar Found. (life, chmn. Mich. chpt. 1988-89); mem. ABA (sect. gen. practice, chmn. 1989-90, exec. coun. 1984-91, ho. of dels. 1979—, chmn. standing com. on membership 1983-89, chmn. fin. com. 1993-94, bd. govs. 1991—, treas. elect 1995-96, treas. 1996—), Detroit Bar Assn. (dir. 1971-80, pres. 1979-80), Detroit Bar Assn. Found. (dir. 1971-84, pres. 1979-80), State Bar Mich. (commr. 1973-83, pres. 1982-83), Mich. State Bar Found. (trustee 1982-83, 85—, chmn. fellows 1986-87), Fellows of Young Lawyers Am. Bar (bd. dirs. 1977-86, chmn. bd. 1984-86, pres. 1983-84), Am. Judicature Soc. (dir. 1971-79, exec. coun. 1986-89), Nat. Conf. Bar Pres. (exec. coun. 1986-89), Am. Bar Ins. Cons. Inc. (bd. dirs. sec. 1988-95), Sixth Cir. Jud. Conf. (life), Orchard Lake Country Club, Detroit Club, Phi Beta Kappa, Omicron Delta Kappa, Phi Eta Sigma, Delta Tau Delta. Home: 1177 Banbury Circle Bloomfield Hills MI 48302 Office: Dickinson Wright Moon Van Dusen & Freeman 500 Woodward Ave Ste 4000 Detroit MI 48226-3423

KRUEGER, ALAN DOUGLAS, communications company executive; b. Little Rock, Dec. 24, 1937; s. Herbert C. and Estelle B. Krueger; m. Betty Burns, Apr. 4, 1975; children: (by previous marriage) Scott Alan, Dane Kieth, Kip Douglas, Bryan Lee. Student, U. Ill., 1956, Wright Coll., 1957-58. Project engr. Motorola, Inc., Chgo., 1956-64; service mgr., field tech. rep. Motorola, Inc., Indpls., 1964-67; pres. Comm. Maintenance, Inc., Indpls., 1967-68, Comm. Unltd., Inc., Indpls., 1968—. Mem. Indpls. Zoologian Soc., Specialized Mobile Radio Wireless Operator Network. Club: Elks. Home: 6242 North 575 East Franklin IN 46131-9538 Office: Comm Unltd Inc 4032 Southeastern Ave Indianapolis IN 46203-1563

KRUEGER, BETTY JANE, telecommunications company executive; b. Indpls., Oct. 4, 1923; d. Forrest Glen and Hazel Luellen (Taylor) Burns; student Butler U., 1948-49; m. Alan Douglas Krueger, Apr. 4, 1975; 1 son by previous marriage—Michael J. Vornehm. Supr., instr. Ind. Bell Telephone Co., Indpls., 1941-54; supr. communications Jones & Laughlin Steel Co., Indpls., 1954-56, Ford Motor Co., Indpls., 1956-64, U.S. Govt., Camp Atterbury, Ind., 1964-66; dir. communications Meth. Hosp. of Ind., Indpls., 1966-79; pres. owner Rent-A-Radio, Inc. of Ind., Indpls., after 1979; sec.-treas. Communications Unltd., Inc. Former pres. Am. Legion Aux.; chmn. for Ind., Girls State U.S.A., 1972-77; probation officer vol., 1973-74; suicide prevention counselor, 1972-73. Recipient award for outstanding community service Ford Motor Co., 1961. Mem. Am. Soc. Hosp. Engring., Am. Hosp. Assn., Nat. Assn. Bus. and Ednl. Radio, Inc., Internat. Teletypewriters for the Deaf, Asso. Public Safety Communications Officers, Inc., Am. Bus. Women. Methodist. Home: RR 2 Box 119 Franklin IN 46131-9538 Office: 4032 Southeastern Ave Indianapolis IN 46203-1563

KRUEGER, BONNIE LEE, editor, writer; b. Chgo., Feb. 3, 1950; d. Harry Bernard and Lillian (Soyak) Krueger; m. James Lawrence Spurlock, Mar. 8, 1972. Student Morraine Valley Coll., 1970. Adminstrv. asst. Carson Pirie Scott & Co., Chgo., 1969-72; traffic coord. Tatham Laird & Kudner, Chgo., 1973-74; traffic coord. J. Walter Thompson, Chgo., 1974-76; prodn. coord., 1976-78; editor-in-chief Assoc. Pubs., Chgo., 1978—; editor-in-chief Sophisticate's Hairstyle Guide, 1978—, Sophisticate's Beauty Guide, 1978—, Complete Woman, 1981—, Sophisticate's Soap Star Hair Styles, 1995; pub., editorial svcs. dir. Sophisticate's Black Hair Guide, 1983—, Sophisticate's Soap Star Styles, 1994. Mem. Statue of Liberty Restoration Com., N.Y.C., 1983; campaign worker Cook County State's Atty, Chgo., 1982; poll watcher Cook County Dem. Orgn., 1983; mem. Chgo. Architecture Found. Mem. Soc. Profl. Journalists, Am. Health and Beauty Aids Inst. (assoc. mem.), Lincoln Park Zool. Soc., Landmarks Preservation Coun. of Ill., Art Inst. Chgo., Sigma Delta Chi. Lutheran. Clubs: Sierra, Headline Club. Office: Complete Woman 875 N Michigan Ave Chicago IL 60611-1803

KRUEGER, DARRELL W., university president; b. Salt Lake City, Feb. 9, 1943; s. William T. and E. Marie (Nelson) K.; m. Verlene Terry, July 1, 1965 (dec. Jan., 1969); 1 child, William; m. Nancy Leane Jones, Sept. 2, 1969; children: Tonya, Amy, Susan. BA summa cum laude, So. Utah State Coll., 1967; MA in Govt., U. Ariz., 1969, PhD in Govt., 1971. Asst. prof. polit. sci. N.E. Mo. State U., Kirksville, 1971-73, v.p. acad. affairs, dean of instrn., 1973-89; pres. Winona (Minn.) State U., 1989—; trainer, practitioner The 7 Habits of Highly Effective People, Missoula, Mont., 1993; mem. adv. bd. 1st Bank of Rochester, Minn. Mem. Gamehaven Coun. Boy Scouts Am., 1989—. Recipient Outstanding Alumnus award, So. Utah State. Mem. Am. Assn. State Colls. and Univs., Am. Assn. Higher Edn., Rotary, Phi Beta Kappa. Mem. LDS Ch. Home: 1411 Heights Blvd Winona MN 55987 Office: Winona State U Somsen 201 8th & Johnson Winona MN 55987

KRUEGER, DONALD ALVIN, publishing executive; b. Sheboygan, Wis., May 26, 1953; s. Arlo Alvin and Meta Ruth (Woelfer) K.; children; Gretchen Marina, David Scott. BA, U. Calif., Santa Barbara, 1977; MS, U. Wis., 1979. Systems analyst Comptek Rsch., Inc., Goleta, Calif., 1983-84; mgr., worldwide product introduction program IBM, Rochester, Minn., 1984-93; gen. mgr. Advanstar Comms., Inc., Duluth, Minn., 1993—; bd. dirs. Datasystems Solutions, Inc., Shawnee Mission, Kans. Recipient Pres.'s Undergrad. fellowship U. Calif., Santa Barbara, 1976; rsch. grantee Sigma Xi, 1980. Mem. IEEE, AMA, ASQC.

KRUEGER, MIKE, agricultural products executive; b. Jamestown, N.D., May 18, 1949. BS, N.D. State U., 1971. Merchandising mgr. Cargill Inc., Mpls., N.D., 1974-82; v.p. Agri-Mark Inc., West Fargo, N.D., 1982—. Contbr. articles to profl. jours. Mem. adv. bd. coll. humanities and social svcs. U. N.D., Fargo. With USAF, 1971-74. Republican. Roman Catholic. Office: Agri-Mark Inc PO Box 716 West Fargo ND 58078-0716

KRUEGER, NEIL L., lawyer, judge; b. Port Washington, Wis., Mar. 27, 1954; s. Verlyn Charles and Doris O. (Janke) K.; m. Antoinette Dee Gall, July 26, 1980; children: Nathan, Nicole, Angela, Alexis. AS, U. Wis., West Bend, 1975; BS, U. Wis., Madison, 1977; JD, La. State U., 1981. Bar: Wis. Atty./devel. exec. Bethesda Luth., Watertown, Wis., 1982-84; found. dir., atty. Northland Found., Marinette, Wis., 1984-88; adminstrv. law judge State of Wis., Milw., 1988—; pvt. practice Cedarburg, Wis., 1982—. Author: 150 Years of Kruegers in America, 1993; co-author: History of the Johann Gottlieb Eberhardt Family, 1992. Del. Rep. Nat. Conv., New Orleans, 1988, state conv., 1973-94; county chmn. Rep, Party, Marinette, 1986-88; mem. ch. coun., bd. edlers Luth. Ch., Marinette and Cedarburg, 1986—. Recipient Exceptional Performance award State of Wis., 1989, 91; named to Outstanding Young Men of Am. Mem. Wis. Bar Assn., County Bar Assn. (sec. 1986, treas. 1987, pres. 1988), Marinette County Bar Assn., First Immanuel Luth. Men's Club. Home: 614 Jefferson St Cedarburg WI 53012 Office: DILHR-WC 819 N 6th #330 Milwaukee WI 53203

KRUG, R. BERNARD, stock and commodities broker; b. Marysville, Kans., Apr. 2, 1944. BBA, Kans. State U., 1966. Lic. NESD Ins. Mktg. rep. Mobile Oil, Fresno, Calif., 1970-77; stockbroker E. F. Hutton, Fresno, 1973-77, Dean Witter, San Modesto, Calif., 1977-80, Amex, San Modesto, 1980-84, Carmel, Calif., 1984-94, Brookstreet Securities, Marysville, 1994—. Treas. Rep. Com., Marysville, 1994—. Capt. USAF, 1966-70. Mem. Am. Legion, Country Club.

KRUG, SHIRLEY, state legislator; b. Milw., Jan. 29, 1958. BS, U. Wis., Milw., 1981, MA, 1983. Mem. from dist. 13 Wis. State Assembly, Madison, 1984-96; former adj. prof. econs. U. Wis., Parkside. Commr. Mils. Met. Sewerage Dist.; former v.p. Jobs with Peace. Address: 6105 W Hope Ave Milwaukee WI 53216 Office: Wis State Assembly State Capitol Madison WI 53702*

KRUGER, VICKI HENRY, elementary education educator; b. Fort Dodge, Iowa, Jan. 23, 1948; d. C. William and Pauline (Hilderbrand) Henry; m. John Edward Kruger, July 24, 1972; children: Kristine, Michael, Kimberly. BA, U. No. Iowa, Cedar Falls, 1971; MA, Concordia Coll., River Forest, Ill., 1975. Tchr. sixth grade East Elem., Ankeny, Iowa, 1970-72; tchr. fifth grade Roosevelt Elem., River Forest, Ill., 1972-73; tchr. sixth grade, 1973-76; tchr. second grade Story City (Iowa) Elem., 1989—. Author: (ednl. game) The War Between the States, 1989, Dinosaurs: Clues to Past, 1992. Mem. NEA, 1970-72, 89-92, Profl. Educators Iowa, 1994—. Mem. Parent Support Group, Women's Club. Home: 1412 Riverhills Dr Story City IA 50248 Office: Roland-Story Elem 900 Hillcrest Story City IA 50248

KRUGER, WILLIAM ARNOLD, consulting civil engineer; b. St. Louis, June 13, 1937; s. Reynold and Olinda (Siefker) K.; m. Carole Ann Hofer, Oct. 17, 1959. BCE, U. Mo.-Rolla, 1959; MS, U. Ill., 1968. Lic. profl. engr., Ill., Mo., Fla., Miss., N.Y., Iowa, Del., Ohio, Ind.; lic. profl. land surveyor, Ill. Civil engr. City of St. Louis, 1959; with Clark, Dietz & Assocs., and predecessors, Urbana, Ill., 1961-79, sr. design engr., 1963-67, dir. transp. div., 1968-79; civil engr. div. hwys. Ill. Dept. Transp., Paris, 1979-83; part-owner ESCA Cons., Inc., Urbana, 1983-88; civil engr. Zurheide-Herrmann, Inc., Champaign, 1988-95, v.p., 1995—; instr. Parkland Coll., Champaign, 1972; mem. Ill. Profl. Engrs. Examining Com., 1982-89; mem. Ill. State Bd. Profl. Engrs., 1990—, vice chmn., 1993-94, chmn., 1995—. With C.E., AUS, 1959-61. Mem. ASTM, ASCE (br. pres. 1982-83, sect. pres. 1988-89, chmn. dist. coun. 1989), NSPE, Ill. Soc. Profl. Engrs. (chpt. pres. 1974, state chmn. registration laws com. 1973, 78), Ill. Assn. Hwy. Engrs., Am. Pub. Works Assn. (sect. dir. 1974-77, 80), Inst. Transp. Engrs., Ill. Profl. Land Surveyors Assn., Soc. Am. Mil. Engrs., Nat. Coun. Examiners for Engring. and Surveying (Disting. Svc. award 1992), U. Mo.-Rolla Acad. Civil Engrs., Ill. Engring. Coun., Ill. Architect-Engr. Coun., U.

Mo.-Rolla Alumni Assn., Champaign Ski Club, Theta Tau, Tau Beta Pi, Chi Epsilon, Pi Kappa Alpha. Home: 1811 Coventry Dr Champaign IL 61821-5239 Office: 2 Henson Pl Ste 1 Champaign IL 61820-7805

KRUH, JANET JACKSON, telecommunications consultant; b. Eureka, Kans., July 27, 1926; d. Elwin A. and Sidney (DeVier) J.; m. Robert F. Kruh, Dec. 19, 1948; children: Lindsay J., Nancy Dee. BA, Washington U., St. Louis, 1948, MA, 1949. Tchr. sci. Mary Inst., St. Louis, 1948-50; staff counselor Washington U., St. Louis, 1960-61; instr. psychology U. Ark., Fayetteville, 1961-62; sch. psychometrician Fayetteville Pub. Schs., 1962-67; dir. Kans. Regents Continuing Edn. Network/Kans. State U., Manhattan, 1977-92; telecommunications cons., 1992—; tech. com. Kans. Dept. Edn., 1985-86; appointed to Judicial Nominating Commn., 21st Dist., Kans.; presenter at pub. confs. Contbr. articles to ednl. publs. Mem. bd. edn. Unified Sch. Dist. 383, Manhattan, 1973-77, pres. bd. edn., 1975-76. Grantee NSF, 1984-86, NEH, 1987-88, 91-92. Mem. AARP (sec. state legis. com. of Kans. 1994-95, vice-chair 1995-96), LWV (pres. Fayetteville local unit 1958-60, Manhattan unit 1968-70, bd. dirs. Manhattan unit 1993—, bd. dirs. Kans. State 1970-72(, Internat. Teleconferencing Assn., Nat. Assn Continuing Edn. Assn., Phi Delta Kappa. Lutheran. Home: 2155 Blue Hills Rd Manhattan KS 66502-4561

KRUIDENIER, DAVID, newspaper executive; b. Des Moines, July 18, 1921; s. David S. and Florence (Cowles) K.; m. Elizabeth Stuart, Dec. 29, 1948; 1 child, Lisa. BA, Yale U., 1946; MBA, Harvard U., 1948; LLD, Buena Vista Coll., 1960, Simpson Coll., 1963; LittD, Luther Coll., 1990; DHL, Drake U., 1990. With Mpls. Star and Tribune, 1948-52; with Des Moines Register and Tribune, 1952-85, pres., pub., 1971-78, chief exec. officer, 1971-85, chmn., chief exec. officer, 1982-85; with Cowles Media Co., 1983-93, pres., chief exec. officer, 1983-84, chmn., chief exec. officer, 1984-85, chmn., 1985-93. Pres. Gardner and Florence Call Cowles Found.; trustee Drake U., Menninger Found., Des Moines Art Ctr., Grinnell Coll. With USAAF, 1942-45. Decorated Air medal with three clusters, D.F.C. Mem. Newspaper Assn. Am., Coun. on Fgn. Rels. , Des Moines Club, Mpls. Club, Sigma Delta Chi, Beta Theta Pi, Beta Gamma Sigma. Home: 3409 Southern Hills Dr Des Moines IA 50321-1318 Office: 715 Locust St Des Moines IA 50309-3724

KRUL, MICHAEL PAUL, electrical engineer; b. Flint, Mich., June 8, 1963; s. John and Betty Jane (Coron) K.; m. Peggy Lynn Alschbach, May 18, 1985; children: Michael Paul II, Thomas Alan, Rebecca Lynn, Alexander Stephen. BSEE, GMI Engring. & Mgmt. Inst., Flint, 1992. Student engr. Tomblinson Harburn & Assocs., Flint, 1988-89, GM (AC Rochester div.), Flint, 1989-92; electrical engr. Lucas Body Systems, Flint, 1992-96; Aisin World Corp. Am., 1996—. With USN, 1981-87. Mem. IEEE, Mich. Soc. Profl. Engrs. Roman Catholic. Home: 818 Frank Ave Flint MI 48504-4859

KRULL, DENNIS KEITH, computer programmer, market analyst; b. Quincy, Ill., Apr. 17, 1963; s. Virgil Peter and Betty Ann (Mueller) K. BS in Computer Sci., U. Ill., 1985. Computer programmer Drexel Burnham Lambert, Chgo., 1985-87, Barnes & Co., Chgo., 1987-89, Citicorp Futures Corp., Chgo., 1989-94; editor The Krull Letter, Roselle, Ill., 1990; computer programmer MS Distbg., Hanover Park, Ill., 1994—. Vol. Vol. Income Tax Assistance, Roselle, 1990. Mem. Nat. Futures Assn. Home: 275 Springhill Dr Apt 303 Roselle IL 60172-2451 Office: MS Distbg 6405 Muirfield Dr Hanover Park IL 60103

KRULL, EDWARD ALEXANDER, dermatologist; b. Oakville, Conn., Oct. 25, 1929; s. Alexander and Marian (Ruppert) K.; m. Joan Marie Adams, Sept. 7, 1955; children: Alisa M., Lael Adams, Edward A., Jr. Student Yale U., 1948-51, MD, 1955. Intern San Francisco City-County Hosp., 1955-56; with Madigan Gen. Hosp., 1959-60; resident Henry Ford Hosp., Detroit, 1960-63, staff physician dept. dermatology, 1965-76, chmn. 1976—; practice medicine specializing in dermatology, Grand Rapids, Mich., 1963-65; bd. dirs. Skin Cancer Found., 1977-80, Found. Internat. Dermatologic Edn., 1980-82; mem. residency rev. com. in dermatology, 1984-94, chmn. residency rev. com., 1987-94. Bd. govs. Henry Ford Hosp., trustee 1986-94, exec. com. bd. trustees, 1986-94. Editorial bd. Jour. Dermatol. Surg. and Oncology, 1976-79, assoc. editor, 1993—. Capt. M.C., U.S. Army, 1957-59, Iran. Fellow Am. Dermatol Assn. (pres. 1995—, Gold award 1996), Am. Coll. Chemosurgery, Am. Acad. Dermatology (editorial bd. jour. 1979-84, chmn. task force on surgery 1978-84, pres. blue ribbon com. 1984, exec. com. adv. bd. 1974-76, chmn. task force surgery Coun. and Lab. Svcs., 1978-80, bd. dirs. 1982-86, exec. com. bd. dirs. 1984-86, v.p. 1986-87, Bronze award exhibit, 1969, coun. sci. assembly 1991—, chmn. 1995—), Am. Bd. Dermotology (diplomate, bd. dirs. 1984-94, v.p. 1992-93, pres. 1994), Am. Bd. Med. Splts. (diplomate, chmn. dermatology sect. 1992-94, bylaws com. 1992, chmn. 1994, com. study evaluation procedures, 1992—), Mich. Dermatol. Soc. (chmn. liaison Blue Cross Blue Shield 1971-72, sec. treas. 1973-75, pres. 1976-77), AMA, Mich. State Med. Soc. (sec. dermatology sect. 1972-73, pres. 1973-74), Wayne County Med. Soc., Am. Soc. Dermatologic Surg. (pres. elect. 1980-81, pres. 1982, bd. dirs., 1973-76, 79-82, chmn. resident com. 1979-84, scholarship com., 1976-81, cons. bd. dirs. 1976-79, chmn. educ. coordinating com., 1978—, Leon Goldman Achievement award 1988), Assn. Professors of Dermatology (bd. dirs. 1988-89), Assn. Acad. Dermatologic Surgeons (pres. 1988-89). Episcopalian. Avocations: tennis, trout fishing, golf. Home: 422 University Pl Grosse Pointe MI 48230 Office: Henry Ford Hosp Dept Dermatology 2799 W Grand Blvd Detroit MI 48202-2608

KRULL, JEFFREY ROBERT, library director; b. North Tonawanda, N.Y., Aug. 29, 1948; s. Robert George and Ruth Otilie (Fels) K.; m. Alice Marie Hart, Apr. 12, 1969; children: Robert, Marla. BA, Williams Coll., Williamstown, Mass., 1970; MLS, SUNY, Buffalo, 1974. Cert. profl. librarian, N.Y., Ohio, Ind. Traffic mgr. New Eng. Telephone Co., Burlington, Vt., 1970-71; tchr. Harrisburg (Pa.) Acad., 1971-72; reference libr. Buffalo and Erie County Pub. Libr., 1973-76; head libr. Ohio U., Chillicothe, 1976-78; dir. Mansfield-Richland County Pub. Libr., Ohio, 1978-86, Allen County Pub. Libr., Ft. Wayne, Ind., 1986—; mem. exec. com. Ft. Wayne Area Libr. Svc. Authority, 1986-90, v.p., 1989; mem. exec. com. Ind. Coop. Libr. Svcs. Authority, 1992—, pres., 1994—; mem. OCLC Pub. Libr. Adv. Coun., 1994—; pres. Ft. Wayne Area INFONET, 1995—. Trustee Ohionet, Columbus, 1984-86. Mem. ALA, Pub. Libr. Assn. (pres. met. librs. sect. 1990-91), Libr. Adminstrn. and Mgmt. Assn., Ohio Libr. Assn. (bd. dirs. 1985-86), Ind. Libr. Fedn. (vice chmn. legis. com. 1987—), Beta Phi Mu (pres. Fort Wayne area InfoNet 1995—). Home: 3017 Oak Borough Run Fort Wayne IN 46804 Offices: Allen County Pub Libr PO Box 2270 900 Webster St Fort Wayne IN 46802-3602

KRUMHANSL, BERNICE ROSEMARY, physical therapist; b. Cleve., Apr. 17, 1922; d. Frank Ralph and Anne Estelle (Pren) K. BA, Notre Dame Coll. of Ohio, Euclid, 1943; Cert. in Phys. Therapy, Cleve. Clinic Found., 1944. Lic. phys. therapist, Ohio. Staff phys. therapist Assn. for Crippled and Disabled, Cleve., 1944-46; phys. therapy dir. St. Alexis Hosp., Cleve., 1946-52, St. Luke's Hosp., Cleve., 1952-86; asst. prof. Ohio Coll. Podiatric Medicine, Cleve., 1986—; phys. therapy cons. Wanless Hosp., Miraj, Maharashtra, India, 1966; phys. therapist in pvt. practice Cleve., 1986—. Author: Opportunities in Physical Therapy Careers; contbr. 57 articles and short stories to profl. jours. Co-founder, past pres. St. Clair Superior Coalition. Notre Dame Coll. of Ohio scholar, 1940-43; Vocat. Rehab. Adminstrn. grantee, 1966. Mem. Am. Phys. Therapy Assn. (chmn. N.E. dist. Ohio chpt. 1952-56, adv. bd. 1956-60, dir. orthopedic study group 1971-78), Am. Orthopedic Phys. Therapy Assn., Internat. Fedn. Orthopedic Manipulative Therapists. Republican. Roman Catholic. Home: 1167 Addison Rd Cleveland OH 44103 Office: Krumhansl Phys Therapy Svcs 1167 Addison Rd Cleveland OH 44103

KRUPA, JOHN HENRY, English language educator; b. Cleve., Aug. 24, 1944; m. Cheryl J. Henninger, May 29, 1971; children: Megan, Chad. BSEd, Kent State U., 1966; postgrad., Goethe German Lang. Inst., Germany, 1967, NDEA German Inst., 1968; MDiv cum laude, Trinity Evang. Div. Sch., 1977. Dealer supr. Hoover Co., Cleve., 1962-64; German tchr. Hampton (Va.) High Sch., 1966-69; tchr. Eli Whitney Elem. Sch., Chgo., 1969-70; mgmt. intern Def. Supply Agy., Alexandria, Va., 1970-71; field staff mem. Campus Crusade for Christ, U. Del., 1971-74; German tchr. Trinity Coll., Deerfield, Ill., 1974-78; pastor Grace Gospel Ch., Chgo., 1977-84; asst. pastor Christian edn. and adult ministries Des Plaines (Ill.) Bible Ch., 1984-89; tchr. ESL Harper Coll., Palatine, Ill., 1989-90, Motorola, Schaumburg, Ill., 1989-94, Oakton Coll., Monnacep-Des Plaines, 1992—; tchr. ESL Triton Coll., 1993—, tchr. ESL and GED math., 1995—; skills enhancement instr. AT&T Alliance, 1993—; tchr. ESL, GED Arthur Andersen: Teach internat. businessmen, 1993—. Mem. Soc. for Accelerated Learning and Teaching, Tchrs. of English to Sprs. of Other Langs. Home: 1039 Walter Ave Des Plaines IL 60016-3332

KRUPER, JOHN GERALD (JACK KRUPER), sales and marketing executive; b. Carbondale, Pa., Feb. 10, 1949; s. John Joseph and Evelyn (Bernosky) K.; B.S. in Bus. Adminstrn. and Accounting, U. Scranton, 1970; postgrad. SUNY, 1974, U. Scranton, 1985; m. Renee Jane Shugg, Aug. 4, 1973; children—Kevin John, Melissa Lynn, Abbey Renee. Store mgr. Endicott Johnson Corp., Schenectady, 1970-71, retail mdse. distbr., Endicott, N.Y., 1971-72, asst. mdse. buyer, 1972-74, full line mdse. buyer, 1974-76, dir. corp. advt. and sales promotion, 1976-79, gen. sales mgr. Ranger divsn., 1979-81, v.p. merchandising, 1981-84, v.p. branded footwear divsn., 1984-86; v.p. Continental Mktg. Group, Inc., 1986-90, v.p. sales and mktg. Lehigh divsn., 1990-92, Iron Age divsn. Childs Corp., 1992-94; nat. sales dir. hy-test divsn. Florsheim Shoe Co., 1994—. Served with Corps. Engrs., U.S. Army, 1970. Home: 1513 S Lake Shore Dr Barrington IL 60010-3533 Office: 130 S Canal St Chicago IL 60606-3900

KRUPINSKI, JERRY W., state legislator; b. Feb. 27, 1941; m. Eileen Krupinski; children: Scott, Erin, Todd. Commr. Jefferson County, Ohio, 1981-86; state rep. Dist. 98 Ohio State Congress, 1987—. Recipient Caritas medal Diocese of Steubenville, Excellence in Govt. award Steubenville C. of C., Consumer of Yr. award Ohio Consumer Coun., 1991. Mem. Polish Nat. Alliance, Gen. George Custer Com., Farm Bur., Indian Club, KC, Moose. *

KRUPOWICZ, THOMAS EDWARD, retired police officer, fingerprint consultant; b. Chgo., Dec. 12, 1938; s. Edward Andrew and Helen Mary (Majerski) K.; m. Patsyann Lois Swenson, May 27, 1961 (dec. May 1989); children: Pamela, Michael, Thomas. Student, Inst. Applied Sci., Chgo., 1962, Bogan Coll., Chgo., 1963-64. Cert. tchr. fingerprint sci., latent print expert, Ill. Courier Swift & Co., Chgo., 1955-57; printing press operator Audit Bur. of Circulations, Chgo., 1957; courier, driver Continental Glass Co., Chgo., 1957-62; police officer, latent print examiner Chgo. Police Dept., 1962-95; author, pub. Terk Books & Pubs., Chgo., 1992—; cons. on fingerprints, 1990-95. Author: (textbook) Fingerprints--The Identity Factors, 1994, (novels) Death Danced at the Boulevard Ballroom, 1992, First Line Defense, 1995, Dead Men Don't Drink Vodka, 1995; contbr. articles to mags. Fellow The Fingerprint Soc.; mem. Internat. Assn. for Identification. Roman Catholic. Home: 8140 S Scottsdale Ave Chicago IL 60652 Office: Terk Books and Pubs PO Box 160 Palos Heights IL 60463

KRUSE, DENNIS K., state legislator; b. Auburn, Ind., Oct. 7, 1946; s. Russell Wayne and Luella Marie (Boger) K.; m. Kay Adele Yerden, 1968; children: Dennis K. II, John Mark, Timothy James, Daniel Webster. Student, Anderson U., 1967-68; BS, Ind. U., 1985; postgrad., Purdue U. Auctioneer Kruse Auctioneers, 1964—; realtor Kruse Realtors, 1968—; asst. to corp. officer Ambassador Steel Corp., 1981—; rep. Dist. 51 Ind. Ho. of Reps., 1990—, ranking mem. county and twp. com., interstate coop. and pub. safety com., mem. ways and means com. Precinct committeeman Jackson Twp. S. DeKalb County, 1968-72; mem. U.S. Electoral Com., Ind., 1972—; trustee Jackson Twp., 1983-89; del. Ind. Rep. State Conv., 1990—; parade marshall Grabili County Fair, Ind., 1990—; bd. dirs. Northeastern Ind. Youth for Christ, 1968—, chmn., 1986—; bd. dirs. Northeastern Ind. Child Evangelism, 1986—; mem. DeKalb County Right to Life; adv. bd. DeKalb County Am. Family Assn., 1988—. Home: 6704 County Road 31 Auburn IN 46706-9635*

KRUSE, LARRY GEORGE, mechanical engineer; b. Oct. 6, 1949. BSME, Iowa State U., 1975. Registered profl. engr., Ia. Mech. engr. Hicklin Engring. Inc., Des Moines, 1975—. With USMC, 1969-70. Roman Catholic. Office: Hicklin Engring Inc 3001 104th St Des Moines IA 50322-3830

KRUSE, WILBUR FERDINAND, architect; b. Selden, Kans., Nov. 4, 1922; s. John Arnold and Kathryn (Zimmerman) K.; m. Mary Teresa Armstrong, Sept. 5, 1949; children: William, Karen, Katherine, Teresa, Peter, Thomas, Ann, Joan. Student, Tex. A&M Mil. Coll., 1943; BS in Architecture, Kans. State U., 1949. Cert. elem. tchr. Assoc. architect Glen H. Thomas & A.B. Harris Architects, Wichita, Kans., 1948-57; architect Kruse, Roberts & Smith Architects, Wichita, 1957-67; owner Wilbur F. Kruse Architects and Assocs., Wichita, 1957-67; owner Kruse Architects and Cons., Wichita, 1967—. Patentee screened veneer vent for masonry, 1986; prin. works include Kans. Vocat. Correctional Tng. Ctr., Topeka, 1983, also numerous jails, detention ctrs, chs., and schs., Wichita Century II Auditorium Complex. Bd. dirs. Community Corrections Wch/Sedgwick Co., Wichita, 1979-83, Kans. chpt. Arthritis Found., 1985-89; advisor to Arthritis Water Exercise Club Inc., 1984-90. Lt. USAF, 1942-45, ETO. Decorated 3 battle stars, pres. unit citation, air medal, 3 clusters; recipient Cert. Appreciation Kans. Dept. Corrections, Topeka, 1983, Honor award for Marshall County govt. complex State Soc. Engrs. Mem. Serra Club (pres. 1988, dist. gov. 1993, regional rep. U.S. and Can. coun. 1995-97). Roman Catholic. Home: 1641 Womer St Wichita KS 67203-1537 Office: Kruse Architects and Cons 1337 N Meridian Ave Wichita KS 67203-4641

KRUSIC, RAYMOND J., financial consultant; b. Escanaba, Mich., Feb. 13, 1964; s. Harold George and Mary J. (Besaw) K.; m. Rebecca A. Davison, July 5, 1986; children: Nicole T., Tyler R., Alexis R. BA with honors, U. Mich., 1986. Project engr. Moore Bus. Forms, Fremont, Ohio, 1986-90; fin. cons. Merrill Lynch, Green Bay, Wis., 1990—. Contbr. articles to profl. jours. Active Jr. Achievement, Green Bay, 1994—; mem. State Planners Coun., Green Bay, 1992—. Republican. Roman Catholic. Home: 3041 Samray Ln Green Bay WI 54313 Office: Merrill Lynch 225 S Monroe Ave Green Bay WI 54301-4011

KRUSICK, MARGARET ANN, state legislator; b. Milw., Oct. 26, 1956; d. Ronald J. and Maxine C. K. BA, U. Wis., 1978; postgrad., U. Wis., Madison, 1979-82. Legal asst. Milw. Law Office, 1973-78; teaching asst. U. Wis., Milw., 1978-79; staff mem. Govs. Ombudsman Program for the Aging & Disabled, Madison, Wis., 1980; adminstrv. asst. Wis. Higher Ednl. Aids Bd., Madison, 1981; legis. aide Wis. Assembly, Madison, 1982-83, state rep., 1983—. Author: Wisconsin Youth Suicide Prevention Act, 1985, Wisconsin Nursing Home Reform Act, 1987, Wisconsin Truancy Reform Act, 1988, Elder Abuse Fund, 1989, Lyme Disease Fund, 1989, Stolen Goods Recovery Act, 1990, Fair Prescription Drug Pricing Act, 1994. Mem. St. Gregory Great Cath. Ch., Milw., 1960—, Dem. Party, Milw., 1980—, Layton Park Assn.; bd. dirs. Alzheimer's Disease Assn., 1986-88. Named Legislator of Yr. award Wis. Sch. Counselors, Madison, 1986; recipient Sr. Citizen Appreciation Allied Coun. for Sr. Milw., 1987, Crime Prevention award Milw. Police Dept., Milw., 1988, Cert. Appreciation, Milw. Pub. Sch., 1989, Friends of Homecare award, 1989, Environ. Decades' Clean 16 award, 1986-90, Badger State Sheriff's Law and Order award, 1993. Mem. Jackson Park Neighborhood Assn., U. Milw. Alumni Assn. (trustee 1986-90). Home: 3426 S 69th St Milwaukee WI 53219-4037 Office: Wis Assembly State Capitol Madison WI 53702

KRUTTER, FORREST NATHAN, lawyer; b. Boston, Dec. 17, 1954; s. Irving and Shirley Krutter. BS in Econs., MS in Civil Engring., MIT, 1976; JD cum laude, Harvard U., 1978. Bar: Nebr. 1978, U.S. Supreme Ct. 1986, N.Y. 1991. Antitrust counsel Union Pacific R.R., Omaha, 1978-86; sr. v.p. law, sec. Berkshire Hathaway Group, Omaha, 1986—. Co-author: Impact of Railroad Abandonments, 1976, Railroad Development in the Third World, 1978; author: Judicial Enforcement of Competition in Regulated Industries, 1979; contbr. articles Creighton Law Rev. Mem. ABA, Phi Beta Kappa, Sigma Xi.

KRUZAN, MARK R., state legislator; b. Hammond, Ind., Apr. 11, 1960. BA, Ind. U., 1982, JD, 1985. Pvt. practice law; state rep. Dist. 61 Ind. Ho. of Reps., 1986—, mem. pub. policy, ethics, vet. affairs and judiciary coms., vice chmn. environ. affairs com., ranking minority mem., mem. ways and means and caucus campaign com., legis coun., chmn. environ. policy com.; adj. prof. Mem. Cmty. Svc. Coun. Mem. Ind. U. Alumni Assn. (life), Ind. State Bar Assn., Greater Bloomington C. of C., Bloomington Press Club, Sigma Delta Chi. Home: 111 E 6th St Bloomington IN 47408-3366*

KRYN, JEANNETTE MIRIAM, music educator, retired research botanist; b. Louisville, May 23, 1913; d. Hyman and Mary (Kohnop) K. BA, U. Cin., 1934, BE, 1935, MA in Botany, 1944; PhD in Botany, U. Mich., 1953. Tchr. Cin. Pub. Schs., 1935-45; asst. prof. botany U. Buffalo, 1947-51; rsch. botanist U.S. Forest Svc. Lab., Madison, Wis., 1952-58; tchr. Madison Pub. Schs., 1959-78; pvt. tutor and tchr. piano Madison, 1978—. Co-author: The Woods of Liberia, 1959; author info. leaflets on fgn. woods, 1952-58. Vol. tutor Madison Pub. Schs., 1978—; vol. worker ARC, 1979—. Recipient Svc. to Mankind award Madison Sertoma Club, 1976, Know Your Madisonian award Wis. State Jour., 1976. Fellow AAAS. Home: 3710 Atwood Ave Madison WI 53714

KRYN, RANDALL LEE, public relations executive; b. Chgo., Oct. 12, 1949; s. Chester N. and Beatrice K. Kryn. AA, Morton Coll., 1970; BS in Journalism, No. Ill. U., 1973. Writer and researcher William M. Young & Assocs., Oak Park, Ill., 1977; asst. pub. rels. dir. Oak Park Festival, 1978; founder Oak Park Ctr. of Creativity, 1978, pres., 1978-90; founder, dir. Reality Communication, Oak Park, 1976-92. Legis. aide to rep. 21st dist. Ill. Gen. Assembly, 1980-83; Rep. candidate for Ill. State Senate, 1982; chmn. 7th Congl. Rep. Coun., 1986-90, Wis. Beyond Beef, 1992—; mem. Ill. Rep. Platform Com., 1986; Dem. Nat. Platform Com., 1992; co-founder Madison EarthSave, 1992. Recipient Golden Trumpet award Publicity Club of Chgo., 1979; named One of 48 Outstanding Young Men of Am. from Ill., Ill. Jaycees, 1980; ambassador for Canberra, Australia, 1982; co-founder EarthSave, Madison, 1992—; dir. Beyond Beef, Madison, 1992—, Earth Save, Madison, 1992. Mem. Pub. Rels. Soc. Am., Seward Gunderson Soc. (co-founder 1978), Ill. Soc. for Psychic Rsch. (bd. dirs. 1975-76, v.p. 1977-79, pres. 1980), Mensa. Author: James Bevel, The Strategist of the 1960s Civil Rights Movement. Home and Office: 146 Langdon St Madison WI 53703-1307

KRYZAK, LINDA ANN, principal; b. Oak Park, Ill., Nov. 3, 1951; d. Eugene Joseph and Helen (Vlahos) K.; children: Melissa Lynn, Heather Rae. BS in Edn., Northern Ill. U., 1973, MS in Edn., 1977. Cert. gen. adminstr., elem. tchr., spl. edn., early childhood spl. edn. tchr., social/emotional disordered tchr., learning disabled, educable and trainable mentally handicapped, supervisory endorsements. Dir. career/life tng., rsch. project leader, ednl. cons. Grove Sch., Lake Forest, Ill., 1974-81; pvt. practice Addison, Ill., 1981-82; tchr. spl. edn. Sch. Dist. 83, Franklin Park, Ill., 1982-85; coord. spl. edn. Leyden Area Spl. Edn. Coop., Franklin Park, Ill., 1985-94; prin. South Elem. Sch., Franklin Park, Ill., 1994—; founder Creative Learning Choices, 1992—. Pub. speaker on computers, assistive technology, software and integration of spl. edn. students into regular classrooms, 1988—. Mem. ASCD, Ill. Computing Educators, Ill. Prins. Assn., Nat. Assn. Elem. Prins.

KRZYSZTOF, SAMBORSKI, engineer; b. Warsaw, Warsaw, Poland, July 26, 1954; came to U.S., 1980; BSME, Marquette U., 1988. Project engr. Stevens Graphics, New Berlin, Wis., 1988-91, Banner Welding Syss., Germantown, Wis., 1991-93, Acro Automation Syss., Inc., Milw., 1993—. Mem. Polonia Soccer Club (Franklin, Wis. 1980—). Office: Acro Automation Syss Inc 2900 W Green Tree PO Box 09401 Milwaukee WI 53209-0401

K-TURKEL, JUDITH LEAH ROSENTHAL (JUDI K-TURKEL), writer, editor, publisher; b. N.Y.C., Jan. 3, 1934; d. Samuel S. and Pauline (Turkel) Rosenthal; divorced; children: Joseph, Jeffrey Kesselman, David, Kevin Peterson. BA, Bklyn. Coll., 1955. Story and mng. editor Dell Publs., N.Y.C., 1955-58, 62-65; editor-in-chief Sterling, Stearn & KMR Publs., N.Y.C., 1959-62; sr. editor Macfadden-Bartell Publs., N.Y.C., 1966-68; freelance writer N.Y.C. and Wis., 1968-89; pres. P/K Assocs., Inc., Madison, Wis., 1977—; instr. adult edn. Great Neck (N.Y.) Pub. Schs., 1973-76, U. Wis., Madison, 1977-82; instr. journalism Madison Area Tech. Coll., 1984-87; lectr. nonfiction writing CW Post Ctr., L.I. U., Manhasset, N.Y., 1976-77; tchr.-in-residence Rhinelander (Wis.) Sch. Arts, 1984-86. Author: (writing as Judi Kesselman) Stopping Out, 1976, (writing as Judi Kesselman-Turkel with Franklynn Peterson) The Do-It-Yourself Custom Van Book, 1977, Vans, 1979, (with others) Eat Anything Exercise Diet, 1979, Snowmobile Maintenance and Repair, 1979, I Can Use Tools, 1981, (textbook) Good Writing, 1980, Test Taking Strategies, 1981, Study Smarts, 1981, Homeowner's Book of Lists, 1981, How to Improve Damn Near Everything Around Your Home, 1981, The Author's Handbook, 1982, rev., 1986, The Grammar Crammer, 1982, Research Shortcuts, 1982, Note-Taking Made Easy, 1982, The Vocabulary Builder, 1982, Getting it Down: How to Get Your Ideas on Paper, 1983, Spelling Simplified, 1983, The Magazine Writer's Handbook, 1983, rev. edit., 1986; syndicated computer newspaper columnist, 1983—; editor (newsletter) CPA Micro Report, 1985-92, CPA's PC Network Advisor, 1991-92; pub. CPA Computer Report, 1994—; contbr. articles to profl. jours. Chmn. non-partisan Citizens Nominating Com., Great Neck, 1972-75. Recipient Bus. Press. award, 1977, Nat. Press Club award, 1984, 85. Mem. Am. Soc. Journalists and Authors, Coun. Wis. Writers (pres. 1982-85), Authors Guild, Authors League, Nat. Press Club, Pen & Brush Club (Madison, publ. chmn. 1978-89). Home and Office: P/K Assocs Inc 3006 Gregory St Madison WI 53711-1847

KUBE, JAMES A., draftsman; b. Milw., Apr. 2, 1936. BS in Mech. Engring., Marquette U., 1962. Chief draftsman, QA engr. ITT AC Pump, Pewaukee, Wis., 1956—. Sgt. U.S. Army, 1958-64. Recipient Engring. Continuation of Standards award Standard Engring. Soc., 1975. Mem. Standard Engring. Soc., Milw. Astronomical Soc., Wehr Astronomical Soc., Jaycees. Roman Catholic. Office: ITT AC Pump N27w23293 Roundy Dr Pewaukee WI 53072-4069

KUBIK, JACK L., state legislator; b. Berwyn, Ill., May 20, 1955; married. BS, DePaul U. Dist. 43 rep. Ill. Ho. Reps., Springfield, 1985—; asst. majority leader Ill. Ho. Reps., mem. exec., elections and state govt., revenue, and rules coms. Recipient Legislator of Yr. award, Suburban Area Agy. on Aging, Meritorious Svc. award, Ill. Assn. of Deaf, Pres.'s award, Viet-Now. *

KUBISTAL, PATRICIA BERNICE, educational consultant; b. Chgo., Jan. 19, 1938; d. Edward John and Bernice Mildred (Lenz) Kubistal. AB cum laude, Loyola U., Chgo., 1959, AM, 1964, AM, 1965, PhD, 1968; postgrad. Chgo. State Coll., 1962, Ill. Inst. Tech., 1963, State U. Iowa, 1963, Nat. Coll. Edn., 1974-75. With Chgo. Bd. Edn., 1959-93, tchr., 1959-63, counselor, 1963-65, adminstrv. intern, 1965-66, asst. to dist. supt., 1966-69, prin. spl. edn. sch., 1969-75, prin. Simpson Sch., 1975-76, Brentano Sch., 1975-87, Roosevelt High Sch., 1987, Haugan Sch., 1989, Cook County Juvenile Temporary Detention Ctr. Sch., Jones Met. High Sch. Bus. and Commerce, 1988-89, Cook County Juvenile Temporary Detention Ctr., 1989-90, adminstr. dept. spl. edn., 1990-93; supr. Lake View Evening Sch., 1982-92, ednl. cons. 1993—; lectr. Loyola U. Sch. Edn., Nat. Coll. Edn. Grad. Sch., Mundelein Coll., 1982-91; coord. Upper Bound Program of U. Ill. Circle Campus, 1966-68. Book rev. editor of Chgo. Prins. Jour., 1970-76, gen. editor, 1982-90. Active Crusade of Mercy; mem. com. Ill. Constnl. Conv., 1967-69; mem. Citizens Sch. Com., 1969-71; mem. edn. com. Field Mus., 1971; ednl. advisor North Side Chgo. PTA Region, 1975; gov. Loyola U., 1961-87. Recipient Outstanding Intern award Nat. Assn. Secondary Sch. Prins., 1966, Outstanding Prin. award Citizen's Shc. Com. of Chgo., 1986; named Outstanding History Tchr., Chgo. Pub. Schs., 1963, Outstanding Ill. Educator, 1970, one of Outstanding Women of Ill., 1970, St. Luke's-Logan Sq. Community Person of Yr., 1977; NDEA grantee, 1963, NSF grantee, 1965, HEW Region 5 grantee for drug edn., 1974, Chgo. Bd. Edn. Prins.' grantee for study robotics in elem. schs.; U. Chgo. adminstrv. fellow, 1984. Mem. Ill. Personnel and Guidance Assn., NEA, Ill. Edn. Assn., Chgo. Edn. Assn., Am. Acad. Polit. and Social Sci., Chgo. Prins. Club (pres. aux.), Nat. Council Adminstrv. Women, Chgo. Council Exceptional Children, Chgo. Council Fgn. Relations, Chgo. Urban League, Loyal Christian Benevolent Assn., Kappa Gamma Pi, Pi Gamma Mu, Phi Delta Kappa, Delta Kappa Gamma (parliamentarian 1979-80, pres. Kappa chpt. 1988-90, Lambda state editor 1982-92, chmn. Lambda state comm. com. 1992, Internat. Golden

Gift Fund award), Delta Sigma Rho, Phi Sigma Tau. Home and Office: 5111 N Oakley Ave Chicago IL 60625-1829

KUBO, GARY MICHAEL, advertising executive; b. Chgo., Aug. 15, 1952; s. Robert S. and Hideko (Nishimura) K.; m. Harriet Davenport, June 14, 1975; children: Michael J., R. Scott. BS, Ill. State U., 1974. Rsch. project dir. Foote, Cone & Belding Communications, Chgo., 1974-76, account rsch. supr., 1976-79, rsch. mgr., 1979-80; assoc. rsch. dir. Young & Rubicam, Chgo., 1980-83; ptnr., group rsch. dir. Tatham, Laird & Kudner Advt., Chgo., 1983-89; v.p., dir. strategic planning and rsch./Midwest, Bozell, Inc., Chgo., 1989-91; sr. v.p., dir. strategic planning and rsch./Midwest, 1991-93; sr. v.p. dir. strategic planning rsch. Ogilvy & Mather, Chgo., 1993-95; prin. KUBO and Ptnrs., Chgo., 1995—. Bd. Dirs. Chgo. Coun. Urban Affairs, 1992—. Mem. Advt. Rsch. Found., Am. Mktg. Assn. (speaker 1983-84, exec. bd.). Avocations: racquet sports, running, music. Home: 2129 Scarlet Oak Ln Lisle IL 60532-2855

KUBO, ISOROKU, mechanical engineer; b. Tokyo, May 16, 1942; came to U.S., 1977; s. Shogo and Sono (Ito) K.; m. Mary Ann Stone, Mar. 17, 1974; children: Tomiko J., Yukari J., Kiyokaz J., Yuri J. PhD in Aero./Mech., Cornell U., 1974; MBA, Ind. U., 1987. Engr. Komatsu Ltd., Tokyo, 1965-73, asst. chief engr., 1973-77; rsch. assoc. Applied Rsch. Lab., Pa. State U., State College, 1977-79; group leader Cummins Engine Co., Columbus, Ind., 1979-82, tech. advisor, 1982-88, dir., 1988—. Recipient Spl. Scholarship Japan Scholarship Assn., 1961-65; Cornell U. fellow, 1969. Mem. ASME (assoc.), Soc. Automotive Engrs. (assoc.), Sigma Xi, Beta Gamma Sigma. Home: 3642 Washington St Columbus IN 47203-1217 Office: Cummins Engine Co PO Box 3005 Columbus IN 47202-3005

KUBY, BARBARA ELEANOR, personnel executive, management consultant; b. Medford, Mass., Sept. 1, 1944; d. Robert William and Eleanor (Frasca) Asdell; m. Thomas Kuby, July 12, 1969. BS in Edn./Psychology, Kent State U., 1966, MEd, 1987. Tchr. Nordonia/Euclid (Ohio) Pub. Schs., 1966-78; mgr. tng. and devel. United Bldg. Factories, Manama, Bahrain, 1979-81, Norton Co., Akron, Ohio, 1981-85; v.p. Kuby and Assocs. Inc., Chagrin Falls, Ohio, 1973-91, pres., 1992—; corp. dir. human resource devel. and systems TransOhio Savs. Bank, Cleve., 1985-88; asst. v.p. human resources and adminstrv. systems Leasing Dynamics, Inc., Cleve., 1988-90; dir. human resources, organizational devel. 60J0 Industries, Akron, 1990-93; v.p. human resources and orgnl. devel. Go-Jo Industries, Akron, 1993—; adj. faculty, cons. Buffalo State U., 1972-92, Lake Erie Coll., Cleve., 1985-95; lectr., cons. Cleve. State U., 1978—; program dir. Ctr. Profl. Adv., East Brunswick, N.J., 1978—. Cons., lectr. Girl Scouts U.S.A., Cleve., 1981-90; colleague Creative Edn. Found.; cons. project bus. Jr. Achievement, 1992-93; bd. trustees Ohio Ballet, 1996. Mem. Am. Mgmt. Assn., Human Resource Planning Soc., Soc. for Human Resource Mgmt., Gestalt Inst. of Cleve., Greenpeace, ACLU. Home: 7236 Chagrin Rd Chagrin Falls OH 44023-1102

KUCERA, DANIEL WILLIAM, retired bishop; b. Chgo., May 7, 1923; s. Joseph F. and Lillian C. (Petrzelka) K. BA, St. Procopius Coll., 1945; MA, Catholic U. Am., 1950, PhD, 1954. Joined Order of St. Benedict, 1944, ordained priest Roman Cath. Ch., 1949. Registrar St. Procopius Coll. and Acad., Lisle, Ill., 1945-49, St. Procopius Coll., Lisle, 1954-56; acad. dean, head dept. edn. St. Procopius Coll., 1956-59, pres., 1959-65; abbot St. Procopius Abbey, Lisle, 1964-71; pres. Ill. Benedictine Coll. (formerly St. Procopius Coll.), Lisle, 1971-76; chmn. bd. trustees Ill. Benedictine Coll. (formerly St. Procopius Coll.), 1976-78; aux. bishop of Joliet, 1977-80; bishop of Salina Kans., 1980-83; archbishop of Dubuque Iowa Iowa, 1983-95; ret., 1995. Mem. KC (4 degree).

KUCERA, KEITH EDWARD, physician; b. Aug. 25, 1960; s. Dale Edward Kucera and Janet Elaine (Livermore) Maciolek; m. Christy Ann Bohl, July 6, 1985; 1 child, Cole Edward. BS, U. Iowa, 1982; DO, Kirksville (Mo.) Coll. Osteo. Medicine, 1987. Diplomate Am. Osteo. Bd. Internal Medicine, Am. Bd. Gastroenterology, Nat. Bd. of Osteo. Med. Examiners. Psychiat. nursing asst. U. Iowa Psychiat. Hosp., Iowa City, 1982-83; intern N.E. Community Hosp., Bedford, Tex., 1987-88; resident in internal medicine Chgo. Coll. Osteo. Medicine, 1988-90, gastroenterology fellow, 1990-92; pvt. practice specializing in gastroenterology Marion, Ind., 1992—; chief internal medicine dept. Marion Gen. Hosp., 1996—. McClymonds Meml. scholar Kirksville Coll. Osteo. Medicine, 1985. Mem. AMA, Am. Osteo. Assn., Am. Coll. Gastroenterology (nat. spkrs. bur.), Am. Soc. Gastrointestinal Endoscopy, Am. Coll. Osteo. Internists, Chgo. Soc. Gastroenterology, Grant County Med. Soc., Delta Chi, Alpha Phi Omega, Sigma Sigma Phi. Home: 1001 W Chapel Pike Marion IN 46952-1844 Office: 123 W Cherry St Marion IN 46952-2655

KUCHAR, KATHLEEN ANN, art educator, artist; b. Meadow Grove, Nebr., Feb. 4, 1942; d. Alvin Charles and Lenora Leona (Bredehoft) K. BA in Edn., U. Nebr. at Kearney, 1963; MA, Ft. Hays State U., 1966; MFA, Wichita State U., 1974. Art instr. Minden (Nebr.) Pub. Schs., 1963-65; prof. art Ft. Hays State U., Hays, Kans., 1967—; consultation panelist Kans. Arts Commn., Topeka, 1984, cons., 1990-91; art exhbn. juror Rocky Mountain Nat. Water Media Exhbn., Golden, Colo., 1992; gov.'s artist of Kans., 1993. Solo exhbns. include Anderson O'Brien Gallery, Omaha, 1991, 93, 96; group exhbns. include Kans. Watercolor Soc., Wichita Art Mus., 1991, 93, 95, Nat. Watercolor Soc. Calif., 1983, 88, Watercolor U.S.A., 1994, Leedy-Voulkos Gallery, 1994, LaPaloma Gallery, Taos, N.Mex., 1995. Recipient Max Beckman Meml. scholarship Bklyn. Art Mus., 1966; fellow in painting Mid-Am. Arts Alliance/Nat. Endowment for Arts, 1986; summer fellow Santa Reparata Graphic Arts Ctr., Florence, Italy, 1991. Mem. Nat. Watercolor Soc., Kans. Watercolor Soc. (charter), Watercolor USA Honor Soc. (charter), Rocky Mountain Nat. Water Media Soc., Hays Arts Coun., Phi Kappa Phi. Office: Fort Hays State U 600 Park St Hays KS 67601-4009

KUCHARIK, KAY E., industrial designer; b. Wickliffe, Ohio, Mar. 2, 1957. AS, C.C. Lakeland, Mentor, Ohio, 1980. Tool designer Kennamental Inc., Cleve., 1977—.

KUCHERA, MICHAEL LOUIS, osteopathic educator; b. Kirksville, Mo., June 25, 1955; s. William Arthur and Natalie Ione (Zange) K.; m. Eva Maria Stahl, Nov. 18, 1978; children: Katherine, Jennifer, Tiffany, David. BA History, BS in Zoology, Iowa State U., 1976; DO, Kirksville Coll. Osteo. Medicine, 1980. Diplomate Nat. Bd. Osteo. Examiners; cert. in osteo. manipulative medicine. Intern Richmond Heights (Ohio) Gen. Hosp., 1980-81; fellow in electromyography Cleve. Clin. Found., 1981; asst. prof. Kirksville Coll. Osteo. Medicine, 1981-87, assoc. prof., 1987-92, prof., 1992—, chmn. dept. osteo. manipulative medicine, 1987—; co-dir. osteo. manipulative medicine residence program Kirkville Coll. Osteo. Medicine, 1989—; dir. Nat. Levitor Ctr., Kirksville, 1983—; cons. Inst. for Gravitational Strain Pathology, Inc., Rangeley, Maine, 1982—; vice chmn. bd., chmn. long range com. Mo. Arthritis Adv. Bd., Jefferson City, 1983-94, chmn., 1994—; chmn. Job Raising Task Force Mo., 1992-93; cons. Nat. Osteo. Bd. Examiners, 1985—, chmn., 1990—; nat. faculty sponsor Undergrad. Acads. Osteopathy, Indpls., 1987-93; editl. cons. Jour. Am. Osteo. Assn., 1992—. Co-author: Osteopathic Considerations in Systematic Dysfunction, 1990, 2d edit., 1991, Osteopathic Principles in Practice, 2d edit., 1991; section editor, chpt. author: Foundations for Osteopathic Medicine, 1996; editor Levitor Networker Quar.; editl. cons. Jour. Am. Osteo. Assn.; contbr. articles to profl. jours. Clk. of vestry Trinity Episcopal Ch., Kirksville, 1982-87, 91-93; bd. dirs., mem. ednl. com. N.E. Mo. Regional Arthritis Ctr., Kirksville, 1984—. Fellow Am. Acad. Disability Evaluating Physicians, Am. Acad. Osteopathy (chmn. undergrad. acads. 1987-93, bd. govs. 1990—, bd. trustees 1993—, chmn. postgrad. stds. and evaluation com. 1992—, Louisa Burns rsch. com., vis. clinician ednl. spkr., pres.-elect 1995, pres. 1996); mem. Am. Osteo. Assn. (vice chmn. bur. rsch. 1991-93, chmn. outsomes rsch. 1993—, pres.'s task force on enhancing osteo. principles and practice/osteo. manipulative treatment 1994-95, faculty Osteo. Med. Edn. Leadership Conf. 1994—), N.Am. Acad. Musculoskeletal Medicine (mem. bd. counsillors 1991-92), Am. Assn. Orthop. Medicine (bd. dirs. 1993—, chmn. edn. com.), Am. Assn. Electrodiagnostic Medicine, Internat. Back Pain Soc., Mo. Assn. Osteo. Physicians and Surgeons (bd. dels. 1990-93, 96, Mo. medallion of honor 1995), Thousand Hills Physicians Network (v.p. 1991-92), N.E. Mo. Osteo. Assn. (pres. 1985-86), Sigma Xi. Republican. Home: 2 Fairlane Kirksville MO 63501-1926 Office: Kirksville Coll Osteo Medicine 800 W Jefferson St Kirksville MO 63501-1443

KUCHTA, JOHN ALBERT, food service manager; b. Chgo., June 3, 1955; s. John and Janet Mary (Ivancak) K.; BS in Math., Northwestern U., 1982. Work coord. Continental Ill. Nat. Bank & Trust Co., Chgo., 1974-78; lab. technician Kasar Labs., Chgo., 1975-76, supr. quality control, 1976-77; supr. weights and measures Bell Chem. Co., Chgo., 1977-78, quality control chemist, 1978-82, mgr. shipping, receiving, distbn., 1982-94; prodn. coord. Bowne, 1994-95; warehouse mgr. Nation Pizza, Schaumberg, Ill., 1995—. Music arranger community theatre. Mem. Am. Soc. Quality Control, Alpha Sigma Lambda. Roman Catholic. Home: 8032 N Wisner St Niles IL 60714-2435 Office: 601 E Algonquin Rd Schaumburg IL 60173

KUCHYNSKI, MARIE, physician; b. Cleve., Sept. 23, 1964; d. Harry Gregory and Albina (Guarnera) K. BA, Case Western Reserve U., 1986, MD, 1990. Diplomate Am. Bd. Internal Medicine. Intern U. Hosps. Cleve., 1990-91, resident, 1991-93; physician pvt. practice, Elyria, Ohio, 1995—. Rheumatology fellow U. Hosps. Cleve., 1993-95. Mem. AMA, Am. Coll. Physicians, Am. Coll. Rheumatology, Cleve. Soc. Rheumatology, Phi Beta Kappa. Democrat. Roman Catholic. Home: 29760 Westminster Dr North Olmsted OH 44070 Office: Elyria Med Group 905 E Broad Elyria OH 44035

KUCINICH, DENNIS J., state legislator; 1 child, Jackie. Student, Cleveland State U.; BA, Case Western Reserve U., MA. Pres. K Comm., Cleve.; v. pres. sales and mktg. Town and Country Printing, Cleve.; councilman City of Cleve., 1969-73, clk. of mcpl. ct., 1975-77, mayor, 1977-79; senator State of Ohio. Named Outstanding Pub. Official, Internat. Eagles.

KUCINSKI, RICHARD J., product designer; b. Cleve., Jan. 6, 1954. AS, Cleve. State U., 1983. Tool and die maker Freeway, Cleve., 1972-76; mgr. product design Kirkwood Industries Inc., Cleve., 1976—. Mem. KC. Office: Kirkwood Industries Inc 4855 W 130th St Cleveland OH 44135-5137

KUCZMARSKI, SUSAN SMITH, management consulting company executive; b. Portland, Oreg., Apr. 24, 1951; d. Fernando Martin and Bula Grace (Weddle) Smith; m. Thomas Dale Kuczmarski, Aug. 2l, 1976; children: John Thomas, James Smith, Thomas Michael. BA, Colo. Coll., 1973; MIA, Columbia U., 1975, MEd, 1978, EdD, 1979. Instr. U. Ill., Chgo., 1976-77, Nat.-Louis U., Evanston, Ill., 1986-88; lectr. Rosary Coll., River Forest, Ill., 1977-78; asst. prof. Concordia U., River Forest, 1977-79; edn. dir. Constl. Rights Found., Chgo., 1979-8l; assoc. dir. devel., instr. Northwestern U., Evanston, 1981-84; exec. v.p. Kuczmarski & Assocs., Chgo., 1984—; trustee Edward Lowe Found., Cassopolis, Mich., 1986—. Author, editor: Youth and Society: Rights and Responsibilities, 2d edit., 1980; co-author: Values-Based Leadership: Rebuilding Employee Commitment, Performance, and Productivity, 1995; book rev. editor Jour. Internat. Affairs, 1973-75. Vol. Harlem Tutorial Program, N.Y.C., 1973-74; trustee Chgo. City Day Sch., Chgo., 1996—. Internat. House fellow, 1974, Columbia U. Sch. Internat. Affairs fellow, 1974-75, Columbia U. internat. fellow, 1975-76. Mem. Com. on Fgn. Affairs, Kappa Alpha Theta. Republican. Roman Catholic. Office: 1165 N Clark St Chicago IL 60610

KUDENHOLDT, SHARON SUE, freelance author; b. Chgo., Aug. 2, 1942; d. Harold Gustavus Adolphus and Thelma (Geen) Soderling; m. John Bernhardt Kudenholdt, Aug. 15, 1970; children: Mara, Kristian, Hannah, Paul. BS, Concordia U., River Forest, Ill., 1964; MA, Loyola U., Chgo., 1968. Cert. tchr., Ill. Art tchr. Walther High Sch., Melrose Park, Ill., 1964-67; asst. tchr. Vogue-Wright Art Studio, Chgo., 1967; English tchr. Kennedy High Sch., Chgo., 1967-72; tchr. Steinmetz High Sch., Chgo.; freelance resumée writer Park Ridge, Ill., 1976—; columnist Park Ridge "Advocate", 1985-87. Mem. Action on Smoking and Health, Washington, 1971—, Christian Found. for Children, Kansas City, Mo., Christian Home Educators Coalition. Home: PO Box 58 Park Ridge IL 60068-0058 Office: Christian Fnd for Chil and Aging 10163 Potter Rd Des Plaines IL 60016-1546

KUDRNA, FRANK LOUIS, JR., civil engineer, consultant; b. Chgo., Sept. 11, 1943; s. Frank Louis Sr. and Helen Georgiana (Malcik) K.; m. Joann Helen Danca, May 3, 1964; children: Karen, Matthew, David. BS in Archtl. Engring., Chgo. Tech. Coll., 1964; MS, Ill. Inst. Tech., 1973, PhD, 1975; MBA, U. Chgo., 1985. Engr. State Dept. Transp., Chgo., 1966-68; supervising engr. Metro. Water Reclamation Dist., Chgo., 1968-76; dir. water resources State of Ill., Chgo., 1976-82; pres. Epstein Civil Engring., Chgo., 1982-86; pres., CEO Kudrna and Assoc., Chgo., 1986—; commr. Great Lakes Commn., Ann Arbor, Mich., 1976—; panel mem. Sea Grant Panel NOAA, Washington, 1992—. Contbr. articles to profl. jours. Mem. DuPage County Regional Plan Commn. Office: Kudrna and Assoc Ltd 400 S Green St Apt 304 Chicago IL 60607-3546

KUEBLER, BARBARA CAMPBELL, science educator; b. Jefferson City, Mo., Aug. 3, 1951; d. Donald Lee and Virginia Lee (Williams) Campbell; m. John Wilson Kuebler, May 15, 1971; children: John Wilson II, Julia Kathryn. BS in Edn., U. Ga., 1973; MEd, Lincoln U., 1993. Tchr. home econs. Madison County H.S., Daniellsville, Ga., 1973-76; tchr. sci. Jefferson City Pub. Schs., 1976—. Mem. ASCD, NSTA (conv. presenter 1996), Nat. Mid. Sch. Assn., Mo. Mid. Sch. Assn. (conv. presenter 1993, 94), Regional Profl. Devel. Com., Delta Kappa Gamma. Mem. Disciples of Christ Ch. Office: Lewis & Clark Mid Sch 325 Lewis & Clark Dr Jefferson City MO 65101

KUEH, THOMAS M., financial consultant; b. Milw., Sept. 13, 1944. BA, St. Norbert Coll., 1971. Salesman Sta. WFMR, Milw., 1979-82; sales mgr. Sta. WBCS, Milw., 1972-79; fin. cons. Smith Barney Inc., Milw., 1982—. With U.S. Army, 1967-69. Office: Smith Barney Inc 411 E Wisconsin Ave Milwaukee WI 53202-4409

KUEHN, ARNOLD E., bank executive; b. Augusta, Wis., Mar. 4, 1915; s. Edward Herman and Wanda Erna (Kromrey) K.; widowed; children: David W., John Edward (dec.), Bruce J. Clk. Peoples State Bank, Augusta, 1936-42; asst. cashier Wittenberg (Wis.) State Bank, 1942-43; cashier Cochrane (Wis.) State Bank, 1943-55; asst. v.p. The State Bank of Viroqua, 1956, exec. v.p., 1956-83, sr. v.p., 1983-85, dir., 1983—; bd. dirs. Vernon Meml. Hosp. Mem. Nat. Fishing Lure Collector Club. Home: 22 Washington Heights Viroqua WI 54665

KUEHNLE, KENTON LEE, lawyer; b. Chgo., Nov. 10, 1945; s. Robert Louis and Mary Caroline (Recktenwald) K.; m. Sherry L. Esposito, June 6, 1970; children: Robert, Amanda, Matthew. BA, Augustana Coll., 1967; JD, Duke U., 1970. Bar: Ohio 1970, U.S. Dist. Ct. (so. dist.) Ohio 1971. Assoc. Dunbar, Kienzle & Murphey, Columbus, Ohio, 1970-77; ptnr. Loveland, Callard & Clapham, Columbus, 1977-80, Scott, Walker & Kuehnle, Columbus, 1980-86, Thompson, Hine & Flory, Columbus, 1986—; mem., lectr. standard forms com. Columbus Bd. Realtors. Co-author: (seminar book) Foreclosure Law, 1989-92, Title Insurance Endorsements, 1991-94; contbr. articles to profl. jours. Mem. Augustana Coll. Alumni Bd., Rock Island, Ill., 1986-89; trustee Madison Plains Scholarship Found., Madison County, Ohio, 1986—; elder First Presbyn. Ch., Grove City, Ohio, 1990-93; pres. Computer Users Group, Columbus, 1985-86. Mem. ABA (sect. real property, probate and trust law 1973—, com. on condominium and coop. housing 1977—), Columbus Bar Assn. (chmn. real property com. 1976-78, chmn. micro computer subcom. 1986-87, 92-94, lectr. for bar assn. seminars), Ohio State Bar Assn. (bd. govs. real property sect. 1979-82, 90—, editor state real property sect. newsletter 1995—, chmn. subcom. to rev. condominium statute 1980-81, lectr. continuing legal edn. programs), Am. Land Title Assn. (lectr. on title aspects of condominium law), Coun. Ethics in Econs., Honesty in Bus., Legal Profession Task Force, Joseph Fletcher Lawyers Conf. (ann. ethics conf., spkr. selection chair). Home: 11325 Big Plain Circleville Rd Orient OH 43146-9301 Office: Thompson Hine & Flory 10 W Broad St Columbus OH 43215-3418

KUELZ, SHERRY LEE, computer professional; b. Janesville, Wis., Oct. 4, 1957; d. Edward Johannes and Dorothy Melvina (O'Kane) Knutson; m. Richard Paul Kuelz, Aug. 21, 1982; children: BrandeNycole Sherry, Scott Richard. Cert. emergency comm., Blackhawk Tech. Coll., 1979; AS, U. Wis., 1992. Sec. Fire Prevention Bur., Janesville Fire Dept., 1975-77; ct. clk. Cook County Cts., Lincoln, Nebr., 1977-78; sec. Nebr. Dept. of Aeronautics, Lincoln, 1978-79; dispatcher Janesville Fire Dept., 1979-80; sec. Milton (Wis.) Coll., 1980-82; reporter Janesville, 1990-95; computer operator Unique Data Svc., Milton, 1993—; cons. Camden Found., Janesville, 1993—, media bd., 1989—. Contbr. poems to profl. publs.; reporter U. Wis. Rock County Paper, Janesville, 1975-76. Active Affirmative Action Program, Janesville, 1988-89; pres. Cmty. Accessibility Medium Dealing with Exceptional Needs, 1989—, Footville Little League, 1995-96. Recipient Vol. award Channel 23-WIFR, 1982. Lutheran. Home: Rt 4 Janesville WI 53545 Office: Camden Found Inc 8441 Mineral Pt Rd Janesville WI 53545-8718

KUENDIG, WILLIAM NORMAN, II, management consultant, actuarial consultant; b. Canton, Ohio, July 11, 1945; s. William N. and Elizabeth Ann (Cox) K.; m. Carol A. Steiger, Dec. 6, 1986; children: Martha, Amy, William, Patricia. BS, Syracuse U., 1967. Enrolled actuary Joint Enrollment Bd. Actuarial trainee Aetna Life & Casualty, Hartford, Conn., 1967-68; asst. actuary Phoenix Mut., Hartford, 1968-74; ptnr. Hooker & Holcombe, Hartford, 1974-76; prin. Towers Perrin, Cleve., 1976-86; v.p. Towers Perrin, Boston, 1986-90; chief actuary Towers Perrin, Cleve., 1990-91, mng. ptnr., 1991—. Pres. Delta Tau Delta Housing Corp., Cleve., 1980. Fellow Soc. Acturaries; mem. Am. Acad. Actuaries (pension com. 1980), Delta Tau Delta. Home: 2861 Broxton Rd Shaker Hts OH 44120-1817 Office: Towers Perrin 1100 Superior Ave E Cleveland OH 44114-2518

KUERBITZ, PATRICIA ANN, writer, poet, artist; b. Bay City, Mich., June 23, 1945; d. Wilfred Joseph and Agnes Irene (Shook) Tacey; m. Ronald Thomas Kuerbitz, July 7, 1990; children: Peggy Burns, Ronald Badgerow Jr., Richard Badgerow, Phyllis Burgett, Merry Baldwin, Edward Baldwin II. AD, Delta Coll., University Center, Mich., 1984. Respiratory therapist Bay City, 1984-94; pres. Pat's Picturesque Poetry, Bay City, 1991—; v.p. Interstate Battery, Bay City, 1990—; calligrapher, writer, artist; instr. calligraphy Burnham Stamp Co., Bay City, 1994—, Pepper Tree Place, Bay City. Author: (poetry) From My Heart, 1985, From My Heart Book II, 1990, From My Heart Parts II Through VI, 1994-96, From My Heart Sampler, 1996. Mem. worship team Faith Center Ch., 1981—; cast mem. Faith Ctr. Prodns., 1988—. Recipient 1st Place award Artex Hobby Products, 1972, 2d Place, 1972, Honorable Mention award World of Poetry, 1987. Home: 901 Murphy Ct Bay City MI 48706 Office: Pat's Picturesque Poetry 901 Murphy Ct Bay City MI 48706

KUHEL, JAMES JOSEPH, information systems analyst; b. Cleve., Apr. 12, 1934; s. Charles and Ann (Mauer) K.; m. Irene Francis Babski, May 12, 1956; children: Lynn, James, Timothy. Grad. high sch., Cleve., 1952. Sales tng. mgr. Bruning div. A.M. Internat., Chgo., 1956-72; regional mgr. OCE Industries Inc., Cleve., 1972-75; pres. Micro Inc., Cleve., 1976-81; territory mgr. A.B. Dick Record Systems Operation, Cleve., 1981-87, mgr. nat. distbr. sales, 1987-88, sales mgr. ea. region, 1988-91, v.p. sales Eastern region, 1991-92; nat. sales mgr., 1992-93; mgr. document imaging products Lake Business Products, Willoughby, Ohio, 1993—. Author: How to Sell Systems in Business, 1969. Served with U.S. Army, 1954-56. Mem. Bus. Equipment Mfrs. Assn. (Man in the Booth 1968), Assn. Info. Image Mgmt. (v.p. 1986—), Soc. Reproduction Engrs. (edn. chmn. 1960-61), Internat. Reprographic Assn. Republican. Roman Catholic. Home: 22691 Briscoe Dr Cleveland OH 44116-3711 Office: Lake Bus Products Operation 38322 Apollo Pkwy Willoughby OH 44094

KUHLMAN, JAMES WELDON, county extension education director; b. Amarillo, Tex., Feb. 13, 1937; s. Herman and Alma Marie (Gerdsen) K.; m. Ann Bullock Davis, Dec. 23, 1967; children: Lisa Ann, Jennifer Shawn. BS, West Tex. State U., Canyon, 1959; MS, U. Nebr., 1962. Teaching asst. West Tex. State U., Canyon, 1958-59; grad. asst. U. Nebr., Lincoln, 1959-62; county ext. agt. U. Nebr., Kearney, 1962-67, Buffalo County ext. agt., chair, 1967-72; Worth County ext. dir. Iowa State U., Northwood, 1972-81; Cerro Gordo County ext. edn. dir. Iowa State U., Mason City, 1981—; farmer Randall County, Tex. and Buffalo County, Nebr., 1955—; spkr. various civic clubs, 1980—, flower garden Buchart Gardens in Victoria, Can., 1990-95. Mem., past pres., past treas. No. Iowa Figure Skating Club, Mason City, 1984—; past vice chair No. Ctrl. Iowa Geneology Club, Mason City, 1992—. With U.S. Army Res., 1961-67. Recipient Disting. Pres. award Sertoma Club Internat., Kearney, Nebr., 1966, Top award Lions Club Internat., Northwood, Iowa, 1979. Mem. Nat. Assn. County Agrl. Agts. (mem. nat. com., voting dir. 1984, 90, Disting. Svc. award 1984), Am. Hereford Assn., Iowa Hereford Assn. (dir. 1991—), Nebr. Hereford Assn., Holstein Assn. Am., North Ctrl. Geneology Club (past vice chair 1992—), Rotary Club Mason City (com. chair 1988—), Mason City C. of C. (agr. com. 1981—, chmn. regional issues com. 1990-91), Iowa State U. Ext. Assn. (dir. 1980's). Presbyterian. Home: 722 N Hampshire Ave Mason City IA 50401-2440 Office: Cerro Gordo County Ext Svc 2023 S Federal Ave Mason City IA 50401

KUHLMAN, KIMBERLY ANN, clinical dietician; b. Toledo, June 30, 1954; d. James Gilbert and Jane Marie (Konczal) Schramm; m. Carl Edwin Kuhlman Jr., May 23, 1981; children: Eric, Christopher. BS in Pub. Health, U. Toledo, 1977; BS in Dietetics, Bowling Green State U., 1978; MEd in Health Edn., U. Toledo, 1988. Cert. diabetes educator. Dietetic intern Good Samaritan Hosp., Cin., 1979; dietitian, tchr. The Toledo Hosp., 1980, clinical dietitian, 1981-83, nutrition support dietitian, 1983-86; dietitian Alcohol Treatment Ctr., Toledo, 1986-87; clin. dietitian Coop. Care Unit, Toledo Hosp., 1987-88; mem. faculty W.W. Knight Family Practice, Toledo, 1988-94; mem. faculty Mercy Coll. N.W. Ohio, 1995—, chief clin. dietitian, 1995—; guest lectr. Toledo Pub. Schs., 1983-84, guest speaker pvt. industry coun., 1989—; instr. Health Aware program Toledo Hosp. Community Health Project, 1980-83. Author: (fact sheet) Home Prental Nutrition; (booklet) Pediatric Nutrition, A Guide to Sensible Eating. Mem. Toledo Art Mus., Toledo Zoo, Toledo Bot. Garden; treas. Presch. Nutrition Coun. N.W. Ohio, Toledo, 1986-89, Am. Cancer Soc. Babe Zaharias Classic; Cub Scout leader Boy Scouts Am. Recipient Patient Care award Am. Acad. Family Physicians, Soc. Tchrs. Family Medicine, Patient Care Mag., 1994. Mem. Nutrition Educators of Health Profls. Practice Group, Sports and Cardiovascular Nutritionists Practice Group of Am. Dietetics Assn., Toledo Dietetic Assn. (chmn. regulations com. 1986-88, co-chmn. membership com. 1983-84, chmn. 1984-85), Toledo Hosp. Corp. Wellness Planning Com., Ann. Conf. on Patient Edn. for AAFP (planning com.), Soc. Tchrs. of Family Medicine. Lutheran. Home: 4264 River Rd Toledo OH 43614-5528

KUHLMAN, THOMAS ASHFORD, American studies educator, writer; b. Cleve., May 24, 1939; s. Orlyn Lee and Catherine Mary (Ashford) K.; m. Mary Louise Haynes, Aug. 22, 1964; children: John Christopher, Katherine Mary. AB with honors, Xavier U., 1961; AM, Brown U., 1963, PhD, 1967. Teaching fellow Brown U., 1963-64; instr. English Georgetown U., 1964-67; asst. prof. English Creighton U., 1967-70, assoc. prof., 1970—, coord. continuing edn., 1973-74; vis. scholar Am. Acad. in Rome, 1981; mem. faculty Inst. Jewish Studies, Omaha, 1974-75; regional dir. Nat. Bicentennial Youth Debates, 1975-76; dir. Copper Hollow Writers WOrkshop, 1977-78; regional humanist Nebr. Com. Humanities, 1976-78. Playwright Each of These Landlords, 1976, Georgian Punch Bowl, Monteith Design, 1982, Idiots Delete, 1987, Hostages of the Court, 1993, fiction in Prairie Schooner Shadows; other literary jours.; author of numerous essays. Mem. coun. Omaha Symphony, 1972-79, mem. exec. com., 1974-77; heritage chmn., bd. dirs. Omaha-Douglas County Bicentennial Commn., 1974-76; sec., bd. dirs. Met. Arts Coun., 1976-78; pres. Landmarks, Inc., 1987-88; bd. dirs. Florence Arts and Humanities Coun., 1979—, pres. 1980; pres. Ponca Sch. PTA, 1976-78. Woodrow Wilson fellow, 1961, Andrew W. Mellon fellow, U. Kans., 1984, NEH fellow, 1989; grantee Office of Edn. Humanities, 1968, Rsch. grantee Creighton U. Faculty, 1969, grantee Nebr. Arts Coun., 1978, grantee Can. Govt. Faculty Devel. Programme, 1979. Mem. Am. Studies Assn., Nebr. Archtl. Found., Omaha Workshop Theater (pres.), Nebr. Humanities Coun., Victorian Soc. Am., Hist. Soc. Douglas County (dir. 1995—), Alpha Sigma Nu. Republican. Roman Catholic. Home: 3650 Burt St Omaha NE 68131-1946 Office: Creighton U Dept English Omaha NE 68178

KUHN, JOHN STEPHEN, drama educator; b. St. Louis, Dec. 1, 1952; s. John Henry and Mary Louise (Reed) K.; m. Patricia Kay Downey, Sept. 16, 1978; children: Rachael, John Christopher. BFA, Southwest Mo. State U., 1981; MFA in Acting, Ohio State U., 1983. Asst. prof. Mo. Western State Coll., St. Joseph, Mo., 1984-85, Tarkio (Mo.) Coll., 1985-86; vis. asst. prof. Oberlin (Ohio) Coll., 1986-87; asst. prof. dept. drama and theater U. Mich., Flint, 1987-93, U. Toledo, 1993—; artistic dir. Mule Barn Theatre, Tarkio,

1985, Creative Arts Prodns., St. Joseph, Mo., 1989; assoc. dir. Oberlin Theatre Inst., 1987; dir. improvisation troup Back Alley Players, Flint, 1989-90; mng. dir. Mich. Shakespeare Festival, Flint, 1989, 90; playwright Blind Sight Buckham Alley Theatre, 1991; dir. promotional videos; festival coord. Midwestern Playwrights Festival, 1994—. Mem. Am. Coll. Theatre Festival, ATHE, ETA. Office: U Toledo Dept Theatre Film and Dance Toledo OH 43606-3390

KUHN, JOSEPHINE M. KELLER, interior decorating business owner; b. Davenport, Iowa, Sept. 27, 1937; d. George Antone and Olive Katherine Keller; m. James Paul, Dec. 27, 1958; children: Christine, Cynthia, George. Student, Am. Inst. Commerce, Davenport, 1958, Coll. DuPage, Glenn Ellyn, 1972, U. Conn., Stamford, 1976, Harvard U., 1990. Pres., owner Timeless Designs, Inc., Lake Forest, Ill., 1984—. Mem. Women's Archtl. League (bd. dirs. 1985-91, 1st v.p. 1989-91).

KUHN, ROBERT HERMAN, city and county official, engineer; b. Canton, Ill., Apr. 10, 1946; s. Orval Jesse Sr. and J. Nellie (Gallien) K.; m. Marlene Elizabeth Shuffer, May 29, 1971; children: Jesse, Regina. BS, U. Ill., 1969, MS, 1975. Registered profl. engr., Mich., Ill. Engr. Crawford, Murphy & Tilley, Springfield, Ill., 1965-68; cons. Grt. Basin Engring., Ogden, Utah, 1973; pub. works engr. City of Bloomington, Ill., 1974; asst. city engr. City of Muskegon, Mich., 1975-78; asst. dir. pub. works County of Muskegon, 1978-85, dir. pub. works and utilities, 1985—; pres. K&S Component Cars, Muskegon, 1978-82; owner BoMar Commodities, Muskegon, 1982—; mem. Solid Waste Planning Bd., 1988-89, Muskegon County Dept. Pub. Works Bd., 1989-96; founder, chmn. Muskegon Internet Coun. Originator and author: City of Muskegon's Internet Home Page. Speaker, facilitator Pre-Cana Marriage Preparation Seminars, 1972—; mem. exec. bd. St. Francis deSales Parish Coun., 1985-88, Muskegon County Cooperating Chs., 1989-92; mem. Charter Study Co., 1979; guitarist ecumenical religious retreats Muskegon Correctional Facilities. With USAF, 1969-73, Panama Canal. Decorated Meritorious Svc. medal; recipient Govt. award Am. City and County Mag., 1987; named One of Outstanding Young Men Am., 1971, Recycler of Yr. Mich. Recycling Coalition, 1989; Harry H. Gunther scholar U. Ill., 1965-69. Mem. ACSE, ASPA, Am. Pub. Works Assn., Am. Water Works Assn., Nat. Assn. Fleet Mgrs., Solid Waste Assn. N.Am. Roman Catholic. Home: 3080 W Sherman Blvd Muskegon MI 49441-1154 Office: City of Muskegon Pub Svc 1350 E Keating Ave Muskegon MI 49442-6106

KUHN, RYAN ANTHONY, media investment banker, investor; b. Framingham, Mass., Sept. 15, 1947; s. Robert Anthony Kuhn and Julia (Scott) McMillan; m. Cynthia Lynn DeVore, June 4, 1988; 1 child, Ryan R. BA in Psychology, Trinity Coll., Hartford, Conn., 1970; MBA, Harvard U., 1979. Mgr. corp. acquisitions McGraw-Hill, N.Y.C., 1979-85; sr. assoc. venture capital Golder, Thoma & Cressey, Chgo., 1985-86; pres. Reid Psychol. Systems, Chgo., 1986-90, Lilly Pulitzer, Chgo., 1990-93; prin. Kuhn & Assocs., Chgo., 1990—. Contbr. articles to profl. publs. and mags.; guest spkr. TV and radio talk show. Bd. dirs. Infant Welfare Soc. Chgo., Harvard Bus. Sch. of Chgo. Republican. Episcopalian. Office: Kuhn and Assocs 205 W Wacker Dr Chicago IL 60606-3538

KUIPERS, JUDITH L., academic administrator. Chancellor U. Wis., La Crosse. Office: University of Wisconsin - La Crosse Office of the Chancellor 1725 State St La Crosse WI 54601-3742

KUKLA, CYNTHIA MARY, artist; b. Chgo., June 23, 1952; d. Stanley A. and Eugenia (Markowski) Cukla; children: Glenn D., Garth A. BFA, Sch. of Art Inst. Chgo., 1973; MFA, U. Wis., 1983. Asst. prof. art No. Ky. U., Highland Heights, 1983-89, assoc. prof. art, 1989-93; assoc. prof. art Ill. State U., Normal, 1993—; lectr. art U. London, 1985, 87, All Hallows Coll., Dublin, 1993; art reviewer Dialogue, Arts in the Midwest, Columbus, Ohio, 1989-92; book reviewer Prentice-Hall, Inc.; art juror Regional Art Exhibits, 1984—; chmn. ann. conf. panel Nat. Coll. Art Assn., 1989, Mid-Am. Coll. Art Assn., 1986, 95,S.E. Coll. Art Assn., 1986, 95. One woman shows at Kortman Ctr. for Design, Rockford, Ill., 1996, Chautauqua (N.Y.) Art Ctr., 1995, Kent State U., Canton, Ohio, 1992, Liberty Gallery, Louisville, 1992, Market Gallery, Rockford, Ill., 1991, Rosewood Art Ctr., Kettering, Ohio, 1990, Headley-Whitney Mus., Lexington, 1987, Cin. Commn. on Arts, 1986, Armory Art Gallery, Blacksburg, Va., 1985, others; exhibited in group shows at Rockford (Ill.) Art Mus., 1995, Peoria (Ill.) Art Ctr., 1995, U. Ky. Art Mus., Lexington, 1995, Arrowmont Ctr. for Arts & Crafts, Gatlinburg, Tenn., 1993-95, Kharkov (Ukraine) Art Mus., 1993, Liberty Gallery, Louisville, 1993, Canton Art Inst., 1992, Galerie Hertz, Louisville, Ohio, 1992, Mus. Ctr. at Union Terminal, Cin., 1991, Mayor's Office Commn. on Culture and Arts, Honolulu, 1991, Solway Coll. Complex, Cin., 1991, Grand European Nat. Ctr. of Arts and Letters, Nationale des Artes, Nice, France, 1990, Am. Embassy, Quito, Ecuador, 1989, Fine Arts Acad., Warsaw, Poland, 1988, Knox Coll. Gallery, Galesburg, Ill., 1988, U. Tenn. travelling exhbn., Knoxville, 1987-89, Ctr. for Contemporary Art, U. Ky., Lexington, 1987, Watertower Art Ctr., Louisville, 1987, Laguna Beach (Calif.) Art Mus., 1983, Springfield (Mo.) Art Mus., 1980, 83, 86, numerous others; works reviewed in (art jour. R.A.M., 1996) New Art Examiner, 1994, Dialogue, 1989, 90, Cin. Enquirer, 1986, 88, 89, Atlanta Art Papers, 1988, Montgomery Ala. Jour., 1987, Louisville Courier-Jour., 1987, 91, 92, Lexington Herald-Leader, 1987, St. Louis Post-Dispatch, 1986, others. Conf. developer, panel chair Gender and Ethnicity in Art, Cin. Art Mus., 1992; mem. exec. bd. Women's Studies program No. Ky. U., 1985-92; mem. Art Inst. Chgo., Contemporary Art Ctr., Cin., Nat. Mus. Women in Art, Washington. Grantee Ill. State U., 1995, Ky. Found. for Women, 1987, 90, Ky. Art Coun., 1988, No. Ky. U., 1985, 87, 90-91, 93, Ill. State U., 1995; Millay Colony/Studios Midwest fellow, 1986, 88; named One of Outstanding Young Women Am., Jaycees, 1983. Mem. AAUW, Nat. Mus. Women in Art (Washington), Art Inst. Chgo., CAC Cin., Coll. Art Assn., Nature Conservancy, Wilderness Soc., Greenpeace Action League. Office: Dept Art 5620 Ill State U Normal IL 61790-5620

KUKUK, ALVIN H., state legislator; b. Macomb, Mich., May 21, 1937. Macomb County C.C. Inspector Macomb Twp., Mich., 1970-78; supr. Macomb Twp., 1980-84, commr., 1988-92; stste rep. Dist. 33 Mich. Ho. of Reps., 1993—; constrn. excavating and real estate sales, 1996—. Precinct del. Rep. Party County & State Convs., 1980, 82, 84, 86, 88, 90, 92. Mem. Nat. Conf. Rep. County Ofcls., New Balt. Hist. Soc., Macomb Twp. Goodfellows (past pres.), Am. Legion Post No. 4 (past dir.). *

KUKULINSKY, NANCY ELAINE, academic administrator; b. Pitts., Feb. 22, 1950; d. Henry Herman and Jennie Loretta (Guzeli) K.; children: Jeremy David Patches, Melissa Ann Patches. BS, U. Pitts., 1971; MPA, Pa. State U., 1981; PhD, U. Pitts., 1987. Rsch. project asst. Penn State U., University Park, Pa., 1971-80; exec. dir. Pathology Edn. & Rsch. Found., Pitts., 1980-90; dir. bus. ops. sch. medicine U. Cin., 1991—; exec. dir. Acad. Pathology Assocs. Inc., Cin., 1991—; cons. Physicians' Adv. Network, Pitts., 1990-91; trustee No. Allegheny Found. for Excellence, Pitts., 1989-91, Path-Tek Diagnostics, Inc., Pitts., 1987-88. Contbr. articles to profl. jours. Mem. Med. Group Mgmt. Assn., Acad. Practice Assn., Pathology Mgmt. Assn., Assn. Women Adminstrs., Grad. Women in Sci. (pres. 1978-79). Democrat. Roman Catholic. Home: 7880 Stonegate Dr # 1208 Cincinnati OH 45255-3181

KULISH, JOHN S., stockbroker; b. Joliet, Ill., Mar. 6, 1946; m. Marie Chumley, Nov. 4, 1984; 6 children. BA, Lovis Inst. Sci. Tech., Lockport, Ill., 1970; MA, Rosewell U., 1972. Sociologist State of Ill., Joliet, 1972-74; v.p. Kemper Securities, Green Bay, Wis., 1987-92; mgr. E G Edwards, Green Bay, Wis., 1992-94; mgmt. dir. Dain Bosworth Inc., Green Bay, 1994—. Author poetry; contbr. articles to newspapers. Bd. dirs. Cath. Social Svcs., 1987-92; leader Cub Scouts. Mem. Kiwanis. Home: 6604 W Slope Ln Oconto WI 54153-9262 Office: Dain Bosworth Inc Ste 8 30 N 18th Ave Sturgeon Bay WI 54235-3207

KULL, STEPHEN R., financial advisor; b. Goshen, Ind., Feb. 12, 1946; s. irvin E. and Eleanor A. (Green) K.; m. Carolyn J. Bullock, July 21, 1973; children: Chadd, Samantha. BS in Fin., Ind. U., 1972. Fin. advisor DuPont, Walston, Elkhart, Ind., 1972-74, McDonnell & Co., Elkhart, 1974, Thompson McKinnen, South Bend, Ind., 1974-89, Prudential Securities, South Bend, 1989—. With USN, 1965-69. Mem. Rotary. Republican. Methodist. Home: 3002 Buckingham Dr South Bend IN 46614-2146 Office: Prudential Securities Inc 431 E Colfax # 10 PO Box 1957 South Bend IN 46634

KULPER, BENJAMIN JACOB, physician; b. Newark, July 17, 1953; s. Benjamin and Mary (Przybeck) K.; m. Susan Mary Dodd, June 20, 1986; 1 child, Michele. BA, Rutgers U., 1975; MD, U. Autonoma De Guadalajara, Mex., 1980. Resident in internal medicine Akron (Ohio) Gen. Med. Ctr., 1982-85; pvt. practice Macedonia, Ohio, 1986-87; bd. dirs. Trumbull-Mahoning Med. Group, Cortland, Ohio, 1987—. Lt. USAR, 1986—. Mem. AMA, Ohio State Med. Assn., Assn. Mil. Surgeons U.S., Assn. U.S. Army, Res. Officer Assn., Napoleonic Soc. Am. Republican. Home: 749 Shadowood Ln SE Warren OH 44484 Office: Trumbull-Mahoning Med Group 2600 Elm Rd Cortland OH 44410

KULTGEN, KIMBERLY JO, university administrator, graphic artist; b. Lansing, Mich., Feb. 3, 1967; d. Gordon and Shirley (Fish) Ewing; m. Kevin Jon Kultgen, Oct. 8, 1994. BA in Visual Comms./Design, Purdue U., 1989. Graphic artist Am. Camping Assn., Martinsville, Ind., 1989-91; graphic designer Butler U., Indpls., 1991-94, art dir., 1994—. Mem. Am. Inst. Graphic Arts, Univ. and Coll. Designers Assn. Office: Butler U 4600 Sunset Ave Indianapolis IN 46208

KUMAR, SUDHIR, biochemistry and neurology educator, researcher; b. Anjhi, India, Sept. 16, 1942; came to U.S., 1965; s. Sita Ram and Sarla (Agarwal) K.; m. Nilima Jain, Jan. 5, 1969; children: Avanti, Anjali. BS in Biology, U. Rajasthan, Jaipur, India, 1959, MS in Biochemistry, 1961; PhD in Biochemistry and Neurochemistry, U. Lucknow, India, 1966; postdoctoral Baylor Med. Sch., 1965-67. Diplomate Am. Bd. Clin. Nutritionists, 1994. Sr. rsch. scientist N.Y. State Res. Inst. of Neurochemistry, Wards Island, 1967-69; chief biochemist Meth. Hosp., Bklyn., 1969-73; rsch. biochemist V.A. Hosp., Bklyn., 1973-75; dir. perinatal lab Christ Hosp., Oak Lawn, Ill., 1975-82; asst. prof. biochemistry and neurology Rush Med. Coll., Chgo., 1976-79, assoc. prof. 1979-83; dir., pres. clin. diagnostics Oak Forest, Ill., 1982-88, dir. clin. regional lab., Hazel Crest, Ill, 1989—; prof. Rush Med. Coll. Chgo., 1983—, Triton Coll., River-Grove, Ill., 1993—, Robert Morris Coll., Chgo., 1994—; cons. scientist V.A. Med. Ctr., Hines, Ill., 1977-80; bd. dirs. Edn. Svcs., Inc., Flossmoor, Ill.; expert UNESCO and Tokten program Govt. of India, 1986-87, 92—. Editor: Biochemistry of Brain, 1980, Perinatal Medicine Vol. 1, 2, and 3, 1979-82, Advances in Brain Biochemistry, 1984, 93; contbr. articles to profl. jours.; patentee in field. Bd. dirs. Festival of India, Ill., 1984-86. Recipient Outstanding New Citizen award Citizenship Coun. of Chgo., 1983; Rsch. fellow C.S.I.R. 1962-65, fellow UNESCO & INSERM, 1971-73, Dreyfus Found. Rsch. fellow, 1971-73; Travel grantee Am. Inst. of Nutrition, 1981. Fellow N.Y. Acad. Scis., Nat. Acad. Clin. Biochemists, Royal Inst. Chemistry, Am. Inst. Chemists; mem. Am. Soc. Biol. Chemists, Am. Soc. Clin. Nutrition, Am. Soc. Neurochemistry, Soc. Pediatric Rsch., Am. Soc. Microbiology, Nat. Acad. Clin. Biochemists, Lucknow U. Alumni Assn. (pres 1976-78, 83-84, Assn. Indians in Am. (nat. v.p. 1983-86, pres. Ill. chpt. 1983-86), Sigma Xi. Jain-Hindu. Club: Flossmoor Country. Lodge: Rotary. Avocations: stamp and coin collecting, tennis, travel. Home: 18901 Springfield Ave Flossmoor IL 60422-1071

KUMMER, MARTY E., mechanical engineer; b. Muncie, Ind., July 29, 1955; s. Donald Eugene and Wilma Virginia (Stockton) K. A in Mech. Drafting, Perdue U., 1975, A in Mech. Drafting Tech., 1976, BS in Mech. Engring., 1978. Registered profl. engr., Ind. Sr. design engr. Dana Corp. Clutch, Auburn, Ind., 1976—. Patentee in field. Mem. Soc. Automotive Engrs. (sub-com. 1981—), Elks (chaplain 1990, esquire 1991, Loyal Knight 1992). Methodist. Office: Dana Corp Spices Clutch 201 Brandon St Auburn IN 46706-1643

KUMMERLE, HERMAN FREDERICK, environmental consulting firm executive; b. N.Y.C., Apr. 25, 1936; s. Herman O. and Edyth K. (Osburg) K.; m. Joan D. Bell, June 1, 1957 (dec. July 1985); children: Anne R. Trachsel, Katherine L. Greenhill; m. Evelyn Hummon Holton, Mar. 1, 1986. BSChemE magna cum laude, NYU, 1957; MSChemE, U. Toledo, 1967. Registered profl. engr., Ohio, Mich., N.Y., Ind. Research engr. Union Carbide Corp., Niagra Falls, N.Y., 1957-61; process engr. Maumee Chem. Co., Toledo, 1962-65; sr. engr., group leader Owens Ill., Toledo, 1965-67, chief chem. engring., 1967-72, mgr. devel. and engring. services, 1972-76, adminstrn. mgr. corp. tech., 1976-79, mgr. energy tech., 1979-84; v.p. tech. and operating services Ann Arbor (Mich.) Cirs., 1985-88; v.p. Midwest Environ. Cons., Toledo, 1988—; mem. tech. rev. team Ohio Dept. Energy, Columbus, 1977-80; mem. environ. and energy subcom. Toldeo Econ. Planning Council, 1979-81. Contbr. articles to profl. jours.; patentee in field. Chmn. bd. dirs. Toledo Met. Mission, 1977-78; mem. exec. com. Toledo Area Council of Chs., 1977-78; bd. dirs. Friendly Ctr., Inc., Toldeo, 1973-76, 80-82; chmn. bd. trustees Toledo dist. United Meth. Ch., 1980-82, lay mem. West Ohio conf., 1981—, chmn. coun. on fin. and adminstrn. West Ohio conf., 1992—. Served to capt. U.S. Army, 1961-62. Mem. Am. Inst. Chem. Engrs. (various offices), NSPE, Ohio Soc. Profl. Engrs., Toledo Soc. Profl. Engrs., Gas Research Inst. (gas firing research task force 1982-83), Glass Packaging Inst. (chmn. energy task force 1976-83), Tau Beta Pi, Phi Kappa Phi, Phi Lambda Upsilon, Sigma Xi. Methodist. Home: 1152 Bernath Pkwy Toledo OH 43615-6743 Office: Midwest Environ Cons 5902 Southwyck Blvd Toledo OH 43614-1521

KUN, JOYCE ANNE, secondary education educator, small business owner; b. Salem, Ohio, Oct. 20, 1946; d. Robert Malvern Slutz and Helen Roberta (Williams) Short; m. James Joseph Kun, June 10, 1978; 1 child, Jessica Erin. BS in Edn., Ohio U., 1969; MA in Tech., Kent State U., 1980. Cert. tchr., Ohio. Tchr. Ridgewood Local, West Lafayette, Ohio, 1970-71, Norton (Ohio) High Sch., 1971—; owner The Norton Pub, Norton, 1992—. Mem. NEA, Nat. Soc. DAR, Ohio Edn. Assn., Ohio Tech. Edn. Assn., N.E. Ohio Tech. Edn. Assn. (officer 1972-78), Norton Classroom Tchrs. Assn. (exec. bd.), Norton Grange, Barberton Moose Lodge, Epsilon Pi Tau. Lutheran. Office: The Norton Pub 4020 Cleve Mass Rd Norton OH 44203-5567 Home: 3500 Greenwich Rd Norton OH 44203-5567 Office: Norton High Sch 4128 Cleve Mass Rd Norton OH 44203-5567

KUNDERT, ALICE E., retired state legislator; b. Java, S.D., July 23, 1920; d. Otto J. and Maria (Rieger) K. Elem. tchr.'s cert., No. State Coll., Aberdeen, S.D., state tchr. cert. Tchr. elem. grades, 1939-43, 48-54; clk., mgr., buyer Gates Dept. Store, Beverly Hills, Calif., Clifton Dress Shop, Hollywood, Calif., 1943-48; dep. supt. schs. Campbell County, S.D., 1954; county cts. clk., 1955-60, register deeds, 1955-69; town treas. Mound City, 1965-69; auditor State of S.D., Pierre, 1969-79; sec. of state, 1980-87; dir. sch. programs S.D. Dept. Edn. and Cultural Affairs, 1987-89; state rep. State of S.D., 1991-93, ret., 1993. Leader 4-H Club, 1949-53, county project leader in citizenship, 1963-64; sec. Greater Campbell County Assn., 1955-57; organizer, leader Mound City Craft and Recreation Club, 1955-60; chmn. Heart Fund, March Dimes, Red Cross, Mental Health drs.; mem. S.D. Gov.'s Study Commn., 1968—; mem. state and local adv. com. region VIII Office Econ. Opportunity; bd. mem., chmn. Black Hills Recreation Lab., 1956-61; exec. sec. Internat. Leaders Lab., Ireland, 1963; Polit. co. vice chmn. Rep. Com., 1964-69, sec-treas. fin. chmn., 1968; mem. State Rep. Adv. Com., 1966-68; state and nat. counselor Teen Age Rep. Club Campbell County, 1964—. Named Outstanding Teenage Rep. adv. in nation, 1970, 71, 76; Recipient Disting. Alumni award No. State Coll., 1975. Home: PO Box 67 Mound City SD 57646-0067 Office: Office Sec of State State Capital Bldg Pierre SD 57501

KUNES, STEVEN MARSHALL, health science association administrator; b. Sparta, Wis., Mar. 8, 1951; s. Gene Duane and Mary Ann (Jacobson) K.; m. Barbara Ann Stetzer, Aug. 26, 1973; children: Heather Leigh, Ryan Lee. BS in Psychology, U. Wis., LaCrosse, 1973. Dir. mktg. Greater LaCrosse Health Plans, 1986-89, asst. plan adminstr., 1989-90, plan adminstr., 1990—. Clk. Holmen (Wis.) Sch. Bd., 1991—, pres., 1995—; pres. Holmen Luth. Ch., 1989—; treas. Holmen Luth. Ch. Trust Found. Mem. Lions. Republican. Home: N6962 Garden St Holmen WI 54636-9407 Office: Grtr LaCrosse Health Plans 1285 Rudy St Onalaska WI 54650-8580

KUNICKI, WALTER JOSEPH, state legislator; b. June 9, 1958. BSN, U. Wis., 1980. Occupational health nurse Louis Allis Mfg., Milw., 1980; mem. Wis. Assembly, Madison, 1980—, speaker of assembly, 1991-94, minority leader, 1995—; mem. joint com. on employment rels., joint com. on legis. orgn.; mem. assembly orgn.; mem. rules com., legis. coun., disablilty bd.; formerly co-chair joint com. on fin., 1989-90, vice chair, 1987-88; mem. com. on audit, 1989-90, legis. coun., 1989-90, claims bd., 1989-90, health and social svcs., 1983-84, legis. coun. com. on home-based pvt. ednl. programs, 1990—, migrant labor coun., 1983-86; chair, legis. coun. com. on regulation fin. insts., 1985-86, legis. coun. com. on bioethics, 1983-84; clin. instr. health restoration program unit U. Wis.-Milw. Active St. Stanislaus Parish. Mem. South Side Businessmen's Club, U. Wis.-Milw. Alumni Assn. Office: PO Box 8952 Madison WI 53708-8952

KUNKEL, RICHARD W., state legislator. BS, Minot State; MEd, U. N.D., EdD; PhD, Columbia U. Retired supt. of schs.; mem. N.D. Ho. of Reps., 1991—, vice chmn. appropriations com., vice chmn. edn. com., vice chmn. environ. divsn. com. Past pres. United Way; exec. coun. Boy Scouts Am. Mem. Elks, Rotary (past pres.), Eagles, Cmty. Concert Assn. (past pres.). Home: 1312 6th St Devils Lake ND 58301-2812*

KUNTZ, DIETER KURT, history educator, researcher, translator; b. Zweibruecken, Germany, Feb. 17, 1951; came to U.S., 1961; s. Kurt Hugo Kuntz and Louise Johanna (Gries) Willbourn; m. Anne Imelda Zimmerman, Oct. 11, 1974; children: Emma Elena, Rudi Paul. BA, Washburn U., 1973; MA, U. Kans., 1983, postgrad., 1984—. Instr. history U. Kans., Lawrence, 1985—. Author: (book and study manual) Inside Hitler's Germany, 1992. Fulbright fellow, Bonn, Germany, 1986; James B. Pearson fellow Kans. Bd. Regents, 1986; Dwight Eisenhower fellow Eisenhower World Affairs Inst., 1990; Jerry Smith scholar Harry S Truman Found., 1986, Lila Atkinson Creighton scholar U. Kans., 1989. Mem. Phi Alpha Theta. Home: 2415 SW 10th Ave Topeka KS 66604-3946 Office: 3001 Wescoe Hall U Kans Dept History Lawrence KS 66045

KUNTZ, KAREN FRANCES, preschool education educator; b. Amery, Wis., May 22, 1952; d. Frank John and Frances Winifred (Carr) Merth; m. James Edward Kuntz, June 22, 1974; children: Sara Jo, Kelli Jean. BS in Elem. Edn., U. Wis., River Falls, 1974. Cert. tchr., Wis. Tchr. 5th grade Albany (Wis.) Pub. Schs., 1974-76; tchr. 2nd grade Clayton (Wis.) Pub. Sch., 1976-85, jr. kindergarten tchr., 1986—; facilitator Student Assistance Program, Clayton, Wis., 1991—; supr. Student Tchrs. U. Wis. Stout. Author, presenter jr. kindergarten curriculum. Bd. dirs. Presch. Playhouse, Turtle Lake, Wis., 1988-90, Dollars for Scholars, Clayton, 1992; mem. Clayton Coronation Com., 1987—, St. Ann's Coun. of Cath. Women, Turtle Lake, 1978—, St. Isadore Cir., Turtle Lake, 1978—, St. Ann Renew Com., Turtle Lake, 1988—. Named Dist. Elem. Tchr. of the Yr. Clayton Pub. Schs., 1991-92; Kohl fellow, 1993. Mem. ASCD, St. Croix Valley Early Childhood Assn., Wis. Early Childhood Assn., Nat. Assn. for Edn. Young Children, St. Croix Valley Reading Coun., Wis. Reading Assn., Internat. Reading Assn., Wis. Fedn. Tchrs., Am. Fedn. Tchrs. Home: 130 70th Ave Clayton WI 54004-3310 Office: Clayton Pub Sch Prentice St Clayton WI 54004

KUNTZ, KENNETH JOSEPH, psychologist, educator; b. Dayton, Ohio, July 4, 1934; s. Walter Frank and Priscilla May (Kammer) K.; m. Micheline Dupuis, July 24, 1971. BA, Washington U., 1956; MA, U. Cin., 1963. Chair dept. psychology U. Dayton, 1976-93, assoc. prof. psychology, 1993-95, faculty devel. dir., 1995—; bd. dirs., v.p. Eastway Corp., Dayton, 1983-89. Mem. exec. com., chair Leadership Dayton, 1981—; mem. class 1992 Leadership Miami Valley, Dayton, 1992—; chair speakers bur. Victory Theatre Vol. Bd., Dayton, 1979-85; bd. dirs., pres. Dayton Bach Soc., 1990—; chair U. Dayton Honorary Degree Com., 1993—; bd. dirs., chair Dayton Vols., 1987-93. Mem. AAUP, Am. Psychol. Assn., Ohio Psychol. Assn., Dayton Area Psychol. Assn. (exec. com., sec. 1976—). Home: 4472 Lotz Rd Dayton OH 45429 Office: U Dayton Dept Psychology Dayton OH 45469

KUNTZ, MARY M. KOHLS, corporate treasurer; b. Chgo., Nov. 25, 1928; d. George William and Myrtle Hansen K.; m. Earl Jeremy Kuntz, July 28, 1957; children: Karen A., Bradford G. Student, Northwestern U., 1946-50. Pvt. practice acctg. Chgo., 1951-63; owner Chgo. Tax Service, 1954-63; controller Gen. Bus. Services, Chgo., 1960-68; v.p., treas. Gen. Tele-Communications, Inc., Chgo., 1968—. Leader Girl Scouts U.S., 1968-71; pres. Wilmette (Ill.) PTA, 1971-75. Mem. Assn. Telemessaging Svcs. Internat., Nat. Soc. Pub. Accts., Chgo. Soc. Clubs, Women's Club Wilmette (bd. dirs. 1975). Office: Gen Tele-Communications Inc 500 N Michigan Ave Chicago IL 60611

KUNTZ, ROBERT ROY, chemistry educator; b. Barry, Ill., Apr. 10, 1937; s. John Henry and Beatrice D. (Borrowman) K.; m. Joan Ruth Baumgartner, July 19, 1959; children: Deborah L., Kenneth W. BS, Culver-Stockton Coll., 1959; MS, Carnegie Inst. Tech., 1962, PhD, 1963. Asst. prof. chemistry U. Mo., Columbia, 1962-66, assoc. prof. chemistry, 1966-71, prof., 1971—; assoc. program dir. NSF, Washington, 1973-74. Mem. AAAS, Am. Chem. Soc., Am. Phys. Soc., Interamerican Photochem. Soc. Office: U Mo 123 Chemistry Bldg Columbia MO 65211

KUNZ, JAMES WILLIAM, systems consultant. BS magna cum laude, U. Mich., 1974, MBA with distinction, 1976. CPA, Mich. Dir. mgmt. consulting svcs. Coopers and Lybrand, Detroit, 1976-92; ptnr. Kunz, Leigh and Assoc., Lathrup Village, Mich., 1992—; mem. Oakland County Bus. Roundtable, Pontiac, Mich., 1993—; speaker in field. Bd. dirs. Red Run Golf Club, Royal Oak, Mich., 1984—. Mem. Mich. Assn. CPAs. Office: Kunz Leigh and Assoc 28081 Southfield Rd Lathrup Village MI 48076-2816

KUNZ, JEFFREY ROBERT MELIUS, health care executive, educator; b. Milw., Jan. 6, 1949; s. Robert Frank and Valerie Olsen Phyllis (Melius) K.; m. Lawren Lee Bergmann, June 16, 1973; children: Kristin E., Karin E., Kathrin A. Student, U. Oslo, 1970; BA with honors, U. Wis., 1971, MA in Adminstrn., 1977, MD, 1977. Asst. dean U. Wis. Med. Sch., Madison, 1982-83, clin. assoc. prof., 1982—; v.p. rehab. McGaw Med. Ctr., Northwestern U., Chgo., 1983-85; mng. ptnr. Rehab. Assocs., Oak Brook, Ill., 1985-87; state health officer State of Wis., Madison, 1987; CEO Monona Grove Clinic, Madison, 1989—; pres. Midwest Health Syss., Inc., Madison, 1993—; chair/mem. Gov.'s Coun. Handicapped Children, Madison, 1982-89; dir. Wis. Pub. Health Assn., Madison, 1987-89. Editor: Family Medical Guide, 1982 (Literary Guild award 1983), Men: How to Understand Your Symptoms, 1986, Women: How to Understand Your Symptoms, 1986, Children: How to Understand Your Symptoms, 1986; sr. editor Jour. AMA, 1980-83; mem. editl. bd. Chest Med. Jour., 1982-85. Exec. bd. mem. U. Wis. Meml. Union Assn., Madison, 1980—; dep. sec. Wis. Dept. Health & Social Svcs., Madison, 1987; treas., dir. Monona (Wis.) Grove Sch. Bd., 1992—; treas. Sigma Phi Ednl. Found., N.Y.C., 1993—. Brittingham Found. scholar, 1970, Marshall Commn. scholar, 1971-72; U. Wis. Vilas Found. fellow, 1975-77, Scholl Med. fellow Northwestern U. Med. Sch., 1978-80. Mem. Bradley Hist. Preservation Found. (trustee 1992—), Brittingham Viking Scholarship Fund (U.S. rep., Skal award 1994), Monona C. of C. (dir. 1994—), University Club. Lutheran. Office: Midwest Health Syss Inc Ste 202 Monona Dr Madison WI 53716

KUNZE, RALPH CARL, savings and loan executive; b. Buffalo, Oct. 31, 1925; s. Bruno E. and Esther (Graubman) K.; m. Helen Hites Sutton, Apr. 1978; children by previous marriage: Bradley, Diane Kunze Cowgill, James. BBA, U. Cin., 1950, postgrad., 1962-63; grad., Ind. U. Grad. Sch. Savs. and Loan, 1956, U. Calif., 1973. With Mt. Lookout Savs. & Loan Co., Cin., 1951-63, sec., mng. officer, 1958-63; with Buckeye Fed. Savs. & Loan Assn., Columbus, Ohio, 1963-77, exec. v.p., sec., 1967-70, pres., sec., vice chmn. bd. dirs., 1970-77; pres., chief operating officer, dir. Gate City Savs. and Loan Assn., Fargo, N.D., 1977-81; chief exec. officer, dir. United Home Fed., Toledo, 1981-91, also chmn. bd. dirs., 1985-91; ret., 1991; former trustee Ohio Savs. and Loan League, Toledo C. of C.; mem. investment adv. com. City of Toledo; mem. media contact group and legis. com. U.S. Savs. League. Mem. Toledo Com. 100, Toledo Zool. Soc., St. Vincent Hosp. Found.; past pres. Toledo Zoo; past pres. coun. Hope Luth. Ch.; pres. Toledo Neighborhood Housing Svcs., 1981-83; pres., chmn. pers. com. United Way Franklin County, Ohio; past pres. Ohio Soc. Prevention Blindness; bd. dirs. Revitalization Corp. Toledo, 1983-84; past mem., trustee Kidney Found. Northwestern Ohio and Luth. Social Svcs., Wesley Glen Retirement Meth. Ctr., Columbus, 1974-77. Served with USNR, 1944-45. Mem. Lambda Chi Alpha. Home: 2606 Emmick Dr Toledo OH 43606-2701

KUO, CHARLES CHANG-YUN, materials science engineer; b. Chiang-Ling, Peoples Republic of China, Dec. 13, 1926; came to the U.S., 1955; s. Hui-Ting and Chin-Yin (Wang) K.; m. Deborah Liu, Dec. 12, 1949; children: Sze-Ping, Sze-Wen, Scot, Stanley. BS in Chem. Engring., Coll. Ordnance Engring., Chungking, Peoples Republic of China, 1949; PhD in Phys. Chemistry, Lehigh U., Bethlehem, Pa., 1961. Asst. prof. Coll. Ordnance Engring., 1949-55; rsch. fellow Lehigh U., 1955-61; mem. tech. staff AT&T Bell Telephone Labs., Allentown, Pa., 1961-67; engring. specialist GTE, Bayside, N.Y., 1967-71; dept. head Engelhard Industries, Newark, N.J., 1971-77; tech. dir. CTS Corp., Elkhart, Ind., 1977—. Author: Engineered Materials Handbook, Vol. 4, 1991; mem. editorial bds. several profl. jours.; tech. editor Jour. Functional Materials, 1990—; author chpts. in books; contbr. over 80 tech. papers. Recipient Best Paper awards Internat. Soc. Microelectronics, 1981, 93, John A. Wagnon Tech. Achievment award, 1987. Home: 7 Swanson Mnr Elkhart IN 46516-5036 Office: CTS Corp 905 N West Blvd Elkhart IN 46514-1875

KUPCHELLA, CHARLES EDWARD, academic administrator, author, educator; b. Nanty Glo, Pa., July 7, 1942; s. Charles Francis and Margaret (Bouite) K.; m. R. Adele Kiel, July 20, 1963; children: Richard Charles, Michele Louise, Jason Charles. BS in Edn., Indiana U. of Pa., 1964; PhD, St. Bonaventure U., 1968. Asst. prof. Bellarmine Coll., Louisville, 1968-72, assoc. prof., 1972-73; assoc. dir. cancer rsch. ctr. Sch. of Medicine, assoc. prof. U. Louisville, 1973-79; prof., chmn. dept. biology Murray (Ky.) State U., 1979-85; dean Ogden Coll. Western Ky. U., Bowling Green, 1985-93; provost S. E. Mo. State U., Cape Girardeau, 1993—; bd. trustees Ky. chpt. The Nature Conservancy, Lexington, 1990-93. Author: Sights/Sounds: Special Senses, 1976, Environmental Science, 1986, 3rd rev. edit., 1993, Dimensions of Cancer, 1987; contbr. chpts. to books, over 50 articles to profl. jours. Bd. dirs. Ky. Ctr. for Pub. Issues, Lexington, 1990-93; mem. cancer edn. rev. com. NIH/Nat. Cancer Inst., 1993—; mem. inst. rsch. grant rev. com. Am. Cancer Soc., 1993-96. NDEA fellow, 1964-68. Mem. AAAS (nominating com. sect. on sci. and engring. 1995—), Ky. Acad. Sci. (pres. 1977), Ky. Sci. and Tech. Coun. (sec., treas. Lexington 1988-93), Am. Assn. Cancer Edn. (chairperson fin. com. 1990-93, treas. 1993—, mem. exec. coun.). Office: SE Mo State U One University Plz Cape Girardeau MO 63701

KUPCINET, IRV, columnist; b. Chgo., July 31, 1912; s. Max and Anna (Paswell) K.; m. Essee Joan Solomon, Feb. 12, 1939; children: Karyn (dec.), Jerry Solomon. AB, Northwestern U., 1930-32; A.B., U. N.D., 1935. Columnist Chgo. Daily Times, 1935-43; columnist Kup's Column, Chgo. Sun Times, 1943—; host TV program Kup's Show, Chgo., 1959—; commentator WBBM-TV, Chgo.; former commentator Chgo. Bears football broadcasts; spl. cons. in charge of columnists for War Fin. Divsn., drives U.S. Treasury Dept. V.p. Dr. Jerome D. Solomon Meml. Found.; originator, host Purple Heart Cruise. Recipient Emmy award, Peabody award, moderator TV show, numerous civic and profl. awards; Wabash Ave. Bridge, Chgo. renamed Irv Kupcinet Bridge, 1986. Mem. Newspaper Guild, Tau Delta Phi, Nat. Press Club (Washington), Chgo. Press Club. Office: Chgo Sun-Times 401 N Wabash Ave Chicago IL 60611-3532

KUPFERLE, ARTHUR TROMMER, telecommunications executive; b. Cin., Aug. 15, 1929; s. Arthur Trommer Sr. and Sarah Elizabeth (Conover) K.; m. Linnett Jane Finneseth, June 16, 1951 (wid. Oct. 1987); children: Margaret Jane, Leonard Trommer; m. Ruth Alice Strimple, June 10, 1995. Diploma in Elec. Engring., U. Cin., 1952. Plant staff asst. Cin. Bell Telephone, 1952-55, engr., 1957-60, toll and power equipment engr., 1960-62, transmission engr., 1963-73, dist. mgr., 1973-92; mem. tech. staff Bell Telephone Labs., Murray Hill, N.J., 1955-57; instr. Am. Tel & Tel, Cooperstown, N.Y., 1962-63; mem. adv. bd. Ohio Coll. of Applied Sci., Cin., 1965-73. Patentee in field. Mem. IEEE, Engr. and Scientists of Cin. (bd. dirs. 1969-72). Episcopalian. Home: 2769 Blackberry Trail Cincinnati OH 45233-1721

KUPPER, BRUCE DAVID, advertising executive; b. Geneva, N.Y., Nov. 17, 1952; s. Alan D. and Leila (Winograd) K.; m. Karen Ryan Kupper, Sept. 12, 1976; children: David, Laura. BA, Bates Coll., 1975. Account exec. Lieberman Advt., St. Louis, 1976-77; account supr. Young & Rubicam, Detroit, 1977-78; sr. ptnr., chief exec. officer Kupper Advt., Inc., St. Louis, 1978—; pres. Kupnic, Inc., 1991—; sr. ptnr. Kupper Parker Communications Inc., 1992—. Author: (Book) French Canadians in Am., 1975. Fellow: Coro Found.; mem. St. Louis Advt. Club, Am. Assn. Advt. Agys. (regional bd. mem.), Westborough Country Club. Office: Kupper Parker Communications Inc 6900 Delmar Blvd Saint Louis MO 63130-4316

KUPPER, JEFF G., company executive; b. Chgo., July 22, 1971. BA in Finance, U. Notre Dame, 1993; MS in Internat. Acctg. and Financing, London Sch. Econs., 1994. Co-owner Globex Inc., Columbus, Ohio, 1993—. Mem. Nat. Policy Forum, Washington, 1994—. Mem. Small Bus. Exporters Assn. Roman Catholic. Home: 1560 Brookeville Ave Columbus OH 43229-1258 Office: Globex Inc 1560 Brookeville Ave Columbus OH 43229-1258

KUPPER, JOHN DOUGLAS, political consultant; b. Milw., Oct. 20, 1957; s. Kenneth M. and Edith B. (Hirsch) K.; m. Janet C. Koestring, June 25, 1988; children: Sara Eleanor, Theodore Joseph. BA magna cum laude, Brandeis U., 1979. Staff asst. U.S. Rep. Henry S. Reuss (Dem.-Wis.), Washington, 1979-82; press sec. U.S. Rep. Lane Evans (Dem.-Ill.), Washington, 1983-88; assoc., polit. cons. Axelrod and Assocs., Chgo., 1988—. Office: Axelrod and Assocs 730 N Franklin St Ste 404 Chicago IL 60610-3526

KUPPER, PHILIP LLOYD, chemist; b. Louisville, Ky., Sept. 7, 1940; s. Louis James and Mary Sylvia (Noonan) K.; m. Lynn Anne Abbinanti, Dec. 28, 1968; children: Nicole Marie, Rachel Ann Mary. BS in Chemistry, U. Md., 1963; MBA, Ga. State U., 1970. Tech. counselor Nat. Soft Drink Assn., Washington, 1964-68; dir., rsch. & devel. Moxie Monarch NuGrape, Atlanta, 1968-69; chief chemist GRAF/S Beverages, Milw., 1970-75; rsch. mgr. Crush Internat., Evanston, Ill., 1975-81; flavor chemist Procter & Gamble, Cin., 1981—. Patentee in field. With USAR, 1963-69. Mem. Soc. Flavor Chemists (cert.), Soc. Soft Drink Techs., Inst. Food Tech. Roman Catholic. Home: 1332 Cryer Ave Cincinnati OH 45208-2807 Office: Procter & Gamble Vinton Hill Tech Ctr 6210 Center Hill Rd Cincinnati OH 45224

KURATKO, BRIAN D., police officer, funeral director; b. Lawton, Okla., June 13, 1969; s. Kenneth Donald Kuratko and Jeanne Kathryn (O'Connell) Sharpe. AAS, Chgo. City-Wide Coll., 1989. Lic. funeral dir., peace officer, Ill. Funeral dir. Kuratko Funeral Dirs., North Riverside, Ill., 1989-95; police officer, detective Village of Lyons (Ill.) Police Dept., 1990—. Mem. Ill. Police Assn. (mem. Honor Guard), Ill. Fraternal Order of Police Lodge, Ill. Funderal Dirs. Assn., Nat. Hostage Negotiators Assn., Lyons Fraternal Order of Police Lodge (sec.). Home: 6340 Americana Dr # 1115 Willowbrook IL 60514 Office: Kuratko Funeral Dirs 2500 S Desplaines Ave North Riverside IL 60546

KURATKO, DONALD F., business management educator, consultant; b. Chgo., Aug. 27, 1952; s. Donald W. and Margaret M. (Browne) K.; m. Deborah Ann Doyle, Dec. 28, 1979; children: Christina Diane, Kellie Margaret. BA in Econs., John Carroll U., 1974; MS in Mortuary Sci. and Adminstrn., Worsham Coll., 1975; MBA in Mktg.-Mgmt., Ill. Benedictine Coll., 1979; DBA in Small Bus. Mgmt., Nova U., 1984. Lic. funeral dir., Ill. Tchr., chmn. bus. dept. Immaculate Conception High Sch., Elmhurst, Ill., 1975-78; prof. bus. Ill. Benedictine Coll., Lisle, 1979-83; prof., dir. small bus.-mgmt. and entrepreneurship Ball State U., Muncie, Ind., 1983—; disting. prof., Ball State U., 1990—; funeral dir. Kuratko Funeral Home, North Riverside, Ill., part-time, 1975—; cons. Kendon Assocs., Riverside, 1983—, Intrapreneurial Group, 1989—; dir. Pathologists Assocs., Acordia Ctrl. Ind., Inc.; cons. Acordia, AT&T, GTE, United Techs., Ameritech, Union Carbide Corp. Author: Management, 1988, 3rd edit., 1991; Effective Small Business Management, 1986, 4th edit. 1995, Entrepreneurship, 1989, 3d edit. 1995, Intrapreneurship and Innovation in the Corporation, 1987; Entrepreneurial Strategy, 1994. Mem. editorial bd. Mid-Am. Bus. Jour., 1985—; consulting editor Entrepreneurship Theory & Practice Jour., Small Bus. Forum, Bus. Case Jour. Contbr. articles in field to profl. jours . Named Outstanding Young Hoosier, Ind. Jaycees, 1985, one of Outstanding Young Men of Am., 1983, 84, recipient George Washington medal of Honor, 1987, Leavey Found. award 1988; named Disting. Teaching Professorship, 1990, Stoops Disting. Prof. Bus., 1990, Entrepreneur of Yr. in Ind., Ernst & Young, Inc. Mag. and Merrill Lynch, 1990, Excellence award N.F.I.B. Found., 1993, Nat. Outstanding Entrepreneurship Educator of the Year award, 1993, Kauffman Found. Entrepreneurship Educator award, 1994. Mem. U.S. Assn. Small Bus. and Entrepreneurship (pres. 1993—), Nat. Acad. Mgmt., Internat. Council for Small Bus., Midwest Bus. Adminstrn. Assn. (pres. entrepreneurship divsn. 1992-93). Roman Catholic. Avocations: weightlifting, jogging. Home: 2309 N Kensington Way Muncie IN 47304-2484 Office: Ball State U Coll Bus Muncie IN 47306

KURIAN, PIUS, physician; b. Arpookara, Kerala, India, May 9, 1959; s. Pylo and Mariamma Kurian; m. Sally Kurian, May 11, 1986; children: Michelle Maria, Matthew Paul, Catherine Tresa. BSc, Kuriakose (India) Elias Coll., 1979; MB, BS, Kottayam (India) Med. Coll., India, 1986. Diplomate Am. Bd. Internal Medicine, Am. Bd. Nephrology. Sr. staff physician Sacred Heart Med. Ctr., Kottayam, 1986; resident physician Nassau County Med. Ctr., East Meadow, N.Y., 1988-91; fellow in nephrology Nassau County Med. Ctr., East Meadow, 1991-94; attending physician in nephrology Mercy Med. Ctr. and Cmty. Hosp., Springfield, Ohio, 1994—. Mem. ACP, AAAS, AMA, Am. Soc. Hypertension, Am. Soc. Nephrology, Am. Coll. Physicians Execs. Roman Catholic. Office: 247 S Burnett Springfield OH 45505

KURIC, JUDI LYNN POPPLEWELL, clinical nurse specialist, consultant; b. Muncie, Ind., Aug. 31, 1961; d. Charlie D. and Bernice Marie (Fowler) Popplewell; m. Steven P. Kuric, May 22, 1982; children: Katelyn, Kyle. BSN, Ind. U., Indpls., 1983; MSN, Wayne State U., 1990. Cert. critical care nurse, rehab. nurse, neuro nurse. Staff nurse Detroit Receiving Hosp.; system coord. S.E. Mich. Spinal Cord Injury System, Detroit; clin. nurse specialist Evansville, Ind.; coor. continuing edn., asst. prof. nursing U. so. Ind. Contbr. articles to profl. jours. Mem. ANA, AACN, Am. Assn. Spinal Cord Injury Nurses (bd. dirs. 1986-91, pres. 1989-90), Am. Assn. Neurol. Nurses (chmn. health policy com. 1989-91), Assn. Rehab. Nurses (founding pres. Heartland chpt., nat. nominating com. 1994—), Nat. Spinal Cord Injury Assn. (bd. dirs. 1985-89, exec. com. bd. dirs. 1987-89, sec.-treas. S.E. Mich. chpt. 1985-87), Am. Spinal Injury Found. (bd. dirs. 1988-90), Nat. Fedn. Splty. Nursing Orgns. (v.p. 1990, pres. 1991), Sigma Theta Tau. Home: 8450 Remington Dr Evansville IN 47711-6321

KURISH, JAMES BRIAN, municipal debt management executive; b. Amherst, Ohio, May 18, 1955; s. Andrew Stefan and Betty Louise (Bryner) K.; m. Mary Lyn Valkenburg, Dec. 23, 1988. BA, The Coll. of Wooster, Ohio, 1977; MS, U. Ill., Champaign, 1980; PhD, 1983; MPPM, Yale U., New Haven, 1989. Mktg. analyst J.M. Smucker Co., Orrville, Ohio, 1976; researcher Dept. Energy, Oak Ridge, Tenn., 1976-79; asst. prof. Econ. U. Hartford, West Hartford, Conn., 1981-84; dir. grad. studies, 1984-85; asst. dean, exec. dir. Paris, 1985-87; assoc. The First Boston Corp., Chgo., 1989-92; dir. Govt. Fin. Officers Assn., Chgo., 1992-94; pres. J.B. Kurish & Assocs., Chgo., 1994-95; exec. dir. Mcpl. Issuer Rsch. and Analysis Ctr., Chgo., 1995—. Author: Debt Issuance, 1993, Pricing Bonds in a Negotiated Sale, 1994; contbr. articles to profl. jours. Mem. Govt. Fin. Officers Assn., Am. Econ. Assn. Home: 1939 N Orchard St Chicago IL 60614 Office: U Ill Coll Bus Adminstrn 2126 University Hall M/C 144 601 S Morgan St Chicago IL 60607

KURTH, TERRY LEE, mechanical engineer; b. Wausau, Wis., Mar. 15, 1947. AAS in Mech. Design, North Ctrl. Tech. Coll., Wausau, 1969. Designer J.I. Case, Wausau, 1972-81; design engr. Gates Rubber Co., Denver, 1981-85; contracts engr./designer GTE Sylvania, Ind., 1985-88; design engr. Orschelen Industries, Moberly, Mo., 1988-91; sr. mech. engr. Mark Andy Inc., Chesterfield, Mo., 1991—. Patentee on drive compotent for auto brake mechanism, 1990. Pres. Right to Life, Adams County, Colo., 1983-84. Mem. Soc. Mfg. Engrs. (hon.). Republican. Office: Mark Andy Inc 18081 Chesterfield Airport Rd Chesterfield MO 63005-1116

KURTICH, JOHN WILLIAM, architect, film-maker, educator; b. Salinas, Calif., Oct. 18, 1935; s. John Joseph and Elizabeth (Lyons) K. BA in Theatre and Cinematography, UCLA, 1957; BArch, U. Calif.-Berkeley, 1966; MS in Architecture and Urban Design (William Kinne fellow, Fgn. Travelling fellow), Columbia U., 1968. Film-maker SMP, Architects, San Francisco, 1960-61; film-maker, archtl. draftsman McCue & Assocs., San Francisco, 1962-66; freelance film-maker, designer Friedberg, N.Y., 1968; instr. Sch. of Art Inst. Chgo., 1968-70, asst. prof., 1970-74, assoc. prof., 1974-82, prof., 1982—, chmn. dept. design and communication, 1981-85, area head interior arch.,1987-94, chmn. undergrad. divsn.; staff architect Am. Excavations, Samothrace, Greece, 1970—; archtl. cons. Fed. Res. Bank Chgo., 1978; William Bronson Mitchell and Grayce Slovet Mitchell endowed chair in Interior Arch, 1995—. Served with USNR, 1957-60. Recipient Architecture medal Alpha Rho Chi, 1966; grantee NEA, 1972, Woman's Bd. Art Inst. Chgo., 1973, Union Independent Colls. Art, 1974, Fulbright-Hays (Eng.), 1976, Fulbright-Hays (Jordan), 1981, Ford Found./Art Inst. Chgo. Faculty Enrichment, 1982, 87, 91, 93, Graham Found. for Advanced Studies in the Fine Arts, 1988. Fellow Royal Soc. Arts (London); mem. AIA (corp. mem.), Soc. Archtl. Historians, Nat. Com. for Interiors, Chgo. Archtl. Club. Multi-media productions include: Hellas, Columbia U., N.Y.C., 1968, Art Inst. Chgo., 1971, 79; Muncie: Microcosm of America (NEA grant), Muncie, Ind., 1972; Legend of the Minotaur, Art Inst. Chgo., 1973; The Seasons, Shapes, Contrasts, Art Inst. Chgo., 1977, 1983, 84; Canal Du Midi, Art Inst. Chgo., 1987; Light: A History of Architecture from Stonehenge to the Fall of Western Civilization, Graham Found., 1988, The Desert of Retz, Graham Found., 1989, The Mysteries of Samothrace, Art Inst. Chgo., 1989, Echoes of Eternity, Art Inst. Chgo., 1989, Porno Versailles, Graham Found., 1990, Monuments and Memorials, State Ill. Art Gallery, 1990, The Art Institute of Chicago: The Corporation, Art Inst. Chgo., 1990, The Seven Wonders of the World, Mus. Contemp. Art, 1991, Design in the Fourth Dimension Space-Time, Neo Con/Chgo. Architecture Found., 1993, The Ancient World, Art Inst. Chgo., 1994, Illumine: The Architecture of Light, Graham Found., 1995, Recent Excavations at Samothrace, Graham Found., 1996. Home: 2054 N Humboldt Blvd Chicago IL 60647-3805 Office: Sch of Art Inst Chgo Office of Interior Arch 37 S Wabash Ave Chicago IL 60603-3103

KURTZ, CARL PAUL, conservationist, writer; b. Marshalltown, Iowa, July 28, 1945; s. Clell Puterbaugh and Hazel Clementine (Dunn) K.; m. Linda Gail Brown, Nov. 19, 1948. BS in Wildlife and Fishery Biology, Iowa State U., 1968. Naturalist St. Anthony, Iowa, 1970—. Photographer 800 photos pub. in over 50 publs., 1971—; author, photographer: Iowa's Wild Places, 1996; photographer photo. exhibits traveling to librs., colls., civic ctrs. and galleries throughout Iowa, 1985—; photo naturalist over 500 lectures, 1970—; restorationist 90 acres tall grass prairie. With U.S. Army, 1968-70. Recipient Gov.'s Vol. Achievement award Iowa Conservation Commn., Des Moines, 1990. Mem. The Nature Conservancy (trustee Iowa chpt. 1973—). Roman Catholic. Home: 1562 Binford Ave Saint Anthony IA 50239-9718

KURTZ, KAREN BARBARA, writer, editor, administrator, consultant; b. Ft. Dodge, Iowa, July 21, 1948; d. Clifford Wenger and Eleanor Marie (Ulrich) Swartzendruber; m. Mark Allen Kurtz, June 25, 1977. AA, Hesston Coll., 1968; BA in Edn., Goshen (Ind.) Coll., 1970; MA in Elem. Edn., Ind. U., 1975. Lifetime cert. elem. tchr. First grade tchr. Fairfield Community Sch., Goshen, 1970-79; asst. editor and advt. copywriter Barth and Assocs., Middlebury, Ind., 1986-87; freelance writer, editor, cons. Kurtz Lens and Pen, Inc., Goshen, 1979-94, pres., 1994—; asst. dir. info. svcs. Goshen Coll., 1987-89; dir. found. rels., 1990-93. Author: Paper, Paint and Stuff, 1984, More Paper, Paint and Stuff, 1989; asst. editor Heritage Country Mag., 1986-87; regular contbr. to Doll World; contbr. articles to various mags. Ch. bd. dirs. Goshen City Ch. of Brethren, 1977, 94, also chmn. stewardship dr., coord. art in the ch. Mem. NEA, NAFE, Nat. Soc. Fund Raising Execs., Ind. State Tchrs. Assn., Fairfield Educators Assn., Soc. Children's Book Writers and Illustrators. Republican.

KURTZ, WILLIAM ALAN, writer; b. Cleve., Feb. 25, 1958; s. Julius and Lillian Kurtz; m. Frances L. Kurtz, Nov. 11, 1990. BA, Miami U., 1980; MS, Ohio U., 1981. Writer, columnist Gameroom Mag., New Albany, Ind., 1989—; instr. Acad. Ct. Reporting, Cleve., 1992—; writer-in-residence Sha Na Na, L.A., 1992—. Contbg. editor Penton Pub., Cleve., 1994—; author: Pinball, The Lure of the Silver Ball, 1988, Slot Machine and Coin-Op Games, 1991, Arcade Treasures, 1994; editor (newsletter) The Sha Na News. Mem. Soc. Profl. Journalists. Home: 34293 Iris Ln Eastlake OH 44095

KURZWEIL, ALAN DENNIS, social worker, marriage and family therapist, consultant; b. N.Y.C., May 27, 1950; s. Raffael and Hilda Molly (Meisel) K.; m. Paula Lee Backstrom, Oct. 24, 1971; children: Jeffrey Michael, Justin Henry. BA in Psychology, Allegheny Coll., 1971; MSSA, Case Western Reserve, 1976. Diplomate Clin. Social Work; lic. ind. social worker, Ohio. Theraeputic activities worker Polk (Pa.) State Sch., 1972-74; planning intern Geauga County Mental Health Bd., Chardon, Ohio, 1974-75; clin. social worker intern Akron Child Guidance Ctr., Barberton, Ohio, 1975-76; clin. social worker Western Reserve Human Services, Akron, Ohio, 1976-88; psychiatric social worker Kaiser-Permanente, Akron, 1988-91, regional coord. of psychiatric social work, Ohio region, 1991—; pvt. practice marriage and family therapist Fairlawn, Ohio, 1983—; co-dir. Stages, Fairlawn, 1984—. Coach N.W. Akron Indoor Soccer, 1986-87; asst. coach Revere Soccer Club, 1991-94; team capt. Summit County Slow Pitch Club, 1984-94. Mem. NASW (dist. sec. 1980-82, dist. treas. 1982-86, mental health chairperson 1980-91, dist. v.p. 1986-89, Social Worker of Yr. 1988), Registry Clin. Social Workers. Democrat. Jewish. Home: 4601 Pinewood Path Akron OH 44321-1246 Office: Fairlawn Med Bldg 3094 W Market St Ste 120 Fairlawn OH 44333

KUSHNER, JEFFREY L., manufacturing company executive; b. Wilmington, Del., Apr. 7, 1948; s. William and Selma (Kreger) K.; m. Carolyn Patricia Hypes, May 2, 1975; children: Tawnya Lynne. BBA summa cum laude, U. Hawaii, 1970; MBA, Columbia U., 1972. Sr. fin. analyst Black & Decker, Towson, Md., 1972-73; div. controller Black & Decker, Solon, Ohio, 1973-74; asst. div. controller Rockwell Internat., Pitts., 1974-75; div. contr. Carborundum Corp., Niagara Falls, N.Y., 1975-77; mgr. fin. planning United Techs. Corp., Hartford, Conn., 1977-80, corp. v.p. fin. planning, 1986-88, corp. v.p. asset mgmt., 1989-92; asst. contr. Sikorsky Aircraft, Stratford, Conn., 1980-82, div. controller, 1982-83, v.p. fin., chief fin. officer, 1983-85; v.p. fin. and adminstrn. MasterBrand Industries Inc., Deerfield, Ill., 1993—. Bd. dirs. ACR, Hartford. 1987-88. Recipient Bronfman Found. fellowship, 1970-71. Mem. Conf. Bd. (coun. 1987-88), Fin. Execs. Inst. Home: 1375 Saunders Rd Riverwoods IL 60015-1745 Office: MasterBrand Industries Inc 510 Lake Cook Rd Deerfield IL 60015-5610

KUSIAK, ANDREW, manufacturing engineer, educator; b. Kozia Wola, Poland, June 14, 1949; came to U.S., 1988; s. Stanislaw and Maria J. (Biernacka) K.; m. Anna B. Rakoczy, July 14, 1974; children: Derek, Dagmar E., Erik N.A. BS, Warsaw Tech. U., 1972, MS, 1974; PhD, Polish Acad. Scis., 1979. Project mgr. Inst. Mgmt. and Orgn., Warsaw, 1979-81; asst. prof. Tech. U. Nova Scotia, Halifax, 1982-85; assoc. prof. U. Manitoba, Winnipeg, 1985-88; prof., chair U. Iowa, Iowa City, 1988—; cons. Rockwell Internat., Iowa City, 1989—, Motorola, Inc., Chgo., 1991—; editor in chief Chapman and Hall, London, 1990—; U.S. editor Taylor and Francis, London, 1990—; chmn. Artificial Intelligence Conf., London, 1990, Hybrid Systems Conf., Budapest, 1993, Prodn. Systems Conf., Winnipeg, 1987. Author: Intelligent Manufacturing, 1990; editor: Intelligent Design, 1992, Artificial Intelligence, 1988, Expert Systems, 1988, Concurrent Engineering, 1993, 94, Handbook of Design Manufacturing and Automation, 1994. Active Iowa City Sci. Ctr., 1992. Recipient Publ. award Internat. Soc. for Productivity Enhancement, 1988, Outstanding Publ. award Inst. Indsl. Engrs., 1993. Mem. Ops. Rsch. Soc. Am., Soc. Mfg. Engrs. (sr., Publ. award 1990), Internat. Fedn. Automation and Control, Internat. Fedn. Info. Processing. Roman Catholic. Home: 2629 Hickory Trl Iowa City IA 52245-3522 Office: U Iowa Dept Indsl Engring Iowa City IA 52242-1527

KUSTER, CHARLES R., communications executive. Staff editor Wallaces Farmer, Des Moines, 1977-80; account exec. C.M.F.Z. Advt., Des Moines, 1980-81; corp. comm. dir. Pioneer Hi-Dred Internat., Johnston, Iowa, 1981—; v.p. Kuster Ltd., Johnston, 1981—. Creator (board games) Balooning, Aggie, 1980; contbr. numerous articles to profl. jours. Coach baseball, softball, soccer and basketball, 1976—; bd. dirs. Des Moines Child Guidance Ctr., Des Moines, 1994—. Mem. Small Bus. Adminstrn. (Small Bus. Advocate award 1984), Nat. Agrl. Mktg. Assn., Agrl. Editors Assn. (chmn. 1981-82, 94-95), Am. Agrl. Editors Assn. (found. bd. dirs. 1994-96). Roman Catholic.

KUSTRA, ROBERT W. (BOB KUSTRA), state official, educator; b. St. Louis, Mar. 21, 1943; s. Walter and Loretto (Shaughnessy) K.; m. Kathleen Breidert, Sept. 10, 1989; children: Jennifer, Stephen; stepchild: Matthew Breidert. BA in Polit. Sci., St. Benedict's Coll., Atchison, Kans., 1965; MA in Pub. Adminstrn., So. Ill. U., 1968; PhD in Polit. Sci., U. Ill., 1975. Prof. Northwestern U., Sangamon State U., U. Ill., Chgo.; exec. asst. to U.S. Senator Charles Percy Chgo., 1978-80; state rep. Ill. Ho. of Reps., 1981-83; state senator Ill. State Senate, 1983-91; lt. gov. State of Ill., Springfield, 1991—. Trustee Village of Glenview, Ill., 1978-80. Named Best Freshman Rep., Ill. Polit. Reporter, 1981, Best Freshman Senator, 1983; Outstanding Legislator, Ill. Assn. Sch. Bds., 1987-88, Friend of Edn., Ill. State Bd. Edn., 1987-88, Heritage award Ill. Divsn. of the Polish-Am. Congress., 1992. Mem. Navy League, Elks. Republican. Roman Catholic. Office: Office Lt Gov Rm 214 Capitol Bldg Springfield IL 62706

KUTRIEH, AHMAD RAMEZ, educator; b. Damascus, Syria, Feb. 18, 1944; came to U.S., 1967; s. Hamdi and Nabiha (Mousli) K.; m. Marcia Geib, June 3, 1972; children: Tarek, Nejim. BA, Damascus U., 1965; MA, Bowling Green (Ohio) State U., 1970, PhD, 1973. Asst. prof. Alcorn State U., Dorman, Miss., 1973-81, U. Qatar, Doha, 1981-89; assoc. prof. King Saud U., Riyadh, Saudi Arabia, 1989—; translator Radio Riyadh, 1992-96. Program writer, presenter radio Saudi Literary Scene, 1994—. Fellow Optimist Internat.; mem. Phi Kappa Phi, Phi Delta Kappa. Islam.

KUZNIK, SUSAN MARIE, management consultant; b. Cleve., Jan. 13, 1956; d. Joseph Stephen and Elizabeth Marie (Horvat) Rerko; m. Robert Joseph Kuznik, Sept. 22, 1979. BS, Cleve. State U., 1978; MS, Case Western Res. U., 1985; PhD, Clayton U., 1987. Info. system specialist Standard Oil of Ohio, Cleve., 1976-80, personnel devel. specialist, 1980-81, supr. sci. svcs., 1981-83, control assoc., 1983-84, sr. project mgr., 1984-85; pres. T.H.E. Assocs., Parma, Ohio, 1985—; adj. prof. Kent (Ohio) State U., 1985-86, Baldwin-Wallace Coll., Berea, Ohio, 1985—, Ursuline Coll., 1990-92, Nova. U., 1990-92; assoc. cons. Daedalean Assocs., Rocky River, Ohio, 1986—; chmn. The Paragon Ctr., North Ridgeville, Ohio, 1986-89; v.p. The Bart Brooks Ctr. for Ethics and Human Values, Houston, 1986—; mem. exec. com. Ctr. for Profl. Ethics, Case Western Res. U., Cleve., 1989—; thesis adv., guest lectr. Ursuline Coll., 1989-93. Mem. Am. Soc. for Tng. and Devel., Orgn. Devel. Network, World Future Soc. Home: 7544 Pleasant Run Dr Seven Hills OH 44131-5900 Office: The Paragon Ctr 32666 Center Ridge Rd # E Elyria OH 44039-2457

KVAALE, THOMAS PAUL, investment company executive; b. Mpls., Mar. 3, 1945; s. Sverre Johannes and Mary (Sushoreba) K.; m. Mary Lee Pratt, Apr. 7, 1979. BS, U. Mpls., 1969. With sales Georgia-Pacific Corp., Mpls., 1969-72; registered rep. Shearson-Hammil, Mpls., 1972-75, E.F. Hutton & Co., Mpls., 1975-89; asst. v.p. Kemper Securities Inc., Mpls., 1989—. Mem. Kemper Million Dollar Club. Office: Kemper Securities Inc 1700 IDG Ctr 80 S 8th St Minneapolis MN 55402-2100

KWAN, CHO-FAI, chemical engineer; b. Hong Kong, Apr. 28, 1965. Bs in Mech. Engring., Cleve. State U., 1988; M in Mech. Engring., 1992. Rsch. asst. Sterling Branch Stirling Engine Br. NASA Lewis Rsch. Ctr., Cleve., 1990-92. Recipient Grad. asst. award Ohio Aerospace Inst., Cleve., 1990-92. Mem. ASME. Home: 26946 Arbor Ln Olmsted Falls OH 44138-3124 Office: MTD Products Tech Ctr PO Box 368022 Cleveland OH 44136-9722

KWAN, MARY P., retail company executive; b. Hong Kong, Dec. 20, 1952; came to U.S., 1971; d. Rocco and Mary (Wong) Y.; m. Tony P. Kwan, June 22, 1974; children: Tammy M., Jonathan M. BS, U. San Francisco, 1974. Sr. mdse. mgr. J.C. Penney, San Francisco, 1974-83; sr. analyst Mervyn's, Hayward, Calif., 1983-84, unit control mgr., 1984-85, buyer, 1985-87, unit control dir., 1987-90, divisional mdse. mgr., 1990-92, divisional v.p., 1992-93; v.p., gen. mdse. mgr. Sears Roebuck & Co., Hoffman Estates, Ill., 1993—. Office: Sears Roebuck & Co 3333 Beverly Rd Hoffman Estates IL 60179

KWAPICH, STEVE E., manufacturing administrator; b. Montreal, Can., June 10, 1954. Machine designer Owens Illinois, Toledo, 1979-85; designer Diana Spicer Universal Joint, Toledo, 1985; CAD supr. Ort Tool & Dye Corp., Erie, Mich., 1985—. Sec. gen. bd. Ch. of Christ, Toledo, 1991—. Mem. Soc. Mfg. Engrs.

KWEIT, ROBERT WILLIAM, political science, public administration educator; b. N.Y.C., July 2, 1946; s. Irving L. and Sylvia (Greenfield) K.; m. Mary Grisez, Nov. 26, 1976. AB, Syracuse U., 1967; MA, U. Pa., 1968, PhD, 1974. Tchg. asst. U. Pa., Phila., 1969-70; instr. St. Joseph's Coll., Phila., 1971-74; asst. prof. Hamilton Coll., Clinton, N.Y., 1974-76; asst. prof. polit. sci. and pub. adminstrn. U. N.D., Grand Forks, 1976-79, assoc. prof. and grad. dir., 1979-83, prof. and grad. dir., 1983-90, prof. and dept. chmn., 1990—; cons. City and County of Grand Forks, 1993; sr. rsch. cons. Bur. of Govtl. Affairs, Grand Forks, N.D., 1994—. Co-author: (books) Concepts and Methods for Political Analysis, 1981, Implementing Citizen Participation, 1981, People and Politics in Urban America, 1990, Public Budgeting, 1995. Pres., v.p., sec. Grand Forks Planning Commn., 1980—; chmn. Grand Forks County Home Rule Committee; mem. Grand Forks Chamber-Govt. Affairs, 1992—, Impact Fee Study Com., 1994—. Mem. AAUP (nat. coun. 1990-93), Am. Soc. for Pub. Adminstrn., Am. Polit. Sci. Assn., Pi Sigma Alpha. Home: 3823 Fairview Dr Grand Forks ND 58201 Office: Univ N D Dept Polit Sci PO Box 8379 Grand Forks ND 58202

KWON, OJOUNG, computer scientist, educator, consultant; b. Taegu, South Korea, Apr. 18, 1955; came to U.S., 1982; s. Hun Sul Kwon and Suk Han Kim; m. Myounghie Kim, July 4, 1986; children: Eunice M., Daniel M., Ruth C.M. BSEE, Yeungnam U., Taegu, South Korea, 1978, MSEE, 1982; MBA, N.H. Coll., 1985; PhD, U. Ala., Tuscaloosa, 1991. Instr. Yeungnam Jr. Coll. of Tech., Taegu, 1982; grad. asst. N.H. Coll., Manchester, 1983-85; systems analyst Info. Resource Group, Inc., Contoocook, N.H., 1985; rsch. asst. Ala. Productivity Ctr. U. Ala., Tuscaloosa, 1989, rsch. asst. Artificial Intelligence Lab., 1985-90; asst. prof. mgmt. info. systems Univ. Ill. at Springfield, 1991-96, assoc. prof. mgmt. info. sys., 1996—. Contbr. articles to profl. jours. With Korean Army, 1978-80. Recipient Competitive Scholarly Rsch. award, 1992, 93, 95, 96; U. Ala. Grad. Coun. rsch. fellow, 1988. Mem. Decision Sci. Inst., Korean Scientists and Engrs. Assn., Am. Assn. for Artificial Intelligence, Soc. of Computer Simulation, Internat. Assn. Knowledge Engrs., Inst. Mgmt. Sci., Beta Gamma Sigma, Mu Sigma Rho. Office: Univ Ill Springfield Dept MIS L-109 Springfield IL 62794-9243

KYLANDER, CHESTER R., retired civilian military employee; b. Terre Haute, Ind., May 4, 1932; s. Clifford R. and Dorothy R. (Gordon) K.; m. Janice E. Bechtol, Feb. 18, 1961; children: Christopher R., Linda E., Elizabeth A. Bus. Edn. Degree, Ind. State U., 1956. Cert. EMT instr. Founder, owner, mgr. Village Office Supply, Nashville, Ind., 1975-82, So. Ind. Ambulance Svcs., Nashville, 1975-83; logistics mgr. Naval Surface Warfare Ctr., Crane, Ind., 1982-93. Founder, pres. Trevlac (Ind.) Vol. Fire Dept., 1973, Brown County EMT Assn., Nashville, 1977; founder Ind. Rivrs and Streams Recreation League, 1992—; mem. exec. bd. Hoosier Trails coun. Boy Scouts Am., 1992—, organizer Campmasters program; trustee Nashville United Meth. Ch., 1992-94, chmn. coun. on ministries, 1988-90; dir. CD, Brown County, 1976-89, mem. adminstrv. bd., 1995—. With USNR, 1951-55. Decorated Bronze Star; recipient Logistician of Yr. award Naval Surface Warfare Ctr., 1989. Mem. Soc. Logistics Engrs. (Ind. state dir. 1990-93, mem. internat. ad hoc com. 1988-90, founder, chmn. So. Ind. chpt. 1988-90, bd. dirs. 1990-93, Logistician of Yr. award 1989, Spl. Recognition award 1990). Home: 1280 E Old State Rd 46 Nashville IN 47448-9212

KYLE, CRAIG HOWARD, mechanical engineer; b. Youngstown, Ohio, Sept. 22, 1968. BS in Mech. Engring., U. Toledo, 1991. Mech. engr. Reichard Indsl. Inc., Columbiana, Ohio, 1992-96. Methodist. Office: Fairfield Machine Co 1143 Lower Elkton Rd Columbiana OH 44408-1509

KYLE, GENE MAGERL, merchandise presentation artist; b. Phila., Oct. 11, 1919; d. Elmer Langham and Muriel Helen (Magerl) K. Student Center for Creative Studies, Detroit, 1938-45. Mdse. presentation artist D. J. Healy Shops, Detroit, 1946-50, Saks Fifth Ave., Detroit, 1950-58, J.L. Hudson Co., Detroit, 1958-84; freelance merchandise presentations for windows, Grosse Pointe, Mich., 1989—; tchr. workshop classes. Exhibited in group shows at Mich. Water Color Soc., 1944, 53, 74, Mich. Artists Exhbn., 1962, 64, Scarab Club, 1948-49, 52, Detroit Artists Market, 1946—, Michigan Gallery, 1989-92, Coach House Gallery, 1980, 90, Cmty. House, Birmingham, Mich., 1993-94, First Fed. Mich. Bank, 1994, 95. Vol. presentation work. Recipient various art awards. Mem. Detroit Inst. Arts Founders Soc., Mich. Water Color Soc., Windsor Art Gallery.

KYLE, RICHARD HOUSE, federal judge; b. St. Paul, Apr. 30, 1937; s. Richard E. and Geraldine (House) K.; m. Jane Foley, Dec. 22, 1959; children: Richard H. Jr., Michael F., D'Arcy, Patrick G., Kathleen. BA, U. Minn., 1959, LLB, 1962. Bar: Minn. 1962, U.S. Dist. Ct. Minn. 1992. Atty. Briggs & Morgan, St. Paul, 1963-68, 1970-92; solicitor gen. Minn. Atty. Gen. Office, St. Paul, 1968-70; judge U.S. Dist. Ct., St. Paul, 1992—. Pres. Minn. Law Rev., Mpls., 1962. Mem. Minn. State Bar Assn., Ramsey County Bar Assn. Republican. Episcopal. Office: US Dist Ct Federal Courts Bldg Saint Paul MN 55101

LAAS, VIRGINIA JEANS, historian; b. Joplin, Mo., Oct. 1, 1943; d. Virgil Edward and Virginia (Kring) Jeans; m. Frederick Hulett Laas, June 22, 1963; children: Andrew, Matthew, Gilbert. BA in History, Kans. State Coll., 1964, MA in History, 1966; PhD in History, U. Ark., 1993. Cert. secondary tchr., history. Jr. high tchr. Joplin (Mo.) Pub. Schs., 1964-65; instr. Mo. So. State Coll., Joplin, 1988-92, asst. prof., 1992—; part-time instr. Pitts. State U., 1980-88, Mo. So. State Coll., 1984-88. Co-author: Lincoln's Lee: The Life of Rear Admiral Samuel Phillips Lee, 1986 (John Lyman Book award of N. Am. Soc. for Oceanic History, 1986, Phi Alpha Theta Best Book award 1986); editor: Wartime Washington: The Civil War Letters of Elizabeth Blair Lee, 1991; contbr. articles to hist. jours. Recipient Southern Outstanding Tchr. award, 1994; rsch. grantee Huntington Libr., 1991, F.D.R. Libr., 1996, State Hist. Soc. Libr., 1996. Mem. Orgn. Am. Historians, So. Hist. Assn., Mo. Hist. Assn., Assn. for Documentary Editing, So. Assn. for Women Historians. Office: Mo So State Coll 3950 Newman Rd Joplin MO 64801-1512

LAATSCH, AUDREY FRIEDA, volunteer, consultant; b. Milw., Aug. 4, 1929; d. Edwin David and Rose Margaret (Kurz) L. BA, U. Wis., 1953; MSW, U. Calif., Berkeley, 1956; cert. child psychotherapy, Inst. for Psychoanalysis, Chgo., 1968; AA in Interior Design, Milw. Area Tech. Coll., 1990. Trainee, social work Wis. Dept. Pub. Welfare, Stevens Point, Wis., 1953-54; caseworker Wis. Dept. Pub. Welfare, Fond du Lac, 1956-59; therapist Lakeside Children's Ctr., Milw., 1959-62, dir. of therapy, 1962-70, assoc. dir., therapy, 1970-77; assoc. dir. Lakeside Children's Ctr. now Lakeside Child & Family Ctr., Milw., 1977-84; dir. treatment foster care Lakeside Child & Family Ctr., Milw., 1984-88; vol. pres. Seth Peterson Cottage Conservancy, Mirror Lake, Lake Delton, Wis., 1989-93; corres. sec. Seth Peterson Cottage Conservancy, Mirror Lake, Lake Delton, Wis., 1993—; treas. Seth Peterson Cottage Conservancy, 1995—; sec. Frank Lloyd Wright/Wis. Heritage Program, 1991-95. Contbr. articles to profl. jours. Mem. Am. Assn. Children's Residential Ctrs. (life mem., program chmn. 1972-73, treas. 1974-75, chmn. nominating com. 1977-79), Assn. Child Psychotherapists, Phi Beta Kappa, Phi Kappa Phi. Democrat. Lutheran. Home: S 1994 Pickerel Slough Rd Wisconsin Dells WI 53965-9783

LABARBERA, ANDREW RICHARD, reproductive biologist; b. Teaneck, N.J., Oct. 6, 1948; s. Mario Richard and Georgine E. (Mart) LaB. BS cum laude, Iona Coll., 1970; MA, Columbia U., 1974, MPhil, 1974, PhD, 1975. Predoctoral USPHS NIH, Washington, 1971-75; staff assoc. Columbia U., N.Y.C., 1975-77; rsch. fellow dept. cell biology Mayo Clinic and Found., Rochester, Minn., 1977-80; asst. prof. dept physiology Northwestern U. Med. Sch., Chgo., 1980-86, dir. radioimmunoassay lab. Ctr. for Endocrinology, Metabolism and Nutrition, 1980-85, asst. prof. dept. ob/gyn., 1985-86, assoc. prof. dept. ob/gyn. and physiology, 1986-88; assoc. prof. tenured dept. ob/gyn. U. Cin., 1988-95, prof., 1995—, adj. assoc. prof. dept. physiology and biophysics, 1988—, vice chmn. dept. ob/gyn., 1989-93; dir. andrology lab. and sperm bank U. Cin. Hosp., 1988—; dir. vitro fertilization lab. Northwestern Meml. Hosp., Chgo., 1985-88; mem. Reproductive Toxicology Working Group, Workshop on Effects of Pesticide on Human Health, Nat. Task Force on Environ. Cancer and Heart and Lung Disease, Keystone, 1988; cons. Nat. Inst. Diabetes, Washington, 1989-90, Diseases and Kidney Spl. Contract Rev. Group, Washington, 1989-90, NIH Reviewers Res., Washington, 1990-94, Nat. Inst. Alcoholism and Alcohol Abuse, 1992, Nat. Inst. Child Health and Human Devel., 1990—. Ad Hoc reviewer Am. Jour. Ob/Gyn., Am. Jour. Physiology, Biology of Reproduction, Endocrinology, Fertiltiy and Sterility, Jour. Andrology, Jour., Clin. Endocrinology and Metabolism, Jour. Pharmacology and Exptl. Therapeutics, NSF, USDA; contbr. chpts. to books and 40 articles to profl. jours. Bd. dirs. West Wellington Condominium Assn., Chgo., 1983-85, pres. Sangamon Lofts Condominium Assn., Chgo., 1986-88. Grantee Population Coun. N.Y.C., 1972-75, faculty Northwestern U., 1981, NIH, 1982-86, 94—, USDA, 1986-92. Mem. AAAS, AAUP, Am. Fertility Soc., Am. Inst. Biol. Scis., Am. Physiol. Soc., Am. Soc. Zoologists, Am. Soc. Andrology, Endocrine Soc., Soc. for Study Reprodcution (chmn. info. mgmt. com. 1983-85, chmn. mem. com. 1987-92), Soc. Exptl. Biology and Medicine, Soc. Gynecologic Investigation, Tissue Culture Assn., Sigma Beta Beta Beta. Home: 1168 Eversole Rd Cincinnati OH 45230-3547 Office: U Cin Coll Medicine PO Box 670526 Cincinnati OH 45267-0526

LA BARGE, WILLIAM JOSEPH, tutor, researcher; b. Portis, Kans., June 27, 1943; s. Louis Joseph and Mary Genevieve (Colton) La B. AB, Ft. Hays State U., Hays, Kans., 1966, postgrad., 1980; postgrad., Cloud County C.C., Concordia, Kans., 1984. Cert. tchr., Kans. Depot agt. Mo. Pacific R.R., Lenora, Kans., 1971-77; correctional officer Kans. Dept. Corrections, Hutchinson, 1977; prodn. worker Becker Mfg. Co., Downs, Kans., 1978-79; ind. study Downs, 1983-88; pvt. tutor world, Am., ancient and military history grade 6 to adult, Downs, 1988—. With USN, 1966-70. Mem. ASCD, Archaeol. Inst. Am., U.S. Naval Inst. Roman Catholic. Home and Office: 519 Blunt St Downs KS 67437-1713

LABOUBE, DEAN R., stockbroker; b. Washington, Mo., Sept. 10, 1949. BS, U. Mo., Rolla, 1973. Stockbroker Houston, 1973-78, Baker Hughes, Houston, 1978-84, IDS, Mpls., 1984-85, A.G. Edwards & Sons Inc., Washington, Mo., 1985—. Leader Boy Scouts Am., Washington, 1988—. Mem. Elks (exalted ruler 1973—). Office: A G Edwards & Sons Inc 1080 Caroline Dr # 1 PO Box 268 Washington MO 63090

LABRUYERE, THOMAS EDWARD, health facility administrator; b. St. Louis, Aug. 2, 1955; s. Thomas Edward and Daisy Lillian (Nussbaum) LaB.; m. Annette Sue Gusoskey, Oct. 27, 1979; children: Thomas Edward III, Christopher John, Sarah Elizabeth. AAS, Maryville Coll., 1979, BS in Mgmt. with honors, 1990; MBA, Maryville U., 1993. Registered respiratory therapist. Coord. insvc. edn. Normandy Hosp., St. Louis, 1977-79; mgr. dept. Lifemark Cardiopulmonary, Houston, 1979-81; from asst. supr. respiratory therapy to adminstrv. dir. St. Anthony's Med. Ctr., St. Louis, 1981-95, adminstrv. dir. Cardiopulmonary and Radiology, 1995—; mem. respiratory care adv. com. Forest Park C.C., St. Louis, 1993—; bd. dirs. Nalco Credit Union, vice chmn., 1995—, mem. supervisory com., 1991-93. Asst. scoutmaster Boy Scouts Am., St. Louis, 1995-96, asst. cubmaster, 1993, 94, troop com. chmn., 1996—; coach CYC Baseball, St. Louis, 1993-96, CYC Soccer, 1993-96. Mem. Am. Coll. Healthcare Execs. (assoc.), Am. Coll. Cardiovascular Adminstrs., Am. Assn. Respiratory Care. Home: 3036 Armona Dr Saint Louis MO 63129 Office: Saint Anthony's Med Ctr 10010 Kennerly Rd Saint Louis MO 63128

LABS, DONALD HERBERT, marketing professional; b. Milw., Sept. 4, 1959; s. Edgar G. and Delores A. (Kanitz) L.; m. Patti A. Ross, Aug. 28, 1982; children: Mathieu D., Kristen A. BA in Mktg., U. Wis., 1981; MBA, No. Ill. U., 1994. Sales rep. Dun & Bradstreet, Milw., 1981-83; sales mgr. Dun & Bradstreet, Chgo., 1983-86, mktg. mgr., 1986-87; dist. mgr. Dun & Bradstreet, Omaha, 1987-90; dir. mktg. Dun & Bradstreet, Naperville, Ill., 1990-95; corp. bus. unit mgr. SPSS Inc., Chicago, 1996—; adj. faculty mktg. dept. Kellstadt Sch. Bus., DePaul U., 1995—; moderator 1995 Chgo. Bus. Mktg. Day Conf. - Chgo. AMA, Global Bus. Mktg. Symposium, Dun and Bradstreet, Chgo., 1994, 95, Global Risk Mgmt. in 90s Conf., Chgo., 1994;. Vol. Batavia (Ill.) River Walk, 1991, Boy Scouts Am., Batavia, 1994. Named World Champion Ice Driller Fox Lake Property Owners Assn., 1980, 2nd Pl., 1981. Mem. Am. Mktg. Assn. (bd. dirs.1994-96, v.p. mktg. rsch. 1996—, v.p.-elect 1994-95, v.p. 1995-96, chairperson events com. 1992-93, Merit award 1993), Chgo. Assn. Direct Mktg., Bus. Mktg. Assn., DePaul U. Mktg. Mgmt. Cert. Exec. Adv. Coun. Lutheran. Home: 438 Meadowrue Ln Batavia IL 60510-2815 Office: SPSS Inc 444 N Michigan Ave Chicago IL 60611

LABSVIRS, JANIS, economist, educator; b. Bilska, Latvia, Mar. 13, 1907; s. Karlis and Kristina L.; Mag.Oec., Latvian State U., 1930; MS, Butler U., 1956; PhD, Ind. U., 1959; Dr. hist. (hon.), Latvian Acad. Scis., 1994. Tchr., Latvia, 1930-36; dir. dept. edn. Fedn. Latvian Trade Unions, 1936-37; v.p. Kr. Baron's U., Extension, Riga, Latvia, 1938-40, also exec. v.p. Filma, Inc., 1939-40; with UNRRA and Internat. Refugee Orgn., Esslingen, Germany, 1945-50; asst. prof. econs. Ind. State U., Terre Haute, 1959-62, assoc. prof., 1963-68, prof., 1969-73, prof. emeritus, 1973—; head dept. pub. and social affairs Latvian Ministry for Social Affairs, 1938-40; dir. Sch. of Commerce and Gymnasium, Tukums, Latvia, 1941-44. Danforth grantee, 1961; Ind. State U. research grantee, 1966; Mem. Am. Latvian Assn., Am. Assn. Advancement Slavic Studies, Assn. Advancement Baltic Studies, Am. Econ. Assn., Royal Econ. Soc. Lutheran. Author: Local Government's Accounting and Management Practices, 1947, 2d edit. 1992; A Case Study in the Sovietization of the Baltic States: Collectivization of Latvian Agriculture 1944-1956, 1959, 2d & 3d edit., 1988, 4th edit. 1989; Atminas un Pardomas, 1984, reprinted in Latvia, 3d edit., 1993; Karlis Ulmanis, 1987, reprinted in Latvia, 2d edit., 1991, Kam Drosme Ir, 1990, reprinted in Latvia, 5th edit., 1992; contbr. articles profl. jours. Recipient Triju Zvaignu Ordenis highest civilian medal President of Latvia, 1995. Home: 2617 Bridgeview Way Apt 1A Indianapolis IN 46220-1438

LABUDDE, ROY CHRISTIAN, lawyer; b. Milw., July 21, 1921; s. Roy Lewis and Thea (Otteson) LaB.; m. Anne P. Held, June 7, 1952; children: Jack, Peter, Michael, Susan, Sarah. AB, Carleton Coll., 1943; JD, Harvard U., 1949. Bar: Wis. 1949, U.S. Dist. Ct. (ea. and we. dists.) Wis. 1950, U.S. Ct. Appeals (7th cir.) 1950, U.S. Supreme Ct. 1957. Assoc. Michael, Best & Friedrich, Milw., 1949-57, ptnr., 1958—; dir. DEC-Inter, Inc., Milw. Western Bank, Western Bancshares, Inc., Superior Die Set Corp., Aunt Nellie's Farm Kitchens, Inc. Bd. dirs. Wis. Hist. Soc. Found.; chmn., bd. dirs. Milw. div. Am. Cancer Soc. Served to lt. j.g. USNR, 1943-46. Mem. Milw. Estate Planning Coun. (past pres.), Wis. Bar Assn., Wis. State Bar Attys. (chmn. tax sch., bd. dirs. taxation sect.), Univ. Club, Milw. Club, Milw. Country Club. Republican. Episcopalian. Home: 4201 W Stonefield Rd Mequon WI 53092-2771 Office: Michael Best & Friedrich 100 E Wisconsin Ave Ste 3300 Milwaukee WI 53202-4107

LACEY, DANIEL S., mechanical engineer; b. Berea, Ohio, Oct. 2, 1963. BS in Mech. Engring., Cleve. State U., 1989. Design engr. Parker Hannifin Value Divsn., Elyria, Ohio, 1984-93, Rex Roth Corp., Wooster, Ohio, 1993—; cons. adv. bd. CAD curriculum Lorrain County C.C., Elyira, 1987—. Office: Rex Roth Corp Value Engr 1700 Old Mansfield Rd Wooster OH 44691-9050

LACEY, HOWARD RAYMOND, food technologist; b. Fitchburg, Mass., Mar. 18, 1919; s. Clarence Frederick and Sarah Lovisa (Hancock) L.; m. Dorothy Louise Daulton, Aug. 23, 1947; children: Howard R. Jr., Janet H. Lacey Wanink. BS in Chemistry, U. Mass., 1942. Processed foods inspector USDA, various locations, 1942-46; tech dir. P.J. Ritter Co. (now Curtice-Burns, Inc.), Bridgeton, N.J., 1946-67; gen. mgr., v.p. mfg. Brooks Foods (now Curtice-Burns, Inc.), Mt. Summit, Ind., 1967-74, tech. dir., 1974-85; pres. Lacey Assocs., Inc., 1985—; cons. Cape May Canners, N.J., Party Tyme Corp., N.Y.C.; instr. Better Process Control Sch., Purdue U., West Lafayette, Ind., 1981-85. Inventor 100% corn sweetner added to catsup, improved method for firming diced red peppers, Stannous chloride added to asparagus. Asst. mgr. Little League Baseball, Bridgeton, N.J., 1958-61; merit badge counselor Cub Scouts, Boy Scouts Am., 1957-67; contbg. mem. U.S. Senatorial Rep. Club, Washington, 1978—, Rep. Nat. Com., 1982—; vol. Ind. Basketball Hall of Fame, 1990—, jr. achievement cons., 1991—. Recipient New Foods award Canner/Packer Mag., 1969, Outstanding Svc. to Food Processing Industry award, Ind. Food Processors Assn., 1985. Mem. Inst. Food Tech. (nat., Hoosier chpt., quality assurance sect.), Phi Tau Sigma (local, nat., internat.). Club: Toastmasters (Bridgeton). Lodges: Masons, Elks. Avocations: tennis, reading, big band music, bicycling.

LACEY, JAMES VINCENT, physician; b. Flint, Mich., Jan. 7, 1944; s. Bernard Francis and Anna Beatrice (Finn) L.; m. Karen A. Prinzing, Dec. 14, 1969; children: John F., James V., Joseph A., Julie J. BS in Chemistry, U. Detroit, 1966; MD, U. Mich., 1970. Diplomate Am. Bd. Internal Medicine and Hematology. Resident in internal medicine U. Mich. Hosp., Ann Arbor, Mich., 1970-72, 74-75, fellow in hematology, 1975-77; physician Prevea Clinic, Green Bay, Wis., 1977—; chief dept. medicine St. Vincent Hosp., Green Bay, 1980-83, v.p. med. staff, 1982-83, chmn. ethics commn., 1995—. mem. bd. dirs., treas. Ctr. Project Inc., Green Bay, 1989—; pres. Brown County Med. Soc., Green Bay, 1992. Lt. Commdr. U.S. Navy, 1972-74. Mem. Am. Coll. Physicians, Am. Soc. Internal Medicine, Am. Soc. Hematology, Wis. Med. Soc., Brown County Med. Soc. Office: Prevea Clinic 1821 S Webster Ave Green Bay WI 54301

LACEY, R. ALTON, academic administrator; b. Oct. 8, 1950; s. Walter L. and Mary Margaret (FEazel) L.; m. Pat Brummett, May 29, 1971; children: Aaron, Brenna. BSChemE, La. Tech. U., 1971; MA in Religious Edn., Southwestern Bapt. Theol. Sem., 1973, PhD, 1977; postgrad., Harvard U., 1990. Minister of youth Royal Ln. Bapt. Ch., Dallas, 1973; instr., evaluator Tarrant County Jr. Coll., Ft. Worth, 1974-75; grad. asst., counselor Bapt. Marriage & Family Couns. Ctr. Southwestern Sem., Ft. Worth, 1975-76; dean of students La. Coll., Pineville, 1976-79, v.p. for devel., 1979-95; pres. Mo. Bapt. Coll., 1995—. Mem. Red River Opera Co.; past bd. dirs., pres. Family Counseling Agy.; bd. dirs., past pres. local YMCA; deacon, Sunday sch. tchr., mem. choir, mem. various coms. 1st Bapt., Pineville. Mem. Coun. for Advancement and Support of Edn., Am. Assn. Higher Edn., Am. Psychol. Assn., Am. Assn. Marriage and Family Therapy. Democrat. Home: 14624 Adgers Wharf Dr Chesterfield MO 63017-5606 Office: Mo Bapt Col One College Park Dr Saint Louis MO 63141

LACH, ALMA ELIZABETH, food and cooking writer, consultant; b. Petersburg, Ill.; d. John H. and Clara E. (Boeker) Satorius; diplome de Cordon Bleu, Paris, 1956; m. Donald F. Lach, Mar. 18, 1939; 1 dau., Sandra Judith. Feature writer Children's Activities mag., 1954-55; creator, performer TV show Let's Cook, children's cooking show, 1955; hostess weekly food program on CBS, 1962-66, performer TV show Over Easy, PBS, 1977-78; food editor Chgo. Daily Sun-Times, 1957-65; pres. Alma Lach Kitchens Inc., Chgo., 1966—; dir. Alma Lach Cooking Sch., Chgo.; lectr. U. Chgo. Downtown Coll., Gourmet Inst., U. Md., 1963, Modesto (Calif.) Coll., 1978, U. Chgo., 1981; resident master Shoreland Hall, U. Chgo., 1978-81; food cons. Food Bus. Mag., 1964-66, Chgo.'s New Pump Room, Lettuce Entertain You, Bitter End Resort, Brit. V.I., Midway Airlines, Flying Food Fare, Inc., Berghoff Restaurant, Hans' Bavarian Lodge, Unocal '76, Univ. Club Chgo.; columnist Modern Packaging, 1967-68, Travel & Camera, 1969, Venture, 1970, Chicago mag., 1978, Bon Appetit, 1980, Tribune Syndicate, 1982; inventor: Curly-Dog Cutting Bd., 1995. Recipient Pillsbury award, 1958; Grocery Mfrs. Am. Trophy award, 1959, certificate of Honor, 1961; Chevalier du Tastevin, 1962; Commanderie de l'Ordre des Anysetiers du Roy, 1963; Confrerie de la Chaine des Rotisseurs, 1964; Les Dames D'Escoffier, 1982, Culinary Historians of Chgo., 1993. Mem. Am. Assn. Food Editors (chmn. 1959). Clubs: Tavern, Quadrangle (Chgo.). Author: A Child's First Cookbook, 1950; The Campbell Kids Have a Party, 1953; The Campbell Kids at Home, 1953; Let's Cook, 1956; Candlelight Cookbook, 1959; Cooking a la Cordon Bleu, 1970; Alma's Almanac, 1972; Hows and Whys of French Cooking, 1974; contbr. to World Book Yearbook, 1961-75, Grolier Soc. Yearbook, 1962. Home and Office: 5750 S Kenwood Ave Chicago IL 60637-1744

LACHANCE, DAVID JOSPEH, geologist; b. Nashua, N.H., Aug. 14, 1951. BA, U. N.H., 1973; MS, Eastern Wash. U., 1978. Cert. petroleum geologist Am. Assn. Petroleum Geologists. Geologist U.S. Dept. Interior, Metairie, La., 1975-76, Washington, 1976-83, Milw., 1983—. Author: (short stories) The Plaza (Japan), 1994, 95, Pleiades, 1994, Art Forum, 1994 (play) Faces in the Raft, 1994. Maj. U.S. Army, 1990-91. Maj. U.S. Army, 1990-91. Republican. Methodist. Home: 1722 N 58th St Milwaukee WI 53202 Office: US Dept Interior 310 W Wisconsin Ave #450 Milwaukee WI 53203

LACHER, JEROME FRANCIS, highway engineer; b. Aberdeen, S.D., Apr. 14, 1942; s. Frank Bernard and Magdelina (Kuntz) L.; m. Shirley Maxine, Feb. 15, 1975; children; Jessica, Cassandra. Student, No. State U., 1960-63; BS in Civil Engring., S.D. State U., 1966. Registered profl. engr. and land surveyor. Hwy. engr. Bur. Indian Affairs, Aberdeen. Chmn. Yankton (S.D.) City Planning Commn., 1976-78; bd. dirs. Wilmot (S.D.) Improvement Assn., 1981-88; pres. Wilmot Cmty. Club, 1983-88; mem. N.E. S.D. Econ. Devel., Aberdeen, 1983-85; lector, Eucharistic min. St. Mary's Ch., Aberdeen, 1989—, mem. ch. coun., 1993—. Named Outstanding Young Man of Milbank, Milbank (S.D.) Jaycees, 1971, Outstanding Young Man of Yankton, Yankton (S.D.) Jaycees, 1976. Mem. Moose, KC, Exch. Club Aberdeen (pres. 1994-95). Roman Catholic. Home: 12883 Fairfield Dr Aberdeen SD 57401-8165 Office: Bur Indian Affairs 115 4th Ave SE Aberdeen SD 57401

LACHES, ROBERT DUANE, vocational educator; b. Elgin, N.D., June 29, 1953; s. Kasper and Elaine (Fraase) L. AAS, N.D. Coll. Sci., Wahpeton, 1980. Cert. trade tech. tchr., N.D.; cert. Citizens Police Acad. Technician KDIX-TV and Radio, Dickinson, N.D., 1973-76, KBMR Music Systems, Inc., Bismarck, N.D., 1976-77; instr. electronics Bismarck Pub. Schs., 1977—; com. mem. MidAm. Vocat. Curriculum, Stillwater, Okla., 1977-80; advisor Bismarck Vocat. Indsl. Clubs Am., 1977—; advisor local chpt. Nat. Vocat.-Tech. Honor Soc. Block capt. Neighborhood Crime Watch, 1995—. Named N.D. VICA Advisor of Yr., 1994-95. Mem. Am. Vocat. Assn., N.D. Vocat. Assn., N.D. Trade Indsl. Technology and Health. Home: 3021 Withers Dr Mandan ND 58554-5225 Office: Bismarck Vo-Tech Ctr 1200 College Dr Bismarck ND 58501-1216

LACHNER, THOMAS F., state legislator. Ill. state rep. Dist. 59. Office: Ste 211 8 N Skokie Hwy Lake Bluff IL 60044

LACIVITA, MICHAEL JOHN, safety engineer; b. Youngstown, Ohio, June 26, 1924; s. John and Carmela (Cacciavillani) L.; m. Margaret Mary Savoia, May 17, 1952; children: Linda Marie Lacivita Krieger, Sandra Marie Lacivita Vicarel. BSBA, Youngstown State U., 1951. Quality control techncian, supr. Republic Rubber div. Aeroquip Corp., Youngstown, 1951-65, mgr. quality control, 1965-67, prodn. supt., 1965-71; quality control mgr. Comml. Shearing Inc., Youngstown, 1971-75, dir. corp. safety, 1975-79, dir. corp. safety and security, 1979-86. Contbr. articles to profl. jours. and newspapers; patentee in field of bicycles; one-man photography shows include Butler Inst. Am. Art, 1984, 89, 92, Apple Gallery, Youngstown, 1985, Youngstown State U. Libr., 1986, Bank One, Youngstown, 1988. With USN, 1943-46. Named to Ohio Sr. Citizens Hall of Fame, 1996. Mem. Am. Soc. Safety Engrs. (safety profl. of yr. award Ohio-Pa. chpt. 1984), Forging Industry Assn. (nat. safety and health com. 1980-83). Home: 3220 Eldora Dr Youngstown OH 44511-1252

LA COUR, LOUIS BERNARD, lawyer; b. Columbus, Ohio, Aug. 12, 1926; s. Louis and Cleo (Carter) La C.; m. Jane Lee McFarland, Mar. 24, 1950; children: Lynne Denise, Avril Rose, Cheryl Celeste. BA, Ohio State U., 1951; LLB, Franklin U., 1961; JD, Capital U., Columbus, 1967. Bar: Ohio 1962. Land commr. U.S. Dist. Ct. (so. dist.) Ohio, Columbus, 1981, spl. master, 1983-87; spl. counsel City of Columbus Atty.'s Office, 1986—. Contbr. articles to profl. jours. Cons. NAACP, N.Y.C., 1975-80; mem. Greater Columbus Arts Coun., Model State Legis. Com.; sec. Mid-Ohio Regional Planning Commn., Columbus, 1978; vice-chmn. Columbus Civic Ctr. Commn., 1979; mem. rural zoning commn. Franklin County, 1994; mem. rural zoning commn. Franklin County, 1994. Mem. ABA, Columbus Bar Assn., Am. Planning Assn. (task force), The Capital Club (spl. com.), New Albany C.C., Internat. Wine and Food Soc., Sigma Pi Phi, Lambda Boulé. Democrat. Roman Catholic. Home: 1809 N Cassady Ave Columbus OH 43219-1520 Office: 400 E Town St Ste 30B Columbus OH 43215-4700

LACOURSE, BARBARA J., financial advisor; b. Traverse City, Mich., Oct. 8, 1959. Paralegal degree, Ferris U., 1985. Lic. series 7, 63, 65 life ins. Paralegal Lowenstein Sandler, Roseland, N.J., 1985-89; fin. advisor E.F. Hutton, Traverse City, 1989-91, Prudential Securities, Traverse City, 1991—; bd. dirs. Desk Derrick, Traverse City. Author: (monthly newsletter) Investing for Women, 1995—. Vol. Easter Seals, Traverse City, 1995—, Am. Cancer Soc., Traverse City, 1995—, Big Bros./Big Sisters, Traverse City, 1990—; pub. speaker various sch. sys., Traverse City. Mem. Zonta. Republican. Roman Catholic. Office: Prudential Securities Inc PO Box 1286 880 Munson Ave Traverse City MI 49685

LA CROIX, ALPHONSE T., entrepreneur; b. Wyandotte, Mich., Nov. 4, 1951; s. Robert A. and Angela (Allumi) La C.; m. Susan Marie Hunt, Apr. 29, 1974; children: Yvonne, Julienne, Aimee, Mark. BS, Marquette U., 1977; MBA, U. Chgo., 1981. Systems analyst Allis-Chalmers, West Allis, Wis., 1976-79; econ. analyst Energy Coop., Inc., Rosemont, Ill., 1979-81; sr. project mgr. Abbott Labs., North Chicago, Ill., 1981-89; project mgr. Kraft Gen. Foods, Deerfield, Ill., 1989-91; pres. ATL System Solutions, Muskegon, Mich., 1991—. With USN, 1969-72, Vietnam. Roman Catholic. Office: ATL System Solutions 3865 Lake Point Dr Muskegon MI 49441

LACROIX, MICHAEL JOHN, librarian; b. Keokuk, Iowa, Sept. 4, 1948; s. John Calvin and Patricia Louise (Hetzer) LaC.; m. Carol Ann Sauer; children: Andrew, Rachel. BA, MacMurray Coll., 1970; MLS, U. Ky., 1972; MBA, U. N.C., Greensboro, 1983. Acquisitions librarian Wake Forest U., Winston-Salem, N.C., 1972-77; coord. tech. svcs. Wright State U., Dayton, Ohio, 1977-80; dir. libr. svcs. Greensboro Coll., 1980-83, Wingate (N.C.) Coll., 1984-91, Albright Coll., Reading, Pa., 1991-94, Creighton U., Omaha, 1995—. Mem. ALA, Spl. Libr. Assn. (treas. N.C. chpt. 1984-86), N.C. Libr. Assn. (treas. 1990-91), Southeastern Libr. Assn. (univ. and coll. libr. sect. vice chmn. 1986-88, chmn. 1988-90). Democrat. Methodist. Club: Toastmasters (Albemarle, N.C.) (sec. 1984-86). Home: 6623 Glenwood Rd Omaha NE 68132-1123 Office: Reinent Alumni Meml Libr Creighton U 2500 Californaia Plaza Omaha NE 68178

LACY, ANDRE BALZ, industrial executive; b. Indpls., Sept. 12, 1939; s. Howard J. II and Edna B. (Balz) L.; m. Julia Lello, Feb. 23, 1963; children: John Andre, Mark William, Peter Lello. BA Econs., Denison U.; DEng (hon.), Rose-Hulman Inst. Various mgmt. positions U.S. Corrugated, Indpls., 1961-69, exec. v.p., 1969-72; exec. v.p., chief ops. officer Lacy Diversified Industries, Indpls., 1972-78, chmn. bd. subs., 1973-78, pres., chief ops. officer, 1978-83; pres., chief exec. officer Lacy Diversified Industries, now LDI, Ltd., Indpls., 1983—, chmn., 1992; bd. dirs. Indpls. Power and Light, Indpls. IPALCO Enterprises, Inc., Indpls., Tredegar Industries, Inc., Richmond, Va., Albemarle Corp., Richmond, Herff Jones, Inc., Indpls., Patterson Dental Co., Mpls., Mid-Am. Capital Resources, Inc. Mem. bd. mgrs. Rose-Hulman Inst., Terre Haute, Ind.; pres. Indpls. Bd. Sch. Commn., Indpls., 1985-86; hon. mem. 500 Festival Assocs., Inc., Indpls.; chmn. United Way Greater Indpls., 1989-91; bd. dirs. Hudson Inst., Indpls. Conv. and Visitors Assn., 1996. Mem. Young Pres. Orgn., Ind. C. of C. (bd. dirs. 1989), Ind. Pres. Orgn., Kiwanis Club of Indpls., Skyline Club, Columbia Club, Meridian Hills Golf and Country Club (Indpls.), Lost Tree Club. Republican. Episcopalian. Home: 5686 N Pennsylvania St Indianapolis IN 46220-3026 Office: LDI Ltd 251 N Illinois St Ste 1800 Indianapolis IN 46204-1945

LACY, HERMAN EDGAR, management consultant; b. Chgo., June 21, 1935; s. Herman E. and Florence L.; m. Mary C. Lacy; children: Frederick H., Carlton E., Douglas H., Jennifer S., Victoria J., Rebecca M. BS in Indsl. Engring., Bradley U., 1957; MBA, U. Chgo., 1966. Cert. mgmt. cons. Plant mgr., indsl. engring. supr. Hammond Organ Co., Chgo., 1961-66; mgr. corp. indsl. engring. Consol. Packaging Corp., Chgo., 1966-68; mgr. mgmt. cons. Peat, Marwick, Mitchell & Co., Chgo., 1968-70; dir. ops. Wilton Enterprises, Inc., Chgo., 1970-77; v.p., gen. mgr. Intercraft Industries Corp., Chgo., 1978-79; pres. Helmco Cons. Assocs., Glenview, Ill., 1979—; instr. Roosevelt U., Oakton Coll., Harper Coll. Served to capt. USAF, 1957-61. Mem. Inst. Indsl. Engrs. (past pres., founder north suburban Ill. chpt.), Am. Mgmt. Assn., Nat. Coun. Phys. Distbn. Mgmt., Soc. Mfg. Engrs., Inst. Mgmt. Cons. Office: Helmco Cons Assocs 1920 Waukegan Rd Ste 212 Glenview IL 60025-1700

LADEHOFF, LEO WILLIAM, metal products manufacturing executive; b. Gladbrook, Iowa, May 4, 1932; s. Wendell Leo and Lillian A. L.; m. Beverly Joan Dreessen, Aug. 1, 1951; children: Debra K., Lance A. B.S., U. Iowa, 1957. Supt. ops. Square D Co., 1957-61; mfg. mgr. Fed. Pacific Electric Co., 1961; v.p. ops. Avis Indsl. Corp., 1961-67; pres. energy products Group Gulf & Western Industries, Inc., 1967-78; chmn. bd., pres., chief exec. officer, dir. Amcast Indsl. Corp., Ohio, 1978-95, also chmn. bd. dirs., 1995—; bd. dirs. Key Bank. With USAF, 1951-54, Korea. Mem. Soc. Automotive Engrs., U. Iowa Alumni Assn., Moraine Country Club, Forest Highlands Country Club, Ventana Canyon Country Club, Alpha Kappa Psi. Republican. Home: 7211 E Desert Moon Loop Tucson AZ 85750-0921 Office: Amcast Indsl Corp PO Box 98 Dayton OH 45401-0098 also: Elkhart Products Corp 1255 Oak St Elkhart IN 46514-2277

LADENSON, ROBERT FRANKLIN, philosophy educator; b. Chgo., Aug. 3, 1943; s. Alex and Inez (Sher) L.; m. Joanne Steiner, Dec. 4, 1982; children: Sarah, Jocelyn. BA, U. Wis., 1965; PhD in Philosophy, Johns Hopkins U., 1970; JD, DePaul Coll. of Law, 1980. Vis. fellow U. Chgo. Law Sch., 1977-78; vis. assoc. prof. U. Colo., Boulder, 1981; asst. prof. philosophy Ill. Inst. Tech., Chgo., 1969-75, assoc. prof. philosophy, 1975-84, prof. philosophy, 1984—; hearing officer, spl. edn. and tenure Ill. State Bd. Edn., 1985—; arbitrator AAA Labor Panel, 1984—. Author: A Philosophy of Free Expression, 1983, Ethics in the American Workplace, 1995; co-author: Ethics and Values in Organizational and Human Systems Development, 1990. Grantee NEH, 1978, NSF, 1979-80. Office: Ill Inst Tech Dept Humanities Chicago IL 60616

LADIGES, LORI JEAN, learning disabilities specialist; b. Sheboygan, Wis., Feb. 25, 1956; d. Donald William and Marion Margaret (Henning) L. BS in Edn., U. Wis., 1978; MA in Learning Disabilities, Cardinal Stritch Coll., 1984. Cert. tchr. elem. (grades 1-8), Cognitive disorders (K-12) and learning disabilities (K-12). Learning disabilities specialist Kohler (Wis.) Pub. Sch., 1978—; part-time instr. Silver Lake Coll., Manitowoc, Wis., 1984-92; tchr. Cardinal Stritch Coll., Milw., 1989, adj. assoc. prof., 1996—; sch. evaluation consortium chair spl. edn. Kohler Pub. Schs., 1989—, learning disabilities specialist, rep. long-range planning com., 1992—, cheerleading advisor, 1981-84, yearbook advisor, 1985-86; reviewer Sch. Evaluation Consortium, 1995. Mem. Sch. to Work com., Alpha Sigma (Grace Alvord award 1978). Lutheran. Home: 2236 N 23rd St Sheboygan WI 53083-4443

LADWIG, BONNIE L., state legislator; b. Dec. 11, 1939; married. Student, U. Wis. Mem. from dist. 63 Wis. State Assembly, Madison, 1992—. Mem. Racine County and Coastal Mgmt. Coun.; mem. County Human Svc. Bd., past chmn. Office: 3516 Marcia Dr Racine WI 53405*

LAETTNER, CHRISTIAN DONALD, professional basketball player; b. Angola, N.Y., Aug. 17, 1969. Student, Duke U. Basketball player Minn. Timberwolves, 1992-1995; now with Atlanta Hawks. Named Most Outstanding Player in NCAA Divsn. 1A Tournament, 1991, Sporting News Coll. Player of Yr., 1992, Sporting News All-Am. First Team, 1992, Naismith award, 1992, Wooden award, 1992; mem. Gold medal Winning Olympic Team, Barcelona, Spain, 1992. Office: Atlanta Hawks 1 CNN Ctr Ste 405 South Tower Atlanta GA 30303*

LAFFERTY, CRAIG T., manufacturing executive; b. Sioux City, Iowa, Apr. 5, 1951. Prodn. machinist Sioux Tools, Sioux City, Iowa, 1973-74, Am. Engring., Sioux City, 1974-75; project coord. Soo Tractor Sweeprake Co., Sioux City, 1975—. Republican. Lutheran. Home: 3530 Aspenwood St Sioux City IA 51104-2304 Office: Soo Tractor Sweeprake Co 1400 W 1st St Sioux City IA 51103-3527

LAFFERTY, NANCY ANN, sociology educator; b. Le Mars, Iowa, Jan. 22, 1936; d. Andrew Raymond and Elizabeth Elnora (Tritz) L.. BA, Viterbo Coll., La Crosse, Wis., 1958; MA, Catholic U. Am., 1970; MSW, Washington U., St. Louis, 1971, PhD, 1974. Cert. secondary edn. tchr., Iowa; mem. Franciscan Sisters of Perpetual Adoration, Roman Cath. Ch. Asst. prof. Washington U., 1971-74, St. Louis U., 1974-77; lectr. Inst. for Edn. in Peace & Justice, St. Louis, 1977-79; coord. edn. Holy Child Jesus, Canton, Miss., 1979-81; asst. prof. St. Ambrose Coll., Davenport, Iowa, 1981-83; assoc. prof. Morningside Coll., Sioux City, 1983-85, Western Iowa Community Coll., Sioux City, 1988-91; prof. sociology Wayne (Nebr.) State Coll., 1991-94; ESL cons. Holy Family Sch., Sioux City, 1995—; lectr. Pastoral Ministry Tng. Program, Jackson, Miss., 1979-81, Global Awareness Through Experience (GATE), Nicaragua, 1989; vis. prof. Providence U., Taichung, Taiwan, 1991, Ednl. Exch., Germany-Tanzania, 1992. Contbr. articles to profl. jours. Bd. dirs. Archway Communities, Inc., St. Louis, 1973-93; mem. Cath. Worker Communities, St. Louis, Davenport and Sioux City, 1976-91, Tri-State Grad. Ctr., 1991-93; active Dorothy Retreat House, 1990-96. Mem. AAUW, Am. Sociol. Assn., Midwest Sociol. Soc., Coun. on Social Work Edn., Nat. Assn. Fine Artists, Am. Watercolor Soc. Home: 1701 S Cecelia St Sioux City IA 51106-2252

LAFFERTY, PETER WILLIAM, product specialist; b. Hartford, Conn., Oct. 24, 1969. BA in Comms., La Salle U., 1992. Account exec., customer svc. Advo, Inc., Milw., 1992-93, sales support, 1994-95; product specialist Weber Marking Sys., Arlington Heights, Ill., 1995—. Vol. emergenty rm. N.W. Cmty. Hosp., Arlington Heights, Ill., 1994—. Mem. Toastmasters, Sigma Phi Epsilon (sec., recruiter 1992—, alumni advisor). Home: # 1 231 S Arlington Heights Rd Arlington Heights IL 60005

LAFFOON, PETER G., investment company executive; b. Cin., June 19, 1956. BA, Lake Forest Coll., 1980. Insurance salesman Mutual Benefit, Cin., 1980-82; ptnr. Seasongood & Mayer, Cin., 1982; chmn. Cin. Mcpl. Bond Club, 1990—. Mem. Cin. Country Club. Republican. Office: Seasongood & Mayer 414 Walnut St Ste 300 Cincinnati OH 45202-3910

LAFLAMME, WILLIAM ROBERT, technical consultant; b. Manchester, N.H., Sept. 20, 1958; s. Albert Joseph Arthur and Constance Ann (Beliveau) LaF.; m. Dianne Elizabeth Smith, Oct. 4, 1986 (div. Aug. 1988); m. Melinda Jean Semetis, Dec. 30, 1988; children: Nicholas Ryan, Alexander Quinn, Garret Benjamin. BS in Computer Sci., Cmty. Colls. of USAF, 1980. Sr. computer operator No. Telecom, Concord, N.H., 1981-85; hardware sys. specialist Medstat Sys., Ann Arbor, Mich., 1985-86; computer sales exec. Compumat, Schaumburg, Ill., 1986-87; computer ops. supr. Pace, Arlington Heights, Ill., 1987-88; tech. support sys. mgr. Arvey Paper and Office Products, Chgo., 1988-89; computer ops. mgr. Reliance Electric, Franklin Park, Ill., 1989-92; sr. sys. mgr. United Stationers, Des Plaines, Ill., 1992-95; client server architect Walgreens, Deerfield, Ill., 1995-96; tech. cons. The Solutions Group, Skokie, Ill., 1996—; computer cons. Creative Output, Inc., Arlington Heights, Ill., 1986—, Home PC, Manhasset, N.Y., 1994-95, Solutions Group, Inc., Skokie, Ill., 1995—; mktg. advisor Peapod, Inc., Evanston, Ill., 1995—. Author, editor mag. Creative Works, 1992; contbr. articles to profl. mags. Mem. Nat. Arbor Day Found., 1990—; mktg. advisor, S.W. tester Peapod, 1995—. Sgt. USAF, 1977-81. Recipient Computer Tech. award Compaq Computer Co., 1987, Sys. Mgmt. cert. Hewlett-Packard, 1991. Mem. Ill. H.S. Assn. Basketball Referees (registered ofcl.), Athletic Ofcls. Svc., Rails-to-Trails Conservancy, Handyman Club of Am. (charter mem.). Republican. Methodist.

LAFLEUR, DAN LEE, stockbroker; b. Madison, Wis., Jan. 31, 1941; s. Alvin Dan and Mae B. (St. John) LaF.; m. Marlene J. Anderson, Dec. 16, 1961; children: Trond, Liv, Neva. BA, U. Wis., 1975. Salesman Midwest Steak Prodn., Davenport, Iowa, 1976-77; stockbroker Kemper Securities Inc., Madison, Wis., 1977—; mem. ESEW, Waukeeshaw, Wis., 1971—. With USN, 1959-63. Mem. Elks, Wis. Fraternity (exec. sec. 1985—). Republican. Lutheran. Office: Everen Securities 426 S Yellowstone Dr PO Box 45500 Madison WI 53744-5500

LAFLEUR, MITCHELL C., state senator, lawyer. Bar: S.D. Mem. S.D. Senate, Pierre, mem. agr., natural rsources, judiciary and local govt. coms. Republican.

LA FOLLETTE, DOUGLAS J., secretary of state; b. Des Moines, June 6, 1940; s. Joseph Henry and Frances (Van der Wilt) LaF. B.S., Marietta Coll., 1963; M.S., Stanford U., 1964; Ph.D., Columbia U., 1967. Asst. prof. chemistry and ecology U. Wis.-Parkside, 1969-72; mem. Wis. Senate, 1973-75; sec. state State of Wis., Madison, 1975-79, 83—. Author: Wisconsin's Survival Handbook, 1971, The Survival Handbook, 1991. Mem. Council Econ. Priorities; mem. Lake Michigan Fed., Wis. Environ. Decade, 1971, S.E. Wis. Coalition for Clean Air, Dem. candidate for U.S. Congress, 1970, for Wis. lt. gov., 1978, for U.S. Senate, 1988. Recipient Environ. Quality EPA, 1976. Mem. Am. Fedn. Tchrs., Fedn. Am. Scientists, Phi Beta Kappa. Office: Office Sec State of Wis PO Box 7848 Madison WI 53707-7848

LAFONTSEE, DANE, ballet company artistic director; b. Lansing, Mich., Nov. 9, 1946; s. Frank and Mary (Braily) LaF.; m. Dana Moore; 1 child, Liane Marie. Student, N.C. Sch. of the Arts, Winston-Salem, 1965-66. Dancer Nat. Ballet of Washington, 1966-67; dancer Pa. Ballet, Phila., 1967-86, ballet master, 1978-80, asst. to artistic dir., 1980-82, assoc. artistic dir., 1982-86; artistic dir. Nashville Ballet, 1986-90, Milw. Ballet, 1990—; bd. dirs. Tenn. Gov.'s Sch. for Arts; choreographer Pa. Ballet, Ballet Okla., Nashville Ballet, Milw. Ballet, Ballet Ariz., Lake Erie Ballet, 1978—; tchr. Nashville Inst. for Arts, 1986—; mem. vis. faculty Med. Coll. Wis. Toured with Rudolf Nureyev, 1973-74; choreographer numerous works for Pa. Ballet Repertory, champion ice dance team, 1986, (musical) Pirates of Penzance, 1988. Office: Milw Ballet 504 W National Ave Milwaukee WI 53204-1746*

LAFORGE, EDWARD, state legislator; b. Nov. 22, 1935. Grad., Bronson Hosp. Sch. Nursing. Rep. Mich. State Dist. 60, 1995—; conservation, environ. & Great Lakes com. Mich. Ho. Reps., human resources & labor com., urban policy com. Address: PO Box 30014 Lansing MI 48909-7514

LAFOUNTAIN, LESLIE JOSEPH, language educator; b. Belcourt, N.D., July 3, 1959; s. Joseph F. and Shirley M. (Gunville) LaF. Student, State Sch. Sci., Wahpeton, N.D., 1977-78; BS, N.D. State U., 1984. Cert. tchr., N.D. Resource tchr. Ojibwa Indian Sch., Belcourt, 1984-85, 87-89; language resource trch. Dunseith (N.D.) Day Sch., 1985—; advisor Indian club Dunseith Day Sch., 1985-86. Chmn. Turtle Mountain Indian Hist. Soc., N.D., 1981—; v.p. Save the Children Fedn., Dunseith, N.D., 1985-86; mem. steering com. H.O.P.E. Orgn./War Against Alchohol and Drug Abusers, Belcourt, 1986; mem. N.D. Council on the Arts. Named One of Outstanding Young Men of Am., 1985. Mem. N.D. Indian Affairs Commn. (rep. 1985-86). Democrat. Roman Catholic. Home: Route 1 Box 229 Endeavor WI 53930

LAGALLY, MAX GUNTER, physics educator; b. Darmstadt, Germany, May 23, 1942; came to U.S., 1953, naturalized, 1960; s. Paul and Herta (Rudow) L.; m. Shelley Meserow, Feb. 15, 1969; children—Eric, Douglas, Karsten. BS in Physics, Pa. State U., 1963; MS in Physics, U. Wis.-Madison, 1965, PhD in Physics, 1968. Registered profl. engr., Wis. Instr. physics U. Wis., Madison, 1970-71, asst. prof. materials sci., 1971-74, assoc. prof., 1974-77, prof. materials sci. and physics, 1977—, dir. thin-film deposition and applications ctr., 1982-93, John Bascom Prof. materials sci., 1986—, E.W. Mueller Prof. materials sci. and physics, 1993—; Gordon Godfrey vis. prof. physics, U. New South Wales, Sydney, Australia, 1987; cons. in thin films, 1977—; vis. scientist Sandia Nat. Lab., Albuquerque, 1975. Editor: Kinetics of Ordering and Growth at Surfaces, 1990, (with others) Methods of Experimental Physics, 1985, Evolution of Surface and Thin-Film Microstructure, 1993; mem. editorial bd., also editor spl. issue Jour. Vacuum Sci. and Tech., 1978-81; rpin. editor Jour. Materials Rsch., 1990-93; mem. editorial bd. Surface Sci., 1994—; contbr. articles to profl. jours.; patentee in field. Max Planck Gesellschaft fellow, 1968, Alfred P. Sloan Found. fellow, 1972, H.I. romnes fellow, 1976, Humboldt Sr. Rsch. fellow, 1992; grantee fed. agys. and industry. Fellow Am. Phys. Soc. (D. Adler award 1994, Davisson-Germer prize 1995), Australian Inst. Physics, Am. Vacuum Soc. (program and exec. coms. 1974-79, M.W. Welch prize 1991, trustee 1995-97); mem. AAAS, Am. Soc. Metals Internat., Am. Chem. Soc. (colloid and surface chemistry divsn.), Materials Rsch. Soc. (medal 1994). Home: 5110 Juneau Rd Madison WI 53705-4744 Office: U Wis Materials Sci & Engring 1509 University Ave Madison WI 53706-1538

LA GATTUTA, JOHN A., stockbroker; b. Buffalo, Jan. 16, 1968; s. Nicholas P. and Mary Ann B. (Bartell) La G.; m. Tamara A. Mattern, Sept. 4, 1993. BA in Econs., John Caroll U., 1990. Stockbroker Merrill Lynch, Cleve., 1990-93, Dean Witter Reynolds, Cleve., 1993—. Active Am. Coun. Blind, 1993—. Republican. Roman Catholic. Office: Dean Witter Reynolds 31st Fl 100 Erieview Plz Cleveland OH 44114-1824

LAGERLUND, TERRENCE DANIEL, neurologist; b. Oak Park, Ill., Aug. 14, 1953; s. Harold and Virginia Marie (Wanamaker) L. BA, Elmhurst Coll., 1970; MS, Va. Poly. Inst. and State U., 1972, PhD in Physics, 1975; MD, U. Miami, Fla., 1982. Diplomate Am. Bd. Psychiatry and Neurology, Am. Bd. Clin. Neurophysiology. Postdoctoral rsch. assoc. MIT, Cambridge, Mass., 1975-78; term physicist Fermi Nat. Accelerator Lab., Batavia, Ill., 1978-80; intern in neurology Mayo Grad. Sch. Medicine, Rochester, Minn., 1982-83, resident in neurology, 1983-86, fellow in electroencephalography, 1986-87; sr. assoc. cons. Mayo Clinic, Rochester, 1987-90, cons. in neurology, 1990—; asst. prof. neurology Mayo Med. Sch., 1987-95, assoc. prof. neurology, 1995—. Contbr.: (chpt.) International Reviews of Neurobiology, 1989, Epilepsy Surgery, 1992, Clinical Neurophysiology, 1996; contbr. articles to profl. jours. including Nuclear Instruments and Methods, Computers in Biology and Medicine, Microvascular Rsch., Am. Jour. Physiology, Jour. of Clin. Neurophysiology, Electroencephalography and Clin. Neurophysiology. Recipient Caton award So. EEG Soc., 1987. Mem. ASTM (electrophysiologic waveforms interchange standards com. 1990—), Am. Epilepsy Soc., Am. EEG Soc. (instrumentation com. 1987—), Am. Acad. Neurology, Cen. EEG Assn., Sigma Xi. Republican. Roman Catholic. Home: 5426 Hawthorn Hill Ln NE Rochester MN 55906-8560 Office: Mayo Clinic 200 1st St SW Rochester MN 55905-0001

LAGUNOFF, DAVID, physician, educator; b. N.Y.C., Mar. 14, 1932; s. Robert and Cicele (Lipman) L.; m. Susan P. Powers, Mar. 8, 1958; children: Rachel, Liza, Michael. MD, U. Chgo., 1957. Rsch. asst. microbiology U. Miami, Coral Gables, Fla., 1951-53; intern U. Calif. San Francisco Hosp., 1957-58; postdoctoral fellow dept. pathology U. Wash., Seattle, 1958-59, trainee in pathology, 1959-60, instr. pathology, 1960-62, asst. prof., 1962-65, assoc. prof., 1965-69, prof., 1969-79; prof. dept. pathology St. Louis U., 1979—, chmn. dept. pathology, 1991-96, asst. v.p., 1989-93; assoc. dean rsch. St. Louis U. Sch. Medicine, 1989-96. Nat. Heart Inst. fellow Carlsberg Laboratorium, Copenhagen, 1962-64, Nat. Cancer Inst. fellow Sir William Dunn Sch. Pathology, Oxford, Eng., 1970. Mem. AAAS, AAUP, Am. Soc. Cell Biology, Am. Assn. Pathologists, Assn. Pathology Chmn., Am. Assn. Immunologists. Office: St Louis Univ Sch Medicine Dept Pathology 1402 S Grand Blvd Saint Louis MO 63104-1004

LAHIRI, DEBOMOY KUMAR, molecular neurobiologist, educator; b. Varanasi, Uttar Pradesh, India, Sept. 9, 1955; came to U.S. 1983.; s. Benoy Kumar and Nilima Rani (Moitra) L.; m. Mithu Mukherjee, Dec. 15, 1991; 1 child, Niloy K. MS, Benaras Hindu U., India, 1975, PhD, 1980. Rsch. fellow Benaras Hindu U., Varanasi, 1975-79; jr. scientist Indian Coun. of Agrl. Rsch., New Delhi, India, 1979-81; postdoctoral fellow McMaster U. Sch. Medicine, Hamilton, Ont., Can., 1982; asst. rsch. scientist NYU, N.Y.C., 1983-86; rsch. assoc. N.Y. State Inst. for Basic Rsch., Staten Island, N.Y., 1987; asst. prof. Mt. Sinai Sch. Medicine, N.Y.C., 1988-90; asst. prof., chief molecular neurogenetics lab. Inst. Psychiat. Rsch. Ind. U. Sch. Medicine, Indpls., 1990—, asst. prof. med. & molecular genetics, 1994-96, assoc. prof. med. neurobiology and med. & molecular genetics, 1996—; presenter in field. Contbr. articles to profl. jours. U.P. Govt. Merit scholar, 1970-75; Univ. Grants Commn. New Delhi jr. rsch. fellow, 1975-79; grantee NIH, 1991—. Mem. AAAS, Am. Soc. Cell Biology, Am. Soc. Human Genetics, Am. Soc. for Neurochemistry, Am. Soc. Biochemistry and Molecular Biology, Genetics Soc. Am., Internat. Soc. for Neurochemistry, Soc. Biol. Psychiatry, Soc. for Neurosci., N.Y. Acad. Scis. Democrat. Hindu. Home: 5731 Arabian Run Indianapolis IN 46208-1684 Office: Inst Psychiat Rsch Ind Univ 791 Union Dr Indianapolis IN 46202-2873

LAHR, JOHN WILLIAM, optometrist; b. Lafayette, Ind., June 11, 1950; s. Willard Keith and Verly Marion (Westfall) L.; m. Mary Jo Geffert, Sept. 11, 1976; children: Brian, Jennifer, Suzanne. BS, Ind. U., 1972, OD, 1974. Assoc. Dr. Earl Doelle, Grand Rapids, Minn., 1974-75; assoc. Dr. G. T. Gibbons, Cambridge, Minn., 1975-77; pres. Cambridge Eye Clinic, 1977—; prin. cons. The Edmonds Group, Phila.; cons. Grand Rapids Vocat. Tech. Inst., 1974-75, Cambridge State Hosp., St. Cloud Vocat. Tech. Inst., 1979-87, Sandstone Fed. Corr. Inst., 1982-88; dir. mktg. Am.'s Doctors of Optometry, Tracy, Minn., 1982—. Fellow Am. Acad. Optometry; mem. Am. Optometric Assn. (eyecare benefits com. 1988—, chmn. coding sub-com., mem. fed. health care entitlement com. 1990—), Minn. Optometric Assn. (pres. 1987—, Optometrist of Yr. 1990-91), Met. Dist. Optometric Soc. (pres. 1982-83), Cambridge C. of C., Rum River Pilots. Republican. Methodist. Home: 707 Sunset Ln Cambridge MN 55008-1019 Office: 120 1st Ave E Cambridge MN 55008-1209

LAHTI, RICHARD IVAR, quality improvement administrator; b. East Chicago, Ind., May 16, 1943; s. Ivar John and Fannie (Panezich) L.; m. Margaret Alethe Dickson, Jan. 24, 1972; children: Sarah, Tom, David, Mari, Susan, John. Student, St. Joseph's Coll., 1969-70. Payroll analyst The Boeing Co., Seattle, 1964-69; mgr. Pare Inc., Madison, Wis., 1969-72; prodn. planner Revlon Co., Phoenix, 1973-78; mgr. The Boeing Co., Wichita, Kans., 1980—. With U.S. Army, 1961-64. Democrat. Congregationalist. Home: 6428 Rodeo St Wichita KS 67226-1414

LAI, JUEY HONG, chemical engineer; b. Taipei, Taiwan, Dec. 4, 1936; came to U.S., 1961, naturalized, 1976; s. Kwo-Wang and Chin-Fong L.; m. Li-Huey Chang, June 30, 1968; children: Eric Yo-Ping, Bruce Yo-Sheng. B.S. in Chem. Engring., Nat. Taiwan U., 1959; M.S. in Chem. Engring., U. Wash., 1963, Ph.D. in Phys. Chemistry, 1969. Rsch. specialist dept. chemistry U. Minn., 1969-73; prin. research scientist Honeywell Phys. Scis. Ctr., Honeywell, Inc., Bloomington, Minn., 1973-78, sr. prin. research scientist, 1978-83; staff scientist Honeywell Tech. Ctr., Honeywell, Inc., 1983-87; pres. Lai Labs., Inc., Burnsville, Minn., 1988—; lectr. SUNY, New Paltz, 1983. Author/editor: Polymers for Electronic Applications, 1989; contbr. articles on solid state chemistry, polymer chemistry and dental materials to tech. jours.; rschr. on polymer materials for electronics, gas removal tech., solid state chemistry and dental materials. Bd. dirs. Chinese Am. Assn. Minn., 1977-79, Minn. Taiwanese Assn., 1995-96. Recipient H.W. Sweatt Tech. award Honeywell, Inc., 1980, Small Bus. Innovation Rsch. award Dept. Health and Human Svcs., 1990, 93, 94. Fellow Am. Inst. Chemists; mem. Am. Assn. Dental Rsch., Am. Chem. Soc., Sigma Xi, Phi Lambda Upsilon. Office: Lai Labs Inc 12101 16th Ave S Burnsville MN 55337-2982

LAIDIG, GARY W., state legislator; b. York, Pa., Aug. 15, 1948; s. Robert Vance and Daisy (Harvey) L.; m. Paula Jane Kinney, 1972; two children. Student, Morningside Coll., 1966-67, U. Wis., River Falls. Dist. 51A rep. Minn. Ho. of Reps., St. Paul, 1972-82; Dist. 56 senator Minn. State Senate, St. Paul, 1982—; mem. ethics and campaign reform, crime prevention fin. divsn., environ. and natural resources and fin. divsn., and fin. and rules and adminstrn. coms., Minn. State Senate. Decorated Nat. Defense Medal, two Vietnamese Svc. ribbons. Named Outstanding Young Man of Stillwater, Minn., 1974; recipient Disting. Svc. awared Stillwater Jaycees, 1975. Mem. VFW, Am. Legion, Jaycees. Office: 855 Eagle Ridge Ln Stillwater MN 55082-9171 also: State Senate State Capital Building Saint Paul MN 55155-1606*

LAINE, ART C., stockbroker; b. Evanston, Ill., Apr. 12, 1952. MBA, Bradley U., 1975. Stockbroker Smith Barney Inc., Peoria, Ill., 1977—. Bd. dirs. Mental Health Assn., Peoria, 1989—.

LAING, JAMES THOMAS, charitable association administrator; b. Charleston, W.Va., Jan. 2, 1934; s. James Tamplin and Claire (Lenila) L.; m. Patricia Ann Boehmer, June 25, 1955 (div. Mar. 1976); children: Michael Thomas, Susan Kay; m. Barbara Jean Crossman, Apr. 20, 1981. AB, Kent

(Ohio) State U., 1955, MA, 1956. Asst. exec. dir. United Cmty. Svcs., Lorain, Ohio, 1959-64; assoc. exec. sec. United Fund, Canton, Ohio, 1964-69; exec. dir. United Fund, St. Joseph, Mo., 1969-73, United Way, South Bend, Ind., 1973-76, United Way of Oaklnad County, Pontiac, Mich., 1976—; instr. sociology Kent State U., St. Mary's Coll., South Bend, Oakland U., Rochester, Mich., 1959-80; field cons. United Health Founds., N.Y.C., 1967-71; mem. profl. adv. com. United Way Am., Alexandria, Va., 1979-84; mem. profl. adv. bd. United Way Internat., 1981—. Bd. dirs. Internat. Bluegrass Music Mus., Owensboro, Ky., 1994—. 1st lt. USAF, 1956-59. Mem. Rotary Club (past pres.), Blue Key, Phi Sigma Kappa, Alpha Kappa Delta, Pi Gamma Mu. Methodist. Home: 3254 Angelus Dr Waterford MI 48329-2512 Office: United Way of Oakland Co 50 Wayne St Pontiac MI 48342

LAIR, HELEN MAY, poet; b. New Castle, Ind., Jan. 3, 1918; d. Harry and Loma D. (Delon) Humphrey; m. Marvin E. Lair, July 2, 1966; children: Michael Lucas, Joan Lucas Krueckegerg, Nancy Lucas (dec.). Student, Anderson Coll., U. Wis., John Herron Sch. Art. Author: (poetry) Lair Of The Four Winds, 1978, Earth Pilgrim, 1981, (column) New Castle Courier Times, 1982—; contbr. numerous poems to anthologies and publs. including Poetry Rev., Our Western World's Greatest Poems, Today's Best Poems, Best Loved Contemporary Poems, Adventures in Poetry, The Criterion, Poet. Past pres. Henry County (Ind.) Art Guild; mem. Hoosier Salon. Recipient Farnell award, N.Y. Poetry Forum, Richard Miller award, Muncie (Ind.) Star 1st place award, Ind. State Fedn. Poetry 1st place award, Golden Poetry award, Campbell Hist. award, Nat. Fedn. Poetry award. Mem. Women in Communication, Acad. Women Poets, Nat. Fedn. Poets, Internat. Poets Achievement, Acad. Leonardo da Vinci, Calif. Fedn. Chaparral Poets, N.E. Ind. Poets, World Congress Poets, Acad. Am. Poets, Ft. Wayne Artists Guild, Unity Writers, Epsilon Sigma Alpha. Roman Catholic. Office: 741 Kenwood Ave Fort Wayne IN 46805-2528

LAIRD, BRADLEY DUANE, social services administrator, psychotherapist; b. Oakland, Calif., Feb. 5, 1956; s. Duane Richard and Eunice Delphine (Glock) L.; m. Elizabeth Lorraine Hughson, Aug. 3, 1985; children: Cameron James, Rhiannon Elizabeth, Quinn Campbell. AA, Concordia Luth. Coll., 1976; BS in Psychology, Valparaiso (Ind.) U., 1978; MSW, Loyola U., 1986; student, Ctr. Psychoanalytic Study, Chgo. Psychiat. technician Porter-Starke Svcs., Inc., Valparaiso, 1978-81; staff therapist II Tri-City Community Mental Health Ctr., East Chicago, Ind., 1981-83, staff therapist IV, 1983-86, program supr., 1986-88, svc. dir., 1988-90; intern U. Chgo. Hosps., 1985-86; pvt. practice psychotherapist Merrillville, Ind., 1989-91; div. dir. Habilitative Systems, Inc., Chgo., 1990-91; assoc. dir. Children's Campus Family and Children's Ctr., Mishawaka, Ind., 1991-95; exec. dir. Family Svc. Assn. LaPorte County, Inc., Michigan City, Ind., 1995—. Gen. mem. Miller and Gary Citizens Corp., 1984-91—, bd. dirs., treas., 1986-88; bd. dirs. Neighborhood Housing Svcs. of South Bend, 1993—; bd. trustees, v.p. First Unitarian Ch. of South Bend, 1994—. Mem. NASW, Nat. Fedn. Socs. for Clin. Social Work, Am. Group Psychotherapy Assn., Am. Soc. Quality Control.

LAKE, BARBARA JOYCE, history and literature educator; b. Winchester, Ky., Dec. 24, 1933; d. James Robert Lake and Hazel Katherine Watkins; m. Graydon Oliver Hambrick, Sept. 9, 1961; children: Diane Elisabeth Pecorari, Jennifer Mary Hambrick. BA in English, U. Ky., 1955, MA in English, 1962; PhD in History, Ohio State U., 1992. Cert. secondary tchr., Ky. Assoc. prof. Capital U., Columbus, Ohio, 1982—; advocate Ohio State U. Advocates, Columbus, 1995—. Pres. Columbus Symphony Youth Orch. Assn., 1985-88. Fulbright fellow U. Liverpool, Eng., 1955-56; internat. devel. grantee Capital U., Beijing, 1995. Mem. Phi Beta Kappa, Phi Alpha Theta, Phi Sigma Iota. Republican. Episcopalian. Office: Capital U 341 Renner Hall Columbus OH 43209

LAKE, CHARLES WILLIAM, JR., retired printing company executive; b. LaPorte, Ind., June 21, 1918; s. Charles William and Jessie Mae (Lyon) L.; m. Louise Safford Sprague, July 4, 1946; children: Charles William III, Elizabeth L. Dolan. Student, U. Wis., 1936-37; BS, Cornell U., 1941; MBA, U. Chgo., 1949. With R.R. Donnelley & Sons Co., Chgo., 1946-90, successively asst. to treas., mgr. mgmt. studies, dir. indsl. engring., 1947-56, dir. engring. rsch. and devel., 1956-58, dir. operating, 1958-59, dir. Chgo. mfg. div., 1959-62, dir. sales div., 1963-64, v.p. co., 1953-63, sr. v.p., 1963-64, pres., 1964-83, chmn. exec. com., 1983-90, chmn. bd., 1975-83, hon. dir., 1990. Mem. vis. com. grad. sch. bus. U. Chgo., libr. vis. com.; mem. devel. adv. com. Cornell U., chmn. emeritus, engring. coun., emeritus trustee, presdl. councillor, univ. coun.; active Northwestern U. Assocs.; bd. dirs. Exec. Svc. Corps.; life trustee Mus. Sci. and Industry; dir. John Crerar Libr. Found. Capt. AUS, 1941-46. Named Grad. Sch. of Bus. Disting. Alumnus, U. Chgo., 1983. Mem. Univ. Club, Sunday Evening Club (hon. trustee), Comml. Club, Chgo. Club, Cornell Club, Hinsdale Golf Club, Old Elm Club, Royal Poinciana Golf Club, Hole in the Wall Golf Club, Naples Yacht Club, Tau Beta Pi, Beta Gamma Sigma. Congregationalist.

LAKE, GAIL ANN, women's health nurse, administrator; b. Detroit, Dec. 4, 1953; d. Frank Allan and Gladys Louise (Turner) Lake; div.; 1 child, Jennifer Lauren Johnson. ADN, Highland Park Community Coll., 1978, AS, AA, 1973; BS, Madonna Coll., Livonia, Mich., 1987, BSN, 1989. Cert. inpatient obstet. nurse. Staff nurse Children's Hosp., Detroit; staff nurse, preceptor Hutzel Hosp., Detroit, clin. mgr., asst. clin. mgr.; also quality assurance coord., mem. Suicide Prevention Task Force; mem., speaker Perinatal Conf. Planning Com. Recipient Detroit News Writing award; finalist Nightengale award, 1994. Mem. Phi Beta Kappa.

LAKEN, NEOMA ANN, retired county recorder; b. Wahpeton, N.D., June 16, 1934; d. Palmer Oscar and Grace Evelyn (Gast) L. Grad. high sch., Breckenridge, Minn. Cert. county recorder. Sec. Wilkin Co. Vets. Svc. Office, Breckenridge, 1952-56; paralegal sec. Korbel & Gospodar Law Office, Breckenridge, 1952-56; dep. register of deeds Wilkin County, Breckenridge, 1956-76, county recorder/registrar of titles, 1976-94; past pres. Wilkin County Ofcls. Orgn., Breckenridge; historian Breckenridge Pub. Sch., local groups, 1976—. Author hist. brochures and booklets; author, prodr. hist. pageants; editor (newsletter) Three Rivers North, 1986-88, The Recorder, 1984-88; contbr. articles to jours. and newspapers. Sec.-treas. Project Breckenridge, 1992—; trustee Dollars for Scholars Found., Breckenridge, 1991-93; head of Red Community Theater, Breckenridge-Wahpeton, 1978—. Mem. Wilkin County Hist. Assn., Minn. Ret. County Recorders Assn., Breckenridge C. of C. (bd. dirs. 1987-89). Lutheran. Home: 404 14th St N Apt 1 Breckenridge MN 56520-1729

LAKES, RODERIC STEPHEN, biomedical engineering educator; b. N.Y.C., Aug. 10, 1948; s. Eric A. and Dorothy E. (Hollweg) L.; m. Diana M. Vezzetti, Aug. 14, 1971. Student, Columbia U., 1964, 65, U. Md., 1969-70; BS, Rensselaer Poly. Inst., 1969, PhD, 1975. NIH predoctoral trainee HEW, 1972-75; rsch. assoc. dept. engring. and applied sci. Yale U., New Haven, 1975-77; asst. prof. physics Tuskegee (Ala.) Inst., 1977-78; asst. prof. biomed. and mech. engring. U. Iowa, Iowa City, 1978-82, assoc. prof., 1982-86, prof., 1986—, prof. laser sci., 1987—; vis. prof. materials dept. Queen Mary Coll., London, spring 1984; vis. prof. engring. mechanics U. Wis., Madison, fall 1990; vis. prof. theoretical and applied mechanics Cornell U., fall 1991; reviewer Allyn and Bacon, 1979-80; external reviewer Nat. Inst. Arthritis Metabolism and Digestive Diseases, NIH, 1979; ad hoc reviewer Pritzker Inst. Med. Engring., Ill. Inst. Tech., Chgo., 1981; workshop participant Am. Acad. Orthop. Surgeons, 1979. Author: (with J.B. Park) Biomaterials, 1992; reviewer, contbr. numerous articles to profl. jours. Recipient Outstanding Faculty award Student Soc. Biomed. Engring., U. Iowa, 1985, 86, 88, 94, award for faculty achievement Burlington No. Found., 1987, Instrnl. Improvement award U. Iowa, 1989; Rensselaer scholar, 1965-69, Univ. Faculty scholar, 1990-93; Old Gold fellow, 1986. Fellow ASME (joint biomechanics com. 1984—, AAAS; mem. Am. Soc. Metals Internat., Am. Phys. Soc., Soc. Photo-Optical Instrument Engrs., Sigma Xi. Episcopalian. Office: U Iowa Dept Biomed Engring Iowa City IA 52242

LAKIN, SCOTT BRADLEY, insurance agent; b. Kansas City, Mo., Dec. 28, 1957; s. John Bradley and Marilyn (Marr) L.; m. Cynthia Kay Wohlgemuth, May 26, 1979; children: Kyle, Caroline, Christopher. BS, William Jewell Coll., 1980. Congl. aide Congressman Richard Bolling, Kansas City, Mo., 1979-82; agt. N.Y. Life Ins. Co., Overland Park, Kans., 1983-84; mgmt. trainee, salesman Plastic Sales and Mfg., Kansas City, 1984-85; agt., registered rep. New Eng. Fin. Svcs., Kansas City, 1986-89, Hokanson, Lehman & Stevens, Inc., Kansas City, 1990—. Treas. Assn. of Clay County Dems., Kansas City, Mo., 1990; com. chmn. Cub Scout Pack 357, Kansas City, 1989-90. Mem. Kansas City Life Underwriters (legis. chmn. 1990—), Sertoma (bd. dirs. 1989-92), Kansas City C. of C. Democrat. Baptist. Home: 3700 NE 49th Ter Kansas City MO 64119-3570 Office: Hokanson Lehman & Stevens 5340 College Blvd Shawnee Mission KS 66211-1621*

LAKSHMAN, MAHESH KUMAR, chemist; b. Poona, India, Mar. 14, 1963. BS in Chemistry, U. Bombay, 1982, MS in Organic Chemistry, 1984; MS in Organic Chemistry, U. Okla., 1987, PhD in Organic Chemistry, 1989. Vis. fellow NIH, Bethesda, Md., 1989-94; sr. scientist Chemsyn Sci. Labs., Lenexa, Kans., 1994—; presenter in field. Contbr. articles and revs. to profl. jours. Karcher fellow U. Okla., 1986-87, Fogarty fellow NIH, 1989-94, Cleo Cross Internat. Student fellow, 1988-89. Mem. Am. Chem. Soc., N.Y. Acad. Scis., Sigma Xi, Phi Lambda Upsilon.

LAKSHMINARAYANAN, VASUDEVAN, physiological optics scientist; b. Madras, India, Apr. 21, 1957; s. Ramabhadra and Jayalakshmi Vasudevan; m. Lorraine L. Janeczko, June 10, 1990. BSc, U. Madras, 1976, MSc, 1978; PhD, U. Calif., Berkeley, 1985. Postgrad. researcher U. Calif., Berkeley, 1985-86, asst. rsch. scientist, 1986-91; prin. clin. rsch. assoc. Allergan Therapeutics, Irvine, Calif., 1991-93; adj. assoc. prof. cognitive sci. U. Calif., Irvine, 1993-94; asst. prof. Sch. Optometry U. Mo., St. Louis, 1993—, adj. assoc. prof. dept. physics and astronomy, 1994—. Contbr. articles and abstracts to profl. jours. and chpts. to books. Fellow Am. Acad. Optometry; mem. Assn. Rsch. in Vision and Ophthalmology, Optical Soc. Am., Sigma Xi.

LALGEE, JOHN CHRISTOPHER, export company executive; b. Swansea, U.K., June 23, 1965. CEO/founder H.S.S., Blackpool, Eng., 1984-89; regional dir. Contract Leads, Rugby, Eng., 1989-93; pres. BCMS Export Devel. Inc., Kenosha, Wis., 1993—. Elder Living Light Christian Ch., Kenosha, 1993—. Office: BCMS Export Devel Inc 5605 6th Ave Kenosha WI 53140-4101

LA LIBERTE, ANN GILLIS, graphic artist, consultant, designer, educator; b. St. Paul, Nov. 10, 1942; d. Edward Robert and Frances Caroline (Sullivan) Gillis; m. Paul Henry La Liberte, Aug. 22, 1964; children: Paul E., Elizabeth La Liberte Collins, Stephen A., Helen C., Peter N., Marc H. Student, Am U., 1963-64, Cardinal Stritch Coll., Milw., 1960-63; BA, Coll. St. Catherine, St. Paul, 1985. Artist, owner Ann La Liberte Papers and Posters, Minnetonka, Minn., 1968-71, A.L. Graphic Design and Drawings, Minnetonka, Minn., 1983-93; artist-in-residence Tara Tonka Studio, Minnetonka, 1988—; artist Arts in Schs., Minn., 1985—; pvt. art tchr., dir. creativity and problem solving seminars, 1991—. Liturgical designer Christian Chs., Mpls. and St. Paul, 1977—; paintings, drawings, photography and sculpture exhibited Mpls. and St. Paul area, 1983—; sculpture Life Exhibit, Paul VI Inst. for the Arts, Washington, 1988, on tour Vt., Ohio, Mo., Ill., Wis., 1988. Del. Minn. Ind. Reps., 1969, vice chmn., 1970; promotional artist Soc. for Preservation Human Dignity, Palatine, Ill., 1973, Minn. Citizens Concerned for Life, 1980-88, Secular Franciscans, St. Paul, 1985; deanery rep. pastoral coun. Archdiocese of St. Paul, Mpls., 1978-82; chmn. devel. task force out-reach program Resurrection Ch., Mpls., 1980-81, cons. artist, 1983—; mem. worship bd. Ch. of Immaculate Heart of Mary, Minnetonka, 1991-95; liturgical art and environ. cons. Mem. Nat. Assn. Liturgical Mins., Mpls. Soc. Fine Arts, Nat. Mus. Women in Arts (charter), Walker Art Ctr., Minnetonka Ctr. for Arts, Coll. of St. Catherine Alumna Assn., Artist for Life Nat. Slide Registry, Delta Phi Delta. Roman Catholic. Home: 13418 Excelsior Blvd Minnetonka MN 55345-4910

L'ALLIER, JAMES JOSEPH, educational multimedia company executive, instructional designer; b. St. Paul, June 24, 1945; s. Charlemagne Joseph and Mildred Marie (LeVasseur) L'A.; m. Susan Kay Margulies, Apr. 28, 1973. BS magna cum laude, U. Wis., River Falls, 1969, MS, 1973; PhD, U. Minn., 1980. Instr. English River Falls Sr. High Sch., 1969-71, Stillwater (Minn.) Sr. High Sch., 1971-80; mgr. computer assisted instrn. Wilson Learning Corp., Mpls., 1980-83, dir. R&D, 1983-86; v.p. R&D Wilson Learning Interactive Tech. Group, Santa Fe, 1986-89; v.p. product devel. Nippon Wilson Learning, Tokyo, 1989-90; v.p. instructional systems Whole Systems International, Cambridge, Mass., 1990-93; v.p. product devel. Nat. Edn. Tng. Group, Naperville, Ill., 1993—; expert witness Universal Tng., Chgo., 1989-91. Author: (video prodns.) Who Shot the Terminal?, 1984, The Tenth Woman, 1987, Working Toward the Future, 1991, America's Workforce: A Vision for the Future, 1992; mem. editorial bd. Learning Age, Mpls., 1987-89; product reviewer Ednl. Tech., N.Y.C., 1981-83; assoc. editor Performance and Instrn., Washington, 1983-85. Curriculum chair Total Info. Ednl. Systems, St. Paul, 1971-76; fund raiser U. Minn. Alliance, Mpls., 1983-89; contbr. Am. Cancer Soc., Washington, 1987—; mem. pub. svc. com. Instructional Systems Assn., Sunset Beach, Calif., 1988—. U. Minn. Grad. Sch. Edn. sr. fellow, 1984; U.S. Dept. Labor grantee, 1991. Mem. U. Wis. Alumni Assn., Instructional Systems Assn. (conf. chair 1980, 84), U. Minn. Alumni Assn., Boston Computer Soc., Pres.'s Club U. Minn., Heritage Soc. U. Wis.; reviewer William H. Donner Found. Inc., N.Y.C., 1993—. Office: Nat Edn Tng Group 1751 W Diehl Rd Naperville IL 60563-1885

LALOR, EDWARD DAVID DARRELL, labor and employment arbitrator, lawyer; b. Madison, Wis., Jan. 29, 1944; s. Edward Richard and Viola (Byrne) Lalor; adult adopted mother: Helen Rose (Litney) Pribble; m. Paula Sue Tompkins, Aug. 12, 1978; children. BBA, U. Wis., 1966, JD, 1969. Bar: Wis., 1969, Minn., 1980, U.S. Dist. Ct. (we. dist.) Wis., 1969, U.S. Supreme Ct., 1979. Gen. atty. NLRB, Kansas City, Mo., Kans., 1969-80; atty. advice divsn., advice br. NLRB, Washington, 1973-74; trial specialist NLRB, Kansas City, 1977-80; arbitrator labor and employment, pres. Pribble Arbitration and Mediation Svcs., Inc., Mpls., 1980-85; arbitrator, pres. Pribble Arbitration and Mediation Svcs., Inc., St. Cloud, Minn., 1985-95; CEO, pres., arbitrator Lalor Arbitration and Mediation, Inc., St. Cloud, Minn., 1995—; mcpl. judge City Countryside (Kans.), 1979-80; mem. arbitration panels Fed. Mediation and Conciliation Svc., 1982—, Am. Arbitration Assn., 1984—, Nat. Mediation Bd., 1991—, Minn. Bur. Mediation Svcs., 1982—, Iowa Pub. Employment Rels. Bd., 1983—; pvt. panel J.I. Case Corp. and I.A. Machinists and Aerospace Workers Local 2525, Fargo, N.D., 1985—; full-day moderator in arbitration, labor and employement law discrimination, alt. dispute resolution, evidence and family law programs Minn. Continuing Legal Edn., 1989—; labor and employment arbitrator Minn. Cts. Alt. Dispute Resolution, 1994—. Contbr. articles to profl. jours. Mem. Minn. Dem. Farm Labor State and Congl. Dist. Ctrl. Com., 1981—, Minn. State Platform Commn., Dem. Farm Labor Party, 1984-85, chmn. senate dist., 1984-85, fundraiser, initiator, co-founder Dr. Guy Stanton Ford Ednl. Found., 1964-69; co-founder Westport Free Health Clinic, Kansas City, Mo., 1970-80; active coun. Land of Lakes coun. Girl Scouts, Minn., 1985—, Leadership Coun. So. Poverty Ctr., Habitat for Humanity Internat. Ptnrs. Coun.; coach Girls Youth Basketball League, St. Cloud, 1992—; bd. dirs. St. Cloud Symphony Orch., 1992-94; chair New Voter registration Drives Senate Dist. 59, 1981-85, Stearns-Benton County Senate Dist.17, 1989-91; historian Lalor Clan for the Ams.; host family for Irish polit. prisoners children's holiday, 1996—; mem. Internat. Hearing Found. Mem. ABA (labor and employment law sects. 1978—), Fed. Bar Assn. (labor and employment law sects. 1974—), Minn. Bar Assn. (labor and employment law sects. 1980—, mock trial program judge 1989—), Nat. Youth Sports Coaches Assn. (cert.), Wis. Bar Assn. (labor and employment law sects. 1969—), Internat. Indsl. Rels. Assn., Soc. Profls. in Dispute Resolution Internat., Indsl. Rels. Rsch. Assn., Theta Delta Chi. Roman Catholic. Office: Lalor Arbitration & Mediation Inc 1220 N 13th St Saint Cloud MN 56303-2733

LAM, NICHOLAS BRIAN, municipal purchaser; b. Holland, Mich., Oct. 13, 1951; s. Donald A. and Martha R. (Van Saun) L.; m. Debra Lee Boven, Dec. 28, 1973; children: Jason, Keith, Heather, Heidi. BA, Hope Coll., Holland, 1974; MPA, We. Mich. U., Kalamazoo, 1980. Cert. purchasing mgr. Dep. county clk. Allegan County, Allegan, Mich., 1974-78; asst. pers./purchasing dir. City of Portage, Mich., 1978-88; dir. purchasing City of Kalamazoo, 1988—. Scout leader Boy Scouts Am., Portage, 1984-90. Mem. Mich. Pub. Purchasing Officers Assn. (bd. dirs.), Nat. Inst. Govtl. Purchasing. Office: City of Kalamazoo 241 W South St Kalamazoo MI 49007

LAMALFA, JOACHIM JACK, clinical psychologist; b. Milw., Aug. 10, 1915; s. Salvatore and Josephine (Foti) L.; m. Constance Zarcone, Dec. 27, 1944; children: Constance Joanne, John Cibik, Jacquelyn Grace, Houston Lee Browne. BS, Marquette U., 1938; MS, U. Wis., 1941; PhD, U. Mich., 1949. Lic. psychologist, Wis. Research asst. U. Mich., Ann Arbor, 1946-47; psychol. intern Milw. County Hosp. for Mental Diseases, 1947-49; instr. psychology Marquette U., Milw., 1951-52; pvt. practice psychology Milw., 1949—; founder, chmn. dept. psychology Milw. County Hosp. for Mental Diseases, 1947, Marquette U. Dept. Psychology, 1947, St. Michael's Hosp. Mental Health Clinic, 1952; mem. affiliate staff St. Mary's Hosp., Ozaukee, Wis., 1994—. Author: (with Henry Viet) Psychosis with Cerebral Arteriosclerosis as Affected by Adrenal Cortical Extract. Mem. Am. Psychol. Assn., Wis. Psychol. Assn., Soc. Clin. Psychologists, Milw. Psychol. Assn., Nat. Register Health Service Providers in Psychology, Phi Kappa Phi, Phi Delta Kappa. Republican. Roman Catholic. Home: 7821 N Lake Dr Milwaukee WI 53217-2911 Office: 121 E Silver Spring Dr Milwaukee WI 53217-4702

LAMAR, MARTHA LEE, chaplain; b. Birmingham, Jan. 2, 1935; d. Alco L. and Anne Lee (Morris) Lee; m. William Fred Lamar, Jr., June 7, 1986; children: Barbara Gayle Martin, Owen Parker Jr. BS, Auburn U., 1955; MA, Christian Theol. Sem., Indpls., 1992. From adminstv. asst. to rsch. coord. Ala. Affiliate Am. Heart Assn., Birmingham, 1977-86; adminstrv. asst. alumni office De Pauw U., Greencastle, Ind., 1986-89; nursing home chaplain Heritage House Health and Rehab. Ctr., Greencastle, 1989—; nursing home chaplain Garfield Park Health Facility, Indpls., 1992-94, Heritage House Health and Rehab. Ctr., Martinsville, Ind., 1992-95; chaplain cons. Oakwood Corp., Indpls., 1991—. Vol. chaplain's office De Pauw U., 1986—, community work for homeless, Greencastle, 1986—, Fountain Sq. Devel. Corp., Indpls., 1992. Mem. ACA, Nat. Interfaith Coalition on Aging, Am. Soc. on Aging, Mental Health and Aging Network and Forum on Religion, Spirituality and Aging, Ind. Health Care Chaplains Assn. Methodist. Office: Heritage House Health & Rehab Ctr 1601 Hosp Dr Greencastle IN 46135

LAMB, GORDON HOWARD, music educator; b. Eldora, Iowa, Nov. 6, 1934; s. Capp and Ethel (Hayden) L; m. Nancy Ann Painter; children: Kirk, Jon, Phillip. B in Music Edn., Simpson Coll., 1956; M of Music, U. Nebr., 1962; PhD, U. Iowa, 1973. Choral dir. Iowa pub. schs., Tama/Paullina, Sac City, 1957-68; asst. prof. music U. Wis., Stevens Point, 1969-70, U. Tex., Austin, 1970-74; prof., dir. divsn. music U. Tex., San Antonio, 1974-79, prof., v.p. acad. affairs, 1979-86; pres. Northeastern Ill. U., Chgo., 1986-95, pres. emeritus, 1996—; Disting. prof. music dept. Western Ill. U., 1996—. Author: Choral Techniques, 1974, 3d edit. 1988; editor: Guide for the Beginning Choral Director; contbr. articles to scholarly and profl. jours.; composer numerous pieces choral music. Served with U.S. Army, 1957-58. Recipient Most Supportive Pres. or Chancellor award Am. Assn. Colls. for Tchr. Edn., 1992. Mem. Am. Assn. Higher Edn., Am. Assn. State Colls. and Univs., Am. Choral Dirs. Assn. (life, chmn. nat. com. 1970-72).

LAMB, LOIS JEAN, English educator; b. Grand Rapids, Mich., Nov. 14, 1931; d. John Remington and Helen Lucille (Forrest) L. BA, Mich. State U., 1954; MA, Western Mich. U., 1960. Cert. sec. edn. Tchr. Kalamazoo (Mich.) Pub. Schs., 1955-56, Niles (Mich.) Pub. Schs., 1956-60, Caledonia (Mich.) Cmty. Sch., 1962-96. Active, former dir., pres. Rockford (Mich.) Theatre, 1972-82. Mem. NEA, Mich. Edn. Assn., Caledonia Cmty. Edn. (sec. 1968-72), Rogue Valley Women's Club (pres., v.p. 1973-75).

LAMB, MARY ANGELA, hospital patient educator, nurse; b. Cin., June 17, 1939; d. Harry C. and Victoria Rose (Wich) Vogelsang; div.; children: Ronald, Catherine, Rod. Diploma in Nursing, Mercy Sch. Nursing, 1960; BSN, Thomas More Coll., 1985. RN, Ohio; cert. CDE, CETN. Staff nurse St. Francis Hosp., Cin., 1960-61, Flagler Hosp., St. Augustine, Fla., 1961, St. Vincent Hosp., Jacksonville, Fla., 1961-63, North Miss. Community Hosp., Tupelo, 1963, Moline (Ill.) Pub. Hosp., 1964-66; staff nurse, head nurse Good Samaritan Hosp., Cin., 1966-72, patient educator, 1973—; cons. United Ostomy Assn., Cin., 1975—. Vol., speaker Am. Cancer Soc., Cin., 1975—; vol. Am. Diabetic Assn., Cin., 1970—. Mem. Am. Assn. Diabetic Edn., Diabetic Educators of Cin. Area (treas. 1992), Internat. Assn. Enterstomal Therapists, Toastmasters. Roman Catholic. Home: 5611 Old Blue Rock Rd Cincinnati OH 45247-2723 Office: Good Samaritan Hosp 375 Dixmyth Ave Cincinnati OH 45220-2475

LAMBERSON, MARY JANE, artist, educator; b. Logan, Iowa, Aug. 10, 1944; d. James Perry and Emma Jane (Skinner) Laughrey; m. Robert Ray Lamberson, Aug. 30, 1964; children: Courtney Kaye, Robert Russell. BFA, Kearney (Nebr.) State Coll., 1988; MA in Edn., U. Nebr., Kearney, 1991. Teaching asst. U. Nebr., Kearney, 1989-91, adj. art instr., 1991; com. chair Dannebrog, Nebr., 1991—; com. chair Art Exit 305, 1991—. Creator Dannebrog Outdoor Hist. Mural, 1991, Kearney's Mayor's Art Project Outdoor Mural, 1993; designer, cons. Cedar Rapids High Sch. Indoor Hist. Mural, 1992. Recipient art awards. Mem. Impact II, Women Artists of Nebr., Kansas City Artist Coalition, Kans. Sculpture Assn., Nebr. Crafts Coun. (bd. dirs. 1988—), Assn. Nebr. Art Club. Home: 688 Liberty Rd Dannebrog NE 68831-3163

LAMBERT, CAROL A., executive search consultant; b. Jacksonville, Fla., Nov. 24, 1941; d. Lucius Luther and Marie Isabel (DeHoff) Estridge; m. Howard J. Lambert; children: David Craig, Bruce Laurence, Eric Ivan. BS in Pharmacy, U. Fla., 1966. Rsch. assoc. G.D. Searle, Skokie, Ill., 1974-76, info. scientist, 1976-77, supr. tech. svcs., 1977-78, mgr. pharm. prodn. ops., 1978-79, dir. pharm. prodn. ops., 1979-81; dir. Nitrodisc mfg. G.D. Searle, Mt. Prospect, Ill., 1981-83; v.p. ops. Hercon Labs., South Plainfield, N.J., 1983-84; pres. Lambert Mgmt. Cons., Inc., Lake Forest, Ill., 1984—. Chmn. Haven-Emergency Shelter for Youth, Northfield, Ill., 1976; bd. dirs. March of Dimes, Chgo., 1974, march chmn. Deerfield, Ill., 1971-73, publicity chmn. Yonkers, N.Y., 1970-71. Recipient Lunsford Richardson Undergrad. Rsch. award, Richardson-Merrell, Inc., 1966. Mem. Am. Assn. Pharm. Scientists (publicity chair we. regional mtg. 1991, chmn. mentoring/networking com., chmn. diversity task force 1993-95), Drug Info. Assn., Regulatory Affairs Profl. Soc., Internat. Soc. Pharm. Engrs., Project Mgmt. Inst., Soc. of Cosmetic Chemists. Office: Lambert Mgmt Cons Inc #1200 831 Oak Knoll Dr Lake Forest IL 60045-2633

LAMBERT, DAVID, physicist; b. Ames, Iowa, Feb. 21, 1952; s. Maurice Reed and Beth (Swainston) L.; m. Janeen Pack, July 8, 1978; children: David, John, Janeen, Rachel, Peter, Michael, Enoch. BA in Physics, U. Calif., Berkeley, 1974, PhD in Physics, 1979. Rsch. asst. Lawrence Berkeley Lab., Berkeley, Calif., 1975-79; rsch. scientist GM Rsch. Labs., Warren, Mich., 1979-80; sr. rsch. scientist GM Rsch. Labs., Warren, 1980-83, staff rsch. scientist, 1983—; adj. prof. dept. physics and astronomy Mich. State U., East Lansing, 1995—. Contbr. articles to Jour. Chem. Physics, Applied Optics, Jour. Applied Physics, Solid State Comms., Phys. Rev., Internat. Jour. Heat and Mass Trans. Com. chmn. Warren Cons. Sch. Dist., 1985. IBM pre-doctoral fellow, 1978; recipient John M. Campbell award, 1988. Mem. Am. Phys. Soc., Am. Chem. Soc., Am. Vacuum Soc., Optical Soc. Am., Electrochem. Soc., Phi Beta Kappa. Mem. LDS Ch. Office: Physics & Physical Chem Dept Bldg I-6 GM R&D Ctr 30500 Mound Rd Warren MI 48090-9055

LAMBERT, LECLAIR GRIER, writer, lecturer, state government publice information administrator; b. Miami, Fla., s. George F. and Maggie (Grier) L.; BS, Hampton Inst., 1959; postgrad. Harvard U., 1959, U. Munich (Germany), 1965-66. Researcher, copy reader Time-Life Books, 1961-64; tchr. biology and Eng. lit., secondary level U.S. Dependent's Schs. Overseas, Tripoli, Libya, 1964-65; biology editor of high sch. textbooks Holt, Rinehart & Winston, N.Y.C., 1966-69; biology editor and writer Ency. Britannica, N.Y.C., 1969; copy editor Russian sci. monographs The Faraday Press, N.Y.C., 1970-71; writer Med. World News, N.Y.C., 1971; pub. rels. writer Nat. Found./March of Dimes, White Plains, N.Y., 1972; lectr. community and human relations, Black cultural heritage at local schs. and colls., 1977-87; guest lectr. Liberty Square (Fla.) 50th Anniversary, 1986, Black History Month Minn. Ho. of Reps., 1990; dir. edn. programs Minn. Ho. Reps.,

1987—, coord. student speakers youth forum, 1992—; radio commentator Sta. KEEY, 1975-80; reporter Twin Cities Courier, Mpls., 1976-86; free lance writer and designer of brochures and pamphlets, 1974—; dir. communications St. Paul Urban League, 1972-80, asst. to exec. dir., 1977-80, 85-86, bd. dirs. 1992—; mem. adv. bd Archie Givens Rare Books Collection, U. Minn., 1988—; exec. dir. African Am. Mus. Art and History, 1980-86; info. officer Mpls. Urban League, 1978-79. Founder, bd. dirs. Summit-University Free Press, 1974-79; bd. dirs. Help Enable Alcoholics to Receive Treatment, 1977-88; adv. bd. Concordia Coll. Minority Program, 1979-85, KARE TV minority adv. bd. 1985-87; U. Minn. Black Learning Resource Center, 1980-83; past mem. Twin Cities Cable Arts Consortium, Roy Wilkins Meml., Com. Civic Ctr., St. Paul, 1985; mem. state meml. com. Martin Luther King; mem. Minn. Martin Luther King Celebration Com., 1987—; mem. Ethiopian Famine Relief Com.; mem. rev. com. Twin Cities Mayors' Public Art Awards, 1981; co-founder West Suburban Annual Black History Month Celebration Com., 1983-86; mem. St. Paul Civic Ctr. Authority Bd., 1985—, vice chair, 1991—; mem. St. Paul City Art Plan Com., 1987-88, Minn. Mus. Art organizational, exhibits plan coms., 1989—, trustee, 1991—, v.p., 1992-93, pres., 1993-94, chair, 1994-95; sgt.-at-arms, officer Minn. Ho. of Reps., 1987-96, coord. ednl. programs, mem. cultural diversity tng. task force, 1992—, dir. pub. info., 1996—; bd. dirs. St Paul Visitors and Conv. Bur., 1990-93. Served to 1st lt., Chem. Corps., U.S. Army, 1959-61. Contbr. articles to profl. jours. Recipient Community Martin Luther King Communications award, 1978, Spl. Recognition award Mpls. St. Acad., 1983; Spl. Achievement award Roosevelt High Sch., 1985, Spl. Recognition award Twin Cities African Am. Mus., 1985, Liberty Square Tenants' Spl. Recognition award, 1986, Vol. Svc. award St. Paul Urban League, 1988. Mem. Pub. Rels. Soc. Am., African-Am. Mus. Assn. (mem. nat. legis. edn. com. 1983, exec. council, Midwest region rep. 1984-89, Achievement award 1985), Minn. Press Club. Author: Reflections of Life--Poems, Prose and Essays, 1981, A Learning Journey Through Black History, 1982; editor, writer: Minnesota's Black Community, 1977; editor: Art in Development: A Nigerian Perspective, 1983. Office: Minn Ho Reps 100 Constitution Ave Saint Paul MN 55155-1409

LAMBERT, MARY PULLIAM, neurobiologist; b. Birmingham, Ala., Apr. 27, 1944; d. Arch and Laura Mae (Cannon) Pulliam; m. Joseph Buckley Lambert, June 27, 1967; children: Laura, Alice, Joseph. BS, Birmingham So. Coll., 1966; PhD, Northwestern U., Evanston, Ill., 1970. Postdoctoral assoc. Northwestern U., Evanston, 1971-73, 1981-83, rsch. assoc. I, 1983-88, rsch. assoc. II, 1988-93; rsch. assoc. III Northwestern U., Evanston, Ill., 1994—. Mem. Soc. for Neuroscience, Phi Beta Kappa, Sigma Xi. Office: Northwestern U Dept Neurobiology/Physiology Hogan Hall 2153 Sheridan Rd Evanston IL 60208

LAMBERT, SALLY RIDEOUT, state legislator; m. Walter Lambert. BS, U. Evansville, 1992. Intern Ind. Senate, 1992; campaign coord. State Senator Greg Server, 1992; intern SOS Group, Inc., 1993; exec. adminstr. Vanderburgh County Rep. Com., 1993-94; mem. Ind. State Ho. of Reps. Dist. 74, mem. ways and means com., vice-chmn. roads and transp. com., vice-chmn. com. economic growth & regulatory relief. Active Ind. Breast Cancer Coalition. Mem. Evansville Area Alumnae (pres.), Warrick County C. of C., Warrick County Farm Bur., Kiwanis, Jaycees, Phi Mu.

LAMBERTI, GARY ANTHONY, biology educator; b. Oakland, Calif., Oct. 5, 1953; s. Antonio A. and Olga C. (Caviglia) L.; m. Donna Packer, June 2, 1990. BS, U. Calif., Davis, 1975; PhD, U. Calif., Berkeley, 1983. Postdoctoral assoc. U. Calif., Berkeley, 1983-84; rsch. assoc. Oreg. State U., Corvallis, 1984-86, asst. prof., 1986-89; asst. prof. dept. biol. scis. U. Notre Dame, Ind., 1989-95, assoc. prof., 1995—, dir. environ. biology grad. tng. program; presenter at profl. confs. Assoc. editor Jour. N.Am. Benthol. Soc., Lawrence, Kans., 1991—; author tech. reports, symposium papers; contbr. 10 chpts. to books, 40 articles to profl. jours. NIH fellow, U. Calif., 1977; grantee NSF, 1990. Mem. AAAS, Am. Inst. Biol. Scis., Ecol. Soc. Am., N.Am. Benthological Soc. (chmn. exec. com. 1986-87, pres.-elect 1996—, Best Paper award 1982). Office: Univ Notre Dame Dept Biol Scis Notre Dame IN 46556

LAMBERTSON, LARRY HALL, psychiatrist; b. Chgo., June 1, 1950; s. Wingate Augustus and Eileen Helen (Hall) L.; m. Anna Marie Schober, May 31, 1980; 1 child, Cynthia Ann. BA, U. Ky., 1972, MD, 1977; postgrad. in Psychiatry, Loma Linda U. Med. Ctr., 1980; fellowship in Child Psychiatry, U. Cin., 1982. Diplomate Am. Bd. Psychiatry and Neurology. Pvt. practice psychiatry Irvine, Calif., 1982-88; psychiatric med. dir. So. Va. Mental Health Inst., Danville, 1989-92; med. dir. Park Ctr. Inc., Ft. Wayne, Ind., 1992—; cons. in nutrition Tyson & Assocs., Santa Monica, Calif., 1984-88; dir. adult program Santa Ana (Calif.) Psychiat. Hosp., 1987-88; mem. courtesy staff Danville Meml. Hosp., 1989-92; forensic psychiat. evaluator Commonwealth of Va., Danville, 1989—; psychiat. cons. Catawba (Va.) State Hosp., 1991-92; assoc. clin. prof. medicine U. Va., 1989-92. Instr. in behavioral emergencies Danville Rescue Squad, 1991. Mem. Chief Med. Officers Assn. (pres. 1992), Danville-Pittsylvania County Acad. Medicine, Monroe Inst. (profl. div.). Home: 2001 Kensington Blvd Fort Wayne IN 46805-4609 Office: Park Ctr Inc 409 E State Blvd Fort Wayne IN 46805

LAMBETH, CLAYTON LEE, agricultural company executive; b. Ridgley, Tenn., July 5, 1939; s. Hugh L. and Pauline (Wooten) L.; m. Margus A. Cardwell, June 22, 1965; children—Kristi M., Troy L. B.S., U. Ariz., 1962, M.S., 1966. Nutritionist Farr Feeds, Greeley, Colo., 1966-68; asst. mgr. Lebsack Feed Lots, Sterling, Colo., 1968-71; v.p. feed lot mgmt. Ceres Inc., Sterling, 1971-76; pres. ranch div. AZL Resources, Phoenix, 1976-79; cons. livestock nutrition, Ft. Morgan, Colo., 1979-80; pres., gen. mgr. Fall River Feed Lots, Hot Springs, S.D., 1980—. Mem. Livestock Mktg. Assn. (bd. govs. 1982—), Am. Nat. Cattlemens Assn. (grading com.), S.D. Stock Growers, Colo. Cattle Feeders Assn. (v.p. 1975-76), Soc. Animal Sci. Club: So. Hills Golf. Lodge: Elks. Home: PO Box 911 Hot Springs SD 57747-0911 Office: Fall River Feed Lots Inc PO Box 892 Hot Springs SD 57747

LAMBOWITZ, SHEILA, state agency administrator; b. Bklyn., June 22, 1947; d. Jack J. and Florence (Lehrman) Mintz. BA in Comparative Lit., Bklyn. Coll., 1969; MBA in Mgmt., St. Louis U., 1981. Customer svc. rep. Conn. Blue Cross, North Haven, 1969-72; HMO coord. Blue Cross & Blue Shield of Greater N.Y., N.Y.C., 1974-75; rsch. analyst Blue Cross Hosp. Svcs., Inc., St. Louis, 1976-78, mgr. product devel. then mgr. govt. programs div., 1978-83, 83-86; hosp. rates & audits chief Ohio Dept. of Human Svcs., Columbus, 1986-90, surveillance & utilization rev. chief, 1990-91; mgr. long term care case mix implementation project Dept. Human Svcs., Columbus, Ohio, 1991-93, chief case mix and sys. adminstrn., 1993—; mem. HCFA joint applications devel. com. Health Stds. Quality Bur., State of Ohio Time Study, coord. HCFA case mix demonstration project, 1994—; State of Ohio coord. MDS2.0 automation project Dept. Human Svcs., 1994—, chmn. Ohio nursing facility Case Mix adv. com., 1994—; chair 1997 Nat. Case Mix and Quality Assurance conf., 1995—. Bd. dirs. League Women Voters Met. Columbus, 1995—. Mem. Phi Alpha Theta. Democrat. Jewish. Office: Ohio Dept of Human Svcs 30 E Broad St Fl 33 Columbus OH 43266-0423

LAMELAS, FRANCISCO J., physicist, educator; b. Havana, Cuba, Feb. 6, 1959. BS in Applied Math., Physics, U. Wis., Milw., 1977-80; MS in Materials Sci., U. Wis., 1980-82; MS in Physics, U. Mich., 1985-87, PhD in Physics, 1985-90. Assoc. engr. IBM, East Fishkill, N.Y., 1982-83, sr. assoc. engr., 1983-84; postdoc. tech. staff mem. AT&T Bell Labs., Murray Hill, N.J., 1990-92; postdoc. fellow U. Mo., 1993-94; asst. prof. physics Marquette (Wis.) U., 1994—. Contbr. articles to profl jours. including Phys. Review. Mem. Am. Phys. Soc. Office: Marquette U Dept of Physics Milwaukee WI 53233

LAMKIN, E(UGENE) HENRY, JR., internist, medical management executive; b. Owensboro, Ky., Feb. 23, 1935; s. Eugene Henry and Nancy Elizabeth (Davidson) L.; m. Martha Savannah Dampf, Aug. 24, 1968; children: Melinda Magness, Matthew Davidson. BA, DePauw U., Greencastle, Ind., 1956; MD, Ind. U., 1960. Diplomate Am. Bd. Internal Medicine. Intern Phila. Gen. Hosp., 1960-61; resident IM IU Med. Ctr., 1961-62, 64-65, fellow in endo. and metab., 1965-66; pvt. practice internal medicine Indpls., 1966-96; pres., CEO Allied Profl. Svcs., Indpls.; founding pres. Agess Med. Clinic, Indpls.; mem. Ind. Ho. of Reps., 16 yrs., majority leader, 4 yrs.; pres. Ind. Employers Healthcare Coalition; asst. clin. prof. medicine Ind. U.Sch. Medicine; formerly med. dir. Millennium Mgmt. Co., Farm Bur. Healthcare Network, Indpls.; past pres. and v.p. med. staff Meth. Hosp. of Ind. Bd. dirs. Physicians Med. Alliance Ind.; mem. organizing com. Ind. Bus. Health Care Coalition. Capt. U.S. Army, 1962-64. Recipient Otis R. Bowen Physician Cmty. Svc. award, Ind. Optometry Assn. award, Appreciation award Ind. Acad. Family Practice, others. Fellow ACP; mem. AMA, Am. Coll. Physician Execs., Nat. Assn. Managed Care Physicians, Nat. Assn. for Health Care Quality. Home: 4145 Washington Blvd Indianapolis IN 46205-2616 Office: Allied Profl Svcs 8250 Haverstick Rd Indianapolis IN 46240

LAMKIN, MARTHA DAMPF, lawyer; b. Talladega, Ala., May 20, 1942; d. Keith J. and Neva (Magness) Dampf; m. E. Henry Lamkin Jr., Aug. 28, 1968; children: Melinda Magness, Matthew Davidson. BA in English, Calif. Baptist Coll., 1964; MA in English and Am. Lit., Vanderbilt U., 1966; JD, Ind. U., 1970. Bar: Ind. 1970. Assoc. Joseph D. Geeslin, Indpls., 1971-72, Lowe, Gray, Steele & Hoffman, Indpls., 1976-82; field office mgr. U.S. Dept. Housing and Urban Devel., Indpls., 1982-87; exec. dir., corp. rep. responsibility and govtl. affairs Cummins Engine Co., Inc., Columbus, Ind., 1987-91; exec. v.p. corp. affairs USA Group, Inc., Indpls., 1991—; pres., bd. dirs. Cummins Engine Found., 1989-91; bd. dirs. Meridian Mut. Ins. Co., Indpls.; pres., bd. dirs. Citizens Gas & Coke Utility, Inc., USA Group, Inc., U.S. Stende Aid Funds, Inc. Commr., sec., chmn. Indpls. Human Rights Commn., 1971-79; commr. Indpls. Housing Authority, 1979-82; chmn. exec. com. S.K. Lacy Exec. Leadership, Indpls., 1986-87; chmn. Ind. Leadership Celebration, Indpls., 1985-87; sec. Gov.'s Mansion Commn., Indpls., 1981-89; bd. dirs. Great Indpls. Progress Commn., 1986-87, Indpls. Symphony Orch., 1983-89, Indpls. Project, 1986-91; bd. dirs., sec. COMMIT, Inc., COMMIT Found., 1990—; chmn. bd. trustees Christian Theol. Sem., Indpls., 1983-93; hon. gov. Richard C. Lugar Excellence Pub. Svc. Series, 1990—; vice-chair, trustee Indpls. Found., 1992—; mem. exec. com. Mayor's Task Force on Housing, 1987. Recipient Presdl. Rank award 1985, Mental Health Initiative Gov. Ind., 1986, Matrix award Women in Communication, 1987. Mem. State Assembly Women (pres. 1977-79), Indpls. Jr. League, Indpls. C. of C. (bd. dirs. 1986-87). Republican. Mem. Disciples of Christ. Office: USA Group Inc PO Box 6180-m597 Indianapolis IN 46206-6180

LAMMERS, MAX P., financial company executive; b. Cin., Apr. 12, 1929. BS, Xavier U., 1951. Dir. br. ops. Berrings Inc., Cleve., 1952-76; v.p. Pre Indsl. Inc., Cleve., 1976-78; pres. Indsl. Internat. Inc., Cleve., 1978-90; exec. v.p. A T Brod & Co. Inc., Cleve., 1990—. 1st lt. USAR, 1951-58. Office: A T Brod & Co Inc # 326 25825 Science Park Dr Ste 340 Cleveland OH 44122-7315

LAMOREAUX, DAVID ALBERT, benefit plans administrator; b. Cleve., Aug. 11, 1924; s. Mark David and Hilda Elizabeth (Schmidt) L.; m. Pamela E. Gordon, June 12, 1948 (dec. 1986); children: David T, Nancy L. Doyle, Mark E, Roy A.; m. Patricia Ermentraudt Wilson, Oct. 21, 1988. AB, U. Mich., 1949, MBA, 1950. Tax pension supr. Kaiser-Frazer Corp., Willow Run, Mich., 1950-54; pension health benefits adminstr. Kaiser Motors Retirement, Wayne, Mich., 1954-76; labor arbitrator Kaiser Motors Retirement, Ann Arbor, Mich, 1960-76; benefit plan adminstr. Internat. Union, UAW, Detroit, 1976—; v.p., bd. dirs. Huron River Area Credit Union, Ann Arbor; treas. bd. dirs. Viva Ventures, 1987-88. Pres. PTO, Ann Arbor, 1968-69. Sgt. USAAF, 1944-46. Mem. Mich. Actuarial Soc., Nat. Assoc. Accts. Ann Arbor Chpt. Democrat. Presbyterian. Home: 3366 Bluett Rd Ann Arbor MI 48105-1557 Office: Internat Union UAW 8000 E Jefferson Ave Detroit MI 48214-3963

LAMPE, KATHERINE EVELYN, physical therapist, educator; b. West Union, Iowa, Feb. 28, 1963; d. Paul Lee and Eloise Therese (McDonald) Kaiser; m. Christopher John Lampe, June 21, 1986; children: Matthew, Samuel, Anna, Sarah. BS, Loras Coll., 1985; M in Phys. Therapy, U. Iowa, 1987. Lic. phys. therapist, Iowa. Phys. therapist St. Luke's Hosp., Cedar Rapids, Iowa, 1987-88, supr., 1988-90, clin. edn., staff devel. coord., 1990-92; lectr. U. Iowa, 1992-94; instr. St. Ambrose U., Davenport, Iowa, 1995—. Mem. adv. bd. Kirkwood PTA, Cedar Rapids, 1985-95. Mem. Am. Phys. Therapy Assn. Home: 1006 Park St Bellevue IA 52031 Office: St Ambrose U 518 W Locust Davenport IA 52803

LAMPERT, LEONARD FRANKLIN, mechanical engineer; b. Mpls., Nov. 13, 1919; s. Arthur John Lampert and Irma (Potter) Smith. BME, U. Minn., 1943, B in Chem. Engring., 1959, MS in Biochemistry, 1964, PhD in Biochemistry, 1969. Registered profl. engr., Minn. With flight measurement rsch. dept. Douglas Aircraft Corp., El Segundo, Calif., 1943-47; researcher, tchr. U. Minn., Mpls., 1947-83; with rsch. engring. dept. Mpls. Honeywell Corp., 1950-55; info. scientist Control Data Corp., Mpls., 1982-88; mech. engr. Leonard Lampert Co., White Bear Lake, Minn., 1988—; scientist Eurasion Watermilfoil Control, White Bear Lake, 1989—; stockholder rep. Lampert Lumber Co., St. Paul, 1988—. Contbr. articles to profl. jours. Mem. Am. Inst. Chem. Engrs. (award 1959), Am. Chem. Soc., U. Minn. Alumni Assn. (advisor) MIT Alumni Assn. (advisor), Phi Gamma Delta (advisor), Gamma Alpha, Phi Lambda Upsilon. Republican. Home and Office: 2467 S Shore Blvd Saint Paul MN 55110-3820

LAMPERT, LEONARD LEE, consulting engineer, land surveyor; b. Mulvane, Kans., July 18, 1906; s. Charles Crockett and Winnie Estelle (Hays) L.; m. Ruth Lillian Currier, Jan. 20, 1934 (dec. 1962); 1 child, Molly Ann Currier; m. Evangeline Virginia Daul Loomis, Aug. 7, 1964; children: Lori Lee, Leonard Lee II. BS in Civil and Irrigation Engring., Colo. State U., 1932. Registered profl. engr., Wis.; registered land surveyor. Br. mgr. Assocs. Investment Co., Stevens Point, Wis., 1934-41; constrn. mgr. Sentry Ins., Stevens Point, 1941-57; owner, pres. Leonard L. Lampert & Assocs., Stevens Point, 1957-84; v.p. Lampert, Lee & Assocs., Wisconsin Rapids, Wis., 1984—; mem. Dept. Agr. Trade and Consumer Protection, Madison, 1990—; chmn. Wis. Exam. Bd. of Architects, Engrs. and Land Surveyors, Madison, 1970-73. Author: Journal Surveying and Mapping, 1990. Chmn. Rep. Party, Stevens Point. Recipient Chmn.'s award Am. Congress on Surveying and Mapping, 1973. Mem. Wis. Soc. Land Surveyors (pres. 1964-65, Cert. of Appreciation 1973), Wis. Soc. Profl. Engrs. (pres. chpt. 1971), Elks (exalted ruler), Sigma Chi. Presbyterian. Office: Lampert Lee & Assocs 10968 Hwy 54E Wisconsin Rapids WI 54494

LAMPINEN, JOHN A., newspaper editor; b. Waukegan, Ill., Nov. 26, 1951; s. Walter Valentine and Patricia Mae Irene (Pruess) L.; m. Belinda Walter, Oct. 20, 1973; children: Amanda Michelle, Heidi Elizabeth. BS in Comm., U. Ill., 1973. Staff writer Paddock Cir. Newspapers, Libertyville, Ill., 1973-75; regional editor The Jour., New Ulm, Minn., 1975-76; various positions Daily Herald, Arlington Heights, Ill., 1976-90; asst. v.p., mng. editor Daily Herald, Arlington Heights, 1990—; adj. prof. Medill Sch. Journalism, Northwestern U., Evanston, Ill., 1995—. Mem. APME, SPJ. Office: Daily Herald 217 W Campbell St Arlington Heights IL 60005-1411

LAMSON, EVONNE VIOLA, therapist, computer software company executive, consultant, pastor, Christian education administrator; b. Ithaca, Mich., July 8, 1946; d. Donald and Mildred (Perdew) Guild; m. James E. Lamson, Nov. 2, 1968; 1 child, Lillie D. Assoc. in Math., Washtenaw C.C., Ypsilanti, Mich., 1977; BS, Ea. Mich. U., 1989; MA in Pastoral Counseling Ashland (Ohio) Theol. Sem., 1993. Lic. profl. counselor, Mich. Data base mgr. ERIM, Ann Arbor, Mich., 1978-81; mgr. product svcs. Comshare, Ann Arbor, 1981-90, project leader, tng. course designer info. techs., 1991-93; founder, pres. G & L Consultants, Brighton, Mich., 1982—; tng. specialist Comshare, Ann Arbor, 1990-93; Assoc. Pastor, dir. Christian edn. Keystone Cmty. Ch., Saline, Mich., 1993-95; founder Living Waters Counseling, 1993—. Study leader Brighton Wesleyan Ch., 1981-93; lic. minister Weseleyan Ch. Am., 1993—; program dir. Wesleyan Womens Assn. of Brighton, 1983-91; clin. staff counselor Women's Resource Ctr., Howell, Mich., 1991-94; clin. supr. counselor Livingston Counseling and Assessment, 1994—, clin. team leader, 1995—. Mem. AACD, NAFE, AACC, Am. Mgmt. Assn., Fairbanks Family of Am., Internat. Platform Assn. Avocations: skiing, motivational speaking, reading. Home: 6708 Calfhill Ct Brighton MI 48116-7419

LANCIONE, BERNARD GABE, lawyer; b. Bellaire, Ohio, Feb. 3, 1939; s. Americus Gabe and June (Morford) L.; m. Rosemary C., Nov. 27, 1976; children: Amy, Caitin, Gillian, Bernard Gabe II, Elizabetta Marie. BS, Ohio U., 1960; JD, Capitol U., 1965. Bar: Ohio 1965, U.S. Dist. Ct. (so. dist.) Ohio 1967, U.S. Supreme Ct., 1969, U.S. Ct. Appeals (4th cir.) 1982, U.S. Dist. Ct. (no. dist.) Ohio, 1989. Pres. Lancione Law Office, Co., L.P.A., Bellaire, Ohio, 1965-87, mng. atty. Cichon Lancione Co., L.P.A., St. Clairsville, Ohio, 1982-85, of counsel Ward, Kaps, Bainbridge, Maurer, Bloomfield and Melvin, Columbus, Ohio, 1987-88; Ohio Asst. Atty. Gen., Columbus, 1988-91; sole practice, 1991—; spl. counsel Ohio Atty. Gen.'s Office, 1991-95; solicitor Bellaire City (Ohio), 1968-72; asst. prosecutor County of Belmont (Ohio), 1972-76; legal counsel Young Democrats Am., 1971-73; pack com. chmn. Pack 961, Westerville, Ohio Cub Scouts of Am., 1992-93. Mem. ABA, Ohio State Bar Assn., Assn. Trial Lawyers Am., Ohio Acad. Trial Lawyers (award of merit 1972). Democrat. Roman Catholic. Home: 1108 Acillom Dr Westerville OH 43081-1104 Office: 647 Park Meadow Rd # E Westerville OH 43081-2878

LANCOUR, KAREN LOUISE, secondary education educator; b. Cheboygan, Mich., June 2, 1946; d. Clinton Howard and Dorothy Marie (Passeno) L. AA, Alpena Community Coll., 1966; BA, Ea. Mich. U., 1968, MS, 1970. Teaching asst. Ea. Mich. U., Ypsilanti, 1968-70; tchr. sci. Utica (Mich.) Community Schs., 1970—. Nat. event supr. Sci. Olympiad, 1986—, mem. nat. rules com., 1987—, state event supr., 1986-91, regional dir., 1987. Recipient Disting. Svc. award Nat. Sci. Olympiad, 1995. Mem. Nat. Sci. Tchrs. Assn., Mich. Sci. Tchrs. Assn., Nat. Assn. Biology Tchrs., Met. Detroit Sci. Tchrs. Assn., Smithsonian Inst., Nat. Geographic Soc., Edison Inst., Mortar Bd., Internat. Biograph. Soc., Am. Biograph. Inst. Rsch. Assn. (dep. gov.), Internat. Platform Assn., Phi Theta Kappa, Kappa Delta Phi. Home: 8378 18 Mile Rd Apt 202 Sterling Heights MI 48313-3034 Office: Henry Ford II High Sch 11911 Clinton River Rd Sterling Heights MI 48313-2420

LANDAUER, CHARLES D., business executive; b. Bronxville, N.Y., May 30, 1934. BA, Dartmouth Coll., 1956. V.p. Landauer Corp., Cumming, Iowa, 1991—. 1st lt. USMC, 1952-58. Office: 12251 Maffitt Rd Cumming IA 50061

LANDER, RUTH A., medical group and association administrator; b. Fitchburg, Mass., Dec. 13, 1948; d. H. Allison and Violet K. (Erickson) Linné; m. C. Stephen Lander, June 28, 1968; children: Timothy, Mary. BA, Ohio State U., 1978; postgrad., Kennedy-We. U., 1995—. Dir. fin. Luth. Svc. Assn. of New Eng., Natick, Mass., 1973-76; gen. mgr. Logos, Columbus, 1976-87; practice adminstr. Columbus Oncology Assocs., Inc., 1987—; pres. elect Adminstrs. in Oncology Hematology Assembly, Englewood, Colo., 1995—, sec., treas., 1994-95, legislative liaison, 1994-95. Editor: Adminstrs. in Oncology Hematology Assembly News, 1994-95; contbr. articles to profl. jours. Tchr. Vineyard Christian Fellowship, Westerville, Ohio, 1995—; grass roots legislative group Ohio Med. Group Mgmt. Assn., Columbus, 1994—. Fellow Med. Group Mgmt. Assn., Am. Coll. Med. Practice Execs.; mem. Am. Coll. Healthcare Execs. (assoc.), Am. Acad. Med. Adminstr., Leading Edge Alliance-Women in Healthcare Leadership, Mid-Ohio Med. Group Mgmt. Assn. (pres. 1993-94, sec. 1992-93, program dir. 1991-92, exec. com. 1990-96), Med. Mgmt. Assn. (sec., exec. com.), Assn. Cmty. Cancer Ctr. Republican. Office: Columbus Oncology Assocs 500 Thomas Ln #3A Columbus OH 43214

LANDERS, PATRICIA ELAINE, nursing supervisor; b. Mason City, Iowa, Jan. 14, 1950; d. Donald Wayne and Donna Louise (Neal) Butler; m. Glenn E. Landers, June 9, 1974; children: Tami Lynn, Terry E., Shawn D. ADN, North Iowa Area C.C., Mason City, 1971. Cert. EMT, paramedic, regional neonatal resuscitation course instr. Staff nurse Floyd County Meml. Hosp., Charles City, Iowa, 1971-73, house supr., 1973—. Nurse ARC; mem. Cmty. Disaster Dr.; tchr. 4-H Club Classes, Ambulance Classes; Sunday sch. tchr. Luth. Ch. Recipient Vol. Svc. award Greene Elem. Sch., 1984, Outstanding Vol. Svc. award Greene Betterment Coun., 1986, Gov.'s Vol. award State of Iowa, 1987, Friend of Edn. award Greene Edn. Assn., 1990. Home: 13273 Jay Ave Greene IA 50636

LANDINI, RICHARD GEORGE, university president, emeritus English educator; b. Pitts., June 4, 1929; s. George R. and Alice (Hoy) L.; m. Phyllis Lesnick, Nov. 26, 1952 (dec. Mar. 1992); children: Richard, Gregory, Matthew, Cynthia, Vincent. A.B., U. Miami, 1954, M.A., 1956; Ph.D., U. Fla., 1959; D.Civil Law, Quincy Coll., 1985; LLD, U. Miami, 1980, Baiko Jo Gakuin Coll., Japan, 1987, Ind. State U., 1996. From asst. prof. to prof. English Ariz. State U., 1959-70, dean, 1968-70; prof. English, acad. v.p. U. Mont., 1970-75; pres. Ind. State U., 1975-92, prof. English, 1975—. Contbr. articles on lit. and higher edn. to profl. jours. Served with U.S. Army, 1948-51. Decorated knight of the Holy Sepulchre Jerusalem, 1996. Mem. Knight of the Holy Sepulchre of Jerusalem, Phi Beta Kappa, Phi Delta Kappa, Phi Alpha Theta, Phi Kappa Phi, Sigma Tau Delta. Roman Catholic. Office: Ind State Univ Dept English Root Hall # A-288 Terre Haute IN 47809

LANDIS, DAVID MORRISON, state legislator; b. Lincoln, Nebr., June 10, 1948; m. Melodee Ann McPherson, June 6, 1969; children: Matthew, Melissa. BA U. Nebr., 1970, JD, 1971, M in Cmty. Regional Planning, 1995, MPA U. Nebr., Omaha, 1984. Bar: Nebr. 1972; practice law, Lincoln, 1972-74; mem. Nebr. Legislature, 1978—, chmn. govt. mil. and vets. affairs com., 1983-87, chmn. banking, commerce and ins., 1988—; instr. Coll. Law U. Nebr., 1990—; adj. faculty mem. dept. pub. adminstrn. U. Nebr., Omaha, 1984, adj. faculty mem. NE Wesleyan U., 1995—; adj. mem. bus. faculty Doane Coll., 1985-95. Named Doane Coll. Tchr. of Yr., 1987, 88, 92. Bd. dirs. Lower Platte S. Natural Resources Dist., 1971-78; officer PTA, 1979-80; adminstrv. law judge Dept. Labor, 1977-78; mem. Nebr. Humanities Council; mem. NE Repertory Theatre. Mem. The Innocents Soc. (hon.), Golden Key Soc. (hon., U. Nebr.). Office: State Legislature State Capitol Lincoln NE 68509

LANDIS, GEORGE HARVEY, psychotherapist; b. Newton, Kans., Dec. 12, 1918; s. Melvin D. and Erie Emma (Byler) L.; m. Lois I. Donaldson, Sept. 26, 1943; children: Judy Carol Landis Forsman, Richard G. Student, Baker U., 1937-38; BA, John Fletcher Coll., 1941; MSW, U. Nebr., 1948. Diplomate Registry of Clin. Social Work; cert. clin. social worker, master social worker, Nebr. Caseworker Family Svc. of Omaha, 1948-50; psychotherapist Midwest Clinic, Omaha, 1950-90; pvt. practice Omaha, 1990—. Served with U.S. Army, 1941-46. Mem. Acad. Cert. Social Workers. Home: 4628 Hascall St Omaha NE 68106-4042 Office: 9239 W Center Rd Ste 200 Omaha NE 68124-1900

LANDIS, LARRY SEABROOK, marketing and communications consultant; b. Princeton, N.J., Nov. 2, 1945; s. Donald Edward and Caroline Ann (Magalhaes) L.; m. Carol Louise Butz, Sept. 28, 1974; 1 child, Christopher Seabrook. AB cum laude, Wabash Coll., 1967; postgrad., U. N.C., 1967-68, Ind. U., 1969-70. Asst. to mayor Richard G. Lugar (now U.S. Senator, R-Ind.), Indpls., 1969-71; press sec. to Otis R. Bowen (Rep. candidate for gov., Ind.) Indpls., 1972; dir. mktg. svcs. Garrison, Jasper Rose & Co., Indpls., 1972-76; v.p. mktg. and media services Hickman & assoc., Indpls., 1976-80; v.p. corp. advt. Am. Fletcher Nat. Bank (Bank One Indpls., N.A.), Indpls., 1980-84; dir. communications PALLM, Inc., Indpls., 1984-85; v.p., dir. account planning Handley & Miller, Inc., Indpls., 1985-91; pres. Marketrends, Inc., 1991—; lectr. polit. sci. Ind. U./Purdue U., Indpls., 1969-71; bd. dirs. Event Techs., Inc. Co-author: How To, 1974; contbr. articles to profl. jours. Active gov.-elect Ad Hoc Com. on Ednl. Fin., Indpls., 1972-73, campaign mgr. Salin for Congress Com., Ft. Wayne, Ind., 1971-72; mem. exec. com. statewide Rep. legis. campaign Victory '90, Ind., 1989-90; mem. mktg. com. United Way Ctrl. Ind., 1992-93; mem. mktg. adv. com. Indpls. Symphony Orch., 1992—; bd. dirs. USCO Adult Edn. Program, Indpls., 1975-82, pres., 1980-82, Citizens Environ. Coun., Inc., Zionsville, Ind., 1984-86, v.p., 1986-96. With U.S. Army, 1968-69. Mem. Am. Mktg. Assn., Acad. Health Svcs. Mktg., Bank Mktg. Assn., Indpls. C. of C., Indpls. Advt. Club, Ind. Hist. Soc. (life, trustee 1995—), Indpls. Press Club, Columbia Club, Econ. Club, Indsl. Computing Soc. (founding), Ind. Software Assn., Nature Conservancy, English-Speaking Union, Pi Delta Epsilon, Delta Sigma Rho, Tau Kappa Alpha, Phi Kappa Psi. Republican. Methodist. Home: 1126 W 77th St South Dr Indianapolis IN 46260 Office: Marketrends Inc Circle Tower Bldg 55 Monument Circle Ste 522 Indianapolis IN 46204-5911

LANDMESSER, HAROLD LEON, tool distributor consultant; b. Mt. Clemens, Mich., Mar. 12, 1917; s. A.R. and Ottilie (Berlin) L.; m. Grace Rae

Valmore, Apr. 27, 1940 (dec. Aug. 1981); children: Frederick, Lawrence; m. Geraldine Gretchine Schaupner, Feb. 12, 1982. Student, U. Detroit, 1936. Salesman Snap-On Tools Corp., Detroit, 1936-40, field salesman, 1940-42, asst. mgr., 1942-56, mgr., 1956-61; owner Landmesser Tools Co., Waterford, 1962-82, cons., 1982—. Mem. Elks (Waterford). Home: 3605 Lakefront St Waterford MI 48328-4332 Office: Landmesser Tools Co 960 S Cass Lake Rd Waterford MI 48328-4121

LANDON, ROBERT GRAY, retired manufacturing company executive; b. Portsmouth, Ohio, Dec. 22, 1928; s. Herman Robert and Hazel Ruth (Tener) L.; m. Sarah A. Newpher, July 2, 1954; children: Geoffrey, Suzanne. Student, Cornell U., 1947-49; BA in Econs., U. Pa., 1955; grad. advanced mgmt. program, Harvard Sch. Bus., 1978. Loan officer Nat. City Bank, Cleve., 1955-60; SEC adminstr. Smith Kline Corp., 1960-64; controller, treas. Grumman Allied Industries, Inc., Garden City, N.Y., 1964-76; v.p. Grumman Allied Industries, Inc., 1977-82; v.p. investment mgmt. Grumman Corp., Bethpage, N.Y., 1978-79; pres. Grumman Ohio Corp., Worthington, Ohio, 1979-88. Served with AC USN, 1949-53. Mem. The Oaks Club.

LANDRUM, PETER FRANKLIN, environmental toxicologist; b. Scotia, Calif., Oct. 15, 1947; s. William Wiesner and Juanita (Lair) Landrum; m. Fawn M. Atkinson, June 24, 1972. BS in Chemistry, Calif. State U., San Bernardino, 1974; PhD in Pharmacology and Toxicology, U. Calif., Davis, 1979. Rsch. assoc. Savannah River Ecology Lab. U. Ga., Aiken, 1980-81; rsch. chemist Gt. Lakes Environ. Rsch. Lab. NOAA, Ann Arbor, Mich., 1981-94, supervisory chemist, 1994—; instr. Eastern Mich. U., Ypsilanti, 1984-91. Contbr. articles to profl. jours; assoc. editor Jour. Great Lakes Rsch., 1992—; mem. bd. editors Chemospher, 1988—. With U.S. Army, 1968-71. Mem. Am. Chem. Soc., Internat. Assn. for Gt. Lakes Rsch., Soc. Environ. Toxicology Chemistry (bd. dirs. 1990-93, charter mem.). Office: Great Lakes Environ Rsch Lab 2205 Commonwealth Blvd Ann Arbor MI 48105-2945

LANDRUM, THOMAS LOWELL, real estate agent, resale shop owner; b. Childress, Tex., July 24, 1935; s. Alton Virgil and Ura (Campbell) L.; m. Margaret Ellen Leslie, Jan. 25, 1959; children: Leslie Christine, Holly Rene, Thomas Lowell Jr., Timothy Louis, James Allen. BS, Tex. A&M U., 1959; MS, Purdue U., 1968, PhD, 1974. Lic. real estate sales rep., Ind. Tech. writer, supr. Mason & Hanger-Silas Mason Co., Amarillo, Tex., 1959-66; specifications engr. Nat. Homes Corp., Lafayette, Ind., 1966; grad. instr., then asst. prof. Purdue U., West Lafayette, Ind., 1966-82, inst. dir., 1982-85; v.p. Ctr. Mgmt. Inst., Lafayette, 1985-86; owner, mgr. The Merry-Go-Round, Lafayette, 1986—; real estate agt. Coldwell Banker Sycamore Realty, West Lafayette, 1991-92, Merit Realty, Lafayette, 1992—; cons., instr. Purdue U., West Lafayette, 1991—. Bd. dirs. Lafayette Sch. Corp., 1978-93; treas. Lafayette Christian Sch. Boosters, 1987-93. Mem. Nat. Assn. Ind. Bus., Ind. Assn. Realtors, Lafayette Bd. Realtors Svc. Corp. (bd. dirs. 1991—), C. of C. Republican. Presbyterian. Home: 40 Valdez Ct Lafayette IN 47905-4050 Office: Merit Realty Inc PO Box 4375 Lafayette IN 47903-4375

LANDRY, MARK EDWARD, podiatrist, researcher; b. Washington, May 24, 1950; s. John Edward and Daphne (Fay) L.; m. Mary Ann Kotey, Sept. 7, 1974; children: John Ryan, Christopher John, Jessica Marie. D in Podiatry, Ohio Coll. Podiatric Medicine, 1975; MS in Edn., U. Kans., 1982. Diplomate Am. Bd. Podiatric Surgery, Am. Bd. Podiatric Orthopedics and Primary Podiatric Medicine. Gen. practice podiatry Kansas City, Mo., 1977—, Overland Park, Kans., 1980—; clin. asst. prof. U. Health Scis., Kansas City, 1985—; clin. assoc. prof. Coll. Podiatric Medicine and Surgery U. Osteo. Medicine and Health Scis., Des Moines, 1985-92; clin. instr. Sch. Medicine U. Mo., Kansas City, 1987-95; founder, bd. dirs. Kansas City Podiatric Residency Program, Kansas City, 1982-91; adv. bd. Rockport Shoe Co. Contbr. articles to profl. jours. Cons. Mid-Am. Track and Field Assn., Lenexa, Kans., 1978-88; com. chmn. Boy Scouts Am., Overland Park, Kans.; coach Johnson County Soccer League, 1987-90, Cath. Youth Orgn. Basketball, 1995-96; sponsor 8 & 11 Baseball League, 1987-90; head coach 6th grade girls' basketball, 1995-96. 1st lt. USAF, 1975-77. Recipient Pres.'s award Ohio Sch. Podiatric Medicine, 1975; USAF scholar Armed Forces Health Professions, 1973-75. Fellow Am. Coll. Foot Surgeons, Acad. Podiatric Sports Medicine, Am. Coll. Primary Podiatric Medicine & Podiatric Orthopedics; mem. Mid-Am. Masters Field and Track Assn., Brit. Podiatry Assn. (hon.), Am. Bd. Primary Podiatric Medicine (founding dir.), Holy Cross Social Club (pres. 1983-84), Brookridge Country Club, Bally Club (Overland Park). Republican. Roman Catholic. Home: 8120 W 99th St Shawnee Mission KS 66212-3444 Office: 10550 Quivira #260 Overland Park KS 66215

LANDSKE, DOROTHY SUZANNE, state senator; b. Evanston, Ill., Sept. 3, 1937; d. William Gerald and Dorothy Marie (Drewes) Martin; m. William Steve Landske, June 1, 1957; children: Catherine Suzanne Jones, Jacqueline Marie Basilotta, Pamela Florence Snyder, Cheryl Lynn Boisson, Eric Thomas. Student St. Joseph's Coll., Ind. U., U. Chgo. Receptionist Cedar Lake Med. Clinic (Ind.) 1959-62; owner, operator Sues Bridal House, 1967-75; dep. clk.-treas., Cedar Lake, 1975; chief dep. twp. assessor Center Twp., Crown Point, Ind., 1976-78, twp. assessor, 1979-84, mem. Ind. Senate, 1984—, chmn. corrections, criminal and civil procedures com. Vice-chmn. Lake County Rep. Cen. Com., 1978-89. Mem. Council State Govts., Nat. Order Women Legislators, Nat. Council State Legislators, Bus. and Profl. Women, League Women Voters, Grange Ind. Farm Bur. Roman Catholic.

LANDWEHR, ARTHUR JOHN, minister; b. Northbrook, Ill., Mar. 8, 1934; s. Arthur John Sr. and Alice Eleanor (Borchardt) L.; m. Avonna Lee, Sept. 19, 1953; children: Arthur J. III, Andrea Lea Askow. BA, Drake U., 1956; BD, Garrett-Theol. Sem., 1959; DD (hon.), North Cen. Coll., 1980. Ordained to ministry Meth. Ch., 1959. Pastor Lyndon (Ill.) United Meth. Ch., 1956-59, Marseilles (Ill.) United Meth. Ch., 1959-65, Faith United Meth. Ch., Lisle, Ill., 1965-69; sr. minister First United Meth. Ch., Elmhurst, Ill., 1969-75, Evanston, Ill., 1975-88; sr. minister Grace United Meth. Ch., Naperville, Ill., 1988—; trustee Garrett-Evang. Theol. Sem., Evanston, 1976—, 1st v.p. bd. trustees, 1977-86; del. to gen. conf. United Meth. Ch., 1976, 80, 84, 88, World Meth. Conf., Nairobi, Kenya, 1986; Wilson lectr., 1987; preacher Adams Sermon Bloomington, Ind., 1991, N.Mex. Ann. Conf., 1992, N.W. Tex. Conf., 1992. Author: In the Third Place, 1972; contbr. articles to profl. jours. Convenor Blue Ribbon Com. for Referendum on Expanded Gambling in Ill., 1994. Recipient citation for human rels. City of Lisle, 1969; study grantee World Coun. Chs., Sri Lanka, 1983, Ecumenical Inst. for Advanced Studies, Tantur, Israel, 1977. Mem. AAAS, Am. Acad. Religion, Am. Theol. Soc., Ill. Bar Assn. (interprofl. cooperation com. 1991-95), Order of St. Luke, Univ. Club (Evanston, Ill., pres. 1986-87). Home: Box 157 Chama NM 87520-0460 Office: Grace United Meth Ch 300 E Gartner Rd Naperville IL 60540-7424

LANDWEHR, BRENDA, state legislator, financial executive. Address: 1927 N Gow Wichita KS 67203

LANE, AL, state legislator; m. Peggy Lane. Grad. Ohio State U. Kans. state rep. Dist. 25, internat. airline capt., ret. Home: 6529 Sagamore Rd Shawnee Mission KS 66208-1946*

LANE, ALFRED L., brokerage executive; b. Appleton City, Mo., Jan. 22, 1938. CPCU. Account exec. Merrill Lynch, Cleve., 1976-79, E.F. Hutton, Cleve., 1979-83; assoc. v.p. Dean Witter Reynolds, Cleve., 1983—. With USMC, 1955-58. Mem. Life Underwriters Tng. Coun. Republican. Home: 342 Bonds Pky Berea OH 44017-1273 Office: Dean Witter Reynolds Galleria Towers at Erie View 31st Fl Cleveland OH 44114

LANE, BRIAN M., management executive; b. Lafayette, Ind., Oct. 12, 1951; s. Robert M. and Juanita J. (Martz) L.; m. Joyce Lynn Hiatt, June 16, 1973; 1 child, Brianne. BSME, Purdue U., 1973. Engr. Logansport (Ind.) Machine Co. Inc., 1973-75, gen. sales mgr., 1973-81, v.p. sales, 1981-84, v.p. engr., 1984-86, exec. v.p., mgr., 1986—; dir. Buck Chuck Co., Kalamazoo, 1987—. Patentee Quick Change Jaw, 1988. Methodist. Home: 730 Cherokee Ave Lafayette IN 47905-1872

LANE, CAROL ELAINE, nurse; b. Omaha, June 28, 1935; d. William Jacob and Alice Marie (Harris) Hatcher; m. Neil Vinton Lane, Aug. 28, 1954 (div. 1976); children: Becky Lane Larson, Mitchel Neil, Paul Bradley. ADN, Iowa We. Community Coll., 1971; BSN, Bishop Clarkson Coll., 1987; grad., Bellevue Univ., 1987. RN, Nebr., Iowa. Nurse Mercy Hosp., Council Bluffs, Iowa, 1971—, staff float nurse, 1982, staff nurse, charge nurse, 1982-84. Phlebotomist Health Fair, Council Bluffs, 1987-91; vol. Council Bluffs Pub. Health Dept., 1975; circle chmn. 1st Presbyn. Ch., Red Oak, Iowa, 1961-62. Mem. Alumni Assn. Bishop Clarkson Nursing Coll. (fund raising com. 1991). Home: 414 Voorhis St Council Bluffs IA 51503-4444

LANE, GARY BARTON, quality assurance professional; b. Mpls., Sept. 1, 1951. Student, U. Minn. With quality control dept. Rosemount Engring., Burnsville, Minn., 1979-86; stockbroker R.J. Steichem & Assocs., Mpls., 1986-90; v.p. QC Inspection Svc., Inc., Burnsville, 1990—. Home: 15898 Harwell Ave Apple Valley MN 55124-4821 Office: QC Inspection Svcs Inc 1121 Riverwood Dr Burnsville MN 55337-1501

LANE, MEREDITH ANNE, botany educator, museum curator; b. Mesa, Ariz., Aug. 4, 1951; d. Robert Ernest and Elva Jewell (Shilling) L.; m. Donald W. Longstreth, Apr. 6, 1974 (div. Feb. 1985). BS, Ariz. State U., 1974, MS, 1976; PhD, U. Tex., 1980. Asst. prof. U. Colo., Boulder, 1980-88, assoc. prof., 1988-89; assoc. prof., curator div. botany Natural History Mus., U. Kans., Lawrence, 1989—; vis. asst. prof. U. Wyo., Laramie, 1985-86; vis. scholar U. Conn., Storrs, 1989; cons. editor McGraw-Hill Ency. of Sci. and Tech., N.Y.C., 1985-92; program dir. Nat. Sci. Found., 1995-97; rsch. assoc. Smithsonian Inst., 1995—. Editor Plant Sci. Bull., 1990-94; contbr. over 25 articles to profl. jours. Mem. Am. Soc. Plant Taxonomists (sec. 1986-88, program dir. 1986-90, councillor 1993-96, Cooley award 1982), Bot. Soc. Am. (sect. chmn. 1984-86, sect. sec. 1986-90), Internat. Orgn. for Plant Biosystematics (councillor 1989-92), Internat. Assn. Plant Taxonomists, Calif. Bot. Soc. Office: R L McGregor Herbarium 2045 Constant Ave Lawrence KS 66047-3729

LANE, PATRICIA PEYTON, nursing consultant; b. Danville, Ill., Oct. 5, 1929; d. Louis Weldon Sr. and Ruth Jeanette (Meyer) Peyton; m. H.J. Lane, Dec. 23, 1950 (div.); children: Jennifer Lane-Carr, Peter Lane, Amelia Ozog. Diploma, St. Elizabeth Hosp., 1950; BA in Psychology magna cum laude, Rosary Coll., 1974; postgrad., Lakeview Coll. of Nursing, Danville, Ill., 1987-88; student, Triton Jr. Coll., River Grove, Ill., 1969-72. Staff nurse St. Elizabeth Hosp., Danville, Ill., 1950; staff nurse nursery Ill. Rsch. and Ednl. Hosp., Chgo., 1951, charge nurse tumour clinic, 1951-54; res. sch. nurse elem. schs., Oak Park, Ill., 1969-78; sta. mgr. Oak Park-River Infant Welfare, Oak Park, Ill., 1972-76; vision and hearing screener suburban elem. schs., Ill., 1980-82; sch. nurse West Subrban Assn. Spl. Edn., Cicero, 1978-80; caseworker, counselor Vermilion County Mental Health and Devel. Disabilities, Inc., Danville, 1983-86; case coord., nurse cons. Crosspoint Human Svcs., Danville, 1986-88; staff nurse psychiat. acute care unit Community Hosp. of Ottawa, Ill., 1988-89; dir. social svcs. Pleasant View Luther Home, Ottawa, 1989-93; clin. case coord. Access Svcs., Inc., Mendota, Ill., 1993—; cmty. ombudsman LaSalle County Alternatives for the Older Adult, Peru, Ill., 1993—; cons. in field. Mem. ANA, Ill. State Nurses Assn. (cert. psychiat./mental nurse). Office: Alternatives for the Older Adult 2000 Luther Dr Peru IL 61354-1205

LANE, ROGER LEE, zoology educator, researcher; b. Mt. Carmel, Ill., July 4, 1945; s. Andy Lee and Flora Baldridge (Walton) L.; m. Paulette Hruban, July 17, 1968; children: Leigh S., Brooke C., Taylor C. BS, U. Nebr., 1968, MS, 1971, PhD, 1974. Lectr. zoology John F. Kennedy Coll., Wahoo, Nebr., 1973-75; asst. prof. Kent State U., Ashtabula, Ohio, 1975-80, assoc. prof., 1980—; mem. long-range planning com. Ashtabula Area City Schs., 1982, sci. adv. com., 1985; mem. citizens adv. panel Chem. Industry, Ashtabula, 1994—; v.p. Ashtabula County Animal Protective League, 1979-90. Contbr. articles to profl. jours. With U.S. Army, 1968-70. Acad. Challenge grantee Ohio Bd. Regents, 1986-92. Mem. Am. Malacological Union, Am. Microscopical Soc., Ohio Acad. Sci., Crustacean Soc. Democrat. Roman Catholic. Home: 2706 Burlingham Dr Ashtabula OH 44004 Office: Kent State U Ashtabula Campus Ashtabula OH 44004

LANE, STEVEN JOSEPH, middle and high school principal, physical education educator; b. Fort Dodge, Iowa, Mar. 23, 1949; s. Joseph LeRoy and Beverly Kay (Yarbrough) L.; m. Rebecca Sue Nelson, Oct. 29, 1948; children: Jason Robert, Michael Joseph. BA, Buena Vista Coll., 1987; MEd, U. S.D., 1993. Farmer Lime Springs, Iowa, 1973-77, Renwick, Iowa, 1977-86; mgr. Pioneer Cheese Coop., Renwick, Iowa, 1985-86; tchr., coach Pomeroy (Iowa) Cmty. Sch., 1987-93; mid. sch. and H.S. prin. Orient (Iowa)-Macksburg Sch., 1993—; v.p. Farmers Coop. Elevator, Renwick, 1984-85. Mem. Pomeroy Town and Country Boosters, 1992-93. Served to sgt. U.S. Army, 1969-70, Vietnam. Mem. ASCD, Pomeroy Edn. Assn. (v.p. 1992-93), Lions, Viona Lodge (Master 1982), Phi Delta Kappa. Democrat. Methodist. Home: 102 E Division St Orient IA 50858-5010 Office: Orient Macksburg Cmty Sch Hwy 25 Orient IA 50858

LANEY, RICHARD BRYANT, marketing executive; b. Akron, Ohio, June 9, 1965; s. Samuel Richard and Sharon Ellaine (Bollinger) L.; m. Leigh Andrea Marshall, May 21, 1990; children: Bryant Cameron, Brendan Richard, Rebecah Leigh. Student, U. Akron, Ohio, 1984-87, Evangel Coll., Springfield, Mo., 1985. Assoc. editor Herald Pub., Akron, 1987-88; editor Akron Bus. Reporter, 1988-90; pres., owner Cambridge Comm., Akron, 1989-92, pres., co-owner, 1994—; dir. mktg. Controlled Power, Canton, Ohio, 1992-94; mktg. cons. Controlled Power, Canton, 1994-95, various pub. schs., Akron/Canton, 1990-95, various businesses, Akron/Canton, 1990-95. Contbr. articles to profl. jours. Campaign mgr. Rep. Mayoral Candidate, Akron, 1988, Rep. State Rep. Candidate, Akron, 1992; event organizer Celebration of Inc., City Green, Ohio, 1992; sch. levy coms. Green Local Schs., City Green, 1988-95. Mem. numerous mktg. and advt. orgns. Office: Richard Laney and Co PO Box 985 Uniontown OH 44685

LANG, CATHERINE LOU, small business owner; b. Hugo, Okla., June 12, 1946; d. John Wilburn Sr. and Velma Lou (Evans) Freeman; m. Laurence Larry Lang, Nov. 20, 1974; children: Tana Louise, Henry Nathan, Gina Elise; 1 stepchild, Michael. BA in Sociology and Econs., Northeastern State U., 1970. Co-owner C&L Jewelry, Waterford, Mich., 1980—; landlord of rental home, Novi, Mich., 1977-93. Active Northwest Child Rescue Women Jr. League, 1975—, League of Women of Detroit; mem. PTA Mercy Sch. for Girls, Farmington, Mich., 1990-94, Walled Lake Mich. Schs., 1981—; mem. Great Decisions, active in leadership, 1988; team parent Team Elan Skating Team, 1991-92; mem. Lakes Assn., Novi, 1992; mem. Covenant Bapt. Ch., 1977—, Am. Bapt. Women. Recipient (with son) Arrow of Light pin Cub Scouts. Mem. AAUW (charter Novi-Northville br.), Internat. Fedn. Univ. Women, Nat. Assn. Investors Corp., Detroit Skating Club, Top Stock Stock Club. Democrat. Home: 1369 E Lake Dr Novi MI 48377-1442 Office: C&L Jewelry 924 W Huron St Waterford MI 48328-3726

LANG, ELVIRA VALENTINA, radiologist, educator; b. Mannheim, West Germany, Oct. 7, 1953; married. MD magna cum laude, U. Heidelberg, Germany, 1978. Diplomate Am. Bd. Radiology, qualified interventional radiology. Intern in radiology, surgery, medicine U. Heidelberg, 1977-78, resident in radiology, 1978-83, jr. faculty radiologist, 1983-84; intern, fellowship in angiography U. Calif., San Diego, 1985-86, resident in radiology, 1986-88; fellowship in interventional and vascular radiology Mallinckrodt Inst. of Radiology, St. Louis, 1988-89; asst. prof. of radiology Stanford U. Sch. of Medicine, 1989-94; assoc. prof. radiology U. Iowa Coll. of Medicine, Iowa City, 1994—, dir. of interventional radiology, 1994—; chief of vascular and interventional radiology VA med. Ctr., Palo Alto, 1989-94, head of radiology rsch. lab., 1989-94. Reviewer Am. Jour. Roentgenology, Jour. Vascular and Interventional Radiology, Investigative Radiology, Acad. Radiology. Rsch. grantee Dept. of Vets. Affairs HSR&D Field Program, 1994—; recipient numerous rsch. grants. Mem. Am. Roentgen Ray Soc., Radiol. Soc. N.Am., Assn. Univ. Radiologists, Soc. Cardiovascular and Interventional Radiology (rsch. com. 1992—), Am. Assn. Women Radiologists, Western Angiographic and Interventional Soc., Am. Coll. Radiology, Soc. Invasive Therapy, Internat. Soc. Exptl. Clin. Hypertension. Office: U of Iowa Hosps and Clinics Dept of Radiology 3890 JPP 200 Hawkins Dr Iowa City IA 52242

LANG, ERNST FREDERICK, radiologist; b. Detroit, Dec. 16, 1916; s. Ernst Frederick and Alice Rhoda (Whitehead) L.; m. Virginia Davis, June 14, 1941; children: William, Carolyn, Elizabeth, Barbara. AB with distinction, U. Mich., 1938, MD, 1941. Diplomate Am. Bd. Radiology (radiology and nuclear medicine); lic. physician, Mich. Intern Harper Hosp., Detroit, 1941, resident in radiology, 1942-45, radiologist, 1945—; radiologist L. Reynolds Assoc., Detroit, 1945—; clin. assoc. prof. radiology Wayne State U. Coll. Medicine, Detroit, 1973-82. Asst., assoc., acting editor Am. Jour. Roentgenology, 1971-80. 1st lt. AUS, 1941. Fellow Am. Roentgen Ray Soc. (exec. coun. 1968-77, 1st v.p. 1976-77)); mem. Radiol. Soc. N.Am., Mich. Radiol. Soc. (sec., treas. 1955-58, pres. 1973-75).

LANG, JOHN ERNEST, lawyer; b. Arkansas City, Kans., Dec. 27, 1936; s. Ernest R. and Ruth (Evans) L.; m. Joleen C. Jilka, Nov. 22, 1959; children: Jill Kay Lang Gobble, Jeffrey R. BS, U. Kans., 1958; JD, Washburn U., 1962. Bar: Kans. 1962, U.S. Dist. Ct. Kans. 1962, U.S. Ct. Appeals (10th cir.) 1969. Mcpl. judge City of Wamego, Kans., 1967-78; county atty. Pottawatomie County, Kans., 1967-70, county counselor, 1977—; sole practitioner Wamego, 1961—; bd. dirs. First Nat. Bank, Wamego. Trustee The Stormont Found., Topeka, 1989-95; trustee Wamego City Hosp., 1969-89, chmn. bd. trustees, 1988-89; chair Gov.'s Com. on Instnl. Mgmt. and Comty. Mental Health, Topeka, 1974-80; mem. Gov.'s Adv. Com. on Criminal Adminstrn., Topeka, 1970-72. With USAR, 1956-62. Mem. Kans. Bar Assn., Pottawatomie County Bar Assn. Democrat. Methodist. Office: PO Box 2 Wamego KS 66547-0002

LANG, KRISTOPHER DOUGLAS, electrical engineer; b. Mt. Vernon, Ohio, Oct. 3, 1965; s. Timothy Jamesen and Veronica Ann (Lafferty) L.; Carol Lynn Sorensen, June 2, 1990; children: Conor Alden. BSEE, GMI Engring. & Mgmt. Inst., 1988; MSEE, Oakland U., 1992. Fire control systems engr. Gen. Dynamics-Land Systems Divsn., Sterling Heights, Mich., 1983-94; project engr. GM-Powertrain Group, Romulus, Mich., 1994—. Republican. Roman Catholic. Home: 3243 Garden Ave Royal Oak MI 48073 Office: GM Powertrain Group 37350 Ecorse Rd Romulus MI 48174

LANG, LOUIS I. (07), state legislator, lawyer; b. Chgo., Nov. 26, 1949; s. Eugene and Shirley (Busel) L.; m. Teri Rosenbaum, 1987; children: David, Adam, Matthew Paul, Chad Paul. BA, U. Ill., 1971; JD, DePaul U., 1974. Ptnr. Feingold, Lang & Levy, 1977—; attorney Niles Twp. Reg. Dem. Orgn., Ill., 1977-87; Dist. 16 rep. Ill. Ho. Reps., Springfield, 1987—; Ill. Ho. Reps. Dem. fl. rep., vice chmn. state govt. adminstrn. com. and judiciary I com., mem. appropriations II, cities and villages, human svcs., higher edn., children, aging and mental health select, health care, real estate law, and rules coms., and spl. com. on flicts of interest. Mem. Mayor's Task Force on Traffic; campaign mgr. Samuel Berger for State Senate, Ill., 1980; bd. dirs. Holocaust Meml. Found., 1987—; bd. dirs. Jewish Cmty. Ctr., 1987—. Named Citizen of the Month, Lerner Newspapers, 1986. Mem. Niles Twp. Dem. Orgn., Decalogue Soc. of Lawyers, Ill. Bar Assn., Chgo. Bar Assn., Hillel Found., Pi Lambda Phi. Home: 5123 Jerome Ave Skokie IL 60077-3359*

LANG, MARY LOU, educational administrator; b. LaJolla, Calif.; d. James O. and Harrie Lu (Jones) E. BA, Columbia Coll., 1986; MA in history, U. Mo., Columbia, 1989. Dir. financial aid Kemper Military Sch., Boonville, Mo., 1989, Columbia Coll., Columbia, Mo., 1989—; staff Columbia Coll., Columbia, 1992—; selector/reader Mo. Tchr. Edn. Scholar., 1992-93. Mem. Mo. Assn. Fin. Aid Pers. (sec. 1994—, chmn. legis. com.), Midwest Assn. fin. Aid Adminstrs., Nat. Assn. Fin. Aid Adminstrs. Office: Columbia Coll 1001 Rogers Columbia MO 65216

LANGA, KENNETH A., physician; b. Mt. Vernon, N.Y., Jan. 21, 1963; s. Robert Michael and Nancy Ruth (Fairstein) L.; m. Lucy Nelson, June 23, 1990; children: Melanie Elizabeth, Daniel Jeffery. BA summa cum laude, Amherst Coll., 1985; PhD, U. Chgo., 1992, MD, 1994. Lic. physician, Mich. Lectr. U. Chgo., 1992-93; resident U. Mich. Med. Ctr., Ann Arbor, 1994—. Pew fellow U. Chgo., 1988-92. Mem. ACP, Soc. Gen. Internal Medicine, Phi Beta Kappa. Office: U Mich Med Ctr Dept Internal Medicine 1500 E Medical Center Dr Ann Arbor MI 48109

LANGBO, ARNOLD GORDON, food company executive; b. Richmond, B.C., Can., Apr. 13, 1937; s. Osbjourn and Laura Marie (Hagen) L.; m. Martha Marie Miller, May 30, 1959; children: Sharon Anne, Maureen Bernice, Susan Colleen, Roderick Arnold, Robert Wayne, Gary Thomas, Craig Peter, Keith Edward. Student, U. B.C. Retail salesman Kellogg Co., Vancouver, 1956-57; dist. mgr. Kellogg Co., Prince George, B.C., 1957-60; supermarket salesman Kellogg Co., Vancouver, 1960; dist mgr. Kellogg Co., Winnipeg, Man., 1964-65; acct. mgr. Kellog Co. of Can., Ltd., Toronto, 1965-67; sales staff asst. Kellogg Co., Battle Creek, Mich., 1967-69, adminstrv. asst. to pres., 1969; exec. v.p. Kellogg Co. of Can. Ltd., London, Ont., 1970; v.p. sales and mktg. Kellogg Salada Can. Ltd., Toronto, 1971-74, sr. v.p. sales and mktg., 1974-76, pres., chief exec. officer, 1976-78; pres. food products div. Kellogg U.S., Battle Creek, 1978-81; past exec. v.p. Kellogg Co., Battle Creek, group exec. v.p., 1983-86, exec. v.p., 1986—; pres. Kellogg Internat., Battle Creek, 1986—; pres. Mrs. Smith's Frozen Foods Co. (subs. Kellogg Co.), Battle Creek, 1983-85, chmn., chief exec. officer, 1985—; pres. Kellogg Internat., 1986—, pres., COO, internat. bd. dirs., 1990—; chmn., CEO Kellogg Co., Battle Creek, 1992—, also dir.; bd. dirs. Johnson & Johnson, Grocery Mfg. Am., Gilmore Int. Keyboard Festival. Vice-pres. Hockey Internat., Battle Creek; trustee Albion Coll.; mem. Canadian-Am. Com., B.C. Premier's Econ. Adv. Coun.; mem. adv. bd. J. L. Kellogg Grad. Sch. Mgmt., Northwestern U.; bd. dirs. Gilmore Internat. Keyboard Festival. Mem. Am. Frozen Food Inst. (bd. dirs., vice chmn. 1985), Grocery Products Mfrs. Can. (bd. dirs.), Tea Council of Can. (bd. dirs.). Office: Kellogg Co Box 3599 1 Kellogg Sq Battle Creek MI 49017-3534*

LANGE, DAVID CHARLES, journalist; b. Natrona Hts., Pa., Oct. 14, 1949; s. Charles Manfred Lange and Helga (Hingst) Faverty; m. Linda Gaiduk, June 29, 1974; children: Erik David, Anthony Charles. BA in Journalism, Kent State U., 1975; postgrad., Akron U., 1980-83. Placement specialist Goodwill Industries Cleve., 1976-77; mng. editor, sports editor Chagrin Valley Times, Chagrin Falls, Ohio, 1977-82; editor Chagrin Valley Times/Solon Times, Chagrin Falls, 1988—; features editor, Sunday editor Lake County Telegraph, Painesville, Ohio, 1982-83; editor Geauga Times Leader, Chardon, Ohio, 1983-84; editor-in-chief Habitat, Cleve., 1984-88. Cub scout den leader, asst. leader Boy Scouts Am. Pack 102, Chagrin Falls, 1992—. With USN, 1968-71, Vietnam. Recipient Democracy in Housing award Cleve. Assn. Real Estate Brokers, 1988. Mem. Soc. Profl. Journalists (Excellence in Journalism award human interest reporting 1981), Ohio Newspaper Assn. (Hooper award for editl. writing 1991-92, 94, 96, 2d place 1990, 93, Hooper award 1993), Chagrin Valley C. of C., Solon C. of C., Cleve. Press Club, Nat. Newspaper Assn., VFW, Am. Legion, Vietnam Vets. Am. (treas. Western res. chpt. 1990—). Home: 8353 Chagrin Rd Chagrin Falls OH 44023 Office: Chagrin Valley Times PO Box 150 Chagrin Falls OH 44022

LANGE, DOUGLAS KEITH, university administrator; b. Seymour, Ind., Apr. 2, 1953; s. John Richard and Hilda Ann (Wolka) L.; m. Suzanne Starr Leitch, May 24, 1981;children: Adam W., Sara C. BS, Ball State U., 1975, MA, 1976; EdD, Vanderbilt U., 1989. Program advisor Greek affairs Iowa State U., Ames, 1976-80; asst. dean student affairs Vanderbilt U., Nashville, 1980-92; dean students S.D. Sch. Mines & Tech., Rapid City, 1992—; cons. U. N.D., 1978, U. Nebr., 1979; bd. dirs. Coun. for Advancement Standards, 1982—, sec., 1996—. Mgr. Little League, Ames, 1979; pres.. Holy Trinity Luth. Ch., Nashville, 1987. Named Vol. of Yr. Tenn. Soc. to Prevent Blindness, 1986. Mem. Nat. Assn. Student Personnel Adminstrs. (bd. dirs. region IV-West 1993—, local arrangements chair for region conf. 1995), Assn. Frat. Advisers (founder, pres. 1981-82), Am. Coll. Personnel Assn., S.D. Coll. Pers. Assn., Nat. Orientation Dirs. Assn., Rapid City C. of C. (svcs. com. 1994—, chair 1996—), Sigma Phi Epsilon. Democrat.

LANGE, FREDERICK EDWARD, JR., computer information systems architect; b. Johnstown, Pa., Oct. 21, 1946; s. Frederick Edward and Jean Louise (Huebner) L.; m. Karen Ann Mawson, Mar. 15, 1975; 1 child, Sharon Ann. BA in Social Scis., Cleve. State U., 1969, MA in Econs., 1978. Cert. secondary tchr., Ohio. Vol. Peace Corps, Liberia and Micronesia, 1969-73; tchr. Cleve. Pub. Schs., 1973-74; dir. Westside Inst. Tech., Cleve., 1974-81;

systems analyst Case Western Res. U., Cleve., 1982-83; systems engr. Profl. Support, Inc., Brecksville, Ohio, 1983-91; analyst Setpoint, Brecksville, 1991-93; prin. cons. Cap Gemini Am., Beechwood, Ohio, 1994—; bd. dirs. Zoe, Inc., Cleve., Fast Refund Svc. Editor: Fuel Efficiency and Safety, 1979; contbr. Data Mgmt. Rev. Mem. Richmond Heights (Ohio) Civic League, 1986, Northeast Ohio Returned Vol. Assn. (Beyond War award 1987), Cleve., 1978—. Mem. Am. Econs. Assn., Data Processing Mgmt. Assn., Assn. Computing Machinery, Instument Soc. Am. (Dedicated Svc. award 1980), Javelin Class Assn. (fleet capt. 1982-83, sec. 1987-88, commodore 1989-91). Home: 4850 Lindsey Ln Cleveland OH 44143-2928 Office: Cap Gemini Am 25800 Science Park Dr Beechwood OH 44122

LANGE, GERALD F., state legislator; m. Alice Lange; 4 children. Student, U. N.D., Georgetown U., U. Navarra, Spain. Mem. S.D. Senate, mem. transp. retirement laws and taxation coms., chmn. local govt. com.; prof., farmer. Home: RR 3 Box 109 Madison SD 57042-9342*

LANGE, KATHERINE JOANN, writer; b. Wyandotte, Mich., Feb. 8, 1957; d. James DiDi and Margaret Ann (Kirk) Putman. Student, Normandale Coll., 1980-82. V.p., artist mgr. The T.S.J. Prodns. Inc., Richfield, Minn., 1975—; mgr., agt. The T.S.J. Booking Agy., Richfield, 1980-96; asst. editor, author Songwriter U.S.A. mag., Atlanta, 1986-87; staff writer Music Mgmt. and Internat. Promotion mag., Copenhagen, 1983—; pres. Katherine's Greetings, 1994—, Internat. Literary Concepts, Mpls., 1996—. Contbr. articles to Sun Newspapers, Songwriter Connection, Woman's Press. Mem. ASCAP, NAFE, Am. Fedn. Musicians. Democrat. Lutheran. Home and Office: Internat Literary Concepts Internat Literary Concepts 422 Pierce St NE Minneapolis MN 55413-2514

LANGE, SCOTT LESLIE, communications company executive, voice professional; b. Chgo., July 10, 1946; s. Harry W. and Evelyn (Udell) L.; m. Linda A. Shoenthal, Mar. 30, 1969; 1 child, Stephen H. BS in Speech, Northwestern U., 1968. Prodn. mgr., announcer WCOG Radio, Greensboro, N.C., 1971-72; writer, producer, dir. ARC, Washington, 1973-78; mgr. audio-visual services Am. Bankers Assn., Washington, 1978-79; writer, producer, dir. AT&T Communications, Washington, 1979-82, Cin., 1982-84; pres. Lange Communications, Inc., Cin., 1984—. Writer, producer, dir. numerous films, videotapes, radio and TV pub. service announcements, slide programs. Served with U.S. Army, 1968-71, Vietnam. Recipient Cert. Outstanding Creativity, U.S. TV Commls. Festival, 1973, 75, Gold Quill of Excellence award Internat. Assn. Bus. Communicators, 1981. Mem. AFTRA, Internat. TV Assn. (pres. D.C. chpt. 1981, Golden Reel of Merit award 1978, Golden Reel of Excellence award 1980), Soc. Motion Picture and TV Engrs. Jewish. Home and Office: Lange Communications Inc 2692 Montchateau Dr Cincinnati OH 45244-3229

LANGEL, ANN ELIZABETH, journalist; b. St. Croix Falls, Wis., July 31, 1963; d. Donald Rae and Clarice Kathryn (Johansen) L. BA, U. Wis., Eau Claire, 1985. Pub. rels. dir. U.S. Water Polo, Colorado Springs, Colo., 1986-87; staff writer Waterloo (Iowa) Courier, 1987-95, Post-Crescent, Appleton, Wis., 1995-96; project coord. Lawrence U., Appleton, Wis., 1996—. Vol. tutor Adult Literacy Program, Waterloo, 1994-95. Mem. Soc. Profl. Journalists, Delta Zeta Sorority (province alumnae dir. 1991-96). Democrat. Roman Catholic. Home: 2116 Henry St #16 Neenah WI 54956

LANGENFIELD, DAVID ALLEN, electrical engineer; b. Washington, Mo., Mar. 15, 1960; s. Arvil H. and Bertha Lee L. BSEE, U. Mo., Rolla, 1983; MSEE, U. Mo., St. Louis, 1989. Registered profl. engr., Mo. Sr. elec. engr. McDonnell Douglas, St. Louis, 1983-88; mgr. product devel. - elec. Mark Andy, Inc., Chesterfield, Mo., 1988—. Mem. Immaculate Conception Ch., Union, Mo., 1993—. Mem. IEEE. Roman Catholic. Home: 40 Lakeshore Ln Union MO 63084 Office: Mark Andy Inc 18081 Chesterfield Airport Rd Chesterfield MO 63005-1116

LANGENHORST, VICKY L., securities trader/dealer; b. Highland, Ill., Mar. 3, 1970. BA, So. Ill. U., Edwardsville, 1992. Sales asst. A.G. Edwards & Sons, Inc., Belleville, Ill., 1991—. Home: PO Box 271 Germantown IL 62245-0271 Office: AG Edwards & Sons Inc PO Box 23918 3601 N Belt W Belleville IL 62223

LANGEVIN, PEGGY ANN, physical therapist, rehabilitation director; b. Bessemer, Mich., Sept. 23, 1945; d. George Mathew and Anita Eloise (LaMarch) Winkowski; m. Ronald George Langevin, Aug.26, 1977. BS, No. Ill. U., 1969; cert. in phys. therapy, Mayo Clinic, 1968. Lic. phys. therapist, N.D., Minn., Calif., Wis. Phys. therapist No. Ill. U. Health Ctr., Dekalb, 1968-69; phys. therapist Dakota Hosp., Fargo, N.D., 1969-81, asst. dir. phys. therapy, 1981-93; dir. phys. therapy Lodi Meml. Hosp., Lodi, Calif., 1981; rehab. dir., phys. therapist Dorchester Nursing Ctr., Sturgeon Bay, Wis., 1994—. Mem. Am. Phys. Therapists Assn. (Wis. chpt., various former positions N.D. chpt.). Republican. Roman Catholic. Home: 1912 Fremont Algoma WI 54201

LANGFORD, CHARLES WESLEY, insurance agent; b. El Centro, Calif., Nov. 28, 1938; s. James Henry and Helen (Torok) L.; children: CHarles Wesley, Randal, Geoffrey, Jacqueline,. Student, U. Nebr., 1956, 57, So. Meth. U., 1960; CLU, Am. Coll. Life Underwriters, 1982. Gen. agt. Lincoln Nat. Life Ins., Cin., 1966-76, Ohio Nat. Life, Alliance, Nebr., 1976—. Mem. Panhandle Assn. Life Underwriters (dir. 1986—). Methodist. Home: 1204 Laramie Ave Alliance NE 69301-2538 Office: Ohio Nat Life PO Box 618 223 Box Butte Alliance NE 69301-0618

LANGHOLZ, ARMIN PAUL, communications educator; b. St. Paul, Minn., June 25, 1929; s. Christian Theodore and Selma Cora (Kamholz) L.; m. Mary Ann Green, Aug. 13, 1955; children: Kevin Dean, Lori Lee Langholz West. BS in Edn., Capital U., 1951; MA, Ohio State U., 1955, PhD, 1965. Instr. Capital U., Columbus, Ohio, 1954-57, asst. prof., 1957-66, assoc. prof., 1966-71, prof., 1971-94, dept. chmn., 1970-75, 80-93, prof. emeritus, 1994—; dir. comm. Met. Area Ch. Bd., Columbus, 1959-70; cons. Luth. Edn. Conf. of North Am., Washington, 1980-94. Prodr.: (children's TV program) Wonderbox, 1959-70, (religious news program) We Want to Know. Bd. dirs., chmn. Luth. Sr. City, Columbus, 1985-90; bd. dirs. cen. Ohio Luth. Social Svcs., 1990—. Sgt. 1st class U.S. Army, 1952-54, Korea. Recipient Stellhorn award, Capital U., 1985, Praestantia award for Disting. Teaching, Capital U., 1986. Mem. Speech Communication Assn., Ohio Speech Communication Assn., Broadcast Edn. Assn., Nat. Acad. TV Arts and Scis. (bd. dirs. Columbus/Dayton/Cin. chpt.), Nat. Collegiate Players, Tau Kappa Alpha. Home: 1348 Haddon Rd Columbus OH 43209-3101

LANGLEY, BRAD SCOTT, travel company executive; b. Goose Bay, Labrador, Can., July 25, 1961; s. Richard Allen and Frances Marguarte (Pyle) L.; m. Carol Anne Nelson, May 4, 1985; children: Scott, Nicholas. BS in Mktg., Ariz. State U., 1983; MBA in Fin., Loyola U., Chgo., 1989. Cert. incentive travel exec. Account exec. Ea. Airlines, Phoenix, 1983-85; mgr. nat. accounts Ea. Airlines, Miami, 1985-86; mgr. nat. conv. and incentive sales United Airlines, Chgo., 1986-90; dir. transp. planning Maritz Travel Co., St. Louis, 1990-91, v.p. product svcs., 1991-93, v.p. western area, 1993—. Mem. Soc. Incentive Travel Execs. (cert. exec.), Toastmasters. Republican. Methodist. Office: Maritz Travel Co 1395 N Highway Dr Fenton MO 63026-1929

LANGLEY, BYRON, state legislator; m. Deloris; 5 children. Mem. transp. com. Mem. N.D. Ho. of Reps., 1973-79; mem. N.D. Senate, 1985—, mem. indsl., bus., and labor com., mem. agr. com., mem. transp. com. farmer, rancher; owner elevator co. N.D. Stockman's Assn., Warwick Rod and Gun Club, Eagles, Elks. Office: RR 1 Box 70 Warwick ND 58381-9650*

LANGLEY, EILEEN ENOLA, accountant; b. Lindsborg, Kans., Mar. 24, 1921; d. Charles Alfred and Teresa Agnes (Nicholson) L. BA in Philosophy, Knas. State U., 1976, MA in Polit. Sci., 1981. Stenographer Burch, Litowich & Royce, Salina, Kans., 1939-40; acct. Fin. Office, Dept. of Army, U.S. Civil Svc., Ft. Riley, Kans., 1940-72; treas. Episcopal Ch., Junction City, Kans., 1961-79. Compiler: (books) Buried Ties to the Old Country, 1983, Abstract of 1905 Atlas of Ellis County, 1984, Genealogy of Konig Family, 1985, Genealogy of Niernberger Family, 1986, Abstract of Funeral Records, Niesley Funeral Home, 1921-1930, 1983, Index of Obituaries, The Ellis Review, 1891-1990, 1991, Genealogy of Nicholson Sisters, 1986, Genealogy of Sebastian J. Trefethen and Elizabeth Locke; & James Isaac Dalrymple and Elizabeth Hazen, 6 vols., 1994, (pamphlets) List of Volga-German Village Founders of Ellis County, 1989, Index, 1967 Canvass of Ellis County Cemeteries, 1983, Cemetery Canvasses of Hyacinth Cemetery, St. Johns Cemetery, St. Anthony Cemetery, 1986, Abstract of Ellis County Naturalization Records, 1872-1906, 1987; contbr. articles to profl. jours. Bd. dirs., treas. Ellis (Kans.) Pub. Libr., 1983-92; exec. com. Ctrl. Kans. Libr. System, Great Bend, 1986-95. Mem. Phi Beta Kappa, Phi Kappa Phi. Democrat. Episcopalian. Home: 107 W 11th St Ellis KS 67637

LANGLEY, GREG A., mechanical engineer; b. Independence, Kans., July 8, 1966. BSME, Kans. State U., Manhattan, 1988. Design engr. Marley Pump, Kansas City, Kans., 1988-92, Great Plains Industries, Wichita, 1993—. Mem. ASME, Soc. Plastic Engrs.

LANGLOIS, ESTHER, marital and family therapist, psychotherapist; b. Lafayette, Ind.. MS, Purdue U., 1938; MA, Ind. U., Indpls., 1957; postgrad., U. Chgo., 1944-46. Lic. ind. social worker, psychologist, Ohio; lic. marriage counselor, Mich.; diplomate Am. Bd. Examiners in Clin. Social Work. Asst. prof. Western Ill. State Tchrs. Coll., Macomb, 1940-48, Pratt Inst., Bklyn., 1949-50, Drexel Inst., Phila., 1952-53; trainee, resident Marriage Coun. Phila., 1950-52; med. social worker Phila. Gen. Hosp., 1953-55; social worker VA Hosp., Indpls., 1957-58; casework supr. Columbus (Ohio) State Hosp., 1958-60; caseworker, supr. Family Counseling Svc., Muncie, 1960-61; pvt. practice marriage and family counseling, Muncie, Ind., 1961-66; asst. prof. Ball State Tchrs. Coll., Muncie, Ind., 1962-63; cons. teens in detention, counselor parents Genesee County, Flint, Mich., 1967-75; conciliation counselor Cuyahoga County Domestic Rels. Ct., Cleve., 1975-82; pvt. practice marital and family therapy and psychotherapy, Lakewood, Ohio, 1982—. Mem. NASW, Acad. Cert. Social Workers, Am. Assn. for Marriage and Family Therapy, Ohio Psychol. Assn., Cleve. Psychol. Assn., AAUW. Episcopalian. Office: 18615 Detroit Ave #207 Cleveland OH 44107-3201

LANGSETH, KEITH, state legislator, farmer; b. Moorhead, Minn., Jan. 20, 1938; s. Norman Clifford and Ruth (Rosenquist) L.; m. Lorraine Mae Ersland, 1957; children: Danny, Gayle, Joy. Farmer; Dist. 9B rep. Minn. Ho. of Reps., St. Paul, 1975-78; Dist. 9 senator Minn. State Senate, St. Paul, 1980—; chmn. agr., transp. and semi-states divsn., Minn. State Senate; mem. Edn., Edn. Funding, Fin., Transp., and Met. Affairs coms. Chmn. Dist. 9 Dem.-Farmer-Labor party, Minn., 1973-74, chmn. Clay County Dem.-Farmer-Labor party, 1974. Office: RR 2 Box 81 Glyndon MN 56547-9631 also: State Senate State Capital Building Saint Paul MN 55155-1606*

LANGSLEY, DONALD GENE, psychiatrist, medical board executive; b. Topeka, Oct. 5, 1925; s. Morris J. and Ruth (Pressman) L.; m. Pauline R. Langsley, Sept. 9, 1955; children: Karen Jean, Dorothy Ruth, Susan Louise. B.A., SUNY, Albany, 1949; M.D., U. Rochester, 1953. Diplomate: Am. Bd. Psychiatry and Neurology (dir. 1976-80), Nat. Bd. Med. Examiners. Intern USPHS Hosp., San Francisco, 1953-54; resident psychiatry U. Calif., San Francisco, 1954-59; NIMH career tchr. in psychiatry U. Calif., 1959-61; candidate San Francisco and Chgo. insts. for psychoanalysis, 1958-67; asst. prof., assoc. prof. psychiatry U. Colo. Sch. Medicine, 1961-68; prof., chmn. dept. psychiatry U. Calif., Davis, 1968-77, U. Cin., 1977-81; prof. dept. psychiatry Northwestern U. Sch. Medicine, Chgo., 1981—; mem. psychiatry edn. com. NIMH, 1969-75; exec. v.p. Am. Bd. Med. Spltys., 1981-91; trustee Ednl. Commn. for Fgn. Med. Graduates, 1983-91; mem. adv. com. on Grad. Med. Edn. Dept. Def., 1986-87; bd. govs. EcuMed, 1983-85; bd. dirs. Nat. Resident Matching Program, 1982, sec. 1984-87, 89-91, pres. 1987-89. Author: The Treatment of Families in Crisis, 1968, Mental Health Education in the New Medical Schools, 1973, Peer Review Manual for Psychiatry, 1976, Handbook of Community Mental Health, 1981, Evaluating the Skills of Medical Specialists, 1983, Legal Aspects of Certification & Accreditation, 1983, Trends in Specialization, 1985, Hospital Privileges & Specialty Medicine, 1986, 2d edit., 1991, How To Evaluate Residents, 1986, How to Select Residents, 1988, Health Policy Issues in Graduate Medicine Education, 1992; contbr. articles to med. jours. Served with AUS, 1943-46; med. officer USPHS, 1953-54. Recipient Spl. awards Colo. Assn. for Mental Health, 1968, Spl. awards Sacramento Area Mental Health Assn., 1973. Fellow Am. Psychiat. Assn. (Hofheimer award 1971, pres. 1980-81, chmn. peer rev. com. 1975-77, Kiewit lectr. 1990, Adminstrv. Psychiatry award 1993), Am. Coll. Psychiatrists; mem. Ctrl. Calif. Psychiat. Soc. (pres. 1973-74), Colo. Psychiat. Soc. (pres.-elect 1967-68), Soc. Med. Adminstrs. Home and Office: 9445 Monticello Ave Evanston IL 60203-1117

LANGWORTHY, ASHER CLINTON, JR., real estate company executive; b. Kansas City, Mo., June 12, 1934; s. Asher Clinton and Georgia Ferree (Hodges) L.; m. Audrey Ione Hansen, Sept. 8, 1962; children: Kristin H., Julia H. AB, Harvard Coll., 1956. Lic. real estate broker, Kans. Pres. Langworthy Cos., Inc., Mission, Kans., 1980—; bd. dirs. UMB/KS Bank, Stagecoach Partnership. With CIC, U.S. Army, 1957-59. Mem. Johnson County Bd. Realtors, Harvard-Radcliffe Club Kansas City. Republican. Episcopalian. Office: Langworthy Cos Inc 6025 Martway St Ste 111 Mission KS 66202-3300

LANGWORTHY, AUDREY HANSEN, state legislator; b. Grand Forks, N.D., Apr. 1, 1938; d. Edward H. and Arla (Kuhlman) Hansen; m. Asher C. Langworthy Jr., Sept. 8, 1962; children: Kristin H., Julia H. BS, U. Kans., 1960, MS, 1962; postgrad., Harvard U., 1989. Tchr. jr. high sch. Shawnee Mission Sch. Dist., Johnson County, Kans., 1963-65; councilperson City of Prairie Village, Kans., 1981-85; mem. Kans. State Senate, 1985—; alt. del. Nat. Conf. State Legislatures, 1985-87, del., 1987—, nominating com., 1990-92, vice chair fed. budget and taxation com., 1994, chair fed. budget and taxation com., 1995-96; del. Midwestern Conf. State Legislatures, 1989. City co-chmn. Kassebaum for U.S. Senate, Prairie Village, 1978; pres. Jr. League Kansas City, Mo., 1977, Kansas City Eye Bank, 1980-82, chmn., 1983-85, bd. mem., 1977—; mem. bd. Greater Kansas City ARC, 1975—, pres., 1984, chmn. midwestern adv. coun., 1985-86, nat. bd. govs., 1987-93; mem. Johnson County C.C. Found., 1989—; mem. Leadership Kans., Germany Today Program, 1991; bd. dirs. Kans. Wildlife & Parks Fund; trustee Found. on Aging, 1992—; mem. nat. adv. panel Child Care Action Campaign, 1988—; mem. adv. com. Coro Found., 1989—; mem. adv. bd. Kans. Alliance for Mentally Ill., 1994—; hon. chair Fund Raiser for Health Partnership of Johnson County, 1995. Recipient Outstanding Vol. award Cmty. Svcs. Award Found., 1983, Confidence in Edn. award Friends of Edn., 1984, Pub. Svc. award as Kans. Legislator of Yr., Hallmark Polit. Action Com., 1991, Clara Barton Honor award Greater Kans. City ARC, Intergovtl. Leadership award League Kans. Mcpls., 1994, Disting. Pub. Svc. award United Cmty. Svcs. of Johnson County, 1995, Outstanding Achievement in Hist. Preservation award Alexander Majors Hist. House, 1995, Kansas City Spirit award, 1996. Mem. LWV, Women's Pub. Svc. Network, U. Kans. Alumni Assn. Episcopalian. Home: 6324 Ash St Prairie Village KS 66208-1369

LANGWORTHY, ROBERT BURTON, lawyer; b. Kansas City, Mo., Dec. 24, 1918; s. Herman Moore and Minnie (Leach) L.; m. Elizabeth Ann Miles, Jan. 2, 1942; children: David Robert, Joan Elizabeth Langworthy Tomek, Mark Burton. AB, Princeton U., 1940; JD, Harvard U., 1943. Bar: Mo. 1943, U.S. Supreme Ct 1960. Practiced in Kansas City, 1943—; assoc., then mem. and v.p. Linde, Thomson, Langworthy, Kohn & Van Dyke, P.C., 1943-91; pres., mng. shareholder Blackwood & Langworthy, P.C., Kansas City, Mo., 1991—; mng. mem. Blackwood & Langworthy, LC, Kansas City, Mo., 1996—; lectr. on probate, law sch. CLE courses U. Mo., Kansas City. Mem. bd. editors Harvard Law Rev., 1941-43; contbr. chpts. to Guardian Desk Book of Mo. Bar. Mem. edn. appeal bd. U.S. Dept. Edn., 1982-86; commr. Housing Authority Kansas City, 1963-71, chmn., 1969-71; chmn. Bd. Election Commrs. Kansas City, 1973-77; chmn. bd. West Ctrl. area YMCA, 1969—; mem. bd. Mid-Am. region YMCA, 1970-83, vice chmn., 1970-73, chmn., 1973-78; pres. Met. Bd. Kansas City (Mo.) YMCA (now YMCA of Greater Kansas City), 1965, bd. dirs., 1965—, mem. nat. bd. 1971-78, 79-83; bd. dirs. YMCA of the Rockies, 1974—, bd. sec., 1994—; chmn. bd. trustees Sioux Indian YMCAs, 1983—; bd. dirs. Armed Svcs. YMCA, 1984-85; pres. Met. Area Citizens Edn., 1969-72; chmn. Citizens Assn. Kansas City (Mo.), 1967, bd. dirs., 1995—; bd. dirs. Project Equality Kans.-Mo., 1967-80, pres., 1970-72, treas., 1972-73, sec., 1973-76; 1st v.p. Human Resources Corp. Kansas City, 1969-71, 72-73, bd. dirs., 1965-73; hon. v.p. Am. Sunday Sch. Union (now Am. Missionary Fellowship), 1965—; vice chmn. bd. trustees Kemper Mil. Sch., 1966-73; U.S. del. YMCA World Coun., Buenos Aires, 1977, Estes Park, Colo., 1981, Nyborg, Denmark, 1985; bd. dirs. Mo. Rep. Club, 1960—; del., mem. platform com. Rep. Nat. Conv., 1960; Rep. nominee for U.S. Congress, 1964; mem. gen. assembly Com. on Representation Presbyn., 1991—, moderator, 1993-94; commr. to gen. assembly Presbyn. Ch., 1984; moderator Heartland Presbyn., 1984. Lt. (j.g.) USNR, 1943-46; now capt. Res. ret. Mem. ABA, Kansas City Bar Assn. (chmn. probate law com. 1988-90, living will com. 1989-91), Mo. State Bar (chmn. probate and trust com. 1983-85, chmn. sr. lawyers com. 1991-93), Lawyers Assn. Kansas City, Harvard Law Sch. Assn. Mo. (v.p. 1973-74, pres. 1974-75, 85-87), Univ. Club (Kansas City), Leawood (Kans.) Country Club. Presbyterian (elder). Home: 616 W 69th St Kansas City MO 64113-1937 Office: 1220 Washington St Ste 300 Kansas City MO 64105-2245

LANIGAN, ROBERT J., packaging company executive; b. Bklyn., Apr. 26, 1928; s. John F. and Katherine (Sheehy) L.; m. Mary Elizabeth McCormick, Dec. 30, 1950; children: Kenneth J., Betty Jane Lanigan Snavely, Kathryn Ann Lanigan Pilewskie, Jeanne Marie Lanigan Schafer, Suzanne Marie Lanigan Georgetti. A.B. in Econs., St. Francis Coll., N.Y.C., 1950; B.A. (hon.), Nathaniel Hawthorne Coll., Antrim, N.H., 1979. Pres. domestic ops. Owens-Ill., Inc., Toledo, 1976-79, pres. internat. ops., 1979-82, pres., 1982-86, chief oper. officer, 1982-84, chief exec. officer, 1984-90, chmn. bd., 1984-91, chmn. emeritus, 1991—; bd. dirs. Chrysler Corp., Detroit, The Coleman Co., Denver, Sonat, Inc., Birmingham, Ala., Dun & Bradstreet Corp., N.Y.C., Sonat Offshore Drilling, Inc., Houston. Pres. Toledo Symphony Orch.; hon. trustee Toledo Mus. Art. Recipient achievement award St. Francis Coll. Alumni Assn., 1980. Mem. Burning Tree (Bethesda, Md.) Club, Quail Creek Country Club (Naples, Fla.), Belmont Country Club (Perrysburg, Ohio). Roman Catholic. Home: 13145 Valewood Dr Naples FL 33999-8506 Office: Owens-Ill Inc 1 Seagate Toledo OH 43666-1000

LANMAN, ROBERT CHARLES, pharmacology and toxicology educator; b. Bemidji, Minn., Oct. 2, 1930; s. Thomas Bradford and Inga Othelia (Engen) L.; m. Dorothy Ann Desnoyers, Nov. 9, 1957; children: Michael Bradford, Dianne Marie, Douglas Robert, Krista Ann. BS in Pharmacy, U. Minn., 1956, PhD in Pharmacology, 1967. Lic. pharmacist Minn. Pharmacologist Nat. Inst. Health, Bethesda, Md., 1961-66; asst. prof. pharmacology, medicine U. Mo., Kansas City, 1966-72; assoc. prof. U. Mo., 1972-81, prof., 1981—, chmn. div. pharmacology, 1987-92, emeritus prof. pharmacology, 1992—; cons. Hoechst Marion Roussel, Inc., Kansas City, 1985—; exec. v.p. Kansas City Analytical Svcs., Shawnee, Kans., 1984—. Contbr. over 20 aricles to profl. jours. With USN, 1948-52. Grantee in field, 1973-90. Mem. Am. Soc. Pharmacology Experimental Therapeutics, Am. Assn. Pharm. Scientists. Republican. Office: Kans City Analytical Svcs 12700 Johnson Dr Shawnee KS 66216-1643

LANNING, RANDALL R., financial consultant; b. Grand Rapids, Mich., Oct. 26, 1954; s. Elmer L. and Jewell (Tygesen) L.; m. Teresa S. Smith, Mar. 13, 1990; children: Samuel Ross, Morgan Terese. B Fin. and Mgmt., Western Mich. U., 1978. Mktg. mgr. Carnation Co., Grand Rapids, 1978-80; fin. cons. E.F. Hutton, Grand Rapids, 1981-89, Prudential Securities Inc., Grand Rapids, 1989—. Mem. steering com. Boy Scouts Am., Grand Rapids, 1988. Mem. Grand Rapids C. of C., Econs. Club Grand Rapids. Republican. Office: Prudential Securities Inc Campau Square Blvd 99 Monroe Ave NW Ste 101 Grand Rapids MI 49503-2639

LANSAW, CHARLES RAY, sales industry executive; b. Middletown, Ohio, Mar. 5, 1927; s. Edward Curtis and Lura (Tyra) L.; m. Joan Betty Kalbaugh, July 4, 1949; children: Charles E., Gail D., Leslie J., Kristi L. Student, Miami U., Oxford, Ohio, 1947-48; student engring., U. Cin., 1949-5l. Chief engr., sales mgr. Dupps Co., Germantown, Ohio, 1950-85; pres. C.R. Lansaw, Inc., Germantown, 1985—. Mem. Germantown Planing Commn.; bd. dirs. Germantown Pub. libr., 1991—; served with VOCA at Saratov and Volgograd, Russia, 1996, Internat. Exec. Svc. Corps, Alexandria, Egypt, 1993. With USNR, 1944-46; with Internat. Exec. Svc. Corp, Alexandria, Egypt, 1993. Mem. U.S. Power Squadron (past officer Dayton), Rotary (pres. Germantown 1987-88). Home: 73 Sue Dr Germantown OH 45327-1628 Office: 45 N Main St Germantown OH 45327-1349

LANSDEN, MICHAEL H., stockbroker; b. Springfield, Ill., June 25, 1970; s. Richard and Mary Sue (Loftus) L. BS, Ill. State U., 1992. Asst. broker Cal Chaney, Morton, Ill., 1992-94; stockbroker A.G. Edwards, Jacksonville, Ill., 1994—. Mem. Jacksonville C. of C., Kiwanis, Greeters Club, Investment Club. Home: 9B Sherwood Eddy Dr Jacksonville IL 62650-2746 Office: AG Edwards & Sons Inc PO Box 817 150 Dunlap Ct Jacksonville IL 62651

LANSWORTH, KAREN ANNE, bookkeeper; b. Hastings, Nebr., Mar. 22, 1952; d. Robert Charles and Opal Irene (Hammer) L. Grad. H.S., Fremont, Nebr. Bookkeeper GAC Fin., Fremont, Nebr., 1972-73, Capital Fin., Fremont, Nebr., 1973-74; clk. Dodge County Assessor's Office, Fremont, Nebr., 1974—; checker Save-Mart, Fremont, 1994—. Vol. Low Income Ministry, Fremont, 1993—. Republican. Lutheran. Home: 345 E 5th Ave Apt 5 Fremont NE 68025

LANTZ, ERIC A., design engineer manager; b. Red Oak, Iowa, Nov. 6, 1950. BS, Iowa State U., 1972. Farmer Red Oak, Iowa, 1972-90; design engr. mgr. Interwest Svcs., Red Oak, 1990—. Office: Interwest Svcs 103 S Broadway St # 93 Red Oak IA 51566-2601

LANTZ, JOANNE BALDWIN, academic administrator emeritus; b. Defiance, Ohio, Jan. 26, 1932; d. Hiram J. and Ethel A. (Smith) Baldwin; m. Wayne E. Lantz. BS in Physics and Math., U. Indpls., 1953; MS in Counseling and Guidance, Ind. U., 1957; PhD in Counseling and Psychology, Mich. State U., 1969; LittD (hon.), U. Indpls., 1985; LHD (hon.), Purdue U., 1994; LLD (hon.), Manchester Coll., 1994. Tchr. physics and math. Arcola (Ind.) High Sch., 1953-57; guidance dir. New Haven (Ind.) Sr. High Sch., 1957-65; with Ind. U.-Purdue U., Fort Wayne, 1965—, interim chancellor, 1988-89, chancellor, 1989-94, chancellor emeritus, 1994—; bd. dirs. Ft. Wayne Nat. Corp., Foellinger Found. Contbr. articles to profl. jours. Mem. Ft. Wayne Econ. Devel. Adv. Bd. and Task Force, 1988-91, Corp. Coun., 1988-94; bd. advisors Leadership Ft. Wayne, 1988-94; mem. adv. bd. Ind. Sml. Bus. Devel. Ctr., 1988-90; trustee Ancilla System, Inc., 1984-89, chmn. human resources com., 1985-89, exec. com., 1985-89; trustee St. Joseph's Med. Ctr., 1983-84, pers. adv. com. to bd. dirs., 1978-84, chmn., 1980-84; bd. dirs. United Way Allen County, sec., 1979-80; bd. dirs. Anthony Wayne Vocat. Rehab. Ctr., 1969-75. Mem. Fort Wayne Ind.-Purdue Alumni Soc. (hon. mem. 1987), Am. Psychol. Assn., AAUW (internat. fellowship com. 1986-88, prog. com. 1981-83, Am. women fellowship com. 1978-83, chmn. 1981-83, trust rsch. grantee 1980), Southeastern Psychol. Assn. (referee conv. papers 1987, 88), Ind. Sch. Women's Club (v.p. prog. chair 1979-81), Pi Lambda Theta, Sigma Xi, Delta Kappa Gamma (editorial bd. 1986-88, gen. chair conv. 1985-86, dir. N.E. region 1982-84, adminstrv. bd., exec. bd. 1982-84, leadership devel. com.).

LAPAN, KARL ROGER, finance and administration executive; b. Mass., Sept. 19, 1965. BS in Bus. Mgmt. summa cum laude, Franklin Pierce Coll., 1986L; MS in Orgn./Human Resources Devel., The Am. U., 1993. Fin. analyst aircraft engine bus. group GE Co., Cin., 1986-88; mgr. fin. analysis and adminstr. industry svcs. engring. GE Co., Charlotte, N.C., 1988-89; mgr. fin. power delivery and control GE Co., Hampton, Va., 1989-91; mgr. competitive and bus. devel. appliances GE Co., Louisville, Ky., 1991-93; mgr. N.Am. fin. ops. capital auto fin. svcs. GE Co., Barrington, Ill., 1993-94; v.p. fin./adminstrn., CFO NBS Imaging Systems, Inc., Ft. Wayne, Ind., 1994-95; sr. v.p., CFO NBS Imaging Syss., Ft. Wayne, Ind., 1995—. Staff mem. St. Michael's Episcopal Youth Conf.; mem. GE Elfun Soc. Mem. Soc. Competitive Intelligence Profls., Pi Alpha Alpha. Home: 1818 Iverness Lakes Crossing Fort Wayne IN 46808 Office: NBS Imaging Systems Inc 1530 Progress Rd Fort Wayne IN 46808

LA PETINA, GARY MICHAEL, lawyer; b. Chgo., Apr. 25, 1955; s. Nicholas J. and Mildred E. (Roth) La P.; m. Donna M. Kulisz, Oct. 9, 1982; children: Patrick James, Nicole Elizabeth. BS, Loyola U., Chgo., 1977; JD,

John Marshall Law Sch., Chgo., 1980. Bar: Ill. 1980. Staff atty. Internat. Assn. Lions Clubs, Oak Brook, Ill., 1982-87, gen. counsel, 1987—. Mem. ABA, Lions. Roman Catholic. Home: 2 S 30th Bristol Ln Warrenville IL 60555 Office: Internat Assn Lions Clubs 300 W 22nd St Oak Brook IL 60521-8815

LAPOSSY, KENNETH A., machine engineer; b. Cleve., Aug. 27, 1948. Machinist, engr. Imperial Die and Mfg. Co., Cleve., 1967—. Office: Imperial Die and Mfg Co 13200 Enterprise Ave Cleveland OH 44135-5104

LARDY, SISTER SUSAN MARIE, prioress; b. Sentinel Butte, N.D., Nov. 9, 1937; d. Peter Aloysius and Elizabeth Julia (Dietz) L. BS in Edn., U. Mary, Bismarck, N.D., 1965; MEd, U. N.D., 1972. Entered Order of St. Benedict, Bismarck, 1957. Elem. tchr. Cathedral Grade Sch., Bismarck, 1958-67, Christ the King Sch., Mandan, N.D., 1967-68, 70-72, St. Joseph's Sch., Mandan, 1968-70; asst. prof. edn. U. Mary, Bismarck, 1972-80; adminstr., asst. prioress Annunciation Priory, Bismarck, 1980-84, prioress, major superior, 1984—; pres., bd. dirs. St. Alexius Med. Ctr., Bismarck, 1984—, Garrison (N.D.) Meml. Hosp., 1984—, U. Mary, Bismarck, 1984—. Chair Health Commn. of Diocese of Bismarck, 1991. Mem. Delta Kappa Gamma. Home: 7520 University Dr Bismarck ND 58504-9681

LARIME, MICHAEL WALL, manufacturing executive; b. Pontiac, Mich., Aug. 24, 1943; s. Carl M. and Jean Elizabeth (Wall) L.; m. Barbara Swartzloff, Aug. 14, 1965; children: Christopher, Matthew. Student, U. Mich., 1961-65; BS in Chemistry, Ea. Mich. U., 1967; cert., Harvard U., 1986, George Washington U., 1974, Stanford U., 1988. Chemist Tecumseh Products Co., Ann Arbor, Mich., 1965-72; rsch. chemist Chem-Trend, Inc., Howell, Mich., 1972-76; chem. engr. Thetford Corp., Ann Arbor, 1976-77, mgr. chem. and prodn. engring., 1977-78, sr. staff engr., 1979-84, gen. mgr. sales and mktg., 1985-86, v.p. sales and mktg., 1986—. Mem. Nat. Marine Mfrs. Soc., Am. Mgmt. Assn., Recreational Vehicle Industry Assn. (mem. show com. 1988—, mem. suppliers com. 1988—, chmn. statis. rsch. com. 1989—, bd. dirs. 1991—, chmn. bd. 1994—), Am. Chem. Soc., Warehouse Distbrs. Assn. Office: Thetford Corp PO Box 1285 Ann Arbor MI 48106-1285

LARKIN, BARRY LOUIS, professional baseball player; b. Cin., Apr. 28, 1964; m. Lisa Davis. Student, U. Mich., 1982-85. Baseball player Cincinnati Reds, 1985—. First baseball player twice named MVP of Big Ten Athletic Conf.; two-time All-Am. honors; named MVP, Rookie of Yr. and to All-Star team, 1988-95, to Topps' Triple-A All-Star team, 1986, All-Star teams by Sporting News, 1988-92, 94-95, AP, 1990, UPI, 1990, Maj. League Baseball, 1988-91, 93, to N.L. Silver Slugger team Sporting News, 1988-92, 95; recipient Gold Glove award, 1994. Office: Cin Reds 100 Riverfront Stadium Cincinnati OH 45202-3590*

LARKIN, BRUCE F., state legislator; m. Judy Larkin. Kans. state rep. Dist. 63, farmer. Home: RR 1 Box 11 Baileyville KS 66404-9705*

LARKIN, ROBERT LEE, protection services official; b. Detroit, Dec. 16, 1966; s. Robert Lee and Rebecca Mae (Laary) L.; 1 child, Brandi Capri. AS, Jordan Coll., 1992. Clk. data processing Mfrs. Nat. Corp., Livonia, Mich., 1988-89; clk. file Dept. Justice, Detroit, 1989-90, ops. asst., 1990—; Res. police officer Detroit Police Dept., 1990—. With USMC, 1985-88.

LARKRIDGE, THEODORE KENNETH, financial manager; b. Chgo., Feb. 14, 1960; s. Theodore and Delilah (Coleman) L. Mgr. Chgo. Bd. Trade, 1978—, instr., 1988—. Active Rep. Presdl. Task Force, Washington, 1989, Presdl. Task Force Campaign Trustee, 1992—. Recipient Medal of Merit Rep. Presdl. Task Force, 1989, Rep. Presdl. Legion of Merit, 1992. Office: Chgo Bd Trade 141 W Jackson Blvd Chicago IL 60604-2904

LAROCCA, PATRICIA DARLENE MCALEER, middle school mathematics educator; b. Aurora, Ill., July 12, 1951; d. Theodore Austin and Lorraine Mae (Robbins) McAleer; m. Edward Daniel LaRocca, June 28, 1975; children: Elizabeth S., Mark E. BS in Edn./Math., No. Ill. U., 1973, postgrad., 1975. Tchr. elem. sch. Roselle (Ill) Sch. Dist., 1973-80; instr. math. Coll. DuPage, Glen Ellyn, Ill., 1988-90; tchr. math. O'Neill Mid. Sch., Downers Grove, Ill., 1995—; pvt. cons., math. tutor, Downers Grove, Ill., 1980-88, 90-95. Bd. dirs. PTA, Hillcrest Elem. Sch., Downers Grove; active Boy Scouts Am.; mem. 1st United Meth. Ch. Ill. teaching scholar, 1969. Methodist. Home and Office: 5648 Dunham Rd Downers Grove IL 60516-1246

LAROSE, MICHAEL H., secondary education educator, coach; b. Bay City, Mich., Dec. 31, 1953; s. Harvey W. and Marilyn (Miller) LaR. BS in Edn., Ctrl. Mich. U., 1977, MA in Ednl. Adminstrn., 1985. Tchr., coach Holy Trinity Sch., Bay City, 1978-79, Cheboygan (Mich.) Cath. Schs., 1979-83; asst. prin., athletic dir. All Saints High Sch., Bay City, 1983-84; asst. men's basketball coach Northwood U., Midland, Mich., 1984-85, 86-87, Emporia (Kans.) State U., 1985-86; K-8 phys. edn. dir. St. Stan's Sch., Bay City, 1986-89; tchr. Gt. Lakes Jr. Coll., Bay City, 1987-89; job developer Delta Coll., University Center, Mich., 1989-92, head men's basketball coach, 1987-92; assoc. prof. humanities and social sci. Great Lakes Jr. Coll., Bay City, 1993-94; tchr., boy's varsity basketball coach Grand Blanc (Mich.) H.S., 1994—; dir. Together We Can Basketball Camp, Olivet, Mich., 1983—, Fairmont, W.Va., 1987—, La-Rose/Washington Basketball Camp, Warrenton, Va., 1989—. Usher, St. Mary's Ch. Named Outstanding Young Educator, Bay City Jaycees, 1989, Tchr. of Yr., Gt. Lakes Jr. Coll., 1989, 94, Men's Basketball Nat. Divsn. II Coach of Yr., Nat. Jr. Coll. Athletic Assn., 1989. Mem. Nat. Assn. Basketball Coaches, Basketball Coaches Assn. Mich.

LARRICK, GEARY HENDERSON, composer; b. Zanesville, Ohio, Nov. 15, 1943; s. Clyde Henderson and Bernice Gail (Geary) L; m. Elizabeth Lee Hatcher, Sept. 23, 1966 (div. Nov. 1973); 1 child, Scott Turner Tielens (dec.); m. Lydia Soon-Soon Fang, Aug. 7, 1981; 1 child, Sulina Yen. BS, Ohio State U., 1965; MusM, Eastman Sch. Music, Rochester, N.Y., 1970; D in Mus. Arts, U. Colo., 1984. Cert. tchr. elem. and secondary music, Ohio. Usher State Theater, Cambridge, Ohio, 1959-61; percussionist Balt. Symphony Orch., 1965-66; tchr. Cambridge City Schs., 1966-68; instr. Muskingum Coll., New Concord, Ohio, 1966-68; percussionist Rochester Philharm., 1968-69; prof. U. Wis., Stevens Point, 1969-85; condr. Stevens Point Symphony Orch., 1971-74; timpanist Ctrl. Wis. Symphony Orch., Stevens Point, 1978-91; composer G and L Pub., Stevens Point, 1985—; grad. asst. Eastman Sch. Music, 1968; writer Peter Lang Pub., N.Y.C., 1989-95; tchr. Conservatory of Music, Stevens Point, 1979-81. Author: Musical References, 1990, Biographical Essays, 1992; also articles; leader Geary Larrick Quartet, Stevens Point, 1972-80. Bd. dirs. Stevens Point Symphony Orch., 1973; mem. scholarship com. U. Wis., 1974, mem. search com., 1984; mem. adminstrv. bd. St. Paul's United Meth. Ch., Stevens Point, 1988. Mem. Wis. Percussive Arts Soc. (pres. 1973), Men's Fellowship Group (chairperson 1985-90), Phi Mu Alpha, Pi Kappa Lambda, Kappa Kappa Psi (chpt. v.p. 1964). Democrat. Home: 2321 Sims Ave Stevens Point WI 54481-3129

LARROWE, VERNON LODGE, electrical engineer; b. Galax, Va., Feb. 21, 1921; s. Eppa Hunton and Jessie Dell (Nichols) L.; m. Florence Cecelia Glinicki, Dec. 26, 1966; 1 child, Victoria. BS, U. Kans., 1950; MS, U. Ill., 1951; PhD, U. Mich., 1964. Assoc. rsch. engr. U. Mich. Inst. Sci. and Tech., Ann Arbor, 1953-57; rsch. engr. U. Mich. Inst., Ann Arbor, 1957-77, hed analog computer lab., 1957-62; lectr. U. Mich., Ann Arbor, 1956-77; rsch. engr. Environ. Rsch. Inst. of Mich., Ann Arbor, 1973-83, sr. rsch. engr., 1983-86, emeritus mem. tech. staff, 1986—. Contbr. articles to profl. jours. Sgt. USAAF, 1943-46. Mem. Soc. Computer Simulation (life), MIdwestern Simulation Coun. (chmn. 1958-59), Sigma Xi. Office: ERIM PO Box 134001 Ann Arbor MI 48113-4001

LARSEN, DENNIS D., design engineer, business executive; b. Winona, Minn., Aug. 2, 1948; s. Darrel Wayne and Doris Marie (Malenke) L.; m. Catherine Donnadean Douglas, May 11, 1967; children: Deana, Jeffrey. Mgr. concrete block plants Shilley Masonry, Mpls., 1978-91; design engr., pres. Block Techs. Inc., Elk River, Minn., 1990—. With U.S. Army Res., 1966-72. Mem. Ducks Unltd. (chpt. chair 1984-87). Republican. Lutheran. Office: Block Techs Inc 12700 206th Ave NW Elk River MN 55330-8923

LARSEN, KATHLEEN MARY, dietitian, program administrator; b. Landstuhl, Germany, Aug. 6, 1956; came to U.S., 1957; d. Walter Augustus and Grace Lillian (Taylor) O'Loughlin; children: Carl Michael, Jill Elizabeth. BA in Dietetics, Coll. St. Scholastica, Duluth, Minn., 1978. Registered and lic. dietitian, Minn. Dietary asst., clin. dietitian St. Luke's Hosp., Duluth, 1977-78, dietary supr., 1979-83; cons. dietitian St. Francis Nursing Home, Superior, Wis., 1983-85; nutrition educator Sr. Dining Program, Duluth, 1983-84, program dir., 1984—; com. mem. Area Agy. on Aging, Duluth, 1988-95. Vol., com. mem. Luth. Ch. of Good Shepherd, Duluth, 1987—, Sunday sch. supt., 1994-95; treas., vol. Lakeside Elem. PTA, Duluth, 1988-93; participant Leadership Duluth, Duluth C. of C., 1991—. Mem. Am. Dietetics Assn., Nat. Assn. Nutrition and Aging Svcs. Programs, Minn. Dietetics Assn. (sec. 1989-90, mem. bylaws com. 1990-94, Recognized Young Dietitian 1987), Minn. Nutrition Dirs. Assn. (vice-chair, treas. 1994—), Head of the Lakes Dist. Dietetic Assn. (sec.-treas. 1982-84, pres. 1986-88). Democrat. Office: Sr Programs 12 E 4th Stll Duluth MN 55805

LARSEN, L. VERNON, retired chemical engineer; b. Paris, Tex., Oct. 9, 1918; s. L. Vernon and May Ella (Furey) L.; m. Helen Ann Worthington, June 22, 1944; 1 child, Claire. BSChE, U. Tex., 1940. Devel. chemist Gen. Electric Co., Pittsfield, Mass., 1941-49; mgr. product devel. Gen. Electric Co., Coshocton, Ohio, 1949-72, mgr. environ. engring., 1972-91; mem. tech. com. 52 Internat. Electrotech. Commn., N.Y.C., 1965-82; mem. Underwriters' Labs. Industry Adv. Groups for Polymeric Insulation and Printed Circuits, 1967-85. Contbr. articles to profl. jours.; patentee in field. Fellow Royal Numismatic Soc.; mem. AIChE, Am. Chem. Soc., Nat. Elec. Mfrs. Assn. (chmn. 1954-80), Br. Numismatic Soc., Coshocton Postal Customer Adv. Coun., Masons, Scottish Rite, York Rite, Shriners, Phi Lambda Upsilon. Republican. Presbyterian. Home: 1136 Kenilworth Ave Coshocton OH 43812-2443

LARSEN, MARY ANN INDOVINA, counselor, English educator; b. Chgo., Aug. 9, 1929; d. Michael and Mary Rosalie (Tamaizzo) Indovina; m. Arthur F. Larsen, Jan. 28, 1956 (dec. June 1989); children: Deborah M. Larsen McIlvain, Michael A., Suzanne M. Larsen Channell. BA, DePaul U., 1951, MA, 1986. 1st grade tchr., music tchr. Whittier Sch., Blue Island, Ill., 1951-53, Graham Sch., Chgo., 1953-59; kindergarten tchr. Twain Sch., Chgo., 1958-59; dental bus. cons. Glenwood, Ill., 1964-87; counselor Glenwood (Ill.) Sch. for Boys, 1987-89; counselor, cord. spl. populations South Suburban Coll, South Holland, Ill., 1987—, also instr. English. Mem. Chgo. Archdiocesal Choral Festival, ch. choir. Mem. Ill. Assn. Counseling and Devel. (writer critiques for manuscripts 1987-90), AACD (book reviewer 1988—), Ill. Sch. Counselors Assn. (chmn. membership com. 1988—). Roman Catholic. Office: South Suburban Coll 15800 State St South Holland IL 60473-1200

LARSEN, MAX D., survey researcher; b. Pratt, Kans., Jan. 23, 1941; s. Harry D. and Deloris Iola (Morgan) L.; m. Lillian M. Grimes, Dec. 22, 1962; children: Michael D., Paul J., Charles D. BA, Kans. State Tchrs. Coll., 1961; MA, U. Kans., 1963, PhD, 1966. Asst. prof. U. Nebr., Lincoln, 1966-69, assoc. prof., 1969-72, prof., 1973-82, dean arts and scis., 1974-82; exec. v.p. The Gallup Orgn., Lincoln, 1982-90, dir. assessment and evaluation divsn., 1990—; bd. dirs. Mid-Continent Regional Edn. Lab., Denver. Author: (books) Introduction to Modern Algebraic Concepts, 1969, Fundamental Concepts of Modern Mathematics, 1970; co-author: (books) Essentials of Precalculus Mathematics, 1971, Multiplicative Theory of Ideals, 1971, Essentials of Elementary School Mathematics, 1974, Understanding Basic Calculus: Applications from Managerial, Social, and Life Sciences, 1978, Brief Calculus with Applications, 1989, Calculus with Applications, 1990; contbr. numerous articles to profl. jours. Elected mem. Nebr. State Bd. Edn., Lincoln, 1984-86. Disting. scholar Nat. Assn. State Bd. Edn., 1994. Mem. Phi Beta Kappa. Democrat. Presbyterian. Home: 641 Haverford Cir Lincoln NE 68510 Office: The Gallup Orgn One Church St 9th Fl Rockville MD 20850

LARSEN, PEG, state legislator; b. Aug. 10, 1949; m. Thomas Larsen; 4 children. BA, U. Slippery Rock. Minn. state rep. Dist. 56B, 1994—; former ednl. asst. spl. needs. Address: 409 Quixote Ave N Lakeland MN 55043

LARSEN, STEVEN, orchestra conductor; b. Oak Park, Ill., Feb. 10, 1951; s. Edwin Earnest and Sylvia Nila Larsen; divorced; children: Vanessa, Krista; m. Martha Jane Bein, Mar. 21, 1993. MusB, Am. Conservatory Music, Chgo., 1975; MusM, Northwestern U., 1976. Cert. Nederlandse Dirigenten Kursus. Instr. music theory, chair instrumental dept Am. Conservatory Music, Chgo., 1976-82, orch. dir., 1978; music dir. Opera Theatre of San Antonio, 1987-90; orch. dir. Rockford (Ill.) Symphony Orch., 1991—; music dir., acting artistic dir. Chgo. Opera Theater, 1981-92; interim artistic dir. Dayton (Ohio) Opera, 1996; music dir. Champaign-Urbana (Ill.) Symphony, 1996—; lectr. opera performance Chgo. Mus. Coll., 1989—. Mem. Rockford Downtown Rotary. Office: Rockford Symphony Orch 711 N Main St Rockford IL 61103-6999

LARSEN, WAYNE DAVID, engineer; b. Peoria, Ill., Oct. 6, 1959; s. Dorwin Ray and Louise Ann (Johnson) L.; m. Susan Jane Carson, June 27, 1987; children: Brett, Jennifer, Steven, Nicholas. BS in Mechanical Engring., U. Ill., 1980, MS, 1982. MTS AT&T, Indpls., 1980—. Home: 7630 Cape Cod Cir Indianapolis IN 46250 Office: AT&T 6612 E 75th St Indianapolis IN 46250

LARSON, ALLAN LOUIS, political scientist, educator, lay church worker; b. Chetek, Wis., Mar. 31, 1932; s. Leonard Andrew and Mabel (Marek) L. BA magna cum laude, U. Wis., Eau Claire, 1954; PhD, Northwestern U., 1964. Instr. Evanston Twp. (Ill.) High Sch., 1958-61; asst. prof. polit. sci. U. Wis., 1963-64; asst. prof. Loyola U., Chgo., 1964-68, assoc. prof., 1968-74, prof., 1974—. Author: Comparative Political Analysis, 1980, (essay) The Human Triad: An Introductory Essay on Politics, Society, and Culture, 1988; (with others) Progress and the Crisis of Man, 1976; contbr. articles to profl. jours. Assoc. mem. Paul Galvin Chapel, Evanston, Ill. Norman Wait Harris fellow in polit. sci. Northwestern U., 1954-56. Mem. AAAS, ASPCA, AAUP, Humane Soc. U.S., Northwestern U. Alumni Assn., Am. Polit. Sci. Assn., Am. Acad. Polit. and Social Sci., Acad. Polit. Sci., Midwest Polit. Sci. Assn., Spiritual Life Inst., Anti-Cruelty Soc., Nat. Wildlife Fedn., Noetic Scis. Inst., Humane Soc. U.S., Kappa Delta Pi, Pi Sigma Epsilon. Roman Catholic. Home: 2015 Orrington Ave Evanston IL 60201-2911 Office: Loyola U 6525 N Sheridan Rd Damen Hall Rm 915 Chicago IL 60626

LARSON, ANDRÉ PIERRE, museum director; b. Little Fork, Minn., Nov. 10, 1942; s. Arne B. and Jeanne F. (Kay) L.; m. Mary Hueschen (div. 1977); 1 child, Nathan; m. Linda S. Hansen; 1 child, Nikolas. MM, U. S.D., 1968; PhD, W.Va. U., 1974. Dir. The Shrine to Music Mus., U. S.D., Vermillion, 1972—; prof. music U.S.D., 1972—. Contbr. articles to profl. jours. Mem. Am. Mus. Instrument Soc. (pres. 1979-87, editor newsletter 1976-94). Republican. Unitarian. Home: 325 Linden Ave Vermillion SD 57069-3227

LARSON, CAL, state legislator, real estate and insurance broker; b. Aug. 10, 1930; m. Loretta Larson; two children. BA, Concordia Coll., Moorhead, Minn. Real estate/ins. broker; state rep. Minn. Ho. of Reps., St. Paul, 1967-74; Dist. 10 senator Minn. State Senate, St. Paul, 1986—; mem. edn.-higher edn. divsn. and edn. funding, fin., commerce and consumer protection, and vet. and gen. legis. coms., Minn. State Senate. Address: 145 State Office Building Bldg Saint Paul MN 55155-1201*

LARSON, CARL SHIPLEY, engineering educator, consultant; b. Chgo., Sept. 23, 1934; s. Carl Uno and Marion Jean Larson; m. Vivian Phylis Peuckert, Dec. 28, 1957; children: Carl, Michael, Daniel. BSME, U. Ill., 1956, MSME, 1958, PhD, 1965. Registered profl. engr., Ill. Engr. Western Electric, Chgo., 1955-56; from instr. to asst. prof. U. Ill., Urbana, 1965-72, assoc. prof., 1972-91, asst. dean, 1974—, prof., 1991-94, prof. emeritus, 1994—; cons. Ruhl and Assocs., Champaign, 1994—; bd. dirs. Capsonic Corp., Elgin, Ill. Contbr. articles to profl. jours. Bd. dirs. United Way, Urbana, 1987. Teaching Fellowship Nat. Sci. Found, Urbana, 1960-64. Mem. Am. Soc. Engring. Edn. (sect. chmn. 1990-91), Nat. Coun. Examiners Engring. (cons., vice-chmn. 1989-92). Office: 411 E Mumford Dr Urbana IL 61801-6230 also: U of Ill 207 Engring Hall 1308 W Green St Urbana IL 61801-2936

LARSON, CAROLE ALLIS, library and information scientist, educator; b. Dayton, Ohio, Aug. 31, 1945; d. Harold Arthur and Myra Barbara (Gwythe) L.; m. Lowel Wilson Eyer, Jr., Nov. 16, 1985. BA in Sociology, Carleton Coll., 1967; MA in Edn., Washington U., 1968; MA in Asian Studies, U. Oregon, 1975; MA in Libr. Sci., U. Denver, 1977. Reference libr. instrnl. svcs. U. Nebr., Kearney, 1978-80; campus libr. Met. Comty. Coll., Omaha, 1980-81; asst. prof. social scis., reference libr. U. Nebr., Omaha, 1981-85, assoc. prof., 1985—; cons. Bellevue Coll. Libr., Omaha, 1982-83. Contbr. articles to profl. jours. Co-recipient Reference Svc. Press award Am. Libr. Assn. Reference and Adult Svcs. Divsn., 1995; Washington U. fellow. Mem. ALA, Assn. Coll. and Rsch. Librs., Nebr. Libr. Assn. Democrat. Home: 2516 N 60 Ave Omaha NE 68104

LARSON, DAVID ALLEN, law educator; b. Libertyville, Ill., Nov. 5, 1954; s. Allen John and Mary Jane (Williams) L. BA magna cum laude, DePauw U., Greencastle, Ind., 1976; JD, U. Ill., 1979; LLM, U. Pa., Phila., 1987. Bar: Minn. 1979, U.S. Dist Ct. Minn. 1980, U.S. Ct. Appeals (8th cir.) 1980, Ill. 1982, U.S. Dist. Ct. (no. dist.) Ill. 1982, Nebr. 1989, U.S. Supreme Ct. 1990. Assoc. Meagher & Geer, Mpls., 1979-81; asst. prof. Loyola U. Chgo. Sch. Bus. Adminstrn., 1981-83; assoc. prof. Millsaps Coll. Sch. Mgmt., Jackson, Miss., 1983-87; prof. Creighton U. Sch. Law, Omaha, 1987-90, 91—; prof.-in-residence appellate div. EEOC, Washington, 1990-91. Contbr. articles to profl. jours. Rsch. scholar Lund (Sweden) U. Law Sch., 1985, 88, 89. Mem. ABA (vice chmn. sect. on internat. law and practice, employment law com.; labor and employment law sect.), Nebr. State Bar Assn. (sec. labor and employment law sect.), Ill. State Bar Assn., Minn. State Bar Assn. Office: Creighton U Sch Law 2133 California St Omaha NE 68178

LARSON, DONALD HAROLD, information systems executive; b. Chgo., Sept. 15, 1959; s. Harold Elmer Jr. and Gladys Betty (Wittenborn) L.; m. Heidi Lynn Lauer, Sept. 15, 1984 (div.); m. Karyn Lynn Gernes, June 26, 1993. BS in Computer Sci., Mktg., DePaul U., Chgo., 1980, MBA, 1982. Acct. exec. Ill. Bell Telephone Co., Rolling Meadows, Ill., 1980-81, communication system rep., 1981-82; midwest area cons. Automatic Data Processing, Harwood Heights, Ill., 1982-83, midwest area supr., 1983-85; network mgr. Automatic Data Processing, Roseland, N.J., 1985-86; telecommunications mgr. Northrop Def. Systems, Rolling Meadows, 1986-88; sr. mgr. telecommunications Kraft, Inc., Glenview, Ill., 1988; dir. telecommunications Kraft Gen. Foods, Inc., Glenview, Ill., 1988-95; dir. client/server arch. Kraft Foods, Northfield, Ill., 1995—. Mem. Nat. Eagle Scout Assn., Pi Sigma Epsilon Alumni Assn. Office: Kraft Gen Foods Inc Three Lakes Dr Three Lakes Dr Northfield IL 60093

LARSON, DONN C., state senator. Farmer, Hudson, S.D.; mem. S.D. Senate, Pierre; mem. com., edn. and local govt. coms. Democrat.

LARSON, ELIZABETH ANN, family and consumer sciences educator; b. Fargo, N.D., Feb. 28, 1958; d. James William and Patricia Marie (Maloney) Friederichs; m. Jeffrey Curtis Larson, June 28, 1980; children: Anthony Clifton, Alexis Leigh. BS in Textiles and Clothing, N.D. State U., 1980, BS in Home Econs. Edn., 1982; MS in Vocat. Edn., Kearney State Coll., 1988. Cert. in family and consumer scis. Sales assoc. Carmichaels, Mc Cook, Nebr., 1983-85; instr. family and consumer scis., chair div. bus. and tech. McCook C.C., 1985-96; chancellor search com. Mid-Plains C.C. area, 1993-94; cons., presenter Kugler Fertilizer Divsn., McCook, 1990; mem. Early Childhood Edn. Task Force, Lincoln, Nebr., 1991—, Base Components Task Force, Lincoln, 1991, others. Bd. dirs., pres. S.W. Nebr. Commun. Theatre, McCook, 1985-88; chmn. com. Chatauqua, McCook, 1990; regional chair Western N.D. Make It with Wool, Grenora, 1982-83. Mem. NEA, Nebr. Edn. Assn., Am. Assn. Family and Consumer Scis. (state advisor 1989-90, state pres. 1995-96, conv. del. 1992, 95), Nebr. Assn. Family and Consumer Scis. (exec. bd. 1989-92, 93-94, New Achiever award 1991), Mid-Plains C.C. Edn. Assn. (pres. 1992-93), Kiwanis (treas., bd. dirs. 1988-92), Phi Delta Kappa, Phi Upsilon Omicron. Republican. Roman Catholic. Home: 809 W 3rd St Mc Cook NE 69001-3164 Office: Mc Cook C C 1205 E 3rd St Mc Cook NE 69001-2631

LARSON, EMILIE GUSTAVA, retired school counselor; b. Northfield, Minn., Apr. 28, 1919; d. Melvin Cornelius and Frieda (Christiansen) L. A.B., St. Olaf Coll., 1940; M.A., Radcliffe Coll., 1946; student U. Chgo., 1951-52. Tchr. Hanska (Minn.) High Sch., 1940-42, Two Harbors (Minn.) High Sch., 1942-45; tchr. J.W. Weeks Jr. High Sch., Newton, Mass., 1946-56, guidance counselor, 1956-79; counselor Warren Jr. High Sch., Newton, 1979-81. Deacon, Univ. Luth. Ch., 1979; bd. dirs. Bus. History and Econ. Life Program, Inc., Northeastern U. Mem. AAUW (state v.p. for program devel., topic chmn. Mass. div. 1975-76, area rep. for internat. rels. Minn. div. 1984-86), Mass. Tchrs. Assn., Newton Tchrs. Assn., St. Olaf Coll. Alumni Assn. (bd. dir. 1982-85), PEO, Va. Gildersleeve Internat. Fund for Univ. Women Inc. (membership com., bd. dirs. 1992), Pi Lambda Theta. Lutheran. Contbr. articles to profl. jours. Address: 1008 1st St W Northfield MN 55057-1614

LARSON, GERALD LEWIS, electrical engineer; b. Pipestone, Minn., June 16, 1940; s. Albert Lewis and Margurite (Kempenich) L.; m. Deana Estep, Sept. 15, 1962; children: Anita, Eric, Christopher. BS in Math., BSEE, Montana State U., 1966; MSEE, Bradley U., 1969. Sr. engr. Caterpillar Co., Peoria, Ill., 1966-71; prin. engr. Eaton Corp., Battle Creek, Mich., 1971-76; mgr. advanced devel. Litton Microwave, Mpls., 1976-80; mgr. electronic controls Trane Corp., LaCrosse, Wis., 1980-85; dir. Autoflex Tech. Ctr., Dearborn, Mich. Mem. IEEE, Instrument Soc. Am. Home: 25012 Cherry Hill St Dearborn MI 48124

LARSON, JEAN ANN, hospital administrator; b. Belleville, Kans., Mar. 4, 1959; d. Verl S. and ELoise E. (Johnson) L.; m. Robert I. Jaramillo, Feb. 27, 1987; children: Danielle Elise, Natalie Elaine. BS in Indsl. Engring., Wichita State U., 1982; M of Internat. Mgmt., Am. Grad. Sch. Internat. Mgmt., 1985. Mgmt. engr. Wesley MEd. Ctr., Wichita, 1982-84; engr. system devel. Electronic Data Systems, Detroit, 1985-86; sr. VIP analyst William Beaumont Hosp., Royal Oak, Mich., 1986-88, asst. dept. mgr., 1988-89, dept. mgr., 1989-93; dir., 1993—; vis. lectr. Oakland U., Rochester, Mich., 1990; presenter in field. Com. mem. Abiding Presence Luth . Ch., 1988—, ch. coun. mem., 1992-93. World Wide fellow Am. Grad. Sch. Internat. Mgmt., 1984. Fellow Healthcare Info. Mgmt. Systems Soc. (nat. edn. com.); mem. Am. Soc. Quality Control, Mich. Hosp. Systems Soc. (bd. dirs., chpt. liaison 1990-91, programs chair 1989-90, pres.-elect 1994-95, various coms. 1987-88), Inst. Indsl. Engrs. (sr. mem.), Amnesty Internat. (local group coord. 1987—). Office: William Beaumont Hosp Mgmt Systems Dept 3601 W 13 Mile Rd Royal Oak MI 48073-6712

LARSON, JERRY L., state supreme court justice; b. Harlan, Iowa, May 17, 1936; s. Gerald L. and Mary Eleanor (Patterson) L.; m. Debra L. Christensen, July 17, 1993; children: Rebecca, Jeffrey, Susan, David. BA, State U. Iowa, 1958, JD, 1960. Bar: Iowa. Partner firm Larson & Larson, 1961-75; dist. judge 4th Jud. Dist. Ct. of Iowa, 1975-78; justice Iowa Supreme Ct., 1978—. Office: Supreme Ct Iowa State Capital Bldg Des Moines IA 50319

LARSON, KEITH DONALD, magazine editor; b. Peoria, Ill., Feb. 19, 1964; s. Donald K. and Joyce Aldys (Erickson) L.; m. Lisa Ann Bircher, Oct. 23, 1992. BS in Chem. Engring. with honors, U. Ill., 1986. Rsch. engr. Amoco Chem. Corp., Naperville, Ill., 1983-88; grad. teaching asst. dept. mech. engring. U. Ill., Urbana, 1988-89; editor-in-chief Control mag. Putman Pub. Co., Chgo., 1989—. Patentee in field; contbr. articles on process control and instrumentation tech. to industry publs. Mem. ASME, AIChE, Instrument Soc. Am. Office: Putman Pub Co 301 E Erie St Chicago IL 60611-3037

LARSON, KEITH WAYNE, printing company executive, industrial engineer; b. Austin, Minn., Oct. 1, 1952; s. Leland B. and Priscilla Jane (Louden) L.; m. Sharon Kay Walker, Aug. 18, 1973; children: Krystal Kay, Nicole Amber. AA, Coll. USAF, San Antonio, 1975; BS in Indsl. Engring.

with honors, U. Wis., 1978; MS in Indsl. Engring., Iowa State U., 1988; cert. internat. mgmt., Internat. Mgmt. Inst., Geneva, Switzerland, 1989. Engring. intern Johnson's Wax, Racine, Wis., summer 1977; dept. mgr. Bounty Towels, robotics engr., contr. Procter & Gamble, Green Bay, Wis., 1978-85; dir. risk mgmt. and human resources Pioneer, Des Moines, 1985-89; v.p. adminstrn. and fin. Brown Printing, Waseca, Minn., 1989—. Contbr. articles to profl. jours. Mem. task force Gov.'s Health Care, Des Moines, 1987-89, Lt. Gov.'s Work Force 2000, Des Moines, 1988; bd. dirs. Young Women's Resource Ctr., Des Moines, 1985-89, Iowa Children's Found., Des Moines, 1987-89, Star City Task Force, Waseca, Minn., 1989-91; counsel Grace Luth., Waseca, 1992—. Sgt. USAF, 1973-76. Mem. Tau Beta Phi. Office: Brown Printing Highway 14 W Waseca MN 56093-2077

LARSON, KEVIN SCOTT, electrical engineer; b. Ann Arbor, Mich., Apr. 23, 1968; s. Levoy E. and Janice R. Larson. BSEE, GMI Engring. & Mgmt. Inst., Flint, Mich., 1991; MSEE, U. Mich., 1993. Assoc. plant elec. engr. GM Willow Run Assembly, Ypsilanti, Mich., 1991; plant elec. engr. GM Willow Run Assembly, 1992; project engr. GM Midsize Car Divsn., Milford, Mich., 1994—. Mem. IEEE, N.Y. Acad. Scis., Eta Kappa Nu, Tau Beta Pi. Office: GM Milford Proving Ground One GM Rd 483 316 236 Milford MI 48380

LARSON, MARIAN GERTRUDE, catalog sales company executive; b. Madison, Wis., Aug. 22, 1927; d. Guy Henry and Gertrude Francis (Everett) L.; m. Edwin B. Roberts, Nov. 22, 1987. BA, U. Wis., 1948; MBA, U. Chgo., 1982. Mgr. continuity, Sta. WISC, Madison, 1948-53; copy chief Spiegel, Inc., Chgo., 1953-58, editor-in-chief women's, 1958-62, catalog mgr., domestics and shoes, 1962-76, group catalog mgr. hardlines, 1976-79, v.p. advt., Oak Brook, Ill., 1979-88; pres. Spiegel Pub. Co., Oak Brook, 1979-88, ret. Bd. dirs. Hinsdale United Way; alumni bd. U. Chgo. Grad. Sch. Bus. Mem. Chgo. Advt. Club, Nat. Assn. Women Bus. Owners, Direct Mktg. Assn.

LARSON, MICHAEL LEN, newspaper editor; b. St. James, Minn., Feb. 3, 1944; s. Leonard O. and Lois O. (Holte) L.; m. Kay M. Monahan, June 18, 1966; children: Christopher, David, Molly. BA, U. Minn., 1966; MBA, Mankato State U., 1986. Mng. editor Paddock Circle Inc., Libertyville, Ill., 1972-74, New Ulm (Minn.) Journal, 1974-76, Republican-Eagle, Red Wing, Minn., 1976-79, Mankato (Minn.) Free Press, 1979-84, 1979-84, editor, 1984-95, editor of editl. page, 1995—. Bd. dirs. Valley Indsl. Devel. Corp., Mankato, 1985-95, also treas.; mem. adv. bd. minn. State U. Bus. Sch. Served with U.S. Army, 1966-68, Vietnam. Recipient five First Place awards for investigative reporting Minn. Newspaper Assn., 1969, 71, 72, 76, 78, First Place award for feature writing, Suburban Newspapers Am., 1974. Mem. Minn. AP (pres. 1988—), Kiwanis. Roman Catholic. Home: 35 University Ct Mankato MN 56001-4182 Office: Mankato Free Press 418 S 2nd St Mankato MN 56001-3727

LARSON, NANCY CELESTE, computer systems manager; b. Chgo., July 17, 1951; d. Melvin Ellsworth and Ruth Margaret (Carlson) L. BS in Music Ed., U. Ill., 1973, MS in Music Edn., 1976; postgrad., Purdue Univ., 1982-86. Vocal music educator Consol. Sch. Dist., Gilman, Ill., 1975-77; elem. vocal music tchr. Sch. Dist. 161, Flossmoor, Ill., 1977-87; instr. Vander Cook Coll., Chgo., 1980-88; systems programmer analyst Sears, Roebuck & Co., Chgo., 1987-92, tech. instr., 1989-90, project leader, 1990-91, sr. systems analyst, 1991-92; sr. systems analyst Trans Union Corp., Chgo., 1992—, project mgr., 1994, mgr., 1994—; tchr. adult computer edn. Homewood-Flossmoor High Sch., 1986-90. Chmn. Faith Luth. Ch., 1982-87, pres. bd., 1988-91, vocal soloist and voice-over performer. Mem. Ill. Music Educators Assn., Music Educators Nat. Conf., Ill. Educators Assn., Nat. Educators Assn., Am. ORFF Schulwerk Assn., Flossmoor Edn. Assn. (negotiator 1983-86). Republican. Lutheran. Office: Trans Union Corp 555 W Adams St Chicago IL 60661-3601

LARSON, PAUL WILLIAM, public relations executive; b. Wilmington, N.C., May 28, 1956; s. Robert WIlliam and Helen Joyce (Hillen) L. BA, U. Calif., Berkeley, 1981; MS in Journalism Medill Sch. of Journalism, Northwestern U., Evanston, Ill., 1991. Reporter Turlock (Calif.) Daily Jour., 1982-84; writer, editor Paul Larson Commns., Modesto, Calif., 1984-90; dir. external affairs and publs. Medill Sch. Journalism, Northwestern U., Evanston, Ill., 1991-96; mgr. strategic comms. AMA, Chgo., 1996—; adj. lectr. Medill Sch. Journalism, Evanston, 1991—; assoc. master Commns. Residential Coll., Northwestern U., Evanston, 1993-96; judge Parenting Publs. of America Contest, Evanston, 1993—. mem. bd. dirs. Housing Options for the Mentally Ill, Evanston, 1993—, Rotary Club of Evanston, Ill., 1994—; docent Evanston Hist. Soc., 1992-95; chair comms. com. Evanston C. of C., 1995—. Recipient Rotary Group Study Exchg. award Rotary Internat., 1986, Rotary Found. Dist. Svc. award, 1995, Leadership Evanston Evanston Cmty. Rels., 1995-96, Vol. of the Yr. award Evanston McGaw YMCA, 1995. Office: AMA 515 N State St Chicago IL 60610

LARSON, RICHARD JAMES, computer network systems executive; b. Davenport, Iowa, Dec. 13, 1954; s. James Kruse and Carol Darlene (Bush) L.; m. Laurel Mae Johnson, Sept. 11, 1982; children: Paul, Jason, Christine. BA in Mass Communications, St. Ambrose Coll., 1977. Audio technician Boom Audio Inc., Davenport, 1971-75; fire equipment insp. Per Mar Security, Davenport, 1975; computer operator Lee Enterprise, Davenport, 1976-77; dir. acad. computer utilization St. Ambrose Coll., Davenport, 1977-78; tech. programmer Montgomery Elevator (name now Montgomery KONE Inc.), Moline, Ill., 1978-87, computer systems mgr. research devel., 1987-90; adminstr. Computer Wide Area Network (WAN), Moline, Ill., 1990—; owner Creative Photography Color Lab. and Studio, Coal Valley, Ill., 1990—. Mem. Nat. Rifle Assn., Masons. Republican. Methodist. Office: Montgomery KONE Inc 1 Montgomery Ct Moline IL 61265-1374

LARSON, ROBERT FREDERICK, public broadcasting company executive; b. Detroit, Mar. 24, 1930; s. Trygve and Solveig Johanna (Larsen) L.; m. Shirley Ann Burch, Aug. 20, 1955; children: Robb Jonathan, Peer Christopher. B.A., Muskingum Coll., 1953; M.Div., Pitts. Theol. Sem., 1956, Th.M, 1960; M.A. in Communications, U. Mich, 1964, Ph.D., 1969. Ordained to ministry Presbyterian Ch. Producer, dir. WITF-TV, Harrisburg, Pa., 1964-68, asst. mgr. program devel., 1968-70, pres., gen. mgr., 1970-83; exec. sec. radio/TV Pa. Council Chs., Harrisburg, 1967-70; pres., gen. mgr. WTVS-TV, Detroit, 1983-95, pres. emeritus for humanities and cmty. devel., 1995—; pres. The Larson Comms. Group, Inc., 1996—; bd. dirs. Am's. Pub. TV Stas., Mich. Pub. Broadcasting, Interlochen Ctr. Arts, Mich's Children, New Detroit Inc., Community Telecom. Network, Neighborhood Renaissance, Inc., Ctrl. Bus. Dist. Assn., New Ctr. Area Coun., William Tynedale Coll.; former vice chmn. bd. dris. PBS. Producer, dir. (TV program) Sons and Daughters, 1967, A Time to Act, 1968, Is Religion Obsolete?, 1969; exec. producer: All About Welfare, No Time To Be A Child, Act Against Violence: Help Wanted; producer: So Where Are You, God?. Mem. Detroit Coun. of Chs., Detroit Presbytery. Mem. Detroit Athletic Club.

LARTEY, VIKTOR AMUGI, design engineer; b. Ghana, Dec. 7, 1950. Student, Brideport U., Conn., 1979; BS in Product Design, Kansas City Art Inst., 1982. Patent law Litman, McMahon & Brown, Kansas City, 1984-85; cons. Jensen Engring., Leewood, Kans., 1985-89; product design analyst AGCO Technidata, Independence, Mo., 1989—; cons. Art Inst. Kansas City, 1993—. Mem. Indsl. Design Soc. Am. Methodist. Office: AGCO Technical Data PO Box 1099 6295 Cottage St Independence MO 64050-4339

LARY, PETER PAUL, probation officer, alderman; b. Danville, Ill., Mar. 16, 1950; s. George F. and Barbara A. (Dugas) L.; m. Michelle S. Mycroft, Oct. 5, 1985. AD, Danville Area C.C., 1974; BA, U. Ill., Springfield, 1977. Probation officer Vermilion County Probation Dept., Danville, 1981—; alderman Danville City Coun., 1991—; chmn. pub. svc. com.; developer, implementor, coord. Pub. Svc. Program, Community Svc. Work Crew. Bd. dirs. Vermilion County Con. on Substance Abuse, Danville, 1982; pres. Vermilion County Young. Reps., 1974; bd. dirs. dist. com. Boy Scouts Am., Danville, 1983. Mem. Danville Area C. of C., Ill. Probation and Ct. Svcs. Assn., Coun. on Social Agys. Christian. Home: 1307 Chandler St Danville IL 61832-2524

LARZELERE, KATHY LYNN, paralegal; b. Sellersville, Pa., Dec. 4, 1955; d. Harold Tyson and Hannah Ruth (Wile) Heckler; m. Lawrence Sollanek, Nov. 1984 (div.); m. Loel Harry Larzelere, Aug. 27, 1992; 1 stepdaughter, Lindsie M. AAS magna cum laude, Columbus State Cmty. Coll., 1991. From sales person to dept. mgr. Macy's New York, North Wales, Pa., 1977-83; store mgr. Bathtique, Wilmington, Del., Towson, Md., 1983-86; customer svc. person Marshall Fields, Chgo., 1987; word processor Franklin County Children Svcs., Columbus, Ohio, 1988-89; legal sec., paralegal M. Cohen and Assocs., Columbus, 1989-94; paralegal Calig and Handelman LPA, Columbus, 1994—. Author: (poetry) American High School Poets, 1973; contbr. articles to newsletter. Ward coord. Amelia Salerno for City Coun., Columbus, 1993. Mem. award Phi Theta Kappa. Mem. Nat. Fedn. Paralegal Asns., Paralegal Assn. Cen. Ohio (formerly Legal Assts. Cen. Ohio, co-chair student outreach com. 1994-95, chair 1995-97, 1st v.p. 1995-96, 96-97, contbr. The Citator newsletter). Lutheran. Home: 2119 Kingsglen Dr Grove City OH 43123 Office: Calig and Handelman 854 E Broad St Columbus OH 43205

LASATER, JOHN ROBERT, lawyer; b. St. Louis, Mar. 12, 1966; s. Donald Eugene and Mary Elizabeth (McGinnis) L. BS, U. Wis., 1988; JD, Washington U., St. Louis, 1991. Bar: Mo. 1991, Ill. 1991. Law clk. Mo. Ct. Appeals, St. Louis, 1991-93; asst. pros. atty. St. Louis County, 1993—. Com. mem. Campaign for Wis., St. Louis, 1992. Mem. ABA, Mo. Bar, Ill. Bar, Bar Assn. Met. St. Louis (com. chair 1992-93, Award of Merit 1993), Wis. Alumni Assn. Office: Office of Pros Atty 7900 Carondelet Ave Clayton MO 63105-1720

LASCARI, NICHOLAS STEPHEN, finance company executive; b. Milw., Nov. 24, 1947; s. Joseph and Angelyn Marie (Gregorich) L.; m. Delores Jane Jendrzejewski, May 30, 1970; children: Scott C., Jeffrey K. BBA, Marquette U., 1970. CPA, Wis. Tax staff Arthur Young & Co., Milw., 1969-76, mgr., 1976-81; v.p. Jannsen & Co., Menomonee Falls, Wis., 1981-82; mgr. Vrakas, Blum & Co., Svc. Corp., Brookfield, Wis., 1982-83; ptnr. Vrakas, Blum & Co., Svc. Corp., Brookfield, 1983-89; v.p. fin. Anderson/Roethle, Milw., 1989-93; ptnr., dir. taxes Conley McDonald & Co., Brookfield, 1993—. Mem. Small Bus. Adminstrn. Adv. Coun., Madison, 1982—, dir. region V, 1982-91; mem. Gov. Thompson Club, Madison, 1986—; sec.-treas. Tuckaway Country Club, Franklin, Wis., 1988-93; dir. Civic Music Assn., Milw., 1994—. With U.S. Army, 1970-76. Named Acct. Adv. of Yr. Small Bus. Adminstrn., 1986; recipient Bell Ringer award Small Bus. Adminstrn., 1989. Mem. AICPA (dir. individual tax com. 1994—), Wis. Inst. CPA's (key person coord., chmn. fed. tax conf. 1986), Ind. Bus. Assn. Wis. (treas. 1986-91, Outstanding Profl. award 1988), Wauwatosa C. of C. Republican. Roman Catholic. Home: 7728 Geralayne Dr Wauwatosa WI 53213 Office: Conley McDonald LLP 19601 W Bluemound Rd Ste 3 Brookfield WI 53045-5974

LASECKI, ROBERT RICHARD, management consultant; b. Dunkirk, N.Y., Apr. 18, 1943; s. Richard R. and Eleanor (Mekus) L.; m. Kathleen D. Soule, July 1, 1967; 1 child, Laura Marie. BSEE, Calif. State U., Pomona, 1964; postgrad., U. So. Calif., 1965-66, UCLA, 1967. Registered profl. engr., Ohio, Ill.; cert. mgmt. cons. Mem. tech. staff Marquardt Corp., Pomona, 1964-65, Hughes Aircraft Corp., Fullerton, Calif., 1965-70; engring. mgr. Eaton Corp., Roanoke, Va., 1970-71; engring. mgr. Otis Elevator Co., Roanoke, 1971-73, Cleve., 1973-75; prin. Booz Allen & Hamilton, Cleve., 1975-83; tech. mgr. Mannesmann Demag Corp., Northbrook, Ill., 1983-85; v.p. Austin Cons., Rosemont, Ill., 1985-90, Knight/Emerson Cons., Chgo., 1990-91; pres. Robert R. Lasecki & Assoc., Libertyville, Ill., 1991—; mem. B56.5 com. Am. Nat. Standards Inst., 1973-84, chmn., 1984—; guest speaker MATPAK Internat. Conf., Sydney, Australia, 1988, 89, Internat. Conf. on Warehousing and Distbn., Toronto, Ont. Contbr. chpts. to books; patentee electronic controls field. Mem. NSPE (sr.), Soc. Mfg. Engrs. (sr., cert.), Inst. Mgmt. Cons. Office: R R Lasecki & Assocs Ste 20 910 Sherwood Dr Lake Bluff IL 60044-2233

LASEE, ALAN J., state legislator. Office: 2259 Lasee Rd De Pere WI 54115-9663 also: RR 2 De Pere WI 54115-9802 also: State Senate State Capitol Madison WI 53702*

LASH, TIMOTHY DAVID, chemistry educator, researcher; b. Salisbury, Eng., Oct. 13, 1953; came to U.S., 1979; s. David and Judith (Spence) L.; m. Susan Shirkey Lash, Feb. 23, 1981. BSc with honors, U. Exeter, Eng., 1975; MSc, U. Wales, Cardiff, 1977; PhD, U. Wales, Cardiff, Eng., 1979. Postdoctoral assoc. U. Tex., Arlington, 1979-81; vis. asst. prof. U. Wis., River Falls, 1981-82; asst. prof. Northern State U., Aberdeen, S.D., 1982-84; asst. prof. Ill. State U., Normal, 1984-88, assoc. prof., 1988-93, prof., 1993—. Grantee NSF, NIH, Petroleum Rsch. Fund. Fellow Am. Inst. Chemists; mem. AAAS, Am. Chem. Soc., Royal Soc. of Chemistry, Internat. Soc. Heterocyclic Chemistry, Ill. State Acad. Sci. (chair chemistry div. 1988-90), Sigma Xi. Office: Ill State Univ Dept Chemistry Normal IL 61790-4160

LASHLEY, CURTIS DALE, lawyer; b. Urbana, Ill., Nov. 3, 1956; s. Jack Dale and Janice Elaine (Holman) L.; m. Tamara Dawn Yahnig, June 14, 1986. BA, U. Mo., Kansas City, 1978, JD, 1981. Bar: Mo. 1981, U.S. Dist. Ct. (we. dist.) Mo. 1981, U.S. Tax Ct. 1982, U.S. Ct. Appeals (8th cir.) 1992. Assoc. Melvin Heller, Inc., Creve Coeur, Mo., 1982; ptnr. Domjan & Lashley, Harrisonville, Mo., 1983-86; asst. gen. counsel Mo. Dept. Revenue, Independence, 1986-89, assoc. gen. counsel, 1989-92, sr. counsel, 1992—, adminstrv. hearing officer, 1995—; spl asst. atty. gen., 1986—; spl. asst. prosecutor Jackson County, Mo., 1990—; city atty., Adrian and Strasburg, Mo., 1985-86. V.p. Cass County Young Reps., Harrisonville, 1985. Mem. ABA, Kiwanis (treas. Harrisonville chpt. 1985-86, Harrisonville Disting. Svc. award 1985), NRA, Phi Alpha Delta. Republican. Presbyterian. Office: Mo Dept Revenue 16647 E 23rd St S Independence MO 64055-1922

LASHLEY, JEFFREY R., financial consultant; b. Leavenworth, Kans., Nov. 12, 1969. BA, Pitts. State U., 1993. Fin. cons. Merrill Lynch, Kansas City, Mo., 1994—. Mem. Phi Kappa Alpha. Republican. Roman Catholic. Office: Merrill Lynch Park Plz # 501 801 W 47th St Kansas City MO 64112-1252

LASHLEY, WILLIAM BARTHOLOMEW, county official; b. Dayton, Ohio, Jan. 2, 1952; s. William Bartholomew and Reta Carolyn (Reicken) L.; m. Loukia Simopoulos, June 30, 1973; children: Nichole E., Felicite D. BA in Econs., Wright State U., 1976; opthomol. sci. degree, Regis U., 1982. Asst. mgr. First Nat. Bank, Dayton, Ohio, 1973-77; mgr. store Kroger Co., Dayton, 1977-80; cashier Frontier Bank, Denver, 1980-82; asst. v.p. Empire Savs., Denver, 1982-85; mgr. investor acctg. Security Pacific Mortgage Corp., Denver, 1985-88; corp. acct. investors Crossland Mortgage Corp., Salt Lake City, 1988-89; fiscal officer Montgomery County Cts., Dayton, 1989—; mem. Montgomery County Fiscal Task Force, Dayton, 1990—. Mem. ABA (assoc.), Am. Bankers Assn., Govt. Fin. Officers Assn., Mortgage Bankers Assn., Ohio State Bar Assn. (assoc.). Home: 3307 Waltham Ave Kettering OH 45429 Office: Montgomery County Cts 41 N Perry St Dayton OH 45422

LASICH, VIVIAN ESTHER LAYNE, secondary education educator; b. Hopewell Twp., Pa., Dec. 17, 1935; d. Charles McClung and Harriette Law (George) Layne; m. William G. Lasich, Apr. 10, 1958; children: C. Laurence, Celeste M., Michelle R. AB, Geneva Coll., 1956; MA in Edn., No. Mich. U., 1970, postgrad. Secondary tchr. Freedom (Pa.) High Sch., 1956-57; elem. educator Gilbert Elem. Sch., Gwinn, Mich., 1967-69; lang. arts educator Gwinn Mid. Sch., 1970—; adv. bd. comty. arts panel Coun. for Arts, Mich., 1979-81; at-large rep. U. Peninsula adv. panel Mich. Dept. Edn./Arts, 1976-79; mem. sch. improvement team, 1988-91, 93-94, mid. sch. concept team, 1992—, co-chair, 1995—, mid. sch. at-risk coord. dist. curriculum coordinating coun., 1995-96; dist. curriculum strategy action team, 1993-94; dist. profl. devel. strategy action team, 1993-94; mem. sounding bd. Mid. Sch., 1994—, dist. sch. improvement team, 1994—; rep. Gwinn Edn. Assn. Mid. Sch., 1995—. Author: Prophets Without Honor: Teachers, Students, & Trust, 1991. V.p. Marquette (Mich.) Community Theatre, 1962-63 bd. dirs. 1963-74, mem. 1961-92; pres. Marquette Arts Coun. 1973-74, v.p. 1972-73, bd. dirs. 1970-78, mem. 1970-84; pres. Upper Peninsula Arts Coordinating Bd. 1976-78, v.p. 1974-76, bd. dirs. 1978-84; bd. dirs. Mich. Community Theatre Assn. 1972-73; bd. dirs. Mich Community Arts Agys., 1976-79. Recipient Committment to Excellence award Marquette Community Theatre, 1965. Devotion to Arts Development award Upper Peninsula (Mich.) Arts Coord. Bd. 1979. Mem. ASCD, NEA, AAUW, Mich. Edn. Assn., Phi Delta Kappa. Presbyterian. Home: 508 Pine St Marquette MI 49855-3838 Office: Gwinn Area Community Schs Gwinn MI 49841

LASLEY, DOUGLAS E., engineering executive; b. Winchester, Ind., Dec. 29, 1957. Sr. design engr. Forge Engring., Muncie, Ind., 1984-87; mfg. design engr. Electronic Data Systems, Anderson, Ind., 1987-89, engring. supr., 1989—. Bd. dirs. local Nazarene Ch. Mem. Soc. Mfg. Engrs. Office: Electronic Data Systems 2401 Columbus Ave Anderson IN 46016-4542

LASLEY, THOMAS J., education educator; b. Delaware, Ohio, July 23, 1947; s. Thomas J. and Anna F. (Cooper) L.; m. Janet L. Olney, Apr. 21, 1973; children—Julianne Marie, Elizabeth Ann. B.S., Ohio State U., 1969, M.A., 1972, Ph.D., 1978. Cert. tchr. and administr., Ohio. Tchr., Upper Arlington, Ohio, 1969-75; research assoc. Ohio State U., 1975-77; cons. Ohio Dept. Edn., 1977-80, asst. dir. tchr. edn. and cert., 1980-83; prof. U. Dayton (Ohio), 1983—, chmn. dept., 1983-92; cons. on sch. research and disruptive student behavior. Mem. Am. Ednl. Research Assn., Assn. Supervision Curriculum Devel., Phi Delta Kappa. Issues in Teacher Education, 1986, Dynamics of Change in Teacher Education, 1986, Teaching Peace, 1994; numerous articles. Office: U Dayton Chaminade Hall Dayton OH 45469

LASLO, DOUGLAS L., electrical engineer, power company administrator; b. Martins Ferry, Ohio, May 21, 1958; s. Daniel William and Margaret Ann (Petrash) L.; m. Mary Ann Dudzik, Oct. 21, 1978; children: Kristina Lynn, Stephanie Ann. BS in Elec. Engring., U. Akron, Ohio, 1987. Registered profl. engr., Ohio. Mechanic Y&O Coal Co., Cadiz, Ohio, 1978-80; electrician Wheeling (W.Va.) Pitts. Steel, 1980-83; distbn. engr. Ohio Edison Co., Youngstown, 1987-89; distbn. maintenance engr. Ohio Edison Co., Akron, 1989-91, project mgr.-automated mapping and facilities mgmt., 1992-93, dir. AM/FM sys., 1994—. Mem. IEEE. Christian. Home: 12320 Milly Dr Doylestown OH 44230 Office: Ohio Edison Co 76 S Main St Akron OH 44308

LASSE, FRANK G., state legislator; b. Dec. 11, 1961. BA, U. Wis., Green Bay. Chmn. Town of Ledgeview. Wis. state assemblyman, Dist. 2, 1994—. Home: 1776 Gordy Ln De Pere WI 54115*

LASSITER, ANTHONY T., neurology; b. Vallejo, Calif., Apr. 13, 1955; s. Harvery G. and Ruby M. (Freeman) L.; m. Jeri J. Schmidt, Apr. 28, 1989; children: Alexis Nicole, Angela Camille, Amanda Patricia. MD, Howard U., 1977. Diplomate Am. Bd. Psychiatry & Neurology. Rsch. assoc. Lovelace Found., Albuquerque, 1982-88; from fellow to asst. prof. U. Pitts., 1989-92; asst. prof. Med. Coll. Ohio, Toledo, 1992-95; dir. Regional Epilepsy Ctr. Northwest Ohio, Toledo, 1996—; mem. bd. dirs. EFA NW Ohio, Toledo, 1993—. Mem. IEEE, Am. EEG Soc., Am. Acad. Neurology, Am. Epilepsy Soc. Office: Toledo Neurol Assoc 3949 Sunforest Ct Ste 105 Toledo OH 43623

LASTER, ATLAS, JR., psychologist; b. Canalou, Mo., Apr. 18, 1948; s. Atlas Sr. and Rose Ella (Brown) L.; m. Janet Lee Rowe, Aug. 22, 1973; Children: Cedric, Marcus, Rosa, Sophia, Leah, Rachel. Student, Wash. U., 1966-69; BD, Union Theology Sem., 1971; MEd, U. Pitts., 1973, PhD, 1976. Staff psychologist Mon-Yough Mental Health Svcs., McKeesport, Penn., 1975-76; cons. psychologist DePaul Health Ctr. Care Unit, Bridgeton, Mo., 1977; program dir. Dept. Corrections, Menard, Ill., 1978; mgmt. cons. Univ. Pk. Group, Palm Beach, Fla., 1980; counseling coord. So. Ill. U., 1981-82; mgr. Comprehensive Counseling and Cons. Svcs., Pitts., 1982-84; dir. of christian edn. Pilgrim Congl. Ch., St. Louis, 1985-86; cons. psychologist Div. of Family Svcs., St. Louis, 1986—; asst. prof. Psychology Mo. Bapt. Coll., St. Louis, 1991—; vocat. rehab. counselor Mo. Divsn. Vocat. Rehab., St. Louis, 1991-93; pvt. practice Clayton, Mo., 1993—; sr. cons. Hanley, Harsche, Roffman and Druch, St. Louis, 1979-80; cons. Dept. Mental Health, St. Louis, 1986—, St. Louis Pub. Schs., 1989—, Ill. Dept. Children and Family Svcs., East St. Louis, 1990—, Health Mgmt. Svcs. Am., East Detroit, Mich., 1990—, Divsn. Children and Family Svcs., Spokane, Wash., 1990—, Decatur, Ga., 1990—. Contbr. articles to profl. jours. Cons. Congress of Racial Equality St. Louis, 1987—. Diplomate Am. Bd. Diability Analysts (sr.); mem. APA, Nat. Assn. Sch. Psychologists, Mo. Psychol. Assn. Baptist. Home: PO Box 16693 Saint Louis MO 63105-1193 Office: Med West Bldg 950 Francis Pl Ste 201 Clayton MO 63105-2465

LATELL, ANTHONY, JR., state legislator; m. Dorothy Kreeger; children: Kurt, Tod. BS, U. Dayton; postgrad., Wright State U., Youngstown State U. Councilman-at-large, coun. pres. Girard City, Ohio, 1976-80; state senator Dist. 32 Ohio State Congress; precinct com. person, mem. Trumbell County Dems., 1970—; commr. Trumbull County, 1980—. Office: 862 Krehl Ave Girard OH 44420*

LATHAM, DUDLEY EUGENE, III (DEL LATHAM), printing and paper converting executive; b. New Rochelle, N.Y., Sept. 28, 1943; s. Dudley E. Latham Jr. and Virginia Lois (Jarman) Latham Brodhagen; m. Kathleen Boylson, Apr. 2, 1965; children: Elizabeth, Clifford, Gregory, Thomas, Mark, John, Andrew. BA, L.I. U., 1967; postgrad., De Paul U., 1969. Sales rep. Hoffman LA Roche, Nutley, N.J., 1967-69, Permacel div. Johnson & Johnson, New Brunswick, N.J., 1969-71, Addison Wesley Pub. Co., Redding, Mass., 1971-72; gen. mgr. Midwest Tape Corp., Madison, Wis., 1972-76; pres. Roll Products, St. Mary's, Kans., 1976—; dir. St. Therese Acad., Madison, Wis., 1974-86. Chmn. Arts in Park, 1993—; city planning commr., 1994-96; mem. St. Mary's C. of C. (bd. dirs. 1993—, sec. 1993-94, pres. 1994-95). Mem. Topeka Country Club, Phi Sigma Kappa. Republican. Roman Catholic. Home: 101 E Mission St Saint Marys KS 66536-1526 Office: Roll Products Inc 511 W Palmer St Saint Marys KS 66536-1627

LATHAM, LAVONNE MARLYS, physical education educator; b. Garrison, Iowa, Mar. 17, 1942; d. Harry August and Vona Irene (Loveless) Hilmer; m. Robert Allen Latham Jr., July 21, 1979. BA, U. Iowa, 1964; postgrad., No. Ill. U., 1985, Western Ill. U., 1970-88, Bemidji State U., 1979. Cert. tchr., Ill. Tchr. phys. edn., elem. computer coord. Erie (Ill.) Community Unit 1, 1964—; head counselor Camp Lenore Owaissa, Hinsdale, Mass., 1964-78. Mem. NEA, AAHPER, Ill. Assn. Health, Phys. Edn. and Recreation, U. Iowa Alumni Assn., Ill. Edn. Assn., Erie Tchrs. Assn. (pres. 1982-83), Nat. Audubon Soc., Nature Conservancy, Delta Kappa Gamma. Baptist. Home: 1002 6th St Erie IL 61250 Office: Erie Community Unit 1 605 6th Ave Erie IL 61250-9452

LATIMORE, RITCHIE R., computer technology educator, consultant; b. Bklyn., Jan. 13, 1954; s. James Charles and Martha Lee (McIntyre) L.; m. Carroll Anne Kisha, June 28, 1985 (div. Aug. 1990); children: Janasia Shaunte, Ritchie Jamaal, Megan Francis, Devon Elliot. AA, U. Md., 1984, BS in computer sci., 1988; MBA, Kent State U., Kent, 1991. Prof. Bryant & Straton Bus. Inst., Richmond Heights, OH, 1991-93, John Carroll U., University Heights, OH, 1992-93; asst. prof. Kent State U., Burton, OH, 1992—; cons. self-employed bus., Cleve., 1991—. Contbr. articles to profl. jours. First Lt., U.S. Army, 1984-88, West Germany. Decorated Army Commendation medal, Disting. Grad. U.S. Army, 1982, W. Germany. Mem. Data Processing Mgmt. Assn., IEEE Computer Soc. Office: Kent State Univ Grauga Campus 14111 Claridon-Troy Rd Burton OH 44021

LA TOURETTE, JOHN ERNEST, academic administrator; b. Perth Amboy, N.J., Nov. 5, 1932; s. John Crater and Charlotte Ruth (Jones) LaT.; m. Lillie M. Drum, Aug. 10, 1957; children—Marc Andrew, Yanique Renee. B.A., Rutgers U., 1954, M.A., 1955, Ph.D., 1962. From asst. prof. to prof. Rutgers U., New Brunswick, N.J., 1960-61, SUNY, Binghamton, 1961-76; chair dept. econs. SUNY, 1967-75, provost grad. studies, 1975-76; dean grad. sch., vice provost grad. studies Bowling Green (Ohio) State U., 1976-79; v.p., provost No. Ill. U., DeKalb, 1979-86; acting pres. No. Ill. U., 1984-85, pres., 1986—; vis. prof. Karlsruhe (W. Ger.) U., 1974; research prof. Brookings Inst., 1966-67; vis. scholar Ariz. State U., 1969, 70; lectr. Econs. Inst., U. Colo., 1966; dir. NSF Departmental Sci. Devel. Grant, 1970-75, First Am. Bank, DeKalb, 1985—, Higher Edn. Stategic Planning Inst., Washington, 1984-88; cons. North Cen. Assn., 1983—. Contbr. articles to profl. jours. Served to capt. USAF, 1955-58. Ford Found. grantee, 1963; SUNY Found. grantee, 1963, 65, 70. Mem. Am. Econ. Assn., Can. Econ.

Assn. (fin. acctg. adv. standards coun. 1991-94). Office: No Ill U Office of Pres De Kalb IL 60115

LATTIMORE, JOY POWELL, preschool administrator; b. Goldsboro, N.C., Jan. 18, 1954; d. Albert and Zudora (Baldwin) P.; m. Vergel L. Lattimore, Dec. 16, 1978; children: V. Alston, Adam V., Alia Joy. BS in Early Child Edn., Barber-Scotia Coll., 1976; MEd in Early and Mid. Child Edn., The Ohio State U., 1977. Dir. alumni affairs Barber-Scotia Coll., Concord, N.C., 1977-79; tchra. Concord Mid. Sch., 1979-80; asst. dir. admissions Kendall Coll., Evanston, Ill., 1980-83; dir. pre-K program Dunbar Ctr. United Way Agy., Syracuse, N.Y., 1987-89; tchr. Hughes Magnet Sch., Syracuse, 1989-90; dir. Busy Bee Day Care, Westerville, Ohio, 1991—. Mem. race adv. com. United Way, 1995-96; vol. benefit com. Columbus Works. Mem. Nat. Assn. Edn. of Young Children, AAUW, NAFE, Internat. Reading Assn., Phi Delta Kappa. Methodist. Home: 610 Olde N Church Dr Westerville OH 43081 Office: Busy Bee Day Care Busy Bee Day Care 610 Olde N Church Dr Westerville OH 43081

LATTS, SANDER MORRIS, psychology educator, counselor; b. Ashland, Wis., Apr. 2, 1935; s. Abraham and Claire Idelle (Frindell) L.; m. Elizabeth Lee Kessel, Mar. 18, 1961; children: Lisa, Allan. BA, U. Minn., 1956; MA, Columbia U., 1959; PhD, U. Minn., 1966. Lic. psychologist, marriage and family therapist, Minn. Assoc. prof. U. Minn., Mpls., 1961—; conseling psychologist, St. Paul, 1966—. Author: (study guide) Human Sexuality, 1986, Violence in the Family, 1989. Mem. APA, Am. Assn. Marriage and Family. Democrat. Jewish. Office: Univ Minn 154 Appleby Hall Minneapolis MN 55455

LAU, MICHELE DENISE, advertising consultant, sales trainer, television personality; b. St. Paul, Dec. 6, 1960; d. Dwyane Udell and Patricia Ann (Yri) L. Student, U. Minn., 1979-82. Pub. rels. coord. Stillwater (Minn.) C. of C., 1977-79; asst. mgr. Salkin & Linoff, Mpls., 1982, store merchandiser, sales trainer, 1982-83; rental agt. Sentinel Mgmt. Co., St. Paul, 1983-84; account exec. Community Svc. Publs., Mpls., 1984-85, frwy. news supr., 1985, asst. sales mgr., 1985-86; asst. sales mgr. St. Paul Pioneer Press Dispatch, 1986-91; pres. Promotional Ptnrs., Eden Prairie, Minn., 1991-96; on-air show host Home Shopping Network, Eden Prairie, 1996—; on-air personality Sta. WCCO II Cable TV Mpls., 1988-89, co-host Afternoon Midwest, 1989-93; co-host Home Shopping Show, host Minn. Voices, Fox 29, 1995; cons. U. Minn. Alumni mag., 1986-89. Author mechandising and sales tng. manuals. Fund-raiser sustaining program YMCA, Mpls., 1986, Jr. Achievement, St. Paul, 1988; cons. Muscular Dystrophy Assn., St. Paul, 1988-89; bd. dirs. St. Paul Jaycees. Mem. NAFE, Nat. Assn. Home Builders, Mpls. Builder Assn. (amb.), Metro-East Profl. Builders Assn. (spl. events com.), Advt. Fedn., The Newspaper Guild, Internat. Platform Assn., Speakeasy Club. Lutheran. Home: Bldg D # 101 4750 Dolphin Cay Ln S Saint Petersburg FL 33711

LAUBER, DARRELL HOWARD, retired county land commissioner; b. Hibbing, Minn., June 24, 1938; s. Howard Benjamin and Ethel May (Anderson) L.; m. Shirley Marie Aho, June 18, 1960; children: Lori, Mark, Paul. AS, Hibbing Jr. Coll., 1958; BS in Forest Resource Mgmt., U. Minn., 1960. State inventory forester Iron Range Resource and Rehab. Bd., Hibbing, 1960-61; forester I Iron Range Resource and Rehab. Bd., Grand Rapids, Minn., 1963; forester II Iron Range Resource and Rehab. Bd., Grand Rapids, 1963-67, conservation mgr. I, 1967-71, natural resource mgr. I, 1971-72, sr. natural resource mgr., 1972-73; natural resource forester specialist I Dept. of Natural Resource, Grand Rapids, 1973-78, natural resource forester specialist III, 1978-83; land commr. Itasca County, Grand Rapids, 1983-95; chmn. Arrowhead Regional Devel. Forestry Com., Duluth, Minn., 1975-85; mem. Minn. Forest Resource Partnership representing Minn. Forestry Assn. Scoutmaster, scout coord. Boy Scouts of Am., Grand Rapids, 1981-87; club leader 4-H, Grand Rapids, 1978-80; elder, tchr., usher, leader First Evang. Luth. Ch., Grand Rapids, 1961—; bd. dirs. Itasca County Park and Recreation Dept., Grand Rapids, 1987—; tech. advisor Environ. Coun., Miss. Headwaters Coun. Mem. Minn. Forestry Assn. (bd. dirs. 1983, chmn. 1995-96), Minn. Land Commrs. Assn. (exec. com. 1993-95), Soc. Am. Foresters (chmn. 1961—), Minn. Generic Environ. Impact Study Commn., Minn. Generic Environ. Impact Study Roundtable, Ruff Grouse Soc. (huntsman), Itasca Gun Club (pres. Most Valuable Mem. 1978), North Ctrl. Beef Growers Assn. (bd. dirs.). Lutheran. Home: 601 La Plant Rd Grand Rapids MN 55744-9199

LAUCK, A. VICTORIA, small business owner, volunteer; b. Cin., Aug. 31, 1955; d. William Louis and Virginia Elizabeth (Hart) Pohl; m. John William Lauck, Nov. 27, 1982; 1 child, Christina Maria. BA in English, Trinity Coll., Washington D.C., 1977; MEd in Public Relations, Xavier U., Cin., 1978; attended, Mount Saint Joseph Coll., Cin., 1984. Public relations, advtg. mgr. Eagle Savings Assn., Cin., 1978-83; owner, ptnr. Make A Statement, Cin., 1991-93; owner V.P. Typesetting, 1988—; mem. bd. dirs. ProKids, Cin., 1990-93, 94-95, Jr. League of Cin., 1992-93, exec. bd. mem. 1994-96. Editor: (book) Cincinnati For Kids, 1990. Vol. catalogue writer Cin. Hist. Soc., 1984-86; printing coord. Cmty. Chest, Cin., Ohio, 1985. Recipient Honor award Assn. of Jr. Leagues, Internat., 1994. Home: 7000 Graves Rd Cincinnati OH 45243

LAUCK, ANTHONY JOSEPH, artist, retired art educator, priest; b. Indpls., Dec. 30, 1908; s. Anthony Peter and Marie Elizabeth (Habig) L. Diploma in fine arts, John Herron Art Sch., 1936; AB, U. Notre Dame, 1942, DFA (hon.), 1980; cert. in carving, painting, Corcoran Sch. Art, 1948. Entered Congregation of Holy Cross, 1937; ordained priest Roman Catholic Ch., 1946; priest aux. St. Martin's Ch., Washington, 1946-48, Holy Cross Ch., N.Y.C., 1948-49; priest aux. univ. ch. U. Notre Dame, Ind., 1950, mem. faculty dept. art univ. ch., 1950-82, assoc. prof. sculpture univ. ch., 1958-70, prof. sculpture, 1970-72, emeritus prof., 1973—, head dept. art, 1960-67, dir. Univ. Art Gallery, 1962-74, dir. emeritus, 1974—; Chmn. art jury Nat. Sacred Heart Drawing Competition, Xavier U., 1956. Exhibited, John Herron Art Inst., Ind. State Fair, Indpls., Corcoran Gallery Art, Nat. Mus. Art, Washington, N.A.D., Audubon Artists, N.Y.C., Pa. Acad. Fine Arts, Phila., Conn. Acad. Fine Art, Hartford, Provincetown (Mass.) Art Assn., Newport (R.I.) Art Assn., sculpture retrospective, U. Notre Dame, 1980-81, Snite Mus.Art, 1993; represented permanent collections, Phila. Mus. Art, Corcoran Gallery Art, Pa. Acad. Fine Arts, Norfolk Mus. Art, South Bend Art Ctr., Indpls. Mus. Art, Snite Mus. Art, Notre Dame U., Ind. State Museum, Indpls., Grand Rapids Art Mus., Evansville Mus. Arts and Sci., Ball State U. Art Mus., Gary Art Center, Hartwick Coll., Krasl Art Ctr., Midwest Mus. of Am. Art, Ind., St. Joseph, Mich., Midwest Mus. of American Art, Elkhart, Ind. ,also pvt. collections.; contbr. articles on sacred art to jours. and mags. Recipient Fairmount Park purchase prize Third Sculpture Internat., 1949, George D. Widener Gold medal for sculpture Am. art exhbn. Pa. Acad. Art, 1953, John Herron Art Inst. citation, 1957, 1st prize for sculpture Newport Art Assn., Peterson Sculpture Purchase award, 1991, Sculpture Purchase prize Midwest Mus. Am. Art, 1992; inducted medalist Ind. Acad., 1973. Mem. Audubon Artists, St. Joseph Valley Watercolor Soc., No. Ind. Artist, Ind. Artists Club, Nat. Sculpture Soc. N.Y. Home: Moreau Seminary Notre Dame IN 46556 Office: U Notre Dame Snite Mus Art Notre Dame IN 46556

LAUENSTEIN, ANN GAIL, librarian; b. Milw., Nov. 8, 1949; d. Elmer Lester Herbert and Elizabeth Renatta (Bovee) Zaeske; m. Mark Lauenstein, Aug. 16, 1986; 1 child, Maria. MA, U. Wis., 1972. Asst. libr. U. Wis., Wausau, 1972-73; cataloger, libr. MacMurray Coll., Jacksonville, Ill., 1973-76; corp. libr. Anheuser-Busch Cos. Inc., St. Louis, 1976—; facilitator Anheuser-Busch Quality Circle, St. Louis, 1984—. Treas. Friends of Kirkwood Libr., 1986—; mem. adv. coun. Sch. Info. Sci. U. Mo., 1987—. Mem. AAUW (editor jour. 1981-84, publicity chmn. 1985-87, scholar 1984), Spl. Librs. Assn. (network liaison 1981-83, chmn. employment com. 1983-84, chmn. hospitality com. 1984-85, membership chmn. 1988-89, newsletter editor 1992-94, advt. editor 1995—), St. Louis Regional Libr. Network (coun. 1981-83), St. Louis Online Users Group, Women in Bus. Network (advt. panel 1980-82, 86-87, programs planner 1987-88, asst. coord. 1988-89), Ohio Coll. Libr. Consortium Acquisitions Users Coun. Office: Anheuser-Busch Co Inc 1 Busch Pl Saint Louis MO 63118-1849

LAUER, ANN RILEY, community volunteer; b. Columbus, Ohio, Jan. 14, 1928; d. John Edgar and Helen Louise (Lacey) Riley; m. Cyril P. Nunley (dec. Aug. 1973); children: Patricia Lacey Nunley, Julia Riley Nunley; m. Harold E. Lauer, June 14, 1975. Student, Case Western Res. U., 1955, Ohio State U., 1976-77. RN, Mich.; cert. religious edn. Diocese Toledo. Mem. citizen bd. Nat. Recreation and Pks. Assn., Washington, 1991-92, Ohio Pks. and Recreation Assn., Columbus; park commr. Johnny Appleseed Metro Pk. Dist., Allen County, Ohio, 1972-92; chmn. commn. State of Ohio, Columbus. Recipient Vol. Ohio Ann. award, 1991, Spl. Recognition award Ohio Pks. and Recreation Assn., 1990, spl. recognition Ohio Senate & Ohio House of Reps., 1991; J.C. Penney Golden Rule grantee, 1989. Mem. Allen County Pk. Dist. Found. (founder, pres. 1992-95), Woman's Club. Roman Catholic. Home: 2614 Shoreline Dr Lima OH 45805 Office: Johnny Appleseed Metro Pk 2355 Ada Rd Lima OH 45801

LAUER, EDWARD MICHAEL, management consultant; b. Sublette, Ill., Dec. 6, 1931; s. Amor Andrew and Isadore (Dwyer) L.; m. Roberta Esther Amfahr, June 28, 1958; children: Larry, Diane, Mary, Mike, Scott. BBA, St. Ambrose Coll., 1958. Office mgr. Black Bros. Co., Mendota, Ill., 1956—. Contbr. articles to profl. jours. Pres. Holy Cross Sch Bd., Medota, 1973-74. Cpl. U.S. Army, 1952-54. Mem. Micrographics Assn. (treas. 1980-81, award 1981), Adminstrv. Mgmt. Assn. (v.p. edn. 1972-73, Key and Scroll Merit award 1978), VFW (quartermaster local chpt.), Elks. Home: 1211 5th St Mendota IL 61342-1915 Office: Black Bros PO Box 310 Mendota IL 61342

LAUFER, CHARLES DAVIS, clinical psychologist; b. Newark, Jan. 22, 1928; m. Dorothy Meyer, Feb. 18, 1969. BA, Wesleyan U., 1949; MA, NYU, 1952; postgrad., U. Tex., 1956; EdD, U. Mich., 1974. Diplomate Am. Psychol. Assn., Am. Bd. Med. Psychotherapists, Am. Assn. Biofeedback Clinicians; lic. psychologist, Mich., Wis., Tenn. Extern, intern Neuropsychiat. Inst., N.Y.C., 1950-51; researcher U. Tex. Speech Clinic, Austin, 1952-56; staff psychologist Tex. State Hosp., Austin, 1953-56; staff-chief psychologist Grand Rapids (Mich.) Child Guidance Clinic, 1956-58; chief clin. psychologist Kent County Juvenile Ct., Grand Rapids, 1958-60; chief psychologist Kent County Spl. Edn. Dept., Grand Rapids, 1960-61; spl. edn. dir. Montcalm County Bd. Edn., Stanton, Mich., 1961-63; interim clin. dir. Woodland Clinic, Petoskey, Mich., 1986-89; pvt. practice psychologist Psychol. Svcs., Grand Rapids, 1963—; cons. Dept. Social Svcs., Kent, Clinton, Ionia Counties, Mich., 1970—; cons. psychologist Care Unit, Glenbeigh, Grand Rapids, 1978-86, Woodland Counseling & Burns Clinic, Petoskey, 1986—, Harbor Hall, Petoskey, 1986-89; adj. prof. Forest Inst. Profl. Psychology, 1986—, Union Inst., 1989—. Contbr. articles to profl. jours. Lic. capt. USCG. Fellow Soc. Personality Assessment, Am. Psychol. Soc.; mem. Am. Acad. Sch. Psychologists, King Strang Assn., Psi Chi, Phi Delta Kappa. Episcopalian. Office: Psychol Svcs 6883 Cascade Rd SE Grand Rapids MI 49546-6869

LAUFMAN, MARK DAVID, securities company official; b. Racine, Wis., May 27, 1944; m. Ilene P. Princer, June 16, 1968; children: Scott, Jonathan, Kimberly. BS, U. Wis., 1966. Dir., mgr. Robert W. Baird & Co. Inc., Madison, Wis., 1969—. Chmn. Jewish Conf., Milw., 1989—; mem. Scott Kuges Campaign Com. Office: Robert W Baird & Co Inc 8000 Excelsior Dr Ste 201 Madison WI 53717-1914

LAUGHLIN, BRUCE, state legislator; b. Finley, N.D., Nov. 25, 1930; s. Harold M. and Johanna Irene (Schroeder)L.; m. Sue Nell Pladson; children: Janice Arlen Rayner, Jody Ann. Mem. N.D. Ho. of Reps., 1971-77, 83—; mem. appropriations com.; mem. govt. oper. divsn. com. N.D. Ho. of Reps.; mem. N.D. Legis. Coun.;. Mem. Econ. Bd., Finley, N.D., Job Devel. Bd., Steele County, Cemetery Bd., Finley. Mem. Comml. Club, Farmers Union, Nat. Farmers Orgn., Farm Bur. Address: PO Box 375 Finley ND 58230-0375*

LAUGHLIN, JAMES DAVID, public finance executive, consultant; b. Indpls., Sept. 23, 1963; s. John Thomas and Eileen Francis (Smith) L. Student, London Sch. Econs., 1984; BA, Wabash Coll., 1985; MBA in Fin., Ind. U., 1987. Sr. rsch. fellow Ind. Econ. Devel. Coun., Indpls., 1989-94; pres. Devel. Analytics, Inc., Indpls., 1994—; cons. J.D. Laughlin & Assocs., Indpls., 1990—. Contbr. articles to profl. jours. Recipient Lilly scholarship Lilly Endowment, Indpls., 1981, Eisenhower scholarship Eisenhower Found., Bloomington, Ind., 1981. Mem. Indpls. Athletic Club. Office: 5863 N Delaware St Indianapolis IN 46220-2529

LAUGHLIN, MARGARET ANN, education educator; b. Kansas City, Mo.; d. James Francis and Frances Meta (Johnson) L. BA, Calif. State U., Sacramento, 1959, MA, 1964; EdD, U. So. Calif., L.A., 1978. Tchr. San Juan Unified Sch. Dist., Sacramento, Calif., 1960-61, Roseville (Calif.) Joint Union High Sch. Dist., 1961-76; asst. prof. Calif. State U., Chico, 1976-79; prof. U. Wis., Green Bay, 1979—; bd. dirs. Nat. Railroad Mus., Green Bay, Wis. Coun. Social Studies, Madison. Contbr. articles to profl. jours. Recipient Svc. award Wis. Coun. Social Studies, 1984, Community Outreach award U. Wis. Green Bay Founders, 1985. Mem. ASCD, Nat. Coun. for Social Studies, Am. Ednl. Rsch. Assn., Comparative and Internat. Edn. Soc., Coun. for Geographic Educators, Social Sci. Ednl. Consortium, Phi Delta Kappa. Office: U Wis Green Bay 2420 Nicolet Dr Green Bay WI 54311-7003

LAUGHLIN, STEVEN L., advertising executive; b. 1948. Copy writer Fuller Biety Connell Agy., Milw., 1968-74, Cramer Krusselt Co., Milw., 1974-75; with Laughlin/Constable Inc., Milw., 1975—, now pres. Office: Laughlin/Constable Inc 207 E Michigan St Milwaukee WI 53202-4905*

LAUGHMAN, LYLE WILLIAM, school superintendent; b. Kansas City, July 2, 1944; s. Basil Delmar and Vivian Lorraine (Martin) L.; m. Sharon Ann Cox, Apr. 2, 1966; children: Christopher Theodore, Roderick Franklin, Konrad Fitzgerald. BS, Ctrl. Mo. State U., 1966, MS in Edn., 1974, EdS, 1978. Cert. tchr., Mo.; cert. sch. adminstr., prin., Mo. Math. tchr. Excelsior Springs (Mo.) Sch. Dist., 1970-71, Lexington (Mo.) Springs Sch. Dist., 1971-74; secondary prin. Wellington-Napoleon R-IX, Mo., 1974-78; supt. of schs. Stet (Mo.) R-XV Sch. Dist., 1978-80, Meadow Heights R-II Sch. Dist., Patton, Mo., 1980-81, Winfield (Mo.) R-IV Sch. Dsit., 1981—; dir., pres. PAL Spl. Edn. Group, Eolia, Mo., 1981-86, I-70 Athletic Conf., Wellington, 1974-78; mem. adv. bd. Pike/Lincoln Vocat. Sch., Eolia, 1981—. Mem. Lincoln County Growth Com., Troy, Mo., 1983-85, Tri-County United Way Bd., St. Charles County, Mo., 1982-86; commr. Lincoln County Planning and Zoning, Troy, 1985-88; elder Troy Presbyn. Ch., 1983-86. Staff Sgt. USAF, 1966-70. Mem. Am. Assn. Sch. Adminstrs., Mo. Assn. Sch. Adminstrs., East Ctrl. Mo. Adminstrs. Office: Lincoln County R-IV Sch Dist 701 Elm St Winfield MO 63389

LAUNDER, YOLANDA MARIE, graphic design director; b. Columbus, Ohio, Mar. 21, 1957; d. Wilbur Winfield and Julia Mary (Moretti) Reifein; m. David Paul Launder, Oct. 14, 1989; 1 child, Jonathan David. BFA in Design Comm., Tex. Tech. U., 1979. Graphic designer Perception, Inc., Chgo., 1980-81; graphic designer Source, Inc., Chgo., 1982-83, assoc. design mgr., 1983-84; sr. graphic designer Oscar Mayer Foods Corp., Madison, Wis., 1984-85, design mgr., 1986-88, group design mgr., 1989-95; assoc. dir., 1995—; lectr. Wis. Dept. Agr., Madison, 1988, Design Mgmt. Inst., Martha's Vineyard, Mass., 1991, Oscar Mayer Foods Corp., Women Career Devel., Madison, 1993-94, Philip Morris Packaging Roundtable, 1995. Co-inventor in field of Oscar Mayer Lunchables Packaging, 1989—. Sunday sch. tchr. St. Bernard's Ch., Dallas, 1973-75; evaluated high sch. portfolios Tex. Tech. U., Chgo., 1982-83; poll watcher David Patt Alderman campaign, Chgo., 1982; graphic design vol. Mental Health Assn. Dane County, 1986, United Way of Wis., Madison, 1992. Recipient Snack Food Package of the Yr. award Food & Drug Packaging Mag., 1989, Sial D'or award Salon International de L'alimentation, Paris, 1990, Bronze award for Excellence in Packaging for Oscar Mayer Lunchables, The Nat. Paperboard Packaging Coun., 1990, Mktg. Creativity award Kraft U.S.A., 1992, 93. Mem. Women in Design/Chgo. (program dir. 1982-83, membership dir. 1983-84, pres. 1984-85), Madison Advt. Fedn. (Addy awards com. 1985, voluntary action com. 1986), Design Madison (programs com. 1989-92), Package Designers Coun. Internat., Design Mgmt. Inst. Office: Oscar Mayer Foods Corp 910 Mayer Ave Madison WI 53704-4256

LAURIE, JOHN ALAN, commercial floor company executive; b. Ft. Wayne, Ind., Nov. 20, 1961; s. Jack J. and Barbara Ann (Seibert) L. BS, Purdue U., 1986; MBA, Harvard U., 1992. Project engr. Nat. Can Corp., Chgo., 1985; mfg. mgr. Procter & Gamble Co., Cin., 1986-88, fin. mgr., 1989, mktg.-brand asst., 1990; strategic cons. Owens-Corning Fiberglas, Brussels, Belgium, 1991; asst. to pres., nat. svc. dir. Cintas Corp., Cin., 1992-94; pres., owner J. Laurie Comml. Floors, Ft. Wayne, 1994—; advisor, co-owner Sweet Treats, Ft. Wayne, 1993—; cons. Free Wind Farm, Ft. Wayne, 1994—; owner, pres., JL Holdings, Ft. Wayne, 1994—. Group leader Jr. Achievement of Cin., 1986-90; vol. Greater Cin. United Way, 1986-90. Mem. Bldg. Constrn. Assn., Beta Theta Pi, Omicron Delta Kappa, Phi Eta Sigma. Home: 7019 Pointe Inverness Way Fort Wayne IN 46804 Office: 1828 S Anthony Blvd Fort Wayne IN 46803

LAURIEN, PHILIP CLARK, city planner, consultant; b. Buffalo, Oct. 23, 1949; s. Ira Morrison and Elsbeth Ann (Murphy) L.; m. Debra Linton, Mar., 1975 (div. July 1980); m. Bonnie Lou Creasy, Aug. 29, 1949; 1 child, Whitney Diana. BA, Miami U., 1971; M of Comty. Planning, U. Cin., 1974. Lic. real estate broker, N.H.; lic. 1 & 2 family bldg. inspectr Coun. Am. Bldg. Ofcls. Planner I No. Ky. Area Planning Commn., Newport, 1974-76; sr. regional planner Nashua (N.H.) Planning Commn., 1976-79; town mgr. Town of Hudson, N.H., 1979-82; cons., ptnr. Piper and Laurien, land planning, Hudson, 1982-86; cons., proprietor Philip Lauren Assocs., land planning, Hudson, 1987-90; dir. devel. dept. Franklin County Commrs., Columbus, Ohio, 1990—; mem. tech. rev. com. Franklin County Subdivsn. Rev., 1990—; mem. GIS com. Franklin County Bd. of Health, 1995—, mem. greenways com. Mid Ohio Regional Planning Commn., 1995—, mem. local govt. com., 1990-95; adj. instr. Chatfield Coll., St. Martin, Ohio, 1974-75, Plymouth (N.H.) State Coll., 1978; lectr. Nat. Bus. Inst., Eau Claire, Wis., 1991-95. Author: (creative land design) Farm Village Ordinance, 1995, (zoning and subdivsn. regulations) Barrington N.H. Master Plan, 1988, Middleton N.H. Master Plan, 1988, (land use plans) Hudson N.H. Master Plan, 1980, Hollis N.H. Master Plan, 1979. Acting chief of police Town of Hudson, 1981. Mem. AM-FM Internat. (pres.-elect IKO chpt. 1993—), Am. Planning Assn., Bldg. Ofcls. and code Adminstrs. Internat., Ohio Code Enforcement Officers Assn. Home: 17578 Raymond Rd Marysville OH 43040 Office: Franklin County Devel Dept 373 S High St Columbus OH 43215

LAURINO, WILLIAM J., state legislator; b. Chgo., Apr. 27, 1941. Student, Wright Jr. Coll., Loyola U., Chgo. State senator Ill. Senate, Springfield; Dist. 15 rep. Ill. Ho. Reps., Springfield, 1971—; asst. majority leader, chmn. ins., pensions and lic. activities com., mem. fin. instn. registration and regulation, horse racing, consumer protection, revenue, transp., and motor vehicles coms., Ill. Ho. Reps. Del. 6th constl. conv., 1970. Home: 5734 N Kingsdale Ave Chicago IL 60646-6623*

LAUSON, JAMES GARFIELD, II, retired fire captain, county supervisor; b. Sheboygan, Wis., June 17, 1943; s. James Garfield Sr. and Ethel Neuschaeffer) L.; m. Barbara J. Newton, Aug. 17, 1963; children: Jefferey James, James Garfield III. Firefighter Neenah (Wis.) Fire Dept., 1967-96; supr. Winnegabo County, Wisc., 1982—. Chmn. steering com. Wis. Counties Assn., 1992-96; pk. and recreation chmn. Winnebago County, 1986—; solid waste mgmt. bd. mem. Winnebago County, 1992—; mem. Neenah H.S. Quarterback Club, 1975-91. Mem. Nat. Assn. Counties (steering com. on energy and environ. land use 1992—, radon/indoor air adv. com. 1995—), Wis. Counties Solid Waste Mgmt. Assn. (mem. exec. bd. 1992—, Winnebago County indsl. devel. bd. 1992—). Democrat. Roman Catholic. Home: 1130 Honeysuckle Ln Neenah WI 54956-3933

LAUZEN, CHRIS, state legislator. MBA, Harvard U. Owner Comprehensive Acct. Svcs., Geneva, Ill.; Dist. 21 senator Ill. Senate, Springfield. Home: 116 S Elmwood Dr Aurora IL 60506-4922*

LAVEAN, MICHAEL GILBERT, advertising agency executive, political consultant; b. Lansing, Mich., Sept. 17, 1954; s. Gilbert Earl and Barbara Ann (Cowels) LaV.; m. Janet Tlapek, Aug. 21, 1992; 1 child, Madeleine. Student, George Mason U., 1972-76. Polit. staff person various Dem. campaigns, 1972-84; mayor City of Saranac, Mich., 1984-86; polit. cons. Polit. Svcs., Inc., Saranac, 1984—; pres. Polit. Svcs., Inc. (merger with A.& N.of Phil.), Saranac, 1985-91; prin. Allan, Drake and LaVean (merger with Drake and Assocs. and, Saranac, Mich., 1991—; bd. dirs. Page Hanes, Inc., Veos, Ltd., Veos, S.A. Co-patentee disposable cervical caps, sustained drug delivery, US and Europe; patentee disposal vaginal device. Vice-chmn. 5th dist. Dem. Com., Grand Rapids, Mich., 1985-87, chmn., 1987-93, vice-chmn. 3d dist., 1993—; mem. Dem. Electoral Coll., 1988; bd. dirs. United Way of Ionia (Mich.) County, 1986-92; exec bd. dirs. Ionia County chpt. ARC, 1987—. Mem. Napoleonic Soc. Am. (bd. dirs. 1991—), Internat. Napoleonic Soc. (bd. dirs. 1995—). Baptist. Home: 108 Mill St Saranac MI 48881-9702 also: 60 Portland Rd West Conshohocken PA 19428-2735

LAVELLE, ELLEN, educational psychologist; b. Oak Park, Ill., Jan. 9, 1949; children: Emily, Stephen. BA, So. Ill. U., 1974, MS in Edn., 1986, PhD, 1990. Asst. prof., dept. chair Teikyo Westmar Univ., LeMars, Iowa, 1991-94; asst. prof., coord. ednl. psych. U. S.D., Vermillion, Iowa, 1995—; cons. in field. Author: Magill's Survey of Social Science, 1993; contbr. articles to profl. jours. Preventative programming Boys' Club of Sioux City. Fellow Postdoctoral Acad. So. Ill. U.; mem. Am. Psychol. Assn., Am. Ednl. Rsch. Assn., Midwest Ednl. Rsch. Assn. Office: U. S.D. Dept. Counseling & Ednl Psy Vermillion SD 57069

LAVERDIERE, VICKI L., business executive; b. East Detroit, Mich., June 2, 1965. Cert. ins. agt., Mich. Agt., cons. Agent Benefits Corp., Warren, Mich., 1991-93; v.p. Consolidated Group Resources, Inc., Bingham Farms, Mich., 1993—. Vol. Salvation Army, Detroit, 1986-91. Office: 30150 Telegraph Rd Ste 161 Bingham Farms MI 48025-4520

LAVEZZI, JOHN CHARLES, art history educator, archaeologist; b. Chgo., July 7, 1940; s. Francis M. and Dorothy M. (Kopal) L. AB magna cum laude, Cath. U. Am., 1962; MA, U. Cin., 1965; postgrad., Am. Sch. Classical Studies, Athens, Greece, 1967-70; PhD, U. Chgo., 1973. Sec. Am. Sch. Classical Studies at Athens, 1968-70; asst. prof. Sch. Art Bowling Green (Ohio) State U., 1973-80, assoc. prof., 1980—; sr. assoc. mem. Am. Sch. Classical Studies at Athens, 1972—, rsch. assoc. Corinth Excavations, 1972—. Contbr. articles to profl. jours. Mem. Toledo Mus. Art. Recipient CUA Stratemeier award, 1962, Medici Circle teaching awards, 1986, 94; grantee Am. Philos. Soc., 1973. Mem. Archeol. Inst. Am., Midwest Art History Soc., Soc. for Preservation of Greek Heritage, Nat. Geog. Soc., Smithsonian Instn. Friends, Cyprus Am. Archeol. Rsch. Inst., Phi Beta Kappa (pres. chpt. 1992), Phi Alpha Theta, Blue Key, Delta Epsilon Sigma, Phi Eta Sigma. Roman Catholic. Office: Bowling Green State U Sch Art Bowling Green OH 43403

LAVIGNA, ROBERT JOHN, state governement executive; b. South Amboy, N.J., Jan. 17, 1952; s. Mario John and Dorothy Irene (Marzacano) L.; m. Patricia Anne McMahon, Oct. 25, 1981; children: Kathleen Rachel, Erin Elizabeth. BA in Pub. Affairs, George Washington U., 1974; MS in Pers./Human Resource Mgmt., Cornell U., 1990. Program evaluator Washington Regional Office, U.S. GAO, 1974-82, sr. program evaluator, 1982-84, dir. human resources, 1984-87; asst. to Asst. Comptr. Gen. of U.S. U.S. GAO, Washington, 1987-91; adminstr. of merit recruitment and selection State of Wis. Dept. Employment Rels., Madison, 1991—; mem. edn. and employment commn. NAACP, Madison, 1993-94; mem. adv. bd. Wis. Cert. Pub. Mgr. Program, Madison, 1995—; mem. manuscript rev. bd. Jossey-Bass Pubs., Inc., San Francisco, 1996. Contbr. articles to profl. jours. Vol. ofcl. Badger State Games, Madison, 1992-96; youth sports coach Recreation Dept., Fitchburg, Wis., 1992-96, McLean (Va.) Youth Assn., 1976-86; vol. South Madison Neighborhood Ctr. Food Pantry, 1993-94. Henry Toll fellow Coun. State Govts., 1994. Mem. Am. Soc. for Pub. Adminstrn. (nat. exec. coun. 1995—, Madison exec. coun. 1995—, Adminstr. of Yr. 1995), Internat. Pers. Mgmt. Assn. (publs. adv. bd. 1992—, com. on standards for ednl. and psychol. testing 1994—, sec.-treas. ctrl. region, 1996—, Agy. Excellence award 1994, Carl K. Wettengel award 1994), Soc. for Human Resource Mgmt. (Masters Thesis award 1990, Best Practices award 1995), Nat. Assn. State Personnel Execs. (Rooney Innovation award 1994), So. Wis. Ofcls. Network, Cornell Alumni Amb. Network. Home: 5845 Woods Edge Rd Madison WI 53711 Office: Divsn Merit Recruitment Dept Employment Rels 137 E Wilson St Madison WI 53702

LAVIN, ROXANNA MARIE, finance executive; b. San Antonio, Sept. 8, 1952; d. Teddy Harold and Cora Ann (Ames) Maddox; m. Michael Paul Lavin, July 11, 1971; children: Sharon Renai, Christopher Michael, Katherine Marie. Student, Ea. Mich. U., 1985, 86, 70; BBA magna cum laude, Cleary Coll., 1992; postgrad, Ctr. Mich. U., 1993, Madonna Univ., 1994; postgrad., U. Mich., 1996. Sales clk. Children's Fashion Shop, Livonia, Mich., 1970; bookkeeping clk. Ypsilanti (Mich.) Savs. Bank, 1970-73; receptionist, acctg. clk. Maize & Blue Properties, Ann Arbor, Mich., 1986-87; acctg. clk. Sensors, Saline, Mich., 1987; office supr., fin. mgr. Great Lakes Coll. Assn., Ann Arbor, 1988-94; fin., pers. mgr. Jackson (Mich.) Libr., 1994—, interim co-dir., 1995. Sec., treas. Old Mill Hills Assn., Pinckney, Mich., 1990-93; mem. Pinckney High and Mid. Sch. Parents, 1990-92; parent vol. Lincoln Cons. Schs., Ypsilanti, 1985-86; mem. Jackson County Literacy Coun. Recipient scholarship Ea. Mich. U., 1970. Mem. AAUW, Mich. Libr. Assn. Office: Jackson Dist Libr 244 W Michigan Ave Jackson MI 49201-2230

LAW, GERALD H., state legislator; b. May 20, 1944; m. Chris; children: Jenney, Katie. MBA, U. Detroit, 1969; MD, Wayne State U. Sch. Law, 1974. Rep. Mich. State Dist. 36, 1983-91, Mich. State Dist. 20, 1995—; trustee Plymouth Twp., Mich.; past Rep. precinct del.; fin. analyst Ford Motor Credit Co. Mem. Kiwanis, K. of C., YMCA, Libr. Soc. Address: PO Box 30014 Lansing MI 48909-7514

LAW, MICHAEL LIEBER, real estate agency executive; b. Neenah, Wis., Feb. 4, 1950. A in Real Estate, Fox Valley Tech. Coll., Appleton, Wis., 1974. Cert. real estate broker, Wis. Pres., owner Law Realty, Appleton, 1974—. With USN, 1968-72. Mem. Nat. Assn. Realtors, Wis. Realtors Assn., Comml. Investment Real Estate Inst. (cert. mem.), Fox Valley Realty Exch. Group, Fox Valley Realtors Assn. (N.E. Wis.). Office: Law Realty 1004 S Olde Oneida St Appleton WI 54915-1399

LAWFER, I. RONALD, state legislator. BA, U. Ill. Dir. Kent Bank; Dist. 74 rep. Ill. Ho. Reps.; mem. Jo Daviess County bd.; bd. dirs. Northwestern Ill. Cmty. Action Agy., Jo Daviess Farm Bur., Jo Daviess Agrl. Extension Coun. Home: 14123 Burr Oak Ln Stockton IL 61085-9514*

LAWLER, GLENN BRUCE, computer software executive; b. Nov. 30, 1952; s. Ward Glenn and Jesse Fairlene (Lane) L.; m. Martha Jo Fisher, June 17, 1976; children: John, Adam. BA, Ill. Wesleyan U., 974. Parts pricing pub. editor Caterpillar Tractor Co., Peoria, Ill., 1974-78; divsn. mgr. Clarklift-West, Inc., Sacramento, Calif., 1978-82; computer sci. faculty Ill. Wesleyan Univ., Bloomington, Ill., 1982-85; pres. Incode Systems, Inc., Peoria, 1983—; acquisition cons. 1st Fed. Savs. and Loan, Spring Valley, Ill.,1990; cons. Cmty. Banks, Peoria, 1990-93, MAGNA Bank, Peoria, 1994—, Dekroyft Metz & Co., Peoria, 1985%. Inventor conv. bus. housing sys., online banking sys., banking payroll sys., direct access svc. sys. Bd. v.p. Luth. Ctrl. Sch. Assn., Peoria, 1991—. Home: 3615 W Chartwell Rd Peoria IL 61615 Office: Incode Systems Inc 2000 W Pioneer Pkwy Ste 7C Peoria IL 61615

LAWLESS, ROBERT, anthropologist, educator; b. Tulsa, Oct. 4, 1937; s. Clarence F. and Virginia (Airy) L.; m. Aida Tijing Arribas, Dec. 27, 1963 (div. May 1978); m. Anita Raghavan, Aug. 8, 1988; children: Ilona Maria, Andrew Airy, Sharmini Karina, Kylen Schaeffer, Tavrick Kinsey. BSJ, Northwestern U., 1959; MA, U. Philippines, 1968; PhD, New Sch. for Social Rsch., 1975. Assoc. prof. anthropology U. Fla., Gainesville, 1976-92; prof. anthropology Wichita (Kans.) State U., 1992—. Author: Societal Ecology in Northern Luzon, 1977, Concept of Culture, 1979, Research Handbook on Haiti, 1990, Haiti's Bad Press, 1992; contbr. articles to profl. jours. With U.S. Army, 1959-62. Recipient Nat. Disting. Course award Nat. Univ. Continuing Edn. Assn., 1988. Fellow Am. Anthrop. Assn.; mem. Sigma Delta Chi, Phi Kappa Phi. Avocation: photography. Office: Wichita State Univ Wichita KS 67260-0052

LAWLOR, WILLIAM JAMES, III, brokerage house executive; b. Chgo., Jan. 30, 1935; s. William James Jr. and Mary Katherine (Fortune) L.; m. Blair Smith, June 16, 1962; children: John, James, Michael, David, Paul. AB in History, Princeton U., 1956; JD, Harvard U., 1959. Bar: Ill. 1960. Analyst Bus. Equity Corp., N.Y.C., 1960-61; analyst, atty. St. Louis Capital, Inc., 1961-62; various positions Loeb, Rhoades, Hornblower and predecessor firms, Chgo., 1962-67, N.Y.C., 1967-80; exec. recruiter Heidrick & Struggles, Chgo., 1980-83; 1st v.p. Smith Barney & Co., Chgo., 1983—; mem. securities law adv. com. Ill. Sec. of State, Chgo., Springfield, 1989-94. Mem. bd. advisors Cath. Charities, Chgo., 1987—; trustee Cath. Theol. Union, Chgo., 1982-95; mem. vis. com. U. Chgo. Dept. Music, 1983—; dir. Chgo. Metro History Edn. Ctr., 1984—, Great Books Found., Chgo., 1995—, overseer Ill. Inst. Tech. Stuart Sch., Chgo., 1982—; dir. Merit Music Program, Chgo., 1994—; trustee Rosary Coll., River Forest, Ill., 1986—. Lt. USCGR, 1959-60. Mem. Bond Club Chgo., Chgo. Club, Econ. Club Chgo., Mid-day Club Chgo. Office: Smith Barney & Co 3 1st Nat Bank Plz Ste 5000 Chicago IL 60602

LAWRENCE, ALICE LAUFFER, artist, educator; b. Cleve., Mar. 2, 1916; d. Erwin Otis and Florence Mary (Menough) Lauffer; m. Walter Ernest Lawrence, Sept. 27, 1941; 1 child, Phillip Lauffer. Diploma in art, Cleve. Inst. Art, 1938; BS in Art Edn., Case Western Res. U., 1938. Grad. asst. in art edn. Kent (Ohio) State U., 1939-40; art tchr. Akron (Ohio) and Cleve. Pub. Schs.; comml. artist B.F. Goodrich Co., Akron, 1942-44; sub. art tchr. Akron Pub. Schs.; sketch artist numerous events Akron, 1945-91. Author numerous poems. Mem. Cuyahoga Valley Art Ctr., Women's Art Mus., Akron Art Mus., 1963-94. Recipient 1st pl., 2d pl. in drawing, Butler Mus. Am. Arts, 1940-41, Cleve. Mus. Art, 1944. Mem. Woman's Art League Akron (sec. 1962), Ohio Watercolor Soc., Internat. Soc. Poets (life). Republican. Home: 861 Clearview Ave Akron OH 44314-2969

LAWRENCE, BARBARA, state legislator; m. Richard Lawrence. Grad., Coll. Emporia. Kans. state rep. Dist. 30, 1993—, tchr. Home: 315 N Roosevelt St Wichita KS 67208-3239 Office: Kans State Senate State Capital Topeka KS 66612*

LAWRENCE, DAVID WILSON, foundation executive; b. Worcester, Mass., June 3, 1942; s. Linwood Reed and Emilie (Wilson) L; m. Susan Gardner Dogherty, June 26, 1965; children: Peter David, Christopher David. AB, Miami U., Oxford, Ohio, 1964; MA in Edn., George Washington U., 1970. Dir. devel. Miami U., 1970-80, assoc. v.p. univ. affairs, 1980-82; chair dept. devel. Mayo Clinic/Found., Rochester, Minn., 1982—; pres. Rochester Airport Commn., 1985—, chair, 1996—; cons. Phi Kappa Tau, Oxford, 1980-83. Mem. exec. com. Rochester Civic Music, 1983-85; bd. dirs. Oxford C. of C., 1979-82; trustee Phi Kappa Tau Found., 1995—. Served to lt. USN, 1964-70; to capt., USNR. Res. Decorated Navy Commendation medal; recipient Admiral Sidney W. Souers award Miami U., 1983. Mem. Assn. Am. Med. Colls., Coun. for Advancement and Support of Edn. Republican. Presbyterian. Lodge: Rotary. Home: Phoenix Farm Salem Rd SW Rochester MN 55902-6655 Office: Mayo Clinic/Found Devel Dept Rochester MN 55905

LAWRENCE, JAMES ROLLAND, retired history educator; b. Omaha, Dec. 5, 1925; s. Herbert Rolland and Margaret Mary (Morrissey) L.; m. Dorothy Margaret Marx, Nov. 13, 1921. BS, Creighton U., 1950; MA in Rsch., St. Louis U., 1962. Mail clk. Omaha World Herald, 1950; mail rm. supr. Am. Embassy, Manila, 1951-52; consular sec. Am. Consulate, Cebu, The Philippines, 1952-53; tchg. fellow Creighton U., Omaha, 1953-54; tchr. Howells (Nebr.) H.S., 1954-55, St. Joseph H.S., Omaha, 1956-60, Viterbo Coll., La Crosse, Wis., 1962-91. With USN, 1944-46, PTO. Decorated Commdr., Disabled Am. Vets., 1995. Mem. Am. Hist. Assn., Orgn. Am. Historians. Roman Catholic.

LAWRENCE, JOAN W., state legislator; m. Wayman; children: David, Anne. RN, L.I. Coll. Hosp. Sch. Nursing; student, Douglass Coll., Rutgers U., Ohio State U. Rep. Dist. 87 Ohio State Congress, 1983-92, rep. Dist. 80, 1993—. Mem. Big Walnut Bd. Edn., 1970-73. Mem. LWV (Ohio pres. 1975-77), YWCA, Women's Polit. Caucus, Mid-Ohio Food Bank, Family Counseling and Crittenton Svc., Farm Bur. Office: Ohio House of Reps Office Of House Mems Columbus OH 43215*

LAWRENCE, JOHN KIDDER, lawyer; b. Detroit, Nov. 18, 1949; s. Luther Ernest and Mary Anna (Kidder) L.; m. Jeanine Ann DeLay, June 20, 1981. AB, U. Mich., 1971; JD, Harvard U., 1974. Bar: Mich. 1974, U.S. Supreme, 1977, D.C. 1978. Assoc. Dickinson, Wright, McKean & Cudlip, Detroit, 1973-74; staff atty. Office of Judge Adv. Gen., Washington, 1975-78; assoc. Dickinson, Wright, McKean, Cudlip & Moon, Detroit, 1978-81; ptnr. Dickinson, Wright, Moon, VanDusen & Freeman, Detroit, 1981—. Exec. sec. Detroit Com. on Fgn. Rels., 1988—; trustee Ann Arbor (Mich.) Summer Festival, Inc., 1990—; patron Founders Soc. Detroit Inst. Arts, 1979—. With USN, 1975-78. Mem. AAAS, ABA, Am. Law Inst., Fed. Bar Assn., State Bar Mich., D.C. Bar Assn., Am. Judicature Soc., Internat. Bar Assn., Am. Hist. Assn., Detroit Club, Detroit Athletic Club, Econ. Club Detroit, Phi Eta Sigma, Phi Beta Kappa. Democrat. Episcopalian. Office: Dickinson Wright Moon VanDusen & Freeman 500 Woodward Ave Ste 4000 Detroit MI 48226-3423

LAWRENCE, JOHN WARREN, business and broadcasting executive; b. Kalamazoo, Mar. 25, 1928; s. William Joseph and Borgia Marie (Wheeler) L.; m. Joanne Myrtle McDonald, Oct. 27, 1956; children: Joni Lawrence Knapper, Jane Lawrence Brogger, John Warren Jr., Jeffrey Michael. BS, Western Mich. U., 1949; MBA, U. Mich., 1950. Gen. mgr. Ill. Envelope, Inc., Kalamazoo, 1958-66, pres., 1958-80, chmn. bd., 1980-85; sec.-treas. Superior Pine Products Co., Fargo, Ga., 1967-93, chmn. bd., 1993—; pres. Channel 41, Inc., Battle Creek, Mich., 1972—; chmn. MCE, Inc., Kalamazoo, 1980-87; co-chmn., 1st health trustee First Health Devel. Corp., Kalamazoo, 1988—, co-chair, 1988-91; founder, pres. chief exec. officer Lawrence Prodns., Inc. (merged with MCE, Inc.), Battle Creek, 1985-89, Galesburg, Mich., 1989—; Trustee Commonwealth Schs., Albion, Mich., 1969-83; trustee Borgess Med. Ctr., Kalamazoo, 1982—, chmn. bd. trustees, 1987-91; trustee Gull Lake Sch. Found., Richland, Mich., 1983-91; bd. dirs. United Way of Mich., 1976-80; trustee Nazareth Coll., Kalamazoo, 1979-91, chmn. bd. trustee, 1983-87; dir., vice chmn. bd. ProMed Healthcare, Kalamazoo, Mich., 1995—; bd. dirs. Greater Kalamazoo United Way, 1970-81, chair fund dr., 1975, pres., 1977-78. Served to lt. (j.g.) USNR, 1952-55. Recipient Mich. Citizen's award Greater Mich. Found., 1963. Roman Catholic. Clubs: Park (Kalamazoo); Gull Lake Country (Richland, Mich.), Pelican Isle Yacht (Naples, Fla.). Office: 1800 S 35th St Galesburg MI 49053-9688

LAWRENCE, JON EDWARD, sales executive; b. Buffalo, Jan. 5, 1965; s. Robert Edward and Jeanne Patricia (Mills) L.; m. Melanie Ann, Oct. 22, 1990; 1 child, Danielle Ann. BS, U. Dayton, 1987. From fin. cons. to v.p. sales Smith Barney, Southfield, Mich., 1987—; lectr. St. Benedict's, Amherst, N.Y., 1993. Fundraiser St. Joseph Coll. Inst., Kenmore, N.Y., 1991-93. Republican. Roman Catholic. Home: 6676 Forest Park Troy MI 48098 Office: Smith Barney Inc 4000 Town Ctr Ste 1600 Southfield MI 48075

LAWRENCE, RALPH WALDO, manufacturing company executive; b. Mineola, N.Y., Sept. 10, 1941; s. Ralph Waldo and Gertrude (Ingles) L.; m. Judith Alice Frost, June 20, 1964; children: Susan, Carolyn. BA, W.Va. Wesleyan Coll., 1963; M in Pub. Adminstrn., Western Mich. U., 1979. Pres. Lawrence Mfrs., Columbus, Ohio, 1970-85; chief automated info. systems contract svcs. Systems Automation Ctr., Columbus, 1980-87, chief plans and mgmt. div., 1987-88; chief ops. Constrn. Supply Ctr., Columbus, 1988-89; chief Info. Ctr. DLA Systems Automation Ctr., Columbus, Ohio, 1989-92, DISA Office of Tech. Integration, Columbus, 1992-93; dep. of def. integration mgr. CALS, Blacklick, Ohio, 1993-95; prin. info. engr. Boeing Info. Systems, Columbus, 1995—; bus. mgr. Computer Sics. Corp., 1995—. Served to capt. U.S. Army, 1963-66. Mem. AFCEA (charter Columbus chpt.), Data Processing Mgmt. Assn. (pres. Columbus chpt. 1987, program dir. Columbus chpt. 1985, bd. dirs. 1987-88), Masons. Republican. Presbyterian. Home: 10201 Covan Dr Westerville OH 43082-9293 Office: Def Info Systems Agy 788 Morrison Rd Blacklick OH 43004

LAWRENCE, ROBERT G., insurance company executive; b. Sheboygan, Wis., Sept. 30, 1932; s. Raymond O. and Mildred (Kahr) L.; m. Phyllis A. Moos, Apr. 15, 1956; children: Cheryll, Daniel, David, Janice, Laura Beth. Grad., Purdue Profl. Mgmt. Inst., Agy. Mgrs. Tng. Coun. CLU, ChFC, fraternal ins. counsellor. Agy. mgr. Modern Woodmen of Am., Brookfield, Wis., 1956—, also bd. dirs.; instr. in field. Contbr. articles to Salesman Mag. Cub scout leader Boy Scouts Am., 1949-50, boy scout leader, 1949-50; chmn. Silver Lake Assn., 1979-84, mem., 1979—; recruiter Jesuir Retreat House, 1979—. Fellow Life Underwriters Tng. Coun. (chmn. 1984); mem. NALU (pres. Ozaukee-Washington chpt. 1968-69, pres. 1979-80, bd. dirs. Milw. chpt.), GAMA (pres. 1989-90, Hall of Fame 1994, 7 Builder of Yr. awards, 8 Nat. Mgmt. awards), Nat. Assn. Fraternal Ins. Counselors (past pres.), Wis. Gen. Agts. and Mgrs. Assn. (past sec.-treas., former bd. dirs., v.p. 1988, pres. 1989), Milw. Fraternal Underwriters Assn. (former pres., past bd. dirs.), Agy. Mgrs. Tng. Coun. (moderator 1986-87, 87-88, 94-95, chmn. 1987-88, mem. coun. Limra chpt. 1993—, chmn. region 6 1994), Pres.'s Club.

LAWS, CAROLYN MARIE RODERICK, medical surgical nurse, pediatrics nurse; b. Anthony, Kans., Feb. 3, 1949; d. Elbert Eugene and Gwendolyn Marie (Moore) R.; m. Gregory Owen Laws, Aug. 1, 1981; 1 child: Jennifer Marie. Diploma, Wesley Sch. Nursing, 1970; BSN cum laude, Wichita State U., 1985. Cert. nursing. Staff RN William Newton Meml. Hosp., Winfield, Kans., 1970-72, 87-89, unit supr., head nurse, 1972-87, 89-95, dir. social svcs., discharge planner, patient educator, 1995—. Recipient Soroptimist Tng. award, 1981. Mem. Nat. Nurses Assn., Sigma Theta Tau. Address: 2704 Morningview Rd Winfield KS 67156

LAWSON, ANITA JEAN, media specialist; b. Flint, Mich., Jan. 16, 1952; d. William Edward and Edna Elizabeth (Bond) L. BS in edn., Ctrl. Mich. U., Mt. Pleasant, 1970-74; postgrad., Western Mich. U., Kalamazoo, 1975—. Cert. tchr., Mich. Media specialist Otsego Pub. Schs., Otsego, Mich., 1974—, media dir., 1990—; cons. St. Margaret's Sch., Otsego, 1985; adv. mem. Instructional Television, Grand Rapids, Mich., 1985-92; bd. dirs. REMC-7, Holland, Mich., 1976—. Big sister Kids Connection, Kalamazoo County, 1982-90; mentor YWCA, Kalamazoo, 1993—. Technology grantee Allegan County Found., 1989. Mem. Mich. Assn. for Media Educators, Mich. Reading Assn., Nat. Wildlife Assn., Mich. Assn. for Computers in Learning, Mich. Edn. Assn., Kalamazoo County Humane Soc. Home: 1716 Roseland Kalamazoo MI 49001 Office: Otsego Pub Schools 540 Washington Otsego MI 49078

LAWSON, DEBRA LEE, physical therapist; b. Harlan, Iowa, Sept. 3, 1960; d. Delmar Lee Von Eschen and Donna Lee Crees Kirkhart; m. Barry E. Lawson, Dec. 6, 1986; 1 child, Alexandra Lee. BS, U. Kans., 1984. Phys. therapist St. Francis Regional Med. Ctr., Wichita, Kans., 1984-85, Tulsa Rehab. Ctr., 1985, Ark. Rehab. Inst., Little Rock, 1985-86; phys. therapist/student coord. Humana Hosp., San Antonio, 1986-87; phys. therapist/office mgr. Occupl. Medicine Assocs., Kansas City, Kans., 1987-90; phys. therapist Am. Rehab. Ctrs., Kansas City, Mo., 1990; phys. therapist, clin. coord. Riverview Ctr. for Ortho Rehab., Columbus, Ohio, 1990—. Sunday sch. tchr., children's coun. Meth. Ch. Mem. Am. Phys. Therapy Assn., Orthopedic Phys. Therapy Assn. Republican. Methodist. Office: Riverview Ctr for Ortho Reh 3600 Olentavey River Rd Columbus OH 43214

LAWSON, JERRY MARSHALL, journalist; b. Anderson, Ind., June 18, 1945; s. Ernest Marshall and Dolores May (Gault) L.; m. Marsha Jean Myers, June 20, 1970; children: Eric Marshall, Kurt Marshall. BS, Ball State U., 1972, MA, 1975; MPA, Ind. U., 1993. Furniture designer, builder Lawson Design, Ft. Wayne, Ind., 1982-87; from sports editor to mng. editor New Haven News/New Allen News, 1987-92; product info. writer Navistar Internat., Ft. Wayne, 1992-93; chair writer's bur. Ft. Wayne Bicentennial Exec. Coun., 1993-94; journalist Herald-Press, Huntington, Ind., 1994; freelance newswriter Ft. Wayne News-Sentinel, 1994—; v.p. Kolor Print, Inc., Ft. Wayne, 1982-83. Newsletter editor Leadership Ft. Wayne Alumni Assn., 1993—, bd. advisors, chair comms. com., Downtown New Haven Task Force, 1991-92. Mem. Writers' Ctr. Indpls., Soc. Profl. Journalists, Ind. Hist. Soc., Allen County-Ft. Wayne Hist. Soc., Canal Soc. Ind., Ft. Wayne Railroad Hist. Soc. Unitarian. Home and Office: 2229 Muskoday Pass Fort Wayne IN 46809-1427

LAWSON, JOYCE J., control clerk, assistant purchasing agent; b. South Bend, Ind., Dec. 12, 1936. Control clk., asst. purchasing agt. Raco Inc, South Bend, Ind., 1979—. Vol. ARC Bloodbank, South Bend. Mem. Am. Secs. Soc. Presbyterian. Home: 263 Rue Bossuet St Apt 1805 South Bend IN 46615-2839 Office: Raco Inc PO Box 4002 South Bend IN 46634-4002

LAWSON, MATTHEW S., securities industry executive; b. New Fairfield, Conn., Aug. 8, 1946; m. Mary Coryn, Jan. 2, 1978. AB, Hamilton Coll., 1968; MBA with honors, U. Chgo., 1985. Account exec. Foote, Cone & Belding Advt., Inc., L.A., 1969-71, account dir., 1971-72; corp. pub. affairs mgr. Mazda Motors Am., Inc., L.A., 1972-74; v.p. Eisaman, Johns and Laws Advt. Inc., L.A., 1975-76; dep. news sec. to Gov. Ronald Reagan Presdl. Campaign, 1976, 80; dir. corp. comm. Computer Scis. Corp., El Segundo, Calif., 1977-82; dir. investor relations Gould Inc., Rolling Meadows, Ill., 1982-85, dir. strategic planning, 1985-86; v.p. NatWest Securities U.S.A., 1987—. Mem. Calif. Rep. Cen. Com., 1969-71; dir. Calif. Rep. Assembly, 1969-73; comm. dir. for Lt. Gov. John Harmer, 1974. Home: 1 S 150th Spring Rd Oakbrook Ter IL 60181 Office: 190 S La Salle St Ste 1050 Chicago IL 60603

LAWYER, VIVIAN JURY, lawyer; b. Farmington, Iowa, Jan. 7, 1932; d. Jewell Everett Jury and Ruby Mae (Schumaker) Brewer; m. Verne Lawyer, Oct. 25, 1959; children: Michael Jury, Steven Verne. Tchr.'s cert. U. No. Iowa, 1951; BS with honors, Iowa State U., 1953; JD with honors, Drake U., 1968. Bar: Iowa 1968, U.S. Supreme Ct. 1986. Home econs. tchr. Waukee High Sch. (Iowa), 1953-55; home econs. tchr. jr. high sch. and high sch., Des Moines Pub. Schs., 1955-61; pvt. practice law, Des Moines, 1972—; chmn. juvenile code tng. sessions Iowa Crime Commn., Des Moines, 1978-79, coord. workshops, 1980; assoc. Lawyer, Lawyer & Assocs., Des Moines, 1981—; co-founder, bd. dirs. Youth Law Center, Des Moines, 1977—; mem. com. rules of juvenile procedure Supreme Ct. Iowa, 1981-87, adv. com. on costs of ct. appointed counsel Supreme Ct. Iowa, 1985-88; trustee Polk County Legal Aid Svcs., Des Moines, 1980-82; mem. Iowa Dept. Human Svcs. and Supreme Ct. Juvenile Justice County Base Joint Study Com., 1984—. Mem. Iowa Task Force permanent families project Nat. Coun. Juvenile and Family Ct. Judges, 1984-88; mem. substance abuse com. Commn. Children, Youth and Families, 1985—; co-chair Polk County Juvenile Detention Task Force, 1988. Editor: Iowa Juvenile Code Manual, 1979, Iowa Juvenile Code Workshop Manual, 1980; co-editor: 1987 Cumulative Supplement, 1993 supplement, Iowa Academy of Trial Lawyers Trial Handbook; author booklet in field, 1981. Mem. Polk County Citizens Commn. on Corrections, 1977. Iowa Dept. Social Svcs. grantee, 1980. Mem. Purple Arrow, Phi Kappa Phi, Omicron Nu. Republican. Home: 5831 N Waterbury Rd Des Moines IA 50312-1339 Office: 427 Fleming Building Des Moines IA 50309-4011

LAXPATI, SHARAD RANJITLAL, electrical engineering educator; b. Bombay, India, July 16, 1938; came to U.S., 1960; s. Ranjitlal P. and Arvinda R. (Zaveri) L.; m. Maureen A. Burns, Nov. 26, 1983. BE, Gujarat U., India, 1957; MS, U. Ill., 1961, PhD, 1965. Jr. sci. officer Atomic Energy Establishment, Bombay, 1958-60; asst. prof. Pa. State U., University Park, 1965-69; assoc. head dept. electrical engrng. and computer sci. U. Ill.-Chgo., 1969—; cons. Symmetron, Inc., Fairfax, Va., 1988—, Naval Research Lab., Washington, 1979-90, Locus Inc., Alexandria, Va., 1984-86, Motorola Inc., Schaumburg, Ill., 1976-77; ptnr. LMS Engring., Chgo., 1986—. Contbr. articles to profl. jours. Mem. IEEE, Instn. Elec. Engrs. (London), Internat. Radio Sci. Union.

LAY, DONALD POMEROY, federal judge; b. Princeton, Ill., Aug. 24, 1926; s. Hardy W. and Ruth (Cushing) L.; m. Miriam Elaine Gustafson, Aug. 6, 1949; children: Stephen Pomeroy (dec.), Catherine Sue, Cynthia Lynn, Elizabeth Ann, Deborah Jean, Susan Elaine. Student, U.S. Naval Acad., 1945-46; BA, U. Iowa, 1948, JD, 1951; LLD (hon.), Mitchell Coll. Law, 1985. Bar: Nebr. 1951, Iowa 1951, Wis. 1953. Assoc. Kennedy, Holland, DeLacy & Svoboda, Omaha, 1951-53, Quarles, Spence & Quarles, Milw., 1953-54, Eisenstatt, Lay, Higgins & Miller, 1954-66; judge U.S. Ct. Appeals (8th cir.), 1966—, chief judge, 1980-92, senior judge, 1992—; faculty mem. on evidence Nat. Coll. Trial Judges, 1964-65, U. Minn. Law Sch., William Mitchell Law Sch.; mem. U.S. Jud. Conf., 1980-92. Mem. editorial bd.: Iowa Law Rev., 1950-51; contbr. articles to legal jours. With USNR, 1944-46. Recipient Hancher-Finkbine medal U. Iowa, 1980. Fellow Internat. Acad. Trial Lawyers; mem. ABA, Nebr. Bar Assn., Iowa Bar Assn., Wis. Bar Assn., Am. Judicature Soc., Assn. Trial Lawyers Am. (bd. govs. 1963-65, Jud. Achievement award), Order of Coif, Delta Sigma Rho (Significant Sig award 1986, Herbert Harley award 1988), Phi Delta Phi, Sigma Chi. Presbyterian.

LAYBOURN, HALE, insurance company executive; b. Cedar Rapids, Iowa, July 20, 1923; s. Harold Hale and Reba S. (Strudevant) L.; BSBA, U. Wyo., 1949; m. Barbara G., Dec. 21, 1947; children—Lillian Louise Laybourn Casares, Constance Grace Laybourn Harb, Deborah Hayle Laybourn Pender, Paul James, Richard Tod, Dorothy M. Asst. bus. mgr. Cheyenne (Wyo.) Newspapers, Inc., 1949-50; fiscal and personnel officer, dir. hosp. facilities Wyo. Dept. Health, 1950-60; dir. internal ops. Blue Cross and Blue Shield, Cheyenne, Wyo., 1960-65; pres. Blue Cross N.D., Fargo, 1965-86; pres., chief exec. officer Dental Service Corp., Vision Service, Inc., 1976-86; Coordinated Ins. Svc., 1982-86; chmn. bd. No. Plains Life Ins. Co., 1983-86, chmn. bd., pres., 1986-88; v.p. Care Plan HMO; bd. dirs. Nat. Blue Cross Assn., 1973-77; chmn. Dist. X Plan Pres's., 1970-73; bd. dir. West Fargo State Bank; pres. Money Concept Internat., Fargo, 1987-93; assoc. cons. Nat. BUs. Cons., Inc., 1989-91. Pres. Fargo-Moorhead Civic Opera Co., 1968-81, chmn. bd., 1981-90; chmn. United Fund, Fargo, 1972. With inf. U.S. Army, 1942-45. Mem. Fargo C. of C. (pres. 1977). Republican. Episcopalian. Clubs: Elks, Kiwanis.

LAYCOCK, GEORGE EDWIN, author, journalist; b. Zanesville, Ohio, May 29, 1921; s. William D. and Hazel D. (Heim) L.; m. Ellen Mae VanAuken, Feb. 14, 1943; children: Elaine Sue, Michael George, Steven Alan. BS in Wildlife Conservation, Ohio State U., 1947. Assoc. editor The Farm Quar., Cin., 1947-51; freelance writer Cin., 1951—; field editor Audubon Mag., 1968-91. Author: Sign of the Flying Goose, 1965, The Alien Animals, 1966, Never Pet a Porcupine (Boys Club award), 1965, Never Trust a Cowbird, 1966, Whitetail-Life of a White-Tailed Deer, 1966, Big Nick, Story of a Remarkable Black Bear, 1967, King Gator, 1968, America's Endangered Wildlife, 1969, Wild Refuge, 1969, Shotgunner's Bible, 1969, Pelicans, 1970, The Diligent Destroyers, 1970, Alaska the Embattled Frontier, 1971, Air Pollution, 1972, Water Pollution, 1972, Wingspread-A World of Birds, 1972, Autumn of the Eagle, 1973, Strange Monsters and Great Searches, 1973, World's Endangered Wildlife, 1973, Wild Animals, Safe Places, 1974, Wild Travelers, 1974, People and Other Mammals, 1975, Squirrels, 1975, Camels-Ships of the Desert, 1975, The Bird Watcher's Bible, 1976, Caves, 1976, Death Valley, 1976, Islands and Their Mysteries, 1977, The Deer Hunter's Bible, 1977, Beyond the Arctic Circle, 1978, Exploring the Great Swamp, 1978, Mysteries, Monsters and Untold Secrets, 1978, Wild Hunters, 1978, How to Buy and Enjoy a Small Farm, 1978, Complete Beginner's Guide to Photography, 1979, Tornadoes, 1979, Does Your Pet Have a Sixth Sense?, 1980, Bats in the Night, 1981, The Kroger Story, 1983, North American Wildlife, 1983, The Wild Bears, 1986, The Mountain Men, 1988, The Hunters and the Hunted, 1990, The Art of John A. Ruthven, 1994; (with Ellen Laycock) Flying Sea Otters, 1970, How the Settlers Lived, 1980, The Ohio Valley, 1983; contbr. articles to profl. jours. Mem. libr. bd. trustees Clermont County, Batavia, Ohio, 1953-63; bd. trustees Cin. Mus. Natural History, 1980-83, Cin. Nature Ctr., 1976-82. 2nd lt. U.S. Army, 1942-45, ETO. Named to Ohio Conservation Hall of Fame Ohio Dept. Natural Resources, 1988; 5 books named as Outstanding Sci. Books for Children, Nat. Sci. Tchrs. Assn. and Children's Book Coun. Joint Com. Mem. Am. Soc. Journalists and Authors, Outdoor Writers Assn. Am. (Jade of Chiefs 1970, Excellence in Craft award 1983, Nat. Book award nomination 1973), Wilderness Soc., Sierra Club.

LAZARUS, M. KAREN, executive director; b. Trenton, N.J., Jan. 5, 1946; d. Bertram Harry and Sydell (Goldfeder) L. BA, Youngstown State U., 1968; postgrad., U. Cin., 1969-70; MBA, Youngstown State U., 1991. Lab. supr. St. Elizabeth Hosp. Med. Ctr., Youngstown, Ohio, 1972-92; exec. dir. Vis. Nurs Assn. Greater Youngstown Area, Youngstown, Ohio, 1992—; instr. Youngstown State U., Youngstown, Ohio, 1980—. Mem. Kiwanis; bd.

dirs. Youngstown Playhouse, 1973-75. Recipient Arthur State Mgrs. award Youngstown Playhouse, 1976. Mem. Am. Soc. Clinical Pathologists. Office: VNA 518 E Indianola Ave Youngstown OH 44502

LAZERSON, EARL EDWIN, academic administrator emeritus; b. Detroit, Dec. 10, 1930; s. Nathan and Ceil (Stashefsky) L.; m. Ann May Harper, June 11, 1966; children from previous marriage: Joshua, Paul. BS, Wayne State U., Detroit, 1953; postgrad., U. Leiden, Netherlands, 1957-58; MA, U. Mich., 1954, PhD, 1982. Mathematician Inst. Def. Analyses, Princeton, N.J., 1960-62; asst. prof. math. Washington U., St. Louis, 1962-65, 66-69; vis. asso. prof. Brandeis U., 1965-66; mem. faculty So. Ill. U., Edwardsville, 1969—, prof. math., 1973—, chmn. dept. math. studies, 1972-73, dean Sch. Sci. and Tech., 1973-76, univ. v.p., provost, 1977-79, pres., 1980-93; pres. emeritus, 1994—. Chmn. Southwestern Ill. Devel. Authority, City of East St. Louis Fin. Adv. Authority; active Leadership Coun. Southwestern Ill., Gateway Ctr. Met. St. Louis, Inc., St. Louis Symphony Soc.; trustee Jefferson Nat. Expansion Meml. Assn., Ill. Econ. Devel. Bd. Recipient Sr. Teaching Excellence award Standard Oil Found., 1970-71. Mem. Am. Math. Soc., Math. Assn. Am., European Math. Soc., London Math. Soc., Soc. Mathematique France, Fulbright Alumni Assn., Sigma Xi. Home: 5 Hidden Valley Ln Edwardsville IL 62025-3706

LAZICH, MARY A., state legislator. Home: 4405 S 129th St New Berlin WI 53151-6901*

LAZZARA, DENNIS JOSEPH, orthodontist; b. Chgo., Mar. 14, 1948; s. Joseph James and Jacqueline Joan (Antonini) L.; m. Nancy Ann Pirhofer, Dec. 18, 1971; children: Kristin Lynn, Bryan Matthew, Matthew Dennis, Kathryn Marie, David Brady. BS, U. Dayton, 1970; DDS, Loyola U., 1974. MS in Oral Biology, 1976, cert. orthodontics, 1976. Practice dentistry specializing in orthodontics, Geneva, Ill., 1976—; mem. dental staff Delnor Community Hosp., Geneva and St. Charles, Ill., 1976—; sec. dental staff, Geneva, 1978-80, v.p., 1980-82, pres., 1982-84, exec. com., 1982-84. Leader Boy Scouts Am., 1988-90. Recipient Award of Merit, Am. Coll. of Dentists, 1974, Harry Sicher honorable mention Council on Research, Am. Assn. Orthodontists, 1977. Mem. Am. Assn. Orthodontists, Midwestern Soc. of Orthodontists, Ill. Soc. Orthodontists, ADA, Fox River Valley Dental Soc. (bd. dirs. 1983-86), Blue Key Nat. Honor Soc. Roman Catholic. Avocations: sailing, golf. Office: PO Box 431 Geneva IL 60134-0431

LAZZARA, JOSEPH J., project engineer; b. Pitts., Dec. 21, 1966; s. Louis J. and Kathleen M. (Kosakowski) L.; m. Ellen M. Noir, Apr. 20, 1990. BS in Mech. Engring., Cannon U., 1988. Project engr. Delco Electronics, Kokomo, Ind., 1993-94, Royal Appliance, Cleve., 1994—. Lt. USN, 1988-93. Office: Royal Appliance Mant 650 Alpha Dr Cleveland OH 44143-2123

LEA, ELEANOR LUCILLE, retired state agency administrator; b. Diller, Nebr., Nov. 6, 1916; d. Edward Richard and Gertrude (Loock) Henrichs; m. Stanley Guy Lea, Mar. 6, 1936; children: Dianna Evenson, Cylesta Peters, Jeffrey, Chad. Student, Fairbury State Coll. Owner Modern Furniture Store, Fairbury, Nebr., 1945-80; dist. mgr. Field Enterprises, Chgo., 1966-80; libr. resource person Fairbury Pub. Libr., 1982-85; job coord. Blue River Area Agy. on Aging, Lincoln, Nebr., 1985-87; Bd. mem. Operation ABLE, Lincoln, 1987-92, Nat. Grandparent Program, Beatrice, Nebr., 1985-87. Pres., dist. v.p. United Meth. Women; Sunday Sch. supt. Meth. Ch., Fairbury; v.p. sch. bd. Fairbury Pub. Sch. Bd., 1956-62; bd. mem. Girl Scouts U.S.A., 1950-56. Mem. Toastmasters (v.p. pub. rels. Lincoln 1992-94). Republican. Home: 2920 S 72nd St Apt 85 Lincoln NE 68506-3681

LEA, LORENZO BATES, lawyer; b. St. Louis, Apr. 12, 1925; s. Lorenzo Bates and Ursula Agnes (Gibson) L.; m. Marcia Gwendolyn Wood, Mar. 21, 1953; children—Victoria, Jennifer, Christopher. BS, MIT, 1946; JD, U. Mich., 1949; grad. Advanced Mgmt. Program, Harvard U., 1964. Bar: Ill. 1950. With Amoco Corp. (formerly Standard Oil Co. Ind.), Chgo., 1949—, asst. gen. counsel, 1963-71, assoc. gen. counsel, 1971-72, gen. counsel, 1972-78, v.p., gen. counsel, 1978-89. Trustee Village of Glenview (Ill.) Zoning Bd., 1961-63; bd. dirs. Chgo. Crime Commn., 1978—, Midwest Council for Internat. Econ. Policy, 1973—, Chgo. Bar Found., 1981—, Chgo. Area Found. for Legal Services, 1981—; bd. dirs. United Charities of Chgo., 1973—, chmn., 1985—. Served with USNR, 1943-46. Mem. ABA, Am. Petroleum Inst., Am. Arbitration Assn. (dir. 1980—), Ill. Bar Assn., Chgo. Bar Assn., Assn. Gen. Counsel, Order of Coif, Law Club, Econs. Club, Legal, Mid-Am. (Chgo.), Glen View, Wyndemere, Hole-In-The-Wall, Sigma Xi. Republican. Mem. United Ch. of Christ.

LEABLE, PHILIP F., township highway commissioner; b. Zion, Ill., Nov. 2, 1926; s. Frank A. and Margarett D. (Winters) L.; m. Margaret A. Pataky, Feb. 19, 1949; children: Penny Fay, Gail Anne. H.s. grad., Gurnee, Ill. Owner, operator Philip F. Leable Trucking, Zion, 1949-54, Philip F. Leable Farm, Zion, 1954-73; foreman Hwy. Dept. Benton Twp., Zion, 1971-77, hwy. commr., 1977—. Sustaining mem. Lake County Rep. Club, Libertyville, Ill., 1977—, Nat. Rep. Com., Washington, 1977—. Mem. Lake County Hwy. Commrs. Assn. (pres. 1984-90), Lake County Twp. Officials (pres. 1993—), Wintthrop Harbor Lions Club, (pres. sec., treas, bd. dirs. Meldin Jones award 1989). Methodist. Office: Benton Twp 40023 N Green Bay Rd Zion IL 60099

LEACH, CHRISTINE ELAINE, technical support executive; b. Riverside, Calif., Aug. 25, 1957; d. Kenneth Orvis and Gwendolyn Eloise (Belew) T.; m. Robert Gary Leach, June 11, 1983; children: Robert Arlan, Jonathan Abraham. Enlisted USAF, 1977, advanced through grades to tech. sgt., 1980, asst. mgr., 1983, adminstrv. supr. battle staff sect., 1984, mgr. force applications adminstrn., 1984-90, resigned, 1988; facility security officer Logicon, Inc., 1990—, assoc. program asst., 1990—; instr. for software Logicon, Inc., Bellevue, Nebr., 1988—. Mem. Air Force Assn. (life). Republican. Baptist. Office: 1408 Fort Crook Rd S Bellevue NE 68005-2969

LEACH, DAVE FRANCIS, editor, musician; b. Iowa City, Iowa, Nov. 12, 1945; s. Joseph Stanley and Thelma Maxine (Strubhar) L.; m. Donna Susan Schoeppner, Dec. 17, 1970 (div. Jan. 1979); children: Arlo Bernard, Cynthia Robin; m. Dorothy Barnes, Dec. 13, 1986. B Music Edn., Drake U., 1967. Band dir. Melcher (Iowa)/Dallas Schs., 1967-68, Coon Rapids (Iowa) Schs., 1970; band instrument repairman Miller Music, Des Moines, 1972—; editor, founder Prayer & Action News, Des Moines, 1989—; producer, host The Uncle Ed Show; trumpet player Des Moines Mcpl. Band, 1963-78; trumpet player, arranger Kingsway Cathedral, Des Moines, 1980's; trumpet player, singer St. Ambrose Cathedral, Des Moines, 1980's; choir dir. Simpson United Meth. Ch., Des Moines, 1988-89; trumpet and violin player St. Augustine's Cathedral, Des Moines, 1989-92. Author, composer: (musical comedy) Werld Klas Ejukashun, 1991; author (book) the Gifts of Governments, 1990. Dem. candidate for state rep., Iowa, 1986, Rep. candidate 1988, 90; active numerous conservative and grass roots groups; pres., edtor Fathers for Equal Rights, Des Moines chpt. 1985-87. Home and Office: 137 E Leach Ave Des Moines IA 50315-3643

LEACH, DAVID CLARK, JR., municipal administrator; b. Evanston, Ill., Jan. 27, 1925; s. David Clark and Della Louise (Carr) L. BSBA, Northwestern U., Evanston, Ill., 1947. Commd. USN, 1943-67, advanced through grades lt. comdr., ret., 1967; dir. mgmt. svcs. Village of Wilmette, Ill., 1968—. Author: Wilmette Nautical Heritage, 1982; editor Wilmette Communicator, 1972—, U.S. Finn Class Assn. Solo newsletter, 1970—. Mem. Wilmette Harbor Assn. (dir. 1989—), Sheridan Shore Yacht Club (chmn. race com. 1974—). Episcopalian. Home: 518 Park Ave Wilmette IL 60091-2552 Office: Village of Wilmette 120 Wilmette Ave Wilmette IL 60091-0040

LEACH, ELEANOR WINSOR, classical studies educator; b. Providence, Aug. 16, 1937; d. Lloyd Moulton and Ruth (Evans) Winsor; m. Peter John Leach, Nov. 15, 1962 (div. 1979); 1 child, Harriet Olney. AB, Bryn Mawr Coll., 1959; MA, Yale U., 1960, PhD, 1963. From instr. to asst. prof. Bryn Mawr (Pa.) Coll., 1962-66; from asst. to assoc. prof. Villanova (Pa.) U., 1966-71; vis. assoc. prof. U. Tex., Austin, 1972-73, Wesleyan U., Middletown, Conn., 1974-76; from assoc. prof. to prof. Ind. U., Bloomington, 1976—, chmn. classical studies, 1978-85; vis. prof. Barnard Coll., Columbia U., 1981-82, U. Md., 1990; resident scholar in classical studies Am. Acad. in Rome, 1983-84; dir. NEH summer seminar for coll. tchrs., 1986, 89; Blegen disting. vis. prof. Vassar Coll., 1987-88; vis. fellow Wolfson Coll., Oxford U., 1996. Author: Virgil's Eclogues: Landscapes of Experience, 1974, The Rhetoric of Space: Artistic and Literary Representations of Landscape in Republican and Augustan Rome, 1988; contbr. more than 40 articles on Roman lit. and art to various publs. Recipient J.S. Guggenheim Meml. fellowship Guggenheim Found., 1976-77, NEH Sr. Rsch. fellowship, 1983-84, ACLS Sr. Rsch. fellowship, 1992-93, Nat. Humanities Ctr. fellowship, 1992-93. Mem. Am. Philog. Assn. (bd. dirs. 1981-84, v.p. for program 1991-94), Virgilian Soc. Am. (v.p., pres. 1991-93), Classical Assn. Midwest and South (exec. com. 1984-88), Archeol. Inst. Am. (pres. Cen. Ind. Soc. 1986-88), Soc. for Promotion of Roman Studies. Home: 417 S Henderson St Bloomington IN 47401-4801 Office: Dept Classical Studies Ind U 547 Ballantine Hall Bloomington IN 47401-5017

LEACH, GREGORY J., metal products company executive; b. Kokomo, Ind., July 30, 1960. Assoc. Indsl. Tech., Purdue U., 1980, Assoc. Mech. Engring., 1987. Prodn. engr. Western Wheel (name now Hayes Wheel Internat.), Huntington, Ind., 1985-91, Bohn Aluminum Corp., Butler, Ind., 1991—. Co-inventor full face modular wheel. Coach Little League Baseball, Cronwell, Ind., 1993-94. Mem. Soc. Automotive Engrs. Lutheran. Home: 1993 N Us Highway 33 Kimmell IN 46760-9783 Office: Bohn Aluminum Corp 6378 US Highway 6 Butler IN 46721-9604

LEACH, JAMES ALBERT SMITH, congressman; b. Davenport, Iowa, Oct. 15, 1942; s. James Albert and Lois (Hill) L.; m. Elisabeth Foxley, Dec. 6, 1975; 1 child, Gallagher. BA, Princeton U., 1964; MA, Johns Hopkins U., 1966; postgrad., London Sch. Econs., 1966-68. Mem. staff Congressman Donald Rumsfeld, 1965-66; U.S. Fgn. Service officer, 1968-69, 70-73; spl. asst. to dir. OEO, 1969-70; mem. U.S. del. Geneva Disarmament Conf., 1971-72, UN Gen. Assembly, 1972, UN Natural Resources Conf., 1975; pres. Flamegas Companies Inc., Bettendorf, Iowa, 1973-76; chmn. bd. Adel Wholesalers, Inc., Bettendorf, 1973-76; mem. 95th-104th Congresses from 1st Iowa dist., 1977—; chmn. banking and fin. svcs. com., mem. internat. rels. com.; mem. U.S. Adv. Commn. Internat. Ednl. and Cultural Affairs, 1975-76. Chmn. Iowa Rep. Directions '76 Com. Episcopalian. Office: 2186 Rayburn Bldg Washington DC 20515-0005*

LEACH, JANET C., publishing executive. Mng. editor The Cin. Enquirer. Office: The Cin Enquirer 312 Elm St Cincinnati OH 45202*

LEACH, JEFFREY DALE, information systems support specialist; b. Salem, Ohio, June 18, 1954; s. Dale Mason and Betty Jane (May) L.; m. Elizabeth Marguerite Short, Aug. 3, 1975; 1 child, Melissa. Electronic tech. mgr. B & L Electronics, Salem, 1976-77; owner, mgr. Leach Electronics, Salem, 1977-78; tool and die maker Sekely Industries, Salem, 1978-86; sr. programmer, tech. support mgr. Integrated Graphic Systems, Salem, 1986-87; mgr. of cad/cam applications Model Pattern Co., Grand Rapids, Mich., 1987-88; tech. support researcher Battelle Meml. Inst., Columbus, Ohio, 1988; asst. system mgr. CAD/CAM program Maghielse Tool Corp., Grand Rapids, Mich., 1988-90; engring. mgr., system adminstr. Gill Tool & Die, Grand Rapids, Mich., 1990-91; systems adminstr. nat. tech. team Ford Motor Co., Dearborn, Mich., 1992-94; project leader Fannie Mae, Washington, 1994—; systems adminstr. Sylvest at Bell Atlantic, Silver Springs, Md., 1994-95, A.C. Coy at Eaton Cutler-Hammer, Pitts., 1995—. With U.S. Army, 1972-75. Office: Ford Motor Co Rm 3720a ae PO Box 2053 Dearborn MI 48123-2053

LEACH, MATTHEW JAMES, informations systems specialist; b. Muncie, Ind., Sept. 29, 1972; s. Timothy James and Jenny Ellen (Vlaskamp) L. Grad. high sch., Muncie, Ind. Data processing asst. Ball State Credit Union, Muncie, Ind., 1989-92; v.p. info. systems Perfect Cir. Credit Union, Hagerstown, Ind., 1992—. Mem. Assn. Systems Mgmt. (pres. users group). Home: 1200 N County Rd 600E Selma IN 47383 Office: Perfect Cir Credit Union 327 E Main St Hagerstown IN 47346

LEACH, NORMAN EDWARD, minister; b. Farmingdale, N.Y., May 17, 1940; s. George Alexander and Irene Alice (Bowen) L. AB, U. Mo., 1962; postgrad., Mo. U. Sch. Social Work, 1962-63; MDiv, San Francisco Theol. Sem., 1970, D in Ministry, 1973. Ordained to ministry Presbyn. Ch., 1971. Mgr. Third Rail Coffee House First Presbyn Ch., San Anselmo, Calif., 1968-70; adj. staff cons. Golden Gate Mission Area Ch. and World Com. United Presbyn. Ch. USA, San Francisco, 1970-72; dir. San Francisco Bay Area Healing Community Program, 1975-89; program adminstr. San Francisco Council Chs., 1976-82, interim acting exec. dir., 1982-84, acting exec. dir., 1984; exec. dir. San Francisco Coun. Chs., 1984-89; with Lincoln Interfaith Coun., Lincoln, Nebr., 1989—; chmn. Presbytery Program Coordinating Council; mem. Presbytery Gen. Council, Presbytery Long-Range Planning Com., Presbytery Nominations Com., Presbytery Permanent Jud. Commn., Interfaith BiCentennial Com., San Francisco, 1975-76, No. Calif. Ecumenical Council, 1975-78, World Council Chs., Vancouver, B.C., Can., 1983; founding mem., pres. Presbyn. Disabilities Concerns Caucus 1981; bd. dirs. World Conf. on Religion and Peace West, 1975-77; founding mem., task force on disabilities Archdiocese of San Francisco, 1975-80. Editor, pub.: Heritage and Hope, 1978, (newspaper) To Free Mankind; mem. editorial bd. Caring Congregation Mag.; contbr. columns to mags., chpts. to books. Mem. Congress on Racial Equality, U. Mo., Columbia, 1958-63, Coalition on Nat. Priorities and Mil. Policy, Washington, 1967-71; bd. dirs. Cambodian-Am. Benevolent Assn., 1975-78, Ind. Living Expn., San Francisco, 1983-87, Am.-Israel Friendship League 1984-89, assoc. United Way Execs., San Francisco, 1982-89; founding mem. San Francisco Intergroup Clearinghouse, 1982-89; founder, pres. emeritus San Francisco Mayor's Council on Disabilities Concerns, 1982—. Recipient God and Country award Boy Scouts Am., 1955, Vigil Honor award, 1974, CORLE/Nat. Council Chs. award, 1977, cert. of merit Mayor Dianne Feinstein, 1985, Freedom award No. Calif. Bd. Rabbis, 1987; named to Gov.'s Hall of Fame for Persons with Disabilities, 1988. Mem. Am. Acad. Polit. and Social Scis., Alpha Sigma Phi, Alpha Phi Omega, Pi Omicron Sigma. Home: 1459 46th Ave San Francisco CA 94122-2902 Office: Lincoln Interfaith Coun 1926 S 17th St Lincoln NE 68502-2701 Office: Lincoln Interfaith Coun Ste 402 Lincoln NE

LEADER, CHRISTOPHER ROBERT, manufacturing executive; b. South Bend, Ind.; s. Robert A. and Dorothy R. L.; m. Linda A. Hoyt; three children. BS in Mech. Engring., U. Notre Dame, 1981; MBA, U. Mich., 1991. Cert. quality engr. Am. Soc. Quality Control. Lt. USN, navigator, dept. head USS England (CG-22), San Diego (home port), 1981-85; statis. process control analyst GM, Saginaw, Mich., 1985-87, sr. quality engr., 1987-91; prodn. supt. Ford Motor Co., Avon Lake, Ohio, 1991-93, vehicle evaluation mgr., 1993-94, prodn. mgr., 1994; v.p. ops. Trek USA Bicycle Corp., Waterloo, Wis., 1994—. Co-author: Quality Engineering Jour., 1989. Lt. USN, 1981-85. Sr. mem. Am. Soc. Quality Control. Office: Trek Bicycle Corp 801 W Madison Waterloo WI 53594

LEAFGREN, FREDERICK ALDEN, human relations consultant; b. Stevens Point, Wis., July 27, 1931; s. George and Elsie (Alden) L.; m. Thomasina Scalise, Jan. 27, 1967; 1 child, Deanna Lynn. BS, U. Ill., 1954; MA, Mich. State U., 1959, PhD, 1968. Dean of men Slippery Rock (Pa.) Coll., 1962-65; dir. housing U. Wis., Stevens Point, 1965-72, assoc. dean students, 1972-75, exec. dir. student life, 1975-79, asst. chancellor student life, 1979—; bd. dirs. Nat. Wellness Inst. Editor: Health Values, 1984, Campus Recreation and Wellness Programs, 1986, (with others) Educational Programming, 1981. Served to lt. U.S. Army, 1956-58. Mem. Am. Coll. Personnel Assn., Nat. Assn. Student Personnel Adminstrs., Assn. Psychol. Type, Internat. Transactional Analysis Assn., Inc., Neurolinguistic Programming, Delta Phi, Phi Delta Kappa. Democrat. Presbyterian. Home and Office: 3734 Oak Moraine Ct Stevens Point WI 54481-9755

LEAKE, RICHARD SCOTT, economics and management educator, tennis coach; b. Denver, Aug. 25, 1948; s. Norman Walton and Delores Luverne (Sandberg) L.; m. Penny Yvonne Johnson, June 7, 1969; children: Scott, Timothy, Tanya. BA, Pacific Luth. U., 1970; MA, Ohio U., 1974; MBA, U. Wis., La Crosse, 1984. Cert. tchr., Wash.; cert. Human Resource Cert. Inst. Tchr., coach Steilacoom (Wash.) Sch. Dist., 1970-73; rsch. asst. Ohio U., Athens, 1973-75; prof. econ., tennis coach Luther Coll., Decorah, Iowa, 1975—, prof. mgmt., 1977—, dir. pers., 1977-81; tennis profl. various camps and clinics, 1976—; propr. Sunrise Racquet Shop, Decorah, 1976-86; cons. N.E. Iowa Small Bus. Devel. Ctr., Dubuque, 1984—. Author: Tennis Instructor's Handbook, 1979, Guidebook for Collegiate Tennis Players, 1985, 2d edit., 1989. Mem. coun. Good Shepherd Luth. Ch., Decorah, 1980, 88-92. Named Tennis coach of Yr., Iowa Intercollegiate Athletic Conf., 1976, 85, 87-91, 93, 94-95; Walton fellow, 1995-96; scholar NSF, 1980-81, Am. Iron and Steel Inst., 1981. Mem. Am. Mgmt. Assn., We. Econ. Assn., U.S. Assn. for Small Bus. and Entrepreneurship, Intercollegiate Tennis Assn., Soc. Human Resource Mgmt., Oneota Valley Tennis Assn. (founder), Omicron Delta Epsilon, Phi Delta Kappa. Republican. Home: 703 Valley View Dr Decorah IA 52101-1021 Office: Dept Econs and Bus Luther Coll Decorah IA 52101

LEAKE, SAM, state legislator, farmer; b. Ralls County, Mo., Feb. 19, 1945; m. Sharon K. Day, 1964; children: Jeff, Scott, Terri, Kevin. Student, Moler Barbar Coll. Farmer, Laddonia, Mo.; mem. Mo. Ho. of Reps., Jefferson City; mem. agr. com., edn. com., social svcs. and medicaid, state parks com., recreation and natural resources com. Del. state and dist. Dem. convs., 1988—. Recipient farm mgmt. award U. Mo., 1982. mem. Twain Lake Assn. Home: RR 2 Box 61A Laddonia MO 63352-9402*

LEAMAN, DAVID CHARLES, management consultant; b. Green Bay, Wis., Mar. 8, 1937. BSEE, Marquette U., 1960, MBA, 1968. Registered profl. engr., Calif. Quality control mgr. battery div. Globe-Union Inc., Milw., 1960-70; dir. profl. devel. Am. Soc. for Quality Control, Milw., 1970-82; v.p., COO McElrath & Assocs., Inc., Mequon, Wis., 1982-94, COO, 1990-94; pres. David C. Leaman & Assocs., Mequon, Wis., 1995—; bd. dirs. numerous orgns.; speaker in field.

LEAMAN, JACK ERVIN, landscape architect, community/regional planner; b. Mason City, Iowa, Jan. 24, 1932; s. Theodore R. and Dorothy M. (Schrum) L.; m. Darlene A. McNary, June 15, 1952; children: Jeffrey A., Danna J., Jay M., Duree K. B.S. in Landscape Architecture and Urban Planning, Iowa State U., 1954, M. Community and Regional Planning, 1982. Registered landscape architect, Calif., Iowa, Minn., N.Mex. Landscape architect Sam L. Huddleston Office, Denver, 1954-55, Phillips Petroleum Co., Bartlesville, Okla., 1955-58; landscape architect for Price Tower and residence with architect Frank Lloyd Wright Bartlesville, Okla., 1957-58; planning technician Santa Barbara County, Calif., 1958-60; planning cons. Engring. Planners, Santa Barbara, 1960-63; planning dir. City of Santa Barbara, 1963-66, City of Mason City, 1966-72; landscape architect, planning cons. Midwest Research Inst., Kansas City, Mo., 1972-74, Hansen, Lind, Meyer, Iowa City, Iowa, 1974-76, Sheffler, Leaman, Rova, Mason City, 1976-78, RCM Assocs., Inc., Hopkins, Minn. and Ames, Iowa, 1978-82; planning dir. City-County Planning, Albuquerque, 1982-86, City of Colorado Springs, Colo., 1986-90; adj. prof. dept. cmty. and regional planning Coll. of Design, Iowa State U., Ames, 1990—; landscape architect, pvt. practice planning cons. Mason City, Iowa, 1990-92; assoc. ptnr., landscape architect, community/regional planner Yaggy Colby Assocs., Mason City, 1992-95; pvt. cons. cmty. and regional planning, landscape architect Mason City, Iowa, 1995—. Recipient Residential Landscape Design award Calif. Landscape Contractors Assn., 1962, Design Achievement award Coll. of Design Iowa State U., 1988. Fellow Am. Soc. Landscape Architects (chpt. pres. 1967-68, 90-91, trustee Iowa 1980-82, N.Mex. 1982-86, Award of Excellence 1954); mem. Am. Inst. Cert. Planners, Am. Planning Assn. (chpt. pres. Iowa 1969-70), Urban Land Inst., Tau Sigma Delta.

LEARNER, HOWARD ALAN, lawyer; b. Chgo., June 1, 1955; s. Donald and Patricia Learner; m. Lauren S. Rosenthal, Oct. 22, 1988; children: Daniel J., Samuel D. AB, U. Mich., 1976; JD, Harvard Law Sch., 1980. Bar: Ill 1980, U.S. Dist. Ct. (no. dist.) Ill. 1980, U.S. Ct. Appeals (7th cir.) 1981, U.S. Supreme Ct. 1993. Gen. counsel Bus. and Profl. People for Pub. Interest, Chgo., 1980-93; pres., exec. dir. Environ. Law and Policy Ctr. Midwest, Chgo., 1993—; chmn., pres., dir. Citizens Utility bd., Chgo., 1984-93; bd. govs. Chgo. Coun. Lawyers, 1986-90. Treas., dir. Ill. Environ., Springfield, 1982-88; legal counsel Ill. chpt. Sierra Club, Chgo., 1984—; dir. Jewish Coun. Urban Affairs, Chgo., 1984-92, Jewish Fund Justice, N.Y.C., 1990—. Environ. fellowship German Marshall Fund U.S. Fellow Leadership Greater Chgo., Royal Soc. Arts, Mfg. and Commerce. Office: Environ Law & Policy Ctr Midwest 203 N La Salle St Ste 1390 Chicago IL 60601-1210

LEARY, RICHARD LEE, museum curator; b. Portsmouth, Va., Sept. 19, 1936; s. Wilbur Talmadge and Mary Katherine (Lee) L.; m. Eleanor Marie Riehl, June 18, 1961; children: Seth Richard, Sara Marie. BS in Geology, Va. Poly. Inst., 1959; MS in Geology, U. Mich., 1961; PhD in Geology, U. Ill., 1980. Field asst. Calif. Oil Co., Colo., 1959, Mobil Oil Co., N.Mex., 1960; part-time asst. Kelsey Mus. U. Mich., Ann Arbor, 1960-61; curator of geology Ill. State Mus., Springfield, 1962—; adj. asst. prof. Sangamon State U., Springfield, Ill., 1973-78, 89—; instr. The Clearing, Ellison Bay, Wis., 1975—; lectr. in field. Contbr. articles to profl. jours. Recipient Fulbright Rsch. award Coun. for Internat. Exch. of Scholars, 1991; grantee NSF, 1981-84, 85, 86, 94, Smithsonian Instn., 1988-89. Mem. Planetary Studies Found. (adv. bd.), Bot. Soc. Am., Geol. Soc. of Am., Ill. State Acad. Sci. (coun. mem. 1974-89, v.p. 1975-76, pres. 1976-77), Internat. Orgn. Palaeobotany, Asociacion Latinoamericana de Paleobotanica y Palinologia. Presbyterian. Office: Ill State Mus Collections 1011 E Ash St Springfield IL 62703-3535

LEARY, ROBIN JANELL, administrative secretary, county government official; b. Hudson, Wis., July 9, 1954; d. Edward James and Marlys Marie (Ensign) L. BA in History, U. Wis., Eau Claire, 1976. From stenographer I to program asst. 3 U. Wis., Eau Claire, 1977—; elected sec. 3rd Congl. Dist./Dem. Party of Wis., 1993-95; elected bd. suprs. Dist. 23, Eau Claire County, 1996—. Chmn. Eau Claire County Dem. Party, 1990-92, sec., 1986-90, mem. ex-officio exec. bd., 1993-95; elected mem. dist. 23 Eau Claire County Bd. Suprs., 1996-98; elected mem. exec. bd. Eau Claire County Dem. Party, 1995—; mem. credentials com. Wis. Dem. Party, 1990-95, chmn. com., 1990-92; mem. elections commn. Wis. Dem. Party, 1990—; del. Dem. Nat. Conv., Atlanta, 1988, N.Y.C., 1992, Chgo., 1996. Named Female Dem. Vol. of Yr., Eau Claire County Dem. Party, 1989. Mem. AFL-CIO (Eau Claire area labor coun., treas. 1986-94, trustee 1994—, sec. 3d congl. dist. com. on polit. edn. 1993—), AFSCME Pub. Employees Organized to Promote Legis. Equality (vice chmn. 3d congl. dist. 1992-93, com. 1993-95, elected vice-chair 3d confl. P.E.O.P.L.E. 1995—, coun. 24 family and gender com. 1990—, tri-coun. state woman's com.). Home: 2104 Providence Ct Eau Claire WI 54703-4103 Office: U Wis 105 Garfield Ave Eau Claire WI 54701-4811

LEATHERBERRY, ANNE KNOX CLARK, interior designer, architectural designer; b. Geneva, Ill., Jan. 19, 1953; d. Donald William and Margaret Lorraine (Johnson) Clark; m. David Boyd Leatherberry, Aug. 5, 1978; children: Elizabeth Anne, Laura Knox. BS in Bus., Miami U., Oxford, Ohio, 1975. With Carson, Pirie, Scott & Co., Chgo., 1975-77; health care sales specialist Gen. Foods Corp., Northlake, Ill., 1977-78; account mgr. Cin., 1978-79; pres., owner Annie's Originals/Kids Collectables, Ltd., Waukesha, Wis., 1979—; mktg. rep./demonstrator mktg. Waukesha, 1988-91; owner Dreamhouse Designs, Waukesha, 1990—, Creative Enterprises Inc., 1990—; cons. Lamb's Quarters, Hartford, Wis., 1982-83, Ungerwear, West Alexandria, Ohio, 1982-84, Little Bits, Waukeshaw, 1984-90, Evelyn's Creations, East Troy, Wis., 1986-90, The Queen's Empire, Inc., Pitts., 1989-90, DRC Co., Mukwonago, Wis., 1990—, Don Belman Builders, 1991-92, Millikin Homes, 1992—, Opportunity Homes, 1993—, Affordable Homes, 1993—, Gemini Homes, 1993, Nelson Remodeling, 1993. Active Waukesha Area Symphonic Band, 1979-93, sec. bd. dirs., 1987-89; active Carroll Coll. Cmty. Orch., 1985-86; vol. tchr.'s aide Clarendon Avenue Sch., Mukwonago, 1988-89; asst. leader Girl Scouts U.S.A., 1988, leader, 1988-89; vol. staff aide Jim Thompson for Gov. Campaign, 1975-76; dir. Children's Choir, 1986; summer music dir. Luth. Ch., 1986, 88; events chmn. Edgewood Golf League, 1988-92; vol. Rose Glen Reading Rams, Waukesha, 1990-92, Health Room, 1990-91, tchr.'s aid, 1991-92; pres. archtl. rev. bd. Red Wing Hills Assn., 1993-96; instr. architecture mentor program Waukesha Sch. Dist., 1995—. Mem. NAFE, PEO (officer 1980-82), Direct Mktg. Assn., Soc. Craft Designers, Met. Builders Assn., Nat. Assn. of Remodeling Industry, Kappa Kappa Gamma. Republican. Lutheran. Home and Office: W241 S5910 Autumn Haze Ct Waukesha WI 53186-9512

LEATHERWOOD, LARRY L., state transportation executive; b. Peoria, Ill., Sept. 7, 1939; s. Larry B.G. and Helen Delpha (Moody) L.; m. Martha Pat Hutchins, May 14, 1938; children: Jeffrey, Stacy. AA, Kellogg C.C., Battle Creek, Mich., 1967; BS, Western Mich. U., 1969, M in Pub. Adminstrn., 1982; sr. exec. fellow, Harvard U., 1985. Dir. minority bus. Mich. Dept. Commerce, Lansing, 1977-83; liason officer Mich. Dept. Transp., Lansing, 1983-85, dep. dir. adminstrn., 1985-92, asst. dep. dir., 1994—; exec. dir. Citizens Coun. Pub. Univs., 1992-94. Bd. dirs., past pres. YMCA of Lansing, 1992-93; bd. dirs. Mich. Pub. Mgmt. Inst., Detroit, 1994-95. Named Mich. Small Bus. Advocate, U.S. Small Bus. Adminstrn., Detroit, 1990, Mich. Pub. Servant of Yr., Am. Soc. Pub. Adminstrn., Lansing, 1992. Mem. The Forum (pres. 1991-92), Black Men, Inc. (chmn. fundraising com. 1992-93), Western Mich. Alumni Assn. (bd. dirs. 1989—), Harvard Univ. Alumni (bd. dirs. 1991-93). Baptist. Home: 812 Canton Dr Lansing MI 48917 Office: Mich Dept Transp 425 W Ottawa St Lansing MI 48909

LEAVENWORTH, PAUL STEPHEN, JR., secondary school educator; b. Grand Rapids, Mich., May 28, 1936; s. Paul Sr. and Dorothy L. (Southwick) L.; m. Patricia J. Nyberg, Sept. 13, 1958; children: Eric Richard, Kristine Amy, Paul Stephen III. AA, Grand Rapids Jr. Coll., 1956; MA, Mich. State U., 1959; postgrad., Western Mich. U., 1980—. Tchr. Newhall Jr. H.S., Wyoming, Mich., 1959-67, Forest Hills H.S., Grand Rapids, Mich., 1967-72; tchr., dept. chair social studies Forest Hills No. H.S., Grand Rapids, 1972—; advisor Sch. State Mock Trial Competition, Grand Rapids, 1986—. Editor: The Civil War Letters of George Miller, 1992; contbr. articles to profl. jours. NEH summer fellow Brown U., 1987, Woodrow Wilson fellow Princeton U., 1992, Stratford Hall fellow R.E. Lee Assn., 1993, Nat. Humanities Ctr. fellow, 1988. Mem. Nat. Coun. for Social Studies, Va. Hist. Soc., Soc. for Historians of Am. Fgn. Rels., Soc. for Mil. History, Assn. for Preservation of Civil Warsites, Delta Tau Delta. Home: 4225 Valley Hollow Dr NE Grand Rapids MI 49505

LEAVITT, JEFFREY STUART, lawyer; b. Cleve., July 13, 1946; s. Sol and Esther (Dolinsky) L.; m. Ellen Fern Sugerman, Dec. 21, 1968; children: Matthew Adam, Joshua Aaron. AB, Cornell U., 1968; JD, Case Western Res. U., 1973. Bar: Ohio 1973. Assoc. Jones, Day, Reavis & Pogue, Cleve., 1973-80, ptnr., 1981—. Contbr. articles to profl. jours. Trustee Bur. Jewish Edn., Cleve., 1981-93, v.p. 1985-87; trustee Fairmount Temple, Cleve., 1982—, v.p. 1985-90, pres., 1990-93; trustee Citizens League Greater Cleve., 1982-89, 92-94, pres., 1987-89; trustee Citizens League Rsch. Inst., Cleve., 1989—, Great Lakes Region of Union Am. Hebrew Congregations, 1990-93; mem. bd. gov. Case Western Res. Law Sch. Alumni Assn., 1989-92; sec. Kulas Found., 1986-88, 93—, asst. treas., 1989-92. Mem. ABA (employee benefits coms. 1976—), Midwest Pension Conf. Jewish. Home: 25961 Annesley Rd Cleveland OH 44122-2437 Office: Jones Day Reavis & Pogue N Point 901 Lakeside Ave E Cleveland OH 44114-1116

LEAVITT, MARTIN JACK, lawyer; b. Detroit, Mar. 30, 1940; s. Benjamin and Annette (Cohen) L.; m. Janice C. (McCreary) Leavitt; children: Michael J., Paul J., David A., Dean N., Keleigh R. LLB, Wayne State U., 1964. Bar: Mich. 1965, Fla. 1967. Assoc. Robert A. Sullivan, Detroit, 1968-70; officer, bd. dirs. Law Offices Sullivan & Leavitt, Northville, Mich., 1970—, pres., 1979—; bd. dirs. Tyrone Hills of Mich., Premiere Video, Inc., The Keim Group, Ltd., Guardian Home Warranty Corp., others. Lt. comdr., USNR, 1959-64. Detroit Edison Upper Class scholar, 1958-64. Mem. ABA, Mich. Bar Assn., Fla. Bar Assn., Transp. Lawyers Assn., ICC Practitioners, Meadowbrook Country Club, Huron River Hunting & Fishing Club (past pres.), Rolls Royce Owners Club (bd. dirs.). Jewish. Office: Sullivan and Leavitt PC PO Box 400 Northville MI 48167-0997

LEAVITT, VICTORIA SEYFERTH, marketing professional; b. Münchweiler, Fed. Republic Germany, May 29, 1959; came to U.S., 1960; d. Blaine H. and Barbara (Geyer) S.; m. William E. Leavitt Jr., June 11, 1983. BS in Human Genetics, U. Mich., 1981, MA in Communications, 1981. Asst. brand Proctor & Gamble Co., Cinn., 1981-82, asst. mgr. brand, 1982-84; assoc. mgr. product Gen. Foods Corp., White Plains, N.Y., 1984-85; mgr. product Gen. Foods Corp., White Plains, 1985-87, sr. mgr. product, team leader, 1987—. Vol. Bruce Mus. Storyhour Jr. League, Greenwich, Conn., 1985—. Home: 4622 Moorland Ave Edina MN 55424-1159 Office: Collins Rapp Agency Group Inc 901 Marquette Ave Minneapolis MN 55402-3205

LEBAMOFF, IVAN ARGIRE, lawyer; b. Ft. Wayne, Ind., July 20, 1932; s. Argire V. and Helen A. (Kachandov) L.; m. Katherine S. Lebamoff, June 9, 1963; children—Damian I., Jordan I., Justin A. A.B. in History, Ind. U., 1954, J.D., 1957. Bar: Ind. 1957, U.S. Ct. Dist. Ct. (no. and so. dists.) 1958, U.S. Supreme Ct. 1963. Sole practice Ft. Wayne, Ind., 1957-68; ptnr. Lebamoff, Ver Wiebe & Snow, Ft. Wayne, Ind., 1968-71; mayor City of Ft. Wayne, 1972-75; sole practice Lebamoff Law Offices, Ft. Wayne, 1975—; U.S. commr. No. Dist. Ind., 1957-62; fgn. service officer USIA Dept. Commerce, Bulgaria, 1964; vis. prof. dept. urban affairs Ind. U.-Purdue, Ft. Wayne, 1976-77. Chmn. Allen County Democratic Com., 1968-75, Ft. Wayne Dept. Parks and Recreation, 1984-88; nat. pres. Macedonian Patriotic Orgn. of U.S. and Can., 1983—. Served with USAF, 1958-64. Mem. ABA, Allen County Bar Assn., Ind. Bar Assn., Am. Trial Lawyers Assn., Ind. Trial Lawyers Assn. Eastern Orthodox. Lodge: Kiwanis. Home: 205 E Packard Ave Fort Wayne IN 46806-1014 Office: Lebamoff Law Offices 918 S Calhoun St Fort Wayne IN 46802-2502

LEBEAU, BERNARD PIERRE, history and foreign language educator; b. Metz, France, Aug. 3, 1932; came to U.S., 1952; s. Pierre and Genevieve (Gallot) L.; m. Patricia Craven, Mar. 17, 1957 (div. Dec. 1969); children: Gabrielle, Brigitte; m. Marcia M. Tolish, June 12, 1974. BA, Ohio U., 1955; MA, Ohio State U., 1957; postgrad., U. Chgo., 1966-69. Asst. prof. French Washington Coll., Chestertown, Md., 1958-61, U.S. Naval Acad., Annapolis, Md., 1961-66; assoc. prof. fgn. lang. North Ctrl. Coll., Naperville, Ill., 1966-81, prof. fgn. lang., 1981-86, chair div. arts and letters, 1978-86, asst. v.p. acad. affairs, 1986-91, prof. history and fgn. lang., 1991—; cons. Naval History div. Office of Chief Naval. Ops., Washington, 1962-66, History div. Ill. Dept. Conservation, 1981-82; dir. Ctr. French Colonial Studies, Prairie du Rocher, Ill., 1985—. Co-author: North Central College and Naperville: A Shared History 1870-1995, 1995; editor, translator French documents in book Naval Documents of the American Revolution, Vol. I, 1965, II, 1966. Pres. Alliance Française de DuPage, Naperville, 1975-80; dir. DuPage County Hist. Soc. Mem. Am. Assn. for State and Local History, Ill. Humanities Coun., Ill. State Hist. Soc., Chgo. Hist. Soc. Roman Catholic. Home: 1150 Iroquois Ave Naperville IL 60563-9321 Office: North Ctrl Coll 30 N Brainard St Naperville IL 60566-7063

LEBLANC, DIANA L., librarian; b. East St. Louis, Ill., Feb. 22, 1952; d. Richard Leland Ninness and Helen Jeanette (Hoy) Hutchison; m. James Kent LeBlanc Sr., Apr. 28, 1972 (dec. Nov. 1987); children: James Kent Jr., Jonathan Brice. Grad. high sch., Collinsville, Ill. Head libr. Caseyville (Ill.) Pub. Libr. Sec. 1st Bapt. Ch. Caseyville, 1986-95, treas., 1974-89. Republican. Office: Caseyville Pub Libr 10 W Morris Caseyville IL 62232

LEBLANC, MICHAEL STEPHEN, insurance and risk executive; b. Perryville, Mo., July 15, 1952; s. Leon John and Marjorie Ann (Whitener) LeB.; m. Dayle Ellen Wingbermuehle, Aug. 13, 1982; children: Luke, Anna, Joseph. EdB, So. Ill. U., Edwardsville, 1979. Head athletic trainer Met. Orthopedic & Sports Medicine, St. Louis, 1979-80, Forest Park Jr. Coll., St. Louis, 1980; sales rep. Cybex, St. Louis, 1980-82; pres. Team Consult, St. Louis, 1982-83; registered rep. Liberty Mut., St. Ann, Mo., 1983-88, Transam. Life Cos., St. Louis, 1988-89, Siegel-Robert, Inc., St. Louis, 1989—. Mem. Cath. Bus. Leaders, St. Louis, 1988; apptd. to St. Ann Commn. for Econ. Devel. and Mcpl. Progress; chmn. St. Ann Commn. for Econ. Devel. Fellow Life Underwriting Tng. Coun.; mem. Nat. Assn. Life Underwriters, St. Louis Baseball Cardinals Club (tng. cons. 1982-83), St. Gregory Athletic Assn. (coach 1986-95), St. Mary's Athletic Assn. (coach 1990-96), Sigma Phi Epsilon Householding Corp. (pres. 1984-86). Republican. Roman Catholic. Home: 3543 St Christopher Ln Saint Ann MO 63074-2834 Office: 8645 S Broadway Saint Louis MO 63111-3810

LEBOS, RICHARD JESSE, accountant, law student; b. Oak Ridge, Tenn., Mar. 18, 1967; s. Richard Jesse Lebos and Elaine Ann (Lewin) Nolan; m. Kimberlee Young, Sept. 11, 1993; 1 child, Alexandra. BBA in Acctg., U. Tex., 1989; MBA, So. Meth. U., 1990; postgrad., Creighton U. CPA, Tex. Acct., sr. acct. Amwest Savs. & Loan, Dallas, 1990-93, contract acct., 1993-94. Republican.

LECAPTAIN, DAVID A., electrical engineer; b. Green Bay, Wis., Jan. 15, 1963; s. Donald N. and Dorothy J. (Skaleski) LeC.; m. Julia K. Kayser, June 4, 1989; children: Michelle, Kevin. BSEE, U. Wis., Platteville, 1985. Product support engr., elec. engr. Norand Corp., Cedar Rapids, Iowa, 1986—. Mem. IEEE. Roman Catholic. Office: Norand Corp 550 2d St SE Cedar Rapids IA 52401-2023

LECHNER, GEORGE WILLIAM, surgeon; b. Denver, July 30, 1931; s. Frank Clifford and Hazel Mae (Elkins) L.; m. Betty Jane Baumbach, Aug. 3, 1952; children: Kathleen Ann, Elaine Marie, Carol Jean, Patricia Louise, James Richard. Student, U. N.Mex., 1948-49; BA, Pacific Union Coll., 1952; MD summa cum laude, Loma Linda U., 1956. Diplomate Am. Bd. Surgery. Intern Pontiac (Mich.) Gen. Hosp., 1956-57; resident in surgery Harper Hosp., Detroit, 1957-58, Wayne State U. Hosp., 1961-64; instr. surgery Wayne State U., 1963-64; practice medicine specializing in gen., vascular and bariatric surgery Kettering, Ohio, 1964-95; mem. faculty and clin. staff Kettering Med. Ctr., Dayton, Ohio, 1967—, also assoc. dir. gen. surgery residency, mem. active staff; clin. assoc. prof. surgery, assoc. dir. emergency medicine residency Wright State U., 1975-78; active staff Sycamore Hosp.; pres. Kettering Emergency Room Corp. Active Big Bros./Big Sisters; bd. elders Seventh-Day Adventist Ch., Kettering; trustee, mem. exec. com. Kettering Med. Ctr., 1971-74; pres. Spring Valley Acad. sch. bd., 1973-75, trustee 1973-78. Served with AUS, 1958-61, Japan. Recipient C.V. Mosby award for acad. excellence, 1956; ACS fellow. Mem. AMA, AAAS, Midwest Surg. Assn., Dayton Surg. Soc., Ohio and Montgomery County Med. Socs., Am. Coll. Emergency Physicians, Soc. Tchrs. Emergency Medicine, Univ. Assn. Emergency Med. Services. Republican. Lodge: Rotary. Home: 1928 Burnham Ln Dayton OH 45429-1102

LECKEY, ANDREW A., financial columnist; b. Chgo., Sept. 22, 1949; s. Alexander and Ellen (Martin) L. B.A., Trinity Coll., Deerfield, Ill., 1971; M.A. in Journalism, U. Mo., 1975; postgrad., Columbia U., 1978-79, Rutgers U., 1981. Fin. editor Oreg. Statesman, Salem, 1975-76; statehouse reporter Phoenix Gazette, 1976-78; fin. columnist Chgo. Sun-Times, 1979-85, Chgo. Tribune and N.Y. Daily News, 1985—; fin. commentator Sta. WBEZ, Chgo., 1981-83, Sta. WLS-TV, Chgo., 1983—; syndicated fin. columnist Los Angeles Times Syndicate, 1983-85, Tribune Media Services, 1985—; fin. commentator WLS-TV. Author: Make Money with the New Tax Laws, 1987. Office: WLS-TV 190 N State St Chicago IL 60601 also: Chgo Tribune Co 435 N Michigan Ave Chicago IL 60611-4001*

LEDER, CYRIL MARTIN, retired English language educator; b. Newark, N.J., Oct. 29, 1926; s. Abraham and Jennie (Albert) L.; m. Ruth Louise Stevenson, Dec. 31, 1923; 1 child, Richard Allen. BA, U. Chgo., 1950, MA, 1953. Cert. secondary tchr., Mich. Tchr. English and French New Buffalo (Mich.) Consolidated Schs., 1953-54; tchr. English Flint (Mich.) Pub. Schs., 1954-56; prof. English and journalism Mott C.C., Flint, 1956-94, ret., 1994. Freelance reviewer jours. With U.S. Army, 1945-47. Mem. Am. Philatelic Soc.

LEDERMAN, LEON MAX, physicist, educator; b. N.Y.C., July 15, 1922; s. Morris and Minna (Rosenberg) L.; m. Florence Gordon, Sept. 19, 1945; children: Rena S., Jesse A., Heidi R.; m. Ellen Carr, Sept. 17, 1981. BS, CCNY, 1943, DSc (hon.), 1980; AM, Columbia U., 1948, PhD, 1951; DSc (hon.), No. Ill. U., 1984, U. Chgo., 1985, Ill. Inst. Tech., 1987. Assoc. in physics Columbia U., N.Y.C., 1951, asst. prof., 1952-54, assoc. prof., 1954-58, prof., 1958-89, Eugene Higgins prof. physics, 1972-79; Frank L. Sulzberger prof. physics U. Chgo., 1989-92; dir. Fermi Nat. Accelerator Lab., Batavia, Ill., 1979-89, dir. emeritus, 1989—; Pritzker prof. sci. Ill. Inst. Tech., Chgo., 1992—; dir. Nevis Labs., Irvington, N.Y., 1962-79; guest scientist Brookhaven Nat. Labs., 1955; cons. Nat. Accelerator Lab., European Orgn. for Nuclear Rsch. (CERN), 1970—; mem. high energy physics adv. panel AEC, 1966-70; mem. adv. com. to div. math. and phys. scis. NSF, 1970-72; sci. advisor to gov. State of Ill., 1989-93. Author: Quarks to the Cosmos, 1989, The God Particle, 1993; also over 200 articles. 1st lt. Signal Corps, AUS, 1943-46. Recipient Nat. Medal of Sci., 1965, Townsend Harris medal CUNY, 1973, Elliot Cresson medal Franklin Inst., 1976, Wolf prize, 1982, Nobel prize in physics, 1988, Enrico Fermi prize, 1992, Rosenblith Lectures in Science and Technology Nat. Acad. of Sciences, 1995; Guggenheim fellow, 1958-59, Ford Found. fellow European Ctr. for Nuclear Rsch., Geneva, 1958-59, fellow NSF, 1967. Fellow AAAS (pres. 1990-91, chmn. 1992-93), Am. Phys. Soc.; mem. NAS, Italian Phys. Soc., Aspen Inst. Physics (pres. 1990-92), Ill. Math. Sci. Acad. (vice chmn. 1985—), Tchrs. Acad. for Math. and Sci. in Chgo. (co-chmn. 1990—). Office: Ill Inst Tech Dept Physics 3300 S Federal St Chicago IL 60616-3732

LEDVINA, CHRISTOPHER THOMAS, geologist, educator; b. Libertyville, Ill., Mar. 25, 1952; s. Steven E. and Lorrain F. (Finley) L.; m. Nancy L. Smith, June 19, 1982. BS in Geology, U. Ill., 1974; MS in Geology, Northeastern Ill. U., 1988; PhD in Mineral Engring., Northwestern U., 1991. Geologist Ill. State Geol. Survey, Urbana, 1974-77; asst. supr. Freeman-United Coal Mining Co., Virden, Ill., 1977-78; examiner Old Ben Coal Co., Benton, Ill., 1978—; assoc. prof. geology Northeastern Ill. U., Chgo., 1989—; chmn. bd., CEO Nat. Coal Mus., West Frankfort, Ill. Contbr. to profl. publs. Mem. AIME, ASME, ASCE, SME, AMC, AAPG, AGU. Office: Northeastern Ill Univ 5500 N Saint Louis Ave Chicago IL 60625-4625

LEE, BENJAMIN LING-HSIAO, industrial technology educator, consultant; b. Ping-Tung, Taiwan, Nov. 16, 1954; came to U.S., 1980; s. Shao-Mu and Kia-Yuan (Lee) L.; m. Esther Jine-Shew Ho, Oct. 22, 1988; 1 child, Alice. BS, Chinese Culture U., Taipei, Taiwan, 1980; MS, Ctrl. Mo. State U., Warrensburg, 1981; D of Indsl. Tech., U. No. Iowa, Cedar Falls, 1992. Cert. Sr. Indsl. Technologist. Technician Cox Ariz. Publs. Inc., Mesa, 1982-83; specialist Vocat. Assistance Commn. Ret. Servicemen Republic of China, Taipei, 1983-84; mgr. China Glory Printing Indsl. Inc., Taipei, 1984-89; mng. dir. Dynasty Color Printing Inc. of Calif., San Francisco, 1986-87; part-time instr. Chinese Culture U., Taipei, 1983-89; asst. prof. Ctrl. Mich. U., Mt. Pleasant, 1992-94, Eastern Mich. U., Ypsilanti, 1994—; mem. adv. com. Mid Mich. C.C., Harrison, 1992-94; cons. Taiwan Printing Industry Assn., Taipei, 1992—. Author: Modern Printing Technology and Management, 1987, 90, The Successful Editor, 1988, 90, 94, To Turn Paper into Gold by Printing, 1988, International Trade of Printing, 1987. Recipient Outstanding Coll. Youth award Republic of China, 1979, Outstanding Alumni award Chinese Culture U., 1984, 1st prize Vocat. Assistance Commn. for Ret. Servicemen, 1984. Mem. China Graphic Arts Assn. (bd. dirs. 1984-90), Chinese Assn. Graphics Sci. and Tech. bd. dirs., Outstanding Article award 1992), Nat. Assn. Indsl. Tech., Graphic Arts Tech. Found., Internat. Graphic Arts Edn. Assn., Kodak Pro Passport Profl. Network. Christian. Home: 3730 Tanglewood Ct Ann Arbor MI 48105 Office: Eastern Mich U 122 Sill Hall Ypsilanti MI 48197

LEE, BENNY Y. C., import and export company executive; b. Taipei, Taiwan, Feb. 23, 1947; s. Ko Kwan and Hsiu Yen (Huang) L.; m. Edith Y.C. Lee, June 25, 1989; children: Jenny I.S., Elizabeth Jordan, Katherine Belinda. Student, Tatung Instn. Tech., Taipei. Staff engr. Bendix Corp., Taipei, 1969-70, Philco Ford Corp., Taipei, 1970; supr. quality control Arvin Corp., Taipei, 1970-72; staff engr. Midland Corp., Taipei, 1972-74, mgr., 1974-77; mgr. elec. dept. Amerex Corp., Taipei, 1977-79; pres., owner Mitco, Taipei, 1979—, Kansas City, Mo. Mem. World Trade Ctr., Kansas City Internat. Trade Club.

LEE, BERNARD SHING-SHU, research company executive; b. Nanking, People's Republic of China, Dec. 14, 1934; came to U.S., 1949; s. Wei-Kuo and Pei-fen (Tang) L.; m. Pauline Pan; children: Karen, Lesley, Tania. BSc, Poly. Inst. Bklyn., 1956, DSc in Chem. Engring., 1960. Registered profl. engr., N.Y., Ill. With Arthur D. Little, Inc., Cambridge, Mass., 1960-65; with Inst. Gas Tech., Chgo., 1965-78, pres., 1978—; chmn. M-C Power Corp., Burr Ridge, Ill.; bd. dirs. NUI corp., Bedminster, N.J., Nat. Fuel Gas Co., Buffalo, Peerless Mfg. Co., Dallas, Energy BioSystems Corp., The Woodlands, Tex., New Eng. Gas Assn.; chmn. SGT, Shanghai, People's Republic of China. Contbr. more than 60 articles to profl. jours. Recipient Outstanding Personal Achievement in Chem. Engring. award Chem. Engring. mag., 1978. Fellow AAAS, Am. Inst. Chem. Engrs. (33d inst. lectr. 1981); mem. AIME, Am. Chem. Soc., Am. Gas Assn. (Gas Industry Rsch. award 1984), Econ. Club Chgo. Office: Inst Gas Tech 1700 S Mount Prospect Rd Des Plaines IL 60018-1804

LEE, BRIANT HAMOR, theatre educator; b. New Haven, May 6, 1938; s. Alfred McClung and Elizabeth Riley (Briant) L.; m. Nancy Jo White, Apr. 21, 1962; children: Guinevere White, Briant Hamor Jr. Cert. de Frequenza, Acad. di Belle Art, Rome, 1960; AB, Adelphi U., Garden City, N.Y., 1961; MA, Ind. U., 1962; PhD, Mich. State U., 1970. Instr. Calif. Western U., San Diego, 1962-63; asst. prof. Bradley U., Peoria, Ill., 1967-68; instr. Bowling Green (Ohio) State U., 1968-75, asst. prof., 1975-78, assoc. prof., 1978-95, prof. theatre dept., 1996—; engr. Kliegl Stage Lighting, N.Y.C., 1963-64. Author: European Post-Baroque Neoclassic Theatre Architecture, 1996, Corrugated Cardboard Scenery, 1993, Theatre Primer, 1991. Mem. ctrl. com. Wood County Dems., Bowling Green, 1970—. Mem. Am. Soc. for Theatre Rsch., Speech Comm. Assn., Assn. for Theatre in Higher Edn., Masons (Shriner). Unitarian. Home: 336 S Church St Bowling Green OH 43402-3719 Office: Bowling Green State Univ 322 South Hall Bowling Green OH 43403-0236

LEE, CATHERINE M., business owner, educator; b. Grand Rapids, Mich., Aug. 21, 1941; m. Gordon Timothy Lee; 4 children. BA, Aquinas Coll., 1963; MA, U. Mich., 1964; postgrad., Wayne State U., 1965-67. mem. Unit Dist. 220 Bd. Edn., 1984-93; sought Dem. nom. Ill. House, 1992; Dem. candidate 16th dist. Ill. U.S. House of Reps., 1996. Roman Catholic. Office: PO Box 204 Cary IL 60013*

LEE, CHARLES C., physicist; b. Szechwan, China, Oct. 8, 1940; came to U.S., 1965; s. James K.C. and Floral (Han) L.; m. Dora Lee, Sept. 5, 1970; children: Andrew, Wendell. BS in Physics, Peking U., Beijing, 1964; MS in Solid State Physics, Purdue U., 1968, PhD in Solid State Physics, 1974. Sr. scientist cen. rsch. lab. 3M Co., St. Paul, 1974-78, rsch. specialist physics and material lab., 1978-82, sr. rsch. specialist engring. systems divsn., 1982-88, divsn. scientist engring. document systems, 1988-93, divsn. scientist comml. graphics, 1993—; tech. auditor 3M Co. Freelance writer Chinese newspaper, N.Y.C.; author: Multi-function CAD Printer, 1984; translator: Optical Electronics, 1980; contbr. articles on laser scanning tech. to profl. jours. Pres. Chinese Am. Assn. Minn., Mpls., 1982; treas. Citizen for S.B. Woo in Minn., Mpls., 1988; organizer Music Festival, St. Paul, Mpls., 1990; chair Friends of Esther Lee Yao in Minn., 1991. Mem. Soc. Photo-Optical Instrumentation Engrs., Soc. Info. Display, Soc. for Imaging Sci. and Tech., Assn. Info. and Image Mgmt. Office: Comml Graphics Divsn 207-BW-09 3M Co Saint Paul MN 55144

LEE, DAVID CHANG, physician; b. Seoul, Republic of Korea, Sept. 14, 1940; s. Young C. Lee and Hae W. (Kim) Kim; m. Margaret C. Park, Sept. 10, 1965; children: Edward, Grace, George. MD, Yon-Sei Sch. Med., Seoul, 1965. Diplomate Am. Bd. Otolaryngology. Intern Howard med. Ctr., Washington, 1965-66; resident gen. surgery Roger's Meml. Hosp., Washington, 1966-67; resident otolaryngology St. Louis City Hosp., 1967-70, U. Md. Hosp., Balt., 1970-71; staff physician Ft. Howard (Md.) Vets. Hosp., 1971-73; asst. prof. U. Ill., Chgo., 1973—. Fellow ACS, Am. Acad. Otolaryncology and Head and Neck Surgery; AMA. Presbyterian. Office: 5320 159th St Oak Forest IL 60452-4705

LEE, DENIS C., medical sculptor and illustrator, educator; b. Chgo., Jan. 8, 1939; s. Donald Charles Lee and Tuberia a. Ruchti; m. Laurel Stordahl, July 30, 1967 (div. 1994); 1 child, Garrick Grant Hilary. BA in Zoology, Ind. U., 1961; MS, U. Ill., Chgo., 1964. Med. illustrator Mayo Clinic, Rochester, Minn., 1964-69; prof. U. Mich., Ann Arbor, 1969-95; chmn. bd. Ctr. Disfigured Childen, Ann Arbor, 1993-94. With U.S. Army, 1964. Recipient Russel Drake award Assn. Med. Illustrators, Charlotte Holt award, Tom Jones award. Mem. Rotary. Republican. Home: 849 Brookside Dr Ann Arbor MI 48105

LEE, DON YOON, publisher, academic researcher and writer; b. Seoul, Korea, Apr. 7, 1936; came to U.S., 1957; s. Yoo-ehn and Ch'i-ho (Kim) L. BA, U. Wash., 1963; MA, St. John's U., Jamaica, N.Y., 1967; MS, Georgetown U., 1971; MA, Ind. U., 1975, 90. Founder, pub. Eastern Press, Inc., Bloomington, Ind., 1981—. Author: History of Early Relation Between China and Tibet, 1981, An Introduction to East Asian and Tibetan Linguistics and Culture, 1981, Learning Standard Arabic, 1988, An Annotated Bibliography of Selected Works on China, 1981, Light Literature and Philosophy of East Asia, 1982, An Annotated Bibliography on Inner Asia, 1983, An Annotated Archaeological Bibliography of Selected Works on Norther and Central Asia, 1983, Traditional Chinese Thoughts: The Four Schools, 1990, others. Office: Eastern Press Inc PO Box 881 Bloomington IN 47402-0881

LEE, JAMES EDWARD, JR., educational administrator; b. Pitts., Mar. 9, 1939; s. Willard and Gladys Hilda (Jenkins) L.; m. Daisy Mae Tibbs, June 29, 1977; children: Stephen Michael, Monica Michelle, Brian Patrick, Priscilla Demone. BS, Wayne State U., 1962, EdS, 1969; MA, U. Mich., 1964; postgrad., Mich. State U., Wayne State U., U. Minn., U. Colo., 1964-95, Ctrl. Mich. U. Cert. tchr., adminstr., Mich. Tchr. Miller, Durfee and Michael Jr. High Schs., Detroit, 1962-67; team leader Nat. Tchr. Corps, Detroit, 1967-69; dept. head Noble Jr. High Sch., Detroit, 1969-74; asst. prin. MacKenzie High Sch., Detroit, 1974-80; asst. prin. Drew Mid. Sch., Detroit, 1980, prin., 1980—; instr. Wayne State U., Detroit, 1967-69, edn. cons., 1970-71; instr. Wayne C.C., 1967-81; prin. adult evening sch., 1974-80, summer gifted program, Detroit, 1986-92; mem. profl. stds. commn. for sch. adminstrs. Mich. Dept. Edn., 1992—, mem. adminstrv. waiver com., 1992-94. Contbg. author: The Development of Micro Teaching as an Evaluative Instrument in Teacher Training, 1969, (manual) The Principalship, 1990. Co-chair ednl. audit com. Oak Park (Mich.) Sch., 1988-90; bd. dirs. Scott Community Ctr., Detroit, 1988—; adv. bd. Adrian/Scott program to inspire readiness for ednl. success, Detroit, 1990—; adv. coun. Christ Child House, Detroit, 1990-92. With USMC, 1956-58. Recipient Prins. and Educators award Booker T. Washington Bus. Assn., Detroit, 1986, 90, Citation for Outstanding Leadership Detroit Bd. Edn., 1986; named finalist Boss of Yr., Detroit chpt. Am. Bus. Women's Assn., 1987. Mem. Nat. Assn. Secondary Sch. Prins., Nat. Mid. Sch. Assn., Mich. Assn. Supervision and Curriculum Devel., Mich. Assn. Secondary Sch. Prins. (exec. bd. 1986-88, Outstanding Mid. Level Prin. of Yr. 1991), Mich. Assn. Mid. Sch. Educators (bd. dirs. 1988-91). Home: 22580 Saratoga St Apt 2102M Southfield MI 48075-5947 Office: Charles R Drew Mid Sch 9600 Wyoming St Detroit MI 48204-4669

LEE, JAMES TRAVIS, JR., surgeon; b. Wichita Falls, Tex., Apr. 20, 1943; s. James Travis and Mary Ann (Walker) L. BA, U. Tex., 1964; MS, PhD, U. Ill., 1968; MD, U. Minn., 1975. Diplomate, Am. Bd. Surgery. Intern U. Minn., Mpls., 1975-76, resident, 1976-81; sr. rsch. scientist 3M Co., St. Paul, 1968-72; staff surgeon VA Med. Ctr., Mpls., 1981—; asst. prof. surgery U. Minn., Mpls., 1981-91, assoc. prof. surgery, 1991—; assoc. chief of surgery VA Med. Ctr., 1991—. Fellow ACS. Office: VA Med Ctr 1 Veterans Dr Minneapolis MN 55417-2300

LEE, JASON HOWARD, pilot; b. New Rockford, N.D., July 8, 1960; s. Kenneth Norman and Sonja Karen (Schmid) L.; m. Pamela Jo Ritterman, Dec. 2, 1995. AA, U. N.D., Devils Lake; Instrument Rated Pilot, Wakefield Flight Svcs., Devils Lake. Profl. pesticide trainer. pres. Maddock (N.D.) Airport Authority, 1992-96. Mem. Nat. Bison Assn., Aircraft Owners and Pilots Assn., N.D. Bison Assn., N.D. Farmers Union, Duk Untld. Inc. Republican. Lutheran. Home: RR 2 Box 126 Maddock ND 58348 Office: Air Agr West Inc RR 2 Box 126 Maddock ND 58348

LEE, JUDY, state legislator; m. Duane Lee; 2 children. BS, U. N.D. Real estate broker; senator Dist. 13 N.D. State Senate, vice chmn. human svcs./polit. subdivsn. coms. Mem. West Fargo (N.D.) Planning and Zoning Com., 1982-94; mem. planning/mktg. com. Dakota Hosp.; mem. parish planning coun. Faith Luth. Ch.; bd. dirs. United Way of Cass-Clay, 1987-93. Named Realtor of Yr., 1988, YMWCA Woman of the Yr. in Vol. Category, 1994. Mem. LWV, West Fargo C. of C. (bd. dirs. 1985-88), Fargo C. of C. (bd. dirs. 1993—), Toastmasters. Office: 808 E Sixth St West Fargo ND 58078

LEE, KEVIN, registered professional engineer; b. Beijing, China, Dec. 5, 1963; came to U.S., 1988; m. Qing Lee, Apr. 14, 1988; children: Anthony Lee, Daniel Lee. BA, Tsing Hua U., China; MS, Rensselaer Polytech. Inst. Engr. Chinese Acad. of Scis., Beijing, 1986-88; engring. mgr. Aviation Lighting Products Sola/Hevi-Duty Electric (unit of Gen. Signal), Lake Geneva, Wis., 1990—. Mem. IEEE. Office: Sola Hevi Duty Electric Co 1101 S Wells St Lake Geneva WI 53147-2425

LEE, MARGARET NORMA, artist; b. Kansas City, Mo., July 7, 1928; d. James W. and Margaret W. (Farin) Lee; PhB, U. Chgo., 1948; MA, Art Inst. Chgo., 1952. Lectr., U. Kansas City, 1957-61; cons. Kansas City Bd. Edn., Kansas City, Mo., 1968-86; guest lectr. U.Mo.-Columbia, 1983, 85, 87, 89, 91, 93-95; one-woman shows Univ. Women's Club, Kansas City, 1966, Friends of Art, Kansas City, 1969, Fine Arts Gallery U. Mo. at Columbia, 1972, All Souls Unitarian Ch. Kansas City, Mo., 1978; two-Woman show Rockhurst Coll., Kansas City, Mo., 1981 exhibited in group shows U. Kans., Lawrence, 1958, Chgo. Art Inst., 1963, Nelson Art Gallery, Kansas City, Mo., 1968, 74, Mo. Art Show, 1976, Fine Arts Gallery, Davenport, Iowa, 1977; represented in permanent collections Amarillo (Tex.) Art Center, Kansas City (Mo.) Pub. Library, Park Coll., Parkville, Mo. Mem. Coll. Art Assn. Roman Catholic. Contbr. art to profl. jours.; author booklet. Home and Studio: 4109 Holmes St Kansas City MO 64110-1127

LEE, MARVA JEAN, counselor, physical education educator, consultant; b. Cleveland, Miss., Feb. 16, 1938; d. Henry Davis and Willie Mae (Caver) Hardy. BS, George Williams Coll., 1960; MA, Northeastern Ill. U., Chgo., 1972; MEdn, Loyola U., Chgo., 1978. Child care worker Inst. Juvenile Rsch., Chgo., 1960-61; phys. educator Chgo. Bd. Edn., 1961-69; instr. George Williams Coll., Downers Grove, Ill., 1969-73; phys. educator Chgo. Bd. Edn., 1973-86, counselor, 1986-94; counselor Olive-Harvey Mid. Coll., 1995—; tchr. trainer family life edn., 1983—. Chmn. Chgo. Pub. Sch. campaign United Negro Coll. Fund, Chgo., 1981, 82, chmn. profl. women's aux., 1983—; bd. dirs. Chgo. com. NAACP Legal Defense and Edn. Fund, 1980—, Akarama Found., 1992-93, 96; sec. bd. dirs. Treshan Youth Found., Chgo., 1977-86; fin. sec. Chgo. Links Found., 1988-90; vol. quarterly pub. United Negro Coll. Fund, 1992; mem. Com. to Elect/Re-elect Roland Burris State Comptr., 1978-90, Com. to Elect Harold Washington Mayor Chgo., 1982-83, inaugural com. for Roland Burris Atty. Gen. State of Ill.; adv. coun. Olive-Harvey C.C. Transition Ctr., 1992—; mem. nat. svcs. youth Links Inc. Named Outstanding Vol., Mid-Am. chpt. ARC, Chgo., 1976, Outstanding Vol., United Negro Coll. Fund, N.Y.C., 1982; recipient Image award Fred Hampton Found., 1979, Svc. to Family Life Edn. award Chgo. Bd. Edn., Leadership Contbn. award United Negro Coll. Fund, 1990, Chgo. Bd. Edn. Svc. award, 1990, UNCF Telethon Leadership award, 1990. Mem. AAHPERD, Ill. Assn. Health, Phys. Edn. and Recreation (mem. exec. com. Chgo. dist.), Ill. Council Family Relations, Am. Assn. Counseling and Devel., Chgo. Guidance and Personnel Assn. Inc., Council Coll. Admissions Counselors, Secondary Sch. Counselors Council, Alpha Kappa Alpha. Avocations: community vol.; community fundraiser; travel. Home: 8300 S Peoria St Chicago IL 60620-3162

LEE, MORDECAI, religious agency adminstrator, political scientist; b. Milw., Aug. 27, 1948; s. Jack Harold and Bernice (Kamesar) L.; 1 child, Ethan. BA, U. Wis., 1970, MPA, Syracuse U., 1972, PhD, 1975. Guest scholar Brookings Instn., Washington, 1972-74; legis. asst. to Congressman Henry Reuss, Washington, 1975; asst. prof. polit. sci. U. Wis.-Whitewater and Parkside, 1976; mem. Wis. Ho. Reps., 1977-82; mem. Wis. Senate, 1982-89; exec. dir. Milw. Jewish Coun. Cmty. Rels., 1990—; adj. prof. govt. U. Wis.-Milw. Jewish.

LEE, PATSY RUTH, retired elementary education educator; b. Mangum, Okla.; d. Caswell Jay Franklin and Elizabeth H. (Epperson) Hinds; m. J. L. Lee, Mar. 4, 1951; children: Scot Franklin, Mark David. BS in Home Econs., Okla. Coll. for Women, 1948; MA in Elem. Edn., Ctrl. Mich. U., 1970. Cert. tchr., Mich. Dietetic intern U. Okla. Hosp., Oklahoma City, 1950; dietitian Elk City (Okla.) Coop. Hosp., 1949-51; dietician Bay County Hosp., Panama City, Fla., 1955-56; dietitian cons. Shawnee (Okla.) Gen. Hosp., 1958-59; dietitian Paxton (Ill.) Gen. Hosp., 1961-65; tchr. Oscoda (Mich.) Area Schs., 1965-91. Sec., chair Oscoda (Mich.) Planning Commn., 1991-95; trustee, treas. Oscoda (Mich.) Sch. Bd., 1995—; vice chair, sec. Iosco Dem. Party, Iosco County Mich.; bus. chair sect., edn. chair United Way of Oscoda, Mich. mem. Oscoda Lioness Club (pres., sec., Lioness of Yr.), Huron Shores Bus. and Profl. Women (legis. chair, Woman of Yr. 1978), Delta Kappa Gamma (pres. chpt. 1982-84). Democrat. Methodist. Home: 5248 Hughes Oscoda MI 48750

LEE, PAULA DEA, business education educator; b. Kewanee, Ill., Jan. 25, 1953; d. William Henry and Elizamae (Peterson) Evans; m. John Patrick Lee, June 1, 1974; children: Melissa Raeanne, Carissa Joeanne. BS in Edn., Ill. State U., Normal, 1974; MS in Edn., Western Ill. U., Macomb, 1985. Cert. tchr., Ill. Bus. edn. tchr. So. Sch. Dist., Stronghurst, Ill., 1975-77; substitute tchr. Atkinson (Ill.) High Sch., 1979-81; prof. Black Hawk Coll., Kewanee, 1983—; pres. Black Hawk Coll. East Campus Faculty Senate, 1990-91, 92-93. Tchr., St. John's Cath. Ch., Galva, Ill., 1987—; sec. Galva High Sch. Music Boosters, 1988-90; mem. Galva High Sch. and Galva Elem. Sch. Adv. Com., 1988—. Named Woman of Yr., Bus. and Profl. Women's Club, Kewanee, 1986; named to Outstanding Young Women of Am., 1986, 87. Mem. Profl. Secs. Internat. (pres. Kewanee chpt. 1992, 93, treas. 1991, sec. 1987-89), Ill. Bus. Edn. Assn. (registration coord. 1991-93, 2d v.p. 1994, 1st v.p. 1995, pres. 1996), Western Ill. Bus. Edn. Assn. (pres. 1990-91), PEO (corr. sec. 1991—), Delta Pi Epsilon. Home: 812 NE 3rd Ave Galva IL 61434-1125 Office: Black Hawk Coll 1501 State Hwy 78 Kewanee IL 61443

LEE, ROBERT, electrical engineering educator; b. Taipei, Taiwan, Apr. 8, 1962; came to U.S., 1967; s. Ming-hsi and Kathleen (Su) L. BSEE, Lehigh U., 1983; MSEE, U. Ariz., 1988, PhD, 1990. Microwave engr. Microwave Semicondr. Corp., Somerset, N.J., 1983-84; mem. tech. staff Hughes Aircraft Co., Tucson, 1984-86; rsch. asst. U. Ariz., Tucson, 1986-90; vis. scientist Sandia Nat. Labs., Albuquerque, 1987-89; asst. prof. elec. engring. Ohio State U., Columbus, 1990—. Contbr. articles to profl. jours. Mem. IEEE (Columbus chair Antennas and Propagation Soc. 1992—), Inst. of the Union of Radio Sci. (Commn. B.), Electromagnetics Acad., Applied Computational Electromagnetics Soc. (short course chair 1994-96). Office: Ohio State U 2015 Neil Ave Columbus OH 43210

LEE, ROGER, state representative, farmer, small business owner. Farmer, De Smet, S.D.; mem. S.D. Ho. of Reps., Pierre, mem. agr., natural resources and transp. coms. Democrat.

LEE, STEPHEN SHENG-HAO, dentist; b. Tao-Yuan Hsien, Taiwan, Dec. 14, 1945; came to U.S., 1972; s. Mao-chi Lee and San-Mei Fan; m. Fei-Jen Lo, Oct. 17, 1973; children: Christopher Stephen, Jennifer Stephanie. BS, Nat. Taiwan U., 1969, MS, 1972; PhD, U. Ill., 1976; DDS, Loyola U., Chgo., 1980. Dentist Stephen Lee Dental Clinic, Berwyn, Ill., 1981—; with curriculum com. dental asst. program Morton Coll., 1988. Author Research Publs., 1972. Bd. mem. Taiwan Benevolent Assn. Chgo., 1983. Mem. ADA, Ill. State Denal Soc., Chgo. Dental Soc. Republican. Office: 3239 Grove Ave Berwyn IL 60402-3468 also: 6550 S Cass Ave Westmont IL 60559-3211

LEE, TIMOTHY EARL, international agency executive, paralegal; b. Seattle, May 23, 1947; s. Charles Augusta and Esther Letty (Young) L.; m. Marcia Lea Wulff, July 6, 1968 (div. May 1976); children: Vincent Dean, Dante' Claude; 1 stepson, Kevin Paul McCorkle; m. Hayne Elizabeth Ashley, Apr. 28, 1984 (div. Apr. 1995). Cert., Ivy Tech., 1981, Am. Inst. Paralegal Studies, 1988. Mgr. Gen. Fin. Corp., Evanston, Ill., 1970-74, FBT Capital Corp., South Bend, Ind., 1974-76; owner Lee's Internat. Investigative Rsch. Agy., Ft. Wayne, Ind., 1978—. Mem. Heritage Foun., Citizens Against Govt. Waste; spl. adv. Allen Superior Ct. With U.S. Army, 1966-68, Vietnam. Recipient Cert. of Appreciation, DAV, 1968. Mem. VFW, Ind. Assn. Pvt. Detectives (v.p. N.E. region Ind. 1984—), Ind. Sheriff's Assn., Ft. Wayne Allen County Security Assn., Coun. for Inter-Am. Security, Nat. Security Ctr., Nat. Def. Inst., 27th Field Artillery Assn. (founding father), Am. Legion, Vietnam Vets, Internat. Platform Assn., Concord Coalition. Home: 8516 River Canyon Dr Fort Wayne IN 46835-1015

LEE, WILLIAM CHARLES, judge; b. Fort Wayne, Ind., Feb. 2, 1938; s. Russell and Catherine (Zwick) L.; m. Judith Anne Bash, Sept. 19, 1959; children—Catherine L., Mark R., Richard R. A.B., Yale U., 1959; J.D., U. Chgo., 1962. Bar: Ind. 1962. Ptnr., Parry, Krueckeberg & Lee, Fort Wayne, 1964-70; dep. pros. atty. Allen County, Fort Wayne, 1963-69, chief dep., 1966-69; U.S. atty. No. Dist. Ind., Fort Wayne, 1970-73; ptnr. Hunt, Suedhoff, Borror, Eilbacher & Lee, Fort Wayne, 1973-81; U.S. Dist. judge No. Dist. Ind., Fort Wayne, 1981—; instr. Nat. Inst. Trial Advocacy. Contbd. numerous publications and lectrs. in the field. Co-chmn. Fort Wayne Fine Arts Operating Fund Drive, 1978; past bd. dirs., v.p., pres. Fort Wayne Philharm. Orch.; past bd. dirs., v.p. Hospice of Fort Wayne, Inc.; past bd. dirs. Fort Wayne Fine Arts Found., Fort Wayne Civic Theatre, Neighbors, Inc., Embassy Theatre Found.; past bd. dirs., pres. Legal Aid of Fort Wayne, Inc.; past mem. ch. coun., v.p. Trinity English Lutheran Ch. Council; past trustee, pres. Fort Wayne Community Schs., 1978-81, pres., 1980-81; trustee Fort Wayne Mus. Art, 1984-90; past bd. dirs., pres. Fort Wayne-Allen County Hist. Soc. Griffin scholar, 1955-59; chmn. Fort Wayne Cmty. Schs Scholarship Com.; bd. dirs. Arts United of Greater Fort Wayne, Fort Wayne Ballet. Weymouth Kirkland scholar, 1959-62; named Ind. Trial Judge of the Yr, 1988. Fellow Am. Coll. Trial Lawyers, Ind. Bar Found.; mem. ABA, Allen County Bar Assn., Ind. State Bar Assn., Fed. Bar Assn., Seventh Cir. Bar Assn., Phi Delta Phi (past bd. dirs., 1st pres.), Benjamin Harrison Am. Inn of Ct., North Side High Alumni Assn. (bd. dirs. pres.), Fort Wayne Rotary Club (bd. dir.). Republican. Lutheran. Office: US Dist Ct 2145 Fed Bldg 1300 S Harrison St Fort Wayne IN 46802-3435

LEE, WILLIAM JOHNSON, lawyer; b. Oneida, Tenn., Jan. 13, 1924; s. William J. and Ara (Anderson) L.; student Akron U., 1941-43, Denison U., 1943-44, Harvard U., 1944-45; J.D., Ohio State U., 1948. Bar: Ohio 1948, Fla. 1962. Research asst. Ohio State U. Law Sch., 1948-49; asst. dir. Ohio Dept. Liquor Control, chief purchases, 1956-57, atty. examiner, 1951-53, asst. state permit chief, 1953-55, state permit chief, 1955-56; asst. counsel, staff Hupp Corp., 1957-58; spl. counsel City Attys. Office Ft. Lauderdale (Fla.), 1963-65; asst. atty. gen. Office Atty. Gen., State of Ohio, 1966-70; adminstr. State Med. Bd. Ohio, Columbus, 1970-85, also mem. Federated State Bd.'s Nat. Commn. for Evaluation of Fgn. Med. Schs., 1981-83; Mem. Flex 1/Flex 2 Transitional Task Force, 1983-84; pvt. practice law, Ft. Lauderdale, 1965-66; acting municipal judge, Ravenna, Ohio, 1960; instr. Coll. Bus. Adminstrn., Kent State U., 1961-62. Mem. pastoral relations com. Epworth United Meth. Ch., 1976; chmn. legal aid com. Portage County, Ohio, 1960; troop awards chmn. Boy Scouts Am., 1965; mem. ch. bd. Melrose Park (Fla.) Meth. Ch., 1966. Mem. Exptl. Aviation Assn. S.W. Fla., Franklin County Trial Lawyers Assn., Am. Legion, Fla., Columbus, Akron, Broward County (Fla.) bar assns., Delta Theta Phi, Phi Kappa Tau, Pi Kappa Delta. Served with USAAF, 1943-46. Editorial bd. Ohio State Law Jour., 1947-48; also articles. Home: Apple Valley 704 Country Club Dr Howard OH 43028-9530

LEESON, JANET CAROLINE TOLLEFSON, cake specialties company executive; b. L'Anse, Mich., May 23, 1933; d. Harold Arnold and Sylvia Aino (Makikangas) Tollefson; children by previous marriage: Warren Scott, Debra Delores; m. Raymond Harry Leeson, May 20, 1961; 1 child, Barry Raymond. Student Prairie State Coll., 1970-76; master decorator degree Wilton Sch. Cake Decorating, 1974; grad. Cosmopolitan Sch. Bus., 1980. Mgr., Peak Svc. Cleaners, Chgo., 1959; co-owner Ra-Ja-Lee TV, Harvey, Ill., 1961-66; founder and head fgn. trade dept. Wilton Enterprises, Inc., Chgo., 1969-75; tchr. cake decorating J.C. Penney Co., Matteson, Ill., 1975; office mgr. Pat Carpenter Assocs., Highland, Ind., 1975; pres. Leeson's Party Cakes, Inc., cake supplies and cake sculpture, Tinley Park, Ill., 1975—; lectr. and demonstrator cake sculpture and decorating; lectr. small bus. and govt. sec., Luth. Ch. Women; active worker Boy Scouts Am. and Girl Scouts U.S., 1957-63; bd. dirs. Whittier PTA, 1962-70, South Suburban Parkinson's Support Group, 1989-90, 91, 92, 93-94; advisory bd. Suburban Parkinson's Support Group, 1993, 94, 95, 96; active Bremen Twp. Rep. Com. Recipient numerous awards for cake sculpture and decorating, 1970—. Mem. Internat. Cake Exploration Soc. (charter, Outstanding Mem. Ill. 1984), Retail Bakers Am., Chgo. Area Retail Bakers Assn. (1st pl. in regional midwest wedding cake competition 1978, 80, 1st pl. nat. 1982, others), Am. Bus. Women's Assn. (chpt. publicity chmn., hospitality chmn. 1982-83, membership chmn. 1988-90, named Woman of Yr. 1986), Ingalls Meml. Hosp. Aux., Lupus Found. Am. (hot line girl Tuesdays Ill. chpt.). Lutheran. Home and Office: 6713 163rd Pl Tinley Park IL 60477-1717

LEESTMA, JAN EDWARD, neuropathologist, medical director; b. Flint, Mich., Nov. 30, 1938; s. Roger A. and Alice J. (Bulman) L.; m. Louise Marsilje, Jan. 8, 1940. BA in Chemistry, Hope Coll., 1960; MD, U. Mich., 1964; MM, Northwestern U., Evanston, Ill., 1986. Diplomate Am. Bd. Pathology. Intern, then resident in pathology U. Colo. Med. Ctr., Denver, 1964-67; fellow neuropathology Einstein Med. Col., Bronx, N.Y., 1967-68; from asst. to assoc. prof. Northwestern U., Chgo., 1971-85; prof., dean students U. Chgo., 1985-87; assoc. med. dir. Chgo. Neurosurg. Ctr., 1987—; cons. neuropathology Beth Naval Hosp. and D.C. Gen. Hosp., Washington, 1968-71, Office of Cook County Med. Examiner, 1977-87, Children's Meml. Hosp., 1982—, Ill. Masonic Med. Ctr., 1991—; attending physician Northwestern Meml. Hosp., Chgo., 1971-85; guest researcher Karolinska Inst., Stockholm, 1981-82. Author: Histological Pathology--Tumor Pathology, 1968, Forensic Neuropathology, 1988; contbr. chpts. to books; contbg. editor books of pathology. Mem. exec. com. Chgo. Coun. Fgn. and Domestic Affairs, 1974-91; bd. dirs. Horizon Hospice, Chgo., 1988-91; v.p., bd. dirs. Juvenile Protective Assn., Chgo., 1977—. Maj. USAF, 1968-71. NIH grantee, 1974-77. Mem. AMA, AAAS, Ill. Med. Soc., Chgo. Med. Soc., Am. Assn. Neuropathologists, N.Y. Acad. Scis., Sigma Xi. Presbyterian. Office: Chgo Neurosurg Ctr 428 W Deming Pl Chicago IL 60614-1719

LEETZ, JOHN RICHARD, health care executive; b. Evanston, Ill., June 5, 1933; s. Richard Carl and Gertrude (Wollenberger) L.; m. Jane Louise Motyka, Oct. 26, 1963; children: John R. II, Trudi Jane, Ruth Anne. Student, Grinnell Coll., 1951-55; grad., Culver Mil. Acad., 1955; student, Art Inst. Chgo., 1955, Northwestern U., 1956-57. With purchasing dept. Am. Hosp. Supply Corp., Evanston, 1956-58, with customer svc. dept., 1958-60, with sales dept., 1960-74; pres., chief exec. officer J.R. Leetz & Assoc. Inc., Evanston, 1974—, Dunlap, Ill., 1978—. Troop comm. chair Evanston area Boy Scouts Am., 1976-78; elder, deacon 1st Presbyn. Ch., Evanston. Recipient Merit Recognition award Health Industry Distbr. Assn., 1975. Mem. Mfr. Agt. Nat. Assn., Health Industry Rep. Assn., Scottish Rite (32d degree), Shriners. Republican. Office: PO Box 277 Dunlap IL 61525-0277

LEFEVRE, DONALD KEITH, electrical engineer; b. Casper, Wyo., Feb. 12, 1956; s. Lorin Durward and Margery Phyllis (Green) L.; m. Susan Lesley Nichols, May 31, 1975; children: Justin, Michelle, Mark, Kristen, Gregory, Sean, Brendan. BS in Physics, Elec. Engring., S.D. Sch. Mines and Technology, 1978; MS in Elec. Engring., U. Utah, 1985. Sr. engr. Sperry Def. Systems, Salt Lake City, 1978-84; chief engr. Anderson Scientific, Rapid City, S.D., 1984-86; asst. prof. elec. engring. S.D. Sch. Mines and Technology, Rapid City, 1986-90; pres. Wesha Technologies, Inc., Rapid City, 1987; pres., founder Cynetics Corp., Rapid City, 1988—; pres., founder Wireless Control Sys., Inc., 1990-94, dir., 1990—; leader of team for world's first multiple-channel compressed digital video broadcast sys.; founder, pres. African TV Investors, LLC. Patentee in field. Mem. bd. advisors Black Hills Bus. Innovation Ctr., Rapid City, 1986-90; founding mem. Black Hills Entrepreneur Network, 1988, dir., 1991-95; chmn. Ptnrs. in Entrepreneurship Com. Rapid City, 1993-95. Recipient Nat. Merit scholar; named Outstanding Recent Grad. in Elec. Engring. award S.D Sch. Mines and Tech., 1989. Mem. IEEE, Soc. Photo-Optical Instrumentation Engrs., Planetary Soc., Soc. Physics Students (chpt. pres. 1977), Eta Kappa Nu, Tau Beta Pi, Sigma Pi Sigma, Pi Mu Epsilon. Republican. Roman Catholic. Lodge: KC. Home: 4911 S Canyon Rd Rapid City SD 57702-1876 Office: Cynetics Corp PO Box 2422 Rapid City SD 57709-2422

LEFF, DEBORAH, foundation executive; b. Washington, Oct. 25, 1951; d. Sam and Melitta (Jerech) L. AB, Princeton (N.J.) U., 1973; Jd, U. Chgo., 1977. Trial atty. Civil Rights divsn. U.S. Dept. Justice, Washington, 1977-79; dir. office of pub. affairs Fed. Trade Commn., Washington, 1980-81; sr. producer Nightline-ABC News, Washington and London, 1983-89, World News Tonight-ABC News, N.Y.C., 1990-91; pres. The Joyce Found., Chgo., 1992—, also bd. dirs.; bd. dirs. CARE, Inc.; chair Midwest Rhodes Scholars Selection Com., Chgo., 1992. Mem. Coun. on Founds. Office: The Joyce Found. Ste 4010 135 S LaSalle St Chicago IL 60603

LEFFEL, JOHN H., financial consultant; b. Evansville, Ind., Nov. 1, 1947. BA, Ind. State U., MBA, 1976. Fin. cons. Dean Witter, Indpls., 1980-82, Smith Barney Inc., Indpls., 1982—. Sgt. N.G., 1967-73. Mem. KC (bd. dirs. 1992—), Kiwanis. Republican. Roman Catholic.

LEFFEL, RUSSELL CALVIN, lawyer; b. Kansas City, Mar. 23, 1948; s. Paul C. and Thelma W. (Wells) L.; children: Brad, Saralyn. BA in Econs., U. Kans., 1970, JD, 1973. Bar: Kans. 1973, U.S. Dist. Ct. Kans. 1973, U.S. Ct. Appeals (fed. cir.) 1986, U.S. Supreme Ct. 1986. Pvt. practice Shawnee Mission, Kans., 1973-75, 77—; ptnr. Wirt & Leffel P.A., Shawnee Mission, 1975-77; pres. Leffel Co. Inc., Kansas City, 1976-86, Rule Realty Corp., Kansas City, 1978—; sec. Mission Hills Homes Co., 1989-91. Mem. Shawnee Mission Edn. Found. Fund, 1991—, founding chmn., 1989-91, co-chmn. alumni assn., 1993-96; asst. scoutmaster Boy Scouts Am., Kansas City, Mo., 1993-94; mem. Unity Temple on the Plaza, 1993—, bd. dirs., 1995-96; shepherd deacon Village Presbyn. Ch., 1989-91; treas. Kans. Reps., Topeka, 1980-82, mem. state com., 1980-88; chmn. Johnson County Reps., Leawood, Kans., 1982-84; candidate Rep. nomination to U.S. Congress from 3d dist. Kans., 1984; mem. Johnson County C.C. Found., 1991-96; mem. devel. com. Kans. U., 1980—. Rusty Leffel Concerned Student award named in his honor U. Kans. Mem. ABA, Kans. Bar Assn., Johnson County Bar Assn. (program chmn. 7 yrs., bd. dirs. 1987-92, pres. 1990-91), Phi Alpha Delta. Home: 700 Ward Pky Apt 801 Kansas City MO 64112-1852 Office: 7315 Frontage Rd Ste 109 Shawnee Mission KS 66204-1658

LEFFLER, CAROLE ELIZABETH, mental health nurse, women's health nurse; b. Sidney, Ohio, Feb. 18, 1942; d. August B. and Delores K. Aselage; children: Veronica, Christopher. ADN, Sinclair Community Coll., Dayton, Ohio, 1975. Cert. psychiat. nurse coord. Nurse Grandview Hosp, Dayton, 1961-76; substitute sch. nurse Fairborn (Ohio) City Schs., 1981-82; dir. nursing Fairborn Nursing Home, 1983; psychiat. nurse coord. Dayton Mental Health Ctr., 1984—; mem. exec. bd. 1199. Vol., instr., disaster health nurse ARC; officer, leader, camp nurse for Girl Scouts, Boy Scouts; Ch. Parish Coun. Recipient Fleur de Lis award Girl and Boy Scouts, Svc. award ARC, Fairborn Mayor's Cert. of Merit for Civic Pride, State of Ohio Govs. award Innovation Ohio. Mem. ANA, Ohio Nurses Assn. Home: 29 W Bonomo Dr Fairborn OH 45324-3407

LEFTWICH, ROBERT EUGENE, oncological nursing educator; b. Lubbock, Tex., July 2, 1940; s. Eugene L. and Georgia (Kirkpatrick) L. BSN, Baylor U., 1963; MS, Northern Ill. U., 1970; PhD, Clayton U., 1977. Head nurse Baylor U. Med. Ctr., Dallas, 1963-64; supr. U.S. Air Force Nurse Corps, Fla., Tex., 1964-67; instr. nursing Cameron State Coll., Lawton, Okla., 1967-68, Rock Valley Coll., Rockford, Ill., 1968-70; dir. ADN program Kankakee (Ill.) Community Coll., 1970-71, dean health edn., 1971-72; chmn. dept. adult nursing Med. Coll. Ga., Augusta, 1972-75; asst. prof. U. Louisville, 1975-77; prof. nursing Governors State U., University Park, Ill., 1977—; bd. mem. Community Health Planning Bd., Kankakee, 1970-72; curriculum cons. Purdue U., Westville, Ind., 1983; oncology nursing cons. Ingalls Hosp., Harvey, Ill., 1979-85; grievance chairperson Univ. Profls. of Ill., University Park, 1981-83. Author: Nursing, Nutrition and the Adult Client, 1974, Humanistic Teaching Strategies and Nursing Students' Attitudes about Death and Dying, 1977, Self-Care Guide for the Cancer Patient, 1989; primary rschr.: Acuity Levels on an Adult Oncology Unit, 1981, Sexual Harrassment in Nursing Education, 1995; contbr. articles to profl. jours. Organist Trinity United Meth. Ch., Chgo., 1985-87; organist, choirmaster Bethel Covenant Ch., Flossmoor, Ill., 1987—. 1st lt. U.S. Air Force, 1963-67. Mem. Univ. Profls. Ill., Am. Guild Organists, Sigma Theta Tau. Office: Governors State U Dept Nursing University Park IL 60466

LEGAN, GREGORY MARK, university development administrator; b. Augusta, Ga., Nov. 4, 1957; s. Alfred Elsworth and Sally Jane (Albee) L.; m. Peggy Lynn Kolosso, Nov. 5, 1982; children: John Francis, Joseph, Michael, Kathleen Ann. BA, Columbia Coll., Chgo., 1979; MS, Ind. Wesleyan, 1991. Sr. community arts coord. Chgo. Coun. on Fine Arts, 1980-84; exec. dir. Tippecanoe Arts Fedn., Lafayette, Ind., 1984-86; dir. devel. computer sci. Purdue U., West Lafayette, Ind., 1986-93; dir. corp. and found. rels. So. Ill. U., Carbondale, 1993-96; exec. dir. John A. Logan Coll. Found., Carterville, Ill., 1996—. Editor Ind. Community Arts Guide, 1986-93. Chair arts subcom. C. of C., Lafayette, 1984-86; pres. Ind. Assembly Local Arts Agys., Indpls., 1985-87, Word City, Chgo., 1982-84; chair local arts agyh. adv. panel Ind. Arts Commn., Indpls., 1986; bd. trustees Ill. Arts Alliance, Chgo., 1983-84. Recipient Community Amb. award Conv. and Visitors Bur., Lafayette, 1991. Mem. Coun. for Advancement and Support of Edn. Methodist. Home: 167 Misty Lake Dr Murphysboro IL 62966-9648 Office: John A Logan Coll Found Dept of Computer Sci Carterville IL 62918

LEGAN, KENNETH, state legislator, farmer; b. Halfway, Mo., Aug. 3, 1946; s. Adolphus J. and June (Jones) L.; m. Rebecca M. Bodenhamer, 1969; children: Brock Alan, Stephanie Kaye. BS, U. Mo., 1969. Owner, mgr. Legan Farms, Halfway, 1971—; mem. Mo. Ho. of Reps., Jefferson City, sr. rep. Mem. Polk County (Mo.) Rep. Ctrl. Com., 1971—, chmn., 1976-80, vice chmn., 1980-86. Recipient Farm Mgmt. award Kansas City C. of C., 1976, Disting. Legislator award MCCA, 1992; named hon. chpt. farmer Halfway Future Farmers Am., 1978. Mem. Farm Bur., Legis. Exch., Lions, Masons, Shriners. Home: RR 2 Box 196 Half Way MO 65663-9666*

LEGENZA, RICHARD ANDREW, lawyer; b. Scranton, Pa., June 26, 1959; s. Jospeh Edward and Genevieve Elizabeth (Zawacki) L.; m. Polly Ann Snyder, Nov. 24, 1984; children: Hanna Virginia, Samuel Richard. BSBA, Ohio No. U., 1981, JD, 1984. Assoc. Palelek, McIlvaine, Foreman & Paul Co., Wadsworth, Ohio, 1984-87; assoc. Sherwin-Williams Co., Cleve., 1987, corp. counsel, 1987-91, sr. corp. counsel, 1991—. Treas. Seville (Ohio) Presbyn. Ch. USA, 1995—. Mem. Am. Corp. Counsel Assn., Ohio Bar Assn. Home: 1097 Oakbrooke Dr Medina OH 44256 Office: Sherwin-Williams Co 101 Prospect Ave NW Cleveland OH 44115

LEGER, DAWN ELIZABETH, newspaper reporter; b. Xenia, Ohio, May 27, 1969; d. James Edward and Verna Mae (Duhan) L. BA in English, Wright State U, 1992, student, 1992—. Reporter Fairborn Daily Herald, Amos Suburban Newspapers, Inc., Fairborn, OH, 1993—. Mem. Soc. of Profl. Journalists. Republican. Roman Catholic. Home: 4500 Wilmington Pike Apt 209 Kettering OH 45440 Office: Fairborn Daily Herald One Herald Sq Fairborn OH 45324

LEGER, ROBERT DAVID, newspaper editor; b. Roswell, N.Mex., June 13, 1957; s. Richard David and Mary Lu (Ford) L.; m. Cynthia Diane Putman, June 8, 1985; children: Andrew, Joshua. BJ, U. Mo., 1978. News editor, chief editorial writer, acting mng. editor Coffeyville (Kans.) Jour., 1979-81; copy editor, asst. news editor Springfield (Mo.) News-Leader, 1981-82, weekend city editor, Sunday editor, 1982-85, metro editor, 1985-88, spl. projects editor, 1988-93, spl. writer (bus.), 1993-94, editorial page editor, 1994—; adj. instr. Drury Coll., Springfield, 1988—; vis. prof. U. Mo. Minority Journalism Workshop, Columbia, 1988. Guitarist, Immaculate Conception Ch. Choir, Springfield, 1982—. Recipient Best of Gannett award for editorial writing Gannett Co. Inc., 1979, 94, 95; 1st place for editorial writing award Mo. Press Assn., 1988, 93. Mem. Soc. Profl. Journalists (pres. S.W. Mo. chpt. 1992-94), Sunrise Rotary Club (program chair 1995-96), Writers Hall of Fame (founding bd. dirs. 1994—). Roman Catholic. Office: Springfield News-Leader 651 Boonville Springfield MO 65806

LEGG, RONALD OTIS, oil company executive; b. Robinson, Ill., Feb. 2, 1945; s. Otis Everett and Hazel Pauline (Simons) L.; m. Connie Darlene Fasig, Nov. 6, 1965; children: Joshua Ronald, Timothy Andrew. Student, U. Ill., 1963-65; BS in Edn., Ea. Ill. U., 1968; MA in Counseling, Liberty U., 1993. Cert. secondary tchr., Ill., nat. cert. counselor. Engring. technician U.S. Geol. Survey, Champaign, Ill., 1965; tchr. math., physics Robinson High Sch., Community Unit Dist. 2 Schs., 1968-75; ptnr. Legg, Sanders & Drake, Robinson, 1975-82; pumper Marathon Oil Co., Bridgeport, Ill., 1982-84, engring. technician, 1984-91; field svcs. mgr. Crete Oil Co., Robinson, Ill., 1991—; individual and family counselor Jasper County Health Dept.,

Newton, Ill., 1992-95. Bd. dirs. New Hebron Water Dist., Robinson, 1970-94, pres.; bd. dirs. Cmty. Unit 2 Sch. Dist., Robinson, 1987—, v.p. bd. dirs., 1987-93; trustee Oak Ridge United Meth. Ch., Flat Rock, Ill., 1980—. Mem. NEA, ACA, Soc. Petroleum Engrs., Am. Assn. Christian Counselors, Internat. Assn. Marriage and Family Counselors, Internat. Assn. Addictions and Offender Counselors, Kappa Mu Epsilon. Democrat. Home: 6659 N 1075th St Robinson IL 62454-9554 Office: Crete OilCo 7005 E 1050th Ave Robinson IL 62454-0902

LEGGE, JOHN CHRISTOPHER, mechanical engineer; b. Denver, Apr. 7, 1964; s. Norman C. and Lynnett J. (Newland) L. BSME, Tri-State U., 1987. Sr. design engr. The Monarch Machine Tool Co., Sidney, Ohio, 1987—. Author: Tales of Christmas Wishes, 1993. Mem. ASME, Kiwanis, Order of the Engr., Kappa Sigma. Republican. Presbyterian. Home: 1406 Grove St Sidney OH 45365-1135 Office: Monarch Sidney 615 Oak Ave Sidney OH 45365-1335

LEGGE KEMP, DIANE, architect, landscape architect; b. Englewood, N.J., Dec. 4, 1949; d. Richard Claude and Patricia (Roney) L.; m. Kevin A. Kemp; children: Alloy Hudson, McClelland Beebe, Logan Roney. BA, Stanford U., 1972; M in Architecture, Princeton U., 1975. Architect Northrop, Kaelber & Kopf, Rochester, N.Y., 1971, Michael Graves, Architect, Princeton, 1972-75, The Ehrenkrantz Group, N.Y.C., 1975-77; ptnr. Skidmore Owings & Merrill, Chgo., 1977-89; prin. Diane Legge Kemp Architecture and Landscape Consulting, Riverside, Ill., 1989-93, pres., 1993—; pres. DLK Architecture, 1993—; chair Princeton U. adv. bd. Sch. Architecture, 1991—; dir. Newhouse Archtl. Found., Chgo., 1991—. Designer, architect: Boston Globe Satellite Printing Plant, 1984, Mfrs. Hanover Plaza, Wilmington, 1987, Herman Miller Showroom, Chgo., 1988, Arlington Internat. Racecourse, 1989, Phila. Newspapers Expansion and Retrofit, 1989, Navy Pier R constrn., 1990, McCormick Place Retrofit and Expansion, 1991, L.A. Times Master Plan, 1992, CRSS capital project mgmt. Chgo. Park Dist., 1993, Chgo. Hist. Blvds. Restoration, 1993, Roosevelt Rd. Reconstruction, Chgo., 1993, Field, Shedd, Adler Mus. Campus, Goodman Theater, Chgo., 1995, Job Corps Tng. Campus, 1995, Chgo. area Circulator Urban Design, 1995, Cook County Hosp., 1996, Chgo. Sun Times, 1996. Mem. bd. govs. Sch. of Art Inst., Chgo., 1991—; dir., past pres. Soc. for Contemporary Art, Chgo., 1991—. Recipient 40 under 40 award N.Y. Archtl. League, 1986; Urban Design award Progressive Architecture, 1984; named one of 100 Most Influential Women in Chgo., Crain's, 1996. Fellow AIA (Disting. Bldg. award 1983, Interiors award 1988, Nat. Urban Design award 1996); mem. NCARB, Am. Soc. Landscape Architects, Urban Land. Inst. Office: DLK Architecture 410 S Michigan Ave Chicago IL 60605-1302

LEGLER, VICTOR W., retired farmer; b. Jamestown, N.D., Nov. 6, 1926; s. Wilbert V. and Kate J. (Mulinex) L.; m. Marlys B. Legler, Aug. 28, 1926; children: Carol, Kent, Paul, Ellen, Jane. BS, N.D. State U., 1950. Asst. county ext. agt. Ext. Svc., Devils Lake, N.D., 1950-51, LaMoure, N.D., 1951; county ext. agt. Sargent Co. Ext. Svc., Forman, N.D., 1951-55; county ext. agt. Griggs Co. Ext. Svc., Cooperstown, N.D., 1955-58; farmer Jamestown, N.D., 1958-92; Stutsman County committeeman Agrl. Stabilization and Conservation Svc., Jamestown, 1977-86; Stutsman County rep. N.D. Wheat Commn., Bismarck, N.D., 1977-81; mem. Agronomy Seed Farm Coun., Casselton, N.D., 1972-84. Corp. USAF, 1946-47. Mem. Landowners Assn. N.D. (dir. 1989—). Home: Rte 1 Box 233 Jamestown ND 58401

LEGO, DANIEL LEE, systems integration engineer; b. Davenport, Iowa, Feb. 13, 1959; s. Cecil Leroy and Delores Mary (Fellner) L.; m. Yeng Chu Yeh, Mar. 16, 1982; children: Mark Daniel, Lori Ann. AS in Electronics Engrng., Hamilton Tech. Coll. Tech. support technician Gateway 2000, North Sioux City, S.D., 1990-91, network adminstr., 1991-92, network supr., 1992-94, sr. network integration engr., 1994—; network cons., Sioux City, 1990—, internet cons., Sioux City, 1992—. With USAF, 1976-88. Mem. IEEE, Nat. Computer Security Assn., Comm. Soc., Computer Soc., Network Profls. Assn., Data Processing Mgmt. Assn., Iowa Sheriffs Deps. Assn. Home: 1118 S Mulberry St Sioux City IA 51106 Office: Gateway 2000 610 Gateway Dr North Sioux City SD 57049

LEHMAN, GEORGE MORGAN, food sales executive; b. Chgo., Apr. 28, 1938; s. George Daniel and Margaret Marie (Cunningham) L.; m. Kathleen Marie Loftus, June 30, 1962; children: Robert Patrick, Daniel Joseph, Kathleen Marie, Michael Francis, William Terrance, Marilyn Elizabeth. BS, Marquette U., 1960; postgrad., Marquette Law Sch., 1962. Salesman, area mgr., city mgr. Am. Dist. Telegram Co., Chgo., 1964-79; security cons. A.I.C. Security Systesm, Chgo., 1981-83; exec. acct. mgr. Murphy Butter & Egg Co., Chgo., 1984-90; acct. exec. Badger/Murphy Food Svc., Chgo., 1990—; assoc. mem. Chef's De Cuisine, Chgo., 1985—. V.p. Sch. Dist. 126, Oak Lawn, Ill.; coach, umpire, v.p. Oak Lawn Little League; coach YMCA Basketball, Oak Lawn Pk. Dist. Basketball. Recipient Those Who Excell in Edn. award Ill. Assn. Sch. Bds., 1991, Cert. of Achievement, 1992. Mem. Beverly Stamp Club, Delta Sigma Pi. Roman Catholic. Home: 10733 Lawler Ave Oak Lawn IL 60453-5113 Office: Badger/Murphy Food Svc 700 N Western Ave Chicago IL 60612-1218

LEHMAN, JEFFREY JOHN, multi-media engineer; b. Detroit, Aug. 13, 1963; s. William James and Patricia Mary Jo (March) L. AS in Mgmt., Macomb C.C., Mt. Clemens, Mich., 1984; BA in Comms., Oakland U., 1987; MA in Bus. Computers, Cen. Mich. U., 1996. Cert. multi-media engr., Sears, Dale Carnegie, Comcast Cablevision. Musician, producer Jim Gold & Gallery, Sterling Heights, Mich., 1987—; mktg. rep. Premier Prodns., St. Clair Shores, Mich., 1987-91, Data Facility, Rochester Hills, Mich., 1988-89; engr. Rockwell Internat., Troy, Mich., 1989-96; pres. LFM Records, Troy, 1992—; pres., engr. Sound Advice Studios, Troy, 1992—; pres. Sound Advice Seminars, Troy, 1995—; multi-media engr. Ford Motor Co./Computer Horizons, 1996—; lectr. Rockwell Computer Club, Troy, 1991—; recording contract with Jim Gold and Gallery, Sussex Records/Mike Theodore and Clarence Avant, N.Y., 1994. Writer/producer: (song) Hard Lovin' Truck Drivin' Man, 1993. Mem. Broadcast Music Industry, Am. Guild of Music (judge 1992—). Home: 5555 Kreger Sterling Heights MI 48310 Office: LFM Records/Sound Advice Ms PO Box 99701 Troy MI 48099

LEHMAN, MICHAEL A., state legislator. Home: 1317 Honeysuckle Rd Hartford WI 53027-2614*

LEHMAN, OTTO ISRAEL H.M., curator emeritus, educator; b. Mar. 6, 1912; came to U.S., 1964; s. Max L. and Constance L. (Münchenburg) L. BLitt, St. Catherines Coll./Oxford U., MA, DPhil. Rabbi, 1938. Asst. to keeper of Oriental manuscripts Bodleian Libr., U. Oxford, Eng.; lectr. Leo Baeck Coll., London; vis. prof. Spertus Coll., Chgo.; curator of manuscripts and spl. collections Hebrew Union Coll., Cin., emeritus curator; adj. prof. dept. religion Miami U., Oxford, ohio. Editor: Handbook of Hebrew and Aramaic Manuscripts; contbr. to Spanish Ency. dela Biblia, 6 vols., 1969, Ency. Judaica, 16 vols., 1962; translator of Chief Rabbi Dr. J.H. Hertz's Pentateuch and Haftorahs into German. Jewish. Home: 3655 Middleton Ave Cincinnati OH 45220

LEHMAN, PRISCILLA LILLIAN, nurse, medical education programs distributing company executive; b. Cleve., July 17, 1945; d. Charles Louis and Jeannette Anne (Karda) L. Diploma Fairview Hosp. Sch. Nursing, Cleve., 1966; B.S. in Nursing, U. Va., 1972; M.S., Case Western Res. U., 1977. Nurse, supr. Parma Community Hosp., Ohio, 1966-69; charge nurse U. Mich. Hosp., Ann Arbor, 1969-70; staff devel. instr. Fairview Gen. Hosp., Cleve., 1972-73, dir. audio visual communications, 1973-82; pres. Lehman & Hall Assocs., Inc., Cleve., 1982—; distbr. Care Video Prodns., Cleve., 1982—; pres. Mailpouch Mailing Service. Writer and producer med. edn. videos. Deacon John Knox Presbyn. Ch. Recipient Golden Reel of Excellence award Internat. TV Assn., 1980, 81; Award of Merit Chgo. Internat. Film Festival, 1981. Republican. Avocations: golf; cross country skiing; swimming; reading. Home: 25730 Hilliard Blvd Westlake OH 44145-3310 Office: Mailpouch Mailing Svc & Care Video Prodns 1650 Crossings Pky Westlake OH 44145-1953

LEHMAN, REBECCA ANN, physical therapist; b. Monroe, Wis., Nov. 3, 1954; d. Paul Reinhard and Karen Ann (Holub) Mueller; m. James Michael Lehman, Aug. 26, 1978; children: Carl James, Daniel James, Pamela Lynn. BS in Phys. Therapy, U. Wis., La Crosse, 1977. Cert. phys. therapist, Wis. Sch. phys. therapist No. Ill. Assn., BiCounty, Ill., 1977-78; staff phys. therapist N.W. Gen. Hosp., Milw., 1978, Milw. Children's Hosp., 1978-80; staff phys. therapist St. Clare Hosp., Monroe, Wis., 1980-92, lead phys. therapist Monroe Clinic, 1992—; cons., mem. Swiss Alps Playground, Monroe, 1993-94. Den leader Cub Scouts, Monroe, 1992—; sec. Ding-a-Dong Presch., Monroe, 1989-90, 93-94, 95-96; coach, asst. coach Green County YMCA, 1994-94, mem. soccer com., 1994—; mem. PTO Parkside Sch., Monroe, 1993—. Mem. Am. Phys. Therapy Assn. Lutheran. Home: 924 2nd St Monroe WI 53566 Office: The Monroe Clinic Hosp Divsn 515 - 22nd Ave Monroe WI 53566

LEHMKUHL, MARGIE MAE, family practice nurse; b. Falls City, Nebr., Aug. 21, 1950; d. Arthur E. and Dora W. (Harper) Jimeson; m. Ronald Joseph Lehmkuhl, June 1, 1968; children: Darcie G., Joseph B. AA with honors, Johnson County C.C., Overland Park, Kans., 1977; BSN with highest distinction, U. Kans., Kansas City, 1979. RN, Kans., Mo. Pediatric and float nurse Humana Hosp., Overland Park, 1979-81, unit mgr., 1981-85; utilization rev. coord. Blue Cross/Blue Shield, Kansas City, Mo., 1985-86; joint venture liaison Blue Cross/Blue Shield and Managed Healthcare Resources, Kansas City, Mo., 1986-87; continuing care provider Managed Healthcare Resources, Overland Park, 1987-88; nursing supr. Hickman Mills Clinic, Kansas City, Mo., 1988-91; asst. adminstr., clin. Hickman Mills Clinic, Kans. City, Mo., 1991-92; coord. occupational health Vis. Nurse Assn. Greater Kansas City, 1993—. V.p. Kans. State Sigma Phi Epsilon Mothers Club, 1992-94; mem. ways and means com. Shawnee Mission West Booster Club, 1983-91; coord. Holy Trinity Religious Edn. Pre-sch., Lenexa, Kans., 1975, 76, instr., 1973-75, bd. dirs., 1975-76. Arthur S. and Leora J. Peck scholar, 1977; Allstate Found. nursing scholar, 1977. Mem. ANA, Kans. State Nurses Assn., U. Kans. Nursing Alumni Assn. (alumni award 1979), Occupational Health Nurses Assn. (chair social and hospitality com. 1995-97, bd. dirs. 1995-97), Sigma Theta Tau, Phi Kappa Phi. Home: 14912 W 89th St Lenexa KS 66215-2908 Office: Vis Nurse Assn Corp 527 W 39th St Kansas City MO 64111-2907

LEIGHTON, ROBERT JOSEPH, state legislator; b. Austin, Minn., July 7, 1965; s. Robert Joseph Sr. and JoAnn (Mulvihill) L. BA, U. Minn., 1988; JD, U. Calif., Berkeley, 1991. Minn. state rep. Dist. 27B, 1995—. Mem. Big Brothers/Big Sisters, bd. dirs., 1994—; mem. Am. Heart Assn., bd. dirs., 1993—. Presdl. and Waller scholar U. Minn., 1988. Mem. ABA, Minn. Bar Assn., Minn. Trial Lawyers Assn., Phi Beta Kappa. Address: 601 N Main St Austin MN 55912

LEINENWEBER, HARRY D., federal judge; b. Joliet, Ill., June 3, 1937; s. Harry Dean and Emily (Lennon) L.; m. Lynn Morley Martin, Jan. 7, 1987; 5 children; 2 stepchildren. AB cum laude, U. Notre Dame, 1959; JD, U. Chgo., 1962. Bar: Ill. 1962, U.S. Dist. Ct. (no. dist.) Ill. 1967. Assoc. Dunn, Stefanich, McGarry & Kennedy, Joliet, Ill., 1962-65, ptnr., 1965-79; city atty. City of Joliet, 1963-67; spl. counsel Village of Park Forest, Ill., 1967-74; spl. prosecutor County of Will, Ill., 1968-70; spl. counsel Village of Bolingbrook, Ill., 1975-77, Will County Forest Preserve, 1977; mem. Ill. Ho. of Reps., Springfield, 1973-83, chmn. judiciary I com., 1981-83; ptnr. Dunn, Leinenweber & Dunn, Joliet, 1979-86; fed. judge U.S. Dist. Ct. (no. dist.) Ill., Chgo., 1986—; bd. dirs. Will County Bar Assn., 1984-86, State Jud. Adv. Coun., 1973-85, sec. 1975-76. Bd. dirs. Will County Legal Assistance Found., 1982-86, Good Shepard Manor, 1981—, Am. Cancer Soc., 1981-85, Joliet (Ill.) Montessori Sch., 1966-74; del. Rep. Nat. Conv., 1980; precinct committeeman, 1966-86. Recipient Environ. Legislator Golden award. Mem. Will County Bar Assn. (mem. jud. adv. coun., 1973-85, sec. 1975-76, bd. dirs. 1984-86), Nat. Conf. Commrs. on Uniform State Laws (exec. com. 1991-93). Roman Catholic. Office: US Dist Ct 219 S Dearborn St Rm 1946 Chicago IL 60604-1706

LEINIEKS, VALDIS, classicist, educator; b. Liepaja, Latvia, Apr. 15, 1932; came to U.S., 1949, naturalized, 1954; s. Arvid Ansis and Valia Leontine (Brunaus) L. BA, Cornell U., 1955, MA, 1956; PhD, Princeton U., 1962. Instr. classics Cornell Coll., Mount Vernon, Iowa, 1959-62, asst. prof. classics, 1962-64; assoc. prof. classics Ohio State U., 1964-66; assoc. prof. classics U. Nebr., Lincoln, 1966-71, prof. classics, 1971—, chmn. dept. classics, 1967-95, chmn. program comparative lit., 1970-86, interim chmn. dept. modern langs., 1982-83. Author: Morphosyntax of the Homeric Greek Verb, 1964; The Structure of Latin, 1975; Index Nepotianus, 1976; The Plays of Sophokles, 1982. Contbr. articles to profl. jours. Mem. AAUP, Am. Classical League, Classical Assn. Middle West and South, Am. Philol. Assn. Republican. Home: 2505 A St Lincoln NE 68502-1841 Office: U Nebr Dept Classics Lincoln NE 68588-0337

LEININGER, LESTER NORMAN, agronomist, consultant; b. Boone, Iowa, Aug. 15, 1925; s. Louis Fredrick and Katherine Emma (Ahrens) L.; m. M. Anita Glasgow, Aug. 7, 1946; children: Linda Kay, Bruce LeRoy. BS, Iowa State U., 1952, PhD, 1959. Cert. profl. crop specialist, soil specialist. Leader, safflower investigation USDA Agrl. Rsch. Svc., Logan, Utah, 1959-65; extension agronomist U. Nebr., Lincoln, 1965-68; dir. rsch. Miller Seed Co., Lincoln, 1968-74; sec., treas. Pest Mgmt. Cons., Inc., Lincoln, 1974-82; pres. Plant Mgmt. Corp., Inc., Lincoln, 1982—, Sun-Tronics, Inc., Lincoln, 1988-90; exec. v.p. Nebr. Cert. Crop. Prodn. Adv. Found., Lincoln, 1988-94; expert witness legal profession, Great Plains, Nebr., 1972—; crop loss cons. Agri-Business, Great Plains, 1978—. Contbr. articles to sci. jours. Leader Boy Scouts Am., Lincoln, 1966-68; exec. com. Explorer Scouts, Lincoln, 1969-75; agrl. com. Nebr. Rep. Party, Lincoln, 1983—. Fellow AAAS; mem. Am. Soc. Agronomy, Crop Sci. Soc. Am., Soil Sci. Soc. Am., Optimist, Alpha Zeta, Gamma Sigma Delta, Sigma XI. Republican. Lutheran. Home: 8148 Sanborn Dr Lincoln NE 68505-2024

LEININGER, MADELEINE MONICA, nurse, anthropologist, administrator, consultant, editor; b. Sutton, Nebr., July 13, 1925; d. George M. S. and Irene (Sheedy) L. BS in Biology, Scholastic Coll., 1950, LHD, 1976; MS in Nursing, Cath. U. Am., 1953; PhD in Anthropology, U. Wash., 1965; DSc (hon., U. Indpls., 1990; PhDN (hon.), Ind. State U., 1990, U. Kuopio, Finland, 1991. RN; cert. transcultural nurse. Instr., mem. staff, head nurse med.-surg. unit, supr. psychiat. unit St. Joseph's Hosp., Omaha, 1950-54; assoc. prof. nursing, dir. grad. program in psychiat. nursing U. Cin. Coll. Nursing, 1954-60; research fellow Nat. League Nursing, Eastern Highlands of New Guinea, 1960-62, 78, 92; research assoc. U. Wash. Dept. Anthropology, Seattle, 1964-65; prof. nursing and anthropology, dir. nurse-scientist PhD program U. Colo., Boulder and Denver, 1966-69; dean sch. nursing, prof. nursing, lectr. anthropology U. Wash., Seattle, 1969-74; dean coll. nursing, prof. nursing and anthropology U. Utah, Salt Lake City, 1974-80; Anise J. Sorell prof. nursing Troy (Ala.) State U., 1981; prof. nursing, adj. prof. anthropology, dir. Ctr. for Health Research, dir. transcultural nursing offerings Wayne State U., Detroit, 1981-95, prof. emeritus, 1995—; adj. prof. anthropology U. Utah, 1974-81; disting. vis. prof. at 75 univs., U.S. and overseas,1970—; cons. Saudi Arabia, Brazil, Europe, Japan, Thailand, China, Burnei, Indonesia, Australia, South Africa, Finland, Sweden, The Netherlands, New Guinea, Australia, Jordan, Iran, Africa, 58 health instns. in U.S. Author: 28 books including Nursing and Anthropology: Two Worlds to Blend, 1970, Contemporary Issues in Mental Health Nursing, 1973, Caring: An Essential Human Need, 1981, Reference Sources for Transcultural Health and Nursing, 1984, Basic Psychiatric Concepts in Nursing, 1960, Care: The Essence of Nursing and Health, 1984, Qualitative Research Methods in Nursing, 1985, Care: Discovery and Clinical-Community Uses, 1988, Ethical and Moral Dimensions of Caring, 1990, Culture Care, Diversity and Universality: A Theory of Nursing, 1991, Care: The Compassionate Healer, 1991, Caring Imperative for Nursing Education, 1991, Transcultural Nursing, 1995; editor Jour. of Transcultural Nursing, 1989—; mem. editl. bd. 10 nat. and internat. jours.; editor or contbr. over 200 articles to profl. jours., 47 chpts. to books; lectr. in field. Disting. vis. scholar at 80 univs., U.S. and overseas; recipient Outstanding Alumni award Cath. U. Am., 1969, Recognition award Am. Assn. Colls. of Nursing, 1976, Nurse of Yr. award Dist. 1 Utah Nurses Assn., 1976, Lit. award Utah Nurses Assn., 1978, Trotter Disting. Pub. Lectr. award U. Tex., 1985, Disting. Faculty Tchg. Recognition award Wayne State U., 1985, Outstanding Faculty Rsch. scholar award Wayne State U. and Gerontology Inst., 1985, Gershenson Rsch. award Wayne State U., 1985, Pace Inst. Rsch. award, 1992, Hewlett Packard Rsch. award, 1992, award for Acad. Excellence AAUW-Detroit, 1986, Disting. award Bd. Govs., 1987, Pres. Excellence in Tchg. award, 1988, Women of Sci. award U. Calif. at Fullerton, 1990, Outstanding Univ. Grad. Mentor award Wayne State U., 1995, Nightingale Rsch. award Oakland U., 1995, outstanding nursing leader Russell Sage Coll, Sigma Theta Tau Intl. Disting. scholar award Russell Sage Coll., 1995. Fellow ANA, Am. Anthropol. Soc. for Applied Anthropology (exec. com. 1980-84), Am. Acad. Nursing; mem. Am. Assn. Humanities, Am. Applied Anthropol. Soc., Mich. Nurses Assn. (Bertha Culp Human Rights award 1994), Ctrl. States Anthropology, Amnesty Internat., Transcultural Nursing Soc. (founder, bd. dirs., pres. 1974-80), Cultural Cmty. Group Assn. (ethics, humanities heritage study group), Nat. Rsch. Care Confs. (leader human care rsch.), Internat. Assn. Human Caring (founder, pres., bd. dirs.), Nordic Caring Soc. Sweden (hon.), Sigma Xi, Pi Gamma Mu, Sigma Theta Tau (Lectr. of Yr. 1987—), Delta Kappa Gamma, Alpha Tau Delta. Office: 11211 Woolworth Plz Omaha NE 68144

LEISING, JEAN, state legislator. Farm owner and operator; indls. nurse Good Samaritan Hosp. Sch. Nursing; state senator from dist. 42 Ind. Senate, 1988—. Trustee Cath. Community Found. Mem. Ind. Corn Growers Assn., Batesville (Ind.) C. of C., Soybean Assn., Pork Producers and Cattlemen's Assn. Republican. Home: 5268 Stockpile Rd Oldenburg IN 47036-9713 Office: Ind State Senate State Capitol Indianapolis IN 46204*

LEISSA, ARTHUR WILLIAM, mechanical engineering educator; b. Wilmington, Del., Nov. 16, 1931; s. Arthur Max and Marcella E. (Smith) L.; m. Gertrud E. Achenbach, Apr. 11, 1974; children: Celia Lynn, Bradley Glenn. BME, Ohio State U., 1954, MS, 1954, PhD, 1958. Engr., Sperry Gyroscope Co., Great Neck, N.Y., 1954-55; rsch. assoc. Ohio State U., 1955-56, instr. engrng. mechanics, 1956-58, asst. prof., 1958-61, assoc. prof., 1961-64, prof., 1964—; vis. prof. Eidgenossische Technische Hochschule, Zurich, Switzerland, 1972-73, USAF Acad., Colorado Springs, Colo., 1985-86; Plenary lectr. 2nd Internat. Conf. on Recent Advances in Structural Dynamics, Southampton, Eng., 1984, 4th Internat. Conf. on Composite Structures, Paisley, Scotland, 1987, Dynamics and Design Conf., Japan Soc. Mech. Engrs., Kawasaki, 1990, Energy Sources and Tech. Conf., ASME, Houston, 1992; cons. in field. Author: Vibration of Plates, 1969, Vibration of Shells, 1973, Buckling of Laminated Composite Plates and Shell Panels, 1985; assoc. editor Applied Mechanics Revs., 1985-93, editor-in-chief, 1993—; assoc. editor Jour. Vibration and Acoustics, 1990-93; mem. editl. bd. Jour. Sound and Vibration, 1971—, Internat. Jour. Mech. Sci., 1972—, Composite Structures, 1982—, Applied Mechanics Revs., 1988-93, Jour. Vibration and Control, 1994—; contbr. over 150 articles to profl. jours. Performer Columbus Symphony Orch. Operas, 1971-79; gen. chmn. Pan Am. Congress Applied Mechanics, Rio de Janeiro, 1989; leader Ohio State U. Mt. McKinley Expdn., 1978. Recipient Recognition plaque Inst. de Mecanica Applicada, Argentina, 1977, Centennial cert., Am. Soc. Engrng. Edn., 1993. Fellow ASME, Am. Acad. Mechanics (pres. 1987-88), Japan Soc. for Promotion Sci.; mem. Am. Soc. for Engrng. Edn., Am. Alpine Club. Home: 1294 Fountaine Dr Columbus OH 43221-1520 Office: 155 W Woodruff Ave Columbus OH 43210-1117

LEISTNER, MARY EDNA, retired secondary education chemistry educator; b. Evanston, Ill., Apr. 13, 1929; d. Joseph W. and Edna C. (Moe) Cox; m. Delbert L. Leistner, Sept. 30, 1950; children: David, Martha, Joseph. BS in Chemistry, Purdue U., 1950; MEd, Miami U., Oxford, Ohio, 1964. Tchr. sci. and math. Cen. Jr. High Sch., Sidney, Ohio, 1962-66; tchr. chemistry, biology, advanced chemistry Sidney High Sch., 1966-93; ret., 1993; mem. high sch. chemistry test com. Nat. Sci. Tchrs. Assn., Am. Chem. Soc., 1983-85. Mem. exec. com. Ohio Dist. Luth. Women's Missionary League, Columbus, 1978-82, convention chmn., 1988; pres. Miami Valley zone, 1985-87; pres. Redeemer Ladies Soc., Sidney, 1980-91, 94—; auxiliary gift shop com. mem. Wilson Meml. Hosp., Sidney, 1994—. Mem. Nat. Sci. Tchrs. Assn. (Cadre 100 award), Western Ohio Sci. Tchrs. Assn. (pres. 1972-73), Sci. Edn. Council Ohio (dist. rep. exec. bd. 1984-86, treas. 1986-90, pres. elect 1991-92, pres. 1992-93, immediate past pres. 1993-94, ch. retirees/historian com. 1995—), Sidney Edn. Assn. (treas. 1980-82, 85-86, tchr. of Yr., 1988), Ohio Acad. Scis. (Jerry Acker Outstanding Tchr. of Yr. 1988-89, Exemplar 1993), Delta Kappa Gamma (2nd v.p. 1992-94, 1st v.p. 1994-96, pres. 1996—). Republican. Lutheran.

LEITCH, DAVID R., state legislator; b. Three Rivers, Mich., Aug. 22, 1948; m. Marlene Leitch; three children. BA, Kalamazoo Coll., 1970. Dist. 47 senator Ill. Senate, Springfield, 1986-87; Dist. 93 rep. Ill. Ho. Reps., Springfield, 1988—; asst. majority leader, mem. appropriations II, utilities, environ. and energy, rules, Medicaid, labor and commerce, reapportionment, and legis. rsch. unit coms., Ill. Ho. Reps. Mem. Rep. ctrl. and fin. coms., Peoria County, Ill., 1975—; v.p. First of Am.-Ill. Named Outstanding Young Man in Peoria; recipient Disting. Svc. award, 1981. Mem. Inst. Physical Medicine, Heartland Health Clinic, United Way, Komen Found., Rotary. Home: 7304 N Manning Dr Peoria IL 61614-1917*

LEITCH, VINCENT BARRY, literary studies educator; b. Hempstead, N.Y., Sept. 18, 1944; s. Eugene Vincent and Lucile Jean (Amplo) L.; m. Jill Robin Berman, May 20, 1970 (div. May 1987); children: Kristin M., Rory G. BA, Hofstra U., 1966; MA, Villanova U., 1967; PhD, U. Fla., 1972. Postdoctoral fellow Sch. Criticism and Theory, U. Calif., Irvine, 1978; interim asst. prof. U. Fla., Gainesville, 1972-73; from asst. prof. to prof. English Mercer U., Macon, Ga., 1973-86; prof. English Purdue U., West Lafayette, Ind., 1986—, co-dir. English and philosophy doctoral program, 1986-93; sr. Fulbright lectr. U. Tampere, Finland, 1979; reviewer NEH, 1985-88; bd. dirs. Purdue U. Press, 1988-90; Moss chair of excellence U. Memphis, 1991; mem. adv. bd. Modern Fiction Studies, 1992—, Symploke, 1995—. Author: Deconstructive Criticism, 1983, American Literary Criticism from the 1930s to the 1980s, 1988, Cultural Criticism, Literary Theory, Poststructuralism, 1992, Postmodernism: Local Effects, Global Flows, 1996; mem. editl. bd. lit. and film series Fla. State U. Press, 1983—, Purdue Univ. Press, 1988-90; mem. staff abstracts of English Studies, 1972-75; mem. editl. bd. South Atlantic Rev., 1985-87. Recipient Outstanding Acad. Book award Assn. Coll. and Rsch. Librs., 1988; Am. Philos. Soc. grantee, 1974; fellow NEH, 1980, Mellon Found., 1981, Am. Coun. Learned Socs., 1985-86, Ctr. for Humanistic Studies, Purdue U., 1989, 96. Mem. MLA (publs. com. 1990-93, assembly del. 1990-92, 93-95, chair organizing com. 1995, chair ad hoc com. on governance issues 1995, mem. 1996, exec. com. lit. criticism divsn. 1994—), Soc. for Critical Exch. (bd. dirs. 1978-83), PEN Am. Ctr., Internat. Assn. for Philosophy and Lit. Office: Purdue U Dept English West Lafayette IN 47907

LEITNER, MARK MATTHEW, lawyer; b. Sheboygan, Wis., Oct. 10, 1958; s. Raymond James and Shirley Mae (Dingeldein) L.; 1 child, Ellen Patricia. BA, Marquette U., 1980; JD, U. Wis., 1985. Bar: Wis. 1985, Ill. 1985, U.S. Dist. Ct. (no. dist.) Ill. 1985, U.S. Dist. Ct. (we. dist.) Wis. 1985, (ea. dist.) Wis. 1988, U.S. Ct. Appeals (7th cir.) 1988. Assoc. Reuben & Proctor, Chgo., 1985-86, Isham, Lincoln & Beale, Chgo., 1986-87, Charne, Clancy & Taitelman, Milw., 1987-91, Charne, Clancy, Krueger & Pollack, Milw., 1991-92; assoc. Kravit, Gass & Weber, Milw., 1992-94, shareholder, 1994—; instr. mass media law Marquette U., 1990—. Co-author: Wisconsin Discovery Law and Practice, 1990. Mem. ABA, Wis. Bar Assn., Milw. Bar Assn., Milw. Young Lawyers Assn., Order of Coif. Democrat. Home: 1217 Pippin Ct Mequon WI 53092-5910 Office: Kravit Gass & Weber 825 N Jefferson St Milwaukee WI 53202-3737

LEITZE, ANNETTE EMILY RICKS, mathematics educator; b. Jacksonville, Ill., May 31, 1951; d. William Brown and Rachel Emily (Husted) Ricks; m. Harold Dean Leitze, Aug. 19, 1972; children: Jason Matthew, Jeremy Michael. BS in Math., Western Ill. U., 1972; MA in Math., Ind. U., 1988, PhD in Math. Edn., 1992. Cert. 6-12 math. tchr., Ill. Tchr. math. Triopia Jr.-Sr. High Sch., Concord, Ill., 1975-80; assoc. instr. dept. math. Ind. U., Bloomington, 1986-88, rsch. asst., assoc. instr. Sch. Edn., 1989-92, instr. math. Sch. Continuing Studies, 1992; prof. Ball State U., Muncie, Ind., 1992—. Contbg. editor: Projects for Real World Problem Solvers, 1991; author software Problem-Solving Data Bank; also articles. Mem. restructuring task force Monroe County Community Sch. Corp., Bloomington, 1989, mem. math. textbook adoption com., 1992. Grad. fellow Ind. U. Sch. Edn., 1989, 90. Mem. Am. Ednl. Rsch. Assn., Spl. Interest Group, Ind. Coun. Tchrs. Math., Math. Assn. Am., Nat. Coun. Tchrs. Math.,

Psychology of Math. Edn., Sch. Sci. and Math. Assn., Kappa Mu Epsilon, Phi Delta Kappa. Office: Ball State U Dept Math Scis Muncie IN 47306

LEITZKE, JACQUE HERBERT, psychologist, corporate executive; b. Watertown, Wis., Dec. 25, 1929; s. Herbert Wilbert and Ruth Valberg (Stavenow) L.; m. Mary Annis Lacey, June 20, 1950 (div. Nov. 1963); children: Keith Alan, Sari Dawn, Thora Jacquelynne. BS, U. Wis., Madison, 1955; MA, Kent State U., 1958. Lic. psychologist, Wis., Ill., N.Y. Sch. psychologist Bur. Child Guidance, N.Y.C., 1959-61; clin. psychologist Bur. of Child Guidance, Neenah, Wis., 1961-64; clin. psychologist, psychotherapist Winnebago County Guidance Ctr., Neenah, Wis., 1961-64; sch. psychologist Waukegan City (Ill.) Sch. Dist. 61, 1965-66; clin. psychologist Wis., Ill., 1967-78; corp. pres., CEO Psychometrics Internat. Corp., Watertown, 1979—. Author: Definitively Incorporeal Human Intelligence Itself; originator intelligence test Abecedarian Measure of Human Intelligence, 1979. Trustee Human Intelligence Rsch. Found. Served with USAF, 1948-51. Mem. APA, Mensa. Home: 1153 Boughton St Apt 807 Watertown WI 53094-3106 Office: Psychometrics Internat Corp PO Box 247 Watertown WI 53094-0247

LEKAN, BRIANA MARKER, photographer; b. Columbus, Ohio, Oct. 9, 1955; d. Daniel Lee and Charlotte (Holley) Marker; m. Thomas James Lekan, Aug. 12, 1978; children: Danelle Kara, Adriana Carol. BA in Art Edn., Ohio State U., 1978. Lic. forensic photographer. Forensic photographer Cuyahoga County, Cleve., 1978-82; free-lance photographer Cin., 1985—; photographer Clev. Basic Police Sch., 1978-82, Cuyahoga County Coroner's Office, 1978-81. Clubs: AMA Aux., United Meth. Women.

LELAND, BURTON, state legislator; b. Detroit, Nov. 24, 1948; s. Morris Leland and Beatrice (Bernstein) L.; m. Rosanne Letvin; children: Zachary Levi, Gabriel Daniel. BS, Wayne State U., 1971; MSW, U. Mich., 1977. Social worker Wayne County Dept. Social Svc., 1972-80; state rep. Dist. 13 Mich. Ho. of Reps., 1981—; mem. Joint Com. on Adminstrv. Rules, Elec. Consumers, Pub. Health & Transp. Coms. Mich. Ho. of Reps.; vice-chmn. Tourism, Fisheries & Wildlife Com. Mem. NASW, Nat. Conf. State Legislators, Alpha Epsilon Pi. Home: 20765 Tireman St Detroit MI 48228-2837*

LELAND, HENRY, psychology educator; b. N.Y.C., Feb. 13, 1923; s. Ida (Miller) L.; m. Helen D. Faitos (div. 1979); children: Colombe, David Jean, Daniel Louis; m. Sherrie Lynn Ireland, Dec. 7, 1980. AB, San Jose State Coll., 1948; PhD, Université de Paris (Sorbonne), 1952. Lic. psychologist, Ohio. Clin. psychologist with Dr. Jean Biro, Paris, 1949-52; sr. clin. psychologist N.Y. State Mental Health Commn., Syracuse, 1952-54; dir. dept. psychol. svc. Muscatatuck State Sch., Butlerville, Ind., 1954-57; chief clin. psychologist Parsons (Kans.) State Hosp. and Tng. Ctr., 1957-63; coord. profl. tng., edn. and demonstration Parsons (Kans.) State Hosp. and Tng. Ctg., 1963-70; assoc. in child rsch. Kansas U. Bur. child Rsch., Lawrence, 1963-70; assoc. prof. psychology Ohio State U., Columbus, 1970-72; prof. Ohio State U., 1972-93, prof. emeritus, 1993—; chief psychology Herschel W. Nisonger Ctr., Columbus, 1970-93; tchg. asst. Ind. U. Extension Svc., 1956-57; assoc. prof. Kansas State Coll., 1958-70; dist. vis. lectr. U. So. Calif., L.A., 1969; prin. investigator Adaptive Behavior Project, Ohio Dept. Mental Health and Mental Retardation, 1972-75, cons., 1972-75; bd. examiners State Bd. Psychology Ohio, 1987-88, 93-94, sec., 1988-89, pres., 1989-90, 94-95, active, 1986-95; cons. Cen. Ohio Psychiat. Hosp., 1986-93; com. on acad. misconduct Ohio State U., 1990-93. Author: (wih D. Smith) Play Therapy with Mentally Subnormal Children, 1965, (with others) Brain Damage and Mental Retardation, 1967, (with others) Handbuch der Kinderpsychotherapie, Vol. II, Germany, 1968, (with others) Social Perceptual Training Kit for Community Living, 1968, Impairment in Adaptive Behavior: A Community Dimension, Tracks, Vols. II, 12, 1960-67, (with others) Social Inference Training of Retarded Adolescents at the Pre-Vocational Level, 1968, (with others) Mental Health Services for the Mentally Retarded, 1972, (with others) Sociobehavioral Studies in Mental Retardation, 1973, (with others) Mental Retardation: Current and Future Perspectives, 1974, (with others) Research to Practice in Mental Retardation and Education and Training, II, 1977, (with others) International Encyclopedia of Psychiatry, Psychology, Psychoanalysis and Neurology, II, 1977, (with others) Psychological Management of Pediatric Problems, 1978, (with Deutsch)Abnormal Behavior, 1980, (with others) Pscychoeducational Assessment of Preschool and Primary Age Children, 1982, (with others) Comprehensive Handbook of Mental Retardation, 1983, (with others) The Foundations of Clinical Neuropsychology, 1983, (with others) Institutions for the Mentally Retarded: A Changing Role in Changing Times, 1986; cons. editor Am. Jour. Mental Deficiency, 1965-70, Profl. Psychology, 1977-95, Mental Retardation, 1980-84; contbr. articles to profl. jours. Sgt. U.S. Army, 1942-45, ETO. Recipient Disting. Svc. in Mental Deficiency award, Am. Assn. on Mental Deficiency, 1985. Fellow AAAS, APA (councilor 1986-90 , Edgar A. Doll Meml. award div. 33 1990), Am. Assn. on Mental Retardation (councilor 1964-68), Ohio Psychol. Assn., Soc. for Pediatric Psychology. Democrat. Jewish. Home: 2120 Iuka Ave Columbus OH 43201-1322

LELLIG, CYNTHIA, public library director; b. Ogden, Iowa, June 29, 1951; d. Robert Emery and Doris Esther (Wiener) M.; m. Donald Leo Lellig, Nov. 30, 1974; children: Matthew Robert, Melanie Ann Lellig. BA in Libr. Sci. and Math., U. No. Iowa, 1973. Cert. pub. libr. level V, State Libr. of Iowa. Jr. sr. h.s. instructional materials ctr. dir. Grundy Ctr. (Iowa) Comty. Schs., 1973-75; elem. and jr. h.s. libr. Jesup (Iowa) Comty. Schs., 1975-80; libr. dir. City of Jesup, 1987—; mem. media adv. coun. Area Edn. Agy. 7, Cedar Falls, Iowa, 1975-77; advisor for design, fund raising, etc. for a new libr. bldg., Jesup, 1990-93; mem. grant rev. com. State Libr. Iowa, Des Moines, 1993. Bd. dirs. ARC, Buchanan County, Iowa, 1995-96; mem. Jesup Middle Sch. Adv. Coun., 1995-96. Mem. Iowa Libr. Assn., Iowa Small Libr. Assn., Cath. Daughters of Am., Jesup C. of C. (bd. dirs. 1994-96). Office: Jesup Pub Libr 721 6th St Box 585 Jesup IA 50648

LEMARBE, EDWARD STANLEY, engineering manager, engineer; b. Chicago Heights, Ill., June 30, 1952; s. Gerald Joseph and Irene Helen (Jelen) LeM.; m. Patricia Ann Czyz, May 28, 1977; children: Kyle Bradford, Randall Jered. BS in Mech. Tech., Purdue U., 1976; MBA, Lewis U., 1984. Field engr. Morrison Constrn. & Engring., Hammond, Ind., 1976-78; sr. engr. Miner Enterprises, Inc., Geneva, Ill., 1978-85; mgr. product devel. Alco Dispensing Systems div. Alco Standard, Torrington, Conn., 1985-88; v.p. engring. Jet Spray Corp., Norwood, Mass., 1988-92; sr. dir. Engring. Multiplex Co., Ballwin, Mo., 1992—; mem. pres.' staff Alco Dispensing/Selmix-Alco, Torrington, 1986-88; mem. exec. com. Jet Spray Corp., Norwood, 1988-92; mem. resource allocation com. Multiplex Co. Inc., 1992—. Mem. ASTM (subcom. 1988—), Am. Mgmt. Assn. (assoc.), Internat. Food Svc. Mfrs. Assn. (corp. mem.), Hickory Bend Condo Assn. (bd. dirs. 1984-85). Republican. Roman Catholic.

LE MASTER, DENNIS CLYDE, forest economics and policy educator; b. Startup, Wash., Apr. 22, 1939; s. Franklin Clyde and Delores Ilene (Schwartz) Le M.; m. Kathleen Ruth Dennis, Apr. 4, 1961; children: Paul, Matthew. BA, Wash. State U., 1961, MA, 1970, PhD, 1974. Asst. prof. dept. forestry and range mgmt. Wash. State U., Pullman, 1972-74, assoc. prof., 1978-80, prof., chair dept., 1980-88; prof., head dept. forestry and natural resources Purdue U., West Lafayette, Ind., 1988—; dir. resource policy Soc. Am. Foresters, Bethesda, Md., 1974-76; staff counsel subcom. on forests Ho. of Reps., Washington, 1977-78; cons. USDA Forest Svc., Washington, 1978, Com. on Agr., Ho. of Reps., 1979-80, Forest History Soc., Durham, N.C., 1979-83, The Conservation Found., 1989-90, Office Tech. Assessment, Washington, 1989-91, Consultative Group on Biol. Diversity, 1991. Author: Decade of Change, 1984; co-editor 8 books; contbr. articles to profl. jours. Bd. dirs. Pinchot Inst. for Conservation. Mem. AAAS, Soc. Am. Foresters (coun. 1988, chair house of soc. dels. 1982), Inland Empire Soc. of Soc. Am. Foresters (chair 1980-81, Forester of Yr. award 1982), Soc. for Range Mgmt., Forest Products Soc., Omicron Delta Epsilon, Beta Gamma Sigma, Xi Sigma Pi. Democrat. Episcopalian. Home: 824 Lazy Ln Lafayette IN 47904-2722 Office: Purdue U Dept Foresty & Natural Resources West Lafayette IN 47907

LEMBERG, STEVEN FLOYD, electrical engineer; b. Mpls., Feb. 4, 1953; s. Floyd Charles and Velma Laura (Kiekow) L.; m. Kathryn Louise Foreman, Aug. 6, 1977; children: Tracie, Kelsey, Shannon, Amanda. Student, North Hennepin Community Coll., Brooklyn Park, Minn., 1971-73; BEE with distinction, U. Minn., 1975. Mgmt. trainee Soo Line R.R., Mpls., 1977-78, engr. signals, 1978-93, mgr. signals, 1993-94, mgr. regulatory affairs, 1994-96; engr. signals & comms. projects south, 1996—. Mem. Assn. Am. R.R.'s (comm. and signal div.), Eta Kppa Nu. Republican. Lutheran. Office: Soo Line RR 105 S 5th St Minneapolis MN 55402-1201

LEMERT, HAROLD WARNER, JR., minister; b. Columbus, Miss., Dec. 4, 1932; s. Harold Warner Sr. and Bess Lee (Nichols) LeM.; m. Carol Ann Ballard, Aug. 27, 1961; children: Elizabeth, Paul William, Jennifer Bess, Amy Ann. BA, U. Mo., 1958; MDiv, Louisville Presbyn. Sem., 1961; D in Ministry, Eden Theol. Sem., 1980. Pastor 1st Presbyn. Ch., Sullivan, Ind., 1961-63, Washington (Mo.) Presbyn. Ch., 1963-66; organizing pastor Christ the King Presbyn. Ch., Jefferson City, Mo., 1966-70, Covenant Presbyn. Ch., Tulsa, 1971-75; assoc. pastor 2d Presbyn. Ch., Bloomington, Ill., 1975-80; pastor, head of staff 1st Presbyn. Ch., Woodstock, Ill., 1980-87, Southminster Presbyn. Ch., Prairie Village, Kans., 1988—; bd. dirs., organizer Project Get Together, Tulsa, 1972; sec. bd. Entrepreneur Assistance Corp., Kansas City, Mo., 1989—. Democrat. Office: Southminster Presbyn Ch 6306 Roe Ave Prairie Village KS 66208

LEMKE, ALAN JAMES, environmental specialist; b. Appleton, Wis., May 22, 1945; s. Edwin R. and Ethel Mae (Noe) L.; m. Joyce Eileen Kruse, May 24, 1975; 1 child, David Edwin. BS in chemistry, Coll. Idaho, 1968. Rsch. chemist Am. Med. Ctr., Denver, 1972-74; chemist U.S. Geol. Survey, Denver, 1975-77; chemist II Occupl. Health Lab., Portland, Oreg., 1977-80, State Hygienic Labs., Des Moines, 1980-82; indsl. hygienist Iowa Divsn. Labor, Des Moines, 1982-88; environ. specialist Iowa Dept. Natural Resources, Spencer, 1988—. Author: The Noe Family's Involvement in the Civil War: A History of Wisconsin's 19th Volunteer Infantry Regiment, 1994. Mem. Am. Indsl. Hygiene Assn. Republican. Evangelical. Home: 1110 15th Ave W Spencer IA 51301 Office: Iowa Dept Natural Resources 1900 N Grand Ave Spencer IA 51301

LEMPKE, MICHAEL WAYNE, water department executive; b. Quincy, Mass., June 13, 1940; s. Henry William and Marjorie E. (Crowell) L.; m. Le Jean Keenan, Mar. 23, 1941; children: Michael D., Shannon R., Shawn L. AA, Citrus Coll.; C in civil engr., Ariz. State U. Mgr. Bullhead City (Ariz.) City Water Dept. United Utilities, 1968-71; v.p., gen. mgr. United Utilities, Payson, Ariz., 1971-73; field serviceman II City Scottsdale (Ariz) Water Dept., 1973-75, pump serviceman, 1975-78, water foreman, 1978-80, water dept. mgr., 1980-83; superintendent water dept. City of West Allis, West Allis, Wis., 1983—. Mem. Am. Water Works Assn. (com. mem.), Am. Pub. Works Assn. (com. mem.), Back Flow Prevention Assn., First Mcpl. Credit Union (bd. dirs.). Office: West Allis Water Dept 6302 W McGeogh Ave West Allis WI 53219

LEMR, JAMES CHARLES, geriatrics nurse; b. Painesville, Ohio, May 24, 1951; s. James Robert and Helene Gloria (Maycroft) L.; m. Sandra Jean Lemr, May 10, 1974; children: Melissa Ann, James Robert. Diploma, Willoughby-Eastlake Sch. Practical Nursing, 1984. Cert. pharmacology, basic life support A.H.A., IV therapy. Charge nurse C.L.P.N. Maple Nursing Home, Chesterland, Ohio, 1991-94, Chardon (Ohio) Quality Care, 1994—. Mem. Lic. Practical Nurse Assn. Ohio. Home: 90 Woodworth Ave Painesville OH 44077-3842

LEMR, SANDRA J., geriatrics nurse, administrator; b. Painesville, Ohio, Aug. 31, 1951; d. Charles J. and Dorothy J. (Vasinosky) Nagy; m. James C. Lemr, May 10, 1974; children: Melissa Ann, James Robert. AAS, Lakeland Community Coll., Mentor, Ohio, 1971; student, Lake Erie Coll., Painesville, Ohio. Nursing supr. Lake Hosp. Systems, Painesville, 1971-86, Heartland of Mentor, 1986-91; asst. dir. nursing Madison (Ohio) Health Care, 1991—. Home: 90 Woodworth Ave Painesville OH 44077-3842

LENARDIC, KENNETH RALPH, systems architect, consultant; b. Cleve., May 18, 1945; s. Ralph and Dolores (Klish) L.; m. Karen Lynn Pierce, Sept. 21, 1968; children: Janis, Kerri. Student, Internat. Data Processing Inst, Cleve., 1966, Kent State U., Euclid, Ohio, 1969. Ops. supr. Towmotor Corp., Cleve., 1969-70; sr. systems analyst Caterpillar Indsl. Inc., Mentor, Ohio, 1978-83, mktg. systems engr., 1983-92; instr. Lakeland C.C., Mentor, 1988-89; systems architect Mitsubishi-Caterpillar Forklift, Mentor, 1992-94; computer cons., Concord, Ohio, 1988-92; pres. Micro Systems Architects, Mentor, 1994—; guest speaker in field. Contbr. articles to profl. jours. Republican. Roman Catholic. Home & Office: Micro Systems Architects 10265 Cherry Hill Dr Concord OH 44077-1515

LENDL, BILL, mechanical engineer; b. Ithaca, N.Y., Feb. 11, 1962; m. René Lendl. BSME, Pa. State U., 1984. Process engr. Procter & Gamble, Mehoopany, Pa., 1984-86, maintenance area mgr., 1986-88; oper. team mgr. Van Leer, Sacramento, 1988-89; internal cons. Van Leer, Belfast, No. Ireland, 1989, Amsterdam, 1990, Waterville, Maine, 1991; ops. mgr. Avery Dennison, Waco, Tex., 1991-94; plant mgr. Avery Dennison-Fasson, Ft. Wayne, Ind., 1994—. Loaned exec. mgr. United Way, Waco, 1992-94. Mem. ASME, KC (grand knight 1994, warden 1993), Mensa. Office: Fasson Roll Div 3011 Independence Dr Fort Wayne IN 46808-1390

LENDT, HAROLD HANFORD, manufacturing representative; b. Boone, Iowa, Jan. 2, 1922; s. Howard Wesley and Hulda Victoria (Tweedt) L.; m. Verna A. Jessen, Nov. 10, 1946 (div. June 1962); children: Cindy Tuttle, Carol Woodbury, Larry. Student, Augustana Coll., 1946-47; BBA, U. S.D., 1948. Salesman Louden Machinery Co., Fairfield, Iowa, 1953-60, Omaha Mut., St. Paul, 1960-62; maintenance supr. Dayton Hudson Corp., Mpls., 1962-79, Towle Real Estate, Mpls., 1979-82; owner, mgr. Harold Lendt Co., St. Paul, 1975—. Trustee Presdl. Task Force, Washington, 1981, life mem.; mem. Rep. Com., Washington, 1974-81; apptd. to Presd. Adv. Commn., 1991; mem. Rep. Senatorial Commn. Served to sgt. U.S. Army, 1942-44, ETO. Recipient Merit award Rep. Task Force, Washington, Senatorial Commn. award, 1996. Home: PO Box 40231 Saint Paul MN 55104-8231

LENEHAN, MICHAEL DANIEL, editor, writer; b. Passaic, N.J., Feb. 3, 1949; s. Daniel Joseph and Eva Ruth (Cavallini) L.; m. Mary Margaret Williams, Oct. 29, 1983; children: John Francis (Jack), Rose Elizabeth. BA in Comm. Arts, U. Notre Dame, 1971. Editorial intern Cue Mag., NYC, 1971; style editor, scriptwriter Ency. Britannica, Chgo., 1971-73; assoc. editor Chgo. Reader, 1975-81, sr. editor, 1982-87, mng. editor, 1987-90, editor, 1990-95, exec. editor, 1995—; contbg. editor Atlantic Monthly, 1984-93. Contbr. articles to mags. and newspapers. Recipient Westinghouse Sci. Writing award AAAS, 1978. Office: Chgo Reader 11 E Illinois St Chicago IL 60611-3540

LENG, MARGUERITE LAMBERT, regulatory consultant, biochemist; b. Edmonton, Alta., Can., Sept. 25, 1926; came to the U.S., 1950; d. Joseph Edouard and Marie (Kiwit) Lambert; m. Douglas Ellis Leng, June 18, 1955; children: Ronald Bruce, Janet Elaine, Douglas Lambert. BSc in Honours Chemistry, U. Alta., 1947; MSc, U. Sask., 1950; PhD, Purdue U., 1956. Rsch. asst. U. Mich. Med. Rsch. Inst., Ann Arbor, 1950-53; sr. rsch. chemist bioproducts Dow Chem. Co., Midland, Mich., 1956-59, sr. registration specialist, product registration mgr., 1966-73, rsch. assoc. for internat. registration agrochems., 1973-86, mgr. internat. regulatory affairs, 1986-90; pres., cons. Leng Assocs., Midland, 1991—. Editor: Pesticide Chemist and Modern Toxicology, 1981, Agrochemical Environmental Fate Studies: State of the Art, 1995; contbr. articles to profl. jours., chpts. in books and encys. Life ins. med. rsch. fellow Equitable Life Assurance Co., 1949-50. Fellow Am. Inst. Chemists (bd. dirs., vice chmn. bd. dirs., exec. com. 1993-95), Am. Chem. Soc. (agrochems. divsn. fellow 1976, chmn. 1981, program chmn. 1980, alt. councilor 1984-91, councilor 1992—); mem. Internat. Soc. for Study Xenobiotics, Assn. Ofcl. Analytical Chemists Internat., Soc. Environ. Toxicology and Chemistry, Sigma Xi. Home and Office: 1714 Sylvan Ln Midland MI 48640-2538

LENKER, FLOYD WILLIAM, farmer; b. Muscatine, Iowa, Dec. 1, 1933; s. Clarence William and Mildred Faye (Noble) L. Grad. high sch., Wilton, Iowa, 1951. Farmer Wilton, 1951—; bd. dirs. Iowa Poland China Assn., 1985—; campaign mgr. Cedar County Farm Bur., 1989-90, pres. 1977-78; treas. Cedar County Extension Coun., 1967. Bd. dirs. Cedar County Rep. Cen. Com., 1980—; pres. Jaycees, 1967, Cedar County Fair, Tipton, Iowa, 1983; trombonist Tri-County Community Band, 1973—, Wilton Drum and Brass Corps, 1961—; sec. ch. bd. United Ch. Christ, 1993. With U.S. Army, 1955-57. Named Outstanding Young Farmer Wilton Jaycees, 1968. Mem. Cedar County Pork Producers (pres. 1967), Cedar County Soybean Assn. (pres. 1991), Wilton Area C. of C., Wilton High Sch. Alumni (pres. 1971, treas. 1975—), Lions (pres. Bennett club 1987, 91, 95). Republican. Mem. United Ch. of Christ. Home: 2053 280th St Wilton IA 52778-9217

LENMAN, TOMAS STIG, engineer; b. Sundsvall, Sweden, July 18, 1945; came to U.S., 1984; . Tor Herman and Elsa Virginia (Johansson) L.; m. Margareta Ingrid Sjolund, Dec. 28, 1968; children: Annica, Susanne. MEng, Royal Inst. Tech., Stockholm, 1971. Devel. engr. Wirsbo Bruks AB, Virsbo, Sweden, 1971-76, mgr. quality assurance, 1976-82, product mgr., 1982-84; v.p. Wirsbo Co., Apple Valley, Minn., 1984-87, pres., 1987-92; dir. Uponor how water divsn., Apple Valley, Minn., 1990-94; pres. Safelink Systems, Inc., 1994—. Author: Water and Pipes, 1984.

LENNES, JOHN BURR, JR., lawyer; b. Temple, Tex., July 10, 1945; s. John Burr and Alma Lee (Parish) L.; m. Karna Louise Lingwall, Aug. 3, 1968; children: Inga, Nels. BA, Wabash Coll., 1966; JD, Columbia U., 1971. Bar: Minn. 1972, U.S. Dist. Ct. Minn. 1981, U.S. Ct. Appeals (8th cir.) 1981, U.S. Supreme Ct. 1981. Spl. term law clk. to judge 4th Dist. Ct., Mpls., 1971-72; counsel State Senate, St. Paul, 1972-76; assoc. Hessian, McKasy, Mpls., 1976-79; gen. counsel Minn. State Chamber, St. Paul, 1979-84; pres. Spano, Lennes & Assocs., St. Paul, 1984-88; dir. legis. affairs Minn. Bus. Partnership, Mpls., 1988-91; commr. labor and industry St. Paul, 1991-95; ptnr. Hillstrom Bale, Mpls., 1995—; bd. regents Internat. Workers' Compensation Coll., 1993-95; pres. Nat. Apprenticeship Program Bd., 1994-95; bd. dirs. State Fund Mut. Ins.; mem. Gov.'s Adv. Com. on Minn. Milestones, 1991-95; mem. Minn. Competitiveness Task Force, 1994-95, Minn. Edn. and Employment Transition Task Force, 1994-95; mem. Ins. Commr.'s Adv. Com. on Workers' Compensation Ins. Rate Deregulation, 1983, many others; lectr. in field. Contbr. articles to profl. jours. Commr. Minn. Dept. Labor and Industry, 1991-95; bd. dirs. Vinland Ctr., Youth Svcs. Bur. Forest Lake; mem. child care task force Commn. on Econ. Status of Women, 1990; founder Minn. Job Stress Coun. Recipient Spl. Recognition award Vinland Ctr., Award of Merit Minn. Safety Coun., 1992, Award of Excellence Minn. Assn. Govt. Communicators, 1993. Mem. Minn. Safety Coun. (exec. com.), Minn. Bar Assn. (corp. counsel, employment law, adminstrv. law, tax law sects.), Soc. Internat. Bus. Fellows, Mensa, Minn. Boat Club. Home: 16720 Norell Ave N Marine MN 55047 Office: Hillstrom Bale Law Firm 607 Marquette Minneapolis MN 55047

LENTZ, CHARLES WESLEY, retired chemical industry executive, consultant; b. Mt. Pleasant, Mich., May 6, 1924; s. James Albert and Laura Belle (Humphrey); m. Elinor Elaine Jessup, June 21, 1947; children: Stephan, James, Joseph, Anthony, Christopher, Mary, Deanne. BS in Chemistry, Mich. State U., 1946. Rsch. chemist Pitts. Plate Glass-Chem. div., New Martinsville, W.Va., 1952-55; rsch. chemist Dow Corning Corp., Midland, Mich., 1955-68, mgr. devel., 1968-73, mgr. corp. rsch., 1973-77, dir. health and environ. scis., 1977-86; ret., 1986; chmn. sci. affair Chem. Specialities Mfg. Assoc., Washington, 1979-81; mem. toxic substances adv. com. EPA, Washington. Contbr. articles to sci. and tech. publs.; inventor in field. Active Big Bros. of Am., Midland, 1956-58; mem., pres. Bullock Creek Bd. Edn., Midland, 1970-78; bd. dirs. Chippewa Nature Ctr., Midland, pres., 1993-94. Mem. Sigma Xi (Sci. excellence award 1965). Home: 5105 Foxcroft Dr Midland MI 48642-3256

LENTZ, LINDA KAY, school psychologist, learning disability educator; b. Dayton, Ohio, Aug. 13, 1936; d. Harry E. and Mary E. (Swinger) Denlinger; m. Paul Dean Lentz, May 5, 1955; children: Lisa Kay Heaton, David Paul. BS, U. Dayton, 1981, MS, 1985; MEd, Wright State U., 1987. Cert. tchr., Ohio. Tchr., owner Springboro (Ohio) Pre-sch., 1974-83; tchr. learning disabilities Franklin (Ohio) City Schs., 1983-87; sch. psychologist Montgomery County Bd. Edn., 1987—. Mem. Springboro Bd. Edn., 1981-84; chairperson Help through Edn. Leads to Prevention, Springboro, 1982-85. Recipient Community Involvement award Springboro Jaucees, 1983, Disting. Service award Springboro Jaycees, 1984, William Holden Jennings Scholar award U. Dayton, 1986-87. Mem. Nat. Assn. Sch. Psychologists, Nat. Assn. for Children with Learning Disabilities, Ohio Assn. for Children with Learning Disabilities, Ohio Assn. for Counseling and Devel. Presbyterian. Home: 7241 Mountain Trl Dayton OH 45459-3151

LENTZ, MARK STEVEN, mechanical engineer; b. Madison, Wis., July 3, 1949; s. Arthur George and Alta Harriet (Miller) L.; m. Duyuan Kay Tremelling, May 17, 1980. BSME, U. Wis., 1978. Registered profl. engr. Wis., Minn., N.J., Alaska, Mass. Engr. Affiliated Engrs., Inc., Madison, 1976-81; project engr. Stanley Cons., Inc., Muscatine, Iowa, 1981-83; sr. mech. engr. Donahue and Assocs., Inc., Sheboygan, Wis., 1983-91; sr. project engr. PSJ Engring., Inc., Milw., 1991-95; pres. Lentz Engring. Assocs., Inc., Kohler, 1995—. With U.S. Army, 1970. Mem. ASHRAE (mem. tech. coms. 1985—, program com. 1988-91, cons. to standard 90 com., Energy award 1988, Energy award Wis. chpt. 1986-87, Energy award region 6 1987, Paper of Yr. award 1991).

LENTZ, RICHARD DAVID, psychiatrist; b. Passaic, N.J., Jan. 27, 1942; s. Harold Arthur and Ruth (Bitterman) L.; m. Joan Ellen Sacks, June 25, 1983; children: Daniel Keith, Andrew Simon. Student, John Hopkins U., 1959-61; AB cum laude, NYU, 1964; MS in Pathology, U. Rochester, 1969, MD with distinction, 1969. Diplomate Am. Bd. Psychiatry and Neurology, Am. Bd. of Pediatrics, Am. Bd. of Pediatric Nephrology. Intern U. Minn. Hosps., Mpls., 1969-70, resident in pediatrics, 1970-71, fellow in pediatric nephrology, 1972-74; resident in neurology and pediatrics Washington U., St. Louis, 1971-72; resident in psychiatry, fellow consultation-liaison U. Minn. Hosps., Mpls., 1979-81; chief pediatric nephrology Walter Reed Army Med. Ctr., Washington, 1974-76; instr. dept. of pediatrics Georgetown Med. Ctr., Washington, 1975; asst. prof. U. Md., Balt., 1978; cons. psychiatrist Park Nicollet Clinic/HSM, St. Louis Park, Minn., 1981—, vice chmn. dept. psychiatry, 1981-85, chmn. patient rels., 1983-95, risk mgmt. com., ops. com., dir. Medctr. Health Plan, 1985-90; chmn. risk mgmt. Health Sys. Minn., St. Louis Park, Minn., 1995—; from clin. asst. prof. to assoc. prof. U. Minn., Mpls., 1981-90; clin. prof. U. Minn., 1990—; chmn. psychiatry Abbott-Northwestern Hosp., Mpls., 1991-92; assoc. dir. profl. assessment program Abbott-Northwestern Hosp., 1993; cons. Courage Ctr., Mpls., Comprehensive Epilepsy Ctr., Bill Kelly House, numerous others. Contbr. articles to profl. jours. Maj. U.S. Army, 1974-76. Mem. Am. Psychiat. Assn., Minn. Med. Assn., Hennepin County Med. Soc. Office: Park Nicollet Med Ctr 2001 Blaisdell Ave Minneapolis MN 55404-2414

LENZEN, LAURA ELAINE, civil engineer; b. Lincoln, Nebr., Apr. 6, 1947; d. George Harry and Esther Ruth (Gies) DeBus; children: Timothy A., Amy L.; m. Louis W. Lenzen, Feb. 15, 1980. Registered profl. engr., Nebr.; cert. profl. mgr. From sec. to traffic engr. supr. Nebr. Dept. Rds., Lincoln, 1969-89, wetlands engr. unit head, 1989—. Recipient Environ. award Fed. Hwy. Adminstrn., 1995, Environ. Excellence award U.S. Dept. Transp., 1995. Mem. Nebr. Mgrs. Assn., Engrs. Club Lincoln (bd. dirs., sec.-treas.). Home: 2017 N 57th St Lincoln NE 68505-1107 Office: Nebr Dept Roads PO Box 94759 Lincoln NE 68509-4759

LEONARD, JACK E., environmental company executive; b. Chickasha, Okla., Feb. 6, 1943; s. C. Adolphe and Emma Lee (Godbey) L.; m. Karen Kay Ball, June 18, 1965; children: Christine, James, Annette. AB in Chemistry, Harvard U., 1965; BD in Theology, So. Meth. U., 1967; PhD in Chemistry and Biology, Calif. Inst. Tech., 1971. Asst. prof. SUNY, Purchase, N.Y., 1971-75; rsch. assoc., asst. prof. Tex. A&M U., College Station, Tex., 1975-83; faculty mem. Blinn Coll., Brenham, Tex., 1983-85; sr. environ. scientist Indpls. Ctr. for Advanced Rsch., 1985-90; pres. Environ. Mgmt. Inst., Indpls., 1990—; vis. rsch. scientist Allied Signal Corp., Morristown, N.J., 1971-75; vis. assoc. prof. U. Tex. El Paso, 1981-82. Harvard nat. scholar Harvard U., 1961-65; Kent fellow Danforth Found., Calif. Inst. Tech., 1967-71, fellow NSF, 1967-71; grantee Welch Found., 1976-79. Mem. AAAS, Am. Chem. Soc., Ind. Acad. Sci. (bd. dirs. Hoosier Safety Coun.).

Methodist. Office: Environ Mgmt Inst Inc 5610 Crawfordsville Rd Ste 15 Indianapolis IN 46224-3714

LEONARD, JOSEPH WESLEY, business educator; b. Webb City, Mo., Feb. 17, 1948. BS, Mo. So. State, 1970; MS, Pittsburgh State U., 1971; MBA, Drury Coll., 1980; PhD, U. Ark., 1983. Contract adminstr. Eagle Picher Industries, Joplin, Mo., 1973-79; instr. U. Ark., Fayetteville, 1979-83; faculty mem. Miami U., Oxford, Ohio, 1983—; cons. Strategic Leadership Forum, Chgo., 1989—. Contbr. articles to profl. jours. Bd. dirs. Cmty. Rels. Bd., Oxford, 1992—. With USNR, 1971-73. Mem. Acad. Mgmt. Democrat. Office: Miami U Dept Mgmt Oxford OH 45056

LEONARD, MICHAEL A., automotive executive; b. Cadillac, Mich., Aug. 3, 1937; s. Hugel A. and Mildred (Johnson) L.; m. Frances Erickson, June 18, 1960; children: Kristin, Anne. MA, Alma Coll., 1959; MBA, Wayne State U., 1964; MS, MIT, 1971. Exec. Chrysler Corp., Highland Park, Mich., 1959-75; group v.p. Bendix Corp., Southfield, Mich., 1975-83; v.p., group exec. Allied Signal Automotive, Bloomfield Hills, Mich., 1983-91; pres. Harman, Inc., Southfield, Mich., 1991-94; mng. ptnr. Exec. Resources Inc., Bloomfield Hills, Mich., 1994—; bd. dirs. Kalyani Brake Co., Pune, India, Bendix France, Paris, Bendix Italy, and fgn. subs. Trustee Alma (Mich.) Coll.; bd. dirs. Presbyn. Villages of Mich. Sloan fellow, MIT. Mem. Soc. Automotive Engrs., Delta Sigma Phi (pres. 1958-59). Presbyterian. Home: 4375 Barchester Dr Bloomfield Hills MI 48302-2116 Office: Executive Resources Inc PO Box 625 Bloomfield Hills MI 48303-9999

LEONARD, RANDAL LEE, stockbroker; b. Milw., Nov. 7, 1954. BS, U. Wis., Stevens Point, 1976. Stockbroker Robert W. Baird & Co. Inc., Milw., 1984—. Office: Robert W Baird & Co Inc PO Box 672 777 E Wisconsin Ave Milwaukee WI 53201

LEONARD, ROBERT DOUGHERTY, communications company executive; b. Chgo., Apr. 15, 1942; s. Robert D. and Ruth Janet (Tankersley) L.; m. Janet Catherine Link, May 10, 1969; children: James Richard, John Banks, Anne Catherine. BS in Gen. Engring., U. Ill., 1964, BS in Communications, 1965. Engr. Teletype Corp., Skokie, Ill., 1965-68, tech. pubs. engr., 1968-72, planning engr., 1972-77; engring. staff mgr. AT&T Network Svcs., Basking Ridge, N.J., 1977-80; staff mgr. AT&T Bus. Svcs., Basking Ridge, 1980-82; dep. chief AT&T Teletype Corp., Skokie, 1982-85; dist. mgr. printers AT&T Computer Systems, Skokie, 1985-87; regional mgr. gateways Mitek Systems Corp., Northfield, Ill., 1987-88; product mgr. broadcast transmission line products Andrew Corp., Orland Park, Ill., 1988—. Contbr. to profl. publs. Mem. Am. Mktg. Assn. (exec.), Numismatic Lit. Guild (life), Am. Numismatic Assn., Am. Numismatic Soc., Am. Israel Numismatic Assn., Token and Medal Soc. (treas. 1993—). Republican. Methodist. Home: 1065 Spruce St Winnetka IL 60093-2169 Office: Andrew Corp 10500 153rd St Orland Park IL 60462-3071

LEONARD, VIRGINIA W., history educator, writer, researcher; b. Willimantic, Conn., Dec. 9, 1941; d. William Norris and Elizabeth Flora (Waugh) L.; m. James Madison Ewing, May 14, 1978. BA in Internat. Rels., U. Calif., Berkeley, 1963; MA in Social Scis., Hofstra U., 1967; PhD in History, U. Fla., 1975. Cert. h.s. tchr. social studies, N.Y., cert. bilingual (Spanish) h.s. tchr. social studies, N.Y.; lic. pvt. pilot. Tchr. social studies Colegio Lincoln, La Lucila, Argentina, 1970, Seward Pk. H.S., N.Y.C., 1975-77; from asst. prof. history to assoc. prof. history Western Ill. U., Macomb, 1977-90; sr. program mgr. Nat. Faculty Exch., Dept. Edn., Washington, 1986-87; prof. history Western Ill. U., Macomb, 1990—; chair univ. pers. com. Western Ill. U., Macomb, 1990-91, chair faculty coun. arts & scis., 1993-95; mem. internat. adv. bd. 5th Internat. Interdisciplinary Congress of Women, 1992-93. Author: Politicians, Pupils, and Priests, 1989, (book chpt.) Los Ensayistas, 1989; contbr. articles to profl. jours. Civilian recreation officer U.S. Army Spl. Svcs., Nuremburg, West Germany, 1963-64; seminar leader Project Dem., LWV, Dubna, Russia, summer 1995; coord. grassroots democracy McDonough County LWV, Ill., 1995; mem. Charlevoix Hist. Soc. Recipient Fulbright Rsch. award Fulbright Com., Argentina, 1983; Orgn. Am. States fellow, 1971-72; Grassroots Democracy grantee LWVEF/AID, 1995. Mem. Am. Hist. Assn., Bus. and Profl. Women (treas. 1994-95), Midwest Assn. Latin Am. Studies (pres. 1984-85), North Cen. Coun. Latin Americanists (chair nominating com. 1990-91, Tchg. award 1990), Berkshire Conf. Women Historians (book prize com. 1990-95), Phi Kappa Phi, Delta Kappa Gamma (legis. com. 1993-94). Unitarian-Universalist. Office: Western Ill U Dept of History Macomb IL 61455

LEONELLI, JOSEPH, laser remote sensing expert and executive; b. Providence, Feb. 21, 1955; s. Joseph and Esther Margret (Grossi) L.; m. Susan Marie Phelan, July 25, 1982; children: Joseph Michael, Stephen James, Kathryn Esther. BA, St. Louis U., 1977, MS in Chemistry, 1978; PhD in Chemistry, Ind. U., 1982. Program mgr. SRI Internat., Menlo Park, Calif., 1985-86, asst. lab. dir., 1987-89, assoc. lab. dir., 1990-92; dir. mktg. Battelle Meml. Inst., Columbus, Ohio, 1992-93, dir. sensor program, 1993-94, v.p. spl. programs, 1995—. Contbr. articles to profl. jours.; patents to procs. Capt. U.S. Army, 1982-85. Mem. Internat. Soc. for Optical Engring. (conf. chair 1993-94), Soc. Photo-Optical Instrument Engrs. (symposium vice-chair sensing com. 1994-95), Air/Waste Mgmt. Assn. (tech. chair, symposium vice chair 1994-95). Home: 893 Cherryfield Ave Columbus OH 43235 Office: Battelle Meml Inst 505 King Ave Columbus OH 43201

LEONETTI, MICHAEL EDWARD, financial planner; b. Oak Park, Ill., Aug. 23, 1955; s. Michael Louis and Dolores Mary (DiOrio) L.; m. Elizabeth Anne Goff, June 16, 1979. BA, St. Marys Coll., 1977. Cert. fin. planner, fund specialist; registered investment advisor. Sales rep. Metropolitan Life, Des Plaines and Rosemont, Ill., 1977-80; fin. planner Money Masters Inc., Buffalo Grove, Ill., 1980-82, Leonetti & Assocs., Buffalo Grove, 1982—; instr. fin. planning Harper Coll., 1982-84. Author: Retire Worry Free: Financial Strategies for Tomorrow's Independence; mem. adv. bd. Practical Fin. Planning; contbr. articles to profl. jours. Named One of Best Fin. Planners in U.S., Money Mag., 1987, One of Top Balanced Style Money Managers in U.S., 1992. Mem. Nat. Assn. Personal Fin. Advisors (pres. 1986-87), United Shareholders Assn., Internat. Assn. Fin. Planning (bd. dirs.), Inst. Cert. Fin. Planners (bd. dirs. 1986—), Registry Fin. Planning Practitioners, Investment Rsch. Inst. (cert. fund specialist), St. Mary Coll. Weight Lifting Club (pres., founder 1973-77). Republican. Roman Catholic. Home: 946 Cambridge Dr Buffalo Grove IL 60089-4310 Office: Leonetti & Assocs 1130 W Lake Cook Rd Ste 105 Buffalo Grove IL 60089-1974

LEONG, G. KEONG, operations management educator; b. Georgetown, Penang, Malaysia, Mar. 10, 1950; s. Eng Loong Leong and Mee Lan Chiew; m. C. Lin Khong; 1 child, Michelle P.Y. BEngring., U. Malaya, Kuala Lumpur, 1973; MBA, U. S.C., 1984, PhD in Bus. Adminstrn., 1987. Trainee exec. Fraser and Neave Co., Kuala Lumpur, 1973-74; project engr. Behn Meyer Engring, Shah Alam, Malaysia, 1974-76, export mgr., 1977; tech. mgr. Behn Meyer Engring., Shah Alam, Malaysia, 1980-82; mgr. Hanseatic Engring. and Trading Co., Bangkok, 1978-80; rsch. asst., teaching asst. U. S.C., Columbia, 1983-87; asst. prof. ops. mgmt. Ohio State U., Columbus, 1987-93; assoc. prof. ops. mgmt. Ohio State U., 1993—; advisor Ohio State U. chpt. Am. Prodn. and Inventory Control Soc., 1989-90, 91—, acad. liaison, 1995-96. Coord. United Way Cen. Ohio, Columbus, 1988, 89, 90, 91. Fellow Inst. of Engrs. Malaysia; mem. Decision Scis. Inst. (chair innovative edn. com. 1994-95, track chair in strategic mgmt. 3d internat. mtg., Best Paper award 1990, Stan Hardy Best Paper award 1995), INFORMS, Acad. of Mgmt., Beta Gamma Sigma. Home: 246 Caren Ave Worthington OH 43085-2525 Office: Ohio State Univ 1775 S College Rd Columbus OH 43210-1309

LEOPOLD, MARK F., lawyer; b. Chgo., Jan. 23, 1950; s. Paul F. and Corinne (Shapira) L.; m. Jacqueline Rood, June 9, 1974; children: Jonathan, David. BA, Am. U., Washington, 1972; JD, Loyola U., Chgo., 1975. Bar: Ill. 1975, U.S. Dist. Ct. (no. dist.) Ill. 1975, Fla. 1976, U.S. Ct. Appeals (7th cir.) 1976, U.S. Ct. Appeals (8th cir.) 1979. Assoc. McConnell & Campbell, Chgo., 1975-79; atty. U.S. Gypsum Co., Chgo., 1979-82, sr. litigation atty., 1982-84; sr. litigation atty. USG Corp., 1985-87, corp. counsel, 1987, sr. corp. counsel, 1987-89; asst. gen. counsel G.D. Searle & Co., 1989-93; sr. gen. counsel Household Internat., Inc., Prospect Heights, Ill., 1993—; adv. bd. Roosevelt U. Legal Asst. Program, 1994—; legal writing instr. Loyola U. Sch. Law, Chgo., 1978-79; pres., bd. dirs. Internat. Policyholders Assn., 1992-93; del. candidate Rep. Nat. Conv., 1996. Mem. Lake County Study Commn. II, Waukegan, Ill, 1989-90; commr. Lake County, Waukegan, Ill., 1982-84, Forest Preserve, Libertyville, Ill., 1982-84, Pub. Bldg. Commn., Waukegan, Ill., 1980-82; chmn. Deerfield Twp. Rep. Cen. Com., Highland Park, Ill., 1984-86, officer, 1981-89; vice chmn. Lake County Rep. Cen. Com., Waukegan, Ill., 1982-84; bd. dirs. Am. Jewish Com., Chgo., 1988-91. Recipient Disting. Svc. award Jaycees, Highland Park, 1983. Mem. ABA (antitrust com. 1976—, litigation com. 1980—, torts and ins. practice com. 1989—), Pi Sigma Alpha, Omicron Delta Kappa. Republican. Office: Household Internat 2700 Sanders Rd Prospect Heights IL 60070-2701

LEPPARD, RAYMOND JOHN, conductor, harpsichordist; b. London, Aug. 11, 1927; came to U.S., 1976; s. Albert Victor and Bertha May (Beck) L. MA, U. Cambridge, Eng., 1955; DLitt (hon.), U. Bath, Eng., 1973; hon. doctorate, U. Indpls., 1991, Purdue U., 1992; hon. degree, Butler U., 1994, Wabash Coll., 1995. Fellow Trinity Coll., Cambridge; univ. lectr. in music U. Cambridge, 1958-68. Mus. dir. English Chamber Orch., London, 1959-77; prin. condr. BBC Philharm., Manchester, Eng., 1972-80; condr. symphony orchs. in Am. and Europe, Met. Opera, N.Y.C., Santa Fe Opera, San Francisco Opera, Covent Garden, Blyndebourne, Paris Opera; prin. guest condr. St. Louis Symphony Orch., 1984-90, music dir. Indpls. Symphony Orch., 1987—, European Tour, 1993; rec. artist, composer numerous film scores; author: (books) Authenticity in Music, 1989, Raymond Leppard on Music/An Anthology of Critical and Personal Writings, 1993. Decorated Commendatore Della Republica Italiana; comdr. Order Brit. Empire. Office: M L Falcone Pub Rels 155 W 68th St Apt 1114 New York NY 10023-5817 also: Indpls Symphony Orch 45 Monument Cir Indianapolis IN 46204-2907

LEPPIK, MARGARET WHITE, state legislator; b. Newark, N.J., June 5, 1943; d. John Underhill and Laura Schaefer White; m. Ilo Elmar Leppik, June 18, 1967; children: Peter, David, Karina. BA, Smith Coll., 1965. Rsch. asst. Wistar Inst., U. Pa., Phila., 1967-68, U. Wis., Madison, 1968-69; mem. Minn. Ho. Reps., St. Paul, 1990, 92, 94. Commr. Golden Valley (Minn.) Planning Com., 1982-90; mem. Golden Valley Bd. Zoning Appeals, 1985-87. Recipient Citizen of Distinction award Hennepin County Human Svcs. Planning Bd. 1992; named Legislator of Yr., U. Minn. Alumni Assn., 1995. Mem. LWV (v.p., dir. 1984-90), Minn. Opera Assn. (pres. 1986-88), Rotary Internat., Optimists Internat. Republican. Home: 7500 Western Ave Golden Valley MN 55427-4849 Office: 393 State Office Bldg Saint Paul MN 55155

LEQUESNE, BRUNO PATRICE BERNARD, research engineer; b. Neuilly-sur-Seine, France, Nov. 2, 1956; came to U.S., 1981; Cert. engring., Ecole Supèrieure d'Elect, Gif-sur-Yvette, 1978; PhD, U. Mo., Rolla, 1984. Rsch. engr. Ecole Supèrieure Electricitè, Gif-sur-Yvette, 1979-81; grad. teaching asst. U. Mo., Rolla, 1982-84; staff rsch. engr. GM R&D Ctr., Warren, Mich., 1984—. Contbr. papers to profl. jours.; patentee in field. Mem. IEEE (sr. mem., Best Paper award 1987, 88, 91, 92). Office: GM R & D Ctr MC 480-106-104 30500 Mound Rd Warren MI 48090

LERMOND, CHARLES AFTON, artist, educator; b. Brunswick, Maine, Aug. 1, 1927; s. Earle and Mabel Elizabeth (Rogers) L.; m. Martha Evelyn (Leeman, Sept. 19, 1948; children: Kent, Nancy. BA, Bowdoin Coll., 1949; MS in Analytical Chemistry, MIT, 1953. Owner, artist The Loom Shed, Oberlin, Ohio, 1981—; lectr., workshop leader, instr. in block-switching, drafting, rug weaving, special overshot techniques, exploration of Theo Moorman techniques; coord. Computers in Weaving; sponsor Ann. Loom Shed Juried Weaving Show. Exhibited in group shows at Mannings Handweaving, 1978-85, Ohio State Fair, 1985, Convergence 1986, 92, 93, Toronto, Can., 1986, Gund Gallery, Columbus, Ohio, 1989; two-man show at Loomworks, Columbus, 1988; contbr. articles to profl. jours. Past pres., founder Firelands Weavers Guild, Oberlin. Recipient Ind. Artist's fellowship in traditional crafts Ohio Arts Coun., 1988. Mem. Firelands Assn. for Visual Arts (founding trustee, sec.). Office: Loom Shed 14301 State Rt 58 Oberlin OH 44074-9471

LERNER, STEPHEN ALEXANDER, microbiologist, physician, educator; b. Chgo., Oct. 4, 1938; s. David G. and Florence (Trace) L.; m. June 6, 1963 (div. 1990); children: Deborah, Daniel, Susan; m. Aug. 18, 1991. AB magna cum laude, Harvard U., 1959, MD magna cum laude, 1963. Intern, then resident Peter Bent Brigham Hosp., 1963-65; rsch. assoc. NIH, 1965-68; postdoctoral fellow Stanford (Calif.) U., 1968-71; asst. prof. then assoc. prof. U. Chgo., 1971-86; prof. of medicine Wayne State U., Detroit, 1986—; convenor Soviet-Am. Symposium Antibiotics and Chemotherapy, Moscow, 1988. Editor: Aminoglycoside Ototoxicity, 1981; mem. editl. bd. Antimicrobial Agts. and Chemotherapy, 1981—, European Jour. Clin. Microbiology and Infectious Diseases, 1992—; contbr. articles to profl. jours. With USPHS, 1965-67. Recipient Borden Rsch. award, 1963. Fellow Infectious Disease Soc. Am., Am. Acad. Microbiology (mem. com. on awards); mem. Am. Soc. Microbiology (chmn. antimicrobial chemotherapy 1987-88, divsn. group rep. 1990-92, councillor 1990-92, chmn. confs. com. 1993—, internat. coord. com. 1993—), Inter-Am. Soc. for Chemotherapy (pres. 1986-88, bd. dirs. 1988—, chmn. 1988-93), Internat. Soc. Chemotherapy (exec. com. 1987-93), Phi Beta Kappa, Sigma Xi, Alpha Omega Alpha. Democrat. Jewish. Office: Harper Hosp Div Infectious Diseases 3990 John Rst Detroit MI 48201-2018

LEROY, JOSEPH F., investment broker; b. Balt., July 17, 1949. BA, U. Wis., 1972. Investment broker Kidder Peabody, Milw., 1986-89; v.p., investment broker A. G. Edwards & Sons Inc., Milw., 1989—. Republican. Office: A G Edwards & Sons Inc Ste #540 700 N Water St Milwaukee WI 53202-4206

LESAGE, JANET BILLINGS, special education educator; b. Oak Park, Ill., Apr. 3, 1947; d. John Joseph and Lorna Betsy (Scott) Billings; m. Richard Alan LeSage, Dec. 6, 1969; children: Laureen, Justin. BS in Edn., No. Ill. U., 1968; MEd, So. Ill. U., 1972, U. Mo., St. Louis, 1994. Tchr. Sch. Dist. 57, Mt. Prospect, Ill., 1968-70; sect. head Morris Libr., So. Ill. U., Carbondale, 1971-72; dir. St. Martin's Sch. for Spl. Children, Ellisville, Mo., 1981-87; tchr. Spl. Sch. Dist. St. Louis County, Town & Country, Mo., 1987—. Active Midwestern Braille Vols., 1974-80. Mem. Mo. Coun. for Exceptional Children (v.p. 1989-90, pres.-elect 1990-91, pres. 1991-92, Tchr. of Yr. 1993), Mo. Divsn. for Early Childhood (founding pres. 1987-90), Pi Lambda Theta.

LESAR, HIRAM HENRY, lawyer, educator; b. Thebes, Ill., May 8, 1912; s. Jacob L. and Missouri Mabel (Keith) L.; m. Rosalee Berry, July 11, 1937 (dec. Oct. 1985); children: James Hiram, Albert Keith, Byron Lee; m. Barbara Thomas, Feb. 12, 1987. AB, U. Ill., 1934, JD, 1936; JSD, Yale U., 1938. Bar: Ill. 1936, Mo. 1954, U.S. Supreme Ct. 1960. Asst. prof. law U. Kans., 1937-40, assoc. prof., 1940-42; sr., prin. atty. bd. legal examiners U.S. CSC, 1942-44; assoc. prof. law U. Mo., 1946-48, prof., 1948-57; prof. law Washington U., St. Louis, 1957-72, dean Sch. Law, 1960-72; founding dean, prof. law So. Ill. U., Carbondale, 1972-80, interim pres. univ., 1974, acting pres., 1979-80, disting. service prof., 1980-82, prof. emeritus, 1982—, vis. disting. svc. prof., 1983—; disting. vis. prof. McGeorge Sch. Law, 1982-83; vis. prof. law U. Ill., summer 1947, Ind. U., summer 1952, U. So. Calif., summer 1959, U. N.C., summer 1961, NYU, summer 1965. Author: Landlord and Tenant, 1957; Contbr. to: Am. Law of Property, 1952, supplement, 1977, also, Dictionary Am. History, Ency. Brit. Bd. dirs. Legal Aid Soc., St. Louis and St. Louis County, 1960-72, pres. 1966-67; mem. Human Rels. Commn., University City, Mo., 1966-71, chmn., 1966, 67; bd. dirs. Land of Lincoln Legal Assistance Found., 1972-82, pres., 1982, vice chmn., 1988—; mem. Fed. Mediation and Conciliation Svc., other arbitration panels; bd. dirs. Bacone Coll., 1981-87; trustee Lincoln Acad. Ill., 1987—. Lt. comdr. USNR, 1944-46. Recipient Pres.' award Mo. Bar, 1968; named Laureate Lincoln Acad. of Ill., 1985. Fellow Am. Bar Found., Ill. Bar Found.; mem. ABA, AAUP, FBA, Am. Arbitration Assn., Am. Law Inst., Ill. Bar Assn., Mo. Bar Assn., St. Louis Bar Assn., Am. Judicature Soc., Univ. Club St. Louis, Yale Club Chgo., Rotary Internat., Jackson Country Club, Masons, K.T., Shriners, Order of Coif, Phi Beta Kappa, Phi Kappa Phi, Phi Delta Phi (hon.). Baptist. Home: 11 Hillcrest Dr Carbondale IL 62901-2444

LESEWSKI, ARLENE, state legislator, insurance agent; b. Apr. 12, 1936; m. Thomas Lesewski; three children. Student, Southwest State U., Minn. Ins. agent; Dist. 21 senator Minn. State Senate, St. Paul, 1993—. Home: PO Box 341-b Marshall MN 56258-0690 Office: Minn State Senate State Capital Building Saint Paul MN 55155-1606*

LESIAK, LUCILLE ANN, graphic designer; b. Chgo., Dec. 31, 1946; d. Walter Joseph and Anna (Cachur) L. BS, Ill. Inst. Tech., 1968. Designer Scott, Foresman & Co., Glenview, Ill., 1968-79, McDougal, Littell & Co., Evanston, Ill., 1979-80; prin. Image Concepts Ltd., Chgo., 1980-82; pres. Lucy Lesiak Design Ltd., Chgo., 1982-91; prin. Lesiak/Crampton Design, Inc., Chgo., 1991—. Mem. Am. Inst. Graphic Arts, Nat. Assn. Women Bus. Owners, Chgo. Book Clinic (cert. of award 1974, 78, 79, 85-90, 94, 95, Desi award 1987, 89). Roman Catholic. Home: 575 W Madison St Chicago IL 60661 Office: 1030 Busse Hwy Park Ridge IL 60068

LESJAK, LISA MARY, secondary school administrator; b. Milw., June 18, 1963; d. Richard Joseph and Mary Barbara (Lezala) L. BA in Journalism/Polit. Sci., U. So. Calif., 1985. Asst. Peter S. Greenberg, L.A., 1984-85; mktg. asst. Mt. Carmel healthcare Ctr., Milw., 1986; dir. devel. St. Mary's Acad., Milw., 1986-90; admissions counselor Marquette U., Milw., 1990-92; devel. dir. Dominican High Sch., Whitefish Bay, Wis., 1992—. Coord. Oak Creek (Wis.) Jr. Miss Program, 1986—, bd. mem. Franklin, Wis., 1989—. Newcomers scholar, 1987. Mem. Coun. for Advancement and Support Edn., Cath. Secondary Sch. Devel. Assn. (pres. 1989-90, 93-96), Women in Comm., Oak Creek Jaycees (Spl. Lady award 1988). Republican. Roman Catholic. Home: 440 E Parkway Estate Dr Oak Creek WI 53154-4525

LESKOW, OLIVE, retired mathematics educator; b. Gary, Ind., June 25, 1919; d. Julian and Antonina (Huminsky) L. AB, Ball State U., 1941; MA, U. Minn., 1947. Tchr. Tolleston Sch., Gary, Ind., 1942-61, Lew Wallace High Sch., Gary, Ind., 1961-84; evaluation team mem. North Cen. Edn. Assn., 1979-83. Author Webster Transparencie Series in Geometry, 1968, pub. play, 1943. Recipient Retiring Outstanding Tchr. award, Ind. State Tchrs. Coun., 1985, Inland Steel Outstanding Tchr. award, 1984. Mem. NEA, AAUW, Nat. Coun. Tchrs. Math. (rep. 1969-91), Ctrl. Assn. Math. and Sci. Tchrs., Gary Classroom Assn., Math. Assn. Am., Sigma Zeta, Delta Kappa Gamma, (Beta Sigma chpt. chmn. fin. com. 1988—, treas. 1988—). Mem. Ea. Orthodox Ch. Home: 1254 Brandywine Rd Crown Point IN 46307-9304

LESLIE, CYNTHIA, mental health nurse; d. John J. and Florence (Traynor) L.; children: Elizabeth, Jennifer. ADN, Triton Coll., River Grove, Ill., 1983; BS, Coll. St. Francis, Joliet, Ill., 1988; MSN, U. Ill., Chgo., 1991. Cert. psychiat./mental health nurse. Program nurse adminstr. HCA River Edge Hosp., Forest Park, Ill.; clin. nurse Elmhurst (Ill.) Meml. Hosp.; clin. nurse specialist adult psychiatry Good Samaritan Hosp., Downers Grove, Ill., clin. nurse mgr. adult psychiat. and chem. dependence svcs. Mem. Am. Psychiat. Nurses Assn., Am. Heart Assn.

LESLY, PHILIP, public relations counsel; b. Chgo., May 29, 1918; m. Ruth Edwards, Oct. 17, 1940 (div. 1971); 1 son, Craig.; m. Virginia Barnes, May 11, 1984. BS magna cum laude, Northwestern U., 1940. Asst. to news editor Chgo. Herald & Examiner, 1935-37; copywriter advt. dept. Sears, Roebuck & Co., Chgo., 1940-41; asst. dir. publicity Northwestern U., 1941-42; account exec. Theodore R. Sills & Co. (pub. rels.), Chgo., 1942; v.p. Theodore R. Sills & Co. (pub. rels.), 1943, exec. v.p., 1945; dir. pub. rels. Ziff-Davis Pub. Co., 1945-46; exec. v.p. Harry Coleman & Co. (pub. rels.), 1947-49; pres. Philip Lesly Co. (pub. rels.), Chgo., 1949—; lectr. pub. rels., pub. opinion to bus. and sch. groups. Co-author: Public Relations: Principles and Procedures, 1945, Everything and the Kitchen Sink, 1955; author: The People Factor, 1974, Selections from Managing the Human Climate, 1979, How We Discommunicate, 1979, Overcoming Opposition, 1984, Bonanzas and Fool's Gold, 1987; bimonthly Managing the Human Climate; editor: Public Relations in Action, 1974, Public Relations Handbook, 3d rev. edit., 1967, Lesly's Public Relations Handbook, 1971, rev. edit., 1978, 83, Lesly's Handbook of Public Relations and Communications, 1991, 96; contbr. articles to bus. publs. Recipient Gold Anvil award Pub. Relations Soc. Am., 1979; voted leading active practitioner Pub. Relations Reporter Survey, 1978. Mem. Pub. Rels. Soc. Am., Phi Beta Kappa. Home and Office: 155 N Harbor Dr Apt 5311 Chicago IL 60601-7326

LESSACK, EDINA, communications company executive; b. Phila., May 10, 1938; d. Irving and Rose (Tiger) Salus; m. Alan Leroy Lessack, Dec. 21, 1958; children: Susan, Lee, Ira. BS in Edn., Temple U., 1960. Sales mgr. George Washington Lodge, King of Prussia, Pa., 1979-80; account exec. Bell of Pa., Phila., 1980-83; account exec. AT&T Communications, Phila., 1983-84, project cons., 1985—; founder, CEO Meetings & Events USA; profl. chorister Opera Co. of Phila., 1965-82; mem. spakers bur. AT&T External Affairs, 1985—. Recipient Cert. of Honor, Temple U., 1975, award for best actress Eastern Pa. Theater Council, 1974. Mem. Temple U. Music Alumni (pres. 1973-76), Meeting Planners Internat., Execs. Club Chgo., Chgo. Soc. Assn. Execs. Avocations: acting; directing; reading. Home: 3200 N Lake Shore Dr 2505 Chicago IL 60657

LESSARD, ROBERT BERNARD, state legislator, recreational facility executive; b. International Falls, Minn., May 18, 1931; s. William O. and Beatrice (Miller) L.; m. Toni Ballon; children: Wendy Jo, Kelly Jo, Brett, Shawn. Owner Spawn Inlet Lodge, Rainy Lake, Minn., 1954-64; mgr. Great Bear Lodge, Can., 1964-67; owner Viking Cruiser, Inc., Rainy Lake, 1970—; Dist. 3 senator Minn. State Senate, St. Paul, 1976—; chmn. environ. and natural resources com., mem. fin., local and urban govt., rules and adminstrn., and vet. and mil. affairs coms., Minn. State Senate. Office: State Senate 111 State Capitol Building Saint Paul MN 55155-1002*

LESSICK, MIRA LEE, nursing educator; b. Hazleton, Pa., Jan. 25, 1949; d. Jack H. and Shirley E. (Frumkin) L. Diploma in nursing, Albany (N.Y.) Med. Ctr., 1969; BSN, Boston U., 1972; MS, U. Colo., 1973; PhD, U. Tex., 1986. Staff nurse Boston City Hosp. and Mass. Gen. Hosp., 1969-72; instr. to asst. prof. nursing, genetics clinician U. Rochester, N.Y., 1973-79; asst. prof. nursing, practitioner Rush U., Chgo., 1986-91, assoc. prof. nursing, 1992—. Contbr. articles to profl. jours. Recipient Bd. of Govs. award, Excellence in Pediatric Nursing award Albany Med. Ctr., 1969, Outstanding Nurse Recognition award March of Dimes Birth Defects Found., 1991, Recognition award for Individual Contbn. to Maternal-Child Health Nat. Perinatal Assn., 1993. Mem. AAAS, ANA, APHA, Internat. Soc. Nurses in Genetics (chair rsch. com.), Assn. Women's Health, Obstetric, and Neonatal Nurses, Am. Soc. Human Genetics, Chgo. Nurses Assn. (legis. com. 1990-91), N.Y. Acad. Scis., Midwest Nursing Rsch. Soc., Sigma Theta Tau (Luther Christman award for excellence in published writing 1993), Phi Kappa Phi. Home: 4180 N Marine Dr Apt 610 Chicago IL 60613-2210 Office: Rush U Coll Nursing 301 SSH Chicago IL 60612

LESSICK-XIAO, ANNE ELSIE, foreign language educator; b. Abington, Pa., Oct. 1, 1956; d. Nestor Lewis and Helen Irene (Scrabis) Lessick; m. Jiahe Xiao, Aug. 30, 1984. BA in Spanish and Latin Am. Studies, Pitzer Coll., Claremont, Calif., 1978; MA in Linguistics, Ohio U., 1983; MA in African Studies, 1984; postgrad. in African Langs. and Lit., U. Wis., 1991-95. ESL instr. Lang. Ctr. of Pacific, Mission Viejo, Calif., 1980-81; Fulbright EFL instr. Lycee Gabriel Faure, Paris, 1983-84; ESL lectr. and acting dir. Intensive English Lang. Ctr. UNR, Reno, 1984-87; instr. Swahili West H.S., Madison, Wis., 1989; project asst. in African art, dept. Afro-Am. studies U. Wis., Madison, 1991, teaching asst. African studies, dept. history, 1991; instr. Swahili U. Wis., Madison, Wis., 1992; inst. Swahili U. Wis.-Madison, 1993-94; ESL instr. Wis. English as a Second Lang. Inst., Madison, 1992—; peace corps vol. Inst. de Nyankunde, Zaire, 1978-80; peer collaborator Madison (Wis.) Metro. Sch. Dist., 1990-94; lang. coord. Wil-Mar Cmty. Ctr., Madison, Wis., 1992; outreach coord. East Asian Studies U. Wis., Madison, 1992-93. Sec. Audubon Soc., Athens, Ohio, 1981-82, Claremont, Calif., 1977-78. Grantee U.S. Dept. Edn., Malindi, Kenya, summer 1988, predissertation Fulbright Assn., Brazzaville, Congo, 1989-90; recipient Excellence in Teaching award Dept. African Lang. and Lit., U. Wis.-Madison, 1993-94. Fellow Nat. Fgn. Lang. Tchrs.; mem. MLA, Fulbright Alumni Assn., African Lit. Assn., African Studies Assn., Coll. English Assn., Am. Comparative Lit. Assn. Democrat. Home: 512 S Brearly St Madison WI 53703 Office: Wis ESL Inst 19 N Pinckney St Madison WI 53701

LESTER, RICHARD LEE, elementary education educator, consultant; b. Omaha, June 30, 1946; s. Joseph Clarence Lester and Ruth Alma (Ward) Bax; m. Peggy I. Amole, Jan. 23, 1971; children: Christopher, Michael, Stephen. BEd, Wright State U., 1976; MEd, Miami U., Oxford, Ohio, 1987. Cert. tchr., Ohio. Head electronics technician Litton Industries, Smyrna, Del., 1967-68; head quality control Advance Devel. Corp., Gardena, Calif., 1968-70; asst. mgr. Katz Drug Co., Springfield, Mo., 1970-71; advt. sales Greenfield (Ohio) Daily Times, 1971-72; tchr. Miami Trace Local Schs., Washington Court House, Ohio, 1976—. Author computer programs. Pres. Fayette County Dem. Club, Washington Court House, 1981; chair Fayette County Dem. Party, 1982. Served with USN, 1964-67, Okinawa. Named Outstanding Young Educator, Washington Court House Jaycees, 1979, Outstanding Life Saving Action awardee Lions Club, 1980; Martha Holden Jennings Found. grantee, 1992, 94, Nat. Ctr. for Sci. Teaching and Learning grantee, 1991-93. Mem. Nat. Sci. Tchrs. Assn., Miami Trace Tchrs. Assn. (pres. 1979-80), Elks. Home: 39 Allen Ave New Holland OH 43145 Office: Miami Trace Jr High Sch 103 Main St Bloomingburg OH 43106

LESTER, ROBIN DALE, educator, author, former headmaster; b. Holdrege, Nebr., Mar. 1, 1939; s. Earl L. and Evelyn Grace (Robinson) L.; m. Helen Sargent Doughty, Aug. 26, 1967; children: Robin Debevoise, James Robinson. Student, St. Andrews U., Scotland, 1958-61; BA, Pepperdine U., 1962, MA, 1963; MAT, U. Chgo., 1966, PhD, 1971. Resident head, dean students office U. Chgo., 1964-72, Ferdinand Schevill fellow dept. history, 1966-68; asst. prof. history Columbia Coll., Chgo., 1966-70; chmn. social scis. dept. Columbia Coll., 1970-72; chmn. history dept. Collegiate Sch., N.Y.C., 1972-75; headmaster Trinity Sch., N.Y.C., 1975-86, San Francisco U. Sch., 1986-88, Latin Sch. of Chgo., 1989-92; tchr. Francis W. Parker Sch., Chgo., 1994—; adj. prof. Columbia Coll., Chgo., 1992—. Author: Stagg's University, 1995, Wuzzy Takes Off, 1995, Roy Foy, 1996; contbr. to N.Y. Times, 1979, 80, 81, Jour. Am. History, 1980, 95, Chgo. Tribune, 1989, Jour. Sports History, 1991, History of Edn. Quar., 1995, U. Chgo. mag., 1995. Mem. Manhattan Borough Dem. Com., N.Y.C., 1977-86; commr. Commn. on Ednl. Issues, 1980-86; mem. edn. com. Chgo. Hist. Soc., 1991-95; mem. Chgo.-Prague Sister Cities Com., 1991; trustee, treas. St. Andrews U. Am. Found., 1985—; precinct capt. Dem. Party, Chgo., 1964. Lauder fellow Aspen Inst., 1985. Mem. Am. Hist. Assn., Am. Studies Assn., N.Am. Soc. Sport Historians (Book Yr. award 1995), Orgn. Am. Historians, Headmaster's Assn., Country Day Sch. Headmaster's Assn., University Club (N.Y.C.), Quadrangle Club. Episcopalian. Home: 2230 N Lincoln Park W Chicago IL 60614-3814 Office: Francis W Parker Sch 330 W Webster Ave Chicago IL 60614-3811

LETARTE, CLYDE, state legislator. BA, Muskegon C.C., Hope Coll.; MA, Mich. State U. Pres. Jackson C.C.; state rep. Mich.; mem. appropriations com. Office: PO Box 30014 Lansing MI 48909-7514*

LETELLIER, ROY, state legislator. Mem S.D. Ho. of Reps.; mem. commerce and taxation coms. Home: 1257 Elkhorn St Belle Fourche SD 57717-1501*

LETSINGER, ROBERT LEWIS, chemistry educator; b. Bloomfield, Ind., July 31, 1921; s. Reed A. and Etna (Phillips) L.; m. Dorothy C. Thompson, Feb. 6, 1943; children: Louise, Reed, Sue. Student, Ind. U., 1939-41; B.S., Mass. Inst. Tech., 1943, Ph.D., 1945; DSc (hon.), Acadia U., Can., 1993. Research assoc. MIT, 1945-46; research chemist Tenn. Eastman Corp., 1946; faculty Northwestern U., 1946—, prof. chemistry, 1959—, chmn. dept., 1972-75, joint prof. biochemistry and molecular biology, 1974—, Clare Hamilton Hall prof. chemistry, 1986-92, Clare Hamilton Hall prof. emeritus chemistry, 1992—; Mem. med. and organic chemistry fellowship panel NIH, 1966-69, medicinal chem. A study sect., 1971-75; bd. on chem. scis. and tech. Nat. Research Council, 1987-90. Mem. bd. editors Nucleic Acids Research, 1974-80; contbr. articles to profl. jours. Guggenheim fellow, 1956; JSPS fellow Japan, 1978; recipient Rosenstiel Medallion, 1985, Humboldt Sr. US Scientist award, 1988, NIH merit award, 1988, Arthur C. Cope scholar award, 1993. Fellow Am. Acad. Arts and Scis., Nat. Acad. Scis., Am. Assn. Arts and Scis.; mem. Am. Chem. Soc. (bd. editors 1969-72, bioconjugate chemistry 1992—, Arthur C. Cope scholar award 1993), Internat. Union Pure and Applied Chemistry, Sigma Xi, Phi Lambda Upsilon (hon. mem.). Home: 316 3rd St Wilmette IL 60091-3461 Office: Northwestern U Chemistry Dept 2145 Sheridan Rd Evanston IL 60208-0834

LEU, JAMES G., project engineer; b. Fondulac, Wis., June 11, 1959. AA in Engring. Tech., Moraine Park Tech. Coll., Fondulac, Wis., 1979. Project engr. Tecumseh Products Co., New Holstein, Wis., 1983—. Roman Catholic. Home: W 265 Foundry Rd Kiel WI 53042 Office: Tecumseh Products Co 1604 Michigan Ave New Holstein WI 53061-1153

LEU, ROBERT W., retired insurance company executive, consultant; b. Peoria, Ill., Aug. 10, 1918; s. Arthur W. and Lillian (Rabe) L.; m. Vivian Kelley, Nov. 15, 1942 (dec. 1973); children: Christine, Connie, Caren; m. Jean Winkelmeyer, July 15, 1974. BSBA, Bradley Univ., 1940. CLU. Pres. Bob Leu Ins. Svc., Peoria, 1940-65; treas., dir. Pioneer Indsl. Park, Peoria, 1956-84; pres. Ins. & Pension Plans, Inc., Peoria, 1966-87; ret., 1987. Author: Good Evening, Bradley Basketball Fans, 1976; mem. editl. bd. CLU Jour.; contbr. articles to Life Ins. Assn. News. Bd. dirs. Highview Nursing Home, Peoria, 1970-79, United Way, Salvation Army, Peoria YMCA, Common Pl. Mission; trustee Peoria Park Dist., Centurion Soc. Bradley U., 1987; mem. Million Dollar Round Table, 1954—. Lt. USN, 1942-45. Recipient Disting. Alumnus award Bradley U., 1977; named to Ill. Basketball Hall of Fame, Ill. Coaches Assn., 1988. Mem. Mt. Hawley Country Club, Island Country Club. Home (summer): 444 W Woodridge Ln Peoria IL 61614 Home (winter): # 703 176 S Collier Blvd Marco Island FL 33937

LEUCK, CLAIRE M., state legislator; m. Richard Leuck. Student, Ind. Vo-Tech. Coll., Ind. State U. Clk. Benton County Cir. Ct., Ind., 1974-82; bailiff, sec. Benton County Cir. Ct., 1984-86; state rep. Dist. 25 Ind. Ho. of Reps., 1986—, chmn. agr. com., mem. natural resources, rds. and transp. com., mem. county and twp. elec., agr. and rural devel. com., ranking minority mem.; farmer. Bd. dirs. Coun. for Acad. Excellence-Dollars for Scholars; mem. St. Anne Soc.; mem. dean's adv. coun. Purdue U. Agr. Mem. Am. Legion Aux., No. Dist. Cir. Ct. Clks., Kappa Kappa Kappa. Home: RR 1 Box 203 Fowler IN 47944-9772 Office: Ind Ho of Reps State Capitol Indianapolis IN 46204*

LEUGERS, THOMAS C., investment executive; b. Cin., July 21, 1946. BA, BS, Xavier U., Cin., 1970. Stockbroker Gradison & Co., Cin., 1974-82, Cetter, Peabody, Cin., 1982-95; investment exec. Painewebber, Cin., 1995—. Sec. Am. Heart Assn., Cin., 1992; chmn. fin. Bethany House, Cin., 1993. With U.S. Army, 1966-68. Mem. Athletic Club. Home: 7381 Ayers Rd Cincinnati OH 45255-3968 Office: Painewebber 312 Walnut St # 2000 Cincinnati OH 45202-4024

LEUNG, PAUL, psychologist, rehabilitation educator; b. Jackson, Mich., Dec. 1, 1941; s. Chiu Sang and Rose (Chan) L.; m. Wendy Lee Ong, Sept. 5, 1965. BS, Calif. Bapt. Coll., Riverside, 1963; MA, Ariz. State U., 1967, PhD, 1970. Cert. rehab. counselor. Asst. prof. U. Ariz., Tucson, 1970-82; rehab. psychologist St. Mary's Hosp./Health Ctr., Tucson, 1975-82; assoc. prof./prof. U. N.C., Chapel Hill, 1982-90; prof. rehab. U. Ill., Champaign/Urbana, 1990—. Editor Jour. Rehab., 1987—; contbr. articles to profl. jours. Mem. Pres.'s Com. on Employment of People with Disabilities, Washington, 1990—. Recipient Outstanding Svc. award Nat. Coun. on Disability, 1993. Mem. APA (pres. divsn. 22 rehab. psychology 1993-94), ACA, AAAS, Am. Rehab. Assn., Nat. Acad. Neuropsychology, Internat. Neuropsychol. Soc., Nat. Coun. on Rehab. Edn. (pres. 1995—, Rehab. Educator of the Yr. 1988). Democrat. Methodist. Home: 2907 Crestridge Dr Champaign IL 61821 Office: Univ of Ill 1207 S Oak St Champaign IL 61820

LEUTH, ANN T., bank executive; b. Dallas, June 30, 1965; d. William and Elizabeth (Stempen) Luther; m. Charles W. Leuth, Dec. 11, 1993. MS, U. Conn., 1987; MBA, Ind. U., 1991. Sales rep. Noxell, N.Y.C., 1987-88; summer assoc. Clairol, N.Y.C., 1990, Kraft Gen. Goods, Chgo., 1991; engagement mgr. McKinsey & Co., Cleve., 1992-95; sr. v.p. institutional asset svcs. KeyCorp., Cleve., 1995—. Address: 300 Greenbriar Dr Avon Lake OH 44012-2158

LEVANDOWSKI, BARBARA SUE, educational administrator; b. Chgo., Mar. 16, 1948; d. Earl F. and Ann (Klee) L.. BA in Edn. and Spanish, North Park Coll., 1970; MS in Elem. Edn., No. Ill. U., 1975, degree in curriculum and supervision/instruction, 1977, EdD, 1979. Cert. elem. tchr.; cert. secondary tchr.; cert. in adminstrv. with supt. endorsement. Tchr. Round Lake (Ill.) Sch. Dist., 1970-75; tchr. Schaumburg (Ill.) Sch. Dist., 1975-87, asst. prin., 1977-87; prin., staff devel. dir. Dist. 200 Northwood Elem. Sch., Woodstock, Ill., 1987-94, dir. curriculum and instrn., 1994—; curriculum cons. Spring Grove (Ill.) Sch. Dist., 1980-81; instr. various courses, Schaumburg, 1984-86; dir. Einstein Sch. Writing Project, 1986-87; dir. Dist. 200 Thinking Skills Task Force, 1988—; co-instr. Dist. 200 Teaching Thinking Skills Across the Curriculum, 1992—, dir. curriculum and instrn.; chair north ctrl. assn. visitation team Huntley Sch. Dist., 1989; presenter various confs. Mem. editorial bd. Ill. Sch. R & D Jour., 1981—; contbr. articles to profl. jours. Mem. staff Round Lake Park Dist., 1973—; chair Computer/Tech. Strategic Action Team, Woodstock, 1988-89. Recipient numerous awards for excellence in teaching, Those Who Excel award State of Ill., 1979; fed. grantee. Mem. NAESP, NAFE, Am. Biog. Inst. Rsch. Assn. (bd. dirs. 1985—, publs. com. 1983), Nat. Staff Devel. Coun., ASCD (inservice presenter 1984-86, presenter state and nat. conv. 1989—), Nat. Coun. of States for InSvc., Ill. Staff Devel. Coun., Ill. Assn. for Supervision and Curriculum Devel. (chair research com. 1982), Ill. Computer Educators, Inst. for Ednl. Rsch. (editorial bd. advisors, co-chair effective teaching characteristics observation 1990—, Omega award), Ill. Prin. Assn., Phi Delta Kappa, Delta Kappa Gamma. Home: 426 Normandie Ln Round Lake IL 60073-3711 Office: Woodstock Sch Dist 200 501 South St Woodstock IL 60098

LEVENTHAL, AARON J., travel writer, fundraiser, publisher; b. Cleve., Oct. 26, 1941; s. Jack A. and Rosalyn (Horowitz) L.; children: Shayne, Danielle. BS in Bus., Ohio State U., 1964, MA in History, 1976; MS Recreation Adminstrn., Ind. U., 1966. Asst. dir. Student Union, Indiana U. Pa., 1965-69; dir. activities Prince Georges Community Coll., Largo, Md., 1969-70; dir. B'nai B'rith Hillel Found., Columbus, Ohio, 1970-80; originator, festival prodr. German Village Oktoberfest, Columbus, 1986—; editor, pub. Kids Connection mag., Columbus, 1983—; founder, dir. Days of Creation Arts Program, Columbus, 1980-86; originator, cons. Cruisin' on the Riverfront, Columbus. Recipient community svc. award Columbus Dispatch, 1984. Mem. Midwest Travel Writers Assn., German Village Bus. League, Internat. Festival Assn.

LEVENTIS, NICHOLAS, chemistry educator, consultant; b. Athens, Greece, Nov. 12, 1957; came to U.S., 1980; s. Spyro and Efrosine (Nenou) L.; m. Chariklia Sotiriou, Nov. 12, 1988. BS in Chemistry, U. Athens, Greece, 1980; PhD in Chemistry, Mich. State U., 1985; grad. cert. in adminstrn. and mgmt., Harvard U., 1992. Grad. asst. Mich. State Univ., East Lansing, 1980-85; rsch. assoc. MIT, Cambridge, Mass., 1985-88; project dir. Molecular Displays, Inc., Cambridge, 1988-90, v.p. of R&D, 1990-93; prof. chemistry U. Mo., Rolla, 1994—; cons. Igen, Inc., Rockville, Md., 1987-94; Hyperion Catalysis Internat., Cambridge, 1988-94, Delta F Corp., Woburn, Mass., 1992-94. Contbr. articles on electrochromic phenomena and devices to Yearbook of Ency. of Sci. & Tech., Jour. Mat. Chem., Chem. of Materials, Jour. Electrochem. Soc. Recipient Greek Inst. State Scholarships awards Greek Govt. Dept. Edn., 1976-79, Katie Y. F. Yang prize Harvard U., Cambridge, 1992; named Ethyl Corp. fellow Mich. State U., East Lansing, 1983, Yates Meml. fellow Mich. State U., East Lansing, 1984. Mem. Am. Chem. Soc. (Arthur K. Doolittle award 1993), Electrochemical Soc., Internat. Union Pure & Applied Chemistry (affiliate mem.), Soc. for Info. Display. Greek Orthodox. Home: 1604 Mccutchen Rd Rolla MO 65401-2651 Office: U Mo Dept Chemistry Rolla MO 65401

LEVETT, JAMES MICHAEL, cardiothoracic surgeon; b. Waterloo, Iowa, Mar. 24, 1949; s. Charles John and Gertrude Clara (Radischat) L.; m. Paula Kathleen Vernon, Sept. 20, 1986; children: Christine, Catherine, Suzanne, Mary. BA, Carleton Coll., 1970; MD, U. Iowa, 1974. Diplomate Am. Bd. Surgery, Am. Bd. Thoracic Surgery. Internship and residency U. Chgo. Hosp. and Clinics, 1974-81, asst. prof. cardiac surgery, 1982-85; postdoctoral fellow Med. Ctr. Duke U., Durham, N.C., 1981-82; asst. prof. surgery Robert Wood Johnson Med. Sch., New Brunswick, N.J., 1985-87, assoc. prof. surgery, 1988; dir. surg. rsch. Deborah Rsch. Inst., Browns Mills, N.J., 1985-88; staff surgeon Deborah Heart and Lung Ctr., Browns Mills, 1985-88; clin. assoc. prof. surgery U. Iowa, Iowa City, 1988-94; cardiothoracic surgeon Surg. Specialists, P.C., Cedar Rapids, Iowa, 1988-94; chmn. dept. of surgery Luth. Gen. Hosp., Park Ridge, Ill., 1994—; clin. prof. surgery U. Chgo. Hosps. and clins., 1995—; bd. dirs. St. Luke's Health Care Found., Cedar Rapids. Contbr. over 80 articles and abstracts to profl. publs. Rsch. grantee Deborah Rsch. Inst., 1987, Am. Heart Assn. N.J., 1988-89, Iowa, 1990-91, Mercy Med. Ctr., Iowa, 1989-92. Mem. ACS, Am. Coll. Cardiology, Am. Assn. Thoracic Surgery, Am. Heart Assn., Soc. Thoracic Surgeons. Home: 1850 S Windridge Dr Lake Forest IL 60045 Office: Dept of Surgery Luth Gen Hosp 1775 Dempster St Park Ridge IL 60068-1143

LEVI, EDWARD HIRSCH, former attorney general, university president emeritus; b. Chgo., June 26, 1911; s. Gerson B. and Elsa B. (Hirsch) L.; m. Kate Sulzberger, June 4, 1946; children: John, David, Michael. PhB, U. Chgo., 1932, JD, 1935; JSD, Yale U., 1938; LLD, U. Mich., 1959, U. Calif., Santa Cruz, 1968, Jewish Theol. Sem. Am., 1968, U. Iowa, 1968, Brandeis U., 1968, Lake Forest Coll., 1968, Dropsie U., 1968, Columbia U., 1968, Yeshiva U., 1968, U. Rochester, 1969, U. Toronto, Ont., Can., 1971, Yale U., 1973, U. Notre Dame, 1974, Denison U., 1974, U. Pa., 1976, U. Nebr., U. Miami, Boston Coll., Brigham Young U., Duke U., Ripon Coll., Georgetown U., Benjamin N. Cardozo Sch. Law, Claremont Ctr. and Grad. Sch., Ind. U.; LHD, Hebrew Union Coll., 1968, Loyola U., 1970, U. Chgo., Bard Coll., 1985, Beloit Coll., DePaul U., 1978; DCL, NYU. Bar: Ill., U.S. Supreme Ct. 1945. Asst. prof. U. Chgo. Law Sch., 1936-40, prof. law, 1945-75, dean, 1950-62; provost U. Chgo., 1962-68, univ. pres., 1968-75, pres. emeritus, 1975—; Karl Llewellyn Disting. Svc. prof. U. Chgo. Law Sch., 1975—, Glen A. Lloyd Disting. Svc. prof., 1977-85, Glen A. Lloyd Disting. Svc. prof. emeritus, 1985—; atty. gen. U.S., 1975-77; Thomas Guest prof. U. Colo., summer 1960; Herman Phleger vis. prof. Stanford Law Sch., 1978; lectr. Salzburg (Austria) Seminar in Am. Studies, 1980; spl. asst. to atty. gen. U.S., Washington, 1940-45; 1st asst. war div. Dept. Justice, 1943, 1st asst. antitrust div., 1944-45; chmn. interdeptl. com. on monopolies and cartels, 1944; counsel Fedn. Atomic Scientists with respect to Atomic Energy Act, 1946; counsel subcom. on monopoly power Judiciary Com., 81st Congress, 1950; trustee Aerospace Corp., 1978-80; Mem. rsch. adv. bd. Com. Econ. Devel., 1951-54; bd. Social Sci. Rsch. Coun., 1959-62, Coun. Legal Edn. and Profl. Responsibility, 1968-74; chmn. 1969-73; mem. Citizens Commn. Grad. Med. Edn., 1963-66, Commn. Founds. and Pvt. Philanthropy, 1969-70, Pres.'s Task Force Priorities in Higher Edn., 1969-70, Sloan Commn. Cable Comm., 1970, Nat. Commn. on Productivity, 1970-75, Nat. Council on Humanities, 1974-75, Nat. Coun. on Legal clinics, 1960-65; chmn. Coun. on Edn. in Profl. Responsibility, 1965-69. Author: Introduction to Legal Reasoning, 1949, Four Talks on Legal Education, 1952, Point of View, 1969; editor: (with J.W. Moore) Gilbert's Collier on Bankruptcy, 1936, Elements of the Law, (with R.S. Steffen), 1950. Hon. trustee U. Chgo.; trustee Internat. Legal Ctr., 1966-75, Woodrow Wilson Nat. Fellowship Found., 1972-75, 77-79, Inst. Psychoanalysis Chgo., 1961-75, Urban Inst., 1968-75, Mus. Sci. and Industry, 1971-75, Russell Sage Found., 1971-75, Aspen Inst. Humanistic Studies, 1970-75, 77-79, Inst. Internat. Edn. (hon.), 1969; public dir. Chgo. Bd. Trade, 1977-80; bd. overseers U. Pa., 1978-82; chmn. bd. Nat. Humanities Ctr., 1979-83, life trustee, 1978—; bd. dirs. MacArthur Found., 1979-84, William Benton Found., 1980-92, Martin Luther King Jr. Fed. Holiday Commn., 1986; bd. of govs. U. Calif. Humanities Rsch. Inst., 1988-91; mem. bd. trustees Skadden Fellowship Found., 1988—. Decorated Legion of Honor (France); recipient Learned Hand medal Fed. Bar Coun. 2nd Cir., 1976, Fordham Stein prize Fordham U., 1977, Louis Dembitz Brandeis medal Brandeis U., 1979; Sterling fellow Yale U., 1935-36; named laureate of Lincoln Acad. Ill., 1976. Mem. ABA, FBA (Honor award 1975), Am. Bar Found., Am. Philos. Soc. (v.p. 1991-94), Ill. Bar Assn. (award of honor 1983), Ill Bar Found. (Disting. Svc. award 1990), Am. Law Inst., Am. Judicature Soc., Chgo. Bar Assn. (Centennial award 1975), Supreme Ct. Hist. Soc., Constl. Rights Found. (Disting. Svc. award 1992), Chgo. Comml. Club, Quadrangle Club, Columbia Yacht Club, Order of Coif, Phi Beta Kappa. Office: U Chgo 1116 E 59th St Chicago IL 60637-1513

LEVIN, CARL, senator; b. Detroit, June 28, 1934; m. Barbara Halpern, 1961; children: Kate, Laura, Erica. BA, Swarthmore Coll., 1956; JD, Harvard U., 1959. Ptnr. Grossman, Hyman & Grossman, Detroit, 1959-64; asst. atty. gen., gen. counsel Mich. CRC, 1964-67; chief appellate defender City of Detroit, 1968-69, mem. coun., 1970-73, pres. coun., 1974-77; ptnr. Schlussel, Lifton, Simon, Rands & Kaufman, 1971-73, Jaffe, Snider, Raitt, Garratt & Heuer, 1978-79; U.S. senator from Mich., 1979—; past instr. Wayne State U., U. Detroit; mem. Armed Svcs. Com., Govtl. Affairs Com., Com. on Small Bus., Senate Dem. Steering & Coordination Com. Mem. Mich. Bar Assn., D.C. Bar. Democrat. Office: US Senate 459 Russell Senate Off Washington DC 20510

LEVIN, CHARLES EDWARD, lawyer; b. Chgo., Oct. 6, 1946; m. Barbara Serwer, Dec. 28, 1975. BA with high honor, DePaul U., 1968; JD cum laude, Northwestern U., Chgo., 1971. Bar: Ill. 1971. Asst. instr. legal writing and rsch. Northwestern U. Law Sch., 1970-71; assoc. D'Ancona & Pflaum, Chgo., 1971-76, ptnr., 1977-90; ptnr. Jenner & Block, Chgo., 1990—; mem. governing bd. Comml. Fin. Assn. Edn. Found., 1990—; asst. instr. legal writing, rsch. Northwestern U., 1970-71. Mem. bd. editors Northwestern U. Law Rev., 1970-71. Mem. aux. bd. Chgo. Architecture Found., 1989—; mem. governing bd. Comml. Fin. Assn. Edn. Found., N.Y. Mem. ABA (bus. sect. 1992—), Chgo. Bar Assn. (vice chmn. architecture and law com. 1974-75, vice chmn. divsn. D, mem. exec. com. fed. tax com. 1983-84, comml. fin. and trans. com. 1990—, Article 9 drafting subcom.), Assn. for Corp. Growth, East Bank Club Chgo., 410 Club. Office: Jenner & Block 1 E IBM Plz Fl 4400 Chicago IL 60611-3586

LEVIN, DAVID L., state legislator. Mem. dist. 82 Mo. Ho. of Reps. Office: Rm 116-3 11208 Sherwood Oak Ct Saint Louis MO 63146

LEVIN, DIANE, public relations consultant, antiques reporter; b. N.Y.C.; d. Harry H. and Goldie L. BA, BJ cum laude, Syracuse U., 1951. Various editl. and reporting positions, 1951-58; acct. supervisor Daniel J. Edelman, Inc., 1958-68; v.p. Harshe-Rotman & Druck, Inc., 1968-75; dir. program underwriting WTTW Pub. TV, Chgo., 1976-88; pub. rels. cons., antiques reporter, 1989—; adj. faculty Columbia Coll., 1989-90, Roosevelt U., 1990-91. Mem. adv. coun. Chgo. Dept. on Aging, 1993—; vol. courtroom mediator Ctr. for Conflict Resolution, 1992—. Fellow Accredited Pub. Rels., Pub. Rels. Soc. Am. (past pres. Chgo. chpt.). Home and Office: 880 N Lake Shore Dr Ste 3C Chicago IL 60611

LEVIN, MARIAN SUNIE, author; b. Kansas City, Mo., Apr. 28, 1931; d. Pro P. and Beatrice (Kurs) Sherman; m. Leon Richard Levin, Feb. 10, 1951; children: Leslie Cheryl, Terry Sue, Patti Ruth. BA, U. Mo., Kansas City, 1951, MA, 1970. Cert. primary and remedial reading tchr. Tchr. Prairie Sch., Shawnee Mission, Kans., 1951-55; dir., head of clinic Midwest Reading and Dyslexia Clinic, Kansas City, Mo., 1970-82; in pub. rels. Marketforce Internat., Kansas City, Mo., 1982-88; author, editor Today's Young Grandparent News, Shawnee Mission, 1989—; pub. speaker to banks, corps., hosps. and chs. Author: Grandparents Little Dividends, 1989, You and Your Grandchildren, 1991, Mingled Roots, 1993; editor newsletter Grandchild, 1995—; columnist Sr. Wire Svc., 1993—; author numerous articles. Mem. Women's Internat., Washington, 1950—, Council of Women, 1950—. Mem. Internat. Reading Assn., Children with Learning Disabilities. Home: PO Box 11143 Shawnee Mission KS 66207

LEVIN, MYLES JEFFREY, marketing and sales executive; b. Balt., July 17, 1966; s. Michael Lee and Judith (Block) L.; m. Lisa Ann Golden, Aug. 21, 1993. BA in English Lit., U. Richmond, 1988, postgrad., 1988-89. Exec. sales Pulse One Comm., Owings Mills, Md., 1989-90; acct. mgr. Profile Inc., Chgo., 1990, mktg. and promotions mgr., 1990-92, dir. sales and mktg., 1992-93; prin. Mye Design, Oak Park, Ill., 1993—; we. regional sales mgr. Karhu U.S.A.-Merrell Footwear/Karhu & Trak Skis, 1994-95, we. sales mgr., 1995-96, nat. sales mgr., 1996—; exec. cons. Wear n Tear Inc., Carmel, Ind., 1992—; cons. Magnani and Assocs. Advt., Chgo., 1993. Named one of Outstanding Young Men in Am., U. Richmond, 1988. Jewish. Home: 12 Fayette Dr Apt 331 South Burlington VT 05403 Office: Rivers West Ste #210 401 S 1st St Minneapolis MN 55401

LEVIN, PAUL JOSEPH, evangelist; b. Rock Island, Ill., Oct. 13, 1914; s. Peter and Hulda (Vromberg) L.; m. Dorothy Hayslip, Mar. 17, 1936 (dec. Oct. 1994). DD (hon.), San Francisco Bapt. Sem., 1969. Radio evangelist 41 stas., throughout U.S., 1957—; pres., founder Bible Tracts, Inc., Carlock, Ill., 1938—; bd. dirs. Bill Rice Ranch, Murfreesboro, Tenn., 1956-96. Author: Pre Wedding Days, 1935, One Step at a Time, 1976, and numerous tracts; recorded albums with Bob Findley, 1933-1975. Republican. Home: PO Box 144 205 E Franklin Carlock IL 61725 Office: Bible Tracts Inc P O Box 188 1925 S Main St Bloomington IL 61702

LEVIN, SANDER M., congressman; b. Detroit, Sept. 6, 1931; s. Saul R. and Bess (Levinson) L.; m. Victoria Schlafer, 1957. B.A., U. Chgo., 1952; M.A., Columbia U., 1954; LL.B., Harvard U., 1957. Supr. Oakland County Bd. Suprs., Mich., 1961-64; mem. Mich. Senate, 1965-70; fellow Kennedy Sch. Govt., Inst. Politics, Harvard U., Cambridge, Mass., 1975; asst. adminstr. AID, Washington, 1977-81; mem. 98th-104th Congresses from 17th (now 12th) Mich dist., 1983—; mem. ways and means com., subcoms. oversight and human resources; adj. prof. law Wayne State U., Detroit, 1971-74. Chmn. Mich. Dem. Com., 1968-69; Dem. Candidate for Gov., 1970, 74. Office: US Ho of Reps 2230 Rayburn HOB Washington DC 20515-2212*

LEVINE, BRUCE CARLAN, history educator; b. N.Y.C., Feb. 23, 1949; s. Seymour William and Harriet L. BA, U. Mich., 1971; MA, U. Rochester, 1973, PhD, 1980. Dir. of rsch. and writing Am. Social History Project, N.Y.C., 1981-86; asst. prof. dept. history U. Cin., 1986-92, assoc. prof. dept. history, 1992-95, prof., 1995—. Author: The Spirit of 1848, 1992, Half Slave and Half Free, 1992; co-author: Who Built America?, 1990, 2d vol., 1992; mem. editorial bd. Internat. Labor and Working Class History, 1990—. Office: U Cin Dept History Cincinnati OH 45221-0373

LEVINE, DONALD PAUL, infectious disease specialist; b. Detroit, Apr. 25, 1945; s. Louis L. and Lily (Lorber) L.; m. Diane Lynn Mendelson, Aug. 1, 1982; children: Miriam T., Carl D., Max N., Hannah R. BA, U. Mich., 1967; MD, Wayne State U., 1972. Diplomate Am. Bd. Infectious Diseases, Diplomate Am. Bd. Internal Medicine. Intern, resident Wayne State U. Affiliated Program; chief sect. infectious diseases Detroit Receiving Hosp.; asst. prof. Wayne State U., Detroit, 1978-83, assoc. prof., 1983-94, prof., 1994—. Editor: Infections Intravenous Drug Abusers, 1990. Office: Detroit Receiving Hosp 4201 Saint Antoine St Detroit MI 48201-2153

LEVINE, GAIL JANICE, publisher; b. Cleve., June 10, 1947; d. Harold and Florence (Bergglas) L.; m. Ronald Byron Rose, Aug. 22, 1968 (div. Nov. 1978); children: David Michael, Danielle Faye, Greg Harrison. BS in Occupational Therapy, Washington U., St. Louis, 1969; MS in Urban Affairs, U. Wis., Milw., 1978. Lic. occupational therapist., Wis. Occupational therapist Therapy Services Inc., Milw., 1974-75; research analyst Med. Coll. Wis., Milw., 1978-79; program dir. Mt. Sinai Hosp., Milw., 1979-80; pub. SingleLife Mag., Milw., 1981—. Vol. returnee Am. Field Service to Brazil, 1964; bd. dirs. Wis. chpt. Amyotrophic Lateral Sclerosis Assn., chair Great Date Auction, 1988. Recipient Successful Mag. Pubs. Group award, 1989; named Health Adv. of Yr. Nat. Womens' Health Network, 1982. Mem. ACLU, Met. Milw. Assn. Commerce, Am. Occupational Therapy Assn., U. Wis.-Milw. Alumni Assn. (life), Milw. Press Club. Democrat. Jewish. Office: SingleLife Enterprises Inc 606 W Wisconsin Ave Ste 1800 Milwaukee WI 53203-1905

LEVINE, JANE, newspaper publisher; b. New Milford, Conn., Apr. 25, 1953; d. David S. and June Ruth (Perry) L.; m. Randy Michael Signor, Mar. 12, 1983. BA summa cum laude, Macalester Coll., 1975. Advt. coord. Chgo. Reader, 1975-78, pub., exec. v.p., COO, 1994—; pub. L.A. Reader, 1978-83; sales mgr. N.C. Ind., Durham, 1984; v.p. advt. and mktg. Sasquatch Pub., Seattle, 1986-94; exec. v.p., COO Washington City Paper, 1994—. Treas. Seattle Advt. Fedn., 1990-92. Mem. Assn. Alternative

Newsweeklies (v.p. 1995), Mktg. and Comms. Execs. Internat. (membership chair 1993-94). Office: Chgo Reader 11 E Illinois St Chicago IL 60611

LEVINE, PHYLLIS, English language educator; b. London, Feb. 9, 1935; arrived in U.S., 1956; d. Joseph and Betty (Joseph) Fleedman; m. Stanley Levine, Apr. 20, 1958; children: Steven R., Julie A. Assoc. degree, Lorain County C.C., 1976; BA in Edn., U. Akron, 1980; MA in Edn., Baldwin Wallace Coll., 1985. Cert. prof. tchr. Salesperson George West Raincoats, London, 1954, Hubbards Dept. Store, London, 1956, Kauffman Dept. Store, Pitts., 1957-58; tchr. Elyria (Ohio) City Schs., 1981—; chem. counselor Elyria Schs., 1990-91; union rep. Elyria Edn. Assn., 1992—. Worker Dem. Party, Elyria, 1995. Mem. AAUW.

LEVINE, STEVEN ALAN, real estate appraiser, environmental consultant; b. Cin., Aug. 28, 1951; s. E. Pike and Beverly Rae (Friedman) L. BA with honors, U. Cin., 1975; postgrad., George Washington U., 1975-77. Appraiser Real Estate Evaluators and Cons., Cin., 1969-75; program asst. U.S. Renegotiation Bd., Washington, 1975; appraiser D.C. Govt., Washington, 1976-77; emergency mgmt. specialist Fed. Emergency Mgmt. Agy., Washington, 1977-80; v.p. Am. Res. and Appraisal Ctr., Cin., 1980—; pres. Steven A. Levine & Assocs., Inc., Cin., 1982—, Am. Inspection Mgmt. Inc., 1990—; v.p., exec. dir. Nat. Assn. Environ. Risk Auditors; cons. U.S. Army, 1982—, U.S. Dept. Interior. Author: Environmental Liabilities Affecting Real Estate, Kuwait: An Environmental Nightmare, The Renegotiation of Defense Contracts, Military Installation Real Property Management, Property Tax Relief Measures for the Elderly. Coord. Henry Jackson for Pres., Washington, 1976; mem. Forum for Urban Studies, Washington, 1977; mem. Common Cause, Washington, 1975-78. Sgt. USAF, 1969-75. Named to Hon. Order Ky. Cols., Louisville, 1979; named lt. col. aide-de-camp Staff of Gov. of Ga., Atlanta, 1979, lt. col. aide-de-camp Staff of Gov. of Ala., Montgomery, 1983. Mem. ASPA, Am. Assn. Cert. Appraisers (sr.), Nat. Assn. Environ. Risk Auditors (v.p., exec. dir., cert. environ, risk auditor). Jewish. Home and Office: Steven A Levine & Assoc Inc 4680 Mission Ln Cincinnati OH 45223-1263

LEVINSON, CHARLES BERNARD, architect; b. Youngstown, Ohio, Dec. 15, 1912; s. Al and Goldye (Davis) L.; m. Doris Mombach, Nov. 10, 1940; children: Ronnie Ann (Mrs. John Shore), Barbara Jean (Mrs. Ronald Stern), Suzanne (Mrs. Ralph Stern). BS in Architecture, U. Cin., 1934. Draftsman Gulf Refining Co., 1934-35; designer Hunt and Allen, 1935-36; pvt. practice architecture Cin., 1936-39, 40—; ptnr. Steelcraft Mfg. Co. div. Prefabricate Bldg. and Bldg. Products, 1940-44, v.p., 1945-51, exec. v.p., 1951-66, pres., 1966-69; v.p. then pres. Bldg. Products div. Knapp Bros. Mfg. Co., 1949-65, Leesburg Realty Co., 1952-76; sec./treas. then v.p./sec. ABCO Tool and Die Co., 1953-70; v.p., sec. Oceanautic Mfg. and Research Co., 1968-70; prof. U. Cin. Coll. Design Archtl. Art, 1970-85; vis. prof. architecture U. Wis., 1973-76, Coll. of the Desert, Palm Springs, Calif., 1976. V.p. Big Bros. Am., Cin., 1957, mem. spl. projects com., 1965, bd. dirs., 1956-66; bd. trustees Big Bros. Assn. Cin., pres., 1953-54, Bob Hope Cultural Ctr., Palm Desert, Calif., 1986—, Cin. Ballet Co.; mem. Nat. Com. Children and Youth, Nat. Com. for Employment of Youth, vice chmn., 1969, bd. dirs. 1962-68; mem. ad hoc adv. steering com. White House Conf. on Children and Youth, 1966-70; bd. dirs. Better Housing League of Cin., 1950—, Jewish Community Ctr., Cin., 1955—, Home for the Jewish Aged, Cin., 1955—, Palm Springs Friends of Los Angeles Philharmonic Orch., 1986—; numerous other civic activities. Mem. AIA, Ohio Soc. Architects. Republican. Jewish. Clubs: Queen City (Cin.), Losantiville Country (Cin.), Desert Island Country (Rancho Mirage, Calif.). Home: 2355 Bedford Ave Cincinnati OH 45208-2656 Office: 9403 Kenwood Rd Ste 103B Cincinnati OH 45242-6820

LEVIS, RICHARD GEORGE, middle school educator; b. Kenosha, Wis., Nov. 20, 1946; s. Elso R. and Valentina (Maraccini) L.; m. Diane Rose Christie, June 12, 1971; 1 child, Maureen R. BS, U. Wis., 1968, MS, 1973. Tchr. social studies Parker Jr. High Sch., Janesville, Wis., 1969, Washington Jr. High Sch., Kenosha, 1969—; mem. com. on vandalism and mid. schs. Kenosha Unified Schs.; jr. h.s. rep. Kenosha Ednl. Found., 1994. Co-author: (with James Hansen) United Nations Resource Materials and Bibliographies, 1974. V.p. Kenosha Tchrs. Union, 1971-73; exec. bd. Kenosha Dem. Party, 1969-86; mem. canvass bd., Kenosha; rep. United Fund, 1985—. Mem. NEA, Nat. Coun. Social Studies, Wis. Social Studies Coun., Wis. Edn. Assn., Kenosha Edn. Assn. (bd. dirs. 1975-77), Phi Delta Kappa. Democrat. Catholic. Home: 3520 14th Pl Kenosha WI 53144-2939 Office: Washington Jr H S 811 Washington Rd Kenosha WI 53140-2846

LEVIT, WILLIAM HAROLD, JR., lawyer; b. San Francisco, Feb. 8, 1938; s. William Harold and Barbara Janis (Kaiser) L.; m. Mary Elizabeth Webster, Feb. 13, 1971; children: Alison Jones, Alexandra Bradley, Laura Elizabeth Fletcher, Amalia Elizabeth Webster, William Harold, III. B.A. magna cum laude, Yale U., 1960; M.A. in Internat. Rels., U. Calif., Berkeley, 1962; LL.B., Harvard U., 1967. Bar: N.Y. 1968, Calif. 1974, Wis. 1979. Fgn. service officer Dept. State, 1962-64; assoc. firm Davis Polk & Wardwell, N.Y.C., 1967-73; assoc., then ptnr. firm Hughes Hubbard & Reed, N.Y.C. and Los Angeles, 1973-79; sec. and gen. counsel Rexnord Inc., Milw., 1979-83; ptnr., dir., chair internat. practice group Godfrey & Kahn, Milw., 1983—; substitute arbitrator Iran-U.S. Claims Tribunal, The Hague, 1984-88; lectr. Practicing Law Inst., ABA, Calif. Continuing Edn. of Bar, State Bar of Wis. Contbr. to: Mergers and the Private Antitrust Suit: The Private Enforcement of Section 7 of the Clayton Act, 1977. Bd. dirs. Wis. Humane Soc., 1980-90, pres., 1986-88; bd. dirs. Vis. Nurse Corp., Milw., 1980-90, chmn., 1985-87; bd. dirs. Vis. Nurse Found., 1986-95, chmn., 1989-91; bd. dirs. Aurora Health Care Inc., 1988-93, Wis. Soc. to Prevent Blindness, 1981-91, Columbia Coll. Nursing, 1992—, Aurora Health Care Ventures, 1993—; rep. Assn. Yale Alumni, 1976-79, 81-84, 90-93; pres. Yale Club So. Calif., 1977-79; mem. neutral advisor panel CPR Inst. for Dispute Resolution. Ford Found. fellow U. Pa., 1961-62, NDEA fellow U. Calif., Berkeley, 1962. Mem. ABA (com. on corp. counsel litigation sect.), Am. Soc. Corp. Secs. (pres. Wis. chpt. 1982-83, dir. 1981-92), Am. Arbitration Assn. (panel arbitrators 1977—), Assn. of Bar of City of N.Y., State Bar Calif. (com. on continuing edn. of bar 1977-79), L.A. County Bar Assn. (ethics com. 1976-79), State Bar Wis. (dir. internat. bus. transactions sect. 1985-92, dist. 2 bd. attys. profl. responsibility com. 1985-94, chmn. 1993-94), Bar Assn. 7th Cir. (gen. chair com. on rules and practice 1995—), Am. Br. Internat. Law Assn., Nat. Assn. Security Dealers (bd. arbitrators 1988—), Chartered Inst. Arbitrators (assoc., London), N.Y. Stock Exch. (panel arbitrators 1988—), N.Am. Coun. London Ct. of Internat. Arbitration, Am. Soc. Internat. Law, Inst. Jud. Adminstrn., Milw. Club, Milw. Athletic Club, Town Club, Phi Beta Kappa. Office: 780 N Water St Ste 1500 Milwaukee WI 53202-3512

LEVITT, PAUL A., financial consultant; b. Chgo., Oct. 21, 1953. BS, U. Ariz., 1976. Pharmacist KMart, Ill., 1976-86; fin. cons. Dean Witter, Schaumburg, Ill., 1986-90, Smith Barney Inc., Northbrook, Ill., 1990—. Office: Smith Barney Inc 5 Revere Dr Fl 5 Northbrook IL 60062-1566

LEVULIS, RAYMOND JOHN, management consultant; b. Glen Lyon, Pa., June 23, 1933; s. Francis John and Helen Telesfora (Osowiecki) L.; m. Maria Soledad Bello Gay, Nov. 16, 1984; children: Diane Lynn Levulis Masseria, Raymond John Jr. BS in Indsl. Engring., Lawrence Tech. U., 1955; MBA, U. Detroit, 1960. Cert. mgmt. cons. Mgr. indsl. engring. Am. Std. Corp., Detroit, 1958-63; mgr. mfg. svcs. A.O. Smith Corp., Charlottesville, Va., 1963-65; prin. A.T. Kearney & Co., Cleve., 1965-72; pres. Corp. Personnel, Charlotte, N.C., 1972-75; sr. v.p. K.W. Tunnell Co., Oak Brook, Ill., 1975-82; sr. ptnr. Case & Co., Chgo., 1982-85; prin. Austin Co., Rosemont, Ill., 1985-88; v.p. Deloitte & Touche, Chgo., 1988-91; founder, owner R.J. Levulis & Assocs., Roselle, Ill., 1991—. Contbr. articles to profl. jours. Mem. Midwest Soc. Profl. Cons. (sr.), Inst. Indsl. Engrs. (life), Am. Prodn. and Inventory Control Soc. (sr.), Soc. Mfg. Engrs. (sr.). Office: RJ Levulis and Assocs 601 Sequoia Trl Roselle IL 60172-1047

LEVY, ARNOLD S(TUART), real estate company executive; b. Chgo., Mar. 15, 1941; s. Roy and Esther (Scheff) L.; m. Eva Cichosz, Aug. 8, 1976; children: Adam, Rachel, Deborah. BS, U. Wis., 1963; MPA, Roosevelt U., 1970. Dir. Neighborhood Youth Corps, Chgo., 1966-68; v.p. Social Planning Assn., Chgo., 1968-70; planning dir. Office of Mayor Chgo., 1970-74; dep. dir. Mayor's Office Manpower, Chgo., 1974-75; sr. v.p. Urban Investment & Devel. Co., Chgo., 1975-93; pres., CEO Stone-Levy, LLC, Chgo., 1994—; mem. S-L Hospitality Group, LLC, 1995—; pres. JMB/Urban Hotels, Hotel and Resort Devel. Group, JMB/Urban Devel. Co., 1985-93; ptnr. Pierce and Co., 1994—; bd. dirs. Hostmark Mgmt. Group, Inc.; mem. Urban Land Inst. Pres. Ark, Chgo., 1970-72, Parental Stress Svcs., Chgo., 1978-79; past lectr. DePaul U., Roosevelt U., Loyola U.; v.p. Inst. Urban Life, Chgo., 1983—. Co-editor: The Professionals' Guide to Commercial Property Development, 1988. Bd. dirs. Mus. Broadcast Communications, Chgo. Coun. of Urban Affairs, Am Shalom, pres. Ill. Humane Soc.; steering com. Radio Hall of Fame; chmn. Spertus Inst. Jewish Studies, Glencoe Plan Commn., Carlton Club (Chgo.), Twin Orchard Club. Home: 535 Park Ave Glencoe IL 60022-1501 Office: Stone-Levy & Co LLC 8700 W Bryn Mawr Ave Ste 900 Chicago IL 60631-3507

LEVY, RONALD T., liquor wholesale distributor; b. St. Louis, June 9, 1932; m. Joyce Hamburg; children: Sharon, Robert, Mark. B in Journalism, U. Ill., 1954. Media rschr. Gardner Advt. Co., St. Louis, 1956-57, media buyer, 1957-58, media rsch. supr. new product intro., 1958-59; sec., gen. mgr. Hamburg Distbg. Co., Inc., Champaign, Ill., 1959-62; v.p., sales mgr. Hamburg Distbg. Co., Inc., 1962-66; pres., CEO, chmn. bd. Hamburg Distbg. Co., Inc., St. Louis, 1966-92; v.p. Union Liquor, Chgo., 1992—; pres. Hamburg Mgmt. Svcs., Inc., 1992—, Ronstone Tech., Champaign, Ill., 1994—; bd. dirs., exec. com. Comml. Bank of Champaign, 1977-85; bd. dirs. BankOne, 1985—; mem. Ill. State Liquor Commn., 1974—; apptd. mem. Dept. Alcohol & Substance Abuse, 1992—. Edn. chmn. Sinai Temple, 1968, fin. com., investment chmn.; v.p. B'nai B'rith, 1966-71; pres. downstate chpt. City of Hope, 1979—; chmn. spl. bus. contbn. Champaign County United Fund, 1969, 75, 81; chmn. Israel Bond Dr., 1974, fin. com., 1985, Champaign-Urbana Century Coalition; dir. C-U Jewish Fedn. Endowment Fund, 1991, 92. Recipient Meritorious Svc. award Champaign County Coun. on Alcoholism and Drug Abuse, 1978, Jameson Civitus award, 1980, Man of Yr. award City of Hope, 1980. Mem. Seagram Family Assn., Wine and Spirits Wholesalers of Am. (assn. svcs. com., budget and adminstrn. chmn. 1984, ins. com. chmn. 1982-84, treas. 1985, sec. 1986, v.p. 1987-88, sr. v.p. 1989, pres. 1990, chmn. 1991), Associated Beer Distbrs. Ill. (area dir. 1964—), Wholesale Liquor Distbrs. Ill. (bd. dirs., past pres.), Champaign-Urbana Beer Distbrs. Assn. (pres., bd. dirs.), Century Coun. (dir. 1991-92, chmn. Champaign-Urbana Century Coalition), Champaign County Elks, Moose, Masons. Office: Hamburg Distbg Co Inc 1206 S Randolph St Champaign IL 61820

LEVY, SAM MALCOLM, advertising executive; b. Henderson, Ky., Nov. 26, 1901; s. Mike Meyer and Hattie Belle (Wile) L.; m. Isabel Helen Cone, Apr. 22, 1929; 1 child, Sue Levy Klau. Student, U. Mo., 1919-21; PhB, U. Chgo., 1921-23; postgrad., Harvard Coll., 1926. Exec. McCann Erickson, N.Y.C., 1923-30; adv. dir. News & Record, Greensborough, N.C., 1930-31; v.p. dir. Keelor & Stites, Cin., 1931-46; lectr. speech U. Cin., 1940-44; pres. Assoc. Adv. Agy., Cin., 1946-71; sr. v.p. Sive Inc. - A Div. Young & Rubicam, 1971-89; ret. Sive Inc.-A Div. Young & Rubicam, 1989; life trustee Clean Cin. Inc., bd. govs. Big Bros. Assn., Glen Manor Home for Aged, 1963—; instr. advt. evening coll. U. Cin., 1945-48. Editor: Socony Monthly Mag., 1925-27. Active Friend of Serengeti Aftrica; mem. Cin. Art Mus. Named to Hon. Order of Ky. Cols., 1984; donated Glass Gallery to Cin. Art Mus., 1980, Floral Clock to Cin. Park Bd., 1988; recipient Key to the City of Cin., 1988, Emerald award, 1993. Mem. Advts. Club Cin., Black Friars Club Chgo., Bankers Club, Losanti Ville Country Club Cin., Founders Soc., Cin. Symphony Orch., Thomas Schippers Soc., Zeta Beta Tau (pres., grad club). Republican. Home: 2444 Madison Rd Cincinnati OH 45208-1256

LEVY, STANLEY ROY, educational administrator; b. Bklyn., July 19, 1934; s. Abraham and Rose (Weinberger) L.; m. Joan Weinberg, June 15, 1963; children: Scott, Marcia. BA, U. Mich., 1955, MA, 1959, PhD, 1964. Assoc. dean students U. Ill., Urbana, 1968-73, asst. vice chancellor, 1973-76, assoc. vice chancellor, 1976-78, acting vice chancellor, 1978-79, vice chancellor, 1979-94; adj. prof. higher edn., 1986—. Bd. dirs. Arrowhead Council Boy Scouts Am., 1983, United Way of Champaign County, 1976-85; mem. Ill. Commn. Cmty. Svc., Ill. Campus Compact, Illini Media Co., Champaign County chpt. ACLU; active Champaign County Crimestoppers, 1986—. Served to 1st lt. U.S. Army, 1955-57, Germany. Mem. Am. Assn. Higher Educ., Nat. Assn. Student Personnel Adminstrs. (v.p. 1976-78), Nat. Assn. State Univ. & Land Grant Colls. (coun. student affairs 1980-94), N. Cen. Assn. Schs. and Colls. (cons., evaluator 1979—). Jewish. Lodges: B'nai Brith. Home: 3006 Meadowbrook Ct Champaign IL 61821-6151 Office: 1310 S Sixth St Champaign IL 61820-5711

LEWAKOWSKI, DEBORAH MARGUERITA, accountant; b. Wayne, Mich., Aug. 21, 1963; d. John Janusz and Margaret Henrietta (Lempicka) L. BS in Acctg. and Mgmt. Info. Sys., Oakland U., Rochester, Mich., 1987; postgrad., U. Mich. CPA, Mich. Staff acct. Straka Jarackas & Co., P.C., Troy, Mich., 1987-88; sr. sys. cons. Derderian Kann Seyferth & Salucci, P.C., Troy, 1988-94; sys. cons. BDO Seidman, LLP, Troy, 1994—. Vol. March of Dimes of Met. Detroit, Acctg. Aid Soc. Met. Detroit, Focus: Hope of Met. Detroit. Mem. AICPAs, Mich. Soc. CPAs (chair info. tech. 1994-96, bd. dirs. Metro Detroit chpt. 1992—), Oakland U. Alumni Assn. (bd. dirs. 1987—), Mich. State U. Alumni Assn. of Oakland County, Bus. and Profl. Women of Rochester (treas. 1993-94), Alpha Kappa Psi. Republican. Roman Catholic. Home: PO Box 1442 Troy MI 48099 Office: BDO Seidman LLP 755 W Big Beaver #1900 Troy MI 48084

LEWANDOWSKI, MICHALENE MARIA, human service consultant, lecturer; b. Hamilton, Ont., Can., June 2, 1920; d. Stanley Casmere and Winifred (Kolodziejski) Doskotch; m. Henry Adam Schultz, Aug. 30, 1939 (dec. July 1940); m. Matthew John Lewandowski, July 27, 1941 (dec. Jan. 1987); children: Adrian, Christopher. Student, Wayne State U. Cert. med. asst.; cert. Am. Coll. Nursing Home Adminstrs., Mich. Health Facilities Assn., various other state health assns. Activity-patient affairs dir. Abbey Nursing Home, Warren, Mich., 1963-70; designated social worker Good Shepherd Nursing Home, Detroit, 1970, Rose-Villa Nursing Home, Roseville, Mich., 1970-81; instr. rehab. and devel. various nursing homes, Warren, 1976—; originator Day Care Ctrs., Macomb County, Mich., 1990-91; cons. various nursing homes, Mich., 1984-87; profl. lectr., 1990—; instr. rehab. and human rels. devel. in nursing homes Macomb County Community Coll., 1976; pres. Macomb County Activity Dirs. Assn., 1975; panelist in field. Author: The Human Island, 1970 (Outstanding Cultural Achievement award, 1976); contbr. articles to profl. pubns. Del. White House Conf. on Aging, Lansing, Mich., Washington, 1971; state commr. on aging State of Mich., Lansing, 1975-80; bd. dirs. Macomb County (Mich.) Coun. on Aging, 1973, spl. cons., 1976. Recipient citation for Care and Therapy of Aged, City of Warren, 1964, Polish Nat. Alliance for Complete Dedication to the Aged, 1970, Spl. Tribute State of Mich., 1974; named Citizen of Week WBRB, 1970; honored for Contbns. to Mankind, Macomb County Commrs., 1973; recipient personal letter from Pres. Nixon for her work; documentary on her work with elderly presented on Sta. WXYZ-TV.

LEWARK, CAROL ANN, special education educator; b. Fort Wayne, Ind., Mar. 8, 1935; d. Lloyd L. and Elizabeth J. (Arthur) Meads; m. Paul N. Lewark, Aug. 20, 1955; children: David P., Laura, Beth, Daniel A. BA, St. mary of Woods, 1978; MS, Ind. U., 1981. Cert. elem. educator, spl. educator mentally retarded K-12, learning disabilities K-12, Ind.; cert. home tng. specialist, Wis. Home tng. specialist Madison Wis. ARC, Madison, 1968-70; nursery sch. cons. Allen County ARC, Ft. Wayne, Ind., 1971-73; early childhood spl. edn. dir. Allen County ARC, Ft. Wayne, 1973—; cons. in field; presenter in field; apptd. by Ind. Gov. to State Interagy. Coordinating Coun. for Infants and Toddlers, 1992-95; apptd. to Higher Ed Coun. for Early Childhood and Spl. Edn. Contbr. articles to profl. jours. Apptd. to Leadership Ft. Wayne, 1994. Named Model Project Site 99-457 Early Intervention Ind. State Dept. Mental Health, 1987; Tech. Assistance grantee Georgetown U., 1991-93. Mem. Ind. Coun. for Exceptional Children (sec. 1990-94), First Steps of Allen County (facilitator 1989—), Leadership Fort Wayne. Home: 910 Kensington Blvd Fort Wayne IN 46805-5312 Office: ARC of Allen County 2542 Thompson Ave Fort Wayne IN 46807-1051

LEWCHANIN, JACQUELINE, manufacturing company executive; b. Chgo., July 9, 1944; d. Quinn Brunson and Edna Mae (McCormick) Thomas; m. Daniel Floyd Lewchanin, Jan. 7, 1965 (div. June 1975); children: John Edward McCormick, Julie Marie, Amber Nicole. Diploma in cosmetology, Approved U., 1963; student, Ky. Christian Coll., 1963-64; fine arts degree, Famous Artist's Sch., 1971; BA, Ind. U., 1989. V.p. Port-O-Stroll Enterprises, Inc., Fairland, Ind., 1971-76, pres., 1976—; med. rsch. asst. Ind. U., Indpls., 1985-88, geology rsch. asst., 1988-89; pre-sentence investigator criminal div. probation dept. Marion Superior Ct., Indpls., 1976-89; rschr. on alcoholism and juvenile delinquency Internat. Graphoanalysis Soc., Chgo., 1980-81; tchr. Free U. and Hoosier Edn. Resource Exch., Indpls., 1977-90; lectr. in field. Author: (poetry) The Fire Within Me, 1985, Smoldering Embers, 1986, Night Talk, 1987, P.S. I Love You, 1989, Odd Lots, 1993, (children's books) Fancy, 1974, Fergasen, 1974, Toby's Gremlin, 1974, The Garden, 1974; contbg. author: (anthologies) On the Threshold of a Dream, 1989 (Nat. Libr. Poetry Editor's Choice award), Best Poems of the 90's, 1991 (Nat. Libr. Poetry Editor's Choice award), Outstanding Poets of 1994, 1994 (Nat. Libr. Poetry Editor's Choice award), Best Poems of 1995, 1995 (Nat. Libr. Poetry Editor's Choice award), Best Poems of 1996, 1996, 14 others; editor newsletter The Hoot, 1983-84; contbr. articles, poems, stories to profl. publs. Trustee Acton (Ind.) United Meth. Ch., 1990—; security vol. Pan Am. Games, Indpls., 1987; vol. Child Protection Team and Task Force for Prevention of Child Abuse, 1983. Recipient Distinguished Poets of Am. award Nat. Libr. of Poetry, 1993. Mem. NAFE, N.Y. Acad. Scis., Internat. Graphoanalysis, Ind. Graphoanalysis (rec. sec. 1977-79, pres., editor 1983-84), Internat. Soc. Poets, Internat. Artist's Soc., Ind. Folk Music and Mountain Dulcimer Soc., Ind. Friends of Bluegrass. Home: 4749 N 550 W Fairland IN 46126-9620

LEWENAUER, JOHN BENJAMIN, investment broker; b. Milw., May 9, 1953. BA in Sci. and Fin. cum laude, U. Colo., 1975. Owner Sturts Women's Apparel, Milw., 1976-86; investment broker Robert W. Baird & Co. Inc., Milw., 1987—. Home: 9624 N Crestwood Ct Mequon WI 53092-5355 Office: Robert W Baird & Co Inc 777 E Wisconsin Ave Milwaukee WI 53201

LEWIN, MITCHELL JOSEPH, die casting engineer; b. Chgo., July 22, 1927; s. Lewis Berkwood and Sadie (Edelstein) L.; m. Sally Louise Bernstein, June 18, 1950; children: Terry Sue, Penny, Jill. BSME, Northwestern U., 1949. Engr. Stewart Die Casting Co., Chgo., 1950-58; prodn. mgr. Paul Krone Die Casting Co., Chgo., 1958-61; dir. rsch. devel. Stewart Die Casting Co., Chgo., 1961-63; chief engr. Superior Die Casting Co., Cleve., 1963-77; v.p. engring. Paul Krone Die Casting Co., 1977-87; pres. Mitchell Lewin Inc., Highland Park, Ill., 1987—; vice chmn. Die Casting Rsch. Found., N.Y.C., 1975-80, ASTM B-6, Phila., 1960—; chmn. DCRF Tech. Coms., N.Y.C., 1969-75. Author: book chpt. on automation, Die Casting; contbr. articles to Die Casting Eng. Mag. Mem. Big Bros. Am., Cleve., 1970-75. Mem. North Am. Die Casting Assn. (Lilligren award 1970, Nysellius award 1975). Home and Office: 1730 Heather Ln Highland Park IL 60035-3718

LEWIN, PEARL GOLDMAN, psychologist; b. Bklyn., Apr. 25, 1923; d. Frank and Anna (Simon) Goldman; m. Seymour Z. Lewin, Oct. 17, 1943; children: David, Jonathan. BA, Hunter Coll., 1943; MS, U. Mich., 1947; PhD, NYU, 1980. Lic. psychologist, N.Y. Insp. chemist quarter master corps U.S. Army, 1943-45; chemist chem. warfare U.S. Army, Edgewood Arsenal, Md., 1945; asst. psychologist Bur. Psychol. Svcs., U. Mich., Ann Arbor, 1947-48; freelance rsch. asst. chemistry N.Y.C., 1955-71; adj. lectr. CUNY, Bklyn., 1973-74, instr., 1974-79, asst. prof., 1979-80; psychologist Creedmore Psychiat. Ctr., N.Y.C., 1980-82; sr. psychologist Manhattan Family Ct., N.Y.C., 1982-87; cons., 1987—; mentor Peer Counseling Orgn., Bklyn. Coll., 1976-80, coord. student svcs. New Sch. Liberal Arts, 1974-76, adminstr. acad. regulations, 1974-76. Author: Sexist Humor, 1979. Mem. APA, Pi Lambda Theta, Phi Kappa Phi. Home and Office: 4231 N Walnut Ave Arlington Heights IL 60004-1302

LEWIN, RHODA GREENE, editor, historian, columnist; b. Mpls., Apr. 6, 1929; d. Louis and Florence (Glick) G.; m. David J. Jacobs, July 23, 1950; m. Thomas M. Lewin, Sept. 19, 1963; children: Ellen, Susan, Kate, Jeffrey. BA in Journalism, U. Minn., 1949, MA in Journalism, 1961, PhD in Am. Studies, 1978. Free lance writer, editor Mpls., 1956—; instr. journalism U. Wis., Superior, 1961-63; instr. communications U. Minn., Mpls., 1963-65, instr. creative writing extension div., 1977-83; mem. acad. coun. Am. Jewish Hist. Soc., 1990—; mem. adv. com. Ind. Scholars Nat. Program, N.Y.C., 1986—; chair archives com. Temple Israel, Mpls., 1986—; pres. Minn. Ind. Scholars Forum, 1983-84; cons., interviewer Mpls. Pub. Libr. Oral History Project, 1983-87; lectr. in field. Editor: Witnesses to the Holocaust: An Oral History (Nat. Jewish Book awards nomination 1990, 91), Security, 1982, Those Were Days of Yesteryear, 1978, Identity mag., 1980-88, Soviet Jewry Action News, 1985-90, Hill and Lake Press, 1978-82; asst. editor: The Legend, 1985-87; contbg. editor Mpls. Star; author: (booklet) Temple Israel: A Brief History, 1987; contbr. numerous articles to profl. jours.; columnist Am. Jewish World, 1988—. Bd. dirs. Mpls. Fedn. for Jewish Svc., 1986-91, B'nai B'rith Chaplaincy at Mayo Clinic, Rochester, Minn., 1987—; mem. exec. bd. Twin Cities chpt. Am. Jewish Com., 1980-90, Oral History Assn. of Minn., 1991—; bd. dirs., chair Capital Campaign Theatre in the Round Players, 1983-86; assoc. chair Kenwood Park Planning Com., 1979-84; mem. Human Devel. Task Force Capital Long-Range Improvement Com., City of Mpls., 1980-82; mem. lake levels adv. com. Mpls. Parks and Recreation Bd., 1979-84; mem. media Fraser Senate Campaign, Minn., 1978. Mem. Minn. Independent Scholars Forum (pres. 1983-84), Oral History Assn., Minn. Hist. Soc. (grantee 1979), Am. Studies Assn., Am. Jewish Hist. Soc., Oral History Assn. Minn. Democrat.

LEWIN, STANTON MORRIS, advertising executive; b. Chgo., Feb. 27, 1959; s. Philip M. and Judith (Langert) L.; m. Terri L. Sugarman, Nov. 12, 1988; children: Alexa, Matthew. BS in Advt., U. Ill., 1981. Account exec. The Schram Co., Chgo., 1982-83; sr. account exec. Jacobs & Clevenger, Chgo., 1984; account supr. Bozell, Jacobs, Kenyon and Eckhardt, Chgo., 1985-87; v.p. Stone & Adler, Chgo., 1988-91; chmn. LKH&S, Chgo., 1992—. Home: 1239 Hohlfelder Rd Glencoe IL 60022 Office: LKH&S 360 N Michigan Ave Chicago IL 60601

LEWIS, ANDRE LEON, artistic director; b. Hull, Que., Can., Jan. 16, 1955; s. Raymond Lincoln and Theresa L. Student, Classical Ballet Studio, Ottawa, Royal Winnipeg (Man.) Ballet Sch., 1975; studies with David Moroni, Arnold Spohr, Rudi van Dantzig, Jiri Kylian, Peter Wright, Hans van Manen, and Alicia Markova, among others. Mem. corps de ballet Royal Winnipeg (Man.) Ballet, 1979-82, soloist, artistic coord., 1984-89, interim artistic dir., 1989-90, assoc. artistic dir., 1990-95, artistic dir., 1995—; staged Danzig's Romeo and Juliet, Teatro Comunale, Florence, Italy, Greek Nat. Opera, Athens. Dancer, soloist (ballets) Song of a Wayfarer, Fall River Legend, Nuages Pas de deux, Lento A Tempo E Appassionatto, Nutcracker, Four Last Songs, Romeo and Juliet, Belong Pas de deux, Ectasy of Rita Joe, (TV and films) Fall River Legend, Giselle, Heartland, Romeo and Juliet, The Big Top, Firebird, Belong Pas De Deux; performed at many events including the opening Gala performance of the Internat. Ballet competition in Jackson, Miss., Le Don Des Etoiles, Montreal, a spl. gala honoring Queen Beatrix of Holland and at a Gala performance in Tchaikovsky Hall, Moscow; appeared as a guest artist throughout N.Am., the Orient and USSR. Office: Royal Winnipeg Ballet, 380 Graham Ave, Winnipeg, MB Canada R3C 4K2*

LEWIS, DANIEL EDWARD, computer company executive, systems engineer; b. Cleve., May 24, 1955; s. Arthur Edward and Vivian Jeanette (Davis) L.; m. Kimber Lea Thacher, Dec. 30, 1993. BSEE, Ohio State U., 1981; MBA, U. Akron, 1988. Registered profl. engr., Ohio. Sys. engr. Firestone Tire & Rubber, Akron, Ohio, 1981-83; software devel. mgr. Diebold Corp., Canton, Ohio, 1983-85; computer product sales Arrow Electronics, Solon, Ohio, 1985-86; sr. sys. analyst Bristol Petroleum, Cleve., 1986-89; product mgr. Telxon Corp., Fair Lawn, Ohio, 1989-93; sr. mktg. mgr. Norand Corp., Cedar Rapids, Iowa, 1993-95, dir. mktg., 1995—. Contbr. articles to profl. jours. Mem. IEEE, Am. Mgmt. Assn., Assn. for Computing Machinery. Home: 3602 Caribou Ct NE Cedar Rapids IA 52402 Office: Norand Corp 550 2d St SE Cedar Rapids IA 52401

LEWIS, DENNIS FRANK, financial executive; b. Hammond, Ind., Apr. 16, 1958; s. Dennis Vivan and Lorraine Cecilia (Austgen) L.; m. Nancy Lou Williams, June 6, 1980; children; Daniel Scott, Robert Patrick, Katrina Elizabeth. Student, Wabash Coll., 1976-78; BSBA, Valparaiso U., 1980. Mgr. Arthur Anderson LLP, Chgo., 1980-93; dir. corp. fin. AM Internat., Mount Prospect, Ill., 1993-94; asst. controller AM Internat., Inc., Mount Prospect, Ill., 1994—. Coach Highland (Ind.) Boys Baseball, 1987—, treas., 1994—; coach Highland Soccer, 1987-94; com. mem. Com. to Elect Dennis

Simala, Highland, 1995—. Recipient Seuoia award Arthur Andersen, 1993. Mem. Frat. Order of Police. Home: 10041 4th Pl Highland IN 46322 Office: AM Internat Inc 1800 W Central Rd Mount Prospect IL 60056

LEWIS, DONALD JOHN, mathematics educator; b. Adrian, Minn., Jan. 25, 1926; s. William J. and Ellanora (Masgai) L.; m. Carolyn Dana Hauf, Dec. 28, 1953. BS, Coll. St. Thomas, 1946; PhD, U. Mich., 1950. Instr. Ohio State U., Columbus, 1950-52; asst. prof. U. Notre Dame (Ind.), 1953-57, assoc. prof., 1957-61; assoc. prof. U. Mich., Ann Arbor, 1961-63, prof. maths., 1963—, dept. chair, 1983-94; dir. Divsn. Math. Scis. Nat. Sci. Found., 1995—; mem. Inst. for Adv. Study, 1952-53, 90-91; vis. scientist U. Manchester (Eng.), 1959-61, Cambridge (Eng.), 1960-61; vis. fellow Trinity Coll., Cambridge, 1965-69, Japanese Soc. for Promotion of Sci., Tokyo, 1974; adv. bd. math. sci. NSF, 1983-86, math panel sci., 1965. Author: Introduction to Algebra, 1965, Calculus and Linear Algebra, 1970; editor: Proceedings of Symposia in Pure Math., 1971; contbr. 55 articles on number theory to profl. jours. Recipient Humboldt Preis award Alexander von Humboldt Soc., Germany, 1980, Disting. Svc. award Am. Math. Soc., 1995; fellow NSF, 1952-53, 59-61. Roman Catholic. Home: 2250 Glendaloch Rd Ann Arbor MI 48104-2832 Office: U Mich Math Dept Ann Arbor MI 48109-1003

LEWIS, ELLEN MILLER (LIN LEWIS), business owner, educator; b. Phila., Mar. 14, 1942; d. Franklin Rush and Ellen (Newhall) Miller; m. Kenneth Dean Lewis, Feb. 25, 1960; children: Debra Lynn Harrington, Kenneth Dean, Christopher L., Sarah E. BA in Biology, Southwestern Coll., Winfield, Kans., 1975. Cert. tchr. biology, chemistry and math., Kans. Lab. technician Snyder Rsch. Found., Winfield, 1975-83; substitute tchr. Douglass (Kans.) High Sch., 1987-91; bus. owner, sec. KSQ Blowmolding Engring. Mfg. Inc., Winfield, 1987—. Contbr. articles to profl. jours. Mem. Unified Sch. Dist. 465 Bd. Edn., Winfield, 1979-95, pres., 1982-83, 90-91, 93-94; mem. Pvt. Industry Coun. Sr. Delivery Area IV, Wichita, Kans., 1989-94; candidate for Kans. Ho. of Reps., 1992; chmn. Cowley County Reps., 1992. Mem. Winfield Swim Club (pres. 1988), Sorosis. Methodist. Office: Engring Mft Inc KSQ Bolwmolding 1st & B Strotherfield PO Box 177 Winfield KS 67156

LEWIS, ERIC D., mechanical engineer; b. Kansas City, Mo., Mar. 4, 1965. B, S.D. State U., 1988, postgrad. Project engr. Rosco Mfg., Madison, S.D., 1988—. Democrat. Office: Rosco Mfg 1001 SW 1st St Madison SD 57042-2619

LEWIS, HUGH B., veterinary medicine educator; b. Cardiff, Wales, U.K., Aug. 23, 1940; m. Mair Harris-Hughes; children: Benjamin, Nicholas. BVMS (DVM), U. Glasgow, Scotland, 1965. Diplomate Am. Coll. Vet. Pathologists; mem. Royal Coll. Vet. Surgeons. Practitioner Somerset, Eng., 1965-66; resident in vet. medicine U. Pa., Phila., 1966-67, NIH postdoctoral fellow in hematology, 1968-70; Cardeza rsch. fellow in hematology Thomas Jefferson Med. Coll., Phila., 1970-71; asst. prof. medicine U. Pa. Sch. Vet. Medicine, Phila., 1971-74, lectr. in medicine, 1974-76; founding ptnr. Willowdale Vet. Ctr., Kennett Square, Pa., 1974-76; assoc. prof. clin. pathology, lab. dir. Purdue U. Sch. Vet. Medicine, West Lafayette, Ind., 1976-77; assoc. dir. pathology Smith Kline & French Labs., Phila., 1977-81, dir. pathology, 1981-82, dir. pathology & toxicology, 1982-85, sr. dir. preclin. devel., 1986—; dean sch. vet. medicine, prof. vet. medicine Purdue U., West Lafayette, 1986—; adj. prof. lab. medicine U. Pa. Sch. Vet. Medicine, Phila., 1979-86. Contbr. over 30 articles to profl. jours.; also monographs, abstracts, chpts. to books. Mem. AAAS, Am. Assn. Lab. Animal Sci., Am. Coll. Vet. Pathologists (examination com. 1975-78, program com. 1983—), Am. Soc. for Vet. Clin. Pathology, (pres. 1983-84, coun. mem. 1980-86, assoc. editor Jour. Vet. Clin. Pathology 1978-86), Am. Hematology Soc., British Vet. Assn., Royal Coll. Vet. Surgeons, N.Y. Acad. Scis., Phila. Hematology Soc., Soc. Toxicologic Pathologists, Society of Toxicology, C.L. Davis Found. (faculty of discussants), Purdue Rsch. Found. Office: Purdue U Sch Vet Medicine West Lafayette IN 47907

LEWIS, JAMES A., state legislator; b. Highland, Ky., Dec. 26, 1930; m. Anna Mae Spencer; children: David, Thomas, Charles. Student, Purdue U. Bldg. contr.; rep. Ind. Ho. of Rep., 1970-72; senator Dist. 45 Ind. State Senate, minority caucus chmn., mem. natural resources, fin., agr. and small bus. coms., mem. labor and pensions com., ranking minority mem., mem. appointments and claims com., mem. consumer affairs com. Mem. City Council, 1960-68; mem. Clark County, Ind. coun., 1981-82; precinct committeeman; scoutmaster Boy Scouts Am. Recipient Best Citizen award Jaycees, 1959. Mem. So. Home Bldrs. Assn., Clark County Conservation Club, Masons, Scottish Rite, Moose. Home: 774 Level St Charlestown IN 47111-1509*

LEWIS, JOHN MENZIES, political science educator; b. Chou Tsun, Shantung, China, Feb. 23, 1941; came to U.S., 1963; s. John L. and Georgina Robb (Menzies) L. BA, Oxford (Eng.) U., 1963, MA, 1969; PhD, Cornell U., 1979. Instr. Cornell U., Ithaca, N.Y., 1967-68; lectr. U. Essex, Colchester, Eng., 1968-73; instr. polit. sci. Ind. U., South Bend, 1973-78, asst. prof., 1978-84, assoc. prof., 1984—, chair dept. polit. sci., 1990—. Mem. Am. Polit. Sci. Assn., Ctr. for the Study of the Presidency. Office: Ind Univ South Bend 1700 Mishawaka Ave South Bend IN 46615-1408

LEWIS, LINDA SUE, elementary education educator; b. San Francisco, Sept. 16, 1947; d. Harry John and Virginia Ruth (Benbow) Walter; m. Danny Morton Lewis, June 28, 1969; children: Mark, Geoffrey. BA in Polit. Sci., U. Calif., 1969. Cert. elem. edn. tchr. Tchr. Effingham Community Unit #40, Edgewood, Ill., 1971—. Assessor Summit Twp., Effingham County, 1986-93; chair Effingham County Edn. Women, 1985; bd. dirs. Effingham Child Devel. Ctr., 1975-78; bd. dirs., adminstrv. bd. Centenary United Meth. Ch., Effingham, 1989-92, trustee, 1992-95. Mem. AAUW (bd. dirs. Ill. state 1981-87, treas. 1990-92, pres.-elect 1992, pres. 1993-95), Ill. Edn. Assn. (membership chair region #7 1985-86, membership com. region #7 1982-86), Effingham Classroom Tchrs. Assn. (sec. 1974-76, regional coun. del. 1990-92). Democrat. United Methodist. Home: 10 Nees Ave Effingham IL 62401-5088 Office: Edgewood Sch PO Box 207 Edgewood IL 62426-0207

LEWIS, LLOYD EDWARD, JR., state legislator; b. Xenia, Ohio, Nov. 17, 1926; s. Lloyd Edward and Ruth (Hamilton) L.; m. Edythe Lenore Mulzac, Apr. 15, 1949; children: James D., Crystal M. BSBA, U. Dayton, 1948; MA in Pub. Adminstrn., Cen. Mich. U., 1976. Vice pres. Lloyd Lewis Sales and Svc. Inc., Dayton, Ohio, 1950-66; program developer SCOPE, Dayton, 1966; gen. mgr. Rikes div. Federated Dept. Stores, Dayton, 1966-75; asst. city mgr. City of Dayton, 1975-80; asst. v.p. Dayton Power & Light Co., 1980-94; mem. Ohio Ho. of Reps., 1994—; treas. Day-Med HMP, Dayton, 1986—; trustee Miami Valley Automobile Assn., Dayton, 1975—, Franciscan Health Systems Dayton, 1986—. Trustee Dayton Found., 1987—; chmn. St. Elizabeth Med. Ctr., Dayton, 1984-86. 2nd lt. U.S. Army, 1948-50. Recipient Outstanding Achievement award Ohio Planning Conf., 1978, Community Svc. award City of Dayton, 1987, Legion of Honor award President's Club, Dayton, 1988; named Marketeer of Yr. Am. Mktg. Assn.-Dayton, 1983. Mem. Am. Assn. Blacks in Energy, Dayton Sales & Mktg. Execs., Breakfast Optimists (pres. 1971-73), Sigma Pi Phi (Dayton, sire archon 1985-86). Home: 800 Oakleaf Dr Dayton OH 45408-1544 Office: Riffe Ctr 77 S High St Fl 11 Columbus OH 43215-6108

LEWIS, LONA LEE, association executive, educator; b. Topeka, Kans., Jan. 18, 1943; d. Walter Lee and Eunice Pearl (Hudson) Moeller; m. Terry Lynn Lewis, May 25, 1962; 1 child, Dawson Lee. BS in Biology, U. Nebr., 1965, MS, 1970. Tchr. Omaha pub. schs., 1965-68, Parkway Schs., Chesterfield, Mo., 1970-81; instr. biology U. Nebr., Omaha, 1967-70; pres. Mo. NEA, Jefferson City, 1979-80, 1981-85; co-owner TDL, Inc.; cons. jr. high sci. program Rand McNally, Chgo., 1967-75. Pres.-elect. Nat. Council of State Edn. Assns., Washington, 1981-85, coordinating v.p., 1981-84, pres., 1985—; dept. leader biology curriculum ind. study project Title V U.S. Govt., 1975-77. Column writer Educationally Speaking, 1981-85. Del. Dem. Nat. Conv., San Francisco, 1984; exec. dir. S.D. Edn. Assn., 1987—; bd. dirs. Horace Mann Ins., Nat. Found. Improvement Edn. Mem. Nat. Sci. Tchrs. Assn., NEA, Nat. Wildlife Fedn. Avocations: reading; stamp collecting, rehabing houses. Home: 232 Neltom Dr Pierre SD 57501-4807 Office: 411 E Capitol Pierre SD 57501

LEWIS, MARTIN EDWARD, shipping company executive, foreign government concessionary; b. Chgo., Dec. 27, 1958; s. Martin Luther and Anna Adlene (Gaines) L. BA, Johns Hopkins U., 1981; postgrad., Rush Med. Coll., 1983-85. Chmn. bd., chief exec. officer Internat. Financier Inc., Chgo., 1987—; co. rep. Assn. S.E. Asia Nations Secretariat Gen., Jakarta, Indonesia, 1995—; co. rep. OPEC, Vienna, 1988—, Supreme Coun. States of Cooperation Coun., Summit Confs. Countries of Cooperation Coun. for Arab States of Gulf, Secretariat Gen., Riyadh, Saudi Arabia, 1989—; corp. amb. plenipotentiary GM Overseas Ops., N.Y.C., 1977, Adam Opel, Russelsheim, Fed. Republic Germany, 1977. Mem. Asia Soc., Japan Soc. Republican.

LEWIS, RONALD LOREN, health care executive; b. Clinton, Mo., Mar. 28, 1946; s. Lester Clark Jr. and Lois Arlene (Sell) L.; m. Nancy Louise Price, Nov. 12, 1966; children: Kimberly Dawn, Matthew Ryan. BBA, Roosevelt U., 1976; MBA, Rosary Coll., River Forest, Ill., 1979. Bus. ofc. mgr. Condell Meml. Hosp., Libertyville, Ill., 1970-72; asst. to adminstr. Rehab. Inst. Chgo., 1972-75; corp. dir. materials mgmt. Evang. Hosps. Corp., Oak Brook, Ill., 1975-81, v.p. materials mgmt., 1981-82, v.p. shared services, 1982-84, v.p. corp. services, 1984—; resource maximization com. Health First Network, Oak Brook, 1985-86. V.p. bd. dirs. St. Matthew United Ch. Christ, Wheaton, Ill., 1986—, chmn. planning com., 1985-86, chmn. personnel com., 1985-86, pres., 1987—, chmn. bldg. com., 1988—; bd. dirs. Peace United Ch. Residences, 1987—, Immanuel Ch. Residences, 1987—. Served with USN, 1965-70, Vietnam. Mem. Am. Hosp. Assn., Am. Soc. for Materials Mgrs., Am. Mgmt. Assn. Office: Evang Hosps Corp 2025 Windsor Dr Hinsdale IL 60521-1586

LEWIS, STEPHEN A, management executive; b. Carthage, N.Y., Oct. 5, 1948. BSME, Ohio U., 1970, MS in Indsl. Engring., 1973. Gen. mgr. Control DATA Corp., Mpls., 1978-89; pres. S.A. Lewis & Assoc., Mpls., 1989-90; CEO Triad Transp., Inc., Mpls., 1990—; pres., CEO Triad Mgmt., Inc., Mpls., 1990—, Trico Energy Systems, Inc., Mpls., 1994—. Contbr. numerous articles to profl. jours. Leader Boy Scouts of Am., Minn., 1990-94. Office: Trico Energy Systems Inc 2 Appletree Sq 335 Minneapolis MN 55425-1612

LEWIS, STEPHEN RICHMOND, JR., economist, academic administrator; b. Englewood, N.J., Feb. 11, 1939; s. Stephen Richmond and Esther (Magan) L.; children: Virginia, Deborah, Mark. BA, Williams Coll., 1960, LLD, 1987; MA, Stanford U., 1962, PhD, 1963; LHD, Doshisha U., 1993. Instr. Stanford U., 1962-63; research advisor Pakistan Inst. Devel. Econs., Karachi, 1963-65; asst. prof. econs. Harvard U., 1965-66; asst. prof. econs. Williams Coll., 1966-68, assoc. prof., 1968-73, prof., 1973-76, Herbert H. Lehman prof., 1976-87, provost of coll., 1968-71, 73-77, spl. asst. to pres., 1979-80, dir. Williams-Botswana Project, 1982-88, chmn. dept. econs., 1984-86; vis. sr. research fellow Inst. Devel. Studies, Nairobi, Kenya, 1971-73; econ. cons. to Ministry of Finance and Devel. Planning, Govt. of Botswana, 1977—; vis. fellow Inst. Devel. Studies, Sussex, Eng., 1986-87; pres., prof. econs. Carleton Coll., Northfield, Minn., 1987—; cons. econs. Ford Found., Edna McConnell Clark Found., World Bank, Orgn. Econ. Coop. and Devel., Govts. of Kenya, Philippines, Botswana; trustee Carnegie Endowment for Internat. Peace, 1988—. Author: (with others) Relative Price Changes and Industrialization in Pakistan, 1969, Economic Policy and Industrial Growth in Pakistan, 1969, Pakistan: Industrialization and Trade Policy, 1970, Williams in the Eighties, 1980, Taxation for Development, 1983, South Africa: Has Time Run Out?, 1986, Policy Choice and Development Performance in Botswana, 1989, The Economics of Apartheid, 1989; editorial bd. Jour. Econ. Lit., 1985-87. Contbr. chpts. to books, articles to profl. jours. Exec. com. Indianhead coun. Boy Scouts Am., 1989—. Decorated Presdl. Order of Meritorious Svc. (Botswana), 1983; Danforth Found. fellow, 1960-63; Ford Found. dissertation fellow, 1962-63; recipient Disting. Eagle Scout award, 1993. Mem. Council on Fgn. Relations, Nat. Tax Assn., Am. Econ. Assn., Phi Beta Kappa. Office: Carleton Coll Office Pres 1 N College St Northfield MN 55057-4001

LEWIS, VIRGINIA LORRAINE, German language educator, musician; b. Wilmington, Del., July 22, 1960; d. Walter David and Carolyn Wyatt (Brown) L. Student, U. Paris, 1979-80; BA in French and Art History, Auburn (Ala.) U., 1981; MA in German, U. Pa., 1986, PhD in German, 1989; postgrad., U. Hamburg, 1987-88. Lectr. U. Pa., Phila., 1988-89; assoc. prof. Drake U., Des Moines, 1989—, study abroad advisor, 1990-92. Author: Flames of Passion/Flames of Greed: Acts of Arson in German Prose Fiction 1850-1990, 1991, Work and Freedom in the Minority Community: Ferdinand von Saar's Die Troglodytin, The German Mosaic, 1993; contbr. articles to profl. jours. Braille transcriber Iowa Dept. for the Blind, Des Moines, 1989—; mem. Iowa Humanities Bd., 1994-97. Annenberg fellow U. Pa., 1983-87, DAAD fellow Govt. Fed. Republic Germany, Hamburg, 1987-88, Am. Coun. of Learned Socs. grantee, 1995, Drake U. rsch. grantee, 1990-96. Mem. MLA, Am. Assn. Tchrs. German, Am. Coun. Tchrs. Fgn. Langs. (cert. oral proficiency tester), Am. Hungarian Educators Assn., Des Moines Musicians Assn., German Studies Assn., Iowa Humanities Bd., Amana Heritage Soc., Am. Philatelic Soc., Phi Kappa Phi, Pi Delta Phi, Delta Phi Alpha, Phi Sigma Iota. Episcopalian. Office: Drake U Dept Modern Langs and Lits 2507 University Des Moines IA 50311-4505

LEWMAN, SANDRA KAY, stockbroker; b. Paris, Ill., Aug. 26, 1946. Sec. Wall St. of Am., Arkansas City, Kans., 1982-85; stockbroker Profl. Investment Svcs., Arkansas City, 1985—. Mem. Arkansas City C. of C., Soroptomist, Beta Sigma Phi. Republican. Office: Profl Investment Svcs PO Box 253 117 W 5th Ave Arkansas City KS 67005

LEY, LINDA SUE, employee benefits company executive; b. Franklin, Ind., Nov. 27, 1949; d. Jiles Rex and Naomi Katherine (Van Horn) Riggs; m. Thomas Alan Ley, Feb. 28, 1987. BS in Edn. with distinction, Ind. U.-Purdue U., 1971, MS in Edn. with highest distinction, 1975. Cert. paralegal; lic. life, accident, health, property and casualty ins. agt., Ind. Elem. tchr. Indpls. Pub. Schs., 1972-74, Center Grove Community Schs., Greenwood, Ind., 1974-81; dir. adminstrn. Brougher Agy., Inc., Greenwood, 1981-84; mgr. claims/customer svc. The Associated Group, Inc., Indpls., 1984-89; v.p. team ops. Key Benefit Adminstrs., Inc., Indpls., 1989-92; regional mgr. ops. rev. Anthem Benefit Svcs. Corp., Indpls., 1992—. Mem. cotillion com. Humane Soc. Indpls., 1991; vol. Riley Run for Children, Indpls., 1985-92. Recipient Good Girl Citizenship award Women's Aux. of Am. Legion, 1968. Mem. Am. Mgmt. Assn., Nat. Assn. Life Underwriters, Nat. Assn. Health Underwriters, Inst. Internal Auditors, Indpls. Paralegal Assn., Toastmasters Internat. Republican. Episcopalian. Home: 6358 Bluff Acres Dr Greenwood IN 46143-9037 Office: Anthem Health Cos 4040 Vincennes Cir Indianapolis IN 46268

LEY, TIMOTHY JAMES, hematologist, molecular biologist; b. Buffalo Center, Iowa, June 17, 1953; s. William Dean and Clara Ruth (Odland) L.; m. Patricia Ann Hohn, Aug. 21, 1986; children: Amelia, James, Anna. BA, Drake U., 1974; MD, Washington U., St. Louis, 1978. Diplomate Am. Bd. Internal Medicine and Hematology. Resident in medicine Mass. Gen. Hosp., Boston, 1978-80; fellow in hematology NIH, Bethesda, Md., 1980-83, sr. investigator, 1984-86; fellow in hematology and oncology Washington U. Med. Sch., St. Louis, 1983-84, asst. prof. medicine and genetics, 1986-90, assoc. prof. medicine, 1990-93, prof. medicine and genetics, 1993—; dir. Hematopsiesis Rsch. Ctr. Hematopoiesis Rsch. Ctr., St. Louis, 1994—. Contbr. more than 70 articles to profl. jours. Secretary, founding mem. Alison Eberlein Found. for Pediatric Cancer Rsch., Buffalo Center and Washington, 1982-91. With USPHS, 1980-86. Mem. Am. Soc. Hematology, Am. Soc. Biochemistry and Molecular Biology, Am. Fedn. for Clin. Rsch., Am. Soc. for Clin. Investigation, Am. Assn. Physicians, Phi Beta Kappa, Alpha Omega Alpha. Democrat. Presbyterian. Office: Washington U Med Sch Box 8007 660 S Euclid Ave Saint Louis MO 63110

LEYDA, MARGARET LARUE, retired educator, bed and breakfast owner; b. Bloomfield, Iowa, Aug. 25, 1923; d. Ray and Pearl Larue (Coffman) Cary; m. Robert Leyda, June 7, 1940 (div. 1975); children: Constance, Carolyn, Richard, Rodney. BA, McKendree Coll., 1965; MA, So. Ill. U., 1976. Cert. elem. and secondary tchr., media specialist. Tchr. 3d, 4th and 5th grades Wolf Branch Sch., Belleville, Ill., 1960-61; kindergarten tchr. Lebanon (Ill.) Grade Sch., 1961-62; tchr. 5th grade gifted Mascoutah (Ill.) Grade Sch., 1963-68; media ctr. coordinator Triad High Sch., St. Jacob, Ill., 1969-84; owner, operator Maggie's Bed and Breakfast, Collinsville, Ill., 1985—; cons. bed and breakfast workshops U. Ill., Champaign, 1990. Author: (cookbook) Wake Up and Smell the Coffee, 1987. Election judge Dem. Party, Collinsville, 1985—. Mem. Ill. Edn. Assn. (bd. dirs. 1977-84, state legis. com. 1988—), Ret. Tchrs. Assn. (legis. chmn. 1986—), Ill. Bed and Breakfast Assn., AAUW, C. of C., Bus. and Profl. Women. Home & Office: Maggie's Bed & Breakfast 2102 N Keebler Ave Collinsville IL 62234-4713

LEYHANE, FRANCIS JOHN, III, lawyer; b. Chgo., Mar. 29, 1957; s. Francis J. and Mary Elizabeth (Crowley) L.; m. Diana M. Urizarri, May 8, 1982; children: Katherine, Francis J. IV, Joseph, Brigid Rose, James Matthew. BA, Loyola U., Chgo., 1977, JD, 1980. Bar: Ill. 1980, U.S. Dist. Ct. (no. dist.) Ill. 1980, U.S. Ct. Appeals (7th cir.) 1986. Assoc. Condon, Cook & Roche, Chgo., 1980-87; ptnr. Condon & Cook, Chgo., 1988—. Contbr. articles to profl. jours. Mem. Sch. bd. Immaculate Conception Parish, Chgo., 1993-96. Fellow Ill. Bar Found.; mem. Appellate Lawyers Assn. Ill., Ill. State Bar Assn. (mem. assembly 1987-90), Chgo. Bar Assn., Blue Key. Office: Condon & Cook 745 N Dearborn St Chicago IL 60610-3826

L'HEUREUX, DENNIS PAUL, chief health system information officer; b. Woonsocket, R.I., Dec. 1, 1950; s. Bertrand Joseph and Alice (Giguere) L'H.; m. Pauline Emelia Lefrançois, July 1, 1972; children: Christopher, Matthew, Sarah, Stephen. BSIE, Northeastern U., 1974, MS in Engring. Mgmt., 1977. Engring. technician Owens-Corning Fiberglas, Ashton, R.I., 1970-71; indsl. engring. asst. Johnson & Johnson, New Brunswick, N.J., 1971-72; dir. mgmt. systems engr. Haricomp Inc., Providence, 1972-80; assoc. vice chancellor info. resources U. Mass. Med. Ctr., Worcester, 1980-86; v.p. clin. and mgmt. support svcs. Leonard Morse Hosp., Natick, Mass., 1986-91; v.p. info. systems, chief info. officer MetroWest Med. Ctr., Framingham, Mass., 1992-94; corp. v.p. and CIO Rockford (Ill.) Health Sys., 1994—; bd. dirs. West Suburban Joint Diagnostics MRI Ctr., S.W. Suburban Emergency Svcs. Fellow Healthcare Info. and Mgmt. Systems Soc. (bd. dirs. 1981-83, 90-91, pres. 1992); mem. Inst. Indsl. Engring. (sr.), Healthcare Fin. Mgmt. Assn. (sr.), Health Industry Bus. Comms. Coun. (bd. govs. 1994—), Alpha Phi Mu, Tau Beta Pi. Roman Catholic. Home: 4834 Crested Butte Trail Rockford IL 61114-7333

LI, BIYUE, mechanical engineer; b. Shanghia, China, Sept. 6, 1956; came to the U.S., 1986; s. Ouru and Xuexie (Luo) L.; m. Tingyu Wang, Jan. 12, 1986; 1 child, Kathryn. BS in Mech. Engring., Huainan Mining Coll., China, 1982; M in Mech. Engring., U. Akron, 1989. Mech. engr. Shanghia (China) Mining Machinery Rsch. Inst., 1982-86; engring. mgr. Underground Tech.-Am. Augers Inc., Wooster, Ohio, 1988-91; engring. project mgr. Bortec Inc., Solon, Ohio, 1992—. Office: Bortec Inc 24100 Hall Ste #39 PO Box 39306 Solon OH 44139-3909

LI, KAM WU, mechanical engineer, educator; b. China, Feb. 16, 1934; came to U.S., 1959; s. Yang Chung and Oy Lan Li; MS, Colo. State U., 1961; PhD, Okla. State U., 1965; m. Shui Mui Chan, Aug. 30, 1956; children: Christopher, Charles. Asst. prof. mech. engring. Tex. A&M U., Kingsville, 1965-67; assoc. prof. N.D. State U., Fargo, 1967-73, prof., 1973—, assoc. dean engring. and arch., 1989-91, chmn. dept. mech. engring., 1994—; cons. Charles T. Main Inc., Boston, 1973-80, Center for Profl. Advancement, East Brunswick, N.J., 1982-84. Recipient cert. appreciation U.S. Navy, 1974; NSF fellow, 1966; Ford Found. fellow, 1972. Mem. ASME, N.Y. Acad Scis., Sigma Xi, Tau Beta Pi, Pi Tau Sigma, Kappa Mu Epsilon. Author: Power Plant System Design and Applied Thermodynamics. Contbr. numerous articles to profl. jours.; govt. engring. research, 1965—. Home: 2516 18th St S Moorhead MN 56560-4811 Office: ND State U University Ave Fargo ND 58105

LI, YAO-EN, chemical engineer; b. Shanghai, People's Republic of China, Oct. 24, 1958; m. Yi-Yin Ku, May 15, 1959; children: Kory, Katherine. MS, U. Ill., Chgo., 1986, PhD, 1988. Scientist Am. Air Liquide, Countryside, Ill., 1988-89, sr. scientist, 1989—. Contbr. articles to AIChE Jour., Jour. of Catalysis, Jour. Phys. Chemistry, Catalysis Letter, Vacuum. James scholar U. Ill., Chgo., 1984; grad. fellow U. Ill., Chgo., 1985-86. Mem. AIChE, Am. Chem. Soc., Tau Beta Pi.

LIANG, CHING (QING), engineering manager; b. Shanghai, China, May 4, 1961. Mgr. engring. Am. Lifts, Greensburg, Ind., 1989—. Mem. ASME, Golden Key Nat. Honor Soc. Office: Am Lifts 601 W McKee St Greensburg IN 47240

LIANNING, DARREL W., managing consultant; b. Deerborn, Mich., Feb. 8, 1948. Mgr. Motorama Engring., Deerborn Heights, Mich., 1967-84; foreman Models & Tools, Inc., Troy, Mich., 1984-89, br. mgr., 1989—. Office: Models & Tools Inc 1880 E Maple Rd Troy MI 48083-4240

LIBBY, GARY A., sales executive; b. Presque Isle, Maine, Mar. 3, 1946; s. Albion Isaac Libby and Elsie Parker Gibson. BA, U. Maine, 1968, MA, 1972. Sr. forecasting analyst Firestone Tire & Rubber, Akron, Ohio, 1972-80; sales exec. Amway, Ada, Mich., 1980—; owner sporting lodges in Maine. Mem. ch. bd. Evangel Temple, Akron, 1990-92, 94, 95. Sgt. U.S. Army, 1968-71. Decorated Bronze Star.

LIBNOCH, JOSEPH ANTHONY, physician, educator; b. South Bend, Ind., Feb. 1, 1934; s. Casimir Louis and Regina (Kaczorowski) L.; m. Irma Lee Lewis, Jan. 14, 1967 (div. 1984); children: Mark Alan Conine, Michael A., Robert Keith, Sharon M., Andrea E. AB in Chemistry, U. Ill., 1955, MD, 1958. Diplomate Am. Bd. Internal Medicine. Rotating intern Cook County Hosp., Chgo., 1958-59; USPHS fellow in rheumatic disorders U. Ill. Rsch. & Ednl. Hosps., Chgo., 1959-60; resident in internal medicine VA West Side Hosp., Chgo., 1960-62, fellow in hematology, 1962-65; asst. chief hematology Clement J. Zablocki VA Med. Ctr., Milw., 1965-66, 68-75; chief hematology oncology sect. Clement D. Zablocki VA Med. Ctr., Milw., 1976—; acting dir. hematology, oncology sects. Med. Coll. Wis., Milw., 1977-78; instr. medicine Med. Coll. Wis., 1965-66, 68-71, asst. prof. medicine, 1972-88, assoc. prof. clin. medicine, 1988—; sr. attending staff Milwaukee County Med. Complex, 1968-95. Contbr. over 43 articles to profl. jours. Lt. comdr. USNR, 1966-68. Mem. AAAS, Am. Soc. Hematology, Internat. Soc. for Exptl. Hematology, Milw. Hematology Oncology Club, Am. Coll. Rheumatology, Phi Beta Kappa, Phi Beta Phi, Omega Beta Pi, Phi Eta Sigma. Home: 2044 N Lake Dr Milwaukee WI 53202-1333 Office: Clement Zablocki VA Med Ctr 5000 W National Ave Milwaukee WI 53295-0001

LIBRETT, JEFFREY SCOTT, foreign language educator, researcher; b. Port Chester, N.Y., Jan. 19, 1958; s. Irving and Paula (Fink) L. BA in Philosophy, Yale U., 1979; MA in English Lit., Columbia U., 1981; PhD in Comparative Lit., Cornell U., 1989. Rsch. asst. Free U. Berlin, 1984-86, comparative lit. instr., 1986-87; asst. prof. German U. Ariz., Tucson, 1987-88; asst. prof. German Loyola U., Chgo., 1988-94, assoc. prof. German, 1995—; lectr. in field, 1987—. Translator: Du Sublime Of The Sublime, 1993; contbr. articles to profl. jours., translator articles, poems. Big Bro., New Haven, Conn., 1975-79; vol. Halfway-House for Ex-Offenders, New Haven, 1978. Fellow NEH, 1988. Mem. Internat. Assn. Philosophy and Lit., North Am. Soc. for Study of Romanticism, Semiotics Soc. Am., Am. Assn. Tchrs. of German, Modern Lang. Assn., Comparative Lit. Assn. Democrat. Jewish. Office: Loyola U 6525 N Sheridan Rd Chicago IL 60626-5311

LICHLYTER, SHARON M., nurse; b. Huntingburg, Ind., Sept. 7, 1952; d. Daniel J. and Jenevea M. (Kraft) L. ADN, Vincennes U., 1973; BSN, U. Evansville, 1987. Staff nurse Good Samaritan Hosp., Vincennes, Ind., 1973-76; staff nurse, med. surg. St. Mary's Med. Ctr., Evansville, Ind., 1976-83, staff nurse, progressive care, 1984-91; staff nurse telemetry unit Deaconess Hosp., Inc., Evansville, Ind., 1990-92; nurse Ind. State Dept. Health, Indpls., 1992—, pub. health nurse surveyor longterm care-complaints divsn., 1994—; adj. prof. Ind. Vocat. Tech. Coll., 1991-92; Pub. Health Nurse surveyor Divsn. Acute Care Svcs. Mem. ANA, Am. Lung Assn. (bd. dirs.), ARC, Ind. Nurses Assn. (mem. sec.). Home: 1731 Bonnie View Dr Evansville IN 47715-6180

LICHT, CHARLES A., mechanical engineer, consultant; b. N.Y.C., Oct. 15, 1924; s. Benjamin Herman and Frances L.; m. Phyllis Aaron, Nov. 25, 1951 (dec. July 1970); children: Heidi Licht, Jonathan Licht, Lisa Licht Glatz; m. Dolores Jean Lewin, Feb. 13, 1971; stepchildren: Richard Hollander, Alan Hollander, Lori Hollander Rusk. BS in Mech. Engring., MIT, 1948, BSBA, 1949. Registered profl. engr. 21 states. Constrn. engr. Am. Steel Foundries, East Chgo., Ill., 1948-50; works mgr. Specialloy, Inc., Chgo., 1950-53; rsch. engr. Apex Smelting Co., Cleve., 1953-54; chief engr. U.S. Reduction Co., East Chgo., 1954-65; plant mgr. U.S. Reduction Co., Ontario, Calif., 1965-66; v.p. tech. svcs. U.S. Reduction Co., East Chgo., 1966-68; pres., chief engr. Chas. Licht Engring. Assocs. Inc., Olympia Fields, Ill., 1968—. Bd. commrs. Olympia Fields park dist., 1960-64; mem. Olympia Fields zoning bd. appeals, 1969-75, Butterfield Creek flood control commn., Flossmoor, Ill., 1990-92. Lt. (j.g.) USNR, 1943-46, PTO. Mem. ASME (life), NSPE, AIME, Air and Waste Mgmt. Assn. (chair environ. mgmt. divsn. 1981-91), Am. Soc. for Metals (life), Am. Assn. Environ. Engrs. (diplomate). Office: Chas Licht Engring Assoc PO Box 315 Olympia Fields IL 60461-0315

LICHTEN, NANCY G., chemical company executive; b. Indpls., Jan. 26, 1960; d. Saul Leonard and Judith Gale (Levine) Thomashow; m. Jeffrey Lichten, Apr. 10, 1988; children: Francine Mills, Sydney Brown. BA, Nat. Coll Edn. M.C. Louis U., 1983. Freelance fundraising and pub. rels. coord., 1983-85; endowment coord. Highland Pk. (Ill.) Hosp., 1985; asst. to dir. acctg. Pioneer Press, Wilmette, Ill., 1985-87; billing coord. Pioneer Press, Wilmette, 1987-88, credit collector, 1988-89, circulation cashier, 1989-90; treas. Black Swan Mfg. Co., Chgo., 1988—. Tchr. North Shore Congregation Israel, Glencoe, Ill., 1976-81, collector, 1985, v.p. young couples club; solicitor Cancer Crusade, Chgo., 1984-85; counselor Drop-in Ctr., Wilmette Youth Orgn., 1983; coord. Mother in Touch, Northbrook, 1990-92. Home: 690 Marion Ave Highland Park IL 60035-5122 Office: Black Swan Mfg Co 4540 W Thomas St Chicago IL 60651-3318

LICHTWARDT, ROBERT WILLIAM, mycologist; b. Rio de Janeiro, Nov. 27, 1924; s. Henry Herman and Ruth Moyer Lichtwardt; m. Elizabeth Thomas, Jan. 27, 1951; children: Ruth Elizabeth, Robert Thomas. AB, Oberlin Coll., 1949; MS, U. Ill., 1951, PhD, 1954. Postdoctoral fellow NSF, Panama, Brazil, 1954-55; postdoctoral rsch. assoc. Iowa State U., Ames, 1955-57; asst. prof. U. Kans., Lawrence, 1957-60, assoc. prof., 1960-65; sr. postdoctoral fellow NSF, Hawaii, Japan, 1963-64; prof. U. Kans., Lawrence, 1965-94, prof. emeritus, 1994—. Author: The Trichomycetes, Fungal Associates of Arthropods, 1986; contbr. 95 articles to profl. jours. Mem. Mycological Soc. Am. (life, pres. 1971-72, editor-in-chief 1965-70, William H. Weston award for tchg. excellence in mycology 1982, Disting. Mycologist award 1991), Brit. Mycological Soc., Japan Mycological Soc. (hon.). Office: U Kans Dept Of Botany Lawrence KS 66045

LICKHALTER, MERLIN EUGENE, architect; b. St. Louis, May 4, 1934; s. Frank E. and Sophia (Geller) L.; m. Harriet Braen, June 9, 1957; children: Debra, Barbara. BArch, MIT, 1957. Registered arch., Mo., Ill., Calif., Fla., Mich., Wis., Nev., Tex., Ala., Okla., Va. Ptnr. Drake Partnership, Architects, St. Louis, 1961-77; pres. JRB Architects, Inc., St. Louis, 1977-81; sr. v.p., mng. dir. Stone, Marraccini & Patterson, St. Louis, 1981-93; sr. v.p., dir. Cannon, 1993—; owner, pres. mgmt. program Harvard U. Bus. Sch., 1992; cons. Dept. Def., Washington, 1977-78; lectr. Washington U. Sch. Medicine, 1989—. Trustee United Hebrew Cong., St. Louis, 1980-88, 93—; exec. com. bd. dirs. Arts & Edn. Coun. St. Louis, 1991—. Capt. U.S. Army, 1957-59. Recipient Renovation Design award St. Louis Producers Coun., 1976, USAF Europe Design Award, 1990. Mem. AIA (nat. acad. architect for health, chmn. 1993), Am. Hosp. Assn., Am. Assn. for Health Planning, St. Louis Regional Growth Assn., Hawthorn Found., St. Louis Club, St. Louis Ambs., Frontenac Racquet Club, Masons. Jewish. Home: 2 Warson Ln Ladue MO 63124-1251 Office: Cannon One City Ctr Saint Louis MO 63101

LIDSTROM, CARL FRANCIS, risk management consultant; b. Fargo, N.D., July 5, 1949; s. C.F. and Frances E. (Lethenstrom) L.; m. Mary Susanne Shuster, Aug. 24, 1972; children: Cal, Sara. BA, Moorhead State U., 1975. CPCU, Am. Inst. for Chartered Property Casualty Underwriters; assoc. in risk mgmt. Ins. Inst. Am.; cert. ins. counselor Soc. of Cert. Ins. Counselors. Asst. state dir. N.D. State Approving Agy., Fargo, 1975-78; pres. CAMM Properties Inc., Ely, Minn., 1978; sales rep. Wausau Ins. Cos., Mpls., 1979-80; mktg. specialist Risk Planners, Inc., Mpls., 1980-83; sales rep. First Ins., Mpls., 1983-84; risk mgmt. cons. Risk Control Inc., Excelsior, Minn., 1984-87, Shea & Lidstrom, Inc., Mpls., 1987-88; pres. Profl. Risk Mgmt., Inc., Eden Prairie, Minn., 1988—; instr. for the assoc. in risk mgmt. program Minn. Chpt. CPCU, Edina, Minn. With USN, 1968-72. Mem. CPCU Soc., Soc. Cert. Ins. Counselors, Minn. Chpt. CPCU (bd. dirs.), Twin Cities Ins. Club, Soc. Risk Mgmt. Cons., Minn. Pub. Risk & Ins. Mgmt. Assn. (assoc. mem.), Minn. Assn. Sch. Bus. Ofcls. Office: Profl Risk Mgmt Inc Ste 255 9979 Valley View Rd Eden Prairie MN 55344

LIE, JOHN JAEHOON, sociology educator; b. Seoul, Korea, Nov. 5, 1959; Came to U.S., 1970.; s. Harry K. and Jane W. (Lee) Lie. AB, Harvard U., 1982, PhD, 1988. Asst. prof. U. Oreg., Eugene, 1989-92; assoc. prof. U. Ill., Urbana, 1992-96, head, sociology dept., 1996—. Editor: The Impoverished Spirit in Contemporary Japan, 1993, (with Nancy Abelmann) Blue Dreams, 1995; contbr. article to prof. jour. Mem. Am. Sociol. Assn. Office: Univ Ill 702 S Wright St 702 S Wright St Urbana IL 61801-3631

LIEBERMAN, DOUGLAS LIONEL, scriptwriter, software writer; b. Detroit, Mich., Dec. 14, 1946; s. Barnard Leon and Mary Elizabeth (McKinney) L.; m. Beverly Anne Berneman,. AB, Columbia U., 1968; MFA, Art Inst. Chgo., 1972. Mem. Cranbrook Sch., Bloomfield Hills, Mich., 1968-70; mem. faculty Art Inst. Chgo., 1970-74; lectr. Northwestern U., Evanston, Ill., 1978-86, Loyola U., Chgo., 1984-86; pres. Rocket Riter, Inc., Skokie, Ill., 1988—; bd. chmn. Imagination Celebration, Chgo., 1973-74. Author: (play) Contemporary Children's Theatre, 1973; editor: Pre-Med: Foundation of a Medical Career, 1968; scriptwriter documentaries including Choosing One's Way (Hugo award Chgo. Film Festival 1994), 1993. Mem. bd. edn., dist. 69, Skokie, IL. Recipient silver medal awards N.Y. FilmFestival, 1979, 1982, bronze medal, 1984, 9 Golden Eagle awards CINE Film Festival, Washington, D.C., 1982, 1985-86, 1989-90, 1992, 1st and 2d place Western Film Showcase, Canada, 1990, Creative Excellence award U.S. Indsl. Film Festival; named Favorite Tchr. Detroit News, 1968. Mem. Halevi Choral Soc. (Chgo.). Office: Rocket Riter Inc 5331 Monroe St Skokie IL 60077-2453

LIEBERMAN, EUGENE, lawyer; b. Chgo., May 17, 1918; s. Harry and Eva (Goldman) L.; m. Pearl Naomi Feldman, Aug. 3, 1947; children: Mark, Robert, Steven. JD, DePaul U., 1940. Bar: Ill. 1940, U.S. Supreme Ct. 1963. Mem. firm Jacobs and Lieberman, 1954-60; sr. ptnr. Jacobs, Lieberman and Aling, 1960-74; spl. hearing officer U.S. Dept. Justice, 1967-78; hearing officer Ill. Pollution Control Bd., 1973—; pvt. practice, Chgo. Contbr. articles to legal publs. With U.S. Army, 1942-45, PTO. Recipient 1st in State award Moot Ct. Championship, 1940, Gold award Philatelic Exhbn., Taipei, 1981, Gold award World Philatelic Exhbn., Melbourne, 1984, Meritorious Svc. medal, others. Mem. Ill. State Bar Assn. (sr. counsellor 1991), Chgo. Bar Assn., Appellate Lawyers Assn., Chgo. Philatelic Soc. (pres. 1964-68), Ill. Athletic Club. Home: 801 Leclaire Ave Wilmette IL 60091-2065

LIEBERTHAL, KENNETH GUY, political science educator; b. Asheville, N.C., Sept. 9, 1943; s. Milton Morton and Naomi Ruth (Burd) L.; m. Jane Lindsay, June 15, 1968; children: Keith, Geoffrey. BA with distinction, Dartmouth Coll., 1965; MA, Columbia U., 1968, PhD, 1972. Instr. to prof. polit. sci. Swarthmore (Pa.) Coll., 1972-83; prof. U. Mich., Ann Arbor, 1983—, rsch. assoc. Ctr. for Chinese Studies, 1983—; Arthur F. Thurnau prof. polit. sci., 1995—; William Davidson prof. bus. adminstrn. U. Mich., Ann Arbor, 1995—, faculty assoc. Ctr. for Russian and East European STudies, 1984—; faculty assoc. William Davidson Inst., 1996—; mem. faculty global leadership program Sch. Bus. Adminstrn. U. Mich., Ann Arbor, 1990—; cons. Rand Corp., Santa Monica, Calif., 1975-82, U.S. Dept. State, Washington, 1978-91, World Bank, Washington, 1987—, Kettering Found., Dayton, Ohio, 1989—; bd. dirs. Nat. Com. on U.S.-China Rels., 1990—. Author: Revolution and Tradition in Tientsin, 1980, Governing China: From Revolution through Reform, 1995; co-author: Policy Making in China, 1988; co-editor, contbg. author: Bureaucracy, Politics and Policy Making in Post-Mao China, 1991, Perspectives on Modern China, 1991; mem. editl. bd. China Econ., 1990—, China Quar., 1991—, Contemporary China, 1995—. Bd. dirs. Hillel Found., Ann Arbor, 1991-93; mem. Econ. Dinner Group, Ann Arbor, 1991—; v.p., bd. dirs. Beth Israel Congregation, Ann Arbor, 1985-90. Rsch. grantee Henry Luce Found., 1988—, NEH, 1991-96. Mem. Am. Polit. Sci. Assn., Assn. for Asian Studies, Coun. on Fgn. Rels. Office: U Mich Ctr for Chinese Studies 104 Lane Hall Ann Arbor MI 48109-1290

LIEBL, DALE JOSEPH, manufacturing engineer; b. Clarkfield, Minn., Oct. 1, 1962. Quality assurance engr. Dale Electronics, Yankton, S.D., 1986-88, quality assurance supr., 1988-90; supr. prodn. Innovex Inc., Montevideo, Minn., 1990-92, supr. engring., 1992—. Cub master Boy Scouts Am., 1995. Roman Catholic. Office: Innovex Inc 1602 Benson Rd Montevideo MN 56265-1118

LIEBMAN, TODD JUSTIN, lawyer; b. Milw., June 28, 1962; s. Albert and Laurel Jeanm (Boalmann) L.; m. Sandra Marie Sorce, Nov. 22, 1986; children: Justin todd, Alyssa Marie. BA, U. Wis., 1987, JD, 1990. Bar: Wis. Law clk. Loeb & Ching S.C., Madison, Wis., 1988-90; assoc. Kissel Law Office, Hartford, Wis., 1993; corp. counsel Sauk County, Baraboo, Wis., 1994—. Capt. U.S. Army, 1990-93. Mem. State Bar Wis. (co-chair), Wis. Assn. County Cour. Counsel (standing com.), Am. Legion, Rotary. Roman Catholic. Home: 526 Naragansett Ave Baraboo WI 53913 Office: Sauk County 515 Oak St Baraboo WI 53913

LIEBOVICH, LOUIS WILLIAM, journalist, educator; b. Rockford, Ill., Jan. 2, 1949; s. Albert Abraham and Dorothy Evelyn (Pollard) L.; m. Shirley Ann Townsend, June 13, 1971; children: Cynthia, Andrew, Rebecca. BA in History, U. Ill., 1971, MS in Journalism, 1972; PhD in Mass Communication, U. Wis., 1986. Reporter Rockford Register-Republic, 1972-76; investigative reporter, asst. city editor Milw. Sentinel, 1976-80; instr. U. Wis., Milw., 1980-81, Whitewater, 1982-85; asst. prof. U. Ill., Urbana, 1985-91, assoc. prof., 1991—. Editor: The Last Jew From Wegrow, 1991; author: The Press and the Origins of the Cold War 1944-47, 1988, Bylines in despair: Herbert Hoover, the Great Depression, and the U.S. News Media, 1994; contbr. articles to profl. jours. Recipient 10 newspaper reporting awards Wis. Newspaper Assn., 1977, 78; grantee Herbert C. Hoover Presdl. Libr., 1989, 92, Harry S. Truman Presdl. Libr., 1984. Mem. Am. Journalism Historians Assn., Assn. for Edn. in Journalism and Mass Comms., 1984—, Sigma Delta Chi. Jewish. Office: U Ill Dept Journalism 119 Gregory 810 S Wright St Urbana IL 61801-3611

LIEBOVICH, SAMUEL DAVID, warehouse executive; b. Rockford, Ill., Sept. 19, 1946; s. Albert A. and Dorothy (Pollard) L.; m. Erna Susan Horewitch, Oct. 1, 1966; children: Elaine Beth, Mitchell Phillip. BS magna cum laude, Bradley U., 1969; postgrad., U. Ill., 1969-70. Dir. purchasing Liebovich Bros. Inc., Rockford, 1970-80, v.p. purchasing and inventory, 1980-82, pres. nat. sales, 1982—. Bd. dirs. Rockford Symphony Orch., 1994-96; mem. allocations com. United Way, Rockford, 1987-88; bus. chmn. Statue of Liberty Com., Rockford, 1986-87; fin. sec., bd. dirs. Temple Beth El, Rockford, 1975-79, treas., 1993-94; v.p. Temple Bethel, 1995-96; chair United Jewish Appeal Greater Rockford Area, 1988-89; pres. Ohave Shalom Synagogue, Rockford, 1977-79, pres. Greater Rockford Jewish Fedn., 1989-92, Wallenberg Com., Rockford, 1988-89. Mem. Nat. Assn. Aluminum Distbrs. (nat. com. 1979-85), Nat. Assn. Steel Distbrs. (bd. dirs. 1990-92, v.p. 1992-93, exec. v.p. 1994-95, pres. 1995-96, Pres. award 1993, 94), Am. Soc. for Metal, Internat. Kiwanis (fellow award), Alpine Kiwanis (bd. dirs., sec., v.p., pres.-elect 1988-95, pres.), Ill.-Iowa Dist. 6 Kiwanis (lt. gov.-elect divsn. 12 1995-96, lt. gov. dist. 12 1996-97), Rockford B'nai B'rith (pres. 1973-76), Masons, Shriners, Mau-Nah-Tee-See Country Club. Republican. Jewish. Home: 5540 Roanoke Rd Rockford IL 61107-1748 Office: Liebovich Bros Inc 2116 Preston St Rockford IL 61102-1975

LIEBSCHUTZ, DAVID H., business consultant; b. Cin., Mar. 19, 1914; s. Leon and Goldie (Fleck) L.; m. Edith Leshner, Aug. 7, 1950; children: Linda, Patricia, Amy. Maj. USAF. Recipient (4) Army Air Force ribbons, 1946-47. Mem. Reform Hebrew Ch. Home: Amberley Village 7460 Aracoma Forest Dr Cincinnati OH 45237

LIEDER, BERNARD L., state legislator, civil engineer; m. Shirley B. Lieder; three children. Student, U. Ill., Purdue U. Engineer; Dist. 2A rep. Minn. Ho. of Reps., St. Paul, 1984—; vice chmn. agr., transp. and semi-state divsn. appropriations com., chmn. transp. fin. divsn. appropriations Minn. Ho. of Reps.; mem. local govt. and met. affairs and transp. coms.; former chmn. ethics com.; mem. capital investments, econ. devel., infrastructure and regulation fin. coms. Home: 911 Thorndale Ave Crookston MN 56716-1150*

LIEM, DARLENE MARIE, secondary education educator; b. Lorain, Ohio, June 25, 1941; d. Frederick August and Mary Jane (Derby) Kubishke; m. Frans Robert Liem; children: Dorothea Saliba, Frans Liem, Raymond Liem, Bryan Liem, Shannon Daniel. BS in Edn., Ohio State U., 1963; ME, Wright State U., 1980. Cert. secondary tchr., Ohio. Sci. tchr. Southwestern City Schs., Grove City, Ohio, 1963-66, Greeneview High Sch., Jamestown, Ohio, 1973—; advisor Quick Recall Team, Jamestown, 1984—, NASA Student Shuttle Projects, Regional winners, 1981, 82; dir. Ramblers Drill Team, Jamestown, 1973-77; adv. TEAMS, 1991—. Contbr. articles to profl. jours. Mem. Huber Heights (Ohio) Community Chorus, 1989-90; girl scout leader Huber Heights Girl Scout Troop, 1976-78; children's choir dir., Huber Heights, 1980-84, Sunday sch. tchr., Huber Heights, 1978-83; summer camp dir. Kirkmont Presbyn. Camp, Bellefontaine, Ohio, 1978-83; ordained elder Presbyn. Ch. Named Outstanding Educator Green County Bd. Edn., 1988-89, 92, Woman of Yr. Am. Bus. Women's Assn., 1988, West Region Project Discovery Tchr.-Leader, 1992—, Tandy Tech. Hon. Mention Tchr., 1994. Mem. Nat. Sci. Tchrs. Assn., Sci. Edn. Coun. Ohio (bd. dirs. 1981-83), Am. Assn. Physics Tchrs. (South Ohio sect.), Western Ohio Sci. Tchrs. Assn. (pres. 1981-83), Delta Kappa Gamma, Phi Delta Kappa, Kappa Delta Pi. Home: 7056 Montague Rd Dayton OH 45424-3044 Office: Greeneview High Sch 53 N Limestone St Jamestown OH 45335-1550

LIEM, KHIAN KIOE, medical entomologist; b. Semarang, Java, Indonesia, Jan. 11, 1942; came to U.S., 1969; s. Coen Ing T and Marie Soei-Nio (Goei) L.; m. Anita Tumewu, Apr. 3, 1980; children: Brian Dexter, Tiffany Marie, Jennifer Amanda, Ashley Elizabeth. BS, Bandung Inst. Tech., Bandung, Indonesia, 1964; MS, Bandung Inst. Tech., 1966, Eastern Ill. U., 1970; PhD, U. Ill., 1975. Registered profl. entomologist, vector ecologist. Grad. teaching asst. Bandung Inst. Tech., 1964-66, grad. instr., 1966-68; grad. rsch./teaching asst. Eastern Ill. U., 1969-70; grad. teaching asst. U. Ill., 1970-74; med. entomologist South Cook County Mosquito Abatement Dist., Harvey, Ill., 1974-76; mgr./dir. med. entomologist South Cook County Mosquito Abatement Dist., Harvey, 1977—; cons. U.S. AID, Washington, 1979--. Recipient Community Svc. award Asian Am. Coalition, 1993. Mem. Am. Mosquito Control Assn. (chmn. resolution com. 1977-78, mem. editorial bd. 1980-83, mem. worldwide com. 1987—), Ill. Mosquito Control Assn. (pres. 1979-81), Entomol. Soc. Am. (com. on book revs.), Am. Tropical Medicine and Hygiene Assn., Am. Registry of Profl. Entomologists, Scientists Inst. Pub. Info., Soc. Vector Ecology, Sigma Xi, Phi Sigma. Roman Catholic. Home: 8012 Binford Dr Orland Park IL 60462-2300 Office: Mosquito Abatement Dist 15440 Dixie Hwy Harvey IL 60426-2801

LIEMMEN, STEVE JAY, engineering manager; b. Green Bay, Wis., Nov. 21, 1963. AD, Northeastern Wis. Tech. Coll., 1984. Mgr. engring. MJR Industries, Menominee, Mich., 1986-91, Piper-Doyon Group, Green Bay, Wis., 1991—. Mem. APEX, Soc. Mfg. Engrs. Office: Piper-Doyon Group 1100 N Irwin Ave Green Bay WI 54302-1543

LIEN, BRUCE HAWKINS, minerals and oil company executive; b. Waubay, S.D., Apr. 7, 1927; s. Peter Calmer and LaRece Catherine (Holm) L.; m. Deanna Jean Browning, May 4, 1978. BS in Bus., Wyo. U., 1953; D of Bus. (hon.), S.D. Sch. Mines & Tech., 1996. Chmn. bd. Pete Lien & Sons, Inc., Rapid City, S.D., 1944-84, bd. chmn., 1984—; chmn. Concorde Gaming Corp., 1990—, Browning Resources U.S., 1989—. Chmn. Community Chest, Rapid City, S.D., 1956; pres., nat. council Boys Club Am., Rapid City, S.D., N.Y.C., 1968; commr. Presdl. Scholars Commn., Washington, 1982; pres. U. Wyo, Found., 1989-90; life bd. dirs. Salvation Army. Served to 1st lt. U.S. Army, 1945-47, 50-52. Recipient Disting. Service award S.D. Sch. Mines, Rapid City, 1972, Disting. Service award Cosmopolitan Internat., Rapid City, 1983; named Disting. Alumnus, Wyo. U., Laramie, 1982. Mem. Internat. Lime Assn. (pres. 1973-75), Nat. Lime Assn. (pres. 1973-75, Merit award 1973, bd. dirs.), VFW, Am. Legion. Republican. Lutheran. Club: Cosmopolitan (Rapid City, S.D.). Lodges: Masons, Elks. Home: PO Box 440 Rapid City SD 57709-0440 Office: Pete Lien & Sons Inc I 90 & Deadwood Ave PO Box 440 Rapid City SD 57709-0440

LIENEMANN, DELMAR ARTHUR, SR., accountant, real estate developer; b. Papillion, Nebr., May 17, 1920; s. Arthur Herman and Dorothea M. (Marth) L.; m. Charlotte Peck, Jun 17, 1944; children: Delmar Arthur Jr., David (dec.), Diane, Douglas, Dorothy, Daniel, Denise. BS, U. Nebr., 1941. CPA, Nebr. Acct. Wickstrom Supply, Lincoln, Nebr., 1941, L.L. Coryell & Sons, Lincoln, 1942, Lester Buckley, CPA, Lincoln, 1943-45; pvt. practice Lincoln, 1945—. Pres., v.p., sec., treas., bldg. chmn., charter mem. Christ Luth. Ch., Lincoln, 1949-70; co-commr. Lancaster County, Lincoln, 1954-58; pres. Lincoln Symphony Orch. Found., 1984—, Ethel S. Abbott Charitable Found. Mem. AICPAs, N.E. Soc. CPAs, Colo. Soc. CPAs, Tex. Soc. CPAs, Sertoma (sec.-treas. Lincoln chpt. 1952-68, Internat. Sertoman of Yr. 1962), Hillcrest Country Club, Nebr. Club, Nebr. Chancelors Club, Nebr. Touchdown Club, Nebr. Power Club, Nebr. Rebounders Club. Republican. Office: PO Box 81407 Lincoln NE 68501-1407

LIER, NANCY JEAN, medical educator, administrator; b. Breckenridge, Mich., Sept. 21, 1942; d. Joseph and Lucinda Martha (Feltman) Smolek; m. James William Lier, June 20, 1964; 1 child, Thomas James. BS, Madonna U., 1964; postgrad., U. Kans., 1976-77; MS in Sci. Adminstrn., Cen. Mich. U., 1985. Supr. immunohematology St. Mary's Med. Ctr., Saginaw, Mich., 1964-66, 67-68, supr. bacteriology, 1968-69, dir. sch. med. tech., 1967—; staff technologist Flint (Mich.) Med. Lab., 1966-67; acad. appointments include Grad Valley State U., Allendale, Mich., 1967—, Ctrl. Mich. U., Mt. Pleasant, 1967-92, Saginaw Valley State U., University Center, Mich., 1967—, Madonna U., Livonia, Mich., 1967—, Mich. Tech. U., Houghton, 1967—. Vol. Boy Scouts Am., Frankenmuth, Mich., 1972-83. Mem. Am. Soc. Clin. Pathologists (cert. med. technologist), Am. Soc. Med. Technologists. Republican. Roman Catholic. Office: St Mary's Med Ctr 830 S Jefferson Ave Saginaw MI 48601-2522

LIESE, CHRISTOPHER A., benefits and financial consulting company owner, state legislator; b. St. Louis, Mar. 24, 1963; s. Albert Joseph and Rose Clare (Kaufmann) L.; m. Sheila Marie Bercier, May 8, 1993. BA, St. Louis U., 1985. CFP. Owner Liese & Assocs., St. Louis; state legislator State of Mo. Legal intern Legal Svcs. for Ea. Mo., Inc., 1984-85; vol. athletic instr. Mo. Athletic Club, 1983—; mem. St. John Bosco Ch., St. Blaise Alumni Com., Mo. River Twp. Dem. Club, N.W. River Twp. Dem. Club, Young Dems. Greater St. Louis. Mem. Mo. Assn. Life Underwriters, Maryland Heights/Westport C. of C. (econ. devel. com. 1990, 91), Jaycees, Delta Sigma Phi (pres. 1983-84). Home: 1948 Marine Terrace Dr Saint Louis MO 63146-2585 Office: State Capital House of Rep House PO Box 65101 Jefferson City MO 65101*

LIETZ, JEREMY JON, educational administrator, writer; b. Milw., Oct. 4, 1933; s. John Norman and Dorothy B. (Drew) L.; m. Cora Fernandez, Feb. 24, 1983; children: Cheryl, Brian, Angela, Andrew, Christopher. BS, U. Wis., Milw., 1961; MS, U. Wis., Madison, 1971; EdD, Marquette U., 1980. Tchr. Milw. Pub. Schs., 1961-63, diagnostic counselor, 1968-71; sch. adminstr., 1971-95; Tchr. Madison (Wis.) Pub. Schs., 1964-65; rsch. assoc. U. Wis., Madison, 1965-67; instr. Marquette U., Milw., 1980-82; lectr. HEW Conf. on Reading, Greeley, Colo., 1973, NAESP Conf. on Reading, St. Louis, 1974, various state and nat. orgns.; co-founder, bd. dirs., cons. Ednl. Leadership Inst., Shorewood, Wis., 1980—; dir. Religious Edn. Program, Cath. Elem. East, Milw., 1985-86. Author: The Elementary School Principal's Role in Special Education, 1982; contbr. numerous articles, chpts., tests, revs. to profl. jours. V.p. PTA, 1961-62. With U.S. Army, 1954-56, ETO. Recipient Cert. of Achievement award NAESP, 1974. Mem. AAAS, Assn. Wis. Sch. Adminstrs. (mem. state planning com. 1977-79, lectr. 1982), Adminstrs. and Suprs. Coun. (mem. exec. bd. dist. 1977-79, mem. contract negotiations com. 1991-95), Filipino Am. Assn. Wis., U. Wis. Alumni Assn. (Madison), Milw. Mcpl. Chess Assn., U.S. Chess Fedn., Phi Delta Kappa. Home: 2205 N Summit Ave Milwaukee WI 53202-1213 Office: Ednl Leadership Inst PO Box 11411 Milwaukee WI 53211-0411

LIETZEN, JOHN HERVY, human resources executive, health agency volunteer; b. Kansas City, Kans., July 17, 1947; s. Walter Edwin and Kathleen Mae (Griffith) L.; children: Gwendolyn Therese, Anne Gabrielle, Sarah Kathleen. BS, Mo. Valley Coll., 1974; MS, U. Mo., 1976; postgrad, U. Nebr., 1982-88. With Union Pacific R.R., 1971—; yard condr. Union Pacific R.R., Kansas City, Kans., 1971-77; pers. officer Union Pacific R.R., Omaha, 1977-78; pers. dir. Union Pacific R.R., Cheyenne, Wyo., 1978-79, sr. tng. officer dept. claims, 1979-83, mgr. staffing, 1983-84, mgr. affirmative action, 1984-86; human resources tng. and devel. cons. Union Pacific R.R., Salt Lake City, 1986-93, Omaha, 1994—. Bd. dirs. Berkshire Village, Kansas City, 1976-77; bd. ministries Valley View Meth. Ch., Overland Pk., Kans., 1976-77; pastor and staff rels. com. Hanscom Pk. United Meth. Ch., 1980-81, lay leader, 1983; asst. leader Wyo. coun. Girl Scouts U.S.A., Cheyenne, 1978-79, asst. leader, Omaha, 1980-89, Salt Lake, 1989—, bd. dirs. Great Plains Girl Scout Coun., 1987-89; exec. bd. Nebr. affiliate Am. Diabetes Assn., 1981-89, pres. Midlands chpt., 1982-84, mem. planning and orgn. com., 1986-87, bd. dirs. Utah affiliate, 1990-94, co-founder Omaha Insulin Pump Club, 1986; loaned exec. United Way of Midlands, 1984. Sgt. U.S. Army, 1968-71, Germany. Mem. ASTD, Am. Soc. Personnel and Guidance Assn., Adult and Continuing Edn. Assn. Nebr. (planning com. 1982-84), Nat. Soc. for Performance and Instrn. Republican. Office: 1416 Dodge-OTC Omaha NE 68179

LIFFNER, GLORIA, food products executive. Pres. Famous Fido's Specialty Foods, Chgo. Office: Famous Fido's Specialty Foods 2560 N Elston Chicago IL 60647*

LIFSCHUTZ, EMANUEL LEWIS, clergy member; b. N.Y.C., June 3, 1907; s. Hyman and Flora (Lewis) L.; married; children: Shelley Lifschutz Bnuch, David, Jonathan. BA, CUNY, 1932; MA, Yeshiva U., N.Y.C., 1952; PhD, Calif. Grad. Sch. Theology, Glendale, 1981; DHL (hon.), Jewish Theol. Sem. Am., N.Y.C., 1969. Ordained rabbi, 1932; cert. psychotherapist, Ill. Rabbi Instnl. Synagogue, N.Y.C., 1937-43; chief rabbi Ottawa (Can.) Jewish Cmty., 1946-51; rabbi Spanish Portugese Synagogue, Phila., 1951-59, Temple Menorah, Milw., 1959-61; cmty. chaplain Milw. Kee Jewish Fedn., 1962-80; pscyiatric chaplain VA Hosp., Milw., 1967-92; retired, 1992—; clin. prof. dept. psychiatry and mental health scis. Med. Coll. Wis., 1980, asst. clin. prof. dept. medicine, 1982-93. Chmn. N.E. Fed. Housing Com., Phila., 1953-55. Chaplain USN, 1943-46. Recipient Anton T. Boisen award Assn. Mental Health, 1980. Mem. Rabbinical Assembly Am., N.Y. Bd. Rabbis, Chgo. Bd. Rabbis, Wis. Coun. Rabbis, Milw. County Chaplains Assn. (chmn. ad hoc com. 1965-66), Assn. Mental Health Chaplains (pres. 1976-78), Zionist Orgn. Am. (pres. Milw. club 1960-61), Masons. Home: 1600 W Green Tree Rd Milwaukee WI 53209-2948

LIFTON, FRED BERNARD, lawyer; b. Detroit, Sept. 24, 1928; s. Isidore and Esther (Zieve) L.; m. Roselle Unatin, June 26, 1949; children: Michelle, Janisse, Claudia, Robert. AB, Wayne U., 1949, JD, 1951. Bar: Mich. 1952, Ill. 1957. Ptnr. Lifton & Lifton, Detroit, 1952; asst. dir. Mich. State Waterways Com., Detroit, 1952-55, dir., 1955-57; legis. coord. Boating Industry Assn., Chgo., 1957-67, exec. dir., 1967-70; prin. Robbins, Schwartz, Nicholas, Lifton & Taylor, Ltd., Chgo., 1970—; advisor Am. Assn. Sch. Adminstrs., Arlington, Va., 1979—. Co-author: (booklet) Bargaining Analyzer, 1974; contbr. articles to profl. jours. Pres. bd. Sch. Dist. 68, Skokie, Ill., 1960-67; bd. edn. Sch. Dist. 219, Skokie, 1967-70. Recipient Boating Safety Man of Yr. award Nat. Assn. State Boating Law Adminstrs., 1970, Outstanding Achievement award Am. Assn. Sch. Pers. Adminstrs., 1989; named Disting. Prof., Nat. Assn. Sch. Execs., 1979. ABA (labor law com.), Ill. Bar Assn. (chair sch. law com.), Mich. Bar Assn., Chgo. Bar Assn.

Office: Robbins Schwartz Nicholas Lifton & Taylor Ltd 29 S La Salle St Chicago IL 60603-1501

LIGGETT, RONALD DAVID, state legislator; m. Frances Liggett. Student, Ball State U., Muncie, Ind., 1963-65. Owner/contr. Liggett Constrn. Co.; rep. Dist. 33 Ind. Ho. of Reps., 1992—, mem. cities and towns, elec. and apportionment coms., mem. labor and employment com.; vice chmn. agr. and rural devel. com. Mem. Pvt. Industry Coun. Mem. Lions, Moose, Masons. Home: RR 1 Box 482 Redkey IN 47373-9797*

LIGGETT, TWILA MARIE CHRISTENSEN, academic administrator, public television company executive; b. Pipestone, Minn., Mar. 25, 1944; d. Donald L. Christensen and Irene E. (Zweigle) Christensen Flesher. BS, Union Coll., Lincoln, Nebr., 1966; MA, U. Nebr., 1971, PhD, 1977. Dir. vocal and instrumental music Sprague (Nebr.)-Martell Pub. Sch., 1966-67; tchr. vocal music, pub. schs., Syracuse, Nebr., 1967-69; tchr. Norris Pub. Sch., Firth, Nebr., 1969-71; cons. fed. reading project, pub. schs., Lincoln, 1971-72; curriculum coord. Westside Community Schs., Omaha, 1972-74; dir. State program Right-to-Read, Nebr. Dept. Edn., 1974-76; asst. dir. Nebr. Commn. on Status of Women, 1976-80; asst. dir. project adminstrn./devel. Great Plains Nat. Instructional TV Libr., U. Nebr., Lincoln, 1980—; exec. prodr. Reading Rainbow, PBS nat. children's series, 1980— (9 Emmy awards 1990-96); cons. U.S. Dept. Edn., 1981; Far West Regional Lab., San Francisco, 1978-79; panelist, presenter AAAS, NEA, NEH, NSF, Corp. Pub. Broadcasting, Internat. Reading Assn., Blue Ribbon panelist, Acad. TV Arts & Scis., 1991-96, final judge Nat. Cable Programming Awards, 1991-92. Author: Reading Rainbow's Guide to Children's Books: The 101 Best Titles, 1994. Bd. dirs. Planned Parenthood, Lincoln, 1979-81. Recipient Grand award N.Y., 1993, Gold medal award Internat. Film and TV Festival, 1996, World Gold medal N.Y. Internat. Film & TV, 1995, Coun. on Internat. Nontheatrical Events Golden Eagle award, 1995, 2 Image awards NAACP, 1996. Mem. NATAS, Internat. Reading Assn. (Spl. award Contbns. Worldwide Literacy 1992), Am. Women in Film and TV,Phi Delta Kappa. Presbyterian. Home: 649 S 18th St Lincoln NE 68508-2681 also: 301 E 79th St Apt 23P New York NY 10021-0944 Office: PO Box 80669 Lincoln NE 68501-0669

LIGHT, CHRISTOPHER UPJOHN, writer, computer musician; b. Kalamazoo, Jan. 4, 1937; s. Richard and Rachel Mary (Upjohn) L.; m. Lilykate Victoria Wenner, June 22, 1963 (div. 1986); children: Victoria Mary, Christopher Upjohn Jr.; m. Margo Ruth Bosker, Jan. 2, 1994. AB, Carleton Coll., 1958; MS, Columbia U., 1962; MBA, We. Mich. U., 1967; PhD, Washington U., 1971. Editor, pub. The Kalamazoo mag., 1963-66; pres. Mich. Outdoor Pub. Co., Kalamazoo, 1965-68; product planner The Upjohn Co., Kalamazoo, 1967-68; asst. prof. U. Utah, Salt Lake City, 1971-72; assoc. prof., chmn. fin. dept. Roosevelt U., Chgo., 1975-78; vis. prof. fin. No. Ill. U., 1978-79; freelance writer, computer musician, 1979—; editor Charles Dickens' Village Coquettes, 1992; mgr. spl. projects Sarasota Music Archive, 1992—. Trustee Harold and Grace Upjohn Found., 1965-85, 94—, pres. 6 yrs.; trustee Kalamazoo Symphony Orch. Assn., 1990—, Sarasota Music Archive, 1990-95, Kalamazoo Coll., 1991-93, Am. Symphony Orch. League, 1992—, sec. 1996—. Recipient ann. press award Mich. Welfare League, 1967. Mem. ASCAP, NARAS (voting com.), Fin. Mgmt. Assn., Soc. Profl. Journalists. Contbr. articles to profl. and microcomputer jours.; music compositions include Ten Polyrhythmic Etudes 1991, Piano Sonata # 1, 1992, record albums include Apple Compote, 1983, One-Man Band, 1985, Ultimate Music Box, Vol. I, 1988, Vol. II, 1993. Mem. U. Club Chicago, Gull Lake Country Club. Office: 136 E Michigan Ave Kalamazoo MI 49007

LIGHT, DOUGLAS BRUCE, biologist, educator; b. N.Y.C., Apr. 9, 1956; s. Jerome E. and Margery R. (Jacobs) L.; children: Erin, Jessica, Rachel. BA in Biology, Colby Coll., 1978; MS in Zoology, U. Minn., 1986, PhD in Physiology, 1986. Cert. 7-12 tchr., Maine. Tchr. biology Winslow (Maine) High Sch., 1978-81; teaching asst., rsch. asst. U. Minn., Mpls., 1981-86; postdoctoral fellow Dartmouth Med. Sch., Hanover, N.H., 1986-88, rsch. assoc., 1988-89; instr. biology Sch. for Life Long Learning, Lebanon, N.H., 1988; prof. Ripon Coll., Wis., 1989—. Contbr. articles to Nature, Sci., Am. Jour. Physiology, Jour. Clin. Investigation, others. Hitchcock Found. grantee, 1988-89; recipient Instrumentation and Lab. Improvement award NSF, 1991, RUI award, 1993. Mem. Am. Physiol. Soc. (Excellence in Rsch. award 1987, Caroline Tum Suden award 1988, May Bumby Severy award 1991, Sr. Class award 1993), Soc. Integrative and Comparative Biology, Biopyhs. Soc., Soc. Gen. Physiologists, Sigma Xi. Office: Ripon Coll Dept Biology 300 Seward St Ripon WI 54971-0248

LIGHT, THEODORE BLAINE, JR., chemical company executive; b. Dayton, Ohio, June 24, 1951; s. Theodore Blaine and Kathleen (Rhea) L.; m. Cynthia Ann Chester, Dec. 28, 1974; children: Theodore Blaine III, William Tyler. BBA, U. Cin., 1974, MBA, 1975, PhD, 1993. Various pos. DuBois Co., Cin., 1975-84, asst. v.p., 1984-87, v.p. corp. mktg., 1987-90; sr. v.p., 1990-91; dir. mktg. DuBois USA, div. Diversey Corp., Cin., 1991—; v.p. DuBois USA div. Diversey Corp., Cin., 1994—. Mem. Beta Gamma Sigma. Home: 3014 Springer Ave Cincinnati OH 45208-2436 Office: DuBois Co 255 E 5th St Cincinnati OH 45202-4700

LIGHTFOOT, JAMES ROSS, congressman; b. Sioux City, Iowa, Sept. 27, 1938; s. Elmer and Altha Lightfoot; m. Nancy Lightfoot; children: Terri, Jamie, Allison, James. Customer engr. IBM, 1957-59; police officer City of Tulsa, 1959-61; broadcaster, 1961-70; Mgr. farm equipment plant Corsicana, Tex., 1970-76; small bus. owner Shenandoah, Iowa, 1976—; mem. 99th-104th Congress from 5th (now 3rd) Iowa dist., 1985—, appropriations com., chmn. treas., postal svc. and gen. govt. subcom., fgn. ops. appropriations subcom., sub. appropriations, trans.; participant numerous world ocnfs. to promote agriculture. Farm editor Sta. KMA-Radio, Shenandoah, Iowa, 1976-84. Served with U.S. Army, then USAR, 1956-64. Mem FAA (Outstanding Svc. award, vol. safety counselor), Farm Bur., U.S. Feed Grains Coun., Soybean Assn., Nat. Agr. Mktg. Assn. (agr. spokesman of the yr. award), Iowa Pork Prodrs. Assn., Iowa Cattleman's Assn. (broadcasting award). Office: US House of Reps 2161 Rayburn Bldg Washington DC 20515-0005

LILBURN, MONTE WAYNE, retail executive; b. Bartlesville, Okla., Jan. 7, 1965; s. James E. and Sandra Kay (Bush) L.; m. Katherine Ann, June 30, 1987; children: Branson Michael Wayne, James Everett II, Alex Christian Monroe. Grad., Winona Sch. Profl. Photography, 1989; BBA in Fin., Pittsburg (Kans.) State U., 1994. Photographer Silver Dollar City, Branson, Mo., 1983-85; gen. mgr. Camera Am. of Bartlesville, 1985-89; pres. Heirloom Photo, Inc., Independence, Kans., 1989-91; owner Monte's Studio, Caney, Kans., 1991-94; mayor City of Caney, 1993-94; CFO Snadon Enterprises, Branson, 1994; dist. mgr. photo divsn. Wal-Mart Stores, Inc., Bentonville, Ark., 1994—; adj. instr. Tri County Vocat. Tech. Sch., Bartlesville, 1986-89, Indpendence Comunity Coll., 1989-91; mem. Southeast Kans. Regional Planning Commn., 1993. Com. mem. Bartlesville Community Light Up the Night, 1989; active Bicknell for Gov. Campaign, Kans. Named Outstanding Young Men of Am., 1989. Mem. Soc. Photofinishing Engrs., Indpendence C. of C., Bartlesville Area C. of C. Republican. Baptist. Home: 415 W Main Madison KS 66860 Office: 413 S Commercial Emporia KS 66801

LILLICH, ALICE LOUISE, retired secondary education educator; b. East Cleveland, Ohio, Aug. 18, 1940; d. Robert Earl and Charlotte Louise (Stewart) L. BS in Home Econs. Edn., Ohio U., 1968. Cert. tchr., Ohio. Quality control Stouffer's Frozen Foods, Cleve., 1961-67; head home econs. dept. Wellston (Ohio) City Schs., 1969-94; with children's dept. Kaufman's Dept. Store, 1995—; Ohio reference person Wagons West tours of Afton, Wyo. Vol. Willoughby Hills United Meth. Ch., mem. nurture com., chair adv. com. Mem. AAUW (2d vice chair 77-80, publicity chair 1985-86, issue chair 1987-90), Ohio Ret. Tchrs. Assn. (Lake County chpt.), Cleve. Audubon Soc., Republican Optimist Club (flag chair 1987-88, 2d v.p. 1989-90), Phi Delta Kappa (found. rep. 1986-87), Delta Kappa Gamma (former v.p., pres. Jackson chpt., mem. Iota-Lake County chpt.). Methodist. Home: 37570 Milann Dr Willoughby OH 44094

LILLY, GEORGE DAVID, broadcasting executive; b. Winchester, Mass., Nov. 4, 1934; s. George M. and Eleanor (Hamlin) L.; children: Brian, Kevin, Kristin. BS in Communication Arts, Boston U., 1956. Mgr. Sta. WGAN-TV, Portland, Maine, 1960-69, Sta. WIVB-TV, Buffalo, 1969-80; v.p. TV ops. Park TV, Ithaca, N.Y., 1980-83; prin., pres. BK&K, Inc., Syracuse, N.Y., 1986—, SJL Broadcast Mgmt. Corp., Billings, Mont. and Montecito, Calif., 1984—; owner SJL Broadcast Mgmt. Corp., Kans., 1988—; prin., dir. Fayetteville, N.C., 1985—; pres. SJL Broadcast Mgmt. Corp., 1984—; owner Sta. KTVQ-TV, Billings, 1984—, Sta. WKFT-TV, Fayetteville, 1985—, Sta. WSTM-TV, Syracuse, 1986—; mem. CBS Affiliates Govt. Relations com., 1986; owner Sta. KSNW-TV, Wichita, Sta. KSNC-TV, Great Bend, Kans., Sta. KSNG-TV, Garden City, Kans., Sta. KSNK-TV, Overlin, Nebr., Sta. KSNT-TV, Topeka, Sta. WJRT-TV, Flint, Mich., 1989. With U.S. Army, 1957-59. Mem. Nat. Assn. Broadcasters. Home: 633 Picacho Ln Santa Barbara CA 93108-1224 Office: KSNW 833 N Main Wichita KS 67203

LILLY, GERALD EDWARD, engineering executive; b. Detroit, July 10, 1939; s. Albert John and Marguerite (Seydel) L.; m. Patricia Meldon Markoff, April 24, 1965 (div. 1979); children: Andren, Eric; m. Elizabeth Sulleau, Aug. 9, 1980; children: Blythe, Allegra. AB, U. Detroit, 1961, Wayne State U., 1966. Mkgt. coord. Eastman Kodak, Co., Rochester, N.Y., 1977-80, nat. accts. mgr., 1980-83, 94-95, acct. mgr., 1983-89, major accts. mgr., 1990-93, mgr. channel mgkt., 1993-94; v.p., COO The Cooke Corp., Bloomfield Hills, Mich., 1995—. Mem. Soc. of Auto Engrs. Episcopalian. Office: Cokke Corp PO Box 0835 Bloomfield Hills MI 48303-0835

LIM, SHUN PING, cardiologist; b. Singapore, Jan. 12, 1947; came to U.S., 1980; s. Tay Boh and Si Moi (Foo) L.; m. Christine Sock Kian Ng; children: Corinne Xian-li, Damien John Xian-ming, Justin David Xian-an. MBBS with honors, Monash U., Clayton, Australia, 1970, PhD, 1981; M in Medicine, Nat. U. Singapore, 1975; M, Royal Australasian Coll. Physicians, 1975. Rsch. scholar Australian Nat. Health and Med. Rsch. Coun., Canberra, 1978-79; fellow in cardiology Michael Reese Hosp., Chgo., 1980-82; chief noninvasive cardiovascular imaging Cin. V.A.M.C., 1982-86; asst. prof. U. Cin., 1982-86; cardiologist Quain and Ramstad Clinic, Bismarck, N.D., 1986-88; clin. asst. prof. U. N.D., Bismarck, 1986-90; pvt. practice cardiovascular diseases, 1988-91; assoc. prof. medicine U. N.D., 1991-93; clin. assoc. prof. Ohio State U., Columbus, 1993—; dir. catheterization lab. Marion (Ohio) Gen. Hosp., 1991-93; med. dir. Cardiovasc. Cons., Columbus, 1993—; pres. Inst. for Advanced Med. Tech., 1990—, Am. Med. Investments, Inc., 1994—; chmn. ICU com. VA Med. and Regional Office Ctr., Fargo, N.D., 1991-93, chief cardiology sect., 1991-93; founder, med. dir. Cardiovascular Cons., Singapore, 1993—. Contbr. articles to profl. jours.; catheter tip polarographic lactic acid and lactate sensor. Fellow ACP, Am. Coll. Cardiology, Internat. Coll. Angiology, Am. Coll. Angiology, Royal Australian Coll. Physicians, Am. Coll. Chest Physicians, Coun. on Clin. Cardiology of Am. Heart Assn., Soc. Critical Care Medicine, Acad. Medicine Singapore; mem. Am. Fedn. Clin. Rsch., Am. Soc. Echocardiography, Am. Heart Assn. (grantee 1984-85), Ohio State Med. Assn., N.Y. Acad. Scis. (life). Methodist. Office: Cardiovascular Cons Ohio Ste 200 & 220 3545 Olentangy River Rd Columbus OH 43214

LIMBAUGH, STEPHEN NATHANIEL, federal judge; b. Cape Girardeau, Mo., Nov. 17, 1927; s. Rush Hudson and Bea (Seabaugh) L.; m. DeVaughn Anne Mesplay, Dec. 27, 1950; children—Stephen Nathaniel Jr., James Pennington, Andrew Thomas. B.A., S.E. Mo. State U., Cape Girardeau, 1950; J.D., U. Mo., Columbia, 1951. Bar: Mo. Prosecuting atty. Cape Girardeau County, Mo., 1954-58; judge U.S. Dist. Ct. (ea. and we. dists.) Mo., St. Louis, 1983—. Served with USN, 1945-46. Recipient Citation of Merit for Outstanding Achievement and Meritorious Service in Law, U. Mo., 1982. Fellow Am. Coll. Probate Counsel, Am. Bar Found.; mem. ABA (ho. of dels. 1987-90), Mo. Bar Assn. (pres. 1982-83). Republican. Methodist. Office: US Dist Ct 1114 Market St Rm 315 Saint Louis MO 63101-2038

LIMMER, WARREN E., state legislator, real estate broker; m. Lori Limmer; two children. BA, Cloud State U. Real estate broker; Dist. 33B rep. Minn. Ho. of Reps., St. Paul, 1988-95; state senator Minn. State Senate, St. Paul, 1995—; former mem. govt. op., labor-mgmt. rels., judiciary, edn.-higher edn. fin. divsn., and environ. and natural resources coms., Minn. Ho. of Reps. Home: 12888 73rd Ave N Maple Grove MN 55369-5247*

LIN, JIMMY TAI-ON, minister; b. Hong Kong, May 23, 1950; came to U.S., 1990; s. Chu Chun and May Fiar (Lo) L.; m. Doris Yuen-Hing Yeung, July 30, 1977; children: Timothy King-Yin, Samuel King-Yu. BS, U. Hong Kong, 1973, grad. dipl. in edn., 1974; MA, Westminster Theol. Sem., 1982, DivM, 1983; ThM, Princeton Theol. Sem., 1984. Ordained to ministry Ch. of Christ, 1984, Christian Reformed Ch. N.Am., 1991. Sr. pastor Hong Kong Hop Yat Ch., 1984-90; min. Chinese Lang. Broadcast Back to God Hour, Chgo., 1990—; mem. adv. bd. Breakthrough Counseling Ctr., Hong Kong, 1987-90, Evang. Reading Room and Pub., Hong Kong, 1986-88; bd. dirs., chmn. Chgo. Chinese Christian Chorale, Westminster Theol. Sem., Phila. Translator (book) The Shorter Catechism, 1979, Perspectives on Pentecost, 1987; editor/translator: Today, 1991—. Home: 7737 W 162 Pl Tinley Park IL 60477 Office: Back to God Hour 6555 W College Dr Palos Heights IL 60463

LIN, PEN-MIN, electrical engineer, educator; b. Liaoning, China, Oct. 17, 1928; came to U.S., 1954; s. Tai-sui and Tse-san (Tang) L.; m. Louise Shou Yuen Lee, Dec. 29, 1962; children: Marian, Margaret, Janice. B.S.E.E., Taiwan U., 1950; M.S.E.E., N.C. State U., 1956; Ph.D. in Elec. Engring., Purdue U., 1960. Asst. prof. Purdue U., West Lafayette, Ind., 1961-66, assoc. prof., 1966-74, prof. elec. engring., 1974-94, prof. emeritus, 1994—. Author: (with L.O. Chua) Computer Aided Analysis of Electronic Circuits, 1975, Symbolic Network Analysis, 1991, (with R.A. DeCarlo) Linear Circuit Analysis, 1995. Fellow IEEE. Home: 3029 Covington St West Lafayette IN 47906-1107 Office: Purdue Univ Sch Of Elec Engring West Lafayette IN 47907

LIN, YUH MEEI, natural product chemist; b. Tainan, Taiwan, Republic of China, Oct. 21, 1941; came to U.S., 1985; s. Teng-Lu and Tseng-Miao L.; m. Po-Jen Wang, Apr. 16, 1966; children: Song-Shung, Iwen. BS, Kaohsiung Med. Coll., Taiwan, 1965; MS, Nagoya City U., Japan, 1969, PhD, 1974. Pharmacist, quality control analyst Hoshen Pharmaceutical Co., Tainan, Taiwan, 1965-66; rsch. asst. Nagoya (Japan) City Univ., 1966-67; asst. researcher Nat. Taiwan U., Taipei, 1970-74; assoc. rsch. fellow Inst. Zoology, Acad. Sinica, Taipei, 1975-82, rsch. fellow, 1982-85; postdoctoral fellow Sch. of Pharmacy, U. N.C., Chapel Hill, 1985-86; rsch. assoc. Coll. Pharmacy U. Ill., Chgo., 1987-88, rsch. assoc. Coll. Medicine, 1988-90; sr. rsch. scientist MediChem Rsch., Inc., Chgo., 1990—; adj. assoc. prof. Kaohsiung Med. Coll., 1972-73, Nat. Taiwan U., 1982-84; adj. assoc. prof. dept. chemistry Chinese Cultural U., Taipei, 1976-77, adj. prof., 1981-84. Contbr. numerous articles to profl. jours. Recipient Award NIH, 1995, Nat. Sci. Coun. award Taiwan, 1977-84, Coun. Agrl. Planning Devel., Taiwan, 1982-84; named one of 10 Outstanding Young Women, Taiwan, 1980. Mem. Am. Chem. Soc., Chinese Chem. Soc., Am. Soc. Pharmacognosy, Pharm. Soc. Japan. Office: MediChem Rsch Inc 12305 New Ave Lemont IL 60439-3687

LINCE, JOHN ALAN, pharmacist; b. Cleve., Sept. 15, 1940; s. John Alexander and Isabelle Stella (Wirbalas) Lincewicz; m. Katherine Ann Hudson, Sept. 9, 1961 (div. Aug., 1984); children: John Jr., Karen, Mark; m. Shirley Ann Baker, Jan. 18, 1985. BS in Pharmacy, Ohio State U., 1964. Registered pharmacist, Ohio. Pharmacist, owner Hill & Dale Pharmacy, Columbus, Ohio, 1964-75, Franklin Park Med. Pharmacy, Columbus, 1975—. Pharmacy Mktg. award Johnson & Johnson, N.J., 1964. Mem. Coop. of Ohio Pharmacies (charter mem., pres. 1991—), Am. Pharm. Assn., Nat. Assn. Retail Druggists, Ohio Pharmacists Assn., Acad. Pharmacy Ctrl. Ohio (trustee 1994-95, pres. 1995-97), Ohio State Alumni Assn., Ohio State U. Coll. Pharmacy Alumni Assn. (charter), Mid-Ohio Combat Shooters Assn. (pres. 1985-88), Rho Chi. Home: 4645 Meekison Dr Columbus OH 43220-3038 Office: Franklin Park Med Pharmacy 1829 E Long St Columbus OH 43203-2066

LINCLAU, DENISE MARIE, nursing administrator; b. Detroit, Oct. 1, 1951; d. Adolph Francis and Marie Yvonne (DeWolf) L.; m. Donald M. Miller, Apr. 11, 1975 (div.); children: Martin Linclau-Miller, Russell Linclau-Miller. BSN, Wayne State U., 1974; MSA, Cen. Mich. U., 1985; student, Wharton Sch. Exec. Mgmt./, Leonard Davis Inst. Health Care Mgmt., U. Pa., 1988, 94. RN, Mich.; cert. nurse adminstr., critical care, trauma nurse. Instr. nursing edn. St. John Hosp., 1973-85; dir. ednl. svcs. Holistic Health Care, Inc., Warren, Mich., 1985-86; clin. mgr. critical care div. Hutzel Hosp. Detroit Med. Ctr., 1986-88; adminstrv. mgr. critical care div. Harper Hosp. Detroit Med. Ctr., 1988-95; dir. critical care nursing svcs. Detroit Receiving Hosp., Detroit Med. Ctr., 1989-95; asst. v.p. critical care and emergency svcs. Sinai Hosp., Detroit, 1995—; instr. advanced courses (ACLS) Am. Heart Assn., 1982—, instr. basic courses BCLS, 1985—. Instr. and mem. U.S. Power Squadron Grosse Pointe, Mich., 1984—; del. People to People Ambassadors Program to People's Republic of China, 1991. Recipient Nat. Disting. Svc. award Registry Nursing Am. Nurses Assn., 1988. Mem. AAUW, ANA, AACN (Pres. award 1975), Am. Assn. Nursing Execs., Am. Orgn. Nurse Execs., Am. Burn Assn., Am. Assn. Female Execs., Sigma Theta Tau, Sigma Iota Epsilon. Roman Catholic. Home: 1375 Grayton St Grosse Pointe MI 48230-1127

LIND, NANCY SUSAN, political science educator; b. Stevens Point, Wis., Feb. 21, 1958; d. Robert M. and Camille R. (Turzenski) L. BS, U. Wis., Stevens Point, 1980; MA, U. Minn., 1982, PhD, 1985. Instr. U. Minn., Mpls., 1985; asst prof. political science Ill. State U., Normal, 1985-82, assoc. prof., 1992—; mem. adv. bd. Grad Programs in Pub. Adminstrn., State of Ill.; mem. dean's adv. coun. Ill. State U., Normal, 1992—, chair curriculum com. Coll. of Arts and Scis., 1990-92, mem. acad. senate, 1993-95, chair coun. Coll. Arts and Scis., 1993-96. Mem. AAUP, Am. Polit. Sci. Assn., Midwest Polit. Sci. Assn., Minn. Alumni Assn. (Instr. of Yr. 1985), U. Wis.-Stevens Point Alumni Assn. Home: 3 Donna Dr Normal IL 61761 Office: Ill State U POS 4600 Normal IL 61790

LIND, REBECCA ANN, mass communication educator; b. Tripoli, Libya, Nov. 18, 1955; came to U.S. 1957; d. Samuel William Jr. and Katherine Joan (Mackichan) L. BA Speech Comm./Journalism cum laude, Humboldt State U., 1987; MA, U. Minn., 1989, PhD in Speech Communication, 1992. Asst. prof. mass communication U. Ill., Chgo., 1992—; freelance voice, on camera, writing and prodn. work, 1981—; program dir./promotion dir./announcer various radio stas. in no. Calif., 1980-87,. Contbr. numerous articles to profl. jours.; regular contbr. Northcoast View Mo. Mag., 1987. Mem. faculty adv. bd. Mus. of Broadcast Comm., Chgo.; bd. dirs. Broadcast Edn. Assn. The Kaltenborn Found. grantee, 1992, Nat. Assn. Broadcasters grantee, 1991-92; U. Minn. Dept. Speech Communication rsch. fellow, 1990, 91; Harold E. Fellows scholar, 1990-91, Presdl. scholar Humboldt State U., 1985-87, Top Scholar award Kappa Tau Alpha, 1987, Don Karshner Meml. scholar, 1986-87, Journalism Alumni scholar, 1986-87, Alfred Piltz Meml. scholar, 1985-86, Speech Communication Dept. scholar Humboldt State U., 1981-82, Elvada Trautmann Estate awardee, 1980-81, others. Mem. Internat. Communication Assn., Speech Communication Assn., Assn. for Edn. in Journalism and Mass Communication, Broadcast Edn. Assn., Phi Kappa Phi, Omicron Delta Kappa, Kappa Tau Alpha, Alpha Lambda Delta. Office: U Ill M/C 132 Rm 1216 at Chgo M/C 132 Dept Comm Chicago IL 60607-7131

LINDAAS, ELROY NEIL, state legislator; m. Janice Roberta Pederson; 7 children. 3d generation farmer; mem. N.D. Senate Dist. 20, 1991—, mem. appropriations com. Past mem. agrl. stblzn. and conservation com. Trail Co.; mem. Farmers Home Adminstrn. Com.; past emergency coord. N.D. Radio; mem. Amateur Civil Emergency Svc. Home: RR 2 Box 91 Mayville ND 58257-9673*

LINDAHL, WESLEY E., academic administrator; b. Chgo., July 12, 1954; s. Elder M. and Muriel R. (Johnson) L.; m. Debra L. Nelson, May 29, 1976; children: Anne L., John W. BA, North Park Coll., 1976; MS, U. Minn., 1980; PHD, Northwestern U., 1990. Cert. secondary educator Ill. Tchr. Glenview (Ill.) Pub. Schs., 1976-78; dir. computer svcs. North Park Coll., Chgo., 1980-84; dir. DAIS Northwestern U., Evanston, Ill., 1984-95; dir. devel. Northwestern U. Dental Sch., Chgo., 1995—; v.p. resource devel. ARNOVA, Indpls., 1994—. Author: Strategic Planning for Fund Raising, 1992 (Grenzebach award 1994). Office: Northwestern U 311 E Chicago Chicago IL 60611

LINDAMOOD, JOHN BEYER, lawyer; b. Columbus, Ohio, Jan. 18, 1941; s. H. Ray and Betty C. (Beyer) L.; children: Jennifer, J. Brad. AB, DePauw U., 1963; JD, Western Res. U., 1966. Bar: Ohio 1966, U.S. Dist. Ct. (no. dist.) Ohio 1968, U.S. Ct. Appeals (6th cir.) 1984, U.S. Supreme Ct. 1986. Assoc. Carson, Vogelgesang & Sheehan, Canton, Ohio, 1966-71; ptnr. Vogelgesang, Howes & Lindamood, Canton, 1971—, Vogelgesang, Howes, Lindamood & Brunn, Canton, 1979—. Editor Western Res. Law Rev., 1965-66. Pres. Canton Exch. Club, 1970; v.p. Canton Jaycees, 1970-71; pres. Stark County Bar Assn., Canton, 1989-90. Fellow Ohio State Bar Found.; mem. ABA, Def. Rsch. Inst., Ohio State Bar Assn. (exec. com. 1982-85), Ohio Assn. Civil Trial Attys. Office: Vogelgesang Howes Lindamood & Brunn 400 Tuscarawas St W Canton OH 44702-2018

LINDAU, JAMES H., grain exchange executive; b. Red Wing, Minn., May 21, 1933; s. Gottfrid and Stasia J. (Holmstrom) L.; m. Barbara Ann Marie Braaten, June 12, 1955; 1 child, James H. Jr. BA, Grinnell Coll., 1955. Mgmt. trainee The Glidden Co., Indpls., 1955-56; adminstrv. asst. Honeywell, Mpls., 1959-60; commodity merchandising v.p. The Pillsbury Co., Fresno, Mpls., 1960-83; mayor City of Bloomington, Minn., 1977-88; pres. Mpls. Grain Exch., 1988—; bd. dirs. Nat. Futures Assn., Chgo., 1988—, mem. exec. com., 1996—; bd. dirs. Nat. Grain Trade Coun., Washington, 1988—, vice chmn., 1996; owner franchise Burger King Restaurant, Burnsville, 1983—; mem. agrl. tech. adv. com. Depts. of Agriculture and Trade, 1990-94. Mem. Bloomington Bd. Edn., 1972-75, chmn., 1973-75; mem. Hennepin County Vo-Tech. Sch. Bd., Mpls., 1972-75, Hennepin Parks Found., 1990-92; candidate for lt. gov. Minn. (Rep., primary), 1982; candidate for gov. Minn. (Rep., primary), 1986; pres. Bloomington Minn. Port Authority, 1982-87. Capt. USAF, 1956-59. George F. Baker scholar Grinnell Coll., 1951-55; recipient Outstanding Leader award City of Bloomington, 1986, Good Neighbor award WCCO Radio, Mpls., 1987. Mem. Am. Swedish Inst., Svenska Sallskapet, Swedish Am. C. of C. (pres. Minn. chpg. 1990-94), Grand Nat. Quail Club (treas. 1986). Lutheran. Office: Mpls Grain Exch 400 Grain Exchange Minneapolis MN 55415-1411

LINDAU, PHILIP, commodities trader; b. 1936. With Pillsbury Co., 1964-93; pres. Pillsbury Flour Milling & Spl. Commodities Ops., Mpls.; pres., CEO Commodity Specialists Co., Mpls. Office: Commodity Specialists Co 301 4th Ave S Minneapolis MN 55415*

LINDBERG, CHARLES DAVID, lawyer; b. Moline, Ill., Sept. 11, 1928; s. Victor Samuel and Alice Christine (Johnson) L.; m. Marian J. Wagner, June 14, 1953; children: Christine, Breta, John, Eric. AB, Augustana Coll., Rock Island, Ill., 1950; LLB, Yale U., 1953. Bar: Ohio 1954. Assoc. Taft, Stettinius & Hollister, Cin., 1953-61, ptnr., 1961-85; mng. ptnr. Taft, Stettinius & Hollister, 1985—; dir. Cin. Bengals Profl. Football Team, Gibson Greetings, Inc., Arga Co., Schonstedt Instrument Co. Editor Nat. Law Jour., 1979-90. Sec. Good Samaritan Hosp., Cin.; bd. dirs. Taft Broadcasting Co., Cin., 1973-87, Dayton Walther Corp., 1986-87; bd. dirs. Augustana Coll., 1978-87, 91—, sec., 1981-82, vice-chmn., 1982-83, chmn., 1983-86; pres. Cin. Bd. Edn., 1971, 74, Zion Luth. Ch., Cin., 1966-69; chmn. policy com. Hamilton County Rep. Com., 1981-90; mem. exec. com. Ohio Rep. Fin. Com., 1989-90; trustee Greater Cin. Ctr. Econ. Edn., 1976-91, pres., 1987-89, chmn., 1989-91; chmn. law firm divsn. Fine Arts Fund, 1985; trustee Pub. Libr. Cin. and Hamilton County, 1982—, pres., 1989-96. Mem. Ohio Bar Assn., Cin. Bar Assn., Greater Cin. C. of C. (trustee 1985, exec. com., vice chmn. govt. and cmty. affairs com. 1989-91), Ohio Libr. Trustees Assn. (bd. dirs. 1986-87), Ohio C. of C. (bd. dirs. 1988-89), Queen City Club (sec. 1989-91), Commonwealth Club, Comml. Club (sec. 1994-96), Cin. Country Club, Optimists. Office: 1800 Star Bank Ctr 425 Walnut St Cincinnati OH 45202-3904

LINDBERG, PAMELA JAN, lithography company executive; b. Rugby, N.D., Jan. 24, 1963; d. Donald Duane and Sara Jean (McDonald) L. BS, Rochester Inst. Tech., 1985. Mng. trainee Malloy Lithographing, Ann Arbor, Mich., 1985-91, quality improvement analyst, 1991-93; mgr. book engring. dept. Malloy Lithographing, Ann Arbor, 1993—. Vol. Mich. Social Svcs., Ann Arbor, Mich., 1987-93. Mem. Am. Bus. Women's Assn. Home: 2140 Garden Homes Ct Ann Arbor MI 48103-2461 Office: Malloy Lithographing P O Box 1124 Ann Arbor MI 48106-1124

LINDBERG, RICHARD CARL, editor, author, historian; b. Chgo., June 14, 1953; s. Oscar Waldemar and Helen Marie (Stone) L.; m. Denise Kay, July 1, 1978. BA, Northeastern Ill. U., Chgo., 1974, MA, 1987. Mgr. Sears Roebuck, Chgo., 1971-84; scriptwriter Signature Group, Schaumburg, Ill., 1984-88; sr. editor Crime Books, Inc., Wilmette, Ill., 1989-92; editor-in-chief Ill. Police and Sheriffs News, Palatine, Ill., 1992—; team historian Chgo. White Sox Baseball Team, 1985—; speaker and lectr. on Chgo. history and baseball, Chgo. Author: Stuck on the Sox, 1978, Who's on Third?, The Chicago White Sox Encyclopedia, 1984, Chicago Ragtime: Another Look at Chicago 1880-1920, 1985, re-pub. as: Chicago by Gaslight: A History of Chicago's Netherworld 1880-1920, 1996, To Serve and to Collect: Chicago Politics and Police Corruption 1855-1960, 1991, Passport's Guide to Ethnic Chicago, 1992, Stealing First in a Two Team Town: The White Sox from Comisky to Reinsdorf, 1994, Quotable Chicago, 1996; contbg. writer Encyclopedia of Major League Team Histories, 1991, The Ballplayers, 1990, A Kid's Guide to Chicago, 1980, Encyclopedia of World Crime, 1990; contbr. articles to Chgo. History, USA Today mag., others. Mem. Soc. Midland Authors (bd. dirs.), Indsl. Rels. Rsch. Assn., Chgo. Crime Commn. Chgo. Press Vet. Assn., Phi Alpha Theta (pres. chpt. 1988-91, Robert Zegger Meml. award 1987). Republican. Methodist. Home: 5915 N Navarre Ave Chicago IL 60631-2628 Office: Combined Cos Police Assn 55 S Northwest Hwy Paltine IL 60067-6230

LINDBLAD, SCOTT A., engineer; b. Benson, Minn., Mar. 7, 1962. BS in Indsl. Tech., U. Wis., Menominee, 1984. Sr. engr. Sheldahl Inc., Northfield, Minn., 1985-91; chief exec. officer, mfg. engr. Automated Assembly Corp., Lakeville, Minn., 1991—. Co-author: Flex Circuits, 1989; patentee in field. Mem. Soc. Mfg. Engrs.

LINDBLAD, WILLIAM JOHN, pharmacologist; b. Glen Head, N.Y., Oct. 14, 1954; s. Herbert Paul and Elizabeth (Kisely) L.; m. Linda Susan Riewald, Aug. 23, 1985; children: Kelsi Anne, Jonathan William. BS, U. Maine, 1976; MS, Cleve. State U., 1977; PhD, U. R.I., 1980. Postdoctoral fellow Med. Coll. Va., Richmond, 1980-81, rsch. asst., 1981-83, asst. prof., 1983-89, assoc. prof., 1989-90; assoc. prof. pharm. scis. Wayne State U., Detroit, 1990—; pres. Yorkshire Pharm. Rsch. Inst., 1996—; pres. Yorkshire Pharms. Rsch. Inst., 1996—. Mng./co-editor: Wound Repair and Regeneration; co-editor: Wound Healing: Biochemical and Clinical Aspects, 1991; contbr. articles to profl. jours., chpts. to books. Community adv. bd. March of Dimes,, Richmond, 1988-90. Recipient Probus Club Acad. Achievement award, 1994. Mem. Am. Assn. for Study of Liver Diseases, N.Y. Acad. Scis., Am. Soc. for Pharmacology and Exptl. Therapeutics, The Wound Healing Soc. Office: Wayne State U Dept Pharm Sci 721 Shapero Hall Detroit MI 48202

LINDBURG, DAYTHA EILEEN, physician assistant; b. Emporia, Kans., June 24, 1952; d. Kenneth Eugene and Elsie Eileen (Smith) L. BS cum laude, Kans. State U., 1974; BS magna cum laude, Wichita State U., 1976. Registered cert. physician asst. Physician asst. in family practice Fredrickson Clinic, Lindsborg, Kans., 1976-93; physician asst. in ob/gyn. Mowery Clinic, Salina, Kans., 1993—; cons. McPherson County (Kans.) Health Dept., 1983—. Mem. adv. bd. Riverview Estates Nursing Home, 1980-86; bd. dirs. McPherson County Humane Soc., 1989-93; choir mem. Messiah Luth. Ch., Lindsborg, 1981—, liturgist, 1991—, mem. Altar Guild, 1976—, mem. music and worship com., 1981-88. Kans. Bd. Regents scholar, 1970-71, Kans. State U. scholar, 1972, 73, Smurthwaite scholar, 1970-74. Mem. Assn. of Physician Assts. in Obstetrics and Gynecology, Kans. Acad. Physician Assts., Am. Acad. Physician Asst.

LINDEMANN, DONALD LEE, utility executive; b. Indpls., Oct. 1, 1936; s. Paul Alexander and Pearl Ann (Raybern) L.; m. Lou Anne Nerge, Dec. 27, 1957; children: Bradford Allen, Dawn Marie. B.S. in Acctg., Butler U., 1958; M.S. in Acctg., St. Louis U., 1961; M.B.A., Harvard U., 1964. C.P.A., Ind. Mgmt. cons. Peat-Marwick-Mitchell, N.Y.C., 1964-65; dir. systems and audit Citizens Gas & Coke, Indpls., 1965-66, controller, 1967-78, sr. v.p., 1978-79, exec. v.p., 1979-80, exec. v.p., chief operating officer, 1981-86, pres., chief exec. officer, 1986—. Bd. dirs. Cmty. Hosp. Indpls., 1994—. 1st lt. USAF, 1959-62. Mem. AICPA, Ind. Assn. CPAs, Am. Gas Assn., Midwest Gas Assn. Republican. Presbyterian. Home: 8612 Emerald Ln Indianapolis IN 46260-1751 Office: Citizens Gas & Coke Utility 2020 N Meridian St Indianapolis IN 46202-1306

LINDEN, HENRY ROBERT, chemical engineering research executive; b. Vienna, Austria, Feb. 21, 1922; came to U.S., 1939, naturalized, 1945; s. Fred and Edith (Lermer) L.; m. Natalie Govedarica, 1967; children by previous marriage: Robert, Debra. BS, Ga. Inst. Tech., 1944; MChemE, Poly. U., 1947; PhD, Ill. Inst. Tech., 1952. Chem. engr. Socony Vacuum Labs., 1944-47; with Inst. of Gas Tech., 1947-78, various rsch. mgmt. positions, 1947-61, dir., 1961-69, exec. v.p., dir., 1969-74, pres., trustee, 1974-78; various acad. appointments Ill. Inst. Tech., Chgo, 1954-86, Frank W. Gunsaulus Disting. Prof. chem. engring., 1987-90, McGraw prof. energy and power engring. and mgmt., 1990—, interim pres., CEO, 1989-90, interim chmn., CEO Ill. Inst. Tech. Rsch. Inst., 1989-90; COO, GDC, Inc., Chgo., 1965-73; CEO Gas Devel. Corp. subs. Inst. Gas Tech., Chgo., 1973-78, also bd. dirs.; pres., dir. Gas Rsch. Inst., Chgo., 1976-87, exec. advisor, 1987—; bd. dirs. Centennial Holdings, Inc., AES Corp., Resources for the Future Inc. Author tech. articles; holder U.S. and fgn. patents in fuel tech. Recipient award of merit oper. sect. Am. Gas Assn., 1956, Disting. Svc. award, 1974, Gas Industry Rsch. award, 1982, R & D award Nat. Energy Resources Orgn., 1986, Homer H. Lowry award for excellence in fossil energy rsch. U.S. Dept. Energy, 1991, award U.S. Energy Assn., 1993, Walton Clark medala Franklin Inst., 1972, Bunsen-Pettenkofer-Ehrentafel medal Deutscher Verein des Gas und Wasserfaches, 1978, Alumni medal Ill. Inst. Tech., 1995; named to Hall of Fame, Ill. Inst. Tech., 1982. Fellow AIChE, Inst. Energy; mem. NAE, Am. Chem. Soc. (recipient H.H. Storch award, chmn. divsn. fuel chemistry 1967, councilor 1969-77), So. Gas Assn. (hon. life). Office: Ill Inst Tech PH 135 10 W 33d St Chicago IL 60616-3730 also: Gas Rsch Inst 8600 W Bryn Mawr Ave Chicago IL 60631-3505

LINDENAU, JUDITH WOOD, real estate professional; b. Zanesville, Ohio, May 22, 1941; d. Vernon Earl Wood and Jean Elizabeth (Hogan) Burkhalter; children: Jonathan, Sarah. BA, Baldwin Wallace Coll., 1963; MA, U. S.D., 1964. Instr. U. S.D., Vermillion, 1963-68; chmn. creative writing dept. Interlochen (Mich.) Arts Acad., 1968-72; supr. Green Lake Twp., Interlochen, 1976-78; exec. v.p. Traverse City (Mich.) Bd. Realtors, 1978—; pres. JWL Assn. Mgmt., Traverse City, 1992—; Bd. dirs. Traverse City Bd. Realtors Sch. Real Estate, 1988—, Homestart! Found., Traverse City, 1989—. Editor Baywatch mag., 1992; contbr. articles to profl. publs. Trustee City Planning Commn., Traverse City, 1986-89; sec. Found. Mental Health, Traverse City, 1987-91. Mem. Am. Soc. Assn. Execs., Kiwanis Club Traverse City (chmn. svc. com. 1990—). Unitarian Universalist. Office: Traverse Area Assn Realtors 852 S Garfield Ave Traverse City MI 49686-3430

LINDESMITH, LARRY ALAN, physician, administrator; b. Amarillo, Tex., July 27, 1938; s. Lyle J. and Imogene Agnes (Young) L.; m. Patricia Ann Brady, June 6, 1959 (div. Mar. 1973); children: Robert James, Lisa Ann; m. Diane Joyce Bakken, Nov. 22, 1973; children: Abigail Arleen, Nathan Lyle, David Alan. BA, U. Colo., 1959; MD, Bowman-Gray Sch. Medicine, Winston-Salem, N.C., 1963. Diplomate Am. Bd. Internal Medicine, Am. Bd. I.M.-Pulmonary Disease; Nat. Inst. Occupational Safety and Health B Reader; provider ACLS, advanced trauma life support. Medical intern U. Chgo. Hosps., Clinics, 1963-64; I.M. resident U. Colo. Med. Ctr., Denver, 1964-66; pulmonary disease fellowship U. Colo. Med. Ctr., Webb-Waring Lung Inst., Denver, 1966-67; asst. dir. infectious and pulmonary disease svc. Madigan Gen. Hosp., Tacoma, Wash., 1967-69; chief pulmonary disease Gundersen Clinic, Ltd., La Crosse, Wis., 1969-87, chief pulmonary and occupational medicine, 1979-89, chmn. dept. medicine, 1987-93; chief occupational health, preventive medicine, 1988—; bd. govs. Gundersen Clinic, Ltd., 1987-93; adj. prof. phys. therapy U. Wis., La Crosse, 1977-92; cons. VA Hosp., Tomah, Wis., 1977-93, Comty. Meml. Hosp., Winona, Minn., 1996—, Tomah Meml. Hosp., 1995—; clin. asst. prof. internal medicine U. Wis., Madison, 1982-92, clin. assoc. prof., 1992—; med. dir. RESTOR U. Wis., La Crosse, 1986-95, Svcs. to Bus. and Industry Gundersen/Luth. Med. Ctr., La Crosse, 1987-94; mem. occupational medicine boardwriting com. Am. Bd. Preventive Medicine, 1992-96. Contbr. book chpts. and articles to profl. publs. Mem. Air Pollution Control Coun. State of Wis. Dept. Natural Resources, 1978-81; vice-chmn. Bd. Control Luther High Sch., Onalaska, Wis., 1990-93. Maj. USAR, 1968-69; chmn. bd. dirs. Greater La Crosse Area C. of C., 1991. Boettcher Found. scholar, 1955-59; named Pagliara Tchr. of Yr. Gundersen Med. Found., 1984; recipient Dist. Svc. award Am. Lung Assn. Wis., 1988. Fellow Am. Coll. Chest Physicians, Am. Coll. Occupational and Environ. Medicine (assoc., chmn. pvt. practice coun., chmn. occupational lung disorders com.); mem. AMA, Am. Bd. Preventive Medicine (occupational medicine com. 1991-95), Am. Assn. Respiratory Therapy, Clin. Sleep Soc., Am. Thoracic Soc. (Wis. counselor 1978-81), Ctrl. States Occupational Medicine Assn. (bd. govs. 1984-95, pres. 1991), Am. Lung Assn. Wis. (pres. 1975-77), Wis. Thoracic Soc. (gen. conf. chmn. 1987), State Med. Soc. Wis. (chmn. environ. and occupational health com. 1989-91). Republican. Lutheran. Home: W 4965 Woodhaven Dr La Crosse WI 54601 Office: Gundersen Clinic Ltd 1836 South Ave La Crosse WI 54601-5429

LINDGREN, KARIN JOHANNA, lawyer; b. Princeton, N.J., July 18, 1960; d. William R. and Abigail H. (Sangree) Schearer. BS in Biology, Ursinus Coll., 1982; JD, Southwestern U., 1985. Bar: Pa. 1985, Calif. 1987, U.S. Dist. Ct. (ctrl., no., so., ea. dists.) Calif. 1987, U.S. Ct. Appeals (9th cir. 1987, Ill. 1994, U.S. Dist. Ct. (no. dist.) Ill. 1995. Assoc. Hillsinger & Costanzo, L.A., 1985-89, Sedgwick, Detert, Moran & Arnold, L.A., 1989-94; spl. counsel Sedgwick, Detert, Moran & Arnold, Chgo., 1994—. Author: Handbook of Medical Liability, 1988; co-author: Healthcare Liability Deskbook, 1992, 4th edit., 1996; contbr. articles to profl. jours., chpts. to books. Mem. Chgo. Bar Assn., Ill. Assn. Def. Trial Counsel, Ill. Assn. Healthcare Attys., Am. Acad. Healthcare Attys., Wilshire Bar Assn. (bd. govs. 1987-93, pres. 1991-92). Office: Sedgwick Detert Moran & Arnold The Rookery 209 S La Salle St Fl 7 Chicago IL 60604-1202

LINDGREN, KERMIT LYLE, nurse; b. Stromsburg, Nebr., Sept. 20, 1953; s. Kermit Lloyd and Agnes Lucille (Black) L. AA, Meth. Coll., 1979; AS, U. Nebr. Med. Ctr., 1982; BS, Nebr. Wesleyan U., 1982; cert. family nurse practitioner, U. N.D., 1985. ACLS, ATLS; cert. physician asst. Teaching assoc. U. Nebr. Coll. Nursing, Lincoln, 1980-82; staff burn/trauma nurse St. Elizabeth Community Health Ctr., Lincoln, 1982-89; RN III Topeka State Hosp., 1989-92, family nurse practitioner, 1992—; instr. prep for parenthood ARC, Lincoln, 1980-89, disaster nurse, 1982-89; nurse practitioner Planned Parenthood, Lincoln, 1985-86; sr. staff nurse II Security Hosp., Lincoln, 1986-88; rural health cons. Johnson County Health Dept., Tecumseh, Nebr., 1984-85; disaster coord. Johnson County Emergency Med. Svc., Tecumseh, 1984-85; BLS instr. Am. Heart Assn., Topeka, 1990—. Capt. U.S. Army Res., 1974—. Decorated Expert Field Med. Badge, Purple Heart. Mem. Am. Burn Assn. Methodist.

LINDLEY, MARALEE IRWIN, county official, consultant, speaker; b. Springfield, Ill., June 30, 1925; d. Oramel Blackstone and Rachel Virginia (Elliott) Irwin; M. Joseph Perry Lindley, Sept. 18, 1948; children—Joseph Perry, Richard Fleetwood. B.S., Northwestern U., 1947; M.A., Sangamon State U., 1973, 79. Cert. tchr., Ill. Bookkeeper, acct. Ill. State Bar Assn., Springfield, 1947-48; curriculum coordinator, tchr. Sch. Dist. 186, Springfield, 1966-80; auditor, trustee Woodside Twp., Springfield, 1977-81; county auditor Sangamon County, Ill., 1980-86, county clk., 1986—; co-author/developer Ill. Elem. Gifted Program, 1977-80 (exemplary citation 1978). Mem. Mayor's Commn. on Internat. Vistors, Springfield, 1964—; sec. Sangamon State U. Found., 1984-86, Symphony Guild, Springfield, 1983-86; treas. Springfield Women's Polit. Caucus, 1983-85; pres. Capitol City Republican Women's Club, Springfield, 1985-87. Recipient hon. Thanks award Land of Lincoln council Girl Scouts U.S., 1958, Appreciation award City of Springfield, 1964, Disting. Citizen award Sch. Dist. 186, Elizabeth Cady Stanton award Springfield Women's Political Caucus, 1987; named to Women of Achievement in Govt., Sangamon State U., 1985, One of 5 Rep. County Ofcls. of Yr., 1985. Mem. Ill. Assn. County Auditors (sec. 1982-84, treas. 1984-86, v.p 1986), Assn. Govt. Accts. (pres. 1984-85), Am. Soc. Pub. Adminstrn., Nat. Assn. Govt. Accts. (regional v.p.), Ill. Women in Govt. (treas.), Women in Mgmt. (Woman of Achievement award 1985), LWV. Lodge: Zonta. Avocations: dulcimer; folk singing; sports; reading; public speaking. Home: 2332 S Noble Ave Springfield IL 62704-4344 Office: Sangamon County Auditor's Office Sangamon County Bldg Springfield IL 62701

LINDLEY, NANCY LONG, marketing professional; b. Columbus, Ohio, Jan. 20, 1954; d. Melvin Eugene and Helen Elizabeth (Schleich) Long; m. Roger Keith Lindley, Dec. 23, 1976. BBA, U. Iowa, 1975; BSME, U. Houston, 1978; cert. master gardener, Mich. State U., 1993. Rsch. engr. Dow Epoxy Resins Tech. Svc., Freeport, Tex., 1978-81; sales specialist Dow Plastic Lined Piping Products, Houston, Tex., 1981-86; product mgr. Dow Oilfield Products, Houston, Tex., 1986-87, Dow Chem. & Metals, Midland, Mich., 1987-90; mktg. mgr. Dow Plastic Lined Piping Products, Bay City, Mich., 1990—; 1990-93, mktg. and customer svc. mgr., 1993—. Contbr. articles to profl. jours. Chmn. citizens review panel United Way, Midland, 1988-90. Mem. Tech. Assn. of Pulp & Paper Industry, Tau Beta Pi, Beta Gamma Sigma, Morter Bd., Omicron Delta Kappa. Methodist. Office: PO Box 1642 Midland MI 48641-1642

LINDNER, ARLON, state legislator; b. Aug. 3, 1935; m. Shirlee Lindner; 4 children. BA, Tex. State U.; MDiv, Cen. Bapt. Theol. Sem., Mpls. Minn. state rep. Dist. 33A, 1993—; self-employed businessman. Address: 19508 Country Cir E Corcoran MN 55374

LINDNER, SCOTT-ERIC, minister; b. Columbus, Ohio, May 15, 1965; s. Lewis Arthur Lindner and Patricia Louise (Copelan) Marie; m. Susan Marie Mills, May 15, 1993. BA, Ohio State U., 1987; MDiv, Trinity Luth. Sem., Columbus, 1991. Ordained to ministry Luth. Ch., 1991. Acquisitions libr. Irene Holm Meml. Libr., Columbus, 1980-83; audio engr. Ottawa Rsch. Corp., Columbus, 1984-87; pastor Grace Luth. Ch.-Evang. Luth. Ch. Am., Vassar, Mich., 1991—; clergy rep. N.W. Mich. Evangelism and Witness Com., Lansing, 1992-96, chmn., 1993-96, ch. cons., coord. Friends of the Future Evangelism Cons., 1994-96; duty chaplain St. Luke's Hosp., Saginaw, Mich., 1991-94. Composer record album: Meditations, 1987, State of the Heart, 1988, Supernatural Jazz, 1995; prodr. record album: New Foundation, 1989, Scenic Route, 1995; author: 5 Steps to an Inner Overhaul, 1994, The Lord's Prayer According to Luke, 1995. Mem. Tuscola County Big Bros./Big Sisters, Caro, Mich., 1992—; steering com. Cass River Habitat for Humanity, 1995—, chairperson family selection com., 1996—. Presdl. scholar, 1987-91; named Big Brother of Yr. Tuscola County, 1995. Mem. Bay Area Pastors' Conf., Vassar Ministeral Assn., Phi Beta Kappa. Home: 857 Saginaw St Vassar MI 48768-1148 Office: Grace Luth Ch 885 Saginaw St Vassar MI 48768-1148

LINDQUIST, EVERETT CARLTON, retired air traffic controller; b. Vasa, Minn., July 25, 1912; s. Charles Fritz and Esther Eleanore (Rundquist) L.; m. Helen Erma Victoria Nelson, July 22, 1939; children: Robert, Richard, Sondra. Grad. high sch., Red Wing, Minn. Clk. Vasa Gen. Store, 1931-33; radio repairman Webber Music Co., Red Wing, 1933-41; movie projectionist Auditorium Theater, Red Wing, 1936-41; comm. operator FAA, various locations, 1941-52; air traffic contr. FAA, Mpls., 1953-71, ret., 1971. Pres. bd. dirs. Vasa Mus., 1989—. Mem. Am. Radio Relay League. Home: 6582 296th St E Cannon Falls MN 55009-9205

LINDQUIST, MARY LOUISE, special education educator; b. South St. Paul, Minn., May 30, 1925; d. Henry Emanuel and Hulda Laura Margaret (Brocker) L. BS in Edn., Minot State Coll., 1962; MS, U. Wis., 1964, PhD, 1969. Cert. psychologist N.D. Missionary in Japan Augustana Luth. Bd. Fgn. Missions, Mpls., 1952-56; elem. sch. tchr. Upham (N.D.) Pub. Schs., 1958-59, Vang Sch. Dist., Ryder, N.D., 1959-61, Minot (N.D.) Pub. Schs., 1961-63; sch. psychologist Madison (Wis.) Pub. Schs., 1966-69; prof. U. N.D., Grand Forks, 1969-95, prof. emeritus, 1995—; cons. Multi-County Spl. Edn., New Rockford, N.D., 1982-85; vis. psychologist Turtle Mountain Schs., Belcourt, N.D., 1978-82; pvt. practice psychologist, Grand Forks, 1980—. Author: Sunday Sch. curriculum/Bd. of Parish Edn., Assn. Free Luth. Congregations. Grantee Office Edn., U. N.D., 1984, 87. Mem. Am. Assn. Christian Counselors, Internat. Coun. Learning Disabilities (N.D. rep. 1992-95), Internat. Platform Assn., No. Lights Coun. Learning Disabilities (pres. 1993-94). Republican. Lutheran. Home and Office: 3720 Cherry G25 Grand Forks ND 58201-7696

LINDSAY, JOHN C., state legislator; b. Omaha, June 27, 1959; m. Mary Beth Barbina, 1988; children: John Jr., Patrick. BA, Creighton U., 1981, JD cum laude, 1984; postgrad., U. Nebr., 1981-82. Ptnr. Lindsay & Lindsay, 1985—; mem. from dist. 9 Nebr. State Senate, Lincoln, 1988—, mem. govt., mil. and vet. affairs coms., mem. banking, commerce and ins. coms., com. on coms., chmn. judiciary com.; vis. asst. prof. bus. law Nebr. Wesleyan U., 1985-86. Named One of Ten Outstanding Young Omahans, 1990. Mem. ABA, ATLA, Nebr. Bar Assn., Omaha Bar Assn., Missouri Valley Profl. Soc., KC, Rotary Club, Omaha Barristers Club (v.p. 1986-87, pres. 1987-88). Home: 120 S 51st St Omaha NE 68132-3524*

LINDSAY, JUNE CAMPBELL MCKEE, communications executive; b. Detroit, Nov. 14, 1920; d. Maitland Everett and Josephine Belle (Campbell) McKee; BA with honors in Speech (McGregor Fund Mich. grantee), U. Mich., 1943; Electronics Engring. certificate Signal Corps Ground Signal Svc., 1943; postgrad. (Inst. Gen. Semantics grantee), U. Chgo., 1944-45, N.Y. U. (Armour grantee), 1945-46, Columbia U., 1946-47, Wayne State U., 1960-64, U. Mich., 1964-70, 78—; MA, Specialist-in-Aging Cert., Inst. of Gerontology, 1982; m. Powell Lindsay, Nov. 25, 1967; 1 child, Kristi Costa-McKee. Coord., activator McKee Prodns., Detroit, 1943-56, Being Unltd., 1957—, InterBeing, Inc., 1979—, M.U.T.U.A.L. A.I.D., 1981—; info. dir. Suitcase Theatre, Inc., Lansing and Ann Arbor, Mich. Cons. Cornelian Corner Detroit, Inc., 1957-63, Islamic Ctr. Found. Soc., Detroit, 1959-62, City Ann Arbor Human Rels. Commn., 1966-68, Urban Adult Edn. Inst., Detroit, 1968-69, Mich. Bell Tel. Co., Detroit, 1969, African Art Gallery Founders, Detroit Inst. Arts, 1964, WKAR-TV, Mich. State U., 1971—. Mem. Nat. Caucus, Ctr. for Black Aged; bd. dirs. Mus. Youth Internat., Saline, Mich., Ann Arbor Community Devel. Corp. Chaplain's asst. Univ. Hosp., Ann Arbor, 1971-72; program dir. People-to-People, Ann Arbor, 1971-72; Suitcase Theatre tour coord. Brit. Empire's Leprosy Relief Assn., 1972—; assembly cons. Baha'i Faith, 1960—; mem. Comprehensive Health Planning Coun. S.E. Mich., Baha'i Internat. Health Agy., Inst. for Advancement of Health, Mission Health, Catherine McAuley Health Ctr. Share and Care Support Group. Recipient Award for Excellence Mich. Ednl. Assn., 1971, Mich. Assn. Classroom Tchrs., 1972; exec. dir. Powell Lindsay Meml. Program in Theatre and Communications, Louhelen Baha'i Sch. and Residential Coll., U. Mich., Flint, Mott Community Coll., 1988—. Mem. ACLU, Soc. for Individual Responsibility, Am. Women in Radio and TV, Broadcast Pioneers, Am. Fedn. Advt., Internat. Platform Assn., Gray Panthers, Planetary Citizens, Am. Assn. Adult and Continuing Edn., Am. Pub. Health Assn., Wellness Assocs., Mich. Assn. Holistic Health, Internat. Health Found., Inst. Study Conscious Evolution, Am. Soc. on Aging, Mich. Health Coun., Nat. Coun. on Aging, U.S., Assn. Humanistic Psychology, Assn. Holistic Health, Internat. Soc. for the Study of Subtle Energies and Energy Medicine, Nat. Inst. for the Clin. Application of Behavioral Medicine, Assn. Baha'i Studies, Mental Health Assn. in Mich., Mich. Soc. Gerontology, Washtenaw County Council on Aging, Nat. Coun. Sr. Citizens, Am. Assn. Ret. Persons, People's Med. Soc., Giraffe Soc., Living Tao Found., World Future Soc., Nat. Trust for Hist. Preservation, Orgn. Devel. Inst. (registered orgn. devel. profl. 1988), UN Assn. of the U.S.A. Home: 2339 S Circle Dr Ann Arbor MI 48103-3442

LINDSEY, ANNE WEST, writer; b. Carterville, Ill., Mar. 29, 1914; d. Jett J. and Lillian Mae (Davis) West; m. Harold L. Zimmerman, Nov. 24, 1959 (dec. 1970); m. Wyatt Allen Lindsey, Dec. 9, 1981 (dec. Nov. 1990). BA, So. Ill. U., 1935; postgrad., U. Mo., 1937. Tchr. Marion Ill. High Sch., 1935-36; newspaper reporter various newspapers, 1937-44; tchr. profl. writing Grad. Sch. So. Ill. U., Carbondale, 1956-60; pres. coun. So. Ill. U.; lectr., speaker in field. Contbr. fiction and articles to 147 nat. mags. including Saturday Evening Post, Holiday, Good Housekeeping, Mademoiselle, Readers' Digest, Ford Times, also fgn. publs., TV dramas for Alcoa Theatre, Fireside Theatre, Robert Montgomery Presents. Bd. dirs. Marion Cultural and Civic Ctr., 1979-90; exec. com., dir., trustee Nat. Friends of Pub. Broadcasting; founder, chmn. bd. dirs. Friends of WSIU-WUSI TV, Carbondale, Olney, Ill.; bd. dirs. State of Ill. Humanities Coun.; mem. adv. bd. Morris Libr., Carbondale, 1961-86; gov. exec. com. So. Ill. U. Found. Bd.; mem. humanities adv. bd. John A. Logan Coll., Carterville, Ill.; mem. State of Ill. Six-Man Steering Com. for the Arts; bd. dirs. Lovejoy Libr., Edwardsville, Ill.; writers aide Nat. Hospitalized Veterans. Recipient Booster award WSUI-TV, 1978, Delta award So. Ill. U., 1982, Alumni award So. Ill. U., 1983, Golden Friend award Morris Libr., 1989, Disting. Svc. award So. Ill. U., 1991, World Affairs Forum, 1992. Home: 1806 W Warren St Marion IL 62959-1406

LINDSEY, JACQUELYN MARIA, editor; b. Buffalo, June 6, 1952; d. George Henry and Patricia Ann (Rott) Bilkey; m. Timothy Paul Murphy, Jan. 29, 1970 (div. May 1981); children: Paul Jeffrey, Jeremy Michael; m. Warren Lee Eckert, Dec. 5, 1987 (div. June 1992); m. Donald J. Lindsey, Nov. 5, 1994. Student, Ind. U., 1984. Adminstrv. asst. Western N.Y. Cath. Visitor, Buffalo, 1979-81; sec. religious edn. Our Sunday Visitor, Huntington, Ind., 1981-84, editorial asst. periodicals dept., 1985, staff editor periodicals and books, editor My Daily Visitor, 1985-91, coord. Diocesan edits., 1986-88, assoc. editor books, 1987-90, editor trade books, 1990-93, acquisitions editor trade books, 1991—, acquisitions editor religious edn., 1991—; co-founder, co-owner Specialty Tool & Engring., LLC, 1995—. Editor, compiler: Photo Directory of U.S. Catholic Hierarchy, 1987, 90, 93; editor Leaves Marianhill Missionaries, 1991—. Candidate for rep. Ind. Gen. Assembly 21st Dist., 1984; mem. LaFontaine Arts Coun., Huntington County, 1985-88; mem. Huntington County Dems., 1986-88. Mem. Cath. Press Assn. Office: Our Sunday Visitor Pub 200 Noll Plz Huntington IN 46750-4310

LINDSEY, JEFFERSON FRANKLIN, III, electrical engineering technology educator; b. East St. Louis, Oct. 9, 1942; s. Jefferson Franklin Jr. and Helen Lucile (Sullenger) L.; m. Sandra S. Skalnik, Dec. 22, 1962; children: Laura L., Jefferson F. IV. BSEE, U. Tex., 1964; MSEE, U. Houston, 1973; DEng, Lamar U., 1974. Registered profl. engr. Elec. engr. NASA, Houston, 1964-68; researcher McDonnell Douglas, Houston, 1974-80, St. Louis, 1985-90; prof. U. Houston, Carbondale, Ill., 1968-80; owner Lindsey Assocs., Carbondale, Ill., 1976—; prof. So. Ill. U., Carbondale, 1980—. Patentee in field; contbr. over 50 articles to profl. jours., chpts. to books, conf. proceedings and tech. reports to profl. publs. Troop com. Boy Scouts of Am., Carbondale, 1980-86; comms. cons. Vol. Fire Dept., Energy, Ill., 1980-83. Recipient Award of Distinction for Ind. Rsch., McDonnell Douglas, 1987, NASA Shuttle Approach and Landing Test award, 1978, Cert. of Merit, NASA, 1971, 76. Mem. IEEE (sr.), Soc. for Advancement Materials and Processes Engring. Office: So Illinois Univ at Carbondale Dept of Tech Carbondale IL 62901-6603 also: Lindsey Assocs 150 E Pleasant Hill Rd Carbondale IL 62901

LINDSEY-HITO, LOIS ELLEN, Spanish language educator, artist; b. Milw., Nov. 29, 1923; d. Fred Crocker and Caroline Buell (Sprowl) Lindsey; m. R.W. Rasmussen (div. 1955); children: David, Dennis; m. O.R. Stiehm (div. 1964) 1 child, Jane; m. Muharrem Hito; 1 child, Zaim. BS in Secondary Edn. with honors, U. Wis., 1964, MS in Secondary Edn. with honors, 1980. Life cert. State of Wis.; cert. Wis. vocat. tech. & adult edn. Spanish lang./English lang. tchr. Brookfield East H.S., Wis., 1964-65, Cudahy (Wis.) Pub. Schs., 1968-91; Spanish lang. tchr. Milw. Area Tech. Coll., Oak Creek, Wis., 1991—. Active in choir, serving meals to needy St. Thomas of Canterbury Ch., Greendale, Wis. Recipient award for oil painting Wis. Edn. Assn., Madison. Mem. NEA, Wis. Edn. Assn., Milw. Area Tech. Coll. Tchrs. Union, Sigma Delta Pi, Kappa Delta Pi. Home: 4236 W Oakwood Rd Franklin WI 53132

LINDSKOG, NORBERT F., business and health administration educator, consultant; b. St. Cloud, Minn., Aug. 2, 1932; s. Magnus Alf and Dorthey Ann (Donken) L. BS, St. Cloud State U., 1954, MS, 1957; MHA, Northwestern U., 1960; DEd, Ariz. State U., 1977. Bus. tchr. Minn. High Schs. and Santa Barbara (Calif.) City Coll., 1954-58; adminstrv. extern Louis A. Weiss Meml. Hosp., Chgo., 1958-59, exec. v.p., 1960-66; adminstrv. resident St. Luke's Hosp., St. Paul, 1959-60; mgmt. cons. in Health & Med. Adminstrn. Booz Allen & Hamilton, Inc., Chgo., 1966-68; cons. in Hosp. adminstr., assoc. for Edn. Ill. Hosp. Assoc., Chgo., 1968-71; faculty assoc.

Ctr. for Health Svcs. Adminstr. Grad. Sch. Bus., Ariz. State U., Tempe, 1974-75; asst. prof. bus. Harold Washington Coll. City Colls. of Chgo., 1968-71, assoc. prof. bus., 1971-76, prof. bus., health adminstrn., 1976—, chmn. dept. bus., 1970-82; bd. dirs. Shoreline Corp., 1988—; lectr. Harold Washington Coll., 1962-68; Cen. YMCA Coll., Chgo, 1973-78, cons. 1978; adj. prof. Internat. Acad. Merchandising & Design, 1978—. Prepub. editor and reviewer for many recent bus. related texts; contbr. to profl. jours. Fellow Royal Soc. Health, Am. Assn. Health Care Execs.; mem. Nat. Assn. Mgmt. Educators, Ill. CPA Found., Am. Soc. for Health Manpower Edn. and Tng., Nat. Bus. Edn. Assn., Ill. Bus. Edn. Assn., Chgo. Bus. Edn. Assn., Am. Hosp. Assn., Northwestern U. Health Adminstrn. Alumni Assn., Ariz. State U. Alumni Assn., St. Cloud State U. Alumni Assn., Masons, Phi Delta Kappa, Delta Pi Epsilon, Alpha Delta Mu, Kappa Delta Pi, Pi Omega Pi, Pi Delta Epsilon, Apha Pi Omega. Home: 6301 N Sheridan Rd Chicago IL 60660-1728 Office: Harold Washington Coll 30 E Lake St Chicago IL 60601-2420

LINDSLEY, JAMES BRUCE, sales and marketing executive; b. Alliance, Ohio, Feb. 28, 1941; s. George Graham and Ruth May (Wilcox) Lindsley; m. Betty Jane Cooper, Aug. 29, 1965. BS in Chemistry, Mt. Union Coll., Alliance, 1964. Lab. technician Hanna Chem. Coatings, Columbus, Ohio, 1965-68; group leader Wm. Armstrong Smith Co., East Point, Ga., 1968-72; chief chemist Progress Paint Mfg. Co., Louisville, 1972-76; product mgr. Freeman Chem. Corp., Port Washington, Wis., 1976-86; sales mgr. Akzo Nobel Resins, East St. Louis, Ill., 1986-91; dir. sales and mktg. Akzo Resins, East St. Louis, Ill., 1991—. Mem. Nat. Paint and Coatings Assn., Fedn. of Socs. for Coating Tech., Honorable Order of Ky. Cols. Office: Akzo Nobel Resins 2904 Missouri Ave East Saint Louis IL 62205-1123

LINDSLEY-GRIFFIN, NANCY, geologist, educator; b. Dallas, Jan. 13, 1943; d. Robert Porter Jr. and Dorothy Gertrude (Johnston) Lindsley; m. John Roy Griffin, June 27, 1968. BS, Colo. Coll., 1964; postgrad., U. So. Calif., 1964-65; MS, U. Calif., Riverside, 1969; PhD, U. Calif., Davis, 1982. Lab. instr., teaching asst. Colo. Coll., Colorado Springs, 1963-64; jr. geologist Signal Oil & Gas Co., L.A., 1965-66; lab. asst. U. Calif., Riverside, 1966-67; geol. asst. U.S. Geol. Survey, Menlo Park, Calif., 1967; field geologist Maine Geol. Survey, Bangor, 1968-71; assoc. instr., teaching asst. U. Calif., Davis, 1972-75; cons. geologist Griffin Resources, Casper, Wyo., 1979-83; asst. prof. U. Nebr., Lincoln, 1983-88, assoc. prof. geology, 1988-94, prof. geology, 1994—, dir. Women Investigating Sci. and Environment Project, 1988—; sedimentologist Ocean Drilling Program, Peru Margin, 1986, structural geologist, Chile Triple Junction, 1991-92; structural geologist Costa Rica Accretionary Margin, 1996; pres., bd. dirs. Gregg Ranch Found., Callahan, Calif., 1990—. Co-author: Ocean Drilling Program Procs., vol. 112, 1990, vol. 141, 1993; contbr. articles to sci. publs. Mem. Am. Assn. Petroleum Geologists, Am. Geophys. Union, Geol. Soc. Am., Soc. Sedimentary Geologists, Assn. for Women Geoscientists (bd. dirs. 1991-93), Am. Geol. Inst., Wyo. Geol. Assn., Sigma Xi, Gamma Phi Beta. Office: Univ Nebr Dept Geology 214 Bessey Hall Lincoln NE 68588-0340

LINDSTROM, LANCE ALAN, electrical engineer; b. Buffalo, Feb. 6, 1970; s. Harvey A. and Lilyan M. L. BSEE, Le Tourneau U., 1993. Engr.-in-tng., Tex. Programmer Vertex Comm. Corp., Kilgore, Tex., 1992; engr. indsl. mgmt. tng. Scot Industries, Pewaukee, Wis., 1993-94; software engr. McDonnell Douglas Aerospace, St. Louis, 1995—; ind. mktg. rep. Watkins Inc., Winona, Minn., 1985—. Designer: (invention) Programmable Split Computer Keyboard, 1992, Digital Anesthesia Monitor, 1993. Vol. counselor Big Sandy Camp, McGregor, Minn., 1992, 93, 94. Recipient Herald of Christ award Christian Svc. Brigade, 1989. Mem. IEEE. Home: 451B Chapel Ridge Hazelwood MO 63042

LINDTEIGEN, SUSANNA, rancher, state official; b. Bismarck, N.D., Oct. 3, 1947; d. Casper J. and Lillian Rose (Gross) Kraft; children: Robin Lee, Rhonda Wendy. BS, Mary Coll., 1979; MPA, U. N.D., 1981. Bookkeeper Cen. Bottling Co., Bismarck, 1966-71; office mgr. Jobbers Warehouse/Allied Van Lines, Bismarck, 1971-72; account clk. Hwy. Patrol, Bismarck, 1972-75, per. sec., 1976-78; legal sec. Pub. Svc. Commn. State of N.D., Bismarck, 1979-80, grants and contracts officer Pub. Svc. Commn., 1980-91. Sec. Dist. 8 Republican Exec. Com., 1995—. Recipient Excellence in Pub. Svc. award Gov. of N.D., 1987, South McLean County Soil Conservation award, 1994. Mem. Pheasants Forever, Westerners Club. Republican. Home and Office: RR 1 Box 115 Turtle Lake ND 58575-9747

LING, KATHRYN WROLSTAD, health association administrator; b. Watertown, Wis., Aug. 3, 1943; d. Jeffrey Harold and Constance Devina (Egre) Wrolstad; stepchildren: Renee Rainey, Roz Harper. BS in History and Polit. Sci., U. Wis., 1965. Supr. recreation ARC, DaNang, Cam Ran Bay, VietNam, 1968; assoc. exec. dir. Am. Cancer Soc., Evanston, Ill., 1968-71, exec. dir., 1971-73; exec. dir. Montgomery County Unit Am. Cancer Soc., Md., 1973-76, cons. income devel., 1976, dir., profl. edn. cancer incidence and end results, 1976-78, dir. income devel., 1978-82; exec. dir. Am. Cancer Soc., Chgo., 1982-84; assoc. exec. dir. Alzheimer's Disease and Related Disorders Assn., Chgo., 1985-87, v.p. community svcs., 1988-91, sr. v.p. chpt. Family Svcs. and Edn. divsn., 1991-93; cons. Nat. Aphasia Assn.; pres. The Leadership Edge, Chgo.; chmn. bd. dirs. Kaleidoscope. Mem. Soc. Non-Profit Orgn. (chmn. bd. dirs.). Home: 1255 N Sandburg Ter Chicago IL 60610

LING, ROBERT WILLIAM, JR., academic director; b. Oakland, Calif., Jan. 31, 1954; s. Robert William Ling and Jacqueline Laura (Roberts) Ling Mullen; m. Beverly Jean Cass, May 5, 1972 (div. Aug., 1994); children: Tami, Sheri, Robin, Cassandra, Amanda. AAS in Med. Tech., C.C. of Air Force, Maxwell AFB, Ala., 1981; BS in Biology, No. Mich. U., 1983, MA in Biology, 1985. Mem. adv. bd. Clear Lake Edn. Ctr., Escanaba, Mich., 1992—, dir., 1993—; mem. adv. bd. Northwoods Math.-Sci. Ctr., Escanaba, 1992—, Delta Menominee Ground Water Edn. Ctr. Escanaba, 1994—. Author: USAFE History of Desert Shield/Storm, 1991; (with others) Clec Master Plan Permit, 1993; contbr. articles to profl. jours. Capt. USAF, 1985-92. Mem. VFW, Soc. for the Study of Amphibians and Reptiles, Kiwanis, Sigma Xi. Democrat. Roman Catholic. Office: Clear Lake Edn Ctr 2525 3d Ave S Escanaba MI 49829

LINGAFELTER, THOMAS W., mechanical engineer; b. Willoughby, Ohio, Mar. 5, 1970. BSME, Ohio State U., 1993. Mem. staff dept. engring. Rapid Design Prototype, Ohio, 1992-93; product engr. Zagar Inc., Cleve., 1993—. Contbr. articles to profl. publs. Mem. ASME, Soc. Mech. Engrs. Republican. Office: Zagar Inc 24000 Lakeland Blvd Cleveland OH 44132-2618

LINGENFELTER, PAUL EUGENE, foundation administrator; b. Duncansville, Pa., Sept. 28, 1945; s. Galen M. and Kathern M. (Rogers) L.; m. Carol E. Gabelmann, Aug. 5, 1966; children: Carl G., Daniel P. BA in Lit., Wheaton (Ill.) Coll., 1967; MA in Higher Edn., Mich. State U., 1968; PhD in Higher Edn., U. Mich., 1974. Dir. Bursley Hall U. Mich., Ann Arbor, 1969-70, dir. couzens program, 1970-71; dept. asst. U. Mich., Ann ARbor, 1971-72, rsch. assoc., grad. sch., 1972-74; asst. dir. fin. planning and analysis Ill. Bd. Higher Edn., Springfield, 1974-76, assoc. dir. fiscal affairs, 1976-80, dep. dir. fiscal affairs, 1980-85; dir. program evaluation John D. & Catherine T. MacArthur Found., Chgo., 1985-93, assoc. v.p. planning and evaluation, 1993—; cons. U.S. Office Edn., Kansas City Region, 1980; adj. faculty pub. policy U. Chgo., 1982-84; evaluation cons. Laidlaw Found., Toronto, Can., 1992-93; sr. advisor Corp. Nat. Svc., Washington, 1993-94. Author: (with others) New Directions in Institutional Research, 1983, Foundation Center Publication, 1995; contbr. articles to newspapers. Bd. dirs. Plymouth Place Retirement Home, LaGrange Park, Ill., 1991-94; treas. Chgo. Childrens Choir, 1992-93; moderator 1st United Ch. of Oak Park, Ill., 1992; profl. singer Chgo. Symphony Chorus, 1986—. Mem. Am. Evaluation Assn., Social Investment Forum, Social Venture Network. Presbyterian. Office: John D and Catherine T MacArthur Found 140 S Dearborn St Chicago IL 60603

LINGLE, MURIEL ELLEN, elementary education educator; b. Sundown Twp., Minn.; d. Harold O. and Carrie H. (Ewald) Anderson; m. Dale A. Lingle, Aug. 21, 1946; children: Barbara Jean, Tamara Jane. BS with distinction, Union Coll., Lincoln, Nebr., 1968; MA, U. Nebr., Lincoln, 1976. Cert. tchr., Nebr. Elem. tchr. Hallam, Nebr., 1959-62; tchr. Cen. Elem. and High Sch., Sprague-Martell, Nebr., 1963-67, Helen Hyatt Elem. Sch., Lincoln, 1968-70; elem. tchr. Crete (Nebr.) Sch. System, 1970-91; ret., 1991. Recipient award for excellence in teaching Cooper Found., 1990-91, Internat. Woman of Yr. award, 1993-94. Home: 4730 Hillside St Lincoln NE 68506-6431

LINK, DEBORAH ANN, nurse; b. Flint, Mich., July 2, 1954; d. Donald Paul and Ruth Ellen (Rubel) L. Cert. practical nursing, Mott C.C., 1974; diploma, Hurley Sch. Nursing, 1980; BS in Health Care, U. Mich., Flint, 1993. Cert. ACLS, BLS provider. Staff nurse Flint Osteo. Hosp., 1980-90, 95—, asst. nurse mgr., 1990-91, staff nurse, 1991-93, clin. coord. family practice, 1993-95. Mem. AAcn (Greater Flint chpt.), Job's Daus. Presbyterian.

LINK, E.G. (JAY) (JAY LINK), corporate executive, financial consultant; b. Portsmouth, Va., Apr. 30, 1952; s. Edward and Hazel (Blalock) L.; m. Pamela Kay Kidwell, Jan. 19, 1955; children: Bethany, Anna, Kara, Lissa. BA, Cin. Bible Coll., 1974; MDiv, Cin. Christian Sem., 1979; BS, Am. Coll. Nutripathy, 1988, MS, 1991; postgrad., Calif. Coast U., 1985-86. Ordained min. Chs. of Christ, 1974. Min. Northern Ky., 1974-79; sales rep. Met. Life Ins., Joplin, Mo., 1979-81, sales mgr., 1981-82; founder, pres. E.G. Link Leasing Co., Inc., Franklin, Ind., 1982-87; founder, dir. Ind. Buying Club, Franklin, 1986—; co-founder, pres. Co-op Svcs., Inc., Franklin, 1990—; founder Shiloh Found., Franklin, 1993—; founder, pres. Philanthro Dynamics, Inc., Franklin, 1982—; nat. seminar spkr. on family wealth counseling; founder, pres. T.E.A.M. Products, Inc., 1993—; cons. to non-profit orgns.; founder, pres. Nat. Assn. Family Wealth Counselors; founder, pres. Family Wealth Counselor's Profl. Mentoring Program. Editor Natural Alternatives, 1990-92, Thinking Beyond..., 1993—; contbr. articles to profl. jours. Founder, dir. Stewardship Ministries, Inc., Franklin, 1984—. Mem. Nat. Assn. Life Underwriters, Nat. Com. Planning Giving, Nat. Alliance Renaissance Assocs., Planned Giving Group Ind., Ind. Assn. Home Educators, Nat. Right to Life, Philanthropy Roundtable, Indpls. Assn. Life, Rutherford Inst., Twenty-Five Million Dollar Internat. Forum, Million Dollar Round Table (Top of the Table award). Republican. Home: 4363 E SR 252 Franklin IN 46131-9137 Office: Philanthro Dynamics Inc 242 E Jefferson Franklin IN 46131-9137

LINK, FRANK ALBERT, retired city manager; b. Sandusky, Ohio, May 11, 1930; s. Frank Anthony and Amelia (Singler) L.; m. Susan Arline Singler, Sept. 9, 1961; 1 child, Jennifer Ann. BA, U. Notre Dame, 1952; postgrad., Gen. Motor Inst., 1957-58. Personnel dir. Aluminium & Magnesium, Inc., Sandusky, 1958-67; mgr. adminstrn. Vulcan Materials Co., Sandusky, 1967-72; city mgr. City of Sandusky, 1972-93; ret., 1993; charter bd. dirs., pres. Erie County Visitors and Conv. Bur., Sandusky. Presiding judge Ct. Equity Cath. Diocese Toledo, 1983-94; past pres. Leadership Enrichment and Devel. Sandusky, 1983, sec., 1983-91, trustee, 1992-96; exec. dir. Miss Ohio Pageant, Sandusky, 1965; bd. dirs., treas. Sandusky Ctrl. Cath. Found., 1986-91, chmn., 1991—; treas. Greater Erie County Mktg. Group, 1988-91; past trustee Merry-Go-Round Mus., Sandusky. Named Outstanding Young Man of Yr. Sandusky Jaycees, 1964, Young Man of Am. U.S. Jaycees, 1965. Mem. Ohio City Mgrs. Assn., Internat. City Mgrs. Assn. Republican. Roman Catholic. Home: 3207 Stonyridge Dr Sandusky OH 44870-5486

LINK, GARY D., university director; b. Wichita, Kans., Nov. 11, 1955; s. Darrell D. and Mildred I. (Dornes) L.; m. Loran D., Landon. BBA, Wichita State U., 1985. Cert. purchasing mgr. Buyer Kans. Gas and Electric, Wichita, 1977-85; dir. purchasing and adminstrv. svcs. Wichita State U., 1985—; cons. in field; officer Kans. Regents Purchasing Adv. Group, 1987-89, 95—; bd. dirs. Kans. Small Bus. Devel. Ctr., Wichita. Coach Little League Baseball. Coach of 1995 World Internat. Basketball Championship team. Mem. Nat. Assn. Ednl. Buyers (membership recruitment com. 1994-95, continuing edn. com. 1995-96, regional exec. com. 1989-94, regional pres. 1992-93), Nat. Assn. Purchasing Mgrs. Republican. Baptist. Home: 2801 N Rock Rd # 702 Wichita KS 67226 Office: Wichita State U 1845 Fairmount Wichita KS 67260-0012

LINKLATER, ISABELLE STANISLAWA YAROSH-GALAZKA (LEE LINKLATER), foundation administrator; b. Chgo., Sept. 15, 1939; d. Baron Stanislaw and Isabelle Lydia (Yarosh) Galazka. BE, Chgo. State U., 1959. Cert. tchr., Ill. Pub. rels. coord. Kelling Co., Chgo., 1955-57; tchr. Chg. Bd. Edn., 1957-89, coord. computer lab., 1989—; founder, pres., exec. dir. Assisi Animal Found. Edn. writer, coord. Elsa Internat. Wild Animal Appeal, Ill., 1985—; writer Lakeland Press, 1992. Bd. dirs. Townsquare Players, Woodstock (Ill.) Opera House, 1989-91. Recipient Outstanding Citizen award CBS Broadcasting, 1992. Mem. McHenry County Defenders (bd. dirs. 1989-91), East African Wildlife Soc. (U.S. rep.). Office: Assisi Animal Found PO Box 143 Crystal Lake IL 60039-0143

LINKNER, MONICA FARRIS, lawyer; b. Detroit, Dec. 2, 1947; d. Bernard and Madelyn (Lederer) Farris; m. Robert V. Linkner, Dec. 27, 1967 (div. May 1973); 1 child, Joshua Morgan Linkner; m. Dennis J. Dlugokinski, June 4, 1984; 1 child, Matthew Scott Dlugokinski. Student, U. Mich., 1965-67; BA magna cum laude, Wayne State U., 1972, JD, 1977. Bar: Mich. 1977, U.S. Dist. Ct. (ea. dist.) Mich. 1977, U.S. Ct. Appeals (6th cir.) 1985. Asst. to reporter State of Mich. Standard Criminal Jury Instrns. Com., Detroit, 1973-74; clin. student atty. Wayne State Univ. Employment Discrimination, Detroit, 1977; clk. Mich. Ct. Appeals, Detroit, 1977-78; assoc. Lampert, Fried & Levitt, PC, Birmingham, Mich., 1978-80, Lopatin, Miller, Freedman, et. al., Detroit, 1980-88; pvt. practice Berkley, Mich., 1988—; prin. atty. Adoption Law Ctr., P.C., 1993—. Editor: Winning Final Arguments, 1985. Advocate Parents for Pvt. Adoption, Lathrup Village, Mich., 1990—; vol. tchr. Peoples Law Sch., Detroit, 1985, Women's Prison Legal Edn. Project, Ypsilanti, Mich., 1975-77. Mem. ATLA, ACLU, Am. Acad. Adoption Attys. (trustee 1995—), Mich. Trial Lawyers Assn. (sustaining; handicappers law reform advocate 1988-90, chair amicus curiae com. 1988-94), State Bar (family law sect. adoltion com.), 1995—, Disability Rights Bar Assn., Women Lawyers Assn. Mich., Family Tree (pres.), Amnesty Internat., Phi Beta Kappa, Alpha Lambda Delta. Office: 3250 Coolidge Hwy Berkley MI 48072-1634

LINN, THOMAS M., investment broker; b. Milw., July 24, 1961; s. John C. and Olive M. (Finnegan) L.; m. Patrice O'Rourke, June 23, 1984; children: Andrew, Emily, Theodore, Maria, Edward. BA, Marquette U., 1983; MBA, U. Wis., Milw., 1986. Mgr. in tng. Badger Savs. Bank, Milw., 1983-84; teaching asst. U. Wis. Bus. Sch., Milw., 1984-86; investment broker Robert W. Baird & Co., Milw., 1986—. Roman Catholic. Home: 2208 E Menlo Blvd Shorewood WI 53211-2606 Office: Robert W Baird & Co Inc 777 E Wisconsin Ave PO Box 672 Milwaukee WI 53201

LINNE, JOHN R., institutional salesperson; b. Grosse Pointe, Mich., May 29, 1958. Student, Mich. State U., 1976-77, Wayne State U., 1977, 80-81. Instnl. salesperson Roney & Co., Detroit, 1978—. Coach, asst. Sports Programs for Children. Mem. Security Traders Assn. (pres. 1991-94). Roman Catholic. Office: Roney & Co 1 Griswold St Detroit MI 48226-3411

LINNERUD, MARK ALAN, secondary education educator; b. Chgo., Mar. 19, 1950; s. Odd Jacob and Mildred (Mjelde) L.; m. Lorraine Kay Bewersdorf, June 10, 1972; children: Christine Ann, Karen Elizabeth. BS in Chemistry, No. Ill. U., 1972; MS in Chemistry, Roosevelt U., 1975. Chemistry tchr. Morgan Park Acad., Chgo., 1975—; participant NSF Inst. at Fermi Nat. Labs., Batavia, Ill., 1984. Recipient award Ill. Sci. Tchrs. Assn., 1995; Tandy Tech. scholar, 1993; fellow NSF, 1986, Woodrow Wilson Nat. Found. Inst., 1989, Dow Chem. Industry Workshop, 1990, Newmast Tchrs. Inst. Stennis Space Ctr., 1992, ChemCom Tchrs. Inst., 1993. Mem. ASCD, Am. Chem. Soc., Nat. Sci. Tchrs. Assn., Argonne Network of Tchrs. Congregationalist. Home: 2201 W 116th Pl Chicago IL 60643-4735 Office: Morgan Park Acad 2153 W 111th St Chicago IL 60643-3959

LINOWES, DAVID FRANCIS, political economist, educator, corporate executive; b. N.J., Mar. 16, 1917; m. Dorothy Lee Wolf, Mar. 25, 1946; children: Joanne Linowes Alinsky, Richard Gary, Susan Linowes Allen (dec.), Jonathan Scott. BS with honors, U. Ill., 1941. Founder, ptnr. Leopold & Linowes (name now BDO Siedman), Washington, 1946-62; cons. sr. ptnr. Leopold & Linowes, 1962-82; nat. founding ptnr. Laventhol & Horwath, 1965-76; chmn. bd, chief exec. officer Mickleberry Comm. Corp., 1970-73; chmn., CEO Perpetual Investment Co., Inc., 1950-88; dir. Horn & Hardart Co., 1971-77, Piper Aircraft, 1972-77, Saturday Rev./World Mag., Inc., 1972-77, Chris Craft Industries, Inc., 1958—, Work in Am. Inst., Inc.; prof. polit. economy, pub. policy, bus. adminstrn. U. Ill., Urbana, 1976—, Boeschensten prof. emeritus, 1987—; cons. DATA Internat. Assistance Corps., 1962-68, U.S. Dept. State, UN, Sec. HEW, Dept. Interior; chmn. Fed. Privacy Protection Commn., Washington, 1975-77, U.S. Commn. Fair Market Value Policy for Fed. Coal Leasing, 1983-84, Pres.'s Commn. on Fiscal Accountability of Nation's Energy Resources, 1981-82; chmn. Pres.' Commn. on Privatization, 1987-88; mem. Council on Fgn. Relations; cons. panel GAO; adj. prof. mgmt. NYU, 1965-73; Disting. Arthur Young Prof. U. Ill., 1973-74; emeritus chmn. internat. adv. com. Tel Aviv U.; headed U.S. State Dept. Mission to Turkey, 1967, to India, 1970, to Pakistan, 1968, to Greece, 1971, to Yugoslavia, 1991; U.S. rep. on privacy to Orgn. Econ. Devel. Intergovtl. Bur. for Informatics, 1977-81, cons., N.Y.C., 1977-81; U.S. State Dept. mission to Chile, Argentina and Uruguay, July, 1988, Yugoslavia, May, 1991. Author: Managing Growth Through Acquistion, Strategies for Survival, Corporate Conscience; commn. report Personal Privacy in Information Society, Fiscal Accountablility of Nation's Energy Resources, The Privacy Crisis In Our Time; editor: The Impact of the Communcation and Computer Revolution on Society, Privacy in America, 1989; contbr. articles to profl. jours. Trustee Boy's Club Greater Washington, 1955-62, Am. Inst. Found., 1962-68; assoc. YM-YWHA's Greater N.Y., 1970-76; chmn. Charities Adv. Com. of D.C., 1958-62; emeritus bd. dirs. Religion in Am. Life, Inc.; former chmn. U.S. People for UN; chmn. citizens com. Combat Charity Rackets, 1953-58. Served to 1st lt. Signal Corps, AUS, 1942-46. Recipient 1970 Human Relations award Am. Jewish Com., U.S. Pub. Service award, 1982, Alumni Achievement award U. Ill., 1989, CPA Distinguished Pub. Svc. award, Washington, 1989. Mem. AICPA (v.p. 1962-63), U. Ill. Found. (emeritus bd. dirs. 1), Coun. Fgn. Rels., Cosmos Club (Washington), Phi Kappa Phi (nat. bd. dirs.), Beta Gamma Sigma. Home: 803 Fairway Dr Champaign IL 61820-6325 Office: U Ill 308 Lincoln Hall Urbana IL 61801 also: 9 Wayside Ln Scarsdale NY 10583-2907

LINSEY, NATHANIEL L., bishop; b. Atlanta, July 24, 1926; s. Samuel and L. E. (Forney) L.; m. Mae Cannon Mills, June 8, 1951; children: Nathaniel Jr., Ricarldo Mills, Julius Wayne, Angela Elise. BS, Paine Coll., 1948, LLD (hon.), 1990; BD, Howard U., 1951; MA in Evangelism, Scarritt Coll., 1974; DD (hon.), Miles Coll., 1975, Tex. Coll., 1985. Ordained to ministry Christian M.E.Ch., 1948. Nat. dir. youth Christian M.E.Ch., 1951-52; pastor Rock of Ages Christian M.E.Ch., 1952-53; presiding elder Columbia (S.C.) dist. Christian M.E.Ch., 1953-55; pastor Vanderhorst Christian M.E.Ch., 1955-56, Mattie E. Coleman Christian M.E.Ch., 1956-62, Thirgood Christian M.E.Ch., 1962-66; gen. sec. evangelism Christian M.E.Ch., 1966-78, chmn. bd. lay activities, 1978-82, chmn. fin. com., 1982-86, elected 39th bishop, 1978—, sr. bishop, CEO, presiding bishop 2d dist., 1994, founder Congress on Evangelism, chmn. dept. fin., 1982-86, chmn. bd. evangelism, missions and human concerns, chmn. Coll. of Bishops, 1980, 92; v.p. Interfaith Christian Coun., Washington, 1979-82; mem. presidium World Meth. Coun.; regional sec. N.Am. sect. world evangelism com. World Methodist Coun. Pres. local chpt. NAACP, Knoxville, Tenn., 1957; trustee Miles Coll., Birmingham, Ala. Recipient Disting. Alumni award Paine Coll., 1978, Presdl. citation Nat. Assn. for Equal Opportunities in Higher Edn., 1979, Disting. Svc. award Govt. D.C., 1984, Pub. Svc. award Tex. Coll., 1984, Disting. Missionary award Calif. conf. M.E.Ch., 1985; chieftancy of Obong Uwanna Ibibio Tribe, Nigeria, 1992—. Mem. World Meth. Coun., So. Calif. Ecumenical Coun. Chs. (pres. L.A. chpt. 1984). Democrat. Home: 5115 Rollman Estate Dr Cincinnati OH 45236

LINSON, ROBERT EDWARD, university administrator emeritus; b. Indpls., Dec. 10, 1922; s. William Albert and Anne Charlotte (Karstedt) L.; m. Nancy Sue Hughes, June 6, 1948; children: Cynthia, Lawrence, LuAnn. BS, Ball State U., Muncie, Ind., 1947; MS, Ball State U., 1948; EdD, U. Denver, 1957. Prin., acting supt. Jonesboro (Ind.) pub. schs., 1948-49; prin J.C. Knight Sch., Jonesboro, 1949-50, 51-52, Spiceland (Ind.) pub. schs., 1952-55; dir. alumni rels. Ball State Tchrs. Coll., Muncie, 1955-75; exec. dir. alumni and devel. Ball State U., Muncie, 1975-80; v.p. univ. relations Ball State U., 1980-87, v.p. univ. relations emeritus, 1987—; cons. in field. Contbr. articles to profl. jours. Bd. dirs. Planned Parenthood of East Ctrl. Ind., 1988-91, United Way of Delaware County, Muncie, 1982-86, Muncie YMCA, 1980-84; mem. task force on govtl. rels. United Way of Ind., Indpls., 1985-91; founder Coun. Advancement and Support of Edn., 1974; bd. dirs. Ind. Basketball Hall of Fame. With USAF, 1943-46, 50-51. Named Outstanding U.S. Advancement Officer, Coun. for Advancement & Support of Edn., 1986; Alumni Disting. Svc. award, Ball State U., 1980, others. Mem. Am. Alumni Coun. (chmn. bd. dirs. 1972-73), Sagamore of the Wabash, Rotary. Democrat. Presbyterian. Home: 909 N Meadow Ln Muncie IN 47304-3326

LINTON, WILLIAM CARL, state legislator; b. Ft. Worth, Tex., Nov. 26, 1929; s. Carl Gustav and Mary Zola (Delashamit) L.; m. Lois Anne Reeder, Dec. 16, 1935; children: David, Rebecca, Angela, Steven. BS in Indsl. Engring., Washington U., 1951; MS in Engring. Mgmt., U. Mo., Rolla, 1974. Registered profl. engr., Mo. Indsl. engr. Laclede Steel, Alton, Mo., 1953-54; sales engr. Nooter Corp., St. Louis, 1954-84; sales rep. Hill Equip. Co., St. Louis, 1984-86; state rep. Mo. Ho. of Reps., Jefferson City, 1986—. Mem. Rockwood Bd. of Edn., St. Louis County, 1976-82, pres., 1981. With U.S. Army, 1951-53. Mem. Nat. Assn. Corrosion Engrs. (chmn. 1964), Eureka C. of C., West St. Louis C. of C. Republican. Presbyterian. Home: 17339 Cougar Trails Dr Grover MO 63040-1014 Office: Ho of Reps State Capitol Building Jefferson City MO 65101-1556*

LINVILLE, JUDITH ANN, writer; b. Tulsa, Jan. 21, 1943; d. James A. and Frances E. (McElyea) Burch; m. Norman D. Linville, Aug. 24, 1968. BA, U. Ark., 1965, MA, 1966. Instr. Pittsburg (Kans.) State U., 1966-70; library asst. Pub. Libr. Denver, 1971-73; freelance writer, St. Louis, 1973-75; features editor Jour. Newspapers, St. Louis, 1975-80, columnist, 1995—; asst. editor Decor mag., St. Louis, 1980-82; sr. info. specialist U. Mo., St. Louis, 1982-85, mgr. news svcs., 1985-87, lectr. Cert. in Writing program, 1987—, advisor student newspaper, 1994—. Author: We Have New Life To Share, 1979, Come, Follow Me, 1989, 2d edit., 1996; contbr. feature articles to newspapers, 1974—, articles to mags., 1980—. Recipient Cert. Leadership YWCA of Met. St. Louis, 1986. Mem. Women in Communications, Phi Beta Kappa. Mem. Disciples of Christ Ch. Office: U Mo Dept English 8001 Natural Bridge Rd Saint Louis MO 63121-4401

LINZ, ANTHONY JAMES, osteopathic physician, consultant, educator; b. Sandusky, Ohio, June 16, 1948; s. Anthony Joseph and Margaret Jane (Ballah) Linz; m. Kathleen Ann Kovach, Aug. 18, 1973; children: Anthony Scott, Sara Elizabeth. BS, Bowling Green State U., 1971; D.O., U. Osteo. Med. and Health Scis., 1974. Diplomate Nat. Bd. Osteo. Examiners; bd. cert., diplomate Am. Osteo. Bd. Internal Medicine, Internal Medicine, Med. Diseases of Chest and Critical Care Medicine. Intern Brentwood Hosp., Cleve., 1974-75, resident in internal medicine, 1975-78; subsplty. fellow in pulmonary diseases Riverside Meth. Hosp., Columbus, Ohio, 1978-80; med. dir. pulmonary svcs. Sandusky (Ohio) Meml. Hosp., 1980-85; med. dir. cardio-pulmonary svcs. Firelands Community Hosp., Sandusky, 1985—; cons. pulmonary, critical care and internal medicine, active staff sect. internal medicine, chmn. dept. medicine, head div. pulmonary medicine Firelands Community Hosp., 1985—; cons. staff dept. medicine Good Samaritan Hosp., 1982-85, sect. internal medicine specializing pulmonary diseases; cons. pulmonary, critical care, and internal medicine Providence Hosp., Sandusky, Mercy Hosp., Willard, Ohio; clin. prof. internal medicine Ohio U. Coll. Osteo. Medicine; clin. prof. medicine Univ. Health Scis. Coll. Osteo. Medicine, Kansas City, Mo.; clin. asst. prof. med. Med. Coll. of Ohio at Toledo; adj. prof. applied scis. Bowling Green State U.; mem. respiratory tech. adv. bd. Firelands Campus, Bowling Green State U., 1983—; med. dir. Respiratory Therapy program, Bowling Green State U., 1984—. Author, contbr. articles and abstracts to profl. jours. Water safety instr. ARC, 1965—; med. dir., clin. rsch. investigator Camp Superkid Asthma Camp, 1984—; bd. trustees Stein Hospice, 1986-90. Recipient Edward Ruff Comty. Svc. award Am. Lung. Assn., 1985, Master Clinician award Ohio U. Coll. Osteopathic Medicine, 1987, Golden Rule award J.C. Penney, 1990, Disting. Alumna/Alumnus award Firelands Coll., Bowling Green State U., 1995. Fellow Am. Coll. Chest Physicians, Am. Coll. Critical Care Medicine, Am. Coll. Osteo. Internists; mem. AAAS, European Thoracic Soc., Am. Osteo. Assn., Ohio Osteo. Assn. (past pres., past v.p., past sec.-treas., acad. trustees

5th dist. acad.), Am. Heart Assn., Am. Thoracic Soc., Ohio Thoracic Soc., Am. Lung Assn. (pres., 1st v.p., med. adv. bd. chmn., exec. bd. dirs., bd. dirs. Ohio's So. Shore sect. 1984—), Nat. Assn. Med. Dirs. Respiratory Care, Ohio Soc. Respiratory Care (med. adviser/dir. 1982—), So. Critical Care Medicine, Am. Coll. Physicians (Ohio chpt.), Found. Critical Care (mem. Founder's Cir.), Sandusky Yacht Club, Sandusky chpt.), Alpha Epsilon Delta, Beta Beta Beta, Pi Kappa Alpha, Atlas Med. Fraternity. Roman Catholic.

LIPINSKI, ANN MARIE, newspaper editor. Assoc. mng. editor for met. news. Chgo. Tribune, now dep. mng. editor. Recipient Pulitzer prize for series on politics and conflicts of interest Chgo. City Coun., 1988. Office: Chgo Tribune PO Box 25340 435 N Michigan Ave Chicago IL 60611

LIPINSKI, MARY J., financial advisor; b. Oak Park, Ill., Aug. 26. BA in Fin., U. Ill., 1990, BA in Econs. Fin. advisor Goldman Sacks, Chgo., Bear Stearns, Chgo., Dean Witter Reynolds, Riverwoods, Ill., 1993—. Mem. Women Employed, Chgo., 1994—. Mem. Bus. and Profl. Women. Office: Dean Witter Reynolds PO Box 765 2500 Lake Cook Rd Riverwoods IL 60015

LIPINSKI, WILLIAM OLIVER, congressman; b. Chgo., Dec. 22, 1937; s. Oliver and Madeline (Collins) L.; m. Rose Marie Lapinski, Aug. 29, 1962; children: Laura, Daniel. Student, Loras Coll., Dubuque, Iowa, 1957-58. Various positions to area supr. Chgo. Parks, 1958-75; alderman Chgo. City Coun., 1975-83; mem. 98th-104th Congresses from 5th (now 3rd) Dist. Ill., 1983—; ranking minority mem., mem. transp. and infrastructure subcom. on railroads. Dem. ward committeeman, Chgo., 1975—; del. Dem. Nat. Midterm Conv., 1974, Dem. Nat. Conv., 1976, 84, 88; pres. Greater Midway Econ. and Community Devel. Com.; mem. Chgo. Hist. Soc., Art Inst., Chgo., pres.'s coun. St. Xavier Coll.; mem. Congl. Competitive Caucus, Congl. Caucus for Women's Issues, Congl. Hispanic Caucus, Congl. Human Rights Caucus, Congl. Populist Caucus, Dem. Study Group, Export Task Force, Inst. for Ill., Maritime Caucus, N.E.-Midwest Congl. Coalition, Urban Caucus. Named Man of Yr. Chgo. Park Dist. 4, 1983; recipient Archer Heights Civic Assn. award 1979, 23d Ward Businessmen and Mchts. award Chgo., 1977, Garfield Ridge Hebrew Congregation award Chgo., 1975-77, Installing Officer award Vittum Park Civic Assn., 23d Ward Minuteman award, Friends of Vittum Park Polish award, Nathan Hale Grand award from S.W. Liberty Soc., S.W. Am. Edn. and Recreation program award, Sentry of Yr. award Stars & Stripes Soc., Ill. State Minuteman award 1991. Mem. Polish Nat. Alliance, Kiwanis (Disting. Svc. award, pres., Peace Through Strength Leadership award 1991). Democrat. Roman Catholic. Office: US Ho of Reps 1501 Longworth House Bldg Washington DC 20515-1303 also: 5832 S Archer Ave Chicago IL 60638-1637*

LIPMAN, DAVID, multimedia company executive; b. Springfield, Mo., Feb. 13, 1931; s. Benjamin and Rose (Mack) L.; m. Marilyn Lee Vittert, Dec. 10, 1961; children: Gay Ilene, Benjamin Alan. BJ, U. Mo., 1953. Sports editor Jefferson City (Mo.) Post-Tribune, 1953, Springfield Daily News, 1953-54; gen. assignment reporter Springfield Leader and Press, 1956-57; reporter, copy editor Kansas City (Mo.) Star, 1957-60; sports reporter St. Louis Post-Dispatch, 1960-66, asst. sports editor, 1966-68, news editor, 1968-71, asst. mng. editor, 1971-78, mng. editor, 1979-92; chmn. Pulitzer 2000 Pulitzer Pub. Co., 1992—; bd. dirs. Pulitzer Charitable Fund, RXL Pulitzer; chmn. oper. com. Ptnrs. Affiliated for Exploring Tech., 1994-96; guest lectr. Am. Press Inst., Columbia U. Journalism Sch., 1967-70; chmn. bd. advisors U. Mo. Sch. Journalism, chmn. bd. dirs. multi-cultural mgmt. program, 1995—; bd. dirs. Columbia Missourian. Author: Maybe I'll Pitch Forever, The Autobiography of LeRoy (Satchel) Paige, 1962, reissued, 1993, Mr. Baseball, The Story of Branch Rickey, 1966, Ken Boyer, 1967, Joe Namath, 1968; co-author: The Speed King, The Story of Bob Hayes, 1971, Bob Gibson Pitching Ace, 1975, Jim Hart Underrated Quarterback, 1977. Bd. dirs. Mid-Am. Press Inst., 1973—, chmn., 1975-77; trustee United Hebrew Congregation, 1975-77; chmn. com. 21st Century, U. Mo., 1993-94; vice chair Mo. Gov.'s Commn. on Info. Tech., 1994-95. 1st lt. USAF, 1954-56. Recipient Univ. Mo. Faculty and Alumni award, 1988, Univ. Mo. Disting. Svc. in Journalism medal, 1989, St. Louis Jermiah award, 1991. Mem. Am. Soc. Newspaper Editors, Newspaper Assn. Am. (industry devel. com. 1993—), Interactive Svcs. Assn. (bd. dirs. 1968), Mo. Editors and Pubs. Assn. (pres. 1990-91), Mo. Soc. Newspaper Editors (bd. dirs. 1990—, vice chmn. 1992-93, chmn. 1993), Mo. Press Assn. (first v.p. 1994—), Mo. AP Mng. Editors Assn., U. Mo. Sch. Journalism Nat. Alumni Assn. (chmn. 1980-83), Press Club of St. Louis (chmn. 1987-94), Sigma Delta Chi (pres. St. Louis chpt. 1976-77), Kappa Tau Alpha, Omicron Delta Kappa. Jewish. Office: Pulitzer Pub Co 900 N Tucker Blvd Saint Louis MO 63101-1069

LIPMAN, JONATHAN, architect, historic preservationist; b. Kenosha, Wis., Apr. 17, 1953; s. William Louis and Anna Lee (Goldstein) L.; m. Pamela Whitworth, Aug. 20, 1989. BArch, Cornell U., 1978. Lic. architect. Prin. Jonathan Lipman Design, Washington, 1983-85; archtl. historian Lipman Davis Architects, Washington, 1987-88; assoc. Lethbridge & Assocs., Washington, 1989-91; prin. Prairie Architects, Fairfield, Iowa, 1991-95, Jonathan Lipman & Assocs., Fairfield, Iowa, 1995—; vis. scholar Cornell U., 1979-82, guest lectr., 1980-82; guest curator H.F. Johnson Mus. Art, Ithaca, N.Y., 1982-86, Nat. Mus. Modern Art, Kyoto, Japan, 1989-91, Renwick Gallery/Smithsonian Instn., Washington, 1986, Wis. Acad. Arts, Scis. & Engring, 1994—; guest lectr. Harvard U., Cambridge, Mass., 1982, Yale U., 1982, Columbia U., 1982, 85, Mus. Modern Art, N.Y.C., 1994, Cath. U., 1996, So. Calif. Inst. of Architecture, 1987, Wis. chpt. AIA, 1994, Iowa chpt. AIA, 1993; outside grant evaluator J. Paul Getty Trust, Malibu, Calif., 1989-94; cons. curator Milw. Art Mus., 1991-92, Mus. Modern Art, N.Y.C., 1979-81, 94; restorer of major bldgs. designed by Frank Lloyd Wright including "Wingspread" and the Johnson Wax Adminstrn. Bldg. Author: Frank Lloyd Wright and the Johnson Wax Buildings, 1986, Frank Lloyd Wright's Pope Leighey House, 1996; essayist: A Frank Lloyd Wright Primer, 1991; archtl. cons. video documentary Uncommon Places: The Architecture of Frank Lloyd Wright, 1985 (Gold medal N.Y. Internat. Video Festival 1985). Active State Iowa Nat. Register Nominations Rev. Com., Jefferson County Hist. Pres. Com. Grantee N.Y. State Coun. on Arts, 1979, Graham Found., 1980; Eidlitz fellow Cornell U., 1981. Mem. AIA, Frank Lloyd Wright Bldg. Conservancy (pres.). Jewish. Home: 205 W Jefferson Ave Fairfield IA 52556-3411 Office: Jonathan Lipman & Assocs 205 W Jefferson Fairfield IA 52556

LIPPERT, ROBERT J., administrator and culinary arts educator, consultant; b. Alma, Mich., May 17, 1932; s. Ackley William Matthew and Myrtle (Boddy) L.; m. Marie Alphonsine Mantei, Apr. 2, 1956; children: Robert Jr., Jeffrey Paul, Mark Edward. BS, Ctrl. Mich. U., 1959, MA, 1965, EdS, 1977. Exec. chef Mt. Pleasant (Mich.) Country Club, 1983-86, Riverwood Golf Course, Mt. Pleasant, 1986-90, The Embers, Inc., Mt. Pleasant, 1957-67; instr. Mt. Pleasant Pub. Schs., 1959-67; dir./culinary arts instr. Mt. Pleasant Tech. Ctr., 1968-95; inst. Ferris State U., Mt. Pleasant, Mich., 1996—; exec. banquet chef The Embers, Inc., 1967—; pres. Lippert Consulting and Svc., Mt. Pleasant, 1983—. Writer, editor, dir. TV program Ask The Chef, 1989-90; contbr. articles to profl. jours. Active ch. fund raisers, Mt. Pleasant, 1973—, State Spl. Olympics, 1982-87; chef banquets for sr. citizens. With USN, 1951-54, Korea. Inducted into Mt. Pleasant Pub. Schs. Hall of Fame, 1994. Mem. Internat. Food Svc. Execs. Assn., Am. Acad. Chefs (Svc. award 1990), Am. Culinary Fedn. (Ctrl. Regional Profl. Chef award 1990), Capitol Profl. Chefs (pres. 1985-89, chmn. of bd. 1990-91, Chef of Yr. award 1987), Food Svc. Tchrs. (pres. 1980, 81, 84, bd. dirs. 1979-89), Golden Toque, Mich. Restaurant Assn. (bd. dirs. 1980-82, 84-85, 93—, Food Tchr. of Yr. award 1981, Disting. Svc. award 1996), Mich. Occupational Edn. Assn. (bd. dirs. 1980-87, Vocat. Tchr. of Yr. award 1986), Mich. Chefs (Jefferson medal 1986). Roman Catholic. Home: 1214 Glenwood Dr Mount Pleasant MI 48858-4328 Office: Ferris State U 1214 Glenwood Mount Pleasant MI 48858

LIPPINCOTT, JONATHAN RAMSAY, healthcare executive; b. Cin., Dec. 26, 1946; s. Morss d'Isay and Virginia Yvonne (Peugnet) L.; m. Nancy Todd Smith, Feb. 22, 1975; children: Jonathan J.E., Michael R.T. BA, Yale U., 1968; MLitt, Oxford U., 1972. Program research analyst human resources adminstrn. City of New York, 1973-76; exec. asst. to dir. med. ctr. U. Cin. Med. Ctr., 1977, asst. sr. v.p., 1977-84; fellow in HMO planning policy & mgmt. Harvard Community Health Plan, Brookline, Mass., 1985-86; assoc. sr. v.p. U. Cin. Med. Ctr., 1984-94; assoc. dir. U. Cin. Hosp., 1993-94; sr. v.p., chief strategic officer Health Alliance Greater Cin., 1994—; exec. dir. bus. devel. Alliance Ptnrs., 1996—; trustee, chmn., bd. Southwestern Ohio Sr. Svcs. Inc., Maple Knoll Village, 1993-96; bd. dirs., sec., treas. Univ. Health Maintenance Orgn., Inc., 1989-93; exec. bd. dirs. The Health Initiative, Cin.; co-dir. U. Cin. Inst. Health Policy and Health Svcs. Rsch., 1993-96. Contbr. articles to cons. and acad. mags. Pres., bd. trustees Little Miami, Inc., Cin., 1984-85; steering com., chmn. health & human svcs. session Leadership Cin., 1983-84; vice chmn. Cin. Transp. Study Com., 1984-85. Mem. Am. Assn. Med. Colls. (midwest regional chmn. group on inst. planning 1991-93), Am. Coll. Health Care Execs., Cin. C. of C. (health care com.). Office: Health Alliance Greater Cin 2060 Reading Rd Ste 400 Cincinnati OH 45202

LIPSCHULTZ, JEREMY HARRIS, communication educator; b. Chgo., Feb. 12, 1958; m. Alexandra (Sandy) Shepherd, Sept. 18, 1983; 1 child, Jeffrey Thomas Shepherd. BA in Polit. Sci., U. Ill., 1980; MA in reporting, Sangamon State U., 1981; PhD in Journalism, So. Ill. U., 1990. News dir., anchor-report Sta. WPGU-FM, Urbana, Ill., 1976-80; technician Sta. WBBM-AM/FM/CBS Radio, Chgo., 1979-81; intern CIB Radio Network, Springfield, Ill., 1981; adj. instr. U. Evansville (Ind.), 1983; news dir., anchor-reporter Stas. WGBF-AM/WHKC-FM, Evansville, 1981-84; grad. asst., instr. So. Ill. U., Carbondale, 1985-88; assoc. prof. U. Nebr., Omaha, 1989—, chair grad. program com., 1995—, comm. dept. Editorial asst.: Journalism Monographs, 1986-87; book reviewer: Communications and the Law; contbr. articles to profl. jours. Mem. AEJMC Tech. Task Force, Assn. for Edn. in Journalism (chair law dvsn. rsch. 1991-92, profl. freedom and responsibility 1992-93, tchr. 1993-94), Investigative Reporters and Editors, Nebr. Writer's Guild. Office: U Nebr Dept Comm Dept Comm 151A Arts and Science Hall Omaha NE 68182

LIPSCHUTZ, MICHAEL ELAZAR, chemistry educator, consultant, researcher; b. Phila., May 24, 1937; s. Maurice and Anna (Kaplan) L.; m. Linda Jane Lowenthal, June 21, 1959; children: Joshua Henry, Mark David, Jonathan Mayer. B.S., Pa. State U., 1958; S.M., U. Chgo., 1960, Ph.D., 1962. Gastdocent U. Bern, Switzerland, 1964-65; asst. prof. chemistry Purdue U., West Lafayette, Ind., 1965-68, assoc. prof., 1968-73, prof., 1973—, chmn. inorganic chemistry, 1978-82, assoc. head dept. of chemistry, 1993—; dir. chemistry ops. Purdue Rare Isotope Measurement Lab. (PRIME), 1990—; vis. assoc. prof. Tel Aviv U., 1971-72; vis. prof. Max-Planck Inst. fuer Chemie, Mainz, Fed. Republic Germany, 1987; mem. panel space sci. experts Com. on Space Rsch., Space Agy. Forum of the Internat. Space Yr., Internat. Coun. Sci. Unions, 1990-92; cons. in field. Assoc. editor 11th Lunar and Planetary Sci. Conf., 3 vols., 1980; fin. editor: Meteoritics and Planetary Sci., 1992—; contbr. numerous articles to profl. jours. Served to 1st lt. USAR, 1958-64. Recipient Cert. of Recognition, NASA, 1979, Cert. of Spl. Recognition, 1979, Group Achievement award, 1983, Cert. Appreciation, Nat. Commn. on Space, 1986; postdoctoral fellow NSF, 1964-65, NATO, 1964-65; Fulbright fellow, 1971-72. Fellow Meteoritical Soc. (treas. 1978-84, mem. joint com. on pubs. of Geochem. and Meteoritical Socs. 1985-93, fin. officer 1985-93, chmn. 1988-90); mem. AAAS, Am. Chem. Soc., Am. Geophys. Union, Planetary Soc., Internat. Astron. Union (U.S. rep. 1988—), Sigma Xi. Office: Purdue U Dept Chemistry West Lafayette IN 47907

LIPSON, CHARLES HENRY, political scientist; b. Clarksdale, Miss., Feb. 1, 1948; s. Harry Mason Jr. and Dorothy (Kohn) L.; m. Susan Linda Bloom, July 13, 1980; children: Michael H., Jonathan S. BA, Yale Coll., 1970; MA, Harvard U., 1974, PhD, 1976. Rsch. assoc. Harvard Ctr. for Internat. Affairs, Cambridge, Mass., 1976-77; asst. prof. U. Chgo., 1977-84, assoc. prof., 1984—; vis. scholar Harvard Ctr. for Internat. Affairs, 1979-80; founding dir. program on internat. politics, econs. and security U. Chgo., 1987—, chair com. on internat. rels., 1992—; vis. fellow London Sch. Econs, 1988-89; mem. Chgo. Com., steering com. Midwest Consortium for Internat. Security Studies. Author: Standing Guard: Protecting Foreign Capital in the 19th and 20th Centuries, 1985; contbr. articles to profl. jours.; mem. bd. editors Internat. Orgn., 1984-90, 96—. Bd. dirs. U. Chgo. Hillel Found., 1990—, mem. exec. com., 1993—, chmn. bd. dirs., 1994—; mem. Hillels of Ill. Governing Commn.; bd. dirs. K.A.M. Isaiah Israel Congregation, Chgo., 1992—. Recipient Faculty Achievement award Burlington-No. Found., 1986; grantee German Marshall Fund U.S., 1983-84; fellow Rockefeller Found., 1979-81. Mem. Am. Polit. Sci. Assn. (sec. 1990-91), Am. Soc. for Internat. Law, Brit.-Am. Conf. for Successor Generation, Chgo. Com., Chgo. Coun. on Fgn. Rels., Internat. Inst. for Stratetic Studies, Internat. Studies Assn., Royal Inst. for Internat. Affairs, Norman Waite Harris Meml. Found. on Internat. Rels. Jewish. Home: 5809 S Blackstone Ave Chicago IL 60637-1855 Office: U Chgo Dept Polit Sci 5828 S University Ave Chicago IL 60637-1515

LIS, MATTHEW J., mechanical engineer; b. Pitts., Nov. 9, 1964. BSME, Ohio State U., 1988. Engr. True Sports, Hilliard, Ohio, 1987-93; sr. engr. Mosler Inc., Hamilton, Ohio, 1993—. Office: Mosler Inc 1561 Grand Blvd Hamilton OH 45012

LISAK, ROBERT PHILIP, physician, researcher, educator; b. Bklyn., Mar. 17, 1941; s. Irving Arthur and Sylvia Lillian (Kadish) L.; m. Deena Freda Penchansky, Aug. 2, 1964; children: Ilene Ann, Michael Loren. BA, NYU, 1961; MD, Columbia U., 1965; MA (hon.), U. Pa., 1976. Diplomate Am. Bd. Neurology. Intern in medicine Montefiore Hosp. and Med. Ctr., Bronx, 1965-66; rsch. assoc. NIMH, Bethesda, Md., 1966-68; resident in medicine Bronx Mcpl. Med. Ctr., 1968-69; resident in neurology Hosp. of the U. of Pa., Phila., 1969-72; with Sch. of Medicine U. Pa., Phila., 1972-87, prof. neurology Sch. of Medicine, 1980-87, vice chmn. dept. neurology Sch. of Medicine, 1985-87; prof., chmn. dept. neurology Sch. of Medicine Wayne State U., Detroit, 1987—; mem. adv. bd. Guillain-Barre Syndrome Internat., Wynnewood, Pa., 1985—; mem. med. adv. bd. Myasthenia Gravis Found., Chgo., 1988—, Nat. Multiple Sclerosis Soc., N.Y.C., 1988—. Co-author: Myasthenia Gravis, 1982; editl. bd. Jour. Neuroimmunology, 1984—, Muscle and Nerve Jour., 1981-86, 92-95, Neurology, 1981-86, Annals of Neurology, 1990-95; contbr. articles to profl. jours. With USPHS, 1966-68. Fulbright rsch. scholar, London, 1978-79; recipient Disting. Teaching award U. Pa., 1985, Drs. award Myasthenia Gravis Found., 1991. Fellow Am. Acad. Neurology (sci. issues com. 1987-93); mem. Am. Neurol. Assn. (membership com. 1989-91, chmn. 1990-91, sci. program com. 1994—), Internat. Soc. Neuroimmunology (exec. com. 1987-91, sec.-treas. 1991-95), Am. Assn. Immunologists, Soc. for Neurosci., Norwegian Neurol. Assn., Royal Soc. Medicine. Office: Wayne State U Sch Medicine 6E-UHC 4201 St Antoine Detroit MI 48201

LISHER, JAMES RICHARD, lawyer; b. Aug. 28, 1947; s. Leonard B. and Mary Jane (Rafferty) L.; m. Martha Gettelfinger, June 16, 1973; children: Jennifer, James Richard II. A.B., Ind. U., 1969, J.D., 1975. Bar: Ind. 1975, U.S. Dist. Ct. (so. dist.) Ind. 1975. Assoc. Rafferty & Wood, Shelbyville, Ind., 1976, Rafferty & Lisher, Shelbyville, 1976-77; dep. prosecutor Shelby County Prosecutor's Office, Shelbyville, 1976-78; ptnr. Yeager, Lisher & Baldwin, Shelbyville, 1977-96; pvt. practice, Shelbyville, 1996—; pros. atty. Shelby County, Shelbyville, 1983-95. Speaker, faculty advisor Ind. Pros. Sch., 1986. Editor: (seminar manual) Traffic Case Defenses, 1982. Bd. dirs. Girls Club of Shelbyville, 1979-84, Bears of Blue River Festival, Shelbyville, 1982—. Recipient Citation of Merit, Young Lawyers Assn. Mem. Nat. Assn. of Criminals, State Bar Assn. (bd. dirs.), Ind. Pub. Defender Assn., Ind. State Bar Assn. (bd. dirs. young lawyer sect 1979-83), Shelby County Bar Assn. (sec./treas. 1986, v.p. 1987, pres. 1988), Ind. Pros. Attys. Assn. (bd. dirs. 1985-95, sec./treas. 1987, v.p. 1988, pres.-elect 1989, pres. 1990). Democrat. Lodges: Masons, Elks, Lions. Home: 106 Western Trce Shelbyville IN 46176-9765 Office: Courthouse Rm 303 Shelbyville IN 46176

LISHER, JOHN LEONARD, lawyer; b. Indpls., Sept. 19, 1950; s. Leonard Boyd and Mary Jane (Rafferty) L.; m. Mary Katherine Sturmon, Aug. 17, 1974. B.A. with honors in History, Ind. U., 1975, J.D., 1975. Bar: Ind. 1975. Dep. atty. gen. State of Ind., Indpls., 1975-78; asst. corp. counsel City of Indpls., 1978-81; assoc. Osborn & Hiner, Indpls., 1981-86; ptnr. Osborn, Hiner & Lisher, 1986—. Vol. Mayflower Classic, Indpls., 1981—; pres. Brendonwood Common Inc.; asst. vol. coord. Marion County Rep. Com., Indpls., 1979-80; vol. Don Bogard for Atty. Gen., Indpls., 1980, Steve Goldsmith for Prosecutor, Indpls., 1979, 83, Sheila Suess for Congress, Indpls., 1980. Recipient Outstanding Young Man of Am. award Jaycees, 1979, 85, Indpls. Jaycees, 1980. Mem. ABA, Ind. Bar Assn., Indpls. Bar Assn. (membership com.), Assn. Trial Lawyers Am., Ind. U. Alumni Assn., Hoosier Alumni Assn. (charter, founder, pres.), Ind. Trial Lawyers Assn., Ind. Def. Lawyers Assn., Ind. U. Coll. Arts and Scis. (bd. dirs. 1983-92, pres. 1986-87), Wabash Valley Alumni Assn. (charter), Founders Club, Presidents Club, Phi Beta Kappa, Eta Sigma Phi, Phi Eta Sigma, Delta Xi Alumni Assn. (charter, v.p., sec., Delta Xi chpt. Outstanding Alumnus award 1975, 76, 79, 83), Delta Xi Housing Corp. (pres.), Pi Kappa Alpha (midwest regional pres. 1977-86, parliamentarian nat. conv. 1982, del. convs. 1978-80, 82, 84, 86, trustee Meml. Found. 1986-91. Presbyterian. Avocations: reading; golf; jogging; Roman coin collecting. Home: 5725 Hunterglen Rd Indianapolis IN 46226-1019 Office: Osborn Hiner Lisher & Orzeska PC Ste 380 8330 Woodfield Crossing Blvd Indianapolis IN 46240-4382

LISHKA, EDWARD JOSEPH, insurance underwriter; b. Chgo., Oct. 8, 1949; s. Edward John and Virginia Nelly (Powers) L.; m. Marie Ann Slawniak, June 7, 1975 (dec. Dec. 1993); 1 child, Ann. BS, Bradley U., 1971, MA, 1972. CPCU. Design engr. Forest Electric Co., Melrose Park, Ill., 1972-73; tech. writer Advance Schs. Inc., Des Plaines, Ill., 1973-74; design engr. Universal Oil Products, Des Plaines, 1974-75; account engr. Oil Ins. Assn., Chgo., 1975-81; policy cons. CNA Ins. Co., Chgo., 1981-85; underwriter Service Ins. Agy., Mount Prospect, Ill., 1985-86; acct. underwriter Arkwright Mut. Inst. Co., Schaumburg Village, Ill., 1986-92; acct. analyst Mack & Parker, Chgo., 1992—; mem. Schaumburg Village Ins. Com., 1983—. Mem. Soc. CPCUs (speaker 1987—, chmn. candidate devel. 1987-88, Profl. Devel. award 1986, 88, 89, 90, 92), Accredited Advisers in Ins. (assoc. in risk mgmt., assoc. in marine ins. mgmt.), Four Winds Ski Club (Itasca, Ill.). Republican. Roman Catholic. Home: 100 Idlestone Ln Schaumburg IL 60194-4044 Office: Mack & Parker 55 E Jackson Blvd Chicago IL 60604-4187

LISS, HERBERT MYRON, newspaper publisher, communications company executive; b. Mpls., Mar. 23, 1931; s. Joseph Milton and Libby Diane (Kramer) L.; m. Barbara Lipson, Sept. 19, 1954; children: Lori-Ellen, Kenneth Allen, Michael David. BS in Econs., U. Pa., 1952. With mktg. mgmt. Procter & Gamble Co., Cin., 1954-63, Procter & Gamble Internat., various countries, 1963-74; gen. mgr. Procter & Gamble Comml. Co., San Juan, P.R., 1974-78; v.p., mgr. internat. ops. InterAm. Orange Crush Co. subs. Procter & Gamble Co., Cin., 1981-84; pres. River Cities (Ohio) Communications Inc, 1985—; pub. The Downtowner newspaper and others, Cin., 1985—. Bd. dirs. Charter Com., Cin., 1958-63, Promotion and Mktg. Assn. U.S., 1978-81, Jr. Achievement, Cin., 1980-87; bd. dirs. Downtown Coun., Cin., 1985-94, treas., 1991-92; bd. dirs. Downtown Cin. Inc., 1995—, mem. retail mktg. com., 1995—. Mem. Manila Yacht Club, Manila Polo, Club Escuela de Equitación De Somos Aquas (Madrid), Rotary Club. (Cin.), Cin. Racquet Club. Home: 8564 Wyoming Club Dr Cincinnati OH 45215-4243 Office: The Downtowner Newspaper 128 E 6th St Cincinnati OH 45202-3211

LIST, CHARLES EDWARD, management and organization development consultant; b. Chgo., May 9, 1941; s. Kermit Paul and Johanna Emma (Staat) L.; B.A., Valparaiso U., 1963; M.A., St. Marys Coll., Winona, Minn., 1980; Ph.D. in Orgn. Devel., Union Coll., Cin., 1984; m. Susan Mary Nelson, July 20, 1968; children—Andrea Sarang, Darcy Young. Mem. personnel staff Control Data Corp., Mpls., 1965-72; mgr. human resource center Supervalu Stores, Mpls., 1973-74; dir. personnel Internat. Dairy Queen, Mpls., 1974-77; mgr. mgmt. and orgn. devel. Cardiac Pacemakers Inc., St. Paul, 1977-82; adj. faculty instr. U. St. Thomas, Cardinal Stritch Coll.; instr. Met. State U., St. Paul, 1972—. Served with USMC, 1963-64. Recipient Instr. Recognition award Met. State U., 1975, 80, 86. Mem. Am. Soc. Personnel Adminstrn., Am. Soc. Tng. and Devel. Episcopalian. Contbr. articles to profl. jours. Home: 4940 Winterset Dr Minnetonka MN 55343-8726

LISZEWSKI, JEFFREY S., financial consultant; b. Grand Rapids, Mich., May 6, 1968. B Fin., Mich. State U., 1991. Fin. cons. Smith Barney Inc., Grand Rapids, 1992—. Republican. Roman Catholic. Office: Smith Barney Inc 99 Monroe Ave NW Ste 200 Grand Rapids MI 49503-2639

LITCHFIELD, JEAN ANNE, nurse; b. Gary, Ind., Oct. 6, 1942; d. Donald Kleine and Helen Louise (Sweet) Eller; m. Norman E. Stone, Dec. 27, 1965 (div. Aug. 1973); children: Diana, David, Julie; m. Frank Litchfield, Jan. 26, 1974. Lic. practical nurse, Ind. U. Vocat. Tech. Coll., 1973; AS in Biology, Richland C.C., 1991; BSN, Millikin U., 1993; MSN, Ind. State U., 1995. RN, Ind., Ill. Nurse asst. St. Anthony Hosp., Terre Haute, Ind., 1960-73, nurse, 1973-74; charge nurse psychiatric ward St. Mary's Hosp., Decatur, Ill., 1974—; instr. allied nursing and health divsn. Richland C.C., Decatur, 1995—; mem. student welfare com. Millikin U., Decatur, 1991-92. Recipient 1st place art award 1984, 85, 86, 2d place art award 1984, 85, 2d place County Fair, 1985, Gold Poet award World of Poetry, 1989, Silver Poet award, 1990; named Most Caring Nurse St. Mary's Hosp. 1990, Clara Compton scholar, St. Mary's Hosp., 1993, 94, scholar Am. Legion, 1992. Mem. Internat. Platform Assn., Barn Colony Artists (treas. 1986-88), Phi Theta Kappa, Beta Sigma Phi (treas. 1976-78), Alpha Tau Delta (treas. 1991-92, pres. 1992-93), Sigma Theta Tau Internat. Home: 1680 N 30th St Decatur IL 62526-5416

LITKE, JAMES ALLAN, columnist; b. Chgo., July 23, 1952; s. Harry and Frida L.; m. Nancy Ellen Klempner, June 12, 1952; children: MatthewRyan, Brian Andrew. BA in Journalism, U. Mo., 1974; MA in English Lang. and Lit., U. Chgo., 1978. Reporter, columnist New Haven (Conn.) Register, 1974-77; reporter The Associated Press, Chgo., 1977-89, nat. sports columnist, 1989—. Contbr. articles to Rolling Stone and Chicago mags. Office: The Associated Press 50 Rockefeller Plz New York NY 10020

LITTLE, CAROL ELIZABETH, journalism consultant; b. Camp Atterbury, Ind., Jan. 31, 1954; d. Ralph Perry and Margaret Ann (Kiel) Owens; m. Gregory James Little, June 1, 1985; children: Joshua Ryan, Sara Christine. BA in Broadcast Journalism, Ind. U., 1982. Programming disc jockey Sta. WCSI-AM and FM Radio, Columbus, Ind., 1974-85; asst. news dir. Stas. WTRE-WRZQ Radio, Greensburg, Ind., 1983; salesperson J.C. Pennys, Columbus, 1984-85; desktop publs. artist Findlay, Ohio, 1986—. Vol. elem. sch. Whittier Sch., Findlay, 1993—; mem. pub. rels. com. Concordia Luth. Ch., Findlay, 1993—. Mem. Soc. Profl. Journalists. Home: 730 Winterhaven Dr Findlay OH 45840

LITTLE, HAROLD EUGENE, physical therapist; b. Burlington, Iowa, Oct. 4, 1951; s. Harold Arthur Little and Rexcena May (Sams) Forrestall; m. Connie Sue Ward Geisendorfer, Aug. 4, 1973 (div. Nov. 1984); children: Kristopher Sean, Erin Marie; m. Kelly Marie McKinney, Apr. 16, 1988; children: Zachary Thomas, Mackenzie Marie, Zeke Patrick. BA, Wartburg Coll., Waverly, Iowa, 1973; Cert. in Phys. Therapy, U. Iowa, 1974; MS, Ill. State U., 1982. Registered phys. therapist, Iowa, Ill., Mo. Adminstrv. dir. PM&R Mennonite Hosp., Bloomington, Ill., 1974-79; dir. phys. therapy McDonough Dist. Hosp., Macomb, Ill., 1979-82; asst. dir. phys. therapy Blessing Hosp., Quincy, Ill., 1982-85; dir. phys. therapy Galesburg (Ill.) Cottage Hosp., 1985-87, Keokuk (Iowa) Area Hosp., 1987-93; rehab. dir. RMI, Salt Lake City, 1993-94, Therapeak, Salt Lake City, 1995—; dir. Tri State Rehab. Svcs., Quincy, Ill., 1995—; rehab. dir. Clark County Health Dept., 1988—, Lewis County Health Dept., 1994—, Blessing Hosp. Homecare, 1996—; back injury cons. Blessing Hosp., Quincy, 1984; trainer Blessing and White, Mennonite Hosp., 1977-78. Vol. sports therapist Quincy Notre Dame H.S., 1982—; organizer med. unit for RAGBRAI at Keokuk, Des Moines Register, 1992. Recipient Recognition award Quincy Notre Dame Basketball Team, 1993. Mem. Am. Phys. Therapy Assn., Ill. Phys. Therapy Assn. (chmn. western dist. of Ill. 1980-84). Republican. Roman Catholic. Home: #2 Sherwood Lake Est Quincy IL 62301

LITTLE, LEWIS H., electrical engineer; b. Clinton, Ind., Oct. 20, 1952. BSEE, U. Notre Dame, 1974. Registered profl. engr., Ind. Elec. engr. Sq D Co., Peru, Ind., 1974-88, Delco, Kokomo, Ind., 1988—. Patentee in field. Acad. coach Odessy of the Mind, Peru, 1995. Mem. KC. Roman Catholic. Home: 432 Egypt Hill Rd Peru IN 46970-3318

LITTLE, STEPHEN JOHN, computer company executive; b. Pontiac, Mich., Sept. 17, 1959; s. John Hammond and Jane Francis (Linehan) L.; m. Pamela K. Little, Dec. 26, 1986; children, Jillian Renee, Stephenie Nicole. Student, Hanover Coll., 1981. Mem. Beta Theta Pi. Home: 55 Lindsey Rd Munroe Falls OH 44262 Office: Quest Integration Svcs 46 Ravenna St Hudson OH 44236

LITTLEFIELD, DANIEL CURTIS, history educator; b. Denison, Tex., Sept. 29, 1941; s. Elroy and Ophelia (Williams) L.; m. Valinda Whitted, June 23, 1990. BA, Sacramento State U., 1964; MA, Johns Hopkins U., 1972, PhD, 1977. Instr. York Coll., CUNY, 1973-77; asst. prof. Va. Commonwealth U., Richmond, 1977-78; assoc. prof. La. State U., Baton Rouge, 1978-88; prof. history U. Ill., Urbana, 1988—; bd. advisors U. S.C. Press, Columbia, 1988—. Author: Rice and Slaves, 1981, Revolutionary Citizens, 1996; contbr. articles to profl. jours. Fellow Nat. Humanities Ctr., 1988-89. Mem. Orgn. Am. Historians, Am. Hist. Assn., So. Hist. Assn., South Caroliniana Soc. Office: U Ill Dept History 810 S Wright St Urbana IL 61801-3611

LITTOOY, FRED NELSON, peripheral vascular surgeon; b. Kansas City, Mo., May 6, 1943; s. Fred Clyde and Helen Virginia (Johnson) L.; m. Martha Sue Gilbert, Aug. 1, 1965 (div.); children: Fred Cameron, Heather Lynn, Chandra Renee, Stephanie Amber. AB, U. Kans., 1965, MD, 1969. Intern, resident U. Calif., San Francisco, 1969-72, 74-76, wound healing rsch., 1972-74, fellow in peripheral vascular surgery, 1976-77; from asst. prof. to prof. surgery Loyola U. Med. Ctr., Maywood, 1977—; staff physician, chief divsn. peripheral vascular surgery Hines VA Med Ctr, Hines, Ill., 1996—. Mem. editl. bd. Vascular Surgery, 1995—. Fellow Am. Coll. Surgeons; mem. Internat. Soc. for Cardiovasc. Surgery, Soc. for Vasc. Surgery, Ctrl. Surgical Assn., Western Surgical Assn., Midwestern Vascular Surg. Soc. (treas. 1985-88, pres. 1991). Office: Loyola U Med Ctr 2160 S 1st Ave Maywood IL 60153 Other: Hines VA Med Ctr Vascular Surgery Divsn Hines IL 60141

LITVAK, RONALD, psychiatrist; b. Cleve., Aug. 11, 1938; s. Albert and Ruth (Jaffe) L.; m. Betty Ann Resnick, Aug. 14, 1960; children: Alan, Diane, Amy. BA, Case Western Res. U., 1960; MD, Ohio State U., 1964, MS, 1968. Diplomate Am. Bd. Psychiatry and Neurology, Am. Bd. Forensic Psychiatry; lic. Ohio. Intern in internal medicine Ohio State U. Hosp., Columbus, 1964-65, resident in psychiatry, 1965-68; chief resident in psychiatry Profl. Staff Ohio State U. Hosp., Columbus, 1967-68; practice medicine specializing in psychiatry Columbus, Ohio, 1964—; dir. outpatient svcs. Harding Hosp., Worthington, Ohio, 1979-83, pres. med. staff, 1980; cons. Ohio Dept. Mental Health and Mental Retardation, 1970-78, Chillicothe VA Hosp., 1970-71, Columbus Police Dept., Worthington Police Dept., Ohio State Hwy Patrol, Indsl. Commn. of Ohio, Ohio Atty. Gen., State Med. Bd. of Ohio, Supreme Ct. of Ohio, Bd. of Commrs. and Grievances and Discipline of the Bar, Columbus City Atty., U.S. Dept. Labor, U.S. Dept. State. Contbr. articles to profl. jours. Served to maj. Med. Service Corps, U.S. Army, 1968-70. Recipient Cert. of Achievement Comdr. U.S. Walson Army Hosp., Ft. Dix, N.J., 1970, Letters of Commendation, Officers in Tng. Brigade, Ft. Dix, N.J. Fellow Am. Psychiat. Assn.; mem. AMA, Ohio State Med. Assn., Ohio Psychiat. Assn., Psychiat. Soc. Cen. Ohio, Acad. Medicine of Columbus and Franklin County, Am. Acad. Psychiatry and the Law. Home: 1195 Circle On The Grn Columbus OH 43235-1208 Office: 1170 Old Henderson Rd # 201 Columbus OH 43220-3661

LITVIN, MARTIN JAY, author, lecturer; b. Galesburg, Ill., Mar. 31, 1928; s. Ben and Sylvia (Gillis) L. BS in Social Studies, U. So. Calif., 1949. lectr. motivational seminars, creative writing and self- pub. Chgo. Pub. Libr. Cultural Ctr., 1986-87; vis. scholar Harvard Divinity Sch., Cambridge, Mass., 1987; cultural corr. The Zephyr, Galesburg, Ill. Author: Sergeant Allen and Private Renick, 1971, Voices of the Prairie Land, 2 Vols., 1972, Black Angel, 1973; Hiram Revels in Illinois, 1974, Chase the Prairie Wind, 1975, The Young Mary, 1976, The Journey, 1981, A Rocking Horse Family, 1982, A Daring Young Man, 1983; Black Earth, 1984, Harvard Index of Julia Fletcher Carney's Lost Writings, 1987, I'm Going to Be Somebody!, a biography of George Fitch, 1991, A Prairie Writer's Life, (novel) The Impresario, 1995, (memoir) Good Morning, Miss Freeman, 1995; editor for George Fitch's book The Big Strike at Siwash; apptd. drama and book critic, The Galesburg Post; host sta. WGPA; commentator Sta. WAIK Radio, 1995; lectr. in field; appears in video tapes. Served with U.S. Army, 1950-52. Recipient Boyd B. Stutler silver medal John Brown Soc., N.Y., 1992. Mem. Dramatists Guild (assoc.), Alumnus of Tau Epsilon Phi. Bondi's Journey, a symphonic piece based on his book, The Journey, was adapted by Bruce Polay. Office: care Bill Butts Ltd 119 S Cherry St Galesburg IL 61401-4527

LITZ, ARTHUR, retired judge; b. N.Y.C., Jan. 9, 1923; s. Benjamin and Sophie Harriet (Madrick) L.; m. Adele Fern Ravitz, June 28, 1953; children: Howard Alan, Robert David, Gwen Robin. BA, Washington U., 1944, MA, 1944; LLB, Harvard U., 1947. Pvt. practice St. Louis, 1947-75; cir. ct. judge State of Mo., St. Louis, 1975-93; arbitrator, mediator St. Louis, 1993—. Book rev. editor St. Louis Bar Jour., 1966—; contbr. articles to profl. jours. Pres. John Marshall Club, St. Louis, 1963; mem. St. Louis County Hist. Bldgs. Commn., 1963-69; chmn. Civil Svc. Commn., St. Louis, 1969-75. Recipient Disting. Svc. award Trial Judges Sect., State of Mo., 1983. Mem. St. Louis County Law Libr. Assn., St. Louis Jewish Cmty. Archives (chair 1993—), St. Louis County Hist. Soc. (chair, Disting. Svc. award 1991). Republican. Home: 17 Heather Hill Ln Saint Louis MO 63132-4105

LIU, BENJAMIN YOUNG-HWAI, engineering educator; b. Shanghai, China, Aug. 15, 1934; s. Wilson Wan-su and Dorothy Pao-ning (Cheng) L.; m. Helen Hai-ling Cheng, June 14, 1958; 1 son, Lawrence A.S. Student, Nat. Taiwan U., 1951-54; B.S. in Mech. Engring., U. Nebr., 1956; Ph.D., U. Minn., 1960. Asso. engr. Honeywell Co., Mpls., 1956; research asst., instr. U. Minn., 1956-60, asst. prof., 1960-67, asso. prof., 1967-69, prof., 1969-93, regent's prof., 1993—, dir. Particle Tech. Lab., 1973-95; dir. Ctr. for Filtration Rsch., 1995—; vis. prof. U. Paris, 1968-69; patentee in field. Contbg. author: Aerosol Science, 1966; editor: Fine Particles, 1976, Application of Solar Energy for Heating and Cooling Buildings, 1977, Aerosols in the Mining and Industrial Work Environment, 1983, Aerosols: Science, Technology and Industrial Application of Airborne Particles, 1984; editor-in-chief: Aerosol Sci. and Tech., 1983-93; contbr. articles to Ency. Chem. Tech. Guggenheim fellow, 1968-69; recipient Sr. U.S. Scientist award Alexander von Humboldt Found., 1982-83. Mem. ASME, ASHRAE, Inst. Environ. Scis. (v.p. 1993-95), Air and Waste Mgmt. Assn., Am. Assn. for Aerosol Rsch. (pres. 1986-88), Chinese Am. Assn. Minn. (pres. 1971-72), Nat. Acad. Engring. Home: 1 N Deep Lake Rd North Oaks MN 55127-6504 Office: U Minn Particle Tech Lab 111 Church St SE Minneapolis MN 55455-0150

LIU, MAW-SHUNG, physiologist, dentist; b. Taiwan, Republic of China, Feb. 2, 1940; came to U.S., 1968; s. Chao-Tung and Chian (Hwang) L.; m. Min-Chau Chang, Sept. 15, 1966; 1 child, Chien-Ye. DDS, Kaohsiung Med. Coll., Taiwan, 1964; PhD, U. Ottawa, Can., 1976. Cert. by Coun. Nat. Bd. Dental Examiners. Intern in pathology U. Ky., Lexington, 1968-69; instr. physiology La. State U. Med. Ctr., New Orleans, 1974-76, asst. prof., 1976-78; assoc. prof. Bowman Gray Sch. Med. Wake Forest U., Winston-Salem, N.C., 1978-82; prof. St. Louis U. Sch. Medicine, 1982—; vis. prof. Beijing Med. U., 1984—, Zhejiang Med. U., 1986, Kaohsiung Med. Coll., 1989—, Chang Gung Med. Coll., 1989—; mem. surgery, anesthesiology and trauma study sect. NIH, 1988-92. Mem. editl. bd. Circulatory Shock, 1982-93, Shock, 1993—; contbr. over 60 articles and 60 papers to profl. jours. Named hon. prof. Nanjing Med. Univ., 1984, Hunan Med. Univ., 1988; grantee Nat. Heart Lung and Blood Inst., Inst. Gen. Med. Sci., 1977—. Mem. Internat. Soc. Heart Rsch., Am. Physiol. Soc., The Shock Soc. Office: St Louis U Sch Medicine Dept Pharm & Physiol Sci 1402 S Grand Blvd Saint Louis MO 63104-1004

LIU, PINGYU, physicist, educator; b. Shanghai, China, May 27, 1941; came to U.S., 1980; s. Shih-Tsan and Wen-Chang (Chen) L.; m. Jiagi Wang, Dec. 22, 1972 (dec. 1983); 1 child, Mei; m. Carolyn Hsu, Oct. 14, 1983; 1 child, Helen Wen. Diploma, Dalian (China) Poly. Inst., 1963; MS, U. Utah, 1982, PhD, 1984. Rsch. asst., postdoctoral rsch. assoc. U. Utah, Salt Lake City, 1981-85; devel. engr. Garrett AiResearch, L.A., 1985-86; sr. engr., engring. specialist, engr. III Allied-Signal Aero. Co., Tucson, Ariz., 1986-92; assoc. prof. imaging sci., dept. radiology Ind. U., Indpls., 1992—. Mem. IEEE, Am. Assn. Physicists in Medicine, Biomed. Optics Soc., SPIE. Office: Ind U Sch Medicine 541 Clinic Dr Indianapolis IN 46202

LIU, YUAN HSIUNG, drafting and design educator; b. Tainan, Taiwan, Feb. 24, 1938; came to U.S., 1970; s. Chun Chang and Kong (Wong) L.; m. Ho Pe Tung, July 27, 1973; children: Joan Anshen, Joseph Pinyang. BEd, Nat. Taiwan Normal U., Taipei, 1961; MEd, Nat. Chengchi U., Taipei, 1967, U. Alta., Edmonton, 1970; PhD, Iowa State U., 1975. Cert. tchr. Tchr. indsl. arts and math. Nan Ning Jr. High Sch., Tainan, Taiwan, 1961-62, 63-64; tech. math. instr. Chung-Cheng Inst. Tech., Taipei, 1967-68; drafter Sundstrand Hydro-Transmission Corp., Ames, Iowa, 1973-75; assoc. prof. Fairmont (W.Va.) State Coll., 1975-80; per course instr. Sinclair Community Coll., Dayton, Ohio, 1985; assoc. prof. Miami U., Hamilton, Ohio, 1980-85, Southwest Mo. State U., Springfield, 1985—; cons. Monarch Indsl. Precision Co., Springfield, 1986, Gen. Electric Co., Springfield, 1988, Fasco Industries, Inc., Ozark, Mo., 1989, 95, Springfield Remfg. Corp., 1990, 92, Ctrl. States Indsl., Intercont Products, Inc., L&W Industries, Inc., ZERCO Mfg. Co., 1994, 95. 2d lt. R.O.C. Army, 1962-63. Recipient Excellent Teaching in Drafting award Charvoz-Carsen Corp., Fairfield, N.J., 1978. Mem. Am. Design Drafting Assn. Office: S W Mo State U Tech Dept 901 S National Ave Springfield MO 65804-0094

LIUZZI, ROBERT C., chemical company executive; b. Boston, 1944; married. AB, Coll. of Holy Cross, 1965; LLB, U. Va., 1968. V.p., gen. counsel U.S. Fin., Inc., 1969-74; with CF Industries, Long Grove, Ill., 1975—, exec. v.p., chief fin. officer, 1977-80, exec. v.p., operating officer, 1980-84, pres., chief exec. officer, 1985—; chmn. ad hoc com. Domestic Nitrogen Prodrs., Washington; chmn., bd. dirs. Can. Fertilizers Ltd., The Fertilizer Inst., Nat. Coun. Farmer Coops., Fla. Phosphate Coun., Tampa; co-chmn. Petrochem. Trade Group, Washington; mem. Nat. Forum Nonpoint Source Pollution sponsored by Nat. Geographic Soc. and Conservation Fund of Washington. Mem. coun. Internat. Exec. Svc. Corps, Stamford, Conn.; mem. bus. adv. coun. Law Sch. U. Va., Charlottesville. Mem. Ill. Bus. Roundtable, Northwestern U. Assocs., Coun. of 100, Tampa Fla. Office: CF Industries Inc One Salem Lake Dr Long Grove IL 60047-8402

LIVASY, JAMES RICHARD, investment broker; b. Champaign, Ill., Aug. 8, 1958. BA, Ill. State U., Bloomington, 1981. V.p., investment broker Stifel Nicolaus & Co., Inc., Decatur, Ill., 1983—. Bd. mem. Boys & Girls Club, Decatur, 1990—, Boy Scouts. Mem. Early Bird Kiwanis Club (pres. 1995-96), Decatur Celebration (v.p. 1985—, pres. 1996). Republican. Office: Stifel Nicolaus & Co 207 N Water St PO Box 1517 Decatur IL 62525

LIVESAY, ROBIN RUCKER, university dean; b. Zanesville, Ohio, Mar. 7, 1939; d. Lloyd and Pearl (Vickers) Rucker; m. Frederick E. Livesay, Sept. 18, 1965; children: Todd, Robert. BS, Ohio U., 1968; MEd, U. Cin., 1969; PhD, Ohio State U., 1974. Registered profl. engr., Ohio.civ. Dean Cen. Ohio Tech. Coll., Newark, 1971-78; pres. LBL Mavericks, Indpls., 1989-96; dean Sch. Bus., endowed chair U. Indpls., 1979—; cons. in field. Author two chpts. in books; contbr. articles to profl. jours. Pres. Youth League, New Palestine, 1986; bd. dirs. Health Net, Indpls., 1990, United Meth. Ch., Greenfield, 1984-86. Mem. IEEE, Assn. Computing Machinery, Indpls. C. of C., Econ. Club Indpls, NY Acad. Sci., Assn. Coll. Business Schs. and Prgms. (bd. commrs. 1995—, pres.-elect 1995—). Republican. Office: U Indpls 1400 E Hanna Ave Indianapolis IN 46227-3630

LIVINGSTON, HOMER J., JR., stock exchange executive; b. Chgo., 1935. BA in Econs., Princeton U., 1957; JD, Chgo. Kent Coll. Law, 1966. With First Nat Bank, Chgo., 1963-79, Lehman Bros. Kuhn Loeb, Chgo., 1979-82, William Blair & Co., Chgo., 1982-84, Algemene Bank Nederland, Chgo., 1984-88, H. Livingston & Co., L.P., Chgo., 1988-92, Livingston Co. Southwest, L.P., Chgo., 1988-92, Midwest Securities Trust Co., Chgo., 1992—; bd. dirs. Peoples Energy Corp., Am. Nat. Can Corp. Office: Midwest Securities Trust Co 440 S La Salle St Chicago IL 60605-1028*

LIVITS, MARIA, mechanical engineer; b. The White River, Russia, Aug. 14, 1954; came to U.S., 1979.; BSME, U. R.R. Transp., Gomel, Russia, 1978. Designer Emerson Electric Co., Hazelwood, Mo., 1980—. Mem. IEEE. Office: Emerson Electric Co Spl Products 8400 Pershall Rd Hazelwood MO 63042-3075

LLEWELLYN, JOHN T., state legislator; m. Becky; children: Evan, Elizabeth, Matthew. BA, Alma Coll. Commr. Newago County, Mich., 1989-92; mem. Pub. Health Bd., 1990-92; mem. Newago County Zoning & Planning Bd., 1990-92; state rep. Dist. 100 Mich. Ho. of Reps., 1993—; owner, operator family orchard Fremont, Mich., 1996—; chair Consumers Com. Mich. Ho. of Reps., vice-chair Ins. Com., 1993—, mem Conservation, Edn. Great Lakes & Higher Edn. Coms., 1993—, mem. task force to study advt. impact, house oversight ethics com., 1996—, chmn. Ins. Com., 1996—, vice chmn. Human Resources & Labor Com., 1996—, co-chair. Mem. Mich. Agrl. Coop. Mktg. Assn. Home: 5588 W 32nd St Fremont MI 49412-9606*

LLITERAS, MARGARITA, Spanish educator; b. Ibiza, Spain, Apr. 7, 1953; came to the U.S., 1982; d. Sebastian and Berta L.; m. Jesus Garcia-Varela, July 20, 1980; children: Nuria, Susana. LLD, U. Barcelona, 1975; MA in Spanish Lit., Ind. U., 1984, PhD, 1991. Assoc. instr. dept. Spanish and Portuguese Ind. U., 1982-89; lectr. dept. classical and modern langs. U. Louisville, 1989-90, vis. asst. prof., 1990-93; asst. prof., coord. Spanish program divsn. humanities Ind. U. S.E., 1993—; atty., Barcelona, 1975-82. Contbr. articles to profl. jours. Mem. MLA, Assn. Doctores y Licenciados españoles en los Estados Unidos. Office: Ind U SE 4201 Grant Line Rd New Albany IN 47150-2158

LLOYD, ED, state legislator; m. Susan Lloyd; 3 children. Pres. AGVISE Lab.; rep. Dist. 19 N.D. Ho. of Reps., mem. fin., taxation and natural resources coms. Mem. new devel. com. N.D. State U.; mem. indsl. tech. transfer com. U. N.D.; bd. dirs. Northwood Deaconess Health Ctr.; mem. Northwood Econ. Devel. Assn. Mem. Soc. Agrl. Cons. N.D., Nat. Alliance Ind. Crop Cons., Northwood Comml. Club, Northwood Lions. Home: PO Box 248 Northwood ND 58267

LLOYD, LEONA LORETTA, judge; b. Detroit, Aug. 6, 1949; d. Leon Thomas and Naomi Mattie (Chisolm) L.; 1 stepson, Joseph Andersen. BS, Wayne State U., 1971, JD, 1979. Bar: Mich. 1981, U.S. Dist. Ct. (ea. dist.) 1981, U.S. Supreme Ct. 1988, U.S. Cir. Ct. (6th cir.) 1983. Speech, drama tchr. Detroit Bd. Edn., 1971-75; instr. criminal justice Wayne State U., Detroit, 1981; sr. ptnr. Lloyd and Lloyd, Detroit, 1982-92; prin. asst., corp. counsel City Detroit Law Dept., 1992-94; judge 36th Dist. Ct., Detroit, 1994—. Co-author, dir. (gospel musical) Freedom Song, 1991. Wayne State U. scholar, 1970, 75; recipient Fred Hampton Image award, 1984, Kizzy Image award, 1985, Nat. Coalition of 100 Black Women Achievement award, 1986, Community Svc. award Wayne County exec. William Lucas, 1986, Merit Black Law Student Assn. cert. U. Detroit, 1986, Spirit of Detroit award, 1991, Martin Luther King Keep This Dream Alive award, 1995, Special Tribute award State of Mich., 1995, Resolution award County of Wayne, 1995, Appreciation cert. City of Detroit, 1995, Bar Assn. award, 1995, B'nai B'rith Barristers award, 1995, Testimonial Resolution award Detroit City Coun., 1995, Woman of Yr. award African Am. Awards Coun., 1996; named to Black Women Hall of Fame. Mem. ABA, Wolverine Bar Assn., Mary McLeod Bethune Assn., Nat. Acad. of Recording Arts & Scis., Mich. State Bar. Office: 421 Madison St Ste 3067 Detroit MI 48226-2358

LLOYD, STEVE, state legislator; b. Apr. 9, 1952; m. Kathe Lloyd, 1993. Grad., Kans. State U., 1976. Kans. state rep. Dist. 64, livestock farmer. Mem. Kans. Farm Bur., Pork Prodrs. Coun. Home: PO Box 101 Palmer KS 66962*

LOBAO, LINDA MARY, sociologist, educator; b. Beverly, Mass., Aug. 9, 1952; d. George and Helen (Baschuk) L.; 1 child, Erick. BA in Sociology, Boston U., 1974; MA in Sociology, U. South Fla., 1981; PhD in Sociology, N.C. State U., 1986. Asst. prof. Ohio State U., Columbus, 1986-90, assoc. prof. dept. agrl. econs. and rural sociology, 1990—. Author: Locality and Inequality: Farm and Industry Structure and Socio-Economic Conditions, 1990; co-author: Beyond the Amber Waves of Grain: An Examination of Social and Economic Restructuring in the Heartland, 1995; contbr. articles to profl. publs. Grantee NSF, 1988, USDA, 1993. Mem. Am. Sociol. Assn., Rural Sociology Soc. (mem. coun. 1985—). Office: Ohio State U Dept of Agrl Econs & Rural Sociology Columbus OH 43212

LOBECK, DAVID R., investment broker; b. Evansville, Ind., May 27, 1963. BS, Ind. State U., 1986. Investment broker Edward D. Jones & Co., New Albany, Ind., 1986—. Bd. dirs. Ronald McDonald Children's Charity Golf Classic, Sellersburg, Ind., 1994-95. Lutheran. Office: Edward D Jones & Co PO Box 8008 2676 Charlestown New Albany IN 47151

LOBODA, MARK JON, physicist; b. Chgo., Jan. 15, 1962; s. Jon A. and Camille R. (Maniszko) L. BS in Physics, DePaul U., 1983, MS in Applied Physics with distinction, 1985. Rsch. scientist, rsch. div. Raytheon Co., Lexington, Mass., 1985-89; sr. rsch. specialist Dow Corning Corp., Midland, Mich., 1989—. Contbr. articles to profl. jours. Recipient Outstanding Transaction Paper award, IEEE Ultrasonics, Ferroelectrics and Frequency Control Soc., 1988. Mem. IEEE, Am. Phys. Soc. Office: Dow Corning Corp MS #CO41A1 Midland MI 48686

LOCH, JOHN ROBERT, educational administrator; b. Sharon, Pa., Aug. 25, 1940; s. Robert Addison and Mary Virginia (Beck) L. Student Waynesburg Coll., 1958; AB, Grove City Coll., 1962; postgrad Pitts. Theol. Sem., 1962; MEd, U. Pitts., 1966, PhD, 1972; cert. Harvard U., 1984. Asst. to dean of men U. Pitts., 1963-64, dir. student union, 1964-70, dir. student affairs rsch., 1970-71, dir. suburban ednl. svcs. Sch. Gen. Studies, 1971-75; dir. continuing edn. and pub. svc. Youngstown (Ohio) State U., 1975-82, dir. continuing edn./edn. outreach, 1982-90, dir. univ. outreach, 1990—, assoc. mem. grad. faculty, 1980-95; rsch. assoc. Pres's Commn. on Campus Unrest, 1970; bd. dirs. Park Vista Retirement Community, 1993—, chmn. program com., 1994-95, vice chair bd. dirs., 1995-96; trustee Ohio Presbyn. Retirement Communities, 1993—, mem. program com., 1993—. Trustee, Mahoning Shenango Area Health Edn. Network, 1976-91, Career Devel. Ctr. for Women, 1978-80; trustee Youngstown Area Arts Coun., 1980-85, pres., 1981-83; bd. dirs. Protestant Family Svcs., 1981-83; active Older Adults Task Force, Mahoning County, 1992—; trustee Mahoning County RSVP, 1983-89, chmn. evaluation com., 1983-84, chmn. pers. com., 1984-85, chmn. bd. trustees, 1986-87; coord. fund raising Nat. Unity Campaign, Mahoning County, 1980; state chmn. Young Rep. Coll. Coun. Pa., 1960. Mem. AAUW, Assn. Continuing Higher Edn., Adult Edn. Assn. USA, Am. Assn. Higher Edn., Nat. U. Continuing Edn. Assn., Ohio Coun. Higher Continuing Edn. (pres. 1979-80), Ohio Continuing Higher Edn. Assn. (hon. life, co-chmn. constn. com. 1982, v.p. state univs. 1984-85, pres.-elect 1985-86, pres. 1986-87, historian 1988-96, chair awards and honors com. 1989-92, editor Voluntary Continuing Edn. Requirements 1993-95, Spl. award 1989), Ohio-Pa. Higher Edn. Network (chair 1989-90), Learning Resources Network Univ. Coun. (Gt. Lakes rep.), Youngstown Traffic Club (hon. life mem.), Youngstown Club, Kiwanis (dir. 1981-82), Omicron Delta Kappa, Kappa Kappa Psi, Phi Kappa Phi (pres. 1980-81, pres. 1995-96), Alpha Phi Omega, Alpha Sigma Lambda, Phi Delta Kappa. Presbyterian. Home: 242 Upland Ave Youngstown OH 44504-1849 Office: Youngstown State U Dept of Education Youngstown OH 44555

LOCH, RANDALL L., sales executive; b. Fairbury, Nebr., Sept. 14, 1947; s. Don L. and Lou Ellyn (Moorg) L.; m. Anita A. Bartling, Sept. 30, 1967; children: Matthew L., Andrew J. BS, U. Nebr., 1972. Market rsch. analyst Maytag, Newton, Iowa, 1972-74; dist. mgr. Maytag, Huntington, W.Va., 1974-76, Worcester, Mass., 1976-78; merchandising mgr. People's Natural Gas, Council Bluffs, Iowa, 1978-80; dist. mgr. Maytag, Yorktown, N.Y., 1980-84; dist. mktg. mgr. Maytag, Randolph, N.J., 1984-87; nat. account mgr. Maytag, NEwton, Iowa, 1987-89; regional sales mgr. Maytag, Chgo., 1989-94, No. divsn. sales mgr., 1994—. 1st lt. U.S. Army, 1967-69. Home: 561 W 81st Burr Ridge IL 60521

LOCHER, DUANE, controller; b. Wash., Nov. 4, 1947; s. Ernst Henry and Gladys Marie (Meyer) L.; m. Jo Ann Johnson, June 6, 1970. BS BA, Southeast Mo. State, 1969; MBA, Southern Ill. U., 1976. Cert. Pub. Accountant. Auditor US Dept. Army, St. Louis, 1969-73; sr. auditor Mercantile Bank, St. Louis, 1973-76; asst. controller Tower Grove Bank & Trust, St. Louis, 1976-77, controller, 1978-83; controller T.G. Bancshares, St. Louis, 1980-81, Commerce Bank St. Louis, 1984—; vol. cons. Inst. Mgmt. Accts., St. Louis, 1980—. Bd. dirs., co-chair funds devel. com. Webster Groves Sch. Found. Mem. AICPA (fin. planners divsn.), Fin. Execs. Inst. (chmn. profl. devel. com. St. Louis chpt. 1991-92), Planning Execs. Internat. (treas. St. Louis chpt. 1980-82), Mo. Soc. CPAs (chair subcom. rels. with educators, nominating com. for Outstanding Educator of Yr. Mo. 1995—). Methodist. Home: 848 Pinetree Ln Saint Louis MO 63119-4136 Office: Commerce Bank St Louis 8000 Forsyth Blvd Saint Louis MO 63105-1707

LOCHER, RALPH SIDNEY, retired state supreme court justice; b. Moreni, Romania, July 24, 1915; s. Ephraim and Natalie (Voigt) L.; m. Eleanor Worthington, June 18, 1939; 1 child, Virginia Lynn. BA with honors, Bluffton Coll., 1936, LLB, Case Western Res. U., 1939. Bar: Ohio bar 1939. Former sec. to Gov. Ohio; former law dir. City of Cleve.; former mayor Cleve.; judge Ohio Ct. Common Pleas Cuyahoga County, 1969-72, Cuyahoga County Ct. Probate Div., 1973-77; justice Supreme Ct. Ohio, 1977-88. Mem. Am. Bar Assn., Bar Assn. Greater Cleve., Cuyahoga County Bar Assn. Democrat. Home: 3280 Green Rd Cleveland OH 44122-4049

LOCHER, RICHARD EARL, editorial cartoonist; b. Dubuque, Iowa, June 4, 1929; s. Joseph John and Lucille (Jungk) L.; m. Mary Therese Cosgrove, June 15, 1957; children: Stephen Robert, John Joseph, Jana Lynne. Student, Loras Coll., 1948, Chgo. Acad. Fine Arts, 1949-51; BFA, Art Center, Los Angeles, 1954, postgrad., 1955-56; DHL (hon.), Ill. Benedictine Coll., 1992. founder, pres. Novamark Corp., Chgo., 1968-72; cons. McDonalds Corp., Oakbrook, Ill.; tchr. art at local high schs. and colls. Asst. writer, artist: Buck Rogers Comic Strip, 1954-57, Dick Tracy Comic Strip, 1957-61, Martin Aerospace co., Denver, 1962-63; art dir. Hansen Co., Chgo., N.Y.C., 1963-68; editorial cartoonist Chgo. Tribune, 1972—; artist Dick Tracy Comic Strip, 1983—; author: Dick Locher Draws Fire, 1980, Send in the Clowns, 1982, Vote for Me, 1988, The Dick Tracy Casebook, 1990, Dick Tracy's Fiendish Foes, 1991, None of the Above, 1992, The Daze of Whine and Neurosis, 1995, (with Michael Kilian) Flying Can Be Fun, 1985; patentee Poker Face device to play poker without cards. Trustee Ill. Benedictine Coll., 1984—. Served with USAF, 1951-53. Recipient Dragonslayer award U.S. Indsl. Coun., 1976, 77, 78, 80, 81, 82, Disting. Health Journalism award, 1981, 82, 83, 84, 85, 92, Overseas Press Club award, 1983, 84, Pulitizer prize, 1983, Sigma Delta Chi award, 1985, World Population Inst. award, 1986, John Fischetti award, 1987, Peter Lisagor award, 1987, 89, 91; Named Ill. FBI Man of Yr., 1993. Mem. Assn. Am. Editorial Cartoonists.

LOCK, ROBERT JOSEPH, accountant; b. Jefferson City, Mo., June 20, 1955; s. Elmer Joseph and Clara Barbara (Luebbert) L.; m. Cheryl Lynne Garoutte, Apr. 20, 1985 (div. Jan. 1988); m. Susan C. Springhower, Nov. 16, 1991. BSBA in Acctg., U. Mo., 1977. CPA, Mo. Sr. Mo. State Auditor's Office, Jefferson City, 1977-82; ptnr. McBride, Lock & Assocs., Kansas City, Mo., 1982—. Pres. Picture Hills Homeowners Assn., 1994-95. Mem. Am. Inst. CPA's, Mo. Soc. CPA's, Assn Govtl. Accts. Roman Catholic. Lodge: KC. Home: 5735 N Polk Dr Kansas City MO 64151-2697 Office: McBride Lock & Assocs 1221 Baltimore Ave Ste 406 Kansas City MO 64105-1913

LOCKHART, GEMMA, producer, writer; b. Rapid City, S.D., Dec. 5, 1956; d. Jim and Teena L.; children: Mica, Nakca, Aaron. BA in English, Creative Writing, Dartmouth Coll., 1979. TV news reporter Duhamel Broadcasting Enterprises, Rapid City, S.D., 1974-80; TV producer Rural Ethnic Inst., Rapid City, 1981-83; instr. Oglala Lakota Coll., Kyle, S.D., 1983-86; horse rider Black Hills, S.D.; TV producer S.D. Pub. TV, Vermillion, 1989-90; ind. producer, 1990—; CEO Wambli Win Prodns., 1994—, Anpao Studio, Rapid City, 1995—; auditor Lakota Elders, Dakota Land, 1975—; freelance columnist various publs. including USA Today. Presdl. scholar, 1975, 85. Mem. NAFE, Dartmouth Coll. Alumni Coun., Nature Conservancy (bd. dirs. 1995-96). Republican. Home: Box 8044 Rapid City SD 57709-8044 also: Dark Canyon Rapid City SD 57702

LOCKHART, LISA HOLMSTROM, artist, librarian; b. Rockford, Ill., Apr. 24, 1959; d. John Theodore and Marcia Lynn (Norton) Holmstrom; m.

Kirk Steven Lockhart, Jan. 2, 1986; 1 child, Loren Felix. BFA, Art Inst. Chgo., 1980; MFA, Cranbrook Acad., 1983. Gallery asst. Klien Gallery, Chgo., 1984-85; mem. exbn. selection com. Near Northwest Arts Coun., Chgo., 1986-88; gallery dir. Gallery Great Lakes Chgo., 1988-90; artist, 1983—; head librarian Onarga (Ill.) Cmty. Pub. Lib. Dist., 1994—; Art dir., Best Promotional Piece/Grafix Can., 1992. Office: Onarga Cmty Pub Lib Dist 209 W Seminary Onarga IL 60955

LOCKHART, ROBERT FREDERICK, electrical engineer; b. Milw., Feb. 18, 1935. BSEE, Milw. Sch. Engring., 1956. Registered profl. engr., Ohio. Elec. engr. Reliance Elec. Co., Cleve., 1961—. Mem. IEEE, Am. Iron & Steel Engrs., Ohio Soc. Elevation of Kites (pres. 1991-94). Lutheran. Office: Reliance Elec Co Sys Divsn 24703 Euclid Ave Cleveland OH 44117-1714

LOCKNER, VERA JOANNE, farmer, rancher, legislator; b. St. Lawrence, S.D., May 19, 1937; d. Leonard and Zona R. (Ford) Verdugt; m. Frank O. Lockner, Aug. 7, 1955; children: Dean M., Clifford A. Grad., St. Lawrence (S.D.) High Sch., 1955. Bank teller/bookkeeper First Nat. Bank, Miller, S.D., 1963-66, Bank of Wessington, S.D., 1968-74; farmer/rancher Wessington, 1955—. Sunday sch. tchr. Trinity Luth. Ch., Miller, 1968-72; treas. PTO, Wessington, 1969-70; treas., vice chmn., chmn., state com. woman Hand County Dems., Miller, 1978—. Named one of Outstanding Young Women of Am., Women's Study Club, Wessington, 1970. Mem. Order of Ea. Star (warder, marshall, chaplain 1970—). Home and Office: RR 2 Box 102 Wessington SD 57381-8932

LOCKWOOD, FRANK JAMES, manufacturing company executive; b. San Bernadino, Calif., Oct. 30, 1931; s. John Ellis and Sarah Grace (Roberts) L.; children from previous marraige: Fay, Frank, Hedy, Jonnie, George, Katherine, Bill, Dena; m. 2d. Crystal Marie Miller, 1986. Student, Southeast City Coll., Chgo., 1955, Ill. Inst. Tech., 1963-64, Bogan Jr. Coll., Chgo., 1966. Foreman Hupp Aviation, Chgo., 1951-60; dept. head UARCO, Inc., Chgo., 1960-68; pres. XACT Machine & Engring., Chgo., 1968—; chmn. bd., pres., bd. dirs. Lockwood Engring., Inc., Chgo.; Ill. Nat. Corp., Chgo., and cons. engr., Chgo. Patentee printing equipment, beverage cans, gasoline pump dispenser "Super Pin", bus. forms equipment. Participant Forest Land Mgmt. Program; mem. Ill. Ambassadors; commr. Econ. Devel. Commn., Mt. Vernon, Ill., 1985; mem. bd. County of Jefferson, Ill., 1992—; mem. exec. com., legis. com. Ill. County Bds. Coun. Named Chgo. Ridge Father of the Yr., 1964. Mem. Ill. Divers' Assn. (pres. 1961-62). Lodge: Masons (32 degree), Shriners (past master 2). Home: RR 1 Texico IL 62889-9801 Office: 7011 W Archer Ave Chicago IL 60638-2201

LOCKWOOD, MICHAEL DACRE, osteopath; b. Express, Alberta, Can., May 17, 1947; came to U.S., 1951; s. Richard Ernest and Edith Armina (Pointon) L. MS, Calif. Polytechnic Inst., 1977; DO, Kirksville (Mo.) Coll. of Osteopathic Medicine, 1981. Bd. cert. Am. Osteo. Bd. of Osteo. Manipulative Medicine; bd. cert. Am. Coll. Family Practitioners. Asst. prof. Kirksville Coll. Osteopathic Medicine, 1982-89, assoc. prof., 1989—; chief of staff Kirksville Osteo. Med. Ctr., 1988-90, 92-94, chair dept. perinatal svcs.; pres. Cranial Acad., 1993-95; life mem. cranial acad. exec. bd. Cranial Acad. Found., 1993—. Trustee N.E. Mo. Osteopathic Charitable Trust. With U.S. Army, 1965-68. Office: 700 W Jefferson St Kirksville MO 63501-1441

LOCKWOOD, WALTER LEE, screenwriter, English language educator; b. St. Joseph, Mich., Aug. 2, 1941; s. Leon W. and Edith E. (Bauer) L.; m. Irene R. Gallacher, Sept. 15, 1962 (div.); children: Ian, Alison, Matthew; m. Pamela B. Broersma, Sept. 31, 1989; children: Susan, Katherine. BA, Mich. State U., 1963; MA, Ind. U., 1964. English prof. Grand Rapids (Mich.) C.C., 1965—; freelance writer, 1970—; advisor Display-A Mag. of the Arts, Grand Rapids, 1965—; mgr. Kent County Poetry Contest, Grand Rapids, 1972-85. Author: (novel) Jones Unbound, 1973, (screenplay-movie) Finnegan Begin Again, 1985 (HBO, Ace award nominee 1985), (documentary) Dyslexia: The Hidden Disability, 1987, (telefilm) Indiscreet, 1988 (CBS Movie of Wk.), Secret Life of Archie's Wife (a.k. Runaway Heart), 1990 (CBS Movie of Wk.), Battling for Baby, 1991 (CBS Movie of Wk.); editor Best of Four, 1970-71. Recipient Woodrow Wilson Found. fellowship, 1963-64. Mem. Writers' Guild Am. West. Democrat.

LOEB, DEANN JEAN, nurse; b. West Union, Iowa, Aug. 1, 1960; d. Dale Alfred and Annagene Helen (Suhr) Ungerer; m. Thomas Allan Loeb, Sept. 1, 1985; children: Ryan, Jennifer, Andrea, Cody. Diploma in nursing, NE Iowa Tech. Inst., 1982. Lic. practical nurse, Iowa. Laundry aide Good Samaritan Ctr., West Union, 1977, kitchen aide, cook, 1977-79, nurses asst., 1979-81, practical nurse, 1982-84; practical nurse Ind. (Ind.) Care Ctr., 1985-89, Dr. Jose C. Aguiar, Waterloo, Iowa, 1989-93, Dr. John Musgrave-Dr. Mary O'Connell, Waterloo, Iowa, 1993-94; nurse Waterloo Asthma and Allergy Clinic, 1994—. Leader Brownies, asst. leader Girl Scouts U.S.; tchr. Bible, Sunday sch., mem. parish bd. edn., mem. parish life com. Zion Jubilee Luth. Ch., Jesup, Iowa. Republican. Home: 7144 Spring Creek Rd Jesup IA 50648-9568

LOEFFLER, ROBERT HENRY, media relations manager; b. Paterson, N.J., Jan. 16, 1947; s. Henry and Erna (Oslau) L.; m. Linda Ray Wilkinson; children: Elizabeth, Gloria. BA, William Paterson Coll., 1972; M Humanities, U. Richmond, Va., 1974; JD, Cleve. State U., 1978. Cert. bus. communicator. Asst. editor Rural Living mag., Richmond, 1972-74; pub. rels. writer Dalton-Dalton-Newport, Shaker Heights, Ohio, 1975; tech. writer Bailey Controls, Wickliffe, Ohio, 1976-78, mgr. media rels., 1985—; mgr. mktg. com. Davy McKee Corp., Independence, Ohio, 1979-83; dir. direct mktg. Predicasts, Cleve., 1984; adj. asst. prof. bus. adminstrn. Baldwin-Wallace Coll., Berea, Ohio, 1982—; adj. prof. bus. adminstr. Notre Dame Coll., Cleve., 1987-94. Author: A Guide to Preparing Cost Effective Press Releases, 1992; contbr. articles to profl. jours. Mem. Mcpl. Cable TV Commn., University Heights, Ohio, 1992, Sch. Dist. Planning Com., University Heights, 1992. With USAF, 1966-70. Mem. Pub. Rels. Soc. Am., Instrument Soc. Am., Bus./Profl. Advt. Assn., Sigma Delta Chi. Home: 2507 Edgerton Rd University Heights OH 44118-4412

LOESCH, KATHARINE TAYLOR (MRS. JOHN GEORGE LOESCH), communication and theatre educator; b. Berkeley, Calif., Apr. 13, 1922; d. Paul Schuster and Katharine (Whiteside) Taylor; student Swarthmore Coll., 1939-41, U. Wash., 1942; BA, Columbia U., 1944, MA, 1949; grad. Neighborhood Playhouse Sch. of Theatre, 1946; postgrad. Ind. U., 1953; PhD, Northwestern U., 1961; m. John George Loesch, Aug. 28, 1948; 1 child, William Ross. Instr. speech Wellesley (Mass.) Coll., 1949-52, Loyola U., Chgo., 1956; asst. prof. English and speech Roosevelt U., Chgo., 1957, 62-65; assoc. prof. communication and theatre U. Ill. at Chgo., 1968—; assoc. prof. emerita speech in communication and theater, U. Ill., Chgo., 1987—. Contbr. writings to profl. jours.; poetry performances. Active ERA, Ill., 1975-76. Am. Philos. Soc. grantee, 1970; U. Ill., Chgo., grantee, 1970. Mem. MLA, Speech Communication Assn. (Golden Anniversary prize award 1969, chmn. interpretation div. 1979-80), Celtic Studies Assn. N.Am., Pi Beta Phi. Episcopalian. Home: 2129 N Sedgwick St Chicago IL 60614-4619 Office: U Ill Dept Performing Arts M/C 255 1040 W Harrison St Chicago IL 60607-7130

LOESCH-FRIES, LORETTA SUE, virology educator; b. Ventura, Calif., Sept. 5, 1947; d. Frank James and Helyn Mildred (Stenson) L.; m. Robert Edward Fries, Feb. 14, 1976; children: Michael, Matthew. BS, Wash. State U., 1969; PhD, U. Wis., 1974. Sr. scientist Agrigenetics, Madison, Wis., 1981-88; asst. adj. prof. U. Wis., Madison, 1987-91; asst. prof. virology Purdue U., West Lafayette, Ind., 1991—; panel mem. for grant rev. panels USDA, 1985, 86, Dept. of Energy, 1988. Asst. editor Molecular Plant Microbe Interactions, 1988-95, Virology, 1993-95, Jour. Virology, 1996—; contbr. articles to profl. jours. Mem. Am. Phytopathological Soc., Am. Soc. Virology, Internat. Soc. Plant Molecular Biology. Office: Purdue U Dept Botany/Plant Pathology Agriculture Rsch Bldg West Lafayette IN 47907-1057

LOFQUIST, JAMES WALLACE, school system administrator; b. Mobridge, S.D., Oct. 26, 1937; s. Palmer Ole and Ella Amanda (Neuman) L.; m. Margaret Lucille DeVries, May 28, 1960; children: Donna Rae, Kraig James, Paul Brian. BS, No. State Coll., 1960, MS, 1964; EdS, U. Nebr., 1972. Tchr., coach, prin. Winfred (S.D.) Pub. Schs., 1960-64, Walthill (Nebr.) Pub. Schs., 1964-66; supt. Conde (S.D.) Pub. Schs., 1966-69, Laurel (Nebr.) Pub. Sch. Dist., 1969-85, Anselmo-Merna (Nebr.) Pub. Sch. Dist. 015, 1985-95, Callaway (Nebr.) Pub. Sch. Dist., 1995—. Mem. Am. Assn. Sch. Adminstrs., Nebr. Coun. Sch. Adminstrs., Nat. Biology Tchrs. Assn., Nebr. Schoolmasters, Merna Area Promoters, Callaway C. of C., Callaway Booster Club, Elks, Masons, Lions, Phi Delta Kappa. Republican. Lutheran. Office: Callaway Pub Sch Dist 101 N Needham PO Box 188 Callaway NE 68825

LOGAN, HENRY VINCENT, transportation executive; b. Phila., Nov. 7, 1942; s. Edward Roger and Alberta (Gross) L.; m. Mary Genzano, Sept. 28, 1963; children: Michele Leah, Maureen Laura, Monica Lynn. BS in Commerce, DePaul U., 1975; M in Mgmt., Northwestern U., 1984. Successively supr. corp. acctg., asst. mgr. gen. acctg., mgr. gen. acctg., dir. corp. acctg. and taxes TTX Co., Chgo., 1962-70, controller, 1970-78, dir. fin. planning, 1978-83, mng. dir., fin. adminstr., 1983-85, v.p., chief fin. officer, 1985-88, sr. v.p. fleet mgmt., 1988—; bd. dirs. Calpro, Co., Mira Loma, Calif., RailGon Co., Chgo.; bd. dirs., fin. com. Railway Supply Assn. Treas. TTX Co. Polit. Action Com., Chgo., 1980; vol Sch. Dist. 87 Task Force, Glen Ellyn, Ill., 1986. Mem. Nat. Freight Transp. Assn., Intermodal Assn. N.Am. (chmn. legis. com. 1992-94), Union League Club (reception com. 1987-92, fin. com. 1993-95), Medinah (Ill.) Country Club. Republican. Roman Catholic. Home: 812 Abbey Dr Glen Ellyn IL 60137-6130

LOGAN, JAMES KENNETH, federal judge; b. Quenemo, Kans., Aug. 21, 1929; s. John Lysle and Esther Maurine (Price) L.; m. Beverly Jo Jennings, June 8, 1952; children: Daniel Jennings, Amy Logan Sliva, Sarah Logan Sherard, Samuel Price. A.B., U. Kans., 1952; LL.B. magna cum laude, Harvard, 1955. Bar: Kans. 1955, Calif. 1956. Law clk. U.S. Cir. Judge Huxman, 1955-56; with firm Gibson, Dunn & Crutcher, L.A., 1956-57; asst. prof. law U. Kans., 1957-61, prof., dean Law Sch., 1961-68; ptnr. Payne and Jones, Olathe, Kans., 1968-77; judge U.S. Ct. Appeals (10th cir.), 1977—; Ezra Ripley Thayer tchg. fellow Harvard Law Sch., 1961-62; vis. prof. U. Tex., 1964, Stanford U., 1969, U. Mich., 1976; sr. lectr. Duke U., 1987, 91, 93; commr. U.S. Dist. Ct., 1964-67. Author: (with W.B. Leach) Future Interests and Estate Planning, 1961, Kansas Estate Administration, 5th edit., 1986, (with A.R. Martin) Kansas Corporate Law and Practice, 2d edit., 1979, The Federal Courts of the Tenth Circuit: A History, 1992; also articles. Candidate for U.S. Senate, 1968. Served with AUS, 1947-48. Rhodes scholar, 1952; recipient Disting. Service citation U. Kans., 1986. Mem. Am., Kans. bar assns., Phi Beta Kappa, Order of Coif, Beta Gamma Sigma, Omicron Delta Kappa, Pi Sigma Alpha, Alpha Kappa Psi, Phi Delta Phi. Democrat. Presbyterian.

LOGAN, LINDA MARY, art education educator; b. Detroit, Dec. 28, 1942; d. Ervin John Moore, Joseph R. Sanson (stepfather) and Helen (Kolczynski) Moore Sanson; divorced; 1 child, Stephen Kelly. BA, Wayne State U., 1965, MA in Tchg., 1971; postgrad., Oakland C.C., 1989—. Cert. tchr., Mich. Instr. art Detroit Bd. Edn., 1967—, instr. gifted art, 1971—; audio-visual asst. Wayne State U., Detroit, 1960-62; clk. Wayne County Treas., Detroit, summers, 1960-63; pvt. decorative painter, Mich., 1962—; pvt. graphic designer logos, Mich., 1971—; tchr. workshops Detroit Schs., 1988—, Children's Mus., Detroit, 1995; advisor Davis Publs., 1990—; developer core curriculum Detroit Art Edn.; judge Free Press Editl. contest. Co-author art appreciation guide; photographer Detroit Zoo Jour., 1991; cons. Art Edn. Text Books, 1988—; exhibited at group shows at Biagus Gallery, Scarab Club, 1995, Oakland C.C., Mich. Coun. of Arts, Mich. Art Edn. Conf., Focus Gallery, 1980—. Vol. Detroit Inst. of Arts, 1992. Mem. Am. Fedn. Tchrs., Mich. Art Edn. Assn., Detroit Art Tchrs. Assn. (treas.), Nat. Art Edn. Assn., Founder's Soc., Greenpeace, Earthwatch. Home: 10705 Nadine Ave Huntington Woods MI 48070-1519

LOGAN, SEAN D., state legislator; b. Salem, Ohio, Feb. 11, 1966; s. Robert C. and Dorothy (Hall) L.; m. Melissa Logan. BA, Muskingum Coll., 1988. Intern Legis. Svc. Commn., 1988; legis. aide Ho. Rep. Ohio State Congress, 1989-90, state reg. Dist. 3, 1990—. Recipient Friendship Pin Beaver Creek Lodge N FOP, Svc. award Columbiana County Fedn. Conservation Club, 1993; named Regional Pub. Servant of Yr. Nat. Soc. Social Workers, 1993. Mem. Nat. Conf. State Legislators, Ohio Farm Bur. (hon.), Sons of Am. Legion (hon.), Ruritan Internat., Jaycee, Columbiana County Twp. Trustees and Clks. Assn. (hon.). *

LOGANI, KULBHUSHAN LAL, civil and structural engineer; b. Mardan, Panjab, India, Oct. 20, 1943; came to U.S., 1965; s. Sulakhan Mal and Shankri Devi L.; m. Suresh Logani, Jan. 24, 1965; children: Sanjay, Monica, Ronica. BSCE, Panjab U., 1961; ME in Structural Engring., Iowa State U., 1970, PhD, 1973. Registered profl. engr., lic. structural engr. Design engr. Bhakra & Beas Design Orgn., New Delhi, 1961-65; engring. cons. Ministry of Agr., Ghana, West Africa, 1965-69; rsch. asst. Iowa State U., Ames, 1969-73; consulting engr. Harza Engring. Co., Chgo., 1973-86; v.p., dir. Facilities Cons. Ltd., Chgo., 1986-93; pres. KL Cons. Ltd., Glenview, Ill., 1991—; cons. dam design and constrn. Dept. Hydraulic Resources, San Juan, Argentina, 1979-83; cons. devel. of instrumentation under artesian conditions Reza Shah Kabir Dam, Iran, 1978-79. Author publs. in field including Proceedings of VII Pan Am. Conf. on Soil Mechanics and Found. Engr.-Can., 1983, Transaction of the 14th Internat. Congress on Large Dams - Brazil, Proceedings of the Internat. Conf. on Recent Advances in Geotechnical Earthquake Engring., U. Mo., Rolla, 1981, various others confs. in field; contbg. author ency. article, 1988; contbr. articles to profl. jours. Founding mem. Assn. of Indian in Am., Chgo. Rsch. grantee Def. Nuclear Agy., Washington, 1970-73. Fellow ASCE; mem. ASTM (com. on soil and rock 1984—), Internat. Soc. Soil Mechanics and Found. Engring., Instn. of Engrs. India. Home and Office: 1144 Bette Ln Glenview IL 60025-2429

LOGIE, JOHN HOULT, mayor, lawyer; b. Ann Arbor, Mich., Aug. 11, 1939; s. James Wallace and Elizabeth (Hoult) L.; m. Susan G. Duerr, Aug. 15, 1964; children: John Hoult Jr., Susannah, Margaret Elizabeth. Student Williams Coll., 1957-59; BA, U. Mich., 1961, JD, 1968; MS, George Washington U., 1966. Bar: Mich. 1969, U.S. Dist. Ct. (we. and ea. dists. 1969) Mich., U.S. Ct. Appeals (6th cir. 1987). Assoc. Warner, Norcross & Judd, Grand Rapids, Mich., 1969-74, ptnr., 1974—; mayor City of Grand Rapids, 1992—; chmn. civil justice adv. group U.S. Dist. Ct. (we. dist.) Mich., 1995—. program coord. condemnation law sect. Inst. Continuing Legal Edn.; guest lectr. Grand Rapids C.C., Grand Valley State U., Western Mich. U., Mich. State U.; legal counsel to 15 West Mich. hosps.; instr. U.S. Naval Acad., 1964-66. Pres. Grand Rapids PTA Council, 1971-73, Heritage Hill Assn., 1976, sec., trustee 1971-84; chmn. Grand Rapids Urban Homesteading Commn., 1975-80, Grand Rapids Hist. Commn., 1985-90, Grand Rapids/Kent County Sesquicentennial Com., 1986-88; MEM. Headlee Blue Ribbon Commn., 1993-94; v.p. bd. dirs. Goodwill Industries, Grand Rapids, 1973-79, Am. Cancer Soc., Grand Rapids, 1970-81; pres., trustee Hist. Soc. Mich., 1984-90. Lt. USN, 1961-66. Mem. ABA (forum com. on health law 1980—), Mich. Bar Assn. (chmn. condemnation com. real property sect. 1985-88), Grand Rapids Bar Assn. (dir. young lawyers sect. 1970), Am. Acad. Hosp. Attys., Mich. Soc. Hosp. Attys. (pres. 1976-77), Nat. Health Lawyers Assn., Univ. Club (dir. 1979-82, pres. 1980-82), Peninsular Club, Williams Club (NYC). Avocations: sailing, hunting, fishing. Home: 601 Cherry St SE Grand Rapids MI 49503-4726 Office: Warner Norcross and Judd 900 Old Kent Bldg Grand Rapids MI 49503 also: Office of Mayor 300 Monroe Ave NW Grand Rapids MI 49503-2206

LOGLI, PAUL ALBERT, lawyer; b. Rockford, Ill., Nov. 20, 1949; s. Albert Joseph and Margaret (Salamone) L.; m. Jodean L. Miller, Oct. 26, 1985; children: Peter Joseph, Benjamin Paul, Jacob Thomas. BA cum laude, Loras Coll., 1971; JD, U. Ill., 1974; LLD (hon.), Loras Coll., 1991. Bar: Ill. 1974, U.S. Dist. Ct. (no. dist.) Ill. 1975. Asst. state's atty. Winnebago County, Rockford, 1974-76; ptnr. North, Ohlson, Logli, Condon & Boyd, Rockford, 1976-81; assoc. judge 17th jud. cir. Winnebago and Boone Counties, Rockford, 1981-86; state's atty. Winnebago County, Rockford, 1986—; govt. appointee to Ill. Motor Vehicle Theft Prevention Coun., 1993—, Ill. Gov.'s Commn. on Gangs, 1996—; chmn. domestic rels. com. Ill. Jud. Conf., 1983-84; mem. faculty Nat. Coll. Dist. Attys., Houston, 1989—; bd. dirs. Amcore Trust Co.; bd. govs. Ill. State Attys. Appellate Profls., 1992—. Apptd. to Ill. Sec. of State's Task Force on Mandatory Ins., 1988-89, Dirs. of Ill. Motor Vehicle Theft Prevention Coun., 1993—; bd. dirs. Rockford Symphony Orch., 1983-87, Rosecrance Meml. Homes for Children, Rockford, 1983—, Rockford Area Conv. and Visitors Bus., 1984-92, Discovery Ctr. Children's Mus., 1986-89, Rockford Crimestoppers, 1986—, Rockford United Way, 1987—; mem. adv. bd. St. Anthony Hosp. Med. Ctr., Rockford, 1983-90. Recipient svc. award Northwest Ill. Chiefs of Police Assn., 1981, New Am. Theater, 1981; Disting. Svc. award Jaycees, 1982; selected one of 10 Oustanding Young Persons State of Ill., Jaycees, 1988. Mem. Ill. State Bar Assn., Winnebago County Bar Assn., Ill. State's Attys. Assn. (pres. 1995), Nat. Dist. Attys. Assn., Rotary (pres. 1991-92). Republican. Roman Catholic. Office: Winnebago County Courthouse 400 W State St Ste 619 Rockford IL 61101-1221

LOGRASSO, DON, state legislator, lawyer; b. Kansas City, Mo., May 31, 1951; m. Leelah Lograsso; children: Chad, Scott. BA, U. Mo., Kansas City, MA, JD. Bar: Mo. Mem. Mo. Ho. of Reps., Jefferson City, 1991—; mem. civil and criminal law, ethics, judiciary and state instn. and property coms. *

LOH, HORACE H., pharmacology educator; b. Canton, Republic China, May 28, 1936. BS, Nat. Taiwan U., Taipei, Republic China, 1958; PhD, U. Iowa, 1965. Lectr. dept. pharmacology U. Calif. Sch. Medicine, San Francisco, 1967; assoc. prof. biochem. Wayne State U., Detroit, 1968-70; lectr., rsch. assoc. depts. psychiatry, pharmacology Langley Porter Neuropsychiatric Inst. U. Calif. Sch. Medicine, San Francisco, 1970-72, assoc. prof. depts. psychiatry, pharmacology Langley Porter Neuropsychiatric Inst., 1972-75, prof. depts. psychiatry, pharmacology Langley Porter Neuropsychiatric Inst., 1975-88; prof., head dept. pharmacology U. Minn. Med. Sch., Mpls., 1989—, Frederick and Alice Stark prof., head dept. pharmacology, 1990—; chmn. annual meeting theme com. on receptors Fedn. Am. Socs. for Exptl. Biology, 1984; mem. exec. com. Internat. Narcotic Rsch. Conf., 1984-87, chair sci. program annual meeting, 1986; mem. adv. com. Nat. Tsing Hua U. Inst. Life Scis., Taiwan, Republic China, 1985-89; mem. exec. com. Com. on Problems of Drug Dependence, Inc., 1985-88; mem. sci. adv. coun. Nat. Found. for Addicitive Diseases, 1987—; cons. U.S. Army R & D Dept. Defense, 1980-84. Mem. editorial adv. bd. Life Scis., 1978—, Substance and Alcohol Abuse, 1980—, Neurochemistry Internat., 1980-88, Neuropharmacology, 1982—, Neurosci. Series, 1982-83, Annual Rev. Pharmacology and Toxicology, 1984-89, Jour. Pharmacology and Exptl. Therapeutics, 1987—; assoc. editor Annual Rev. Pharmacology and Toxicology, 1990-95, CRC Critical Rev. in Pharmacological Scis., 1987-88; author 56 book chpts; editor 1 book; contbr. 300 articles to profl. jours. Recipient Career Devel. award USPHS, 1973-78, 78-83, Rsch. Scientist award, 1983-88, 1989-94, Humboldt award for sr. U.S. scientists (Fed. Republic Germany), 1977. Mem. Am. Coll. Neuropsychopharmacology (honorific awards com. 1988—), Am. Soc. Pharmacology and Exptl. Therapeutics (program com. 1976-86, trustee bd. publs. 1987-93, com. on confs. 1990-93), Soc. Chinese Bioscientists in Am. (pres. 1985-86), Western Pharmacology Soc. (councilor 1980-83, pres. 1984-85). Office: U Minn Med Sch Dept Pharmacology 3 249 Millard Hall Minneapolis MN 55455

LOHMANN, JOAN GARDNER JENKINS, writer; b. Chgo., May 14, 1930; d. Richard Leos and Gladys (Gardner) Jenkins; m. Karl Baptiste Lohmann Jr., June 30, 1951; children: Kathleen Lohmann Baumann, Kenneth John, Sara Lohmann Kirk. BA, U. Ill., 1951; MA, Ind. U., 1953. Rsch. asst. Union Coll., Schenectady, N.Y., 1952-53, U. Mich., Ann Arbor, Mich., 1953-56; freelance writer West Lafayette, Ind., 1957-76, 92—; writer, editor Sch. Edn. Purdue U., West Lafayette, 1973-76, devel. dir. Sch. Nursing, 1976-92. Author children's fiction, poetry, articles, ednl. TV scripts; editor tech. reports, newsletters, brochures, reports. Mem. LWV (Citizen Edn. grantee 1987-88, bd. dirs. 1985-90, 94-96).

LOHR, DAVID L., state legislator; m. Linda Lohr. BS, Ind. U., MS. Tchr. Gibault Sch. Boys; mem. Ind. State Ho. of Reps. Dist. 46, mem. aged and aging com., edn., pub. policy, ethics com., vice chmn. agr. and rural devel. com.

LOIUDICE, THOMAS ANTHONY, gastroenterologist, researcher; b. Wilmington, Del., Dec. 3, 1942; s. Dominick and Carmela (Vignola) LoI.; m. Jean Anne Lang, June 20, 1970; children: Christopher, Mark. BS, St. Joseph's U., 1966; DO, Chgo. Coll., 1972. Diplomate Am. Bd. Family Practice, Am. Bd. Internal Medicine, Am. Bd. Nutrition; lic. physician Tenn., Pa., Ind., Ohio, N.Y., Fla. Intern U. Health Ctr. Pitts. Hosp., 1972-73, jr. asst. resident in internal medicine, 1973-74, sr. asst. resident in internal medicine, 1974, fellow cardiology, 1975; fellow gastroenterology and clin. nutrition Union U., Albany, N.Y., 1975-77; pres. Akron (Ohio) Gastroenterology Assocs., Inc., 1978—; instr. Northeastern Ohio U., Akron, 1977-83, asst. prof., assoc. prof. gastroenterology, 1983-91, prof., 1991—, head subsect. nutrition, 1986—; sec.-treas. Tri-County Emergency Med. Svc., Inc., 1983—; clin. rsch. assoc. Smith, Kline & French Labs., 1983—; mem. sr. teaching staff St. Thomas Med. Ctr., Akron, chief nutrition, head nutritional support team, 1989—; mem. courtesy staff Barberton Citizens Hosp., Barberton, Ohio, Cuyahoga Falls (Ohio) Gen. Hosp.; mem. jr. staff Akron Gen. Med. Ctr.; mem. staff Akron City Hosp.; speaker in field. Contbr. numerous articles to So. Med. Jour., Gastroeterology, Ob/Gyn., Am. Jour. Gastroenterology, Am. Jour. Digestive Diseases, Am. Jour. Clin. Nutrition, N.Y. Jour. Medicine, and other. Grantee William H. Rorer, Smith Kline and French, Ortho Pharm. Corp., Glaxo Pharm. Fellow ACP, Am. Coll. Angiology, Am. Coll. Gastroenterology, Am. Coll. Nutrition, Royal Soc. Medicine (Eng., affiliate); mem. AMA, AAAS, Am. Coll. Emergency Physicians, Am.Soc. Contemporary Medicine and Surgery, Am. Soc. Internal Medicine, Am. Gastroenterology Assn., Am. Assn. for Study Liver Disease, Am. Soc. Gastrointestinal Endoscopy, Am. Fedn. Clin. Rsch., Ohio Med. Assn., Ohio Soc. Internal Medicine, Northeastern Ohio Soc. Gastrointestinal Endoscopy, Summit County Med. Soc. Roman Catholic. Office: Akron Gastroenterology Assoc 444 N Main St Ste 324 Akron OH 44310-3110

LOKEN, LANCE GABRIEL, geologist, soil scientist; b. Rugby, N.D., Aug. 19, 1963; s. Gordon Larry and Charlotte Eunice (Sundell) L. BS in Geology, N.D. State U., 1985, MS in Soil Sci., 1991. Cert. monitoring well contractor, N.D. Grad. rsch. asst. soils dept. N.D. State U., Fargo, 1985-87; soil scientist USDA Soil Conservation Svc., Bottineau, N.D., 1987-88; soil conservationist USDA Soil Conservation Svc., Bottineau, 1988-89; indsl. hygienist technician Braun Engring. Testing, Inc., Bismarck, N.D., 1989-90; environ. geologist Braun Environ. Labs., Inc., Bismarck, 1990-91; environ. scientist Braun Intertec Environ., Inc., Bismarck, 1991-92; CEO, pres. High Plains Consortium Inc., Bismarck, 1993—. Chmn. environ. policy sect. White House Conf. on Small Bus., Bismarck, 1994. Mem. N.D. Geol. Soc., N.D. Groundwater League, Profl. Soil Classifiers Assn. N.D., Bus. Opportunities Assn. (bd. dirs.), Amateur Trapshooting Assn., Japan karate Assn. U.S. Democrat. Lutheran. Office: High Plains Consortium Inc PO Box 1292 Bismarck ND 58502-1292

LOLIE, ALLAN F., JR., lawyer; b. Staunton, Ill., Nov. 19, 1966; s. Allan F. Lolie, Sr. and Carol Marie (Sturm) Rehmstedt. BS in Law Enforcement Adminstrn., Western Ill. U., 1988; JD, Southern Ill. U., 1991. Law clk. to Justice Carl Lund Ill. Appellate Ct., Paris, 1991; state's atty. Edgar County State Atty.'s Office, Paris, Ill., 1992-95. Mem. Paris Kiwanis Club (pres. 1995—), Paris Elks Lodge # 812 (lecturing knight 1995—). Democrat. Lutheran. Home: 601 E Court Paris IL 61944 Office: Edgar County State's Attorney 115 W Court Paris IL 61944

LOLLAR, ROBERT MILLER, management consultant; b. Lebanon, Ohio, May 17, 1915; s. Harry David and Ruby (Miller) L.; m. Dorothy Marie Williams, Jan. 1, 1941; children: Janet Ruth (Mrs. Frank Schneider), Katherine Louise. BChemE, U. Cin., 1937, MS, 1938, PhD, 1940. Cereal analyst Kroger Food Found., Cin., 1935-37; devel. chemist Rit Product div. Corn Products, Indpls., 1937-39, 40-41; assoc. prof. U. Cin., 1941-59; tech. dir. Armour & Co., Chgo., 1959-73; mgmt. and tech. cons., pres. Lollar and Assocs., 1973—; tech. dir. Leather Industries Am., Cin., 1975-86, cons., 1986—. Dir. OSRD, 1942-45. Recipient Alsop award Am. Leather Chemists Assn., 1954, Disting. Svcs. award, 1985, 86, Fraser Muir Moffat medal Leather Industries Am. Mem. Am. Leather Chemists Assn. (pres., editor-in-chief), Inst. Food Technologists, Am. Chem. Soc. (nat. councillor), Am. Soc. Quality Control, World Mariculture Soc., Sigma Xi, Tau Beta Pi, Alpha Chi Sigma. Address: 5960 Donjoy Dr Cincinnati OH 45242-7508

LOLLI, DON R(AY), lawyer; b. Macon, Mo., Aug. 9, 1949; s. Tony and Erma Naomi (Gerlich) L.; m. Deborah Jo Mrosek, May 29, 1976; children:

Christina Terese, Joanna Elyse, Anthony Justin. BA in Econs., U. Mo., 1971, JD, 1974. Bar: Mo. 1974, U.S. Dist. Ct. (we. dist.) Mo. 1974, U.S. Ct. Appeals (8th cir.) 1976, U.S. Ct. Appeals (10th cir.) 1979, U.S. Supreme Ct. 1979, U.S. Tax Ct. 1981, U.S. Ct. Appeals (3rd cir.) 1992, U.S. Dist. Ct. (ea. dist.) Mo. 1996. Assoc. Beckett & Steinkamp, Kansas City, Mo., 1974-79, ptnr. Beckett, Lolli, & Bartunek, 1980—; lectr. continuing legal edn. seminar U. Mo. Sch. Law, Kansas City, 1984, 89. Vol. coach Visitation Sch. Mem. ABA, Mo. Bar Assn., Kansas City Bar Assn., Lawyers Assn. Kansas City, U. Mo. Alumni Assn., Beta Theta Pi Alumni, Phi Delta Phi (pres. Tiedman Inn 1973-74, Merit cert. 1974). Roman Catholic. Clubs: Kansas City (Mo.), 611 Club. Home: 645 W 62nd St Kansas City MO 64113-1501 Office: Beckett Lolli & Bartunek PO Box 13425 Kansas City MO 64199-3425

LOMBARD, ARTHUR J., judge; b. N.Y.C., Nov. 30, 1941; s. Maurice and Martha (Simons) L.; m. Frederica Koller, Aug. 18, 1968; children: David, Lisa. BS in Acctg. magna cum laude, Columbia U., 1961; JD, Harvard U., 1964. Bar: N.Y. 1964, U.S. Ct. Appeals (2d cir.) 1965, U.S. Supreme Ct. 1970, U.S. Ct. Appeals (6th cir.) 1972, Mich. 1976. Law clk. to J. Edward Lumbard chief judge U.S. Ct. Appeals (2d cir.), N.Y.C., 1964-65; teaching fellow law sch. Harvard U., Cambridge, Mass., 1965-66; instr. Orientation Program in Am. Law, Assn. Am. Law Schs., Princeton, N.J., 1966; prof. law Wayne State U., Detroit, 1966-87, assoc. dean law, 1978-85; prof. Detroit Coll. Law, 1987-94, dean, chief adminstrv. officer, 1987-93; judge Wayne County (Mich.) Cir. Ct., 1994—; chmn. revision of Mich. class action rule com. Mich. Supreme Ct., 1980-83; reporter rules com. U.S. Dist. Ct. (ea. dist.) Mich., 1978-94. Contbr. articles to profl. jours. Mem. Mich. Civil Rights Commn., 1991-94, co-chmn., 1992-93, chmn. 1993-94. Office: 1913 City County Bldg Detroit MI 48226

LOMBARDI, FREDERICK MCKEAN, lawyer; b. Akron, Ohio, Apr. 1, 1937; s. Leonard Anthony and Dorothy (McKean) L.; m. Margaret J. Gessler, Mar. 31, 1962; children: Marcus M., David G., John A., Joseph F. BA, U. Akron, 1960; LLB, Case Western Res., 1962. Bar: Ohio 1962, U.S. Dist. Ct. (no. dist.) Ohio 1964, U.S. Ct. Appeals (6th cir.) 1966. Prin., shareholder Buckingham, Doolittle & Burroughs, Akron, 1962—, chmn. comml. law and litigation dept., 1989—. Bd. editors Western Res. Law Rev., 1961-62. Trustee, mem. exec. com., v.p. Ohio Ballet, 1985-93; trustee Walsh Jesuit H.S., 1987-90, Akron Golf Charities; chmn. formation com., 1st pres. St. Hilary Parish Coun., trustee, 1976-78; past chmn. World Series of Golf. Mem. Ohio Bar Assn. (coun. of dels. 1995-97), Akron Bar Assn. (trustee 1991-94), Case Western Res. U. Law Alumni Assn. (bd. govs. 1995-98), Soc. Benchers (bd. govs. 1995-98), Fairlawn Swim and Tennis Club (past pres.), Portage Country Club (fin. com.), Akron City Club, Rotary (fin. com. Akron), Pi Sigma Alpha. Democrat. Roman Catholic. Office: Buckingham Doolittle & Burroughs 50 S Main St Akron OH 44308-1828

LOMBARDO, DAVID ALBERT, actor, writer, speaker, aviation educator; b. Chgo., Jan. 31, 1947; s. Ignace Palmeri and Diane Marion (Balducci) L. BS, U. Ill., 1974, MEd, 1977. Tchr. York Community High Sch., Elmhurst, Ill., 1974-75; instr. Coll. Edn., U. Ill., Urbana, 1975-77, asst. dir. career devel. and placement, 1977-79; with Accelerated Ground Schs., Urbana, 1978-81, dir. Nat. Flying Inst. refresher clinics; pres. Flying Illini, Inc., Savoy, Ill., 1972-80; curriculum devel. cons. CFI Programs, 1979-82; dir. program devel. Airmanship, Inc., Rockford, Ill., 1981-82; gen. aviation cons. Lombardo & Assocs., 1981—; asst. prof. profl. aviation La. Tech. U., Ruston, 1982-85; dir. tng. Frasca Internat., Urbana, Ill., 1985-88; asst. prof., aerotech. program leader Bowling Green (Ohio) State U., 1988-91; assoc. dean aviation Lewis U., Romeoville, Ill., 1991-93; chief instr. Greater St. Louis Flight Instrs. Assn., 1980-81; accident prevention counselor FAA, 1980—. Author: Aircraft Systems: Understanding Your Airplane, 1988, Advanced Aircraft Systems, 1993; assoc. editor Images, 1988-90; editor Simulation Newsletter, 1985-91, contbg. editor Pvt. Pilot Mag., 1984-87; contbr. articles to profl. jours. Bd. dirs. Ruston Community Theater, 1983-85; founder, bd. dirs. Hill Country Arts Coun., 1983-85. With AUS, 1966-69, Vietnam. Decorated Vietnamese Gallantry Cross; recipient Flying Col. award Delta Air Lines, 1978, Ark. Traveler award Gov. of Ark., 1978, Flight Inst. Proficiency award Phases I, II, III, IV, FAA, 1980, Plaque of Appreciation, Greater St. Louis Flight Instrs. Assn., 1981, Excellence award La. Tech. U., 1984, Instr. Yr. award Aerotech Program Bowling Green State U., 1989, numerous others. Mem. Aircraft Owners and Pilots Assn., Univ. Aviation Assn. (chmn. FAA/Univ. Aviation Assn. flt. tng. device task force 1990-93, chmn. simulation com. 1987-93, mem. publs. com. 1985-88, nat. treas. 1992-93), Aviation/Space Writers Assn. (Midwest region Journalism award of Excellence 1989), Assn. Aviation Psychologists, Human Factors Soc., Soc. Automotive Engrs., Alpha Eta Tho (advisor 1983-85, 88-91), Chi Gamma Iota, Phi Delta Kappa, Epsilon Pi Tau. Republican. Roman Catholic. Home and Office: 1113 S Raven Rd Shorewood IL 60436-9650

LOMBARDO, PHILIP JOSEPH, broadcasting company executive; b. Chgo., June 13, 1935; s. Joseph Pete and Josephine (Franco) L.; m. Marilyn Ann Tellefsen, June 22, 1963; children: Dean, Jeffrey. Student, U. Ill., 1953-55; BA in Speech, Journalism and Radio/TV, U. Mo., 1958, postgrad. speech, 1958; grad. advanced mgmt. program, Harvard U., 1976. Account exec. Sta. WWCA, Ind., 1959-60; producer-dir. Sta. WBBM-TV, Chgo., 1960-65; program mgr., acting gen. mgr. Sta. WLWT, Cin., 1965-67; v.p., gen. mgr. Sta. WGHP-TV, N.C., 1968-73; pres., chief exec. officer Corinthian Broadcasting Corp., N.Y.C., 1973-82; chmn., pres., chief exec. officer Champlain Communications Corp., N.Y.C., 1982-84; mng. gen. ptnr. Citadel Communications Co. Ltd., N.Y.C., 1982—; chmn., pres., chief exec. officer Citadel Communications, Co. Ltd., C.C.C. Communications Corp., Lombardo Communications II, Inc., P.J.L. Investments, Inc., N.Y.C., 1984—; mng. gen. ptnr., nat. sales rep. U.S. and Can. TV stas. Can. Communications Co., Toronto, 1985—; mng. gen. ptnr. Coronet Communications Co., N.Y.C., 1985—, Capital Comm. Co., Inc., 1994—, Citadel Comm., LLC, 1995—; bd. dirs. The Gabelli Group, The Lynch Corp., N.Y.C. Mem. adv. bd. Salvation Army; com. budget, bd. dirs. United Fund; mem. com. High Point (N.C.) United Schs.; 1st vice chmn. Central Carolina chpt. Nat. Multiple Sclerosis Soc., 1968-73; bd. dirs. High Point Arts Council, 1968-73. Served with AUS, 1959, 62. Recipient Disting. Svc. award Freedom Found., Am. Legion, High Point (N.C.) Youth Coun. Mem. Dirs. Guild Am., Internat. Radio and TV Soc. (bd. govs.). Clubs: Winged Foot Golf, Marco Polo, Board Room, Bronxville Field, Chgo. Press. Lodges: Rotary, Kiwanis. Home: 24 Masterton Rd Bronxville NY 10708-4804 Office: Citadel Comm Co 17 Kraft Ave Bronxville NY 10708-4103

LOMBARDO, RICHARD JAMES, emergency physician; b. Manchester, Conn., July 22, 1944; s. Corado James and Constance Marie (Sapienza) L.; m. Sandra Lee Haag, May 24, 1969 (dec. Jan. 1975); children: Terri Lyn, Karin Michelle; m. Sandra Lynn Rockneberg, May 21, 1976; 1 child, Amanda Lee; stepchildren: Michael DeHaan, Darrin DeHaan. BS, Trinity Coll., Hartford, Conn., 1966; MD, U. Medicine and Dentistry N.J., Newark, 1970. Family practice staff physician Tipton County Hosp., Covington, Tenn., 1973-78, Randolph County Med. Ctr., Pocahontas, Ark., 1979-86; emergency physician, med. dir. emergency dept. Springfield (Mo.) Cmty. Hosp., 1987-92; emergency physician Rsch. Belton (Mo.) Hosp., 1992—, Rsch. Med. Ctr., Kansas City, Mo., 1992—; chief of staff Tipton County Hosp., 1978, Randolph County Med. Ctr., 1984. Lt. USN, 1971-73. Mem. Met. Med. Soc., Mo. State Med. Assn. Home: 705 Sandpiper Raymore MO 64083 Office: Rsch Belton Hosp 17065 S 71 Hwy Belton MO 64012

LONDON, TERRY, state legislator; b. Apr. 15, 1940; married 1980. Rep. Mich. Ho. of Rep., 1985-86, state rep. Dist. 81, 1988—; chmn. St. Clair County Rep. Com. Home: 1020 Illinois St Marysville MI 48040-1575*

LONE, RITA JOAN, retired linen service manager; b. New Castle, Ind., Jan. 29, 1938; d. Alva Dale and Edna Jane (Walker) L. BS in Edn., Ind. Wesleyn U., 1961. Registered exec. housekeeper, laundry and linen dir. Tchr. Avilla (Ind.) High Sch., 1961-63, Peru (Ind.) Jr. High and High Sch., 1963-66, R.J. Basket Jr. High Sch., Jonesboro, Ind., 1966-67; asst. chemist Marion (Ind.) Gen. Hosp., 1967-71, supr. 2nd shift, 1971-79, med. technologist, 1979-81, instr. ednl. svcs., 1981-88, mgr. environ. and linen svcs., 1988-94; instr. Ind. Wesleyan U., Marion, 1976-78. Vol. Am. Cancer Soc., Marion, 1981-87; instr. Arthritis Found., Marion, 1985-88; active, instr. CPR, Am. Heart Assn. Mem. Nat. Assn. Instnl. Linen Mgmt. (chair ednl. affairs com. 1995—), Ind. Assn. Instnl. Linen Mgmt. (treas.), Nat. Exec. Housekeepers Assn. (chpt. pres.,, 2d vice gov. Cen. dist., gov. 1995—). Home: 11959 Lancewood Dr Roscommon MI 48653-9001

LONG, EDWIN TUTT, surgeon, data base company executive; b. St. Louis, July 23, 1925; s. Forrest Edwin and Hazel (Tutt) L.; m. Mary M. Hull, Apr. 16, 1955; children: Jennifer Ann, Laura Ann, Peter Edwin. AB, Columbia U., 1944, M.D., 1947. Diplomate Am. Bd. Surgery, Am. Bd. Thoracic Surgery. Rotating intern Meth. Hosp., Bklyn., 1947-78; surg. intern U. Chgo. Clinics, 1948-49, resident in gen. surgery, 1952-55, resident in thoracic surgery, 1955-57; asst. prof. surgery U. Chgo., 1957-59; thoracic and cardiovascular surgeon, chief surgery dept. Watson Clinic, Lakeland, Fla., 1960-69; asso. prof. surgery U. Pa., Phila., 1970-73; thoracic and cardiovascular surgeon Allegheny Cardiovascular Surg. Assocs., Pitts, 1973-88; exec. v.p. Mailings Clearing Ho. and Roxbury Press, Inc., 1988-90, pres., 1990—, chmn., bd. dir., 1991—; dir. Watson Clinic Rsch. Found., 1965-69; bd. dirs. Roxbury Press, Inc., Cardiac Telecom, Inc., Pitts. Pressure Vectorography Rsch. grantee Alfred P. Sloan Found., 1963; patentee gas sterilizer, 1969. Capt. USAF, 1950-52. Mem. ACS, Am. Coll. Cardiology, Internat. Soc. for Cardiovascular Surg., Allegheny Vascular Soc. (pres. 1987), Ea. Vascular Soc. (founding mem.), Soc. Thoracic Surgery (founding mem.), Direct Mktg. Assn., Midwest Bioethics Ctr., Kansas City Club, Rotary, Sigma Xi, Beta Theta Pi. Home and Office: 1415 Torrey Pines Dr Columbia MO 65203-4830 Office: Roxbury Press Inc 601 E Marshall St Sweet Springs MO 65351-0295

LONG, ELIZABETH L., state legislator, small business owner; m. Kent Long; children: Amie, Dana, Sarah. Student, Drury Coll. County clk. Laclede County, Mo., 1982-90; owner, mgr. retail gift shop, Lebanon; mem. Mo. Ho. of Reps., Jefferson City, 1991—; mem. election fed.-state rels. and vet. affairs, fees and salaries, state parks, recreation and natural resources and tourism, recreation and cultural affairs coms. Mem. Lebanon Area Found. Mem. Lebanon C. of C. Republican. Home: RR 2 Box 39 Lebanon MO 65536-9602*

LONG, ERIC CHARLES, biochemist; b. Reading, Pa., Nov. 20, 1962; s. Ronald Barry and Carole Kay (Mauger) L. BS in Biochemistry, Albright Coll., 1984; PhD, U. Va., 1988. Rsch. fellow Columbia U., N.Y., 1988-89; fellow Jane Coffin Childs Meml. Fund for Med. Rsch. Calif. Inst. Tech., Pasadena, Calif., 1989-91; mem. rsch. faculty Calif. Inst. Tech., Pasadena, 1989-91; asst. prof. chemistry Ind. U., Purdue U., Indpls., 1991—. Contbr. articles to profl. jours. Recipient MDS Labs. award Albright Coll., 1984, Trustee Grant award, 1980-84. Mem. AAAS, Am. Chem. Soc., Am. Peptide Soc. Office: Ind U Purdue U Indpls 402 N Blackford St Indianapolis IN 46202-3272

LONG, JAN MICHAEL, state legislator; b. Pomeroy, Ohio, May 31, 1952; s. Lewis Franklin and Dorothy (Clatworthy) L.; m. Susan Louise Custer, May 12, 1978; children: John D., Justin M., Jason M. BA, Ohio State U., 1974; JD, Capital U., 1979. Adminstrv. asst. Congressman Doug Applegate, Washington, 1974-77; asst. prosecuting atty. Pickaway County, Circleville, Ohio, 1979-80; mem. Ohio State Senate, Columbus, 1987—; asst. minority whip Ohio Senate, Columbus, 1995—. Named one of Outstanding Young Men Am. U.S. Jaycees, 1987. Mem. Pickaway County Bar Assn. (treas. 1985-86, sec. 1986-87). Democrat. Home: 522 Glenmont Dr Circleville OH 43113-1523 Office: Ohio Senate Rm 134 Statehouse Columbus OH 43215

LONG, JIM, state legislator; m. Margaret E. Long. Kans. state rep. Dist. 38, fire chief. Home: 1803 N 126th St Kansas City KS 66109-4520*

LONG, JOHN FREDERICK, veterinary pathobiology educator; b. Napoleon, Ohio, May 30, 1924; s. George Emerson and Emily Mary (Lynas) L.; m. Sarah Elizabeth Brackney, June 15, 1948; children: George Lynas, Helen Lucille Long Corcoran, Harold Roy, Clara Alice Long Lawrence, Nancy Carol Long Sieber. BA, Ohio State U., 1947, MSc, 1948, DVM, 1955, PhD, 1966. Grad. asst. dept. zoology Ohio State U., Columbus, 1947-49, rsch. asst. dept. surg. rsch., 1950-51, rsch. asst. dept. dairy sci., 1951-55, NIH postdoctoral fellow dept. vet. pathology, 1964-66, instr. dept. vet. pathology, 1966-67, NIH spl. rsch. fellow, 1967-68, asst. prof. dept. vet. pathobiology, 1968-71, assoc. prof. dept. vet. pathobiology, 1971—; assoc. prof. dept. vet. biosci. Ohio State U., 1995—; vet. diagnostician Ohio Dept. Agr., Reynoldsburg, 1955-63. Contbr. articles to profl. jours., chpt. to book. Cpl. U.S. Army, 1943-46. NIH grantee, 1968, 86. Mem. Am. Vet. Med. Assn., Am. Assn. Avian Pathologists, Ohio Vet. Med. Assn., Gerontol. Soc. Am., Am. Chem. Soc. (affiliate), Ohio Hist. Soc., Phi Zeta. Office: Ohio State U Dept Vet Bioscis 1925 Coffey Rd Columbus OH 43210-1005

LONG, JOHN HAMILTON, historian, editor; b. Brockton, Mass., Mar. 3, 1937; s. Samuel and Elizabeth H. (Lewis) L.; m. Sally F. Tufts, Aug. 29, 1964; 1 child, Faith E. Student, Princeton U., 1955-58; BA with high honors, Northeastern U., 1966; MA in History, Clark U., 1970. Lectr. Assumption Coll., Worcester, Mass., 1970-71; asst. editor Newberry Libr., Chgo., 1971-75, project dir., 1975-82; freelance researcher Chgo., 1984-86; program dir. Chgo. Metro History Fair, Chgo., 1987; asst. dir. for rsch. and edn. Newberry Libr., Chgo., 1987-88, project dir. Atlas of Hist. County Boundaries, 1988—; panelist NEH, Washington, 1985; chair staff fund drive Newberry Libr., Chgo., 1980; instr. adult history courses, 1978, 88, 92, 94-95, summer inst. for tchrs., 1980-82, 92, 95, 96. Joint editor, author: Atlas of Early American History, 1976, The Settling of North America, 1995; editor joint author: Historical Atlas and Chronology of County Boundaries, 1788-1980, 5 vols., 1984, County Boundaries of Selected States, 1790-1980 (datafile), 1982, Atlas of Historical County Boundaries, 7 vols., 1993—; contbr. articles to profl. jours. Councilor Ill. Hist. Sites Adv. Coun., Springfield, Ill., 1980-82; pres. North Pk. Tower Cooperative, Chgo., 1975-76. With U.S. Army, 1959-62. Grantee NEH, 1977, 79, 88, 90, 92, 95; NDEA Title IV fellow Clark U., 1966-69. Mem. Am. Hist. Assn., Orgn. Am. Historians, Nat. Coun. on Pub. History, Nat. Trust for Hist. Preservation, Nat. Computer Graphics Assn., Chgo. Map Soc. (pres. 1978-80, treas. 1977-78, v.p. 1992-93). Office: Newberry Libr 60 W Walton St Chicago IL 60610-3305

LONG, JOHN P., broker; b. Jackson, Mich., Mar. 16, 1946. BA in Econs., Aquinas Coll., 1969. Asst. v.p. City Bank & Trust, Jackson, 1968-78; ins. agt. Equitable Life Ins. of Iowa, Jackson, 1978-86; broker Smith Barney Inc., Jackson, 1986—. With USAR, 1968-74. Roman Catholic. Office: Smith Barney Inc PO Box 1387 1 Jackson Sq Jackson MI 49204

LONG, KAREN DRAUT, librarian; b. Middletown, Ohio, Aug. 25, 1939; d. Arthur William and Estelle (Lowe) Draut; m. Kenneth Robert Long, Feb. 2, 1962; children: Kristin E., Keith T. BA, Ohio Wesleyan U., 1961; MA, U. Ill., 1962; MLS, U. Pitts., 1988. Dir. Childhood League Nursery Sch., Columbus, Ohio, 1963; asst. dean of women Ohio Wesleyan U., Delaware, Ohio, 1964, lectr. in politics and govt., 1965; tchr. Oxford (Ohio) City Schs., 1967, Highline Pub. Schs., Washington, 1967-70; freelance calligrapher Pitts., 1973-87; head fgn. lit. Cleve. Pub. Libr., 1990—. Mem. Play Readers, Cleve., 1988. Mem. AlA, Ohio Libr. Coun. (action coun. 1992—), Pub. Libr. Assn., Mortar Bd. Soc. Phi Beta Kappa, Beta Phi Mu. Home: 2976 Manchester Rd Shaker Heights OH 44122

LONG, KEVIN JAY, medicolegal consultant; b. Chgo., May 19, 1961. Student, Chgo. Med. Sch., 1983-86; BS in Math./Stats., Loyola U., Chgo., 1985; postgrad., John Marshall Law Sch., 1988-90. Researcher Cons. in Neurology, Ltd., Skokie, Ill., 1981-84, Assn. for Women's Health Care, Ltd., Chgo., 1982-83; researcher dept. neurology U. Ill., Chgo., 1985-86; law clk. Steven K. Jambois, Chgo., 1989; med. paralegal Hilfman & Fogel, P.C., Chgo., 1989-92; internal medicolegal cons. Robert A. Clifford & Assocs., Chgo., 1992; medicolegal cons. Chgo., 1992—. Contbr. articles to Current Problems in Obstetrics and Gynecology, Archives of Neurology, Archives of Internal Medicine, Pediatrics, Clin. Electroencephalography, Am. Jour. Medicine, Hosp. Pharmacy, Pediatric Emergency Care, Quality Management in Health Care, Houston Medicine, Nursing Quality Connection. Mem. Nat. Hon. Soc. Secondary Schs., Assn. Trial Lawyers Am., Am. Med. Student Assn., N.Y. Acad. Scis., Blue Key Nat. Hon. Frat., Beta Beta Beta Biol. Honor Soc., Alpha Epsilon Delta Premed. Honor Soc. Jewish. Home and Office: Ste 3-South 1325 W North Shore Ave Chicago IL 60626-4763

LONG, SARAH ELIZABETH BRACKNEY, physician; b. Sidney, Ohio, Dec. 5, 1926; d. Robert LeRoy and Caroline Josephine (Shue) Brackney; m. John Frederick Long, June 15, 1948; children: George Lynas, Helen Lucille Corcoran, Harold Roy, Clara Alice Lawrence, Nancy Carol Sieber. BA, Ohio State U., 1948, MD, 1952. Intern Grant Hosp., Columbus, Ohio, 1952-53; resident internal medicine Mt. Carmel Med. Ctr., Columbus, 1966-69, chief resident internal medicine, 1968-69; med. cons. Ohio Bur. Disability Determination, Columbus, 1970—; physician student health Ohio State U., Columbus, 1970-73; sch. physician Bexley (Ohio) City Schs., 1973-83; physician advisor to peer rev. Mt. Carmel East Hosp., Columbus, 1979-86, med. dir. employee health, 1981-96; physician cons. Fed. Black Lung program U.S. Dept. Labor, Columbus, 1979—. Mem. AMA, Gerontol. Soc. Am., Ohio Hist. Soc., Ohio State Med. Assn., Franklin County Acad. Medicine, Alpha Epsilon Delta, Phi Beta Kappa. Home: 2765 Bexley Park Rd Columbus OH 43209-2231

LONG, TIMOTHY J., money manager; b. Cleve., June 1, 1965. BA, U. Mich., 1987; MA, St. Johns U., N.Y.C., 1991. Mgr. Mobile Oil, N.Y.C. and Grand Rapids, Mich., 1987-93; money mgr. Merrill Lynch, Grand Rapids, 1994—. Home: 1782 Rivere Ridge Grand Rapids MI 49546 Office: Merrill Lynch Frey Bldg 300 Ottawa Ave NW Grand Rapids MI 49503-2304

LONGARDNER, CRAIG THEODOR, manufacturing executive; b. Ft. Wayne, Ind., June 2, 1955; s. Joseph Bernell and Dolores Waneta (Kiel) L.; m. Marsha Elaine Lessig, July 9, 1983; children: Joseph Simon, Jacob Kiel. BA, Ind. U., 1977; MBA, Butler U., 1985. Cert. purchasing mgr. Divisional buyer Eaton Corp., Cleve., 1977-80; purchasing mgr. Hurco Cos., Inc., Indpls., 1980-85; materials mgr. Ransburg Corp., Indpls., 1985-88; purchasing mgr. Nucor Steel Corp., Crawfordsville, Ind., 1988-94; mgr. materials & transp. Steel Dynamics, Inc., Butler, Ind., 1994—; instr. bus. statistics Kellogg Community Coll., Battle Creek, Mich., 1977. Mem. John Wayne Found. (life); fundraiser Nat. Leukemia Soc. Jr. Achievement. Mem. Assn. MBA Execs., Nat. Assn. Purchasing Mgrs., Ind. U. Alumni Assn. (life). Republican. Presbyterian. Home: 3016 Wilderness Rd Fort Wayne IN 46845-1652 Office: Steel Dynamics Inc 4500 County Rd 59 Butler IN 46721

LONGAS, MARIA OLIVA, chemistry educator, researcher; b. Medellin, Antioquia, Columbia; came to U.S., 1965; d. Francisco de Paula and Maria Ignacia (Carmona) L. MS, NYU, 1973, PhD, 1978. Rsch. assoc. Columbia U. Coll. of Physicians & Surgeons, N.Y.C., 1979-81; postdoctoral fellow Mt. Sinai Sch. Medicine, N.Y.C., 1982-83, asst. prof., 1983-87; assoc. prof. Purdue U. Calumet, Hammond, Ind., 1990-96, prof. chemistry, 1996—. Contbr. articles to profl. jours. Recipient Alumni award Hunter Coll., CUNY, 1971; grantee Nat. Inst. Aging, 1983-87; grantee Purdue Rsch. Found., summers 1988, 90-91, travel grantee, 1989, 91, 93. Mem. Am. Chem. Soc., Am. Chem. Soc. for the Biol. Chemist, N.Y. Acad. Sci., Soc. Complex Carbohydrates, Soc. for Applied Spectroscopy, Glycobiology. Office: Purdue Univ Calumet 2233 171st St Hammond IN 46323-2094

LONGHENRY, JOHN CHARLES, social studies educator, human resources specialis; b. Rockford, Ill., Oct. 27, 1948; s. Helen Janice (Weingartner) Willfong; m. Carol Ann Carroll, Dec. 18, 1971; 1 child, Ethan R. AA, Rock Valley Coll., 1972; BA, No. Ill. U., 1976; MBA, Rockford Coll., 1993. Cert. human resources specialist. Major assembler Chrysler Corp., Belvidere, Ill., 1969-75; social studies tchr. Belvidere H.S., 1975-76, Rockford Luth. H.S., 1977-79; sales/human resources Sundstrand Corp., Rockford, 1979-92; world/U.S. history/govt. tchr. Rockford Auburn H.S., 1992—; Class of 1995 advisor Auburn H.S., 1992-95, co-sponsor Key Club, 1993-95, Jr. Engring. Tech. Soc. coach, 1993-94; capital fund drive bd. dirs. Barbara Olson Sch. of Hope, Rockford, 1989. Exec. bd. mem.-at-large Blackhawk Area coun. Boy Scouts Am., Rockford, 1988-95, chmn. Nat. Eagle Scout Assn., 1985-88, cubmaster Pack 21, 1988-92, scoutmaster troop 21, 1994—, commr. dist. and unit, 1977-85. Served with U.S. Army, 1967-69, Vietnam. Recipient Disting. Svc. award Jaycees, 1982, Silver Wreath award Nat. Eagle Scout Assn., 1983, numerous other awards, 1982-92. Mem. NEA. Presbyterian. Office: Auburn HS 5110 Auburn St Rockford IL 61101

LONGHOFER, RONALD STEPHEN, lawyer; b. Junction City, Kans., Aug. 30, 1946; s. Oscar William and Anna Mathilda (Krause) L.; m. Elizabeth Norma McKenna; children: Adam, Nathan, Stefanie. BMus, U. Mich., 1968; JD, 1975. Bar: Mich. 1975, U.S. Dist. Ct. (ea. dist.) Mich., U.S. Ct. Appeals (6th cir.), U.S. Supreme Ct. Law clk. to judge U.S. Dist. Ct. (ea. dist.) Mich., Detroit, 1975-76; ptnr. Honigman, Miller, Schwartz & Cohn, Detroit, 1976—, chmn. litigation dept., 1993-96. Editor Mich. Law Rev., 1974-75. Served with U.S. Army, 1968-72. Mem. ABA, Detroit Bar Assn., Fed. Bar Assn., Detroit Club, Detroit Econ. Club, U. Mich. Pres. Club, Order of Coif, Phi Beta Kappa, Phi Kappa Phi, Pi Kappa Lambda. Home: 46401 W Main St Northville MI 48167-3035 Office: Honigman Miller Schwartz & Cohn 2290 1st National Bldg Detroit MI 48226

LONGNECKER, RICHARD MAYNE, molecular virologist; b. Chgo., Oct. 22, 1959; s. Richard S. and Josephine A. (Quesnel) L. BS, U. Mich., 1982; PhD, U. Chgo., 1987. Rsch. fellow U. Chgo., 1987-88, Harvard Med. Sch., Boston, 1989-93; prof. Northwestern U., Chgo., 1993—. Author: Prototype HSV Vaccines, 1987, Genetic Engineering of HSV, 1988, HSV As Vectors, 1989. Rsch. grantee U. Mich., 1979-82, NIH U. Chgo., 1987, Leukemia Soc., 1988—; Regent Alumni scholar U. Mich., 1980. Mem. AAAS, Assn. Microbiology. Home: 401 E Ontario # 2002 Chicago IL 60611-9999 Office: Northwestern U Med Sch 303 E Chicago Ave Chicago IL 60611-3008

LOOMER, GERALD EARL, secondary school science educator; b. Hot Springs, S.D., May 5, 1947; s. Myron Henry and Pauline Ann (Miller) L.; m. Lynn Clar Lilevjen, June 7, 1974 (div. Dec. 1993); children: Michael Franklin, Myra Francine. BS in Physics, St. John's U., 1969; MS in Physics, S.D. Sch. Mines and Tech., 1972. Cert. tchr., S.D., Minn., W.Va., Tex. Physics instr. S.D. Sch. Mines and Tech., Rapid City, 1969-72; sci. tchr. Philip (S.D.) H.S., 1972-74, Lakefield (Minn.) H.S., 1974-78, Rapid City (S.D.) Ctrl. H.S., 1978-87, Rapid City Stevens H.S., 1988—; tchr., cons. TI-IN Network, San Antonio, 1987-88. Contbr. articles to profl. jours. and mags.; co-author conf. procs. Internat. Conf. on Thermal Conductivity. Precinct chmn. Rep. Party, Rapid City, 1982-87; parish rep. MayFest, Rapid City, 1984-86. Named Nat. Tchr. of Yr., S.D. Dept. Edn., 1983; recipient Presdl. award for excellence in sci. tchg. U.S. Dept. Edn., 1984, Alumni Achievement award St. John's U.; Tchr. in Space finalist NASA, 1985; Christa McAuliffe fellow U.S. Nat. Sci. Found., 1987-88. Mem. S.D. Sci. Tchrs. Assn. (pres., newsletter editor 1978—, Outstanding Svc. award 1994), Nat. Sci. Tchrs. Assn. (v.p. Uniserve 1978—, Nat. Tchr. of Yr.), KC (chancellor, lector 1975—), Phi Delta Kappa (pres., v.p., sec., Pres.' award 1991, 75 Outstanding Leaders in Edn. award 1980). Roman Catholic. Home: 435 Viking Dr # WW Radid City SD 57701-9558 Office: Rapid City Stevens HS 1200 44th St Mail Stop WW Rapid City SD 57702

LOOMIS, HOWARD KREY, banker; b. Omaha, Apr. 9, 1927; s. Arthur L. and Genevieve (Krey) L.; AB, Cornell U., 1949, MBA, 1950; m. Florence Porter, Apr. 24, 1954; children: Arthur L. II, Frederick S., Howard Krey, John Porter. Mgmt. trainee Hallmark Cards, Inc., Kansas City, Mo., 1953-56; sec., controller, dir. Mine Svc. Co., Inc., Ft. Smith, Ark., 1956-59; controller, dir. Electra Mfg. Co., Independence, Kans., 1959-63; v.p., dir. The Peoples Bank, Pratt, Kans., 1963-65, pres., 1966—; pres., dir. Gt. Plains Leasing, Inc., Pratt, 1966-80, Central States Inc., Pratt, 1970-76, Krey Co. Ltd., Pratt, 1978—; fin. chmn. Econ. Lifelines, Topeka; bd. dirs. All Ins., Inc., Pratt, Kans. Devel. Credit Corp., Topeka, Kans. Wildscape Found.; past dir. Fed. Reserve Bank of Kansas City, Mo.; past pres. Pratt County United Fund. Past chmn. Cannonball Trail chpt. ARC; bd. dirs., past comdg. gen. Kans. Cavalry; past pres. Investment Com., Kanza coun. Boy Scouts Am. With AUS, 1950-52. Mem. Kans. C. of C. and Industry (past transp. chmn., dir., v.p.), Pratt Area C. of C. (past pres., dir.), Kans. Bankers Assn. (past dir.), Fin. Execs. Inst. (Wichita chpt.), Sigma Delta Chi, Chi Psi. Republican. Presbyterian. Club: Park Hills Country (past pres.). Lodges: Elks, Rotary. Home: 502 Welton St Pratt KS 67124-0928 Office: The Peoples Bank 222 S Main St Pratt KS 67124-1102

LOOMIS, JAMES PRENTICE, aeronautical engineer; b. Canton, Ohio, June 2, 1934; s. Eugene Abner and Annabel (Baum) L.; m. Hallie Maud

Hall, Sept. 16, 1956; children: Leslie Jean Loomis Stoll, Laurie Jean Loomis Monnier. B Aero. Engring., Ohio State U., 1958. Registered profl. engr., Ohio. Researcher Battelle, Columbus, Ohio, 1958-68, assoc. div. chief, 1968-72, program office mgr., 1972-74, sect. mgr., 1974-86, ctr. dir., 1986-89, v.p., 1989-94; retired, 1994. Editor: High Speed Commercial Flight: The Coming Era, 1987, High Speed Commercial Flight: From Inquiry to Action, 1989. Chmn. Columbus Metro Airport/Aviation Commn., 1985-90; vice chmn. Columbus Mcpl. Airport Authority, 1990—. 1st lt. U.S. Army, 1958-59. Mem. AIAA (assoc. fellow), System Safety Soc. (sr.). Republican. Methodist. Home: 1007 Kenway Ct Columbus OH 43220-4159

LOOMIS, ROBERT ARTHUR, sales executive; b. Oelwein, Iowa, June 27, 1936; s. Irving McArthur and Elsie Pauline (Brickman) L.; m. Karen Lee McKiney, Dec. 27, 1958; children: Duane Robert, Debra Lee, David Craig, Douglas Irving. Grad. high sch., Arlington, Iowa, 1954. With Rath Packing Co., Waterloo, Iowa, 1954-62; salesman Firestone Tire & Rubber Co., Waterloo, 1961-64; plant mgr. Firestone Tire & Rubber Co., Aberdeen, S.D., 1964-66, Wichita, Kans., 1966-70; asst. br. mgr. Myers Tire Supply, Kansas City, Mo., 1970-71; sales devel. mgr. Bandag, Inc., Kansas City, 1971—. Cubmaster Boy Scouts Am., Excelsior Springs, Mo., 1971-74; asst. scoutmaster 1974-78. With U.S. Army, 1955-57. Mem. Elks. Republican. Lutheran. Home: 305 Virginia Rd Excelsior Springs MO 64024-1226

LOOMIS, SALORA DALE, psychiatrist; b. Peru, Ind., Oct. 21, 1930; s. S. Dale Sr. and Rhea Pearl (Davis) L.; m. Carol Marie Davis, Jan 3, 1959; children: Stephen Dale, Patricia Marie. AB in Zoology, Ind. U., 1953, MS in Human Anatomy, 1955, MD, 1958. Diplomate Am. Bd. Psychiatry and Neurology. Intern Cook County Hosp., Chgo., 1958-59; resident in psychiatry Logansport (Ind.) State Hosp., 1959-60, Ill. State Psychiat. Inst., Chgo., 1960-62; staff psychiatrist Katharine Wright Psychiat. Clinic, Chgo., 1962-65, dir., 1965-92; cons. Ill. Youth Commn. 1962-64; instr. psychiatry Northwestern U. Med. Sch., Chgo., 1962-64, assoc. 1964-67; asst. dir. Northwestern U. Psychiat. Clinics, Chgo., 1963-65; attending psychiatrist, vice chmn. dept. psychiatry St. Joseph Hosp., Chgo., 1964—; lectr. psychiatry and neurology Loyola U. Med. Sch. Chgo., 1964-65, assoc. 1965, asst. prof. 1965-73, lect. 1980-89, clin. assoc. prof., 1989—; psychiat. cons. Ill. Dept. Pub. Health, 1967—; sr. attending psychiatrist, chmn. dept. psychiatry Ill. Masonic Med. Ctr., Chgo. 1970-92, chmn. emeritus, 1992—; assoc. prof. psychiatry U. Ill. Coll. Medicine, Chgo., 1973—. Fellow Am. Coll. Psychiatrists, Am. Psychiat. Assn. (life), Acad. Psychosomatic Medicine; mem. AMA, Ill. State Med. Soc. (chmn. council on mental health and addiction 1974-75, chmn. joint peer rev. com. 1975-76), Ill. Psychiat. Soc. (chmn. ethics com. 1974-75, chmn. peer rev. com. 1976-78), Chgo. Med. Socs. Office: 8 S Michigan Ave Chicago IL 60603-3302

LOOSER, DEVONEY KAY, English educator; b. St. Paul, Minn., Apr. 11, 1967; d. LeRoy Joseph and Sharon LeAnn (Sarslow) L.; m. George Lewis Justico, 1996. BA, Augsburg Coll., 1989; PhD, SUNY, Stony Brook, 1993. Instr. English SUNY, Stony Brook, 1989-93; asst. prof. English Ind. State U., Terre Haute, 1993—. Editor: Jane Austen and Discourses of Feminism, 1995; contbr. articles to profl. jours. NEH fellow, 1994. Mem. MLA, Am. Soc. Eighteenth Century Studies, N.Am. Soc. Study Romanticism. Office: Dept English Ind State U Terre Haute IN 47809

LOPARO, CHARLES A., SR., educator; b. Wadsworth, Ohio, July 10, 1933; s. Anthony and Frances (DiBianca) L.; m. Kathryn Ward, June 4, 1960; children: Anne, Charles A. Jr. BS in Edn., Kent State U., 1956, MEd, 1961, PhD, 1982; postgrad., Tufts U., 1966, Carnegie Mellon U., 1977. Supr. social studies Ohio Dept. Edn., Columbus, 1965-68; dir. curriculum Cleveland Heights (Ohio)-University Heights City Schs., 1968-74; asst. supt., interim supt. Brecksville (Ohio)-Broadview Heights City Schs., 1975-79; dir. field experience and Univ. sch., Kent (Ohio) State U., 1979-84, asst. prof., 1987—; dir. elem. edn. Westlake (Ohio) City Schs., 1984-86; prin. Our Lady of Good Counsel Sch., Cleve., 1986-87; adminstrv. officer Huffmaster Assocs., 1990-93; ednl. cons. Cedar, Inc. Contbg. author: Our American Heritage. Bd. dirs. Ohio Thespians Assn. Wall Street Jour. fellow. Mem. Assn. for Supervision and Curriculum Devel., Ohio Assn. for Elem. Adminstrn., Buckeye Assn. for Sch. Adminstrs., Internat. Reading Assn., Phi Delta Kappa (bd. dirs.).

LOPER, JOHN CAREY, molecular genetics and environmental toxicology, research scientist, educator; b. Hadley, Pa., June 21, 1931; s. Clark M. and Anna B. (Carey) L; m. Dorothy L. Moredock, Dec. 23, 1956; children: John T., Robert D., Christopher L. BA, Western Md. Coll., 1952; MS, Emory U., 1953; PhD, The Johns Hopkins U., 1960. Instr. to asst. prof. St. Louis U. Sch. Medicine, 1960-63; asst. prof. U. Cin. Coll. Medicine, 1963-66, assoc. prof., 1966-74, prof. microbiology, 1974-88, prof. environ. health, 1979—, prof., assoc. dir. dept. molecular genetics, biochemistry and microbiology, 1988—; environ. cons., 1984—; prin. investigator U. Cin./Nat. Inst. Environ. Health Scis. Superfund Basic Rsch. Program, 1991—. Contbr. articles to profl. jours. 1st lt. Med. Svc. Corp, 1954-56. Vis. fellow genetics Australian Nat. U., Camberra, 1971; Grad. Sch. fellow U. Cin; Rsch. grantee. Mem. Am. Genetics Soc., Am. Soc. Microbiology, Am. Chem. Soc., Am. Soc. Biochem. Molecular Biology. Democrat. Office: U Cin Coll Medicine Dept Molecular Genetics Biochem Microbio Cincinnati OH 45267-0524

LOPEZ, CAROLYN CATHERINE, physician; b. Chgo., Oct. 13, 1951; d. Joseph Compean and Angela (Silva) L. BS, Loyola U., Chgo., 1973; MD, U. Ill., 1978. Diplomate Am. Bd. Family Practice. Intern, resident Rush/Christ Hosp., Chgo., 1978-81; med. dir. Wholistic Health Ctr., Oak Lawn, Ill., 1981-82; clin. dir. Anchor HMO, Oak Brook, Ill., 1982-84, assoc. med. dir., 1984-87; med. dir. Chgo. Pk. Dist., 1987-91; v.p. Rush Access HMO, Chgo., 1992-93; asst. dean Rush Med. Coll., 1990-93; med. dir. Rush Access HMO, Chgo., 1991-93, v.p., 1992-93; v.p. for profl. affairs Rush Anchor HMO, 1993; sr. v.p. and chief med. officer Rush-Prudential Health Plans, 1993-95; chair dept. family practice Cook County Hosp., 1996—. Primary Care Policy fellow USPHS, 1993. Mem. AMA, APHA, Am. Acad. Family Physicians, Chgo. Med. Soc., Ill. State Med. Soc., Am. Coll. Physician Execs., Ill. Acad. Family Physicians (bd. dirs. 1987-89, speaker 1990-91, bd. chair 1990-91, pres.-elect 1991-92, pres. 1992-93, alt. del. to Am. Acad. Family Physicians 1992—), Am. Med. Women's Assn. Roman Catholic. Office: Cook County Hosp Dept Family Practice 1900 W Polk Chicago IL 60612

LOPEZ, JACQUELINE, dance therapist; b. Chgo., Jan. 21, 1962; d. Manuel and Ernestine (Sandoval) L.; m. Anthony Perez, June 5, 1983 (div. Dec. 1991); children: Noel Antionette, Gabriel Edward. BA, Barat Coll., 1983; MA, Columbia Coll., 1991; BSN, St. Xavier U., 1996. Dance therapist, cons. Chgo. Assn. of Retarded Citizens, 1985-89; psychology cons. C.A.R.C., Chgo., 1986-90. Author: The Koala Bear Family, 1986; director/writer: Southwest Xmas Chows, 1986-89. Dir. children's choir. Mem. Student Nurse Assn. (v.p. 1993-94, pres. 1994-95), Ill. Hispanic Nurse Assn. Home: 5732 S Homan Ave Chicago IL 60629-3114

LOPEZ-COBOS, JESUS, conductor; b. Toro, Spain, Feb. 25, 1940; m. Alicia Ferrer, May 15, 1987; 3 children. PhD in philosophy and music, U. Madrid, 1964; diploma composition, Madrid Conservatory, 1966; diploma conducting, Viennna (Austria) Acad., 1969. Gen. music dir. Deutsche Oper Berlin, 1981-90; prin. guest condr. London Philharm., 1981-86; prin. condr., artistic dir. Spanish Nat. Orch., 1984-89; music dir. Cin. Orch., 1986—; music dir. Orchestre de Chambre de Lausanne, Switzerland, 1990, condr.; also condr. concerts Edinburgh Festival, London Symphony, Royal Philharm., N.Y. Philharm., L.A. Philharm., Chgo. Symphony, Cleve. Orch., Phila. Orch., Berlin Philharm., Berlin Radio Orch., Amsterdam Concertgebouw, Vienna Philharm., Swiss Romande, Muncih Philarharm., Hamburg NDR, Oslo Philharm., Zurich Tonhalle, Israel Philharm., opera prodns. at Royal Opera House, Covent Garden, London, La Scala, Milan, Italy, Met. Opera, N.Y.C., Paris Opera, others; recs. include Lucia di Lammermoor New Philham. Orch., Otello, recital and operatic disc with José Carrera and London Symphony Orch., Liszt's Dante Symphony with Swiss Romande, Falla's Three-Cornered Hat, R-K Capricio Espagnole, Chiabrier's Espana with L.A. Philharm., others. Recipient 1st prize Besancon Internat. Condr.'s Competition, 1969, Prince of Astrurias award Spanish Govt., 1981, 1st Class Disting. Svc. medal Fed. Republic of Germany, 1989. Office: Cin Symphony Orch 1241 Elm St Cincinnati OH 45210-2267 also: Orchestre de Chambre de Lausanne, Chemin de devin 72, CH-1012 Lausanne Switzerland*

LOQUASTO, KLAUS WOLFGANG, writer, editor; b. Bremen, Fed. Republic of Germany, Feb. 19, 1946; came to U.S., 1948; s. Fred Sr. and Waltraud (Suessmann) L.; m. Valerie Jean Soriano, Apr. 26, 1985. BA in English and German, Wilkes Coll., 1969; cert. in Journalism, Newspaper Inst., Mamaroneck, N.Y., 1991. Writer, editor The Liberator, Forest Lake, Minn., 1990—; sect. editor Men's Rights Assn., Forest Lake, 1989—. Author short stories. With USN, 1969-71, Vietnam. Recipient Sandy Ninninger award Key Club, 1965. Republican. Home: 6109 Little Foxes Run Columbia MD 21045-5642 Office: The Liberator RR 6 Forest Lake MN 55025-9806

LORA, RONALD GENE, history educator; b. Bluffton, Ohio, Aug. 10, 1938; s. Milo August and Mabel (Luginbihl) L.; m. Alice Chumbley, Mar. 22, 1975; children: Jacqueline, Cynthia, Leah, Jeff. BS, Bluffton Coll., 1960; PhD, Ohio State U., 1967. Tchr. Fostoria (Ohio) High Sch., 1960-62; instr. history Bluffton (Ohio) Coll., 1964-66; teaching asst. Ohio State U., Columbus, 1966-67; prof. history U. Toledo, 1967—; trustee Bluffton Coll., 1987—. Author: Conservative Minds in America, 1971; editor: America in the '60s, 1974, The American West, 1980. Solicotor United Way, 1993—; mem. Toledo Mus. Art, 1994—. Mem. AAUP, Am. Hist. Assn., Orgn. Am. Historians, Ohio Acad. History (exec. coun. 1966—), Pres. Club Bluffton Coll., Phi Alpha Theta. Democrat. Office: U Toledo History Dept 2801 W Bancroft St Toledo OH 43606

LORD, JAMES GREGORY, marketing and fundraising consultant; b. Cleve., Aug. 23, 1947; s. James Nelson and Esther L.; children: Michael Richard, Rebecca Esther. Student U. Md., Far East Campus, 1966-68, Cleve. State U., 1968-72; m. Wendy Franklin, July 10, 1977. TV news prodr. Far East Network, Tokyo, 1965-68; wire editor News-Herald, Willoughby, Ohio, 1968-69; pub. rels. assoc. United Way, Cleve., 1969-70; free-lance pub. rels. person, Cleve., 1970-72; dir. pub. rels. Ketchum, Inc., Pitts., 1972-77; cons. mktg., devel. philanthropic instns., Cleve., 1977—; chief devel. officer Cleve. Mus. Art, 1984-85; vis. fellow St. Mary's Coll., 1993; chair Mgmt. of Change Think Tank, 1993; disting. fellow Mt. Vernon Inst., 1995; developer The Philanthropic Quest Methodology, 1995-96; del. United Religious Charter Writing Summit, 1996; frequent keynote spkr.; sponsor Crossing Boundaries: Building Creative Partnerships Conf., 1996. With USN, 1964-68, Japan. Author: Philanthropy and Marketing, 7th edit., 1981, The Raising of Money, 1983 (nat. and internat. bestseller), Communicating with Donors, 1984, Building Your Case, 1984, The Campaign Manuals, 1985, The Development Consultant, 1985, Guide for the Professional, 2d edit., 1986, Philanthropic Quest series of 9 books, 1996, others; editor: Results! Time Management System, 1986, Market Smart, 1988, The Campaign Letter, Non-Profit Mgmt. Report; contbr. numerous articles on philanthropy, mktg. and quality of life in Am. cities to various publs.; developed one-man photography exhbns., 15 worldwide sites, 1968-72. Home: 28050 S Woodland Rd Cleveland OH 44124-4538 Office: Care of Third Sector Press PO Box 18044 Cleveland OH 44118-0044

LORD, STUART C., dean. BA, Tex. Christian U., 1982; MDiv, Princeton Theol. Sem., 1986, M of Theology, 1987; D of Ministry, United Theol. Sem., 1993. Student asst. min. Holy Trinity-Bethlehem Presbyn., Phila., 1982-83; intern pastor A&M Presbyn. Ch., College Station, Tex., 1984-85; instr. health fitness Princeton (N.J.) U., 1985-87; univ. chaplain dir. DePauw U., Greencastle, Ind., 1987-94, assoc. dean. acad. affairs, 1994—; co-chmn. DePauw Minority Task Force, 1995—; mem. adv. bd. Benner Found., 1995—. Contbr. articles to profl. jours. Bd. dirs. Putnam County Mental Health Assn., Greencastle, 1995—, Ind. Campus Compact, 1995, Greencastle Opportunity Housing, 1995, Companion Cmty. Devel. Opportunities, 1995; vol. Boy Scouts Am. Mem. NAACP, Nat. Assn. Ptnrs. Edn., Nat. Ctr. Svc. Learning-Early Adolscence, Nat. Soc. Exptl. Edn., Nat. Assn. coll. & Univ. Chaplains (past pres.), Alliance Svc. Learning Edn. Reform. Office: DePauw U 500 E Seminary St Greencastle IN 46135

LORD, SUZANNE MOLINET, advertising executive; b. N.Y.C., Oct. 26, 1961; d. Roland Kenesaw and Anne (Dow) Molinet; m. Keith Edward Lord, Oct. 27, 1990. BS, Duke U., 1983; MBA, Columbia U., 1985. Rsch. analyst Rsch. Arts, Inc., Chgo., 1985-86; asst. account exec. Tatham-Laird & Kudner (name changed to Tatham Euro RSCG), Chgo., 1986, account exec., 1987-88, account supr., 1988-92, ptnr., acct. supr., 1992-94; mgmt. supr. Tatham Euro RSCG, Chgo., 1994—. Vol. Jr. League Chgo., 1987—; treas. Loyola Beach Neighborhood Assn. Mem. Beta Gamma Sigma. Office: Tatham Euro RSCG 980 N Michigan Ave Chicago IL 60611-4501

LORD, WILLIAM HERMAN, performing arts educator, theatre consultant; b. Providence, Feb. 28, 1931; s. Herman Maurice and Gertrude Elizabeth (Thompson) L.; m. Catherine Lynn Ball, Sept. 14, 1957; children: Jennifer Lynn, Louise Giovanna. BA, Evansville Coll., 1953; MA, R.H.M. Stage Equipment, Evanston, Ill., 1961. Installation/sales R.H.M. Stagg Equipment, Indpls., 1955-57; scenic carpenter WFBM-TV, Indpls., 1957-60; prodn. supr. Avondale Playhouse, Indpls., summer 1957-63; tchr. tech. theatre North Ctrl. H.S., Indpls., 1958-96, dept. chmn., 1985-96; theatre cons. William H. Lord, Inc., Indpls., 1960—; pres. Theatre Assocs., Inc., Indpls., 1958—. Author: (textbook) Stagecraft 1: Your complete guide to backstage work, 1978, 2nd edit., 1991, (manual) Installing a Stage Lighting System, 1977, (workbook) Stagecraft 1, 1985; contbr. articles to profl. jours. Deacon Northminster Presbyn. Ch., Indpls., 1958-60, elder, 1971-73, 90-93. Served to sgt. U.S. Army, 1953-55. Mem. Ednl. Theatre Assn. (inducted into Hall of Fame 1995), Ind. Theatre Assn. (v.p. 1990-92). Home and Office: William H Lord Inc 9210 N College Ave Indianapolis IN 46240

LORE, MARY J., accountant; b. St. Louis, Dec. 10, 1956. BBA, U. Mich., 1979. CPA, Mich. Controller Manley, Bennet & MacDonald, Detroit, 1984; dir. fin. and adminstrn. Med-Stat Systems, Ann Arbor, Mich., 1984-86; v.p, CFO Venture, Detroit, 1987-94; v.p., CFO Cellex Bio-scis., Inc., Mpls., 1987—; pres., owner McFarland Florist and Greenhouses, Inc., Farmington Hills, Mich., 1992—; bd. dirs. Regenerex, Mpls. Sec., bd. dirs. Farmington Area Philharmonic, 1994—; mem. adv. bd. U. Mich. Sch. Mgmt., Dearborn, 1994—. Named Floral Marketer of Yr. Soc. Am. Florists, 1994. Mem. AICPA, Mich. Assn. CPAs, Nat. Assn. Career Women, Nat. Assn. Women Bus. Owners, Greater Detroit C. of C. (amb. bd. 1992—, Future 50 Co. of Greater Detroit 1994). Office: McFarland Florists Greenhou 28915 Grand River Ave Farmington MI 48336-5831

LORENZ, RICHARD CARL, biologist; b. Buffalo, Jan. 12, 1954; s. James Henry and Mary Jean (Burton) L.; m. Maureen Lynn Carver, Dec. 1, 1979; children: Krysten Elizabeth, Ellen Marie. BA in Botany, Miami U., 1976; MS in Environ. Biology, Ohio State U., 1981. Lic. water plant operator. Rsch. microbiologist Columbus (Ohio) Div. of Water, 1981-85, chief biologist, 1985-93; supt. of water City of Westerville, Ohio, 1993—. Contbr. chpt. to Biogeography at the Island Region of Western Lake Erie, 1988; contbr. articles to various jours. Pres. Friends of Stone Lab., Put-In-Bay, Ohio, 1988. Grantee U.S. EPA, 1979-81. Mem. Am. Water Works Assn. (mem. governing bd. Ohio sect. 1989-95, chairperson Ohio sect. 1993-94), Nat. Mgmt. Assn. (v.p. 1987), Am. Soc. for Microbiology, Ohio Lake Mgmt. Soc., Water Mgmt. Assn. Ohio. Office: Westerville Water Plant 21 S State St Westerville OH 43081-6800

LORENZ, RONALD THEODORE, manufacturing executive; b. Chgo., Apr. 9, 1936; s. Raymond W. and Olga (Hagel) L.; m. Elizabeth L. Lehning, Nov. 26, 1960 (div. 1970); children: Dane B., Drenna D.; m. Phyllis J. Scordato, May 5, 1972 (div. May 1989); children: Amy J., Adam R. Cert. stationary engr. Asst. engr. Conrad Hilton Hotel, Chgo., 1953-55, engr., 1957-59; engr. Kemper Ins. Co., Chgo., 1959-67; pres. Capitol Music Ctrs., Elgin, Ill., 1967-81, Rapco Internat., Jackson, Mo., 1982-91, Allied Industries, Cape Girardeau, Mo., 1992—. Served with U.S. Army, 1955-57. Mem. Jackson C. of C. (officer 1987-88), Nat. Assn. Music Mchts. (officer trade show com. 1987-90). Republican. Home and Office: 3819 Stonebridge Dr Cape Girardeau MO 63701

LORENZI, JOHN CHARLES, computer analyst, musician; b. Lincoln, Ill., Mar. 24, 1959; s. John Bart and Eva Victoria Lorenzi. AS in Computer Sci., LLCC, Springfield, Ill., 1980. Computer analyst State of Ill., Springfield, 1980—. Musician, playing piano and drums. Home: 830 S Walnut Springfield IL 62704-2526

LORGE, CHARN TERESA MARIA, elementary education educator, real estate agent; b. Gorseinon, Wales, May 15, 1963; came to U.S., 1982; d. Surjit and Daya Wanti (Khrey) Lotay; m. Robert Gerald Lorge, Nov. 6, 1982. Student, U. Lancaster, England, 1981-82; BA in Econs., U. Wis., 1986, BS in Edn., 1991, M in Elem. Edn., 1994. Cert. elem. tchr., reading tchr., Wis.; lic. real estate broker, Wis. Real estate broker Lorge Sales, Bear Creek, Wis., 1985—; customer contact rep. Bank One Appleton, Appleton, Wis., 1986-89; tchr. Madison (Wis.) Met. Sch. Dist., 1991—; bd. dirs. Welcome Co. Treas. Legal Aux. Wis., Outagamie County, 1988-89, pres., 1989—; sponsor Children Internat., Kansas City, 1991—; mem. WYOU Cmty. TV, Inc. Mem. NEA, Wis. Edn. Assn. (coun.), Madison Area Reading Coun., Madison Tchrs. Inc., U. Wis. Meml. Union (life), U. Wis. Alumni Assn., Princeton Club, Golden Key, Pi Lambda Theta, Phi Kappa Phi. Roman Catholic. Home: PO Box 14704 Madison WI 53714-0704 Office: Lorge Sales 204 Railroad St Bear Creek WI 54922-0047

LORGE, WILLIAM D., state legislator, farmer, real estate broker; b. Bear Creek, Wis., Aug. 31, 1960; s. Gerald D. and Christina C. (Ziegler) L.; m. Molly Marie McGinty, Apr. 11, 1996. BA in Internat. Rels., U. Wis., 1983. Real estate broker W. Lorge Sales, Bear Creek, Wis., 1988—; mem. Wis. State Assembly, Madison, 1989—; chairperson Assembly state affairs com.; vice-chair Assembly state fed. rels. com., Assembly ins. securities and corp. policy com.; vice chair assembly ins., securities and corp. policy com., mem. excise and fees com., mem. tourism, hwys., consumer affairs com., criminal justice com., corrections com. Wis. State Assembly; vice chair assembly Fed. State Rels. Com.; mem. Wis. Trust for Hist. Preservation. Sponsor Christian Children's Fund, 1979—. Named outstanding young man in Am., 1990, legislator of yr. Wis. Conservation Congress, 1992. Mem. Nat. Conf. Ins. Legislators (exec. com. mem.), U.S. Jaycees, Lions, KC. Republican. Roman Catholic. Home: Rt 1 Bear Creek WI 54922

LOSCHEIDER, PAUL HENRY, academic administrator; b. Joliet, Ill., Nov. 24, 1954; s. John H. and Marian T. (Mantel) L.; m. Mary Susan Futterer, Aug. 1, 1976; children: Eric, Brian, Scott. BA in Acctg., Lewis U., Romeoville, Ill., 1976. CPA, Ill. Staff auditor Cooper & Lybrand, Aurora, Ill., 1976-78; comptroller N. Cen. Coll., Naperville, Ill., 1978-83, v.p. bus. affairs, 1983—. Mem. Nat. Assn. Coll. and Univ. Bus. Officers, Ctrl. Assn. Coll. and Univ. Bus. Officers, Ednl. and Instl. Ins. Adminstrs. (trustee student ins. program). Roman Catholic. Home: 824 Magnolia Ln Naperville IL 60540-7311 Office: North Cen Coll 30 N Brainard St Naperville IL 60540-4607

LOSCHKY, HELEN MORRIS, retired English literature educator; b. Greenwich, Conn., Nov. 1, 1933; d. Harold McLellan and Madeleine Emilie (de Russy) Johnson; m. David John Loschky, Dec. 29, 1956 (div. 1985); children: Lester Christian, Theresa Helen. BA in English, Pembroke Coll., 1955; MA in English, Brown U., 1965, PhD in English, 1970. Asst. prof. English Lincoln U., Jefferson City, Mo., 1969-74, assoc. prof. English, 1974-84, dir. honors program, 1978-93, prof. English, 1984—; grantwriter Title 3, Washington, 1980-81; cons. Little Brown Handbook, N.Y.C., Mo. R.E. Bd., Jefferson City. Contbr. articles to profl. jours. Bd. dirs. Maplewood Barn Theatre, Columbia, Mo., 1979-83, Thomas Jefferson Libr., Jefferson City, 1992-93; bd. dirs., chair Unity Ch., Jefferson City, 1992-93; judge speech and theatre Jefferson City H.S., 1990—. Fellow Danforth Found., 1955-56, Brown U., 1963-67; scholar Pembroke COll., 1951-55. Mem. AAUP, AAUW (sec. investment club 1994—), Nat. Collegiate Honors Coun., Great Plains Honors Coun. (past pres., Lifetime Member award 1995). Democrat. Home: 1010 Lafayette St Jefferson City MO 65101-3505

LOSEE, JOHN FREDERICK, JR., manufacturing executive; b. Milw., Apr. 27, 1951; s. John Frederick and Helen (Joslyn) L.; m. Jane Agnes Trawicki, Aug. 25, 1973; children: Nicole Marie, John Michael. BSME, Marquette U., 1973, MS in Indsl. Engring., 1982. Registered profl. engr., Wis.; cert. numerical control mgr., Wis. Mfg. engr. OMC-Evinrude div. Outboard Marine Corp., Milw., 1975-78, mfg. engr. supr., 1978-80, mgr. tool engring., 1980-85, mgr. process and tool engring., 1985-86, dir. mfg. engring., 1986-88; v.p. ops. Rytec Corp., Jackson, Wis., 1988-90; v.p. adminstrn. Custom Products Corp., 1990-91; part-owner Nat. Mfg. Co. Inc., Milw., 1991-96; owner JFL Mfg., 1996—. Mem. Numerical Control Soc., Soc. Mfg. Engrs., Computer and Automated Systems Assn. Republican. Roman Catholic. Home: W264n6565 Hillview Dr Sussex WI 53089-3452

LOSS, JOHN C., architect, retired educator; b. Muskegon, Mich., Mar. 6, 1931; s. Alton A. and Dorothy Ann (DeMars) Forward; m. LaMyrna Lois Draggoo, June 7, 1958. B.Arch., U. Mich., 1954, M.Arch., 1960. Registered architect, Md., Mich. Architect Eero Saarinen & Assocs., Bloomfield Hills, Mich., 1956-57; owner John Loss & Assocs, Detroit, 1960-75; prof., acting dean Sch. Architecture, U. Detroit, 1960-75; prof., head dept. architecture N.C. State U., Raleigh, 1975-79; assoc. dean. Sch. Architecture U. Md., College Park, 1981-83, prof. architecture, 1979-93, prof. emeritus architecture, 1993—; dir. Architecture and Engring. Performance Info. Ctr., 1982-93; pvt. practice, Annapolis, College Park, 1979-93, Whitehall, Mich., 1993—; mem. com. NRC-NAS, 1982-93; mem. bldg. diagnostics com. Adv. Bd. on Build Environ., 1983-93; mem. com. on earthquake engring. NRC, 1983-93; leader survey team for tornado damage in Pa. and Ohio, 1985. Author: Building Design for Natural Hazards in Eastern United States, 1981, Identification of Performance Failures in Large Structures and Buildings, 1987, Analysis of Performance Failures in Civil Structures and Large Buildings, 1990, Performance Failures in Buildings and Civil Works, 1991; works include med. clinic, N.C.; Aldersgate Multi Family Housing, Oscoda, Mich. Advisor Interfaith Housing Inc., Detroit, 1966-74; advisor Detroit Mayor's Office, 1967-69, Interim Housing Com. Mich. State Housing Devel. Authority, Lansing, 1969-71, Takoma Park Citizens for Schs. (Md.), 1981-82; advisor, cons. Hist. Preservation Commn., Prince George's County, Md.; mem. planning commn. Blue Lake Twp., Mich., 1994—. With U.S. Army, 1954-56. NSF grantee, 1978-81, 1982-84, 86-87, 88-90; named one of Men of Yr., Engring. News Record, 1984. Fellow AIA. Democrat. Roman Catholic.

LOTT, JOHN ALFRED, chemist, educator; b. Germany, Oct. 30, 1936; came to U.S., 1947; s. Richard F. and Ethel M. Lott; m. Gerlinde B. Lott; 1 child, Christopher Martin. BS summa cum laude, Rutgers U. Coll. Pharmacy, 1959, MS, 1961; PhD, Rutgers U. Sch. Chemistry, 1965. Diplomate Am. Bd. Clin. Chemistry; registered pharmacist, N.J. Asst. prof. U. Mich., Flint, 1965-68; asst. prof., assoc. prof. Ohio State U., Columbus, 1968-81, prof., 1981—. Contbr. numerous chpts. in books and articles to profl. jours. Fellow Am. Found. Pharm. Edn., 1959-61, Johnson & Johnson, 1964; grantee CDS, 1981, duPont Corp., 1983, 95, BMD, 1984, Kodak Co., 1986, 88, 93, Ames Co., 1987, Ciba-Corning, 1988, Miles Lab., 1989, 91, 93, Isolab, 1992, 94, Bremer Fund, 1992, Bayer Corp. Mem. AAUP, Am. Chem. Soc., Am. Assn. Clin. Chemistry (Bernard J. Katchman award Ohio Valley sect. 1979, Miriam Reiner award Capital sect. 1994), Nat. Acad. Clin. Biochemistry (Presdl. Recognition award 1983), Assn. Clin. Scientists. Office: Starling Loving M-368 Ohio State Univ Med Ctr Columbus OH 43210-1240

LOTUACO, LUISA GO, pathologist; b. Gapan, Nueva Ecija, Philippines, Jan. 29, 1938; d. Galicano Yuzon and Alicia (Go) L.; m. George Garrett Shepherd; 1 child, Lara. Student, U. Santo Tomas, Manila, Philippines, MD cum laude, 1960. Diplomate Am. Bd. Coll. Am. Pathology. Pathologist, Manila Sanitarium and Hosp., Manila, Philippines, 1969-72; mem. pathology faculty Kansas U., Kansas City, 1972, 1974-94; pathologist St. Catherine Hosp., East Chgo., Ind., 1973-74, VA Med. Ctr., Kansas City, Mo., 1974-94; chief pathology and lab. medicine John Pershing VA Med. Ctr., Poplar Bluff, Mo., 1994-96, chief of staff, 1995—. Paul Harris fellow, 1996. Fellow Coll. Am. Pathology, Am. Assn. of Clin. Pathologists; mem. U.S. and Canadian Acad. Pathologists, Am. Assn. Blood Banks, Philippine Med. Soc. of Kansas City (pres. 1981-83), Am. Med. Women's Assn., Philippine Med. Soc. Avocations: stamps; ceramics; antiques, opera, classical music. Home: 14111 Christy Ln Poplar Bluff MO 63901 Office: John Pershing VA Med Ctr 1500 N Westwood Blvd Poplar Bluff MO 63901-3318

LOTURCO, RAYMOND ANDREW, industrial designer, consultant; b. Tarrytown, N.Y., Mar. 5, 1936; s. Andrew Moses and Glendora Esther (Plimpton) LoT.; m. Muriel Josephine Bahner, Sept. 1, 1960 (dec. Jan. 1995); m. Marga Wolf, June 29, 1996. BFA, R.I. Sch. of Design, 1958. Staff designer Chris Craft Corp., Pompano Beach, Fla., 1959-62; assoc. designer PMMA Assocs., Pitts., 1962-68; mgr. design Cosco Inc., Columbus, Ind., 1968-75; cons. designer RAL Indsl. Design, Columbus, Ind., 1975—; pres. Paramed Corp., Columbus, Ind., 1994—. Patentee in field. With U.S. Army, 1958-59. Mem. Indsl. Designers Soc. Am. (dir. 1985, regional rep. consumer com. 1970-72; co-founder, chmn. Ind. chpt. 1984-85, Cert. of Appreciation 1986), Soc. Plastics Engrs., Ind. Mfrs. Assn., Harrison Lake Country Club (chmn. house com. 1976-78). Republican. Office: 1111 E 54th St Indianapolis IN 46220

LOTVEN, HOWARD LEE, lawyer; b. Springfield, Mo., Apr. 8, 1959; s. Isadore and Gytel (Tuchmeier) L.; m. Charlotte Lotven. BA, Drake U., 1981; JD, U. Mo., Kansas City, 1984. Bar: Mo. 1984, U.S. Dist. Ct. (we. dist.) Mo. 1984. Pvt. practice Kansas City, 1984—; asst. prosecutor City of Kansas City, 1985; prosecutor City of Harrisonville (Mo.), 1989-91, atty., 1989-91; chief ops. Integra Systems & BNDBL, 1989-90; mem. exec. bd. KCESP, Inc., 1991-92; criminal law com., co-chmn. 1991-92, gen. practice law com. 1993—, law day speaker, 1986—, lectr. Mem. Kansas City Men's Sr. Baseball League, 1990-96, exec. bd., divsn. dir., 1991-96; mem. B'nai B'rith Dist. II, 1977—; vol. Hunger Project, 1985—; judge Mo. State H.S. Moot Ct. Competition, 1992; Hyde Park Crime Patrol, 1985-91, Hyde Park Assn. Zoning and Planning Commn., 1993—; vol. Heartland United Way, 1995. Mem. ABA, Mo. Bar Assn. (young lawyer's coun. 1986-88, lectr. 1987-90, criminal law com. 1989—, gen. practice law com. 1990—, co-chair criminal law com. 1991-92, exec. coun. gen. practice law com. 1993—, Law Day spkr. 1990-95, lectr. 1987-90, 92), Kansas City Bar Assn. (mcpl. cts. com., Vol. Atty. Project, 1992—, Vol. Atty. Project award winner 1994), Delta Theta Phi, Omicron Delta Kappa, others. Democrat. Jewish. Office: 417 E 13th St Ste 400 Kansas City MO 64106-2878

LOTZ, EDWARD L., JR., sales and marketing professional; b. Louisville, Apr. 21, 1958; s. Edward L. and Doris J. (Temple) L. BA in Chemistry, U. Louisville, 1992. Tech. svc. mgr. Interez, Inc., Louisville, 1986-87, Avery Chem. Divsn., Mill Hall, Pa., 1987-90; technician Celanese Specialty Resins, Louisville, 1987-92; polymer chemist Celanese Specialty Resins, 1986-92; tech. svc. mgr. Rohm and Haas Co., Phila., 1990-92; tech. sales rep. Rohm and Haas Co., Chgo., 1992-95; mkt. mgr. polymer Wacker Chemicals, Chgo., 1995—; Conn. Patentee in field. Home: 2421 W Pratt Ste 889 Chicago IL 60645

LOU, ZHENG (DAVID), mechanical engineer, biomedical engineer; b. Changshu, Jiangsu, Peoples Republic China, Apr. 25, 1959; came to U.S., 1982; s. Gui-Xin and Pei-Ling (Wang) L.; m. Min Yu, 1984; children: Katherine Hua, Paul Anjun, Craig Ankai. BE, Zhejiang U., Hangzhou, China, 1982; PhD, U. Mich., 1990. Asst. rsch. scientist Transp. Rsch. Inst. U. Mich., Ann Arbor, 1990-93; mfg. tech. engr. Ford Motor Co., Ypsilanti, Mich., 1993—. Contbr. articles to Jour. Rheology, Jour. Biomechanics, others. Grantee NASA, 1992-94, U.S. Army, 1992-94. Mem. ASME, Soc. Rheology, SAE, N.Y. Acad. Scis., SME, Tau Beta Pi, Sigma Xi. Home: 1613 Old Salem St Plymouth MI 48170-1026 Office: Ford Motor Co EFHD PO Box 922 McKean and Textile Rds Ypsilanti MI 48197

LOUCKS, STEVEN R., environmental management executive; b. Ft. Sam Houston, Tex., June 27, 1946. BS in Chemistry, U. Minn., 1968, BSEE, 1975. Registered profl. engr. Lab. mgr. Minn. Dept. of Health, Mpls., 1968-76; safety and health mgr. Medtronic, Inc., Mpls., 1976-81; pres. Environ. Mgmt. & Tech., Mpls., 1981—. Contrb. article to profl. jour. Mem. Profl. Engring. Group. Office: Environ Mgmt & Tech P O Box 32333 Minneapolis MN 55432-0333

LOUCKS, VERNON R., JR., healthcare products and services company executive; b. Evanston, Ill., Oct. 24, 1934; s. Vernon Reece and Sue (Burton) L.; m. Linda Kay Olson, May 12, 1972; 6 children. B.A. in History, Yale U., 1957; M.B.A., Harvard U., 1963. Sr. mgmt. cons. George Fry & Assos., Chgo., 1963-65; with Baxter Travenol Labs., Inc. (now Baxter Internat. Inc.), Deerfield, Ill., 1966—, exec. v.p., 1976, also bd. dirs., pres., chief oper. officer, 1980, chief exec. officer, chmn., 1987—; bd. dirs. Dun & Bradstreet Corp., Emerson Electric Co., Quaker Oats Co., Anheuser-Busch Cos.; bd. advisors Nestlē U.S.A. Trustee Rush-Presbyn.-St. Luke's Med. Ctr.; assoc. Northwestern U. 1st lt. USMC, 1957-60. Recipient Citizen Fellowship award Chgo. Inst. Medicine, 1982, Nat. Health Care award B'nai B'rith Youth Svcs., 1986, William McCormick Blair award Yale U., 1989, Semper Fidelis award USMC, 1989, Disting. Humanitarian award St. Barnabas Found., 1992, Alexis de Tocqueville award for community svc. United Way Lake County, 1993; named 1983's Outstanding Exec. Officer in the healthcare industry Fin. World; elected to Chgo.'s Bus. Hall of Fame, Jr. Achievement, 1987. Mem. Health Industry Mfrs. Assn. (chmn. 1983), Bus. Roundtable (conf. bd., mem. policy com.), Bus. Coun. Clubs: Chgo. Commonwealth, Commercial, Mid-America; Links (N.Y.C.). Office: Baxter Healthcare Corp One Baxter Pkwy Deerfield IL 60015

LOUDEN, WILLIAM FRANK, librarian; b. New Castle, Pa., Oct. 8, 1947; s. William Lawrence and Jean Rose (McCready) L. BA, Mount Union Coll., Alliance, Ohio, 1969; MDiv, Duke U., 1973; MLS, U. Pitts., 1974. Catalog libr. Heidelberg Coll., Tiffin, Ohio, 1974-78; head catalog libr. Baylor U., Waco, Tex., 1978-81, asst. libr. dir., 1982-86; asst. dean librs. U. Cin., 1986-94; libr. U. Evansville, Ind., 1994—. Mem. ALA, Ind. Coop. Libr. Svcs. Authority (bd. dirs. 1994—), Assn. Coll. and Rsch. Librs (bylaws com. 1993—), State U. Libr. Autmoation Network (bd. dirs. 1994—), Baylor U. Librs. Sys. (adv. bd., bd. dris. 1994—), Lita/Lama (1996 nat. conf. program com. 1995—). Office: U Evansville 1800 Lincoln Ave Evansville IN 47722

LOUDERBACK, JEFFREY DALE, journalist, publishing executive; b. Xenia, Ohio, July 1, 1968; s. Frank Dale and Rebecca A. (Stillwell) L. BA in Comm., Wright State U., 1990. Cert. profl. writer. Staff writer Fairborn (Ohio) Daily Herald, 1989-90, Xenia (Ohio) Daily Gazette, 1990-93, Skywrighter, Wright-Patterson AFB, Ohio, 1993-96; pub. Outrider Publications, Dayton, Ohio, 1996—; Contbg. writer Dayton Daily News, 1989—; freelance writer, 1990—. Author: Dayton: Cradle of Inventions, 1995; editor Pet Tails, 1995—. Mem. Soc. Profl. Journalists, Pub. Rels. Soc. Am. Democrat. Home: 1519 Valley Heights Rd Xenia OH 45385

LOUDERBACK, KEVIN WAYNE, business owner; b. Mt. Vernon, Ill., Mar. 10, 1971; s. Richard Lynn and Wilberta Maxine (Anderson) L. Draftsman, civil engr. Finley Engring. Co., Inc., Lamar, Mo., 1988-91; civil engr. GTE North, Sun Prairie, Wis., 1991-92; with Empiregas Corp., Lebanon, Mo., 1992-93; EMT-A Breech Paramedics Ambulance Svc., Lebanon, Mo., 1993-94; EMT Lake of the Ozarks Ambulance Svc., 1994—; owner, chmn., pres. Ozark Jerky Co., Inc., Conway, 1992—; vol. EMT-P Conway Rescue Group, 1993-95, EMT-P Dallas County Rescue, 1995—. Vol. fireman Barton County Alert Squad, Lamar, 1989-92; mem. Barton County Disaster Team, 1989-92, Barton County Haz-Mat Squad, 1988-92, Mo. Emergency Preparedness Assn., 1989-92. Baptist. Home: Rte 3 Box 132E Buffalo MO 65622 Office: Ste 100 Rte 3 Box 132E Buffalo MO 65622-9112

LOUDERMELT, LAURA ALENE, mental health nurse; b. Chattaroy, W.Va., Nov. 12, 1940; d. Ermel and Edith (Presley) Stepp; m. James D. Loudermelt, June 29, 1957; children: Natalie, Lisa, Jim. ADN, Kalamazoo Valley C.C., 1984; BSN, U. Mich., 1988; MS in Nursing Adminstrn., Andrews U., 1993. Cert. mental health nurse ANA. Staff nurse Borgess Med. Ctr., Kalamazoo, 1984; shift supr. Total Living Ctr., Kalamazoo, 1985; shift supr. Kalamazoo Reg. Psychiatric Hosp., 1985—, unit mgr. male and female admissions, utilization rev. nurse; participant Internat. Nursing Rsch. Conf., 1992; mem. Kalamazoo Nursing Rsch. Collective. Mem. Southwestern Mich. Psychiat. Nursing Coun. (co-chair 1988-90), Eta Zeta chpt. Sigma Theta Tau. Home: 5641 Meredith Dr Kalamazoo MI 49002-2254

LOUDON, DONALD HOOVER, lawyer; b. Kansas City, Kans., Nov. 20, 1937; s. Donald Charles and Berenice (Hoover) L.; m. W. Sue Cantrell, Aug. 17, 1958; children: Donald H. Jr., Kurt William. BJ, U. Mo., 1959; LLB, U. Kans., 1962. Bar: Mo. 1962, U.S. Supreme Ct. 1977. Reporter Kansas City Times, 1959; assoc. Blackmar, Swanson & Midgley, Kansas City, Mo., 1962-65; asst. gen. counsel Commerce Bank of Kansas City (Mo.), 1965-68; dir., shareholder Morris, King, Stamper & Bold, Kansas City, Mo., 1968-87, Shughart, Thomson & Kilroy, P.C., Kansas City, Mo., 1987—; sec. Torotel, Inc., Grandview, Mo., 1984—. Elder, Presbyn. Ch. Mem. ABA, Met. Bar Assn. Kansas City, Lawyers Assn. Kansas City, Delta Tau Delta (pres., bd. dirs. Columbia, Mo. chpt.). Office: Shughart Thomson & Kilroy 12 Wyandotte Plz 120 W 12th St Kansas City MO 64105-1902

LOUDON, JOHN, state legislator. Mem. dist. 88 Mo. Ho. of Reps. Office: 134 Burtonwood Dr Rm 115-G Ballwin MO 63011

LOUDON, KAREN LEE, physical therapist; b. Kansas City, Mo., July 25, 1958; d. Walter Raymond and Clarice Frances (Washburn) L. BS in edn., U. Kans., 1980; BS in physical therapy, U. Kans. Medical Ctr., 1985; MS in edn., U. Kans., 1987. Registered physical therapist, Kans., Mo. Physical therapist Watkins Ctr. Univ. Kans., Lawrence, Kans., 1985—; adv. Pre Physical Therapy Club/Students, Lawrence, 1986—; mem./presenter Kans. City Orthopaeric Study Group, Kans. City., 1987—; athletic trainer, Sunflower State Games, Lawrence, 1990-92; clinical instr. Univ. of Kans. Medical Ctr., Lawrence, 1987—. Contbr. articles to profl. jours. Mem. Am. Phys. Therapy Assn. (Kans. leg. com. 1983-84, Kans. Disting. Clin. Svc. award 1995), Nat. Athletic Trainer Assn., Am. Coll. Sports Medicine, Phi Kappa Phi. Office: Watkins Health Ctr U Kans Lawrence KS 66045

LOUGH, RICK LEO, sales and marketing professional; b. Belleville, Ont., Can., Sept. 15, 1948; came to U.S., 1990; s. Leslie Robert and Jessie Pearl (Logue) L. BA, U. Western Ont., London, Can., 1971; BS with honors, U. Guelph, Ont., 1972, DVM, 1976. Toxicologist Bio Rsch. Labs. Ltd., Montreal, Que., Can., 1976-78, head gen. toxicology, 1978-81, head gen. toxicology and animal health, 1981-83, assoc. dir. toxicology, 1983-84, dir. mktg., 1984-87, sr. dir. pacific rim bus. Devel., 1987-90; v.p. internat. sales and mktg. Internat. Rsch. and Devel. Corp., Mattawan, Mich., 1991-95; cons. environ. toxicology specialist Calif. State Pub. Health, L.A., 1984-87; cons. in regulatory toxicology Consultra Internat. Ltd., Tokyo, 1990-91. Hastings County Vet. scholarship Ont. Vet. Assn., 1972. Mem. Soc. of Toxicology of Can., European Soc. of Toxicology, Occupational Hygiene Assn. of Ont. (pub. rels. com. 1985-87), Am. Mgmt. Assn., Ont. Vet. Assn. Home: 631 Carrington Ct Kalamazoo MI 49009-2463 Office: Internat Rsch & Devel 500 N Main Mattawan MI 49071

LOUGHARY, THOMAS MICHAEL, dentist; b. Beardstown, Ill., June 13, 1959; s. Thomas Giels and Beverly Ann (Marshall) L.; m. Vicki Lynne Shaneman, May 25, 1986 (div.); children: Thomas Michael II, Victoria Paige. Student, Knox Coll., 1977-80; DMD, So. Ill. U., Alton, 1984. Dentist Pla. Dental Ctr., Jacksonville, Ill., 1984-90, Dental Assocs. of Jacksonville, 1991—; gen. practice dentistry Beardstown Dental Assocs., 1985—; staff dentist Passavant Hosp., Jacksonville, Ill.; cons. Cass County Cancer Assn., Virginia, Ill., 1986—, Beardstown Board Edn., 1980—. Soloist Jacksonville Symphony Soc., 1984, 87; dir. Beardstown Community Theater, 1990-91, Jacksonville Theater Guild, 1990; chmn. Cass County Cancer Soc., 1989—. Recipient monetary cert. Phi Gamma Delta Ednl. Found., 1980. Mem. ADA, Chgo. Dental Soc., G.V. Black Dental Soc., Jacksonville C. of C., Kiwanis, Elks. Republican. Lutheran. Home: 5 Guy Dr Jacksonville IL 62650-9400 Office: Dental Assocs Jacksonville 1515 W Walnut Blvd # 10 Jacksonville IL 62650-1910

LOUGHRAN, GERARD ANDREW, chemistry consultant, polymer scientist; b. Mt. Vernon, N.Y., Sept. 10, 1918; s. George Andrew and Harriet Willhelmenia (Reiss) L.; m. Kathleen Pearse O'Connor, Aug. 11, 1945; children: Maura, Kathleen, Gerard Jr., Judith Ann. BS in Chemistry, Fordham U., 1941; MS in Chemistry, N.Y.U., 1948. Analytical chemist N.Y. Quinine & Chem. Works, Bklyn., 1941-43; grad. asst. chemistry Fordham U., Bronx, N.Y., 1943-44; rsch. chemist Am. Cyanamid Co., Stamford, Conn., 1946-56, R.T. Vanderbilt Co., East Norwalk, Conn., 1956-59; rsch. scientist USAF Materials Lab., Wright-Patterson AFB, Ohio, 1960-86; cons. Kettering, Ohio, 1986—; cons. Universal Tech. Corp., Dayton, Ohio, 1989; presenter in field. Contbr. 15 articles to profl. jours. With U.S. Navy, 1944-46. Fellow Am. Inst. Chemists (profl. chemist accredited); mem. AAAS, Am. Chem. Soc. (Dayton sect., polymeric materials div., sci. and engring. div., polymer chemistry div., rubber div.), Nat. Assn. Retired Fed. Employees, N.Y. Acad. Scis, Am. Legion. Home: 4575 Irelan St Dayton OH 45440-1548

LOUGHRAN, ROBERT P., electrical engineer; b. Milwaukee, Wis., Apr. 1, 1952. BA in Journalism, Anthropology cum laude, U. Wis., Milw., 1975, BSEE cum laude, 1990. Engr. asst. Environmental Dynamics, Sharon, Wis., 1982-87; instrumentation engr. Aqua-Chem, Milw., 1990-92; elec. project engr. Anguil Environmental, Milw., 1992—. Musician: Cedarburg (Wis.) Civic Band, Lakeshore Symphonie Band, N.E. Greater Milw., 1991—. Chmn. Lake Camus Protection & Rehab. Dist., Delavan, Wis., 1980-86. Mem. IEEE, Tau Beta Pi.

LOUREY, BECKY J., state legislator; b. 1943; m. Gene Lourey; 11 children. Student, Asbury Coll., U. Minn. Mem. Minn. Ho. of Reps., 1990—, mem. various coms., vice-chair health and housing fin. divsn., mem. internat. trade, tech. and econ. devel. divsn., mem. Legis. Commn. Health Care Access. Democrat. Home: Box 100 Star Rte Kerrick MN 55756 Office: Minn Ho of Reps 421 State Office Bldg Saint Paul MN 55155-1606

LOURIE, ALEXANDER, lawyer; b. Boston, Mar. 8, 1957; s. Marvin Herbert and Joan Eleanor (Beckel) L.; m. Mary Elizabeth Sterk, Sept. 2, 1990; 1 child, Katherine. BS, Duke U., 1979; JD, U. Chgo., 1983, MBA, 1983. Bar: Ill. 1983. Assoc. Jenner & Block, Chgo., 1983-90, ptnr., 1991—; fgn. atty. Mori Sogo Law Offices, Tokyo, 1990-91. Dir. Performing Arts Chgo., 1994—. Office: Jenner & Block One IBM Plz Chicago IL 60611

LOURWOOD, DAVID LEE, JR., pharmacotherapist, educator; b. St. Louis, Nov. 20, 1956; s. David Lee Sr. and Nancee Joan (Spradling) L.; m. Arlene Louise Holloman, June 2, 1990; 1 chld, Darryl Christopher. BS in Pharmacy, St. Louis Coll. Pharmacy, 1979; PharmD, Wayne State U., 1982. Bd. Cert. Pharmacotherapy Specialist, 1992. Pharmacy intern Jewish Hosp., St. Louis, 1976-79; pharmacist Hutzel Hosp., Detroit, 1980-81; clin. pharmacist Cook County Hosp., Chgo., 1981-85, clin. pharmacy coord., 1985-89; asst. dir. pharmacy Edgewater Med. Ctr., Owen Healthcare Inc., Chgo., 1989-90; pharmacotherapist Columbia/ Michael Reese Hosp. and Med. Ctr.-Columbia/HCA, Chgo., 1990—; clin. asst. prof. dept. pharmacy practice Coll. Pharmacy, U. Ill., Chgo., 1990—, clin. asst. prof. dept. ob-gyn. Coll. Medicine, 1990—; cons. Profl. Drug Systems, Inc., St. Louis, 1982—. Author: Antibiotic Drug Interactions in Evaluations of Drug Interactions, 1982—; mem. editl. bd. Annals of Pharmacotherapy, 1986-94. Dist. commr. Boy Scouts Am., Oak Park, Ill., 1982-85, La Grange, Ill., 1985-89; pres. Lombard (Ill.) Pk. Dist., Swim and Dive Team, 1994—. O.J. Cloughly Grad. fellow St. Louis Coll. Pharmacy, 1979. Mem. Am. Soc. Health-Systems Pharmacists, Am. Coll. Clin. Pharmacy, Ill. Coll. Clin. Pharmacy, Ill. Coun. Health-Systems Pharmacists, St. Louis Coll. Pharmacy Alumni Assn., No. Ill. Soc. Hosp. Pharmacists. Home: 352 W Madison St Lombard IL 60148-3218 Office: Columbia Michael Reese Hosp Med Ctr 2929 S Ellis Ave Chicago IL 60616

LOUSBERG, PETER HERMAN, lawyer; b. Des Moines, Aug. 19, 1931; s. Peter J. and Otillia M. (Vogel) L.; m. JoAnn Beimer, Jan. 20, 1962; children: Macara Lynn, Mark, Stephen. AB, Yale U., 1953; JD cum laude, U. Notre Dame, 1956. Bar: Ill. 1956, Fla. 1972, Iowa 1985; cert. mediator, Iowa. Law clk. to presiding justice Ill. Appellate Ct., 1956-57; asst. states atty. Rock Island County, Ill., 1959-60; ptnr. Lousberg, Kopp, Kutsunis and Weng, P.C., Rock Island, Ill.; opinion commentator Sta. WHBF, 1973-74; lectr., chmn. Ill. Inst. Continuing Edn.; lectr. Ill. Trial Lawyers seminars; chmn. crime and juvenile delinquency Rock Island Model Cities Task Force, 1969; chmn. Rock Island Youth Guidance Coun., 1964-69; mem. adv. bd. Ill. Dept. Corrections Juvenile Divsn., 1976; Ill. commr. Nat. Conf. Commrs. Uniform State Laws, 1976-78; treas. Greater Quad City Close-up Program, 1976-80; mem. nominations commn. U.S. Senate Judicial Nominations Commn. Ctrl. Dist., Ill., 1993—; bd. visitors No. Ill. U. Coll. Law. Contbr. articles to profl. jours. Bd. dirs. Rock Island Indsl.-Comml. Devel. Corp., 1977-80; bd. govs. Rock Island Cmty. Found., 1977-82; U.S. Sen. Jud. Nominations Commn. cen. dist. Ill., 1993—. 1st lt. USMC, 1957-59. Fellow Am. Bar Found. (rsch. adv. com., chair 1993-96, Ill. chair of fellows 1995—), Am. Coll. Trial Lawyers, Ill. Bar Found. (bd. dirs. 1986-93, chmn. fellows 1987-88); mem. ABA (ho. of dels. 1990-93), Am. Law Inst., Ill. State Bar Assn. (bd. govs. 1969-74, 88-94, chmn. spl. survey com. 1974-75, com. on mentally disabled 1979-80, spl. com. on professionalism 1986-87, task force on professionalism 1987-89, atty.'s fees 1988, bd. dirs. 1989—, pres. 1992-93, pres./chair bd. Mutual Ins. Co. 1993-94), Rock Island Bar Assn., Assn. Trial Lawyers Am., Ill. Trial Lawyers Assn. (bd. mgrs. 1974-78), Am. Judicature Soc., Nat. Legal Aid and Defenders Assn. (regional coord. 1989-90), Ill. Inst. Continuing Legal Edn. (bd. dirs. 1980-83, chmn. 1981-82), Lawyers Trust Fund Ill. (bd. dirs. 1984-88), Fla. Bar Assn. (chmn. out-of-state practitioners com. 1985-86), Rock Island C. of C. (treas. 1975, pres. 1978), Quad Cities Coun. of C. of C. (1st chmn. 1979-80), Notre Dame Club, Quad Cities Club, Rotary (bd. dirs. Quad Cities). Roman Catholic. Home: 740 51st Ave East Moline IL 61244-4447 Office: 1515 4th Ave Ste 101 Rock Island IL 61201-8651

LOUTZENHISER, CAROLYN ANN, elementary education educator; b. Rochester, Minn., Sept. 18, 1942; d. Frank Arnold and Mae Nellie (Walters) Mahnke; m. John William Loutzenhiser, July 1, 1967; 1 child, Amy. BS, Wis. State U., 1966. Lic. tchr., Minn. First grade tchr. St. Paul Pub. Schs., 1966-67; first grade tchr. Dist. 535 Rochester Pub. Schs., Rochester, Minn., 1967-73; reading tchr. Rochester Pub. Schs., 1974—; presenter Chpt. I tchr. aides, Rochester, 1974-76; speaker, presenter Chpt. I workshop for parents, Rochester, 1974-88, So. Minn. Edn. Coop. Svc. Unit, Rochester, 1984, 91, 92. Legis. chmn. PTA, Churchill Sch., Rochester, 1982-84; mem. PTA, Rochester; guardian coun. mem. Jobs Daughters Bethel 13, Rochester, 1971, 86-88. Mem. NEA, AAUW (study group chmn. 1973-74), Minn. Edn. Assn., Rochester Edn. Assn., Order Eastern Star (worth matron Rochester chpt. 1975-76), White Shrine of Jerusalem (worthy high priestess Rochester chpt. 1981-82), Alpha Delta Kappa (pres. Delta chpt. 1990-92). Republican. Congregationalist. Home: 706 Northern Hills Dr NE Rochester MN 55906-4081 Office: Hawthorne Sch 700 4th Ave SE Rochester MN 55904-7306

LOVE, JEFFREY WILLIAM, commercial banker; b. Harvey, Ill., Apr. 6, 1966; s. Wesley Merwin and Rebecca (Carino) L. Diploma, Culver Mil. Acad., 1984; BS in Econs., Purdue U., 1988. Career assoc. Norwest Bank Ft. Wayne (Ind.), N.A., 1988-89, corp. svcs. specialist, 1989-91, corp. svcs. rep., 1991-92, corp. svcs. officer, 1992-95; 2d v.p. NBD Bank, N.A., Ft. Wayne, 1995—; dir. Treasury Mgmt. Assn. Ind., Indpls., 1991-95. Mem. Masons (lodge pres. 1995), Shriners, Summit Club, Kappa Alpha Order (regional dir. 1991—).

LOVE, JOHN C., finance company executive; b. Saynor, Wis., July 8, 1932. BA in Acctg., U. Wis., 1954. Ptnr. Arthur Anderson & Co., Milw., 1956-81; mem. First LaSalle Capital L.L.C., Milw., 1991—. Lt. U.S. Army, 1954-56. Home: 5150 N Port Washington Rd Milwaukee WI 53217-5462 Office: Low & Assocs 3431 Surrey Dr Saline MI 48176-9571

LOVE, MICHAEL JONATHAN, retail company executive; b. Front Royal, Va., Nov. 25, 1952; s. Enoch Walden and Virginia (Nickens) L.; m. Karen Cobb, Nov. 4, 1978; children: Diana M., Michael Jonathan II. BA in Psychology, Randolph Macon Coll., Ashland, Va., 1975; ThD, Emmaus Sem., Bristol, Tenn., 1984. Credit mgr. trainee Sears Credit, Richmond, Va., 1976-77; credit mgr. Sears Credit, Gary, Tenn., 1977-85; card svc/prodigy mgr. Sears Payment Systems Trans. Svcs., Inc., Gary, 1985-89; client svcs. adminstr. Sears Payment Systems Trans. Svcs., Inc., Riverwoods, Ill., 1989-90, client svcs. mgr., 1990—; quality program chmn. SPS Transactions, Inc., Riverwoods, 1990-92, Black Exec. Exch. Program coord. Urban League, 1990—, Inroads coord., 1990—. Bd. dirs. Johnson City (Tenn.) Girl's Club, 1988-90, Washington County Commn. on Sch. Consol., Johnson City, 1981-82, Jonesboro (Tenn.) Pks. and Recreation Commn., 1981-83, Johnson City Red Cross, 1982-86, Evangel. Child and Family Agy., 1996—; founding pastor Trinity Bapt. Cmty. Ch., Cary, Ill., 1991—; mem. adv. bd. Vets. Upward Bound, East Tenn. State U., Johnson City, 1985-89, C.A.S.A. East Tenn. State U., Johnson City, 1988-89; chmn., founder Trinity African-Am. Mentoring Program, 1995—, Trinity Charity Golf Classic, 1991—, Trinity Gospelfest in the Pk., 1995—. Named Hon. Staff Mem. Tenn. Ho. of Reps., Nashville, 1987; recipient Tenn. Office of Minority Bus. Enterprise Achievement award State of Tenn., Nashville, 1988, Cert. of Appreciation Nat. Urban League Black Exec. Exch. Program, N.Y.C., 1991; named to Leadership 200 Johnson City C. of C., 1989. Mem. Johnson City NAACP (pres. 1979-89), Cary Ministerial Alliance, Omega Psi Phi (chaplain 1979-89, Citizen of Yr. 1980, Man of Yr. 1982, Scholar of Yr. 1984). Home: 505 Surrey Ridge Dr Cary IL 60013-3221

LOVEJOY, STEPHEN B., environmental policy analyst; b. Kokomo, Ind., June 16, 1949; s. Peter Alfred and Shirley Janet (Cole) L.; m. Catharine Loise Webb, Jan. 16, 1969 (div. July 1983); 1 child, Brittany Anne; m. Margaret Mary Cain, Jan. 1, 1986; children: Kelly, Howard, Steven, Gail and Douglas Kochell. BS, Purdue U., 1971; MA, Mankato (Minn.) State U., 1975; PhD, Utah State U., 1980. Rsch. scientist U. Wis., Madison, 1977-80; asst. prof. Purdue U., West Lafayette, Ind., 1980-84, assoc. prof., 1984-90; sr. policy analyst U.S. EPA, Washington, 1987-88; coord. Ctr. for Alternative Agr. Sys., West Lafayette, 1989-93; prof. dept. agrl. econs. Purdue U., 1990—; sr. ptnr. L&L Assocs., West Lafayette, 1991—; chair Purdue Employees Fed. Credit Union, West Lafayette, 1991—; bd. dirs. Ind. Inst. on Recycling, Terre Haute, Ind., 1990—; panel mem. Office of Tech. Assessment, U.S. Congress, Washington, 1994-95; assoc. dir. Natural Reservoir and Environ. Sci., 1995—; faculty advisor Purdue Coll. Republican, 1996—. Editor: Conserving Soil, 1985, Agriculture and Water Quality, 1989; assoc. rsch. editor Jour. Soil and Water Conservation, 1993—. Mem. West Lafayette Recycling Com., 1992—; mem. West Lafayette Rep. Com., 1994—. Recipient award of merit Soil Conservation Soc. Am., 1987, Bronze award U.S. EPA, 1987, Profl. Excellence award Am. Agrl. Econs. Assn., 1993. Mem. Lions Club. Office: Purdue U Dept Agrl Econs 1145 Krannert Bldg West Lafayette IN 47907-1145

LOVELL, EVAN MCCULLOCH, international development group manager; b. Berlin, Vt., Sept. 26, 1969; s. Christopher Ward and Ellen (McCulloch) L. BA, U. Vt., 1992. Dir. spl. projects E-II Mgmt., Washington, 1992-93; asst. to chmn. for internat. devel. Astrum Internat., N.Y.C., 1993-94; mgr. internat. devel. group Culligan Internat., Northbrook, Ill., 1995—. Fundraiser Clinton for Pres., Washington, 1992. Mem. Asia Soc., Princeton Club. Democrat. Office: 1 Culligan Pky Northbrook IL 60062

LOVELL, HARRY RHYS, university administrator; b. Chgo., Dec. 9, 1936; s. Glenn Ayres and Mona Elizabeth (Williams) L.; m. Uretta Ruth Mounts, June 25, 19611 Rhys William, Thad Christopher, Megan Ruth, Mollie Ann. BFA, Ill. Wesleyan U., 1960. Cert. fund raising exec. Elem. tchr. Pontiac (Ill.) Sch. Dist., 1959-68, Bloomington (Ill.) Sch. Dist. 87, 1968-73; dir. ann. funds and alumni affairs Ill. Wesleyan U., Bloomington, 1973-89, dir. maj. gifts, 1989-90, dir. rsch., 1990-93, dir. rsch./maj. gifts, 1994—. Trustee Cmty. Players, Bloomington, 1991—; co-founder Vermillion Players, Pontiac, 1965-68; treas. Coun. Advancement & Support Edn. Dist. 5, Washington, 1994—. Mem. Nat. Soc. Fund Raising Execs. (ctrl. Ill. chpt. pres.-elect 1994—), Mason, Scottish Rite Consistory (scholarship chair 1992—). Methodist. Home: 302 Margaret Ave Normal IL 61761 Office: Ill Wesleyan U PO Box 2900 1312 N Park St Bloomington IL 61702

LOVELL, MARY ANN, secondary education educator; b. Magnolia, Ark., May 30, 1943; d. Dezzy and Priscilla (Glover) Biddle; m. Clearence Edward Lovell, June 4, 1966 (div. 1975); children—Clearesia Ann, Delia Marie, Dezzy Aquib. BA, U. Ark., 1965; MS, Ouachita Bapt. U., 1972. Tchr. high sch., Stutgart, Magnolia, Arkadelphia and Eudora, Ark., 1964-75, Milw., 1981—; tchr. Ethan Allen Sch., Dept. Health and Human Svcs. State of Wis., 1986; job svc. specialist CETA, Wis. Dept. Industry, 1975-76; spl. project, coord. Milwaukee County Civil Svc. Commn., 1976-78. Mem. Internat. Reading Assn., Wis. State Reading Assn., Wis. Edn. Assn. (coun. 1989-90), Milw. Tchrs. Edn. Assn., Milw. Inner City Arts Council, Inc., Milw. Area Reading Coun., Educators' Politically Involved Coun., Am. Mgmt.

Assn., State of Wis. Edn. Profls. (Local 3271). Democrat. Pentecostal. Club: Playboy (Chgo.).

LOVY, ANDREW, osteopathic physician, psychiatrist; b. Budapest, Hungary, Mar. 15, 1935; came to U.S., 1939; s. Joseph and Elza (Kepecs) L.; m. Madeline Rotenberg, Aug. 16, 1959 (div. Sept. 1991; children: Daniel, Jordan, Howard, Jonathan, Elliot, Richard, Mickey. Student Wayne State U., 1956; BS, Ill. Coll. Optometry, 1957, OD, 1958. DO, Chgo. Coll. Osteopathy, 1962. Diplomate Am. Bd. Psychiatry and Neurology. Intern, Mt. Clemens (Mich.) Hosp., 1962-63; resident VA Hosp., Augusta, Ga., 1971-74; practice medicine specializing in psychiatry, Detroit, 1982; prof. psychiatry, chmn. dept. psychiatry Chgo. Coll. Osteo. Medicine, 1981-82; dir. psychiat. tng. program Mich. Osteo. Med. Ctr., Detroit, 1982-86; adj. prof. psychiatry W.Va. Coll. Osteo. Medicine, 1984; clin. prof. psychiatry N.Y. Coll. Osteo. Medicine, 1984; med. dir. Eastwood Clinics, 1987-90; clin. prof. psychiatry N.D. Coll. Medicine, 1990; prof., chmn. dep. psychiatry Chgo. Coll. Osteopathic Medicine, 1990-92; med. dir. behavioral medicine Saginaw Community Hosp., 1992-94; clin. prof. psychiatry Mich. State U., 1995—; dir. psychiatric residency program Midwestern U., 1995—. With M.C., U.S. Army, 1966-68, Vietnam. Decorated Air medal, Bronze Star with oak leaf cluster, Purple Heart, Army Commendation medal. Fellow Am. Coll. Neuropsychiatry; mem. Am. Osteo. Assn., Am. Heart Assn. (mem. stroke com. 1987-89), Am. Psychiat. Assn., Am. Acad. Pain Mgmt., Assn. Clin. Hypnosis, Am. Osteo. Coll. Neuropsychiatry (pres.-elect 1982-83, pres. 1983-84), Am. Med. Joggers Assn. Author: Vietnam Diary, 1971. Office: 3340 Hospital Rd Saginaw MI 48608

LOW, LOUISE ANDERSON, consulting company executive; b. Saline, Mich., May 1, 1944; d. Harry Linné and Rose Josephine (Chvala) Anderson; m. James Thomas Low, Dec. 30, 1967; children: James William, Eric Linné, Kari Louise, Antony Anderson. BA in Biology, U. Mich., 1966. Permanent teaching cert., Mich.; cert. master gardener Coop. Ext. Svc. Tchr. secondary sci. Novi (Mich.) Community Schs., 1966-67; rsch. asst. U. Mich. Med. Sch., Ann Arbor, 1967-68; tchr. secondary sci. Livonia (Mich.) Pub. Schs., 1968-72; tax preparer H&R Block, Saline, 1991; sr. exec. asst. Low & Assocs., Saline, 1991—. apptd. mem. long-range planning com. Saline Area Schs., 1990-94, apptd. mem. gifted and talented com., 1996—; mem. Saline H.S. PTO, 1995—; treas. youth bd. Zion Luth. Ch., Ann Arbor, 1993—; mem. St. Joseph Hosp. Ball Com., 1994; active Friends of the Saline Dist. Libr. Mem. AAUW (life, bd. dirs., com. chairperson), Washtenaw County Alliance for Gifted Edn. (v.p., bd. dirs.), U. Mich. Conger Alumnae Group (bd. dirs., mem. exec. bd.), Alumni Assn. U. Mich. (life), Interlochen Ctr. for Arts Alumni Orgn. (life), Ann Arbor Area Panhellenic Alumnae (pres. 1976-77), Wayne State U. Faculty Wives, Travis Pointe Country Club, Huron Valley Swim Club, Sigma Kappa (alumnae pres. 1970-72), Alpha Mu Sigma Kappa (mem. corp. bd., mem. adv. bd.). Lutheran. Home and Office: Low & Assocs 3431 Surrey Dr Saline MI 48176-9571

LOWDER, JAMES DANIEL, writer, editor, educator; b. Quincy, Mass., Jan. 2, 1963; s. John Joseph and Edna (Hayes) L.; m. Debra Ann Davidson, Aug. 9, 1986. BA, Marquette U., 1985; postgrad., U. Ill., 1985-87. Instr. dept. English U. Ill., Champaign, 1985-87; asst. editor (vol.) Fine Tuning mag., Milw., 1987-88; editor book dept. TSR, Inc., Lake Geneva, Wis., 1988-92; freelance writer, editor New Berlin, Wis., 1987—; instr. dept. arts and humanities Marian Coll., Fond du Lac, 1995—. Author: (novels) Crusade, 1991, Knight of the Black Rose, 1991, Ring of Winter, 1992, Prince of Lies, 1993, Name Your Nightmare, 1995; editor (anthologies) Realms of Valor, 1993, Realms of Infamy, 1994; contbr. articles, book revs., film revs. to profl. jours. Mem. Sigma Tau Delta, Phi Alpha Theta. Home and Office: 15120 W Mayflower Ct New Berlin WI 53151-6748

LOWE, ALLEN, state legislator. Rep. Dist. 105 Mich. Ho. of Rep., 1993—. Home: 1101 Ottawa St Grayling MI 49738-1323*

LOWE, CLAYTON KENT, visual imagery, cinema, and video educator; b. Endicott, N.Y., July 10, 1936; s. Clayton Edwin and Loretta Arlene (Terry) L.; m. Janet E. Snider, 1957 (div. 1977); children: Steven Scott, Kim Ann Parker, David William, Rebecca Michelle Sobel; m. Robin S. McKell, 1980 (div. 1993). BA, Bethany Coll., 1958; MS, Butler U., 1967; PhD, Ohio State U., 1970; BD, Christian Theol. Sem., Indpls., 1962. Pastor Bellaire (Ohio) Christian Ch., 1957-58, Beallsville (Ohio) Christian Ch., 1958, Russellville (Ind.) Christian Ch., 1958-60, Montclair (Ind.) Christian Ch., 1960-61; youth dir. St. Paul United Ch. of Christ, Columbus, 1967-70; asst. prof. journalism U. Ga., 1970-72; asst. prof. comm. Ohio State U., Columbus, 1972-73, asst. prof. photography and cinema, 1973-74, assoc. prof., 1974—, chairperson photography and cinema, 1974-78, dir. grad. studies photography and cinema, 1989-92; assoc. prof. emeritus Ohio State U., 1992—; comml. TV prodr., dir., writer Stas. WISH-TV, 1960-66, WLWI-TV, 1966-67, WOSU-TV, 1967-70; moderator World Film Classics, Educable TV-25, 1991—, also bd. dirs.; E.R.I.C. evaluator-film theory, 1973-78; juror Columbus Internat. Film and TV Festival, 1993, 94. Book reviewer The Arts Edn. Rev. of Books; editor: The Movies on Media Catalog, 1995; host: Columbus Mus. of Art "Movies on Media" film series, 1995, 96. Eli Lilly Found. grantee, 1961-63, Ohio State U. Devel. of Media on Media Study Collection grantee, 1985; Recipient Casper award for A Thing Called Hope, WISH-TV, 1966, Regional Emmy for A Tribute to Dr. King, WOSU-TV, 1968; nominated for regional Emmys for Lucasville, WOSU-TV, 1970, High Street, WOSU-TV, 1975. Mem. AAAS, NATAS (bd. govs. Ohio chpt. 1973-74), Univ. Film and Video Assn., Ohio State U. Dept. Photography and Cinema Alumni Assn. (pres. 1994-95, bd. dirs. 1994—), Kiwanis. Home: 68 Walhalla Rd Columbus OH 43202-1441

LOWE, JOHN BURTON, molecular biology educator, pathologist; b. Sheridan, Wyo., June 13, 1953; s. Burton G. and Eunice D. Lowe. BA, U. Wyo., 1976; MD, U. Utah, 1980. Diplomate Am. Bd. Pathology. Asst. med. dir. Barnes Hosp. Blood Bank, St. Louis, 1985-86; instr. Sch. of Medicine Washington U., St. Louis, 1985, asst. prof. Sch. of Medicine, 1985-86; asst. investigator Howard Hughes Med. Inst., Ann Arbor, Mich., 1986-92, assoc. investigator, 1992—; asst. prof. Med. Sch. U. Mich., Ann Arbor, 1986-91, assoc. prof. Med. Sch., 1991-95, prof. Med. Sch., 1995—. Contbr. articles to Jour. Biol. Chemistry, Genes and Devel., Nature, Cell. Office: U Mich Howard Hughes Med 1150 W Medical Center Dr Ann Arbor MI 48109-0650

LOWE, RALPH EDWARD, lawyer; b. Hinsdale, Ill., Nov. 24, 1931; s. Charles Russell and Eva Eleanor (Schroeder) L.; m. Patricia E. Eichhorst, Aug. 23, 1952; children: John Stuart, Michael Kevin, Timothy Edward. BA, Depauw U., 1953; LLB, U. Ill., 1956. Bar: Ill. 1956, U.S. Dist. Ct. (no. dist.) Ill. 1957, Ga. 1974, U.S. Dist. Ct. (no. dist.) Ga. 1980, S.C. 1990. Assoc. Ruddy & Brown, Aurora, Ill., 1956-58; ptnr. Lowe & Richards, Aurora, 1959-62, Vincent, Lowe & Richards, Aurora, 1963-71; pvt. practice Aurora, 1972-74, Aurora and Atlanta, 1974-85; prin. Lowe & Steinmetz, Ltd., Aurora and Atlanta, 1985-91; chmn. Inter-Am. Devel. Corp., Ill., 1965-67. Office: 407 W Galena Blvd Aurora IL 60506-3946

LOWE, ROY GOINS, lawyer; b. Lake Worth, Fla., Apr. 8, 1926; s. Roy Sereno and May (Goins) L.; A.B., U. Kans., 1948, LL.B., 1951. Admitted to Kans. bar, 1951; gen. practice, Olathe, 1951—; mem. firm Lowe, Farmer, Bacon & Roe and predecessor, 1951—. Served with USNR, 1944-46. Mem. Bar Assn. State Kans., Johnson County Bar Assn., Am. Legion, Phi Alpha Delta, Sigma Nu. Republican. Presbyn. Home: 701 W Park St Olathe KS 66061-3137 Office: Colonial Bldg Olathe KS 66061

LOWE, WILLIAM CURTIS, historian; b. Savannah, Ga., Nov. 24, 1947; s. William Robert and Louise (Moore) L.; m. Flora Stith, June 14, 1969; 1 child, Elizabeth Nell. AB in History, Coll. William and Mary, 1969; MA in History, Emory U., 1972, PhD in History, 1975. Vis. asst. prof. Auburn (Ala.) U., 1976-78, Marshall U., Huntington, W.Va., 1978-79, Black Hawk Coll., Moline, Ill., 1979-80; chmn. history dept. Mt. St. Clare Coll., Clinton, Iowa, 1980—, chmn. social scis. div., 1986-92, acad. dean, 1992—. Author: Blessings of Liberty: Safeguarding Civil Rights, 1992; contbr. articles to profl. jours. Vestryman St. John's Episc. Ch., Clinton, 1990-94. Maj. USAR, 1969-91. Ford fellow Emory U., 1972. Mem. Am. Hist. Assn., N.Am. Conf. Brit. Studies, Ga. Hist. Soc., So. Hist. Soc., Va. Hist. Soc. Democrat. Episcopalian. Home: 1143 Galbraith Dr Clinton IA 52732-3369 Office: Mt St Clare Coll 400 N Bluff Blvd Clinton IA 52732-3910

LOWE, WILLIAM DANIEL, automotive company research executive, consultant; b. Oklahoma City, Dec. 23, 1949; s. Daniel Potter and Nova Jene (Werrell) L.; children: Kellie Christine, William Matthew. BA, Baylor U., 1972; MS, Cen. Mich. U., 1991; PhD, Walden U., 1994. Asst. office mgr. Oldsmobile Divsn., GMC, L.A., 1972-74; dist. mgr. Oldsmobile Divsn. GM, Mpls., L.A., Houston, 1975-83; office mgr. Oldsmobile Divsn., GMC, Kansas City, 1984-88; asst. field mktg. mgr. Oldsmobile divsn. GMC, Lansing, Mich., 1989-90; mktg. mgr. Oldsmobile divsn. GMC, Washington, 1991; consumer rsch. mgr. GMC, Lansing, 1992-95, rsch. mgr. Oldsmobile Divsn., 1996—. Republican. Baptist. Home: 3033 Ingersoll Rd Lansing MI 48906-9152 Office: Oldsmobile Divsn GMC 920 Townsend St Lansing MI 48921-0001

LOWENBERG, LORRAINE LYNETTE, psychiatric and mental health nurse; b. Donnellson, Iowa, Apr. 20, 1940; d. Arnold H. and Frances (Neff) L. BA in Biology, Bluffton (Ohio) Coll., 1962; MBA, Ind. U., South Bend, 1984; ADN, Southwestern Mich. Coll., 1991. RN, Ind.; cert. psychiat. mental health nurse. Adminstrv. sec. Miles Labs., Inc., Elkhart, Ind., 1969-86; exec. sec. Elkhart County Health Dept., 1987-88; asst. to the pres. Goshen (Ind.) Coll., 1988-89; staff nurse Oaklawn Hosp., Goshen, 1991, Elkhart Gen. Hosp., 1991-92; staff nurse inpatient unit Otis R. Bowen Ctr. Human Svcs., Warsaw, Ind., 1993—. Mem. Ind. Sheriff's Assn., Chronic Fatigue Immune Dysfunction Syndrome Assn. Am., Am. Soc. for Prevention of Cruelty to Animals, Am. Psychiatric Nurses Assn., Am. Holistic Nurses Assn. Home: 612 University St Donnellson IA 52625

LOWENHAUPT, CHARLES ABRAHAM, lawyer; b. St. Louis, May 19, 1947; s. Henry Cronbach and Cecile (Koven) L.; m. Rosalyn Lee Sussman, Dec. 28, 1969; children: Elizabeth Anne, Rebecca Jane. BA cum laude, Harvard U., 1969; JD magna cum laude, U. Mich., 1973. Bar: Mo. 1973, U.S. Dist. Ct. (ea. dist.) Mo. 1975, U.S. Ct. Appeals (8th cir.) 1975, U.S. Tax Ct. 1975, U.S. Ct. Claims 1975, U.S. Supreme Ct. 1987. Law clk. to presiding justice U.S. Tax Ct., Washington, 1973-75; ptnr. Lowenhaupt, Chasnoff, Armstrong & Mellitz, St. Louis, 1977-94; advisor Inst. for Pvt. Investors, 1991-93; mem. Lowenhaupt & Chasnoff, LLC, St. Louis, 1994—; speaker Nat. Assn. Ind. Schs., St. Louis Assn. Legal Assts., Washington U. Bus. Sch., Inst. for Pvt. Investors, numerous others; mem. adv. bd. dirs. Cottonwood Gulch Found., Thoreau, N.Mex., Textile Mus., Washington. Bd. dirs. Ctrl. West End. Assn., Inc., St. Louis, 1976-80, Temple Emanuel, St. Louis, 1982-89, Craft Alliance St. Louis, 1987-90, Helicon Found., San Diego, 1989—, St. Louis Regional Med. Ctr. Found., 1993—, chmn. bd. dirs., 1995—; bd. dirs. St. Louis Zoo Found., 1993—, sec., 1995—; mem. What Works com. St. Louis Bus. Jour., 1994—; sec. Gladys & Henry Crown Ctr. for Sr. Living, 1996—; mem. entrepreneurial planning com. St. Louis Met. Assn. for Philanthropy, 1996—. Mem. ABA (tax section, estate and gift section, real property section, probate and trust law, task force legal financial planning, chmn. generation-skipping transfer tax subcom., estate and gift tax com. tax sect. 1995—), Mo. Bar Assn. (tax section, probate and trust section), Bar Assn. of Met. St. Louis (tax section, real property and development sect.), Order of the Coif, St. Louis Estate Planning Coun., Mo. Athletic Club, Harvard Club of N.Y.C., Noonday Club. Home: 58 Kingsbury Pl Saint Louis MO 63112-1859 Office: Lowenhaupt & Chasnoff L L C 10 S Broadway Ste 600 Saint Louis MO 63102-1733

LOWNSDALE, GARY RICHARD, mechanical engineer; b. Poplar Bluff, Mo., Nov. 2, 1946; s. Edward Lee and Margie Lee (Tesreau) L.; m. Paulette Ann Wermuth, Nov. 30, 1968; children: Charles Edgar, Larissa Renee. BSME, U. Cin., 1970. Registered profl. engr., Mich. Trainee engring. mgmt. Chrysler Corp., Highland Park, Mich., 1965-69; contact engr. Chrysler Corp., Hamtramck, Mich., 1970-71; prin. design engr. Ford Morot Co., Dearborn, Mich., 1971-82; exec. dir. advance programs Schlegel Corp., Madison heights, Mich., 1982-86; mgr. automotive design ctr. GE, Pittsfield, Mass., 1986-87; mgr. strategic projects GE, Southfield, Mich., 1990; v.p. design and engring. Autopolymer Design inc., Auburn Hills, Mich., 1987-88; chief engr. polymer body Saturn corp., Troy, Mich., 1988-90; industry dir. Hercules Incorp., Troy, Mich., 1990-92; dir. mktg. automotive systems group Johnson Controls, Inc., Plymouth, Mich., 1992; dir. comml. bus. APX Internat., Madison Heights, Mich., 1993-94; v.p., COO TRANS 2 Corp., Livonia, Mich., 1994-96; v.p. ops. Mastercraft Boat Co., Vonore, Tenn., 1996—. Presenter internat. and tech. papers; patentee in field. Sec. Coventry Gardens Homeowners Assn., Livonia, Mich., 1976-86; dist. leader Boy Scouts Am., Livonia, 1977—; pres. PTA, Livonia, 1982-84. Mem. ASME (sr.), Am. Soc. Body Engrs., Engring. Soc. Detroit (vice chmn. 1972-82), Soc. Plastics Engrs., Soc. Automotive Engrs. (co-chmn. com. 1991-92), Elfen Soc., Hadley Hills Homeowners Assn. (pres. 1990—), Sports Car Club Am. (solo chmn. 1972-76, Solo Nat. Champion award 1974). Home: 4221 Meadow Pond Ln Metamora MI 48455-9751 Office: Mastercraft Boat Co 100 Cherokee Cove Dr Vonore TN 37885

LOWRIE, PAMELA BURT, educator, artist; b. Geneva, Ill., May 12, 1937; d. Morris Nathan and Helyn (Beetlestone) B.; children: Edmund Gale, Matthew Burt; m. Michael Hammer, Aug. 14, 1982. BA, U. Mich., 1959; MS in Edn., No. Ill. U., Dekalb, 1970; MA, Claremont Grad. Sch. (Calif.), 1979. One person shows: Loyola U. Gallery, Chgo., U. Ill. Med. Ctr. Gallery, 1978, Elmhurst (Ill.) Coll. Gallery, 1980, Kankakee (Ill.) Coll. Gallery, 1982, The Edge Gallery, Villa Park, Ill., 1984, Gahlberg Gallery Coll. of DuPage, 1986, 87, 92, Elmhurst Art Mus., 1994, Am. Headquarters of the Theosophical Soc., 1995 Schafer Gallery; group shows include: Five Women Artists from Ill., Notre Dame U., 1979, Springfield (Ill.) Art Assn. Gallery, 1981, Am. Cultural Ctr., Taipei, Taiwan, 1982, Campanille Gallery, Chgo., Limelight-Abstract Art, Riverwalk Gallery, Naperville, Ill., David Adler Cultural Ctr., Libertyville, Ill., Norris Gallery, St. Charles, Ill., Gov. State U., Park Forest, Ill.; represented in permanent collections: Coll. DuPage, Glen Ellyn, Ill., AT&T, Naperville, Eastman Pharms., Malvern, Pa., Getty Synthetic Fuel, Chgo., Monte Christo Condominiums, Fla., Nara Jr. Coll., Japan, No. Trust Bank, Chgo., Plan Corp., Wheaton, Ill.; art cons. Sch. Dist. 41, Glen Ellyn, Ill., 1970-72; prof. art Coll. DuPage, Glen Ellyn, 1972-94; ret. 1994. Dir., staff Nat. Great Tchrs. Seminars, Williams Bay, Wis., 1976-94; staff Calif. Great Tchrs. Seminar, Santa Barbara, 1979, Hawaii Great Tchrs. Seminar, 1990; vis. prof. Christ Ch. Coll., Canterbury, Eng., 1990. Bd. dirs. Fine Arts Rev. Com., DuPage County, Ill., 1982. Home and Studio: 926 N Scott St Wheaton IL 60187-3862

LOWRIE, WILLIAM G., oil company executive; b. Painesville, Ohio, Nov. 17, 1943; s. Kenneth W. and Florence H. (Strickler) L.; m. Ernestine R. Rogers, Feb. 1, 1969; children: Kristen, Kimberly. BChemE, Ohio State U., 1966. Engr. Amoco Prodn. Co. subs. Standard Oil Co. (Ind.), New Orleans, 1966-74, area supt., Lake Charles, La., 1974-75, div. engr., Denver, 1975-78, div. prodn. mgr., Denver, 1978-79, v.p. prodn., Chgo., 1979-83; v.p. supply and marine transp. Standard Oil Co. (Ind.), Chgo., 1983-85; pres., Amoco Can., 1985-86; sr. v.p. prodn., Amoco Prodn. Co., 1986-87, exec. v.p. USA, 1987-88; exec. v.p. Amoco Oil Co., Chgo., 1989-90, pres., 1990-92; pres. Amoco Prodn. Co., 1992-94; exec. v.p. E&P sector Amoco Corp., 1994-95, pres. 1996—. Bd. dirs. Jr. Achievement, Northwestern Meml. Corp.; trustee, bd. dirs. Nat. 4-H Coun. Named Outstanding Engring. Alumnus, Ohio State U., 1979, Disting. Alumnis Ohio State U., 1985. Mem. Am. Petroleum Inst., Soc. Petroleum Engrs., Mid-Am. Club (Chgo.). Republican. Presbyterian. Office: Amoco Corp PO Box 87703 Chicago IL 60680-0703

LOWRY, BOB BILL, manufacturers executive; b. Columbus, Ohio, Apr. 2, 1934; s. Franklin and Dorothy Mae L.; m. Joan Dondrea, June 15, 1957; 1 child, Christopher Scott. BS, Baldwin-Wallace Coll., 1956; MA, W.Va. U., 1959. Asst. W.Va. U., Morgantown, 1959; sales Ohio Nut & Bolt Co., Berea, Ohio, 1962-68; tchr., coach Brookside High Sch., Sheffield Lake, Ohio, 1959-62; pres. C.J. Scott Co., Bay Village, Ohio, 1968—. Recipient Merit award Baldwin Wallace Coll., 1996. Mem. NRA, Am. Trapshooting Assn., Kiwanis (officer 1959-62), Dover Bay Gun Club (pres. 1971-95), Amherst-Beaver Creek Hunt Club, Ducks Unltd. Roman Catholic. Home: 578 Yarmouth Ln Bay Village OH 44140

LOWRY, EDDIE ROUNTREE, JR., classical studies educator; b. Fredericksburg, Va., Nov. 18, 1945; m. Astride Hazemann; children: Sophie, Carolyn. BA, Hampden-Sydney (Va.) Coll., 1968; MDiv, Harvard U., 1971, PhD, 1980. Lectr. Yale U., New Haven, Conn., 1978-80, asst. prof. classics, 1980-82; asst. prof. fgn. lang. U. Dayton, Ohio, 1982-88; Uihlein chair classical studies Ripon (Wis.) Coll., 1988—, assoc. prof., 1988-94, prof., 1994—, chair dept. Romance and classical langs., 1992-96. Author: Thersites A Study in Comic Shame, 1991. Woodrow Wilson fellow, 1968. Mem. Am. Philol. Assn. (mem. joint com. on classics in Am. edn. with Am. Classical League 1995—), Am. Classical League, Archaeol. Inst. Am., Classical Assn. Mid. West and South (chairperson coll. awards com. 1992—), Wis. Latin Tchrs. Assn. (pres. 1991-94, mem. exec. com. 1995—), Wis. Assn. Fgn. Lang. Tchrs. (mem. exec. com. 1991-94, mem. task force on block scheduling 1994-95), Phi Beta Kappa. Home: 646 Woodside Ave Ripon WI 54971-1641 Office: Ripon Coll Dept Romance Classical Lang 300 Seward St Ripon WI 54971

LOWRY, JOAN MARIE DONDREA, broadcaster; b. Weirton, W.Va., June 8, 1935; d. Rudolph and Mary (Telmanik) Dondrea; m. Robert William Lowry, June 15, 1957; 1 child, Christopher Scott. BS in Edn., Baldwin-Wallace Coll., 1956; student Ohio Sch. Broadcasting, 1977-79. Gen. mgr., news dir. Sta. WLRO, Lorain, Ohio, 1980-82; host 35 Live, Cinemavidio TV, Elyria, Ohio, 1980-83; TV show host Continental Cable, Cleve., 1983—; pub. rels. dir. Sta. WZLE, Lorain, 1982-83; broadcaster, cmty. rels. dir. Sta. WRKG, Lorain, 1983—, news dir., 1988—; govt. and pub. affairs mgr. No. Ohio Continental Cablevision, 1991—; treas. bd. dirs. Better Hearing Inst., Washington, 1992—; spkr. in field. Appeared in motion pictures: Those Lips Those Eyes, 1982, One Trick Pony, 1982; performer commls. Mem. steering com. Nat. Coun. Better Hearing and Speech, 1985—, mem. coun. better hearing and speech month, Washington, 1985—, Lorain County coun., 1986—, nat. pres. better hearing and speech month, 1995; mem. cmty. resource coun. Leadership Lorain County, 1988-89; trustee Delta Zeta Found., 1983-95, pres., 1987-95; active Women in Cable, 1993, Lorain Litter Control Bd., 1981-83; comms. and mktg. com. United Way, 1987—; bd. dirs. Lorain Conty Sr. Citizens Assn., 1982-85, Lorain Consumers Coun., 1980—; v.p. Bay Village PTA Coun., 1973-75; mem. Martin Luther King Steering Com., 1987—; chmn. adv. bd. Lorain County Heart Assn., 1988; trustee N.E. affiliate Am. Heart Assn., also active Leadership Coun., 1988—, trustee; active Multiple Sclerosis Soc., Am. Cancer Soc., Muscular Dystrophy Assn., Founders Meml. Found, others; chair Lorain County Mothers March of Dimes, 1988; grand marshal numerous parades. Named Woman of Achievement, Nat. YWCA and Lorain County Bus. and Industry Assn., 1983, Ohio Delta Zeta Alumnae Woman of Yr., 1995; recipient USAF award, 1982, USN award, 1981, Media award Am. Cancer Soc., 1982, Comm. award Easter Seals Soc., 1981, Cmty. Svc. award Lorain County chpt. Am. Heart Assn., 1981, Service to Mankind award Sertoma Internat., 1988, Baldwin-Wallace Coll. Alumni Merit award, 1996; ofcl. hostess for U.S. Army in Lorain County, 1980-83; Mayor's Proclamation, 1982; hon. recruiter award U.S. Army, 1981; recognition award Ohio House Reps., nat. Delta Zeta Woman of Yr. award, 1995. Mem. Bus. and Profl. Women, Lorain County Arts Coun., Leadership Lorain County Alumni Assn. (bd. dirs. 1990—), Baldwin-Wallace Alumni Assn. (nat. pres. 1979-81), LWV (chpt. pres. 1966-67), Cleve. Amateur Fencers (pres. 1965-67), Internat. Platform Assn. Byzantine Catholic. Home: 578 Yarmouth Dr Cleveland OH 44140-1753

LOWRY, KEVIN M., manufacturing executive; b. Lorain, Ohio, Aug. 8, 1957. AA, Lorain (Ohio) C.C., 1983. Assembler Ford Motor Co., Lorain. 1981-83; foreman U.S. Steel, Lorain, 1983-85; dept. supr. Lorain Products, 1985—. Vol. Amherst (Ohio) Parks Dept. Mem. Calibration Systems Orgn. Office: Lorain Products 1122 F St Lorain OH 44052-2255

LOWTHER, JAMES E., state legislator; m. Virginia Lowther. Kans. state rep. Dist. 60, ret. banker. Home: 1549 Berkeley Rd Emporia KS 66801-5559*

LOWTHIAN, PETRENA, college president; b. London; d. Leslie Irton and Petrena Lowthian; m. Clyde Hennies (div.); children: David L. Hennies, Geoffrey L. Hennies; m. Misson Mandel, 1987. Dip. Royal Acad. Dramatic Art, London, 1952. Retail career with various orgns., London, Paris, 1949-57; founder, pres. Lowthian Coll. divsn. Lowthian Inc., Mpls., 1964. Mem. adv. council Minn. State Dept. Edn., Mpls., 1974-82; mem. adv. bd. Mpls. Community Devel. Agy., Mpls., 1983-85; mem. Downtown Council Mpls., 1972, chmn. retail bd., 1984-92; mem. Bd. Bus. Indsl. Advisors U. Wis.-Stout, Menomonie, 1983-89. Mem. Fashion Group, Inc. (regional bd. dirs. 1980), Rotary (mem. career and econ. edn. 1991). Home: 10 Creekside St Long Lake MN 55356-9431 Office: Lowthian Coll 825 2nd Ave S Minneapolis MN 55402-2808

LOY, RICHARD FRANKLIN, civil engineer; b. Dubuque, Iowa, July 6, 1950; s. Wayne Richard and Evelyn Mae (Dikeman) L.; m. Monica Lou Roberts, Sept. 2, 1972 (div.); children: Taneha Eve, Spencer Charles. BSCE, U. Wis., Platteville, 1973. Registered profl. engr., Wis., Ohio. Engr. aid Wis. Dept. of Transp., Superior, 1969; asst. assayer Am. Lead & Zinc Co., Shullsburg, Wis., 1970; asst. grade foreman Radandt Construction Co., Eau Claire, Wis., 1970; air quality technician U. Wis., Platteville, 1972-73; asst. city engr. City of Kaukauna, Wis., 1973-77; asst. city engr. City of Fairborn, Ohio, 1977-89, city engr., 1989-93; pub. works dir. City of Fairborn, 1993—. Bd. dirs. YMCA Fairborn, 1990-95; mem. coun. Trinity United Ch. of Christ, Fairborn, 1989-92; chmn. Chillicothe dist. Tecumseh coun. Boy Scouts Am., 1991-93. Recipient Blue Coat award, 1983; named to Exec. Hall of Fame, N.Y., 1990. Mem. ASCE, NSPE, Am. Pub. Works Assn., Am. Water Works Assn., Inst. Transp. Engrs.

LOY, ROBERT E., mechanical engineer; b. Bucyrus, Ohio, Mar. 11, 1944. BS in Mech. Engring., Ohio State U., 1970. Registered profl. engr., Ohio; cert. fluid power engr. Sr. project engr. KDC Corp., Galion, Ohio, 1976-85; sr. engr. Nat. Machinery Co., Tiffin, Ohio, 1985—. Patentee in field. Mem. Fluid Power Soc. Office: Nat Machinery Co 161 Greenfield St Tiffin OH 44883-2422

LOY, WILLIAM ALEXANDER, lawyer; b. Robinson, Ill., Mar. 8, 1929; s. Clarence Henry and Jean Emmons (Alexander) L.; m. Anne Rooney, June 7, 1952; children: Thomas Vincent, James Stephen, Lee Anne Loy Reindl. AB, U. Notre Dame, 1954, JD, 1958. Bar: Ind., U.S. Dist. Ct. Ind., U.S. Ct. of Claims, U.S. Ct. Mil. Appeals, U.S. Supreme Ct. Ptnr. firm Wallace, Wallace & Loy, Covington, Ind., 1958-63; lawyer USAF Judge Advocate Dept., 1963-80; individual practice law Peru, Ind., 1980—; pers. officer, fin. officer USAF REs., 1953-63. County chmn. Young Reps., Fountain County, Ind., 1962-63. Lt. col. USAF, 1980. Mem. Ret. Officers Assn. (life), Nat. Eagle Scout Assn., Am. Legion, KC, VFW. Roman Catholic. Home: 20 Farview Peru IN 46970 Office: 1 1/2 S Broadway Peru IN 46970

LU, JAMES J., SR., electrical engineer; b. Shanghai, China, Mar. 9, 1941; s. Zhidao L. and Peiying Feng; m. Zaizhu Xia; 1 child, Jinghuan Lu. PhD, Zhejiang U., Hangzhou, China, 1969; student, Va. Tech., 1983-85. Sr. Elect. Engr. Cert. Elec. engr. Elec. Power Rsch. Inst., Beijing, 1970-83; rsch. scientist Va. Tech., Blacksburg, 1983-85; sr. elec. engr. Nanjing (China) Auto Rsch. Inst., 1985-90; rsch. scholar Ohio State U., Columbus, 1991-93; analytical engr. Power Technologies, Inc., Schenectaday, N.Y., 1993-94; elec. engr. Joslyn Hi-Voltage Corp., Cleve., 1994-96; sr. elec. engr. Parker Hannifin Corp., Cleve., 1996—. Author: Digital Protective Relay, 1989; contbr. articles to profl. jours.; designer: static busbar protection, 1983 (2d prize 1984); designer, patentee, MP-based transformer relay, 1989 (1st prize, Energy Ministry of China, appraisal com. sci. and tech., 1991). Mem. (sr.) IEEE. Office: Parker Hannifin Corp 257 Huddleston Ave Cleveland OH 44221

LUBAR, SHELDON BERNARD, venture capitalist; b. Milw., May 21, 1929; s. Joseph J. and Lottie (Stern) L.; m. Marianne Segal, Aug. 31, 1952; children: Kristine, David, Susan, Joan. BBA, U. Wis., 1951, LLB, 1953; DCS, U. Wis., Milw., 1988. V.p. Marine Nat. Exch. Bank, Milw., 1953-61; pres. Marine Capital Corp., Milw., 1961-65; chmn., pres. Mortgage Assocs., Inc., Milw., 1966-73; asst. sec., commr. FHA, Dept. HUD, U.S. Govt., Washington, 1973-74; pres. Midland Nat. Bank, Milw., 1975-76; chmn. Lubar & Co., Inc., Milw., 1977—, Christiana Co., Inc., Milw., 1987—; bd. dirs. Mass. Mut. Life Ins. Co., Springfield, Firstar Bank Corp., Milw., MGIC, Milw., Christiana Cos., Inc., Milw., Ameritech, Inc., Chgo. Author: (with others) Financing Economic Development, 1990. Pres. Milw. Art Mus., 1977-80, Wis. Policy Rsch. Inst., Milw., 1987—; trustee Marquette U., Milw., 1985-91; regent U. Wis. System, 1991—. Office: Lubar & Co Inc 777 E Wisconsin Ave Milwaukee WI 53202-5302

LUBBERS, AREND DONSELAAR, academic administrator; b. Milw., July 23, 1931; s. Irwin Jacob and Margaret (Van Donselaar) L.; m. Eunice L. Mayo, June 19, 1953 (div.); children—Arend Donselaar, John Irwin Darrow, Mary Elizabeth; m. Nancy Vanderpol, Dec. 21, 1968; children—Robert Andrew, Caroline Jayne. AB, Hope Coll., 1953; AM, Rutgers U., 1956; LittD, Central Coll., 1977; DSc, U. Sarajevo, Yugoslavia, 1987; LHD, Hope Coll., 1988; DSc, Akademia Ekonomiczna, Krakow, Poland, 1989, U. Kingston Univ., Eng., 1995. Research asst. Rutgers U., 1954-55; research fellow Reformed Ch. in Am., 1955-56; instr. history and polit. sci. Wittenberg U., 1956-58; v.p. devel. Central Coll., Iowa, 1959-60; pres. Central Coll., 1960-69, Grand Valley State U., Allendale, Mich., 1969—; mem. Am. Assn. State Colls. and Univs. seminar in India, 1971, Fed. Commn. Orgn. Govt. for Conduct Fgn. Policy, 1972; USIA insp., Netherlands, 1976; mem. pres.'s commn. NCAA, 1984-87, 89—, pres. com., 1989-95; bd. dirs. Grand Bank, Grand Rapids, Mich. Sutdent Cmty. amb. from Holland (Mich.) to Yugoslavia, 1951; bd. dirs. Grand Rapids Symphony, 1976-82, Butterworth Hosp., 1988; chmn. divsn. II NCAA Pres.'s Commn., 1992-95. Recipient Golden Plate award San Diego Acad. Achievement, 1962, Golden-Emblem Order of Merit Polish Peoples Republic, 1988; named 1 of top 100 young men in U.S. Life mag., 1962. Mem. Mich. Coun. State Univs. Pres. (chmn. 1988), Grand Rapids World Affairs Council (pres. 1971-73), Phi Alpha Theta, Pi Kappa Delta, Pi Kappa Phi. Home: 801 Plymouth Ave SE Grand Rapids MI 49506-6555 Office: Grand Valley State U Coll Landing 1 Campus Dr Allendale MI 49401-9401

LUBBOCK, JAMES EDWARD, retired writer, photographer, publicity consultant; b. St. Louis, Sept. 12, 1924; s. Winans Fowler and Hildegard Beauregard (Whittemore) L.; m. Charlotte Frances Ferguson, Aug. 24, 1947; children: Daniel Lawrason (dec.), Brian Wade, Kathleen Harper. BA in English, U. Mo., 1949. Asst. editor St. Louis County Observer, 1949-51; staff writer St. Louis Globe-Democrat, 1951-53, state editor, 1954-56; mng. editor Food Merchandising mag., 1956-57; free-lance indsl. writer-photographer, cons., St. Louis, 1958-89; pres. James E. Lubbock, Inc., 1981-89. With Signal Corps, U.S. Army, 1943-46. Mem. Soc. Profl. Journalists, St. Louis Press Club, ACLU, Common Cause. Democrat. Home and Office: 10734 Clearwater Dr Saint Louis MO 63123-4911

LUBENSKY, EARL HENRY, anthropologist, archaeologist; b. Marshall, Mo., Mar. 31, 1921; s. Henry Carl and Adele Gertrud (Biesemeyer) L.; m. Anita Ruth Price, June 27, 1942 (dec. July 1992); children: Tom, Gerald, John Christopher; m. Margot Truman Patterson, Mar. 26, 1994. BA, Mo. Valley Coll., 1948, LLD (hon.), 1968; BS, Georgetown U., 1949; MS, George Washington U., 1967; MA, U. Mo., 1983, PhD, 1991. Mgr. Tavern Supply Co., Marshall, Mo., 1938-42; real estate salesman Mitchell Quick Realtor, Silver Spring, Md., 1948; rsch. analyst Georgetown U., Washington, 1949; reference asst. Libr. of Congress, Washington, 1949; fgn. svc. officer Dept. of State, Washington, 1949-79; adj. rsch. assoc. U. Mo., Columbia, 1992—. Contbr. articles to profl. jours. Pres. Muleskinners, Columbia, 1995; treas. The Theatre Soc., Columbia, 1993—, The Mo. Archeol. Soc., Columbia, 1981-90; pres. Anthropology Student Assn., Columbia, 1981-82. With Mo. N.G. 1937-40. 2d lt. U.S. Army, 1942-45, lt. col. USAR, 1945-81. Eagle Scout Boy Scouts Am., 1939. Mem. Mos. Archaeol. Soc. (charter, trustee, Appreciation award 1991), Soc. for Am. Archaeology (Presdl. Recognition award 1991), Inst. Andean Studies, Fgn. Svc. Assn., Diplomatic and Consular Officrs Retired, Boone County Hist. Soc., others. Democrat. Home: 1408 Bradford Dr Columbia MO 65203 Office: Dept Anthropology Univ Mo Columbia MO 65211

LUCAL, MARTHA JANE, judge; b. Weston, W.Va., June 9, 1938; d. James Cledith and Mary Elizabeth (Ocheltree) Bleigh; m. Dean S. Lucal, May 4, 1962; children: Katherine Ann, Mary Elizabeth. AA, Stephens Coll., Columbia, Mo., 1958; BA, Ohio State U., 1961, JD, 1961. Atty. ICC, Washington, 1962-63; tchr. Erie County Sch. Sys., Ohio, 1964-67; asst. pros. atty. Erie County, Sandusky, Ohio, 1976-78; solicitor Village of Berlin Heights, Ohio, 1983-84; pvt. practice law Sandusky, 1972-84; judge probate divsn. Erie County Common Pleas Ct., Sandusky, 1985—. Contbr. articles to profl. publs. Recipient Superior Judicial award Ohio Supreme Ct., 1986. Mem. AAUW, nat. Judicial Coll., Ohio Bar Assn., Nat. Coll. Probate Judges, Ohio Probate Judges Assn. Methodist. Home: 404 Cedar Brook Ln Sandusky OH 44870-5433 Office: Erie County Common Pleas Court 323 Columbus Ave Sandusky OH 44870-2602

LUCARELL, WILLIAM R., electrical engineer; b. Youngstown, Ohio, Apr. 25, 1945. B in Elec. Engring., Youngstown State U., 1969. Controls engr. Reliance Electric, Cleve., 1972-77; asst. chief elec. engr. Taylor Winfield Corp., Brookfield, Ohio, 1977—. Patentee in field. Cpl. U.S. Army, 1969-71. Roman Catholic. Office: Taylor Winfield Corp PO Box 500 Brookfield OH 44403-0500

LUCAS, BERT ALBERT, pastor, social services administator, consultant; b. Hammond, Ind., Mar. 26, 1933; s. John William and Norma (Gladys) Graham; m. Nanci Dai Hindman, Sept. 10, 1960; children: Bradley Scott, Traci Dai. BA, Wheaton Coll., 1956; BD, No. Bapt. Theol. Sem., 1960, ThM, 1965; MSW, U. Mich., 1971; D in Marriage and Family, Ea. Bapt. Theol. Sem., 1988. Lic. social worker, Ohio; ordained clergyman Am. Baptist Conv.; cert. family life educator. Chaplain Miami Children's Ctr., Maumee, Ohio, 1967-83; assoc. pastor First Bapt. Ch., La Porte, Ind., 1959-62; pastor Maumee Bapt. Ch., 1963-67; adminstrv. social work supr. Lucas County (Ohio) Children Svcs., 1967—; pastor Holland (Ohio) United Meth. Ch., 1979-90, Broadway United Meth. Ch., 1994—; adj. prof. Bowling Green (Ohio) State U., 1972-79; family life cons. New Horizon's Acad., Holland, 1984-86, co-dir. family svcs. 1985-86; cons. parenting, marriage enrichment, Toledo, 1986—. Rep. precinct capt., Toledo, 1984. Bert A. Lucas Day proclaimed City of Holland, 1984. Mem. AACD, Am. Assn. Marriage and Family Therapy (assoc.), Assn. for Couples in Marriage Enrichment, Hist. Preservations of Am. (Community Leader and Noteworthy Ams. award 1976-77), Council Family Rels.

LUCAS, JUANITA GLASSCO, realtor, systems analyst; b. Waverly, Ohio; d. Harold Frank and Lillie Meredith (Harris) Glassco; 1 child, Carol Brynne. BS, Franklin U., Columbus, Ohio, 1976; grad., Def. Logistics Supply Mgmt. Program, U.S. Dept. Def., 1978; MA, Cen. Mich. U., Mt. Pleasant, Mich., 1979; postgrad., Columbia Pacific U., 1993—. Sec. State of Ohio, Columbus, 1951-57; registration clk. Wittenberg U., Springfield, Ohio, 1957-60; asst. to registrar U. Chgo., 1960-62; local bd. clk. Selective Svc. Sys., Columbus, 1962-66; supply sys. analyst Def. Sys. Automation Ctr., U.S. Dept. Def., Columbus, 1966-89; realtor Saxton Real Estate, Columbus, 1976—, Saxton Realtors, 1993—; interior designer Transdesigns, Atlanta, 1983-87; fashion cons. Worldwide Images, Boston, 1989-94; cons. Mary Kay Cosmetics, 1994—. Mem. Hope Luth. Ch., Columbus, 1969—, Impressarios Opera, Columbus, 1988—. Mem. Nat. Assn. Realtors, Ohio Assn. Realtors, Women's Coun. Realtors (mem. leadership tng. designation program), Ctrl. Mich. U. Alumni, Am. Contract Bridge League, Internat. Platform Assn., Internat. Pageant Assn. (cert. pageant judge), Sigma Iota Epsilon. Home: PO Box 30127 Gahanna OH 43230-0127

LUCAS, JUNE H., state legislator; children: Deven Armeni, Adrien. Student, Youngstown State U. Mem. Ohio Ho. of Reps., 1986—, mem. energy and environment, judiciary and criminal justice coms.; Mem. adv. com. ohio child support guidelines, women's policy and rsch. Com.; ranking minority mem. family svcs. com. Contbr. articles to Warren Tribune Chronicle. Active Animal Welfare League. Named Woman of Yr., Coalition Labor Union Women, YWCA, 1988. Mem. NOW (Trumbull County chpt.), LWV, Ohio Bus. and Profl. Women, Ohio Farm Bur., Mosquito Creek Devel. Assn., Farmer's Union, Sierra Club. Democrat. Home: 1435 Locust St Mineral Ridge OH 44440-9721 Office: Ohio House of Reps Office of House Mems Columbus OH 43215

LUCAS, LARRY JAMES, state legislator; m. Debera Lucas; 4 children. Student, S.D. State U., 1969-74. Mem. S.D. Ho. of Reps., 1993—, mem. edn. and state affairs coms.; tchr. Todd County Sch. Dist., 1975—. Home: PO Box 182 Mission SD 57555-0182*

LUCAS, LEONARD L., deputy sheriff, poet and storyteller; b. Chgo., July 22, 1933; s. Steve Sanders and Jessie Lucas; m. Aretha Lucas, Jan. 2, 1955; children: Marilyn Diana Jefferson, Leonardo, Randy, Renee Losardo, Kenyetta. BA, Chgo. State U., 1972; MA, Chgo. Northeastern U., 1972. Phys. instr. Chgo. Park Dist., 1959-72, playground supr., 1959-72; dir. Cmty. of United People, Chgo., 1972-74; tchr. City Coll. Adult Edn., Chgo., 1974-77; substitute tchr. Chgo. Pub. Schs., 1974-77; manpower planner Mayor's Office of Employment Tng., Chgo., 1977-92; dep. sgt. Sheriff's Office, Chgo., 1992—; mem. adv. bd. Freedom for Hungry Found., Washignton, 1972-74, Urban Life Ctr., Chgo., 1972-75. Author: (poetry) Run Don't Cry, 1973, Tell the Children the Truth, 1995; African historian and story teller. V.p., precinct organizer, cons. 28th Ward Dem. Orgn., Chgo., 1991. Served with USAF, 1951-54. Recipient Chgo. 1st Brian Piccolo essay award, 1969. Home: 11349 S Indiana Chicago IL 60628

LUCAS, PATRICIA LYNN, financial executive; b. Memphis, Apr. 22, 1962; d. James Devoughn Harrington and Joyce Marie Horn Raiolo; m. Robert Warren Lucas, May 4, 1957; 1 child, Matthew Robert. Student, DePaul U., 1987. Lic. broker, Ill. Asst. mgr. McDonald's, South Chicago Heights, Ill., 1981, Taco Bell, Chgo., 1982, Brown's Chicken, Chicago Heights, Ill., 1983; customer svc. rep. Am. Nat. Bank, Chgo., 1983-85; bank mktg. rep. Kemper Fin. Svcs., Inc., Chgo., 1985-88; investment exec. Pathway Fin., Chicago Heights, 1988-90; mgr. INVEST Fin. Corp. Calumet Fed. Savs. & Loan, Dolton, Ill., 1990—. Vice pres., treas. Cedarwood Coop., Inc., Park Forest, 1990-92. DePaul U. scholar, 1982-86. Mem. Kemper Exec. Coun., Moose. Home: 3501 Dale Dr Crete IL 60417-1354 Office: Calumet Fed Savs & Loan 1350 E Sibley Blvd Dolton IL 60419-2965

LUCAS, SHIRLEY AGNES HOYT, management executive; b. Chicago, Aug. 21, 1921; d. Howard L. and Lucille P. (Von Krippenstapel) Hoyt; m. William H. Lucas, Feb. 2, 1952; 1 child, Lucille Shirley. Student, Northwestern U., 1941-42. V.p. Lucas Co., Chgo., 1980—. Mem. Ill. Hosp. Assn. (Leadership award 1975), Aux. Christ Hosp. and Med. Ctr. (life, past bd. dirs., cotillion chmn., housewalk chmn.). Republican. Lutheran. Office: Lucas Co 9127 S Kedzie Ave Evergreen Park IL 60642-1606

LUCAS, WAYNE LEE, sociologist, educator; b. Joliet, Ill., Jan. 6, 1947; s. Cecil Elmer and Mabel (Torkelson) L.; m. Nancy Jean Floyd, Aug. 23, 1969; children: Jeffrey, Keri. BS, Ill. State U., 1969, MS, 1972; PhD, Iowa State U., 1976. Assoc. prof. U. Mo. Kansas City, 1976—. Contbr. articles to profl. jours. Mem. Acad. Criminal Justice Scis., Am. Soc. Criminology, Soc. for Study of Social Problems, Midwestern Criminal Justice Assn., Midwest Sociol. Soc. Democrat. Presbyterian.

LUCCHESI, LIONEL LOUIS, lawyer; b. St. Louis, Sept. 17, 1939; s. Lionel Louis and Theresa L.; m. Mary Ann Wheeler, July 30, 1966; children: Lionel Louis III, Marisa Pilar. BSEE, Ill. Inst. Tech., 1961; JD, St. Louis U., 1969. Bar: Mo. 1969. With Emerson Electric Co., 1965-69; assoc. Polster, Polster & Lucchesi, St. Louis, 1969-74, ptnr., 1974—; city atty. City of Ballwin (Mo.), 1979-85, 92—. Alderman City of Ballwin, 1977-79, mem. Zoning Commn., 1971-77. Served to lt. USNR, 1961-65. NROTC scholar, 1957-61; recipient Am. Jurisprudence award St. Louis U., 1968-69. Mem. ABA, Am. Patent Law Assn., Assn. Trial Lawyers Am., St. Louis Met. Bar Assn. (exec. com., pres.-elect 1984, pres. 1985-86), Newcomen Soc. N.Am. Republican. Roman Catholic. Clubs: Forest Hills, Rotary (St. Louis) (pres. elect 1991-92, pres. 1992-93). Office: 763 S New Ballas Rd Saint Louis MO 63141-8704

LUCE, PRISCILLA MARK, public affairs executive; b. N.Y.C., Feb. 4, 1947; d. S. Carl and Patricia (Greenfield) Mark; m. Robert Warren Luce, July 19, 1969; children: James Warren, David Mark. BA, U. Pa., 1968. Adminstrv. asst. Phila. Mus. Art, 1968-69; asst. dir. pub. info. Mt. Holyoke Coll., South Hadley, Mass., 1969-71; v.p. Barnes & Roche, Inc., Phila., 1971-82; mgr. civic programs TRW Inc., Cleve., 1982-85; mgr. community relations TRW Inc., 1985-88, mgr. external communications, 1988-90, dir., pub. affairs and advt., 1990-92; v.p. info. sys. and svcs. comms., cons. United Way Svcs., Cleve., 1983-85, 92-94, v.p. mktg. and orgn. comms., 1994—; cons. United Way Svcs., Cleve., 1983-85. Trustee New Orgn. for the Visual Arts, Cleve., 1983—, Community Info. Vol. Action Ctr., Cleve., 1984-86, Albert M. Greenfield Found., Phila., 1989—; trustee Ohio Chamber Orch., Cleve., 1986-92, chmn. devel. com. 1987-88, chmn., trustee, 1991-92, exec. v.p., 1990-91; pres. New Orgn. for the Visual Arts, Cleve., 1984-86; mem. steering com. Cleve. Art Festival, 1983-84, Mayor's Cultural Arts Planning Task Force, Cleve., 1985-87; trustee Ret. Sr. Vol. Prog., 1991; leadership devel. prog. participant United Way Svcs., Cleve., 1983; mem. steering com. Bus. Volunteerism Coun. of Cleve., 1984-92, comm. adv. com. Work in NE Ohio Coun., 1991—. Recipient Woman of Profl. Excellence award YWCA of Cleve., 1990. Mem. Pub. Rels. Soc. Am., Cleve. Advt. Club. Republican. Office: TRW Inc 1900 Richmond Rd Cleveland OH 44124-3719

LUCE, STANFORD LEONARD, retired French language and literature educator; b. Boston, May 19, 1923; s. Stanford Leonard and Agnes Wilson (Foote) L.; m. Frances Alleman, Aug. 30, 1947 (div. Oct. 1970); children: Stanford C., Marian E., Richard L., James J.D.; m. Louise Ann Fiber, July 6, 1973. BA, Dartmouth Coll., 1947; MA, Yale U., 1948, PhD, 1953. Grad. asst. Yale U., New Haven, 1949-51; instr. Clark U., Worcester, Mass., 1951-52; from asst. prof. to prof. emeritus Miami U., Oxford, Ohio, 1952-88; vis. scholar Harvard U., Cambridge, Mass., 1986. Editor: Céline and His Critics, 1986; translator: Entretiens avec le Prof. Y, 1986. Bldg. coord. Habitat for Humanity, Oxford, 1995; bd. dirs. United Campus Ministry, Oxford, 1987-89; bd. dirs., field worker PUSH, Oxford, 1987—. Sgt. U.S. Army, 1943-46. Mem. MLA, Am. Assn. Tchrs. French, Kiwanis. Episcopalian. Home: 169 Shadowy Hills Oxford OH 45056

LUCEY, PAULA ANN, health facility administrator; b. Milw., Mar. 21, 1954; d. Thomas G. and Joan Mary (Rathburn) L. BSN, U. Wis., Milw., 1976; MSN, Marquette U., 1988; grad., Wharton Nurse Exec. Fellowship, 1994. Staff nurse John L. Doyne Hosp., 1977-81, clin. supr., 1981-88, dir. nursing, 1988-91, dir. acute care svcs., 1991-92, assoc. adminstr. patient care svcs., 1992-95; dir. health-related programs Milw. County, 1995—; clin. preceptor Marquette U., Milw. Mem. ANA, Am. Orgn. Nurse Execs. (Baxter Quality award for Inovative Patient Care Leadership), Acad. of Healthcare Execs., Sigma Theta Tau. Roman Catholic. Office: Milw County Health Programs 802 N 94th Wauwatosa WI 53226

LUCIANO, GWENDOLYN KAYE, planning specialist, utility rates administrator; b. Cleve., Feb. 26, 1954; d. Charles Wayne and Lila (Cole) Rhodes. BA in Math. and Mktg., Lake Erie Coll., 1975, MBA, 1988. cert. project mgmt. profl. Scheduling engr. A.G. McKee & Co., Independence, Ohio, 1975-78; project scheduling supr. Perry Nuclear Plant Raymond Kaiser Engrs., Perry, Ohio, 1978-85; maintenance planning supr. Cleve. Electric Illuminating Co., 1985-89; mgmt. cons. Liberty Cons. Group, Balt., 1989-91; outage planning coord. Cleve. Electric Illuminating, 1991-94; mgr. fed. regulation Centerior Energy Corp., Independence, Ohio, 1994-96, mgr. fed. reg. and pricing, 1996—; instr. Inst. Nuclear Power Ops., Atlanta, 1993-94; bd. dirs. Learning About Bus., 1992-96. Mem. Am. Assn. Cost Engrs., Project Mgmt. Inst., Lake Erie Coll. Nat. Alumni Assn. (pres. 1996—). Republican. Episcopalian. Office: Centerior Energy Corp 6200 Oak Tree Blvd Independence OH 44131-2510

LUCKER, RAYMOND ALPHONSE, bishop; b. St. Paul, Feb. 24, 1927; s. Alphonse and Josephine (Schiltgen) L. B.A., St. Paul Sem., 1948, M.A., 1952; S.T.L., U. St. Thomas, Rome, 1965, S.T.D., 1966; Ph.D., U. Minn., 1969; LHD honoris causa, Coll. St. Catherine, 1993. Ordained priest Roman Cath. Ch., 1952, bishop, 1971. Asst. dir. Confrat. of Christian Doctrine, Archdiocese of St. Paul, 1952-58, dir., 1958-68; prof. catechetics St. Paul Sem., 1957-68; dir. dept. edn. U.S. Cath. Conf., Washington, 1969-71; consecrated bishop, 1971; aux. bishop of St. Paul and Mpls., 1971-76; bishop of New Ulm, Minn., 1976—. Author: Aims of Religious Education, 1966, Some Presuppositions on Released Time, 1969, My Experience: Reflections on Pastoring, 1988; editor: The People's Catechism, 1995; contbg. author: Catholic Social Thought, 1990, The Universal Catechism Reader, 1990, Living the Vision, 1992. Recipient Nat. Catechetical award, 1991. Home: 1400 6th St N New Ulm MN 56073-2057 Office: Catholic Pastoral Ctr 1400 6th St N New Ulm MN 56073-2057

LUCKING, PETER STEPHEN, marketing consultant, industrial engineer; b. Kalamazoo, Oct. 11, 1945; s. Henry William, Sr., and Mary (Lynn) L.; m. Marilyn Barbara Jensen, Dec. 18, 1971. BA, Western Mich. U., 1968; BS in Indsl. Engring., 1973. Indsl. engr. Motorola, Phoenix, 1974, Revlon, Inc., Phoenix, 1974-75; indsl. engr. Hooker Chem. and Plastics Co., Niagara Falls, N.Y., 1975-76, sr. corp. indsl. engr., 1976-77; indsl. engr. Carborundum Co., Niagara Falls, 1977-78; cons. H.B. Maynard and Co., Pitts., 1978-85; mgr. indsl. engring. Carrier, Tyler, Tex., 1985-88; cons. H.B. Maynard and Co., Pitts., 1988-92; pres., mktg. cons. MARPET Systems, Inc., 1992—; lectr. in field, 1989. Advisor, Jr. Achievement, Niagara Falls, 1977. Author chpts. to books. Served with U.S. Army, 1969-70, Vietnam. Mem. Inst. Indsl. Engrs. (sr. mem., region v.p. 1983-85), Inst. Indsl. Engrs. (pres. Niagara Frontier chpt. 1977-78, paper presented fall conf.). Democrat. Roman Catholic. Home: 12826 Weatherstone Dr Florissant MO 63033-4045 Office: MARPET Systems Inc 11220 W Flossant Ste 141 Saint Louis MO 63033

LUCKNER, HERMAN RICHARD, III, interior designer; b. Newark, Ohio, Mar. 14, 1933; s. Herman Richard and Helen (Friednour) L. BS, U. Cin., 1957. Cert. interior designer and appraiser. Interior designer Greiwe Inc., Cin., 1957-64; owner, internat. designer Designers Loft Interiors, Cin., 1964—; owner Designer Accents, Cin., 1991—. Mem. bd. adv. Ohio Valley Organ Procurement Ctr., Cin., 1987—, U. Cin. Fine Arts Collection and Hist. Southwest Ohio. Mem. Am. Soc. Interior Designers, Appraisers Assn. Am., Metropolitan Club. Republican. Home and Office: 555 Compton Rd Cincinnati OH 45231-5005

LUEBBERS, JEROME F., state legislator; m. Judy Luebbers; children: Joe, Jerry, Jim, Julie, Jill, Jesse. Student, Quincy Coll. State rep. Dist. 21 Ohio State Congress, 1979-92, state rep. Dist. 33, 1993—; trustee Delhi Twp., 1970-78; pres. Cin. Newsmonth Inc. Recipient Certificate Support Ohio Farmers Union, 1990, Appreciation award Boy Scouts Am. Troop 483, 1991, Things Keep Looking Up award Downs Syndrome Assn. Greater Cin., 1991, Jack Wolf Meml. award Ohio Sec. State, 1991, Legis. Appreciation award Ohio Right to Life, 1991, Guardian of Small Bus. Nat. Fedn. Ind. Bus., 1992; named Legislator of Yr. Hamilton County Assn. Trustees and Clks., 1985, Hamilton County Twp. Assn., 1990. Mem. Delhi Twp. Civic Assn., Prince Hill Civic Assn., Easter Seals (Mary Schloss award selection com.), Oak Hills Local Sch. Dist. (Hall Honor selection com.), Cath. Soc. Svc. Bd. Cin. Archdiocese, Delhi/Riverview Kiwanis, Diamond Oaks Adv. Com. *

LUECKE, ELEANOR VIRGINIA ROHRBACHER, civic volunteer; b. St. Paul, Mar. 10, 1918; d. Adolph and Bertha (Lehman) Rohrbacher; m. Richard William Luecke, Nov. 1, 1941; children: Glenn Richard, Joan Eleanor Ratliff, Ruth Ann. Student, Macalester Coll., St. Paul, 1936-38, St. Paul Bus. U., 1938-40. Author lit. candidate and ballot issues, 1970—; producer TV local issues, 1981—; contbr. articles to profl. jours. Founder, officer, dir., pres. Liaison for Inter-Neighborhood Coop., Okemos, Mich., 1972—; chair countrywide special edn. millage proposals, 1958, 1969; trustee, v.p., pres. Ingham Intermediate Bd. Edn., 1959-83; sec., dir. Tri-County Cmty. Mental Health Bd., Lansing, 1964-72; founder, treas., pres. Concerned Citizens for Meridian Twp., Okemos, 1970-86; mental health rep. Partners of the Americas, Belize, Brit. Honduras, 1971; trustee Capital Area Comprehensive Health Planning, 1973-76; v.p., dir. Assn. Retarded Citizens Greater Lansing, 1973-83; chair, mem. Cmty. Svcs. for Developmentally Disabled Adv. Coun., 1973—; dir., founder, treas. Tacoma Hills Homeowners Assn., Okemos, 1985—; facilitator of mergers Lansing Child Guidance Clinic, Clinton and Easton counties Tri-County Cmty. Mental Health Bd., Lansing Adult Mental Health Clinic, founder. Recipient Greater Lansing Cmty. Svcs. Coun. "Oscar," United Way, 1955, state grant Mich. Devel. Disabilities Coun., Lansing, 1983, Disting. award Mich. Assn. Sch. Bds., Lansing, 1983, Pub. Svc. award C.A.R.E.ing, Okemos, 1988, Earth Angel award WKAR-TV 23, Mich. State U., East Lansing, 1990, Cert. for Cmty. Betterment People for Meridian, Okemos, 1990, 2nd pl. video competition East Lansing/Meridian Twp. Cable Comm. Commn., 1990, 1st pl. award video competition, 1992; Ingham Med. Hosp. Commons Area named in her honor, Lansing, 1971. Mem. Advocacy Orgn. for Patients and Providers (dir. 1994—). Home: 1893 Birchwood Dr Okemos MI 48864-2766

LUEDER, DIANNE CAROL, library director; b. Racine, Wis., Aug. 5, 1944; d. James Richard and Margaret Ann (Eick) Helland; m. Roland Herman Lueder, Aug. 29, 1981 (dec. July 1993); children: Daniel Lee Bertelsen, Barbara Marie Bertelsen. BA, U. Wis.-Parkside, Kenosha, 1979; MLS, U. Wis., Milw., 1972. Ref./outreach libr. Elk Grove Village (Ill.) Libr., 1979-80; dir. Bartlett (Ill.) Pub. Libr., 1980-84; asst. exec. dir. DuPage Libr. Sys., Geneva, Ill., 1984-88; pres. Lueder Enterprises, Inc., Wauconda, Ill., 1988—; exec. dir. Roselle (Ill.) Pub. Libr., 1990—. Author: Administrator's Guide to Library Building Maintenance, 1992. Vice pres. Roselle Pub. Libr. Found., 1994-96. Mem. NAFE, ALA, AAUW, Ill. Libr. Assn., Libr. Adminstrs. Coun. No. Ill. Roselle C. of C. (program dir. 1994-95). Lutheran. Home: 27798 N Forest Garden Wauconda IL 60084 Office: Roselle Pub Libr Dist 40 S Park St Roselle IL 60172

LUEKE, DONNA MAE, national retail company manager; b. Toledo, Sept. 18, 1946; d. Herbert Henry and Margery Alberta (Welsh) L. BA, Adrian Coll., 1968. Tchr. Anchor Bay Schs., New Baltimore, Mich., 1968-74; salesperson Jacobson's, Birmingham, Mich., 1974-76; sales rep. Stark & Co., Detroit, 1976-80; regional retail supr. Norwich-Eaton Consumer Pharms., Louisville, 1980-83; territory rep. Procter & Gamble, Louisville, 1983-84; dir. Progressive Retail, Raleigh, N.C., 1984-89; nat. retail mgr. CIBA Consumer Pharms. and CIBA Vision Corp., Wayne, Pa., 1989-92. Student govt. v.p. Adrian Coll., 1966, 67. Mem. Nature Conservancy, Sierra Club.

LUEPKER, RUSSELL VINCENT, epidemiology educator; b. Chgo., Oct. 1, 1942; s. Fred Joseph and Anita Louise (Thornton) L.; m. Ellen Louise Thompson, Dec. 22, 1966; children: Ian, Carl. BA, Grinnell Coll., 1964; MD with distinction, U. Rochester, 1969; MS, Harvard U., 1976; MD (hon.), U. Lund, Sweden, 1996. Intern U. Calif., San Diego, 1969-70; resident Peter Bent Brigham Hosp., Boston, 1973-74; cardiology fellow Peter Bent Brigham Hosp./Med., Boston, 1974-76; asst. prof. divsn. epidemiology med. lab. physiol. hygiene U. Minn., Mpls., 1976-80, assoc. prof., 1980-87, prof. divsn. epidemiology and medicine, 1987—, dir. divsn. epidemiology, 1991—; cons. NIH, Bethesda, Md., 1980—, U. So. Calif., L.A., 1985—, Armed Forces Epidemiology Bd., 1993—; vis. prof. U. Goteborg, Sweden, 1986, Ninewells Med. Sch., Dundee, Scotland, 1995. Lt. comdr. USPHS, 1970-73. Harvard U. fellow, 1974-76, Bush Leadership fellow, 1990; recipient Prize for Med. Rsch. Am. Coll. Chest Physicians, 1970, Nat. Rsch. Svc. award Nat. Heart, Lung and Blood Inst., Bethesda, 1975-77, Disting. Alumni award Grinnell Coll., 1989. Fellow ACP, Am. Coll. Cardiology, Am. Heart Assn. Coun. on Epidemiology (chmn. 1992-94), Am. Heart Assn. Sci. Sessions (program com. chair 1995—), Am. Coll. Epidemiology; mem. Delta Omega Soc. (Nat. Merit award 1988). Office: Univ Minn Sch Pub Health Div Epidemiology 1300 S 2nd St Ste 300 Minneapolis MN 55454-1015

LUERSSEN, FRANK WONSON, retired steel company executive; b. Reading, Pa., Aug. 14, 1927; s. George V. and Mary Ann (Swoyer) L.; m. Joan M. Schlosser, June 17, 1950; children: Thomas, Mary Ellen, Catherine, Susan, Ann. BS in Physics, Pa., State U., 1950; MSMetE, Lehigh U., 1951; LLD (hon.), Calumet Coll.; DPS (hon.), Xavier U. Metallurgist research and devel. div. Inland Steel Co., East Chicago, Ind., 1952-54; mgr. various positions Inland Steel Co., 1954-64, mgr. research, 1964-68, v.p. research, 1968-77, v.p. steel mfg., 1977-78, pres., 1978-85, chmn., 1983-92; bd. dirs. Morton Internat., Inc. Contbr. articles on steelmaking tech. to various publs. Trustee Northwestern U., 1980—; trustee, sec., treas. Munster Sch. Bd., 1957-66. With USNR, 1945-47. Named disting. alumnus Pa. State U. Fellow Am. Soc. Metals; mem. AIME (Disting. life mem., B.F. Fairless award, Howe meml. lectr. 1988-91), Am. Iron and Steel Inst. (Gary medal, chmn. 1989-90), Nat. Acad. Eng. Home and Office: 8226 Parkview Ave Munster IN 46321-1419

LUETKENHAUS, WILLIAM JOSEPH, state legislator; b. Josephville, Mo., Sept. 15, 1962; s. Elmer William and Marilyn (Jenkins) L.; m. Patricia Ann Schulte; 1 child, Katie. Attended, Ranken Tech Coll., 1982-84. Lic. real estate broker, Mo. Plumber Lic. Journeymen, 1984—; owner, pres. Luetkenhaus Plumbing Co. Inc., Josephville, 1988—, Luetkenhaus Comml. Investment Inc., 1989—; village trustee Town Bd., Josephville, 1989-90; county commr. St. Charles County, 1991-92; mem. Mo. Ho. of Reps. 12th

Dist., Jefferson City, 1992—. Active St. Joseph Ch., Josephville; mem. Dardenne Dem. Club, O'Fallon, Mo., 1991—. Mem. Plumbers Local 35, Ranken Alumni Club, Lions. Catholic. Home: 742 Hancock Rd Josephville MO 63385 Office: Ho of Reps State Capital Jefferson City MO 65101*

LUETTGEN, MICHAEL JOHN, engineer; b. Milw., May 14, 1960; s. Donald Robert and Nancy Carol (Boede) L. BSME, U. Wis., Milw., 1983; MSME, U. Wis., 1988. Registered profl. engr., Wis. With advanced mech. devel. Delco Electronics Corp., Kokomo, Ind., 1984-88; with product design engring. Ford Motor Co., Dearborn, Mich., 1989—. Inventor integrated pressure sensor and pressure sensor package, automotive elect. module. Office: Ford Motor Co Electronics Div 17000 Rotunda Dr Dearborn MI 48120-1168

LUGAR, RICHARD GREEN, senator; b. Indpls., Apr. 4, 1932; s. Marvin L. and Bertha (Green) L.; m. Charlene Smeltzer, Sept. 8, 1956; children: Mark, Robert, John, David. B.A., Denison U., 1954; B.A., M.A. (Rhodes scholar), Oxford (Eng.) U., 1956. Mayor Indpls., 1968-75; vis. prof. polit. sci. U. Indpls., 1976; mem. U.S. Senate, 1977—, chmn. com. fgn. relations, 1985-86, chmn. com. on agr.nut. and forestry, 1995—; chmn. Nat. Rep. Senatorial Com., 1983-84; Treas. Lugar Stock Farm, Inc.; mem. Indpls. Sch. Bd., 1964-67, v.p., 1965-66; vice chmn. Adv. Commn. on Intergovtl. Relations, 1969-75; pres. Nat. League of Cities, 1970-71; mem. Nat. Commn. Standards and Goals of Criminal Justice System, 1971-73; Del., mem. resolutions com. Republican Nat. Conv., 1968, del., mem. resolutions com., 1992, Keynote speaker, 1972, del., speaker, 1980; mem. internat. adv. council Inst. Internat. Studies. Author: Letters to the Next President, 1988. Trustee Denison U., U. Indpls.; bd. dirs. Nat. Endowment for Democracy, Am. Running and Fitness Assn.; bd. dirs. Youth for Understanding. Served to lt. (j.g.) USNR, 1957-60. Pembroke Coll., Oxford U. hon. fellow. Mem. Blue Key, Phi Beta Kappa, Omicron Delta Kappa, Pi Delta Epsilon, Pi Sigma Alpha, Beta Theta Pi. Methodist. Club: Rotary. Office: US Senate 306 Hart Senate Bldg Washington DC 20510

LUHMAN, WILLIAM SIMON, community development administrator; b. Belvidere, Ill., May 15, 1934; s. Donald R. and H. Elizabeth (Rudberg) L. AB, Park Coll., 1956; MA, Fla. State U., 1957. City planner City of Moline, Ill., 1959-64; planning dir. Rock Island County, Ill., 1964-66; exec. dir. Bi-State Met. Planning Commn., Rock Island, 1966-71; dir. regional devel. Northeastern Ill. Planning Commn., Chgo., 1971-74, assoc. dir., 1975-76, dep. dir., 1977-79, acting exec. dir., 1979-80, asst. dir., 1980-81; v.p. Pub. Mgmt. Info. Svc., Chgo., 1981; asst. dir. No. Ill. U. Ctr. Govt. Studies, DeKalb, 1981-91, program coord., 1991; exec. dir. Growth Dimensions for Belvidere-Boone County, Ill., 1991—, pres., 1982-86; vis. instr. Augustana Coll., Rock Island, 1967, 69. Mem. Boone County Regional Planning Commn., 1986—, chmn., 1986-90; mem. Belvidere-Boone County Regional Planning Commn., 1986—, chmn., 1990-92; bd. dirs. Sch. Dist. 100 Found. for Excellence in Edn., 1992—; mem. Boone County Arts Coun., Friends of Ida Pub. Libr. Mem. Am. Soc. Pub. Adminstrn., Am. Planning Assn., Internat. City Mgmt. Assn., Ill. Devel. Coun. Home: 1538 Fremont St Belvidere IL 61008-5939 Office: 419 S State St Belvidere IL 61008-3706

LUHTA, CAROLINE NAUMANN, airport manager, flight educator; b. Cleve., Mar. 26, 1930; d. Karl Henry and Fannie Arletta (Harlan) Naumann; m. Fred Harlan Jones, July 2, 1955 (div. 1961); m. Adolph Jalmer Luhta, Dec. 12, 1968 (dec. 1993); 1 child, Katherine Louise. BA, Ohio Wesleyan U., 1952; BS magna cum laude, Lake Erie Coll., Painesville, Ohio, 1977. Rsch. chemist Standard Oil Co. Ohio, Cleve., 1952-68; office mgr. Adolph J. Luhta Constrn. Co., Painesville, 1968-83; acct. Thomas Y. Ellis, CPA, Painesville, 1978; bd. dirs. Painesville Flying Svc., Inc., 1968—, flight instr., 1970—, pres., 1993—, 1993—; bd. dirs. Concord Air Park, Inc., Painesville, 1968—, pres. 1993—; accident prevention counselor FAA, Cleve., 1975-85. Contbr. articles to profl. jours. Trustee Northeastern Ohio Gen. Hosp., Madison, 1973-83, chmn. bd. 1980-82; trustee Internat. Women's Air and Space Mus., Centerville, Ohio, 1989-96, treas. 1991-95; trustee Concord Twp., 1992—. Recipient Aerospace award Cleve. Squadron, Air Force Assn., 1966. Mem. Nat. Assn. Flight Instrs., Exptl. Aircraft Assn., Aircraft Owners and Pilots Assn., Ninety-Nines (life, chmn. All-Ohio chpt. 1969-70, Achievement award 1965, Amelia Earhart Meml. scholar 1970), Silver Wings (life), Order Ea. Star, Alpha Delta Pi (life). Office: Painesville Flying Svc Inc 12253 Concord Hambden Rd Painesville OH 44077-9566

LUISIER, DENNIS LEE, engineer design specialist; b. Saukville, Wis., June 18, 1955; s. Irvin O. and Dolores May (Schwalbe) L. AD in Design, U. Wis., Washington County, 1977. Engr. design specialist Leeson Electric, Grafton, Wis., 1976—. Mem. The Leeson Employees Credit Union, Grafton, 1979—; coun. mem. St. John's Luth. Ch., Port Washington, Wis., 1980—. Office: Leeson Electric PO Box 241 Grafton WI 53024-0241

LUKEN, RONALD LEIGH, consultant; b. Peoria, Ill., Dec. 2, 1941; s. Walter Edward and Mildred (Martin) L.; m. Judith Ann Siddle, Aug. 31, 1963; children: Christopher S., Douglas L., Steven M. BS, U. Ill., 1963; MBA, Bradley U., 1967. Mgr. Arthur Andersen & Co., Chgo., 1970-79; ptnr. Andersen Cons., Chgo., 1979-90; prin. Productivity Cons. Group, Oak Brook, Ill., 1991—; mem., past chmn. Nat. Coun. Advisors Coll. Bus. Bradley U., Peoria, 1984—. Treas., past pres., past sec. Naperville (Ill.) Evening Lions, 1975-95. Mem. Midwest Soc. Profl. Cons., Chgo., 1995. Home: 2290 Sutton Ln Aurora IL 60504

LULAY, GAIL C., human resources and corporative outplacement executive, consultant; b. Evanston, Ill., Feb. 13, 1938; d. Earl Albert and Helen Marie (Blackwell) Minnich; m. Wayne L. Lulay, Aug. 15, 1959; children: Michael Brent, Catherine Marie. BS, Elmhurst Coll., 1970; MS, Roosevelt U., 1972. Cert. counselor, Ill. Instr. Dist. #181, Hinsdale, Ill., 1970-74; corp. bus. devel. Continental Bank, Chgo., 1974-79; pres., owner Lulay & Assocs., Inc., Downers Grove, Ill., 1979—; instr. Elmhurst Coll. Adult Edn., 1982, Coll. of DuPage, Glen Ellyn, Ill., 1983-86; lectr., cons. in field., 1980—. Author: Nelson Eddy, America's Favorite Baratone, Authorized Biographical Tribute, 1992; contbr. articles to profl. jours. Bd. dirs. Crisis Homes, Des Plaines, Ill., 1984-86. Mem. Am. Assn. Counseling and Devel., Am. Soc. Personnel Adminstrn., Assn. Outplacement Cons. Firms, Inc., Human Resources Mgmt. Assn. of Chgo., Roosevelt U. Alumni Assn., Chi Omega. Office: Lulay & Assocs Inc 1431 Opus Pl Downers Grove IL 60515-1166

LUMPE, SHEILA, state legislator; b. Apr. 17, 1935; m. Gustav H. Lumpe, 1958. AB, Ind. U.; postgrad., Johns Hopkins U.; MA, U. Mo. Mem. Mo. Ho. of Reps. Trustee Mo. Consol. Health Care Plan; active Civil Liberties Union; bd. dirs. People to People. Democrat. Home: 6908 Amherst Ave Saint Louis MO 63130-3124 Office: Mo Ho of Reps State Capitol Building Jefferson City MO 65101-1556

LUMPKIN, BEATRICE, mathematics educator; b. N.Y.C., Aug. 3, 1918; d. Morris Abraham and Dora (Chernin) Shapiro; m. Frank Lumpkin; children: Carl, Jeanleah, Paul, John. MS, Noreastern Ill. U., 1969, Ill. Inst. Tech., Chgo., 1973. Mgr. electronics manuals Knight Electronics-Allied Radio, Chgo., 1951-64; tchr. math., writer Chgo. Pub. Schs., 1965-67, 88-90; pvt. practice Detroit, Milw., Portland, 1990—; assoc. prof. math. Chgo. City Colls., 1967-82. Author: Senefer and Hatshepsut, 1983, Young Genius in Old Egypt, 1977, rev. edit., 1992, (curriculum) African and African-American Contributions to Mathematics, 1987, (lessons) Algebra Framework in Chicago Public Schools, 1990, African Roots of Benjamin Banneker's False Position Solutions, 1992, Multicultural Science and Math Connections, 1995, Math—A Rich Heritage, 1995. V.p. Coalition Labor Union Women, 1994. Mem. AAAS, Am. Women in Math., Internat. Study Group for Ethnomath., Nat. Coun. Tchrs. Math., Ill. Coun. Tchrs. Math., History and Pedagogy of Math., Benjamin Banneker Assn. Home: 7123 S Crandon Ave Chicago IL 60649-2507

LUMPKIN, JOHN ROBERT, public health physician, state official; b. Chgo., July 28, 1951; s. Frank and Beatrice (Shapiro) L.; m. Mary S. Blanks, Jan. 28, 1984; children: Alia, John R. Jr. BS, Northwestern U., Evanston, Ill., 1973; MD, Northwestern U., Chgo., 1974; MPH, U. Ill., Chgo., 1985. Diplomate Am. Bd. Emergency Medicine. Intern U. Chgo. Hosps., 1975, resident anesthesiology, 1976-78, vice chmn. emergency medicine, 1981-84; asst. prof. U. Chgo., 1978-84; asst. dir. emergency medicine South Chgo. Hosp., 1984-85; staff physician St. Mary of Nazareth Hosp., Chgo., 1985; assoc. dir. Ill. Dept. Pub. Health, Springfield and Chgo., 1985-90, dir., 1990—; cons. Egyptian Ministry Health, Cairo, 1986-90; mem. sec.'s adv. com. on injury control Ctrs. for Dis. Control, Atlanta, 1989-93. Fellow Am. Coll. Emergency Physicians (bd. dirs. 1987-93); mem. Soc. Tchrs. Emergency Medicine (pres. 1981-82), Ill. Coll. Emergency Physicians (pres. 1982-83, Bill B. Smiley award 1986), Assn. State and Territorial Health Ofcls. (pres. 1995-96). Office: Ill Dept Pub Health 100 W Randolph St Ste 6-600 Chicago IL 60601-3219

LUMPKINS, ROBERT L., business executive; b. Lawrenceburg, Tenn., Jan. 25, 1944; s. Robert L. and Maude (Holthouse) L.; m. Sara Jane O'Connell, Dec. 29, 1966; 1 child, Christine Jane. BS in Math. magna cum laude, U. Notre Dame, 1966; MBA, Stanford U., 1968. Fin. analyst Cargill Inc., Mpls., 1968-70, mgr. fin. info. svcs. dept., 1970-73, gen. mgr. Cargil Leasing corp., 1973-75, group contr., 1975-82, sec., fin. com., 1975-82, pres. fin. svcs. divsn., 1983-88; chief fin. offficer Cargill Europe Cargill Inc., London, 1988-89; CFO Cargill Inc., Mpls., 1989-95, vice chmn., 1995—; bd. dirs. Continental Airlines, Houston. Mem., vice chmn. sci. adv. coun. U. Notre Dame, 1994—; bd. dirs. Minn. Orch. Assn., Mpls., 1993—; trustee Minn. Med. Found., Mpls., 1992—; bd. dirs. Greater Mpls. Met. Housing Corp., 1996. Mem. Minikahda Club. Roman Catholic. Office: Cargill Inc Box 5724 Minneapolis MN 55440

LUND, DORIS HIBBS, retired dietitian; b. Des Moines, Nov. 10, 1923; d. Loyal Burchard and Catharine Mae (McClymond) Hibbs; m. Richard Bodholdt Lund, Nov. 9, 1946; children: Laurel Anne, Richard Douglas, Kristi Jane Lund Lozier. Student, Duchesne Coll., Omaha, 1941-42; BS, Iowa State U., 1946; postgrad., Grand View Coll., Des Moines, 1965; MS, Iowa State U., 1968. Registered dietitian, lic. dietitian. Clk. Russell Stover Candies, Omaha, 1940-42; chemist Martin Bomber Plant, Omaha, 1942-43; dietitian Grand Lake (Colo.) Lodge, 1946; tailoring instr. Ottumwa Pub. Schs., 1952-53; cookery instr. Des Moines Pub. Schs., 1958-62; dietitian Calvin Manor, Des Moines, 1963; home economist Am. Wool Coun./Am. Lamb Coun., Denver, 1963-65, The Merchandising Group of N.Y., 1965-68, Thomas Wolff, Pub. Rels., 1968-70; home economist weekly TV program Iowa Power Co., 1968-70; cons. in child nutrition programs Iowa Dept. Edn., Des Moines, 1970-95; ret. Nutritioneering, Ltd., 1995; Mem. Iowa Home Economists in Bus. (pres. 1962-63), PEO, Pi Beta Phi (Iowa Gamma chpt. pres. 1945-46). Pres. Callanan Jr. H.S. PTA, 1964, Roosevelt H.S. PTA, 1966; pres., mem. Ctrl. Presbyn. Mariners, Des Moines; ruling elder, clk. of session Ctrl. Presbyn. Session, Des Moines, 1972-78; bd. dirs. Ctrl. Found., 1996; amb. Friendship Force Internat., 1982—. Duchesne Coll. 4 yr. scholar. Mem. Iowa Home Economists in Bus. (pres. 1962-63), PEO, Pi Beta Phi (pres. 1945-46). Republican. Home: 105 34th St Des Moines IA 50312-4526

LUND, ERIC RUDOLPH, journalist, educator; b. Chgo., Nov. 1, 1925; s. John Eric and Edith Sofia (Strom) L.; m. Florence Johannsen, Sept. 7, 1947 (dec. 1989); m. Grace Lillian Welch Carlson, Nov. 17, 1990. BS in Journalism, Northwestern U., 1949. Reporter Evanston (Ill.) Rev., 1946-56, editor, 1961-66; reporter, asst. city editor Chgo. Daily News, 1957-61, asst. city editor, Saturday editor, asst. mng. editor, 1966-77; free-lance writer, instr. North Park Coll., Chgo., 1978-84; dir. journalism grad. program Columbia Coll., Chgo., 1984-94; adj. grad. faculty mem. Northwestern U. Medill Sch. Journalism, Evanston, 1977-78. Editorial cons., columnist: Chgo. Reporter, 1986-91; contbr.: Swedish-American Life in Chicago, 1850-1930, 1991. Past trustee Evanston Hist. Soc.; past mem. Evanston Plan Commn. Sgt. U.S. Army, 1944-46, PTO. Recipient Bicentennial medal King Carl XVI Gustaf of Sweden, 1976, named Royal Order of North Star Knight First Class, 1978. Mem. Swedish-Am. Hist. Soc. (pres. 1976-82, chmn., dir.), Swedish Coun. Am. (dir.), Soc. Profl. Journalists, Chgo. Headline Club (past dir.). Episcopalian. Home and Office: 2547 Ridgeway Ave Evanston IL 60201-1159

LUND, JAMES BERNARD, financial advisor; b. St. Paul, Oct. 12, 1963; s. Robert Joseph and Mildred Ellen (Smith) L.; m. Dawn Denise Behm, Sept. 6, 1986; children: Christina Joan, Melissa Ellen. BS, Mankato (Minn.) State U., 1985, MBA, 1986; cert., Coll. Fin. Planning, Denver, 1992. CFP. Adminstrv. asst. Mankato Multi-Specialty Health Care Clinic, 1985; auditor, adminstrv. asst. divsn. fiscal affairs Mankato State U., 1985-86; pers. and bus. fin. planner IDS Fin. Svcs., Mpls., 1986—, field mgr., 1988-92, gold team fin. planner, sr. fin. advisor, 1992—; ptnr. Cardnet Midwest, St. Paul, 1991-94; pres. James B. Lund, Inc., New Brighton, Minn., 1993—; sr. fin. advisor, bus. fin. advisor Am. Express Fin. Advisors, Inc., New Brighton, Minn., 1986—. Author: Marketing of Health Care Services Especially by Hospitals, 1986, Physician Assistants Within the Health Care Industry With Specific Reference to Group Practice, 1986; co-author: Hospital Services Market, 1986. Bd. dirs., sec. Minn. State U. Sys., St. Paul, 1985-89; bd. dirs. Student Exch., Student Assn. Mankato State U.; chmn. health svc. adv. com. Mankato State U., 1985-86; mktg. coord., treas. planning and program com. worksite health promotion/Heart at Work program Am. Heart Assn., Mankato, 1986; tchr. Sunday sch., assisting min., lector, other positions Beautiful Savior Ch., Mpls., 1987—, chmn. pers., fellowship and stewardship coms., 1990—, bd. dirs., 1989-92; senator, v.p., pres. Mankato State U., 1982-85; vol. ARC, Mpls. and St. Paul, bd. dirs. St. Paul chpt.; vol. Congressman Penny Re-election Campaign, Mankato, 1984; founding mem., bd. dirs. Penny Fellowship, 1988-90; bd. dirs. Missing Children Minn., Mpls., 1994—; precinct del. Dem. Party, Mankato, 1984; sec. strategic planning com. for Greater Mankato Area ACT 2000 Health & Med. Svcs. Task Force; active Tyrone Guthrie Cir., Mpls., 1992-93; divsn. leader Top Fin. Planner Awards, 1987—, Master Planner Awards, 1990—; IDS pres. Adv. Coun., 1993, Honor Scholarship Mankato State U., 1981-82. Recipient Disting. Svc. award Minn. State U. Student Assn., 1988, Minn. State U. Sys., 1989, Academic Excellence award DAR, 1981, Cert. of Appreciation Mankato State U. Student Assn., 1989; USAF scholar, 1981, HECB scholar, 1981-85. Mem. Inst. CFPs, Internat. Assn. Fin. Planning, Assn. Life Underwriters, Assn. Health Ins. Agts., Soc. Human Resource Mgmt., Nat. Planned Giving Coun., Minn. Planned Giving Coun., Mankato Area C. of C. (bd. dirs. 1983-85). Office: Am Express Fin Advisers Inc 900 Long Lake Rd # 300 New Brighton MN 55112

LUND, KARL S., engineer; b. Hamilton, Ont., Can., Sept. 13, 1950. B, No. Mich. U., 1973. Chief engr. Tool-Rite, Warren, Mich., 1974—.

LUND, VIRGINIA LLEGO, museum director, curator, chemistry educator; b. Dagupan, Philippines, Jan. 23, 1939; came to U.S., 1981; d. Moises Permolan and Cristina Rosario (Bautista) Llego; m. Dennis Wayne Lund, Feb. 21, 1979; 1 child, Tina Ruth. BS in Chemsitry, Silliman U., Dumaguete, Philippines, 1970; MS in Food Chemsitry, U. Philippines, 1977. Analyst, cosmetics dept. FDA, Manila, Philippines, 1971-72; instr. chemistry Foundation U., Dumaguete, 1972-77; acting chair dept. chemistry Foundation U., 1977-79; dir., curator The Frank House, U. Nebr., Kearney, 1990—; tech. cons. Pap Food Products, Manila, 1971-72; dir. cultural affairs Found. U., 1976-77; chem. lab. supr. U. Nebr., Kearney, 92-94. Bd. dirs. Buffalo County ARC, Kearney, 1990—, vol. ARC, 1988—. Named Vol. of Yr., AMI Westpark Community Hosp., Hammond, La., 1987. Mem. NAFE, AAUW, Nat. Trust Historic Preservation, Victorian Soc., buffalo County Hist. Soc., Nebr. Mus. Assn., Kearney Hospitality Group. Home: 2010 W 24th St Kearney NE 68847-4908 Office: Frank House 905 W 25th St Kearney NE 68849-0001

LUNDBY, MARY A., state legislator; b. Carroll County, Feb. 2, 1948; d. Edward A. and Elizabeth Hoehl; m. Michael Lundby, 1971; 1 child, Daniel. BA in History, Upper Iowa U., 1971. Former staff asst. Senator Roger Jepsen; mem. Iowa State Senate. Active Solid Waste Adv. Com. Republican. Home: 1240 14th St Marion IA 52302-2562 Office: Iowa State Senate State Capitol Des Moines IA 50319*

LUNDGREN, RALPH EDWARD, foundation officer; b. LaCrosse, Wis., June 14, 1935; s. Henry Victor and Esther Bernice (Nelson) L.; m. Nancy Charlotte Schwarz, June 27, 1959; children: Craig H., Jennifer E., Eric J. BA, Elmhurst Coll., 1957; M in Edn., Loyola U., 1961, PhD., 1966. Instr. Loyola U., Chgo., 1962, St. Marys Coll., Winona, Minn., 1964; dir. counseling and guidance St. Joseph High Sch., Westchester, Ill., 1961-65; asst. dir. Ill. Dept. Edn., Springfield, 1965-66; dir. Ill. Dept. Edn., 1966-67, Springfield, 1967-69; dep. dir. Ill. Bd. Higher Edn., Chgo., 1969-73; program dir. Lilly Endowment, Inc., Indpls., 1973-95, v.p. edn., 1994—; mem. Elmhurst Coll. Bd. of Trustees, 1974-94. Contbr. articles to profl. jours. Pres., mem. Carmel-Clay Ednl. Found., 1978-83; mem. Carmel-Clay Pub. Libr., 1993—; v.p., mem. Carmel Symphony Orch. Bd., 1985-88; treas. Ind. Ky. Conf., United Ch. of Christ, 1985-88. Cpl. U.S. Army, 1957-59. Mem. Am. Assn. of Higher Edn. Home: 11826 Rolling Springs Dr Carmel IN 46033-3272 Office: Lilly Endowment Inc 2801 N Meridian St Indianapolis IN 46208-0068

LUNDIN, ROBERT KING, freelance journalist, photographer; b. Utica, N.Y., May 1, 1956; s. Robert William and Margaret Mary (Waitt) L. Student, Exeter (Eng.) U., 1976-77; BA, Kenyon Coll., 1978. Corr. Glen Ellyn (Ill.) News, 1991—, The Daily Herald, Arlington Heights, Ill., 1995; freelance reporter Chgo. Tribune, 1994—. Author: (play) Martha! Oh Martha!, 1987, Will the South Please Rise Again, 1995; (poetry) Main Street Café, 1991. Bd. dirs. Alliance Mentally Ill, Springfield, Ill., 1995—, Alliance Mentally Ill DuPage, Wheaton, Ill., 1995—; v.p. Ill. Consumer Coun., 1995—. Mem. Nat. Press Photographers Assn., Soc. Profl. Journalists. Home and Office: 417 N Main #1 Glen Ellyn IL 60137

LUNDQUIST, VIRGINIA ARETA, public affairs executive; b. Cleve., Oct. 8, 1949; d. Roger E. and Margaret A. (Grober) Kerr; m. Eric Christopher Lundquist, Apr. 14, 1972. BA in English Lit., U. Detroit, 1971, MBA in Mktg., 1978. Asst. editor FTD news Florists Transworld Delivery Assn., Detroit, 1971-74; copy editor Campbell-Ewald Advt., Detroit, 1974-78; advt. & promotion mgr. Am. Motors Corp., Southfield, Mich., 1978-87; European advt. mgr. Chrysler Motors Corp., Highland Park, Mich., 1987-88; v.p. comm. United Technologies Automotive, Dearborn, Mich., 1988-92; v.p. pub. affairs AlliedSignal Automotive, Southfield, 1992—. Trustee Detroit Symphony Orch., Detroit, 1991—. Mem. Adcraft Club Detroit, Econ. Club Detroit, Pub. Rels. Soc. Am. Office: Allied Signal Automotive 20650 Civic Center Dr Southfield MI 48076-4110

LUNDSTROM, GILBERT GENE, banker, lawyer; b. Gothenburg, Nebr., Sept. 27, 1941; s. Vernon G. and Imogene (Jackett) L.; m. Joyce Elaine Ronin, June 26, 1965; children: Trevor A., Gregory G. BS, U. Nebr., 1964, JD, 1969; MBA, Wayne State U., 1966. Bar: U.S. Dist. Ct. (1st dist.) Nebr. 1969, Nebr. 1969, U.S. Ct. Appeals (5th cir.) 1970, U.S. Ct. Appeals (10th cir.) 1971, U.S. Ct. Appeals (8th cir.) 1974, U.S. Ct. Appeals (3d cir.) 1986. Ptnr. Woods & Aitken, Lincoln, Nebr., 1969-93; pres., CEO First Fed. Lincoln Bank, 1994—; part-time faculty law sch. U. Nebr.-Lincoln, 1970-74; dir. First Fed. Lincoln Bank, TMS Corp. of Ams., First Fin. Corp.; bd. dirs. Sahara Enterprises, Inc., Sahara Coal Co., Chgo.; dir. Fed. Home Loan Bank Topeka. Bd. dirs. Folsom Children's Zoo, Lincoln, 1979-83, St. Elizabeth Hosp. Found. Fellow Nebr. State Bar Assn.; mem. ABA, ATLA, Lincoln Bar Assn., Nebr. Bar Assn., Newcomer Soc. U.S. Republican. Methodist. Club: Country Club of Lincoln. Lodge: Masons, Scottish Rite (33 degree). Home: 7441 N Hampton Rd Lincoln NE 68506-1633 Office: First Fed Lincoln 1235 N St Lincoln NE 68508-2008

LUNDSTROM, WILLIAM JOHN, academic administrator; b. Chgo., June 20, 1944; s. Gustav Wilhelm and Alice Linea L.; m. Susan Creveling, Mar. 13, 1976; children: Lara Danielle, Kristin Alyce. BS, Purdue U., 1965; MBA, Ind. U., 1967; DBA, U. Colo., 1974. Lectr. Calif. State U., Fullerton, 1968-71; vis. prof. Colo. State U., Ft. Collins, Colo., 1973-74; prof. So. Meth. U., Dallas, 1974-77, U. Miss., Oxford, 1977-81; chair dept. mktg. and dir. Inst. for Internat. Bus. Old Dominion U., Norfolk, Va., 1981-92; dean, spl. asst. to pres., prof. mktg. Coll. Bus. Adminstrn. Cleve. State U., 1992—; cons. Primm Advt., Norfolk, 1983-85, Atlantic Permanent Savs. and Loan, Norfolk, 1982-83; rsch. dir. KCB&N Advt., Dallas, 1975-77; dir. Va. Ctr. for World Trade, Norfolk, 1987-88. Author: More than 100 books, articles, papers, 1973—. Bd. dirs. ARC of Tidewater, Norfolk, 1986-88; vol. United Way, Hampton Roads, Va., 1983-88; ch. deacon. Named Outstanding Researcher, Old Dominion U., Norfolk, 1984, U. Miss., Oxford, 1978, Outstanding Tchr., U. Miss., Oxford, 1979; recipient Fgn. Exchange grant, Ind. U., Paris, France, 1967. Fellow Acad. Mktg. Sci. (v.p. 1978-89); mem. Am. Mktg. Assn., So. Mktg. Assn., Southwestern Mktg. Assn. (v.p. 1981-82). Republican. Home: 32049 Pinetree Rd Cleveland OH 44124-5943 Office: Cleve State U Coll Bus Cleveland OH 44115

LUNDY, DALE ALLEN, telecommunications company administrator; b. Alvin, Tex., Nov. 20, 1950; s. James R. and Betty L. (Helm) L.; m. Evelyn Crowe, May 1, 1971; children: Ryan, Alisa, Jordan. BS in Math., Okla. Christian U. Sci. & Arts, Oklahoma City, 1973. Cert. cost analyst; cert. cost estimator/analyst. Acctg. supr. Southwestern Bell Telephone, St. Louis, 1974-79, area mgr. cost studies, 1979-84, dist. mgr. cost analysis, 1984—; lectr., expert witness in field. Contbr. articles to profl. jours. Elder, Mid-County Ch. of Christ, Webster Groves, Mo., 1989—. Mem. Soc. for Cost Estimating and Analysis (editorial award 1990). Home: 762 Winding Bend Ln Manchester MO 63021-7044 Office: Southwestern Bell 1 Bell Ctr # 37 Q 1 Saint Louis MO 63101-3002

LUNDY, RICHARD BRUCE, computer system company; b. Moline, Ill., July 12, 1941; s. Alvin S. and Dorothy M. (Klingbiel) L.; m. Ellen M. Wade, July 18, 1964; children: Elizabeth Ann, Peter John William. BSEE, U. Mich., 1964. Project engr. Info. Instruments, Ann Arbor, 1963-68, group mgr., 1969-71; founder, pres., CEO Com, Inc., Ann Arbor, 1972—; founder, bd. dirs., officer Com 2, Saline, Mich., 1985-92; sect. dir. Mich. Tech. Coun., Ann Arbor, 1988-92; presenter workshops and seminars. Trustee, officer Dexter (Mich.) Cmty. Schs., 1979—, United Meth. Retirement Cmtys., Chelsea, Mich., 1983—; bd. dirs. Washtenaw United Way, Ann Arbor, 1987-95, Ann Arbor Hands on Mus., 1982-86, mem. adv. coun., 1986—; bd. dirs., officer Huron Valley Ambulance Co., Ann Arbor, 1987—. Mem. IEEE. Home: PO Box 247 Dexter MI 48130-0247 Office: Com Inc PO Box 489 Dexter MI 48130-0489

LUNDY, SADIE ALLEN, small business owner; b. Milton, Fla., Mar. 29, 1918; d. Stephen Grover and Martha Ellen (Harter) Allen; m. Wilson Tate Lundy, May 17, 1939 (dec. 1962); children: Wilson Tate Jr., Houston Allen, Michael David, Robert Douglas, Martha Jo-Ellen. Degree in acctg., Graceland Coll., 1938. Acct. Powers Furniture Co., Milton, Fla., 1939-40, Lundy Oil Co., Milton, 1941-52; controller First Fed. Savs. & Loan, Kansas City, Mo., 1953-55, Herald Pub. Co., Indepenence, Mo., 1956-58; mgr. Baird & Son Toy Co., Kansas City, Mo., 1959-62; regional mgr. Emmons Jewelers of N.Y., Kansas City, 1963-65; owner, pres. Lundy Tax Service, Independence, 1965-85; corporate sec., purchasing mgr. Optimation, Inc., Independence, 1974-85, mgr., 1985—; v.p. Lundy Oil Co., Milton, 1941-52. Contbr. articles to profl. jours. Mem. com. Neighborhood Council, Independence, 1985. Mem. Am. Bus. Women's Assn., Independence C. of C. (mem. com. 1965-85). Republican. Mem. Reorganized Ch. of Jesus Christ of Latter Day Saints. Club: Independence Women's. Home: PO Box 520238 Independence MO 64052-0238 Office: Optimation Inc 300 N Osage St Independence MO 64050-2705

LUNGREN, JOHN HOWARD, law educator, oil and gas consultant, author; b. Chgo., Feb. 11, 1925; s. Charles Howard and Edna Hughes (Edwards) L.; m. Phyllis Joan Jolidon, Dec. 12, 1953 (div.); 1 son, John Eric; m. Susan Jeanette Whitfield, Sept. 22, 1984. B.A., Beloit Coll., 1948; J.D., Marquette U., 1952; M.A., U. Wis.-Milw., 1974. Bar: Wis. 1952, Ill. 1975, Kans. 1980. Assoc. gen. counsel A. O. Smith Corp., 1964-74; gen. atty. Clark Oil & Refining Corp., 1954-64; prof. law Lewis U., Glen Ellyn, Ill., 1975-80; assoc. prof. law Washburn U. Sch. Law, Topeka, 1980-85; practice, Chgo., from 1977; with Turner & Boisseau Ltd., Wichita, Kans., 1985-88; of counsel Lungren and Whitfield-Lungren, Wichita, 1987—; cons. oil and gas; Kans. rep. legal com. Interstate Oil Compact. Chmn., Milwaukee County Republican Party, 1966-70; justice of peace, Wauwatosa, Wis., 1964-68. Served with USN, 1943-46. Mem. ABA, Ill. Bar Assn., Wis. Bar Assn., Kans. Bar Assn., Wichita Bar Assn.

LUOMA, JUDY, ranching executive. Office: Luoma Egg Ranch Inc 2535 State Hwy 18 Finlayson MN 55735*

LUPKE, DUANE EUGENE, insurance company executive; b. Ft. Wayne, Ind., July 17, 1930; s. Walter Herman and Lucy (Bell) L.; married, Sept. 14, 1957; children: Diane Carol, Mark Duane, David Burgess, Andrea Lucy. BS, Ind. U., 1952. CPCU. With Lupke Rice Clancy Assocs., Ft. Wayne, Ind., 1954—, pres., 1969—. Bd. dirs. Concordia Ednl. Found., Ft. Wayne; dir., treas. Luth. Health Found. Ind., 1995. Lt. U.S. Army, 1952-54. Lutheran. Home: 1407 Hawthorne Rd Fort Wayne IN 46802-4957 Office: Lupke Rice Clancy Assocs PO Box 11309 Fort Wayne IN 46857-1309

LUPO, BARBARA JANE, cosmetics specialist; b. Tilden, Nebr., Nov. 3, 1953; d. Elwyn LeRoy and Jacqueline Joyce (Vaughan) Church; m. David Anton Lupo, Apr. 20, 1985; children: Christopher, Michael. BS in Bus. Adminstrn., Dickinson (N.D.) U., 1985. Various positions Dickinson, 1972-76; receptionist, sec. Holiday Inn, Bismarck, N.D., 1976-77, sales and catering dir., 1977-79; sec., receptionist Butler Machinery, Bismarck, 1979-81; desk clk. Oasis Motel, Dickinson, 1981-85; sales and catering dir. Hospitality Inn and Conv. Ctr., Dickinson, 1985-88, asst. mgr., sales dir., 1985-95; ind. beauty cons. Mary Kay Cosmetics, 1995—; student Citizen Police Acad., Dickinson, 1991, guest speaker, 1992. Mem. Hotel-Motel Assn., Dickinson C. of C.-Ambs. Office: 741 8th Ave E Dickinson ND 58601

LUPULESCU, AUREL PETER, medical educator, researcher, physician; b. Manastiur, Banat, Romania, Jan. 1, 1923; came to U.S., 1967, naturalized, 1973; s. Peter Vichentie and Maria Ann (Dragan) L. MD magna cum laude, Sch. Medicine, Bucharest, Romania, 1950; MS in Endocrinology, U. Bucharest, 1965; PhD in Biology, Faculty of Scis., U. Windsor, Ont., Can. Diplomate Am. Bd. Internal Medicine. Chief Lab. Investigations, Inst. Endocrinology, Bucharest, 1950-67; research assoc. SUNY Downstate Med. Ctr., 1968-69; asst. prof. medicine Wayne State U., 1969-72; assoc. prof., 1973—; vis. prof. Inst. Med. Pathology, Rome, 1967; cons. VA Hosp., Allen Park, Mich., 1971-73. Author: Steroid Hormones, 1958, Advances in Endocrinology and Metabolism, 1962, Experimental Pathophysiology of Thyroid Gland, 1963, Ultrastructure of Thyroid Gland, 1968, Hormones and Carcinogenesis, 1983, Hormones and Vitamins in Cancer Treatment, 1990; reviewer for various sci. jours.; contbr. chpts., numerous articles to profl. publs.; research on hormones and tumor biology; studies regarding role of hormones and vitamins in carcinogenesis. Fellow Fedn. Am. Socs. for Exptl. Biology; mem. Electron Microscopy Soc. Am., Soc. for Investigative Dermatology, N.Y. Acad. Sci., AMA (physician's recognition award 1983, 86), Am. Soc. Cell Biology, Soc. Exptl. Biology and Medicine, AAAS. Republican. Home: 21480 Mahon Dr Southfield MI 48075-7525 Office: Wayne State U Sch Medicine 540 E Canfield St Detroit MI 48201-1928

LURTON, H. WILLIAM, retired retail executive; b. Greenwich, Conn., Sept. 18, 1929; s. William Pearl and Elizabeth (McDow) L.; m. Susan Harvey, Oct. 26, 1980; children: Scott, Carrie, Nancy, Jennifer, Barbara, Diana, Deborah, Sarah. B.A., Principia Coll., 1951. Sales rep. Jostens Inc., Mpls., 1955-61; yearbook sales and plant mgr. Jostens Inc., Visalia, Calif., 1961-66; gen. sales mgr. yearbook div. Jostens Inc., v.p., gen. mgr. yearbook div., 1969-70, corp. exec. v.p., 1970-71, mem. exec. com., 1970-72, pres., 1971-75, chief operating officer, 1971-72, chief exec. officer, 1972-94, chmn. bd., 1975-94, also dir.; ret., 1994; dir. Deluxe Inc., Pentair, Inc. Bd. dirs. U.S. C. of C., Mpls. YMCA. Served with USMC, 1951-53. Mem. Quail Ridge Country Club (Boynton Beach, Fla.), La Quinta Resort Country Club (Calif.), Tammaron Country Club (Durango, Colo.), Mpls. Clubl. Clubs: Wayzata (Minn.) Country, Minneapolis. Home: 3135 Jamestown Rd Long Lake MN 55356-9648

LUSTENADER, BARBARA DIANE, human resources executive; b. Albany, N.Y., Nov. 26, 1953; d. Charles Elmer and Janet Barbara (Bergh) Setzer; m. Robert Alan Lustenader, May 20, 1972. BA in English, Coll. St. Rose, Albany, 1974; MA in English, SUNY, Oswego, 1979. Cert. sr. in profl. human resources (SPHR). Tchr. English Port Byron (N.Y.) Cen. Schs., 1974-79; saleswoman Miller/Hahn, Auburn, N.Y., 1979-80; exec. asst. to v.p. devel. Wells Coll., Aurora, N.Y., 1980-83, adminstrv. asst. to pres., 1983-85; assoc. dir. admissions Wells Coll., Aurora, 1985-87; asst. div. mgr. human resources Yaskawa Electric Am., Inc., Northbrook, Ill., 1987-89; div. mgr. corp. adminstrn. and human resources Yaskawa Electric Am., Inc., 1989-90, dir. adminstrn. and human resources, br. mgr., 1990-94; pres. Lake Assocs., Inc., Mundelein, Ill., 1994—; spkr. in field, 1994—. Bd. dirs. Lake County (Ill.) Youth Conservation Corps, 1993-96, chmn. 501(3) (c) com., 1993-94; bd. dirs., vol., co-chmn. Friends Schweinfurth Meml. Art Ctr., Auburn, 1983; bd. dirs., sec., chmn. human resource com., nominating com. YWCA Lake and McHenry Counties, 1995—. Mem. LWV (bd. dirs., fin. chmn. Cayuga County, N.Y. chpt. 1984-86, Mundelein chpt. 1988-90, 96—), Soc. Human Resource Mgmt. (fin. com. 1990, cert. com. 1995-96, program com. 1996-97, Profl. Excellence award 1995), No. Ill. Bus. Assn. (co-chmn. pers. generalists roundtable 1987—, mem. compensation com. 1989—, mem. human resources policies and practices com. 1989—, Outstanding Individual Contbr. award 1995), Am. Compensation Assn., Chgo. Compensation Assn., Basically Bach (devel. com. 1991), Lake County Women in Mgmt. (awards com. 1991, 94, 95, chair 1996, chair program com. 1994-96, Women of Achievement award 1996, Nat. Charlotte Danstrom award 1996), Japan Soc. Am. Home and Office: Lake Assocs Inc 472 Killarney Pass Cir Mundelein IL 60060-1259

LUSTIG, EDITH PERKINS, freelance photographer; b. Warren, Mass., Sept. 20, 1929; d. Bertram Webster and Edith Madeleine (Pettengill) Perkins; m. Edgar Lloyd Lustig, Apr. 18, 1952; children: Susan Janell, Carol Anne. AA, Stephens Coll., 1949. Photographer Stephens Coll., Columbia, Mo., 1950-51; freelance photographer Warren, 1951-52, St. Louis, 1987—; freelance writer, 1995—. Columnist, St. Anthony's Med. Ctr. Aux. Newsletter, 1992—. Instr. first aid ARC, St. Louis, 1963—, instr. CPR, 1977—, blood program aide, 1975—; vol. St. Anthony's Med. Ctr., St. Louis, 1975—, mem. blood drive com., 1988—, life mem.; leader Girl Scouts U.S., 1960-68; mem. bd. deaconesses Affton Presbyn. Ch., 1965-67, chair, 1966-67; active DAR, 2d v.p., 1989-92. Recipient Vol. ARC Group award St. Anthony's Med. Ctr., 1979, Clara Barton award ARC, 1987, Lindbergh Leaders award Lindberg Sch. Dist., St. Louis, 1991, Citizen of Yr. award Crestwood-Sunset Hills Area C. of C., 1995. Mem. Stephens Coll. Afternoon Alumnae Club (bd. dirs. 1958-71), Brentwood Figure Skating Club (bd. dirs. 1974-82, pres. 1979-82), Kappa Alpha Mu. Presbyterian.

LUTE, RICHARD CALVIN, JR., mechanical design engineer; b. Barberton, Ohio, May 18, 1953; s. Richard Calvin Sr. and Betty Jean (Miller) L. Student, Akron Tech. Inst., U. Akron. Mgr. engring. Ferriot Corp., Akron, Ohio, 1973-87; mech. design engr. Telxon Corp., Akron, 1987-93, Interbold Plant 9, Canton, Ohio, 1993—. Author design manuals; patentee in field. Bd. dirs. Mogadore (Ohio) Baseball Bd., 1987—, coach, 1987—. Democrat. Home: 3460 Curtis St Mogadore OH 44260-1049 Office: Interbold Plant 9 5995 Mayfair Rd North Canton OH 44720-1550

LUTER, NOVELLA MARIE, credit union administrator; b. Brodhead, Wis., Nov. 27, 1939; d. Werner Marvin and Lois W. (Shaw) Badertscher; m. Paul Albert Luter, July 11, 1958; children: Kathleen Marie, Renee Anne. A in Bus., A in Computer Sci., Rock Valley Jr. Coll., Rockford, Ill., 1973; B, Western Ill. U., 1994. Paraprofl. Harlem Sch. Dist., Loves Park, Ill., 1970-73; clk. WF and John Barnes Credit Union, Rockford, Ill., 1978-80; sec. First Bapt. Ch. of Machesney Park, Ill., 1978-80; office mgr. Gunite Employees Credit Union, Rockford, 1980—; bd. gov. Western Ill. Univ. Treas. First Bapt. Ch. Machesney Park, 1984—, Rockford Area Svc. Assn., 1991—; leader Luters Looter 4-H Club, 1966-79. Mem. Forest City Am. Bus. Women (treas. 1990-92, Woman of Yr. 1991), Loves Park Homemakers (chmn. 1987-91, spl. activities com. 1970-92, Woman of Yr. 1988), Accent on Homemaking. Office: Gunite Employees Credit Union 816 Marchesano Dr Rockford IL 61102-3522

LUTER, TERRI LEE, human resources consulting company executive; b. Detroit, Nov. 5, 1953. Cert. sr. profl. in human resources. Systems analyst ANR Pipeline, Detroit, 1977-82; cons. Ciber, Dearborn, Mich., 1982-85; v.p. Arbor Cons. Group Inc., Plymouth, 1985—. Mem. Bd. of Human Resources Systems Profls. (fin. officer, past pres., others), Womens Econ. Club. Democrat. Office: Arbor Cons Group Inc 711 W Ann Arbor Trl Plymouth MI 48170-1677

LUTH, JAMES CURTIS, systems consultant; b. Fairmont, Minn., May 19, 1961; s. Richard H. and Doris M. (Shockley) L.; m. Susan Marie Euteneuer, Aug. 6, 1994. BA, Wartburg Coll., Waverly, Iowa, 1983; MBA, U. Minn., 1992. Programmer, analyst Grinnell (Iowa) Mut. Reins Co., 1984-86; systems cons., Analyst Internat. Corp., Rochester, Minn., 1986-88; analyst Internat. Corp., Mpls., 1988-89; systems cons. Analytical Techs., Inc., St. Paul, 1989-94; sys. cons. AstroTek Inc., Savage, Minn., 1994-95; ind. sys. cons., 1995—. George A. Hormel Co. merit scholar, 1979; Wartburg Coll. scholar, 1979. Methodist. Home: 15038 Monterey Ave S Savage MN 55378-4642

LUTHER, DARLENE, state legislator; b. 1947; m. Bill Luther; 2 children. BA, U. St. Thomas. Mem. Minn. Ho. of Reps., 1993—. Home: 6809 Shingle Creek Dr Brooklyn Park MN 55445-2647 Office: Minn Ho of Reps State Capital Building Saint Paul MN 55155-1606

LUTHER, GEORGE AUBREY, orthopedic surgeon; b. Keokuk, Iowa, Dec. 11, 1933; s. George August and Leda (Galbraith) L.; m. Dorothy Gould Luther, Aug. 18, 1956; children: Melinda, George Bradley. AB, Cen. Meth. U., 1955; MD, Vanderbilt U., 1959. Diplomate Am. Bd. Orthopaedic Surgery. Intern Vanderbilt U. Hosp., Nashville, 1959-60, resident, 1961-64, instr., 1964; resident St. Louis City Hosp., 1960-61; pres. St. Louis Orthopedic Inst., 1965—; pres. med. staff St. Joseph Hosp., St. Louis, 1982-83; trustee St. Joseph Hosp., 1981-84. Contbr. article profl. jours. Served to maj. U.S. Army, 1967-69. Fellow Am. Acad. Orthopedic Surgery, ACS (admissions com. 1982—); mem. AMA, Mo. Orthopedic Soc. (v.p. 1985-86, pres. 1986-87), St. Louis Metro. Med. Soc. (counselor 1983-85), Vanderbilt Orthopedic Soc. (pres. 1981-82), Tenn. Soc. of St. Louis. Republican. Methodist. Club: Bellerive Country. Home: 177 Ladue Oaks Ct Saint Louis MO 63141-8128

LUTHI, RAY, state legislator; m. Vivian F. Luthi. Mem. from dist. 76 Kans. State Ho. of Reps., Topeka; rancher Lamont, Kans. Address: PO Box 76 Lamont KS 66855

LUTHRINGSHAUSEN, WAYNE, brokerage house executive; b. 1945. Commodities sys. analyst Howard, Weil, Labouesse, Friedricks, Inc., New Orleans, 1968-70; planning specialist Chgo. Bd. Trade, 1970-72; with Options Clearing Corp., Chgo., chmn., CEO. Office: Options Clearing Corp 440 S La Salle St Chicago IL 60605*

LUTTNER, EDWARD F., consulting company executive; b. Cleve., Feb. 16, 1942; s. John J. and Angela (Haberbosch) L.; m. Nancy E., July 15, 1977; children: Amy, Mark. BA, Loyola U., 1966, MDiv, 1974; MA, U. Detroit, 1970. Cert. NASD. Dir. standards-devel. Bernard Haldane Assocs., Boston, Internat. Career Consulting Corp., Waltham, Mass.; v.p. career mgmt. svcs. Bernard Haldane Assocs., Cleve.; dir. profl. svcs. Right Assocs., Phila.; pres. Elby Career Group, Inc., Cleve. V.p. Rotary, Fairview Park, 1988-89. Mem. AACD, Nat. Career Devel. Assn.

LUTTRULL, SHIRLEY JOANN, protective services official; b. Fordland, Mo., Feb. 26, 1937; d. Thomas Marion and Pauline (Sherrow) Pirtle; m. Leslie Allen Luttrull, June 3, 1956 (div. May 1978); children: Vicki Lynn, Ricki Allen; m. Orben Lowell Clark, Dec. 31, 1982 (div. Oct. 1987); m. Barry Mabe, June 1992 (div. Oct. 1994). Student, Southwest Mo. State U., 1979. Checker person Lea's Market, Fordland, Mo., 1955-56; plant supr. Mellers Photo Lab., Springfield, Mo., 1968-82; shopper Hopper and Hawkins, Dallas, 1982-83; crew leader Sentinal Security, Okla. City, Shrink Control Corp., Houston, 1984-86; sales mgr. Shrink Control Corp., 1986-88; owner Internal Theft Control, Springfield, 1988--. Mem. Mo. Retail Grocers Assn., Springfield C. of C. Republican. Home and Office: 1347 S Airwood Dr Springfield MO 65804-0520

LUTZ, DAVID JOHN, psychology educator; b. Denver, Sept. 20, 1953; s. Joseph Herbert and Eleanor Josephine (Canacari) L.; m. Ellen Scott McLean, Aug. 8, 1978; children: Britton McLean, Kellen McLean. BA in Psychology and Sociology, U. Kans., 1975, MA in Psychology, 1978, PhD in Clin. Psychology, 1980. Therapist Psychology Clinic, U. Kans., 1976-78, asst. instr., 1977-79; intern in profl. psychology Peabody Coll., Vanderbilt U., 1979-80; assoc. prof. dept. psychology Calif. State U., San Bernardino, 1980-87, supr. grad. students Community Counseling Ctr., 1980-87, faculty cons. computer ctr., 1981-84, assoc. dean, 1984-86; therapist Inland Counties Family Learning Ctr., Grand Terrace, Calif., 1982-87, Ctr. for Individual and Family Therapy, Colton, Calif., 1984-87; prof. S.W. Mo. State U., Springfield, 1987—; psychologist Associated Psychol. Svcs., Springfield, 1987-91, Ctr. for Profl. Counseling, 1991—; Cons. Patton State Hosp., 1981-84, Omnitrans tranp. system, 1981-82, Behavior Mgmt. Cons., Inc. Contbr. articles to profl. jours. Active Social Sci. Rsch. and Instructional Coun., State of Calif., 1981-84; active planning and adv. coun. Calif. State U., San Bernardino, 1983-84, mem. faculty senate, 1983-86; bd. dirs. The Boys Club San Bernardino, 1985-86. Mem. APA (clin. psychology divsn., tchg. divsn., sec.-treas. cons. psychology divsn. 1986-92, pres. cons. psychology divsn. 1993-94, psychotherapy divsn., psychologists in ind. practice divsn., sport and exercise psychology divsn., treas. Soc. for Psychol. Study of Men and Masculinity divsn. 1995-97), Assn. Advancement Psychology, Mo. Psychol. Assn., Ozark Area Psychol. Assn. Home: 2240 E Belmont Ct Springfield MO 65802-2860 Office: SW Mo State U Dept Psychology 901 S National Ave Springfield MO 65804-0027

LUTZ, L. JACK, retail executive, congressman; b. Anderson, Ind., Dec. 26, 1945; s. Parmer Luther and AllaFrances (Dolenski) Lutz; m. Marietta Mason, Sept. 9, 1967 (div. 1985); children: Alastasia, Michael L., Christopher J.; m. Susan Kramer, Aug. 30, 1986; 1 child, Jennifer J. Student, Ind. U., 1963-67. Active Madison County Industry Coun., 1983-91, Ind. Gen. Assembly, 1991—. Named Boy of Yr. Am. Legion, 1963. Mem. Anderson Country Club, Columbia Club, Nat. Exch. Club (bd. dirs. 1985-89). Republican. Methodist. Home: 5070 Stonespring Way Anderson IN 46012-9717

LUTZ, LARRY EDWARD, state legislator; b. Evansville, Ind., Oct. 28, 1938; s. Edward George and Bertha (Eberhardt) L.; m. Mary Lotus Toelle, 1961; 1 child, Chris Edward. Student, Lockyears Bus. Coll., Evansville, Ind., 1963, U. so. Ind., 1985. Lt. Evansville Fire Dept., 1963-65, inspector, 1966-68, dist. chief, 1979-83; master firefighter State of Ind., 1979; assessor Perry Twp., Vanderburgh County, Ind., 1979-82; rep. Dist. 76 Ind. Ho. of Reps., 1982—, chmn. environ. affairs com., mem. ins. corp. and sml. bus. com., mem. pub. safety com., labor com., rds. and transp. com. Named Hon. State Fire Marshal, 1980-83, Firfighter of Yr., Kiwanis, Ind., 1980. Mem. Ind. Firefighters Assn. (pres. 1976-77), Ind. Assessors Assn. (v.p. 1981), Kiwanis. Home: 2736 W Virginia St Evansville IN 47712-5617*

LUTZ, SANDRA JEANIENE, family nurse practitioner; b. Pekin, Ill., Apr. 1, 1937; d. Howard Frederick and Wanda Sue (Weber) Rohrs; m. Eugene Harold Lutz, Jan. 19, 1957; children: Eric H., Karl E., April D., Matthew D., Peter J., Camilia J., Charles W. ADN, Ill. Ctrl. Coll., 1977; BSN, Bradley U., 1986; MSN, U. Ill., Chgo., 1989. Cert. family nurse practitioner; cert. Tai Chi Chih instr.; cert. healing touch practitioner; cert. H.T. instr. Staff nurse/charge nurse ob-gyn. Pekin (Ill.) Meml. Hosp., 1977-81; community health nurse Tazewell County Health Dept., Pekin, 1981-84; staff nurse obstetrics Saint Francis Med. Ctr., Peoria, Ill., 1984-85; dir. home health, DON nursing home Hopedale (Ill.) Med. Ctr., 1985-86; charge nurse nursing home Americana Health Care, Peoria, 1986-87; staff nurse progressive cardiac care unit St. Francis Med. Ctr., Peoria, 1987-89; supr., nurse practitioner med. svcs. Peoria (Ill.) County Jail/Saint Francis Med. Ctr., 1989-92; supr., nurse practitioner Bradley U. Health Ctr./Saint Francis Med. Ctr., Peoria, 1992-94; full-time nurse practitioner St. Francis Community Clinic, 1994—; instr. health sci. Illinois River Correctional Facility, Canton, 1991; part-time nurse practitioner St. Francis Cmty. Clinic, 1992-94. Pres. Tazewell Toastmasters, Pekin, 1990. Mem. Am. Acad. Nurse Practitioners, Am. Holistic Nurses Assn. (north ctrl. regiona dir. 1994—), Ill. Assn. Coun. Nurse Practitioners (exec. sec. 1992-94), Bradley U. Hilltop Nurses Alumni Assn. (v.p. 1985-90, pres. 1990-92, 92-94), Sigma Theta Tau (Epsilon Epsilon sec. 1990-92, pres. elect 1992-94, pres. 1994—), Altrusa Internat. (v.p. 1994), Nurse Healers Profl. Assn. Lutheran. Home: 1514 Summer St Pekin IL 61554-5643 Office: St Francis Cmty Clinic 530 NE Glen Oak Peoria IL 61637

LUUS, GEORGE AARNE, physician; b. Estonia, Apr. 23, 1937; s. Edgar and Aili (Poldmaa) L.; M.D., U. Toronto (Ont., Can.), 1962; m. Margit Jaanusson, Sept. 14, 1962 (div. 1983); children—Caroline Anna Elizabeth, Clyde Gregory Edgar, Lia Esther Isabelle; m. 2d, Donna Gervais Martell, Oct. 1, 1983. Intern Toronto East Gen. and Orthopaedic Hosp.; practice medicine specializing in family medicine, Sault Sainte Marie, Ont., 1963—; mem. Algoma Dist. Med. Group, 1966—; sec. med. staff Gen. Hosp., 1972—, v.p., bd. dirs., 1973. Adv. bd. Can. Scholarship Trust Found., 1976-77. Mem. Algoma West Med. Acad. Lodge: Rotary. Home: 42 Linstedt St, Sault Sainte Marie, ON Canada P6B 3H9 Office: 240 McNabb St, Sault Sainte Marie, ON Canada P6B 1Y5

LUZKOW, JACK LAWRENCE, history educator, writer, consultant; b. Detroit, Dec. 18, 1941; s. Irving and Sally (Eagle) Farber; m. Susan Frankel, Mar. 27, 1964 (div. Dec. 1973); 1 child, Catherine Alexis; m. Virginia Ann Trieglaff, May 15, 1976; 1 child, Frank Jason. BA, Wayne State Univ., 1966; MA, St. Louis Univ., 1975, PhD, 1981. Bibliographic specialist Southern Ill. Univ., Carbondale, 1979-81; history prof. Union Coll., Barbourville, Ky., 1981-84, Marycrest Coll., Davenport, Iowa, 1984-90, Teikyo-Marycrest Univ., Davenport, Iowa, 1990—; pres. Cons. Global Learning, Davenport, 1992—; v.p. Lonetree Enterprises, Davenport, 1991—; v.p. Marycrest Acad. Senate, Davenport, 1990-91; past pres. Inst. Ednl. Seninars, Davenport, 1988; speaker Vis. Artists Series, Davenport, 1985. Contbr. articles to profl. jours. V.p. Latin Am. Human Rights Action Ctr., Iowa City, Iowa, 1988-90. Recipient Mellon-James Still fellowship, Univ. Ky., 1982, 84, rsch. grant Ky. Humanities Coun., Barbourville, 1984, dean's grant Marycrest Coll., 1986, 89, 90, Teikyo Marycrest Univ., 1991. Mem. Nat. Soc. Sci. Assn. (nat. governing & edn. bd. 1990—), European Studies Assn., Radical Historians of Am., Mo. Valley Hist. Assn. Office: Teikyo Marycrest U 1607 W 12th St Davenport IA 52804-4034 Home: 1804 Pershing Ave Davenport IA 52803-4327

LYALL, KATHARINE C(ULBERT), academic administrator, economics educator; b. Lancaster, Pa., Apr. 26, 1941; d. John D. and Eleanor G. Lyall. BA in Econs., Cornell U., 1963, PhD in Econs., 1969; MBA, NYU, 1965. Economist Chase Manhattan Bank, N.Y.C., 1963-65; asst. prof. econs. Syracuse U., 1969-72; prof. econs. Johns Hopkins U., Balt., 1972-77; dir. grad. program in public policy Johns Hopkins U., 1979-81; dep. asst. sec. for econs. Office Econ. Affairs, HUD, Washington, 1977-79; v.p. acad. affairs U. Wis. System, 1981-85; prof. of econ. U. Wis., Madison, 1982—; acting pres. U. Wis. System, Madison, 1985-86, 91-92, exec. v.p., 1986-91, pres., 1992—; bd. dirs. Kemper Ins. Cos.; mem. bd. Carnegie Found. for Advancement of Teaching. Author: Reforming Public Welfare, 1976, Microeconomic Issues of the 70s, 1978. Mem. Mcpl. Securities Rulemaking Bd., Washington, 1990-93. Mem. Am. Econ. Assn., Assn. Am. Univs., Phi Beta Kappa. Home: 6021 S Highlands Ave Madison WI 53705-1110 Office: U Wis System Office of Pres 1720 Van Hise Hall 1220 Linden Dr Madison WI 53706-1525

LYBROOK, TIM C., business executive, real estate executive; b. Kokomo, Ind., Feb. 5, 1959. AS, Purdue U., 1979. Lic. real estate broker, Ind. Cons. Indpls., 1979-89; pres. Pointe Realty, Bloomington, Ind., 1989—, Teletron Inc., Bloomington, 1989—. Contbr. articles to profl. jours. Republican. Office: Teletron Inc 2200 E Pointe Rd Bloomington IN 47401-9075

LYBYER, MIKE JOSEPH, state legislator, farmer; b. Waynesville, Mo., Feb. 23, 1947; m. Mary Jane Rockill, 1981. BS, U. Mo., 1969. Farmer Huggins, Mo., 1969—; mem. Mo. Senate, Jefferson City, 1976—; mem. edn. and transp. bill coms., chmn. agr., conservation and parks com. Mem. Masons, Shriners, Odd Fellows. Democrat. Office: Rte 9 Box 200 Huggins MO 65484 also: State Senate State Capitol Building Jefferson City MO 65101-1556*

LYDEEN, JERRY BRUCE, state offical; b. Fergus Falls, Minn., Dec. 7, 1936; s. Lloyd G. and Agnes M. Lydeen; m. Doris M. Perkins, June 26, 1965; children: Michelle M. Rutherford, Brian J. BS in Bus. Edn., St. Cloud (Minn.) State U., 1958; MS in Bus. and Vocat. Edn., U. N.D., Grand Forks, 1963, postgrad., 1963—. Bus. edn. tchr. Lone Rock (Wis.) H.S., 1958-59, Moose Lake (Minn.) H.S., 1959-61; chmn. bus. edn. dept. Thief River Falls (Minn.) Area Tech. Coll., 1961-66, Bemidji (Minn.) Area Tech. Coll., 1966-69; N.D. state supr. bus. and office tech. N.D. State Bd. Vocat. and Tech. Edn., Bismarck, 1970—; bd. dirs. nat. Future Bus. Leaders Am.-Phi Beta Lambda, 1993—; mem. Policy Com. Bus. and Econ. Edn., 1993—. Editor adminstrn. and supervision sect. Bus. Edn.Forum, 1992-93; editor, pub. North Dakota's State Suprevisor's Newsletter, 1970—. Mem. NEA, Nat. Bus. Edn. Assn., Am. Vocat. Assn., Nat. Assn. Bus. Edn. State Suprs., Mountain Plains Bus. Edn. Assn., N.D. Bus. and Office Edn. Assn., N.D. Vocat. Assn., Delta Pi Epsilon. Presbyterian. Office: ND State Bd Vocat/Tech Edn Capitol Bldg 15th Fl 600 E Boulevard Ave Bismarck ND 58505-0610

LYLE, MARY KAY, order buying company executive; b. St. Joseph, Mo., Jan. 22, 1943; d. Ralph and Lydia Margurite (Nuckols) Roderick; m. Kenneth G. Hughes, Sept. 16, 1962 (div. Mar. 1968); 1 child, Kenna Kay McCracken; m. Joe Max Lyle, July 14, 1973; 1 child, Marty Joe Patrick. Diploma, North Andrew High Sch., 1961. Teller, bookkeeper Farmers State Bank, Rosendale, Mo., 1961-64; billing clk. Crouch Bros. Trucking, St. Joseph, 1964-65; clk. Am. Nat. Bank, St. Joseph, 1965-69; adminstr. Pleasant Hill Nursing Home, Oregon, Mo., 1969-72; bookkeeper John Clay & Co. Order Buying, Savannah, Mo., 1972—; real estate agt. Landmark, Inc., Savannah, 1981-89, Excel Realty, Savannah, 1989-94; Realty Execs., Savannah, 1994—. Mem. bd. elders First Christian Ch., Savannah, 1989-92, 94-96, youth group leader, 1985-86. Mem. DAR, Mo. Cattle Women (pres. 1992-94, Cattle Woman of Yr. 1994), Andrew County Cattle Women (pres. 1980, 93-96, sec.-treas. 1981-94, Recognition award), Xi Zeta Epsilon (pres. chpt. 1989, 92, Sweetheart 1987, 93, Girl of Yr. 1987, 89). Republican. Home: PO Box 207 Savannah MO 64485-0207 Office: John Clay & Co Order Buying PO Box 207 Savannah MO 64485-0207

LYLES, JEAN ELIZABETH CAFFEY, journalist, church worker; b. Abilene, Tex., Mar. 2, 1942; d. Wiley Luther and Pauline Linn (Marlin) Caffey; m. James Vernon Lyles, Aug. 23, 1969 (div. Aug. 1987). Student, McMurry Coll., 1960-61; BA with honors, U. Tex., 1964. Copy editor Christian Century mag., Chgo., 1972-74, assoc. editor, 1974-84, editor at large, 1984—; assoc. editor Religious News Svc., N.Y.C., 1984-87; sr. news editor The Lutheran, Chgo., 1987-91; news dir. United Meth. News Svc., Evanston, Ill., 1991-94; freelance photojournalist, 1995—, freelance organist, 1995—. Author: A Practical Vision of Christian Unity, 1982; contbg. author: The First Amendment in a Free Society, 1979, Fearfully and Wonderfully Weird, 1990; contbg. editor Wittenburg Door, 1982-87; columnist Inside the Am. Religion Scene, 1985-87, The Underground Ecumenist, 1989-92; mem. editl. bd. Mid-Stream, Indpls., 1984—; mem. exec. com. Associated Ch. Press, 1989-91. Church organist. Mem. Religion Newswriters Assn., Am. Guild Organists, Hymn Soc. Am., United Meth. Assn. of Communicators. Democrat. Episcopalian. Home: 922 North Blvd Oak Park IL 60301-1243

LYMAN, ARTHUR JOSEPH, financial executive; b. Evergreen Park, Ill., May 18, 1953; s. Arthur Edward and Margaret (O'Conner) L.; m. Janet Lee Wenzel, Sept. 9, 1984; children: Christina Lee, Alissa Mary, Arthur Joseph Jr. BA, Knox Coll., 1975; M in Mgmt., Northwestern U., 1977. CPA, Ill.; CFP. Audit supr. Arthur Andersen & Co., Chgo., 1977-83; fin. planning analyst Montgomery Ward & Co., Chgo., 1983-84; dir. fin. and adminstrn. ctrl. region Coopers & Lybrand, Chgo., 1984-88, CFO Midwest region, 1989-93, nat. dir. fin. field ops., 1993—. Mem. AICPA, Fin. Execs. Inst. (bd. dirs. Chgo. chpt. 1992—), Ill. Inst. CPA's, Pi Sigma Alpha, Tau Kappa Epsilon (honor award 1988, chmn. bd. trustees 1988-93). Roman Catholic. Home: 3 Cornell Dr Lincolnshire IL 60069-3222 Office: Coopers & Lybrand 203 N La Salle St Chicago IL 60601-1210

LYNCH, DANIEL C., state legislator; b. Omaha, Aug. 9, 1929; m. Jane Lynch, 1950; children: Debby, Julia, Marrianne, Maureen, Dan Jr. Student, Loras Coll. Pres. Lynch Plumbing & Heating Co.; mem. from 13th dist. Nebr. State Senate, Lincoln, 1984—, chmn. rules com., past mem. com. on coms., appropriations com., past mem. Nebr. retirement sys. com.; v.p. consumer and govt. affairs Blue Cross/Blue Shield, Nebr. Commr. Douglas County, 1960-81; mem. Pres.' Coun. on Intergovtl. Affairs; mem. adv. com.

Ea. Nebr. Office on Aging. Mem. Assn. Counties, Omaha Comml. Club. Office: Nebr State Senate State Capitol Rm 2107 Lincoln NE 68509 also: Nebr State Legislature State Capital Lincoln NE 68516*

LYNCH, DAVID WILLIAM, physicist, educator; b. Rochester, N.Y., July 14, 1932; s. William J. and Eleanor (Fouratt) L.; m. Joan N. Hill, Aug. 29, 1954 (dec. Nov. 1989); children: Jean Louise, Richard William, David Allan; m. Glenys R. Bittick, Nov. 14, 1992. BS, Rensselaer Poly. Inst., 1954; MS, U. Ill., 1955, PhD, 1958. Asst. prof. physics Iowa State U., 1959-63, assoc. prof., 1963-66, prof., 1966—, chmn. dept., 1985-90, disting. prof. liberal arts and scis., 1985—; on leave at U. Hamburg, Germany; dir. microelectronics rsch. ctr. Iowa State Univ., 1995—; and U. Rome, Italy, 1968-69; sr. physicist Ames Lab. of Dept. of Energy; acting assoc. dir. Synchrotron Radiation Ctr., Stoughton, Wis., 1984; vis. prof. U. Hamburg, summer 1974; dir. Microelectronics Rsch. Ctr., Iowa State U., 1995—. Fulbright scholar U. Pavia, Italy, 1958-59. Fellow Am. Phys. Soc.; mem. AAAS, Optical Soc. Am. Home: 3315 Ross Rd Ames IA 50014-3959

LYNCH, LELAND T., advertising executive. Co-founder, chmn., CEO Carmichael Lynch, Mpls., 1962—; co-founder Leading Ind. Agy. Network. Bd. dis. Planned Parenthood Minn., Minn. Pub. Radio; chair-elect Mpls. Downtown Coun., 1996—. Mem. Am. Assn. Advt. Agys. (regional pres., nat. sec./treas.). Office: Carmichael Lynch Inc 800 Hennepin Ave Minneapolis MN 55403-1803*

LYNCH, PRISCILLA A., nursing educator, therapist; b. Joliet, Ill., Jan. 8, 1949; d. LaVerne L. and Ann M. (Zamkovitz) L. BS, U. Wyo., 1973; MS, St. Xavier Coll., Coll., 1981. RN, Ill. Staff nurse Rush-Presbyn.-St. Luke's Med. Ctr., Chgo., 1977-81, psychiat.-liaison cons., 1981-83, asst. prof. nursing, unit leader, 1985—; mgr. and therapist Oakside Clinic, Kankakee, Ill., 1987—; mem. adv. bd. Depressive and Manic Depression Assn., Chgo., 1986—; mem. consultation and mental health unit Riverside Med. Ctr., Kankakee, 1987—; speaker numerous nat. orgns. Contbr. numerous abstracts to profl. jours., chpts. to books. Bd. dirs. Cornerstone Svcs. Recipient total quality mgmt. award Rush-Presbyn.-St. Luke's Med. Ctr., 1991. Mem. ANA, Ill. Nurses Assn. (coms.), Coun. Clin. Nurse Specialists, Profl. Nursing Staff (sec. 1985-87, mem. coms.). Presbyterian. Home: 606 Darcy Ave Joliet IL 60436-1673

LYNCH, TONY A., mechanical engineer; b. Columbus, Ind., Sept. 6, 1969. BSME, Purdue U., Indpls., 1993. Mech. technician Arvin N.Am. Automotive, Columbus, 1993-94, process engr., 1994—. Served with Ind. Army N.G., 1988—. Mem. Soc. Mfg. Engrs.

LYNCH, WILLIAM THOMAS, JR., advertising agency executive; b. Evergreen Park, Ill., Dec. 3, 1942; s. William T. and Loretta J. L.; m. Virginia Louise Venteicher, Aug. 21, 1965; children: Kelly, Maureen, Kim, Meagan, Molly. BA, Loras Coll., 1964; MBA, U. Iowa, 1966. Media trainee Leo Burnett Co. Inc., chgo., 1966-68, asst. account exec., 1968-76, v.p., 1976-79, sr. v.p., 1979-82, exec. v.p., 1981-85; vice chmn. Leo Burnett USA, chgo., 1985-89; chmn., CEO Leo Burnett USA, Chgo., 1987-91; pres. Leo Burnett Co., Inc., Chgo., 1992-93; pres., CEO Leo Burnett Worldwide, Chgo., 1993; CEO, pres. Leo Burnett Worldwide, Leo Burnett Co. Inc., Chgo., 1993—. Mem. coun. U. Chgo. Grad. Sch. Bus.; bd. dirs. Chgo. United, Northwestern Meml. Hosp., Chgo. Mem. Econ. Club Chgo. Roman Catholic. Office: Leo Burnett Co Inc 35 W Wacker Dr Chicago IL 60601*

LYNES, JAMES WILLIAM, SR., communications company executive; b. Waverly, Iowa, July 26, 1928; s. James Kendall and Lenore Clara (Kuethe) L.; m. Opal Marie Kerdus, Aug. 24, 1954; 1 child, James William Jr. Student, U.S. Mil. Acad., 1946-47; BA in History, Wartburg Coll., 1950. Rural letter carrier U.S. Postal Svc., Plainfield, Iowa, 1951-86; corp. sec. Butler-Bremer Mut. Telephone Co., Plainfield, Iowa, 1962—, also bd. dirs.; pres. Iowa Rural Letter Carriers Assn., 1981-83, v.p., 1979-81, state bd. dirs. 1976-83. Vice chmn. Bremer County Bd. Health, Waverly, Iowa, 1969-84, Waverly-Shell Rock Hospice, 1989-93, pres., 1992-93; fin. chmn. Bremer County Rep. Ctrl. Com., Waverly, 1987-92; mayor pro-tem City of Plainfield, Iowa, 1985-89, 91-94, mayor, 1994—, coun. mem., 1983-94; pres. Bremer County Hist. Soc., 1966—. With U.S. Army, 1951-53. Named Lion of Yr. Waverly Lions Club, 1988; Melvin Jones fellow, 1994. Mem. Plainfield Lions (sec. Plainfield chpt. 1971-72, pres. Waverly chpt. 1982-83, editor bulletin 1978—), Kopper Klowns (pres. 1980-81), Waterloo German-Am. (v.p., 1979-80), A.F. & A.M., Shriners. Lutheran. Home: 219 Main St # 218 Plainfield IA 50666-9753

LYNETT, WILLIAM RUDDY, publishing, broadcasting company executive; b. Scranton, Pa., Jan. 18, 1947; s. Edward James and Jean O'Hara L.; children: Scott, Jennifer, Christopher P. B.S., U. Scranton, 1972. Pub. Scranton Times, 1966—; pres., chief exec. officer Shamrock Communications, Inc., 1971—; pres. Towanda Daily Rev., 1977-81, Owego Pennysaver Press, Inc., 1977-81; owner, Pres. Mgmt. Program, Harvard U., 1990. Bd. dirs. Community Med. ctr., Scanton; chmn. Mayor's Libr. Fund Drive, 1974; chmn. spl. gifts divsn. Heart Fund, 1975; bd. govs. Scranton Area Found.; trustee U. Scranton, 1990—; chmn. Steamtown Nat. Pk. Grand Opening com. Mem. Nat. Assn. Broadcasters, Pa. Assn. Broadcasters, Am. Newspaper Pubs. Assn., Pa. Newspaper Pubs. Assn., Greater Scranton C. of C. (chmn. membership drive 1980-81). Democrat. Roman Catholic. Clubs: Scranton Country, Elks, K.C. Office: 149 Penn Ave Scranton PA 18503-2022

LYNN, JOHN ALBERT, history educator; b. Glenview, Ill., Mar. 18, 1943; s. Judd Benjamin and Adelle (Savage) L.; m. Andrea Ellen Kramer, June 13, 1965; children: Daniel Morgan, Nathanael Greene. BA, U. Ill., 1964; MA, U. Calif., Davis, 1967; PhD, UCLA, 1973. Vis. asst. prof. Ind. U., Bloomington, 1972-73; asst. prof. U. Maine, Orono, 1973-77; asst. prof., assoc. prof., prof. history U. Ill., Champaign/Urbana, 1978—; Oppenheimer chair of warfighting strategy Marine Corps U., Quantico, Va., 1994-95; chmn. Midwest Consortium on History, Urbana, 1987—. Author: Bayonets of the Republic, 1984 (Best 1st Book award 1985), Lessons in the History of Western Civilization, 1987; co-author: Lessons in American History, 1988, A Guide to Sources in European Military History, 1991; editor: Tools of War, 1990, Feeding Mars, 1993; also articles. NEH summer grantee, Paris, 1980, 87, grantee U. Ill., Urbana, 1989-90. Mem. Soc. Mil. History (Midwest regional coord. 1989—), Midwest Consortium Mil. History (chmn. 1987—). Home: 910 W Hill St Champaign IL 61821-2706

LYNN, MICHAEL ROBERT, chemical engineer; b. Chgo., Apr. 17, 1957; s. George John and Selma Ruth (Lehning) L.; m. Cindy Lynn Polovitch, June 19, 1982; 1 child, Jessica Anne. BSChemE, U. Ill., Chgo., 1981; MEM, Northwestern U., 1989. Engr. U.S. EPA, Chgo., 1980-82; staff mem. U.S. Gypsum Co., Des Plaines, Ill., 1981-84; rsch. staff mem. U.S. Gypsum Co., Libertyville, Ill., 1984-87, sr. rsch. staff mem., 1987-88, mem. tech. staff III, 1988-92, acting program mgr., 1992-93, program mgr., 1993—. Dem. precinct worker, Park Ridge, Ill., 1976. James scholar U. Ill., 1975-79. Mem. Am. Inst. Chem. Engrs. and Forest Products. Lutheran. Office: US Gypsum Co 700 N US Highway 45 Libertyville IL 60048-1268

LYNN, ROBERT WILLIAM, gas and electric utility company official; b. N.Y.C., Jan. 27, 1943; s. William Ernest and Jeannette (Reardon) L.; m. Sara E. Davis, Aug. 26, 1961 (dec. Nov. 1980) children: Robert, John, William, David, Michelle; m. Roberta Periolat, July 5, 1992. A.A.S. in Supervision, Purdue U., 1974, B.S. in Indsl. Engring., 1976, MBA Ind.-Wesleyan U., 1991. Engr. No. Ind. Pub. Service Co., Crown Point, 1968-77, engring. supr., Gary, 1977-79, sr. cons., Hammond, 1979-82, mgr., 1982-89, asst. to sr. v.p. and gen. mgr. energy distrbn., 1989-90; mgr. strategic planning, 1990—, lectr., 1992-93; advisor Purdue U.-Hammond, 1979. Served with USN, 1960-67. Mem. Inst. Indsl. Engrs. (sr. project award 1976). Avocations: sailing, sculpture. Home: 218 N 375 W Valparaiso IN 46383-7726 Office: NIPSCO 5265 Hohman Ave Hammond IN 46320-1722

LYON, BARBARA WEBER, marketing professional; b. Trenton, N.J.; d. Charles Maurice and Dolores Miriam (Little) Weber; m. Dale Alvah Lyon, Aug. 4, 1979; children: Brett Alexander, Zachary James. AA, Am. Fashion Coll., Lucerne, Switzerland, 1975. Retail mgr. Strawberry Jam, New Hope, Pa., 1975-78; tech. asst. Ednl. Testing Svc., Princeton, N.J., 1978-87; owner Lyon Share Word Processing Svc., Menomonie, Wis., 1986-94; exec. officer Dunn-Pepin Bd. Realtors, Menomonie, 1987-94; actress Fanny Hill Dinner Theater, Eau Claire, Wis., 1994-96; office mgr. Brakken Vet. Clin., Menomonie, WI, 1994—; mktg. exec. Melaleuca, Inc., Idaho Falls, Idaho, 1994—; vocalist Reunion Blues. Pres. Menomonie Theatre Guild, 1989-91, membership chair, 1988, 94-96, props chair, 1986-87; coord. Mothers Offering Mothers Support, Menomonie, 1987-89. Unitarian Universalist (religious edn. chair 1993-94). Home: 1231 Meadow Hill Dr Menomonie WI 54751-1726 Office: Brakken Vet Clin Rm 309 2215A Schneider Ave Menomonie WI 54751-2509

LYON, JEFFREY, journalist, author; b. Chgo., Nov. 28, 1943; s. Herbert Theodore and Lyle (Hoffenberg) L.; m. Bonita S. Brodt, June, 20, 1981; children: Lindsay, Derek. BS in Journalism, Northwestern U., 1965. Reporter Miami (Fla.) Herald, 1964-66, Chgo. Today, 1966-74; reporter Chgo. Tribune, 1974-76, columnist, 1976-80, 94—, feature writer specializing in sci., 1980—; creative writing adj. prof.; coord. joint sci. and journalism programs Columbia Coll., Chgo., 1987—, dir., 1988—. Author: Playing God in the Nursery, 1985, Altered Fates: Gene Therapy and the Retooling of Human Life, 1995; also newspaper series Altered Fates, 1986 (Pulitzer Prize 1987). Mem. State of Ill. Perinatal Adv. Com., Springfield, 1986-90; mem. pediat. ethics com. U. Chgo. Hosps., 1985-90; bd. dirs. Shore Cmty. Svcs. to Retarded Citizens, Evanston, Ill., 1985-90; mem. bd. Little City, Palatine, Ill., 1979—. Recipient Nat. Headliner award Atlantic City Press Club, 1984, Citizen Fellow award Inst. Medicine of Chgo., 1987, Peter Lisagor award, 1990. Office: The Chgo Tribune 435 N Michigan Ave Chicago IL 60611-4001

LYON, JOANNE B., psychologist; b. Little Rock, June 2, 1943; d. F. Ike and Marie (Graham) Beyer; m. Jas. Sherod Lyon, Dec. 1971 (div. Sept. 1975), m. John M. Lofton, May 22, 1983 (dec. Feb. 1990). BA, Webster U., 1966; MEd, U. Mo., St. Louis, 1976, PhD, 1986. Lic. psychologist, Kans. Reading specialist Rockwood Sch. Dist., St. Louis, 1976-79; psychology cons. handicapped component St. Louis Head Start, 1982-83; intern Topeka State Hosp., 1983-84; dir. partial hosp. programs Family Svc. & Guidance Ctr., Topeka, 1985-89; pvt. practitioner and joint owner Shadow Wood Clin. Assocs., Topeka, 1989—; clin. supr. Family Svc. & Guidance Ctr., Topeka, 1989-93. Mem. exec. bd. Interfaith of Topeka, I Have a Dream Coalition, Psychology Advisory Bd. Behavioral Sci. Regulatory Bd.; bd. dirs. Temple Beth Sholom Sisterhood. Sherman scholar U. Mo., St. Louis, 1982. Mem. APA, Kans. Psychol. Assn., Am. Orthopsychiatric Assn., Soc. for Personality Assessment. Jewish. Home: 3030 SW Arrowhead Rd Topeka KS 66614-4134 Office: Shadow Wood Clin Assocs 2933 SW Woodside Dr Topeka KS 66614-4181

LYON, JOHN JOSEPH, liberal arts and education educator, administrator, translator; b. Chgo., Sept. 18, 1932; s. William Bridgman and Mary Catherine (Sullivan) L.; m. Jacqueline Theresa Woods (div.); children: Thomas, Siobhan, Nora, Matthew, Geoffrey, Mark, Arthur, Kathleen; m. Elizabeth Lenore Booker; children: Jean, Christopher, Brendan, Sheilagh, Patrick. BA in History and Lit., U. Notre Dame, 1954; student, Emory U., 1955; tchrs. cert., Bowling Green U., 1959; MA in History and Lit., U. Notre Dame, 1955; PhD in History and Lit., U. Pitts., 1966. Tchr. Fostoria (Ohio) Secondary Sch., 1956-60; instr., asst. prof., assoc. prof. Duquesne U., Pitts., 1960-67; asst., assoc. prof. U. Notre Dame, Ind., 1967-83, chmn. gen. program liberal studies, 1973-79, chmn. grad. program in history, philosophy of sci., 1973-76; ednl. advisor St. Mary's Coll., Winona, Minn., 1983-84; prof., dean Ky. State U., 1985-86; assoc. prof. dept. lang. and lit. Lakeland Coll., Sheboygan, Wis., 1986-90; chmn. humanities div. Ind. Acad. for Sci., Math. and Humanities, 1990, Ball State U., 1990; assoc. prof., dir. edn. programs Hillsdale (Mich.) Coll., 1990-93. Author: (with others) Episodes in American History, 1973 (with Phillip Sloan) From Natural History to the History of Nature, 1981; translator: From Aristotle to Darwin and Back Again (Etienne Gilson), 1986, Linguistics and Philosophy (Etienne Gilson), 1988, German Science (Pierre Duhem), 1991; contbr. articles to profl. jours. Scholar Emory U., 1955; Danforth grantee, 1965-66, Nat. Endowment for Humanities grantee, 1971-72; Wilbur Found. fellow, 1984-85. Mem. Nat. Assn. Scholars. Republican. Roman Catholic.

LYON, MICHAEL WILLIAM, utility company executive; b. Watseka, Ill., June 16, 1954; s. C.W. and Betty Charlotte (Hall) L.; m. Barbara Lynn Parry, July 31, 1982; children: Jonathan Christian William, Jennifer Ashley Lynn. AA, SUNY, Albany, 1983; BS in Psychology, SUNY, 1988; postgrad., Ill. State U., 1988-93, U. Ill., 1996—. Lic. sr. reactor operator. Tng. instr. Ill. Power Co., Clinton, 1983-84, sr. instr. ops., 1984-85, lead instr. ops., 1985-87, supr. lic. tng., 1987-89, supr. requalification and ops. tng., 1989-91, dir. emergency response, 1991-94, dir. ops. tng. and emergency response, 1994—. Pres. DeWitt County United Way Bd., Clinton, 1989-90; site coord. Clinton Power Sta. United Way, 1990—. With USN, 1976-83. Mem. Midwest Nuclear Tng. Assn., Am. Psychol. Assn., Am. Soc. Tng. and Devel. Republican. Methodist. Home: 705 E Florida Ave Urbana IL 61801-8617 Office: Ill Power Co Nuclear Tng & Support PO Box 678 Clinton IL 61727-0678

LYON, THOMAS L., agricultural organization administrator; b. Toledo, Iowa, Sept. 12, 1940; m. Barbara Lyon; children: Jeff, Melissa, Scott. BS in Dairy Sci., Iowa State U., 1962. Exec. sec. Iowa State Dairy Assn.; with 21st Century Genetics, gen. mgr., 1976-93; pres. Coop. Resources Internat., Shawano, Wis., 1993—. Bd. dirs. Am. Farmland Trust, Coop. Bus. Internat., Coop. Devel. Found.; chmn. Nat. Coop. Bus. Assn.; mem. Nat. Rural Devel. Task Force & Coop. 2000 com., Dairy Shrine Club, steering com. Wis. Dairy Inititative 2020, Kellogg Found. Food Systems; bd. advisors U. Wis., Eau Claire; bd. visitors U. Wis., Madison; trustee Grad. Inst. Coop. Leadership, Coop. Found.; cons. U. Wis. Bus. Schs. Review. Recipient Friend of Extension award U. Wis., 1981, Wis. Friend of County Agents award, 1984, Dairy Industry Person of Yr. award World Dairy Expo, 1985, Nat. Coop. Pub. Svc. award, 1991, Disting. Citizen Shawano award, 1993, Agribus. award Iowa State U. Coll. Agr. Alumni Soc., 1995. Office: Coop Resources Internat 100 MBC Dr Shawano WI 54166

LYON, WAYNE BARTON, manufacturing company executive; b. Dayton, Oct. 26, 1932; m. Maryann L., 1961; children: Karyn, Craig, Blair. B-SChemE, U. Cin., 1955; MBA in Mktg., U. Chgo., 1969. Registered profl. engr., Mich. Tech. rep. Union Carbide, Chgo., 1955-62; product devel. mgr., v.p. bus. devel. Ill. Tool Works, Chgo., 1962-72; group v.p., exec. v.p. Masco Corp., Taylor, Mich., 1972-85, pres., coo, 1985—, also bd. dirs.; bd. dirs. Masco Corp., Taylor, Mich., Payless Cashways, Inc.; lectr. AMA. Patentee in field. Bd. govs., trustees Cranbrook Kingswood Schs., Bloomfield Hills, Mich., 1984—, Orchard Lake Country Club, Mich., 1985-90. Capt. U.S. Army, 1955-63. Mem. Fairlane Club (Dearborn, Mich.), TPC of Mich. Club, Orchard Lake Country Club, Bloomfield Hills Country Club. Office: Masco Corp 21001 Van Born Rd Taylor MI 48180-1340*

LYONS, ARTHUR, economist. Dir. Ctr. for Econ. Policy Analysis, Chgo. Office: Ctr Econ Policy Analysis 202 S State St Chicago IL 60604

LYONS, DAN A., computer engineer; b. Xenia, Ohio, Sept. 23, 1955. B, Cin. Bible Coll., 1977. Engr. Thomas A. Moser & Assocs., Cin., 1979-89; chief engr. Systecon Incorp., West Chester, Ohio, 1989—, also bd. dirs. With USAF, 1972-74. Mem. ASHRAE. Office: Systecon Incorp 9750 Crescent Park Dr West Chester OH 45069-3894

LYONS, EILEEN, state legislator; b. N.Y.C., July 3, 1941. Ill. state rep. Dist. 47, 1995—. Office: 1030 S LaGrange Rd La Grange IL 60525

LYONS, J. ROLLAND, civil engineer; b. Cedar Rapids, Iowa, Apr. 27, 1909; s. Neen T. and Goldie N. (Hill) L.; BS, U. Iowa, 1933; m. Mary Jane Doht, June 10, 1924; children: Marlene R. Sparks, Sharon K. Hutson, Mary Lynn Lyons. Jr. hwy. engr. Works Projects Adminstrn. field engr. Dept. Transp., State Ill., Peoria, 1930-31, civil engr. I-IV Cen. Office, Springfield, 1934-53, civil engr. V, 1953-66, municipal sect. chief, civil engr. VI, 1966-72. Civil Def. radio officer Springfield and Sangamon County (Ill.) Civil Def. Agy., 1952—. Recipient Meritorious Service award Am. Assn. State Hwy. Ofcls., 1968, 25 Yr. Career Service award State Ill., 1966, Cert. Appreciation Ill. Mcpl. League, 1971. Registered profl. engr., Ill.; registered land surveyor, Ill. Mem. NSPE, Nat. Soc. Profl. Engrs., Ill. Soc. Profl. Engrs., Ill. Assn. State Hwy. Engrs., State Ill. Employees Assn., Am. Pub. Works Assn., Am. Assn. State Hwy. Ofcls., Amateur Trapshooters Assn., Sangamon Valley Radio Club, Lakewood Golf and Country Club, KC, Abe Lincoln Gun Club, South Fork Conservation Club (Ill.). Address: 3642 Lancaster Rd Springfield IL 62703-5022

LYONS, JERRY LEE, mechanical engineer; b. St. Louis, Apr. 2, 1939; s. Ferd H. and Edna T. Lyons. Diploma in Mech. Engring., Okla. Inst. Tech., 1964; MSME, S.W. U., 1983; PhD in Engring. Mgmt., Southwest U., 1984. Registered profl. engr., Calif. Project engr. Harris Mfg. Co., St. Louis, 1965-70, Essex Cryogenics Industries, St. Louis, 1970-73; mgr. engring. rsch. Chemetron Corp., St. Louis, 1973-77; cons. fluid controls Wis. U., 1977—; pres., chief exec. Yankee Ingenuity, Inc., St. Louis, 1974—; v.p., gen. mgr. engring. R & D Essex Fluid Controls divsn. Essex Industries, Inc., St. Louis, 1977-90; pres. Lyons Pub. Co., St. Louis, 1983—; pres., CEO Innovative Controls divsn. Yankee Ingenuity, Inc., Ft. Wayne, Ind., 1991—; chmn. exec. bd. continuing engring. edn. in St. Louis for U. Mo., Columbia, 1980-81; bd. dirs. Intertech., Inc., Houston; cons. fluid power dept. Bradley U., Peoria, 1977-84. Author: Home Study Series Course on Actuators and Accessories, 1977, The Valve Designers Handbook, 1983, The Lyons' Encyclopedia of Valves, 1975, 93, The Designers Handbook of Pressure Sensing Devices, 1980, Special Process Applications, 1980; co-author: Handbook of Product Liability, 1991; contbr. articles to profl. jours.; patentee in field. With USAF, 1957-62. Recipient Winston Churchill medal, 1988, Dwight D. Eisenhower Achievement award of honor, 1990; named Businessman of Week (KEZK radio), Eminent Churchill fellow Winston Churchill Wisdom Soc. Fellow ASME; mem. N.Y. Acad. Scis., Soc. Mfg. Engrs. (cert. product design, chmn. mo. registration com. 1975-90, chmn. St. Louis chpt. 1979-80, internat. dir. 1982-84, 85-87, engr. of yr. 1984, internat. award of merit 1985), Nat. Soc. Profl. Engrs., Mo. Soc. Profl. Engrs., St. Louis Soc. Mfg. Engrs. (chmn. profl. devel., registration and cert. com. 1975-79), Instrument Soc. Am. (control valve stability com. 1978-84), Computer and Automated Sys. Assn. (1st chmn. St. Louis chpt. 1980-81), St. Louis Engrs. Club (award of merit 1977, wisdom award of honor 1987, Wisdom Hall of Fame 1987), Am. Security Coun. (committeeman 1976—), Nat. Fluid Power Assn. (com. on pressure ratings 1975-77), Am. Legion. Lutheran. Home and Office: 2607 Northgate Blvd Fort Wayne IN 46835-2986

LYSON, HAL CURTIS, investigator; b. Minot, N.D., Nov. 8, 1953; s. Harlan Marvin and Genevieve Mathilda (Woessner) L.; m. Paulette Marie Neigum, July 28, 1973; children: Curtis John, Paula Jean, Brian Harlan. Student, Bismarck Jr. Coll., U. Cinn. Firefighter, lt. Bismarck (N.D.) Fire Dept., 1974-79, inspector, investigator, 1979-86; investigator Robins, Kaplan, Miller & Ciresi, Mpls., 1986—. Author: (with others) Fire Investigation Manual, 1992. Coach Bismarck Youth Hockey, 1986-93, Burnsville Baseball, 1990—. Mem. Internat. Assn. Arson Investigators (cert., bd. dirs. Minn. chpt. 1989—, cert. com. and liaison 1991—), Nat. Fire Protection Assn. (adv. bd. 1988—), Nat. Assn. Fire Investigators, Eagles (Eagle of Yr. 1984), Am. Legion. Roman Catholic. Office: Robins Kaplan Miller Ciresi 800 Lasalle Ave Minneapolis MN 55402-2006

LYTAL, PATRICIA LOU, art educator; b. Ft. Wayne, Ind., Sept. 11, 1936; d. George F. and Geraldine (Beck) Heingartner; m. Wayne Earl Lytal; Sept. 16, 1956; children: Michael Wayne, Patrick Allen (dec.), Terry Lee, Shawn David. Tchr. oil painting Ft. Wayne Park Sch. Bd, 1980-83, Ind. U.- Purdue U. Continuing Edn., Ft. Wayne, 1986—; ind. tchr. oil painting Ft. Wayne, 1976—; instr. Ft. Wayne Sr. Ctr., Decatur (Ind.) Park Bd., Ft. Wayne Park and Recreation Dept. 1 tchr. oil painting for Chpt. 2 through St. Joseph Med. Ctr.; judge Ft. Wayne Women's Club Ind. Art Contest, 1989-90, 94. Artist: (murals) Diehm Mus. Natural History, 1981, Grace United Meth. Ch. Home, 1983, La Margarita Restaurant. Recipient 3d pl. china painting State of Ind., Best of Show award Ft. Wayne Woman's Club Ind. Artist Show, award Montpelier Brass Latch Art Show, 1993, 94, 95, Judges award Huntington Coll. Arts Contest, 1993. Mem. Brown Country Art Soc., Park County Art Soc., Ft. Wayne Artist Guild, Torrence Artist Guild. Democrat. Home and Office: 1625 N Glendale Dr Fort Wayne IN 46804-5851

LYTLE, GENE E., marketing executive; b. East Pitts., Pa., Jan. 8, 1937. Dist. mgr. KFC Corp., Iowa City, 1968-82; pres. Mktg. Syss. Unlimited Corp., Iowa City, 1982—. Sgt. U.S. Army, 1956-59. Protestant. Home & Office: 60 Arbury Dr Iowa City IA 52246

LYTLE, JAMES ROBERT, product design engineer; b. Mishawaka, Ind., June 7, 1953. Student, S.W. Mich. U., 1971-73; A in Mech. Tech., Perdue U., 1983. Product design engr. Wayne Home Equipment, Fort Wayne, Ind., 1980-91; sr. product designer Patton Electric, New Haven, Ind., 1991-93; product design engr. The Bargman Co., Albion, Ind., 1993—. Patentee in field. Coach Little League Boys, Osceola and Ft. Wayne, Ind., 1971-94. Mem. Soc. Automotive Engrs. Republican. Roman Catholic. Office: The Bargman Co 211 E Park Dr Albion IN 46701-1440

LYTLE, MARK L., state legislator. Student, Oakland City Coll., Ball State U., Muncie, Ind.; grad., Ky. Sch. Mortuary Sci. Mng. dir. Lytle-Gans-Andrew Funeral Home; state rep. Dist. 69 Ind. Ho. of Reps., 1992—, mem. county and twp. ways and means com., vice chmn. natural resources com. Mayor, City of Madison Ind.; recorder Jefferson County, Ind.; precinct committeeman; mem. Southeastern Ind. Regional Planning Commn. Mem. Sons of Legion, Elks. Home: 423 W Main St Madison IN 47250-3736*

LYTTLE, BRADFORD JANES, political scientist; b. Chgo., Nov. 20, 1927; s. Charles Harold and Marcia Taft (Janes) Lyttle; m. Mary Suzuki, Dec., 1967 (div. 1969). BA in Philosophy, Earlham Coll., 1949; MA in English Lit., U. Chgo., 1951; MA in Polit. Sci., U. Ill., Chgo., 1976. Political activist, coordinator numerous peace walks, anti Vietnam War demonstrations. various locations, 1952-74. Author: You Come With Naked Hands: The Story of the San Francisco to Moscow Walk for Peace, 1962; (booklets) National Defense Through Nonviolent Resistance, 1958, Washington Action, 1969, May Ninth, 1970, The Apocalypse Equation, 1982, The Flaw in Deterrence, 1982, The Chicago Anti-Vietnam War Movement, 1988; publisher Midwest Pacifist Commentator; also numerous articles. Imprisoned for mil. draft refusal, 1954-55. Home: 5729 S Dorchester Ave Chicago IL 60637-1726

MA, JIANNENG, microbiologist, researcher; b. Dongyong, Zhejiang, Peoples Republic of China, Jan. 18, 1958; came to the U.S., 1986; s. Shichun and Chune (Jin) M.; m. Danghua Zhou, July 18, 1984; children: Kevin Quansheng, Susan Zhou. DVM, Huazhong Agrl. U., 1982; MS, Jiangsu Acad. Agrl. Sci., 1984; PhD, Va. Poly. and State U., 1991. Rsch. asst. Jiangsu (Peoples Republic of China) Acad. Agrl. Sci., 1982-84; rsch. assoc. Wash. State U., Pullman, 1986-87, Va. Poly. Inst. & State U., Blacksburg, 1987; rsch. scientist Cambridge Biotech Corp., Worcester, Mass., 1992-94; rsch. sci. Mallinckrodt Vet., Inc., Mundelein, Ill., 1995—. Contbr. chpt. to book, articles to profl. jours.; patentee in field. Mem. AAAS, Am. Soc. for Microbiology (Grad. Student Travel award 1991), Conf. Rsch. Workers in Animal Diseases. Home: 1641 Belle Haven Dr Grayslake IL 60030 Office: Mallinckrodt Vet Inc 421 E Hawley St Mundelein IL 60060

MAASS-MORENO, ROBERTO, physiologist, educator, engineer.; b. Phila., Aug. 11, 1952; s. Roberto Maass-Escoto and Lilia M.; m. Christina Gómez-Bellengè, July 13, 1985; children: Sebastian R., Julien T., Sophie E. BS in Physics, U. Mexico, Mexico City, 1979; MS in Biomed. Engring., Case Western Res. U., 1982, PhD in Biomed. Engring., 1987. Postdoctoral fellow Ind. U. Sch. of Medicine, Indpls., 1987-91, rsch. assoc., 1991-92, asst. scientist, instr., 1992-93; asst. prof., scientist Ind. U. Sch. Medicine, Indpls., 1993—. Contbr. articles to profl. jours. Mem. IEEE, Am. Physiol. Soc., Biomed. Engring. Soc., Microcirculatory Soc. Office: Ind U Sch of Medicine 635 Barnhill Dr Indianapolis IN 46202-5126

MAATMAN, RUSSELL WAYNE, retired chemistry educator; b. Chgo., Nov. 7, 1923; s. John and Cora (Van Proyen) M.; m. Jean Sherrard, Dec. 27, 1948; children: John, Susan Meyers, Rebecca, Deborah Baker, Ruth Carter. AB, Calvin Coll., 1946; PhD, Mich. State U., 1950. Asst. prof. chemistry DePauw U., Greencastle, Ind., 1949-51; sr. rsch. chemist Mobil

Oil Co., Paulsboro, N.J., 1951-58; assoc. prof. chemistry U. Miss., Oxford, 1958-63; prof. chemistry Dordt Coll., Sioux Center, Iowa, 1963-90. Author: The Bible, Natural Science, and Evolution, 1970, The Unity in Creation, 1978, The Impact of Evolutionary Theory: A Christian View, 1993; contbr. tech. articles to profl. jours. Rsch. grantee AEC, Petroleum Rsch. Fund, Rsch. Corp., 1960-80. Fellow Am. Sci. Affiliation; mem. Am. Chem. Soc., Kiwanis (pres.-elect 1995-96). Mem. Christian Reformed Ch. Home: 401 Fifth Ave SE Sioux Center IA 51250

MABEN, BURTON FREEMAN, financial planner, analyst; b. Nashville, Nov. 13, 1961; s. Hayward Clinton and Carrie Mae (Harris) M. BA in Sociology, Albion Coll., 1983; MS in Pub. Policy Analysis, U. Rochester, 1985. Program analyst City of N.Y., 1984; dir., pub. policy First Cir. Assocs., Inc., Detroit, 1985-88; sr. planner City of Detroit, 1987-94; mng. rep. Fortis Advisors, Inc.; acad. coord. Detroit Acad. Finance; mayoral appointee Detroit Assn. Commn., 1987-88. Mem. 1st Congressional Young Dems., So. Christian Leadership Conf. Assn. Recipient Profl. Devel. award U. Rochester, 1983; Sloan Found. fellow U. Rochester. Mem. Nat. Assn. Securities Profls., Assn. Pub. Policy Mgmt., NAACP. Office: Fortis Fin Group 15999 W 12 Mile Rd Ste 220 Southfield MI 48076-7161

MABRY, CELIA ELAINE HALES, librarian; b. Ayden, N.C., Sept. 6, 1946; d. Thomas Edwin and Joyce Elaine (Hill) H.; m. Paul Davis Mabry Jr., July 12, 1986. BA, Duke U., 1968, MA, 1970; MLS, East C. U., 1975; PhD, Fla. State U., 1982. Instr. Stratford Coll., Danville, Va., 1970-72; media coord. New Hanover County Pub. Schs., Wilmington, N.C., 1976-78; lectr. East Carolina U., Greenville, N.C., 1980-81; reference libr., English bibliographer U. N.C., Charlotte, 1983-86; reference instr., libr., religion bibliographer U. Minn., Mpls., 1986—. Author: (monograph) The World of the Aging: Information Needs and Choices, 1993; contbr. articles to profl. jours. Mem. LWV, Wilmington, 1976-78, Tallahassee, 1978-79; bd. dirs. Mental Health Assn. Minn., 1991-96, sec., 1993-96; co-pres. U. St. Thomas Women's Assn., 1990-91. Mem. ALA (bd. dirs. reference and adult svcs. divsn. 1988-90, sec. English and Am. lit. discussion group 1986, chmn. libr. svcs. aging population com. 1985-88), Beta Phi Mu, Kappa Delta Pi. Democrat. Methodist. Home: 28 Mississippi River Blvd N Saint Paul MN 55104-5713 Office: U Minn Wilson Libr 309 19th Ave S Minneapolis MN 55455-0438

MABUS, CATHERINE ADAM, adminstrative assistant; b. Chgo., Mar. 3, 1948; d. Adam Harry and Helen George (Kichkaylo) Wanaski. BA in Music, So. Ill. U., 1990. Adminstrv. asst. fgn. langs. and lit. So. Ill. U., Carbondale, 1984—, co-chmn. women's caucus, 1989-90, 94-95. Chorus dir. Sweet Adelines Internat., Carbondale, 1979-92; mem. Civil Svc. Employee's Coun., Carbondale, 1989—, sec., 1994—; mem. steering com. Women's Bus. Coun. So. Ill., Carbondale, 1991. Recipient Univ. Woman of Distinction award, 1990, Civil Svc. Outstanding Svc. award, 1992. Mem. Am. Philatelic Soc., So. Ill. Choral Soc. (hon. life), Jackson County So. Ill. U.-Carbondale Alumni Assn. (bd. dirs. 1994—), Soc. for Preservation and Encouragement Barbershop Quartet Singing in Am. (coach 1981-92), Bus. and Profl. Women's Club (pres. Carbondale chpt. 1991-92, dist. dir. 1995-96, state bylaws chair 1996—, state bd. dirs. 1995—), So. Ill. Stamp Club (pres. 1985-87, 91), Mu Phi Epsilon, Gamma Beta Phi. Eastern Orthodox. Office: So Ill U Dept Fgn Langs & Lits Carbondale IL 62901

MACARUSO, VICTOR MAURICE, academic administrator; b. Providence, Apr. 1, 1944; s. Mario George and Teresa Elinore (Christopher) M.; m. Linda Lee Wuethrich, Nov. 24, 1973; children: Melissa, Mario, Monica. BA, Providence Coll., 1966; MA, U. Kans., Lawrence, 1970; DA, U. Mich., 1992. Prof. English Mt. Senario Coll., Ladysmith, Wis., 1968—, v.p. acad. affairs, 1995—; chair fin. com., bd. mem. Higher Edn. Consortium for Urban Affairs, Mpls., 1982—, Kinship, Ladysmith, 1988—; mem. planning com. Collaboration for Advancement of Tchg., Mpls., 1995—; cons. Drevco Corp., Milw., 1996. Pres. Our Lady of Sorrows Sch. Bd., Ladysmith, 1974-75; chairperson Helmet Safety Com., Ladysmith, 1994—; bd. mem. Flambeau Valley Arts, Ladysmith, 1994—. Mem. Kiwanis Internat. (pres. 1996-97), Jaycees (Outstanding Tchr. 1982). Democrat. Roman Catholic. Home: 70 River Ave Ladysmith WI 54848 Office: Mt Sinerio Coll 1500 College Ave Ladysmith WI 54848

MACAULAY, ALLEN F., radio broadcasting executive; b. L.A., Oct. 30, 1949; s. Peter Frank and Margaret M. (McGifford) M. D in Divinity, Internat. Bible Inst., St. Louis, 1976, M in Evangelism, 1976, M in Biblical Teaching, 1976; MA in Ministry, San Diego Bible Seminary, 1989. From tape technician to pub. affairs dir. Sta. KTOF-FM, Cedar Rapids, Iowa, 1971—; tape technician Sta. KCDR (now Sta. KMRY), Cedar Rapids, Iowa, 1984—. Composer: (song) My Friend; singer The Masters Quartet; soloist The Hauskins Singers; founder Sta. KNGR; bd. advisors The Blackwood Bros.; violinist New Bern Consort. Club: Ham Radio.

MACCORMACK, LAWRENCE LEE, chemicals marketing executive; b. N.Y.C., May 4, 1945; s. Donald George and Mary Louise (Flanagan) MacC.; m. Bonnie Lindsey Hall, June 10, 1967; children: Christopher Edward, Chad Eric. AB in History & Polit. Sci., Wagner Coll., 1967; MBA, U. Conn., 1974. Underwriting & programming trainee Great Am. Ins. Co., N.Y.C., 1967-68; systems analyst Am. Can. Co., Greenwich, Conn., 1970-73; sales mgr. Image Carrier Corp., N.Y.C., 1974; mng. dir. Dixie products Am. Can Co., 1975-81; dir. mktg. Lily-Tulip Cup Co., Augusta, Ga., 1982-85; v.p., gen. mgr. Ecolab Inc., St. Paul, 1985-96; exec. v.p., gen. mgr. Orchem Corp., Fairfield, Ohio, 1996—; mktg. cons. pvt. practice, New Fairfield, 1981. Mem. mgmt. decision lab. bd. NYU, Manhattanville, 1979-81; coach soccer and basketball Minnetonka (Minn.) Youth Assn., 1986-90; scoutmaster Boy Scouts Am., Excelsior, Minn., 1986-90. Sgt. U.S. Army, 1968-70.

MACDONALD, DAVID RICHARD, industrial psychologist; b. Dowagiac, Mich., May 20, 1953; s. Jerrold Brewster and Shirley Ann (Shaffer) MacD.; m. Mary Elizabeth Olson, Dec. 20, 1975 (div. Sept. 5, 1995); 1 child, Sarah Ann. AS, Southwestern Mich. Coll., 1973; BBA, Western Mich. U., 1975, MA, 1976, EdS, 1979; PhD, Mich. State U., 1986. Announcer, boardman WDOW AM/FM, Dowagiac, Mich., 1969-72; mgmt. devel. specialist Interstate Motor Freight System, Grand Rapids, Mich., 1977-79; sr. mgmt. tng. instr. GTE Gen. Telephone Co. Mich., Muskegon, 1979-82; cons. human resources devel. Steelcase, Inc., Grand Rapids, 1982-86, mgr. performance devel., 1986—; asst. prof. grad. mgmt. Aquinas Coll., Grand Rapids, 1983—; cons., speaker in field; facilitator, program dir. Devel. Dimensions Internat., Pitts., 1981; facilitator Alamo Learning Systems, Southfield, Mich., 1983, 86, Wilson Learning Corp., Eden Prairie, Minn., 1983; job analysis program mgr. Barry M. Cohen & Assocs., Largo, Fla., 1985. Co-chair United Way Steelcase campaign, Grand Rapids, 1986. Mem. ASTD (sec. W. Mich. chpt. 1977-79), Soc. Indsl.-Orgnl. Psychology, Am. Psychol. Assn., Nat. Soc. for Performance and Instrn., Mensa, Phi Kappa Phi. Republican. Home: 2306 Prospect Ave SE Grand Rapids MI 49507-3159 Office: PO Box 1967 Grand Rapids MI 49501-1967

MACDONALD, GARY BRUCE, communications executive; b. Spokane, Wash., Apr. 17, 1950; s. William and Thelma (Wilhelm) MacD.; m. Joy Bea Fukumoto, June 1973 (div. Dec. 1980). BA, Fairhaven Coll., 1973. Fgn. svc. officer U.S. Info. Agy., Washington, 1976-84; asst. cultural attache U.S. Embassy, Rabat, Morocco, 1977-78; dir. Am. Cultural Ctr., Damascus, Syria, 1978-82; planning officer Office Acad. Programs, Washington, 1982-83; country affairs officer Office of N. African Near Eastern and South Asian Affairs, Washington, 1983-84; exec. dir. AIDS Action Coun., Washington, 1984-87; coord. Asia/Near East programs AIDSCOM Acad. Ednl. Devel., Washington, 1987-91; dep. dir. Acad. Ednl. Devel. AIDS Communication Support, Washington, 1991-93; sr. program officer social devel. programs Acad. Ednl. Devel., Washington, 1993-95; Midwest rep. Acad. Ednl. Devel., Indpls., 1995—; cons. World Bank, India, 1992—, U.S. Agy. for Internat. Devel., Washington, 1987-89, WHO, Geneva, 1987, Pan Am. Health Orgn., Mexico City, 1987, govts. of Philippines, Thailand, Indonesia, 1987-89. Editor: Five Experimental Colleges, 1973; contbr. articles to profl. jours. Clark county coord. Youth for McCarthy, Vancouver, Washington, 1968; v.p. Gay Activists Alliance, Washington, 1983-84; chmn. com. on human rels. Met. Police, Washington, 1985. Recipient Pub. Svc. award Franklin E. Kameny, 1985, Cert. of Honor City and County of San Francisco, 1986, Harvey Milk Pub. Svc. award Nat. Gay and Lesbian Health Found., 1987, Alumni Fellow award Fairhaven Coll., 1991. Office: Acad Ednl Devel 902 N Meridian Ste 311 Indianapolis IN 46204

MACDONALD, MIKE J., mechanical design engineer; b. Vn Nuys, Calif., Aug. 29, 1957. BSME, U. Wis. Plattville, 1980. Sr. design engr. Gilman, Giddings & Lewis, Janesville, Wis., 1980-91; project mgr. Giddings & Lewis, Janesville, Wis., 1991—. Republican. Roman Catholic.

MACFARLANE, MALCOLM HARRIS, physics educator; b. Brechin, Scotland, May 22, 1933; came to U.S., 1956; s. Malcolm P. and Mary (Harris) M.; m. Eleanor Carman, May 30, 1957; children: Douglas, Kenneth, Sheila, Christine. M.A., U. Edinburgh, Scotland, 1955; Ph.D., U. Rochester, 1960. Research asso. Argonne (Ill.) Nat. Lab., 1959-60; asst. prof. physics U. Rochester, 1960-61; asso. physicist Argonne Nat. Lab., 1961-68, sr. physicist, 1968-80; prof. physics U. Chgo., 1968-80, Ind. U., Bloomington, 1980—; vis. fellow All Souls Coll., Oxford (Eng.) U., 1966-67; mem. nuclear scis. adv. com. Dept. Energy-NSF, 1983-87; cons. Ency. Brit. Contbr. articles of theoretical nuclear physics to profl. jours. Guggenheim fellow physics, 1966-67; Alexander von Humboldt Found. sr. scientist award, 1985. Fellow Am. Phys. Soc.; mem. Nuclear Physics sect. Am. Phys. Soc. (mem. exec. com. 1969-71). Home: 3510 E Homestead Dr Bloomington IN 47401-4217 Office: Dept Physics Indiana U Bloomington IN 47405

MACFARLANE, WILLIAM NOBLE, JR., foundation executive; b. Montclair, N.J., Oct. 1, 1962; s. William Noble Sr. and Patricia Irene (Mack) Mac.; m. Marie Christine Te Pas, Dec. 8, 1990; 1 child, Jude Thaddeus II. BA cum laude, Univ. Notre Dame, 1984. Nat. product mgr. Packaging Systems, Hyannis, Mass., 1985-87; social studies dir. Legion of Christ Sch., Center harbor, N.H., 1987-89; dir. govt. rels. and new product mgmt. Plastic Safety Systems, Cleve., 1990-93; exec. dir. The Mary Found., Lakewood, Ohio, 1993—, St. Jude Media, Lakewood. Author: (novel) Pierced by a Sword, 1995. Founder Knights of Immaculata Religious Group, Notre Dame, 1984; dir. Human Life Internat. Conf., Cleve., 1991. Mem. KC, Cleve. Knights Immaculata (pres. 1990—). Republican. Roman Catholic. Home: PO Box 614 Lakewood OH 44107-0914

MACHASKEE, ALEX, newspaper publishing company executive; b. Warren, Ohio; m. Carol Machaskee. Degree, Cleve. State U. Sports reporter The Warren (Ohio) Tribune; dir. labor rels. and personnel The Plain Dealer, Cleve., asst. to pub., promotion dir., v.p., gen. mgr., 1985-90, pres., pub., 1990—. V.p. Mus. Arts Assn. (Cleve. Orch.); chmn. Greater Cleve. Roundtable; bd. dirs. Ohio Arts Coun., Cleve. Found., Univ. Hosps. Health Sys., Inc., Univ. Cir., Inc., Greater Cleve. Growth Assn., Cleve. Tomorrow, Nat. Conf., Gt. Lakes Sci. Mus., Cleve. Coun. on World Affairs, United Way Svcs., Cleve. Initiative for Edn., Rock and Roll Hall of Fame and Mus., Mus. Coun. of Cleve. Mus. Art and St. Vladimir's Orthodox Theol. Sem., Crestwood, N.Y.; mem. vis. com. Weatherhead Sch. Mgmt., Case Western Res. U.; mem. adv. com. Newspaper Mgmt. Ctr., Northwestern U. Mem. Newspaper Assn. Am. (mem. labor rels. subcom.). Office: Plain Dealer Pub Co 1801 Superior Ave E Cleveland OH 44114-2107

MACHULAK, EDWARD LEON, real estate, mining and financial corporation executive; b. Milw., July 14, 1926; s. Frank and Mary (Sokolowski) M.; BS in Accounting, U. Wis., 1949; student spl. courses various univs.; m. Sylvia Mary Jablonski, Sept. 2, 1950; children: Edward A., John E., Lauren A., Christine M., Paul E. Chmn. bd., pres., Commerce Group Corp., Milw., 1962—, San Luis Estates, Inc., 1973—, Homespan Realty Co., Inc., 1974—, Universal Developers, Inc., 1972—, Picadilly Advt. Agy., Inc., 1974—; chmn. bd., chief exec. officer, Gen. Lumber & Supply Co., Inc., 1949—; bd. dirs., v.p., San Sebastian Gold Mines, Inc., 1969-73, chmn. bd., pres., 1973—; bd. dirs, sec., LandPak, Inc., 1985—; bd. dirs. Edjo Ltd., 1974—, sec., 1976—; ptnr., Weem Assocs., 1974—; bd. dirs., designee Comseb Joint Venture Woodcreek Devel. Corp., 1987. Mem. nat. adv. coun. SBA, 1972-74, co-chmn. 1973, 74. Recipient Recognition award U.S. SBA, 1975, N.W. Festival Corp., 25 Yr. Recognition award San Sebastian Community, Santa Rosa de Lima, El Salvador, 1991, San Sebastian Community El Salvador award, 1992, El Salvador Ministry Edn. award, 1992. Edward L. Machulak Day proclaimed by students of Canton San Sebastian, El Salvador, May 9, 1992; recipient recognition award for valuable consideration of support and svc. to San Sebastian Community, 1992, Cmty. Recognition award Santa Rosa De Lima, 1994. Mem. Nat. Assn. Small Bus. Investment Co's (nat. chmn. legis. com. 1968-73, bd. govs. 1970-74, exec. com. 1971-74, sec. 1972-74, Disting. Service award to Am. Small Bus. 1970), Midwest Regional Assn. Small Bus. Investment Cos. (bd. dirs. 1968-74, v.p. 1970-71, pres. 1971-72, Outstanding Services award 1972), State of Wis. Council on Small Bus. Investment (chmn. 1973-74), Wis. Bd. Realtors (various coms. 1955-88), Milw. Bd. Realtors (various coms. 1955-88). Pres.' Council Marmion Mil. Acad., Aurora, Ill., 1966-79, lay life trustee, 1972, fin. advisor 1967-71, chmn. spl. fund raising com. 1966-67, planning com. 1972-79; chmn. adv. bd. Jesuit Retreat House, Oshkosh, Wis., 1966-68; chmn., bd. dirs. Spencarian Coll. of Bus., 1973-74; chmn. St. John Cathedral Symphony Concert Com., Milw., 1978; sustaining mem. Met. Mus. Art, 1974—. Served with AUS, 1945-46. Recognized bus. leader in Congl. Record, 1976; named Hon. Life Mem., Mid-Continental Railway, 1963. Clubs: Tripoli Golf (Milw.); Lodge: KC (4th degree 1971—, recognition award 1989). Home: 903 W Green Tree Rd Milwaukee WI 53217-3716 Office: 6001 N 91st St Milwaukee WI 53225-1721

MACIEJ, JAMES VALENTINE, commercial real estate consultant; b. Little Falls, Minn., Feb. 13, 1950; s. Leo Lewis and Jennie (Sobieck) M.; m. Ann Marie Julia Miller, June 10, 1972. BA in Urban Affairs, St. Cloud State U., 1973. Cert. indsl. developer. Field rep. Minn. Dept. of Econ. Devel., St. Paul, 1973-75, mgr. indsl. devel., 1975-77; bus. cons. U.S. SBA, Mpls., 1977; v.p. Woodward & Assoc., Inc., Mpls., 1977-81, Ac'cent Real Estate Co., Ltd., Edina, Minn., 1981-95; pres. The Ac'cent Cos., Inc., Edina, 1990-95; v.p. Griffin Cos., Mpls., 1995—; pres. Minn. Indsl. Devel. Assn., 1982; chmn. Comml.-Indsl. Divsn., Mpls. Area Assn. realtors, 1995; chmn. Orgn. of Comml. Realtors, Mpls., 1983. Mem. Minn. Shopping Ctr. Assn., Nat. Assn. of Indsl. and Office Properties, Minn. Assn. of Relators, Mpls. Assn. of Realtors, Econ. Devel. Assn. of Minn. Republican. Roman Catholic. Office: Griffin Cos Ste 300 510 Marquette Ave Minneapolis MN 54021

MACINTOSH, BETTY ARLENE, state community services administrator; b. Dover, Ohio, July 14, 1938; d. Brady Burrell and Juanita (Scott) Ballard; m. Thomas Eugene Ellwood, Nov. 2, 1957 (div. Sept. 1976); children: Sharon Kay Mahaffey, Scott Thomas; m. Larry David Macintosh, Dec. 23, 1976. BS in Edn., Ohio State U., 1970, MA in Edn., 1975. Social worker Franklin County Welfare Dept., Columbus, Ohio, 1970-71; dir. day care ctr. Amerikid, Columbus, 1971-72; supr. day care unit Ohio Dept. of Welfare, Columbus, 1972-74, mgr. child care unit, 1974-79; early childhood and supportive home svcs. specialist State of Ohio, Columbus, 1979-81; chief Office Early Childhood/Sch. Age Programs Ohio Dept. Mental Retardation/Devel. Disabilities, Columbus, 1986-88, dep. dir., 1988—. Chairperson bd. Action for Children, Columbus. Mem. Profl. Assn. for the Retarded. Methodist. Office: OH Dept Mental Retardation Devel Disability 30 E Broad St Fl 12 Columbus OH 43215-3414

MACIOCH, JAMES EDWARD, investment consultant, financial planner; b. Cleve., Mar. 30, 1947. Cert. fin. planner, Coll. for Fin. Planning, Denver, 1992; BS, U. Dayton, 1969. Lic. series 7, Nat. Assn. Securities Dealers. Registered floor broker Mid-Am. Commodity Exch., 1988-90; registered floor broker, mem. Chgo. Bd. Trade, 1990—; investment cons. Montano Securities Corp., Chgo., 1993-94, Dickinson & Co., Rosemont, Ill., 1995—. Mem. Internat. Soc. for Fin. Planning. Office: Dickinson & Co 5600 N River Rd Ste 180 Rosemont IL 60018-5184

MACK, ALAN WAYNE, interior designer; b. Cleve., Oct. 30, 1947; s. Edmund B. and Florence I. (Oleksa) M. BS in Interior Design, Case Western Res. U., 1969. Designer interior design dept. Halle's, Cleve., 1969, 71-73; designer Nahan Co., New Orleans, 1973-75, Hemenway's Contract Design, New Orleans, 1975-76; ptnr. Hewlett-Mack Design Assocs., New Orleans, 1976-85; sr. assoc., dir. interior design Hansen Lind Meyer, Inc., 1985—; mem. adv. com. interior design dept. Delgado Jr. Coll., New Orleans; mktg./merchandising adv. coun. St. Mary's Dominican Coll., New Orleans; mem. friends devel. coun. U. Iowa Mus. Art, 1986-91, chair, 1990-91; chmn. adv. com. interior design program Iowa State U., 1991—; bd. dirs. Johnson County United Way, 1991—; mem. design review com., City of Iowa City, 1992-93. Served with U.S. Army, 1969-71. Co-author audiovisual presentation Nat. Home Improvement Coun. Conf., 1981. Mem. ASID (profl. mem., presdl. citation, 1980, treas. La. dist. chpt. 1984), Vis. Nurse Assn. (bd. dirs. 1991—), Found. for Interior Design Edn. Rsch. (standards com., 1972-76, bd. visitors 1977-80, accreditation com., 1981-95, trustee 1996—). Home: 3800 N Lake Shore Dr Apt 2G Chicago IL 60613

MACK, DORIS ANN, data processing systems supervisor; b. Clinton, Iowa, Jan. 9, 1945; d. Stuart Herman and Anita Dorothy (Todtz) Gibson; m. John Willard Mack, May 6, 1967; children: Noel John, Kristine Doris. AA, Clinton (Iowa) Community Coll., 1965; BA, U. Iowa, 1967, St. Ambrose Coll., 1981. Keypunch operator, acctg. clk. Wagner Printers, Davenport, Iowa, 1973-82; computer programmer, systems analyst, systems supr. Modern Woodmen of Am., Rock Island, Ill., 1982—. Mem. planning com. United Way, Rock Island, 1991—. Mem. AAUW (sec. 1989-90, 3d v.p. 1992-93), Data Processing Mgmt. Assn. (sec. 1991-93, exec. v.p. 1993, pres. 1994), Planned Parenthood Cmty. Coun. Office: Modern Woodmen of Am 1701 1st Ave Rock Island IL 61201-8724

MACK, KIRBIE LYN, municipal official; b. Chgo., Jan. 3, 1953; d. Robert Lee and Luvonia (Cheatham) Green; m. Jeffery Frazier Mack, Aug. 10, 1974; children: Maaina, Jeffery Jr., Anisha. BA in Psychology, Northeastern Ill. U., 1975; MA in Policy Analysis and Pub. Adminstrn., U. Wis., 1995. Pers. specialist City of Madison, Wis., 1975-76; program asst. planning budget analysis dept. natural resource State of Wis., Madison, 1976-79, dir. conservation corps, 1979-80, equal opportunity officer, mgr., 1980-85, chief negotiator employment rels., 1985-89; dir. affirmative action dept. City of Madison, 1989—. Co-host, prodr. (cable TV program) Focus On Equality, 1989—. Pres. Southside Raiders Football Booster Club, Madison, 1995. Recipient Gov.'s Orchid award State of Wis., 1987, Exemplary Leadership award Wis. Assn. Black State Employees, 1993, Leadership in Affirmative Action award Am. Soc. for Pub. Adminstrs., 1992, 93, Outstanding Cmty. Svc. award Prevention and Intervention Alcohol and Drug Abuse, 1992, Spirit of Am. Woman award Sta. WISC-TV, 1994, Pub. Svc. for Students award Links, Inc. and Madison Pub. Schs., 1994; named one of 100 Most Alluring Creative Influential and Entrepreneurial People Madison Mag., 1995. Mem. NAACP (life, 1st v.p. 1993—, 2d v.p., Outstanding Svc. award Madison br. 1990, 92, Unsung Heroine award 1993), Am. Contract Compliance Assn., Wis. Assn. Black State Employees (past pres. 1985, Pres.'s award 1989-90). Office: City of Madison Ste 130/MMB 215 Martin Luther King Jr Blvd Madison WI 53701

MACK, SHANE LEE, professional baseball player, olympic athlete; b. L.A., Dec. 7, 1963. Student, UCLA. With San Diego Padres, 1987-88; outfielder Minn. Twins, 1990—; player U.S. Olympic Baseball Team, 1984. Office: Minn Twins 501 Chgo Ave S Minneapolis MN 55415

MACK, STEPHEN W., financial planner; b. Chgo., Mar. 4, 1954; s. Walter M. and Suzanne (Charbonneau) M.; m. Dayle A. Rothermel, Nov. 19, 1983; children: Michael, Veronica, Kevin. BBA in Fin., U. Mich., 1976; cert., Coll. Fin. Planning, Denver, 1987. NASD Lic. Series 63 Uniform Securities Agent State Law Exam., Series 7 Gen. Securities Rep., Series 5 Interest Rate Options, Series 8 Gen. Securities Sales Supr., Series 15 Fgn. Currency Options, Series 24 Gen. Securities Prin., Series 4 Registered Options Prin., Series 53 Municipal Securities Prin. Gen. sales mgr. Mack Cadillac Corp., Mt. Prospect, Ill., 1976-81; sales rep. Merrill Lynch Co., Chgo., 1981-84; resident mgr. Merrill Lynch Co., Rockford, Ill., 1984-85; asst. v.p. Merrill Lynch Co., Skokie, Ill., 1985-86; pres., chief exec. officer Mack Investment Securities, Inc., Glenview, Ill., 1986—; editor, distributor Mack Tracks, monthly newsletter; creator Trend Managed Account. Developer Trend Managed Account (TMA) (svc. mark); creator Turning Point Account (TPA). Mem. Inst. Cert. Fin. Planners, Internat. Assn. registered Fin. Planners, Nat. Assn. Securities Dealers, Internat. Assn. Fin. Planners, Am. Assn. Cert. Fin. Planners, Am. Assn. Registered Fin. Planners, Am. Assn. Registered Investment Advisers, Mensa. Office: Mack Investment Securities Inc 1939 Waukegan Rd Glenview IL 60025-1715

MACK, WILLIAM JOSEPH, psychotherapist, rehabilitation specialist; b. Evergreen Park, Ill., Mar. 5, 1943; s. Arol Ruth (Tallut) M.; m. Margaret Crace McCullom, Jan. 8, 1966 (div. Aug. 1979); children: William, Amy; m. Joan Kinnon, May 22, 1987; stepchildren: Margaret, Wendy, Douglas, Suzanne. BA, U. Dayton, 1965; cert., Ind. State U., Terre Haute, 1980; MA, Ball State U., 1983; M Health Scis., Governors State U., 1994; Doctorate, Am. Inst. Hypnotherapy, 1995. Lic. social worker, Ill.; cert. addictions counselor, clin. hypnotherapist, Ill.; nat. cert. master addictions counselor; lic. clin. profl. counselor, Ill. Mktg. rep. Texaco Inc., Lockport, Ill., 1969-73; med. rep. Merrell-Dow, Kokomo, Ind., 1973-82; program coordinator Pilsen Vocat., Chgo., 1983-85; dir. sheltered workshop Edgewater Community Mental Health Ctr., Chgo., 1985-88; mem. staff Edgewater Uptown Community Mental Health Ctr., Chgo., 1988-92; program dir. Community Counseling Ctrs. Chgo., 1992-96; mgr. adult health ctr. Chgo. Commons, 1996—; adj. faculty mem. Kendall Coll.; therapist Vet. Ctr., Chicago Heights, Ill., 1984-85. Instr. first aid ARC, Chgo., 1986. Served with U.S. Army, 1965-68; Res. ret. Mem NASW, Internat. Assn. PsychoSocial Profls., Am. Assn. Profl. Hypnotherapists, Mktg. Execs. for Sheltered Workshops, Chgo. Soc. Clin. Hypnosis, Am. Legion, Ret. Officers Assn. Democrat. Roman Catholic. Home: 2755 W Farragut Ave Chicago IL 60625-3508 Office: Chgo Commons Adult Health Ctr 1258 W 51st St Chicago IL 60609

MACKEL-RICE, GWENDOLYN ROSETTA, social worker, foundation program officer; b. Natchez, Miss., Jan. 21, 1941; d. Audley Maurice and Rosetta Libian (Lloyd) Mackel; m. Leon N. Rice, Aug. 8, 1963 (div. Aug. 1971); children: Leon McKinley, Laura Gweneth, Lloyd Hoskins. BA, Bennett Coll., 1961; AM, U. Chgo., 1992. Supervising caseworker Cook County Dept. Pub. Aid, Chgo., 1962-68; social worker Ill. Dept. Children Family Svcs., Chgo., 1971; svc. dir. programs for sr. citizens Hull House Assn., Chgo., 1971-74; assoc. dir. U. Chgo. Office Spl. Programs, Chgo., 1974-78; dir. devel. Meth. Youth Svcs., Chgo., 1981-84; founding exec. dir. Project IMAGE, Chgo., 1984-90; social worker, orgnl. devel. cons. Chgo., 1990-93; exec. dir. The Youth Consortium of Greater Grand Boulevard, 1993-94; sr. program officer Polk Bros. Found., 1994—. Active St. Mark Meth. Ch., Chgo.; dir. United Voices for Children, Chgo., 1985-89, Big Buddies Youth Svcs., Inc., 1986-91. Recipient Black Rose award social svc. League of Black Women Chgo., 1988; community svc. fellow Chgo. Community Trust, Chgo., 1990. Mem. NASW, Blacks in Devel. (founding dir.), Inst. for Athletics and Edn. (steering com. 1984—), Assn. Black Social Workers, Alfreda Wells Duster Civic Club (pres. 1994—). Methodist. Home: 8600 S Prairie Ave Chicago IL 60619-6044

MACKENZIE, GEORGE ALLAN, diversified company executive; b. Kingston, Jamaica, Dec. 15, 1931; s. George Adam and Annette Louise (Maduro) MacK.; m. Valerie Ann Marchand, June 30, 1971; children from previous marriage: Richard Michael, Barbara Wynne. Student, Jamaica Coll., Kingston, 1944-48. Commd. flying officer Canadian Air Force, 1951, advanced through grades to lt. gen., 1978; comdr. Canadian Forces Air Command, Winnipeg, Man., 1978-80; resigned Canadian Forces Air Command, 1980; exec. v.p., COO Gendis Inc., 1980-89, pres., COO, 1989—, also bd. dirs.; bd. dirs. Sony of Can. Ltd., Willowdale, Ont., Can.; pres. Gendis Bus. Svcs.; chmn. exec.com. MMG MGmt. Group, Saan Stores Ltd.; bd. dirs. Tundra Oil and Gas Ltd., Chauvco Resources Ltd., Gendis Inc., bd. dirs.; pres. COO Met. Stores of Can. Ltd. Bd. dirs. St. Boniface Gen. Hosp. Rsch. Found.; coun. mem. Duke of Edinburgh's Award in Can.; mem. regional adv. bd. Carleton U.; mem. jud. coun. Province of Manitoba. Decorated comdr. Order of Mil. Merit, Order St. Johns, Can. Decoration, Knight of St. Lazarus of Jerusalem. Mem. United Services Inst. Can. (hon. v.p.), Canadian Corps Commissionaires (gov.), Police Chiefs Research Found. (co-chmn.), Pan Am. Games Soc. (hon.). Clubs: Rotary (Winnipeg); Lakewood Country (Delta); Manitoba; St. Charles Golf and Country. Home: Box 9, 383 Christie Rd, St Germain, MB Canada ROG 2A0 Office: Gendis Inc, 1370 Sony Pl, Winnipeg, MB Canada R3T 1N5

MACKEY, BENJAMIN FRANKLIN, JR., lawyer, consultant; b. Little Rock, Jan. 26, 1935; s. Benjamin Franklin and Maxie (Walker) M.; m. Diane

Stoakes, June 24, 1958 (div. May 1995); children: Benjamin Franklin III, Stuart Stoakes, Sarah Dryden. Student, U. Ark., Little Rock, 1955; BA, Northwestern U., 1957; JD, U. Ark., Little Rock, 1975. Bar: Ark. 1975, Tex. 1988, U.S. Dist. Ct. (ea. and we. dists.) Ark. 1975, U.S. Ct. Appeals (8th cir.) 1975, U.S. Supreme Ct. 1993. Personnel asst. brand mgmt. Proctor & Gamble, Cin., 1957-64; cons. Booz, Allen & Hamilton, Chgo., 1964; exec. asst. Ark. Power & Light, Little Rock, 1965-72; assoc. Spitzberg, Mitchell & Hays, Little Rock, 1975-77; sole practice Little Rock, 1977-94. Bd. dirs., sec. Inglewood Found., Little Rock, 1971-93; mem. Little Rock Dist. Sch. Bd., 1983-86; mem. ct. of rev. Episc. Ch. Province VI for States of Ark., Kans., Mo., Okla. and Tex., 1984-94; chancellor Diocese of Ark., 1988-94; pres. bd. dirs. U. Ark. for Med. Scis. Found., 1985-87; pres. Ark. Cmty. Found., Little Rock, 1985-86. Mem. ABA (various sects.), Ark. Bar Assn. (ho. of dels. 1981, ethics and grievances com. 1980-83, Meritorious Svc. award 1981), Pulaski County Bar Assn. (bd. dirs. 1982, Outstanding Contbn. award 1980), Inst. Internat. Edn. Southern (bd. dirs. 1985-94), Little Rock Country Club. Democrat. Home and Office: 900 N Lake Shore Dr 1802 Chicago IL 60611

MACKEY, CHARLES RALPH, benefits firm executive; b. Belvidere, Ill., Dec. 24, 1947; s. Ralph Winfield and Anne Patricia (Belmont) M.; children: Stuart, Shaun; m. Janice L. Kalsted, May 17, 1991; children: Sarah C., Steven C. BS in Urban Studies, Elmhurst (Ill.) Coll., 1980, BS in Polit. Sci., 1980. CFP, Life Underwriters Tng. Coun. I and II; registered rep. Nat. Assn. Securities Dealers; cert. employee benefit cons. Agt. Occidental/Transam. Life, Oakbrook, Ill., 1973-78; owner Key Fin., Carol Stream, Ill., 1978-83; broker, mgr. Brodsky Agy., Palatine, Ill., 1983-89; pres. Mackey Benefits Group, Inc., Palatine, 1983—. Pres. Heritage Lake Estates Assn., Wheaton, Ill., 1976-78. Mem. Internat. Found. Employee Benefit Plans, Nat. Assn. Life Underwriters, Nat. Assn. Health Underwriters, Internat. Assn. Fin. Planners. Presbyterian. Home: 147 W Fullerton Ave Glendale Heights IL 60139-2669 Office: Mackey Benefits Group Inc 865 E Wilmette Rd Ste G Palatine IL 60067-6493

MACKEY, ELIZABETH JOCELYN, music educator; b. Corbin, Ky., Oct. 30, 1927; d. Elbert Thomas (dec.) and Flora (Bryant) M. BS in Music Edn., Peabody Coll., 1948; MusB in Voice, Greensboro (N.C.) Coll., 1953; MusM in Music History, U. Mich., 1956, PhD in Musicology, 1968. Instr. Indiana (Pa.) State Coll., 1956-58; assoc. prof. Minot (N.D.) State Coll., 1964-67; asst. prof. Ball State U., Muncie, Ind., 1969-74, assoc. prof., 1974-80, prof., 1980-94, prof. emerita, 1994—. Contbr. articles to profl. publs. Fulbright scholar, 1961-62; AAUW fellow, 1963-64. Mem. Pi Kappa Lambda, Sigma Alpha Iota (Province pres. 1978-87, various awards). Lutheran. Home: 1205 W Riverside Ave Muncie IN 47303-3651

MACKEY, ROBERT JOSEPH, business executive; b. Detroit, Apr. 28, 1946; s. Robert and Bridget (Degnan) M.; m. Regina E. Richmond, July 27, 1968; children: Robert, Scott. BS in Indsl. Mgmt., Lawrence U., Southfield, Mich., 1971; MBA, Wayne State U., 1979. Dir. bus. affairs Harper Grace Hosp., Detroit, 1975-79; v.p. Nat. Health Corp., Southfield, 1979-83; v.p., founder Health Resources Mgmt., Southfield, 1983-86; pres., founder Medview, Inc., Farmington Hills, Mich., 1986-91, CompPro, Inc., Farmington Hills, Mich., 1986-91, CompPro Calif., Inc., Long Beach, 1986-91; founder, owner Regulation Enterprises, Inc., Southfield, 1991—; founder, dir., officer Laser Eye Ctrs. of N.Am., 1994—. Bd. dirs. Am. Cancer Soc., Southfield, 1986-91, Dad's Club, Cath. Cen. High Sch., Redford, 1987-93; mem. Gov.'s Task Force on Health Care Cost Containment, Mich., 1989, 90. Mem. Am. Assn. Profl. Providers, Detroit Econ. Club, Marina City Club. Home: 33905 Schulte St Farmington MI 48335-4162 Office: Laser Eye Ctrs NAm 28530 Orchard Lake Rd # 106 Farmington Hills MI 48334

MACKIE-MASON, JEFFREY KING, economics educator; b. N.Y.C., Aug. 22, 1959; s. John Huey and Janice Ruth (Auman) Mason; m. Jane Lillian MacKie, Aug. 23, 1980; children: Brian Alexander, Andrew Reid. AB, Dartmouth Coll., 1980; MPP, U. Mich., 1982; PhD, MIT, 1986. Cons., lobbyist Nat. Audubon Soc., Washington, 1979; rsch. resident Dept. of Energy, Washington, 1981; spl. cons. Nat. Econ. Rsch. Assocs., Cambridge, Mass., 1984-87; asst. prof. econs. U. Mich., Ann Arbor, 1986-92, assoc. prof. econs. and pub. policy, 1992—, assoc. prof. info., 1996—; anti-trust cons. TVA, 1982-84, Bristol Myers, 1986, Pacific Telesis, 1986, Intel, 1988, Virtual Maintenance, Inc., 1989-90, Grumman System Support Corp., 1990, Systemcare Inc., 1991, Comm-Tract, Inc., 1991, Datastat Co., 1992, ITS, 1994-95, Sun Microsystems, 1995, AT&T, 1995, Am. Online, 1995, EDS, 1995, ASI, 1996, Bell Atlantic, 1996, Disc Mfg. Inc., 1996. Mem. editl. bd. RAND Jour. of Econs., 1996—, Telecomm. Sys., 1996—; referee Jour. Polit. Economy, Am. Econ. Rev., Jour. Fin., others; contbr. articles to profl. jours. Paul R. Richter fellow, 1979-80, Andrew W. Mellon Nat. Resource Econs. fellow, 1980, Phoenix Meml. Lab. Energy Rsch. fellow, 1981-82, NSF, 1982-85, Alfred P. Sloan Found. fellow, 1985-86, Collegiate Coun. fellow, 1987-88, Nat. fellow Hoover Instn. Stanford U., 1990-91, faculty rsch. fellow Nat. Bur. Econ. Rsch., 1987-93, rsch. assoc., 1993—; Joseph A. Livingston Rsch. scholar, 1989-90; Rackham Faculty Rsch. grantee, 1987-88, 89-99, Rsch. Partnership grantee U. Mich., 1988-90, Faculty Assistance Fund grantee, 1990, Faculty Recognition Fund grantee, 1990—, NSF grantee, 1990-91, 91-93, 93—. Mem. Econometric Soc., Am. Fin. Assn., Am. Econs. Assn. Office: U Mich Dept Econs 462 Lorch Hall Ann Arbor MI 48109

MACKLIN, MARTIN RODBELL, psychiatrist; b. Raleigh, N.C., Aug. 27, 1934; s. Albert A. and Mitzi (Robbell) M.; m. Ruth Chimacoff (div.); children: Meryl, Shelley; m. Anne Elizabet Warren, May 25; children: Alicia, Aaron. BME, Cornell U., 1957, M in Indsl. Engring., 1958; PhD in Biomed. Engring., Case Western Res. U., 1967, MD, 1977. Diplomate Am. Bd. Psychiatry and Neurology; cert. in alcoholism and other drug dependencies Am. Soc. Addiction Medicine. Investigator Am. Heart Assn., Cleve., 1969-74; vis. fellow U. Sussex, Brighton, England, 1970; assoc. prof. biomed. engring. Case Western Res. U., 1972-81, asst. prof. psychiatry, 1981—; clin. dir. Horizon Ctr. Hosp., Warrensville Township, Ohio, 1981-83; adminstrv. dir. Riverview Psychiat. Assocs., 1983-94; med. dir. Woodside Hosp., 1989-94; v.p. med. affairs Geauga Hosp., Chardon, Ohio, 1994—; psychiat. cons. Glenbeigh Hosp., Ohio and Fla.; cons. various indsl. cos. Contbr. articles to profl. jours; patentee in field. NIH rsch. grantee Kellogg Found., Cleve., 1967-81; Laughlin fellow Am. Coll. Psychiatry, 1980. Mem. Am. Psychiat. Assn., Am. Coll. Physician Execs., Cleve. Acad. Medicine, Cleve. Psychiat. Soc. Home: 348 N Chestnut St Jefferson OH 44047-1130

MACKLIN, WILLIAM EDWARD, state legislator, lawyer; b. Lindsborg, Kans., Dec. 29, 1945; s. William Edward and Marion (Beckstrom) M.; m. Paige Evelyn Hatfield, 1967; children: Sarah Kathryn, Daisy Erin, Molly Evelyn. BA, U. Minn., 1968; JD, William Mitchell Coll. Law, St. Paul, 1965. Attorney, shareholder Nord & Macklin, 1982-89; Dist. 37B rep. Minn. Ho. of Reps., St. Paul, 1989—; mem. taxes, judiciary, local govt. and metropolitan affairs coms., Minn. Ho. of Reps. Mem. Lakeville (Minn.) C. of C., Lions. Office: 307 State Office Bldg Saint Paul MN 55155-1201*

MACLANE, SAUNDERS, mathematician, educator; b. Taftville, Conn., Aug. 4, 1909; s. Donald Bradford and Winifred (Saunders) MacL.; m. Dorothy M. Jones, July 21, 1933 (dec. Feb. 1985); children: Margaret Ferguson, Cynthia M. Hay; m. Osa Skotting Segal, Aug. 16, 1986. PhB, Yale U., 1930; AM, U. Chgo., 1931; DPhil, Goettingen, Fed. Republic Germany, 1934; DSc (hon.), Purdue U., 1965, Yale U., 1969, Coe Coll., 1973, U. Pa., 1977, Union Coll., 1990; LLD (hon.), Glasgow U., Scotland, 1971. Sterling Research fellow Yale U., 1933-34; Benjamin Peirce instr. Harvard U., 1934-36; instr. Cornell U., 1936-37, U. Chgo., 1937-38; asst. prof. Harvard U., 1938-41, assoc. prof., 1941-46, prof., 1946-47; prof. math. U. Chgo., 1947-63, chmn. dept., 1952-58, Max Mason Disting. Service prof. of math., 1963-82, prof. emeritus, 1982—; exec. com. mem. Internat. Math. Union, 1954-58; research mathematician Applied Math. Group, Columbia, 1943-44, dir., 1944-45; Mem. Nat. Sci. Bd., 1974-80. Author: (with Garrett Birkhoff) Survey of Modern Algebra, 1942, Homology, 1963, Algebra, 1967, Categories for the Working Mathematician, 1971, Mathematics: Form and Function, 1985, (with I. Moerdijk) Sheaves in Geometry and Logic, A First Introduction to Topos Theory, 1992; editor: Bull. Am. Math. Soc., 1943-46, mng. editor, 1946-47; editor: Trans. Am. Math. Soc., 1949-54; chmn. editorial com., editor Carus Math. Monographs, 1940-45; contbr. articles to Annals Math., other jours. Recipient Nat. Medal of Sci. Nat. Sci. Found., 1989; John Simon Guggenheim fellow, 1947-48, 72-73. Mem. Am. Math. Soc. (coun. mem. 1939-41, v.p. 1946-47, pres. 1973-74, Leroy P. Steele prize 1986), Math. Assn. Am. (v.p. 1948-49, pres. 1950-52, Chauvenet prize for math. expn. 1941, Disting. Svc. award 1975, Proctor prize 1979), Nat. Acad. Sci. (coun. mem. 1958-61, 69-72, v.p. 1973-81, chmn. editorial bd. procs. 1960-68), Royal Danish Acad. Scis. (fgn. mem.), Am. Philos. Soc. (mem. council 1960-63, v.p. 1968-71), Akademie der Wissenschaften (Heidelberg), Royal Soc. Edinburgh, Assn. for Symbolic Logic (exec. com. 1945-47), Am. Acad. Arts and Sci. (coun. mem. 1981-85), Phi Beta Kappa, Sigma Xi. Congregationalist. Home: 5712 S Dorchester Ave Chicago IL 60637-1727

MAC LAREN, DAVID SERGEANT, manufacturing corporation executive, inventor; b. Cleve., Jan. 4, 1941; s. Albert Sergeant and Theadora Beidler (Potter) MacL.; children: Alison, Catherine, Carolyn. AB in Econs., Miami U., Oxford, Ohio, 1964. Chmn. bd., pres., Jet Inc., Cleve., 1967—; founder, chmn. bd., pres. Air Injector Corp., Cleve., 1966-78; founder, pres., chmn. bd. Fluid Equipment, Inc., Cleve., 1966-72; founder, chmn. bd., pres. T&M Co., Cleve., 1966-71, Alison Realty Co., Cleve., 1966—; chmn. bd., pres. Sergeant Realty, Inc., 1979-86; bd. dirs. Gilmore Industries, Cleve., 1975-77, MWL Systems, L.A., 1979-85; mem. tech. com. Nat. Sanitation Found., Ann Arbor, Mich., 1967-90. Patentee in field. Mem. Rep. State Cen. Com., 1968-72; bd. dirs. Cleve. State U. Found., 1986-90. Served with arty. AUS, 1964-66. Fellow Royal Soc. Health (London); mem. Nat. Environ. Health Assn., Am. Pub. Health Assn., Nat. Water Pollution Control Fedn., Cen. Taekwondo Assn. (2d Dan), Jiu-Jitsu/Karati Black Belt Fedn. (black belt instr.), Mercedes Benz Club N.Am. (pres. 1968), H.B. Leadership Soc. (sch. headmaster soc., devel. com. 1976-78), SAR, Soc. Mayflower Descendants, Delta Kappa Epsilon (nat. bd. dirs. 1974-86, dir. Kappa chpt. 1969—), Mentor Harbor Yachting Club, The Country Club, Cotillion Soc., Union League Club (N.Y.C.), Yale Club (N.Y.C.), Deke Club (N.Y.C.), N.Y. Acad. Scis. Home: West Hill Dr Gates Mills OH 44040 Office: Jet Inc 750 Alpha Dr Cleveland OH 44143-2125

MACLAUGHLIN, HARRY HUNTER, federal judge; b. Breckenridge, Minn., Aug. 9, 1927; s. Harry Hunter and Grace (Swank) MacL.; m. Mary Jean Shaffer, June 25, 1958; children: David, Douglas. BBA with distinction, U. Minn., 1949, JD, 1956. Bar: Minn. 1956. Law clk. to justice Minn. Supreme Ct.; ptnr. MacLaughlin & Mondale, MacLaughlin & Harstad, Mpls., 1956-72; assoc. justice Minn. Supreme Ct., 1972-77; U.S. sr. dist. judge Dist. of Minn., Mpls., 1977—; part-time instr. William Mitchell Coll. Law, St. Paul, 1958-63; lectr. U. Minn. Law Sch., 1973-86; mem. 8th Cir. Jud. Council, 1981-83. Bd. editors: Minn. Law Rev, 1954-55. Mem. Mpls. Charter Commn., 1967-72, Minn. State Coll. Bd., 1971-72, Minn. Jud. Council, 1972; mem. nat. adv. council Small Bus. Adminstrn., 1967-69. Served with USNR, 1945-46. Recipient U. Minn. Outstanding Achievement award, 1995. Mem. ABA, Minn. Bar Assn., Hennepin County Bar Assn., Beta Gamma Sigma, Phi Delta Phi. Congregational. Office: US Dist Ct 684 US Courthouse 110 S 4th St Minneapolis MN 55401-2221

MACLEAN, HUGH CAMERON, bridge professional, international bridge master; b. Mpls., Feb. 24, 1938; s. Hugh Cameron and Clare Amelia (McClelland) MacL.; m. Mary Anne Nelson, May 22, 1991. Represented U.S. in Open Pair Olympiad, Las Palmas, 1974. Nat. awards include 2d pl. Advanced Sr. Masters, NAC, 1962, 1st pl. Life Master Mens Pairs, 1970, 1st pl. Men's Team, 1974, 2d pl. Open Pairs, 1974, 2d pl. Blue Ribbon Pairs, 1975, 2d pl. Vanderbilt, 1977, 1st pl. Golden Cup Masters Pairs, 1978; regional awards include Mid. Am.-Can. Teams, 1962, 64, 65, Mens, 1963, Mixed Pairs, 1965, Masters, 1966, Gopher Mens Pairs, 1966, 71, Gopher Knockouts, 1967, 71, Can. Prairie Masters, 1970, Champagne Mens Pairs, 1970, Pheasant Knockouts, 1970, 72, 75, Tri Unit Mixed Pairs, 1971, Can. Prairie Mens, 1972, Can. Prairie Knockouts, 1972, Iowa Knockouts, 1972, Gopher Master Pairs, 1973, Iowa Mens Pairs, 1973, Tri Unit Knockouts, 1974, Can. Prairie Knockouts, 1975, Can. Prairie Open, 1975, Can. Prairie Masters, 1975, Pheasant Mens Pairs, 1975, Iowa Masters, 1975, Summer Open Teams, 1975, Dist. 15 Open Teams, 1975, Mo. Valley Knockouts, 1975, Thunderbay Knockouts, 1975, Thunderbay Swiss Teams, 1975, Thunderbay Masters Pairs, 1975, Cambrian Shield Open Teams, 1976, Can. Prairie Knockouts, 1976, Can. Prairie Open Pairs, 1976, Can. Prairie Mens Swiss Teams, 1976, Pitts. Open Teams, 1976, Pitts. Knockouts, 1976, Great Lakes Masters, 1976, Motor City Masters, 1976, So. Calif. Knockouts, 1976, Gopher Swiss Teams, 1976, Iowa Open Teams, 1976, Dist. 8 Open Pairs, 1977, Dist. 8 Masters Pairs, 1977, Tri Unit Mens Swiss Teams, 1977, Intermountain Open Pairs, 1977, Pacific N.W. Knockouts, 1977, Polar Knockouts, 1977, Bellville Masters Pairs, 1977, Bellville Open Pairs, 1977, Puget Sound Knockouts, 1977, Dist. 20 Knockouts, 1977, Cambrian Shields Knockouts, 1977, 83, Ctrl. States Winter Open Teams, 1977, Ctrl. States Men's Swiss Teams, 1978, Mpls. Knockouts, 1978, Champagne Open Pairs, 1978, 79, Dist. 14 Knockouts, 1983, Cambrian Shield Open Teams, 1983, Madison Flight A Swiss Tams, 1983, Des Moines Knockouts, 1983, Canadian Prairie Open Pairs, 1984, Dist. Grand Nat. Teams, 1986, 87, 88, Canadian Prairie Men's, 1986, Ctrl. States Open Pairs, 1987, Gopher Masters Pairs, 1988, 89, Fargo Swiss Tams, 1990, Winnipeg Flighted Open, 1992, Winnipeg Flighted Team, 1992, Omaha Regional KO, 1993, Gopher Flighted KO, 1993, Green Bay Regional KO, 1993, Cedar Rapids Regional KO, 1994. Home: 9200 Poplar Bridge Rd Bloomington MN 55347-1841

MACLENNAN, JOHN DUNCAN, state official; b. Boston, June 10, 1943; s. John T. and Clara Isabell (MacKenzie) M.; m. Bette B. Krombholz, Dec. 19, 1970; children: David Andrew, Maureen Renee. BA, Boston U., 1965; MA, Roosevelt U., Chgo., 1973; D in Pub. Adminstrn., Nova Southeastern U., 1983. Asst. commr. Chgo. Dept. Planning, 1989-92; assoc. dir. edn. Internat. Assn. Assessing Officers, 1993-96; state dir. bus. tech. programs Ill. Dept. Commerce and Cmty. Affairs, 1996—; faculty Roosevelt U., Chgo., 1992. Author: (play) Ft. Dearborn, 1989. Mem. Cmty. Devel. Adv. Bd., Chgo., 1988.Capt. USAF, 1965-69. Mem. Am. Soc. for Pub. Adminstrn. (bd. dirs. Chgo. chpt. 1988-95). Home: 7305 A N Campbell Ave Chicago IL 60645 Office: DCCA Office Bus Technology 100 W Randolph St Ste 3-400 Chicago IL 60601

MACON, IRENE ELIZABETH, interior designer, consultant; b. East St. Louis, Ill., May 11, 1935; d. David and Thelma (Eastlen) Dunn; m. Robert Teco Macon, Feb. 12, 1954; children: Leland Sean, Walter Edwin, Gary Keith, Jill Renee Macon Martin, Robin Jeffrey, Lamont. Student Forest Park Coll., Washington U., St. Louis, 1970, Bailey Tech. Coll., 1975, Lindenwood Coll., 1981. Office mgr. Cardinal Glennon Hosp., St. Louis, 1965-72; interior designer J.C. Penney Co., Jennings, Mo., 1972-73; entrepreneur Irene Designs Unltd., St. Louis, 1974—; vol. liaison Pub. Sch. System, St. Louis, 1980-82; cons. in field. Inventor venetian blinds for autos, 1981, T-blouse and diaper wrap, 1986; cons., bus. mgr. Anything and Everything Store, St. Louis; Author 26th Word newsletter, 1986, (songs) My God's Child Teach Free Will, God is Hiring Now, 1993. Committeewoman Republican party, St. Louis, 1984; vice chair 4th Senatorial Dist. of Mo., 1984, vol. St. Louis Assn. Community Orgns., 1983; instr. first aid Bi-State chpt. ARC, St. Louis, 1984, mem. speakers bur., 1991; cubmaster pack #80 Keystone dist. Boy Scouts Am.; block capt. Operation Brightside, St. Louis, 1984; co-chair status and role of women Union Meml. United Meth. Ch., 1986—, program resource sec., 1990—; trustee Wofit Found., 1989; spokesperson Minority Affairs Initiative Program Am. Assn. Retired Persons, 1991; sec. to block Fedn. Block Units St. Louis Urban League, 1994; mem. Notary Pub. Commn., 1994—; Rep. election judge 26.8 pct Ward, 1994; pub. speaker, story teller prayer breakfast Grace Chapel Ministries, 1994; gospel radio program host Sta. KSTL Radio; transl. bible stories Old Testament and New Testament, It's Gospel Time; volunteer Northside Preservation Commission 1996; speaker at Black Alcoholic/Drug Svc. Info. Center, 1996. Composer religious music. Named One of Top Ladies of Distinction St. Louis, 1983. Mem. NAACP, Am. Soc. Interior Designers (assoc.), Nat. Mus. Women in the Arts (charter), Nat. Stroke Assn., Internat. Platform Assn., Nat. Coun. Negro Women (1st v.p. 1984), Invention Assn. of St. Louis (subcom. head 1985), Coalition of 100 Black Women, St. Louis Assn. Fashion Designers, Pres. Club. Methodist. Achievements include invention of Irene's Autoshade, an accordian type of pleated material designed to adhere to automobile windows for the purpose of protecting it from the sun. Avocations: reading, designing personal wardrobe, modeling, horseback riding, boating. Home: PO Box 775641 Saint Louis MO 63112-5641

MADDEN, BARTLEY JOSEPH, economist; b. N.Y.C., Nov. 3, 1943; s. Bartley Joseph and Genevieve Helen (Ghehan) M.; m. Maricela Elizondo, 1995; children by previous marriage: Gregory, Jeffrey. BS in Mech. Engring., U. So. Calif., Los Angeles, 1965; MBA, U. Calif., Berkeley, 1970. V.p. Callard, Madden & Assocs., Chgo., 1970-83; sr. v.p. Harbor Capital Advisors, Chgo., 1983-92; ptnr. Holt Value Assocs., Chgo., 1993—. Author: Economics in Your Interest, 1984. With U.S. Army, 1966-68. Mem. Tau Beta Pi, Beta Gamma Sigma. Home: 216 Middaugh Rd Clarendon Hills IL 60514-1004 Office: Holt Value Assocs 300 S Riverside Plz Ste 1400N Chicago IL 60606-6615

MADDEN, CHERYL BETH, state legislator; b. Burke, S.D., Nov. 15, 1948; d. Herman and Ida Denker; m. Michael K. Madden, 1977; children: Pamela, Jessica, Rachel.; Grad. high sch. Mem. S.D. Ho. of Reps., mem. edn., health and human svc. coms. Chaplain, chmn. Fedn. Rep. Women. *

MADDEN, JAMES DESMOND, forensic engineer; b. Jersey City, Mar. 1, 1940; s. Louis A. and Ann (Desmond) M. BSChemE, U. S.C., 1963, ME, 1966. Lic. profl. engr., Ohio; cert. diplomate forensic engr. Process engr. Monsanto Co., Alvin, Tex., 1966-67; process and project engr. Union Carbide Corp., Houston, 1967-70; systems engr. M.W. Kellogg Co., Houston, 1970-73, prin. systems engr., 1974-77; sr. process engr. Litwin Co., Houston, 1973-74; sr. project engr. Davy Powergas, Houston, 1977-78, supervising project engr., 1978-79; mgr. equipment engring. DM Internat., Houston, 1979-80, project engring. mgr., 1980-83; owner, forensic engr. Madden Forensic Engring., Parma, Parma Heights and Brecksville, Ohio, 1983—. Pres. Houston Young Adult Rep. Club, 1970-73; chmn. Tex. Young Adult Rep. Clubs, 1973. NSF rsch. grantee, 1963; NASA fellow, 1963-65. Mem. ASTM, ASME, NSPE, Soc. Automotive Engrs., Nat. Fire Protection Assn., Am. Chem. Soc., Am. Inst. Chem. Engrs., Inst. Transp. Engrs., Transp. Rsch. Bd. (individual assoc.), Nat. Acad. Forensic Engrs., Sigma Xi, Sigma Pi Sigma, Tau Beta Pi, Omicron Delta Kappa. Office: 10175 Brecksville Rd Cleveland OH 44141-3205

MADDOX, LINDA GAY NELSON, freelance writer; b. Kansas City, Mo., Apr. 29, 1945; d. Roy Monroe and Mildred Arlene (Petersen) Nelson; m. Donald Lee Maddox, Jan. 30, 1965 (div. Apr. 1976); children: Guy Geoffrey, Margot Justine, Gregory Owain. BA summa cum laude, Duke U., 1970; MA, Northwestern U., 1993. Cert. h.s. tchr., French and English, Ill., Mo., Kans. Paralegal Shook, Hardy Bacon, Kansas City, Mo., 1977; estate analysis specialist Mutual Benefit Life, Kansas City, Mo., 1978-81; asst. mgr. mktg., advanced underwriter Capitol Bankers Life/Miller-Tarrolly Ins. Group, Milw., 1981-83; paralegal Azulay & Azulay, P.C., Chgo., 1983-86; tchr. Dist. 203 New Trier H.S., Winnetka, Ill., 1994; piano tchr., Kansas City, 1975-80; author tax outline on exec. ins. for presentation of paper at bus. ins. seminar Seattle Estate Planning Coun., 1981; freelance writer Mid-Mo. Bus. Jour., Columbia, 1996. Sunday sch. tchr., 1st Congl. Ch., Santa Barbara, Calif., 1973; vol. tchr's aide, El Rancho Elem., Goleta, Calif., 1973-74. Mem. MLA, AAUW, Nat. Coun. Tchrs. of English, Duke U. Alumni Assn., Northwestern U. Alumni Assn., Phi Beta Kappa, Kappa Delta Pi.

MADDY, COLEEN, quality assurance professional; b. Wilkinsburg, Pa., July 24, 1964; d. Jimmy Joe and Agnes (Prosser) M. BA in English Lit., U. N.Mex., 1987; MA in English lit., U. Iowa, 1989. Software tester Am. Coll. Testing, Iowa City, 1989-93; mgr. software quality assurance Breakthrough, Inc., Oakdale, Iowa, 1993—; adj. prof. Kirkwood C.C., 1992—. Bood rev. editor Iowa Woman, 1990-95; contbr. articles to ency. and mags. Mem. Phi Kappa Phi, Phi Beta Kappa. Roman Catholic.

MADER, WILLIAM STEVEN, systems analyst, operations specialist; b. Detroit, Nov. 3, 1943; s. William J. and Mary M. (Zielinski) M.; m. Martha Kasper, Aug. 2, 1980; children: Leeanne, Curtis Cooper, William A. Grad. high sch., Detroit. State cert. marine law enforcement officer, instr. for water safety, snowmobile safety, hunter safety. Programmer Chatham Supermarkets, Warren, Mich., 1972-74, program analyst, 1974-75, sr. analyst, 1975-80, bus. systems specialist, 1980-84, program mgr., 1984-85, acting dir. MIS, 1985-86; program analyst GARB-KO, Inc., Saginaw, Mich., 1986-87, ops. mgr., 1987-89, systems support mgr., 1989—; owner WSM Svcs., Omer, Mich., 1986—. Res. officer Frankenmuth (Mich.) Mounted Police, 1986-95; sr. vice commdr. Am. Legion Post 104, Standish, Mich., 1987-88, commdr., 1988-89, judge advocate, 1992-94; capt. Arenac County Sheriff Res., Standish, 1990—. With USN, 1961-64. Voted Officer of the Yr., Frankenmuth Mounted Police, 1992. Mem. Amvets (charter post 104). Roman Catholic. Home: 4030 Kocot Rd Omer MI 48749-9726 Office: GARB-KO Inc 3925 Fortune Blvd Saginaw MI 48603-2287

MADICH, BERNADINE MARIE HOFF, savings and loan executive; b. Duluth, Minn., Mar. 4, 1934; d. Palmer and Esther (Anderson) Hoff; m. Michael Madich, May 23, 1955 (div. 1986); children: Michael R.H., Tina B. Watts, Rory G. (dec.). Student, Inst. Fin. Edn., 1972, 73, 77-78, 83-84, 86-87, cert. real estate law, 1984. Teller St. Louis County Fed. Savs. and Loan, 1972-73, sec., ins. mortgage counselor, 1973-83, loan servicing specialist, 1983-86, asst. mgr. loan servicing dept., 1986—. Pack leader Boy Scouts Am., Duluth, 1964-68; leader Girl Scouts U.S., Duluth, 1972-74; chmn. Duluth Hall of Fame, 1983—; docent Glensheen U. Minn., 1979-85; vol. St. Luke's Hosp., Duluth, 1968-72; asst. treas. Port Cities Luncheon, Duluth, 1984-86, treas., 1987—, co-chair, 1989—, chmn., 1989-90; chairperson Duluth East High Sch. All-Sch. Reunion, 1986; active Lakeside Presbyn. Ch. Mem. Duluth Area Ins. Women (treas. 1977-79, v.p. 1979-80, pres. 1980-82, advisor 1991—), Duluth Bus. and Profl. Women (treas. 1976-88, 2d v.p. 1986, 1st v.p. 1987, pres. 1988—), Ambassadors of Duluth, Duluth C. of C. (Twin Ports Woman of Yr. 1995), Duluth Curling Club, Duluth Figure Skating Club, Altrusa Internat. Home: 6520 W Hunter Lake Rd Duluth MN 55803-9424 Office: St Louis Bank for Savs Fed Savs & Loan PO Box 115 Duluth MN 55801-0115

MADIGAN, JOHN WILLIAM, publishing executive; b. Chgo., June 7, 1937; s. Edward P. and Olive D. Madigan; m. Holly Williams, Nov. 24, 1962; children: Mark W., Griffith E., Melanie L. BBA, U. Mich., 1958, MBA, 1959. Fin. analyst Duff & Phelps, Chgo., 1960-62; audit mgr. Arthur Andersen & Co., Chgo., 1962-67; v.p. investment banking Paine, Webber, Jackson & Curtis, Chgo., 1967-69; v.p. corp. fin. Salomon Bros., Chgo., 1969-74; v.p., CFO, dir. Tribune Co., Chgo., 1975-81, exec. v.p., 1981-91, pub., 1990-94, pres., CEO, 1991-94, pres., COO, 1994-5, chmn., pres., CEO, 1996—, 1996—. Trustee Rush-Presbyn.-St. Luke's Med. Ctr., Mus. TV & Radio in N.Y., Northwestern U., Ill. Inst. Tech. Mem. Chicagoland C. of C. (bd. dirs.), Chgo. Coun. on Fgn. Rels. (bd. dirs.), Robert R. McCormick Tribune Found. (bd. dirs.), Newspaper Mgmt. Ctr. at Northwestern U. (exec. com.), Econ. Club Chgo., Comml. Club Chgo. Home: 1160 Laurel Ave Winnetka IL 60093-1820 Office: Tribune Co 435 N Michigan Ave Chicago IL 60611-4001

MADIGAN, MICHAEL JOSEPH, state legislator; b. Chgo., Apr. 19, 1942; m. Shirley Roumagoux; children: Lisa, Tiffany, Nicole, Andrew. Ed., U. Notre Dame, Loyola U., Chgo. Mem. Ill. Ho. of Reps., 1971—, majority leader, 1977-80, minority leader, 1981-82, house speaker, 1983-94, Dem. leader, 1995—; lawyer. Sec. to Alderman David W. Healey; hearing officer Ill. Commerce Commn.; del. 6th Ill. Constnl. Conv.; trustee Holy Cross Hosp.; ex officio mem. adv. com. to pres. Richard J. Daley Coll.; adv. com. Fernley Harris Sch. for Handicapped; committeeman 13th Ward Democratic Orgn. Mem. Council Fgn. Relations, City Club Chgo. Office: House Reps State Capital Bldg Springfield IL 62706

MADIGAN, ROBERT A., state legislator; b. Lincoln, Ill., Nov. 28, 1942; m. to Connie Madigan; two children. BS, Millikin U., 1966. Dist. 45 senator Ill. Senate, Springfield, 1987—; mem. agr. and conservation, labor and commerce, elem. and secondary edn., pensions and licensed activities, welfare and corrections, pub. health, welfare and corrections coms., Ill. Senate; mem. joint coms. on intergovernmental cooperation, regulation of professions and occupations, consumer banks, Ill. pension funds in Northern Ireland; bd. dirs. Comprehensive Health Ins. Plan, Geologic Map Task Force. Home: 618 N Chicago St Lincoln IL 62656-2131*

MADORE, JOYCE LOUISE, gerontology nurse; b. Madison, Kans., Dec. 15, 1936; d. Lionel Wiedmer and Mary Elizabeth (Piley) Murphy; m. Robert

Madore, Aug. 15, 1969; children: Carl, Clay. BS, Emporia State U., 1980; diploma, Newman Hosp., 1981. RN, Kans., Mo.; cert. gerontol. nurse, non profit adminstr., nursing home adminstr. Med. charge nurse St. Mary's Hosp., Emporia, Kans., 1971-72; dir. nursing Madison (Kans.) Manor, 1974-81, 82-83; staff nurse Newman Meml. Hosp., Emporia, 1981-82; dir. Daybreak Adult Day Svcs., dir. HELP program Springfield (Mo.) Area Coun. of Chs., 1983—; mem. Gov.'s Com. to Establish Rules and Regulations on Adult Day Care Patients State of Mo.; cons. U. Mo. Coop. Extension Svc. Program Guides on Adult Day Care. Contbr. video Understanding Aging Program; developer Home Guide for the Homebound, 1996. Named one of Outstanding Nurses in Mo. St. Louis U., 1989. Mem. NANA, AFE, Adult Day Care Assn. (past sec., exec. past v.p. 1989-91), Mo. Nurses Assn., Mo. Adult Day Care assn. (pres. 1991-95, Exec. award 1995), Mo. League of Nursing. Home: 171 Hilltop Oaks Ln Sparta MO 65753-8911

MADSEN, DOROTHY LOUISE (MEG MADSEN), writer; b. Rochester, N.Y.; d. Charles Robert and Louise Anna Agnes Meyer; BA, Mundelein Coll., Chgo., 1978; m. Frederick George Madsen, Feb. 17, 1945 (dec.). Pub. rels. rep. Rochester Telephone Corp., 1941-42; feature writer Rochester Democrat & Chronicle, 1939-41; exec. dir. LaPorte (Ind.) chpt. ARC, 1964; dir. adminstrv. svcs. Bank Mktg. Assn., Chgo., 1971-74; exec. dir. The Eleanor Women's Found., Chgo., 1974-84; founder Meg Madsen Assocs., Chgo., 1984-88; women's career counselor; founder, Clearinghouse Internat. Newsletter; founder Eleanor Women's Forum, Clearinghouse Internat., Eleanor Intern Program Coll. Students and Returning Women. Served to lt. col. WAC, 1942-47, 67-70. Decorated Legion of Merit, Meritorious Svc. award. Mem. Res. Officers Assn., Mundelein Alumnae Assn., Phi Sigma Tau (charter mem. Ill. Kappa chpt.). Home and Office: 1030 N State St Chicago IL 60610-2844 also: 3902 Joliet Rd La Porte IN 46350

MADSEN, GEORGE FRANK, lawyer; b. Sioux City, Iowa, Mar. 24, 1933; s. Frank O. and Agnes (Cuhel) M.; m. Magnhild Norstog, June 28, 1959; 1 child, Michelle Marie. BA, St. Olaf Coll., 1954; LLB, Harvard U., 1959. Bar: Ohio 1960, Iowa 1961, U.S. Dist. Ct. (no. and so. dists.) Iowa, U.S. Ct. Appeals (8th cir.), U.S. Supreme Ct. 1991. Trainee Cargill, Inc., Mpls., 1954; assoc. Durfey, Martin, Browne & Hull, Springfield, Ohio, 1959-61; assoc., then ptnr. Shull, Marshall & Marks, Sioux City, 1961-85; ptnr. Marks & Madsen, Sioux City, 1985—. Author, editor: Iowa Title Opinions and Standards, 1978; contbg. author: The American Law of Real Property, 1991. Sec., bd.dirs. Sioux City Boys Club, 1969-76; mem. Sioux City Zoning Bd. Adjustment, 1963-65; past pres. Morningside Luth Ch., Sioux City; active Iowa Mo. River Preservation and Land Use Authority, 1992—. Lt. USAF, 1954-56. Fellow Iowa State Bar Found.; mem. ABA, Iowa Bar Assn., Woodbury County Bar Assn., St. Olaf Coll. Alumni Assn. (past pres. Siouxland chpt.), Nat. Wildlife Assn., Mont. Wildlife Assn., Rocky Mountain Elk Found., Pheasants Forever, Phi Beta Kappa (past pres. Siouxland chpt.), Rotary Internat. Office: 700 4th St Ste 303 PO Box 3226 Sioux City IA 51102-3226

MADSEN, MICHAEL J., mechanical engineer; b. Mpls., Dec. 30, 1957. BS in Mech. Engrng., U. Minn., 1982. Mfrs. rep. Pall Inc., Glen Cove, N.Y., 1984-87, Satorius Inc., East Granby, Conn., 1987-88, Miessner Inc., Calif., 1989-90; sr. filtration devel. engr. Osmonics, Hopkins, Minn., 1990—. Mem. ASTM, Am. Filtration Soc. Office: Osmonics 5951 Clearwater Dr Hopkins MN 55343-8990

MADSEN, PHILIP DANA, development consultant; b. Frederic, Wis., July 9, 1954; s. Lester Leroy and Coral Barbara (Barnish) M.; m. Cynthia Ann Frink, Aug. 28, 1987 (div. Mar. 1991); m. Linda Marie Gunderson, Sept. 3, 1977 (div. 1984). BA cum laude, Augsburg Coll., Mpls., 1979; diploma, Dunwoody Inst., Mpls., 1981; postgrad., Luther Sem., St. Paul, 1981-82; disting. mil. grad., U.S. Army Officer Candidate, Sch., 1984. CFP. Automotive technician Dynotech, Mpls., 1982-83; maintenance technician Midland Bldg. Svcs., Mpls., 1983-84; sales mgr. Home Rental Systems, Mpls., 1985; registered rep. 1st Investors Corp., Edina, Minn., 1984-86, LPL Fin. Svcs., Edina, 1986-91; propr. Integrity Fin. Svcs., Edina, 1991-95; proprietor Minn. Mainstream, 1996—. Contbr. articles to trade jours. and newspapers. Active Richfield (Minn.) Cmty. Edn. Adv. Coun., 1992-94; dir. ops. Minn. for Perot, Richfield, 1992; founder Independence Party of Minn., 1992, chmn., 1992-93, state sec., 1995—; chmn. rules com. Nat. Patriot Party, 1995—. With U.S. Army, 1972-75, 1st lt. Minn. Army N.G., 1984-90. Mem. Pi Gamma Mu. Lutheran. Home: 7117 Rice Lake Ln Lino Lakes MN 55014 Office: Minn Mainstream 7117 Rice Lake Ln 3601 Minnesota Dr Ste 880 Lino Lakes MN 55014

MADSON, PAULETTE KAY, home economics educator; b. Spencer, Iowa, Mar. 26, 1957; d. Harry Martin and Marjorie Elizabeth Nielsen; m. Larry Lee Madson, Aug. 3, 1990. BS, Iowa State U., 1979. Family and consumer sci. tchr. Walnut (Iowa) Community Sch., 1979—. Treas. Patterns for Progress, Des Moines, 1986-89; cons. Shelby County Econ. Devel. Coun., Harlan, Iowa, 1988; active Rep. Women, Walnut, 1989—, Questers, 1990—, Danish Immigrant Mus., 1987—, FHA Hero-Master Advisor, 1993; mem. planning com. for Home Econs. Educators Conf., 1993, 94; fair judge 4-H, 1981—, state fair judge, 1991—; county voting del. Rep. Ctrl. Com., 1994. Recipient 4-H Alumni award Shelby County, 1993, Outstanding H.S. Tchr., Optimists, 1995. Mem. ASCD, FHA (hon.), Am. Vocat. Assn., Family and Consumer Sci. Edn. Assn., Iowa State U. Alumni Assn., Coll. Family and Consumer Scis. Alumni Assn., Delta Kappa Gamma. Republican. Lutheran. Home: 1832 400th St Walnut IA 51577-6002

MAERSCH, NANCY KAY, laboratory manager; b. Norfolk, Nebr., May 11, 1942; d. Ambrose Pryor and Angela Gertrude (Goergen) Jordan; m. Frank C. Maersch, May 11, 1968; 1 child, Todd F. BS in Med. Tech., Mt. Marty Coll., 1963; MA in Health Care Adminstrn., Cen. Mich. U., 1981. Diplomate Lab. Medicine; clin. lab. scientist; specialist in hematology. Med. technologist Madison (Wis.) Gen. Hosp. Lab., 1963-64, hematology sect. head, 1964-72, hematology specialist, 1973-79, hematology sect. head, 1979-80, lab. customer svc. rep., 1980-82, mgr. adminstrv. svc. and mktg., 1982-85; mgr. mobile diagnostics Meriter Gen. Med. Labs., Madison, 1985-87, mgr. client svcs., 1987-89, mgr. lab. ops., 1990—; bd. dirs. Dane County Cytology Ctr., Madison. Chair Edgefest event Edgewood H.S. Aux., 1987-92; mem. Bus. Forum, Madison, 1989—; vol. Ronald McDonald House; bd. dirs. parents assn. Marquette U., 1993—. Mem. Am. Soc. Clin. Lab. Sci., Wis. Soc. Clin. Lab. Sci. (sec. 1967-70, 76-80), Clin. Lab. Mgmt. Assn., Wis. chpt. Clin. Lab. Mgmt. Assn. (bd. dirs., pres.-elect 1995-96), Madison Area Lab. Suprs., Madison Civics Club. Roman Catholic. Home: 3105 Nottingham Way Madison WI 53713-3457 Office: Gen Med Labs 36 S Brooks St Madison WI 53715-1304

MAFFEI, ROCCO JOHN, lawyer; b. Portland, Maine, Nov. 23, 1949; s. Rocco and Grace Marie (Bartlett) M; m. Susan Marie Farrell, June 23, 1973; children: Rocco Francis, Christopher Matthew. BA in History, Trinity Coll., 1972; JD, U. Maine, 1975. Bar: Maine 1975, Mass. 1975, U.S. Dist. Ct. Maine 1975, Ohio 1977, U.S. Ct. Claim 1980, U.S. Supreme Ct. 1980, Minn. 1981, U.S. Dist. Ct. Minn. 1981. Ptnr. Briggs & Morgan Law Firm, St. Paul, 1980-83, Hart & Bruner Law Firm, Mpls., 1983-85; v.p. gen. counsel Computing Devices Internat., a Ceridian Co., Bloomington, Minn., 1985—; adj. prof. law William Mitchell Sch. Law, St. Paul, 1982—, Air Force Inst. Tech., 1983—. Contbr. articles to profl. jours. Served to capt. USAF, 1975-80, lt. col. Res. Fellow Nat. Contract Mgmt. Assn. (pres. Twin Cities chpt. 1985-86, regional v.p. 1990-91, Charles J. Delaney award 1986, bd. dirs.); mem. ABA (chmn. com. pub. contract law sect. 1984-88, 93—), Fed. Bar Assn., Minn. Bar Assn., Huber Hts. Jaycees (Jaycee of Yr. 1978). Republican. Roman Catholic. Home: 1161 Tiffany Cir N Saint Paul MN 55123-1871 Office: Computing Devices Internat M/S BLCSID 8800 Queen Ave S Bloomington MN 55431-1908

MAGAFAS, DIANIA LEE, geriatrics nurse consultant, administrator; b. Chgo., Oct. 17, 1963; d. Alec and Jacqueline Magafas; 1 child, Jason. BS, St. Xavier Coll., Chgo., 1986, MSN, 1991. Staff nurse Ingalls Meml. Hosp., Harvey, Ill., 1986-88; asst. DON Wedgewood Nursing Pavilion, Chgo., 1988-90; nursing cons. long term care Dynamics Healthcare Cons., Inc., Skokie, Ill., 1990—. Mem. Sigma Theta Tau.

MAGEE, THOMAS HENRY, medical doctor, medical educator; b. Newport, R.I., Nov. 26, 1958; s. Francis Robert and Anne Louise (Moriarty) M; m. Christina Marie Lapolla, June 7, 1987. BA, Wesleyan U., 1977-81; MD, N.Y. Med. Coll., 1982-86. Diplomate Am. Bd. Radiology. Staff radiologist Bethesda (Md.) Naval Hosp., 1991-94; asst. prof. medicine Uniformed Svcs. Sch. of Med., Bethesda, 1991-94, Kansas U. Sch. of Med., Kansas City, 1994—; staff radiologist Menorah Med. Park, Overland Park, Kans., 1994—. Contbr. articles to profl. jours. including Radiology, Jour. of Computer Assisted Tomography, also others. Lt. comdr. USNR, 1991-94. Recipient Jonas N. Muller award N.Y. Med. Coll., 1986. Mem. Am. Roentegen Ray Soc., Radiologic Soc. of N. Am. (cert. of merit 1990). Home: 4304 W 126th Terrace Leawood KS 66209 Office: Menorah Med Park 5721 W 119th St Leawood KS 66209

MAGGIO, MICHAEL JOHN, artistic director; b. Chgo., July 3, 1951; s. Carlo and Genevieve (Sparacino) M.; m. Janice St. John, Sept. 7, 1974 (div. June 1977); m. Julie Carol Jackson, Mar. 29, 1980 (div. Dec. 1994); 1 child, Ben. BA, U. Ariz., 1973, MA, 1974. Artistic dir. Woodstock (Ill.) Music Theatre Festival, 1980-82, Northlight Theatre, Evanston, Ill., 1983-87; assoc. artistic dir. Goodman Theatre, Chgo., 1987—; artistic advisor Columbia Coll., Chgo., 1987—. Directed Another Midsummer Night, Brutality of Fact, Black Snow, Wings, Shakespeare's A Midsummer Night's Dream, Romeo and Juliet, Uncle Vanya, 1989-90, A Flea In Her Ear, A Christmas Carol, Sunday In The Park With George, Cyrano De Bergerac, The Front Page, The Dining Room; artistic dir. Northlight Theatre premieres of Dealing, City On The Make, Heart of A Dog, (Am. premiere) Ballerina, (world premiere) Sondheim Suite; dir. The Real Thing, West Memphis Mojo, Highest Standard of Living, Endgame, The Winter's Tale, Travesties, Tartuffe, Spokesong, Ladies In Waiting; dir. prodn. of Titus Andronicus for N.Y. Shakespeare Festival; prodns. include McCarter Theatre, Guthrie Theater in Mpls., The Cleve. Playhouse, Ariz. Theatre Co., Actors Theatre of Louisville, Seattle Repertory Co. chmn. Michael Merritt Award and Endowment Fund, Columbia Coll, Chgo. Recipient Joseph Jefferson "Jeff" Citation 1975-76. 78, 93-94, Father of Yr. award, Chgo. Father's Day Com., 1986, Excellence in Arts award De Paul U. Theatre Sch., 1993, Obie award, 1993,. Office: Goodman Theatre 200 S Columbus Dr Chicago IL 60603-6402

MAGLIOCCA, LARRY ANTHONY, education educator; b. New Castle, Pa., Sept. 3, 1943; s. Anthony Norman Magliocca and Madeline Rose Ross; m. Judie Alene Kerr, Sept. 1, 1964 (div.); children: Jeannine Marie, Seth Bryan; m. Phyllis Marion Gentry, May 9, 1981; 1 child, Nicholas Rossi. BSEd, Slippery Rock State Coll., 1967; MEd, U. Pitts., 1970; PhD, Ohio State U., 1978. Dir. Youth Devel. Ctr. of Pa., New Castle, 1967-70; state cons. S.D. Dept. Pub. Inst., Pierre, S.D., 1970-73; coord. Balt. City Pub. Schs., 1973-76; exec. dir. Ctr. for Spl. Needs Population, Columbus, Ohio, 1979-92; assoc. prof. Ohio State U., Columbus, 1988—; vis. lectr. Melbourne (Australia) State Coll., 1978-79; adj. faculty Johns Hopkins U., Balt., 1974-76; blue ribbon task force, Chgo. City Pub. Schs., 1985. Author three books in spl. edn. field, 1978-92; contbr. articles to profl. jours.; editor: The Directive Teacher jour., 1976-84; author/designer instructional materials in math. problem solving, 1992. Founder Young Scientists Club, Westerville, Ohio, 1990-92; rsch. fellow Interant. Sys. Inst., 1994-96. Mem. Soc. for Gen. Systems Rsch., Am. Assn. for Artificial Intelligence, Coun. for Exceptional Children. Democrat. Unitarian-Universalist. Office: Ctr Spl Needs Populations 700 Ackerman Rd Ste 440 Columbus OH 43202-1559

MAGNAGHI, RUSSELL MARIO, education educator; b. San Francisco, Oct. 12, 1943; s. Mario Vincent and Grace Helen (Mendiara) M.; m. Caryl Sheridan, Nov. 23, 1973 (div. 1979); 1 child, Emily; m. Diane Kordich, Feb. 14, 1993. BA, U. San Francisco, 1965; MA, St. Louis U., 1967, PhD, 1970. Prof. No. Mich. U., Marquette, 1969—, univ. historian, 1994—; mem. Mich. Quincentervary Jubilee Commn., Lansing, 1990-92; bd. trustees Hist. Soc. Mich., 1996-97. Author: Miners, Merchants, 1987, Indians of Upper Peninsula, 1984, Way It Happened, 1982; editor: Hasinai, 1987. Chmn. Heritage Com., Marquette, Mich., 1992. Recipient Helen Longyear Paul award Marquette County Hist. Soc., Marquette, 1988; Peter White Scholar, No. Mich. U., 1989; NEH grantee Mich., 1982. Mem. Am. Hist. Assn., Orgn. Am. Hist., Western Hist. Assn. Democrat. Roman Catholic. Office: No Mich U Dept History 1401 Presoue Isle Ave Marquette MI 49855-5352

MAGSIG, JUDITH ANNE, early childhood education educator; b. Saginaw, Mich., Nov. 9, 1939; d. Harold Howard and Catherine Louise (Barstow) Gay; m. George Arthur Magsig, June 22, 1963; children: Amy Catherine, Karl Joseph. BA, Alma Coll., 1961. Cert. tchr., early childhood tchr., Mich. 1st grade tchr. Gaylord (Mich.) Schs., 1961-64, spl. edn. tchr., 1965-67, kindergarten tchr., 1968—. instr. Suzuki violin method; second violinist Traverse (Mich.) Symphony Orch., 1985-92. Mem. ASCD, NEA, Mich. Edn. Assn., Gaylord Edn. Assn., Assn. for the Edn. of Young Children, Assn. for Childhood Edn. Internat., Suzuki Assn. Am., Am. String Tchrs. Assn., Order Eastern Star, Voyageurs, Alpha Delta Kappa (pres. Beta Rho chpt. 1980-82, 84-86). Methodist. Home: 2130 Evergreen Dr Gaylord MI 49735 Office: S Maple Multi Age Program 590 W Fifth St Gaylord MI 49735

MAGUIRE, DANIEL CHARLES, ethics educator; b. Apr. 4, 1931. STD, Gregorian U., Rome, 1969. Extraordinary prof. St. Mary's Sem. and Univ., 1964-66; interim asst. prof. Cath. U., 1966-67, from asst. prof. to assoc. prof., 1967-71; assoc. prof. Marquette U., Milw., 1971-78, prof., 1978—; part-time instr. Villanova U., 1960-64; vis. John A. O'Brien prof. U. Notre Dame, 1983-84; vis. prof. Trinity Coll., Dublin, Ireland, 1985. Author: Moral Absoluteness and the Magisterium, 1970, Death by Choice, 1973, 2d edit., 1984, The Moral Choice, 1978, paperback edit., 1979 (Best Book of Yr. 1979, Best Scholarly Book of Yr. 1979), A New American Justice: Ending the White Male Monopolies, 1980, paperback edit. titled A New American Justice: A Moral Proposal for the Reconciliation of Personal Freedom and Social Justice, 1981, 2d edit. titled A Case for Affirmative Action, 1992, The New Subversives: Anti-Americanism of the Religious Right, 1982, The Moral Revolution, 1986, On Moral Grounds: The Art/Science of Ethics, 1991, The Moral Core of Judaism and Christianity, 1993; editl. cons., mem. editl. bd.: Eglise et Theologie, 1981—; contbr. articles to profl. jours. including Listening: Jour. of Religion and Culture, Bull. of Acad. for Health Svcs. Mktg., Christianity and Crisis, N.Y. Times, Conscience, Cath. Bill of Rights; TV appearances include David Susskind Show, 1981, 82, Donohue show, 1984, Dan Rather Pre-Election Spl., 1984. Named one of 40 Male Heroes of Past Decade, Men Who Took a Chance and Made a Difference, Ms. Mag., 1982, one of Civil Libertarians of Yr., Wis. Civil Liberties Union, 1984, one of Most Interesting People in Milw., Milw. Mag., 1984; recipient Torch Bearer award Cream City Bus. Assn., Milw., 1983, award for prophetic leadership in lesbian/gay ministry Consultation on Homosexuality, Social Justice and Roman Catholic Theology, San Francisco, 1985. Mem. Soc. Christian Ethics (bd. dirs., v.p., pres.), Cath. Theol. Soc. Am., Coll. Theology Soc. (bd. dirs.), Moral Alternatives (co-founder), Soc. Christian Ethics (pres. 1981), Religious Consultation on Population, Reproductive Health and Ethics (pres.). Office: Marquette U Dept Theology Milwaukee WI 53233

MAGUIRE, DAVE, real estate manager; b. Macomb, Ill., Dec. 11, 1949; s. Davis and Martha Mae (Jennings) M. BA, So. Ill. U., 1973. Mgr. Chapman's Bookstore, Inc., Macomb, 1973-78; real estate mgr. Westbrook Village, Macomb, 1978—. Pres. McDonough County Bd. Health, Macomb, 1985—; chmn. City/County Transit Commn., Macomb, 1982-89; alderman Macomb City Coun., 1979-89; precinct committeeman McDonough County Rep. Cen. Com., Macomb, 1977-94; trustee Spoon River Coll., Canton, Ill., 1993—, chmn. bd. dirs. 1995—. Mem. Ill. C.C. Trustees Assn. (bd. reps. 1993—, vice chmn. state rels. com. 1995—), Macomb Area Indsl. Devel. Corp. (exec. com. 1996—), Macomb Area C. of C. (bd. dirs. 1989—, pres.), Assn. Fraternity Advisors, Ill. DeMolay (Legion of Honor 1978, Cross of Honor 1980), Elks, Masons, Delta Upsilon (internat. sec. 1988-91, Meritorious Svc. award 1981). Methodist. Home: 554 W Murray St Macomb IL 61455-1316 Office: Westbrook Village 900 Linden Ln Macomb IL 61455-1074

MAHAFFEY, JOHN CHRISTOPHER, association executive; b. Jefferson City, Mo., July 20, 1953; s. Fred Turner and Betty Cord (Woodfill) M.; m. Leslie Anne DenUyl Mahaffey, Oct. 24, 1987; children: Michael, Katherine. BA, Western Ill. U., Macomb, 1975. Legis. aide Congressman Harold R. Collier, Washington, 1972-73; legis. asst. Nat. Assn. Retail Druggists, Washington, 1975-76; dir. Commn. and Meetings Nat. Assn. Bds. of Pharmacy, Chgo., 1976-80; exec. dir. Chgo. Soc. Assn. Execs., Chgo., 1980—; mem. assn. com. of 100, U.S. C. of C., 1995—. Commr. City of Park Ridge Econ. Devel. Commn., Park Ridge, Ill., 1990-94, 96—; mem. exec. com. Chgo. Conv. and Tourism Bur., 1993—. Recipient Disting. Alumni award Western Ill. U., Macomb, 1993. Fellow Am. Soc. Assn. Execs. (mem. cert. commn. 1989-91, Key award 1994); mem. The Tower Club. Presbyterian. Office: Chicago Soc Assn Execs 20 N Wacker Dr Ste 3000 Chicago IL 60606

MAHAR, SHANNON NEAL, sales executive; b. Detroit, Jan. 25, 1945; s. Walter Vincent and Jean Jaculine (Shusta) M.; children: Sean, Adam, Jaime. BA, Wayne State U., 1963, MA, 1971, postgrad. Pres. Southeastern Mich. Svcs., Inc., Jackson. Office: Southeastern Mich Svcs Inc 1514 4th St Jackson MI 49203-4071

MAHAR, WILLIAM F., JR., state legislator; b. Chicago Heights, Ill., Feb. 13, 1947; m. Elizabeth Mahar; two children. BA, So. Ill. U.; MS, Purdue U. Trustee Village of Homewood, Ill., 1979-85; Dist. 19 senator Ill. Senate, Springfield, 1985—; mem. election and reapportionment, local govt., appropriations I, energy and environment, econ. devel., fin. and credit regulations, pub. health, welfare and corrections, and state govt. orgn. and adminstrn. coms., Ill. Senate. Home: 8612 Wheeler Dr Orland Park IL 60462-4704 also: 17950 Halsted St Homewood IL 60430-2014 Office: State Senate State Capital Springfield IL 62706*

MAHER, DAVID WILLARD, lawyer; b. Aug. 14, 1934, Chgo.; s. Chauncey Carter and Martha (Peppers) M.; BA Harvard, 1955, LLB, 1959; m. Jill Waid Armagnac, Dec. 20, 1954; children: Philip Armagnac, Julia Armagnac. Bar: N.Y. 1960, Ill. 1961; pvt. practice Boston, N.Y.C., 1958-60; assoc. Kirkland & Ellis, and predecessor firm, 1960-65, ptnr. 1966-78; ptnr. Reuben & Proctor, 1978-86, Isham, Lincoln and Beale, 1986-88, Sonnenschein, Nath & Rosenthal, 1988—; gen. counsel BBB Chgo. and No. Ill.; lectr. DePaul U. Sch. Law, 1973-79, Law Sch. of Loyola U., Chgo., 1980-84. Mem. vis. com. to the Div. Sch., U. Chgo., 1986—. Served to 2d lt. USAF, 1955-56. Fellow Am. Bar Found. (lifetime); mem. ABA, Am. Law Inst., Ill. Bar Assn., Chgo. Bar Assn., Bull Valley Hunt Club, Chgo. Lit. Club, Union League Club, Tavern, Club. Roman Catholic. Home: 311 W Belden Ave Chicago IL 60614-3817 Office: Sonnenschein Nath & Rosenthal 233 S Wacker Dr Ste 8000 Chicago IL 60606-6404

MAHER, FRANK ALOYSIUS, research and development executive, psychologist; b. Jamaica, N.Y., Mar. 31, 1941; s. Frank A. and Gertrude F. (Peterson) M.; m. Barbara A. Eggers, Aug. 14, 1965 (div. 1978); children: B. Kelly, F. Scott, Erin K.; m. Karen S. Adcock, June 28, 1980. BA, U. Dayton, 1966, MS, 1971. Lic. psychologist, Ohio. Research psychologist Ritchie Inc., Dayton, Ohio, 1965-68, Bunker Ramo, Dayton, 1968-70; lectr., research assoc. Wright State U., Dayton, 1970-71; research psychologist USAF, Wright Patterson AFB, Ohio, 1971-84; dir. Perceptronics, Inc., Dayton, 1984-87; rsch. and devel. exec. Unisys, Dayton, 1987-92, bus. devel. cons., 1992-94; v.p. Black Tech. Corp., Dayton, 1994—; counseling psychologist Eastway Mental Health Ctr., Dayton, 1974-75, Good Samaritan Mental Health Ctr., Dayton, 1979. Conbtg. author: Perceptions in Information Sciences; editor: Developmental Learning Handbook. Bd. dirs. Miami Valley Mental Health Assn., Dayton, 1974-77, Greene Mental Health Assn., Xenia, Ohio, 1977. Roman Catholic. Home: 7881 Stanley Mill Dr Dayton OH 45459-5152 Office: Black Tech Corp 4130 Linden Ave Ste 305 Dayton OH 45432

MAHER, TERRY MARINA, religious organization administrator; b. Phila., Oct. 13, 1955; d. Thomas Michael and Marion Teresa (Corbett) M. BA in History and Religious Studies, U. San Diego, 1977; M in Theol. Studies, Cath. Theol. U., Chgo., 1989. Dir. religious edn. Diocese of San Diego, 1977-80; dir. religious edn. Archdiocese of Cin., 1982-84, assoc. dir. youth ministry, 1984-87; pastoral assoc. Diocese of Toledo, 1989-95; state chancellor Internat. Educators for Peace Edn. Sec. social concerns bd. Met. Chs. United, Dayton; mem. justice com. Sisters of the Precious Blood; active tour to explore conditions in Nicaragua, New Orleans, 1983, 10-day tour of Guatemala, 1991; founder, v.p., bd. dirs. Care and Share Ctr. City of Sandusky, Ohio; Ohio state chancellor Internat. Educators for World Peace; v.p. Care and Share, Inc. of Erie County, 1993-95. Mem. Sanctuary, Pledge of Resistance, Internat. Assn. Educators for Peace (state chancellor). Democrat. Home: 72 Dorvid Rd Rochester NY 14617-2104 Office: Saints Peter & Paul Ch 510 Columbus Ave Sandusky OH 44870-2730

MAHLER, VINCENT A., political science educator; b. Chgo., Nov. 26, 1949; s. Albert A. and Irene A. (Yog) M.; m. Mary Duda, Sept. 10, 1972; children: Stephen, David, Katherine. BA, Loyola U., Chgo., 1971; MA, Loyola U., 1973; PhD, Columbia U., 1978. Asst. prof. Loyola U., Chgo., 1979-84, assoc. prof., 1984-90, prof., 1990—. Mem. Am. Polit. Sci. Assn., Internat. Studies Assn., European Cmty. Studies Assn., Midwest Polit. Sci. Assn. Democrat. Roman Catholic. Home: 1025 S Prospect Ave Park Ridge IL 60068-4728 Office: Loyola U Chgo 6525 N Sheridan Rd Chicago IL 60626

MAHNKE, KURT LUTHER, psychotherapist, clergyman; b. Milw., Feb. 18, 1945; s. Jonathan Henry and Lydia Ann (Pickron) M.; m. Dana Moore, Mar. 19, 1971; children: Rachel Lee, Timothy Kurt, Jonathan Roy. BA, Northwestern Coll., Watertown, Wis., 1967; MDiv, Wis. Luth. Sem., 1971; MA, No. Ariz. U., 1984. Cert. profl. counselor, marriage and family therapist, ind. clin. social worker. Pastor Redeemer/Grace Luth. Chs., Phoenix & Casa Grande, Ariz., 1971-75, St. Philips Luth. Ch., Milw., 1975-78, 1st Luth. Ch., Prescott, Ariz., 1978-82; counselor NAU Counseling/Testing Ctr., Flagstaff, Ariz., 1983-84, Wis. Luth. Child & Family Svc., Wausau, Wis., 1984-86; area adminstr. Wis. Luth. Child & Family Svc., Appleton, Wis., 1986-89; founder, psychotherapist Family Therapy & Anxiety Ctr., Menasha, Wis., 1989—; part-time min. St. Paul Luth. Ch., Appleton, 1993-94; presenter Nat. Police Week, Washington, 1995-96, 13th Nat. Conf. on Anxiety Disorders, Charleston, S,C., 1993; cons. editor Northwestern Pub. House, Milw., 1990—; adj. faculty Fox Valley Tech. Coll., Appleton, 1993—. Cons. editor Counseling at the Cross, 1990; contbr. articles to profl. publs. Cons. Wis. Evang. Luth. Synod, Milw., 1986—; cons. crisis counselor Fox Valley Luth. H.S., Appleton; crisis counselor Critical Incident Stress Debriefing Team, Fox Cities, 1991—; active Fox Cities Cmty. Counsel. Mem. ACA, Am. Mental Health Counselors Assn., Anxiety Disorders Assn. Am., (charter), Internat. Assn. Marriage and Family Counselors, Assn. Specialists in Group Work, Nat. Anxiety Found., Obsessive Compulsive Found., Wis. Outpatient Mental Health Facilities. Republican. Lutheran. Office: Family Therapy/Anxiety Ctr 1477 Kenwood Ctr Menasha WI 54952-1160

MAHON, MARK P., state legislator; b. Apr. 30; m. Florence Mahon; four children. Ret. labor union officer; Dist. 40A rep. Minn. Ho. of Reps., St. Paul, 1993—. Home: 8435 Portland Ave Bloomington MN 55420-2405*

MAHONEY, JOHN, state legislator; m. Ann; 4 children. BS, U. N.D., JD. Mem. N.D. Ho. of Reps., 1991—, mem. indsl., bus. and labor com., mem. transp. com.; Oliver County States Atty., 1979—. Mem. KC, Elks, Lions. Home: PO Box 355 Center ND 58530-0355*

MAHONEY, RICHARD JOHN, manufacturing company executive; b. Springfield, Mass., Jan. 30, 1934; m. Barbara Marsden Barnett, Jan. 26, 1956; 3 children. BS in Chemistry, U. Mass., 1955, LLD (hon.), 1983. Product devel. specialist Monsanto Co., 1962; market mgr. new products Monsanto Co., St. Louis, 1965-67; plastic products and resins div. Monsanto Co.; market mgr. bonding products, div. sales dir. Monsanto Co., Kenilworth, N.J., 1967-71; sales dir. Agrl. div. Monsanto Co., St. Louis, 1971-74, dir. internat. ops., 1974-75, gen. mgr. overseas div., 1975; corp. v.p., mng. dir. Monsanto Agrl. Products Co., 1975-76; group v.p., mng. dir. Monsanto Plastics & Resins Co., 1976-77, exec. v.p., 1977-80, pres., 1980, chief operating officer, 1981, bd. dirs., 1979—; pres., chief exec. officer Monsanto Co., St. Louis, 1983-86; chmn., chief exec. officer Monsanto Co., 1986-95; bd. dirs. Met. Life Ins. Co., Union Pacific Corp., G.D. Searle & Co., Nutra Sweet Co. Bd. dirs. U.S.-Russia Bus. Coun.; trustee Washington U., St. Louis. Recipient Frederick S. Troy Alumni Achievement award U.

Mass., Amherst, 1981; hon. fellowship Exeter Coll., Oxford, 1986. Mem. Chem. Mfrs. Assn., Soc. Chem. Industry, Bus. Coun., Bus. Round Table, Log Cabin Club, St. Louis Club, Bellerive Country Club, Met. Club. Office: Monsanto Co 800 N Lindbergh Blvd Saint Louis MO 63141-7843*

MAIDA, ADAM JOSEPH, cardinal; b. East Vandergrift, Pa., Mar. 18, 1930. Student, St. Vincent Coll., Latrobe, Pa., St. Mary's U., Balt., Lateran U., Rome, Duquesne U. Ordained priest Roman Cath. Ch., 1956, consecrated bishop, 1984. Bishop Green Bay, Wis., 1984-89; archbishop Detroit, 1990-95; cardinal, 1995—. Home: 75 E Boston Blvd Detroit MI 48202-1318 Office: Archdiocese of Detroit 1234 Washington Blvd Detroit MI 48226-1825

MAIESE, KENNETH, neurologist; b. Audubon, N.J., Dec. 5, 1958; s. Charles and Margaret (Fioretti) M. BA summa cum laude, U. Pa., 1981; MD, Cornell U., 1985. Intern N.Y. Hosp., 1985-86, resident in neurology, 1986-89, asst. attending physician, 1989-94; asst. prof. Cornell U. Med. Coll., N.Y.C., 1989-94; assoc. prof. Sch. Medicine Wayne State U., Detroit, 1994—, dir. Lab. Molecular and Cellular Cerebral Ischemia, 1994—; with, 1995—; dir. neurol. diagnosis N.Y. Hosp., 1991-94. Author: Neurology and General Medicine, 1989, Neurological and Neurosurgical ICU Medicine, 1988; contbr. articles to Neurology, Jour. Cerebral Blood Flow and Metabolism, Jour. Intensive Care Medicine, Jour. Neurosci., Jour. Neurosci. Rsch., Neurosci. Lett., Jour. Brain Rsch. doseph Collins scholar, 1981-85, Grupe Found. scholar, 1985; grantee NIH, 1990—, Nat. Stroke Assn., 1992-94, Am. Heart Assn., 1995—, United Cerebral Palsy Found., 1995—, Janssen Found., 1995—; recipient Young Scientist award Jours. Cerebral Blood Flow, 1991, Hoechst Investigaror award, 1993, Robert G. Siekert award in stroke, 1994, Johnson and Johnson Disting. Investigator award, 1996. Mem. Am. Acad. Neurology, N.Y. Acad. Scis., Assn. for Rsch. in Nervous and Mental Diseases, Am. Neurol. Assn., Soc. Neurosci. Roman Catholic. Office: Wayne State U Sch Medicine 6E-19 Univ Health Ctr Dept Neurology 4201 Saint Antoine St Detroit MI 48201-2153

MAILES, KIM(BER DEAN), automotive executive; b. Abilene, Tex., Jan. 20, 1956; s. Harold Dean and Carmen Dale (Burr) M.; m. Carol Jean Carnes, May 19, 1979; 1 child, Colton Dean. Postgrad., Nova U., 1987-89; student, Mo. So. State Coll., 1977-79; BA, Ctrl. Bible Coll., 1983; MA, Assemblies God Theol. Sem., 1986. Announcer Radio Sta. KBTN, Neosho, Mo., 1972-74; sales rep. Burr Motor Co., Neosho, 1974-84, mgr., 1989—; founder, pastor Abundant Life Assembly God, Neosho, 1980-86; founder, gen. mgr. Radio Sta. KNEO (FM), Neosho, 1984-86; dist. youth dir. So. Mo. Dist. Assemblies God, Springfield, 1986-89; field dir. Gen. Coun. Assemblies God Internat., Springfield, 1988-89; founder, pres. Trinity Christian Fellowship, Neosho, 1990—; v.p. Joplin Metro 2000, 1983-86; baccalaureate speaker Neosho High Sch. Commencement, 1986, 93, East Newton (Mo.) High Sch., 1994, Assembly God Theol. Sem., Springfield, 1986; cons. Ch. God Apostolate Faith, Tulsa, 1989-91; speaker in field. Author: Destined for Hell, 1986; contbr. articles to mags. Precinct com. Newton County Rep. com., Neosho, 1974-86; commr. Mo.-Kans. coun. Boy Scouts Am., Joplin, Mo., 1982-86, leader, 1993—; bd. dirs. Crowder Coll. Found., Neosho, 1982-86; bd. dirs., v.p. Mid. Am. Concern Internat., Inc., Grand Haven, Mich., 1995—; v.p. MIA-Am.; v.p. Neosho Bd. Edn., 1983-86; mem. White River Band of No. Cherokee Nation; cub master Cub Scout Pack 100, Neosho, Mo. Mem. Trinity Christian Fellowship (pres. 1990), Victory Fellowship Ministries, Mo. Master Gardeners, Kiwanis (bd. dirs. 1987-89), Neosho C. of C. (bd. dirs. 1995—). Republican. Office: PO Box 15 Neosho MO 64850-0015

MAINARDI, CESARE ROBERTO GIOVANNI, management consultant; b. Rome, Italy, Nov. 17, 1962; s. Cesare Camillo and Marilyn G. (Gates) M.; m. Elizabeth Jane Shillington, June 19, 1986; children: Cesare Evan Shillington, Avery Kent Shillington, Amelia Jane Shillington. BS in Indsl. Engring., Northwestern U., Evanston, Ill., 1984; M of Mfg. Engring., Northwestern U., 1985, M of Mgmt., 1986. Engr. Gestioni Radio TV, S.P.A., Milan, Italy, 1983, Videoresearch, Milan, 1983-84; assoc. Booz-Allen & Hamilton, Cleve., 1986-89, sr. assoc., 1989-91, prin., 1991-93, v.p., 1993—. Whirlpool mfg. fellow Northwestern U., 1984-85; Fawco Found. scholar, 1981. Mem. Alpha Lambda Delta. Roman Catholic. Office: Booz Allen & Hamilton 1375 E 9th St Cleveland OH 44114-1724

MAINS, DOUGLAS BENJAMIN, orthopaedic surgeon; b. Aurora, Ill., July 25, 1934; s. Douglas Landis and Faith E. (Jess) M.; m. Frances Franks, June 14, 1956; children: Sheryl Elizabeth, Sheila Lynn. BS, Wheaton Coll., 1956; MD with honors, U. Ill., Chgo., 1960. Diplomate Am. Bd. Orthopaedic Surgeons. Intern USPHS Hosp., San Francisco, 1960-61; resident in orthopaedic surgery Hines VA Hosp. and Shriners Crippled Children Hosp., Chgo., 1963-67; clin. assoc. prof. Loyola U. Stritch Sch. Medicine, Maywood, Ill., 1972—; asst. prof. orthopaedics U. Iowa, Iowa City, 1973-74; Pres. Mona Kea Med. Condominium, Carol Stream, Ill., 1972-89. Patentee surgical instrument for proximal tibial osteotomy. Pres. Conservation Found. of DuPage, 1988-89. With USPHS, 1960-63 Dem. candidate for U.S. house form I.L.,1996. Fellow ACS, Am. Acad. Orthpaedic Surgeons; mem. Alpha Omega Alpha. Presbyterian. Office: Orthopaedic Assocs of DuPage 515 Thornhill Dr Carol Stream IL 60188-2703

MAIORIELLO, RICHARD PATRICK, otolaryngologist; b. Phila., Mar. 17, 1936; s. Gesumino Theodore and Angelina (Del Rossi) M.; A.B., U. Pa., 1960; M.D., Jefferson Med. Coll., 1964; M.S., Thomas Jefferson U., 1972; m. Susan Hemenway, Mar. 6, 1979; children—Gabriel, Angela, Richard. Commd. 2d lt., U.S. Air Force, 1963, advanced through grades to col., 1977; ret., 1979; intern Keesler Hosp., 1965-67; chief flight medicine USAF Base, Bitburg, W. Ger., 1965-68; resident in otolaryngology Thomas Jefferson Hosp., Phila., 1968-71, 72-73; fellow in physiology Thomas Jefferson U., 1971-72; dir. med. edn. Andrews AFB, 1974-78; assoc. prof. uniformed services Univ. Health Scis., 1978-79; assoc. prof. Northeastern Ohio U. of Medicine, 1983—; mem. staff Aultman Hosp., 1979—; assoc. staff Timken Mercy Med. Ctr., 1981—, Union Hosp., 1988—; cons. otolaryngology to Surgeon Gen., 1977—; pres. Mid-Ohio Dressage Assn. Served with USNR, 1954-58. Decorated Air Force Commendation medal; diplomate Nat. Bd. Med. Examiners, Am. Bd. Otolaryngology. Fellow ACS, Am. Soc. Head and Neck Surgery; mem. Am. Acad. Otolaryngology, Am. Acad. Facial Plastic and Reconstructive Surgery, Am. Assn. Cosmetic Surgery, Vail Cosmetic Surg. Soc., Hanoverian Soc. (exec. v.p.), U.S. Dressage Fedn. (chmn. all-breeds coun.), Centurion Club. Republican. Roman Catholic. Office: 1445 Harrison Ave NW Canton OH 44708-2620

MAIOTTI, DENNIS PAUL, manufacturing company executive; b. Cleve., Oct. 14, 1950; s. Raymond Joseph and Shirley Mae (Lang) M.; m. Rebecca Mueller, Aug. 11, 1973; children: Jennifer, David. BA, Baldwin-Wallace Coll., 1972; postgrad., Ohio U., 1972-73, Northwestern U., 1974. Cert. secondary tchr. Asst. employee relations Eaton Corp., Cleve., 1973-74, mgr. prodn., 1974-76, v.p. mktg., 1976-84, exec. v.p., 1984-86; pres. Lennon Wallpaper Co., Joliet, Ill., 1986-88, Mokena (Ill.) Mills Inc., 1988—. Editor, columnist South Life met. newspapers, Cleve., 1968-72. Mem. Wallcovering Mfgrs. Assn., Kappa Delta Pi, Delta Phi Alpha. Republican. Lutheran. Office: Mokena Mills Inc 19806 Wolf Rd Mokena IL 60448-1316

MAIR, BRUCE LOGAN, interior designer, company executive; b. Chgo., June 5, 1951; s. William Logan and Josephine (Lee) M. BFA, Drake U., 1973; postgrad., Ind. Wesleyan U., 1990—. Mgr., head designer Reifers of Indpls., 1973-79; pres. Interiors Internat., Indpls., 1979-87; sr. designer Kasler Group, Indpls., 1987-89; dir. devel. Tillery Interiors and Imports, Greenwood, Ind., 1990; v.p. Tillery Interiors and Imports, Indpls., 1990-92; owner Mair Interior Design Group, Indpls., 1992—; pres. Tokens Inc., Indpls., 1982-88, Meg-A-Wat Enterprises Inc., Indpls., 1985-87, Luxury Ice Creams Inc., Indpls., 1986-87. Cover designer Indpls. Home and Garden mag., 1978, feature designer 1980; feature designer Builder mag., 1979; co-designer feature Indpls. At Home mag., 1979. Campaigner Anderson for Pres., 1980. Mem. Am. Soc. Interior Designers (treas. Ind. chpt. 1982-83, Pres. awards 1981-82), U.S. Rowing Assn. (master 1987—), St. Joseph Hist. Neighborhood Assn., Columbia Club (rowing crew coxswain 1986—), Highland Model A Club, Tower Harbor Yacht Club (Douglas, Mich.), Alpha Epsilon Pi. Home: 219 E 10th St Indianapolis IN 46202-3303 Office: Mair Interior Design Group 219 E 10th St Indianapolis IN 46202-3303

MAISEL, DARRELL KEITH, manufacturing executive; b. East St. Louis, Ill., Mar. 5, 1947; s. Charles Earl and Lonah Belle (Harrison) M.; m. Darlyn Marie Range, Nov. 27, 1974; children: Tracy, Richard, Donald, James. Student, Wash. U., St. Louis, 1975-81, Belleville Area Coll., 1975-79, U. Mo., 1981-82; cert., Ranken Tech. Trade Sch., St. Louis, 1969-71. Assembly line worker Chevrolet div. GM, St. Louis, 1965-66; mgr. svc. sta. Standard Oil Co., Cahokia, Ill., 1966-67; millwright Cerro Copper Products Co., Sauget, Ill., 1967-70, electrician, 1970-72, maintenance supr., 1972-76, elec. engr., 1976-78; maintenance supt. Cerro Copper Products Co., Sauget, 1978-81; tech. mgr. Cerro Copper Products Co., Shelbina, Mo., 1981-82; plant gen. mgr. Cerro Copper Tube Co., Shelbina, Mo., 1982-88; v.p. Cerro Copper Tube Co., Shelbina, 1988-90; exec. v.p. The Folding Bleacher Co., Altamont, Ill., 1990-91; pres. Hannibal (Mo.) Cabinet Works, Inc., 1992-93; dir. ops. Reading Tube Corp., Hannibal, 1993-94; v.p. ops. Cerro Copper Tube Co., Shelbina, Mo., 1994—. Active St. Johns Luth. Ch., Hannibal. Office: Cerro Copper Tube Co PO Box 168 Shelbina MO 63468-9999

MAISEL, MICHAEL, clothing executive; b. Newark, Oct. 19, 1947; s. Irving and Betty (Markin) M.; m. Arlette Bernstein, Oct. 18, 1980; children: Ian Albert, Alicia Beth, Noah Shawn, Bette Gabrielle, Melissa Ann, Eunice Blanca. B.S. in Mktg., B.A. in Gen. Bus. Adminstrn., Ariz. State U., 1969. Asst. sales mgr. Mid-Atlantic Shoe Co. div. Beck Industries, N.Y.C., 1969-71; dir. imports Felsway Corp., Totowa, N.J., 1972-73; exec. v.p. Carber Enterprises, N.Y.C., 1973-80; v.p. S.R.O. div. Caressa, N.Y.C., 1980-84; pres. Sandler of Boston, N.Y.C., 1984-85, chmn. bd., 1986—; v.p. Lowell Shoe, Inc., Hudson, N.H., 1992-93; v.p. Selby, U.S. Shoe, Cin., 1993—; cons. in field. Mem. 210 Shoe Industry (life), Nat. Shoe Retailers Assn. (bd. dirs.), Nat. Shoe Mfrs. Assn. Republican. Jewish. Designer Carber's shoe, displayed in Met. Mus. Art; nominated for Coty design award, 1974-78; recipient Friendship award City of Cin. Human Rels. Commn., 1994. Office: 9 West Group 1 Eastwood Dr Cincinnati OH 45227-1197

MAITLAND, JOHN W., JR., state legislator; b. Normal, Ill., July 19, 1936; m. Joanne Sieg; three children. Student, Ill. State U. Grain farmer; Dist. 44 senator Ill. Senate, Springfield, 1979—; asst. majority leader, Ill. Senate; mem. elem. and secondary edn. appropriations I, energy and environment, and appropriations II coms.; minority spokesman; mem. commn. intergovernmental cooperation, con. and fiscal commn., task force on sch. fin. Office: 525 N East St Bloomington IL 61701-4060 Home: RR 3 Box 279 Bloomington IL 61704-9554*

MAJOR, MARY JO, dance school artistic director; b. Joliet, Ill., Dec. 5, 1955; d. George Francis and Lucille Mae (Ballun) Schmidberger; m. Perry Rex Major, June 9, 1979. AA, Joliet Jr. Coll., 1976; BA, Lewis U., 1978; MS, Ill. State U., 1983; postgrad., No. Ill. U., Nat. Lewis U. and Gov.'s State U. Cert. tchr., Ill. Tchr., softball coach St. Rose Grade Sch., Wilmington, Ill., 1977-78; tchr., coach volleyball, basketball, softball Reed Custer High Sch., Braidwood, Ill., 1978-79; pvt. tutor, 1979; tchr. Coal City (Ill.) Middle Sc, 1980—, basketball coach, 1980-84; owner, dir., choreographer Major Sch. Dance, Inc., Coal City, 1984—; owner Technique Boutique, 1991; founder Major Motion Dancers, 1984—; aerobics instr. Wilmington Park Dist.,1977-82, Coal City Shape Shoppe, 1980-82; cheerleading sponsor Joliet Jr. Coll., 1976-77, aerobics instr., 1980-81; pvt. dance instr., Coal City, 1981; dancer, choreographer Coal City Bi-Centennial Celebration, 1981, Coal City Community Celebration, 1982; founder Major Motion Dancers, 1984-95; tchr., Russia, 1990; dancer, choreographer various performances for ch. and civic orgns.; televised half-time performance and tour Citrus Bowl. Commd. to choreograph and appear in video prodn.: Jacinta, Not an Ordinary Love, The Patty Waszak Show A Bit of Branson, 1995-96. Mem. Arts Coun. Co-op. Recipient Proclamation of Achievement award Dance Olympus, Chgo., 1986, 87, 88, 89, 90, 91, 92, 93, 94, 95, 96, Best Choreographer award 1990, Merit award Tremaine Dance Conv., 1991-92; named Best Actress, Joliet Kiwanis, 1989, Best Musician, 1990. Mem. NEA, Ill. Edn. Assn., Coal City Cmty. Unit Edn. Assn. Office: Major Sch Dance Inc 545 E 1st St Coal City IL 60416-1635

MAJORS, RICHARD GEORGE, psychology educator; b. Ithaca, N.Y.; s. Richard G. II and Fannie Sue Majors; legal guardian: Lillian A. McGill. AA, Auburn (N.Y.) Community Coll., 1974; BA in History, Plattsburgh State Coll., 1977; PhD in Ednl. Psychology, U. Ill., 1987. Various social svc. positions, 1976-79; probation officer, ct. investigator Plattsburgh, 1979; clin. intern McKinley Health Ctr., Urbana, Ill., 1981; rsch. asst. U. Minn., Mpls., 1981, U. Ill., Urbana, 1981-84; instr. Parkland Community Coll., Champaign, Ill., 1985; rsch. asst. U. Ill., Champaign, 1985-86; postdoctoral fellow U. Kans., Lawrence, 1987-89; postdoctoral fellow, clin. fellow Harvard Med. Sch., Boston, 1989-90; asst. prof. psychology U. Wis. System, 1990-93; sr. rsch. assoc. The Urban Inst., Washington, 1993-95; vis. fellow, scholar The David Walker Rsch. Inst., Mich. State U., 1995—; vis. fellow, scholar David Walker Rsch. Inst. Mich. State U.; presenter in field. Co-author: Coolpose: The Dilemmas of Black Manhood in America, 1992, The American Black Male: His Present Status and Future, 1994; founder Jour. of African Am. Men. Named one of Outstanding Young Men of Am., 1987. Fellow APA (predoctoral minority fellow 1984); mem. Nat. Coun. African Am. Men (chmn., co-founder), Soc. for Psychol. Study of Ethnic Minority Issues, Am. Orthopsychiat. Assn., Greenpeace, Kappa Delta Pi, Phi Delta Kappa. Office: David Walker Rsch Inst Mich State U B421 West Fee Hall East Lansing MI 48824

MAJURE, OLIVER DAVIS, marketing professional; b. Newton, Miss.. BFA cum laude, U. Kansas City and Art Inst., 1951. Art dir. Skelly Oil Co., Kansas City, Mo., 1952-54, Fleming Foods Inc., Oklahoma City, 1954-60; creative dir. Old Am. Ins. Co., Kansas City, 1960-72; copy writer Brewer Divsn. Young & Rubicam, Kansas City, 1972-73; cons. direct mktg. Dave Majure, Direct Mktg., Shawnee Mission, Kans., 1973-89; direct mktg. cons. Foley Mfg. Co., Mpls., 1973-87, Am. Fidelity Ins. Co., Oklahoma City, 1974-89, Physicians Mutual Ins. Co., Omaha, 1974-76, Shopsmith Tools, Tipp City, Ohio, 1976-78, Babson Mutual Funds, Kansas City, 1978-83, Hallmark Cards, Kansas City, 1979. Author: Direct Hit, 1994. With USAAF, 1942-46, ETO. Fellow Soc. of Fellows Nelson Art Gallery and Mus. Home: 12600 Mohawk Ln Leawood KS 66209

MAKEPEACE, DARRYL LEE, consulting company executive; b. Pitts., Oct. 24, 1941; s. Thomas Henry Makepeace and Nevada Ruth (Wagener) Desin. BS in Indsl. Engring., Pa. State U., 1969; MBA, Pepperdine U., 1982. Dept. mgr. Procter & Gamble, Cin., 1969-72; plant mgr. CBS Mus. Instruments, Fullerton, Calif., 1972-76; dir. mfg. Frigid Coil/Wolf Range, Whittier, Calif., 1977-79; mgr. materials mgmt. Nat. Supply, Los Nietos, Calif., 1979-85; assoc. prof. mgmt. Calif. State U., Fullerton, 1982-86; mgr. mfg. Nat. Supply, Los Nietos, Calif., 1985-86; program mgr. Armco Cumberland Group, Middletown, Ohio, 1986; ptnr., cons. Armco Cumberland Group, Mason, Ohio, 1986-87; prin., owner Cumberland Group, Cin., 1988—; owner Phoenix Cons., Inc., Cin., 1991—; owner, pres. D.L. Makepeace & Assocs., Mason, Ohio, 1991—; assoc. prof. mgmt. Wright State U., Dayton, Ohio, 1987-88, Miami U., Oxford, Ohio, 1988-89. Author: The System, American Iron and Steel Institute, Steel Body Panel Performance Characteristics, 1991; contbr. articles to profl. jours. Served with U.S. Army, 1960-61. Named to Honorable Order of Ky. Cols. Mem. Am. Prodn. and Inventory Control Soc., Inst. Indsl. Engrs., Alpha Pi Mu, Tau Beta Pi, Sigma Tau.

MAKO, WILLIAM LAWRENCE, manufacturing executive; b. Cleve., June 16, 1958; s. Lawrence M. and Margret E. (Borchard) M.; m. Bonnie M. Schultz; 1 child, Brokke A. BA in Bus., Wittenberg U., 1981; MBA, Cleveland State U., 1989. V.p. Conmak, Inc., Conneaut, Ohio, 1981-82; pres. Le Bears' Inc., Moreland Hills, Ohio, 1982-83; mgr. Wendy's Old-Fashioned Hamburgers, Bozeman, Mont., 1984; exec. v.p. Great Lakes Properties Corp., Conneaut, 1984-88; v.p. Conneaut Harbor Devel. Co., Ohio, 1988-90; exec. v.p. Def-Tec Corp., Rock Creek, Ohio, 1990-95; pres., gen mgr. MFG Justin Tanks Inc., Georgetown, Del., 1995-96; corp. ops. specialist Molded Fiberglass Co., Ashtabula, Ohio, 1996—. Mem. Safari Club Internat., N.Am. Hunting Club (life). Republican. Roman Catholic. Home: 222 Elliot Ave Jefferson OH 44047 Office: Molded Fiverglass Co PO Box 675 1315 W 47th St Ashtabula OH 44004

MAKOWSKI-JESTER, SUSAN, pharmaceuticals company administrator; b. Milw., July 16, 1960; d. Ralph Frank and Rosemarie Jean (Rupcich) Makowski; m. Joseph Leo Jester, Dec. 2, 1990. BA with honors, Alverno Coll., Milw., 1987; MS, Cardinal Stritch Coll., Milw., 1995. Mgr. clin. rsch. program Med. Coll. Wis., Milw., 1988-95; instr. computer sci. Alverno Coll., 1995; mgr. rsch. ops. Lorex Pharms., Skokie, Ill., 1995—; speaker on women in sci. Mem. Assn. Clin. Pharmacology, Greenpeace. Republican. Roman Catholic. Home: 2032 E Howard Ave Saint Francis WI 53235

MAKSYMOWICZ, WESLEY, design engineer; b. Poland, Dec. 25, 1951. BEE, Warsaw Poly. Inst., Poland, 1977. Mech. design engr. G.W. Electric, Blue Island, Ill., 1981-84, Marvel Metal Co., Chgo., 1984-87, Roland Borg Corp., Chgo., 1987-90, Total Controls Products, Melrose Park, Ill., 1990—. Roman Catholic. Home: 4841 Weyland Ave Chicago IL 60641 Office: Total Control Products 2001 Janice Ave Melrose Park IL 60160-1010

MALANY, LE GRAND LYNN, attorney general, lawyer, engineer, bank executive; b. Chgo., May 14, 1941; s. LeGrand Franklin and Marion (Jaynes) M.; m. Barbara Bumgarner, June 26, 1965; children: LeGrand Karl, Siobhan, Carleen. BS in Engring. Physics, U. Ill., 1964, JD, 1970. Bar: Ill. 1970, U.S. Dist. Ct. (cen. dist.) Ill. 1970, Ill. Supreme Ct., 1970, U.S. Dist. Ct. (so. dist.) Ill. 1974, U.S. Dist. Ct. (no. dist.) Ill. 1981, U.S. Ct. Appeals (7th cir.) 1972, U.S. Supreme Ct. 1975, U.S. Ct. Mil. Appeals 1971; registered profl. engr., Ill.; lic. real estate broker; lic. bldg. inspector, mgmt. planner, and asbestos project designer, Ill. Asst. astronomer Adler Planetarium, Chgo., 1960-63; rsch. asst. Portland Cement Rsch. Assn., Skokie, Ill., 1964; instr. dept. gen. engring. U. Ill., 1965-70, instr. Office Instrn. Resources, 1967-68, instr. Hwy Traffic Safety Ctr., 1968-69; lectr. Police Tng. Inst., Urbana, Ill., 1969-70; project dir. driver control program U.S. Dept. Transp., 1971-73, project dir., author driver license examiner tng. curriculum, 1973; assoc. drivers license adminstr. State of Ill., Springfield, 1973-74, asst. auditor gen., 1977-83, asst. atty. gen., dir. policy, planning and tech. State of Ill., 1983-85, chief internal audito

MALECKI, DAVID MICHAEL, airport manager; b. Ft. Leavenworth, Kans., Sept. 10, 1948; s. John Adam and Marylee Kathryn (Fogle) M.; m. Janice Adele Mayse, Sept. 2, 1972; children: Joshua Gerald, Madeline Elizabeth. BS, Cen. Mo. State U., Warrensburg, 1973; MPA, U. Mo.-Kansas City, 1977. Probation and parole officer Mo. Bd. Probation and Parole, Independence, 1973-76; rsch. asst. budget and systems office City of Kansas City (Mo.), 1976-77, budget analyst, 1977-80, adminstrv. officer, asst. airport mgr. aviation dept. Richards-Gebaur Meml. Airport, 1980-89, airport mgr., 1994—; asst. mgr. Ground Transp., Kansas City Internat. Airport, 1989-94. Mem. Independence Neighborhood Coun., 1974-75. With U.S. Army, 1969-71, N.G., 1972—. Decorated Army Res. Achievement Medal with oak leaf clusters (2). Mem. N.G. Assn., Mo. N.G. Assn., Aircraft Owners and Pilots Assn., Pi Sigma Alpha. Home: 5774 Bower Ave Kansas City MO 64133-3637 Office: Richards-Gebaur Meml Airport 15405 Maxwell Ave Kansas City MO 64147

MALEK, REZA SAID, urological surgeon; b. Aug. 22, 1940; s. Said and Banoo (Rais) M.; m. Haleh F. Rassa, Feb. 9, 1980. MB, BS, U. London, 1964; MS in Urology, U. Minn., 1971. Diplomate Am. Bd. Urology. Intern St. Mary's Hosp., Eastbourne, Eng., 1964-65, Lister Hosp., Hitchin, Eng., 1964-65; resident, sr. house officer St. Thomas's Hosp., U. London, 1965-66, Mayo Grad. Sch. Medicine, Rochester, Minn., 1967-71; rsch. fellow in calculous disease of urinary tract, vis. clin. surgeon Bowman-Gray Sch. Medicine, Winston-Salem, N.C., 1971-72; instr. urology Mayo Clinic, Rochester, 1972-74, asst. prof., 1974-76, assoc. prof., 1976-91, prof., 1991—; adviser to regional dir. WHO, 1972; cons. urology Mayo Clinic, 1972—. Fellow ACS, Royal Coll. Physicians and Surgeons of Can., Am. Soc. for Laser Medicine and Surgery; mem. AMA, Minn. Med. Assn., Zumbro Valley Med. Soc., Sigma Xi. Home: 1523 Camelback Ct NE Rochester MN 55906-8960 Office: Mayo Clinic 200 1st St SW Rochester MN 55905-0001

MALEWICKI, DEBRA SUZANNE, state official, educator; b. Monroe, Wis., July 23, 1954; d. Raymond Lester Miskimon and Dorothy Rose (Youngwith) Sewell; m. Robert Allen Malewicki, May 22, 1987; children: Marissa, John Ryan. BA, East Tex. State U., 1980; MBA, U. Wis., Whitewater, 1984. Dir Wis. Innovation Svc. Ctr., Whitewater, 1985—; instr. Lakeland Coll., Sheboygan, Wis., 1986—. Author (with others) Marketing Ingenuity and Invention, 1989. Advisor Phi Gamma Nu, Whitewater, 1986—; chmn. Wis. Gov.'s Task Force on Innovation and and Rsch. and Devel., Small Bus. Conf., Madison, 1987. Mem. Small Bus. Innovations Rsch. Com. (chairperson 1987—), Wis. Bus. Women's Coalition (chairperson conf. 1987—). Office: Wis Innovation Ctr 402 McCutchan Hall U Wis Whitewater WI 53190

MALEWSKI, JENNIFER JEAN, clergy member; b. Deshler, Ohio, Dec. 31, 1946; d. David Edwards and Alberta Elsa (Ostrand) Parr; m. Charles William Malewski, Dec. 22, 1972; children; David Frank, John Charles, Jenelle Alberta. BA, U. Nebr., 1967; MDiv, St. Paul Sch. Theology, Kansas City, Mo., 1987. Ordained to ministry Christian Ch. (Disciples of Christ). Tchr. correlated studies Omaha Pub. Schs., 1967-70; tchr. English Independence (Mo.) Pub. Schs., 1970-74; ministerial intern Overland Park (Kans.) Christian Ch., 1986-87; chaplain intern Bethany Med. Ctr., Kansas City, Kans., 1987-89; staff chaplain U. Kans. Med. Ctr., Kansas City, 1989—, mem. pediatrics ethics com., religion and medicine symposium cmty. planning sensitivity com.; dir. interim pastoral care Spofford Home, Kanasas City, 1988; presenter on spiritual care of dying patients and their loved ones of diverse religious traditions U. Kans. Med. Ctrs. Religions and Medicine Symposium, U. Nebr. Rites and Rituals Seminar, Omaha, King's Coll. of U. Western Ont. 14th Annual Bereavement Conf. Contbr. articles to profl. jours. Disciples Women's scholar, 1984-86. Mem. Funeral & Meml. Soc. Am. (bd. dirs. Kansas City chpt. 1996—), Kans. Assn. Chaplains (sec. 1991-92, treas. 1994—), Kansas City Assn. Chaplains (treas. 1996—), Disciples Ministers Assn., Coll. of Chaplains.

MALICKI, GREGG HILLARD, engineer; b. Chgo., Feb. 13, 1947; s. Hillard Lawrence and Virginia Valerie (Vosen) M.; 1 child, James Michael. BSBA, U. Ill., Champaign, 1975; MBA, U. Iowa, 1985; student, Coll. DuPage, Glen Ellyn, Ill., 1972-73, Ill. Inst. Technol., 1965-68. First lt. U.S. Army, 1969-72; sr. engring. analyst Deere & Co., Moline, Ill., 1975-87; sr. cons. engr. Deere & Co., Ill., 1987-94; regional mgr. Internat. Supply Mgmt. Svcs., 1994—; pres. Inst. Indsl. Engrs., Moline Ill., 1987--. Lt. col. USNG, 1975—. Recipient Letter of Commendation Nat. Merit 1965. Sr. mem. Inst. Indsl. Engrs. (pres. 1987—); mem. Am. Prodn. & Inventory Control Soc., Phi Theta Kappa, Chi Gamma Iota. Roman Catholic. Home: 3418 49th St Moline IL 61265-8219 Office: Deere & Co John Deere Rd Moline IL 61265

MALIK, AZFAR MOHAMMED, psychiatrist, medical administrator; b. Karachi, Sind, Pakistan, Dec. 16, 1953; came to U.S., 1981; s. Akhter and Shamin (Rahman) M.; m. Maheen Mubarak, Sept. 12, 1953; children: Samir, Zayir, Areeb. MB BS, Dow Med. Coll., Karachi, Pakistan, 1978; Cert., Ednl.Commn. Foreign Med. Grads, 1981. Diplomate Am. Bd. Psychiatry and Neurology, Am. Bd. Geriatric Psychiatry, Am. Bd. Addictive Psychiatry. Resident physician surgery Civil Hosp., Karachi, Pakistan, 1978-79; resident physician medicine St. Luke's Univ. Hosp., Malta, 1979; asst. cons. psychiatry Mt. Carmel Hosp., Malta, 1979-81; resident physician dept. psychiatry St. Louis U. Hosp., 1982-85, chief resident dept. psychiatry, 1984-85; psych. assoc. dept. psychiatry St. John's Med. Ctr., St. Louis, 1985-86, med. dir., 1986—; pres. Lencor, Inc., St. Louis, 1987—; psychiat. cons. Psychiat. Cons., St. Louis, 1986—; pres. Kromal Inc., 1993—; v.p. Highland Devel. Corp., 1994—; mem. quality assurance com. Dept. Psychiatry St. John's Mercy Med. Ctr., 1985-90, asst. clin. prof. St. Louis U. Hosp., 1992; chmn. quality assurance com., allied health profls. com. St. Anthony Med. Ctr., St. Louis, 1990—; v.p., bd. dirs. St. Louis CISD, 1990-92, med. dir. St. Louis Regional CISD, 1991—, Diagnostic Neurology, Inc. 1992—. Contbr. articles to profl. jours.; presenter stress workshops, St. Louis. Mem. AMA (Physician Recognition award), So. Med. Assn., Am. Psychiat. Assn., Eastern Mo. Psychiat. Soc., N.Y. Bellevue Med. Soc., Assn. Pakistani Physicians N. Am., Forest Hills Country Club. Home: 17025 Orville Rd Chesterfield MO 63005-6910 Office: Psychiat Cons Ltd 621 S New Ballas Rd Ste 398 Saint Louis MO 63141-8241

MALIK, RAYMOND HOWARD, economist, scientist, corporate executive, inventor, educator; b. Lebanon, Feb. 4, 1933; came to U.S., 1948, naturalized, 1963; s. John Z. and Clarice R. (Malik) M. BA, Valparaiso U., 1950; BSBA and Econs., Simpson Coll., 1951; MSBA, So. Ill. U., 1956, PhD in Electronics and Econs., 1959. Supr. Arabian Am. Oil Co., Beirut, 1952-54; mem. grad. faculty, advisor Ill. State U., 1954-59; prof., head world trade programs Central YMCA Community Coll., Chgo., 1966-74; pres. Malik Internat. Enterprises Ltd., Chgo., 1959—; advisor U.S. Congl. Adv. Bd. Author: The Guide to Youth, Health and Longevity, 1980, Do You Really Need Glasses, 1988; inventor selectric typing elements and mechanism, 1959, heater-humidifier-dehumidifier, 1963, ednl. math toy, 1965, circle of sound concept of sound propogation, 1967; designed, introduced Computer and Others, 1962; introduced molecular concept in color TV (system-three and others), 1973, gamma ray breast cancer detector, 1976, auto-ignition instant hot water heater, 1981, water filter, purifier and softener, 1984, no doze warner, 1985, indoor-outdoor barbeque grill, 1985, infra-red heat massager, 1986; designed and introduced telephone shoulder rest with adjustable mechanism, 1962, electronic telephone (Trimline, others), 1964, modular telephone, 1975, video phone, 1991; pioneer developer interplanetary communications system, 1961. Deacon, mem. pastor-congl. com., youth and young adult ednl. com. St. George Orthodox Ch., Cicero, Ill.; fundraiser March of Dimes, St. Jude Hosp., Am. Cancer Soc., Am. Heart Fund, numerous others; mem. Am. Task Force for Lebanon, 1992—. Named to Wisdom Hall of Fame, 1987, Personality of Yr. 1995; Fulbright scholar, 1948-50, Meth. Ch. scholar, 1950-51; So. Ill. U. fellow, 1954-59. Mem. IEEE, AAAS, Am. Mgmt. Assn., Am. Econ. Assn., Am. Mktg. Assn., Import Clubs U.S., Internat. Bus. Coun., Internat. Platform Assn., Pres.'s Assn., Nat. Assn. Self-Employed, Imperial Austrian Legion of Honor, Internat. Students Assn., Soc. Mfg. Engrs., Am. Legion, Highlander Club, Phi Beta Kappa, Sigma Xi, Delta Rho, Beta Gamma Sigma, Alpha Phi Omega. Address: PO Box 3194 Chicago IL 60654-0194

MALINOWSKI, DENNIS EDMUND, government consultant; b. Sheboygan, Wis., Mar. 18, 1948; s. Edmund Thomas and Delores Rose (Zientarski) M.; m. Linda Ann Paulinski, June 15, 1968; children: Patrick, Melanie, Anne. BBA, U. Notre Dame, 1970. Analyst Dun & Bradstreet, Chgo., 1970-72; prodn. supr. Ball Brothers Corp., Mundelein, Ill., 1972-74; adjudicator, specialist, personnel dir. State of Wis., Madison, 1974-81; asst. mgr. claims Wis. Physicians Svc., Madison, 1981-84; fin. dir. Walworth County, Elkhorn, Wis., 1984-90; mgr. David M. Griffith and Assocs., Madison, 1990—; part-time instr. Madison Area Tech. Coll., Madison, 1973-89. Cub master Cub Scouts Am., Boy Scouts Am., Madison, 1978; basketball coach St. Dennis Parish and YMCA, Madison, 1979-81; active local ch. groups. Nelson Mufflen scholar, 1966. Mem. Wis. Counties Fin. Officers Assn. (v.p. 1984—), Notre Dame Alumni Assn. South Ctrl. Wis. (pres. 1979-82, exec. bd. 1990-93), Nat. Notre Dame Alumni Assn. (senate rep. 1981-82, 87). Roman Catholic. Home: 4323 Sprecher Rd Madison WI 53704-6537 Office: David M Griffith and Assocs 2445 Darwin Rd Ste 201 Madison WI 53704

MALKOFF, SOLOMON, lawyer; b. Youngstown, Ohio, Apr. 24, 1918; s. Isadore and Tillie (Chaimovich) M.; m. Shirley Glick, Aug. 3, 1947; children: Wendy Marcia Malkoff Blume, Marc David. BA, Ohio State U., 1940, JD, 1942. Atty. Capital Improvement, Youngstown, 1950-52, Urban Renewal, Youngstown, 1952-55, Traxler, Malkoff, Boyd, Rummell & Zamary Co. L.P.A., Youngstown, 1955—. Pres. Mahoning Co. Welfare, Youngstown, 1950-61; comdr. Jewish War Vets., Youngstown, 1959—; active B'nai B'rith, Youngstown, 1946—. Cpl. U.S. Army, 1942-45, ETO. Decorated Am. Campaign medal, European medal, African medal, Middle East medal, Bronze Battle Stars (5). Mem. ABA, ATLA, Ohio Bar Assn., Mahoning County Bar Assn., Trumbull County Bar Assn., Ohio Acad. Trial Lawyer Assn. Office: Traxler Malkoff Boyd Rummell Zamary Co LPA PO Box 6565 400 Mahoning Bank Bldg Youngstown OH 44501

MALLETT, SUSAN MARIE, nurse; b. Cambridge, Ohio, June 29, 1954; d. Everett Frederick and Sylvia Victoria (Goodall) M. ASN, Sinclair Community Coll., 1975; BSN summa cum laude, U. Cin., 1991; MS summa cum laude, Wright State U., 1993. Staff relief nurse Med. Personnel Pool, Dayton, Ohio, 1975-84, Staff Builders, Dayton, Ohio, 1984; staff nurse Miami Valley Hosp., Dayton, Ohio, 1984-89, shift mgr., 1989-93; trauma rsch. coord. Miami Valley Hosp., Dayton, 1993—. Mem. health adv. bd. Head Start, Dayton, 1992—. Mem. Am. Assn. Neurosci. Nurses, Sigma Theta Tau. Home: 1197 Tralee Trl Dayton OH 45430-1233 Office: Miami Valley Hosp 1 Wyoming St Dayton OH 45409-2722

MALLIN, SANFORD RICHARD, medical science educator; b. Milw., Jan. 12, 1933. BS, U. Wis., 1954, MD, 1957. Diplomate Am. Bd. Internal Medicine. Intern Mt. Sinai Hosp., Milw., 1957-58; resident in internal medicine Hahnemann Hosp. and Med. Coll., 1958-60; fellow in metabolic and endocrine rsch. Michael Reese Hosp., Chgo., 1960-62; instr. medicine Chgo. Med. Sch., 1961-62; clin. instr. medicine Marquette (Wis.) Sch. Medicine, 1962-68; asst. clin. prof. mediicne, then assoc. clin. prof. Med. Coll. Wis., Milw., 1968-81, clin. prof. medicine, 1981—; assoc. clin. prof. medicine U. Wis. Sch. Medicine, Madison, 1975-80, clin. prof. medicine, 1980—, preceptor, 1968-75. Contbr. numerous articles to profl. jours. Fellow ACP, Am. Coll. Endocrinology; mem. AMA, Am. Fedn. Clin. Rsch., Endocrine Soc. (clin. endocrinology initiatives com., postgrad. edn. com.), Am. Assn. Clin. Endocrinologists, Am. Diabetes Assn. (ctrl. coun. 1973-75, pres. 1974, bd. dirs. 1964-82, 85-90), Milw. Acad. Medicine (pres. 1976), Am. Soc. Internal Medicine, Wis. State Med. Soc., Med. Soc. Milw. County (pres. 1991), N.Y. Acad. Scis., Milw. Internists Club.

MALLMANN, ALEXANDER JAMES, physics educator, researcher; b. Sheboygan, Wis., Dec. 8, 1937; s. Alexander Bernard and Anne Frances (Govek) M.; m. Jean Louise Kowalsky, Aug. 10, 1968 (div. 1981); children: James Steven, David Louis; m. Roberta Belle Daellenbach, May 25, 1991. BS, U. Wis., Milw., 1965, MS, 1968; PhD, Marquette U., 1977. Instr. Milw. Sch. Engring., 1968-69, asst. prof., 1969-72, assoc. prof., 1972-78, prof. physics, 1978—, R.D. Peters prof. materials sci., 1990—. Co-author: Physics: Principles and Applications, 1990, Experiments in Physics, 1990; referee Am. Jour. Physics, 1977—, Jour. the Optical Soc. Am., 1977—; contbr. articles to profl. jours. With USAF, 1955-59. Recipient Outstanding Teaching award Inland Steel-Ryerson Found., 1983, Karl O. Werwath Engring. Rsch. award, 1996. Mem. Optical Soc. Am. (tech. program com. on meteorol. optics 1982-83), Wis. Assn. Physics Tchrs. (pres. 1981-82), Physics Club Milw. (pres. 1982-83, 88-89, sec.-treas. 1990—). Democrat. Home: 20250 Jeffers Dr New Berlin WI 53146-2522 Office: Milw Sch Engring Dept Physics and Chemistry 1025 N Broadway Milwaukee WI 53202-3109

MALLON, FLORENCIA ELIZABETH, history educator; b. Santiago, Chile, Oct. 28, 1951; d. Richard Dicks and Ignacia (Bernales) M.; m. Steve Jefferey Stern; children: Ramon Joseph, Ralph Isaiah. BA, Harvard U., 1973; MA, Yale U., 1975, M of Philosophy, 1976, PhD, 1980. Asst. prof. Marquette U., Milw., 1981-82; asst. prof. U. Wis., Madison, 1982-84, assoc. prof., 1984-88, prof., 1988—. Editl. bd. Latin Am. Perspectives, 1982—, Political Power and Social Theory, 1990—, L.Am. Rsch. Rev., 1992—; author: The Defense of Community in Peru's Central Highlands, 1983 (Bolton hon. mention award 1984), Peasant and Nation, 1995 (Bryce Wood Book award 1995); contbr. articles to profl. jours. Fellow Ctr. for Advanced Study, Stanford, Calif., 1990-91, fellow NEH, 1990-91, John Simon Guggenheim Meml. fellow, 1996, RISM Landes Sr. fellow, 1996; Rsch. grantee Social Sci. Rsch. Coun., 1981, Fulbright Found., 1984-85. Mem. Am. Hist. Assn., Conf. on Latin Am. History, Latin Am. Studies Assn. Office: Univ Wisconsin/History Dept 3211 Humanities Bldg 455 N Park St Madison WI 53706-1405

MALLORY, MARK L., state legislator, librarian. Student, Cin. Acad. Math. & Sci.; BS, U. Cin. Dept. mgr. Hamilton County Pub. Libr. Graphic Prodn., Cin.; rep. dist. 31 Ohio Ho. Reps., Columbus. Mem. NAACP, Libr. Staff Assn., Black Male Coalition, Friends of Pub. Libr., Urban League of Cin., Pub. Libr. Staff Assn., Internat. TV Assn.

MALLORY, TROY L., accountant; b. Sesser, Ill., July 30, 1923; s. Theodore E. and Alice (Mitchell) M.; m. Magdalene Richter, Jan. 26, 1963. Student So. Ill. U., 1941-43, Washington and Jefferson Coll., 1943-44; BS, U. Ill., 1947, MS, 1948. Staff sr. supr. Scovell, Wellington & Co., CPA's, Chgo., 1948-58; mgr. Gray Hunter Stenn, CPAs, Quincy, 1959-62, ptnr., 1962—. Mem. fin. com. United Fund, Adams County, 1961-64. Bd. dirs. Woodland Home for Orphans and Friendless, 1970—, pres., 1981-84, 87-90. With 84th Inf. Div. AUS, 1942-45. Decorated Purple Heart, Bronze Star. Mem. AICPA, Ill. CPA Soc., Quincy C. of C. (bd. dirs. 1970-76), Rotary (bd. dirs. Quincy 1967-70, pres. 1978-79), Shriners (bd. dirs. Quincy 1982-85, pres. 1988), Royal Order of Jesters (Ct. 20), Railsplitters Soc. (pres. 1993). Home: 49 Wilmar Dr Quincy IL 62301-6847 Office: 500 Maine St Quincy IL 62301-3932

MALLOY, EDWARD ALOYSIUS, priest, university administrator, educator; b. Washington, May 3, 1941; s. Edward Aloysius and Elizabeth (Clark) M. BA, U. Notre Dame, 1963, MA, 1967, ThM, 1969; PhD, Vanderbilt U., 1975. Joine Congregation Holy Cross, 1963, ordained priest Roman Cath. Ch., 1970. Instr. U. Notre Dame, Ind., 1974-75, asst. prof., 1975-81, assoc. prof., 1981-88, prof. theology, 1988—, assoc. provost, 1982-86, pres. elect, 1986, pres., 1987—; bd. regents U. Portland, Oreg., 1985—. Author: Homosexuality and the Christian Way of Life, 1981, The Ethics of Law Enforcement and Criminal Punishment, 1982, Culture and Commitment: The Challenge of Today's University, 1992; contbr. articles to profl. jours. Chmn. Am. Coun. on Edn.; bd. dirs. NCAA Found., 1989—; mem. Bishops and Pres.' com. Assn. Cath. Colls. and Univs., 1988—; bd. dirs. Internat. Fedn. Cath. Univs., 1988—; mem. Pres.'s Adv. Coun. on Drugs, 1989—; mem. adv. bd. AmeriCorps and Nat. Civilian Community Corps, 1994—; interim chmn. Ind. Commn. on Community Svc., 1994—; bd. dirs. Points of Light, Campus Compact. Mem. Cath. Theol. Soc., Am. Soc. Christian Ethics, Bus.-Higher Edn. Forum, Assn. Governing Bds. of Univs. and Colls. (vice chair 1996—), The Conf. Bd. Office: U Notre Dame Office Pres Notre Dame IN 46556

MALLOY, JAMES JOSEPH, real estate manager; b. Milw., Feb. 25, 1941; s. Joseph James Malloy and Olga Ida (Heuiter) Auerbach; m. Kathleen Mary Vanden Elsen, Oct. 5, 1974; children: Steven, Scott. BS, U. Wis., Stevens Point, 1965; MS, No. Ill. U., 1969; postgrad., U. Iowa, 1969-73. Dir. cartographic svcs. No. Ill. U., Dekalb, 1965-68, instr. geography, 1968-69; transp. planning coord. East Cen. Wis. Regional Planning Commn., Neenah, Wis., 1973-80; dir. sales and mktg. Wis. & So. RR Co., Horicon, 1980-82, asst. gen. mgr., 1982-85, gen. mgr., 1985-86, sr. v.p., gen. mgr., 1986-88; exec. v.p., COO Wis. & So. R.R. Co., Horicon, 1988-94; realtor Prudential Preferred Properties, Brookfield, Wis., 1994—. Bd. dirs. Midwest Adv. Bd., Homewood, Ill., 1985-94; prog. devel. coun. Operation Lifesaver, Inc., Alexandria, Va., 1987-90. Staff sgt. U.S. Army Nat. Guard, 1965-72. Mem. Midwest Adv. Bd. (pres. 1990-91, bd. dirs. 1985-94, Am. Shortline RR Assn. (regional v.p. 1990-94, bd. dirs. 1986—), Am. Assn. RR Supts., Wis. Operation Lifesaver Com. Home: 885 Rocky Pt # C Brookfield WI 53005-5739 Office: Prudential Preferred Properties 17345 W Bluemound Rd Brookfield WI 53045

MALLOY, KATHLEEN SHARON, lawyer; b. Evergreen Park, Ill., Apr. 7, 1948, d. Clarence Edmund and Ruth Elizabeth (Petrini) M.; m. Randall Kleinman, Aug. 5, 1978; children: Brighid, Ellena, Grant. BA in Psychology, St. Louis U., 1970; JD, Loyola U., Chgo., 1976. Bar: Ill. 1976, Calif. 1977. CPCU; assoc. in reinsurance. Account exec. Complete Equity Mkts., Wheeling, Ill., 1970-76, corp. counsel, 1976-80, v.p., gen. counsel, 1980-83, exec. v.p., gen. counsel, 1983, chief oper. officer, gen. counsel, 1984-85, vice chmn. bd., gen. counsel, 1986-90; founding ptnr. firm Malloy & Kleinman, P.C., Des Plaines, Ill., 1985—. Vol. atty. legal aid orgns., Calif., 1976-79; dir. Keep Des Plaines Beautiful, Inc., 1990-92. Mem. ABA, Calif. State Bar Assn., Mensa, Women's Bar Assn., Nat. Legal Aid and Defender Assn. (exofficio mem. ins. com. 1986-94), Am. Soc. Chartered Property Casualty Underwriters. Office: Malloy & Kleinman PC 640 Pearson St Ste 206 Des Plaines IL 60016-4624

MALM, ROGER CHARLES, lawyer; b. Hot Springs, S.D., July 8, 1949; s. Harry Milton and Angeline Mae (Johnson) M.; m. Sandra M. Metz, July 15, 1972; children: Andrew, Elliott, Nicholas. BA, St. Olaf Coll., 1971; JD, U. N.D., 1974. Bar: N.D. 1974, Ariz. 1975, Minn. 1980, U.S. Dist. Ct. N.D. 1974, U.S. Dist. Ct. Ariz. 1976, U.S. Ct. Appeals (9th cir.) 1981, U.S. Supreme Ct. 1981, U.S. Ct. Appeals (8th cir) 1982, U.S. Dist. Ct. Minn. 1985, U.S. Claims Ct. 1985, U.S. Tax Ct. 1988. Ptnr. Brink, Sobolik, Severson, Malm & ALbrecht, P.A., Hallock, Minn., 1980—; county atty. Kittson County, Minn., 1995—. Hospice dir. Kittson County Hospice, Inc., 1984—; bd. dirs. Cmty. Theatre, Hallock, 1987—, Greater Grand Forks Cmty. Theater, 1991-95. Mem. ABA, Ariz. Bar Assn., N.D. Bar Assn., Minn. Bar Assn. (bd. govs. 1993—), Am. acad. Hosp. Attys. Lutheran. Office: Brink Sobolik Severson Vroom & Malm 217 S Birch Box 790 Hallock MN 56728

MALMQUIST, CARL PHILLIP, psychiatrist; b. St. Paul, Mar. 10, 1934; s. Phillip C. and Lillian Viola (Kahler) M.; m. Arlyn Virginia Bodal (dec. 1984); children: Derek, Jay. BA summa cum laude, U. Minn., 1954, MD, 1958, MS in Philosophy of Sci., 1961. Diplomate Am. Bd. Psychiatry and Neurology, Am. Bd. Child Psychiatry, Am. Bd. Adult Psychiatry; cert. forensic psychiatry, added qualification in forensic psychiatry. Intern U. Minn., 1962-63, Columbia Med. Ctr., N.Y.C., 1963-64; assoc. prof. dept. psychiatry U. Mich., 1965-67; assoc. prof. Inst. Child Devel. U. Minn., Mpls., 1967-70, prof., dir. child and adolescent psychiatry, 1971-72, prof. criminal justice, 1972-80, prof. social psychiatry, dept. sociology, 1980—; cons. Hennepin County, Mpls., 1967—, Dist. Ct., 1969—; mem. commn. of mentally disabled ABA, 1985. Author: Adolescent Development, 1980, Homicide: Psychiatric Perspectives, 1996; mem. editl. bd. Psychiat. Anns., 1981; contbr. articles to profl. jours. Fellow Am. Psychiat. Assn. (mem. commn. on jud. action 1994—), Am. Coll. Psychiatrists, Am. Orthopsychiat. Assn., Am. Acad. Child Psychiatry, Am. Acad. Psychiatry and Law, Am. Coll. Forensic Psychiatry; mem. Group for Advancement Psychiatry. Episcopalian. Home: 5010 Bruce Ave Minneapolis MN 55424-1318 Office: U Minn 6600 France Ave S Ste 545 Minneapolis MN 55435-1804

MALNASSY, LOUIS STURGES, public relations counselor; b. Chgo., May 11, 1952; s. Louis Allen and Valear Lucille (Henry) M.; m. Suzy Eileen Harrison, Dec. 20, 1975 (div. 1979); m. Kathleen Nancy Kunimoto, Nov. 15, 1980. BJ, U. Mo., 1974. Announcer Sta. WIKY-AM/FM, Evansville, Ind., 1974; host Sta. WKYX-AM, Paducah, Ky., 1974-75; program dir. Sta. WKYQ-FM, Paducah, 1974-75; prodn. dir. Sta. WPAD-AM/FM, Paducah, 1975-79; copywriter George Johnson, Advt., St. Louis, 1979; sr. writer Stix, Baer and Fuller, St. Louis, 1979-81; acct. exec. Shandwick USA (formerly Dorf & Stanton Comm.), St. Louis, 1981-85, sr. writer, 1985-90, acct. supr., 1990—; freelance journalist, 1974-75. Co-author: Growing for the Future, 1985; contbr. articles to profl. jours. Mem. Nat. Agri Mktg. Assn. (Best of NAMA award 1983), Nat. Assn. Farm Broadcasters, Pub. Rels. Soc. Am. Office: Shandwick USA Comm Communications 515 Olive St Ste 1900 Saint Louis MO 63101

MALNORY, MARGARET ELLEN, perinatal clinical nurse specialist, nurse researcher; d. John W. and Lina E. (Whalen) Malnory; m. Thomas Silbernagel; children: Shannon, Colin. BSN, U. Wis., 1973, MSN, 1978. Staff nurse U. Wis. Hosp., Madison, 1973, Madison Gen. Hosp., 1973-78; asst. adj. prof. parent/child nursing Marquette U., Milw., 1978-81; perinatal clin. nurse specialist St. Michael Hosp., Milw., 1979-81; dir. family centered maternity care/perinatal CNS Mt. Sinai Med. Ctr., Milw., 1981-87, dir. labor/deliver, NICU, FCNU, 1987-88; mgr. FCNU/labor and deliver, perinatal CNS Sinai Samaritan Med. Ctr., Milw., 1988-89, mgr. WCC and perinatal CNS, 1989-92; nurse adminstr. Tokos Med. Corp., 1992-95; nurse rschr. U. Wis. Med. Sch., Milw., 1995—; prenatal case mgr., home care coord. Sinai Samaritan Med. Ctr., Milw., 1995—; lectr. and cons. in field; adv. bd. Nat. Perinatal Nurses Conf., 1989-91. Contbr. articles to profl. jours.; co-editor Perinatal Nursing Link Newsletter, 1991. Named Maternal-Child Nurse of Yr., Wis. Nurses Assn./March of Dimes, 1991. Mem. NAACOG, ANA, Milw. Dist. Nurses Assn., Wis. Assn. for Prenatal Care, Sigma Theta Tau (treas. 1991). Office: Sinai Samaritan Med Ctr 2000 W Kilbourn St Milwaukee WI 53213

MALONE, DANIEL LEE, controller; b. Decatur, Ill., Aug. 2, 1949; s. Henry E. and Shirley E. (Frank) M.; m. Linda S. Hunter, Nov. 20, 1971; children: John, Megan. AAS, Wright Jr. Coll., 1972; BS in Bus. Adminstrn., Roosevelt U., 1977. Cost analyst Western Electric, Cicero, Ill., 1969-73; staff acct. Fred Landau and Co. CPA's, Chgo., 1973-74; asst. to v.p. of adminstrn. Magnecraft Electric., Chgo., 1974-77; ops. mgr. Bliss and Laughlin-Waco Midwest, Addison, Ill., 1977-78; internal auditor FHC Enterprises, Inc., Rosemont, Ill., 1978-80; controller FHC Enterprises, Inc., Rosemont, 1980-83, v.p. fin., 1983-87, sr. v.p., 1987-89, chief fin. officer, 1990—. Treas. Our Saviors Luth. Ch., Burbank, Ill., 1979-80; Fin. adv. 1986—; mem. Gov.'s Task Force on Nursing Homes, Ill., 1983-85, CPA's For Pub. Interest, Chgo., 1987—. Mem. AICPA, IBCFP, Ill. CPA Soc. (long term care inst. com. chmn. 1987-88, mem. svc. 1980), Franklin Honor Soc., Roosevelt Univ., Marriage Encounter, Beta Gamma Sigma. Office: FHC Enterprises Inc 10700 W Higgins Rd Ste 301 Des Plaines IL 60018-3724

MALONE, JAMES WILLIAM, retired bishop; b. Youngstown, Ohio, Mar. 8, 1920; s. James Patrick and Katherine V. (McGuire) M. AB, St. Mary Sem., Cleve., 1945; MA, Cath. U. Am., 1952, PhD, 1957. Ordained priest Roman Catholic Ch., 1945; asst. pastor Youngstown, 1945-50; supt. schs. Diocese of Youngstown, 1952-65; instr. ednl. adminstrn. St. John's Coll., Cleve., 1953; aux. bishop of Youngstown, 1960-68; bishop, 1968-96; ret. Diocese Youngstown, 1996; v.p. Nat. Conf. cath. Bishops, 1980-83; pres. Nat. Conf. Cath. Bishops, 1983-86, mem. Bishops' Com. Ecumencial and Interreligious Affairs; cons. Com. on Socia Devel. & World Peace; ad hoc com. on health care NCCB, ex corde ecclesiae com.; mem. Nat. Interfaith Com. for Worker Justice. consultor Com. on Social Devel. and World Peace; mem. ad. hoc com. on health care, ex corde ecclesiae com. Nat. Conf. Cath. Bishops; mem. Nat. Interfaith Commn. for Worker Justice. Trustee Cath. U. Am.

MALONE, LAURENCE ADAMS, economist, consultant; b. Cleve., Dec. 4, 1911; s. Cornelius Fitzgerald and Grace Adams (True) M.; m. Ethel Whatley, Jan. 2, 1962 (dec. 1987); m. Nettie Allen, July 24, 1987. LLB, Chgo. U., 1962; PhD, Columbia Pacific U., 1967. Contracting officer USN Sea Systems Command, Washington, 1941-79; economist Direct Answer Publishing Inc, Chagrin Falls, Ohio. Author: An Evolving World, 1972, Restoration, 1972, Our Debt Money Systems, 1985, How to Stop Foreclosure, 1982; patentee in field. Decorated Order of St. John, Knights of Malta. Roman Catholic. Home: 332 Hamlet Hills Dr Chagrin Falls OH 44022-2807

MALONEY, CHERYL ANN, author, photographer; b. St. Paul, Aug. 30, 1949; d. Arlie Chester and Mary Dawn (Holm) M. AA, U. Minn., 1969, BA in Speech and Theatre, 1972; MA in Theology/Spirituality, Coll. St. Catherine, St. Paul, 1989, MA cert. in Pastoral Ministry, 1990; postgrad., Calif. Inst. Integral Studies, 1994—. Dir. Women's Network, Mpls., 1975-76; dir. cultural arts City of Bloomington, Minn., 1977-78; community organizer Mpls. Crime Prevention Program, 1979-80; bus. adminstr. Al's Auto Crushing, Inc., Mpls., 1980-81; rsch. assoc. St. Paul Ramsey Med. Ctr., 1981-83; adjustor Dependable Auto Appraisal, Inc., Bloomington, 1983; dir. mktg. and devel. Health Recovery Center, Mpls., 1983-85; cons. Autowoman, Inc., Mpls., 1985—; mktg. rep. Dashe and Thomson, Mpls., 1987-89; dir. sales and mktg. Fredrickson Communications, Mpls., 1989-91; freelance photographer, Mpls., 1971—; quality cons., 1991—; ofcl. photographer Internat. Women's Ecumenical Decade Chs. Solidarity Women, 1993; speaker U. Bethlehem, Israel, 1993; tchr. Holy Childhood H.S., Jamaica, 1992; presenter M.R.A. Internat. Conf., Caux, Switzerland, 1996. Author: Housing Resource Book for Minneapolis, 1974, Women's Network Directory, 1976; photographer: Goodwill Designer Showcase Magazine, 1975. State Dem. del., St. Paul, 1976; coach and youth leader Unity South Ch., Bloomington, 1967-93; coach Ind. Ch., Mpls., 1984-92; chaplain U. St. Thomas, St. Paul, 1989-92, chair women and religion com.; outreach min., ch. developer Unity of Valley, Minn., 1990-93; U.S. rep. Gov. Gen.'s Conf., Jamaica, 1992; lay consociate Sisters St. Joseph, 1992, appt. peace and justice commn., 1993—; chair 125th Anniversary Celebration Sisters of the Holy Family; presenter Internat. Youth Leadership Conf., Brazil, Uruguay, Argentina, 1993. Recipient Celtic Studies award Coll. St. Catherine, St. Paul, 1988; honoree Hamnline U., St. Paul, 1993; Great Lakes Region scholar, 1986. Mem. AAUW, Mpls. Women's Rotary (bd. dirs. 1990-94), Minn. Coun. for Quality (editor newsletter 1993-94, Sales and Mktg. Execs. Am., Theol. Insights Prog. Coll. St. Catherine, M.R.A. Caux Bus. Roundtable Internat. (nat. team planners for N.Am. and S.Am. activities), Self-Employed Womens Club (co-dir., 1992-94), Le Group, Nat. Fedn. Ind. Bus. Home: 5501 Queen Ave S Minneapolis MN 55410-2532 Office: Sisters of the Holy Family Dir of Devel 159 Washington Blvd Fremont CA 94539-0324

MALONEY, VINCENT JOHN, lawyer, social worker, psychotherapist; b. Bryn Mawr, Pa., June 21, 1949; s. Vincent John and Mary Margaret (Lavelle) M.; m. Kathaleen Joanne Carpenter, Dec. 3, 1988; children: Kimberly Kenny, Jennifer Kenny. BA, U. Mich., 1972, MSW, 1976; JD, Wayne State U., 1987. Bar: Mich. 1987, Colo. 1992; cert. social worker; registered clin. social worker. Camp dir. Hemophilia of Mich., Ann Arbor, 1976-77; clin. supr. Cornerstone Counseling, Belleville, Mich., 1978-84; psychotherapist Community Care Svcs., Belleville, 1984-87; assoc. atty. Hyman, Gurwin Nachman Gold and Alterman, Southfield, Mich., 1987-88; pvt. practice Farmington Hills, Mich., 1988—; mem. Com. to Establish Friend of the Ct. Guidelines for Custody Disputes, State Ct. Adminstrv. Office, 1990-91; field instr. U. Mich. Sch. Social Work, 1978-85. Co-author: Consumer Guide to Divorce, 1990. Mem. State Bar Colo., Nat. Assn. Social Workers, State Bar Mich. (family law sect.). Office: 30445 Northwestern Hwy Ste 200 Farmington Hills MI 48334-3175

MALOOLEY, DAVID JOSEPH, electronics and computer technology educator; b. Terre Haute, Ind., Aug. 20, 1951; s. Edward Joseph and Vula (Starn) M. B.S., Ind. State U., 1975; M.S., Ind. U., 1981, doctoral candidate. Supr., Zenith Radio Corp., Paris, Ill., 1978-79; assoc. prof. electronics and computer tech. Ind. State U., Terre Haute, 1979—; cons. in field. Served to 1st lt. U.S. Army, 1975-78. Mem. ASCD, Soc. Mfg. Engrs., Nat. Assn. Indsl. Tech., Am. Vocat. Assn., Instrument Soc. Am. (sr.), Phi Delta Kappa, Pi Lambda Theta, Epsilon Pi Tau. Democrat. Christian. Home: 11420 Spring Creek Rd Terre Haute IN 47805-9679 Office: Ind State U Computer Sci Dept Terre Haute IN 47809

MALOON, JERRY L., lawyer, physician, medicolegal consultant; b. Union City, Ind., June 23, 1938; s. Charles Elias and Bertha Lucille (Creviston) M.; children: Jeffrey Lee, Jerry Lee II. BS, Ohio State U., 1960, MD, 1964; JD, Capital U. Law Sch., 1974. Intern Santa Monica (Calif.) Hosp., 1964-65; tng. psychiatry Cen. Ohio Psychiat. Hosp., 1969, Menninger Clinic, Topeka, 1970; clin. dir. Orient (Ohio) Devel. Ctr., 1967-69, med. dir., 1971-83; assoc. med. dir. Western Electric, Inc., Columbus, 1969-71; cons. State Med. Bd. Ohio, 1974-80; pvt. practice law, Columbus, 1978—; pres. Jerry L. Maloon Co., L.P.A., 1981—; medicolegal cons., 1972—; pres. Madison, Maloon & Barclay Co., L.P.A., 1990-95; guest lectr. law and medicine Orient Devel. Ctr. and Columbus Devel. Ctr., 1969-71; dep. coroner Franklin County (Ohio), 1978-84. Served to capt. M.C., AUS, 1965-67. Fellow Am. Coll. Legal Medicine; mem. AMA, ABA, Ohio Bar Assn., Columbus Bar Assn., Am. Trial Lawyers Assn., Ohio Trial Lawyers Assn., Columbus Trial Lawyers Assn., Ohio State U. Alumni Assn., U.S. Trotting Assn., Am. Profl. Practice Assn. Clubs: Ohio State U. Pres.'s, Buckeye. Home: 2140 Cambridge Blvd Upper Arlngtn OH 43221-4104 Office: Jerry L Maloon Co LPA 475 E Town St Columbus OH 43215-4706

MALOTT, ROBERT HARVEY, manufacturing company executive; b. Boston, Oct. 6, 1926; s. Deane W. and Eleanor (Thrum) M.; m. Elizabeth Harwood Hubert, June 4, 1960; children: Elizabeth Malott Pohle, Barbara Holden, Robert Deane. A.B., U. Kans., 1948; M.B.A., Harvard U., 1950; postgrad., N.Y. U. Law Sch., 1953-55. Asst. to dean Harvard Grad. Sch. Bus. Adminstrn., 1950-52; with FMC Corp., 1952—; asst. to exec. v.p. chems. div. FMC Corp., N.Y.C., 1952-55; controller Niagara Chem. div. FMC Corp., Middleport, N.Y., 1955-59; controller organic chems. div. FMC Corp., N.Y.C., 1959-62; asst. div. mgr. FMC Corp., 1962-63, div. mgr., 1963-65, v.p., mgr. film ops. Am. Viscose div., 1966-67, exec. v.p., mem. president's office, 1967-70; mgr. machinery divs. FMC Corp., Chgo., 1970-72; pres. FMC Corp., from 1972, chief exec. officer, 1972-91, chmn., 1973-91, chmn., exec. com., 1991—; dir. FMC Corp., Amoco Corp., United Techs. Corp. Trustee U. Chgo.; bd. govs. Argonne Labs.; bd. overseers Hoover Instn.; mem. Nat. Bd. of Nat. Mus. of Nat. Hist. Smithsonian Inst.; bd. dirs. Nat. Park Found. Served with USNR, 1944-46. Mem. Explorers Club, Bus. Coun., U.S. C. of C., Econ. Club, Mid-Am. Club, Indian Hill Club,

Bohemian Club, Phi Beta Kappa, Alpha Chi Sigma, Beta Theta Pi. Office: FMC Corp 200 E Randolph St Chicago IL 60601-6436

MALTZ, ROBERT, surgeon; b. Cin., July 21, 1935; s. William and Sarah (Goldberg) M.; m. Sylvia Moskowitz, Aug. 24, 1958; children: Mark Edward, Deborah Lynn, Steven Alan, David Stuart. BS in Zoology, U. Cin., 1958, MD, 1962. Diplomate Am. Bd. Otolaryngology, 1970. Intern Cin. Gen. Hosp., 1962-63; resident Barnes Hosp., St. Louis, 1965-69; asst. prof. surgery Stanford U. Med. Ctr., Palo Alto, Calif., 1969-71; asst. prof. otolaryngology U. Cin. Med. Ctr., 1971-75, assoc. prof. otolaryngology, 1975—; dir. dept. otolaryngology Jewish Hosp., Cin., 1992—; chief, div. head and neck surgery, dept. otolaryngology and maxillofacial surgery U. Cin. Med. Ctr., 1972-76; bd. dirs. Cancer Control Council, U. Cin. Med. Cntr.; cons. Bur. Crippled Children's Svcs., State of Ohio; mem. med. records com. Cin. Gen. Hosp., utilization rev. com., tissue com., Holmes Hosp., Med. Audit Com., Tissue Com., Cin. Gen. Hosp., med. records com. Jewish Hosp.; on staff VA Hosp., Cin., Children's Hosp. Med. Ctr., Holmes Hosp., Bethesda Hosp., Cin., Christ Hosp., Shriners Burn Inst., Cin., Our Lady of Mercy Hosp.; del. to numerous profl. confs.; mem. health affairs adv. com. Cmty. Mut. Ins. Co.; mem. mng. bd. PIE Mut. Ins. Co.; bd. dirs. UCATS, 1995—; instr. short term courses in field. Contbr. articles to profl. jours. Bd. dirs. Jewish Community Rels. Coun.; mem. faculty adv. com. U. Cinn., mem. med. alumni exec. coun. Capt. USAF, 1963-65, PTO. USPHS fellow, 1968-69; grantee Eli Lilly Co. grantee, 1971-76, Burroughs Wellcome Co., 1972. Fellow ACS, Am. Acad. Facial and Reconstructive Surgery (edn. com. 1972, future plans com. 1973-75, sci. program com., budget and fin. com. 1975, chmn. credentials com., no. sect. 1980-85), Royal Soc. Health, Internat. Cosmetic Surgeons, Am. Acad. Cosmetic Surgeons, Am. Assn. Cosmetic Surgeons (sec.-treas. 1976-81); mem. Am. Acad. Otolaryngology and Head and Neck Surgery, Am. Coun. Otolaryngology, Soc. Univ. Otolaryngologists, Pan-Am. Assn. Oto-Rhino-Laryngology and Broncho-Esophagology, Ohio State Med. Assn., Cin. Acad. Medicine (chmn. pub. rels. com. 1980, trustee 1992-95, legis. com. 1985—, treas. 1993-95, chmn. commn. com. 1994—, pres. 1996, editl. bd. 1994—, chmn. specialty soc. com. 1995), U. Cin. Alumni Assn. (bd. govs., sec. 1994, fin. v.p. 1995, 1st v.p. 1996), Cin. Ear, Nose and Throat Soc., Ulex Club, Metro Club, Losantiville Country Club, Queen City Racquet Club, Omicron Delta Kappa, Sigma Sigma, Sigma Alpha Mu. Home: 2601 Willowbrook Dr Cincinnati OH 45237-3725 Office: 10496 Montgomery Rd Cincinnati OH 45242-5220

MAMAT, FRANK TRUSTICK, lawyer; b. Syracuse, N.Y., Sept. 4, 1949; s. Harvey Sanford and Annette (Trustick) M.; m. Kathy Lou Winters, June 23, 1975; children: Jonathan Adam, Steven Kenneth. BA, U. Rochester, 1971; JD, Syracuse U., 1974. Bar: D.C. 1976, U.S. Ct. Appeals (D.C. cir.) 1976, Fla. 1977, U.S. Supreme Ct. 1979, US. Dist. Ct. (ea. dist.) 1983, U.S. Ct. Appeals (6th cir.) 1983, Mich. 1984, U.S. Dist. Ct. (no. dist.) Ind. 1984. Atty. NLRB, Washington, 1975-79; assoc. Proskauer, Rose, Goetz & Mendelsohn, Washington, N.Y.C. and L.A., 1979-83; assoc. Fishman Group, Bloomfield Hills, Mich., 1983-85, ptnr., 1985-87; sr. ptnr. Honigman, Miller, Schwartz and Cohn, 1987-94; pres. Morgan Daniels Co., Inc., West Bloomfield, Mich., 1995—; ptnr. Clark Klein & Beaumont, P.L.C., Detroit, 1995-96, Clark Hill, P.L.C., Detroit, 1996—; bd. dirs. Mich. Food and Beverage Assn., Air Conditioning Contractors of Am., Air Conditioning Contractors of Mich., Associated Builders and Contractors, Am. Subcontractors Assn., Mich. Mfrs. Assn. Labor Counsel. Gen. counsel Rep. Com. of Oakland County, 1986-89, 93—, Constrn. Code commn. Mich., 1993—; bd. dirs. 300 Club, Mich., 1984-90; pres. 400 Club, 1990-93, chmn., 1993—; mem. Associated Gen. Contractors Labor Lawyers Coun.; mem. Rep. Nat. Com. Nat. Rep. Senatorial Com., Presdl. Task Force, Rep. Labor Coun., Washington; city dir. West Bloomfield, 1985-87; pres. West Bloomfield Rep. Club, 1985-87; fin. com. Rep. Com. of Oakland County, 1984-93; pres. Oakland County Lincoln Rep. Club, 1989-90; bd. dirs. camping svcs. and human resources com. YMCA, 1989-93, Anti-Defamation League, 1989—; vice chmn. Lawyers for Reagan-Bush, 1984; v.p. Fruehauf Farms, West Bloomfield, Mich., 1985-88; mem. staff Exec. Office of Pres. of U.S. Inquiries/Comments, Washington, 1981-83. Mem. ABA, Fed. Bar Assn., Mich. Bar Assn., Fla. Bar Assn. (labor com. 1977—), Mich. Bus. and Profl. Assn., Am. Subcontractors Assn. (Southeastern Mich., bd. dirs.), Founders Soc. (Detroit Inst. Art), D.C. Bar Assn., Detroit Bar Assn., Oakland County Bar Assn., B'nai B'rith (v.p. 1982-83, trustee Detroit coun. 1987-88, bd. dirs. Detroit Barristers unit 1983-91, pres. 1985-87), Detroit Club, Oakpointe Country Club, Detroit Soc. Clubs, Skyline Club, Fairline Club, Renaissance Club. Office: Clark Hill PLC 1600 First Fed Bldg Detroit MI 48226 also: Morgan Daniels Co Inc 5484 Crispin Way Rd West Bloomfield MI 48323

MAMMEL, RUSSELL NORMAN, retired food distribution company executive; b. Hutchinson, Kans., Apr. 28, 1926; s. Vyvian E. and Mabel Edwina (Hursh) M.; m. Betty Crawford, Oct. 29, 1949 (dec. Oct. 1994); children: Mark, Christopher, Elizabeth, Nancy. BS, U. Kans., 1949. With Mammel's Inc., Hutchinson, 1949-57, pres., 1957-59; retail gen. mgr. Kans. divsn. Nash Finch Co., Hutchinson, 1959-61; retail gen. mgr. Iowa divsn. Nash Finch Co., Cedar Rapids, 1961-66; dir. store devel. Nash Finch Co., Mpls., 1966-75, v.p., 1975-83, exec. v.p., 1983-85, pres., COO, 1985-91; also bd. dirs. Nash Finch Co., Mpls., Mpls., 1991; pvt. investments, 1991—. With AUS, 1944-46. Home: 6808 Cornelia Dr Minneapolis MN 55435-1608 Office: Nash Finch Co 7600 France Ave S Minneapolis MN 55435-5924

MAMUT, MARY CATHERINE, retired entrepreneur; b. Calabria, Italy, Oct. 17, 1923; came to U.S., 1928; d. Carmelo Charles and Caterina (Tripodi) Cogliandro; m. Michael Matthew Mamut, May 15, 1954; children: Anthony Carl, Charles Terrance. Student, Stenotype Comml. Coll., 1946-50. Sec. to pres. Thomas Goodfellow, Inc., Detroit, 1942-50; asst. to v.p. R.G. Moeller Co., Detroit, 1951-52; sec. to pres. United Steel Supply Co., Detroit, 1952-54; sec. to libr. Farmington (Mich.) Schs., 1962-68; real estate agt., 1969; owner, mgr. Crystal Fair, Birmingham, Mich., 1969-88; ret. Crystal Fair, Mich.; tchr. Stenotype Comml. Coll., Detroit, 1952-54. Vol. Henry Ford Mus., Dearborn, Mich., 1989-90, Greenfield Village, 1989-90, West Bloomfield Libr., 1993-95. Recipient World Lifetime Achievement award Am. Biog. Inst. U.S.A., 1993. Mem. Am. Bus. Women's Assn., Birmingham-Bloomfield C. of C., Profl. Secs. Internat, NAFE. Roman Catholic. Home: 7423 Coach Ln West Bloomfield MI 48322-4022

MANCHESTER, CAROL ANN FRESHWATER, psychologist; b. Coshocton, Ohio, Sept. 30, 1942; d. James M. and Kathleen C. (Call) Freshwater; m. Crosby Manchester, Mar. 16, 1963 (dec. 1973). BS, Ohio State U., 1963, MS, 1973, PhD, 1977. Diplomate Internat. Soc. Psychotherapy and Behavioral Medicine, Am. Bd. Forensic Examiners. Elem. counselor Columbus (Ohio) Pub. Schs., 1973-79; counselor Regional Alcoholism & Tng. Ctr., Columbus, 1977-79; therapist Beechwold Clinic, Columbus, 1977-80; counselor Gifted and Talented Program, Columbus, 1979-81; dir. Freshwater Mental Health Clinic, Columbus, 1982—; asst. clin. prof. Coll. Medicine Ohio State U., 1990-95; instr. psychology Urbana Coll., Columbus, 1977-79; dir. Freshwater Clinic, Columbus, 1983—; bd. dirs. Ecole Francaise, Columbus, 1985—; cons. Columbus Cmty. Hosp., 1988—, Mt. Carmel Med. Ctr., Park Med. Ctr., Columbus, 1990—; presenter in field. Author: Affective Model The Gifted and Talented Handbook for Columbus Public Schools, 1981. Active Gov.'s Task Force on Child Abuse, Columbus. Recipient Disting. Svc. award Ohio Counselor's Assn., Valley Forge Freedom award. Mem. ACLU, AOA, Am. Acad. Cert. Neurotherapists (v.p. 1993, 94, diplomate, exec. bd. dirs.), Am. Acad. Neurobrainwave Therapists (v.p.), Soc. of Neuronal Regulation (v.p.), Nat. Soc. Clin. Hypnosis, Meninger Soc., Internat. Soc. Post Traumatic Stress, Internat. Soc. Multiple Personality Disorder, Assn. Applied Psychophysiology and Biofeedback, Ohio Psychol. Assn., Delta Omicron, Tau Beta Sigma. Office: Freshwater Clinic 6065 Glick Rd Ste C Powell OH 43065-9604

MANCHESTER, DIANA, writer; b. Columbus, Ohio, Aug. 7, 1955; d. Robert William Sr. and Ruth Evelyn (Price) Short; m. Jason Hewitt Manchester, Aug. 7, 1982. Grad. Human Nutrition summa cum laude, Ohio State U., 1995, postgrad., 1995—. With First Columbus Corp., 1973-78; with DaNite Sign Co., Columbus, 1978-79; treas. Guardian Nat. Corp., Columbus, 1979-81; stamp dealer Quality Topical Supply, Columbus, 1981-82, E.M. Ellman & Assocs., Columbus, 1982-85; vol. philatelic activities Columbus, 1985—; ptnr. Shortbread Pub., 1994—; instr. dept. nutrition Ohio State U., 1995—. Author: GPS 40th Anniversary Anthology, 1989, Postage Rates of Germany, 1906-1923, 1991; editor Inflation Study Group Bull. of the German Philatelic Soc., 1984—. Mem. Am. Dietetic Assn., Am. Home Econs. Assn., Am. Philatelic Soc. (chmn. activities com. 1988—, Unit 30 writers coun. mem. 1987-91), Columbus Philatelic Club Inc. (COLOPEX show chmn. 1987-91, medal of honor 1988, Carl Sachs award 1989), German Philatelic Soc. (bd. dirs. 1989-93), Am. Philatelic Congress (coun. mem. 1988-91), Phi Upsilon Omicron, Kappa Omicron Nu, Phi Kappa Phi. Republican.

MANCINOTTI, CRAIG JOHN, financial executive; b. Genoa, Ohio, Aug. 8, 1961. BBA in Fin., U. Toledo, 1983, MBA, 1984. Exec. v.p., prin. Austin Assocs., Inc., Toledo, 1982—; bd. dirs. Peoples State Bank. Contbr. articles to profl. jours. Office: Austin Assocs Inc 7205 W Central Ave Toledo OH 43617-1118

MANCUSO, JOSEPH EDWARD, medical psychotherapist; b. Rockford, Ill., Dec. 1, 1955; s. Robert Fredrick and Anne Mancuso. Student, Bradley U., Peoria, Ill., 1974-76; BA in Psychology, Marquette U., 1984, MEd in Ednl. Psychology, 1987. Cert. alcohol and drug abuse counselor, Wis. and nat.; cert. clin. assoc. med. psychotherapist, nat.; cert. ind. clin. social worker, Wis. Child care worker Community Care Svcs. Inc., Milw., 1984; day care dir. Mich. Street Day Care, Milw.; adminstrv. unit clk. Milw. Jewish Nursing Home; day care tchr. St. Mary's Children's Sch., Milw.; psychotherapist Wis. Correctional Svcs., Milw.; coord. alcohol and other drug abuse St. Mary's Psychiat. Hosp., Milw., 1990-92; cons. social worker St. Mary's Med. Hosp., Milw., 1990-91; pvt. practice, 1993—; emergency rm. social worker Sinai Samaritan Med. Ctr., Milw., 1994—; presenter in field. Cartoonist, published and shown in galleries throughout Milw. Mem. Am. Psychol. Assn. (assoc.), Wis. Psychol. Assn. (assoc.), Am. Ednl. Rsch. Assn. Home: 2490 N Fredrick Ave Milwaukee WI 53211-4419 Office: 2577 N Downer Ave Ste 210 Milwaukee WI 53211-4253

MANDECKI, WLODEK, molecular biologist; b. Warsaw, Poland, Aug. 29, 1951; s. Stefan Mandecki and Cecylia (Sobolewska) Mandecka; m. Wanda Michalska, Apr. 24, 1977; children: Michael, Thomas, Joanna. MS, U. Warsaw, 1975; PhD, Polish Acad. Scis., 1979. Postdoctoral researcher UCLA, L.A., 1980, U. Wis., Madison, 1980-81, U. Colo., Boulder, 1981-83; group leader, lab. head Abbott Labs., Abbott Park, Ill., 1983—. Contbr. over 50 articles to profl. jours. Mem. Protein Soc., AAAS. Office: Abbott Labs Viral Discovery D90D 1401 Sheridan Rd North Chicago IL 60064

MANDEL, KARYL LYNN, accountant; b. Chgo., Dec. 14, 1935; d. Isador J. and Eve (Gellar) Karzen; m. Fredric H. Mandel, Sept. 29, 1956; children: David Scott, Douglas Jay, Jennifer Ann. Student, U. Mich., 1954-56, Roosevelt U., 1956-57; AA summa cum laude, Oakton Community Coll., 1979. CPA, Ill. Pres. Excel Transp. Service Co., Elk Grove, Ill., 1958-78; tax mgr. Chunowitz, Teitelbaum & Baerson, CPA's, Northbrook, Ill., 1981-83, tax ptnr., 1984—; sec-treas. Lednam, Inc., Coffee Break, Inc.; mem. acctg. curriculum adv. bd. Oakton Community Coll., Des Plaines, Ill., 1987—. Contbg. author: Ill. CPA's News Jour. Recipient State of Israel Solidarity award, 1976. Mem. AICPA, Am. Soc. Women CPA, Women's Am. ORT (pres. Chgo. region 1972-74, v.p. midwest dist. 1975-76, nat. endowment com., nat investment adv. com.), Ill. CPA Soc. (chmn. estate and gift tax com. 1987-89, legis. contact com. 1981-82, pres. North Shore chpt., award for Excellence in Acctg. Edn., Bd. dirs. 1989-91), Chgo. Soc. Women CPA, Chgo. Estate Planning Coun., Nat. Assn. Women Bus. Owners, Lake County Estate Planning, Coun., Greater North Shore Estate Planning Coun. Office: 401 Huehl Rd Northbrook IL 60062-2300

MANDELKER, DANIEL ROBERT, law educator; b. Milw., July 18, 1926; s. Adolph Irwin and Marie (Manner) M.; divorced; children: Amy Jo, John David. BA, U. Wis., 1947, LLB, 1949; JD, Yale U., 1956. Bar: Wis. 1949. Asst. prof. law Drake U., 1949-51; atty. HHFA, Washington, 1952-53; asst. prof., then assoc. prof. law Ind. U., 1953-62; mem. faculty Washington U., St. Louis, 1962—; prof. law Washington U., 1963-74, Howard A. Stamper prof. law, 1974—; Walter E. Meyer rsch. prof. law Columbia U., 1971-72; Ford Found. law faculty fellow, London, 1959-60; cons. State of Hawaii Dept. Planning and Econ. Devel., 1972-78, State of Hawaii Office of State Planning, 1993-94; legal resources adv. group Transp. Rsch. Bd., 1991-94; mem. local govt. adv. bd. intergovtl. rels. U.S. Adv. Commn., 1985-88; mem. devel. regulations coun. Urban Land Inst., 1980-96; cons. housing subcom., banking and currency com. U.S. Ho. of Reps., 1970-71, cons. policy studies, ins. subcom., banking, fin., urban affairs coms., 1989-91; cons. state and local govts. on land use regulation; Nat. Disting. lectr. Fla. State Jour. Land Use and Environ. Law, 1992; 15th Denman lectr. U. Cambridge, Eng., 1992. Author: Green Belts and Urban Growth: English Town and Country Planning in Action, 1962, Controlling Planned Residential Developments, 1966, Managing Our Urban Environment-Cases, Text and Problems, 1966, 2d edit., 1971, Case Studies in Land Planning and Development, 1968, The Zoning Dilemma, 1971, (with W.R. Ewald) Street Graphics and the Law, 1971, 2d edit., 1988, (with R. Montgomery) Housing in America: Problems and Perspectives, 1973, 2d edit., 1979, Housing Subsidies in the United States and England, 1973, New Developments in Land and Environmental Controls, 1974, Environmental and Land Controls Legislation, 1976, supplement, 1982, (with D. Netsch) State and Local Government in a Federal System, 1977, supplement, 1981, (with D. Netsch and P. Salsich) 2d edit., 1983, supplement, 1987, (with Netsch, Salsich and Wegner) 3rd edit., 1990, supplement, 1992, (with R. Cunningham) Planning and Control of Land Development, 1979, 3d edit., 1990, (with R. Cunningham and J. Payne) 4th edit., 1995, Environment and Equity, 1981, (with others) Cases and Materials on Housing and Urban Development, 1981, 2d edit., 1989, Land Use Law, 1982, 3d edit., 1993, supplement, 1995, (with F. Anderson and D. Tarlock) Environmental Protection Law and Policy, 2d edit., 1990, NEPA Law and Litigation, 2d edit., 1992, supplement, 1996, (with J. Gerard and T. Sullivan) Federal Land Use Law, 1986, supplement, 1995; mem. editl. adv. bd. various land use jours. Mem. nat. adv. com. on outdoor advt. and motorist info. Dept. Transp., 1980-81; mem. adv. com. on housing Dem. Caucus, U.S. Ho. of Reps., 1981-82; pres. Nat. Coalition for Scenic Beauty, 1987-88; sr. fellow Urban Land Inst., 1989-95; mem. law sch. editl. bd. Michie Co., 1989—. Mem. NAS (com. social and behavioral urban rsch. 1967-68), Am. Planning Assn. (bd. dirs. 1981-84, Housing Policy Task Force 1990-93, property rights task force 1994-95), Order of Coif, Phi Beta Kappa, Phi Kappa Phi. Office: Washington U Sch Law Campus Box 1120 Saint Louis MO 63130

MANDERS, KARL LEE, neurosurgeon; b. Rochester, N.Y., Jan. 21, 1927; s. David Bert and Frances Edna (Cohan) Mendelson; m. Ann Laprell, July 28, 1969; children: Karlanna, Maidena; children by previous marriage; Karl, Kerry, Kristine. Student, Cornell U., 1946; MD, U. Buffalo, 1950. Diplomate Am. Bd. Neurol. Surgery, Am. Bd. Clin. Biofeedback, Am. Bd. Hyperbaric Medicine, Am. Bd. Pain Medicine, Nat. Bd. Med. Examiners. Intern U. Va. Hosp., Charlottesville, 1950-51, resident in neurol. surgery, 1951-52; resident in neurol. surgery Henry Ford Hosp., Detroit, 1954-56; pvt. practice Indpls., 1956—; med. dir. Cmty. Hosp. Rehab. Ctr. for Pain, 1973—; chief hosp. med. and surg. neurology Cmty. Hosp., 1983, 93; coroner Marion County, Ind., 1977-85, 92-96. Served with USN, 1952-54, Korea. Recipient cert. achievement Dept. Army, 1969. Fellow ACS, Internat. Coll Surgeons, Am. Acad. Neurology; mem. Am. Assn. Neurol. Surgery, Congress Neurol. Surgery, Internat. Assn. Study of Pain, Am. Assn. Study of Headache, N.Y. Acad. Sci., Am. Coll. Angiology, Am. Soc. Contemporary Medicine and Surgery, Am. Holistic Med. Assn. (co-founder), Undersea Med. Soc., Am. Acad. Forensic Sci., Am. Assn. Biofeedback Clinicians, Soc. Cryosurgery, Pan Pacific Surg. Assn., Biofeedback Soc. Am., Acad. Psychosomatic Medicine, Pan Am. Med. Assn., Internat. Back Pain Soc., North Am. Spine Soc., Am. Soc. Stereotaxic and Functional Neurosurgery, Soc. for Computerized Tomography and Neuroimaging, Ind. Coroners Assn. (pres. 1979), Royal Soc. Medicine, Nat. Assn. Med. Examiners, Am. Pain Soc., Midwest Pain Soc. (pres. 1988), Am. Acad. Pain Medicine, Cen. Neurol. Soc., Interurban Neurosurg. Soc., Internat. Soc. Aquatic Medicine, James A. Gibson Anat. Soc., Am. Bd. Med. Psychotherapists (mem. profl. adv. council), James McClure Surg. Soc., Brendonwood Country Club, Highland Country Club. Home: 5845 High Fall Rd Indianapolis IN 46226-1017 Office: 7209 N Shadeland Ave Indianapolis IN 46250-2021

MANDERSCHEID, LESTER VINCENT, agricultural economics educator; b. Andrew, Iowa, Oct. 9, 1930; s. Vincent John and Alma (Sprank) M.; m. Dorothy Helen Varnum, Aug. 29, 1953; children: David, Paul, Laura, Jane. BS, Iowa State U., 1951, MS, 1952; PhD, Stanford U., 1961. Grad. asst. Iowa State U., Ames, 1951-52, Stanford (Calif.) U., 1952-56; asst. prof. Mich. State U., East Lansing, 1956-65, assoc. prof., 1965-70, prof., 1970-73, prof., assoc. chmn., 1973-87, prof., chmn., 1987-92, prof., 1992—; reviewer Tex. A&M Agrl. Econ. Program, College Station, 1989; con. Consortium Internat. Earth Sci. Info. Network, Ann Arbor, 1990. Co-author: Improving Undergraduate Education, 1967; contbr. articles to jours. in field. Pres. parish coun. St. Thomas, East Lansing, 1984-87; coll. coord. United Way, East Lansing, 1983-84. Recipient Disting. Faculty award Mich. State U., 1977. Mem. Am. Agrl. Econ. Assn. (pres. 1988-89, bd. dirs. 1982-85, excellence in teaching award 1974), Am. Statis. Assn., Am. Evaluation Assn., Am. Econ. Assn., University Club, Sigma Xi (pres. 1986-87), Phi Kappa Phi (pres. 1979-80). Roman Catholic. Home: 2372 Burcham Dr East Lansing MI 48823-7242 Office: Mich State U Dept of Agrl Econs Circle Dr East Lansing MI 48824-1039

MANDIA, PATRICIA MARIE, English language and literature educator, writer; b. Alliance, Ohio; d. John and Ladene Elizabeth (Haidet) M. BA summa cum laude, Kent State U., 1981, MA in English, 1983, PhD in English, 1987. Instr. English Kent (Ohio) State U., 1987—; dir. Kent State Writing Ctr., 1986-87. Author: Comedic Pathos: Black Humor in Twain's Fiction, 1991; contbr. articles to profl. jours. and mags. Recipient Finley award for light verse Stark County Poetry Soc., 1990. Mem. MLA, Sigma Tau Delta. Office: Kent State U Dept English 113 Satterfield Hall Kent OH 44242-0001

MANDRELL, GENE DOUGLAS, logistician; b. Clinton, Okla., Jan. 7, 1944; s. Glen Douglas and Mary Emma (Spears) M. BA, U. Okla., 1966; MS, Ctrl. Mich. U., 1995; diploma, Indsl. Coll. Armed Forces, 1976, Armed Forces Staff Coll., 1977. Logistics officer Hdqrs. AF Logistics Command, Wright-Patterson AFB, Ohio, 1971-79; asst. for supply policy Office Sec. AF, Washington, 1979-81; congl. fellow U.S. Ho. of Reps., Washington, 1981; dep. dir. command policy and current issues Hdqrs. AF Logistics Command, Wright-Patterson AFB, Ohio, 1982-87, dep. dir. concept devel. and integration, 1987; spl. asst. strategic planning DCS/Communication Computer Systems, Hdqrs. AF Logistics Command, Wright-Patterson AFB, Ohio, 1988-89, dir. strategic planning & policy, 1989-93; dep. dir. corp. info. HQ AF Materiel Command, 1993-95; dir. sys. engrng. Hdqrs. Material Sys. Group, Wright-Patterson AFB, Ohio, 1995, tech. dir., 1996—; vis. lectr. Air War Coll., Maxwell AFB, Ala., 1977-85. Co-author: Public Policy for the 1980's, 1981. Chmn. City Planning Commn., Huber Heights, Ohio, 1983-93. Served to sgt. U.S. Army, 1967-70. Named one of Outstanding Young Men of Am., U.S. Jaycees, 1982. Mem. Internat. Inst. Forecasters, Soc. Logistics Engrs. (life, Dayton chpt. vice-chmn. 1977-78), Am. Def. Preparedness Assn. (life, v.p.), Air Force Assn. (life), World Future Soc. (Dayton chpt. bd. dirs. 1984-93, pres. 1987-88), Am. Planning Assn., Am. Acad. Polit. and Social Scis., Am. Acad. Polit. Sci., Logistics Edn. Found., Ohio Soc. SAR, Huber Heights C. of C., Engrs. Club. Republican. Home: 5261 Coco Dr Dayton OH 45424-5701 Office: HQ Material Sys Group Wright-Patterson AFB OH 45433

MANFRO, PATRICK JAMES (PATRICK JAMES HOLIDAY), radio artist; b. Kingston, N.Y., Dec. 30, 1947; s. Charles Vincent and Anna Agnes (Albany) Manfro; Assoc. Sci. in Acctg., Ulster Coll., 1968; diploma Radio Electronics Inst., 1969; student St. Clair Coll., 1974—; m. Janice Lynn Truscott, July 5, 1975; children: Wesley Patrick, Whitney Dawn. Program dir., radio artist WKNY, Kingston, 1966-70; radio artist WPTR, Albany, N.Y., 1970, WPOP, Hartford, Conn., 1970, CKLW, Detroit, 1970-71, WORFM, N.Y.C., 1971-72; radio artist CKLW Radio, Detroit, 1972—, asst. program dir., 1978-80, program dir., 1980-83; v.p. programming CKLW/CFXX, Detroit, 1983-84 ; pres. Musicom Inc., radio cons. co., Detroit; pres., chief exec. officer Internat. Data Corp., Wilmington, Del.; pres., pub. Broadcast Solutions, Detroit; adviser New Contemporary Sch. Announcing, Albany, 1973—; comml. announcer radio, television, 1970—. Judge, Miss Mich. Universe Pageant, 1970. Mem. N.Y. State N.G., 1968-74. Recipient 5 Year Service ribbon N.Y. State, 1973; named Runner-up Billboard Air Personality awards, 1971, Can. Radio Programmer of Yr., 1992, 93. Mem. AFTRA, Screen Actors Guild, Smithsonian Assos., BMI Songwriters Guild. Club: Dominion Golf and Country. Home: 3466 Wildwood, Windsor, ON Canada N8R 1X2 Office: PO Box 186 Dearborn MI 48121-0186

MANGES, HARRY LEO, agricultural engineer; b. Rice County, Kans., June 18, 1928; s. Elmer Fern and Charlotte Emily (Scott) M.; m. Elaine Hope Whitney, Sept. 5, 1948; children: Charlotte, Rodney, James, David. BS in Agrl. Engring., Kans. State U., 1949, MS, 1959; PhD, Okla. State U., 1969. Registered profl. engr., Kans. Agrl. engr. USDA-SCS, Mankato, Kans., 1949-51; soil conservationist USDA-SCS, Sublette, Kans., 1951-53; area engr. USDA-SCS, Beloit, Kans., 1953-56; instr. Kans. State U., Manhattan, 1956-63, asst. prof., 1963-71, assoc. prof., 1971-77, prof., 1977-93, prof. emeritus, 1993—; mem. solid waste adv. coun. Kans. Dept. Health, Topeka, 1971-72; cons. natural gas rates Kans. Corp. Commn., Topeka, 1976-77; cons. irrigation Heifer Project Internat., Puebla, Mex., 1990; cons. acad. programs Gheorghe Asachi Politech, Iasi, Romania, 1991; vis. prof. Cath. U., Leuven, Belgium, 1985, 86, 89, 91. Contbr. articles to profl. jours. Mem. adv. bd. Teen Outreach, Manhattan; mem. troop com. Boy Scouts Am., Manhattan. Named Hon. State Farmer Future Farmers Am., 1977; recipient Award of Excellence Halliburton Edn. Found., 1982. Mem. Am. Soc. Agrl. Engrs. (dist. dir. 1990-92, Engr. of Yr. Kans. sect. 1983), Kans. Engring. Soc. (chmn. tri-valley chpt. 1989-90), Kiwanis (circle K advisor 1991-94). Methodist. Home: 1424 University Dr Manhattan KS 66502-3446

MANGLA, KISHAN C., systems engineer; b. Delhi, India, Sept. 20, 1940. BEE, BIT, Pilani, India, 1963; MEE, Rutgers U., 1979. Control engr. Midland Ross, Sommerset, N.J., 1972-78; sys. engr. Reliance Electric Co., Cleve., 1978—. Hindu. Home: 430 Lassiter Dr Cleveland OH 44143-3612 Office: Reliance Electric Co 24703 Euclid Ave Cleveland OH 44117-1714

MANHAL-BAUGUS, MONIQUE, counselor; b. St. Louis, May 18, 1963; d. Harvey Charles and Sandra Jean (Glenzer) Manhal; m. Donald Alan Baugus, Sept. 1, 1991; children: Dominique, Aungelique, Jacquelyne, Quincey. MA, U. Cin., 1993, EdD, 1996. Cert. chem. dependency counselor, Ohio; cert. criminal justice specialist; lic. social worker, Ohio. Chem. dependency counselor Ctrl. Cmty. Health Bd., Cin., 1994—; rschr. Women's Residential Addiction Program, Covington, Ky., 1994—. Contbr. articles to profl. jours. U. Cin. scholar, 1991—. Mem. ACA, Nat. Assn. Alcohol and Drug Abuse Counselors, Inst. Control Theory Reality Therapy Quality Mgmt., Nat. Assn. Forensic Counselors, Ky. Coalition Women Substance Abuse Treatment (steering com. 1993—).

MANHEIM, WERNER, language educator; b. Berlin, Germany, Feb. 17, 1915; came to U.S., 1937; s. Martin and Else (Schindler) M.; m. Eliane Housiaux, Aug.18, 1951 (dec. 1994). BEd, U. Berlin, 1935; MusB, Cin. Conservatory Music, 1940, MusM, 1941; DFA, Chgo. Musical Coll., 1950; LittD (hon.), World Acad. Arts & Culture, 1993. Asst. prof. Ind. U., E. Chgo., 1947-54; rsch. asst. Inst. for Sex Rsch., Bloomington, Ind., 1955-58; from asst. prof. to prof. French and German Ind. U., Fort Wayne, 1958—; instr. music St. Francis Coll., Fort Wayne, 1969-77. Author 20 vols. poetry; contbr. articles to profl. jours. With U.S. Army, 1941-45. Recipient medal studiosis humanitatis, 1979, Poetenmünze zum Halbenbogen, 1980, certificate of merit Cambridge Adolf Bartels Commemoration honor, 1980, Dr. Heinrichmock medal, 1982, Eminet Poet Internat. Poets Acad., 1986, Golden Poet award, 1989, 90, 91. Mem. Internat. Authors Plesse, Internat. Culture Coun. (sec.), World Poetry Soc., German Haiku Soc. (hon.). Home: 2906 Hazelwood Ave Fort Wayne IN 46805

MANICKE, MICHAEL DON, automobile service owner; b. Watertown, Wis., Feb. 23, 1951; s. Daniel Eugene and Dorothy Ester (Hackbarth) M.; m. Donna Marie Kaminski, June 28, 1980; children: Carissa, Bryan, Shari, Bruce. Grad. h.s., Oshkosh, Wis. Sign maker Dan's Sign Shop, Marshfield, Wis.; owner Fgn. Auto Svc., Marshfield, 1977—. With USN, 1969-73, Vietnam. Roman Catholic. Office: Fgn Auto Svc 10519 County A Marshfield WI 54449

MANION, DANIEL ANTHONY, federal judge; b. South Bend, Ind., Feb. 1, 1942; s. Clarence E. and Virginia (O'Brien) M.; m. Ann Murphy, June 29, 1984. BA, U. Notre Dame, 1964; JD, Ind. U., 1973. Bar: Ind., U.S. Dist. Ct. (no. dist.) Ind., U.S. Dist. Ct. (so. dist.) Ind. Dep. atty. gen. State of Ind., 1973-74; from assoc. to ptnr. Doran, Manion, Boynton, Kamm & Esmont, South Bend, 1974-86; judge U.S. Ct. Appeals (7th cir.), South Bend, 1986—. Mem. Ind. State Senate, Indpls., 1978-82. Home: 20725 Riverlan Rd South Bend IN 46637-1029 Office: US Ct Appeals 301 Federal Bldg 204 S Main St South Bend IN 46601-2122

MANION, PAUL THOMAS, lawyer; b. Decatur, Ill., Apr. 7, 1940; s. Charles F. and Jeannette (Kaufman) M.; m. Bonnie J. Rivard, Aug. 12, 1961; children: Christine, Sheila, Tessy, Michael, Brian, Daniel. BBA in Fin., Notre Dame U., 1961; JD, DePaul U., 1964. Bar: Ill 1964, U.S. Ct. Appeals (7th cir.) 1975. Ins. investigator Hooper Holmes Bur., South Bend, Ind., 1958-61; supr. U.S. Dist. Ct., Chgo., 1961-64; asst. states atty. Iroquois County, Watseka, Ill., 1964-67; sr. ptnr. Manion, Devens & McFetridge, Ltd., Hoopeston, Ill., 1967—. Author: With Friends Like These, 1985. Mem. exec. com. Vermilion County Dem. Party, Danville, Ill., 1974—, county chmn. 1983-87; pres. Vermilion Mental Health Ctr., Danville, 1975-78. Mem. Ill. Bar Assn., Assn. Trial Lawyers Am., Ill. Trial Lawyers Assn. Democrat. Roman Catholic. Home: RR 2 Box 80 Hoopeston IL 60942-9706 Office: Manion Devens & McFetridge 216 S Market St Hoopeston IL 60942-1508

MANIS, MELVIN, psychologist, educator; b. N.Y.C., Feb. 18, 1931; s. Alex and Hanna (Oyle) M.; m. Jean Denby, May 28, 1954; children: Peter Eugene, David Denby. AB in Psychology, Franklin and Marshall Coll., 1951; PhD, U. Ill., 1954. Instr. psychology U. Pitts., 1956-58; rsch. psychologist Ann Arbor VA Med. Ctr., Mich., 1958-89; prof. psychology U. Mich., Ann Arbor, 1966—, assoc. chair dept. psychology, 1990-91. Author: Cognitive Processes, 1966, An Introduction to Cognitive Psychology, 1971; editor Jour. Personality and Social Psychology, 1980-84. Served with USPHS, 1954-56. Mem. APA, Am. Psychol. Soc., Midwestern Psychol. Assn., Soc. Exptl. Social Psychology, AAUP, Phi Beta Kappa, Sigma Xi. Democrat. Jewish. Club: Racquet (Ann Arbor). Home: 20 Harvard Pl Ann Arbor MI 48104-1726 Office: U Mich Dept Psychology Ann Arbor MI 48109

MANJI, KURBANALI MOHAMED, real estate company executive, architect; b. Mwanza, Tanzania, Apr. 19, 1950; came to U.S., 1983; s. Mohamed and Fatma (Khimji) M. Diploma, U. East London, 1974; post-grad. diploma, N.E. London Poly., 1976; MPPM, Yale U., 1985. Registered architect, Eng. Asst. London Borough of Newham, 1971-74; architect B.E.P. Partnership, London, 1976-77, London Borough of Brent, 1977-78; sr. architect Zuhair Fayez & Assocs., Jeddah, Saudi Arabia, 1978-79; prin. K.M. Manji, Architect, London, 1979-81; designer architect Crang and Boake, Toronto, Ont., Can., 1981-83; v.p. Meta Ptnrs., Cleve., 1985-93, Med. Facilities Devel. & Mgmt. Co., Mpls., 1986-89, Retirement Developers, Inc., Mpls., 1986-93, The Townsend Group, Cleve., 1993-95. Bd. dirs. YMCA, Mayfield, Ohio, 1992-93. Mem. Royal Inst. Brit. Architects, Architects Rgistration Coun. U.K., Nat. Assn. Real Estate Investment Trusts, Ont. Assn. Architects, Yale U. Alumni Assn. (sec. Cleve. 1987-93), Yale Careers (vice chmn. Cleve. 1989-93). Muslim.

MANLEY, DAVID THOMAS, employment benefit plan administration company executive; b. Youngstown, Ohio, Apr. 13, 1938; s. Harry T. and Margaret M. (Stein) M.; m. Virginia Borcik, Sept., 1961 (div. 1975); children: Kelly A., Scott D., Lynne M., Brian D., Leslie; m. Ruth Ann Osterhage, Dec. 31, 1975; children: David Louis, Mollie O. Student, Youngstown U., 1956-60. Dist. sales mgr. Res. Life, Dallas, 1960-63, Guarantee Res. Life, Hammond, Ind., 1963-64; mgr. brokerage CNA Ins. Group, Chgo., 1964-68; pres. Greater Del. Corp., Dover, 1981-85; pres. Variable Protection Adminstrn., Cleve., 1968—, also bd. dirs.; pres. VPA Ins., Ltd., 1985—, also bd. dirs.; with VPI, Inc. Rep. precinct committeeman, 1966-72, ward leader, 1970-72; mem. Cuyahoga County Rep. Com., 1970-72; mem. bd. Zoning Appeals, Hinckley, Ohio Twp.; pres. Our Lady of Grace Bd. Fin., 1980-89. Mem. Soc. Profl. Benefit Adminstrs., Mass Market Ins. Inst., Internat. Found. Employee Benefits, Am. Mgmt. Assn., KC. Roman Catholic. Home: 2485 Bethany Ln Hinckley OH 44233-9741 Office: Variable Protection Adminstrs Inc 6902 Pearl Rd Ste 500 Cleveland OH 44130-3621

MANLEY, JANET ZEEGERS, retired small business owner; b. Grosse Pointe, Mich., July 4, 1933; d. Frank and Maria Elisabeth (Voncken) Zeegers; m. Richard Edward Manley, Dec. 3, 1955; 1 child, David Richard. A in Bus., Mich. State U., 1953. Owner, ptnr., mgr. Zeegers Electric, Center Line, Mich., 1950-91; sec., stenographer Mopar divsn. Chrysler Corp., Center Line, 1953-55; sec., stenographer Oldsmobile divsn. GM, Lansing, Mich., 1956-63; libr. aide Houghton Lake Pub. Libr., Mich., 1970-94; mgr., salesperson Carolyn's Book Nook, Houghton Lake, Mich., 1980-88. Sec. bd. edn., Houghton Lake, Mich., 1976—, Mid-Mich. Libr. League Bd., Cadillac, 1970—, Mich. Libr. Assn., Lansing, 1985—. Recipient award of Distinction Mich. Assn. Sch. Bds., 1994, Master Bd. Mem. award, 1996. Mem. Am. Bus. Women's Assn. (com. chair 1987—, Woman of Yr., 1995). Home: 6119 W Nestel Rd Houghton Lake MI 48629

MANN, BENJAMIN HOWARD, information management company executive; b. Ashland, Ky., July 10, 1958; s. James Edward and Nancy Ann (Riddle) M. BSBA, Ohio State U., 1980. Fin. analyst Bison Mfg. and Fabrication, Buffalo, 1980-82; fin. contr. Bush Plastics, Inc., Salamanca, N.Y., 1982-83; pres. Bison Leasing Co., Inc., Cleve., 1983-94; CFO golf course devel. and mgmt. The Van Cleef Cos., Beachwood, Ohio, 1994; CFO The Van Cleef Cos., Cleve., 1994-95; COO, CFO Secured Paper Solutions, Ltd., Cleve., 1995—; vice chmn. Buffalo Holdings, Inc., 1985-94. Mem. NRA, Buffalo Club, Canterbury Golf Club, Crag Burn Golf Club, Sand Hills Golf Club. Republican. Episcopalian. Office: Secured Paper Solutions Inc 5875 Landerbrook Dr Ste 200 Cleveland OH 44124

MANN, DAVID SCOTT, lawyer; b. Cin., Ohio, Sept. 25, 1939; s. Henry M. and Helen Faye M.; m. Elizabeth Taliaferro, Oct. 5, 1963; children: Michael, Deborah, Marshall. AB cum laude, Harvard Coll., 1961, LLB magna cum laude, 1968. Bar: Ohio 1968. Assoc. Dinsmore & Shohl, Cin., 1968-74, ptnr., 1974-83; ptnr. Taliaferro and Mann, Cin., 1983-92; councilman City of Cin., 1974-92, mayor, 1980-82, 91; mem. 103d Congress 1st Ohio dist., Washington, 1993-94; mem. armed svcs. com., mem. jud. com. Washington; of counsel Thompson, Hine and Flory, Cin., 1995—; vis. prof. Coll. of Law, U. Cin., 1995—. Editor Harvard Law Rev., 1966-68, notes editor, 1967-68; contbr. articles to profl. jours. Mem., chmn. Cin. Bd. Health, 1972-74. With USN, 1961-65. Mem. Cin. Bar Assn. Democrat. Methodist. Home: 568 Evanswood Pl Cincinnati OH 45220-1527

MANN, DAVID WILLIAM, minister; b. Elkhart, Ind., Apr. 17, 1947; s. Herbert Richard and Kathryn (Bontrager) M.; m. Brenda Marie Frantz, June 7, 1969; children: Troy, Todd, Erika. BA, Bethel Coll., 1969; MS, Nat. Louis U., 1986. Ordained to ministry Missionary Ch., 1978. Campus life dir. Youth for Christ, Elkhart, 1969-77; denominational youth dir. Missionary Ch., Ft. Wayne, Ind., 1977-81, Christian edn. dir., 1981-88, U.S. dir. missions, 1990—; assoc. dir. World Ptnrs., Ft. Wayne, 1988-90; dir. Missionary Ch. Vol. Svc., Ft. Wayne, 1983—. Author: (with others) Youth Leaders Source Book, 1985; contbr. articles to profl. jour. Mgr. Little League, Ft. Wayne, 1981-89, bd. dirs. 1986. Mem. Nat. Assn. Evangelicals, Evangelical Fgn. Mission Assn., Denominational Execs. in Christian Edn. (chmn. 1988), Aldersgate Pub. Assn. (bd. dirs. 1985, 87), Nat. Christian Edn. Assn. (exec. com. 1987-89). Home: 10025 Crown Point Dr Fort Wayne IN 46804-4391 Office: Missionary Ch 3811 Vanguard Dr Fort Wayne IN 46809-3304

MANN, DONNA MARIE, extension educator; b. Macomb, Ill., Apr. 22, 1949; d. Gene Wendell and Eva Alleyne (Moore) Beck; m. John A. Mann (div. Sept. 1974); 1 child, Toria Shawn Ellis. BS in Home Econs., U. Ill., 1971, M of Extension Edn., 1980. Cert. hospitality educator. Extension advisor Calhoun County U. Ill. Coop. Extension Svc., Hardin, 1971-73; extension advisor home econs. Ogle County U. Ill. Coop. Extension Svc., Oregon, 1973-92; extension educator St. III Cmty. Leadership and Volunteerism U. Ill. Coop. Extension Svc., Freeport, 1992—; pres. Ill. Spl. Events Network, Champaign, 1994—. Bd. dirs., pres. Autumn on Parade Festival, Oregon, Ill., 1990—; sec. Oregon Competitive Cmtys., 1994—; founder Hometown Holidays Event, Oregon, 1985—; state pres. Internat. Festival and Events Assn. Recipient Superior Svc. award USDA. Mem. Extension Assn. Ill. (bd. dirs. 1993—), Ill. Assn. Extension Home Economists (pres. 1990-91, awards), Cmty. Devel. Soc., Oregon C. of C., Epsilon Sigma Phi. Home: 807 Webster St Oregon IL 61061 Office: Freeport Extension Ctr 773 W Lincoln Ste 403 Freeport IL 61032

MANN, GREGORY LEE, real estate appraiser, tax tribunal referee; b. Flint, Mich., Sept. 23, 1953; s. Harold Ross and Carol Maxine (Kile) M.; m. Judith Ann Markusse, Apr. 11, 1992; 1 child, David Harold. AB, U. Mich., 1975. Lic. appraiser, Mich. Sr. econ. devel. analyst Ho. Rsch. Staff Mich. Ho. of Reps., Lansing, 1977-93; referee Mich. Tax Tribunal, Lansing, 1993-95; appraiser West Mich. Appraisal Svcs., Kalamazoo, Mich., 1994—; bd. dirs., sec. Mich. Tax Info. Coun., Lansing, 1988—. Bd. dirs. Blue Care Network/Health Ctrl., Lansing, 1990-93; mem. exec. bd. Greater Lansing ACLU, 1991-93; vice chmn. Kalamazoo Dems., 1994—, mem. state ctrl. com., Lansing, 1995. Mem. Kalamazoo Torch, 1990—. Home: 1216 Franklin St Kalamazoo MI 49001 Office: W Mich Appraisal Svcs Inc 821 W South St Kalamazoo MI 49007

MANN, PHILLIP LYNN, data processing company executive; b. Charleston, W.Va., July 26, 1944; s. Clarence Edward and Virginia Charlotte (Rupe) M.; m. Edith Jane Dewell, Dec. 28, 1966 (div. 1977); 1 child, Cynthia Lynn; m. Phyllis Anita Berg, May 18, 1979; children: Stacia Lynn, Brandon Granville. BSEE, Purdue U., 1970; MBA, U. Chgo., 1975. Devel. engr. Western Electric Co., Inc., Lisle, Ill., 1970-77; v.p. Uniq Digital Techs., Inc., Batavia, Ill., 1977-88; pres. ProTech Computer Group, Inc., Batavia, 1988—. Served with USN, 1962-66. Home: 428 Meadowrue Ln Batavia IL 60510-2815 Office: ProTech Computer Group Inc 143 1st St Batavia IL 60510-2452

MANNELLA, LARRY, manufacturing engineer; b. Tarentum, Pa., June 2, 1942. B, Pa. State U., 1969. With Diebold, Inc., Canton, Ohio, 1969—, mgr. engring., 1992—. Patentee in field. With USN, 1960-64. Office: Diebold Inc 818 Mulberry Rd SE Canton OH 44707-3256

MANNING, PETER KIRBY, sociology educator; b. Salem, Oreg., Sept. 27, 1940; s. Kenneth Gilbert and Esther Amelia (Gibbard) M.; m. Victoria Francis Shaughnessy, Sept. 1, 1961 (div. 1981); children—Kerry Patricia, Sean Peter, Merry Kathleen; m. Betsy Cullum-Swan, Aug. 4, 1991. B.A., Willamette U., 1961; M.A., Duke U., 1963, Ph.D., 1966; M.A. (hon.), Oxford U., Eng., 1983. Instr. sociology Duke U., 1964-65; asst. prof. sociology U. Mo., 1965-66, Mich. State U., East Lansing, 1966-70; assoc. prof. sociology and psychiatry Mich. State U., 1970-74, prof., 1974—; prof. criminal justice, 1993—; Beto chair lectr. Sam Houston State U., 1990; Ameritech lectr. E. Ky. U., 1993; cons. Nat. Inst. Law Enforcement and Criminal Justice (now Nat. Inst. Justice), U.S. Dept. Justice, Rsch. Triangle Inst., NSF, Nat. Health and Med. Rsch. Coun., Australia, 1980—, Social Sci. Rsch. Coun. Eng., AID (Jamaica), 1991, Sheehy com. Police Pay and Performance, Eng., 1993. Author: Sociology of Mental Health and Illness, 1975, Police Work, 1977, The Narcs' Game, 1980, Semiotics and Fieldwork, 1987, Symbolic Communication, 1988, Organizational Communication, 1992, other books; also book chpts., articles in profl. jours.; cons. editor series: Principal Themes in Sociology; co-editor Sage Series in Qualitative Methods, Communications and Social Order Aldine/deGruyter; adv. editor, mem. editorial bd. numerous jours. in social scis. Recipient Bruce Smith Sr. award Acad. Criminal Justice Scis., 1993, Charles H. Cooley award Mich. Sociol. Assn., 1994; NDEA fellow, 1962-64, NSF fellow, 1965, fellow Balliol Coll., Oxford U., 1982-83, vis. fellow Wolfson Coll., Oxford U., 1981, 82-83, fellow, 1984-86. Mem. Am. Soc. Criminology, Am. Sociol. Assn., Brit. Soc. Criminology, Internat. Sociol. Assn., Midwest Sociol. Soc., Soc. Study of Social Problems, Soc. for the Study of Symbolic Interaction (spl. recognition award 1990, v.p. 1992-93, program chair 1993), Internat. Soc. for Semiotics and Law. Office: Mich State U 516 Baker Hall East Lansing MI 48824-1118

MANNING, ROBERT HENDRICK, development director; b. Soerabaja, Java, Indonesia, Aug. 23, 1941; s. William and Gertrude (Unk) M. BS, No. Mich. U., 1974. Instr. sailing USCG Acad., New London, Conn., 1959-63; dir. audio visual svcs. No. Mich. U., Marquette, 1965-93; dir. devel. Bresnan Comm. Co., Marquette, 1993—; ind. media cons., Marquette, 1969—. Pub. TV host PBS Sta. WNMU-TV, 1977—. Hon. mem. Marquette-Alger County Med. Soc. (exec. dir. 1970—, capt. U. Rsch. Vessel 1977-79). Home: PO Box 309 Marquette MI 49855-0309 Office: Bresnan Comm Co PO Box 190 Marquette MI 49855-0190

MANNING, RONALD LEE, banker; b. Hillsboro, Ohio, Jan. 15, 1951; s. George Charles and Margaret Alice (Hail) M. BSBA, Bowling Green State U., 1973; Cert., U. Okla., 1984. Teller, collection coordinator Bank of Wood County, Bowling Green, Ohio, 1972-73; mgr. Park Nat. Bank, Newark, Ohio, 1973-76; mgr., asst. v.p. BancOhio Nat. Bank, Cin., 1976-78, br. adminstr., 1978-81, mgr. comsumer credit, 1981-83; v.p., dist. lending mgr. BancOhio Nat. Bank, Newark, 1983-88; pres. BancOhio Nat. Bank, Bellefontaine and Kenton, 1988-92, Nat. City Bank, Newark-Licking, Perry, 1993—; mem. adv. com. Ctrl. Ohio Tech. Coll., Newark, 1983-90; lectr. U. Cin., 1978-85, Camp Enterprise, Newark, 1993—; chmn. Manningstead Farms, Howard, Ohio, 1986—. Mem. adv. com. Am. Cancer Soc., Newark, 1976—, lay trustee Ohio div., 1990; mem. United Way of Licking County, 1993—; pres. Mann, Inc., 1990—; mem. Hardin County Literacy Coun., Inc., 1990—; mem. adv. com. Ohio Hi Point JVS Bus. Mgmt., 1989-92; mem. governing com. Licking County Found., 1993—; mem. bus. and industry coun. Licking Meml. Hosp., 1993—. Named to Hon. Order of Ky. Col., 1972. Mem. Mental Health Assn., Newark Area C. of C. (dir. 1993—), Am. Inst. Banking, Ohio Oil & Gas Assn., Rotary, Valley of Cin., Masons. Avocations: sports, hunting. Home: 88 N 33rd St Newark OH 43055-2040 Office: Nat City Bank 68 W Church St Newark OH 43055-5044

MANNING, SUSAN HARRIET HINMAN, procurement analyst; b. Dayton, Ohio, Jan. 19, 1943; d. Willis Henry and Marian Florence (Roberts) Hinman; m. Gary Lee Manning, May 16, 1963 (div. May 1977); children: 1 child, Katherine Joanne Manning Rodriguez. Diploma in clerical bookkeeping, Miami Jacobs Jr. Coll., Dayton, 1963; student, Air War Coll., Maxwell AFB, Ala., 1984. Cert. in contract mgmt. With Civil Air Patrol, 1959—; cadet program devel. officer CAP Ohio Wing, Columbus, 1973-77; dep. chief staff for tng. CAP Great Lakes Region, 1977-83; comdr. group II CAP Oakland County, Royal Oak, Mich., 1986-87; computer officer CAP Mich. Wing, Trenton, 1987-89, dir. comm., 1989-90; contracting officer & procurement instr. Def. Elecs. Supply Ctr., Kettering, Ohio, 1982-84; procurement analyst U.S. Army Tank Automotive Command, Warren, Mich., 1984—; founder, staff mgr. Great Lakes Region CAP Region Staff Coll., Ky., Mich., Ohio, Wis., Ind. & Ill., 1978-84; sr. tng. officer, instr. Great Lakes Region CAP Comm. Coll., various locations, 1980—. Author (guide) Preparation Procurements 25K, 1983; co-author (booklet) Staff College Directors Guide, 1977. Republican. Office: US Army-TACOM Attn AMSTA-AQ-DAC (Manning) Warren MI 48397-5000

MANNING, SYLVIA, English studies educator; b. Montreal, Que., Can., Dec. 2, 1943; came to U.S., 1967; d. Bruno and Lea Bank; m. Peter J. Manning, Aug. 20, 1967; children—Bruce David, Jason Maurice. B.A., McGill U., 1963; M.A., Yale U., 1964, Ph.D. in English, 1967. Asst. prof. English Calif. State U.-Hayward, 1967-71, assoc. prof., 1971-75, assoc. dean, 1972-75; assoc. prof. U. So. Calif., 1975-94, prof., assoc. dir. Ctr. for Humanities, 1975-77, assoc. dir. Ctr. for Humanities, 1975-77, chmn. freshman writing, 1977-80, chmn. dept. English, 1980-83, vice provost, exec. v.p., 1984-94; prof. English U. Ill., 1994—, v.p. for acad. affairs, prof. English, 1994—. Author: Dickens as Satirist, 1971; Hard Times: An Annotated Bibliography, 1984. Contbr. essays to mags. Woodrow Wilson fellow, 1963-64, 66-67. Mem. MLA, Dickens Soc. Office: U of Ill 377 Henry Adm Bldg 506 S Wright St Urbana IL 61801-3614

MANNWEILER, PAUL S., state legislator. Mem. Ho. of Reps. Ind. 49th Dist.; Republican floor leader. Office: 3543 Delaware Commons South Dr Indianapolis IN 46220-3742

MANOOGIAN, RICHARD ALEXANDER, manufacturing company executive; b. Long Branch, N.J., July 30, 1936; s. Alex and Marie (Tatian) M.; children: James, Richard, Bridget. B.A. in Econs, Yale U., 1958. Asst. to pres. Masco Corp., Taylor, Mich., 1958-62, exec. v.p., 1962-68, pres., 1968-85, chmn. bd., CEO, 1985—; chmn., dir. Mascotech, Inc., Trimas Corp.; dir. NBD Bancorp, Inc., Detroit Renaissance, Am. Bus. Conf. Trustee U. Liggett Sch., State Dept. Fine Arts Comsn., Founder's Soc., Detroit Inst. Arts, Center for Creative Studies; trustee coun. Nat. Gallery Art. Mem. Young Presidents Orgn., Yale Alumni Assn. Clubs: Grosse Pointe Yacht, Grosse Pointe Hunt, Country Club Detroit, Detroit Athletic. Office: Masco Corp 21001 Van Born Rd Taylor MI 48180-1340

MANOS, GEORGE P., state agency administrator; b. Akron, Ohio, Apr. 14, 1933; s. Paul J. and Carolyn Manos; m. Jeanette Manos, June 23, 1957; children: Paul, Carolyn, Elena. BS in BA, U. Akron, 1962; BS in Mil. Planning, Army Command & Staff Coll., Ft. Leavenworth, Kans., 1973; MBA in Econ. Planning, Indsl. Coll. Armed Forces, Washington, 1975; MBA in Govt. Adminstrn., Calif.-Pacific U., San Diego, 1979. Purchasing agt. Pflueger Corp., Akron, 1960-64; stockbroker Merrill Lynch, Akron, 1964-70; asst. bus. mgr. Akron City Schs., 1970-78; purchasing dir. City of Akron, 1978-90; stockbroker Equitable Ins. Co., 1990-93; internat. export counselor Ohio Devel. Agy., Kirtland, 1993—. Lt. col. U.S. Army, 1980-84. Mem. Ret. Officers Assn. (chpt. v.p. 1994-95), Res. Officers Assn. (chpt. sec. 1990-94, chpt. pres. 1974-76), Assn. U.S. Army (chpt. pres. 1990-92), United We Stand Am. (v.p. 1994-95), Theta Chi (chpt. alumni pres. 1990-92). Republican. Greek Orthodox.

MANSBRIDGE, JANE JEBB, political scientist, educator; b. N.Y.C., Nov. 19, 1939; d. Ronald and Georgia St. Claire (Mullen) M.; m. Christopher Jencks; 1 child, Nathaniel Mansbridge Jencks. BA, Wellesley Coll., 1961; MA, Harvard U., 1966, PhD, 1971. Asst. prof. polit. sci. U. Chgo., 1973-80; assoc. prof. Northwestern U., Evanston, Ill., 1980-86, prof. polit. sci., 1986-91, Jane W. Long prof. arts and scis., 1991-96; prof. J.F. Kennedy Sch. Govt. Harvard U., 1996—. Author: Beyond Adversary Democracy, 1980, Why We Lost the ERA, 1986, (with Susan M. Okin) Feminism 2 vols., 1994; editor : Beyond Self-Interest, 1990; mem. editorial bd.: Signs, Jour. Polit. Philosophy. Scholar Russell Sage Found., 1991-92; fellow Inst. for Advanced Study, 1985-86, Rockefeller Humanities, 1982-83, NSF, 1971-72. Mem. Am. Polit. Sci. Assn. (v.p. 1992-93, exec. com. 1987-89, coun. 1987-89, program chair 1990), Am. Acad. Arts and Scis. Office: JF Kennedy Sch Govt 79 JFK St Cambridge MA 02138

MANSFIELD, KAREN LEE, lawyer; b. Chgo., Mar. 17, 1942; d. Ralph and Hilda (Blum) Mansfield; children: Nicole Rafaela, Lori Michele. BA in Polit. Sci., Roosevelt U., 1963; JD, DePaul U., 1971; student U. Chgo., 1959-60. Bar: Ill. 1972, U.S. Dist. Ct. (no. dist.) Ill. 1972. Legis. intern Ill. State Senate, Springfield, 1966-67; tchr. Chgo. Pub. Schs., 1967-70; atty. CNA Ins., Chgo., 1971-73; law clk. Ill. Apellate Ct., Chgo., 1973-75; sr. trial atty. U.S. Dept. Labor, Chgo., 1975—, mentor Adopt-a-Sch. Program, 1992-95. Contbr. articles to profl. jours. Vol. Big Sister, 1975-81; bd. dirs. Altgeld Nursery Sch., 1963-66, Ill. div. UN Assn., 1966-72, Hull House Jane Addams Ctr., 1977-82, Broadway Children's Ctr., 1986-90, Acorn Family Entertainment, 1993-95; mem. Oak Park Farmers' Market Commn., 1996—; rsch. asst. Citizens for Gov. Otto Kerner, Chgo., 1964; com. mem. Ill. Commn. on Status of Women, Chgo., 1964-70; del. Nat. Conf. on Status of Women, 1968; candidate for del. Ill. Constl. Conv., 1969. Mem. Chgo. Council Lawyers, Women's Bar Assn. Ill., Lawyer Pilots Bar Assn., Fed. Bar Assn. Unitarian. Clubs: Friends of Gamelan (performer), 99's Internat. Orgn. Women Pilots (legis. chmn. Chgo. area chpt. 1983-86, legis. chmn. North Cen. sect. 1986-88, legis. award 1983, 85). Home: 204 S Taylor Ave Oak Park IL 60302-3307 Office: US Dept Labor Office Solicitor 230 S Dearborn St Fl 8 Chicago IL 60604-1505

MANSKE, BRADLEY WILLIAM, computer engineer; b. North Platte, Nebr., Feb. 20, 1961; s. Marlin William and Sandra Kay (Dempsy) M.; m. Ginny Marie Hayes, Dec. 31, 1986; children: Miranda Lyn, Conrad William, Karissa Rae. BS in Computer Engring., Iowa State U., 1983. Computer engr. Montgomery Elevator Co., Moline, Ill., 1984—. Patentee elevator self-diagnostic control. Mem. IEEE. Office: Montgomery Koné Elevator 1800 River Dr Moline IL 61265

MANSON, CAREY MARC, mechanical engineer; b. Indpls., Apr. 24, 1957. BS in Mech. Engring., U. Minn., 1979. Sr. engr. Fisher-Rosemount Sys. Inc., Burnsville, Minn., 1979—. Patentee passive cooling device. Mem. Toastmasters Interant. (competent toastmaster). Office: Fisher-Rosemount Sys Inc 12000 Portland Ave Burnsville MN 55337-1522

MANTEY, PAUL, electrical engineer; b. Milw., Nov. 13, 1958. Assoc. Machinery Repair & Rebuilding, Waukesha County Tech. Coll., 1980. Elec. engr. Quadra, Inc., Racine, Wis., 1991—. Mem. Antique Power and Collectibles Soc. (bd. dirs. 1992—). Office: Quadra Inc 1833 Oakdale Ave Racine WI 53406-4711

MANTHEI, ROBIN DICKEY, research technician; b. Tucson, May 16, 1956; d. Wilbur Dunbar French and Barbara Dickey; m. Joel Robert Manthei, Sept. 4, 1976; children: Nicholas Robert, Charles Dickey. AS, Augsburg Coll., 1976; cert. med. lab. technician, Med. Inst. Minn., 1978; BS, U. Minn., 1994. Med. lab. technician Lufkin Med. Lab., Mpls., 1978-82; jr. scientist U. Minn., Mpls., 1982-86; rsch. tech. Mayo Found., Rochester, Minn., 1986-89; chpt. leader Young Astronaut Program, 1987-94; jr. scientist Inst. Human Genetics U. Minn., 1989-90; rsch. asst. Mpls. Med. Rsch. Found., 1990-93; lab. instr. North Hennepin C.C., Brooklyn Park, Minn., 1994—. Contbr. articles in field. Mem. DAR. Episcopalian. Home: 7630 Lanewood Ln N Maple Grove MN 55311-2670

MANTOVANI, JOHN FRANCIS, neurologist, educator; b. St. Louis, Jan. 17, 1949. BA cum laude, U. Evansville, 1971; MD, U. Mo., 1974. Diplomate Am. Bd. Pediatrics, Am. Bd. Psychiatry and Neurology. Resident pediatrics, neurology, fellow child neurology Washington U. & St. Louis Childrens Hosp., 1974-79; practitioner adult & child neurology Dean Clinic, Madison, Wis., 1979-84; dir. child neurology, vice chmn. dept. pediatrics St. John's Mercy Med. Ctr., St. Louis, 1984—; clin. asst. prof. neurology U. Wis., Madison, 1980-84; instr. clin. pediatrics and neurology Washington U., St. Louis, 1985-95, asst. prof. clin. pediatrics. and neurology, 1995—. Contbr. articles to profl. jours. Mem. AMA, Am. Acad. Pediatrics, Am. Acad. Cerebral Palsy and Developmental Medicine (com. mem. 1985-87, 1989-91, bd. dirs. 1994—), Am. Acad. Neurology, Am. Bd. Electroencephalography, Child Neurology Soc., Alpha Omega Alpha. Office: Ste 5009 621 S New Ballas Rd Saint Louis MO 63141-8200

MANTZELL, BETTY LOU, school health administrator; b. Brookville, Pa., Oct. 16, 1938; d. Elmer William and Wilda Mae (Enterline) M. Diploma, Ind. (Pa.) Hosp. Sch. Nursing, 1959; BSN, Case Western Res. U., 1969, MA, 1978; cert. supr. ednl. adminstrn., Cleve. State U., 1983; cert. supr., John Carroll U., 1989. RN, Ohio, Pa. Oper. rm. nurse Univ. Hosps. of Cleve., 1963-69; sch. nurse various locations Cleve. Pub. Schs., 1969-85, coord. sch. nurses, 1976-85, acting asst. supr. health svcs., 1985-86, supr. health svcs., 1986—; mem. adv. com. to baccalaureate nursing program Cleve. Stae U.; prevention of blindness adv. com. Cleve. Sight Ctr.; active All Kids County Consortium Cleve. Dept. Pub. Health; mem. sch. health com. Acad. Medicine Cleve.; Frances Payne Bolton Sch. Nursing, mem. alumni assn.; clin. instr. cmty. health nursing Case We. Res. U., Cleve., 1988-90, women's connection; mem. coun. econ. opportunities Greater Cleve.; mem. adv. com. Headstart Health Svcs. Mem. Am. Sch. Health Assn., Nat. Assn. Sch. Nurses, Ohio Assn. Sch. Nurses, Northeastern Ohio Assn. Sch. Nurses, Ohio Assn. Secondary Sch. Adminstrs., Cleve. Coun. Adminstrs. and Suprs., Cleve. Med. Libr. Assn. Office: Jane Addams Bus Careers Ctr Office Health Svcs Rm 206 2373 E 30th St Cleveland OH 44115

MANUEL, DENNIS LEE, real estate broker; b. Flint, Mich., May 30, 1945; s. Wilbur O. and Helen (Baumgartner) M.; m. Carol Ann Peterson, Oct. 8, 1965 (div. Oct. 1973); children: Mary Lynn, Annette Leigh; m. Darlene Kay Bernethy, Sept. 10, 1976; 1 child, Tracy Michelle Sanford. BS, Cen. Mich. Coll., 1969; grad., Real Estate Inst., 1988; student, Mich. Inst. Real Estate, 1989. Lic. real estate broker, Mich. Sales assoc. Blanche Bekkering Realtors, Flint, 1969-71; office mgr. Gosline Realtors, Grand Blanc, Mich., 1971-73; gen. mgr. Hallmark REaltors, Grand Blanc, 1973-78; dist. mgr.

Real Estate One Lakeshore, Traverse City, Mich., 1978-79; v.p., broker Real Estate One Hallmark, Grand Blanc, 1979-80; pres., broker Real Estate One Regency, Fenton, Mich., 1980—. Spl. dep. Flint Sheriff Dept., 1986. Mem. Nat. Assn. Realtors, Mich. Assn. Realtors, Flint Bd. Realtors, Nat. Write Your Congressman, Moose, Elks. Republican. Roman Catholic. Home: 12329 Margaret Dr Fenton MI 48430-8850 Office: Real Estate One Regency 425 Rounds Dr Fenton MI 48430-1717

MANZULLO, DONALD A, congressman, lawyer; b. Rockford, Ill., 1944; s. Frank A. Sr. and Kathryn M.; m. Freda Teslik; children: Neil, Noel, Katie. BA in Polit. Sci./Internat. Rels., American U., 1967; JD, Marquette U. Law Sch. Atty., 1970—; mem. 103th Congress from 16th Ill. Dist., 1993—; mem. House Com. on Internat. Rels., subcom. econ. policy, trade and environ., subcom. on Asia and the Pacific, House Com. on small bus., chmn. on subcom. on procurement exports and bus. opportunity, Joint Econ. Commn. Mem. No. Ill. Alliance for Arts, Friends of Severson Dells, Citizens Against Govt. Waste, Rep. Nat. Com. Recipient George Washington honor medal for excellence in pub. comm. Freedoms Found., Valley Forge, Pa., 1991. Mem. ABA, Ill. Bar Assn., Ogle County Bar Assn. (pres. 1971, 73), Nat. Legal Found., Acad. Polit. Sci., Ill. Press Assn., Ill. C. of C., Oregon City C. of C., Nat. Land Inst., Nat. Fedn. Ind. Bus., Ogle County Hist. Soc., Aircraft Owners and Pilots Assn., Ogle County Pilots Assn., Ill. Farm Bur., Ogle County Farm Bur. Office: US Ho of Reps 426 Cannon House Office Bld Washington DC 20515-1316

MAPEL, PATRICIA JOLENE, farmer, consultant; b. Lake City, Iowa, June 24, 1933; d. John Gilbert and Blanche Evelyn (Taylor) Sharkey; m. J.R. Mapel, Sept. 1, 1952 (dec. 1992); children: Pati Jo, Mark L., Grant L., Penelope R., Kay Collene. Student, Wesley Meml. Hosp. Sch. of Nursing, 1951-52. Ptnr. farming Lake City, Iowa, 1953-92; ptnr., pres. Mapel Farms Ethanol, Inc., Lake City, Iowa, 1984-92; house dir. Delta Delta Delta Simpson Coll., Indianola, Iowa, 1993—; cons. Dept. of Energy, Kansas City, 1981; demonstrator, educator Iowa Cen. Community Coll., Ft. Dodge, Iowa. Contbr. articles to profl. jours. Bd. dirs. Cen. Sch. Preservation, Inc., Lake City, 1984-90. Mem. Entre Nous Music Club, Eastern Star. Democrat. Mem. Ch. of Christ. Home: 705 N C St Indianola IA 50125-1274

MARAN, MICHAEL JOSEPH, publisher, writer, lawyer; b. Mt. Pleasant, Mich., Nov. 19, 1952; s. Anthony John and Lucile Mildred (Newton) M. BA, Mich. State U., 1973; JD, U. Wis., 1977. Bar: Mich. 1977, Wis. 1977. Pvt. practice law Mt. Pleasant, 1977-79; asst. prof. bus. law and regulation Ctrl. Mich. U., Mt. Pleasant, 1979-80; campaign coord. Ferency for Gov., Lansing, Mich., 1981-82; staff atty. UAW-GM Legal Svcs., Lansing, 1983-84; pub. Grand River Press, Lansing, 1985—. Author: Michigan Divorce Book, 1986, Make Your Own Will, 1990, Michigan Power of Attorney Book, 1991. Bd. dirs. Mt. Pleasant Zoning Bd., 1978-81, East Lansing (Mich.) Zoning Bd., 1991-95. Mem. Mich. State Bar Assn., Phi Beta Kappa (Mich. State U. chpt.). Home: 1850 Abbott # C-11 East Lansing MI 48823 Office: Grand River Press 3401 E Saginaw # 103-F Lansing MI 48912

MARAZITA, ELEANOR MARIE HARMON, secondary education educator; b. Madison County, Ind., Oct. 25, 1933; d. William Houston Harmon and Martha Belle (Savage) Hinds; m. Philip Marazita; children: Mary Louise, Frank, Dominic, Vincent, Elizabeth Faye, Candice Marie, Daniel William. BS in Home Econs., Ctrl. Mich. U., 1955; MA in Human Ecology, Mich. State U., 1971. Cert. vocat. home econs. tchr., K-Jr. Coll., cert. speech correction tchr. Tchr. adult edn. Mt. Pleasant, Mich., 1956; substitute tchr. North Branch (Mich.) Schs., 1961-64; tchr. Pied Piper Cooperative Nursery Sch., Lansing, Mich., 1964-69, Lansing C.C., 1971-81, Grand Ledge (Mich.) H.S., 1969—; debate coach, forensic coach, student congress advisor Grand Ledge H.S., 1984—; Mich. tchr. del. World Conf. Tchg. Profls., 1985; adv. mem. Mich. Tchr. Competency Testing Program, 1992. Bd. dirs. Greater Lansing chpt. U.N., 1995—; vol. St. Lawrence Mental Health Hosp., 1972-73, Listening Ear Crisis Intervention Ctr., 1973-77, Capital City Convalescent Home, 1969-73; chmn. study com. Delta Twp. Libr., 1969-73, Jr. League, 1969—; interviewer Youth for Understanding, 1978-83; active exch. student orientation program Mich. State U., 1977, exch. trips, 1979-82; mem. adv. bd. Mich. League Human Svcs., 1988-91, Eaton County Extension Svcs., 1988-91, Mich. Women's Assembly, 1986-91; mem. Friends of Waverly Libr.; participant 3rd Congress Educators Caucus, 1986-92; 4-H leader, 1950-65. Recipient State Tchr. Multicultural award, 1989, UN Global Educator award, 1991, State Tchr. Maureen Wyatt feminist award, 1996. Mem. NEA, Mich. Edn. Assn. (mem. polit. action exec. bd. 1986—, v.p. women's caucus 1986-93, Liz Siddell State Internat. Cultures award 1992), Internat. Platform Assn., Circumnavigators Club (travel around world in one trip 1993), Century Club (travel in 100 countries outside U.S. 1994), Mich. Speech Coaches Assn. (scholarship com. 1984—), Mich. Assn. Speech Coaches, Delta Kappa Gamma (co-chairperson State World Fellowship 1993-95, chpt. Women of Distinction award 1993), Phi Delta Kappa (Tchr. of Yr. Mich. State U. 1992, State Tchr. Mayreen Wyatt Feminist award 1996). Home: 214 Farmstead Ln Lansing MI 48917-3015

MARBLE, GARY, state legislator. Mem. dist. 130 Mo. Ho. of Reps. Office: 214 E Main Rm 135 AC Neosho MO 64850

MARCANTONIO, ARTHUR, quality assurance executive; b. N.Y.C., Apr. 12, 1936; s. Anthony and Marie (Salerni) M.; m. June Fisher, June 25, 1957. BS in Metal. Engring., Lehigh U., 1957; MBA in Fin., Kent State U., 1961. Corp. dir. tech. Republic Steel, Cleve., 1978-84, LTU Steel, Cleve., 1984-91; quality assurance corp. dir. Fosecu, Cleve., 1991—. Contbr. steel making and steel product articles to profl. jours. Mem. AIME (v.p. 1981, Austin award), Iron and Steel Soc. (pres., Disting. Mem.), Am. Soc. for Quality Control. Home: 2256 Herrick Cir Hudson OH 44236-2355

MARCH, LEE ANTHONY, computer specialist; b. Carlisle, Pa., June 26, 1967; s. Lee Albert and Roberta Lee (Neff) M. BS in Sci. Electronic Engring. Tech., DeVry Inst. Tech., 1989. Network adminstr. Nationwide Mut. Ins. Co., Columbus, Ohio, 1988-91; systems devel. specialist Fin. Horizons Distbrs. Agy., Inc., Columbus, Ohio, 1992—; electronic comms. specialist Nationwide Ins. Co., 1996—. Youth leader Parkview United Meth. Ch., Columbus, 1991—. Methodist. Office: Nationwide Ins Co 1 Nationwide Plz 2-05-01 Columbus OH 43215

MARCH, ROBERT HERBERT, physicist, writer; b. Chgo., Feb. 28, 1934; s. Herbert and Jacinta Virgilia (Grbac) M.; m. Georgianna Bennington Pugh, Jan. 5, 1953 (div. 1973); 1 child, Thomas; m. Kathryn Ann Holtgrauer, Dec. 15, 1979 (div. 1995). BA, U. Chgo., 1952, MS, 1955, PhD, 1960. Instr. U. Chgo., 1959-60; lectr. Midwest U., Madison, Wis., 1960-61; instr. U. Wis., Madison, 1961-62, asst. prof., 1962-65, assoc. prof., 1965-71, prof., 1971—, chmn. Integrated Liberal Studies, 1987-90, 96—; vis. sci. Lawrence Berkeley Lab, Calif., 1964, Cern Geneva Switzerland, 1967, Ferilab, Chgo., 1973, SLAC Menlo park, Calif., 1975; vis. prof. UCAL Irvine, 1978. Author: Physics for Poets, 1970, contbr. articles to profl. jours. Mem. Fedn. of Am. Sci., Washington, 1956-67, Union of Concerned Sci., Boston, 1994—. Shell Oil fellow, U. Chgo., 1956—; recipient sci. writing award Am. Inst. Physics, 1971, 73. Mem. Am. Physcial Soc., Am. Assoc. U. Prof. (chpt. pres.). Office: U Wis 1150 University Ave Madison WI 53706

MARCHESE, RONALD THOMAS, ancient history and archaeology educator; b. Fresno, Calif., Mar. 17, 1947; s. John Anthony and Julie Rita (Ferrarese) M.; m. Marcia Lynn Schneider, Apr. 6, 1974 (div. Apr. 1980); children: Stephanie Jo, Kayla Marie. BA summa cum laude, Calif. State U., Fresno, 1970; MA, N.Y.U., 1972, PhD with distinction, 1976; postgrad., Columbia U., 1972-73. Asst. prof. Va. Poly. Inst., Blacksburg, 1976-77; asst. to assoc. prof. ancient history and archaeology U. Minn., Duluth, 1977-87, prof., 1987—; rsch. assoc. dept. classics NYU, 1972-74; evaluator grant proposals NEH, HSF; excavator numerous sites in Israel and Turkey; lectr. in field. Author 4 books; contbr. articles to profl. jours. Recipient Fulbright-Hays Sr. Research fellowship, Turkey, 1984-85, 91-92, The Am. Council Learned Socs. fellowship, 1977-78, NDEA Title VI Fgn. Languages fellowship, 1972-75, Spl. Commendation for Excellence award Phi Alpha Theta, 1979; grantee NEH, 1978, 80, nat. Geographic Soc., 1974, Andrew Mellon Found., NSF, Ford Found., 1971-72, U. Minn., others. Mem. NEH, Nat. Assn. Scholars, Coun. for Internat. Exchange, Am. Coun. Learned Socs., Fulbright Alumni Assn., Phi Alpha Theta, Sigma Xi. Roman Catholic. Home: 5789 220th St N Forest Lake MN 55025-9677

MARCIL, WILLIAM CHRIST, SR., publisher, broadcast executive; b. Rolette, N.D., Mar. 9, 1936; s. Max L. and Ida (Fuerst) M.; m. Jane Black, Oct. 15, 1960; children: Debora Jane, William Christ Jr. BSBA, U. N.D., 1958. Br. mgr. Community Credit Co., Mpls., 1959-61; with Forum Comms. Co., Fargo, N.D., 1961—, pres., pub., CEO, 1969—. Pres. Forum Comm. Found.; past bd. dirs. North Ctrl. region Boy Scouts Am. With U.S. Army, 1958-59. Mem. Inland Newspaper Press Assn., N.D. Press Assn., Am. Newspaper Pubs. Assn. (past dir., chmn.), Fargo and Morehead C. of C., N.D. State C. of C. (past pres.), U.S. C. of C. (past chmn.), Sigma Delta Chi, Lambda Chi Alpha. Republican. Lodges: Masons, Shriners, Elks, Rotary. Home: 1618 8th St S Fargo ND 58103-4240 Office: Forum Comm Co 101 Fifth St N Fargo ND 58102-4826

MARCINIAK, CLAUDIA NOELLE, real estate company executive; b. Chgo., Dec. 2, 1959; d. Edward Allen and Virginia Ceil (Volini) M.; m. Steven Michael Puiszis, Oct. 13, 1984; children: Stephen Edward, Claire Elizabeth, Michael Colin. Student, U. Ill., 1977-78; BA in Bus. Adminstrn., Loyola U., 1981; MA in Mgmt., Northwestern U., 1984. Supr. records audit Cook County States Atty.'s Office, Chgo., 1981-82; asst. mgr. Laventhol & Horwath, Chgo., 1984-88; v.p. Citicorp Real Estate, Chgo., 1988—. Treas. West Suburban Spl. Recreation Found., Franklin Pk., Ill., 1994—, trustee, 1994—. Mem. Real Estate Fin. Forum. Office: Citicorp Real Estate 200 S Wacker 32nd Fl Chicago IL 60606

MARCINIAK, DAVID BUSTER, engineer, consultant; b. Milw., July 21, 1939; s. Boleslaus Joseph and Florence (Szydlowski) M.; m. Mary Clair Beyer, Oct. 18, 1968; children: Michael David, Christine Renee, Joseph Andrew. Student, U. Wis., Milw., 1957-58; BSEE, Milw. Sch. Engring., 1961. Registered profl. engr., Wis., Calif. Assoc. engr. U.S. Cold Regulation Research and Engring. Lab., Hanover, N.H., 1962-64; staff engr. Cleaver Brooks Co., Milw., 1964-66; reliability engr. Astronautics Corp. Am., Milw., 1966-68; engr. Louis Allis Co., New Berlin, Wis., 1968-75, sr. engr., cons., 1983—; reliability engr. Siemens Allis, West Allis, Wis., 1975-79, chief quality assurance engr., 1980-81; quality assurance rep. Grumman Aerospace, Bethpage, N.Y., 1979-80; mgr. reliabiltiy and product safety Allis Chalmers Corp., West Allis, 1981-83; sr. engr., mgr. Magnetek, New Berlin, Wis., 1983-95; freelance cons. engring., St. Francis, Wis., 1995—. Served with U.S. Army, 1962-64. Mem. IEEE, Soc. Reliability Engrs. (internat. rep. 1979—, v.p. Milw. chpt. 1978, pres. 1979-95), Inst. Environ. Scis., Am. Legion. Roman Catholic. Home: 3633 E Tesch Ave Saint Francis WI 53235-4837 Office: Louis Allis Co 427 E Stewart St Milwaukee WI 53207-9999

MARCO, GUY ANTHONY, librarian, educator; b. N.Y.C., Oct. 4, 1927; s. Gaetano Mongelluzzo and Evelyn Capobianco; m. Karen Csontos, July 23, 1949; 1 son, Howard William. Student, DePaul U., 1947-50; B.Mus., Am. Conservatory Music, Chgo., 1951; M.A. in Music, U. Chgo., 1952, M.L.S., 1955, Ph.D. in Musicology, 1956. Librarian, instr. musicology Chgo. Mus. Coll., 1953-54; asst. classics library U. Chgo., 1954; asst. librarian, instr. music Wright Jr. Coll., Chgo., 1954-56; librarian, instr. music Amundsen Jr. Coll., Chgo., 1957-60; asso. prof. library sci., chmn. dept. Kent State U., 1960-66; prof., dean Kent State U. (Sch. Library Sci.), 1966-77; chief gen. reference and bibliography div. Library of Congress, Washington, 1977-78; dir. for N.Am., Library Devel. Cons.'s, London, 1979-81; prof., dir. div. library sci. San Jose State U., 1981-83; exec. dir. Global Research Services, Washington, 1984-85; chief libr. activities U.S. Army, Ft. Dix, N.J., 1985-89; sr. fellow, adj. prof. libr. sci., editor Third World Librs. Rosary Coll., River Forest, Ill., 1989—; vis. lectr. library sci. U. Wis., summer 1955; reference librarian Chgo. Tchrs. Coll., summer 1957; vis. prof. library sci. N.Y. State Coll. Tchrs., Albany, summer 1956, 58; guest lectr. library sci. U. Denver, summer 1959; vis. prof. U. Okla., summer 1960, Coll. Librarianship, Wales, summer 1974, 76, 77, U. Md., summer 1978. Author: The Earliest Music Printers of Continental Europe, 1962, An Appraisal of Favorability in Current Book Reviewing, 1959, (with Claude Palisca) The Art of Counterpoint, 1968, Information on Music, vol. I, 1975, vol. II, 1977, vol. III, 1984, Opera: A Research and Information Guide, 1984, Ency. of Recorded Sound in the United States, 1993; contbr. 150 articles to profl. jours., also book revs. Served with AUS, 1946-47. Mem. ALA, Am. Musicological Soc. Home: 3450 N Lake Shore Dr Apt 3508 Chicago IL 60657-2864 Office: Rosary Coll Libr Sch River Forest IL 60305

MARCUM, BRADLEY DALE, English educator; b. Portsmouth, Ohio, Mar. 26, 1960; s. Norman Leon and Rosemary (Sexton) M. BA, Ohio U., 1986; MA, Wright State U., 1988. Instr. of English Ctrl. State U., Wilberforce, Ohio, 1990-94, dir. The Writing Lab., 1994—; adj. prof. English Ind. U. East, Richmond, 1988-89; adj. prof. developmental English Wright State U., Dayton, 1988-90, adj. prof. English, 1988-90, Urbana U., London, Ohio, summer 1992, 93. Mem. Dayton Free Net Poet Soc. Democrat. Home: 4959 Effingham Pl Dayton OH 45431 Office: Ctrl State U Brush Row Rd 235 Wesley Hall Wilberforce OH 45384

MARCUM, JOSEPH LARUE, insurance company executive; b. Hamilton, Ohio, July 2, 1923; s. Glen F. and Helen A. (Stout) M.; m. Sarah Jane Sloneker, Mar. 7, 1944; children: Catharine Ann Marcum Lowe, Joseph Timothy (dec.), Mary Christina Marcum Manchester, Sarah Jennifer Marcum Shuffield, Stephen Sloneker. B.A., Antioch Coll., 1947; M.B.A. in Fin, Miami U., 1965. With Ohio Casualty Ins. Co. and affiliates, 1947—, now chmn. bd., also bd. dirs.; bd. dirs. First Nat. Bank S.W. Ohio; bd. dirs., chmn. exec. com. First Fin. Bancorp., Monroe, Ohio. Chmn. bd. trustees Miami U., Oxford, Ohio. Capt., inf. U.S. Army. Mem. Soc. CPCU, Queen City Club, Bankers Club, Princeton Club N.Y., Little Harbor club, Walloon Lake Country Club, Mill Reef Club. Presbyterian. Home: 475 Oakwood Dr Hamilton OH 45013-3466 Office: Ohio Casualty Corp 136 N 3rd St Hamilton OH 45025-0002

MARCUS, JACQUELINE BRASNICK, nutritionist; b. Buffalo, June 17, 1949; d. Edward Herman and Rose (Abrams) Brasnick; m. Harvey Steven Marcus, Aug. 13, 1972; children: Meredith Emily, Morgan Ian, Mason Douglas. BS, No. Ill. U., 1971, MS, 1979. Cert. nutrition specialist; registered and lic. dietitian. Nutrition therapist, health educator good health program Skokie (Ill.) Valley Comty. Hosp., 1979-83; editor, pub. Sports-Nutrition News Healthmere Press, Inc., Evanston, Ill., 1982-91; dir. nutrition svcs. Physicians Weight Loss Ctrs., Akron, Ohio, 1987-91; pvt. practice as consulting nutritionist Wilmette, Ill., 1979—; cons. to maj. bus., food-related cos., advt. and pub. rels. firms including 1996 Olympics/U.S. Olympic Com., Brunswick Corp., Quaker Oats, Kelloggs, Best Foods, McDonald's, J. Walter Thompson, Burson-Marsteller, Daniel J. Edelman P.R., IBM, Inland Steel Union 76. Editor-in-chief: Sports-Nutrition: A Guide for the Professional Working with Active People, 1986; author, pub.: Wooden Door Diet Plan and Cookbook, 1983, More Recipes from Wooden Door, 1984; author: Healthwalk, 1990, Manual of Behavior Modification, 1991; scriptwriter: Women and Fitness. Bd. dirs. McKenzie Elem. Sch., Wilmette, 1985-95, Highcrest Mid. Sch., Wilmette, 1995—, Wilmette Jr. H.S., 1993—, Beth Emet Synagogue, Evanston, 1995—. Recipient Excellence award for pvt. practice and consultation Am. Dietetic Assn. Found., 1989; named one of Outstanding Young Women Am. Restaurants and Instns. Mag. Fellow Am. Dietetic Assn. (registered dietitian); mem. Ill. Dietetic Assn. (lic. dietitian), Ohio Dietetic Assn. (lic. dietitian), Jr. League of Evanston-North Shore (chairperson numerous coms., bd. dirs., Vol. of the Month award), Sports and Cardiovasc. Nutritionists (chairperson, sec.), Ill. Dietetic Assn., Chgo. Dietetic Assn. (pres.-elect), North Suburban Dietetic Assn. (chair various coms., bd. dirs. 1996), Entrepreneurial Nutritionists. Home: 1414 Forest Ave Wilmette IL 60091

MARCUS, JOYCE LYNN, marketing executive; b. Chgo.; d. David D. and Alyce (Kramer) M. BS in Edn., No. Ill. U., 1969. Artist R.R. Donelly, Des Plaines, Ill., 1969-70; creative dir. United Bankers Assn., Chgo., 1970-73; pres. Marcus Design, Inc., Wheeling, Ill., 1973—, Marcus Advt., Inc., Wheeling, 1978—; bd. dirs. First Colonial Bank N.W., First Colonial Investment Svcs. Bd. dirs., sec. Y-Me Nat. Breast Cancer Orgn., Chgo., 1989—, chmn. comm. com.; pres. Timbers Residents Assn., Riverwoods, Ill., 1993—. Recipient Excellence award Y-Me Nat. Breast Cancer Orgn., 1994. Mem. Bus. Mktg. Assn., Riverwoods Residents Assn. Office: Marcus Inc 401 S Milwaukee Ave Wheeling IL 60090

MARCUS, LARRY DAVID, broadcasting executive; b. N.Y.C., Jan. 27, 1949; s. Oscar Moses and Sylvia (Ackerman) M.; m. Noreen Mary Marcus, Dec. 24, 1975; children: Julia Ilene, Barbara Maureen. BBA, CUNY, 1970, postgrad. studies Bus. Admistrn., 1970-72. Acctg. mgr. Sta. WPLG-TV, Miami, Fla., 1974-75; v.p., bus. mgr. Sta. KPLR-TV-Koplar Communications, Inc., St. Louis, 1976-82; chief fin. officer Koplar Communications, Inc., St. Louis, 1982-88, River City Broadcasting Co., St. Louis, 1988-96; gen. ptnr. Marcus Investments, L.P., 1996—; bd. dirs. Citation Sys. Inc. Mem. Broadcast Cable Fin. Mgmt. Assn. (bd. dirs. 1976-89, treas. 1989-90, sec. 1990-91, v.p. 1991-92, pres. 1992-93). Jewish. Office: KDNL TV 1215 Cole St Saint Louis MO 63106-3818

MARCUS, STEVEN ERIC, sales executive, musician; b. Phila., Dec. 21, 1956; s. Sheldon Marcus and Naomi Marlene (Sher) Zebrick; m. Patricia Michal Davis Marcus, May 1, 1983; children: Jonathan David, Shira Rose. B Music Edn. summa cum laude, Temple U. Esther Boyer Coll. Music, Phila., 1978, MusM, 1979. Music tchr. Pennsbury Sch. Dist., Fallsington, Pa., 1978-79, Phila. Sch. Dist., 1978-79; grad. teaching asst. Music Theory Temple U. Coll. Music, Phila., 1978-79; piano and organ sales counselor Taylor Music Co. Inc., Willow Grove, Pa., 1978-85; dist. sales mgr. Baldwin Piano and Organ Co. Inc., Loveland, Ohio, 1985-91; retail divsn. mgr., 1991-94; dir. sales Steinway Piano The Beautiful Sound, Inc., Burr Ridge, Ill., 1994—; pres. Barrington (Ill.) Area Bus. Network, 1993—, Chicagoland Study of Piano Enhances Learning and Life Success, Inc., Burr Ridge, Ill., 1995—; dir. Chgo. String Ensemble, 1994-95, Palatine (Ill.) Concert Band, 1994-95; adv. bd. Ars Viva, 1995—. Composer: Choral Composition Adon Olam, 1977, Sonata for Symphonic Band, 1974; arranger: When I Fall in Love, 1994. Mem. The New Oratorio Singers, Palatine Concert Band, Barrington Brass Quintet, Tubists Universal Brotherhood Assn., Lyric Opera of Chgo. Barrington Chpt., Phi Mu Alpha Sinfonia Profl. Music. Home: 756 Concord Ln Barrington IL 60010 Office: The Beautiful Sound Inc 120 Burr Ridge Pkwy Burr Ridge IL 60521

MARCUSE, MANFRED JOACHIM, paper products executive; b. Berlin, Apr. 17, 1927; came to U.S., 1947, naturalized, 1951; s. Bruno and Hedwig Elisabeth (Ettling) M.; m. Charlotte Kraemer, Sept. 23, 1950. Grad. high sch., Berlin. Export clk. ERICO Corp., N.Y.C., 1947-49; sales rep. Roseda Mills, Buffalo, 1950, various companies, 1953-58; systems engr. Nebr. Salesbook Co., Lincoln, 1958-64; prin., owner, chmn. Marc Bus. Forms Inc., Chgo., 1964—. Contbr. articles to profl. jours. Supporting mem. Selfhelp Home for the Aged, Chgo., 1988—, Chgo. Symphony, Lyric Opera, Chgo. United Jewish Appeal. With U.S. Army, 1951-52. Jewish. Office: Marc Business Forms Inc 2722-26 W Peterson Ave Chicago IL 60659

MARES, HARRY, state legislator; b. Dec. 21, 1938; m. Geri Mares; 7 children. BA, Loras Coll., Dubuque, Iowa; MS, Winona State U. Minn. state rep. Dist. 55A, 1994—; former tchr. Address: 2592 Crown Hill Ct White Bear Lake MN 55110

MARGOLIS, FRED SHELDON, pediatric dentist, educator; b. Lorain, Ohio, Mar. 31, 1947; s. Benjamin Barnett and Zelma (Bordo) M.; m. Susan Kreiter, Sept. 12, 1971; children: David S., Adam R. BS, Ohio State U., 1969, DDS, 1973; cert. pediatric dentistry U. Ill.-Chgo., 1976. Dental intern Mt. Sinai Hosp., Chgo., 1973-74; practice dentistry North Suburban Dental Assocs., Skokie, Ill., 1974-84; practice dentistry, Arlington Heights, Ill., 1979-96, Buffalo Grove, Ill., 1996—; chief of dentistry Northwest Community Hosp., 1989-90, Arlington Heights; asst. prof. pediatric dentistry Loyola U. Dental Sch., Maywood, Ill., 1982-83, guest lectr. pediatric dentistry, 1983-87; dental cons. Delta Dental Plan, Chgo., 1983; staff dentist Glenkirk Schs., Glenview, Ill., 1984—; pres. Smile Makers Seminars, 1984—. Contbr. articles to profl. pubs. Cubmaster N.E. Ill. coun. Boy Scouts Am., 1984, 87-91, Den Leader, 1986-87; mem. human rights com. Glenkirk Schs.; pres., bd. dirs. Ill. Found. Dentistry Handicapped, 1995—. Mem. ADA, Am. Acad. Pediatric Dentistry, Ill. State Dental Soc. (bd. trustees 1996—), Am. Soc. Dentistry for Children, Chgo. Dental Soc. (v.p. North Side br. 1987-89, pres.-elect North Side br. 1989-90, pres., 1990, chmn. access to care com. 1989-90, bd. dirs. 1992-94), Alpha Omega (sec. 1995-96, v.p. 1996—). Jewish. Avocations: photography, piano, tennis. Home: 365 Moraine Rd Highland Park IL 60035

MARGOLIS, MICHAEL STEPHEN, political science educator, consultant; b. Chgo., Mar, 27, 1940; s. Ralph Victor and Annette (Krassner) M.; m. Ellen Louise Freedman, Dec. 26, 1964; children: Karen, Jennifer, Abby, Max, Nicola; m. Elaine Cajano Camerota, June 23, 1990. AB, Oberlin Coll., 1961; MA, U. Mich., 1962, PhD, 1968. Lectr. Politics U. Strathclyde, Glasgow, Scotland, 1965-67; instr. polit. sci. U. Pitts., 1967-68, asst. prof., 1968-73, assoc. prof., 1973-85, prof., 1985-90; prof. U. Cin., 1990—, dept. head, 1990-95; lectr. politics U. Glasgow, 1973-74; cons. in field. Author: (with others) Political Stratification and Democracy, 1972, Viable Democracy, 1979; editor: (with G. Mauser) Manipulating Public Opinion, 1989, (with John Green) Machine Politics, Soundbites & Nostalgia, 1993, Free Expression, Public Support & Censorship, 1994; mem. Allegheny County Democratic Com., Pa., 1971-73. Mem. Am. Polit. Sci. Assn., Am. Assn. Pub. Opinion Rsch., Midwest Polit. Sci. Assn., So. Polit. Sci. Assn. Avocations: sports; travel; reading. Home: 658 Pointe Benton Ln Covington KY 41014-1100 Office: U Cin Dept Polit Sci ML 0375 Cincinnati OH 45221-0375

MARIANI, CARLOS, state legislator; b. July 13, 1957; m. Maritza Mariani; two children. Student, Macalester Coll.; postgrad., UJ. Miami. Social issues program dir.; Dist. 65B rep. Minn. Ho. of Reps., St. Paul, 1990—; former vice chmn. econ. devel., infrastructure and regulations fin. com., Minn. Ho. of Reps.; asst majority leader; mem. edn.-higher edn., and housing and transp. and transit coms. Office: 232 Stevens St W Saint Paul MN 55107-2735*

MARIK, KAREN L., manufacturing company executive; b. St. Louis, Sept. 26, 1967; d. Thomas Richard and Donna Jean M. BSBA, U. Mo., 1989. Mgmt. trainee Caterpillar Inc., Peoria, Ill., 1989-90, inventory rsch. analyst inventory mgmt., 1990-92, tng. analyst human resources, 1992-93, graphic artist, pub. affairs asst., 1992-95; mktg. coord. City of Coral Springs, Fla., 1995; graphics prodn. specialist Maritz Mktg. Rsch. Inc., Fenton, Mo., 1996—. Editor: Caterpillar Manifold Newsletter. Coord. United Way Campaign, 1994; bus. cons. Jr. Achievement of Ill., Peoria, 1991, 92; youth counselor Woodland Bapt. Ch., Peoria, 1990. Recipient O'Connor-Carey Bus. award Stephens Coll., 1987. Me. U. Mo. Alumni Assn., Pub. Relations Soc. of Am. Office: Maritz Marketing Research Inc 1297 N Highway Dr Fenton MO 63099 Office: Maritz Mktg Rsch Inc 1297 N Highway Dr Fenton MO 63099

MARIN, VINCENT ARUL, infosystems executive; b. Sangeethamangalam, Tamil Nadu, India, Sept. 9, 1959; s. Mariappan and Arulmary M.; m. Thelma Mabel Sophiya. B in Commerce, Loyola Coll., Madras, India, 1982; MBA, Loyola Coll., Balt., 1983; MS in MIS, No. Ill. U., 1985. Cert. systems profl. Instr. No. Ill. U., DeKalb, Ill., 1985-86; info. ctr. mgr. Nat. Assn. Realtors, Chgo., 1987, dir. infosystems rsch., 1989-91, dir. bus. systems devel., 1992-94; mgr. info. sys. McKinsey & Co. Inc., Chgo., 1994—; adj. prof. DePaul U. Treas. Chgo. Tamil Sangam Orgn. Mem. Beta Gmma Sigma. Office: McKinsey & Co Inc 1 First Nat Plz Ste 2900 Chicago IL 60607

MARINI, MARGARET MOONEY, social sciences educator; b. Spangler, Pa., Apr. 21, 1947; d. William Henry and May (Howson) Mooney; m. John Joseph Marini, June 13, 1970. BA summa cum laude, Goucher Coll., 1969; PhD, Johns Hopkins U., 1974. Rsch. scientist Battelle Meml. Inst., Seattle, 1974-83; affiliate asst. prof. U. Wash., Seattle, 1976-83; assoc. prof. Vanderbilt U., Nashville, 1983-88; prof. U. Minn., Mpls., 1988—; mem. peer rev. panel NSF, Arlington, Va., 1993-94, NIH, Bethesda, Md., 1976-77, 80-85. Cons. editor Am. Jour. Sociology, 1984-86, 92-94; adv. editor Sociol. Methodology, 1987-92. Recipient Rsch. Career Devel. award NIH, 1985-90; predoctoral fellow NIMH, 1969-73. Mem. AAAS, Internat. Sociol. Assn.,

Am. Sociol. Assn., Sociol. Rsch. Assn., Population Assn. Am. (bd. dirs. 1990-92), Am. Statis. Assn., Socio-Econs. Soc.

MARINO, CHARLES JOSEPH, arbitrator; b. Gillespie, Ill., May 30, 1926; s. Joseph and Lucille (Valerio) M.; m. Laura Donadon, Apr. 15, 1950; 1 child, Charles Joseph Jr. BS in Commerce, St. Louis; BA in Mgmt., Webster U. Indsl. rels. Kroger Co., St. Louis, 1946-47; dir. pers. St. Louis U., 1949-67; dir. manpower mgmt. Blue Cross Hosp. Svcs. Inc., St. Louis, 1967-75; exec. asst. to the dir. health and hosps. City of St. Louis, 1975-77; cons. to exec. dir. Urban League St. Louis, 1977-79; auditor dept. revenue State of Mo., 1979-85; pvt. practice, 1979—; arbitrator ABA, St. Louis, 1994; panel mem. Fed. Mediation and Conciliation, 1979—; panel arbitrator dist. 12 United Mine Workers of Am. and Consol. Coal Cos., 1994—. Chmn. compliance divsn. St. Louis Coun. on Human Rels., 1968-76; mem. adv. bd. Minority Econ. Devel. Assn., 1970-77; bd. dirs. Opportunities Industrializatio O.I.C., 1972-75; bd. dirs. Consumer Credit Counseling Svc., 1977-78; mem. labor and indsl. rels. com. State of Mo., 1972-75; mem. adv. com. Bd. Edn. Work-Study PRogram, 1972-75; bd. dirs., exec. com. nominating com., fin. and endowment com., chmn. pers. policy com. Urban League of St. Louis, 1968-77. With U.S. Navy, 1944-46. Mem. Internat. Rels. Rsch. Assn., Am. Arbitration Assn., Internat. Pers. Mgmt. Assn., Nat. Assn. Accts., Indsl. Rels. Rsch. Assn., Am. Soc. for Pers. Adminstrn., Am. Mgmt. Assn., St. Louis Pers. and Guidance Assn., Am. Inst. of Mgmt. Roman Catholic. Home: 7161 Lindenwood Pl Saint Louis MO 63109-1116

MARINO, WILLIAM FRANCIS, telecommunications industry executive, consultant; b. Phila., Dec. 28, 1948; s. William F. and Edith Ellen (Dougherty) M.; m. Mary Ellen Klems, Sept. 29, 1979; children: Kiersten Leigh, Meghan Lyn. Student, Ohio State U., 1967; BS in Fin. and Acctg., Widener U., 1970; MBA, NYU, 1976. Sr. acctg., fin. positions U.S. Steel Corp., Pitts., 1970-83; v.p. U.S. Steel Credit Corp., Pitts., 1983-85; dir. fin. programs CIS Corp., Syracuse, N.Y., 1985, v.p. instl. sales, 1986; pres. CIS Credit Corp., Syracuse, N.Y., 1987, v.p. fin., 1988; v.p., chmn. reorganization com. Continental Info. Systems Corp., Syracuse, N.Y., 1989; v.p. fin., CFO ITEC Corp., Lake Bluff, Ill., 1990-91; pres., CEO ITEC Corp., Lake Bluff, 1991—; chmn. The Telecare Group, Inc.; advisor, cons. Chong & Assocs., N.Y.C., 1989. Advisor Hiawatha coun. Boy Scouts Am., Syracuse, 1987; dir. Cystic Fibrosis Found., Syracuse, 1987-88. Recipient Century award Boy Scouts Am., Syracuse, 1988. Mem. Am. Assn. Equipment Lessors, Am. Mgmt. Assn., Fin. Execs. Inst., Aircraft, Owners & Pilots Assn. Republican. Home: 1280 Thornbury Ln Libertyville IL 60048-2361 Office: ITEC Corp 999 Sherwood Dr Lake Bluff IL 60044

MARINO ANGSTADT, MARLENE, fine artist, artist agent; b. N.Y.C., Jan. 1, 1947; d. Michael John and Anne (Bisogno) Marino; m. Robert David Angstadt, Dec. 29, 1972. Student, Caldwell Coll., 1965-66; BA, So. Ill. U., 1966-69, Teaching Cert., 1970. Free-lance art dir. J. Walter Thompson; Foote, Cone & Belding; Michael Marino & Assocs., N.Y.C., 1970-72; art dir. Sun Printing Corp., Naperville, Ill., 1973-79; art dir./prodn. mgr. New World Pub. Co., Chgo., 1980-86; pres., owner FDM Prdons., Inc./Marlene Marino Mktng. and Creative Svcs., Chgo., 1986—; lectr. career seminar North Cen. Coll., Naperville, 1978; pvt. tutor art creativity, Chgo. area, 1985—; tchr. Columbia Coll., Chgo., 1992. Mem. The Art Inst. of Chgo., Nat. Mus. of Women in the Arts, Am. Craft Coun. Office: FDM Prodns Inc 75 E Wacker Dr STe 2500 Chicago IL 60601

MARIOTTI, JOHN LOUIS, plastics and rubber manufacturing company executive; b. Toluca, Ill., Apr. 12, 1941; s. Faustino L. and Lillian E. (Gallagher) M.; m. Maureen, Aug. 22, 1964; children: Lisa, Michael, Susan. BSME, Bradley U., Peoria, Ill., 1963; MSME, U. Wis., 1964. Process engr., staff engr., staff supr. Automatic Electric Co., 1964-67; mfg. mgr. L.R. Nelson Corp., Peoria, Ill., 1967-76, v.p. planning and devel., 1976-79; pres., gen. mgr. Okla. Bicycle Div., Ponca City, 1979-83, Huffy Bicycle Co., Dayton, Ohio, 1983—. Chmn. bd. Productivity Communication Ctr., Chapel Hill, N.C.; chmn. bd. Goodwill Industries Dayton, 1990-93. Mem. Bicycle Inst. Am. (pres. 1991-92). Republican. Roman Catholic. Office: Huffy Corp 7701 Byers Rd Miamisburg OH 45342-3657

MARIS, CHARLES ROBERT, surgeon, otolaryngologist; b. Champaign, Ill., Nov. 24, 1948; s. Harold Franklin and Marjorie Ellen (Beermann) M.; m. Karen Lynne Richardson, Dec. 27, 1970; children: Katherine, Emily, Charles Jr. BS, Eastern Ill. U., 1971; MD, U. Ill., 1975. Diplomate Am. Bd. Surgery, Am. Bd. Otolaryngology. Resident in otolaryngology U. Nebr. Med. Ctr., Omaha, 1982; chief of surgery Sarah Bush Lincoln Health Ctr., Mattoon, Ill., 1984-85, chmn. exec. com., 1985, 89, 94, chief of staff, 1986, 90, 95; bd. dirs. 1st Mid-Ill. Bank & Trust. Mem. Charleston Community Unit Dist. #1 Sch. Bd., 1984-88. Lt. Col. U.S. Army Reserve, 159th Mash (Operation Desert Storm) 1990-91. Named one of Outstanding Young Men in Am., 1985. Fellow Am. Coll. Surgeons, Am. Acad. Otolaryngology-Head and Neck Surgery, Am. Acad. Facial Plastic and Reconstructive Surgery. Republican. Methodist. Office: 200 Lerna Rd South Mattoon IL 61938-9252

MARK, PETER, director, conductor; b. N.Y.C., Oct. 31, 1940; s. Irving and Edna M.; m. Thea Musgrave, Oct. 2, 1971. BA (Woodrow Wilson fellow), Columbia U., 1961; MS, Juilliard Sch. Music, 1963. Prof. music and dramatic art U. Calif., Santa Barbara, 1965-94; fellow Creative Arts Inst., U. Calif., 1968-69, 71-72; guest condr. Wolf Trap Orch., 1979, N.Y.C. Opera, 1981, L.A. Opera Theater, 1981, Royal Opera House, London, 1982, Hong Kong Philharm. Orch., 1984, Jerusalem Symphony Orch., 1988, Tulsa Opera, 1988, Compania Nacional de Opera, Mexico City, 1989, 92, N.Y. Pops, Carnegie Hall, 1991. Concert violist U.S., S.Am., Europe, 1961-67; artistic dir., condr. Va. Opera, Norfolk, 1975—, gen. dir., 1978—; condr.: Am. premier of Mary, Queen of Scots (Musgrave), 1978; World premier of A Christmas Carol (Musgrave), 1979, of Harriet, the Woman Called Moses (Musgrave), 1985, of Simon Bolivar (Musgrave), 1984, Porgy and Bess, Buenos Aires, Mexico City and São Paulo, 1992, Orlando Opera co., 1993, Richmond Symphony, 1993, Krakow Opera, 1995, Pacific Opera Victoria (Can.), 1996, Cleve. Opera, 1996, Festival Pucciniano-Torre del Lago, Italy, 1996. Recipient Elias Lifchey viola award Juilliard Sch. Music, 1963; named hon. citizen of Norfolk (Va.). Mem. Musicians Union, Phi Beta Kappa. Office: Va Opera PO Box 2580 Norfolk VA 23501-2580

MARKEE, KATHERINE MADIGAN, librarian, educator; b. Cleve., Feb. 24, 1931; d. Arthur Alexis and Margaret Elizabeth (Madigan) M. AB, Trinity Coll., Washington, 1953; MA, Columbia U., 1962; MLS, Case Western Res. U., 1968. Employment mgr., br. store tng. supr. The May Co., Cleve., 1965-67; assoc. prof. libr. sci., data bases libr. Purdue U. Libr., West Lafayette, Ind., 1968—. Contbr. articles to profl. jours. Mem. ALA, AAUP, Spl. Librs. Assn., Ind. Online Users Group, Sigma Xi (Rsch. Support award 1986). Office: Purdue U Libr West Lafayette IN 47907-1530

MARKEL, FRANK LEWIS, JR., retired actuary; b. Hillsboro, Ill., Jan. 20, 1925; s. Frank Lewis and Blanch Nelle (Watkins) M.; m. Elizabeth Kaster, Oct. 8, 1955; 1 child, Karen Elizabeth Markel Uthe. BS, Northwestern U., 1950. Asst. actuary Continental Assurance Co., Chgo., 1952-68; sr. actuary Gen. Bd. Pensions, Evanston, Ill., 1968-90. Staff sgt. U.S. Army, 1943-46, 50-51. Mem. SAG.

MARKING, T(HEODORE) JOSEPH, JR., transportation and urban planner; b. Shelbyville, Ind., June 28, 1945; s. Theodore Joseph and Alvena Cecelia (Thieman) M.; BA, So. Ill. U., 1967, M. City and Regional Planning, 1972; m. Kathy K. Hagerman, Nov. 25, 1969. Intelligence research specialist Def. Intelligence Agy., Washington, 1967-68; planner I, St. Louis City Plan Commn., 1970; transp. planner Alan M. Voorhees & Assocs., St. Louis, 1970-74, sr. transp. planner, 1974-78, assoc., 1978; sr. transp. planner Booker Assocs., Inc., St. Louis, 1978-80, chief traffic and transp. sect., 1980-85; mgr. transit planning East-West Gateway Coordinating Coun., St. Louis, 1985-88 ; mgr. planning dept., Harland Bartholomew & Assocs., St. Louis, 1988-91; sr. transp. planner Burns & McDonnell Engrng. Co., St. Louis, 1992-95; sr. transp. planner Booker Assoc., Inc., St. Louis, 1996—; planner-in-charge, Mo.; guest lectr. St. Louis C.C. Dist., Webster U., St. Louis U. Mem. Am. Inst. Cert. Planners (charter), Am. Planning Assn. (charter, treas. transp. planning divsn., past pres., pres., sec., dir. St. Louis sect.), Inst. Transp. Engrs., Traffic Engrs. Assn. Met. St. Louis (past pres.). Office: 1139 Olive St Saint Louis MO 63101

MARKLE, GERALD ELLIOTT, sociology educator; b. Detroit, Nov. 14, 1942; s. Sidney and Rose (Bachrach) M.; m. Frances McCrea; 1 child, Linus. BA, Wayne State U., 1964, MA, 1966; MA, Fla. State U., 1969, PhD, 1971. Prof. Western Mich. U., Kalamazoo, 1971—. Author: Meditations of a Holocaust Traveler, 1995; co-author: Cigarettes: Battle Over, 1984, Japanese transl., Minutes to Midnight, 1989; editor: Handbook of Science and Technology Studies, 1995. Office: Western Mich U Dept Sociology Kalamazoo MI 49008

MARKLEY, LYNN MCMASTER, rubber and plastics company executive; b. Carrollton, Ohio, Aug. 18, 1938; s. Charles Sparks and Florence Elizabeth (McMaster) M.; m. Ina Marie Hogsed, Nov. 1, 1958; children: Jerry Lynn, David Alan, Margaret Elisabeth. BS in Chemistry, Mt. Union Coll., Alliance, Ohio, 1960; MBA, Akron U., 1966. Rsch. chemist PPG Chem., Barberton, Ohio, 1960-62; lab. mgr. Gen. Tire Co., Akron, 1962-66; mgr. matls. Dunlop Tire Co., Buffalo, 1966-74; mgr. passenger matls. Uniroyal Inc., Tire div., Troy, Mich., 1974-76; mgr. quality assurance Uniroyal Inc., Tire div., 1976-78, dir. quality assurance, 1978-80, dir. matls., 1980-81, dir. product engrng., 1981-86, dir. ops. staff, 1986; dir. mfg. quality assurance Uniroyal/Goodrich Tire Co., Akron, 1986-94; mgr. quality and tech. Bailey Transp. Products, Inc., Conneaut, Ohio, 1994—. Mem. Am. Soc. Quality Control. Office: PO Box 500 333 Gore Rd Conneaut OH 44030

MARKO, SHARON, state legislator; b. Mar. 2, 1953. BS, Ind. U.; post-grad., U. Minn. Minn. state rep. Dist. 57B, 1994—; comms. cons. Address: 121 10th St Newport MN 55055

MARKOS, CHRIS, real estate company executive; b. Cleve., Nov. 25, 1926; s. George and Bessie (Papathatou) M.; m. Alice Zaharopoulos, Dec. 11, 1949; children: Marilyn, Irene, Betsy. BA, Case Western Reserve, Cleve., 1960; LLB, LaSalle U., Chgo., 1964. Cert. gen. real estate appraiser, Ohio. Vice-pres. Herbert Laronge Inc., Cleve., 1963-76; v.p. Calabrese, Racek and Markos Inc., Cleve., 1976-83; v.p. Herbert Laronge Inc., Cleve., 1983-87, pres., 1987-88; v.p. Cragin Lang, Inc., Cleve., 1989-91; sr. cons. Grubb & Ellis, Cleve., 1991-93; sr. v.p. Realty One Appraisal Divsn., Independence, Ohio, 1993—; pres. Alcrimar Inc., 1989—. Co-author: Ohio Supplement to Modern Real Estate Practice, 5th-7th edits.; cons. editor, co-author: Modern Real Estate Praactice in Ohio, 1st-3rd edits. Bd. dirs. David N. Meyers Coll., Cleve., 1984—. With U.S. Army, 1945-46. Named Realtor of the Year, Cleve. Bd Realtors, 1976. Mem. Am. Soc. Appraisers (sr., pres. 1973, state dir. 1976), Cleve. Bd. Realtors (pres. 1974, Realtor of Yr. 1976). Republican. Greek Orthodox. Home: 6731 Hidden Lake Trail Brecksville OH 44141-3189 Office: Realty One 6000 Rockside Woods Blvd Cleveland OH 44131-2330

MARKOVIC, JOHN JOVAN, modern European historian, educator; b. Ćubrija, Serbia, Yugoslavia, June 21, 1949; came to U.S., 1969; s. Elijah and Budimka (Pavlovic) M.; m. Vesna Zlatanovska, July 28, 1959; children: John-Philip Thomas, Christianna. BA, Andrews U., 1982; MA, Bowling Green State U., 1986, PhD, 1990. Instr. U. Toledo, 1989; asst. prof. Andrews U., Berrien Springs, Mich., 1990-96, assoc. prof., 1996—. Editor East/West Edn., 1992—. Home: 7201 N US 31 Berrien Springs MI 49103 Office: Andrews Univ History Dept Berrien Springs MI 49104

MARKS, ESTHER L., metals company executive; b. Canton, Ohio, Oct. 3, 1927; d. Jacob and Ella (Wisman) Rosky; m. Irwin Alfred Marks, June 29, 1947; children: Jules, Howard, Marilyn. Student, Ohio State U., 1945-46, Youngstown State U., 1946-47. V.p. Steel City Iron & Metal, Inc., Youngstown, Ohio. Pres. Jr. Hadassah, Youngstown, 1943-45, Pioneer Women, Youngstown, 1951, Anshe Emeth Sisterhood, Youngstown, Broadway Theatre League, Youngstown, 1958, B'nai B'rith Women, Youngstown, 1962, Dist. 2 B'nai B'rith Women, Cleve., 1969-70, Jewish Cmty. Ctr., Youngstown, Youngstown Area Jewish Fedn., 1988-90; v.p. United Way, Youngstown, 1991, chmn., 1996; grad. Leadership Youngstown, 1991; bd. Akiva Acad. Commn. for Jewish Edn., Temple El Emeth, Stambaugh Auditorium. Named Guardian of the Menorah B'nai B'rith, Youngstown, 1978; recipient BBG Alumna award B'nai B'rith Girls, Washington, 1989. Mem. LMV, YWCA, Ohio Hist. Soc. Democrat. Jewish. Home: 3511 5th Ave Youngstown OH 44505-1907 Office: 703 Wilson Ave Youngstown OH 44506-1445

MARKS, FLORENCE CARLIN ELLIOTT, nursing informaticist; b. Louisville, Ky., Oct. 15, 1928; d. David Carlin and Anna Marie (Lance) Elliott; m. George Edward Marks, Mar. 18, 1961; children: Mary Ellen Marks Fox, Ruth Ann, Charles Douglas. BS in Chemistry, Zoology, U. Cin., 1949; BSN, U. Minn., 1953, M of Nursing Adminstrn., 1956. RN, Minn. From staff nurse to asst. head nurse U. Minn. Hosps., Mpls., 1953-54; staff nurse Marseilisbog Hosp., Aarhaus, Denmark, 1954-55; nursing supr. U. Minn. Hosps., Mpls., 1956-61, spl. asst. to dir. of nursing svc., 1962; rsch. asst. Hill Family Found. Nursing Rsch. Project, Mpls., 1966-69; writer U. Minn. Sch. of Nursing, Mpls., 1976; cons. U. Minn. Sch. of Nursing, 1976, 1978; nursing program specialist Hennepin County Med. Ctr., Mpls., 1978-84, nursing info. systems dir., cons., 1987—; nursing utilization system coord. U. Minn. Hosps., Mpls., 1984-87; cons. Creative Nursing Mgmt., 1992—; speaker, lectr. various nursing confs. in U.S. Contbr. articles to profl. publs., chpts. to profl. books, posters, abstracts; co-author: (with Joan Williams) (TV series) TLC, 1953 (McCall's award 1954); editor: Tomorrow's Nurse, 1960-62; Minn. Nursing Accent (commemorative issue 60th anniversary) May, 1965. Prin. flutist St. Anthony Civic Orch., 1975—, bd. dirs., 1988-92, adminstrv. bd. Hennepin Ave. United Meth. Ch., 1974-77, tchr., 1966-83 intermittently, cmty. outreach ministry, chair adv. com., 1992-95; mem. U. Minn. Sch. Nursing Densford Recognition Com., 1992-96; troop leader Mpls. coun. Girl Scouts USA, 1971-85, bd. dirs., 1977-79, svc. unit mgr., 1973-77; den leader Cub Scouts Webelo den, Viking coun. Boy Scouts Am., 1977-79; v.p. Wilshire Park PTSA, 1975-76, pres., 1976-77. Recipient Thanks Badge Greater Mpls. Girl Scout Coun. Mem. Minn. Nurses Assn. (various coms., bd. dirs. 1959-61), Minn. League for Nursing, Minn. Heart Assn. (profl. edn. com. 1959-61), Nursing Info. Discussion Group (chmn. Twin City program com. 1985-91, 95—), U. Minn. Sch. Nursing Alumni Assn. (bd. dirs. 1963-67, pres. 1965-66), Mortar Bd., Zeta Tau Alpha, Tau Beta Sigma, Sigma Theta Tau (bd. dirs. Zeta chpt. 1969-73, 89-91, pres. 1972-73, heritage com. 1990). Home: 3424 Silver Lake Rd NE Minneapolis MN 55418-1605

MARKS, GARY A., business executive; b. Chgo., Aug. 11, 1952. BFA, U. Ill., 1975. Exec. v.p. Levy Organize, Chgo., 1978-84; pres. Devel. Resources, Inc., Chgo., 1984—. Fundraiser Jewish United Fund, Chgo., 1985—; campaign supporter 42nd Ward Dem. Orgn., Chgo., 1985—. Recipient Svc. award Chgo. Coun. of Builders, 1987. Mem. Std. Club of Chgo. Office: Devel Resources Inc 439 N Wells St Chicago IL 60610-4512

MARKS, MARIE SCHULZ, investment service president; b. Youngstown, Ohio, Sept. 25, 1957; d. Alvin James and Mary Ann (Webber) Schulz; m. Paul R. Marks, June 20, 1981; children: Sean M. Ryan N. Kaylyn M. Cert., Ind. Ctrl. U.; student, Coll. for Fin. Planning, Denver, 1990—. CFP; lic. br. mgr. Investment specialist Robert W. Baird & Co., Inc., Indpls., 1988—; annuity specialist Northwestern Mut. Life, Indpls., 1994—; agt. Northwestern Mut. Life, 1988—; pres. Comprehensive Investments, Indpls., 1990—; cons. Firstmark Investor Svcs., Inc., 1981-88; asst. v.p., dir. ops., cons. Firstmark Securities Inc., N.Y.C., 1984-86. Co-author, editor: Creative Investment Library for Overseas Missionary Group, 1991. Vice precinct committeeman Rep. Party, Indpls., 1979-80; voter registrar Rep. Party, Indpls., 1979-80. Recipient All Am. Team sales award Am. Funds, 1990—. Mem. Securities Industry Assn., Builders Assn. of Greater Indpls. Women's Aux. (v.p. 1986, v.p. property owners assn. 1988-89), Mademoiselle Career Mktg. Bd. Republican. Roman Catholic. Office: Bank One Ctr Tower 3800 Indianapolis IN 46204

MARKS, MARTHA ALFORD, author; b. Oxford, Miss., July 27, 1946; d. Truman and Margaret Alford; m. Bernard L. Marks, Jan. 27, 1968. BA, Centenary Coll., 1968; MA, Northwestern U., 1972, PhD, 1978. Tchr. Notre Dame High Sch. for Boys, Niles, Ill., 1969-74; teaching asst. Northwestern U., Evanston, Ill., 1974-78, lectr., lang. coord., 1978-83; asst. prof. Kalamazoo (Mich.) Coll., 1983-85; writer Riverwoods, Ill., 1985—; cons. WGBH Edn. Found., Boston, 1988-91, Am. Coun. on the Tchg. of Fgn. Langs., 1981-92, Ednl. Testing Svcs., 1988-90, Peace Corps., 1993. Co-author: Destinos: An Introduction to Spanish, 1991, Al corriente, 1989, 93, Que tal?, 1986, 90; author: (workbook) Al corriente, 1989, 93; contbr. articles to profl. jours. Mem. Lake County (Ill.) Bd., Forest Preserve Commn., 1992—, Lake County Conservation Alliance; vice chmn. Friends of Ryerson Conservation Area Bd.; co-founder Reps. for Environ. Protection. Mem. AAUW. Home: 2940 Cherokee Ln Riverwoods IL 60015-1609 Office: County Bd Office County Bldg Rm 1001 18 N County St Waukegan IL 60085-4304

MARKUS, JOEL SETH, data processing management executive; b. Kansas City, Mo., Oct. 11, 1950; s. Milton Jerome and Ethel (Ginsberg) M.; m. Glenna Rae Shinkle, Apr. 1, 1984. Student, Bradley U., 1968-71; cert. in data processing, U. Mo., 1972; A in Applied Sci., Penn Valley Community Coll., 1975. Data processing clk. United Mo. Bank Kansas City, 1973-74, programmer, 1975-76, systems programmer, 1977-81, project mgr., 1982-83, v.p. communication systems, 1984-90, v.p. tech. systems, 1990—. Mem. Jewish Com. on Scouting, Kansas City, 1984—, scholarship chmn., 1985-86, 90—, sec.-treas., 1987, treas., 1990—; active adult edn. com. Beth Shalom Congregation, Kansas City, 1987; v.p. Morningview Homes Assn., Overland Park, Kans., 1987, treas., 1988-90, bd. dirs., 1993-96, editor, 1993-96. Recipient Shofar award Jewish Com. on Scouting, 1986; named to Eagle Scouts Boy Scouts Am., 1966. Mem. Kansas City IMS Users Group (sec. 1978-79). Democrat. Home: 9742 Antioch Rd Shawnee Mission KS 66212-4027 Office: UMB Bank NA 928 Grand Blvd Box 419226 Kansas City MO 64141-6226

MARKWOOD, ALAN JEFFREY, health association administrator; b. Yonkers, N.Y., July 7, 1954; s. Ira M. and Alice Markwood; m. Beth Grube, July 28, 1985; children: Carolyn M., Emily A. BA in Psychology, U. Rochester, 1976; MA in Psychology, Alfred U., 1977; cert. of advanced grad. study, Boston U., 1991. Cert. sch. psychologist. Sch. psychologist Sangamon Area Spl. Edn. Dist., Springfield, Ill., 1978-80, Sutton (Mass.) Pub. Schs., 1980-81; spl. edn. tutor Brookline (Mass.) Schs., 1982; teaching and field supervision fellow Boston U./Chelsea (Mass.) Schs., 1982; sch. psychologist Stoneham (Mass.) Schs., 1983-86; prevention area coord. Chestnut Health Systems, Inc., Bloomington, Ill., 1987-95, prevention projects coord., 1995—; governing bd. mem. Operation Snowball, Inc., Ill., 1988-91, pres., 1990; liaison bd. mem. Ill. Drug Edn. Alliance, 1991—; governing bd. mem., youth violence prevention com. chair Ill. Coun. for Prevention of Violence, 1995-96. Cmty. mediator Children's Hearings Project, Cambridge, Mass., 1985-87; state del. Drug Watch Internat., Ill., 1992—. Prevention Coalition grantee Ctr. for Substance Abuse Prevention, 1995. Mem. Nat. Assn. Mediation in Edn. (reviewer 1988—), Ill. Assn. Prevention (founding mem.), Ill. Assn. Student Assistance Profls. (founding mem.), Phi Delta Kappa. Office: Chestnut Health Systems Inc 702 W Chestnut Bloomington IL 61701

MARLEY, ANNE HARDER, small business owner; b. Topeka, Jan. 22, 1959; d. Robert Clarence and Dorothy Lou (Welty) H.; m. Dennis G. Marley, May 30, 1981; children: Eric, Claire. BS, Baker U., 1981. CPA, Kans. Auditor Grant Thornton, Kansas City, Mo., 1981-86; controller Profl. Rehab. Mgmt., Olathe, Kans., 1986-87, parttime controller, 1987-88; v.p. Occudata, Inc., Overland Park, Kans., 1987—. Youth group sponsor Valley View United Meth. Ch., Overland Park, Kans., 1981-90; vol. Pets for Life, Kansas City, Mo., 1986—; tchr. Sunday Sch. Valley View United Meth. Ch., 1990—; mem. Cultural Brige com., 1991—. Mem. Alpha Delta Sigma, Phi Mu (treas. corp. bd. 1989-90). Democrat. Office: Occudata Inc 5700 Broadmoor Ste 310 Mission KS 66202-2405

MARQUES, JOSÉ D., SR., communications specialist; b. Braga, Portugal, Sept. 18, 1959; came to U.S., 1981; s. Joaquim Fernandes and Maria Conceicao (Pereira) M.; m. Deborah Widder, Mar. 25, 1995. MA, MDiv., Cath. Theol. Union, Chgo., 1985; MA in Journalism, Ohio State U., 1989. Assoc. editor Comboni Missionaries, Cin., 1986-90, editor, media dir., 1990-91; pub. rels. specialist Choicecare, Cin., 1992-93, sr. comms. specialist, 1993—. Mem. Pub. Rels. Soc. Am., Cin. Editors Assn., Soc. Profl. Journalists, Ohio State U. Alumni Assn., Kappa Tau Alpha. Office: Choicecare 655 Eden Park Dr Cincinnati OH 45202

MARR, KATHLEEN MARY, biologist, educator; b. Sheboygan, Wis., Sept. 20, 1954; d. David William Rath and Gloria Agnes (Carus) Otto; m. Philip Dean Marr, Jan. 3, 1976; children: Amanda, Samantha, Cornelius, Emerson. BS, Lakeland Coll., 1976; MS, Marquette U., 1986, postgrad. Instr. U. Wis., Sheboygan, 1978-82, Manitowoc, 1982; teaching asst. Marquette U., Milw., 1982-85; asst. prof. Divine Word Coll., Epworth, Iowa, 1985-87; asst. prof. Lakeland Coll., Sheboygan, 1987—, chair dept. biology, dir. pre-med. program. Author Lab Studies in Intro Biology, Lab Studies in Human Anatomy & Physiology. Educator Elderhostels, Lakeland Coll., 1989-91; accordianist Cedar Grove (Wis.) Klompen Dancers, 1982-91; ethicist Speakers Bur., Union of Concerned Scientists, Washington, 1990-91. Mem. AAAS, Am. Soc. Zoologists, Midwest Coll. Biology Tchrs. Roman Catholic. Office: Lakeland Coll County Trunk M Sheboygan WI 53082

MARRA, SAMUEL PATRICK, retired pharmacist, small business owner; b. Sault Ste Marie, Mich., Apr. 15, 1927; s. Leonard and Nancy (Clement); m. Jeanette L. Rohr, Sept. 2, 1949; children: Rebecca, Nancy, David, Dana, Janet. BS in Pharmacy, Ferris State Coll., 1949. bd. dirs. Chem. Bank, No. States Bancshares, Chem. Bank North. Bd. dirs. Houghton Lake Edn. Found.; pres. Houghton Lake Grenadier Band; co-chmn. Scheutte for Congress, Roscommon County, 1984, 86. Mem. Nat. Assn. Retail Druggists. Republican. Home: 10672 W Houghton Lake Dr Houghton Lake MI 48629-9725

MARRAZZI, MARY ANN, pharmacologist, pharmacology educator; b. Ann Arbor, Mich., Dec. 22, 1945; d. Amedeo S. and Rose Florence (Netter) M. BA in Chemistry, U. Minn., 1966; student, U. Pitts., 1962-64; postgrad., U. Minn., 1966-69; PhD in Pharmacology, Washington U., St. Louis, 1972. NIH (NINCDS) postdoctoral fellow pharmacology dept. Sch. Medicine, Washington U., 1972-74; asst. prof. pharmacology Sch. Medicine, Wayne State U., Detroit, 1974-78, assoc. prof., 1978—; assoc. pharmacologist dept. psychiatry Harper-Grace Hosps., Detroit, 1981—; vis. investigator div. neuropharmacology U. Mo. Inst. Psychiatry, St. Louis, 1974; presenter profl. orgns. including 4th Ann. Conf. on Prostoglandins, Vail, Colo., 1975, 2nd Internat. Conf. on Eating Disorders, 1986, Biol. Psychiatry Meeting, 1986, 4th Internat. Conf. on Eating Disorders, 1990. Contbr. chpt. to: Hunger: Basic Mechanisms and Clinical Implications, 1976, Iontophoresis and Transmitter Mechanisms in the Mammalian Central Nervous System, 1977, Food Intake and Chemical Senses, 1977; co-contbr. chpt. to: The Prostoglandins, vol. 2, 1974, The Brain as an Endocrine Organ, 1990; contbr. articles on eating disorders and related rsch. to profl. publs. USPHS tng. grantee, 1966-69, 69-72. Mem. Am. Soc. Pharmacology and Exptl. Therapeutics, Soc. for Neurosci., Am. Soc. Neurochemistry, Soc. Biol. Psychiatry, Det. Physiol. Soc., Sigma Xi. Home: 962 Lochmoor Blvd Grosse Pointe MI 48236-4010 Office: Wayne State U Sch Medicine Dept Pharm 540 E Canfield Ave Detroit MI 48201

MARSDEN, DAVID LAWRENCE, psychiatric technician, writer; b. Dayton, Ohio, May 17, 1954; s. Francis Joseph and Elizabeth Ann (Mueller) M.; m. Kim McConnel, June 12, 1981 (div. May 1986); children: Angela Marie, Jefferey David, Ryan Lawrence and David Alexander (twins), Joseph Edward. Student, Ivy Tech. Coll., Ft. Wayne, Ind., Purdue U., Ft. Wayne, 1987-90, C.C., Las Vegas, nev., 1991-94. Cert. mental health technician. Psychiat. attendant The State Sch., Ft. Wayne, 1983-84; alcoholism technician Washington House, Inc., Ft. Wayne, 1984-85; counselor Bashor Childrens Home, Ft. Wayne, 1986, Crossroads Childrens Home, Ft. Wayne, 1986-87; psychiat. technician Assn. for Retarded Citizens, Ft. Wayne, 1988-89, Nev. Mental Health Ctr., Las Vegas, 1990-94, The Stress Ctr., Decatur, Ind., 1995—. Songs written include Wasn't it Yesterday, You Got the Wrong Man, You Were There. Served with U.S. Army, 1978-86. Roman Catholic. Home: 6510 Covington Rd Apt E-237 Fort Wayne IN 46804

MARSDEN, STEPHEN JAMES, agricultural consulting company executive; b. Fall River, Mass., Oct. 22, 1942; s. James and Avis (Bolderson) M.; m. Josefina G. DeGuzman, Jan. 11, 1991. Traveling salesman Stuppy Greenhouse Co., North Kansas City, Mo., 1968-72; sales mgr. Hummert Internat., St. Louis, 1972-79; owner, cons. S.J. Marsden & Coy Inc., Rogersville, Mo., 1979—; owner Herbal Advantage, Inc., Rogersville, 1995—,

Goodlife Industries, Inc., Turners, Mo., 1987—; internat. agr. cons. Office: SJ Marsden & Co Inc Rt 3 Box 93 Rogersville MO 65742-9214

MARSH, CLARE TEITGEN, retired school psychologist; b. Manitowoc, Wis., July 7, 1934; d. Clarence Emil and Dorothy (Napiezinski) Teitgen; m. Robert Irving Marsh, Jan. 30, 1955; children: David, Wendy Marsh Tootle, Julie Marsh Domino, Laura Marsh Beltrame. MS in Ednl. Psychology, U. Wis., Milw., 1968. Sch. psychologist Milw. Pub. Schs., 1975-76; lead psychologist West Allis (Wis.)-West Milw. Pub. Schs., 1968-95; sch. psychologist Wauwatosa (Wis.) Pub. Schs., 1987; instr. Milw. Sch. Engring., 1989-90, Alverno Coll., 1990-95. NDEA fellow, 1966-68. Mem. Internat. Sch. Psychologists Assn., Nat. Assn. Sch. Psychologists (del.), Suburban Assn. Sch. Psychologists (pres. 1976-77, 86-87), Wis. Assn. Sch. Psychologists (pres. 1990-91, chmn. membership com. 1980-84, sec. 1985-89, chmn. conv. 1987), Wis. Fedn. Pupil Svcs., Phi Kappa Phi, Pi Lambda Theta (pres.), Kappa Delta Pi, Phi Delta Kappa, Sigma Tau Delta, Alpha Chi Omega. Home: 14140 W Honey Ln New Berlin WI 53151-2442

MARSH, CLAYTON EDWARD, retired army officer, information systems specialist; b. Worthington, Minn., Jan. 24, 1942; s. Cecil Eugene and Edna Luella (Clausen) M.; m. Carol Ruth Lundmark Franz, June 30, 1962 (div. 1979); children: Tracey Diane, Julie Doreen, Leslie Dawn, Lori Dion; m. Kyong Hui Yi, Aug. 28, 1979; 1 child, Rebecca Lee. BA, St. Cloud State U., 1974; MS, U. So. Calif., 1979. Commd. 2d lt. U.S. Army, 1967, advanced through grades to lt. col., 1985; v.p., mgr. systems devel. dept., data automation divsn. 1st Nat. Bank Omaha, 1989—. Decorated Def. Superior Svc. medal, DFC, Bronze Star, Army Commendation medal, Air medal. Mem. Data Processing Mgmt. Assn., Internat. Assn. Approved Basketball Ofcls. Republican. Mem. Ch. of Christ. Home: 3103 Rahn Blvd Omaha NE 68123-2641 Office: 1st Nat Bank Omaha 1 First National Ctr Omaha NE 68102

MARSH, FRANK (IRVING), former state official; b. Norfolk, Nebr., Apr. 27, 1924; s. Frank and Delia (Andrews) M.; m. Shirley Mac McVicker, Mar. 5, 1943; children: Sherry Anne Marsh Tupper, Corwin Frank, Stephen Alan (dec.), Mitchell Edward, Dory Michael, Melissa Lou. BS, U. Nebr., 1950; hon. degree in commerce and bus., Lincoln Sch. Commerce, 1975. Builder, businessman, part-time instr. Lincoln Sch. System, 1946-52; sec. of state State of Nebr., Lincoln, 1953-71, lt. gov., 1971-75, state treas., 1975-81, 87-91; state dir. Farmers Home Adminstrn., Lincoln, 1981-85; with Tabitha, Inc., Lincoln, 1986; ptnr. Lincoln Landscaping and Landscape Interiors Inc., 1983—; organizer, CEO Lincoln FoodNet, Inc. Ops., 1985—; U.S. State Dept. escort, interpreter, cons. Ctr. Continuing Edn., U. Nebr., 1986-87; mem. Foodchain Assn. (prepared perishable food rescue programs); bd. dirs. Ultras Pharmaceuticals; founder/CEO Agates Etc. Bd. dirs. Lincoln Mayor's Com. Internat. Friendship, 1967—; affiliate mem., past pres. Nat. Coun. Internat. Visitors, Washington, 1967; bd. dirs. Nebraskaland Found., Inc., Lincoln, 1970—, Lincoln-Lancaster Food and Hunger Coalition, Good Neighbor Ctr.; hunger coord. Lincoln Dist. United Meth. Ch.; port insp., past fleet adm. Soc. Nebr. Adms. With AUS, 1943-46, ETO. Recipient Gov.'s Citation, State of Nebr., 1984, Outstanding Svc. award U.S. Info. Agy., 1990, Lincoln Parks and Recreation award, 1991, Mayor's Waste and Recycling award, 1993, Lincoln Dist. Outstanding Laity award United Meth. Ch., 1993, Citation of Achievement Nebr. Game and Parks Commn., 1993, Unsung Hero award United Way, 1996. Mem. VFW (life), Internat. Livestock Identification Assn. (life), Am. Legion, Disabled Am. Vets. (life), Nebr. Alumni Assn. (Outstanding Alumni award 1975, life), Nebr. Nut Growers Assn., Nebr. Hist. Soc. (life), Alpha Phi Omega (life), Sertoma (past pres. Gateway Club). Republican. Methodist. Home: 2701 S 34th St Lincoln NE 68506-3211 Office: 1911 R St Lincoln NE 68503-2931

MARSH, ROBERT CHARLES, writer, music critic; b. Columbus, Ohio, Aug. 5, 1924; s. Charles L. and Jane A. (Beckett) M.; m. Kathleen C. Moscrop, July 4, 1956 (div. 1985); m. Ann Noren, Feb. 25, 1987; 1 child, James MacArtain. BS, Northwestern U., 1945, AM, 1946; postgrad., U. Chgo., 1948; EdD, Harvard U., 1951; postgrad., Oxford U., 1952-53, Cambridge U., 1953-56. Instr. social sci. U. Ill., 1947-49; lectr. humanities Chgo. City Jr. Coll., 1950-51; asst. prof. edn. U. Kansas City, 1951-52; vis. prof. edn. SUNY, 1953-54; humanities staff U. Chgo., 1956-58, lectr. in social thought, 1976; music critic Chgo. Sun-Times, 1956-91; dir. Chgo. Opera Project, Newberry Libr., 1983—. Author: Toscanini and the Art of Orchestral Performance, 1956, rev. edit., 1962, The Cleveland Orchestra, 1967, Ravinia, 1987, James Levine at Ravinia, 1993; editor: Logic and Knowledge, 1956. Co-recipient Peabody award for ednl. broadcasting, 1976; Ford Found. fellow, 1965-66. Mem. Harvard U. Faculty Club. Roman Catholic. Home and Office: 1001 7th St New Glarus WI 53574-0790

MARSHALEK, EUGENE RICHARD, physics educator; b. N.Y.C., Jan. 17, 1936; s. Frank M. and Sophie (Weg) M.; m. Sonja E. M. Lennhart, Dec. 8, 1962; children: Thomas, Frank. BS, Queens Coll., 1957; PhD, U. Calif., Berkeley, 1962. NSF postdoctoral fellow Niels Bohr Inst., Copenhagen, Denmark, 1962-63; rsch. assoc. Brookhaven Nat. Lab., Upton, N.Y., 1963-65; asst. prof. U. Notre Dame, Ind., 1965-69, assoc. prof., 1969-78, prof., 1978—. Contbr. articles to profl. jours. Recipient Alexander von Humboldt sr. scientist award, 1985. Mem. AAAS, Am. Phys. Soc., Sigma Xi. Office: U Notre Dame Dept Physics Notre Dame IN 46556

MARSHALL, CAROLYN ANN M., church official, consultant; b. Springfield, Ill., July 18, 1935; d. Hayward Thomas and Isabelle Bernice (Hayer) McMurray; m. John Alan Marshall, July 14, 1956 (dec. Sept. 1990); children: Margaret Marshall Bushman, Cynthia Marshall Kyrouac, Clinton, Carol. Student, De Pauw U., 1952-54; BSBA, Drake U., 1956; D of Pub. Svc. (hon.), De Pauw U., 1983; LHD (hon.), U. Indpls., 1990. Corp. sec. Marshall Studios, Inc., Veedersburg, Ind., 1956-89, exec. cons., 1989-93; sec. Gen. Conf., lay leader South Ind. conf. United Meth. Ch., 1988—; Carolyn M. Marshall chair in women studies Bennett Coll., Greensboro, N.C., 1988; fin. cons. Lucille Raines Residence, Inpls., 1977—. Pres. Fountain Ctrl. Band Boosters, Veedersburg, 1975-77; del. Gen. Conf., United Meth. Ch., 1980, 84, 88, 92, 96, pres. women's divsn. gen. bd. global ministries, 1984-88; bd. dirs. Franklin (Ind.) United Meth. Ch. Home: 204 N Newlin St Veedersburg IN 47987-1358

MARSHALL, DALLAS RAY, college marketing agent; b. Neligh, Nebr., Sept. 13, 1955; s. James Kenneth and Dorothy Mae (West) M. BA, U. Nebr., Lincoln, 1984; practical English, Career Inst., Fairfield, N.J., 1990. Independent agent Am. Passage Media Corp., Seattle, 1983—, Am. Ednl. Svcs., Lansing, Mich., 1984—, Collegiate Poster Network, Inc., Chgo., 1986—, On Campus Promotions, Inc., Harriman, N.Y., 1987—. Author: (poems) Christmas Concerto, 1990 Pains Descending In Autumn, 1990, Out of the Catacombs, 1991, Victorious Glory, 1992, Back Pages of Joy, 1993, If Left To My Wretchedness, 1993, End of the Siege, 1994, Sealed Within The Shiedl of the Son, 1994, Nothing of Mine Alone, 1995; contbr. chpt. to This Is His!. Grace I. Grace I. Bridge scholar U. Nebr., Lincoln, 1980-81, 82-83. Democrat. Mem. Evangelical Free Ch. Home: PO Box 131 Norfolk NE 68702-0131

MARSHALL, IRL HOUSTON, JR., residential and commercial cleaning company executive; b. Evanston, Ill., Feb. 28, 1929; s. Irl H. and Marjorie (Greenleaf) M.; m. Barbara Favill, Nov. 5, 1949; children: Alice Marshall Vogler, Irl Houston III, Carol Marshall Allen. AB, Dartmouth Coll., 1949; MBA, U. Chgo., 1968; cert. franchise exec., La. State U., 1991. Gen. mgr. Duraclean Internat., Deerfield, Ill., 1949-61; mgr. Montgomery Ward, Chgo., 1961-77; pres., chief exec. officer Duraclean Internat., 1977—. Inventor/patentee in field. Pres. Cliff Dwellers, Chgo., 1977; exec. com., treas., dir. Highland Park Hosp., 1971-80; dir. Continential Ill. Bank Deerfield, 1982-90; bd. dirs. Better Bus. Bur. Chgo. & No. Ill., Chgo., 1988—. Mem. Internat. Franchise Assn. (bd. dirs. 1981-90, pres. 1985, chmn. 1985-86), Econ. Club Chgo., Exmoor Country Club, Univ. Club Chgo. Presbyterian. Home: 1248 Ridgewood Dr Northbrook IL 60062-3725

MARSHALL, LINDA RAE, cosmetic company executive; b. Provo, Utah, Aug. 1, 1940; d. Arvid O. and Tola V. (Broderick) Newman; children: James, John. Student Brigham Young U., 1958-59, U. Utah, 1960-61. Buyer, Boston Store, 1961-62; sec. Milw. Gas & Light Co., 1962-64; mktg. rep. Elysee Cosmetics, Madison, Wis., 1971-75, pres., 1975—; v.p., Dionne, Inc., 1987—, ptnr. Pres. Falk Sch. PTA, Madison. Author: Discover the Other Woman in You, 1980; monthly beauty columnist Beauty Fashion mag.; contbg. author Cosmetic Industry Sci. and Regulatory Found., 1984. Mem. Aestheticians Internat. Assn. (adv. bd.), Cosmetic, Toiletry and Fragrance Assn. (exec. com., bd dirs., chmn. voluntary program, chmn. small cosmetic com., membership com. task force), Cosmetic Exec. Women. Address: PO Box 4084 Madison WI 53711

MARSHALL, PETER E., pastor; b. Massillon, Ohio, Sept. 13, 1926; s. Louis E. and Irene M. (Francis) M.; m. Patricia Helene Stromp, Oct. 25, 1947; children: Peter C., Thomas J., Steven F., Katherine H., David L., Mary Ann. Student, Kent State U.; DDiv, Utah Bible Coll. Sales rep. Ford Motor Co., Canton, Ohio; electrician United Engring., Canton; famer Middle Branch, Ohio; builder Thomas Homes, Massillon, Ohio; pastor Temple of Healing Stripes, Middle Branch. Author: Build Your Own Log Home, 1990, Conversations with God, 1991, Small Farm Sheep Breeding, 1992, Peace of Mind, 1994. With U.S. Marines, 1951-53. Decorated Purple Heart, Bronze star.

MARSHALL, ROBERT LOGAN, safety engineer, educator; b. Haverhill, Kans., June 2, 1925; s. Ira Thomas and Abbie Bertha (Covert) M.; m. Mary Anne Martin, Nov. 2, 1946; children: Suzanne, Robert Craig. BS in Math., U. Kans., 1948, EdD, 1961; MA in Edn., U. Wichita, 1956. Cert. safety profl., Ill. Tchr. driver edn. Pub. Schs., Hill City, Kans., 1948-51; dir. safety edn. Pub. Schs., Eldorado, Kans., 1953-56; supr. safety edn. Pub. Schs., Kansas City, Mo., 1956-61; assoc. exec. sec. Nat. Commn. Safety Edn., Washington, 1961-67; dean sch. pub. svcs. Ctrl. Mo. State U., Warrensburg, 1967-90; pres. Safety, Health, and Environ. Resource Ctr., Warrensburg, 1990—; cons. film prodn. Ford Motor Co., 1986; mem. rsch. studies Pacific Inst. for Rsch. and Evaluation, 1992—. Author: Safe Performance Driving, 1975. Capt. USN, 1943-46, 51-53. Fellow Vets. of Safety, 1987; recipient Kaywood award Am. Driver and Traffic Safety Edn. Assn., 1990, Disting. Svc. award Nat. Safety Coun., 1991. Fellow Am. Acad. Safety Edn.; mem. Am. Soc. Safety Engrs. (editl. bd. 1980-89), Internat. Com. on Alcohol, Drugs and Traffic Safety, Elks, Shrine, Rotary (area coord. Polio Plus 1986-88), Phi Kappa Phi. Democrat. Methodist. Home: 307 Jones Ave Warrensburg MO 64093 Office: Internat Safety Health & Environ Resource Ctr Hum 202 CMSU Warrensburg MO 64093

MARSHALL, THOMAS W., state legislator; b. Marshall, Mo., Jan. 30, 1940. BS, Ctrl. Mo. State U. Tchr., artist, Marshall; mem. Marshall City Coun., 1976-83; mayor pro tem City of Marshall, 1983; mem. Mo. Ho. of Reps., Jefferson City, 1983—. Democrat. Home: 318 E Vest St Marshall MO 65340-2254*

MARSHALL, WILLIAM G., state legislator; b. Greenfield, Mo., Oct. 28, 1942; m. Janice Rae Marshall; children: Jeffrey, Tony, Lisa. BS, U. Mo., 1965. Real estate and ins. broker, farmer Greenfield; mem. Mo. Ho. of Reps., Jefferson City, 1986—, mem. transp., ins., tourism and agr.-bus. coms. Mem. Masons, Shriners. Republican. Home: RR 2 Box 72 Greenfield MO 65661-9603*

MARSIGLIO, LORRIE (DOLORES WALTERS MARSIGLIO), public relations and marketing executive; b. Chgo., Oct. 2, 1948; d. Walter and Olga Maximena; m. John Thomas Marsiglio. Columnist Pulitzer Lerner Voice, Schaumburg, Ill., 1983-90, Pioneer Press Newspaper, Barrington, Ill., 1990-94; owner Lorimar, Wasco, Ill., 1980—; instr. pub. rels. Coll. of Du Page, Glen Ellyn, Ill., 1980—, Elgin (Ill.) C.C., 1987-88, Roosevelt U., Chgo., 1987-88, William Rainey Harper Coll., 1993; tchr. H.S. Dist. 211, Palatine, Ill., 1980-93, H.S. Dist. 214, Arlington Heights, Ill., 1983-93, Mundelein (Ill.) H.S. Dist., 1987-88; co-host Savvy Shopper weekly show Sta. WFXW, Geneva, Ill. Author: 101 Free Publicity, Marketing and Networking Ideas That Get Results, 1994, 2d edit., 1995; contbr. articles to profl. publs. Recipient TCI Casey Cable TV award, 1992. Mem. N.W. Suburban Assn. of Commerce and Industry, Roselle C. of C., Hoffman Estates C. of C., Phi Theta Kappa. Office: PO Box 284 Wasco IL 60183-0284

MARTEL, PETRA JEAN HEGSTAD, elementary school educator; b. Oakland, Calif., May 27, 1944; d. Lorentz Reginald and Hazel Dorothy (Danielson) Hegstad; m. Curtis Wayne Martel, Apr. 30, 1966 (div. 1989); children: Christopher W., Peter L., Loren R. BS in Elem. Edn. and German, Concordia Coll., Moorhead, Minn., 1966; MS in Elem. Edn., Bemidji (Minn.) State U., 1989. Cert. German, elem. edn., reading cons., remedial and devel. reading tchr. K-12, Minn. 2d grade tchr. Rice Creek and Hayes Elem. Schs., Fridley, Minn., 1966-72; chpt. 1 reading tchr. Chief Bug-O-Nay-Ge-Shig Sch., Cass Lake, Minn., 1986-92; tchr. English/reading Rochester (Minn.) Pub. Schs., 1992-93; Chpt. I lead reading tchr. English/reading Moorhead (Minn.) Jr. H.S., 1993—, student newspaper advisor, 1993—. Vol. den mother Cub Scouts, Bismarck, N.D., 1976-77; vol. com. to establish kindergarten Bismarck Pub. Schs., 1974-75; vol. com. to help refugees relocate Bismarck, 1976; vol. Bemidji Sch. System, 1985. Mem. NEA, Northland Reading Coun. (pres. 1985-86, honor coun. 1986), Minn. Reading Assn. (sec. 1993—), Internat. Reading Assn., Minn. Edn. Assn., Kappa Delta Pi. Home: 2333 Calihan Ave NE Bemidji MN 56601-2333

MARTELLARO, JOSEPH ALEXANDER, economics educator; b. Rockford, Ill., July 20, 1924; s. Vito and Maria Enza (Ciaccio) M.; m. Loretta W. Kowalski, Aug. 25, 1945; children: Joseph M., Charles S., David M. AB in Econs., U. Notre Dame, 1956, MA in Econs., 1958, PhD in Econs., 1962. From lectr. to asst. prof. Ind. U., South Bend, 1961-66, dept. chair, 1964-67, assoc. prof., 1966-67; prof. No. Ill. U., DeKalb, 1967—, assoc. dean grad. sch., 1967-73, acting dean grad. sch., 1973-74; mem. coun. deans No. Ill. U., 1969-74, univ. coun., 1973-74, univ. pers. com., 1973-74, grad. coun., 1969-74, dept. rules com., 1985-86, grad. faculty admissions com., 1984-86, chmn. grade rev. bd., 1975-93, mem., 1982—, dept. exec. com., 1979-82, 85, 90, 91, numerous others; vis. prof. Università degli Studi di Milano, Italy, 1982; adj. prof. Nat. Chung Hsing U., 1982-83; Fulbright rsch. lectr. Nat. Taiwan U., 1982-83, appointed to spl. chair of prof. econs., 1988; vis. rsch. prof. Istituto di Economia Università degli Studi di Milano, 1984; pres., chmn. bd. Martell Radio and Appliances, Inc., South Bend, Ind.; pub. rels. advisor several organizations. Author: Economic Development in Southern Italy 1950-60, 1965; contbg. author: A Handbook on Latin America for Teachers, 1968, Economic Reform in China, Hungary, and USSR, 1989; author: (with others) Studi in Memoria di Tullio Bagiotti, 1988, Perspectives for Teachers of Latin American Culture, 1970; reviewer, referee The Chinese Econ. Rev.; edit. columnist DeKalb Daily Chronicle, 1968-69; columnist Sycamore Rep., 1976-78; mem. internat. edit. bd. Jour. Econs. and Internat. Rels., 1987-91; book reviewer in field; contbr. 55 articles to profl. jours. Fundraiser for retarded children; election poll judge, active in nat. and local elections; active Cub Scouts, Little League baseball. With U.S. Army, 1960-61, served to adj. gen. div. level USAR, 1972-78. Fulbright grantee Argentina, 1964-65, Nat. Taiwan U., 1982-83, nominated Yugoslavia, 1992; grad. fellow U. Notre Dame, 1958-60; rsch. grantee No. Ill. U., 1966-67. Fellow Internat. Ctr. Asian Studies; mem. Assn. Comparative Econs. (charter), U.S. Normandy Com. (charter, coun. mem. 50th Anniversary of Battle of Normandy Found.), European Comparative Econ. Assn. (charter), Am. Air Mus., Am. Legion, DAV, K.C., Am. Air Mus. Eng. (charter). Home: 1702 Margaret Ln De Kalb IL 60115-1806 Office: No Ill U Dept Econs De Kalb IL 60115

MARTEN, DENNIS LEE, retail executive, financial planner; b. Tomah, Wis., Nov. 23, 1957; s. Eugene Norbert and Joyce Shirley (Lawrence) M.; m. Beth Ann Ruettinger, Oct. 17, 1980; children: Robert Lee, David Eugene, Philip Glen. BS, Ariz. State U., 1980. Pres., store mgr. Marten Crafts, Inc. dba Ben Franklin Crafts, Manhatten, Kans., 1985—; v.p. Eugene Marten Enterprises, Cottonwood, Ariz., 1990-93; pres. Eugene Marten Enterprises, Cottonwood, 1993—; gen. ptnr. Marten Land, Ltd., 1994—; small employer rep., bd. mem. Kan. Small Employer Health Reinsurance Program., 1992—; chair retail counsel Hobby Industries Assn., 1993-95. Co-contbr. software reviews to profl. jour. Asst. scout master Boy Scouts Am. troop 223; bd. dirs. Kansas C. of C. and Industry, 1992-94, regional v.p., 1995—; Rep. Precinct Man, 1990-94; chair Social Svcs. Adv. Bd., Manhattan, 1992-95; mem. Kan. Guardian Adv. Council, 1993—; mem. Small Bus. Adv. Council, Congressman Sam Brownback, 1995—. Capt. U.S. Army, 1980-85, Germany. Named among most influential retailers Craftrends Mag., 1995. Mem. Westloop Merchants Assn., Westside Bus. Assn., Manhattan C. of C. (bd. dirs. 1994—), Manhattan Solar Kiwanis (sec. 1990-93). Lutheran. Office: Marten Crafts Inc dba B Franklin Crafts 1101 Westloop Place Manhattan KS 66502

MARTENS, DONALD MATHIAS, orthodontist; b. Coleman, Wis., June 25, 1925; s. Harry Alfred and Emma Genevive (Laurent) M.; m. Fern Ann Krejcarek, June 24, 1950; children: Daniel, Nance, Dean, Cathy, Cynthia, Linda, James, Jeffrey, Michele. DDS, Marquette U., 1952. Diplomate Internat. Bd. Orthodontics. Practice dentistry specializing in orthodontics Green Bay, Wis., 1952—; pres. San Luis Manor, Inc., Green Bay, 1973-86. Pres. Martens Found., Green Bay, 1982—. Served with USAAF, 1943-46. Fellow Am. Acad. Orthodontics (pres. 1971-72); mem. Brown Door Kewaunee Dental Soc. (pres. 1964), Fedn. Orthodontics Assn. (pres. 1979-81). Republican. Roman Catholic. Lodge: Optimist (pres. Green Bay club 1964). Home: 3853 Tamarack Dr Green Bay WI 54313-4816

MARTENS, PATRICIA FRANCES, adult education educator; b. St. Louis, Nov. 27, 1943; d. John William and Mary Ruth (Bolds) Martens; m. George Joseph Miller, Aug. 7, 1965 (div.); children: Nicolette, George Jr., Jeffrey. BS in Psychology, So. Ill. U., 1975; MA in Counseling, St. Louis U., 1990, PhD in Psychol. Founds., 1996. Cert. sexuality educator. Primary, intermediate tchr. St. Hedwig Sch., St. Louis, 1961-66; jr. high tchr. Assumption Sch., St. Louis, 1976-81; tchr. trainer grad. students Paul VI Cathechetical Inst., St. Louis, 1986-88; nat. tchr. trainer St. Louis, 1989—; cons. Archdiocese L.A., Archdiocese St. Louis, Nat. Coun. Cath. Bishops, 1991; del. Nat. Cath. Ednl. Del. to Russia and Lithuania, 1993; frequent spkr. and presenter at schs., parishes ednl. confs., nat. and internat. religious edn. mtgs.; TV appearances on ABC and CTNA; nat. ednl. cons. Tabor Pub. Author: (videos) In God's Image: Make and Female, 1989, God Doesn't Make Junk, 1989 (Cath. Audio Visual Educators award 1991), (books) Parent to Parent, 1989, Sex Is Not A Four-Letter Word!, 1994. Recipient Award Cath. Press Assn., 1995. Mem. AACD, Nat. Cath. Educators Assn., Am. Assn. Sex Educators, Counselors, Therapists, Assn. for Religious Values in Counseling, Am. Sch. Counselor Assn., Am. Coll. Personnel Assn., Soc. for Sci. Study of Sex, Pi Lambda Theta. Home and Office: 8061 Daytona Dr Apt 1E Saint Louis MO 63105-2549

MARTENSON, EDWARD ALLEN, theater manager; b. Paris, Ky., May 4, 1949; s. Milton A. and Bettye (Hudnall) M.; m. Gina Franz, Mar. 18, 1979; children: Benn, Hallie. AB, Princeton U., 1971. Mgr. McCarter Theater, Princeton, N.J., 1973-79; mng. dir. Yale Repertory Theater, New Haven, 1979-82; dir. theater program NEA, Washington, 1982-86; exec. dir. Guthrie Theater, Mpls., 1986—; adj. assoc. prof. Sch. Drama Yale U., New Haven, 1979-82, co-chmn. adminstrn., 1979-82. Home: 102 Farmdale Rd W Hopkins MN 55343-7183 Office: Guthrie Theater 725 Vineland Pl Minneapolis MN 55403-1139*

MARTH, MARY ELLEN (KIM MARTIN), entertainer; b. Atkinson, Minn., July 15, 1936; d. Sigvard B. Kanikkeberg and Beatrice M. (Lundberg) Wangen; m. Luther H. Marth (div.); children: Mitzie, Leslie, Tina, Allen. Entertainer The Kim Martin Show, 1960—; band leader Kim Martin Show, 1960—; real estate owner Marth Properties, Mpls., 1972—. Author of poems, songs, articles, short stories., historian. Sec. Hennepin County Adult Foster Care, Mpls, 1983—; mem. Summit Ministries, Colo, 1995, Columbia Heights Owners Assn., 1990—, Multi-Housing Assn., Mpls, 1993—, Vesterheim Geneal. Mus., 1990, Norwegian Am. Mus., 1988—. Named Queen of Country Music, Country Entertainers Assn., Mpls., 1977, Entertainer of Yr. 1978, Female Vocalist of Yr., 1978, Best Band of Yr., 1979, Songwriter of Yr., 1980. Mem. Winnesheik Geneal. Soc., Fillmore County Hist. Soc., Vesterheum Geneal. Soc. Baptist.

MARTIN, ALAN ROBERT, legislative staff member; b. Akron, Ohio, May 21, 1968; s. Robert Allen and Andrea (Bacca) Martin; m. Katherine Ann Jakubko, June 5, 1993. BA, Cert. of Applied Politics, U. Akron, 1990. Gov.'s honors intern Ohio Dept. Human Svcs., Columbus, 1989; Bliss Inst. of Applied Politics intern Ohio Senate Reps., Columbus, 1990; legis. asst. State Rep. Tom Watkins/Joy Padgett, Columbus, 1991-93; legis. rsch. asst. Ohio House Rep. Caucus, Columbus, 1993-95; campaign mgr. Kerry Metzger for State Rep., Columbus, 1994; legis. aide State Rep. Bill Schuck, Columbus, 1995-96; interim dir. Joint Com. on Agy. Rule Rev. Ohio Ho. of Reps., Columbus, 1996, asst. dir. Joint Com. on Agy. Rule Rev., 1996—. Campaign vol. Ohio House/Senate, Columbus, 1989, 91-95; mem. Coll. Reps., Akron, Ohio, 1988-90; mem. Columbus Outdoor Pursuits, 1995—. Office: Ohio Ho of Reps 77 S High St 13th Fl Columbus OH 43266

MARTIN, BARBARA JEAN, elementary school principal; b. Mt. Vernon, Tex., May 17, 1940. BA, Fisk U., Nashville, 1961; MEd, U. Ill., Chgo., 1979, PhD, 1992. Cert. tchr. kindergarten to 3rd grade, type 75 adminstr., Ill. Tchr. Chgo. Pub. Schs., 1969-93, prin., 1993—. Mem. Nat. Alliance Black Sch. Educators, Delta Kappa Gamma (sec. 1992—), Pi Lambda Theta, Alpha Kappa Alpha. Home: 825 E Drexel Sq Chicago IL 60615-3705 Office: O W Holmes Sch 955 W Garfield Blvd Chicago IL 60621-2240

MARTIN, BARBARA LEE, computer programmer, analyst; b. Warsaw, N.Y., Feb. 11, 1941; d. Eldon Merritt Glor and Ora Elizabeth (Putney) Newton; m. Brent Robert Martin, July 7, 1962 (div. Jan. 1979); children: Dane Robert, Dale Eldon. BS, Otterbein Coll., 1962; postgrad., Marion (Ohio) Tech. Coll., 1977-78. Tchr. math. Avon (Ohio) High Sch., 1962, Taft Jr. High Sch., Marion, 1962-66; computer programmer Nationwide Ins. Co., Columbus, Ohio, 1978-80; lead programmer/analyst The Scotts Co. (formerly O.M. Scott & Sons Co.), Marysville, Ohio, 1980—. Sec. bd. zoning appeals Delaware (Ohio) Twp., 1988-92, chair, 1993, 94, 95, 96; chair outreach com. Olentangy River Valley Assn., Del., 1988-90, chair assn. 1990, 91. Mem. AAUW (membership v.p. Del. br. 1993, 94, 95). Unity. Office: The Scotts Co 14111 Scottslawn Rd Marysville OH 43040-9506

MARTIN, CHERI CHRISTIAN, health services administrator; b. Nashville, Mar. 9, 1956; d. Jesse Thomas and Eloise (McClain) Christian; m. George A. Martin, June 25, 1977 (div. May 1995); children: Matthew Alexander, Kristin Leigh. BS in Family Resources and Consumer Scis., U. Wis., 1977; cert. healthcare mgmt., U. St. Thomas, 1991. Asst. buyer Dayton Hudson, Mpls., 1978-79, assoc. buyer, 1979-81; instr. Nat. Coll., Mpls., 1981-82; mgr. store Connco Shoes, Inc., Mpls, 1982-83; patient svcs. rep. Group Health, Inc., Mpls., 1984-89, dental mgr., 1989-94, regional mgr., 1994—; cert. facilitator the Seven Habits of Highly Effective People, 1996. Cert. facilitator (seminar) The Seven Habits of Highly Effective People, 1996. Mem. Minn./Dakota Assn. Patient Reps. (v.p. 1989-90), U. Wis. Alumni Assn., Group Health Social Club Mpls. (pres. 1987-89).

MARTIN, CLARA RITA, elementary education educator; b. Steubenville, Ohio, Oct. 14, 1953; d. Robert Emmett and Mary Agnes (Flynn) Joyce; m. Gary Dean Martin, July 8, 1978; children: Bradley A., Douglas A. BS in Elem. Edn., Coll. Steubenville, 1975; MS in Interdisciplinary Skillls, U. Dayton, 1984. Cert. tchr., Ohio. Reading specialist Steubenville City Sch. Dist., 1975; tchr. elem. schs. Harrison Hills City Sch. Dist., Jewett and Hopedale, Ohio, 1975—; coord. spelling bee Harrison News Herald Spelling Bee, Cadiz, Ohio, 1984—. Jump Rope for Heart coord., asst. coord. Meml. Day Program, 1992. Mem. Harrison Hills Tchrs.' Assn. (grievance chair, chief negotiator 1980—, bldg. rep. 1985—, del. Ohio Edn. Assn. Conv., 1981—), Ladies Ancient Order Hibernians (sec. 1991-92). Roman Catholic. Home: PO Box 184 Bloomingdale OH 43910-0184

MARTIN, CLARENCE F., farmer, state legislator; b. Lefor, N.D., May 3, 1929; s. Paul P. and Katie (Hollinger) M.; m. Viola Mayer; children: Francis, Laurie, Lynn. Farmer N.D., 1951—; rep. N.D. Ho. of Reps., Bismarck, 1975—, chmn. legis. commn., 1990—, chmn. constl. com., 1988—, mem. legis. coun., 1993-94, spkr., 1994-95; bd. dirs. West Plains Electric, N.D. State Electric Co-op, Mandan, vice-chmn. Mem. KC (State Oustanding Citizenship award 1974-75, sec. 1967-70, dist. dep. 1963-67, state dept. 1971-72), Elks. Home: PO Box 54 # 011 Lefor ND 58641

MARTIN, DAVID ROBERT, purchasing agent, business owner; b. Cleve., Aug. 24, 1960; s. Paul P. and Rose Marie (Kvocak) M. BS, Ohio State U., 1982; MBA, Lake Erie Coll., 1989. Buyer CEI Perry Nuclear Plant, North Perry, Ohio, 1984-95; owner Nat. Pastime Video and Sports, Fairport Harbor, Ohio, 1991—. Mem. East End Purchasing Agts. (sec. 1991-92, treas. 1992-93, chmn. 1993-94). Republican. Roman Catholic. Office: Nat Pastime Video & Sports 306 High St Fairport Harbor OH 44077

MARTIN, DEBBIE MARY KRECKLOW, critical care nurse; b. Eau Claire, Wis., Dec. 30, 1956; d. Ralph Otto and Lenore Vivian (Lawler) Krecklow; m. David Glenn Martin, Oct. 7, 1989; 1 child, Michael Jerald. Diploma, St. Joseph's Hosp. Sch. Nursing, Marshfield, Wis., 1978; student, Viterbo Coll. RN, Minn., Wis.; cert. provider BLS, ACLS, PALS, Neonatal Resuscitation Program, BTLS, EPA, ATLS, ACS, Am. Heart Assn.; cert. Flight RN. Staff-charge nurse cardiovasc. ICU, preceptor St. Joseph's Hosp., Marshfield, Wis., 1978-80; staff-charge nurse trauma and mobile ICU U. Madison (Wis.) Hosp. and Clinics, 1980-83; staff-charge nurse CCU Fairview Ridges Hosp., Burnsville, Minn., 1984-85; helicopter flight team leader Life Link III, St. Paul, Minn., 1985-89; flight nurse Med-Link Air/Tec/Luth. Hosp., LaCrosse, Wis., 1989-93; preceptor The Spirit of Marshfield (Wis.), St. Joseph's Hosp., 1993—; nurse lectr. LaCrescent (Minn.) Fire Dept. Co-author: Rev. Trauma/Life Support Center Orientation Manual, 1983; author Core Curriculum, Nat. Flight Nurses Assn., 19956. Vol. RN, LaCrescent City Health Commn., 1991-92. Mem. AACN (cert. CCRN; CCRN com. 1984, symposium com. 1984, pub. rels. com. 1985-86, chmn. 1986-87), Nat. Flight Nurses Assn. (charter, North Ctrl. Regional chpt. 1990, nat. conf. program com. 1987, sec. 1993-94, Wis. bd. dirs. 1995-96, cert. flight registered nurse). Roman Catholic. Home: M313 Birch St Marshfield WI 54449-9107 Office: Spirit of Marshfield MTS c/o St Josephs Hosp 611 Saint Joseph Ave Marshfield WI 54449-1832

MARTIN, DONALD CREAGH, surgeon; b. Port Chester, N.Y., Mar. 7, 1937; s. Donald Creagh and Margaret Eleanor (Dobson) M.; m. Jacqueline Anne Poole, Sept. 25, 1965; children: Samuel, Joseph. BA in Econs., Yale U., 1958; MD, U. Pa., 1962. Diplomate Am. Bd. Surgery. Intern, Pa. Hosp., Phila., 1962-63, resident in gen. surgery and pathology, 1965-67, 69-71, 72-74, instr. anatomy, 1968-69, 71-72; practice gen. surgery, White Plains, N.Y., 1974-78, Toledo, 1978—; rsch. asst. dept. surgery Guy's Hosp., London, 1967-68; mem. staff Toledo, Mercy, Riverside, St. Charles hosps.; clin. asst. prof. surgery Med. Coll. Ohio, Toledo, 1980—. Trustee Toledo Community Hosp. Oncology Program, 1987-93; bd. dirs. Lucas County chpt. Am. Cancer Soc., 1983-90; med. adv. bd. Aetna of NW Ohio, 1993—. Served with M.C., USNR, 1963-65. Fellow ACS, Am. Coll. Nutrition; mem. AMA, AAAS, Toledo Surg. Soc. (councillor 1992-95, pres. 1995-96), Soc. Internat. Chiurgie, World Assn. for Hepato-Pancreato-Biliary Surgery (founder), Am. Hepato-Pancreato-Biliary Assn., 1994—; Republican. Club: Shadow Valley. Contbr. articles to med. jours. Office: 2109 Hughes Dr Ste 600 Toledo OH 43606-5104

MARTIN, DOROTHY REGINA, biology educator; b. Vergennes, Ill., Sept. 13, 1943; d. James Louis and Lorene Jo (Schneider) M. BA in Zoology, So. Ill. U., 1965, MA in Zoology, 1967; DA in Biology, Idaho State U., 1988. Instr. biology Monmouth (Ill.) Coll., 1967-68; sr. rsch. technician U. Chgo., 1969-70; instr. biology Black Hawk Coll., Moline, Ill., 1968-69, prof., 1970—, dir. Teaching/Learning Ctr., 1992-95; presenter ann. meeting Am. Assn. Higher Edn., 1993; cons. evaluator North Ctrl. Assn., Chgo., 1990—; mem. North Ctrl. Acceditation Rev. Coun., 1995—; coord. classroom assessment program Black Hawk Coll., 1995. Author: Anatomy-Physiology Lab Manual, 1980, 87, 91, 95, Anatomy-Physiology Test Bank, 1991, 94; contbr. articles to profl. publs. Bd. dirs. Cath. Social Svcs., Rock Island, Ill., 1980-92; keyperson United Way, Moline, 1985. Mem. Nat. Dir. of Arts Assn. (charter), Ill. State Acad. Sci. (coun. mem. 1980-91, chair sci. talent search com. 1982-91, 95—), Human Anatomy Physiology Soc., Nat. Assn. Biology Tchrs., Sigma Xi, Phi Kappa Phi, Phi Delta Kappa, Beta Beta Beta, Alpha Lambda Delta. Roman Catholic. Office: Black Hawk Coll 6600 34th Ave Moline IL 61265-5870

MARTIN, EARL DEAN, physical therapist; b. Mammoth Springs, Ark., July 30, 1959; s. Earl Eudell and Ruth (Standley) M.; m. Mary Ellen Eckstein, June 10, 1989; children: Tyler Joseph, Jenny Catherine, Kelsey Elizabeth, McKenzie Mae. BS in Biology, U. Ill., 1982; MS in Phys. Therapy, Boston U., 1987. Lic. phys. therapist, Ill.; bd. cert. pediatric clin. specialist. Phys. therapist Carle Hosp., Urbana, Ill., 1987-88; prin. phys. therapist Phys. Therapy Svcs. for Children, Philo, Ill., 1988—; phys. therapist Champaign Children's Home, 1988-90, Devel. Svc. Ctr., Champaign, 1988-90, 1996—; sch. phys. therapist Urbana Schs., 1988-95, Ford-Iroquois Assn. for Spl. Edn., Gilman, Ill., 1988-89, Vermilion County Assn. for Spl. Edn., Danville, Ill., 1992-95, Champaign Cmty. Schs., 1994-95, Champaign County Rural Coop., Rantoul, Ill., 1994-95; clin. instr. phys. therapist. asst. program Lakeland Coll., Effingham, Ill., 1993—; clin. instr. phys. therapy program Midwestern U., Downers Grove, Ill., 1996—; ind. evaluator State of Ill. Registry Ind. Sch. Evaluators, Springfield, Ill., 1993—; pediat. phys. therapist Cerebral Palsy Clinic, Vermilion County, Danville, 1994-95; mem. adv. bd. Champaign County Arthritis Found., Urbana, Ill. 1995—. Vol. Champaign Park Dist., 1984, Spl. Olympics, Boston, 1986, Grand Prairie Olympics, Watseka, Ill., 1989. Mem. Am. Phys. Therapy Assn, Ill. Phys. Therapy Assn. (mem. pediats. sect.). Home: 808 S Garfield St Philo IL 61864 Office: Phys Therapy Svc for Children 808 S Garfield St Philo IL 61864

MARTIN, GARY J., retired manufacturing executive, mayor; b. Des Moines, Feb. 8, 1957; s. William Carl Martin and Mary Louise (Festner) Sweeney; m. Carolyn J. Karau, July 28, 1956; children: Victoria, Cheryl, Dennis. BBA, Marquette U., 1972. CPA Wis., 1973. Mfr. GM, Milw., 1957-68, engring. mgr., 1968-73; CFO Miller Brewing Co., Milw., 1974-76, dir. corp., 1977-78; pres. Better Brands of N.Y., N.Y.C., 1978-79; exec. v.p. Seven Up Co., St. Louis, 1979-85; v.p. mktg. Schenley Industries, Dallas, 1985-86; cons. Martin & Assocs., Dallas, 1986-89; mayor Osage Beach, Mo., 1992-95. With USN, 1954-57. Named Area Gov. of Yr., Toastmasters, Inc., 1968. Home: RR 3 Box 4991 Osage Beach MO 65065-9611 also: 2166 Springmeadow Dr Spring Hill FL 34606

MARTIN, JOANNE LUTHER, library director; b. Shaker Heights, Ohio, Nov. 15, 1945; d. Fred William and Laurette Jean (Phillips) Luther; m. Jonathan Bruce Martin, Nov. 18, 1972; children: Laura, David, Douglas. BA, Geneva Coll., 1968; MS, Syracuse U., 1969. Reference libr. Robert Morris Coll., Pitts., 1969-70; libr. Reformed Presbyn. Sem., Pitts., 1970-73; substitute work supr. Big Lakes Developmental Ctr., Inc., 1989; children's libr. Clay Ctr. (Kans.) Pub. Libr., 1991-93, libr. dir., 1994—; also advisortrustees bd. Office: Clay Ctr Carnegie Libr 706 6th Clay Center KS 67432

MARTIN, JOHN GUSTIN, investment banker; b. Bay Port, Mich., Dec. 25, 1928; s. Rig and Phoebe (Ballard) M.; m. Patricia Jean Martell, Nov. 16, 1957; children: James Martell, John Douglas. BA, Mich. State Coll., 1952; student, U. Detroit Law Sch., 1952-54. With First of Mich. Corp., Detroit, 1952—; sr. v.p. First of Mich. Corp., 1966-69, exec. v.p., 1969, pres., 1970—, dir., 1966—; trustee Renaissance Assets Trust; mem. regional firms adv. com. N.Y. Stock Exch. Chmn. bd. Bon Secours Health System Found., Grosse Pointe, Mich. Mem. Bond Club Detroit (pres. 1961), Security Traders Detroit (pres. 1963), Investment Bankers Am. (nat. com. 1969—), Nat. Assn. Security Dealers (nat. com. 1973), Security Industry Assn. (bd. dirs. 1986-89), Mich. State U. Bus. Alumni Assn. (dir., recipient Outstanding Alumni award 1974). Clubs: Detroit, Grosse Pointe Yacht, Renaissance. Home: 794 N Saint Joseph St #44 Suttons Bay MI 49682-9755 Office: First of Michigan Corp 100 Renaissance Ctr Fl 26 Detroit MI 48243-1003

MARTIN, JOHN THOMAS, physician, author, educator; b. Cleve., June 8, 1924; s. Clarence Henry and Clara May (Feeney) M.; m. Marion Elizabeth George, Feb. 18, 1946; children: Thomas R., David B., Richard G., Janet E., Patricia L., Robert W. MD, U. Cin., 1948. Commd. 1st lt. USAF, 1949, advance through grades to maj., 1953; resident in anesthesiology Lackland AFB Hosp., San Antonio, 1953-55; asst. chief USAF Sch. Anesthesiology, Lackland AFB, 1955-57; attending anesthesiologist Baylor U. Hosp., Dallas, 1957-58; cons. dept. anesthesiology Mayo Clinic, Rochester, Minn., 1958-72; head Meth sect. anesthesiology Mayo Clinic, 1966-72; chmn. dept. anesthesiology Ochsner Med. Ctr., New Orleans, 1972-74; clin. assoc. prof. anesthesiology Tulane U. Sch. Medicine, New Orleans, 1972-74; prof. anesthesiology Med. Coll. Ohio, Toledo, 1974-90; chmn. dept. anesthesiology Med. Coll. Ohio, 1980-89, emeritus prof. anesthesiology, 1990—. Editor, author: Positioning Patients Anesthesia/Surgery, 1978, 2d edit., 1987, 3d edit., 1996; editor ASA Handbook of Hosp. Facilities for Anesthesia, 1972, 2d edit., 1974; contbr. articles to profl. jours. Chmn. conductor selection com. Rochester Symphony Orch., 1963-66; pres. Rochester Civic Music, 1965. Mem. Internat. Anesthesia Rsch. Soc. (chmn. 1979-81, trustee 1965-90), Minn. Soc. Anesthesiologists (pres. 1966-67), Ohio Soc. Anesthesiologists (pres. 1988-89), Am. Med. Writers Assn. (pres. Minn. chpt. 1970-71), Assoc. Physicians Med. Coll. Ohio (bd. dirs. 1974-89), Am. Soc. Anesthesiology, Sigma Xi, Alpha Omega Alpha, Sigma Chi, Phi Chi. Republican. Home: 4605 Woodland Ln Sylvania OH 43560-3221 Office: Med Coll of Ohio Toledo PO Box 10008 Toledo OH 43699

MARTIN, JOHN WILLIAM, educator, antiquarian bookseller; b. Palo Alto, Calif., Feb. 21, 1946; s. Norman J. and Betty G. (Fawcett) M.; m. Diane Elizabeth Hirsch, Dec. 29, 1968; children—Molly E., Jamie S. B.A., U. Minn., 1968; M.A., U. Oreg., 1972, D.A. in English, 1973. Instr., U. Oreg., Eugene, 1972; mem. faculty Moraine Valley Coll., Palos Hills, Ill., 1972—, prof., 1985—; owner/mgr. John Wm. Martin--Bookseller, La Grange, Ill., 1973—; owner, mgr. Twice Read Books, La Grange, 1989—; tech. writing cons., 1972—; lit. property appraiser, 1973—. Co-author: Township Trustees, 1980; literary editor Bullfrog Mag., 1971-72. Contbr. articles to profl. jours. Pres., trustee LaGrange Pub. Library Bd., 1982-90. Mem. Bibliog. Soc. Am., Bibliog. Soc., Dickens Soc., Victorians Inst., Oxford Bibliographical Soc., William Morris Soc., Pvt. Libraries Assn., MLA. Unitarian. Avocations: travel; hiking.

MARTIN, KIM See **MARTH, MARY ELLEN**

MARTIN, LAURA BELLE, real estate and farm land manager, retired educator; b. Jackson County, Minn., Nov. 3, 1915; d. Eugene Wellington and Mary Christina (Hanson) M. BS, Mankato State U., 1968. Tchr. rural schs., Renville County, Minn., 1937-41, 45-50, Wabasso (Minn.) Pub. Sch., 1963-81; pres. Renville Farms and Feed Lots, 1982—. Pres. Wabasso (Minn.) Edn. Assn., 1974-75, publicity chmn., 1968-74; sec. Hist. Renville Preservation Com., 1978—; publicity chmn. Town and Country Boosters, Renville, 1982-83. Mem. Genealogy Soc. Renville County, Am. Legion Aux. Democrat. Lutheran. Home and Office: 334 NW 1201 Holden MO 64040-9804

MARTIN, LEE, mechanical engineer; b. Elkhart, Ind., Feb. 7, 1920; s. Ross and Esther Lee (Schweitzer) M.; m. Geraldine Faith Fitzgarrald, July 20, 1945; children: Jennifer L., Casper, Rex, Elizabeth L. SBME, SMME, MIT, 1943. With GE, 1940-42; with NIBCO Inc., Elkhart, 1943—, pres., 1957-76, chmn., 1975—. Chmn. Samaritan Inst., Denver, 1980-86; dir. Interlochen (Mich.) Ctr. for Arts, 1983-94; trustee Tri-State U., Angola, Ind., 1973-88. Mem. Union League Club (Chgo.).

MARTIN, MARSHALL ALLEN, agricultural economist; b. Kewanee, Ill., Dec. 16, 1943; s. Marion R. and Lucille (Myers) M.; m. Berdine R. Kipp, June 5, 1966; children: Melanie A., Matthew A. BS, Iowa State U., 1966; MS, Purdue U., 1972, PhD, 1976. Dir, tchr. Instituto Rural de Montero, Santa Cruz, Bolivia, 1966-71; grad. rsch. asst. Purdue U., West Lafayette, Ind., 1971-73; from asst. prof. to prof. Purdue U., West Lafayette, 1976-90, prof. agrl. econs., 1990—; assoc. head dept. agrl. econ., 1995—; vis. scholar U. Sao Paulo, Brazil, 1974-75; cons. Ford Found., Brazil, 1978, World Bank, Brazil, 1979, U.S. C. of C., Mexico, 1990; mem. adv. bd. Fed. Res. Bank of Chgo., 1989-90; dir. Ctr. for Agrl. Policy and Tech. Assessment, Purdue U., 1988—; mem. biotech. com. Nat. Assn. State Univs. and Land Grant Colls., 1988—; mem. oper. com. Nat. Agrl. Biotech. Coun., 1991—. Author: Commercial International Agricultural Policies, 1991; author/editor: Agricultural Biotechnology, 1991; contbr. articles to profl. jours. Sch. supt. search com., West Lafayette Community Sch. Corp., 1989; pres., bd. dirs. Global Ministries of the North Ind. Conf., United Meth. Ch., 1980-85. Recipient Rsch. Grant German Marshall Fund, 1987, rsch. awards Am. Agrl. Econs. Assn., 1981, 82, 83, 92. Mem. AAAS, Nat. Acad. Sci. (Russia), Atlantic Econ. Soc. (exec. com. 1995—), Sigma Xi (chpt. pres. 1987). Home: 108 Crimson Ct West Lafayette IN 47906-1602 Office: Purdue U Dept Agrl Econs 1145 Krannert Rm 655 West Lafayette IN 47907-1145

MARTIN, MARY KAYLENE, librarian; b. Lafayette, Ind., Sept. 18, 1955; d. Harold Clifton and Helen Nora (Dewitt) M. BS, Ball State U., 1978, MLS, 1983. Cert. Ind. libr. I Ind. State Library. Tchr., libr. Cannelton (Ind.) City Schs., 1978-81; tchr. North Newton H.S., Morocco, Ind., 1981-82; grad. asst., abstractor Ball State U., Muncie, Ind., 1982-83; historian Ball Meml. Hosp., Muncie, 1983; libr. Jasper County Pub. Libr., Rensselaer, Ind., 1983-94; libr. dir. Newton County Pub. Libr., Lake Village, Ind., 1994—; cmty. tchg. fellow St. Joseph's Coll., Rensselaer, 1995—; com. chair Incolsa Membership Adv. Coun., Indpls., 1994—. Spkr. in field. Cmty. rels. com. mem. Jasper County Hosp., Rensselaer, 1993—; fed. fin. aid forms asst. Purdue U. Calumet, Hammond, Ind., 1995—. Recipient Margaret McNamara Reading award Rensselaer Ctr. Mid. Sch., 1988; named Woman of Yr. Am. Bus. Women's Assn., 1989. Mem. Nat. Hot Rod Assn., Tech. Svc. Librs. (Ohio Valley group), Andy Griffith Show Rerun Watchers Club (pres. Pucka Pucka Pucka chpt. 1995—), Morocco Ladies Literary Club (pres. 1994-95), Kappa Kappa Kappa Beta Upsilon chpt. Democrat. Office: Newton County Pub Libr 9458 N 315 W PO Box 206 Lake Village IN 46349

MARTIN, MICHAEL MCCULLOCH, biology and chemistry educator; b. Junction City, Kans., Mar. 21, 1935; s. Thomas Lyle and Malvina (Rucks) M.; m. Joan Stadler, Dec. 10, 1965; children—Jeffrey Thomas, Linda. A.B., Cornell U., 1955; Ph.D., U. Ill., 1958. Mem. faculty U. Mich., Ann Arbor, 1959—, prof. biology and chemistry, 1970-85, prof. biology, 1985—, assoc. dean Coll. Lit., Sci. and the Arts, 1991-95, chmn. div. biol. scis., 1982-85. NSF postdoctoral fellow, 1958-59; NSF faculty fellow in sci., 1976-77; Sloan Found. fellow, 1966-68; Fulbright research scholar, 1986-87. Mem. AAAS, Am. Inst. Biol. Scis., Internat. Soc. Chem. Ecology. Home: 5530 Warren Rd Ann Arbor MI 48105-9425

MARTIN, PHIL, state legislator; m. Patricia Martin. Kans. state rep. Dist. 13, real estate, antiques exec. Office: 403 W Euclid St Pittsburg KS 66762-5011 also: State Senate State Capitol Topeka KS 66612*

MARTIN, PHILLIP DWIGHT, banking consulting company executive, mayor; b. Nevada, Mo., Jan. 4, 1943; s. E. Dwight and Berniece E. (Leedy) M. BS, U. Mo., 1964, MBA, 1965, cert. math. and bus. edn., 1966. Tchr. Warson (Mo.) Pub. Schs., 1966-68; investment analyst Bus. Men's Assurance Co. Am., Kansas City, Mo., 1968-70; exec. v.p. Farmer's Bank Walker, Mo., 1970-71; banking cons. Howard J. Blender Co., Dallas, 1971-84; chmn. Profit Motivators Internat., Inc., Boulder, Colo., 1984—; mayor City of Walker, 1986—. Home: 214 E Marvin Ave Walker MO 64790-0069 Office: Profit Motivators Internat 2146 Linden Dr Boulder CO 80304-0428

MARTIN, QUINN WILLIAM, lawyer; b. Fond du Lac, Wis., Mar. 12, 1948; s. Quinn W. and Marcia E. (Petrie) M.; m. Jane E. Nehmer; children: Quinn W., William J. BSME, Purdue U., 1969; postgrad., U. Santa Clara, 1969-70; JD, U. Mich., 1973. Bar: Wis. 1973, U.S. Dist. Ct. (ea. dist.) Wis. 1973, U.S. Ct. Appeals (7th cir.) 1973. Sales support mgr. Hewlett-Packard, Palo Alto, Calif., 1969-70; assoc. Quarles & Brady, Milw., 1973-80, ptnr., 1980—; bd. dirs. Associated Bank Milw., U-Line Corp., Altim, Inc., Tomahawk, Wis., Martin Comm., Inc., Kaukauna, Wis., ALTIM, Inc., Tomahawk, Wis., Gen. Timber and Land, Inc., Fond du Lac. Active McCallum for Lt. Gov., Wis., U. Mich. Law Sch. Fund; bd. dirs. Milw. Zool. Soc., Found. for Wildlife Conservation. Mem. ABA, Wis. Bar Assn., Milw. Bar Assn., Milw. Club, Ozaukee Country Club, Chaine des Rottiseurs, Delta Upsilon (sec.), Milw. Alumni Club. Office: Quarles & Brady 411 E Wisconsin Ave Milwaukee WI 53202-4409

MARTIN, RAYMOND BRUCE, plumbing equipment manufacturing company executive; b. N.Y.C., Oct. 23, 1934; s. Raymond M. and Margaret (Lennon) M.; m. Suzanne Ruth Longpre, Sept. 3, 1960; 1 son, Christopher Haines. A.B., Villanova U., 1956. With Corning Glass Works (N.Y.), 1956-68, nat. plumbing sales mgr., 1966-68; v.p. mktg. Briggs Mfg. Co., Warren, Mich., 1968-69, v.p., gen. mgr. plumbing fixture div., 1969-72; pres., chief exec. officer Water Control Internat. Inc., Troy, Mich., 1972-91; dir. Internat. Tech. Corp., Cash Control Products Inc.; pres., chief exec. officer W/C Technology Corp., 1991; mem. plumbing harmonization Fed. North Am. Free Trade Delegation, 1992. Served with AUS, 1957-58. Mem. Am. Soc. Plumbing Engrs., Plumbing Mfrs. Inst. (chmn. HUD Task Group 1981-82, chmn. communications com. 1983-86, chmn. fed. water conservation com. 1988-90), Am. Soc. Sanitary Engrs., ASME (panel 19, chmn. definitions task group 1993-94, chmn. water closet hyraulic performance task group 1993-94), Republican. Roman Catholic (trustee 1982-86). Clubs: Orchard Lake Country, L'Arbre Croche (chmn. archtl. com. 1989—, bd. dirs.). Patentee in field. Office: 2820 W Maple Rd Troy MI 48084-7011

MARTIN, ROBERT EDWARD, architect; b. Dodge City, Kans., Mar. 17, 1928; s. Emry and Alice Jane (Boyce) M.; m. Billie Jo Lange, Aug. 16, 1952 (div. Feb. 1970); m. Kathryn M. Arvanitis, June 26, 1971; children: Lynn, Amy, Blaine. Student, McPherson Coll., 1946-48; BArch, U. Cin., 1954. Registered architect, Ohio. Architect Samborn, Steketee, Otis & Evans, Inc., Toledo, 1956-58; prin. Schauder & Martin, Toledo, 1958-72, The Collaborative, Inc., Toledo, 1972-93; mem. Bd. Examiners Archs., Ohio, 1985-95, pres., 1989-94; bd. examiners Nat. Coun. Archtl. Registration Bds., 1986—, edn. com., 1992; chmn. site design divsn. Archtl. Registration Exam., 1989, 90, 91; mem. Nat. Coun. Archtl. Registration Bds. Grading, 1987-94; chmn. study of Toledo Fire & Rescue Dept., Corp. for Effective Govt., 1994. Artist numerous paintings. Mem. Toledo Planning Commn., 1971-74, Toledo Zoning Appeals Bd., 1973, Toledo Bd. Bldg. Stds., 1967-84, Citizens Fire Adv. Commn., 1974-80, Citizens Urban Area Adv. Commn., 1962, Toledo Area Coun. Govts., 1977-80, Com. of 100, Toledo, 1987-89, Spectrum Friends Fine Arts, Inc., Toledo; chmn. bd. Toledo Area Govtl. Rsch. Assn., 1981-90; chmn. Corp. for Effective Govt., Study of Toledo Fire and Rescue Dept., 1994; chmn. Cystic Fibrosis, Toledo. 1985. Seved to capt. USAF, 1954-56. Recipient numerous watercolor awards. Fellow AIA (pres. Toledo chpt. 1966, Arch. of Yr. 1993), Archs. Soc. Ohio (pres. 1975), Ohio Watercolor Soc., N.W. Ohio Watercolor Soc., Toledo Fedn. Art Socs. (pres. 1989, 90), Spectrum, Tile Club, Toledo Artists Club, Toledo Artists Club, Sylvania Country Club, Rotary, Masons, Shriners, Jesters. Mem. Ch. of Brethren. Home: 5119 Regency Dr Toledo OH 43615-2946 Office: 1700 N Reynolds Rd Toledo OH 43615-3628

MARTIN, RUSSELL LEE, social service executive; b. West Plains, Mo., Dec. 22, 1947; s. Harold L. and Dorothy M. (Pendleton) M.; m. Shirley Cory, June 8,1968; children: Brian, Trevor, Jordan. BS, Coll. of Ozarks, 1969; MBA, S.W. Mo. State U., 1977. Cert. fin. planner. Registrar Coll. of Ozarks, Point Lookout, Mo., 1968-70; asst. treas. Coll. of Ozarks, Point Lookout, 1972-77; v.p. Mo. Bapt. Children's Home, Bridgeton, 1977—. Mem. Internat. Assn. Fin. Planning, Inst. Cert. Fin. Planners, Coll. of Ozarks Alumni Assn. (treas. 1992-94, pres.-elect 1996—). Baptist. Office: Mo Bapt Children's Home 11300 Saint Charles Rock Rd Bridgeton MO 63044-2793

MARTIN, TRIPP, quality assurance professional; b. Springfield, Mass., Dec. 20, 1950; s. William Jr. and Jane (Godley) M.; m. Mary Lee Koll, July 15, 1978; children: Sarah Natanya, William Evan. BA, Dickinson Coll., 1972; MA in Religion, Westminster Sem., Phila., 1978. Cert. quality engr., cert. mech. insp. Mgr. prodn. control Atlantic Spring Co., Phila., 1980-82; mgr. quality control Atlantic Spring Co., Flemington, N.J., 1982-84, mgr. quality assurance, 1985-86, plant mgr., 1986-87, mgr. engring., 1987-88; supr. quality assurance Chempump div. Crane Co., Warrington, Pa., 1984-85; dir. quality Peterson Am. Corp., Southfield, Mich., 1988-93, 94—; gen. mgr. Peterson Spring, Southfield, Mich., 1993-94. Contbr. articles to profl. jours. Mem. Am. Soc. for Quality Control (sr., exec. com. automotive div. 1989—), Am. Prodn. and Inventory Control Soc. (cert. prodn. and inventory mgr.). Republican. Presbyterian. Office: Peterson Spring Corp Office PO Box 5059 Southfield MI 48086-5059

MARTIN, VALENTINA KUCHYNKA, real estate company executive, consultant; b. Traer, Iowa, Feb. 11, 1925; d. Jerry Frank and Albina (Vojtech) Kuchynka; m. Merle R. Martin, Dec. 15, 1941; 1 child, Jerald L. Grad., Realtors Inst., 1981; BA, U. No. Iowa, 1982, MA, 1989. Lic. Realtor, Iowa, CPM. Instr. Hawkeye Community Coll., Waterloo, Iowa, 1978-83; sec. Martin Inc. Realtors, Waterloo, Iowa, 1975-90; pres. Martin Inc. Realtors, Waterloo, 1990—; cons. Mt. Village I 202 Direct Loan Project, Waterloo, 1990-92; past dir. Iowa Woman mag. Author: Soldiers Orphans Home, 1863-1879, 1983; reporter No. Iowa, Cedar Falls. Mem. Waterloo Planning and Zoning Commn., 1990—; chmn. Waterloo Human Rights Commn., 1987—; active fund drive Salvation Army, Waterloo. Recipient Cert. Recognition Iowa State Hist. Soc., 1984, Realtors Community Svc. award 1993; nominee Athena award Waterloo C. of C., 1989-91. Mem. AAUW (pres. 1994-96, Grant award 1994), SBA (regional dir. 1980—), LWV, Nat. Assn. Realtors, Iowa Assn. Realtors, Waterloo-Cedar Falls Bd. Realtors (pres. 1975, Realtor of Yr. 1977), Cath. Order Foresters (sec. 1990-93), Altrusa (pres. Waterloo chpt. 1967-68). Democrat. Roman Catholic. Home: 3433 Rosehill Ter Waterloo IA 50701-4713

MARTIN, WILLIAM E., agricultural economist, educator; b. Modesto, Calif., Apr. 12, 1933; s. Marion A. and Dorothy C. (Garnett) M.; m. Marjorie L. Ashcroft, Jan. 1953 (div. 1965); children: Jon W., Tom A., Jane A., Amy M.; m. Jean C. Rush, Oct. 21, 1983; stepchildren, Benjamin E., Samuel C., Joseph H., Margaret R. BS, U. Calif., Davis, 1954; PhD, U. Calif., Berkeley, 1961. Rsch. assoc. U. Calif., Berkeley, 1958-61; asst. prof. U. Ariz., Tucson, 1961-63, assoc. prof., 1963-68, prof., 1968-89, prof. emeritus, 1989—; prof. U. Ill., Champaign, 1990-92; agrl. economist, cons., 1992—; rschr., tchr. in natural resource econs. and agrl. econs. to various orgns., including NSA, U.S. Sec. of Interior. Co-author: Farmers, Workers and Machines, 1965, Water Supplies and Economic Growth in an Arid Environment, 1973, Saving Water in a Desert City, 1984; contbr. articles to profl. jours.; assoc. editor Am. Jour. Agrl. Econs., 1986-91. Lt. (j.g.) USNR, 1954-57. Hon. rsch. assoc. water program Harvard U., 1967; Fulbright Sr. scholar, 1985; sr. fellow East-West Food Inst., 1975. Fellow Am. Agrl. Econs. Assn. (exec. bd. 1980-83); mem. Western Agrl. Econs. Assn. (v.p. 1974-75, pres.-elect 1975-76, pres. 1976-77, Outstanding Published Rsch. award 1963, 66, 70, 74, 76, 85), Ariz. Acad. Sci., Phi Beta Kappa. Home: RR 2 Box 59 Heyworth IL 61745

MARTIN-BOWEN, (CAROLE) LINDSEY, freelance writer; b. Kansas City, Kans., Aug. 4, 1949; d. Lawrence Richard and V. Marie (Schaffer) Pickett; m. Frederick E. Nicholson, July 3, 1971 (div. 1977); 1 child, Aaron Frederick; m. Edwin L. Martin, June 18, 1980 (div. 1987); 1 child, Ki Elise; m. Michael L. Bowen, Dec. 23, 1988. BA in English Lit., U. Mo., Kansas City, 1972, MA in English and Creative Writing, 1988, postgrad., 1991-94; postgrad., U. Mo. Kansas City Sch. Law, Kansas City, 1995—. Tech. editor Office Hearings and Appeals, U.S. Dept. Interior, Washington, 1976-77; reporter, photographer Louisville Times, 1982-83; reporter, features editor Sun Newspapers, Overland Park, Kans., 1983-84; assoc. editor Modern Jeweler, Overland Park and N.Y.C., 1984-85; writer Coll. Blvd. News, Overland Park, 1985-89, KC View, Kansas City, Mo., 1988-89; editor Number One, Kansas City, Mo., 1986-88, cons., 1988-89; copywriter Sta KXEO/KWWR Radio, Mexico, Mo., 1989; editorial asst. New Letters, 1985—; features writer, columnist The Squire, Prairie Village, Kans., 1990-95; instr. English U. Mo., Kansas City, 1986-88, Johnson County C.C., 1988-95; tchr. English and fiction Longview C.C., 1988-95; instr. writing and mass comm. Webster U., 1990—; instr. world lit., Am. lit., women in lit., creative writing Penn Valley C.C., 1993—, faculty sponsor The Penn; owner, writer Paladin Freelance Writing Svc., Kansas City, 1988—; prodn. editor Nat. Paralegal Reporter, 1992-95, editor 1994—; staff writer, editor Nat. Fedn. Paralegal Assns., Inc. books and pubs.; writing contest judge New Letters, 1987—. Author: (novel) The Dark Horse Waits in Boulder, 1985, (poetry) Waiting for the Wake-Up Call, 1990, Second Touch, 1990, (fiction) Cicada Grove and Other Stories, 1992; contbr. poems, book revs., features, cartoon artwork, and photographs to numerous publs. including New Letters, Lip Service and Contemporary Lit. Criticism. Campaigner McGovern for Pres. Campaign, Kansas City, 1971-72. Regents scholar, 1967; GAF fellow, 1986. Mem. U. Mo.-Kansas City Alumni Assn. (media com. 1983-84), Phi Kappa Phi. Roman Catholic. Home: 7109 Pennsylvania Ave Kansas City MO 64114-1316 Office: Nat Paralegal Reporter Hdqs. 32 W Bridlespur Ter. Kansas City MO 64114

MARTINDALE, LARRY RICHARD, computer services company consultant; b. Grove City, Ohio, Nov. 18, 1938; s. Lawrence Thomas Hoyt and Thelma Elizabeth (Strickler) M.; m. Carol Sue Woods, Dec. 22, 1959; children: Larry Richard, Lynnette Carolita, Kyle Edgar, Connie Beth, Tanya Sue. AS, Franklin U., 1972, BS, 1973. Sales analysis clk. Scoa Industries Inc., Columbus, Ohio, 1956-64, computer operator, 1964-65, computer programmer, 1965-66, systems programmer, 1966-68, programmer/analyst, 1968-73; sr. programmer/analyst Ohio State Dept. Pub. Welfare, Columbus, 1973-75; sr. analyst Cutler-Williams Inc., Dayton, Ohio, 1975-76; sr. programmer/analyst Blue Cross/Blue Shield Ind., Indpls., 1976-78; sr. staff cons. Cap Gemini Am. (formerly CGA Computer Assocs.), Holmdel, N.J., 1978-95; cons. Profl. Data Dimensions, Indpls., 1995—, U.S. Dept. Def., Indpls., 1995, Eli Lilly Co., 1995-96, Anthem Health, 1996—; cons. Blue Cross/Blue Shield Ind., 1975-76, Blue Cross/Blue Shield N.W. Ohio, Toledo, 1978, Federated Dept. Stores Inc., Cin., 1878-81, Dayton Newspapers, Inc., 1981, 84, Delco Electronics, Inc., Kokomo, Ind., 1981-84, Procter & Gamble, Inc., Cin., 1984-95. Jr. high basketball coach Muhlenberg Twp. Sch., Darbyville, Ohio, 1956-57; coach, bd. dirs. Derby (Ohio) Little League baseball, 1972-75, Rush County Youth basketball league, Rushville, Ind., 1978-81; coach Rush County Youth football league, Rushville, 1982-83; bd. dirs. Rushville Babe Ruth baseball league, 1981; youth pres. Darbyville Ch. Nazarene, 1958-60, trustee, 1968-75, treas., 1970-75, fin. sec., 1970-75; fin. sec. Rushville Ch. Nazarene, 1977-95, trustee, 1980-87, dir. youth ministries, 1983, chmn. bd. Christian life, 1987-95; chmn. bd. Sunday sch. ministries Shelbyville (Ind.) First Ch. of the Nazarene, 1996—. With U.S. ARmy, 1961-63. Mem. Am. Legion. Republican. Home: 2402 N 900 W Arlington IN 46104-9558 Office: Profl Data Dimensions 200 S Meridian St Ste 200 Indianapolis IN 46225

MARTINEK, FRANK JOSEPH, chemical company executive; b. Cleve., Apr. 10, 1921; s. Michael Joseph and Sophie Anna (Fortuna) M.; B.S. in Chemistry, Ohio State U., 1950; m. Julianne Christine Radics, Oct. 9, 1954; children—Frank Joseph, Janet Arlene. Chemist, Diamond Alkali Co., Painesville, Ohio, 1950, Sherwin Williams Co., Cleve., 1950-52; group supr. Sherwin Williams, Cleve., 1953-63, tech. mgr., 1964-72; pres. Mar-Bal, Inc., Cleve., 1972-78; pres. Mid-Am. Chem. Corp., Cleve., 1978—. Served with AUS, 1942-45. Decorated Bronze Star (2). Mem. Am. Chem. Soc., Soc. Plastics Industries, Cleve. Soc. Coatings Tech., Cleve. Chem. Assn. Roman Catholic. Home: 1745 Jonathans Trce Cleveland OH 44147-3288 Office: 4701 Spring Rd Cleveland OH 44131-1025

MARTINEZ, BENJAMIN A., state legislator; b. Chgo.; m. Hortense Martinez; three children. Dist. 2 rep. Ill. Ho. Reps., Springfield, 1987—; co-chmn. urban redevel. com., chmn. exec. and vet. affairs com., mem. rules, housing, small bus., transp. and motor vehicles, fin. instns., elections, human svcs. appropriations, reappointment registration and regulation coms., mem. commn. on intergovernmental cooperation, Ill. Ho. Reps. Home: 1818 W 18th St Chicago IL 60608-1944*

MARTINEZ, PENNY CAROL, small business owner; b. Lexington, N.C., Aug. 25, 1959; d. Samuel Harding and Kathryn Levena (Smith) Courtney; m. Ervin Leory Jackson, June 20, 1983 (div. Mar. 1984); 1 child, Chaz Courtney; m. Raul Martinez, Jan. 26, 1991. Grad., Grandview (Mo.) Beauty Coll., 1979; diploma in gen. edn., So. Mo. State U., 1984; student, State Fair C.C., Sedalia, Mo., 1994—. Lic. cosmetologist, Mo.; lic. barber, Calif.; lic. economist, Mo. Cashier Courtney's Five and Dime, Warsaw, Mo., 1969-78; owner, operator A-1 Styling Salon, Warsaw, Mo., 1985-90; mgr., operator Fantastic Sam's Salon, Walnut, Calif., 1990-91, Dillards Beauty Salon, Kansas City, Mo., 1991-93; owner A-P.M. Salon, Warsaw, 1992—; owner P.C.M. Publ., Warsaw, 1993—; land rschr. Benton County Property, Warsaw, 1993-95. Author: Blow Ark, 1995; author poems and plays; dir. movie and play The Haunting of a Driveway, 1994; patentee in field. Recipient comml. recording contract Rainbow Records, 1993. Republican. Baptist. Home: 104 W Osage St Warsaw MO 65355 Office: A-P M Salon at P I Investigations Rt 3 Box 2 C Warsaw MO 65355

MARTINSON, ROBERT WILLIAM, state legislator; b. Bismarck, N.D., Dec. 28, 1946; s. Edward L. and Josephine (Saldin) M.; 3 children. AA, Bismarck Jr. Coll., 1967; BS, Mary Coll. N.D., 1972. Pres. Brock Lee Films; mem. N.D. Ho. of Reps., 1973—, chmn. state and fed. govt. com., mem. indsl., bus. and labor com., mem. appropriations and govt. oper. divsn. com., majority whip; pres. Brock Lee Graphics, The Tracker Film Prodn. Co.; owner O'Brian's Tavern. Recipient Virgil R. Kottsick award. Mem. Am. Legion, Elks, Alpha Tau Omega. Home: PO Box 2296 Bismarck ND 58502-2296*

MARTON, LAURENCE JAY, clinical pathologist, educator, researcher; b. Bklyn., Jan. 14, 1944; s. Bernard Dov and Sylvia (Silberstein) M.; m. Marlene Lesser, June 27, 1967; 1 child, Eric Nolan. BA, Yeshiva U., 1965, DSc (hon.), 1993; MD, Albert Einstein Coll. Medicine, 1969. Intern Los Angeles County-Harbor Gen. Hosp., 1969-70; resident in neurosurgery U. Calif.-San Francisco, 1970-71, resident in lab. medicine, 1973-75, asst. research biochemist, 1973-74, asst. clin. prof. depts. lab. medicine and neurosurgery, 1974-75, asst. prof., 1975-78, assoc. prof., 1978-79, prof., 1979-92, asst. dir. div. clin. chemistry, dept. lab. medicine, 1974-75, dir. div., 1975-79, acting chmn. dept., 1978-79, chmn. dept., 1979-92; dean med. sch. U. Wis., 1992-95, prof. pathology and lab. medicine and oncology, 1992—; prof. dept. human oncology U. Wis., Madison, 1993-95. Co-editor: Polyamines in Biology and Medicine, 1981; Liquid Chromatography in Clinical Analysis, 1981; Clinical Liquid Chromatography, vol. 1, 1984, vol. 2, 1984. Served with USPHS, NIH, 1971-73. Recipient Rsch. Career Devel. award Nat. Cancer Inst., Disting. Alumnus award Albert Einstein Coll. Medicine, 1992. Mem. Am. Assn. Cancer Rsch., AAAS, Acad. Clin. Lab. Physicians and Scientists, Am. Investigative Pathology, Am. Soc. Clin. Pathologists, Soc. Analytical Cytology, Alpha Omega Alpha. Jewish. Home: 5810 Tree Line Dr Fitchburg WI 53711-5826 Office: U Wis Med Sch McArdle Lab Cancer Rsch 1400 University Ave Madison WI 53706

MARTY, JOHN, state senator, writer; b. Evanston, Ill., Nov. 1, 1956; s. Martin E. and Elsa Louise (Schumacher) M.; m. Connie Jaarsma, Nov. 29, 1980; children: Elsa, Micah. BA in Ethics, St. Olaf Coll., 1978. Researcher Minn. Ho. of Reps., St. Paul, 1980-82, com. adminstr. com. criminal justice, 1982-84; corp. found. grant adminstr., 1984-86; mem. Minn. State Senate, St. Paul, 1987—. Dem. Farm Labor gubernatorial candidate, 1994.

MARTY, MARTIN EMIL, religion educator, editor; b. West Point, Nebr., Feb. 5, 1928; s. Emil A. and Anne Louise (Wuerdemann) M.; m. Elsa Schumacher, 1952 (dec. 1981); children: Frances, Joel, John, Peter, James, Micah, Ursula; m. Harriet Lindemann, 1982. MDiv, Concordia Sem., 1952; STM, Luth. Sch. Theology, Chgo., 1954; PhD in Am. Religious and Intellectual History, U. Chgo., 1956; LittD (hon.), Thiel Coll., 1964; LHD (hon.), W.Va. Wesleyan Coll., 1967, Marian Coll., 1967, Providence Coll., 1967; DD (hon.), Muhlenberg Coll., 1967; LittD (hon.), Thomas More Coll., 1968; DD (hon.), Bethany Sem., 1969; LLD (hon.), Keuka Coll., 1972; LHD (hon.), Willamette U., 1974; DD (hon.), Wabash Coll., 1977; LLD (hon.), U. So. Calif., 1977, Valparaiso U., 1978; LHD (hon.), St. Olaf Coll., 1978, De Paul U., 1979; DD (hon.), Christ Sem.-Seminex, 1979, Capital U., 1980; LHD (hon.), Colo. Coll., 1980; DD (hon.), Maryville Coll., 1980, North Park Coll. Sem., 1982; LittD (hon.), Wittenberg U., 1983; LHD, Rosary Coll., 1984; LHD (hon.), Rockford Coll., 1984; DD (hon.), Va. Theol. Sem., 1984; LHD (hon.), Hamilton Coll., 1985, Loyola U., 1986; LLD (hon.), U. Notre Dame, 1987; LHD (hon.), Roanoke Coll., 1987, Mercer U., 1987, Ill. Wesleyan Coll., 1987, Roosevelt U., 1988, Aquinas Coll., 1988; LittD (hon.), Franklin Coll., 1988, U. Nebr., 1993; LHD (hon.), No. Mich. U., 1989, Muskingum Coll., Coe Coll., Lehigh U., 1989, Hebrew Union Coll. and Governors State U., 1990, Whittier Coll., 1991; Calif. Luth. U., 1993; DD (hon.), St. Xavier Coll. and Colgate U., 1990, Mt. Union Coll., 1991, Tex. Luth. Coll., 1991, Aurora U., 1991, Baker U., 1992; LittD (hon.), U. Nebr., 1993; LHD (hon.), Luth. U., 1993; Litt.D, U. Nebr., 1993; LHD, Calif. Luth. U., 1993, Midland Luth. Coll., 1995; DD, Hope Coll., 1993, Northwestern Coll., 1993; LHD (hon.), George Fox Coll., 1994, Drake U., 1994, Centre Coll., 1994; DD, Yale U., 1995, Yale U., 1995. Ordained to ministry Luth. Ch., 1952. Pastor Washington, 1950-51; asst. pastor River Forest, Ill., 1952-56; pastor Elk Grove Village, Ill., 1956-63; prof. history of modern Christianity Div. Sch. U. Chgo., 1963—, Fairfax M. Cone Disting. Service prof., 1978—; assoc. editor Christian Century mag., Chgo., 1956-85, sr. editor, 1985—; co-editor Ch. History mag., 1963—; pres. Park Ridge (Ill.) Ctr.: An Inst. for Study of Health, Faith and Ethics, 1985-89; dir. fundamentalism project Am. Acad. Arts & Scis., 1988—. Author: A Short History of Christianity, 1959, The New Shape of American Relicion, 1959, The Improper Opinion, 1961, The Infidel, 1961, Baptism, 1962, The Hidden Discipline, 1963, Second Chance for American Protestants, 1963, Church Unity and Church Mission, 1964, Varieties of Unbelief, 1964, The Search for a Usable Future, 1969, The Modern Schism, 1969, Righteous Empire, 1970 (Nat. Book award 1971), Protestantism, 1972, You Are Promise, 1973, The Fire We Can Light, 1973, The Pro and Con Book of Religious America, 1975, A Nation of Behavers, 1976, Religion, Awakening and Revolution, 1978, Friendship, 1980, By Way of Response, 1981, The Public Church, 1981, A Cry of Absence, 1983, Health and Medicine in the Lutheran Tradition, 1983, Pilgrims in Their Own Land, 1984, Protestantism in the United States, 1985, Modern American Religion, The Irony of it All, Vol. 1, 1986, An Invitation to American Catholic History, 1986, Religion and Republic, 1987, Modern American Religion. The Noise of Conflict, Vol. 2, 1991, (with R. Scott Appleby) The Glory and the Power, 1992; editor: (with Jerald C. Brauer) The Unrelieved Paradox: Studies in the Theology of Franz Bibfeldt, 1994; editor (jours.) Context, 1969—, Second Opinion, 1990; sr. editor The Christian Century, 1956—; contbr. articles to religious publs. Chmn. bd. regents St. Olaf Coll. Sr. scholar-in-residence The Park Ridge Ctr., 1989—. Fellow Am. Acad. Arts and Scis. (dir. fundamentalism project 1988-94), Soc. Am. Historians; mem. Am. Phil. Soc., Am. Soc. Ch. History (pres. 1971), Am. Cath. Hist(pres. 1981), Am. Acad. Religion (pres. 1987-88), Am. Antiquarian Soc. Home: 239 Scottswood Rd Riverside IL 60546-2223

MARTY, MYRON AUGUST, historian, educator; b. West Point, Nebr., Apr. 10, 1932; s. Emil Adolph and Anna Louise (Wuerdemann) M.; m. Shirley Lee Plunk, July 31, 1954; children: Miriam, Timothy, Elizabeth, Jason. BS, Concordia Coll., River Forest, Ill., 1954; M.A. in Edn., Washington U., St. Louis, 1960; MA, St. Louis U., 1965; PhD in History, 1967. Tchr. Trinity Luth. Sch., Ft. Wayne, Ind., 1954-57, Luth. H.S., St. Louis, 1957-65; prof. history, adminstr. Florissant Valley C.C., St. Louis, 1966-80; dep. dir. div. edn. programs NEH, Washington, 1980-84, acting dir., 1981, cons., 1977-80; dean Coll. Arts and Scis., prof. Drake U., Des Moines, 1984—, dean Coll. Arts and Scis., 1984-94, Ann G. and Sigurd E. Anderson U. prof. and prof. history, 1994—; mem. com. Coll. Bd. and Ednl. Testing Service, 1967-76; accreditation cons., evaluator N. Central Assn., 1969-80, 84—, mem. exec. bd. Commn. on Instns. Higher Edn., 1977-80. Author: Lutherans and Roman Catholicism: The Changing Conflict, 1968; Retracing Our Steps: Studies in Documents from the American Past, 1972; co-author: Nearby History: Exploring the Past Around You, 1982; Your Family History: A Handbook for Research and Writing, 1978. Book reviewer St. Louis Post-Dispatch, 1969—. NEH fellow, 1972-73; Newberry Library fellow, 1979. Mem. Orgn. Am. Historians (exec. bd. 1985-88), Am. Hist Assn., Soc. History Edn., Am. Soc. Ch. History, Nat. Trust for Hist. Preservation, Phi Beta Kappa. Democrat. Lutheran. Home: 2028 Elm Cir West Des Moines IA 50265-4294 Office: Coll Arts and Scis Drake U Des Moines IA 50311

MARTZ, DONALD S., environmental services administrator. BS in Physics, N.M. Inst. Mining and Tech.; M in Tech., Ea. Mich. U. Mgr. The Dragun Corp., Farmington Hills, Mich. Contbr. articles to profl. jours. Mem. AAAS, Air and Waste Mgmt. Assn., Source Evaluation Soc. Office: The Dragun Corp 30445 Northwestern Hwy Farmington Hills MI 48334

MARVIN, DAVID EDWARD SHREVE, lawyer; b. Lansing, Mich., Jan. 6, 1950; s. George Charles Marvin and Shirley Mae (Martin) Schaible; m. Mary Anne Kennedy, Sept. 16, 1972; 1 child, John. BS cum laude, Mich. State U., 1972; JD cum laude, Wayne State U., 1976. Bar: Mich. 1976, U.S. Dist. Ct. (ea. dist.) Mich. 1976, U.S. Dist. Ct. (we. dist.) Mich. 1978, U.S. Ct. Appeals (7th cir.) 1977, U.S. Ct. Appeals (6th cir.) 1979, U.S. Supreme Ct. 1979, U.S. Ct. Appeals (D.C. cir.) 1982, D.C. 1982. Asst. mgr. Alta Supply Co., Lansing, 1972-73; rsch. asst. Wayne State U., Detroit, fall 1975; jud. intern. U.S. Dist. Ct., Detroit, summer, 1975; shareholder Fraser Trebilcock Davis & Foster, P.C., Lansing, 1976—, chair., Govt. Law Dept., 1992—; pres. Red Rock Prodns., Inc., 1990-94; lectr. Inst. Continuing Legal Edn., 1989. Exec. editor Wayne Law Rev., 1975-76; contbr. articles to law jours. Commr. Mich. Solar Resource Adv. Panel, Lansing, 1978-81, Mich. Commn. Profl. & Occupational Licensure, 1981-83; chmn. Ingham County Energy Commn., Mason, Mich., 1978-80 (state bar rep. assembly 1985-88); dir., corp. sec. Friends Mich. Hist. Ctr., Inc., 1988—; treas. Lansing Lawyer Referral Svc., 1981; state del. Nat. Solar Congress, Washington, 1978; hearing officer City of East Lansing, 1985; Tri-County Coun. of Bar Leaders (chmn. 1986); bd. dirs. East Lansing Edn. Found., 1990-92; bd. dirs. Impression Five Sci. Mus., 1991—; regional fin. chmn. Abraham for U.S. Senate, 1993-94. Recipient Disting. Vol. award Tri-County Voluntary Action Ctr., 1990, Gov's. Minuteman award, 1990, John W. Cummiskey award State Bar Mich., 1990, George Washington Honor medal Freedoms Found., 1990; named Outstanding Young Man Am., 1984, The Outstanding Young Lawyer in Mich., 1985-86, Small Bus. Adv. Yr., C. of C., 1991; Wm. D. Traitel scholar, 1975. Fellow Mich. State Bar Found. (life); mem. ABA, State Bar Mich. (com. chmn., sect. coun. 1982—, state chmn. 1988-89), Mich. Soc. Assoc. Execs., Ingham County Bar Assn. (pres. 1985-86), Pro Bono Lawyers Svc. (pres. 1982-83), Lansing Regional C. of C. (v.p. 1987), Mich. Audubon Soc. (bd. dirs. 1991—), Mich. State Univ. Alumni Assn. (nat. bd. dirs. 1992—), State Capital Law Firm Group (nat. bd. dirs. 1989—, chmn. com. Can. 1990—, co-chair pub. utility, energy and comm. sect. 1994—), Downtown Coaches Club (bd. dirs., pres. 1987), Nat. Resource Ctr. on State Laws and Regulations (nat. bd. dirs. 1993—), Mich. State U. Pres.'s Club, Rotary, Phi Alpha Delta, Phi Eta Sigma, Theta Delta Chi (pres. 1972). Republican. Home: 1959 Groton Way East Lansing MI 48823-1347 Office: Fraser Trebilcock Davis & Foster PC Michigan Nat Towers Fl 10 Lansing MI 48933

MARVIN, JAMES CONWAY, librarian, consultant; b. Warroad, Minn., Aug. 3, 1927; s. William C. and Isabel (Carlquist) M.; m. Patricia Katharine Moe, Sept. 8, 1947; children: Heidi C., James Conway, Jill C., Jack C. B.A., U. Minn., 1950, M.A., 1966. City librarian Kaukauna, Wis., 1952-54; chief librarian Eau Claire, Wis., 1954-56; dir. Cedar Rapids (Iowa) Pub. Library, 1956-67, Topeka Pub. Library, 1967-92; Am. Library Assn.-Rockefeller Found. vis. prof. Inst. Library Sci. U. Philippines, 1964-65; vis. lectr. dept. librarianship Emporia (Kans.) State U., 1970-80; chmn. Kans. del. to White House Conf. on Libraries and Info. Services, Gov.'s Com. on Library Resources, 1980-81; mem. Kans. State Libr. Adv. Commn., 1992—. Served with USNR, 1945-46. Mem. ALA, Iowa Libr. Assn. (past pres.), Kans. Libr. Assn., Philippine Libr. Assn. (life), Mountain Plains Libr. Assn. Home: 40 SW Pepper Tree Ln Topeka KS 66611-2055

MARVIN, RICHARD WALTER, company executive; b. Chgo., May 31, 1930; s. Donald Thomas and Lucille Florence (Newbanks) M.; m. Florence Marie Hilton June 6, 1954; 1 child, Marjorie Ann. Office: Emcorp 25840 S Sunset Dr Monee IL 60449-9190

MARX, HAZEL RUTH, retired primaary school educator; b. Holland, Mich., June 1, 1912; d. William Ivar and Pearl Maud (Souter) Dick; m. George Fielden Marx June 21, 1939 (dec. July 1994)); children: Russell Fielden and Lowell Eldon. Student, Hope Coll., Holland, 1930-33; AB in Edn., U. Mich., 1934; student, Ohio State U., 1962-70. Cert. tchr., Mich., Ohio. Tchr. public schs., St. Louis, Mich., 1934-39, South Western City Schs., Grove City, Ohio, 1951-74. Compiler: The Peter Dick Family, 1979, The Descendants of John Frederick Wilhelm Marx, 1982, The Descendants of George Harley Souter, 1988, Some Descendants of Samuel Fredericks Collins, 1994. Active Hoge Meml. Presbyterian Ch. Mem. Columbus & Franklin County Fedn. of Women's Clubs (edn. com.).

MARYFIELD, JOHN ARTHUR, manufacturing company executive; b. St. Louis, Sept. 24, 1955. BSBA, U. Mo., 1979; MBA, Northwestern U., 1991. CPA, Ill., Hawaii, Mo. Auditor Grant Thorton, Kansas City, Mo., 1977-79; cons. Grant Thorton, Honolulu, 1979-83; mgr. cons. Grant Thorton, Chgo., 1983-85; asst. contr. Field Corp., Chgo., 1985-87; v.p., group contr. Ill. Tool Works, Glenview, Ill., 1987—; mem. alumni adv. bd. U. Mo. Bus. and Pub. Adminstrn., 1994—. Trustee Kenilworth (Ill.) Libr. Bd., 1994—. Mem. AICPA, Ill. Inst. CPAs, Fin. Execs. Inst. Office: Ill Tool Works 3600 W Lake Ave Glenview IL 60025

MARZ, MICHAEL BLASE, electrical engineer; b. South Bend, Ind., June 6, 1961; s. Paul A. and Jane Ann (Gember) M. BSEE, U. Notre Dame, 1983; MSEE, Purdue U., 1984; MBA, U. Minn., 1989. Registered profl. engr., Minn. Rsch. asst. Purdue U., West Lafayette, Ind., 1983-84; sys. performance engr., sys. planning engr. Minn. Power, Duluth, 1985-89; staff engr. Cooper Power Systems, Franksville, Wis., 1989—. Coach little league. Mem. IEEE (sr. mem., working group, task force com. 1990—). Roman Catholic. Home: 1021 Echo Ln Racine WI 53406 Office: Cooper Power Systems 11131 Adams Rd Franksville WI 53126

MARZANO, MARY KAY, physical therapist; b. Toledo, Nov. 25, 1963; d. Augustine and Jane Mary (Comes) M. BS, Marquette U., 1986; postgrad., U. Wis., Milw., 1990—. Staff phys. therapist Zablocki VA Med. Ctr., Milw., 1986—. Coord. Milw. Teens Encounter Christ Retreat Program, Milw., 1994—; 2d grade catechist Gesu Ch., Milw., 1987—, mem. parish coun., 1990-94; mem. Am. Heart Assn., 1991—. Mem. Am. Phys. Therapy Assn. (VA sect. 1986-87, 89—, cardiopulmonary sect. 1988—), Wis. Phys. Therapy Assn. Roman Catholic. Home: 3719 N 86th St Milwaukee WI 53222 Office: Zablocki VA Med Ctr 5000 W National Ave Milwaukee WI 53295

MARZINSKI, LYNN ROSE, oncological nurse; b. Milw., Mar. 15, 1951; d. Anthony A. and Delores D. (Moczynski) Miller; m. Ronald M. Marzinski, Aug. 26, 1972; children: Nicholas, Benjamin. BSN, U. Wis., 1973; MSN, U. Wis., 1992. RN, Wis.; cert. gerontol. and oncology nurse. Relief supr. Manpower Temp. Nursing, Wauwatosa, Wis.; mgr. St. Camillus Health Ctr., Wauwatosa; staff nurse St. Luke's Med. Ctr., Milw.; oncology rsch. coord. Sinai Samaritan Med. Ctr., Milw.; lectr. U. Wis., Milw. Mem. Oncology Nursing Soc., Wis. Nurse's Assn., Southeastern Wis. Oncology Nursing Soc. (rsch. com.), Am. Assn. Therapeutic Humor, Sigma Theta Tau. Home: 2620 N 68th St Wauwatosa WI 53213-1310

MASCHKA, DENNIS LEE, parks and recreation director; b. Wabasha, Minn., July 12, 1945; s. Leroy John and Margaret LaRue (McDonough) M.; m. Linda Ann Becchetti, Aug. 1, 1970; children: Brian Louis, Megan Anne. BS, Mankato State U., 1972, M, 1992. Dir. cmty. edn. Litchfield (Minn.) Pub. Schs., 1972-76; asst. dir. parks, recreation and forestry City of Austin, Minn., 1976-92, exec. dir. parks, recreation and forestry, 1992—. Author: The Coaches Book, 1985. Bd. dirs. Austin Youth Football, 1980—, Spruce Up Austin Com., 1989—; pres. Austin Jaycees, 1980-82; commr. Dist. 1 Softball, So. Minn., 1985—; chairperson Convention Visitors Bur., Austin, 1990-94; chair Ctrl. Catholic Sch. Bd., 1982-84. Recipient Leadership award Blanden Found., 1993; named Ten Outstanding Young Minnesotans, 1982, Outstanding Young Men Am., 1983. Mem. Minn. Park and Recreation (con. com. 1991, pres. So. chpt. 1988-90), Nat. Parks and Recreation, Austin Sports Commn. (chairperson), Austin Youth Football, Rotary Internat. Republican. Roman Catholic. Home: 2105 7th Ave SW Austin MN 55912 Office: City of Austin Parks Recreation & Forestry 121 4th Ave NE Austin MN 55912

MASCIA-STRICKLER, MARTHA, special education educator; b. Detroit, Dec. 26, 1947; d. George Amedio and Evelyn Henrietta (Jacques) Mascia; m. Jerold Strickler, Sept. 17, 1988. BS, Wayne State U., 1971; MA, Oakland U., 1977. Cert. vocat. evaluator, tchr., guidance counselor, sex edn. educator, Mich. Para-profl. Oakland Intermediate Schs., Waterford, Mich., 1966-71, tchr. spl. edn., 1971-78; curriculum cons. Pontiac (Mich.) Schs., 1978-81, vocat. evaluator, 1981—; curriculum sponsor Oakland Schs., Waterford, 1979. Author (handbook) Teacher Assistants Handbook, 1968; co-author (manual) Career Education Model, 1981. Program v.p. Oakland Audubon Soc., 1979-82, pres., editor, 1989; chpt. rep. Mich. Audubon Soc., 1990—, life mem. Recipient Cert. of Appreciation Vocat. Studies Ctr., U. Wis., 1986; scholar Alhambra Orgn., 1967-68. Mem. Mich. Assn. Vocat. Evaluation Specialists in Edn. (co-founder), Mich. Assn. Learning Disabilities Educators, Oakland County Assn. Spl. Svcs. Vocat. Cons.

MASEK, BARRY MICHAEL, accountant; b. Beatrice, Nebr., Nov. 18, 1955; s. Charles Joseph and Patricia Anne (Hynek) M.; m. Mary Ellen McNamara, Nov. 27, 1981; children: Katherine Marie, Caroline Christine, Amanda Elizabeth. BS in Acctg., U. Nebr., 1979. CPA, Nebr., Ill. Staff asst. Arthur Andersen & Co., Chgo., 1979-81, sr. acct., 1981-84, mgr. acctg. and auditing, 1984-88, sr. mgr. auditing and fin. cons., 1988-93, ptnr., 1993—. Mem. Am. Inst. CPA's, Nebr. State Soc. CPA's, Ill. State Soc. CPA's. Roman Catholic. Home: 1024 S Hamlin Ave Park Ridge IL 60068-4368 Office: Arthur Andersen & Co 33 W Monroe St Chicago IL 60603-5302

MASEK, MARK JOSEPH, laboratory administrator; b. Joliet, Ill., June 13, 1957; s. Glenn James and Helen Margaret (Gleason) M.; m. Theresa Marie Norton, Oct. 24, 1987. BJ, U. Ill., 1979. Reporter The Daily Illini, Champaign, 1976-79, Joliet Herald-News, 1978-79; columnist, editor Elgin (Ill.) Daily Courier-News, 1979-88; editor The Daily Herald, Arlington Heights, Ill., 1988-90; publs. mgr. Argonne (Ill.) Nat. Lab., 1990—. V.p. Recycle Now-Joliet, 1991—; active City of Joliet Environ. Commn., 1993-96; bd. dirs. Will County Habitat for Humanity, 1994—. Recipient 1st pl. pub. svc. award Ill. AP Editor's Assn., 3d pl. pub. svc. award, 1980, 2d pl. columns award No. Ill. Newspaper Assn., 1982, 1st pl. columns award Nat. Newspaper Assn., 1982. Mem. Soc. Profl. Journalists, Mensa. Democrat. Roman Catholic. Office: Argonne Nat Lab 9700 Cass Ave Argonne IL 60439-4803

MASON, BRUCE, advertising agency executive; b. Chgo., Dec. 20, 1939; s. William G. and Maryellen (Robb) M.; m. Diana Albery, Sept. 14, 1963; children: Jennifer, Kristin, Amy. BA, St. John's U., 1961; MBA, U. Chgo., 1963. Account exec. Leo Burnett, Chgo., 1965-69; with Foote Cone & Belding, Chgo., 1969—, dir. account mgmt., 1979-81, gen. mgr., 1981-87, pres. cen. region, 1987-88, chmn. cen. region, 1988, chmn. bd., chief exec. officer, 1991—; bd. dirs. Foote, Cone & Belding, 1987—. Capt. U.S. Army, 1963-65. Mem. Am. Assn. Advt. Agys. (reg. bd. 1987—). Office: Foote Cone & Belding Commns Inc Hdqrs 101 E Erie St Chicago IL 60611-2811

MASON, DAVID JAMES, English language educator; b. Bellingham, Wash., Dec. 11, 1954; s. James Cameron Mason and Evelyn Mae (Peterson) Brueggeman; m. Jonna Heinrich, Apr. 1, 1978 (div. 1986); m. Anne Harriet Lennox, Oct. 16, 1988; 1 stepchild, Darcy. BA, Colo. Coll., 1978; MA, U. Rochester, 1985, PhD, 1989. Screenwriter Trans World Internat., L.A., 1981-82; poetry fellow Wesleyan Writers Conf., Middletown, Conn., summer 1985; vis. instr. Colo. Coll., Colorado Springs, 1983, 87, vis. prof., 1986, 87, 88; instr. U. Rochester, N.Y., 1989—; asst. prof. English Moorhead (Minn.) State U., 1989-93, assoc. prof., 1993—. Author: (poetry) Blackened Peaches, 1989, Small Elegies, 1990, The Buried Houses, 1991, The Country I Remember, 1996; contbr. articles, poems, stories, essays and translations to profl. jours. Recipient Nicholas Roerich poetry prize, 1991, Alice Fay Di Castagnola award, 1994; Raymond Ball fellow U. Rochester, 1988. Mem. Wystan Hugh Auden Soc., Phi Beta Kappa, Phi Kappa Phi. Home: 1333 5th Ave S Moorhead MN 56560-2947 Office: Moorhead State U Dept English Moorhead MN 56563

MASON, DAVID STEWART, political science educator; b. Washington, Nov. 23, 1947; s. Richard S. and Sheila M. Mason; m. Sharon Ann Wood, June 17, 1970; children: Dana Kathryn, Melanie Elizabeth. BA, Cornell U., 1969; MA, Johns Hopkins U., 1971; PhD, Ind. U., 1978. Asst. prof. Butler U., Indpls., 1975-82, assoc. prof., 1982-90, prof., 1990—, dept. chair, 1991—. Author: Public Opinion and Political Change in Poland, 1985 (Quincy Wright award 1986), Revolution in East-Central Europe, 1992, rev. edit., 1996. Rsch. grantee Nat. Coun. for Soviet and East European Rsch., 1990-92, 96-97, Social Sci. Rsch. Coun., 1990, Am. Coun. Learned Socs., 1983. Mem. Am. Polit. Sci. Assn., Am. Assn. for Advancement of Slavic Studies, Internat. Studies Assn.-Midwest (pres. 1986-87). Democrat. Office: Butler U 4600 Sunset Ave Indianapolis IN 46208-3443

MASON, DONALD ROGER, protective services official, city official; b. Kalamazoo, June 30, 1942; s. Donald R. and Mary Jane (Anderson) M.; m. Judith Gay Thompson, Feb. 24, 1964 (div. July 1981); children: Chad A., Bredt P.; m. Katherine M. Compton, Nov. 25,1981; children: Meg E. Krueger, Stephanie Shepherd. BS in Criminal Justice, Nazareth Coll., Kalamazoo, 1980; grad., FBI Acad., Quantico, Va., 1988. Cert. EMT, police officer, firefighter, Mich.; lic. bldg. contractor, Mich.; reg. bldg. inspector, Mich. Police officer City of Otsego, Mich., 1966, City of Plainwell, Mich., 1977, City of Battle Creek, Mich., 1970-71; youth officer Portage (Mich.)

Police Dept., 1971-78; chief police City of Mendon, Mich., 1978-80; chief police, dir. emergency med. svcs. City of Belding, Mich., 1980-92, dir. pub. safety, 1992—; advisor criminal justice program Grand Valley State U., Allendale, Mich., 1984—; chmn. Emergency Dispatch Fire and Emergency Med. Svcs. Com., Ionia, Mich., 1990—. Trustee Belding Bd. Edn., 1988—; chmn., founder Miss Belding Pageant, 1988—. Sgt. USAF, 1966-70. Recipient Chief's Achievement award City of Belding, 1984, achievement award Mich. Mcpl. League, 1985. Mem. Internat. Assn. Chiefs Police, Mich. Assn. Chiefs Police (rep. 1985), West Mich. Assn. Chiefs Police (chmn. 1987), Mich. Assn. Sch. Bds., Belding Area C. of C. (pres. 1984-85, 87, 92), FBI Acad. Assocs., Masons. Republican. Methodist. Home: 207 W Congress St Belding MI 48809-1609 Office: Belding Police Dept 120 Pleasant St Belding MI 48809-1644

MASON, DORIS ANN, county official; b. Storm Lake, Iowa, Sept. 30, 1943; d. Joseph and Agnes (Zelenka) Vodicka; m. Gary Lee Smith, Mar. 21, 1962 (div. 1980); children: Barry Dee Smith, Brenda Lee Esquitin; m. Donald Ray Mason, Aug. 25, 1990. Grad. high sch., Fairmont, Nebr. Typist, clk. Hall County Treas.'s Office, Grand Island, Nebr., 1962-76; dep. treas. Hall County Treas.'s Office, Grand Island, 1976-90, treas., 1990—. Active Hall County Rep. Party, Hall County Rep. Women, Grand Island. Mem. Internat. Tng. Comm. (LaGrande chpt.), Nat. Assn. County Treas. and Fin. Officers, Nebr. Assn. County Ofcls., Grand Island C. of C., Nebr. Rep. Party Booster Club, Grand Island Luncheon Bus. and Profl. Women's Club (corr. sec. 1992), Eagles Aux., Grand Island Women's Bowling Assn. Office: Hall County Treasurer 121 S Pine St Grand Island NE 68801-6076

MASON, DOUGLAS MICHAEL, environmental scientist; b. Phila., Apr. 20, 1950; s. Clayton Douglas and Veronica Mary (Doyle) M.; m. Peng Keokamsorn, Apr. 1, 1973 (div. 1983); children: Frank, Penny; m. Josephine Ruth Joliet, June 30, 1990 (div. 1993); children: Wendy, Jonathan, Kimberly. BS, Del. Valley Coll., 1978; M in Agr., Pa. State U., 1982; PhD, U. Pa., 1993. Lab. asst. Community Coll., Phila., 1973-77; soil conservationist USDA Soil Conservation Svc., Somerset, Pa., 1977-79; rsch. asst. Pa. State U. Dept. of Agronomy, State Coll., 1979-82; soil scientist Pa. Dept. Environ. Resources, Norristown, 1982-87; agronomist/soil scientist Nat. Ctr. for Appropriate Tech., Memphis, 1987-88; soil scientist Ozark Soil Svcs., Inc., Springfield, Mo., 1988-89; dir. pollution prevention Hoosier Environ. Coun., Indpls., 1989-92; soil scientist Hoosier Soil Svcs., Inc., Indpls., 1992-93, Ind. Dept. Environ. Mgmt., Indpls., 1993-94; exec. dir. Hoosier UNCED Watch, Indpls., 1994—; environ. sci. Specialty Sys. Hazardous Waste, Inc., Indpls., 1995—; bd. dirs., Found. for Global Sustainability, Knoxville, Tenn., 1987-92, Hoosier Alliance for Consumer Rights, Indpls., 1989-92, Citizens Action Coalition, Indpls., 1990-91, Indpls. Peace and Justice Ctr., 1994—. Contbr. articles to profl. jours. Candidate, U.S. Ho. Reps., State Coll., Pa., 1980; environ. rep., Fin. AssuranceBd., Indpls., 1992; lobbyist, Hoosier Environ. Coun., Indpls., 1989-92. Sgt. USAF,1969-73. Mem. Am. Soc. Agronomy, Crop Sci. Soc. Am., Soil Sci. Soc. Am., Internat. Soc. Soil Sci., World Assn. Soil & Water Conservation, Soil & Water Conservation Soc.,Am. Registry of Cert. Profls. in Agronomy, Crops & Soils. Roman Catholic. Office: SSHW Inc Hoosier UNCED Watch 310 S State St Indianapolis IN 46201

MASON, EARL JAMES, JR., pathologist, educator b. Marion, Ind., Aug. 26, 1923; s. Earl James and Grace A. (Leer) M.; student Marion Coll., 1940-41; B.S. in Medicine, Ind. U., 1944, A.B. in Chemistry, 1947, M.A. in Bacteriology, 1947; Ph.D. in Microbiology, Ohio State U., 1950; M.D., Western Res. U., 1954; m. Eileen Gursansky, Dec. 2, 1967. Diplomate Am. Bd. Nuclear Medicine. Teaching asst. dept. bacteriology Ind. U., 1945-47; research fellow depts. ophthalmology and bacteriology Ohio State U., Columbus, 1947-48, teaching asst. dept. bacteriology, 1948-50; Crile research scholar Western Res. U., Cleve., 1951-53; Damon Runyon cancer research fellow dept. pathology Western Res. U.-Cleve. City Hosp., 1951-56; dept. chief dept. pathology USPHS Hosp., San Francisco, 1956-58; fellow pathology U. Tex. Postgrad. Sch. Medicine, M.D. Anderson Hosp. and Tumor Inst., Houston, 1958-59; asst. prof. dept. pathology Baylor U. Coll. Medicine, 1959-60; asst. pathologist Jefferson Davis Hosp., 1959-60; asst. pathologist Michael Reese Hosp. and Med. Center, Chgo., 1960-61; assoc. dir. dept. pathology, dir. dept. biol. scis. Mercy Hosp., 1960-65; dir. labs. St. Mary Med. Ctr., Gary and Hobart, Ind., 1965—; assoc. prof. pathology Chgo. Med. Sch., 1966—; clin. prof. pathology Ind. U. Med. Sch., 1976—. Diplomate Am. Bd. Pathology in anat. and clin. pathology, radioisotopic pathology and dermatopathology, Am. Bd. Nuclear Medicine. Mem. Coll. Am. Pathologists, Am. Assn. Pathologists and Bacteriologists, Am. Soc. Clin. Pathologists, Internat. Acad. Pathologists, Am. Soc. Exptl. Pathology, Am. Assn. Cancer Research, Am. Assn. Blood Banks, Am. Soc. Hematology, Am. Acad. Dermatology, Soc. Nuclear Medicine, Lake County Med. Soc., Am. Soc. Cytology, Sigma Xi. Research on cellular origin of antibodies and virus-cell interactions. Home: 64465 Via Risso Palm Springs CA 92264-0236 Office: 1500 S Lake Park Ave Hobart IN 46342-6638

MASON, JAMES W., lawyer, state legislator; b. Aug. 5, 1948; m. Betsy Mason; children: Jim, Julie, Katie. BS, St. Louis U.; JD, Ohio No. U. State rep. Dist. 25 Ohio Ho. of Reps.; mem. Bexley Bd. Zoning Appeals, Franklin County Reps. exec. com.; lawyer; adj. prof. Capital U. Law Sch.; adminstrv. dir. Ohio Supreme Bd. Commrs. Mem. adv. bd. St. Charles H.S. Mem. Ohio State Bar Assn., Columbus Bar Assn., Franklin County Trial Lawyers Assn., Bexley Lions Club, Bexley/Whitehall Rotary Club. *

MASON, LINDA, physical education educator, softball and basketball coach; b. Indpls., Jan. 29, 1946; d. Harrison Linn and Hazel Marie (Bledsoe) Crouch; divorced; children: Cassandra, Andrew. BS, Ind. U., 1968, MS, 1977. Cert. phys. edn. tchr., K-12, Ind. Tchr. phys. edn. Woodview Jr. H.S., Indpls., 1968-71; tchr. phys. edn., coach Ind. U.-Purdue U. of Indpls., 1972-76; basketball coach Butler U., Indpls., 1976-84; head softball coach, asst. basketball coach Westfield Washington High Sch., Westfield, Ind., 1985; tch. phys. edn., basketball coach Orchard Park Elementary Sch., Carmel, Ind., 1985—; elem. physical edn. tchr., Carmel-Clay Schs., Carmel, 1985—; asst. varsity coach softball, Carmel H.S., 1993-95, head varsity softball coach, 1996—; head coach Ind. Girls' H.S. All-Stars, Indpls., 1980. Named Coach of Yr. Dist. 4, Nat. Collegiate Athletic Assn., 1983. Mem. Delta Psi Kappa.

MASON, MARILYN GELL, library administrator, writer, consultant; b. Chickasha, Okla., Aug. 23, 1944; d. Emmett D. and Dorothy (O'Bar) Killebrew; m. Carl L. Gell, Dec 29 1965 (div. Oct. 1978); 1 son, Charles E.; m. Robert M. Mason, July 17, 1981. B.A., U. Dallas, 1966; M.L.S., N. Tex. State U., Denton, 1968; M.P.A., Harvard U., 1978. Libr. N.J. State Libr., Trenton, 1968-69; head dept. Arlington County Pub. Libr., Va., 1969-73; chief libr. program Metro Washington Coun. Govts., 1973-77; dir. White House Conf. on Librs. and Info. Svcs., Washington, 1979-80; exec. v.p. Metrics Rsch. Corp., Atlanta, 1981-82; dir. Atlanta-Fulton Pub. Libr., Atlanta, 1982-86, Cleve. Pub. Libr., 1986—; trustee Online Computer Library Ctr., 1984—; Evalene Parsons Jackson lectr. div. librarianship Emory U., 1981. Author: The Federal Role in Library and Information Services, 1983; editor: Survey of Library Automation in the Washington Area, 1977; project dir.: book Information for the 1980's, 1980. Bd. visitors Sch. Info. Studies, Syracuse U., 1981-85, Sch. of Libr. and Info. Sci. , U. Tenn.-Knoxville, 1983-85; trustee Coun. on Libr. Resources, Atlant, 1992—. Recipient Disting. Alumna award N. Tex. State U., 1979. Mem. ALA (mem. council 1986—), Am. Assn. Info. Sci., Ohio Library Assn., D.C. Library Assn. (pres. 1976-77). Home: 12427 Fairhill Rd Cleveland OH 44120-1015 Office: Cleve Pub Libr 325 Superior Ave E Cleveland OH 44114-1205

MASON, MARK ALAN, physical therapist; b. Omaha, Nebr., Dec. 1, 1955; s. Robert Emmett and Evelyn Pauline (Adams) M.; m. Shelley Morreen Schunk; children: Scott Andrew, Lee Alan. B.Biology, Bowling Green (Ohio) State U., 1977; B.Phys. Therapy, Ohio State U., 1980. Phys. therapist Rehab. Assocs., Cin., 1980—; tchr. kinesiology Mt. St. Joseph U., Cin., 1981-90; cons. Multiple Sclerosis Soc., Cin., 1981—. Named Care Giver of the Yr., Home Health Care Mgmt. Assn., 1990. Mem. Am. Phys. Therapy Assn. Home: 3375 Algus Ln Cincinnati OH 45248-2823

MASON, ROBERT THOMAS, theatrical lighting designer, writer; b. Detroit, Aug. 5, 1949; s. Herbert William and Edna Helen (Coll) M. BA in English and Creative Writing, U. Mo., 1975. Light bd. operator/designer Tiffany's Attic, Kansas City, Mo., 1988-90; light bd. operator Mo. Repertory Theatre, Kansas City, 1992; lighting designer Plaza Dinner Playhouse, Kansas City, 1992-94; audio engr. The New Theatre, Overland Park, Kans., 1994-95, Am. Heartland Theatre, Kansas City, 1995-96. Author: Fakin' the Blues, 1992, (screenplay) Escape From Earth, 1983, (play) Last Exit, 1976, (play adaptation) The Fall of the House of Usher, 1986. Mem. Am. Contract Bridge League (life master). Democrat.

MASON, STEPHEN OLIN, academic administrator; b. Fresno, Calif., July 11, 1952; s. Olin James and Mary Edna (Moyer) M. BA, Bridgewater (Va.) Coll., 1974; MEd, James Madison U., 1979; PhD, Loyola U., Chgo., 1991. Asst. to the dir. student ctr. Bridgewater Coll., 1974-76; guidance counselor Woodlawn Elem. Sch., Sebring, Fla., 1976-77; asst. dean for student devel. Bridgewater Coll., 1977-81; dir. student life Roger Williams Coll., Bristol, R.I., 1981-83; assoc. dean for residential svcs. Dickinson Coll., Carlisle, Pa., 1983-84; v.p., dean student affairs Westmar Coll., LeMars, Iowa, 1984; rsch. assoc. to pres. Elmhurst (Ill.) Coll., 1986-87; v.p. student affairs Felician Coll., Chgo., 1987-88; dean students Huntingdon Coll., Montgomery, Ala., 1988-90; dir. devel. McPherson (Kans.) Coll., 1990-94, v.p. fin. svcs., 1994—. Participant ARC Blood Drive, 1978-79; mem. allocations com. United Way, Carlisle, 1984; mem. adv. bd. LeMars chpt. Siouxland Coun. for Alcoholism and Drug Abuse, 1984; site coord. for coat drive Mental Health Greater Chgo., 1985; dir-at-large Bridgewater Coll. Alumni Bd., 1987-91; v.p. McPherson Habitat for Humanity, 1993, 94, bd. dirs., 1993-96, pres., 1994; bd. dirs. McPherson Mus. and Arts Found., 1992-94, Assn. Brethren Caregivers, 1993—. Mem. Am. Assn. for Higher Edn., Assn. for Study of Higher Edn., Coun. for Advancement and Support of Edn. Home: 1502 E Sharp St Mc Pherson KS 67460-3851 Office: McPherson Coll 1600 E Euclid St Mc Pherson KS 67460-3847

MASON, STEVEN CHARLES, forest products company executive; b. Sarnia, Ont., Can., Feb. 22, 1936. B.S., MIT, 1957. Pres. div. Mead Corp., Dayton, Ohio, 1978-79, group v.p., 1979-82, sr. v.p. ops., 1982, pres., chief oper. exec., 1990-92, vice chmn., 1992—, chmn., CEO, 1992—. Office: Mead Corp Courthouse Plz NE Dayton OH 45463

MASON, THOMAS ALEXANDER, historian; b. Port Huron, Mich., Oct. 29, 1944; s. Frank Hallgren and Charlotte (Hamilton) M.; m. Christine Huguette Guyonneau, Aug. 11, 1984; 1 child, Charlotte Guyonneau. BA in History with highest honors, Kenyon Coll., 1966; MA, U. Va., 1970, PhD, 1975. Asst. prof. history Pembroke (N.C.) State U., 1976-79; assoc. editor Papers of James Madison, U. Va., 1979-86, acting editor, 1986-87; dir. publs. Ind. Hist. Soc., 1987—. uthor: Serving God and Mammon: William Juxon, 1582-1663, 1985; exec. editor: Traces of Indiana and Midwestern History, 1989—; editor: Documentary Editing, 1989-93, Mag. of Albemarle County History, 1984-86; co-editor: Papers of James Madison, congl. series, vols. 14-16, 1983-89, Presidential Series, vol. 1, 1984; project dir.: Papers of Lew Wallace, 1992—; mem. editl. bd. Jour. of the Early Republic, 1991-95, Ency. of Indpls., 1990-94; contbr. articles to encys. and scholarly jours. Served with USMC, 1966-68. Mem. Am. Assn. for State and Local History, Am. Hist. Assn., N.Am. Conf. on Brit. Studies, So. Hist. Assn., Assn. Documentary Editing (dir. publs. 1995—, Disting. Svc. award 1993), Hist. Soc. of the Episcopal Ch. (sec. 1995—), English-Speaking Union (pres. Indpls. br. 1989—, chmn. region VI 1996—, Lily Dabney scholar 1972), Raven Soc., Rotary (Indpls.), Athletic Club (Indpls.), Colonnade Club (Charlottesville), Royal Commonwealth Soc. (London), Omicron Delta Kappa, Alpha Delta Phi. Episcopalian. Home: PO Box 20331 Indianapolis IN 46220-0331 Office: Ind Hist Soc 315 W Ohio St Indianapolis IN 46202-3299

MASON, WILLIAM G., state legislator; m. Betty Mason. Kans. state rep. Dist. 75, 1993—. Home: 1661 Arizona St El Dorado KS 67042-4202*

MASSENGALE, MARTIN ANDREW, agronomist, university president; b. Monticello, Ky., Oct. 25, 1933; s. Elbert G. and Orpha (Conn) M.; m. Ruth Audrey Klingelhofer, July 11, 1959; children: Alan Ross, Jennifer Lynn. BS, Western Ky. U., 1952; MS, U. Wis., 1954, PhD, 1956; LHD (hon.), Nebr. Wesleyan U., 1987; DS (hon.), Senshu U., Tokyo, 1995. Cert. profl. agronomist, profl. crop scientist. Research asst. agronomy U. Wis., 1952-56; asst. prof., asst. agronomist U. Ariz., 1958-62, assoc. prof., assoc. agronomist, 1962-65, prof., agronomist, 1965-76, head dept., 1966-74, assoc. dean Coll. Agr. assoc. dir. Ariz. Agr. Expt. Sta., 1974-76; vice chancellor for agr. and natural resources U. Nebr., 1976-81; chancellor U. Nebr.-Lincoln, 1981-91, interim pres., 1989-91; pres. U. Nebr., 1991-94, pres. emeritus, 1994, found. prof. and dir. Ctr. for Grassland Studies, 1994—; chmn. pure seed adv. com. Ariz. Agrl. Expt. Sta.; past chmn. bd., pres. Mid-Am. Internat. Agrl. Consortium; coord. com. environ. quality EPA-Dept. Agrl. Land Grand U.; past chmn. bd. dirs. Am. Registry Cert. Profls. in Agronomy, Crops and Soils; bd. dirs. Ctr. for Human Nutrition, Agronomic Sci. Found., U. Nebr. Found.; mem. exec. com. U. Nebr. Tech. Park, LLC. Chmn. NCAA Pres.'s Commn., 1988-91; distbn. revenue com., standing com. on appointments North Ctrl. Assn. Commn. on Insts. Higher Edn., 1991; trustee Nebr. State Hist. Soc.; bd. govs. Nebr. Sci. and Math. Initiative; active Knight Found. Commn. on Intercollegiate Athletics. Named Midlands Man of Yr., 1982, to We. Ky. U. Hall of Disting. Alumni, 1992, Outstanding Educator of Am., 1970; recipient faculty recognition award Tucson Trade Bur., 1971, Ak-Sar-Ben Agrl. Achievement award, 1986, Agrl. Builders Nebr. award, 1986, Walter K. Beggs award, 1986, hon. state farmer degrees Ky., Ariz., Nebr. Future Farmers of Am. Assns. Fellow AAAS (sect. chmn.), Crop Sci. Soc. Am. (past dir., pres. 1972-73, past assoc. editor), Am. Soc. Agronomy (past dir., vis. scientist program, past assoc. editor Agronomy Jour., past chmn. bd. dirs., Disting. Svc. award 1984); mem. Am. Grassland Coun., Ariz. Crop Improvement Assn. (bd. dirs.), Am. Soc. Plant Physiology, Nat. Assn. Colls. and Tchrs. Agr., Soil and Water Conservation Soc. Am., Ariz. Acad. Sci., Nebr. Acad. Sci., Agrl. Coun. Am. (bd. dirs., issues com.), Coun. Agrl. Sci. and Tech. (bd. dirs. 1979-82, 94—), Nat. Assn. State Colls. and Land Grant Univs. (chmn. com. on info. tech. 1987-94, exec. com. 1990-92, bd. dirs. 1992-94), Edn. Enging. Professions (mem. commn.), Coll. Football Assn. (chmn., bd. dirs. 1986-88), Am. Assn. State Coll. and Univs. (task force instl. resource allocation), Assn. Am. Univs. Rsch. Librs. (steering com. 1992-94), Nebr. C. of C. and Industry, Nebr. C.C. Assn. (hon.), Lincoln C. of C., Nebr. Vet. Med. Assn. (hon.), Sigma Xi, Phi Kappa Phi, Gamma Sigma Delta, Alpha Zeta, Phi Sigma, Gamma Alpha, Alpha Gamma Rho, Phi Beta Delta, Golden Key Nat. Honor Soc. Office: U Nebr 220 Keim Hall Lincoln NE 68583

MASSEY, ANDREW JOHN, conductor, composer; b. Nottingham, Eng., May 1, 1946; came to U.S., 1978; s. Henry Louis Johnson and Margaret (Park) M.; m. Sabra Ann Todd, May 29, 1982; children: Colin Sebastian, Robin Elizabeth. BA, Oxford U., 1968, MA, 1981; MA, Nottingham U., 1969. Asst. condr. The Cleve. Orch., 1978-80; assoc. condr. New Orleans Symphony, 1980-86, San Francisco Symphony, 1985-88; music dir. Fresno (Calif.) Philharmonic, 1986-93, R.I. Philharmonic, Providence, 1986-91; music dir. Toledo Symphony Orch., 1991—, also condr.; vis. scholar Brown U., Providence, 1986—. Composer incidental music (stage prodns.) Murder in the Cathedral, 1968, King Lear, 1971, A Midsummer Night's Dream, 1972. Office: care Toledo Symphony Two Maritime Plz Toledo OH 43604-1868

MASSEY, ELLEN FRANCES GRAY, language educator; b. Nevada, Mo., Nov. 14, 1921; d. Chester Harold and Pearl (Welch) Gray; m. Lane Massey, Sept. 26, 1947 (dec. Sept. 1959; children: David, Ruth, Frances. AB, U. Md., 1943; BS, U. Mo., 1945; MEd, Drury Coll., 1960. Tchr. elem. Conway (Mo.) Schs., 1957-60; tchr. h.s. Hartville (Mo.) Sch. Dist., 1960-63; tchr. English Lebanon (Mo.) Schs., 1963-86; adj. faculty Drury Coll., Springfield, Mo., 1986—; instr. elderhostel program YMCA of the Ozarks, Potosi, Mo., 1989—; spkr. Mo. Humanities Coun., 1991-93. Author: Moonsilver, 1991, award, 1991, Too Many Secrets, 1992, award, 1992, The Bequest, 1993, award, 1993, EquestriCat, 1994, A Grave Situation, 1994; editor: Bittersweet Country, 1978, Bittersweet Earth, 1985, Briarwood, 1987-89. Recipient Award of Merit Am. Assn. State and Local Historians, 1980, Ozark Heritage award Greene County (Mo.) Hist. Soc., 1980, Svc. to Edn. award Phi Delta Kappa, 1986; inducted Writers Hall of Fame, 1995. Mem. Mo. Folklore Soc. (bd. dirs.), Mo. Writers Guild, Ozark Writers League, Heartland Writers Guild, We. Writers Am., Delta Kappa Gamma (parliamentarian 1980—). Home and Office: 126 Maple Dr Lebanon MO 65536

MASSEY, JAMES EARL, clergyman, educator; b. Ferndale, Mich., Jan. 4, 1930; s. George Wilson and Elizabeth (Shelton) M.; m. Gwendolyn Inez Kilpatrick, Aug. 4, 1951. Student U. Detroit, 1949-50, 55-57; BTh, BRE, Detroit Bible Coll., 1961; AM, Oberlin Grad. Sch. Theology, 1964; postgrad. U. Mich., 1967-69; DD, Asbury Theol. Sem., 1972, Ashland Theol. Sem., 1991, Huntington Coll., 1994; Hum. D. Tuskegee U., 1995; DD Warner Pacific Coll., 1995; LittD Anderson U., 1995; postgrad. Pacific Sch. Religion, 1972, Boston Coll., 1982-83. Ordained to ministry Church of God, 1951. Assoc. minister Ch. of God, Detroit, 1951-53; sr. pastor Met. Church of God, Detroit, 1954-76, pastor-at-large, 1976; speaker Christian Brotherhood Hour, 1977-82; prin. Jamaica Sch. Theology, Kingston, 1963-66; campus minister Anderson Coll., Ind., 1969-77, asst. prof. religious studies, 1969-75, assoc. prof., 1975-80, prof. N.T. and homiletics, 1981-84; dean of chapel and univ., prof. religion and society Tuskegee U., Ala., 1984-89; dean, prof. preaching and bibl. studies Anderson (Ind.) Sch. of Theology, 1989-95, dean emeritus and disting. prof.-at-large, 1995—; chmn. Commn. on Higher Edn. in the Ch. of God, 1968-71; vice chmn. bd. publs. Ch. of God, 1968-78; dir. Warner Press, Inc. Author: When Thou Prayest, 1960; The Worshipping Church, 1961; Raymond S. Jackson, A Portrait, 1967; The Soul Under Siege, 1970; The Church of God and the Negro, 1971; The Hidden Disciplines, 1972; The Responsible Pulpit, 1973; Temples of the Spirit, 1974; The Sermon in Perspective, 1976; Concerning Christian Unity, 1979; gen. editor: Christian Brotherhood Hour Study Bible, 1979; Designing the Sermon, 1980; co-editor Interpreting God's Word for Today, 1982; editor Educating for Service, 1984; The Spiritual Disciplines, 1985, The Bridge Between, 1988, Preaching From Hebrews, 1992, The Burdensome Joy of Preaching, 1996; mem. editl. bd. The Christian Scholar's Rev. Leadership mag.; mem. editorial bd., contbg. editor Vol. I New Interpreter's Bible, 1990—; contbg. editor Preaching mag.; sr. editor Christianity Today Mag. Mem. Corp. Inter-Varsity Christian Fellowship; bd. dirs. World Vision. Served with AUS, 1951-53. Rsch. scholar Christianity Today Inst. Mem. Nat. Assn. Coll. and Univ. Chaplains, Nat. Com. Black Churchmen, Nat. Negro Evang. Assn. (bd. dirs. 1969-86). Office: 201 Mill Stream Ln Anderson IN 46011-1916

MASSEY, JAMES L., investment banker; b. Cairo, Ga., Feb. 9, 1943; s. Robert L. and Grace P. (Pinson) M.; m. Sue Ann Jameson, Oct. 9, 1971; children—Vaughn Elizabeth, Lee Jameson. BA, Fla. State U., 1965; MBA, Emory U., 1967. With Salomon Bros. Inc., 1967—; instnl. sales rep N.Y.C., 1967-74; regional mgr. Atlanta, 1974-79; nat. sales mgr., gen. ptnr. N.Y.C., 1979-82, exec. com., 1982—, vice chmn., 1988—; chmn., CEO Salomon Bros. Europe Ltd., London, 1988—; honorary managing dir. Salomon Bros., N.Y.C., 1992—. Trustee Greenwich Acad., 1984—, vice chmn. bd.; bd. dirs. Film Soc. of Lincoln Ctr., N.Y.C. Republican. Episcopalian. Home: 99 Round Hill Rd Greenwich CT 06831-3722

MASSEY, TODD A., investment banker, consultant; b. Mankato, Minn., Nov. 5, 1962; s. Ronald Gene and Karen Diane (Rand) M. BA in English Lit., Beloit (Wis.) Coll., 1985. Editor Grant Thornton, Chgo., 1986-87; owner Beloit Trading Group, Palatine, Ill., 1987-95; v.p., owner Practice Support Corp., Wisconsin Rapids, 1990-95; ptnr. Massey-Ehredt, Ltd., Princeton, Ill., 1991-95; pres. Rand Bros. and Co., Inc., Princeton, Ill., 1995; dir. Beloit Trading Group, Princeton, Ill., 1993-95. Dir. Ill. Valley Youth Symphony, Ogelsby, 1994-95; co-mgr., campaign Johnson Bur. County Sheriff, Princeton, Ill., 1994, Clayton Mayor of Princeton, Ill., 1995. Mem. Optimist Club, Elks Lodge. Home: 410 N Putnam Princeton IL 61356 Office: Massey-Ehredt Ltd 28 E Marion St Princeton IL 61556

MASSEY, VINCENT, biochemist, educator; b. Berkeley, New South Wales, Australia, Nov. 28, 1926; s. Walter and Mary Ann (Mark) M.; m. Margot Grunewald, Mar. 4, 1950; children: Charlotte, Andrew, Rachel. BSc with honors, U. Sydney, Australia, 1947; PhD, U. Cambridge, Eng., 1953; DSc (hon.), U. Tokushima, 1994. Mem. research staff Henry Ford Hosp., Detroit, 1955-57; lectr. to sr. lectr. U. Sheffield, 1957-63; prof. Med. Sch. U. Mich., Ann Arbor, 1963-95, J. Lawrence Oncley Disting. U. prof., 1995—; mem. biochemistry-biophysics rev. panel NSF, 1980-84; mem. fellowship rev. panel NIH, 1965-69, mem. biochemistry study sect. NIH, 1972-76, chmn. 1974-76. Contbg. author numerous books.; co-editor Flavins and Flavoproteins, 1982; contbr. numerous articles, chiefly on oxidative enzymology, to profl. jours. Recipient Alexander von Humboldt U.S. Sr. Scientist award, 1973-74, 86; Imperial Chem. Industries Research fellow, 1953-55. Fellow Royal Soc. London; mem. NAS, Biochem. Soc., Am. Soc. Biochemistry and Molecular Biology (membership com. 1970, nominating com. 1978-80, chmn. 1979-80, chmn. program com. 1992-93), Am. Chem. Soc. (exec. bd. divsn. biol. chemistry 1975-77). Home: 2536 Bedford Rd Ann Arbor MI 48104-4008 Office: U Mich Med Sch Dept Biol Chemistry Ann Arbor MI 48109

MASSIE, SAMUEL PROCTOR (TREI), III, insurance company executive; b. Nashville, May 28, 1958; s. Samuel Proctor Jr. and Gloria Belle (Thompkins) M.; m. Michelle Kyle Anderson, May 28, 1988; 1 child, Victoria Michelle. BA, Amherst Coll., 1980; MBA, Vanderbilt U., 1984, JD, 1984. Fin. analyst Ryder Systems Inc., Miami, Fla., 1984-85; fin. mgr. IBM, Lexington, Ky., 1985-90; product mgr. Progressive, Richmond Heights, Ohio, 1990—. Cluster leader YMCA Black Achievers, Lexington, 1987-90. Recipient Young Achievers award Black Young Christians Assn., Miami, 1985, Black Achievers award UMCA, 1990; NSF grantee Yale U., 1981-82. Mem. Am. Mgmt. Assn., Kappa Alpha Psi. Episcopalian. Home: 906 Nela View Rd Cleveland OH 44112-2353

MASSINGILL, JOHN LEE, JR., research director; b. Lufkin, Tex., Aug. 18, 1941; s. John Lee Massingill and Bernice (King) Hartley; m. Janice Lee Massingill, Mar. 23, 1963; children: John Lee III, Joseph Lee. BA in Chemistry, Tex. Christian U., 1963, MS in Analytical Chemistry, 1965, PhD in Organic Chemistry, 1968. Sr. rsch. chemist Basic Rsch. Dow Chem., Freeport, Tex., 1968; devel. assocs. Resins R&D Dow Chem., Freeport, Tex., 1970-93; dir. Coatings Rsch. Inst. Ea. Mich. U., Ypsilanti, 1993—; dir. Paint Rsch. Assoc. Labs. Inc., 1993-94; cons. Exxon Chem. Co., Baytown, Tex., 1994. Contbr. articles to profl. jours.; patentee in field. Capt. U.S. Army, 1968-70. Mem. Am. Chem. Soc., Detroit Soc. Coatings Tech. Republican.

MASSMANN, ROBERT, mechanical engineer; b. Williamsburg, Va., Dec. 27, 1948. BS in Mech. Engring., Ohio No. U., 1977. Mech. engr. Warner Swaysey, Cleve., 1977-83, Cin. (Ohio) Milacron, 1984—. Patentee in field. With USN, 1972-75.

MASSURA, EILEEN KATHLEEN, family therapist; b. Chgo., July 25, 1925; d. John William and Loretta (Feil) Statemeier; m. Edmund Karamanski, July 24, 1948 (dec.); children: John, Kathleen; m. Alfred Massura, Aug. 30, 1963; children: Michael, Kathryn, Mark. BS in Nursing, DePaul U., 1963; MS in Nursing, St. Xavier Coll., 1971. RN; cert. family therapist. Dir. nurses Franklin Blvd. Hosp., Chgo., 1958-62; adminstr. Mich. Ave Hosp., Chgo., 1962-64; instr. St. Xavier Coll., Chgo., 1972-74, Joliet (Ill.) Jr. Coll., 1972-81; family therapist Oak Lawn (Ill.) Family Svc., 1978-88; prof. nursing Govs. State U., University Park, Ill., 1981-89; family therapist McCarthy & Assocs., Oak Lawn, 1982-93, Massura & Assocs., Oak Lawn, 1994—; preceptor to grads. St. Xavier Coll., 1980-90, Govs. State U., 1980-89; co-leader Clin. Study Med./Surg. Nursing, Moscow, 1984; presenter Am. Nursing Rev., Ala., Fla., Va., Pa., Tex., Md., 1985-86. Leader Campfire Girls, Oak Lawn, 1964-74; co-leader Orient/Am. Med./ Surg. Nursing, 1987; mem. Marist Women's Bd., Chgo., 1978-82, Bro. Rice Women's Bd., Chgo., 1969-72; Luth. Family Svc. Bd. Day Care for Srs., 1988-89. Grantee HEW, 1969-71; named Disting. Nurse Alumnae, St. Xavier Coll., 1985; named Nursing Prof. of Yr., Govs. State U., 1983. Mem. Am. Nurses Assn. (nominating com. 1982-87), Ill. Nurses Assn. (program com. 1980-84), Am. Assn. Marital and Family Therapists, Cath. Order Foresters, Sigma Theta Tau (v.p. 1971-75). Roman Catholic. Office: 5660 W 95th St Oak Lawn IL 60453-2380

MAST, KANDE WHITE, artist; b. St. Louis, Mar. 10, 1950; d. Elliott Maxwell and Mary (Barritt) W. Student, U. Mo., 1968-70, Longview Community Coll., Kansas City, Mo., 1970-71. Free-lance artist Albany, N.Y., 1973-74, Kansas City, 1974—; dir., tchr. Studio Kande, Sch. Fine Arts, Kansas City, 1983-86; founder, exec. dir. Art Ctr. Kansas City, 1986-90. Pres., bd. dirs. Advocates for Children, Inc., 1996—; vol. Ozanam Home for Boys, Kansas City, 1987—, mem. adv. bd., 1991—. Mem. Nat. Mus. Women in the Arts, Greater Kansas City Art Assn. Home and Office: 10243 Cedarbrooke Ln Kansas City MO 64131-4209

MAST, MAE JERENE, nurse; b. Drenthe, Mich., Feb. 13, 1922; d. Henry R. and Hattie (Brouwer) M. Diploma in Nursing, Blodgett Meml. Sch. Nursing, 1953; Diploma, Frontier Nursing Service/Midwifery, 1960. Grad. nurse Blodgett Meml. Hosp., Grand Rapids, Mich., 1953; missionary RN Sudan United Mission Nigeria (West Africa) Christian Reformed Bd. World Missions, 1954-79; staff RN geriatrics nursing home Zeeland, Mich., 1980—. Tchr. Spl. Edn. MInistries, Zeeland, 1984-91. Home: Apt 119 230 S State St Bldg 18 Zeeland MI 49464

MASTELLER, BRUCE ALLEN, exercise specialist; b. Atlantic, Iowa, June 19, 1961; s. Curtis Campbell and Rosalie E. (Schaaf) M. BA in Edn., Buena Vista Coll., 1983; 1985-88. Student activities coord. Buena Vista Coll., Storm Lake, Iowa, 1983-85; grad. asst. St. Cloud (Minn.) State Univ., 1986-88; exercise specialist Our Lady of Lourdes Hosp., Norfolk, Nebr., 1988—; treas. Student Health Fund, Norfolk, 1991—. With Planned Approach to Community Health, Norfolk, 1991—; bd. dirs. Madison County Div. Am. Heart Assn., Norfolk, 1990—, pres. 1993—; with Norfolk United Way, 1993—. Mem. Norfolk Jr. C. of C. Presbyterian. Office: Our Lady of Lourdes Hosp 1500 Koenigstein Ave Norfolk NE 68701-3664

MASTERS, BRUCE ALLEN, biostratographer, micropaleontologist; b. Terre Haute, Ind., Nov. 3, 1936; s. Cletus Hunter and Eva Lee (Osburn) M.; m. Shirley Ann Howard, Apr. 11, 1963 (dec.); m. Linda Maureen Branson, Apr. 29, 1996. BS, Valparaiso U., Ind., 1959; MA, U. Calif.-Berkeley, 1962; PhD, U. Ill.-Urbana, 1970. Assoc. geologist Humble Oil and Refining Co., Houston, 1962-65; assoc. prof. Hartwick Coll., Oneonta, N.Y., 1969-74; spl. rsch. assoc. Amoco Prodn. Co., Tulsa, 1974-92; pres. MasterStrat Internat., Fairbanks, Ind., 1992—; biostratigraphic cons.; mem. adv. bd. Micropaleontology Press Am. Mus. Natural Hist. Author: Oceanic Micropalaeontology, 1977. Contbr. articles to profl. jours. Mem. Am. Assn. Petroleum Geologists, Paleontol. Rsch. Instn., Paleontol. Assn., Cushman Found., Brit. Micropalaeontology Soc., Swiss Geol. Soc.

MASTERS, WILLIAM ALAN, agricultural economist; b. Chgo., Apr. 23, 1961; s. Roger Davis Masters and Judith Anne (Rubin) Bush; m. Mia Lewis, Sept. 10, 1988; children: Zoe, Beatrice. BA, Yale Coll., 1984; MA, Stanford U., 1986, PhD, 1991. Rsch. assoc. U. Zimbabwe, Harare, 1988-90; asst. prof. Purdue U., West Lafayette, Ind., 1991-96, assoc. prof., 1996—; cons. ICRISAT, Bulawayo, Zimbabwe, 1989, World Bank, Harare, 1990, U.S. AID, Harare, 1992, 95. Author: Government and Agriculture in Zimbabwe, 1994; contbr. articles to profl. jours. Harry S. Truman Found. scholar, 1981-87; Fulbright grantee, 1988-89; rsch. fellow Rockefeller Found., 1990. Mem. Am. Agrl. Econs. Assn., Am. Econs. Assn., African Studies Assn., Internat. Agrl. Trade Rsch. Consortium. Office: Purdue U Dept Agrl Econs West Lafayette IN 47907

MASTIN, TIMOTHY JAY, public relations professional; b. Rochester, N.Y., Mar. 14, 1965; s. William Carlton and Viola May (Rohring) M. Student, U. Rochester, 1983-84; BA, So. Nazarene U., 1988; postgrad., Nazarene Theol. Sem., 1989. Teller Guaranty Bank and Trust, Oklahoma City, 1985-86; v.p. campus ministries So. Nazarene U., Bethany, Okla., 1986-88; coord. program and promotion Nazarene Compassionate Ministries, Kansas City, Mo., 1988-95; asst. to dir. Nazarene Compassionate Ministries Resource Devel., Kansas City, 1995—; program dir. Coll. and Univ. Students Serving &Enabling, Kansas City, Mo., 1990—. Editor newsletter The Bridge, 1988—; contbr. articles to religious publs. Vol. Rep. Hdqrs., Oklahoma City, 1984, Kansas City, 1992; social coord. Bethany First Ch. of Nazarene, 1986-88; denomination liaison Kansas City Crop Hunger Walk, 1988; vol. Kansas City Rescue Mission, 1991; coord. Youth in Mission program Nazarene Youth Internat., Kansas City, 1994-95. Office: Nazarene Compassionate Ministries 6401 Paseo Blvd Kansas City MO 64131-1213

MASTRIANA, ROBERT ALAN, architect; b. Youngstown, Ohio, July 6, 1949; s. Fred Paul and Rose L. (Fusco) M.; m. Kathy Ann Peloe, June 26, 1971; children: Robert Byron, Kathryn Olivia. BArch, Kent State U., 1972, U. D'Florence (Italy), 1972. Registered profl. architect, Fla., N.J., Ohio, Pa., Tenn., Tex., W.Va., Va.; cert. gen. contractor, Fla. Project architect Allan M. Sveda, Architect, Cuyahoga Falls, Ohio, 1972-75; pvt. practice architect Poland, Ohio, 1976-78; ptnr., architect 4M Co., Youngstown, 1978—; mem., past chmn. City of Youngstown Design Rev. Bd.; past chmn. Poland Village Design Rev. Bd.; past asst. chmn. Poland Bd. Appeals; tchr. archtl. awareness class to realtors for continuing edn. Trustee Circle of Butler Art; past trustee Poland Twp. Hist. Soc.; patron Youngstown Symphony Soc.; past asst. chmn. bd. trustees 1st Covenant Ch.; mem. adv. bd. YMCA, Kent State U. Sch. Arch.; mem. Nat. Trust Histo. Preservation. Recipient Builder award Poland Masonic Lodge, 1988, Charles Marr award Archtl. Soc. Ohio Found., 1990, Barvikski Meml. award, 1983; Paul Harris fellow Boardman Rotary, 1988. Mem. AIA (past pres. Ohio chpt., past treas., state conv. chmn., design awards chmn., past pres. Ea. Ohio chpt., past v.p., bd. dirs.), Am. Archtl. Found., Ohio Archtl. Found. (bd. dirs.), Youngstown Warren Region C. of C. (civic improvements award com.), Dover Club, Rotary, Fellowship Christian Athletes, Phi Gamma Delta. Home: 34 Botsford St Youngstown OH 44514-1755 Office: 4M Company 4251 Glenwood Ave Ste 3 Youngstown OH 44512-1062

MASTROROCCO, KEVIN SAMUEL, mechanical engineer; b. Greenburg, Jan. 14, 1965. BSME, U. Cin., 1991. Mech. engr. Mutlifold Internat., Milford, Ohio, 1991—. Office: Multifold Internat 1300 US 50 Milford OH 45150

MATANKY, ARNIE, publisher; b. Oak Park, Ill., June 25, 1930; s. Harry and Mary (Jakobowsky) M. AA, Wright Coll., 1950; postgrad., U. Chgo., 1954-55. City desk asst. Chgo. Sun, 1947; with Chgo. Jour. of Commerce, 1948; editor radio news Community News Service, Chgo., 1948-51; news editor CBS News, Chgo., 1953-59; owner, operator Info. Cons., Chgo., 1959-71, 80—; dir. pub. info. Chgo. Park Dist., 1971-80; pub. Near North News, Chgo., 1956—. Contbg. editor Public Relations, 1970; editor Africa File. Pres. Lincoln Park Villas Condominium Assn., Chgo., 1978-91, Park Synagogue, Chgo., 1970-72, Sandburg Village Coun., Chgo., 1970-72; chmn. 18th Dist. Community Police Coun., Chgo., 1969-71; bd. dirs. Internat. Visitors Ctr., 1972-82; bd. overseers Nat. Ctr. for Freedom of Info. Studies. Sgt. 1st class U.S. Army, 1951-53. Mem. Am. Legion (comdr. 1958-59, vice chmn. fgn. rels. coun., vice comdr. dept. of France, pres. Fgn. and Outlying Depts. and Posts), Nat. Am. Vets. Press Assn. (pres. 1977-79), Internat. Press Club Chgo. (pres. 1991—), Chgo. Coun. on Fgn. Rels., Libr. of Internat. Rels., Psywar Soc. (U.K.), Jewish War Vets., Am. Topical Assn., Am. Philatelic Soc., UN Philatelists, Brit. Am. Postal Cover Soc., Amnesty Internat., Assn. of Former Intelligence Officers, Hugo's Companions (pres. 1991), Arthur Conan Doyle Soc., Chinese Passenger Traffic Club (v.p.), Travelers Century Club, Kiwanis (pres. Near North Chgo.), B'nai B'rith (pres. 1965-67), Near North Assn. Condominium Pres. (sec. 1990—). Home: 10 E Ontario St Chicago IL 60610-2756 Office: Near North News 502 222 W Ontario St Chicago IL 60610-3695

MATANKY, ROBERT WILLIAM, lawyer; b. Chgo., Dec. 26, 1955; s. Eugene and Gertrude (Shiner) M.; m. Lee Mindy Frankel, Sept. 1, 1985; chldren: Ruth Michele, Eugene David, Kathryn Sarah, Ariella Aliza, Jacob Edward. BS in Engring., U. Ill., 1977; JD, Ill. Inst. Tech., 1980; A in Hebrew Lit., Hebrew Theol. Coll., 1980; MBA in Fin., U. Chgo., 1990. Bar: Ill. 1980, U.S. Dist. Ct. (no. dist.) Ill. 1980, U.S. Ct. Appeals (7th cir.) 1980, U.S. Supreme Ct. 1984; lic. real estate broker, Ill.; lic. ins. broker, Ill. Traffic coord. Chgo. Rock Island & Pacific R.R. Co., Chgo., 1978-79; assoc. Holobow & Taslitz, Chgo., 1980-81; corp. counsel Matanky Realty Group, Chgo., 1981-84, asst. v.p., 1984-86, v.p., 1987—; ptnr. Kreisler & Matanky, Chgo., 1982—. Editor Decalogue Jour., 1985-92. Co-chmn. lawyers divsn. Jewish United Fund, 1983-90; bd. dirs. Hebrew Theol. Coll., Skokie, Ill., 1985—, Jewish Nat. Fund, Chgo., 1984—, Congregation Ezras Israel, Chgo., 1983—, Congregation K.I.N.S. of West Rogers Park, 1994—; bd. dirs. Assoc. Talmud Torahs, Chgo., 1983—, v.p., 1986—; mem. bd. govs. The Hillels of Ill., 1986—, State of Israel Bonds, 1987—; mem. bd. advisors Mt. Sinai Hosp. North, 1988; co-founder, bd. dirs. Chgo. Eruv, Inc., 1992—, pres., 1994—. Recipient Pub. Svc. award Assoc. Talmud Torahs, 1993. Mem. Nat. Assn. Realtors (comml. investment mem. Real Estate Inst. 1992), Chgo. Bar Assn. (real estate tax com. 1993—), Decalogue Soc. Lawyers (bd. mgrs. 1979—, pres. 1986-87, Intra-Soc. award 1985), Inst. Indsl. Engrs., Chgo. Bd. Realtors (active prin. 1985—), Real Estate Securities and Syndication Inst. (designations rev. bd. 1986-90), Ill. Assn. Realtors (State Legis. contact), Chgo. Bd. Realtors Peer Rev. Panel (arbitration com. 1986—). Office: Kreisler & Matanky 1332 N Halsted St Ste 300 Chicago IL 60622-2637

MATASOVIC, MARILYN ESTELLE, business executive; b. Chgo., Jan. 7, 1946; d. John Lewis and Stella (Butkauskas) M. Student, U. Colo. Sch. Bus., 1963-69. Owner, pres. UTE Trail Ranch, Ridgway, Colo., 1967—; pres. MEM Equipment Co., Mokena, Ill., 1979—; sec./treas. Marlin Corp., Ridgway, 1991—, v.p., sec.-treas., 1991—; sec.-treas. Linmar Corp., Mokena, 1991-93, pres., 1994—; ptnr. Universal Welding Supply Co., New Lenox, Ill., 1964-90; v.p. OXO Welding Equipment Co, Inc., New Lenox, 1964-90; ptnr. Universal Internat., Mokena, Ill., 1990—; ind. travel agt. Ideal Travel Concepts, Mokena, Ill., 1994—. Co-editor newsletters. U.S. rep. World Hereford Conf., 1964, 68, 76, 80, 84, 96. Mem. Am. Hereford Aux. (charter, bd. dirs. 1989-94, historian 1990-92, v.p. 1992, pres.-elect 1993, pres. 1994), Am. Hereford Assn., Am. Hereford Women (charter, pres. 1994, bd. dirs. 1994—), Am. Agri-Women, Colo. Hereford Aux., Ill. Hereford Aux. (v.p. 1969-70), U. Colo. Alumni Assn., Ill. Agri-Women, Las Vegas Social Register.

MATCHETT, ANDREW JAMES, mathematics educator; b. Chgo., Jan. 30, 1950; s. Gerald James and Margaret Ellen (Stump) M.; m. Nancy Valentine Stasack, Aug. 7, 1976; children: Gerald Albert, Philip Joseph, Melanie Jeanne. BS, U. Chgo., 1971; PhD, U. Ill., 1976. Grad. teaching asst. U. Ill., Urbana, 1971-76; asst. prof. Tex. A&M U., College Station, 1976-82; asst. prof. U. Wis., La Crosse, 1982-86, assoc. prof., 1986—; dir. Consortium for Core Math. Curriculum, Wis., 1987-88. Contbr. articles to profl. jours. Chmn. troop 18 com. Boy Scouts Am., La Crosse, 1990, charter rep. troop 18, 1992-94, scoutmaster, 1994—. Mem. AAAS, Am. Math. Soc., Am. Statis. Assn., Math. Assn. Am. (sec.-treas. Wis. sect. 1989—). Unitarian. Home: 327 24th St N La Crosse WI 54601-3850 Office: U Wis Dept Math 1725 State St La Crosse WI 54601-3742

MATCHETTE, PHYLLIS LEE, editor; b. Dodge City, Kans., Dec. 24, 1921; d. James Edward and Rose Mae (McMillan) Collier; A.B. in Journalism, U. Kans., 1943; m. Robert Clarke Matchette, Dec. 4, 1943; children: Marta Susan, James Michael. Reporter, Dodge City Daily Globe, 1944; tchr. English, Dodge City Jr. High Sch., 1944-45; asst. instr. Coll. Liberal Arts, U. Kans., Lawrence, 1945-47; dir. Christian edn. Southminster United Presbyn. Ch., Prairie Village, Kans., 1963-65; editor publs., dir. communications, supr. in-plant printing Village United Presbyn. Ch., Prairie Village, 1965-86 ; freelance journalist, 1987-91. Hon. mem. Commn. of Ecumenical Mission and Relations, hon. mem. Program Agy., Presbyn. Ch., U.S.A.; ordained elder Village Presbyn. Ch., 1964, elected elder, 1988-90. Mem. D.A.R., Women in Communications, Kans. U. Dames (pres. 1946), Kansas City Young Matrons, P.E.O., Alpha Chi Omega (pres. edn. found. Phi chpt. 1951). Republican. Club: Order of Eastern Star. Home: 7405 El Monte St Shawnee Mission KS 66208-2968

MATERNE, DAVID, software and distribution company executive; b. Detroit, Jan. 20, 1956; s. Roland Albert and Marian Johanna (Kane) M.; m. Carolyn Lee Carlton, Dec. 6, 1980. BS in Acctg. and Bus. summa cum laude, Wayne State U., Detroit, 1978. CPA, Mich. Acct. KPMG Peat, Marwick, Detroit, 1978-82; asst. v.p., corp. contr. Perry Drug Stores, Pontiac, Mich., 1982-85; pres. equipment and supply divsn. Domino's Pizza, Inc., Ann Arbor, Mich., 1985-92; pres. Ptnrs. in Dough, Inc., Anchorage, 1991-92; v.p. Domino's Pizza Distbn. Corp., Ann Arbor, 1986-92; v.p. fin. and adminstrn. New World Sys. Corp. Computer Software, Troy, Mich., 1992—; cons. Innovation Network, Ann Arbor, 1989-92. Author: Keeping Score: Improving Quality With An Innovative Bonus System, 1989. Treas., Holy Redeemer Ch., Warren, Mich., 1979-80. Mem. AICPAs, Mich. Assn. CPAs, Nat. Assn. Chain Drug Stores (fin. stds. com. 1983-85). Home: 10279 Lakeside White Lake MI 48386-2241 Office: New World Sys Corp Ste 1100 888 W Big Beaver Rd Troy MI 48084-9999

MATHAY, JOHN PRESTON, elementary education educator; b. Youngstown, Ohio, Jan. 27, 1942; s. Howard Ellsworth and Mary Clara (Siple) M.; m. Sandra Elizabeth Rhoades, June 9, 1973 (div. Jan. 1986); children: Elizabeth Anne, Sarah Susannah; m. Judith Anne Matthy, June 19, 1988; 1 child, Andrew Micah. B History, Va. Mil. Inst., Lexington, 1964; Cert. Teaching, Cleve. State U., 1972; postgrad., Mich. State U., 1964-65; MEd, Westminster Coll., New Wilmington, 1986. Cert. asst. supt., elem. tchr., elem. prin., high sch. prin. Cabinet maker Artisian Cabinet, Orwig Cabinets, Cleve. and Howland, Ohio, 1970-72; tchr. Urban Community Sch., Cleve., 1972-73, Pymatuning Valley Schs., Andover, Ohio, 1973—; cross country coach, 7th and 8th grade track coach, Andover. Bd. mem. Badger Sch. Bd., Kinsman, Ohio; trustee Kinsman Libr.; trustee, elder Kinsman Presbyn. Ch. Capt. U.S. Army Res., 1966-69. Martha Holden Jennings Found. scholar, Cleve., 1976. Mem. ASCD, Pymatuning Valley Edn. Assn. (pres. 1975-76, 91-92, 94-95), Ohio Edn. Assn., Am. Legion, Rotary (pres. 1991-92, sec. 1992-93, Paul Harris fellow), Masons (jr. deacon 1984-85, 32d deg., York Rite commandery), Ashtabula County Antique Engine Club, Phi Delta Kappa. Republican. Presbyterian. Home: 8424 Main St Kinsman OH 44428-9409 Office: Pymatuning Valley Schs W Main St Andover OH 44003

MATHER, GEORGE ROSS, clergy member; b. Trenton, N.J., June 1, 1930; s. Samuel Wooley and Henrietta Elizabeth (Deardorff) M.; m. Doris Christine Anderson, June 28, 1958; children: Catherine Anne Mather-Grimes, Geoffrey Thomas. BA, Princeton U., 1952; MDiv, Princeton Theol. Sem., 1955; DD, Hanover Coll., 1986. Ordained to Ministry, 1955. Asst. pastor Abington (Pa.) Presbyn., 1955-58; pastor 1st Presbyn. Ch. Ewing, Trenton, 1958-71; sr. pastor 1st Presbyn. Ch. Ft. Wayne, Ind., 1971-86; pastor 3d Presbyn. Ch. Ft. Wayne, Ind., 1987-95. Author: Frontier Faith: The Story of the Pioneer Congregations, 1992; co-editor: On the Heritage Trail, 1994; contbr. articles to profl. jours. Pres. Allen County Libr. Trustees, Ft. Wayne, Allen County Libr. Found., Ft. Wayne, Clergy United for Action, Ft. Wayne; trustee Hanover (Ind.) Coll.; chmn. Bicentennial Religious Heritage Commn., 1994; bd. dirs. Smock Found., 1971-85. Mem. Ind. Religious History Assn. (bd. dirs.), Allen County Ft. Wayne Hist. Soc. (bd. dirs.), The Quest Club (pres.). Home: 6669 Quail Ridge Ln Fort Wayne IN 46804

MATHER, ROGER FREDERICK, music educator, freelance technical writer; b. London, England, May 27, 1917; came to U.S., 1938; s. Richard and Marie Louise (Schultze) M.; m. Dorothea Meinen, Sept. 11, 1943 (div. Sept. 1971); children: Arielle Diane, Christopher Richard; m. Betty Louise Bang, Aug. 3, 1973. BA with honors, Cambridge U., 1938; MSc, MIT, 1940; MA in Metallurgy, U. Cambridge, 1941. Registered profl. engr., Ohio, Mich., Pa. Rsch. metallurgist Inland Steel Co., East Chicago, Ind., 1940-42; chief metallurgist Willys-Overland Motors, Toledo, 1942-46, Kaiser-Frazer Corp., Willow Run, Mich., 1946-50; project mgr. U.S. Steel Corp., Pitts., 1950-61; dir. rsch. engring. Mine Safety Appliances Co., Pitts., 1961-62; rsch. staff Du Pont Co., Wilmington, Del., 1962-63; chief nuclear power tech. br. NASA, Cleve., 1963-73; adj. prof. music U. Iowa, Iowa City, 1973-96; instr. pub. speaking and stage fright U. Iowa, 1983-85, Kirkwood C.C., Iowa City, 1983-85; cons. Miyazawa Flutes, U.S.A., Coralville, Iowa, 1985-90; lectr. U. Toledo; Mich. state examiner Registration of Profl. Engrs.; condr. numerous workshops, clinics, classes, and flute recitals regionally, nationally, and abroad. Author: The Art of Playing the Flute, 1980, 2d vol., 1981; author chpts. in Woodwind Anthology and Fluting and Dancing; pub., exec. editor The Romney Press, 1980—; contbr. numerous articles to sci. and music jours. Mem. Nat. Flute Assn. (life, coms.), Nat. Assn. Coll. Wind and Percussion Instrs., Am. Mus. Instrument Soc., Nat. Assn. Mus. Instruments Techs., Am. Recorder Soc., Galpin Soc., Brit. Flute Soc., Soc. Automotive Engrs., AIME, Am. Soc. Metals, ASTM, ASME, AIAA, Soc. Experimental Stress Analysis, Air Force Assn., Army Ordnance Assn., NAM (rsch. com.), The Pa. Assn., Mensa. Episcopalian. Home: 308 4th Ave Iowa City IA 52245-4613 Office: U Iowa Sch Music Iowa City IA 52242

MATHERN, TIM, state senator, social worker; b. Edgeley, N.D., Apr. 19, 1950; s. John J. and Christina (Wolf) M.; m. Lorene Randall Mathern, Feb. 12, 1971; children: Rebecca, Tonya, Joshua, Zachary. BA, N.D. State U., 1971; MSW, U. Nebr., Omaha, 1980. Dir. of devel. Cath. Family Svc., Fargo, N.D., 1972—; mem. N.D. State Senate, Bismarck, 1986—, chmn. health and comms. com., 1993-95, mem. legis. mgmt. com., 1993—, asst. minority leader, 1993-95, 95—; mem. political subdivsn. com., N.D., 1995—. Mem. Fargo-Cass County Econ. Devel. Corp., 1993—, Nat. Family Life Ministries; asst. minority leader N.D. Senate, 1992—, Judicial Standards Com. Named Legislator of Yr., Red River Valley Mental Health Assn., 1989, 91, Legislator of Yr., N.D. Children's Caucus, 1993. Mem. NASW (Social Worker of Yr. award 1987), Mental Health Assn. Democrat. Roman Catholic. Home: 406 Elmwood Fargo ND 58103-4315 Office: 2537 S University Fargo ND 58103-5736

MATHESON, MAX SMITH, physical chemical researcher; b. McGill, Nev., May 24, 1913; s. Henry Thompson and Ethel (Smith) M.; m. Gladys Mulchahey, Sept. 30, 1939 (div. 1965); children: Linda J., Marc E.; m. Georgine M. Modica, Apr. 29, 1967 (dec. Dec. 1995); 1 child, Jean S. Fornango. AB, U. Utah, 1936; PhD, U. Rochester, 1940. Rsch. chemist Gen. Labs., U.S. Rubber Co., Passaic, N.J., 1940-50; assoc. chemist Argonne (Ill.) Nat. Lab., 1950-52, sr. chemist, 1952-79, dir. chem. div., 1965-71, group leader, 1971-79, cons., 1979-90; temporary employee Argonne (Ill.) Nat. Lab., Lemont, Ill., 1990—; adj. prof. U. Utah, Salt Lake City, 1982-85; chmn. Gordon Conf. Radiation Chem., New Hampton, N.H., 1960; vis. prof. Hebrew U., Jerusalem, 1972. Author: (with others) Photocatalysis in Organized Assemblies, 1989; contbr. articles to profl. jours. Fellowship Guggenheim Found., 1960-61. Mem. AAAS, Am. Chem. Soc. (com. internat. activities 1968-73), Am. Phys. Soc., Radiation Rsch. Soc. (council 1975-78), Phi Beta Kappa, Phi Kappa Phi. Office: Argonne Nat Lab 9700 Cass Ave Lemont IL 60439-4803

MATHEW, MARTHA SUE CRYDER, retired education educator; b. Hallsville, Ohio, Feb. 21, 1928; d. Earl and Minnie Ada (Hough) Cryder; m. Guy Wilbur Mathew, Mar. 25, 1949; children: John G., Jeffrey Bruce. BS, Ohio No. U., 1966. Cert. tchr., Ohio. Tchr. Immaculate Conception Sch., Celina, Ohio, 1961-64, Zane Trace Local Sch., Chillicothe, Ohio, 1964-93; ret., 1993; mem. Juvenile Ct. Rev. Bd., Ross County, Chillicothe. Vol. ARC; band mem. Cicleville Pumpkin Show. Named Educator of Yr., Zane Trace Local, Ross County, 1993. Mem. Order Ea. Star (Worthy Matron 1976, 88, Evergreen chpt. 169, Adelphi), Ladies Oriental Shrine (treas., sec., v.p., pres.), Delta Kappa Gamma (com.). Republican. Methodist. Home: 8995 State Route 180 Kingston OH 45644-9546

MATHEWS, GEORGE MEPRATHU, accounting executive; b. Taiping, Perak, Malaysia, Feb. 23, 1960; came to U.S., 1985; s. Mathews and Annamma Chempanal; m. Asha Henry, May 29, 1993; 1 child, Reishma Ann. B of Commerce, U. Kerala, Trivandrum, South India, 1982; MBA, U. Dallas, 1987. Acctg. asst. AGK Acctg. & Mgmt., Butterworth, Penang, West Malaysia, 1982-83; acctg. officer Sabah Rubber Fund Bd., Kota Kinabula, Sabah, East Malaysia, 1984; acctg./LAN mgr. Karol Media, Wilkes-Barre, Pa., 1988-94; internat. acctg. specialist Amway Corp., Ada, Mich., 1994—. Mem. Am. Mgmt. Assn., Sigma Iota Epsilon. Office: Amway Corp 7575 E Fulton St Ada MI 49301-9173

MATHEWS, MARY BETH, nursing educator; b. Kansas City, Kans., July 3, 1942; d. Leon Ward and Mary Elizabeth (McManis) Zimmerman; m. Richard H. Strauss, Oct., 1967 (div.); 1 child, Scott Christopher Stauss; m. C. Weldon Mathews, Nov., 1989; stepchildren: Cynthia Elaine, Terri Mathews Ely. BSN, Cornell U., 1965; M in Nursing, U. Wash., 1969; PhD, Ohio State U., 1983. Cert. staff devel. and continuing edn. Instr. Sch. Nursing U. Pa., Phila., 1970-72; dir. continuing edn. Sch. Nursing Boston U., 1975-78; asst. prof. nursing, dir. Office Continuing Edn. Coll. Nursing Ohio State U., Columbus, 1981-90; assoc. prof. nursing, dean Sch. of Nursing Ashland (Ohio) U., Columbus, 1990-93; dir. nursing edn. devel and rsch. Riverside Meth. Hosps., Columbus, 1993—. Contbr. articles to profl. jours. Mem. ANA (chair coun. continuing edn. 1978-80, chair constituent assembly 1988-90, bd. dirs. 1992-94), Ohio Nurses Assn. (pres. 1985-89), MAIN, MNRS, NNSDO, Sigma Theta Tau, Phi Delta Kappa, Phi Kappa Phi.

MATHEWS, PAUL JOSEPH, allied health educator; b. Washington, Aug. 17, 1944; s. Paul Joseph and Ruth Irene (O'Malley) M.; m. Loretta Jeanne Calvo; children: Heather Marie, Amy Elizabeth, Timothy Hunter. AS, Quinnipiac Coll., 1971, BS, 1975; MPA, U. Hartford, 1978; EdS, U. Mo., Kansas City, 1989. Registered respiratory therapist; lic. respiratory therapist, Kans. Instr., clin. coord. New Britain (Conn.) Gen. Hosp., 1971-74; instr. Quinnipiac Coll., Hamden, Conn., 1974-76; chief respiratory therapy dept. Providence Hosp., Holyoke, Mass., 1974-80, dir. cardiology/neurology, 1977-80, asst. dir. planning, 1980-81; asst. prof. U. Kans. Sch. Allied Health, Kansas City, 1981-88, assoc. prof. respiratory care edn., 1988—, chmn. dept. respiratory care edn., 1981-93, assoc. prof. phys. therapy Grad. Sch., 1992—; U. Kans.; adj. assoc. prof. Ctr. on Aging U. Kans. Med. Ctr., 1987—; hon. prof. U. Costa Rica, San Jose, 1987—; cons. FDA, 1988, NIH, 1988, 89, SUNY, Stony Brook, 1990, USPHS, 1994, 95. Mem. editl. bd. Nursing, 1989—, Neonatal Intensive Care, 1990, Jour. Respiratory Care Edn., 1993—, Respiratory Therapy, 1988, Respiratory Therapy Intern, 1991; author audio tapes in field; contbr. articles to profl. jours., chpts. to books. Recipient Creative Achievement award Puritan-Bennett Corp., 1984, 85, A. Gerald Shapiro award N.J. Soc. for Respiratory Care, 1990; internat. fellow Project HOPE, 1987, 92. Mem. Am. Assn. Respiratory Care (bd. dirs. 1984-87, v.p. 1987, pres.-elect 1988, pres. 1989), Am. Coll. Chest Physicians, Sigma Xi, Lambda Beta, Phi Lambda Theta. Home: 8844 Hemlock Dr Overland Park KS 66212-2946 Office: U Kans 39th and Rainbow Blvd Kansas City KS 66103

MATHEWS, ROBERT EARL, II, insurance company executive; b. Cleve., 1932; s. Robert Ellsworth and Dorothy Marie (Boyle) M.; m. Jean Mizer, 1941; children: Heather Lynn, Holly Katherine. BS, Kent State, 1955. Assoc. R. Earl Mathews Agy., Cleve., 1956—; pres. Louisville Title Ins., Cleve., 1961. Trustee Cleve. Play House, 1975-87, Cleve. Mus. Natural History, 1987—, Am. Mus. Fly Fishing, 1993—. Mem. Rowfant Club, Union Club.

MATHEWS-GRAHAM, CARLA, English language educator; b. Chgo., Feb. 21, 1952; d. Carl Young and Katherine ELizabeth (Gifford) Mathews; m. Bruce Alan Graham, Oct. 27, 1990; children: Greg, Scott. BS in Secondary Edn., U. Wis., Milw., 1979, MS in Cultural Edn., 1990. Cert. secondary tchr., Wis. English tchr. Germantown Dist. Schs., Germantown, Wis., 1980—, Marquette U., Milw., 1981-83, Norris Adolescent Ctr., Mukwonago, Wis., 1983-88, Carroll Coll., Waukesha, Wis., 1991. Mem. AAUW, NEA, Wis. Edn. Assn., Germantown Edn. Assn. (negotiator 1985-92), Nat. Abortion Rights League, Planned Parenthood of Wis., Nat. Women's Art Mus. N.Y.C. Democrat.

MATHEWSON, HUGH SPALDING, anesthesiologist, educator; b. Washington, Sept. 20, 1921; s. Walter Eldridge and Jennie Lind (Jones) M.; m. Dorothy Ann Gordon, 1943 (div. 1952); 1 child, Jane Mathewson Holcombe; m. Hazel M. Jones, 1953 (div. 1978); children: Geoffrey K., Brian E., Catherine E. Brock, Jennifer A. Jehle; m. Judith Ann Mahoney, 1979 (div. 1990). Student, Washburn U., 1938-39; A.B., U. Kans., 1942, M.D., 1944. Intern Wesley Hosp., Wichita, Kans., 1944-45; resident anesthesiology U. Kans. Med. Ctr., Kansas City, 1946-48; pvt. practice specializing in anesthesiology Kansas City, Mo., 1948-69; chief anesthesiologist St. Luke's Hosp., Kansas City, 1953-69; med. dir., sect. respiratory therapy U. Kans. Med. Ctr., 1969-92, assoc. prof., 1969-92, prof., 1975-92, prof. anesthesiology emeritus, respiratory care edn., 1992—; examiner schs. respiratory therapy, 1975—; oral examiner Nat. Bd. Respiratory Therapy; mem. Coun. Nurse Anesthesia Practice, 1974-78; prof. phys. therapy edn., 1993—. Author: Structural Forms of Anesthetic Compounds, 1961, Respiratory Therapy in Critical Care, 1976, Pharmacology for Respiratory Therapists, 1977; contbr. articles to profl. publs.; mem. editorial bd. Anesthesia Staff News, 1975-84; assoc. editor: Respiratory Care, 1980—, cons. editor, 1980—, editor-in-chief Respiratory Mgmt., 1989-92. Trustee Kansas City Mus., Kansas City Conservatory of Music, 1993—. Served to lt. comdr. USNR, 1956. Recipient Bird Lit. prize Am. Assn. Respiratory Therapists, 1976. Mem. Mo. Soc. Anesthesiologists (pres. 1963), Kans. Soc. Anesthesiologists (pres. 1974-77), Kans. Med. Soc. (council), Phi Beta Kappa, Sigma Xi, Lambda Beta (hon.). Office: Kans Med Ctr 39th and Rainbow Blvd Kansas City KS 66103

MATHEWSON, JAMES L., state legislator; b. Warsaw, Mo., Mar. 16, 1938; m. Doris Angel Mathewson, 1964; 3 children. Student, Redding Jr. Coll., Calif. State U. Real estate appraiser Sedalia, Mo.; mem. Mo. Ho. of Reps., Jefferson City, 1974-80; mem. Mo. Senate, Jefferson City, 1980—, majority floor leader, 1984-88, pres. pro teme, 1989—. Mem. Sedalia C. of C., Am. Legion, Masons, Elks, Moose. Democrat. Office: RR 4 Box 183A Sedalia MO 65301-9447 also: 113 E 4th St Sedalia MO 65301-4401 also: 142 S Limit Ave Sedalia MO 65301-3655*

MATHIAS, MARGARET GROSSMAN, manufacturing company executive, leasing company executive; b. Detroit, June 26, 1928; d. D. Ray and Lila May (Skinner) Grossman; children: Deborah, Robert, Lesley, Jennifer, Mary. BA, Mt. Holyoke Coll., 1949; cert., Am. Acad. Art, 1951. Artist and co-mgr. Mary Chase Marionettes, N.Y.C., 1951-54; exec. v.p. Star Five Corp., Elkhart, 1975-88, pres., treas., chmn. bd., 1985-90; sec., chmn. bd. L & J Press Corp., Elkhart, Ind., 1985-91, also chmn. bd. dirs.; chmn. MAGCo Inc., Elkhart, 1986—; pres. Tech Products, Inc., Elkhart, 1992—. Mem. fin. com. United Fund, Elkhart, 1960-64, parents adv. bd. Furman U., Greenville, S.C., 1978-83, art adv. bd. Mount Holyoke Coll., South Hadley, Mass., 1982—; pres. Tri Kappa Service Orgn., Elkhart, 1965-66; trustee Stanley Clark Sch., South Bend, Ind., 1977-87. Recipient Lawson Top Sculpture Purchase award Midwest Mus. Am. Art, 1990. Mem. Elkhart C. of C. Republican. Clubs: Elcona Country (Elkhart), Woman's Athletic (Chgo.), Thursday (Elkhart) (pres. 1976). Home and Office: 1077 Greenleaf Blvd Apt 209 Elkhart IN 46514-3563

MATHIAS, MARK ROBERT, chemical company executive; b. Uhrichsville, Ohio, Oct. 28, 1951; s. Robert William and June Beth (Miller) M.; m. Sarah Rea Huebner, Feb. 16, 1971; children: Beth, Sharon, Junelle, Matthew. BS in Zoology, Kent State, 1976. Lab. dir. U.S. Chem., Gnadenhutten, Ohio, 1976-77, 2 shift supr., 1977-78, 1 shift supr., 1978-79, plant mgr., 1978-81, tech. sales, 1981-83; pres., owner Marvin Custom Initiator Mixing, Inc., 1983—. Scoutmaster, Boy Scouts Am., Gnadenhutten, Ohio, 1990—; soccer coach, County YMCA, 1990—.

MATHIESEN, THOMAS JAMES, musicology educator; b. Roslyn Heights, N.Y., Apr. 30, 1947; s. James Christian and Edris Elva (Leatherman) M.; m. Penelope Jay Price, Sept. 11, 1971. Student, Stanford U., 1965, 67; MusB, Willamette U., 1968; MusM, U. So. Calif., L.A., 1970, D. Musical Arts, 1971. Lectr. musicology U. So. Calif., L.A., 1971-72; prof. music Brigham Young U., Provo, Utah, 1972-88, assoc. dean honors, 1986-88; prof. music Ind. U., Bloomington, 1988-96, dist. prof., 1996—; project dir. Thesaurus Musicarum Latinarum, Ind. U., Bloomington, 1990—. Author: Bibliography of Sources for the Study of Ancient Greek Music, 1974, Aristides Quintilianus on Music, 1983, Ancient Greek Music Theory, 1988 (Duckles award 1989); editor: Festa Musicologica: Essays in Honor of George J. Buelow; gen. editor Greek and Latin Music Theory, 1982—; editor 10 vols.; contbr. articles to profl. jours. Pres. Holiday Hills Assn., Springville, Utah, 1978-84. Grantee Am. Coun. Learned Socs., 1977, NEH, 1992-96; fellow NEH, 1985-86, Guggenheim fellow, 1990-91. Mem. AAUP, Am. Musicological Soc., Soc. for Music Theory, Music Libr. Assn., Am. Philol. Assn., Theta Alpha Phi, Omicron Delta Kappa, Pi Kappa Lambda, Phi Mu Alpha. Home: 1800 N Valley View Dr Ellettsville IN 47429-9487 Office: Ind U Sch Music Bloomington IN 47405

MATHIESON, CAROL ANN FISHER, music educator; b. Lansing, Mich., July 16, 1948; d. Vernon Jacob and Verna Josephine (Berry) Fisher; m. Robert John Mathieson, Jan. 15, 1977; children: Kristina Margaret, Andrew David (dec.). BA cum laude, Maryville Coll., 1970; MusM, U. Tenn., 1974; DMA, U. Iowa, 1981. Dir. instrumental music Blount County Pub. Schs., Maryville, Tenn., 1970-72; instr. music and art Damavand Coll., Tehran, Iran, 1972-74; instr. music Culver-Stockton Coll., Canton, Mo., 1975-77, asst. prof., 1977-84, assoc. prof., 1984-92, prof., 1992—; dir. opera workshop Culver-Stockton Coll., 1979—; cons. Arts Edn. Task Force, Jefferson City, Mo., 1991—. Author: Selected Repertoire for Voice and Obbligato Instruments, 1981. Comty. song leader Canton Area Arts Coun., 1988—, program com., 1990-91, bd. dirs., 1992—, dir. Gt. River Women's Chorus, 1991—; mem. adv. bd. Muddy River Opera Co., Quincy, Ill., 1990—; bd. dirs. Quincy Area Children's Chorus, 1995—; min. music Quincy Unitarian Ch., 1977—. Mem. AAUP, AAUW (coll. rep. 1990—), Presbyn. Assn. Musicians, Am. Guild Organists, Coll. Music Soc., Music Educators Nat. Conf., Unitarian Musician's Network, Nat. Assn. Tchrs. Singing. Office: Culver-Stockton Coll Div Fine Arts Canton MO 63435

MATHIEU, THOMAS C., state legislator; b. Sheboygan, Wis., Dec. 2, 1936; m. Luan J. Lanning; children: Susan, Thomas, Jeffrey, Lori. Dir. cmty. devel., Kent Cmty. Action Program; state rep., Mich. Ho. of Reps. Dist. 92, 1974-94, Mich. Ho. of Reps. Dist. 76, 1995—. majority whip Mich. Ho. of Reps., 1975-76, asst. majority leader, 1977-84, mem. Appropriations com., co-chmn. judiciary com., mem. Joint Legis. Retirement Com. Named Conservation Legislator of the Yr, Mich. United Conservation Clubs, 1979, Outstaanding Svc. award Grand Rapids Jr. Coll., 1980, Outstanding Svc. award Assn. Ind. Colls. and Univs., 1984, Outstanding Legislator of the Yr. AAUP, 1982. Mem. Nat. Assn. Civilian Conservation Corpps. *

MATHIOUDAKIS, MICHAEL ROBERT, life insurance and estate planning executive; b. Indpls., Sept. 3, 1963; s. Robert G. and Annabel M. (Pattison) M.; m. JoLee Katherine Pilarski, Dec. 27, 1986. BBA, U. Notre Dame, 1985. CLU; ChFC; lic. renaissance advisor. Acct. Price Waterhouse, Indpls., 1985-87; account exec. Anderson Assocs., Indpls., 1987-88; v.p. Exec. Fin. Group Inc., Indpls., 1988-94; founder, pres. The GENESIS Group, LLC, Indpls., 1995—. Deacon East 91st St. Christian Ch., Indpls., 1988-90, trustee East 91st St. Christian Ch. Found.; bd. dirs. Ind. Fellowship Christian Athletes, 1989-91; mem. adv. bd. Student Venture of Greater Indpls., 1989-92. Mem. Nat. Assn. Life Underwriters, Indpls. Estate Planning Coun., Am. Soc. CLU and ChFC (cert.), Indpls. Bus. Connection (founder, pres. 1987-90). Republican. Home: 10555 Chestnut Hill Cir Fishers IN 46038-9431 Office: The GENESIS Group LLC Ste 555 9000 Keystone Crossing Indianapolis IN 46240

MATHIS, DAVID B., insurance company executive; b. Atlanta, Ga.. BA, Lake Forest Coll., 1960. Chmn. Kemper Corp., Long Grove, Ill., 1992-96; chmn., pres., CEO Kemper Nat. Ins. Cos., Long Grove, Ill., 1996—; also bd. dirs. Kemper Corp. Office: Kemper Nat Ins Cos 1 Kemper Dr Long Grove IL 60049

MATHIS, JACK DAVID, advertising executive; b. La Porte, Ind. Nov. 27, 1931; s. George Anthony and Bernice (Bennethum) M.; student U. Mo., 1950-52; BS, Fla. State U., 1955; m. Phyllis Dene Hoffman, Dec. 24, 1971; children: Kane Cameron, Jana Dene. With Benton & Bowles, Inc., 1955-56; owner Jack Mathis Advt., 1956—; cons. films, including That's Action!, 1977, Great Movie Stunts: Raiders of the Lost Ark, 1981, The Making of Raiders of the Lost Ark, 1981, An American Legend: The Lone Ranger, 1981; Heroes and Sidekicks: Indiana Jones and the Temple of Doom, 1984, The Republic Pictures Story, 1991, The Making of The Quiet Man, 1992, Roy Rogers: King of the Cowboys, 1992, Cliffhangers: Adventures from the Thrill Factory, 1993, The Making of Sands of Iwo Jima, 1993, Gene Autry: Melody of the West, 1994. Mem. U.S. Olympic Basketball Com. Recipient citation Mktg. Research Council N.Y., inducted Ill. Basketball Hall of Fame. Mem. Alpha Delta Sigma. Author: Valley of the Cliffhangers, Republic Confidential, Valley of the Cliffhangers Supplement. Office: PO Box 3580 Barrington IL 60011-3580

MATHIS, JAMES BENNETT, engineer; b. Louisville, Mar. 10, 1954. AS, U. Cin., 1995. Circuit bd. engr. Audio Sys., Louisville, 1980-85; engr. Cin. Dynacomp, Milford, Ohio, 1985-95, engrng. project mgr., 1995—. With USN, 1976-79. Mem. Inst. Packaging and Interconnecting Electronic Circuitry Designers Coun. Office: Cin Dynacomp 502 Techne Center Dr Milford OH 45150-2763

MATHIS, LOIS RENO, retired elementary education educator; b. Vinson, Okla., June 10, 1915; d. William Dodson and Trudie Frances (Brady) Reno; m. Harold Fletcher Mathis, June 6, 1942 (dec.); children: Robert F., Betty Mathis Sproule. BS, Southwestern Okla. U., 1939; MA, U. Pitts., 1945; PhD, Ohio State U., 1965. Cert. elem. tchr.; cert. elem. supr. Tchr. Okla. Pub. Schs., Tea Cross, 1936-39, Tipton, 1939-42; tchr. Ohio County Schs., Wheeling, W.Va., 1944-45, Norman (Okla.) Pub. Schs., 1951-52, Kent (Ohio) State U., 1954-60, Ohio State U., Columbus, 1961-62, Columbus (Ohio) Pub. Schs., 1967-80; ret., 1980; ednl. cons. in field, 1965—. Mem. Women's Round Table, Columbus, 1986-88; mem. data collection com. 100 Good Schs., Columbus, 1982-84. Mem. AAUW (pres. 1986-88), Ohio State Univ. Women's Club, Phi Delta Gamma (pres. 1980-82), Pi Lambda Theta, Alpha Delta Kappa, Kappa Delta Pi (counselor 1976—, alumni counselor exec. coun. internat. 1990-92, Honor Key 1991). Democrat. Baptist. Home: 2905 Halstead Rd Columbus OH 43221-2917

MATHISEN-REID, RHODA SHARON, international communications consultant; b. Portland, Oreg., June 25, 1942; d. Daniel and Mildred Elizabeth Annette (Peterson) Hager; m. James Albert Mathisen, July 17, 1964 (div. 1977); m. James A. Reid Sr., Jan. 1, 1991. BA in Edn., Music, Bible Coll., Mich., 1964. Community Rels. officer Gary-Wheaton Bank, Wheaton, Ill., 1971-75; br. mgr. Stivers Temporary Personnel, Chgo., 1975-79; v.p. sales Exec. Technique, Chgo., 1980-83; prin. Mathisen Assocs., Clarendon Hills, Ill., 1983—; presenter seminars; featured speaker Women in Mgmt. Oak Brook Chpt., 1988.; cons. Haggai Inst., Atlanta; adv. mem. Nat. Bd. Success Group, 1986. Pres. chancel choir Christ Ch. of Oak Brook, 1985-87, chmn. 1st Profl. Women's Seminar, 1995; mem., 1992—, bd. dirs. Career Devel. Inst., Oak Brook, 1992; judge Mrs. Ill., USI Pageant, 1994. Mem. NAFE, Bus. and Profl. Women (charter mem. Woodfield chpt.), Execs. Club Oak Brook, Assn. Commerce and Industry (named Ambassador of Month N.W. suburban chpt. 1979), Oak Brook Assn. Commerce and Industry (mem. membership com.), Women Entrepreneurs of DuPage County (membership chmn., featured speaker Jan. 1988), Art Inst. Chgo., Willowbrook/Burr Ridge C. of C. Republican. Office: Mathisen Assocs 17 Lake Shore Dr Clarendon Hills IL 60514-2221

MATHISON, THOMAS RICHARD, architect; b. Traverse City, Mich., June 28, 1951; s. Richard Frank and Joan Frances (Fouch) M.; m. Denise Louise Seguin, Aug. 31, 1974; children: Evan, Lauren, Bryan. BArch, U. Mich., 1973, MArch, 1975. Registered architect, Mich., Fla. Asst. to v.p. Coxe Assocs., Phila., 1974; architect GBKB Assocs., Traverse City, Mich., 1975-84; prin. Bell Assocs., Clearwater, Fla., 1984-88, WBDC Group, Grand Rapids, Mich., 1988-93; v.p. Tower Pinkster Titus Assoc., Grand Rapids, Mich., 1993—. Choir mem. Calvary Bapt. Ch., Grand Rapids, 1988—, Heartsong, 1991—. Recipient Design award Assn. Builders & Contractors West Mich. chpt. 1991, 92. Mem. AIA (pres. Mich. chpt. 1996, pres. Grand Valley chpt. 1992, v.p. 1991, treas. 1989-90, Design award 1992). Office: Tower Pinkster Titus Assoc Ste 255 678 Front St NW Grand Rapids MI 49504

MATIA, PAUL RAMON, federal judge; b. Cleve., Oct. 2, 1937; s. Leo Clemens and Irene Elizabeth (Linkert) M.; m. Nancy Arch Van Meter, Jan. 2, 1993. BA, Case Western Res. U., 1959; JD, Harvard U., 1962. Bar: Ohio 1962, U.S. Dist. Ct. (no. dist.) Ohio 1969. Law clk. Common Pleas Ct. of Cuyahoga County, Cleve., 1963-66, judge, 1985-91; asst. atty. gen. State of Ohio, Cleve., 1966-69; adminstrv. ast. to atty. gen. State of Ohio, Columbus, 1969-70; senator Ohio State Senate, Columbus, 1971-75, 79-83; ptnr. Hadley, Matia, Mills & MacLean Co., L.P.A., Cleve., 1975-84; judge U.S. Dist. Ct. (no. dist.) Ohio, 1991—. Candidate Lt. Gov. Rep. Primary, 1982, Ohio Supreme Ct., 1988; vice chmn. exec. com. Cuyahoga County Rep. Orgn., Cleve., 1971-84. Named Outstanding Legislator, Ohio Assn. for Retarded Citizens, 1974, Watchdog of Ohio Treasury, United Conservatives of Ohio, 1979; recipient Heritage award Polonia Found., 1988. Mem. FBA, Am. Judicature Soc., Ohio Bar Assn., Cleve. Bar Assn. (President's award 1988), Cuyahoga County Bar Assn., Athletic Club Columbus, Club at Society Ctr. Office: US Dist Ct 201 Superior Ave E Cleveland OH 44114-1204

MATIS, BONNIE LEAH, health care administrator; b. Battle Creek, Mich.; d. Edward James and Miriam Charlotte (Bedrosian) Brown; m. Jeffery Scott Matis, Nov. 9, 1991. Student, Kent (Ohio) State U., 1986, Macomb Coll., Mt. Clemens, Mich., 1987; BA in Communication Arts, Health Sci., Oakland U., Rochester, Mich., 1990. Cert. phys. fitness specialist 1986. Instr., lectr. YMCA, Warren, Mich., 1986-90; regional dir., adminstr. Pro Therapy of Am., Inc., Birmingham, Mich., 1994—; med. asst. Rochester, 1988-89; profl. model, 1984-90; apprentice tchr. TV prodn. Oakland U., Rochester, 1990; TV/video producer KDN Videoworks, Comcast Cable, Oakland U., 1989-91; mgr., counselor Trim 4 Life Clinic, Sterling Hts., Mich., 1989-90; founder, pres. Future Perfect of Mich., Mt. Clemens, 1990—; program dir., mgr. Crittenton Hosp., Rochester, 1991-92; adminstr. Total Therapy Mgmt., Inc., Farmington Hills, Mich., 1993, Sterling Phys. Therapy and Rehab., P.C., Warren, Mich., 1994; regional dir. outpatient svcs./adminstrn. Pro Therapy of Am., Inc., Birmingham, Mich., 1994-96, dir. mktg., 1996—; lectr. in field; cons. in field; script writer; theatre performer, actor, dancer choregrapher Detroit Dance Co. Workshops, F&R Dance Co., Macomb Ctr. for Performing Arts, Meadowbrook Estate, 1971-86; comml./indsl. actor internat. agencies. Author/creator Fit Facts Community Newsletter, 1987-89. Vol. ARC, Roseville, Mich., 1983-84; mem. Women's Sports Found., 1987; com. mem. Community Outreach Networking, Quality Assurance, 1991-92. Recipient Excellent Leadership award, Health Occupation Students of Am., 1984, Community Svc. Appreciation award, ARC/Martin Pl. Hosp., 1984, Award of Excellence, Model of the Yr., USA, 1990. Mem. NAFE, Women in Comm., Birmingham/Bloomfield C. of C., Oakland U. Alumni Assn.

MATLOW, LINDA MONIQUE, photographic agency executive, publishing executive; b. Chgo., July 24, 1955; d. Charles and Milly Matlow. Grad. high sch., Chgo.; student, Sch. Modern Photography, N.Y.C., 1977-79. Promotions and pub. relations staff Jaydee Enterprises, Chgo., 1971-73; mgr. First Venture, Inc., Chgo., 1973-77; photographer, pub. relations staff Bands & Mags., Chgo., 1977—; photographer, writer, editor Pix Internat., Chgo., 1982—; pub. variety of monthly mags. on disk including Retro, ARTchive, Cre-8, Event; photo editor Beat. Chgo. Sounds; bur. chief Praire Sun; electronic pub. and image design Internet Pub. Contbr. photographs to pubs. including N.Y. Times, Chgo. Tribune, Boston Globe, Harper's Bazaar, Redbook. Vol. telethon Variety Club of Chgo., 1986, Spl. Childrens' Charities, Little City Found., Chgo. Acad. for the Arts. Named Rock Photographer Night Rock newspaper, Chgo., 1980, 81, one of Chgo.'s Most Successful and Eligible Bachelorettes Today's Chgo. Woman mag., 1989; recipient Hon. mention Internat. Photographer Mag., 1990, winner B&W Print of Ray Charles, 1991; finalist Photographers Forum B&W Print, 1991. Mem. Nat. Press Photographers Assn., NARAS, Internat. Freelance Photographers Orgn., Chgo. Women in Pub., Chgo. Area Internet Soc. Roman Catholic.

MATNEY, MALINDA MAE, housing director; b. Wichita, Kans., Apr. 22, 1966; d. Therold F. and Linda Joan (Hay) M. BA, Wichita State U., 1988; MMus, U. Colo., 1992. Coord. United Govt. Grad. Schs., Boulder, Colo., 1990-91; exec. U. Colo. Student Union, Boulder, 1991-92; asst. to dir. Family Learning Ctr., Boulder, 1992-93; housing dir. Kansas City Art Inst., 1993—. Mem. Nat. Assn. Parliamentarians, Coll. and Univ. Housing Officers Internat. (assoc.), Kappa Kappa psi (nat. v.p. 1995—, midwest dist. gov. 1992-95).

MATSON, PEGGY KEPURAITIS, software engineer; b. Chgo., Feb. 21, 1961; d. Edward Donald and Therese Dolores (Mooney) Kepuraitis; m. John Christopher,July 27, 1991. BSEE, U. Ill., 1984; MSEE, U. Ill., Chgo., 1989; MBA, U. Chgo., 1995. Elec. engr. II hardware Motorola, Schaumburg, Ill., elec. engr. I hardware, elec. engr. I software, sr. engr. software, group leader software, sect. mgr. software, engrng. mgr. software. Patentee on communication console sta. with priority queing, 1992. Chair various projects Chgo. Jaycees, 1984-89. Mem. IEEE, Motorola Tech. Women's Network (vice chair 1992-93). Office: Motorola 3701 E Algonquin Rd Rolling Meadows IL 60008

MATSON, WESLEY JENNINGS, educational administrator; b. Svea, Minn., June 25, 1924; s. James and Ettie (Mattson) M.; m. Doris Cragg; 1 child, James Jennings. BS with distinction, U. Minn., 1948; MA, U. Calif., Berkeley, 1954; EdD, Columbia U., 1960. High sch. tchr. Santa Barbara County Pub. Schs., Santa Maria, Calif., 1948-50; instr. U. Calif., Berkeley, 1950-54, Columbia U., N.Y.C., 1954-55; lectr. Fordham U., N.Y.C., 1955-56; asst. prof. U. Md., College Park, 1956-59; prof., asst. dean U. Wis., Milw., 1959-72; dean emeritus Winona (Minn.) State U., 1972-88; vis. prof. U. P.R., Rio Peidras, Western Wash. U., Bellingham, San Diego State U., U. Minn., Mpls., U. Hawaii; adj. faculty St. Olaf Coll., Northfield, Minn., 1990-95; cons. U.S. Dept. Edn., Washington, Ill., Wis.; bd. regents Wis. Dept. Pub. Instruction; examiner Nat. Coun. Accreditation Tchr. Edn., North Ctrl. Assn., Chgo. Editorial bd.: Jour. Instructional Psychology; contbr. articles to profl. jours. Exec. com. Minn. Alliance of the Arts, Mpls.; mem. Minn. Com. Certification Stds., St. Paul; bd. dirs. Ft. Snelling Meml. Chapel Found. Served to capt. USAAF, 1943-46, ETO. Decorated Bronze star; recipient Disting. Service award Wis. Assn. Tchr. Edn., 1972. Mem. Minn. Assn. Colls. for Tchr. Edn. (pres. 1983-85, hon. life award of merit 1985), Nat. Assn. Tchr. Educators (exec. com. 1970-72), Nat. Edn. Assn. (life), Assn. Higher Edn., Minn. Edn. Assn., Minn. Hist. Soc., U. Minn. Alumni Soc. (Outstanding Educator award 1984), Rotary, Phi Delta Kappa, Kappa Delta Pi, Alpha Sigma Phi. Home: 6615 Lake Shore Dr S Minneapolis MN 55423-2273

MATTESON, CLARICE CHRIS, artist, educator; b. Winnipeg, Man., Can., Sept. 2, 1918; came to U.S., 1922; d. Sergis and Nina (Balter) Alberts; m. D.C. Matteson, 1956 (dec. 1976); children: Kemmer, Gretchen. BA, Met. State U., 1976; MA in Liberal Studies, Hamline U., 1986; PhD in Humanities, LaSalle U., 1995. Mem. Orson Welles' staff, Hollywood, Calif., 1945-46; owner Hilde-Gardes Co., L.A., 1947-56; instr. art North Hennepin C.C., Brooklyn Park, Minn., 1975-81; prodr., host Accent on Art TV Program, St. Paul, 1979—; instr. art Lakewood C.C., U. Minn., Normandale C.C., Bloomington (Minn.) Sch. Dist., Mpls. Sch. Dist., St. Paul Sch. Dist., 1981—. Exhibited in group shows at Mpls. Inst. Art, 1994-95, Govs. 1006 Soc., 1994—; represented in permanent collections Richard James Gallery, Mpls., Gallery 416, Mpls.; corr. Schaumburg (Ill.) Newspapers, 1962-68; prodr., host TV series Kids Art, Mpls.-St. Paul, 1995; prodr. series program Internat. Cafe Internet Arts, 1996; patentee plastic products. Active Minn. Orch. (WAMSO), Mpls., 1972—, vol. Recipient award for creative leadership Minn. Assn. for Continuing Adult Edn., 1977, Gold Cup award Bloomington Cable, 1989, Gov.'s Letter of Commendation, 1994; Park Cable TV grantee, 1982, Minn. Humanities Commn. grantee, 1985. Mem. ASCAP (award 1996), AAUW (dir. arts com. 1989-90, bd. dirs. 1990-92), Am. Pen Women (v.p. Minn. chpt. 1994-96), Am. Composers Forum, Minn. Artists Assn., Minn. Territorial Pioneers (bd. dirs. 1995—), Internat. Alliance for Women in Music, St. Paul Neighborhood Network, N.Y. Neighborhood Network. Home and Office: 2119 Sargent Ave Saint Paul MN 55105-1126

MATTHEWS, C(HARLES) DAVID, real estate appraiser, consultant; b. Anniston, Ala., June 15, 1946; s. James Boyd and Emma Grace (McCullough) M.; m. Stephanie Ann Woods, Dec. 28, 1968; children: Alison Paige, Dylan McCullough. BS, U. Tenn., 1968. County appraiser Assessor's Office, Freeport, Ill., 1969-71; staff appraiser Ill. Dept. Highways, Springfield, 1971-72; appraiser, dir. counseling Norman Benedict Assocs., Hamden, Conn., 1972-76; mgr. appraisal dept. Citizens Realty & Ins., Evansville, Ind., 1976-80; owner, mgr. David Matthews Assocs., Evansville, 1980—; adj. real estate faculty U. Conn., 1974-76, U. Evansville, 1978-87, Appraisal Inst., 1989—; citizen amb. to Russia on Urban Valuation Team, 1993. Tympanist Chattanooga Symphony; drummer Templeaires Big Band; author: (with others) Downtown Master Plan of Evansville, Indiana, 1984, The Appraisal of Real Estate, 10th edit. Mem. Leadership Evansville, 1982; arbitrator Am. Arbitration Assn., 1986—; v.p. Corp. for Housing Opportunities in City of Evansville, 1989-92; chmn. bd. trustees Meth. Temple, 1994-96. Recipient merit award Willard Libr. Photog. Contest, 1988. Mem. Am. Inst. Real Estate Appraisers (vice chmn. nat. admissions 1990, state pres. 1987, governing councillor 1989-90), Appraisal Inst. (chmn. gen. appraiser bd. 1991-92, exec. com. 1991-92, 95-96, chmn. pub. rels. 1993, chmn. comm. 1995-96, Percy Wagner award 1992), Soc. Real Estate Appraisers (local pres. 1981), Evansville Bd. Realtors (pres. 1986, Realtor of Yr. award 1987), Counselors of Real Estate, Evansville C. of C., Mensa, Rotary. Home: 430 S Boeke Rd Evansville IN 47714-1616 Office: 123 NW 4th St Rm 711 Evansville IN 47708-1719

MATTHEWS, DAN, state legislator. Sales and rentals exec.; mem. from dist. 20 S.D. State Ho. of Reps., Pierre, mem. health and human svc. com., mem. judiciary and ret. laws coms. Address: 1301 W Norway Mitchell SD 57301

MATTHEWS, GERTRUDE ANN URCH, retired librarian, writer; b. Jackson, Mich., July 16, 1921; d. Charles P.A. and Amy (Granville) Urch; student Albion Coll., 1940-41; AA, Jackson Jr. Coll., 1939; BS, MS in Library Arts, U. Mich., 1959; m. Geoffrey Matthews, June 30, 1942 (dec.). Adult services librarian Jackson, Mich., 1959-63; asst. dir., librarian Franklin Sylvester Library, Medina, Ohio, 1963-81, dir. older adults facility library, 1977-93. Pres., Hist. Soc., 1966-67; active Dollars for Scholars Com., 1966-86; mem. Bicentennial Com.; officer diocesean leval Episcopal Ch.; mem. vestry St. Paul's Ch., Medina, 1981-84. Mem. ALA, Ohio Library Assn., AAUW (dir., Community Service award 1985, Woman of Yr.), LWV (dir.). Republican. Contbr. articles to profl. and popular publs.; weekly newspaper columnist, 1958-81; bookreviewer The Nat. Librarian. Home: 750 Weymouth Rd Medina OH 44256-2038

MATTHEWS, LORI, data processing executive, accountant; b. Kansas City, Mo., Apr. 16, 1947; d. Joseph Garland and Irene Mildred (Nunn) Mills; m. Duane Carlson Matthews Jr., Feb. 12, 1971; children: Jason Andrew, Jodi Ann. AS in Gen. Bus., Johnson County Community Coll., Overland Park, Kans., 1976. Payroll clk. Burstein-Applebee Co., Kansas City, 1965-69; acctg. clk. S-G Metals, Kansas City, 1969-71; equipment acct. Reno Constrn. Co., Overland Park, 1971-79; office mgr. Cen. States Structures, Inc., Overland Park, 1980; acct. City of Shawnee, Kans., 1980-83, dir. data processing div., 1983—. Mem. Flint PTA, Shawnee, 1981-93, Shawnee Mission North High PTA, 1991—; den leader Boy Scouts Am., 1984-86; parent sponsor Just Say No Club, 1987-88; parent leader Girl Scouts USA, 1989-92. Mem. Shawnee Mission Assn. for the Gifted, Computer Profls. Unltd. (treas. 1993—). Democrat. Home: 6351 W 49th St Mission KS 66202-1714 Office: City of Shawnee 11110 Johnson Dr Shawnee Mission KS 66203-2750

MATTHEWS, NORMAN EAKES, obstericican, gynecologist, medical director; b. Chgo., Dec. 20, 1933; s. Warren Bond and Martha Nancy (Eakes) m.; m. Rubie Elizabeth Wells, Aug. 29, 1958 (div. 1971); m. Adrianne Price, July 13, 1980; children: Samuel Eakes, Mary Martha. AB, Haverford Coll., 1954; MD, Harvard U., 1958. Diploma Am. Bd. Ob-Gyn. Internship, residency in gen. surgery U. Cin. Hosps., 1958-63; med. missionary Am. Friends Bd. of Missions, Kaimosi, Kenya, 1963-65; residency in ob-gyn U. Cin., 1966-69, asst. prof. ob-gyn, 1970-71; pvt. practice Cin., 1971-74, 1977—; asst. prof. Med. Coll. Va., Richmond, 1970-74; med. dir. Planned Parenthood Assn. of Cin., 1977—. Mem. Assn. of Reproductive Health Profls., Nat. Abortion Fedn., Cin. Acad. of Medicine, Cin. Ob-Gyn Soc. Mem. Soc. of Friends. Home: 2509 Observatory Ave Cincinnati OH 45208 Office: Planned Parenthood Ohio Ky 2314 Auburn Ave Cincinnati OH 45219

MATTHEWS, WILLIAM EDMUND, newspaper and travel magazine publisher; b. Shelbyville, Ky., Apr. 30, 1930; s. Robert Foster and Zerelda Tribble (Baxter) M.; m. Else Vivien Bender Jorgensen, June 13, 1952; children: Lisa Gaines, William E. II, Ellen Matthews Oetinger, Bland Ballard. BA, U. Mich., 1952. Info. specialist C.I.A., Washington, 1953-61; owner, pubr. The Shelby Sentinel, Shelbyville, Ky., 1961-68; pres., gen. mgr. Newspapers Inc., Shelbyville, Ky., 1968-73; pres. Landmark Community Newspapers, Shelbyville, Ky., 1973-76; pubr./gen. mgr. Scripps Howard Community News, Cin., 1976-82; v.p., editor Mid-Continent Devel. & Tourism, Huntingburg, Ind., 1982-93, pres., editor, 1993—; editor The Huntingburg Press, 1987—, pub., 1993—. Editor/pubr.: The Relentless Reds, 1976, The Royal Reds, 1977. 2d lt. U.S. Army, 1952. Mem. Ky. Press Assn. (pres. 1977), Ky. Weekly Newspaper Assn. (pres. 1975), Rotary. Christian Ch. (Disciples of Christ). Home: 467 Cove Rd Shelbyville KY 40065-8924 Office: The Huntingburg Press 423 E 4th St Huntingburg IN 47542-1339

MATTILA, MARY JO KALSEM, elementary and art educator; b. Canton, Ill., Oct. 26, 1944; d. Joseph Nelson and Bernice Nora (Milbauer) Kalsem; m. John Peter Mattila, Jan. 27, 1968. BS in Art, U. Wis., 1966; student, Ohio State U., 1972, Drake U., 1981; MS in Ednl. Adminstrn., Iowa State U., 1988. Cert. tchr., prin., supr., adminstr., art tchr., secondary tchr., Iowa. Tchr. 2d grade McHenry (Ill.) Pub. Schs., 1966-67, Wisconsin Hts. Schs.,

Black Earth, Wis., 1967-69; substitute tchr. Columbus (Ohio) City Schs., 1969-70; elem. art tchr. Southwestern City Schs., Columbus, 1972-73; adminstrv. intern Ames, Iowa, 1984-86; lead tchr. at Roosevelt Sch. Ames Cmty. Schs., 1986-87, art vertical curriculum chair, 1983-89, art educator, elem. and spl. edn., 1973—. Author articles. Active LWV, Ames, 1982—; fundraiser Altrusa, Ames, 1992—. Recipient Very Spl. Svc. award for Disting. Svc. in Very Spl. Arts, Gov. of Iowa, 1984. Mem. ASCD, NEA, Nat. Assn. Elem. Sch. Prins., Nat. Art Edn. Assn. Home: 2822 Duff Ave Ames IA 50010-4710 Office: Ames Cmty Schs 120 S Kellogg Ave Ames IA 50010-6719

MATTINGLY, KEITH EDWARD, clergyman, educator; b. Cin., Aug. 19, 1974; s. John Charles and Eulalie Vincetta (Reed) M.; m. Margarita Claudia Krieghoff, June 7, 1970; children: Sean Elliott, Claudine Yvette. BA, Andrews U., Berrien Springs, Mich., 1969, MDiv, 1972, postgrad., 1994—. Ordained to ministry Seventh-day Adventist Ch., 1972. Min. Ark.-La. Conf. Seventh-day Adventists, Gentry, Ark., 1971-72, Fayetteville, Ark., 1972-75, Malvern, Ark., 1975-77; min. Fla. Conf. Seventh-day Adventists, Cocoa, 1977-79; min., prof. Andrews U., 1979—; chaplain USAR, Gary, Ind., 1980-85, Mich. Army Res., Battle Creek and Jackson, 1985—; chaplainRotary Club, Malvern 1975-77, Civitan, Malvern, 1975-77. Author: (book/syllabus) Christian Beliefs, 1986, Issues in the Great Controversy, 1987, Early and Later Prophets, 1990. Lt. col. U.S. Army, 1990-91, Desert Storm. Mem. Soc. Bibl. Studies, Theta Alpha Kappa. Home: 10853 Ridgewood Tr Berrien Springs MI 49103 Office: St Andrews U Dept Religion Berrien Springs MI 49104

MATTISON, ROBERT MYRON, consultant, author, researcher; b. Key West, Fla., Nov. 23, 1954; s. Clarence L. and Eleanor (Kelly) M.; m. Brigitte Kilger, Nov. 10, 1979; children: Stephanie, Chris, Dustin, Peter. BS, U. Ill., Chgo., 1984. Cert. office automation profl. Cons. Matside, Inc., Des Plaines, Ill., 1976-85, AT&T, Skokie, Ill., 1985-87, Cap Gemini Am., Westchester, Ill., 1987-92, DRT Sys. Internat., Westchester, 1992-94; EDS, 1994—; co-chair Unix Internat. Perfomance Mgmt. Work Group. Author: Understanding DBMS, 1992; contbr. articles to profl. jours. Bd. dirs. ALANO of Des Plaines, 1991—. Mem. IEEE, Assn. for Computing Machinery, Nat. Assn. Systems Programmers. Republican. Home: 9316 N Western Ave Des Plaines IL 60016-3972

MATTRISCH, DAN D., product designer; b. Ft. Atkinson, Wis., June 29, 1968. AS in Mech. Design, Blackhawk Tech. Coll., 1989. Draftsman Schlueter Co., Janesville, Wis., 1989-90; product designer Weiler & Co., Inc., Whitewater, Wis., 1990—. Office: Weiler and Co Inc 1116 E Main St Whitewater WI 53190-2103

MATTSON, CAROL LINNETTE, social services administrator; b. Frederic, Wis., Oct. 3, 1946; d. Clarence Waldemar and Lucille Anna Mathilda (Bengtson) Hedlund; m. Wesley Harlan Mattson, June 24, 1967; 1 child, Aaron Ray. BS, U. Wis., Menomonie, 1968. Home econs. tchr. Luck (Wis.) High Sch., 1968-72; clk. Daniels Twp., Siren, Wis., 1973-75; family living instr. Wis. Indianhead Tech. Inst., New Richmond, 1974-77; aging program dir. Polk County, Balsam Lake, Wis., 1977—; sec., bd. dirs. Polk County Transp. for the Disabled and Elderly, Inc., Balsam Lake, 1978—; sec., mem. com. Long Term Support Com., Balsam Lake, 1985-90. Mem. Wis. Assn. Nutrition Dirs., Wis. Assn. Aging Unit Dirs. Lutheran. Office: Polk County Aging Programs PO Box 605 Balsam Lake WI 54810-0605

MATTSSON-BOZE, DANIEL WINSTON, missionary; b. Chgo., Apr. 8, 1945; s. Joseph D. and Daga A. (Erlandsson) Mattsson-B.; m. Arleta R. Yoder, Mar. 25, 1967 (dec. Jan. 1968); m. Ingrid E. Obrink, Apr. 26, 1969; children: Peder, Karl, Katrina, Phillip. BA, U. Ill., 1965; MEd, No. Ill. U., 1968. Pres. Herald of Faith, Inc., Anoka, Minn., 1982—; ins. sales N.Y. Life, Corpus Christi, Tex., 1976-87; field assoc. Billy Graham Evangelistic Assn., 1993-95; cons. Anoka Cmty. Ch., 1992-93; v.p. Assemblies of God Internat. Fellowship, San Diego, 1987—; bd. dirs. Romanian Mission, Chgo., 1992—. Office: Herald of Faith PO Box 7 Anoka MN 55303

MATUS, MARK THOMAS, industrial engineer; b. Chgo., July 11, 1966. AA in Engring., Wright Coll., Chgo., 1987. Retail asst. mgr. Sears, Niles, Ill., 1984-86; engr. M&R Printing Equipment Inc., Glen Ellyn, Ill., 1992—.

MATUSKA, FRANK M., project manager; b. Chgo., July 14, 1952. BS, So. Ill. U., 1976. Manufacturing engr. Ford Motor Co., Sterling Heights, Mich., 1976-84; project mgr. Fanutic Robotics N.A., Inc., Auburn Hills, Mich., 1984—. With AFR, 1970-76. Office: Fanuc Robotics NA Inc 2000 S Adams Rd Auburn Hills MI 48326-2800

MATZKE, GERALD E., state legislator; b. Seward, Nebr., Mar. 16, 1931; m. Lee Ellen Matzke; children: Jay, Jane (Matzke) Christofferson, Doran, Dana. BA, U. Nebr., 1952; JD, NYU, 1955. Bar: Nebr. Tchg. assoc. and asst. to dean Coll. of Law U. Nebr., Lincoln, 1955-56; ptnr. Martin, Mattoon, Matzke & Mattoon Law Firm, Lincoln, 1956—; senator State of Nebr., Lincoln, 1956—; magistrate apptd. by Nebr. Fed. Ct., 1970-74; mem. com. on inquiry 6th Supreme Ct. Dist.; vice chmn. Health and Human Svc. Com., Nebr. State Senate, mem. rules and transp. coms.; bd. dirs. Sidney Fed. Savings and Loan Assn.; part owner 400 acre Family Farm, Seward County, Nebr. Formerly bd. dirs. Cheyenne County Hosp. Assn., Sidney United Fund Drive; past pres. Sidney Sch. Bd. Assn.; former mem. adv. coun. U. Nebr. Pres. and program adv. com. Nebr. Ednl. TV Commn.; trustee U. Nebr. Found.; elder Light Meml. Presbyn. Ch. Mem. ABA, Nebr. State Bar Assn., Nebr. Bar Assn., We. Nebr. Bar Assn. (past pres.), Masons, Elks (Sidney).

MAUCH, JEANNINE ANN, elementary education educator; b. Scribner, Nebr., Apr. 17, 1944; d. Oscar Herman Frederick and Viola Fredricka (Backhus) M. BS in Luth. Teaching, Concordia Coll., 1966, MEd, 1988. Cert. tchr., Nebr. Tchr. 1st, 2d, 3d and 4th grades St. Paul Luth. Ch., Perham, Minn., 1966-68; tchr. 3d and 4th grades Wheat Ridge (Colo.) Luth. Ch., 1968-70; tchr., prin. St. Mark Luth. Ch., Yonkers, N.Y., 1970-86; tchr. 3d, 4th and 5th grades Zion Luth. Ch., Plainview, Nebr., 1987—. Recipient 25-Yr. Svc. plaque Zion Luth. Ch., Plainview, 1992, others. Mem. Luth. Edn. Assn. Home: PO Box 218 Plainview NE 68769-0218

MAUGANS, JOHN CONRAD, lawyer; b. Miami County, Ind., May 10, 1938; s. Willis William and Evelyn Jeannette (Mills) M.; m. Judith M. Gallagher, Jan. 24, 1960 (dec. June 1984); children: Lisa Denise, Stacy Erin, Kristen Cherie; m. Jo Ella Middlekauff, June 7, 1985. AB, Manchester Coll., 1960; LLB with distinction, Ind. U., 1962, JD, 1969. Bar: Ind. 1962. Assoc. Barnes, Hickam, Pantzer & Boyd, Indpls., 1962-63; practice in Kokomo, 1966—; ptnr. firm Bayliff, Harrigan, Cord & Maugans, P.C., 1969—; guest lectr. Coll. Bus., Manchester Coll., 1966-80. Chmn. Howard County fund dr. Manchester Coll., 1971; bd. dirs. Tribal Trails council Girl Scouts U.S.A., 1977-85, Vols. in Community Service, 1978-84, Home Health Care of Central Ind., Inc., 1983-89; trustee Western Sch. Corp., 1986—, pres., 1991-93; bd. dirs. Kokomo Park Band Inc., 1989—; chmn. Christian Edn. com., Main St Christian Ch., 1993—; mem. asset devel. com. Cmty. Found. Howard County, Inc., 1994—. Served to capt. AUS, 1963-66. Fellow Ind. Bar Found., Am. Trial Lawyers Found. (Roscoe Pound chpt.); mem. Ind. Bar Assn., Howard County Bar Assn. (pres. 1989), Assn. Trial Lawyers Am., Ind. Trial Lawyers Assns., Manchester Coll. Alumni Assn. (chmn. area chpt. 1970, 88, 89, 90, 91), Manchester Coll. M. Alumni Assn. (pres. 1972), Order of Coif, Phi Delta Phi. Contbr. articles to legal jours. Home: 1890 S 820 West Russiaville IN 46979 Office: PO Box 2249 123 N Buckeye Kokomo IN 46904-2249

MAULDIN, WILLIAM HENRY (BILL MAULDIN), cartoonist; b. Mountain Park, N.Mex., Oct. 29, 1921; s. Sidney Albert and Edith Katrina (Bemis) M.; m. Norma Jean Humphries, Feb. 28, 1942 (div. 1946); children—Bruce Patrick, Timothy; m. Natalie Sarah Evans, June 27, 1947 (dec. Aug. 1971); children—Andrew, David, John, Nathaniel; m. Christine Ruth Lund, July 29, 1972; children: Kaja Lisa, Samuel Lund. Ed. pub. schs. and high schs., N.Mex. and Ariz.; studied art, Chicago Acad. of Fine Arts; M.A. (hon.), Conn. Wesleyan U., 1946; Litt.D. (hon.), Albion Coll., 1970, N.Mex. State U., Las Cruces, 1972; L.H.D. (hon.), Lincoln Coll., 1970, Wash. U., St. Louis, 1984, Coll. of Santa Fe, 1986. Cartoonist St. Louis Post-Dispatch, until 1962, Chgo. Sun-Times, 1962-91. Tech. adviser, actor film Teresa, 1950; actor film The Red Badge of Courage, 1950; author or cartoonist: Star Spangle Banter, 1941, Sicily Sketch Book, 1943, Mud, Mules and Mountains, 1943, This Damn Tree Leaks, 1945, Up Front (Book of the Month selection), 1945, Back Home (Book of the Month seleaction), 1947, A Sort of a Saga, 1949, Bill Mauldin's Army, 1951, Bill Mauldin in Korea, 1952, What's Got Your Back Up?, 1961, I've Decided I Want My Seat Back, 1965, The Brass Ring, 1971 (Book of Month Club selection), Mud and Guts, 1978: Let's Declare Ourselves Winners and Get the Hell Out, 1985; illustrator: Bradley: A Soldier's Story, 1978; author, illustrator numerous articles Sports Illus., Life, Collier's. Served with U.S. Army, 1940-45, 45th Inf. Div. and Stars and Stripes; campaigns Sicily, Italy, France, Germany. Decorated Purple Heart, Legion of Merit; recipient Pulitzer prize for cartoons 1944, 59, Sigma Delta Chi award for cartoons 1963, 69, 72; Prix Charles Huard de dessin de presse Fondation pour l'Art et la Recherche Paris, 1974, Walter Cronkite award for journalistic excellence Ariz. State U., 1985. Fellow Sigma Delta Chi. Home: Watkins-Loomis Agy 133 E 35th New York City NY 10016

MAURER, BEVERLY BENNETT, school administrator; b. Bklyn., Aug. 23, 1940; d. David and Minnie (Dolen) Bennett; m. Harold M. Maurer, June 12, 1960; children: Ann Maurer Rosenbach, Wendy Maurer Rausch. BA, Bklyn. Coll., 1960, postgrad., 1961; postgrad., U. Richmond, 1980-90, Va. Commonwealth U., 1980-90. Cert. tchr., N.Y., Va. Math. tchr. Col. David Marcus Jr. High Sch., Bklyn., 1960-61, Pomona (N.Y.) Jr. High Sch., 1967-68; math. tchr. Hebrew day sch. Rudlin Torah Acad., Richmond, Va., 1969-80, asst. prin., 1980-86, prin., 1986-89; dir. edn. Jewish Community Day Sch. Ctrl. Va., Richmond, 1990-93; ednl. cons., 1993—; propr. East Coast Antiques. Developed talented and gifted program, pre-admission program for children at Med. Coll. Va., 1982. Bd. dirs. Jewish Comty. Ctr., Richmond, 1980s; bd. dirs. Aux. to Med. Coll. Va., Richmond, 1980s, Aux. to U. Nebr. Med. Ctr., 1994—, Uta Hallee, 1994—. Recipient Master Tchr. award Rudlin Torah Acad., 1983. Mem. Jewish Community Day Sch. Network, Anti-Defamation League, Jewish Women's Club. Republican.

MAURER, EDGAR A., mechanical engineer; b. Dover, Ohio, July 29, 1943. BSME, Tri-State U., 1964. Staff design engr. Hoover Co., North Canton, Ohio, 1968—. Patentee in field. Office: Hoover Co 101 E Maple St North Canton OH 44720

MAURER, EDWARD LANCE, chiropractor, radiologist; b. Rahway, N.J., June 4, 1937; s. Frank Eugene and Charlotte Marian (Crook) M.; m. Jean Carol Qutten, Feb. 14,1960 (dec. 1995); children: Lance P., Terry L. D of Chiropractic, Lincoln Chiropractic Coll., Indpls., 1958; student, Western Mich. U., 1970-72, Upper Iowa U., 1974-76. Diplomate Am. Chiropractic Bd. Radiology. Pvt. practice, 1961—; editor-in-chief ACA Press Pub.; pres. Chiro/Net. Ltd., Valhalla Enterprises, land devel. co.; mem. postgrad. faculty in radiology Nat. Coll. Chiropractice, past mem. bd. dirs. Mem. editl. bd. Jour. Manipulative and Physiol. Therapeutics, Am. Jour. Chiropractic Medicine, D.C. Tracts periodical; author: (textbook) Practical Applied Roentgenology, 1983, Selected Ethics and Protocols in Chiropractic, 1991; contbr. articles to profl. jours., chpt. to book. Bd. dirs., chmn. Lincoln Coll. Edn. and Rsch. Fund, others. Fellow Can. Chiropractic Coll. Radiologists, Internat. Coll. Chiropractic; mem. Am. Chiropractic Assn. (bd. govs., exec. com., radiol. health cons., state del.), Kalamazoo County Chiropractic Assn. (past pres.), Mich. Chropractic Assn. (past dist. v.p., Chiropractor of Yr. award 1981), Am. Chiropractic Coun. Roentgenology (past dist. bd. dirs. and pres.), Am. Chiropractic Registry Radiol. Techs. (exec. v.p.). Republican. Office: Kalamazoo Chiropractic Ctr 2330 Gull Rd Kalamazoo MI 49001-1432

MAURER, MICHAEL DEAN, secondary school educator; b. Wichita, Kans., Aug. 12, 1961; s. Frederick and Patricia Ann (Felzien) M.; m. Joyce Marie Payne, June 14, 1985; children: Anthony Paul, Abigail Marie. BS in Secondary Edn., Kans. Newman Coll., 1984; postgrad., Wichita State U., 1994—. Cert. math. and phys. edn. tchr., Kans. Math. tchr. Renwick Unified Sch. Dist., Andale, Kans., 1984-86, Haysville (Kans.) Unified Sch. Dist., 1986—. Baseball umpire Metro Umpires Assn., Wichita, Kans., 1991—; football referee, Wichita, 1995—. Mem. NEA (Kans. negotiations commr. 1992-94), Haysville Edn. Assn. (chief negotiator 1991—, pres. 1993-94). Republican. Roman Catholic. Office: Haysville Campus HS 2100 W 55th St S Wichita KS 67217

MAURITZ, FORREST F., engineering manager; b. Denison, Iowa, Oct. 10, 1948. AS, Iowa State U., 1968. Project engr. Gen. Filter Corp., Ames, Iowa, 1981-86; asst. chief engr. Seabee Hampton, Hampton, Iowa, 1986-91; engring. mgr. Energy Mfg. Co., Monticello, Iowa, 1991—; mem. com. Nat. Fluid Power Assn., 1991—. Inventor patent on ctr. flow bypass valve, 1995; co-inventor patent on steam-trap valve, 1977. Vol. Troop 91, Boy Scouts Am., Dubuque, Iowa, 1994—. With U.S. Army, 1969-71. Republican. Baptist. Office: Energy Mfg Co 204 Plastic Ln Monticello IA 52310-9404

MAURO, ARTHUR V., investment executive, university chancellor; b. Thunder Bay, Ont., Can., Feb. 15, 1927; s. Arthur George and Maria (Fortezza) M.; m. Nancie June Tooley, Sept. 1, 1951; children: Barbara, Christine, Jennifer, Gregory. BA, St. Paul's, Winnipeg, 1949; LLB, Univ. Man., 1953, LLM, 1956. Bar. Manitoba Can. 1953. Spl. counsel Province of Manitoba, 1958-69, chmn. royal commn. on northern transp., 1967-69; lect. transp. and comm. law Univ. Manitoba, Can., 1967-69; chmn., dir. Investors Group Inc., 1985—; also chancellor Univ. Manitoba; bd. dirs. Investors Syndicate Ltd., Investors Group Trust Co. Ltd., Investors Syndicate Property Corp., I.G. Investment Mgnt. Ltd., Power Fin. Corp., PWA Corp., Fed. Industries Ltd., Can. Pacific Hotels Corp. Named knight of St. Gregory, 1967. Mem. Manitoba Bar Assn. Roman Catholic. Office: U Manitoba, Off of Chancellor, Winnipeg, MB Canada R3T 2N2*

MAURSTAD, DAVID INGOLF, insurance agency executive; b. North Platte, Nebr., Aug. 25, 1953; s. Ingolf Byron and Marilyn Sophia (Gimble) M.; m. Karen Sue Micek, Sept. 7, 1974; children: Ingolf, Derek, Laura. A. in Fine Arts, Platte Community Coll., Columbus, Nebr., 1973; BSBA, U. Nebr., 1989. Asst. golf profl. Country Club of Lincoln (Nebr.), 1973-76; head golf profl. Westward Ho Country Club, Sioux Falls, S.D., 1977; ins. agt. Maurstad/Zimmerman Ins., Beatrice, Nebr., 1978-84; ins. agy. mgr. Maurstad Ins. Svcs., Inc., Beatrice, 1984-90, pres., 1990—. Pres. Beatrice YMCA, 1982-83, Gage County United Way, Beatrice, 1985, founding trustee, 1st pres. Beatrice Ednl. Found., 1988—; mem. Nebr. Rep. State Cen. Com., Lincoln, 1985-90, 95—, elected Bd. Edn. Sch. Dist. #15, Beatrice, 1988-90; candidate Nebr. Legisalture, Lincoln, 1986; elected mayor City of Beatrice, 1991-94, chmn. Highway 77 Improvement Assn., 1991-94; elected state senator Nebr. Dist. 30, 1994—. Named Outstanding Young Man of Am., Beatrice Jaycees, 1985, Citizen of Yr. Beatrice C. of C., 1993, Outstanding Amateur Golfer Nebr. Golf Assn., 1981; recipient Young Alumnus award U. Nebr. Alumni Assn., 1993, Disting. Svc. award Nat. Fedn. Interscholastic Ofcls. Assn., 1989. Mem. Ind. Ins. Agts. Nebr. (Young Agt. of Yr. 1985), Blue Valley Life Underwriters (bd. dirs. 1988-94), Beatrice C. of C. (bd. dirs. 1985-87), U. Nebr.-Lincoln Coll. Bus. Adminstrn. Alumni Bd. (bd. dirs. 1989—, pres. 1994-95, Leadership award 1994), Nebr. Diplomate, Shriners, Rotary, Elks, Eagles, Mason. Lutheran. Home: 1604 S 3rd St Beatrice NE 68310-4819 Office: 121 N 6th St Beatrice NE 68310-3908

MAUST, JOSEPH J., agricultural products supplier. Pres. Active Feed Co. Office: Active Feed Co 7564 Pigeon Rd Pigeon MI 48755*

MAUTINO, FRANK J., state legislator; b. Spring Valley, Ill., Aug. 7, 1962. BS, Ill. State U. Dist. 76 rep. Ill. Ho. Reps., Springfield, 1991—; mem. housing ins., pub. safety,and infrastructure appropriations coms., Ill. Ho. Reps. Home: Webster Park Pl 108 W Saint Paul St Spring Valley IL 61362-1951*

MAUZEY, ELIZABETH MOWRY, technical education educator; b. St. Joseph, Mo., Oct. 16, 1951; d. Robert Eugene and Letha Marie (Shull) Mowry. BS in Edn., N.W. Mo. State U., Maryville, 1973; MEd, U. Mo., 1981. Cert. tchr., Mo. Instr., chairperson dept. bus. N.W. Tech. Sch., Maryville, 1976—, tech. coord., 1995—; cons. to various govt., pub. and pvt. agys., 1985—; software developer Dogwood Applications Devel., Maryville, 1989—. Contbg. author: Secretarial Technology, 1986; co-author software systems. Mem. Am. Vocat. Assn. (v.p. 1992-95, bd. dirs. 1992-95), Mo. Vocat. Assn. (bd. dirs. 1983-91, Tchr. of Yr. 1991), Mo. Bus. Edn. Assn. (pres. 1985-86, Tchr. of Yr. 1990), Maryville Tchrs. Assn. (pres. 1981-82), Internat. Assn. Rebekah Assemblies (chaplain 1988-89), Rebekah Assembly Mo. (pres. 1981-82). Office: NW Tech Sch 1515 S Munn Ave Maryville MO 64468-2757

MAXSON, JOHN EUGENE, land surveyor; b. Jackson, Mich., Dec. 8, 1945; s. John Wilbur Maxson and Betty Jane (Eash) Maxson Crisenbery; m. Gail Marie Poole, Aug. 8, 1966 (div. 1972); children: John Leonard, Karri Marie; m. Edna Lydia Krutsch, Dec. 6, 1975 (dec. Sept. 1984); m. Nancy Marie Gorczyca, Oct. 12, 1985 (div. 1996); 1 child, Gregory Michael. Student Jackson Community Coll., 1964-66 cert. Internat. Corr. Schs., 1974. Registered land surveyor, Mich., Alaska, Wis., N.D., S.D., Miss., Calif. Draftsman Commonwealth Assocs., Jackson, 1964-69, designer, 1969-73, surveyor, 1973-79; project coordinator Gilbert/Commonwealth, Jackson, 1979-82, project mgr., 1982-88; pres. Geodetic Cons. Inc., Lansing, Mich., 1988-89; pres., owner J.E. "Skip" Maxson & Assoc. Inc., Jerome, Mich., 1989—. Pres. Mirror Lake Property Owners Assn., Jerome, Mich., 1980-83, 93—, Liberty Twp. Planning Com., 1990—; trustee Mich. Mus. Surveying. Mem. Nat. Soc. Profl. Surveyors, Surveyors Hist. Soc. (bd. dirs. 1992—, Mich. Soc. Registered Land Surveyors (sec. cen. chpt. 1981-82, pres. 1984-87, state bd. dirs. 1987-93), Am. Congress Surveying and Mapping. Republican. Roman Catholic. Avocations: hunting, fishing, trapping. Home and Office: JE Skip Maxson & Assocs Inc PO Box 129 Somerset Center MI 49282

MAXSON, NANCY M., librarian; b. Detroit; d. Paul H. and Margaret L. (Warsop) Peterson; children: Michelle Maxson, Bryan Maxson. BA, Hillsdale Coll., 1960; MLS, Wayne State U., 1973. Tchr. Royal Oak (Mich.) Schs., 1962-63; libr. Van Dyke Schs., Warren, Mich., 1970—. Office: Lincoln High Sch 22500 Federal Ave Warren MI 48236

MAXWELL, EVELYN MAE, whole health educator and consultant; b. Morse, Kans., Mar. 7, 1932; d. Harry Lewis and Florence (Moore) Westhoff; m. Gordon E. Maxwell, May 31, 1952; children: Gregory, Mary Snitow, Cynthia Maxwell, Stephanie Louise. BSN, U. Kans., 1955, MN in Mental Health Nursing, 1985. RN, Kans. Pvt. duty nurse Milw.; staff nurse oper. rm. St. Luke's Hosp., Milw., Confederate Meml. Hosp., Shreveport, La.; instr. Marymount Coll. Nursing, Salina, Kans., 1984-87; vice mayor Salina City, 1995—; individual, family, group, and orgn. cons., Salina; task force Salina Prevention Partnership on Crime and Violence, 1995. Mem. subcom. on intensive supervision Salina County Corrections Com., 1988, Salina Prevention Partnership Task Force on Health; mem. Scholarship Found. Alcohol and Chem. Dependency Treatment Svcs., 1992, Housing Resource Bd., 1989-91, United Meth. Ch. Missions; resource for eating disorder support groups; Salina City Commr., 1993—, Mayor, 1996-97. Mem. ANA, Kans. State Nurses Assn. (mem. peer asssitance com. 1989). Home and Office: 414 E Wayne Ave Salina KS 67401-6778

MAXWELL, FLORENCE HINSHAW, civic worker; b. Nora, Ind., July 14, 1914; d. Asa Benton and Gertrude (Randall) Hinshaw; BA cum laude, Butler U., 1935; m. John Williamson Maxwell, June 5, 1936; children: Marilyn Maxwell Grissom, William Douglas. Coord., bd. dirs. Sight Conservation and Aid to Blind, 1962-73, nat. chmn., 1969-73; active various fund drives; chmn. jamboree, hostess coms. North Cen. High Sch., 1959, 64; Girl Scouts U.S., 1937-38, 54-56; mus. chmn. Sr. Girl Scout Regional Coun., 1956-57; scorekeeper Little League, 1955-57; bd. dirs. Nora Sch. Parents' Club, 1958-59, Eastwood Jr. High Sch. Triangle Club, 1959-62, Ind. State Symphony Soc. Women's Com., 1965-67, 76-79, Symphoguide chmn., 1976-79; vision screening Indpls. innercity pub. sch. kindergartens, pre-schs., 1962-69, also Headstart, 1967—; asst. Glaucoma screening clinics Gen. Hosp., Glendale Shopping Ctr., City County Bldg., Am. Legion Nat. Hdqrs., Ind. Health Assn. Conf., 1962-73; chmn. sight conservation and aid to blind Nat. Delta Gamma Found., Indpls., Columbus, Ohio, 1969-73; mem. telethon team Butler U. Fund, 1964; symphoguide hostess Internat. Conf. on Cities, 1971, Nat. League of Cities, 1972; mem. health adv. com. Headstart, 1976—, sec., 1980—, mem. social svcs. com., 1987—, coord. vision rescreening and referrals, assessment team of compliance steering com., 1978-79, 84, 86, 87, 88, 91, 92 (appreciation award 1983); founder People of Vision Aux., 1981, bd. dirs., 1981—, v.p., 1990-92, mem. coordinate vision and glaucoma screenings and office svcs.; initiated vision screening and eye safety education at Jameson Camp for Children:, 1987; trainer vision screening, 1988—. Recipient Key to City of Indpls., 1972, Those Spl. People award Women in Communication, 1980, Jefferson award for disting. pub. svc. Indpls. Star, 1991, Cmty. Action Head Start Outstanding Vol. award, 1996. Mem. Nat. Soc. to Prevent Blindness (now Prevent Blindness Am.), Ind. Audubon Soc., Ind. Hist. Soc., Ind. Soc. to Prevent Blindness (now Prevent Blindness Ind., dir. 1962—, exec. com. 1971—, v.p. 1983-86, sec., 1971-83, asst. sec.-treas., 1987-92), Ind. del. to nat. 3-yr. program planning conf. 1985, internal analysis task force for svcs. 1987, Sight Saving award 1974, life hon. v.p. 1983—), Jameson Camp Auxiliary, Ind. State Symphony Soc. Women's Com. (vol. Indpls. symphony orch.'s discovery concerts, vol. Indpls. noontime concerts, vol. Yuletide coffee concerts), People of Vision, Delta Gamma (chpt. golden anniversary celebration decade and communication chmn. 1975, treas. Alpha Tau house corp. 1975-78, nat. chmn. Parent Club Study Com. 1976-77, instr. province leadership seminar workshop 1989, Cable award 1969, Outstanding Alumna award 1973, Svc. Recognition award 1977, Shield award 1981, scholarship honoree 1981, Stellar award 1986, Oxford award, 1992). Republican. Address: 1502 E 80th St Indianapolis IN 46240-2706

MAXWELL, JACK ERWIN, manufacturing company executive; b. Cleve., July 17, 1926; s. Fred A. and Gertrude F. (Haug) M.; m. Martha Jane Miller, Dec. 28, 1966; children by previous marriage: Laura Jane, Fredric, Elizabeth Grant, Carla Moore, Linda Hanson. B.S., Case Inst. Tech., 1949; M.B.A., Harvard U., 1952. Indsl. engr. Lincoln Electric Co., Cleve., 1952-53; mgr. purchase analysis Ford Motor Co., Dearborn, Mich., 1953-57; v.p. Booz, Allen & Hamilton, Inc., Detroit, 1957-69; v.p. corp. devel. Am. Motors Corp., Detroit, 1969-71; v.p. adminstrn. Am. Motors Corp., 1971-76, v.p. non-automotive subsidiaries, 1976-79, v.p. diversified ops., 1979-80; chmn., pres. Wheel Horse Products, Inc., South Bend, Ind., 1974-80; chmn. Ingersoll Products Corp., Chgo., 1980-86; pres. Wellmax, Inc., 1976—. Served with USNR, 1944-46. Mem. Case Inst. Tech. Alumni Assn., Harvard Bus. Sch. Alumni Assn., Tau Beta Pi, Theta Tau. Clubs: Detroit Athletic, Economics, Chicago, Old Club. Home: 3541 Bradway Blvd Bloomfield Hills MI 48301-2409 Office: 6905 Telegraph Rd Ste 330 Bloomfield Hills MI 48301-3160

MAXWELL, JOE, state senator; b. Kirksville, Mo., Mar. 17, 1957; s. Robert E. and Molly B. Maxwell; m. Sarah Maxwell; children: Megan, Shannon. BS in Secondary Edn., Social Studies, U. Mo., 1986, JD, 1990. Farmer Rush Hill, Mo., 1976-78; ptnr., operator Maxwell Svc., Laddonia, Mo., 1978-84; rural mail carrier U.S. Postal Svc., Rush Hill, 1980-84; outstate field coord. Travis Morrison's Campaign for State Auditor, Mo., 1986; Mo. state field coord. Richard Gephardt for Pres., 1986-87; atty. Mexico, Mo., 1992—; mem. Mo. Senate, 1990-94, 1994—; mem. Senate Appropriations, Commerce and Environment, Edn., Judiciary, Labor and Indsl. Rels., Pub. Health and Welfare coms.; vice chair Elections, Pensions and Vet.'s Affairs coms. Assoc. editor-in-chief Mo. Jour. of Dispute Resolution, 1989. Mem. Am. Legion, 1982—, adj. Post 510, 1982-84; mem. Young Dem. Clubs Mo., 1982—, jud. coun. Young Dems. Am., 1985, pres., 1984-87, 9th Congl. Dist. chmn., 1982; mem. Laddonia Bapt. Ch., 1975—, Sunday Sch. tchr., 1990-91, pulpit com.; bd. dirs. Handi-Shop Inc., Mexico, 1981-84, chmn. mfg. and mktg. com., 1982-84; bd. dirs. Boy Scouts Am. Troop 94, 1980-82. Recipient St. Louis Globe Dem. award for outstanding achievement, 1979, Cert. of Appreciation, Troop 94, Boy Scouts Am., 1982, Mo.'s Outstanding Male Young Dem. award, 1987, George B. Freeman award for outstanding svc., 1987, Appreciation award Mo. Bar, 1992, Mo. Ho. of Reps. Resolution # 624 for exceptional svc. Mo., 1987, Mo. State Senate Resolution # 382 for exceptional svc. Mo., 1987; named one of Outstanding Young Men of Am., 1983, 85. Mem. Moose, Jaycees (Laddonia chpt. pres. 1978-79, coord. Laddonia Area Blood Drive, coord. Laddonia City Clean-up Day, chmn. Mexico Soybean Festival 1989, chmn. Lenten Breakfast 1990, Presdl. award of honor 1979), Kappa Delta Pi, Golden Key Nat. Honor Soc. Office: State Senate Rm 329 Capitol Bldg Jefferson City MO 65101

MAXWELL, KIMBERLY ANN, critical care nurse; b. Zanesville, Ohio, Apr. 25, 1956; d. William Allen and Shirley Ann (Walpole) Robison; m. Myron D. Maxwell, Aug. 17, 1980. AS, Ohio U., Zanesville, 1980. Cert. ACLS, ACLS instr., CCRN, PALS. Staff med.-surg. RN Springfield (Ohio) Community Hosp., 1980-81; charge med.-surg. RN Medina (Ohio) Community Hosp., 1981-82; staff med.-surg. RN Bethesda Hosp., Zanesville, 1982-86; staff RN ICU Grant Med. Ctr., Columbus, Ohio, 1986—. Mem. AACN. Republican. Methodist.

MAXWELL, PATRICIA JOY, fund raising executive; b. Belle Plaine, Iowa, Feb. 7, 1937; d. Verne Edwin and Julia Inez (Beem) M. Student Pepperdine Coll., 1954-55; BS, Iowa State Tchrs. Coll., 1958; MPA, Roosevelt U., 1982. Dir. resource devel. Boys Clubs Am., 1978-81; exec. dir. Westlake Health Svcs. Found., 1981-84; assoc. dean devel. and alumni affairs U. Ill. Coll. Medicine, 1984-91; sr. maj. gifts officer U. Ill., 1991-93; v.p. devel. Orlando (Fla.) M.D. Anderson Cancer Ctr., 1993; assoc. dir. spl. gifts nat. hdqs. Alzheimer's Assn., Chgo., 1995; exec. dir. Friendly Hills Healthcare Found., La Habra, Calif., 1996—; cons. Ency. Britannica Ednl. Corp., Prentice Hall Inc., U.S. State Dept. Mem. N.Y. Acad. Scis., Am. Mktg. Assn., Chgo. Area Pub. Affairs Group, Univ. Club (Chgo.), Balboa (Calif.) Bay Club, Lake Nona Club (Orlando). Address: PO Box 5916 Newport Beach CA 92662-5916

MAXWELL, RICHARD EUGENE, educational association administrator; b. Jackson Center, Ohio, Nov. 21, 1940; s. Merton E. and Ruth Mary (Zehner) M.; m. Rosemary Forestal, Aug. 25, 1962; children: Susan, R. Kevin, John. BA, Coll. of Wooster, 1962; MA in Edn., U. Akron, 1968; postgrad., Kent State U. Cert. tchr., sch. supt., Ohio. Tchr. Cloverleaf Local Schs., Seville, Ohio, 1962-68; asst. prin., fed. coord. West Holmes Local Schs., Millersburg, Ohio, 1968-70; supt. of schs. West Holms Local Schs., Millersburg, Ohio, 1970-81, Holmes County Schs., Millersburg, 1981-93; dir. leadership devel. Buckeye Assn. Sch. Adminstrs., 1993—; cons. sch. fin. Buckeye Assn. Sch. Adminstrs., Westerville, Ohio, 1980-92, Ohio Dept. Edn., Columbus, 1980-92; prof; Ashland (Ohio) U., 1981—. Author: Practitioners Guide to School Finance, 1992. Mem. Juvenile Attention Ctr. Planning Com., Canton, Ohio; mem. Holmes County Cmty. Players, Millersburg. Recipient Dick Maxwell Edn. award Berlin (Ohio) Area Bus. Assn., 1987. Mem. Am. Edn. Fin. Assn., Am. Assn. Sch. Adminstrs. (com. mem.), Buckeye Assn. Sch. Adminstrs. (pres. 1985-86, Exemplary Leadership award), Rotary Internat. (pres. Millersburg chpt.), Phi Delta Kappa. Democrat. Roman Catholic. Home: 1269 Gemstone Sq W Westerville OH 43081-4562 Office: 750 Brooksedge Blvd Westerville OH 43086-6138

MAXWELL, RUTH ELAINE, artist, interior designer, decorative painter; b. Cleve., Oct. 7, 1934; d. Norman Lee and Katherine Ellen (Hamilton) Brown; m. Clarence LeRoy Maxwell, June 25, 1955; children: Lisa Maxwell Callahan, Lynne Maxwell Quinn, Laura Maxwell Jochem, James. BFA, Ohio State U., 1956, teaching cert., 1956. Cert. elem. sch. tchr., Ohio. Tchr. Hilliard (Ohio) Elem. Sch., 1956-58; comptr. Callahan Family Golf Ctr., Hilliard, 1989—. Pres. Capa Colleagues, Ohio Theatre, Columbus, 1986; pres., governing bd. Theatre Shop, 1988, buyer, 1995—; vol. Columbus Assn. Performing Arts Colleagues, 1981—; mem. Hilliard Arts Coun., 1989-91; vocalist Damenchor of Columbus Maennerchor, 1975—, treas., 1979-81, fin. sec., 1991-94; sec. Canterbury Unit of Columbus Symphony Orch. Women's Assn., 1993-94, treas., 1995-96, project chairperson, 1996—, v.p., 1996—; mem. Women's Guild of Opera, Columbus, 1994—. Mem. Gamma Alpha Chi (hon., sec. Ohio State U. chpt. 1954), Gamma Phi Beta. Republican.

MAY, ALAN ALFRED, lawyer; b. Detroit, Apr. 7, 1942; s. Alfred Albert and Sylvia (Sheer) M.; m. Elizabeth Miller; children: Stacy Ann, Julie Beth. BA, U. Mich., 1963, JD, 1966. Bar: Mich. 1967, D.C. 1976; registered nursing home adminstr., Mich. Ptnr. May and May, Detroit, 1967-79, pres. May & May, P.C., 1979—; spl. asst. atty. gen. State of Mich., 1970—; of counsel Charfoos & Christensen P.C. and predecessor firm Charfoos, Christensen & Archer, P.C. (name changed to Charfoos & Christensen P.C.), Detroit, 1970—; pres., instr. Med-Leg Seminars, Inc., 1978; lectr. Wayne State U., 1974; instr. Oakland U., 1969. Chmn. Rep. 18th Congl. Dist. Com., 1983-87, now chmn. emeritus; chmn. 19th Congl. Dist. Com., 1981-83; mem. Mich. Rep. Com., 1976-84; del. Rep. Nat. Conv., 1984, mem. platform com., 1988; former chmn. Mich. Civil Rights Commn., Mich. Cancer Found.; past mem. Mich. Civil Svc. Commn.; trustee NCCJ (mem. exec. bd. of Nat. Conf.), Temple Beth El Birmingham, Mich., also v.p., mem. exec. bd.; mem. Electoral Coll.; bd. dirs., exec. bd. Detroit Round Table, Charfoos Charitable Found. Mem. The Nat. Conf. (exec. bd.), Detroit Bar Assn., Oakland County Bar Assn., Victors Club, Franklin Hills Country Club (past pres., bd. dirs.), Presidents Club (trustee). Contbr. article to profl. jours. Home: 4140 Echo Rd Bloomfield Hills MI 48302-1941 Office: May & May PC 3000 Town Ctr Ste 2600 Southfield MI 48075-1211

MAY, BRIAN HENRY, state legislator; b. St. Louis, Nov. 22, 1962. BS in Edn. summa cum laude, Harris-Stowe State Coll., 1986; JD, St. Louis U., 1989. Mem. dist. 108 Mo. Ho. of Reps.; with firm Casserly, Jones & Brittingham, P.C., St. Louis, 1990-95, Larsen, Feist & Bedell, P.C., St. Louis, 1995—. Office: 5816 Pennsylvania Saint Louis MO 63111

MAY, BRYCE JON, computer consultant; b. Audubon, Iowa, June 26, 1948; s. Anthony W. and Marie J. (Rasmussen) M. BS, Western Mich. U., 1987. Cert. radiation protection technologist. Congl. aide/counselor Hon. Ron Dellums, Berkeley, Calif., 1973-75; health physics/chemistry engr. Mgmt. Support Svcs., Grand Junction, Mich., 1975-85, pres., 1985—. Treas. Columbia Twp., Van Buren County, Mich., 1995—. With USN, 1968-73. Mem. Bangor Lions (dir. 1992—). Democrat. Office: Mgmt Support Svcs 10083 County Rd 215 Grand Junction MI 49056

MAY, FRANK BRENDAN, JR., lawyer; b. Bronx, N.Y., Oct. 17, 1945; s. Frank Brendan and Margaret (Borza) M.; m. Mary Frances Fitzsimmons, June 19, 1976; children: David Brendan, Brian Christopher. BA in Econs., NYU, 1973, postgrad., 1973-75; JD, John Marshall Law Sch., Chgo., 1978. Bar: Ill. 1979, U.S. Dist. Ct. (no. dist.) Ill. 1979, U.S. Ct. Appeals (7th cir.), 1979, U.S. Supreme Ct. 1995. Legal intern criminal div. Cook County State's Atty.'s Office, Chgo., 1977-78; legal intern juvenile div. DuPage County State's Atty.'s Office, Wheaton, Ill., 1978; sr. assoc. atty. Lillig, Kemp & Thorness, Ltd., Oak Brook, Ill., 1978-81; v.p., gen. counsel Coldwell Banker, Oak Brook, 1981-90, Prudential Preferred Properties, Des Plaines, Ill., 1991—; arbitrator 18th Jud. Cir. Ct., Dupage County, Ill., 1993—. Sgt. USAF, 1963-67. NYU Coun. scholar, 1971-73; David Davis Meml. scholar, 1970-71. Mem. ABA (real estate sect.), Ill. State Bar assn. (real estate sect.), DuPage county Bar Assn. (real estate law com., lic. Ill. real estate broker 1994), Medinah Country Club. Home: 2064 Stonebridge Ct Wheaton IL 60187-7177 Office: Prudential Pref Properties 2700 S River Rd Ste 415 Des Plaines IL 60018-4108

MAY, LARRY, philosophy educator; b. Pitts., Apr. 26, 1952; s. Lawrence S. and Frances J. (Zoller) M.; m. Marilyn Friedman, Feb. 8, 1988; 1 child, Elizabeth Nichole. BSFS, Georgetown U., 1973; MA in Philosophy, New Sch. Social Rsch., 1976, PhD, 1977. Asst. prof. philosophy U. Conn., Storrs, 1977-79; vis. asst. prof. philosophy U. Wis., Madison, 1979; from asst. prof. to prof. philosophy Purdue U., West Lafayette, Ind., 1979-91; prof. philosophy Washington U., St. Louis, 1991—; cons. Ind. State Senate, Indpls., 1981. Author: The Morality of Groups, 1987, Sharing Responsibility, 1992, The Socially Responsive Self, 1996; co-editor: Collective Responsibility, 1991, Rethinking Masculinity, 1992, Applied Ethics: A Multicultural Approach, 1993, Mind and Morals, 1995, Hannah Arendt: Twenty Years Later, 1996; mem. editl. bd. Bus. Ethics Quar., 1990—, Jour. Social Philosophy, 1993—. Mem. ethics com. St. Louis Children's Hosp., 1991—. Grantee Exxon Edn. Found., 1982, Eli Lilly Endowment, 1990, 91, NSF, 1993-95. Mem. Am. Philos. Assn. Office: Washington U Dept Philosophy 1 Brookings Dr Saint Louis MO 63130-4862

MAY, LINDA KAREN CARDIFF, safety engineer, nurse; b. San Mateo, Calif., Oct. 26, 1948; d. Leon Davis and Jane Vivian (Gallow) Cardiff; m. Donald William May, Dec. 7, 1969 (div. Feb. 1988); children: Charles David, Andrew William. Student in nursing So. Ill. U., 1969, Ill Wesleyan U., 1989; AAS, Parkland Coll., 1977; BS in Pub. Health and Safety Engring. with honors, U. Ill., Urbana, 1987; RN, BSN, Lakeview Coll., 1990. RN, Ill., Ind., Mo., N.Mex., Tex., Wis.; registered profl. nurse; nat. registered EMT, Ill.; OSHA accredited instr. constrn. safety and health. Indsl. nurse C.S. Johnson Co., Champaign, Ill., 1978-79; safety dir. Solo Cup Co., Urbana, Ill., 1979-84; safety engr. Clinton Nuclear Power Plant, Ill. Power Co., 1984-86, occupational safety and health specialist Danville Vet.'s Med. Ctr., 1986—; with LKM Health and Safety Cons., Inc., Champaign, Ill. Mem. Champaign County Crime Prevention Coun., 1978-83, bd. dirs., 1980-82; active Champaign County Task Force on Arson, 1981—, Mercy Hosp. Aux., Covenant Hosp Auxiliary, 1977—. Ill. State Gen. Assembly scholar, 1967. Mem. AACN, APHA (mem. occupational health and safety sect.), Am. Soc. Safety Engrs. (vice chair Ctrl. Ill. sect. 1985-86), Am. Nuclear Soc. (mem. biology and medicine divsn., mem. radiopharm. and isotope product stds. com.), Am. Assn. Occupational Health Nurses, Nat. Registery EMT, Ill. Environ. Health Assn., Ill. Soc. Pub. Health Educators, Associated Ill. Milk, Food and Environ. Sanitarians, Pre-Hosp. Care Providers Ill., Ill. EMTs Assn., N.Y. Acad. Sci, U. Ill. Alumni Assn. (life), Parkland Coll. Almuni Assn. (life, bd. dirs. 1987—, v.p. 1992—), Parkland Coll. Found. Bd. (alumni assn. liason bd. dirs. 1993), Ill. Wesleyan U. Alumni Assn., Lakeview Coll. Nursing Alumni Assn., Eta Sigma Gamma. Methodist. Home: PO Box 3954 Champaign IL 61826-3954

MAY, MARGRETHE, allied health educator; b. Tucson, Ariz., Oct. 6, 1943; d. Robert A. and Margrethe (Holm) M. BS in Human Biology, U. Mich., 1970, MS in Anatomy, 1986. Cert. surg. technologist. Surg. technologist Hartford (Conn.) Hosp., 1965-68, U. Mich. Hosps., Ann Arbor, 1968-70; asst. operating room supr. U. Ariz. Med. Ctr., Tucson, 1971-72; coord. operating room tech. program Pima Coll., Tucson, 1971-76; prof., coord. surg. tech. and surg. first asst. programs Delta Coll., University Center, Mich., 1978—; commr. Commn. on Accreditation of Allied Health Ednl. Programs, Chgo., 1994—, Coun. Accreditation and Unit Recognition, 1994—. Editor: Core Curriculum for Surgical Technology, 3d edit., 1990, Core Curriculum for Surgical First Assisting, 1993; contbr. articles to profl. jours. Mem. Assn. Surg. Technologists (bd. dirs. 1987-89, pres.-elect 1989-90, pres. 1990-91, on-site visitor program accreditation 1974—, chmn. exam writing com. 1981, liaison coun. on cert. co-chmn. 1977, chmn. 1978, sec.-treas. 1979, chmn. accreditation review com for edn. in surg. tech. 1994—), Am. Soc. Law, Medicine and Ethics, Mich. Assn. Allied Health Professions (sec. 1994—), Nat. Network Health Career Programs in Two-Year Colls. Home: 2506 Abbott Rd Apt P-2 Midland MI 48642-4876 Office: Delta Coll Dept Surgery University Center MI 48710

MAY, PHYLLIS JEAN, financial executive; b. Flint, Mich., May 31, 1932; d. Bert A. and Alice C. (Rushton) Irvine; m. John May, Apr. 24, 1971. Grad. Dorsey Sch. Bus., 1957; cert. Internat. Corr. Schs., 1959, Nat. Tax Inst., 1978; MBA, Mich. U., 1970. Registered real estate agt; lic. life, auto and home ins. agent. Office mgr. Comml. Constrn. Co., Flint, 1962-68; bus. mgr. new and used car dealership, Flint, 1968-70; contr. various corps., Flint, 1970-75; fiscal dir. Rubicon Odyssey Inc., Detroit, 1976-87, Wayne County Treas.'s Office, 1987-93; exec. fin. office Grosse Pointe Meml. Ch., 1993—; acad. cons. acctg. Detroit Inst. Commerce, 1980-81; pres. small bus. specializing in adminstrv. cons. and acctg., 1982—; supr. mobile svc. sta., upholstery and home improvement businesses; owner retail bus. Pieces and Things. Pres. PTA Westwood Heights Schs., 1972; vol. Fedn. of Blind, 1974-76, Probate Ct., 1974-76; mem. citizens adv. bd. Northville Regional Psychiat. Hosp., 1988, sec. 1989-90. Recipient Meritorious Svc. award Genesee County for Youth, 1976, Excellent Performance and High Achievement award Odyssey Inc., 1981. Mem. NAFE (bd. dirs.), Am. Bus. Women's Assn. (treas. 1981, rec. sec. 1982, v.p. 1982-83, Woman of Yr. 1982), Womens Assn. Dearborn Orch. Soc., Dearborn Community Art Ctr., Mich. Mental Health Assn., Internat. Platform Assn., Guild of Carillonneurs in N.Am., Pi Omicron (officer 1984-85). Baptist.

MAYANS, CARLOS, state legislator; m. Linda K. Mayans. Kans. state rep. Dist. 100, 1993—, chmn. health and human svcs. com., owner ins. agy. Home: 1842 N Valleyview St Wichita KS 67212-6738*

MAYER, DONNA MARIE, management information systems manager; b. Cicero, Ill., Apr. 21, 1949; d. Edward J. and Valerie I. (Laskowski) Veverka; m. Scott H. Mayer, Jan. 30, 1971. BS in Math., U. Ill., 1971; MBA, U. Calif., Irvine, 1975. Rsch. asst. U. Ill., Urbana, 1969-71; office mgr., tax preparer H & R Block, Calif., 1972; campus stats. info. coord., project mgr., sys. analyst U. Calif., Irvine, 1972-80; project mgr. Northrop, Hawthorne, 1980-83; cons. self-employed Ill., 1983—; tax cons. in field, 1972—; guest spkr. in field. Statis. info. coord.: Mgmt. Info. Systems, 1972-79, Leadership Info. coordination, 1979, Student & Workload Computerized Estimation System Model, 1973-80. Campus statis. info. coord. U. Calif., Irvine, 1972-80; cmty. fund raising for charities, Panhellenic Scholarship Fund; pres. Alpha Xi Delta Long Beach Alumnae, v.p., treas., sec., 1977-80, mem., 1968—; charity funding U.S. Navy Wives Club, Nuclear U.S. Navy Wives membership recognition, 1975; fall festival com. Friends of Danada Forest Preserve, Ill., 1989-95; mem. PTA, Ill., 1990-95; mem. Girl Scouts USA, 1958-67, 71-72, 90-95, leader, 1971-72, 90-95; ch. organist, 1963-71, 71-77. James scholar U. Ill., 1967—, Dean's list U. Ill., 1967-71; recipient Silver award for Excellence in Income Tax Preparation, 1972, Good Sportsmanship award, 1979, U. Employee Scholarship award, 1973-75. Mem. AAUW (corp. del. U. Calif. Irvine 1976-79, Nat. Leadership award 1979, univ. del. nat. conv. 1979, hon. bd. dirs. scholarship com. 1975-81), LWV (state budget com. vice chmn. 1975-76, state study com. 1976-78, bd. treas. Orange Coast League 1979-80, treas. 1977-79, com. chmn. 1975-81), Northrop Mgmt. Group, U. Calif. Faculty Club, Am. Statis. Assn., Acad. of Mgmt., Calif. Women in Higher Edn., Assn. Systems Mgmt., Assn. Computing Machinery, Grad. Sch. Mgmt. Alumnae, U. Calif. Alumnae Assn., U. Ill. Alumnae Assn., Internat. Toastmistress Clubs (area. coun. bd. dirs. 1978-80, coun. treas. 1979-80, Speech Contest award 1979, pres., v.p. 1978-79, treas., sec. 1977-78, parliamentarian com. chmn., recording sec. 1978-79, Internat. Mag. recognition 1979, regional rep. 1980), Panhellenic Coun. (bd. dirs. 1969-71, scholarship chmn. 1969-71), Naperville H.S. Alumnae. Home: 601 Arboretum Cir Wheaton IL 60187

MAYER, MARK E., engineering executive; b. Milw., Mar. 21, 1961; s. Eugene A. and Daisymae L. (Sallis) M. BSME, Mich. Technol. U., 1984. Registered profl. engr., Wis. Engr. Marinette (Wis.) Marine, 1985-88, Marathon Engrs., Menasha, Wis., 1989-94; project mgr. Omnni Assocs., Appleton, Wis., 1994—. Commr. Menasha Bd. Edn., 1994—; trustee Menasha Edn. Endowment Fund, 1994—; councilman Bethel Evang. Luth. Ch., Menasha, 1992-94; bd. dirs. Bethel Elem. Sch., Menasha, 1995. Mem. ASME (sect. pres. 1992), TAPPI. Home: 519 First St Menasha WI 54952 Office: Omnni Associates 303 S Bluemound Dr Appleton WI 54914

MAYER, ROBERT ANTHONY, college president; b. N.Y.C., Oct. 30, 1933; s. Ernest John and Theresa Margaret (Mazura) M.; m. Laura Wiley Christ, Apr. 30, 1960. BA magna cum laude, Fairleigh Dickinson U., 1955; MA, NYU, 1967. With N.J. Bank and Trust Co., Paterson, 1955-61; mgr. advt. dept. N.J. Bank and Trust Co., 1959-61; program supr. advt. dept. Mobil Oil Co., N.Y.C., 1961-62; asst. to dir. Latin Am. program Ford Found., N.Y.C., 1963-65; asst. rep. Ford Found., Brazil, 1965-67; asst. to v.p. adminstrn., 1967-73; officer in charge logistical services Ford Found., 1968-73; asst. dir. programs N.Y. Community Trust, N.Y.C., 1973-76; exec. dir. N.Y. State Council on the Arts, N.Y.C., 1976-79; mgmt. cons. N.Y.C., 1979-80; dir. Internat. Mus. Photography, George Eastman House, Rochester, N.Y., 1980-89, mgmt. cons., 1989-90; pres. Cleve. Inst. of Art, 1990—. Mem. editorial adv. bd.: Grants mag., 1978-80; author: (plays) La Borgia, 1971; Alijandru, 1971, They'll Grow No Roses, 1975. Mem. state program adv. panel NEA, 1977-80; mem. Mayor's Com. on Cultural Policy, N.Y.C., 1974-75; mem. pres.'s adv. com. Bklyn. campus, L.I. U., 1978-79; bd. dirs. Fedn. Protestant Welfare Agys., N.Y.C., 1977-79, Arts for Greater Rochester, 1981-83, Garth Fagan's Dance Theatre, 1982-86; trustee Internat. Mus. Photography, 1981-89, Lacoste Sch. Arts, France, 1991—, sec., 1994—; mem. dean's adv. com. Grad. Sch. Social Welfare, Fordham U., 1976; mem. N.Y. State Motion Picure and TV Devel. Adv. Bd., 1984-87, N.Y. State Martin Luther King Jr. Commn., 1985-90, Cleve. Coun. Cultural Affairs, 1992-94; chmn. Greater Cleve. Regional Transit Authority Arts in Transit Com., 1992-95. Recipient Nat. award on advocacy for girls Girls Clubs Am., 1976. Mem. Nat. Assembly Art Agys. (bd. dirs. 1977-79, 1st vice chmn. 1978-79), Alliance Ind. Colls. Art (bd. dirs. 1983-91, vice chmn. 1986-87, sec. 1987-89), N.Y. State Assn. Museums (bd. councilors 1983-86, pres. 1986-89), Assn. Ind. Colls. Art and Design (bd. dirs. 1991—, exec. com. 1991-93). Home: 20201 N Park Blvd Apt 101 Shaker Heights OH 44118-5024 Office: Cleve Inst Art 11141 East Blvd Cleveland OH 44106-1710

MAYERS, DOUGLAS BRUCE, anesthesiologist, medical director; b. Coral Gables, Fla., May 24, 1949; s. Isadore Rhett and Le Ann (Rozran) M.; m. Ruth Ellen Schwartz Mayers, Aug. 5, 1973; children: Debra Beth, Joshua Kenneth, David Isaac. AB, Washington U., St. Louis, 1971; PhD in Pharmacology, 1977, MD, 1977. Diplomate Am. Bd. ANesthesiologists. Resident physician U. Hosp. Cleve., 1978-81; staff physician Mt. Sinai Med. Ctr. Cleve., 1981—; med. dir. Ambulatory Surgery and Endoscopy, 1993—; cons. Med. malpractice Cases, Cleve., 1985—. Chmn. Physicians Divsn. Jewish Welfare Fund, Cleve., 1994-96. Mem. AMA, ACP, Physician Execs. Northeast Ohio, Am. Soc. Anesthesiologists. Jewish. Office: Mt Sinai Integrated Med Campus 26900 Cedar Rd Ste 30N Beachwood OH 44122

MAYES, BILL EDWIN, educational administrator; b. Hamilton, Mo., Oct. 1, 1934; s. Lawrence and Ada May (Smith) M.; m. Loraine Martha Lampman, June 24, 1962; children: Mark, Todd, Karin. BS in Edn., Cen. Mich. U., 1961, MA, 1981. Cert. secondary tchr. Advt. clk. Am. Motors, Detroit, 1953-54, 54-56; factory worker Bathey Mfg., Plymouth, Mich., summers 1959-61; secondary tchr. St. Louis (Mich.) Pub. Schs., 1961-82; lic. residential builder L&M Builders, St. Louis, 1970-81; regional career tech. edn. adminstr. Gratiot Isabella Regional Edn. Svc. Dist., Ithaca, Mich., 1982—; chmn. Career Edn. Adv. Commn., Lansing, 1992; bd. dirs. Employability Skills Adv. com., State of Mich., Strategic Planning for Career Tech. Edn., Vocat. Tech. Edn. Curriculum Consortium. Sec. Greater Gratiot Devel., Ithaca, 1991; bd. dirs. St. Louis Downtown Devel. Authority, 1992; exec. bd. United Way, Gratiot County, 1983-89. With U.S. Army, 1954-56. Recipient Mich. Leadership award State of Mich., 1987. Mem. Mich. Occupational Edn. Assn. (pres. 1991-92), Mich. Congress Sch. Adminstrs., Mich. Coun. Vocat. Adminstrs. (pres. 1988, exec. com.), Mich. Assn. Career Edn. (pres. 1984, bd. dirs. Disting. Svc.), St. Louis Lions Club (pres. 1970), Mich. Occupational Info. Svc. (adv. bd.), Phi Delta Kappa (pres. 1992-93). Republican. Methodist. Home: Orchard Pointe Saint Louis MI 48880 Office: Gratiot Isabella RESD Box 310 1131 E Center St Ithaca MI 48847-1603

MAYES, JEAN MARIE KEALLY, global education and foreign language educator; b. Pitts., July 11, 1942; d. Walter Edward and Pauline Gertrude (Hughes) Keally; m. David Lincoln Mayes, June 12, 1971; 1 child, Paul B. BA, Seton Hill Coll., Greensburg, Pa., 1964; MA, U. Pitts., 1970, U. Iowa, 1987. Conversational English tchr. Lycée Jeanne d'Arc, Clermont-Fd, France, 1964-65; tchr. 6th grade St. Mary's Sch., Joplin, Mo., 1965-66; instr. French Seton Hill Coll., 1966-71; tchr. French Villa Maria High Sch., Erie, Pa., 1972-78; asst. prof. French Tenn. State U., Nashville, 1980-81; substitute tchr. various schs., Mt. Pleasant/Iowa City, Iowa, 1982-84; tchr. French Regina High Sch., Iowa City, 1984-85; program designer Sac and Fox Settlement Sch., Tama, Iowa, 1988-89; program coord. Iowa Peace Inst., Grinnell, Iowa, 1989-94; ESL instr. Briar Cliff Coll., 1995—. Freelance writer Internat. Travel mag. and Sioux City Jour. Coord. Grinnell Peace Links, 1991-94; co-chair LeMars Sister Cities Assn., 1995—. Mem. AAUW, Grinnell LWV (bd. dirs. 1989-91), Am. Assn. Tchrs. French. Home: 646 Lee Dr Le Mars IA 51031

MAYES, MAUREEN DAVIDICA, physician, educator; b. Phila., Oct. 16, 1945; d. David M. and Marguerite Cecilia (Fineran) M.; m. Charles William Houser, Dec. 18, 1976; children: David Steven, Edward Charles. BA, Coll. Notre Dame, 1967; MD, Ea. Va. Med. Sch., 1976; MA in Pub. Health, U. Mich., Ann Arbor, 1994. Resident in internal medicine Cleve. Clinic Found., 1977-79, fellow in rheumatology, 1979-81; asst. prof. medicine W.Va. U., Morgantown, 1981-85; asst. prof. medicine Wayne State U., Detroit, 1985-90, assoc. prof. medicine, 1990—; dir. scleroderma unit Wayne State U., Detroit, 1991—. Contbr. articles to profl. jours. Pres. bd. United Scleroderma Found., 1988-89, mem. med. adv. bd., 1995—; bd. trustees Mich. chpt. Arthritis Found. Robert Wood Johnson scholarship EVMS, 1972, NIH fellow, 1993-94, NIAMS Sr. Rsch. fellowship, 1994; recipient Lower award Cleve. Clinic Found., 1981. Fellow Am. Coll. Rheumatology (mem. ctrl. region coun. 1995—), Am. Coll. Physicians; mem. Am. Fedn. Clin. Rsch., Mich. Rheumatism Soc. Office: Wayne State U Hutzel Hosp 4707 Saint Antoine St Detroit MI 48201-1427

MAYFIELD, HAROLD FORD, biology educator; b. Mpls., Mar. 25, 1911; s. John Edwin and Ida Mathilda (Thorberg) Blegen; m. Virginia Gaby Duval, June 14, 1936; children: Sigrid Christina, John Eric, Sheryl Melinda, Charles Frederick. BS, Shurtleff Coll., 1933; MA in Math., U. Ill., 1934; DSc (hon.), Occidental Coll., 1968, Bowling Green State U., 1975. Dir. pers. Owens-Illinois Inc., Toledo, 1936-71, ret., 1971; adj. prof. biology U. Toledo, 1982—. Author: The Kirtland's Warbler, 1960; contbr. articles to profl. jours. Coun. mem. President's Com. on Equal Opportunity, Washington, 1962-68; mem. Toledo Bd. Community Rels., 1968-71, Toledo-Lucas County Libr. Bd., 1971, Recovery Team Kirtland's Warbler, Washington, 1975-90. Recipient U.S. Forest Svc. 75th Anniversary award, 1980, Disting. Svc. award Detroit Audubon Soc., 1960, Disting. Svc. award Audubon Soc. Western Pa., 1978, Arthur A. Allen award Cornell U., 1990; named to Ohio Conservation Hall of Fame, 1978. Fellow AAAS, Am. Ornithologists Union (pres. 1966-68); mem. Wilson Ornithol. Soc. (pres. 1961-62), Cooper Ornithol. Soc. (pres. 1974-75). Home: 1614 Gronlund Cir Toledo OH 43614

MAYNARD, JOAN, education educator; b. Louisa, Ky., Oct. 18, 1932; d. Macon Scott and Jeanette (Thompson) Chambers; m. Frank Maynard Jr., June 15, 1951 (dec. Oct. 1988); children: Mark Steven, Julia Beth Maynard McFann, Robert Blake. BA, Wittenberg U., 1977; MEd, Wright State U., 1980, Wright State U., 1984. Tchr., reading specialist Mechanicsburg (Ohio) Exempted Village Schs., 1976—; pres. TOTT Publs. Inc., Bellbrook, Ohio, 1988—; rep. Career Edn., Mechanicsburg, 1981-88, mem. Thompson Grant Com., Mechanicsburg, 1987-88. Author: Mud Puddles, 1988, Mud Pies, 1989. Vol. Mechanicsburg Schs. Levy, 1980, 82, 88, Congl. Race, Campaign County, Ohio, 1982, 84, 86; cons. Urbana U., Ohio, 1988-90, 91, 92, 93; tutor Laubach Lit. Action, Urbana, 1989-90, 91-93, 94. Recipient Thompson grant, 1982, 88, 92. Mem. AAUW (edn. chmn. Champaign County chpt. 1988-89, treas. 1989-90), Internat. Reading Assn., Champaign County Reading Coun. (treas. 1990-91), Midwestern Assembly Lit. Young People (treas. 1989-93), Kappa Delta Pi. Home: 1546 Parkview Rd Mechanicsburg OH 43044-9779 Office: Exempted Village Schs 60 High St Mechanicsburg OH 43044-1003

MAYNARD, JOHN M., manufacturing executive; b. Waukasha, Wis., Nov. 15, 1948. Assoc. Electronics Engring. Tech., Waukasha County Tech. Inst., 1969. Product specialist GTE Automatic Electric, Waukasha, 1968-81, Graham Co., Milw., 1981—. Light and sound technician Waukasha Civic Theater, 1964-69, 75-78, First United Meth. Ch., 1975—; cons. First United Meth. Ch., West Allis, Wis., 1988—. Staff sgt. USAF, 1970-74. Republican. Methodist. Office: Graham Co PO Box 23880 Milwaukee WI 53223-0880

MAYNARD, ROBERT HOWELL, lawyer; b. San Antonio, Feb. 15, 1938; s. William Simpson Sr. and Lillian Isabel (Tappan) M.; m. Joan Marie Pearson, Jan. 6, 1962; children: Gregory Scott, Patricia Kathryn, Alicia Joan, Elizabeth Simms. BA, Baylor U., 1959, LLB, 1961; LLM, Georgetown U., 1965. Bar: Tex. 1961, D.C. 1969, Ohio 1973. Trial atty. gen. litigation sect. lands div. U.S. Dept. Justice, Washington, 1964-65; spl. asst. to solicitor U.S. Dept. Interior, Washington, 1965-69; legis. asst. U.S. Senate, Washington, 1969-73; ptnr., dept. head Smith & Schnacke, Dayton, Ohio, 1973-83; dir. Ohio EPA, Columbus, Ohio, 1983-85; ptnr., environ. policy and stategy devel., tech. law Vorys, Sater, Seymour and Pease, Columbus, 1985—. Trustee Ohio Found. for Entrepren. Edn., Business Technology Ctr., Episcopal Cmty. Svcs. Found. USNR, 1962-65. Episcopalian. Office: Vorys Sater Seymour & Pease PO Box 1008 52 E Gay St Columbus OH 43216-1008

MAYPOLE, DONALD EUGENE, social work educator; b. Boise, Idaho, July 7, 1934; s. Walter Maypole and Isabel (Wray) McKay; m. Mary Jane Rosnow, July 18, 1964; children: Nathan, Kristen. AA, Boise Jr. Coll.,

1954; BS in Psychology, Idaho State Coll., 1957; MSW, U. Wis., 1961; PhD, U. Minn., 1979. Cons. div. mental hygiene Bur. Community Resources, Madison, Wis., 1965-69, asst. dir., 1969-71; exec. dir. Miss. River Human Svcs. Ctr., Independence, Wis., 1971-76; coord. social work program Coll. St. Teresa, Winona, MN, 1977-79; assoc. prof., dept. dir. U. No. Iowa, Cedar Falls, 1979-86; dir. dept. social work U. Minn., Duluth, 1986—; cons., Duluth, 1986—; vis. prof. Social Svc. Inst., Porto, Portugal, 1992. Co-author: Relationships in Social Service Practice, 1983; contbr. over 30 articles to profl. jours., also chpts. to books, presentations in field; mem. editorial bd. Jour. Edn. for Social Work, 1983-86, Jour. Activities, Adaptation and Aging, 1985—; manuscript reviewer State and Local Govt. Rev., 1988; mem. editorial com. The Haworth Press. Bd. Ctr. for Alcohol and Drug Treatment, 1986-93. Lt. Col. USAF and USANG, 1952-83. Fulbright scholar, 1985, 88, Salzburg seminar fellow, 1986; recipient letter of commendation Warren P. Knowles, Alumni Achievement award Idaho State U., 1990. Mem. Nat. Assn. Social Workers, Coun. on Social Work Edn., Inter-Univ. Consortium for Social Devel., Fulbright Assn., Nat. Guard Assn. Home: 10774 E EFAW Ln Lake Nebagamon WI 54849-9025 Office: U Minn Dept Social Work Duluth MN 55812

MAYR, JAMES JEROME, fertilizer company executive; b. Beaver Dam, Wis., Aug. 19, 1942; s. Alfred A. and Maxine E. (Kuehl) M.; m. Carol Ann Kaufman, Sept. 4, 1965; children: Christin and Carin (twins), Cathy, Conni. BS in Agrl. Econs., U. Wis., 1964. Mgr. trainee Oscar Mayer, Madison, Wis., 1964-65; v.p. Mayr's Seed and Feed, Beaver Dam, 1966-78; product mgr. Chem. Enterprises, Houston, 1978-80; gen. mgr. Coash, Inc., Bassett, Nebr., 1981-88, v.p., 1989; mgr. Blicks Agri-Farm Ctr., Inc., Scott City, Kans., 1990-91; area mgr. Rosen's Inc., Fairmont, Minn., 1992-95, Helena Chem. Co., Rochester, Minn., 1995—; cons. Beaver Dam, 1971-75; speaker fertilizer orgns., Wis. Advisor U. Wis. Coll. Agriculture; mem. com. Upper Elk Horn Natural Resources Dist., Oneill, Nebr., 1985-86. Mem. Wis. Fertilizer Assn. (bd. dirs. 1970-74), Nat. Fertilizer and Solutions Assn., Nebr. Fertilizer and Chem. Assn. Republican. Roman Catholic. Lodge: KC (dep. grand knight 1978-80, 81-85, Man of Yr. 1982). Home: 2550 Oak Hills Dr SW Rochester MN 55902-1263

MAYS, CAROL JEAN, state legislator; b. Independence, Mo., July 16, 1933; m. Ronald H. Mays; children: Terri, Melanie, Hugh. Student, Baker U. State rep., chmn. consumer protection edn. appropriations com., mem. transp., ways & means & comm. coms. Mo. Ho. of Reps., Jefferson City; restaurant owner. Mem. Mo. Restaurant Assn., Independence C. of C., Fairmount Comml. Club, Alpha Chi Omega. Democrat. Methodist. Home: 3603 S Hedges Ave Independence MO 64052-1167 Office: Mo Ho of Reps State Capitol Building Jefferson City MO 65101-1556*

MAYS, LESTER LOWRY, broadcast executive; b. Houston, July 24, 1935; s. Lester T. and Virginia (Lowry) M.; m. Peggy Pitman, July 29, 1959; children: Kathryn Mays Johnson, Linda Mays McCaul, Mark P., Randall T. BS in Petroleum Engring., Tex. A&M U., 1959; MBA, Harvard U., 1962. Comml. recorder San Antonio; with Sta. KTTU-TV, Tucson, Sta. KOKI/KTFO-TV, Tulsa, Sta. WMPI/WJTC-TV, Mobile and Pensacola, Okla., Sta. WAWS-TV, Jacksonville, Fla., Sta. KSAS-TV, Wichita, Kans., Sta. KLRT/KASN-TV, Little Rock, Sta. WFTC-TV, Mpls., Sta. WFTC-TV, WLMT/WMTU-TV, WLMT/WMTU TV, Memphis, Sta. WXXA, Albany, Sta. WQUE-AM-FM, New Orleans, Clear Channel Sports, Des Moines, Okla. News Network, Oklahoma City, Va. News Network, Stas. KJYO and KTOK, Oklahoma City, Sta. KEBC, Oklahoma City, Sta. WELI, New Haven, Sta. WKCI-WAVZ, New Haven, Sta. KPEZ, Austin, Tex., Stas. KHYS, KALO, KBXX, KMJQ, KPRC, KSEV and KYOK, Houston and Point Arthur, Tex., KMOD & KAKC, Tulsa, KTAM & KORA, Bryan and College Station, Tex., WHAS & WAMZ, Louisville; with radio and TV broadcasting WOAI, KQXT, and KAJA, San Antonio; pres., CEO Clear Channel Comms., Inc., San Antonio; past chmn. bd. CBS Radio Affiliates Bd. Bd. dirs., trustee Tex. Rsch. Pk.; bd. dirs., mem. exec. com. United Way; chmn. United Way San Antonio and Bexar County, 1995; regent emeritus Tex. A&M U. Sys.; trustee Tex. Rsch. and Tech. Found.; mem. deve. bd. U. Tex. Health Sci. Ctr.; adv. dir. Permanent Univ. Fund Tex. Mem. Nat. Assn. Broadcasters (past chmn. joint bd.), Greater San Antonio C. of C. (past chmn.), Rotary. Home: 400 Geneseo Rd San Antonio TX 78209-6127 Office: Clear Channel Comm PO Box 659512 San Antonio TX 78265-9512

MAYS, M. DOUGLAS, state legislator, financial consultant; b. Pittsburg, Kans., Aug. 18, 1950; s. Marion Edmund and Lilliemae Ruth (Norris) M.; m. Lena M. Krog, June 10, 1971; children: Jessica, Aaron. BFA, Pittsburg State U., 1972; postgrad., Washburn U., 1973—. Registered rep. Waddell & Reed, Inc., Topeka, 1981-83, Paine Webber Jackson & Curtis, Topeka, 1983-85, Columbian Securities, Topeka, 1985-87; commr. securities State of Kans., Topeka, 1987-91; pres. Mays & Assocs., Topeka, 1991—; mem. Kans. Ho. Reps., Topeka, 1993—; adminstrv. law judge various securities proceedings, 1987—; with securities and commodities fraud working group U.S. Dept. Justice, 1988-90; with penny stock task force SEC, 1988-90; del. Commonwealth Secretariat Symposium Comml. Crime, Cambridge, Eng., 1989; securities arbitrator, 1991—. Rep. precinct committeeman Shawnee County, Kans., 1976—, county chmn., 1978-82; mem. 2d Dist. Rep. State Com., Kans., 1976-86, 92—; mem. Kans. Rep. State Com., 1976-87; Senate steering com. Kassebaum for Senate campaign, 1978; chmn., mgr. Hoferer for Senate campaign, 1984; campaign coord., dir. fin. Hayden for Gov., 1986; mem. pub. bldg. commn. City of Topeka, 1985-86, bldg. and fire appeals bd. , 1986-89, dep. mayor, 1987-88; mem. Topeka City Coun., 1985-89; exec. bd. Topeka/Shawnee County Interngovtl. Coun., 1986-89; adv. bd. Topeka Performing Arts Ctr., 1989-90; active Topeka/Shawnee County Met. Planning Commn., 1992—, chmn., 1994—. Mem. North Am. Securities Adminstrs. Assn. (chmn. enforcement sect. 1988-89, pres.-elect, bd. dirs. 1989-90, pres. 1990-91), Nat. Assn. Securities Dealers, Nat. Futures Assn. (bd. arbitrators), Internat. Orgn. Securites Commns. (inter-Am. activities consultative com. 1990, pres.'s com. 1990, del. 1990). Methodist. Home: 1920 SW Damon Ct Topeka KS 66611-1926 Office: Kans Ho Reps State Capitol Topeka KS 66612

MAYWOOD, PAUL STANLEY, geologist, educator; b. Salt Lake City, Sept. 17, 1952; s. Stanley W. and Katherine F. (Forcade) M. BS in Environ. Geosci., Mesa Coll., Colo., 1978; MS in Geology, Portland State U., 1988. Registered profl. geologist Del., Ky., Mo., Pa., Tenn., Wis., Wyo.; cert. profl. geologist Ind. Night warehouse mgr. Perington Wholesale, Inc., Denver, 1973-75; computer operator First Nat. Bank Denver, Grand Junction, 1978-79; drafting technician Agapito & Assocs., Inc., Grand Junction, 1979; computer geologist NERCO, Inc., Portland, Oreg., 1980-82; staff geologist NERCO Mining Co., Sheridan, Wyo., 1982-84; mine geologist Bridger Coal Co./Pacific Minerals, Rock Springs, Wyo., 1984-91; cons., 1991-92; sr. geologist Atlantic Environ. Svcs., Inc., 1992—; affiliate instr. in geology Western Wyo. Coll., Rock Springs, 1985. State of Colo. grantee, 1978; recipient Achievement award NASA, 1970. Mem. Am. Inst. Profl. Geologists, Nat. Assn. Geology Tchrs., Am. Assn. Petroleum Geologists, Geol. Soc. Am. Home: 1844 High Sun Dr Florissant MO 63031-2754 Office: Atlantic Envir Svcs 2232 Welsch Industrial Ct Saint Louis MO 63146-4222

MAZZELLA, PATRICIA ANNE, public health nurse; b. Huntington, W.Va., Aug. 29, 1946; d. J. Shelby and Ethel V. (Taylor) Christian; m. Joseph E. Mazzella, Aug. 26, 1967 (div. Jan. 21, 1975); 1 child, Joseph Michael. Diploma, St. Mary's Sch. of Nursing, 1967; postgrad., Mt. St. Joseph Coll., Cin., 1986—. Cert. gerontol. nurse, ANCC. Charge nurse, asst. head nurse St. Mary's Hosp., Huntington, W.Va., 1967-71; charge nurse Cabell-Huntington Hosp., Huntington, W.Va., 1971-72; nursing supr. The Huntington Hosp., Inc., Huntington, W.Va., 1972-77; dir. nursing Parke Care Nursing Homes, Cin., 1978-80; pub. health nurse II Cin. Health Dept. 1980-84, pub. health nurse III, 1984-88, dir. nursing home licensure program, 1988—; adv. bd. mem. Pro-Seniors Long Term Care Ombudsman, Cin., 1989—, Senior Citizen Adv. Coun., Cin., 1990—; presenter of workshops in field. Mem. adv. bd. Live Oaks Vocational Sch. Spl. Edn. Programs, 1993—. Recipient Scholastic Achievement award St. Mary's Sch. of Nursing, 1967, Nurse of Yr. award Cin. Bd. of Health, 1986. Mem. Assn. for Learning Disabilities (bd. dirs. 1978—). Home: 1421 Maple Ave Cincinnati OH 45215-2115 Office: Cincinnati Health Dept 3101 Burnet Ave # 202 Cincinnati OH 45229-3014

MAZZOTTI, RICHARD RENE, pharmacist; b. Taylorville, Ill., Dec. 8, 1937; s. Rene and Elizabeth Lenore (Gordon) M.; m. Jerri Lynn VanVleet, July 28, 1962; children: Ann Elizabeth, Lisa Lyn. BS, St. Louis Coll., 1961. Lic. registered pharmacist, Mo., Ill.; lic. registered real estate broker, Ill.; registered securities salesperson, Ill.; designated cert. comml. investment mem. Pharmacist, ptnr. Rene's Drug Store, Taylorville, 1957-73; pharmacist, owner Bach's Gen. Discount, Taylorville, 1970-75; owner Ricks Stereo Ctr., Taylorville, 1975-79; pharmacist, owner Union Prescription Ctr., Springfield, Ill., 1973-89; broker Craggs Adams Realtors, Springfield, 1981—; owner Capitol Pharmacy, Springfield, 1989-94. Pres. Taylorville Assn. Commerce and Industry, 1978-79; asst. instr. Real Estate Securities and Syndication Inst., Nashville, 1979; pres. Retail Mchts. Assn., Taylorville, 1967. Mem. Ill. Pharm. Assn. (v.p. 1995—), Springfield Pharmacists Assn. (pres. 1990—), Mo. Pharm. Assn., Am. Pharm. Assn., Nat. Assn. Retail Druggists, Ctrl. Ill. Bd. Realtors (C.C.I.M.) Retailers Nat. Mktg. Inst., Ill. Chpt. Cert. Comml. Investment Mems., Real Estate Securities and Syndication Inst., Ill. Chpt. Real Estate Securities and Hyndication Inst., Capitol Club Ill., Realtors Polit. Action Com. Democrat. Roman Catholic. Home: 1203 Roosevelt Rd Taylorville IL 62568-8909 Office: Ill Dept of Pub Aid 201 S Grand Ave E 3d Fl Springfield IL 62763-0001

MAZZUCA, ROBIN LYNN, nurse, paramedic; b. Berwyn, Ill., July 16, 1958; d. Robert Walter and June Emily (Tvrz) Hass; m. Dale Charles Mazzuca, Nov. 6, 1982. Student, Northland Coll., Ashland, Wis., 1976-77, Morton Coll., Cicero, Ill., 1978-79, U. Ill., Chgo., 1979; BS in Nursing and Psychology, Elmhurst (Ill.) Coll., 1995. Apprentice pharmacist, asst. mgr. Golden Drugs, Berwyn, 1978-79; accounts payable, receivable clk. Transp. Engring., Inc., Oak Brook, Ill., 1979-80; adminstrv. asst. Chgo. Haulage, Inc., Schiller Park, Ill., 1980-84; emergency med. svc. coord. Lyons (Ill.) Fire Dept., 1980-90; owner, pres., instr. Phoenix Emergency Care Tng., Inc., Lyons, 1985—; code enforcement officer, paramedic, firefighter Western Springs (Ill.) Fire Dept., 1987-92, pub. edn. coord., 1987-92; specialty care technician, Ill. Dept. Pub. Health trauma registry LaGrange (Ill.) Meml. Hosp., 1991-95, trauma coord., 1995—; emergency med. svcs. coord. McCook (Ill.) Police and Fire Dept., 1985—; emergency med. svc. instr. Forest Park (Ill.) Fire Dept., 1985-90, Reynolds Metals, McCook, 1989—; mem. Gov.'s Emergency Med. Svc. Adv. Coun., Ill., 1989-91, upstate quality improvement subcom. Ill. Dept. Pub. Health adv. bd., 1995—. Editorial bd. Jour. Emergency Care, 1987-89. Instr./trainer Am. Heart Assn., Westchester, 1985—; mem. standards com. Gov.'s EMS Adv. Coun., Ill., 1989-91; mem. task force focusing on chem. wastes in schs. U.S. Fire Adminstrn., 1990; mem. upstate quality improvement subcom. Ill. Dept. Pub. Health, 1995—. Mem. Ill. EMT Inst. Coords. Soc. (sec. 1985-87), Nat. Assn. EMT, Nat. Fire Protection Assn., Am. Trauma Soc., Ill. Fire Safety Alliance, Ill. Nurses Assn., Emergency Nurses Assn., Chgo. Met. Trauma Soc., ACLS Inst. Am. Heart Assn., Sigma Theta Tau, Zeta Beta, Psi Chi. Lutheran. Office: La Grange Meml Hosp 5101 Willow Springs Rd La Grange IL 60525-2600

MCAFEE, ROD DALE, electrical engineer; b. New Philadelpia, Ohio, Sept. 4, 1967; s. Dale and Lynda (Garber) McA. BS in Elec. Engring., U. Akron, 1990. Project engr. Gradall, New Philadelphia, Ohio, 1990—. Deacon Jerusalem United Ch. of Christ, New Philadelphia, 1993; mem. York Twp. (Ohio) Vol. Fire Dept., 1987—. Office: 406 Mill Ave SW New Philadelphia OH 44663-3835

MCALEY, DAVID WILLIAM, broadcasting executive; b. Blue Island, Ill., Nov. 12, 1949; s. William Matthew McAley and Eleanor Mary (Weisenburger) Potter; m. Lynette Christine Johnson, June 9, 1984; children: Elizabeth Mary, Matthew Carl. BS in Journalism, No. Ill. U., DeKalb, 1971. Account exec. WMRO Radio, Aurora, Ill., 1971-73, sports dir., 1973-75; pres. Huskie Broadcast Properties, Aurora, 1975-77; v.p., sta. mgr. Stevens Broadcasting Corp., Aurora, 1977-83; sta. mgr. Midwest TV, Inc., Peoria, Ill., 1983-89; exec. v.p. Airplay Broadcasting Corp., Rockford, Ill., 1989—; instr. Bradley U., Peoria. Committeeman Ill. Broadcaster's Legis. Lobbying Com., Springfield, 1990—; campaign cabinet United Way, Aurora, 1980-83; with community rels. Bradley U., Peoria, 1986-89. Named Outstanding Sportscaster Nat. Assn. Softball Writers and Broadcasters, 1974, Ill. Radio Broadcaster of Yr., 1994. Mem. Ill. Broadcasters Assn. (v.p. 1994-96, pres. 1996-97). Roman Catholic. Office: Airplay Broadcasting Corp 2830 Sandy Hollow Rd Rockford IL 61109-2369

MCALINDON, MARY NAOMI, healthcare information administrator; b. Ebensburg, Pa., Oct. 16, 1935; d. S. David and Genevieve (Little) Solomon; m. James Daniel McAlindon, Nov. 25, 1961; children: Robert, Donald, James, Peter, M. Catherine. BSN, Georgetown U., 1957; MA, U. Mich., 1979; EdD, Wayne State U., 1992. RN, Mich. Staff nurse Georgetown U. Hosp., Washington, 1957-59; instr. St. Joseph Hosp., Flint, 1959-62; clin. instr. Mott. C.C., Flint, 1980-81; asst. DON McLaren Hosp., Flint, 1980-89, adminstrv. asst., 1989-92, asst. v.p., 1992-95; clin. informatics mgr. McLaren Health Care Corp., Flint, 1995—. Mem. bd. trustees United Way Genesee County, Flint, 1988-95. Mem. ANA (cert. advanced nursing adminstr., mem. exec. com. 1991-93), Am. Med. Informatics Assn. (chairperson nursing group 1993-94), Nat. League Nursing (cons. 1986-89, mem. exec. com. 1988, 93-95, 95-97), Vis. Nurses Assn. (pres., bd. dirs. 1986-89), Dist. Nurses Assn. (pres. 1993-96), Nursing Honor Soc. U. Mich. (pres. 1996—). Office: McLaren Health Care Corp 401 S Ballenger Hwy Flint MI 48532-3638

MCALLISTER, ROBERT DALE, judge; b. St. Louis, Oct. 8, 1930; s. Hudson William and Marie Edna (Gross) McA.; m. Sondra Sue Faupel, July 6, 1960 (div. 1970); m. Julianne States, Dec. 12, 1970; children: Terry Sue, David Lee, Melissa Ann, Jennifer Marie. BA in Elem. Edn., Harris Tchrs. Coll., 1953; JD, St. Louis U., 1965. Bar: Mo. 1965, Iowa 1965. Asst. city atty. City of Des Moines, 1965-70; ptnr. Spaulding & McAllister, St. Louis, 1970-78; judge 21st Jud. Ct. Mo., St. Louis, 1979—. Author: Murphy's Law, 1990, The College, 1992. With U.S. Army, 1953-55. Mem. United Ch. of Christ. Home: 274 Ridge Trail Dr Chesterfield MO 63017-3030

MCANDREW, FRANCIS THOMAS, psychology educator; b. Augsburg, Germany, Jan. 27, 1953; came to U.S., 1953; s. John Francis Paul and Jane Ann (Tuman) McA.; m. Maryjo Ann McCarthy, July 29, 1978; children: Timothy Ned, Maura Jill. BS in Psychology, King's Coll., 1974; PhD in Exptl. Psychology, U. Maine, Orono, 1981. Prof. psychology Knox Coll., Galesburg, Ill., 1979—, chair dept. Psychology, 1993—; head wrestling coach Knox Coll., Galesburg, 1985-89, 92—, program chair environ. studies, 1993—. Author: Environmental Psychology, 1993; reviewer NSF, profl. jours.; contbr. articles to prol. jours. Fellow U. Maine, Orono, 1974-75. Mem. Am. Psychol. Soc., Animal Behavior Soc., Midwestern Psychol. Assn., Ea. Psychol. Assn., Internat. Soc. for Human Ethology, Soc. for Personality and Social Psychology, Coun. Undergrad. Tchrs. of Psychology. Home: 733 Bateman St Galesburg IL 61401-2822 Office: Dept Psychology Knox Coll Galesburg IL 61401-4999

MCAULIFFE, ROGER P., state legislator, police officer; b. Chgo., July 6, 1938; five children. Graduate, Chgo. Police Acad. Police officer Chgo.; Dist. 14 rep. Ill. Ho. Reps., Springfield, 1973—; asst. majority leader, Ill. Ho. Reps.; mem. pers. and pensions, transp., consumer protection and profl. regulations coms. Named Legislator of Yr., Ill. Nurse Assn., 1983, 84. Mem. Moose, Bass. Home: 4660 N Austin Ave Chicago IL 60630-3100*

MCBEE, ROBERT LEVI, retired federal government official, writer, consultant; b. Braymer, Mo., Aug. 25, 1927; s. Calvin Levi and Wavah E. (Tripp) McB.; m. Lucymae A. Armijo, June 13, 1959; children: Martin Christopher, Mark Antony Christian, Mathew Alfonso Calvin. BA, Westminster Coll., Fulton, Mo., 1952. Advt. mgr. Battenfeld Grease and Oil Corp., Kansas City, Mo., 1952-53; asst. to advt. mgr. Ash Grove Lime and Cement Co., Kansas City, Mo., 1953-57; publicity dir. Am. Campaign Svcs., Kansas City, Mo., 1957; freelance writer Chelan, Wash., 1957-58; reporter Kansas City (Mo.) Times Star, 1958-61; assoc. editor Bailey Publs., Independence, Mo., 1961-63; editor Nat. Cath. Register, Denver, 1963-64; mng. editor Pleasant Hill (Mo.) Times, 1964-67; community affairs specialist Region 7 Job Corps, Kansas City, Mo., 1967-69; pub. info. officer Region 7 Office Econ. Opportunity, Community Svc. Adminstrn., Kansas City, Mo., 1969-81; pub. affairs specialist Kansas City Dist. Army C.E., 1981-85; chief community rels. Fifth U.S. Army, San Antonio, 85-88; acting dir. Chgo. Regional Office Pub. Affairs Dept. Vet. Affairs, 1989-90, asst. dir., 1988-94; acting dir. dept. vets. affairs Chgo. Regional Office Pub. Affairs, 1989-91. Sec., asst. treas. Kansas City Area Transp. Authority, 1965-70; pres. Pleasant Hill (Mo.) C. of C., 1966-67; sec. City Planning and Zoning Commn., Pleasant Hill, 1966; bd. dirs. Cath. Info. Svcs., Kansas City, 1966-72; adv. trustee Rsch. Med. Ctr., Kansas City, 1967-82. Mem. Westminster Coll. Alumni Coun. (life), Pi Delta Epsilon, Eta Sigma Phi, Kappa Alpha. Democrat. Roman Catholic.

MCBRIDE, GENEVIEVE GARDNER, public relations educator, author; b. Milw., Aug. 26, 1949; d. Raymond E. and Marian B. (Dunne) McB.; m. John E. Caspari, Mar. 17, 1973 (div. June 1986); children: John McBride Caspari, Catherine Southmayd Caspari. BS in Edn. and History, U. Wis., Milw., 1971; MA in Journalism, Marquette U., 1983; PhD in Mass Comm., U. Wis., 1989. Accredited pub. rels. cons. Columnist Milw. Sentinel, Milw., 1969-71; prodn. editor Milw. Star & Courier, Milw., 1971-72; asst. news editor Waukesha (Wis.) Freeman, 1972-74; dir. pub. rels. Carroll Coll., Waukesha, 1974-83; instr., lectr. U. Wis. (various campuses), Marquette U., Milw., Waukesha, 1980-88; instr. U. Wis., Milw., 1988-89, asst. prof., 1990-94, assoc. prof., 1994—, Fromkin lectr., 1995; cons. Univ. Sch. of Milw., Milw. Jour., 1980—, others. Author: On Wisconsin Women: Working For Their Rights From Settlement to Suffrage, 1994 (Book of Merit award 1994). Recipient Kenneth Kingery Scholarly Book award Coun. for Wis. Writers, 1995. Mem. Pub. Rels. Soc. Am., Assn. for Edn. in Journalism and Mass Comm., State Hist. Soc. Wis., Orgn. Am. Historians. Office: Mass Comm Dept PO Box 413 Milwaukee WI 53201-0413

MCBRIDE, JERRY E., state legislator; b. Licking, Mo., May 20, 1939; m. Deloris Pearl Harris, 1971; children: Heather, Jarrett, Ginger Dee. Grad. high sch., Rolla, Mo. Mem. Mo. Ho. of Reps., Jefferson City, 1974-76, 78-80, 1982—; chmn. state parks, recreation and natural resources com., mem. agribus., rules and joint rules and appropriations, natural and econ. resources com. Mem. SAR, Mo. Sch. Mines-U. Mo. Rolla Alumni Assn. (life), Order of Stars and Bars. Democrat. Home: PO Box 292 Edgar Springs MO 65462-0292*

MC BRIDE, ROBERT DANA, steel company executive; b. Decatur, Ill., Nov. 5, 1927; s. Glen Clovis and Winifred Audrey (Spates) McB.; m. Gloria Jean Haefner, July 8, 1950; children: Scott, Dana, Kelly, Kitty. B.S., U.S. Mil. Acad., 1950; grad., Advanced Mgmt. Program, Harvard U., 1974. V.p. ops. Granite City Steel Co., Ill., from 1966; pres. Granite City Steel div. Nat. Steel Corp., 1976-77; pres. Great Lakes Steel div. Nat. Steel Corp., Detroit, 1977-82; pres. Nat. Steel Corp., Pitts., 1983-86; sr. cons. Genix Corp., Pitts., 1987-89; pres. Trebbi Cons., Washington, 1989-90; pres., CEO McLouth Steel, Trenton, Mich., 1991-92, chmn., CEO, 1993-94, chmn., 1995—, also bd. dirs.; bd. dirs. The Dreyfus/Laurel Funds, Pitts., Salem Corp., Pitts.; mem. bd. visitors Marine Biol. Lab., Woods Hole, Mass. Served with U.S. Army, 1950-56. Decorated Purple Heart, Silver Star, Bronze Star. Mem. Am. Iron and Steel Inst., Assn. Iron and Steel Engrs. (dir., past pres.). Roman Catholic. Home: 15 Waverly Ln Grosse Pointe MI 48236-3039

MCBRIDE, VICKIE DARLENE, geriatrics nurse; b. Tampa, Fla., Jan. 17, 1944; d. Harold Victor Burch and Dorothy June (Higley) Keen; m. Dennis McBride, July 12, 1969 (div. June 1980); m. John Lawrence Petonic Jr., Mar. 20, 1982 (div. Dec. 1993); children: Elizabeth, Christopher. BSN, Marycrest Coll., Davenport, Iowa, 1966; MBA, Baldwin-Wallace Coll., Berea, Ohio, 1986. Cert. rehab. nurse, dir. nursing. Charge nurse Mercy Hosp., Davenport, 1966; staff devel. for critical care Cleve. Clinic, 1969-73; dir., med. svcs. coord. Free Clinic West, Cleve., 1973-74; DON Cuyahoga Falls (Ohio) Gen. Hosp., 1974-76; DON Kaiser Found. Hosp., Cleve., 1976-79, regional coord. staff devel., 1979-83; DON Forest Hills Nursing Home, Cleve., 1983-86; sr. cons. Clemens Nelson & Assocs., Worthington, Ohio, 1986-88; corp. cons. Altercare Inc., Navarre, Ohio, 1988—; CEO, pres. New Beginnings, Inc., 1996—; course coord. critical care Cleve. State U., 1973-75; trustee Free Med. Clinics of Cleve., 1972-73; affiliate faculty Capital U., 1976-79. Lt. USN, 1966-69. Mem. AACN, Nat. Dirs. Nursing Long Term Care, Ohio Dirs. Nursing Long Term Care, Am. Healthcare Assn., Nat. League for Nursing, Am. Rehab. Nurses. Roman Catholic. Home: PO Box 1053 Medina OH 44258-1053 Office: Altercare 7222 Day Ave SW Navarre OH 44662-9404

MCCABE, DONALD JAMES, educational research director; b. Flint, Mich., Oct. 4, 1932; s. Lemuel Cicero and Bernice Agnes (Webb) McCabe; m. Ann Louise Smith; children: Robert James, Linda Carol. AA, Flint Jr. Coll., 1950-52; PhB, U. Detroit, 1954, MA, 1962. Tchr. L'Anse Creuse Schs., Mt. Clemens, Mich., Mt. Morris (Mich.) Bd. Edn., 1959-61; tchr. reading Flint Bd. Edn., 1962-74; research dir. AVKO Ednl. Research Found., Birch Run, Mich., 1974—, pres., 1974-76; advisor Decade of Progress com. Mich. Dept. Edn., 1980. Author: Reading Via Typing, 1980, (weries) Sequential Spelling I-VII, 1982, (dictionary) Word Families Plus, 1984, For Adults Only, 1986, AVKO Spelling "Difficulty" Dictionary, 1988, Helping Anyone Overcome Reading/Spelling Problems, 1988, The Patterns of English Spelling, 1990, To Teach A Dyslexic, 1995; contbr. numerous articles to profl. jours. Served as sgt. U.S. Army, 1954-57. Recipient Mary Scott award AVKO Ednl. Research Found. Inc., 1982, Disting. Leadership award ABI, 1988. Mem. Internat. Reading Assn., Correctional Edn. Assn., Coalition of Literacy, Orton Dyslexia Soc. Roman Catholic. Clubs: Clio (Mich.) Golf; Flint Duplicate Bridge. Lodges: Rotary, Lions. Home: PO Box 83 Birch Run MI 48415-0083 Office: AVKO Ednl Rsch Found Inc 3084 Willard Rd Clio MI 48420

MCCABE, GARY FRANKE, bank hospitality manager; b. Salisbury, Md., Jan. 27, 1945; s. John Walter and Elsie Mae (Benson) McC.; m. Janice Christine Colona, Feb. 2, 1969; 1 child, Andrea Christine. Student, Va. Tech. Inst., 1963-64. Electronics technician USN, 1965-72; with mgmt. and sales divsn. Marriott Corp., Washington and Chgo., 1972-83; with mgmt. divsn. Canteen Corp., Chgo., 1984-86, Harris Trust & Savs. Bank, Chgo., 1987-95; regional dir. dining svcs. Forum Group, Inc., Fairfax, Va., 1995—; Marriott Internat., 1995—; cons. Performex Systems, Mpls., 1980-89. Author, narrator (tng. video) How to do a Presentation, 1989 (1st Place award), (video) Beef Around the World, 1990 (1st Place). Mem. various coms. Our Redeemers United Meth. Ch., Schaumburg, Ill., 1979—; v.p. personal devel. Ill. Jaycees, Streamwood, 1979—; chmn. Streamwood Fire and Police Commn., 1983-89, 93-95. Named one of Outstanding Young Men of Am., Ill. Jaycees, 1982, Amb., 1984. Mem. Nat. Restaurant Assn., Soc. for Food Svc. Mgmt. (regional conf. 1989, edn. com. 1990, nat. conf. com. 1995). Republican. Home: 51 N Walnut Ct Streamwood IL 60107-6609 Office: Forum Group Inc Ste 400 11320 Random Hills Rde Fairfax VA 22030

MCCABE, GENE JEROME, dean; b. Davenport, Iowa, Jan. 23, 1962; s. Gene T. McC. and Anne M. (Bergthold) Hamann; m. Cassie E. Helgesen, May 29, 1993; 1 child, Maggie J. BS in Computer Sci., U. Iowa, 1984; MBA, U. Ill., 1991. Cert. computing profl. Analyst, programmer State Farm Ins. Co., Bloomington, Ill., 1985-89; cons. Office Info. Mgmt. U. Ill., Urbana, 1989-91; instr. Scott C.C., Davenport, Iowa, 1991-92; coord. acad. microcomputing St. Ambrose U., Davenport, Iowa, 1992-93; dean info. systems Lincoln Land C.C., Springfield, Ill., 1993—. Mem. Data Processing Mgmt. Assn., CAUSE. Home: 2205 Renwick Dr Springfield IL 62704 Office: Lincoln Land CC 5250 Shepherd Rd Springfield IL 62794

MCCABE, RONALD BRIAN, library director; b. Cedar Falls, Iowa, Sept. 28, 1948; s. William Harold and Joyce Marguerite (Bertness) McC.; m. Deborah Jean Martin, Aug. 22, 1970. BA, Luther Coll., 1971; MSLS, U. Ky., 1975. Br. libr. Rockingham County Pub. Libr., Rerdsville, N.C., 1975-78; libr. dir. LeMars (Iowa) Pub. Libr., 1979-82; head ext. svcs. Moline (Ill.) Pub. Libr., 1982-83, libr. dir., 1983-86; libr. dir. Champaign (Il.) Pub. Libr. and Info. Ctr., 1986-91, McMillan Meml. Libr., Wisconsin Rapids, Wis., 1991—; apptd. chairperson Libr. Svc. and Constrn. Act Com., 1995-96. Mem. govtl. affairs com. Wis. Rapids Area C. of C., 1994, chairperson; campaign chairperson United Way South Wood County, Wisconsin Rapids, 1995. Mem. Wis. Libr. Assn., Lincoln Trails Libr. Sys. (chairperson automated librs. coun. 1987-88), Wisconsin Rapids Cmty. Theatre. Democrat. Episcopalian. Home: 321 Woodland Dr Wisconsin Rapids WI 54494 Office: McMillan Meml Libr 490 E Grand Ave Wisconsin Rapids WI 54494

MCCABE, STEVEN LEE, structural engineer; b. Denver, July 11, 1950; s. John L. and M. Leora (Shaw) McC.; m. Ann McCabe, Aug. 10, 1974; 1 child, Stephanie A. BSME, Colo. State U., 1972, MSME, 1974; PhD in Civil Engring., U. Ill., 1987. Registered profl. engr., Colo., Kans., Okla. Engr. Pub. Svc. Co. of Colo., Denver, 1974-77; sr. engr. R.W. Beck and Assocs., Denver, 1977-78; engr., project engr. Black & Veatch Cons. Engrs., Kansas City, Mo., 1978-81; asst. prof. civil engring. U. Kans., Lawrence, 1985-91, assoc. prof., 1991—, tchg. fellow, 1994—; vis. prof. structural engring. Norwegian Inst. Tech., Trondheim, 1995-96. Contbr. articles to profl. jours. Named Fulbright scholar U.S. Govt. to Norway, 1995-96, Ill. fellow, 1981-82; grantee Am. Inst. Steel Constrn., 1990-91, NSF, 1989-91, 91—, Civil Engring. Rsch. Found., 1991—; recipient Mech. Coupler Industry Testing Consortium Funding, 1992-95, Structural Rsch. Paper award Am. Concrete Inst., 1996. Mem. ASME (pressure vessels and piping divsn. honor paper award 1989, cert. of recognition for svc. 1993), ASTM, ASCE (assoc. editor Jour. Structural Engring. 1992-94), ACI (pres. Kans. chpt. 1992), IEEE Computer Soc., Am. Soc. Engring. Edn., Earthquake Engring. Rsch. Inst., European Assn. Concrete, Sigma Xi, Sigma Tau, Pi Tau Sigma, Phi Kappa Phi, Chi Epsilon. Republican. Roman Catholic. Office: U Kans 2015 Learned Hall Lawrence KS 66045-7526

MCCAFFERTY, CHARLES TERRENCE, architect; b. Detroit, Dec. 30, 1934; s. Eugene Francis and Mary Henrietta (LaChapielle) McC.; m. Marilyn Elizabeth Doonan, Nov. 19, 1960; children: Melanie, Matthew, Ann Mary. BArch, U. Notre Dame, 1958; M of Urban Planning, Wayne State U., 1964. Prin. planner Detroit City Plan Commn., 1959-67; asst. design dept. head Giffels & Rossetti, Detroit, 1967-69; v.p. Rossetti Assocs., Detroit, 1969-76; pres. CTMA Architects, Detroit, 1976-92, Riverside Design Group, Grosse Pointe Woods, Mich., 1992—; commr. Sts. & Traffic Commn, Detroit, 1971-73. With USMCR. Mem. AIA, Nat. Coun. Arch. Registration Bds., Detroit Boat Club. Roman Catholic. Office: Riverside Design Group Inc 20311 Mack Ave Grosse Pointe Woods MI 48236

MCCAFFERTY, JOHN MARTIN, real estate executive, commodities trader; b. Detroit, May 28, 1956. AA, Northwestern Mich. Coll., 1976; BS with honors, No. Mich. U., 1978; BSBA with honors, U. Denver, 1982. Staff acct. Patrick J. McCafferty & Co. CPA's, Traverse City, Mich., 1978-81; investment analyst Beaumont Investment Co., Traverse City, 1982-84; v.p. Beaumont/McCafferty Devel. Group, Traverse City, 1984-89; pres. Mitchell Creek Investors, Traverse City, 1985—; v.p. McCafferty Real Estate Group, Traverse City, 1985-88; mng. ptnr. J.M. McCafferty & Assocs. L.L.C., 1996—. Kenneth M. Good scholar Opportunity Found., 1982. Mem. Nat. Assn. Realtors, Mich. Assn. Realtors, Traverse City Bd. Realtors. Republican. Roman Catholic. Home: 10281 E San Remo Dr Traverse City MI 49686-8563 Office: PO Box 1427 Traverse City MI 49685-1427

MCCAFFERTY, MARLYN JEANETTE, elementary education educator; b. Montgomery County, Ill., Nov. 27, 1945; d. James Daniel and Mary Elizabeth (Miller) Lentz; m. Gary Ray McCafferty, July 23, 1966; children: Kay Jean, Dawn Jeanette. BS in Elem. Edn., Greenville Coll., 1966; MS in Elem. Edn., So. Ill. U., 1977. Cert. k-9th grade tchr. Tchr. elem. Hillsboro (Ill.) Community Unit Dist. 3, 1966—; mem. gifted edn. com. Hillsboro Community Unit Dist. 3, 1979-80. Active ARC bloodmobile, Hillsboro, 1971-93; chmn. bd. Christian edn. Hillsboro 1st Bapt. Ch., 1965-93, jr. ch. dir., 1975—, tchr. bible sch., 1980—, mem. libr. com., choir pianist, 1990; dir. Montgomery County swim team, Litchfield, Ill., 1988-90; co-chmn. sewing booth Hillsboro Hosp. bazaar, 1991; mem. Hillsboro Hosp. scholarship com., 1993-95. Mem. Hillsboro Unit Edn. Assn. (sec., bd. mem.), Student Tchr. Adv. Coun. Greenville Coll. Baptist. Office: Beckemeyer Sch 1035 Seymour Ave Hillsboro IL 62049-1060

MCCAFFERTY, OWEN EDWARD, accountant, dental-veterinary practice consultant; b. Cleve., Sept. 5, 1952; s. Owen James and Ann Theresa (Barrett) McC.; m. Colleen Maura Mullen, Aug. 3, 1974; children: Owen Michael, Hugh Anthony, Maura Kathleen, Bridget Colleen. AB, Xavier U., 1974. CPA, Ohio. Mem. staff to sr. accountant Deloitte, Haskins, & Sells, Cleve., 1974-78; ptnr., pres. Douglas, McCafferty & Co., Inc., Rocky River, Ohio, 1978-86; pres. Owen E. McCafferty, CPA, Inc., North Olmsted, Ohio, 1986—, McCafferty/Beach Devel., Inc., North Olmsted, 1989—; lectr. various vet. and dental assns.; cons. in field; mng. ptnr. McCafferty/Beach Real Estate Ventures, 1988—. Co-author: The Business of Veterinary Practice, 1993; mem. editorial adv. bd. Vet. Econs. Mag.; contbr. articles to acctg. and vet. jours. Mem. fin. com. St. Richard Paris, 1987-95, chmn. budgeting com., 1991-95. Recipient Meritorius Service award Ohio Vet. Med. Assn., 1986, Am. Animal Hosp. Assn. award, 1988. Mem. AICPA (pvt. cos. practice sect.), Ohio Soc. CPAs (chmn. mgmt. adv. svcs. com. Cleve. chpt. 1987-89), mem. liaison com.), Vet. Hosp. Mgrs. Assn. (pres. 1993), Vet. Practice Mgrs. Assn. Gt. Britain and Republic of Ireland (hon. life). Democrat. Roman Catholic. Office: PO Box 839 North Olmsted OH 44070-0839

MCCAFFREY, LAWRENCE JOHN, historian, educator; b. Riverdale, Ill., Aug. 10, 1925; s. John Thomas and Alma Ellen (Kelly) McC.; m. Joan Elizabeth McNamara, Sept. 3, 1949; children: Kevin, Sheila, Patricia. BA, St. Ambrose Coll., 1949; MA, Ind. U., 1950; PhD, U. Iowa, 1954; HHD (hon.), St. Ambrose Coll., 1982; D of Lit. (hon.), Nat. U. Ireland, Dublin, 1987. Instr. humanities Mich. State U., East Lansing, 1954-55; assoc. prof. history Coll. of St. Catherine, St. Paul, 1955-58; vis. lectr. history U. Iowa, Iowa City, 1958-59; assoc. prof. history U. Ill., Urbana, 1959-64; prof. history Marquette U., Milw., 1964-69, U. Maine, Orono, 1969-70; prof. emeritus Loyola U., Chgo., 1970-91; vis. prof. U. Iowa, Iowa City, 1960, 63, 66, Sch. Irish Studies, Dublin, Ireland, 1970, U. Coll. Cork, Ireland, 1979, 80, 83, Concordia U., Montreal, Can., 1988. Author: Irish Federalism in the 1870s: A Study in Conservative NAtionalism, 1962, Daniel O'Connell and the Repeal Yeat, 1966, The Irish Question, 1800-1922, 1968, The Irish Diaspora in America, 1976, 84, Ireland From Colony to Nation State, 1979, Textures of Irish-America, 1992, The Irish Question: Two Centuries of Conflict, 1995; co-author: The Irish in Chicago, 1987, The Irish Experience, 1996; editor and contbr.: Irish Nationalism and the American Contribution, 1976; co-editor and contbr.: Perspectives on Irish Nationalism, 1988. With U.S. Coast Guard, 1943-46. Mem. Am. Cath. Hist. Assn. (pres. 1990-91), Am. Conf. for Irish Studies (co-founder, sec. 1959-66, pres. 1976-79). Democrat. Roman Catholic. Home: 1227 Maple Ave Evanston IL 60202-1216 Office: Loyola U History Dept 6525 N Sheridan Rd Chicago IL 60626-5311

MCCALLISTER, RICHARD ANTHONY, business consulting company executive; b. Newark, Ohio, Apr. 10, 1937; s. Ward C. and LeDema McC.; B.S., Ill. State U., 1960; postgrad. U. So. Calif., 1960-62; m. Trina D. Gordon, Sept. 1, 1979; children: Todd, Mark. Indsl. cons. Sci. Rsch. Assocs., 1964-66; v.p. Mgmt. Psychologists, Inc., Chgo., 1966-68; dir. Price Waterhouse & Co., Chgo., 1968-75; pres. William H. Clark Assocs., Inc., Chgo., 1975-89; sr. v.p., dir. Boyden Internat., Chgo, 1989-91; mng. dir. Boyden Midwest, 1991—; mng. dir., bd. dirs. Boyden World Corp.; chmn. WHCA Ptnrs., 1986—; bd. dirs. sec. Mid Am., 1992—; adv. bd. mem. Fuduciary Management, Inc., former bd. dirs. Calumet Industries Inc.; mem. adv. bd. Lionheart Trust Co., 1988-93. Former pres. Dist. 113 Bd. Edn., Deerfield, Ill.; bd. dirs., exec. com. Grant Hosp., Chgo.; bd. dirs., exec. com. House of Vision, 1975-82. Mem. Glen View Club, Racquet Club, Chgo. Club, Mid-Am. Club (bd. dirs., treas.). Republican. Office: 180 N Stetson Ave # 5050 Chicago IL 60601-6710

MC CALLUM, CHARLES EDWARD, lawyer; b. Memphis, Mar. 13, 1939; s. Edward Payson and India Raimelle (Musick) McC.; m. Lois Ann Gowell Temple, Nov. 30, 1985; children: Florence Andrea, Printha Kyle, Chandler Ward, Sabra Nicole Temple. B.S., MIT, 1960; J.D., Vanderbilt U., 1964. Bar: Mich., Tenn. 1964. Assoc. Warner Norcross & Judd LLP, Grand Rapids, Mich., 1964-69; ptnr. Warner, Norcross & Judd, Grand Rapids, Mich., 1969—, mng. ptnr., 1992—; rep. assemblyman State Bar Mich., 1973-78; dir. Rsch. and Tech. Inst. West Mich., 1986—, chmn., 1989-91; lectr. continuing legal edn. programs; chmn., bd. dirs. Butterworth Ventures, 1987—; mem. West Mich. World Trade Week Com., 1988—, chmn., 1990-91; mem. Mich. Dist. Export Coun., 1990—, chmn., 1992—. Chmn. Grand Rapids Area Transit Authority, 1976-79, mem., 1972-79; regional v.p. Nat. Mcpl. League, 1978-86, mem. coun., 1971-78; pres. Grand Rapids Art Mus., 1979-81, trustee, 1976-83, 94—; chmn. Butterworth Hosp., 1979-87, trustee, 1977-87; chmn. Butterworth Health Corp., 1982-89, dir., 1982—, vice chmn., 1989-91, sec., 1991—; vice chmn. Citizens Com. for Consolidation of Govt. Svcs., 1981-82; chmn. Kent County Cultural Svcs. Woodrow Wilson fellow, 1960-61; Fulbright scholar U. Manchester, Eng., 1960-61. Mem. ABA (com. on law firms bus. law sect. 1982-94, chmn. com. on law firms bus. law sect. 1994—, chmn. subcom. on firm mgmt. 1988-95, mem. fed. regulation of securities com. 1982—, mem. internat. bus. law com.), Am. Law Inst., Tenn. Bar Assn., Mich. Bar Assn. (mem. coun. bus. law sect. 1983-89, sect. chmn. 1988-89, ex-officio coun. bus. law sect. 1989—, chmn. takeover laws subcom. 1986-88, co-chmn. internat. bus. law com., internat. law sect. 1988-89), Grand Rapids Bar Assn., Interant. Bar Assn., Grand Rapids c. of C. (pres. 1975, bd. dirs. 1970-76), Univ. Club, Peninsular Club, Order of Coif, Sigma Xi. Home: 110 Bittersweet Ln NE Ada MI 49301-9552 Office: 111 Lyon St NW Grand Rapids MI 49503-2404

MCCALLUM, LAURIE RIACH, lawyer, state government; b. Virginia, Minn., Aug. 19, 1950; d. Keith Kelvin and Maybelle Louella (Hanson) Riach; m. J. Scott McCallum, June 19, 1979; children: Zachary, Rory, Cara. BA, U. Ariz., 1972; JD, So. Meth. U., 1977. Bar: Wis. 1977. Consumer atty. Office of Commr. of Ins., Madison, Wis., 1977-79; asst. legal counsel Gov. of Wis., Madison, Wis., 1979-82; mng. ptnr. Petri and McCallum Law Firm, Fond du Lac, Wis., 1979-80; exec. dir. Wis. Coun. on Criminal Justice, Madison, 1981-82; commr. Wis. Pers. Commn., Madison, 1982—, chairperson, 1988—; mem. gov.'s jud. selection com. Supreme Ct., 1993; dir. State Bar Labor Law Sect., Madison, 1988-91; faculty U. Wis. Law Sch., Madison, 1992, 93. Chair vol. com. Wis. Spl. Olympics, Madison, 1981; dir. Off-the-Square Club, Madison, 1981, Met. Madison YMCA, Madison, 1982-88. Republican. Office: State Pers Commn Ste 1004 131 West Wilson St Madison WI 53703-3233

MCCALLUM, RALPH WILLIAM, materials scientist; b. Pasadena, Calif., June 5, 1947; s. Robert E. and Grace (Glenn) McC.; m. Virginia L. Morehouse, July 14, 1973; children: Kendall, Ethan. BA in Math. and Physics, Carleton Coll., 1969; PhD in Physics, U. Calif., San Diego, 1977. NSF postdoctoral fellow U. Calif., San Diego, La Jolla, 1977-78; sci. staff IFF-KFA Julich, Fed. Republic of Germany, 1978-82; sr. scientist Energy Conversion Devices, Inc., Troy, Mich., 1982-86; sr. scientist Ames (Iowa) Lab. Iowa State U., 1986—, adj. prof. materials sci. and engring., 1987—, dir. Rare Earth Info. Ctr., Ctr. for Rare Earth & Magnetics, 1996—. Contbr. articles to Jour. of Metals, Phys. Rev. B., Jour. of Materials Sci., Physica C. Mem. Am. Phys. Soc. Materials Rsch. Soc.; Minerals, Metals and Materials Soc. Office: Iowa State U Ames Lab Ames IA 50011

MCCALLUM, SCOTT, state official; b. Fond du Lac, Wis.; m. Laurie McCallum; children: Zachary, Rory, Cara. BA, Macalester Coll.; MA in Internat. Studies, Johns Hopkins U. Property developer Fond du Lac; mem. Wis. State Senate; lt. gov. State of Wis.; dir. Workplace Child Care Clearinghouse; chair Repeat Offenders Task Force State of Wis., Trauma and Injury Prevention Task Force; coord. Gov.'s Conf. on Small Bus.; presdl. appointee to Internat. Trade Policy Adv. Com.; past chair Nat. Conf. of Lt. Govs.; gov.'s appointee to Nat. Aerospace States Assn. Office: Lt Gov Rm 22 East State Capitol Madison WI 53702*

MCCALMONT, PAUL E., engineering analysis supervisor; b. Youngstown, Ohio, June 7, 1952. BS, U. Cin., 1975. Engring. Siemens-Allis, Norwood, Ohio, 1975-84; sr. rsch. engr. Cin. Milacran Inc., Cin., 1984-88; mech. engring. mgr. Welco, Cin., 1988-90; analysis supr. Cin. Milacron, Inc., Cin., 1990—; v.p. McCalmont & Assocs., Cin., 1980—. Patentee in field. Mem. Acoustical Soc. Am., A.O.P.A. Home: 3848 Marburg Ave Cincinnati OH 45209-1838

MCCAMMACK, MIKE, business executive; b. Indpls., Apr. 9, 1953; s. John David and Billy Jean (Sharp) McC.; m. Karen Kay Jurey, July 26, 1975; children: Lisa Sue, Bradley Michael. BS in Indsl. Engring., Purdue U., 1975, MS in Indsl. Adminstrn., 1978. Indsl. engr. Rockwell, Inc., Cedar Rapids, Iowa, 1975-77; materials mgr. Rockwell, Inc., Melbourne, Ill., 1978-79; staff asst. AMP, Inc., Harrisburg, Pa., 1979-80, mgr. indsl. engring., 1980-81, mgr. mfg. engring., 1981-84, product mgr., 1984-86; mgr., cons. A.T. Kearney, Chgo., 1986-87; product mgr. Molex, Inc., Lisle, Ill., 1987-89, v.p., gen. mgr., 1989—. Office: Molex Inc 2222 Wellington Ct Lisle IL 60532

MCCAMPBELL, WANDA MAE HENNECKE, vocational school administrator; b. Cape Girardeau, Mo., Oct. 3, 1951; d. Alvin E. and Esther E. (Best) Hennecke; m. Russell E. McCampbell, June 30, 1980. BS in Edn., S.E. Mo. State U., 1974, MS in Edn., 1979; EdD, U. Mo., 1989. Placement specialist Perry County Sch. Dist. No. 32, Perryville, Mo., 1974-80; adult supr./placement Columbia (Mo.) Pub. Schs., 1980-87, asst. dir. vocat., 1987—. Recipient Outstanding Placement Specialist Mo. Placement Assn., 1983, Outstanding Svc. award City of Columbia, 1988. Mem. ASCD, Mo. Vocat. Assn., Am. Vocat. Assn., Mo. State Tchrs. Assn., Mo. Coun. for Local Adminstrs. (co-chair 1991-93), Nat. Coun. for Local Adminstrs., Mo. Vocat. Adminstrs. Acad. (co-chmn. 1991-93), Columbia C. of C. (Leadership Columbia 1989), Alpha Delta Kappa (state pres. 1992-94). Office: Columbia Career Ctr 4203 S Providence Rd Columbia MO 65203-7157

MCCANDLESS, BARBARA J., auditor; b. Cottonwood Falls, Kans., Oct. 25, 1931; d. Arch G. and Grace (Kittle) McCandless; m. Allyn O. Lockner, 1969. BS, Kans. State U., 1953; MS, Cornell U., 1959; postgrad. U. Minn., 1962-66, U. Calif., Berkeley, 1971-72. Cert. family and consumer scientist; enrolled agt. IRS. Home demonstration agt. Kans. State U., 1953-57; teaching asst. Cornell U., 1957-58, asst. extension home economist in marketing, 1958-59; consumer mktg. specialist, asst. prof. Oreg. State U., 1959-62; instr. home econs. U. Minn., 1962-63, research asst. agrl. econs., 1963-66; asst. prof. U. R.I., 1966-67; assoc. prof. family econs., mgmt., housing, equipment dept. head S.D. State U., 1967-73; asst. to sec. Dept. Commerce and Consumer Affairs, S.D., 1973-79, tax cons., 1980-91, revenue auditor, 1991—. Mem. Nat. Council Occupational Licensing, dir., 1973-75, v.p., 1975-79. Mem. Am. Agrl. Econs. Assn., Am. Assn. Family and Consumer Scis., Am. Coun. Consumer Interests, Assn. Govt. Accts., Inst. Internal Auditors, Nat. Coun. on Family Rels., LWV, Kans. State U. Alumni Assn., Pi Gamma Mu. Research on profl. and occupational licensing bds. Address: 2114 SW Potomac Dr Topeka KS 66611-1445

MCCANN, SHEILA KAY, landman; b. Michigan City, Ind., Dec. 17, 1963; d. Robert Louis Blankenship and Sharon Lee (Buchanan) Ungerank; m. Kenneth Martin McCann, May 28, 1983; children: Eric Robert, David Allen. Grad. high sch., Michigan City, Ind. Landscaper La Porte, Ind., 1989—. Missionette leader La Porte Assembly of God Ch., 1989-90; mem. health and safety com. PTA Sch. Bd., 1992—. Recipient Bronze medal Vocat. Indsl. Clubs Am., 1982. Office: 243 Rockwood St La Porte IN 46350-3037

MCCANN-TURNER, ROBIN LEE, child, adolescent analyst; b. Spokane, Wash., Sept. 27, 1945; d. Robert Allen McCann and Mary Lavelle Wilson; m. C. F. Turner, Sept. 10, 1975. BA, U. Mont., 1967; MSW, Wash. U., 1969; cert. child-adolescent psychoanalysis, Hampstead Ctr., London, Eng., 1979. Asst. clin. prof., child and adolescent medicine St. Louis U. Med. Sch., 1984—, Cardinal Glennon Children's Hosp., 1984—; pvt. practice; mem. faculty St. Louis Psychoanalytic Inst., 1982—, chmn. child study group, 1994—, dir. child devel. project, 1994—; mem. ho. of dels. U. Mont., Missoula, 1990—. Mem. APA, NASW, Assn. Child Psychoanalysis, Am. Psychoanalytic Assn. Office: 141 N Meramec Ave Ste 208-209 Clayton MO 63105-3750

MCCARROLL, KATHLEEN ANN, radiologist, educator; b. Lincoln, Nebr., July 7, 1948; d. James Richard and Ruth B. (Wagenknecht) McC.; m. Steven Mark Beerbohm, July 10, 1977 (div. 1991); 1 child, Palmer Brooke. BS, Wayne State U., 1974; MD, Mich. State U., 1978. Diplomate Am. Bd. Radiology. Intern/resident in diagnostic radiology William Beaumont Hosp., Royal Oak, Mich., 1978-82, fellow in computed tomography and ultrasound, 1983; radiologist, dir. radiologic edn. Detroit Receiving Hosp., 1984—, vice-chief dept. radiology, 1988-96, chief dept. radiology, 1996—; pres.-elect med. staff Detroit Receiving Hosp., 1992-94, pres., 1994-96; mem. admissions com. Wayne State U. Coll. Medicine, Detroit, 1991—; officer bd. dirs. Dr. L. Reynolds Assoc., P.C., Detroit, 1991-94, 96—; presenter profl. confs.; assoc. prof. radiology Wayne State U. Sch. Medicine, Detroit, 1995—; bd. trustees Detroit Med. Ctr., 1996—. Editor: Critical Care Clinics, 1992; mem. editorial bd. Emergency Radiology; contbr. articles to profl. publs. Trustee Detroit Med. Ctr., 1996—. Mem. AMA, Am. Coll. Radiology (Mich. chpt. sec. 1995—), Radiol. Soc. N.Am., Assn. Univ. Radiologists, Am. Roentgen Ray Soc., Am. Soc. Emergency Radiologists (bd. dirs. 1996—), Mich. State Med. Soc., Wayne/Oakland County Med. Soc., Phi Beta Kappa. Office: Detroit Receiving Hosp 3L-8 4201 Saint Antoine St Detroit MI 48201-2153

MCCARRON, JOHN FRANCIS, columnist; b. Providence, Jan. 20, 1949; s. Hugh Francis and Katherine Anne (Brooks) McC.; m. Janet Ann Velsor, Sept. 3, 1971; children: Veronica, Catherine. BS in Journalism, Northwestern U., 1970, MS in Journalism, 1973. Gen. assignment reporter Chgo. Tribune, 1973-80, urban affairs writer, 1980-91, fin. editor, 1991-92, editorial bd. columnist, 1992—. Contbr. to Planning mag., World Book Ency., Preservation mag. Lt. USNR, 1970-72. Recipient Editors award AP, 1983, 84, Ann. Journalism award Am. Planning Assn., 1983, Heywood Broun award Am. Newspaper Guild, Washington, 1989, Peter Lisagor award Soc. Profl. Journalists, 1994. Home: 1425 Noyes St Evanston IL 60201-2639 Office: Chicago Tribune Chicago IL 60611

MCCART, MARIAN LONGACRE, minister; b. Exeter, N.H., Nov. 21, 1938; d. Andrew (dec.) and Marian (Sykes) (dec.) L.; m. Bruce R. McCart, July 8, 1961; children: Anne Drolet, Marian Motz, Daniel James, Jennifer (dec. 1985). BA, Carleton Coll., Northfield, 1960; MS of elem. edn., Syracuse U., Syracuse, 1961; MDiv, U. Dubuque Theological Sem., Dubuque, 1983. Cert. elem. tchr., N.Y., Iowa, Ill. Ordained to ministry Presbyn. Ch. U.S., 1994. Tchr. Ames Cmty. Sch., Ames, Iowa, 1961-65; tchr. St. Katharine's Sch., Davenport, Iowa, 1965-75, Rock Island, Ill., 1965-75; dir. of Christian edn. South Park Ch., Rock Island, 1977-79, First United Meth. Ch., Moline, Ill., 1979-82; interim min. First Presbyn., Davenport, Iowa, 1984, Viola Presbyn., Ill., 1985-86, Gloria Dei Presbyn., Rock Island, Ill., 1986-88, United Presbyn., Alexis, Ill., 1988-89, Edgington Presbyn., Taylor Ridge, Ill., 1990; installed min. West Park Presbyn., Davenport, 1991—; Synod commr. Great Rivers Presbyn., Peoria, 1990-92, Gen. Assembly commr. 1988; com. on ministry East Iowa Presbyn., Iowa City, 1994—; PROBE Ch. Redevelopment Presbytery, Louisville, 1993—. Active local PTA. Democrat. Presbyterian. Home: 4109 44th St Rock Island IL 61201 Office: West Park Presbyn Church 4209 W Locust St Davenport IA 52804

MCCARTER, WILLIAM J., JR., broadcasting executive; b. Phila., June 10, 1929; s. William J. and Julia R. (Miller) McC.; m. Emma Linda Warner, Jan. 19, 1952; children—Julianne, William J. II, Amy, James Andrew. B.A., Lafayette Coll., 1951; postgrad., Temple U. Sch. Communication, 1957-58. Dir. WFIL-TV, Phila., 1953-57; program dir. WHYY-TV, Phila., 1957-62; program devel. officer Nat. Ednl. Television, N.Y.C., 1962-64; pres., gen. mgr. WETA-TV/FM, Washington, 1964-71, WTTW-TV, Chgo., 1971—; lectr. U. Pa., Am. U., Northwestern U.; TV cons. Govt. V.I.; pres. Eastern Ednl. TV Network, 1968-71. Mem. Pres.'s Commn. on Human Rights, 1968; telecommunications adviser to mayor of Washington.; Trustee St. John's Coll., Washington; bd. mgrs. Pub. Broadcasting Service, mem. Chgo. com. bd. dirs. Served to 1st lt. AUS, 1951-53. Decorated Bronze Star medal, Purple Heart.; Recipient Bd. Govs.' award Washington Acad. Television Arts and Scis., 1971. Mem. Nat. Acad. Televison Arts and Scis. (v.p. 1967-69), Washington Acad. Television Arts and Scis, pres. 1966-68), Public TV Mgrs. Council, Nat. Assn. Ednl. Broadcasters (dir. 1970-72, vice chmn. 1970-72), Radio and TV Corrs. Assn., Chgo. Council Fgn. Relations (dir.). Clubs: National Press (Washington), International (Washington); Mid-Am. (Chgo.), Union League (Chgo.). Office: Sta WTTW-TV 5400 N Saint Louis Ave Chicago IL 60625-4623*

MCCARTHY, ALICE ROSS, communications executive; b. Cooperstown, N.Y., Apr. 23, 1924; d. David Nelson and Amanda (Carlson) Ross; m. Walter John McCarthy, Sept. 3, 1949 (div. 1988); children: W.J. III, David N., Sharon A., James H., William H. BS, Cornell U., 1944, MS, 1947; PhD, Wayne State U., 1986. Asst. placement sec., instr. N.Y. State Coll. Human Ecology, Cornell U., Ithaca, 1947-49; pub. affairs coord. Common Ground, Birmingham, Mich., 1972-78; instr. Oakland U., Rochester, Mich., 1977-78; program assoc., cons. Community Found. Southeastern Mich., Detroit, 1986-88; dir. adv. bd. Parent Talk, Detroit Free Press, Detroit, 1987-93; founder, pres. Ctr. for Advancement Family, Grosse Pointe Woods, Mich., 1988—, Bridge Communications, Birmingham, 1988—; editor, adv. bd. column Detroit Free Press, 1987-93; editor newsletter probate ct. Oakland County, Pontiac, 1987-92; writer The Am. Family in Edn. and the Family, 1992; cons Wayne (Mich.) County Regional Svc. Ctr., 1990—; researcher State Dept. of Edn. and Dept. Pub. Health, Mich., 1991—; rschr., editor, publ. Oakland Schs., Mich., 1992—; mem. internat. network Ctr. Families, Cmtys. and Schs., Children's Learning, Boston U., 1993—; researcher comprehensive sch. health edn. State Dept. Pub. Health, Mich., 1993. editor: Health Guides, 1990-92; editor: PREVCO Newsletter, 1992-95, Suburban Comm., 1994—; exec. editor, pub.: Healthy Newsletters, 1992—; exec. editor, pub.: Healthy Newsletters, 1992—, Healthy Prescholers at School-At Home, 1994, 2nd edit., 1995, Teacher-Mades and Redi-Mades, 1995; exec. editor., rschr.: Healthy Family Families Healthy Children, 1994-95; editor: Tuning Into Twenty-First Century Schools and Teens, 1995; exec. editor, pub. Healthy Teens: Success in High School and Beyond, 1996. Mem. bd. regents Lake Superior State U., Sault Ste. Marie, Mich., 1986-94, pres., 1991-92, chmn. pres. search com., 1991-92; mem. adv. coun. Cornell U., 1986-91; chairperson bd. dirs. Merrill Palmer Inst., Wayne State U., 1992-95; co-chmn. PREVCO, Southfield, Mich., 1991-93, bd. dirs., 1993—; bd. dirs. Mich. Health Edn. Found., 1994—. Recipient Health Children award Comp. Health Assn., AWD City. award Merrill-Palmer Inst. Wayne State U., 1989, Pub. Svc. award Coll. of Human Ecology Cornell U., Great Am. Trad. award B'nai B'rith, 1985, Award of Excellence, Internat. Assn. Bus. Communicators, 1993, 94, 95, Health Info. award Health Info. Ctr., 1994, 95. Mem. Nat. Coun. Family Rels., Nat. Assn. Edn. Young Children, Mich. Coun. Family Rels. (bd. dirs., Profl. award 1990), Oakland Family Svcs. (bd. dirs.), Rainbows for All God's Children (adv. bd.). Methodist. Home and office: 1450 Pilgrim Ave Birmingham MI 48009-1006

MCCARTHY, JOHN CARROLL, transportation company executive; b. Berwyn, Ill., June 9, 1950; s. Justin Thomas and Charlotte Carroll (Smith) McC.; m. Jane Ellen Torri, Oct. 14, 1978; children: Quin, John Jr. BS in Commerce, DePaul U., 1972; MBA in Mgmt., Loyola U., 1980. Mgmt. trainee Continental Air Transport, Chgo., 1972-73, dir. mktg., 1973-74, dir. mktg. and sales, 1974-76, v.p., 1976-78, exec. v.p., dir., 1978-87, major shareholder, 1983—, pres., CEO, 1987—; pvt. sector bd. rep. Chgo. Area Transp. Study, 1989—; bd. dirs. GROUNDNET, Washington. Bd. dirs. Travelers & Immigrants Aid, Chgo., 1985—, Chgo. Conv. Bur., 1994—, Mercy Hosp. & Med. Ctr., Chgo., 1994—; trustee St. Xavier U., Chgo., 1991—; mem., pres. St. Clement Sch. Bd., 1993-96. Recipient Dennis Kelly Svc. award Cath. Charities, 1991, Pres.'s award St. Ignatius Coll. Prep, 1993; named Outstanding Young Citizen, Chgo. Jaycees, 1988. Mem. Airport Ground Transp. Assn. (dir., past pres. 1980—), Met. Transp. Assn. (dir., pres. 1983—), Young Pres.'s Orgn., Cath. Charities (bd. of advisors 1986—), Irish Fellowship Club. Roman Catholic. Home: 900 W Castlewood Chicago IL 60640 Office: Continental Air Transport 730 W Lake St Chicago IL 60661

MCCARTHY, KAREN P., congresswoman, former state representative; b. Mass., Mar. 18, 1947. BS in English, Biology, U. Kans., 1969, MBA, 1985; MEd in English, U. Mo., Kansas City, 1976. Tchr. Shawnee Mission (Kans.) South High Sch., 1969-75, The Sunset Hill (Kans.) Sch., ., 1975-76; mem. Mo. House of Reps., Jefferson City, Mo., 1977-94; cons. govt. affairs Marion Labs., Kansas City, Mo., 1986-93; congresswoman, Mo. 5th Dist. U.S. Congress, Washington, D.C., 1995—; rsch. analyst pub. fin. dept. Stearn Bros. & Co., 1984-85, Kansas City, Mo.; rsch. analyst Midwest Rsch. Inst., econs. and mgmt. scis. dept., Kansas City, 1985-86. Del. Dem. Nat. Conv., 1992, Dem. Nat. Party Conf., 1982, Dem. Nat. Policy Com. Policy Commn., 1985-86. Recipient Outstanding Young Woman Am. award, 1977, Outstanding Woman Mo. award Phi Chi Theta, Woman of Achievement award Mid-Continent Coun. Girl Scouts U.S., 1983, 87, Annie Baxter Leadership award, 1993; named Conservation Legislator of Yr., Conservation Fed. Mo., 1987. Fellow Inst. of Politics; mem. Nat. Inst. of Politics;

mem. Nat. Conf. on State Legis. (del. on trade and econ. devel. to Fed. Republic of Germany, Bulgaria, Japan, France and Italy, mem. energy com. 1978-84, fed. taxation, trade and econ. devel. com. 1986, chmn. fed. budget and taxation com. 1987, vice chmn. state fed. assembly 1988, pres.-elect 1993, pres. 1994), Nat. Dem. Inst. for Internat. Affairs (instr. No. Ireland 1988, Baltic Republics 1992, Hungary 1993). Office: US House Reps House Office Bldg 1232 Longworth Washington DC 20515-2505

MCCARTHY, KEVIN BART, lawyer; b. Washington, May 7, 1948; s. Frank Jeremiah and Frances Patricia (Bilderback) McC.; m. Patrice Borders, Apr. 3, 1971; children: Kevin Patrick, Charles Ryan, Molly Virginia, Bridget Louise, Moira Patrice. BBA, U. Notre Dame, 1970; JD, Ind. U., Indpls., 1973. Bar: Ind. 1973, U.S. Dist. Ct. (so. dist.) Ind. 1973, U.S. Ct. Appeals (7th cir.) 1974, Ill 1976, U.S. Dist. Ct. (cen. dist.) Ill. 1985, U.S. Ct. Appeals (6th cir.) 1985. Bail commr. Mcpl. Ct. Marion County, Indpls., 1972-73; asst. regional counsel Fed. Hwy. Adminstrn., Homewood, Ill., 1973-75; 1st asst., chief counsel Ill. Dept. Transp., Springfield, 1975-77; counsel com. on interstate and fgn. commerce, subcom. on transp. and commerce Ho. Reps., Washington, 1977-79, asst. counsel com. on pub. works and transp., 1979-82, counsel com. on pub. works and transp., 1982; pvt. practice law Springfield, 1982-87; acting U.S. trustee Dept. Justice, Springfield, 1987-88; U.S. trustee Dept. Justice, Indpls., 1988—; pvt. practice Indpls. and Springfield. Mem. Ill. State Bd. Agrl. Advisors, 1987-88. Mem. Ill. Bar Assn., Ind. Bar Assn., Am. Judicature Soc. Home: 5619 Surrey Hill Rd Indianapolis IN 46226-1561

MCCARTHY, MICHAEL M., construction executive. CEO McCarthy, St. Louis. Office: McCarthy Bldg Cos 1341 N Rock Hill Rd Saint Louis MO 63124-1441

MC CARTHY, WALTER JOHN, JR., retired utility executive; b. N.Y.C., Apr. 20, 1925; s. Walter John and Irene (Trumbl) McC.; m. Linda Lyon, May 6, 1988; children by previous marriage: Walter, David, Sharon, James, William. B.M.E., Cornell U., 1949; grad., Oak Ridge Sch. Reactor Tech., 1952; D.Eng. (hon.), Lawrence Inst. Tech., 1981; D.Sc. (hon.), Eastern Mich. U., 1983; LHD, Wayne State U., 1984; LLD, Alma (Mich.) Coll., 1985. Engr. Public Service Electric & Gas Co., Newark, 1949-56; sect. head Atomic Power Devel. Assos., Detroit, 1956-61; gen. mgr. Power Reactor Devel. Co., Detroit, 1961-68; with Detroit Edison Co., 1968-90, exec. v.p. ops., 1975-77, exec. v.p. divs., 1977-79, pres., chief operating officer, 1979-81, chmn., chief exec. officer, 1981-90; bd. dirs. Comerica Bank Calif., Energy Conversion Devices Inc. Author papers in field. Past chmn., bd. dirs. Inst. Nuclear Power Ops. Fellow Am. Nuclear Soc., Engring. Soc. Detroit; mem. ASME, NAE. Methodist.

MCCARTNEY, N.L., investment banker; b. Jameson, Mo., Oct. 12, 1923; m. Helen M. Walsh, Feb. 11, 1950; children: Patricia, Deborah, Patrick. BS, U. Md., 1956; MBA, Syracuse U., 1959; MPA, George Washington U., 1963. Enlisted U.S. Army, 1944, advanced through grades to col., ret., 1972; dir. S.W. Mo. Health Care Foun., Springfield, 1974-88; pres. Resource Mgmt. Co., Springfield, 1988-96; exec. v.p. Spencer and Assocs., Springfield, 1990-94; instr. Southwest Mo. State U., Springfield, 1972-82. Pres. S.W. Mo. Adv. Coun. Govts., Ozarks Crime Prevention Coun., 1983-93, Vis. Nurse Assn.; mayor of Springfield, 1993-95. Mem. Rotary. Methodist. Home: 1233 E Loren St Springfield MO 65804-0041 Office: PO Box 389 Springfield MO 65801

MC CARTNEY, RALPH FARNHAM, lawyer; b. Charles City, Iowa, Dec. 11, 1924; s. Ralph C. and Helen (Farnham) McC.; J.D., U. Mich., 1950; B. Sci., Iowa State U., 1972; m. Rhoda Mae Huxsol, June 30, 1950; children: Ralph, Julia, David. Bar: Iowa 1950. Mem. firm Miller, Heuber & Miller, Des Moines, 1950-52, Frye & McCartney, Charles City, 1952-73, McCartney & Erb, Charles City, 1973-78; judge Dist. Ct. Iowa, Charles City, 1978-87; chief judge 2d. Judicial Dist., 1987-92; sr. judge Ct. Appeals, 1992—; mem. jud. coordinating com. Iowa Supreme Ct. Chmn. Supreme Ct. Adv. Com. on Adminstrn. of Clks. Offices; mem. Iowa Ho. of Reps., 1967-70, majority floor leader, 1969-70; mem. Iowa Senate, 1973-74. Bd. regents U. Iowa, Iowa State U., U. No. Iowa, Iowa Sch. for Deaf, Iowa Braille and Sight Saving Sch. Served with AUS, 1942-45. Mem. Iowa Bar Assn., Iowa Judges Assn. Home: 1828 Cedar View Dr Charles City IA 50616-9129 Office: Cty Chambers Courthouse Charles City IA 50616

MCCARTNEY, RHODA HUXSOL, farm manager; b. Floyd County, Iowa, June 30, 1928; d. Julius Franklin and Ruth Ada (Carney) Huxsol; m. Ralph Farnham McCartney, June 25, 1950; children: Ralph, Julia, David. AA, Frances Shimer, 1948; BA, U. Iowa, 1950. Mng. dir. McCartney-Huxsol Farms, Charles City, Iowa, 1969—; prin. trustee J.F. Huxsol Trusts, Charles City, Iowa, 1984—. Pres. Nat. 19th Amendment Soc., Charles City, 1991—; mem. Terace Hill Commn., Des Moines, 1988-94; bd. dirs. Iowa Children and Family Svcs., Des Moines, 1963-68; mem. Iowa. Arts Coun., Des Moines, 1974-78. Mem. AAUW, Iowa LWV, PEO. Congregationalist. Home: 1828 Cedar View Dr Charles City IA 50616-9129 Office: McCartney-Huxsol Farms 117 N Jackson St Charles City IA 50616-2002

MCCARTY, RICHARD JOSEPH, consulting engineer; b. Warren, Ohio, Apr. 15, 1948; s. Ralph Edward and Ann Katheerine (Nelms) McC.; m. Cathy Rae Reid, May 12, 1970 (div.); children: Michelle Rae, Erica Ann; m. Nora Elaine Jennings, Dec. 5, 1981; 1 child, Trillion Nora. BA, Hiram Coll., 1991; MBA, Baldwin-Wallace Coll., 1993; postgrad., Nova U., 1993—. Cert. K-12 tchr., adult tchr., spl. edn. tchr., Ohio. Engr. United Telephone Co., Warren, Ohio, 1969-70; cons. engr. Henkels & McCoy, Inc., Blue Bell, Pa., 1970-78, Lambic Telecom, Inc., N.Y.C., 1978-83; regional mgr. Lambic Telecom, Inc., Warren, Ohio, 1985-88; v.p. McAreg Enterprises, Inc., Pocono Lakes, Pa., 1983-84; computer instr. Trumbull County Joint Vocat. Sch., Warren, 1988-90; pres., adminstr. Trillion Inst., Warren, 1990-91; cons. engr. E.G. Keller and Assocs., Elkhart, Ind., 1991—; spkr. Steelworkers Reemployment Challenger, Youngstown, Ohio, 1990-92; edn. cons. to GM Corp. for Warren City Schs. state and fed. programs, 1994-95. Contbr. articles to profl. publs. Democrat. Home: 1914 W Market St Warren OH 44485-2643 Office: EG Keller & Assocs PO Box 964 Elkhart IN 46515-0964

MC CARTY, THEODORE MILSON, business executive; b. Somerset, Ky., Oct. 10, 1909; s. Raymond Andrew and Jennie (Milson) McC.; m. Elinor H. Bauer, June 14, 1935 (dec. Oct. 1989); children: Theodore F., Susan McCarty Davis. Comml. Engr., U. Cin., 1933, postgrad., 1934-35. Asst. store mgr. Wurlitzer Co., Rochester, N.Y., 1936-38, mgr. real estate div. Cin. and Chgo., 1939-41, dir. procurement, DeKalb, Ill., 1942-44, mdse. mgr. retail div., Chgo., 1945-48; pres., gen. mgr., dir. Gibson Inc., 1948-66; owner, pres., treas., dir. Bigsby Accessories Inc., Kalamazoo, 1966—; owner, pres., dir. Flex-Lite, Inc.; v.p., dir. Command Electronics, Kalamazoo. Patentee in music field. Bd. dirs. Glowing Embers council Girl Scouts U.S., 1968-74. Inducted Hollywood Rock Walk of Fame (guitar innovator); recipient Leo award Guitar Player Mag., 1992. Mem. Am. Music Conf. (pres., adminstr. 1961-63, 70-77, dir. 1956—, hon. life dir.), Guitar and Accessory Mfrs. Assn. (past pres., hon. life dir.), Kalamazoo Symphony Soc. (past pres.), S.A.R. (charter mem.), Alpha Kappa Psi, Alpha Tau Omega, Omicron Delta Kappa. Presbyterian. Clubs: Masons, Rotary (past pres.), Kalamazoo Country (past pres.), Park. Home: Bronson Woods 1028 Essex Cir Kalamazoo MI 49008-2349 Office: Bigsby Accessories Inc 3521 E Kilgore Rd Kalamazoo MI 49002-1939 also: Menehune Shores 760 S Kihei Rd #609 Kihei Maui HI 96753

MCCASKEY, MICHAEL B., professional football team executive; b. Lancaster, Pa., Dec. 11, 1943; s. Edward B. and Virginia (Halas) McCaskey; m. Nancy McCaskey; children: John, Kathryn. Grad., Yale U., 1965; PhD, Case Western Res. U. Tchr. UCLA, 1972-75, Harvard U. Sch. Bus., Cambridge, Mass., 1975-82; pres., chief exec. officer Chgo. Bears (NFL), 1983—. Author: The Executive Challenge: Managing Change and Ambiguity. Named Exec. of Yr. Sporting News, 1985. Office: Chgo Bears Halas Hall 250 Washington Rd Lake Forest IL 60045-2471

MCCASLIN, TERESA EVE, human resources executive; b. Jersey City, Nov. 22, 1949; d. Felix F. and Ann E. (Golaszewski) Hrynkiewicz; m. Thomas W. McCaslin, Jan. 22, 1972 (div.). BA, Marymount Coll., 1971; MBA, L.I. U., 1981. Adminstrv. officer Civil Service Commn., Fed. Republic Germany, 1972-76; personnel dir. Oceanroutes, Inc., Palo Alto, Calif., 1976-78; mgr., coll. relations Continental Grain Co., N.Y.C., 1978-79, corp. personnel mgr., 1979-81, dir. productivity, internal cons., 1981-84; dir., human resources Grow Group, Inc., N.Y.C., 1984-85, v.p. human resources, 1985-86, v.p. adminstrn., 1986-89; corporate v.p. human resources Avery Dennison Corp., Pasadena, Calif., 1989-94, Monsanto Co., St. Louis, 1994—; adv. bd. St Johns Mercy Med. Ctr., Goodwill Industries of Mo., St. Louis U. Internat. Sch. Bus. Career counselor Marymount Coll. Career Ctr., Tarrytown. Recipient Sustained Superior Performance award U.S. Civil Service Commn., Fed. Republic Germany. Mem. Am. Mgmt. Assn., Human Resources Coun. Roman Catholic. Office: Monsanto Co 800 N Lindbergh Blvd Saint Louis MO 63167

MCCASLIN, WC, products and packaging executive. Office: Douglas Products & Packaging 1550 E Old 210 Hwy Liberty MO 64068*

MCCAUL, JOSEPH PATRICK, chemical engineer; b. N.Y.C., May 11, 1952; s. Joseph and Marion (Sheehan) McC.; separated Kathleen Anne Crowley, Aug. 3, 1974; children: Kenneth, Christine. BSChemE, Poly. Inst. Bklyn., 1973, M in Polymer Sci. and Engring., 1977; MBA, Case Western Res. U., 1987. Registered ofcl., class I baseball umpire Ohio H.S. Athletic Assn. Prodn. supr. Mobay Chem. Corp., Bayonne, N.J., 1973-77; process engr. Borg Warner Chems., Parkersburg, W.Va., 1977-78; process control engr. Borg Warner Chems., Ottawa, Ill., 1978-79, process control mgr. Linmar plant, 1979-82; mgr. tech. svc. Standard Oil Co., Cleve., 1982-87; mgr. internat. sales and tech. svc. Barex Group BP Chems., Cleve., 1987—. Contbr. articles to profl. publs., mags., ency.; patentee in field. Exec. bd. dirs. Mentor Lake Area Baseball, Mentor on the Lake, Ohio, 1988-89, pres. Mentor McMinn Area Baseball League, 1989-91; trustee Pinegate Homeowners Assn., Mentor, Ohio, 1988-89. Mem. Soc. Plastics Engrs. (award 1987), Pinegate Homeowners Assn. (past trustee). Republican. Roman Catholic. Home: 8733 Applewood Ct Mentor OH 44060-2213 Office: BP Chems H225F 4440 Warrensville Center Rd Cleveland OH 44128

MCCAULEY, DANIEL F., electrical engineer; b. Des Moines, Dec. 18, 1944. BSEE, Iowa State U., 1966. Engring. sect. mgr. elec. engring. Ametek Inc., Kent, Ohio, 1968—. Patentee in field. Bd. mem. Kent (Ohio) City Bd. Zoning Appeals, 1979-85, chmn., 1984-85. Mem. IEEE. Office: Ametek Inc Lamb Elec 627 Lake St Kent OH 44240-2646

MCCHESNEY, SAMUEL PARKER, III, real estate executive; b. Oakland, Calif., July 30, 1945; s. Samuel Parker and Edna Margaret (McCorkle) McC.; m. Vicki Storrie, June 21, 1969; children: Nathan, Amanda, Jed. BA, Washington and Lee U., 1967; JD, Case Western Res. U., 1970. Lic. real estate broker, Mo., Kans. Urban intern and multifamily housing rep. HUD, Chgo., 1970-71; project loan mgr. 1st Home Investment Corp., Overland Park, Kans., 1971-72; v.p. devel. Northland Bldg. Corp., Gladstone, Mo., 1973-74; cons. Urban Equities, Kansas City, Mo., 1975; pres., co-owner McChesney Devel. Co., Inc., Edwardsville, Kans., 1976-78; pres., owner McChesney, Inc., Kansas City, 1978—; Managed Maintenance Inc., 1990—. Pres. Lake Quivira (Kans.) Homeowners Assn. Inc., 1983-85; mem. planning and zoning com. City of Lake Quivira, 1983, mem. planning commn., 1992—; mem. real estate com. Quivira, Inc., 1986, nominating com., 1987-88, 90, restrictions & covenants update com., 1993—; mem. patron's com. Tom Watson Golf Classic, Kansas City, 1984-85; mem. Lake Quivira Long Range Planning Com., 1987-88. Mem. Met. Kansas City Bd. Realtors, Johnson County Bd. Realtors, Assisted Housing Mgrs. Assn. (dir. region 7 1995—), Lake Quivira Country Club (pres. 1983-85). Home: 510 Hillcrest Rd E Lake Quivira KS 66106-9781 Office: 9403 W 119th Terr Overland Park KS 66213

MCCLAIN, RICHARD EUGENE, osteopath; b. Evanston, Ill., July 25, 1961; s. Richard Eugene Sr. and Nara Mary (Roberts) McC.; m. Anita Maire Lande, Sept. 2, 1985; children: Austin James, Garrett Andrew. BS, UCLA, 1984; postgrad., Ohio U. Coll. Osteo. Medicine, 1993—. Rsch. asst. dept. med. biochemistry Tex. A&M U., College Station, 1992-93; extern Ohio U. Coll. Osteo. Medicine, Massillon, 1995—. Vol. Habitat for Humanity, Athens, Ohio, 1995. With USN, 1984-92. Mem.Am. Med. Student Assn. (legis. affairs officer 1993—), Am. Osteo. Assn., Student Osteo. Surg. Assn. (nat. liaison officer 1993—), Sigma Sigma Phi. Republican. Office: Doctors Hosp 400 Austin Ave Massillon OH 44646

MCCLAIN, RICHARD WAGNER, state legislator; m. Barrie L. Brandt. BS, Purdue U., 1970. Sales mgr. east coast CTS Microelectronics; owner, mgr. The Spogge Shoppe, The Capt. Logan Hotel and Office Bldg.; sales and mktg. mgr. Controls, Inc.; trustee Jefferson Twp., 1978-80; city engr. Logansport, 1980-84; mem. Ind. Ho. Reps. Dist. 24; me. roads and transp. com., ways and means com. Active Boy Scouts Am., Red Cross, United Way, Farm Bur. Mem. Am. Legion, C. of C.

MCCLAIN, THOMAS E., communications executive; b. East Liverpool, Ohio, July 26, 1950; s. Thomas E. and Helen Marie (Polinski) McC. BA, Case Western Reserve, Cleve., 1972; MA, Kans. State U., 1973. With intergovtl. rels. Ohio EPA, Columbus, 1974-77; legis. liaison Ohio Consumers Counsel, Columbus, 1977-80; dep. dir. Ohio Consumers Counsel, 1980-81; press sec. Ohio Atty. Gen., Columbus, 1982-83; asst. dir. Pub. Utilities Commn., Columbus, 1983; with instnl. rels. dept. Battelle Project Mgmt. Div., Chgo., 1983-84; mgr. instl. rels. Battelle Project Mgmt. Div., 1984-86; mgr. comms. Battelle, Columbus, 1986-88, dir. corp. comms., 1989-95, v.p. corp. comms., 1995—; sec. devel. bd. Children's Hosp., Columbus, 1990—. Vol. Ohio Youth Commn., Columbus, 1975-76; active ARC-Cen. Ohio chpt., 1986-87. Warren Lahr scholar Case Western Reserve U., 1971-72. Mem. Rotary (chmn. program com. 1991-93, bd. dirs. 1994-95, 2d v.p. 1996—). Presbyterian. Home: 2689 Camden Rd Upper Arlington OH 43221-3221 Office: Battelle 505 King Ave Columbus OH 43201-2696

MCCLAIN, WILLIAM ANDREW, lawyer; b. Sanford, N.C., Jan. 11, 1913; s. Frank and Blanche (Leslie) McC.; m. Roberta White, Nov. 11, 1944. AB, Wittenberg U., 1934; JD, U. Mich., 1937; LLD (hon.), Wilberforce U., 1963, U. Cin., 1971; LHD, Wittenberg U., 1972. Bar: Ohio 1938, U.S. Dist. Ct. (so. dist.) Ohio 1940, U.S. Ct. Appeals (6th cir.) 1946, U.S. Supreme Ct. 1946. Mem. Berry, McClain & White, 1937-58; dep. solicitor, City of Cin., 1957-63, city solicitor, 1963-72; mem. Keating, Muething & Klekamp, Cin., 1972-73; gen. counsel Cin. Br., SBA, 1973-75; judge Hamilton County Common Pleas Ct., 1975-76; judge Mcpl. Ct., 1976-80; of counsel Manley, Burke, Lipton & Cook, Cin., 1980—; adj. prof. U. Cin., 1963-72, Salmon P. Chase Law Sch., 1965-72. Exec. com. ARC, Cin., 1978—; bd. dirs. NCCJ, 1975—. Served to 1st lt. JAGC, U.S. Army, 1943-46. Decorated Army Commendation award; recipient Nat. Layman award, A.M.E. Ch., 1963; Alumni award Wittenberg U., 1966; Nat. Inst. Mcpl. Law Officers award, 1971. Fellow Am. Bar Found.; mem. Am. Judicature Soc., Cin. Bar Assn., Ohio Bar Assn., ABA, Fed. Bar assn., Nat. Bar Assn., Alpha Phi Alpha, Sigma Pi Phi. Republican. Methodist. Clubs: Bankers, Friendly Sons of St. Patrick Lodge: Masons (33 deg.). Home: 2101 Grandin Rd Apt 904 Cincinnati OH 45208-3346

MCCLANAHAN, CONNIE DEA, pastoral minister; b. Detroit, Mar. 1, 1948; d. Manford Bryce and Dorothy Maxine (Keely) McC. BA, Marygrove Coll., 1969; MRE, Seattle U., 1978; D Ministry, St. Mary Sem. and U., Balt., 1988. Cert. in spiritual direction, youth ministry, advanced catechist. Campus minister Flint (Mich.) Newman Ctr., 1970-80; coord. religious edn. Blessed Sacrament Ch., Burton, Mich., 1981-84; pastoral assoc. Good Shepherd Cath. Ch., Montrose, Mich., 1984-90; pastor Sacred Heart Ch., Flint, 1990—; music min. New Light Prayer Cmty., Flint, 1979—; co-chaplain Dukette Cath. Sch., Flint, 1991—; ind. spiritual dir., 1988—; resp. Diocesan Regional Adult Edn., 1993-96; mem. Nat., State and Lansing Diocese Catholic Campus Ministry Assns., 1970-80; mem. campus ministry task force Interfaith Metro. Agy. for Planning, 1974-76; mem. Lansing Diocesan Liturgical Commn., 1977-80; mem. Flint Cath. Urban Ministry, 1977-80, 90—, co-chair, 1992-94; mem. Flint Cath. Healing Prayer Team, 1977-84; coord. nat. study week Cath. Campus Ministry Assn., 1978; mem. steering com. All-Mich. cath. Charismatic Com. on Lay Ministry, 1984-86; convener Diocesan Lay Ministry Com. on Cert./Continuing Edn./Spirituality, 1985-86; mem. Diocesan Com. to Update Catechist Formation Handbook, 1989-91; mem. Diocesan All Family Conf. Steering Com., 1990—; mem. Lansing Diocese svc. com. of Cath. Charismatic Renewal, 1979-85, 95—. Mem. Assn. Cath. Lay Ministers (co-chair Region III 1986-87), Profl. Pastoral Ministers Assn. (co-chair 1988-90). Roman Catholic. Office: Sacred Heart Ch 719 E Moore St Flint MI 48505-3905

MCCLELLAN, KEITH, editor, writer; b. Iowa City, Dec. 17, 1936; s. Kenneth and Alice Mae (Arford) McC.; m. Barbara Alice Miller, June 7, 1958 (div. Dec. 1989); children: Michael Keith, Bethany Alice McClellan Brennan, Timothy Keith. BA in Edn./Social Sci., U. No. Iowa, 1959; postgrad., Williams Coll., Williamstown, Mass., 1960, U. Chgo., 1959-67. Tchr., chair negotiating com. Hammond (Ind.) Pub. Schs., 1959-64; asst. to dir. Ctr. for Urban Studies U. Chgo., 1964-67; asst. dir. Met. Housing & Planning Coun. Chgo., 1967-68; v.p. Social Planning Assn., Chgo., 1968-70; project dir. Welfare Coun. Chgo., 1970-71; dep. area mgr. Abt Assocs., Cambridge, Mass., 1971-73; dir. rsch. and govt. rels. United Torch (United Way), Cleve., 1973-75; dir. United Labor Agy., Cleve., 1975-79; exec. dir. Tri-County EAP, Akron, Ohio, 1980-87; dir. health interventions Coun. on Health Costs, Charlotte, N.C., 1987-89; editor Employee Assistance Quar. Haworth Press, Binghamton, N.Y., 1983—; mem. internal rev. group Nat. Inst. Alcohol Abuse and Alcoholism, Washington, 1976-81; mem. adv. com. Nat. Inst. on Drug Abuse Office of Workplace Initiatives, Washington, 1988-89. Author: Sunday Football, 1997; monthly columnist U.S. Jour. of Drug and Alcohol Dependence, 1983-89; contbr. articles to scholarly jours. Bd. dirs. Founders Found., Akron, 1985-91; organizer 50th Anniversary Celebration Alcoholics Anonymous, Akron, 1984-85; bd. dirs. 15 civic orgns., 1968-95; adv. com. 8 state adv. coms., 1980-93. Recipient Peter Bommarito award for outstanding voluntary comty. svc., 1987, award for pre-eminent contbns. to EAP Rsch., Ga. Inst. Tech., 1989; John Hay scholar Williams Coll., 1960, William Murphy scholar U. Chgo., 1965-66; Bowman C. Lingle fellow U. Chgo., 1966-67, Harry Baime fellow Ill. Regional Coun. on Planning, 1968. Mem. Adminstrs. and Cons. on Assn. Labor-Mgmt. Alcoholism, Employee Assistance Soc. N.Am. (co-founder, pres., v.p. 1983-94, Lifetime Achievement award 1992), Kenny Found. Mich. (bd. dirs. 1992-95), Cleve. Labor Coun. (rep., del. 1975-77). Democrat. Lutheran. Home: 14100 Balfour St Oak Park MI 48237

MCCLELLAND, EMMA L., state legislator; b. Springfield, Mo., Feb. 26, 1940; m. Alan McClelland; children: Mike, Karen. BA, U. Mo., 1962. Dir. field office, corp. divsn. Mo. Sec. of State, St. Louis; committeewoman Gravis Township; mem. St. Louis County Rep. Cent. Com., Mo. Rep. State Com.; mem. Mo. State Ho. Rep., 1991—, mem. appropriations, edn., budget, and mcpl. corps. coms. Bd. dirs. Epworth Children's Home, Family Support Network; elder Webster Groves Presbyn. Ch. Recipient Silver Svc. award Nat. Soc. Autistic Children, Outstanding Svc. award Am. Assn. Mental Deficiency, Spl. Leadership award for govt. YWCA of St. Louis. Mem. Webster Groves C. of C., Pi Lambda Theta. Republican. Presbyterian. Home: 455 Pasadena Ave Webster Grove MO 63119-3126 Office: Mo Ho of Reps State Capitol Building Jefferson City MO 65101-1556

MCCLELLAND, HELEN, music educator; b. Chgo., Dec. 5, 1951; d. Leon Leroy and Willie Jo (Darnell) McC.; (div. Sept. 1981); 1 child, Tasha Renee. Diploma in arts, Kennedy-King Coll., 1971; cert. in voice, Sherwood Music Coll., 1971-73; BS, Chgo. State U., 1975, MA in Adminstrn., 1983; D in Adminstrn. and Supervision, U. Calif., 1993. Tchr. Faulkner Sch., Chgo., 1975-78; tchr. music Harvey (Ill.) Pub. Sch. Dist. 152, 1978—; dir. music Pleasant Green Missionary Bapt. Ch., Chgo., 1971—; mem. sch. bd. New World Christian Acad., Chgo., 1988—; bd.d irs. South Shore Drill Team, Chgo. Author: operetta So You Want to Be a Star, 1987. Cmty. worker People United to Save Humanity, Chgo., 1973, Harold Washington Orgn., Chgo., 1987; cmty. educator Chgo. Planned Parenthood, 1988; cmty. counselor Lincoln Cmty. Ctr., Chgo., 1975; mem. sch. bd. Dist. 160, 1994. Named Tchr. of the Yr., Faulkner Sch., 1976. Mem. Ill. Edn. Assn., NEA, Harvey Edn. Assn., Tennis Club, Traveling Club, Phi Delta Kappa, Pi Lambda Theta. Democrat. Baptist. Home: 18029 Ravisloe Ter Country Club Hills IL 60478-5169

MCCLELLEN, BURNELL HOMER, engineer, military officer; b. North Platte, Nebr., Sept. 10, 1955; s. Walter H. and Ila M. (Daniels) McC.; m. Sonda Kay Johnson, May 25, 1991. BS, U. Nebr., 1980, MS, 1986. Plant foreman KAW Dehydrating, Brady, Nebr., 1975-80; commd. 2d lt. U.S. Army, 1980, advanced through grades to maj., 1993; maintenance mgr. U.S. Army, Schofield Barracks, Hawaii, 1980-84; facility mgr. Nebr. Mil. Dept., Lincoln, 1986—. Mem. Nat. Guard Assn., Nat. Guard Hist. Soc. Home: 2nd St Box 184 Garland NE 68360 Office: Nebr Mil. Dept 1300 Military Rd Lincoln NE 68508-1051

MCCLOSKEY, JOHN, environmental engineer; b. Belfast, Ireland, Nov. 29, 1937; came to U.S., 1957; s. Joseph and Mary Bernadette (Keenan) McC.; m. Margaret McKenna, Apr. 1, 1956; children: Joseph, Sean, Patrick, Lisa. Student, Rutgers U., 1957-61, Newark Coll. Engring., 1960-67. Registered profl. engr., Nebr., N.J. Pres., design dir. McCloskey Enterprises, Omaha, 1986-93, cons., 1993—; v.p. govtl. affairs Tecrep Inc., Salt Lake City, 1984-88; safety dir. Control Data Corp., Omaha, 1974-84, radiation safety officer, 1978-84; v.p., tech. dir. Terminal Svcs., Columbus, Nebr., 1983-85. Author: Crush Grinding, 1974. Recipient J.L. Higgins award State of Nebr., 1979-80. Mem. Numerical Control Soc. (cert.), Soc. Mfg. Engrs., Control Data Corp. (pres. 1974-76), KC. Democrat. Roman Catholic. Home and Office: 5134 Decatur Omaha NE 68104

MCCLOW, ROGER JAMES, lawyer; b. St. Johns, Mich., July 23, 1947; s. Jack Gordon and Madalene V. (Mahaffy) McC.; m. Suzanne Terese Posler, July 13, 1978. BA in Polit. Sci. with distinction, U. Mich., 1969; JD magna cum laude, Wayne State U., 1976. Bar: Mich. 1977, U.S. Dist. Ct. (ea. dist.) Mich. 1977, U.S. Ct. Appeals (6th cir.) 1985, U.S. Ct. Appeals (8th cir.) 1987, U.S. Supreme Ct. 1988. Assoc. Miller, Cohen, Marten & Sugerman, Detroit, 1977-81, Klimist, McKnight & Sale, P.C., Southfield, Mich., 1981-83; ptnr. Klimist, McKnight, Sale, McClow & Canzano, P.C., Southfield, 1983—. Tutor Children's Ctr., Detroit, 1990—; bd. dirs. Hemid (Sr. Citizen's Agy.), Detroit, 1982—; mem. gun safety com. Alliance for Greater, Safer Detroit, 1993—; vol. Hospice Legal Aid, Detroit, 1991—. Mem. State Bar Mich. (labor law and employment sect. 1992—), Detroit Bar Assn., Oakland County Bar Assn., Assn. Trial Lawyers Am., Mich. Trial Lawyers Assn., Indsl. Rels. Rsch. Assn., Phi Sigma Alpha. Democrat. Office: Klimist McKnight Sale McClow & Canzano 400 Galleria Officentre Ste 11 Southfield MI 48034-8473

MCCLURE, ALVIN BRUCE, computer programmer and analyst; b. Cin., Mar. 2, 1953; s. Alphonso Bruce McClure and Jewel Lee (Smith) Yates; m. Katherine Shenkar, Nov. 7, 1979; children: Jaina, Randi. Student, U. Mich., 1971-73, 76-77, Fanshawe Coll., London, Ont., Can., 1974-75, Coll. of St. Thomas, 1989-91. Programmer Mfg. Data Systems, Ann Arbor, Mich., 1978-79; systems software specialist Mpls. Star and Tribune, 1979-81; systems analyst NCR COMTEN, Inc., Roseville, Minn., 1981-84; software systems support programmer INTRAN Corp., Bloomington, Minn., 1984-85; programmer/analyst Minn. Dept. Natural Resources, St. Paul, 1985—; mem. mgmt. info. services tech. com., St. Paul, 1987—. Community adv. bd. Sta. WCAL-FM, 1988-90. Mem. IEEE, Am. Inst. Physics, Audio Engring. Soc., Internat. Platform Assn., Mgmt. Info. Svcs., Aikido Yoshinkai Mpls.-St. Paul (4th degree black belt, head instr.). Home: 2104 24th Ave S Minneapolis MN 55406-1014 Office: Minn Dept Natural Resources 500 Lafayette Rd Ste 7 Saint Paul MN 55155-4002

MCCLURE, ARTHUR FREDERICK, II, history educator, archivist; b. Leavenworth, Kans., Jan. 24, 1936; s. Arthur Frederick and Dorothy Louise (Davis) McC.; m. Judith Hallaux, Jan. 20, 1959; children—Allison, Arthur Kyle, Amy Louise, Steven Anderson. B.A., U. Kans., 1958; Ph.D., 1966; M.A., U. Colo., 1960. Asst. prof. history Central Mo. State U., Warrensburg, 1965-69, assoc. prof., 1969-72, prof., 1972—, chmn. dept. history, 1971-81, chmn. dept. history and anthropology, 1981—, univ. archivist, 1985—; vis. prof. history Sch. Humanities and Social Scis. U. Glamorgan, Pontypridd, Wales, 1994. Author: The Truman Administration and the Problems of Postwar Labor, 1945-48, 1969; The Versatiles: A Study of Supporting Players in the American Motion Picture, 1930-55, 1969; The Films of James Stewart, 1970; The Movies; An American Idiom, Readings in the Social History of the American Motion Picture, 1971; Heroes, Heavies, and Sagebrush: A Pictorial History of the " B" Western Player, 1973; Hollywood at War: The American Motion Picture and World War II, 1939-1945, 1973; The Fulbright Premise: Senator J. William Fulbright and Presidential Power in Foreign Policy, 1973; Star Quality: Screen Actors from the Golden Age of Film, 1974; Character People: Supporting Players in the American Motion Picture, 1976; Remembering Their Glory: Sports Heroes of the 1940s, 1977; Character People: Supporting Players in the American Motion Picture, 1979; International Film Necrology, 1981; William Inge: A Bibliography, 1982; Research Guide to Film History, 1983; More Character People: Supporting Players in the American Motion Picture, 1984, Education for Work: The Historical Evolution of Vocational and Distributive Education in America, 1985, Ronald Reagan: His First Career, A Bibliography of the Movie Years, 1988, Memories of Splendor: The Midwestern World of William Inge, 1989, William Inge: A Bibliographical Guide, 1991; contbr. articles to profl. jours. Mem. film adv. com. Mo. Council on Arts, 1972-73; hon. commr. Mo. Am. Revolution Bicentennial Commn., 1975; mem. Mo. Health Coordinating Council, 1976-79; mem. Mo. Health Facilities Rev. Com., 1981-82; mem. Mo. Commn. on Status of Women, 1982-85; mem. nat. adv. com. William Inge Collection, Independence Community Coll., Kans., 1982—; mem. Mo. Com. for Humanities, 1984-85. bd. dirs. Warrensburg Youth Services, Inc., 1982-83; mem. community adv. bd. Sta. KMOS-TV, 1980-83. Served with U.S. Army, 1958. Recipient Disting. Faculty award Sch. Arts and Scis., Central Mo. State U., 1979; grantee Harry S. Truman Library Inst., 1964, 71, Kansas City Regional Council for Higher Edn., 1969-70; hon. fellow Harry S. Truman Library Inst. Nat. and Internat. Affairs, 1970; NEH grantee Northwestern U., 1979; Herbert Hoover scholar, 1980, Moody grantee, Lyndon B. Johnson Library, 1980-81. Mem. Soc. Am. Archivists (audio-visual records com. 1971-73), Popular Culture Assn., Nat. Film Soc., Am. Film Inst., Soc. Cinema Studies, State Hist. Soc. Mo., Orgn. Am. Historians, Am. Hist. Assn., Brit. Film Inst., Phi Kappa Phi. Republican. Episcopalian. Avocation: history of motion pictures. Home: 1405 Charleston Ct Warrensburg MO 64093 Office: Central Mo State U Dept History and Anthropology Warrensburg MO 64093

MCCLURE, LAURA, state legislator; m. John D. McClure. Kans. state rep. Dist. 119, 1993—. Home: 202 S 4th St Osborne KS 67473-2426 Office: Kans Ho of Reps State Capitol Topeka KS 66612*

MCCLURE, MARY VIRGINIA, consumer products company executive; b. Sedalia, Mo., Apr. 29, 1954; d. Stevens Williams and Sarah Catherine (Jones) McC. BS, U. Mo., 1976; MBA, Harvard U., 1981. Dir. communications Dairy Coun., Omaha, 1976-79; staff asst. Hallmark Cards, Kansas City, Mo., 1981-82, mktg. planner, 1982-84, mfg. sect. mgr., 1984-85, product mgr., 1985-87, gen. mgr., 1987-95, v.p., gen. mgr., 1995—. Bd. mem. Mo. Artisans Bus. Devel. Assn., Columbia, 1991—, Keller Grad. Sch., Kansas City, 1990—, Ctr. for Mgmt. Assistance, Kansas City, 1992. Home: 1004 W 70th Ter Kansas City MO 64113-2047 Office: Hallmark Cards 2525 Gillham Rd Kansas City MO 64108-2622

MCCLURE, MATTHEW K., secondary education educator; b. Anderson, Ind., Sept. 20, 1963; s. M. Kenneth and Noma Joan (Prince) McC.; m. Nancy Lee Waymire, July 14, 1984; 1 child, Katherine. BS, Ball State U., 1984; CAS, U. Chgo., 1985, MA, 1986; MS, Northwestern U., 1987. Cert. educator K-12. Social sci. Maine H.S. Dist. 207, Park Ridge, Ill., 1987—; edn./tech. cons. Motorola, Schaumburg, Ill., 1994—; co-chair Writing Across the Curriculum Dist. 207, 1989-92, social science audio-visual libr., 1987—. Mem. ASCD, Coun. for Am. Studies Edn., Phi Delta Kappa. Office: Maine West HS 1755 S Wolf Rd Des Plaines IL 60018

MCCLUSKEY, ANITA, technician; b. Hamilton, Ohio, May 10, 1964; d. Jimmie Helen (Henderson) McGuire; m. James Brandoc Turner McCluskey, May 2, 1986; children: Jamaal Brandon, Ky'Juan Justin Turner. Grad. h.s., 1982. Cert. stenographer. Various positions Ohio Casualty Ins. Co., Hamilton, 1984—, input display clk., 1991-94, CD&E technician, 1994—. Contbr. poetry to anthologies. Home: 1141 Central Ave Hamilton OH 45011

MCCLUSKEY, MATTHEW CLAIR, physical chemist; b. New Kensington, Pa., Jan. 2, 1957; s. John J. and Carole Sue (Hilliard) McC.; m. Cornelia Mary Sanders, Sept. 26, 1981. BS, Ohio State U., 1985; PhD, U. Va., 1990. Post-doctoral fellow in chemistry Dept. Energy Lawrence Berkeley Lab., Berkeley, 1990-92; cons. Annapolis Rsch. Assocs., Fontana, Calif., 1991—; historic ho. preservationist The Ridge, Manchester, Ohio, 1992—; pres., founder YogaWorks, 1994—; cons. Hopewell Farm, 1993—. Contbr. articles to profl. jours. Mem. Inter-Tribal Indian Coun., 1993—. Mem. Ohio Archeol. Soc., Integral Yoga Tchrs. Assn. Home: 5151 US Highway 52 Manchester OH 45144-9753

MC COIN, JOHN MACK, social worker; b. Sparta, N.C., Jan. 21, 1931; s. Robert Avery and Ollie (Osborne) McC.; BS, Appalachian State Tchrs. Coll., Boone, N.C., 1957; MS in Social Work, Richmond (Va.) Profl. Inst., 1962; postgrad. U. N.C., 1959-60; PhD, U. Minn., 1977. Lic. master social worker. Social svc. worker Broughton State Hosp., Morganton, N.C., 1958-59, John Unstead State Hosp., Butner, N.C., 1960-61; clin. social worker Dorothea Dix State Hosp., Raleigh, N.C., 1962-63; child welfare case worker Wake County Welfare Dept., Raleigh, 1963-64; psychiat. social worker Toledo Mental Hygiene Clinic, 1964-66; sr. psychiat. social worker N.Y. Hosp.-Cornell U. Med. Ctr. Westchester Divsn., White Plains, 1966-68; social worker VA Hosp., Montrose, N.Y., 1968-73, also vol. mental health worker Westchester County Mental Health Assn. and Mental Health Bd., White Plains, N.Y.; seminar instr. Grad. Sch. Social Work, U. Minn., Mpls., 1973-74; social worker F.D.R. VA Health Care Facility, Montrose, 1975-77; asst. prof. social work U. Wis., Oshkosh, 1977-79, chmn. dept. cmty. liaison com., 1978-79; assoc. prof. social work Grand Valley State Colls., Allendale, Mich., 1979-81; social worker VA Med. Ctr. Battle Creek, Mich., 1981-83; supr. social worker Dept. VA Med. Ctr., Leavenworth, Kans., 1983-94; cons. 44th Gen. Hosp., USAR, Menasha, Wis., 1978-79, 5540th Support Command, USAR, Grand Rapids, Mich., 1979-83; cons. in field; adj. faculty mem. social scis. dept., Kansas City C.C., 1985-89, St. Mary Coll., 1984, Kellogg C.C., Battle Creek, 1981-83; adj. faculty mem. sch. social welfare, U. Kans., Lawrence, 1992. With USMC, 1948-52, USMCR, 1957-72; lt. col. USAR, 1972-91. Recipient Outstanding Performance award VA, 1971, Superior Performance award, 1982, Outstanding Performance award, 1983; grantee NIMH, 1974; cert. social worker, N.Y. Mem. Nat. Assn. Social Workers (social action com. W. Mich. br. 1980-81), Alpha Delta Mu. Democrat. Baptist. Author: Adult Foster Homes: Their Managers and Residents, 1983; founder (with Human Scis. Press), editor Adult Foster Care Jour., 1987-88, Adult Residential Care Jour., 1989-91, independent jour., 1992—; contbr. articles to profl. jours.; presenter in field. Home: 4913 Colonial Way Lawrence KS 66049-3723

MCCOLLUM, BETTY, state legislator; b. July 12, 1954; m. Douglas McCollum; 2 children. BS in Edn., Coll. St. Catherine. Retail store mgr. Minn.; mem. Minn. Ho. Reps., 1992—, mem. edn. com., environ. and natural resources com., mem. gen. legis. com., vet. affairs and elections com., mem. transportation and transit com., asst. majority leader, chair Legis. Commn. on Econ. Status of Women. Mem. St. Croix Valley Coun. Girl Scouts, Greater East Side Boy Scouts. Democrat. Home: 2668 4th Ave E North Saint Paul MN 55109-3116 Office: Minn Ho of Reps State Office Bldg 100 Constitution Ave Rm 501 Saint Paul MN 55155-1606

MCCOLLUM, JEAN HUBBLE, medical assistant; b. Peoria, Ill., Oct. 21, 1934; d. Claude Ambrose and Josephine Mildred (Beiter) Hubble; m. Everett Monroe Patton, Sept. 4, 1960 (div. Jan. 1969); 1 child, Linda Joanne; m. James Ward McCollum, Jan. 2, 1971; 1 child, Steven Ward. Student, Bradley U., Ill. Cen. Coll. Stenographer Caterpillar Tractor Co., Peoria, 1952-53, supr. stenographer pool, 1953-55, adminstrv. sec., treas., 1955-60, sec., asst. dept. mgr., 1969-71; med. staff sec. Proctor Cmty. Hosp., Peoria, 1978-82; med. asst. Drs. Taylor, Fox and Morgan, Peoria, 1982-84; freelance med. asst. Meth. Hosp. and numerous physicians, Peoria, 1984-89; office mgr. Dr. Danehower, McLelland and Stone, Peoria, 1989—. Vol. tutor Northmoor Sch., Peoria, 1974-78; bd. dirs., mem. exec. com., com. chmn. Planned Parenthood, Peoria, 1990-92. Recipient Outstanding Performance award Proctor Hosp., 1981, also various awards for svc. to schs., ch. and hosps. for mentally ill. Mem. Nat. Wildlife Fedn., Mensa Internat. (publs. officer, editor 1987-89), Mothers League (treas. 1977), Willow Knolls Country Club (social com. 1989-90), Nature Conservancy, World Wildlife Fund, Forest Park Found., Jacques Cousteau Soc., Wilderness Soc. Methodist. Home: 2822 W Pine Hill Ln Peoria IL 61614-3256

MCCOLLUM, TIMOTHY A., financial planner; b. East Pointe, Ga., Sept. 5, 1958; s. Hugh A. and Norma C. (Dyer) McC.; m. Janice K. Parker, May 28, 1980; children: Brandon Jon, Lindey Ellen, Ryan Timothy. BA, Jones U., 1980, MA, 1982. CLU, lic. ins. counselor. Mgr. Capital Holding Corp., Columbus, Ohio, 1982-85; ptnr. Fin. Architects, Inc., Southfield, Mich., 1985-96; pres. McCollum and Assocs., Inc., Bloomfield Hills, Mich., 1996—. Mem. Nat. Assn. Life Underwriters (nat. quality award 1995). Office: McCollum & Assocs Inc Seven W Square Lake Rd Bloomfield Hills MI 48302

MCCONAGHY, GEORGE ALOYSIUS, chemistry research manager; b. Chgo., Apr. 19, 1945; s. George A. and Mary E. (Morris) McC.; m. Kathleen M. Downey, Aug. 12, 1972; children: Christine, Jennifer. B-SChemE, U. Ill., 1967; MSChemE, U. Wash., 1968; PhD in Chem. Engring., U. Ill., 1974. Rsch. engr. Amoco Corp.-Chem. Sector, Whiting, Ind., 1968-70; rsch. engr. Amoco Corp.-Chem. Sector, Naperville, Ill., 1974-77, rsch. supr., 1977-83, rsch. dir., 1983-93, sr. rsch. supr., 1993-94, rsch. mgr., 1994—; lectr. chemistry for execs. Duke U., Durham, N.C., 1994—; mem. adv. bd. Mfg. Rsch. Ctr., U. Ill., Urbana, 1990, Nat. Ctr. for Composite Materials, 1988. Mem. AIChE (chair Chgo. sect. 1983, chair Thiele Award com. 1985-90), Am. Chem. Soc. (petroleum rsch. fund 1989-92), Sigma Xi. Home: 962 Merrimac Cr Naperville IL 60540 Office: Amoco Rsch Ctr PO Box 3011 Naperville IL 60566

MCCONNELL, E. HOY, II, advertising executive; b. Syracuse, N.Y., May 14, 1941; s. E. Hoy and Dorothy R. (Schmitt) McC.; m. Patricia Irwin, June 26, 1965; children: E. Hoy, III, Courtney. B.A. in Am. Studies magna cum laude with high honors, Yale U., 1963; M.B.A. in Mktg, Harvard Bus. Sch., 1965. With Foote, Cone & Belding, 1965-76; v.p. account supr. Foote, Cone & Belding, Chgo., 1971-72, 74-76, Phoenix, 1972-74; with D'Arcy-MacManus & Masius, Chgo., 1976-85, sr. v.p., dir. client services, then vice chmn., 1978-80, pres., 1980-84, chmn., 1984-85; mng. dir. D'Arcy Masius Benton & Bowles, Chgo., 1986-96; sr. v.p., acct. dir. Leo Burnett Co., 1996—; also bd. dirs. D'Arcy Masius Benton & Bowles, Chgo.; sr. v.p., account dir. Leo Burnett Co., Chgo., 1996—. Bd. dirs. Evanston (Ill.) United Way, 1980-83, Evanston Youth Hockey Assn., 1980-89, pres. 1981-83; bd. dirs. Off-the-Street Club, 1980-90, Bus. Profl. People for Pub. Interest, 1981-83, 96—, v.p. 1984-89, pres. 1990-95; bd. dirs. Harvard Bus. Sch. Club, 1990-92; mem. Chgo. Coun. on Fgn. Rels., 1989—. Mem. Am. Assn. Advt. Agys. (gov.-at-large Chgo. coun. 1984, sec. 1986, vice chmn. 1987, chmn. 1988-89), BBB Chgo. (advt. rev. bd.), Tavern Club, Glen View Country Club (bd. dirs. 1992—), Dairymen's Country Club, Chgo. Club (membership comm. 1994—), Yale Club Chgo. (bd. dirs. 1996—). Democrat. Unitarian. Home: 2703 Colfax St Evanston IL 60201-2035 Office: Leo Burnett Co 35 W Wacker Dr Chicago IL 60601

MCCONNELL, GEORGE ALAN, electrical engineer; b. Detroit, May 15, 1929. BS in Physics, Wayne State U., Detroit, 1952; MSEE, U. Mich., 1962. Staff engr. specialist Vickers Inc., Rochester Hill, Mich., 1954—. Patentee: Valve Driver, Hydraulic Trainer. Cpl. U.S. Army, 1952-54. Mem. Detroit Yacht Club. Roman Catholic. Office: Vickers Inc 2730 Research Dr Rochester Hills MI 48309-3574

MCCONNELL, JOHN, manufacturing executive. With Worthington Industries, Inc., 1953—, chmn. bd., 1973. Office: JMAC Inc 150 E Wilson Bridge Rd Worthington OH 43085-2328

MCCONNELL, JOHN THOMAS, newspaper executive, publisher; b. Peoria, Ill., May 1, 1945; s. Golden A. and Margaret (Lyon) McC.; 1 child, Justin. B.A., U. Ariz., 1967. Mgr. Fast Printing Co., Peoria, 1970-71; mgmt. trainee Quad-Cities Times, Davenport, Iowa, 1972-73; asst. gen. mgr., then v.p., gen. mgr. Peoria Jour. Star, 1973-81, pub., 1981—, pres., 1987—. Bd. dirs. Peoria Downtown Devel. Council, Peoria Devel. Corp.; past trustee Methodist Hosp., Peoria. Served with USAR, 1967-69. Named Young Man of Year Peoria Jaycees, 1979. Mem. Peoria Advt. and Selling Club, Peoria C. of C. Congregationalist. Club: Peoria Country. Office: Peoria Jour Star Inc 1 News Plz Peoria IL 61643-0001

MCCONNELL, JOSEPH FREDRICK, sportscaster; b. Rochester, Ind., Mar. 10, 1939; s. Joseph Wilson and Josephine (Rowe) McC.; m. Jane Ann Leffert, June 22, 1963 (div. 1972); children: Colleen, Michael, Kent; m. Susan Jane Graves, Feb. 13, 1982. BA in Phys. Edn., Franklin (Ind.) Coll., 1962. Voice of Denver Broncos, Phoenix Suns, Ind. Pacers, 1969-77, 78-79, Minn. Vikings, 1971-76, 85-87, Minn. Twins, 1978-79, Chgo. Bears, 1977-84, Chgo. WhiteSox, 1980-84, PIA/Sears Coll. Football Game of Week, 1989-91, NBA Game of Week, Chgo., 1989-91; with NBA Radio, N.Y.C., 1991-95; voice of Indpls. Colts NBA, N.Y.C., 1991-95; with Purdue Radio Network, 1995—. With Army N.G., 1955-62. Named Ind. Broadcaster of Yr., AP, 1973-76, Ind. Press Club, 1977, Ill. Broadcaster of Yr., UPI, 1980-83; recipient Athletic Achievement award Franklin Coll. Alumni Assn., 1979. Fellow Am. Sportscasters Assn., Nat. Sportscasters and Sportwriters Assn. (Ill. Broadcaster of Yr. award 1981). Republican. Presbyterian. Home and Office: 3411 E Banta Rd Indianapolis IN 46227-7607

MCCONNELL, PATRICIA ANN, health facility administrator; b. Bklyn., Feb. 28; d. Philip P. and Dagney C. (Petersen) Powers; m. Alexander McConnell, Jan. 15; children: Francis X., Robert M., Bonnie J., Douglas P. AAS in Nursing, Milw. Area Tech. Coll., Milw., 1978; student, U. Wis., 1980; BA, Nat. Lewis U., 1989. RN, Ill., Ind., Wis., Inc.; registered profl. nurse; cert. case mgr.; cert. pain mgr.; cert. ins. rehab. specialist; cert. occupational hearing conservationalist. Nurse, oncology dept. St. Luke's Hosp., Milw., 1976-79; supr. employee health dept. Harnisfeger P&H, Cudahy, Wis., 1979-82; staff nurse employee health dept. 1st Wis. Nat. Bank, Milw., 1982-83; med. svcs. cons. Crawford Risk Mgmt. Svcs., Schaumburg, Ill., 1983-86; case mgmt. specialist Nat. Rehab. Cons., Westmont, Ill., 1986-87; pres., dir. Mid-State Health and Rehab., Westmont, 1987—; bd. dirs. Women in Workers Compnsation of Ill., vice chmn. 1993-94, sponsor chair 1994-95. Founding mem. Rape Recovery Project Hot Line, vol. support group, Chgo., 1989—, bd. dirs. 1990—; active Ill. Coalition Against Sexual Assault, 1990; vol. literacy tutor World Relief Orgn. and Literacy Vols. Am., 1990—; den mother Cubs, Boy Scouts of Am., 1966-68; health and safety svcs. instr. ARC, 1993-94; religion instr. St. Helena Cath. Ch., Greendale, Wis. 1973-75. Mem. LWV, Am. Assn. Occupational Health Nurses Group (treas. 1990-91, pres. 1992-93), Assn. Rehab. Nurses, Am. Acad. Pain Mgmt. (clin. assoc. 1991—), Assn. Vocat. Rehabilitationists in Ill., Women in Workers Compensation of Ill. (mem. bd. 1993-96), Oak Brook Assn. Commerce and Industry (small bus. com. 1989-90), Dolton Regional Hosp. Aux. (charter, nominating com., publicity chair 1965), Women in Mgmt. (hospitality chair). Roman Catholic. Home: 821 Oakwood Dr Westmont IL 60559-1035 Office: 504A E Ogden Ave Ste 249 Westmont IL 60559-1228

MCCONNELL, RICHARD L., state legislator; s. James and Mary M. McConnell; m. Jill Gentry; 4 children. Student, U. Evansville, Oakland City Coll.; grad. Sch. Banking, U. Wis. Fin. cons.; state rep. Dist. 64 Ind. Ho. of Reps., 1990—, chmn. pub. policy, ethics and vet. affairs coms., ranking minority mem., mem. Agr. and rural Devel. Fin. Inst. and natural resources. Precinct committeeman Gibson County, councilman-at-large, 1987-90. Home: PO Box 1304 Princeton IN 47670-0704*

MCCONVILLE, LYNN CUPPINI, school system director; b. Rockford, Ill., Feb. 4, 1950; d. Gino M. and Helen Virginia (Salamone) Cuppini; m. Thomas B. McConville, Nov. 27, 1992. BA, Coll. St. Teresa, 1972; MEd in Adminstrn., No. Ill. U., 1989. Tchr. St. Bernadette Sch., Rockford, 1973-81; tchr. Boylan Catholic High Sch., Rockford, 1981-85, dir. devel. and alumni, 1985—; adv. bd. Spectrum Sch., Rockford, 1987-88. Contbr. articles to newsletter Accent on Excellence, jour. NCEA. Mem. Catholic Women's League. Roman Catholic. Office: Boylan Catholic High Sch 4000 St Francis Dr Rockford IL 61103

MCCOOL, RICHARD BUNCH, real estate developer; b. Kokomo, Ind., Jan. 2, 1925; s. James Victor and Margaret (Bunch) M.C.; m. Victoria R. Middleton, Dec. 23, 1977; children: Kathryn, Suzanne, Rick; 1 stepchild, April. AB in Govt., Ind. U., 1950. Chmn., chief exec. officer Holida Corp., Indianapolis, 1950-70, Great Lakes Homes, Indpls., 1970-77, Am. Investment, Indpls., 1971—; bd. dirs. Am. Investment Group, Indpls., Investor Fin. Services, Indpls.; dir., gen. ptnr. Manor Group, Ind., Ky., 1977—; cons. Wickes Corp., 1970-77. Author: Real Estate Investments, 1981; contbr. articles to mags., newspaper column on contract bridge, 1966-74. Pres., chmn. various civic orgns., 1960-77; permanent mem. Nat. Rep. Senate Com., 1984. Recipient Geisenbier award Kokomo Jaycees, 1960; named to the Hon. Order Ky. Col. Served to capt., U.S. Army, 1943-46, PTO. Mem. Am. Contract Bridge League (life master 1972), No. Ind. Bridge Assn. (pres. 1974), Pvt. Pilot Assn. (pres. 1969), Nat. Contractors Assn. (founding pres. 1970, Contractor of Yr. 1974), Apt. Assns., Cert. Mgmt. Group (pres. 1980), Ind. U. Alumni Club, Sigma Nu. Congregationalist. Clubs: Columbia, Skyline (Indpls.). Lodges: Masons, Shriners. Office: 14904 Greyhound Ct Carmel IN 46032-1091

MCCORCLE, MARCUS DUANE, obstetrician, gynecologist; b. Bassett, Nebr., Jan. 28, 1951; s. Milton Flynn and Mary Ann (Oatman) McC.; m. Brenda Jo Fulbright, June 16, 1974; children: Christa, Matthew, Louisa, Megan. BS in Biology, Evangel Coll., 1973; MD, U. Mo., 1977. Diplomate Am. Bd. Ob-Gyn. Resident in ob-gyn St. John's Mercy Hosp., St. Louis, 1977-81; practice medicine specializing in ob-gyn Springfield, Mo., 1981—; chmn. Ob-Gyn dept. Lester E. Cox Med. Ctrs., 1987-89. Bd. deacons Ctrl. Assembly of God Ch., Springfield, 1983-90; bd. dirs. Evangel. Coll., 1992—. Fellow Am. Coll. Ob-Gyn. (sec., treas. Mo. chpt., treas. Mo. sec., vice chmn. 1992—); mem. Mo. State Med. Assn. (del.), Greene County Med. Soc. (treas. exec. coun.), Evangel. Coll. Alumni Assn. (pres. 1990-91), Mo. State Bd. Healing Arts. Republican. Office: 1000 E Primrose St Springfield MO 65807-7005

MCCORMICK, JAMES HALL, social services administrator; b. Midland, Mich., May 28, 1952; s. Norbert Gerald and LaRene (Hall) McC.; m. Susan Kay Moore, Sept. 9, 1972; 1 child, Jennifer Helen. BS, Mich. State U., 1974; MPA, Western Mich. U., 1980. Lic. nursing home adminstr. Caseworker, fundraiser Big Bros./Big Sisters, Ionia, Mich., 1974-76; adult svcs. case mgr. Montcalm County Dept. Social Svcs., Stanton, Mich., 1976-77, Barry County Dept. Social Svcs., Hastings, Mich., 1977-78; adult facility devel. specialist Mich. Dept. Social Svcs., Lansing, Mich., 1978-80; social svcs. specialist Eaton County Dept. Social Svcs., Charlotte, Mich., 1980-85; program specialist Mich. Dept. Social Svcs., Lansing, 1985-89; acting dir. Shiawassee County Dept. Social Svcs., Owosso, Mich., 1989; dir. Newaygo County Dept. Social Svcs., White Cloud, Mich., 1989—, also bd. dirs. Pres. Fremont (Mich.) Area Elderly Needs Fund, 1993—; trustee, mem. exec. com. The Fremont Area Found., 1990—. Home: 661 Seminole Dr Fremont MI 49412 Office: Newaygo Co Dept Social Svcs PO Box 864 1025 James St White Cloud MI 49412

MCCORMICK, KATHLEEN MARIE, medical surgical nurse; b. McKeesport, Pa., Sept. 20, 1962; d. Raymond P. Jr. and Eileen M. (Roper) Kerrigan; m. Dennis J. McCormick, May 23, 1992; children: Mallory Elizabeth, Amanda Mary. BSN, Coll. of Mt. St. Joseph, Cin., 1984. RN, Ohio; cert. med.-surg. nurse, BLS instr. Asst. mgr. and educator peripheral vascular/gen. surgery unit Park Med. Ctr., Columbus, Ohio. Mem. Acad. Med. Surg. Nurses, Sigma Theta Tau.

MCCORMICK, MICHAEL DEL, business executive; b. Crawfordsville, Ind., Nov. 6, 1950; s. Ralph Cecil and Jessie Elizabeth (Bass) McC.; m. Nancy Lynn Wilkinson, Apr. 6, 1974; children: Carrie Elizabeth, Benjamin Wilkinson. BA, Wheaton Coll., 1973. Cert. ins. counselor. Sales mgr. Meridian Ins. Co., Ind., 1973-77; agt. ins. McCormick-Metsker, Inc., Crawfordsville, Ind., 1977—, pres. adminstrv., 1981—; sec.-trustee Ind. Pub. Employers Plan, 1989—; commr. I.P.S.R.M.C., State of Ind., 1986-89; trustee, sec. Ind. Pub. Employers' Plan, 1989—. Chmn. United Fund, Montgomery County, Ind., 1994; pres., trustee Crawfordsville Cmty. Sch., 1988—; chmn., trustee Michael Com. for Good Govt., Crawfordsville, 1988—. Fellow Acad. Producer Ins. Studies (advanced coverage facility instr. 1984—); mem. Ind. Ins. Agts. of Am. (dir. 1988—, Educator of Yr. 1990, 93), Profl. Ins. Agts. Am. (trustee 1973-88, Profl. Agt. of Yr. 1987, Presdl. Citation 1987), Ind. Soc. Chgo., Pub. Risk Mgmt. Assn. Am., Young Agts. Assn. (lifetime), Crawfordsville Kiwanis Club (dir. 1984-86). Office: McCormick-Metsker Inc 302 E Market St Crawfordsville IN 47933

MCCORMICK, WILLIAM EDWARD, environmental consultant; b. Potters Mills, Pa., Feb. 9, 1912; s. George H. and Nellie (Mingle) McC.; m. Goldie Stover, June 6, 1935; children: John F. (dec.), Kirk W. B.S., Pa. State U., 1933, M.S., 1934. Tchr., Centre Hall (Pa.) High Sch., 1934-37; chemist Willson Products, Inc., Reading, Pa., 1937-43; indsl. hygienist Ga. Dept. Pub. Health, Atlanta, 1946; mgr. indsl. hygiene and toxicology B.F. Goodrich Co., Akron, Ohio, 1946-70; pres. WRC Environ., 1966—; mgr. environ. control B.F. Goodrich Co., 1970-73; mng. dir. Am. Indsl. Hygiene Assn., Akron, 1973-83; exec. sec. Soc. Toxicology, 1976-83; chmn., treas. Envirotox Mgmt., Inc., 1983-93; pres. WRC Environmental, 1996—; mem. exec. com. rubber sect. Nat. Safety Coun., 1955-73, gen. chmn., 1971-72; mem. environ. health com. Chlorine Inst., 1968-73; mem. food, drug and cosmetic chems. com. Mfg. Chemists Assn., 1960-73, chmn., 1967-69, also mem. occupational health com., 1965-73; mem. adv. com. on heat stress U.S. Dept. Labor, 1973; mem. Nat. Adv. Com. Occupational Safety and Health, 1983-85; pres. Am. Indsl. Hygiene Found., 1984, trustee, 1982-89. Contbr. articles to profl. jours. Served to capt. USPHS, 1943-46. Recipient Borden award Am. Indsl. Hygiene Assn., 1993. Mem. AAAS, Am. Chem. Soc., Soc. Toxicology, Am. Indsl. Hygiene Assn. (pres. 1964, charter), Indsl. Hygiene Roundtable (charter), Am. Acad. Indsl. Hygiene (charter), Mason (33 degree), Shriner. Republican. Episcopalian. Home and Office: 419 Dorchester Rd Akron OH 44320-1315

MCCOY, BERNARD ROGERS, television anchor; b. Cortland, N.Y., Dec. 24, 1955; s. Donald Richard and Vivian Alicia (Rogers) McC.; m. Joanne Louise Lohr, Apr. 29, 1989; children: Emily Louise, Marian Alicia. BS in Journalism, U. Kans., 1979; postgrad., Mich. State U. Mgmt. trainee Garney Constrn. Co., Kansas City, Mo., 1979-80; reporter, anchor Sta. WIBW-AM-FM-TV, Topeka, 1979-80, Sta. KCTV-TV, Kansas City, 1980-89; anchor Sta. WKBD-TV, Detroit, 1989-93, WILX-TV, NBC, Lansing, Mich., 1993—; chmn. Earthwork Environ. Adv. Bd., Southfield, Mich., 1989—. Bd. dirs. Judson Ctr.; celebrity fundraiser Salvation Army, Detroit, 1989, March of Dimes, Detroit, 1989, hon. co-chair Mid-Mich. WalkAmerica, 1996; celebrity fundraiser Cancer Soc., Detroit, 1989, The Sanctuary, Royal Oak, Mich., 1989; mem. YMCA, 1991—; mem. Sparrow Hosp. Children's Miracle Network Com., 1996, Mid-Mich. Environ. Action Coun., 1996; project coord. News-10 Computer Edn., 1996. Recipient Spot News awards Mo. Broadcasters Assn., 1987, Kansas City Press Club, 1987, Kans. Broadcasters Assn., 1987, Disting. Environ. Reporting awards Detroit Audubon Soc., 1991, Mich. Audubon Soc., 1992, Ben East award Mich. United Conservation Clubs, 1991, 93, Mich. Outstanding Individual Reporting award UPI, 1991, Emmy award for Outstanding Reporting in Mich., 1994. Mem. Nat. Acad. of TV Arts and Scis. (bd. dirs. Mich. chpt.), Nat. Geo. Soc., Soc. Environ. Journalists (charter, planner nat. conf.). Office: WILX-TV PO Box 30380 Lansing MI 48909-7880

MCCOY, HENRIKA, social worker; b. Chgo., May 8, 1971; d. Henry and Ida Carolyn (Hood) McC. BA, Washington U., St. Louis, 1991; M in Social Work, U. Pa., 1993. Lic. clin. social worker, Ill., type 73 sch. social worker, Ill. Social work intern Phila. Schs. Collaborative, 1991-92, Pa. Sch. for the Deaf, Phila., 1992-93; family worker Ada S. McKinley Comty. Svcs., Chgo., 1993; clin. therapist St. Joseph's Carondelet Child Ctr., Chgo., 1993-95; substance abuse counselor BRASS Found., Inc., Chgo., 1995—; individual family therapist Midwest Family Resource Assocs. Lt., Evergreen Park, Ill., 1995—; social worker Met. Family Svcs., Chgo., 1995—. Quadrennial vol. United Way of Chgo., 1996. Mem. Nat. Assn. of Social Workers, Nat. Assn. Black Social Workers (cert. of recognition 1993), Delta Sigma Theta. Home: 9612 S Wentworth Ave Chicago IL 60628 Office: Met Family Svcs SW # 108 14535 John Humphrey Dr Orland Park IL 60462

MCCOY, JEANIE SHEARER, analytical chemist, consultant; b. Mancelona, Mich., May 27, 1921; d. Theophil R. and Goldie Margaret (Halladay) Schroeder; m. Theodore R. Shearer, June 14, 1958 (div. 1964); 1 child, Blair Barnett; m. George Altha McCoy, July 23, 1966. AA, North Pk. coll., 1941; BS, Northwestern U., 1944; MS, No. Ill. U., 1970. Jr. analytical chemist Buick Motor divsn. GM, Melrose Park, Ill., 1944-45; asst. rsch. chemist Hodson Oil Corp., Chgo., 1945-47; asst. analytical chemist

Internat. Harvester Co., Melrose Park, 1947-49, analytical chemist, 1949-60, prin. chemist, 1960-74, supr. metal process control, 1974-82; cons. cutting fluid mgmt. divsn. JMT, Inc., Lombard, Ill., 1983—. Author: (monograph chpt.) Metalworking Fluids, 1993; editor: Lubrication Engring. Mag., 1980—. Fellow Soc. Tribologists and Lubrication Engrs. (P.M. KU award 1991, Allan Mantenfel award Chgo. sect. 1987); mem. AAUW, Soc. Automotive Engrs., Am. Chem. Soc., Abrasive Engring. Home: 654 West Rd Lombard IL 60148 Office: JMT Inc Cutting Fluid Mgmt Divsn PO Box 756 Lombard IL 60148

MCCOY, JOENNE RAE, psychiatric clinic administrator; b. Detroit, Jan. 26, 1941; d. Harlan and Dorothy (Simpson) Heinmiller; children: Harlan Craig, Cathi-Jo. BA, Mich. State U., 1966; MSW, U. Mich., 1983. Tchr. pub. schs., Owosso and Garden City, Mich., 1962-73; psychotherapist, group leader Wayne County Hosp., Mich., 1981-82; psychotherapist East Point, Westland, Mich., 1982-83, Midwest, Dearborn, Mich., 1982-83; owner, dir. Personal Devel. Ctrs., Inc., Plymouth, Mich., 1981—, Co-Dependency Specialists S.E. Mich. Ltd., Livonia, Mich., 1988—, Intergrated Health, 1994—; bd. dirs. Hospice Suport Svcs., Inc., Livonia; cons. Westland (Mich.) Convalescent Ctr., 1983-89; supr. grad. students U. Mich., 1986—; cons., facilitator Women-the Emerging Entrepreneurs, Wayne State U. and Small Bus. Assn., 1985—; chmn. Substance Abuse Com., Plymouth Schs., 1982; cons. Salvation Army, Plymouth. Mem. bd. advisors (newsletter) Personal Performance, Balt., 1986—. Mem. steering com. for neighborhood programs YWCA. Soroptimist scholar, 1982. Mem. NAFE, Internat. Assn. Pediatric Social Workers, Internat. Platform Assn., Mich. Assn. Bereavement Counselors, Families in Crisis: Domestic Violence Inc., Nat. Assn. Social Workers (cert.), Am. Entrepreneurs Assn., Women's Network (pres.), Acad. Cert. Soc. Workers, Agora Club, Passport Club, Agora Club. Avocation: international business and finance. Home: 37644 N Laurel Park Dr Livonia MI 48152-2662 Office: Co-Dependency Specialist SE Mich Ltd Pc 37677 Professional Dr Livonia MI 48154

MCCOY, KIRK JAY, human resources and public affairs manager; b. Columbus, Ohio, Oct. 2, 1961; s. Ralph Edward and Carolyn Sue (Tope) McC. BSLHR, Ohio State U., 1983. Asst. to pers. adminstr. City of Columbus, Ohio, 1983-85; pers. analyst City of Columbus, 1985-86, pers., pub. info. mgr., 1986-93; human resources and pub. affairs mgr. Solid Waste Authority, Grove City, Ohio, 1993—; mem. adv. bd. Nat. Mgmt. Assn., Columbus, 1993—, Ohio State U. Sch. of Pub. Policy, Columbus, 1993—. Pres. NMA, Buckeye Coun., Ohio, 1991-92; chmn. new income Prevent Blindness, Columbus, 1993-94, Hugh O'Brian Youth Found., Columbus, 1993—; mem. Leadership Columbus, 1994-95; ops. dir. Hugh O'Brian Youth Found. Tng. Inst., Phoenix, 1994. Named Mem. of Yr., NMA, Buckeye Coun., 1994. Republican. Home: 133 Price Ave Columbus OH 43201-5407 Office: Solid Waste Authority Ctrl Ohio 3011 Columbus St Ste 203 Grove City OH 43123

MCCOY, LAWRENCE EDWARD, paper company executive; b. Springfield, Ohio, June 14, 1935; s. George Albert and Olive E. (Ross) McC.; m. Carole A. Holmes, June 8, 1957; children: Melissa L. McCoy Horn, Larry Scott. BA, Wittenberg U., 1957, postgrad., 1960-62. Asst. sales mgr. Omco Prodn. Corp., Springfield, Ohio, 1957-65; v.p. sales Thomas Tape Co., Springfield, Ohio, 1965-83; v.p., gen. mgr. Eastern Coated Papers, Springfield, Ohio, 1983-85; product mgr. Rexford Paper Co., Milw., 1985—; pres. Gummed Industry Assn., N.Y.C., 1978-80. Bd. dirs. exec. com. Wittenberg Alumni Assn., Springfield, 1960-63; pres. Cmty. Planning Coun., Springfield, 1962-64; bd. dirs. Clark County United Way, Springfield, 1964-71; chmn. Clark County Mental Health Bd., Springfield, 1975-83; pres. 1stL uth. Ch., Springfield, 1989-92. Recipient Alumni citation Wittenberg U., 1993. Mem. Kiwanis, Masons. Republican. Home: 2104 Cheviot Hills Dr Springfield OH 45505 Office: Rexford Paper Co 3100 W Mill Rd Milwaukee WI

MCCOY, MATTHEW WILLIAM, state official, human resource manager; b. Des Moines, Mar. 29, 1966; s. William Paul and Mary Ann (Kenneally) McC.; m. Jennifer Ann Stitt, May 29, 1993. BA in History and Polit. Sci., Briar Cliff Coll., 1988. Human resources mgr. Ruan Transp. Mgmt. Systems, Des Moines, 1989-92; state rep. State of Iowa, Des Moines, 1992—. Bd. dirs. Polk County (Iowa) Conservation Bd. Democrat. Roman Catholic. *

MCCOY, RICHARD JAMES, jeweler, real estate developer, broker; b. Saint Joseph, Mich., Oct. 1, 1946; s. Robert J. McCoy and Claredean Grace Seel. BA, Ariz. State U., 1968; MA, Andrews U., 1970. Lic. real estate developer. Retail exec., 1972—, real estate developer, 1976—. Contbr. articles to profl. jours. 2d lt. USN, 1970-72, Vietnam. Mem. Nat. Assn. Realtors. Home: 2719 Lakeview Ave Saint Joseph MI 49085 also: 37 N Shore Dr South Haven MI 49090-1164 Office: McCoy Bros Inc 787 Miners Rd Saint Joseph MI 49085-9604

MCCOY, TERRY, educator, community activist; b. N.Y.C., Apr. 3, 1939; d. Robert John and Mary Frances (Harris) Wallace; m. David Ormsby McCoy, July 1, 1961; children: Stephen Andrew, Elizabeth Anne. AB in French, Wells Coll., Aurora, N.Y., 1961; MA in French, NYU, 1966; MA in Theoretical Linguistics, Ohio State U., 1984. Cert. secondary tchr. French, elem. tchr., Ohio. Tchr., chair fgn. lang. dept. Lawrence (N.Y.) Jr. H.S., 1961-64; tchr., founder The Treehouse Nursery Sch., Xenia, Ohio, 1968-71; tchr. Keene (N.H.) Elem. Sch., 1972-73; tchr. math. and sci. Columbus (Ohio) Torah Acad., 1974-83; grad. teaching asst. Ohio State U., Columbus, 1983-85; coord. state ballot issue Merit Selection of Judges, Columbus, 1986-87; adv. for social ministry Luth. Social Svcs., Columbus, 1988-90; dir. Hunger Network in Ohio, Columbus, 1990—; cons. Episc. Diocese of So. Ohio Hunger Task Force, 1993—, West Ohio Unit Meth. Hunger Divsn., 1990—; mem. Have a Heart Ohio, Columbus, 1986—; mem. adv. bd. Ch. World Svc.-Ohio, Columbus, 1992—. Co-editor: Escol '84, 1984, Escol '85, 1985. Bd. dirs. LWV Met. Columbus, 1982-89, LWV-U.S., Washington, 1994—; legis. dir. LWV Ohio, 1987-91; pres. LWV Met. Columbus, 1991-94. Episcopalian. Home: 2021 Indianola Ave Columbus OH 43201 Office: Hunger Network in Ohio 82 E 16th Ave Columbus OH 43201

MC COY, THOMAS LARUE, mathematician, educator; b. Seville, Ohio, Jan. 16, 1933; s. Calvin Armstrong and Irene Rosemund (LaRue) McCoy; m. Leslie Helene Reiwitch, Nov. 29, 1957 (div. 1985); children: Bruce Duncan, Clare Ann; m. Brenda Lee, 1988; children: Anna Chang, Jenny Chang. B.A., Oberlin Coll., 1954; M.S., U. Wis., 1956, Ph.D., 1961. With Inst. Air Weapons Research, Chgo., 1960; instr. Ill. Inst. Tech., 1961-62, asst. prof., 1962-64; asst. prof. Mich. State U., East Lansing, 1964-67; asso. prof. Mich. State U., 1967-77, prof. math., 1977—. Contbr. articles to math. jours. Mem. NCTM, Am. Math. Soc., Soc. Indsl. and Applied Math., Math. Assn. Am. Office: Dept Math Mich State U East Lansing MI 48824

MCCRACKEN, CARON FRANCIS, computer company executive, consultant; b. Detroit, Jan. 12, 1951; d. WIlliam Joseph and Constance Irene (Kramer) McC. AS, Mott C.C., 1971; BS, Ctrl. Mich. U., 1973; MA, U. Mich., 1978; postgrad., Wayne State U., 1979-81, 93—. Tchr. Elkton, Pigeon, Bayport (Mich.) High Sch., 1973-74, Davison (Mich.) Jr. High Sch., 1974-75; instr. Mott C.C., Flint, Mich., 1974-78; planning and rsch. specialist Flint Police Dept., 1977-79; campus coord., programmer Systems & Computer Tech. Corp., Detroit, 1981-82; acad. specialist, 1982-83, mgr. acad. computing systems, 1983-84, mgr. adminstrv. computing systems, 1984-85; communications analyst Fruehauf Corp., Detroit, 1985-86, sr. comms. analyst, 1986-87; account cons. US Sprint Communications Co., Detroit, 1987-89; account mgr. US Sprint Communications Corp., Detroit, 1989-90; sr. mgr. Technology Specialists, Inc., Phila., 1990-91; sr. tech. cons. Digital Mgmt. Group, Detroit, 1991-92; sr. assoc. info. tech. practice, tech. delivery svcs. Coopers & Lybrand, Detroit, 1992—; adv. bd. CONTEL Bus. Networks, Atlanta, 1987. Contbr. articles to profl. jours. Vol. charitable and homeless orgns., including COTS - Coalition on Temporary Shelter, Core Cities, Paint the Town; vol. computer project Wayne State U., 1993-95; vol. tech. advisor on 1992 elections project City of Detroit; vol. St. Joseph's Mercy Hosp., Pontiac, Mich., 1995; bd. dirs. Bloomfield Hills Condominium Assn., 1996—. Mem. Data Processing Mgmt. Assn., Assn. Computing Machinery, Detroit Inst. Arts, Alumni Assn. U. Mich., Alumni Assn. Wayne State U., Smithsonian Instn. (assoc.), Adventure Cycling Assn. (Missoula, Mont.). Home: 100 W Hickory Grove H4 Bloomfield Hills MI 48304-2169 Office: Coopers & Lybrand 400 Renaissance Ctr Detroit MI 48243-1507

MCCRACKEN, CHARLES, mathematician, educator; b. Santa Monica, Calif., Nov. 12, 1927; s. Charles and Madge (Lorenz) McC.; m. Mary Jane Foster, Dec. 18, 1977. BSc, U. Cin., 1950, MA, 1952. Engr. Boeing Co., Wichita, Kans., 1980-84; mem. tech. staff Logicon, Inc., Dayton, Ohio, 1984-85; ops. analyst Northrop Corp., Ventura, Calif., 1985-88; lectr. math. Capital U., Dayton, 1989—, Sinclair Coll., Dayton, 1992—. Contbr. articles on math. to profl. jours. Candidate Dayton City Commn., 1991, Dayton Bd. Edn., 1993; founder, chmn. People for Parks and Playgrounds, Dayton, 1990-94; dir. Camp Emanuel, Dayton, 1991—; mem. ctrl. com. Montgomery County Dem. Party, 1994—. Mem. Math. Assn. Am., Sch. Sci. and Math. Assn., Optimists, Masons. Democrat. Mem. Ch. of Christ. Home: 451 Watervliet Ave Dayton OH 45420-2466

MCCRACKEN, CHARLES JAMES, philosophy educator; b. L.A., Apr. 17, 1933; s. Charles James and Alice (Henderson) McC.; m. Katherine Polutanowitsch, Dec. 1956; children: Theresa, Peter. BA, UCLA, 1955; MA, Fordham U., 1959; PhD, U. Calif., Berkeley, 1969. Instr. philosophy Mich. State U., East Lansing, 1965-68, asst. prof., 1968-71, assoc. prof., 1971-80, prof., 1980—. Author: Malebranche and British Philosophy, 1983; contbr. articles to profl. jours. Ephraim Weiss scholar, 1963-64; James Sutton fellow, 1964-65. Mem. AAUP, Am. Philos. Assn. Home: 509 Cowley Ave East Lansing MI 48823 Office: Mich State U 503 S Kedzie Hall East Lansing MI 48824

MCCRACKEN, INA, business executive; b. Highland Park, Mich., Oct. 7, 1939; d. James Howard and Lodaskia (Smoot) Smith; children: Michalene, Colet, Paulet, Pauleta. BA, Mich. State U., 1961, MEd, 1980; Edn. Specialist cert., Wayne State U., 1982, EdD, 1994. Cert. tchr., adminstr., supt., Mich. Pres. Career Mgmt. Systems, Inc., Detroit; instr. Highland Park Bd. Edn. Bus. trainer Detroit Self-Employment Project. Mem. Minority Bus. Inc. (corr. sec.), Nat. Alliance of Black Sch. Educators, Wayne State U. Coll. Edn. Alumni (chmn. bd. govs.), Phi Delta Kappa. Office: PO Box 04721 Detroit MI 48204-0721

MCCRACKEN, MICHAEL DALE, customer services representative; b. Belleville, Ill., Oct. 13, 1951; s. William Lee and Myrna Louise (Lezotte) McC.; m. Patricia Sue Koller, Aug. 24, 1974; 1 child, Steven Michael. BBA in Acctg., Nat. U., 1980; BS in Mgmt., Dyke Coll., Cleve., 1990. Adjutant-pers. officer USMC, Findlay, Ohio, 1975-82; A/P supr. Hancor, Inc., Findlay, Ohio, 1982-84; customer svcs. rep. LTV Steel Co., Cleve., 1986—. Author: Memories from the Rain, 1993, Shadows in the Moonlit Sky, 1995. Lt. col. USMCR. Mem. Nat. Assn. Accts., Am. Legion, AMVETS. Republican. Lutheran. Home: 7804 Barnes Rd Vermilion OH 44089 Office: LTV Steel Co. 1549-GH Prospect Ave Cleveland OH 44115

MC CRACKEN, PAUL WINSTON, economist, business educator; b. Richland, Iowa, Dec. 29, 1915; s. Sumner and Mary (Coffin) McC.; m. Emily Ruth Siler, May 27, 1942; children—Linda Jo, Paula Jeanne. Student, William Penn Coll., 1937; MA, Harvard U., 1942, PhD, 1948. Faculty Found. Sch., Berea Coll., Ky., 1937-40; economist Dept. Commerce, Washington, 1942-43; fin. economist, dir. research Fed. Res. Bank of Mpls., 1943-48; assoc. prof. Sch. Bus. Adminstrn., U. Mich., 1948-50, prof., 1950-66, Edmund Ezra Day Univ. prof. bus. adminstrn., 1966-86, prof. emeritus, 1986—; chmn. Nat. Bur. Econ. Rsch.; trustee Earhart Found.; mem. pub. oversight bd. AICPA. Author: monographs Can Capitalism Survive?; articles on financial, econ. subjects. Fellow Am. Statis. Assn.; mem. Am. Econ. Assn., Am. Finance Assn., Royal Econ. Soc., Harvard Grad. Soc. (coun.). Presbyn. Clubs: Cosmos (Washington); Harvard (N.Y.C.). Home: 2564 Hawthorne Rd Ann Arbor MI 48104-4032

MC CRAY, BILLY QUINCY, newspaper owner, former state senator, real estate broker; b. Geary, Okla., Oct. 29, 1927; s. John Joel and Ivory Beatrice (Jessie) McC.; m. Wyvette M. Williams, Oct. 12, 1952; children: Frankie Leen, Anthony, Melody, Kent. Mem. Kans. Ho. of Reps., Wichita, 1967-72, Kans. Senate, 1973-84; real estate broker; dir. minority bus. div. Kans. Dept. Econ. Devel., 1984-86; commr. Sedgwick County Wichita, Kans., 1987-94; owner newspaper Cmty. Voice, 1994—; chmn. County Commn., 1991; with Kans. Healthy Kids Corp., 1992-93. Mem. Wichita Human Relations Comm., 1961-63, Mayor's Adv. Com., Wichita, 1964—, Sedgwick County Commn., 1986—. Served with USAF, 1947-51. Mem. African Methodist Episcopal Ch. Democrat. Home: 2801 N Rock Rd # 901 Wichita KS 67226 Office: PO Box 20804 Wichita KS 67208

MCCREA, STEVE C., automotive executive; b. Montgomery, Ala., Mar. 24, 1950. Student, Belleville (Ill.) Jr. Coll., S. W. Mo. State U., Springfield, Mo. Salesman Am. Nat. Ins. Co., Springfield, Mo., 1971-73; sales mgr. Reliable Chevrolet, Springfield, 1973-89; pres. Automotive Resources Devel., Springfield, 1989—. Office: Automotive Resources Devel 3754 S Glenstone Ave Springfield MO 65804-4416

MCCROHON, CRAIG, lawyer; b. Harvey, Ill., Oct. 17, 1961; s. Maxwell and Nancy McCrohon. BA, Harvard U., 1984, London Sch. Econs., 1988; JD, U. Pa., 1989, MBA, 1989. Bar: Ill. 1989, U.S. Dist. Ct. (no. dist.) Ill. 1989. Assoc. Winston & Strawn, Chgo., 1989-91, Freeborn & Peters, Chgo., 1991—. Editor: Let's Go: USA, 1983. Mem. strategic planning com. Econ. Devel. Commn. City of Chgo., 1991; pres. bd. dirs. Cook County Transition Team-Econ. Devel. Mem. Ill. C. of C. (working group econ. devel. com.), Chgo. Bar Assn. (chmn. com. consumer fin. svcs. 1991-92), Cook County Bar Assn., Bus. Execs. for Econs. Justice (exec. com.), Com. to Lower Utility Bills (chmn. 1984), Dem. Leadership for the Twenty-First Century (mem. bd. dirs.), Phi Alpha Delta. Home: 200 E Chestnut St Apt 907 Chicago IL 60611-2317 Office: Freeborn & Peters 311 S Wacker Dr Chicago IL 60606-6618

MCCUEN, JOHN JOACHIM, financial company executive; b. Washington, Mar. 30, 1926; s. Joseph Raymond and Josephine (Joachim) McC.; m. Gloria Joyce Seidel, June 16, 1949; children: John Joachim Jr., Les Seidel. BS, U.S. Mil. Acad., 1948; M of Internatl. Affairs, Columbia U., 1961; grad., U.S. Army War Coll., 1968. Commd. 2d. lt. U.S. Army, 1948, advanced through grades to col.; dir. internal def. and devel. U.S. Army War Coll., Carlisle Barracks, Pa., 1969-72; chief U.S. Def. Liaison Group, Jakarta, Indonesia, 1972-74; chief field survey office U.S. Army Tng. and Doctrine Command, Ft. Monroe, Va., 1974-76; ret. U.S. Army, 1976; mgr. tng. Chrysler Def., Center Line, Mich., 1977-82; mgr. modification ctr. Land Systems div. Gen. Dynamics, Sterling Heights, Mich., 1982-83; mgr. field ops. Land Systems div. Gen. Dynamics, Warren, Mich., 1983-94; pres. Mich. Econ. Devel. Corp., Birmingham, 1994—, The Magic Christmas Tree, Inc., Birmingham, 1994—; owner Adventure and Exotic Travel Outfitters, Inc., Birmingham, 1995—; pres. First Internat. Corp., Birmingham, 1995—; ptnr. East West Connection, Birmingham, Mich.; past pres. Energy Resource Mgmt. Sys., Inc., Birmingham; armor advisor 3d Royal Thai Army, Utaradit, 1957-58; U.S. rep. users' com. NATO Missile Firing Installation Crete, Paris, 1964-66; advisor Vietnamese Nat. Def. Coll., Saigon, 1968-69; spkr. on terrorism and counter insurgency. Author: The Art of Counter Revolutionary War-The Strategy of Counter Insurgency, Faber 1966, Stackpole, 1967, Circulo Militar, 1967. Pres. Troy (Mich.) Cmty. Concert Assn., 1985—, bd. dirs., 1992; past pres. Mich. Oriental Art Soc., Birmingham; pres. Grander View Found. Sr. Housing and Nursing, Milford, Mich., 1984—; past 1st reader First Ch. of Christ Scientist, Birmingham, 1989-92; past chmn. region VI N.E. unit Detroit United Way Campaign. Mem. Soc. Logistics Engrs., Nat. Mgmt. Assn., Assn. U.S. Army, Oriental Art Soc. Republican. Home: 32863 Balmoral St Beverly Hills MI 48025-3008 Office: Mich Econ Devel Corp 700 E Maple Rd Ste 203 Birmingham MI 48009

MCCULLAGH, GRANT GIBSON, architect; b. Cleve., Apr. 18, 1951; s. Robert Ernest and Barbara Louise (Grant) McC.; m. Suzanne Dewar Folds, Sept. 13, 1975; children: Charles Weston Folds, Grant Gibson Jr. BArch, U. Ill., 1973; MArch, U. Pa., 1975; MBA, U. Chgo., 1979. Registered architect, Ill. Project designer Perkins & Will, Chgo., 1975-77; dir. mktg. The Austin Co., Chgo., 1977-83, asst. dist. mgr., 1983-84, dist. mgr., 1984-88, v.p., 1987-88; chmn., chief exec. officer McClier Corp., Chgo., 1988—. Contbr. articles to various indsl. publs. Bd. dirs. Friends of Prentice Hosp. Mem. FAIA, Chgo. Architecture Found. (pres. 1988-91, adv. bd. trustee 1994—, dir. Design/Build Inst. Am. 1994—, treas. 1995-96), Econ. Club, Chgo. Club, Comml. Club, Casino Club, Univ. Club, Indian Hill Country Club, Comml. Club. Republican. Episcopalian. Home: 43 Locust Rd Winnetka IL 60093-3725 Office: McClier Corp 401 E Illinois St Chicago IL 60611-4363

MCCULLOUGH-WIGGINS, LYDIA STATORIA, pharmacist, consultant; b. Chgo., May 14, 1948; d. George Robert and Isabell (King) Boulware; m. Robert Dale McCullough, Aug. 1, 1970 (div. Oct. 1977); m. 2d, James Calvin Wiggins, Nov. 3, 1979. Student Wis. State U.-Whitewater, 1966-69; B.S. in Pharmacy, U. Ill.-Chgo., 1972; cert. UCLA, 1976-78. Registered pharmacist, Ill. Registered pharmacy apprentice Lefel Drugs, Chgo., 1971-72; pharmacy mgr. Fernwood Pharmacy, Chgo., 1972-73, Sapstein Bros. Pharmacy, Chgo., 1973-74; dir. pharmacy Martin Luther King Neighborhood Health Ctr., Chgo., 1974-80; pharmacist in charge Walgreens, Chgo., 1980-89; mgr. East End Pharmacy, Oak Park, Ill., 1989-90; rep. The Prudential, La Grange, Ill., 1991-95; registered pharmacist OSCO Drugs, Oak Park, 1995—. Bd. dirs. Nia Comprehensive Ctr. Developmental Disabilities, Inc.; mem. coalit. Labor Union Women Exec. Bd. Author: M.L.K. Drug Formulary, 1978. Recipient Cert. of Leadership, YMCA Met. Chgo., 1979; Kizzy award 1980 Black Women Hall of Fame Found., Chgo., 1981; Ann. Med. Achievement award Greater Chgo. Met. Community, 1981. Mem. NAFE, Chgo. Pharmacists Assn., Am. Pharm. Assn., Ill. Pharm. Assn., Nat. Pharm. Assn. (exec. bd.), U. Ill. Alumni Assn. Democrat. Baptist. Club: Christian Novice (pres. 1977-78) (Chgo.). Home: 618 Marshall Ave Bellwood IL 60104-1839

MCCULLY, WILLIAM CRAIG, library administrator; b. Richmond Heights, Mo., Sept. 15, 1947; s. William Craig and Amelia Agnes (Kearns) McC.; m. Nancy Louise Buddenbaum, June 19, 1976; children: Claire Louise, Edward William. BA in History, U. Notre Dame, 1969, MAin Modern European History, 1970, PhD, 1973; MLS, U. Ill., 1975. Dir. Everett M. Dirkson Congressional Leadership Rsch. Ctr., Pekin, Ill., 1975-78, Pekin (Ill.) Pub. Lib., 1975-82; exec. librarian Park Ridge (Ill.) Pub. Lib., 1982—; chmn. dir.'s adv. coun. Ill. Valley Lib. Sys., Pekin, 1980-81; chmn., Ill. State Lib. Adv. Com. and Subcoms., Springfield, 1982-88; sec., Regional Adv. Coun., North Suburban Lib. Sys., Wheeling, Ill., 1988-89; pres., Coop. Computer Svcs., Arlington Heights, Ill., 1991-92; mem. study com. lib. fin., Ill. Gen. Assembly, Springfield, 1993—. Book reviewer: Library Journal, 1980-92. Mem. literature adv. panel, Ill. Arts Coun., Springfield, 1984-87. Capt. USAR, 1973-74. Mem. ALA, Ill. Lib. Assn., Kiwanis. Home: 1321 Peachtree Ln Mount Prospect IL 60056 Office: Park Ridge Pub Lib 20 S Prospect Ave Park Ridge IL 60068

MCCURDY, DAVID B., healthcare ethics consultant, educator; b. Peoria, Ill., Dec. 2, 1946; s. Clarence Donald and Mary Louise (Shearer) McC.; m. Susan Patricia Gohl, Nov. 18, 1978; children: Margaret Anne, Maureen Elizabeth (dec.), Douglas Dustin. BA, Elmhurst Coll., 1968; MDiv, Union Theol. Sem., N.Y.C., 1972; D Ministry, Bethany Theol. Sem., Oak Brook, Ill., 1989. Ordained to ministry United Ch. of Christ, 1972. Pastor Gackle (N.D.)-Jud Congl. Parish, 1973-76; chaplain Elmhurst (Ill.) Coll., 1976-79, mem. adj. faculty dept. theology and religion, 1980-83, 85—; staff chaplain Good Samaritan Hosp., Downers Grove, Ill., 1980-84; chaplain supr. Good Samaritan Hosp. of Evang. Health Systems, Downers Grove, Ill., 1984-91, dir. religion and health, 1991-92; v.p. religion and health, 1992-95; co-dir. clin. healthcare ethics support svcs. Park Ridge Ctr. for Study of Health, Faith and Ethics, Chgo., 1995—; ethics cons. Evang. Health Sys., Oak Brook, Ill., 1988-95; chmn. Ill. United Ch. of Christ Chaplains, 1986-87; bd. dirs. Chgo. Clin. Ethics Programs, 1996—. Bd. editors Jour. Supervision and Tng. in Ministry, 1989—, co-editor jour. symposium, 1990, editor clin. vignettes sect., 1992—; editl. advisor biomedical ethics CareGiver Jour., 1995—. Chmn. Hosp. Vol. Chaplaincy Program, Elmhurst, 1978-79. Fellow. Coll. Chaplains (bd. cert.); mem. Assn. Clin. Pastoral Edn. (cert. supr., chmn. theol. edn. com. North Ctrl. region 1989-94, stds. com. 1995-96), Soc. for Bioethics Consultation, Soc. for Health and Human Values, Am. Assn. of Bioethics, Am. Soc. Law, Medicine and Ethics, Met. Ecumenical Chgo. Chaplains Assn., Lions (sec. Gackle 1974-76). Office: Pk Ridge Ctr Study Hlth Faith & Ethics 211 E Ontario Ste 800 Chicago IL 60611-3215

MCCURDY, KURT BASQUIN, real estate corporation officer; b. Portsmouth, Ohio, Dec. 24, 1952; s. Robert Kurt and Sue Ann (Basquin) McC.; m. Eileen Wirtz, May 21, 1977; children: Andrew Kurt, Patrick Robert, Meghan Eileen. Student, Ohio No. U., Ada, 1971-72; BA, Ohio State U., 1976. Cert. residential specialist. Sales assoc. HER Realtors, Inc., Columbus, Ohio, 1975—, also bd. dirs.; appraiser Franklin County Probate Ct., Columbus, 1978—; guest lectr. Ohio State U., 1981, Franklin U., 1982-83. Contbr. articles to real estate mags. Mem. Realtors Polit. Action Com., Columbus, 1978—, Chmn.'s Club, Rep. Party, Franklin County, 1980-85; v.p., bd. dirs. Culver (Ind.) Mil. Summer Schs., 1979-84. Named nat. sales winner The Dozen, 1984-94, 96; recipient The Dozen award, 1995. Mem. Ohio Assn. Realtors Assn. (Profl. of Yr. award 1979, 83, 84, president's sales award 1986-94), Bldg. Industry Assn. (15 Million Dollar Club, bd. dirs. 1994—, panelist Floyd Wickman Master Sales Acad. 1995, 96, Realtor of Yr. award 1992), Columbus Bd. Realtors 25 Million Dollar Club, Delaware County Bd. Realtors 25 Million Dollar Club, Westerville Athletic Club, Lakes Golf and Country Club. Home: 3295 Glen Oaks Ct Lewis Center OH 43035-9344 Office: HER Realtors Inc 5888 Cleveland Ave Columbus OH 43231-6883

MCCURRY, MARGARET IRENE, architect, educator; b. Chgo., Sept. 26, 1942; d. Paul D. and Irene B. McC.; m. Stanley Tigerman, Mar. 17, 1979. BA, Vassar Coll., 1964. Registered architect, Ill., Mass., Mich.; registered interior designer, Ill. Design coord. Quaker Oats Co., Chgo., 1964-66; sr. interior designer Skidmore, Owings & Merrill, Chgo., 1966-77; pvt. practice architect Margaret I, Chgo., 1977-82; ptnr. Tigerman, McCurry, Chgo., 1982—; vis. studio critic Art Inst. Chgo., 1985-86, 88, lectr., 1988, bd. dirs. Archtl. Soc., 1988—, adv. bd. textile dept., 1992—; vis. studio critic U. Ill., Chgo., Miami U., Oxford, Ohio, 1990; juror Internat. furniture awards Progressive Architecture mag., N.Y.C., 1986, advt. awards, 1988; juror design grants Nat. Endowment for Arts, Washington, 1983; NEA Challenge Design Rev., 1992; peer reviewer design excellence program Gen. Svcs. Administrn., 1992—; juror, Wis., Minn., Calif., Va., Washington, Pitts., Ky., Conn. Soc. Architects, Detroit, N.Y.C., Memphis, Austin, L.A. chpts. AIA, Am. Wood Coun., Am. Inst. Architecture Students Design Competition, 1993. Contbr. Chgo. Archtl. Club Jour.; designer, contbr. archtl. exhibit Art Inst. Chgo., 1983-85, 93, Chgo. Hist. Soc., 1984, Gulbenkian Found., Lisbon Portugal, 1989, Chgo. Athenaeum, 1990, Gwenda Jay Gallery, 1992, Women of Design Traveling Exhbn., 1992-96; archtl. drawings and models in permanent collection Art Inst. Chgo. and Deutsches Architektur Mus., Frankfurt. Chmn. furniture sect. fundraising auction Sta. WTTW-TV, PBS, Chgo., 1975-76; mem. Chgo. Beautiful Com., 1968-70; mem. alumni coun. Grad. Sch. Design, Harvard U.; bd. mem. Architecture and Design Soc. Art Inst. Chgo., mem. textile adv. bd. textile dept. Loeb fellow Harvard U., 1986-87; recipient Builders Choice Grand award Builders Mag., 1985, Interior Design award Interiors Mag., 1983, Dean of Architecture award Chgo. Design Source and the Merchandise Mart, 1989; inducted into Interior Design Hall of Fame, Interior Design Mag., 1990. Fellow AIA (v.p. bd. dirs. Chgo. chpt. 1984-89, chairperson 1993, nat. design com., lectr. Colo. chpt. 1985, nat. conv. 1988, Monterey Design Conf. 1989, Washington Design Ctr. 1989, Nat. Honor award 1984, Nat. Interior Architecture award 1992, Disting. Bldg. award Chgo. chpt. 1984, 86, 91, 94, Disting. Interior Architecture award 1981, 83, 88, 91, product display Neocon award 1985, 88), Coll. of Fellows AIA, Internat. Interior Design Assn., Chgo. Network, Am. Soc. Interior Designers (Nat. Design award 1992, 94, Ill. chpt. Design award 1994, Ill. chpt. Merit award 1994, v.p. bd. dirs. Chgo. chpt.), Chgo. Archtl. Club, Arts Club Chgo., Womens Athletic Club. Episcopalian. Office: Tigerman McCurry Archs 444 N Wells St Chicago IL 60610-4522

MCCUSKEY, MICHAEL PATRICK, judge; b. Peoria, Ill., June 30, 1948; s. Frank Morgan and Margaret Gertrude (Watkins) McC.; m. Linda A. Weers, July 1, 1978 (div. July 1985); 1 child, Melinda; m. Brenda Huber, Dec. 3, 1990; 1 child, Ryan Michael. BSEd, Ill. State U., 1970; JD, St. Louis U., 1975. Tchr. Ottawa (Ill.) Twp. High Sch., 1970-72; ptnr. Pace, McCuskey and Galley, Lacon, Ill., 1975-88; pub. defender Marshall County

State of Ill., Lacon, 1976-88; judge 10th Jud. Circuit of Ill., Peoria, 1988-90; justice 3d Dist. Appellate Ct., Ottawa, 1990—. Bd. dirs. Cen. Ill. chpt. ARC, Peoria, 1989-95, Ill. State U. Alumni Assn., Normal, 1995—. Mem. Ill. Judges Assn., Ill. State Bar Assn. (gen. practice sect. coun. 1991—, assembly 1992—, criminal justice sect. coun. 1994—), Peoria County Bar Assn., Rotary (Paul Harris fellow 1985—). Democrat. Methodist. Home: 212 E State St PO Box 69 Washburn IL 61570-0069 Office: Third Dist Appellate Ct Ste 595 124 SW Adams St Peoria IL 61602-1320

MCCUTCHAN, NEIL J., communications educator; b. Evansville, Ind., Oct. 31, 1938; s. Henry Jason and Laura Helen (Swope) McC.; m. Judith Katherine Grunow, Feb. 17, 1962; 1 child, Allen Neil. BFA, Coll. Conserv. Music, Cin., 1960; MA, U. Cin., 1972. Film editor WKRC-TV, Cin., 1956-61, film editor, buyer, 1970-72; rescue helicopter pilot USAF, Tampa, Thailand, Turkey, 1962-67; prodn. asst. WTVW-TV, Evansville, Ind., 1967-68; producer, dir. Ky. Ednl. TV, Lexington, 1968-70; grad. asst. Ohio State U., Columbus, 1972-76; asst. prof. U. N.D., Grand Forks, 1976-96; ret., 1996. dir. (film) That My People Might Live, 1978; dir., editor Classroom Follies, 1988. Maj. USAFR (ret.), 1962-67. Grantee: U ND Instructional Devel., Moss, Norway, 1993. Mem. Speech Comms. Assn., Internat. TV Assn., Broadcast Edn. Assn., Nat. Assn. TV Program Execs., Masons (Master Acacia Lodge 1985-86, patron Acacia chpt. OES 1992, 93, 95-96, venerable master Scottish rite 33 degree Scottish Rite, Grand Forks valley 1991-92). Office: Univ ND PO Box 7169 Grand Forks ND 58202

MCCUTCHAN, WILLIAM MARK, banker; b. Evansville, Ind., Apr. 10, 1954; s. Harold O. and Carol A. (Blackman) McC.; m. Donna D. Mushrush, Aug. 11, 1984 (div. July 1990); 1 child, William A. BS, Ind. U., 1976; diploma comml. lending, Am. Inst. Banking, 1986; loan rev. cert., Bank Adminstrn. Inst., 1990. Mgmt. trainee Citizens Nat. Bank, Evansville, 1977-79; with Old Nat. Bank, Evansville, 1979-86, loan review officer, 1984-86; dir. loan review, asst. v.p. Old Nat. Bancorp, Evansville, 1986-96, mgr. loan adminstrn., 1996—. Trustee, treas. Willard Libr., Evansville, 1986—; mem. exec. com. Buffalo Trace coun. Boy Scouts Am., Evansville, 1995—; sec.-treas. McCutchanville (Ind.) Cemetery Assn., 1980—; bd. dirs. So. Ind. Higher Edn.; chmn. Old Nat. Bank Polit. Action Com.; chmn. fin. com. McCutchanville United Meth. Ch. Mem. Am. Mensa Ltd., Evansville Country Club, Evansville Kennel Club. Republican. Methodist. Home: 10351 Browning Rd McCutchanville IN 47711-9204 Office: Old Nat Bancorp PO Box 718 Evansville IN 47705-0718

MCCUTCHEON, HOLLY MARIE, accountant; b. Pitts., Aug. 14, 1950; d. George and Ruth (Bradburn) Rudawski. Student, Ohio Dominican Coll., 1968-69, Wittenburg U., 1979-81; BS in Acctg. and Fin. magna cum laude, Wright State U., 1983. Cert. mgmt. acct. Acct. Morris Bean & Co., Yellow Springs, Ohio, 1983-86; contr. Speco Aerospace Corp., Springfield, Ohio, 1986-96, AIDA-Dayton (Ohio) Techs. Corp., Dayton, Ohio, 1996—; cons. Glenwood Tng. Ctr., Yellow Springs, 1983-86. Coach City Recreation Youth Soccer, Springfield, 1982-85; mem. st. Raphael Adult Choir, Springfield, 1986-89. Mem. Inst. Mgmt. Accts. (pres. Dayton chpt. 1994-95). Office: AIDA-Dayton Techs Corp 3131 S Dixie Dr Ste 401 Dayton OH 45439

MC CUTCHEON, JOHN TINNEY, JR., journalist; b. Chgo., Nov. 8, 1917; s. John Tinney and Evelyn (Shaw) McC.; m. Susan Dart, Feb. 1, 1943; children: Anne McCutcheon Lewis, Mary, John Tinney III. BS, Harvard U., 1939. Reporter City News Bur., Chgo., 1939-40; Reporter Chgo. Tribune, 1940-51, editor column A Line O' Type or Two, 1951-57, editorial writer, 1957-71, editor editorial page, 1971-82, columnist, 1967-70. Pres. Lake Forest (Ill.) Libr., 1970-72. Served with USNR, 1941-46. Mem. Soc. Midland Authors, Am. Soc. Newspaper Editors, Nat. Conf. Editorial Writers, Geog. Soc. Chgo. (pres. 1955-57), Chgo. Zool. Soc. (hon. trustee), Chgo. Hist. Soc. (life trustee), Inter Am. Press Assn. (dir., freedom of press com. 1978-87), Sigma Delta Chi. Clubs: Onwentsia (Lake Forest), Tavern (Chgo.), Wayfarers (Chgo.). Home: PO Box 689 Lake Forest IL 60045-0689 also: 99 Holbert Cove Rd Saluda NC 28773-9502

MCCUTCHEON, RONALD EUGENE, social studies educator; b. Zanesville, Ohio, July 31, 1940; s. Ralph Dale and Helen Irene (Combs) McC.; m. Catherine Marie Jorgensen; Apr. 2, 1966; children: Lois Sevim McCutcheon Tsardoulias, Karin Elizabeth McCutcheon Pavlovic. BS in soc. studies edn., Ohio State U., 1965; MS, U. Oreg., 1971. Houseparent, cmty. devel. U.S. Peace Corps, Istanbul, Turkey, 1965-67; soc. studies tchr. Clev. Pub. Schs., 1967-68, Lakewood (Ohio) Pub. Schs., 1968-75, 76-94; geography and English tchr. Fulbright Exch. Program, Newton Aycliff, Eng., 1975-76. Co-creator: (ednl. game) Industrialization, 1968. Mem. Nat. Coun. Soc. Studies, N.E. Ohio Returned Vols. Assn. (Beyond War award, 1987, Outstanding Svc. award, 1992), Turkish Am. Soc. No. Ohio, West Side Irish Am. Club, Ohio Norsemen (initiator, facilitator, 1993, membership chairperson, 1993-95), Clan Donald U.S.A.

MCDADE, LINNA SPRINGER, retired academic program administrator; b. Lincoln, Ill., May 18, 1932; d. Clifford Harry and Lois Mae (Lovett) S.; m. Wesley Dale McDade, June 13, 1951; children: Kimberly Rachel, Chance Linnea, Wesley Dale Jr., Bryan Anthony, Darby Erin. Student, Northwestern U., 1950; AB with honors, U. Ill., 1971. Cert. tchr., Ill. Substitute tchr. Sch. Dist. 116, Urbana, Ill., 1972-74; mng. editor Am. Sociol. Rev., Am. Sociol. Assn., Urbana, 1977-80; asst. to head dept. sociology U. Ill., Urbana, 1980-90; ret., 1990; grants coord. The Reading Group, Urbana, Ill., 1995-96. Chorus mem. Ill. Opera Theatre, 1979-82; pres. Evening Etude Music Club, 1958-60; dir. children's choir 1st Presbyn. Ch., Urbana, 1977, deacon, 1985—, elder, 1989—; co-pres. Washington Sch. PTA, Urbana, 1963-64; bd. dirs. Frances Nelson Health Ctr., Champaign, Ill., 1989-93; vol. fundraising coord. New Hope Jobs, Champaign, 1994—; bd. dirs. Adoption Studies Inst., Washington, 1995-96. Recipient " So Proudly We Hail" Community Svc. award The Exch. Club Urbana, 1990. Mem. Phi Alpha Theta. Home: 2433 County Road 1225 N Saint Joseph IL 61873-9727

MCDANIEL, CHARLES-GENE, journalism educator, writer; b. Luxora, Ark., Jan. 11, 1931; s. Charles Waite and Edith Estelle (Kelly) McD. B.S., Northwestern U., 1954, M.S. in Journalism, 1955. Reporter Gazette and Daily, York, Pa., 1955-58; sci. writer Chgo. bur. A.P., 1958-79; assoc. prof. journalism dept. Roosevelt U., Chgo., 1979-83, prof., 1984-96, chmn. dept., 1979-93, head faculty of journalism and communication studies, 1993-95, prof. emeritus, 1996—. Contbg. editor Libido; contbr. to anthologies, poems, Ency. Britannica, World Book Ency.; contbr. articles to profl. jours.; Chgo. corr. The Med. Post, Toronto, 1979—. Trustee Roosevelt U., 1985-94; bd. dirs. Internat. Press Ctr. Chgo., 1993—; mem. Ill. Gay and Lesbian Task Force. Recipient writing awards Erikson Inst. for Early Edn., 1972, writing award AMA, 1974, writing awards Chgo. Inst. for Psychoanalysis, 1971, 73, writing awards Ill. Med Soc., 1972, 73, writing awards ADA, 1975, Am. Psychol. Assn., 1982. Mem. ACLU, Fellowship of Reconciliation, War Registers League, Art Inst. Chgo. (life), Mus. Contemporary Art (charter), Nat. Lesbian and Gay Journalists Assn., Ill. Arts Alliance, Handgun Control Inc. Home and Office: 5109 S Cornell Ave Chicago IL 60615-4215

MCDANIEL, CRAIG MILTON, art educator; b. Norfolk, Va., Sept. 14, 1948; s. John Milton and Edith Lord (Rang) McD.; m. Jean Ellis Robertson, June 12, 1976. BS in Econs., U. Pa., 1970; MFA, U. Mont., 1975; MS in Urban Mgmt., Drexel U., 1976; MFA, Ohio State U., 1986. Curator performing arts John Michael Kohler Arts Ctr., Sheboygan, Wis., 1976-78; founder, dir. So. Ohio Mus., Portsmouth, 1978-84; dir. programs Columbus (Ohio) Mus. Art, 1985-88; dir. Turman Art Gallery Indiana State U., Terre Haute, 1988-94, assoc. prof. art, 1994—; artist-in-residence Millay Colony for Arts, Austerlitz, N.Y., 1994; mem. visual artists fellowship panel Ohio Arts Coun., Columbus, 1992, chairperson artists in edn. panel, 1986-87, chairperson individual artists fellowship program, 1980; mem. bd. trustees Ohio Mus. Assn., 1981-88; panelist Arts in Edn. Ind. Arts Commn., Indpls., 1993, 94, site evaluator, 1990, 92; project cons. Nat. Endowment for Arts, 1976-80. One-man shows include Purdue U., West Lafayette, Ind., 1994, Jan Cicero Gallery, Chgo., 1995, Swope Art Mus., Terre Haute, 1994, Gov. Ohio's State Residence, 1987. Mem. Coll. Art Assn. Office: Indiana State Univ Dept Art 7th & Chestnut Sts FA 108 Terre Haute IN 47809

MCDANIEL, GEORGE WILLIAM, priest; b. Washington, Iowa, May 4, 1942; s. Merritt Eugene and Dolores Marie (Keifer) McD. BA, St. Ambrose U., Davenport, Iowa, 1966; MA, Aquinus Inst. Theology, Dubuque, Iowa, 1974, U. Iowa, 1977; PhD, U. Iowa, 1985. Ordained priest Roman Cath. Ch., 1970. Assoc. pastor St. Peter's Cath. Ch., Keokuk, Iowa, 1970-73, St. Patrick's Cath. Ch., Ottumwa, Iowa, 1973-74; dean students St. Ambrose U., Davenport, 1974-76, assoc. dir. devel., 1976-77, instr. history, 1977-82, asst. prof. history, 1982-89, assoc. prof. history, 1989—; rector St. Ambrose Sem., Davenport, 1989-96; mem. Nat. Com. Rituals & Emblems, 1982-84, Lambda Chi Alpha. Hoover scholar, 1982, 85. Mem. Orgn. Am. Historians, State Hist. Soc. Iowa (pres. 1984-86, trustee 1981-86, 88-91), U.S. Capitol Hist. Assn., Victorian Soc. Iowa, Lambda Chi Alpha (pres. alumni bd. 1983-86, bd. dirs. 1992—). Home: 518 W Locust St Davenport IA 52803-2829 Office: St Ambrose U 518 W Locust St Davenport IA 52803-2829

MC DANIEL, JAMES EDWIN, lawyer; b. Dexter, Mo., Nov. 22, 1931; s. William H. and Gertie M. (Woods) McD.; m. Mary Jane Crawford, Jan. 22, 1955; children: John William, Barbara Anne. AB, Washington U., St. Louis, 1957, JD, 1959. Bar: Mo. 1959. Assoc. firm Walther, Barnard, Cloyd & Timm, 1959-60; assoc. firm McDonald, Barnard, Wright & Timm, 1960-63, ptnr., 1963-65; ptnr. firm Barnard, Timm & McDaniel St. Louis, 1965-73; ptnr. firm Barnard & Baer, St. Louis, 1973-82; ptnr. Lashly & Baer, St. Louis, 1982—, prosecuting atty., 1968—; city atty. City of Glendale, Mo., 1996—; bd. dirs. Eden. Theol. Sem., Airtherm Mfg. Co.; lectr. Latvian U., Riga, Inst. Fgn. Rels., Banking in Am., 1992-93. Leader legal del. Chinese-Am. Comparative Law Study, People's Republic China, 1988, Russian-Am. Comparative Law Study, USSR, 1990; trustee, past chmn., past treas. 1st Congl. Ch. St. Louis. With USAF, 1951-55. Fellow Am. Bar Found. (life), St. Louis Bar Found. (life); mem. ABA (ho. of dels. 1976-80, 84-92, state del. 1986-92, chmn. lawyers conf., jud. adminstrn. divsn. 1985-86, 8th cir. rep. standing com. on fed. judiciary 1992-95), The Mo. Bar (pres. 1981-82, bd. govs. 1974-83, mem. standing com. on jud. qualification, tenure and compensation 1996—), Mo. Assn. Def. Counsel, Bar Assn. Met. St. Louis (pres. 1972), Internat. Assn. Ins. Counsel, Assn. Def. Counsel St. Louis (past pres.), Phi Delta Phi. Home: 767 Elmwood Ave Saint Louis MO 63122-3216 Office: Lashly & Baer 714 Locust St Saint Louis MO 63101-1603

MCDANIEL, LAURALYN, marketing professional; b. Flint, Mich., Jan. 27, 1963; d. Norman Dale and Donna Lou (Dixon) McD. BA, Oakland U., 1985; MBA, U. Notre Dame, 1987. Market rsch. S.W. Mich. Commn., St. Joseph, 1986; cons. pvt. practice, Flint, 1987-89; mktg. asst. IBA Health & Life Assurance, Kalamazoo, Mich., 1989-91, mktg. specialist, 1991-92; mktg. specialist, mgmt., 1992-95; tech. program adminstr. Soc. of Mfg. Engrs., 1996—. Planning com. Jingle Bell Run Arthritis Found., Kalamazoo, 1991, planning com. star waiter dinner, 1992, public relations com., 1995—; spl. events com. Greater Kalamazoo united Way, 1991, spl. events chair, mem. comm. cabinet, 1992-93; mem. corp. olympic festivls com. YMCA, 1992; decorating com. Gilmore Young Artists Showcase Opening Night Gala, 1993; mem. K.C.I.L. Kalamazoo Ctr. for Ind. Living; mem. Independence Open Planning Com., 1994; chair Disability Resource Ctr. 1994-95, barrier bash planning com., 1995. Mem. Women in Comm., Inc. (bd. dirs., spl. events chair West Mich. chpt. 1990-93), Inter Com. Home: 25701 W 12 Mile Rd #804 Southfield MI 48431 Office: Soc of Mfg Engrs One SME Dr PO Box 930 Dearborn MI 48034

MCDANIEL, RANDALL CORNELL, professional football player; b. Phoenix, Dec. 19, 1964. BPE, Ariz. State U., 1988. Offensive guard Minn. Vikings, 1988—. Named NFL All-Pro Team Guard by Sporting News, 1991-93. Office: Minn Vikings 9520 Viking Dr Eden Prairie MN 55344-3825*

MCDANIELS, JOHN LOUIS, retired mathematics educator; b. Alton, Ill., Oct. 3, 1933; s. John Clarence and Carrie Elizabeth (Kortkamp) McD.; m. Betty Lou Verble, June 20, 1964. BS, U. Mo., Rolla, 1960; MS, So. Ill. U., 1977. Registered profl. engr., Ill., Mo. Engr. McDonnell Douglas Corp., St. Louis, 1960-74; prof. Lewis and Clark Community Coll., Godfrey, Ill., 1975-96; dist. TEAMS competition coord. Ill. Jr. Engring. Tech. Soc., Lewis and Clark C.C., 1987-96, pre-engring. coord., 1975-96, water tech. coord., 1975-92. Bd. dirs. Alton (Ill.) Mus. History and Art, 1984-86. With U.S. Army, 1954-56. Mem. Am. Soc. Engring. Edn., Ill. Math. Assn. Cmty. Colls., Kiwanis (Alton-Godfrey pres. 1989-90, Disting. Pres. award 1990), Sigma Pi Sigma, Tau Beta Pi, Kappa Delta Pi. Presbyterian. Home: 3208 Greenwood Ln Godfrey IL 62035-1815

MCDANIELS, PEGGY ELLEN, special education educator; b. Pulaski, Va., Jan. 4, 1945; d. James H. and Gladys M. (Hurd) Fisher; m. Robert A. McDaniels, Feb. 17, 1973; children: Dawn Marie, Robert C. A Gen. Studies, Schoolcraft Coll., 1976; BA, Ea. Mich. U., 1980, MA, 1985. Cert. adminstr. Woodcock Johnson Psychoednl. Battery (Orton-Gillingham Tng). Payroll sec. Otto's Painting and Drywall, West Bloomfield, Mich., 1964-75; office mgr., closing sec. Bing Constrn. Co., West Bloomfield, 1964-75; substitute tchr. Wayne-Westland Schs., Westland, Mich., 1980-83, Farmington (Mich.) Schs., 1980-83; tchr. spl. edn. Romulus (Mich.) Community Schs., 1983-85, Cros-Lex Schs., Croswell, Mich., 1985-87, Pointe Tremble Elem. Sch., Algonac, Mich., 1987—; organizer, recorder Tchr. Assistance Team, Algonac, 1991—. Mem. Coun. Exceptional Children, Learning Disability Assn. (treas. 1988-90), Mich. Assn. Learning Disability Edn., ASCD. Home: 2406 Military St # 1 Port Huron MI 48060-6665

MCDERMAND, DOUGLAS DAVID, county official; b. Milw., Sept. 1, 1952; s. David Charles and Grace Jane (Powers) McD.; m. Charlotte S.E. Keim, June 7, 1975; children: Kelly Alison, Ryan Douglas. BA in Libaral Arts and Scis., U. Ill., 1975; MPA, Sangamon State U., 1981. Mgr./planner cmty. devel. assistance program Ill. Dept. Commerce and Cmty. Affairs, Springfield, 1976-84; exec. dir. North Ctrl. Ill. Coun. of Govts., Princeton, 1984-91, Coles County Regional Planning and Devel. Commn., Charleston, Ill., 1991—. Editor manual: Community Development Grants Management Manual, 1995. Mem. Am. Planning Assn., Ill. Devel. Coun., Ill. Rural Water Assn., Ill. Assn. Regional Couns. (sec.-treas. 1989-91, pres. 1992-93). Presbyterian. Home: 2108 Sarah's Ln Charleston IL 61920

MCDERMOTT, MOLLY, lay minister; b. Cloquet, Minn., Aug. 19, 1932; d. Harry W. McD.; children: Elizabeth Sanders Hellenbrand, Sarah Sanders, Mary Sanders Day, Margaret Kathleen Sanders Lorfeld. Student, Oreg. State Coll., 1951, U. Minn., Duluth, 1953. Claims specialist Cuna Mut. Ins. Soc., Madison, Wis., 1975—; propr. Molly's Garden. Storyteller, ventriloquist St. Bernard's Parish, mem. faith cmty. commn., liturgical environ. com.; mem. Friends of Aboretum. Mem. Perennial Soc., Toastmasters, The Rose Soc. (storyteller, ventriloquist). Roman Catholic. Home: 1724 Parmenter St Middleton WI 53562-3153

MCDONALD, BRONCE WILLIAM, community activist, advocate; b. Dayton, Ohio, Mar. 21, 1949; s. Lawrence and Pauline Elizabeth (Macknight) McD. Student, Wright State U., 1968-71, U. Dayton, 1971, Dayton Art Inst., 1967-68. Trainer, cons. Nat. Assn. Youth Orgns. United, Washington, 1971-73; program assoc. Dayton (Ohio) Model Cities, 1973-74; child care worker II Montgomery County Children's Svcs. Bd., Dayton, 1974-78; inventory control Mark Morris Tires, San Francisco, 1979-82; office mgr. Bio-Feedback Internat., San Francisco, 1978-84; speaker, bd. dirs. Dayton Area AIDS Task Force, 1987—, AIDS Found. Dayton, 1988-92; community activist People With AIDS, Dayton, 1987—; co-chair Dayton HIV Prevention Cmty. Planning Group Montgomery County Combined Health Dist.; com. mem. Direct Svcs. Dayton Area AIDS Task Force, 1987-92, speaker bur., 1987-92, edn. com., 1987-92, AIDS Found. Miami Valley, 1992—, speaker bur., 1992—, edn. com., 1992—, Pub. Policy and Conflict Mgmt., Ohio Statewide HIV Prevention Cmty. Planning Group, Ohio Dept. Health, The Prevention Summit: HIV Prevention Cmty. Planning Co-chairs meeting, Ctr. for Disease Control and Prevention, Nat. Alliance of State & Territorial AIDS Dirs., Nat. Minority AIDS Coun., Atlanta, 1995—; hotline vol. Dayton Lesbian & Gay Ctr., 1988—; mem. minority AIDS coalition Montgomery County Health Dept., Dayton, 1987—, minority health and social issues coalition, 1988—; bd. dirs. The African Am. Forum on AIDS, Dayton, 1990—, nat. AIDS awareness program So. Christian Leadership Conf., Dayton, 1993—; speaker numerous orgns. on AIDS; bd. dirs. Miami Valley AIDS Partnership, mem. membership, outreach, and needs assessment coms., 1995—. Founding mem., treas. Dayton Area People with AIDS Coalition, 1987-92, Men of All Colors Together, Dayton, 1988-90; co-chair Regional Cmty. Prevention Coord. Com., 1996—. Recipient Pres.'s Citation, 1989, Ohio AIDS Svc. award Ohio Dept. Health, 1990, Cert. of Merit Ohio Dept. Health, Columbus, 1994, Plaque of Vol. Outstanding Merit Montgomery County Combined Health Dist., Dayton, 1995, Outstanding Vol. Svc. Plaque Ohio Dept. Health, 1995, Man of Yr. award Met. Cmty. Ch., Cmty. Unity Health and Wholeness Project, Dayton, 1995. Mem. Nat. Assn. Black and White Men Together. Home: 39 Central Ave Apt 323 Dayton OH 45406-5514

MCDONALD, BRUCE A., financial consultant; b. Evanston, Ill., Apr. 24, 1934; s. John Miller and Florence (Merrill) M.; m. Elizabeth A. Bowler, Dec. 28, 1955 (dec. 1981); children: Bruce A. Jr., Robert G., Scott A., Susan E.; m. Pamela A. Spencer, Sept. 6, 1982. BA, Colgate U., 1955. Banker No. Trust Co., Chgo., 1955-94; pres. McDonald Fin. Svcs., Glencoe, Ill., 1994—. Lt. USAF, 1956-58. Mem. Inst. Cert. Bankers (cert. trust and fin. advisor). Republican. Home: 502 Monroe Ave Glencoe IL 60022

MCDONALD, CAROLYN ANN, dance educator, choreographer; b. Blytheville, Ark., Aug. 27, 1963; d. Travis Eugene and Barbara Jean (Myers) McD. BA in Dance, U. Calif., Irvine, 1987; postgrad., U. Iowa, 1995—. Instr. dance Kirkwood C.C., Cedar Rapids, Iowa, 1987-90; choreographer Kirkwood C.C., Cedar Rapids, 1987—, artistic dir., 1990-96, 1996—; Choreographer Colorguard dance ensemble Wash. H.S., Cedar Rapids, 1996—; instr. dance Coe Coll., Cedar Rapids, 1989—; owner, pres. McDonald Arts Ctr., Marion, Iowa, 1988—; choreographer Washington H.S. Color Guard, Cedar Rapids, 1996—; cons. Jane Boyd Cmty. House, Cedar Rapids, 1993-94; choreographer, color guard dance ensemble Washington H.S., Cedar Rapids, 1996—. Office: 105 Southview Dr Marion IA 52302-3055

MCDONALD, DAVID EUGENE, package car driver; b. Decatur, Ill., July 6, 1956; s. Robert Alexander McDonald and Ida Jane (Varvil) Hall; m. Lynda Jean Christensen McDonald, Apr. 23, 1983; 1 child, Melanie Ann. BS in History, Ill. State U., Normal; student in Bus., Parkland Cmty. Coll., Champaign, Ill. Asst. mgr. Gen. Cinema Corp., Decatur, Champaign, Chgo., 1978-81; mgr. Classic Cinemas, Elmhurst, Ill., 1981-83, World Mgmt. Inc., Downers Grove, Ill., 1983-87; package car driver UPS, Addison, Ill., 1987—. Mem. Jr. Achievement, 1971-75, Dupage County Rep., Wheaton, Ill., 1993—. Named Mr. Exec. Jr. Achievement, Decatur, Ill., 1975; recipient Internat. Literary award Manuscripts Internat., Dayton, Wash., 1988. Republican. Lutheran. Home: 717 S Lodge Ln Lombard IL 60148 Office: UPS 150 Lombard Ave Addison IL 60101

MCDONALD, GLENA JUNE, elementary education educator; b. Lubbock, Tex., Aug. 26, 1947; d. Glen Armstrong Egan Jr. and June Eve (Malouf) Wellman; m. John Freeman McDonald, June 24, 1967; 1 child, Elizabeth Clare. BA, Albertus Magnus Coll., 1969; MEd, U. Ill., Chgo., 1976; cert. advanced studies, Concordia Coll., River Forest, Ill., 1989. Cert. elem. edn., sch. counselor; nat. cert. counselor. Tchr. Chgo. Pub. Schs., 1973-89, sch. counselor, 1989—; adj. prof. psychology, Concordia U., River Forest, Ill., 1994—. Mem. Oak Park-River Forest (Ill.) Infant Welfare Soc., 1989—. Recipient Gov.'s Master Tchr. award State of Ill., 1984; named Finalist for Human Devel. award Oppenheimer Family Found., 1991. Mem. ACA, Am. Sch. Counselor Assn., Ill. Counseling Assn., Ill. Sch. Counselor Assn., Phi Delta Kappa. Episcopalian. Home: 1443 Lathrop Ave River Forest IL 60305-1119

MCDONALD, HAL MARK, music educator, pianist; b. Sikeston, Mo., Feb. 7, 1956; s. Louie and Thelma (Beck) McD. B of Music Performance, So. Ill. U., 1978; M of Music Performance, So. Ill. U., Edwardsville, 1983. Organist 1st United Meth. Ch., Sikeston, 1974-76; organist, min. music 1st Presbyn. Ch., Wood River, Ill., 1977-83; organist St. Paul's Episcopal Ch., Sikeston, 1985—; piano and organ instr. Three Rivers C.C., Poplar Bluff, Mo., 1984—, Hal Mark McDonald Keyboard Studio, 1974—. Named one of Outstanding Young Men of Am., 1989, one of Men of Achievement, 1994. Mem. Piano Tchrs. Soc. Am., Nat. Fedn. Music Clubs, Nat. Guild Piano Tchrs. (pres. Alton, Ill. aux. 1981-84), St. Louis Piano Tchrs. Forum, S.E. Mo. Coun. on Arts, Alton Area Piano Tchrs. Guild, S.E. Area Music Tchrs. Assn., Mo. Music Tchrs. Assn., Music Tchrs. Nat. Assn., Mo. Music Educators Assn., Music Educators Nat. Conf., Sikeston Little Theatre, Allegro Music Club. Home and Office: 424 Johanna Place Dr Saint Louis MO 63021-6495

MCDONALD, HUGH JOSEPH, biochemist; b. Glen Nevis, Ont., Can., July 27, 1913; came to U.S., 1935; s. Roderick J. and Annie Sarah (McDonell) McD.; m. Margaret B. Taylor, Feb. 14, 1942 (dec. Jan. 1963); children: George Gordon, Jean Margaret, Gail Margaret; m. Avis Eugenia Nieman, Aug. 8, 1964. BSc with 1st class honors, McGill U., 1935; MS, Carnegie Mellon U., 1936, DSc, 1939; hon. grad., Universidade Catolica, Rio de Janeiro, 1961. Diplomate Am. Bd. Clin. Chemistry. Instr. chemistry Ill. Inst. Tech., Chgo., 1939-41, asst. prof., 1941-42, assoc. prof., 1943-46, prof., 1946-48; prof., chmn. biochemistry Loyola U., Stritch Sch. Medicine, Maywood, Ill., 1948-79, prof. emeritus, 1979—; prof. chemistry Kendall Coll., Evanston, Ill., 1981-86; rsch. scientist Manhattan Project, Columbia U., N.Y.C., 1943-44; cons. Argonne Nat. Lab., Lemont, Ill., 1946-79, State of Ill. Dept. Pub. Health, Springfield, 1967-81. Author: Ionography: Electrophoresis in Stabilized Media, 1955; co-author: Nutrition for the Prime of Life, 1993; mem. editorial bd. Atherosclerosis, 1970; assoc. editor Analytical Biochemistry, 1960-70. Fellow AAAS, Nat. Acad. Clin. Biochemistry; mem. Am. Chem. Soc., Am. Assn. Clin. Chemistry (pres. 1953, nat. award in edn. 1979) Am. Soc. Biochem. and Molecular Biology. Roman Catholic. Home: 5344 Cleveland St Skokie IL 60077-2414 Office: Loyola U Stritch Sch Medicine 2160 S 1st Ave Maywood IL 60153-3304

MCDONALD, JAMES MICHAEL, employee counselor; b. Detroit, Aug. 1, 1931; s. James Michael and M. Ruth (Doran) McD.; m. Lillian Patricia Canjar, Sept. 24, 1977. BA, Sacred Heart Sem., Detroit, 1953; Theology Lic., St. John's Sem., Plymouth, Mich., 1957. Cert. employee assistance profl., Mich. Priest Archdiocese of Detroit, 1957-74; employee counselor GM Corp., Detroit, 1974—; chmn. treatment com. Detroit EAPA, 1975-85; adv. bd. Robinwood Clinic, Detroit, 1976-80, Health Mgmt. Systems, Southfield, Mich., 1988-90. Office: GM Corp Med Dept 30001 Van Dyke Warren MI 48090

MCDONALD, JAY BRIGGS, sales executive; b. Chgo., Sept. 30, 1957; m. Valerie J. Wolosz, Sept. 22, 1979; 1 child, Samantha Ann. BA in Econs., Ripon Coll., 1979. Regional sales mgr. Speed Queen, Cin., 1979-85; nat. accounts mgr. Speed Queen, Ripon, Wis., 1986-88, nat. mdse. mgr., 1988-91; nat. sales mgr. Huebsch Originators divsn. Raytheon, Ripon, 1992—. Bd. dirs. Ripon Jaycees, 1988-89, Ripon Area Svc. Corp. Mem. Am. Mgmt. Assn. Roman Catholic. Office: Huebsch Originators Shepard St Ripon WI 54971

MCDONALD, JUDITH LOUISE, dean; b. Rockville, Nebr., Jan. 17, 1939; d. D.E. and Gladys V. (Anderson) McD.; children: Candee McDonald Murtland, Sandee McDonald Osmundson. BS, U. Nebr., 1965, MS in Edn. Adminstrn., 1968, PhD in Interdisciplinary Studies, 1980; MA in Acad. Librarianship, U. Denver, 1972. Dir. sch. svc. div. Milford (Nebr.) Pub. Schs., 1965-68; libr. sci. program Chadron (Nebr.) State Coll., 1968-74; coord. learning ctr. State U. Nebr., Scottsbluff, 1974-76; adminstrv. asst. to dept. chair U. Nebr., Lincoln, 1975-77; dir. librs. Bemidji (Minn.) State U., 1977-80, dean libr. and libr. scis., 1980-84, acting dean humanities and fine arts, 1982-84, dean Coll Arts and Letters, 1984—; invited participant Am. Coun. Edn., 1986. Editor, researcher, writer TV documentary Song of the Plains, 1979 (Eudora Welty award). Mem. long range planning com. Pub. Libr., Bemidji, 1980-84; mem. adv. bd. Minn. Youth Svc., St. Paul, 1983-88, Minn. State Arts Bd., St. Paul, 1984-85; bd. dirs. Minn. Pub. Radio, St. Paul, 1985-86, Minn. Humanities Commn., 1991—. Bush Summer fellow Am. Coun. Edn., 1982; named to Gallery of Grads. U. Nebr., Lincoln., 1984. Mem. MLA, Assn. Ednl. Communications and Tech., Assn. Gen. and Liberal Studies, Coun. on Colls. Arts and Scis. Office: Bemidji State U 1500 Birchmont Dr NE Bemidji MN 56601-2600

MCDONALD, LARRY WILLIAM, neuropathologist educator; b. Louisville, Nebr., May 25, 1928; s. Clifford Marion and Tessie Margaret (Higgens) McD.; m. Dorothy Ann Baumgartner, Dec. 26, 1955; children: Laura Ann (dec.), Susan Helen, Lawrence Clifford. BA, U. Calif., Berkeley, 1950; MD,

Northwestern U., 1955. Resident in pathology Pondville State Hosp., Walpole, Mass., 1959-60; instr. Harvard U. Med. Sch., Boston, 1961-62; rsch. assoc. U. Calif., Berkeley, 1963-67; assoc. prof. of pathology U. Calif., Davis, 1968-74; prof. Wright State U., Dayton, Ohio, 1975-77; prof. neuropathology U. Ill., Chgo., 1978-94, ret., 1994, prof. emeritus, 1994—. Contbr. articles to Jour. of Neurosurgery, Lab. Investigation, Exptl. and Molecular Pathology, Am. Jour. Pathology. Capt. USAF, 1957-58. Recipient 1st place award Electron Micro Exhibit, Electron Microscopy Soc. of N.Am., 1967. Mem. Internat. Acad. Pathology, AMA (Gold Medal Hektoen award 1968), Am. Assn. Neuropathologists, Coll. Am. Pathologists. Office: Univ Ill Dept Pathology M/C 847 1819 W Polk St Rm 446 Chicago IL 60612-7335

MCDONALD, ROBERT DELOS, manufacturing company executive; b. Dubuque, Iowa, Jan. 30, 1931; s. Delos Lyon and Virginia (Kolck) McD.; m. Jane M. Locher, Jan. 16, 1960 (div. Jan. 1970); children: Jean, Patricia, Maria, Sharon, Rob; m. Marilyn I. Miller, July 4, 1978. BA in Econs., U. Iowa, 1953. With A.Y. McDonald Mfg. Co., Dubuque, 1956—, salesman, 1956-60, sales mgr., 1961-64, mgr. Dubuque wholesale br., 1965-72, v.p., 1971-72, v.p., corp. sec., 1972-83, sr. v.p., corp. sec., 1983-85, pres., 1985-95, chmn. bd., chief exec. officer, 1987—, also bd. dirs., 1964—; bd. dirs. Brock-McVey Co., Lexington, Ky., A.Y. McDonald Supply Co., Inc., Dubuque; sr. v.p., bd. dirs. A.Y. McDonald Industries, Inc., Dubuque, 1983—; chmn. bd., pres., CEO, bd. dirs. A.Y.M. Inc., Albia, Iowa. Trustee, bd. dirs. A.Y. McDonald Mfg. Co. Charitable Found., 1978—, pres., 1982—; bd. dirs. Stonehill Care Ctr., Dubuque, 1984-92, chmn. bd., 1991-92; mem. Stonehill Renovation and Financing Task Force, 1992—; bd. dirs. Dubuque Boys Club, 1989—, Save Iowa's Civil War Monument Restoration Fund, 1995—, Dubuque County Hist. Soc., 1996—; trustee United Way Svcs., Inc., Dubuque, 1989—; vice chmn. Stonehill Benevolent Found., Dubuque, 1988-92; mem. adv. coun. region VII SBA, Cedar Rapids, 1984—; mem. adv. bd. Jr. Achievement Tri-States, Inc., 1991—, Iowa State Fair Blue Ribbon Found., 1993—. Lt. USNR, 1953-56, Korea. Mem. Am. Mgmt. Assn., Am. Supply Assn., Am. Water Works Assn., Nat. Assn. Mfrs., Dubuque Area C. of C., Am. Legion, Dubuque Shooting Soc., Dubuque Golf and Country Club, Sigma Alpha Epsilon. Republican. Roman Catholic. Home: Fountain Hill 3399 Eagle Point Dr Dubuque IA 52001 Office: AY McDonald Mfg Co PO Box 508 Dubuque IA 52004-0508

MCDONALD, SUSAN B., psychologist; b. Ft. Erie, Ont., Can., July 15, 1956; d. Charles A. and Doris F. (Staples) McD. BA Honours magna cum laude, Queens U., Kingston, Ont., 1978; MS, Fla. State U., 1982. Lic. psychologist, Wis. Intern Wis. Dept. Corrections, Madison, 1983-84, cons., 1984-85, project specialist, 1985-86; psychologist Waupun (Wis.) Correctional Instn., 1986-89, Genesis Counseling Svcs., Ltd., Janesville, Wis., 1989—; psychol. cons. Wis. Div. Probation and Parole, Janesville, 1991—. Vol. Janesville High Schs., 1991, 92. Fellow Wis. Sex Offender Treatment Network (grad.); mem. APA (assoc.), Assn. Treatment Sexual Abusers (clin.), Am. Profl. Soc. on Abuse of Children, Am. Coll. Forensic Examiners, Phi Kappa Phi, Mu Alpha Theta. Office: Genesis Counseling Svcs 2020 E Milwaukee St Janesville WI 53545-2600

MCDONALD, SYLVIA EICHNER, neuro-rehabilitation clinical nurse specialist; b. Milw., May 26, 1956; d. Thomas Lee and Sylvia Mary (O'Malley) Eichner; m. Donald James McDonald, June 30, 1989. BSN, St. Scholastica Coll., 1979; MS, Boston Coll., 1986. RN, Wis.; CRRN. Neurosurg. nurse Milwaukee County Med. Complex, Milw., 1979-80; nurse neurosci. ICU Froedtert Hosp., Milw., 1980-82, clin. nurse specialist spinal cord injury, 1986-93; neuro-rehab. clin. nurse specialist Mercy Med. Ctr., Oshkosh, Wis., 1993—. Co-author: Informational Guide for Persons with Spinal Cord Injury, 1987; contbg. author: Pathophysiology: Concepts of Altered Health States, 1991, 3rd edit., 1993. Mem. Nat. Spinal Cord Injury Assn. (bd. dirs. Milw. chpt. 1990-91), Am. Assn. Spinal Cord Injury Nurses (bd. dirs. 1988-92, pres. 1990-91, mem. standards and guidelines subcom. 1990—, content chair for devel. of sexuality guideline for individuals with spinal cord injury 1994—, chairperson stds. and guidelines com. 1991-94), Am. Assn. Rehab. Nurses. Office: Mercy Med Ctr 631 Hazel St Oshkosh WI 54901

MCDONALD, W. R., employee benefits consultant, developer; b. Mt. Vernon, Ill., Nov. 1, 1929; s. Archie R. and Vernadean Pearl (Bailey) McD. BS, Ind. State U., 1953. Pres. Youth, Inc., Terre Haute, Ind., 1947; dist. mgr. New Eng. Life Ins. Co., Sacramento, 1958-62; v.p. Sutter Sq., Inc., Sacramento, 1960-62, Southland Trust Co., Tucson, 1963-65, Am. Equity Group, Inc., Indpls., 1966-68; sr. ptnr. Ins. Investors' Guidance Systems, Mt. Vernon, 1972—; pres. Interstate Investors & Growers Syndicate, Inc., Indpls., 1975—; mng. ptnr. Halia Crest Land Trust, Mt. Vernon, 1977-79; pres. Intermed. Self-Ins. Group, Mt. Vernon, 1979—; sr. gen. ptnr. Interstate Investors Golf and Garden Solar Lodges, 1980—, Investors Strategies Group, St. Louis, 1982-85, Internat. Benefits Adv. Group, St. Louis, 1984; mng. gen. ptnr. Sundowners' Retirement Resorts, 1986—; bd. dirs. Southland Trust Life Ins. Co., Phoenix, 1964; cons. So. Ill. U., Carbondale, 1973, 84—; mktg. cons. Total Health Care, Inc., Centralia, Ill., 1986-88. Chmn. United Crusade, Sacramento, 1960; chmn. bd. dirs. Salvation Army, Sacramento, 1961; bd. dirs. USO, 1962. Served with USAF, 1951-57. Recipient Outstanding Flight Officer Achievement cert. USAF, 1957; named Disting. Grad., Aviation Cadets, 1952, U.S. Rookie of Year, New Eng. Life Ins. Co., 1959. Mem. Mt. Vernon C. of C. Republican. Lodge: Civitan (Sacramento Internat. chpt. pres. 1961). Office: PO Box 946 Mount Vernon IL 62864-0946 also: 11 S Meridian St Ste 810 Indianapolis IN 46204-3506

MCDONELL, EDWIN DOUGLAS, information systems executive, consultant, writer; b. Johnson City, N.Y., Aug. 16, 1953; S. Alex Edwin and Loretta Arlene (Terry) McD. BA in English Lit., U. Cin., 1976; MSLS in Info. Sci., Case Western Reserve U., 1978; MBA in Mgmt. Info. Systems, Ind. U., 1983. Cert. mgmt. cons. Assoc. Crowe Chizek & Co., CPAs, Indpls., 1983-88, prin., 1989-92; dir. office automation svcs. USA Group, Fishers, Ind., 1992-95; ind. cons. and writer, 1995—; com. chairperson Fin. Mgrs. Soc., Chgo., 1989-92; cons., spkr. Lafferty Group Confs., London, 1992—. Author: (books) Creating a Customer-Driven Retail Bank, 1991, Handbook of Systems Management, 1992, Rebuilding the Retail Bank, 1992, Document Imaging Technology, 1993. Mem. Inst. Mgmt. Cons., Beta Gamma Sigma, Sigma Iota Epsilon. Republican. Presbyterian. Office: 8403 La Habra Ln Indianapolis IN 46236

MCDONNELL, JOHN FINNEY, aerospace and aircraft manufacturing executive; b. Mar. 18, 1938; s. James Smith and Mary Elizabeth (Finney) McD.; m. Anne Marbury, June 16, 1961. BS in Aero. Engring., Princeton U., 1960, MS in Aero. Engring., 1962; postgrad. in bus. adminstrn., Washington U., St. Louis, 1962-66. Strength engr. McDonnell Aircraft Co. (subs. McDonnell Douglas Corp.), St. Louis, 1962, corp. analyst, 1963-65, contract coord., adminstr., 1965-68; asst. to v.p. fin. Douglas Aircraft Co. (subs. McDonnell Douglas Corp.), 1968; v.p. McDonnell Douglas Fin. Corp. (subs. McDonnell Douglas Corp.), 1968-71; staff v.p. fiscal McDonnell Douglas Corp., 1971-75, corp. v.p. fin. and devel., 1975-77, corp. exec. v.p., 1977-80, pres., 1980—, mem. exec. com., 1975—, chmn., 1988—, past CEO, also bd. dirs.; bd. dirs. Ralston Purina Co. Bd. commrs. St. Louis Sci. Ctr.; trustee KETC, Washington U., also chmn. nat. coun. faculty arts and scis. com. Office: McDonnell Douglas Corp PO Box 516 Saint Louis MO 63166-0516*

MCDONNELL, ROSEMARY CYNTHIA, special populations programmer; b. Washington, July 31, 1969; d. Joseph Patrick and Judith Ann (Bruscino) McD. BS, Bradley U., Peoria, Ill., 1991; postgrad., Ill. Ctrl. Coll., 1993. Qualified mental retardation profl. Team leader Community Workshop and Tng. Ctr., Peoria, 1989-92; polit. sci. intern City of Peoria, 1991; undergrad. teaching asst. Bradley U., Peoria, 1991; family support coord. Tazewell County Resource Ctr., Pekin, Ill., 1992-93, early intervention asst., 1993-94; spl. populations programmer Pekin Pk. Dist. Recreation Office, 1994—. Asst. coach Spl. Olympics, Peoria, 1992. Olive B. White scholar Bradley U., 1990. Mem. NOW, Pi Gamma Mu, Phi Alpha Theta. Roman Catholic. Home: PO Box 363 Pekin IL 61555-0363

MCDONOUGH, PATRICK DENNIS, academic administrator; b. Virginia, Minn., Jan. 30, 1942; s. James Morris and Vivian S. (Knudtson) McD.; children: Jeffrey, Anne; m. Karen Howe, June 27, 1981. BA cum laude, Moorhead State U., 1964; MA, U. Kans., 1969; PhD, U. Minn., 1972. Asst. prof. theatre Emporia (Kans.) State U., 1966-70; dir. sales, mktg. Guthrie Theater, Mpls., 1971, 72; asst. prof. speech, dir. of forensics Moorhead (Minn.) State U., 1972-73; assoc. prof., mng. dir., chair Marshall Performing Arts Ctr. U. Minn., Duluth, 1973-76; dean fine arts, prof. U. Evansville (Ind.), 1976-81; vice chancellor, prof. U. Wis., Stevens Point, 1981-84; program dir. (edn. and leadership) W.K. Kellogg Found., Battle Creek, Mich., 1984-89; 15th pres., prof. theatre and mgmt. Marietta (Ohio) Coll., 1989-95, exec. dir. McDonough Ctr. for Leadership and Bus.; assoc. vice chancellor planning and analysis Calif. State U. Sys., Long Beach, 1995—; pres. Emporia chpt. AAUP, 1969; cons. Lexington (Ky.) Children's Theatre, 1979; festival evaluator Am. Coll. Theatre Festival, 4 states, 1975, 76; mem. theatre panel Ind. Arts Commn., Indpls., 1977-79; mem. arts orgn. panel Mich. Arts Bd., Detroit, 1985-89; presenter workshops, conv. programs. Producer, dir. 100 plays and musicals, 1964-84; contbr. articles to profl. publs. Bd. visitors U. Wis., Stevens Point, 1988-90; dist. organizer Eugene McCarthy Presdl. Campaign, Emporia, 1968; mem. leadership commn. Am. Coun. Edn., 1989-94; mem. exec. com. Campus Compact, 1990-95; bd. dirs. numerous civic and arts orgns., 1973-90; chmn. govs. adv. com. on vol. svc., Ohio, 1990-93; mem. leadership studies project U. Md., 1994—. Recipient Disting. Alumnus award Moorhead State U., 1989; grantee Minn. Arts Bd., 1974-76, Ind. Arts Commn., 1976-79. Mem. Am. Assn. Higher Edn., Univ. and Coll. Theatre Assn. (v.p. 1982-83), Marietta Country Club, Stevens Point Country Club, Athletic Club of Columbus. Democrat. Episcopalian. Office: Calif State U Sys 400 Golden Shore Long Beach CA 90802-4275

MCDOUGAL, ALFRED LEROY, publishing executive; b. Evanston, Ill., Feb. 12, 1931; s. Alfred L. and Mary (Gillett) McD.; m. Gudrun Fenger, May 7, 1960 (div. 1982); children: Thomas, Stephen; m. Nancy A. Lauter, Mar. 1, 1986. BA, Yale U., 1953; MBA, Harvard U., 1957. Asst. to pres. Rand McNally & Co., Skokie, Ill., 1962-65, mgr. sch. dept., 1965-69; pres. McDougal, Littell & Co., Evanston, Ill., 1969-91, chmn., CEO, 1991-94; dir. Houghton Mifflin Co., Boston, 1994—; CEO Alth Corp., 1994—; chmn. McDougal Family Found. Trustee Hadley Sch. for Blind, Winnetka, Ill., 1980-83; chmn. budget com. Evanston United Fund, 1974-76, bd. dirs.; bd. dirs. Evanston YMCA, 1988-94, Youth Job Ctr., 1987—, chmn., 1989-91, Opportunity Internat., 1994—, Literacy Chgo., 1992—, treas., 1994—. With U.S. Army, 1953-55. Mem. Assn. Am. Pubs. (exec. com. sch. divsn. 1981—, chmn. 1988-89, 92-94, dir. 1987-89), No. Ill. Assn. (1st v.p. 1984, chmn. 1985). Office: ALM Corp 401 N Michigan Ave 27th Fl Chicago IL 60611

MCDOUGAL, MARIE PATRICIA, English and psychology educator; b. Mt. Clemens, Mich., Apr. 10, 1946; d. Allan Charles and Dorothy Nadine (Berger) Ling; m. Douglas Stevens McDougal, Aug. 23, 1969. BA, Cen. Mich. U., 1968. Lic. tchr., Mich. Tchr. L'Anse Creuse High Sch., Harrison Twp., Mich., 1969—; mem. L'Anse Creuse High Crisis Team, 1988-93, S.A.F.E. Task Force, Harrison Twp., 1986—. Columnist The Jour. Newspaper, Mt. Clemens, 1983-90; speaker in field. Mem. L'Anse Creuse Athletic Boosters; chair Harrison Twp. Hist. Commn. Recipient Appreciation award Macomb County Hist. Soc., 1989, Pres. award for lit. excellence The Nat. Authors Registry, 1994. Mem. Soc. Children's Book Writers, Romance Writers Am., Venice Shores Property Owners (bd. dirs. 1990—, corr. sec. 1994—), Detroit Women Writers, Bay Area Writers' Guild, L'Anse Creuse Public Schs. Alumni Assn. (steering com. 1996). Lutheran.

MCDOWELL, DANIEL QUINCE, JR., airline executive, state transportation technician, aeronautics coordinator, state aviation planner; b. Bklyn., Dec. 6, 1949; s. Daniel Quince and Amelia (DeFreese) McD.; AS, Ill. Ctrl. U., 1977; BS, Bradley U., 1979; diploma U.S. Air Force Region Staff Coll., Colorado Springs, Colo., 1984; cert. Air Force Aux. Corp. Learning Course, Mpls., 1984, Nat. Staff Coll., Maxwell AFB, Ala., 1994. Sr. ground svcs. rep. Overseas Nat. Airways, JFK Airport, N.Y., 1967-70; asst. carrier U.S. P.O., Roosevelt, N.Y., part-time 1969-70; weapons sys. tech. USAF, 1970; weapons sys. officer USAF, 1971; maj. USAFR, 1968-93; sta. agt. Ozark Air Lines, Peoria, Ill., 1971-81, Mpls., 1981-85; customer svc. mgr., 1985-86; Westinghouse Electric, 1987-88, Minn. Dept. of Transp. Dist. 5, Golden Valley, Mn., 1988-90; spl. programs coord., pub. affairs coord., milit. liaison, aviation planner Office of Aeronautics Minn. Dept. of Transp., St. Paul, 1990—; dual aux. video bd. design cons. TriImage Tactical Sys., Sacramento, 1982-88; dir. Minnesota Aviation Symposium, 1991; coord. Minn. Aviation Symposium, 1992. Author: The Sign of the Eagle, 1982; editor: Minn./DOT Aeronautics Tech. Bull. Decorated Air medal with oak leaf clusters. Squadron comdr. CAP/U.S. Air Force Aux., Peoria, 1980-82, Group III staff officer, Mpls., 1983-86, Minn. wing dir. aerospace edn., 1986—, Minn. wing liaison officer AFROTC/CAP Flight Program, 1989-94, support unit comdr. Minn. Air Nat. Guard Mus., 1992—. With USAF, 1970-71. Recipient Outstanding Achievement award Ozark Air Lines, 1985, Exceptional Svc. medal U.S. Air Force Aux.-CAP, 1985, Disting. Svc. medal, 1986, Find Ribbon, 1987, Air Search and Rescue Ribbon and award, 1987, Grover Loening Aerospace, Aerospace Edn. awards, 1985, USA Today Crystal Globe, 1991, Disting. Speaker award U. Minn., 1993, Northern Lights Merit award, 1993. Mem. AIAA, Res. Officers Assn. (reserve officer award), Am. Def. Preparedness Assn., Aerospace Edn. Found. (life), Air Force Assn. (life, sec. 1990, v.p. 1990-91, E.W. Rawlings chpt., v.p. membership and recruiting 1991-93, Medal of Merit 1991, Ira Eaker fellow 1991, state sec. 1994—, nat. advisor to the pres. on cap affairs), Associated Photographers Internat., Internat. Freelance Photographers Orgn., Minn. Air N.G. Mus., North Cen. Region Aerospace Edn. Assn., Global Access Devel. Assn. (exec. bd. advisor), Am. Legion (aviation post 511) AMVETS (aviation post 25). Avocations: creative writing, reading, freelance photography, listening to classical music, travel. Office: Office of Aeronautics 222 Plato Blvd E Saint Paul MN 55107-1618

MCDOWELL, GEORGE EDWARD, manufacturing executive; b. St. Louis, Feb. 15, 1944; s. Frank and Mary Elizabeth (Neal) McD. BA, Washington U., St. Louis, 1966; MBA, Drury Coll., 1968. CPA, Hawaii. Cost analyst Ford Motor Co., St. Louis, 1968-73; acctg. supr. ITT Grinnell Corp. subs Internat. Telephone and Telegraph Corp., Elmira, N.Y., 1973-74; acctg. mgr. Emerson Electric, St. Louis, 1974-76; data processing mgr. Ethyl Corp., St. Louis, 1976-84; v.p. Clayton Corp., St. Louis, 1984—; instr. Belleville (Ill.) Area Coll., 1982—. Contbr. articles to profl. jours. Served with U.S. Army, 1968-70. Mem. Am. Inst. CPA's, Mo. Soc. CPA's. Home: 657 Craigwoods Dr Saint Louis MO 63122-5514 Office: Clayton Corp 866 Horan Dr Fenton MO 63026-2416

MCDOWELL, JACK BURNS, professional baseball player; b. Van Nuys, Calif., Jan. 16, 1966. Grad., Stanford U. Baseball player Chgo. White Sox, 1987-88, 90-95, N.Y. Yankees, 1995, Cleve. Indians, 1996—. mem. Am. League All-Star Team, 1991-93; Sporting News All-Star Team, 1992, 93; Am. League Complete Games Leader, 1991-92; recipient Cy Young award Baseball Writers Assn. Am., 1993; named Sporting News Pitcher of Yr., 1993. Office: Cleveland Indians 2401 Ontario St Cleveland OH 44115*

MCELROY, DAN, state legislator; b. July 15, 1948; m. Mary McElroy. BA, U. Notre Dame. Minn. state rep. Dist. 36B, 1994—; former mgmt. cons. Address: 12805 Welcome Ln Burnsville MN 55337

MCELROY, LAURINCE DEAN (LARRY MCELROY), theater director, educator, consultant; b. Des Moines, Mar. 15, 1962; s. Raymond Dean and Mary Louise (Brockway) McE.; m. Lisa Maureen Bubon, July 1, 1987. AA, Grand View Coll., Des Moines, 1982, BA, 1984; MFA, U. S.D., 1991. Mgr. box office Purple Cow Players, Ltd., Des Moines, 1984-85; adminstrv. asst. Black Hills Playhouse, Custer, S.D., 1989; adminstrv. asst. U. S.D. Theatre, Vermillion, 1988-89, pub. dir., 1989-90, grad. teaching asst., 1990-91; adj. instr. Simpson Coll., Indianola, Iowa, 1994-96; T'ai Chi instr. Des Moines Pub. Schs. Continuing Edn., 1994—; co-founder Iowa Com. for Arts, Recreation and Entertainment's Theatre Project, Des Moines, 1984-85, Shakespear on the Loose Assn., Des Moines, 1987-88; directing coach arts outreach program U. S.D., 1988-90, co-founder student theatre coop., 1988-89, mem. theatre dir. search com., spring 1989, mem. theatre season selection com., spring 1990. Author: (stage adaptation) Voices That Care: Stories and Encouragements for People with AIDS/HIV and Those Who Love Them, 1996; dir. plays Treasure Islands, 1983, P.S. Your Cat is Dead!, 1985, Warren, 1989, Land of Little Horses, 1989, Burn This, 1990, Bedsheets and Breakfast Meats, 1990, Prelude to a Kiss, 1992, Shadowlands, 1993, As Is, 1995; playwright, dir. There is No Time, 1989; appeared in plays Cloud 9, 1985, The Boys in the Band, 1987, Glengarry Glen Ross, 1987, A Midsummer Night's Dream, 1988, Corpse!, 1989, Romeo and Juliet, 1990, God's Country, 1991. Mem. com. U. S.D. AIDS Task Force, 1988-90. Recipient Youth Direct Svcs. award United Way Cen. Iowa, Des Moines, 1982, Cert. Appreciation, Gay Coalition Des Moines, 1988; Weber scholar U. S.D. Theatre, 1989. Democrat. Home and Office: 818 18th St # 1 Des Moines IA 50314-1135

MCENIRY, ROBERT FRANCIS, education educator; b. Milw., Feb. 22, 1918; s. Frank Michael and Mary (Brown) McE. BA, St. Louis U., 1941, Philosophiae Licentiatus cum laude, 1944, Theologiae Licentiatus cum laude, 1953, PhL, ThL cum laude, 1953; PhD, Ohio State U., 1972. Instr. classics St. Louis U. High Sch., 1944-47, Creighton Prep. Sch., Omaha, 1947-48; asst. prof., chmn. classics Rockhurst Coll., Kansas City, Mo., 1953-58; retreat dir. White House Retreat, St. Louis, 1958-68; assoc. research prof. Creighton U., Omaha, 1972-89; dir., facilitator Growth for Couples, 1975-89; lectr. Creighton Natural Family Planning Ctr.; facilitator groups Adult Children of Alcoholism and Dysfunctional Families, 1989-93; vis. lectr. San Francisco Sch. Theology, San Anselmo, Calif., 1985; presenter over 700 lectrs., seminars and workshops in 43 states and 12 fgn. countries on value decisions during high anxiety and stress; exec. dir. Studies Adult Survivors of Abuse, 1993—; tchr., counselor in marriage and family issues. Editor and pub. Interaction Review, 1982-89; editor Scholar and Educator, 1974-76; mem. editorial bd. Counseling and Values, 1976-82; editor (book) Pastoral Counseling, 1977, Premarriage Counseling, 1978; contbr. over 180 articles to profl. jours.; literary agent, 1992—. Mem. Bd. of Pastoral Ministry, Omaha, 1972-78. Research grantee Council for Theol. Reflection, 1975-77; recipient Research award Creighton U., 1977. Fellow Nat. Acad. Counselors and Family Therapists (editor book rev. 1979-91); mem. APA, Am. Assn. for Religious Values in Counseling (editor newsletter 1982-89, Outstanding Svc. award 1985, Meritorious Svc. award 1989), Phi Delta Kappa (exec. com. 1977-83, del. 1981-83). Home: 3016 Paddock Rd Apt 12B Omaha NE 68124-2942 Office: Creighton U Dept of Education 2500 California St Omaha NE 68178

MCEWEN, LARRY BURDETTE, retired English and theater arts educator, author; b. Clay Center, Nebr., Aug. 4, 1934; s. Gerald E. and Marie L. (Pennington) McE.; m. Charlotte E. Alloway, Feb. 14, 1978; children: Diana J., Sheila J. AB, Augustana Coll., Rock Island, Ill., 1962; MS, Ill. State U., 1968. Cert. tchr., Nebr. Prof. theatre arts Blackburn Coll., Carlinville, Ill., 1969-75; counselor div. vocat. rehab. Nebr. Dept. Edn., Lincoln, 1976-82; tchr. English Hastings (Nebr.) Sr. High Sch., 1983-92; vis. lectr. Mt. Senario Coll., Ladysmith, Wis., 1971, Knox Coll., Galesburg, Ill., 1974, Hastings (Nebr.) Coll., 1976. Author: Much Ado About Shakespeare, 1992, Goose and Fables, 1994, To Honor Our Fathers and Mothers, 1996; author Apple Software; dir. 63 theatrical prodns.; contbr. numerous articles to profl. publs. With USAF, 1951-52. Grad. fellow Ind. U., 1968-69; Quad-City Music Guild scholar, 1961-62. Mem. NEA, Neb. State Edn. Assn., Acad. Computers in Eng., Apple Programmers and Developers Assn., Nat. Apple Users Group, Nat. Coun. Tchrs. English, Alpha Psi Omega, Alpha Phi Omega. Home and Office: 603 E 5th St Hastings NE 68901-5336

MCFADDEN, JAMES FREDERICK, JR., surgeon; b. St. Louis, Dec. 5, 1920; s. James Frederick and Olivia Genevieve (Imbs) McF.; m. Mary Cella Switzer, Sept. 15, 1956 (div. Sept. 1969); children: James Frederick, Kenneth Michael, John Switzer, Mary Cella, Joseph Robert; m. Deanne Nemec Puls, Apr. 29, 1989. AB, St. Louis U., 1941, MD, 1944. Intern Boston City Hosp., 1944-45; ward surgeon neorsurg. and orthopedics McGuire Gen. Hosp., Richmond, Va., 1945; ward surgeon in internal medicine Regional Hosp., Fort Knox, Ky., 1946; ward surgeon plastic surgery Valley Forge Gen. Hosp., Phoenixville, Pa., 1946-47; intern St. Louis City Hosp., 1947-48; resident in surgery VA Hosp., St. Louis, 1948-52; clin. instr. surgery St. Louis U., 1952-62; gen. practice medicine specializing in surgery St. Louis, 1952—; mem. staff St. Mary's Hosp., 1952-77, St. John's Mercy Hosp., 1952-74, Desloge Hosp., 1952-62, Frisco RR Hosp., 1953-64, DePaul Hosp., 1954—, Christian Hosp., 1955-66, 83—. Mem. St. Louis Ambassadors, 1979-81; officer St. Louis County Aux. Police, 1973-75. Served to capt. AUS, 1945-47. Recipient Eagle Scout award, Order of the Arrow Honor award Boy Scouts Am. Fellow ACS, Royal Soc. Medicine, Internat. Coll. Surgeons; mem. St. Louis Med. Soc., Am. Coll. Occupl. and Environ. Medicine, Am. Soc. Clin. Hypnosis, Internat. Soc. Hypnosis, Am. Assn. RR Surgeons, St. Louis U. Student Conclave, Alpha Sigma Nu, Phi Beta Pi. Roman Catholic. Home: PO Box 411933 Saint Louis MO 63141-1933 Office: 11500 Olive Blvd Saint Louis MO 63141-7143

MCFADDEN, NADINE LYNN, secondary education Spanish educator; b. Cleve., May 13, 1947; d. Frank and Helen (Senich) Mancini; m. Francis Joseph McFadden, Aug. 22, 1970; children: Ian Mancini, Kevin Mancini. BS in Edn., Ohio U., 1969; MA in Edn., Kent State U., 1990. Lic. tchr., Ohio. High sch. tchr. Spanish Parma (Ohio) City Schs., 1969—; chaperone European cultural trips Parma City Schs., 1973-76, 80, 92, 95, 96, strategic planning com., 1991-92; chmn. textbook com. Strongsville (Ohio) City Schs., 1990-92; program presenter in-svc. fgn. lang. tchrs., Parma; adj. prof. Fresno Pacific Coll. Mem. NEA, Am. Assn. Tchrs. Spanish and Portuguese, Ohio Modern Lang. Tchrs. Assn., Ohio Edn. Assn., Parma Edn. Assn. Home: 17536 Brandywine Dr Strongsville OH 44136-7034 Office: Parma City Schs Ridge Rd Parma OH 44129

MCFALLS, JACQUELYN KAY, obstetrics nurse; b. Freeport, Ill., Nov. 23, 1946; d. Eugene L. Bower and Phyllis E. (Weems) Bower Thomasson; m. Randall L. McFalls, June 4, 1966; children: Melinda R., Michelle L. Degree in Nursing, Rockford Meml. Sch., 1967; BSN, Rockford Coll., 1985; MS, No. Ill. U., 1989. Head nurse alcholoism Singer Zone Ctr., Rockford, Ill., 1967-72; staff nurse obstetrics Rockford Meml. Hosp., 1972-74, nurse mgr. post-partum, 1976-87, perinatal outreach, 1987-91, nurse mgr. perinatology, 1988-91; head nurse Sojourn House, Freeport, Ill., 1974-76; head nurse labor and delivery LDS Hosp., Salt Lake City, 1991-92, Rockford Meml. Hosp., 1992—. Contbr. articles to profl. jours. Co-chmn. United Way, Rockford, 1985; bd. dirs. Stephenson County Assn. for Prevention Child Abuse, Freeport, Ill., 1985-91. Mem. Am. Orgn. Nurse Execs. (bd. dirs., nurse mgr. coun. 1988-91), Am. Bus. Women (Lamplighter chpt.), Ill. Orgn. Nurse Execs. (co-chmn. coun. nurse mgrs. 1987, pres. 1994), Utah Orgn. Nurse Execs. (steering com. 1991—, nurse mgr. coun.), Utah Perinatal Assn., No. Ill. Regional Perinatal Adv. Bd., Assn. Women's Health Obstet. and Neonatal Nurses, Healthy Mothers/Healthy Babies Coalition, Sigma Theta Tau. Home: 1422 Lacresta Dr Freeport IL 61032-6138 Office: Rockford Meml Hosp 2400 N Rockton Ave Rockford IL 61103-3655

MC FARLAND, H. RICHARD, food company executive; b. Hoopeston, Ill., Aug. 19, 1930; s. Arthur Bryan and Jennie (Wilkey) McF.; m. Sarah Forney, Dec. 30, 1967. BS, U. Ill., 1952. With Campbell Soup Co., Camden, N.J., 1957-67; mgr. purchasing Campbell Soup Co., 1961-67; dir. procurement Keebler Co., Elmhurst, Ill., 1967-69; v.p. purchasing and distbn. Ky. Fried Chicken Corp., Louisville, 1969-74; v.p. food svcs., sales and distbn. Ky. Fried Chicken Corp., 1974-75; pres., dir. Mid-Continent Carton Co., Louisville, 1974-75, Ky. Fried Chicken Mfg. Corp., Nashville, 1974-75; owner, pres., dir. McFarland Foods Corp., Indpls., 1975—; bd. dirs. Fountain Trust Co., Ind., Covington Svc. Corp., Ind.; pres., bd. dirs. Ky. Fried Chicken Advt., Inc., Ind., 1975-87, exec. coun., 1988-91; mem. exec. coun., nat. franchise coun. Ky. Fried Chicken, 1979-85; bd. dirs. Ky. fried Chicken Nat. Purchasing Coop., 1981-85, chmn. ins. com., 1982-84; chmn. processed foods com. World's Poultry Congress, 1974; dir. nat. advt. coun. Ky. Fried Chicken, 1985-91, exec. com., 1988-90, chmn., 1989-90; mem. devel. com. U. Ill., 1989—. Mem. U. Ill. Found., 1992—, bd. dirs., 1993—; chmn. U. Ill. Nat. Advocates, 1994—; life pres. U. Ill. Sr. Class of '52; bd. dirs. Ind. Fedn. Children and Youth, 1983-84; chmn. campaign Ind. Ky. Fried Chicken March of Dimes, 1978-87; nat. trustee McCormick Theol. Sem., 1993—. 1st lt. USAF, 1952-54, Korea. Recipient Award of Merit U. Ill. Coll. Agr., 1988, Achievement award U. Ill. Alumni Assn., 1996. Mem. Ky. Restaurant Asns. (bd. dirs. 1970-75), Nat. Broiler Coun. (bd. dirs. 1971-74), Ind. Restaurant Assn., Am. Shorthorn Breeders Assn., Great Lakes Ky. Fried Chicken Franchise Assn. (bd. dirs. 1975-91, 1st v.p. 1978-79, pres. 1979-80), Delta Upsilon. Presbyterian. Clubs: Main Line Ski (Phila.) (pres. 1964); Hillcrest Country. Home: 6361 Avalon Ln Indianapolis IN 46220-5009 Office: 6284 Rucker Rd Ste M Indianapolis IN 46220-4851

MCFARLAND, MARY A., elementary and secondary school educator, administrator; b. St. Louis, Nov. 12, 1937; d. Allen and Maryann (Crawford)

Mabry; m. Gerald McFarland, May 30, 1959. BS in Elem. Edn., S.E. Mo. State U., 1959; MA in Secondary Edn., Washington U., St. Louis, 1965; PhD in Curriculum and Instrn., St. Louis U., 1977. Cert. tchr. elem., secondary, supt., Mo. Elem. tchr. Berkeley Sch. Dist., St. Louis, 1959-64; secondary tchr. Parkway Sch. Dist., St. Louis, 1965-75, social studies coord. K-12, 1975—, dir. staff devel., 1984—; adj. prof. Maryville U., St. Louis, 1990—; cons. pvt. practice, Chesterfield, Mo. Co-author: (text series) The World Around Us, 1990, 3d rev. edit., 1995; contbr. articles to profl. jours. Nat. faculty Nat. Issues Forum, Dayton, Ohio. Mem. ASCD, Social Sci. Edn. Consortium, Nat. Coun. for Social Studies (pres. 1989-90), Mo. Coun. for Social Studies (pres. 1980-81). Democrat. Methodist. Office: Parkway Schs Dist Instrnl Svcs 12657 Fee Fee Rd Saint Louis MO 63146-3855

MCFARLAND, ROBERT EDWIN, lawyer; b. St. Louis, July 25, 1946; s. Francis Taylor and Kathryne (Stevens) M.; m. Jeannine M. Ghekiere, Feb. 26, 1982. B.A., U. Mich. 1968, J.D., 1971. Bar: Mich. 1971, U.S. Dist. Ct. (ea. dist.) Mich. 1971, U.S. Ct. Appeals (6th cir.) 1974, U.S. Supreme Ct. 1975, U.S. Ct. Appeals (D.C.) 1978. Law clk. to chief judge Mich. Ct. Appeals, 1971-72; assoc. William B. Elmer, St. Clair Shores, Mich., 1972-74, James Elsman, Birmingham, Mich., 1974-75; ptnr. McFarland, Schmier, Stoneman & Singer, Troy, Mich. 1975-77; sr. ptnr. McFarland & Bullard, Bloomfield Hills, Mich., 1977-90; sr. ptnr. McFarland & Niemer, Farmington Hills, Mich., 1990-91; shareholder, Foster, Swift, Collins & Smith, P.C., Farmington Hills, Mich., 1992—. Chmn. bd. of govs. Transp. Law Jour., U. Denver Coll. of Law, 1981-83; mem. rulemaking study com. Mich. Pub. Svc. Commn., 1983-84, Motor Carrier adv. bd., 1984-88; mem. bd. of control Intercollegiate Athletics, U. Mich., 1966-68. Served to capt. USAR, 1971-80. Mem. Transp. Lawyers Assn., Assn. Interstate Commn. Practioners, ABA, State Bar Mich. (vice-chmn. transp. law com. adminstrn. law sect. 1990—, sect. coun. aol law sect. 1994—), Am. Judicature Soc.

MCFATE, KENNETH LEVERNE, trade association administrator; b. LeClaire, Iowa, Feb. 5, 1924; s. Samuel Albert and Margaret (Spear) McF.; m. Imogene Grace Kness, Jan. 27, 1951; children: Daniel Elliott, Kathryn Margaret, Sharon Ann. BS in Agrl. Engring., Iowa State U., 1950; MS in Agrl. Engring., U. Mo., 1959. Registered profl. engr., Mo. Agrl. sales engr. Ill. No. Utility Co., Aledo, 1950-51; extension agrl. engr. Iowa State U., Ames, 1951-53, rsch. agrl. engr., 1953-56; prof. agrl. engr. U. Mo., Columbia, 1956-86, prof. emeritus, 1986; dir. Mo. Farm Electric Coun., Columbia, 1956-75; exec. mgr. Nat. Farm Electric Coun., Columbia, 1975-86; pres., exec. mgr. Nat. Food and Energy Coun., Columbia, 1986-91, pres. emeritus, 1991; mgr. Electrotechnology Rsch., 1991-93; bd. dirs. Internat. Congress Agrl. Engrs., Brussels, 1989-94. Editor, author: (with others) Handbook for Elsevier Science, Electrical Energy in World Agriculture, 1989; mem. editl. bd. Energy in Agriculture for Elsevier Sci., Amsterdam, The Netherlands, 1981-88. 2d lt. USAAF, 1943-45. Recipient Outstanding Svc. awards Nat. Safety Coun., 1975, MOFEC, 1976, Nat. 4-H Coun., 1982, Nat. Hon. Extension Frat., 1984, Hon. award Future Farmers Assn., 1991. Fellow Am. Soc. Agrl. Engrs. (George Kable elec. award 1974); mem. Alpha Epsilon, Gamma Sigma Delta. Republican. Presbyterian. Home: 9450 E Highway HH Hallsville MO 65255-9724

MCGAGHIE, THOMAS JAMES, adult educator; b. Chgo., Aug. 29, 1949; s. William and Vivian Iona (Skoglund) McG. BA, Western Mich. U., 1979, MA, 1986. Cert. tchr. Mich. Instr. Kalamazoo (Mich.) Adult/Alternative Edn., 1980—; instr. Western Mich. U., 1988—, Kellogg C.C., Battle Creek, Mich., 1989—; mem. Mich. Coun. on Learning for Adults, 1985—, Literacy Network Kalamazoo County, 1990—, Supt.'s Leadership Com., 1990-92. Bd. dirs. Big Brothers/Big Sisters, Kalamazoo, 1990—; mem. Leadership Kalamazoo, 1993—, Vision 2000, Kalamazoo Pub. Schs., 1993-94. Mem. Mich. Acad. Scis., Arts & Letters. Home: 1551 Concord # 2D Kalamazoo MI 49009 Office: Cmty Edn Ctr 714 S Westnedge Kalamazoo MI 49001

MCGAGHIE, WILLIAM CRAIG, medical educator; b. Chgo., June 28, 1947; s. William and Vivian Iona (Skoglund) M.; m. Pamela Wall, Mar. 13, 1976; children: Michael Craig, Kathleen Ann. BA, Western Mich. U., 1969; MA, Northwestern U., 1971, PhD, 1973. Lectr., Northwestern U., Evanston, Ill., 1973-74; asst. prof. U. Ill., Chgo., 1974-78; asst. prof. U. N.C., Chapel Hill, 1978-81, assoc. prof. sch. of medicine, 1981-89, prof., 1989-92; prof. preventive medicine and prof. med. edn. Northwestern U. Med. Sch., 1992—. Author: Competency-Based Curriculum Development, 1978; editor: Handbook for the Academic Physician, 1986; cons. editor College Teaching, Review Edn. Rsch.; mem. editl. bd. Evaluation and the Health Professions, 1981—; contbr. numerous articles to profl. jours. Lic. lay reader Episcopal Ch. Grantee USPHS, Culpepper Found., Wash. Sq. Health Found. Mem. APA (v.p.), Am. Ednl. Research Assn. Avocations: running, gourmet cooking. Home: 2153 Beechwood Ave Wilmette IL 60091-1505 Office: Northwestern U Med Sch Office Med Edn 3-130 Ward Bldg W117 303 E Chicago Ave Chicago IL 60611-3008

MCGANNON, JOHN BARRY, university administrator; b. Humboldt, Kans., Apr. 18, 1924; s. Patrick Joseph and Jane Clare (Barry) McG. AB magna cum laude, St. Louis U., 1947, MA, 1952, PhD, 1963. Joined Soc. of Jesus, 1942, ordained priest Roman Catholic Ch., 1955. Dean Coll. Arts and Scis. St. Louis U., 1963-73; v.p. Rockhurst Coll., Kansas City, 1973-77; v.p. for devel. St. Louis U., 1977-90, chancellor, 1990—; cons., examiner North Ctrl. Accrediting Assn., Chgo., 1958-80. Truste Loyola U., New Orleans, 1988-94, St. Peter's Coll., Jersey City, 1991—, U. San Francisco, 1991—. Mem. Jesuit Advancement Adminstrs. (pres. 1985-87), Coun. for Advancement and Support of Edn., Nat. Soc. Fund Raising Execs., Nat. Coun. for Planned Giving, Rotary. Office: St Louis U 221 N Grand Blvd Saint Louis MO 63103-2097

MCGARRY, ANNE PRITCHARD, real estate salesman; b. Mpls., June 13, 1935; d. Manion John and Elizabeth Marian (McCann) Pritchard; m. Kevin Vincent McGarry, Sept. 15, 1956; children: Elizabeth Moore, John Manion, Kevin Vincent Jr., Peter Thomas, Anne Julia. Student, Manhattanville Coll., 1953-56. Real estate sales Rayner, First United, Winnetka, Ill., 1979-91, Baird and Warner, Winnetka, Ill., 1992—. Mem. Jr. League of Chgo., Benton Settlement House (bd. dirs.). Republican. Roman Catholic. Home: 2629 Kenilworth Ave Wilmette IL 60091-1372 Office: Baird and Warner 714 Elm St Winnetka IL 60093-2506

MCGARRY, KEVIN VINCENT, retired magazine executive; b. Bayside, N.Y., May 18, 1929; s. John James and Julia (McCarthy) McG.; m. Anne Pritchard, Sept. 15, 1956; children—Elizabeth Moore, John Manion, Kevin Vincent, Peter Thomas, Anne Julia. BS, Fordham U., 1952; postgrad. Wharton Sch., U. Pa., 1954-55. With IBM, 1955-56, Honeywell Corp., 1956-59; advt. mgr. Wall St. Jour., Mpls., 1959-67; advt. mgr. Nat. Observer, Detroit, 1967-73; assoc. Midwest advt. mgr. Wall St. Jour., Chgo., 1973-78; Midwest advt. mgr. Wall St. Jour., Chgo., 1978-89; cons. Midwest ops. Am. City Bus. Jours., Chgo., 1989-95. 1st lt. arty. AUS, 1952-54. Mem. Thoroughbred Club Am., AdCraft Club, Tavern Club, Westmoreland Country Club, Penn Club (N.Y.), Delta Sigma. Republican. Roman Catholic.

MCGARVEY, SCOTT ALLEN, marketing professional, consultant, educator; b. New Haven, Conn., Apr. 18, 1955; s. David Carter and Ann Jeannette (Williams) McG. BA in Social Scis., U. Chgo., 1977, MA in Econs., 1978, MBA, 1981. Group project mgr. Brand Group, Chgo., 1980-82; cons. WEFA Group (formerly Chase Econometrics), Chgo., 1982-85; sr. cons. Price Waterhouse, L.A., 1985-86; mktg. mgr. Landis & Gyr Powers, Buffalo Grove, Ill., 1986-92; pres., owner Scott McGarvey Assocs. Mktg. Cons., Homewood, Ill., 1992—; instr., adj. faculty MBA program Sch. Grad. Studies, Olivet Nazarene U., Kankakee, Ill., 1994—. Mem. Sales and Mktg. Execs. (v.p. mktg. 1994-95), Chgo. Assn. Direct Mktg. (various coms.), Bus. Mktg. Assn., MIT Enterprise Forum, Planning Forum. Republican. Office: Scott McGarvey Assocs 1000 Holbrook Rd Unit N Homewood IL 60430

MCGARVEY, WILLIAM K., otolaryngologist, surgeon; b. Marion, Ind., Aug. 3, 1937; s. Eugene J. and Rosemary (Kelley) McG.; m. Janet Lee Prentice, Feb. 27, 1975; children: Erika, Kevin. AB in Anatomy and Physiology, Ind. U., 1959, MD, 1962. Diplomate Bd. Otolaryngolgy and Head and Neck Surgery. Intern San. Francisco Gen. Hosp., 1962-63; resident in otolaryngology and head and neck surgery Ind. U. Med. Sch. and assoc. hosps., Indpls., 1963-67; practice medicine specializing in otolaryngology and head and neck surgery San Francisco, 1969-74, Indpls., 1974—; asst. prof. otolaryngology and head and neck surgery Ind. U. Sch. Medicine, 1974; asst. prof. otolaryngology and head and neck surgery, U. Calif. Med. Sch., San Francisco, 1969-74; chmn. dept. otolaryngology and head and neck surgery, Community Hosp., Indpls., 1976-78. Served with maj. U.S. Army, 1967-69, Vietnam. Fellow ACS, Am. Acad. Otolaryngology and Head and Neck Surgery, Am. Acad. Facial Plastic and Reconstructive Surgeons; mem. Am. Acad. Otolaryngic Allergy, Undersea Med. Soc. Hyperbaric Medicine. Republican. Methodist. Clubs: Meridian Hills (Indpls.) Country, Skyline (Indpls.). Lodge: Masons. Home: 1816 Wood Valley Dr Carmel IN 46032-3561 Office: Ind Otolaryngology-Head and Neck Surgery 5508 E 16th St Indianapolis IN 46218

MCGARY, DARIA L., foreign languages educator; b. Antwerp, Belgium, Aug. 1, 1930; came to U.S., 1954; d. William Reynolds and Daria Louise (Bowles) Marshall; m. Frank Joseph McG., Oct. 6, 1951; children: Sharon, Kevin, Marc, Christopher. Interpreter to gen. Mil. Assistance Adv. Group, Brussels, 1950-54; tchr. German, French, Spanish Padua Franciscan Sch., Cleve., 1974-79; tchr. Bishop Ready H.S., Columbus, Ohio, 1979-82; tchr. French, Spanish, dept. chair The Wellington Sch., Columbus, 1982-94; lectr. French Club, Columbus, 1951-89. Home: 3367 Durkin Cir Dublin OH 43017

MC GARY, THOMAS HUGH, lawyer; b. Milburn, Ky., Mar. 6, 1938; s. Ollie James and Pauline Elizabeth (Tackett) McG.; A.B., Elmhurst Coll., 1961; J.D., U. Chgo., 1964; m. Madalyn Maxwell, July 4, 1968. Admitted to Ill. bar, 1964; asst. atty. gen. State of Ill., 1965-67, supr. consumer credit, 1967-71; ind. practice law, Springfield, Ill., 1971—; v.p., dir. Citizens Bank of Edinburg (Ill.), 1971—, Bank of Kenney (Ill.), 1977-92, Bank of Springfield; instr. Lincolnland Coll., 1970-73; asso. prof. med. humanities So. Ill. U. Sch. Medicine. Mem. Springfield Symphony Assn.; mem. Springfield Election Commn.; bd. dirs., chmn. Cen. Ill. Youth Services Bur.; bd. dirs. Springfield Urban League; vestryman St. Paul's Cathedral. Mem. Am., Ill., Sangamon County bar assns., Am. Judicature Soc.. Democrat. Clubs: Sangamo (Springfield). Home: 2018 Briarcliff Dr Springfield IL 62704-4126 Office: 600 S 4th St Springfield IL 62703-1603

MCGAUGHEY, ALBERT WAYNE, retired mathematics educator; b. Russellville, Ind., July 16, 1914; s. Walter Lee and Belva Jane (Harbison) McG.; m. Margie V. Silverthorn, July 11, 1940; children: Stanley W., Dennis M., Lynn D. McGaughey Kearney, Donna J. McGaughey Defenbaugh. AB in Liberal Arts, Wabash Coll., 1935; MS in Physics, State U. Iowa, 1937; PhD in Math., U. Cin., 1940. Instr. math. Purdue U., West Lafayette, Ind., 1940-41; asst. prof. U.S. Naval Acad., Annapolis, Md., 1941-46; prof., chmn. dept. Westminster Coll., New Wilmington, Pa., 1946-48; prof., chmn. dept. Bradley U., Peoria, Ill., 1948-79, dir. NSF Summer Inst., 1961-66; ret., 1979; part-time prof. Eureka (Ill.) Coll., 1954-81; tchr.-trainer Indian high sch. math. tchrs. AID Summer Inst., Burdwan U., 1967; assoc. dir. secondary edn. dept. NSF, Washington, 1968-69. Mem. Cen. Ill. Coun. on Aging, 1970—, also past coun. chmn. and dept. chmn.; bd. dirs., vol., treas., com. chmn. Common Place, 1970—. Mem. Phi Beta Kappa, Sigma Psi, Math Assoc. America (sec. treas. Ill. sect.). Republican. Mem. Christian Ch. (Disciples of Christ). Home: 2703 N Kingston Dr Peoria IL 61604-2142

MCGAVIC, JUDY L., coal company official; b. Evansville, Ind., June 29, 1944; d. M. Galen and Helen L. (Sims) Barclay; m. Ronald R. McGavic, Aug. 22, 1962; 1 child, Michael D. Student, Ky. Wesleyan Coll., 1965-66, Murray (Ky.) State U., 1968, U. Ky., 1969; B of Liberal Arts, U. Evansville, 1994. Mine clk. Peabody Coal Co., Centertown, Ky., 1973-78, chief mine clk., 1978-81, sr. mine clk., 1981-86, panel technician, 1986, sr. coord. employee rels., 1987-88, employee rels. rep., 1988-92; sr. employee rels. rep. Peabody Coal Co., Lynnville, Ind., 1993-95. Peabody Coal Co. campaign chmn. United Way, 1992, 93, also chmn. blood drive. Mem. NAFE. Home: 7600 Edgedale Dr Newburgh IN 47630-3062

MCGEE, JOHN EDWARD, retired gynecologist; b. Granite City, Ill., Nov. 25, 1928; s. James Anthony and Anna Elizabeth McGee; m. Margaret Ann Grems, Oct. 17, 1953; children: Michael, Joseph, Ann, Jane, Brian, Robert, James, Maureen. BS, St. Louis U., 1949, MD, 1953. Cert. Am. Bd. Ob-Gyn. Intern Ancker Hosp., St. Paul, 1953-54; resident in internal medicine U. Minn., Mpls., 1954; resident in ob-gyn St. Louis U. Hosp., 1957-60; chief dept. ob/gyn Ft. Madison (Iowa) Hosp., 1965; chief dept. maternal child health Burlington (Iowa) Med. Ctr., 1983, chief of staff, 1986; pres. S.E. Iowa Health Sys. Agy., 1975, Burlington Preferred Provider Orgn., 1991-94. Pres. Ft. Madison Sch. Bd., 1969. Lt. comdr. USNR, 1955-57. Fellow Am. Coll. Ob/Gyn; mem. AMA, Am. Urogynecological Soc., Iowa Med. Soc. Republican. Roman Catholic. Home and Office: 1005 Denmark Hilltop Fort Madison IA 52627-2749

MCGEE, PATRICK EDGAR, postal service clerk; b. Chgo., Jan. 13, 1944; s. Ralph and Minnie Odelia (Crutcher) McG. Machine clk. U.S. Postal Svc., Chgo., 1977—. Author of poems. Mem. The Art Inst. Chgo., Mus. Sci. & Industry, Chgo. Mem. Internat. Soc. Poets. Democrat. Roman Catholic. Office: US Postal Svc Chicago IL

MCGEHEE, BRYAN KEITH, information systems manager, systems analyst; b. Burlington, Wash., Oct. 8, 1958; s. Thomas Bryan and Edith Belle (Esary) McG.; m. Jayne Marie Abraham, May 21, 1984 (div. July 1987); 1 child, Michael Bryan; m. Karen Jean Uebinger, Aug. 3, 1987; children: Jennifer Nicole, Jessica Lynn, Thomas Bryan, Samantha Anne. BBA and BA in Mktg., Carthage Coll., Kenosha, Wis., 1992. Combine operator Nat. Canneries, Burlington, 1975-77; warehouseman Bellingham (Wash.) Cold Storage, 1977-78; enlisted USMC, 1978, advanced through grades to staff sgt., 1984; avionics technician USMC, Tustin, Calif., 1978-81; computer programmer USMC, Kansas City, Mo., 1981-86; resigned USMC, 1986; staff analyst Cap Gemini Am., St. Louis, 1986-87, Milw., 1987-88; lead programmer U.S. Sprint, Dallas, 1987; sr. sys. analyst S.C. Johnson & Son, Inc., Racine, Wis., 1988-94, info. sys. cons. bus. applications, 1994—; mem. natural sub-com. Application Devel. Council, Racine, 1991-93, chmn., 1994—. Mem. Racine Area Users Group (sec. 1988-89, v.p. 1989-91, pres. 1991-94). Home: 3418 93rd St Sturtevant WI 53177 Office: SC Johnson & Son Inc 1525 Howe St Racine WI 53403

MC GEHEE, H(ARRY) COLEMAN, JR., bishop; b. Richmond, Va., July 7, 1923; s. Harry Coleman and Ann Lee (Cheatwood) McG.; m. June Stewart, Feb. 1, 1946; children: Lesley, Alexander, Harry III, Donald, Cary. BS, Va. Poly. Inst., 1947; JD, U. Richmond, 1949; MDiv, Va. Theol. Sem., 1957, DD, 1973. Bar: Va. 1949, U.S. Supreme Ct. 1954; ordained to ministry Episcopal Ch., 1957. Spl. counsel dept. hwys. State of Va., 1949-51, gen. counsel employment svc., 1951, asst. atty. gen., 1951-54; rector Immanuel Ch.-on-the-Hill, Va. Sem., 1960-71; bishop Diocese of Mich., Detroit, 1971-90; adv. bd. Nicaraguan Network, Ctr. for Peace and Conflict Studies, Wayne State U.; bd. dirs. Mich. Religious Coalition for Abortion Rights, 1976-84; trustee Va. Theol. Sem., 1978-93; pres. Episc. Ch. Pub. Co., 1978-85. Columnist: Detroit News, 1979-85; weekly commentator pub. radio sta. WDET-AM, Detroit, 1984-90. Mem. Gov.'s Commn. on Status of Women, 1965-66, Mayor's Civic Com., Alexandria, 1967-68; sponsor Nat. Assn. for ERA, 1977-85; pres. Alexandria Legal Aid Soc., 1969-71; bd. dirs. No. Va. Fairhousing Corp., 1963-67; pres. Mich. Coalition for Human Rights, 1980-89; chmn. Citizens' Com. for Justice in Mich., 1983-84; sponsor Farm Labor Orgn. for Children, 1983-85; bd. dirs. Pub. Benefit Corp., Detroit, 1988-90, Mich. Citizens for Personal Freedom, 1989-92, Poverty and Social Reform Inst., Detroit, 1989—, Bread for the World, 1990-94, Ams. United for Separation of Ch. and State, 1990, ACLU Oakland County, Mich., 1991-94; co-chair Lesbian-Gay Found. Mich., 1991—. 1st lt. C.E., U.S. Army, 1943-46. Named Feminist of Yr., Detroit NOW, 1978; recipient Humanitarian award Detroit ACLU, 1984, Phillip Hart medal Mich. Women's Studies Assn., 1984, Sayre award for justice and peace Episc. Peace Fellowship, 1988, Spirit of Detroit award, 1989, Archbishop Romero award Mich. Labor Com., 1990, Brotherhood award AME Ch., Detroit, 1993, Ira Jayne award Detroit br. NAACP, 1993, Martin Luther King, Jr. award United Ch. of Christ, 1995. Mem. Detroit Econ. Club (bd. dirs.). Home: 1496 Ashover Dr Bloomfield Hills MI 48304-1215 Office: Diocese of Mich 4800 Woodward Ave Detroit MI 48201-1310

MCGILL, JAMES TERRY, academic administrator; b. Portland, Oreg., Feb. 24, 1943; s. James Woodrow and Thelma Blanche (Wright) McG.; m. Sylvia Postl, Mar. 17, 1944; children: Brian J., Bradley J., Amy L. BA, BS in Math. with honors, Oreg. State U., 1965; PhD in Ops. Rsch., Stanford U., 1969. Part-time ops. analyst Stanford Rsch. Inst., Menlo Park, Calif., 1966-69; mem. prof. staff Inst. for Def. Analyses, Arlington, Va., 1969-72; dep. dir. acad. and health affairs Ill. Bd. Higher Edn., Springfield, 1972-76; assoc. vice chancellor for resource planning U. Ill. Med. Ctr., Chgo., 1976-80; v.p. Oreg. Health Sci. Univ., Portland, 1980-86; v.p. adminstrv. affairs U. Mo., Columbia, 1986-95, exec. v.p., 1995—. Trustee Stephens Coll., Columbia, 1990-96, vice chair fin., 1991-96; bd. dirs. Advent Enterprises, Columbia, 1994—. Mem. Ops. Rsch. Soc. Am., Nat. Assn. State Univ. and Land Grant Colls. (mem. exec. com. coun. on bus. affairs 1991—, chair 1994-95), Nat. League Nursing (mem. fin. com. 1993—, bd. govs. 1995—), Sigma Xi, Phi Kappa Phi, Pi Mu Epsilon, Phi Eta Sigma. Office: U Mo Sys 215 University Hall Columbia MO 65211

MCGILL, KARLEEN A., occupational health nurse; b. Muncie, Ind., Aug. 9, 1948; d. William E. and Elizabeth (Samaniego) Koger; m. Keith V. McGill, Feb. 19, 1984; children: Thomas, Robin, Kelly, Kevin. Diploma, St. Vincents Sch. Nursing, 1969; BSN, Ball State U., 1988; MS, Ind. Wesleyan U., 1996. Cert. occupational health nurse, family nurse practitioner. Staff nurse, labor/delivery dept. Ireland Army Hosp., Ft. Knox, Ky., 1972-73; charge nurse, newborn nursery Goshen (Ind.) Gen. Hosp., 1973-75, staff nurse, surgery recovery rm., 1975-78; company nurse Starcraft, Topeka., Ind., 1978-79; employee health nurse St. Joseph Hosp., Ft. Wayne, Ind., 1979-80; asst. charge nurse IV team Community Hosps. of Indpls., 1980-81, oper. rm. nurse, 1981-86, occupational edn. coord., health mgr., 1986-89, nurse mgr., immediate care facility, 1989-90; employee occupational health nurse Community Hosp. East, Indpls., 1990-92; occupational health nurse cons. workmed Riverview Hosp., Noblesville, Ind., 1992-94; pvt. family practice Greenfield, Ind., 1996—. Capt. USAR ANC, 1986—. Mem. Am. Assn. Occupational Health Nurses, Am. Oper. Rm. Nurses, Assn. Mil. Surgeons U.S., Sigma Theta Tau.

MCGILL, MICHAEL JOHN, computer/information scientist; b. Detroit; s. Jack Arthur and Margaret Mary (Woodcock) McG.; m. Jennifer Joan Kuehn, Dec. 2, 1977; children: Erin Kuehn, Andrew Kuehn. BA, Syracuse U., 1968, PhD, 1973. Asst. prof. SUNY, Oswego, 1972-74; assoc. prof. Syracuse U., 1974-80; sr. info./computer advisor U.S. EPA, Washington, 1980-81; program dir. NSF, Washington, 1981-83; v.p. OCLC Inc., Dublin, Ohio, 1983-90; v.p. ind. mktg. Ameritech Info. Systems, Dublin, Ohio, 1990-92; dir. network systems U. Mich., Ann Arbor, 1992—; Author: Modern Information Retrieval, 1983; contbr. articles to profl. jours. Author: Modern Information Retrieval, 1983; contbr. articles to profl. jours. bd. dirs. Arthritis Found. Cen. Ohio, Columbus, 1988—. NSF grantee, 1976—. Fellow AAAS (coun. mem. 1990—); mem. ACM (Spl. Interest Group for Info Retrieval, editor, treas., vice chmn.). Home: 8055 Golfview Ct Columbus OH 43235-1230 Office: U Mich Med Ctr 1500 E Medical Center Dr Ann Arbor MI 48109-0999

MCGINN, PATRICIA FERRIS, professional counselor; b. Riverside, Calif., July 30, 1938; d. John Mark and Kathryn (Miller) Ferris; m. Bernard John McGinn, July 10, 1971; children: Daniel Ferris, John Ferris. BA magna cum laude, St. Mary's Coll., Notre Dame, Ind., 1960; MA, U. Notre Dame, 1965, U. D.C., 1972. Lic. clin. profl. counselor. Tchr. St. Joseph's High Sch., South Bend, Ind., 1962-63; tchr. St. Cecilia's Acad., Washington, 1965-68, sch. counselor, 1969-71; tchr. St. Patrick's Acad., Washington, 1968-69; family therapist The Depot, Chgo., 1972-78; dir. counseling ctr. St. Mary's Coll., 1978-80; pvt. practice Chgo., 1980—. Mem. ACA, Am. Mental Health Counselors Assn., Ill. Counseling Assn., Ill. Mental Health Counselors Assn. (exec. dir. 1993—, co-chair govt. rels. com. 1989-93), Coalition Ill. Counseling Orgns. (exec. dir. 1994—). Democrat. Roman Catholic. Office: 5847 S Blackstone Ave Chicago IL 60637-1818

MCGINNIS, KENNETH L., state official. Dir. Corrections Dept., Lansing, Mich. Office: Corrections Dept Grandview Plz PO Box 30003 Lansing MI 48909*

MCGIVERIN, ARTHUR A., state supreme court justice; b. Iowa City, Iowa, Nov. 10, 1928; s. Joseph J. and Mary B. McG.; m. Mary Joan McGiverin, Apr. 20, 1951; children: Teresa, Thomas, Bruce, Nancy. BSC with high honors, U. Iowa, 1951, JD, 1956. Bar: Iowa 1956. Pvt. practice law Ottumwa, Iowa, 1956; alt. mcpl. judge Ottumwa, 1960-65; judge Iowa Dist. Ct. 8th Jud. Dist., 1965-78; assoc. justice Iowa Supreme Ct., Des Moines, 1978-87, chief justice, 1987—. Mem. Iowa Supreme Ct. Commn. on Continuing Legal Edn., 1975. Served to 1st lt. U.S. Army, 1946-48, 51-53. Mem. Iowa State Bar Assn., Am. Law Inst. Roman Catholic. Office: Iowa Supreme Ct State Capital Bldg Des Moines IA 50319*

MCGLONE, EDWARD LEON, dean, consultant, academic administrator; b. Athens, Ohio, Sept. 20, 1941; s. Charles Edward and Alice Aileen (Giles) McG.; m. Sarah Leona Chapman; children: Matthew Steven, Andrew Edward. BA summa cum laude, MA, Ohio State U., 1963; PhD, Ohio U., 1967. Asst. prof. No. Ill. U., DeKalb, 1964-68, Wash. State U., Pullman, 1968-70; assoc. prof. Wayne State U., Detroit, 1970-74; dir. Detroit Speech and Hearing Ctr., 1974-75; chmn. So. Ill. U., Carbondale, 1975-80; dean Miss. State U., Starkville, 1980-87; v.p. acad. affairs Emporia (Kans.) State U., 1987-89, dean, 1991—. Author: Understanding Oral Communication, 1972; contbr. articles to profl. jours. Founding pres. Miss. Council Colls. of Arts and Scis., Jackson, 1982-84. Recipient Outstanding Tchr. award Cen. States Speech Assn., 1967, Top Three Rsch. Papers award Speech Communication Assn., 1970; Woodrow Wilson fellow Ohio U., 1962. Home: PO Box 507 Emporia KS 66801-5918 Office: Emporia State Univ Off of Dean Emporia KS 66801

MCGLOSHEN, THOMAS HILTON, JR., marriage and family therapist; b. Louisville, May 17, 1938; s. Thomas Hilton and Lorean Frances (Hopper) McG.; m. Joan Carmellia Carter, Oct. 10, 1965; children: Kimberly, Kristin. BA, Centre Coll., 1960; MDiv., McCormick Theol. Sem., 1963; MA, Western Ky. U., 1974; PhD, Ohio State U., 1985. Lic. profl. clin. counselor, Ohio; ordained to ministry, Presbyn. Ch., 1963; cert. family life educator. Pastor First Presbyn. Ch., Russellville, Ky., 1963-68; outpatient therapist Barren River Comprehensive Care Ctr., Bowling Green, Ky., 1968-77; career counselor Midwest Career Devel. Svc., Columbus, Ohio, 1978-81; pvt. practice Dublin, Ohio, 1981—; instr. U. Ky. C.C., Hopkinsville, 1966-67; adj. faculty Vanderbilt U. Div. Sch., Nashville, 1971-77, Ohio State U. Coll. of Medicine, Columbus, 1989—, Trinity Luth. Seminary, Columbus, 1987—; grad. faculty Western Ky. U., Bowling Green, 1974-77. Editorial bd., select panel of reviewers Career Devel. Quar., 1983-91; contbr. articles to profl. jours. Chmn., bd. dirs. Dublin Counseling Ctr., 1980. Fellow Inst. for Humanities and Medicine, 1988-89. Mem. Ohio Assn. for Marriage and Family Therapy (Award of Honor 1988), Nat. Coun. on Family Rels., Ohio Coun. on Family Rels. (pres. 1991-92), Am. Group Psychotherapy Assn., Assn. for Psychol. Type (pres. ctrl. Ohio chpt. 1992-94), Am. Counseling Assn., Am. Assn. for Marriage and Family Therapy (clin. mem., approved supr.), Omicron Delta Kappa, Omicron Nu, Phi Upsilon Omicron. Office: 5178 Blazer Meml Pkwy Dublin OH 43017-1339

MCGLOTHLIN, JAMES DUAYNE, research industrial hygienist, ergonomist; b. Dearborn, Mich., July 29, 1951; s. John Henry and Bernadeen (Babnaw) McG.; m. Nancy Kay Snoeyink, Aug. 21, 1948; children: Malia Anne, Jaime Lynn. BA in Psychology, U. Hawaii, 1975, MPH in Epidemiology, MS in Environ. Health, 1977; PhD in Indsl. Health, U. Mich., 1988. Cert. profl. ergonomist. Legis. asst. Hawaii State Ho. of Reps., Honolulu, 1976-77; environ. cons. Hawaii Med. Clinic, Honolulu, 1977-78; mgr. criteria document USPHS, Cin., 1978, rsch. indsl. hygienist, 1978-81; ergonomics program coord. USPHS, Morgantown, W.Va., 1984; chief accident analysis sect. USPHS, Morgantown, 1984-85; rsch. occupational ergonomist, hygienist USPHS, Cin., 1985—; asst. prof. Kettering Labs., U. Cin., 1987—, assoc. prof. dept. indsl. and mech. engring., 1988—; adj. prof. dept. indsl. engring. Ohio State U., Columbus, 1990—; course dir. and instr. in ergonomics Northwestern U. Sch. of Engring. and Applied Sci., Evanston, Ill., 1990—. Developer methods for indsl. containment investigation and real time sampling, 1987; editor: Manual Material Handling: Understanding and Preventing Back Trauma, 1989; contbr. over 80 articles to profl. jours. Vice chmn. profl. adv. com. Surgeon Gen.'s Health Svcs., Washington, 1991—, chmn., 1992-93; chmn. ergonomics com. Ohio Safety and Health Congress, Columbus, 1989—. Recipient two Commendations, USPHS, 1990, Surgeon Gen.'s Explemplary Svc. medal, 1992, 93, exemplary svc. award Nat. Inst. Occupl. Safety and Health Ctrs. for Disease Control and Prevention, 1995, cert. of excellence, 1995. Mem. Nat. Commd. Officers Assn. (v.p. 1988, pres. 1989—), Am. Indsl. Hygiene Assn. (chmn. ergonomics com. 1987, 95-96, program chmn. 1993-94), Am. Conf. Govtl. Indsl. Hygienists, Human Factors and Ergonomics Soc., Internat. Indsl. Ergonomics (program chmn. safety com. 1989), Cin. Origami Guild (internat. corp. sec. 1989—), Toastmasters (pres. 1992-93, ednl. v.p. 1991—). Methodist. Home: 1006 Markley Rd Cincinnati OH 45230-4105 Office: Nat Inst Occupational Safety/Health 4676 Columbia Pky Cincinnati OH 45226-1922

MCGOVERN, DIANNE, legal administrator; b. Pitts., Feb. 26, 1948; d. John David and Mary Elizabeth (Shirk) McG. BA, Millsaps Coll., Jackson, Miss., 1970; MS in Mgmt., Baker U., 1992. Docket clk. Popham Law Firm, Kansas City, Mo., 1972-78, paralegal, 1978-81, legal adminstr., 1981—. Bd. dirs. Kansas City Zoo Docents, 1994-96. Mem. ABA (assoc.), Assn. Legal Adminstrs. (asst. regional v.p. 1991), Kansas City Assn. Legal Adminstrs. (pres., bd. dirs. 1987-90). Democrat. Roman Catholic. Home: 4425 Jarboe St Apt 10 Kansas City MO 64111-3555 Office: The Popham Law Firm PC 922 Walnut St Kansas City MO 64106-1809

MCGOVERN, JUDY ANN, food products executive; b. Meriden, Conn., Aug. 14, 1956. Mgr. Expresso Experience, Portland, Oreg., 1989-92; v.p. MainStream Expresso Inc., Ann Arbor, Mich., 1993—. Roman Catholic. Office: Main Stream Expresso Inc 1612 Greenview Dr Ann Arbor MI 48103-5706

MCGOWAN, DAVID ALLEN, real estate broker; b. Chgo., Jan. 17, 1952; s. James Francis and Elizabeth (DeMoon) McG.; 1 child, Victoria Lynn. BS, Ill. State U., 1975; postgrad., John Marshall Law Sch., 1982, Keller Sch. Mgmt., 1987—. V.p. DeMoon Realty, Inc., Chgo., 1977-80; dir. edn. Chgo. Bd. Realtors, 1980-84; pres. Century 21 Phoenix, Inc., Schaumburg, Ill., 1984-87, Land of Lincoln Real Estate, Inc., Glendale Heights, 1987-93; fin. mgr., human resource mgr. Century 21 ABC Schiro Group, Schaumburg, Ill., 1993. Mem. Real Estate Educators Assn. (v.p. 1984-85), Assn. Ill. Real Estate Educators (v.p. 1983-85), Sigma Pi. Office: D Allen & Assocs PO Box 872 Saint Charles IL 60174-0872 also: Century 21 ABC Schiro Grp 1732 W Wise Rd Schaumburg IL 60193

MCGRAIL, MICHAEL JOSEPH, communications specialist; b. Chgo., Jan. 26, 1954. BA in Polit. Sci., Loyola U., 1976; MPA, Roosevelt U., 1978. Tax svc. rep. IRS, Chgo., 1976-79, taxpayer svc. specialist, 1979-87, pub. affairs specialist, 1987-94, tax law specialist, 1994—; tng. instr. IRS, 1980—, spokesperson, 1987-94, quality facilitator, 1990-93; tax cons., fin. analyst Terry Savage Books. Host: (info. series) Taking the Fear Out of Filing, 1989—, (live call-in show) IRS Tax Talk, 1989-94. Vol. tutor various social orgns.

MCGRATH, JOHN JULIAN, writer, communication consultant; b. N.Y., Aug. 2, 1944; s. John Joseph and Dolores Marie McG.; m. Sylvia Salinas, July 10, 1971; children: John Joseph, James Louis. BS in History, Political Science, Sul Ross State U., Alpine, Tex., 1972; MS in Bus. with honors, Cardinal Stritch Coll., Milw., 1993. Editor AT Pub. Co., Washington, D.C., 1968-70; correspondent Associated Press, Alpine, 1970-72; night city editor San Antonio (Tex.) Express-News, 1970-76; dir. external rels. MCAIR McDonnell Douglas Corp., St. Louis, 1976-82; mgr. comms. svcs. Miller Brewing Co., Milw., 1982-88; creative dir. Ford Motor Maritz Comms., Detroit, 1988-89; prin. McGrath & Assocs., Chgo., 1989—; dir. mgmt. comms. Argonne Nat. Lab., Chgo., 1993—; cons. Ford Motor Co., Detroit, 1990-95, Johnson Controls, Milw., 1992—. Contbr. articles to jours. in field. Lt. Comdr. USNR, 1964-68. Recipient Silver Trumpet award Publicity Club of Chgo., 1995. Mem. Pub. Rels Soc. Am. (vice chmn. Chgo. suburban chpt. 1993-95), Nat. Press Club, Nat. Writer's Union, Nat. Assn. Sci. Writers, The Producer's Guild (ethics com. 1984-88), Profl. Journalism Soc. Office: Argonne Nat Lab 9700 S Cass Ave OPA/201 Argonne IL 60439

MCGRATH, LEE UPTON, school rings and yearbooks company executive; b. Roslyn, N.Y., June 7, 1956; s. Joseph U. and Antoinette (Marchese) McG.; m. Bonnie Speer, Dec. 30, 1988. Student, U. Catolica del Ecuador, Quito, 1977; BSBA, Georgetown U., 1978; MBA, U. Chgo., 1984. Mktg. analyst Productos Lacteos del Cribe, Barranquilla, Colombia, 1978; treasury analyst Westinghouse Electric, N.Y.C., 1979-81; internat. banker First Nat. Bank, Chgo., 1981-83; fin. analyst GM, N.Y.C., 1984-89; asst. treas. H.B. Fuller Co., St. Paul, 1989-95; v.p., treas. Jostens, Inc., Mpls., 1995—. Mem. Cato Inst., Washington, 1990—; mem. adv. coun. Minn. Pub. Radio, St. Paul, 1993; bd. dirs. HIRED, Mpls., 1993. Mem. Inst. Mgmt. Accts.

MCGRATH, MICHAEL ALAN, state government officer; b. Trenton, N.J., Oct. 27, 1942; s. Lyman Levitt and Ada Frances (Hofreiter) McG.; m. Marsha Louise Palmer, Aug. 6, 1966; children: David Patrick, Stephen Gregory, Christopher Andrew. AA, Daytona Beach Jr. Coll., 1967; BA, Stetson U., 1969. Supr. 1st Trust Co., St. Paul, 1969-72; v.p. Internat. Dairy Queen, Inc., Bloomington, Minn., 1972-84; dir. ops. WISCECO, Inc., Bloomington, 1984; bus. mgr. McGraw-Hill, Inc., Edina, Minn., 1985; pres. Policy Advisors, Inc., Bloomington, 1986; treas. State of Minn., St. Paul, 1987—; mem. State Bd. Investment, State Exec. Coun., 1987—; bd. dirs. Minn. State Retirement Systems, St. Paul; Minn. rep. Pub. Fin. Network, 1989—. Mem. editorial bd. Pension Fund News, 1988-90. Chmn. bd. dirs. Urban Concerns Workshop, Inc., St. Paul, 1984-86; sec. League Minn. Human Rights Commn., Mpls., 1985-86; chmn. sen. dist. 41 Dem. Farm Labor Party, 1984-86, treas. 3d congl. dist., New Hope, Minn., 1986, pres. Dem. Farm Labor Club, Bloomington, 1982-84. Served with USAF, 1962-66. Mem. Nat. Assn. State Treas. (midwest v.p. 1988-89, sec.-treas. 1990-94, sr. v.p. 1994-95, pres. 1995-96, coun. of state govts., fin. com. 1993-94, long-range planning com. 1995, exec. com. 1995-96), Coun. of Instnl. Investors, Govt. Fin. Officers Assn., Nat. Assn. State Auditors, Comptrs. and Treas. (exec. com. 1995-96, nat. electronic benefits transfer coun., 1995—). Office: Office of Treasury State Minn 50 Sherburne Ave Ste 303 Saint Paul MN 55155-1402

MCGRAW, VINCENT DEPAUL, manufacturing executive; b. Kansas City, Mo., July 19, 1930; s. Edwin John and Gertrude Catherine (McKean) McG.; m. Mildred Queen, 1953 (div. 1955); m. Rose Marie Taffe, Feb. 13, 1964; children: Michele Marie, Catherine Veronica. BA, Met. State U., St. Paul, 1976. Mgr. Pinkerton's Inc., various locations, 1956-66; pres. McGraw Security Systems Inc., Mpls., 1966-70; dir. security Applebaums Food Markets Inc., St. Paul, 1969-72; pres. Acad. and Range Inc. for Maximum Safety and Security, Mpls., 1972-74; gen. mgr. Jesco Indsl. Supplies inc., New Hope, Minn., 1977-92; pres. Economy Sales & Svc., Inc., Mpls., 1992—. Author: McGraw Book of Antique Inkwells, 1972, (booklet) Property Inventory, 1971, Inkwell & Accessories: A Collector's Guide to Useful Resources, 1989; pub. newsletter The Stained Finger, 1981. Bd. dirs. Elderfriend's Inc., Mpls., 1975—, Cath. Ctr. Separated and Divorced, Mpls., 1979-84, Cath. Charities Corp. Bd., Mpls., 1982-84; presentor We're In Svc. Edn., Mpls., 1984—; vol. Hennepin County Hist. Soc., Cath. Charities Seton Child Weldfare, 1991—; vol. Tribunal officer, field advocate Archdiocese of St. Paul and Mpls., 1975—. Mem. Soc. Inkwell Collectors (pres., researcher 1980—), Twin Cities Purchasing Mgmt. Assn. Inc., Adminstrv. Mgmt. Soc., Am. Legion, Navy League, Assn. Naval Aviation, Inc., KC. Democrat. Home: 5136 Thomas Ave S Minneapolis MN 55410-2241 Office: Economy Sales & Svc Inc 6417 Penn Ave S Richfield MN 55423-1142

MCGREW, PATRICIA ANN, geriatrics nurse; b. Ind., Mar. 4, 1955; d. William M. and Bonnie B. (Guysinger) Barton; m. Michael E. McGrew, July 23, 1977; children: Marianne, Samantha. Diploma, Parkview Meth. Sch. Nursing, 1978. RN, Ind. Staff nurse, supr. then asst. DON Riverview Care Ctr., Ft. Wayne, Ind., 1987-89; DON Heritage Manor N., Ft. Wayne, 1989-90; staff nurse labor, delivery, post-partum Parkview Meml. Hosp., Ft. Wayne, Ind., 1990-94; perinatal nurse clinician Caremark Healthcare, 1992-93; acute renal dialysis nurse NE Ind. Kidney Ctr., 1994—; perinatal nurse clinician Caremark Healthcare, 1992-93; cons. in field.

MCGRUDER, ROBERT, newspaper publishing executive. Exec. editor Detroit Free Press. Office: 321 W Lafayette Blvd Detroit MI 48226-2705

MCGUINNESS, BARBARA SUE, food products executive; b. Lansing, Mich., Feb. 8, 1947; d. William Harrison and Gertrude Esther (Parker) Coleman; m. Michael L. Mueller, Aug. 12, 1965 (div. June 1973); children: Meredith Sue, Matthew Parker; m. John McGuinness, Dec. 8, 1978. Student, Meramec Community Coll., 1975-77, Florissant Valley Community Coll., 1984-87. Instr. Lindbergh Sch. Dist., St. Louis, 1975-77; surp. Velvet Freeze Ice Cream Co., St. Louis, 1977-81, v.p., 1981—. Chmn. Fin. Com. Chesterfield (Mo.) Transition Com., 1988—, campaign chmn. Chesterfield Inc. Com., 1988—, chmn. Chesterfield Planning & Zoning Commn., 1988-95, chmn. Chesterfield Inaugural Commns., 1988; rep. State Mo. Electoral Coll. U.S., 1988; apptd. vice chmn. Selective Svc. System Draft Bd. #20, 1981-91, chmn., 1991-92; state parliamentarian Mo. Fedn. Women's Dem. Clubs, 1989-91, 93-95; del. Dem. Nat. Conv., 1972, 80, 92; mem., grad. Leadership St. Louis, 1991—, St. Louis County Pvt. Industry Coun., 1991-92, St. Louis County DARES Bd., 1991-94, Mayor;s Chester Valley Flood Recovery Task Force, 1993-94, Chesterfield Valley Rebuilding Task Force, 1993-94, St. Louis County Boundary Commn., 1995-2000, chmn., 1995; mem. Chesterfield Intergovernmental Rels. Com., 1993-94; campaign mgr. Robert McCulloch for county prosecuting atty., St. Louis, 1990-94, Howard Wagner Mo. Sec. of State, 1992; active Chesterfield Econ. Devel. Coun., 1990-91; chmn. St. Louis County Inaugural Commn., 1991. Recipient Key to City award City Govt. Crestwood, Mo., 1974, Key to City Chesterfield, 1988, Distinguished Service award, 1988, St. Louis County Dem. of Yr. award, 1986, Planning Comsnr. or Yr. award Dwight Davis Am. Planning Assn., 1993, Excellence in Community Devel. award Chesterfield Civ. Progress, 1993, Humanitarian award 1993, End Hunger award U.S. Mayors, 1993, Disting. Svc. awad Mid-East Area Agy. on Aging, 1994; named Chesterfield Citizen of Yr., 1989. Mem. Am. Planning Assn., Area Ice Cream Retailers Assn. (pres. 1979-84), Chesterfield C. of C. (Civic award 1988). Democrat. Baptist. Home: 95 River Bend Dr Chesterfield MO 63017-2671 Office: Velvet Freeze Ice Cream Co 7355 W Florissant Ave Saint Louis MO 63136-1348

MCGUIRE, ANTHONY BARTHOLOMEW, engineering executive; b. Bklyn., Jan. 19, 1945; s. Edward Sylvester and Frances Mary (Wojciechowicz) M.; m. Lynn Marie Andersen, Mar. 16, 1968; children: Christopher, Hillary, Kathryn, Susan. BE, Manhattan Coll., 1966. Registered profl. engr., Ill., Ind., N.Y., Ohio, Mich., Wis., Mass., N.J., Mo., Conn., Md., Ky., Minn., Va., Pa., Nebr., Nev., Iowa, others. Project mgr., engr. various firms, 1966-80; v.p. Perkins and Will, Chgo., 1980-83, Environ. Systems Design, Chgo., 1983-86; pres. McGuire Engrs., Chgo., 1986—. Contbr. articles to profl. jours. Mem. Ill. regional insulation adv. com. City of Chgo. code rev. com. Named Outstanding Engrng. Grad., Manhattan Coll., 1992. Mem. ASHRAE (award of Merit 1975, chpt. pres. 1988-90), NSPE (Young Engr. of Yr. award 1975), Am. Soc.Plumbing Engrs., Chgo. Architecture Found., Stewart Club, Chgo. Hist. Soc., Western Trade Assn., Chgo. Bldg. Congress. Home: 1615 N Cleveland Ave Chicago IL 60614-5647 Office: McGuire Engrs PC 300 S Riverside Plz Chicago IL 60606-6613

MCGUIRE, JOHN C., state legislator; b. Joliet, Ill.; m. Marilyn McGuire; four children. Student, Joliet (Ill.) Jr. Coll.; BA, Colo. State Coll. Trustee, supr. Joliet Twp.; tchr., coach; Dist. 86 rep. Ill. Ho. Reps., Springfield, 1991—; mem. labor and commerce, transp. and motor vehicles, econ. and urban devel., elem. and secondary edn., gen. svc. appropriations, and aging coms., Ill. Ho. Reps. Mem. VFW, Irish Am. Soc. Home: 1510 Glenwood Ave Joliet IL 60435-5832*

MCGUIRE, JOHN W., SR., advertising executive, marketing professional, author; b. Chgo., May 12, 1952; s. Eugene H. Sr. and Marjorie (Bolger) McG.; m. Mary Sue Roper, June 17, 1972 (div. 1977); 1 child, John William Jr.; m. Lynn L. Rembos, June 21, 1984 (div. April 1991); children: Kelly Lynn, Ryan Michael. AA, Chgo. City Colls., 1972; BA, Northeastern Ill., Chgo., 1974. Janitor Bd. of Edn., Chgo., 1970-74; sales rep. Motorola Comms., Inc., Schaumburg, Ill., 1974-76, Pattis Group, Chgo., 1976-77; midwest sales mgr. Harcourt Brace Jovanovich Pub. Co., N.Y.C., 1977-79; account sales mgr. Cosmopolitan Mag. Hearst Pub. Co., N.Y.C., 1979-81; midwest acct. mgr. Psychology Today Mag. Ziff-Davis Pub. Co., N.Y.C., 1981-82; midwest regional mgr. Pennwell Pub. Co., Tulsa, Okla., 1982-84; western regional sales mgr. SN Pub. Co., West Dundee, Ill., 1984-91; western regional sales mgr., midwest regional sales mgr. Jobson Pub. Co., N.Y.C., 1991—. Author: (book) One Man's Life: A Poetic Review, 1995, singer (cassette tapes), designer (creative posters). With USN, hon. discharge 1970. Mem. VFW, Midwest Healthcare Mktg., Arlington Poetry Project. Republican. Roman Catholic. Home: 41W585 Golden Oaks Saint Charles IL 60175

MCGUIRE, MARK ALAN, chemical engineer; b. Omaha, Sept. 6, 1968; s. Alvin Verdell and Barbara Frances (Rihanek) McG. BA in Math., Peru (Nebr.) State Coll., 1991, BA in Phys. Sci., 1991; MS in Chem. Engrng., U. Kans., 1993. Teaching asst. Peru State Coll., 1988-91; chemistry intern Omaha Pub. Power Dist., Nebraska City, Nebr., 1991; rsch. asst. Tertiary Oil Recovery Project, Lawrence, 1991-93; rsch. asst. chemistry U. Kans., Lawrence, 1990; sales rep. process divsn. Davis Water & Waste Industries, Inc., Tellevast, Fla., 1993—. Recipient scholarship Phillips Petroleum Corp., 1991-93. Mem. NEA (rep. to higher edn. com. 1989-90, del. 1989), Am. Inst. Chem. Engrs. (grad. rep. 1992-93), Student Edn. Assn. Nebr. (southeastern regional rep. 1989-90), Peru Student Edn. Assn. (pres. 1989-91, Outstanding Achievement award 1990). Republican. Mem. Assembly of God Ch. Home: RR 2 Box 172 Blair NE 68008-9760 Office: Davis Process Divsn 2650 Tellevast Rd PO Box 29 Tellevast FL 34270-0029

MCGUIRE, MARY JO, state legislator; b. 1956. BA in Bus. Adminstrn., Coll. of St. Catherine; JD, Hamline U.; postgrad., Harvard U., 1995—. Mem. Minn. Ho. of Reps., 1988-94, mem. judiciary com., judiciary fin. divsn., vice chair local govt. and met. affairs; mem. labor and mgmt. rels. com. Democrat. Home: 1529 Iowa Ave W Saint Paul MN 55108-2128 Office: Minn Ho of Reps State Ho Office Bldg Saint Paul MN 55155

MCGUIRE, MICHAEL G., music therapist, educator; b. St. Louis, May 6, 1949; s. William W. and Reathel M. (Hill) McG. MusB, Cen. Meth. Coll., 1971, Mich. State U., 1974; MM, SUNY, Fredonia, 1978. Registered, bd. cert. music therapist. Music therapist Buffalo Psychiat. Ctr., 1974-76; dir. music therapy Nazareth Coll., Rochester, N.Y., 1978-82, Ea. Mich. U., Ypsilanti, 1983—. Founding editor: (jour.) Music Therapy Perspectives, 1981-89. Mem. Lesbian, Gay, and Bisexual support svcs. adv. bd. Ea. Mich. U., Ypsilanti, 1993-95. Mem. Nat. Assn. for Music Therapy (chair profl. competencies 1994—). Office: Ea Mich U Dept of Music Ypsilanti MI 48197

MCGUIRE, NORA E., account executive; b. Evanston, Ill., Nov. 5, 1966. BBA, Loyola U., 1989. Mktg. exec. JMB Realty, Chgo., 1989-90; sr. acct. exec. James E. Frick, Hopkins, Minn., 1990—. Vol. Boys and Girls Clubs, Mpls., 1994—. Mem. Employers Assn., Am. Payroll Assn., Minn. C. of C.

MCGUIRE, TIMOTHY JAMES, lawyer, county and state official; b. Mount Pleasant, Mich., Mar. 24, 1949; s. James Edward and Anita Matilda (Starr) McG.; m. T. Jean Fannin, May 10, 1975; children: Tracy, Jason, Jeffrey. BA, Aquinas Coll., Grand Rapids, Mich., 1971; JD cum laude, William Mitchell Coll. Law, St. Paul, 1987. Bar: Minn. 1987. Mng. editor Ypsilanti Press, Mich., 1973-75, Corpus Christi Caller, Tex., 1975-77, Lakeland Ledger, Fla., 1977-79, Mpls. Star, 1979-82; mng. editor features and sports Mpls. Star and Tribune, 1982-84, mng. editor, 1984-91, exec. editor, 1991-93; editor, gen. mgr. reader customer unit, 1993—; Pulitzer Prize juror, 1988-89, 95-96. Lay preacher St. Joseph Roman Cath. Ch., Mpls., 1995—. Mem. Am. Soc. Newspaper Editors (bd. dirs. 1992—, chmn. change com. 1994-95, chmn. program com. 1996—), Minn. State Bar Assn. Roman Catholic. Home: 3645 Rosewood Ln N Minneapolis MN 55441-1127 Office: Star Tribune 425 Portland Ave Minneapolis MN 55488-0001

MCGUIRE, TIMOTHY JAMES, refrigeration technician; b. Detroit, Dec. 13, 1948; s. James Thomas and Glenna Doreen (Elkins) McG. Student, Monroe County Cmty. Coll., Monroe, Mich., 1967; HVAC diploma, Nat. Inst. of Tech., Toledo, Ohio, 1983; student, Henry Ford Cmty. Coll., Dearborn, Mich., 1984. Cert. Refrigeration Engr. First Class, Mich. Refrigeration tech. McLouth Steel Products, Trenton, Mich., 1972—. Author: How to Collect Antique American Bottles (Inexpensively), 1990. Mem. Phi Theta Kappa. Democrat. Roman Catholic. Home: 24854 Strewing Rd Flat Rock MI 48134

MCGUIRE, TIMOTHY JOSEPH, physical therapist, video consultant; b. Iron Mountain, Mich., Mar. 12, 1963; s. Maynard Francis and Marcella Janet (Zambon) McG.; m. Kathleen Mari Westerheide, May 18, 1991; 1 child, Casey. BS in Biology, U. Mich., Ann Arbor, 1985; BS in Phys. Therapy, U. Mich., Flint, 1987. Lic. phys. therapist, Ill. Phys. therapist Ingam Med. Ctr., Lansing, Mich., 1987-90; contract therapist R.W. Rausch and Assocs., Inc., Chgo., 1990-91; mgr. River Forest Phys. Therapy R.W. Rausch Rehab. Svc., River Forest, 1991—; co-owner Absolute Rehab. Video Inc., Lansing, Mich., 1992—. Editor, cameraman rehab. videos, 1992. Mem. Am. Phys. Therapy Assn., Am. Running and Fitness Assn., Ill. Phys. Therapy Assn. (ctrl. dist. rep. 1993—), Chgo. Sports Medicine Soc., U. Mich. Alumni Assn. Roman Catholic. Office: River Forest Phys Therapy Ctr 7321 W North Ave River Forest IL 60305

MCGURN, GEORGE WILLIAM, lawyer; b. Chgo., May 10, 1914; s. George William and Margaret Anna (Gavin) McG.; m. Margaret Mary Daley (dec. Oct. 1967); children: Margaret Mary (dec.), George, Anne, Jane, Mary, Michael, Susan; m. Antoinette Margaret Feuce, Nov. 28, 1970. Student, Clemson U., 1932-34; JD, Ill. Inst. Tech., 1938; LLM, U. Chgo., 1946. Bar: Ill. 1938, U.S. Dist. Ct. (no. dist.) Ill. 1951, U.S. Supreme Ct. 1955, U.S. Ct. Appeals (7th cir.) 1974. Assoc. LaRochelle, Brooks & Beardsley, Chgo., 1938-40; asst. gen. counsel Pabst Brewing Co., Chgo., 1946-48; ptnr. Reum, Casello and McGurn, Chgo., 1948-51; asst. counsel Chgo. Dist. Engr. Office U.S. Army, Chgo., 1951-53; asst. atty. gen. Office of Ill. Atty. Gen., Springfield, Ill., 1953-54; chief counsel and sec. Ill. State Toll Highway Commn., Chgo. and Oak Brook, Ill., 1954-63; ptnr. Healy and McGurn, Chgo. and Oakbrook, 1963-82; ret. Healy and McGurn, 1982-88; counsel Law Offices of Michael McGurn, Warrenville, Ill., 1988—. Editor Chgo.-Kent Law Rev., 1936-38. Rep. committeeman, Elmhurst, Ill., 1960-63. Served to maj. U.S. Army, 1941-46; col. res. ret. Postgrad scholar Chgo.-Kent Coll. Law Ill. Inst. Tech., 1938; recipient Citizenship award Ill. Inst. Tech., 1988. Mem. ABA, Ill. State Bar Assn. (sr. counselor 1988), DuPage County Bar Assn., Rotry (sec. Oak Brook club 1962-63, v.p 1963-64), K.C., Delta Theta Phi (scholarship key). Roman Catholic. Home: 1572 S Prospect St Wheaton IL 60187-7750 Office: McGurn & Assocs Ltd Unit 101 29W140 Butterfield Rd Warrenville IL 60555

MC HENRY, MARTIN CHRISTOPHER, physician, educator; b. San Francisco, Feb. 9, 1932; s. Merl and Marcella (Bricca) McH.; m. Patricia Grace Hughes, Apr. 27, 1957; children: Michael, Christopher, Timothy, Mary Ann, Jeffrey, Paul, Kevin, William, Monica, Martin Christopher. Student, U. Santa Clara, 1950-53; MD, U. Cin., 1957; MS in Medicine, U. Minn., 1966. Intern, Highland Alameda County (Calif.) Hosp., Oakland, 1957-58; resident, internal medicine fellow Mayo Clinic, Rochester, Minn., 1958-61, spl. appointee in infectious diseases, 1963-64; staff physician infectious diseases Henry Ford Hosp., Detroit, 1964-67; staff physician Cleve. Clinic, 1967-72, chmn. dept. infectious diseases, 1972-92, sr. physician infectious diseases, 1992—. Asst. clin. prof. Case Western Res. U., 1970-77, assoc. clin. prof. medicine, 1977-91, clin. prof. medicine, 1991—; assoc. vis. physician Cleve. Met. Gen. Hosp., 1970—; cons. VA Hosp., Cleve., 1973—. Chmn. manpower com. Swine Influenza Program, Cleve., 1976. Served with USNR, 1961-63. Named Disting. Tchr. in Medicine Cleve. Clinic, 1972, 90; recipient 1st ann. Bruce Hubbard Stewart award Cleve. Clinic Found. for Humanities in Medicine, 1985, Nightingale Physician Collaboration award Cleve. Clinic Found. Divsn. Nursing, 1995. Diplomate Am. Bd. Internal Medicine. Fellow ACP, Infectious Diseases Soc. Am., Am. Coll. Chest Physicians (chmn. com. cardiopulmonary infections 1975-77, 81-83), Royal Soc. Medicine of Great Britain; mem. Am. Soc. Clin. Pharmacology and Therapeutics (chmn. sect. infectious diseases and antimicrobial agts., 1970-77, 80-85, dir.), Am. Thoracic Soc., Am. Soc. Clin. Pathologists, Am. Fedn. Clin. Rsch., Am. Soc. Tropical Medicine and Hygiene, Am. Soc. Microbiology, N.Y. Acad. Scis. Contbr. numerous articles to profl. jours., also chpts. to books. Home: 2779 Belgrave Rd Pepper Pike OH 44124-4601 Office: 9500 Euclid Ave Cleveland OH 44195-0001

MCHENRY, TIMOTHY HOWARD, elementary education educator; b. Colunbus, Ohio, Dec. 19, 1945; s. Howard Almond and Bettie Marie (Summers) McH.; m. Marianne L. Moehle, April 26, 1980 (div.). BS in Education, Miami U., Ohio, 1967; MA in Education, Kent State U., 1970. Cert. elem. tchr., prin., Ohio. Tchr. grade 4 Lorain City Schs., Ohio, 1967-68, Clearview Local Schs., Lorain, Ohio, 1968-70; tchr. grade 5 Grandview Heights City Schs., Ohio, 1970-73; tchr. grade 6 Madison Local Schs., Groveport, Ohio, 1973-75; head tchr., grade 6 tchr. Midview Local Schs., Grafton, Ohio, 1975-76; elem. substitute tchr. Elyria City Schs., Ohio, 1976-81; agent Banker's Life Ins. Co., Avon Lake, Ohio, 1977; hourly employee, inspector metall. dept. U.S. Steel Co., Lorain, Ohio, 1977-82; tchr. grade 1 Cleveland Pub. Schs., Ohio, 1982-85, tchr. grade 3, 1985—. Scoutmaster Boy Scouts Am., Avon Lake, 1967-70, 76-88, Columbus, 1970-76, Sheffield Lake, 1988-90, asst. scoutmaster, 1988—; mem. Church Choir, Lorain, 1980—; tchr. grade 1-3, Church Sch., Lorain, 1984—. Recipient Commendation cert. Ohio House Rep., Columbus, 1988, Scouter's key Boy Scouts Am., 1970, 93, God and Svc. Adult Religious award Boy Scouts Am., 1992, Dist. award of Merit Boy Scouts Am., 1992. Mem. Internat. Reading Assn., Ohio Council I.R.A., Assn. Supervision and Curriculum Devel., Lillian Hinds Reading Assn. (sec. 1985-88, v.p. 1988-90, pres. 1990-92, program com. 1993—). Home: 4880 Greenwood Dr Sheffield Lake OH 44054-1517

MCHUGH, EARL STEPHEN, dentist; b. Colorado Springs, Colo., Feb. 27, 1936; s. Earl Clifton and Margaret Mary (Higgins) M.; m. Joan Bleckwell, Aug. 24, 1957; children: Kevin, Stacey, Julie. BA, Cornell U., 1958; DDS, U. Mo., 1962. Pvt. practice, Kansas City, Mo., 1964—; lectr. U. Mo. Dental Sch., Kansas City, 1988, clin. staff, 1989, 90, 91, 92, 93, 94, 95, ethics seminar faculty staff, addiction in dentistry faculty, 1995; cons. Hallmark, Inc., Kansas City, 1988; adv. dir. Rsch. Hosp., Kansas City. Contbr. articles to profl. jours. Deacon Presbyn. Ch. Prairie Village, Kans., 1982-84; vol. Shawnee Mission Hosp. Kans., 1985-88; lectr. Drug Recovery Program, Kansas City, Kans., 1988-89, 92, 93, 94. Capt. Dental Corp, U.S. Army, 1962-64. Mem. Valley Hope Assn. (rsch. hos. adv. bd. 1995-96), Audubon Soc. (Ortnithologist of Yr. award Kansas City chpt. 1990), Kans. Ornithol. Soc. (v.p. 1989-90, pres. 1990-91), Internat. Coun. Bird Preservation (Kans. del. 1990, coord. Kans. Breeding Bird Atlas 1992, 93, 94, 95, chmn. Kans. bird records com.), Omicron Kappa Upsilon, Chi Psi.

MCHUGH, JOSEPH EDWARD, motion control device application engineer; b. Cleve., Jan. 16, 1938; s. Joseph James and Larue Goldia (Edwards) McH.; m. Carol Ann Kadis, Oct. 24, 1964; children: Michelle Lynn, David Michaele, Kelly Ann. Ohio State U., 1956-59, Cuyahoga C.C., 1975, Lakeland C.C., 1984, 95; Degree in mech. engring., Columbia Pacific U., 1985; Materials Engring. Inst., 1989. R&D tech. Stock Equipment Co., Chagrin Falls, Ohio, 1964-66; design engr. Bailey Meter Co., Wickliffe, Ohio, 1966-71; project engr. W.L. Tanksley Co., Wickliffe, Ohio, 1971-77, Motorola, Inc., Phoenix, 1977-79; design engr. Allen-Bradley Co., Inc., Highland Heights, Ohio, 1979-83; program mgr. Cyberex, Inc., Mentor, Ohio, 1983-87; project leader Associated Enterprises, Painesville, Ohio, 1987-91; mgr. design engring. Victoreen Corp., Solon, Ohio, 1991-93; application engr. Thermotion Corp., Willoughby, Ohio, 1993—; pres., CEO COMDESCO, 1984-95. Inventor in field, with patents for latching actuator, flue damper, and residential wheelchair ramp. Pres., CEO Gt. Lakes Preservation Found., Mentor, Ohio, 1989-95; mem. URSBA, Northern Ohio, 1993. With USAF, 1959-65. Mem. Am. Soc. Metals, Gas Appliance Mfrs. Assn., Am. Gas Assn. Republican. Home: 8790 Norwood Dr Mentor OH 44060 Office: Thermotion Corp 4399 Hamann Pkwy Willoughby OH 44094

MCHUGHES, BRIAN ANDREW, commercial real estate executive; b. St. Louis, Nov. 5, 1963; s. Dennis Patrick and Helen (Ruth) McH.; m. Kim Dawn Andrews, May 24, 1991. BA in Comm., U. No. Iowa, 1987. Owner, propr. Brian's Car Detailing Svc., Des Moines, 1979-91, Winning Edge Resumés, Des Moines, 1987-91; sales agt., agt. trainer Life Investors Ins.

Co., West Des Moines, Iowa, 1987-88; placement specialist ADIA Pers. Svcs., Des Moines, 1988-90; sales assoc., trainer Hubbell Realty Co., Des Moines, 1990-94; broker assoc., dir. recruiting and tng. Iowa Realty Comml., West Des Moines, Iowa, 1994—. Vol. firefighter Clive (Iowa) Vol. Fire Dept., 1992-94; amb. City of Clive, 1991; state del. Iowa Rep. Com., Des Moines, 1984. Mem. Internat. Coun. Shopping Ctrs., Greater Des Moines Bd. Realtors, Embassy Club. Roman Catholic. Home: 652 61st St West Des Moines IA 50266 Office: Iowa Realty Comml 4949 Westown Pkwy Ste 145 West Des Moines IA 50266

MCINDOO, WALTER ROLLA, electronics executive; b. Terre Haute, Ind., Nov. 16, 1934; s. Chester Lewis and Marjoie Ruth (Fry) McIn.; m. Shirley Ann Genung, June 10, 1956; children: Nancy Jean McIndoo Periman, Timothy Paul, Susan Jeanine McIndoo McLaughlin. BSEE, Rose Polytech. Inst., 1956; MS in Engring. Sci., Purdue U., 1965. Trainee Delco Radio Div., G.M., Kokomo, Ind., 1956-57, product supr., 1957-58, 58-60, design engr., 1958, process engr., 1960-65, supr. engring., 1965-68; supt. mfg. Delco Electronics Div., G.M., Kokomo, 1968-78, plant mgr., 1978-83; dir. semiconductor bus. unit Delco Electronics Cori, G.M., Kokomo, 1983-92; retired, 1992; bd. dirs. Semiconductor Rsch. Corp., Raleigh, N.C.; task force mem. Rose Hulman Curriculum, Terre Haute, 1991-92. Mem. adv. coun. Sch. Tech., Purdue U., Lafayette, Ind., 1987-92; bd. dirs. YMCA, Kokomo, 1982-96, pres., 1991-92; bd. dirs. Howard Cmty. Hosp. Endowment, Kokomo, 1980-86; deacon Alto Rd. Ch. of Christ, Kokomo, 1964-71, elder, 1971-79, 83-96; indsl. task force to Gov. Ind., 1993-94; chmn. of career svcs. Rose Hulman Alumni Bd., 1993-95. Recipient Disting. Svc. award Ind. Electronics Mfrs. Assn., 1991. Republican. Home: 5003 Pavalion Dr Kokomo IN 46901-3652

MCINERNY, RALPH MATTHEW, philosophy educator, author; b. Mpls., Feb. 24, 1929; s. Austin Clifford and Vivian Gertrude (Rush) McI.; m. Constance Terrill Kunert, Jan. 3, 2953; children: Cathleen, Mary, Anne, David, Elizabeth, Daniel. BA, St. Paul Sem., 1951; MA, U. Minn., 1952; PhD summa cum laude, Lval U., 1954; DHL, St. John Fisher Coll., 1993, St. Anselm Coll., 1995. Instr. Creighton U., 1954-55; prof. U. Notre Dame, Ind., 1955—, Michael P. Grace prof. medieval studies, 1988—, dir. dept., 1978-85; vis. prof. Cornell U., 1988, Cath. U., 1971, Louvain, 1983, 95; founder Internat. Catholic Univ. Author: (philos. works) The Logic of Analogy, 1961, History of Western Philosophy, vol. 1, 1963, vol. 2, 1968, Thomism in an Age of Renewal, 1966, Studies in Analogy, 1967, New Themes in Christian Philosophy, 1967, St. Thomas Aquinas, 1976, Ethica Thomistica, 1982, History of the Ambrosiana, 1983, Being and Predication, 1986, Miracles, 1986, Art and Prudence, 1988, A First Glance at St. Thomas: Handbook for Peeping Thomists, 1989, Boethius and Aquinas, 1989, Aquinas on Human Action, 1991, The Question of Christian Ethics, 1993, Aquinas Against the Averroists, 1993; (novels) Jolly Rogerson, 1967, A Narrow Time, 1969, The Priest, 1973, Gate of Heaven, 1975, Rogerson at Bay, 1976, Her Death of Cold, 1977, The Seventh Station, 1977, Romanesque, 1977, Spinnaker, 1977, Quick as a Dodo, 1978, Bishop as Pawn, 1978, La Cavalcade Romaine, 1979, Lying Three, 1979, Abecedary, 1979, Second Vespers, 1980, Rhyme and Reason, 1981, Thicker than Water, 1981, A Loss of Patients, 1982, The Grass Widow, 1983, Connolly's Life, 1983, Getting Away with Murder, 1984, And Then There Were Nun, 1984, The Noonday Devil, 1985, Sine Qua Nun, 1986, Leave of Absence, 1986, Rest in Pieces, 1985, Cause and Effect, 1987, The Basket Case, 1987, Veil of Ignorance, 1988, Abracadaver, 1989, Body and Soil, 1989, Four on the Floor, 1989, Frigor Mortis, 1989, Savings and Loan, 1990, The Search Committee, 1991, The Nominative Case, 1991, Sister Hood, 1991, Judas Priest, 1991, Easeful Death, 1991, Infra Dig, 1992, Desert Sinner, 1992, Seed of Doubt, 1993, The Basket Case, 1993, Nun Plussed, 1993, Mom and Dead, 1994, The Cardinal Offense, Law and Ardor, 1995; editor The New Scholasticism, 1967-89; editor, pub. Crisis, 1982-96; pub. Catholic Dossier, 1995—. Exec. dir. Wethersfield Inst., 1989-92; bd. govs. Thomas Aquinas Coll., Santa Paula, Calif., 1992—. With USMCR, 1946-47. Fulbright rsch. fellow, Belgium, 1959-60, NEH fellow, 1977-78, NEA fellow, 1983, Fulbright scholar, Argentina, 1986, 87. Fellow Pontifical Roman Acad. St. Thomas Aquinas; mem. Am. Philos. Assn., Am. Cath. Philos. Assn. (past pres., recipient medals), Am. Metaphys. Soc. (pres. 1992), Internat. Soc. for Study Medieval Philosophy, Medieval Acad., Mystery Writers Am., Authors Guild, Fellowship Cath. Scholars (pres. 1992-95). Home: 2158 Portage Ave South Bend IN 46616-2035 Office: U of Notre Dame Dept of Philosophy 336 O Shaugnessy Hall Notre Dame IN 46556-5639

MCINNIS, JAMES MILTON, publishing company executive; b. Repton, Ala., Jan. 8, 1934; s. Clarence W. and Ada Mae (Owens) McI.; m. Joan Horton, May 17, 1953; children: Deborah Lynn, Cynthia Jane, Daniel Paul, Brenda Joyce. BA, Am. U., 1959, LLB, 1962, JD, 1963. Gen. agt., ins. broker, 1958-61; staff asst. U.S. Senate, Washington, 1961-62; with FBI, 1962-63; jr. atty. So. Ry. System, Washington, 1964-65; mgmt. exec. Public Utilities Reports, Arlington, Va., 1965—, advt. sales mgr., 1965-68, asst. gen. mgr., asst. v.p., 1968-69, v.p., asst. sec., treas., 1970-72, v.p. adminstrn., 1972-76, v.p. ops., 1976-79, exec. v.p., gen. mgr., 1980-81, pres., chief exec. officer, 1981-93, chmn. bd. dirs., 1993—, also exec. sec. utilities publ. com., 1981-93, chmn., 1993—; mem. Washington legal com. Am. Bus. Press, Washington; substitute instr. U. Tubingen (Germany), 1955; past chmn. Assn. Paid Circulation Publs. Officer, Arlington County (Va.) PTA, 1973-75; mem. adv. com. Arlington County Sch. Bd., 1973-75; bd. deacons First Bapt. Ch., Washington, 1969—; bd. dirs. Arlington Heart Assn. Served with U.S. Army, 1953-55. Mem. Delta Theta Phi. Republican. Clubs: Nat. Potomac Yacht (past commodore), Arlington Forest. Contbr. articles to Life Ins. Salesman mag.; top ins. salesman in U.S., Mut. and United of Omaha Life Ins. Co., 1961.

MCINTEE, TERRI LEE, disability advocate; b. Cleve., Nov. 9, 1955; d. Edward Franklin and Janet Rae (Porter) McI.; m. Romulo David Larenas, Jan. 3, 1980 (div. June 1993); children: Derek Tyrone, Tirrell Daniel. BA in Humanities, Ohio State U., 1978; MA in Human Resource Mgmt. & Devel., New Sch. for Social Rsch., 1990. Benefit approver Equitable Life Assurance Soc., Cleve., 1978-79; equiclaims project team Equitable Life Assurance Soc., N.Y.C., 1979-82; hosp. adminstr. Lenox Hill Hosp., N.Y.C., 1982-84; human resource info. analyst Securities Industry Automation Corp., N.Y.C., 1984-90; regional cons. Family Info. Network, Burton, Ohio, 1994—; regional cons. N.E. Ohio Arc of Ohio, 1996—; chair family concerns com. Lake County Early Intervention Collaborative, Mentor, Ohio, 1994—; co-chair family resource com. Geauga County Early Invervention Collaborative, Chardon, Ohio, 1994—. Active Burton (Ohio) Congl. Ch., 1994—; charter mem. Geauga Leadership Class, 1995-96; apptd. gov. Ohio's Disability Planning Coun., 1996—. Recipient Svc. award Lake County Early Intervention Collaborative, Mentor, 1995. Mem. NAFE, AAUW, Nat. Down Syndrome Congress, Mid Hudson Valley Down Syndrome Congress (sec. 1993, Disting. Svc. award 1992), Upside of Downs, Schs. are for Everyone (bd. dirs. 1995—), The Arc, Internat. Order Ea. Stars. Home: 13754 Ford Ln #1 Burton OH 44021-9536 Office: Family Info Network 13754 Ford Ln #1 Burton OH 44021-9536

MCINTOSH, CALVIN EUGENE, retired small business owner; b. Jakes Prairie, Mo., Mar. 4, 1926; s. Benjamin Louis and Mary Margaret (Calvin) McI.; m. Mary Frances Gravatt, Nov. 30, 1947; children: Dennis Eugene, Gail Sue. Student, St. Louis U., 1950. Clk. U.S. Post Office, St. Louis, 1950-52; salesman Skelly Oil Co., Kans. City, Mo., 1952-60; mgr. Skelly Oil Co., Kans. City, 1960-62; merchant McIntosh Furniture Co., Salem, Mo., 1962-88. Bd. dirs. Dent County Fire Protection Dist., Salem, 1983—. Sgt. USAAF, 1944-46. Republican.

MCINTOSH, CAROLYN MEADE, retired educational administrator; b. Waynesburg, Ky., Oct. 21, 1928; d. Clarence Hobert and Sarah Letitia (Bentley) Meade; m. Edgar G. McIntosh, Aug. 21, 1948; children: Wayne, Jeanne, Penny, Jimmi, Carol. BS, Miami U., Oxford, Ohio, 1962; MEd, Xavier U., Cin., 1966. Elem. tchr. Ohio, 1961-79; prin. New Richmond (Ohio) Sch. Dist., 1980-91; ret., 1991; tchr. Clermont County Adult Edn. Program, 1970-95, Clermont County dir.of Headstrart 1971-72, Clearmont County Rep. to Ohio elem. adminstr., 1985-87, Pres. Clermont and Brown County adminstr., 1988-89. Editor Ret. Tchrs. Newsletter. Pres. New Richmond Bd. Edn.; v.p. U.S. Grant Vocat. Sch. Bd. Edn.; mem. Clermont County Excellence in Edn. Com.; mem. edn. adv. com. Clermont Coll.; mem. adv. bd. Bethany Children's Home; mem. Clermont 2001 Com.; mem. Rep. Ctrl. Com. of Clermont County. Recipient New Richmond Adminstr. of the Yr. award City of New Richmond, 1989. Mem. AAUW, ASCD, NAESP, Nat. Sch. Bd. Assn., Ohio Sch. Bd. Assn., Ohio Assn. Elem. Sch. Adminstrs. (all county legis. liaison), Ohio County Ret. Tchrs. Assn., Clermont County Ret. Tchrs. Assn. (pres.), Order Eastern Star, Phi Delta Kappa, Delta Kappa Gamma (pres. chpt.). Baptist.

MCINTOSH, DAVID M., congressman; b. June 8, 1958; m. Ruthie McIntosh. Grad., Yale Coll., 1980, U. Chgo., 1983. Bar: Ind., U.S. Supreme Ct. Spl. asst. domestic affairs to Pres. Reagan; spl. asst. to Atty. Gen. Meese; liaison Pres.'s Commn. on Privatization; spl. asst. to V.P. Quayle, dep. legal counsel to; exec. dir. Pres.'s Coun. on Competitiveness; sr. fellow Citizens for a Sound Economy; founder Federalist Soc. for Law & Pub. Policy, now co-chmn.; mem. U.S. Ho. of Reps., 104 Congress, Washington, 1995—, mem. Govt. Reform & Oversight Com., chmn. panel's Econ. Growth, Natural Resources and Regulatory Affairs Subcom. Mem. State Bar of Ind. Republican. Office: US House Reps 1208 Longworth House Office Bldg Washington DC 20515-1402

MCINTOSH, RICKY, electrical design engineer; b. Oceola, Iowa, Dec. 9, 1966. BS in Computer Sci., Iowa State U., 1989, MS in Computer Sci., 1991. Engr. rsch. asst. Dent Energy Ames Lab., Ames, Iowa, 1991-94; elec. design engr. Ryko Mfg., Grimes, Iowa, 1994—; cons. in field. Office: Ryko Mfg 11600 NW 54th Ave Grimes IA 50111

MCINTRYE, GERALDINE K., training center administrator; b. Kansas City, Mo., Nov. 21, 1929. BS, Ctrl. Mo. State U., 1954; M, U. Kansas City, 1960. Cert. secondary tchr., Eng. lang., Mo. Tchr. Metro Cmty. Coll. Dist., Kansas City, 1960-71; v.p. McIntrye Prodns., Kansas City, 1971-88, Nat. Law Enforcement Tng. Ctr., Kansas City, 1988—. Editor: ednl. filmstrips, videos, 1971-88.

MC INTURF, FAITH MARY, engineering company executive, thoroughbred harness racing executive; b. Grand Ridge, Ill., Aug. 22, 1917; d. Lynne E. and Margaret (Garver) McInturf; grad. high sch. With The J.E. Porter Corp., Chgo., 1939-65, v.p., 1951-65, sec., 1951-65, also dir.; with Potomac Engring. Corp., 1941—, now pres., treas., bd. dirs.; dir. Chgo. Harness Racing Inc., also Balmoral Jockey Club, Inc., 1967-72, sec., dir., 1974-78; sec., treas., dir. Balmoral Park Trot, Inc., 1969-72; sec., dir. Horse Racing Promotions, Inc., 1974-77. Roman Catholic. Home: 1360 N Lake Shore Dr Chicago IL 60610-2181 Office: 919 N Michigan Ave Chicago IL 60611-1601

MCINTURFF, FLOYD M., retired state agency administrator; b. Greenback, Tenn., May 1, 1923; s. Samuel Floyd and Hazel Agnes (Vaden) M.; m. Merle Celeste Sosna, May 27, 1950; children: Judith Margaret, Laura Ellen, Melissa Ann. BS, U. Tenn., Knoxville, 1950. Asst. to the chief engr., missiles Rockwell Internat., Columbus, 1957-73; chief, targeted jobs tax credit program Ohio Bur. Employment Svcs., Columbus, 1974-88; ret., 1988. Commd. officer U.S. Army Signal Corps., 1942-46, 51-52. Mem. Opera Columbus, Columbus Astron. Soc., Soc. Separationists, Sons of Revolution. Home: 4985 Beatrice Dr Columbus OH 43227-2114

MCINTYRE, MICHAEL TRUETT, university administrator; b. Highland Park, Ill., May 9, 1961; s. Tommy Dewane and Sheryll E. (Neewbrough) McI.; m. Marcie Lea Coleman; children: Coleman Truett, Delaney Rhea. BA in Gen. Bus. Mgmt., U. Wyo., 1984. Mgr. food svc. U. Wyo., Laramie, 1984-87; food svc. dir. Svc. Am. Corp., Dayton, Ohio, 1987-90; dir. aux. svcs. Northeastern Ill. U., Chgo., 1990—. Trustee Congl. Ch. of Deerfield, Ill., 1995—. Mem. Nat. Assn. Coll. Aux. Svcs. Home: 1026 Central Deerfield IL 60015 Office: Northeastern Ill U 5500 N St Louis Ave Chicago IL 60625

MCKAY, EUGENE HENRY, JR., food company executive; b. Battle Creek, Mich., June 25, 1929; s. Eugene Henry and Ella Florence (Everest) McK.; m. Beverly June Blakeman, Nov. 6, 1951 (div. 1981); children: Eugene Henry III, John Blakeman, Heather Melinda; m. Janice Lee Rook, 1989. BA, Mich. State U., 1951. Prodn. mgr. Battle Creek Food Co., 1955-60; franchise mgr. Archway Cookies, Inc., 1960-65, v.p., 1965-75, exec. v.p., 1975-85, pres., ptnr., 1985-96, ptnr., co-chmn., CEO, 1996—. Maj. U.S. Army, 1951-54. Republican. Presbyterian. Office: Archway Cookies Inc 5451 W Dickman Rd Battle Creek MI 49015-1034

MCKAY, LAURIE MARIE, special education educator; b. Cadillac, Mich., Sept. 10, 1960; d. Leonard Max and Mary Ann (Pierzina) Tykwinski; m. John William McKay, June 27, 1992; 1 child, Abbe Rose; stepchildren: David John, Chad Richard. BA in Psychology, Mich. State U., 1983; cert., Ctrl. Mich. U., 1990; postgrad., Grand Valley State U., 1992—. Cert. tchr. elem. edn., emotionally impaired, Mich. Tchr. spl. edn. Reed City (Mich.) Pub. Schs., 1990-91; instrl. aide Wexford-Missaukee Intermediate Sch., Cadillac, Mich., 1983-89, tchr. spl. edn., 1991—; rep., mem. student assistance program com., CCD instr. grade 4 Wexford-Missaukee Profl. Assn.; water safety instr. ARC, 1995. Cookie mgr. Crooked Tree Girl Scout Coun., Cadillac, 1989. Mem. Mich. Assn. of Tchrs. of Emotionally Disturbed Children, Coun. for Exceptional Children, Wexaucola Reading Coun. Democrat. Roman Catholic. Home: 121 Henderson Pl Cadillac MI 49601-9633 Office: Wexford Missaukee Sch Dist 9905 S 13 Rd Cadillac MI 49601-9352

MCKEAGUE, DAVID WILLIAM, district judge; b. Pitts., Nov. 5, 1946; s. Herbert William and Phyllis (Forsyth) McK.; m. Nancy L. Palmer, May 20, 1989; children: Mike, Melissa, Sarah, Laura, Elizabeth, Adam. BBA, U. Mich., 1968, JD, 1971. Bar: Mich. 1971, U.S. Dist. Ct. (we. dist.) Mich. 1972, U.S. Dist. Ct. (ea. dist.) 1978, U.S. Ct. Appeals (6th cir.) 1988. Assoc. Foster, Swift, Collins & Smith, Lansing, Mich., 1971-76, ptnr., 1976-92; sec.-treas. Foster, Swift, Collins & Smith, 1990-92; judge U.S. Dist. Ct., Western Dist. Mich., Lansing, 1992—. Mem. nat. com. U. Mich. Law Sch. Fund, 1980-92; gen. counsel Mich. Rep. Com., 1989-92; mem. adv. coun. Wharton Ctr., Mich. State U., 1996—. Mem. FBA (bd. dirs. Western Mich. chpt. 1991—), Mich. Bar Assn., Ingham County Bar Assn., Country Club Lansing (bd. govs. 1988-92, 96—). Roman Catholic. Office: US Dist Ct 315 W Allegan St Lansing MI 48933-1514

MCKEAN, MERYL LIN, television news reporter; b. Warrensburg, Mo., Dec. 1, 1957; d. Meryl M. and Willa Mae (Fellhauer) McK. BS, Cen. Mo. State U., 1980. News reporter Sta. KWQC-TV, Davenport, Iowa, 1980-81, Sta. KTUL-TV, Tulsa, 1981-85, Sta. WDAF-TV, Kansas City, Mo., 1985—. Bd. dirs. Western Mo.-Greater Kansas City chpt. Arthritis Found., 1988-93; co-host telethon, 1988, pub. edn. chmn., 1993; bd. dirs. Kansas City region Easter Seal Soc., 1990-94; co-host telethon, 1989-92; bd. dirs. Mo. Easter Seal Soc., 1992, vice chmn. pub. rels., 1992-93; guest spkr. to ch., bus. and sch. orgns.; mem. adv. coun. Kansas City Harvest, 1991-93. Recipient Russell L. Cecil award for journalism Arthritis Found., 1985, 2d place award for TV journalism Am. Acad. Family Physicians, 1987, Pub. Edn. award Mo. divsn. Am. Cancer Soc., 1987. Mem. Order of Rainbow for Girls (grand cross of color), Phi Kappa Phi, Delta Zeta (dir. collegiate chpt. 1986-90, v.p. Kansas City alumnae chpt. 1986-87, pres. 1987-88, historian 1991-92, Greater Kansas City Woman of Yr. award 1988, internat. chmn. alumnae programs 1994—). Methodist. Office: Sta WDAF-TV 3030 Summit St Kansas City MO 64108-3312

MCKEAND, PATRICK JOSEPH, newspaper publisher, educator; b. Anderson, Ind., June 10, 1941; s. William Dale and Iva Pearl (Shaw) McK. BA, Ind. U., 1963; MA, Ball State U., 1983. Staff writer The St. Petersburg (Fla.) Times, 1963; mng. editor The Anderson (Ind.) Herald, 1968-79; adminstr. analyst Ind. Medicaid Program, Indpls., 1980-81; assoc. prof. Defense Info. Sch., Ft. Ben Harrison, Ind., 1981-89; owner p.m. ink!, Indpls., 1989—; pub. bd. dirs. Student Pub. at Ind. U., Purdue U. at Indpls., 1992—; bd. dirs. Miss Indpls. Scholarship Pageant, Indpls, 1994—. Capt. U.S. Army, 1964-68. Decorated Bronze Star, Army Commendation medal with 1 Oak leaf cluster. Mem. Soc. Profl. Journalists (bd. dirs., v.p.), Soc. Newspaper Design, Assn. Educators in Journalism and Mass Comm., Associated Press Mng. Editors Assn., Ind. Collegiate Press Assn. (bd. dirs.), Coll. Media Advisors. Home: 4450 E 56th St Indianapolis IN 46220 Office: Sch of Journalism 902 W New York St Indianapolis IN 46202

MCKECHNIE, ED, state legislator; b. July 31, 1963; m. Kristy McKechnie. Kans. state rep. Dist. 3. Mem. Lions. Address: 224 W Jefferson St Pittsburg KS 66762-5140*

MC KEE, GEORGE MOFFITT, JR., civil engineer, consultant; b. Valparaiso, Nebr., Mar. 27, 1924; s. George Moffitt and Iva (Santrock) McK.; student Kans. State Coll. Agr. and Applied Sci., 1942-43, Bowling Green State U., 1943; B.S. in Civil Engring., U. Mich., 1947; m. Mary Lee Taylor, Aug. 11, 1945; children—Michael Craig, Thomas Lee, Mary Kathleen, Marsha Coleen, Charlotte Anne. Draftsman, Jackson Constrn. Co., Colby, Kans., 1945-46; asst. engr. Thomas County, Colby, 1946; engr. Sherman County, Goodland, Kans., 1947-51; salesman Oehlert Tractor & Equipment Co., Colby, 1951-52; owner, operator George M. McKee, Jr., cons. engrs., Colby, 1952-72; sr. v.p. engring. Contract Surety Consultants, Wichita, Kans., 1974—. Adv. rep. Kans. State U., Manhattan, 1957-62; mem. adv. com. N.W. Kans. Area Vocat. Tech. Sch., Goodland, 1967-71. Served with USMCR, 1942-45. Registered profl. civil engr., Kans., Okla., registered land Surveyor, Kans. Mem. Kans. Engring. Soc. (pres. N.W. profl. engrs. chpt. 1962-63, treas. cons. engrs. sect. 1961-63), Kansas County Engr's. Assn. (dist. v.p. 1950-51), N.W. Kans. Hwy. Ofcls. Assn. (sec. 1948-49), Nat. Soc. Profl. Engrs., Kans. State U. Alumni Assn. (pres. Thomas County 1956-57), Am. Legion (Goodland 1st vice comdr. 1948-49), The Alumni Assn. U. Mich. (life), Colby C. of C. (v.p. 1963-64), Goodland Jr. C. of C. (pres. 1951-52). Methodist (chmn. ofcl. bd. 1966-67). Mason (32 deg., Shriner); Order Eastern Star. Home: 8930 Suncrest St # 502 Wichita KS 67212-4069 Office: 6500 W Kellogg Dr Wichita KS 67209-2212

MCKEE, GLENN ALLEN, business owner; b. Detroit, Dec. 6, 1948; s. Kenneth and Lanora C. (Anderson) McK.; m. Charlotte S. Morgan, Feb. 14, 1970 (div. Sept. 1984); children: Kelly, Logan; m. Sandra J. Morse, Aug. 18, 1990; stepchildren: Stephanie Wensmann, Brian Wensmann, Breanna Wensmann. BS in Mgmt., Oakland U., Rochester, Mich., 1974. Sales rep. Burroughs Corp., Troy, Mich., 1974-76; br. mgr. Paychex, Bloomington, Minn., 1976-81; pres., owner Payroll Gen., Bloomington, 1981-87, McKee Investments dba Games By James, Edina, Minn., 1987—. Mem. Burnsville (Minn.) City Coun., 1987—; commr. Minn. Valley Transit Authority, Burnsville, 1991—, Econ. Devel. Authority, Burnsville, 1991—. With U.S. Army, 1970-71. Home: 13508 Knob Hill Rd Burnsville MN 55337 Office: Games By James 3610 W 70th St Edina MN 55420

MCKEE, SUSAN PARK, meeting planner, writer; b. Ill., Nov. 18, 1945. BA, UCLA, 1968; MS, Ind. U., 1974; MA, Purdue U., 1994. Reporter Indpls. Star, 1968-73, fashion editor, 1973-83; meeting planner, freelance writer AGENDA: Indy, Inc., Indpls., 1980—; contbg. editor Indpls. Monthly mag., 1983-88; cons. Ind. U. Ctr. on Philanthropy of Ind. U.-Purdue U., Indpls., 1988, mem. adv. bd. com. Am. Studies. Mem. editl. bd. Indy's Child mag., 1989-94; contbg. editor Indpls. Register, 1995—. Pres. Indpls. Coun. for Internat. Visitors, 1985-89, Ind. Internat. Coun., 1990—; founder, bd. dirs. Internat. Ctr. Indpls., pres. 1976-77. Mem. Am. Coun. Germany, Orgn. Am. Historians, Am. Hist. Assn., Am. Acad. Religion, Am. Studies Assn., Ind. Assn. Historians, Chgo. Area Group Study Religious Cmtys., Soc. Profl. Journalists. Office: AGENDA: Indy Inc PO Box 68466 Indianapolis IN 46268-0466

MCKELVY, NATALIE ANN, writer, novelist, poet; b. Evanston, Ill., Feb. 8, 1950; d. Glen Edward and Alice Adeline (Izmer) DeViney; m. Charles Kenneth McKelvy, Aug. 13, 1977. BA in History, U. Chgo., 1972, MBA, 1980. Real estate specialist Gen. Svcs. Adminstrn./U.S. Govt., Chgo., 1972; mortgage analyst Rhoads-Baxter Inc., Western Springs, Ill., 1972-74; mortgage broker Advance Mortgage Corp., Chgo., 1974-75; real estate analyst Lehndorff Real Estate Investors, Chgo., 1975-76; reporter Pensions and Investment Age Mag., Chgo., 1976-78; fin. reporter Chgo. Tribune, 1978-79; speechwriter U.S. League of Savs. Insts., Chgo., 1980-85; writer McKelvy Communications/Dunery Press, Harbert, Mich., 1985—; speaker on real estate investing, 1984. Author: Pension Fund Investments in Real Estate, 1983, Where's Ours?, 1987, My California Friends: and Other Works, 1988, Party Chicks: and Other Works, 1990 (Quality Paperback book selection 1990), Mona and the Arabs: and Others Works, 1991, Cream Tortes: and Other Works, 1992, The Golden Book of Child Abuse: and Other Works, 1993, Dead Babies: and Other Stories, 1994, Eddie & Mike: and Other Works, 1995, Croz and Ray: and Other Works, 1996; resident playwright Actors & Playwrights Initiative Theater, Kalamazoo, Mich., 1994-95. Recipient award for Fiction Reading, Mich. City (Ind.) Pub. Libr., 1989, Houston Booksellers Assn. Reading Series, Houston, 1989. Home and Office: PO Box 116 Harbert MI 49115-0116

MCKENNA, ANDREW JAMES, paper distribution and printing company executive, baseball club executive; b. Chgo., Sept. 17, 1929; s. Andrew James and Anita (Fruin) McK.; m. Mary Joan Pickett, June 20, 1953; children: Suzanne, Karen, Andrew, William, Joan, Kathleen, Margaret. B.S., U. Notre Dame, 1951; J.D., DePaul U., 1954. Bar: Ill. CEO Schwarz Paper Co. (name now Schwarz), Morton Grove, Ill., 1964—; dir. Chgo. Nat. League Ball Club Inc., Chgo. Bears.; bd. dirs. Dean Foods Co., 1st Nat. Bank Chgo., Skyline Corp., Tribune Co., AON Corp., McDonald's Corp. Chmn. bd. trustees U. Notre Dame, Mus. Sci. & Industry, Chgo.; bd. dirs. Cath. Charities of Chgo., Children's Meml. Med. Ctr. Chgo. Mem. Chgo. Athletic Assn., Econ. Club, Lyric Opera (bd. dirs.), Chgo. Club, Comml. Club, Econs. Club., Execs. Club Chgo. (chmn.), Glenview Golf Club, Old Elm Club, Merit Club, Casino Club, The Island Club. Home: 60 Locust Rd Winnetka IL 60093-3751 Office: Schwarz 8338 Austin Ave Morton Grove IL 60053-3209

MCKENNA, KATHLEEN KWASNIK, artist; b. Detroit, Nov. 6, 1946; d. John J. and Eleanor H. (Ciosek) K.; m. Frank J. McKenna, Jr., Mar. 16, 1968. Cert., Cooper Sch. Art, Cleve., 1973; student, Art Students' League, N.Y.C., 1972, 74. Instr. portrait painting Baycrafters, Bay Village, Ohio, 1976-79; self-employed painter, 1972—. One-person shows include Ctrl. Nat. Bank, Cleve., 1975, Women's City Club Gallery, Cleve., 1979, Kennedy Ctr. Art Gallery, Hiram, Ohio, 1980, Chime Art Gallery, Summit, N.J., 1985, Bolton Art Gallery, Cleve., 1986, 91, Lakeland C.C. Gallery, Kirtland, Ohio, 1996; group shows include Butler Inst. Am. Art, 1981, 89, 91, 93, Mansfield (Ohio) Art Ctr., 1990, Circle Gallery, N.Y.C., 1978, Canton (Ohio) Art Inst., 1990, others. Recipient Pres.'s award Am. Artists Profl. League, 1993, other awards. Mem. New Orgn. for the Visual Arts, Catharine Lorillard Wolfe Art Club (Pastel Soc. plaque 1989, Mae Berlind Bach award 1983, Cert. of Merit 1981), Allied Artists Am. (assoc.; Gold medal of Honor 1989). Roman Catholic. Studio: 15914 Chadbourne Rd Shaker Heights OH 44120

MCKENNA, WILLIAM JOHN, textile products executive; b. N.Y.C., Oct. 11, 1926; s. William T. and Florence (Valis) McK.; m. Jean T. McNulty, Aug. 27, 1949 (dec. Nov. 1984); children: Kevin, Marybeth, Peter, Dawn; m. Karen Lynne Hilgert, Aug. 6, 1988; children: Katherine Lynne, William John IV. BBA, Iona Coll., 1949; M.S. (Univ. Store Service scholar), NYU, 1950. V.p. Hat Corp. Am., N.Y.C., 1961-63, v.p. mktg., 1961-63, exec. v.p., 1963-67; pres. Manhattan Shirt Co., N.Y.C., 1967-74, Lee Co., Inc., Shawnee Mission, Kans., 1974-82, also dir.; pres., dir. Kellwood Co., St. Louis, 1982—, chief exec. officer, 1984—, also bd. dirs., chmn., CEO, 1991—; dir. Genovese Drug Stores, Melville, N.Y., United Mo. Bancshares, Kansas City, Mo., United Mo. Bank of St. Louis, Cardinal Ritter Inst. Trustee St. Louis U., Boys Hope; permanent deacon Archdiocese St. Louis. With USN, 1944-46, PTO. Mem. Sovereign Mil. Order Malta, St. Louis Club, Bellerive Country Club. Roman Catholic. Office: Kellwood Co PO Box 14374 Saint Louis MO 63178-4374

MCKENNA, WILLIAM P., state legislator; b. St. Louis, Aug. 29, 1946. BS, S.E. Mo. State U.; postgrad., St. Louis U. In constrn. field, Barnhart, Mo.; mem. Mo. Ho. of Reps., Jefferson City, 1983-93, Mo. Senate, Jefferson City, 1993—. Democrat. Home: 6969 Dipple Ln Barnhart MO 63012-1410*

MCKENNON, KEITH ROBERT, chemical company executive; b. Condon, Oreg., Dec. 25, 1933; s. Russel M. and Lois E. (Edgerton) McK.; m. Patricia Dragon, Sept. 30, 1961; children: Brian, Marc, Kevin. B.S., Oreg. State U., 1955. Rsch. chemist Dow Chem. Co., Pittsburg, Calif., 1955-67; sales mgr. Dow Chem. Co., Houston, 1967; research mgr. Dow Chem. Co., Midland,

Mich., 1968-69, bus. mgr., 1969-80, v.p., 1980-83, group v.p., 1983-87, exec. v.p., 1987-92, also bd. dirs.; pres. Dow USA, 1987-90; chmn., chief exec. officer Dow Corning Corp., 1992-94, also bd. dirs.; chmn. PacifiCorp, Portland, Oreg., 1994—; bd. dirs. PacifiCorp, Tektronix. Patentee. Recipient Chemical Industry medal Soc. of Chemical Industry, 1994. Republican. Presbyterian. Home: PO Box 5542 Stateline NV 89449-5542 Office: PacifiCorp Ste 1600 700 NE Multnomah St Portland OR 97232-4116

MCKENZIE, ANDREW, union administrator; b. Oct. 23, 1937; m. Dorothy Marsh, July 19, 1964; 1 child, Andre'. Framer Fenwick Fashion, St. Louis, 1957-62; from organizer to exec. sec. Local 160, St. Louis, 1962—; exec. mgr., chmn. Midwest Joint Bd., St. Louis, 1978-89, mgr., chmn., 1989-92; pres. Internat. Health & Welfare, St. Louis, 1992—; v.p. exec. coun. AFL-CIO. Active Calvary Missionary Bapt. Ch., Cardinal Ritter H.S. Prep. With U.S. Air Force, 1952-56. Baptist. Office: Internat Leather Goods Un 300 S Grand Blvd Ste 241 Saint Louis MO 63103

MCKENZIE, CAROLYN CALDWELL (CARRIE), telecommunications executive; b. Milw., Mar. 25, 1964; d. Arno Arthur Schubert Jr. and Susan Ann (Graaskamp) Martin; m. Daniel Lee McKenzie, May 10, 1962; children: Alison Leigh, Connor Caldwell. BA, Marquette U., 1986. Devel. assoc., auction coord. KNCT-TV 46, Killeen, Tex., 1986-87; account exec. Cellular One/McCaw Comm., Temple, Tex., 1987-90; indirect sales team leader Cellular One/McCaw Comm., Temple, 1990-91; retail mktg. specialist Cellular One/Bell South, Milw., 1991-94; team leader Cellular One/Bell South, Sheboygan, Wis., 1994; retail merchandising supr. Cellular One/Bell South, Waukesha, Wis., 1994-96; sales mgr. retail accts. PrimeCo. Personal Comms., Milw., 1996—; publicity chairperson Ft. Hood (Tex.) Officer's Wives' Club, 1986-87. Mem. Planned Parenthood of Wis., Milw., 1992—; choir mem., publicity coord. St. Sebastian Ch., Milw., 1992—; mem. Roosevelt PTA, Wauwatosa, Wis., 1992—. Roman Catholic. Home: 2421 N 67th St Wauwatosa WI 53213-1440 Office: PrimeCo Personal Comm 700 W Virginia St Ste 300 Milwaukee WI 53204

MCKENZIE, TERRY P., systems engineer; b. Dayton, Ohio, Nov. 10, 1951. Machinist/engr. Cardinal Tools, Englewood, Ohio, 1974-87; systems engr. Process Equip. Co., Tipp City, Ohio, 1988—; cons. in field. Jehovah Witness. Office: Process Equip 4191 US Route 40 Tipp City OH 45371-9283

MCKEOWN, MARY ELIZABETH, educational administrator, medical office manager; d. Raymond Edmund and Alice (Fitzgerald) McNamara; BS, U. Chgo., 1946; MS, DePaul U., 1953; m. James Edward McKeown, Aug. 6, 1955. Supr. high sch. dept. Am. Sch., 1948-68, prin., 1968—, trustee, 1975—, v.p., 1979, exec. v.p., 1992—. Mem. ASCD, LWV, Nat. Assn. Secondary Sch. Prins., North Cen. Assn. Colls. and Schs. (exec. bd. 1990-93). Assn., Nat. Home Study Coun. (chairperson rsch. and edn. com. 1988-93). Author study guides for algebra, geometry and calculus. Home: 5120 Deblin Ln Oak Lawn IL 60453 Office: 2200 E 170th St Lansing IL 60438

MCKERNAN, JOHN B., sales executive; b. Detroit, Jan. 23, 1949. BA, Ea. Mich. U., 1976. Sr. acct. exec. Xerox Corp., Southfield, Mich., 1975-80; regional sales dir. Elexsis, Inc., Livonia, Mich., 1980—. Mem. PTA. Served to sgt. USAF, 1970-73. Republican. Roman Catholic.

MCKERNAN, LEO JOSEPH, manufacturing company executive; b. Phila., Feb. 17, 1938; s. Leo Joseph and Mary (Dever) McK. Student, Iona Coll., 1956-59, NYU, 1961-62, U. Bridgeport, 1962-64. With Eaton Corp., Carol Stream, Ill., 1959-74, mgr. mfg. Controls div., 1974; v.p., gen. mgr. Axle div. Clark Equipment Co., Buchanan, Mich., 1974-77, group v.p., 1977-83, sr. v.p., then exec. v.p., then chief oper. officer, 1983-86; pres., chief exec. officer Clark Equipment Co., South Bend, Ind., 1986—, chmn., 1988—, also bd. dirs.; mem. supervisory bd. VME Group N.V.; bd. dirs. 1st Source Corp., Lincoln Nat. Corp., Nat. Assn. Mfrs. Bd. dirs. St. Joseph Community Found., Ind.; mem. U. Notre Dame Engrng. Adv. Coun., 1985—, corp. grants com., 1988—.

MCKIM, SAMUEL JOHN, III, lawyer; b. Pitts., Dec. 31, 1938; s. Samuel John and Harriet Frieda (Roehl) McK.; children: David Hunt, Andrew John; m. Eugenia A. Leverich. AA cum laude, Port Huron Jr. Coll., 1959; BA cum laude, U. Mich., 1961, JD cum laude, U. Mich., 1964. Bar: Mich. 1965, U.S. Dist. Ct. (so. dist.) Mich. 1965, U.S. Ct. Appeals (6th cir.) 1969, U.S. Supreme Ct., 1994. Assoc. Miller, Canfield, Paddock and Stone, P.L.C., Detroit, Bloomfield Hills, Howell, Kalamazoo, Lansing, Monroe, Traverse City and Grand Rapids, Mich., Washington, N.Y.C., Pensacola, St. Petersburg, Fla., Gdansk, Warsaw, Poland, 1964-71, sr. mem., 1971—, head state and local tax sect., 1985—, chmn. tax dept., 1989-94, mng. ptnr., 1979-85, chmn., mng. ptnr., 1984-85; mem. tax coun. State Bar Mich., 1981-84, chmn. state and local tax com. real property sect., 1982-90; adj. prof. law sch. Wayne State U., 1993—. Bd. dirs., past chmn. Goodwill Industries of Greater Detroit, 1970—; dir. Goodwill Industries Found., 1982-95; elder Presbyn. ch., Stevens min.; coun. mem. at large Detroit area coun. Boy Scouts Am., 1987—. Fellow Am. Coll. Tax Counselors; mem. ABA, Mich. Bar Assn., Detroit Bar Assn., Detroit Club, Barrister's Soc., Ostego Ski Club, Port Huron Golf Club, Order of Coif, Phi Delta Phi. Assoc. editor Mich. Law Rev. Home: 32778 Friar Tuck Ln Beverly Hills MI 48025 Office: Miller Canfield Paddock & Stone 150 W Jefferson Ave Ste 2500 Detroit MI 48226-4415

MCKINLEY, CAMILLE DOMBROWSKI, psychologist; b. Buffalo, May 6, 1922; d. Eugene Anthony and Anne Victoria (Sliwinska) Dombrowski; m. Thomas Leroy Smith, Dec. 30, 1944 (div. 1977); children: Thomas Dan, Cynthia Camille (dec.), Pamela Susan; m. William Frank McKinley, Oct. 7, 1984 (dec. Mar. 1985). BA, Syracuse U., 1943; MA, Boston U., 1947; edn. specialist, Mich. State U., 1970, PhD, 1978. Acad. advisor Mich. State U., East Lansing, 1966-70, dir. Career Ctr., 1970-81, counseling psychologist Counseling Ctr., 1981-91; pres. Priam Pubs., 1978—; mem. Career Planning and Placement Coun. Mich. State U., 1970-91. Editor: The Mich. State Univ. Referral Directory, 1970-91, The Gracious Reader, 1970-80; editor, publisher The CAM Report, 1978—. Founding pres. Greater Lansing chpt. Planned Parenthood, Mich., 1967; v.p. Opera Co. of Mid-Mich., 1983-85; bd. dirs. Wharton Ctr. for Performing Arts and Dean's Cmty. Coun., Mich. State U., mem. Platinum Cir. Mem. Mich. State U. Pres.'s Club and Beaumont Tower Soc., Pontiac Yacht Club, Mackinac Island Yacht Club, Zonta Internat., Zeta Tau Alpha. Home: PO Box 1862 East Lansing MI 48826-1862

MCKINLEY, NORMA ELIZABETH, education educator; b. N.Y.C., Jan. 26, 1939; d. Mongor Nobel and Florence Emma (Werner) Anderson; m. Michael Robert McKinley, June 8, 1959; 1 child, Scott Alan. BS in Edn., Ohio U., 1960; MEd, Ashland U., 1978. Cert. elem. educator, Ohio, N.J.; supr., Ohio. Tchr. Johnstown (Ohio)-Monroe Local Schs., 1960-61, Whitehall (Ohio) City Schs., 1961-62, Ashland (Ohio) City Schs., 1962-91; adj. prof. U. Cin., 1978-81; instr. Ashland U., 1987-91, adj. prof., 1991—; cons. law-related edn. Ashland County, chem. awareness. Mem. Athena Study Club, Ashland, Rep. Women's Club, Ashland. Recipient ABA First Pl. Pub. Svc. award for Law Day/Citizenship Project of Ashland City Sch. Dist., 1986, First Pl. award of Ohio Coun. of Econ. Edn., 1985-86, 80-81, Exemplary Juvenile Justice Program award of Ohio Assn. Juvenile Ct. Judges for Ashland City Sch. Dist. Law-Related Edn. Project, 1985, Award of Merit, Ohio State Bar Assn., 1978-79, Am. Lawyers Cert. of Appreciation, 1989; named Jennings scholar, 1974-75. Mem. NEA, AAUP, Ohio Edn. Assn., Ohio Coun. Social Studies, Alpha Delta Kappa. Home: 404 Lake Shore Dr #4 Ashland OH 44805-9200 Office: Ashland U 101 Kates Ctr Ashland OH 44805

MCKINLEY BALFOUR, STEPHANIE ANN, learning resources director, librarian; b. Galesburg, Ill., Mar. 27, 1948; d. William Chester and Virginia Ann (Clugsten) McKinley; m. James Robert Miller, Mar. 2, 1968 (div. Mar. 1978); 1 child, Christopher Antonin Miller; m. David Alan Balfour, Nov. 23, 1991. BA in Speech, Drama, Western Ill. U., 1970; MLS, Drexel U., 1974. Cert. tchr., Ill., media specialist, Ill. Libr. William McKinley Elem. Sch., Phila., 1971-76, Regional Jr. H.S., Amherst, Mass., 1976-77, Garfield Elem. Sch., Monmouth, Ill., 1977-79; dir. learning resources Spoon River Valley Sch. Dist., London Mills, Ill., 1979-95; dir. librs. Spoon River Valley Sch. Dist./Avon Sch. Dist., Ill., 1995—; dir. summer reading program Avon (Ill.) Pub. Libr., 1980-95. Leader 4-H, Avon, 1983-92; vol. EMT Galesburg Hosp. Ambulance Svc., Galesburg/Avon, 1978—; dir. religious edn. Avon Federated Ch., 1984—. Named Outstanding Young Educator by Monmouth Jaycees, 1979. Mem. Am. Found. Vision Awareness Ill. Affiliate (pres.), Nat. Edn. Assn., Ill. Edn. Assn., Ill. Sch. Libr. Media Assn., Phi Delta Kappa, Gamma Lambda-Delta Kappa Gamma Soc. Internat. (pres. 1992-94, 1st v.p. 1990-92, recording sec. 1988-92). Republican. Mem. United Ch. of Christ. Home: RR2 274 Funcheon Ct Avon IL 61415 Office: Spoon River Valley Sch Dist RR 1 London Mills IL 61544-9801

MCKINNEY, DENNIS, state legislator; m. Jean McKinney. Farmer, stockman Coldwater, Kans.; mem. from dist. 108 Kans. State Ho. of Reps., Topeka, 1993—. Address: HC 72 Box 40 Coldwater KS 67029

MCKINNEY, JANET KAY, law librarian; b. Kansas City, Mo., Feb. 15, 1959; d. Charles Durward and Helen Jean (Bost) Freeman; m. Larry Emmett McKinney, July 11, 1981. BA, Avila Coll., 1981; MA in Libr. Sci., U. Mo., 1989. Circulation libr. Midwestern Bapt. Theol. Sem., Kansas City, 1981-84, acquisitions libr., 1984-85, reference libr., 1985-90; environ. divsn. libr. Black & Veatch, Kansas City, 1990-91; acquisitions/serials libr. U. Mo. Leon E. Bloch Law Libr., Kansas City, 1991—. Mem. ALA, Am. Assn. Law Librs. (com. on rels. with info. vendors 1994-96, editl. bd. Tech. Svcs. Law Libr. 1994-96), Mid-Am. Assn. Law Librs. (newsletter adv. mgr. 1993-94), Southwestern Assn. Law Librs., N.Am. Serials Interest Group, Spl. Librs. Assn. (chpt. employment com. chmn. 1990-91, chpt. treas. 1991-94, chpt. pres.-elect 1994-95, chpt. pres. 1995-96). Office: U Mo Kansas City Leon E Bloch Law Libr 5100 Rockhill Rd Kansas City MO 64110-2446

MCKINNEY, SUSAN DAWN, librarian; b. Danville, Ind., Feb. 13, 1965; d. Michael Harold and Janet Kay (Hogue) Conger; m. Donald Eugene McKinney, May 19, 1989; 1 child, Michael Arthur. BA in History, DePauw U., 1987; MLS, U. Ill., 1989. Librarian St. Joseph Twp. (Ill.) Lib., 1990—. Mem. Urbana (Ill.) Assembly of God., 1993—. Mem. Ill. Libr. Assn., Order of the Amaranth, White Shrine of Jerusalem (Noble Shepherdess 1994-95, Worthy Chaplain 1996—), Order of the Eastern Star (conductress, 1994-95, assoc. matron 1995-96), St. Joseph C. of C. (sec.). Republican. Home: Box 1012 304 E Sherman Saint Joseph IL 61873 Office: St Joseph Twp Libr Box 259 201 N Third St Saint Joseph IL 61873

MCKINNEY-KELLER, MARGARET FRANCES, retired special education educator; b. Houston, Mo., Nov. 25, 1929; d. George Weimer and Thelma May (Davis) Van Pelt; m. Roy Calvin McKinney Sr., Nov. 11, 1947 (dec. Feb. 1990); children: Deanna Kay Little, Roy Calvin Jr.; m. Clarence Elmore Keller, June 8, 1991; 1 child, Dennis Lee Keller. BS with honors, Bradley U., 1963, MA in Counselor Edn., 1968, postgrad., 1992; postgrad., U. Ill., 1993—, Aurora Coll., Ill. Ctrl. Coll. In real estate Peoria, Ill., 1951-57; tchr. Oak Ridge Sch., Willow Springs, Mo., 1947-48, pvt. kindergarten, Washington, Ill., 1957-59, Dist. 50 Schs., Washington, Ill., 1959-67; tchr. socially maladjusted Washington Twp. Spl. Edn. Coop., 1967-70; tchr. behavior disordered Tazewell-Mason Counties Spl. Edn., Washington, Ill., 1970-78; resource tchr. Dist. 50 Schs., Washington, 1978-94; ret., 1994. Cons. moderator Active Parenting Group, Washington, 1972—; adv. bd. to establish Tazewell County Health Dept., 1960s; pres. gov. bd. Faith Luth. Day Care Ctr., Washington, 1970—, Washington Sr. Citizens, 1982-91; coach Spl. Olympics, Washington, 1979—; pres. Faith Luth. Ch. Coun., Washington, 1985-86; laity v.p. No. Conf. Evang. Luth. Ch. Am., Ctrl. Ill., 1986-92; vol. Proctor Hosp., 1994—. Mem. AAUW, Washington Bus. and Profl. Women (pres. 1979-80, 88-89, dist. 9 dir. 1995-96), Am. Legion Aux., German-Am. Soc., Alpha Delta Kappa (state office, ctrl. region). Home: 603 Sherwood Park Rd Washington IL 61571-1828

MCKINSEY, THOMAS MICHAEL, philosopher, educator; b. Fayette, Mo., Aug. 19, 1941; s. John Paul and Clarice Kathryn (Stark) McK.; m. Pamela Elaine Sears, July 5, 1969; children: Daniel Nicholas, Gabriel Lawrence. BA, So. Meth. U., 1963; MA, Kans. State U., 1966; PhD, Ind. U., 1976. Instr. philosophy Ohio U., Chillicothe, 1972-75; asst. prof. philosophy Wayne State U., Detroit, 1976-82, assoc. prof., 1982-91, chair dept. philosophy, 1987-91, prof., 1991—; lectr. philosophy Moscow State U., 1991-92. Contbr. articles to Philos. Rev., Midwest Studies in Philosophy, Philos. Studies, Philos. Perspectives, others. NEH summer stipend awardee, 1980; ACLS fellow, 1982-83; Fulbright grantee, 1991-92. Mem. AAUP, Am. Philos. Assn. Democrat.

MCKNIGHT, SUSAN COLEMAN, dean, academic director; b. St. Louis, June 22, 1960; d. John Joseph and Ruth Bee (Coleman) McK. BA, Washington U., St. Louis, 1982, JD, 1985. Bar: Mo. 1985. Paralegal studies program coord. Sanford-Brown Coll., Hazelwood, Mo., 1990-93, dean instruction, 1992-93; dir. br. campus Fontbonne Coll., St. Louis, 1994-95; campus dir. Sanford-Brown Coll., 1995—. Mem. Bar Assn. Met. St. Louis. Democrat. Home: 1332 NE Parvin Rd # 104 Kansas City MO 64116

MCKOWEN, DOROTHY KEETON, librarian; b. Bonne Terre, Mo., Oct. 5, 1948; d. John Richard and Dorothy (Spoonhour) Keeton; m. Paul Edwin McKowen, Dec. 19, 1970; children: Richard James, Mark David. BS, Pacific Christian Coll., 1970; MLS, U. So. Calif., 1973; MA in English, Purdue U., 1985, postgrad., 1991—. Libr.-specialist Doheny Libr., U. So. Calif., L.A., 1973-74; asst. libr. Pacific Christian Coll., 1974-78; serials cataloger Purdue Univ. Librs., 1978-88; head children's and young adult svcs. Kokomo-Howard County Pub. Libr. (Ind.), 1988-89, coord. children's and tech. svcs., 1989-91; cataloger, network libr. Ind. Coop. Libr. Svcs. Authority, 1991—; vice chairperson Christian Edn. Com., Brady Lane Ch. of Christ, 1986-87, chairperson, 1987-88, pianist, 1978—, adult Sunday Sch. tchr., 1989—, choir dir., 1990—, organist, 1992—; bd. dirs. Good Shepherd Learning Ctr., 1990—, vice-chairperson, 1991-92, chairperson, 1992-94; bd. dirs. Purdue Christian Campus House, 1985-90, v.p., 1986-88, pres., 1988-90. Mem. ALA, Modern Lang. Assn., Soc. Early Americanists, Assn. for Libr. Collections and Tech. Svcs. (bd. dirs. 1986-90, 95—, vice chairperson, chairperson elect coun. of regional groups 1986-88, chairperson 1988-90, conf. program com. 1986-88, internat. rels. com. 1986-88, micropub. com., 1986-87, subject analysis com., subcom. to rev. Dewey 621.38, 1987, membership com. 1988-90, libr. resources and tech. svcs. editorial bd. 1988-90, planning and rsch. com. 1988-90, planning com. 1990-91, program initiatives com. 1991-93, chairperson 1991-93, orgn. and bylaws com. 1991-92), Ind. Libr. Fedn. (vice chmn. tech. svcs. div. 1983-84, chmn. 1984-85), Ohio Valley Group Tech. Svcs. Librs. (vice chmn. 1984-85, chmn. 1985-86). Republican. Home: 7625 Summit Ln Lafayette IN 47905-9729 Office: INCOLSA 6202 Morenci Trail Indianapolis IN 46268-2536

MCKOWN, LESLIE HENRY, minister; b. Shoals, Ind., May 7, 1934; s. Edgar Monroe and Mary Elizabeth (Eicholz) McK.; m. Martha Ann Powell, June 22, 1957; children: Karen Marie, Liana Jane. BA, U. Evansville, 1954; S.T.B., Boston U., 1957, MA, 1959; D of Ministry, Christian Theol. Sem., 1984. Ordained deacon United Meth. Ch., 1955, elder, 1957. Pastor Nashville Meth. Ch., 1959-62, Mitchell (Ind.) Meth. Ch., 1962-65, Blue Grass United Meth. Ch., Evansville, Ind., 1965-70, Gatun Union Ch., Panama Canal Zone, 1970-72, Grace United Meth. Ch., Terre Haute, Ind., 1972-76, New Life United Meth. Ch., Shelbyville, Ind., 1976-79, Owensville (Ind.) United Meth. Ch., 1979-86, Johnson United Meth. Ch., New Harmony, Ind., 1986-89, First United Meth. Ch., Petersburg, Ind., 1989—; chairperson South Ind. Conf. Divsn. of Global Ministries, 1978-86, Evansville Area Coun. Schs. Bd. Edn., 1967-70; coord. Vols. in Mission, 1991—; v.p. Intersharing North Ctrl. Jurisdiction of United Meth. Ch., 1988-96. Mem. Mayor's Com. on Housing, Evansville, 1968; bd. dirs. Vigo County Community Action Program, Terre Haute, 1974-76, pres., 1975-76. Methodist. Office: First United Meth Ch PO Box 81 Petersburg IN 47567-0081

MCKOWN, RICHARD DALE, sales and marketing executive; b. Columbia City, Ind., Apr. 2, 1947; s. Ralph O. and Itha J. McK.; m. Dawn Marie Nunes; 1 child, Kelley L. BS in Bus. Mgmt. and Adminstrn. with dist., Ind. U., Ft. Wayne, 1971; MS in Bus. Adminstrn., St. Francis Coll., Ft. Wayne, 1978. Cert. trade specialist. Sales coord., job analyst, wage/salary adminstr., pers. mgr. Sun Metal Products, Inc., Warsaw, Ind., 1971-76; gen. mgr. Hamelin Industries, Inc. (formerly SunCrest, Inc.), Warsaw, Ind., 1976-79; exec. v.p., gen. mgr. Lyall Internat., Inc., Kendallville, Ind., 1980; internat. account exec., dir. internat. sales, product mgr. Flint & Walling and Am. Dryer divsn. Masco, Inc., Detroit, 1980-84; v.p. sales and mktg., sales mgr. Sun Metal Products, Inc., 1984-93; dir. bus. devel. Persons-Majestic Mfg. Co., Monroeville, Ohio, 1994—; Am. agt. Sturmey-Archer Ltd. (U.K.). Served in Vietnam, 1966-68. Mem. Cycle Parts Accessories Assn. (pres.), Mensa.

MCLAREN, RICHARD WELLINGTON, JR., lawyer; b. Cin., May 15, 1945; s. Richard Wellington and Edith (Gillett) McL.; m. Ann Lynn Zachrich, Sept. 4, 1971; children: Christine, Richard, Charles. BA, Yale U., 1967; JD, Northwestern U., 1973. Bar: Ohio 1973, U.S. Dist. Ct. (no. dist.) Ohio, 1973, U.S. Ct. Appeals (6th cir.) 1978, U.S. Supreme Ct. 1981. Assoc. Squire, Sanders & Dempsey, Cleve., 1973-82, ptnr., 1983-87; prin., counsel Ernst & Whinney, Cleve., 1988-89; assoc. gen. counsel Ernst & Young, 1989-93; prin. counsel Centerior Energy Corp., 1994—. 1st lt. U.S. Army, 1967-70. Mem. ABA (litigation and corp. law), Am. Judicature Soc., Ohio Bar Assn., Def. Rsch. Inst., Cleve. Athletic Club. Home: 20 River Stone Dr Chagrin Falls OH 44022-1142 Office: Centerior Energy Corp 6200 Oak Tree Blvd Independence OH 44131

MCLARNEY, CHARLES PATRICK, lawyer; b. Hemple, Mo., Mar. 28, 1942; s. Charles Joseph and Owatonna Mary (Sayles) McL.; m. Martina Borkowski, Aug. 28, 1965; children: Ellen, Megan, Michael. BS, St. Benedict's Coll., 1964; JD, U. Mo., 1968. Bar: Mo. 1968, U.S. Dist. Ct. (we. dist.) Mo. 1968, U.S. Ct. Appeals (8th cir.), U.S. Supreme Ct. 1968. Assoc. Shook, Hardy & Bacon, Kansas City, Mo., 1968-72, ptnr., 1972-93, mng. ptnr., 1985-88, 91—; shareholder, pres. Shook, Hardy & Bacon, P.C., Kansas City, 1993-96; mng. ptnr. Shook, Hardy & Bacon L.L.P., Kansas City, 1996—. Active Friends of Art, Kans. City, 1980—. Fellow Internat. Soc. Barristers (bd. dirs. 1989-94), Am. Coll. Trial Lawyers; mem. Kansas City Met. Bar, Lawyers Assn. Kansas City (pres. 1987-88), Mo. Bar (bd. govs., bd. dirs. 1991-94), Kansas City Soc. Fellows, Eight Twenty-Two Club, Kansas City Club, Plaza Bus. Breakfast Club (pres. 1983-84). Democrat. Roman Catholic. Office: Shook Hardy & Bacon PC 1200 Main St Ste 2200 Kansas City MO 64105-2100

MCLAUGHLIN, CHARLES HUGH, JR., technolgy educator; b. Providence, Aug. 29, 1956; s. Charles Hugh and Marguerite Mary (Mourningham) McL.; Belinda Ann Mummert, Nov. 4, 1989; children: Meaghan Elizabeth, Charles Hugh III. BS, R.I. Coll., 1978, MEd, 1984; PhD, U. Md., 1991. Indsl. arts tchr. Providence Sch. Dept., 1978-84; grad. asst. R.I. Coll., Providence, 1983-84; grad. asst. U. Md., Coll. Park, 1985-86, rsch. asst., 1984-85, instr., 1986-90; asst. prof. Ball State U., Muncie, Ind., 1990—; cons. Pub. Svc. Ind., Indpls., 1993-94; curriculum devel. ITT Edn. Svcs., Indpls., 1991; curriculum cons. Md. State Dept. Higher Edn., Annapolis, 1989-90. Contbr. articles to profl. jours. Eisenhower Math./Sci. grantee Ind. Commn. Higher Edn., Indpls., 1991, 92, 95. Mem. Internat. Tech. Edn. Assn. (chair spl. events com., 1995—), N.Am. Assn. Environ. Edn., Ind. Math. Sci. Tech. Edn. Alliance, Coun. Tech. Edn., Phi Delta Kappa (2nd v.p. 1995-96). Home: 8405 Lone Beech Dr Muncie IN 47304 Office: Ball State U Dept Industry & Tech Muncie IN 47306-0255

MCLAUGHLIN, DEBORAH ANN, public relations and marketing executive; b. Hoisington, Kans., Nov. 12, 1952; d. Kenneth Theodore and Mildred Marie (Steiner) Siebert; m. Donald Raymond McLaughlin, July 17, 1976; 1 child, Kalla Dawn. AS, Barton County Coll., Great Bend, Kans., 1972; BS, Kans. State U., 1975. News editor Great Bend Tribune, 1975-76; deposition indexer Turner & Boisseau, Great Bend, 1976-77; feature editor Mid-Kans. Ruralist, Hoisington, 1977-78; copywriter, audio-editor Advt. Assocs., Great Bend, 1978-79; photographer, sales mgr. Clay Ward Color Portraits, Great Bend, 1979-80; news editor, photographer St. John (Kans.) News, 1980-83; freelance writer, photographer Great Bend, 1984-85; pres., owner McLaughlin Pub. Rels. Agy., Great Bend, 1985-87; owner Cen. Kans. Sunrise mag., Great Bend, 1987-88, Creative Mktg. Svcs., Great Bend, 1988—; dir. pub. info. Unified Sch. Dist. 428, Great Bend, 1991-93. Editor Ellinwood Leader, 1995—; contbr. articles and photographs to various publs. Mem. Coalition for Prevention Child Abuse, Great Bend, 1986-87; mem. 75th anniversary com. Kansas State U. Coll. Journalism and Mass Communications, Manhattan, 1986. Mem. Kans. State U. Alumni Assn. Roman Catholic. Home and Office: 381 Grove Ter Great Bend KS 67530-9710

MCLAUGHLIN, STANLEY A., JR., travel company executive; b. Jersey City, Mar. 7, 1943; s. Stanley A. and Virginia (Lesnevich) Mc.; m. Silvia Marlene Stessl, July 30, 1966; children: Mark, Matthew. BS, U.S. Mil. Acad., West Point, N.Y., 1964; postgrad., U. Mich., 1969-70. Travel dir. Maritz Travel Co., Fenton, Mo., 1971-72; travel account exec. Maritz Travel Co., 1972-73; account mgr. Maritz Motivation Co., Detroit, 1973-78; v.p. and regional mgr. Maritz Motivation Co., Detroit, Dallas, 1979-86; corp. v.p. and area mktg. mgr. Maritz Motivation Co., Fenton, 1987-91; exec. v.p. Maritz Travel Co., Fenton, 1991-94; corp. v.p., dir. bus. devel. divsn. Maritz Performance Improvement Co., Southfield, Mich., 1994-95, corp. v.p., dir. corp. devel., 1995—. Bd. dirs. West Point Soc. North Tex., Dallas, 1986, Vietnam Meml. Orgn. of Tex.,Dallas, 1987, Boys Club of St. Louis, 1992. Capt. U.S. Army, 1964-70, Vietnam. Home: 5 Vaughan Crossing Bloomfield Hills MI 48304 Office: Maritz Performance Improve 1000 Town Ctr Ste 1200 Southfield MI 48075

MCLAWHON, RONALD WILLIAM, pathology educator, biochemist; b. Chgo., Sept. 10, 1957; s. William Columbus and Esther Shirley (Bukowski) McL. AB in Biol. Scis., U. Chgo., 1979, MS in Biochemistry, 1980, PhD in Biochemistry, 1982; MD, Rush Med. Coll., 1986. Diplomate Am. Bd. Pathology. Rsch. assoc. pediat. Joseph P. Kennedy Jr. Mental Retardation Rsch. Ctr., Chgo.; rsch. assoc. pediatrics U. Chgo. Pritzker Sch. Medicine, 1982-83; resident in pathology Rush-Presbyn.-St. Luke's Med. Ctr., Chgo., 1986-87, pathologist, 1987-88; instr. Rush Med. Coll., Chgo., 1986-87, asst. prof., 1987-88; resident in pathology U. Chgo. Med. Ctr., 1988-90; asst. prof. U. Chgo. Pritzker Sch. Medicine, 1990-96, prof., 1996—; dir. clin. chemistry, attending physician U. Chgo. Med. Ctr., 1990—. Contbr. articles to Jour. Biol. Chemistry, Molecular Pharmacology, Jour. Neurochemistry, Jour. Membrane Biology, Procs. of NAS. U.S. Pub. Health Predoctoral fellow NIH, 1981-82; James B. Herrick scholar Rush Med. Coll., 1986-87; recipient Young Investigator award Acad. Clin. Lab. Physicians and Scientists, 1990. Mem. AAAS, Am. Soc. for Biochemistry and Molecular Biology, Am. Soc. for Cell Biology, Am. Assn. Pathologists, Coll. Am. Pathologists, Am. Soc. Clin. Pathologists, Sigma Xi. Office: U Chgo Pritzker Sch Medicine Dept Pathology 5841 S Maryland Ave MC 0004 Chicago IL 60637-1470

MCLEAN, GARY NEIL, educator, management consultant; b. Sarnia, Ont., Can., Nov. 25, 1942; came to U.S., 1965; s. Leslie Neil and Minnie Irene (Robbins) McL.; m. Lynn Jensen Harvey, June 23, 1968; children: Katherine, Laird, Melissa, Paul, Cynthia, Brian. AA in Commerce, Graceland Coll., Lamoni, Iowa, 1961; BA in Bus. Admin./Secretarial Studies, U. Western Ont., London, Can., 1964; MA, Columbia U., 1965, EdD, 1971; MDiv. in Theology, United Theol. Sem., 1983. Instr. bus. adminstrn. and secretarial studies Quinsigamond C.C., Worcester, Mass., 1965-67; project dir. CUNY, 1967-69; instr. Coumbia U., 1968-69; asst. prof. U. Minn., Mpls., 1969-72, assoc. prof., 1972-81; prof., coord. human resource devel. U. Minn., St. Paul, 1981—, head bus. and mktg. edn., 1990-92, coord. adult edn., 1995—; pres. CompuKeys, St. Paul, 1985-90; ind. cons., St. Paul, 1970—; assoc. editor Human Resource Devel. Quar., San Francisco, 1989-93, editor, 1993—; cons. and exec. editor Jour. Edn. for Bus., Washington, 1984—. Author: (with others) Workplace Success: General Business, 1991, Electronic Keyboarding, 1992, Comprehensive Word Processing: A Complete Program in Machine Transcription, 1994; author, editor: (with others) Practicing Organization Development: A Guide for Consultants, 1995; editor: (with others) Performance Appraisal: Perspectives on a Quality Management Approach, 1990, The Role of Organization Development in Quality Management and Productivity Improvement, 1988; editor: Korean Philately, 1995—; mem. editl. bd., chair Jour. Vocat. Edn. Rsch., 1978-81; contbr. articles to profl. jours. Bd. dirs. Block Nurses Program, Inc., St. Paul, 1986-89; pastor Reorganized Ch. of Jesus Christ of Latter Day Saints, Apple Valley and No. St. Paul. Recipient Robert E. Slaughter award McGraw-Hill Co., 1975, Outstanding Vol. of Yr. award Planned Parenthood Minn., 1983, Horace T. Morse-Amoco Found. award for Outstanding Contbns. to Undergrad. Edn., U. Minn., 1986. Mem. ASTD (rsch. com. 1993—), Minn. Bus. Educators (pres.-elect 1974-76, pres. 1976-77, past pres. 1977-78, Outstanding Postsecondary Bus. Educator award 1986), North Ctrl.

Bus. Edn. Assn. (exec. bd. dirs. 1974-76), Minn. Vocat. Assn. (exec. bd. dirs. 1975-77), Minn. Coun. for Gifted and Talented (sec., bd. dirs. 1980-81), Acad. Human Resource Devel. (bd. dirs. 1994-96), Korea Stamp Soc. (bd. dirs. 1995—), Clan McLean Minn. (asst. commr. 1992-96, commr. 1996—). Office: U Minn 1954 Buford Ave Saint Paul MN 55108-6196

MCLEAN, LARRY R., biochemist; b. Detroit, Aug. 21, 1954; s. Raymond D. and June A. (Matthews) McL.; m. Wendy E. Crandall, Aug. 13, 1977; children: Elizabeth, Shannon, Joshua. BS, Mich. State U., 1976; PhD, Med. Coll. Pa., Phila., 1981. Postdoctoral fellow Royal Free Hosp. Sch. Medicine, London, 1981-82, U. Cin., 1982-85; scientist Hoechst Marion Roussel, Cin., 1985—. Contbr. articles to profl. jours. Med. Coll. Pa. Rsch. fellow, 1978; NATO fellow, 1981, Muscular Dystrophy Assn. fellow, 1982; NIH Postdoctoral fellow, 1982; recipient Alumnae citation Med. Coll. Pa., 1990. Mem. Biophys. Soc., Am. Soc. Biochemistry and Molecular Biology, Am. Heart Assn., Nat. Sci. Tchrs. Assn. Office: Hoechst Marion Roussel 2110 E Galbraith Rd Cincinnati OH 45237-1625

MCLENDON, JESSE LAWRENCE, protective services official; b. Kansas City, Mo., Aug. 6, 1950; s. Jessie Lewis and Sara (Boyd) McL.; m. Jean Creason Wilhelm, Sept. 24, 1982. AAS in Criminal Justice Adminstrn., Maple Wood C.C., 1984; BS in Criminal Justice Adminstrn. summa cum laude, Park Coll., 1988, BS in Pub. Adminstrn. summa cum laude, 1988, M in Pub. Affairs with honors, 1993; grad., FBI Nat. Acad., 1993. Cert. police officer Mo. Dept. Pub. Safety, P.O.S.T. tng. instr. U. Mo.'s Law Enforcement Tng. Inst., 1991—. Chief communications officer Dept. Police, Riverside, Mo., 1969-70; patrolman Dept. Police, Lake Waukomis, Mo., 1971-72; corporal Dept. Police, Platte Woods, Mo., 1970-72; patrolman Dept. Police, North Kansas City, Mo., 1972-76, detective, 1976-86, sgt., 1986-90; lt., comdr. support svcs. divsn., 1990-92; capt., comdr. investigation divsn. Dept. Police, North Kansas City, 1992-94, maj., asst. chief of police, comdr. patrol divsn., 1994—; instr. tng., outreach program Kansas City Regional Acad., 1985-86, North Kansas City Police Res. Unit, 1977-78; grad. Ctrl. States Law Enforcement Exec. Devel. seminar FBI, 1995; adj. instr. criminal justice adminstrn. and pub. adminstrn. Park Coll., 1988—; investigator Clay County Med. Examiner, Liberty, Mo., 1976-90, Kansas City Major Case Squad, 1976—, Clay County Prosecutor's Office, Liberty, 1976-87. Recipient Valor award Met. Chiefs and Sheriffs, 1978, 83, Profl. Svc. award North Kansas City Kiwanis, 1984; named Outstanding Law Enforcement Officer, So. Clay County Jaycees, 1977. Mem. ASPA, Am. Criminal Justice Assn., Internat. Assn. Chiefs of Police, Mo. Soc. for Pub. Adminstrn., FBI Nat. Acad. Assocs., Internat. Assn. Identification (Mo. divsn.), Mo. Peace Officers Assn., Am. Soc. Law Enforcement Trainers, Mo. Profl. Photographers Assn., Delta Tau Kappa. Democrat. Episcopalian. Home: 3613 N Wabash Ave Kansas City MO 64116-2882 Office: North Kansas City Police Dept 2010 Howell St Kansas City MO 64116-3526

MCLENNAN, ROBERT GORDON, management company executive; b. Chgo., Aug. 13, 1943; s. Robert G. and Grace (Anderson) McL.; m. Rebecca Ann Martin, Aug. 14, 1965; children: Robert Martin, Douglas Andrew. BA, Cornell Coll., 1965; JD, U. Ill., 1968. Bar: Ill. 1968. Atty. Amoco Oil Co., Chgo., 1968-70; ptnr. McLennan Co., Park Ridge, Ill., 1970-81; pres. Beacon Mgmt. Co. (formerly, Legacy Mgmt. Corp.), Ill., 1981—; chmn. bd. dirs. Plainsbank of Ill., Des Plaines. Chmn. bd. dirs., chmn. exec. com. Advocate Health Care, Oak Brook, Ill., 1988—; trustee Village of Glenview, Ill.; chmn. caucus Glenview Elem. Sch., 1972-73. Mem. Chief Execs'. Org., World Pres.'s Org., Chgo. Pres.'s Org.

MCLEOD, BRUCE M., sports association executive; b. Fort Frances, ON, Canada; m. Sande Halstad; children: Leah, Shannon. Grad., U. Minn., Duluth. Commr. Western Collegiate Hockey Assn., 1994—. Office: Western Colligate Hockey Assoc 10 University Dr Duluth MN 55812

MCLEOD, PHILIP ROBERT, publishing executive; b. Winnipeg, Man., Can., May 4, 1943; s. Donald G. and Phyllis (Brown) McL.; m. Cheryl Amy Stewart, Sept. 25, 1965 (div. 1992); children: Shawn Robert, Erin Dawn; m. Virginia Mary Corner, Nov. 6, 1992. Journalist Bowes Pub., Grande Prairie, Alta Truro, N.S., 1962-76; journalist, dep. mng. editor Toronto (Ont., Can.) Star, 1976-87; editor-in-chief London (Ont.) Free Press, 1987—. Southam fellow Southam Newspapers, 1970. Mem. The London Club. Office: The London Free Press, 369 York St, London, ON Canada N6A 4G1

MCLEVIE, JOHN GILWELL, education educator; b. Masterton, Wairarapa, N.Z., Nov. 2, 1929; came to U.S., 1968.; s. Edward Mitchell and Gwendoline Mary (Faire) McL.; m. Elaine Marianne Foote, May 7, 1955; children: Anne, Karen, Lynne. BA in History, Victoria U., Wellington, N.Z., 1955, MA in Edn., 1957; PhD in Edn., Mich. State U., 1970. Tchr. Rongotai Coll., Wellington, 1953-57; tchr., housemaster Alexandra Grammar Sch, Singapore, 1958-63; lectr. U. Hong Kong, 1963-68; chief of party Calif. Brazil Project, Brasilia, 1973-76; prof. edn. San Diego State U., 1970-84, chmn. dept., 1978-84; assoc. dean U. Houston-Clear Lake, 1984-89; cons. Calif. Commn. on Tchr. Credentialing, Sacramento, 1989-94; prof. edn. No. Ill. U., DeKalb, 1994-96; dir. Ctr. for Grad. Study Nat. U., San Diego, 1996—; integration analyst San Diego Unified Sch. Dist., 1980-81. Contbr. articles to profl. jours. Mem. Assn. for Tchr. Educators (past pres. State of Calif. chpt.), Phi Delta Kappa (Leadership award 1981, Educator of Yr. award 1988). Episcopalian. Home: 2936 Cacatua St Carlsbad CA 92009

MCLIN, NATHANIEL, JR., civic worker; b. Chgo., June 19, 1928; s. Nathaniel and Anna (Polk) McL.; m. Lena Mae, July 18, 1952; children—Nathaniel Gerald, Beverly Jane. Student Wilson Jr. Coll., Chgo., 1946-50, Roosevelt U., 1950-52; M.A. Govs. State U.; postgrad. (fellow), Walden U., 1976. Technician, Michael Reese Hosp., 1951-52, U. Chgo. Goldblatt Clinic, 1952-53; bus driver Chgo. Transit Authority, 1953-64; pub. relations dir. Opera Theater of Chgo., 1959-60; mgr. McLin Opera Co., Chgo., 1960-71; salesman Watkins Products Co., 1964-65; tchr. Chgo. Com. on Urban Opportunity, 1965-71; soloist Park Dist. Opera Guild, Chgo., 1964-68; creator, developer All Souls Universalist Childrens Theatre and Opera Workshop, 1986; dir. Centarus II Prodn. Co. Active Beatrice Caffrey Found., Chgo.; soloist Trinity United Ch. Mens Chorus, Chgo., 1962-66; active fund raising campaign pub. rels. YMCA, 1963-64; cultural coord., dir. Halsted Urban Progress ctr., Chgo., 1966-71; dir. Faces of Crime Symposium All Souls Ch., Chgo., also lay leader, 1980—; establisher Far South Opera Guild Pullman Presbyn. Ch., Chgo, 1991; creator The Pullman Opera, 1992; parole supr. State of Ill., ret. 1993; active combined arts program Centarus II and Pullman Presby. Ch. Pullman Roseland Cultural Complex, 1988. Served with U.S. Army, 1946-47. Recipient Wheelers Social Club citation for efforts in nations cultural devel., 1962; named one of Outstanding Civic Leaders Am., 1967. Lodge: Fraternal Order of Police (pres. lodge 83 1980-81). Author: Parole: The Ex-offender's Last Hope, 1983; creator, developer The Monthly Cultural Series, 1988—. Home and Office: 7630 S Hoyne Ave Chicago IL 60620-5737

MCLIN, RHINE LANA, state legislator, funeral service executive, educator; b. Dayton, Ohio, Oct. 3, 1948; d. C. Josef, Jr., and Bernice (Cottman) McL. B.A. in Sociology, Parsons Coll., 1969; M.Ed., Xavier U., Cin., 1972; postgrad. in law U. Dayton, 1974-76, AA in Mortuary Sci., Cin. Coll., 1988. Lic. funeral dir.; cert. tchr., Ohio. Tchr. Dayton Bd. Edn., 1970-72; divorce counselor Domestic Relations Ct., Dayton, 1972-73; law clk. Montgomery Common Pleas Ct., Dayton, 1973-74; v.p., dir., embalmer McLin Funeral Homes, Dayton, 1972—; instr. Central State U., Wilberforce, Ohio, 1982—; mem. Ohio Ho. of Reps., 1988-94; state senator Ohio State Senate, 1994—. com. mem. Human Svcs. and Aging Com., Agrl. Com., Hwys. and Transp. Com., Energy, Natural Resources and Environ. Com. Mem. Democratic Voters League, Dayton, Dem. Nat. Com.; mem. inspection com. V.C. Correctional Instn. Mem. Nat. Funeral Dirs. Assn., Ohio Funeral Dirs. Assn., Montgomery County Hist. Soc., NAACP (life), Nat. Council Negro Women (life), Delta Sigma Theta. Home: 1130 Germantown St Dayton OH 45408-1465 Office: Ohio State Senate State House Columbus OH 43215

MCLINDEN, JAMES HUGH, molecular biologist; b. Marion, Kans., July 29, 1949; s. James Edward and Lenora Ann (Waner) McL. BA with honors, Emporia State U., 1971; PhD, U. Kans., 1983. Postdoctoral rsch. asst. biology Ohio State U., Columbus, 1983-87; sr. scientist Am. Biogenic Scis., Inc., Notre Dame, Ind., 1987-89, dir. molecular biology, 1989-91, v.p. molecular biology, 1991—. Author: (with others) Viral Hepatitis, 1990; contbr. articles to Jour. Virology, CRC Critical Revs. in Biotech., Biochem.-Biophysica ACTA, Applied and Environ. Microbiology. Mem. AAAS, Am. Soc. Microbiology, Am. Soc. Virology, N.Y. Acad. Sci., Soc. Indsl. Microbiology, Beta Beta Beta. Home: 4232 Hickory Rd Apt 3A Mishawaka IN 46545-2581 Office: Am Biogenetic Scis Inc 1539 N Ironwood Dr South Bend IN 46635

MCLUCKIE, STEVE, state legislator; b. Midland, Mich., July 17, 1956; s. Robert Frost and Gladys (Wilson) McL.; married. BSW cum laude, Western Mich. U., 1978. Field rep. Mo. Fedn. Tchrs., 1985—; mem. Mo. Ho. of Reps., Jefferson City, 1993—. Bd. dirs. Mo. Citizen Action, 1981—, Com. for County Progress, 1988—, Kansas City Progress, 1989—; former mem. transition team for Marsha Murphy for County Exec.; Mo. labor coord. Mondale for Pres., 1984. Democrat. Home: 9738 Shepards Dr Kansas City MO 64131*

MCMAHAN, GALE ANN SCIVALLY, school system administrator; b. Anna, Ill., Oct. 19, 1946; d. George Oliver and Jessie Lee (Johnson) Scivally; m. Joe Henry McMahan, Dec. 14, 1963; children: Randy Scott, Joseph Paul. BS, So. Ill. U., 1971, MS, 1974, PhD, 1994. Cert. tchr., supr., adminstr., Ill. Resource tchr. Jonesboro (Ill.) Sch. Dist. 43, 1971-73, dir. early intervention, 1991-94; resource tchr. Anna Sch. Dist. 37, 1973-94; supt. Lick Creek Sch. Dist. 16, Buncombe, Ill., 1994-95, Vienna (Ill.) Pub. Sch. Dist. 55, 1995—; lectr. Shawnee C.C., Ullin, Ill., 1986-88, So. Ill. U., Carbondale, 1990, 92, 93; reader U. Ill. Bd. Edn., Springfield, 1989, 92; mem. adv. bd. for early intervention Anna Interagy. Coun., 1991—, Ill. Interagy. Coun., Springfield, 1991—; mem. peer monitor spl. edn. dept. Ill. Bd. Edn., 1993—, mem. monitoring team for tchr. preparation programs; mem. content adv. com. Ill. Cert. Testing Sys., 1994—. Co-author: (video) Jenny...Our Child of Today!, 1991; editor: Churches in Clear Creek Association, 1988. Recipient Those Who Excel in Edn. award of recognition Ill. Bd. Edn., 1992, grantee, 1990—. Mem. Coun. Exceptional Children (presenter 1991), Ill. Supt. Assn., Ill. Prin. Assn., Ill. Women Adminstrs., Anna Elem. Edn. Assn. (pres. 1992-94), DAR, Delta Kappa Gamma (scholar 1989-90, co-contbr. article to Bull. 1993), Phi Kappa Phi, Kappa Delta Phi, Phi Delta Kappa. Baptist. Home: 4890 State Rte 146 E Anna IL 62906

MCMAHON, PHYLLIS OLIVER, physical therapist; b. Culver, Kans., Mar. 29, 1926; d. George Macklin Oliver and Bessie Mabel Rarig; m. Thomas E. McMahon, June 10, 1950; children: Gregory, Timothy, Samuel, Paul. BS in Physical Therapy, Kansas U., 1948. Registered physical therapist. Physical therapist Dixon and Dively Orthopedic Clinic, Kansas City, Mo., 1948-50, Midwest Rehab., Kansas City, Mo., 1982-86, Phonex-Hudson, Overland Pk., Kans., 1983-88; pvt. practice physical therapy Topeka, 1971-96. Mem. Am. Physical Therapy Assn. (legis. chmn. Kans. chpt. 1972-78). Republican. Presbyterian. Home & Office: 5600 SW 23rd St Topeka KS 66614-1730

MCMANAMAN, KENNETH CHARLES, lawyer; b. Fairfield, Calif., Jan. 25, 1950; s. Charles James and Frances J. (Holys) McM.; m. Carol Ann Wilson, Apr. 15, 1972; children: Evan John, Kinsey Bridget, Kierin Rose. BA cum laude, S.E. Mo. State U., 1972; JD, U. Mo., Kansas City, 1974; grad. Naval Justice Sch., Newport, RI., 1975; MS in Bus. Mgmt. summa cum laude, Troy State U., Montgomery, Ala., 1978. Bar: Mo. 1975, Fla. 1976, U.S. Dist. Ct. (we. dist.) Mo. 1975, U.S. Dist. Ct. (ea. Dist.) Mo. 1978, Fla. 1976, U.S. Dist. Ct. (no., mid. dists.) Fla. 1976, U.S. Ct. Mil. Appeals 1977, U.S. Ct. Appeals (5th, 8th cirs.) 1977, U.S. Supreme Ct. 1978, D.C. 1991; cert. mil. judge. Ptnr. firm O'Loughlin, O'Loughlin & McManaman, Cape Girardeau, Mo., 1978—; prof. bus. law Troy State U., Ala., 1976-78; prof. bus. law S.E. Mo. State U., Cape Girardeau, 1978-84; instr. Mo. Dept. Pub. Safety, S.E. Mo. Regional Law Enforcement Tng. Acad., 1979—, Cape Girardeau Police Res., 1983-93; mcpl. judge City of Jackson, Mo., 1980-89, 94—; spl. mcpl. judge City of Cape Girardeau, 1981-89; atty. Ct. Apptd. Spl. Advs./Guardians in Ct. for Children, 1994—; spl. mcpl. judge City of Fredricktown, Mo., 1995. Mem. Cape Girardeau County Coun. on Child Abuse, 1980-89; membership dir. S.E. Mo. Scouting coun. Boy Scouts Am., 1980-82; mem. Cape Girardeau County Mental Health Assn., 1982-92; active local and state Dem. Party, del. Nat. Dem. Conv., San Francisco, 1984, chmn. County Dem. Com., 1984-86; mem. 8th Congl. Dist. Dem. Com., 1984-86, 27th State Dem. Senatorial Com., 1984-86, ward committeeman, 1984-94; bd. dirs. Area wide Task Force on Drug and Alcohol Abuse, 1984-87; sponsor drug edn./prevention program in schs.; bd. dirs. Cape County chpt. Nat. Kidney Found, 1988-93; pres. Jackson Area Soccer Assn., 1987-93. Capt. JAGC, USNR, 1994—. Recipient Robert Chilton award City of Jackson for leadership, integrity, and responsibility, 1995—; named One of Outstanding Young Men of Am. 1981, 82, 84, 85. Mem. ABA (Mo. del. for young lawyers div. 1982-83)., Mo. Bar Assn. (chmn. trial advocacy task force 1982, psychology and the law task force 1983), Mo. Bar (young lawyers sect. council, rep. dist. 13, 1980-85), Fla. Bar Assn., Kansas City Bar Assn., Assn. Trial Lawyers Am., Fed. Bar Assn., Nat. Coll. Dist. Attys., Cape Girardeau County Bar Assn. (founder, pres. young lawyers sect. 1981-82), Naval Res. Assn. (v.p. Southeast Mo.-So. Ill. chpt. 1980-85), S.E. Mo. State U. Alumni Coun., Sigma Chi (numerous awards), Sigma Tau Delta, Pi Delta Epsilon. Roman Catholic. Home: 400 Oak Forest Dr Jackson MO 63755-3504 Office: O'Loughlin O'Loughlin McManaman 1736 N Kingshighway St Cape Girardeau MO 63701-2122

MCMANUS, GEORGE ALVIN, JR., state senator, cherry farmer; b. Traverse City, Mich., Dec. 12, 1930; s. George Alvin and Frieda Anna (Fromholz) McM.; m. Clara Belle Kratochvil, Aug. 16, 1949; children: Eliza J. Saints, Molly S. Agostinelli, Margaret L. Egelus, Kathleen E. Nurohammed, Kerry E. Canellos, George A., John K., Bridgett E. Popp, Matthew R. BS, Mich. State U., 1952, MS, 1953. Fruit grower pvt. practice, Traverse City, Mich., 1953—; coop. extension agt. Mich. State U., 1956-82; senator Mich. State Senate, Lansing, Mich., 1991—. Trustee Northwestern Mich. Coll., Traverse City, 1970-90; pres. Traverse City C.of C., 1982, Traverse City Rotary, 1993. Named Citizen of Yr. Traverse City C. of C., 1984. Mem. KC, Elks Club, Rotary Club. Republican. Roman Catholic. Office: Mich State Senate 605 Farnum Bldg Lansing MI 48913

MCMANUS, JANE H., reporter; b. Würzberg, Germany, Nov. 6, 1955; came to U.S., 1956; d. John Thomas and Ann (Thompson) Hackett; m. Gregg Mauzy McManus, Oct. 6, 1989. A, Colby-Sawyer Coll., New London, 1975; BS, Colgate U., Hamilton, 1977. Admissions counselor Franklin Coll., Franklin, Ind., 1979-89; bank officer Bank One, Indianapolis, 1979-89; reporter Evansville Press, Evansville, Ind., 1995—.

MCMANUS, MARTIN JOSEPH, lawyer, priest; b. Toledo, Mar. 24, 1919; s. Martin Joseph and Elizabeth Marie (McDermott) McM. AB, John Carroll U., 1939; LLB, Georgetown U., 1942; LLM, U. So. Calif., 1946; D in Juridical Sci., NYU, 1961; B in Canon Law, Cath. U. Am., 1964; Licentiate in Canon Law, D in Canon Law, The Pontifical Univ. Lateran, 1965; Licentiate in Sacred Theology, The Pontifical Univ. Urbanianum, 1966; DST, The Pontifical Univ. Angelicum, 1967. Bar: Calif. 1947, U.S. Supreme Ct. 1960; ordained priest Roman Cath. Ch., 1959. Pvt. practice L.A., 1947-54; prof. law Southwestern U., L.A., 1947-57; prof. law U. San Diego, 1959-63, dean Law Sch., 1960-63; atty.-advisor U.S. Govt., Washington, 1977-82; counsel to bishop 2d Vatican Coun., Rome, 1962-65; advisor, cons. Republican Nat. Com., Washington, 1968-73; adminstrv. law judge HHS, Southfield, Mich., 1982—.

MCMICHAEL, JEANE CASEY, real estate corporation executive; b. Clarksville, Ind., May 7, 1938; d. Emmett Ward and Carrie Evelyn (Leonard) Casey; m. Norman Kenneth Wenzler, Sept. 12, 1956 (div. 1968); m. Wilburn Arnold McMichael, June 20, 1978. Student Ind. U. Extension Ctr., Bellermine Coll., 1972-73, Ind. U. S.E., 1973—, Kentuckiana Metroversity, 1981—; Grad. Realtors Inst., Ind. U., 1982; grad. Leadership Tng., Clark County, Ind.; lic. real estate broker, Ind., Ky.; master Grad. Realtors Inst., Cert. Residential Specialist, Cert. Real Estate Broker, Leadership Tng. Grad. Owner, pres. McMichael Real Estate, Inc., Jeffersonville, 1979-88, 90-96; mgr., owner Buzz Bauer Realtors, Clark County, 1989-91; mng. broker Parks & Weisberg Realtors, Jeffersonville, Ind., 1989-91; instr. pre-license real estate Ivy Tech. State Coll., 1995-96, real estate Tng. Concepts, Inc. Pres. of congregation St. Mark's United Ch. of Christ, 1996, pres., Mr. and Mrs. Class, chmn., fin. trustee and bus. adv., chmn. devel. com., 1993, 94; chmn. bd. trustees, Brooklawn Youth Svcs., 1988-94, chmn. 1994-95; chmn. social com. Rep. party Clark County (Ind.); v.p. Floyd County Habitat for Humanity, 1991, 94/95. Recipient cert. of appreciation Nat. Ctr. Citizen Involvement, 1983; award Contact Kentuckiana Teleministries, 1978. Mem. Nat. Assn. Realtors (nat. dir. 1989—), Ind. Assn. Realtors (state dir. 1987—, quick start speaker 1989-91), Nat. Women's Council Realtors (state pres., chmn. coms., state rec. sec., 1984, state pres. 1985-86, Nat. Achievement award 1982, 83, 84, 85, 86, 87, 88, 89, 90, nat. gov. Ind. 1987, v.p. region III 1988, Ind. Honor Realtor award 1982—), Women's Council of Realtors (speaker 1990-94, Mem. of Yr. 1988), Ky. Real Estate Exchange, So. Ind. Bd. Realtors (program chmn. 1986-87, bd. dirs., pres., 1988—, Realtor of Yr. 1985, instr. success series, 1989-92, Snyder Svc. award 1987, Omega Tau Rho award 1988, Excellence in Edn. award 1989), Ind. Assn. Realtors (state dir. 1985—, bd. govs., instr./trainer, speaker 1989-94, chair bd. govs. 1991), Toastmasters (pres. Steamboat chpt.), Psi Iota Xi. Office: McMichael Real Estate Inc 1402 Blackiston Mill Rd Jeffersonville IN 47129-1227 Address: 23 Arctic Springs Rd Jeffersonville IN 47130

MCMILLAN, HUGH HOPKINS, environmental engineer; b. Chgo., Dec. 23, 1936. BSEE, Valparaiso U., 1962. Registered profl. engr., Ill., 1967. Gen. supt. Metro Sanitary Dist., 1962-83; v.p. Paschen Contractors, Chgo., 1983-87, M&O Environ., East Hazel Crest, Ill., 1992-95, Hydrodynamics, Inc., LaGrange, Ill., 1994-95; gen. supt. Metro Water Reclamation Dist., Chgo., 1995—; cons. Glenview, Ill., 1987-92. With U.S. Army, 1954-57. Mem. IEEE, WEF, IWEA, Am. Acad. Environ. Engrs., Am. Legion. Office: Met Water Reclamation Dist 100 E Erie St Chicago IL 60611

MCMILLAN, JAMES, popcorn company executive; b. Chgo., Aug. 13, 1929; s. James and Coretta (Kemp) McM.; m. LaNore Vanda Reynolds, July 13, 1952; children: Joseph, Steven, Douglas. BS, Roosevelt U., 1974; MS in Edn., Chgo. State U., 1975. Cert. tchr., Ill. Photo offset supr. Remco Sporting Goods, Inc., Chgo., 1957-59; supr. hotel graphics Morrison Hotel, Chgo., 1959-64; supr. graphics Sheridan-Peter Pan Studios, Chgo., 1964-69; dir. graphics and prodn. Bostrom Trade Mgmt. Corp., Chgo., 1969-71; v.p. Harry Franklin Sch. Photographers, Chgo., 1971-73; sales rep. ITT, Chgo., 191973-74; merchandiser Braun N.Am., Boston, 1974-75; edn. adminstr. Ill. Dept. Corrections, Joliet, 1977-87; pres. Mrs. Mac's Popcorn Shop Ltd., Chgo., 1987—; co-founder, The Insider prison newspaper; mem. grad. assistanceship Chgo. State U.; gen. contractor, Chgo. Bus. mgr., Marquette Ave. Block Club, 1979-81; nominee local sch. coun. With USN, 1944-46, PTO. Mem. So. Chgo. C. of C. (bd. dirs. 1990—, v.p. 1992), Graphic Arts Tchrs. Assn. (sec.-treas. 1984-85), Ill. Vocat. Assn. (sch. community rep.), Ill. Assn. for Advancement Black Ams. in Vocat. Edn., Ill. Correctional Assn., Epsilon Pi Tau. Democrat. Office: Mrs Mac Popcorn Shop Ltd 2906 E 83rd St Chicago IL 60617-2133

MCMILLAN, KENNETH GORDON, farm organization executive; b. Macomb, Ill., Sept. 7, 1942; s. Keith Edward and Opal Leone (Dimmitt) McM. BS in Agriculture, U. Ill., 1967, MS in Agrl. Econs., 1969, postgrad., 1975. Nat. pres. Future Farmers Am., Washington, 1962-63; asst. dir. legislation Ill. Farm Bur., Bloomington, 1968-70, asst. to pres., 1970-72; confidential asst. U.S. Sec. Agr., Washington, 1972; spl. asst. U.S. Congressman L.C. Arends, Washington, 1973; chief speech writer U.S. Sec. Agr., Washington, 1973-74; state senator 47th Dist. Ill., 1977-83; asst. prof. polit. economy and commerce Monmouth (Ill.) Coll., 1989-94; corp. sec., asst. to pres. Ill. Farm Bur., Bloomington, 1994—; dir., past pres. Ill. Agrl. Leadership Found., Macomb, 1980-93; dir. Ill. Tax Found., Springfield, 1984-93; v.p. Nat. Suffolk Sheep Assn., Columbia, Mo., 1978-90; pres. Bushnell (Ill.) Econ. Devel. Corp., 1986-94. Candidate for Ill. Congress, 1982, 84; trustee Wesley Found., United Meth. Ch., U. Ill., Urbana, 1968-78. Mem. Rotary (dir. 1975-94). Republican. Home: PO Box 5100 Bloomington IL 61702 Office: Ill Farm Bur Box 2901 Bloomington IL 61702

MC MILLAN, R(OBERT) BRUCE, museum executive, anthropologist; b. Springfield, Mo., Dec. 3, 1937; s. George Glassey and Winnie Mae (Booth) McM.; m. Virginia Kay Moore, Sept. 30, 1961; children: Robert Gregory, Michael David, Lynn Kathryn. B.S. in Edn, S.W. Mo. State U., 1960; M.A. in Anthropology, U. Mo., Columbia, 1963; Ph.D. in Anthropology (NSF fellow), U. Colo., Boulder, 1971. Rsch. assoc. in archaeology U. Mo., 1963-65, 68-69; assoc. curator anthropology Ill. State Mus., Springfield, 1969-72; curator anthropology Ill. State Mus., 1972-73, asst. mus. dir., 1973-76, mus. dir., 1977—; exec. sec. Ill. State Mus. Soc., 1977—; lectr. in anthropology Northwestern U., 1973; bd. dirs. Found. Ill. Archaeology, 1978-83. Editor: (with W. Raymond Wood) Prehistoric Man and His Environments, 1976. Mem. Ill. Spl. Events Commn., 1977-79, program chmn., 1977-78; commr. Ill. and Mich. Canal Nat. Heritage Corridor Commn., 1988—. NSF grantee, 1971, 72, 80; Nat. Endowment for Humanities grantee, 1978. Fellow AAAS, Am. Anthrop. Assn.; mem. Am. Assn. Mus. (council 1982-86), Midwest Mus. Conf. (pres.), Soc. Am. Archaeology, Current Anthropology (asso.), Am. Quaternary Assn., Sigma Xi. Office: Ill State Mus Spring and Edwards Sts Springfield IL 62706 also: Dickson Mounds Museum Lewistown IL 61542

MCMILLIAN, THEODORE, federal judge; b. St. Louis, Jan. 28, 1919; m. Minnie E. Foster, Dec. 8, 1941. BS, Lincoln U., 1941, HHD (hon.), 1981; LLD, St. Louis U., 1949; HHD (hon.), U. Mo., St. Louis, 1978. Mem. firm Lynch & McMillian, St. Louis, 1949-53; asst. circuit atty. City of St. Louis, 1953-56; judge U.S. Ct. Appeals (8th cir.), 1978—; judge Circuit Ct. for City St. Louis, 1956-72, Mo. Ct. Appeals eastern div., 1972-78; asso. prof. adminstrn. justice U. Mo., St. Louis, 1970—; asso. prof. Webster Coll. Grad. Program, 1977; mem. faculty Nat. Coll. Juvenile Justice, U. Nev., 1972—. Served to 1st lt. Signal Corps U.S. Army, 1942-46. Recipient Alumni Merit award St. Louis U., 1965, ACLU Civil Liberties award, 1995, Disting. Lawyer award Bar Assn. Met. St. Louis, 1996. Mem. Am. Judicature Soc., Am. Bd. Trial Advs. (hon. diplomate), Lawyers Assn. Mo., Mound City Bar Assn., Phi Beta Kappa, Alpha Sigma Nu. Office: US Ct Appeals 8th Circuit 526 US Ct & Custom House 1114 Market St Saint Louis MO 63101-2043

MCMILLIN, MOLLY ODIORNE, reporter; b. Wichita, Kans., May 17, 1955; d. Harold E. and Viola (Freitag) Odiorne; m. Michael L. McMillin, Jan. 11, 1974; children: Scott, Ashley, Andrew. BA in Comms., Wichita State U., 1994. Mng. editor Kans. Bus. Report, Topeka, 1993; reporter Wichita Bus. Jour., 1994, Wichita Eagle, 1995—. Recipient 2nd and 3rd place awards Kans. Press Assn., 1994. Mem. Soc. Profl. Journalists (1st place in-depth reporting award 1994), Women in Comms. (past pres. 1993-94). Home: 1334 W 30th St Wichita KS 67217 Office: Wichita Eagle 825 E Douglas Wichita KS 67202

MCMINN, VIRGINIA ANN, human resources consulting company executive; b. Champaign, Ill., Apr. 7, 1948; d. Richard Henry and Esther Lucille (Ellis) Taylor; m. Michael Lee McMinn, Dec. 29, 1973. BA in Teaching of English, U. Ill., 1969; MS in Indsl. Rels., Loyola U., Chgo., 1985. Pers. sec. Solo Cup Co., Urbana, Ill., 1972-74; pers. asst. Rust-Oleum Corp., Evanston, Ill., 1974-75, asst. pers. mgr., 1974-80; mgr. employee rels. Rust-Oleum Corp., Vernon Hills, Ill., 1980-81, mgr. human resources, 1981-84; dir. human resources Field Container Corp., Elk Grove Village, Ill., 1984-87; regional mgr. human resources Hartford Ins. Corp., Chgo., 1987-90; owner, pres. McMinn & Assocs., Ltd., Palatine, Ill., 1988—; founder S.W. Human Resources Group, Chandler, Ariz., 1995; instr. bus. and mgmt. divsn. Trinity Coll., Deerfield, Ill., 1984-85; instr. bus. and social scis. Harper Coll., Palatine, Ill., 1990-93; bd. dirs. Nierman's Hard-To-Find Sizes Shoes, Chgo.; spkr. on legal issues, terminations, employment at will, career planning, job search, and human resources function to area colls., industry and profl. and women's groups. Bd. dirs. Ill. Crossroads coun. Girls Scouts USA, Elk Grove, 1988-92; mem. Ill. Com. to Implement Clean Indoor Air Act, Chgo., 1990-91; past mem. adv. bd. Coll. of Lake County, 1982-84. Mem. Soc. for Human Resource Mgmt., Nat. Network Sales Profls. (program chmn. 1990-93), Women in Mgmt. (chpt. Leadership award corp. category, past pres.), Palatine C. of C., Rotary Club Palatine. Office: 1423 Michele Dr Palatine IL 60067-5656

MCMINN, WILLIAM LOWELL, JR., engineer; b. Wilmington, N.C., Apr. 1, 1943; s. William Lowell McMinn Sr. and Elma Dell (Jordan) Higgins; m. Dorothy Ellen Kochert, Apr. 26, 1967; children: Jeffery Allan, Lori Ellen. Grad. high sch., Peru, Ind. Registered profl. engr., 1966. Locomotive engr. C.S.X. Transp., Riverdale, Ill., 1963—. Mem. Main St. United Meth. Ch., Peru. Mem. Brotherhood Locomotive Engrs. (sec. Peru chpt. 1977—, treas. 1991—), Peru Male Chorus, Elks, Moose. Home: 439 Riverview Rd Peru IN 46970-3122

MCMORROW, MARY ANN G., judge; b. Chgo., Jan. 16, 1930; m. Emmett J. McMorrow, May 5, 1962; 1 dau., Mary Ann. Student Rosary Coll., 1948-50; J.D., Loyola U., 1953. Bar: Ill. 1953, U.S. Dist. Ct. (no. dist.) Ill. 1960, U.S. Supreme Ct. 1976. Atty. Riordan & Linklater Law Offices, Chgo., 1954-56; asst. state's atty. Cook County, Chgo., 1956-63; sole practice, Chgo., 1963-76; judge of Cir. Ct. Cook County, 1976-85, Ill. Appellate Ct., 1985-92, Supreme Ct. Ill., 1992—. Contbr. articles to profl. jours. Faculty adv. Nat. Jud. Coll., U. Nev., 1984. Mem. Chgo. Bar Assn., Ill. State Bar Assn., Women's Bar Assn. of Ill. (pres. 1975-76, bd. dirs. 1970-78), Am. Judicature Soc., Northwestern U. Assocs., Ill. Judges Assn., Nat. Assn. Women Judges, Advocates Soc., Cath. Lawyers Guild (bd. dirs. 1980—), Northwest Suburban Bar Assn., West Suburban Bar Assn., Loyola Law Alumni Assn. (bd. govs. 1985—), Ill. Judges Assn. (bd. dirs.), Cath. Lawyers Guild (v.p.), The Law Club of the City of Chgo., Inns of Ct. Office: Supreme Ct of Ill 160 N La Salle St Chicago IL 60601-3103

MCMULLEN, DAVID WAYNE, education educator; b. Canton, Ill., Apr. 6, 1957; s. Earl Eugene and Juanita Elaine (Estep) McM.; m. Faye Anne Whitaker, Mar. 28, 1981; 1 child, James Earl. BS, Bradley U., 1980, MS, 1984; PhD, U. Ill., 1989. Cert. sec. tchr., Ill. Tchr. 7th and 8th grade sci. Bartonville (Ill.) Grade Sch., 1980-83; grad. asst./instr. U. Ill., Urbana, 1985-89; instr. Bradley U., Peoria, Ill., 1987-89, assoc. prof. tchr. edn., 1989-95; dir. Ctr. Rsch. and Svc. Coll. Edn. and Health Scis. Bradley U., Peoria, 1995—; instr. gifted program Bradley U. Inst. for Gifted and Talented Youth, Peoria, summers 1984, 85, 88—; computer cons. MicroComputer Cons., Morton, Ill., 1984-85; instr. Computer Terminal, Peoria, 1984; system operator Free Ednl. Electronic Mail, Peoria, 1991—. Author computer software: Science Fair Success, 1984. Sec. bd. Common Place, Peoria, 1992. Mem. ASCD, Assn. Computing Machinery, Assn. Advancement Computing Edn., Internat. Soc. for Tech. in Edn., Phi Delta Kappa, Phi Kappa Phi, Phi Alpha Theta. Mem. Christian Ch. (Disciples of Christ). Office: Bradley Univ 208 Westlake Hall Peoria IL 61625

MCMUNN, ALAN STUART, business executive, artist; b. Kittaning, Pa., Feb. 25, 1948; s. Raymond Stuart and Gladys Elenore (Porter) McM.; m. Linda Jean Grey, Oct. 21, 1949 (div. June 12, 1972); m. Pamela E. Goellnitz, June 27, 1966. A in Bus., Am. Inst. Commerce, 1992. Enlisted USN, 1966, ret., 1976; owner McMunn Trucking, L.A., 1976-79; warehouse mgr. Carter Sexton, North Hollywood, Calif., 1979-83; office mgr. Stanton Constrn., North Hollywood, Calif., 1983-85; pres. McMunn and Co., Davenport, Iowa, 1986—. Mem. Oxford Club. Republican. Presbyterian. Office: McMunn and Co PO Box 2056 Davenport IA 52809

MCNALLY, ANDREW, IV, publishing executive; b. Chgo., Nov. 11, 1939; s. Andrew and Margaret C. (MacMillin) McN.; m. Jeanine Sanchez, July 3, 1966; children: Andrew, Carrie, Ward. BA, U. N.C., 1963; MBA, U. Chgo., 1969. Bus. mgr. edn. divsn. Rand McNally & Co., Chgo., 1967-70, exec. v.p., sec., 1970-74, pres., 1974—, CEO, 1978—, also chmn. bd. dirs., 1993—; bd. dirs. Mercury Fin. Inc., Hubbell Inc., Morgan Stanley Funds, Zenith Electronics Corp., Allendale Ins., Borg Warner Securities Corp. Trustee Newberry Libr.; bd. dirs. Children's Meml. Hosp.; active vis. com. of libr. U. Chgo. With Air Force N.G., 1963-69. Mem. Chgo. Club, Saddle and Cycle Club, Commonwealth Club, Glen View Golf Club, Links (N.Y.C.). Office: Rand McNally & Co 8255 Central Park Ave Skokie IL 60076-2908

MCNAMARA, ANN DOWD, medical technologist; b. Detroit, Oct. 17, 1924; d. Frank Raymond and Frances Mae (Ayling) Sullivan; m. Thomas Stephen Dowd, Apr. 23, 1949 (dec. 1980); children: Cynthia Dowd Restuccia, Kevin Thomas Dowd; m. Robert Abbott McNamara, June 15, 1985. BS Wayne State U., 1947. Med. technologist Woman's Hosp. (now Hutzel Hosp.), Detroit, 1946-52, St. James Clin. Lab., Detroit, 1960-62; supr. histo-pathology lab. Hutzel Hosp., Detroit, 1962-72, Mt. Carmel Mercy Hosp., 1972-87, ret., 1987; docent Domino's Ctr. for Architecture & Design, Ann Arbor, Mich., 1988. Mem. Am. Soc. Clin. Pathologists, Am. Soc. Med. Technology, Mich. Soc. Med. Tech., Nat. Soc. Histotechnology, Mich. Soc. Histotechnologists, Wayne State U. Alumni Assn., Smithsonian Assocs., Detroit Inst. Arts Founders Soc. Home: 29231 Oak Point Dr Farmington Hills MI 48331-2774

MCNAMARA, DAVID JOSEPH, financial and tax planning executive; b. Osceola, Iowa, Feb. 6, 1951; s. Loras Emmett and Nadine Evelyn (DeLancey) McN.; m. Ruth Ellen Hanken, Oct. 4, 1974; children: Benjamin, Shawna, Heather. BGS, U. Iowa, 1974. Cert. fin. planner Coll. Fin. Planning, 1985; registered prin. Nat. Assn. Securities Dealers. Pres. The Planners, 1985—; ptnr. VF Realty Ptnrs., West Des Moines, Iowa, 1987—. Mem. Internat. Assn. Fin. Planners (bd. dirs. Iowa chpt. 1984-85). Republican.

MCNAMEE, JAMES MICHAEL, police officer; b. Chgo., May 8, 1957; s. Graham Fritzgerald and Catherine Mary (Quirk) McN.; m. Denise Ann Discannio, Oct. 27, 1990. Counselor Maryville Acad., Des Plaines, Ill., 1978-79; police officer Village of Barrington (Ill.), 1979-82, 83—; dep. sheriff Los Angeles County, L.A., 1982-83; pres. Barrington Police Pension Bd. Co-author: Illinois Police Pension Handbook, 1988. Dem. committeeman Kane County, 1985, McHenry County, 1990. With U.S. Army, 1974-76. Recipient Creative Excellence award Internat. Found. of Employee Benefit Plans, 1994. Mem. Ill. Police Pension Fund Assn. (pres. 1985—), Nat. Fire and Police Pension Fund Assn. (bd. dirs. 1993—), Barrington Police Benevolent Assn. (v.p. 1989—), Am. Legion, Fraternal Order of Police. Roman Catholic. Office: Ill Police Pension Fund Assn 800 Lee St Ste 3 Des Plaines IL 60016

MCNEAL, PALMER CRAIG, governmental consultant; b. Columbus, Ohio, July 3, 1950; s. James E. and Carmella (DiPietro) McN.; m. Barcy Francis McNeal, May 10, 1991. BS in Polit. Sci., Ohio State U., 1973; MS in Adminstrn., Ctrl. Mich. U., 1988. County recorder Franklin County, Columbus, 1981-85, country auditor, 1985-92; pres. J. Kensington Grey & Co., Inc., Columbus, 1992—, Ohio Govtl. Svcs., Columbus, 1992—. Elected committeeman Rep. Ctrl. Com., Columbus, 1982-91; chmn. Ohio League Young Reps., Ohio, 1982-83; bd. trustees Internat. Visitors Coun., Columbus, 1987-92, Columbus Coun. on World Affairs, 1988-92. Lt. col. U.S. Army, 1973—. Mem. Am. Acad. Polit. Sci., Columbus Met. Club (mem. membership com. 1995—), Ohio Delta Co. (bd. trustees, advisor), Capital Club (amb.'s coun.), Athletic Club Columbus, Sons of Italy. Roman Catholic. Home: 5456 Blue Cloud Ln Westerville OH 43081

MC NEILL, CARMEN MARY, business broker; b. Charles City, Iowa, July 16; d. Benjamin T. and Mary (Orvis) McN. MBA, U. Chgo., 1957. Sec.-treas., Old Rep. Life Ins. Co., 1943-62; cons., officer life cos., 1962-70; broker-finder, owner Am. Cons., Chgo., 1970—. Methodist. Home: 918 Argyle Ave Flossmoor IL 60422-1257 Office: 18118 Martin Ave Ste 1 Homewood IL 60430-2120

MCNEILL, DONALD AUBREY, labor union administrator; b. Granite City, Ill., Apr. 4, 1947; s. Aubrey and Mary Ellen (Gough) McN.; m. Karen Shirleen Schickendanz, May 8, 1971; children: Shannon Marie McNeill Thompson, Jennifer Beth. BA, McKendree Coll., 1978. Machine operator Combustion Engring., St. Louis, 1965-83; inventory control specialists Marsh Co., Belleville, Ill., 1983—; pres. St. Clair Lodge IAMAW, Belleville, Ill.; v.p. Southwestern Ill. Ctrl. Labor Coun., Belleville, 1996—; del. AFL/CIO Union Label Coun., Belleville, 1995—. Union rep. United Way, 1993—. Mem. Ill. State Coun. Machinists, Vietnam Vets Am. Democrat. Methodist. Home: 2711 E Main St Belleville IL 62221-5033 Office: St Clair Lodge 353 IAMAW 2711 E Main St Belleville IL 62221-5033

MC NELLY, FREDERICK WRIGHT, JR., psychologist; b. Bangor, Maine, Apr. 14, 1947; s. Frederick Wright and E. Frances (Cutter) McN.; 1 adopted son, Roger; foster children: Joseph, Ronald, Michael, Jeffrey. BA magna cum laude, U. Minn., 1969; MA, U. Mich., 1971, PhD, 1973. Registered clin. psychologist, Ill., Wis.; lic. foster parent, Ill., 1973-86. Rsch. coord. NSF project U. Minn., Morris, 1968-69, lab. instr., 1969; trainee USPHS, 1969-70, 72; teaching fellow psychology U. Mich., Ann Arbor, 1970-72; ednl. examiner Ann Arbor Pub. Schs., 1971; dir. psychol. svcs. Children Devel. Ctr., Rockford, Ill., 1972-82, program dir., 1982-86; cons. psychologist, 1986—; lectr. Rock Valley Coll., Rockford, 1974-75; part-time pvt. practice psychology, Rockford and Belvidere, Ill., 1980-86, Beloit, Wis., 1985-86, full time 1986—; mental health cons. Rockford Head Start, 1982—, United Cerebral Palsy, Blackhawk Region, 1986—, Access Svcs., Mendota, Ill., 1992—; mem. health svcs. adv. com. human resources dept., City of Rockford, 1985—; presenter state and regional workshops and confs. Contbr. articles to profl. jours. Active Boy Scouts Am.; chmn. spl. edn. regional advisory com. Bi-County Office of Edn., Rockford, 1976-78; mem. Nat. and Ill. Com. on Child Abuse; co-chmn. Winnebago County Child Protection Assn., 1980; elder Willow Creek United Presbyn. Ch., Rockford, 1980-83; mem. stronghold renovation session com. Presbytery of Blackhawk, Oregon, Ill., 1985. Named U.S. Jaycees Outstanding Young Man of 1977. Mem. APA, Midwestern Psychol. Assn., Ill. Psychol. Assn., No. Ill. Psychol. Assn. (chmn. 1976-77), No. Ill. Pvt. Practice Mental Health Assn. (v.p. 1993-94, pres. 1994-96), Coun. for Exceptional Children, Soc. Rsch. in Child Devel., Nat. Assn. Retarded Citizens, Ill. Assn. Retarded Citizens, Am. Humane Assn. (children's div.), Nat. Register Health Svc. Providers in Psychology, Nat. Assn. of Disability Examiners, Nat. Foster Parents Assn., Ill. Foster Parents Assn. Home: 11591 Beverly Ln Belvidere IL 61008-8708 Office: Childrens Devel Ctr 650 N Main St Rockford IL 61103-6921 Office: 972 N Main St Rockford IL 61103-7061

MCNENNAMIN, MICHAEL J., bank executive. Exec. v.p. Bank One, Columbus. Office: Bank One of Columbus 100 E Broad St Columbus OH 43271*

MCNENNY, KENNETH G., state legislator; m. Herrietta; 4 children. Mem. S.D. Ho. of Reps., 1993—, vice chmn. agr. and natural resources, mem. appropriations com.; rancher. Home: HC 75 Box 192 Sturgis SD 57785-8909*

MCNEW, FRANCES WILKINS, nursing administrator; b. Newport News, Va., Mar. 23, 1930; d. Irvin C. and Doris (Saunders) Wilkins; m. Richard E. Lollar, Nov. 24, 1956 (dec. Jan. 1964); children: William C., Catherine A.; m. Virgil H. McNew, Mar. 4, 1972 (dec. July 1982). Student, James Madison U., 1947-49; BSN, Med. Coll. Va., 1952; MSN, Ohio State U., 1965. RN, Va., Ohio. Coord. Med. Coll. Va., Richmond, 1952-53; dir. Sch. Nursing, Riverside Hosp., Newport News, 1954-56; from head nurse to dir. Ohio State U. Hosps., Columbus, 1957-88, instr. emeritus, 1988—; dir. Life Ctr.: Adult Day Care, Reynoldsburg, Ohio, 1983-95. Recipient Outstanding Sr. Citizen award Columbus Jr. C. of C., 1990. Mem. ANA, Ohio State U. Alumni Assn., Civitans, Sigma Theta Tau, Alpha Sigma Alpha. Methodist. Home: 1204 Carrousel Dr Reynoldsburg OH 43068

MCNULTY, DIANE ROSE, library director; b. Belleville, Ill., Mar. 1, 1956; d. Kenneth Edgar and Ethel Mae (Boettcher) Poll; m. Richard J. McNulty, Jr., Nov. 26, 1988; children: Deirdre Claire, Connor Kenneth. BS, Ill. State U., 1978; MLS, No. Ill. U., 1982. Children's libr. Broadview (Ill.) Pub. Libr., 1979-80; children's libr. Barrington (Ill.) Area Pub. Libr. Dist., 1980-82, head tech. svcs., 1982-94; libr. dir. Cary (Ill.) Area Pub. Libr. Dist., 1994—. Mem. ALA, Ill. Libr. Assn., Pub. Libr. Assn. Office: Cary Area Pub Libr Dist 255 Stonegate Rd Cary IL 60013

MCNULTY, PATRICK JAMES, magistrate; b. L'Anse, Mich., May 18, 1922; s. William James and Marie Albertine (Duchenni) McN.; m. Gladys Bird LaFave, Aug. 14, 1952; children: Pamela, Patricia, Priscilla. Student, St. Thomas Coll., 1940-43; BSL, U. Minn., 1947, JD, 1949. Bar: Minn. 1949, U.S. Dist. Ct. Minn. 1949, U.S. Ct. Appeals (8th cir.) 1949. Assoc. Royal G. Bouschor, Duluth, 1950-52; ptnr. Bouschor & McNulty, 1952-68; ptnr. Patrick J. McNulty & Assocs., 1968-78; U.S. magistrate, 1978—; spl. asst. to atty. gen. State of Minn., 1960-64; judge U.S. Bankruptcy Ct., 1968-75. Mem. St. Louis County Bd. Freeholders, Duluth Bd. Zoning Appeals. Served with USAAF, 1943-46. Mem. Minn. State Bar Assn., ABA, Nat. Conf. U.S. Bankruptcy Judges, Nat. Conf. U.S. Magistrates, Order of Coif. Roman Catholic. Clubs: Northland Country. Office: Suite 412 Federal Bldg Duluth MN 55802

MCNULTY, ROBERTA JO, educational administrator; b. Cin., July 17, 1945; d. Edward Norman and Ruth Marcella (Glass) Stuebing; children: Meredith Corinne, Brian Edward, Stephen Barrett. BS in Edn., U. Cin., 1967; MA in Edn., Coll. of Mount St. Joseph, 1989; PhD in Ednl. Adminstrn. and Supervision, Bowling Green State U., 1993. Elem. tchr. St. Mary Sch., Urbana, Ohio, 1968; elem. tchr. Urbana (Ohio) City Schs., 1968-70, middle sch. tchr., 1970-71; off-campus liaison Mt. St. Joseph Coll., 1987-89; adj. faculty Bowling Green State U., 1990—; gen. edn. supr., testing 540 coord. curriculum devel. and implementation Fulton County Ednl. Svc. Ctr., Wauseon, Ohio, 1992—; Lamaza instr. Scioto Meml. Illustrated Lamaze Edn., Portsmouth, Ohio, 1983-84, Tiffin (Ohio) Childbirth Edn. Assn., 1984-87; edn. symposium com. chair Project Discovery, 1995—; proficiency test rev. com. Ohio Dept. Edn., 1993-94. Grad. editor Am. Secondary Edn., 1989-92. Mem. sch. bd. St. Mary Sch., Urbana, 1971-75; mem. parent adv. com. Wheelersburg (Ohio) Local Schs., 1978-84; mem. parents coun. U. Evansville, 1990-93; exec. dir. Am. Cancer Soc., Tiffin, Ohio, 1985; treas. Parents' Boosters Club, Portsmouth YMCA, 1979-84; chmn. Y-wives com. Tiffin-Cmty. YMCA, 1984-87; mem. Archbold (Ohio) Teen Issues Adv. Com., 1995—. Recipient Doctoral fellowship Bowling Green State U., 1989-92, Svc. Appreciation award Cub Scouts, 1990-92. Mem. ASCD, Ednl. Leadership Assn., N.W. Ohio Assn. for Supervision and Curriculum Devel., Ohio Sch. Suprs. Assn., Ohio Coun. Tchrs. English Language Arts, Assn. Tchr. Educators, Ohio Assn. Tchr. Educators (nat. del.), Phi Delta Kappa. Office: Fulton County Ednl Svc Ctr 602 S Shoop Ave Wauseon OH 43567-1712

MCNULTY-MAJORS, SUSAN ROSE, special education administrator; b. Fargo, N.D., Oct. 5, 1944; d. Leo G. McNulty and Jane Lyon (McDonald) McNulty-Schmallen; d. Herbert G. Schmallen (stepfather); m. B. Joseph Majors II, Aug. 23, 1975. BS, N.D. State U., 1966; MA, U. Mich., 1969. Lic. tchr., Mass., Minn.; lic. ind. clin. social worker; cert. chem. dependency practitioner. Tchr. sci. Incarnation Sch., Mpls., 1966-67; tchr. English George Daly Jr. High Sch., Flint, Mich., 1967-68; tchr. New Boston (Mich.) Elem. Sch., 1969-70; tchr. home econs. Newton (Mass.) Jr. High Sch., 1970-73; program adminstr. Bell Hill Recovery Ctr., Wadena, Minn., 1973-80, exec. dir., 1980-85; coord. emotionally and behavior disordered edn. Wadena Pub. Schs. TOW Spl. Edn. Coop., 1985-94; dir. spl. edn. PAWN Spl. Edn. Coop., Park Rapids, Minn., 1994-95; educator, cons. emotional/behavioral disorders Northland High, Remer, Minn., 1995—; therapist Neighborhood Counseling, Wadena, Minn., 1995—; emotional/behavioral disorders educator, dir. spl. edn. Remer-Longville Dist. 118, Remer, Minn., 1996—; mem. Wadena Tech. Adv. Bd., 1978—. Mem. adv. bd. Todd-Wadena Community Corrections, Long Prairie, Minn., 1975—; mem. Woodview adv. bd., 1990—; mem. fund adminstrn. bd. Ctrl. Minn. Initiative, 1996—. Fresh Air Camp fellow U. Mich., 1968; recipient Ashland Oil Golden Apple Achievement award. Roman Catholic. Home: 843 7th St SW Wadena MN 56482-1934 Office: Northland High Remer MN 56672

MCNUTT, JAMES, state legislator; b. Jan. 1935; m. Mary Jane; three children. BA, Mich. State U., MA. Sheriff Midland County, 1976-90; state rep. Dist. 102 Mich. Ho. of Reps., 1990-95, state rep. Dist. 98, 1995—; mem. Corrections & Mental Health Coms. Mich. Ho. of Reps.,. Recipient Liberty Bell award Mich. Bar Assn. Mem. Mental Health in Mich Assn., Mich. Sheriff's Assn. (pres.), Midland Sheriff's Assn., Kiwanis, C. of C. Home: 4000 Haskin Dr Midland MI 48640-2265*

MCPHAIL WHITAKER, SANDRA SUE, vocalist, educator; b. South Bend, Ind., June 20, 1949; d. William George and Bertha May (Culp) McPhail; m. Audie Dale, Aug. 22, 1970; children: Audie David, Andrea, Alexandra. BA in Music Edn., Olivet Nazarene U., 1974; MusM in Voice, Ball State U., 1993, Am. Conservatory of Music, Chgo., 1995; postgrad., Ball State U., 1993-96. Instr. choral and gen. music Joliet (Ill.) Pub. Schs., 1974-77; profl. singer SW for the Arts, Muncie, Ind., 1977—; vocal tchr. Muskegon Heights, Mich., 1977-90, Blue Lake Comty. Sch. for Fine Arts, Whitehall, Mich., 1978-81, Ball State U., Muncie, 1991-95; 0000, 1991-96; with music dept. Ind. Wesleyan U., Marion, Ind., 1996—; lectr., demonstrator Integration of Arts, Norton Shores, Mich., 1977-90; spl. program in arts SPARK, Grand Haven, Mich., 1978, 89; guest artist internat. travel Revival for our Day, Parker City, Ind., 1975—. Participant cmty. theater Muskegon Civic Opera, 1979; vol. tchr. West Shore Christian Acad., Muskegon, 1977-79, 89. Grantee Ball State U., 1991-96. Mem. Nat. Assn. Tchrs. Singing, Sonneck Soc., Coll. Music Soc., Sigma Alpha Iota (nat. voice scholar 1993). Republican. Home: 1705 N Tillotson Muncie IN 47304 Office: Ind Wesleyan U Music Dept Marion IN 46953

MCPHERSON, MELVILLE PETER, academic administrator, former government official; b. Grand Rapids, Mich., Oct. 27, 1940; s. Donald and Ellura E. (Frost) McP.; m. Joanne McPherson; 1 child, Donald B.; 1 stepchild, Michael D. Kircher. JD, Am. U., 1969; MBA, Western Mich. U., 1967; BA, Mich. State U., 1963. Peace Corps vol. Peru, 1965-66; with IRS, Washington, 1969-75; spl. asst. to pres. and dep. dir. Presdl. Pers. White Ho., Washington, 1975-77; mng. ptnr. Washington office Vorys, Sater, Seymour & Pease, 1977-81; adminstr. AID, Washington, 1981-87; dep. sec. Dept. Treasury, Washington, 1987-89; group exec. v.p. Bank of Am., San Francisco, 1989-93; pres. Mich. State U., East Lansing, 1993—. Mem. D.C. Bar Assn., Mich. Bar Assn. Republican. Methodist. Office: Office of the Pres Mich State U 450 Administration Bldg East Lansing MI 48824-1046

MCPHERSON, ROBERT EUGENE, dentist; b. Neligh, Nebr., June 27, 1932; s. Verne Edgar and Hilah (Fisher) McP.; m. Betty Lou Barnes, July 17, 1952 (div. Feb. 1977); children: Kathryn Louise, Scott Allen; m. Kathleen Ann Jacoby. BS in Dentistry, U. Nebr., 1954, DDS, 1956. Pvt. practice dentistry, Hastings, Nebr., 1958—. Pres., Hastings Libr. Bd., 1991-92; mem. Nebr. Libr. Commn., Lincoln, 1991—. With Dental Corps, USF, 1956-58. Miller scholar Donald Walters Miller Found., 1956; state fluoridation grantee USPHS, 1967. Fellow Internat. Coll. Dentists; mem. ADA (del. 1979-81), Nebr. Dental Assn. (pres. 1980-81, editor Jour.), Am. Assn. Dental Practice Adminstrn. (pres. Found. 1991-92), Hastings C. of C. (pres. 1992), Lions. Office: 2217 W 12th St Hastings NE 68901

MCQUEARY, FRED M., pharmaceutical executive; b. Springfield, Mo.; s. William L. and Jennie McQueary; m. Ramona A. Frazier, June 25, 1952; children: Fred G., Mark L., David B. BSBA, U. Mo., 1952. Treas. McQueary Bros., Springfield, Mo., 1954-68; v.p. then pres. McQueary Bros. Drug Co., Springfield, Mo., 1968—. With U.S. Army, 1952-54. Mem. Nat. Wholesale Drug Assn. (bd. dirs. 1989-94, vice chmn. 1994-95, chmn. 1995-96), Rotary (pres. 1985). Republican. Presbyterian. Office: McQueary Bros Drug Co 500 W Olive St Springfield MO 65806

MCREYNOLDS, ALLEN, JR., investment company executive; b. Carthage, Mo., Dec. 25, 1909; s. Allen and Maude (Clark) McR.; m. Virginia Madeliene Hensley, Jan. 17, 1946; children: Sharron Anne, Amy Elizabeth, Mary Armilda, Allen IV. Student, N.Mex. Mil. Inst., 1926-29, U. Mo., 1929-31. Pres. Joplin (Mo.) Stockyards, Inc., 1945-83; v.p., dir. First Nat. Bank, Monett, Mo., 1943-80; v.p., cashier First Nat. Bank, Golden City, Mo., 1950-56; dir. First Nat. Bancorp, Joplin, 1982-87. Pres. Jasper County Assn. for Soc. Services, 1976-78, Mo. State Southern Coll. Found., Joplin, 1984-85. Mem. Sigma Nu. Democrat. Episcopalian. Home: 1202 Mississippi Ave Joplin MO 64801-5344 Office: Mercantile Bank Bldg Rm 513 Joplin MO 64801

MCSHANE, LAWRENCE EDWARD, paralegal advocate; b. Waukegan, Ill., July 28, 1952; s. Edgar Lee and Betty Lucille (Riehl) McS. BA, Carthage Coll., Kenosha, Wis., 1975; Legal Asst. Cert., Roosevelt U., Chgo., 1984. Sales rep. Dun & Bradstreet, Glen Ellyn, Ill., 1983-84, Focal Point Fotographics, Waukegan, Ill., 1985-87; paralegal advocate Prairie State Legal Svc., Waukegan, 1987—. Co-editor newsletter Lake County Democrat, 1995—. Precinct committeeman, treas. Waukegan Dems., 1994—; treas./campaign staff Friends of Terry Link, Vernon Hills, Ill., 1995—; v.p. bd. trustees Waukegan Pub. Libr., 1993—; mem. Dem. Nat. Com., 1987—; mem. Dem. Leadership for the 21st Century,1994—; newsletter chmn. Lake County Dem. Party, 1994—. Recipient Cmty. Spirit award United Way of Lake County, Ill., 1992. Mem. Ill. State Bar Assn., Ill. Paralegal Assn., Ill. Libr. Assn. Methodist.

MCSHERRY, JAMES FRANCIS, small business owner, management consultant; b. Chgo., Apr. 18, 1953; s. John Patrick and Evelyn Agatha (Donohoe) McS.; m. Peggy Ann Prunty, Oct. 16, 1976; children: Kathleen, Patrick, Meghan, Erin. BS in Bus. Mgmt., John Carroll U., 1975. Mktg. mgr. Union Carbide Corp., Chgo., 1975-77; mgr. ter. sales Union Carbide Corp., Indpls., 1977-79; mgr. regional sales Union Carbide Corp., Milw., 1979-81; v.p. exec. search McSherry & Assocs., Inc., Chgo., 1981-83; prin. exec. search Dieckmann & Assocs., Ltd., Chgo., 1983-94; sr. v.p., gen. mgr. midwest Battalia Winston Internat., Chgo., 1994—. Regional sch. chmn. Joliet (Ill.) Cath. Diocese, 1983-86; pres. St. Margaret Mary Parish Coun., Naperville, Ill., 1986-89, mem. corp. fundraising com. Mental Health Assn., Chgo., 1984-87; bd. dirs. Family Svc. DuPage, 1989—; devel. bd. United Charities of Chgo., 1991—. Mem. Am. Mktg. Assn., Sales and Mktg. Execs. Chgo., Human Resource Mgmt. Assn., Employment Mgmt. Assn. Chgo., Assn. Exec. Search Cons., Execs. Club of Chgo., Univ. Club. Republican. Home: 837 Turnbridge Cir Naperville IL 60540-8341 Office: Battalia Winston Internat 180 N Wacker Dr Ste 600 Chicago IL 60606-3418

MCSPADDEN, WILLIAM A., financial systems executive; b. Athens, Tenn., Nov. 14, 1952; s. James Harris Jr. and Anna Mae (Archer) McS.; m. Janeyl Ann Harris, June 8, 1974; children: Scott, Ashley, Zachary. BS, USAF Acad., 1974; MA, Ctrl. Mich. U., 1976. Cert. info. sys. auditor. Project leader Panhandle Eastern Corp., Kansas City, Mo., 1979-85; office mgr. We-Mac Mfg., Kansas City, 1985-87; EDP auditor TWA, Kansas City, 1987-88; sr. auditor Mut. Benefit Life, Kansas City, 1988-89; project mgr. Sprint Corp., Kansas City, 1989—. Treas., elder Antioch Cmty. Ch., Kansas City, 1989—. Capt. USAF, 1974-79. Libertarian. Home: 9709 N Harrison St Kansas City MO 64155

MCSWINEY, CHARLES RONALD, lawyer; b. Nashville, Apr. 23, 1943; s. James W. and Jewell (Bellar) Mc.; m. Jane Detrick McSwiney, Jan. 2, 1970. BA, Kenyon Coll., Gambier, Ohio, 1965; JD, U. Cin., 1968. Assoc. Smith & Schnacke, Dayton, Ohio, 1968-72, ptnr., 1972-89, pres. and mng. ptnr., 1984-89; sr. v.p., gen. counsel The Danis Cos., Dayton, 1989-92; vice chmn. Carillon Capital, Inc., Dayton, 1992—; chmn., CEO Crysteco, Inc., Wilmington, Ohio, 1995—; pres. interchange exec. Presdl. Commn. on Personnel Interchange, Washington, 1972-73. Chmn., pres. bd. trustees Dayton Ballet Assn., 1985-88; trustee Columbus (Ohio) Symphony Orch., 1981-84; chmn. Dayton Performing Arts Fund, 1989-92, Dayton Devel. Coun., 1987-90, Wright State U. Found., Dayton, 1988-94, Miami Valley Sch., Dayton, 1988-94, Arts Ctr. Found., 1986—; mem. bd. advisors Wright State U. Coll. Bus. Adminstrn., 1988—; bd. vis. U. Cin. Coll. Law, 1987-89. Recipient Bronze Medal for Performance U.S. EPA, 1973. Mem. ABA, Ohio Bar Assn., Dayton Bar Assn., Dayton Area C. of C. (trustee 1987-90). Republican. Presbyterian. Home: 3780 Ridgeleigh Rd Dayton OH 45429-1253 Office: Carillon Capital Inc Kettering Tower Ste 1480 Dayton OH 45423-1480

MCTERNAN, ANN CIBUZAR, adult nurse practitioner; b. Brainerd, Minn., Nov. 26, 1950. BS in Family Social Sci., U. Minn., 1973; BSN, U. N.C., Greensboro, 1976; MSN-N.P., George Mason U., Fairfax, Va., 1990. RN, Va., Md., Calif., Minn., Washington; cert. adult nurse practitioner. Mem. nursing staff U.S. Naval Hosp., Beaufort, S.C., 1976-77, Eskaton Monterey Hosp., Monterey, Calif., 1977-78; staff Drug Enforcement Adminstrn., Bangkok, 1978-80; mem. nursing staff US Naval Hosp., Okinawa, Japan, 1981-82; mem. nursing staff. St. Joseph's Med. Ctr., Brainerd, 1986-87, Potomac Hosp., Woodbridge, Va., 1980-81, 87-90, Marymount U., Arlington, Va., 1989-90; low impact/expectant mothers aerobic instr. Saratoga Dance Ctr., Springfield, Va., 1990-94; adult nurse practitioner Prime Care, Annandale, Va., 1991-95; master mem. IDEA Found., San Diego, 1990—; aerobic fitness instr. Am. Coun. on Exercise, San Diego, 1990—. Mem. AAUW, Am. Coll. Sports Medicine, Am. Coun. on Exercise, Exer-Safety Assn., Am. Acad. Nurse Practitioners. Home: c/o Cibuzar #202 727 SW 4th St Brainerd MN 56401

MCTIGUE, PATRICK J., advertising executive, publishing executive. Pres. Frank J. Corbett, Inc., Chgo. Office: Frank J Corbett Inc 211 E Chicago Ave Chicago IL 60611-2616*

MCTYRE, ROBERT EARL, publishing executive; b. Detroit, Aug. 2, 1955; s. Earl Melvin and Barbara Jean (shorter) McT.; m. Earn Diane Fortune, Mar. 1975 (div. Jan. 1977); m. Dianne Denise Ball, Nov. 1978 (div. Feb. 1982); m. Carmela Ann Baldwin, Sept. 22, 1990; stepchildren: DuJuan Robinson, Tamika Baldwin. Student, Wayne State U., 1988-90. EMT Mich. EMT Detroit Gen. Hosp., 1975-77, Detroit Fire Dept., 1977-85; freelance writer, 1978-86; intern, classified sales Met. Times, Detroit, 1985-86; gen. mgr. Eastside Citizens News, Detroit, 1986-87; reporter Mich. Chronicle, Detroit, 1987-89, assoc. editor, 1989-93, exec. editor, 1993—; pres., CEO BenWil Creative Mgmt. Svcs., Detroit, 1993—; speaker in field. Author and editor of poems. Assoc. minister New Resurrection Bapt. Ch., Detroit, 1988—. Mem. Soc. Environ. Journalists. Republican. Baptist. Office: Mich Chronicle 479 Ledyard Detroit MI 48201

MCVAY, W. WELDON, insurance agent, farmer; b. Sycamore Valley, Ohio, Apr. 21, 1930; s. Fred J. and Minnie Odessa (Christy) McV.; m. Nina May Newman, Oct. 19, 1958 (div. 1983); children: Rhonda Jo, McHenry, Gene; m. Ethel Cordell Bramble Etchison, Aug. 17, 1985. Student, So. Ill. U., 1955-57. Teamster Pure Oil Co., Clay City, Ill., 1948-50, teamster, roustabout, 1953-55; roughneck Don Slape Drilling Co., Olney, Ill., 1950-51; ins. trainee Am. Republic Ins. Co., Springfield, Ill., 1958-61; ins. agent State Farm Ins. Cos., Bloomington, Ill., 1961—. Staff sgt. U.S. Army, 1951-53, Korea. Decorated Combat Infantry Badge, Silver and Bronze Battle Stars, Purple Heart. Mem. Am. Legion, Elks, Moose, Masons. Republican. Baptist. Office: State Farm Ins 220 E 2d St PO Box 699 Flora IL 62839

MCVICAR, RICHARD LEE, journalist; b. Ft. Leavenworth, Kans., Oct. 25, 1955; s. John Franklin and Jean Arlene McV. BA with high distinction, Ohio No. U., 1978; MDiv, Vanderbilt Divinity Sch., 1982; postgrad., Ohio State U., 1991-92. Ordained minister, Disciples of Christ Ch., 1982. VISTA vol. Adult Basic & Literacy Edn., Logan and Dayton, Ohio, 1992-93; reporter Madison Press, London, Ohio, 1993—. Mem. Soc. Profl. Journalists. Office: The Madison Press 30 S Oak St London OH 43140

MCVICKER, MARY ELLEN HARSHBARGER, museum director, art history educator; b. Mexico, Mo., May 5, 1951; d. Don Milton and Harriet Pauline (Mossholder) Harshbarger; m. Wiley Ray McVicker, June 2, 1973; children: Laura Elizabeth, Todd Michael. BA with honors, U. Mo., 1973, MA, 1975, PhD, Columbia, Mo., 1989. Instr. Columbia U., Mo., 1977-78, Cen. Meth. Coll., Fayette, Mo., 1978-85, mus. dir., 1980-85; project dir. Mo. Com. for Humanities, Fayette, 1981-85, Mo. Dept. Natural Resources Office Hist. Preservation, 1978-85; owner, Memories of Mo. & Tour Tyme, Inc., 1986—; prof. history Kemper Mil. Coll., 1993—. Author: History Book, 1984. V.p. Friends Hist. Boonville, Mo., 1982-87, pres., 1989-90; bd. dirs. Mus. Assocs. Mo. U., Columbia, 1981-83, Mo. Meth. Hist. Soc., Fayette, 1981-84; chmn. Bicentennial Celebration Methodism, Boonville, Mo., 1984; pres. Arts & Sci. Alumni, U. Mo., 1992—; bd. dirs. Mo. Humanities Coun., 1993—. Mem. Mo. Alliance for Hist. Preservation (charter), AAUW (treas. 1977-79), Am. Assn. Museums, Centralia Hist. Soc. (project dir. 1978), Mus. Assocs. United Meth. Ch. (charter, bd. dir. 1981-83), Phi Beta Kappa, Mortar Bd. Democrat. Clubs: Women's (treas. 1977-79), United Meth. Women's Group (charter mem.). Avocations: collecting antiques, gardening, family farming, singing, travelling. Home: 22151 Highway 98 Boonville MO 65233 Office: Tour Tyme PO Box 72 Columbia MO 65205

MCVOY, KIRK WARREN, physicist, educator; b. Mpls., Feb. 22, 1928; s. Kirk Warren and Phyllis (Farmer) McV.; m. Hilda A. Van Der Laan, Aug. 15, 1953; children—Christopher, Lawrence, Annelies. B.A., Carleton Coll., 1950; B.A. (Rhodes scholar), Oxford U., Eng., 1952; Dipl., U. Gottingen, Germany, 1953; Ph.D., Cornell U, 1956. Research asso. Brookhaven Nat. Lab., Upton, N.Y., 1956-58; asst. prof. Brandeis U., 1958-62; assoc. prof. physics U. Wis., Madison, 1963-67, prof., 1967-93, prof. emeritus, 1993—; vis. distinguished prof. physics Bklyn. Coll., 1970-71; vis. prof. Ind. U., 1971-72. Fulbright research grantee U. Utrecht, Netherlands, 1960-61; sr. scientist awardee A. von Humboldt Found., Max-Planck-Institut für Kernphysik, Heidelberg, W. Ger., 1980-81. Fellow Am. Phys. Soc. Office: U Wis Dept Physics 1150 University Ave Madison WI 53706-1302

MCWHORTER, JOHN FRANCIS, manufacturing engineer; b. Cleve., June 20, 1941; s. John Francis and Daisy Alice (Morrell) M. B.S. in Mgmt. Sci., Case Inst. Tech., 1963. With TRW Inc., Cleve., 1963-87 , process planning engr., 1963-64, tool evaluation engr., 1964-67, Jr. Achievement adv., 1965-67; computer applications engr., 1967—, prodn. engr., 1972—; pres. John McWhorter & Assocs., Inc., 1989—. mem. info. systems conf., 1982. Chmn. Cuyahoga County Youth for Goldwater, 1964; Republican precinct Committeeman, 1964-68; mem. Shaker Heights (Ohio) Rep. Club, 1964-72, sec., 1970; coordinator Ward 32 Cleve. Mayoral Campaign; 1969; mem. ARC Gallon Club, 1971. Mem. Kirley Investment Club (pres. 1982, 86), English Speaking Union (dir. Cleve. br. 1980-85), Sigma Nu. Developer more than 300 computer software applications for company. Home and Office: 20900 Claythorne Rd Cleveland OH 44122-1959

MCWHORTER, LAWRENCE JAMES, design draftsman, township trustee; b. Washington Twp., Ohio, Dec. 21, 1939; s. James Floyd and Dorsa (Bates) McW.; m. Carolyn Lucille Camp, Mar. 18, 1965; 1 child: Cynthia Dawn McWhorter Brunton; 1 stepchild, Tamara Faith Marcum. Draftsman McNally Pittsburg Mfg. Inc., Wellston, Ohio, 1958-65, lead design draftsman, 1965-87, project coord., 1987; design draftsman Hamden, Ohio, 1987-91; owner Southeastern Drafting, Hamden, Ohio, 1991—; twp. trustee Clinton Twp.-Vinton County, Hamden, Ohio, 1989—. Pres. Vinton County Hist. Geneal. Soc., Hamden; mem. adv. com. GJMV Four County Solid Waste Dist., Wellston, 1993—; chmn. exec. bd. Vinton County Emergency Mgmt. Agy., 1994—. Republican. Home: PO Box 312 32 W Elm St Hamden OH 45634-0312 Office: Southeastern Drafting 71 Stanton Ave Hamden OH 45634

MCWILLIAMS, CYNTHIA LYNN, public health nurse; b. Indpls., June 7, 1957; d. Edward Lee and Annie Victoria (Gordon) Thomas; divorced. Practical nurse cert., Indpls. Pub. Schs., 1976; BSN, Ind. U., 1985. RN, Ind. Practical nurse Wishard Meml. Hosp., Indpls., 1977-85; nurse VA Hosp., Indpls., 1985-86, St. Vincents Hosp., Indpls., 1986-87; nurse Marion County Health Dept., Indpls., 1987—, cert. care coord., 1992—; pub. speaker, health educator Marion County Health Dept., Indpls., 1987—; mem. Marion County Coun. on Adolescent Pregnancy, Indpls. Domestic Violence Network. Mem. APHA, Ind. Pub. Health Assn. (treas. ctrl. chpt. 1993-96), Sigma Theta Tau. Home: 3426 Admar Ct # H Indianapolis IN 46205

MEACHAM, JEFFREY WAYNE, computer programmer; b. Memphis, Aug. 31, 1941; s. William Harvey and Ruby Louise (Britnell) M.; m. Melani Denise Paganoni, June 23, 1990; 1 child, Bethany Jelene. Grad., State Tech. Inst., 1991. Head computer operator Nat. Safety Assn., Memphis, 1988-94; programmer, analyst Moline (Ill.) Paint Mfg., 1994—; cons. in field. Republican. Bpatist. Home: 5206 N Brown St Davenport IA 52804 Office: Moline Paint Mfg 5400 23d Ave Moline IL 61265

MEAD, PRISCILLA, state legislator; m. John L. Mead; children: John, Willian, Neel, Sarah. Student, Ohio State U. Councilwoman Upper Arlington, Ohio, 1982-90, mayor, 1986-90; mem. Ohio Ho. of Reps. Mem. Franklin County Child Abuse and Neglect Found., Coun. for Ethics and Econs. Recipient Svc. award Northwest Kiwanis, Woman of Yr. award Upper Arlington Rotary, Citizen of Yr. award U.S. C. of C. Mem. LWV, Upper Arlington Edn. Found., Jr. League Columbus, Upper Arlington C. of C., Delta Gamma. Republican. Home: 2281 Brixton Rd Columbus OH 43221-3117 Office: Ohio Ho of Reps State House Columbus OH 43215

MEADE, PATRICIA SUE, marketing professional; b. Columbus, Ohio, Mar. 14, 1960; d. Harold Eugene and Glenna Rhae (Croaff) M. BS in Communications, Ohio U., 1982, M in Sports Administrn., 1984, MS in Communications, 1986. Dir. advt. The Pensacola (Fla.) Civic Ctr., 1984-85; asst. dir. mktg. Ohio Ctr. Co., Columbus, 1985-86; asst. v.p. mktg. Doctors Hosp., Columbus, 1986-88; regional mgr. mktg. Jacobs, Visconsi & Jacobs Co., Cleve., 1988-89; dir. bus. devel. and pub. affairs Deaconess Hosp., Cleve., 1989-91; div. head mktg. and pub. affairs Lake Metroparks, Concord Township, Ohio, 1991-93; sr. health care cons. Cohen & Co., Cleve., 1993—; pres. Creative Works, Inc., Cleve., 1995—; bd. trustees Mooreland Estate Inc. Mem. NAFE, Am. Mktg. Assn., New Orgn. Visual Artists, Ohio Hosp. Assn., Ctr. for Contemporary Art, Cleve. Mus. Art, Garden Club Cleve.

MEADORS, GAYLE MARLEEN, lawyer; b. Chgo., Sept. 13, 1946; d. Howard C. and Eileen M. (Baker) M.; m. William Frank Fortuna II, June 11, 1983. AB in English Lit. with honors, U. Ill., 1969; MA in Libr. Sci., U. Chgo., 1973; JD magna cum laude, DePaul U., 1977. Bar: Ill. 1977. Cons. Hewitt Assocs., Lincolnshire, Ill., 1976-83; sr. counsel Am. Hosp. Supply Corp., Evanston, Ill. 1983-84; assoc. Katten, Muchin, Zavis, Pearl, Greenberger & Galler, Chgo., 1984-87; assoc. Pope, Ballard, Shepard & Fowle, Ltd., Chgo., 1987-90; ptnr. Martin, Craig, Chester & Sonnenschein, Chgo., 1990—. Columnist for Jour. Med. Practice Mgmt. Mem. Am. Heart Assn. of Metro. Chgo. (vol. mgmt. svcs, human resources com.), Ill. State Bar Assn., Chgo. Bar Assn., Network Profls. Working in Employee Benefits, Phi Beta Kappa. Home: 530 E Prospect Ave Lake Bluff IL 60044-2616 Office: Martin Craig Chester & Sonnenschein 2215 York Rd # 550 Oak Brook IL 60521

MEADOWS, AMY LYNN, newspaper copy chief; b. Meade County, S.D., Aug. 4, 1972; d. Kenneth Lee and Susan Clair (Congleton) M. BA in Journalism, Ind. U., 1994. Editorial asst. Ind. Builder Mag., Bloomington, 1990-94; graphic designer Johnson County Daily Jour., Franklin, Ind., 1994; copy editor Johnson County Daily Jour., Franklin, 1994-95, copy chief, 1995—. Home: 4055 Peacful Pl Greenwood IN 46142 Office: Johnson County Daily Jour 2575 N Morton St Franklin IN 46131

MEAD ROSEN, CLARE, journalist, consultant; b. Green Bay, Wis., Mar. 27, 1941; d. Ralph and Anna (McKeough) Mead; m. Herbert H. Rosen, Mar. 21, 1971; children: Mollie Rosen, Michael Rosen. BA in History and English, Dominican Coll., Houston, 1963; MA in Am. History, U. Notre Dame, 1966. Contbg. editor Time Mag., N.Y.C., 1970-74; asst. to editor-in-chief Time Inc. Publs., N.Y.C., 1978-82; producer broadcast documentaries Minn. Pub. Radio, Mpls., 1984-86; freelance reporter/writer Time, Life, Discover, Picture Week, People and other mags., 1975—; tchr. U.S. history and drama in various high schs. in Tex., Minn., Tenn., Mich., 1964-67, also vol.; vol. tchr. Cornerstone Sch., Detroit, 1995-96; editorial cons. Lofy Assocs., Mpls., 1987-94. Rschr., reporter editor; producer, writer, performer film for Title III. Bd. dirs. Internat. Wolf Ctr., Minn., 1987-89, Memphis Friends of the Libr., 1992-94, Women's Com. for Hospice Care, Detroit, 1995—. Recipient Corp. for Pub. Broadcasting news and info. award, 1985; named to Outstanding Young Women of Am., 1972. Mem. Friends of Libr., So. Poverty Law Ctr., others. Home and Office: 1370 Bramblebush Run Bloomfield Hills MI 48304-1501

MEAL, LARIE, chemistry educator, researcher, consultant; b. Cin., June 15, 1939; d. George Lawrence Meal and Dorothy Louise (Heileman) Fitzpatrick. BS in Chemistry, U. Cin., 1961, PhD in Chemistry, 1966. Rsch. chemist U.S. Indsl. Chems., Cin., 1966-67; instr. chemistry U. Cin., 1968-69, asst. prof., 1969-75, assoc. prof., 1975-90, prof., 1990—, researcher, 1980—; cons. in field. Contbr. articles to sci. jours. Mem. AAAS, N.Y. Acad. Scis., Am. Chem. Soc., Internat. Assn. Arson Investigators, NOW, Planned Parenthood, Iota Sigma Pi. Democrat. Home: 2231 Slane Ave Norwood OH 45212-3615 Office: U Cin 2220 Victory Pky Cincinnati OH 45206-2822

MEANS, GEORGE ROBERT, organization executive; b. Bloomington, Ill., July 5, 1907; s. Arthur John and Alice (Johnson) M.; m. Martha Cowart, Aug. 5, 1950. B.Ed., Ill. State U., 1930; A.M., Clark U., 1932; HHD (hon.), Rikkyo U., Tokyo; H.H.D. (hon.), Ill. State U.; HHD (hon.), Ill. Wesleyan U., Ky. Wesleyan Coll. Cartographer, map editor, 1932-35; with Rotary Internat., 1935—; beginning as conv. mgr., successively head Middle Asia office Rotary Internat., Bombay, India; asst. gen. sec. Rotary Internat., 1948-52, gen. sec., 1953-72; sec. Rotary Found., 1953-72; hon. dir. Washington Nat. Corp.; dir. Hertzberg-New Method, Inc., Ind. State Retirement Home Guaranty Fund, 1982-95. Author: Rotary's Return to Japan, also numerous articles. Mem.-at-large nat. council Boy Scouts Am. Served as comdr. USNR, 1942-46. Decorated Legion of Honor France; Chilean Order of Merit; Japanese Order of Rising Sun; Italian Order of Merit; recipient Disting. Service award Geog. Soc. Chgo., 1972; Paul Harris fellow The Rotary Found. Fellow Am. Geog. Soc.; mem. Rotary Club (Evanston, Bloomington, Ill., Sydney, Australia, Kyoto, Osaka and Tokyo, Japan, Seoul, Korea, Cape Town, South Africa, Ituzaingo, Saavedra, Argentina, Greenwood, Ind.), Gamma Theta Upsilon. Home: 1067 Smock Dr Greenwood IN 46143-2426

MEARS, ORUM GLENN, III, automotive executive; b. Canton, Ohio, Jan. 19, 1958; s. O. Glenn Jr. and Dana Arlene (Christman) M.; m. Mary Kay Wallick, May 6, 1995. BBA magna cum laude, U. Cin., 1981. CPA, Ohio. Acct., auditor Deloitte, Haskins & Sells, Cin., 1981-85; comptroller Park Honda, Canton, 1985-86; salesperson Sunshine Acura, Farmington Hills, Mich., 1986; gen. mgr. Park Honda South, New Philadelphia, Ohio, 1987, pres., owner, 1987—; chmn. Dist. 4C Honda Dealer Coun., 1995-97. Mem. agy. adminstrn. com. United Way, New Philadelphia, 1989—. Recipient Am. Honda Motor Co.'s Master of Customer Satisfaction, 1991, 92, 93, 94, Acad. Dept. award in French lang. Kent State U., 1996. Mem. AICPA, Ohio Soc. CPAs, Nat. Automobile Dealers Assn., Lions (treas. New Philadelphia Club 1992-94, 3rd v.p. 1994-95, 2d v.p. 1995-96), Tuscarawas County C. of C., Beta Gamma Sigma, Alpha Lambda Delta. Office: Park Honda South 512 4th St NW New Philadelphia OH 44663-1743

MEARS, PATRICK EDWARD, lawyer; b. Flint, Mich., Oct. 3, 1951; s. Edward Patrick and Estelle Veronica (Mislik) M.; m. Geraldine O'Connor, July 18, 1981. BA, U. Mich., 1973, JD, 1976. Bar: N.Y. 1977, U.S. Dist. Ct. (so. and ea. dists.) N.Y. 1977, Mich. 1980, U.S. Dist. Ct. (we. and ea. dists.) Mich. 1980, U.S. Ct. Appeals (6th cir.) 1983. Assoc. firm Milbank, Tweed, Hadley & McCloy, N.Y.C., 1976-79, ptnr. Warner, Norcross & Judd, Grand Rapids, Mich., 1980-91; sr. mem. Dykema Gossett PLLC, Grand Rapids, 1991—; adj. prof. Grand Valley State U., Allendale, Mich., 1981-84. Author: Michigan Collection Law, 1981, 2d edit., 1983, Basic Bankruptcy Law, 1986, Bankruptcy Law and Practice in Michigan, 1987; contbr. articles to profl jours. Chairperson legis. com. East Grand Rapids Parent-Tchr. Assn., 1992-94; dir. Children's Law Ctr., 1994, Grand Rapids Ballet, 1994—, East Grand Rapids Pub. Sch. Found., 1994—. Fellow Am. Coll. Bankruptcy; mem. ABA (vice chmn. workouts, enforcement of creditors rights, and bankruptcy com. ABA real property sect. 1995—), Mich. State Bar Assn. (mem., sec. coun. real property sect. 1993—), Am. Bankruptcy Inst., Fed. Bar Assn. (chairperson bankruptcy sect. We. Mich. chpt. 1992-94), Comml. Law League Am., Am. C. of C. in France, Grand Rapids Rotary, World Affairs Coun. of West Mich., West Mich. World Trade Assn., Peninsular Club (Grand Rapids), East Hills Athletic Club. Office: Dykema Gossett 200 Old Town Riverfront Bu Grand Rapids MI 49503

MEARS, SANDRA A., state agency administrator, lawyer, educator; b. Kansas City, Mo., Oct. 31, 1954; d. Thomas Robert and Tinnie Irene (Sample) M. AB magna cum laude, St. Louis U., 1976, JD, 1979. Atty. S.E. Mo. Legal Svcs., Inc., Caruthersville, Mo., 1980-81; exec. dir. Sojourner Truth Ctr. for Women, Caruthersville, 1981-82, Women's Ctr. & Safe House, Cape Girardeau, Mo., 1982-83; prin. Sandra A. Mears, Atty., Cape Girardeau, 1983-87; sr. counsel Mo. Dept. Revenue, Jefferson City, 1987-93, dept. dir. divsn. motor vehicle and drivers licensing, 1993—; adadj. prof. Lincoln U., Jefferson City, 1988-93, 94—; mem. Nat. Commn. on Unifo Traffic Laws & Ordinances, Chgo., 1991-95. Author: (booklet) Handbook on Municipal Court, 1990, Department of Revenue Cases--A Guide for Courts and Prosecutors. Mem. Nat. Fedn. Bus. and Profl. Women, Washington, 1980-89; bd. dirs. Mo. Fedn. Bus. & Profl. Women, Columbia, 1986-89. Named Woman of the Yr., River City Bus. & Profl. Women, 1985. Mem. ABA, Am. Assn. Motor Vehicle Adminstrs. (chair region III legal svcs. com. 1991-93, vice chair internat. legal svcs. com. 1994—), Mo. Bar Assn. (vice-chair aviation and transp. law com. 1993—, writer booklets). Office: Mo Dept of Revenue 301 W High St Rm 470 Jefferson City MO 65105-0629

MECKLENBURG, GARY ALAN, hospital executive; m. Lynn Kraemer; children: John, Sarah. BA, Northwestern U., 1968; MBA, U. Chgo., 1970. Adminstrv. resident Presbyn.-St. Luke's Hosp., Chgo., 1969-70, adminstrv. asst., 1970-71, asst. supt., 1971-76, assoc. supt., 1976-77; assoc. supt. U. Wis. Hosps., Madison, 1977-80; adminstr. Stanford U. Hosp. Clinics, Calif.; pres., CEO St. Joseph's Hosp., Milw., 1980-85; pres., dir. Franciscan Health Care Inc., Milw., 1985; pres., CEO Northwestern Meml. Hosp., Northwestern Meml. Corp., Chgo., 1985—; preceptor, guest lectr., mem. adv. bd. Kellogg Sch. Mgmt., chgo., 1986—; pres., chief exec. officer, dir. Northwestern Healthcare Network, 1990-92. Recipient Harold M. Coon, M.D. Merit award Wis. Hosp. Assn., 1974. Mem. Am. Hosp. Assn. (sect. met. hosps., mem. bd. trustees 1996—, chmn. sect. 1991, mem. regional policy bd., #5 1984-85, 87-94, 95—, mem. ho. dels. 1984, 87, mem. com. on med. edn. 1987-90), Ill. Hosp. Assn. (bd. dirs. 1988—, chmn. 1994, mem. steering com. coun. tchg. hosps. 1985—), U. Chgo. Hosp. Adminstrn. Alumni Assn. (pres. 1985-86), Econ. Club Chgo., Comml. Club Chgo. Office: Northwestern Meml Hosp Superior St & Fairbanks Ct Chicago IL 60611

MEDEMA, JEFFREY S., mechanical engineer; b. Fulton, Ill., June 19, 1968. BSME, U. Ill., 1990; MSME, Purdue U., 1991. Product engr. Delco Remy, Anderson, Ind., 1991—. Gen. Motors fellow, 1990-91. Mem. Soc. Automotive Engrs., Soc. Exptl. Mechanics. Christian. Office: Delco Remy 2401 Columbus Ave Anderson IN 46016-4542

MEDHI, DEEPANKAR, computer science educator; b. Guwahati, Assam, India, June 17, 1962; came to U.S., 1983; s. Jyotiprasad and Prity (Chowdhury) M.; m. Karen Thompson, Aug. 15, 1987; children: Neiloy M., Robby S. BSc in Math., Gauhati U., Assam, India, 1981; MS in Math., U. of Delhi, India, 1983; MS in Computer Sci., U. Wis., 1985, PhD in Computer Sci., 1987. Teaching and rsch. asst. U. Wis., Madison, 1983-87; mem. tech. staff AT&T Bell Labs., Holmdel, N.J., 1987-89; rsch. asst. prof. U. Mo., Kansas City, 1989-91, asst. prof. computer sci., 1991-96, assoc. prof., 1996—. Mem. bd. editors Jour. of Network and Systems Mgmt.; contbr. papers to sci. confs. Mem. IEEE, Assn. Computing Machinery, Ops. Rsch. Soc. Am. (pres. Kansas City chpt. 1991-92), Soc. Indsl. Applied Math. Home: 4009 W 100th Ter Shawnee Mission KS 66207-3740 Office: U Mo Kansas City Computer Sci Tele Program 5100 Rockhill Rd Kansas City MO 64110-2446

MEDIN, LOWELL ANSGARD, security company executive; b. Shafer Twp., Minn., Aug. 28, 1932; s. Ansgaard Phillip Magnus and Adelaide Marie Christine (Grandstrand) M.; m. Frances Irene Knutson, Sept. 13, 1958; children: Kimberly June, James Lowell. AS in Liberal Arts, U. Minn., 1957, BBA, 1959. Dairy farmer Medin Farm, Franconia Twp., 1951-53; silo builder Lindstrom Silo, 1956-58; employment mgr. John Wood Co., St. Paul, 1959; salesperson Diversey Co., LaCrosse, Wis., 1959-60; rebuyer, inventory mgr. Montgomery Ward, St. Paul, 1960-67; rebuyer, rebuyer mgr. Montgomery Ward, Chgo., 1967-85; with sales dept. J.T. Gen. Store, Palatine, Ill., 1986; rebuying mgr. Sportsmen's Guide, Golden Valley, Minn., 1987; inventory mgr. Donald Bruce and Co., Chgo., 1988-91; supr. Pinkerton Security Ops., 1992—; pics coord. Hickory Farms, Itasca, Ill., 1995—. Author: (with others) Shafer Swamp to Village, 1978, The Pioneers of Chisago County 1838-1870, 1992, The Knutson/Stavenau Family Roots, 1994. Candidate for polit. office, Mpls., 1967; del. Minn. State Dem.-Farm Labor Conv., 1956, 58; chmn. cancer drive Village of Palatine, 1968, mem. dist. 6 adv. coun., 1989—; mem. Homeowners Coun., Palatine, 1976-77; mem. coun. Christ Luth. Ch., Palatine, 1981-86; officer Chicago County DFL Party, 1956-60; del. Chicago County DFL Conv., 1956, 58; pres. Palonis Park Homeowners Assn., Palatine, 1976-82. Cpl. U.S. Army, 1953-55, ETO. Mem. No. Ill. Civil War Roundtable (chartered officer 1983-86, trustee, sec., 2d v.p.), VFW (life, post 981, Arlington Hts.), Am. Legion (life, post 690, Palatine), Alpha Phi Omega. Republican. Lutheran. Home: 121 S Linden Ave Palatine IL 60067-6342

MEDLAND, TIMOTHY JOSEPH, broadcast executive; b. Logansport, Ind., Jan. 7, 1948; s. Thomas Galagher and Mary (Hassett) M.; m. Joanna Lynn White, Nov. 10, 1984; children: Drew, Kirk, Tim, Chris, Matt. BA, Ball State U., 1970; postgrad., U. Pa., 1982. Acct. exec. Am. Fletcher Nat. Bank, Indpls., 1970-73; from acct. exec. to gen. sales mgr. Radio Sta. WIBC, Indpls., 1973-83; gen. sales mgr. Radio Sta. WIBC-WKLR, Indpls., 1983-88; v.p., gen. mgr. Radio Sta. WZTR, Milw., 1988-90; pres., gen. mgr. Radio Sta. WTPI/WZPL/WMYS, Indpls., 1990—. Bd. dirs. United Christmas Svcs., Indpls., 1985-88; mem. exec. bd. Clean City Com., Indpls., 1992—; mem. adv. bd. Indpls. Zoo. Named one of Outstanding Young Men of Am., 1984. Mem. Ball State Telecomm. Alumni Soc. (bd. dirs.). Office: MyStar Communications Corp WTPI/WZPL/WMYS 9245 N Meridian Indianapolis IN 46260

MEEK, FORREST BURNS, educational administrator, trading company executive; b. Tustin, Mich., June 11, 1928; s. Robert B. and Electa I. (Gallup) M.; m. Jean R. Grimes, June 26, 1953; children: Sally, Thomas, Nancy, Charles. AA, Spring Arbor Coll., 1950; AB, Mich. State U., 1953; postgrad., U. Ga., 1965; MA, Cen. Mich. U., 1967. Asst. supt. Tranter Mfg. Co., Lansing, Mich., 1951-53; pres. Pioneer Mortgage Co., Clare, Mich., 1966-74; exec. sec., chmn. bd. Edgewood Press, Clare, 1971—; gen. mgr. Blue Water Imports, 1985; dir. Hanover Ednl. Ctr., Clare, 1986—, Ctr. for Chinese-Am. Scholarly Exchs., Inc., 1989—; gen. mgr. Blue-Water Internat. Trading Co., Inc.; vis. prof. Wuhan U., People's Republic China, 1986, 87; dist. office mgr. Fed. Decennial Census, 1990; hon. headmaster Xiaohe H.S., Hubei Province, China, 1994—; CFO AM. Petroleum Corp., 1996; pres. MGF Drilling USA, Inc., 1996—. Author: Michigan Timber Battleground, 1976, Michigan Heartland, 1979, One Year in China, 1988, Michigan Logging Railroad Era, 1850-1963, 1989, Railways and Tramways, 1990, Lumbering in Eastern Canada, 1991, Pearl Harbor Remembered, 1991, Heroes of The Twentieth Century, 1996. Coordinator Clare County Bicentennial Com., 1975-76; Rep. fin. chmn., Clare County, 1966-71, asst. treas. 10th dist. Mich, 1967-69; trustee local sch. bd.; chmn. local county jury bd. Served to staff sgt. U.S. Army, 1946-48. Mem. Am. Entrepreneur Assn., Mich. Sci. Tchrs. Assn., Mich. Hist. Soc., Heartland Mich. Geneal. Soc., White Pine Hist. Soc. (exec. sec.), Ctr. for Chinese-Am. Scholarly Exchs. Republican.

MEEK, VIOLET IMHOF, dean; b. Geneva, Ill., June 12, 1939; d. John and Violet (Krepel) Imhof; m. Devon W. Meek, Aug. 21, 1965 (dec. 1988); children: Brian, Karen; m. Don M. Dell, Jan. 4, 1992. BA summa cum laude, St. Olaf Coll., 1960; MS, U. Ill., 1962, PhD in Chemistry, 1964. Instr. chemistry Mount Holyoke Coll., South Hadley, Mass., 1964-65; asst. prof. to prof. Ohio Wesleyan U., Delaware, Ohio, 1965-84, dean for ednl. svcs., 1980-84; dir. annual programs Coun. Ind. Colls., Washington, 1984-86; assoc. dir. sponsored programs devel. Rsch. Found. Ohio State U., Columbus, 1986-91; dean, dir. Ohio State U., Lima, 1992—; vis. dean U. Calif., Berkeley, 1982, Stanford U., Palo Alto, Calif., 1982, reviewer GTE Sci. and Tech. Program, Princeton, N.J., 1986-92, Goldwater Nat. Fellowships, Princeton, 1990-96. Co-author: Experimental General Chemistry, 1984; contbr. articles to profl. jours. Bd. dirs. Luth. Campus Ministries, Columbia, 1988-91, Luth. Social Svcs., 1988-91, Americom Bank, Lima, 1992—, Lima Symphony Orch., 1993—, Art Space, Lima, 1993—, Allen Lima Leadership, 1993—, Am. House, 1992—, Lima Vets. Meml. Civic Ctr. Found., 1992—; chmn. synodical coms. Evang. Luth. Ch. Am., Columbus, 1982; bd. trustees Trinity Luth. Sem., Columbus, 1996—; chmn. Allen County C. of C., 1995—. Recipient Woodrow Wilson Fellowship, 1960. Mem. Nat. Coun. Rsch. Adminstrs. (named Outstanding New Profl. midwest region 1990), Am. Assn. Higher Edn., Phi Beta Kappa. Home: 209 W Beechwold Blvd Columbus OH 43214-2012 Office: Ohio State U 4240 Campus Dr Lima OH 45804-3576

MEEKER, DAVID ANTHONY, public relations executive; b. Akron, Ohio, June 1, 1939; s. Charles Anthony and Lucia Pauline (Schweikert) M.; m. Anita Marie De Jacimo, June 24, 1961; children: Christine Marie, Elizabeth Ann, Eileen Louise, David Edgerton. BS in Indsl. Journalism, Kent State U., 1961, postgrad., 1963-64. Editor Recordak Record, Eastman Kodak Co., N.Y.C., 1961-62; journalist Akron Beacon Jour., 1962-66, St. Louis Post-Dispatch, 1966-69; exec. sec. to mayor City of St. Louis, 1969-71; asst. dir. Ohio Dept. Natural Resources, Columbus, 1971-73; exec. dir. Ohio Dem. Party, Columbus, 1973-74; pres. Urbanistics, Inc., 1974-76; ptnr. Meeker-Mayer Pub. Rels., 1976-84; pres. David A. Meeker & Assocs., Inc., Akron, 1984-89; exec. v.p., gen. mgr. Edward Howard & Co., Akron, 1989—. Bd. dirs. Akron Regional Devel., St. Edward Home; Dem. candidate for mayor City of Akron, 1987; mem. pub. rels. adv. coun. Kent State U. Sch. Journalism, regional environ. priorities project pub. com.; chmn. Summit County charter commn., 1995. Recipient Con Lee Kelliher award Kent State U., 1966, Disting. Alumnus award Sch. Journalism, 1983. Mem. Pub.

Rels. Soc. Am. (nat. honors and awards com. 1981-83, chmn. 1983, nat. membership com. 1980-81, chmn. 1984, past del.-at-large nat. assembly, chmn. Counselors Acad. spring conf. 1987, pres. Akron chpt. 1982, immediate past chmn. and dir. environ. sects.), PROhio Network (founder), Internat. Pub. Rels. Assn., Soc. Profl. Journalists (past pres. Buckeye chpt.), SAR. Roman Catholic. Home: 269 S Rose Blvd Akron OH 44313-7843 Office: One Cascade Pla 19th Fl Akron OH 44308

MEEKISON, MARYFRAN, writer, photographer; b. Napoleon, Ohio, Apr. 9, 1919; d. Frank J. and Elizabeth (Keyes) Shaff; m. David Meekison, June 17, 1939; children: Maureen Meekison Houppert, David Francis, Beth Ann. Student, St. Mary's Coll., Notre Dame, Ind., 1936-39. Hist. writer, photographer, Napoleon, 1963—, St. Augustine Ch., 1983—. Author: (photographer) Canal Days to Modern Ways Revisited, 1984; (brochure) Canal Days to Modern Ways, 1963; mem. editorial adv. bd. Courier mag., 1989-91; contbr. articles to numerous mags. Steering com. Napoleon Susquicentennial, 1984; trustee Napoleon Pub. Lib., 1976—. Recipient Spl. citation Courier Alumnae mag., also numerous photography and writing awards; named Citizen of the Yr., Napoleon Area C. of C., 1990; recipient Pres.'s medal, St. Mary's Coll., Notre Dame, Ind., 1991. Mem. Alumnae Assn. St. Mary's Coll. (bd. dirs. 1985-91), Literary Club. Democrat. Roman Catholic. Home: PO Box 253 Napoleon OH 43545-0253

MEEKS, CLAYTON BREWSTER, automotive industry executive; b. Tulsa, Okla., July 10, 1942; s. Clayton Wert and Helen Virginia (Brewster) M.; m. Elizabeth Ann Lunsford, June 25, 1963; children: Richard Lee, Virginia Ann. BSBA, U. S.C., 1967, MBA in Ops. Mgmt., 1974. Plant and area acct. Internat. Minerals and Chems., Hartsville, S.C., 1967-70; divsn. staff acct. Alamac Divsn. Westpoint-Pepperell, Lumberton, N.C., 1970-72; analyst, officer mgr. Mfg. divsn. MacAndrews & Forbes, McBee, S.C., 1972-73; plant contr. United Plastics divsn., Internat. Telephone and Telegraph, Bainbridge, Ga., 1975-76; dir. mfg., cost acct. United Plastics divsn., Internat. Telephone and Telegraph, Madison Heights, Mich., 1976-79; pres. Automotive Products (USA), Inc., 1979-87; v.p. ops. Transtechnology Corp., 1988-90; gen. mgr. Teleflex Inc., 1990-92; v.p. ops. Hi-Lex Corp., Battle Creek, Mich., 1992-95; All-Lock Co. Inc. (sub. Gen. Automotive Specialty Co., Inc.), Selma, Ala., 1995—. Sgt. U.S. Army, 1967. Mem. Am. Mgmt. Assn., SME, Newcomen Soc., Beta Gamma Sigma. Methodist. Home: 621 Union St Selma AL 36701 Office: Gen Automotive Specialty Co 4555 Water Ave Selma AL 36701

MEEKS, ROBERT L., state legislator; b. Ft. Wayne, Ind., Feb. 3, 1934; m. Carol Meeks; children: Denise Schrock, Kevin, Layne, Kent. Senator Dist. 13, Ind. State Senate, 1988—, mem. appointment & claims, fin., natural resources, pub. policy coms.; pres. Meeks Agy. Past trustee Lakeland Sch. Bd. Recipient Maddox award FOP Life Savers Club, Allen County. Mem. Am. Legion, C. of C., Masons (Shriner). Home: RR 3 Box 51 Lagrange IN 46761-9803*

MEESE, ERNEST HAROLD, thoracic and cardiovascular surgeon; b. Bradford, Pa., June 23, 1929; s. Ernest D. and Blanche (Raub) M.; m. Rockell D. Dombar, Aug. 30, 1985; children: Donyel Hindee, Nathan Samuel; children from previous marriage: Constance Ann, Roderick Bryan, Gregory James. BA, U. Buffalo, 1950, MD, 1954. Diplomate Am. Bd. Surgery, Am. Bd. Thoracic Surgery. Resident in gen. surgery Millard Fillmore Hosp., Buffalo, 1955-59; resident in thoracic surgery U.S. Naval Hosp., St. Albans L.I., N.Y., 1961-63; group practice thoracic and cardiovascular surgery, Cin., 1965-88; pvt. practice, Cin., 1988—; asst. clin. prof. surgery Cin. Med. Ctr., 1972—; head sect. thoracic and cardiovascular surgery St. Francis-St. George Hosp., Deaconess Hosp.; mem. staff Good Samaritan Hosp., Bethesda Hosp., Christ Hosp., Providence Hosp., Childrens Hosp., Jewish Hosp. Kenwood, Jewish Hosp. of Cin. Contbr. articles to profl. jours. and textbooks. Pres. bd. dirs., chmn. service com. Cin.-Hamilton County unit Am. Cancer Soc., v.p., trustee, mem. exec. bd., chmn. service com.; pres., bd. trustees, exec. bd. Ohio div. Am. Cancer Soc.; trustee Southwestern Ohio chpt. Am. Heart Assn. Comdr. M.C., USN, 1959-65. Fellow ACS, Internat. Coll. Surgeons; mem. Soc. Thoracic Surgeons, Am. Coll. Chest Physicians, Am. Coll. Angiology, Cin. Surg. Soc., Am. Coll. Cardiology, Gibson Anat. Hon. Soc., AMA, Am. Thoracic Soc., Assn. Mil. Surgeons U.S., Acad. Medicine Cin., Assn. Advancement Med. Instrumentation, N.Am. Soc. Pacing and Electrophysiology, Am. Soc. Laser Medicine and Surgery, Med. Found. Cin. (pres. 1996), Phi Beta Kappa, Phi Chi (treas. 1952-54). Clubs: Western Hills Country, Queen City, Mediclub (pres. 1983-85) (Cin.). Lodge: Masons. Home: 174 Pedretti Ave Cincinnati OH 45238-6025 Office: 5049 Crookshank Rd Cincinnati OH 45238-3349

MEESE, ROBERT ALLEN, architect; b. St. Paul, Mar. 16, 1956; s. Lloyd George and Drusilla (Deis) M.; m. Nancy Ann Jensen, July 16, 1988. BArch, U. Minn., 1981. Registered architect, Minn. Job capt., draftsman James Cooperman & Assoc., Mpls., 1979-80; assoc. architect Ellerbe Assoc., Mpls., 1981-86; project architect Boarman Assoc., Mpls., 1986-87; project mgr. Heise, Reinen, MacRae & Assocs. Inc., Mpls., 1987-88; project architect Opus Corp., Mpls., 1988-89; project mgr., assoc. v.p. Hammel Green & Abrahamson, Inc., Mpls., 1989—. Prin. works include St. Paul Winter Carnival Ice Palace (Progressive Architecture award 1986), U. Minn. Hosps. Unit J, ConAgra Product Devel. Facility, Brian Coyle Cmty. Ctr. Bd. dirs. Westbrooke West Condominium Assn., 1990-95, treas. Mem. AIA (Minn. Honor award 1986). Mem. United Church of Christ. Club: Afton (Minn.) Alps Ski Patrol (advisor 1985). Home: 6150 Concord Hill Ln Hopkins MN 55345-6092 Office: Hammel Green & Abrahamson Inc 1201 Harmon Pl Minneapolis MN 55403-1920

MEFFORD, DARRELL, physicist, engineer; b. Palestine, Ill., Feb. 17, 1945. BA in Physics, So. Ill. U., 1967; MA in Physics, Wayne State U., 1969. Quality mgr. Sarkes-Tarzan, Bloomington, Ill., 1972-78; quality and product engr. RCA, Findlay, Ohio, 1979-86, GE, Findlay, 1986-89; lead engr. Harris Co., Findlay, 1989—. Served with U.S. Army, 1970-72. Republican. Baptist. Office: Harris 1700 Fostoria Ave Findlay OH 45840-6220

MEGARD, ROBERTA ANN (BOBBI MEGARD), city official; b. Boise, Idaho, Sept. 15, 1936; d. Roy Wilson and Georgia Leah (Scott) McNeal; m. Robert O. Megard, July 3, 1958; children: Jason, Allison, Rachel. BA, U. Oreg., 1958; MA, Ind. U., 1962. Tchr. Springfield (Oreg.) H.S., 1958-59, Spencer (Ind.) City Schs., 1960-61, Washburn H.S., Mpls., 1964-67; exec. dir. LWV, St. Paul, 1984-85; cmty. organizer St. Anthony Park Cmty. Coun., St. Paul, 1985-93; councilmember City of St. Paul, 1994—; citizen rep. St. Paul Pub. Schs., 1979-84, mem. citizen budget adv. com., 1992-93; chair region 11 Ednl. Cooperative Svcs. Unit, 1982-83; mem. pub. info. officer task force Ramsey County, 1985, chair jail facilities com., 1989-90, mem. home rule charter commn., 1992-94; chair qualifications and examining commn. St. Paul Police Chief, 1992; mem. legis. task force for sewer rate relief St. Paul City Coun., 1992-93; mem. asst. city engr. selection com. City of St. Paul, 1995; mem. St. Paul liaison/exec. bd. mem., legis. com. Ramsey County League of Local Govt.; active Children's Initiative Governance Bd., Mpls./St. Paul Family Housing Fund, Mpls./St. Paul Housing Fin. Bd., Twin City Area Labor Mgmt. Coun. Bd., St. Paul City DFL Ctrl. Com. Exec. Bd. Active Parents for Integrated Edn., 1970-74, St. Anthony Park Elem. Sch. PTSA, 1976-78, St. Anthony Park Assn., 1978-80, St. Paul Neighborhood Energy Consortium, 1986-88, St. Anthony Park Block Nurse Program, 1985-93; vice chair Minn. Election 96 Task Force, League of Minn. Cities, 1996; mem. adv. com. Met. Coun. Land use, 1996; bd. dirs. Women in City Govt., 1996. Mem. LWV (pres. St. Paul 1983-85, bd. dirs. Minn., so. Minn. liaison 1987-89, budget chair 1988-93, Faye Lyksett award 1988), League of Minn. Cities (bd. dirs. 1995—, mem. improving our cmty. life com.), Greater Mpls. C. of C. (mem. bldg. our future task force), Assn. Met. Municipalities (mem. housing and econ. devel. com.), St. Paul Area C. of C. (Leadership St. Paul 1988-89). Episcopal. Home: 1439 Hythe St Saint Paul MN 55108 Office: City of St Paul 310 City Hall Saint Paul MN 55102

MEHAFFEY, KAREN RAE, library director; b. Ann Arbor, Mich., Mar. 16, 1959; d. Donald Robert and Betty Jane (Pond) Forsyth; m. Colin Henry Mehaffey, Oct. 21, 1989. AB in Music History, U. Mich., 1981, MLS, 1982. Rsch. asst. U. Mich., Ann Arbor, 1981-82; libr. asst. archives U. Mich., Dearborn, 1985; rsch. asst. Gale Rsch., Detroit, 1982-83, rsch. coord., 1983-84; libr. St. Hedwig High Sch., Detroit, 1986-88; asst. libr. Sacred Heart Major Sem., Detroit, 1988-92, dir. Szoka libr., 1992—; spkr. Nat. Women's History Project, 1993—, Greenfield Village & Henry Ford Mus., 1996—. Author: Victorian American Women 1840-1880, 1992, The After Life: Mourning and the Mid-Victorians, 1993; contbg. editor: Camp Chase Gazette, 1988—, Citizens Companion Mag., 1994—; contbr. of book revs. to Library Journal 1996—, Choice 1996—; contbr. articles to Civil War Lady Mag., 1992-93. Vol. Greenfield Village, Dearborn, 1988—, Historic Fort Wayne, Detroit, 1988-92. Mem. ALA, Mich. Libr. Assn., Assn. Coll. and Rsch. Librs., Libr. Adminstrn. and Mgmt. Assn. Methodist. Office: Sacred Heart Major Sem 2701 W Chicago Detroit MI 48206

MEHARRY, RONALD LEE, real estate investor, inn keeper; b. Mt. Vernon, Ohio, May 26, 1950; s. Thomas Earl and Evelyn Glades (Magley) M.; m. Joyce Ann Gonce, Aug. 15, 1975 (div. 1981); 1 child, Chad Michael. Cert. in paramedicine, Muskingum Area Tech. Coll., 1977; student bus., Mt. Vernon Nazarene Coll., 1987-88. Cert. paramedic, emergency med. technician, Ohio. Paramedic Mt. Vernon Life Support Team, 1971-84, Knox Community Hosp., Mt. Vernon, 1984-85, Delaware County Emergency Med. Svc., Mt. Vernon, 1985-91; with Meharry & Benner Properties, Mt. Vernon, 1989—; pres. Meharry & Assocs., Mt. Vernon, 1993—; co-owner Scoops Sweet Shop Deli, Mt. Vernon, 1991-92; owner, inn keeper The Stauffer House/Bed and Breakfast Inn, Mount Vernon; instr. CPR, Am. Heart Assn., Mt. Vernon, 1972-83; instr. first aid ARC, Mt. Vernon, 1974-75. Deacon Zion Luth. St., North Jellaway, Ohio, 1986-87; mem. ch. coun. faith Luth. Ch., Mount Vernon, chmn. social & economical outreach bd.; bd. dirs. Knox County Habitat for Humanity, 1996—, publicity & sight selection coms. Mem. Knox County-Mt. Vernon C. of C. Republican. Home and Office: The Stauffer House 304 N Mulberry St Mount Vernon OH 43050-2056

MEHL, SCOTT ANDREW, quality assurance engineer; b. Huntington, N.Y., Aug. 10, 1967; s. Ronald Walter Mehl and Margaret Mary (Hren) Hodor. BSEE, U. Wis., 1993. Quality assurance engr. Alliant Tech Systems, Accudyne Ops., Janesville, Wis., 1995—. With USN, 1985-87. Mem. IEEE, Optical Soc. of Am., Naval Inst., Am. Soc. of Quality Control, Am. Legion. Republican. Lutheran. Home: 1905 Jackson St Stoughton WI 53589

MEHLER, BARRY ALAN, humanities educator, journalist, consultant; b. Bklyn., Mar. 18, 1947; s. Harry and Esther Mehler; m. Jennifer Sue Leghorn, June 2, 1982; 1 child, Isaac Alan. BA, Yeshiva U., 1970; MA, CCNY, 1972; PhD, U. Ill., 1988. Rsch. assoc. Washington U., St. Louis, 1976-80, instr. history, 1977; NIMH trainee racism program U. Ill., Champaign, 1981-85, rsch. asst. IBM EXCEL project, 1986-88; asst. prof. humanities Ferris State U., Big Rapids, Mich., 1988-93, assoc. prof., 1993—; media cons. Scientist's Inst. for Pub. Info., N.Y.C., 1980—; cons. Calif. Humanities Coun., 1995, ZDF/arte (Zweite Deutsches Fernshen--German pub. TV), 1995, House Subcom. on Consumer Protection, 1994, McIntosh Commn. for Fair Play in Student-Athlete Admissions, 1994, Can. Broadcast Svc., Toronto, Ont., 1985-92; judge Women's Caucus Awards for Excellence, St. Louis, 1989-91, 93. Contbr. over 100 articles and revs. to profl. jours. Rsch. fellow NSF, 1976-80, Babcock fellow U. Ill., 1985-86; grantee Rockefeller Found., 1977; Ferris State Bd. of Control cert. of Recognition, 1994; structure learning assistance program grantee Office of Minority Affairs, Lansing, Mich., 1994—. Mem. Am. Hist. Soc., Behavior-Genetics Assn., NAACP, Soc. for Study Social Biology, Ctr. for Dem. Renewal, History of Sci. Soc., B'nai B'rith (Anti-Defamation League). Jewish. Home: 216 Rust Ave Big Rapids MI 49307-1726 Office: Ferris State U 901 S State St Big Rapids MI 49307

MEHLINGER, HOWARD DEAN, education educator; b. Hillsboro, Kans., Aug. 22, 1931; s. Alex and Alice Hilda (Skibbee) M.; m. Carolee Ann Case, Dec. 28, 1952; children: Bradley Case, Barbara Ann, Susan Kay. BA, McPherson (Kans.) Coll., 1953; MS in Edn, U. Kans., 1959, PhD, 1964. Co-dir. social studies project Pitts. pub. schs., 1963-64; asst. dir. fgn. relations project North Central Assn. Schs. and Colls., Chgo., 1964-65; mem. faculty Ind. U., Bloomington, 1965—, prof. history and edn., 1974—, dean Sch. Edn., 1981-90, dir. Ctr. for Excellence in Edn., 1990—; social studies adviser Houghton Mifflin Pub. Co.; cons. U.S. Office Edn. Co-author: American Political Behavior, 2d edit., 1977, Count Witte and the Tsarist Government in the 1905 Revolution, 1972, Toward Effective Instruction in the Social Studies, 1974, School Reform in the Information Age, 1995; editl. bd. Education and Society, history tchr.; editor: UNESCO Handbook on the Teaching of Social Studies, 1981; co-editor: Yearbook on the Social Studies, 1981. STAG grantee Dept. State, 1975. Mem. NEA, Nat. Council Social Studies, Am. Edn. Research Assn., Am. Hist. Assn., Am. Assn. for Advancement Slavic Studies, Phi Beta Kappa, Phi Alpha Theta, Pi Sigma Alpha, Phi Delta Kappa. Home: 3271 Ramble Rd E Bloomington IN 47408-1094 Office: Ind Univ Ctr Excellence Edn 230 N Rose St Bloomington IN 47405-1004

MEHTA, RAJENDRA, chemist, researcher, administrator; b. Jodhpur, India, May 15, 1955; came to U.S., 1981; s. Moti Mal and Puspha (Bhandari) M.; m. Kamala Parkah, Nov. 28, 1981; children: Nidhi, Neeray. BSc, U. Jodhpur, 1974, MSc in Organic Chemistry, 1976, PhD in Chemistry, 1981. Postdoctoral rsch. fellow Gaylord Rsch. Inst., Whippany, N.J., 1981-83, sr. rsch. chemist, 1983-86; mgr. R & D Epolin Inc., Paterson, N.J., 1987-89; project scientist Standard Register Co., Dayton, Ohio, 1989-90, sr. project scientist, 1990—, mgr., 1991—. Patentee for protective coating on thermal paper, 1990, radiation curable receptive coating for thermal transfer, 1990, dual adhesive, 1994, bonding adhesive under pressure, 1995, trasnparentization of celluloric fibers, 1995. Mem. ASTM, Am. Chem. Soc., Red-Tech Orgn. Home: 220 Estates Dr Dayton OH 45459-2838 Office: Standard Register Co 120 Campbell St Dayton OH 45408-1977

MEIDL, KEVIN, music educator; b. Manitowoc, Wis., Dec. 10, 1960; s. Kenneth John LeRoy and Bernita Ann (Pritzl) M. MusB, Lawrence U., 1983; MusM in Music Edn. summa cum laude, Northwestern U., 1991; PhD in Edn. summa cum laude, LaSalle U., 1995. Tchr. music Einstein Jr. High Sch., Appleton, Wis., 1983-85, Appleton (Wis.) High Sch. W., 1985—. Conductor, Fox Valley Symphony Chorus, Appleton, 1983-85, St. Edward's Ch. Choir, Mackville, Wis., 1983-88, Appleton Boy Choir, 1983—; bd. dirs. A Better Chance, Appleton, 1985-91. Named Secondary Educator of Yr., Mielke Found., 1994-95. Mem. Am. Choral Dirs. Assn. (mem. state bd. 1980—), Internat. Fedn. Choral Music, Music Educators Nat. Conf., Soc. Acad. Achievement, Wis. Choral Dir. Assn. (pres.-elect 1992, pres. 1995—), Nat. Honor Soc., Mortar Bd., Pi Kappa Lambda, Phi Mu Alpha (pres. 1982-83). Roman Catholic. Home: 916 S Park Ave Neenah WI 54956-4259 Office: Appleton High Sch W 610 N Badger Ave Appleton WI 54914-3405

MEIER, DAVID TIMOTHY, utility company specialist; b. Anderson, Ind., Sept. 16, 1968; s. Paul David and Charlene Frances (Roberts) M. BSEE, Purdue U., 1990; MBA, Butler U., 1996. Lic. profl. engr., Ind. Computer programmer Fisher Guide div. GM, Anderson, 1985-86; transmission line engr. Indpls. Power and Light Co., 1991-96, corp. strategist, 1996—. Mem. IEEE, NSPE, Golden Key, Mensa, Eta Kappa Nu, Tau Beta Pi, Phi Eta Sigma. Republican. Home: 7422 Blue Creek South Dr Indianapolis IN 46256-3903 Office: Indpls Power & Light Co One Monument Cir Indianapolis IN 46204-2936

MEIER, ROBERT FRANK, sociology educator; b. Madison, Wis., Sept. 10, 1944; s. Frank and Eileen (Thompson) M.; m. Lee Jane Schoenfeld, Sept. 10, 1971; children: Jennifer, Chrissy, Michael. BS, U. Wis., 1967, MS, 1972, PhD, 1974. Probation officer Dane County Probation Office, Madison, 1967-70; asst. prof. U. Calif., Irvine, 1974-78; asst. prof., assoc. prof., prof. sociology Wash. State U., Pullman, 1978-90, dept. chmn., 1984-89, assoc. dean, 1989-90; prof. sociology, chmn. dept. Iowa State U., Ames, 1990-94; cons. Nat. Inst. Justice, Washington, 1980—, NSF, Washington, 1985—. Author: Crime and Society, 1989; co-author: Sociology of Deviant Behavior, 1979, 4th edit., 1995, Crime and Its Social Context, 1994; editor: Theoretical Methods in Criminology, 1985; co-editor: White-Collar Crime, 1995. Capt. USAR, 1967-77. Mem. Am. Soc. Criminology, Am. Sociol. Assn., Midwest Sociol. Assn. Home: 818 Idaho Ave Ames IA 50014-3021 Office: Iowa State U Dept Sociology Ames IA 50011

MEIER, ROBERT JOSEPH, JR., software engineer; b. St. Marys, Pa., Aug. 7, 1959; s. Robert Joseph and Joán (Kerner) M. BS in Physics, Villanova U., 1981, BEE, 1981; MEE, Stanford Coll., 1982; PhD in Elec. Engring., Stanford U., 1988. Registered profl. engr., Ind. Physics rschr. Villanova (Pa.) U., 1979; software engr. Radio Corp. Am., Somerville, N.J., 1980; cons. NSF, Villanova, 1981; sci. group leader Project Pleides Space Sta., Stanford, 1982; software engr. Harris Corp., Melbourne, Fla., 1983; rsch. physicist NASA, Moffett Field, Calif., 1984-88; sr. software engr. proCASE, Inc., Santa Clara, Calif., 1988-89; sr. software engr., cons. Bell Labs. AT&T, Naperville, Ill., 1989-91; sr. software engr. Graphics Software Lab. AT&T, Indpls., 1992-93; cons. Custom Tools, Indpls., 1993—; webmaster FANUC Robotics, 1995—; comml. pilot, 1993. Author: Spaceborne Flotilla Servicing, 1986; inventor in field. Instr. water safety ARC, Santa Clara, 1979-84; capt. Emergency Mgmt. Agy. Radio Unit, Naperville, Ill., 1989-91. Recipient Cert. of Recognition, Ill. Ho. of Reps., 1991; fellow Charles LeGeyt Fortescue, 1981, NSF, 1982-84. Mem. IEEE (pub. referee 1984-89), Usenix Assn., White River Aviation Club, KC (treas. 1986-91), Phi Kappa Phi, Tau Beta Pi, Sigma Pi Sigma. Libertarian. Roman Catholic. Home: # 307 740 Ironwood Dr Apt 307 Rochester MI 48307-1322 also: 2536 Greenwich Rd Winston Salem NC 27104-4143 Office: Fanuc Robotics NAm Inc 2000 S Adams Rd Auburn Hills MI 48326-2800

MEILICKE, WARREN A., mechanical designer; b. Milw., Dec. 2, 1934. Assoc. Mech. Engring., Milw. Area Tech. Coll., 1961, Assoc. Photography, 1961; Assoc. Comml. Art, Famous Artist Sch., 1967. Owner, operator Texaco Svc. Sta., South Milwaukee, Wis., 1961-62; layout draftsman J.I. Case, Racine, Wis., 1964-66, Allis-Chalmers, Milw., 1966-67, Simplicity, Port Washington, Wis., 1968-69; sr. designer Jacobsen Textron, Racine, 1970—. Chmn. Lake Arrowhead Golf Course, Nekoosa, Wis., 1987—; ofcl. photographer Wis. Jr. Miss Inc., South Milwaukee, 1974-82. With USN, 1957-59. Methodist. Home: 706 Lakeview Ave South Milwaukee WI 53172-3852 Office: Jacobsen Textron 1721 Packard Ave Racine WI 53403-2561

MEINER, SUE ELLEN THOMPSON, gerontologist, nursing educator and researcher; b. Ironton, Mo., Oct. 24, 1943; d. Louis Raymond and Verna Mae (Goggin) Thompson; m. Robert Edward Meiner, Mar. 5, 1971; children: Diane Thompson Bubb, Suzanne Elaine. AAS, Meramec C.C., 1970; BSN, St. Louis U., 1978, MSN, 1983; EdD, So. Ill. U., Edwardsville, 1991. RN, Mo.; cert. med./surg. clinician; cert. gerontol. nurse practitioner; cert. clin. specialist in gerontol. nursing. Staff RN St. Joseph's Hosp., St. Charles, Mo., 1976-78; nursing supr. Bethesda Gen. Hosp., St. Louis, 1975-76, 71-74; adult med. dir. Family Care Ctr.-Carondelet, St. Louis, 1978-79; program dir., lectr. Webster Coll./Bethesda Hosp., Webster Groves, Mo., 1979-82; diabetes clin. specialist Washington U. Sch. Medicine, St. Louis, 1982; chmn. dept. nursing, asst. prof. St. Louis C.C., 1983-88, Barnes Hosp. Sch. Nursing, 1988-89; instr. U. Mo., St. Louis, 1989; assoc. prof. St. Charles County C.C., St. Peters, Mo., 1990-92, Deaconess Coll. of Nursing, 1991-93; patient care mgr. Deaconess Hosp., St. Louis, 1993-94; assoc. prof. Jewish Hosp. Coll. of Nursing and Allied Health, 1994-96; gerontol. nurse, instr. Wash. U. Sch. Med., St. Louis, 1996—; nat. dir. edn. Nat. Assn. Practical Nurse Edn. and Svc., Inc., St. Louis, 1984-86; mem. task force St. Louis Met. Hosp. Assn., 1987-88; mem. adv. com. Bd. Edn. Sch. Nursing, St. Louis, 1986-90; project dir. NIH Grant Washington U., St. Louis, 1996—. Contbr. articles to profl. jours. and books. Chmn. bd. dirs. Creve Coeur Fire Protection Dist. Mo., 1984-89; vice chmn. Bd. Cen. St. Louis County Emergency Dispatch Svc., 1985-87; asst. leader Girl Scouts U.S., St. Louis, 1975; treas. Older Women's League, St. Louis, 1992-93. Recipient Woman of Worth award Gateway chpt. Older Women's League, 1993. Mem. ANA, Am. Nurses Found., Nat. League for Nursing, Am. Soc. of Aging, Mid-Am. Congress on Aging, Creve Coeur C. of C., Order Ea. Star (chaplain 1970), Jobs Daus. (guardian 1979-80), Sigma Theta Tau (fin. chmn. 1984, archivist 1985-87), Sigma Phi Omega (pres. 1990-91), Kappa Delta Pi. Home and Office: 700 Wren Path Ct Ballwin MO 63021-4794

MEINERS, PHYLLIS HENRI, publisher, training consultant, author; b. Boston, Nov. 8, 1940; d. Samuel Henry and Edith (Salvin) Bloom; m. William F. Meiners Jr.; 1 child, Hilary Henri Tun-Atz. BA, U. Calif., Berkeley, 1962; postgrad., MIT, 1971-72, Rockhurst Coll., 1980-83. Cert. fund raising exec. Dir. rsch. Harbridge House, Boston, 1964-70; rsch. assoc. MIT, Cambridge, 1970-71; advocate planner Urban Planning Aid, Cambridge, 1972-73; program adminstr. U. Hawaii, Honolulu, 1974-79, Mo. div. Community Devel., Kansas City, 1980-82; founder, pres. Corp. Resource Cons., Kansas City, Mo., 1982-95; founder libr. corp. philanthropy Corp. Resource Ctr., 1988; founder, pres. CRC Publ. Co., 1993—. Mem. Nat. Com. of Responsive Philanthropy, South Town Coun., Kansas City, Friends of Art, Kansas City; staff coord. Mayor Charles B. Wheeler Campaign, Kansas City, 1979. Mem. Nat. Soc. Fundraising Execs. (bd. dirs.), Greater Kansas City C. of C. (entrepreneurs coun.), Greater Kansas City Coun. Philanthropy, Native Ams. in Philanthropy, Brookside Neighborhood Assn., Kansas City Consensus, Nat. Coun. Jewish Women, Pub.'s Mkgt. Assn., Mid Am. Pubs. Assn. Democrat. Jewish. Office: PO Box 22583 Kansas City MO 64113-2583

MEIS, NANCY RUTH, marketing and development executive; b. Iowa City, Aug. 6, 1952; d. Donald J. and Theresa (Dee) M.; m. Paul L. Wenske, Oct. 14, 1978; children: Alexis Meis Wenske, Christopher Meis Wenske. BA, Clarke Coll., 1974; MBA, U. Okla., 1981. Cultural program supr. City of Dubuque, Iowa., 1974-76; community services dir. State Arts Council of Okla., Oklahoma City, 1976-78, program dir., 1978-79; mgr. Cimarron Circuit Opera Co., Norman, Okla., 1979-82, bd. dirs., 1982-86; account exec. Bell System, Kansas City, Mo., 1982; mgr. spl. svcs. Children Internat., Kansas City, 1983-86; dir. mktg. and fund raising, 1986-87, dir. devel., 1987-88, v.p. devel., 1988-90; dir. mktg. and consulting svcs, Unimedia div. Universal Press Syndicate, Kansas City, 1990-95; dir. mktg. Universal New Media divsn. Universal Press Syndicate, 1996—; cons., copywriter; speaker in field; co-founder Sage Enterprises, Inc. Co-founder Girls to Women; founder The Garnet Ring.

MEISCH, JANENE KAY, women's health nurse; b. Caledonia, Minn., Aug. 10, 1950; d. Charles Arvid and Alma Leota (Kannenberg) Rollins; m. Arnold Leo Meisch, Nov. 2, 1968; children: Kelly, Abigail. ADN, Western Wis. Tech. Coll., LaCrosse, 1979. Cert. reproductive endocrinology/infertility NAACOG. Staff nurse ob/gyn. Luth. Hosp. LaCrosse, 1979-86; staff nurse ob/gyn. Gundersen Clinic, LaCrosse, 1986-87, staff nurse infertility, 1987-91, nurse clinician, 1991—; cons. Infertility Support Group, 1988—. Mem. Nurses Profl. Group Am. Soc. Reproductive Medicine, Am. Fertility Soc. Office: Gundersen Clinic Ltd 1836 South Ave La Crosse WI 54601-5429

MEISNER, MARY JO, editor; b. Chgo., Dec. 24, 1951; d. Robert Joseph and Mary Elizabeth (Casey) M.; 1 child, Thomas Joseph Gradel. BS in Journalism, U. Ill., 1974, MS in Journalism, 1976. Copy editor Wilmington (Del.) News Jour., 1975-76, labor and bus. reporter, 1975-79; labor and gen. assignment reporter Phila. Daily News, 1979, city editor, 1979-83, met. editor, 1983-85; PM city editor San Jose (Calif.) Mercury News, 1985-86, met. editor, 1986-87; city editor The Washington Post, 1987-90; mng. editor The Ft. Worth Star-Telegram, 1991-93; editor and v.p. The Milw. Jour., 1993-95; editor, sr. v.p The Milw. Jour. Sentinel, 1995—. Mem. AP Mng. Editors (bd. dirs. 1992-95), Am. Soc. Newspaper Editors, Internat. Press Inst. (bd. dirs. 1994—, Pulitzer prize juror 1994, 96). Office: The Milw Jour Sentinel 333 W State St Milwaukee WI 53201-0371

MEISSNER, ANN LORING, psychologist, educator; b. Richland Center, Wis., Nov. 26, 1924; d. Frank Gilson Woodworth and Leona Bergman; m. Hans Meissner, July 4, 1946 (div. 1953); children: Edie, John Arthur; m. Corbin Sherwood Kidder, Oct. 28,1979. BS, U. Mich., 1953; MS, U. Wis., 1960, PhD, 1965; MPH, U. Calif., Berkeley, 1969; diploma, Gestalt Inst., Cleve., 1974, U. Minn., 1993. Lic. psychologist, Minn. Assoc. dir. Coop. Sch. Rehab. Ctr., Mpls., 1965-72; assoc. prof. W.Va. U., 1972-74; psychologist Alternative Behavior Assn., Mpls., 1974-79, Judson Family Ctr., Mpls., 1979-84; pvt. practice St. Paul, 1984—; dir. nursing Augsburg U., Mpls., 1974-76; adj. prof. St. Mary's Coll., Mpls., 1979—; mem. staff Gestalt Inst. Twin Cities, Mpls., 1978-88; dir. Today Per., Mpls., 1980-91; mem. State Bd. Psychology, Mpls., 1982-86; adv. bd. doctoral program U. St. Thomas, St. Paul, adj. faculty, 1993. Recipient Disting. Human Svc. Profl. award N. Hennepin C.C., Mpls., 1981. Mem. APA, Minn. Women Psychologists. Episcopalian. Home: 111 Kellogg Blvd E Apt 1501 Saint Paul MN 55101-1214 Office: 1360 Energy Park Dr Ste 330 Saint Paul MN 55108-5252

MEISSNER, SUZANNE BANKS, pastoral associate; b. Flint, Mich., July 12, 1943; d. Leon J. and Eunice Alberta (Conners) Banks; m. Edward J. Meissner, Aug. 20, 1966 (div. Sept. 1975). BA, North Park Coll., 1965; MA, Ea. Mich. U., 1979; M in Pastoral Studies, Loyola U., New Orleans, 1991. Cert. secondary educator, Mich., spiritual dir., Mich. Tchr. Flint (Mich.) Cmty. Schs., 1965-94; pastoral assoc. St. Michael Ch., Flint, 1985—; mem. listening ministries adv. bd. Diocese of Lansing, Mich., 1994—, co-chair Profl. Pastoral Mins. Assn., 1994—, chair diocesan pastoral coun., 1986-88. Mem. Phi Kappa Phi, Phi Delta Kappa. Democrat. Home: 7217 N McKinley Rd Flushing MI 48433 Office: Saint Michael Church 609 E 5th Ave Flint MI 48503

MEISTER, BERNARD JOHN, chemical engineer; b. Maynard, Mass., Feb. 27, 1941; s. Benjamin C. M. and Gertrude M. (Meister); m. Janet M. White, Dec. 31, 1971; children: Mark, Martin, Kay Ellen. B.S. in Chem. Engring., Worcester Poly. Inst., 1962; Ph.D. in Chem. Engring., Cornell U., 1966. Engring. researcher Dow Chem. Co., Midland, Mich., 1966—, sr. rsch. specialist, 1978-81, assoc. scientist, 1981-85, sr. assoc. scientist, 1985-92, rsch. scientist, 1992—. Contbr. articles to profl. jours. Mem. Am. Inst. Chem. Engrs., Am. Chem. Soc., Soc. Plastics Engrs., Soc. Rheology, Sigma Xi. Mem. Ch. of Nazarene. Home: 2925 Chippewa Ln Midland MI 48640-4181 Office: Dow Chem Co 438 Bldg Midland MI 48640

MELCHIORRE, ERIK BALDWIN, geochemist, educator; b. Cin., Feb. 14, 1968; s. Richard George and Wilma (Baldwin) M. BS in Geol. Scis., U. So. Calif., 1990; MS in Geology, Ariz. State U., 1993; leadership devel. cert., U. Calif., Davis, 1994; postgrad., Washington U., St. Louis, 1995—. Registered geologist, Mo. Tchg. asst. Ariz. State U., Tempe, 1990-92, head tchg. asst., 1992-93; tchg. and rsch. asst. U. Calif., 1993-94; tchg. and rsch. assoc. Washington U., 1995—; geologist Cyprus Bagdad (Ariz.) Cooper Corp., summer 1991; field mapper Ariz. Geol. Survey, Tucson, 1991, 92; geologist Phelps Dodge Morenci (Ariz.), Inc., summer 1992, hydrogeologist, summers 1993, 94. Editor: The History of Camp Wolfeboro, 1986; contbr. articles to profl. jours. Found. grantee Soc. Profl. Well Log Analysts, 1994; rsch. grantee North Coast Geol. Soc., 1994, 95. Mem. Am. Assn. Petroleum Geologists, Geol. Soc. Am., Soc. for Mining, Metallurgy and Exploration, Am. Inst. Profl. Geologists, Delta Sigma Phi. Office: Wash U Dept Earth & Planetary Sci One Brookings Dr CB 1169 Saint Louis MO 63130

MELE, JOANNE THERESA, dentist; b. Chgo., Dec. 5, 1943; d. Andrew and Josephine Jeanette (Calabrese) M. Diploma, St. Elizabeth's Sch. Nursing, Chgo., 1964; diploma in Dental Hygiene, Northwestern U., 1977; A.S., Triton Coll., 1979; D.D.S., Loyola U., 1983. Registered nurse, dental hygienist. Staff nurse in medicine/surgery St. Elizabeth's Hosp., Chgo., 1964-66, operating room nurse, 1966-67; head nurse operating room Cook County Hosp., Chgo., 1967-76, head nurse ICU, 1976-77; dental hygienist Mele Dental Assocs., Ltd., Oakbrook, Ill., 1977-79, practice dentistry, 1983—; clinical asst. prof. Loyola U., Chgo., 1988. Recipient Northwestern U. Dental Hygiene Clinic award, 1977; Dr. Duxler Humanitarian award scholar Loyola U., 1982. Mem. Chgo. Dental Soc., Ill. State Dental Soc., Acad. Gen. Dentistry, Am. Assn. Women Dentists, Acad. Operative Dentistry, Am. Prosthodontic Soc., Psi Omega (Kappa chpt.). Roman Catholic. Avocations: reading; music; golfing; jogging; skiing.. Office: Mele Dental Assocs Ltd 120 Center St Ste 610 Hinsdale IL 60521

MELI, DAVID, program manager; b. Detroit, Sept. 2, 1964. B, L.I.T., 1986. Program mgr. Minowitz Mfg. Co., Roseville, Mich., 1986—. Office: Minowitz Mfg Co 27941 Groesbeck Hwy Roseville MI 48066-5221

MELIN, ROBERT ARTHUR, lawyer; b. Milw., Sept. 13, 1940; s. Arthur John and Frances Magdalena (Lanser) M.; m. Mary Magdalen Melin, July 8, 1967; children: Arthur Walden, Robert Dismas, Nicholas O'Brien, Madalyn Mary. B.A. summa cum laude, Marquette U., 1962, J.D., 1967. Bar: Wis. 1966, U.S. Dist. Ct. (ea. dist.) Wis. 1966, U.S. Ct. Appeals (7th cir.) 1966, U.S. Ct. Mil. Appeals 1967, U.S. Supreme Ct. 1975. Law clk. U.S. Dist. Ct. Eastern Dist. Wis., 1966; instr. bus. law U. Ga., Hinesville, 1968, also lectr. bus. law U. Md., Asmara, 1970; lectr. law Haile Selassie I U. Law Faculty, Addis Ababa, Ethiopia, 1971-72; mem. firm Walther & Halling, Milw., 1973-74, Schroeder, Gedlen, Riester & Moerke, Milw., 1974-82; ptnr. Schroeder, Gedlen, Riester & Melin, Milw., 1982-84, Schroeder, Riester, Melin & Smith, 1984—. lectr. charitable solicitations and contracts Philanthropy Monthly 9th Ann. Policy Conf., N.Y.C., 1985. Chmn. Milw. Young Democrats, 1963-64. Served to capt. JAGC, AUS, 1967-70. Mem. Wis. Acad. Trial Lawyers, ABA, Wis. Bar Assn., Milw. Bar Assn., Am. Legion, Friends of Ethiopia, Delta Theta Phi, Phi Alpha Theta, Pi Gamma Mu. Roman Catholic. Author: Evidence in Ethiopia, 1972; contbg. author to Annual Survey of African Law, 1974; contbr. numerous articles to legal jours. Home: 8108 N Whitney Rd Milwaukee WI 53217-2752 Office: 135 W Wells St Milwaukee WI 53203-1807

MELLEMA, DONALD EUGENE, radio news reporter and anchor; b. Chgo., Mar. 30, 1937; s. Raymond Cornelius and Dorothy Sofia (Miller) M.; m. Freda Dieterlen Mellema, Sept. 23, 1961; children: Darryl Emerson, Duane Edward. BA in Speech, Beloit (Wis.) Coll., 1959. News dir. WGEZ Radio, Beloit, 1959; evening host, newsman WOSH Radio, Oshkosh, Wis., 1959-63; morning host, newsman WANE Radio, Ft. Wayne, Ind., 1963-65; news dir. WATI Radio, Indpls., 1965-67; news writer WGN Radio, Chgo., 1967-69; news reporter, anchor WBBM Radio, Chgo., 1969—; mem. publs. adv. bd., pres's adv. coun., cons. Beloit Coll., 1996—, also profl.-in-residence. Speaker, motivator Chgo. Pub. Sch. Youth Motivation Program, 1993—; advisor, cons. media rels. to various police and civic orgns.; commr., unit leader Boy Scouts Am., 1971-81; ch. deacon Park Ridge (Ill.) Presbyn. Ch., 1980-83. Recipient Regl. award Radio TV News Dirs. Assn., 1994, Newsfinder award AP, 1995; named to Taft H.S. Hall of Fame, 1995. Mem. Ill. News Broadcasters Assn. (Silver Dome 1st Place award 1994), Soc. Profl. Journalists (Peter Lisagor award 1991), Am. Legion. Republican. Office: WBBM/CBS 630 N McClurg Ct Chicago IL 60611

MELLEMA, GREGORY FRANK, philosophy educator; b. Chgo., June 22, 1948; s. Julius Franklin and Alyce Grace (VandeRiet) M.; m. Nancy Ann Larson, July 6, 1973; children: Adam Franklin Mellema, Jenna Emily Mellema. BA, Calvin Coll., 1970; PhD, U. Mass., 1974; MBA, U. Mich., 1978. Instr. St. Olaf Coll., Northfield, Minn., 1974-75; asst. prof. Calvin Coll., Grand Rapids, Mich., 1975-76, 78-80; assoc. prof. Calvin Coll., Grand Rapids, 1980-84, prof., 1984—; asst. editor Philosopher's Index, Bowling Green, Ohio, 1976-79; writer test materials Am. Coll. Testing Svc., Princeton, N.J., 1981-82; adj. prof. Aquinas Coll., Grand Rapids, Mich., 1991-93. Author: Beyond the Call of Duty, 1991, Individuals, Groups and Shared Moral Responsibility, 1988; contbr. articles to profl. jours. Mem. Am. Philo. Assn., Soc. for Bus. Ethics, Soc. Christian Philosophers. Mem. Christian Reformed Ch. Home: 4834 Curwood Ave SE Kentwood MI 49508-4816 Office: Calvin Coll Calvin Coll Grand Rapids MI 49506

MELLION, MORRIS BERNARD, physician, educator; b. Providence, Dec. 24, 1939; s. Frank and Yvette Gladys (Shaset) M.; m. Irene Mabel Conner, June 6, 1970; children: Rose Conner, Frank Bruce. BA with honors, Cornell U., 1961; postgrad., Tulane U., 1964-66; MD, Yale U., 1970. Diplomate Am. Bd. Family Practice (relevancy com. 1988-89, cons. sports medicine com. 1988). Intern, resident U. Vt. Sch. Medicine, Burlington, 1970-74; pvt. practice, Moran and Teton Village, Wyo., 1971-72, Jackson, Wyo., 1974-82; asst. and assoc. prof. Sch. Health, Phys. Edn.-Recreation, U. Nebr., Omaha, 1986-90, supr. practicum worksite, 1986—, adj. assoc. prof., 1990—; coord., dir. family practice fellowship in sports medicine U. Nebr. Med. Ctr., Omaha, 1988-90, clin. assoc. prof. family practice and orthopaedic surgery, 1990—; med. dir. Sports Medicine Ctr., Omaha, 1990—, HMO Nebr. Inc. (Blue Cross Blue Shield managed care subs.), 1996—; clin. asst. prof. preventive and family medicine U. Colo. Sch. Medicine, Denver, 1980-92; del. Coun. Med. Splty. Socs., Lake Forest, Ill., 1991-92; mem. rev. panel Am. Family Physician, 1988—, Physician and Sportsmedicine, 1988—, Medicine and Sci. in Sports and Exercise, 1990—, Jour. Musculoskeletal Medicine and Exercise, 1990—; mem. exec. bd. Midwest Youth Coaches Assn., Omaha, 1991, cons., 1992—; tournament physician NCAA, Omaha, 1988; med. advisor Dept. Vocat. Rehab., Teton County, 1976-82. Editor, author: Office Management of Sports Injuries and Athletic Problems, 1988, The Team Physician's Handbook, 1990, Sports Medicine Secrets, 1994, Office Sports Medicine, 1995; mem. editl. bd. Family Practice Bull., 1988-90; assoc. editor Heart Disease and Stroke, 1991-94; also articles. Bd. dirs. Athletes Fighting Substance Abuse, Omaha, 1990; med. cons. Teton Community Mental Health Ctr., Jackson, 1975, bd. dirs., 1976-79, pres. bd., 1977-78; med. advisor Teton County chpt. Am. Cancer Soc., Jackson, 1974-76; mem. Nat. Ski Patrol, Grand Targhee Ski Area, Alta, Wyo., 1977-81; mem. adv. bd. Jackson Hole Arts Ctr., 1982, Dignity, Inc., Jackson, 1981-82; mem. bd. Community Children's Project, Jackson, 1976-78; also others. Lt. (j.g.) USN, 1961-65. Recipient Cornell Aero. Lab. award Cornell U., 1965, Spl. Recognition award U. Nebr., 1988-89; scholar Naval ROTC, 1961-65; Woodrow Wilson fellow Princeton U., 1965. Fellow Am. Acad. Family Physicians (vice speaker Congress of Dels. 1984-88, speaker Congress of Dels. 1988-90, pres.-elect 1990-91, pres. 1991-92, exec. com. 1990—, chair Com. on Health Edn. 1984-87, chair Task Force on Sports Medicine 1988-89); mem. AMA, Soc. Tchrs. Family Medicine, Nebr. Acad. Family Physicians, Nebr. Med. Assn., Metro Omaha Med. Soc., Am. Acad. Allergy, Am. Coll. Sports Medicine, Am. Orthopaedic Soc. for Sports Medicine (affiliate), Am. Heart Assn. (coun. on arteriosclerosis), Nat. Strength and Conditioning Assn., Nat. Athletic Trainers Assn. (adv.), Cycling Rsch. Assn., Am. Med. Soc. for Sports Medicine (charter), Phi Beta Kapa, Pi Sigma Alpha. Jewish. Office: Sports Medicine Ctr 2255 S 132nd St Omaha NE 68144-2501

MELLOTT, ROBERT VERNON, advertising executive; b. Dixon, Ill., Jan. 1, 1928; s. Edwin Vernon and Frances Rhoda (Miller) M.; m. Sarah Carolyn Frink, June 11, 1960; children: Lynn Mellott Finzer, Susan Mellott Dodge, David Robert. BA, DePauw U., 1950; postgrad. Grad. Sch., Ind. U., 1950-51, Law Sch., 1959-61, MA, 1983. TV producer, dir. Jefferson Standard Broadcasting Co., Charlotte, N.C., 1951-59; asst. dist. mgr. GM., Flint, Mich., Chgo., 1961-62; TV and radio comml. supr. NW Ayer & Son, Chgo., 1962-65; TV and radio producer Foote, Cone & Belding Advt. Inc., Chgo., 1965-67, mgr. midwest prodn., 1967-69, mgr. comml. coordination, 1969-74, v.p., mgr. comml. svcs., Chgo., 1974-93 (ret.); cons. speech and broadcasting comm. Mem. media adv. com. Coll. of Dupage, Glen Ellyn, Ill., 1971-82; chmn. Cub Scout Com., Wheaton, Ill., 1978-79; bd. dirs. Chgo. Unltd., 1969-71. Mem. Am. Assn. Advt. Agys. (broadcast adminstrn. policy com., broadcast talent union rels. ANA-AAAA joint policy com. 1984-93), World Communication Assn., Internat. Platform Assn., Phi Delta Phi, Alpha Tau Omega. Republican. Mem. Evang. Christian Ch. Clubs: DePauw U. Alumni Assn., Ind. U. Alumni. Home: 26w130 Tomahawk Dr Wheaton IL 60187-7823

MELNIKOFF, SARAH ANN, gem importer, jewelry designer; b. Chgo., Feb. 12, 1936; d. Harry E. and Marie Louise (Straub) Caylor; m. Casimir Adam Jestadt, Feb. 27, 1959 (div. Sept. 1972); 1 child, Christina Marie Jestadt-Russo; m. Sol Melnikoff, July 31, 1981. Student Gemol. Inst. Am., 1968-69, Am. Acad. Art, Chgo., 1952-56, Art Inst. Chgo., 1953, Mundelein Coll., Chgo., 1953-54. Pres., Casmira Gem, Inc., Chgo., 1963—; comml. artist, Chgo., 1957-78; owner Acorn Antiques and Uniques, Chgo. U.S. del. Internat. Colored Gemstone Dealers Assn., W.Ger., 1985; lectr., cons. in field. Mem. Chgo. Salesman's Alliance, MINK Inc., Women's Jewelry Assn., Am. Gem Trade Assn. (nat. sec. 1982-86, 88—, dir. 1988-92), Chgo. Jewelers Assn. (bd. dirs. 1994—), Women's Jewelry Assn., Inc., Am. Horse Show Assn., Am. Saddlebred Horse Show Assn., Mid-Am. Horse Show Assn. (dir. 1980-83). Republican. Roman Catholic. Avocation: horses, antiques.

MELOCHE, JOSEPH LAWRENCE, mechanical engineer; b. Detroit, June 27, 1971. BSME, G.M.I. Engring. & Mgmt. Inst., 1994. Assoc. engr. Numatics, Inc., Highland, Mich., 1989-94; sr. project engr. Ingersoll-Rand ARO Corp., Bryan, Ohio, 1994—. Mem. Soc. Mfg. Engring., Nat. Fluid Power Assoc. Office: ARO Corp 1 Aro Ctr Bryan OH 43506-1100

MELSON, ROBERT FRANK, political science educator; b. Warsaw, Poland, Dec. 27, 1937; came to U.S., 1947; s. William John and Nina (Ponczek) M.; m. Gail C. Freedman, Sept. 22, 1964; children: Sara, Joshua. BS, MIT, 1959, PhD, 1967. Asst. prof. Mich. State U., East Lansing, 1967-71; prof. Purdue U., West Lafayette, Ind., 1971—. Author: Nigeria: Modernization and the Politics of Communalism, 1971, Revolution and Genocide, 1992. Recipient Ford Found. fellowship, Nigeria, 1964-65, Human Rights award Leiden U., The Netherlands, 1993; fellow Ctr. for Advanced Study U. Ill., 1969-70; rsch. assoc. Truman Inst., Jerusalem, 1977-78, 83. Mem. Am. Polit. Sci. Assn., Am. Hist. Assn., Soc. for Armenian Studies, Midwest Jewish Studies Assn. Office: Purdue U Polit Sci Dept Lafayette IN 47907

MELSTED, MARCELLA H., retired administrative assistant, civic worker; b. Mayville, N.D., Mar. 3, 1922; d. Hans Morris and Betsy (Stenerson) Hanson; m. Alvin K. Melsted, June 6, 1965 (dec. June 1994). BS in Commerce, U. N.D., 1946, postgrad. Sec. Off. Sci. R&D, Washington, 1943-45; adminstrv. asst. Am. Embassy (Marshall Plan), Oslo, 1948-50, Paris, 1950-52; adminstrv. asst. N.D. Geol. Soc., Grand Forks, 1953-65. Co-editor: Memories of Homemakers, 1988. Pres. Borg Home Auxiliary, 1984—; apptd. cons. rep. State Plumbing Bd.; chmn. needlepointing dining room chairs N.D. Gov.'s mansion; parliamentarian N.D. Extension Homemakers, Women of Evang. Luth. Ch. Am., v.p., bd. dirs., 1985-91; mem. N.D. Humanities Coun., 1985-91; bd. dirs. Friends of N.D. Mus.; mem. Quad County Cmty. Action Bd., 1995—. Mem. AAUW (parliamentarian N.D. State divsn., 2 fellowships, author branch history, state pres. 1962-64, nat. membership com. 1964-66), N.D. State Fedn. Garden Clubs (state pres., life, tree chmn. nat. bd., state treas. 1991—), Four Seasons Garden Club (sec.-treas. 1987—), Homemakers Clubs (various coms.), China Painters Guild (various coms.). Democrat. Home: 7862 127th Ave NE Edinburg ND 58227-9604

MELTON, EDWARD JOSEPH, commercial banker; b. Louisville, Feb. 24, 1957; s. Edward C. and Francis H. Melton; m. Cheryl A. Melton, June 14, 1980; children: Jennifer Marie, James Edward. BS, Northeastern Ill. U., Chgo., 1979; M Mgmt., Northwestern U., Evanston, Ill., 1981. Banking officer Continental Bank, Chgo., 1981-88; sr. v.p., sr. loan officer 1st Midwest Bankcorp., Inc., Itasca, Ill., 1988—; dir. Material Space Handling Corp., Northbrook, Ill., 1990—; instr. Keller Grad. Sch. Mgmt., Lincolnshire, 1991—. V.p. bd. Holy Cross Sch., Deerfield, Ill., 1992—; mem. Habitat for Humanity, Waukegan, Ill., 1991—. Mem. Deerfield C. of C. Republican. Roman Catholic. Home: 1280 Warwick Ct Deerfield IL 60015-3009 Office: First Midwest Bank NA 725 Waukegan Rd Deerfield IL 60015-4326

MELTON, EMORY LEON, lawyer, publisher, state legislator; b. McDowell, Mo. June 20, 1923; s. Columbus Right and Pearly Susan (Wise) M.; student Monett Jr. Coll., 1940-41, S.W. Mo. State U., 1941-42; LLB, U. Mo., 1945; m. Jean Sanders, June 19, 1949; children: Stanley Emory, John Russell. Admitted to Mo. bar, 1944; individual practice law, Cassville, Mo., 1947—; pres. Melton Publs., Inc., pub. 2 newspapers, 1959—; pros. atty. Barry county (Mo.), 1947-51; mem. Mo. Senate, 1973—. Chmn., Barry County Republican Com., 1964-68. Served with AUS, 1945-46. Recipient award for meritorious public service St. Louis Globe-Democrat., 1976. Mem. Mo. Bar Assn. Baptist. Clubs: Lions, Masons. Office: PO Box 488 Cassville MO 65625-0488

MELTON, JEAN EDITH, retired elementary education educator; b. Monticello, Iowa, Nov. 17, 1926; d. James Calvin and Edith C. (Schneider) Bender; m. Thomas Greenleaf Melton, Sept. 9, 1947; children: Nance Jean, Thomas Mark, David Myron. AA, Dubuque (Iowa) U.; BA, Ctrl. Mo. State U., 1971; MA in Edn., U. Mo., Kansas City, 1978. Cert. elem. tchr. Mentor new tchr., Independence; hon. mem. PTA, Independence. Mem. Mo. State Tchrs. Assn. (mem. local bd.), Internat. Reading Assn., Delta Kappa Gamma (bd. dirs.), Presbyn. Women's Orgn. (hon. Christian edn. mem.), P.E.O. Home: 305 N Delaware Independence MO 64050

MELTZER, SHARON BITTENSON, English language and humanities educator; b. Bklyn., Feb. 22, 1940; d. Abraham and Lena Yetta (Bienstock) Bittenson; m. Herbert Yale Meltzer, June 12, 1960; children: David Owen Meltzer, Danielle Beth Meltzer. AB, Barnard Coll., 1961; AM, Yale U., 1962, PhD, 1970. Lectr. CUNY, 1963; instr. Tufts U., Medford, Mass., 1965-66; lectr. U. Chgo., 1970-71, asst. prof., 1971-76, asst. dean of students, social scis., 1977-80; assoc. prof. Chgo. City-Wide Coll., 1981-85, prof., 1985-91; prof. English Richard J. Daley Coll., Chgo., 1991—. Recipient Woodrow Wilson fellowship Yale U., 1961, 64, Jr. Sterling fellowship Yale U., 1962, U. Chgo. Outstanding Tchr. award, 1989, 90, 95. Mem. Modern Lang. Assn., Nat. Coun. Tchrs. English, C.C. Humanities Assn., Internat. Assn. for Philosophy and Lit., Soc. for Critical Exch., Phi Beta Kappa. Home: 83 Altentann Nashville TN 37215 Office: Richard J Daley Coll 7500 S Pulaski Rd Chicago IL 60652-1242

MELVIN, BILLY ALFRED, clergyman; b. Macon, Ga., Nov. 25, 1929; s. Daniel Henry and Leola Dale (Seidell) M.; m. Marcia Darlene Eby, Oct. 26, 1952; children: Deborah Ruth, Daniel Henry II. Student, Free Will Baptist Bible Coll., Nashville, 1947-49; B.A., Taylor U., Upland, Ind., 1951; postgrad., Asbury Theol. Sem., Wilmore, Ky., 1951-53; B.D., Union Theol. Sem., Richmond, Va., 1956; D.D., Azusa (Calif.) Coll., 1968; LL.D. (hon.), Taylor U., 1984; DD, Huntington Coll., 1995. Ordained to ministry Free Will Baptist Ch., 1951; pastor First Free Will Baptist Chs., Newport, Tenn., 1951-53, Richmond, 1953-57; pastor Bethany Ch., Norfolk, Va., 1957-59; exec. sec. Nat. Assn. Free Will Baptists, 1959-67; exec. dir. Nat. Assn. Evangelicals, 1967-95.

MENCHHOFER, ROBERT HENRY, sales professional; b. Milan, Ind., July 31, 1948; s. Paul Henry and Berta Jean (Black) M.; m. Donna Lee Garner, Mar. 1, 1969; children: Christopher, Angela. Student, GM Inst., Flint, Mich., 1966-68; BS in Indsl. Mgmt., Purdue U., 1972. Systems analyst Packard Electric div. GMC, Warren, Mich., 1972-74; coord. svc. ctr. Link Belt divsn. FMC Corp., Indpls., 1974-80; field sales rep. Stewart Warner South Wind Corp., Indpls., 1980-88, sales mgr., 1988-94; nat. sales mgr. Champ Products Inc., Sarasota, Fla., 1994-95; v.p. N.W. Awards and Recognition Products Inc., Indpls., 1995—. Pres. Brownsburg (Ind.) Jaycees, 1978-79; state chmn. Ind. Jaycees, 1979-84; mem. 500 Festival Assocs. Mem. Soc. Automotive Engrs., Appaloosa Horse Club, Cen. Ind. Appaloosa Horse Club (treas. 1987, pres. 1988-89), U.S. Jaycees Senate, Phi Gamma Delta. Home: 9281-C Notre Dame Dr Indianapolis IN 46240

MENCO, BERNARD, biologist; b. Arnhem, The Netherlands, Jan. 9, 1946; came to U.S., 1982; s. A. and A. (Hakkert) M. BSc, Agrl. U., Wageningen, The Netherlands, 1968, MSc, 1972, PhD, 1977. Rsch. officer U. Warwick, Coventry, U.K., 1972-75; sr. rsch. assoc. State U. Utrecht, The Netherlands, 1975-81, Klinikum Essen, Fed. Republic Germany, 1981-82; from rsch. assoc. to rsch. assoc. prof. Northwestern U., Evanston, Ill., 1982—. Contbr. articles to profl. jours.; editor: Microscopy Rsch. and Technique, 1990—. Recipient Takasago award European Chemoreception Orgn., 1990; finalist Hennessey-Moet-Louis Vuitton prize; Hasselblad Found. fellow, 1988. Mem. Am. Chemoreception Orgn., Soc. Neurosci., Soc. Cell Biology. Office: Northwestern U Dept Neurobiol Physiol Evanston IL 60208

MENDELSOHN, ZEHAVAH WHITNEY, data processing executive; b. Houston, Nov. 22, 1956; d. Alfred Peter and Sarah (Carsey) Whitney; m. Avrum Joseph Mendelsohn, June 27, 1982. AA, College of DuPage, 1988; BA, Nat. Louis U., 1989. Cert. quality analyst. Mgmt. analyst U. Ill., Abraham Lincoln Sch. Medicine, Chgo., 1976-83; sr. analyst quality assurance Ofcl. Airline Guides, Oak Brook, Ill., 1983-95; mgr. process mgmt. U.S. Cellular, 1995—; cons. Polic Cons., Westmont, Ill. Mem. Quality Assurance Inst., Am. Soc. for Quality Control, Chgo. Quality Assurance Assn. (dir. cert.), Chicagoland Handicapped Skiers (pres. 1986-87, 89-91), Profl. Ski Instrs. Am. Office: United States Cellular 8410 W Bryn Mawr Chicago IL 60631

MENDELSON, DAVID FREY, neurology educator; b. St. Louis, Feb. 25, 1925; s. Harry and Lorine Esther (Korngold) M.; m. Mary Ann Lavis, June 21, 1956 (div. Mar. 1978); children: Lorine Ann, David Frey, Helen Elizabeth, Jonathan Joseph. BA, U. Calif., Berkeley, 1946; MD, Ind. U., Indpls., 1948. Diplomate Am. Bd. Psychiatry and Neurology. Intern Ind. U., Indpls., 1948-49; resident Barnes Hosp., St. Louis, 1950-51; fellow neurology U. Minn., Mpls., 1953-58, instr. neurology, 1956-58; practice medicine specializing in neurology St. Louis, 1958—; clin. asst. prof. St. Louis U., 1958-83, Washington U., St. Louis, 1983—. Bd. dirs. Mo. Blue Shield, St. Louis, 1964-72, trustee, 1972-85, corp. bd. 1985—. Served to capt. USAF, 1951-53. Fellow Am. Acad. Neurology; mem. Am. Med. Electroencephalography Soc., St. Louis Met. Med. Soc., St. Louis Soc. Neurol. Scis., Rocky Mountain Traumatologic Soc. Jewish. Club: St. Louis Racquet. Home: 7906 Kingsbury Blvd Saint Louis MO 63105-3824 Office: 141 N Meramec Ave Saint Louis MO 63105-3750

MENDENHALL, GORDON LEE, secondary school educator; b. Winchester, Ind., Sept. 8, 1947; s. Paul G. and Evelyn N. (Pursley) M.; m. Susan Matchett, June 23, 1973; children: Tyler G., Erin E. BA in Zoology, Chemistry, Taylor U., 1969; MA in Secondary Edn., Ball State U., 1972, EdD in Sci. Edn., 1995. Tchr. Union City (Ind.) H.S., 1969-70, Craig Middle Sch., Indpls., 1970-75, Lawrence Ctrl. H.S., Indpls., 1975-90; teaching asst. Ball State U., Muncie, 1990-92; tchr. biology, human genetics Lawrence North H.S., Indpls., 1992—; instr. U. Indpls., summer, 1985-95, U. St. Thomas, Houston, summer 1987-90; cons. NSF, Washington, 1984—; cons. Videodiscovery, Inc., Seattle, 1994—; edn. com. Great Lakes Regional Genetics Group, Madison, Wis., 1989-95. Co-editor Genetic Messenger newsletter, 1993-94; contbr. articles to profl. jours. Recipient Ind. Presdl. Award in Sci., NSF, 1986; Lilly Open fellow, 1982, Access Excellence fellow Genentech Inc., 1994; Tandy Tech. scholar, 1990. Mem. Nat. Sci. Tchrs. Assn., Nat. Assn. Biology Tchrs. (Ind. Outstanding Biology Tchr. 1989), Hoosier Assn. Sci. Tchrs. Methodist. Home: 8741 Ginnylock Dr Indianapolis IN 46256-1161

MENDENHALL, HANS, graphic designer; b. Chgo., Mar. 27, 1952; s. Lawrence and Jacqueline France (Stewart) M.; m. Janet Schneider, May 13, 1972 (div. Apr. 1976). Student, Chgo. State U., 1969-71. Printer Canteen Corp., Chgo., 1970-73; graphic coord. Beltone Electronics, Chgo., 1973—. Vol. staff cat records database Best Friends Animal Sanctuary, Kanab, Utah, 1994-95. Home: 2000 W Morse Chicago IL 60645

MENEFEE, FREDERICK LEWIS, advertising executive; b. Arkansas City, Kan., Oct. 22, 1932; s. Arthur LeRoy and Vera Mae (Rather) M.; m. Margot Leuze, Sept. 16, 1955; children: Gregory S., Christina Menefee-Anderson. AA, Arkansas City Jr. Coll., 1952; BA, U. Wichita, 1958. Sports editor, bus. mgr. Ark. Light and Tiger Tales, 1950-52; Sports reporter Ark. City Daily Traveler, 1950-52; advt. mgr. Derby Star, Haysville Harold and Sedgewick County News, 1956-57; vice-pres., account exec. Asso. Advt. Agy., 1958-64; with McCormick-Armstrong Advt. Agy. (name changed to Menefee and Ptnrs., Inc. in 1989), Wichita, 1964—, agy. mgr., 1964—, account supr., 1965—, gen. mgr., 1972—, pres., chief exec. officer, 1979—, chmn. bd., 1984—, pres., chmn. bd., 1989—. Pub. relations chmn. Wichita Centennial Nat. Art Show and Exhibit, 1969-70. Served with AUS, 1953-55. Named Advt. Man of Yr., Advt. Club of Wichita, 1964, Advt. Man of Yr., 9th Dist. Am. Advt. Fedn., 1965; Adm. Windwagon Smith III award Wichita Festivals Inc., 1976. Mem. Am. Advt. Fedn. (nat. bd. dirs. 1969-70, dist. gov. 1968-69, chmn. nat. coun. govs. 1969-70, Wichita Wagonmasters (capt. 1974-75, dir.; charter), Wichita Advt. Club (pres. 1963-64), PAWS, Inc. (pres. 1985-88), Alpha Delta Sigma (pres. 1957-58, Outstanding Svc. award 1958). Home: 2235 Red Bud Ln Wichita KS 67204-5346 Office: Menefee & Ptnrs Inc 1065 N Topeka St Wichita KS 67214-2913

MENKEDICK, JOHN RICHARD, research scientist; b. Cin., Aug. 15, 1951; s. Earl Henry and Mildred (Yeager) M.; m. Margaret Helen Strunk, Oct. 5, 1987; 1 child, Mary Sarah. BA in English, U. Cin., 1974, BS in Edn., 1974, MS in Math., 1984. Statistician Computer Scis. Corp., Cin., 1984-87, site mgr., 1987-90; dir. computing Hanover (Ind.) Coll., 1990-92; sr. rsch. scientist Battelle Meml. Inst., Columbus, Ohio, 1992—. Contbr. articles to profl. jours. Mem. Sierra Club, Ohio, 1984-95. Mem. Am. Statis. Assn. Office: Battelle 505 King Ave Columbus OH 43201

MENNINGER, ROY WRIGHT, medical foundation executive, psychiatrist; b. Topeka, Oct. 27, 1926; s. William Claire and Catharine (Wright) M.; m. Beverly Joan Miller, Mar. 4, 1973; children: Heather, Ariel, Bonar, Eric, Brent, Frederick, Elizabeth. AB, Swarthmore (Pa.) Coll., 1947; MD, Cornell U., 1951; DHL, Ottawa (Kans.) U., 1977; LittD, William Jewell Coll., Liberty Mo., 1985. Diplomate Am. Bd. Psychiatry and Neurology, 1959. Intern N.Y. Hosp., 1951-52; resident in psychiatry Boston State Hosp., 1952-53, Boston Psychopathic Hosp., 1953-56; from resident psychiatrist to assoc.

med. psychiatrist Peter Bent Brigham Hosp., Boston, 1956-61; teaching and rsch. fellow Harvard U. Med. Sch., Boston, 1956-61; staff psychiatrist Menninger Found., Topeka, 1961-63, dir. dept. preventative psychiatry, 1963-67, pres., CEO, 1967-93; chmn., 1991—; bd. dirs. Bank IV Topeka N.A., CML Corp., The New Eng., U.S. Behavioral Health; mem. Karl Menninger Sch. Psychiatry, Topeka, 1972—, Ind. Sector, 1990—; clin. prof. psychiatry U. Kans. Med. Ctr., Wichita, 1977—; cons. Colmery-O'Neil VA Med. Ctr., Topeka, 1979—. Author: Trends in American Psychiatry: Implication for Psychiatry in Japan; co-author: The Medical Marriage, 1988, The Psychology of Postponement in the Medical Marriage; cons. editor Jour. Medical Aspects Human Sexuality, 1967-90; editor adv. bd. Parents mag., 1966-80, Clin. Psychiatry News, 1973—; reviewer Am. Jour. Psychiatry, 1980—. Mem. sponsoring com. Inst. Am. Democracy, 1967-70; mem. adv. group Horizons '76 Am. Revolution Bicentennial Commn.; adv. bd., steering com. Topeka Inst. Urban Affairs, 1967-70; adv. bd. Highland Park-Pierce Neighborhood House, Topeka, 1967-70; bd. dirs. Shawnee council Campfire Girls, Topeka, 1962-69, A.K. Rice Inst., Washington, Sex Info. and Edn. Council U.S., 1972-73, mem. edn. com., long range planning com., 1972-73; bd. dirs. Goals for Topeka, Topeka Inst. Urban Affairs, 1969-74, v.p., 1973; med. adv. com. VA Hosp., 1972-78; mem. Gov.'s Com. on Criminal Adminstrn., 1971-74; trustee People-to-People, Kansas City, Mo., 1967-69, Baker U., 1968-72, Midwest Research Inst., 1967-1986, 86—, mem. exec. com., 1970-86; vis. lectr. Fgn. Service Inst., State Dept., 1963-66; chmn. social issues com. Group Advancement Psychiatry, 1972-82; community adv. bd. Kans. Health Workers Union, 1968-70; adv. com. to bd. dirs. New Eng. Mut. Life Ins. Co., 1968-70. With U.S. Army, 1953-55. Recipient Disting. Svs. citation U. Kans., 1985; Pacific Rim Coll. Psychiatry fellow. Fellow Am. Psychiat. Assn. (life), Joint Info. Svc. (exec. com.), Am. Coll. Psychiatry, Am. Orthopsychiat. Assn., Am. Coll. Mental Health Adminstrs.; mem. AAAS, Northeastern Group Psychotherapy (hon.), Physicians Social Responsibility, Kans. Psychiat. Soc., Greater Topeka C. of C. (dir.). Episcopalian. Office: Menninger Found PO Box 829 Topeka KS 66601-0829

MENTEL, MICHAEL CHRISTOPHER, lawyer; b. Columbus, Ohio, Nov. 27, 1961; s. James Michael and Victoria K. (Haslett) M.; m. Marisa Ann Rotolo, Oct. 7, 1989; children: Angela, Connor. BA, Capital U., 1984, JD, 1987. Bar: Ohio 1988, U.S. Supreme Ct. 1992, U.S. Ct. Appeals (6th cir.) Ohio 1994, U.S. Dist. Ct. (so. and no. dists.) Ohio 1995. Intern U.S. Sen. John Glenn/Washington Workshops, Washington, summer 1980; account clk. Ohio Atty. Gen., Columbus, 1981-82; intern Columbus City Atty., 1983-84; legal intern Franklin County Pub. Defender, Columbus, 1987-88, staff atty., 1988-89; atty. Ohio EPA, Columbus, 1990-93, supr. atty., 1993-94; atty. Crabbe, Brown, Jones, Potts & Schmidt, 1994—; bd. dirs. Hilliard Edn. Found., 1996—. Mem. Ohio Dems for 90's, 1990—; vol. Operation Feed Columbus, 1990. Mem. ABA, Ohio State Bar Assn., Columbus Bar Assn. (environ. law coms.), Ancient Order of Hibernians, Shamrock Club. Democrat. Roman Cathlic. Home: 3152 Rockfence Dr Columbus OH 43221-4726

MENYHERT, STEPHAN, retired chemist; b. Nagyatad, Hungary, Sept. 18, 1937; came to U.S., 1952; s. Steven and Elfriede A. (Brockmann) M.; m. Roberta Powers, May 27, 1962 (div. Feb. 1978); children: Oleg A., Piroska L., Steven R., George M. BSChemE, U. Cin., 1962; MBA, Xavier U., 1981. Process rsch. chemist Emery Industries, Inc., Cin., 1962-74, mgr. pilot plant, 1974-82; quality assurance chemist II Henkel, Emery Group (formerly Emery Industries, Inc.), Cin., 1982-93; ret., 1994. Tech. advisor Colerain Twp. Vol. Fire Dept., Cin., 1964-76. Mem. AIChE, Am. Chem. Soc., Am. Soc. for Quality Control, Germania Soc. (chmn. bldg. com. Cin. chpt. 1974-77, pres. 1985-87, 94-95). Presbyterian. Office: 3435 Statewood Dr Cincinnati OH 45251-2383

MERCER, BETTY DEBORAH, electrologist, poet, writer, proofreader; b. N.Y.C., Sept. 10, 1926; d. Cecil Boyce and Martha (Romanoff) Fishbein; m. Frank Berthold Mercer, Dec. 22, 1957 (dec. Aug. 1979); children: Kenneth Arnold, Stephen Harry. BS, NYU, 1948; cert. in psychology, child guidance, vocat. guidance, Cornell U., 1951; cert. in libr. sci., Queens Coll., 1954, 55; cert., Hoffman Inst. Electrolysis, N.Y.C., 1955; cert. piano and honors theory II, Royal Conservatory of Music, Toronto, 1965. Pvt. tutor English N.Y.C., 1948, proofreader, copyholder various firms, 1951-54; freelance book reviewer Viking Press, N.Y.C., 1954; clin. electrologist, 1955—; pvt. tchr. piano Muskegon, Mich., 1967—; sales rep. Beauty Counselor, Studio Girl, Sudbury, Ont., Can., 1963-64, Blair Products, Muskegon, 1967-68, 78-80; chair Muskegon Writers, 1979-80; freelance proofreader, 1988, 89; invited Third Coast Writers Conf. Western Mich. U. Author: (poetry book) Toward A Brighter Tomorrow!, A First Collection of Twenty-Seven Published Poems, 1980; contbr. poetry to mags., anthologies including New Writers Mag., Carmichael Pubs. Leader Girl Guides, Sudbury,1958, local chpt. Girl Scouts U.S.A., Muskegon, 1967; libr., cart Sudbury Meml. Hosp., 1963-65; libr. Temple B'nai Israel, Muskegon,1969-78; vol. Hospice Respite Svc., Muskegon, 1989; chairperson Muskegon Hadassah, 1971-72. Recipient Silver Poet award, 5 Golden Poet awards, 10 Merit awards World of Poetry, Sacramento, 1984—, Editors Choice award Nat. Library Poetry, Owings Mills, Md., 1988, 89, Poet of Yr. award Nat. Poetry Pubs. Assn., L.I., N.Y., 1974, 76, Bronze cert. Creative Enterprises, Carson City, Nev., 1986, 87, 5th pl. prize Poetry Unltd., 1991. Fellow World Lit. Assn.; mem. AAUW (pub. com. 1987-88, membership com. 1985-86), Clover Internat. Poetry Assn. (life, DANAE title cert. 1974-75), Am. Electrology Assn., Internat. Guild Profl. Electrologists, Electrolysis Assn. Mich., Region II Electrolysis Assn., Internat. Platform Assn., NYU Alumni Assn., Muskegon Writers, Poetry Soc. of Mich., Hadassah Women's Zionist Orgn. (life), NYU Club. Jewish. Home: 1422 New St Muskegon MI 49442-5372

MERCER, DAVID ROBINSON, cultural organization administrator; b. Van Nuys, Calif., Aug. 14, 1938; s. Samuel Robinson and Dorothy (Lenox) M.; m. Joyce Elaine Dahl, Aug. 23, 1958; children: Steven, Michael, Kimberly. BA, Calif. State U., L.A., 1961. Exec. dir. YMCA of L.A., 1963-69, sr. v.p., 1969-80; reg. mgr. Am. City Bur., Hoffman Estates, Ill., 1980-82; pres. YMCA of San Francisco, 1982-90; nat. exec. dir. YMCA of USA, Chgo., 1990—; cons. fin. devel. YMCAs throughout U.S., 1975—. Mem. The Family, Rotary (bd. dirs. 1987-89). Republican. Methodist. Office: YMCA of USA 101 N Wacker Dr Chicago IL 60606-1718

MERCER, JOHN WHITTY, state agency executive; b. Madison, Fla., Aug. 28, 1942; s. Dalton and Ethel Berenice (Whitty) M.; m. Leslie Joan Klug, Dec. 20, 1969; children: Ashley Nicole, Hillary Elizabeth. AA, North Fla. Jr. Coll., 1962; BA, Fla. State U., 1964, MS, 1966; PhD, U. Minn., 1979. Polit. sci. instr. U. Wis., River Falls, 1966-69, U. Nebr.-Kearney, 1969-70; gen. mgr. Walvern Manor Supper Club, River Falls, 1971-73; rsch./planning asst. Macalester Coll., St. Paul, 1974-75; rsch. fellow Coll. Edn., U. Minn., Mpls., 1975-79; sr. edn. planner State Planning Agy., St. Paul, 1979-82; exec. dir. State Coun. on Vocat. Tech. Edn., St. Paul, 1982-93; dep. commr. edn. Minn. Dept. Edn., Saint Paul, 1993-95; dir. orgn. devel. Minn. Dept. Children, Families and Learning, St. Paul, 1995—; mng. ednl. change fellow U. Minn., 1973-74, ednl. policy fellowship program mem., 1980-81. Co-author: (monographs) Entrepreneurial Graduates, 1987, Fifty Indices of Effectiveness, 1991, Career Planning and Development, 1991, Technology Competence, 1992, Giving Meaning to Cultural Diversity in Education and Work: A Position Statement, 1992, The Condition of Correctional Education in Minnesota: Toward a Vision for Learning, 1993, Making the First Chance a Real Chance: Bridging Education and Work for All Minnesota Youth and Adults, 1993, Harnessing the Dynamics of Educational Change: Learning is What Education is All About, 1993, Focus on Process Improvement: An Evaluation of the Use of the RFP Process in the Distribution of Federal Workforce Education Funds in Minnesota, 1993. Chmn. Minn. Task Force on Edn. and Employment Transitions, 1991-93; chmn. Minn. Edn. and Employment Transitions Coun., 1993-95; chair Minn. Citizens Panel on Content Learner Outcomes, 1993; chmn. Minn. Task Force on Tech. Competence, 1991-95, Minn. State Multicultural Edn. Adv. Com., 1993—; vice chair, chair goverance com. Minn. Edn. Telecomm. Coun., 1995-96; mem. edn. com. Minn. Coun. on Econ. Edn., 1995—; chair State Vocat. H.S. Planning Com., 1995—; mem. cmty. adv. coun. Tele-Commuter Resources, Inc., 1995—; treas., mem. exec. com., bd. dirs. Ramsey Hill Assn., St. Paul, 1978-83, 96—; mem. vestry Ch. of St. John the Evangelist, St. Paul, 1983-87; facilitator Visioning Convocation, Episcopal Diocese of Minn., 1992; mem. bd. mgrs. Midway br. St. Paul YMCA, 1993—, mem. exec. com., chair devel. com., chair strategic planning group, 1995. Recipient Disting. Svc. award Minn. Vocat. Assn., 1992, Good Neighbor award Ramsey Hill Assn., 1983. Mem. Am. Assn. for Higher Edn., Politics of Edn. Assn., Assn. for Quality and Participation, World Future Soc., Phi Delta Kappa. Home: 596 Holly Ave Saint Paul MN 55102-2210 Office: Minn Dept Children Families & Learning 550 Cedar St Saint Paul MN 55101-2233

MEREDITH, MERI HILL, reference librarian; b. Riverside, Calif., May 30, 1943; d. William Beans and Marie Louise (Zantzinger) Hill; m. William Rinehardt Meredith, Mar. 17, 1970 (div.); children William Rinehardt III, Sarah Daingerfield Meredith. AB in French, George Washington U., Washington, 1967; MLS, Ind. U., 1980. Cataloger Ind. U., Bloomington, 1980-81; bus. libr. Cummins Engine Co., Columbus, Ind., 1981-88; pres. Info. and Comm. Rsch., Inc., Columbus, 1989-92; reference libr. Ohio State U. Bus. Libr., 1992—; bd. dirs. Sch. of Libr. and Info. Sci., Ind. U., Bloomington; pres., co-founder Ind. On-Line Users Group, Indpls. Mem. AAUP, Spl. Librs. Assn., Acad. Libr. Assn. of Ohio. Republican. Roman Catholic. Home: 1800 Lafayette Pl Apt A1 Columbus OH 43212 Office: Ohio State U Bus Libr 110 Page Hall 1810 College Columbus OH 43210

MERGENOVICH, SHIRLEY ANN, educator; b. Clinchco, Va., July 13, 1938; d. Floyd Fuller and Cara Mae (Deel) Fuller; m. Carl Mullins (div. 1963); children: Roger Dean, Rex Dale; m. Peter Mergenovich, May 1, 1971 (dec.). AA, Community Coll. St. Louis, 1973; BA in History summa cum laude, Maryville Coll., St. Louis, 1975; MEd in Adminstrn., U. Mo., 1980; cert. in small bus. mgmt., C.C. St. Louis, 1989. Cert. lifetime secondary prin. and tchr. Sales Libson Shops, St. Louis, 1960-61; inventory control and customer svc. Precision Auto Components Co., St. Louis, 1961-64; exec.sec. Precision Auto/TRW, St. Louis, 1964-65; city clk. City of Ballwin (Mo.), 1965-66; exec. dir. Charter Rev. Commn., St. Louis County, Mo., 1966-67; admisntrv. asst. Planning Dir. of St. Louis County, 1968-69; asst. econ. researcher Reg. Ind. Devel. Co., Clayton, Mo., 1969-70; tchr. Eastern history and culture N.W. R-1 Sch. Dist., House Springs, Mo., 1975-90; founder/dir. adult edn. prog. Jefferson Coll. R-1 Schs., House Springs, 1985-86; founder, prin. cons. Performance Builders, St. Louis, 1989; mem. adj. faculty C.C. St. Louis, Webster U., Maryville U., St. Louis; dir. adult continuing edn. Jefferson Coll., 1985-86; part-time mgmt. cons., 1970-79; designer, facilitator numerous tng. programs; designer, implementor pilot study for tchrs. on tchg. and learning styles in pub. schs. Author: A Statistical Summary of Vocational Technical Programs in St. Louis Metro Area, 1970; co-author: Analysis and Projection of Manpower Requirements in St. Louis Metro Area, 1970, Discipline Handbook, 1978; contbr. articles to profl. jours. Tchr. Sunday sch. Ballwin Bapt. Ch.; active Mentoring Women in Transition, Working with Execs. and Mgrs. Out of Work. Named Woman Entrepreneur, Small Bus. Adminstrn., 1989, others; Fulbrightscholar Korea on quality exch. tchr. program, 1982. Mem. NEA, ASTD (bd. dirs., v.p. 1984-88, editor/pub. Torch newsletter 1984-88), Am. Soc. Quality Control, Mo. Cmty. Edn. Assn. (bd. dirs. 1979-81), St. Louis Woman's Commerce Assn. (mem. gov.'s adv. coun. on vocat. edn. 1968-70), N.W. St. Louis Hons. Assn., Woman Entrepreneurial Alumnae Assn.

MERICLE, ROBERT BRUCE, mathematics educator; b. Omaha, June 4, 1938; s. Robert Bruce and Olga Lorrayne (Dyba) M.; m. Gael Tonia Sylce, Aug. 24, 1963; children: Erik Bruce, Andrea Lyn, Melanie Anne. BS in Math., Iowa State U., 1960; MS, U. Md., 1964; PhD, Wash. St. U., 1970. Instr. U. Maine, Orono, 1964-66, Wash. State U., Pullman, 1966-70; asst., assoc. prof. Mankato (Minn.) State U., 1970-74; dir., acad. computer svc. Mich. Tech. U., Houghton, 1974-77; prof. math. Mankato State U., 1977—. Mem. Am. Math. Soc., Math. Assn. Am. Office: Mankato State U Dept Math MSU 41 PO Box 8400 Mankato MN 56002-8400

MERIDEN, TERRY, physician; b. Damascus, Syria, Oct. 12, 1946; came to U.S., 1975; s. Izzat and Omayma (Aidi) M.; m. Lena Kahal, Nov. 17, 1975; children: Zina, Lana. BS, Sch. Sci., Damascus, 1968; MD, Sch. Medicine, Damascus, 1972, doctorate cum laude, 1973. Diplomate Am. Bd. Internal Medicine. Resident in infectious diseases Rush Green Hosp., Romford, Eng., 1973; house officer in internal medicine and cardiology Ashford (Eng.) Group Univ. Hosps., 1973-74; sr. house officer in internal medicine and neurology Grimsby (Eng.) Group Univ. Hosps., 1974; registrar in internal medicine and rheumatology St. Annes Hosp., London, 1974-75; jr. resident in internal medicine Shadyside Hosp., Pitts., 1975-76, sr. resident in internal medicine, 1976-77; fellow in endocrinology and metabolism Shadyside Hosp. and Grad. Inst., Pitts., 1976-77; clin. asst. prof. U. Ill., Peoria, 1979; pres. Am. Diabetes Assn., Peoria, 1982-84; dir. Proctor Diabetes Unit, Peoria, 1984—, 1984—; adviser to the Gov. of Ill. on Diabetes. Mem. editorial bd. Diabetes Forecast mag., Clin. Diabetes, 1990; contbr. articles to profl. jours. Fellow ACP, FACE, Am. Coll. Endocrinology; mem. AMA (Recognition award 1985, ADA (chmn. profl. edn. and rsch. 1980—, mem. editl. bd. and Spanish lit. bd. nat. bd. dirs. 1986—, vice chmn. nat. com. on diabetes edn. and affiliate svcs. 1986—, Outstanding Svc. award 1984, Outstanding Diabetes Educator award 1986), Am. Cancer Soc. (Life Line award 1983), Am. Assn. Clin. Endocrinology (founding), Am. Coll. Endocrinology, The Obesity Found. (Century award 1984, Recognition award 1985). Home: 115 E Coventry Ln Peoria IL 61614-2103 Office: 900 Main St Ste 300 Peoria IL 61602-1005

MERIWETHER, HEATH J., newspaper publisher; b. Columbia, Mo., Jan. 20, 1944; s. Nelson Heath and Mary Agnes (Immele) M.; m. Patricia Hughes, May 4, 1979; children: Graham, Elizabeth. BA in History, BJ, U. Mo., 1966; MA in Teaching, Harvard U., 1967. Reporter Miami (Fla.) Herald, 1970-72, editor Broward and Palm Beach burs., 1972-77, exec. city editor, 1977-79, asst. mgr. editor news, 1979-80, mng. editor, 1981-83, exec. editor, 1983-87; exec. editor Detroit Free Press, 1987-95, publisher, 1996—. Trustee Greenhills Sch., 1995—; bd. dirs. Detroit Symphony Orch., 1996—. Served to lt. USNR, 1967-70. Journalism fellow Stanford U., 1980. Roman Catholic. Office: Detroit Free Press 321 W Lafayette Blvd Detroit MI 48226-2705

MERLENO, TONI AUTUMN, personnel executive; b. Garfield Heights, Ohio, Jan. 16, 1954; d. Anthony and Joyce Irene (Price) M. BA in English, King's Coll., Briarcliff Manor, N.Y., 1976. Cert. secondary tchr., Ohio. Tchr. English, Heritage Christian Sch., Cleve., 1976-77, 1st Bapt. Christian Sch., Elyria, Ohio, 1977-84; pers. asst. May Dept. Stores Co., Cleve., 1984-85; coord. human resources cen. credit dept. May Co., Parma, Ohio, 1985-86, mgr. human resources Parmatown br., 1986-89; pers. mgr. Green Cir. Growers, Inc., Oberlin, Ohio, 1989—. Soloist Weymouth Community Ch., Medina, Ohio, 1985—. Home: 4189 Hamilton Rd Medina OH 44256-9087 Office: Green Circle Growers Inc 15650 State Route 511 Oberlin OH 44074-9465

MERLIS, ANTHONY LOGAN, neuroradiologist; b. Detroit, July 24, 1943; s. Jerome K. and Grace Mary (Logan) M.; m. Ellen Bernice Kowalczyk, Jan. 3, 1970; children: Jennifer, Abigail. AB, Johns Hopkins U., 1964; MD, U. Md., 1968. Dilpomate Am. Bd. Radiology. Intern in medicine Northwestern U. Med. Ctr., Chgo., 1968-69; resident in radiology Mallinckrodt Inst. Radiology, St. Louis, 1969-70, 72-73, fellow in neuroradiology, 1973-75; from asst. prof. to assoc. prof. radiology Dartmouth Hitchcock Med. Ctr., Hanover, N.H., 1975-85; dir. residency radiology programs, 1980-85; neuroradiologist Madison (Wis.) Radiologists, S.C., 1985—; asst. prof. radiology U. Wis., Madison, 1985—; chmn. credentials com., vice-chief staff St. Mary's Hosp. Med. Ctr., Madison, 1992-94, chief of staff, 1994-96. Lt. commdr. USN, 1970-72. Mem. Am. Soc. Neuroradiology (sr.), Am. Soc. Head and Neck Radiology, Am. Coll. Radiology, Radiologic Soc. N.Am. Office: Madison Radiologists SC 6601 Grand Teton Plz Madison WI 53719-1049

MERNALYN, actress, writer, producer; b. Detroit, July 23; d. Irwin and Myldred (Kolb) Hamburger. GPA with highest honors, Northwood of Mich. Profl. internat. model, freelance fashion cons.; creator, producer for pvt. Clubs Art Deco Fashion Shows; former fashion commentator Radio Luxembourg; nat. spokesperson GM; internat. spokesperson Jaguar; concierge L'Ermitage Hotel Group; customer cons. Tiffany & Co., Beverly Hills; pub. rels. Bunny Playboy Club Internat.; radio personality various USA stas.; creator, pres. PillowTalk Ltd., U.K. and U.S. Producer, writer, narrator nationally syndicated radio shows In a Word Mood, BabyTalk, The Children's Corner, FlashBack, The Veneration Generation, Today's Woman, Movie Moments; recurring role ABC-TV primetime sitcom New World Television, others; frequent guest nat. TV and radio talkshows; author: My Book, two volumes Philosophy/Humanity, contbg. author poetry anthology to profl. journals; dir. creator, instr. of Improving Quality of Humanity and Personal Certitude Classes; Shakespearean lead actress The Globe Theatre, American debut, A Yorkshire Tragedy, Much Ado About Nothing, Twelfth Night, Taming of the Shrew, Man of La Mancha, and many others. Active Am. Lung Assn., Friends of Animals. Named the Most Perfect Girl, Miss Budweiser Anheuser-Busch, Miss Internat. MG Brit. Leyland Eng.-USA. Mem. Screen Actors Guild, Am. Film Inst., Museum of the City of New York, Los Angeles County Museum of Art, Northwood of Mich. Alumni Assn., Art Deco Soc. N.Y. and L.A., Smithsonian.

MERRELL, ED, JR., historical society administrator. BA in Polit. Sci., U. South Ala., 1973; M of Recreation and Park Adminstrn., Clemson U., 1974. Interpreter Ninety Six (S.C.) Historic Site, 1974; costumed host, interpreter dept. exhbn. bldgs. Colonial Williamsburg (Va.) Found., 1976; instr. environ. interpretation dept. recreation/pk adminstn. Coll. of Forest and Recreation Resources, Clemson (S.C.) U., 1974-78; substitute tchr. Mobile (Ala.) County Pub. Sch. System, 1978-79; historic site adminstr. Historic Jefferson Coll., 1979-81; character interpreter at the gov.'s palace Colonial Williamsburg Found., 1981; dir. mus. svcs. Ga. Agrirama in Tifton, 1982-83; mgr. of interpretation Henry Ford Mus. and Greenfield Village, Dearborn, Mich., 1983-90; dir. New Market (Va.) Battlefield Hist. Park and Hall of Valor Civil War Mus., 1990-94; exec. dir. Olmsted County Hist. Soc., Rochester, Minn., 1994—. Mem. Am. Assn. for State and Local History, Am. Assn. of Mus. (accreditation commn. vis. com. mem., mus. assessment program, MAP I surveyor), Assn. for Living Hist. Farms and Agrl. Mus., Inst. of Mus. Svcs. (peer rev. for gen. operating support grants). Home: 3730 Mayowood Rd SW Rochester MN 55902-4261 Office: Olmsted County Hist Soc 1195 County Road 22 SW Rochester MN 55902-6619

MERRELL, RICHARD G., executive recruitment company official; b. Bald Knob, Ark., Jan. 16, 1937; s. Leroy G. and Callie I. (Beavers) M.; m. Aprildawn D. Messerschmidt, June 22, 1963; children: Christopher G., Kelly E. Student, Purdue U., 1955-57; BSEE, Valparaiso Tech. Inst., 1962; BSEE with distinction, Ill. Inst. Tech., 1970, MSEE, 1974. Electronic engr. Motorola, Inc., Chgo., 1962-68; sr. cons. engr. Zenith Electronics Corp., Glenview, Ill., 1968-78, electronic engring. mgr., 1981-91; electronic engring. mgr. Oak Industries, Crystal Lake, Ill., 1978-81; tech. recruiter Exec. Search Network, Arlington Heights, Ill., 1991-92, TSC Mgmt. Svcs. Group, 1993—; part-time instr. Ill. Inst. Tech., 1974-82. Contbr. articles to profl. jours.; numerous patents in field. Coach girls softball and Little League baseball, Hebron, Ill., 1984-91; v.p. Ill. Dist. 19 Bd. Edn., Hebron, 1991-93, mem., 1985-93, 95—. With USN, 1954-55. Mem. IEEE (sr. mem., adminstrv. com. consumer electronics group 1988-95). Home: 11212 Vanderkarr Rd Hebron IL 60034-9695 Office: TSC Mgmt Svcs Group PO Box 384 Barrington IL 60011-0384

MERRIAM, GENE, state legislator, accountant; b. Minn., Nov. 1, 1944; s. George C. and Frances (Couillard) M.; m. Maureen Elizabeth Brown, 1965; children: Jeffrey Vincent, Brian Patrick, Kathryn Jean. BSBA, U. Minn., 1967. Councilman-at-large Coon Rapids, Minn., 1973-74; Dist. 49 senator Minn. State Senate, St. Paul, 1975—; CPA Minn., 1970—; chmn. fin. com., mem. crime prevention, environ. and natural resources, and rules and adminstrn. coms., Minn. State Senate. Mem. Beta Alpha Psi. Office: 10451 Avocet St NW Minneapolis MN 55433-4872 also: State Senate State Capital Building Saint Paul MN 55155-1606*

MERRIER, HELEN, actress, writer; b. Chgo., Mar. 10, 1932; d. Miner Thompson and Helen (Hembree) Coburn; m. Tim Meier, Dec. 23, 1954; 1 child, William Frank. BA, Mills Coll., 1954; BS, Northwestern U., 1955. Actress (radio) Ma Perkins, One Man's Family, Standard School House of the Air, 1934-52, (stage) Lady Lucinda's Scrapbook, Edinburgh Fringe Festival, Scotland, 1996, New Am. Conservatory Theater, San Francisco, 1996, Time and the Conways, Remains Theater, 1991, Cinderella, Milw., 1991, Chgo. theatres including Second City ETC, Organic Theatre, Center Theatre, Court, Drury Lane Oakbrook, Hull House, Kingston Mines, other theatres, including Cleveland Play House, Coconut Grove Playhouse, Fla., Evergreen Stage Co., L.A., M & W Prodns., Milw., Guthrie Theatre, Mpls., (musicals) Woman of Year, Drury Lane, Evergreen Park, Ill., 1989, Sweeney Todd, Calo Theater, Chgo., 1991, Dreams of Defiance, N.Y.C., Chgo. and Ohio, Aristophanes' The Birds, Wisdom Bridge Theatre, Chgo., 1993, Dreams of Defiance, Theatre Bldg., Chgo., 1994, (film) Women in Treatment, 1990; dir. (stage) Center, Chgo., 1993. Women's bd. dirs. No. Ill. divsn. Salvation Army, 1965—; bd. dirs. Chgo. chpt. Prin. Found., 1972—, Women's Coll. Bd., 1956-66, Scottish Cultural Soc., 1976—; mem. Gaelic League, 1981-86, Celtic League, 1985—, Clan Irvine Assn., 1992—, Am. Anthrop. Soc., 1955-70, Am. Folklore Soc., 1955-70, Primitive Art Soc., 1975-85; mem. Apollo Chorus of Chgo., 1982-87, bd. mgmt., 1984-85. Mem. AFTRA, Actors Equity Assn. (Midwest adv. bd. 1983-84), Screen Actors Guild, Mills Coll. Club Chgo. (bd. dirs. 1962-81), Brit. Club Chgo., The Arts Club Chgo. Home: 915 Linden Ave Wilmette IL 60091-2712

MERRILL, ARTHUR LEWIS, retired theology educator; b. Tura, Assam, India, Sept. 14, 1930; s. Alfred Francis and Ida (Walker) M.; m. Barbara Jean Mayer, Aug. 18, 1951 (dec. June 1978); children: Margaret Jean, Katherine Merrill Nelson, Robert L.; m. Margaret Z. Morris, Sept. 11, 1985. BA, Coll. of Wooster, 1951; BD with distinction, Berkeley Bapt. Div. Sch., 1954; PhD, U. Chgo., 1962. Ordained to ministry United Ch. of Christ, 1954. Asst. prof. Bapt. Missionary Tng. Sch., Chgo., 1957-58; assoc. prof. Mission House Theol. Sem., Plymouth, Wis., 1958-62; assoc. prof. United Theol. Sem. Twin Cities, New Brighton, Minn., 1962-67, prof., 1967-95, prof. emeritus, 1995—. Author: United Theological Seminary of the Twin Cities: An Ecumenical Venture, 1993; co-author: Biblical Witness and the World, 1967; co-editor: Scripture in History and Theology, 1977; contbr. articles to profl. publs. ATS-Lilly postdoctoral fellow, 1966-67. Mem. Soc. Bibl. Lit., Am. Schs. Oriental Rsch., Israel Exploration Soc., Minn. Theol. Libr. Assn. (pres. 1994-95). Home: 1601 Bessmore Park Rd Rochester IN 46975

MERRILL, FRANK WAYNE, mail order sales executive; b. Ann Arbor, Mich., Aug. 7, 1947; s. Frank W. and Thelma Mae (Smith) M. BBA in Bus. Adminstrn., U. Mich., 1969. Acct. Com-Share, Inc., Ann Arbor, Mich., 1970; auditor Defense Contract Audit Agy., Toledo, 1970-78; proprietor, owner Saturday Night Records, Toledo, 1978-85, Macomb, Ill., 1985—. Home and Office: Saturday Night Records PO Box 669 Macomb IL 61455 Office: Saturday Night Records PO Box 669 Macomb IL 61455

MERRILL, KENNETH COLEMAN, retired automobile company executive; b. South Bend, Ind., Feb. 20, 1930; s. Kenneth Griggs and Helen Shapley (Coleman) M.; m. Helen Jean Tagtmeyer, June 10, 1956; children: Barry, Diane, John. B.A., Cornell U., 1953; M.B.A., Ind. U., 1956. With Ford Motor Co., Dearborn, Mich., 1956-91; asst. controller Ford Motor Co., Dearborn, 1967-71, gen. asst. controller, 1971-73, controller N.Am. automotive ops., 1973-79, exec. dir. parts ops., 1979-80, exec. dir. bus. planning and trust mgmt., 1980-87; pres. Ford Motor Credit Co., Dearborn, 1987-91, ret., 1991; bd. dirs. Am. Dental Techs., 1990—; v.p. Wadsworth (Ohio) Ford, 1992—. Pres. Plymouth (Mich.) Symphony Soc., 1969-70; vice chmn. bd. dirs. Detroit Inner City Bus. Improvement Forum, 1977-79; bd. dirs. Schoolcraft Coll. Found., 1982-94, pres., 1984-86; bd. dirs. Crossroads, 1992-94, 96—, treas., 1994. Mem. Fin. Execs. Inst., Greater Detroit C. of C. (bd. dirs. 1988-91, exec. com. 1990-91), Detroit Econ. Club, Barton Hills Country Club, Oaks Club (Sarasota, Fla.), Beta Gamma Sigma, Psi Upsilon. Episcopalian (treas. 1973-74, 79—). Home: 1450 Maple St Plymouth MI 48170-1516 also: Apt 306H 8779 Midnight Pass Rd Sarasota FL 34242-2850

MERRILL, MICHELLE C., science educator, health educator; b. Yankton, S.D., Nov. 1, 1969; d. Thomas Orville and Dorothea Helga (Kube) M. BS in Biology, Buena Vista Coll., 1992; MA, U. Nebr., 1996. Cert. tchr., Nebr. Biology tchr. Roncalli Cath. H.S., Omaha, Nebr., 1992-94, Skutt Cath. H.S., Omaha, Nebr., 1995; instr. U. Nebr., Omaha, 1995, grad. asst., 1995-96. Asst. editor: Jour. Alcohol and Drug Edn., 1994—. Instr., ARC, 1995—. Mem. Eta Sigma Gamma, Alpha Omega (pres. 1995—).

MERRITT, DORIS HONIG, pediatrics educator; b. N.Y.C., July 16, 1923; d. Aaron and Lillian (Kunstlich) Honig; children: Kenneth Arthur, Christopher Ralph. B.A., CUNY, 1944; M.D., George Washington U., 1952.

Diplomate Am. Bd. Pediatrics, Nat. Bd. Med. Examiners. Pediatric intern Duke Hosp., 1952-53; teaching and rsch. fellow pediatrics George Washington U., 1953-54; pediatric asst. resident Duke U. Hosp., 1954-55, cardiovascular fellow pediatrics, 1955-56, instr. pediatrics, dir. pediatric cardiorenal clinic, 1956-57; exec. sec. cardiovascular study sect., gen. medicine study sect. div. rsch. grants NIH, 1957-60; dir. med. rsch. grants and contracts Sch. Medicine Ind. U., 1961-62, asst. prof. pediatrics Sch. Medicine, 1961-68, asst. dean med. rsch. Sch. Medicine, 1962-65, asst. dir. med. rsch., aerospace rsch. application ctr. Sch. Medicine, 1963-65, assoc. dir. med. rsch. Sch. Medicine, 1965-68, asst. dean for rsch., office v.p. rsch. and dean advanced studies Sch. Medicine, 1965-67, dir. sponsored programs, asst. to provost Sch. Medicine, 1965-68, assoc. dean for rsch. and advanced studies, office v.p. and dean for rsch. and advanced studies Sch. Medicine, 1967-71, assoc. prof. pediatrics Sch. Medicine, 1968-73, prof. Sch. Medicine, 1973-80, assoc. dean Sch. Medicine, 1987—, prof. pediatrics, assoc. dean Sch. Medicine, 1988—; spl. asst. to dir. NIH, 1978-87, rsch. tng. and rsch. resource officer, 1980-87, acting dir. Nat. Ctr. Nursing Rsch., 1986-87; acting dean Sch. Engring. and Tech. Purdue U., 1995—; bd. dirs. Ind. Health Industry Reform; cons. USPHS, NIH div. rsch. grants Div. Health Rsch. Facilities and Resources, Nat. Heart Inst., 1963-78, Am. Heart Assn., 1963-67, Ind. Med. Assn. Commn. Vol. Health Orgns., 1964-67, Bur. Health Manpower, Health Profession's Constrn. Program, 1965-71, Nat. Library Medicine, Health Ctr. Libr. Constrn. Program, 1966-72; dir. office sponsored programs Ind. U.-Purdue U. Indpls. Office Chancellor, 1968-71, dean rsch. and sponsored programs, 1971-79; mem. Nat. Library Medicine biomed. communications rev. com., 1970-74; mem. com. to study rsch. capabilities acad. depts. ob-gyn Inst. Medicine, 1990-91. Contbr. articles to profl. jours. Chmn. Indpls. Consortium for Urban Edn., 1971-75; v.p. Greater Indpls. Progress Com., 1974-79; mem. Community Svc. Council, 1969-75; bd. dirs. Bd. for Fundamental Edn., 1973-77, Ind. Sci. Edn. Found., 1977-78, Community Addiction Svc. Agy., Inc., 1972-74; trustee Marian Coll., 1977-78; exec. com. Nat. Council U. Rsch. Adminstrs., 1977-78; bd. regents Nat. Library Medicine, 1976-80; chmn. adv. screening com. for life scis. Council Internat. Exchange of Scholars, 1978-81; bd. dirs. Community Svc. Coun. Cen. Ind., 1989-94, Univ. Hosp. Consortium, Tech. Assessment Ctr., 1990-93; mem. Ind. Health Industry Forum, 1993—; chmn. scientific and tech. review bd. on biomedical and behavioral rsch. facilities NIH Ctr. for Rsch. Resources, 1994—. Served to lt. (j.g.) USNR. Fellow Am. Acad. Pediatrics; mem. AAAS, George Washington U., Duke U. Med. Alumni Assns., Phi Beta Kappa, Alpha Omega Alpha., NIHNCRR (chair scientific and tech. rev. bd. on biomed. and biobehavioral rsch. facilities 1994-97). Office: Dean's Office ET 219 Purdue Sch E & T 799 W Michigan St Indianapolis IN 46202-5132

MERRITT, GARRY A., state legislator; m. Gretchen Merritt. Real estate and mortgage broker Overland Park, Kans.; mem. from dist. 20 Kans. State Ho. of Reps., Topeka. Address: 10301 Granada Overland Park KS 66207

MERRITT, JIMMIE ALCO, chemical company executive, sales and marketing; b. Alma, Ga., June 24, 1927; s. Jessie Littleton and Sally Ester (Talbert) M.; m. Florence Narcissus Harger; children: Norrie Lee Merritt Loomis, Sally Rebecca Merritt Merk, James Alco, Edgar Littleton. AB, U. N.C., 1957. Rschr. The Rohm & Haas Co., Phila., 1957-58; salesman The Rohm & Haas Co., Louisville, 1958-59; salesman The Rohm & Haas Co., Cin., 1959-80, sr. accts. mgr., 1980-87; pres., owner The Meritech Co., Cin., 1987—; bd. advisors, dir. Med. Diagnostic Internat., Miami, Fla., 1990—; spkr. in field. Lay leader Shiloh United Meth. Ch., Delhi Hills, Ohio, 1970-80, Sunday sch. tchr. Mem. Am. Assn. Textile Chemists and Colorists (midwest chmn. 1994—), Fedn. Socs. Coating Tech. (edn. chmn. 1993), Delhi Hills Masonic Lodge No. 775 (master 1975-76, sec. 1976-77, trustee 1976-81). Republican. Home: 5120 Old Oak Trail Cincinnati OH 45238

MERRITT, RICHARD LAWRENCE, political scientist, educator; b. Portland, Oreg., Aug. 8, 1933; s. Raymond Arlie and Sarah Elizabeth (Cook) M.; m. Anna Johanna Gode-von Aesch, Aug. 9, 1958; children—Christopher Eugene, Geoffrey Andreas, Theodore Aleyn. BA, U. So. Calif., 1955; MA, U. Va., 1956; postgrad., Free U. Berlin, 1956-57; PhD, Yale U., 1962. Instr. polit. sci. Yale U., 1962-63, asst. prof., 1963-67; assoc. prof. polit. sci., research assoc. prof. communications U. Ill., Urbana, 1967-69; prof. polit. sci., research prof. communications U. Ill., 1969—, head dept. polit. sci., 1978-84; Fulbright rsch. prof. Free U. Berlin, Berlin, Germany, 1969-70; vis. prof. internat. rels. Free U. Berlin, 1976; vis. scholar Sci. Center Berlin, 1976-83; Fulbright rsch. prof. Humboldt U., Berlin, 1962-63; cons. UN, USIA, Fed. Republic Germany; vis. prof. internat. rels., Rhodes U., Grahamstown, Republic of South Africa, 1991. Author: Symbols of American Community, 1735-1775, 1966, Comparing Nations, 1966, Systematic Approaches to Comparative Politics, 1970, Public Opinion in Occupied Germany, 1970, Public Opinion in Semisovereign Germany, 1980, From National Development to Global Community, 1981, Innovation in the Public Sector, 1985, Living with the Wall, 1985, Berlin between Two Worlds, 1986, Communication and Interaction in Global Politics, 1987, Science, Politics, and International Conferences, 1989, International Event-Data Developments: DDIR Phase II, 1993, Democracy Imposed: U.S. Occupation Policy and the German Public, 1945-1949, 1995; editor books and series in field. Recipient Wakefield award for outstanding service U. Ill., Urbana, 1975. Mem. Internat. Polit. Sci. Assn. (program chmn. 1976-79, v.p. 1979-82, book series editor 1980-91), Am. Polit. Sci. Assn. (program chmn. 1970, council mem. 1969-70), Internat. Studies Assn. (program chmn. 1973, v.p. 1980-81, pres. Midwest sect. 1984-85), Peace Sci. Soc., Conf. Group on German Politics (pres. 1986-88). Democrat. Office: Dept Polit Sci U Ill 702 S Wright St Urbana IL 61801-3696

MERSHART, RONALD VALERE, history educator; b. Chgo., Mar. 24, 1932; s. Pascal Girard and Margaret Elizabeth (DeBender) Meerschaert; m. Eileen DeGrand, Sept. 4, 1965 (div. 1989); children: Marielle Anne, Paul Valere. BA, DePaul U., 1954, MA, 1964; PhD, U. Chgo., 1969. Headmaster St. Louis Acad., 1957-59; fin. analyst Chem. Bank/N.Y. Trust Co., N.Y.C., 1959-61; instr. Ind. U., Gary, 1964, Roosevelt U., Chgo., 1965-67; prof. history U. Wis., Superior, 1967—, chair Dept. History, Politics and Society, 1994—. Author: S.N.H. Linguet: Reluctant Revolutionary, 1969, Centennial, 1989; editor NOW Newsletter, 1992-95. V.p. AAUP, Wis., 1972-73; pres. Assn. U. Wis. Faculties, Madison, 1980-82; clk. Superior Bd. Edn., 1985-91; active Gov.'s Commn. on Status of Women, Madison, 1977-79, Wis. Citizens Conf. on Jud. Orgn., Madison, 1973; mem. Am. Fedn. Tchrs. Higher Edn. Commn., Washington, 1981-84. Democrat. Home: 6-A Hayes Ct Superior WI 54880 Office: Univ Wisconsin 1800 Grand Ave Superior WI 54880-2873

MERSHON, JERRY LEWIS, judge; b. Oakley, Kans., Sept. 25, 1933; m. Jacqueline L. Page, Apr. 21, 1957; children: Diane, Michelle, Daniel. BS, Kans. State U., 1955; JD, Washburn U., 1961. Bar: Kans. 1961, U.S. Dist. Ct. Kans. 1961. Pvt. practice Manhattan, Kans., 1961-65; probate judge 21st Jud. Dist. Kans. Riley County Ct., Manhattan, 1965-76, assoc. dist. judge, 1977-78, dist. judge div. 2, 1978—, adminstrv. judge, 1982—; apptd. mem. Dist. Magistrate Manual and Cert. com. Kansas Supreme Ct., 1977-78; mem. Dist. Ct. Records com. Kans. Jud. Coun., 1977-78, Standing Family Law Adv. com. and others; past mem. Gov.'s Com. on Criminal Adminstrn. and others; bus. law instr. Kans. State U., 1963-64; lectr. various summer colls. and tng. sessions nationwide; Kans. del. to Nat. Conf. of Spl. Ct. Judges, 1973. Contbr. articles to Washburn Law Jour., Juvenile and Family Ct. Jour., Nat. Coun. Juvenile and Family Ct. Judges Textbook, Kans. Family Law Quar., others. Bd. dirs. Kans. Corp. for Change-Children's Issues, Riley County Family Svcs. Coun., Riley County Cmty. Corrections; past pres., advisor Manhattan unit Nat. Coun. on Alcoholism and Drug Edn.; past mem., past vice chmn. bd. dirs. Meml. Hosp., Manhattan; mem. bd. fellows Nat. Ctr. for Juvenile Justice, Pitts., 1996. 1st lt. USAF, 1955-58. Recipient Disting. Svc. award City of Manhattan, 1967, Outstanding Young Man award, 1967, Outstanding Participant award Summer Coll. II, Nat. Coll. Juvenile Justice, Reno, Nev., 1975, Lawyers Helping People award Kans. Trial Lawyers, 1986, Svc. to Children award Govs. Conf. for Prevention of Child Abuse, 1987, Faculty Meritorious Svc. award Nat. Coll. Juvenile and Family Law, 1995, Kans. Supreme Ct. Justice award for disting. contbns. to improvement of justice in Kans., 1996, others; named to Outstanding Young Men in Am., 1967. Mem. ABA (jud. adminstrn. divsn., nat. conf. state trial judges, Juvenile and Family Law Com.), Nat. Coun. Juvenile and Family Ct. Judges (publs. policy group, editl. reader Juvenile and Family Court Jour., Meritorious Svc. to Juvenile Cts. of Am. award 1992), Nat. Conf. State Trial Ct. Judges, Nat. Coll. Probate Judges, Nat. Assn. Probate Judges, Internat. Assn. Probate Judges, Kans. Bar Assn. (svc. award 1984), Kans. Dist. Judges Assn. (exec. com., sec.-treas. 1987, pres. 1989), Kans. Coun. on Crime and Delinquency, Kans. Probate, County and Juvenile Ct. Judges Assn. (past pres.), Riley County Bar Assn. (past pres.), Clay County Bar Assn., Masons, Shriners, Lions, Elks, Phi Alpha Delta. Mem. Christian Ch. Home: 1905 Indiana Ln Manhattan KS 66502-2325 Office: 21st Jud Dist Ct 100 Courthouse Plz Manhattan KS 66502-6018

MERTES, CHRISTOPHER PATRICK, newspaper editor; b. St. Paul, Nov. 27, 1963; s. Daniel George and Dee Louise (Trainor) M. BA in Journalism, U. Wis., Eau Claire, 1987. Reporter Clark County Press, Neillsville, Wis., 1988-89; mng. editor The Star, Sun Prairie, Wis., 1989—. Mem. Wis. Newspaper Assn. (1st prize for in-depth reporting 1992, 93). Roman Catholic. Home: 1510 Sunfield St Sun Prairie WI 53590-2652 Office: The Star 114 Columbus St Sun Prairie WI 53590-2926

MERTINS, JAMES WALTER, entomologist; b. Milw., Feb. 18, 1943; s. Walter Edwin and Harriet Ellen (Sockett) M.; m. Marilee Eloise Joeckel, Dec. 8, 1979. BS in Zoology, U. Wis., Milw., 1965; MS in Entomology, U. Wis., 1967, PhD in Entomology, 1971. Project assoc. dept. entomology U. Wis., Madison, 1971-75, rsch. assoc. dept. entomology, 1975-77; asst. prof. dept. entomology Iowa State U., Ames, 1977-84; entomol. cons. Ames, 1984-89; entomologist Nat. Vet. Svcs. Labs. USDA Animal and Plant Health Inspection Svc., Ames, 1989—. Co-author: (textbook) Biological Insect Pest Suppression, 1977, Russian edit., 1980, Chinese edit., 1988; contbr. articles to profl. jours. NSF Grad. fellow, 1970. Mem. Entomol. Soc. Am. (Insect Photgraphy award 1984, 86), Entomol. Soc. Can., Mich. Entomol. Soc., Wis. Entomol. Soc. (pres., sec., treas., bd. dirs.), Cyclone Corvettes, Inc. (co-founder, pres. 1978, 79, sec., treas., bd. dirs., Mem. of Yr. 1982), Am. Mensa. Office: USDA APHIS VS NVSL PL PO Box 844 Ames IA 50010-0844

MERTZ, DOLORES MARY, farmer, legislator; b. Bancroft, Iowa, May 30, 1928; d. John Francis and Gertrude (Erickson) Shay; m. H. Peter Mertz (dec. 1983), Dec. 27, 1951; children: Peter, Mary Simpson, David, Ann Cornicelli, Helen Powell, Janice, Carol. AA, Briar Cliff Coll., 1948. Pres. Coun. Cath. Women, Sioux City, Iowa, 1986-88; state regent Cath. Daughters of Am., Iowa, 1988—; county supr. Kossuth County, Iowa, 1983-89; legislator Iowa Ho. of Reps.(15th dist.), 1989—. Dem. precinct com. person, Kossouth County, Iowa, sec. 1975—. Recipient Womens Leadership award Iowa Lakes Community Coll., 1988; named Woman of Yr. Beta Sigma Phi Internat., West Bend, Iowa, 1989; recipient Iowa Lakes Community Coll. Disting. Svc. award, 1992, Guardian of Small Businsess award. Mem. Soroptomist Internat. (Woman of Distinction award 1987), Drama Club (pres. 1970's). Roman Catholic. Home: 607 110th St Ottosen IA 50570-8504 Office: Iowa Ho of Reps State Capitol Des Moines IA 50319*

MERTZ, FRED J., transportation executive; b. St. Louis, Aug. 31, 1938; s. Joseph Edward and Vita Rose (Passanante) M.; divorced; children: Michael, Michelle, Nicole. Student, St. Louis U., 1957-62. Asst. div. controller Brunswick Corp., DeLand, Fla., 1967-69; plant controller Brunswick Corp., Saint Joseph, Mo., 1969-72; plant mgr. Brunswick Corp., Saint Joseph, 1972-75; exec. v.p. Midwestern Distbn., Inc., Fort Scott, Kans., 1976-80; pres. United Services Inc., Nashville, 1980-81; exec. v.p. Prime, Inc., Springfield, Mo., 1981—; pres. Transp. Investments, Inc., Springfield, 1984—, MAM Inc., Springfield, 1984—; gen. mgr. Affordable Home Ctrs., Springfield, 1985—. Served with U.S. Army, 1962. Home and Office: 4125 E Canyon Dr Springfield MO 65809

MERVILDE, MICHAEL JOHN, clinical social worker; b. Mishawaka, Ind., Mar. 7, 1947; s. Armond Emil and Amelia (Canarecci) M.; m. Karen Sue Selig, Aug. 3, 1974; children: Lisa Marie, Michael John Jr. AB, St. Edwards U., Austin, Tex., 1969; MSW, Washington U., St. Louis, 1975. Acting exec. dir. Hotline, South Bend, Ind., 1973; clin. assoc. Drug Info. Ctr., St. Louis, 1973-74, Social Health Assn., St. Louis, 1975; mental health coord. Kewaunee County Unified Bd., Algoma, Wis., 1975-78; clin. social worker Bay Psychiat. Clinic, Green Bay, Wis., 1978-86; ptnr., clin. social worker Green Bay Wellness & Behavioral Health Clinic, 1985—; mem. adv. bd. Upjohn Home Health Care, Green Bay, 1980-85. Mem. NASW (bd. dirs. Wis. chpt. 1981-85), Acad. Cert. Social Workers, Acad. Family Mediators (assoc.), Optimists (charter, sec. Green Bay). Roman Catholic. Office: Green Bay Wellness & Behavioral Hlth Clinic 125 S Jefferson St Green Bay WI 54301-4500

MERWIN, HARMON TURNER, retired regional planner; b. Middlefield, Ohio, July 10, 1920; s. Harry Elverton and Ora (Turner) M.; m. Eldred Louise Merwin, Apr. 10, 1954; children: Elaine, Brian, Kathryn (dec.). B in Landcape Architecture, Ohio State U., 1950. Planner, then dir. Franklin County Regional Planning Commn., Columbus, Ohio, 1951-69; dep. dir. Mid-Ohio Regional Planning Commn., Columbus, 1970-74; program mgr. Mid-Ohio Regional Planning Commn., 1975-80, spl. projects sr. cons., 1975-80, sr. cons., 1981-91; retired, 1991; cons. in field. Bd. dirs., Columbus Met. Area Community Action Orgn., 1963-65; mem. facilities com., environ. health subcom., Mid-Ohio Health Planning Fedn., Columbus; pres. Ohio Planning Conf., 1963-65. Sgt. USAAF, 1942-46, ETO. Mem. Am. Inst. Cert. Planners (past pres. Ohio chpt.). Republican. Methodist. Home: 2325 Lytham Rd Columbus OH 43220-4637

MERZ, JAMES LOGAN, electrical engineering and materials educator, researcher; b. Jersey City, Apr. 14, 1936; s. Albert Joseph and Anne Elizabeth (Farrell) M.; m. Rose-Marie Weibel, June 30, 1962; children: Kathleen, James, Michael, Kimarie. BS in Physics, U. Notre Dame, 1959; postgrad., U. Göttingen, Fed. Republic Germany, 1959-60; MA, Harvard U., 1961, PhD in Applied Physics, 1967; PhD (hon.), Lingköping U., Sweden, 1993. Mem. tech. staff Bell Labs., Murray Hill, N.J., 1966-78; prof. elec. engring. U. Calif., Santa Barbara, 1978-94, prof. materials, 1986-94, chmn. dept. elec. and computer engring., 1982-84, assoc. dean for rsch. devel. Coll. Engring., 1984-86, acting assoc. vice chancellor, 1988, dir. semiconductor rsch. corp. core program on GaAs digital ICs, 1984-89, dir. Compound Semiconductor Rsch. Labs., 1986-92, dir. NSF Ctr. for Quantized Electronic Structures, 1989-94; Freimann prof. elec. engring. U. Notre Dame (Ind.), 1994—, v.p. for grad. studies and rsch., 1996—; NATO Advanced Study Inst. lectr. Internat. Sch. Materials Sci. and Tech., Erice-Sicily, Italy, 1990; mem. exec. com. Calif. Microelectronics Innovation and Computer Rsch. Opportunities Program, 1986-92; mem. NRC com. on Japan, NAS/NAE, 1988-90; mem. internat. adv. com. Internat. Symposium on Physics of Semiconductors and Applications, Seoul, Republic of Korea, 1990, Conf. on Superlattices and Microstructures, Xi'an, China, 1992; participant, mem. coms. other profl. confs. and meetings. Contbr. numerous articles to profl. jours.; patentee in field. Fulbright fellow, Danforth Found. fellow, Woodrow Wilson Found. fellow. Fellow IEEE, Am. Phys. Soc.; mem. IEEE Lasers and Electro-Optics Soc. (program com. annual mtg. 1980), IEEE Electron Device Soc. (sec. 1994, 95), Am. Vacuum Soc. (exec. com. electronic materials and processing divsn. 1988-89), Electrochem. Soc., Materials Rsch. Soc. (editl. bd. jour. 1984-87), Soc. for Values in Higher Edn., Inst. Electronics, Info. and Comm. Engrs. (overseas adv. com.), Sigma Xi, Eta Kappa Nu. Office: U Notre Dame Dept Elec Engring 275 Fitzpatrick Hall Notre Dame IN 46556-5637

MESCHKE, HERBERT LEONARD, state supreme court justice; b. Belfield, N.D., Mar. 18, 1928; s. G.E. and Dorothy E. Meschke; m. Shirley Ruth McNeil; children: Marie, Jean, Michael, Jill. B.A., Jamestown Coll., 1950; J.D., U. Mich., 1953. Bar: N.D. Law clk. U.S. Dist. Ct. N.D., 1953-54; practice law Minot, N.D., 1954-85; justice N.D. State Supreme Ct., 1985—; mem. N.D. Ho. of Reps., 1965-66, N.D. Senate, 1967-70. Mem. ABA, Am. Law Inst., Am. Judicature Soc., N.D. Bar Assn. Office: ND State Supreme Ct State Capitol 600 E Boulevard Ave Bismarck ND 58505-0660

MESHBESHER, RONALD I., lawyer; b. Mpls., May 18, 1933; s. Nathan J. and Esther J. (Balman) M.; m. Sandra F. Siegel, June 17, 1956 (div. 1978); children: Betsy F., Wendy S., Stacy J.; m. Kimberly L. Garnaas, May 23, 1988; 1 child, Jolie M. BS in Law, U. Minn., 1955, JD, 1957. Bar: Minn. 1957, U.S. Supreme Ct. 1966. Prosecuting atty. Hennepin County, Mpls., 1958-61; pres. Meshbesher and Spence Ltd., Mpls., 1961—; lectr. numerous legal and profl. orgns.; mem. adv. com. on rules of criminal procedure Minn. Supreme Ct., 1971-91; cons. on recodification of criminal procedure code Czech Republic Ministry of Justice, 1994. Author: Trial Handbook for Minnesota Lawyers, 1992; mem. bd. editors Criminal Law Advocacy Reporter; mem. adv. bd. Bur. Nat. Affairs Criminal Practice Manual; contbr. numerous articles to profl. jours. Mem. ATLA (bd. govs. 1968-71), ABA, Minn. Bar Assn., Internat. Acad. Trial Lawyers, Am. Coll. Trial Lawyers, Am. Bd. Trial Advs., Am. Bd. Criminal Lawyers (v.p. 1983), Am. Acad. Forensic Scis., Nat. Assn. Criminal Def. Lawyers (pres. 1984-85), Minn. Trial Lawyers Assn. (pres. 1973-74), Minn. Assn. Criminal Def. Lawyers (pres. 1991-92), Trial Lawyers for Pub. Justice, Calif. Attys. for Criminal Justice. Home: 2010 Sugarwood Dr Orono MN 55356-9339 Office: Meshbesher & Spence 1616 Park Ave Minneapolis MN 55404-1631

MESHEL, HARRY, state senator, political party official; b. Youngstown, Ohio, June 13, 1924; s. Angelo and Rubena (Markakis) Michelakis; children: Barry, Melanie. BSBA, Youngstown Coll., 1949; MS, Columbia U., 1950; LLD (hon.), Ohio U.; Youngstown State U.; LLD (hon.), Ohio Coll. Podiatric Medicine; LHD (hon.), Youngstown State U. Exec. asst. to mayor City of Youngstown, Ohio, 1964-68; urban renewal dir. City of Youngstown, Ohio, 1969; mem. 33d district Ohio Senate, Columbus, 1971-93; Dem. minority leader Ohio Senate, 1981-82, 85-90, pres. and majority leader, 1983-84, com. mem. econ. develop., sci. & tech., state & local govt., ways & means, commerce & labor, controlling bd., state employment compensation bd., fin. chmn., 1974-81, rules chmn., 1983-84, com. mem. rules, reference & oversight, 1985-90; state chair Ohio Dem. Party, 1993—; real estate broker; adj. prof. polit. sci. Ohio U.; faculty mem. (limited svc.) Youngstown State U.; div. mgr. investment firm; Ohio Senate special com. mem. Task Force on Drug Strategies, Ohio Acad. Sci. Centennial Celebration Commn., Motor Vehicle Inspection & Maintenance Program, Legis. Oversight Com., Ohio Boxing Commn., Correctional Inst. Inspection Com., Ohio Small Bus. & Entrepreneurship Coun., Gov.'s Adv. Coun. Travel & Tourism, Legis. Svc. Commn., Capital Sq. Rev. & Adv. Bd., others. Past pres., past lt. gov. Am. Hellenic Ednl. Prog. Assn. (AHEPA); precinct committeeman Mahoning County Dem. Party, ward captain, mem. exec. com.; campaign mgr. local candidates, county campaign mgr. presdl. candidates; del. Dem. Mid-Term Conv., 1981; founder Great Lakes/N.E. Legis. Coalition; chmn., founder Nat. Dem. State Legis. Leaders Assn.; dir. State Legis. Leaders Found.; state/fed. assembly, mem. communications com. Nat. Conf. State Legis., legis. mgmt. com., govt. opers. com.; chair fiscal affairs com. Midwest Conf. Coun. State Govts., task force on econs. & fiscal affairs; del., exec. com. Dem. Nat. Com.; mem. Dem. Leadership Coun., State Dem. Exec. Com.; exec. com. Assn. State Dem. Chairs; bd. trustees Nat. Hall of Fame for Persons with Disabilities; mem. St. Nicholas Greek Orthodox Ch. With USN, 1943-46. Decorated two Bronze Battle Stars; recipient Dist. Svc. award Office of Pres., Top Legislator award Ohio Union Patrolmen Assn., Dist. Citizen award Med. Coll. Ohio, City of Hope Leadership award, 1993, Legis. Leadership award Ohio Coalition for Edn. of Handicapped Children, Phillips Medal of Pub. Svc., Ohio U., John E. Fogarty award Gov.'s Com. of Employment of Handicapped, Gov.'s award, 1992, U. Cin. Award for Excellence, Lamp of Learning award Ohio Edn. Assn., Black Cultural Soc. award East Liverpool, Mahoning Valley Man of Yr. award, Mahoning Valley Econ. Devel. Corp., Office Holder of Yr. award Truman-Johnson Dem. Women, Best Interest of Children award Fathers of Equal Rights, Founders Day award Circle of Friends Found., Helping Hand award Easter Seal Soc., Honorary Riverboat Captain award Mahoning County Dem. Party, Community Svc. and Special Svcs. awards Eastern Orthodox Men's Soc., Periclean award AHEPA, Academy of Achievement award Nat. AHEPA Ednl. Found., Nat. Svc. Dem. award AHEPA, 1994, Disting. Citizen award Youngstown State U. Alumni Assn., numerous appreciation and recognition awards; recipient Outstanding Legislator awards Ohio Acad. Trial Lawyers, Ohio Assn. Pub. Sch. Employees, Ohio Rehab. Assn., League Ohio Sportsmen; recipient Dist. Svc. awards Youngstown State U., Ohio Edn. Assn., Ohio Union Patrolmen Assn., Ohio Disabled Vets., AFL-CIO Ohio Barbers Union, AFL-CIO Nat. Assn. of Theatre Owners of Ohio; named Guardian of the Menorah, Youngstown B'nai B'rith, Outstanding Dem., Fairfield Dem. Club, 1993. Mem. (life) NAACP, ACLU, AMVETS (Legislator of Yr. 1993), VFW, Am. Legion, Cath. War Vets (Dist. Legislator award), Vet. Boxers Assn. Mercer County, Pa., Trumbull County Boxers' Legends of Leather (Man of Yr. award Hall of Fame), William Holmes McGuffey Hist. Soc., Buckeye Elks Lodge (hn.); mem. Kiwanis Internat., Urban League, Alliance C. of C., Southern Community Jaycees (hon.), Soc. for Preservation of Greek Heritage, Greek Am. Progressive Assn., Pan Cretan Assn., Arms Hist. Mus. Soc., Eagles, Moose, The Stambaugh Pillars.

MESHII, MASAHIRO, materials science educator; b. Amagasaki, Japan, Oct. 6, 1931; came to U.S., 1956; s. Masataro and Kazuyo M.; m. Eiko Kumagai, May 21, 1959; children: Alisa, Erica. BS, Osaka (Japan) U., 1954, MS, 1956; PhD, Northwestern U., 1959. Lectr., rsch. assoc. dept. materials sci. and engring. Northwestern U., Evanston, Ill., 1959-60, asst. prof., assoc. prof., then prof., 1960-88, chmn. dept. materials sci. and engring., 1978-82, John Evans prof., 1988—; vis. scientist Nat. Rsch. Inst. Metals, Tokyo, 1970-71; NSF summer faculty rsch. participant Argonne (Ill.) Nat. Lab., 1975; guest prof. Osaka U., 1985; Acta/Scripta Metallurgica lectr., 1993-95. Co-editor: Lattice Defects in Quenched Metals, 1965, Martensitic Transformation, 1978, Science of Advanced Materials, 1990; editor: Fatigue and Microstructures, 1979, Mechanical Properties of BCC Metals, 1982; contbr. over 225 articles to tech. publs. and internat. jours. Recipient Founders award Midwest Soc. Electron Microscopists, 1987. Fellow ASM (Henry Marion Howe medal 1968), Japan Soc. Promotion of Sci.; mem. AIME, Metallurgical Soc., Japan Inst. Metals (Achievement award 1972). Home: 3051 Centennial Ln Highland Park IL 60035-1017 Office: Northwestern U Dept Materials Sci Eng Evanston IL 60208

MESHINESH, KHADER, mechanical engineer; b. Damascus, Syria, Oct. 14, 1962. Student, Damascus Civil Engring., 1981-83; BS in Mech. Engring., S.D. State U., Brookings, 1988; M of Engring. Mgmt., Milw. Sch. Engring., 1994. Mech. engr. Sencore Electronics, Sioux Falls, S.D., 1987-88, Lytton Microwave, Sioux Falls, 1988-90; product engr., mech. engr. Speed Queen, Ripon, Wis., 1990—. Mem. Arab Anti Discrimination Com., Washington, 1987—. Mem. ASME. Republican. Moslem. Office: Speed Queen PO Box 990 Ripon WI 54971-0990

MESNARD, DARRELL DEAN, SR., insurance agent; b. Decatur, Ill., Apr. 4, 1923; s. Harvey I. and Hazel Cora (Painter) M.; m. Grace Hannah Nelson, Nov. 18, 1945; children: Linda K. Mesnard Phegley, D. Dean Jr., Kathleen A. Mesnard Evans, Karen L. Mesnard Muir. BS, Millikin U., 1949; cert., The Am. Coll., Bryn Mawr, Pa., 1958, The Am. Coll., Bryn Mawr, Pa., 1983. CLU, ChFC. Agt. Met. Life, Decatur, 1950-84, Conn. Mut., Decatur, 1984—. Author: (book) Plain Talk About Retirement and Money, 1977, Empire Express, 1991. 1st lt. USAAF, 1943-45, PTO. Mem. Ctrl. Ill. Estate Planning Coun., Ctrl. Ill. CLUs, Decatur Assn. Life Underwriters (past pres.), Nat. Heritage and Wildlife Found., Kiwanis (past bd. dirs.), Mason (life), Am. Legion, Shriners, Million Dollar Round Table (life). Republican. Home: 757 W Harold Cir Decatur IL 62526-1118 Office: Mass Mut 1999 W Grand Ave Decatur IL 62522-1311

MESSER, ALLEN, insurance consultant, trainer, educator; b. Hamilton, Ohio, Apr. 28, 1949; s. Oscar Bishop Messer, Sr. and Alena (Richardson) Lathery. BA, U. Evansville, 1971. Cert. ins. counselor; CPCU. Claims rep. United Farm Bur. Mut. Ins. Co., Indpls., 1971-74, gen. agt., 1974; dist. sales mgr. Meridian Mut. Ins. Co., Indpls., 1974-77; br. mgr. Mich. Mut. Ins. Co., Indpls., 1977-81; v.p. M.J. Schuetz Agy., Indpls., 1981-87; account exec. Waterfield Ins. Agy., Inc., Indpls., 1987-90; v.p. Comprehensive Fin. Svcs., Muncie, Ind., 1990-91, Jackson-McCormick Ins., Lebanon, Ind., 1991-92; exec. dir. Soc. Cert. Ins. Counselors, Austin, Tex., 1992-93; pres. Ins. Concepts & Svcs., Inc., Indpls., 1989—. Editor: PF&M, The Rough Notes Company, 1993-94. Mem. Soc. CPCU, Soc. Cert. Ins. Counselors, Elks, Masons, Highland Golf & Country Club. Home and Office: 205 Woodside Ln Valparaiso IN 46383-6035

MESSERLI, GARY ROBERT, air terminal executive; b. Colorado Springs, Colo., June 16, 1955; s. Robert Vincent and Florence Margaret (Nowack) M.; m. Mary Margaret Short, Apr. 19, 1991; children: James K. Baker, Heather Baker. BSBA, U. N.D., 1977; MBA, U. S.D., 1985. Sta. supr. Frontier Airlines, Kansas City, Mo., 1977-86; supr. accounts payable Frontier Airlines, Denver, 1986-87; customer svc. rep. United Airlines, Rapid

City, S.D., 1987-88; dep. dir. airport Sioux Falls (S.D.) Regional Airport, 1988—. Author: Sabre Reservations and Ticketing, 1988. Advisor Sioux Coun. Boy Scouts Am., 1992-93; cons. Jr. Achievement, Sioux Falls, 1993-95. Mem. Am. Assn. Airport Execs. (cert.). Office: Sioux Falls Reg Airport 2801 Jaycee Ln Sioux Falls SD 57104

MESSING, CAROL SUE, communications educator; b. Bronx, N.Y.; d. Isidore and Esther Florence (Burtoff) Weinberg; m. Sheldon H. Messing; children: Lauren, Robyn. BA, Bklyn. Coll., 1967, MA, 1970. Tchr. N.Y.C. Bd. Edn., 1967-72; prof. lang. arts Northwood U., Midland, Mich., 1973-93, prof., 1993—; owner Job Match, Midland, 1983-85; cons. Mich. Credit Union League, Saginaw, 1984-87, Nat. Hotel & Restaurant, Midland, 1985-89, Univ. Coll. program, Continuing Edn. program, Northwood U., 1986—, Dow Chem. Employee's Credit Union, 1988—. Author: (anthology) Symbiosis, 1985, rev. edit., 1987, Controlling Communication, 1987, rev. edit., 1993, Creating Effective Team Presentations, 1995; co-author: PRIMIS, 1993. Mem. LWV, Nat Coun. Tchrs. English, Kappa Delta Pi, Delta Mu Delta (advisor). Office: Northwood U 3225 Cook Rd Midland MI 48640-2311

MESSINGER, SUSAN FRANCESCA, city planner; b. Vienna, Austria; came to U.S., 1938; d. Emil Oskar and Rosl (Bauer) M. Student, U. Ill., 1940-41, Temple U., 1942; BA, U. Chgo., 1944, MA, 1953; postgrad., New Sch. Social Rsch., 1945-46, Ill. Inst. Tech., 1961-62. Rsch. asst. Nat. Labor Bur., Chgo., N.Y.C., 1944-46; archaeol. asst. U. Chgo. Expdn., 1947; rsch. asst. U. Chgo., 1953-54; archaeol. asst. U. Okla. Expdn., Norman, 1948; rsch. analyst Mayor's Housing & Redevel. Coordinator, Chgo., 1954; planning analyst, asst. to dep. exec. dir. Chgo. Land Clearance Commn., 1954-62; city planner, dir. rsch. Dept. Urban Renewal, Chgo., 1962-77; city planner, project mgr. Dept. Planning, City and Cmty. Devel., Chgo., 1978-82; city planner, mgr. Dept. Econ. Devel., Chgo., 1982-87; sr. planner Dept. Planning, Chgo., 1988-91; sr. city planner Dept. Planning and Devel., Chgo., 1992—; instr. Dept. Planning, Chgo., 1992. Mem. Friends of Downtown, Chgo., Chgo. Archtl. Found., Lyric Opera, Chgo. Symphony, Art Inst. Chgo. Hattie M. Strong Found. grantee. Fellow Am. Anthropol. Assn., Soc. for Applied Anthropology; mem. Am. Planning Assn. (law and internat. divsns. co-chairm program com. 1986-87, ann. meeting mobile workshop 1993), Am. Assn. of U. Women (past bd. dirs.), UN Assn., Nat. Trust for Historic Preservation, Soc. of Archtl. Historians, Am. Statis. Assn., Am. Assn. for the Advancement of Sci., History of Sci. Soc., City Club of Chgo., Sierra Club, Alpha Lambda Delta. Home: 1400 N Lake Shore Dr Chicago IL 60610 Office: Dept Planning and Devel 1000 City Hall 121 N LaSalle Chicago IL 60602

MESSNER, JAMES W., advertising executive; b. 1939. Attended, 1959-61. With Sta. WCSM, Celina, Ohio, 1961-63, Sta. WTOD, Toledo, 1961-63, Detroit Advt. Agy., 1965-68, Norman, Navan, Moore & Bard, 1968-77; chmn. bd. dirs. J.W. Messner Inc., Grand Rapids, Mich., 1977—. Office: JW Messner Inc 161 Ottawa Ave NW Ste 403 Grand Rapids MI 49503*

MESTAD, GARY ALLEN, education educator; b. Mason City, Iowa, Feb. 14, 1946; s. Orval Alden and Trina W. (Linne) M.; m. Merikay Linda Marth, Aug. 15, 1970. BS, Mankato State U., 1970. Cert. tchr., Iowa. Tchr. social studies Garner-Hayfield Schs., Garner, Iowa, 1970—; head coach jr. high sch. varsity girls' softball Garner Hayfield Schs., Iowa; head coach jr. high girls' basketball and softball. Sports writer Garner Leader and Signal, 1971—; contbr. articles on basketball instruction to profl. publs. Mem. NEA, Iowa State Edn. Assn., Iowa Mid. Sch. Assn., Garner-Hayfield Tchrs. Assn., Iowa Athletic Coaches Assn. Home: 520 Grove Ave Garner IA 50438-1452 Office: Garner Hayfield Sch 1080 Division St Garner IA 50438-1740

MESULAM, MARSEL, neurologist, educator; b. Istanbul, Turkey, Apr. 7, 1945; came to U.S., 1964; s. Mose and Fani (Rozanes) M.; m. Sandra Weintraub, June 17, 1984; 1 child, Semra. BA, Harvard U., 1968, MD, 1972. Intern Hosp. of U. Pa., 1971-73; resident Boston City Hosp., 1973-76; asst. prof. Harvard Med. Sch., Boston, 1977-80, assoc. prof., 1986-94, prof., 1986—; Ruth and Evelyn Dunbar prof. neurology and psychiatry Northwestern U. Med. Sch., 1994—, dir. behavioral neurology and Alzheimers program, 1994—; dir. behavioral neurology Beth Israel Hosp., Boston, 1979-93. Author: Principles of Behavioral Neurology, 1985. Recipient Javits Neurosci. award NIH, 1985, MnKnight Dir.'s award McKnight Found. Fellow Am. Acad. Neurology (Wartenberg lectr. 1991), Am. Neurol. Assn. Office: Northwestern U Med Sch Behav/Cog Neurol Rm 11-450 320 W Superior St Chicago IL 60610-3516

METCALF, ROBERT CLARENCE, architect, educator; b. Nashville, Ohio, Nov. 7, 1923; s. George and Helen May (Drake) M.; m. Bettie Jane Sponseller, Sept. 15, 1943. Student, Johns Hopkins U., 1943; B.Arch., U. Mich., 1950. Draftsman G.B. Brigham, Jr., Architect, Ann Arbor, Mich., 1948-52; pvt. practice architecture Ann Arbor, 1953—; lectr. architecture U. Mich., Ann Arbor, 1955-58; asst. prof. U. Mich., 1958-63, asso. prof., 1963-68, prof., 1968-91, chmn. dept., 1968-74; dean U. Mich. (Coll. Architecture and Urban Planning), 1974-86; Emil Lorch prof. emeritus U. MIch., 1991—, dean emeritus, 1991—; sec. Mich. Bd. Registration for Architects, 1975-79, chmn., 1980-82. Designer 127 bldgs., Ann Arbor, 1953—. Served with U.S. Army, 1943-46, ETO. Decorated Silver Star; recipient Sol King award for excellent teaching in architecture U. Mich., 1974; named Emil Lorch Professor of Architecture, 1989. Fellow AIA; mem. Mich. Soc. Architects, Assn. Collegiate Schs. Architecture, Phi Kappa Phi, Tau Sigma Delta. Home: 1052 Arlington Blvd Ann Arbor MI 48104-2816 Office: U Mich 2150 Art Architecture Bldg Ann Arbor MI 48109 also: 2211 Medford Rd Ann Arbor MI 48104-5004

METER, KAREN SHELLEY, music educator, veterans advocate; b. Crawford, Nebr., June 4, 1946; d. Alfred Arnold and Betty Jean (Connell) Thompson; m. Charles Louis Meter, Apr. 19, 1980; 1 child, Christopher Vincent. BS, N.D. State U., 1971. Cert. secondary tchr., N.D. Enlisted USN, 1965, stationed at Beaufort (S.C.) Naval Hosp., 1965-73; tchr. choral music Watford City (N.D.) H.S., 1971-73; singer Chgo. Symphony Chorus and Chgo. Chamber Choir, 1974-76; owner Music Par Elegance, Crystal Lake, Ill., 1980-95; organist St. Thomas the Apostle, Crystal Lake, 1987-94; owner Burley Hollow, Crystal Lake, 1995—; chmn. sch. lobbyist LINK, Pub. Sch. Dist. 47, Crystal Lake, 1988-91; nat. bd. dirs. VietNow, Rockford, Ill., 1993-94, dir. dist. 2 Ill. dept., 1994, chair VA Nursing Home Ill. Dept., West Chicago, 1994—; Am. Legion svc. officer VA Med. Ctr., North Chicago, Ill., 1994—, mem. women's vet.'s com., 1995—. Jr. v.p. McHenry Co. V.A.C., Crystal Lake, 1994—, sr. v.p., 1995—; treas. McHenry County Dem. Party, 1994—; chmn. Stand Down, Chgo. 1994—. Mem. Amvets (VA liaison, post 269, 1993), DAR (1st vice regent 1993), Am. Guild of Organists, Am. Legion, VietNam Vets. Am. Methodist. Home: 266 Dartmoor Dr Crystal Lake IL 60014

METHENY, JAN WALTER, business manager, chief financial officer; b. Fort Dodge, Iowa, Apr. 29, 1952; s. Vincent Raymond and Dora Irene (Cornelius) M.; m. Joanne Kathleen Hickman, June 1, 1974; children: Jessica, Jack, Jeffrey, Joel, Julie, Jared, Jason, Jan-Michael, Jonathan, Justin. BA, Faith Bapt. Bible Coll., 1974, ThB, 1974. Pastoral staff Olivet Bapt. Ch., Shawnee Mission, Kans., 1974-76; asst. bus. mgr. Faith Bapt. Bible Coll., Ankeny, Iowa, 1978-84; regional sales mgr. Moody Press, 1984-88; bookstore mgr. Faith Bapt. Bible Coll., Ankeny, 1988-92, v.p. fin., CFO, 1992—, adj. faculty, 1988-91. Bd. deacons Fellowship Bapt. Ch., 1995. Named one of Outstanding Young Men in Am., 1979. Mem. Assn. Bus. Adminstrs. of Christian Colls. (bd. dirs. 1995-98, treas. 1995-98). Republican. Baptist. Office: Faith Bapt Bible Coll & Theol Seminary 1900 NW 4th St Ankeny IA 50021

METRES, PHILIP JOHN, JR., psychologist; b. Bklyn., Nov. 11, 1942; s. Philip and Lily (Boulos) M.; m. Katherine Sheila Dannemann, Aug. 30, 1969; children: Philip J. III, Katherine Marie, David Michael. AB in Psychology, Coll. of Holy Cross, 1964; MA in Social Psychology, U.S. Internat. U., 1971, PhD in Profl. Psychology, 1975. Licensed clin. psychologist, Ill. Instr. psychology San Diego Evening Coll., 1971-73; research psychologist Naval Health Research Ctr., San Diego, 1971-76; clin. psychologist N. Shore Ctr. for Counseling and Therapy, Northbrook, Ill., 1978—, Old Orchard Hosp., Skokie, Ill., 1978-80. Co-editor: Family Separation and Reunion: Adjustment of POW's and MIA's, 1975; contbr. articles to profl. jours. Commr. Spring Lakes Sports League, Lincolnshire, Ill., 1979-80; founding pres. Lincolnshire Citizens for Drug Awareness, 1981-82; bd. dirs. Christian Laity Chgo., vice chmn. 1986-89. Served to lt. USN, 1964-69, capt. Res., 1969-91, ret. 1991. Decorated Bronze Star, combat V-device. Fellow Interuniv. Seminar on Armed Forces and Soc.; mem. APA, Am. Assn. Marriage and Family Therapy, Assn. Christian Therapists, Naval Res. Assn. (life), Ret. Officers Assn. Roman Catholic. Office: North Shore Ct Counseling & Therapy 655 Landwehr Rd Northbrook IL 60062-2311

METS, LISA ANN, academic administrator; b. Lapeer, Mich., Feb. 24, 1954; d. Harald and Meeta Alexandra (Linnas) M. BA, U. Mich., 1976, postgrad., 1984-87, 90-95; MA, Ind. U., 1978. Asst. prof. Vincennes (Ind.) U., 1979-83, dept. chair, 1981-85, assoc. prof., 1983-85; sr. asst. to v.p. adminstrn. and planning Northwestern U., Evanston, Ill., 1987-90; sr. adminstr. Ctr. for Rsch. on Learning and Tchg., U. Mich., 1995—. Co-editor: Key Resources on Higher Education Governance, Management, and Leadership, 1987, (monograph) Improving Teaching and Learning through Research, 1988, (monograph) Using Academic Program Review, 1995; editor News from SCUP, 1988-91; contbr. chpt. to book. Mem. Am. Assn. for Higher Edn., Assn. for the Study Higher Edn., Assn. for Instnl. Rsch., Soc. for Coll. and Univ. Planning, Profl. Orgnl. Devel. Network, Phi Delta Kappa. Lutheran.

METTA, DAVID KEITH, government official; b. Oak Park, Ill., Feb. 12, 1953; s. Donald Nash and Joanne Helen (Nicolosi) M.; m. Gail Diane Ross, Sept. 13, 1980. Student, Coll. of Dupage, Glen Ellyn, Ill., 1971-72, Northwestern U., 1987. Police officer DuPage County Sheriff's Dept., Wheaton, Ill., 1974-79; fed. officer Argonne (Ill.) Nat. Lab., 1979-83, sgt., 1983-85, lt., 1985-86, capt., 1986-88, tng. mgr., 1988-89, mgr. security programs, 1989—, ANL-E site classification officer, ops. security mgr., acting mgr. safeguards and security, 1995—; mem. firearms safety com. Argonne Nat. Lab., 1988—; mem. U.S. delegation to counries of former Soviet Union. Recipient Franklin M. Kreml Leadership award, Northwestern U. Traffic Inst., 1987; recipient numerous commendations and ltrs. of recognition. Mem. Alumni Assn. Northwestern U. Traffic Inst., Nat. Tactical Officers Assn., Ill. Police Combat Assn. Republican. Methodist. Office: Argonne Nat Lab 9700 Cass Ave Lemont IL 60439-4803

METTERS, THOMAS WADDELL, sports writer; b. Columbus, Ohio, Apr. 17, 1939; s. Thomas Hammond and Charlotte Ann (Waddell) M. BS in Journalism, Ohio U., 1965. Sports editor The Traveller, Ft. Lee, Va., 1960-62; sports writer The Athens (Ohio) Messenger, 1965—; asst. to officials Legion Baseball, Athens, 1962—. Contbr.: Ohio Interscholastic Athletic Media Guide, 1985. Bd. dirs. Athens H.S. Booster Club, 1975—; official scorekeeper Am. Legion World Series, Millington, Tenn., 1989. With U.S. Army, 1959-62. Named to Ohio H.S. Basketball Coaches Assn. Hall of Fame, 1993; recipient Contributor award Ohio H.S. Track & Field Coaches Assn., 1995. Mem. Soc. Profl. Journalists (Recognition plaque 1973), Ohio Associated Press Sports Writers Assn. (pres. 1984), Green & White Club (sec. 1983—, Jonesy Sams award 1987), Ohio Prep Sports Writers Assn. (Hall of Fame 1990), Ky. Colonels, Am. Legion. Republican. Home: 71 Sunnyside Dr Athens OH 45701 Office: The Athens Messenger Rt 33 N and Johnson Rd Athens OH 45701

METZ, DONALD LEHMAN, sociology educator; b. Chambersburg, Pa., July 2, 1935; s. Abram Lehman and Mary Elizabeth (Diffenderfer) M.; m. Mary Coale Haywood, July 31, 1965; children: David Haywood, Michael Lehman. BA, Pa. State U., 1957; STB, Harvard U., 1960; MA, U. Calif., Berkeley, 1965, PhD, 1971. Rsch. asst. Mt. Zion Hosp. and Med. Ctr., San Francisco, 1962-63; teaching asst. U. Calif., Berkeley, 1963-64; rsch. asst. Survey Rsch. Ctr., Berkeley, 1964; rsch. assoc. Bur. Cmty. Rsch., Berkeley, 1964-65; asst. prof., chair dept. sociology Earlham Coll., Richmond, Ind., 1969-75; asst. prof. sociology Marquette U., Milw., 1975-83, chair dept. social and cultural scis., 1988-93, assoc. prof. sociology, 1983—; emergency med. tech.-ambulance, Milw., 1978-80. Author: New Congregations, 1967, Running Hot, 1982; contbr. chpts. to book, poetry to anthologies. Bd. dirs., sec. Funeral and Meml. Soc., Greater Milw., 1978-84; bd. dirs. United Ministries in Higher Edn., Milw., 1977-83; project support Fair Housing Coun., met. Milw., 1988. Danforth Sem. fellow, 1960-61, Kent fellow, 1965-68, NEH fellow in ethics edn., 1989-90. Fellow Soc. for Sci. Study of Religion; mem. AAUP (sec.-treas.), Am. Sociol. Assn., Assn. Practical and Profl. Ethics, Wis. Sociol. Assn., Pi Gamma Mu. Democrat. Mem. United Ch. of Christ. Home: 2952 N Stowell Ave Milwaukee WI 53211 Office: Marquette U Box 1881 Milwaukee WI 53201-1881

METZ, PHILIP STEVEN, surgeon, educator; b. Omaha, May 12, 1945; s. Roman A. and Gwanetha (Hamilton) M.; m. Dianne Pearson, July 11, 1970; children: Amy Michelle, Wendy Marie, Stephanie Joy, Philip Robb. BS, Loras Coll., 1965; MD, U. Nebr., 1969. Diplomate Am. Bd. Surgery and Bd. Plastic Surgery with spl. qualification in hand surgery. Commd. USN, 1969; intern Nat. Naval Med. Ctr., Bethesda, Md., 1969-70; resident gen. surgery Oakland (Calif.) Naval Hosp., 1970-74; resident plastic and reconstructive surgery U. Utah, 1974-76; fellow hand surgery Derbyshire Royal Infirmary, Derby, Eng., 1980; dir. cleft palate team Nat. Naval Med. Ctr., Bethesda, 1977-79, chmn. plastic surgery, 1978-79; chmn. plastic surgery Bethesda Naval Hosp., Washington, 1979-80; pvt. practice Denver, 1980-82, Lincoln, Nebr., 1982—; chmn. plastic surgery Lincoln Gen. Hosp., 1986-87, mem. bd. med. examiners State Nebr., 1988—; cons. cleft palate team State of Nebr., 1986; asst. clin. prof. U. Nebr.; mem. Nebr. State Bd. Examiners. Contbr. articles to profl. jours. Capt. USNR, 1980—. Fellow ACS, Internat. Coll. Surgeons; mem. Am. Soc. Plastic and Reconstructive Surgery, Assn. Mil. Surgeons U.S., Assn. Mil. Plastic Surgeons, British Assn. for Surgery of the Hand, Royal Soc. Medicine, Am. Cleft Palate Assn., AMA, Am. Soc. Maxillo-Facial Surgery, Am. Assn. Hand Surgery, Lancaster County Med. Soc. Office: 801 S 48th St Lincoln NE 68510-3726

METZEN, JAMES P., state legislator, banker; b. Oct. 1943; m. Sandie Metzen; two children. Student, U. Minn. Banker; state rep. Minn. Ho. of Reps., St. Paul; Dist. 39 senator Minn. State Senate, St. Paul, 1986—; chmn. govt. op. and reform com.; mem. jobs, energy and cmty. devel., fin. divsn. consumer protection, rules and adminstrn., and vet. and gen. legis. coms., Minn. State Senate. Office: 312 Deerwood Ct South Saint Paul MN 55075-2102 also: State Senate State Capital Building Saint Paul MN 55155-1606*

METZENBAUM, HOWARD MORTON, former U.S. senator; b. Cleve., June 4, 1917; s. Charles I. and Anna (Klafter) M.; m. Shirley Turoff, Aug. 8, 1946; children: Barbara Jo, Susan Lynn, Shelley Hope, Amy Beth. B.A., Ohio State U., 1939, LL.D., 1941. Chmn. bd. Airport Parking Co. Am., 1958-66, ITT Consumer Services Corp., 1966-68; chmn. bd. ComCorp, 1969-74; mem. War Labor Panel, 1942-45, Ohio Bur. Code rev., 1949-50, Cleve. Met. Housing Authority, 1968-70, Lake Erie Regional Transit Authority, 1972-73, Ohio Ho. of Reps., 1943-46, Ohio Senate, 1947-50; chmn. anti-trust sub-com., labor sub-com. U.S. Senate; mem. intell com., budget com., environ. and pub. works com., judiciary com., labor and human resources, energy and natural resources, dem. policy com. Trustee Mt. Sinai Hosp., Cleve., 1961-73, treas, 1966-73; bd. dirs. Coun. Human Rels., United Cerebral Palsy Assn., Nat. Coun. Hunger and Malnutrition, Karamu House, St. Vincent Charity Hosp., Cleve., St. Jude Rsch. Hosp., Memphis; nat. co-chmn. Nat. Citizen's Com. Conquest Cancer; vice chmn. fellows Brandeis U.; chmn. Am. Friend Rabin Ctr., Tel Aviv, Israel; mem. Bd. Nat. Peace Garden Found. Mem. ABA, Ohio Bar Assn., Cuyahoga Bar Assn., Cleve. Bar Assn., Am. Assn. Trial Lawyers, Order of Coif, Phi Eta Sigma, Tau Epsilon Rho. Office: Consumer Federation of America 1424 16th St NW Ste 504 Washington DC 20036-2211

METZGER, KERRY R., state legislator; m. Karen Metzger; children: Robert, Ryan. BS, Juniata Coll.; DDS, Temple U. Dentist pvt. practice, New Phila., Ohio; councilman City of New Phila., 1988-94; pres. City Coun. of New Phila., 1992-94; rep. dist. 97 Ohio Ho. of Reps., Columbus, 1994—. Mem. Tuscarawas County Rep. Exec. Com. Named Internat. Senator Jaycees; recipient Presidential award of honor, Ohio Jaycees. Mem. Am. Dental Assn., Ohio Dental Assn., Tuscarawas County Dental Soc., Soc. Forensic Odontology, Tuscarawas C. of C., Tuscarawas Valley Civil War Roundtable.

METZLER, ERIC HAROLD, state agency administrator; b. Albion, Mich., Nov. 13, 1945; s. Clarence Harold and Lois Marian (Bastian) M.; m. Patricia Ann (Trescott), Aug. 26, 1967; 1 child, Meredith Gene. BS, Mich. State U., 1968. Ops. mgr. ODNR div. Watercraft, Columbus, Ohio, 1973-80, dep. chief, 1980-96; rsch. assoc. Ohio Agrl. Rsch Ctr., Wooster, 1974-78, Ohio Biol. Survey, Columbus, 1980-84, Fla. State Collection Arthropods, Gainesville, 1985—, Cleve. Mus. Natural History, 1985—, Carnegie Mus. Natural History, 1992—. Contbr. articles to profl. jours. Pres. Columbus Matural History Soc., 1981, treas. 1985—. Mem. Ohio Parks and Recreation Assn. (treas. 1978-80, 3d v.p. 1981), Ohio Lepidopterist (sec. treas. 1979, pres. 1980, newsletter editor 1980—), Lepidopterists Soc. (treas. 1985-87, pres. 1996-97). Home: 1241 Kildale Sq N Columbus OH 43229-1306

METZNER, BARBARA STONE, university counselor; b. St. Louis, June 9, 1940; d. Wendell Phillips and Lois Custer (Rake) Metzner. AB, Ind. U., 1962, MS, 1964, EdD, 1983; BA, Purdue U., 1979. Asst. dean students U. Ill., Urbana, 1964-68; undergrad. advisor UCLA, 1968-69; asst. dean students Ohio State U., 1969-72; student affairs officer San Diego State U., 1972-76; sr. counselor Ind. U. - Purdue U., Indpls., 1976—; supr. Ednl. Testing Svc., Indpls., 1980-90; cons. editorial bd. Nat. Acad. Advising Assn., Manhattan, Kans., 1987-93; adj. prof. Ind. U., 1987—; mgr. Info. Svcs., Ind. U.-Purdue U., 1989-91. Contbr. articles to profl. jours. Mem. Marion County Precinct Election Bd., 1980—; exec. com. Ind. Allied Health Assn., 1983-84; VIP escort Pan Am. Games, 1987. Spencer Found. grantee, 1985. Mem. APA, Am. Edn. Rsch. Assn., Nat. Acad. Advising Assn., Assn. Instl. Rsch., Assn. Study Higher Edn., Kappa Alpha Theta (vol. charity benefits 1980—). Office: IUPUI 620 Union Dr Unit 242 Indianapolis IN 46202-5130

MEYER, BRENDA SUE, critical care and home health nurse; b. Ft. Wayne, Ind., Apr. 16, 1954; d. Herbert Carl and Marilyn Ruth (Nagel) M. Grad., Ft. Wayne Commun. Schs., 1975; AAS, Purdue U., 1983, BSN, 1989; MSN in Comty. Health with honors, Ind. U., Indpls., 1995. RN, Ind.; cert. ACLS. Various nursing positions Parkview Hosp., Ft. Wayne, 1970—, intensive care nurse, 1976—, founding mem. Code Blue com., 1981—; chmn., 1992-95; post masters nurse practitioner St. Francis Coll., 1995—; rsch. asst. Nat. Heart Risk Study, 1991-95; exec. bd. dirs. Super Shot Saturday, A.J. Bloesing Ctr. Vol., Allen County Bd. Health Immigration Clinic, Ft. Wayne, 1987—, Allen County Med. Response Team for Disaster Relief, Ft. Wayne, 1990-95, Focus on Health, Ft. Wayne, 1987—. Recipient Nurses Who Care award, 1992. Mem. Ind. State Nurses Assn. (exec. bd. 1991—, vice chmn. staff nurse coun. 1995), Sigma Theta Tau (Xi Nu St. Francis chpt., presenter master's rsch. 1995 confs.). Lutheran. Home: 1206 Pemberton Dr Fort Wayne IN 46805-5332

MEYER, ERIC KENT, journalism educator and consultant; b. Marion, Kans., Aug. 23, 1953; s. Otto William Jr. and Joan Aileen (Wight) M.; divorced; 1 child, Nathaniel Jeremy Meyer-Gleason. BS, U. Kans., 1975; MA, Marquette U., 1996. Sunday editor, reporter, copy editor The Daily Pantagraph, Bloomington, Ill., 1975-77; news photo and graphics editor, asst. news editor, copy editor, reporter Milw. Jour., 1977-94; instr. Marquette U., Milw., 1993-96, U. Ill., Urbana, Wis., 1996—; mng. ptnr., editor on-line resource Newslink Assocs., 1995—. Author: Tomorrow's News Today: Strategic Guide to Online Publishing, 1995, Graphics Journalism, 1996. Pres. Spring Terrace Homeowners, Milw., 1981-83. Recipient awards UPI, 1983-85, photography award, reporting award AP, Ill., 1976-77. Mem. Soc. Profl. Journalists (bd. dirs. Milw. chpt. 1995-96, treas.), Soc. Newspaper Design, Assn. for Edn. in Journalism. Republican. Methodist. Home: 1508 Devonshire Dr Champaign IL 61821 Office: U of Ill 017 Johnston Hall Gregory Hall Urbana IL 61801

MEYER, FRED ALBERT, JR., political science educator; b. Milw., Oct. 7, 1942; s. Fred Albert and Rose Henrietta (Hafemann) M. BA, U. Wis., 1964; MA, U. Wis., Milw., 1966; PhD, Wayne State U., 1974. Instr. Carroll Coll., Waukesha, Wis., 1970-71; prof. Polit. Sci. Ball State U., Muncie, Ind., 1971—; editor Ind. Jour. Polit. Sci. Co-editor: Determinants of Law Enforcement Policies, 1979, Evaluating Alternative Law Enforcement Policies, 1979; co-author: The Criminal Justice Game, 1980; co-editor: State Policy Problems, 1993. Chair Gender Fairness Coalition of Ind., Indpls., 1988-93, sec., 1994—; chair Ind. Found. on Gender-Based Edn., Indpls., 1988-93; sec. Healthy Mothers Healthy Babies of Delaware County, 1995—; mem. coun. Policy Studies Orgn., 1994—. Recipient grant to produce videotape on access to prenatal care in Delaware County, Ind. Hoosier Heartland chpt. March of Dimes, Muncie, 1990. Mem. Am. Polit. Sci. Assn., Policy Studies Orgn., Midwest Polit. Sci. Assn., Western Polit. Sci. Assn., So. Polit. Sci. Assn., Audubon Soc., Sierra Club. Office: Polit Sci Dept Ball State U Muncie IN 47306

MEYER, FRED WILLIAM, JR., memorial parks executive; b. Fair Haven, Mich., Jan. 7, 1924; s. Fred W. and Gladys (Marshall) M.; m. Jean Hope, Aug. 5, 1946; children—Frederick, Thomas, James, Nancy. AB, Mich. State Coll., 1946. Salesman Chapel Hill Meml. Gardens, Lansing, Mich., 1946-47; mgr. Roselawn Meml. Gardens, Saginaw, Mich., 1947-49; dist. mgr. Sunset Meml. Gardens, Evansville, Ind., 1949-53; pres., dir. Memory Gardens Mgmt. Corp., Indpls., Hamilton Meml. Gardens, Chattanooga, Covington Meml. Gardens, Ft. Wayne, Ind., Chapel Hill Meml. Gardens, Grand Rapids, Mich., Forest Lawn Memory Gardens, Indpls., Lincoln Memory Gardens, Indpls., Sherwood Meml. Gardens, Knoxville, Tenn., Chapel Hill Meml. Gardens, South Bend, Ind., White Chapel Meml. Gardens, Springfield, Mo., Nebo Meml. Park, Martinsville, Ind., Mercury Devel. Corp., Indpls., Quality Marble Imports, Indpls., Quality Printers, Indpls., Am. Bronze Craft, Inc., Judsonia, Ark. Mem. C. of C., A.I.M., Am. Cemetery Assn., Sigma Chi, Phi Kappa Delta. Clubs: Columbia, Meridian Hills Country, Woodland Country. Home: 110 E 111th St Indianapolis IN 46280-1051 Office: 3733 N Meridian St Indianapolis IN 46208-4305

MEYER, GEORGE HERBERT, lawyer; b. Detroit, Feb. 19, 1928; s. Herbert M. and Agnes F. (Eaton) M.; m. Carol Ann Jones, 1958 (div. 1981) children: Karen Ann, George Herbert Jr.; m. Katherine Palmer White, Nov. 12, 1988. A.B., U. Mich., 1949; J.D., Harvard U., 1952; cert., Oxford (Eng.) U., 1955; LL.M. in Taxation, Wayne State U., 1962. Bar: D.C. bar 1952, Mich. bar 1953. Assoc. firm Fischer, Franklin & Ford, Detroit, 1956-63; mem. firm Fischer, Franklin & Ford, 1963-74; established firm George H. Meyer, 1974-78; sr. mem. firm Meyer and Kirk, 1978-85; sr. mem. Meyer, Kirk, Snyder & Safford PLLC, Bloomfield Hills and Detroit, Mich., 1985—; curator Step Lively exhibit Mus. Am. Folk Art, N.Y.C., 1992; lectr. Am. Folk Art. Author: Equalization in Michigan and Its Effect on Local Assessments, 1963, Folk Artists Biographical Index, 1986, American Folk Art Canes: Personal Sculpture, 1992. Chmn. Birmingham (Mich.) Bd. Housing Appeals, 1964-68; vice chmn. Birmingham Bd. Zoning Appeals, 1966-69; mem. Birmingham Planning Bd., 1968-70; trustee, Bloomfield Village, Mich., 1976-80, pres., 1979-80; trustee Mus. Am. Folk Art, N.Y.C., 1987—; mem. exec. bd. Detroit Area coun. Boy Scouts Am., 1976—, counsel, 1986—; mem. nat. adv. bd. Folk Art Soc. Am., 1994—; trustee Detroit Sci. Ctr., 1985—. 1st lt. JAG, USAF, 1952-55, maj. Res. ret. Recipient Silver Beaver award Detroit Area coun. Boy Scouts Am., 1989. Mem. ABA, Detroit Bar Assn., Oakland County Bar Assn., State Bar Mich., Harvard Law Sch. Assn. Mich. (dir. 1959—, pres. 1970-78), Detroit Sci. Mus. Soc. (pres. 1961-74, chmn. 1974—), Am. Folk Art Soc., Prismatic Club, Scarab Club, Harvard Club (N.Y.C.), Detroit Club, Masons, Rotary, Phi Beta Kappa, Alpha Phi Omega. Republican. Unitarian. Home: Meyer Kirk Snyder & Stafford PLLC Ste 100 100 W Long Lake Rd Bloomfield Hills MI 48301-2242 Office: Meyer Kirk Snyder & Stafford 100 W Long Lake Rd Ste 100 Bloomfield Hills MI 48304-2773

MEYER, HENRY LEWIS, III, banker; b. Cleve., Dec. 25, 1949; s. Henry Lewis and Anne (Taylor) M.; m. Jane Kreamer, July 15, 1978; children: Patrick Harrison, Andrew Taylor, Christopher Bicknell. BA, Colgate U., 1972; MBA, Harvard U., Boston, 1978. Asst. v.p. Soc. Nat. Bank, Cleve., 1972-76, v.p., 1978-81, sr. v.p., 1981-83; exec. v.p. Soc. Bank, N.Am., Dayton, Ohio, 1983-85, pres., chief operating officer, 1985-87; sr. exec. v.p. Soc. Bank, N.Am., Cleve., 1987-89, vice chmn. bd., 1989—; exec. v.p. Soc. Corp., 1987—; bd. dirs. Soc. Bank, Columbus, Soc. Investor Svcs. Corp., Nat. Fin. Svcs. Corp., Soc. Mortgage Co. Trustee Am. Cancer Soc. (Cuyahoga County Unit), Fedn. for Neighborhood Progress, Inc., A.M. McGregor Home, Cleve. Mus. Nat. History. Republican. Episcopalian. Clubs: Kirtland Country (Cleve.), The Union (Cleve.).

MEYER, J. THEODORE, lawyer; b. Chgo., Apr. 13, 1936; s. Joseph Theodore and Mary Elizabeth (McHugh) M.; m. Marilu Bartholomew, Aug. 16, 1961; children: Jean, Joseph. B.S., John Carroll U., 1958; postgrad. U. Chgo.; J.D., DePaul U., 1962. Bar: Ill. 1962, U.S. Dist. Ct. (no. dist.) Ill. 1962. Ptnr. Bartholomew & Meyer, Chgo., 1963-83; mem. Ill. Gen. Assembly, House of Rep., 28th Legis. Dist., 1966-72, 74-82, chmn. House environ. study com., 1968; chmn. energy environ. com. and natural resources com.; mem. appropriations and exec. com.; chmn. Joint House/Senate com. to review state air and water plans, 1968; mem. Fed. State Task Force on Energy; chmn., founder Midwest Legis. Coun. on Environ., 1971; mem. State of Ill. Pollution Control Bd., Chgo., 1983—; mem. Joint Legis. Com. on Hazardous Waste in Lake Calumet Area, 1987; lectr. in field. Recipient Appreciation award Ill. Wildlife Fedn., 1972, Environ. Quality award Region V, EPA, 1974, Pro Bono Publico award Self-Help Action Ctr., 1975, Merit award Dept. Ill. VFW, 1977, Environ. Legislator of Yr. award Ill. Environ. Coun., 1978-79; Disting. Lawyer Legislator of Yr.; commd. hon. lt. aide-de-camp Ala. State Militia; commd. Hon. Tex. Citizen. Fellow Chgo. Bar Found.; mem. ABA, Ill. Bar Assn., Chgo. Bar Assn., Nat. Rep. Legis. Assn., Nat. Trust Hist. Preservation, Nat. Wildlife Fedn., Ill. Hist. Soc., Beverly Tennis Club, Beverly Hills Univ. Club. Republican. Roman Catholic. Office: State of Ill Ctr 100 W Randolph St Ste 11500 Chicago IL 60601-3220

MEYER, JAMES PHILIP, secondary education social studies educator; b. Berwyn, Ill., May 2, 1946; s. Albert Fred and Eleanore Ann (Szydlowski) M.; m. Candice Marie Richter, Dec. 19, 1970; children: Teri Lynn, David Philip. Student, Athenaeum of Ohio, 1964-66, Maryknoll Coll., 1966-67; BA in Classics, Loyola U., Chgo., 1969; postgrad., Roosevelt U., 1972-76, U. Ill., 1990, Bradley U., 1994. Cert. tchr. 6-12, Ill. Tchr. Cass Sch. Dist. # 63, Darien, Ill., 1969—; football coach Cass Sch. Dist. #63, Darien, Ill. 1969-84, basketball and softball coach, 1969-87; official scorekeeper and statistician at Downers Grove N. Girls Basketball, 1988—. Campaign mgr. Citizens for Donohue 13th dist. U.S. Congress, Naperville, Ill., 1984; campaign. coord. County Bd. candidate, Lombard, Ill., 1986, sec. DuPage County Dems., Lombard, 1986-90; bd. dirs., program com. Jr. Achievement, Chgo., 1987—. Recipient Excellence in Teaching award Ill. Math. and Sci. Acad., Aurora, Ill., 1991, Bus.-Edn. Partnership award Ill. State Bd. Edn., 1994. Mem. Ill. Norsk Rosemalers Assn. (computer records com., Swedish days com.). Roman Catholic. Home: 4216 Elm St Downers Grove IL 60515-2115 Office: Cass Sch Dist # 63 8502 Bailey Rd Darien IL 60561-5333

MEYER, JOHN CHARLES, religious studies educator; b. Dubuque, Iowa, Aug. 12, 1934; s. George Walter and Mary Helen (Schmitt) M.; m. Mary Claire Wesenberg, July 22, 1970; 1 child, John David. BA, Loras Coll., Dubuque, Iowa, 1956; MA, STG, U. Louvain, Belgium, 1960; PhD, Cath. U. Am., 1968; postgrad., Ill. State U., 1971-72. Latin and religion tchr. Columbus H.S., Waterloo, Iowa, 1960-62; prof. theology Loras Coll., 1962-69; prof. religious studies Bradley U., Peoria, Ill., 1969—; cons. Nat. Conf. Cath. Bishops, Washington, 1975-76, St. Francis Med. Ctr. Care Decisions, Peoria, 1985-89, Cath. Diocese of Peoria, 1985-92; adv. bd. Heart of Ill. Infant Devel. Ctr., Peoria, 1984-86. Author: Christian Beliefs and Teachings, 1981; contbr. articles to profl. jours. Pres. bd. dirs. Peoria Assn. Retarded Citizens, 1984-85; v.p. bd. dirs. Parc Devel. Homes, Inc., Peoria, 1983—; chmn. advocacy com. Parc, Inc., Peoria, 1991-95; pres. edn. commn. St. Vincent de Paul Sch., Peoria, 1993-95. Named Outstanding Educator of Am., 1975; recipient Francis C. Mergen award for pub. svc. Bradley U., 1985. Mem. AAUP, Am. Assn. Retarded Citizens, Am. Assn. on Mental Retardation, Cath. Theol. Soc. Am., Coll. Theology Soc., Am. Acad. Religion. Roman Catholic. Office: Bradley Univ Theology Dept Peoria IL 61625

MEYER, JOHN JAY, computer systems analyst; b. Warren, Ohio, Feb. 7, 1950; s. John Jacob and Thelma Ida (Force) M.; m. Cynthia Diane Jacobs, Dec. 20, 1975; children: Jon David, Timothy Lane, Jeremy Todd, Jason Thomas. BS in Math., Case Western Res. U., 1973. Programmer Sperry-Univac, Washington, 1973-76; programmer analyst Sperry-Univac, Eagan, Minn., 1976-80, software cons., 1980-82; prin. software engr. Unisys, Roseville, Minn., 1982-95, staff software engr., 1995—. Active Boy Scouts Am. Mem. IEEE. Home: 16773 Ides Cir Lakeville MN 55044 Office: Unisys PO Box 64942 Saint Paul MN 55164

MEYER, JON KEITH, psychiatrist, psychoanalyst, educator; b. Springfield, Ill., May 6, 1938; s. Samuel Barclay and Finela Hermoine (Roehl) M.; m. Eleanor Fumie Yamashita, June 6, 1964; children: David Christopher, Laura Tamiko. AB summa cum laude, Dartmouth Coll., 1960; MD, Johns Hopkins U., 1964; grad., Washington Psychoanalytic Inst, 1980. Intern internal medicine Johns Hopkins Hosp., Balt., 1964-65, resident in psychiatry, 1965-67, 69; resident in psychiatry St. Elizabeth's Hosp., Washington, 1968; spl. asst. to dir. NIMH, Bethesda, Md., 1969-71; asst. prof. psychiatry Johns Hopkins Med. Sch., Balt., 1971-76, assoc. prof., 1976-83; prof. psychiatry Med. Coll. Wis., Milw., 1983—, prof. psychoanalysis in psychiatry, 1987—, prof. family medicine, 1990—; tng. and supervising analyst Chgo. Inst. for Psychoanalysis, 1987—; vice chmn. Dept. of Psychiatry, 1993—; chief psychiatry Froedtert Meml. Luth. Hosp., Milw., 1994—; med. dir. Wis., Psychoanalytic Found., Milw., 1987-91, sec. bd. dirs., 1988-91; bd. dirs. DePaul Hosp. Author books; contbr. chpts. to books, numerous articles to profl. jours. Comdr. USPHS, 1967-71. Daniel Webster Nat. scholar Dartmouth Coll., 1960, sr. fellow, 1959-60, Dennison rsch. fellow Johns Hopkins Med. Sch., 1964; Erik Erikson scholar-in-residence Austen Riggs Ctr., Stockbridge, Mass., 1991-92. Fellow Am. Psychiat. Assn.; mem. Internat. Psychoanalytic Assn., Am. Psychoanalytic Assn., (exec. councilor 1993—, chmn. com. on coun. structure and function 1995—), Internat. Acad. Sex Rsch., Am. Coll. Psychiatrists, Am. Coll. Psychoanalysts, Wis. Psychoanalytic Soc. (founding pres. 1989-91). Office: Med Coll Wis 2321 E Stratford Ct Milwaukee WI 53211-2631

MEYER, JUDITH LOUISE, obstetrician-gynecologist; b. East Grand Rapids, Mich., Feb. 26, 1933; d. George and Evangeline (Boerma) M. AB, Calvin Coll., Grand Rapids, 1955; postgrad., Mich. State U., 1955-56; MD, Women's Med. Coll. Pa., 1961. Intern Blodgett Meml. Med. Ctr., Grand Rapids, 1961-62; resident Med. Coll. Pa., Phila., 1962065; pvt. practice Grandville, Mich., 1965—; asst. clin. prof. coll. human medicine Mich. State U., Grand Rapids, 1970—. Violinist Grand Rapids Symphony, 1961, 65-74, West Shore Symphony, Muskegon, Mich., 1976-81, Kent Philharmonic, Grand Rapids, 1989—; singer Park Congl. Choir, Grand Rapids, 1987—. Fellow Am. Coll. Ob-gyn., Am. Fertility Soc.; mem. Am. Women Surgeon's Assn., Mich. State Med. Soc., Kent County Med. Soc. (legis. com.), Woman's City Club, Ladies Literary Club. Republican. Mem. Reformed Ch. Am. Office: 3181 Prairie St SW Grandville MI 49418-2076

MEYER, MARK, state legislator. Home: 920 16th St S La Crosse WI 54601-4903*

MEYER, MICHAEL A., mechanical engineer; b. Milw., June 20, 1961. A in Mech. Design, Milw. Area Tech. Coll., 1985. Design engr. Dri Tec, Inc., Milw., 1992—; owner Michael Meyer Designs, Oak Creek, Wis., 1992—. Republican. Methodist. Office: Dri Tec Inc PO Box 23888 Milwaukee WI 53223-0888

MEYER, PAUL S., counselor; b. Cin., 1940; s. Charles E. and A. S. Meyer. BA, U. Cin., 1962, MA, 1967; MS, DePaul U., 1979. Nat. cert. counselor; cert. rehab. counselor, vocat. evaluator, Ohio. Owner, mgr. and predecessors Paul S. Meyer Assocs., Cin., 1977—; cons. editor Jour. Rehab. Adminstrn., 1989-91. Guest editor Jour. Rehab., 1979. 1st lt. U.S. Army, 1962-68. Decorated Nat. Def. Svc. medal; Paul S. Meyer award established by Ohio Vocat. Evaluation and Work Adjustment Assn., 1989. Mem. Nat. Rehab. Assn. (W.F. Faulkes award 1986), Vocat. Evaluation and Work Adjustment Assn. (pres. 1979, Paul R. Hoffman award 1983), U.S. Armor Assn. (Armor Assn. award 1962), The Am. Legion. Office: One Lytle Pl Cincinnati OH 45202

MEYER, ROBERT PAUL, quality assurance executive, consultant, foundation executive; b. Cin., Jan. 3, 1945; s. Raymond J. and Magdalen (Muenchen) M.; m. Kathleen Marie Wirtz, Aug. 9, 1969; children: Daniel, Maureen, Melanie, Gregory. BS in Physics, Xavier U., 1967; MBA in Mgmt., U. Akron, 1972. Cert. quality engr. Scientist PPG Industries, Akron, Ohio, 1967-71; quality engr. Hoover Co., North Canton, Ohio, 1971-73; quality mgr. Hunt-Wesson Foods Ohio Match Co., Wadsworth, Ohio, 1973-75; dir. tech. svc. Club Alumninum Co., Cleve., 1975-78; productivity dir. Babcock & Wilcox Co., Akron, 1978-82; pres. Work in NE Ohio Coun., Independence, Ohio, 1982—; pres. Cleve. Assn. for Quality and Participation, Cin., 1983. Mem. Leadership Cleve., 1990-91, Greater Cleve. Growth Assn., 1985—. Named Leader of the Week, Sta. WDOK-Radio and East Ohio Gas Co., Cleve., 1990; recipient Malcolm Baldrige Nat. Quality award Examiner, 1991. Mem. Am. Soc. for Quality Control (sr. mem., local chmn. 1978), Network of Quality and Productivity Ctrs. (chmn. 1991), Assn. for Quality and Participation (local chmn. 1983), Nat. Assn. Area Labor-Mgmt. Coms. (bd. dirs. 1990—). Roman Catholic. Office: Work in NE Ohio Coun 2600 Rockside Woods Blvd # 300 Cleveland OH 44131

MEYER, RONALD J., business executive; b. Detroit, Mar. 27, 1950. PhD in Theology, U. Md., 1970. Cert. record mgmt. cons. V.p. Energy Info. Data, Inc., Berkley, Mich., 1980—; CEO Am. Info. Svcs. Inc., Berkley, 1981—, Am. Imaging Systems Inc., Berkley, 1988—, Medicine Microfilm, Berkley, 1987—, Microfilm Svcs. of Mich. Inc., Berkley, 1989—. Named Citizen of Yr. City of Berkley, 1991. Mem. Berkley Mens Club. Office: PO Box 721411 Berkley MI 48072-0411

MEYER, RUSSEL WILLIAM, JR., aircraft company executive; b. Davenport, Iowa, July 19, 1932; s. Russell William and Ellen Marie (Matthews) M.; m. Helen Scott Vaughn, Aug. 20, 1960; children: Russell William, III, Elizabeth Ellen, Jeffrey Vaughn, Christopher Matthews, Carolyn Louise. B.A., Yale U., 1954; LL.B., Harvard U., 1961. Bar: Ohio 1961. Mem. firm Arter & Hadden, Cleve., 1961-66; pres., chief exec. officer Grumman Am. Aviation Corp., Cleve., 1966-74; exec. v.p. Cessna Aircraft Co., Wichita, Kans., 1974-75; chmn. bd., chief exec. officer Cessna Aircraft Co., 1975—; bd. dirs. Western Resources, Boatman's Bancorp, Vanguard Airlines; presdl. appointee Aviation Safety Commn., 1987—; mem. Pres.' Airline Commn., 1993. chmn. bd. trustees 1st Bapt. Ch., Cleve., 1972-74; bd. dirs. United Way, Wichita and Sedgwick County, Wichita State U. Endowment Assn.; trustee Wesley Hosp. Endowment Assn., Wake Forest univ.; bd. govs. United Way Am., 1993—. Served with USAF, 1955-58. Recipient Collier trophy Nat. Aeronautic Assn., 1986, George S. Dively award Harvard U., 1992, Wright Bros. Meml. trophy, 1995. Mem. ABA, Ohio Bar Assn., Kans. Bar Assn., Cleve. Bar Assn., Gen. Aviation Mfrs. Assn. (chmn. bd. dirs. 1973-74, 81-82, 93-94), Wichita C. of C. (chmn. 1988—, bd. dirs.). Clubs: Wichita, Wichita Country, Castle Pines, Isleworth, Latrobe Country. Home: 600 N Tara Ct Wichita KS 67206-1830 Office: Cessna Aircraft PO Box 7704 1 Cessna Blvd Wichita KS 67215-1400

MEYER, RUTH KRUEGER, museum administrator, educator, art historian; b. Chicago Heights, Ill., Aug. 20, 1940; d. Harold Rohe and Ruth Halbert (Bateman) Krueger; m. Kenneth R. Meyer, June 15, 1963 (div. 1978); 1 child, Karl Augustus. B.F.A., U. Cin., 1963; M.A., Brown U., 1968; Ph.D., U. Minn., 1980. Lectr. Walker Art Ctr., Mpls., 1970-72; instr. U. Cin., 1973-75; curator Contemporary Arts Ctr., Cin., 1976-80; dir. Ohio Found. Arts, Columbus, 1980-83, Taft Mus., Cin., 1983-93; prof. Miyazaki (Japan) Internat. Coll., 1994—; adj. prof. The Union Inst., Cin., 1994. Pub. Dialogue Mag., Columbus, 1980-83; author: (exhbn. catalogues) Sandy Rosen Vestal Vases, 1986, Oblique Illusion: An Installation by Rick Paul, 1986, David Black an American Sculptor, 1985, Brad Davis: The Pines, 1984, The American Weigh, 1983, New Epiphanies, 1982, (with others) The Tafts Collection: The First Ten Years of Its Development, 1988, The Tafts of Pike St., 1988, (exhbn. catalogue) The History of Travel: Paintings by William Wegman, 1985-90, 1990, The Artist Face to Face: Two Centuries of Self-Portraits from the Paris Collection of Gerald Shurr, 1989, Tributes to the Tafts, 1991, The Taft Museum: Its Collection and Its History, 1995; contbr. articles to profl. jours. Recipient rsch. award Kress Found., 1967, 76; named Chevalier in the Order of Arts and Letters, Govt. of France, 1989. Mem. Internat. Assn. Art Critics, Coll. Art Assn. Democrat. Office: Miyazaki Internat College, 1405 Kano Kiyotake-Cho, Miyazaki 88916, Japan

MEYER, THOMAS J., mathematics educator; b. Rochester, Minn., Aug. 14, 1949; s. Donald Joseph and Jean Ann (Gerleman) M.; m. Nancy Mae Lewis, Jan. 3, 1986. BS, Ea. Mich. U., 1971, MA, 1974, 83. Tchr. math. Van Buren Schs., North Jr. High Sch., Belleville, Mich., 1972-83; tchr. math. Belleville High Sch., 1983—, chmn. math. dept., 1989—. Mem. Nat. Council Tchrs. Math., Mich. Council Tchrs. Math., Math. Assn. Am., Van Buren Edn. Assn. (trustee 1974-86, crisis com. chmn. 1982-85). Home: 708 Collegewood St Ypsilanti MI 48197-2133 Office: Van Buren Pub Schs 501 W Columbia Ave Belleville MI 48111-2611

MEYER, WILBUR L., manufacturing engineer; b. Lancaster, Ohio, Mar. 12, 1950. AS in Tool Engring. Tech., ITT Tech., 1970; AS in Mfg. Tech., Ohio U., 1987, BS in Indsl. Tech., 1991. Tchr. Lancaster (Ohio) City Schs., 1977-86; tool engr. H.B.I. Automotive Glass, Lancaster, 1986-91; mfg. prodn. engr. Diamond Electronics Inc., Lancaster, 1992—. Mem. adv. bd. Vocat. Drafting, Lancaster, 1992—. Mem Soc. Mfg. Engrs. (cert.). Mem. Ch. of Christ Christian Union. Office: Diamond Electronics Inc PO Box 200 Lancaster OH 43130-0200

MEYERS, KAREN HOPKINS, management consultant; b. N.Y.C., Oct. 23, 1948; d. Richard Anthony and Jeanne Frances (O'Brien) Hopkins; m. John Walter Wingate, June 21, 1969 (div. 1972); m. Robert Bernard Meyers, Jan. 29, 1983; 1 child, Elizabeth. BA, Mich. State U., 1970; post grad., UCLA, 1970-72; MA, Bowling Green (Ohio) State U., 1974; PhD, Bowling Green State U., 1982. Writer Allstate Ins. Co., Northbrook, Ill., 1977-79; dir. tng. Ins. Co. N. Am., Kalamazoo, 1979-81; career devel. specialist Owens Ill., Inc., Toledo, 1981-83; pers. staff specialist First Nat. Bank, Toledo, 1983-84, dir. tng., 1984-86, mgmt. cons., 1986-88; dir. mgmt. devel. The Employers' Assn. of Toledo, 1988-89; prin. mgmt. cons. bus. Toledo, 1990—; dir. Heidelberg Coll. Tiffin, Ohio, 1994—. Contbr. articles to profl. jours. Mem. allocation com. United Way, Toledo, 1983; pres. Westmoreland Assn., 1985. Fellow Woodrow Wilson Found., 1970. Mem. Phi Beta Kappa. Democrat. Roman Catholic.

MEYERS, LOUISA ANN, business and communications consultant; b. Omaha, July 5, 1956; d. V. William and Darinka Stephania (Shuput) M. BA in Liberal Studies magna cum laude, U. Nebr., Omaha, 1983. Wardrobe asst. Royal Shakespeare Theatre, Stratford-upon-Avon, Eng., 1977-78, asst. adminstr., 1978-79; stage/asst. co. mgr. Omaha Cmty. Playhouse, Nebr. Theatre Caravan, 1979-80; stage/prodn. mgr. Firehouse Dinner Theater, Omaha, 1980-81; pers. benefits technician Bergan Mercy Hosp., Omaha, 1981-82, unit sec., 1981-83; planning mgr. Mercy Health Sys. of Midlands, Omaha, 1984-85; staff asst. Omaha City Coun., 1985-86; mayoral aide City of Omaha, 1986-87; cmty. devel. mgr. City of Omaha, 1987-89, mayor's spl. projects mgr., 1989; exec. dir. Neighborhood Housing Svcs., Omaha, 1989-90; dir. Office Comms., legis. liaison Nebr. Dept. Health, Lincoln, 1993-95; co-founder, mng. ptnr. Mercury Bus. Comms., Omaha, 1990—; presenter on pub. policy to various comty. orgns.; flood disaster coord. Nebr. Dept. Health, 1993; state rep. Nat. Coun. Pub. Health Info. Coalition, 1993-95; film. commr. City of Omaha, 1986-89, rep. to League of Nebr. Municipalities, 1986-87; festival coord. City of Omaha, 1985-86; adminstr. City of Omaha Cable TV, 1985-86; writer various grants, reports for City of Omaha; mem. efficiency task orce City of Omaha. Contbr. articles to profl. jours.; reporter Gateway newspaper, 1982; author, co. mgr., stage mgr. dramatic touring prodn. Nebraska Heritage, 1974-75. Mem. chancellor's adv. com. U. Nebr., Omaha, 1974, bicentennial com., 1975; chair Joslyn Chamber Music Series, 1986-87; coord. fundraiser Queen Elizabeth Hosp., Birmingham, Eng., 1979; exec. dir. Omaha Coalition for Homeless, 1990-91; campaign mgr. Horgan for Legislature, Omaha, 1990; vol. Jesse Rasmussen for Legislature Campaign, Omaha, 1994. Medill Sch. Journalism scholar, 1973, Margaret Builta scholar, 1983; recipient Admiralty award Nebr. Navy, 1993. Mem. LWV, NOW, Nat. Mus. Women in Arts (charter mem.), Phi Kappa Phi, Alpha Psi Omega. Home: 4927 Pinkney St Omaha NE 68104 Office: Mercury Bus Comms PO Box 31397 Omaha NE 68131-0397

MEYERS, LYNN BETTY, architect; b. Chgo., Dec. 2, 1952; d. William J. and Dorothy (King) M.; m. Dana Terp, May 17, 1975; children: Sophia, Rachel. Student, Royal Acad. Architecture, Copenhagen, Denmark, 1971; BArch, Washington U., St. Louis, 1974, MArch, 1977. Registered architect, Ill., Fla. Architect Holabird & Root Architects, Chgo., 1973, 76, Jay Alpert Architects, Woodbridge, Conn., 1976, City of Chgo. Bur. Architects, 1978-80; sole practice architecture Chgo., 1980-82; prin., architect Terp Meyers Architects, Chgo., 1982—; real estate salesman, Ill., 1991, Fla.; v.p. Paradise Grove Devel. Corp., 1991—. Exhbns. include: Centre George Pompidou, Paris, 1978, Fifth Internat. Congress Union Internat. Des Femmes Architects, Seattle, 1979, Frumkin Struve Gallery, Chgo., 1981, Art. Inst. Chgo., 1983, Inst. Francais d'Architecture, Paris, 1983, Mus. Sci. and Industry, Chgo., 1985, Hyde Park Art Ctr., 1990, 91, Chgo. Architecture and Design Art Inst. 1923-1993, 1993; pub. in profl. jours. including Progressive Architecture, Modo Design, Inland Architect, 1984, Chgo. Archtl. Jour., 1983, L.A. Architect; work featured in various archtl. books; exhibited 150 Yrs. of Chgo. Architecture, Mus. Sci. and Industry, Chgo., 1985, Chgo. Women in Architecture - Progress and Evolution, Chgo. Hist. Soc., 1974-84. Recipient Progressive Architecture mag. award, 1980, citation Archtl. Design, 1980. Mem. AIA (task force com. for 1992 World's Fair, 1st place award L.A. Real Problems Competition 1986, Art By Architects award 1989, Art award 1990), Union Internat. Des Femmes Architects, Chgo. Women in Architecture (v.p. 1980-81, Allied Arts award 1974), Young Chgo. Architects. Office: Terp Meyers Architects 919 N Michigan Ave Chicago IL 60611-1601

MEYERS, MATTHEW FRANK, advertising executive; b. Iowa City, May 26, 1967; s. Virgil Dwight and Peggy Ann (Welch) M.; m. Marcella Kay Bender, Sept. 1, 1990. A in Journalism, Muscatine (Iowa) C.C., 1988; B in Journalism, U. Iowa, 1990. Advt. rep. Muscatine Jour., 1987-88, The Daily Iowan, Iowa City, 1989, Iowa City Press Citizen, 1990; advt. exec. Madison (Wis.) Newspapers, Inc., 1990-95; gen. mgr. Sunshine Wheels for You, Madison, 1995—. Account exec. United Way, Madison 1994. Mem. Wis. Auto/Truck Dealers Assn., Apt. Assn. Methodist. Home: 2209 Wagon Trl Madison WI 53716 Office: Sunshine 1019 Jonathan Dr Madison WI 53713

MEYERS, MICHAEL NEAL, telecommunications industry executive; b. Sherman, Tex., Oct. 15, 1945; s. H. Neal and Annetha F. (Ullrick) M.; m. Sandra R. McKellip, Jan. 29, 1967; children: Melissa E., Heather A. BA in Math., U. Ill., 1967; MS in Info. Sci., U. Chgo., 1969, MBA, 1984. With AT&T/Lucent Technologies Bell Labs., Naperville, Ill., 1967—; devel. dir. AT&T Bell Labs., Naperville, Ill., 1993—. Contbr. numerous articles to profl. jours. Home: 108 Pembroke Rd Naperville IL 60540-5625

MEYERS, PAMELA SUE, lawyer; b. Lakewood, N.J., June 13, 1951; d. Morris Leon and Isabel (Leibowitz) M.; m. Gerald Stephen Greenberg, Aug. 24, 1975; children: David Stuart Greenberg, Allison Brooke Greenberg. AB with distinction, Cornell U., 1973; JD cum laude, Harvard U., 1976. Bar: N.Y. 1977, Ohio 1990. Assoc. Stroock & Stroock & Lavan, N.Y.C., 1976-80; staff v.p., asst. gen. counsel Am. Premier Underwriters, Inc., Cin., 1980—. Mem. Am. Soc. Corp. Secs. (membership chmn. 1990-91, adv. com. 1991—), Cin. Bar Assn., Greater Cin. Women Lawyers Assn., Harvard Club of Cin. (bd. dirs. 1993—), Phi Beta Kappa. Jewish. Home: 3633 Carpenters Creek Dr Cincinnati OH 45241-3824 Office: Am Premier Underwriters 1 E 4th St Cincinnati OH 45202-3717

MEYERSICK, SHARON KAY, insurance administrator, nurse; b. Waynesville, Mo., Mar. 19, 1945; d. James Monroe and Fannie Mae (Williams) Atkinson; m. Bernard William Meyersick Jr., July 27, 1974 (dec. May 1992). AD in Nursing, Mercamec Community Coll., St. Louis, 1970; BS in Nursing, Tarkio Coll., Mo., 1983; postgrad., Webster Coll., St. Louis, 1988. Staff nurse Normandy Osteopathic Hosp., St. Louis, 1970-76, head nurse, 1976-79, instr. nursing edn., 1979-81; quality assurance nurse Barnes Hosp., St. Louis, 1981-84; review analyst Blue Cross-Blue Shield of Mo., St. Louis, 1985-87, supr. program review, 1987-91; patient care coord. Prudential Ins. Co. Am./St. Louis Health Care Mgmt., St Louis, 1991—. Office: Prudential Ins Co Am Saint Louis Health Care Mgmt 12312 Olive Blvd Saint Louis MO 63141-6448

MICALLEF, JOSEPH STEPHEN, lawyer; b. Malta, Oct. 19, 1933; came to U.S., 1949; s. John E. and Josephine (Brownrigg) M.; m. Jane M. Yungers, Sept. 5, 1959; children: Lisa R., Maura J. Fisk, Sara M. Hulse, Amy A., Joseph S. Jr. BA cum laude, U. St. Thomas, 1958, LLB, JD, 1962. Pres., CEO Fiduciary Counselling, Inc., St. Paul, 1961—; trustee Gt. No. Iron Ore Properties Trust, St. Paul, The Charles A. Lindbergh Fund, Mpls.; mem. bd. visitors U. Minn. Law Sch., Mpls. Past pres., mem. exec. com. Minn. Hist. Soc., St. Paul; bd. dirs. Minn. Air NG Hist. Found., Inc.; bd. overseers Hill Monastic Manuscript Libr.; past regent St. John's U., Collegeville, Minn.; mem. investment adv. com. Archdiocese St. Paul/Mpls.; mem. fin. coun. Cathedral of St. Paul; dir. emeritus Sci. Mus. Minn., St. Paul; trustee James Jerome Hill Ref. Libr., St. Paul. Decorated Knight of the Sovereign Mil., Order of Malta, 1981, Knight of the Equestrian Order of Holy Sepulchre of Jerusalem, Hon. Consul Gen. of Malta, St. Paul/Mpls. Mem. ABA (com. on real property, probate and trust law), Minn. Bar Assn. (subcom. on the Minn. nonprofit corp. act trust law com.), Minn. Coun. on Founds. (govt. rels. com.), Minn. Club, Town & Country Club, Casino Maltese Club, The Union Club (Malta). Office: Fiduciary Counselling Inc Ste 2100 332 Minnesota St Saint Paul MN 55101

MICCOLIS, DOMINIC JON, publishing advisor, consultant; b. Oak Park, Ill., July 22, 1940; s. Dominic Louis and Anna Constance (Griggaitis) M.; m. Phyllis Ann Fioramonti, Dec. 4, 1966; children: Michelle Anna, Jon Michael, Patrick Joseph. BA, Elmhurst Coll., 1964; MA, Roosevelt U., 1978; grad. Exec. Bus. Adminstrn. Program, U. Va., 1986. Dept. chmn., instr. Mendel Cath. Prep. Sch., Chgo., 1964-70; editor Benefic Press div. Harcourt Brace, Westchester, Ill., 1970-72; sr. editor Rand McNally, Skokie, Ill., 1972-74; project dir. Laidlaw div. Doubleday, River Forest, Ill., 1974-77; v.p., exec. editor World Book Pub., Chgo., 1977-94; prin., owner PDM Assocs., Roselle, Ill., 1994—; assoc. Profl. Pub. Svcs., Westport, Conn., 1994—; cons. Consumer Mktg. Svcs., Hollywood, Fla., 1994—; cons., electronic pub. Scott Fetzer/World Book, Inc., Westlake, Ohio, 1994—. Editor: (book and electronic) World Book-Thorndike Barnhart Dictionary, 1985-94 (Best Gen. Dictionary 1988), (set) Childcraft-The How and Why Library, 1985-94 (Best Children's Set 1984), (video) How th Study, 1986 (Am. Video Assn. award 1987-88), (mixed-media) Early World of Learning, 1987 (PTA citations 1987—). Mem. ASCD, Phi Alpha Theta. Republican. Roman Catholic. Office: PDM Assocs 10699 E Willow Rd Stockton IL 61085-9541

MICH, CONNIE RITA, mental health nurse, educator; b. Nebr., Feb. 5, 1926; d. Henry B. and Anna (Stratman) Redel; m. Richard Mich. BSN, Alverno Coll.; postgrad., Marquette U.; MSN, Cath. U. Am. Asst. clin. dir. in-patient svcs. Fond du Lac (Wis.) County Health Ctr., 1974-78; head nurse, program coord. acute psychiat. unit St. Agnes Hosp., Fond du Lac, 1979-83; mental health clinician Immanuel Med. Ctr., Omaha, 1984-89; instr., clin. supr., asst. prof. psychiat. mental health Coll. St. Mary, Omaha, 1989-93; med. programs dir. Inst. Computer Sci. Ltd., 1989—; program dir. med. programs Gateway Coll., Omaha, 1995; chairperson Examining Coun. on RNs; writer items State Bd. Test Pool Exam.; pres. Milw. Coun. Cath. Nurses; vice chairperson Wis. Conf. Group Psychiat. Nursing Practice. Mem. Sigma Theta Tau, Pi Gamma Mu.

MICHAEL, BRIAN P., mechanical engineer; b. Hartford City, Ind., Dec. 1, 1960. BSME, Tri State U., Angola, Ind., 1984. Prodn. engr. Square D Co., Huntington, Ind., 1984-88; v.p. engring. Marshall Electronic Co., Rochester, Ind., 1989-92; mech. engr. Thomson Consumer Electronics, Indpls., 1992—. Coach, adminstr. Boys and Girls Club, Greenfield, Ind., 1993-95. Mem. NSPE. Republican.

MICHAEL, MICHAEL SHLEMON, programmer analyst; b. Baghdad, Iraq, Feb. 9, 1957; came to the U.S., 1973; s. Shlemon S. and Nanny O. (Mackou) M.; m. Jackline Michael, Apr. 26, 1986; children: Paul William, Matthew Bejan. BS in Computer Sci., BS in Bus. & Mgmt., Northeastern Ill. U., 1982. Data entry operator Uptown Fed. Savs., Chgo., 1977-80; computer operator Bank of Ravenswood, Chgo., 1980-86; sr. computer operator Leath Furniture, Lincolnwood, Ill., 1986-87; computer ops. mgr. Maurice Sporting Goods, Northbrook, Ill., 1987-90; jr. programmer Interim Sys. Corp., Northbrook, 1990-91; syhs. programmer Handy Andy Corp., Schaumburg, Ill., 1991-92; tech. support/programmer Hardis Corp., Schaumburg, 1992-93; programmer analyst Armstrong Blum Mfg. Co., Mt. Prospect, Ill., 1993—. Mem. Assyrian Athletic Club (treas. 1990-92, Merit award 1992). Democrat. Roman Catholic. Home: 8850 Prospect Niles IL 60714

MICHAELS, MARION CECELIA, writer, editor, news syndicate executive; b. Black River Falls, Wis.; d. Leonard N. and Estelle O. (Payne) Doud; m. Charles Webb (div.); children: Charles, David, Robert; m. Mark J. Michaels (div.); 1 child, Merry A. Student, MIT, 1962-64, U. Wis., 1971-76; BS in Bus. Edn., U. Wis., 1978, MS in Spl. Edn., 1981. Mgr., instr. bus. program Blackwell Job Corps Ctr., 1987-89; mgr. Michaels Secretarial Svc., Black River Falls, Wis., 1979-83; columnist, editor Michaels News, Black River Falls, 1983—, pres., 1989—. Columnnist: Single Parenting, 1983-94, Parenting Plus, 1990—; editor, contbr. (column) Surviving Single, 1990-95, To Read or Not, Report From Planet Earth, 1989—, Travel Tidbits, 1991—, Surviving Sane, 1995—. Chmn. Brockway Community Orgn., 1969-71; chair, counselor Brockway Youth Group, 1970-72; chmn. labor com. Dem. Platform Com., Wis., 1975-76; candidate State Assembly, 1978, 82. Mem. Bus. Edn. Honor Soc., Edn. Hon. Soc. Office: Michaels News RR 5 Box 367 Black River Falls WI 54615-9160

MICHAK, HELEN BARBARA, educator, nurse; b. Cleve., July 31; d. Andrew and Mary (Patrick) M. Diploma Cleve. City Hosp. Sch. Nursing, 1947; BA, Miami U., Oxford, Ohio, 1951; MA, Case Western Res. U., 1960. Staff nurse Cleve. City Hosp., 1947-48; pub. health nurse Cleve. Div. Health, 1951-52; instr. Cleve. City Hosp. Sch. Nursing, 1952-56; supr. nursing Cuyahoga County Hosp., Cleve., 1956-58; pub. information dir. N.E. Ohio Am. Heart Assn., Cleve., 1960-64; dir. spl. events Higbee Co., Cleve., 1964-66; exec. dir. Cleve. Area League for Nursing, 1966-72; dir. continuing edn. nurses, adj. assoc. prof. Cleve. State U., 1972-86; asst. regional cons. Ohio Bd. Nursing, 1991—. Trustee N.E. Ohio Regional Med. Program, 1970-73; mem. adv. com. Dept. Nursing Cuyahoga C.C., 1967-87; mem. long term care com. Met. Health Planning Corp., 1974-76, plan devel. com. 1977; mem. policy bd. Ctr. Health Data N.E. Ohio, 1972-73; mem. Rep. Assembly and Health Planning and Devel. Commn., Welfare Fedn. Cleve., 1967-72, Cleve. Cmty. Health Network, 1972-73, United Appeal Films and Speakers Bur., 1967-73; mem. adv. com. Ohio Fedn. Lic. Practical Nurses, 1970-73; mem. tech. adv. com. No. Ohio Lung Assn., 1967-74, 90-93; mem. Ohio Commn. on Nursing, 1971-74; mem. citizens com. nursing homes Fedn. Community Planning, 1973-77; mem. com. on home health services Met. Health Planning Corp., 1973-75; mem. profl. adv. com. on home care Fairview Gen. Hosp., 1987-91. Mem. Nat. League Nursing (mem. com. 1970-72), Am. Nurses Assn. (accreditation visitor 1977-78, 83-88) Ohio Nurses Assn., (com. continuing edn. 1974-79, 82-87, 89-92, chmn. 1984-86), Greater Cleve. (joint practice com. 1973-74, Greater Cleve. Nurses Assn. (trustee 1975-76) , Cleve. Area Citizens League for Nursing (trustee 1976-79, v.p. 1988-90), Zeta Tau Alpha, Sigma Theta Tau. Home and Office: 4686 Oakridge Dr North Royalton OH 44133

MICHAL, PHILIP QUENTIN, veterinarian, mayor; b. Rensselaer, Ind., May 15, 1940; s. Robert John and Doris Maurine (Yost) M.; m. Judith Lynn Price, June 9, 1963; children: David Scott, Richard Joseph, Christopher Thomas. DVM, Purdue U., 1964. Sole vet. practitioner in mixed practice Wingate, Ind., 1965-69, Crawfordsville, Ind., 1969-74; sole propr. small animal practice Crawfordsville, 1974-87; owner N.W. Vet. Hosp., Crawfordsville, 1987—; mayor of Crawfordsville, 1987—. Elder, chmn. evangelism, 1st Christian Ch., 1992. Mem. AVMA, Ind. Vet. Med. Assn., Kiwanis (past pres. Crawfordsville club), Moose. Mem. Christian Ch. (Disciples of Christ). Home: 102 N Davis St Crawfordsville IN 47933-1206 Office: 300 E Pike St Crawfordsville IN 47933-2537

MICHALAK, MICHAEL VINCENT, physician assistant; b. Berea, Ohio, May 26, 1951; s. Joseph Michalak and Dorothy (Stawicki) M.; m. Pranee, May 1, 1975; children Paul, Diana. ADN, Cuyahoga Community Coll., Cleve., 1980; APA, Cuyahoga Cmty. Coll., 1983; BSN, SUNY, 1986. Physician's Asst. Nursing asst. Cleve. Clinic Found., 1976-80, staff RN, 1981-87; nurse clinician cardiology Cleve. Clinic Found., Cleve., 1987-92; physician's asst. Lakewood (Ohio) Hosp., 1989; physician asst. Midland Internal Medicine Assocs., 1995—. Staff sgt. USAF and Ohio Air N.G., 1972-84; 2d lt. USAR, 1987-93; capt. USAFR, 1993-95. Mem. Am. Acad. of Physician's Assts., Ohio Assn. of Physician's Assts., Mich. Acad. Physician Assts. Home: 6183 Moreland Ln Saginaw MI 48603-2726

MICHALSKI, (ŻUROWSKI) WACŁAW, adult education educator; b. Pierzchnica, Poland, Sept. 14, 1913; came to the U.S., 1951; s. Antoni and Józefa (Skrybuś) M.; m. Urszula Lewandowska, Nov. 12, 1959 (dec. 1986); 1 child, Anthony Richard. MA, Tchr.'s Coll., Poland, 1934; grad., Officer's Mil. Sch., Poland, 1934-35; postgrad., U. Wis. M.A.T.C., 1951-55. Lic. real estate broker, Wis. Tchr. jr. high sch. Poland, 1936-39; mgr. acctg. Ampco Metal Co., Milw., 1951-84; tchr., educator Marquette U., U. Wis. Ext., Milw., 1962-90, Milw. Area Tech. Coll., 1963—; real estate agt. Wauwatosa Realty Co., Milw., 1955—. Contbr. articles to profl. jours. Archivist Holy Cross Brigade and Nat. Armed Forces of Poland, 1991—. With underground resistance, Poland, 1939-45; officer Holy Cross Brigade, Poland, 1944-55, which joined U.S. 3rd Army, Czechoslovakia, 1945; Polish guard U.S. Army, Germany, 1945-47; officer Internat. Refugee Orgn., Germany, 1947-51. Recipient Polish Heritage award Pulaski Coun. Milw., 1992, Cert. of Appreciation State Hist. Soc. Wis., 1987, Vol. Svc. award Inner Agy. Coun. Volunteerism, 1986, Cert. of Commendation for Exemplary Work as an Older Worker in Our Community Milw. Com. for Nat. Older Work Week, 1995. Mem. Polish Am. Congress, N.Am. Polish Ctr. Study, Polish Western Assn. Am. (Diploma of Merit 1988), Vets. Orgns. WWI, WWII. Roman Catholic. Home: 5505 Bentwood Ln Greendale WI 53129-1314 Office: Wauwatosa Realty Co 5300 S 108th St Hales Corners WI 53130-1368

MICHEEL, DONALD EARL, construction engineer, therapist; b. Gordon, Nebr., Oct. 15, 1944; s. Earl H. and Mae (Wells) M.; m. Juanita L. Bak Micheel, Aug. 31, 1985; 1 child Shawn. Degree in Bus. Admin., Nebr. State U., Kearney, 1962-65. Constrn. inspector S.D. Dept. Hwys., Martin, 1969-75; inspector Pierce & Harris Engrs., Huron, S.D., 1975-79; surveyor Great Plains Engrs., Valentine, Nebr., 1979-81; region materials and radiol. safety officer S.D. Dept. Transp., Pierre, 1981—; mem. S.D. State Employees Orgn., Pierre, 1981—. Mem. Jaycees, Martin, S.D., 1970-73. Sgt. USAF, 1965-69, Vietnam. Mem. AF&A Masons, Order of Eagles, Am. Legion, VFW. Home: 220 S Grant Ave Pierre SD 57501

MICHELS, ADAM W., shop foreman; b. Waterloo, Iowa, Nov. 8, 1966. AAS, Hawkeye Inst. Tech., 1987. Shop foreman, programmer Hawkeye Tool and Die Inc., Jesup, Iowa, 1984—. Office: Hawkeye Tool & Die Inc 730 Main St Jesup IA 50648-1008

MICHELSEN, JOHN ERNEST, software services company executive; b. New Brunswick, N.J., May 11, 1946; s. Ernest Arnold and Ursula (Hunter) M.; B.S., Northwestern U., 1969; M.S., Stevens Inst. Tech., 1972; M.B.A. in Fin. with honors, U. Chgo., 1978; m. Ruth Ann Flanders, June 15, 1969; children—Nancy Ellen, Rebecca Ruthann. Real-time programmer Lockheed Electronics Co., Plainfield, N.J., 1969-72; control system designer Fermi Nat. Accelerator Lab., Batavia, Ill., 1972-75; chief system designer Distributed Info. Systems Corp., Chgo., 1975-78, v.p., 1978-79; mgr. M.I.S. adminstrn. FMC Corp., Chgo., 1979-82; pres. Infopro, Inc., 1982—. Mem. Assn. Computing Machinery, Phi Eta Sigma, Tau Beta Pi, Beta Gamma Sigma. Office: 2625 Butterfield Rd Oak Brook IL 60521-1234

MICHETTI, SUSAN JANE, media relations director, video producer, communications consultant; b. Kenosha, Wis., Dec. 20, 1948. BA cum laude, U. Wis., 1981; Cert. A, B, C for real estate law, appraisal and mktg., Gateway Tech. Inst., Kenosha, 1979; postgrad., Carthage Coll., Kenosha, 1984. Pub. rels. and media dir. Big Bros./Big Sisters of Kenosha County, Wis., 1978-79; newspaper editor U. Wis., Parkside, 1979-81; news reporter, newscaster Sta. WRJN Radio, Racine, Wis., 1982-84; pub. info. specialist, graphic designer Kenosha Unified Sch. Dist., 1983-84; book editorial and prodn. coord. Scott, Foresman and Co., Glenview, Ill., 1985-88; instr. profl. devel. U. Wis., Parkside, 1988-89; fin. svcs./pub. rels. editor Phillips Pub., 1986-95; propr. Michetti Multi-Media Assocs., Kenosha, 1981—; cons. in field. Contbr. articles to profl. jours. Media cons. Friends of Peter Barca for State Legislature, Kenosha, 1985-92; art fair asst. Friends of Kenosha Pub. Mus., 1986-92; mem. program devel. com. Racine Hist. Soc. and Pub. Mus., 1984-85. Scholar, Kenosha Found., 1979-81, Kenneth L. Greenquist, 1980, Vilas, 1968-71, Ida D. Altemus, 1969-70. Mem. NAFE, Am. Soc. Profl. and Exec. Women, Internat. Soc. Unified Sci. Home and Office: Michetti Multi-Media Assocs PO Box 54 Kenosha WI 53141-0054

MICHLIN, ARNOLD SIDNEY, finance executive; b. Altoona, Pa., Sept. 2, 1920; s. John Mandel and Zelda (Solomon) M.; m. Florence Karbal, Aug. 17, 1941; children: Leslye Joyce Borden, Kenneth Brian, Steven Bruce, Joan Mindy Ennis. BS in Chemistry, Detroit Inst. Tech., 1944. Salesman Michlin Co., Detroit, 1934-41; chemist Ford Motor Co., Dearborn, 1941-44; chief chemist Continental Aviation and Engrng., Detroit, 1944-45; chemist U.S. Dept. of Chem. Warfare, Edgewood, Md., 1945-46; ptnr. Michlin Surplus Co., Detroit, 1947-83; pres. Michlin Indsl. Finishes, 1954-81; chem. cons. Michlin Chem. Corp., Madison Heights, Mich., 1981-82; fin. planner PA Securities, Southfield, Mich., 1980-83, Korn Womack Stern & Assocs., Southfield, 1983-89; registered rep. Titan Value Equities Group, Southfield, 1989—; cons. Project Equality, Archdiocese Detroit, 1970, Michlin Computer Cons., Ann Arbor, 1986—, LaserLand, Sylvan Lake, Mich., 1991—. Patentee in field. Bd. dirs. Ecumenical Inst. for Jewish and Christian Study, 1983, pres., 1992-93; founder Am. Arabic and Jewish Friends, Detroit, 1981; mem. Detroit Com. for Soviet Jewry, 1970—, co-founder, 1979, Materials for People of Palestine, 1946, co-founder, 1946, Muslim Christian Jewish Trialog, 1986—, co-founder. Recipient Heart of Gold award United Found., 1988. Mem. NCCJ (bd. dirs. Interfaith Roundtable, nat. bd. mem.), Internat. Assn. Fin. Planners, B'nai B'rith (pres. Detroit coun. 1982), Zionist Orgn. Am., Anti Defamation League, Cong. Shaarey Zedek Men's Club (program chmn. 1985—, Man of Yr. award 1994). Home: 31460 Stonewood Ct Farmington Hills MI 48334

MICKELSON, STACEY, state legislator. BA, Minot State U. Asst. mgr. Wild Things Gallery; rep. Dist. 38 N.D. Ho. of Reps., mem. judiciary and transp. coms.; mem. Interim Govt. Budget and Finance com. Mem. Minot Symphony Assn. (bd. dirs., 2nd v.p.), Minot Adult Literacy Vols., B.I.L.L.D. Fellow. Home: 2017 Ida Mae Ct Minot ND 58703

MICKLEY, G. ANDREW, psychologist, neuroscientist, educator, retired air force officer; b. Pitts., Feb. 28, 1948; s. Gordon Andrew and Martha Elizabeth (Myers) M.; m. Jacqueline Ruth Mansour, Aug. 15, 1970; 1 child, Katherine Ruth. BA, Gettysburg Coll., 1970; MA, U. Va., 1972, PhD, 1978. Commd. 2d lt. USAF, 1970, advanced to maj., 1983, advanced to lt. col., 1988-93, ret., 1993; test/rev. psychologist Occupational Measurement Ctr., San Antonio, 1972-76; prin. investigator Armed Forces Radiobiology Rsch. Inst., Bethesda, Md., 1976-79, chief exptl. psychology div., 1984-89; dep. chief radiation physics br. USAF Sch. Aerospace Medicine, 1989-90; sci. dir. Radiofrequency Radiation Divsn., Armstrong Lab., 1990-93; assoc. prof. USAF Acad., Colorado Springs, 1981-83; adj. assoc. prof. Uniformed Svcs. U. of Health Scis., 1983-89, U. Colo., 1981-83, life sci. div. U. Tex., San Antonio, dept. radiology U. Tex. Health Scis. Ctr., 1989-93; assoc. prof. dept. psychology, dir. neurosci. program Baldwin-Wallace Coll., Berea, Ohio, 1993—;chm. dept. psychology, Baldwin-Wallace Coll., Berea, Ohio, 1996—; grant reviewer NSF, 1983—, USPHS, 1985—, NIH, 1992—. Cons. editor Science, Pharmacology, Biochemistry and Behavior, Radiation Rsch., Life Sci.; assoc. editor Transplantation and Neural Plasticity; contbr. articles to profl. jours., chpts. to books. USAF Sch. Aerospace Medicine grantee, 1978-80, Def. Nuclear Agy. grantee, 1980-83, NSF grantee, 1994—; recipient Rsch. and Devel. award USAF, 1981. Mem. AAAS, Soc. for Neurosci., Radiation Rsch. Soc., Soc. Toxicology, Internat. Behavioral Neurosci. Soc., Sigma Xi, Psi Chi, Phi Sigma. Lutheran. Avocations: tennis, skiing, running, reading. Office: Baldwin-Wallace Coll Dept Psychology Carnegie Hall 275 Eastland Rd Berea OH 44017-2088

MICZUGA, MARK NORBERT, metal products executive; b. Chgo., Feb. 14, 1962; s. Norbert and Rita (Kamper) M.; m. Maria Del Carmen Caballero, Sept. 19, 1992; children: Angelica Pamela, Henry. BS, DePaul U., 1984, MBA, 1989. Mgr. steel products Mitsubishi Internat. Corp., Chgo., 1985-93; v.p. sales MC Fabrication Industries, Inc., Oak Brook Terrace, Ill., 1993—. Mem. Assn. MBA Execs. Office: MC Fabrication Industries 1 Lincoln Ctr Ste 1670 Villa Park IL 60181-4273

MIDDAUGH, JAMES (MIKE), state legislator; b. Paw Paw, Mich., Sept. 4, 1946; s. Orson William and Phyllis Jean M.; m. Mary Ann. Student, Ferris State Coll., 1965-68; BS in Edn., Western Mich. U., 1969. Rep. Mich. Dist. 45, 1983-92, Mich. Dist. 80, 1993—; del. Van Buren County Mich. State Rep. Conv., 1965-73; adminstrv. asst. Mich. State Sen. Harry Gast, 1970—; chmn. issues com. Mich. Ho. Reps., 1974—, asst. minority whip, vice chmn. conservation, recreation & environ. com., mem. corps. and fin. com., pub. utilities & liquor control com. Mem. NRA, Farm Bur., N.Am. Hunting Club, Ferris State Coll. Alumni Assn. (pres. 1975), Southwestern Mich. Assn. Law Enforcement Officers. Home: 603 W Michigan Ave Paw Paw MI 49079-1050 Address: State Capitol PO Box 30014 Lansing MI 48909-7514*

MIDDEKE, RICHARD JOSEPH, accountant; b. St. Charles, Mo., Aug. 28, 1960; s. James Allen Middeke and Carol Ann (DeCoster) LaBarge; m. Lynda Claudine Hanrahan, Oct. 4, 1986; children: Tanner Christian, Arick Joseph, Jack Gardner, Samuel Paul. BS in Acctg., S.W. Mo. State U., 1984. CPA, Mo. Acct. Coopers and Lybrand, Kans. City, Mo., 1984-87, St. Louis, 1987-90; internat. acctg. mgr. Caboline Co., St. Louis, 1990—. Treas. Asthma and Allergy Found., St. Louis, 1988-92. Mem. AICPA, Mo. Soc. CPAs. Home: 30 Downfield Dr Saint Charles MO 63304-7588 Office: Caboline Co 350 Industrial Ct Saint Louis MO 63144

MIDDLETON, BETH ANN, wetland ecology educator; b. Madison, Wis., Aug. 18, 1955; d. Harry Willard and Eva Mae M. BS in Botany, U. Wis., 1978; MS in Biology, U. Minn., Duluth, 1983; PhD in Botany, Iowa State U., 1989. Botanist U.S. Park Svc., Bayfield, Wis., 1979-81; instr. Northland Coll., Ashland, Wis., 1979-82; postdoctoral assoc. Iowa State U., Ames, 1989-90; assoc. prof. wetland ecology So. Ill. U., Carbondale, 1990—. Contbr. articles to Aquatic Botany, Jour. Ecol. Soc., Jour. Tropical Ecology, Wildfowl, Can. Jour. Botany, Biotropica, Jour. Vegetation Sci., Vegetatio, Bull. Torrey Bot. Club, Restoration Ecology; assoc. editor: Wetlands-Bd. Orgn. of Tropical Studies. MacMillan fellow Delta Waterfowl, Man., Can., 1984; grantee Fulbright Coun. Internat. Exch., India, 1990-91. Mem. Soc. Wetland Scientists, Ecol. Soc. Am. Orgn. Tropical Studies (bd. dirs.), Assn. Tropical Biologists. Office: Dept Plant Biology So Ill Univ 411 Life Sci Carbondale IL 62901

MIDDLETON, MARC STEPHEN, corporate insurance specialist; b. Louisville, Dec. 7, 1950; s. Joseph Scott and Virginia Marie (Schuler) M.; m. Carmen Teresa Fauscette, Feb. 22, 1969; 1 child, Marc Christopher. AA, Dalton Jr. Coll., 1970; BBA, U. Ga., 1972. Sr. risk analyst Deere and Co., Moline, Ill., 1973-78, mgr. corp. claims, 1978-79, mgr. corp. ins. dept., 1980-86; v.p. risk mgmt. svcs. John Deere Ins. Group, Moline, Ill., 1987-91; dir. risk mgmt. Deere and Co., Moline, Ill., 1992—; v.p. bd. dirs. Tahoe Ins. Co., Reno, 1981-83, Sierra Gen. Life Ins. Co., Reno, 1981-83, Continental Guaranty, Ltd., Hamilton, Bermuda, 1981-83; v.p. John Deere Ins. Co., Rock River Ins. Co., Tahoe Ins. Co., 1990-91, John Deere Life Ins. Co., Sierra Gen. Life Ins. Co., 1991. Mem. Citizen's Adv. Council to East Moline (Ill.) Sch. Bd., 1978-80; coach YMCA Youth Basketball, Moline, 1978. Mem. Risk and Ins. Mgmt. Soc., Risk Mgmt. Council of Machinery and Allied Products Inst., Captive Ins. Cos. Assn., ESIS (Delphi panel 1985—), Internat. Platform Assn. Roman Catholic. Home: PO Box 369 6 Eagle Pointe Pass Rapids City IL 61278 Office: Deere & Co John Deere Rd Moline IL 61265-6785

MIDDLETON, MARY, secondary education educator; b. Lackawana, N.Y., Nov. 13, 1942; d. Arthur Jordan and Kathryn (Sternburg) M. BS in Edn., Ohio State U., 1965; postgrad., Akron U., 1970, Cleve. State U., 1981-84. Profl. cert. in edn. Tchr. Columbus (Ohio) Schs., 1966-68, Brooklyn (Ohio) Schs., 1968—; co-dir. C.A.R.E. (Chem. Abuse Reduced through Edn.), Brooklyn (Ohio) City, 1986—, Englist dept. chair, acad. team advisor Brooklyn (Ohio) Schs., 1987—; mem. dimensions of learning task force Bklyn. Schs., Advisor: English hon. 1990—. Contbr. articles to profl. jours. Campaign worker North Olmsted (Ohio) Dem. club, 1988, 92, 96; recreation dir. Country Club Condominiums, 1992—. Recipient N.E. Ohio Writing Project fellowship Martha Holden Jennings, Cleve. State U., 1985. Mem. ASCD, NEA, AAUW, Ohio Edn. Assn., Brooklyn (Ohio) Edn. Assn. (sec.), Ohio Coun. Tchrs. English and Lang. Arts, Cinnamon Woods Condominiums Assn. (bd. dirs.), Re-elect the Pres. Com., Ohio State U. Alumni Assn., Phi Mu. Methodist. Home: 7127 Bayberry Cir North Olmsted OH 44070-4765 Office: Brooklyn City Schs 9200 Biddulph Rd Brooklyn OH 44144-2614

MIDDLETON, THOMAS F., state legislator; b. Mich., July 29, 1945; m. Kathy; children: Amy, Jason, Ted. Student, Mich. State U. Rep. Mich. Dist. 61, 1991-94, Mich. Dist. 46, 1995—; asst. floor leader house Rep. caucus Mich. Ho. Reps., 1993—, appropriations com., mil. & vet. affairs subcom., chair pub. health com., vice chair corrections com., vice chair transp. com., vice chair K-12 sch. aid & dept. edn. com.; owner, operator Kay Belle Farms. Mem. Optimist. Home: 641 N Hurd Rd Ortonville MI 48462-9787 Address: PO Box 30014 Lansing MI 48909-7514*

MIDEI, RICHARD ALLEN, financial services executive, entrepreneur; b. Martins Ferry, Ohio, Nov. 8, 1947; s. Angelo James and Yolanda (Camillozzi) M.; m. Mary Jo Spanner, July 12, 1969; 1 child, Jeremy Richard. AS in Ins., Jefferson Tech. Coll., Steubenville Tech. Coll., 1969; BS in Bus., Youngstown State U., 1972. Pres. Midei Svc. Ctrs. Inc., Tiltonsville, Ohio, 1972—; registered rep. Walnut Street Securities Inc., St. Louis, 1986—; assoc. Diversified Fin. Svcs., Dallas, W.Va., 1986—. Bd. dirs. Family Svc. Upper Ohio Valley, Wheeling, W.Va., 1986-89; mem. fin. com. St. Joseph Cath. Ch., Tiltonsville, 1988-95. Mem. Nat. Assn. Security Dealers (registered). Democrat. Home: 58635 Eileen St Rayland OH 43943 Office: 58635 Eileen St Rayland OH 43943

MIELKE, JON ALAN, elementary school administrator; b. Racine, Wis., Mar. 29, 1954; s. Paul Gilbert and Gloria Ester (Bronson) M.; m. Judy Mae Pelz, June 16, 1979; children: Jeremy, Justin, Jonathan. BA, Concordia Coll., 1979, MA, 1986. Lic. elementary administrator, Wis. Tchr. Grace Luth. Sch., St. Petersburg, Fla., 1979-84; adminstr. First Immanuel Luth. Sch., Cedarburg, Wis., 1986—. Mem. Ea. Ofcls. Assn., Luth. Educators Assn., Assn. for Supervision and Curriculum Devel. Republican. Home: W67n787 Franklin Ave Cedarburg WI 53012-1180 Office: First Immanuel Lutheran Sch W67n622 Evergreen Blvd Cedarburg WI 53012-1848

MIELKE, SUSAN KAY, mental health nurse; b. Saginaw, Mich., Apr. 4, 1963; d. Walter John Jr. and Sally Jane (Spiekerman) Hetzner; m. Gary Alan Mielke, Aug. 16, 1986; children: Caroline, Elizabeth, Trevor. BSN, Mich. State U., 1985. Staff nurse Weight Loss Clinic, Saginaw, 1987, St. Mary's Hosp., Saginaw, 1985-88; RN III supr. psychiat. nursing Caro (Mich.) Ctr., 1987—; co-dir., co-owner CM Med.-Legal Cons. Inc, Saginaw, 1990—. Mem. Mich. State U. Nursing Alumni Assn. Lutheran. Home: 2855 S Sheridan Rd Caro MI 48723-9623 Office: Caro Ctr 2000 Chambers Rd Caro MI 48723

MIGALA, GEORGE WESLY, broadcast executive; b. Chgo., Nov. 15, 1948; s. Joseph and Estelle (Suwala) M.; m. Grazyna Anna Barszczyk, Sept. 27, 1980; 1 child, Stephen Joseph. BA in Philosophy, Loyola U., 1970. Restricted radio telephone operators permit, FCC. Sta. mgr. Sta. WCEV-Radio, Chgo., 1979—; producer, announcer Voice of Polonia Radio Program, Chgo., 1981—, announcer, 1970—; travel agt. Europe Travel Bur., Chgo., 1970-79. Pres. Bd. Local Improvements, Chgo., 1990—, active, 1986—; advisor on Polish Am. affairs Sen. Paul Simon, Chgo., 1984-96; bd. dirs. Copernicus Found., Chgo., 1972-95, Polish Am. Congress, Chgo., 1973—, nat. v.p., 1973-88. Named one of Outstanding Young Men Am., 1981, 82, Honorary Knight Knights of Dabrowski, 1984; recipient Disting. Svc. award Polish Am. Congress, 1977. Mem. Polish Nat. Alliance, N.W. Action Coun. (bd. dirs. 1985—). Democrat. Roman Catholic. Office: Sta WCEV-Radio 5356 W Belmont Ave Chicago IL 60641-4103

MIGALA, LUCYNA JOZEFA, broadcast journalist, arts administrator, radio station executive; b. Krakow, Poland, May 22, 1944; d. Joseph and Estelle (Suwala) M.; came to U.S., 1947, naturalized, 1955; student Loyola U., Chgo., 1962-63, Chicago Conservatory of Music, 1963-70; BS in Journalism, Northwestern U., 1966. Radio announcer, producer sta. WOPA, Oak Park, Ill., 1963-66; writer, reporter, producer NBC news, Chgo., 1966-69, 1969-71, producer NBC local news, Washington, 1969; producer, coord. NBC network news, Cleve., 1971-78, field producer, Chgo., 1978-79; v.p. Migala Communications Corp., 1979—; program and news dir., on-air personality Sta. WCEV, Cicero, Ill., 1979—; lectr. City Colls. Chgo., 1981, Morton Coll., 1988. Columnist Free Press, Chgo., 1984-87. Founder, artistic dir., gen. mgr. Lira Ensemble (formerly The Lira Singers), Chgo., 1965—, Artist-in-Residence, Loyola U. Chgo.; mem., chmn. various cultural coms. Polish Am. Congress, 1970-80; bd. dirs. Nationalities Svcs. Ctr., Cleve., 1973-78; bd. dirs., v.p. Cicero-Berwyn Fine Arts Coun., Cicero, Ill.; mem. City Arts I and II panels Chgo. Office of Fine Arts, 1986-89, 94; v.p. Chgo. chpt. Kosciuszko Found., 1983-86; bd. dirs. Polish Women's Alliance Am., 1983-87, Ill. Humanities Coun., 1983-89, mem. exec. com., 1986-87; bd. dirs. Ill. Arts Alliance, 1989-92; founder, gen. chmn. Midwest Chopin Piano Competition (now Chgo. Chopin Competition), 1984-86; founding mem. ethnic and folk arts panel Ill. Arts Coun., 1984-87, 92-94. Recipient AP Broadcasters award, 1973, Emmy award NATAS, 1974, Cultural Achievement award Am. Coun. for Polish Culture, 1990, Award of Merit Advocates Soc. Polish Am. Attys., 1991, Human Rels. Media award City of Chgo., 1992, Outstanding Achievement in Polish Culture award Minister of Fgn. Affairs, Rep. of Poland, 1994; Washington Journalism Ctr. fellow, spring 1969. Mem. Soc. Profl. Journalists. Office: Sta WCEV 5356 W Belmont Ave Chicago IL 60641-4103 also: The Lira Ensemble 6525 N Sheridan Rd # SKY 905 Chicago IL 60626

MIGLIORINO, CAROLINE MILANO, nursing consultant; b. Shaker Heights, Ohio; d. Albino and Albina (Tognaccini) Milano; m. Mauro A. Migliorino; children: Paul P., Monica M., Marc J., Laura E. ADN, Prairie State Jr. Coll., Chicago Heights, Ill., 1974; BSN, Gov.'s State U., University Park, Ill., 1977, MSN, 1984. Cert. in addictions. Dir. health svcs. Art Inst. Chgo.; managed care specialist dept. psychiatry Christ Hosp., Oak Lawn, Ill.; counselor chem. dependence and addictions Oak Lawn; prof. med. psychiatry & addictions; adj. prof. clin. psychiatry South Suburban Jr. Coll., 1994—, Joliet (Ill.) Jr. Coll., 1994—; managed care specialist Christ Hosp., Oak Lawn; adj. prof. South Suburban Jr. Coll., Joliet Jr. Coll. Recipient Acad. award Gov.'s State U. Alumni Assn., 1984. Mem. ANA, Ill. Nurses Assn., Nat. Nurses Soc. on Addictions. Home: 37 S Stough St Hinsdale IL 60521-3014

MIGNACCA, EGIDIO CARMEN, principal; b. Detroit, May 19, 1931; s. Luigi and Antonietta (Lato) M.; m. Joann Veronica Oddo, July 31, 1965; 1 child, Briana. BS in Edn., Wayne State U., 1957, EdD in Adminstrn., 1988; MA in Edn., U. Detroit, 1962; EdS in Adminstrn., Ea. Mich. U., 1975. Tchr. Detroit Bd. Edn., 1957-68; tchr. Warren (Mich.) Consol. Schs., 1968-70, 81-83, 84-86, asst. prin., 1970-75, 83-84, community edn. specialist, 1980-81, prin., 1975-80, 86—; instr. U. Detroit, 1975-77. Mem. Optimists (treas. Sterling-Warren, Mich. 1990), Phi Delta Kappa (v.p. 1978-79). Democrat. Roman Catholic. Home: 14562 Carmel Dr Sterling Heights MI 48312-4306 Office: Pearl Lean Elem Sch 2825 Girard Dr Warren MI 48092-1840

MIHALAS, DIMITRI MANUEL, astronomer, educator; b. Los Angeles, Mar. 20, 1939; s. Emmanuel Demetrious and Jean (Christo) M.; m. Alice Joelen Covalt, June 15, 1963 (div. Nov. 1974); children: Michael Demetrious, Genevieve Alexandra; m. Barbara Ruth Rickey, May 18, 1975 (div. Dec. 1992). B.A. with highest honors, UCLA, 1959; M.S., Calif. Inst. Tech., 1960, Ph.D., 1964. Asst. prof. astrophys. scis. Princeton U., 1964-67; asst. prof. physics U. Colo., 1967-68; asso. prof. astronomy and astrophysics U. Chgo., 1968-70, prof., 1970-71; adj. prof. astrogeophysics, also physics and astrophysics U. Colo., 1972-80; sr. scientist High Altitude Obs., Nat. Center Atmospheric Research, Boulder, Colo., 1971-79, 82-85; prof. astronomy U. Ill., 1985—; astronomer Sacramento Peak Obs., Sunspot, N.Mex., 1979-82; cons. Los Alamos Nat. Lab, 1981—; vis. prof. dept. astrophysics Oxford (Eng.) U., 1977-78; sr. vis. fellow dept. physics and astronomy Univ. Coll., London, 1978; mem. astronomy adv. panel NSF, 1972-75. Author: Galactic Astronomy, 2d edit, 1981, Stellar Atmospheres, 1970, 2d edit., 1978, Theorie des Atmospheres Stellaires, 1971, Foundations of Radiation Hydrodynamics, 1984; assoc. editor Astrophys. Jour, 1970-79, Jour. Computational Physics, 1981-87, Jour. Quantitative Spectroscopy, 1984—; mem. editorial bd. Solar Physics, 1981-89. NSF fellow, 1959-62; Van Maanen fellow, 1962-63;

Eugene Higgins vis. fellow, 1963-64; Alfred P. Sloan Found. Research fellow, 1969-71; Alexander von Humboldt Stiftung sr. U.S. scientist awardee, 1984. Mem. U.S. Nat. Acad. Sci., Internat. Astron. Union (pres. commn. 36 1976-79), Am. Astron. Soc. (Helen B. Warner prize 1974), Astron. Soc. Pacific (dir. 1975-77). Home: 1924 Blackthorn Dr Champaign IL 61821-6300 Office: Dept Astronomy U Ill 1002 W Green St Urbana IL 61801-3074

MIHM, MICHAEL MARTIN, federal judge; b. Amboy, Ill., May 18, 1943; s. Martin Clarence and Frances Johannah (Morrissey) M.; m. Judith Ann Zosky, May 6, 1967; children—Molly Elizabeth, Sarah Ann, Jacob Michael, Jennifer Leah. B.A., Loras Coll., 1964; J.D., St. Louis U., 1967. Asst. prosecuting atty. St. Louis County, Clayton, Mo., 1967-68; asst. state's atty. Peoria County, Peoria, Ill., 1968-69; asst. city atty. City of Peoria, Ill., 1969-72; state's atty. Peoria County, Peoria, Ill., 1972-80; sole practice Peoria, Ill., 1980-82; U.S. dist. judge U.S. Govt., Peoria, Ill., 1982—; chief U.S. dist. judge U.S. Dist. Ct. (ctrl. dist.) Ill., 1991—; chmn. com. internat. jud. rels. U.S. Jud. Conf., 1994-96, mem. exec. coun., 1995—;, mem. com. jud. br., 1987-93; adj. prof. law John Marshall Law Sch., 1990—. Past mem. adv. bd. Big Brothers-Big Sisters, Crisis Nursery, Peoria; past bd. dirs. Salvation Army, Peoria, W.D. Boyce council Boy Scouts Am., State of Ill. Treatment Alternatives to Street Crime, Gov.'s Criminal Justice Info. Council; past vice-chmn. Ill. Dangerous Drugs Adv. Council; trustee Proctor Health Care Found., 1991—. Recipient Good Govt. award Peoria Jaycees, 1978. Mem. Peoria County Bar Assn. (former bd. dirs., past chmn. entertainment com.). Roman Catholic. Office: US Dist Ct 204 Federal Bldg 100 NE Monroe St Peoria IL 61602-1003

MIKAELIAN, MARISA GEDERIAN, physical therapist, business owner; b. East Chicago, Ind., Apr. 5, 1963; d. Charles and Isabelle (Babikian) Gederian; m. Brian Bedros Mikaelian, Feb. 24, 1961; 1 child, Thaddeus Samuel. Student, Purdue U., 1981-84; BS in Phys. Therapy, U. Health Sci.-Chgo. Med. Sch., 1986; MS in Phys. Therapy, 1993. Lic. phys. therapy, Ill., Ind. Staff phys. therapist St. Margaret Hosp., Hammond, Ind., 1986-87, Condell Med. Ctr., Libertyville, Ill., 1987-90, Buffalo Grove (Ill.) Phys. Therapy Clinic, 1990-92; pvt. practice Lake County, Ill., 1992-93, MGM Phys. Therapy, Libertyville, Ill., 1993—. Mem. Am. Phys. Therapy Assn. Armenian Christian Orthodox. Office: MGM Phys Therapy 1105 W Park Ave Ste 3 Libertyville IL 60048

MIKE, EDWARD JOSEPH, psychologist, consultant; b. Grand Rapids, Mich., Oct. 7, 1935; s. Edward Peter and Beatrice (Lang) M.; m. Suzanne Rita Megel, May 3, 1973; children: Deborah Jacqueline, Karen Rebecca. BA, Athenaeum of Ohio, 1958; STL, U. Gregoriana, 1962; MA, U. Detroit, 1972, PhD, 1980. Lic. psychologist, lic. marriage counselor, cert. social worker, Mich. Psychologist Profl. Counseling Ctr., West Bloomfield, Mich., 1975-79, Meredith Counseling Ctrs., Farmington Hills, Mich., 1979-90; pres. Brighton (Mich.) Counseling, 1990-96, Northwood Counseling, Harrison, Mich., 1995-96. Bd. dirs. Big Bros. Big Sisters, Howell, Mich., 1989-96; trustee Dyslexia Resource Ctr., Howell, 1991-96. Mem. APA. Home: 5135 Glenway Dr Brighton MI 48116

MIKELSON, JOHN DAVID, career officer; b. Hamilton, Ohio, Jan. 30, 1960; s. David Lee Mikelson and Betty Susan (Popp) Hernstrom; m. Madonna Odilia Seydel Lynch, Feb. 14, 1982; children: Brenna L. Lynch, Cassie A. Lynch, Maxwell A., Donovan J. Student, U. Iowa, Iowa City, 1978-80, Kirkwood Cmty. Coll., Cedar Rapids, 1981-83. Psychol. aide U. Hosp. & Clinic, Iowa City, 1979-84; med. specialist 1st BN 410th Infantry, Iowa City, 1978-84; recruiter U.S. Army Recruiting Cmd., Iowa City, 1984-91, 234th Signal BN IA ARNG, Cedar Rapids, Iowa, 1991-93; supply sgt. 109th Area Sup. Med. Bn., Iowa City, 1993—; mem. Johnson Co. Military Affairs, Iowa City, 1984—. Lector St. Mary's Cath. Ch., Iowa City, 1992—. Mem. Am. Soc. of Mil. Insignia Collectors, Am. Legion, KC (knight 3rd degree). Republican. Roman Catholic. Home: 204 Dartmouth St Iowa City IA 52245 Office: HSC 109th Area Sup Med Battalion 925 S Dubuque St Iowa City IA 52240

MIKESELL, JASON LEE, programmer analyst; b. Corydon, Iowa, Feb. 15, 1970; s. Steven G. and Doris K. (Hockensmith) M. AAS in Computer Sci., Indian Hills C.C., Ottumwa, Iowa, 1992; BA in Mgmt. Sci., Buena Vista Coll., 1992. Program dir. KELR-FM Radio Sta., Chariton, Iowa, 1985—; programmer analyst Hy-Vee, Inc., West Des Moines, Iowa, 1992—. Republican. Home: PO Box 713 Chariton IA 50049-0713 Office: KELR-FM Radio PO Box 693 927 1/2 Braden Chariton IA 50049

MIKIEWICZ, ANNA DANIELLA, marketing and sales representative; b. Chgo., Dec. 22, 1960; d. Zdislaw and Lucy (Magnusewska) K. BS in Mktg., Elmhurst Coll., 1982; postgrad. Triton Coll. Asst. to Midwestern regional mgr. Meister Pub. Co., Chgo., 1983; sales rep. First Impression, Elk Grove, Ill., 1984; mktg. and customer svcs. rep. Airco Ind. Gases, Broadview and Carol Stream, Ill., 1985, Yamazen USA, Inc., Schaumburg, Ill., 1985-88; nat. sales and mktg. coord. Kitamura Machinery U.S.A. Inc., 1988-95; mktg. mgr. Beth Lee Boutique, 1995—. Named Chgo. Polish Queen Polish Am. Culture Club, 1983-84; nominated White House Fellowship Program. Mem. NAFE. Republican. Roman Catholic.

MIKKELSON, RAYMOND CHARLES, physics educator; b. Blue Earth, Minn., Mar. 22, 1937; s. Henry and Ruth Alberta (Furland) M.; m. Helen Ann Gunderson, Aug. 28, 1960; 1 child, Susan Marie. BA, St. Olaf Coll., 1959; MS, U. Ill., 1961, PhD, 1965. Prof. of physics Macalester Coll., St. Paul, 1965—, dept. chair, 1976-79, 94—; application analyst Sperry Univac, St. Paul, 1968; vis. scientist Argonne (Ill.) Nat. Lab., 1971-72, 3M Co., St. Paul, 1985-86, 92-93; vis. scholar U. Minn., Mpls., 1979; cons. in field. Editor newsletter Digital Equipment Users Soc., 1982-85; contbr. articles to profl. jours. Mem. Am. Assn. Physics Tchrs. (v.p., pres. Minn. sect. 1968-70), Am. Phys. Soc., Optical Soc. Am. Lutheran. Office: Macalester Coll Physics Dpt 1600 Grand Ave Saint Paul MN 55105-1801

MIKRUT, JOHN JOSEPH, JR., labor arbitrator, educator; b. Erie, Pa., Mar. 23, 1944; s. John Joseph and Helen Frances (Dorobiala) M.; BS, Edinboro U. of Pa., 1966; postgrad. U. Mass., 1966-68; EdD, U. Mo., Columbia, 1976; m. Lois Ann Leonard, Aug. 26, 1968. Intern edn. dept. United Steelworkers Am., Pitts., 1967-68; instr. labor studies Pa. State U., 1968-69; labor specialist, assoc. prof. labor edn. U. Mo., Columbia, 1969-88; labor arbitrator Nat. Rail Adjustment Bd., Am. Nat. Can Co., Steelworkers' Union, Continental Can. Co. and Steelworkers Union, U.S. Postal Svc., Am. Postal Workers Union, FAA, Nat. Air Traffic Contrs. Assn., Nat. Assn. Letter Carriers, TWA, Machinists Dist 142-Midwest Discharge Panel, S.W. Airlines and Machinists Dist. 142 Sys. Bd. Adjustment; mem. labor arbitration panels Fed. Mediation Conciliation Svc., Nat. Mediation Bd., Am. Arbitration Assn; appointed spl. arbitrator AMTRAK/Machinists negotiations impass. Chmn., City of Columbia Pers. Adv. Bd., 1976—; chmn. Columbia Mayor's Spl. Labor Negotiations Rev. Com. Mem. Nat. Acad. Arbitrators, Soc. Profls. Dispute Resolution, Iowa Pub. Employee Relations Bd., Kans. Pub. Employee Relations Bd., Ill. Edn. Employee Relations Bd., Ill. Pub. Employees Arbitration Panel, Univ. and Coll. Labor Edn. Assn., Indsl. Relations and Research Assn., Ctr. for Employment Dispute Resolution (bd. dirs.). Contbr. articles to profl. jours. Home and Office: 2236 Country Ln Columbia MO 65201-6334

MILBERT, ROBERT P., state legislator; b. June 1949; m. Vicky Milbert; three children. BA, Dartmouth Coll. Dist. 39B rep. Minn. Ho. of Reps., St. Paul, 1986—; former vice chmn. gaming divsn. gen. legis., judiciary, vet. affairs and gaming coms., Minn. Ho. of Reps.; vice chmn. internat. trade, tech. and econ. devel. divsn. com. on commerce and econ. devel.; mem. taxes com. Office: 579 State Office Bldg Saint Paul MN 55155-1201*

MILBY, DOUGLAS K., electrical engineer; b. Dayton, Ohio, May 14, 1963. BSEE, U. Dayton, 1985. Tech. staff Hughes Aircraft, Long Beach, Calif., 1985-88; radar sys. engr. Sverndrup Tech., Inc., Dayton, 1988-89; project supr. Sys Rsch. Lab., Beaver Creek, Ohio, 1989-91; logics engr. RJO Inc., Dayton, 1992-93; project engr. Crane Pumps & Sys., Inc., Piqua, Ohio, 1993—. Office: Crane Pumps and Systems Inc PO Box 603 Piqua OH 45356-0603

MILES, ALFRED LEE, real estate broker, educator; b. Eaton, Ohio, Aug. 4, 1913; s. James Sampson and Grace Blanche (Bittner) M.; m. Margaret Lucille Saul, Mar. 18, 1936 (div. Mar. 1949); children: Ronald Lynn, Walter Whitney; m. Virginia Null Engelman, Feb. 24, 1951; children: Victoria Ellen, Kimber Lee, Bethany Laine, Christopher, Kent; stepchildren: Dianne Fogle, Norbert Nicholas Engelman, Jr. Student Ohio State U., 1930-33, Sinclair Coll., 1945, Miami-Jacobs Coll., 1954-56. Instr. pvt. courses in real estate prins. and real estate law, Dayton, Ohio, 1949—; instr. real estate Miami Jacobs Jr. Coll. Bus., 1983—; instr. short courses Spl. Sessions Div. U. Dayton, 1971-77. Violinist, Dayton Civic Orch., 1927-29, Ohio State U. Symphony, 1930-33, Columbus Symphony, 1930-33. Named Ky. col. Mem. Internat. Platform Assn., Real Estate Educators Assn., Cin. Bankers Club. Republican. Home: 1629 Far Hills Ave Dayton OH 45419-3133 Office: 2185 S Dixie Dr Dayton OH 45409-2016

MILES, CHARLENE, small business owner; b. Pine City, Ark., Dec. 4, 1928; d. Albert and Katherine (Coakes) Banks; m. James Dixon Jr., Jan. 5, 1947 (div. 1955); children: James Walter II, Shirley; m. Joe Miles, Apr. 21, 1955 (dec.); 1 child, Donell. AA, Shorter Coll., Little Rock, Ark., 1946; cert., Buffalo (N.Y.) Beauty Coll., 1960. Lic. cosmetologist. Technician Posner Beauty Products, N.Y.C., 1960-63; instr. Peter Piccolo Beauty Sch., Buffalo, 1974-75; founder, pres. Charlene's Unisex Salon of N.Y., Detroit, 1975—; judge Student Cosmetology Assn., Buffalo, 1980—; founder, advisor Charlene Katherine Nat. Hair Network; advisor, cons. Waiting 2 Exhale Salon Inc. Pres. Profls. Against Drugs, Detroit, 1988—; corp. dir. Op. Push, Chgo., 1987—; mem. St. John Bapt. Ch., St. James Bapt. Ch. Named Pres. of Yr. CUS Bd. Dirs., 1984. Mem. Nat. Hairdressers Assn., Pacesetters (outstanding service award 1984), Mary B. Tolbert Assn., Beverly Area Planning Assn., Coalition of 100 Women. Democrat. Home: PO Box 7518 Bloomfield Hills MI 48302-7518 Office: Charlenes Unisex Salon NY 433 5th Ave New York NY 10016-2207

MILES, WENDELL A., federal judge; b. Holland, Mich., Apr. 17, 1916; s. Fred T. and Dena Del (Alverson) M.; m. Mariette Bruckert, June 8, 1946; children: Lorraine Miles, Michelle Miles Kopinski, Thomas Paul. AB, Hope Coll., 1938, LLD (hon.), 1980; MA, U. Wyo., 1939; JD, U. Mich., 1942; LLD (hon.), Detroit Coll. Law, 1979. Bar: Mich. Ptnr. Miles & Miles, Holland, 1948-53, Miles, Mika, Meyers, Beckett & Jones, Grand Rapids, Mich., 1961-70; pros. atty. County of Ottawa, Mich., 1949-53; U.S. dist. atty. Western Dist. Mich., Grand Rapids, 1953-60; U.S. dist. judge Western Dist. Mich., 1974—, chief judge, 1979-86, sr. chief judge, 1986—; cir. judge 20th Jud. Cir. Ct. Mich., 1970-74; instr. Hope Coll., 1948-53, Am. Inst. Banking, 1953-60; adj. prof. Am. constl. history Hope Coll., Holland, Mich., 1979—; mem. Mich. Higher Edn. Commn.; apptd. Fgn. Intelligence Surveillance Court, Washington, 1989—. Pres. Holland Bd. Edn., 1952-63. Served to capt. U.S. Army, 1942-47. Recipient Liberty Bell award, 1986. Fellow Am. Bar Found.; mem. ABA, Mich. Bar Assn., Fed. Bar Assn., Ottawa County Bar Assn., Grand Rapids Bar (Inns of Ct. 1995—), Am. Judicature Soc., Torch Club, Rotary Club, Masons. Office: US Dist Ct 236 Fed Bldg 110 Michigan Ave NW Grand Rapids MI 49503-2313

MILETICH, IVO, library and information scientist, bibliographer, educator, linguist, literature research specialist; b. Pucisca, Yugoslavia, Apr. 18, 1936; came to U.S., 1966, naturalized, 1972; s. Josip and Mandina (Bagich) M.; m. Mira Pilja, Mar. 11, 1967; children: George Edward, Marina Julie. AB, Acad. Edn., Split, Yugoslavia, 1960; AM in History, U. Skopje, Macedonia, Yugoslavia, 1966; cert. advanced study, English Inst., Chgo., 1969; MA in Libr. Sci., Rosary Coll., River Forest, Ill., 1971. Cert. libr., Va. Tchr. various schs. Yugoslavia, 1959-65; asst. bibliographer Slavic langs. and lit. Joseph Regenstein and Sam Harper Librs., U. Chgo., 1967-71; tchr. Croatian lang. co-edn. YMCA Community Coll., Chgo., 1969-71, 74—; bibliographer Old Dominion U., Norfolk, Va., 1971-74; assoc. prof. libr. sci., bibliographer Chgo. State U., 1974—; translator, interpreter English, Latin, Croatian, Serbian, Macedonian, Bulgarian, Old Ch. Slavic, Slovene, 1969—; interpreter Berlitz Trans. Ctr. Sch. Langs.; lectr. South Slavonic langs., lit., history and culture, Balkan states culture, heritage and folk lit., transl. techniques. Contbr. various confs., seminars, workshops, jours., transl. of articles, studies, work on dictionary, Berlitz Transl. Svc. transl. and interpretion. Recipient cert. of appreciation YMCA C.C., Chgo., 1976, cert. Beta Phi Mu, U. Pitts., 1972, Am. Translators Assn., 1980, Assn. Coll. and Rsch. Librs., 1986. Mem. ALA, Am. Fedn. Tchrs., Assn. Coll. and Rsch. Librs., Chgo. Acad. Libr. Coun. Libr. of Congress (assoc.), Soc. Scholarly Pub., Beta Phi Mu. Home: 618 Exchange Ave Calumet City IL 60409-3903 Office: Chgo State U Rm Lib 203 95th St at King Dr Chicago IL 60628

MILEWSKI, BARBARA ANNE, pediatrics nurse, neonatal intensive care nurse; b. Chgo., Sept. 11, 1934; d. Anthony and LaVerne (Sepp) Witt; m. Leonard A. Milewski, Feb. 23, 1952; children: Pamela, Robert, Diane, Timothy. ADN, Harper Coll., Palatine, Ill, 1982; BS, Northern Ill. U., 1992; postgrad., North Park Coll. RN, Ill.; cert. CPR instr. Staff nurse Northwest Community Hosp., Arlington Heights, Ill., Resurrection Hosp., Chgo.; nurse neonatal ICU Children's Meml. Hosp., Chgo.; day care cons. Cook County Dept. Pub. Health; CPR instr. Stewart Oxygen Svcs., Chgo.; instr., organizer parenting and well baby classes and clinics; vol. Children's Meml. Hosp.; health coord. CEDA Head Start; cons. day care Cook County Dept. Pub. Health. Vol. first aid instr. Boy Scouts Am.; CPR instr. Harper Coll., Children's Meml. Hosp.; dir. Albany Park Cmty. Ctr. Head Start, Chgo.; day care cons. Cook County Dept. Pub. Health. Mem. Am. Mortar Bd., Sigma Theta Tau.

MILKMAN, ROGER DAWSON, genetics educator, molecular evolution researcher; b. N.Y.C., Oct. 15, 1930; s. Louis Arthur and Margaret (Weinstein) M.; m. Marianne Friedenthal, Oct. 18, 1958; children: Ruth Margaret, Louise Friedenthal, Janet Dawson Milkman Lussenhop, Paul David. A.B., Harvard U., 1951, A.M., 1954, Ph.D., 1956. Student, asst., instr., investigator Marine Biol. Lab., Woods Hole, Mass., 1952-72, 88-96; instr., asst. prof. U. Mich., Ann Arbor, 1957-60; assoc. prof., prof. Syracuse U., N.Y., 1960-68; prof. biol. scis. U. Iowa, Iowa City, 1968—, chmn. univ. genetics PhD program, 1992-93; vis. prof. biology Grinnell (Iowa) Coll., 1990; mem. genetics study sect. NIH, 1986-87; NSF panelist, 1996—. Translator: Developmental Physiology, 1970; editor: Perspectives on Evolution, 1982, Experimental Population Genetics, 1983, Evolution jour., 1984-86; mem. editl. bd. Molecular Phylogenetics and Evolution; contbr. articles to profl. jours. Sec. Soc. Gen. Physiologists, 1963-65, Am. Soc. Naturalists, 1980-82; alumni rep. Phillips Acad., Andover, Mass., 1980-94. NSF grantee, 1959—; USPHS grantee, 1984-87. Fellow AAAS; mem. Am. Soc. for Microbiology, Genetics Soc. Am., Corp. Marine Biol. Lab., Soc. for Gen. Microbiology (U.K.), Soc. Study Evolution, Soc. Molecular Biology and Evolution, Internat. Soc. for Molecular Evolution. Jewish. Home: 12 Fairview Knoll NE Iowa City IA 52240-9147 Office: U Iowa Dept Biol Scis 138 Biology Building Bldg Iowa City IA 52242-1324

MILLARD, CHARLES PHILLIP, manufacturing company executive; b. Janesville, Wis., Apr. 21, 1948; s. Duane Francis and Mary Lou (Ganley) M.; m. Mary Franzen, Oct. 7, 1967 (div.); children: Katherine, Laura. Student, U. Wis., Janesville, 1966-67. Spot welder Gen. Motors Corp., Janesville, 1966-67; plant mgr. Insta-Foam Products, Addison, Ill., 1967-72; warehouse mgr. Ram Golf Corp., Elk Grove, Ill., 1972-77; master scheduler Gandalf Data Inc., Wheeling, Ill., 1977-84; corp. mfg. coord. Gandalf Data Inc., Wheeling, 1984-85; corp. mktg. coord. Gandalf Technologies Inc., Wheeling, 1985-87, corp. strategist, 1988-89; internat. rsch. analyst Gandalf Data Inc., Wheeling, 1989-90; asst. mgr. safety/security Fellowes Mfg. Co., Itasca, Ill., 1990-93; process specialist, cons. Janesville, Wis., 1993-94; asst. mgr. Janesville Travel Ctr., Janesville, Wis., 1994-95; prodn. material coord. Alliant TechSystems, Janesville, Wis., 1995—. Patrol Officer Des Plaines (Ill.) Police Res., 1987-89. Mem. Am. Mgmt. Assn., Am. Mktg. Assn., Furniture Workers Union, Am. Fedn. Police, Nat. Rifle Assn.

MILLARD, KEN M., automotive executive; b. Omaha, Nebr., May 1, 1928; s. Martin and Louise (VomWeg) M.; m. Shirley Meth, Sept. 3, 1947; children: Deborah J. Millard Cizek, Scott. Student, U. Nebr., 1948-52. Sales rep. B.F. Goodrich, Omaha, 1952-54; v.p. Hook-Millard Tire, Omaha, 1954-57; sales rep. Danlop Tire, Waterloo, Iowa, 1957-63; v.p. Carl A. Anderson, Inc., Omaha, 1963-70; pres. Replacement Parts Whse., Omaha, 1970-77, Millard's Inc., Omaha, 1977—; v.p. Alpha Am. Ltd., Omaha, 1977—; adv. coun. Wagner Brake, St. Louis, 1964—, Goodyear Tire, Lincoln, Nebr., 1964—; bd. dirs. Auto Value, Chattanooga, Tenn. Bd. elders Jaynes St. Ch., 1967. With U.S. Army, 1946-48. Named One of Automotive Mktgs. Top 100 Retailers Automotive Mktg., 1989—. Mem. Auto Value Assocs. (treas. 1991, bd. dirs.), Happy Hollow Club, Shriner, Campions Club, C. of C. Home: 1011 Mason St Omaha NE 68108 Office: Millards Inc 1011 Mason Omaha NE 68108-3219

MILLER, ANGELA PEREZ, bilingual, special education, and educational leadership educator; b. Chgo., Oct. 1, 1936; d. Jesse and Emily (Ibarra) P.; m. John F. Miller, May 6, 1961 (div.); 1 son, Dion. BA, U. Ill., 1958; MA, Northeastern Ill. U., 1975; MEd, De Paul U., 1984; PhD, U. Ill.-Chgo., 1990. Cert. elem. tchr., spl. edn., bilingual edn., adminstrn., Ill. Tchr. Chgo. pub. schs., 1962-70; exchange tchr. Mexico City schs., 1970-71; asst. prin. Burns Elem. Sch., Chgo., 1972-77; asst. prin. Benito Juarez H.S., Chgo., 1977-85; field adminstr. Chgo. Pub. Schs., 1985-88, prin., 1988-89, adminstr. Office of Reform Implementation, 1989-91, dir. staff training and devel., 1991-94; asst. prof. DePaul U., Chgo., 1994—; vis. asst. prof. U. Ill., Chgo., 1992, 93. Pres., bd. dirs. Latino Inst.; co-chair Consortium Chgo. Sch. Rsch. Mem. ASCD, Nat. Staff Devel. Coun., Am. Ednl. Rsch. Assn., Coun. Exceptional Children, Nat. Assn. Bilingual Edn. Office: 2320 N Kenmore Ave Chicago IL 60614-3210

MILLER, ARNOLD, newspaper editor; b. Cleve., May 24, 1931; s. Ben and Fanny (Keller) M.; m. Loretta Cooney, June 29, 1957 (div. 1977); children: Anita, Adrienne, Evan, Bryn, Alyssa. BS in Journalism, Kent State U., 1956. Copy editor News-Sentinel, Fort Wayne, Ind., 1956; asst. city editor Beacon Jour., Akron, Ohio, 1957-65; mng. editor Morning Herald, Hagerstown, Md., 1965-69; reporter, columnist, asst. news editor Cleve. Press, 1969-72; mng. editor Chronicle-Telegram, Elyria, Ohio, 1972—. With U.S. Army, 1953-54. Mem. Assoc. Press Mng. Editors Assn., Md.-Del. Press Assn., Ohio UPI Editors Assn. (pres. 1978), Assoc. Press Soc. Ohio (adv. bd. 1992-93). Jewish. Home: 1550D Cedarwood Dr Cleveland OH 44145-1806 Office: Chronicle-Telegram 225 East Ave Elyria OH 44035-5634

MILLER, ARTHUR HAWKS, JR., librarian, consultant; b. Kalamazoo, Mar. 15, 1943; s. Arthur Hawks and Eleanor (Johnson) M.; m. Janet Carol Schroeder, June 11, 1967; children: Janelle Aileen, Andrew Hawks. AB, Kalamazoo Coll., 1965; student U. Caen, Calvados, France, 1963-64, Lake Forest Grad. Sch. Mgmt., 1990-91; AM in English, U. Chgo., 1966, AM in Librarianship, 1968; PhD, Northwestern U., 1973. Reference libr. Newberry Libr., Chgo., 1966-69, asst. libr. pub. svcs., 1969-72; coll. libr. Lake Forest (Ill.) Coll., 1972-94, archivist and libr. for spl. collections, lectr. English dept., 1993—; mem. Ill. Libr. Computer Sys. Policy Coun., Chgo., 1982-87, 92-94. Pres. Lake Forest/Lake Bluff Hist. Soc., 1982-85, Lake County Hist. Soc., 1985—, Ill. Ctr. for Book Bd., 1992-93, v.p. 1993—; trustee Ragdale Found., 1986—, sec., 1987-92, pres., 1992-93, v.p., 1993-94, bd. dirs., 1990—. Mem. ALA (chmn. history sect. 1982-83, chmn. coll. sect. 1986-87), Melville Soc. Am., Ill. Libr. Assn. (chmn. pub. policy com. 1988-90), Pvt. Acad. Librs. of Ill. (v.p. 1988-90, pres. 1990-92), Caxton Club (pres. 1978-80, coun. mem. 1988-91). Presbyterian. Home: 169 Wildwood Rd Lake Forest IL 60045-2462 Office: Lake Forest Coll Donnelley Library 555 N Sheridan Rd Lake Forest IL 60045-2338

MILLER, ARTHUR J., JR., state legislator; b. Detroit, July 11, 1946; m. Marsha Ann; children: Holly A., Nicole M., Arthur J. III, Derek E. Student, Eastern Mich. U. Dem. leader Mich. State Senate Dist. 10, 85—; city coun. Warren, Mich., v.p., pres.;. Office: 11139 Olive St Warren MI 48093-6557 Address: State Senate 11139 Olive St Warren MI 48093*

MILLER, BENJAMIN K., state supreme court justice; b. Springfield, Ill., Nov. 5, 1936; s. Clifford and Mary (Luthyens) M. BA, So. Ill. U., 1958; JD, Vanderbilt U., 1961. Bar: Ill. 1961. Ptnr. Olsen, Cantrill & Miller, Springfield, 1964-70; prin. Ben Miller-Law Office, Springfield, 1970-76; judge 7th jud. cir. Ill. Cir. Ct., Springfield, 1976-82, presiding judge Criminal div., 1977-81, chief judge, 1981-82; justice Ill. Appellate Ct., 4th Jud. Dist., 1982-84, Ill. Supreme Ct., Springfield, 1984—; chief justice Ill. Supreme Ct., 1991-93; adj. prof. So. Ill. U., Springfield, 1974—; chmn. Ill. Cts. Commn., 1988-90; mem. Ill. Gov.'s Adv. Coun. on Criminal Justice Legis., 1977-84, Ad Hoc Com. on Tech. in Cts., 1985—. Mem. editorial rev. bd. Illinois Civil Practice Before Trial, Illinois Civil Trial Practice. Pres. Cen. Ill. Mental Health Assn., 1969-71; bd. govs. Aid to Retarded Citizens, 1977-80; mem. Lincoln Legals Adv. Bd., 1988—. Lt. USNR, 1964-67. Mem. ABA (bar admissions com. sect. of legal edn. and admissions to bar 1992—), Ill. State Bar Assn. (bd. govs. 1970-76, treas. 1975-76), Sangamon County Bar Assn., Women's Bar Assn. of Ill., Ctrl. Ill. Women's Bar Assn., Am. Judicature Soc. (bd. dirs. 1990-95), Abraham Lincoln Assn. (bd. dirs. 1988—). Office: Supreme Ct Ill 1st Of America Ste 560 Springfield IL 62701

MILLER, BERNARD J., III, advertising executive; b. 1949. BS in Mktg., Ind. U., 1971; M in Advt., Northwestern U., 1972. With brand mgmt. Alberto Culver, Chgo., 1972-74; with Columbian Advt. Del, Chgo., 1974—. Office: Columbian Advt Del 201 E Ohio St Chicago IL 60611-3202*

MILLER, BERNARD JOSEPH, JR., advertising executive; b. Louisville, July 31, 1925; s. Bernard J. Sr. and Myrtle (Herrington) M.; m. Jayne Hughes, Aug. 7, 1948 (div. Oct. 1970); children: Bernard J. III, Jeffrey, Janet Marie.; m. Brita Naujok, Nov. 24, 1970; 1 child, Brian. BS, Ind. U., 1949. Merchandising mgr. Brown-Forman Distillers, Inc., Louisville, 1949-54; v.p. Phelps Mfg. Co., Terre Haute, Ind., 1954-60; pres. Columbian Advt. Inc., Chgo., 1960-87, chmn., 1987—. 2d lt. USAF, 1943-46, PTO. Mem. Point of Purchase Advt. Inst. (bd. 1970-73), Saddle and Cycle Club (bd. dirs. 1987-90). Office: Columbian Advt Inc 201 E Ohio St Chicago IL 60611-3202*

MILLER, BERTIN, priest, social administrator; b. Joliet, Ill., May 15, 1936; s. William Sumner Ellsworth and Mary Marguerite (Hanrahan) M. BA, Quincy Coll., 1960; STB, Antonianum, Rome, 1964. Ordained priest Roman Cath. Ch., 1964. Chaplain Mo. State Correction Farmington/Pacific, Hillsboro, Mo., 1988-92; exec. dir. Evergreen Hills Homes, Dittmer, Mo., 1973—; dir. II Ritiro, Dittmer, 1977—; spiritual dir. St. Michael's Inst., Sunset Hills, Mo., 1986-88; lectr. Marsh, Curtis, McCall, St. Louis, 1986—. Chaplain Cedar Hill (Mo.) Fire Dept., 1989-92; assoc. mem. Nat. Coun. on Sexual Addiction, Inc.; founder, exec. dir. Wounded Bros. Project, 1992—; Catholic chaplain Jefferson County Sheriff's Dept., 1995—. Mem. Lions, Elks, KC (4th deg.). Home: PO Box 400 Dittmer MO 63023 Office: PO Box 220 Dittmer MO 63023

MILLER, CALLIX EDWIN, manufacturing executive, consultant; b. South Bend, Ind., Mar. 27, 1924; s. Callix Edwin and Marguerite Cash (Sweeney) M.; m. Theresa Ann Pirchio, June 25, 1949; children—Madeline, Callix, John, David, Thomas. B.S. in Archtl. Engring., U. Notre Dame, 1949. Mgr. engring. Internat. Mining and Chem. Corp., Chgo., 1951-61; exec. dir. Sperry Rand Corp., N.Y.C., 1961-64; v.p. Internat. Minerals & Chem. Corp., Chgo., 1964-72; v.p. Assocs. Corp. N.Am., Dallas, 1972-78; corp. v.p. tech. resources Clark Equipment Co., Buchanan, Mich., 1978-85, consulting services covering design, planning, feasibility studies, econ. devel. Bd. dirs. Chgo. Area council Boy Scouts Am., 1967-70, Alexian Bros. Hosp., Chgo., 1966-68. Served with USNR, 1943-45. Mem. AIA, ASCE, Soc. Am. Mil. Engrs., Am. Concrete Inst. Republican. Roman Catholic. Clubs: Knollwood Country; Northbrook (Ill.) Sport; Faculty (U. Notre Dame). Lodges: Elks, K.C. Home: 16174 Baywood Ln Granger IN 46530-9716

MILLER, CANDICE S., state official; b. May 7, 1954; m. Donald G. Miller; 1 child, Wendy Nicole. Student, Macomb County C.C., Northwood Inst. Sec., treas. D.B. Snider, Inc., 1972-79; trustee Harrison Twp., 1979-80, supr., 1980-92; treas. Macomb County, 1992-95; sec. of state State of Mich., Lansing, 1995—; chair Mich. State Safety Commn., 1995—; mem. M-59 Task Force Strategy Com. Mem. community coun. Selfridge Air Nat. Guard Base. Mem. Boat Town Assn., Ctrl. Macomb C. of C., Harrison Twp. Indsl. Corridor. Office: Treasury Building 430 W Allegan, 1st Fl Lansing MI 48918-9900

MILLER, CHARLES, business management research and measurements consultant; b. Crowley, La., Nov. 1, 1959; s. Rufus Paul and Rose (Lacombe) M.; m. Monica Lynn Habetz, Aug. 10, 1985. BS, La. State U.,

1981, MS, 1985; PhD, Ohio State U., 1989. Rsch. asst. horticulture dept. La. State U., Baton Rouge, 1977-78, La. State Soil Testing Lab., Baton Rouge, 1978-81; rsch. assoc. La. Rice Rsch. Sta., Crowley, 1982; agriculture tchr. Acadia Parish Sch. Bd., Crowley and Iota, 1982-87; rsch. assoc. Ohio State U., Columbus, 1987-89, asst. prof., 1989-92; sr. cons., mgr. measurements Shaffer Sherman Sperry & Swaddling, Inc., Westerville, Ohio, 1992—. Minister, lector St. John Neumann Ch., Sunbury, Ohio, 1992—. Recipient project grant for tchr. prep. program U.S. Dept. Edn., 1990, Am. Farmer award Nat. Future Farmers Am., 1979. Mem. Am. Soc. for Quality Control, Omicron Tau Theta (editor 1991-92, Outstanding Svc. award 1992), Phi Delta Kappa, Gamma Sigma Delta, Alpha Zeta. Democrat. Roman Catholic. Office: Shaffer Sherman Sperry & Swaddling Inc 575 Copeland Mill Rd Westerville OH 43081-8977

MILLER, CHARLES KENT, electrical engineer; b. Dardanelle, Ark., Jan. 4, 1932. B, U. Ark., 1960. Registered profl. engr., S.D., Ark. From jr. design engr. to sr. design engr. & mgr. prodn. Ctrl. Moloney, Inc., Pine Bluff, Ark., 1960-75; chief engr. T & R Electric Supply Co., Colman, S.D., 1975—. With USNG, 1950-77. Mem. IEEE (sr.), NSPE. Republican. Mem. Ch. of Christ. Home: PO Box 126 Colman SD 57017-0126 Office: T & R Electric Supply Co PO Box 180 Colman SD 57017-0180

MILLER, DANIEL G., corporate executive; b. Cambridge, Mass., Mar. 16, 1949; s. Francis Marion and Marjorie Lee (Rickman) M.; m. Amy Elizabeth Carr, May 25, 1971; children: Rebecca Carr, Katherine Gordon. BS in Chemistry, Bucknell U., 1971; PhD in Pharm. Biochemistry, U. Wis., 1975. Asst. prof. pharmacognosy U. Minn., Mpls., 1975-80, assoc. mem., grad. studies program in pharmacognosy, 1978-81; sr. immunologist 3M Cen. Rsch. Lab., St. Paul, Minn., 1980-81, rsch. specialist immunology, 1981; rsch. mgr., biotechnology 3M Life Scis. Sector Lab., St. Paul, Minn., 1981-83, tech. mgr., biotechnology, 1983-84, lab. mgr., biotechnology, 1984-88; dir. R&D DIANON Systems, Inc., Stratford, Conn., 1988-90, v.p. R&D, 1990-93; pres. Regenerex, Inc., Mpls., 1994—. Contbr. articles to profl. jours. and publs. Mem. Am. Chem. Soc., AAAS, Am. Assn. Colls. Pharmacy, AAUP, Sigma Xi. Unitarian. Office: Regenerex Inc 8500 Evergreen Blvd Minneapolis MN 95433

MILLER, DANIEL MARTIN, surgeon, oncologist; b. Edmonton, Alberta, Can., Dec. 16, 1917; came to U.S., 1922; s. David and Lena (Horwich) M.; m. Harriet R. Rosen, Mar. 7, 1973; children: Neil L., Craig R., Alexander R. BS in Medicine, Creighton U., 1938, MD, 1942. Attending surgeon Meth. Hosp., Omaha, 1952-95, Bishop Clarkson Hosp., Omaha, 1952-95; asst. prof. surgery U. Nebr. Med. Sch., Omaha, 1952-55, assoc. prof. surgery, 1955-95; med. dir. Bishop Clarkson Hosp., 1985-94. Maj. USAF, 1942-46. Mem. AMA, Am. Coll. Surgeons, Am. Assn. Cancer Rsch., Nebr. Med. Assn., Omaha Douglas County Med. Soc., Assn. Clin. Oncology, Ewing Soc. Independent. Jewish. Home: Apt 4-A-2 8405 Indian Hills Dr Omaha NE 68114

MILLER, DANIEL RAYMOND, prosecutor; b. Evansville, Ind., Sept. 20, 1963; s. Daniel Edgar and Virginia Sue (Baumgart) M. BA magna cum laude, DePauw U., 1985; JD cum laude, Ind. U., 1989. Bar: Ind. 1989. Clk. to presiding judge William I. Garrard Ind. Ct. of Appeals, Indpls, 1989-90; dep. pros. atty. Vanderburgh County Pros.'s Office, Evansville, 1990—. Chmn. com. Substance Abuse Coun. Vanderburgh County, 1993—; chmn. pastoral coun. St. John Cath. Ch., Evansville, 1995-96. Meml. Ind. Bar Assn., Ind. Drug Enforcement Assn., 4-H Club Assn. (bd. dris. 1995-96, leader Energetics club 1991—), St. Vincent DePaul Soc. (sec. conf. 1994, 95—). Republican. Roman Catholic. Home: 13521 N Green River Rd Evansville IN 47711 Office: Vanderburgh Co Pros Office Rm 108 City County Adm Bldg Evansville IN 47708

MILLER, DAVID GIBBS, electrical contractor; b. Chgo., May 12, 1946; s. Arthur John and Carolyn (Raymond) M.; m. Kathryn Powell, Aug. 23, 1969; children: Marcy Gibbs, Thomas Duncan. BS in Bus. Mgmt., Bradley U., Peoria, Ill., 1973. Exec. v.p. The Powell Electric, Inc., Newark, Ohio, 1973-83; pres. Buckeye Elec. Constrn. & Maintenance, Newark, 1983—. Chmn. comml. div. United Way of Licking County, Newark, 1986. Served with U.S. Army, 1970-72. Mem. Am. Subcontractors Assn. (pres. Ctrl. Ohio chpt. 1987-88, nat. pres. 1991-92, bd. dirs., John Hampshire award 1994), Newark Rotary Club. Republican. Office: Buckeye Elec Constrn & Maintenance Inc 111 S 21st St Newark OH 43055

MILLER, DAVID HARRY, physics educator; b. St. Mellion, Cornwall, Eng., Mar. 3, 1939; came to U.S., 1963; s. Harry John and Inez Miller; m. Isobel Elizabeth Stuart, Aug. 23, 1961; children: Scott David, Steven James. BS, London U., 1960, PhD, 1963. Rsch. prof. Purdue U., West Lafayette, Ind., 1963-65; asst. prof. Purdue U., West Lafayette, 1965-68, assoc. prof., 1968-76, prof. physics, 1976—; vis. scientist CERN, Geneva, 1972-73; vis. fellow Cornell U., Ithaca, N.Y., 1991—, prin. investigator, 1971—. Contbr. articles to sci. jours. John Simon Guggenheim Found. fellow, 1972-73. Fellow Am. Phys. Soc.; mem. AAAS, Royal Coll. of Sci. (assoc.). Office: Purdue U Physics Dept West Lafayette IN 47907

MILLER, DEBORAH JEAN, computer training and document consultant; b. Elmhurst, Ill., Oct. 2, 1951; d. Thomas Francis and Ruthe Conn (Johnston) M. BFA, Ill. Wesleyan U., 1973; MA, Northwestern U., 1974. Pres. Miller & Assocs., Evanston, Ill., 1980—. Mem. AAUW, NOW, Internat. Interactive Comm. Soc., Soc. Tech. Comm., Ind. Writers Chgo. (bd. dirs. 1985-86), Chgo. Coun. Fgn. Rels., Internat. Soc. Performance and Instrn. (Chgo. chpt.), Northwestern U. Alumni Assn. Office: 814 Mulford St Evanston IL 60202-3331

MILLER, DENNIS DIXON, economics educator; b. Chillicothe, Ohio, May 1, 1950; s. Kermit Baker and Martha (Ralston) M. BA, Heidelberg Coll., 1972; MA, U. Colo., 1979, PhD, 1985. Instr. in econs. Am. U., Cairo, Egypt, 1982-84; internat. economist USDA, Washington, 1985-86; assoc. prof. Baldwin-Wallace Coll., Berea, Ohio, 1987—; rsch. assoc. Internat. Ctr. Energy and Econ. Devel., Boulder, Colo., 1979-82, 84-85; vis. scholar Hoover Instn., Stanford U., Palo Alto, fall 1986; acad. advisor Heartland Inst., Chgo., 1988—, Buckeye Ctr.; book reviewer Choice mag., 1984—; , manuscript reviewer Dryden Press, 1994—; pub. policy advisor Heritage Found.'s Listing, Washington, 1991—, econ. cons. gen., 1991—; vis. prof. Mithibai Coll., U. Bombay, India, summer and fall 1991; coord. agy. Air Quality Pub. Adv. Task Force, 1993; v.p. Adam Ferguson Inst., 1996—. Earhart Found. fellow, 1977-78. Mem. AAAS, Am. Econs. Assn., Cleve. Coun. on World Afairs, Assn. Pvt. Enterprise Edn., Intertel, Nat. Assn. Forensic Economists, Assn. for Study of Grants Edn., N.Am. Econ. and Fin. Assn., Middle East Inst., Sierra Club, Nature Conservancy, Mensa. Home: 12 Adelbert St Apt 2 Berea OH 44017-1753 Office: Baldwin Wallace Coll Dept Of Econs Berea OH 44017

MILLER, DIANE KAY, nursing educator; b. Ithaca, N.Y., Oct. 24, 1953; d. Wallace R. and Shirley L. (Withers) Nark; m. Gordon W. Miller, June 26, 1971; children: Stacey L., Brian S. AAS in Nursing, Broome Community Coll., 1978; BSN, Purdue U., 1988; MSN, Ball State U., 1995. CRRN, BLS, Ind.; RN, Ind., N.Y. Staff nurse, supr. Endicott (N.Y.) Nursing Home, 1979-81; charge RN rehab. and med.-surg. United Health Svcs. Wilson Hosp., Binghamton, N.Y., 1981-85; telemetry-rehab. nurse Parkview Hosp., Fort Wayne, Ind., 1985-88; med. svc. cons. Crawford & Co. Health & Rehab., Fort Wayne, 1988; dir. nursing Unicare Health System, Fort Wayne, 1989; nursing instr. Ivy Tech State Coll., Ft. Wayne, 1990—. Mem. Assn. Rehab. Nurses, Phi Theta Kappa, Sigma Theta Tau. Home: 5621 Albany Ct Fort Wayne IN 46835-4294 Office: Ivy Tech State Coll 3800 N Anthony Blvd Fort Wayne IN 46805-1430

MILLER, DONALD MUXLOW, accountant, administrator; b. Luverne, Minn., Feb. 21, 1924; s. Henry Clay and Mildred Eva (Muxlow) M.; m. Eunice Jean Gibson, Feb. 19, 1944; children: SueRilla M., Donna Jean Eichten, Patsy Ann Pushee. Student, Metro State, St. Paul, Minn., 1973-84. Lic. pub. acct. Mgr. Hines & Paulus, CPA, Worthington, Minn., 1952-65; commandant Minn. Vets. Home, Mpls., 1965-68; prin. D.M. Miller, Acct., 1968-70, 76-78; asst. sec. Minn. State Senate, St. Paul, 1970-72; comptr. Western Oil Co., Mpls., 1972-76; commr. Dept. Vet. Affairs, State of Minn., St. Paul, 1978-81; prin. D.M. Miller & Assoc., Ltd., Mpls., 1981—; chief exec. officer MARD, Inc., Mpls., 1985-95; v.p. Miller, Micketts & Assocs. Ltd., Mpls., 1993—. Trustee Heart Professorship Found., 1987-91; pres. Legionville Sch. Patrol Camp, Brainerd, Minn., 1963-64; pres. bd. govs. Big Island Vets. Camp, Mpls., 1986-88. 2nd lt. USAAC, 1942-46; 1st lt. USAF, 1951-52. Recipient Volunteer of the Year award Kidney Found., 1975. Mem. VFW, Nat. Soc. Pub. Accts., Minn. Assn. Pub. Accts., Nat. Assn. State Vets. Homes (hon. life mem., reg. v.p. 1967-68), Nat. Assn. State Dirs. Vets Affairs (reg. v.p. 1978-79), Minn. Gaming Assn. (exec. sec. 1987-92), Am. Legion (hon life mem., comdr. Minn. 1962-63, com. chmn. 1980-84, pres. Minn. Found. Bd. 1990-91), Masons, Shriners. Presbyterian. Office: Miller Micketts & Assocs Ltd 9033 Lyndale Ave S Ste 201 Minneapolis MN 55420-3537

MILLER, DORIS MAYHILL, accountant; b. Arkansas City, Kans., Apr. 30, 1947; d. Samuel Walter and Ferne Etta (Nellis) M.; m. James M. Dent, Aug. 3, 1971 (div. Dec. 31, 1982); m. Albert Raymond Miller, July 1, 1984; stepchildren: Michelle, Debra, Lynda. BS in Elem. Edn., Kans. State U., 1969; M in Sec. Edn., Emporia State U., 1980; math. student, Johnson County C.C., Lenexa, Kans., 1975-83; bus. and acctg. student, Cowley County C.C., Arkansas City, Kans., 1984-91. Cert. tchr., Kans. Tchr. 5th grade Olath (Kans.) Unified Sch. Dist., 1969-70; tchr. Shawnee Mission (Kans.) Unified Sch. Dist., 1970-84; field trip coord., counselor Live and Learn Group Home Boys, Olathe, summer 1983; tchr. jr. h.s. Arkansas City Unified Sch. Dist., Arkansas City, 1984-86; instr., bookkeeper, office mgr. H&R Block Profl. Bus. Svc., Arkansas City, 1986-88; acct. Winfield (Kans.) Correctional Facility, 1988—; mem. tng. adv. bd. Winfield Correctional Facility, Winfield, 1990—. Singer ch. and cmty. choirs, Lenexa, Olathe, Arkansas City, 1973—; vol. youth diversion Cmty. Accountability Bd., Olathe, 1982-84; 4-H judge Coop. Ext. Coun., Sedgwick County, 1991—; bd. dirs., trustee, treas. Meth. Ch., 1993-94, acct., treas., 1994—.

MILLER, DWIGHT RICHARD, cosmetologist, corporate executive, hair designer; b. Johnstown, Pa., Jan. 24, 1943. Grad., Comer & Doran Sch., San Diego; DSci. (hon.), London Inst. for Applied Rsch., 1973. Cert. aromatherapist; lic. cosmetologist., instr.; Brit. Mastercraftsman. Styles dir. Marinello-Comer, Hollywood, Calif., 1965-67; expert Pivot Point Internat., Chgo., 1967-68; styles dir. Lapins, L.A., 1969; dir. Redken, L.A., 1970, Vidal Sassoon, London, 1971-74; world amb. Pivot Point, New Zealand and Australia, 1974-75; internat. artistic dir. Pivot Point, Chgo., 1975-78; internat. dir., co-founder Hair Artists Inst. & Registry, 1978-81; internat. artistic dir. Zotos Internat., Darien, Conn., 1981-87, Matrix Essentials, Inc., Solon, Ohio, 1987-92; bd. dirs., v.p. creative, internat. artistic dir. Anasazi Exclusive Salon Products, Inc., Dubuque, Iowa, 1992—; judge hairdressing competitions including Norwegian Masters, Australian Nat. Championships; pres. Intercrimpers, London, 1974-75. Author: Sculptic Cutting Pivot Point 75, Prismatics, 1983; prod., dir. 15 documentaries, numerous tech. and industry videos; contbr. articles, photographs to popular mags.; developer several profl. product lines including Vidal Sassoon-London, Design Freedom, Bain de Terre, Ultra Bond, Vavoom!, Systeme Biolage, Anasazi. With USMC, 1960-64. Named Artistic Dir. Yr. Am. Salon mag.; presented with Order of White Elephant, 1976; recipient London Gold Cup for Best Presentation London Beauty Festival, 1982, Dr. Everett G. McDonough award for Excellence in Permanent Waving, World Master award Art and Fashion Group, 1992. Mem. Cercle des Arts et Techniques de la Coiffure, Intercoiffure, Haute Coiffure Franchaise, Soc. Cosmetic Chemists, Hair Artists Great Britain, Internat. Assn. Trichogists, Nat. Cosmetologists Assn. (HairAmerica), Am. Soc. Phytotherapy and Aromatherapy, HairChicago (hon.), Art and Fashion Group (pres. 1993), 'Dressers MC (pres. 1990—), London's Alternative Hair Club (patron). Address: 13900 Watt Rd Novelty OH 44072-9741

MILLER, ESTHER SCOBIE POWERS, real estate appraiser, professional watercolorist; b. Peninsula, Ohio, Apr. 16, 1929; d. John Henry and Hazel Blanche (Appleton) Scobie; m. Elmer Duane Powers, June 13, 1948 (div. 1965); m. Kenneth Ward Miller, Aug. 26, 1980; children: Terrance, Michael, Susan, Jennifer. Student, Kansas City (Mo.) Art Inst., 1948-50, Bethel Coll., 1965-67, Ind. U., South Bend, 1965-67. Designated SRA-real estate appraiser. Owner brokerage Powers Realty, Culver, Ind., 1967-76; pvt. practice fee appraising South Bend, 1978-84, Culver, 1984-88, Plymouth, Ind., 1988-90; profl. watercolorist. Mem. St. Joe Valley Water Color Soc. Methodist.

MILLER, EUGENE, university official, business executive; b. Chgo., Oct. 6, 1925; s. Harry and Fannie (Prosterman) M.; m. Edith Sutker, Sept. 23, 1951 (div. Sept. 1965); children: Ross, Scott, June; m. Thelma Gottlieb, Dec. 22, 1965; stepchildren: Paul Gottlieb, Alan Gottlieb. BS, Ga. Inst. Tech., 1945; AB magna cum laude, Bethany Coll., 1947, LLD, 1969; diploma, Oxford (Eng.) U., 1947; MS in Journalism, Columbia U., 1948; MBA, NYU, 1959; postgrad., Pace U., 1973—. Reporter, then city editor Greensboro (N.C.) Daily News, 1948-52; S.W. bur. chief Bus. Week mag., Houston, 1952-54; assoc. mng. editor Bus. Week mag., N.Y.C., 1954-60; dir. pub. affairs and communications McGraw-Hill, Inc., 1960-63, v.p., 1963-68; sr. v.p. pub. rels. and investor rels., exec. com. N.Y. Stock Exch., N.Y.C., 1968-73; sr. v.p. CNA Fin. Corp., Chgo., 1973-75; chmn. Eugene Miller & Assocs., Glencoe, Ill., 1975-77; v.p. USG Corp., Chgo., 1977-82, sr. v.p., 1982-85, mem. mgmt. com., 1982-91, exec. v.p., CFO, 1985-87, elected vice chmn., CFO, 1987-91, mem. exec. com., also bd. dirs.; prof., asst. dean Coll. Bus., Fla. Atlantic U., 1991—; chmn., CEO Ideon Group, Inc., Jacksonville, Fla., 1996—; adj. prof. mgmt. NYU, 1963-65; prof. bus. adminstrn. Fordham U., 1969-75; prof. fin., chmn. dept. Northeastern Ill. U., 1975-78; lectr. to bus. and ednl. groups; bd. dirs. MRFI, Inc., Chgo., Teletech Holding Inc., Denver; bd. dirs., mem. adv. bd. dirs. Nationwide Acceptance Corp., Chgo.; cons. to sec. Dept. Commerce, 1961-66; editor-in-residence U. Oreg., 1992; exec.-in-residence U. Ill., 1991, U. Wis., 1991, U. Toronto, 1992; exec.-in-residence, POHL fellow U. Wyo., 1992; mem. adv. bd. CFO mag., 1991—. Author: Your Future in Securities, 1974, Barron's Guide to Graduate Business Schools, 1977, 9th edit., 1995; contbg. editor: Public Relations Handbook, 1988, Boardroom Reports, 1986—; writer syndicated bus. column., 1964-86. Trustee Bethany Coll.; mem. alumni bd. Columbia U. Sch. Journalism. Comdr. USNR, World War II, ret. Recipient outstanding achievement award Bethany Coll., 1963, 50th anniversary award Sch. Journalism Columbia U., also honors award, 1963, Sch. Journalism Ohio U., 1964, disting. svc. award in investment edn. Nat. Assn. Investment Clubs, 1980, Roalman award Nat. Investor Rels. Inst., 1987. Fellow Pub. Rels. Soc. Am.; mem. Nat. Assn. Bus. Economists, Soc. Am. Bus. Editors and Writers (founder), Fin. Execs. Inst., Arthur Page Soc., Mid-Am. Club, St. Andrew's Country Club, Sigma Delta Chi, Alpha Sigma Phi. Home: 7351 Ballantrae Ct Boca Raton FL 33496-1423 Office: Fla Atlantic U 777 Glades Rd Boca Raton FL 33431-0991 Office: Ideon Group Inc 7596 Centurion Pkwy Jacksonville FL 32256

MILLER, FRANK WILLIAM, legal educator; b. Appleton, Wis., May 15, 1921; s. Frank Paul and Ruth Margaret (Arft) M.; m. Lucille Gloria Rinnan, Sept. 8, 1945; children: Deborah Lynn, Patrica Elizabeth. B.A., U. Wis., 1946, LL.B., 1948, S.J.D., 1954. Bar: Wis. 1948. Mem. faculty Washington U., St. Louis, 1948-91, Coles prof. criminal law and adminstrn., 1962-64, James Carr prof. criminal jurisprudence, 1964-91, prof. emeritus, 1991—; Dan Hopson Disting. prof. So. Ill. U., Carbondale, 1992; summer vis. prof. law U. Ark., 1952, 54, 56, Stetson U., 1955, U. Wis., 1957, U. Tex., 1975, 85; vis. prof. law So. Ill. U. at Carbondale, 1973-74, summers 1976-81; chmn. round table council criminal law Assn. Am. Law Schs., 1961; chmn. Pub. Defender Adv. Com. St. Louis County, 1962. Author: (with A.C. Becht) Factual Causation in Negligence and Strict Liability Cases, 1961, Prosecution: The Decision to Charge a Suspect with a Crime, 1969; editor: (with R.O. Dawson, George E. Dix, Raymond I. Parnas) Criminal Justice Administration, 1976, 4th edit., 1991, (with Dawson, Dix, Parnas) The Police Function, 1982, 5th edit., 1991, Sentencing and The Correctional Process, 1976, The Juvenile Justice Process, 1976, 3d edit., 1985, The Mental Health Process, 1976, Prosecution and Adjudication, 1982, 4th edit., 1991. Served with AUS, 1942-45. Recipient citation for outstanding teaching Washington U. Alumni Fedn., 1965, Washington U. Law Alumni Assn., 1991. Mem. ABA, Am. Law Inst. (Guttmacher award 1977), Order of Coif. Democrat.

MILLER, FREDERICK WILLIAM, publisher, lawyer; b. Milw., Mar. 18, 1912; s. Roy W. and Kathryn (Oehlers) M.; m. Violet Jane Bagley, Mar. 31, 1939. B.A., U. Wis., 1934, LLB, 1936. Bar: Wis. 1936. Assoc. Tenney & Davis, Madison, 1935-36; atty. State of Wis., Madison, 1936-77; pub. The Capital Times Co., Madison, 1979—, also dir.; dir. Madison Newspaper, Inc., 1970—, chmn. bd., 1980—; dir. Evjue Found., Inc., Madison, 1957—. Trustee Evjue Charitable Trust, Madison, 1970—. Mem. Wis. Bar Assn. Clubs: Madison Club, Univ. Club. Home: 2810 Arbor Dr Madison WI 53711-1826 Office: Capital Times Co PO Box 8056 1901 Fish Hatchery Rd Madison WI 53713-1248

MILLER, GARY ALLEN, financial planner; b. Redding, Calif., Nov. 28, 1960; s. Orland Lee and Velma Bernice (Hess) M.; m. Sherry Lee Starr, Nov. 2, 1979 (div. Aug., 1981); 1 child Sharon Danielle; m. Teresa Lynn Rice, June 4, 1983 (div. July 1992); children: Justin, Allen, Chelsea. Chartered fin. cons. cert., Am. Coll., Bryn Mawr, Pa., 1989. Owner, mgr. Miller TV and Electronics, Topeka, Kans., 1982-86; fin. planner Tantillo and Miller, Inc., Topeka, 1986—. Mem. Toastmasters, Million Dollar Round Table. Home: 6446 SW 21st Ter Topeka KS 66614-5605 Office: Tantillo & Miller Inc 3706 SW Topeka Blvd Ste 400 Topeka KS 66609-1239

MILLER, GEORGE DEWITT, JR., lawyer; b. Detroit, Aug. 20, 1928; s. George DeWitt and Eleanor Mary Miller; m. Prudence Brewster Saunders, Dec. 28, 1951; children: Margaret DeWitt, Joy Saunders. BA magna cum laude, Amherst Coll., 1950; JD with distinction, U. Mich., 1953. Bar: Mich. 1953, U.S. Dist. Ct. (so. dist.) Mich. 1953, U.S. Ct. Appeals (6th cir.) 1960, U.S. Tax Ct. 1960. Assoc. Bodman, Longley & Dahling, Detroit, 1957-61, ptnr., 1962—. Trustee, mem. Matilda R. Wilson Fund, 1993—; trustee Maplegrove Ctr./Kingswood Hosp., Henry Ford Health Sys., 1995—. Capt. USAF, 1953-56. Recipient Commendation medal. Mem. ABA, State Bar Mich., Detroit Bar Assn., Detroit Club, Detroit Athletic Club, Orchard Lake Country Club, Order of Coif, Phi Beta Kappa. Episcopalian. Home: 320 Dunston Rd Bloomfield Hills MI 48304-3415 Office: Bodman Longley & Dahling 100 Renaissance Ctr Ste 34 Detroit MI 48243-1003

MILLER, HAROLD ARTHUR, lawyer; b. St. Marie, Ill., Aug. 18, 1922; s. Arthur E. and Luletta (Noé) M.; m. Michele H. Rogivue, Nov. 23, 1947; children: Maurice H., Jan Leland, Marc Richard. BS in Acctg., U. Ill., 1942, JD, 1950. Bar: Ill. 1950, U.S. Dist. Ct. Ill. 1950, U.S. Tax Ct. 1950. Fgn. svc. officer U.S. State Dept., Paris, France, 1945-48; ptnr. Filson, Williamson & Miller, Champaign, Ill., 1950-60, Williamson & Miller, Champaign, 1960-72, Miller & Hendren, Champaign, 1972—; atty. Christie Clinic Assn., Champaign, 1960-88; atty. pub. schs. dists., Champaign & Vermilion Counties, Ill., 1960—; atty. for municipalities in Champaign County, Ill., 1970—. Author: Estate Planning for Doctors, 1961. Bd. dirs., officer Urbana Sch. Dist., 1957-69; chmn., trustee Parkland Coll., Champaign, 1971-91; founding bd. mem. CCDC Found., Champaign-Urbana Ednl. Found., Moore Heart Found., Christie Found.; life mem. PTA. With inf. U.S. Army, 1942-45, ETO. Mem. ABA, Am. Judicature Soc., Ill. and Local Bar Assns., Ill. Trial Lawyers Assn., Alpha Kappa Psi. Presbyterian. Office: Miller & Hendren Attys 30 E Main St # 300 Champaign IL 61820-3629

MILLER, HAROLD LOUIS, real estate developer; b. Chgo., Mar. 28, 1921; s. Louis H. and Minnie (Smith) M.; m. Beatrice Rochell Kraus, Jan. 4, 1950; children: Judith B. Schechtman, Steven A., Robert F. JD, John Marshall Law Sch., 1954. Bar: Ill. 1955, U.S. Supreme Ct. 1959. Co-owner Miller Furniture Co., Chgo., 1939-42; pres. All State Piano Co., Chgo., 1945-54; pvt. practice Chgo., 1955—; founder, CEO First Condominium Devel. Co., Chgo., 1964—; pres. Res. Savs. & Loan, Elmhurst, Il., 1970-73, Concorde Enterprises, Inc., Chgo., 1982—, Harold L. Miller & Co., Chgo., 1990—; adj. prof. U. Ill., Chgo., 1994—; cons. FHA, Washington, 1964. Contbr.: Weinberg on Family Law, 1956. Originator nat. campaign Save A Cambodian Child Now, Chgo., 1981; trustee Beth Emet Synagogue, Evanston, Ill., 1963-70, Beth Hillel Synagogue, Wilmette, Ill., 1952-55. Staff sgt. USAF, 1942-45. Recipient award City of Hope, 1981, State of Israel Bonds, 1982. Mem. ABA, Chgo. Bar Assn., Ill. Bar Assn., B'nai B'rith, Carlton Club. Home: 3750 N Lake Shore Dr # 9C Chicago IL 60601

MILLER, HARRY JOHNSON, hematology educator, oncologist; b. Miles City, Mont., Feb. 19, 1926; s. Harry G. and Harriet R. (Wildish) M.; m. Lucia Taylor, Dec. 31, 1947; children: Sally, Elizabeth, Katherine, Patricia, Blair. BS, Northwestern U., 1950, MD, 1952. Diplomate Am. Bd. Internal Medicine Hematology and Med. Oncology. Instr. Med. Sch. Northwestern U., Chgo., 1959-62, assoc. Med. Sch., 1962-70, asst. prof. Med. Sch., 1970-76, assoc. prof. Med. Sch., 1976-94; attending physician Evanston (Ill.) Hosp., 1959—, head hematology div., 1965-94, pres. profl. staff, 1974-75. Contbr.: (book) Fundamentals of Cancer Management, 1982. Chmn. bd. Unitarian Ch., Evanston, 1976; pres. bd. Hospice of the North Shore, Evanston, 1988-90. Sgt. USAAF, 1944-46. Named Physician of the Yr., Evanston Hosp., 1978, Vol. of the Yr., Northshore mag., 1990. Recipient Henry P. Russe Citation for Exemplary Compassion in Healthcare, Inst. of Med. of Chicago, 1993. Fellow ACP; mem. Am. Soc. Hematology, Am. Fedn. Clin. Rsch., Am. Soc. Clin. Oncology, Internat. Soc. Hematology, Eastern Coop. Oncology Group.

MILLER, HARVEY ALFRED, botanist, educator; b. Sturgis, Mich., Oct. 19, 1928; s. Harry Clifton and Carmen (Sager) M.; m. Donna K. Hall, May 9, 1992; children: Valerie Yvonne, Harry Alfred, Timothy Merk, Tanya Merk. B.S., U. Mich., 1950; M.S., U. Hawaii, 1952; Ph.D., Stanford U., 1957. Instr. botany U. Mass., 1955-56; instr. botany Miami U., 1956-57, asst. prof., 1957-61, assoc. prof., curator herbarium, 1961-67; prof., chmn. program in biology Wash. State U., 1967-69; vis. prof. botany U. Ill., 1969-70; prof., chmn. dept. biol. scis. U. Cen. Fla., 1970-75, prof., 1975-94; v.p. Marine Research Assocs. Ltd., Nassau, 1962-65; assoc. Lotspeich & Assocs., natural systems analysts, Winter Park, Fla., 1979—; botanist U. Mich. Expdn. to Aleutian Islands, 1949-50; prin. investigator Systematic and Phytogeographical Studies Bryophytes of Pacific Islands, NSF, 1959, Miami U. Expdn. to Micronesia, 1960; dir. NSF-Miami U. Expdn. to Micronesia and Philippines, 1965; prin. investigator NSF bryophytes of So. Melanesia, 1983-86; research assoc. Orlando Sci. Ctr., Orlando; vis. prof. U. Guam, 1965; cons. tropical botany, foliage plant patents, also designs for sci. bldgs.; adj. prof. botany Miami U., 1985—, vis. prof. botany, 1994—; field researcher on Alpine meadows in Irian Jaya, 1991, 1992. Author: (with H.O. Whittier and B.A. Whittier) Prodromus Florae Muscorum Polynesiae, 1978, Prodromus Florae Hepaticarum Polynesiae, 1983; Field Guide to Florida Mosses and Liverworts, 1990; editor: Florida Scientist, 1973-78; contbr. articles to sci. jours. Mem. exec. bd. and chem. scholarship and grant selection com. Astronauts Scholarship Found. (formerly Mercury Seven Found.), 1985—. Recipient Acacia Order of Pythagoras; recipient Acacia Nat. award of Merit; Guggenheim fellow, 1958. Fellow AAAS, Linnean Soc. London; mem. Pacific Sci. Assn. (chmn. sci. com. for botany 1975-83), Assn. Tropical Biology, Am. Inst. Biol. Scis., Am. Bryol. Soc. (v.p. 1962-63, pres. 1964-65), Brit. Bryol. Soc., Bot. Soc. Am., Internat. Assn. Plant Taxonomists, Internat. Assn. Bryologists, Mich. Acad. Sci. Arts and Letters, Hawaiian Acad. Sci., Am. Soc. Plant Taxonomists, Fla. Acad. Sci. (exec. sec. 1976-83, pres. 1980), Nordic Bryol. Soc., Acacia, Explorers Club, Sigma Xi, Phi Sigma, Beta Beta Beta. Home: PO Box 6004 Oxford OH 45056-6004 Office: Miami U Dept Botany Oxford OH 45056

MILLER, HUGH THOMAS, computer consultant; b. Indpls., Mar. 22, 1951; s. J. Irwin and Xenia S. Miller; m. Linda Anderson, 1975 (div. 1987); 1 child, Jonathan William; m. Katherine McLeod, 1988 (div. 1995). BA, Yale U., 1976; SM in Mgmt., MIT, 1985. Owner Hugh Miller Bookseller, New Haven, 1976-83, Hugh Miller Cons., New Haven; ind. cons. microcomputers, 1981-85; supr. decision technologies divsn. Electronic Data Sys., Inc., Troy, Mich., 1985-86, supr. product and mfg. engring. divsn., 1986-90; product mgr. Indsl. Bus. Devel. Electronic Data Sys., Inc., Troy, supr. Packard Electric Acct., 1990-92, acct. mgr. GM Chassis Sys. Ctr., 1992-93; with mfg. profl. devel. program Electronic Data Sys., Inc., Troy, Mich., 1993, requirements mgr. Consistent Engring. Environ., 1994—. Editor, ptnr. The Common Table, pub. firm. Bd. dirs. Irwin-Sweeney-Miller Found., Columbus, Ind.,1972—; bd. of govs. MIT Sloan Sch. Mgmt., 1989-94; IT adv. com. Yale U., 1996—. Mem. IEEE, Assn. Computing Machinery, Am. Mensa Ltd. Home: 1173 Lake Angelus Rd Lake Angelus MI 48326-1028 Office: EDS Ste 200 3310 W Big Beaver Rd Troy MI 48084

MILLER, IRVING FRANKLIN, chemical engineering educator, academic administrator; b. N.Y.C., Sept. 27, 1934; s. Sol and Gertrude (Rockkind) M.; m. Baila Hannah Milner, Jan. 28, 1962; children: Eugenia Lynne, Jonathan Mark. BS in Chem. Engring., NYU, 1955; MS, Purdue U., 1956; PhD, U.

Mich., 1960. Research scientist United Aircraft Corp., Hartford, 1959-61; from asst. prof. to prof., head chem. engring. Poly. Inst. Bklyn., 1961-72; prof. bioengring., head bioengring. program U. Ill., Chgo., 1973-79, acting head systems engring. dept., 1978-79, assoc. vice chancellor for research, dean Grad. Coll., 1979-85, prof. chem. engring., head chem. engring., 1986-95, dir. Ctr. for Advanced Edn. and Rsch., 1989-90, dir. Office of Spl. Projects, 1990-92, dir. bioengring. program, 1992-95; dean Coll. Engring. U. Akron, Ohio, 1995—; cons. to industry, also Nat. Acad. Scis., NIH. Editor: Electrochemical Bioscience and Bioengineering, 1973; Contbr. articles profl. jours. Mem. Am. Inst. Chem. Engrs., Am. Chem. Soc., AAAS, Biomed. Engring. Soc., N.Y. Acad Scis. Home: 23299 Shaker Blvd Shaker Heights OH 44122-9999 Office: ASEC 201 Akron OH 44325-3901

MILLER, JANET LOUISE, education educator, consultant; b. Ottumwa, Iowa, Jan. 16, 1945; d. William Otto and Clara Vinese (Hueckendorf) M.; m. Phillip Hunter Fassett, Aug. 31, 1966 (div. July 1974). AB, Grove City (Pa.) Coll., 1966; MA, U. Rochester, N.Y., 1974; PhD, Ohio State U., 1977. Cert. secondary tchr., N.Y. English tchr. Massena (N.Y.) Ctrl. H.S., 1966-72, Wayne Ctrl. H.S., Ontario Ctr., N.Y., 1973-74; rschr. Battelle Mem. Inst., Columbus, Ohio, 1977-79; asst. prof. English Old Dominion U., Norfolk, Va., 1979-82; assoc. prof. St. John's U., Jamaica, N.Y., 1982-88, Hofstra U., Hempstead, N.Y., 1988-92; prof. Nat.-Louis Lab., Beloit, Wis., 1992—; cons. Verona (Wis.) area pub. schs., 1992—; rshr. Coalition of Essential Schs., Providence, R.I., 1992-95. Author: Creating Spaces and Finding Voices: Teachers Collaborating for Empowerment, 1990 (Stessin award 1992, Britton award 1992); contbr. articles to profl. jours. including Ednl. Theory, English Edn., also others. Home: 4144 Hwy 78 N Mt. Horeb WI 53572 Office: Nat Louis Lab 501 Prospect St Beloit WI 53511

MILLER, JOHN R., construction company executive; b. Ft. Jennings, Apr. 6, 1943; s. Carolus J. and Mary M. (Fortman) M.; m. Margaret M. Kehres; children: Michelle, Scott. Grad. high sch., Ottoville, Ohio. Sales mgr. Kahle-Langhals Redi-Mix, Kalida, Ohio, 1962—. Trustee Jennings Twp., Ft. Jennings, Ohio, 1969—; mem. planning commn. Putnam County, Ottawa, Ohio, 1978—; bd. dirs. Emergency Med. Svc., 1973-93, Ft. Jennings Park; mem. Putnam Twp. Assn., 1969—; Ft. Jennings vol. fireman; ctrl. committeeman Putnam County Rep. Ctrl. Mem. Elks. Roman Catholic. Home: 220 Maple Ln Fort Jennings OH 45844

MILLER, KAREN LYNN, clinical social worker; b. Trenton, Mo., Mar. 3, 1956; d. Arthur Leon and JoAnn (Ellis) Sawyer; m. Stuart W. Miller, May 31, 1975; children: Matthew A., and Michael A. AA, Longview C.C., Lees Summit, Mo., 1992; BSW, Ctrl. Mo. State U., 1994; postgrad. in social work, U. Kans., 1994—. Accts. payable clk. Panhandle Ea. Pipeline, Kansas City, Mo., 1975-81; hairdresser The Hairdresser, Independence, Mo., 1984-87; self employed hairdresser Independence, 1987-93, 94-95; case mgr. intern Hope House, Independence, 1994; clin. social worker, intern Heart Am. Family Svcs., Kansas City, 1994—, Western Mo. Mental Health Ctr., Kansas City, 1989—; vol. hotline Hope House Battered Women's Shelter, Independence, 1989—; mem. adv. bd. home econs. dept. Independence Schs., 1990—. Vol. Juvenile Family Ct., Kansas City; sec. Assn. S.W. Students Ctrl. Mo. State U., 1992-93. Mem. Nat. Assn. S.W., Phi Alpha (sec. 1994—), Phi Theta Kappa. Home: 4815 S Kendall Dr Independence MO 64055-5344

MILLER, KEITH LLOYD, lawyer; b. Harvey, N.D., July 27, 1951; s. Lloyd Vernie and Marian A. (Leintz) M.; m. Linda Suzanne Nelson, Aug. 7, 1971; children: Christopher Nelson, Ann Elizabeth. BA, Concordia Coll., Moorhead, Minn., 1972; JD, U. N.D., 1975. Bar: Minn. 1976, U.S. Dist. Ct. Minn. 1976, U.S. Ct. Appeals (8th cir.) 1976, N.D. 1982, U.S. Dist. Ct. N.D. 1982. Assoc. Stefanson, Landberg & Alm, Moorhead, 1976-78; ptnr. Miller, Norman & Assocs., Ltd., Moorhead, 1978—; cons. Nat. Legal Svcs. Corp., Washington, 1984-86; dir. Northwestern Minn. Legal Svcs. Corp., Moorhead, 1981-87, chmn. bd., 1983-86. Bd. dirs. Clay County Dem. Farm Labor Party, Moorhead, 1984-86; advisor Nat. Moot Trial Competition Team Concordia Coll., 1986-96; mem. organizing com., 1st pres. Judge Ronald N. Davies Inn of Ct., 1996—. Mem. ATLA, Minn. Trial Lawyers Assn. (bd. govs. 1987—, treas. 1995—, sec. 1996—, contbr. to jour.), Minn. State Bar Assn. (cert. civil trial specialist), N.D. Trial Lawyers Assn. (lectr. ann. spring seminar 1991), State Bar Assn. N.D., Am. Arbitration Assn. (arbitrator 1980—), Acad. Cert. Trial Lawyers of Minn. Lutheran. Office: Miller Norman & Assocs Ste 201 403 Center Ave Moorhead MN 56560

MILLER, KEVIN D., security executive; b. Chgo., Feb. 7, 1949; s. Donald D. and Anna Agnes (Long) M.; m. Patricia D. Hallberg, Sept. 5, 1995; children: Angela Christy, Jenny Lynne Hallberg, Julie Anne Judd, Suzanne Michelle. BSBA cum laude, Upper Iowa U., 1984. Cert. info. sys. security profl., cert. disaster recovery planner. Detective Dolton (Ill.) Police Dept., 1970-78; systems analyst United Airlines, Chgo., 1978-88; mgr. info. security and bus. continuance Apollo Travel Svcs., Rolling Meadows, Ill., 1989—. Mem. Am. Soc. Indsl. Security, Info. Sys. Security Assn. (past pres. Chgo. chpt.). Home: 236 Skylark Ct Bartlett IL 60103-2024

MILLER, KIMBERLY CLARKE, human services manager; b. Cleve., Apr. 28, 1965; d. Byron William and Diane Lee (Bodovetz) Smith; m. Kenneth J. Magalong, Oct. 20, 1984 (div. Sept. 1986); 1 child, Amanda Lynn; m. Anthony A. Miller, Aug. 31, 1991; stepchildren: Dixie Ann, Anthony V. Grad. high sch., Bainbridge, Ohio. Asst. mgr. Just Kids, Stafford, Va., 1983-85; credit mgr. Lenders Loan, Beauford, S.C., 1986; customer rep. Equisystems, Rancho-Cordova, Calif., 1986-87; administrn. mgr. Occupational Urgent Health Systems, Sacramento, 1987-88; operation supr. Tex. region Occupational Urgent Health Systems, Ft.Worth, 1988-89; Co-author tng. manual, 1989. Co-Author: (book) Training Manuel, 1989. Recipient Art awards, Grahmsville, N.Y., 1981. Democrat. Home: 3218 State Route 82 Lot 120 Mantua OH 44255-9326

MILLER, KRISTIE, writer; b. Chgo., Dec. 9, 1944; d. Maxwell Peter Miller, Jr. and Ruth Elizabeth (McCormick) Tankersley; m. Thomas L. Hawkins, Aug. 11, 1986; m. William Hartshorne Twaddell, June 11, 1966 (div. Dec. 1984); children: William Sanderson, Ellen Johnson. BA, Brown U., 1966; MA, Georgetown U., 1977. Cert. secondary English tchr., Md. Edn. rsch. specialist U.S. Info. Agy., Washington, 1972-73; acting pub. affairs officer U.S. Info. Agy., Maputo, Mozambique, 1980-81; tchr. English various schs., U.S./Arabia/Venezuela/Africa, 1969-84; columnist News Tribune, La Salle, Ill., 1984—; dir. Tribune Co., Chgo. Author: (book) Ruth Hanna McCormick, 1992 (Friends of Lit. award 1992); editor: (book) ESL in Bilingual Education, 1976. Mem. Orgn. of Am. Historians, Am. Hist. Assn., Fgn. Svc. Spouse Oral History (sec. 1990-94). Democrat. Home: 5907 Frazier Lane McClean VA 22101 Office: News Tribune New Tribune 426 Second St La Salle IL 61301

MILLER, LESLIE ADRIENNE, English language educator, poet; b. Medina, Ohio, Oct. 22, 1956; d. Ray Glen and Martha Ann (Ferguson) M. BA, Stephens Coll., Columbia, Mo., 1978; MA, U. Mo., 1980; MFA, U. Iowa, 1982; PhD, U. Houston, 1991. Dir. creative writing Stephens Coll., 1983-87; vis. poet U. Oreg., Eugene, 1991; assoc. prof. English U. St. Thomas, St. Paul, 1991—. Author: (poems) Fortissimo, 1978, No River, 1988, Staying Up for Love, 1990, Ungodliness, 1993; co-author: Hanging on the Sunburned Arm of Some Homeboy, 1982. Mem. MLA, Assoc. Writing Programs, Ohio Libr. Assn., Poets and Writers, Poetry Soc. Am. Home: 168 College Ave W Apt 2 Saint Paul MN 55102-1962 Office: U Saint Thomas 2115 Summit Ave Saint Paul MN 55105-1048

MILLER, MALCOLM HENRY, manufacturing sales executive, real estate developer; b. Elgin, Ill., Feb. 6, 1934; s. Carl Theodore and Alice Lucy (Garbisch) M. BA, U. Wis., 1957; postgrad., Am. Inst. Fgn. Trade, 1961, U. N.Mex., 1963. Sales engr. Fairbanks Morse Corp., Beloit, Wis., 1962; pvt. practice real estate Albuquerque, 1964-75; supt., v.p. Walworth Foundries, Inc., Darien, Wis., 1959-61, exec. v.p. sales, co-owner, 1975—; v.p. sales, co-owner Waukesha Specialty Co., Inc., Darien, 1975—; treas. Fastcast, Inc., Albuquerque, 1993—. Loan advisor, developer Community Assn. for Sr. Housing, Albuquerque, 1967-70; Rep. candidate for state senator N.Mex., 1970; active fin. com. Bernalillo County Reps., N.Mex., 1970-80, Walworth County Reps., Wis., 1976-77. Served to 1st lt. U.S. Army, 1957-59. Mem. Am. Foundrymen's Assn., Dairy Food Industries Supply Assn., Dairy Food Industries Supply Assn. (bd. dirs. 1992-95), Santa Fe Opera Guild, Big Foot Country Club, Nat. "W" Club, Masons, Sigma Alpha Epsilon. Republican. Episcopalian. Home: 223 Fremont St PO Box 37 Walworth WI 53184 Office: Walworth Foundries Inc PO Box 160 Hwy 14 and Hwy 15 Interchange Darien WI 53114

MILLER, MARIE CATHERINE, music educator; b. Manitowoc, Wis., Oct. 5, 1947; d. Winston V. and Betty M. (Stephani) M.; m. Roger Wright, Feb. 24, 1989. MusB, Silver Lake Coll., Manitowoc, Wis., 1974; MusM, Northwestern U., Evanton, Ill., 1976; PhD in Music Edn., Fla. State U., 1990. Cert. music tchr., Wis. Tchr. music Antigo (Wis.) Sch. Sys., 1969-73, Green Bay (Wis.) Schs., 1973-75; asst. prof. music Silver Lake Coll., Manitowoc, 1976-83; instr. music S.E. Mo. State U., Cape Girardeau, 1983-86; assoc. prof. music Emporia (Kans.) State U., 1990-94, assoc. chair music, 1992—, chair divsn. music, 1994—. Author: (with others) Music Materials and Activities, 1992; contbr. articles to profl. jours. inst. adult literacy Emporia Adult Lit. Program, 1991—; adjudication Piano Festivals, Wis., Mo., Kans., Fla., 1970—; chmn. bd. Humane Soc. Flint Hills, Emporia, 1992—; mem. programming com. Emporia Arts Coun., 1994—. Named Outstanding Young Women of Am., 1974. Mem. Kans. Conf. Music Tchrs. Edn. Profs. (program chiar 1992—, treas. 1995—), Music Educators Nat. Conf. (advisor local chpt. 1990—), Music Tchrs. Nat. Conf. (state bd. dirs. 1976-82), Emporia C. of C. (edn. com. 1994—), Pi Kappa Lambda, Sigma Alpha Iota. Office: Emporia State Univ 1200 Commercial Emporia KS 66801

MILLER, MARK, newspaper editor. BA in English, Grinnell Coll., 1976. Mng. editor Crain's Chgo. Bus., 1983-89, editor, 1989-93; dep. mng. editor, columnist Chgo. Sun-Times, 1993—; mem. exec. com. Com. on Fgn. Affairs. Guest radio and TV shows including Chicago Tonight with John Callaway, Sta. WTTW. Office: Chgo Sun Times 401 N Wabash Ave Chicago IL 60611-3532

MILLER, MERTON HOWARD, finance educator; b. Boston, Mass., May 16, 1923; s. Joel L. and Sylvia F. (Starr) M. AB, Harvard U., 1943; PhD, Johns Hopkins U., 1952. With Treasury Dept., 1944-47, Fed. Res. Bd., 1947-49; asst. lectr. London Sch. Econs., 1952; asst. prof., then assoc. prof. Grad. Sch. Indsl. Adminstrn., Carnegie Inst. Tech., Pitts., 1958-61; prof. banking and fin. Grad. Sch. Bus. U. Chgo., 1961—. Co-author: Theory of Finance, 1972, Macroeconomics, 1974, Financial Innovation and Market Volatility, 1991. Recipient Nobel prize in econs., 1990. Fellow Econometric Soc.; mem. Am. Fin. Assn. (pres. 1976), Am. Econ. Assn., Am. Statis. Assn. Office: U Chgo Grad Sch Bus 1101 E 58th St Chicago IL 60637-1511*

MILLER, MICHAEL MICHEL, physician, addiction medicine clinician, health facility administrator, educator; b. Alexandria, La., Nov. 1, 1952; s. Richard Earl Calvit and Virginia (Bowers) M.; m. Kathleen Marie Etlicher, June 4, 1977; children: Andrea Kathleen, Courtney Allyce. BS, Georgetown U., 1972; MD, Tulane U., 1979. Diplomate Am. Bd. Psychiatry and Neurology; cert. of added qualification in addiction psychiatry. Tchr. Holy Savior Menard Ctrl. H.S., Alexandria, 1974-76; resident in psychiatry Med. Coll. Wis., Milw., 1979-81, U. Minn. Hosps. and Clinics, Mpls., 1981-83; fellow in chem. dependency U. Minn., 1982-83; pvt. practice, Eau Claire, Wis., 1983-89; med. dir. Eau Claire Regional Detoxication Ctr., 1983-89; med. dir. Genesis adolescent alcohol and drug treatment program Luther Hosp., Eau Claire, 1987-89; med. dir. Newstart Addiction Medicine Meriter Hosp., Madison, Wis., 1989—, med. dir. Meriter Behavioral Svcs., 1996—; asst. clin. prof. U. Wis. Med. Sch., Eau Claire, 1987-89; asst. clin. prof. dept. family medicine and practice, dept. psychiatry and dept. internal medicine U. Wis., Madison, 1989—; mem. mng. com. Statewide Physicians Health Program, Madison, 1985—. Contbg. author: Addictive Disorders: A Practical Guide to Treatment, 1991, Principles of Addiction Medicine, 1994; contbr. articles to profl. jours. Mem. AMA (del. ho. of dels. 1996—), Am. Psychiat. Assn., Am. Soc. Addiction Medicine (cert. 1986, 94, chmn. reimbursement com. 1990-94, chmn. managed care com. 1994-95, chmn. quality improvement com. 1994—), Am. Acad. Addiction Psychiatry, AMERSA, Wis. Psychiat. Assn. (chair com. on addiction psychiatry 1995—), Wis. Soc. Addiction Medicine (pres. 1993-95), State Med. Soc. Wis. (chair commn. on addictive diseases 1996—). Democrat. Roman Catholic. Office: Meriter Behavioral Svcs Meriter Hosp 309 W Washington Ave Madison WI 53703

MILLER, NANCY ELLEN, computer consultant; b. Detroit, Aug. 30, 1956; d. George Jacob and Charlotte M. (Bobroff) M. BS in Computer and Comm. Sci., U. Mich., 1978; MS in Computer Sci., U. Wis., 1981. Product engr. Ford Motor Co., Dearborn, Mich., 1977; computer programmer Unique Bus. Systems, Inc., Southfield, Mich., 1978; tchg. asst. computer sci. dept. U. Wis., Madison, 1978-82; computer scientist Lister Hill Nat. Ctr. for Biomed Comm. Nat. Libr. Medicine, NIH, Bethesda, Md., 1984-88; knowledge engr. Carnegie Group, Inc., Dearborn, 1989; computer cons. West Bloomfield, Mich., 1993—. Mem. Nat. Abortion and Reproductive Rights Action League, Washington, 1984—, Nat. Women's Polit. Caucus, 1984—, Jewish Fedn. Met. Detroit, 1991—. Recipient Jour. of Am. Soc. for Info. Sci. Best Paper award, 1988. Mem. IEEE Computer Soc., Assn. for Computing Machinery (sec. S.E. Mich. spl. interest group on artificial intelligence 1993-94), Am. Assn. for Artificial Intelligence and Spl. Interest Groups in Mfg. and Bus., Assn. for Logic Programming, U. Wis. Alumni Club (life), U. Mich. Alumni Club (life). Democrat. Jewish. Home and Office: 6220 Village Park Dr #104 West Bloomfield MI 48322

MILLER, PATRICIA LOUISE, state legislator, nurse; b. Bellefontaine, Ohio, July 4, 1936; d. Richard William and Rachel Orpha (Williams) Miller; m. Kenneth Orlan Miller, July 3, 1960; children: Tamara Sue, Matthew Ivan. RN, Meth. Hosp. Sch. Nursing-Indpls., 1957; BS, Ind. U., 1960. Office nurse A.D. Dennison, MD, 1960-61; staff nurse Meth. Hosp., Indpls., 1959, Community Hosp., Indpls., 1958; representative, State of Ind., Dist. 50, Indpls., 1982-83, senator, State of Ind., Dist. 32, Indpls., 1983—, mem. edn. com., 1984-90, health welfare and aging com. 1983-90, labor and pension com. 1983-94, legis. apportionment and elections coms., chmn. interim study com. pub. health and mental health Ind. Gen. Assembly, 1986; chair Senate Environ. Affairs, 1990-92, Health and Environ. Affairs, 1992—; mem. election com., 1992—; mem. budget subcom. Senate Fin. Com., 1995— . Mem. Bd. Edn., Met. Sch. Dist. Warren Twp., 1974-82, pres., 1979-80, 80-81; mem. Warren Twp. Citizens Screening Com. for Sch. Bd. Candidates, 1972-74, 84, Met. Zoning Bd. Appeals, Div. I, appointed mem. City-County Council, 1972-76; bd. dirs. Central Ind. Council on Aging, Indpls., 1977-80; mem. State Bd. of Voc. and Tech. Edn., 1978-82, sec., 1980-82; mem. Gov.'s Select Adv. Commn. for Primary and Secondary Edn., 1983; precinct committeeman Republican Party, 1968-74, ward vice chmn., 1975-78, ward chmn., 1978-85, twp. chmn., 1985-87; vice chmn. Marion County Rep., 1986—; del. Rep. State Conv., 1968, 74, 76, 80, 84, 86, 88, 90, 92, 94, sgt. at arms, 1982, mem. platform com., 1984, 88, 90, 92, co-chmn. Ind. Rep. Platform Com., 1992; del. Rep. Nat. Conv., 1984, alternate del., 1988, Rep. Presdl. Elector Alternate, 1992; active various polit. campaigns; bd. dirs. PTA, 1967-81; pres. Grassy Creek PTA, 1971-72; state del. Ind. PTA, 1978; mem. child care adv. com. Walker Career Center, 1976-80, others; bd. dirs. Ch. Fedn. Greater Indpls., 1979-82, Christian Justice Center, Inc., 1983-85, Gideon Internat. Aux., 1977—; mem. United Meth. Bd. Missions Aux. of Indpls., 1974-80, v.p., 1974-76; bd. dirs. Lucille Raines Residence, Inc., 1977-80; exec. com. S. Ind. Conf. United Meth. Women, 1977-80, lay del. S. Ind. Conf. United Meth. Ch., 1977—, fin. and adminstrn. com., 1979-88, planning and research com., 1980-88, co-chmn. law adv. com., chmn. health and welfare, conf. council ministries, also mem. task force, bd. ordained ministry, also panel, chmn. com. on dist. superintendency, dist. council on ministries; sec. Indpls. S.E. Dist. Council on Ministries, 1977-78, pres., 1982; chmn. council on ministries Cumberland United Meth. Ch., 1969-76; chmn. stewardship com. Old Bethel United Meth. Ch., 1982-85, fin. com., 1982-85, adminstrv. bd., mem. council on ministries, 1981-85; co-chair Evangelism Com., 1994—; jurisdictional del. United Meth. Ch., 1988, 92; alternate del. United Meth. Ch. Gen. Conf., 1988, delegate, 1992; mem. health and human svcs. com. Midwest Legis. Conf., 1995. Recipient Phi Lambda Theta Honor for outstanding contbr. in field of edn., 1976; Woman of the Year, Cumberland Bus. and Profl. Women, 1979; Ind. Voc. Assn. citation award, 1984, others. Mem. Indpls. Dist. Dental Soc. Women's Aux., Ind. Dental Assn. Women's Aux., Am. Dental Assn. Women's Aux., Council State Govt. (intergovtl. affairs com.), Nat. Conf. State Legislatures (health com. vice chmn. 1994—), Warren Twp. Rep. Franklin Rep., Lawrence Rep., Center Twp. Rep., Fall Creek Valley Rep., Marion County Council Rep. Women, Ind. Women's Rep., Indpls. Women's Rep., Ind. Fedn. Rep. Women, Nat. Fedn. Rep. Women, Beech Grove Rep., Perry Twp. Rep. Home: 1041 Muessing Rd Indianapolis IN 46239-9614

MILLER, PATRICIA PALMER, environmental professional; b. Columbus, Ohio, Oct. 4, 1941; d. Dwight Miller and Edith Virginia (Gray) Palmer; m. Michael I. Walling, Aug. 3, 1963 (div. 1979); children: Sabrina Marie, Tristan Corbett Palmer, Rebecca Arabella; m. Robert Page Miller, Mar. 2, 1991. BA with honors, Denison U., 1963. Rsch. assoc. Parke-Davis Pharm. Co., Ann Arbor, Mich., 1963-65; environ scientist Ohio EPA, Columbus, 1979-85, div. chief, 1985-92; mgr. state-wide air quality program Hazardous Substance Rsch. Ctr., Mich. State U., East Lansing, 1992—; tech. transfer specialist Hazardous Waste Rsch. Ctr., Mich. State U., East Lansing, 1992—; cons. in field. Contbr. to profl. publs. Bd. dirs. Youngstown (Ohio) Symphony Orch., 1978-79, Mid-Mich. Tech. Coun., Air Waste Mgmt. Assn. East Ctrl. Sect., 1992—, sec., 1996; adult vol. Boy Scouts Am., Girl Scouts. Leadership fellow Mich. State U., 1996. Mem. Air and Waste Mgmt. Assn. (bd. dirs. Mich. chpt. 1992—), vol. WKAR, Audubon Soc., PEO Sisterhood, State and Territorial Air Pollution Profls. Assn. (funding chmn. 1988-91, pub. freelance writer). Office: Hazardous Substance Rsch A124 Engring Rsch Complex East Lansing MI 48824

MILLER, PATRICK WILLIAM, research administrator, educator; b. Toledo, Sept. 1, 1947; s. Richard William and Mary Olivia (Rinna) M.; m. Jean Ellen Thomas, Apr. 5, 1974; children: Joy, Tatum, Alex. BS in Indstrl. Edn., Bowling Green State U., 1971, MEd in Career Edn. and Tech., 1973; PhD in Indstrl. Tech. Edn., Ohio State U., 1977. Tchr. Montgomery Hills Jr. High Sch., Silver Spring, Md., 1971-72, Rockville (Md.) High Sch., 1973-74; asst. prof. Wayne State U., Detroit, 1977-79; assoc. prof., grad. coord. indstrl. edn. and tech. Western Carolina U., Cullowhee, N.C., 1979-81; assoc prof. U. No. Iowa, Cedar Falls, 1981-86; dir. grad. studies practical arts and vocat.-tech. edn. U. Mo., Columbia, 1986-89; devel. editor Am. Tech. Pubs., Homewood, Ill., 1989-90; proposal mgr. Nat. Opinion Rsch. Ctr. U. Chgo., 1990—; pres. Patrick W. Miller and Assocs., Munster, Ind., 1981—; presenter, advisor and cons. in field. Author: Nonverbal Communication: Its Impact on Teaching and Learning, 1983, Teacher Written Tests: A Guide for Planning, Creating, Administering and Assessing, 1985, Nonverbal Communication: What Resarch Says to the Teacher, 1988, How To Write Tests for Students, 1990; mem. editl. bd. Jour. Indsl. Tchr. Edn., 1981-88, Am. Vocat. Edn. Rsch. Jour., 1981-85, 94—, Tech. Tchr., 1982-84, Jour. Indsl. Tech., 1984—, Jour. Vocat. and Tech. Edn., 1987-90, Human Resource Devel. Quar., 1989—; also articles. Sec. U. No. Iowa United Faculty, Cedar Falls, 1983-84, pres., 1984-86. Lance cpl. USMC, 1966-68, Vietnam. Recipient editl. recognition award Jour. Indsl. Tchr. Edn., 1984, 86, 88; named One of Accomplished Grads. of Coll. Tech., Bowling Green State U., 1995. Mem. ASTD, Am. Ednl. Rsch. Assn., Am. Vocat. Assn., Am. Vocat. Edn. Rsch. Assn., Nat. Assn. Indsl. Tech. (chmn. rsch. grants 1982-87, pres. industry div. 1991-92, chmn. exec. bd. 1992-93, past pres. 1993-94, Leadership award 1992, 93), Nat. Assn. Indsl. and Tech. Tchr. Educators (pres. 1988-89, past pres. 1989-90, trustee 1990-93, Outstanding Svc. award 1988, 90), Nat. Assn. Vocat. Edn. Spl. Needs Pers., Internat. Tech. Edn. Assn., Coun. Tech. Tchr. Edn., Epsilon Pi Tau, Phi Delta Kappa. Office: Univ Chgo Nat Opinion Rsch Ctr 1155 E 60th St Chicago IL 60637-2745

MILLER, PEGGY MCLAREN, management educator; b. Tomahawk, Wis., Jan. 12, 1931; d. Cecil Glenn and Gladys Lucille (Bame) McLaren; m. Richard Irwin Miller, June 25, 1955; children: Joan Marie, Diane Lee, Janine Louise. BS, Iowa State U., 1953; MA, Am. U., 1959; MBA, Rochester Inst. Tech., 1979; PhD, Ohio U., 1987. Instr. Beirut Coll. for Women, 1953-55, U. Ky., Lexington, 1964-66, S.W. Tex. State U., San Marcos, 1981-84; home economist Borden Co., N.Y.C., 1955-58; cons. Consumer Cons., Chgo., Springfield, Ill., 1972-77; sr. mktg. rep. N.Y. State Dept. Agr., Rochester, 1978-79; asst. prof., coord. bus. and mgmt. Keuka Coll., Keuka Park, N.Y., 1979-81; lectr. mgmt. Ohio U., Athens, 1984—. Co-editor: Fifty States Cookbook, 1977; contbr. articles to profl. jours. Mem. Soc. for Advancement of Mgmt. (advisor campus chpt.), Mortar Bd., Phi Kappa Phi. Home: 17 Briarwood Dr Athens OH 45701-1302 Office: Ohio U Copeland Hall Athens OH 45701

MILLER, PHILIP WILLIAM, airport executive; b. Elkhart, Ind., Feb. 5, 1948; s. William Philip and Ruth (Putman) M. BS, USAF Acad., 1971; MBA, U. No. Colo., 1977. Commd. 2d lt. USAF, 1971, advanced through grades to capt., 1975; instr. pilot 49th Tactical Fighter Wing, Alamogordo, N.Mex., 1976-79, King Abdulaziz Air Base, Dhahran, Saudi Arabia, 1979-81; retired, 1981; br. mgr. flight ops. support McDonnell Douglas, Dhahran, 1981-83; owner Miller Enterprises, Denver and Hickory, N.C., 1984-87; pres. Cannon Aviation Inc., Hickory, 1985, Miller Theatres, Inc., Elkhart, 1987-90; owner Main St. Prodn., Inc., Elkhart, 1991-92; mgr. Elkhart Mcpl. Airport, 1992-94; pres. SkyQuest Flight Ctr., Inc., Elkhart, Ind., 1995—; bd. dirs. Elkhart Ctr., Inc. Author ednl. materials. Bd. dirs. Downtown Merchant's Assn., Elkhart, 1987-88; chmn. Elkhart Jazz Festival, 1987-90. Mem. Am. Assn. Airport Execs., Nat. Bus. Aircraft Assn., Exptl. Aircraft Assn., Aircraft Owners and Pilots Assn., Internat. Aerobatic Club, Elks. Republican. Methodist. Office: SkyQuest Flight Ctr Inc 1211 C R 6 West Elkhart IN 46514

MILLER, ROBERT ARTHUR, state supreme court chief justice; b. Aberdeen, S.D., Aug. 28, 1939; s. Edward Louis and Bertha Leone (Hitchcox) M.; m. Shirlee Ann Schlim, Sept. 5, 1964; children: Catherine Sue, Scott Edward, David Alan, Gerri Elizabeth, Robert Charles. BSBA, U. S.D., 1961, JD, 1963. Asst. atty. gen. State of S.D., Pierre, 1963-65; pvt. practice law Philip, S.D., 1965-71; state atty. Haakon County, Philip, 1965-71; city atty. City of Philip, 1965-71; judge State of S.D. (6th cir.), Pierre, 1971-86, presiding judge, 1975-86; justice S.D. Supreme Ct., Pierre, 1986—, now chief justice; bd. dirs. Nat. Conf. of Chief Justices; trustee S.D. Retirement Sys., Pierre, 1974-85, chmn., 1982-85; mem. faculty S.D. Law Enforcement Tng. Acad., 1975-85. Mem. S.D. State Crime Commn., 1979-86; mem. adv. commn. S.D. Sch. for the Deaf, 1983-85, Communications Svcs. to Deaf, 1990—; cts. counselor S.D. Boy's State, 1986—. Mem. State Bar of S.D., S.D. Judges' Assn. (pres. 1974-75). Roman Catholic. Lodge: Elks. Office: SD Supreme Ct 500 E Capitol Ave Pierre SD 57501-5070

MILLER, ROBERT HASKINS, retired state chief justice; b. Columbus, Ohio, Mar. 3, 1919; s. George L. and Marian Alice (Haskins) M.; m. Audene Fausett, Mar. 14, 1943; children: Stephen F., Thomas G., David W., Stacey Ann (dec.). A.B., Kans. U., 1940, LL.B., 1942; grad., Nat. Coll. State Trial Judges, Phila., 1967. Bar: Kans. 1943. Practice in Paola, 1946-60; judge 6th Jud. Dist. Kans., Paola, 1961-69; U.S. magistrate Kans. Dist., Kansas City, 1969-75; justice Kans. Supreme Ct., Topeka, 1975-88, chief justice, 1988-90, ret., 1990; chmn. Kans. Jud. Coun., 1987-88. Contbg. author: Pattern (Civil Jury) Instructions for Kansas, 2d edit, 1969. Served with AUS, 1942-46. Mem. Kans. Bar Assn., Wyandotte County Bar Assn., Shawnee County Bar Assn., Am. Legion, Phi Gamma Delta, Phi Delta Phi. Presbyterian. Office: Supreme Ct Kans-Jud Ctr 301 SW 10th Ave Topeka KS 66612-1502

MILLER, ROBERT HUGH, lawyer; b. Phila., Feb. 16, 1941; s. Joseph Harold and Beatrice Gertrude Miller; m. Bonnie Deborah Moss, Mar. 27, 1977; 1 son, Jason Scott. B.S., Pa. State U., 1962; LL.B., Dickinson Sch. Law, 1965; postgrad. in labor law Georgetown U., 1965-67. Bar: Calif. 1974, Pa. 1965. Atty., Dept. Labor, Washington, 1965-67; field atty. Regions 6 and 21, NLRB, Pitts. and Los Angeles, 1967-71, supervisory atty. Region 21, 1971-77, regional atty. Region 20, San Francisco, 1977-82, regional dir. Region 20, 1982—. Served with Pa. Air N.G., 1966-71. Mem. ABA (labor law sect.). Author articles. Office: Ware & Freidenrich 400 Hamilton Ave Palo Alto CA 94301-1809

MILLER, ROBERT MICHAEL, publishing executive; children: Jeremy Richard, Eric Robert. AAS in Graphic Design Tech., Invor Hills C.C., 1994. Account mgr. Webb Pub. Co., Maxwell Group, St. Paul, 1977-88; account exec. Russ Moore Assocs., Eagn, Minn., 1988-89; pres. Jeric Pubs., Inc., Inver Grove Heights, Minn., 1989-91; pub., owner Jeric Pub. Group, Inc., South Saint Paul, Minn., 1992-95; cons., bd. dirs. Auto Ctr. St. Paul, 1990-91, J&E Constrn., Inver Grove Heights, 1990-92. Pub., account mgr. Explore Minn. Calendar, 1988; pub., account exec. Sr.'s Choice Mag., 1989; pub. There is No November, 1991. Office: Jeric Pub Inc PO Box 108 South Saint Paul MN 55075-0108

MILLER, ROBERT RUSH, retired biology educator; b. Colorado Springs, Colo.; s. Ralph Gifford and Lucy Bond (Morgan) M.; m. Frances Voorhees Hubbs, Oct. 11, 1940 (dec.); children: Frances, Gifford, Roger, Lawrence, Benjamin. AB, U. Calif., Berkeley, 1938; MA, U. Mich., PhD. Assoc. curator of fishes Smithsonian Inst., Washington, 1944-48; assoc. curator of fishes U. Mich., Ann Arbor, 1948-59, asst. prof. zoology, 1948-53, assoc. prof. zoology, 1954-59, prof. zoology, 1960-86, prof. emeritus of biology, 1986—, curator emeritus of fishes, 1986—; cons. on endangered species, Anheuser-Busch Cos., St. Louis, 1988. Co-author: (book) Ichthyology, 1962, 2d edit., 1977. Skywatch warden Civilian Def. Agy., Ann Arbor, 1942-43. Guggenheim fellow Guggenheim Found., Smithsonian Inst., 1973-74. Fellow AAAS; mem. Am. Fisheries Soc. (award of excellence), Ariz.-Nev. Acad. of Sci. (hon.), Soc. Mexicana de Zoologia (hon.), ASIH (Gibbs Meml. award 1994), Am. Soc. Ichthyologists (pres. 1950-55). Office: Mus of Zoology Univ Mich 1109 Geddes Ave Ann Arbor MI 48109-1049

MILLER, ROBIN J., computer engineer; b. Peoria, Ill., July 14, 1959; m. Katie L. Kroenlein; 2 children. Attended, Ill. Ctrl. Coll., 1977-80. Candidate for Ill. State Senate. Address: PO Box 5424 Peoria IL 61601*

MILLER, ROGER L., financial planner; b. Cin., Feb. 22, 1949. BS, Miami U., 1971. CFP. Sales rep. Prudential Ins., Cin., 1973-74; v.p. Fin. Planning Cons. Inc., Middletown, Ohio, 1974-84, Integrated Profl. Fin. Planning, Middletown, 1984—. Republican. Baptist. Office: Integrated Profl Fin Planni 1046 Summitt Dr Middletown OH 45042-3400

MILLER, RONALD CARL, dermatologist, educator; b. Saginaw, Mich., Aug. 17, 1946; s. Fred Walter Miller and Henrietta (Pabst) Dubay; m. Diane Kay Berger, Dec. 10, 1966; children: Matthew, Michelle, Jolee. Student, Saginaw Valley State Coll., 1972-77, Mich. State U., 1977-84. Pattern maker GM, Saginaw, 1966-82; intern Flint (Mich.) Osteo. Hosp., 1984-85; gen. practice physician Deckerville, Mich., 1985-90; preceptorship Am. Osteo. Coll. Dermatology, 1990-93; pvt. practice dermatologist Lansing, Mich., 1993—; asst. clin. prof. Mich. State U., East Lansing, 1988—. Mem. Am. Osteo. Coll. Dermatology (bd. cert.), Am. Osteo. Assn., Ea. Osteo. Med. Soc. (pres. 1987-88), Sanilac County Med. Soc. (pres. 1988-89). Lutheran. Home: 3215 Cardiff Ct Lansing MI 48911 Office: 1515 Lake Lansing Lansing MI

MILLER, ROY RAYMOND, optician, ocularist; b. Delta, Ohio, Sept. 20, 1929; s. Roy Draton and Ethel Bernice (Shaffer) M.; m. Evelyn Frances Birsen, Jan. 16, 1954; children: Stephanie, Christopher, Neil Benjamin. Student, Burnham High Sch., Sylvania, Ohio. Lic. Optician. Optician Miller Opticians Inc., Lima, Ohio, 1961-88; pres. Miller Opticians and Miller, Lima, 1961-88, Artificial Eye Lab., Toledo, 1961-88; lic. ocularist Miller Artificial Eye Lab., Toledo; appointed to Ohio Optician and Oculorist Bd., Gov. Vonivoich. Lectr. Nat. Convention, 1978, 1987. Candidate U.S. Congress, Lima 1984, zoning appeals bd. Shawnee Twp., 1980-88, lic. bd. Ohio Optical Dispensing Bd., 1979-85. Cpl. US Army, 1951-52. Fellow Nat. Acad. Opticianry (Contbn. to Edn. of Opticianry award 1995); mem. Am. Soc. Ocularists, Opticians Assn. Am. (past bd. dirs., Optician of Yr. 1995), Guild Prescription Opticians of Am. (bd. dirs.), Optician Assn. Ohio (past pres.), Sertoma (pres. 1983-84), Kiwanis (pres. 1973-74). Republican. Roman Catholic. Office: Miller Opticians Inc 825 W Market St Lima OH 45805-2742

MILLER, SCOTT JOSEPH, software executive; b. Milw., Feb. 15, 1964; s. James Russell and Gloria (Welter) M.; m. Jeanette Luczko, Aug. 9, 1986; children: Nicholas Scott, Maxine Loren. AA in Applied Scis., Milw. Sch. Engring., 1984, BS in Elec. Engring. Tech., 1986. MIS dir. ArcRon Ltd., Menomonee Falls, Wis., 1986; application engr. ICOM, Inc., West Allis, Wis., 1986-88, support engr., 1988-90; prodn. mgr., 1990-91; pres. WM Investments, Inc., Milw., 1992-93; ops. mgr. ICOM, Inc., West Allis, 1991-94, ICOM, Inc./Rockwell Software Inc., 1994—, Rockwell Software Inc., Milw., 1994—. Mem. IEEE, Consumer Electronics Soc., Computer Soc., Engring. Mgmt. Soc. Home: 98N 9435 W Huntington Dr Mequon WI 53092

MILLER, SHELBY ALEXANDER, chemical engineer, educator; b. Louisville, July 9, 1914; s. George Walter and Stella Katherine (Cralle) M.; m. Jean Adele Danielson, Dec. 26, 1939 (div. May 1948); 1 son, Shelby Carlton; m. Doreen Adare Kennedy, May 29, 1952 (dec. Feb. 1971). B.S., U. Louisville, 1935; Ph.D., U. Minn., 1943. Registered profl. engr., Del., Kans., N.Y. Asst. chemist Corhart Refractories Co., Louisville, 1935-36; teaching, rsch. asst. chem. engring. U. Minn., Mpls., 1935-39; devel. engr., rsch. chem. engr. E.I. duPont de Nemours & Co., Inc., Wilmington, Del., 1940-46; assoc. prof. chem. engring. U. Kan., Lawrence, 1946-50; prof. U. Kan., 1950-55; Fulbright prof. chem. engring. King's Coll. Durham U., Newcastle-upon-Tyne, Eng., 1952-53; prof., chem. engring. U. Rochester, 1955-69, chmn., 1955-68; assoc. lab. dir. Argonne (Ill.) Nat. Lab., 1969-74; dir. Ctr. Ednl. Affairs, 1969-79, sr. chem. engr., 1969-84; ret. sr. chem. engr., cons., 1984—; vis. prof. chem. engring. U. Calif., Berkeley, 1967-68; vis. prof. U. of Philippines, Quezon City, 1986. Editor: Chem. Engring. Edn. Quar, 1965-67; sect. editor: Perry's Chem. Engring. Handbook, 5th edit., 1973, 6th edit., 1984; contbr. articles to tech., profl. jours. Sec. Kans. Bd. Engring. Examiners, 1954-55; mem. adv. com. on tng. Internat. Atomic Energy Agy., 1975-79; treas. Lawrence (Kans.) League for Practice Democracy, 1950-52; sec. Argonne Credit Union, 1994—. Fellow AAAS, Am. Inst. Chemists, Am. Inst. Chem. Engrs. (past chmn. Kansas City sect.); mem. Am. Chem. Soc. (past chmn. Rochester sect.), Soc. Chem. Industry, Am. Soc. Engring. Edn. (past chmn. grad. studies div.), Am. Nuclear Soc., Filtration Soc., Triangle, Sigma Xi, Sigma Tau, Phi Lambda Upsilon, Tau Beta Pi, Alpha Chi Sigma. Presbyn. Home: 825 63rd St Downers Grove IL 60516-1962 Office: Argonne Nat Lab Chem Tech Divsn Argonne IL 60439

MILLER, STANLEY MANFRED, systems engineer; b. Hopewell, N.J., Nov. 29, 1956. BSME, Wentworth Inst. Tech., 1985; postgrad., U. Ill., 1995—. Lead sys. engr. Graco Inc., Franklin Park, Ill., 1986—; rep. 3-A Dairy Equip., Dairy & Food Industry Assn. Supply, Inc., Rockville, Md., 1988—. Patentee bin evacuation sys. Episcopalian. Office: Graco Inc 9451 Belmont Ave Franklin Park IL 60131-2811

MILLER, STEPHEN BRYAN, social worker, marriage counselor; b. Clare, Mich., Aug. 1, 1951; s. Bryan David and Shirley Jean (Dull) M.; m. Nancy Marie Brandau, Aug. 24, 1974; children: Jennifer Marie, Adam Bryan. AA, Ferris State U., Big Rapids, Mich., 1972; BS, Western Mich. U., 1974, MSW, 1978. Lic. marriage counselor. Social worker Ionia (Mich.) Intermediate Schs., 1974-76, Sanilac County Dept. Social Svcs., Sandusky, Mich., 1976; clin. social worker Caro (Mich.) Regional Mental Health Ctr., 1978; sch. social worker Tuscola Intermediate Schs., Caro, 1978-81, Allegan (Mich.) County Schs., 1981-83, Thornapple-Kellogg Pub. Schs., Middleville, Mich., 1983—; field instr. Western Mich. U., Kalamazoo, 1988—; pvt. marriage counselor, Kentwood, Mich., 1989—; family and marriage cons. John Knox Presbyn. Ch., Grand Rapids, Mich., 1989—. Chairperson Kentwood Activities Com., 1988-89; deacon John Knox Presbyn. Ch., Grand Rapids, 1987-90. Mem. NASW, Acad. Cert. Social Workers (cert.), Mich. Nat. Edn. Assn. (region IX del. 1986-88), Mich. Assn. Tchrs. of Emotionally Disturbed Children. Democrat. Home: 5642 Juanita Dr SE Grand Rapids MI 49508-6427 Office: Thornapple-Kellogg Schs 509 W Main St Middleville MI 49333-9772

MILLER, SUSAN KAY, nursing administrator; b. Souix City, Iowa, June 1, 1959; d. Roger Burnett and Verna May (Cirks) M.; children: Gregory Lee, Michael Jon. BA in Nursing, Gustavus Adolphus Coll., 1981. RN, Minn. RN student nurse tng., oncology St. Lukes Hosp., Duluth, Minn., 1981-83; RN, nurse mgr. Seldon Nelson, DO, Williamston, Mich., 1983-85; staff RN Noran Neurological Clinic, Fridley, Minn., 1985-87; RN, clin. ops. mgr. Associated Med. Cons., Coon Rapids, Minn., 1987—, asst. adminstr., 1993-94; adminstr. Met. Cardiology COns., Mpls., 1994—; RN advisor North Suburban Home Infusion Therapy, Coon Rapids, 1991-93. Mem. Am. Assn. Office Nurses, Upper Midwest Ambulatory Nursing Adminstrs. Group, Am. Heart Assn. Anoka Inc., Minn. Med. Group Mgmt. Assn., Med. Group Mgmt. Assn. Lutheran. Office: Met Cardiology Cons 3960 Coon Rapids Blvd # 206 Minneapolis MN 55433

MILLER, SUZANNE KAY, corporate educator; b. Greensburg, Pa., June 21, 1951. BS in Elem. Edn., Clarion U., 1973; MEd, Pa. State U., 1976, PhD, 1985. Tchr. Cranberry Sch., Seneca, Pa., 1973-78; sch. adminstr. Valley Sch., Ligonier, Pa., 1978-83; instr., instrl. designer Pa. State U., University Park, 1983-85; supr. edn. devel. Alcoa, Alcoa Center, Pa., 1985-88; mgr. engring. and quality tng. Alcoa, Pitts., 1988-91, mgr. Alcoa edn., 1992-95; dir. corp. edn. Bandag, Inc., Muscatine, Iowa, 1996—, v.p. tng. & devel. Mem. Internat. Soc. for Performance Improvement, Am. Soc. for Tng. and Devel., Pa. State Alumni Assn. (bd. dirs., chair publicity 1995), Muscatine C. of C. (bd. dirs., pres. 1995—). Home: 1 Chestnut Dr Blue Grass IA 52726 Office: Bandag Inc 2905 N Hwy 61 Muscatine IA 52761

MILLER, TAMARA DEDRA, psychologist; b. Cleve., Jan. 13, 1961; d. Taswill Taylor and Ethel (Midgett) M.; stepd. Gwendolyn (Hicks) M. BA in Psychology, Wittenberg U., 1982; D in Psychology, Wright State U., 1987. Lic. clin. psychologist, Ohio. Chief psychol. svc. USAF, Altus, Okla., 1987-89; chief psychol. testing USAF, Dayton, Ohio, 1989-92; dir. PTSD program Dept. VA, Dayton, 1992—; clin. prof. Wright State U., Dayton, 1992—; cons. Jackson County Youth, Altus, 1987-89, Ctr. for Retardation, Altus, 1987-89; adj. prof. Ctrl. State U., Wilberforce, 1991—; mem. panel Women's Fed. Program, Dayton, 1991; clin. advisor Les Femmes Concerned Citizens for Cancer, Dayton, 1992—. Consulting editor: Professional Psychology: Research and Practice, 1994. Capt. USAF, 1986-89. Mem. Nat. Coun. Negro Women Inc., VA Psychologists, Delta Sigma Theta. Home: 5670 Olive Tree Dr Dayton OH 45426-1313 Office: Dept VA Affairs Med Ctr 4100 E 3rd St Dayton OH 45403-2244

MILLER, TERRY ALAN, chemistry educator; b. Girard, Kans., Dec. 18, 1943; s. Dwight D. Miller and Rachel E. (Detjen) Beltram; m. Barbara Hoffmann, July 16, 1966; children: Brian, Stuart. BA, U. Kans., 1965; PhD, Cambridge (Eng.) U., 1968. Disting. tech. staff Bell Telephone Labs, 1968-84; vis. asst. prof. Princeton U., 1968-71; vis. lectr. Stanford U., 1972; vis. fgn. scholar Inst. Molecular Sci., Okazaki, Japan, summer 1983; Ohio eminent scholar, prof. chemistry Ohio State U., Columbus, 1984—; chair Molecular Spectroscopy Symposium, Columbus, 1992—. Mem. editl. bd. Jour. Chem. Physics, 1978-81, Jour. Molecular Spectroscopy, 1982-87, Laser Chemistry, 1986—, Rev. of Sci. Instruments, 1986-89, Jour. Phys. Chemistry, 1989-95, Jour. Optical Soc. Am., 1989-95, Chemtracts, 1989-90, Ann. Revs. Phys. Chemistry, 1989-94, Jour. Molecular Structure, 1996—; contbr. more than 250 articles to profl. jours. Marshall fellow Brit. Govt., 1965-67, NSF fellow, 1967-68; William F. Meggard Awd., 1993, Optical Soc. Am. Fellow Optical Soc. Am. (Meggars award 1993), Am. Phys. Soc.; mem. Am. Chem. Soc. (councilor), Coblentz Soc. (Bomen-Michaelson award 1995). Office: Ohio State U 120 W 18th Ave Columbus OH 43210-1106

MILLER, TERRY ELLIS, ethnomusicologist; b. Dover, Ohio, Feb. 19, 1945; s. Max Troendley and Anna Lou (Ellis) M.; m. Elizabeth Limkemann, May 29, 1966 (div. 1982); children: Sonia Elizabeth, Esther; m. Sara Margaret Stone Miller, May 26, 1985. BM, Coll. of Wooster, Ohio, 1967; MM, Ind. U., 1971, PhD, 1976. Instr. to asst. prof. to assoc. prof. to prof. Kent State U., Ohio, 1975—; co-dir. Ctr. for Study of World Musics, Kent, Ohio, 1981—. Author: Traditional Music of the Lao, 1985, Folk Music in America: A Reference Guide, 1986, An Introduction to Playing the Kaen, 1980, A History of Siamese Music, 1995. Panelist Ohio Arts Coun., Columbus, Ohio, 1983-87, 96. Fellow Fgn. Area Ford Found., Thailand, 1972-74, U. Edinburgh, 1988, Thailand, 1982. Mem. Soc. Ethnomusicology (treas. 1995—), The Siam Soc., Soc. Asian Music (pres. 1994—), Coll. Music Soc., The Sonneck Soc., Am. Musicol. Soc. Office: School of Music Kent State Univ Kent OH 44242

MILLER, THERESA ANN, management consultant; b. St. Charles, Mo., Apr. 1, 1945; d. Ford Emmett Wilkins and Alice Mary (Faerber) Wilkins Burrow. Cert. secretarial, N.E. Mo. State Tchrs. Coll., 1964; AA, St. Louis Community Coll., 1976; BSBA, Lindenwood Coll., 1983, MBA, 1990; MBA Cert. Internat. Bus., 1991. With McDonnell Douglas Aerospace-East, St. Louis, 1985—, supr. master files dept., 1984—, sect. mgr. office svcs., 1987—, auditor self-governance audit program, 1991—, sr. analyst command media, 1993-95, sr. analyst, investigations/corp. human resource, 1995—. Mem. NAFE, Nat. Notary Assn., Lindenwood Coll. Alumni Club (past pres. St. Charles chpt.), Mgmt. Club McDonnell Douglas Aerospace. Roman Catholic. Home: 15618 Coventry Farm Dr Chesterfield MO 63017-7386 Office: McDonnell Douglas Aerospace PO Box 516 Saint Louis MO 63166-0516

MILLER, THOMAS B., educational administrator; b. Grand Rapids, Mich., June 2, 1933; s. Charles Henry Miller and Edith A. (Aldrich-Cleland) Vachon; m. Carol Unger, Aug. 3, 1957 (div. Sept. 1970); children: Tom, Tammie, Michael, Michelle; m. Leona Faye Strecker Baier, July 29, 1972; children: Judy, Janice, Joan. AA, Grand Rapids Jr. Coll., 1957; BA, Hope Coll., 1959; MA, U. Nebr., 1981. Tchr. history Fennville (Mich.) High Sch., 1959-60, Jackson (Mich.) High Sch., 1960-61, Coopersville (Mich.) High Sch., 1961-65; spl. agt. FBI, nationwide, 1965-85; dir. Nebr. Law Enforcement Tng. Ctr., Grand Island, 1985—; class counselor new agts. tng. FBI Acad., Quantico, Va., 1982-83; tng. coord. FBI, 1983-85. Contbr. articles to profl. jours. Sgt. USMC, 1952-55, Korea. Mem. Am. Soc. Law Enforcement Trainers, Police Officers Assn. Nebr., Nebr. Sheriff's Assn., Nebr. Drug Policy Bd., Nebr. Soc. Former FBI Agts., Assn. Chiefs of Police, Internat. Assn. Dirs. Law Enforcement Standards and Tng., Riverside Country Club (bd. dirs.), Saddle Club, Rotary (bd. dirs.), Am. Legion (Cert. of Commendation North Platte chpt. 1973), Optimist (Law Enforcement award North Platte chpt. 1973). Lutheran. Office: Nebr Law Enforcement Ctr 3600 N Academy Rd Grand Island NE 68801-9200

MILLER, THOMAS J., state attorney general; b. Dubuque, Iowa, Aug. 11, 1944; s. Elmer John and Betty Maude (Kross) M.; m. Linda Cottington, Jan. 10, 1981; 1 child, Matthew. B.A., Loras Coll., Dubuque, 1966; J.D., Harvard U., 1969. Bar: Iowa bar 1969. With VISTA, Balt., 1969-70; legis. asst. to U.S. rep.John C. Culver, 1970-71; legal edn. dir. Balt. Legal Aid Bur., also mem. part-time faculty U. Md. Sch. Law, 1971-73; pvt. practice McGregor, Iowa, 1973-78; city atty. McGregor, 1975-78, Marquette, Iowa; atty. gen. of Iowa, 1979-91, 95—; ptnr. Faegre & Benson, Des Moines, 1991-95. Pres. 2d Dist. New Democratic Club, Balt., 1972. Mem. Am. Bar Assn., Iowa Bar Assn., Common Cause. Roman Catholic. Office: Office of the Atty Gen Hoover State Office Bldg 2nd Fl Des Moines IA 50319

MILLER, THOMAS MICHAEL, physical therapist, educator; b. Elgin, Ill., Oct. 26, 1959; s. William J. and Viola M. (Adamowski) M.; m. Kirsten Marlene, Aydt, Mar. 20, 1982; children: Rita, Christopher, Matthew, Naomi. BA in Physiology, So. Ill. U., 1981; BA in Phys. Therapy, Northwestern U., Chgo., 1983. Registered phys. therapist, Ill. Coord. phys. therapy Burnham Hosp., Champaign, Ill., 1983-88; mgr. phys. therapy St. Joseph Meml. Hosp., Murphysboro, Ill., 1988-89, Carbondale (Ill.) Clinic, 1989-93, Delta/Tip of Ill., Carterville, 1993—; adj. faculty So. Ill. U., Carbondale, 1994. Mem. Am. Phys. Therapy Assn. (orthopedic sect.). Republican. Presbyterian. Office: Delta Rehab Clinic One Tip Dr Carterville IL 62918

MILLER, THOMAS MILTON, banker; b. Corydon, Ind., Mar. 2, 1930; s. R. Earl and Catherine (Hudson) M.; m. Kathryn Janet Owens, Aug. 28, 1954; children: Kimberleigh Kathryn, Thomas Milton, Jennifer Allen. B.S. in Bus, Ind. U., 1952; postgrad., U. Wis. Grad. Sch. Banking, 1961. With Ind. Nat. Bank, Indpls., 1954—; head Ind. div. Ind. Nat. Bank, 1964-68, sr. v.p., head met., 1968-71, exec. v.p., head comml. banking div., 1971-76, pres., from 1976, chmn., chief exec. officer, 1979—; chmn. INB Nat. Bank, INB Fin. Corp.; dir. State Life Ins. Co., Indpls. Water Co., Boehringer Mannheim U.S. Holdings, Inc. Mem. exec. com. Indpls. Conv. and Visitors Assn., chmn. bd.; mem. adv. bd. Ind. U.-Purdue U., Indpls.; dir., mem. exec. com. Ind. U. Found. Served to 1st lt. AUS, 1952-54. Mem. Am. Bankers Assn., Res. and City Bankers, Assn. Bank Holdings Cos. (dir.), Ind. C. of C. (dir., mem. exec. com.), Indpls. C. of C., Ind. U. Alumni Assn., Ind. Soc. Chgo., Ind. U. Varsity Club, Meridian Hills Country Club (Indpls.), Economic Club (Indpls., past pres.), Masons, Sigma Chi. Republican. Methodist. Home: 10691 Winterwood Carmel IN 46032-8258 Office: NBD Indiana Inc 1 Indiana Sq Ste 501 Indianapolis IN 46204-2004

MILLER, TICE LEWIS, theatre educator; b. Lexington, Nebr., Aug. 11, 1938; s. Tice M. and Thyra V. (Lewis) M.; m. Carren J. Miller, Sept. 6, 1963; children: Dane, Graeme. BA, Kearney State Coll., 1960; MA, U. Nebr., 1961; PhD, U. Ill., 1968. Instr. Kansas City (Mo.) Jr. Coll., 1961-62; asst. prof. U. West Fla., Pensacola, 1968-72; from assoc prof. to prof., chair U. Nebr., Lincoln, 1972—; mem. commn. on accreditation Nat. Assn. Schs. of Theatre. Author: Bohemians and Critics, 1981; co-editor: Shakespeare Around the Globe, 1986, Cambridge Guide World Theatre, 1988 (Hewitt award 1989), Cambridge Guide American Theatre, 1993, The American Stage, 1993. Bd. dirs., ATHE, 1987-89, Lincoln Midwest Ballet Co., 1989-91, Theatre Arts for Youth, Lincoln, 1975-76, Pensacola Theatre, 1970-71. Lt. comdr. USNR 1963-65. Am. Theatre fellow. Fellow Great Plains Assn.; mem. Am. Soc. for Theatre Rsch. Democrat. Unitarian. Office: U Nebr Dept Theatre Arts Danc Lincoln NE 68588

MILLER, TOM C., mechanical engineer; b. Cin., Jan. 13, 1951. B, U. Cin., 1974. Chief engr. Cin. Gear Co., 1974—. Vol. local ch. activities. Office: Cincinnati Gear Co 5657 Wooster Pike Cincinnati OH 45227-4120

MILLER, TRUDY JOYCE, retail executive, publisher; b. Chgo.; d. Leonard John and Evelyn Grace (Winter) Clarke; m. William Robert Miller, Oct. 8, 1960; children: William, James, Brian, Catherine. Student, Marycrest Coll., 1959; student in Interior Design, Art, Prairie State Coll., 1975; student in Publishing, Northwestern U., 1983. Reporter, feature writer Hammond (Ind.) Times, 1967-73, Village Press, South Holland, Ill., 1973-75; owner The Emporium, Glenwood, Ill., 1975-76, Second Thoughts, Chicago Heights, Ill., 1976—; pres. retail outlet Second Thoughts Inc., Chicago Heights, 1984—; editor Second Thoughts Publishing, Chicago Heights, 1982—; bd. dir. Fashion Consortium, Chgo., 1984-86; speaker in field. Author: 1983 Guide to Suburban Resale and Thrift Shops, Where to Find Everything For Practically Nothing in Chicagoland, 1984, 86. Bd. dirs. econ. devel. Thornton Coll., South Holland, 1983-85; mem. small bus. adv. bd. Prairie State Coll., Chicago Heights, 1984-85; fashion show coordinator Operation ABLE Past 50 Job Fair, Chicago Heights, 1985. Mem. Nat. Assn. Resale and Thrift Shops (founder, bd. dirs., sec. 1984-86, pres. 1986-93, exec. dir. 1993-94, editor newsletter 1987-94, coord. 1st, 2d, 3d and 4t h ann. confs. 1988-90), Internat. Assn. Ind. Pubs., Chgo. Women in Pub., Nat. Assn. Women Bus. Owners, South Suburban Assn. Commerce and Industry, Women in Mgmt., So. Suburban Network (bd. dirs., editor newsletter 1984-85), Toastmasters (v.p. 1984-85). Roman Catholic. Office: Second Thoughts Inc 153 Halsted Chicago Heights IL 60411-1249

MILLER, VALERIE LYNN, transportation executive; b. Independence, Mo., Mar. 10, 1948; d. Arthur Stewart and Mary Genevieve (Hill) Kistler; m. David Harrison Miller, June 13, 1970; children: Ian Harrison, Whitney Stewart. BS in Home Econs., U. Mo., 1970. County home economist U. Mo. Ext., Ray County, Mo., 1975-79; substitute tchr. Richmond (Mo.) RXVI Schs., 1980-83; exec. dir. Ray County Transp., Richmond, 1987—; seminar presenter Mo. Met. Planning Orgn. conf., Columbia, 1994, Mo. Assn. for Developmental Disabilities, Columbia, 1991; legis. advocat4e for rural transp. Mo. Pub. Transp. Assn., Jefferson City, 1991—. Treas., grant adminstr. Light House Presch. for Exceptional Chidlren, Wood Heights, Mo., 1979-84; trustee United Meth. Ch., Richmond, 1988-94; mem. steering com. Youth Job Corp, Ray County, 1994—; Mem. sch. bd., v.p. Richmond RXVI Schs., 1987-94; cmty. rep. Mo. Valley Human Resources/Head Start, Marshall, 1994—. Mem. Mo. Pub. Transit Assn. (bd. dirs., v.p. 1989—), Cmty. Transp. Assn. Am. (Mo. state del. 1994—), Mid. Am. Regional Coun. (bd. dirs., spl. transp. adv. com., Ray county rep. 1989—, pub. transp. task force 1994-95). Home: 216 Park Ave Richmond MO 64085 Office: Ray County Transp 201 E Lexington Richmond MO 64085

MILLER, WAYNE CLAYTON, student services assistant director; b. Columbus, Ohio, Feb. 23, 1949; s. Eugene H. and Beulah M. (Stoll) M. BA, Owosso Coll., 1971; MA, Mich. State U., 1979. Mgr. adminstrv. svcs. John Wesley Coll., Owosso, Mich., 1972-75, instr., social sci., 1975-78, dir., career planning, 1978-79; acad. advisor Spring Arbor (Mich.) Coll., 1979-81, instr., history, 1979-81; acad. counselor Franklin U., Columbus, 1981-83, asst. dir. acad. advising, 1983-85, dir., acad. advising, 1985-92, instr. Film Appreciation, 1985—; advisor Franklin U. Student Senate, Columbus, 1982-84; inst. creative activities program Ohio State U., Columbus, 1990—; discussion panelist Educable TV-25 World Film Classics series, 1990—; juror social issues category The Columbus Internat. Film and Video Festival, 1994, chair edn. category, 1995, 96; mem. spkrs. bur. Franklin U. Editor: (newsletter) New Directions, 1985-91; assoc. editor: Movies on Media Handbook. Bd. trustees Film Coun. of Greater Columbus; co-host: Columbus Museum of Art Film series, 1996. Named one of Outstanding Young Men in Am., 1982, 85. Mem. Nat. Acad. Advising Assn. (cert. of merit award 1986, Outstanding Instnl. Advising award 1994), Nat. Film Soc. (life), Am. Film Inst., Ohio Coll. Pers. Assn., Nat. Euchre Players Assn. (dir. adminstrn.), Columbus Kiwanis (chair career guidance com.). Home: 2729 Brittany Oaks Blvd Hilliard OH 43026-8575 Office: Franklin U 201 S Grant Ave Columbus OH 43215-5301

MILLER, WILLIAM ALVIN, clergyman, author; b. Pitts., Jan. 1, 1931; s. Christ William and Anna Ernestine (Wilhelm) M.; m. Marilyn Mae Miller, Aug. 8, 1953; children: Mark William, Eric Michael. BA, Capital U., 1953; MDiv, Luth. Theol. Sem., Columbus, Ohio, 1957; MST, Andover Newton Theol. Sch., Newton Centre, Mass., 1958, D of Ministry, 1974. Ordained to ministry Luth. Ch.; lic. marriage & family therapist, Minn. Pastor St. James Luth. Ch., Balt., 1958-66; chaplain Fairview Hosp., Mpls., 1966-73, dir. dept. religion & health, 1973-87; instr. Fairview Sch. Nursing, Mpls., 1967-75, Luther Northwestern Theol. Sem., St. Paul, 1973-85; pres. Woodland Pub. Co., Wayzata, Minn., 1979—; dir. Woodland Pastoral Assocs., Mpls., 1987—; assoc. pastor Cen. Luth. Ch., Mpls., 1989-94; chair bd. dirs. Luth. Social Svcs. Md., Balt., 1963-65; adminstr. Dialogue 88, Mpls., 1987-88. Author: Why Do Christians Break Down?, 1973, Big Kids' Mother Goose, 1976, When Going to Pieces Holds You Together, 1976, You Count, You Really Do!, 1976, Mid Life, New Life, 1978, Conversations, 1980, Make Friends With Your Shadow, 1981, Prayers at Mid Point, 1983, The Joy of Feeling Good, 1986, Your Golden Shadow, 1989, 91, Meeting the Shadow, 1991; assoc. editor Jour. Pastoral Care, Decatur, Ga., 1984-88; contbr. articles to profl. jours. Chaplain, Jr. C. of C., Randallstown, Md., 1962-64; bd. dirs. Am. Protestant Health Assn., Schaumburg, Ill., 1983-89. Fellow Coll. Chaplains (pres. 1985-87), Assn. Mental Health Clergy (Anton T. Boisen award 1989); mem. Assn. Clin. Pastoral Edn. (supr.), Am. Assn. Marriage & Family Therapy. Home and Office: 2005 Xanthus Ln N Minneapolis MN 55447-2053

MILLER, WILLIAM PAUL, psychologist; b. Elyria, Ohio, Nov. 15, 1943; s. John Paul and Madalene Helen (Schultheis) M.; m. Karen Ellen Muetzel, July 17, 1971; children: Carson, Colin. BA in Psychology, Ohio State U., 1965; MEd in Sch. Psychology, Kent State U., 1971. Lic. psychologist, Ohio. Psychologist Mentor (Ohio) Schs., 1970-71; sch. psychologist Perkins Local Schs., Sandusky, Ohio, 1971—; instr. psychology Tiffin (Ohio) U., 1987—. Mem. Mental Health Bd. of Seneca, Sandusky and Wyandot Counties, Tiffin, Ohio, 1986-88. Mem. Ohio Sch. Psychologists Assn., Seneca Stargazers Club. Lodges: Lions, Masons. Home: 38 E Cherry Ave Tiffin OH 44883-3407 Office: Perkins Local Schs 1210 E Bogart Rd Sandusky OH 44870-6411

MILLER, WORTH ROBERT, history educator; b. Tucson, Sept. 19, 1943; s. Worth Franklin and Vena (Wood) M. BA, U. Tex., 1971; MA, Trinity U., 1977; PhD, U. Okla., 1984. Instr. U. Okla., Norman, 1984-85; vis. asst. prof. East Tex. State U., Commerce, 1985-86; asst. prof. Southwest Mo. State U., Springfield, 1987-90, assoc. prof., 1990-95, prof. history, 1995—; vis. asst. prof. Tex. A&M U., Coll. Sta., 1986-87; conv. coord. program dir. Thirteenth Mid-Am. Conf. on History, 1991, Sventeenth Conf., 1995; presenter in field. Author: Oklahoma Populism: A History of the People's Party in the Oklahoma Territory, 1987; author: (with others) American Populism, 1994, The Gilded Age: Essays on the Origins of Modern America, 1996; co-editor: A List of References for the History of the Farmers' Alliance and Populist Party, 1989; contbr. articles to scholarly jours. including Kansas History: A Journal of the Ctrl. Plains, Jour. of Southern History, Chronicles of Okla., Jour. of Urban History, Locus: Regional and Local History of the Americas.; contbr. 9 biographies to Handbook of Tex., 1986. Recipient Faculty Achievement award for Excellence in Rsch. Southwest

Mo. State U., 1991-92. Office: Southwest Mo State U 901 S National Springfield MO 65804

MILLHOLLEN, GARY LLOYD, geology educator; b. Ft. Benning, Ga., Oct. 14, 1941; s. Lloyd F. and Dorothy F. (Huggins) M.; m. Anne Sheila Mertl, June 25, 1978; children: Emily Louise, Michael Alexander. BS, U. Oreg., 1963, MA, 1965; PhD, Pa. State U., 1970. Grad. asst. U. Oreg., Eugene, 1963-65, Pa. State U., University Park, 1965-70; rsch. assoc. U. Chgo., 1970-71; asst. prof. U. S.C., Columbia, 1971-74; rsch. assoc. Purdue U., West Lafayette, Ind., 1974-75, asst. prof., 1975-78; assoc. prof. Ft. Hays (Kans.) State U., 1978-92, prof., 1992—; cons. in field. Mem. Am. Geophys. Union, Nat. Assn. Geoscience Tchrs., Geol. Soc. Am., Mineral Soc. Am., Kans. Acad. Scis. Home: 1303 Steven Dr Hays KS 67601-2629 Office: Ft Hays State U 600 Park St Hays KS 67601-4099

MILLIGAN, AMANDA LEIGH, marketing executive, editor; b. Columbia, S.C., July 21, 1975; d. Larry and Marji Milligan. Student, U. Ala., 1993—. Editl. classified asst. Press-Rep Newspapers, St. Charles, Ill., 1994; student life editor The Crimson White, Tuscaloosa, Ala., 1995; mktg. intern Crain's Chgo. Bus., 1995, 96. Buford Boone Meml. scholar, 1995. Mem. Soc. Profl. Journalists (pres. 1996—), Advt. Fedn., Gamma Beta Phi.

MILLIGAN, ROBERT LEE, JR., computer company executive; b. Evanston, Ill., Apr. 4, 1934; s. Robert L. and Alice (Connell) M. BS, Northwestern U., 1958; m. Susan A. Woodrow, Mar. 23, 1957; children: William, Bonnie, Thomas, Robert III. Account rep. IBM, Chgo., 1957-66; sr. cons. L.B. Knight & Assocs., Chgo., 1966-68; v.p. mktg. Trans Union Systems Corp., Chgo., 1968-73; sr. v.p. sales mktg., sec. Systems Mgmt. Inc., Rosemont, Ill., 1973-87, dir., 1980-87; pres., CEO, owner Target Data, Inc., Northbrook, Ill., 1987; pres. CEO Wireless Spectrum Tech., Inc., Northbrook, Ill., 1993—; mng. dir. L. William Teweles & Co., 1996—; treas. Systems Mgmt. Inc. Svc. Corp., 1981-84; dir. Nanofast, Inc., Chgo., 1982—. Div. mgr. North Suburban YMCA Bldg. Fund, 1967; area chmn. Northfield Twp. Rep. Party, 1965-71. Bd. dirs. United Fund, Glenview, Ill., 1967-69, Robert R. McCormick Chgo. Boys Club, 1974—; pres. Glenview Amateur Hockey Assn., 1974-79, bd. mgrs., 1982-86; gen. mgr. Glenbrook South High Sch. Hockey Club, 1973-78. With AUS, 1953-55. Mem. Data Processing Mgmt. Assn., Assn. for Info. and Image Mgmt., Chgo. High Tech. Assn., Info. Industry Coun. of Met. Chgo., Consumer Credit Assn. (bd. dir., sec. 1969-70), Cellular Telecomm. Industry Assn., Personal Comm. Industry Assn., Telecomms. Industry Assn., Winforum, Phi Kappa Psi. Presbyterian. Clubs: Northwestern (bd. dir. 1973-75) (Chgo.); Glenview (Ill.). Home: 1450 Lawrence Ln Northbrook IL 60062-4704 Office: Wireless Spectrum Tech Inc PO Box 1417 Northbrook IL 60065-1417

MILLION, KENNETH RHEA, management consultant; b. Trenton, Ohio, July 3, 1939; s. Clara (Poff) Gardner; divorced; 1 child, Kimberley Rhea Stang. BSBA, U. Cin., 1963. With human resources mgmt. dept. Bendix Corp., Hamilton, Ohio, 1962-65, Cin., 1965-69; dir. pers. Lunkenheimer Co., Cin., 1969-73; v.p. human resources Clopay Corp., Cin., 1973-75; pres. Mgmt. Performance Inc., Cin., 1975-78; pres., owner Million & Assocs., Inc., Cin., 1978—. Internat. amb. People to People and Am. Soc. Pers. Adminstrn., 59 countries. Mem. Kiwanis (v.p. Cin. 1985-86). Republican. Home: 1412 Two Garfield Pl Cincinnati OH 45202 Office: 1831 Carew Tower Cincinnati OH 45202

MILLON, DELECTA GAY, nursing educator; b. Flint, Mich., Aug. 4, 1943; d. Rudolph Albert Spaleny and Odessa Mae (Bergeron) Kelley; divorced; children: Daniel Lawrence, Christopher Matthew. ADN, Flint Community Jr. Coll., 1963; BS in Edn. and Human Svcs., U. Detroit, 1981; MA in Classroom Teaching, Mich. State U., 1986, cert. in vocat. edn., 1986; postgrad., Mary Grove Coll. RN, Mich.; lic. emergency med. tech.; cert. emergency med. technician instr.-coord., firefighter I. Nurse McLaren Gen. Hosp., Flint, 1963-64, Flint Osteo. Hosp., 1974-76; tchr. Mott Adult High Sch., 1971-75, Flint Comm. Schs., 1974—; occupational nurse GM, 1986—; evaluator emergency med. tech. practical exam. State of Mich., nurse's assisting cert. exam. Vol. tchr. Mundy Twp. Fire Dept., Swartz Creek, Mich., 1986—. Mem. Soc. Mich. Emergency Med. Technician Instrs. and Coords. (sec. 1980-87, outstanding contbn. award 1987). Roman Catholic. Office: Genesee Area Skill Ctr G-5081 Torrey Rd Flint MI 48507

MILLOY, FRANK JOSEPH, JR., surgeon; b. Phoenix, June 26, 1924; s. Frank Joseph and Ola (McCabe) M.; BS, Notre Dame U., 1946; MS, Northwestern U., 1949, M.D., 1947. Intern, Cook County Hosp., Chgo., 1947-49, resident, 1953-57; practice medicine, specializing in surgery, Lake Forest, Ill., 1958—; asso. attending staff Presbyn.-St. Lukes Hosp.; attending staff Cook County Hosp.; mem. staff U. Ill. Rsch. Hosp.; clin. asso. prof. surgery, U. Ill. Med. Sch.; asso. prof. surgery Rush Med. Sch. Cons. West Side Vet. Hosp. Served as apprentice seaman USNR, 1943-45; lt. M.C., USNR, 1950-52; PTO. Diplomate Am. Bd. Surgery and Thoracic Surgery. Mem. A.C.S., Chgo. Surg. Soc., Internat. Soc. Surgery, Am. Coll. Chest Physicians, Soc. Thoracic Surgeons, Phi Beta Pi. Clubs: Metropolitan, University (Chgo.). Home: 574 Jackson Ave Glencoe IL 60022-2036

MILLS, CARL RHETT, linguist, educator; b. Hillsboro, Oreg., May 5, 1942; s. John LeRoy and Phyllis Elaine (Christener) M.; m. Judith Anne Golly, Dec. 18, 1968; children: Megan Elaine, Jessica Lee. AAS, Columbia Basin Coll., 1967; BA with honors, Cen. Wash. State Coll., 1969; DA, U. Oreg., 1972, PhD, 1975. Instr. U. Cin., 1975-76, asst. prof. English, 1976-81, assoc. prof. English, 1981—; mem. planning com. Evergreen State Coll., Olympia, Wash., 1968-70; cons. Am. U. in Cairo, Egypt, 1982-83, Sirkin, Penales and Mezibov, Cin., 1987-88; prof. English Inst., Istanbul, Turkey, summer, 1983, Estonian Bus. Sch., Tallinn, Estonia, 1995. Author: American Grammar, 1990; contbr. articles to profl. jours. Sgt. USMC, 1961-67. Danforth Found. fellow, 1969, Woodrow Wilson Found. fellow 1971; Fulbright grantee Troms, Norway, 1977-78, Cairo, 1982-83. Mem. AAAS, Linguistic Soc. of Am., Linguistic Assn. Can. and the U.S., Smithsonian Assocs., Southeastern Conf. on Linguistics. Democrat. Home: 7800 Diven Rd Hillsboro OH 45133-7969 Office: U Cin Dept English ML 069 Cincinnati OH 45221-0069

MILLS, CRAIG J., chemical engineer; b. Dennison, Iowa, June 16, 1963. Electronic assembly Electrosound Equipment Co., Council Bluffs, Iowa, 1984-87; planning engr. Radio Engring., Omaha, 1987-92; supr. Spectronics Corp., Lincoln, 1992—. Office: Spectronics Corp 4645 Hartley St Lincoln NE 68504-1652

MILLS, LOIS JEAN, company executive, former legislative aide, former education educator; b. Chgo., Oct. 20, 1939; d. Martin J. and Annabelle M. (Hrabik) Rademacher; m. Frederick V. Mills, Dec. 1, 1974; children: Todd, Susan, Randal, Merre, Mollie, Michael, Mark (dec.). BS in Edn., Ill. State U., Normal, 1962, MS in Edn., 1969. Lectr. elem. curriculum Ill. State U.; in-svc. advisor for elem., gifted, critical thinking and study skills, coop. learning Title I State Bd. Edn., Springfield, Ill.; elem. tchr., supr. Metcalf Lab. Sch. Ill. State U.; legis. aide to Asst. Majority Leader Senator John Maitland, Jr., Ill. Gen. Assembly, 1991-95; pres., ptnr. Mills Design Assocs.; mem. state rep. Dan Rutherford's house task force for statute repeal, adv. roundtable, legis. task force for cmty. residential svcs. deaf adults; campaign coord. Asst. Majority Leader Senator John Maitland, Jr.; county campaign coord. for Ill. Comptroller Loleta Didrickson. Contbr. articles to profl. jours. Pres. Leadership Ill.; past pres. governing bd. Lake Bloomington Assn.; mem. mgmt. com. McLean County 21st Century commn., commr. McLean County Regional Planning cmmn. (vice chair 1994-95); bd. govs. Ill. Lincoln Excellence in Pub. Svc. Series, other civic activities. Recipient Exemplary Tchr. awards Ill. State U. Student Elem. Edn. Bd., Women of Distinction award YWCA of McLean County. Mem. NAFE, Ill. State U. Alumni Assn. (bd. dirs., past pres.), McLean County Rep. Women's Club (past pres.), Ill. Rep. Committeewoman's Roundtable, Ill. Fedn. Rep. Women, Nat. Fedn. Rep. Women, Internat. Platform Assn. Home: K-162 Lake Bloomington RR 2 Box 60A Hudson IL 61748-9414

MILLS, NANCY ANNE, elementary education educator; b. Madisonville, Ky., Oct. 2, 1937; d. Leslie Owen and Ruby A. (Baker) Hawkins; m. Orton Leroy Mills, May 11, 1957; children: Charles Leroy, Roy Leslie. BS in Edn., Ind. U., South Bend, 1970, MS in Edn., 1972; Ednl. Specialist dergree, Ind. U., 1978. Cert. elem. tchr., Ind. Tchr. elem. South Bend Schs., 1972—; gifted cadre' Purdue U-For Ind., Lafayette, 1988—; presenter workshops; cons. econ. edn. Chmn. new ch. com. Nazarene Ch., South Bend, 1990; supr. students with Student Exch., France, 1991-95. Named Woman of Yr., Profl. and Bus. Womans Club, 1989; Inst. for Chem. Edn. grantee, 1989. Mem. Ind. Coun. Econ. Edn. (cons. 1987—, Tchr. of Yr. for State of Ind. 1992), Delta Kappa Gamma. Home: 16320 Wellington Pky Granger IN 46530-8309 Office: Muessel Sch 1213 California Ave South Bend IN 46628-2701

MILLS, PETER RICHARD, advertising executive; b. Nanango, Queensland, Australia, Mar. 28, 1939; s. Frederick Richard and Muriel Estelle (Fischer) M.; m. Nicole Poulin, July 2, 1982; children: Duncan, David, Alexander, Maxine. Student, York U., Toronto, 1964-65. Copy/contact Jackson Wain Publicity Ltd., Brisbane, Australia, 1957-60; copywriter T. Eaton Co., Toronto, Can., 1960-62; bus. mgr. Southam Publs. Inc., Toronto, 1962-66; account exec. J. Walter Thompson, Vancouver, Toronto, 1966-70; gen. mgr. J. Walter Thompson, Montreal, Can., 1970-75; chief oper. office J. Walter Thompson, Toronto, Can., 1975-79; gen. mgr. J. Walter Thompson, N.Y.C., 1979-82; chmn., chief exec. officer J. Walter Thompson, Australia, 1982-88; pres., chief exec. officer Comcore/BBDO, Toronto, Can., 1986-91; pres., No. Am. div. BBDO Worldwide Inc., Southfield, Mich., 1991-93; chmn., pres., CEO Roy Ross Comms. Inc., Bloomfield Hills, Mich., 1993—. Mem. Nat. Yacht Club, Toronto. Office: Roy Ross Comms Inc 100 Bloomfield Hills Pky Bloomfield Hills MI 48304-2949*

MILLS, RICHARD HENRY, federal judge; b. Beardstown, Ill., July 19, 1929; s. Myron Epler and Helen Christine (Greve) M.; m. Rachel Ann Keagle, June 16, 1962; children: Jonathan K., Daniel Cass. BA, Ill. Coll., 1951; JD, Mercer U., 1957; LLM, U. Va., 1982. Bar: Ill. 1957, U.S. Dist. Ct. Ill. 1958, U.S. Ct. Appeals 1959, U.S. Ct. Mil. Appeals 1963, U.S. Supreme Ct. 1963. Legal advisor Ill. Youth Commn., 1958-60; state's atty. Cass County, Virginia, Ill., 1960-64; judge Ill. 8th Jud. Cir., Virginia, 1966-76, Ill. 4th Dist. Appellate Ct., Springfield, Ill., 1976-85, U.S. Dist. Ct. (cen. dist.) Ill., Springfield, 1985—; adj. prof. So. Ill. U. Sch. Medicine, 1985—; mem. adv. bd. Nat. Inst. Corrections, Washington, 1984-88, Ill. Supreme Ct. Rules Com., Chgo., 1963-85. Contbr. articles to profl. jours. Pres. Abraham Lincoln coun. Boy Scouts Am., 1978-80. With U.S. Army, 1952-54, Korea, col. res.; maj. gen. Ill. Militia. Recipient George Washington Honor medal Freedoms Found., 1969, 73, 75, 82, Disting. Eagle Scout Boy Scouts Am., 1985. Fellow Am. Bar Found.; mem. ABA (joint com. profl. sanctions), Ill. Bar Assn., Chgo. Bar Assn., Cass County Bar Assn. (pres. 1962-64, 75-76), Sangamon County Bar Assn., 7th Cir. Bar Assn., Am. Law Inst., Fed. Judges Assn., Army and Navy Club (Washington), Sangamo Club, Masons (33 degree). Republican. Home: 2112 Augusta Dr Springfield IL 62704-3103 Office: US Dist Ct 319 US Courthouse Springfield IL 62701

MILLS, RILLA DEAN, university administrator, consultant; b. Mt. Pleasant, Iowa, Dec. 16, 1942; s. Chester Jimmie and Leora Mae (Riley) M.; m. Sue Veranne Cornick, June 6, 1965; children—Jason Cornick, Jesse Nelson. Student, Talladega Coll., 1964; B.A., U. Iowa, 1965; A.M., U. Mich., 1967; Ph.D., U. Ill., 1981. Editor The Daily Iowan, Iowa City, 1963-64; reporter The Evening Sun, Balt., 1967-69; Moscow and Washington corr. The Sun, Balt., 1969-75; instr. U. Miss., Oxford, 1976; asst. prof., lectr. U. Ill., Urbana, 1976-79; lectr., assoc. prof. Calif. State U.-Fullerton, 1979-83; dir. Sch. Journalism Pa. State U., University Park, 1983—; cons. various newspapers. Contbr. articles to popular and scholarly jours. Gannett teaching fellow, Ind. U., 1977; adminstrv. fellow Columbia U., 1985. Mem. Assn. for Edn. in Journalism and Mass Communication, Speech Communication Assn., Phi Kappa Phi. Home: 640 Royal Cir State College PA 16801-6459

MILLSAP, BARBARA ANN, clinical social worker; b. Detroit, June 15, 1940; d. John Edward and Irene Julia (Turowski) Wojtylo; m. Claude Millsap, Dec. 14, 1974. BS in Social Work, Mich. State U., 1963; MSW, Wayne State U., 1966. Cert. social worker. Clinician Northeast Guidance Ctr., Detroit, 1966-73, Cabin Fever Clinic, Anchorage, 1975-76; clinician Anchorage Community Mental Health Ctr., 1976-79, supr. adult svcs., 1979-82; social worker Bloomfield (Mich.) Hills Sch. Dist., 1986—. Mem. NASW, Soc. Clin. Social Workers, Mich. Sch. Social Workers Assn. Home: 3284 Schoolhouse Dr Waterford MI 48329-4331 Office: Bloomfield Hills Sch Dist 4200 Andover Rd Bloomfield Hills MI 48302-2000

MILNE, ROBERT DAVID, investment management company executive; b. East Grand Rapids, Mich., Dec. 28, 1930; s. Robert Kenneth and Alice Elfrieda (Youngberg) M.; m. Alma Jean Zimmerman, Dec. 15, 1960; children: R. John, Thomas D., Ruth J., Mary E. Jamba. BA, Baldwin-Wallace Coll., Berea, Ohio, 1952; JD, Cleve. State U., 1957. Analyst, Boyd, Watterson & Co., Cleve., 1952-54, portfolio mgr., 1954-79; pres. Duff and Phelps Investment Mgmt. Co., Cleve., 1979—, pres., CEO Duff & Phelps Selected Utilities Inc., 1987—. Editor: Investment Values in a Dynamic World, 1974. Assoc. editor Fin. Analysts Jour., 1966-83. Served with USAF, 1949-50. Mem. Inst. Chartered Fin. Analysts (pres. 1974-75, C. Stewart Sheppard award 1978), Cleve. Soc. Security Analysts (pres. 1962-63), Greater Cleve. Bar Assn. Clubs: Union, Print of Cleve. (treas. 1991—). Avocation: jogging. Home: 4455 Valley Forge Dr Cleveland OH 44126-2826 Office: Duff & Phelps Utilities Income 55 E Monroe St Ste 3800 Chicago IL 60603*

MILOSAVLJEVIC, ALEKSANDAR DUŠAN, computer scientist; b. Banja Luka, Yugoslavia, Apr. 12, 1961; s. Dusan and Vera Milosavljevic; m. Aysen Kutly, Aug. 4, 1990 (div. Nov. 1991). Diploma in Elec. Engring., Belgrade (Yugoslavia) U., 1984; MS in Computer Sci., Santa Clara U., 1986; PhD in Computer Sci., U. Calif., Santa Cruz, 1990. Scientist, engr. Linus Pauling Inst., Palo Alto, Calif., 1990-92; asst. scientist Argonne (Ill.) Nat. Lab., 1992—. Contbr. articles to profl. jours. Mem. IEEE, Am. Assn. for Artificial Intelligence, Biomatrix Soc. Christian Orthodox. Home: 300 W 60th St Apt B506 Westmont IL 60559 Office: Argonne Nat Lab 9700 S Cass Ave Bldg 202 Argonne IL 60439

MILOSCIA, STEVE, cement company foreman; b. Biloxi, Miss., Sept. 28, 1959; m. Beverly Miloscia; 7 children. BS, USAF Acad., 1982. Rep. candidate for U.S. House 3rd Dist., Mo., 1996. With USAF, 1982-88. Roman Catholic. Office: PO Box 453 Barnhart MO 63012*

MILSTEIN, ROBERT ARLEN, fund development administrator, consultant; b. Tucson, May 17, 1949; s. Victor Mills and Rebecca (Rosen) M.; m. Ruth Milstein, July 19, 1981; 2 daughters. Student, Atlantic Coll., 1966; BA in Edn., U. Ariz., 1971; MA, Ariz. State U., 1975; student, U. Tenn., 1976-77. Sales mgr. Tandy Corp., Chgo., 1978-85; dir. customer svc. U.S. and Can. London House/McMillan Sch. Pub. House, Rosemont, Ill., 1985-92; dir. devel./religion, cmty. health Advocate Health Care, Oakbrook, Ill., 1985-92; sr. assoc. Nat. Com to Prevent Child Abuse, Chgo., 1995—. Bd. dirs. Citizens Police Oversight Com., Oak Park, Ill., 1995—; trustee, endowment Oak Park Temple, 1995—; bd. adv. Child Sexual Abuse Treatment Ctr., 1992-95, South Side Health Care Project, Chgo., 1992-93, Interfaith Coun. for the Homeless, Chgo., 1994. Named Vol. of Yr., Ill. Profl. Soc. Abuse of Children, 1994. Mem. Phi Kappa Phi. Democrat. Jewish. Office: Nat Com Prevent Child Abuse 332 S Mich Ave Ste 1600 Chicago IL 60604

MILTON, LEONHARDA LYNN, elementary and secondary school educator; b. Minneota, Minn., Apr. 7, 1924; d. John and Mathilde (Bockman) Hinderlie; m. John Ronald Milton, Aug. 3, 1946; 1 child, Nanci. BA, U. Minn., 1949. Cert. tchr., Minn., Colo., S.D. Visual art tchr. Humboldt High Sch., St. Paul, 1949-57, Vermillion (S.D.) Middle Sch., 1972—; tchr. Kuns Miller Jr. High Sch., Denver, 1960-61; occupational therapist N.D. State Hosp., Jamestown, 1959-60. Exhibited prin. works in numerous shows in Minn., N.D., S.D. Mem. Nat. Art Edn. Assn. (State Art Educator award 1983), S.D. Art Educators (pres. 1980-83), S.D. Alliance for Art Edn. (pres. 1985-88). Democrat. Lutheran. Home: 630 Thomas St Vermillion SD 57069-3631 Office: Vermillion Mid Sch Princeton St Vermillion SD 57069

MIMS, ALBERT, safety consultant, executive, educator; b. Keyser, Ky., Feb. 28, 1924; s. Albert and lelia F. Mims; m. margie L. Kolbe, Apr. 12, 1985; children: John Albert, Rebecca Fern. AB, U. N.C., 1953, MS, 1954; MBA, U. Cin., 1962, PhD, 1973. Profl. safet engr.; cert. safety profl., hazard control mgr., safety specialist, safety mgr., safety exec. Safety engr. Procter & Gamble, Cin., 1957-72; assoc. prof. indsl. safety U. Wis., 1973—; safety cons., CEO, chm. bd. A. Mims Assocs., Madison, Wis., 1972—; active hazardous materials tng. program for compliance officers U.S. Dept. Labor OSHA Tng. Inst., 1973-74; expert witness in field. Mem. editorial bd. Profl. Safety, 1979-84, World Safety jour., 1989—; presented papers to local, nat., and internat. groups on occupational safety; contbr. articles to profl. jours. Active United Appeal/Way, Little League baseball, football, basketball, Dan Beard coun. Boy Scouts Am., 1962-67. With USN Air Corps, 1942-46. Mem. Am. Soc. Safety Engrs. (visitation team mem. for accreditation of colls. and univs.), Am. Indsl. Hygiene Assn., Nat. Safety Mgmt. Soc., Human Factors Soc., System Safety Soc., World Safety Orgn., Nat. Safety Coun. (exec. com., gen. chmn. chem. sect. 1979-80, Disting. Svc. Safety award 1989). Republican. Office: PO Box 2102 Appleton WI 54913-2102

MINCKLER, LEON SHERWOOD, forestry and conservation educator, author; b. New Milford, N.Y., May 7, 1906; s. Walter Harmon and Eva Lena (Williams) M.; m. Althea Mae Singleton, Mar. 31, 1929 (dec. 1946); children: L. Sherwood, C. Christine, E. Maxine; m. Edith Adair Springer, Mar. 7, 1947; children: Sandra Gayle, Walter David; adopted children: William, Jean. BS in Forestry, N.Y. State Coll. Forestry, 1928, PhD in Plant Physiology, 1935. Jr. forester U.S. Forest Svc., Kans., Okla., Tex., 1935-36; rsch. forester U.S. Forest Svc., Asheville, N.C., 1936-45; rsch. ctr. leader U.S. Forest Svc., Buckingham, Va., 1945-46; forester U.S. Forest Svc., Carbondale, Ill., 1946-68; prof. agr. Va. Poly. Forestry Coll., Blacksburg, Va., 1968-70; adj. prof. forestry SUNY, Syracuse, 1970-77; cons., writer Blacksburg, 1977-91; adj. prof. So. Ill. Forestry Coll., Carbondale, 1991—. Author: Woodland Ecology, 1975; contbr. over 170 articles to profl. jours. Recipient 50 Yr. Award of Merit, N.Y. State Coll. Forestry. Fellow AAAS; mem. Soc. Am. Foresters, Nat. Parks and Conservation Assn. (bd. dirs. 1970-80, adv. bd. 1991—). Democrat. Unitarian. Home: 211 Violet Ln Carbondale IL 62901

MINEKA, SUSAN, psychology educator; b. Ithaca, N.Y., June 2, 1948; d. Francis Edward and Muriel Leota (McGregor) M. BA in Psychology magna cum laude, Cornell U., 1970; PhD, U. Pa., 1974. Lic. psychologist, Ill. Prof. psychology U. Wis., Madison, 1974-85, U. Tex., Austin, 1986-87; prof. Northwestern U., Evanston, Ill., 1987—; co-dir. Panic Treatment Ctr., EvanstonHosp., 1988—; mem. NIH Panic Consensus Panel, 1991. Editor Jour. Abnormal Psychology, 1990-94; contbr. articles to profl. jours. Grantee NSF and NIMH, 1977-89. Fellow APA (bd. sci. affairs 1992-94, chair 1994, pres. divsn. 12, sect. 3 1995), Am. Psychol. Soc.; mem. Psychonomic Soc., Assn. for Advancement Behavior Therapy, Midwestern Psychol. Assn. (pres.-elect 1995-96, pres. 1996—), Internat. Primatol. Soc., Internat. Soc. for Rsch. on Emotion, Soc. for Rsch. in Psychopathology (mem. exec. bd. 1992-94), Phi Beta Kappa, Sigma Xi. Democrat. Home: 1825 N Lincoln Plz Apt 1609 Chicago IL 60614-5337 Office: Northwestern U Psychology Dept Evanston IL 60208

MINER, FERN PIPPENGER, librarian; b. Nappanee, Ind.; d. Stanley Morris and Dorothy Lorene (Miller) Pippenger; m. James Robert Miner, Aug. 7, 1966; 1 child, Jill Rene. BS, Manchester Coll., 1964; MS, Purdue U., 1968; MLS, Ind. U., 1986. cert. elem. tchr., Ind; libr. III, Ind. Elem. tchr. TriCreek Schs., Lowell, Ind., 1965-66, Lakeland Schs., Syracuse, Ind., 1966-67, North Montgomery Schs., Linden, Ind., 1968-73; children's librn. Lebanon (Ind.) Pub. Libr., 1978-85, libr. dir., 1985-92, adult svcs. librn., 1992—. Bd. dirs. Boone County Performing Arts, Lebanon, 1993-94, choir mem., 1991—, Project Literacy: Boone County, 1987—; founding mem. Friends of the Libr., 1986—. Recipient Literacy award Govs. Voluntary Action Program, Ind., 1993. Mem. Pub. Libr. Assn., Am. Libr. Assn., Ind. Libr. Fed. (mem. advisory bd. 1991-94), Ambassadair Travel Club, Zonta (dist. chair 1994-96). Republican. Mem. Christian Ch. Office: Lebanon Pub Libr 104 E Washington Lebanon IN 46052

MINGE, DAVID, congressman, lawyer, law educator; b. Clarkfield, Minn., 1942; m. Karen Aaker; children: Erik, Olaf. BA in History, St. Olaf Coll., 1964; JD, U. Chgo., 1967. Atty. Faegre & Benson, Mpls., 1967-70; prof. law U. Wyo., 1970-77; atty. Nelson, Oyen, Torvik, Minge & Gilbertson, 1977-93; mem. 103d-104th Congresses from 2nd Minn. Dist., 1993—; mem. agrl. com.; cons. Ho. Jud. Com., Subcom. Adminstrv. Law U.S. Congress, 1975; formerly atty. Minn. Valley Coop. Light and Power Assn., 1984-93; chair Agrl. Law Sect., Minn. State Bar Assn. 1990-92, adv. bd. Western Minn. Legal Svcs., 1978-84; bd. dirs. Legal Advice Clinics, Ltd., Hennepin County, Western Minn. Vol. Atty. Program. Clk. Montevideo Sch. Bd., 1989-92; dir. Montevideo Community Devel. Corp.; steering com. Clean Up the River Environ., 1992 ; co-coord. Montevideo area CROP Walk for the Hungry, Multi-church Vietnamese Refugee Resettlement Com., Montevideo, 1978-90; bd. dirs. Montevideo United Way, Model Cities Program, Kinder Kare; chair AFS Montevideo chpt. Mem. Minn. Bar Assn., Chippewa County Bar Assn. (chair), Montevideo C. of C., Kiwanis (pres.). Office: 1415 Longworth HOB Washington DC 20515-2302

MINNESTE, VIKTOR, JR., retired electrical company executive; b. Haapsalu, Estonia, Jan. 15, 1932; s. Viktor and Alice (Lembra) M.; B.S. in Elec. Engring., U. Ill., 1960. Electronic engr. Bell & Howell Co., 1960-69, microstatics div. SCM Co., 1969-71, Multigraphics div. A-M Co., 1972-73; electronic engr. bus. products group Victor Comptometer Co. (merged with Walter Kidde Corp. 1977), Chgo., 1973-74, service mgr. internat. group, 1974-75, then supr. electronics design group, to 1982; project engr. Warner Electric, 1982-84; systems engr. Barrett Electronics, 1984-85; phone engr. Williams Electronics, 1986-88, cons. engr., 1988-92; ind. contractor, 1993-95, ret., 1995; pub. Motteid/Thoughts, 1962-68; chmn., Estonian-Ams. Polit. Action Com., 1968-72. Served with AUS, 1952-54. Home and Office: 3134 N Kimball Ave Chicago IL 60618-6856

MINNICH, DANIEL HAROLD, television news reporter; b. Elyria, Ohio, July 1, 1962; s. Harold Frederick and Eileen (Downie) M.; m. Kathleen Ann McKinley, Apr. 25, 1992. BA cum laude in Journalism, Ohio State U., 1984, BS cum laude in English Edn., 1985. With dept. promotions, rschr. Sta. WMJI-FM, Sta. WBBG, Cleve., 1985; news reporter Sta. WEOL, Sta. WBEA-FM, Elyria, 1985-86; traffic reporter Metro Traffic Control, Cleve., 1985-86; news reporter Sta. WCPN-FM, Cleve., 1985-87, Sta. WRQC-FM, Cleve., 1987-88; news anchor, producer Cablevision of Ohio, Cleve., 1988-89; news anchor, reporter Sta. WBOY-TV, Clarksburg, W.Va., 1989; news reporter, producer Sta. WTVQ-TV, Lexington, Ky., 1990-93; news reporter Sta. WHIO-TV, Dayton, 1994—; tchg. asst. U. Ky., Lexington, 1992-93. Vol. Am. Cancer Soc., 1994—. Mem. Ohio State U. Alumni Assn. Democrat. Roman Catholic. Home: 2573 Marscott Dr Centerville OH 45440 Office: Sta WHIO-TV 1414 Wilmington Ave Dayton OH 45401

MINOGUE, JOHN P., academic administrator, priest, educator; b. Chgo.. B in Philosophy, St. Mary's Sem.; MDiv, Deandreis Inst. Theology, 1972; M in Theology, DePaul U., 1975; D in Ministry, St. Mary of the Lake Sem., 1987. Ordained Vincentian priest, 1972. Vincentian priest Congregation of the Mission; instr. theology, dir. clin. pastoral placement programs St. Thomas Sem., Denver, 1972-76; instr. grad. theology, asst. then acad. dean DeAndreis Inst., 1976-83; pres. DePaul U., Chgo., 1993—; trustee DePaul U., 1991—; bd. mems. DePaul U. Corp., 1981-91; adj. prof. Sch. New Learning DePaul U., 1984—, instr. law and med. ethics Coll. Law DePaul U., 1989—; asst. prof. clin. ob.-gyn. Northwestern U.; instr. health care ethics St. Joseph Coll. Nursing, Joliet, Ill., Northwestern Sch. Nursing, Chgo.; cons. nat. heatlh care ethics, patient decision-making. Office: De Paul U 25 E Jackson Blvd Chicago IL 60604-2218

MINOR, HUGH DAVID, draftsman; b. Omaha, July 29, 1955; s. John William and Betty Ann (Roush) M. AAS, Iowa We. C.C., 1975. Archtl. technician Dana Larson Roubal & Assocs., Omaha, 1972-73; lab. technician Nebr. Testing Labs., Omaha, 1975-76; engring. technician USDA, Soil Conservation Svc., Council Bluffs, Iowa, 1976-77; civil draftsman Leo A. Daly Co., Omaha, 1977-78; project designer Automatic Sprinkler Corp., Omaha, 1978-81; sr. engring. technician HGM Assocs., Inc., Omaha, 1983—. Hon. mem. nat. steering com. Clinton/Gore '96 Campaign; mem. John F. Kennedy Libr., Historic Gen. Dodge House; mem. Council Bluffs Cmty. Schs. Vocat. Edn. Adv. Coun., Tucker Center, 1995—. Fellow Internat. Biog. Assn.; mem. AIA (assoc., sec.-treas. S.W. Iowa sect. 1994-96), Am. Design Drafting Assn., Nat. Trust for Historic Preservation, Libr. of Congress Assocs., The Cousteau Soc., Sherlock Holmes Soc. London, Frank Lloyd Wright Home and Studio Found. Democrat. Presbyterian. Home: 5644 S 94th Pl #16 Omaha NE 68127-3439 Office: HGM Assocs Inc 1104 Douglas on the Mall Omaha NE 68102

MINOR, MELVIN G., state legislator; b. Aug. 24, 1937; m. Carolyn Minor. Student, Emporia State U. Kans. state rep. Dist. 114, farmer. Mem. Masons, Shriners (Wichita Consistory). Home: RR 2 Box 31 Stafford KS 67578-9315*

MIRABELLO, MARK LINDEN, history educator; b. Toledo, May 6, 1955; s. Paul Joseph and Regina Joan (Baranski) M. BA, U. Toledo, 1977; MA, U. Va., 1979; PhD, U. Glasgow (Scotland), 1988. Instr. honors program U. Toledo, 1984-87; sr. instr. European history Shawnee State U., Portsmouth, Ohio, 1987-88, asst. prof. European history, 1988-93, chair honors program, 1990—, assoc. prof. European History, 1993—; vis. assoc. prof. European history Nizhni Novgorod State U., Russia, 1994; dir. Ian B. Cowan Award for Outstanding Work in Hist. Studies, Shawnee State U., Portsmouth, 1990—; cons. The Open Air, Shawnee State U. newspaper, Portsmouth, 1992—, The Univ. Chronicle Shawnee State Univ. Newspaper, Portsmouth, 1992—; co-founder, advisor Ar Tyr Ar Fraternity Shawnee State U., Portsmouth, 1992—. Author: The Odin Brotherhood: A True Narrative of a Dialogue with a Mysterious Secret Society, 1992. Co-founder, adviser Delta Tau Omega fraternity, Shawnee State U., Portsmouth, 1992—. Mem. Am. Hist. Assn., Ohio Acad. History, Fortean Soc. (London), Internat. Fortean Orgn., Planetary Soc.. Home: 940 2nd St Portsmouth OH 45662 Office: Dept History Shawnee State U Portsmouth OH 45662

MIRANDA, MARIO JAVIER, economics educator; b. Havana, Cuba, Sept. 23, 1954; came to U.S., 1961; s. Mario Santiago and Ofelia (Luis) M.; m. Barbara A. Lucey, May 13, 1986; children: Olivia K., M. Alexander, Cristian B. BA, Coll. of Wooster, 1976; MS, U. Wis., 1984, PhD, 1985. Asst. prof. U. Conn., Storrs, 1986-88; asst. prof., assoc. prof. Ohio State U., Columbus, 1988—; cons. USDA, Washington, 1987—, Chgo. Bd. Trade. Contbr. articles to profl. jours. Mem. Am. Econs. Assn., Am. Agrl. Econs. Assn., Sigma Xi, Phi Kappa Phi. Home: 1807 Riverhill Rd Columbus OH 43221-1334 Office: Ohio State U 2120 Fyffe Rd Columbus OH 43210-1099

MIRCHANDANEY, ARJAN SOBHRAJ, mathematics educator; b. Hydrabad, Sind, India, Aug. 13, 1923; s. Sobhraj Gurmukhdas and Jamuna Mohanlal (Advani) M.; m. Padma Kalachand Lalwani, Oct. 20, 1958; 1 child, Haresh. BS, U. Bombay, India, 1943; MS, U. Bombay, 1946; PhD, U. Conn., 1984. Asst. prof. math. D.G. Nat. Coll., U. Bombay, 1943-47; lectr. Jai Hind Coll. U. Bombay, 1949-60, lectr. postgrad. classes, 1953-78, prof. math. Jai Hind Coll., 1960-69, prof., head dept. math. Jai Hind Coll., 1969-78; asst. prof. math. No. Ill. U., DeKalb, 1979-80, Knox Coll., Galesburg, Ill., 1982-85; prof. math. Defiance (Ohio) Coll., 1986—; coord. math. coll. sci. improvement program for Bombay colls., 1971-74; vis. prof. math. St. Lawrence U., Canton, N.Y., 1978; vis. asst. prof. Cornell U., Ithaca, N.Y., 1985-86; postgrad. lectr. U. Bombay, 1953-78; external examiner Shivaji U., Kolhapur, India, 1972-74; presenter Internat. Congress on Relativity and Gravitation, Munich, 1988, Internat. Congress History of Sci., Munich, 1989. Author: A Course in Elementary Trigonometry, 1954, 3d edit., 1965; contbr. to profl. jour. and book. Mem. Nat. Ctr. for Performing Arts, Bombay, 1969-78. Grantee Defiance Coll., 1989. Mem. Am. Math. Soc., Math. Assn. Am. Home: 700 Ralston Ave Apt 36 Defiance OH 43512-1567 Office: Defiance Coll 701 N Clinton St Defiance OH 43512-1610

MIRTALLO, JAY MATTHEW, pharmacist, educator; b. Stamford, N.Y., Oct. 29, 1953; s. Leonard and Betty Louise (Clapper) M.; children: Karissa Wesley, Taylor Jay. BS in Pharmacy cum laude, U. Toledo, 1976; MS in Hosp. Pharmacy, Ohio State U., 1978. Resident in hosp. pharmacy Ohio State U. Hosps., Columbus, 1978, clin. pharmacist, 1978—, clin. assoc. prof. coll. pharmacy, 1985—; grad. faculty Coll. Pharmacy Ohio State U., 1983, adj. asst. prof. dept. surgery, 1984; lectr. rsch. ednl. audiences; cert. nutrition support pharmacist, 1994—; chmn. Clin. Nutrition Panel. Mem. editl. bd. Ann Pharmacother, 1982—, Clin. Pharmacy, 1983-95, Nutrition in Clin. Practice, 1986-90; contbr. articles to profl. jours. Fellow Am. Soc. Hosp. Pharmacists; mem. Am. Soc. Parenteral and Enteral Nutrition (Disting. Pharmacist award 1993), Ohio Soc. Hosp. Pharmacists (Hosp. Pharmacist of Yr. 1985), Ctrl. Ohio Soc. Hosp. Pharmacists (Outstanding Svc. award 1983). Roman Catholic. Office: Ohio State U Med Ctr Dept Pharmacy DN 368 410 W 10th Ave Columbus OH 43210-1240

MISCHKE, CARL HERBERT, religious association executive, retired; b. Hazel, S.D., Oct. 27, 1922; s. Emil Gustav and Pauline Alvina (Polzin) M.; m. Gladys Lindloff, July 6, 1947; children: Joel, Susan Mischke Blahnik, Philip, Steven. B.A., Northwestern Coll., Watertown, Wis., 1944; M.Div., Wis. Luth. Sem., Mequon, 1947. Ordained to ministry Evang. Lutheran Ch. Parish pastor Wis. Synod, 1947-79; pres. Western Wis. Dist. Evang. Luth. Ch., Juneau, 1964-79; v.p. Wis. Luth. Synod, Milw., 1966-79, pres., 1979-93; retired, 1993.

MISCHKE, CHARLES RUSSELL, mechanical engineering educator; b. Glendale, N.Y., Mar. 2, 1927; s. Reinhart Charles and Dena Amelia (Scholl) M.; m. Margaret R. Bubeck, Aug. 4, 1951; children: Thomas, James. BSME, Cornell U., 1947, MME, 1950; PhD, U. Wis., 1953. Registered mechanical engr. Iowa, Kans. Asst. prof. mech. engring. U. Kans., Lawrence, 1953-56; assoc. prof. mech. engring. U. Kans., 1956-57; prof., chmn. mech. engring. Pratt Inst., N.Y.C., 1957-64; prof. mech. engring. Iowa State U., Ames, 1964—, Alcoa Found. prof., 1974. Author: Elements of Mechanical Analysis, 1963, Introduction to Computer-Aided Design, 1968, Mathematical Model Building, 1972; editor: Standard Handbook of Machine Design, 1986, 1996, Mechanical Engineering Design, 5th edit., 1989, 8 Mechancal Designers Workbooks, 1990, Fundamentos de Diseno Mechanico, 4 vols., 1994. Scoutmaster Boy Scouts Am., Ames. With USNR, 1944-75, mem. Res. ret. Recipient Ralph Teetor award Soc. Automotive Engrs., 1977, best book award Am. Assn. Pubs., 1986, Legis. Teaching Excellence award Iowa Assembly, 1990, Ralph Coates Roe award Am. Soc. for Engring. Edn., 1991. Fellow ASME (life, Machine Design award 1990); mem. Am. Soc. Engring. Edn. (Centennial cert. 1993), Am. Gear Mfrs. Assn., Scabbard and Blade, Cardinal Key, Sigma Xi, Phi Kappa Phi, Pi Tau Sigma. Office: Iowa State U Dept Mech Engring Ames IA 50011

MISSMAN, JEFFREY STEPHAN, bank executive; b. Dixon, Ill., July 29, 1944; s. Clifford Elmer and Arletta Rachael (Downing) M.; student U. Ill., 1962-63; BA, Coe Coll., 1966; student London Sch. Econs. and Polit. Scis., 1964-65; MBA (Scholar award), Washington U., 1968; CPA, Mo.; m. Kathleen Frances Vaughan, Aug. 8, 1970. Auditor, Arthur Andersen & Co., St. Louis, 1968-70, sr. auditor, 1970-72, sr. auditor, Kansas City, Mo., 1972-74; asst. controller spl. projects Commerce Bank of Kansas City, 1974-75, asst. controller, mgr. audit dept., 1975-79, v.p., asst. sec., mgr. corp. trust dept., 1979-81, v.p., mgr. securities services group, 1981-85, mgr. treasury services group, 1985-87; v.p., dir. compliance and control Commerce Bancshares Inc., 1988—; individual trustee First Mortgage Bonds of Kansas City Power and Light Co.; adj. faculty econs. and acctg. Rockhurst Coll., 1978-79. Coach Johnson County Amateur Hockey Assn., 1974-79; trustee Westport Allen Center, 1982—, treas., 1985-87; mem. community adv. bd. Sta. KCPT, 1991—. Mem. AICPA, Mo. Soc. CPAs, Beta Gamma Sigma. Republican. Methodist.

MISUREC, RUDOLF, physician, surgeon; b. Dobre Pole, Czechoslovakia, June 27, 1924; came to U.S., 1967; s. Gustav and Hilda (Safar) M.; m. Miluse Kisil, 1951 (div. 1978); children: Peter Clyde, Rudolph Carl; m. Stanislava Coufal, 1978. MD, Masaryk's U., Brno-Czechoslovakia, 1950. Diplomate Am. Bd. Urology, gen. surgery (Czechoslovakia), thoracic surgery (Czechoslovakia). Intern U. Ill., Chgo., 1967-68, resident in urology, 1968-71, clin. asst. prof. urology, 1975—. Mem. Rep. Presdl. Task Force, 1984, Rep. Presdl. Legion of Merit, 1992. Capt. Czechoslovakia Army, 1950-55. Recipient Cert. of Achievement U.S. Army, 1967, Letter of Appreciation, 1967. Fellow ACS, Internat. Coll. Surgeons, Am. Urol. Assn.; mem. AMA, Chgo. Med. Soc., N.Y. Acad. Scis., Czechoslovak Soc. Arts and Scis. (U.S.). Roman Catholic. Office: 3340 Oak Park Ave Berwyn IL 60402-3420

MITCHELL, ALTON JAY, software engineer; b. Washington, Nov. 9, 1960; s. Alton Evander and Lillie Mae (Talley) M. AA in Computer Sci., Prince George's C.C., 1980; BS in Computer Sci., U. Md., 1982; MS in Computer Sci. and Math., U. Waterloo, Ont., 1984. Programmer Nat. Weather Svc., Suitland, Md., 1977-81; scientific programmer Systems Applied Scis. Corp., Riverdale, Md., 1981-82; software engr. AT&T Bell Labs., Naperville, Ill., 1982—. Election judge DuPage County, 1993—; exploring advisor Boy Scouts Am., District Heights, Md., 1976-86. Mem. IEEE, Assn. of Computing Machinery. Democrat. Home: 530-606 Riverfront Circle Naperville IL 60540 Office: AT&T Labs 2000 N Naperville Rd Naperville IL 60566

MITCHELL, BEVERLY ANN BALES, agency owner, women's rights advocate; b. Fremont, Nebr., July 27, 1944; d. Richard Lee Roy Stillwell Bales and Thelma May (Nelson) Lemen (dec.). BA, Midland Luth. Coll., 1967; postgrad., U. Iowa, 1970, 71. Reporter, film columnist, entertainment sect. editor Fremont (Nebr.) Daily Guide and Tribune, 1961-66; tchr. H.S. English Cedar Bluffs (Nebr.) Valley PUb. Schs., 1967-71; dir. quality control, dir. field ops. Frank N. Magid Assocs., Marion, Iowa, 1971-76; employment specialist U.S. Dept. Labor, Cedar Rapids, Iowa, 1976-78; owner, gen. agy. Mitchell Ins., Cedar Rapids, 1978—. Founder, editor: (monthly periodical) Lilith Speaks, 1971-76, 88—; contbr.: Strong Minded Women, 1992. Co-founder, pres. Cedar Rapids (Iowa) Womens Caucus, 1971-76; commr. Cedar Rapids Civil Rights Commn., 1976-80, Cedar Rapics Charter Commn., 1995-96; pres. Linn County (Iowa) Women's Polit. Caucus, 1977-79; mem. Linn County Bd. Condemnation and Compensation, 1994—. Recipient Creighton By-Line award Creighton U., Omaha, 1963, Best Editorial award Nebr. Press Assn., Lincoln, 1963; named Women of the Yr., Cedar Rapids (Iowa) Women's Orgns., 1977. Mem. NRA, NOW (coord. Iowa state divsn. 1973-76, pres. Cedar Rapids chpt. 1994—), Bus. and Profl. Women (bd. dirs. 1994-95), Dodge County Humane Soc. Lutheran. Unitarian. Office: Mitchell Ins 1000 Maplewood Dr NE Cedar Rapids IA 52402-3807

MITCHELL, DAVID ANDREW, electrical engineer; b. Columbus, Ohio, Sept. 17, 1963; s. William and Roberta (Leonard) M.; m. Anita M. Baljak, June 23, 1984; children: Sarah, Ryan. Carmen. Bs in elec. engring., Ohio State U., 1991. Registered profl. engr.-in-tng., Ohio. Elec. engr. Worthington Industries Buckeye Steel Castings Divsn., Columbus, 1991-94; mfg. systems engr. Worthington Industries, Worthington Steel Corp., Columbus, 1994—. Sgt. U.S. Army, 1983-87. Mem. IEEE, Industrial Systems Soc. Republican. Roman Catholic. Office: Worthington Steel MIS 7404 Worthington Galena Rd Columbus OH 43085

MITCHELL, DONALD E., rehabilitation counselor, transition counselor; b. Kansas City, Mo., Jan. 19, 1948; s. Rosa E. Mitchell. BA, Southwestern Coll., 1970; MS in Community Counseling, Emporia State U., 1983, MS in Vocat. Rehab. Counseling, 1986; postgrad., U. Kans., Pitts. State U., Emory U. Svc. technician, sales and sheet metal installer Lee's Cooling and Heating, Independence, Kans., 1976-82; dir. partial hosp. facility, case mgr. Iroquis Ctr. for Human Devel., Greensburg, Kans., 1983-85; job coach Kans. Social Rehab. Svc., Topeka, 1985-86; title IV counselor Independence Community Coll., 1986-87; vocat., rehab. counselor II, transition counselor Kans. Rehab. Svcs., Chanute, 1988—; program dir. Magdeline Group Home, Kans. City, 1995—. Bd. dirs. Helping Hearts Heal. Mem. Nat. Eagle Scout Assn., Helping Hearts Heal (bd. dirs.), Kans. Vocat. Evaluator and Assessment Assn. (membership chmn., pres.), Nat. Rehab. Assn., Kans. Rehab. Assn., Chi Sigma Iota.

MITCHELL, ERNST KERN, security systems company executive; b. Detroit, June 11, 1955; s. Maurice Alexander and Ernestine (Kern) M. BA, Albion (Mich.) Coll., 1977. Dir. engring. R&D Computerized Security Sys., Madison Heights, Mich., 1977—. Patentee in field. Mem. Soc. Mfg. Engrs. (sr. mem.), Sugar Springs Country Club. Home: 36528 Briarcliff Sterling Heights MI 48312

MITCHELL, FRANK R., electrical engineer; b. Madison, Wis., Dec. 4, 1933. BSEE, U. Ill., 1956. Sr. engr. Knowles Electronics, Itasca, Ill., 1980—. Mem. IEEE. Office: Knowles Electronics 1151 Maplewood Dr Itasca IL 60143-2058

MITCHELL, GEORGE ALLEN, public policy consultant; b. Denver, Oct. 8, 1946; s. George Withee and Mary Mitchell; m. Susan Miller, Oct. 28, 1973; children: Maggie, Nellie. Student, U. Wis., 1964-69. Reporter Wis. State Jour., Madison, 1967-71; bus. reporter Wall Street Jour., Chgo., 1972; polit. reporter Riverside (Calif.) Press Enterprise, 1972-73; asst. sec. revenue State of Wis., Madison, 1974-76, asst. state budget dir., 1976-78; spl. asst. to Congressman Les Aspin, Janesville, Wis., 1978; dir. govt. contracts Carley Capital Group, Madison, 1979-82; pres. Carley Mgmt. Co., Milw., 1982-85; ptnr. The Mitchell Co. Inc., Milw., 1986-93; dir. pub. works Milwaukee County, Milw., 1993-94; ptnr. The Mitchell Co., Inc., Milw., 1994—; cons. facility plan Milw. Pub. Schs., 1992; mem. adv. com. U. Wis. Sch. Edn., Milw. Mem. Gov.'s Task Force on Corrections, 1996, Greater Milw. Com., 1983-85; chmn. Wis. Study Commn. on Quality Pub. Edn. in Met. Milw., 1984-85; past trustee Pub. Policy Forum, Milw., former mem. 2020 project; former chmn. Shorewood Sch. Dist. Chpt. 220 Planning Coun.; bd. dirs. Milw. Symphony Orch. Evans scholar U. Wis., 1964-69' Medill fellow Northwestern U. Sch. Journalism, 1970. Office: 2025 N Summit Ave Milwaukee WI 53202-1319

MITCHELL, GEORGE TRICE, physician; b. Marshall, Ill., Jan. 20, 1914; s. Roscoe Addison and Alma (Trice) M.; m. Mildred Aletha Miller, June 21, 1941; children: Linda Sue, Mary Kathryn. BS, Purdue U., 1935; MD, George Washington U., 1940. Intern Meth. Hosp., Indpls., 1940-41; gen. practice medicine Marshall, 1946—; mem. courtesy staff Union and Regional Hosps., Terre Haute, Ind.; clin. assoc. Sch. Basic Medicine U. Ill.; chmn. bd. dirs. First Nat. Bank, Marshall. Author: Dr. George-An Account of the Life of a Country Doctor, 1993. Mem. adv. coun. premedicine Eastern Ill. U., 1965-69; alt. del. Rep. Conv., 1968, del., 1972; trustee Lakeland Jr. Coll., 1978-92. Lt. col. USAAF, 1941-45. Named Health Practitioner of Yr. Ill. Rural Health Assn., 1993, Nat. Health Practioner of Yr. Nat. Rural Health Assn., 1995. Fellow Am. Acad. Family Physicians (Family Physician of Yr. 1993); mem. AMA, Ill. med. Soc. (2d v.p. 1980-81), Clark County Med. Soc. (pres.), Aesculapian Soc. of Wabash Valley (pres. 1965), Nat. Rural Health Assn. (Practitioner of Yr. 1995), Clark County Hist. Soc. (pres. 1968-70), Masons (32 degree), Shriners. Methodist. Home: RR 2 Marshall IL 62441-9802 Office: 410 N 2nd St Marshall IL 62441-1010

MITCHELL, GERALD L., state legislator; b. June 18, 1942; m. Janet L. Mitchell; 3 children. BS, Eureka Coll., 1968; MS, Ill. State U., 1974; EdS, Western Ill. U., 1992. Tchr., coach, 1968-74, prin. elem., mid., and h.s., 1974-86; dir. evaluation and edn. svc. Dixon Dist., 1986-92; asst. supt., 1992-93, supt., 1993-94; Ill. state rep. Dist. 73, 1995—. Mem. ASCD, Nat. Staff Devel., Coun., Am. Assn. Sch. Adminstrs., Ill. Assn. Sch. Bd. Office: 100 E Fifth St Rock Falls IL 61071

MITCHELL, JAMES W., state legislator; b. Springfield, Mo., June 30, 1950; s. James Robert and Shirley (Sharp) M.; m. Terri Lea Starmer; 1 child, Mona. BA, Drury Coll., 1973, MA, 1081. Pres. Mitchell Bros. Farms, Richland, Mo., 1980-86; owner, mgr. Jim Mitchell Ins. Agy., Richland, 1984—; mem. Mo. Ho. of Reps., Jefferson City, 1883—. Alderman City of Richland, 1978-83; bd. dirs. Mo. Ozarks Econ. Opportunity Corp., 1983—; pres. Cmty. Assn., 1976-79. Recipient award of merit Mo. Tchrs. Assn., 1979, Meritorious Svc. award St. Louis Globe Dem., 1984-86; named Outstanding Rural Freshman Legislator, 1982-84. Mem. NRA, Pulaski County Landowners Assn., Phi Delta Kappa, Sigma Nu. Republican. Home: PO Box 741 201 Chestnut Richland MO 65556*

MITCHELL, JOHN DAVID, journalism educator; b. Chgo., Jan. 22, 1924; m. Mila Agnes Johnston, Sept. 12, 1947 (div. 1981); children: Justin, Alexandra. AB, Oberlin Coll., 1950; MS in Journalism, Kans. State U., 1959. Sports editor Elgin (Ill.) Courier-News, 1946-47; reporter/desk man Rockford Morning Star, Ill., 1950-52, Lima News, Ohio, 1952-56; temp. instr. Kans. State U., 1956-58; asst. prof., assoc. prof. Univ. Colo., 1958-73; mag. dept. acting chair Newhouse Sch., Syracuse (N.Y.) Univ., 1973-79, newspaper dept. chair, 1973-83, journalism divsn. acting asst. dean, 1980-81, journalism prof., 1973-94, prof. emeritus, 1994—; Fulbright lectr. Thammasat Univ., Bangkok, 1962-63; exec. sec. N.Y. State Soc. of Newspaper Editors, Syracuse, 1973-80. Co-author: Mass Communication Resources in Thailand, 1965; contbr. chpt. to The Asian Newspapers Reluctant Revolution, 1971; contbr. articles to profl. jours. Mem. Assn. for Edn. in Journalism and Mass Communication (charter mem. newspaper div., head 1976-79, minorities and communications div. charter mem., sec. 1977-79), Soc. Profl. Journalists, Syracuse Press Club (Svc. award 1984). Democrat. Home: 101 Sun Harbor Dr Liverpool NY 13088-4323

MITCHELL, JOHN DAVID, public relations executive; b. St. Joseph, Mo., Dec. 4, 1959; s. John Bushnell and Shirley May (Jones) M.; m. Charlotte Ann Christensen, Oct. 20, 1984; children: John Heming, Molly Ann. Student, Mo. Western State Coll., 1978-80; BS in Journalism, U. Kans., 1982. Reporter, anchor, sports anchor KQTV-TV, St. Joseph, Mo., 1982-87; reporter, anchor, mng. editor KMIZ-TV, Columbia, Mo., 1987-89; prodr., reporter KYTV-TV, Springfield, Mo., 1989-92; asst. dir. pub. rels. Drury Coll., Springfield, 1992—. Vol. Ozarks Pub. TV, Springfield, 1993-94; mem. Vision 20/20 Econ. Devel. Task Force, Springfield, 1995-96; crew mem. Children's Miracle Network Telethon, Springfield, 1992-93, 96. Mem. Pub. Rels. of the Ozarks, Soc. Profl. Journalists, Leadership Springfield. Office: Drury College 900 N Benton Ave Springfield MO 65802

MITCHELL, KENDALL, writer, literary critic; b. Chgo.; s. John Kendall Southgate and Ann (Leichsenring) M. BA, Yale U., 1946. Instr. Am. U. of Beirut, 1946-49; pub. rels. dir., dir. publs. Bldg. Owners and Mgrs. Assn. Internat., Chgo., 1951-76; cons. Bldg. Mgrs. Assn., Chgo., 1976-85; writer, reviewer Chgo. Tribune and Chgo. Sun Times, 1977—; lectr. journalism Roosevelt U., Chgo., 1981—. Author: A Chair By The Fire, 1951; translator: Lebanon, 1949. With USAAF, 1942-43. Mem. Nat. Book Critics Circle, Elizabethan CLub, Alpha Delta Phi. Episcopalian. Home: 318 South Blvd Evanston IL 60202-3019

MITCHELL, KIERON BREON, financial analyst; b. Oxford, Eng., Sept. 8, 1968; s. Bert Breon and Lynda Diane (Fink) M.; m. Courtney Joanne Ridge, May 12, 1990. BA in Computer Sci., German, Philosophy, Ind. U., 1990. Scientific anlayst Eli Lilly and Co., Indpls., 1990-94. Author: Who's Who Among Play-by-Play Mail Gamers, 1989. Congress-Bundestag Exch. scholar, Germany, 1986; recipient Computer Sci. Achievement award, 1990. Office: Eli Lilly and Co Lilly Corp Ctr DC 1866 Indianapolis IN 46185

MITCHELL, LEE MARK, communications executive, investment fund manager, lawyer; b. Albany, N.Y., Apr. 16, 1943; s. Maurice B. and Mildred (Roth) M.; m. Barbara Lee Anderson, Aug. 27, 1966; children: Mark, Matthew. A.B., Wesleyan U., 1965; J.D., U. Chgo., 1968. Bar: Ill. 1968, D.C. 1969, U.S. Supreme Ct. 1972. Assoc. Leibman, Williams, Bennett, Baird & Minow, Chgo. and Washington, 1968-72; assoc. Sidley & Austin, Washington, 1972-74, ptnr., 1974-84, 92-94; exec. v.p. and gen. counsel Field Enterprises, Inc., Chgo., 1981-83, pres. and chief exec. officer, 1983-84; pres., chief exec. officer Field Corp., 1984-92; prin. Golder, Thoma, Cressey, Rauner, Inc., Chgo., 1994—; bd. dirs. Paging Network, Inc., Washington Nat. Corp., Chgo. Stock Exch., Inc., PTN Pub. Co.; chmn. Learning Scis. Corp., NOTIS Systems, Inc., 1987-91. Author: Openly Arrived At, 1974, With the Nation Watching, 1979; co-author: Presidential Television, 1973. Mem. LWV PResdl. Debates Adv. Com., Washington, 1979-80, 82; U.S. del. Brit. Legis. Conf. on Covt. and Media, Ditchley Park, Eng., 1974; bd. visitors U. Chgo. Law Sch., 1984-86, Medill Sch. Journalism, Northwestern U., 1984-91; bd. govs. Chgo. Met. Planning Coun., pres., 1988-91; mem. midwest regional adv. bd. Inst. Internat. Edn., 1987—; trustee Ravinia Festival Assn., Northwestern U. Mem. ABA, Fed. Comm. Bar Assn., Econ. Mid-Am. Club (trustee), Chgo. Club, Comml. Club Chgo. Home: 135 Maple Hill Rd Glencoe IL 60022-1252 Office: Golder Thoma Cressey Rauner Inc 6100 Sears Tower Chicago IL 60606-6402

MITCHELL, MILTON EDWARD, librarian; b. Wausaukee, Wis., Jan. 2, 1945; s. Siegel Joseph and Emma Marie (Steinbrecher) M.; m. Barbara Jean Johanek, June 25, 1966 (div. 1978); m. Rosemary Justine Kilbridge, Mar. 10, 1980. BA, U. Wis., 1966, MALS, 1968. Cert. grade I libr., Wis. Libr. Milw. Pub. Libr., 1966-68, U. Wis., Oshkosh, 1968-72, Oshkosh Pub. Libr., 1972-78; libr. system dir. Indianhead Libr. System, Eau Claire, Wis., 1978—; chmn. Coun. of Wis. Librs.; mem. Coun. on Librs. and Network Devel. Mem. Wis. Libr. Assn. (pres. 1985), Libr. Adminstrs. Assn. (chmn. 1980-81). Office: Indianhead Libr System Ste 101 3301 Golf Rd Eau Claire WI 54701

MITCHELL, PHILIP MICHAEL, aerospace engineer, consultant; b. Mobile, Ala., Feb. 12, 1953; s. Philip Augustus and Betty J. (Hardy) M. BS in Aeros. magna cum laude, Embry-Riddle Aero. U., Daytona Beach, Fla., 1980, MS in Aeros., 1987; postgrad., Wright State U., 1995—. Radar systems engr. ITT, Van Nuys, Calif., 1980-82; commd. 2d lt. USAF, 1982, advanced through grades to maj., 1994; bomber br. chief 42d Orgnl. Maintenance Squadron, Loring AFB, Maine, 1983-86; officer-in-charge weapons br. 520th Aircraft Generation Squadron, RAF Upper Heyford, Eng., 1986; asst. maintenance supr. 20th Equipment Maintenance Squadron, RAF, RAF Upper Heyford, 1986-87, 88-90; weapons safety officer 20th Tactical Fighter Wing, RAF Upper Heyford, 1986-87; chief standardization and tng. div. 42d Bomb Wing, Loring AFB, 1990-91; chief of maintenance 42d Maintenance Squadron, Loring AFB, Maine, 1991-92; maintenance mgmt. officer 42d BMW, 1992-94; dir. spl. projects and policies Aero. Sys. Ctr., Wright-Paterson AFB, Ohio, 1994-95; grad. rsch. asst. Wright State U., 1995—; adj. prof. European div. Embry-Riddle Aero. U., 1988-90; aerospace cons., 1987—. Recipient Meritorious Svc. medal with cluster, Commendation medal with one oak leaf cluster, Air Force Achievement medal. Fellow Brit. Interplanetary Soc.; mem. AIAA (sr.), Soc. Logistics Engrs., Am. Prodn. and Inventory Control Soc., Air Force Assn., Royal Scottish County Dance Soc., Masons (32 deg.), Scottish Rite. Episcopal. Home and Office: 6305 Longford Rd Dayton OH 45424-3573

MITCHELL, ROBERT HOWARD, quality engineer; b. St. Paul, Jan. 11, 1958; s. Robert Howard Sr. and Sharon Rose (Bechner) M.; m. Lori Jane Beaver, Oct. 2, 1982; children: Jacob B., Kyle R. BS, U. Minn., Morris, 1980. Quality engr. 3M, St. Paul, 1981-91; statis. cons. 3M, Hutchinson, Minn., 1991-94; mfg. tech. supr. 3M, 1994—. Quality mgmt. cons. City of Hutchinson, Minn., 1994, Mihead County Commrs., Glencoe, Minn., 1995. Mem. Am. Soc. Quality Control (cert. quality engr., sec. stats. divsn. 1996—). Republican. Roman Catholic. Home: 106 Century Ave SE Hutchinson MN 55350 Office: 3M Tape Mfg 915 Hwy 22 South Hutchinson MN 55350

MITCHELL, STEVEN THOMAS, mine superintendent; b. Deadwood, S.D., Dec. 30, 1953; s. Albert Blair and Aili Marie (Penttila) M.; m. Cynthia Rose Collins, Oct. 8, 1976; children: Brian Albert, Sheryl Lynn. BS in Mining Engring., S.D. Sch. of Mines & Tech., 1976, MS in Mining Engring., 1977. Mine planning engr. Homestake Mining Co., Lead, S.D., 1977-79, bulk mining foreman, 1980-81, gen. service foreman, 1981-83; contract adminstr. Homestake Mining Co., Jardine, Mont., 1981; ragged top project mgr. Homestake Mining Co., Lead, 1984, open cut project coordinator, 1985-86, deep level project supt., 1986-87, mine supt., 1988-95; mine supt. Open Cut, 1995—. Chmn. Black Hills sect. AIME, Rapid City, S.D., 1985-86; pres. ch. coun. First Luth. Ch. Lead, 1993-95; co-chmn. We. Regional Conf. on Precious Metals, Coal and Environment, Rapid City, 1987, program co-chmn., 1990. Named Outstanding Young Men of Am., Jaycees, 1981, 83, Boss of the Yr., Lead-Deadwood Jaycees, 1990; recipient Outstanding Recent Grad. award S.D. Sch. of Mining & Tech., Rapid City, 1984. Mem. Soc. Explosive Engrs., S.D. Mining Assn., Soc. Mining Engrs., Rod and Gun Club, Lead Country Club, Tau Beta Pi, Pi Mu Epsilon. Republican. Lutheran. Home: PO Box 534 Deadwood SD 57732-0534 Office: Homestake Mining Co 630 E Summit St Lead SD 57754

MITCHELL, VERNICE VIRGINIA, nurse, poet, author; b. Scott, Miss., Mar. 11, 1921; d. Isaiah and Martha Magdalene (Edwards) Smith; m. Willis Mitchell, Aug. 17, 1940; children: Elaine, Kenneth, Liethia, John, Ransom, Paul. Diploma, Princeton Continuation Coll., 1955. Nurse Cook County Sch. Nursing, Chgo., 1951-59, U. Ill. Hosp., Chgo., 1959-67, Grant Hosp., Chgo., 1967-78, Northwestern Meml. Hosp., Chgo., 1979-84; with U. Ill. Hosp. Aetna Nurse's Registry, Chgo., 1984—. Author: The Book Success

Through Spiritual Truths, 1987, Details Through Rose-Colored Glasses, 1995, (poems) A Woman, chicago, The 12 Months; also numerous poetry and musical lyrics; poems submitted to Dial-A-Poem, Chgo., 1988-89. Chmn. cookbook project 1988-89. Recipient merit cert. Am. Poetry Assn., 1982, merit cert. World of Poetry, 1983, 85, Golden Poet award 1986, 87, 88, Silver Poet award, 1989, 90; inducted into the Hall of Fame for Sr. Citizens, Chgo., 1991. Mem. 6700 Emerald Ave. Block Club (pres. 1971-92).

MITCHELSON, BONNIE ELIZABETH, Canadian politician, nurse; b. Winnipeg, Man., Can., Nov. 28, 1947; d. Henry Alfred and Millie Christine (Leslie) Bester; m. Donald Mitchelson, Aug. 30, 1969; children: Michele, Scott. Diploma in nursing, Winnipeg Sch. Nursing, 1968, ICU course, 1969. Nurse various hosps., Winnipeg, 1968-86; legis. dep. health critic Urban Affairs Critic, 1986-87; min. responsible for status of women and for lotteries, 1988-93; min. Ministry of Culture, Heritage and Citizenship, Winnipeg, 1988-93, Ministry of Family Svcs., Winnipeg, 1993—.

MITSTIFER, DOROTHY IRWIN, honor society administrator; b. Gaines, Pa., Aug. 17, 1932; d. Leonard Robert and Laura Dorothy (Crane) Irwin; m. Robert Mitchell Mitsifer, June 17, 1956 (dec. Aug. 1984); children: Kurt Michael, Brett Robert. BS, Mansfield U., 1954; MEd, Pa. State U., 1972, PhD, 1976. Cert. home economist. Tchr. Tri-County High Sch., Canton, Pa., 1954-56, Loyalsock Twp. Sch. Dist., Williamsport, Pa., 1956-63; exec. dir. Kappa Omicron Phi, Williamsport, Pa., 1964-86, Kappa Omicron Phi, Omicron Nu, Haslett, Mich., 1986-90, Kappa Omicron Nu, East Lansing, Mich., 1990—; prof. continuing edn. Pa. State U., University Park, 1976-80; prof. Mansfield (Pa.) U., 1980-86, pres.'s intern, 1984-86. Editor Kappa Omicron Nu Forum, 1986—; contbr. articles to profl. jours. Pres., bd. dirs. Profl. Devel. Ctr. Adv. Bd., Vocat. Edn., Pa. State U., 1980-86. Mem. ASCD, Am. Home Econs. Assn., Mich. Home Econs. Assn. (exec. dir. 1986—), Am. Vocat. Assn., Am. Soc. Assn. Execs., Nat. Soc. Fund Raising Profls., Coll. Edn. Alumni Soc. Pa. State U. (pres. 1986-88, bd. dirs. 1980-90), Kappa Delta Pi. Home: 1425 Somerset Close St East Lansing MI 48823-2435 Office: Kappa Omicron Nu 4990 Northwind Dr Ste 140 East Lansing MI 48823-5031

MITTON, MICHAEL PAUL, nurse anesthesist; b. Fayetteville, Ark., Jan. 17, 1955; s. Robert Charles Mitton and Norma Jean (Henderson) Douglas; m. K. Denise Walls, Dec. 6, 1991. Diploma in nursing, St. Joseph Hosp. Sch. Nursing, Lancaster, Pa., 1976; diploma in anesthesia, St. Joseph Hosp. Sch. Anesthesia, Lancaster, Pa., 1979. Cert. registered nurse anesthetist. From staff anesthetist to sr. anesthetist Paris (Ill.) Cmty. Hosp., 1979-93; sr. anesthetist WSM Hosp., Shelbyville, Ind., 1993—; pres. Profl. Edn. Svcs., Shelbyville, 1993—. Mem. Anesthesia & Critical Care Assn. (pres. 1981-93). Office: JEM Sys 1943 N Riverwood Dr Shelbyville IN 46176

MITZEL, RICHARD J., management consultant, purchasing manager; b. Hague, N.D., May 2, 1942; s. Lawrence F. and Cecilia (Johs) M.; m. Arlyce A. Anfinson, Dec. 27, 1969; children: Derek J., Heidi A., Heather M., Holly L. BBA, No. State U., 1969. CEO, co-owner Anfinson's Inc., Dickenson, N.D., 1969-92; purchasing mgr. Fisher Industries, Dickenson, N.D., 1993—; owner DAK Enterprises, Dickenson, N.D., 1994—; bd. dirs. Mid-State Distbn. Co. Inc., St. Paul, Minn., 1984-86, pres. 1985. Mem. finance coun. St. Wenceslaus Ch., Dickinson, 1990—; pres. Dickinson H.S. PAC com., 1995. With U.S. Army, 1964-66. Mem. Knights of Columbus, Elks. Republican. Roman Catholic. Home: 10875 24th St S.W. Dickinson ND 58601-9003

MITZELFELD, JIM, lawyer, journalist; b. Royal Oak, Mich., Apr. 26, 1961; s. Thomas Henry and Audrey Mae (Howard) M.; m. Lisa Jeanne Grayson, Sept. 28, 1985. BA in Journalism, Mich. State U., 1984; JD, U. Mich., 1996. Intern newspaper reporter The Times, Hammond, Ind., 1981; editor-in-chief The State News, East Lansing, Mich., 1982-83; intern reporter Democrat & Chronicle, Rochester, N.Y., 1983; newspaper reporter The Oakland Press, Pontiac, Mich., 1984-85, The Flint (Mich.) Jour., 1985-86, UP Internat., Lansing, 1986, AP, Lansing, 1986-88, The Detroit News, Dearborn, Mich., 1988-90; state capitol reporter The Detroit News, Lansing, 1990-93; intern law clk. to Judge David W. McKeague U.S. Dist. Ct. for We. Dist. Mich., 1994; summer assoc. Butzel Long, Lansing, 1994; law clk. Holland & Hart, Denver, 1995, Miller, Canfield, Lansing, Mich., 01995; law clk. to Judge David W. McKeague U.S. Dist. Ct. (we. dist.) Mich., 1996—. Polit. commentator Off the Record Pub. TV, 1986-93. Recipient Nat. Best of Gannett Runner-up award, 1991, Top Well Done prize Best of Gannett, 1993, 2d place prize Mich. Assn. Press Editl. Assn., 1994, Pulitzer prize for beat reporting, 1994; honored by Mich. State Senate for pub. svc., 1993. Mem. Soc. Profl. Journalists (Journalist of Yr. Detroit Chpt. 1994), Mich. State U. Alumni Assn., State News Alumni Assn. (pres., co-founder 1991-93). Episcopalian. Home: 1905 Anderson Ave Ann Arbor MI 48104-4747 Office: U Mich 5395 Wild Oak Dr East Lansing MI 48823-7252

MIU, RICHARD A, engineer; b. Galion, Ohio, Oct. 6, 1961. BS in Computer Sci., Ohio State U., 1983. Software engr. Autocall, Shelby, Ohio, 1983-85, ITT Power Syss., Galion, Ohio, 1985-88, Cooper Industries, Inc., Mt. Vernon, Ohio, 1988—.

MIXER, RONALD WAYNE, minister; b. Mpls., Jan. 22, 1954; s. Joseph William and Faith Amour (Minor) M.; m. Glenda Renae Fjordbak, June 22, 1974; children: Rachelle Renae, Danielle Kaye. BA, North Cen. Bible Coll., 1977; M in Ministry, Internat. Bible Sem., 1983. Ordained to ministry. Dir. ch. ministry Rock River Christian Ctr., Rock Falls, Ill., 1977-79; dir. christian edn. Cen. Assembly of God, Tulsa, 1979-80; sr. pastor Manchester (Iowa) Assembly of God, 1980-83, Richmond (Mo.) Assembly of God, 1983-84, Odessa (Mo.) First Assembly of God, 1984-87; field rep. Am. Bible Soc., N.Y.C., 1988—. Commr. Olathe (Kans.) Human Rels. Commn., 1990—, chair, 1996—. Named one of Outstanding Young Men in Am., U.S. Jaycees, 1986. Mem. Internat. Platform Assn., Assemblies of God Ministers (Kansas City, Kans. chpt.). Republican. Office: Am Bible Soc 15720 W 150th Ter Olathe KS 66062-4732

MIYAMOTO, RICHARD TAKASHI, otolaryngologist; b. Zeeland, Mich., Feb. 2, 1944; s. Dave Norio and Haruko (Okano) M.; m. Cynthia VanderBurgh, June 17, 1967; children: Richard Christopher, Geoffrey Takashi. BS cum laude, Wheaton Coll., 1966; MD, U. Mich., 1970; MS in Otology, U.So. Calif., 1978. Diplomate Am. Bd. Otolaryngology. Intern Butterworth Hosp., Grand Rapids, Mich., 1970-71, resident in surgery, 1971-72; resident in otolaryngology Ind. U. Sch. Medicine, 1972-75; fellow in otology and neurotology St. Vincent Hosp. and Otologic Med. Group, L.A., 1977-78; asst. prof. Ind. U. Sch. Medicine, Indpls., 1978-83, assoc. prof., 1983-88; prof. 1988—; chmn. 1987, chief Otology and Neurotology dept. Otolaryngology, Head and Neck Surgery, Ind. U., 1982—, chmn. dept. Otolaryngology, 1987—, Arilla DeVault prof., 1991; chief Otolaryngology, Head and Neck Surgery Wishard Meml. Hosp., 1979—. Mem. editorial bd. Laryngoscope, Am. Jour. of Otology, Otolaryngology-Head and Neck Surgery, European archives of Oto-Rhino-Laryngology, Anales de Otorrinolaringologia Mexicana; contbr. articles to profl. jours. Mem. adv. coun. Nat. Inst. Deafness and other communication disorders, 1989—; mem. med. adv. bd. Alexander Graham Bell Assn. for the Deaf, The Ear Found. Served to maj. USAF, 1975-77. Named Arilla DeVault Disting. investigator Ind. U., 1983. Fellow Am. Acad. Otolaryngology (gov. 1982—), ACS, Am. Otological, Rhinological, and Laryngological Soc. (Thesis Disting. for Excellence award), Am. Neurotology Soc. Am. Auditory Soc. (mem. exec. com. 1985—); mem. Otosclerosis Study Group (coun. 1993—), Am. Otol. Soc. (coun. 1992—), Marines Meml. Assn., Wheaton Coll. Scholastic Honor Soc., Cosmos Club of Washington, Columbia Club of Ind., Royal Soc. Medicine London, Collegium Oto-Laryngologicum Amecitiae Sacrum; Alpha Omega Alpha. Avocation: tennis. Office: Indiana U Sch Med 702 Barnhill Dr Indianapolis IN 46202-5128

MIZEL, GERALD M., financial company executive; b. Mitchell, S.D., Nov. 18, 1933; s. Phillip E. and Esther (Martinisky) M.; m. Liora Katzengord, Nov. 1, 1966; children: Michelle, Elliana. BBA, U. Miami, 1957. Exec. v.p., sec., treas. Midland Fin. Co., Chgo., 1957—; v.p. Mercury Fin. Co., 1994—; bd. dirs. AVGOL, Tel-Aviv. Mem. exec. com. Cmty. Assistance for Secondary Edn., Chgo., 1988-93; bd. dirs. Bur. of Jewish Employment Problems, Chgo., 1989-96, Coun. for Jewish Elderly, 1989-92, Friends of Israel Def. Forces in Midwest, 1987-96, chmn. 1991-92, Jewish Fedn. Met. Chgo./Jewish United Fund Met. Chgo., 1992-93, Am. Jewish Congress, Chgo., 1992—, v.p., devel. chair. Named Honoree Community Assistance for Secondary Edn. in Israel, 1988. Mem. Ind. Fin. Assn. Ill. (bd. dirs., sec.-treas. 1992-95). Home: 15 Country Ln Northfield IL 60093 Office: Midland Fin Co 7541 N Western Ave Chicago IL 60645-1510

MLOCEK, SISTER FRANCES ANGELINE, financial executive; b. River Rouge, Mich., Aug. 4, 1934; d. Michael and Suzanna (Bloch) M. BBA, U. Detroit, 1958; MBA, U. Mich., 1971. CPA, Mich. Bookkeeper Allen Park (Mich.) Furniture, 1949-52, Gerson's Jewlery, Detroit, 1952-53; jr. acct. Meyer Dickman, CPA, Algaze, Staub & Bowman, CPAs, Detroit, 1953-58; acct., internal auditor Sisters, Servants of Immaculate Heart of Mary Congregation, Monroe, Mich., 1959-66, asst. gen. treas., 1966-73, gen. treas., 1973-76; internal auditor for parishes Archdiocese of Detroit, 1976-78; asst. to exec. dir. Leadership Conf. of Women, Silver Spring, Md., 1978-83; dir. of fin. Nat. Conf. of Cath. Bishops/U.S. Cath. Conf., Washington, 1989-94; CFO Sisters Servants of the Immaculate Heart of Mary, Monroe, Mich., 1994—; trustee Sisters, Servants of Immaculate Heart of Mary Charitable Trust Fund, Monroe, 1988—. Author: (manual) Leadership Conference of Women Religious/Conference of Major Superiors of Men, 1981. Treas. Zonta Club of Washington Found., Washington, 1983-88, pres., 1992-93; bd. dirs. Our Lady of Good Counsel High Sch., Wheaton, Md., 1983-89. Mem. AICPA, D.C. Inst. CPAs (mem. not-for-profit com. 1992-94, CFOs com. 1990-94. Democrat. Roman Catholic. Office: Sisters Servants Immaculate Heart Mary 610 W Elm Ave Monroe MI 48162-7909

MOAN, JODI ANN, rehabilitation services professional and camp director; b. Olney, Ill., Sept. 6, 1964; d. Larry Edward and Donna Kay (Crawford) M. AS, Vincennes U., 1984; BS, Ind. State U., 1987. Asst. mgr. Triple B Farms, Sumner, Ill., 1982-86; camp idr. Happiness Bag, Inc., Terre Haute, Ind., 1986-87, program/camp dir., 1987—; A.R.C. of Vigo County Habilitation Trainer, Terre Haute, 1989—; human rights chair Melita, Inc., Terre Haute, 1990—; pres. Handicapable Scouting, Terre Haute, 1988-92; dir. of competition Area 7 Spl. Olympics, Indpls., 1992—. Bd. dirs. T.H. South Little League (v.p. 1992—). Named Jr. Coll. All-Am., Women's Basketball Coaches' Assn., 1984, Vol. of Yr., Dist. 4 Little League, 1994; recipient scholarship Fred and Hilda White Fund, Ind. State U., 1986. Mem. Am. Camping Assn., Vigo County Assn. for Retarded Citizens, Ind. Spl. Olympics, Women's Internat. Bowling Congress. Office: Happiness Bag Inc 1519 South 7th St Terre Haute IN 47802

MOBERG, DAVID FORREST, journalist; b. Galesburg, Ill., Sept. 27, 1943; s. Forrest Wilbert and Ruby Tennena (Kjellander) M.; m. Deborah Jo Patton, May 23, 1981; children: Carl, Sarah. BA, Carleton Coll., Northfield, Minn., 1965; MA, U. Chgo., 1971, PhD, 1978. Reporter Newsweek mag., N.Y.C., 1965-66; lectr. various colls. and univs., Chgo., 1972-76; from assoc. editor to nat. affairs editor to sr. editor In These Times mag., Chgo., 1976—. Editor Mother, A Jour. of New Lit., 1964-65; contbr. articles and reviews to newspapers and popular mags. NIMH grantee, 1968-73. Mem. Phi Beta Kappa. Home: 5731 S Blackstone Ave Chicago IL 60637-1823

MOBLEY, EMILY RUTH, library dean, educator; b. Valdosta, Ga., Oct. 1, 1942; d. Emmett and Ruth (Johnson) M. AB in Edn., U. Mich., 1964, AM in Libr. Sci., 1967, postgrad. Tchr. Ecorse (Mich.) Pub. Schs., 1964-65; adminstrv. trainee Chrysler Corp., Highland Park, Mich., 1965-66, engring. libr., 1966-69; libr. II Wayne State U., Detroit, 1969-72, libr. III, 1972-75; staff asst. GM Rsch. Labs. Libr., Warren, Mich., 1976-78, supr. reader svcs., 1978-81; libr. dir. GMI Engring. & Mgmt. Inst., Flint, Mich., 1982-86; assoc. dir. for pub. svcs. & collection devel., assoc. prof. libr. sci. Purdue U. Librs., West Lafayette, Ind., 1986-89, acting dir. librs., assoc. prof. libr. sci., 1989, dean librs., prof. libr. sci., 1989—; adj. lectr. U. Mich. Sch. Libr. Sci., Ann Arbor, 1974-75, 83-86; mem. editorial bd. Reference Svcs. Rev., 1989—; grants reader Libr. of Mich., 1980-81; project dir. Mideastern Mich. Region Libr. Cooperation, 1984-86; cons. Libr. Coop. of Macomb, 1985-86, Clark-Atlanta U., 1990, 91; mem. search com. for new dir. of libr. Smithsonian Instn., 1988; mem. GM Pub. Affairs Subcom. on Introducing Minorities to Engring. Author numerous publs.; mem. editl. bd. Infomanage, 1993—; presenter in field. Mem. corp. vis. com. for librs. MIT, 1990—; mem. Ind. Statewide Libr. Automation Task Force, 1989-90; mem. state tech. strategy subcom. on info. tech. & telecommunications Ind. Corp. for Sci. & Tech., 1989; mem. nat. adv. com. Libr. of Congress, 1988; trustee Libr. of Mich., 1983-86, v.p., 1986, long range plan com., 1979-82, task force on document access and delivery, 1977-79; info. project mem. Rep. Nat. Conv., 1980; bd. dirs. Small Farms Assn., Southfield, Mich. Recipient Bausch & Lomb award for Scientific Achievement, 1960, Cert. for Outstanding Performance in Acad. Achievement State of Mich. Ho. of Reps., 1976, Spl. Tribute for Outstanding Contbns. Libr. of Mich. Bd. Trustees, 1986, Disting. Alumnus award U. Mich. Sch. Info. & Libr. Studies, 1989; U. Mich. Regents Alumni scholar, 1960-64; CIC doctoral fellow in libr. sci., 1973-76. Mem. ALA (com. on accreditation, subcom. to rev. 1972, standards for accreditation 1988-89, OLOS minority internship com. 1988-89, nominating com. 1992-93, mem. coun. resolutions com. 1993—), Assn. Coll. & Rsch. Librs. (task force on libr. sch. curriculum 1988-89, com. on profl. edn. 1990-92), Libr. Adminstrn. & Mgmt. Assn., Assn. Rsch. Librs. (bd. dirs. 1990-93), Spl. Librs. Assn. (pres. 1987-88, fellow 1991, numerous coms. and other offices), Alpha Kappa Alpha. Office: Purdue U Librs Stewart Ctr West Lafayette IN 47907

MOCK, DEAN R., state legislator. Owner, operator, Mock's TV Sales and Svc.; mem. from 48th dist., Ind. State Ho. of Reps., 1976—. mem. pub. policy com., ethics com., vets. affairs com., county and twp. com., labor and employment com., age and agine com., chmn. rds. and transp. com.; pres. Ind. Electric Svc. Assn. Del. Ind. Rep. State Conv., 1978-80. Mem. Elkhart C. of C., Am. Fedn. Musicians, Masons, Shriners, Scottish Rite, Moose. Home: 54135 County Road 7 Elkhart IN 46514-3076*

MOCKABEE, M(ARION) EUGENE, minister; b. Concordia, Kans., June 17, 1940; s. Owen Eugene Brewer and Velda Evon (Cherington) Mockabee; m. Sondra Sue Stanton, June 8, 1963; 1 child, Tabitha Joy Mockabee Coykendall. BSEE, Kans. State U., 1963; MDiv, Lexington Theol. Sem., 1967, D Ministry, 1977. Ordained min. Christian Ch. Pastor First Christian Ch., Dos Palos, Calif., 1967-71, Plattsmouth, Nebr., 1971-79; talk show host Radio KOTD, Plattsmouth, Nebr., 1976-78; sr. pastor Ctrl. Christian Ch., Kalispell, Mont., 1980-88; owner, software developer Nova Computers, Kalispell, Mont., 1984-89; sr. pastor Wyatt Pk. Christian Ch., St. Joseph, Mo., 1989—; moderator Christian Ch. Mont., Great Falls, 1984-86; mem. gen. bd. Christian Ch. in U.S. & Can., Indpls., 1985-90, adminstrv. com., 1988-90, commn. fin., 1990-96. Chaplain Flathead County Sheriff's Dept., Kalispell, 1985-86, Kalispell Police Dept., 1987-88. Decorated Admiral Nebr. Navy, 1979. Mem. High Twelve Club (chaplain 1993), Freemasons (Scottish rite), Shriners, Rotary (chaplain 1984-90). Democrat. Home: 2502 Francis St Saint Joseph MO 64501 Office: Wyatt Pk Christian Ch 2623 Mitchell Ave Saint Joseph MO 64507

MOCKUS, JOSEPH FRANK, electrical engineer; b. Chgo., Nov. 17, 1965; s. Joseph John and Jean Frances (Widmar) M. BS Gen. Engring., Washington Nat. U., 1995. Cert. engr.-in-tng. Mich., cert. quality sys. auditor, RAB. Asst. engr. C. Cretors and Co., Chgo., 1987; dir. engring. Andrew Corp. Wireless Products Group, Itasca, Ill., 1989—. Patentee in field. Mem. ASTM, IEEE, Am. Soc. Quality Control (sr., cert. quality technician), Antennas and Propagation Soc., Vehicular Tech. Soc., No. Ill. Deming User Group, Mensa. Home: 2321 S 11th Ave No Riverside IL 60546-1124 Office: Antenna Co 1100 Maplewood Dr Itasca IL 60143-3205

MODANO, MICHAEL, professional hockey player; b. Livonia, Mich., June 7, 1970. Right wing/center Minn. North Stars, 1988-93, Dallas Stars, 1993—; player World Hockey League East All-Star Game, 1988-89, NHL All-Rookie Game, 1989-90, NHL All-Star Game, 1993. *

MODER, KENNETH PHILIP, chemist; b. Chgo., Dec. 21, 1954; s. William Edward and Marie Ann (Novak) M.; m. Jill Ann Unger, May 16, 1992; 1 child by previous marriage, Jennifer Anne. BS, DePaul U., 1976; PhD, U. Ill., 1981. Sr. chemist Eli Lilly & Co., Lafayette, Ind., 1981-90, rsch. scientist, 1990—. Contbr. articles and referee for several profl. jours.; patentee in field. Mem. AAAS, N.Y. Acad. Sci., Am. Chem. Soc. (organic div.). Office: Eli Lilly & Co PO Box 685 DC TL12 Lafayette IN 47502

MODERY, RICHARD GILLMAN, marketing and sales executive; b. Chgo., Sept. 20, 1941; s. Richard Gustave Modery and Betty Jane (Gillman) Perok; m. Kay Francis Whitby, July 31, 1966 (div. July 1977); children: Stacey Lynn, Marci Kay; m. Anne-Marie Lucette Arsenault, Feb. 27, 1979. Student, Joliet (Ill.) Jr. Coll., 1959-61, Aurora (Ill.) Coll., 1963-65, Davenport Bus. Coll., Grand Rapids, Mich., 1969-71, Northwestern U., Evanston, Ill., 1987. Mktg. products mgr. Rapistan, Inc., Grand Rapids, 1964-75; mgr. estimating, project mgmt., customer svc. E.W. Buschman Co., Cin., 1975-78; exec. v.p. Metzgar Conveyor Co., Grand Rapids, 1979-84; mng. dir. Metzco Internat (cen. and S.Am.), Grand Rapids, Mich., 1981-84, Transfer Technologies, Inc., Grand Rapids, 1984-87; gen. ptnr., pres., chief exec. officer Nat. Monument Co., Grand Rapids, 1986—; v.p. Translogic Corp., Denver, 1987-88; corp. officer, v.p. mktg., field ops. and sales S.I. Handling Systems, Inc., Easton, Pa., 1988-91; v.p. mktg., sales and engring. Integrated Material Handling Co., Tomkins Industries, Inc., Oshkosh, Wis., 1991-93; pres. Handling Concepts, Inc., Chgo., Can., 1993—. Patentee in field. Commr. City of East Grand Rapids, Mich. Traffic Commn., 1983-86. Served with USNG, 1963-69. Mem. Internat. Material Mgmt. Soc., Am. Mgmt. Assn., Material Handling Inst. Am., Material Handling Inst. (speaker nat. confs.), Am. Mktg. Assn., Conveyor Equipment Mfrs. Assn., Material Handling Equipment Distbrs. Assn., Masons (32 degree). Home: 2255 Palmer Cir Naperville IL 60564-5672 Office: Handling Concepts Inc 2255 Palmer Cir Naperville IL 60564-5672

MOE, ROGER DEANE, state legislator, secondary education educator; b. Crookston, Minn., June 2, 1944; s. Melvin Truman and Matheldia (Njus) M.; m. Paulette Moe; four children. BS, Mayville State Coll., 1966; student, Moorhead State Coll., 1969, N.D. State U., 1970. Tchr. Ada (Minn.) H.S., 1966—; v.p. Coleman, Christison Advt. Agy.; Dist. 2 senator Minn. State Senate, St. Paul, 1970—; chmn. rules and adminstrn. com., mem. ethics and campaign reform, edn., and higher edn. coms., Minn. State Senate. Ward del. Ada, Minn., 1970; state del. Minn. Dem.-Farmer-Labor Conv., 1970. Mem. NEA, Ada Edn. Assn., Jaycees. Office: RR 3 Box 86A Erskine MN 56535-9532 also: State Senate State Capital Building Saint Paul MN 55155-1606*

MOE, VIDA DELORES, civic worker; b. Ryder, N.D., Feb. 29, 1928; d. John Nelson and Inga Marie (Lewis) Ahlgran; m. Placido Ferdinand, July 28, 1950 (div.); children: Terrence Paul, Star Marie; m. Edgar Louis Moe, May 24, 1970 (dec. 1983). Student, Minot State U., 1964-66; diploma interior decorating, LaSalle Extension U., 1976. Sec. Raleigh Ins., Tacoma, 1949-50; clk. stenographer Army Transp. Office, San Francisco, 1951-51; clk.-typist Base Supply, Minot AFB, N.D., 1960-61, clk.-stenographer Base Housing, 1961-62, 74, sec. MIADS Direction Ctr., 1962-63, sec. QC Br., 1963-64, sec. dept. acctg. and fin., 1964-65, med. sec. USAF Regional Hosp., 1965-66, sec. Minuteman AFSC, 1966-67, 74-75, sec. 5th Bomb Wing, 1967-70, sec. 1st Missile Wing, 1973-74, sec. dept. mil. personnel, 1975-76, sec. disaster preparedness, 1987-93; sec., salesperson Allen Realty, Minot, 1980-85. Pres. City Art League, 1977-79, 86-87; chmn. Carnegie Restoration and Art Ctr. Project, 1980-87; bd. dirs. Patrons of Libr., Minot, 1978-87, sec., 1979-80, v.p., 1981, pres., 1982-83; v.p. 40/50 Rep. Women Minot, 1982, chair decorations com., 1983; historian Minot Rep. Women, 1984-86. Recipient Superior Performance award 5th Bomb Wing, Minot AFB, 1968, Devotion to Vol. Duty award USAF Regional Hosp., Minot, 1983, 86, Superior Performance Cash award Dept. of Air Force 857 Combat Support Group, 1988-91. Mem. AARP (dir. 1995-96), Nat. Assn. Retired Fed. Employees, N.D. Bus. and Profl. Women's Club (rec. sec. 1978-79, 81-82), Minot Bus. and Profl. Women's Club (pres. 1981-82), Am. Legion Aux. (judge jr. art posters contest 1980-82, pres. 1982-84), Minot Shrine Hosp. Aux. (v.p. 1984, 85, pres. 1986, 87), Beta Sigma Phi (v.p. Laureate Epsilon chpt. 1981-82, pres. 1983-85, Valentine Queen 1985, Girl of Yr. 1985, preceptor Eta chpt., Girl of Yr., 1980, life), MidState Porcelain Artists Guild (v.p. 1983 89, pres. 1984), Order Eastern Star (North Dakota Grand chpt., grand rep. 1979-81, dist. dep. 1982-83, chair credentials com. 1983-84, Grand Martha 1984-85, Grand Electa 1985-86, chmn. registration com. 1986-87, assoc. Grand Conductress 1987-88, Grand Conductress 1989-90, assoc. Grand Matron 1990-91, Worthy Grand Matron 1991-92, Worthy Matron Minot Venus chpt. 1976, 87, 88-89, sec. 1993-94, chaplain 1994-95, assoc. conductress 1995-96, conductress 1996—), Elketts (2nd. v.p. 1988-89, sec. 1993-94), Sons Norway (social dir. 1993-94, chmn. social dirs. 1994), Eagles Aux. (conductor 1993-94, chaplain 1994-95, v.p. 1995-96, pres. 1996—). Lutheran. Avocations: porcelain painting, oil painting, sewing, tennis, embroidery. Home: 705 25th St NW Minot ND 58703-1733

MOEHR, JOHN E., electrical engineer; b. Plymouth, Wis., June 7, 1947. BSEE in Tech., Milw. Sch. Engring., 1976. Software engr. Kearney & Trecker, Milw., 1980-87; project engr. Brady U.S.A., Inc., Milw., 1987—. With USNR, 1966-68. Lutheran.

MOELHMAN, AMY JO, social worker; b. Lafayette, Ind., Mar. 18, 1954; d. Charles and Marian (Young) Moelhman. BS, Ball State U., 1976; MSW, U. Denver, 1979. Cert. clin. social worker, Ind. Social worker Adolescent Crisis Team, Adams County Social Svc., Denver; counselor adolescent boys prog. Pleasant Run Children's Home, Indpls.; group therapist Mothers of Victims of Sexual Abuse, Mid-Town Mental Health, Indpls.; supr. foster care and counseling prog. Children's Bur., Indpls.; mgr. Family Connection Ctr., 1989-90; dir. family programs Vis. Nurse Svc., Indpls., 1990—; chair Ind. Coalition of Family-based Svcs., 1992-94; co-chair family preservation com. Marion County Stepahead; part-time faculty masters in social work program Ind. U.-Purdue U., Indpls. Contbr. articles to profl. jours. Mem. NASW, Acad. Cert. Social Workers. Home: 818 E 53rd St Indianapolis IN 46220-3104

MOEN, RODNEY CHARLES, state senator, retired naval officer; b. Whitehall, Wis., July 26, 1937; s. Edwin O. and Tena A. (Gunderson) M.; m. Catherine Jean Wolfe, 1959; children: Scott A., Jon C., Rodd M., Catherine J., Daniel M. Student Syracuse U., 1964-65; BA, U. So. Calif., 1972; postgrad. Ball State U., 1975-76. Contbg. editor Govt. Photography, 1970-74; gen. mgr. Western Wis. Communications Coop., Independence, Wis., 1976-83; mem. Wis. Senate, 1983—, mem. health, human svcs. and aging com., 1983—. Lt. USN, 1955-76, Vietnam. Democrat. Home: 2119 Dewey St Whitehall WI 54773-9591 Office: State Capitol PO Box 7882 Madison WI 53707-7882

MOENS, THOMAS ODIN, lawyer, computer consultant; b. Moline, Ill., Dec. 11, 1961; s. Arlen L. and Judith E. (Minick) M. AA, Black Hawk Coll., Moline, 1986; BS, U. Iowa, 1988, JD, 1992. Bar: Ill. 1992, Iowa 1993, U.S. Ct. Appeals (7th cir.) 1993, U.S. Dist. Ct. (ctrl. dist.) Ill. 1993. Entertainer, musician, Moline, 1982-89; mng. editor Transnat. Law and Contemporary Problems, Iowa City, 1990-92; assoc. Blackwood, Nowinski, Huntoon & Swanson, P.C., Moline, 1991—; computer applications cons. Ipse Dixit Pub., Moline, 1988—. Mem. ABA, Ill. State Bar Assn., Iowa State Bar Assn., Scott County Bar Assn., Rock Island County Bar Assn., Rock Island Jaycees (bd. dirs. 1994—), Ill. Quad Cities Rotary, Quad Cities Credit Assn., Quad City Bicycle Club, Iowa Trails Coun., Rails to Trails Conservancy, Cornbelt Running Club, Phi Theta Kappa. Office: Blackwood Nowinski Huntoon & Swanson 1000 36th Ave Ste 100 Moline IL 61265-7126

MOERDYK, CHARLES CONRAD, school system administrator; b. Kalamazoo, Sept. 4, 1948; s. Vernon Frank and Eileen Marie (Riverside) M.; m. Cheryl Ann Rudge, July 29, 1967 (div. 1984); children: Paulette Ann, Carie Ann; m. Cynthia Marie Peters, Sept. 1, 1984. BBA, Western Mich. U., 1970; M of Edn. Adminstrn., Northern Mich. U., 1990. CPA Mich. 1974. Acct. J.R. Rugg & Co., Grand Rapids, Mich., 1970-71; controller Newman Visual Edn. Inc., Grand Rapids, Mich., 1971-73; asst. auditor gen. State of Mich., Lansing, 1973-74; ptnr. Goodman deMink & Cerutti, Kalamazoo, 1974-79; cons. pvt. practice, Kalamazoo & Crystal Falls, Mich., 1980-85; interim dir. support svcs. Planned PArenthood Assn., Chgo., 1981-82; bus. mgr. Breitung Twp. Schs., Kingsford, Mich., 1985-89, Alma (Mich.) Pub. Schs., 1989—; adj. prof. Davenport Coll., Alma, 1991—; dir., treas. Gra Co Fed. Union, Alma, 1991-94. Mem. World Future Soc. Home: PO Box 305 Alma MI 48801-0305 Office: Alma Pub Schs 1500 Pine Ave Alma MI 48801-1275

MOFFATT, DAVID ROBERT, freelance writer; b. Newport, R.I., July 17, 1963; s. Robert Bruce and JoAnn (Vosika) M.; m. Joan Margaret Zurn, Jan. 12, 1994. Pvt. practice as writer and photographer Eveleth, Minn., 1981—; poetry editor Star Triad Mag., Vero Beach, Fla., 1992-93. Author: The Folded Paper Dream, 1993, Explorations in the Ordinary, 1996, (computer software) Four Text Adventures and Moffatt's Adventure, 1987-88; columnist: Seasons, 1990-92. Recipient first place award for photography Celebrate Minn., 1990. Mem. MENSA. Libertarian. Home: 710 Harrison St Eveleth MN 55734

MOFFITT, DONALD L., state legislator; b. Knox County, Feb. 18, 1947; s. Russell Wellington and Gertrude (Johnson) M.; m. Carolyn J. Lock; children: Linda J., Justin L., Amanda H. BS, U. Ill., 1969. Tchr.; Dist. 94 rep. Ill. Ho. Reps., Springfield, 1993—; treas. West Ill. Police Tng. Orgn.; mem. Knox County bd., 1978-84, chmn. 1982-84, treas. 1984-93; mem. Agr. Housing and Edn. Com. Ill. Ho. Reps., 1993—; sec. Agr. and Edn. Twp. and County Com., 1995—. Mem. Carver Cmty. Action Agy. recipient Friend of Agr. award Ill. Farm Bur., 1994—. Mem. Ill. Farm Bur., Lions Club, Masons, Alpha Zeta, Omicron Delta Kappa. Home: RR 1 Box 160 Gilson IL 61436-9707*

MOGHISSI, KAMRAN S., obstetrician, gynecologist, educator; b. Tehran, Iran, Sept. 11, 1925; came to U.S., 1959, naturalized, 1965; s. Ahmad and Monireh (Rohani) M.; m. Ida Laura Tedeschi, Jan. 2, 1952; children: Diana J., Soraya R. ChB, MB, U. Geneva, 1951, MD, 1952. Diplomate Am. Bd. Ob-Gyn., Am. Bd. Reproductive Endocrinology. Intern, Univ. Hosp., Geneva, 1951-52, Horton Gen. Hosp., United Oxford Hosps., Banbury, Eng., 1952-53; resident in ob-gyn. Gloucestershire Royal Hosp., Eng., 1953-54, St. Helier Hosp., London, 1954-55, Leeds Regional Hosp. Bd., Yorkshire, Eng., 1955-56, Detroit Receiving Hosp., 1961, attending gynecologist, 1962; assoc. prof. ob-gyn. U. Shiraz Med. Sch., Iran, 1957-59; rsch. assoc. ob-gyn. and physiol. chemistry, Wayne State U., Detroit, 1959-61, asst. prof., 1962-66, assoc. prof., 1966-70, prof., 1970—, dir. div. reproductive endocrinology and infertility, 1970-94; vice chmn., 1983-88, chmn. dept. ob-gyn., 1988-91; sr. attending physician ob-gyn. Hutzel Hosp., Detroit, 1963, vice chief, 1978-82, 83-89, chief, 1982-83, 88-91, chief of staff, 1991-93, attending surgeon, chief ob-gyn. Harper-Grace Hosp., 1983-84, attending surgeon, emeritus, chief ob-gyn. emeritus, 1991—; obstetrician, gynecologist, chief, Detroit Med. Ctr., 1988-91; cons. and lectr. in field. Contbr. chpts. to books, articles to profl. jours. Developer exhibits in medicine, movies and teaching prodns.; mem. numerous editorial bds.; cons. in field. Fellow ACS, Am. Coll. Ob-Gyn. Am. Gynecol. and Obstetric Soc.; mem. AMA (ho. of dels. 1992—), AAAS, Am. Soc. Reprodn. Medicine (formerly Am. Fertility Soc., pres. 1990-91), Soc. Study Reprodn., Am. Soc. Andrology, Wayne County Med. Soc., Mich. Soc. Ob-Gyn, Central Assn. Ob-Gyn., N.Y. Acad. Scis., Soc. Reproductive Endocrinologists (charter mem., pres. 1990), Soc. Reproductive Surgeons (charter mem.), Soc. for Assisted Reproductive Tech. (charter mem.), Lochmoor Club (Grosse Pointe), Renaissance Club (Detroit). Home: 56 Moorland Dr Grosse Pointe Shores MI 48236-1112 Office: Hutzel Hosp 4707 St Antoine Blvd Detroit MI 48201-1427

MOGIELSKI, PHYLLIS ANN, health association administrator, psychotherapist; b. Chgo., Mar. 5, 1964; d. Edward John and Carmella (Iovino) M. BA, Coll. St. Francis, Joliet, Ill., 1986; MS, Ill. Benedictine Coll., 1990. Cert. drug and alcohol abuse counselor. Sr. counselor PEER Svcs., Inc., Evanston, Ill., 1987-90; project mgr. Am. Acad. Pediatrics, Elk Grove Village, Ill., 1991—; youth worker Dept. Youth Svcs., Highland Park, Ill., 1989; supr., dir. social svcs. Bonaventure House, Chgo., 1989-91, instr. Moraine Valley C.C., Palos Hills, Ill., 1991; assoc. psychotherapist Healy & Assocs., Naperville, Ill., 1991-92, Brook Clinic Assocs., Oak Brook, Ill., 1992—. Mem. NASW, Employee Assistance Profls. Assn., Inc., Ill. Alcohol and other Drugs Profl. Cert. Assn., Inc. Office: Am Acad Pediatrics 141 NW Point Blvd Elk Grove Village IL 60007-1019

MOGLER, ROBERT WAYNE, banker; b. Elgin, Ill., Jan. 21, 1941; s. Clarence Robert and Ruth Lucille (Hoagland) M.; m. RuthAnn Marie Lobben (dec.); children: Cynthia Ann Myroth, Deborah R., Rebecca. From cashier to v.p. Elgin (Ill.) Nat. Bank, 1959-76; v.p. Elgin Fed. Fin. Ctr., 1976—; pres. Elgin (Ill.) Agy., Inc., 1985—. Dir. Sr. Svcs. Assocs., Inc. 1988-94, treas., 1990-93; mem. exec. bd. Elgin Neighborhood Watch, 1993-95; active Elgin Leadership Conf., 1995. Recipient Golden Heart award Heartland Blood Ctr., 1959-95, Appreciation award City of Elgin, 1994; named Ill. Citizen of Yr., Ill. Crime Prevention Assn., 1995. Mem. Fin. Instns. Mktg. Assn., Fin. Instns. Ins. Mgrs., Am. Mktg. Assn. Presbyterian. Office: Elgin Fed Fin Ctr 850 Summit St Elgin IL 60120

MOHLER, TERENCE JOHN, psychologist; s. Edward F. and Gertrude A. (Aylward) M.; m. Carol B. Kulczak; children: Renee, John, Timothy. BE, ME, EdS, Toledo U.; PhD, Walden U., Union Inst., 1979. Psychologist, Toledo Bd. Edn., 1969-89; sr. ptnr. Psychol. Assocs., Maumee, Ohio, 1970—; assoc. fellow Inst. for Advanced Study in Rational Psychotherapy, N.Y.C. Served with U.S. Army, 1951-53; Korea. Lic. psychologist, Ohio. Mem. Am., Ohio, Northwestern Ohio, Maumee Valley Psychol. Assns., Soc. Behaviorists, Toledo Acad. Profl. Psychology, Nat. Registry Mental Health Providers, Am. Pers. and Guidance Assn., Ohio Pers. and Guidance Assn., Coun. for Exceptional Children, Rotary (Paul Harris Fellow), Kappa Delta Phi. Home: 1904 Glen Ellyn Dr Toledo OH 43614-3256 Office: 5757 Monclova Rd Maumee OH 43537-1837

MOHN, WALTER ROSING, metallurgical engineer, researcher; b. Fairmont, W.Va., Mar. 20, 1948; s. Norman Carroll and Edna Louise (Rosing) M.; m. Tracey Davison, Oct. 15, 1977; children: Kristin, Lindsay. BS in Aerospace Engring., Tex. A&M U., 1972; MS in Metallurgy, U. Conn., 1974. Materials engr. Pratt & Whitney Aircraft, East Hartford, Conn., 1974-76; rsch. metallurgist R&D dept. R&D ctr. GE, Schenectady, N.Y., 1976-78; pilot plant supr. Allied-Signal Corp., Morristown, N.J., 1978-83; dir. advanced tech. Advanced Composite Materials Corp., Greer, S.C., 1983-90; prin. engr. Babcock & Wilcox, Alliance, Ohio, 1990—. Inventor, patentee mirror optic article, rapid solidification processing, heat exchanger tube design; contbd. articles to profl. jours. Pres. Powderhorn Homeowners Assn., Simpsonville, S.C., 1984-86. Recipient 2nd honorable mention, 1984, prin. developer r&d 100 award, 1987, R&D Mag., Des Plaines. Mem. ASM Internat. (chpt. chmn. 1989-90, 94-95), Wilderness Ctr., Astronomy Club. Home: 7836 Campton Cir NW North Canton OH 44720-8327 Office: Babcock & Wilcox R & D Div 1562 Beeson St NE Alliance OH 44601-2165

MOHR, EILEEN THERESA, environmental geologist; b. Buffalo, Feb. 21, 1957; d. Jacob Carl and Marjorie Mary (McDonald) M. BA magna cum laude in geology, SUNY, Buffalo, 1979; MS summa cum laude, Kent State U., 1983. Cert. profl. geologist, hazardous materials mgr.; lic. profl. geologist, Pa. Intern U.S. Geol. Survey, Flagstaff, Ariz., 1978; grad. tchg. asst. Kent (Ohio) State U., 1979-81; geologist Ohio Environ. Protection Agy., Twinsburg, 1982-87, project mgr., 1990—; co-facilitator H.M. Environ. Reflection Action Group, Villa Maria, Pa., 1989-91. Head coach Challenger Baseball, Streetsboro, Ohio, 1994—; vol. AIDS Holistic Health Svcs., Akron, Ohio, 1990—, H.M. Life Opportunity Svcs., Akron, 1990—, Villa Maria Organic Farm, 1995—, various others. Recipient 1st and 2nd place Randolph Portage County Fair photography contest, 1986. Mem. N.E. Ohio Cert. Hazardous Materials Mgr.'s chpt., Kent State Newman Ctr. Democrat. Roman Catholic. Office: Ohio Environ Protection Agy 2110 E Aurora Rd Twinsburg OH 44087

MOHR, ELLEN G., English language educator; b. Mt. Pleasant, Iowa, Dec. 5, 1942; d. F.W. and Martha Margaret (Desenberg) Grube; m. Jan A. Mohr, Aug. 18, 1972; children: Jon, Jennifer. BS in Edn., N.W. Mo. U., 1964, MA in English, 1970. English instr. George Washington Middle Sch., Ridgewood, N.J., 1968-69, Excelsior Springs (Mo.) High Sch., 1970-71, Greenfield Middle Sch., Cin., 1972-73; writing ctr. dir. Johnson County Community Coll., Overland Park, Kans., 1980—; staff devel. intern Johnson County Comm. Coll., Overland Park, Kans., 1994-95, faculty dir. Ctr. for Teaching and Learning, 1995—. Author: Midwest Writing Center Association Proceedings Book, Writing Lab., Newsletter. Recipient Faculty Recognition award Mich. Consortium for C.C.'s, 1991-92, Disting. Status award Johnson County C.C., 1994-96. Mem. Midwest Writing Ctr. Assn. (chair bd. dirs. 1986-91), Nat. Writing Ctr. Assn. (exec. bd. 1989-92, named peer tutor cons.), Kans. Assn. Tchrs. of English, Phi Delta Kappa. Home: 10826 King St Shawnee Mission KS 66210-1267

MOHR, JAMES LEGRAND, accountant; b. Indpls., May 20, 1950; s. George William and Joan Eillen (Goldsmith) M.; m. Aline Mary Lindquist, Dec. 29, 1973; children: Stephen, Eric, Mark, Michael. BS, Ind. U., 1972, JD, 1975. CPA, Wis. Ptnr. KPMG Peat Marwick, Milw., 1975—. Mem. planned giving coun. Children's Hosp., Milw. Mem. Am. Inst. CPA's, Wis. Inst. CPA's, Wis. Retirement Plan Profl. Ltd. (v.p. 1985-88)., Milw. Estate Planning Coun., Ltd. (bd. dir. 1990—). Presbyterian. Clubs: Milw. Yacht, Ozaukee Country (Mequon, Wis.).

MOHR, KAREN, accounting executive; b. Adrian, Mich., June 11, 1963; d. Archie and Arda (Tressler) Bragg; m. David Mohr, June 1, 1985; children: Timothy, Eric David, Eddie Allen. A in Acctg., Jackson Bus. Inst., 1983. Data entry clk. Credit Bur. Lenawee County, Adrian, 1985, Merrilats, Adrian, 1986; circulation clk. Adrian Daily Telegram, 1987-89; pres. Golden Sunshine Products, Adrian, 1989—. Home and Office: 705 N Locust St Adrian MI 49221-2241

MOILANEN, THOMAS ALFRED, construction equipment distributor; b. Hancock, Mich., Sept. 3, 1944; s. A. Edward and Elsie E. (Karkanen) M.; m. Kathleen Ann Maibach, Sept. 18, 1965; children: Todd Alan, Karl Edward. Cert., Wayne State U., 1967. Licensed funeral dir., Mich. Funeral dir. Ross B. Northrop & Son, Inc., Redford, Mich., 1967-68; sales mgr. Cloverdale Equipment Co., Oak Park, Mich., 1971; v.p., gen. mgr. Cloverdale Equipment Co., Oak Park, 1972-78, pres., chief exec. officer, bd. dirs., 1978—; pres., chief exec. officer, bd. dirs. Hasper Equipment Co., Muskegon, Mich., 1980—, SunBelt Crane & Equipment, Sarasota, Fla., 1982-90, Armstrong/Cloverdale Equipment Co., Columbia, S.C., 1987-89; pres. Air Cloverdale, Inc., 1996—. Treas., bd. dirs. Livonia Hockey Assn., 1981-82. Mem. Associated Equipment Distbrs. Am. (equipment distbn. com. 1984, lt. dir. region 7 1993), Mich. Constrn. Equipment Dealers Assn. (pres. 1983, 88, 94), Concrete Improvement Bd. (bd. dirs. 1978-79), Kiwanis (bd. dirs. Redford 1967-69, pres. 1969-70), Skyline Club (Southfield, Mich.). Republican. Home: 18332 Laraugh Dr Northville MI 48167-3504 Office: Cloverdale Equipment Co 13133 Cloverdale St Oak Park MI 48237-3205

MOKARI, MOHAMMED EBRAHIM, electrical engineer; b. Azarshahr, Iran, Feb. 19, 1943; came to U.S., 1984; s. Hossein and Ghamar (Budagi) M.; m. Ashraf S. Hashemi Davani, Oct. 6, 1971; children: Babak, Atabak, Amir. BS in Physics, U. Tabriz, Iran, 1964; MSEE, Mich. Tech. U., 1968; PhD in Elect. Engring., U. Ill., 1970. Registered profl. engr., Ohio. Prof., dept. chmn. Sharaz (Iran) U., 1970-84; assoc. prof. U. Ill., Urbana, 1984-86; assoc. prof. Ohio U., Athens, 1986-90, prof., 1990—; rschr., cons. Wright Patterson Airforce Base, Dayton, Ohio, 1987—; vis. rsch. assoc. Cornell U., Ithaca, N.Y., 1974-75; participant Tokten program UN, N.Y.C., 1991, 93; reviewer and presenter in field. Contbr. articles to profl. jours. Recipient Outstanding Rsch. award Ohio U. Sch. Engring. and Tech., 1989. Mem. IEEE (sr. mem.). Home: 13 Coventry Ln Athens OH 45701 Office: Ohio Univ Stocker Ctr 345 Athens OH 45701

MOLARO, ROBERT S, state legislator, lawyer. BS, Loyola U.; JD, John Marshall Law Sch. Dem. committeeman Ward 12 Chgo.; Dist. 12 senator Ill. Senate, Springfield, 1993—; del. Dem. Nat. Conv. 1988. Home: 4655 S Springfield Ave Chicago IL 60632-4043*

MOLDENHAUER, KENNETH LEE, training executive; b. Independence, Kans., Aug. 6, 1964; s. Frank L. and Dorothy (Tallman) M.; m. Marcine L. Shaner, Sept. 3, 1988. AA, Coffeyville (Kans.) C.C., 1984; BS in Agrl. Edn., Kans. State U., 1986; MS in Agrl. Edn., 1987. Grad. teaching asst. Kans. State U., Manhattan, 1986-87; human resources trainee Excel Corp., Dodge City, Kans., 1987-88, human resources tng. asst., 1988-89, coord. hourly employee tng., 1989-91, coord. hourly employee tng. corp., 1991-93; mgr. ops. tng. Excel Corp., Wichita, Kans., 1993—. Mem. Am. Mgmt. Assn., Toastmasters (treas. 1992-93). Office: Excel Corp 151 N Main St Wichita KS 67201

MOLENBEEK, ROBERT GERRIT, accountant, realtor; b. Grand Rapids, Mich., Feb. 7, 1944; s. Gerrit John and Jean (Wierenga) M.; m. Marsha Lee Rockel, Mar. 23, 1966; children: Rebecca, Tammy, Brian, Brent. AS in Bus. Adminstrn. with honors, Davenport U., 1964; BBA in Acctg. with honors, Ferris State U., 1966; MBA, Grand Valley State U., 1976. CPA, Mich.; cert. comml. investment mem.; cert. exch. consular; cert. buyer broker; cert. internat. property specialist; accredited land consular. Staff acct. various firms Grand Rapids, 1969-72; staff acct., ptnr. Tuori Jacobson, CPA, Muskegon, Mich., 1972-73; sr. internal auditor Wolverine Worldwide, Rockford, Mich., 1973-75; pvt. practice acctg. Grand Rapids, 1975—; controller Sq. Real Estate, Grand Rapids, 1976-87, real estate salesman, 1976—; cons. Property Corp. Am., 1976-94, S & S Supplies, Grand Rapids, 1986—, Ea. Gardens, Inc., 1987-89. Active West Mich. R.R. Hist. Soc., Grand Rapids, 1986—, Muskegon R.R. Hist. Soc., 1985—, Trade exch. Am., 1985—; active Realtors Land Inst., 1987—, dir., 1990, sec.-treas., 1991-92, v.p. 1993, pres., 1995—, nat. gov.-at-large, 1991—, nat. market session com. chmn. 1995, nat. v.p. fin. 1996; gov. Comml. Indsl. Group Mich. Assn. of Realtors, 1993, chmn.-elect, 1995, chmn. 1996. Mem. AICPA, Mich. Assn. CPAs, Nat. Assn. Realtors, Mich. Assn. Realtors, Grand Rapids Assn. Realtors (mem. comm./indsl. com. 1989-92), Grand Rapids Exchangers and Traders, Comml. Investment Real Estate Inst. (Multimillion Sales award 1976—, Ten Million Sales award 1980, Top Ten Sales award 1980), Internat. Real Estate Fedn., Mich. Bus. Brokers Assn., Mich. Assn. Real Estate Exchangers (assoc., sec. 1989, pres. 1990), Ind. Real Estate Exchangers (affiliate), Chgo. Area Real Estate Exchangers (affiliate). Home: 4440 7 Mile Rd NE Belmont MI 49306-9650 Office: SJ Wisinski & Co 2618 E Paris Ave SE Grand Rapids MI 49546-6137

MOLER, DONALD LEWIS, educational psychology educator; b. Wilsey, Kans., Jan. 12, 1918; s. Ralph Lee and Bessie Myrtle (Berry) M.; B.S., Kans. State Tchrs. Coll., Emporia, 1939; M.S., U. Kans., Lawrence, 1949, Ph.D., 1951; m. Alta Margaret Ansdell, Nov. 6, 1942; 1 son, Donald Lewis Jr. Tchr., Centralia (Kans.) High Sch., 1939-42, Carthage (Mo.) High Sch., 1946-48; asst. dir. Reading Clinic, U. Kans., 1948-51; dir. reading program Ea. Ill. U., 1951-70, prof. dept. ednl. psychology and guidance, 1963—, chmn. dept., 1963-84, dean Sch. Edn., 1980; vis. scholar U. Fla., 1965. Served with Signal Corps, U.S. Army, 1942-46. Recipient C.A. Michelman award, 1974; Disting Svc. award Ill. Assn. Counselor Educators, 1985. Mem. Ill. Guidance and Pers. Assn. (pres. 1968-69), Ill. Counselor Educators and Suprs., Ill. Coll. Pers. Assn., Am. Pers. and Guidance Assn. (senator 1970-71), Assn. Counselor Edn. and Supervision, Assn. Humanistic Edn. and Devel., Phi Delta Kappa, Xi Phi, Pi Omega Pi, Pi Kappa Delta, Sigma Tau Gamma. Methodist. Assoc. editor Ill. Guidance and Pers. Assn. Quar., 1970-84, mng. editor, 1984—. Home: 407 W Hayes Ave Charleston IL 61920-3303 Office: Ea Ill U Dept Ednl Psychology and Guidance Charleston IL 61920

MOLFESE, VICTORIA J., research administrator; b. Palo Alto, Calif., Aug. 27, 1946; d. James Frederick and A. Victoria (Parsons) Jones; m. Dennis L. Molfese, Sept. 11, 1971; children: David L., Peter J. BA, San Francisco State U., 1968, MA, 1970; PhD, Pa. State U., 1974. Asst. prof. So. Ill. U., Carbondale, 1973-78, assoc. prof., 1978-85, prof., 1985—, assoc. dir., 1986, acting dir., 1986-88, assoc. dean/dir., 1988—. Author: Perinatal Risk and Infant Development, 1989. Bd. dirs. Archway, Carbondale; active Boy Scouts of Am., Carbondale, 1989—. Grantee Ill. Groundwater Consortium, Washington, 1990, Neonatal Predictors of Lang., Washington, 1986—, Kellogg Found., Mich., 1994-95. Mem. Soc. Rsch. Adminstrs., Nat. Coun. of Univ. Rsch. Adminstrs., Midwest Soc. of Rsch. Adminstrs. (pres. 1992-93), Coun. of Grad. Schs., Nat. Assn. State U. and Land Grant Colls., Am. Psychol. Soc. Office: So Ill Univ Woody Hall C-206 Carbondale IL 62901

MOLIERE, JEFFREY MICHAEL, cardio-pulmonary administrator; b. San Pedro, Calif., Nov. 22, 1948; s. Dwight Hedrick and Geraldine Stabile. AA, L.A. Harbor Coll., 1968; postgrad., Calif. State U., Long Beach, 1968-69; cert. in respiratory care, Calif. Coll. for Health Sci., 1982, Biosystems Inst., 1984; assoc. degree, Ind. U., Indpls., 1987, B in Gen. Studies, 1990; MS in Cmty. Health Adminstrn., Calif. Coll. for Health Sci., 1994. Registered respiratory therapist, respiratory care practitioner; cert. pulmonary tech. Alt. supr. Good Samaritan Hosp., Vincennes, Ind., 1976-79; critical care technician Winona Meml. Hosp., Indpls., 1979-80; neonatal ICU-critical care technician Mercy Hosp., Urbana, Ill., 1980-82; cardio-pulmonary supr. Winona Meml. Hosp., Indpls., 1982-92; dir. pulmonary svcs. MidWest Med. Ctr., Indpls., 1992-93; mgr., bronchoscopy, pulmonary function testing, respiratory care VA Med. Ctr., Indpls., 1993—, ednl. coord., EEO counselor, 1993—; mem. adj. faculty Ind. Vocat.-Tech. Coll., 1993—; adv. bd. Allied Health Ind. U., 1995—. Mem. adv. bd. allied health Ind. U., 1996—, Ind. Vocat. Tech. Coll., 1987—. Mem. Nat. Bd. Respiratory Care, Am. Assn. for Respiratory Care (clin. practice guideline rev. bd.), Ind. Soc. for Respiratory Care, Nat. Bd. for Respiratory Care, Alpha Sigma Lambda (charter, Membership award 1990).

MOLL, JOSEPH EUGENE, chemical engineer, chemical company executive; b. Evansville, Ind., Sept. 3, 1950; s. Jacob Eugene and Mary Ann (Zenthoefer) M., m. Karen Jean Pennington, Aug. 20. 1977; children: Laura, Angela, Jared. BS in Chem. Engring., Purdue U., 1972. Cert. ofcl. USS Swimming. Mem. mfg. mgmt. staff GE, Selkirk, Danville, N.Y., Ill, 1972-74; product devel. engr. GE, Pittsfield, Mass., 1974-75; tech. specialist Betz Labs., Kokomo, Ind., 1975-78; account mgr. Betz Labs., Evansville, Ind., 1978-88; account exec. Betz Indsl., Evansville, 1988-90, area mgr., 1990—; mem. Mayor's Tech. Adv. Com., Mt. Vernon, Ind., 1983—. Instr. ARC, Evansville, 1971-73; ofcl. Ill. High Sch. Assn., Danville, 1972-73; min. of the word St. Matthew's Ch., Mt. Vernon, Ind., 1980—; amb. Promise Keepers Men's Ministry, 1994—, Sunday sch. tchr., 1996—; asst. cubmaster Boy Scouts Am., 1993—. Mem. AICE (v.p. 1971-72), Tech. Assn. of Pulp and Paper Industry, Am. Water Works Assn., Purdue Alumni Assn. (life), John Purdue Coaches Club, Elks, Omega Chi Epsilon, Triangle Fraternity. Roman CAtholic. Home: 28 Parkridge Dr Mount Vernon IN 47620-9405 Office: Betz Labs 3751 Pennridge Dr Ste 116 Bridgeton MO 63044

MOLL, WILLIAM GENE, broadcasting company executive; b. Sikeston, Mo., Dec. 25, 1937; s. John Alexander and Letha Ann (McDowell) M.; m. Marilyn Lewis, Aug. 2, 1957; children: David William, Craig Lewis. Student, So. Ill. U., 1955-57, Anderson Coll., 1957-58; B.S. in Edn., S.E. Mo. State Coll., 1960; M.A., U. Tex., 1963. Announcer, program dir. Sta. KSIM, Sikeston, Mo., 1954-57, 58-59; announcer Sta. WCBC, Anderson, Ind., 1957; announcer, writer, dir., news anchor KFVS-TV, Cape Girardeau, Mo., 1959-62; producer, dir., writer KLRN-TV, Austin, Tex., 1962-64; mgr. sta. ops. KLRN-TV, San Antonio, 1964-69; v.p., gen. mgr. WSMW-TV, Worcester, Mass., 1969-72; with KENS-TV, San Antonio, 1972-87, pres., gen. mgr., 1977-81, chmn., 1981-87; pres., chief exec. officer Harte-Hanks TV Group, 1979-81; pres., chief exec. officer Harte-Hanks Broadcasting & Entertainment, 1981-87, chmn. TV group, 1981—; sr. v.p. Harte-Hanks Communications, Inc., 1981-87. Bd. dirs. San Antonio Art Inst., 1974—, chmn., 1978-81; bd. dirs. Goodwill Industries, 1973-87, pres., 1987-88; bd. dirs. San Antonio Symphony Soc., 1979-85, United Way San Antonio, 1979-82, Friends of the McNay, 1979-81, Media-Advt. Partnership for Drug-Free Am., 1987—; exec. bd. Alamo Area council Boy Scouts Am. Mem. Tex. Assn. Broadcasters (dir. 1976—, sec.-treas. 1981—, pres. 1983), TV Bur. of Advt. (bd. dirs. 1980—, sec. 1981-83, chmn. 1983-85, pres./chief exec. officer 1987—), CBS TV Affiliates Assn. (bd. dirs. 1980-83), Internat. Radio TV Found. (bd. dirs. 1985-88), Advt. Council (bd. dirs. 1987—), Electronic Media Rating Council (bd. dirs. 1987—). Clubs: Torch (San Antonio), Giraud (San Antonio); Oak Hills Country. Office: WKRC-TV 1906 Highland Ave Cincinnati OH 45219-3104*

MOLLENKAMP, GAYLE L., state legislator; m. Marilyn Mollenkamp. Rep. dist. 118 State of Kans. Republican. *

MOLLOFF, FLORENCE JEANINE, speech and language therapist; b. St. Louis, Aug. 28, 1959; d. Lawrence Allan and Rietta Gertrude (Fiegenbaum) M. BS, Fontbonne Coll., St. Louis, 1983; MEd summa cum laude, Nat. Louis U., St. Louis, 1989; student, Project ACCESS Inst., 1992, Judevine Ctr. Autistic Children Tng., 1992. Cert. speech correctionist, Mo. Intern St. Louis State Sch. for Profoundly Retarded, 1983-84; speech therapist St. Louis Pub. Schs., 1984—; Judvine Ctr. for Autistic Children Tng., 1992; speech/lang. therapist St. Louis Pub. Schs./Autism Program, 1992-93; speech/lang. therapist Michael Sch. Medically Fragile and Multiply Handicapped St. Louis Pub. Schs., 1993—, speech, lang. therapist St. Louis Pub. Schs./Michael Sch. for Medically Fragile and Multiply Handicapped, 1993—; ednl. cons. program devel. Mo. Coalition for Environ., St. Louis, Columbia, Kansas City, 1990—; cons., trainer in puppetry Kids on the Block, St. Louis Pub. Schs., 1988—; vol. grant writer West End Restoration Corp. Author, creator transition curriculum: Consultative Resource Program, 1989; creator puppet program: Save Our Astonishing Plantet, 1990; ednl. cons. program devel. young St. Louis audiences (adapted program for severe to profoundly handicapped children "Arabian Nights", 1994; contbr. artist St. Louis Internat. Jazz Mus.; vol. grant writer West End Restoration Corp. Educator, lobbyist Coalition for the Environ., St. Louis, 1990; activist, lobbyist Housing Now, St. Louis, 1989; foster paranet Christian Children's Fund, 1986—; activist Habitat for Humanity Internat., 1994—; mem., fundraiser Gateway I Have a Dream Found., 1995—; mem. nat. steering com. (hon.) Pres. Clinton's Re-election, 1995; vol. grant writer West End Restoration Corp.; mem. Emily's List. Mem. AAUW, Coun. Exceptional Children (state rep. Mo. divsn. for children with communicative disorders 1988-89, presenter nat. conv. 1989), Internat. Platform Assn., Am. Fedn. Tchrs. (bldg. rep. 1992), Nat. Arbor Day Found., Nat. Parks and Conservation Assn., Nat. Women's Polit. Caucus, Mo. Assn. for Augmentative Comm. Systems, Met. St. Louis Women's Polit. Caucus, Emily's List, Am. Med. Writers Assn., Soc. for Technical Communication. Democrat. Home: 9823 Lullaby Ln Saint Louis MO 63114-2510

MOLNAU, CAROL, state legislator; b. Sept. 17, 1949; m. Steven F. Molnau; 3 children. Attended, U. Minn. Mem. Minn. Ho. of Reps., 1992—. Active Our Saviors Luth. Ch., 4-H, Chaska City Coun. Mem. Agrl. Com., Econ. Devel., Infrastructure & Regulation Fin.-Transportation Fin. Divsn., Fin. Inst. & Ins.: Internat. Trade & Economic Devel. Republican. Home: 495 Pioneer Trl Chaska MN 55318-1151 Office: 287 State Office Bldg Saint Paul MN 55155

MOLTZ, MARSHALL JEROME, lawyer; b. Chgo., May 22, 1930; s. Nathan and Rose (Nathanson) M.; m. Rita G., Dec. 26, 1954; m. 2d, Mary Ann, Nov. 4, 1967; children: Alan J., Michelle S. Yastrow, Marilyn F. Moltz-Hohmann, Julie A., Steven E., Rachel N. BS, Northwestern U., 1951, JD, 1954. Bar: Ill. 1954, Mo. 1954. Assoc., John B. Moser, Chgo., 1957; assoc. Goldberg, Devoe, Shadur & Mikva, Chgo., 1957-58; assoc. Lester Plotkin, Chgo., 1958-59; sole practice, Chgo., 1959-65; ptnr. Moltz & Spagat, Chgo., 1966-67; sole practice, Chgo., 1967-68; ptnr. Moltz & Wexler, Chgo., 1968-80; sole practice Chgo. 1980—; pres. Mercury Title Co.; faculty mem. profl. liab. in real estate transactions ABA Regional Inst., 1993; mem. Blue Ribbon com. Cook County Recorder of Deeds; speaker real estate law; atty. Counseling Ctr. of Lake View Mental Health Orgn., Chgo. With M.I., U.S. Army, 1955-56; ETO. Recipient Louden Wigmore prize Northwestern U. Law Sch., 1954. Mem. ABA, Am. Coll. Real Estate Lawyers, Ill. State Bar Assn., Chgo. Bar Assn. (mem. real property law com. 1958—, chmn. Torrens sub-com. 1968-75, vice chmn. real property law com. 1974-75, chmn. real property law com. 1975-76, speaker and faculty mem. various seminars 1993-96, faculty mem. residential real estate seminar, 1995, 96), VFW, Phi Alpha Delta (law fraternity). Author course outlines Ill. Inst. Continuing Legal Edn., 1972, 73; editorial bd. Northwestern U. Law Rev., 1953-54. Home: 112 Harvard Ct Glenview IL 60025-5917 Office: 77 W Washington St Ste 1620 Chicago IL 60602-2903

MOLZEN, CHRISTOPHER JOHN, lawyer; b. Manhattan, Kans., Sept. 5, 1961; s. Gilbert John and Janice Molzen; m. Robin Larson. BA in Polit. Sci., U. Mo., 1983, JD, 1987. Bar: Mo. 1987, U.S. Dist. Ct. (we. dist.) Mo. 1987, U.S. Tax Ct. 1994, U.S. Supreme Ct. 1994. Assoc. Crouch, Spangler & Douglas, Harrisonville, Mo., 1989-95, Shughart Thomson & Kilroy, Kansas City, 1995—. Co-author, editor The Judicial Handbook of Kansas City, 1993. Pegasus scholar Inner Temple, London, 1991, William L. Bradshaw scholar, 1982. Mem. ATLA, Mo. Assn. Trial Attys., Kansas City Met. Bar Assn., Young Lawyer's (pres. 1996—), Federalist Soc., Ross T. Roberts Inn of Ct., Order of Barristers, Phi Delta Phi. Republican. Methodist. Home: PO Box 6938 Lees Summit MO 64086-5942 Office: Shughart Thomson & Kilroy Twelve Wyandotte Plz 120 W 12th St Kansas City MO 64105

MOMA, NANCY MAE, librarian; b. Bethany, Ill., Sept. 9, 1936; d. Charles A. and Zenith Mae (Taylor) Reider; children; Kevin, Lyle. Grad., Sullivan (Ill.) H.S., 1954. Clk. typist Gen. Electric, Decatur, Ill., 1955-59; typist Franklin Life Ins., Springfield, Ill., 1960-67; rep. Avon Products, Inc., Marton Grove, Ill., 1972—; libr. Stonington Twp. (Ill.) Libr., 1982—. Home: 301 S Main St Box 305 Stonington IL 62567 Office: Stonington Twp Libr 501 E North Stonington IL 62567

MONAGHAN, M. PATRICIA, university administrator, writer, poet; b. Bklyn., Feb. 15, 1946; d. Edward Joseph and Mary Margaret (Gordon) M. BA in English, U. Minn., 1967, MA in English, 1970; MFA, U. Alaska, 1980; PhD, The Union Inst., 1995. News editor U. Alaska, Fairbanks, 1970-71; pub. rels. dir. Walker Art Ctr., Mpls., 1972; editor Minn. Monthly Minn. Pub. Radio, St. Paul, 1973-74; women's editor Daily News miner, Fairbanks, 1975; lectr., head English dept. Tana Valley C.C., Fairbanks, 1976-87; instr. writing The Neighborhood Inst., Chgo., 1987-89; dir. cont. edn. St. Xavier U., Chgo., 1990—; resident faculty DePaul U. Sch. for New Learning, Chgo.; Booklist reviewer ALA, Chgo., 1987—. Author: Book of Goddesses and Heroines, 1981, 90, Working Wisdom, 1994, O Mother Sun New View of Feminine, 1994, (poetry) Seasons of the Witch, 1992 (Friends of Lit. award 1992). Exec. bd. mem. South Shore Cultural Ctr., Chgo., 1989-92. Recipient Rsch. award NUCEA, 1993, Univ. Alaska, 1987. Mem. Am. Conf. on Irish Studies, Soc. Midland Authors (bd. mem.), Authors Guild. Democrat. Quaker. Office: DePaul Univ Sch for New Learning 243 S Wabash 7th Fl Chicago IL 60604

MONAHAN, EDWARD JOSEPH, III, orthodontist; b. Great Falls, Mont., July 31, 1942; s. Edward Joseph and Helen Jeanette (Winter) M.; m. Saundra Louise Yost, June 17, 1967; children: Heather Kathryn, Shannon Kelly. DDS, U. of Minn., Mpls., 1967; MSD, U. of Minn., 1972. Dentist USAF, Ankara, Turkey, 1968-70; orthodontic resident U. of Minn., Mpls., 1970-72; orthodontist Alexandria, Minn., 1972—. Ch. coun. pres. First Luth. Ch., 1979-82. With USAF, 1967-70. Mem. Hon. Dental Soc., W. Cent. Dist. Soc., Minn. Dental Assn., ADA, Minn. Assn. of Orthodontists, Midwestern Soc. of Orthodontists, Am. Assn. of Orthodontists, Rotary. Home: 1724 E Lake Geneva Rd NE Alexandria MN 56308-7965 Office: 1106 Broadway St Alexandria MN 56308-2530

MONAHAN, LEONARD FRANCIS, musician, singer, composer, publisher; b. Toledo, Aug. 19, 1948; s. Leonard Francis and Theresa Margaret (Geraldo) M.; m. Elaine Ann Welling, Oct. 14, 1978. B.S. in Psychology and Philosophy, U. Toledo, 1980. Musician, writer Len Monahan Prodns., Toledo, 1971-75; musician, composer, publisher World Airwave Music, Toledo, 1975—; founder Red Dog Records Label. Recipient Internat. Recognition of Christmas Music. Mem. Broadcast Music Inc., Internat. Platform Assn., Nat. Assn. Independent Recording Distbrs. Author: If You Were Big and I Were Small, 1971, The Land of Echoing Fountains, 1972, Sending You My Thoughts, 1987, Another Road, 1987, Tapping at Your Window, 1988; composer numerous songs. Home: 620 Masonic Way # E Belmont CA 94002-2730 Office: F-Hall 8535 8-1 Delta OH 43515

MONARCH, JOEL R., lawyer; b. Chgo., Feb. 5, 1950; s. Abe and LaVille M. (Morris) M.; m. Constance M. Baznik, Apr. 1, 1989; 1 child, Mars. BA, U. Ill., Chgo., 1977; JD, Northwestern U., 1980. Bar: Ill. 1980. Pvt. practice Chgo., 1980-83; dep. commr. Cook County Bd. Tax Appeals, Chgo., 1983-86; taxpayer's advocate City of Chgo., 1987-95; dep. dir. Chgo. Dept. Revenue, 1989—. Pres. Food for People Food Coop., Chgo., 1983, Logan Sq. Neighborhood Assn., Chgo., 1988, Unity Playlot Adv. Coun., Chgo., 1996. Home: 3431 W Drummond Pl Chicago IL 60647-1211 Office: City of Chgo Dept Revenue Rm LL30 333 S State St Chicago IL 60604

MONBERG, JAY PETER, management consultant; b. N.Y.C., Aug. 19, 1935; s. Carl-Johannes and Maria Anna Sophie (Haugwitz-Hardenberg-Reventlow) Hammerich-Monberg; B.B.A., Northwestern U., 1962, M.B.A., 1968. Corp. controller Furnas Elec. Co., Batavia, Ill., 1966-67; sr. v.p., dir. Logan Mfg. Co., Chgo., 1967-72; exec. v.p. Moser Industries, Inc., Naperville, Ill., after 1972; pres., chief exec. officer, dir. Wickman Machine Tools Inc., Elk Grove Village, Ill., also sector exec. John Brown Co., Ltd., London, 1977-80; internat. mgmt. cons., 1980—. Mem. dean's council Grad. Sch. Mgmt., Northwestern U., 1973— . Fellow Inst. Dirs. of U.K., , Inst. Mktg., British Inst. Mgmt.; mem. European Planning Fedn., Inst. of Mktg., Strategic Planning Soc., Internat. Soc. Planning and Strategic Mgmt., Am. Mgmt. Pres. Assn. Scandinavian-Am. Found., Rebild Nat. Park Soc. (v.p.), Dania Soc., Danish Nat. Com. (trustee), Sheffield Hist. Soc., Danish Am. Lang. Found. (pres.), Danish-Am. C. of C. (v.p., dir.), Chgo. Council on Fgn. Relations, Chgo. Com., Internat. Trade Club of Chgo. Clubs: Execs., Mid-Am., Internat., 100 Club of Cook County, Union League (Chgo.); The Am. Club (London, Eng.), The English Speaking Union (London). Home: 5201 S Torrey Pines Dr Unit 1249 Las Vegas NV 89118 also: 1 Passage du Cedre Saint Marceau, 45100 Orleans France Office: 100 Kenilworth Rd, Coventry CV4 7AH, England also: Lerchenborgvej 1 Vanlose, Copenhagen Denmark

MONCHER, DANIEL JOSEPH, hospital executive, accountant; b. Detroit, Nov. 3, 1960; s. James Charles and Elizabeth Ann (Smilnak) M.; m. Mary Kathryn Kasten, June 2, 1984; children: Nicholas Daniel, Benjamin Charles. BS in Bus., Miami U., Oxford, Ohio, 1982; MBA, Tiffin (Ohio) U., 1994. CPA, Ohio. Mgr. audit staff Ernst & Whinney, Toledo, 1982-86; dir. fin. Mercy Hosp., Toledo, 1986-88; v.p. fin., chief fin. officer Mercy Hosps., Tiffin and Willard, Ohio, 1988—, interim pres., CEO, 1993. Trustee Dental Dispensary N.W. Ohio, 1987-88, Tiffin Health Found., 1989—, Am. Heart Assn., Seneca County Div., 1991—, Mercy Tiffin Physician Hosp. Orgn., 1993—. Mem. AICPAs, Ohio Soc. CPAs, Healthcare Execs., Soc. for Healthcare Planning and Mktg. (sect. for managed care), Healthcare Execs. of N.W. Ohio, Am. Acad. Med. Adminstrs., Healthcare Fin. Mgmt. Assn., Am. Coll. Healthcare Execs., Evans Scholars Found. (par Club 1982—). Roman Catholic. Office: Mercy Hosp 485 W Market St Tiffin OH 44883-2611

MONDALE, JOAN ADAMS, wife of former vice president of U.S.; b. Eugene, Oreg., Aug. 8, 1930; d. John Maxwell and Eleanor Jane (Hall) Adams; m. Walter F. Mondale, Dec. 27, 1955; children—Theodore, Eleanor Jane, William Hall. BA, Macalester Coll., 1952. Asst. slide librarian Boston Mus. Fine Arts, 1952-53; asst. in edn. Mpls. Inst. of Arts, 1953-57; weekly tour guide Nat. Gallery of Art, Washington, 1965-74; hostess Washington Whirl-A-Round, 1975-76. Author: Politics in Art, 1972. Mem. bd. govs. Women's Nat. Dem. Club; hon. chmn. Fed. Coun. on Arts and Humanities, 1978-80; bd. dirs. Associated Coun. of Arts, 1973-75, Reading Is Fundamental, Am. Craft Coun., N.Y.C., 1981-88, J.F.K. Center Performing Arts, 1981-90, Walker Art Ctr., Mpls., 1987-93, Minn. Orch., Mpls., 1988-93, St. Paul Chamber Orch., 1988-90, Northern Clay Ctr., 1988-93, St. Paul, 1988-93, Nancy Hauser Dance Co., Mpls., 1989-93, Minn. Landmarks, 1991-93; trustee Macalester Coll., 1986—. Presbyterian. Office: Unit 45004 Box 200 APO AP 96337-5004

MONDALE, THEODORE ADAMS, state senator; b. Mpls., Oct. 12, 1957; s. Walter Frederick and Joan (Adams) M.; m. Pamela Burris, June 12, 1988; children: Louis F., Amanda J., Berit C. BA in History, U. Minn., 1985; JD, William Mitchell Coll. Law, 1988. Assoc., law firm Larkin, Hoffman Daly & Lindgren, 1988-91; state senator Minn. State Senate, St. Paul, 1990—; v.p. pub. programs United HealthCare; legal counsel United HealthCare Corp., Mpls. Press aide Carter for Pres. Com., 1976; surrogate speaker Carter Reelection Com., 1979-80, Mondale for Pres. Com., 1983-84; midwest dir. Dukakis for Pres. Com., 1988. Home: 3800 France Ave S Saint Louis Park MN 55416-4912 Office: Minn Senate 226 State St Saint Paul MN 55107-1611

MONDALE, WALTER FREDERICK, former vice president of United States, diplomat, lawyer; b. Ceylon, Minn., Jan. 5, 1928; s. Theodore Sigvaard and Claribel Hope (Cowan) M.; m. Joan Adams, Dec. 27, 1955;children: Theodore, Eleanor, William. BA cum laude, U. Minn., 1951, LLB, 1956. Bar: Minn. 1956. Law clk. Minn. Supreme Ct.; pvt. practice law, 1956-60; atty. gen. State of Minn., 1960-64; U.S. senator from Minn., 1964-77, v.p. of U.S., 1977-81; mem. Nat. Security Council, 1977-81; mem. firm Winston & Strawn, 1981-87; ptnr. Dorsey & Whitney, Mpls., 1987-93; U.S. amb. to Japan Tokyo, 1993—. Author: The Accountability of Power—Toward a Responsible Presidency, 1975; mem. Minn. Law Rev. Dem. nominee for Pres. U.S., 1984. With U.S. Army, 1951-53. Mem. Minn. Law Review. Presbyterian.

MONDUL, DONALD DAVID, lawyer; b. Miami, Fla., Aug. 24, 1945; s. David Donald and Marian Wright (Heck) M.; children: Alison Marian, Ashley Megan. BS, U.S. Naval Acad., 1967; MBA, Roosevelt U., 1976; JD, John Marshall Law Sch., 1979. Bar: Ill. 1979, Fla. 1980, U.S. Patent Ct. 1980, U.S. Supreme Ct. 1990. Mktg. rep. Control Data Corp., Chgo., 1977-79; patent atty. Square D Co., Palatine, Ill., 1979-81, Ill. Tool Works, Chgo., 1981-87, Cook, Wetzel & Egan, Ltd., Chgo., 1987-89, Foley & Lardner, Chgo., 1989-95, IBM, Hopewell Junction, N.Y., 1995—; mem. adj. faculty W.R. Harper Coll., Palatine, Ill., 1979-83, Roosevelt U., Chgo., 1979-80. Comdr. USNR, 1967-77, ret. Mem. ABA, Ill. Bar Assn., Fla. Bar, Chgo. Bar Assn., Patent Law Assn. Chgo. Presbyterian.

MONETTE, LOUIS GAYLE, small business owner, consultant, writer; b. Baton Rouge, Jan. 13, 1925; s. Arthur Gayle and Laura Eloise (Perreand) M.; m. Patricia Ann Penny, Nov. 29, 1957 (div. 1970); 1 child, David Page; m. Charlotte Marie Fradette, Sept. 19, 1971; children: Jacolia Marie, Kelly Amos, Laura Waunita, James Louis-Albert. BS, La. State U., 1952. Organ installer Aeolian-Skinner Organ Co., Boston, 1954-57; tonal finisher Casavant Frères, St. Hyachinthe, 1958-63; chief tonal finisher Casant Frères, St. Hyachinthe, 1960-63; organ builder, svc. Charlotte, N.C., 1963-68; svc. mgr. N.Y.C. office M.P. Möller Inc., Hagerstown, Md., 1968-69; organ builder, svc. Sauk City, Wis., 1970—; cons. Sauk City, 1991—. Author: Organ Tonal Finishing and Fine Tuning, 1981, The Art of Organ Voicing, 1992, Index: L'Art du Facteur D'Orgues, 1993. With U.S. Army, 1943-46, ETO. Mem. Am. Guild of Organists. Democrat. Roman Catholic.

MONEY, MARGARET SARAH, primary education educator; b. Detroit, Feb. 1, 1942; d. William Anton and Margaret Melville (Mitchell) Niemetta; m. Robert McGuffey Money, May 30, 1964; children: Thomas Andrew, Elizabeth Anne. BA, Alma Coll., 1964; MA, Mich. State U., 1969. Cert. elem., early childhood tchr., Mich. Tchr. Lansing (Mich.) Pub. Schs., 1964-69; substitute tchr. Sault Ste. Marie (Mich.) Area Pub. Schs., 1979-92; preschool tchr. C.L.M. Community Action Agy., Sault Ste. Marie, 1991—. Treas. Chippewa Unit Am. Cancer Soc., Sault Ste. Marie, 1986-91; trustee First United Presbyn. Ch., Sault Ste. Marie, 1991-94. Mem. AAUW, Nat. Assn. Edn. Young Children. Democrat. Office: CLM Community Action Agy 524 Ashmun St Sault Sainte Marie MI 49783-1908

MONICAL, ROBERT DUANE, consulting structural engineer; b. Morgan County, Ind., Apr. 30, 1925; s. William Blaine and Mary Elizabeth (Lang) M.; m. Carol Arnetha Dean, Aug. 10, 1947 (dec. 1979); children: Mary Christine, Stuart Dean, Dwight Lee; m. Sharon Kelly Eastwood, July 13, 1980; 1 stepson, Jeffrey David Eastwood. B.S.C.E., Purdue U., 1948, M.S.C.E., 1949. Engr. N.Y.C. R.R., Cin., 1949-51, So. Rwy., Cin., 1951; design engr. Pierce & Gruber (Cons. Engrs.), Indpls., 1952-54; founder, partner Monical & Wolverton (Cons. Engrs.), Indpls., 1954-63; founder, partner Monical Assocs., Indpls., 1963—, pres., 1975—; v.p. Zurwelle-Whittaker, Inc. (Engrs. and Land Surveyors), Miami Beach, Fla., 1975-90; Mem. Ind. Adminstrv. Bldg. Council, 1969-75; chmn., 1973-75; mem. Meridian St. Preservation Commn., 1971-75, Ind. State Bd. of Registration for Profl. Engrs. and Land Surveyors, 1976-84, chmn., 1979, 83. Served with USNR, 1943-46, USAR, 1948-53. Mem. ASCE (Outstanding Civil Engr. award Ind. sect. 1987), Cons. Engrs. Ind. (pres. 1969, Cons. Recognition award 1986), Am. Cons. Engrs. Council (pres. 1978-79), Ind. Soc. Profl. Engrs. (Engr. of Yr. 1980), Nat. Soc. Profl. Engrs., Prestressed Concrete Inst., Am. Concrete Inst., Post-Tensioning Inst., Am. Inst. Steel Constrn., Am. Arbitration Assn., Indpls. Sci. and Engring. Found. (pres. 1992-93), Am. Legion, Lions, Masons, Shriners. Mem. Christian Ch. Home and Office: 14238 Skipper Ct Carmel IN 46033-8715

MONNIN, FRANK JOSEPH, retired program analyst; b. Russia, Ohio, Apr. 17, 1935; s. Albert Jules and Eva Monnin; m. Barbara Ann Pitstick, Dec. 29, 1962 (dec. Aug. 1966); m. Barbara Jane Gundolf Bayard, May 11, 1968; 1 child, Lisa; stepchildren: Gary Bayard, Steven Bayard, Robert Bayard, Alan Bayard. BA, U. Dayton, 1958; MEd, Xavier U., 1966; postgrad., U. Madrid, 1965, U. Lyons, France, 1965-66, Ohio State U., 1969-72. Cert. tchr., Ohio. Tchr. Ohio Pub. Schs., Dayton and Cin., 1960-65; program analyst USAF, Wright-Patterson AFB, Ohio, 1966-67, tech. info. specialsit, 1967-72, computer systems analyst, 1977-94, ret., 1994. Editor jour. Nuntius Aulae, 1956-60; translator jour. Philosophy Today, 1956-62. Fredin scholar, 1965-66. Mem. KC. Republican. Roman Catholic. Home: 561 Lohnes Dr Fairborn OH 45324

MONROE, HASKELL M., JR., university educator; b. Dallas, Mar. 18, 1931; s. Haskell M. and Myrtle Marie (Jackson) M.; m. Margaret Joan Phillips, June 15, 1957; children: Stephen, Melanie, Mark, John. B.A., Austin (Tex.) Coll., 1952, M.A., 1954; Ph.D., Rice U., Houston, 1961. From instr. to prof. Tex. A&M U., 1959-80; asst. dean Tex. A&M U. (Grad. Sch.), 1965-68, asst. v.p. acad. affairs, 1972-74, dean faculties, 1974-80, assoc. v.p. acad. affairs, 1977-80; pres. U. Tex., El Paso, 1980-87; chancellor U. Mo., Columbia, 1987-91; prof. history U. Mo., 1987—; instr. Schreiner Inst., Kerrville, Tex., summer 1959; vis. lectr. Emory U., summers 1967, 72; faculty lectr. Tex. A&M U., 1972; alumni lectr. Austin Coll., 1980; bd. dirs. Southwestern Bell Corp., Boone County Nat. Bank. Contbr. articles, revs.; editor: Papers of Jefferson Davis, 1964-69; adv. editor: Texana, 1964-71; bd. editorial advisers: Booker T. Washington Papers, 1965-85 . Bd. dirs. Brazos Valley Rehab. ctr., 1975-77, Salvation Army, El Paso, 1984-87, Columbia, Mo., 1988—, Crime Stoppers of El Paso, United Way Columbia, 1988-94; trustee Bryan Hosp., 1976-79, chmn., 1979; bd. ch. viss. Austin Coll., 1977-78; deacon First Presbyn. Ch., Bryan, 1961-63, elder, 1965-67, 69-71, 73-74, clk. of session, 1973-74, chmn. pulpit nominating com., 1971-72; mem. presbytery's coun. Presbytery of Brazos, 1969-71, mem. resources for the 80s steering com., 1978-80; elder 1st Presbyn. Ch., El Paso, 1984-87, 1st Presbyn. Ch., Columbia, 1994—; mem. exec. bd. Grat Rivers coun. Boy Scouts Am., 1990—; mem. Pres. Coun. NCAA, 1986-87. Recipient Citation of Appreciation, LULAC, 1982, also numerous achievement awards; grantee Social Sci. Rsch. Coun., Tex. A&M U., Huntington Libr. Mem. Am. Hist. Assn., Orgn. Am. Historians, So. Hist. Assn. Hist. Found. Presbyn. and Reformed Chs. (pres. 1970-72), Coll. Football Assn. (chmn. bd. 1989-90, bd. dirs.), Truman Scholarship Panel, Soc. Conf. Deans Faculties and Acad. V.P.s (pres. 1978), Rotary (El Paso, hon. Columbia, Mo.). Home: 3200 Westcreek Cir Columbia MO 65203-0904 Office: U Mo 306 Reynolds Ctr Columbia MO 65211

MONROE, JEFF, state legislator. Rep. S.D. State Dist. 24; health and human svcs. com. S.D. Ho. Reps., local govt. com.; pvt. practice chiropractic neurology. Address: 207 E Capitol Pierre SD 57501

MONROE, LOREN E., business executive; b. Thomasville, Ga., Apr. 5, 1932. LLM, Wayne State U., 1980. CPA, Mich. Auditor Mich. Dept. of Treasury, Detroit, 1959-70; tax mgr. Coopers & Lybrand, Detroit, 1970-76; atty. Mosley & Monroe, P.C., Detroit, 1976-78; treas. State of Mich., Lansing, 1978-82; v.p. Pierce, Monroe & Assocs., Detroit, 1985—; bd. dirs. Aurora Hosp., Detroit. With U.S. Army, 1953-55. Mem. Masons. Republican. Office: Pierce Monroe & Assocs Ste 2200 Buhl Bldg Detroit MI 48226

MONROY, THOMAS GERALD, management consulting executive, educator; b. Little Rock, Dec. 11, 1944; s. Martin Jacques and Theresa Antonio (Marchigiano) M.; m. Duane Elizabeth LaVigne; children: Margaret Lang, Thomas Anthony. BSBA, St. Leo Coll., 1978; MBA, Rutgers U., PhD. COO Lo Conte Constrn. & Real Estate, Bloomfield, N.J., 1961-65, TJL Media, Inc., N.Y.C., 1978-92; founder, chmn. Tomon Importing, Phu Hiep, Vietnam, 1968-71; officer U.S. Army, 1967-78; pres. Mutual Credit N.J., Bloomfield, 1976-78; CEO Thomas G. Monroy & Assoc. Inc., Cleve., N.Y.C., El Paso, Tex., 1978—; chmn., trustee Monroy Ednl. Systems, Inc., Cleve., 1992—; adv. bd. Students in Free Enterprise, Berea, Ohio, 1986—; exec. dir.Family/Small Bus. Inst., Berea, 1992—. Author: Activity Guide for Youth Entrepreneurship, 1994; editor: Art & Science of Entrepreneurship Education, vol. I, 1993, vol. II, 1994, vol. III, 1995; contbr. articles to profl. jours. Youth Entrpreneurship mentor Sun Media Group, Cleve., 1992—, Lions Club Internat., Cleve., 1992—. Endowed chairholder in entrepreneurship Figgie Internat./Balwin Wallace Coll.. Bera, 1992-94; recipient Best Paper on Entrepreneurship award Coleman Found., Chgo., 1993, 94, Youth Edn. grantee, 1993, 94, 95; recipient Regional Supporter Entrpreneurship Inc. Mag./Ernst & Young, Cleve., 1994. Mem. U.S. Assn. Small Bus. & Entrepreneurs (directorship 1992—, youth entrepreneurship mentor, 1992—, edit. bd. 1994—), U.S. Acad. Mgmt. (entrepreneur divsn., bd. dirs., newsletter editor), Internat. Coun. Small Bus., Assn. Pvt. Entrepreneurship Edn., Family Firm Inst./Family Bus. Rev. (edit. bd., 1994—), Project Excelence in Entrpreneurial Edn. (founder). Republican. Roman Catholic. Office: 1931 W 25th St Cleveland OH 44113

MONSON, DAVID CARL, school superintendent, farmer, state legislator; b. Langdon, N.D., July 30, 1950; s. Carl Arthur and Shirley Jean (Klai) M.; m. Mary Kathryn Greutman, July 8, 1972; children: Cordell Carl, Cale David, Jared Arthur. Cert. tchr., adminstr., N.D. Sci. tchr. Hankinson (N.D.) Pub. Sch., 1972-75; tchr. Nekoma (N.D.) Pub. Sch., 1975-76; tchr., prin. NeKoma (N.D.) Pub. Sch., 1976-79; tchr., supt. Nekoma (N.D.) Pub. Sch., 1979-80; tchr., prin. Milton (N.D.)-Osnabrock High Sch., 1981-84; supt. Adams (N.D.) Pub. Schs., 1984-88; ins. agt. N.Y. Life, Fargo, N.D., 1988-95; farmer Osnabrock, 1975—; state rep. N.D. State Legis., Bismarck, 1993—; supt. Edinburg (N.D.) Pub. Schs., 1995—; bd. dirs. No. Canola Growers, Langdon, N.D. Mem. sch. bd. dirs. Osnabrock Sch. Bd., 1989—; leader Bobcats 4-H Club, 1988—. Mem. N.D. Farm Bur., N.D. Coun. Sch. Adminstrs., Nat. Assn. Life Underwriting (Quality award 1992, 93, 94) Eagles, Knights of Pythias of N.D. and Sask. (grand sec. 1985-93, award 1990). Republican. Lutheran.

MONSON, DIANNE LYNN, literacy educator; b. Minot, N.D., Nov. 24, 1934; d. Albert Rachie and Iona Cordelia (Kirk) M. BS, U. Minn., 1956, MA, 1962, PhD, 1966. Tchr., Rochester Pub. Schs. (Minn.), 1966-59, U.S. Dept. Def., Schweinfurt, W.Ger., 1959-61, St. Louis Park Schs. (Minn.), 1961-62; instr. U. Minn., Mpls., 1962-66; prof. U. Wash., Seattle, 1966-82; prof. literacy edn. U. Minn., Mpls., 1982—, chmn. Curriculum and Instrn., 1986-89. Co-author: New Horizons in the Language Arts, 1972; Children and Books, 6th edit., 1981; Experiencing Children's Literature, 1984; (monograph) Research in Children's Literature, 1976; Language Arts: Teaching and Learning Effective Use of Language, 1988; Reading Together: Helping Children Get A Good Start With Reading, 1991; assoc. editor Dictionary of Literacy, 1995. Recipient Outstanding Educator award U. Minn. Alumni Assn., 1983, Alumni Faculty award, 1991, (associate editor) The Literacy Dictionary, 1995. Fellow Nat. Conf. Rsch. in English (pres. 1990-91); mem. Nat. Coun. Tchrs. of English (exec. com. 1979-81), Internat. Reading Assn. (dir. 1980-83, Arbuthnot award 1993), ALA, U.S. Bd. Books for Young People (pres. 1988-90). Lutheran. Home: 740 River Dr Saint Paul MN 55116-1069 Office: U Minn 350 Peik Hall Minneapolis MN 55455

MONTALBANO, DANIEL CLARENCE, jeweler; b. Chgo., July 14, 1950; s. Clarence Benjerman and Betty Christine (Robertson) M.; m. Sally Ann Kaufman, Apr. 6, 1973; children: Andrew Matthew, Katie Lynn. Cert. in jewelery repair & fabrication, Milw. Area Tech. Coll., 1994. Fire fighter City of Menasha (Wis.) Fire Dept., 1974-91; goldsmith Dan's Jewelry Repair, Menasha, 1994—. Packmaster Boy Scouts of Am., Menasha, 1984-87; chmn. hospitality ministry St. Bernards, Appleton, Wis., 1995—. Home: 380 Frances St Menasha WI 54952

MONTELLO, RAPHAEL RANDOLPH, vocational school educator, culinary executive; b. Dayton, Ohio, Oct. 3, 1951; s. R. V. and W. J. (Jacobs) M.; m. Bettina Burrell, June 3, 1971 (div.); 1 child, Amber Ginger. Student, Culinary Inst. Am., 1971; BA in English and Psychology, U. Wis., 1990, MS in Ednl. Psychology, 1995. Youth programmer U. Wis. Extension, Madison, 1991-93; study skills trainer Help at Student Housing, Madison, 1990-94; youth programmer Bayview Ctr., Madison, 1993-95; tchr., coord. Madison Area Tech. Coll., 1993—; exec. dir. We're Cooking Now, Madison, 1994-96; program developer/coord. Bayview Ctr., Madison, 1996—; edn. cons. Project Opportunity, Madison, 1993-94, U. Wis. Sch. Nursing, Madison, 1994; presenter at confs., Tex. and Wis., 1995. Vol. tutor Urban League, Madison, 1987; mem. Landlord-Tenant Task Force, Fitchburg, Wis., 1988. Named Tutor of Yr., Greater Univ. Tutoring Svc., U. Wis., Madison, 1989. Mem. Phi Beta Kappa. Buddhist. Home: 1814 Greenway Cross # 8 Madison WI 53713 Office: Bayview Ctr 601 Bayview Madison WI 53715

MONTENARO, REGINA LYNNE, secondary education educator; b. Huntington, W.Va., Sept. 17, 1947; d. Oscar Edward and Peggie Lee (Miser) Jeffers; m. Donald J. Montenaro, July 2, 1982; 1 child, Joshua Aaron. BA, Marshall U., 1971, MA, 1974; postgrad., Ashland U., Coll. of Mt. St. Joseph, Marshall U., Bowling Green State U., Ohio State U. Reading tchr. Prichard (W.Va.) Elem. Sch., 1971-74; tchr. English, theater and speech, chair lang. arts dept. Buffalo H.S., Kenova, W.Va., 1974-83; tchr. English and theater Westerville (Ohio) South H.S., 1983-89; facilitator lang. arts dept. Heritage Mid. Sch., 1989—, Westerville City Schs.; W.Va. state dir. All-Am. Drill Team and Flag Corps, 1978-81; W.Va. state dir. Internat. Thespian Soc., 1978-81; mem. planning team Ctrl. Ohio Regional Profl. Devel. Ctr. Lang. Arts. Mem. ASCD, Nat. Coun. Tchrs. English (com. on media), Nat. Mid. Sch. Assn., Internat. Reading Assn., Assembly on Media Arts (exec. bd. dirs.), Nat. Telemedia Coun., Ohio Mid. Sch. Assn., Showcase Am. Aux. (judge), Ohio Coun. Tchrs. English Lang. Arts (coord. pre-K-8 writing awards, exec. bd. dirs.). Home: 1826 Calico Ct Powell OH 43065-9518

MONTGOMERY, ANDREW STUART, financial advisor; b. Decorah, Iowa, May 25, 1960; s. Henry Irving and Barbara Louise (Hook) M. Student bus. adminstrn., Escola Rua de Jardim, Sao Paulo, Brazil, 1978-79; BA in Econs. and Bus. Adminstrn. magna cum laude, Coe Coll., 1983. CFP. Registered rep. 1st Investors Corp., Mpls., 1983-84; fin. adviser Planners Fin. Svcs., Inc., Mpls., 1984—, asst. to pres., 1984-85, dir. computer dept., 1984-87, investment analyst, 1985—, chairperson investment mgr. selection com., 1986—, v.p., 1989-93, exec. v.p., 1993-94, pres., 1994—. Active Mpls. Estate Planning Coun., pres., 1992-93, program chairperson, 1991-92. Mem. Inst. CFP (cert. program v.p. local chpt. 1993-94, program adv. 1995-96, mem. lic. practitioner divsn.), Nat. Assn. Life Underwriters, Internat. Assn. Fin. Planning, Toastmasters (sec. Mpls. chpt. 1986, treas. 1987), Audubon Soc., Phi Beta Kappa, Phi Kappa Phi. Office: Planners Fin Svcs Inc 7710 Computer Ave Ste 100 Minneapolis MN 55435-5417

MONTGOMERY, BETTY D., state official, former state legislator. BA, Bowling Green State U.; JD, U. Toledo, 1976. Former criminal clk. Lucas County Common Pleas Ct.; asst. pros. atty. Wood County, Ohio, pros. atty., 1980-88; pros. atty. City of Perrysburg, Ohio; mem. Ohio Senate, 1989-94; atty. gen. State of Ohio, Columbus, 1995—. Mem. Nat. Dist. Atty. Assn., Ohio Bar Assn., Toledo Bar Assn., Wood County Bar Assn. Address: 1164 Dawn Dr Reynoldsburg OH 43068-9999 Office: Attorney Generals Office State Offical Tower 30 E Broad St Columbus OH 43215-3428

MONTGOMERY, CHARLES BARRY, lawyer; b. Latrobe, Pa., Apr. 17, 1937. BA cum laude Muskingum Coll., 1959; JD U. Mich., 1962. Bar: Ill. 1962, U.S. Dist. Ct. (no. dist.) Ill., 1982, U.S. Supreme Ct. 1971. Atty. Jacobs & McKenna, 1962-67; founder, ptnr. Jacobs, Williams and Montgomery, Ltd., 1967-85; sr. ptnr. Williams and Montgomery, Ltd., Chgo., 1985—; instr. advocacy inst. U. Mich., Ann Arbor, 1985, advanced program Nat. Inst. Trial Advocacy, 1986, trial acad. Internat. Assn. Def. Counsel, 1987, law inst. program Def. Rsch. Inst; pub. speaker ins. litigation; contbr. articles to profl. jours. Fellow Internat. Acad. Trial Lawyers; mem. ABA (vice-chair medicine and law com. 1989-90), Am. Arbitration Assn., Chgo. Bar Assn., Def. Rsch. Inst., Ill. Assn. Def. Trial Counsel, Ill. Assn. Hosp. Attys., Ill. State Bar Assn., Internat. Assn. Def. Counsel, Nat. Assn. R.R. Trial Counsel, Soc. Trial Lawyers, Legal Club of Chgo., Trial Lawyers Club of Chgo. Office: Williams and Montgomery Ltd 20 N Wacker Dr Chicago IL 60606-2806

MONTGOMERY, GARY, dentist; b. Buffalo, Oct. 14, 1957; s. Roderick Frederick and Agnes H. (Debolock) M.; m. Annegret Susanne Herrmann, Nov. 2, 1985 (div. July 17, 1994); children: Robert Frederick, Peter Erich. BSChemE cum laude, Washington U., St. Louis, 1979; DMD, Harvard U., 1984. Gen. dentist lic. practitoner clinic Sch. Dental Medicine Harvard U., Boston, 1983-84; resident in gen. dentistry U. Md. Hosp., Balt., 1984-85; pvt. practice Cleve., 1985—; mem. courtesy staff Fairview Gen. Hosp., Cleve., 1990-92; mem. courtesy staff St. Vincent Charity Hosp. and Health Ctr., Cleve., 1991-93, mem. assoc. ative staff in oral surgery, 1993-95, active med. staff in dentistry, 1995—. Recipient Community Svc. award HELP Found., 1992. Mem. ADA, Ohio Dental Assn., Cleve. Dental Soc., Alpha Lambda Delta, Tau Beta Pi. Lutheran. Home: 3900 Spencer Rd Rocky River OH 44116-3866 Office: 1148 Euclid Ave Ste 317 Cleveland OH 44115-1604

MONTGOMERY, GRETCHEN GOLZÉ, secondary education educator; b. Washington, Sept. 16, 1941; d. Alfred Rudolph and Marjorie (Lodge) Golzé; m. Charles Williams, Jan. 25, 1963 (div. Oct. 1975); children: Rebecca, Matthew; m. Jerry L. Montgomery, May 14, 1977. BA, Marietta Coll., 1963. Cert. tchr., Ohio. Tchr. Warren Local Sch. Dist., Vincent, Ohio, 1963-67; dir. Betsey Mills Club, Marietta, Ohio, 1975-80; tchr. Wolf Creek Sch. Dist., Waterford, Ohio, 1980—; mem. lang. arts course of study com. Washington County, Marietta, 1985—, mem. competency based edn. testing com., 1985—; mem. ednl. planning com. Wolf Creek Edn., Waterford, 1988-91, mem. testing com., 1988—, mem. textbook com., 1989-90; mentor tchr. Washington County, 1991—, mentor tchr. trainer, 1994—. Jennings scholar Martha Holden Jennings Found., 1982. Mem. NEA, Nat. Coun. Tchrs. English, Ohio Coun. Tchrs. English Lang. Arts, Wolf Creek Local Tchrs. Assn. (sec. 1985—), Ohio Edn. Assn., Ohio Tchr. Leader Network. Home: 105 Rathbone Ter Marietta OH 45750-1443 Office: Wolf Creek Schs PO Box 45 Waterford OH 45786-0045

MONTGOMERY, HENRY IRVING, financial planner; b. Decorah, Iowa, Dec. 18, 1924; s. Harry Biggs and Martha Grace (Wilkinson) M.; m. Barbara Louise Hook, Aug. 14, 1948; children: Barbara Ruth, Michael Henry, Kelly Ann, Andrew Stuart. Student U. Iowa, 1942-43, 47-48; B.B.A., Tulane U., 1952, postgrad., 1952; postgrad. U. Minn., 1976. Cert. fin. planner, Colo. Field agt. OSS, SSU, CIG, CIA, Central Europe, 1945-47; pres. Nehi Bottling Co., Decorah, Iowa, 1952-64; prin. Montgomery Assocs., Mktg. Cons., Trieste, Italy and Iowa, 1965-72; pres. Planners Fin. Svcs., Inc., Mpls., 1972-95, chmn., 1995—; prin. Montgomery Investment Mgmt., 1992—. Author: Race Toward Berlin, 1945. Served with U.S. Army, 1943-46; ETO. Mem. Inst. Cert. Fin. Planners (bd. dirs. 1977-82, pres. 1980-81, chmn. 1981-82, Cert. Fin. Planner of Yr. 1984, chmn. Fin. Products Standards Bd. 1984-88), Nat. Assn. Securities Dealers (mem. dist. 8 com. 1988-91, vice chmn. 1990), Internat. Assn. Fin. Planning (internat. dir. 1976-81), Mpls. Estate Planning Coun., Met. Tax Planning Group (pres. 1984-87), Twin City Fin. Planners (pres. 1976-78), Twin Cities Soc. of Inst. Cert. Fin. Planners, Am. Legion, Elks (Decorah), Beta Gamma Sigma. Avocations: Italian and German langs. Office: Planners Fin Svcs Inc 7710 Computer Ave Ste 100 Minneapolis MN 55435-5417

MONTGOMERY, JAMES HUEY, state government administrator, consultant; b. New Albany, Miss., Dec. 2, 1942; s. James Columbus and Ethel Louise (Todd) M.; divorced; children: Angela Lee, Leslie Louise. B degree, Wayne State U., 1991. Border patrol agt. U.S. Border Patrol, Calexico, Calif., 1964-66, Miami, Fla., 1969-71; spl. agt. U.S. Immigration and Naturalization, San Francisco, 1971-75, Chgo., 1975-76; spl. agt. U.S. Immigration and Naturalization, Ft. Snelling, Minn., 1976-78, asst. regional commr., 1978-82; dist. dir. U.S. Immigration and Naturalization, Detroit, 1982-93, ret., 1993; pres. Guard Well Inc., 1994—; dir. comml. enforcement BOPR, Mich. Commerce Dept., Lansing, 1995—. Mem. Leadership Detroit, 1991—; mem. Mich. polit. leadership program Mich. State U., 1993—. 1st lt. U.S. Army, 1966-69. Recipient Appreciation award Korean Soc. Detroit, 1987, Chaldean Fedn. Am., 1988, Chaldean Kiwanis Club, 1988, Cmty. Appreciation award TV Orient, 1993, Appreciation award Arab Am. Chaldean Assn., 1993. Mem. Immigration Dirs. Assn. (chmn. 1988-91, dep. chmn. 1985-88), Internat. Border Assn. (pres. 1986, bd. dirs. 1982-93), Southeastern Mich. Chiefs of Police, Golden Key, Fed. Exec. Bd. (policy com. 1985-93, quality mgmt. com. 1992-93), Arab Am. C. of C. Detroit (bd. dirs. 1994), Internat. Inst. of Detroit (bd. dirs. 1995—). Baptist. Home and Office: 2516 Royce Ct East Lansing MI 48823-2965

MONTGOMERY, JAMES V., state legislator; b. Cabool, Mo., Sept. 5, 1937; s. Clyde Andrew and Ruby (Tilley) M.; m. Karen Kay Cooper, Apr. 23, 1961; children: James V. Jr., Diana Kay. Student, S.W. Mo. State U., 1959-60, U. Va., 1961-62, U. Mo., 1988. Paper boy Kirkman Svc., Cabool, 1950-58; funeral home attendant Gorman-Schaupfe, Aprngfield, Mo., 1958-60; planner McDonnell-Douglas, St. Louis, 1963-73; owner, operator Jim's Svc. Sta., Cabool, 1973-78; mgr. Ozarko Oil Co., Cabool, 1978-88; legislator Mo. Ho. of Reps., Jefferson City, Mo., 1988—; mem. adv. bd. S.W. Mo. State U., West Plains, 1988—; vice chmn. hwy. and transp. com., parks and natural resources com. Mo. Legis., 1991-92. Treas. Cabool Devel. Corp., 1986-87; committeeman Twp. of Burdine, Cabool, 1980-88; vice chair Tex. County Dems., Houston, Mo., 1984-88. With U.S. Army, 1961-63. Mem. Cabool C. of C. (pres. 1987-88), Am. Legion, NRA, Lions. Baptist. Home: RR 1 Box 136 Cabool MO 65689-9706 Office: Mo State Legislature Capitol Office Rm 111 Jefferson City MO 65101*

MONTGOMERY, JEFFREY THOMAS, professional baseball player; b. Wellston, Ohio, Jan. 7, 1962. BS Computer Sci., Marshall Coll., 1984. With Cin. Reds, 1983-88, Kansas City Royals, 1988—; mem. Am. League All-Star Team, 1992-93, 96. Names Am. League Fireman of Yr., Sporting News, 1993. Office: Kansas City Royals PO Box 419969 Kansas City MO 64141-6969*

MONTGOMERY, JOHN GREY, publisher, television executive; b. N.Y.C., Aug. 8, 1940; s. John David and Mary (Kennedy) M.; children: Carol Michele Rowe, John D. II, Robert Grey; m. Sue Ann Cooper. BA, Yale U., 1962; MBA, Stanford U., 1964. Asst. to pres. San Francisco Newspaper Agy., 1964-73; pres. Montgomery Comms., Junction City, Kans., 1973—; bd. dirs. AP, N.Y.C., First Nat. Bank, Sprint/United Telephone Midwest. Civilian aide to Sec. U.S. Army, Washington, 1981, 95—; former chmn. Kans. Bd. Regents, Topeka, 1993-94; lt. gov. nominee Dem. Party, Topeka, 1986; mem. adv. bd. Assn. U.S. Army, Arlington, Va., 1985-92. Recipient Outstanding Kansan award Kans. Jaycees, 1976. Mem. Am. Newspaper Pubs. Assn. (bd. dirs. 1984-92), Auto Club Kans. (chmn. bd. 1993-95), Junction City C. of C. (bd. dirs. 1992-95), William Allen White Found., Rotary, Beta Theta Pi, Mason and Shriner. Democrat. Episcopalian. Home: 510 Redbud Dr Junction City KS 66441-3342 Office: Montgomery Comms Inc 222 W 6th St Junction City KS 66441-3047

MONTGOMERY, MARIANNE BEATTY, primary education educator; b. Rockford, Mich., Apr. 7, 1931; d. C. Earl and Hazel Marian (Cowles) Beatty; m. Robert M. Montgomery, Sept. 24, 1954 (div. Dec. 1986); children: Robert B., Megan A. AB, Wayne State U., 1954; MA, U. Ky., 1965; cert. in early childhood edn., Ea. Ky. U., 1973. Tchr. Fayette County Pub. Schs., Lexington, Ky., 1967-94; ret., 1994. Chairperson Coalition for the ERA, Lexington, 1982; mem. Leadership: Edn., 1987-88; mem. Nat. Tchr. Corps., 1965-66. Named to Hon. Order Ky. Colonel, 1985. Mem. DAR, AAUW (pres. Lexington chpt., Edith Weill award 1982, bd. dirs.), NEA, Ky. Edn. Assn., Fayette County Edn. Assn. (bd. dirs., v.p. 1967—), Soc. Richard III, Jane Austen Soc. N.Am. Democrat. Congregationalist. Home: 518 Wealthy St SE Grand Rapids MI 49503-5449

MONTI, ROBERT KEITH, resort executive; b. Boston, Oct. 14, 1956; s. Raymond Maurice and Marilyn (Wood) M.; m. Rhonda Lynn Maas, June 7, 1992; 1 child, Ian Marcel. Culinary Arts, Greater Lawrence VocTech, Andover, Mass., 1974. Line cook DiGivani's Restaurant, Lawrence, Mass., 1972-74; banquet cook Sheraton Rolling Green, Andover, Mass., 1974-80; constrn. Audrey Constrn., Bow, N.H., 1980-84; sales mgr. Tex. Clearing House, Austin, 1984-87; drilling and blasting Bangor, Maine, 1987-89; mktg. mgr. Long Lines, Sioux City, Iowa, 1990-91, sales assoc., 1991-92, sales mgr., 1992-93; project dir. Leisure Property Specialists, Dakota Dunes, S.K., 1992—; cons. Leisure Property Specialists, Iowa, Minn., 1993-95. Recipient Del Pirello award Voke Tech, Andover, 1974. Mem. Iowa Dart Assn. Home: 813 7th St S Virginia MN 55792 Office: Leisure Property Specialist Box 469 Biwabik MN 55708

MONTUORI, DEBORAH JANE, English language educator; b. Detroit, Aug. 26, 1948; d. Walter F. and Virginia S. (Wheeler) Lusky; m. Dominic A. Montwori, Mar. 21, 1970 (div. Nov. 1985); 1 child, Ellen. BA, U. Mich., 1985, MA, 1987, PhD, 1991. Asst. prof. English, U. Mo., Columbia, 1991—; assoc. mem. Humanities Inst., U. Mich., 1990—. Mem. editorial bd. Moving Out: A Feminist Lit. Jour., 1982-86. Founding mem., pres., treas. Midwest Renaissance Theatre Co., Columbia, 1992-94, dir. Hamlet, 1993. Fellow Andrew Mellon-Woodrow Wilson Found., 1985-91, NEH, 1992-93, rsch. fellow U. Mo., 1992. Mem. MLA, Mo. Modern Lang. Assn., Soc. for Values in Higher Edn., Marlowe Soc. Am., Shakespeare Soc. Am., Renaissance Soc. Am., Ctrl. Renaissance Conf., Phi Beta Kappa. Office: U Mo Dept English 107 Tate Hall Columbia MO 65211

MONTY, MITCHELL, landscape company executive. Pres. Suburban Landscape Assocs., Inc. Office: Suburban Landscape Associates Inc 20875 N Brady Davenport IA 52809*

MONYAK, WENDELL PETER, pharmacist; b. Chgo., Sept. 14, 1931; s. Wendell and Mary Elizabeth M.; m. Lorraine Mostek, Aug. 29, 1964. BS in Chemistry, Roosevelt U., 1957; BS in Pharmacy, St. Louis Coll. Pharmacy, 1961. Asst. chief pharmacist Little Co. of Mary Hosp., Chgo., 1961-66; chief pharmacist MacNeal Meml. Hosp., Berwyn, Ill., 1966-72; dir. pharmacy Ill. Masonic Med. Ctr., Chgo., 1972, dir. pharm. services, 1972-87; dir. pharmacy services St. Anne's Hosp., Chgo., 1987-88; adminstr., 1989—; teaching assoc. U. Ill., 1972-87. Author: Hospital Formulary and Therapeutic Guide for Residents and Interns, 1974, 3d edit. 1986. Pres., chmn. bd. dirs. Bohemian Home for Aged, 1986—. With M.C., AUS, 1955-57. Mem. Am. Pharm. Assn., Am. Soc. Hosp. Pharmacists, Ill. Pharm. Assn. (Spl. Recignition award), No. Ill. Soc. Hosp. Pharmacists, Chgo. Hosp. Coun. Club: Oakbrook Exec. Home: 19 W 059 Chateau N Oak Brook IL 60521 Office: 1347 Crystal Naperville IL 60563

MOODY, J(OHN) WILLIAM, natural resources executive; b. Zanesville, Ohio, Aug. 15, 1947; s. John R. and Velma B. (Wilson) M.; m. Karen S. Lane, Sept. 3, 1967; children: Robin R. Moody McClay, Bart A. BS, Ohio State U., 1969. Livestock mktg. staff Prodrs. Livestock Assn., Mt. Vernon, Ohio, 1970-75; county auditor Knox County, Mt. Vernon, 1975-91; chief fiscal officer Ohio Dept. Natural Resources, Columbus, Ohio, 1991-94; asst. dir. Ohio Dept. Natural Resources, Columbus, 1995—; sec. County Auditors Assn. Ohio, Columbus, 1978-91; bd. mem. Govt. Fin. Officers Assn. Ohio, Columbus, 1991-93. Mem. exec. com. Gt. Lakes Commn., 1996—; rep. to Ohio Water Devel. Authority, 1995—. Mem. Ohio Farm Bur., Ch. Pastor-Parish Com. Republican. United Methodist. Home: 18405 Roberts Rd Fredericktown OH 43019 Office: Ohio Dept Natural Resources 1930 Belcher Dr Columbus OH 43224-1387

MOODY-ADAMS, MICHELE MARCIA, philosophy educator; b. Chgo., Aug. 31, 1956; d. Harold Lee and Shirley (McDonald) M.; m. James Eli Admas, Jr., June 16, 1984; 1 child, Katherine Claire. BA, Oxford U., 1980, Wellesley Coll., 1978; MA and PhD, Harvard U., 1986. Asst. prof. Wellesley (Ma.) Coll., 1986-88, U. Rochester, Rochester, N.Y., 1988-91, Ind. U., Bloomington, Ind., 1991—; mem. of com., Marshall scholarship selection com., Boston, 1987-90, Chgo., 1993—; mem. editorial bd. Public Affairs Quarterly, 1992-94. Contbr. articles to profl. jours. Recipient Marshall scholarship British Marshall Commn., 1978-80, fellowship U. Tchrs., Nat. Endowment For Humanities, 1991-92. Mem. Am. Philosophical Assn., Soc. Philosophy & Pub. Affairs. Office: Ind U Dept Philosophy Sycamore Hall 026 Bloomington IN 47405

MOON, CINDI A., critical care nurse; b. Indpls., Apr. 23, 1957; d. Donald G. and Anne E. (Stephenson) M. Student, Ball State U., 1975-77; LPN, IVTC, Indpls., 1983; ADN, Marian Coll., 1987. RN, QMRP, QMHP. Lic. practical nurse psychiat. patient care Meth. Hosp. Inc., Indpls., staff nurse med. patient care, staff nurse emergency med. trauma ctr.; poison info. specialist Ind. Poison Ctr., Meth. Hosp. Inc., Indpls.; specialist infusion therapy, neuro psychology specialist; clin. support nurse infusion therapy Corinthian Healthcare Syss.; dir. nursing Lockerbie ICF for Mentally Ill, New Horizon Devel. Ctr. ICF/MR-DD; med. staff Indpls. Motor Speedway. Coord. first aid Ind. State Fair. Named ARC Vol. of the Yr. Health Svcs., 1988; recipient Commentation, Gov. of Ind., 1988, 89. Mem. Emergency Nurse Assn., Am. Urologic Assn. Allied, Indpls. chpt. ARC, Ind. State Nurses Assn. (bd. dirs. dist. 5, del. 1993-95 convention, Ind. Intravenous Nurse Soc., Ind. Spina Bifida Assn., Marian County Mental Health Assn. Home: 9949 Montery Rd Indianapolis IN 46236-1698

MOORE, ALBERT LAWRENCE, investment company executive, investment broker; b. Marion, Ind., Feb. 12, 1956; s. John Calvin and Alta Marie (Glandt) M.; m. Diane Kay Poe, Feb. 28, 1982; children: Wesley Calvin, Lisa Michelle. BA, Ind. U., Kokomo, 1978. Claims rep. Social Security Adminstrn., 1978-83; from investment broker to v.p. J.J.B. Hilliard W.L. Lyons, Inc., Greensburg, Ind., 1983—. Pres. Decatur County Dem. Club, Greensburg, 1984-89, Decatur County United Fund, 1989-90; chmn. Greensburg Dem. Com., 1987; vice chmn. Decatur County Dem. Ctrl. Com., 1983—; bd. dirs. Decatur County Meml. Hosp., chmn. bd., 1991-94, vice chair, 1996—; mem. Decatur County Election Bd., 1990—; mem. local coordinating com. Gov.'s Coun. for Drug Free Ind., 1991-93. Mem. Masons, Scottish Rite, Indpls. Urban League, Interfaith Alliance. Presbyterian. Home: 807 E Erdmann Rd S Greensburg IN 47240-8661 Office: JJB Hilliard WL Lyons Inc 101 E Main St Greensburg IN 47240-2031

MOORE, ANDREA S., state legislator; b. Libertyville, Ill., Sept. 2, 1944. Attended, Drake U. m. William Moore; 3 children. Mem. Ill. Ho. of Reps., 1993—; mem. com. on elections and state govt., mem. com. on aging, mem. cities and villages com., mem. environ. and energy com., mem. labor and commerce com. Republican. Home: 361 S Saint Marys Rd Libertyville IL 60048-9407 Office: Ill Ho of Reps State Capitol Springfield IL 62706 also: 2014-H Stratton Bldg Springfield IL 62706 also: 733 N Milwaukee Ave Libertyville IL 60048-1913

MOORE, ANNE K., medical surgical nurse; b. Sioux Falls, S.D., Aug. 10, 1962; d. Darrel Pershing and Joyce Irene Drake; m. Roger Walter Moore, Nov. 14, 1987. B of Arts and Sci., Augustana Coll., Sioux Falls, 1987. RN. Nurse intern Sioux Valley Hosp., Sioux Falls; staff nurse McKennan Hosp., Sioux Falls; head nurse, supr. Prince of Peace Hosp., Sioux Falls; nurse Crippled Children's Hosp. & Sch., Sioux Falls; cardiac rehab. edn. nurse Worthington (Minn.) Regional Hosp.; staff nurse Pipestone (Minn.) County Med. Ctr., St. Mary's Hosp., Superior, Wis. Home: N14480 Island View Rd Minong WI 54859

MOORE, CAROLYN LANNIN, video specialist; b. Hammond, Ind., Aug. 14, 1945; d. William Wren and Julia Audrey (Mathews) Lannin; m. F. David Moore, Oct. 21, 1967; children: Jillian Winter Moore Mirise, Douglas Mathew, Owen Glen. BA, Ind. U., 1967; MA, Purdue U., 1991. Stockholders corr. Sears Roebuck and Co., Chgo., 1967-68; caseworker Lake County Dept. of Pub. Welfare, Hammond, Ind., 1968-71; field dir. Campfire Girls Inc., Highland, Ind., 1975-77; project dir. Northwest Ind. Pub. Broadcasting, Highland, 1984-85, interim exec. dir., 1985-87; cons. Telecommunications and Grant Writing, Munster, Ind., 1981-85; prin. Carolyn Moore and Assocs.-Laughing Cat Prodns., Munster, Ind., 1987—; instr. Purdue U.-Calumet, Ind., 1989; instr. Valparaiso (Ind.) U., 1990-91; lectr. in field. Prodr. TV series Visclosky Viewpoint, 1985-87; video prodr. A Kid's Eye View of the Symphony, 1987; vol. on-air talent WYIN Channel 56; co-host This Week in Munster. Mem. Munster Cable TV Commn., 1984—; bd. dirs. N.W. Ind. Literacy Coalition, Inc.; mem. Lake County Master Gardeners; bd. dirs. Ednl. Referral Ctr.. Mem. AAUW, NAFE, Alliance for Cmty. Media, Assn. Ind. Video and Filmakers Inc., Munster C. of C., Communicators N.W. Ind. (treas. 1996), N.W. Ind. World Trade Coun., Ind. U. Alumni Assn., Scherwood Ladies Golf Leagues, Wicker Park Ladies Golf League (pres.). Democrat. Catholic. Home and Office: Carolyn Moore & Assocs Laughing Cat Prodns 9604 Cypress Ave Munster IN 46321-3418

MOORE, DAVID JOSEPH, design engineer; b. Fostoria, Ohio, July 9, 1941; s. Paul David and Gladys Lucille (Bennett) M.; m. Jacqueline Kay Marshall, Nov. 23, 1963; children: Nicole Marie, Danielle Renee. Student, Ohio State U., 1959-61; Assoc. in Machine Design, Chgo. Tech. Coll., 1967. Designer Excello Corp., Fostoria, 1967-72; owner Sportsman Shop, Fostoria, 1972-79; process engr. United Aircraft Products, Forest, Ohio, 1979-81; design engr. Autolite div. Allied Automotive, Fostoria, 1981—. Inventor manufacture method of platinum spark plug (2). Bd. dirs. Fostoria Athletic Boosters, 1973-79. Recipient Allied Signal Tech. Achievement award, 1991. Mem. Soc. Mfg. Engrs., Machine Vision Internat., Fostoria Area C. of C. (bd. dirs. 1976-79), Am. Soc. Quality Control (cert. quality engr.), Lions (youth com. 1965-75), Elks (trustee 1974-79). Republican. Methodist. Office: Allied Signal Filter and Spark Plug Div 1600 N Union St Fostoria OH 44830-1958

MOORE, DAVID ROBERT, lawyer; b. Champaign, Ill., Jan. 1, 1959; s. Robert P. and Barbara L. (James) M. BA, Butler U., 1980; JD, Ind. U., 1982. Bar: Ill. 1983, Ind. 1983, U.S. Dist. Ct. (ctrl. dist.) Ill. 1983, (so. dist.) Ind. 1988. Assoc. Moore & Assocs., Champaign, 1983-90; ptnr. David R. Moore, P.C., Urbana, Ill., 1990-93, Follmer & Moore, Urbana, 1993—. Mem. Ind. State Bar Assn., Ill. State Bar Assn., Dram Shop Def. Bar Assn. Office: 1717 Philo Rd Urbana IL 61801-6044

MOORE, DENNIS FREDERIC, physician; b. Kansas City, Mo., Apr. 10, 1936; s. Frederic Dillon and Rhetta Louise (Dowling) M.; m. Mary Jane O'Malley, Sept. 3, 1960; children: Dennis Frederic, Thomas Allen, Timothy Joseph, Michael Christopher. BA, Westminster Coll., Fulton, Mo., 1958; MD, Tulane U., 1962. Diplomate in internal medicine, hematology and med. oncology Am. Bd. Internal Medicine. Intern St. Francis Hosp., Wichita, Kans., 1962-63; resident in medicine VA Hosp. and Affil. Hosps., Wichita, 1963-66; chief outpatient svcs. USPHS Hosp., Galveston, Tex., 1966-67, dep. chief medicine, 1967-68; advanced clin. fellow in medicine (hematology) U. Tex./M.D. Anderson Hosp. and Cancer Rsch. Inst., Houston, 1968-69; clin. prof. medicine Kans. Sch. Medicine, Wichita, 1970—; chmn. dept. hematology and med. oncology Wichita Clinic, P.A., 1989—; clin. investigator S.W. Oncology Group, Wichita, 1972—; clin. investigator CCOP, Wichita, 1982—. Fellow ACP; mem. AMA, Internat. Cancer Congress, Am. Soc. Clin. Oncology, Am. Soc. Hematology, Am. Fedn. Clin. Rsch., N.Y. Acad. Scis., Kans. Soc. Clin. Oncology (treas. 1994—), Kans. Med. Soc., Sedgwick County Med Soc. Republican. Roman Catholic. Office: Wichita Clinic PA 3311 E Murdock Wichita KS 67208

MOORE, DIANNE J. HALL, insurance claims administrator; b. Wadsworth, Ohio, June 9, 1936; d. Glenn Mackey and Dorothy Laverne (Broomall) Hall; widowed; children: Christine M. Gardner Fiocca, Jon R. Gardner. BA in Speech, Heidelberg Coll., Tiffin, Ohio, 1958. Receptionist Buckeye Union Ins. Co., Akron, Ohio, 1966-67; adjuster Liberty Mut. Ins. Co., Akron, 1967-69; claims liaison Ostrov Agy., Akron, 1969-70; underwriter Clark Agy., Wadsworth, 1971-72; adjuster Celina Group, Wadsworth, 1972-73, Nationwide, Canton, Ohio, 1973-77; asst. claim mgr. Motorist Mut. Ins. Co., Akron, 1977-87; claim rep. Ohio Casualty Ins. Co., San Diego, 1987-88; claims adminstr. Riser Foods, Inc. Risk Mgmt., Bedford Heights, Ohio, 1989—. Mem. Ohio Hist. Soc., Friends of Gettysburg. Mem. Ohio State Claims Assn., Akron Claims Assn. (pres. 1985), Canton Claims Assn. Office: Riser Foods Inc 5300 Richmond Rd Bedford OH 44146-1335

MOORE, DICK, controls engineering manager; b. Saginaw, Mich., July 20, 1948. AS, Delta Coll., Univ. Ctr., Mich., 1975. Controls engrng. mgr. Saginaw (Mich.) Machine Systems, 1975—; mem. 4-yr. com. S.V.S.U. 1979, tech. adv. bd. Delta Coll., University Park, 1988-93. Mem. E.S.D. Office: Saginaw Machine Systems 800 N Hamilton St Saginaw MI 48602-4354

MOORE, DONALD LYNN, economic planner; b. Kansas City, Mo., Jan. 17, 1947; s. George and Edna Marie (Hockett) Sanders; m. Nellie Mae McKinzy, July 2, 1976; 1 stepson, Phillip Ray McKelvy. AA, Kansas City Jr. Coll., 1967; BBA, Wichita State U., 1970; MPA, U. Mo., Kansas City, 1974. Economist Mid-Am. Reg. Council, Kansas City, Mo., 1970-74; mktg. specialist Black Econ. Union of Greater Kansas City, 1974; econ. devel. adminstr. Jackson County Econ. Devel. Commn., Independence, Mo., 1976-91; sr. planner Econ. Devel. Corp. Kansas City, Mo., 1991—. Mem. Gov.'s Gen. Motors Leeds task force, Kansas City, 1987-88, others. Mem. Mo. Indsl. Devel. Coun. (v.p. 1988, pres. 1989-90). Democrat. Methodist. Home: 7325 Lydia Ave Kansas City MO 64131-1813 Office: Econ Devel Corp Kansas City 10 Petticoat Ln Ste 250 Kansas City MO 64106-2103

MOORE, DONALD PAUL, retired electrical engineer; b. Dayton, Ohio, Aug. 14, 1926; s. Walter Jennings and Dora (Hill) M.; m. Elizabeth Gerretje Derksen, Dec. 18, 1949; children: Anne, Donald, Dora, Peter, William, Richard, Norman, Emily. BEE, Ohio State U., 1954; B in Indsl. Mgmt., Franklin U., 1969, B in Real Estate, 1981; M in Indsl. Mgmt., Cen. Mich. U., 1974. Profl. elec. engr., Ohio; lic. steam engr., radio operator. Nuclear rsch. tech. Ohio State U., Columbus, 1949-54; microwave antenna engr. Ohio State U. Rsch. Found., Columbus, 1954-58; prof. electronics and computers Franklin U., Columbus, 1958-78, plant engr., 1978-88; tech. writer Liebert Corp., Columbus, 1991; chief engr. City of Columbus, 1991-92; cons. x-ray instrumentation Riverside Meth. Hosp., Columbus, 1971; cons. computer instrn. Western Electric Co., Columbus, 1969; cons. engr. Halmar Electronics, Columbus, 1959-64. Sci. judge Ohio Jr. Acad. Sci., Columbus, 1960-70; vol. instr. Columbus Met. Libr., 1978; rsch. chmn. Franklin County Geneal. Soc., Columbus, 1992. With USN, 1944-46. Rsch. grantee NSF, 1948. Mem. IEEE (editor 1984-87), Ohio Soc. Profl. Engrs. (editor 1991-92), Engrs. Club Columbus, Nat. Mgmt. Assn., Eta Kappa Nu. Presbyterian. Home: 1300 Fairview Ave Columbus OH 43212-3309

MOORE, EDWIN H., electric metering company executive; b. Bklyn., Aug. 31, 1951; s. Dorothy J. (Mixson) Douglas; m. Kathleen Armstrong, June 1, 1974; children: Cason A., Allison K., Ashley E., Brady E. AA, Broward C.C., Ft. Lauderdale, 1971; BA, Fla. State U., 1973, MSPA, 1975. Mem. legis. staff Fla. House of Reps., Tallahassee, 1973-76; mem. cabinet staff Comptroller of Fla., Tallahassee, 1976-77; exec. dir. Broward County Mental Health Bd., Ft. Lauderdale, 1977-78; v.p. Electric Metering Co., Arlington Heights, Ill., 1978-89, pres., 1990—; mem. small bus. adv. bd. Ill. Commerce Commn., Chgo.; mem. state bd. Nat. Fedn. of Ind. Bus., Springfield, Ill., 1984—, state chmn. 1989-91. mem. bd. dirs. Ill. Bd. Higher Edn., Springfield, 1991—, Ill. Joint Edn. Com., Spring Lake Sports Bd., Lincolnshire, Ill., 1990—, Gov's. Pvt. Enterprise Adv. Bd., Springfield; cert. referee (soccer) Ill. H.S. Assn., 1995—, Ill. Youth Soccer Assn., 1994—; state soccer coach, 1992—. Office: Electric Metering Co 406 W Campus Dr Arlington Heights IL 60004

MOORE, EUGENE, state legislator. Dist. 7 rep. Ill. Ho. Reps., Springfield; sr. acct. exec. Met. Life.; mem. affirmative action com. 7th congr. dist. (Ill.); Dem. coord. Maywood (Ill.); trustee Proviso (Ill.) Twp. Bd.; mem. Cmty. Econ. Devel. Assn. Cook County, Ill. Home: 1423 S 11th Ave Maywood IL 60153-1961*

MOORE, GARRY A., state legislator; b. Yankton, S.D., May 14, 1949; m. Connie Moore; 4 children. Student, S.D. State U. Mem. S.D. Ho. of Reps., 1993—; mem. judiciary and taxation coms. Home: 2310 Western Ave Yankton SD 57078-1419*

MOORE, GARY RAY, small business owner; b. Madera, Calif., Feb. 12, 1948; s. Walter Columbus and Betty June M.; m. Mary Carlene Byrd, June 23, 1966; children: John, Phillip, Paul, David. AA in Electronics, Crowder Coll., 1988; Diploma in Christian Edn., Ozark Bible Coll., 1984. Food processor Cadahy Cheese Co., Neosho, Mo., 1966-67; rail worker Kansas City Southern, Neosho, 1967-68; pump maintenance worker Sperry Rand, Joplin, Mo., 1968-71; enlisted USAF, 1971, advanced through ranks to staff sgt., 1974, missile maintaineence worker, 1971-79, resigned, 1979; drill operator La-Z-Boy Chair Co., Neosho, 1980-92; owner Global Products Co., Neosho, 1989—; cons. Inventors Counselors, Neosho, 1989—; bus. advisor Starting Smart newsletter, Ops. and Fulfillment Mag. Author: Pyrotechnics, 1970; contract inventor: Underwater Direction Finder, 1991. Mem. Specialty Merchandisers Assn., Phi Beta Kappa. Republican. Assembly of God. Home: 1103 S Lafayette St Neosho MO 64850-2363 Office: Global Products 1103 S Lafayette PO Box 315 Neosho MO 64850-0315

MOORE, GWENDOLYNNE, state legislator. Home: 4043 N 19th Pl Milwaukee WI 53209-6806 Office: Wis State Assembly State Capital Madison WI 53702*

MOORE, HELEN ELIZABETH, reporter; b. Rush County, Ind., Dec. 19, 1920; d. John Brackenridge and Mary Amelia (Custer) Johnson; m. John William Sheridan, July 6, 1942 (dec. Jan. 1944); m. Harry Evan Moore, May 15, 1954; 1 child, William Randolph. BS, Ind. U., 1972, MS, 1973. Ofcl. ct.

reporter 37th Jud. Cir., Brookville, Ind., 1950-60; freelance reporter Rushvile, Ind., 1960—; conv. reporter various assns. With USMC, 1943. Recipient Sagamore of the Wabash award Gov. Ind., 1984. Mem. Women Marines Assn. (charter, nat. pres. 1966-68), Am. Legion Aux. (various offices 1950— including Eight Forty nat. sec.-treas., pres. Ind. dept. 1966-67, conv. reporter), Bus and Profl. Women (dist. dir., various offices 1967—), Nat. Shorthand Reporters Assn. (registered profl. reporter), Ind. Shorthand Reporters Assn. (state treas., editor Hoosier Reporter, chmn. legal directory), German Geneal. Soc. Am., Ind. German Heritage Soc. (state dir. 1984-92, pres. 1990-92), Ind. U. Alumni Assn. Democrat. Methodist. Home and Office: PO Box 206 Rushville IN 46173-0206

MOORE, JOHN EDWARD, marketing professional, freelance writer; b. Watertown, Wisc., Sept. 18, 1920; s. John Martin and Grace Marie (Dent) M.; m. Barbara J. Gates, Sept. 21, 1947 (div. 1957); m. Sally Elizabeth Bond, Oct. 18, 1958; children: Gerald Ian, Helen Louise, Jeffrey Craig, Tracy Patricia. U. Wisc., 1946. Mktg. rsch. mgr. Procter & Gamble (Manila) Phillippines, 1949-57; staff assignment Overseas Div. Procter Gamble, Cin., 1958-62; mkt. rsch. mgr. Procter & Gamble Scandinavia, Newcastle, Tyne, U.K., 1962-64, Export & Spl. Ops., Procter & Gamble A.G., Geneva, Switzerland, 1964-75; assoc. mgr. mkt. rsch. Procter & Gamble, Cin., 1976-79, internat. mktg. rsch. mgr., 1980-84; com. J.E. Moore, Cin., 1984-95; freelance writer, 1990—; pres. Philippine (Manila) Radio Broadcasting Corp., 1952-54, mem. European Opinion and Mktg. Congress, 1964-75; cons. J.E. Moore, Cin., 1984-94. Contbr. articles to profl. jours. Chmn. Boy Scouts of Am. Geneva, 1975, pres. Cin. Youth Symphony Orch. 1980-82, Men's com. Cin. Art Mus. 1984—, fund raiser Art Acad., Cin. 1987. With U.S. Army-ETO. Recipient Market Rsch. Pioneer award, Philippines, 1987. Mem. Am. Assn. Individual Investors, Smithsonian Assocs., Am. Assn. Retired Persons, Internat. Visitors Ctr., Racquet Club. Episcopalian. Home and Office: 7972 Shelldale Way Cincinnati OH 45242-6431

MOORE, JOHN L., judge; b. Ortonville, Minn., Sept. 27, 1931; s. Harold L. and Lilian O. (Rudd) M.; m. Carol A. McDonald, Sept. 22, 1956; 1 dau., Mary Kathryn. B.A., Beloit (Wis.) Coll.; J.D., Northwestern U. Bar: Ill. 1957, U.S. Dist. Ct. (no. dist.) Ill. 1958, U.S. Ct. Apls. (7th cir.) 1961. Sole practice, 1957-64; state's atty. County of Ogle, Ill., 1964-68; magistrate 15th Cir., 1968-70, cir. judge, Oregon, Ill., 1970—; mem. faculty State's Atty.'s Law Tng. Assn. Mem. ABA, Ill. Bar Assn. Roman Catholic. Office: 201 N 3rd St PO Box 338 Oregon IL 61061

MOORE, JOHN RONALD, manufacturing executive; b. Pueblo, Colo., July 12, 1935; s. John E. and Anna (Yesberger) M.; m. Judith Russelyn Bauman, Sept. 5, 1959; children: Leland, Roni, Timothy, Elaine. BS, U. Colo., 1959; grad. advanced mgmt. program, Harvard Grad. Sch. Bus., 1981. Mgmt. trainee Montgomery Ward & Co., Denver, 1960-65; distbn. mgr. Midas Internat. Corp., Chgo., 1965-71; v.p., gen. mgr. Midas, Can., Toronto, Ont., 1972-75; pres. Auto Group Midas Internat. Corp., Chgo., 1976-82, pres., chief exec. officer, 1982—, also bd. dirs.; bd. dirs. Midas Australia Pty. Ltd., Melbourne. Served with U.S. Army, 1953-55. Mem. Ill. Mfr.'s Assn., Motor Equipment Mfrs. Assn. (pres.'s council 1982—), Internat. Franchising Assn., Econ. Club of Chgo., Comml. Club Chgo., Harvard Bus. Sch. Alumni Assn., U. Colo. Alumni Assn. Republican. Office: Midas Internat Corp 225 N Michigan Ave Chicago IL 60601-7601

MOORE, JOHN W., academic administrator. Pres. Ind. State U., Terre Haute. Office: Indiana State U Office of President Terre Haute IN 47809*

MOORE, JOSEPH ARTHUR, alderman, lawyer; b. Chgo., July 22, 1958; s. Max Dale and Marilyn Ruth (Herzog) M.; m. Elaine Carol Weiss, Sept. 24, 1988; 1 child, Nathan Alexander. BA, Knox Coll., Galesburg, Ill., 1980; JD, DePaul U., Chgo., 1984. Bar: Ill. Atty. City of Chgo. Dept. of Law, 1984-91; alderman 49th Ward, Chgo., 1991—; mem. adv. bd. Rogers Park Cmty. Action Network, Chgo., 1991—, Dev Corp. North, Chgo., 1993—. Pres. Network 49, Chgo., 1987-90; bd. dirs. Citizen Action, Washington, 1994—, Ill. Pub. Action, Chgo., 1991—, Ind. Voters Ill., Chgo., 1986-90. Dan Coman scholar DePaul U. Coll. Law, 1984. Democrat. Roman Catholic. Office: 7356 N Greenview Chicago IL 60626

MOORE, LARRY EMMETT, television news reporter, horse breeder; b. Edina, Mo., July 26, 1942; s. Robert Emmett and Mary Leona (Clark) M.; m. Ruth Ann Winter, June 15, 1968; children: Jeff, Jennifer, Monica, Greg, Jessica. BA, N.E. Mo. State U., Kirksville, 1967; MA in Journalism, U. Mo., Columbia, 1968; AD (hon.), State Fair C.C., Sedalia, Mo., 1978. News anchor, reporter, editor KMBC-TV, Kansas City, Mo., 1968—; bd. dirs. Univ. Health Scis., Kansas City, Mo.; mem. adv. bd. Dream Factory, Kansas City, 1984—. Author: 20 x 30 Backyard Gardening Guide, 1978. Bd. govs. Am. Royal, Kansas City, 1984—; mem. adv. bd. Cystic Fibrosis Found., Kansas City, 1974—, St. Patrick's Parade, Kansas City, 1976—; bd. dirs. Am. Cancer Soc., Kansas City, 1972—. Recipient Stephen Douglas Vol. award, 1992, Amb. of Hope award Am. Cancer Soc., 1992, Humanitarian award Park Lane Found., 1990. Mem. Kansas City Press Club. Roman Catholic. Home: 200 W 54th St Kansas City MO 64112 Office: KMBC-TV 1049 Central Kansas City MO 64105

MOORE, MARJORIE ANN, physical therapist educator; b. Spokane, Wash., Apr. 29, 1951; d. Howard Eugene and Pauline Marie (Dunmire) M.; m. Robert Paul Block, June 17, 1994. BS, U. Wash., 1974, MS, 1978; PhD, U. Iowa, 1987. Registered phys. therapist, Wash. Instr. U. Wash., Seattle, 1979; teaching assoc., rsch. asst. UCLA, 1979-81; clin. phys. therapist Hilhaven Home Health, Seattle, 1982; instr. U. Iowa, Iowa City, 1988; asst. prof. U. R.I., Kingston, 1988-91; asst. prof. Coll. of St. Catherine, Mpls., 1991-94, assoc. prof., 1994—. Contbr. articles to profl. jours.; book content editor Human Kinetics Pub., 1995—. Recipient Acad. scholarship Kinesiology Dept. UCLA, 1979-80, McCloy scholarship Exercise Sci. Dept. U. Iowa, 1987. Mem. Am. Phys. Therapy Assn. (jour. reviewer 1990—, book reviewer 1989—, mem. edn. sect. 1991—, mem. orthopedic sect. 1991—, mem. rsch. section 1996—), Internat. Assn. for Dance, Medicine & Sci., Am. Coll. Sports Medicine. Home: 2204 Seabury Ave Minneapolis MN 55406 Office: Coll of St Catherine 601 25th Ave S Minneapolis MN 55454

MOORE, MARY JOHNSON, women's and children's health nurse; b. West Point, N.Y., Feb. 8, 1940; d. Robert Philip and Edith (Carr) Johnson; m. Prentis M. Moore, Dec. 28, 1960 (dec. Jan. 1990); children: Carol Edith, Tracey Marie. Diploma nursing, Boston City Hosp. Sch. Nursing, 1960; student, Dominican Coll. Sacred Heart, 1961-62, Univ. Without Walls, 1973-75, U. Houston, 1987—. Lic. nurse, Mass., N.Y., Tex., Ill. Staff nurse Lyons Health Ctr. City of Houston Health Dept., 1982-85; staff nurse Inst. Rsch. and Rehab., Houston, 1976-78, supr. unit clks., 1980-82; clinic nurse Tex. Sch. for Deaf, Austin, 1985-86; charge nurse maternity and well baby clinics City of Houston Health Dept., 1982-85; staff nurse pediatrics Ben Taub Gen Hosp., Houston, 1987-92; ob-gyn. clin. telephone nurse MacGregor Med. Assocs., Houston, 1992-93; pediat. nurse Grant Hosp., Chgo., 1994—. Active ARC. Mem. Assn. Rehab. Nurses (bd. dirs. 1980-82, chpt. sec. 1983, chpt. newsletter com., creative writing 1992), Soc. Pediatric Nurses.

MOORE, MCPHERSON DORSETT, lawyer; b. Pine Bluff, Ark., Mar. 1, 1947; s. Arl Van and Jesse (Dorsett) M. BS, U. Miss., 1970; JD, U. Ark., 1974. Bar: Ark. 1974, Mo. 1975, U.S. Patent and Trademark Office 1977, U.S. Dist. Ct. (ea. dist.) Mo. 1977, U.S. Ct. Appeals (8th, 10th and Fed. cirs.). Design engr. Tenneco, Newport News, Va., 1970-71; assoc. Rogers, Eilers & Howell, St. Louis, 1974-80; ptnr. Rogers, Howell, Moore & Haferkamp, St. Louis, 1981-89; ptnr. Armstrong, Teasdale, Schlafly & Davis, St. Louis, 1989-95; ptnr. Polster, Lieder, Woodruff & Lucchesi, St. Louis, 1995—. Bd. dirs. Legal Services of Eastern Mo., 1984—. With USAR, 1970-76. Mem. ABA, Bar Assn. Met. St. Louis (chmn. young lawyers sect. 1981-82, sec. 1984-85, v.p. 1985-86, chmn. trial sect. 1986-87, pres. 1988-89), Ark. Bar Assn., St. Louis Bar Found. (sec. 1984-85, v.p. 1988-89, pres. 1989-90), The Mo. Bar (chmn. patent, trademark and copyright law com. 1992-94, co-chmn. 1994-95), St. Louis County Bar Assn., Women Lawyers Assn., Am. Intellectual Property Law Assn., Mound City Bar Assn., Phi Delta Theta Alumni (treas. St. Louis chpt. 1987-88, sec. 1988-89, v.p. 1989-90). Episcopalian. Club: Univ. (St. Louis). Home: 33 Deerfield Rd Saint Louis MO 63124-1412 Office: Polster Lieder Woodruff & Lucchesi 763 S New Ballas Rd Saint Louis MO 63141-8750

MOORE, MICHAEL THOMAS, mining executive; b. Bklyn., Oct. 10, 1934; s. Michael Joseph and Lucille M. (Wild) M.; m. Beatrice Lorraine Quinto, Sept. 10, 1960; children: Teresa, Stephanie, Jennifer, Elisabeth. BS in Bus., Indiana U. of Pa., 1956; postgrad., U. Pitts., 1959-63, Am. U., 1963-64, NYU, 1964-66. Fin. analyst, supr. U.S. Steel Corp., Duquesne, Pa., 1956-63; plant controller Am.-Standard, Balt., 1963-64; sr. fin. analyst Celanese Corp., N.Y.C., 1964-66; asst. controller to controller Cleve.-Cliffs Inc., 1966-72, v.p. controller, 1972-75, sr. v.p., 1975-83, exec. v.p., CFO, 1983-86, pres., dir., 1986, pres., dir., CEO, 1987, pres., CEO, 1987—, chmn., CEO, 1988—; bd. dirs. KeyCorp, LTV Corp. Bd. dirs. Cleve. Tomorrow, 1989—; trustee Fairview Health Sys., Cleve., 1990—. With U.S. Army, 1957-58. Named Outstanding Alumnus Indiana U. of Pa., 1981, Mining Industry CEO of Yr., 1993. Mem. Am. Iron and Steel Inst. (bd. dirs. 1987—), Nat. Mining Assn. (bd. dirs. 1987—), Bus. Roundtable, Am. Iron Ore Assn. (bd. dirs. 1987—), Union Club, The Fifty Club, Westwood Country Club, Pepper Pike Club, Rolling Rock Club, Quail Creek Country Club, Laurel Valley Golf Club. Roman Catholic. Office: Cleveland Cliffs Inc 1100 Superior Ave E Cleveland OH 44114-2518

MOORE, MITCHELL JAY, lawyer, law educator; b. Lincoln, Nebr., Aug. 29, 1954; s. Earl J. and Betty Marie (Zimmerlin) M.; m. Sharon Lea Campbell, Sept. 5, 1987. BS in Edn., U. Mo., Columbia, 1977, JD, 1981. Bar: Mo. 1981, U.S. Dist. Ct. (we. dist.) Mo. 1981, Tex. 1982. Sole practice Columbia, Mo., 1981—; coordinating atty. student legal svcs. ctr. U. Mo., Columbia, 1983-89. Mem. Columbia Substance Abuse Adv. Commn., 1989—; bd. dirs. Planned Parenthood of Ctrl. Mo., Columbia, 1984-86, Opportunities Unltd., Columbia, 1984-86, ACLU of Mid-Mo., 1991—; Libertaian candidate for Atty. Gen. of Mo., 1992, for 9th congl. dist. U.S. Ho. of Reps., 1994; mem. Probation and Parole Citizens Adv. Bd., 1995—. Mem. Boone County Bar Assn., Assn. Trial Lawyers Am., Mo. Assn. Trial Attys., Phi Delta Phi. Libertarian. Unitarian. Office: 1210 W Broadway Columbia MO 65203-2126*

MOORE, PAUL BRIAN, geophysical sciences educator; b. Stamford, Conn., Nov. 24, 1940; s. George Joseph and Bessie Mina (Biddick) M. BS, Mich. Tech. U., Houghton, 1962; SM, U. Chgo., 1964, PhD, 1965. Instr. U. Chgo., 1966-67, asst. prof., 1967-69, assoc. prof., 1969-71, prof. geophys. sci., 1971—; cons. to approximately 20 industries, 1966-92. Co-editor: The Phosphate Minerals, 1983; sr. author over 200 profl. papers, 1966-92. Recipient award Sloan Found., 1969-71; Dreyfus Found. grantee, 1973-74. Fellow Mineral. Soc. Am. (life, councillor 1975-78, award 1974); mem. Am. Chem. Soc., Mineral. Soc. Gt. Britain, N.Y. Acad. Scis., Lepidopterist's Soc., Explorer's Club. Lutheran. Home: 5559 S Blackstone Ave # 3 Chicago IL 60637-1833 Office: U Chgo Geophys Scis Dept 5734 S Ellis Ave Chicago IL 60637-1434

MOORE, PEGGY SUE, corporation financial executive; b. Wichita, Kans., June 16, 1942; d. George Alvin and Marie Aileene (Hoskinson) M. Student, Wichita State U., 1961-63, Wichita Bus. Coll., 1963-64. Contr. Mears Electric Co., Wichita, 1965-69; exec. v.p., sec., treas., chief fin. officer CPI Corp., Wichita, 1969—, also bd. dirs.; Trustee Fringe Benefits Co., Kansas City, Mo., 1984-85. Active Rep. Nat. Com., Washington, 1985-86, task force, 1986—; treas., bd. dirs. Good Shepherd Luth. Ch., Wichita, 1980-85, mem., 1977—; active Wichita Commn. on Status of Women, 1988. CPI Corp. recipient of Blue Chip Enterprise prize U.S. C. of C., 1996. Mem. NAFE, DAR, Nat. Assn. of Women Bus. Owners, Wichita C. of C., Women's Nat. Bowling Assn. (bd. dirs., pub. com. 1969-76), Internat. Platform Assn., Kans. Purveyors Assn. (bd. dirs. 1988-89), Women's Speakers Bur. Office: CPI Corp 816 E Funston St Wichita KS 67211-4309

MOORE, RICH BLAISE, radio station official, music researcher; b. Elkhart, Ind., Nov. 25, 1961; s. Richard Devon and Mary Jo (DelPrete) M. Student, Elk Career Ctr., Elkhart, 1980-82. Program and music dir. Sta. WVPE, Elkhart, 1980-82; announcer Sta. WAMJ, Mishawaka, Ind., 1983-84, Stas. WKAM-WZOW, Goshen, Ind., 1984-88, Sta. WAOR, Niles, Mich., 1990-92; music dir. WZOW, Elkhart, 1988-90; program and music dir. Sta. WKAM, Goshen, 1990—; announcer Sta. WAMJ, Mishawaka, Ind., 1983-84. Home: 4 Sunrise Dr Elkhart IN 46517-1608

MOORE, RICHARD ALAN, optometrist; b. La Harpe, Ill., Jan. 6, 1948; s. Emory Royal and Betty Jane (Baldwin) M.; divorced; children: Shannon Louise, David Matthew. BA in Philosophy, Drake U., 1970; BS in Optometry, Pacific U., 1972, OD, 1974. Lic. optometrist Ill., Oreg., Calif. Pvt. practice optometry Portland, Oreg., 1974-79, Carthage, Ill., 1980—; mem. clin. faculty Pacific U., Forest Grove, Oreg., 1978-79; lectr. Ill. Paraoptometric Soc. State Seminar, 1984. Editor: (newsletter) Southwester (Service Above Self award 1978-79). Mem. planning commn. City of Carthage, 1982-90; bd. dirs. Hancock Ctrl. Sch. Dist., Carthage, 1985-90, pres., 1987-90; v.p. Coll. Edn. Found., Inc., 1989—, Carthage Pk. Dist., 1982-88; organizer, pres. Hancock Transp. Coalition, 1990-92; organizer, pres. protem Hancock County Sch. Bd. Assn., 1990; Rep. candidate for state rep. from 95th dist., 1990, Hancock County Bd., 1990-94, chmn. legis. com., 1993; mem. Hancock County Rep. Ctrl. Com., 1990-92; precinct committeeman Hancock Twp., 1990-92. Mem. Am. Optometric Assn. (Best Non-Tech. Article award 1988, Recognition award 1989, Best Guest Editorial award 1991), Ill. Optometric Assn. (exec. coun. 1985-91, organizer, 1st chmn. soc. pres.'s coun. 1987, v.p. govtl. rels. 1987-91, chmn. polit. action com. 1987-91, mem. pres.'s cabinet 1987-91, chmn. resolutions com. 1991), West Ctrl. Ill. Optometric Soc. (pres. 1985-87), Carthage C. of C. (pres. 1983-84), Kiwanis (pres. Carthage chpt. 1981-82). Republican. Home: 517 W Adams St Macomb IL 61455-1323 Office: Carthage Optometric Office PO Box 457 Carthage IL 62321-0457

MOORE, SCOTT, state official; b. York, Nebr., 1960; m. Danene Tushar, 1989. BA in Polit Sci., U. Nebr. Legis. aide Nebr. Legislature, 1981-86, mem., 1986-94, chair appropriations com.; sec. of state State of Nebr., 1995—; with Moore & Sons. Office: State Capitol # 2300 PO Box 94608 Lincoln NE 68509-4608 Address: 2025 B St Lincoln NE 68502 also: State Legislature State Capital Lincoln NE 68516

MOORE, STEPHEN FREDERICK, manufacturing engineer; b. Battle Creek, Mich., Jan. 24, 1953. AS, Ferris State U., Big Rapids, Mich., 1972. Designer Sutter Products, Holly, Mich., 1972-74; contact man Century Engring., Grand Blanc, Mich., 1974-85; project mgr. Atlas Tech., Fenton, Mich., 1985—; mem. quality control com. Atlas Tech., Fenton. Inventor: patents on press room automation. Mem. Am. Mgmt. Assn. Office: Atlas Tech 201 S Alloy Dr Fenton MI 48430-1703

MOORE, STEPHEN JAMES, lawyer; b. Kansas City, Mo., Aug. 9, 1947; s. James Andrew and Frances Clare (Kennedy) M. BSBA, Rockhurst Coll., 1969, BA, 1975; JD, U. Mo., Kansas City, 1977, postgrad., 1990—. Bar: Mo. 1978, U.S. Dist. Ct. (we. dist.) Mo. 1978, U.S. Ct. Appeals (8th cir.) 1980, U.S. Ct. Appeals (10th cir.) 1981, U.S. Claims Ct. 1991. Law intern Mo. Atty. Gen.'s Office, Kansas City, 1976-77, asst., 1978; assoc. Popham, Conway, Sweeny, Fremont & Bundschu PC, Kansas City, 1978-84, Freilich, Leitner & Carlisle, P.C., Kansas City, 1985, Herrick, Feinstein, Kansas City, 1985-86, Freilich, Leitner, Carlisle & Shortlidge, Kansas City, 1986-90; ptnr. Freilich, Leitner & Carlisle, Kansas City, Dallas, L.A., 1987—; adj. prof. law U. Mo., Kansas City, 1995—. Mem. Friends of Art, Nelson-Atkins Mus. Art, Kansas City, 1988—, Smithsonian Inst., Washington, 1985—, Nat. Trust for Historic Preservation, Washington, 1988—. Mem. ABA, Assn. Trial Lawyers Am., Kansas City Metro Bar Assn., Sports Car Club Am., Am. Mus. Nat. History, Porsche Club Am., Lake Ozarks Yacht Assn., Boat Owners Assn. U.S., Delta Theta Phi, Tau Kappa Epsilon. Roman Catholic. Home: 5840 Mcgee St Kansas City MO 64113-2132 Office: Freilich Leitner & Carlisle 4600 madison Ave Ste 1000 Kansas City MO 64112-3012

MOORE, STEVEN DANA, editor, publisher, critic; b. South Gate, Calif., May 15, 1951; s. Maurice Perry and Mary Myles (McNeil) M. BA, U. No. Colo., 1973, MA, 1974; PhD, Rutgers U., 1988. Owner bookstore, Littleton, Colo., 1978-82; teaching asst. Rutgers U., New Brunswick, N.J., 1984-88; sr. editor Dalkey Archive Press, Normal, Ill., 1988-96. Author: A Reader's Guide to William Gaddis's "The Recognitions," 1982, William Gaddis, 1989, Ronald Fairbank: An Annotated Bibliography of Secondary Materials, 1996; editor: (with John Kuehl) In Recognition of William Gaddis, 1984; also numerous articles.

MOORE, TERRY LEE, organized labor administrator; b. Omaha, Feb. 24, 1943; s. Charles Franklin and Helen Elizabeth (Remer) M.; m. Mary Jean Kolo, June 13, 1964 (div. Dec. 1983); children: Tawni (dec.), Terry, Tara; m. Tania Shapiro, July 13, 1984; children: Jill Abrahamson, Nicole Abrahamson. Butcher Swift & Co., Omaha, 1961-66; spindle line operator Control Data Corp., Omaha, 1969; machine operator Kellogg Corp., Omaha, 1969-76; pres. Omaha Fedn. Labor, 1976—; chmn. SeptemberFest, Omaha, 1977—. Chmn. Tree of Lights campaign Salvation Army, 1990, 91, v.p., 1992, 93; chmn. edn. Nebr. Coun. Econ. Edn.; v.p., trustee Omaha Schs. Found.; bd. dirs. Wellness Coun.; bd. dirs. Work Net; bd. dirs. United Catholic Social Svcs., pub. rels., pub. dept. com.; v.p., vice chmn. labor United Way Midlands, campaign cabinet; v.p. Douglas County Recreation Corp.; spl. events adv. bd. Jewish Nat. Fund. Served in USAR, 1961-66. Recipient vol. action award St. Vincent DePaul Emergency Shelter. Mem. AFL/CIO (exec. bd. Nebr., cmty. svc. com., del. Nebr.), Nebr. Coun. Indsl. Unions, Am. Fedn. Grainmillers, Top 50 Ctrl. Bodies of U.S. Office: Omaha Fedn Labor AFL/CIO 3000 Farnam St Ste 5 E Omaha NE 68131

MOORE, THOMAS EARL, public relations executive; b. Charlotte, Mich., Sept. 24, 1956; s. Stanton Garrison and Alberta Vhay (Durfee) M.; m. Karen Marie Voinovich, July 14, 1995. B of Applied Arts, Ctrl. Mich. U., 1977. News dir. WIBM Radio, Jackson, Mich., 1977-79, WBCM Radio, Bay City, Mich., 1979-81; news anchor, reporter WDEL Radio, Wilmington, Del., 1981-84; news dir. WSBY/WQHQ Radio, Salisbury, Md., 1984-87, WBKC Radio, Painesville, Ohio, 1987-88; news anchor/reporter WERE Radio, Cleve., 1988-93; pub. info. dir. Substance Abuse Initiative, Cleve., 1993—; news anchor WWWE Radio, Cleve., 1995—. Recipient Excellence in Journalism award Press Club Cleve., 1992, Best Spot News award Ohio AP, 1992. Mem. Soc. Profl. Journalists (bd. dirs. 1994—). Home: 4337 Chanticleer Dr Fairview Park OH 44126 Office: Substance Abuse Initiative 614 Superior Ave W Ste 300 Cleveland OH 44113

MOORE, THOMAS JAMES, III, data processing executive; b. Detroit, Nov. 3, 1942; s. Thomas James and Marjorie Ruth (Kaiser) M. BS in Acctg., Wayne State U., 1964, MBA in Adminstrv. Svcs., 1967. Mgmt. cons. Arthur Andersen & Co., Detroit, 1966-72; project leader J.L. Hudson Co., Detroit, 1972-74; project mgr. Nat. Bank Detroit, 1974-77, mgr. data security and privacy, 1977-79; mgr. computer systems Mich. Cancer Found., Detroit, 1979-81; mgr. data processing Harper-Grace Hosps., Detroit, 1981-82, mgr. systems devel. and computer svcs., 1982-83, acting dir. mgmt. info. svcs., 1983-84; mgr. systems devel., 1984-85; systems engr. mgr. Electronic Data Systems, 1985—. Active Founders Soc. of Detroit Inst. Arts. Mem. Wayne State U. Alumni Assn., Patrons of Wayne State U. Theaters, Detroit Econ. Club, Assn. Systems Mgmt., Data Processing Mgmt. Assn., Delta Sigma Pi, Omicron Delta Kappa. Home: 2285 Golfview Dr Apt 205 Troy MI 48084-3914 Office: Electronic Data Systems 26533 Evergreen Rd Ste 437 Southfield MI 48076-4240

MOORE, THOMAS PAUL, broadcast executive; b. Danville, Ill., Feb. 29, 1928; s. Lester Rufus and Mabel Ellen (Jackson) M.; m. Jean LaVonne Sather, Aug. 31, 1952; children: Randyl Ellen, Patricia Kay, Gregory Sather. BA, North Cen. Coll., Naperville, Ill., 1952; postgrad., Denver U., 1952-53. Newscaster Sta. KFEL-AM-FM-TV, Denver, 1952-54; sales rep. Sta. KGMC, Englewood, Colo., 1954-56; sales mgr. Sta. KDEN-AM-FM, Denver, 1956-62; pres. Stas. WBCO, WQEL, Bucyrus, Ohio, 1962—; bd. dirs. First Fed. Savings and Loan, Bucyrus, 1990—. Lay leader, mem. program council Ohio Sandusky Conf., United Methodist Ch., 1966-69 (pres. gen. laity bd. and laymen's found. 1968-72); mem. Gen Council on Ministries, 1980-84, N.W. Ohio Water Devel. Adv. Com., 1967-69, Sandusky River Basin Water Pollution Study Com., 1968-69; v.p., bd. mgrs. EUB Men, Evang. United Brethren Ch., 1958-68; pres. Rocky Mountain Conf., 1957-61; mem. gen. bd. Nat. Council Christian Chs. Am., 1968-72; charter pres. Bucyrus Bratwurst Festival, Inc., 1968; adv. bd. Bucyrus Salvation Army, 1964-68; mem. planning com. East Ohio Conf., 1972-76 (chmn. commn. on minimum salaries, 1968-72, lay leader, 1972-76); vice chmn. council ministries, mem. episcopal com., 1972-76, head. del. to gen. conf., Portland, Oreg., 1976, Balt., 1984; head del. to Jurisdictional Conf., Sioux Falls, 1976, Duluth, Minn., 1984; pres. United Meth. Communications, 1972-76, mem. gen. council fin. and adminstrn., 1976-80; mem. communications commn. Nat. Council Chs., 1972-76; mem. communications con. Ohio Council Chs.; mem. Episc. com., chmn. New Vision Task Group, both East Ohio Conf., North Cen. Jurisdiction, United Meth. Ch.; mem. exec. com. Council on Ministries, 1980-86; mem. World Meth. Council, 1986-91; trustee United Theol. Sem., 1972-80; trustee Ohio Northern U., 1986—, mem. exec. com., 1991—, chair student affairs com., 1991-95, chair, 1995—; mem. exec. com. East Ohio del. to United Meth. Gen. Conf. and Jurisdictional Conf., 1987-91; v.p. Community Improvement Corp., Bucyrus, 1989-91; mem. Overall Econ. Devel. Com. of Crawford County; chmn. Crawford County Traffic Safety Council, 1979-89; pres. Crawford County Econ. Devel. Adv. Coun., 1992—; mem. Crawford County Devel. Bd., Inc.; mem. exec. com. of del. to 1988 Gen. Conf. United Meth. Ch., St. Louis; bd. dirs. Bucyrus Community Hosp., 1992-96, mem. fin. com., 1993-96, chair nominating com., 1993-96, campaign dir., chair fundraising com., 1993-96, v.p. bd. dirs., 1994-96; chmn. N. Ctrl. Ohio Health Sys., 1996—. Served with USN, 1946-48. Named a Civic Leader of Am., 1968. Mem. Nat. Assn. Broadcasters (legis. liaison 1984-91, mem. small market radio com.), Ohio Assn. Broadcasters (pres. 1982-85), North Ctrl. Ohio Broadcasters Assn. (pres. 1983-84, 96—, v.p. 1985-96), Bucyrus Area C. of C. (chmn. airport study com. 1967-68, bd. dirs. 1964-67, pres. 1989-91), Rotary (pres. Bucyrus chpt. 1992-93). Office: SA-MOR Stas 403 E Rensselaer St Bucyrus OH 44820-2438

MOORE, VERNON JOHN, JR., pediatrician, lawyer, medical consultant; b. Chgo., Mar. 18, 1942; s. Vernon John Moore; m. Rutheva deVera Dizon, Feb. 27, 1979; children: Christopher, Joseph. BS, Loyola U., Chgo., 1964, JD, 1986; MD, U. Ill.-Chgo., 1968. Bar: Ill. 1986, U.S. Dist. Ct. (no. dist.) Ill. 1986. Intern St. Joseph Health Care Ctrs. and Hosp., Chgo., 1968-69; resident in pediatrics St. Joseph Hosp., Chgo., 1971-74, chief resident, 1972-74; pvt. practice Chgo., 1974-76; ped. med. cons. Hartgrove Hosp., Chgo., 1996—; asst. dir. pediat. edn. St. Joseph Health Care Ctrs. and Hosp., 1974-76, co-dir., 1978-86, acting chmn. dept. pediats., 1985-86; clin. assoc. prof. Pediats. Loyola U., Maywood, Ill., 1981-87; med. cons. CNA Ins. Cos., Chgo., 1987-94. Part-time staff Chgo. office Sen. Everett M. Dirksen, 1961-64. With USN, 1969-71, 76-78; capt. USNR, 1983—. Fellow Am. Acad. Pediat., Am. Coll. Legal Medicine; mem. Ill. Bar Assn. (chmn. standing com. on interprofl. coop. 1991-92), U. Ill. Alumni Assn. (bd. dirs. 1983-89), Alumni Assn. Coll. Medicine U. Ill. (alumni councillor 1989—), U. Ill. Pres. Coun. Republican. Roman Catholic. Home: 146 Park Ave River Forest IL 60305-2040 Office: Hartgrove Hosp 520 N Ridgeway Ave Chicago IL 60624

MOORE, WALTER EMIL, JR., financial planner; b. Pawtucket, R.I., May 26, 1925; s. Walter Emil and Gladys (Hobson) M.; m. Alta Tarbell Wilson, Sept. 25, 1948; children: Kathy Louise, Richard Emil, John Emil. BS, MIT, 1948; MS, Case Inst. Tech., 1960. Cert. fin. planner, investment advisor. With Firestone Tire & Rubber Co., Akron, Ohio, 1948-86; founder Moore & Assocs, 1990—. Served with USNR, 1943-45. Republican. Congregationalist. Avocations: flying, music, woodworking. Home: 1330 Taft Ave Cuyahoga Falls OH 44223-2246 Office: Moore & Assocs 3618 W Market St Akron OH 44333-2425

MOORE MOIF, FLORIAN HOWARD, electronics engineer; b. Shelby, Ohio, Aug. 23, 1929; s. Carl Leslie and Mona Pearl (Dearth) M.; m. Dorothy Elizabeth Morse, Dec. 19, 1950. AA, Harvard U., 1974. Cert. indsl. maint. electrician; tchg. cert. indsl. electricity, indsl. electronics. With Diebold Inc., Boston, 1955-56; mem. electronics R & D staff Radio Corp. Am., Burlington, Mass., 1956-59; mem. electronics/mech. R & D staff MIT, Cambridge, 1959-74; mem. electricity/electronics/electromech. R & D staff Charles Stark Draper Labs., Cambridge, 1974-76; tchr. indsl. electronics Ashland County Joint Vocat. Sch., Ashland, Ohio, 1976-78; buyer Autocall divsn. Fed. Signal Corp., Shelby, 1978-79; journeyman electrician Excel Wire & Cable divsn. United Tech., Tiffin, Ohio, 1980-86; tchr. indsl. electricity Madison Comprehensive H.S., Mansfield, Ohio, 1986-88; pres., CEO Florian H. Moore & Assocs., Shelby, 1988—. Vol. Ohio Geneal. Libr., Mansfield; foster parent Commonwealth of Mass., 1962-82 (38 children). With USAF, 1948-52. Mem. Ohio Geneal. Soc. (v.p. Richland-Shelby gen. chpt. 1993-95, 95—), Am. Contingent 10th Foot Royal Lincolnshire Regtl. Assn. (life), DAV (life), Order Internat. Fellowship (charter, U.S. rep. 1995), Masons

(32d degree), Kappa Delta Phi (life). Home and Office: 6234 State Route 61 N Shelby OH 44875-9575

MOORE-RIESBECK, SUSAN, osteopathic physician; b. Joliet, Ill., Jan. 23, 1963; d. Roy W. and Rita M. (Gondek) Moore; m. David E. Riesbeck. BS in Chemistry, Loyola U., Chgo., 1984; DO, Kirksville Coll. Osteo. Med., 1990. Diplomate Am. Bd. Family Practice. Chief resident in family practice Michiana Cmty. Hosp., South Bend, Ind., 1990-92, asst. residency dir., 1993—; med. dir. Transitional Health Svcs. Shamrock Gardens, South Bend, Ind., 1994—, Healthwin Nursing Home, South Bend, Ind., 1995—; Healthwin, South Bend; chair family practice dept. St. Mary Cmty. Hosp., South Bend, Ind., 1994—; med. advisor House Call, Mishawaka, Ind. Ann Wright Hazen scholar, 1987-90, Quad City Osteo. Assn. scholar, 1987; recipient Janet M. Glasgow Meml. Achievement citation AMA, 1990. Mem. Am. Osteo. Assn., Ind. Assn. Osteo Physicians and Surgeons, Am. Coll. Family Practitioners in Osteo. Medicine and Surgery, Phi Sigma Alpha. Office: 2515 E Jefferson Blvd South Bend IN 46615-2635 also: 150 W Angela South Bend IN 46617-1101

MOORING, F. PAUL, physics editor; b. Pitt County, N.C., Feb. 6, 1921; s. Benjamin Arthur and Amanda Elizabeth (Congleton) M.; m. Jean Louise Carpenter, Aug. 28, 1948; children: Cecily Hamm, Carol Larson, Margaret. BA, Duke U., 1944; PhD, U. Wis., 1951. Instr. Duke U., Durham, N.C., 1943-46; teaching asst. U. Wis., Madison, 1946-50, rsch. asst., 1950-51; physicist Argonne (Ill.) Nat. Lab., 1951-83; editor, cons. Am. Inst. Physics, Argonne, 1983—; adj. prof. St. Louis U., 1966-83. Contbr. articles to profl. jours. Pres. The Ill. Prairie Path, Wheaton, Ill., 1971-93, Ill. Audubon Soc., Wayne, Ill., 1978-81. Fulbright Rsch. fellow U. Helsinki, 1962-63. Mem. AAAS, Am. Phys. Soc. Democrat. Home: 295 Abbotsford Ct Glen Ellyn IL 60137-4803

MOORSHEAD, JOHN EARL, porcelain manufacturing executive; b. Chgo., June 20, 1939; s. Robert Fletcher and Helen (Rahm) M.; m. Jo Ann Morgan; m. Mary Margaret Maras (div.); children: Brett, Chad; m. Susan A. Tryner (div.); children: Pamela, John Jr. BSChemE, Ill. Inst. Tech., 1963, MBA, 1970. Sales mgr. Chi-Vit div. Eagle-Picher Industries, Chgo., 1963-67, dist. mgr., 1967-76; dist. mgr. Chi-Vit div. Eagle-Picher Industries, Altoona, Iowa, 1976-80; sales mgr. Chi-Vit div. Eagle-Picher Industries, Oakbrook, Ill., 1980-82; v.p. sales and service Chi-Vit div. Eagle-Picher Industries, Urbana, Ohio, 1982-84, div. pres., 1984-88; pres. Chi-Vit Corp. (formerly div. of Eagle-Picher Industries), Urbana, Ohio, 1988—; pres. Chgo. Vitreous Can., Ltd. div. Eagle-Picher Industries, Ingersoll, Ont., 1984—. Mem. Porcelain Enamel Inst. (bd. dirs. 1983—, chmn. bd. dirs. 1990-92). Republican. Lutheran. Home: PO Box 658 Urbana OH 43078-0658 Office: Chi-Vit Corp 720 S Edgewood Ave Urbana OH 43078-9603

MOOTY, JOHN WILLIAM, lawyer; b. Adrian, Minn., Nov. 27, 1922; s. John Wilson and Genevieve (Brown) M.; m. Virginia Nelson, June 6, 1952 (dec. 1964); children: David N., Bruce W., Charles W.; m. Jane Nelson, Jan. 15, 1972. B.S.L., U. Minn., 1943, LL.B., 1944. Bar: Minn. 1944. Ptnr. Gray, Plant, Mooty & Bennett, Mpls., 1945—; chmn. bd. Internat. Dairy Queen, Inc.; bd. dirs. Bur. of Engraving, Inc., Riverway Co. and subs., Rio Verde Svcs., Inc., Ariz., Turnquist, Inc. Author: (with others) Minnesota Practice Methods, 1956. Chmn. Gov.'s Task Force on Edn., 1981; pres. Citizens League Mpls., 1970; acting chmn. Republican Party of Minn., 1958. Mem. ABA, Minn. Bar Assn., Hennepin County Bar Assn., U. Minn. Alumni Assn. (pres. 1982). Clubs: Interlachen (Mpls.), Lafayette (Mpls.), Minikahda (Mpls.), Mpls. (Mpls.). Home: 6601 Dovre Dr Minneapolis MN 55436-1711 Office: 3400 City Ctr 33 S 6th St Minneapolis MN 55402-3601

MORALES, JOHN RUEDA, corporate accounting executive; b. Chgo., Oct. 16, 1956; s. Juan Santa Maria and Elena (Rueda) M.; m. Carla Ann Cosentino, Apr. 19, 1980; 1 child, Samantha. BA, St. Xavier U., 1979. CPA, Ill. Mgmt. analyst Chgo. Water Reclamation Dist., 1980-85; sr. auditor Ernst & Young, Chgo., 1985-87; prin. auditor Am. Nat. Can Co., Chgo., 1987-90; supr. internal audit Square D Co., Palatine, Ill., 1990-93, contr. corp. acctg., 1993-95, sr. fin. analyst mktg. group, 1996—. Sponsor Chgo. Tng. Alliance, 1992, 93, 94, 95, 96. Mem. AICPA, Ill. Soc. CPAs, Inst. Internal Auditors. Office: Square D Co Executive Pla Palatine IL 60067

MORALES-GALARRETA, JULIO, psychiatrist, child psychoanalyst; b. Trujillo, Peru, Dec. 1, 1936; came to U.S., 1973; s. Julio Morales-Fernandez and Lidia (Galarreta) Morales; (div.); children: Lourdes Lydia, Julio Fernando. MD, U. Trujillo, 1966; grad., St. Louis Psychoanalytic Inst., 1984, grad. in child psychoanalysis, 1985. Diplomate Am. Bd. Psychiatry and Neurology; cert. psychoanalyst.; cert. child psychoanalyst. Resident in psychiatry Ministry of Pub. Health, Peru, 1965-68; supr. psychiat. tng. program Ministry Pub. Health, Peru, 1970-72; physician and surgeon U. Trujillo, 1966; instr. psychaitry St. Marcos U., Peru, 1968-72; resident in psychiatry Fairfield Hills Hosp., Newtown, Conn., 1972-74; fellow in child psychiatry Washington U., St. Louis, 1974-76, instr. child psychiatry, 1976-82; dir. child devel. project St. Louis Psychoanalytic Inst., 1982-94; dir. child and adolescent psychotherapy program, 1993—; assoc. clin. prof. psychiatry and pediatrics St. Louis U., 1983-96, clin. prof. psychiatry and pediatrics, 1996—; faculty psychoanalysis and child analysis St. Louis Psychoanalytic Inst., 1984—, supervising analyst in child analyst, 1988, tng. and supervising analyst in adult and child psychoanalysis, 1991—. Fellow Peruvian Psychiat. Assn., Am. Psychiat. Assn.; Am. Psychol. Assn.; mem. St. Louis Met. Med. Soc., Am. Acad. Child Psychiatry, Am. Psychoanalytic Assn., Am. Soc. Adolescent Psychiatry, Assn. Child Psychoanalysis. Home: 665 S Skinker Blvd Saint Louis MO 63105-2300 Office: 141 N Meramec Ave Saint Louis MO 63105-3750

MORAN, JAMES BYRON, federal judge; b. Evanston, Ill., June 20, 1930; s. James Edward and Kathryn (Horton) M.; children: John, Jennifer, Sarah, Polly; stepchildren: Katie, Cynthia, Laura, Michael. AB, U. Mich., 1952; LLB magna cum laude, Harvard U., 1957. Bar: Ill. 1958. Law clk. to judge U.S. Ct. of Appeals (2d cir.), 1957-58; assoc. Bell, Boyd, Lloyd, Haddad & Burns, Chgo, 1958-66, ptnr., 1966-79; judge U.S. Dist. Ct. (no. dist.) Ill., Chgo., 1979—. Dir. Com. on Ill. Govt., 1960-78, chmn., 1968-70; vice chmn., sec. Ill. Dangerous Drug Adv. Coun., 1967-74; dir. Gateway Found., 1969—; mem. Ill. Ho. of Reps., 1965-67; mem. Evanston City Council, 1971-75. Served with AUS, 1952-54. Mem. Chgo. Bar Assn., Chgo. Council Lawyers, Phi Beta Kappa. Clubs: Law, Legal. Home: 117 Kedzie St Evanston IL 60202-2509 Office: US Dist Ct 219 S Dearborn St Chicago IL 60604-1702

MORAN, JERRY, state legislator; m. Robba A. Moran. Senator dist. 37 State of Kans. Republican. Home: 2758 Thunderbird Dr Hays KS 67601-1419*

MORAN, JOAN JENSEN, physical education and health educator; b. Chgo., Sept. 25, 1952; d. Axel Fred and Mary J. (Maes) J.; m. Gregory Keith Moran. BS in Edn., Western Ill. U., 1974; MS in Edn., No. Ill. U., 1978. Cert. tchr., Ill. Tchr., coach East Coloma Sch., Rock Falls, Ill., 1974—; part-time recreation specialist Woodhaven Lakes, Sublette, Ill., 1975-79; cons. Ill. State Bd. Edn., Springfield, 1984—; instr. NDEITA, Ill., 1988—; facilitator Project Wild, Ill., 1990—. Instr. ARC, Rock Falls, 1978—, Am. Heart Assn., Rock Falls, 1978—; exec. bd. East Coloma Cmty. Club; fitness del. to Russia and Hungary, 1992; cons. Alcohol Awareness & Occupant Restraint Ill. State Bd. Edn., Substance Abuse Guidance Edn. Com., Rock Falls Drug Free Cmty. Grant com., Whiteside County CPR Coord. com. Recipient Western Ill. U. Alumni Achievement award, 1993, Western Ill. Master Tchr. award, 1993, Svc. award Ill. Assn. Health, Phys. Edn., Recreation and Dance, 1991, 92, Outstanding Young Woman award, 1986, Phys. Educator of Yr. award, 1988; named Mid. Sch. Phys. Edn. Tchr. of Yr. Midwest AAHPERD, 1993, Ill. Assn. Health, Phys. Edn., Recreation and Dance, 1992, Gov.'s Coun. Health and Phys. Edn. award, 1991, Am. Tchr. of Yr. award Walt Disney Co., 1993, Excel award ISBE, 1995. Mem. AAHPERD, NEA, Ill. Assn. Health, Phys. Edn., Recreation and Dance (v.p. teenage youth 1988-90, pres. 1994, past pres., conv. coord. 1995), No. Dist. Ill. Assn. Health, Phys. Edn., Recreation and Dance, Ill. Edn. Assn. (newsletter editor 1984-85, exec. bd. 1985-90, treas. 1985-90), East Coloma Edn. Assn. (pres., pub. rels., v.p. 1993-94, Environ. Edn. Assn. Ill. Democrat. Lutheran. Home: 1903 E 41st St Sterling IL 61081-9449

MORAN, JOHN THOMAS, JR., lawyer; b. Oak Park, Ill., Mar. 15, 1943; s. John T. and Corinne Louise (Dire) M.; m. Catherine Casey Pyne, May 16, 1981; 1 child, Sean Michael Pyne-Moran. AB cum laude, U. Notre Dame, 1965; JD, Georgetown U., 1968. Bar: Ill. 1969, Colo. 1976, U.S. Supreme Ct. 1973. Chief appeals div. Pub. Defender Cook County, Ill., 1970-82; gen. counsel Pub. Defender Cook County, Chgo., 1984-86; chief litigation atty. Frank & Flaherty, Chgo., 1982; cons. ABA, Chgo., 1982-83; sole practice Chgo., 1986-93; founder Law Offices of John Thomas Moran;, 1993-95. Editor: Gideon Revisited, 1983. Bd. dirs. Lawyers for the Creative Arts, 1973—. Ford Found. grantee Internat. Common Law Colloquium, London, 1976, NEH grantee, Harvard Law Sch., 1977. Mem. Ill. State Bar Assn., Appellate Lawyers Assn., Nat. Legal Aid and Defenders Assn., Am. Soc. Internat. Law, Georgetown U. Law Ctr. Alumni Soc., Sorin Soc. U. Notre Dame. Home: 930 Oakwood Ave Wilmette IL 60091-3320 Office: The Delaware Bldg 36 W Randolph St Ste 800 Chicago IL 60601-3516

MORAN, THOMAS J., public library director; b. Rock Island, Ill., Sept. 17, 1948; s. John Paul and Betty Louise (McGonigle) M.; m. Barbara Ann Yager, June 12, 1971; children: Brendan, Ryan, Zachary. Student, Georgetown U., 1966-69; BA, U. Ill., Chgo., 1972; MLS, Rosary Coll., 1977. Patient svc. coord. Wesley Meml. Hosp., Chgo., 1971-73; circulation supr. U. Md. Libr., College Park, Md., 1973, U. Ill. Med. Ctr. Libr., Chgo., 1974; reference libr. Northwestern U. Law, Chgo., 1974-78; libr. Am. Bar Found., Chgo., 1978-81; ptnr. James A. Moran Agy., Rock Island, Ill., 1981-83; asst. dir. Davenport (Iowa) Pub. Libr., 1983-88; libr. dir. Moline (Ill.) Pub. Libr., 1988—; instr. Black Hawk Coll., Moline, 1993—; Moline devel. bd. Moline Devel. Group, 1994-95; pres. Coun. on Cmty. Svc., Moline, 1993-94; sec. City Club of the Quad Cities, Davenport, 1992-93. Leader Great Books Program, Moline, 1991-95. Mem. ALA, Iowa Libr. Assn. (chair intellectual freedom com. 1984-88), Ill. Libr. Assn. (chair pub. libr. mgrs. forum 1994), Moline Rotary. Home: 3218 14th St Rock Island IL 61201 Office: Moline Pub Libr 504 17th St Moline IL 61265

MORCOTT, SOUTHWOOD J., automotive parts manufacturing company executive; b. 1939; married. Student, Davidson Coll.; MBA, U. Mich. Pres. Dana Corp., Toledo, 1963—; sales engineer, plant mgr. Dana Corp., Tyston, Ind., 1963-75; pres. Dana World Trade Corp., 1969; v.p. ops. Hayes Dana Ltd. Dana Corp., 1975-77, exec. v.p., gen. mgr., 1977-78, pres. Hayes-Dana Ltd., 1978-80, group v.p. Dana svc. parts group, 1980-84, pres. N.Am. ops., 1984-86, pres., chief operating officer, 1986—, chief exec. officer, 1989—, also chmn., dir., 1990—. Office: Dana Corp 4500 Dorr St Toledo OH 43615*

MORDINI, MARILYN HEUER, physical education educator; b. Waukegan, Ill., Aug. 23, 1936; d. Lester and Evelyn (Scott) Heuer; m. Robert D. Mordini, Feb. 24, 1962; children: Robert Jr., Bruce, Beth. BS in Phys. Edn., Ill. State U., 1958; MS in Phys. Edn., Chgo. State U., 1984; MS in Adminstrn., Northeastern Ill. U., 1994. Tchr. phys. edn. Libertyville (Ill.) Pub. Schs., 1958-63, Highland Park (Ill.) Pub. Schs., 1978-81; tchr. phys. edn. North Chicago (Ill.) Sch. Dist. 187, 1981—, dir. intramural sports, 1985-92; tchr. phys. edn. Highland Park Summer Migrant Program, 1981-90; adv. bd. Park Dist. Highland Park, 1982-84. Rep. United Way, North Chicago, 1990-92; bd. dirs. Lake County divsn. Am. Heart Assn., 1992—, chmn. Highland Park/Highwood br. Lake County divsn., 1995—. Mem. AAHPERD, Ill. Assn. Health, Phys. Edn., Recreation and Dance (pres. N.E. dist. 1995-96, Elem. Phys. Educator of Yr. 1991), Am. Fedn. Tchrs. Home: 2035 Grange Ave Highland Park IL 60035-1719

MORDY, JAMES CALVIN, lawyer; b. Ashland, Kans., Jan. 3, 1927; s. Thomas Robson and Ruth (Floyd) M.; m. Marjory Ellen Nelson, Nov. 17, 1951; children: Jean Claire Mordy Jongeling, Rebecca Jane Mordy King, James Nelson. AB in Chemistry, U. Kans., 1947; JD, U. Mich., 1950; postgrad., George Washington U., 1950-51. Bar: Kans. 1950, Mo. 1950; cert. in bus. bankruptcy law Am. Bankruptcy Bd. Cert. Assoc. Morrison, Hecker, Buck, Cozad & Rogers, Kansas City, Mo., 1950-59; ptnr. Morrison & Hecker, Kansas City, 1959—. Contbg. author: Missouri Bar Insurance Handbook, 1968, Missouri Bar Bankruptcy Handbook, 1991, 2d edit., 1995; contbr. articles to profl. jours. Chmn. bd. Broadway United Meth. Ch., Kansas City, 1964-70, chmn. bd. trustees, chmn. fin. com., 1988-90, 94; bd. dirs., exec. com. Della C. Lamb Neighborhood House, Kansas City, 1973-80; coun. mem. St. Paul Sch. Theology, Kansas City, 1986-96; del. 17th World Meth. Conf., Rio, 1996. Comdr. USNR, 1945-46, 51-53. Summerfield scholar, 1943-47; recipient Shepherd of the Lamb award Della C. Lamb Neighborhood House, 1980. Fellow Am. Coll. Bankruptcy, Am. Bar Found. (life); mem. ABA, Am. Judicature Soc., Am. Bankruptcy Inst., Mo. Bar Assn., Kans. Bar Assn., Kansas City Met. Bar Assn., Lawyers Assn. Kansas City, Workout Profs. Assn. Kansas City, Univ. Club (v.p., bd. dirs. 1983, 86), Barristers Soc., Phi Beta Kappa, Delta Tau Delta (pres. Kansas City alumni chpt. 1965-72, pres. U. Kans. House Corp. 1966-72), Alpha Chi Sigma, Phi Alpha Delta. Home: 8741 Ensley Ln Leawood KS 66206-1615 Office: Morrison & Hecker 2600 Grand Ave Kansas City MO 64108-4606

MOREHEAD, JOHN WOODSON, management consultant; b. Owensboro, Ky., July 22, 1948; s. Clarence Grinstead and Cora Elizabeth (Binion) M.; m. Carolyn Marie Kelley; children: Kelley Anne, Kathleen Elizabeth, Shannon Marie, Robert Patrick. BA, U. Ky., 1970. Tech. adminstr. MGA Tech., Inc., Chgo., 1971-74; assoc. Intercon Rsch. Assocs., Ltd., Evanston, Ill., 1974-81; pres. Tech. Search Internat., Inc., Elk Grove Village, Ill., 1981—; cons. Scottish Devel. Agy., Glasgow, 1988—, Coun. of 100, Rockford, Ill., 1987—; dir. Inventor's Coun., Chgo., 1985—. Author: Finding and Licensing New Products and Technology from U.S.A., 1982, (with Hubert J. Stitt and Samuel R. Baker) The Licensing and Joint Venture Guide, 1984. Mem. Inst. Internat. Licensing Practitioners, Licensing Execs. Soc. (chmn. Chgo. chpt. 1988—), Licensing, Innovation and Tech. Cons. Assn., Midwest Soc. Profl. Cons., Chgo. High Tech. Assn. Methodist. Office: Tech Search Internat Inc 225 N Arlington Heights Rd Elk Grove Village IL 60007-1017

MOREHOUSE, LAWRENCE GLEN, veterinarian, emeritus professor; b. Manchester, Kans., July 21, 1925; s. Edwy Owen and Ethel Merle (Glenn) M.; m. Georgia Ann Lewis, Oct. 6, 1956; children: Timothy Lawrence, Glenn Ellen. BS in Biol. Sci., Kans. State U., 1952, DVM, 1952; MS in Animal Pathology, Purdue U., 1956, PhD, 1960. Lic. vet. medicine. Veterinarian County Animal Hosp., Des Peres, Mo., 1952-53; supr. Brucellosis labs. Purdue U., West Lafayette, Ind., 1953-60; staff veterinarian lab. svcs. USDA, Washington, 1960-61; discipline leader in pathology and toxicology, animal health divsn. USDA Nat. Animal Disease Lab., Ames, Iowa, 1961-64; prof., chmn. dept. veterinary pathology Coll. Vet. Medicine U. Mo., Columbia, 1964-67, 84-86; dir. Vet. Med. Diagnostic Lab., 1968-88; prof. emeritus Coll. Vet. Medicine U. Mo., Columbia, 1986—; cons. USDA, to comdg. gen. U.S. Army R & D Command, Am. Inst. Biol. Scis., NAS, Miss. State U., St. Louis Zoo Residency Tng. Program, Miss. Vet. Med. Assn., Okla. State U., Pa. Dept. Agr., Ohio Dept. Agr. Co-editor: Mycotoxic Fungi, Mycotoxins, Mycotoxicoses: An Encyclopedic Handbook , 3 vols., 1977; contbr. numerous articles on diseases of animals to profl. jours. Active Trinity Presbyn. Ch., Columbia, 1989-92; bd. dirs. Mo. Symphony Soc., Columbia, 1989-92. With USN, 1943-46, PTO, U.S. Army, 1952-56. Recipient Outstanding Svc. award U.S. Dept Agr., 1959, Merit Cert., 1963, 64, Disting. Svc. award Coll. Vet. Medicine U. Mo., 1987. Fellow Royal Soc. Health London; mem. Am. Assn. Vet. Lab. Diagnosticians (E.P. Pope award 1976, chmn. lab. accreditation bd. 1972-79, 87-90, pres. 1979-80, sec.-treas. 1983-87), World Assn. Vet. Lab. Diagnosticians (bd. dirs. 1984—), N.Y. Acad. Sci., U. S. Animal Health Assn., Am. Assn. Lab. Animal Sci., Mo. Soc. Microbiology, Am. Assn. Avian Pathologists, N.Am. Conf. Rsch. Workers in Animal Diseases, Mo. Univ. Retirees Assn. (v.p. 1996—). Presbyterian. Home: 916 Danforth Dr Columbia MO 65201-6164 Office: U Mo Vet Med Diagnostic Lab PO Box 6023 Columbia MO 65201

MORELAND, MICHAEL JOSEPH, state representative; b. Ottumwa, Iowa, Dec. 9, 1962; s. John Norbert and Mary Margaret (Donnelly) M.; m. Sheri Lynne Strauss, Sept. 18, 1992. BS, Creighton U., 1985; JD, U. Iowa, 1990. Bar: Iowa 1991, U.S. Dist. Ct. (no. and so. dists.) Iowa 1991. Assoc. McKay, Moreland & Webber, P.C., Ottumwa, Iowa, 1991-92, ptnr., 1992—; state rep. State of Iowa, Des Moines, 1992—. Bd. dirs. Ottumwa Planning and Zoning Commn., 1990-92. Mem. Iowa Bar Assn. (dist. rep. Young Lawyers div. 1991-93), Wapello County Bar Assn. (treas.), Ottumwa Area C. of C. (bd. dirs.), Pi Mu Epsilon. Democrat. Roman Catholic. Home: 2716 Clearview St Ottumwa IA 52501-1154 Office: McKay Moreland & Webber 129 W 4th St Ottumwa IA 52501-2510*

MORELLI, ANTHONY FRANK, pediatric dentist; b. Chgo., Aug. 10, 1956; s. Frank A. and Josephine M. (Cerniglia) M.; m. Tina Makris, July 24, 1982; children: Deanna Nicole, Michelle Tina. BS, Loyola U., Chgo., 1976; DDS, Loyola U., Maywood, Ill., 1984, postgrad., 1986. Cert. specialist pediatric dentistry, Ill; Diplomate Am. Bd. Pediatric Dentistry. Pediatric dentist Infant Welfare Soc. Chgo., 1984-90; chief resident dept. pediatric dentistry sch. denistry Loyola U., Maywood, 1985-86, assoc. prof. pediatric dentistry, 1986-91; pvt. practice La Grange, Ill., 1988—; mem. staff Children's Meml. Hosp., Chgo. and Westchester, Ill., Mt. Sinai Hosp., Chgo., MacNeal Hosp., Chgo. Mem. ADA, Chgo. Dental Soc., Am. Soc. Dentistry Children, Am. Acad. Pediatric Dentistry, Am. Bd. Pediatric Dentistry (diplomate), Ill. Soc. Pediatric Dentistry. Home: 524 Banyon Ln La Grange IL 60525-1904 Office: 4727 S Willow Springs Rd La Grange IL 60525

MORELLI, WILLIAM ANNIBALE, SR., aerospace manufacturing company executive; b. Cin., July 2, 1938; s. Annibale and Angiolina (DiPietro) M.; m. Velma Lois Hammond, May 12, 1962 (div. Sept. 1974); children: Paula Anne, Cathi Susan, Melissa Anne; m. Beverly Ann Bulmer, Feb. 14, 1975 (div. 1995); 1 child, William A. Jr.; stepchild, Stacey Dawn Watson. BBA, U. Cin., 1960. Fin. analyst Federated Dept. Stores, Cin., 1961-66; mfrs. rep. Hyde Corp., Cin., 1966-75; sales mgr. Clipper Industries, Roseville, Mich., 1975-76, Bachan Aerospace Corp., Madison Heights, Mich., 1976-83; pres. Caratron Industries, Inc., Warren, Mich., 1983—, Norwood Precision Products, 1991—; v.p. TKO Sports Prodn. Ltd., 1992-95; pres. Caratron RDM, L.C., 1994—, TKO Sports Prodn. Ltd., 1991-93. Apptd. to Gov.'s Entrepreneurial and Small Bus. Commn., 1988-91, bd. dirs. Macomb-St. Clair Pvt. Industry Coun. Ill.; chmn. bd. Mich. Found., Inc. Mem. Am. Gear Mfrs. Assn., Warren C. of C. (bd. dirs., chmn. 1988-90), Italian Am. C. of C., Phoenix Ctr. (bd. dirs., treas. 1988-89, v.p. 1990-91), Masons, Shriners. Office: Caratron Industries Inc 27955 College Park Dr Warren MI 48093-4877

MORELLI-SCHROTH, PAULA A., biologist; b. Cin., July 11, 1962. BS in Biology, No. Ky. U., 1985. Indsl. hygienist Nat. Occupational Inst. Safety and Health, Cin., 1981-85; compliance officer OSHA, Cin., 1985-86; indsl. hygienist PEI Assocs. Inc., Cin., 1986-87; v.p. Ungers & Assocs. Inc., Cin., 1987—. Mem. Am. Indsl. Hygiene Assn. (profl. devel. com. Ohio Valley sect. 1988—). Office: Ungers & Assocs Inc 1136 Saint Gregory St Cincinnati OH 45202-1724

MORENO, SUSAN JAYNE, foundation adminstrator; b. Gary, Ind., Mar. 10, 1946; d. William Franklin and Edna Mae (Parker) Sykes; m. Marco Antonio Reyes Moreno, Apr. 5, 1969; children: Elizabeth Ann, Kathryn Amanda. BS in Bus. Adminstrn., Wittenberg U., Springfield, Ohio, 1968; MA in Applied Behavioral Sci., Valparaiso (Ind.) U., 1988. Editor The Maap, Crown Point, Ind., 1984—; founder, pres. Maap Svcs., Inc., Crown Point, Ind., 1976—; lectr. on autism, nationwide, 1976—; mem. nat. adv. bd. St. Joseph Coll., Rensselaer, Ind., 1994—; mem. adv. bd. Ind. Resource Ctr. on Autism, Bloomington, 1994—. Author: High Functioning Individuals with Autism: Advice and Information, 1991; contbr. chpt. to book. Co-founder ARRISE, Forest Park, Ill., 1978; founder Spl. Recreation Program, Lake Zurich, Ill., 1977. Mem. PEO Sisterhood, Tri Kappa, Chi Omega. Presbyterian. Office: Maap Svcs Inc PO Box 524 Crown Point IN 46307

MORETTI, ROBERT JAMES, psychologist, educator; b. Chgo., Aug. 28, 1949; s. James John and Elva Eve (Bonini) M.; m. Carol L. Curt, Dec. 6, 1986. BS in Psychology, Loyola U., Chgo., 1971, PhD in Clin. Psychology, 1982; MA in Behavioral Sci., U. Chgo., 1976. Lic.clin. psychologist, Ill.; Rsch. fellow Ill. State Psychiat. Inst., Chgo., 1974-76; clin. asst. prof. Loyola U. Sch. Dentistry, Chgo., 1976-81; asst. prof. behavioral scis. Northwestern U. Dental Sch., Chgo., 1981-91, assoc. prof, 1991—. chmn., 1981-88; asst. prof. psychiatry Northwestern U. Med. Sch., 1983-91, assoc. prof., 1991—; asst. dir. clin. tng., dir. health psychology, 1988-93; asst. prof. Grad. Sch., 1986-91, assoc. prof. 1991-91; faculty mem. C.G. Jung Inst. Chgo., 1993—; staff Charter Barclay Hosp., Chgo., Northwestern Meml. Hosp.; sr. faculty AIDS Mental Health Edn. and Evaluation Project, 1986-89, dir. relaxation and epilepsy project, 1991—. Mem. editl. bd. Jour. of Am. Analgesia Soc., 1987—; contbr. articles to profl. jours. Served with Ill. Army Nat. Guard, 1971-77. Kellogg fellow Am. Fund Dental Health, 1981. Mem. APA, Ill. Psychol. Assn., Am. Assoc. Applied and Preventive Psychology, Soc. Behavioral Medicine, Assn. Applied Psychophysiology and Biofeedback, Soc. Personality Assessment, Internat. Stress Mgmt. Assn., Am. Pain Soc. Home: 3458 N Normandy Ave Chicago IL 60634-3717 Office: Northwestern U Medical Sch 625 N Michigan Ave Ste 1730 Chicago IL 60611-3109

MOREY, SHARON LYNN, psychotherapist, mediator; b. Cherokee, Iowa, Apr. 8, 1948; d. Joseph Glenn and Annie (Bush) M.; m. Edward Devere Beck, July 23, 1988; stepchildren: Mark Edward, Bruce David. Cert. in bus., Mpls. Bus. Coll., 1968; BA in Psychology, Adminstrn., Met. State U., 1988; PhD in Clin. Psychology, The Union Inst., 1992. Exec. dir. Iowa Lakes Regional Orgn., Spirit Lake, 1982-86; peer acad. advisor Met. State U., St. Paul, 1986-88; appointed to mktg. task force Minn. State U. System, St. Paul, 1987-88; crisis phone counselor Lovelines Counseling Ctr., Mpls., 1987-88; mediator North Hennepin Mediation Project, Brooklyn Center, Minn., 1988-93; pvt. practice St. Anthony Mental Health Ctr., Mendota Heights, Minn., 1988-93; intern in clin. psychology Richfield (Minn.) High Sch., 1990-91; psychotherapist, mediator St. Anthony Mental Health Clinic, St. Paul, 1990-93; cons. Iowa Lakes Regional Orgn., Spirit Lake, 1986-90; group facilitator Toughlove Orgn., Eagan, Minn., 1987-90. Mem. Okoboji Area After 5 Christian Bus. Women, Spirit Lake, 1978-82, Okoboji Lakes Bible and Missionary Conf., Spirit Lake, 1978—, Grad. Sch. of Union Inst. Exec. Learner Coun., Cin., 1990-92; bd. dirs. N.W. Iowa Singles Weekend Conf., Spirit Lake, 1978. Met. State U. scholar, 1987, Highland Park Bus. and Profl. Women scholar, 1987; grantee Dept. Vocat. Rehab., 1986-87, Alliss Edn. Foun., 1986, Pell, 1986-87. Mem. APA, N.Am. Soc. Adlerian Psychologists, Minn. Coun. Mediators (interim v.p. 1990-91), Minn. Psychol. Assn., Grad. Sch. of Union Inst. Alumni Assn., Met. State U. Alumni Assn., Minority and Women Doctoral Directory, Soc. Profls. in Dispute Resolution, Assn. Family and Conciliation Cts. Mem. Christian Ch.

MORFORD-BURG, JOANN, state senator, investment company executive; b. Miller, S.D., Nov. 26, 1956; d. Darrell Keith Morford and Eleanor May (Fawcett) Morford-Steptoe; m. Quinten Leo Burg, Nov. 12, 1983. BS in Agrl.-Bus., Comml. Econs., S.D. State U., 1979; cert. in personal fin. planning, Am. Coll., 1992. Agrl. loan officer 1st Bank System, Presho, S.D., 1980-82, Wessington Springs, S.D., 1982-86; agrl. loan officer Am. State Bank, Wessington Springs, 1986; registered investment rep. SBM Fin. Svcs. Inc., Wessington Springs, 1986—; mem. S.D. State Senate, Wessington Springs, 1990—, majority whip, 1993-94, minority whip, 1994—; mem. senate appropriations com. 1993—; chair senate ops. and audit com. 1993, 94; mem. ops. and audit com., 1995—; active Nat. Conf. State Legislators' Assembly of Fed. Issues Environ. Com., 1995—. Mem. Midwestern-Can. task force Midwest Conf., 1990-94; mem. transp. com., commerce com., taxation com. S.D. State Senate, Pierre, 1990-92; treas. twp. bd. Wessington Springs, 1990-92; mem. Wessington Springs Sch. Improvement Coun. Mem. Future Farmers Am. (adv. bd. Wessington Springs chpt.), S.D. State U. 4-H Alumni Assn., Nat. Life Underwriters Assn. (Huron chpt.), Order Ea. Star (various offices 1980—). Democrat. Methodist. Home and Office: 38678 SD Highway 34 Wessington Springs SD 57382-5806

MORGAN, ANNETTE N., state legislator; b. Kennett, Mo., Aug. 31, 1938; m. William P. Morgan, 1961; children: John, Katherine. BA, U. Mo., MA. Tchr. adult edn.; mem. Mo. Ho. of Reps. Mem. Adult Edn. Assn. Democrat. Presbyterian. Home: 221 W 48th St #1601 Kansas City MO 64112 Office: Mo Ho of Reps State Capitol Building Jefferson City MO 65101-1556

MORGAN, ARDYS NORD, superintendent of schools; b. South Bend, Ind., Nov. 1, 1946; d. Arthur August and Janet Ardis (Eide) Nord; children: Elizabeth Elayne, Matthew Richard. BS in Elem. Edn., Ind. U., Bloomington, 1968; MS in Elem. Edn., Ind. U., Indpls., 1972; reading cert., Ind. U., South Bend, 1982; EDS, Ind. U., Bloomington, 1992; adminstr. lic., Ind. U.-Purdue U., Indpls., 1989; EdD in Curriculum and Sch. Adminstrn., Ind.

U., 1994. Tchr. South Bend, 1968-69, 73-87, adminstr. dept. instrn. and curriculum, 1987-90; tchr. Indpls., 1969-70; resident lectr. Ind. U./Purdue U., Indpls., 1970-73, adminstr., 1989; mem. adj. faculty Ind. U., South Bend, 1985-90, acting program dir. elem. and secondary edn., 1990-92; asst. supt. schs. Michigan City (Ind.) Area Schs., 1992-94; supt. Union North United Schs. Corp., 1995—; cons. on implementation of tech., mid. grades and effective teaching strategies, elem. curriculum, reading and lang. arts, fed. and state projects, staff devel. Recipient Disting. Alumni award div. edn. Ind. U., South Bend, 1990. Lilly Endowment fellow, 1987. Home: 51550 Stratton Ct Granger IN 46530 Office: Union North United Schs 22607 Tyler Rd Lakeville IN 46536-9733

MORGAN, ARTHUR THOMAS, steel company executive; b. Rochester, N.Y., Mar. 13, 1928; s. Joseph and Elizabeth (Perrone) Mitrano; m. Heidi Kopper, July 23, 1960; 1 child, Audrey Christina. BSMetE, Purdue U., 1951; MBA, U. Chgo., 1960. Research metallurgist Inland Steel Co., East Chicago, Ind., 1951-60, sr. metallurgist, 1961-63; chief metallurgist Borg-Warner Corp., Chicago Heights, Ill., 1964-72; works mgr. Calumet Steel Co., Chicago Heights, Ill., 1973-74, v.p., 1975-81; v.p., gen. mgr. Spencer Clark Metal Industries Inc., South Holland, Ill., 1982-93, also bd. dirs.; pres., chmn. bd. dirs. Resources Metals Svcs., Inc., South Holland, Ill., 1994—; cons. metallurgy, South Holland, 1982—; bd. dirs. FREMA, Inc., Highland, Ind. Patentee in field. Mem. ASTM, Am. Soc. for Metals, Am. Inst. Mining and Metall. Engrs. (chmn. Chgo. sect. 1978), Steel Bar Mills Assn. (chmn. 1978-79). Republican. Lutheran. Home: 16038 Minerva Ave South Holland IL 60473-1754 Office: Resources Metals Svcs Inc PO Box 731 South Holland IL 60473-0731

MORGAN, BRUCE BLAKE, banker, economist; b. Kansas City, Mo., Feb. 3, 1946; s. Everett Hilger and Dorothy Aletha (Blake) M.; children: Bruce Blake, Denise Dawn. BS, Mo. Valley Coll., 1968; MS, U. Mo., Columbia, 1973; MA, U. Mo., Kansas City, 1977, PhD, 1979; diploma in banking U. Wis., 1987. Community devel. specialist U. Mo. Extension, Columbia, 1968-73; community devel. specialist Midwest Rsch. Inst., Kansas City, 1973-83, also mgr. regional econs., assoc. dir., dir. econs. and social sci., sr. adv. for mgmt.; adj. grad. prof. sch. bus. and pub. adminstrn. U. Mo., Kansas City, 1975-93; v.p., exec. v.p. Kansas City Bancshares, 1984-86; dir. fin. svcs. Coopers & Lybrand, 1986-89; pres. Profl. Bank Cons., 1989—; exec. v.p., dir. Winterset State Bank, 1991-92; chmn., pres., CEO, dir. Valley State Bank, 1993—; adj. prof. Benedictine Coll., 1993—; mem. staff Mo. Girls State, 1976-90; chmn. Pres's. Adv. Coun. on Univ. Extension, 1987-90; bd. dirs. Johnson County Bank, 19994. Bd. govs. Community Mental Health Ctr. South, 1984—. Office: 5115 Roe Blvd Roeland Park KS 66205-2368

MORGAN, DENNIS BRENT, minister, psychologist; b. Kansas City, Mo., Dec. 28, 1949; s. Ira Pershing and Josephine (Langworthy) M. BA, Pittsburg (Kans) State U., 1971, MS, 1976; postgrad., U. Kans., 1976; PsyD in Psychology, Western Colo. U., 1978. Diplomate Am. Bd. Psychotherapy (bd. dirs. 1982—); ordained to ministery Internat. Ministerial Fellowship, 1989. Chief psychologist Sierra Vista Psychol. Hosp., Highland, Calif., 1980; psychol. asst. Ctr. for Active Psychology, Riverside, Calif., 1981—; chief psychologist HSA Heartland Hosp., Nevada, Mo., 1983-84, Profl. Psychol. Svc., Kansas City, Mo., 1976—; sr. pastor Heartland Ch., Kansas City, 1989—; v.p. psychol. svcs. Group Dynamics, Dallas, 1978—; mem. staff Kellogg Psychiat. Hosp., Corona, Calif., Long Beach Neuropsychiat. Inst., Charter Baywood Hosp., Coll. Hosp., Cerritos, Calif., 1983—; mem. faculty Crystal Cathedral Lay Mins. Tng. Ctr., mini-seminary, San Juan Capistrano Community Ch. Author: Manage Your Stress Before It Manages You, 1983. Maj. U.S. Army, 1971-89. Mem. Nat. Psychiat. Assn. (life), Am. Assn. Christian Counselors, Nat. Assn. Disability Examiners, Mo. Assn. Disability Examiners, Mo. State Psychol. Assn., Ret. Officers Assn., U.S.A., U.S. Navy League, Kansas City Club, Univ. Club of Kansas City, Psi Chi, Lambda Chi Alpha (pres. Kansas City alumni assn. Pittsburg). Office: 4050 Broadway St Ste 220 Kansas City MO 64111-2611

MORGAN, DENNIS RICHARD, lawyer; b. Lexington, Va., Jan. 3, 1942; s. Benjamin Richard and Gladys Belle (Brown) M. BA, Washington and Lee U., 1964; JD, U. Va., 1967; LLM in Labor Law, NYU, 1971. Bar: Ohio 1967, Va. 1967, U.S. Ct. Appeals (4th cir.) 1968, U.S. Ct. Appeals (6th cir.) 1971, U.S. Supreme Ct. 1972. Law clk. to chief judge U.S. Dist. Ct. Ea. Dist. Va., 1967-68; mem. Marshman, Snyder & Seeley (now Marshman, Snyder & Corrigan), Cleve., 1971-72; dir. labor rels. Ohio Dept. Adminstrv. Svcs., 1972-75; asst. city atty. Columbus, Ohio, 1975-77; dir. Ohio Legis. Reference Bur., 1979-81; assoc. Clemans, Nelson & Assocs., Columbus, 1981; pvt. practice, Columbus, 1978-92; lectr. in field; guest lectr. Cen. Mich. U., 1975; judge moot ct. Ohio State U. Sch. Law, 1981, 83, grad. div., 1973, 74, 76, Baldwin-Wallace Coll., 1973; legal counsel Dist. IV Communications Workers Am., 1982-88; pers. dir. Pub. Utilities Commn. Ohio, 1989-91; asst. atty gen. State of Ohio, 1991—. Vice-chmn. Franklin County Dem. Party, 1976-82, dem. com. person Ward 58, Columbus, 1973-95; chmn. rules com. Ohio State Dem. Conv., 1974; co-founder, trustee Greater West Side Dem. Club; negotiator Franklin County United Way, 1977-81; regional chmn. ann. alumni fund-raising program U. Va. Sch. Law; commr. Greater Hilltop Area Commn., 1989—; pres. Woodbrook Village Condominium Assn., 1995—. Robert E. Lee Rsch. scholar, summer, 1965; recipient Am. Jurisprudence award, 1967. Capt. U.S. Army, 1968-70. Mem. Indsl. Rels. Rsch. Assn., ABA, Fed. Bar Assn., Am. Judicature Soc., Pi Sigma Alpha. Roman Catholic. Clubs: Shamrock, Columbus Metroplitan (charter). Home: 1261 Woodbrook Ln # G Columbus OH 43223-3243

MORGAN, DONALD CRANE, lawyer; b. Detroit, Sept. 17, 1940; s. Donald Nye and Nancy (Crane) M.; m. Judith Munro, June 23, 1962; children: Wendy, Donald. BA, Ohio Wesleyan U., 1962; JD, U. Mich., 1965. Bar: Mich. 1966, U.S. Dist. Ct. (ea. dist.) Mich. 1966, U.S. Ct. Appeals (6th cir.) 1967, U.S. Supreme Ct. 1971. Ptnr. Kerr, Russell and Weber, Detroit, 1965-87; of counsel Draugelis & Ashton, Plymouth, Mich., 1988-93; pvt. practice Plymouth, Mich., 1993—; twp. atty. Plymouth Twp., 1970-85, Northville Twp., 1972-85; city atty. City of Plymouth, 1995—; mediator Wayne County Mediation Tribunal, Detroit, 1981—, Oakland County Mediation Tribunal, Pontiac, Mich., 1992—; hearing panelist Mich. Atty. Discipline Bd., 1981—. Chmn. Wayne County II congl. Dist. Rep. Party, 1979-81; bd. dirs. Growth Works, Inc., treas., 1992-95, pres. 1995—; ruling elder 1st Presbyn. Ch., Plymouth, 1976-79, 90-93. Paul Harris fellow, 1980. Mem. ABA, Mich. Def. Trial Counsel, State Bar of Mich. (rep. assembly 1979-85, 89-95), Detroit Assn. Def. Trial Counsel, Plymouth Rotary (pres. 1985-86), Phi Alpha Delta, Sigma Alpha Epsilon. Republican. Presbyterian. Home: 1440 Woodland Pl Plymouth MI 48170-1569 Office: 134 N Main St Plymouth MI 48170-1250

MORGAN, HOWARD CAMPBELL, banker; b. Phila., June 14, 1935; s. Howard Moody and Margaret (Lyon) M.; m. Patricia H. Morgan (dec.); children: Pamela Ann, Kimberly Joy, Jennifer Lee; m. Judith P. Sanderson, 1994. BA in History, Lafayette Coll., Easton, Pa., 1957; postgrad., Harvard U., 1967. Comml. banker Citicorp, N.Y.C., 1957-79, sr. v.p., 1979-80; midwest sr. exec. Citicorp, Chgo., 1981—; mem. Govt. Commn. Fin. Insts., Chgo., 1984. Councilman Borough of Waldwick, N.J., 1964-68; trustee St. Ignatius Coll. Pres., Chgo., 1986-88, Lyric Opera Co., Chgo., 1987-95; chmn. Lincoln Pk. Zool. Soc., Chgo., 1987-90; bd. dirs., 1984—; bd. dirs. Exec. Svc. Corps, Chgo. Mem. Chgo. Econ. Club, Chgo. Club. Home: 5727 S Kenwood Ave Chicago IL 60637-1718 Office: Citicorp 500 W Madison St Chicago IL 60661-2511

MORGAN, JERRY, physical education educator, consultant; b. LaGrange, Ga., Oct. 18, 1953; s. Charlie and Mary Morgan; m. Susan Wilkerson Morgan, Sept. 15, 1979; children: Sherry, Christina, Jerrick. BS in Edn., Cleve. State, 1979, M in Edn., 1985. Cert. in physical edn., health, exercise physiology. Coach St. Ignatius H.S., Cleve., 1979-80; master tchr. East Cleve., 1979—; dir. youth program Case Western Reserve U., Cleve., 1980-83, 1980-83; teacher Shaw High School, 1979—. Author: How To Get Money For College, 1993. Pres. Lotus Drive Street Club, 1983-90, Lee Harvard Cmty., Cleve., 1985-89. Recipient Coach of the Yr. award Coaches Assn. Mem. Cleve State Alumni (chmn. 1989-92, Super Alumni award 1991). Office: J&M Consultants 3691 Lee Rd # 106 Shaker Heights OH 44120

MORGAN, RHELDA ELNOLA, secondary school educator; b. St. Louis, June 10, 1947; d. Harry and Lillie Bertha (Citizen) Marbry; m. Edward Lee Morgan; 1 child, Tawanna Ka-Rheida. BA in Edn., Harris-Stowe Coll., 1968; MA in Teaching, Webster U., 1981; postgrad., St. Louis U., 1989—. Primary tchr. Brunswick Elem. Sch., Gary, Ind., 1969-72, Walbridge Sch., St. Louis, 1972-84; lang. arts tchr. Ford Mid. Sch., St. Louis, 1984-87; lang. arts tchr., lang. dept. chairperson Marquette Visual & Performing Arts Mid. Sch., St. Louis, 1987-88; English tchr. Cen. Visual & Performing Arts High Sch., St. Louis, 1988-89, social studies tchr., 1989-90, English/fgn. lang. dept. chairperson, 1989-93; counselor Hugh O'Brian Youth Seminar, St. Louis, 1992, 93; English tchr. Soldan Internat. High Sch., St. Louis, 1993—; cons. for scholarship pageant edn. dept. Ch. of God in Christ, Jurisdiction 1, St. Louis, 1988-89; mem. adj. faculty Harris-Stowe State Coll., 1994—; mem. edn. adv. com. Principia Coll., 1993—; supervising tchr. for apprentices and practice tchrs. Recipient Trophy for 14 Yrs. as Aux. Treas. Mem. Nat. Coun. Tchrs. English, Popular Culture/Am. Culture, Ladies Aux. VFW (treas. 2910, 1972-86). Pentecostal.

MORGAN, ROBERT ANTHONY, optical physicist, research scientist; b. Eau Claire, Wis., June 16, 1962; s. David and Mary Ann (Derouin) M.; children: Kali Rose, Bria Elaine. BS in Physics summa cum laude, U. Wis., Eau Claire, 1984; MS, U. Ariz., 1986, PhD in Optical Scis., 1988. Teaching and rsch. asst. U. Wis., Eau Claire, 1981-84; from rsch. asst. to rsch. assoc. Optical Scis. Ctr. U. Ariz., Tucson, 1984-88; mem. tech. staff AT&T Bell Labs., Murray Hill, N.J., 1988-94; prin. sr. rsch. scientist Honeywell Tech. Ctr., Plymouth, Minn., 1994—; vis. scientist Applied Optics Univ. Erlangen, Germany, 1993. Contbr. numerous articles to profl. jours. IBM fellow, 1987-88; SPIE scholar, 1987-88. Mem. Optical Soc. Am., Laser and Electroptic Soc. Mem. Christian Ch. Office: Honeywell Tech Ctr 12001 State Hwy 55 Plymouth MN 55441-4479

MORGAN, ROBERT DALE, federal judge; b. Peoria, Ill., May 27, 1912; s. Harry Dale and Eleanor (Ellis) M.; m. Betty Louise Harbers, Oct. 14, 1939; children—Thomas Dale, James Robert. A.B., Bradley U., 1934; J.D., U. Chgo., 1937. Bar: Ill. 1937. Practice in Peoria, 1937-42, 46-67, Chgo., 1946-50; partner firm Morgan, Pendarvis & Morgan, Peoria, 1946-57, Davis, Morgan & Witherell, Peoria, 1957-67; U.S. judge So Dist Ill. (became Central Dist. 1979), Peoria, 1967—, sr. status U.S. judge, 1982. Contbr. articles to law revs. Mayor, Peoria, 1953-57; Bd. dirs. YMCA, Peoria, 1940-72, pres., 1947-53; Trustee Bradley U. Served from 1st lt. to maj. AUS, 1942-46. Mem. ABA, Am. Judicature Soc., Ill. Bar Assn., Peoria County Bar Assn. Presbyterian. Clubs: Creve Couer (Peoria), Rotary (Peoria) (pres. 1962-63), Country (Peoria). Office: US Dist Ct 228 Fed Bldg 100 NE Monroe St Peoria IL 61602-1003

MORGAN, ROGER JOHN, research scientist; b. Manchester, England, Nov. 2, 1942; came to U.S., 1968; s. Leslie Budworth and Hilda May (Bevins) M.; m. Anne Christine Cheetham, Sept. 23, 1967; children: Jacqueline, Nicholas, Melissa. BS in Chemistry with honors, U. of London, 1965; PhD in Polymer Phyics, U. of Manchester, 1968. Asst. rsch. prof. Washington U., St. Louis, 1968-72; scientist McDonnell Douglas Rsch. Labs., St. Louis, 1972-78; group leader Lawrence Livermore (Calif.) Nat. Lab., 1978-85; mem. tech. staff Rockwell Internat., Thousand Oaks, Calif., 1985-93; head of composites Mich. Molecular Inst., Midland, 1986-93; dir. Advanced Materials Engring. Experiment Sta., Mich. State U., Midland, 1993—. Co-editor: Advanced Composites Bull., 1989-96; mem. editl. adv. bd. Jour. Composite Materials, 1985—, Jour. Advanced Materials, 1991—; contbr. over 130 articles to profl. jours. Mem. Am. Chem. Soc., Soc. for Advancement of Materials and Process Engrs. Office: Mich. State U. Materials Engring Expt Sta 2203 Eastman Ave Midland MI 48640-2608

MORGAN, STANLEY LEINS, pharmaceutical company executive, consultant; b. Sandyville, Ohio, Jan. 28, 1918; s. Eben T. and Nora (Leins) M.; B.S. in Chem. Engring., Case Inst. Tech., 1939; m. Eloise Morkel, Feb. 22, 1941; children: Susan, Patricia, Ann. Chem. engr. Ben Venue Labs., Inc., Bedford, Ohio, 1940-42, mgr. blood plasma lab., 1942-44, gen. mgr., chief engr., 1944-61, v.p., 1961-63, exec. v.p., 1963—, also dir.; dir. Duramed Pharm. Co. Registered profl. engr., Ohio. Fellow Am. Inst. Chemists; mem. Am. Chem. Soc., Health Industries Mfrs. Assn., Am. Inst. Chem. Engrs., N.Y. Acad. Sci., Cryobiology Soc., Parental Drug Assn., Cleve. Engring. Soc., Assn. Ofcl. Racing Chemist. Methodist. Clubs: Acacia Country (Cleve.). Home: 31051 Northwood Dr Cleveland OH 44124-5411 Office: 270 Northfield Rd Cleveland OH 44146-4642

MORGAN, STEPHEN CARL, communications educator; b. Chattanooga, Mar. 18, 1941; s. Ralph and Dorothy Spracklin (Polson) M.; m. Erika Matuza, Mar. 9, 1963; children: Stephen Erik, Cynthia Selene. BA in English, U. Omaha, 1965; MA in English, U. Nebr. Omaha, 1968. Instr. English Dana Coll., Blair, Nebr., 1966-68, Southwest Mo. State U., Springfield, 1968-71, Hashell Indian Nations U., Lawrence, Kans., 1972-73; asst. dir. Univ. News Office Kans. State U., Manhattan, 1973-77; dir. pub. info. U. Wis. Eau Claire, 1977-82; editor Kans. Agrl. Experiment Sta. Kans. State U., Manhattan, 1982-95, mgr. spl. projects Dept. Comm., 1995—. Author poem in Defunct Mag., 1971; contbr. articles to profl. jours. With USN, 1959-61. Mem. N.H. Coun. for Advancement of Edn. (various awards), Internat. Mediating Soc., Gamma Sigma Delta (pub. rels. dirs. 1983). Office: Dept Comm Umberger Hall Kansas State Univ Manhattan KS 66506

MORGANROTH, FRED, lawyer; b. Detroit, Mar. 26, 1938; s. Ben and Grace (Greenfield) M.; m. Janice Marilyn Cohn, June 23, 1963; children: Greg, Candi, Erik. BA, Wayne State U., 1959, JD with distinction, 1961. Bar: Mich. 1961, U.S. Dist. Ct. (ea. dist.) Mich. 1961, U.S. Ct. Claims 1967, U.S. Supreme Ct. 1967; trained matrimonial arbitrator. Ptnr. Greenbaum, Greenbaum & Morganroth, Detroit, 1963-68, Lebenbom, Handler, Brody & Morganroth, Detroit, 1968-70, Lebenbom, Morganroth & Stern, Southfield, Mich., 1971-78; sole practice Southfield, 1979-83; ptnr. Morganroth & Morganroth P.C., Southfield, 1983-94, Morganroth, Morganroth, Alexander & Nye, P.C., Birmingham, Mich., 1994—. Mem. ABA (family law sect. 1987—), Mich. Bar Assn. (hearing panelist grievance bd. 1975—, Oakland County family law com. 1988—, vice chmn. 1992-93, chair 1993—), State Bar Mich. (mem. family law coun. of family law sect. 1990—, treas. 1993-94, chmn.-elect 1994-95, chmn. 1995-96), Detroit Bar Assn., Oakland Bar Assn. (cir. ct. mediator 1984—), Am. Arbitration Assn. (Oakland County family law com. 1985—, vice chmn. 1992-93, chmn. 1993-94, trained matrimonial arbitrator), Detroit Tennis Club (Farmington, Mich., pres. 1978-82), Charlivaux Country Club. Jewish. Home: 30920 Woodcrest Ct Franklin MI 48025-1435 Office: 300 Park St Ste 410 Birmingham MI 48009

MORGANROTH, MAYER, lawyer; b. Detroit, Mar. 20, 1931; s. Maurice Jack Morganroth and Sophie (Reisman) Blum; m. Sheila Rubinstein, Aug. 16, 1958; children: Lauri, Jeffrey, Cherie. JD, Detroit Coll. Law, 1954. Bar: Mich. 1955, U.S. Dist. Ct. Mich. 1955, Ohio 1958, U.S. Dist. Ct. (no. dist.) Ohio 1958, U.S. Ct. Appeals (6th cir.) 1968, U.S. Supreme Ct. 1971, N.Y. 1983, U.S. Dist. Ct. N.Y. 1985, U.S. Tax Ct. 1985, U.S. Ct. Appeals (4th cir.) 1985, U.S. Ct. Claims 1986, U.S. Ct. Appeals (2d cir.) 1986, U.S. Ct. Appeals (fed. cir.), U.S. Ct. Appeals (8th cir.) 1994. Sole practice Detroit, 1955—, N.Y.C., 1983—; ptnr. Morganroth & Morganroth, 1989—; cons. to lending instns.; lectr. on real estate NYU, 1980—, bus. entities and structures Wayne State U., 1981—; trial atty. in fed. and state jurisdictions, nationwide. Served with USN, 1948-50. Mem. ABA, FBA, N.Y. State Bar Assn., Southfield Bar Assn., Oakland Bar Assn., Assn. Trial Lawyers Am., Assn. Trial Lawyers Mich., Am. Judicature Soc., U.S. Supreme Ct. Hist. Soc., Nat. Criminal Def. Assn., West Bloomfield (Mich.) Club, Fairlane Club (Dearborn, Mich.), Knollwood Country Club, Edgewood Athletic Club (pres. 1963-65). Democrat. Jewish. Office: Ste 1500 3000 Town Ctr Southfield MI 48075-1153 also: 444 Madison Ave Ste 2801 New York NY 10022-6903

MORGANROTH, PATRICIA ANN, nursing educator; b. Bayonne, N.J., Jan. 14, 1948; d. Anthony and Veronica Lombardi; m. Joseph H. Morganroth, Dec. 4, 1971; children: Joseph, Stacy. BSN, Villanova U., 1969; MSN, U. Cinn., 1985. Cert. diabetes educator, CPR instr. Psychiat. staff nurse Vets. Hosp. Med. Ctr., Cin., 1970-72; dir. nursing Byars Nursing Home, Cin., 1972; instr. Good Samaritan Hosp., Cin., 1972-74; staff nurse Providence Hosp., Cin., 1982-83; dir. CNS Bethesda Hosp. Diabetes Care Ctr., Cin., 1985-90; OPT instr. Bethesda Clin. Staff Devel., Cin., 1990—; instr. Cin. State Tech. and Cmty. Coll., 1990—; OPT staff nurse Bethesda Lithotripsy Ctr., Cin., 1994-95. Contbr.: Diabetes: Education is the Key, 1988. Speaker Bethesda Hosp. Speakers Bur., Cin., 1985-92; vol. ARC, Cin., 1992— (Pat on the Back award 1994); v.p. Green and White Club, Cin., 1994—. Capt. nurse corps. U.S. Army, 1968-70. Mem. Nat. League Nursing, Nat. Student Nurse Assn. (advisor 1994—), Am. Diabetes Assn., Am. Assn. Diabetes Educators, Diabetes Educators Cin. Area (bd. dirs. 1988-90, pres.-elect 1990-91, pres. 1991-92). Home: 5541 Foxrun Ct Cincinnati OH 45239

MORHARD, ALBERT J., lawyer; b. Cleveland Heights, Ohio, Oct. 6, 1929; s. Albert and Josephine Morhard; children: Susan, Albert Jr., Kathleen. BA, Case Western Res. U., 1952; JD, Cornell U., 1956. Bar: Ohio 1956, U.S. Dist. Ct. 1956, U.S. Ct. Appeals 1972. Atty. Payntor & Green, Cleve., 1956-58, Bremer Morhard & Black, Cleve., 1958-60, Bremer Thompson Morhard & Cayne, Cleve., 1960-83, Webster Morhard & Koch, Cleve., 1983-86, Vanaken & Bond, Cleve., 1986-88, Rhoa Follen & Rollin, Cleve., 1988—; acting judge, magistrate, trial referee Lyndhurst Mcpl. Ct., 1979—. Mem. Ohio State Bar Found. (trustee 1988), Cuyahoga County Bar Assn. (pres. 1974-75, trustee 1974—), Cleve. Acad. Trial Attys. (pres. 1972-73), Cleve. Law Libr. Assn. (trustee 1974-94), Omicron Delta Kappa. Office: Rhoa Follem & Raiolen 1850 Midland Bldg Cleveland OH 44115

MORIARTY, JUDITH KAY SPRY, state official; b. Fairfield, Mo., Feb. 2, 1942; d. Earl Price and Blanche May (McDavitt) Spry; children: Derek David, Michael Price, Timothy John. Student Central Mo. State U., State Fair C.C.; tng. cert. Elections and County Clks. Assn., Mo., 1985. Motor Vehicle agt. Sedalia Motor Vehicle Registration, Mo., 1977-81; county clk. Pettis County, Sedalia, 1982-93; sec. of state State of Mo., 1993—. Vice regent Daus. Isabella, Sedalia, 1985-86; del. Mo. Dem. Conv., 1980, 84; active Women's Dem. Club Pettis County, Sacred Heart Cath. Ch., Mo. Coun. Econ. Edn., Mo. Hist. Recs. Preservation Bd., Friends of Archives, Local Recs. Bd., State Recs. Commn., Literacy Investment for Tomorrow; bd. dirs. Salvation Army, Sedalia, 1978—, Am. Cancer Soc., Sedalia, 1982—, Sedalia Area Council for Arts, 1980-84. Named Outstanding Young Woman Sedalia, Sedalia Jaycees, 1959. Mem. LWV, Bus. and Profl. Women (legis. chmn. 1984-86), Sedalia Area C. of C. (v.p., bd. dirs. 1982-85), Women's Aglow. Avocations: reading; physical fitness; walking; pen and ink sketching; baking. Office: Office Sec of State PO Box 778 Jefferson City MO 65102-0778*

MORICE, SANDRA KAY, librarian; b. Rolla, Mo., Sept. 9, 1951; d. Courtney Ray and Evelyn Elizabeth (Tesreau) Harris; m. Michael Lee Morice, July 11, 1970; children: Kindra E., Keith E. Student, S.E. Mo. State Coll., Cape Girardeau, Mo., 1969-70. Libr. aide Butzbach (Germany) Army Libr., 1986-88, libr., 1988-89; libr. Wakefield (Kans.) Pub. Libr., 1990—. Chmn. Pride, Wakefield, 1991-94, treas. 1994—; bd. dirs., Pride, Inc., Topeka, 1993-95, Family Cmty. Leadership, Kans. Mem. Wakefield Libr. Club, Madura Congl. Ch. Office: Wakefield Pub Libr 207 Third St Wakefield KS 67487

MORIN, PATRICK JOYCE, advertising executive; b. Manila, Philippines, June 10, 1938; (parents Am. citizens); s. Martin Joseph and Janet (Westwater) M.; m. Deborah E. O'Brien, Apr. 7, 1993; children: Martin, Sarah. BA, Ohio State U., 1961, JD, 1964. Account exec. J. Walter Thompson Co., N.Y.C., 1964-66, Chgo., 1966-69; pres. Ky. Roast Beef div. Ky. Fried Chicken Inc., Louisville, 1969-71; v.p., account dir. Grey Advt. Co., Detroit, 1971-75; pres. Griswold Eshleman Inc., N.Y.C., 1976-79; pres., CEO Griswold Eshleman, Cleve., 1979—; pres. Ross Roy Advt., Detroit, 1991-93; bd. dirs. Nat. Advt. Rev. Bd. With U.S. Army, 1956. Mem. Am. Assn. Advt. Agys. (Cleve. coun., past pres.), N.E. Ohio Squash Racquet Assn. (bd. dirs.), Ohio State U. Alumni Assn. (former mem. adv. coun.), Ohio State U. Pres.'s Club, Cleve. Advt. Club (pres. 1986-87), Hermit Club, Shorery Club, Muirfield Village Club. Home: 13 Shoreby Dr Bratenahl OH 44108-1161 Office: Griswold Eshleman 101 W Prospect Ave Cleveland OH 44115-1027*

MORIN, WILLIAM RAYMOND, bookstore chain executive; b. Escanaba, Mich., Apr. 19, 1949; s. Raymond Louis and Naomi Rita (Flynn) M.; m. Yvonne Catherine Singleton, Aug. 7, 1971; children: Timothy Raymond, Kathryn Naomi. BS in Bus. summa cum laude, No. Mich. U., 1974; MBA, Mich. State U., 1979. Grad. teaching assoc. Mich. State U., East Lansing, 1977-79; instr. U. Wash., Seattle, 1979-80; regional franchise rep. Taco John's, Cheyenne, Wyo., 1981-87; dir. franchising Dawn Donut Systems, Inc., Flint, 1987-91; sr. rep. leasing and rsch. Family Bookstores, Grand Rapids, Mich., 1991-93, dir. real estate and legal, 1993—. Contbr.: (book) Principles of Modern Management, 1980. Staff sgt. U.S. Army, 1967-70. Home: 1207 Fallingbrook Dr SE Kentwood MI 49508-6247 Office: 5300 Patterson Ave SE Grand Rapids MI 49530

MORING, WALTER G., product engineer; b. Toledo, Jan. 29, 1947. B, U. Toledo, 1976. Chief product engr. A.P. Parts Co., Toledo, 1970—. Patentee in field.

MORITZ, JOHN REID, lawyer; b. Hamilton, Ohio, Nov. 30, 1951; s. Edward and Betty (Reid) M.; m. Darla F. Winter, July 26, 1986; children: Alexander R., Andrew F., Kathryn Ann. BA, Alma Coll., 1978; JD, Thomas M. Cooley Sch. Law, 1982. Bar: Mich. 1982. Law clk. Mich. 30th Jud. Cir., Lansing, 1981, Mich. 20th Jud. Cir., Grand Haven, 1982-83; legis. aide to rep. Mich. Ho. of Reps., Lansing, 1981-82; assoc. Swaney, Thomas & Moritz P.C., Holland, Mich., 1983—. With U.S. Army, 1973-76. Mem. ABA, Mich. Bar Assn., Ottawa County Bar Assn., Mich. Trial Lawyers Assn. Home: 4345 Lakeshore Dr N Holland MI 49424-5650 Office: Swaney Thomas & Moritz PC 30 E 9th St Holland MI 49423-3508

MORK, GORDON ROBERT, historian, educator; b. St. Cloud, Minn., May 6, 1938; s. Gordon Matthew and Agnes (Gibb) M.; m. Dianne Jeannette Muetzel, Aug. 11, 1963; children: Robert, Kristiana, Elizabeth. Instr. history U. Minn., Mpls., 1966; lectr., asst. prof. U. Calif., Davis, 1966-70; mem. faculty Purdue U., West Lafayette, Ind., 1970—; assoc. prof. Purdue U., West Lafayette, 1973-94; prof. history, 1994—; dir. honors program in the humanities Purdue U., West Lafayette, 1985-87, dir grad. studies in history, Am. studies, 1987-93; resident dir. Purdue U.-Ind. U. Program, Hamburg, Fed. Republic Germany, 1975-76; rsch. fellow in humanities U. Wis., Madison, 1969-70; mem. test devel. com., advanced placement European history Ednl. Testing Svc., 1993—, chair, 1995—. Author: Modern Western Civilization: A Concise History, 3d edit., 1994, Instructor's Manual: A History of Civilization, 1988, 96; mem. adv. bd. Teaching History, 1983—, History Tchr., 1986—. Mem. citizens task force Lafayette Sch. Corp., 1978-79; bd. dirs. Ind. Humanities Coun., 1986-89; bd. dirs., sec. Murdock-Sunnyside Bldg. Corp., 1980—; elder Cen. Presbyn. Ch., Lafayette, 1973-75, deacon, 1996-99. Mem. Internat. Soc. History Didactics (v.p. 1991-95), Am. Hist. Assn., Conf. Group on Ctrl. European History, Soc. History Edn., Leo Baeck Inst., Com. for History in the Classroom (treas. 1990-93), Phi Beta Kappa. Home: 1521 Cason St Lafayette IN 47904-2642 Office: Purdue U Dept of History West Lafayette IN 47907-1358

MORLAN, GORDON ELLIOTT, secondary school educator; b. Odessa, Tex., Oct. 12, 1936; s. Clarence Elmer and Lona (Elliott) M.; m. Judith Jeannette Green, June 18, 1960; children: Christopher E., Andrew B. BS, Ottawa U., 1959; MA, Western Mich. U., 1962, U. N.H., 1967. Tchr. Mattawan (Mich.) H.S., 1959-60, Kimball High Sch., Royal Oak, Mich., 1960-64, Univ. High Sch., Kalamazoo, Mich., 1964-65; tchr. chemistry Grosse Pointe (Mich.) Pub. Schs., 1968—, chmn. sci. dept., 1970—. Mem. flood plan commn. Grosse Pointe Park City Coun., 1988. Recipient Excellence in Edn. award Lakeshore Optimists, Grosse Pointe, 1987, 92, Golden Apple award Wayne County Ind. Sch. Dist., Detroit, 1989; named Newsweek Outstanding Tchr., Detroit, 1989. Mem. Am. Chem. Soc. (edn. com. 1989—), Mich. State Tchrs. Assn., Grosse Pointe Sail Club. Home: 723 Barrington Rd Grosse Pointe MI 48230 Office: Grosse Pointe North High Sch 707 Vernier Rd Grosse Pointe MI 48236

MORLEY, JOHN EDWARD, physician; b. Eshowe, Zululand, South Africa, June 13, 1946; came to U.S., 1977; s. Peter and Vera Rose (Phipson)

M.; m. Patricia Morley, Apr. 4, 1970; children: Robert, Susan, Jacqueline. MB, BCh, U. Witwatersrand, Johannesburg, South Africa, 1972. Diplomate Am. Bd. Internal Medicine, subspecialty cert. endocrinology and geriatrics. Asst. prof. Mpls. VA Med. Ctr. and U. Minn., 1979-81; assoc. prof. U. Minn., Mpls., 1981-84; prof. UCLA San Fernando Valley, 1985-89; dir. GRECC Sepulveda (Calif.) VA Med. Ctr., 1985-89; Dammert prof. gerontology, dir. div. geriatric medicine St. Louis U. Med. Ctr., 1989—; dir. geriatric rsch., edn. and clin. ctr. St. Louis VA Med. Ctr., 1989—; mem. adv. panel of geriatrics and endocrinology U.S. Pharmacopeial Conv., Inc., Rockville, Md., 1990—. Author: (with others) Nutritional Modulation of Neuronal Function, 1988, Neuropeptides and Stress, 1988, Geriatric Nutrition, 1990, 2d edit., 1995, Medical Care in the Nursing Home, 1991, Endocrinology and Metabolism in the Elderly, 1992, Memory Function and Aging Related Disorders, 1992, Aging and Musculoskeletal Disorders, 1993, Aging, Immunity and Infection, 1994, Sleep Disorders and Insomnia in the Elderly, 1993, Quality Improvement in Geriatric Care, 1995, Focus on Nutrition, 1995, Applying Health Services Research to Long-Term Care, 1996, As We Age, 1996; mem. editl. bd. Peptides, 1983—, Internat. Jour. Obesity, 1986-89, Jour. Nutritional Medicine, 1990—, Clinics in Applied Nutrition, 1990-92; editor geriatrics sect. Yearbook of Endocrinology, 1987—, Nursing Home Medicine, 1992—, Clin. Geriatrics, 1992—, others. Mem. adv. bd. Alzheimer's Assn., St. Louis, 1990-92; mem. adv. com. for physicians Mo. Divsn. Aging, Jefferson City, 1990—; bd. dirs. Mo. Assn. Long Term Care Physicians, 1991—, Long Term Care Ombudsman Program, St. Louis, 1992, Fund for Psychineuroimmunology, 1990—, Hamilton Hts. Health Resource Ctr., 1992—. Recipeint Mead Johnson award Am. Inst. Nutrition, 1985. Mem. ACP (geriatrics subcom. 1991-92), Am. Soc. Clin. Investigation, Endocrine Soc., Am. Fedn. Clin. Rsch., Am. Acad. Behavioral Sci., Am. Geriatrics Soc. (assoc. editor jour. 1989-93, pres. Mo.-Kans. affiliate 1996—), Am. Fedn. Clin. Rsch., Gerontology Soc. Am., Am. Diabetes Assn., Am. Soc. Pharmacy and Therapeutics, Soc. for Neurosci., La Asociacion de Gerontologica y Geriatrica, A.C. (hon.), Assn. Dirs. Geriatric Acad. Programs. Office: Saint Louis U Sch Medicine 1402 S Grand Blvd Rm M238 Saint Louis MO 63104-1004

MORRELL, WAYNE MARKLEY, computer engineer; b. Camden, N.J., Dec. 13, 1936; s. Philip Wayne and Mildred (Morris) M.; m. Kathleen Fitzgerald, Nov. 18, 1961 (div. 1983); children: Jeanette Anne Morrell Huang, Daniel Lawrence, Ruth Ellen Morrell Saenz, David Michael, Andrew Wayne. Tech. instr. def. systems Burroughs Corp., Paoli, Pa., 1958-62, systems engr., 1962-68; systems support mgr. Burroughs Machines , Ltd., Houslow, Middlesex, Eng., 1968-77; data communications support mgr. Burroughs Corp., Detroit, 1977-82, sr. product mgr., 1982-85; sr. elec. engr. Herstal Automation, Ltd., Berkley, Mich., 1987-89. With USAF, 1955-58. Mem. Math. Assn. Am., Mensa. Republican. Home: 627 Sedgefield Dr Bloomfield Hills MI 48304

MORRIS, ANN HASELTINE JONES, social welfare administrator; b. Springfield, Mo., Feb. 3, 1941; d. Mansur King and Adelaide (Haseltine) Jones; m. Ronald D. Morris, Nov. 29, 1963 (div. 1990); children: David, Christopher. BA in Edn. and Art, Drury Coll., 1963. Art instr. Ash Grove (Mo.)/Bois D'Arc Pub. Sch. Dist., 1963-64; instr. Drury Coll., Springfield, 1966-67; tchr. Springfield R-12 Sch. Dist., 1974-86; exec. dir. S.W. Ctr. for Ind. Living, Springfield, 1986—; adv. com. Springfield R-12 Spl. Edn., 1993—; tech. cons. and alternative dispute resolution mediator Ams. with Disabilities Act EEOC, Dept. of Justice Network, 1993—. Bd. dirs. Ozark Greenways, 1991-93, Springfield Deaf Relay, 1988-90; adv. task force Allied Health Program Devel. S.W. Bapt Univ., 1988; mem. Drury Coll. Women's Aux., 1984—, conservator of the peace, handicap parking enforcement action team, 1991—; bd. treas. Mo. Parent Act, 1989-91, Diversity Network of the Ozarks, 1990—; svc. coord. Youthnet, 1990—; community adv. bd. Rehab. Svcs., St. John's Regional Health Care Ctr., 1988-91; mem. Springfield Homeless Network, 1989—, others; apptd. to Mo. Gov.'s Coun. on Disability; pres. Statewide Ind. Living Coun. Mem. NOW (sec. 1991), P.E.O., Mo. Assn. of Ctrs. for Ind. Living (v.p. 1990—), Mo. Assn. for Social Welfare (bd. treas. 1989-95), Nat. Assn. of Ind. Living Ctrs. (AIDS task force 1993—), Assn. of Programs for Rural Ind. Living, Nat. Soc. of Fund Raising Execs., Mo. Rehab. Assn., C. of C. (healthcare divsn.), Zeta Tau Alpha. Home: 1748 E Arlington Rd Springfield MO 65804-7742

MORRIS, BARBARA KATHERINE, renal, cardiac, vascular nurse; b. Omaha, Oct. 7, 1941; d. Albert Joseph and Rosemary (Cloidt) Ulrich; m. Gary David Toman, Oct. 7, 1961 (div. 1988); children: Cindy Penke, Bob Toman, Kim Volwiler, Vicki Toman; m. Gary Morris, Nov. 7, 1992. Nursing diploma, Creighton Meml. Hosp., 1961. RN, Nebr. Staff nurse St. Joseph Hosp., Omaha, 1961-70, Am. Med. Inst., Omaha, 1975-88, 90—; night supr. Nebr. Masonic Home, Omaha, 1988-90; bd. dirs. Am. Diabetic Assn.; Retainment, Recruitment Com., Omaha, 1990—. Bd. mem. Cass County 4-H Coun., Weeping Water, N.C., 1976-86; leadership club mem., Plattsmouth, N.C., 1976-86; spl. events. chmn. Cass County Dem., Plattsmouth, 1986—. Roman Catholic. Home: 15506 6th St Plattsmouth NE 68048-7716

MORRIS, CANDACE L., state legislator. Student, Ind. U. Owner, dir. daycare; mem. Ind. State Ho. of Reps. Dist. 94, mem. commerce and econ. devel. com., mem. judiciary and pub. safety com., vice-chmn. families, children and human affairs com. Mem. MIBOR, Circle City Child Care Assn., N.W. Roundtable, Pike, Wayne, Washington and Eagle Creek GOP Clubs.

MORRIS, GREG JAMES, advertising executive; b. Topeka, Jan. 25, 1956; s. James A. and Patricia A. (Souders) M.; m. Joyce L. Izynski, Feb. 25, 1978; children: Chad, Jason, Jonathon. BA in Telecomm., Ind. U., 1978. Account exec. WIBC Radio, Indpls, 1978-81, 85-88, WNDE Radio, Indpls, 1981-84; nat. sales mgr. WIBC/WKLR Radio, Indpls, 1988-89; gen. sales mgr. WKLR Radio, Indpls, 1989-91; advt. dir. Indpls. Bus. Jour., 1991—; sales mgr. WTPI/WMUS radio, Indpls., 1996—. Mem. Advt. Club Indpls., Phi Delta Theta. Republican. Home: 11853 Stoney Bay Cir Carmel IN 46033-9501 Office: Indpls Bus Jour 431 N Pennsylvania St Indianapolis IN 46204-1806 Other Office: WTPI/WMUS Radio 9245 N Meridian St Inidianapolis IN 46260

MORRIS, HUBERT ANDREW, auditor; b. Des Moines, June 30, 1946; s. Hubert Andrew Sr. and Mary Louise (Coppola) M. BA in Acctg., Loras Coll., 1970; AA in Computer Programming, Des Moines Area Community Coll., 1987. Cert. info. systems auditor, cert. internal auditor, Iowa. Acct. John S. Oden Co., CPAs, Des Moines, 1970-72; controller Randolph Investment, Des Moines, 1972-78; audit supr. Wausau Ins. Cos., Des Moines, 1978-83; programmer, analyst Hawkeye Investment Mgmt., Des Moines, 1983-85; with quality assurance Employers Mut. Cos., Des Moines, 1985-87; info. systems auditor Fed. Home Loan Bank Des Moines, 1987-95; internal audit dir. ITS, Inc., Des Moines, 1995—; pres. SAO, Inc., Des Moines, 1974-78; co-owner Hayen & Morris, Des Moines, 1980—. Chmn. Washington Sch. Zoning Commn., Des Moines, 1986. Named one of Outstanding Young Men in Am. , U.S. Jaycees, 1980. Mem. Electronic Data Processing Auditors Assn. Am. (founder Iowa chpt., pres. 1986-88), Inst. Internal Auditors, Data Processing Mgmt. Assn. Roman Catholic. Home: 2010 S Union St Des Moines IA 50315-7138 Office: 6700 Pioneer Pkwy Johnston IA 50131

MORRIS, JEFFREY SELMAN, orthopedic surgeon; b. Johannesburg, South Africa, June 26, 1948; arrived in Can., 1979; came to U.S., 1990; s. Israel and Anna Riva (Belikoff) M.; m. Carol Parker, Jan. 21, 1973 (div. 1986); children: Amit, Leora. BSc, U. Witwatersrand, Johannesburg, 1970, B of Medicine, B of Surgery, 1973. Rotating intern Natalspruit Hosp., South Africa, 1974, surg. resident, 1975-76; resident in orthopedic surgery Cen. Emek Hosp., Afula, Israel, 1977-79, Queen's U., Kingston, Ont., Can., 1979-82; orthopedic surgeon Port Arthur Clinic, Thunder Bay, Ont., 1983-86, Joseph Brant Meml. Hosp., Burlington, Ont., 1986-90, Beachwood (Ohio) Orthopedic Assocs., 1990—; mem. staff Meridia South Pointe Hosp., Cleve.; assoc. staff Meridia Hillcrest Hosp., Cleve., Mt. Sinai Hosp. Cleve. Contbr. articles to profl. jours., chpt. to book. Med. advisor Arthritis Soc., Thunder Bay, 1983-86. Mem. ACS, Can. Med. Assn., Ont. Med. Assn., Can. Orthopedic Assn., Ont. Orthopedic Assn., Ohio Orthopedic Soc., Cleve. Orthopedic Soc., Cleve. Acad. Medicine, Royal Coll. Physicians and Surgeons (Can.), Can. Soc. Surgery of the Hand, Ohio Med. Assn. Jewish. Office: Beachwood Orthopedic Assocs 23250 Mercantile Rd Beachwood OH 44122-5928

MORRIS, JOAN TAUBE, personnel administrator; b. East Detroit, Mich., Feb. 12, 1965. BBA, Mich. State U., 1987. Purchasing mgr. ops. W.A. Kates Co., Ferndale, Mich., 1988-93; v.p. pers. mgmt. Taube Family of Cos., Inc., Ferndale, 1988—. Mem. Am. Mgmt. Assn. Republican. Office: Taube Family of Cos Inc 1450 Jarvis St Ferndale MI 48220-2064

MORRIS, JOHN DAVID, museum fundraiser; b. Peoria, Ill., June 2, 1968; s. Pettus Thomas Morris Jr. and Helen Inez (Cox) Ferguson; m. Cynthia Renee Maloney Morris, Oct. 19, 1991; 1 child, Jordan Ambrose. BA in Radio and TV, The George Washington U., 1990; MPA, 1993. Presdl. intern The George Washington U., 1990-92; dir. Devel. Lakeview Mus. Arts and Sci., Peoria, Ill., 1992—. Congl. intern U.S. House Rep. Minority Leader, Washington, 1987; White House intern, Washington, 1988; bd. dirs. Ctrl. Ill. Youth Symphony, Peoria, 1993—; pres. Richwoods H.S. Alumni Assn., 1995—; mem. Peoria County Rep. Ctrl. Com., Rep. committeeman. Recipient George Washington award, 1992; named in 40 leaders under 40, Peoria area, 1995. Mem. Rotary Club Peoria, Pi Alpha Alpha. Republican. Presbyterian. Home: 4104 N Chelsea Pl Peoria IL 61614 Office: Lakeview Museum Arts & Scis 1125 W Lake Ave Peoria IL 61614

MORRIS, LESTER A., insurance company executive; b. 1938. With Peat, Marwick, Mitchell & Co., Chgo., 1960-64, IRS, Chgo., 1964-65; chmn. bd. Mesirow Fin. Holding Inc., Chgo., 1965—. Office: Mesirow Ins Svcs Inc 350 N Clark St Chicago IL 60610-4712*

MORRIS, MELANIE MARIE, nurse; b. Lima, Ohio, Aug. 3, 1963; d. Andrew J. and Helen (Kaniclides) Menegos. BS in Nursing, U. Akron, 1986, MBA in Mgmt., 1993. RN, Ohio. Home health aid Nurses' Ho. Calls, Akron, Ohio, 1985, Portamedic, Akron, 1985; intravenous technician Akron City Hosp., 1985-86, nurse, 1987-88; nurse Vis. Nurse Svc., Akron, 1988-89; nurse Akron Gen. Med. Ctr., 1989—, clin. mgr. SICU/MICU, 1994—. Mem. Young Adult League, Akron; mem. Annunciation Ch. Choir, Akron, sec. 1989-90, 92-94, pres. 1995—. Mem. Daus. of Penelope (treas. 1988-90). Republican. Greek Orthodox.

MORRIS, PHYLLIS SUTTON, philosophy educator; b. Quincy, Ill., Jan. 25, 1931; d. John Guice and Helen Elizabeth (Provis) Sutton; m. John Martin Morris, Feb. 4, 1950; children: William Robert, Katherine Jill. Student, U. Mich., 1948-51; AB, U. Calif., 1953; MA, Colo. Coll., 1963; PhD, U. Mich., 1969. Instr. humanities Mich. State U., East Lansing, 1968-69; from lectr. to assoc. prof. Kirkland Coll., Clinton, N.Y., 1969-78; assoc. prof. Hamilton Coll., Clinton, 1978-83; adj. assoc. prof. LeMoyne Coll., Syracuse, N.Y., 1983-85; rsch. assoc. in philosophy Oberlin (Ohio) Coll., 1995—; vis. prof. philosophy Oberlin Coll., 1989-91, 93, 94-95, U. Mich., Ann Arbor, 1996. Author: Sartre's Concept of a Person, 1976; revs. editor Sartre Studies Internat. jour., 1995; contbr. articles to profl. jours. Travel grantee Am. Coun. Learned Socs., 1988, Summer Seminar grantee NEH, 1974, 82. Mem. Am. Philos. Assn., Sartre Cir., Sartre Soc. N.Am. (co-founder 1985, exec. com. 1985-91), Soc. for Phenomenology and Existential Philosophy, Soc. for Women in Philosophy. Democrat. Home: 2116 Runnymede Blvd Ann Arbor MI 48103-5034

MORRIS, RICHARD JEFFERY, plastic extrusion company executive; b. Peoria, Ill., Feb. 23, 1953; s. Gordon Dale and Selma Ann (Ferguson) M.; m. Patricia Ann Boarman, Apr. 23, 1977; children: Michael Christopher, Christine Elizabeth. BFA, U. Ill., 1975. Elec. engr. Hatfield Electric Co., Mossville, Ill., 1975-76; designer Internat. Paper Co., Peoria, 1976-79, Champion Internat., St. Paul, 1979-80; indsl. designer Liberty Diversified Industries, Mpls., 1980-81, rsch. specialist, 1981-82; gen. mgr. Diversi-Plast Products, Mpls., 1982-96, v.p., gen. mgr., 1996—; freelance artist, 1970-81; graphics instr. Ill. Cen. Coll., Peoria, 1978-79; com. mem. Home Ventilating Inst. Patentee bldg. and packaging methods. Mem. ch. coun. St. Mark Luth. Ch., Chillicothe, Ill., 1972; coach youth athletics, Mpls., 1987—, fundraiser Mpls. YMCA, Mpls. United Way; bd. dirs., dir. basketball Prior Lake Athletics for Youth. Mem. Soc. Plastics Engrs., Phi Theta Kappa. Home: 15987 Island View Rd NW Prior Lake MN 55372-1606 Office: Diversi Plast Products 7425 Laurel Ave Minneapolis MN 55426-1501

MORRIS, RICHARD LOUIS, healthcare company executive; b. Piits., Apr. 15, 1940; s. Robert Edwin and Marina (Hegeman) M.; m. Roberta Christine Pavlik, Jan. 26, 1963; children: Richard Jr. Tracy, Anne, John. Student, Duquesne U., Pitts., U. Md. Sales rep. Procter and Gamble, Washington D.C., 1976-70, Nat. Chemsearch Corp., Washington, 1970-71, Sherwood Med., Washington D.C., 1971-72; v.p. LaBarge Inc., St. Louis, 1972-81, Mon-A-Therm, Inc., St. Louis, 1981--; founder, pres., bd. dirs. Innovation Med. Techs., Inc., St. Louis, 1990—; founder, dir. Mon-A-Therm, Inc., St. Louis, 1981-88; dir. sales Mallinckrodt Anesthesia Products, Mallinckrodt, Inc., 1988-90. Mem. Lions Club Internat. Republican. Roman Catholic. Home: 1751 Baxter Forest Ct Chesterfield MO 63005-4659 Office: 750 Goddard Ave Chesterfield MO 63005-1100

MORRIS, ROBERT JULIAN, JR., art gallery owner; b. Decatur, Ill., Jan. 12, 1932; s. Robert J. and M. Letitia (Ross) M.; m. J. Jean Nelson Morris, June 6, 1952; children: R. Thomas, Debora L., Charles A., Sandra J. BS in Chemistry, U. Ill., 1954; MS in Chemistry, Marshall U., 1961. Analytical chemist Union Carbide Chemicals, South Charleston, W.Va., 1954-61; sr. research chemist U.S. Gypsum Co., Des Plaines, Ill., 1961-63; research mgr. MacAndrews and Forbes Co., Camden, N.J., 1963-66; tech. dir. Nat. Can Corp., Chgo., 1966-73; v.p. corp. engring. Coachmen Industries Inc., Middlebury, Ind., 1973-74; pres. Coachmen Homes Corp., 1974-76; chmn. bd., chief exec. officer Medallion Plastics Inc., Elkhart, Ind., 1976-93; owner Robert Morris Gallery, Goshen, Ind., 1993—. Contbr. articles to profl. jours. Bd. dirs. Career Ctr., Elkhart, 1983-89, Ind. Voc. Tech. Coll., Plastics R&D Ctr. Ball State U., 1987-94. Mem. Rotary. Republican. Methodist. Home: 113 E Madison St Goshen IN 46526 Office: Robert Morris Gallery 113 E Madison Goshen IN 46526

MORRIS, STEPHEN R., state legislator; m. Barbara Morris, 1968; children: Stephanie, Susan, Sara Beth. BS, Kans. State U., 1969. Farmer Hugoton, Kans.; mem. from dist. 39 Kans. State Senate, vice chmn. agr. com., mem. energy and natural resources com., mem. emergency med. svc. bd., coord. coun. on early childhood devel. svc. With USAFR, 1974—. Mem. Kans. State U. Alumni Assn.

MORRIS, SUSAN MARIE, librarian; b. Marshalltown, Iowa, Oct. 28, 1955; d. Donald Leroy and Lorena Pearl (Mitchell) M. BME, Wartburg Coll., 1977; MALS, U. Iowa, 1983. Tchr. vocal music Ayrshire (Iowa) Consol. Sch., 1978-80, Fayette (Iowa) Community Sch., 1980-81; libr. I Quincy (Ill.) Coll., 1983-85; cons. Great River Libr. System, Quincy, 1985-87; cataloging libr. Wartburg Coll., Waverly, 1987-92; head tech. svcs. Cedar Falls (Iowa) Pub. Libr., 1992-94; dir. Le Mars (Iowa) Pub. Libr., 1994—. Contbr. articles to profl. jours. Mem. ctrl. com. Bremer County Dems., Waverly, 1988-92; pres. Wartburg Symphony Assn., 1990-91; treas. Friends of the Waverly Pub. Libr., 1989-92, v.p. 1992-94. State of Iowa scholar, 1977. Mem. ALA, AAUW, Iowa Libr. Assn. (chair tech. svcs. forum 1991, chair pub. rels. com. 1990-91). Office: Le Mars Public Library 46 1st St SW Le Mars IA 51031-3696

MORRIS, VINCENT EDWIN, religious association administrator; b. Sterling, Ill., Feb. 8, 1967; s. Clark Edwin and Virginia (Crossett) M.; m. Ellen Rising, June 1, 1991. BA in Bibl. Studies, Gordon Coll., Wenham, Mass., 1988, BA in Youth Ministries, 1988. Dir. youth Immanuel Presbyn. Ch., Warrenville, Ill., 1989—. Home: 501 E Willow Ave Wheaton IL 60187-5522 Office: Immanuel Presbyn Ch 29 W 260 Batavia Rd Warrenville IL 60555

MORRISON, CAROLE LYNNE, community volunteer; b. Longmont, Colo., Oct. 29, 1946; d. Joseph Jefferson and Calvena Hale (Dunnell) Hastings; m. Ivan Lavern Morrison, July 3, 1970; children: Brett Alan, Brian Lavern. BSE, Abilene Christian U., 1969. Food server Catchings Cafeteria Abilene (Tex.) Christian U., 1964-67, switchboard operator Zellner Hall, 1967-69; sec., bookkeeper Mountain States Children's Home, Longmont, Colo., 1969-76; bookkeeper Citizen Newspaper, Longmont, Colo., 1978, Dan's Nautilus, Longmont, Colo., 1980; aide Burlington Elem. Sch., Longmont, Colo., 1986-87; paraprofl. Rose Hill (Kans.) High Sch., 1991-96. Vol. rose Hill H.S. and Elem. Sch., 1988-91, Rose Hill Stoll Media Ctr., 1992, Burlington Elem. Schs., Longmont, 1980-86; Bible class tchr. Ch. of Christ, Longmont, Coloc. and andover, Kans., 1974-96; parent vol. Sch. Improvement Leadership Team, Rose Hill H.S., 1993-96; spkr. ladies retreats and lectureships, Akron Colo. Ch. of Christ, 1994, Winfield, Kans. Ch. of Christ, Andover, Kans. Ch. of Christ, 1995. Named Outstanding Young Woman in Am., 1983. Home: 1630 N Main St Rose Hill KS 67133-9313

MORRISON, CONSTANCE FAITH, state legislator, realtor; b. Washington; d. Graham Edward and Cora E. (Smith) Wilson; m. George H. Morrison, May 14, 1955; 4 children. AA, Normandale C.C., 1980. Photojournalist Dakota County Tribune, 1970-76; pub. affairs writer, pub. info. coord. Ind. Sch. Dist. 191, 1976-80; ind. realtor, 1980—; mem. I-R caucus Minn. Ho. of Reps., 1986-94; sec.-treas. I-R caucus, 1993-94; mem. Minn. Ho. of Reps., 1986-94. Mem. Burnsville City Coun., 1977-82; mayor City of Burnsville, 1982-86, chairwoman chem. health com., 1987-92; bd. dirs. Minn. League Cities, 1983-86, Mpls. Area United Way, 1988—, Minn. Citizens League Bd., 1995—, Dakota County Libr. Bd., 1995—, Dakota County Planning Com., 1995—; chair adminstrv. bd. Grace United Meth. Ch., Burnsville, 1986-90, 95—; co-chairwoman Com. to Elect Rep. Women, St. Paul, 1987-91. Mem. Burnsville C. of C., Rotary. Home: 909 W 155th St Burnsville MN 55306-5405

MORRISON, DENNIS PATRICK, psychologist; b. Warren, Ohio, Mar. 11, 1949; s. Frank Joseph and Ruby (Shaver) M.; m. Marsha Gay Smith, Dec. 21, 1977; children: Michael, Christopher. BS, Ball State U., 1973, MA, 1974; MA, Ball State U., 1984, PhD, 1986. Psychologist So. Ark. Regional Health Ctr., El Dorado, Ark., 1974-76, Gallahue Mental Health Ctr., Indpls., 1976-80; doctoral fellow Ball State U., Muncie, Ind., 1980-82; aerospace physiologist USN, Pensacola, Fla., 1982-83; doctoral intern Ctr. for Mental Health, Anderson, Ind., 1983-84; coord. St. Francis Hosp. Ctr., Indpls., 1984-87; dir. community svcs. Quinco Consulting Svcs., Columbus, Ind., 1987-89; mgr. North Kans. City (Mo.) Hosp., 1989; mgr. market planning Nat. Computer Systems, Minnetonka, Minn., 1989-90, dir., 1990-92; dir. Medco Behavioral Care, Inc., 1993-94; CEO South Ctrl. Cmty. Mental Health Ctr., Bloomington, Ind., 1995—; asst. prof. So. Ark. U., El Dorado, 1975-76, Ball State U., 1986; ind. cons. exercise & sports orgns., 1981-92. Author mag. column The Human Factor, 1983-84; contbr. articles to profl. jours.; patentee in field. Mem. Gov.'s Task Force for Alzheimers, Indpls., 1987-89; mem. Smoking Cessation Task Force Govs. Project, Indpls., 1987. Lt. USN, 1982-83. Mem. APA, Am. Assn. Partial Hospitalization (outcomes task force 1993), Minn. Psychol. Assn., Assn. for Sports Psychology in Ind. (co-founder 1988), Managed Health Care Assn. (quality com. 1991-92). Office: 645 S Rogers St Bloomington IN 47403

MORRISON, EMILY, property manager; b. Mpls., Aug. 25, 1961; d. John G. and Helene Jayme; m. Frederick Anders Friedman, July 12, 1989; 1 child, Carissa Cloe. BA with honors, U. Minn., 1983. Mgmt. trainee Carlson Corp., Mpls., 1983-84, sect. mgr., 1984-86, divsn. head, 1986-89; property mgr. Werik Apts., Cin., 1990-95; building and property mgr., 1995—. Vol. Cin. Home Schooling Assn., 1992—. Mem. Am. Assn. Home Schooling Parents. Democrat. Roman Catholic. Home: 2330 Kemper Ln Cincinnati OH 45206-2611

MORRISON, GARY BRENT, hospital administrator; b. Anamosa, Iowa, Aug. 30, 1952; s. Kenneth Dale and Norma Elizabeth (Higgens) M.; children: Daniel, Lindsay. BA Polit. Sci., U. Mich., Dearborn, 1975; M Health Svc. Adminstrn., U. Mich., 1978. With Univ. Hosp. Univ. Mich., Ann Arbor, 1975-78, Robert Packer Hosp., Sayre, Pa., 1978-88; assoc. adminstr. St. Mary's Hosp., Rochester, Minn., 1988-90, adminstr., 1990-93; exec. v.p., COO Scott & White Meml. Hosp., Temple, Tex., 1993—. Dir. Tex. State Tech. Coll.; mem. Airport Adv. Bd.; bd. dirs. Better Bus. Bur., Temple Free Clinic, Temple Edn. Found. Mem. Am. Coll. Healthcare Execs. (diplomate), Tex. Assn. Pub. and Not-for-Profit Hosps. (bd. dirs.). Office: Scott & White Meml Hosp 2401 S 31st St Temple TX 76508-0001

MORRISON, JAMES FRANK, optometrist, state legislator; b. Colby, Kans., Apr. 11, 1942; s. Lloyd Wayne and Catherine Louise (Beckner) M.; m. Karen Jean Carr, Aug. 25, 1963; children: Mike, Jeff, Scott. Student, U. Kans., 1960-64; BS, So. Coll. Optometry, 1967, OD, 1967. Pvt. practice, 1969-75; founder, chief staff N.W. Kans. Ednl. Diagnostic and Referral Ctr. Children, Inc., Colby; asst. chief engr. Sta. KXXX-FM, 1977-80, chief engr., 1980-82; prof. vision dept. Colby Community Coll., 1979-84; mem. Kans. Ho. Reps., Topeka, 1992—. Cubmaster pack 140 Cub Scouts Am., 1970-80, dist. chmn., 1977-79. Fellow Am. Acad. Optometry, Coll. Optometrists in Vision Devel.; mem. Am. Optometric Assn., Am. Soc. Broadcast Engrs., Kans. Soc. Broadcast Engrs. (founder, pres. 1970-71), Kans. Optometric Assn., Kans. Assn. Children with Learning Disabilities, Mo. Optometric Assn., Thomas County Assn. Retarded Children, Rotary, Lions , Kiwanies (pres. 1971-72), Masons, Shriners. Rotary. Mem. Assemblies of God. Ch. Home: 3 Cottonwood Dr Colby KS 67701-3902 Office: Morrison Optometric Assocs 180 W 6th St Colby KS 67701-2315

MORRISON, JOSEPH FRANCIS, JR., communications company executive; b. Chgo., Jan. 20, 1943; s. Joseph F. and Eileen V. (Colleran) M.; m. Mary Ellen Brennan, Dec. 27, 1974; children: Deborah Anne, Mary Eileen, Maureen. BS, U. Ill., Chgo., 1969, MS, 1973. Adminstr. U. Ill., Chgo., 1965-76; sales rep. No. Telecom, Chgo., 1976-79; br. mgr. Datapoint Corp., Chgo., 1979-81; gen. mgr. United Techs., Chgo., 1981-83; v.p. IBM/ROLM, Chgo., 1983-89; pres., CEO Darome Teleconf., Chgo., 1989-93, Morrison Comms., Elk Grove, Ill., 1993—; trustee Darome Teleconf., 1989-92. Bd. dirs. St. Patrick H.S., Chgo., 1990—. Served with USN, 1961-65. Republican. Roman Catholic. Home: 2227 Shetland Rd Barrington IL 60010 Office: Morrison Comms 1000 Thorndale Ave Elk Grove Village IL 60007

MORRISON, JOSEPH YOUNG, transportation consultant; b. Flushing, N.Y., Jan. 4, 1951; s. William Barrier and Barbara Helen (Lowe) M.; m. Sally Jo Ormston, Dec. 19, 1976; children: Susan Parker, Travis Barrier. AS, Montreat (N.C.)-Anderson Coll., 1971; BA, Oglethorpe U., 1989. Dept. head J.C. Penny & Co., Atlanta, 1971-74; uniform patrol officer City of Atlanta, 1974-80; spl. agt. U.S. Dept. Transp., Atlanta, 1980-82; group dir. safety and ins. Western Express, Atlanta, 1982-85; dir. safety Taylor Maid Transp., Albany, Ga., 1985-86; v.p. risk mgmt. Burlington Motor Carriers, Inc., Daleville, Ind., 1986-96; pres. Motor Carrier Safety Cons. Inc., Noblesville, Ind., 1996—. Contbg. author: Guide to Handling Hazardous Material, 1986. Mem. Am. Trucking Assn. (hazardous materials com. 1982-86, chmn. injury control com. 1984-88, safety mgmt. coun. 1982—, interstate carrier conf. 1985—, nat. freight claims and security coun. 1985—, Safety Improvement awards, Accident Reduction awards, Injury Reduction awards), Kenilworth Civic Club (treas. Stone Mountain Ga. chpt. 1981-83, pres. 1983-84), Sertoma Club, Sigma Alpha Epsilon. Republican. Methodist. Home: 7111 Oakview Cir Noblesville IN 46060-9419 Office: Motor Carrier Safety Cons 136 S 9th St PO Box 2067 Noblesville IN 46060

MORRISON, MICHAEL GORDON, university president, clergyman, history educator; b. Green Bay, Wis., Mar. 9, 1937; s. Gordon John and Gertrude (Crilly) M. A.B., St. Louis U., 1960, M.A., 1965, Ph.L., 1965, S.T.L., 1969; Ph.D., U. Wis., 1971. Ordained priest Roman Catholic Ch., 1968. Joined S.J., 1955; asst. v.p. acad. affairs Marquette U., Milw., 1974-77; v.p. acad. affairs Creighton U., Omaha, 1977-81, acting pres., 1981, pres., 1981—, dir.; mem. governing bd. Creighton Prep. Sch., 1993—. Bd. dirs. Health Future Found., 1983—, Xavier U., 1992—, Omaha 100 Inc., 1991—; mem. cons. com. SAC, 1988—; mem. adv. bd. Salvation Army, 1992—; trustee Duchesne Acad. of Sacred Heart, 1995—. Recipient Human Rights award Anti-Defamation League, 1982, Humanitarian award Nat. Conf. Christians and Jews, 1989. Mem. Assn. Jesuit Colls. and Univs. (bd. dirs.), Assn. Ind. Colls. and Univs. Nebr. (bd. dirs. 1981—), Nat. Assn. Ind. Colls. and Univs. (bd. dirs. 1993—),Greater Omaha C. of C. (bd. dirs. 1993—), Alpha Sigma Nu, Beta Alpha Psi. Office: Creighton U 2500 California St Omaha NE 68178-0001

MORRISON, ROBERT SCHECK, food processing company executive; b. Flushing, L.I., N.Y., Apr. 4, 1942; s. Forrest John Morrison and Grayce

Morrison (Scheck) Hopkins; m. Susan E. Brennan, Oct. 1988; children: R. Scott, Stephen L., James F., Emily E., Catherine A. BS in English, Coll. Holy Cross, 1963; MBA, U. Pa., 1969. Asst. brand mgr. Procter & Gamble, Cin., 1969-72, brand mgr., 1972-75, assoc. advt. mgr., 1975-81, div. mgr., 1981-83; v.p. mktg. Kraft Inc., Glenview, Ill., 1983-85, group v.p., pres. refrigerated products group, 1985-89; pres. Kraft Gen. Foods Can., Toronto, Ont., 1989-91, Gen. Foods U.S.A., White Plains, N.Y., 1991-95; chmn., CEO, Kraft Foods, Inc., Northfield, Ill., 1995—. Mem. bd. dirs. Lyric Opera of Chgo., Ravinia Festival, Highland Park, Ill. Decorated Silver Star, Purple Heart. Mem. Chgo. Club, Comml. Club Chgo. Clubs: Glen View (Golf, Ill.), Stanwich (Greenwich, Conn.), Chgo. Club, Comml. Club of Chgo. Office: Kraft Foods Inc Three Lakes Dr Northfield IL 60093-2753

MORRISSEY, JOHN FRANCIS, accountant; b. Lee County, Ill., Feb. 3, 1940. Pres., owner John Morrissey Accts., Rockford, Ill., 1972—; co-owner, treas. Staff Mgmt. Inc., Rockford, 1983—. Contbr. articles to local publs. Mem. Nat. Assn. Profl. Employers Orgns. (nat. speaker). Office: 5919 Spring Creek Rd Rockford IL 61114-6447

MORRIS-TATUM, JOHNNIE, state legislator. Address: 3711 W Douglas Ave Milwaukee WI 53209-3620*

MORROW, BRENT, mechanical engineer; b. Independence, Mo., Jan. 10, 1967. BSME, U. Mo., Kansas City, 1990; MBA, Rockhurst Coll., Kansas City, Kans., 1994. Quality control engr. Smith & Lovelace, Lenexa, Kans., 1990; facilities engr. Royal Mech., Overland Park, Kans., 1991; constrn. engr. Jensen Constrn., Independence, 1992; mech. engr. Harlan Corp., Kansas City, Kans., 1992—. Mem. ASME, Engring. Alumni Assn. U. Mo. Office: Harlan Corp 27 Stanley Rd Kansas City KS 66115-1330

MORROW, ELIZABETH, business owner, sculptress, museum association administrator, educator; b. Sibley, Mo., Feb. 28, 1947; d. Elman A. and Lorine (Hostetter) Morrow; married, 1970 (div. 1979); children: Jan Pawel, Lorentz Arthur. Student, William Jewell Coll., 1958-59, Colo. Coll., 1959-60, U. Okla., 1960-62; BFA, U. Kans., 1964, MFA, 1967; postgrad., U. Minn., 1965, U. Kans., 1968. Pres. E. Morrow Co., Kansas City, Mo., 1966-67; head dept. art U. Hawaii, Honolulu, 1968-69, Tarkio (Mo.) Coll., 1970-74; exec. dir. Pensacola (Fla.) Mus. Art, 1974-76; pres., owner Blair-Murrah Exhbns., Sibley, Mo., 1980—; pres. bd. trustees, chief exec. officer Blair-Murrah, Inc., 1991—; sec.-treas. Coun. for Cultural Resources, 1995—. Del. White House Conf. on Small Bus., 1986. Lew Wentz scholar U. Okla., 1960-62. Mem. AAUW, Internat. Coun. of Mus., Internat. Coun. Exhbn. Exch., Internat. Soc. Appraisers, Am. Assn. Mus., Nat. Orgn. of Women Bus. Owners, Nat. Assn. Mus. Exhibitions, Ft. Osage Hist. Soc., Friends Art, Internat. Com. Fine Arts, Internat. Com. Conservation, Internat. Sculpture Ctr., DAR, Delta Phi Delta. Republican. Home: Vintage Hill Orch Sibley MO 64088 Office: Blair-Murrah Vintage Hill Orch Sibley MO 64088 also: 7 rue Muzy, PO Box Nr 554, 1211 Geneva 6 Switzerland

MORROW, JAMES DAVID, business owner; b. Bristol, Pa., Apr. 29, 1955. BS in Indsl. Design, U. Cin., 1978. V.p. Robert Case & Assocs., Chgo., 1983-94; co-owner PODD Morrow Design, Chgo., 1994—. Co-inventor 15 patents in the medical healthcare field. Vol. YMCA Indian Guides, Chgo., 1995. Recipient The Good Design award Chgo. Antheniam, 1993, The R-n-D 100 award R&D Mag., 1993. Roman Catholic. Office: 1440 N Dayton St Ste 303 Chicago IL 60622-2604

MORROW, MARY JANE, critical care nurse; b. Louisiana, Mo., Sept. 24, 1962; d. John Beauchamp and Jane Evelyn (Wallace) M. ADN, St. Mary's Coll., O'Fallon, Mo., 1983. Cert. pediatric advanced life support provider, trauma nurse core course provider. Staff and charge nurse Pike County Meml. Hosp., Louisiana, 1983-84, house supr., 1984-88, ICU supr., 1988-91, staff nurse obstetrics and emergency room, 1991-92; emergency room staff nurse Children's Hosp., St. Louis, 1992—, aux. charge nurse emergency rm., 1994-95, charge nurse, 1995—; instr. IV therapy Eolia (Mo.) Area Vo-tech Sch., 1989—; ACLS instr. Am. Heart Assn., St. Louis, 1989—. Mem. AACN. Home: 414 N 4th St Louisiana MO 63353-1730

MORROW, RICHARD MARTIN, retired oil company executive; b. Wheeling, W.Va., Feb. 27, 1926; married. B.M.E., Ohio State U., 1948. With Amoco Corp., 1948-91; v.p. Amoco Prodn. Co., 1964-66; exec. v.p. Amoco Internat. Oil Co., 1966-70; exec. v.p. Amoco Chem. Corp., 1970-74, pres., 1974-78; pres. Amoco Corp., 1978-83, chmn. chief exec. officer, 1983-91; ret., 1991; bd. dirs. Potlatch Corp., Marsh & McLennan Cos., Inc., Seagull Energy Corp. Trustee U. Chgo. and Rush-Presbyn. St. Luke's Med. Ctr. Office: Amoco Corp 200 E Randolph St Ste 7909 Chicago IL 60601-6436

MORSE, A(LBERT) REYNOLDS, corporate executive; b. Oct. 20, 1914; s. Bradish P. and Anna (Reynolds) M.; m. Eleanor Reese, Mar. 20, 1942; 1 child, Brad Goodell. BA, U. Colo., 1938; MBA, Harvard U., 1939; PhD (hon.), Rollins Coll., 1985. Dist. mgr. Reed Prentice Corp., Cleve., 1940-49; pres. IMS Co., Cleve., 1949-93, Salvador Dali Mus., St. Petersburg, Fla., 1992—. Named to Order of Isabella Catolica by King of Spain, 1989. Mem. Knights of Malta, Phi Beta Kappa. Office: IMS Co 10373 Stafford Rd Chagrin Falls OH 44023-5237

MORSE, LEON WILLIAM, traffic, physical distribution and transportation management executive, consultant; b. N.Y.C., Nov. 13, 1912; s. Benjamin and Leah (Shapiro) M.; m. Goldie Kohn, Mar. 30, 1941; children: Jeffrey W., Saul J. BS, NYU, 1935; grad. Acad. Advanced Traffic, 1937, 1954; DBA, Columbia Pacific U., 1979. Registered practitioner STB, Fed. Maritime Commn. Individual bus., traffic mgmt. cons., Phila., 1950-58; gen. traffic mgr. W.H. Rorer, Inc., Ft. Washington, Pa., 1958-78; adj. prof. econs. of transp., logistics Pa. State U., Ogontz campus, 1960-82; owner Morse Assocs.; course leader seminars in freight traffic mgmt., phys. distbn. mgmt., transp. contract negotiations and freight claims for univs. in the U.S.; bd. dirs. Sr. Security Assocs., Inc.; Bd. trustees Temple B'rith Shalom. Author: Practical Handbook of Industrial Traffic Management, 1980, 87, (manuals) Job of the Traffic Manager, Effective Traffic Management, Fundamentals of Traffic Management, Transportation Contract Negotiations and Freight Claims. Capt. transp. corps, AUS, World War II. Recipient Del. Valley Traffic Mgr. of Yr. award, 1963. Mem. Traffic and Transp. Club of Phila., Traffic Club of Phila., Traffic Club of Norristown, Am. Soc. Internat. Execs. (past pres., bd. dirs., sec., cert.), Assn. Transp. Practitioners, Am. Soc. Transp. and Logistics (emeritus), Council Logistics Mgmt., Transp. Research Forum, Health & Personal Care Distribution Conf. (pres. 1973-75, chmn. bd. 1975-77), Sr. Security Assn., Inc. (bd. dirs.), Delta Nu Alpha Transp. Fraternity, Mason, Shriner.

MORSE, SAUL JULIAN, lawyer; b. N.Y.C., Jan. 17, 1948; s. Leon William and Goldie (Kohn) M.; m. Anne Bruce Morgan, Aug. 21, 1982; children: John Samuel, Elizabeth Miriam. BA, U. Ill., 1969, JD, 1972. Bar: Ill. 1973, U.S. Dist. Ct. (so. dist.) Ill. 1976, U.S. Ct. Appeals (7th cir.) 1983, U.S. Supreme Ct. 1979, U.S. Tax Ct. 1982. Law clk. State of Ill. EPA, 1971-72; law clk. Ill. Commerce Commn., 1972, hearing examiner, 1972-73; trial atty. ICC, 1973-75; asst. minority legal counsel Ill. Senate, 1975, minority legal counsel, 1975-77; mem. Ill. Human Rights Commn., 1985-91; dir. Ill. Comprehensive Health Ins. Plan, treas., chair grievance com.; gen. counsel Ill. Legis. Space Needs Commn., 1978-92; sole practice, Springfield, Ill., 1977-79; ptnr. Gramlich & Morse, Springfield, Ill., 1980-85; prin. Saul J. Morse and Assocs., 1985-87; ptnr. Morse, Giganti and Appleton, 1987-92; v.p., gen. counsel Ill. State Medical Soc., 1992—; lectr. in continuing med. edn. 1986-90; counsel symposia; bd. dirs. Springfield Ctr. for Ind. Living, 1984-89, Ill. Comprehensive Health Ins. Plan Bd., United Cerebral Palsy Land of Lincoln, United Way Sangamon County, mem., bd. dirs. Springfield Jewish Fedn., 1992-95; mem. task force on transp. Republican Nat. Com., 1979-80, Springfield Jewish Community Rels. Coun., 1976-79, 82; mem. spl. com. on zoning and land use planning Sangamon County Bd., 1978. Named Disabled Adv. of Yr., Ill. Dept. Rehab. Svcs., 1985; recipient Chmn.'s Spl. award Ill. State Med. Soc., 1987, Susan S. Suter award as outstanding disabled citizen of Ill., 1990. Mem. Nat. Health Lawyers Assn., Am. Soc. Law and Medicine, ABA (vice chmn. medicine and law com. 1988-90, tort and ins. practice sect., forum com. on health law), Ill. State Bar Assn. (spl. com. on reform of legis. process 1976-82, spl. com. on the disabled lawyer 1978-82, young lawyers sect. com. on role of govt. atty. 1977-80, chmn. 1982, sect. council adminstrv. law, vice chmn. 1981-82), Sangamon County Bar Assn., Am. Soc. Med. Assn. Counsel, Phi Delta Phi. Home: 1701 S Illini Rd Springfield IL 62704-3301 Office: Ill State Med Soc 600 S 2nd St Ste 200 Springfield IL 62704-2542

MORSE, STEVEN, state legislator, farmer; b. Apr. 22, 1957. Student, U. Wis., U. Minn., Mich. State U. Apple grower and processor; Dist. 32 senator Minn. State Senate, St. Paul, 1986—; chmn. environ. and natural resources fin. divsn., mem. agr. and rural devel., fin. (state govt. divsn.), and govt. op. and reform coms., Minn. State Senate. Office: PO Box 175 Dakota MN 55925-0175*

MORTENSEN, MARY ELLEN, pediatrician, educator, medical administrator; b. Austin, Minn., Oct. 9, 1951; d. Jerry Sheehan and Mary Jean (Daugherty) Lund; m. Brian Kim Mortensen, Mar. 15, 1980; children: Lindsey, Brian. BA, Smith Coll., 1974; MD, Emory U., 1978; MS, U. Ariz., 1983. Diplomate Am. Bd. Med. Toxicology, Am. Bd. Pediatrics. Resident in pediatrics U. Ariz., Tucson, 1978-81, fellow in clin. pharmacology, 1981-83; with epidemiology intelligence svc. Ctrs. for Disease Control, Atlanta, 1983-85; clin. asst. prof. dept. pediatrics Emory U., Atlanta, 1984-87; med. epidemiologist Agy. for Toxic Substance and Disease Registry, Atlanta, 1985-87; med. dir. Cen. Ohio Poison Ctr., Columbus, 1987-92; med. dir. Ohio health ops. Nationwide Life Ins. Co., 1995—; asst. prof. pediats. Ohio State U., Columbus, 1987-92, assoc. prof., 1992-95, clin. assoc. prof., 1995—; cons. Nat. Libr. Medicine, Washington, 1990-95; dir. Ctrl. Ohio Lead Clinic, Columbus, 1989-95, mem. med. toxicology sub-bd., 1992-95; reviewer U.S. Pharmacopial Drug Info., Washington, 1989—. Contbr. articles and revs. to profl. jours. and chpts. to books. Lt. comdr. USPHS, 1983-87. Fellow Am. Acad. Clin. Toxicology, Am. Acad. Pediatrics (cons. com. on drugs 1987-92, chmn. exec. com. sect. on clin. pharmacology and therapeutics 1990-93, com. on environ. health 1990-92, chmn. com. on environ. health Ohio chpt. 1990-95); mem. Am. Assn. Poison Control Ctrs. (bd. dirs. 1987-92). Office: Nationwide Health Plans 200 E Campus View Blvd Ste 300 Columbus OH 43235-4678

MORTENSEN, STANLEY JOHN, automotive executive; b. Clinton, Iowa, Feb. 28, 1949; s. Mark Axel and Ruth Evelyn (Sloan) M.; m. Sharron Rae Pendleton, June 13, 1981; children: Carl, Glenn, Sean, Laurel. Student, U. Iowa, 1967-68. Mgr. new car sales Coral Honda, Highland, Ind., 1988; sales rep. Bob Rohrman Enterprises, Lafayette, Ind., 1983-94, Schaumburg and Palatine, Ill., 1985-88, 89-92; asst. lease mgr., sales rep. Schaumburg Honda, Schaumburg, Ill., 1991-92; lease mgr. Indy Honda, Indpls., 1992-94; sales and lease specialist Tom Wood Lexus, Indpls., 1994-95; sales and lease cons. Tutwler Cadillac, Indpls., 1995; gen. mgr. Bob Rohrman Mitsubishi-Hyundai, Lafayette, 1995-96; cons. A&B Sales Support Sys., Crystal Lake, Il., 1988. Dem. candidate Ind. Senate from dist. 23, 1982. Mem. Foursquare. Home: 6574 Crystal Springs Dr Plainfield IN 46168-8733 Office: Blossom Chevrolet 1850 N Shadeland Ave Indianapolis IN 46219

MORTENSEN-SAY, MARLYS (MRS. JOHN THEODORE SAY), school system administrator; b. Yankton, S.D., Mar. 11, 1924; d. Melvin A. and Edith L. (Fargo) Mortensen; BA, U. Colo., 1949, MEd, 1953; adminstrv. specialist U. Nebr., 1973; m. John Theodore Say, June 21, 1951; children: Mary Louise, James Kenneth, John Melvin, Margaret Ann. Tchr. Huron (S.D.) Jr. High Sch., 1944-48, Lamar (Colo.) Jr. High Sch., 1950-52, Norfolk Pub. Sch., 1962-63; sch. supt. Madison County, Madison, Nebr., 1963—. Mem. NEA (life), AAUW, Am. Assn. Sch. Adminstrs., Dept. Rural Edn., Nebr. Assn. County Supts., N.E. Nebr. County Supts. Assn., Assn. Sch. Bus. Ofcls., Nat. Orgn. Legal Problems in Edn., Assn. Supervision and Curriculum Devel., Nebr. Edn. Assn., Nebr. Sch. Adminstrs. Assn. Republican. Methodist. Home: 4805 S 13th St Norfolk NE 68701-6627 Office: Courthouse Madison NE 68748

MORTIBOY, CLARA LOUISE BECK, educator; b. Eldora, Iowa, Sept. 1, 1928; d. Arthur Rudolph and Hazel Esther (Callaway) Beck; m. Forrest Edmund, May 30, 1970 (dec. Jan. 1979). MusB, Simpson Coll., 1948; MA, U. Iowa, 1956. Instr. piano St. Katharine's Sch., Davenport, Iowa, 1948-51; band dir. Bettendorf (Iowa) Community Schs., 1951-67, Davenport (Iowa) Community Schs., 1967-91; retired, 1991—. Mem. Nat. Flute Assn., Iowa Band Masters, Callaway Family Assn., Quad Cities Plus 60 Club, Friends of Art, Putnam Mus., Davenport Area Ret. Tchrs., Shrine Widows Club. Home: 2610 E Pleasant St Davenport IA 52803-3449

MORTIMER, LAWRENCE PATRICK, sales executive; b. Chgo., Mar. 17, 1948; s. Evon Joseph and Lois Jean (Carlson) M.; m. Michele Marie Reese; 1 child, Kyle Patrick. BS in Journalism and Comms., Point Park Coll., Pitts., 1971. Newspaper pub.rep. Mathews, Shannon & Cullen, Cleve., 1972-76; regional sales mgr. Gannett Newspaper Advt. Sales, Atlanta, 1976-77; Midwest regl mgr. Gannett Newspapers, Chgo., 1977-82; Chgo. sales exec. USA Today, 1982-84; v.p., we. sales mgr. Gannett Media Sales, San Francisco, 1984-87; v.p., assoc. dir. advt. USA Weekend, Chgo., 1987-89; v.p., group sales mgr. ActMedia, Chgo., 1989—; bd. dirs., pres.-elect. Cmty. Youth Newspapers, Chgo., 1983-84; bd. dirs. Midwest Golf Nat. Pro-Am, Chgo., 1995. Bd. dirs. Spl. Olympics, St. Charles, Ill., 1995—. Served with U.S. Army, 1971-72/. Mem. Food Mktg. Inst., Promotional Mktg. Assn. Republican. Roman Catholic. Home: 1524 Falcon Dr Wheaton IL 60187 Office: ActMedia 1011 E Touhy Des Plaines IL 60018

MORTON, CRAIG RICHARD, real estate investor; b. Mpls., Dec. 8, 1942; s. William Charles and Patricia Louise (Hare) M.; children: Kelly McCall, Bradley Winslow. Student, U. Philippines, Quezon City, 1961-62; BA in Geography of Southeast Asia, U. Minn., 1966; postgrad., St. John's Coll., Annapolis, 1966. Vol. U.S. Peace Corps, Philippines, 1966-68; v.p. Rent Mgmt., Inc., Mpls., 1970-80; pres. Diversified Hawaiian Investments, Inc., Mpls., 1981—, Craig R. Morton & Assoc., Inc., Mpls., 1980—; founder numerous real estate ltd. partnerships, Minn., N.Mex., Hawaii, Tex.; real estate developer Enchanted Lakes, Minn., 1990; pres. Am. Forex Corp., 1995. Am. Field Svc. scholar to Pakistan, 1960. Mem. Soc. Mayflower Descs., Jaguar Club Minn., Rotary (Paul Harris fellow 1982), Order of DeMolay, Boy Scouts Order of Arrow. Republican. Lutheran. Home: Rt 8 Box 605 Aitkin MN 56431-9106

MORTON, STEPHEN DANA, chemist; b. Madison, Wis., Sept. 7, 1932; s. Walter Albert and Rosalie (Amlie) M.; B.S., U. Wis., 1954, Ph.D., 1962. Asst. prof. chemistry Otterbein Coll., Westerville, Ohio, 1962-66; postdoctoral fellow water chemistry, pollution control U. Wis., Madison, 1966-67; water pollution research chemist WARF Inst., Madison, 1967-73; head environ. quality dept., 1973-76; mgr. quality assurance Raltech Sci. Services, 1977-82; pres. SDM Cons., 1982—. Served to 1st lt. Chem. Corps, AUS, 1954-56. Mem. AAAS, Am. Chem. Soc., Am. Water Works Assn., Am. Soc. Limnology and Oceanography, Water Environ. Fedn. Author: Water Pollution—Causes and Cures, 1976. Home: 1126 Sherman Ave Madison WI 53703-1620

MOSAK, BARBARA MARCIA, designer; b. Chgo., Nov. 14, 1950; d. Joseph and Anna (Rabinovitz) M.; m. David Parker, Apr. 2, 1995. BA in Design with honors, U. Ill., Chgo., 1976. Tchr. art Temple Emanuel, Chgo., 1973-74; graphic designer Beham & Assocs., Inc., 1974-76, Sta. WFLD-TV, Fox TV, Chgo., 1976-77; graphic artist Sta. WBBM-TV, CBS, Chgo., 1977-87, art dir., 1987-88, design dir., 1988-92; freelance designer Chgo., 1992—. Contbg. author: TV Guide Tune-In Advertising, 1988 (Judge's Choice award 1988). Vol. video artist Communication for Social Change, Chgo., 1974; vol. designer Kidney Found. Ill., 1974-76, NOW, Chgo., 1975; vol. designer, tutor Jewish Vocat. Svc., Chgo., 1981-82. Recipient Desi award Graphics Design: USA, 1981, cert. of leadership YWCA, Chgo., 1983. Jewish. Home and Office: 901 S Plymouth Ct Chicago IL 60605-2059

MOSBY, JOHN SINGLETON, JR., clinical administrator, educator, consultant; b. Memphis, Tenn., Aug. 15, 1950; s. John Singleton Sr. and Corinne (Mellard) M.; m. Donna Marie Redding, June 15, 1978; 1 child, John Singleton III. BA, Hendrix Coll., 1972; BS, Palmer Coll. Chiropractic, Davenport, Iowa, 1976; DC, Palmer Coll. Chiropractic, 1976; MD, Am. U./Caribbean Sch. Medicine, B.W.I., 1984. Pvt. practice Osceola, Ark., 1976-79; educator Tex. Chiropractic Coll., Pasadena, 1979-80; educator, clin. cons. diagnosis pathology dept. Palmer Coll. Chiropractic, Davenport, 1985-89, faculty mem. spl. programs, 1988—, clin. cons. staff, educator continuing edn., coord. clinic acad. curriculum, 1989-92, spl. care unit coord., 1991—. Vol. Ark. Children's Colony, Conway, Ark., 1971. With USMC, 1972. Named to Outstanding Young Men Am. 1977, 88. Mem. Ark. Chiropractic Assn. (bd. dirs. 1977-80), SAR, Am. Chiropractic Assn., Osceola C. of C., Palmer Internat. Alumni Assn., Rotary, Phi Lambda Kappa (nat. soc.). Methodist. Home: 3201 Somerset Dr Bettendorf IA 52722-2732

MOSCO, SCOTT M., retail business owner; b. Park Ridge, Ill., Oct. 7, 1962; s. Owen Nathaniel Mosco and Barbara Joyce (Ordman) Palermo; m. Marcela Madeline Apolo, Dec. 13, 1986; children: Nathaniel, Daniel. Student, Harry S. Truman City Coll., De Paul U. Trading fl. phone clk. Lind Waldock & Co., Chgo., 1982-84, Chgo. Corp., 1984; trading fl. mgr. Chgo. .RSch. & Trading Group, 1984-87; trading fl. phone clk. Merrill Lynch Commodites, Chgo., 1987, Mocatta Metals Inc., Chgo., 1987-88; rsch. analyst asst. G.N.P. Commodities Inc., Chgo., 1988-89; pres. Jewelry As Art Inc., Valparaiso, Ind., 1989—. Republican. Office: Jewelry As Art Inc 1304 Gibraltar Ct Valparaiso IN 46383

MOSELEY-BRAUN, CAROL, senator; b. Chgo., Aug. 16, 1947; d. Joseph J. and Edna A. (Davie) Moseley; m. Michael Braun, 1973 (div. 1986); 1 child, Matthew. BA, U. Ill., Chgo., 1969; JD, U. Chgo., 1972. Asst. U.S. atty. U.S. Dist. Ct. (no. dist.) Ill., 1973-77; mem. Ill. Ho. of Reps., 1979-88; recorder of deeds Cook County, Ill., 1988-92; U.S. senator from Ill. Washington, 1993—; mem. fin. com., subcom. on social security and family policy, subcom. on medicare, long-term care and health ins., mem. com. on banking, housing and urban affairs, subcom. on HUD oversight and structure, subcom. on internat. fin. and monetary policy, subcom. on fin. instns. and regulatory relief. Office: US Senate 320 Hart Senate Bldg Washington DC 20510

MOSEMAN, MILDRED MAE, retired elementary school educator and principal; b. Humboldt, Nebr., Dec. 12, 1917; d. Jesse Edwin and Lydia L. (Smerchek) Nemechek; m. Arthur George Moseman, Dec. 13, 1942; children: Michael Joh, Lanny Joe. Cert. in teaching, U. Nebr., 1942; BS, Morningside Coll., 1957; postgrad., U. S.D. Cert. elem. tchr., secondary social studies tchr., Nebr., Iowa. Rural sch. tchr. Richardson County, Nebr., 1935-38; kindergarten tchr. Dawson (Nebr.) schs., 1938-42; 1st and 2d grade tchr. Beatrice (Nebr.) schs., 1942-43; 5th grade tchr., high sch. registrar El Reno (Okla.) schs., 1943-46; substitute tchr., 1946-51; 3d grade tchr. South Sioux City (Nebr.) schs., 1951-57; 4th - 6th grade tchr. Sioux City (Iowa) schs., 1957-84; ret.; presenter workshops Nat. Sci. Convention, nationwide. Editor centennial book South Sioux Star, 1967; contbr. articles to profl. publs. Organizer Friends of Libr., South Sioux City, 1985, pres., 1985-90; organizer Jr. Red Cross, Sioux City, 1984—; active Adult Basic Edn., South Sioux City, 1986-93; pres. Ret. Sioux City Educators, 1987-89; mem. com. Am. 2000, South Sioux City Schs., 1992-93; bd. dirs. Siouxland Comty. Found., 1992-93, Women of Excellence, 1991-93; pres. South Sioux City Woman's Club, 1975, Am. Bus. Women, 1980, AAUW, 1976, Sioux City Edn. Assn., 1972-84; chair South Sioux City Arboretum Com., 1993-94; mem. South Sioux City Chamberetts, 1994, pres., 1996; mem. Tree Bd. South Sioux City Parks and Recreation, 1993-94; presenter storytimes So. Sioux City Libr., travelogues to schs., chs., svc. groups, nursing homes. Recipient Profl. award Sioux City Woman's Club, 1975, Sioux City Edn. Assn., 1983-84, Am. Bus. Women, 1980, AAUW, 1976, Soil Conservation Tchr. award State of Iowa, 1973, Internat. award U. Western Ill., 1974, Ann. award Rotary, 1990, Outstanding Citizen award Ext. Club, 1972, Women of Excellency Vols. award, 1989, J.C. Penney Vols. award, 1989, Vol. Svc. to Children Merit award KTIV, 1992, Adult Edn. Vol. of Yr. award N.E. C.C., 1990, Spl. citation for exceptional vol. svc. ARC, 1992, Eyes on Nebr. award Nebr. Optometric Assn., 1994, Omicron Delta Kappa Outstanding Cmty. award, Morningside Coll., 1995, Vol. Svc. award Sioux City Parks and Recreation, 1995, others. Lutheran. Home: 123 Fairview Dr South Sioux City NE 68776-3562

MOSENA, DAVID R., transportation executive. M in City Planning, U. Tenn. Dir. rsch. Am. Planning Assn., Chgo.; mem. staff City of Chgo., 1984-89, planning commr., 1989-91, chief of staff, 1991-92, aviation commr., 1992-96; pres. CTA, 1996—. Chmn. bd. dirs. U. Chgo. Lab. Schs. Office: CTA Merchandise Mart Plz PO Box 3555 Chicago IL 60654

MOSER, GREGG ANTHONY, career officer; b. Holton, Kans., Aug. 6, 1954; s. Paul Robert and Ila Rose (Jenkins) M.; m. Shari Ann Larson, Nov. 3, 1984. BS in Constrn. Sci., Kans. State U., 1979; MS in Safety, Ctrl. Mo. State U., 1984. Commd. 2d lt. USAF, 1980, advanced through grades to maj., 1991. Mem. Air Force Assn. (pres. Lt. Erwin R. Bleckley chpt. 1992-93, Medal of Merit 1994), Lions (pres. Wichita Flying Lions chpt. 1992-93, zone 1 chmn. dist. 17-SE region II 1993-94, dir. Scott Comty. Lions Club 1994-95, v.p. Scott Comty. Lions Club 1995-96). Republican. Methodist. Home: 625 W 5th St Holton KS 66436-1406 Office: 607th Air Support Squadron/LGS Osan AB ROK APO AP 96278-2047

MOSER, JEFFERY RICHARD, state official; b. Miller, S.D., Feb. 8, 1961; s. Richard and Ardessa Joan (Yost) M. Student, U. Minn., 1979-84; postgrad., Duke U., 1995. Exec. intern pub. affairs dept. Target Corp., Mpls., 1982; intern asst. for legis. and policy Minn. Agri-Growth Coun., Bloomington, 1984-85; field dir. U.S. Congressman Thomas A. Daschle, Aberdeen, S.D., 1986; pvt. cons., 1986-89, artist, small bus. owner, 1990—; exec. dir., chief lobbyist on state and nat. issues S.D. Assn. Towns and Twps., 1990-95; dep. state treas. State of S.D., Pierre, 1995—; participant 4-H/UN/USAID Presdl. young adult exch. program to Kenya and Botswana, Africa, summer 1985. Gen. election poll watcher Hand County Rural precincts, 1988; past mem. Beadle County Dems.; mem. Hughes County Dems.; del. State Dem. Conv., 1990, 92, 94; sec. State Dem. Party Govt. Reform platform subcom., 1992, mem. State Dem. Party Econ. Devel. platform subcom., 1994; temporary precinct committeeman N.E. Huron, 1992, Clinton for Pres., 1992; nom. Dem. candidate State Auditor, 1994; donor Dem. Nat. Com.; Dem. Nat. Senate Task Force; chmn. Dem. Congl. Campaign Com. Dem. Nat. Conv., 1996, Clinton-Gore, 1996; at. del. Dem. Nat. Conv., 1996; vol. leader, advisor, and state fair judge S.D. 4-H Program, 1981—; bd. dirs. S.D. Rural Devel. Coun., 1993-95, S.D. State Adv. Com. for Green Thumb, Inc., 1993-95; mem. task force Nat. Urban Comparative Risk Environ., 1994, Common Cause S.D., 1991-94; dist. dir. S.D. Farmers Union, 1988-93, Golden Razor Hair Salon, Inc., Mpls., 1983-84; mem. Rose Hill Presbyn. Ch., S.D. Com. for World Food Day, S.D. Bread for the World, S.D. Project Prosperity Coalition, S.D. Health Care Reform Coalition, S.D. Artists Network, S.D. Hist. Soc.; sec. Presbytery of S.D. Advocacy Devel. Ministry unit, 1992-93, ch. camp dean; vol. coord. Bread for the World Hunger Awareness event, Huron, 1993; mem. planning com. 1993 Regional 4-H Leaders Forum, Sioux Falls; past del. rep. S.D. Nat. 4-H Congress, Nat. Farmers Union Nat. conf., Presbyn. Ch. USA Gen. Assembly, Nat. 4-H Coun. Master Communicators Conf., Common Cause Nat. Leadership conf., Sharing Global Harvests Nat. Tng., Nat. Assn. Towns and Twps. Am.'s Town Meeting; bd. co-chair Huron Postal Customer Adv. Bd., 1993-95; bd. dirs. S.D. Peace and Justice Ctr., sec.-treas., 1994, v.p., 1995. Mem. Huron C. of C. (govt. affairs com. 1991), Phi Beta Kappa, Omicron Delta Kappa, Mortar Bd. Office: Office of State Treas SD State Capitol Bldg #212 500 E Capitol Ave Pierre SD 57501-5070

MOSES, ROBERT KENNETH, computer technician; b. Chgo., Sept. 6, 1952; s. Kenneth Lee and Jean Elizabeth (Kulp) M.; m. Peggy Lyn Tibbits, Dec. 30, 1984 (div. June 1994). BA, North Cen. Coll., Naperville, Ill., 1974. Maint. engr. J.C. Penney Co., Schaumburg, Ill., 1974-75; bar mgr. Hoffman Lanes, Hoffman Estates, Ill., 1975-76; pres. Tech Theatre Inc., Lisle, Ill., 1975-83; maint. mgr. Naperville Park Dist., 1976-81; projectionist/stagehand West Plaza Cinemas/Paramount Arts, Aurora, Ill., 1981-94; computer technician Valcom/PCC, Itasca, Ill., 1994—; co-founder, pres. Riverfront Playhouse, Aurora, 1979-81. Mem. Internat. Alliance of Theatrical State Employees and Motion Picture Machine Operators U.S. and Can., Soc. Motion Picture and TV Engrs. Home: 454 Seminary Ave Aurora IL 60505-4720

MOSES, WINFIELD C., JR., state legislator; b. Ft. Wayne, Ind., Feb. 20, 1943; s. Winfield C. and Helen A. (O'Neil) M.; children: Elizabeth, Christopher. A.B. in Econs, Ind. U., 1964, M.B.A. in Fin, 1966. Apt. builder Ft.

Wayne, Ind., 1966-80; mem. City Council Ft. Wayne, 1972-79; mayor City of Ft. Wayne, 1980-87, state rep., 1992—. Founding pres. Washington House, 1973-76, Citizen Energy Coalition, 1974-75; active Am. Heart Assn. Mem. C. of C., Rotary. Democrat. Unitarian. Office: 6000 N Oak Blvd Fort Wayne IN 46818-2438

MOSHMAN, DAVID STEWART, educational psychology educator; b. Bklyn., May 9, 1951; s. Howard and Ruth (Silver) M.; m. Sara Anderson, Sept. 26, 1987; children: Eric Schroeder, Michael. BA, Lehigh U., 1971; PhD, Rutgers U., 1977. Asst. prof. ednl. psychology U. Nebr., Lincoln, 1977-82, assoc. prof., 1982-89, prof., 1989—, chmn. ednl. psychology dept., 1994—; mem. exec. com. Acad. Freedom Coalition Nebr., 1988—, pres., 1993. Author: Developmental Psychology, 1987, Children, Education and the First Amendment, 1989; editor: (book) Children's Intellectual Rights, 1986, (jour.) Devel. Rev., 1996—. Bd. dirs. ACLU Nebr., 1982—, pres., 1987-89, 93-95. Mem. APA, Soc. Rsch. Child Devel., Soc. Rsch. Adolescence, Jean Piaget Soc. (bd. dirs. 1995—). Democrat. Home: 1901 Pepper Ave Lincoln NE 68502-3044 Office: U Nebr Dept Ednl Psychology Lincoln NE 68588-0345

MOSKAL, ROBERT M., bishop; b. Carnegie, Pa., Oct. 24, 1937; s. William and Jean (Popivchak) M. BA, St. Basil Coll. Sem., Stamford, Conn., 1959; lic. sacred theology, Cath. U. Am., 1963; student, Phila. Mus. Acad. and Conservatory of Mus., 1963-66. Ordained priest Ukrainian Cath. Ch. 1963. Founder, pastor St. Anne's Ukrainian Cath. Ch., Warrington, Pa., 1963-72; sec. Archbishop's Chancery, Phila., 1963-67; apptd. vice-chancellor Archeparchy of Phila., 1967-74; pastor Annunciation Ukrainian Cath. Ch., Melrose Park, Phila., 1972-74; named monsignor, 1974; chancellor archdiocese, pastor Ukrainian Cath. Cathedral of the Immaculate Conception, Phila., 1974-84; apptd. bishop, 1981; Ordained titular bishop of Agathopolis and aux. bishop Ukrainian-Rite Archeparcy of Phila., 1981-83; first bishop Diocese of St. Josaphat, Parma, Ohio, 1983—; pro-synodal judge Archdiocesan Tribunal, Phila., 1965-67; founder Ukrainian Cath. Hour: God is with Us, Sta. WIBF-FM, Phila, 1972-77, Christ Among Us, Sat. WTEL, 1975—; mem. Ukrainian Cath. Ch. Liturgical Subcommn., 1980; host to His Holiness Pope John Paul II. Bd. dirs. Ascension Manor, Inc., Phila., 1964-84, sec.-treas., 1964-78, exec. v.p., 1977-84. Office: PO Box 347180 5720 State Rd Parma OH 44134-7180

MOSLEY, ALBERT G., philosophy educator; b. Dyersburg, Tenn., Oct. 28, 1941; s. Harry and Jo Ella (Johnson) M.; m. Betty Emirita Cheek, 1974 (dec. 1978); children: Jason, Jo Ella, Kayode; m. Kathleen Ramona Simms, July 1980; children: Amelia, Charles. BS, U. Wis., Madison, 1963, PhD, 1975. Instr. Howard U., Washington, 1968-69; asst. prof. Fed. City Coll., Washington, 1969-74; from assoc. prof. to prof. U. D.C., 1974-89; prof. Ohio U., Athens, 1990—. Home: 22 Canterbury Dr Athens OH 45701 Office: Philosophy Dept-Ohio U Athens OH 45701

MOSLEY, JEAN BELL, columnist; b. Elvins, Mo., Sept. 21, 1913; s. Wilson LeRoy and Myrtle (Casey) B.; m. Edward Price Mosley (dec. Jan. 1977); 1 child, Stephen Price. BS in Edn., Southeast Mo. State U., 1937. Tchr. Graniteville (Mo.) Sch., 1934-36; sec., mgr. Arnold Roth Ins. Agy., Cape Girardeau, Mo., 1937-44; columnist Southeast Missourian, Cape Girardeau, Mo., 1955—; freelance writer, 1948—. Author: The Mockingbird Piano, 1953 (Mo. Writers Guild award), Wide Meadows, 1960, The Crosses at Zarin, 1967, The Deep Forest Award, 1985 (C.S. Lewis Silver medal), Seeds on the Wind, 1995; contbr. short stories to books and articles to profl. jours. and mags. Mem., past pres. Quest Club, Cape Girardeau, 1956—; mem. pub. libr. bd. of publs. Cape Girardeau, 1968; bd. publs. Southeast Mo. U., Cape Girardeau, 1967. Mem. Mo. Writers Guild (pres. 1956), Cape Girardeau Writers Guild (pres. 1953). Methodist. Home: 703 E Rodney Cape Girardeau MO 63701

MOSS, CHARLES JOSEPH, III (CHUCK MOSS), writer, broadcaster; b. Norfolk, Va., Aug. 31, 1953; s. Charles Joseph Jr. and Sally Jane (Brown) M.; m. Alice Northrop Heaton, June 30, 1979; children: Elizabeth Northrop, Carolyn Woods. BA, Mich. State U., 1975; JD, U. Detroit, 1979. Bar: Mich. 1979. Asst. prosecuting atty. Genesee County, Flint, Mich., 1979-81; pvt. practice law Ferndale, Mich., 1981-85; polit. writer/columnist Birmingham, Mich., 1985—; talk show host Sta. WXYT-AM, 1993—; co-host WTVS TV56, 1996—. Mem. Birmingham Traffic Safety Bd., Oakland County Pub. Transit Auth. Bd., 1996—. Recipient award for radio commentary UPI, 1989. Mem. Optimists (Birmingham, Mich. chpt. dir.). Address: 1184 Dorchester Dr Birmingham MI 48009-5900

MOSS, GERALD S., dean, medical educator; b. Cleve., Mar. 4, 1935; s. Harry and Lillian (Alter) M.; m. Wilma Jaback, Sept. 1, 1957; children: William Alan, Robert Daniel, Sharon Lynn. BA, Ohio State U., 1956, MD cum laude, 1960. Diplomate Am. Bd. Surgery (apptd. assoc. examiner com. 1989); lic. Ill. Intern Mass. Gen. Hosp., Boston, 1960-61, resident, 1961-65; from asst. prof. to assoc. prof. dept. surgery Coll. Medicine U. Ill., Chgo., 1968-72, prof., 1973-77, 89—, head dept. surgery, 1989, dean, 1989—; prof. dept. surgery Pritzker Sch. Medicine U. Chgo., 1977-89; prof. dept. surgery U. Ill., Coll. of Medicine, 1989—; tutor in surgery Manchester (Eng.) Royal Infirmary, 1964; asst. chief surgical svcs. VA West Side Hosp., Chgo., 1968-70; attending surgeon dept. surgery Cook County Hosp., Chgo. 1970-72, chmn. 1972-77; dir. surgical rsch. Hektoen Inst. for Med. Rsch., Cook County Hosp., 1972-77, Micheal Reese Hosp. and Med. Ctr., Chgo., 1977-89, chmn. dept. surgery, 1977-89, chief svc. 1989, trustee, 1981, and numerou coms.; appointed to Nat. Rsch. Coun., NAS, 1966-68, Ad Hoc Subcom., NAE, 1970, Ad Hoc Study Sect., 1970, del. to Third Joint U.S-USSR Symposium, 1983, Blood Diseases and Resources Adv. Com., 1984-88, Planning Com. for discussing key blood problems, Nat. Heart and Lung Inst., 1987, chmn. Plasma and Plasma Products Com., 1979, bd. dirs., 1983, v.p., 1985, Ad Hoc Transition Com., Am. Blood Commn., 1989, Panel on Rsch. Opportunities, Office Naval Rsch. Program, 1987, exec. com., coord. com., Nat. Blood Edn. Program, 1988, Tech. Adv. Task Force Am. Hosp. Assn., 1988, chmn. review panel contract proposals, NIH, 1975, program project site visit, 1976, chmn. site-visit review group, 1977, adv. com. Blood Resources Work group, 1978, Planning Com. for Consensus, 1987, Small Bus. Innovation Rsch., 1988, Med. Rsch. Scv. Merit Review Bd. VA, 1978-81, Liaison Com. Graduate Med. Edn. AMA, 1979, and numerous other coms. for various med. organizations; cons. Nat. Heart and Lung Inst., Transfusion Medicine Acad. Awardees Program; vis. prof. Montefiore Med. Ctr. Bronx, N.Y., 1986, Ohio State U., 1988, U. N.Mex., Albuquerque, 1989, Seton Med. Ctr., Austin, Tex., 1990, U. Ill. Coll. Medicine, Peoria, 1991; guest lectr., participant numerous meetings, symposiums; cons. in field. Contbr. numerous articles to profl. jours., chpts. to books.. With U.S. Army, 1965-68, Vietnam. Teaching fellow Harvard Med. Sch., 1962; receipient Stitt Lectr. award Assn. Mil. Surgeons U.S.A., 1981; grantee U.S. Navy, 1969-84, U.S. Army, 1971-74, 75-78, NIH, 1969, 83-84, Dept. Pub. Health, 1973, HEW, 1974-77, UpJohn, 1974, Northfield Labs. 1985-89. Fellow ACS (pre and postoperative care com. 1975-83, rep. Am. blood commn. 1977—, mem. various coms., speaker various symposiums), Am. Soc. Surgery Trauma; mem. Am. Surgical Assn. (rep. Nat. Soc. Med. Rsch. 1984-88), Am. Trauma Soc., Am. Physicians Fellowship (rep. Israel Med. Assn.), Assn. Acad. Surgery (chmn. membership selection com. 1973-75, pres. elect 1974-75, pres. 1975-76, exec. coun. 1977-79), Soc. Univ. Surgeons (rep. Nat. Soc. Med. Rsch. 1973-77, com. Surgical Edn. 1979-81), Ctrl. Surgical Soc. (rep. Nat. Soc. Med. Rsch 1973-77), Shock Soc. (chmn. planning com. 1986, chmn. program com. 1986, pres. elect 1986-87, pres. 1987-88), Soc. for Surgery Alimentary Tract (mem. com. west north ctrl. region 1978-82), Internat. Soc. Blood Transfusion, SurgicalBiology Club II, Nat. Soc. for Med. Rsch., Collegium Internationale Chirugiae Digestivae, Societe Internationale de Chirugie, Sigma XI, Alpha Omega Alpha (faculty advisor 1972-73). Office: U Ill Coll Medicine 1853 W Polk St # C 784 Chicago IL 60612-4316

MOSS, LESLIE OTHA, justice administrator; b. Detroit, Mar. 8, 1952; s. Lonnie and Emma (Robinson) M. BA, U. Mich., 1982, postgrad., 1990—. Technician oper. rm. Sinai Hosp., Detroit, 1972-75; nurses' technician Detroit Osteo. Hosp., 1976-83; supr. Southfield (Mich.) Placement Ctr., 1983-85; rsch. asst. Wayne County Commr.'s Office, Detroit, 1985-86; fin. aid counselor Wayne State U., 1986-87; probation officer Dept. Corrections State of Mich., 1988—; exec. asst. Human Rights Dept., City of Detroit; rsch. asst. Law Dept. City of Detroit, 1990; asst. pers. mgr. Detroit Osteo. Hosp., 1991-93, Highland Pk. C.C., 1991-93; mental health worker Mich. Health Ctr.-Adult Mental Health and New Ctr. Hosp., Detroit, 1992-94; legal technician Ptnrs. Against Crime, Detroit, 1994; social work technician, 1994; sgt. of arms Detroit Police Res., 1987—; intern, assoc. prodr. local TV sta., Detroit, 1993; mem. bd. advisors, mem. bd. govs. Am. Biog. Rsch. Inst., dep. gov., 1994; exec. cons. in field., 1993—; asst. pers. mgr., 1993—. Bd. advisors Am. Biog. Inst., 1994; active re-election com. Mayor Coleman A. Young, Detroit, 1989-93; patient care counselor; adv. various causes, including industrialized Am., higher edn., automotive quality. Recipient Twentieth Century Achievement award Biog. Centre, 1994, Spl. Recognition award Detroit Pub. Sch. Sys., 1992, Internat. Man of Yr. award, 1992-93; award for mass media svc. participation Barden Cable Vision, Detorit, 1991, Man of the Yr. award, 1996, Disting. Alumni Award Mumford H.S. Detroit, 1996; named Most Admired Man of Decade, 1994, Disting. Alumnus, Detroit Pub. Schs. Mich., 1995, Most Admired Man of the Yr., State of Mich., 1995. Mem. NAFE, NAACP (advisor 1989), Internat. Order of Merit, Assn. Pre-Med Students (cons. 1988—), Assn. Psychologists, Am. Biog. Rsch. Inst. Assn. (mem. bd. govs. 1993, dep. gov.), Internat. Platform Assn., U. Mich. Alumni Assn., Golden Key (life), Kappa Alpha Psi. Home & Office: 2020 Witherell St Ste 735 Detroit MI 48226-1618 Address: 1581 Kendall Detroit MI 48238

MOSS, LISA ANN, critical care nurse; b. Unionville, Mo., Dec. 17, 1964; d. Homer Lee and Rose Marie (McDowell) Pickering; m. James Edward Moss, Aug. 13, 1983. ADN, North Cen. Mo. Coll., 1985. Cert. CEN, BLS, ACLS, PALS, BTLS, TNCC, TNS, PALS instr., emergency nurse's pediat. course. RN, shift supr. Wayne County Hosp., Corydon, Iowa, 1985-87; RN emergency dept., ICU, house supr. Grim Smith Hosp., Kirksville, Mo., 1987-92; RN emergency room Kirksville Osteo. Med. Ctr., 1992—; RN pediatrics U. Hosp. & Clinics, Columbia, Mo., 1992-93; RN emergency dept. U. Hosp. & Clinics, Columbia, 1993—; traveling nurse Nurses Unltd., Inc., Kirksville, 1989-94. Mem. Emergency Nurses Assn. Baptist. Home: RR 5 Box 342 Unionville MO 63565-9804

MOSS, RANDY HAYS, electrical engineering educator; b. Searcy, Ark., Aug. 7, 1953; s. Roy Pearson and Lillian Lorene (Hays) M.; m. Mary Grace Anderson, Aug. 5, 1978; children: Benjamin Roy, Andrew Paul. BSEE, U. Ark., 1975, MSEE, 1977; PhDEE, U. Ill., 1981. Registered profl. engr., Mo. Vis. instr. U. Ill., Urbana, 1979, vis. lectr., 1980; asst. prof. of elec. engring. U. Mo., Rolla, 1981-86; assoc. prof. of elec. engring. U. Mo., 1986-91, prof. elec. engring., 1991—; bd. dirs. Mo. Enterprise, Rolla. Contbr. articles to profl. jours. Bd. dirs. United Ministries in Higher Edn., Rolla, 1983-88, Wesley Found., Rolla, 1983-88. Recipient Lindbergh award AIAA, 1985, Outstanding Young Mfg. Engr. award Soc. of Mfg. Engrs., 1987, Ralph R. Teetor Ednl. award Soc. of Automotive Engrs., 1988. Mem. IEEE (sec., treas. of Rolla subsect. 1982-84), Rolla Kiwanis Club (pres. 1994-95, sec. 1983-84), Sigma Xi (pres. U. Mo. chpt. 1987-88), Eta Kappa Nu. Methodist. Home: 12901 County Road 3000 Rolla MO 65401-8144 Office: U Mo Rolla Electrical Engring Dept Rolla MO 65409-0040

MOSS, STEVEN C., electrical engineer; b. St. Louis, Aug. 23, 1959. BS in Elec. Tech., Washington U., 1992. Designer Westinghouse Electric, St. Louis, 1978-88, McDonnell Douglas, St. Louis, 1988-91; elec. engr. Killark Electric, St. Louis, 1991—. Office: Killark Electric 3940 M L King Dr Saint Louis MO 63113

MOSS, SUSAN, nurse, retail store owner; b. Youngstown, Ohio, Aug. 17, 1940; d. Jarlath G. and Sara G. (Curley) Carney; divorced; children: John P., Jerri Ann Moss Williams. Lic. nurse, Choffin Sch., 1973; AS in Am. Bus. Mgmt., Youngstown State U., 1992. Surg. scrub nurse St. Elizabeth Hosp., Youngstown, 1972-78; office mgr. Moss Equipment Co., North Jackson, Ohio, 1978-83; pvt. duty nurse Salem, Ohio, 1979—; night nurse supr. Gateways for Better Living, Youngstown, 1982-84; owner Laura's Bride and Formal Wear, Salem, 1987—; CEO Strawberry Sunshine Svcs. Co., Salem, 1994—; cons. Edith R. Nolf, Inc., Salem. Author: (novelette) Turlaleen. Water therapy aide Easter Seal Soc., Youngstown, 1970-75, bd. trustees, 1973-75; mem. Hear, Now, Denver, 1989. Mem. LPN Assn. Ohio, Bus. and Profl. Women, Youngstown State U. Alumni Club, Short Hills Lit. Soc., Beta Sigma Phi (v.p., Silver Circle award 1986, Order of the Rose 1987). Democrat. Roman Catholic. Office: Laura's Bride & Formal Wear 1271 E Pidgeon Rd Salem OH 44460-4364

MOSS, THOMAS HENRY, science association administrator; b. Cleve., June 27, 1939; s. Joseph Harold and Elsa Margaret (Lemkau) M.; m. Kathleen Goddard, May 31, 1965; children: Ellen, Joseph, Cheryl, David. AB, Harvard U., 1961; PhD, Cornell U., 1965. Cons. analyst govtl. sci. policy U.S. Govt. Office Mgmt. and Budget, Washington, 1963-67; research physicist IBM Corp., Yorktown, N.Y., 1967-74, 75-76; staff dir., sci. advisor Office of Congressman George E. Brown, Washington, 1976-79; staff dir. subcom. sci., research and tech. Ho. of Reps., Washington, 1979-82; prof. physics, dean grad. studies and research Case Western Res. U., Cleve., 1982-96; exec. dir. Govt.-Univ.-Industry Roundtable, 1996—; with Nat. Acad. Scis, Washington; adj. prof. physics Columbia U., N.Y.C., 1966-76; mem. nat rev. com. Office of Nuclear Waste Isolation, Columbus, 1983—; bd. dirs. Univ. Tech. Inc., Cleve.; bd. dirs. Ctr. Great Lakes, Chgo., 1985—; v.p. Edison Poymer Innovation Corp., Independence, Ohio, 1986-90. Editor: The Three Mile Island Nuclear Accident-Lessons, 1981; asst. editor Environ. Profl. mag.; cons. editor Sci, Tech. and Human Values Environ. mag.; contbr. articles to profl. jours. Treas. Lake Bancroft Cmty. Assn., Falls Church, Va., 1980; mem. adv. bd. Small Bus. SBIR Program, Cleve., 1983-85; mem., v.p. Shaker Heights (Ohio) Bd. Edn., 1989-96; chmn. N.E. Region Ohio Systemic Statewide Initiative in Sci. and Math. Edn., 1992-95. ASME fellow, 1995-96, NSF fellow Nobel Instn., 1966-67. Fellow Am. Phys. Soc. (chmn. forum on physics and soc. 1990-91), Nat. Coun. Univ. Rsch. Administrs. (Nat. Innovation Program award 1987), Scientists Inst. Pub. Info. (Disting. Svc. award Harlem Prep. Sch. 1971); mem. AAAS (chmn. com. on sci., engring. and pub. policy 1989-91). Office: NAS Rm 340 2101 Constitution Ave Washington DC 22312

MOSSMAN, DOUGLAS, psychiatrist, educator; b. East Grand Rapids, Mich., Oct. 10, 1954; s. Sidney and Agnes (Daye) M.; m. Nancy Elizabeth Hoevenaar, Sept. 4, 1983 (div. Mar. 1989); 1 child, Rachel; m. Kathleen Joan Hart, Oct. 29, 1989; 1 child, Sarah. BA, Oberlin Coll., 1976; MD, U. Mich., 1981. Instr. Med. U. S.C., Charleston, 1986-88; vol. asst. prof. U. Cin., 1980-90, assoc. prof. clin. psychiatry, 1990-93; assoc. clin. prof., dir. divsn. forensic psychiatry Wright State U. Sch. Medicine, Dayton, Ohio, 1993—; adj. prof. U. Dayton Sch. Law, 1994—. Contbr. more than 40 articles to profl. jours. Recipient Levine Essay awards U. Cin., 1984, 85, 86, Mental Health Media award Cin. Mental Health Assn., 1990; Ohio Dept. Mental Health rsch. fellow, 1990-91. Mem. Am. Psychiat. Assn., Ohio Psychiat. Assn., Am. Acad. Psychiatry and the Law, Soc. for Med. Decision Making, Assn. for Advancement of Philosophy and Psychiatry, Phi Beta Kappa. Democrat. Jewish. Office: Wright State U Dept Psychiatry PO Box 927 Dayton OH 45401-0927

MOSSMAN, ROBERT GILLIS, IV, civil and environmental engineer; b. Youngstown, Ohio, Jan. 28, 1960; s. Robert Gillis III and Carol (Hoyt) M. B Engring., Youngstown State U., 1984. Engr. Lynn, Kittenger & Noble, Inc., Warren, Ohio, 1984-85, Thomas Fok & Assocs., Ltd., Youngstown, 1985-86, Daniel C. Baker Assocs., Inc., Beaver, Pa., 1986-87; cons. Youngstown, 1987—. Mem. Water Pollution Control Fedn. Home and Office: 58 Norwick Dr Youngstown OH 44505-1626

MOST, MARVIN CONRAD, electrical engineer; b. Chicago Heights, Ill., June 10, 1964; s. Marvin Ervin and Mildred Caroline (Becker) M. BSEE, U. Ill., Chgo., 1987. Avionics engr. USAF, Ohio, 1987—. Mem. IEEE, Soc. Info. Display (treas. 1995). Home: 455 Towanda Circle Dayton OH 45431 Office: ASC/YPRX 2 1981 Monohan Way Wright Patterson AFB OH 45433

MOSTYN, MARGE LOIS IRWIN, secondary school educator; b. Joliet, Ill., Jan. 16, 1947; d. Robert L. and Edith V. (Bertino) Irwin; m. John P. Mostyn Jr., Sept. 28, 1968; children: Mollie Mostyn, Jay Mostyn. BA, Lewis U., 1977; MS in Edn. in Ednl. Psychology, No. Ill. U., 1993. Tchr. St. Joseph Grade Sch., Lockport, Ill., 1977-81; tchr. (sewing) Stretch and Sew, Joliet, 1981-83; tchr. Joliet Jr. Coll., 1988 (fall); tchr. math. Providence Cath. High Sch., New Lenox, Ill., 1983—; mem. vis. faculty Ea. Ill. U.; tchr. Ill. Math and Sci. Acad., Aurora, Ill., summers 1989-95; instr. Lewis U., Romeoville, Ill., 1992-93; workshop leader St. Mary's Press, Winona, Mich., 1995-96. Speaker South Suburban Math. Coun., Park Forest, Ill., 1991. Impact II grantee, Aurora, 1990, Newmast NSF, 1991. Fellow Ill. Math. and Sci. Acad.; mem. Nat. Coun. Tchrs. Math., Ill. Coun. Tchrs. Math. Roman Catholic. Home: 1012 Garfield St Lockport IL 60441-3641 Office: Providence Cath High Sch 1800 W Lincoln Hwy New Lenox IL 60451-3533

MOTSINGER, LINDA SUE, university official; b. Scottsburg, Ind., Sept. 13, 1947; d. Edwin Wardie and Laurel Imogene McKnight; m. Gary L. Motsinger, Oct. 22, 1966. Postgrad., Ind. U., Bloomington, 1979—. Dictaphone typist O.P. Link Handle Co., Salem, Ind., 1965-66; sec. Tex. Instruments Credit Union, Dallas, 1966-67, John Erb Ins., Merritt Is., Fla., 1968-69; Teller First Nat. Bank of Niceville, Fla.; sec. Ind. U., Bloomington, 1971-73, sr. sec., 1973-80, prin. sec., 1980-81, adminstrv. sec., 1980-83, adminstrv. asst., 1983-92, asst. to v.p., 1992-96, asst. to pres. Advanced Rsch. and Tech. Inst., 1996—. Editor: ACAP Computing Conf., 1979-80. Named Woman of the Year, Am. Bus. Women's Assn., 1986, Girl of the Year Beta Sigma Phi, 1988. Republican. Home: 5120 N Echo Bnd Bloomington IN 47404-9003 Office: Ind U Showers Rsch Park Bloomington IN 47408-4144

MOTSINGER, LINDA SUSAN BAUMGARDNER, commercial printing firm owner; b. Chgo., Mar. 14, 1941; d. Bryan Burdette and Chrystal Lucille (Adams) Baumgardner; m. Larry Lee Motsinger, Oct. 2, 1959; 1 child, Eric Lee. Cert. of completion life ins. underwriting Northwestern Mut. Life Ins. Co., Milw., 1962. Bookkeeper Busey Bank Corp., Urbana, Ill., 1959-60; bookkeeper Northwestern Mut. Life Ins. Co., Champaign, Ill., 1960-62, asst. office mgr.-bookkeeper, 1962-65; tech. typist-sec. U. Ill. Coll. Engring., Urbana, 1965-70; entrepreneur pub. rels. L & L Printing Svc., St. Joseph, Ill., 1975—. Co-author, editor, pub.: A Genealogical Record of the Family Baumgardner, 1971; editor, pub.: (reunion handbooks) UHS--20 Years Later, 1979, UHS--30 Years Later, 1989, UHS--Thirty-Five Years Older and Still a Tiger!, 1994; editor, pub. (ann. alumni newsletter) Tiger Pause, 1989—. Organizer, co-chair Reunion Com. UHS, 1959, Urbana, 1978—. Republican. Office: L & L Printing Svc PO Box 543 Saint Joseph IL 61873-0543

MOTTLEY, JAMES DONALD, state legislator, lawyer; b. Alamogordo, N.Mex., Aug. 29, 1954; s. Harry Edward Mottley Jr. and Linnie Sue (Tate) Johnson; m. Patricia Chris Cooper, June 30, 1980 (div. May 1984). BA in Polit. Sci. magna cum laude, Wright State U., 1975, MS in Econs., 1976; JD, Salmon P. Chase Coll. of Law, 1991. Bar: Ohio, 1991, U.S. Dist. Ct. (so. dist.) Ohio 1992. Fin. mgr. NCR Corp., Dayton, Ohio, 1977-81; mgr. cash mgmt. and investment banking NCR Corp., Dayton, 1982-84; asst. to county commr. Montgomery County, Dayton, 1981-82; treas. NCR Credit Corp., Dayton, 1984-87; chief dep. county auditor Montgomery County Auditors Office, Dayton, 1987-91; assoc. Taft, Stettinius & Hollister, Cin., 1991-92; ptnr. Flanagan, Lieberman, Hoffman & Swaine, Dayton, 1993—; mem. Ohio Ho. of Reps., Columbus, 1993—. Mem. ctrl. and exec. coms. Orgn. Montgomery County Rep. Party, Dayton, 1985—. Mem. Optimists, Masons (master). Presbyterian. Home: 1641 Longbow Ln West Carrollton OH 45449-2344 Office: Ohio Ho of Reps 77 S High St Columbus OH 43266

MOUL, MAXINE BURNETT, state official; b. Oakland, Nebr., Jan. 26, 1947; d. Einer and Eva (Jacobson) Burnett; m. Francis Moul, Apr. 20, 1972; 1 child, Jeff. BS in Journalism, U. Nebr., 1969; DHL (hon.), Peru State Coll., 1993. Sunday feature writer, photographer Sioux City Iowa Jour., 1969-71; reporter, photographer, editor Maverick Media, Inc., Syracuse, Nebr., 1971-73, editor, pub., 1974-83, pres., 1983-90; grant writer, asst. coord. Nebr. Regional Med. Program, Lincoln, 1973-74; lt. gov. State of Nebr., Lincoln, 1991-93; dir. Dept. Econ. Devel., Lincoln, 1993—. Mem. Dem. Nat. Com., Washington, 1988-92, Nebr. Dem. State Ctrl. Com., Lincoln, 1974-88; del. Dem. Nat. Conf., 1972, 88, 92; mem. exec. com. Nebr. Dem. Party, Lincoln, 1988-93. Recipient Margaret Sanger award Planned Parenthood, Lincoln, 1991, Champion of Small Bus. award Nebr. Bus. Devel. Ctr., Omaha, 1991, Toll fellowship Coun. State Govts., Lexington, Ky., 1992. Mem. Bus. and Profl. Womem, Nebr. Mgmt. Assn. (Silver Knight award 1992), Nat. Conf. Lt. Govs. (bd. dirs. 1991-93), Nebr. Press Women, Women Execs. in State Govt., Cmty. Devel. Soc., U. Nebr.-Lincoln Journalism Alumni. Democrat. Office: State of Nebr PO Box 94666 Lincoln NE 68509-4666

MOULDER, T. EARLINE, musician; b. Buffalo, Mo., Oct. 11; d. Earl Young and Ruby M. (Philpott) M.; m. R. David Plank, Dec. 21, 1980; children: Jeannine Stanton, Jon Stanton, Timothy Stanton. AB in Biology and French, Drury Coll., 1973; M in Music magna cum laude, Ind. U., 1963; D in Musical Arts, U. Kansas, 1991; pvt. organ study, Andre Marchal, Paris, France, 1971. Organist St. Paul Meth. Ch., Springfield, Mo., 1961-81; concert organist U.S., Europe, Middle East, 1964—; exec. editor Drury Coll. Mirror, Springfield, Mo., 1971-73; journalist U.S. Naval Res., Springfield, Mo., 1975-77; organist King's Way Meth. Ch., Springfield, Mo., 1983-93; chair organ dept. Drury Coll., Springfield, Mo., 1968—, coll. organist, 1991—; lectr. recitals on Jewish music, 1991—; translator, Profl. documents, 1990—. Composer organ composition, 1971—; contbr. articles to profl. jours. Charter mem. Nat. Mus. Am. Indian, 1994—. Recipient Teaching fellow U. Kans., Drury Mirror award Rank I Mo. Coll. Newspaper Assn. Mem. Sigma Alpha Iota, Alpha Lambda Delta, Pi Delta Phi, Beta Beta Beta, Pi Kappa Lambda, Organ Hist. Soc., Am. Guild Organist. Home: 3563 E Linwood Dr Springfield MO 65809 Office: Drury Coll 900 N Benton Springfield MO 65802

MOULTON, JOY WADE, genealogist, writer; b. Oxnard, Calif., Nov. 30, 1928; d. Merle E. and Elouise (Morgan) Wade; m. Edward Quentin Moulton, Jan. 2, 1954; children: Jennifer Fairchild Moulton Look, Charles Wade, David Frederick II, Alison Joy Moulton Papanikos. AB, U. Calif., Berkeley, 1950; MS, Wellesley Coll., 1953. Cert. genealogist. Instr. Ohio State U., Columbus, 1954-66, 73-83; spl. writer Columbus Dispatch, 1975—; lectr., 1981—; workshop and seminar leader, 1986—. Author: Genealogical Resources in English Repositories, 1988, Supplement to Genealogical Resources in English Repositories, 1992; columnist Find Your Ancestors, Columbus Dispatch, 1975—, Western Res. Family Tree, Western Res. mag., 1977-79. Pres. women's bd. Columbus Mus. Art, 1982-83; mem. Upper Arlington (Ohio) Arts Commn. (vice chmn., 1979-81); chmn. Greater Columbus Arts Festival, 1974. Fellow Soc. Genealogists (London); mem. Women in Comms., Nat. League Am. Pen Women, Internat. Soc. Brit. Genealogy and Family History (pres. 1989-93, editor newsletter 1986-95, Nat. Geneal. award 1987), Coun. Genealogy Columnists (pres. 1989-92, Excellence in Writing 1st and 3d Pl. awards 1993), Nat. Geneal. Soc. (Excellence in Gen. Methods and Sources Book award 1993), Ohio Geneal. Soc., Ohio Hist. Soc. (trustee 1976-79), New Eng. Hist. Geneal. Soc. (trustee 1979-81), Assn. Profl. Genealogists (trustee 1985-87), Geneal. Spkrs. Guild (charter). Home: 1303 London Dr Columbus OH 43221-1541

MOUNTZ, LOUISE CARSON SMITH, retired librarian; b. Fond Du Lac, Wis., Oct. 20, 1911; d. Roy Carson and Charlotte Louise (Scheurs) Smith; m. George Edward Mountz, May 4, 1935 (dec. Oct. 3 1951); children: Peter Carson, Pamela Teeters Mountz McDonald. Student, Western Coll., 1929-31; AB, The Ohio State U., 1933; MA, Ball State U., 1962; postgrad., Manchester Coll., 1954, Ind. U., 1960-61. Cert. tchr., Ind. Tchr. Monroeville (Ind.) High Sch., 1953-54, Riverdale High Sch., St. Joe, Ind., 1954-55; libr. High Sch., Avilla, Ind., 1955-58; head libr. Penn High Sch., Mishawaka, Ind., 1958-67, Northwood Jr. High Sch., Ft. Wayne, Ind., 1967-69, McIntosh Jr. High Sch., Auburn, Ind., 1969-74; dir. Media Ctr. DeKalb Jr. High Sch., Auburn, Ind., 1974-78; ret., 1978; cons. media ctr. planning Penn-Harris-Madison Sch. Corp., Mishawaka, 1966-67. Author: Biographies for Junior High Schools and Correlated Audio-Visual Materials, 1970; contbr. articles to profl. jours. Bd. dirs. DeKalb County chpt. ARC, 1938-42, 51-53, DeKalb County Heart Assn., 1946-52, DeKalb County Cmty. Concert Assn., 1946-58, Am. Field Svc. Mishawaka chpt., 1960-67; active Ft. Wayne Philharmonic Orch. Assn., Ft. Wayne Art Mus., Ft. Wayne Hist. Soc., DeKalb County Hist. Soc., Garrett Hist. Soc., DeKalb County Genealogy Soc., Preservation of DeKalb County Heritage Assn., DeKalb Meml. Hosp. Women's Guild, also life mem. Mem. AAUW, ALA, NEA, World Confedn. Orgns. Teaching Professions, Nat. Coun. Tchrs. English, Ind. Sch. Librarians Assn. (dir. 1963-67), Internat. Assn. Sch. Librarianship, Ind. Assn. Ednl. Communication and Tech., Assn. Ind. Media Educators,

Nat. Ret. Tchrs. Assns., Nat. Trust Hist. Preservation, Hist. Landmarks Found. Ind., Delta Kappa Gamma (charter mem., Beta Beta chpt.), Kappa Kappa Kappa (pr. officer 1941-45, pres. Alpha Chi chpt. 1938-40, Garrett Assoc. chpt. 1971-73), Delta Delta Delta (house pres.). Methodist. Lodge: Order Ea. Star. Clubs: Greenhurst Country, Ft. Wayne Women's, Athena Lit. (hon. mem.), Ladies Lit. of Auburn. Home: 19 Castle Ct Auburn IN 46706-1439

MOUSSEAU, DORIS NAOMI BARTON, retired elementary school principal; b. Alpena, Mich., May 6, 1934; d. Merritt Benjamin and Naomi Dora Josephine (Pieper) Barton; m. Bernard Joseph Mousseau, July 31, 1954. AA, Alpena Community Coll., 1954; BS, Wayne State U., 1959; MA, U. Mich., 1961, postgrad., 1972-75. Profl. cert. ednl. adminstr., tchr. Elem. tchr. Clarkston (Mich.) Community Schs., 1954-66; elem. sch. prin. Andersonville Sch., Clarkston, 1966-79, Bailey Lake Sch., Clarkston, 1979-94; ret., 1994. Cons., rsch. com. Youth Assistance Oakland County Ct. Svcs., 1968-88; leader Clarkston PTA, 1967-94; chair Clarkston Sch. Dist. campaign, United Way, 1985, 86; mem. allocations com. Oakland County United Way, 1987-88. Recipient Outstanding Svc. award Davisburg Jaycees, Springfield Twp., 1977, Vol. Recognition award Oakland County (Mich.) Cts., 1984. Fellow ASCD, MACUL (State Assn. Ednl. Computer Users); mem. NEA (del. 1964), Mich. Elem. and Middle Sch. Prins. Assn. (treas., regional del. 1982—, pres.-elect Region 7 1988-89, program planner, pres. 1989-90, sr. advisor 1990-91, Honor award Region # 7 1991), Mich. Edn. Assn. (pres. 1960-66, del. 1966), Clarkston Edn. Assn. (author, editor 1st directory 1963), Women's Bowling Assn., Elks, Spring Meadows Gold Club, Phi Delta Kappa, Delta Kappa Gamma (pres. 1972-74, past state and nat. chmn., Woman of Distinction 1982). Republican. Home: 6825 Rattalee Lake Rd Clarkston MI 48348-1955

MOUZAKES-SILER, HELEN HARRIET (ELENA MOUZAKES-SILER), retired executive secretary, lyric soloist; b. Detroit, Nov. 16, 1929; d. Constantine Demetrios and Alexandra (Poulos) Mouzakes; m. John Floren Siler, Oct. 12, 1980 (dec. Oct. 1988). Pvt. student Hellenic lang., 1940-45; student, Detroit Conservatory Music, 1944-47, Wayne U., 1950-52, Detroit Bus. Inst., 1948-49. Choir dir., soloist Greek Orthodox Annunciation Cathedral, 1948-52; exec. sec. Ford Motor Co. World Hdqrs., Dearborn, Mich., 1949-82; profl. lyric soprano Elena the Singing Sec'y, 1978—. Soloist Nat. Anthem, Detroit Tigers, Detroit Lions, Detroit Ethnic Festival, 1978—. Asst. choir dir. St. Nicholas Greek Orthodox Ch., 1960-92; Holy Cross Greek Orthodox Choir, 1993—; active Farmington Hills Libr., 1994—. Mem. Founders Soc. Detroit Inst. Arts, Daus. of Penelope (pres. 1964-65, 89-91, pres. Doris chpt. 1996—), Am. Hellenic Ednl. Progressive Assn., St. Nicholas Philoptohos Soc., Elks (exec. bd. Viviens 1994—).

MOWBRAY, CAROL BEATRICE THIESSEN, mental health researcher, social work educator; b. Boston, Aug. 20, 1948; d. Peter Isaac and Jessamine Beatrice (Olpin) Thiessen; m. Charles Sherman Mowbray, June 1, 1970; children: Orion, Nicholas. BS, Tufts U., 1970, MS, 1971; PhD, U. Mich., 1975. Lectr. dept. psychology Mich. State U., East Lansing, 1974-75; social rsch. analyst Mich. Dept. Mental Health, Lansing, 1975-76, dir. spl. analytical studies, 1976-77, exec. asst. to dir., 1977-78, dir., program and grants coord., 1978-80, dir. rsch., evaluation and demonstration, 1980-90; assoc. prof. social work Wayne State U., Detroit, 1990-94; assoc. prof. social work U. Mich., Ann Arbor, 1994—, assoc. dir. Risk Poverty and Mental Health Rsch. Ctr., 1995—, assoc. dean rsch., 1996—; cons. grant rev. NIMH, Rockville, Md., 1981—. Author: Women and Mental Health, 1984; mem. editorial bd. Evaluation and Program Planning, Psychiat. Rehab. Jour.; consulting editor: SW Rsch.; contbr. articles to profl. jours. Rsch. grantee dual diagnosis NIMH, 1989-95, supported edn. grantee Substance Abuse-Mental Health Svcs. Adminstrn., 1992—, mentally ill mothers grantee NIMH, 1994—. Fellow APA (sect. chmn. 1990-92, Disting. Svc. award div. 18 1988); mem. NASW, Internat. Assn. Psychosocial Rehab. Svcs. (rsch. com. 1994—), Am. Evaluation Assn., Midwest Psychol. Assn. Home: 5460 Prairie Vw Brighton MI 48116-7715 Office: U Mich Sch Social Work 1065 Frieze Bldg Ann Arbor MI 48109-1285

MOWERY, MARK ROTH, chemist; b. Gaylord, Mich., Jan. 9, 1960; s. Roth Delmar and Janice Mae (Mahn) M.; m. JoAn Marie Wieckowski, Sept. 1, 1990. AS, Alpena Community Coll., Alpena, Mich., 1982; BS, Central Mich. Univ., 1985, MS, 1990. Rsch. assoc. Mich. Molecular Inst., Midland, Mich., 1986-89; assoc. scientist Bristol-Myers Squibb, Wallingford, Conn., 1989-91; assoc. chemist The UpJohn Co., Kalamazoo, Mich., 1991—. Mem. N.Y. Acad. Sci., Am. Chem. Soc., Sigma Pi Sigma. Lutheran. Home: 7402 Quail St Portage MI 49002-4214 Office: The UpJohn Co 7000 Portage Rd # 2 Kalamazoo MI 49001-0102

MOYER, GEORGE HAMILTON, JR., lawyer; b. Omaha, May 17, 1937; s. George Hamilton and Eunice Francesca (Geiger) M.; m. Marilyn Jean De Groot, June 5, 1965; children: Michael Christopher, Eric Hamilton. BA, U. Nebr., 1959, LLB, 1962. Bar: Nebr. 1962, U.S. Ct. Appeals (8th cir.) 1979, U.S. Supreme Ct. 1991; cert. Am. Bd. Trial Advocacy. Ptnr. Moyer, Moyer Egley, Gulher & Warnemunde, Madison, Nebr.; bd. dirs. Bank of Madison & Trust Co.; prevailing counsel U.S. Supreme Ct., 1992. Chmn. Madison County Republicans, 1964-66; treas. Nebr. Young Republicans, 1964-66. Fellow Am. Bd. Trial Advocacy; mem. Nebr. Bar Assn., Nebr. State Hist. Soc., Am. Assn. Trial Attys. (nat. gov. 1979-81), Nebr. Assn. Trial Attys. (bd. dirs. 1977-79, 92-95, treas. 1995—, trustee 1989—), Nebr. Hist. Soc. Found. (trustee 1990—, bd. dirs. 1993—). Democrat. Methodist. Office: Moyer Moyer et al Box 510 114 W 3d Madison NE 68748

MOYER, JOHN L., electrical designer, control engineer; b. Galion, Ohio, June 16, 1947. BS in Electronic Tech., U. Akron, 1993. Elec.designer PF&K Assocs., Akron, Ohio, 1988-91; elec. designer, control engr. Guild Internat., Cleve., 1992—. Served with U.S. Army, 1968-74. Home: 238 Edgerton Rd Akron OH 44303-1523 Office: Guild Internat. 7273 Division St Cleveland OH 44146-5405

MOYLAN, STEPHEN CRAIG, architect; b. Chgo., Mar. 4, 1952; s. Martin James and Shirley Ann (Randazzo) M.; m. Cynthia Kathleen LoPresti, June 9, 1974. BArch, U. Notre Dame, 1975. Registered architect, Ill.; cert. Nat. Coun. Archtl. Registration Bds. Supr. engrng. Roper-IBG, Wheeling, Ill., 1975-79; architect Skidmore, Owings & Merrill, Chgo., 1979-82; project mgr. Harmon Contractors, Elk Grove Village, Ill., 1982-84; architect Blumenthal & Assocs., Chgo., 1984-85, Loebl, Schlossman & Hackl, Chgo., 1985-86, Groggs & Assocs., Chgo., 1986-87, CRS Sirrine, Inc., Chgo., 1987-88, Teng & Assocs., Chgo., 1988-90, IDEA Design/Build, Lake Forest, Ill., 1990—; instr. Oakton C.C., Des Plaines, Ill., 1989-93. Mem. AIA (chmn. young archs. com., Chgo. intern arch. com., profl. devel. com., assoc. dir. Ill. chpt. 1983-87, bd. dirs. 1993), Soc. Am. Mil. Engrs., U.S. Judo Assn. (silver life, patron life, 4th degree black belt), Kiwanis, Notre Dame Monogram Club. Roman Catholic. Home: 780 E Green Briar Ln Lake Forest IL 60045-3217 Office: IDEA Design/Build 225 E Deerpath Rd Ste 130 Lake Forest IL 60045-1970

MROCZKIEWICZ, KENNETH J., design draftsman; b. South Bend, Ind., Jan. 7, 1951. Assoc. in Machine Design, Tri State U., 1972. Sr. design draftsman Wells Electronic Inc., South Bend, 1972—. Baptist. Office: Wells Electronic Inc 1701 S Main St South Bend IN 46613-2211

MRUK, CHRISTOPHER J., psychologist, educator; b. Mt. Clemens, Mich., May 21, 1949; s. Joseph and Veronica (Harris) M; m. Marsha Jean Oliver, Dec. 24, 1983. BS, Mich. State U., 1971; MA, Duquesne U., 1974, PhD, 1981. Lic. clin. psychologist, Ohio, Pa. Staff psychologist Mon Valley Mental Health Ctr., Monessen, Pa., 1981-82; dir. counseling St. Francis Coll., Loretto, Pa., 1982-83; prof. Firelands Coll., Bowling Green State U., Huron, Ohio, 1984—; cons. psychologist Firelands Cmty. Hosp., Sandusky, Ohio, 1988—. Author: Self-Esteem: Research, Theory and Practice, 1995; contbr. chpts. to books and articles to profl. jours. Bd. dirs. Safe Harbour Domestic Violence Ctr., Sandusky, 1992. Mem. Am. Psychol. Assn.

MRVAN, FRANK, JR., state legislator; m. Jean Mrvan. Asst. v.p. First Nat. Bank East Chgo.; mem. Ind. State Senate, 1978—, asst. chmn. minority caucus, 1981-82; mem. health and environ. affaris com., ins. and fin. instns. com., edn. comm., appt. and claims com., govt. and regulatory coms. Mem. Hammond Planning Commn.; mem. Ind. State Commn. for Handicapped; mem. Hammond City Coun. Mem. KC, PTA (past pres.), Hammond Young Dems., Lake County Fish and Game Protective Assn., Am. Legion. Home: 6732 Maryland Ave Hammond IN 46323-1825 also: State Senate State Capital Indianapolis IN 46204*

MUCCIANTE, MARY F., state official; b. Springfield, Ill., Feb. 11; d. Donald R. and Frances Iverne (Cline) M. BA in Legal Studies, Sangamon State U., Springfield, 1984, MPA, 1989. Program planner Ill. Dept. on Aging, Springfield, 1984-86, civil rights coord., 1986-87, program planner, 1987-88; mgr. occupational disease registry Ill. Dept. Pub. Health, Springfield, 1988-92, mgmt. analyst, 1992—. Precinct committeeman Springfield Rep. Com., 1992; bd. dirs. Capital City Rep. Women, 1996—; grad. Leadership Springfield, 1996. Mem. APHA, ASPA (bd. dirs. 1987-89), Ill. Pub. Health Assn. (exec. coun. com. 1991-94), Ill. Women in Mgmt. (bd. dirs., sec. 1996-97), Springfield C. of C., Leadership Springfield Alumni Assn. (bd. dirs. 1996-99). Roman Catholic. Home: 1918 Jeanette Ln Springfield IL 62702-4643

MUCHMORE, DENNIS C., governmental affairs consultant; b. Charleston, Ill., Nov. 23, 1946; s. Maurice Leo and Rose Catherine (Driscoll) M.; 1 child from previous marriage, Shane. BS in Edn., Ea. Ill. U., 1968; M in Pub. Adminstrn., Mich. State U., 1982. Tchr. Fitzgerald Pub. Schs., Warren, Mich., 1969-73; pres. Fitzgerald Edn. Assn., Warren, 1969-73; cons. Mich. State Senate, Lansing, 1975-77, adminstrv. asst., 1973-80; mgr. of tax and labor Mich C. of C., Lansing, 1980; v.p. Mich. C. of C., Lansing, 1980-84; cons. GCSI, Lansing, 1984-88; prin. Dennis Muchmore & Assoc., Lansing, 1988-93; pres. Muchmore Harrington Assoc., Lansing, 1993—. Bd. dirs. Ea. Ill. U. Found., Charleston, 1992—, Lansing C.C. Found., Lansing, 1993—, Lansing Symphony Orch., 1992—, Mich. Festival, East Lansing, 1986-94; host com. Am. Legis. Exch. Coun., Lansing, 1993-94; adv. bd. Mid Mich. Opera Theatre, Lansing, 1994—. Mem. Am. Assn. of Polit. Cons., Mongoose Moguls, Mountain Men, Am. Soc. of Publ Adminstrs. (bd. dirs. capital chpt. 1982-86). Roman Catholic. Home: PO Box 20114 Lansing MI 48901 Office: Muchmore Harrington Assocs 500 Michigan Nat Tower Lansing MI 48933

MUDD, MICHAEL SIDNEY, public relations executive; b. New Rochelle, N.Y., June 9, 1951; s. Sidney Peter and Ada Marie (Herbermann) M.; children: Graham, Claire; m. Nancy A. Nevin, Mar. 29, 1994. BA in English, Coll. of the Holy Cross, Worcester, Mass., 1973. Reporter News Recorder, Worcester, Mass., 1973-74; reporter, editor Gannett Westchester Newspapers, White Plains, N.Y., 1974-77; v.p. Siegel & Gale Inc., N.Y.C., 1977-78, BBDO Inc., N.Y.C., 1979-84; dir. corp. communications Gen. Foods Corp., White Plains, 1984-89; v.p. corp. communications Kraft Gen. Foods Inc., Glenview, Ill., 1989—. Republican. Office: Kraft Gen Foods Three Lakes Dr Northfield IL 60093

MUELLER, DON SHERIDAN, retired school administrator; b. Cleve., Nov. 4, 1927; s. Don P. and Selma Christina (Ungericht) M.; B.S., Mt. Union Coll., 1948; M.A., U. Mich., 1952; Ed.S., Mich. State U., 1968; Ph.D., Clayton U., 1977; m. Vivian Jean Santrock, Aug. 27, 1947 (dec. 1993); children—Carl Frederick, Cathy Ann. Tchr., Benton-Harbor Fair Plain (Mich.) Schs., 1947-52; dir. music edn. Okemos (Mich.) Pub. Schs., 1952-64; jr-sr. high prin. Dansville (Mich.) Schs., 1964-68; prin. DeWitt (Mich.) High Sch., 1968-73; supt. Carsonville-Port Sanilac Schs., Carsonville, Mich., 1973-94; ret., 1994. Recipient Community Leader of Am. award, 1968, 72, 73-74; Acad. Am. Educators award, 1973-74. Mem. Am., Mich. assns. sch. adminstrs., Mich. Assn. Sch. Bds., NEA, Assn. Supervision and Curriculum Devel., Clinton Prins. Assn. (pres. 1972-73), Ingham Prins. Assn. (pres. 1967-70), Mich. Sch. Band/Orch. Assn. (sec. 1962-63, pres. dist. 5 1958-60), Okemos Edn. Assn. (pres. 1962-63), River Area Supts. Assn. (pres. 1979-80). Home: 188 S High St Box 257 188 S High St Box 257 Carsonville MI 48419-0257

MUELLER, GEORGE BERNARD, contracting company executive; b. Evergreen Park, Ill., Sept. 9, 1939; s. Marc John and Violet Louise (Dillman) M.; m. Jean Marie Hoban, Oct. 31, 1964; children: Marc, Matthew, Mary, Kurt. Student, DePaul U., 1958-62. Regional sales rep. Ludowici Celadon, Chgo., 1958-65; v.p. Archtl. Engring. Prodns., San Diego, 1965-81; regional mgr. AEP/Span, San Diego, 1981-83; mfrs. rep. Span Metals Corp., Dallas, 1981-87, Overly Mfg., Greensburg, Pa., 1985—; cert. applicator Hickman Constrn. Prodns., N.C., 1986--; cons., rep. RTS System, San Diego, 1972--; pres. Mueller Shirt Co., Richton Park, Ill., 1986--, Specified Roofing, Inc., Richton Park, 1968--; cons. Strata Oil Co., Evergreen Park, 1987-89. Contbr. articles to profl. jours.; owner U.S. and fgn. patents in shirt constrn. and metal roof panels. Bd. dirs., chmn. Joliet (Ill.) Diocesan Sch. Bd., St. Liborius Sch. Bd., Steger, Ill.; mem. adv. bd. Marian Cath. High Sch., Chicago Heights, 1988-91; parish bd. pres. Fin. Bldg. and Devel. Coms., Steger, 1988—. Mem. Paulist Choir Alumni (co-founder, pres. 1969--), Paulist Choir Alumni Chorale (co-founder, dir., officer 1971--), KC. Home: 3540 Chalet Ln Crete IL 60417-1109 Office: Specified Roofing Inc 22307 Ridgeway Ave Richton Park IL 60471-2048

MUELLER, KEITH JOHN, political science educator. BA, U. Wis., Milw., 1973, MA, 1975; PhD, U. Ariz., 1979. From asst. prof. to assoc. prof. polit. sci. U. Nebr., Lincoln, 1979-91, prof., 1991—; dir. sect. health svcs. rsch. U. Nebr. Med. Ctr., Omaha, 1990—. Contbr. articles to profl. jours. HHS grantee, 1992. Mem. Nat. Rural Health Assn. (pres. 1996—). Home: 5319 Howard St Omaha NE 68106-1324 Office: U Nebr Med Ctr 600 S 42nd St Omaha NE 68105-1002

MUELLER, WALT, state legislator; b. Springfield, Mo., Dec. 12, 1925. BS, U. Kans. Mem. Mo. State Ho. of Reps. Dist. 93, 1973-93, Mo. State Senate Dist. 15, 1993—. Address: 12325 Manchester Rd Saint Louis MO 63131-4316*

MUELLER, WILLYS FRANCIS, JR., pathologist; b. Detroit, July 15, 1934; s. Willys Francis and Antoinette Frances (Stimac) M.; M.D., U. Mich., 1959; m. Dolores Mae Vella, Aug. 25, 1956; children: Renee Ann, Willys Francis, Paul E., Mark A., Maria D., Beth M., Matthew P. Intern, Providence Hosp., Detroit, 1959-60, resident, 1960-62; resident Wayne County Gen. Hosp., Eloise, Mich., 1962-64; asst. pathologist Grace Hosp., Detroit, 1964; asso. pathologist Hurley Hosp., Flint, Mich., 1964-66; asso. pathologist Hurley Med. Ctr., Flint, 1968—, dir. lab., 1981—; chief dep. med. examiner Genesee County, Mich., 1971—; pres. Pathology Assos. Inc.; assoc. clin. prof. Coll. Human Medicine, Mich. State U.; med. dir. blood svcs. Wolverine region/ Grant Lakes region ARC, 1981-96. Served with M.C., U.S. Army, 1966-68. Fellow Am. Soc. Clin. Pathologists, Coll. Am. Pathologists, Am. Acad. Forensic Scis.; mem. AMA (Physician's Recognition award 1974-77, 78-81, 81-84, 85-87, 87-90, 91, 93—), Mich. State Med. Soc., Mich. Soc. Pathologists (sec.-treas. 1981-83, pres. elect 1984, pres. 1985), Genesee County Med. Soc. (pres. 1987), Mich. Assn. Blood Banks (bd. dirs., pres. 1992), Nat. Assn. Med. Examiners. Republican. Roman Catholic. Club: K.C. Editor: Bull. of Genesee County Med. Soc. Home: 13335 Pomona Dr Fenton MI 48430-1223 Office: Hurley Med Ctr Dept Pathology Flint MI 48502

MUELLNER, JOHN PHILLIP, librarian, educator; b. Chgo., June 20, 1936; s. John William and Catherine (McMahon) M.; divorced; children: April, Phillip, Erich, Owen. AA, Wright Jr. Coll., 1957; BE, Chgo. State U., 1960, ME, 1963; postgrad. Loyola U., Chgo., 1964. Cert. libr., H.S. English tchr., elem. tchr., Ill. Tchr.-libr. Chgo. Pub. Schs., 1958-94, head, Schiller Park Pub. Libr., 1964-92; ret. Home: 2717 N Racine Ave Chicago IL 60614-1205

MUGNAINI, ENRICO, biobehavioral sciences and psychology educator, researcher, consultant; b. Colle Val d'Elsa, Italy, Dec. 10, 1937; came to U.S., 1969.; children: Karin E., Emiliano N.G. MD summa cum laude, U. Pisa, Italy, 1962. Microscopy lab. rsch. fellow Dept. Anatomy U. Oslo Med. Sch., 1963, asst. prof., head of electron microscopy lab., 1964-66, assoc. prof., 1967-69; prof. biobehavioral scis. and psychology, head lab. of neuromorphology U. Conn., Storrs, 1969-95; dir. inst. for neurosci. Northwestern U., Chgo., 1996—; vis. prof. Dept. Anatomy Harvard U., Boston, 1969-70; traveling lectr. Grass Found., spring 1986, fall 1990. Mng. editor USA Anatomy and Embryology Jour., 1989—; contbr. more than 100 articles to books and jours. Recipient Decennial Camillo Golgi award Acad. Nat. dei Lincei, 1981, Sen. Javits Neurosci. Rsch. Investigator award NIH, 1985-92. Mem. AAAS, Am. Assn. Anatomists, Am. Soc. Cell Biology, Internat. Brain Rsch. Orgn., Internat. Soc. Developmental Neurosci., N.Y. Acad. Scis., Norwegian Nat. Acad. Scis. and Letters, Soc. Neurosci., Cajal Club (pres. 1987-88). Office: U Northwestern Inst Neurosci 5-474 Searle Bldg 320 E Superior St Chicago IL 60611-3010

MUHA-RONNEAU, CAROL, medical surgical nurse, critical care nurse; b. East Chgo., Ind., July 24, 1950; d. Joseph Peter and Victoria Magdelene (Biernacki) Muha; m. John Evan Ronneau, Nov. 11, 1989; 1 child, Heather. AAS, Purdue U., 1972, BSN, 1976, MSN, 1988. RN, Ind., Ill.; cert. BLS, ACLS. Staff nurse St. Catherine's Hosp., East Chgo., Ind., 1972-75, unit dir., 1975-76; cardiovascular nurse practitioner Cardiovascular and Renal Cons., Homewood, Ill., 1976-83; vis. instr. Purdue U. North Cen., Westville, Ind., 1984-88, asst. prof., 1988-93, assoc. prof., 1994—; vis. instr. Purdue U./Calumet, Hammond, Ind., 1976-77; cons. On Course Seminars, Valparaiso, Ind., 1991; bd. dirs. ednl. adv. com. Porter County Sch. Corp., 1992-93; chairperson Heartbeats Health Festivals, Westville, Ind., 1989-90, 91. Author: (abstract) Cooperative Learning, 1992, 93, Pocket Care Plans, 1989. Bd. dirs. Am. Cancer Soc., Laporte County, Ind., 1988-90; bd. dirs., officer, Porter County, Ind., 1989—; bd. dirs. Am. Cancer Soc., 1988-90, Am. Heart Assn., Porter County, 1989—, v.p., 1994—. Recipient Best Lect. of Yr. award Purdue U., 1986-87, Vol. of Yr. award Am. Heart Assn., 1991-92, Outstanding Svc. award Am. Heart Assn., 1990-91. Mem. Ind. State Nurses Assn., Purdue U. Nursing Honor Soc. (chairperson elections 1989-92), Sigma Theta Tau. Roman Catholic. Office: Purdue U North Cen 1401 S Us Highway 421 Westville IN 46391-9543

MUHLENBRUCH, CARL W., civil engineer; b. Decatur, Ill., Nov. 21, 1915; s. Carl William and Clara (Theobald) M.; m. Agnes M. Kringel, Nov. 22, 1939; children: Phyllis Elaine (Mrs. Richard B. Wallace), Joan Carol (Mrs. Frederick W. Wenk). BCE, U. Ill., 1937, CE, 1945; MCE, Carnegie Inst. Tech., 1943; LLD, Concordia U., River Forest, Ill., 1995. Research engineer Aluminum Research Labs., Pitts., 1937-39; cons. engring., 1939-50; mem. faculty Carnegie Inst. Tech., 1939-48; assoc. prof. civil engring. Northwestern U., 1948-54; pres. TEC-SEARCH, Inc. (formerly Ednl. and Tech. Consultants Inc.), 1954-67, chmn. bd., 1967—; Pres. Profl. Centers Bldg. Corp., 1961-77. Author: Experimental Mechanics and Properties of Materials; Contbr. articles engring. publs. Treas., bd. dirs. Concordia Coll. Found.; dir. Mo. Lutheran Synod, 1965-77, vice chmn. 1977-79. Recipient Stanford E. Thompson award, 1945. Mem. Am. Econ. Devel. Coun. (cert. econ. developer), Am. Soc. Engring. Edn. (editor Ednl. Aids in Engring.), NSPE, ASCE, Sigma Xi, Tau Beta Phi, Omicron Delta Kappa. Club: University (Evanston). Lodge: Rotary (dist. gov. 1980-81, dir. service projects Ghana and the Bahamas). Home and Office: Tec-Search Inc 4071 Fairway Dr Wilmette IL 60091-1005

MUIR, JIM R., business executive; b. Ilford, Essex, U.K., Dec. 25, 1939. Cert., S.E. London Politechnic, London, 1960; BA in Bus. Mgmt., U. South Africa, 1981. Engr. Ford Motor Co., Dunton, Eng., 1956-74, Nissan, Pretoria, 1974-85; v.p. Troy Design and Mfg., Redford, Mich., 1991-93; CEO Troy Design, Inc., 1993—. Soccer coach Lake Orion Soccer League, 1991—. Mem. Soc. of Automotive Engrs., Inst. of the Motor Industry. Office: 2653 Industrial Row Dr Troy MI 48084-7038

MUIR, WILLIAM LLOYD, III, academic administrator; b. Norton, Kans., Mar. 20, 1948; s. John Thomas and Rosalie June (Benton) M. BBA, Kans. State U., 1977. Asst. sec. of state State of Kans., Topeka, 1971-72, fin. adminstr. atty. gen. office, 1972-79, comptroller, gov.'s office, 1979-87; dir. econ. devel. Kans. State U., Manhattan, 1987-91, asst. to v.p., 1991—; Faculty rep., senator, Kans. State U. student govt. assn., 1992—. Bd. dirs. United Way of Riley County, 1989—, chair, 1992; mem. task force City of Manhattan/Riley County Blank Page Econ. Devel., 1989-91; trustee Kans. State U. Found., 1993—; mem. Leadership Kans., 1989. Named to Outstanding Young Men in Am., 1983, 84, 85. Mem. Friends of Cedar Crest Assn., Inc., Nat. Geog. Soc., Sierra Club, Masons, Alpha Tau Omega (nat. officer), Alpha Kappa Psi. Episcopalian. Home: 2040 Shirley Ln Manhattan KS 66502-2059 Office: Kansas State U 122 Anderson Hall Manhattan KS 66506-0100

MULCAHY, CHARLES CHAMBERS, lawyer, educator; b. Milw., Oct. 5, 1937; s. Thomas Lawrence and Mary (Chambers) M.; m. Judith Ann Schweiger, June 29, 1963; children: Mary Mulcahy Muth, Meg Mulcahy Ekmark, Beth. BS, Marquette U., 1959, JD, 1962. Bar: Wis. 1962, Fla. 1987. Atty., pres. Mulcahy & Wherry, Milw., 1966-91; atty. Whyte Hirschboeck Dudek S.C., Milw., 1991—; adj. prof. Marquette U. Law Sch., Milw., 1975-90; hon. consul Belgium, Milw., 1985—; pres. Pub. Policy Forum, 1992-94; bd. dirs. Wis. Mfrs. and Commerce, 1988-95; mem. Wis. Coun. on Mcpl. Collective Bargaining, 1993—; bd. dirs. Med. Coll. Wis., 1980—, Greater Milw. Com., 1976—. Author: Public Employer Managers Manual, 1968; co-editor: Public Employment Law , 1974, 2nd edit., 1979, 3rd. edit., 1988. County supr. Milw. County, 1964-76; pres. Milw. Tennis Classic, 1975—; chmn. War Meml. Corp., 1976-84; pres. Wis. World Trade Ctr., 1987-91 (Meritorious Svc. award 1991). With USAF, 1962-68. Recipient County Achievement award Nat. Assn. Counties, 1976; named Father of Yr. Children's Outing Assn., 1984; named to Marquette U. Athletic Hall of Fame, 1988. Mem. Milw. County Hist. Soc. (pres. 1980-81), Marquette Law Alumni Assn. (pres. 1971-72). Republican. Roman Catholic. Home: 1820 E Fox Ln Fox Point WI 53217-2858 Office: Whyte Hirschboeck Dudek SC 111 E Wisconsin Ave Ste 2100 Milwaukee WI 53202-4809

MULDER, DONALD R., telecommunications executive; b. Grand Rapids, Mich., July 23, 1944; s. William H. and Alice L. Meines; m. Carole Grevengoed, Mar. 23, 1944; children: Gregory, Karen, Joel. BS, Calvin Coll., 1967; MSEE, U. Mich., 1968; MBA, U. Chgo., 1982. Mem. staff Bell Labs., Naperville, Ill.; v.p. tech. Centel, Chgo., v.p. mktg.; prin. Booz, Allen, Hamilton, Bethesda, Md.; v.p. market devel. No. Telecom, Schaumberg, Ill.; v.p. strategic planning U.S. Robotics, Skokie, Ill.; Mem. exec. adv. bd. NFC, Chgo.; chmn. rsch. consortium NSF. Active U. Ill. Coll. Engring. bd., Champaign, Ill. Mem. IEEE. Office: US Robotics 8100 N McCormick Blvd Skokie IL 60076

MULDER, PATRICIA MARIE, education educator; b. South Bend, Ind., Dec. 28, 1944; d. Ervin James and Carmen Virginia (Sheeley) Anderson; m. James R. Mulder, Dec. 27, 1964; children: Todd Alan, Scott Robert. BA, Western Mich. U., 1967. Freelance writer, photographer Berrien Springs, Mich., 1980—; tchr. Eau Claire (Mich.) Pub. Schs., 1969-70; staff writer, sales rep. Jour. Era, Berrien Springs, 1979-81; sales rep. Berrien County Record, Buchana, Mich., 1981-82; account exec. WHFB Radio Palladium Pub. Co., St. Joseph, Mich., 1982-86; substitute tchr. Berrien County Intermediate Dist., 1986-89; instr. Southwestern Mich. Coll., Dowagiac, 1989—. Editor The Positive Image newsletter, 1980—, The F Stop, 1982-90; author: Poetry Anthologies, 1989—; staff writer Decision Point, 1988-89; newsletter editor Fernwood Nature Photographers, 1980—. Ofcl. photographer Ind. and Internat. Spl. Olympics, Notre Dame, 1986. Named Emerging Artist Ind. Coun. for the Arts, 1989, Honor award Southwestern Coun. of Camera Clubs, 1988, Photographer of the Yr. Berrien County Photographic Artists, 1987, 90. Mem. AAUW, Nat. Authors Registry, Meth. Profl. Women (sec. 1990—), Berrien County Artists (v.p. 1986), Berrien County Photographic Artists (v.p. 1984), Southwestern Mich. Coun. Camera Clubs, Berrien Springs Camrea Club (v.p. 1980—). Methodist. Home: 10252 Castner Dr Berrien Springs MI 49103-9602 Office: Southwestern Mich Coll 58900 Cherry Grove Rd # 316L Dowagiac MI 49047-9726

MULDER, RICHARD DEAN, state legislator; b. Rock Valley, Iowa, May 8, 1938; m. Ruth Maxine Van Buren; 4 children. BS, S.D. State U., 1960; MD, U. Iowa, 1968. Minn. state rep., 1994—; family physician. Address: PO Box A Ivanhoe MN 56142

MULDOWNEY, KERRY PHILLIP, psychologist, sociologist, educator; b. Rockford, Ill., May 6, 1950; s. Glenn and Bernadette (Myers) M.; m. Christine E. Hehir, May 19, 1973; children: Emily, Timothy. AA, Rock Valley Coll., 1975; BS, No. Ill. U., 1977, MS in Edn., 1981. Cert. educator/

counselor, Ill. Tchr. Woodstock (Ill.) Marian Cath., 1977-81; tchr., counselor Hononegah H.S., Rockford, 1981—; adj. prof. Nat.-Louis U., Evanston, 1988—; cons. Motivation Assoc., Rockford, 1981-96; pub. spkr. motivational, inspirational, self-esteem topics, 1986-95. Author: Barriers to Success, 1995-96; co-author: World of School 1995. Pres. parish coun. St. Peter's Ch. Coun., South Beloit, Ill., 1995-96. Named No. Ill. Tennis Coach of Yr., NIC 10-NIC 9 Coaches, 1983-92. Mem. ASCD, NEA, Ill. Edn. Assn., Ill. Tennis Coaches Assn., Hononegah Edn. Assn. (pres. 1994-97). Republican. Roman Catholic. Home: 6850 Heirloom Ct Roscoe IL 61073 Office: Hononegah H S 307 Salem Rockton IL 61072

MULHOLLAN, PAIGE ELLIOTT, academic administrator emeritus; b. Ft. Smith, Ark., Dec. 10, 1934; s. Paige Elwood and Ruth Dickinson (Berry) M.; m. Mary Bess Flack, July 8, 1956; children: Paige E. Jr., Kelly V. BBA, U. Ark., 1956, MA in History, 1962; PhD in History, U. Tex., 1966. From asst. to assoc. prof. history U. Ark., Fayetteville, 1963-70; assoc. dean arts and scis. Kans. State U., Manhattan, 1970-73; dean arts and scis. U. Okla., Norman, 1973-78; provost, v.p. acad. affairs Ariz. State U., Tempe, 1978-81, exec. v.p., 1981-85; pres. Wright State U., Dayton, Ohio, 1985-94; ret., 1994; cons. examiner North Ctrl. Assn., Chgo., 1972-94; chair Interuniv. Coun. Ohio, 1993-94. Mem. Okla. Humanities Com., 1974-77, chmn., 1975-77; bd. dirs. Pub. Sta. WPTD-TV, Dayton Art Inst., Miami Valley Rsch. Found.; mem. adv. com. Air Force ROTC, 1989-93. 1st lt. U.S. Army, 1956-57. Mem. nat. Assn. State Univs. and Land Grant Colls. (commn. on arts and scis. 1973-78, chmn. 1974-76), Am. Assn. State Colls. and Univs. (bd. dirs. 1991-92), Coun. Colls. Arts and Scis. (bd. dirs. 1976-78, sec.-treas. 1977-78), Dayton Area C. of C., Ohio Coll. Assn. (pres. 1989). Home: 24 Big Woods Dr Hilton Head Island SC 29926

MULHOLLAND, SUSAN COLLINS, archaeologist, researcher; b. Springfield, Mass., July 2, 1955; d. Irwin and Florence Mary (Jahn) Collins; m. Stephen Leigh Mulholland, Aug. 1, 1981. BA, Bridgewater State Coll., 1976; MS, U. Minn., 1979, PhD, 1987. Sr. scientist U. Minn., Duluth, 1987—. Jr. editor: Phytolith Systematics, 1992. Mem. Soc. for Am. Archaeology, Soc. of Profl. Archaeologists, Soc. for Phytolith Rsch. (pres. 1993), Sigma Xi. Office: U Minn 10 University Dr Duluth MN 55812

MULICH, STEVE FRANCIS, safety engineer; b. Kansas City, Mo., Apr. 23, 1934; s. Stephen Francis and Mary Margret (Mish) M.; m. m. Apr. 5, 1974 (div.); children: Michael Francis, Mischelle Marie, Merko Mathew, Cherie Regina, Michael Klaus, Gary John, Josette Marie. BS in Gen. Sci., U. Notre Dame, 1956. Phys. chemist high altitude combustion Army Rocket and Guided Missile Agy., Huntsville, Ala., 1957-59; ballistics facility mgr. Aerojet Gen. Corp., Sacramento, 1960-65; chief engr. minute man penetration aids MB Assoc., Bollinger Canyon, Calif., 1968-72; lab mgr. hazardous materials and ballistics Martin Marietta, Waterton, Colo., 1966-75; plant mgr. smog sampler collectors mfg. Gen. Tex. Corp., Santa Clara, Calif., 1976-77; chief engr. auto airbag plant mgr. Talley Industries, Mesa, Ariz., 1978-84; prin. engr., engring. unit mgr. high energy test labs. FMC Corp., Mpls., 1984-95; v.p. ops. NEI Corp., Rock Island, Ill., 1995—. Author: Solid Rocket Technology, 1967; inventor stun gun, combustion augemented plasma gun, semiconductor initiator. With U.S. Army, 1957-59. Recipient Acad. Achievement award Bausch & Lomb, Kenosha, Wis., 1952. Mem. IEEE, AIAA (assoc.), Am. Def. Preparedness Assn., Navy League. Home: 1325 104th Pl NE Minneapolis MN 55434-3620 Office: NEI Corp 4900 Wapello Rd Davenport IA 52802

MULL, SANDRA SUE, health, physical education and recreation educator; b. W. Frankfort, Ill., June 1, 1943; d. Henry Richard and Opal I (Gibbins) M. BA (cum laude), Lincoln Christian Coll., Lincoln, Ill., 1965; MA, Peabody Coll., Nashville, 1968. Elem. tchr. pvt sch., Toronto, Ont., Can., 1966-67; tchr. phys. edn. Metcalf Sch., Ill. State U., Normal, 1968-69; instr., then asst. prof. N.W. Mo. State U, Maryville, 1969—; coach gymnastic team N.W. Mo. State U., Maryville, 1969-79, also resource persons for drugs, nutrition and fitness; dir. community gymnastics and camp, 1975-85, gymnastic cons. for pub. schs. Contbr. articles to profl. jours. Bd. dirs., tchr., elder, area lay pastor 1st Christian Ch., 1973-95, bd. dirs., 1980-94, bd. moderator, 1992; active Sch. and Cmty. Drug Free Task Force, 1989-94, Wellness Works Task Force, 1994—. Mem. AAUW (bd. dirs., sec. 1990—), AAHPERD (spkr. nat., state and dist. convs., divsn. chair-elect health edn. of ctrl. dist., sect. chair health edn. divsn. ctrl. dist.), ASCD, Mo. AHPERD, Am. Sch. Health Assn. (spkr. nat., state and dist. convs.), U.S. Gymnastic Fedn., Soroptomists (sec. Maryville, Mo. chpt. 1975-85), Phi Delta Kappa. Mem. Christian Ch. Home: 720 W Cooper St Maryville MO 64468-2122 Office: Northwest Mo State U Martindale # 206 Maryville MO 64468

MULL, THERESA DIANE, physical therapist; b. Indpls., Nov. 17, 1962; d. William Michael Mull and Judith Gale (Kolp) Spurgeon. BS, Ind. U., 1988; M in Health Sci., U. Indpls., 1993. Lic. phys. therapist, Ind. Phys. therapist Advanced Phys. Therapy, Indpls., 1988-90, Ind. Ctr. for Rehab. Medicine, Indpls., 1990-93; dir. phys. therapy Libr. Pk. Rehab. Ctr., Greenwood, Ind., 1993-94; phys. therapy Rehab. Hosp. of Ind., Indpls., 1994—. Mem. Am. Phys. Therapy Assn. Office: Rehab Hosp of Indiana 4141 Shore Dr Indianapolis IN 46254

MULLALLY, PIERCE HARRY, retired steel company executive; b. Cleve., Oct. 6, 1918; s. Pierce Harry and Laura (Lynch) M.; student U. Western Ont., 1935; B.S., John Carroll U., 1939; M.D., St. Louis U., 1943; m. Mary Eileen Murphy, Feb. 22, 1943; children—Mary Kathleen, Pierce Harry. Intern, St. Vincent Charity Hosp., Cleve., 1943, resident in surgery, 1944, 47-50, staff surgeon, 1951-62, head peripheral vascular surgery, 1963-76, dir. med. edn., 1967-73, dir. dept. surgery, 1968-75, trustee, 1977-86 ; plant physician Republic Steel Corp., Cleve., 1952-68, med. dir., 1968-76, corp. dir. occupational medicine, 1976-84; cons. LTV Steel Co., 1984-86; med. dir., chmn. med. adv. bd. Ohio Health Choice Plan Inc. Vice-chmn. Cleve. Clinic-Charity Hosp. Com. Surg. Residency Tng., 1970-78; health com. Bituminous Coal Operators Assn.; trustee Wood Hudson Cancer Research Labs., Inc., 1984—; bd. dirs. Phoenix Theatre Ensemble, 1982-86. Served to capt. U.S. Army, 1944-46; PTO. Diplomate Am. Bd. Surgery. Fellow ACS, Am. Coll. Angiology; mem. Am. Iron and Steel Inst. (chmn. health com. 1977-79), Am. Acad. Occupational Medicine, Am., Ohio occupational med. assns., Acad. Medicine, Cleve. (dir. 1969-72), Cleve. Surg. Soc., Western Res. Med. Dirs., Soc. Clin. Vascular Surgery. Roman Catholic. Clubs: Cleve. Skating, Cleve. Playhouse, Serra. Home: 2285 Harcourt Dr Cleveland OH 44106-4614

MULLEN, THOMAS EDGAR, real estate consultant; b. Hackensack, N.J., Feb. 10, 1936; s. Luke B. and Jean (Edgar) M.; m. Sarah Lee Huff, Aug. 17, 1984. BS in Engring., Va. Poly. Tech., 1954; grad mgmt. program, Harvard U., 1964. Cons. in field. Mgr. mktg. Eastern Airlines, N.Y.C., 1954-69; pres. Profl. Sprits Mktg., N.Y.C., 1969-72, Shelter Devel. Corp. Am., N.Y.C., 1972-79; supr. ops. Gen. Mills, Orlando, Fla., 1980-86; cons., exec., realtor A.H.M. Graves Co. Inc., Indpls., 1986-92; pres. Pegasus Assocs. Ltd., 1992—. Inventor TV Guider Holder, patent, 1971. Fundraiser Am. Cancer Soc., Miami, 1967-70, Westchester Hosp., N.Y.C., 1967-70; pres. Brighton Found. Mem. Met. Bd. Realtors, Builders Assn. Greater Indpls. (bd. dirs.), Ind. Builders Assn. (bd. dirs.), Nat. Assn. Realtors, Inst. Residential Mktg. (pres. sales & mktg. coun., bd. dirs.). Republican. Roman Catholic. Home: 6251 Behner Way Indianapolis IN 46250-1494

MULLENAX, CHARLES HOWARD, veterinarian, researcher; b. Sterling, Colo., Feb. 5, 1932; s. Guy William and Evelyn Irene (Simpson) M.; m. Phyllis Jean Brown, June 11, 1954 (div. 1972); children: Mark David, Craig Collins, Jean Gail, Nancy Alba; m. Lidia Hincapie, Nov. 7, 1974. BS, Colo. State U., 1953, DVM, 1956; MS, Cornell U., 1961; diploma de honor, Ctrl. U., Quito, Ecuador, 1966. Cert. in epidemiology Ctrs. for Disease Control, USPHS. Owner Mt. Pks. Vet. Hosp., Evergreen, Colo., 1956-59; teaching and rsch. asst. Cornell U., Ithaca, N.Y., 1959-61; rsch. veterinarian Nat. Animal Disease Ctr., Agrl. Rsch. Svc., USDA, Ames, Iowa, 1961-64; Fulbright prof., dir. of clinics Ctrl. Univ., Quito, 1964-66; pathologist, tng. leader Rockefeller Found., Internat. Ctr. for Tropical Agriculture, Bogotá and Cali, Colombia, 1966-71; project dir., cons. World Bank, Washington, 1971-74; prof., rschr. Tech. U. Llanos, Villavicencio, Colombia, 1974-84; mem. acad. staff Univ. Calif. and Univ. Mo., 1985-87; rsch. assoc. Rural Devel. Inst., Univ. Wis., River Falls, 1988—; cons. Bahamas Livestock Co., Eleuthera, 1956-57, U.S. Agy. Internat. Devel., Washington, 1985-87; ofcl. rep. Colombian Ministry Agr., Bogotá, 1972-73, Livestock Prodrs. Assn. of Meta, Villavicencio, 1982-83. Contbr. more than 50 articles to sci. jours. Lay min. Presbyn. Bd. Nat. Missions, Lapwai, Idaho, 1955; pres. grad. student bd. Cornell U., 1960-61; pres. sch. bd. Am. Sch., Quito, 1965. Recipient Medal of Merit, Colombian Vet. Pharm. Inst. and Livestock Prodrs. Assn. of Meta, Bogotá, 1985. Mem. Soc. Tropical Vet. Medicine, N.Y. Acad. Scis., Internat. Soc. for Ecosys. Health. Home: N7003 710th St Beldenville WI 54003-5426

MULLER, H(ENRY) NICHOLAS, III, foundation executive; b. Pitts., Nov. 18, 1938; s. Henry N. Jr. and Harriet (Kerschner) M.; m. Nancy Clagett, June 20, 1959 (div. 1985); children: Charles T., Brook W.; m. Carol A. Cook, Jan. 4, 1986. BA, Dartmouth Coll., 1960; PhD, U. Rochester, 1968. Instr. Dartmouth Coll., Hanover, N.H., 1964; lectr. Mt. Allison U., Sackville, N.B., Can., 1964-66; asst. prof. history U. Vt., Burlington, 1966-69; assoc. prof. history, 1970-73; prof. history U. Vt., Burlington, 1974-78, asst. dean Coll. Arts and Scis., 1969-70, assoc. dean Coll. Arts and Scis., 1970-73, dir. Living/Learning Ctr., 1973-78; pres. Colby-Sawayer Coll., New London, N.H., 1978-85; dir. State His. Soc. Wis., Madison, 1985-96; pres., CEO Frank Lloyd Wright Found., Spring Green, Scottsdale, Wis. Ariz., 1996—; chmn. State Hist. Records Adv. Bd., 1985-96, Wis. Burial Sites Bd., 1988-96, Wis. Submerged Cultural Resources, 1993-96, Standex Internat. Corp., Salem, N.H., Nat. Trust for Hist. Preservation, 1989—; mem. Gov. Coun. on Tourism, 1987-96. Co-author: An Anxious Democracy, 1982; co-editor: Science, Technology and Culture, 1974, In a State of Nature, 1982; sr. editor Vt. Life mag., 1975-87; editor Vt. History, 1977-85. Chmn. Bicentennial Com., Burlington, 1976, Vt. Coun. Hist. Preservation, 1975-78; fin. chmn. Vt. Bicentennial Commn., 1970-77; mem. Wis. Sesquicentennial Commn., 1995—; mem. N.H. Postsecondary Edn. Commn., 1983-85; trustee Vt. Hist. Soc., 1972-85, v.p., 1975-82; bd. dirs. USS Wisconsin, 1989-93, Wis. Preservation Fund Inc., 1989—; trustee, vice chmn., sec. Taliesin Preservation Commn., 1990—. Fellow Ctr. for Rsch. on Vt.; mem. Nat. Coun. on Pub. History (bd. dirs. 1988-90), Am. Assn. State and Local History (councillor 1988-91), Vt. Archeol. Soc. (pres. 1971-74), Madison Club. Office: Frank Lloyd Wright Found Taliesin-West Scottsdale AZ 85261-4430 Other Office: Frank Lloyd Wright Found Taliesin Scottsdale AZ 85261

MULLER, MARCEL W(ETTSTEIN), electrical engineering educator; b. Vienna, Austria, Nov. 1, 1922; came to U.S., 1940; s. Georg and Josephine (David) M.; m. Esther Ruth Hagler, Feb. 2, 1947; children: Susan, George, Janet. BSEE, Columbia U., 1949, AM in Physics, 1952; PhD, Stanford U., 1957. Sr. scientist Varian Assocs., Palo Alto, Calif., 1952-66; prof. elec. engring. Washington U., St. Louis, 1966-91, prof. emeritus, rsch. prof., 1991—; vis. lectr. U. Zurich, Switzerland, 1962-63; vis. prof. U. Colo., Boulder, summer 1969; vis. scientist Max Planck Inst., Stuttgart, Fed. Republic of Germany, 1976-77; cons. Hewlett-Packard Labs., Palo Alto, 1985-89, SRI Internat., Menlo Park, Calif., 1986—. Sgt. U.S. Army, 1943-46. Recipient Humboldt prize Alexander von Humboldt Soc., 1976; Fulbright grantee, 1977, grantee NSF, 1967—. Fellow IEEE, Am. Physical Soc. Home: 4954 Lindell Blvd Saint Louis MO 63108-1500 Office: Washington Univ Campus Box 1127 1 Brookings Dr Saint Louis MO 63130-4862

MULLIGAN, ROSEMARY ELIZABETH, paralegal; b. Chgo., July 8, 1941; d. Stephen Edward and Rose Anne (Sannasardo) Granzyk; children: Daniel R. Bonaguidi, Matthew S. Bonaguidi. AAS, Harper Coll., Palatine, Ill., 1982; student, Ill. State U., 1959-60. Paralegal Miller, Forest & Downing Ltd., Glenview, Ill., 1982-91; ind. contractor mcpl. law, 1991—; paralegal seminar educator Harper Coll. Pro-choice activist and mem. Ill. Ho. of Reps., 1993—, chmn. human svcs. appropriations com.; gov.'s workgroup on early childhood. Recipient Disting. Alumnus award Ill. C.C. Trustee Assn., 1993, Legislator of Yr. award Ill. Assn. Cmty. Mental Health Agys., 1995, Heart Start award Nat. Ctr. Clin. Infant Programs. Mem. LWV, Ill. Paralegal Assn., Nat. Women's Polit. Caucus, Ill. Fedn. Bus. and Profl. Women, Ill. Women in Govt., Chgo. Women in Govt. Rels., Ill. Fedn. Bus. and Profl. Women (nat. legis. platform rep. 1991-92, chair Outstanding Working Women of Ill. 1991-92, state membership chair 1989-90, state legis. co-chair, nat. platform rep. 1988-89, state legis. chair, nat. platform rep. 1987-88). Roman Catholic. Home: 856 E Grant Dr Des Plaines IL 60016-6260 Office: Ill Ho of Reps State Capitol Springfield IL 62706 also: 932 Lee St Ste 204 Des Plaines IL 60016

MULLIKIN, THOMAS WILSON, mathematics educator; b. Flintville, Tenn., Jan. 9, 1928; s. Houston Yost and Daisy (Copeland) M.; m. Mildred Virginia Sugg, June 14, 1952; children—Sarah Virginia, Thomas Wilson, James Copeland. Student, U. South, 1946-47; A.B., U. Tenn., 1950; postgrad., Iowa State U., 1952-53; A.M., Harvard, 1954, Ph.D., 1958. Mathematician Rand Corp., Santa Monica, Calif., 1957-64; prof. math. Purdue U., 1964-93, interim v.p., dean grad. sch., 1991-93, dean grad. sch., prof. math emeritus, 1993—. Served with USNR, 1950-52. Mem. Am. Math. Soc., Soc. for Indsl. and Applied Math., AAAS, Sigma Xi. Home: Cape Carteret 104 Club Ct Swansboro NC 28584-9736

MULLINS, CONNIE RAE, school board executive; b. Neillsville, Wis., Aug. 26, 1948; d. Allen Oren and Lydia Agnes (Schlinsog) Montgomery ; m. Raymond Allen Mullins, Sept. 14, 1968; children: Tonya, Joel, Colette. Grad., high sch., 1966. Keypunch operator Am. Can Co., Neenah, Wis., 1966-70; owner Mullins Cheese Factory, Spencer, Wis., 1970-81; mem. sch. bd. Colby (Wis.) Sch. Dist., 1990-93, 94—; receptionist Clark-Marathon Vet. Clinic, Colby, 1992, Dr. R.G. Frank, 1992-93; owner The Colby Cheese Factory, 1993—; outreach corr. Nightsounds, 1987—; pub. spkr. Lions and Eye Bank, State of Wis., 1974—; music dir. Abbotsford (Wis.) Bible Ch., 1990-92; caretaker for elderly ladies, 1995—. Singer in gospel group Hope of Glory, 1986-89. Pres., sec., treas. Clark County Ext. Homemakers, 1976-87, family chmn., 1980; singer, announcer Clark County Choraliers, 1976-86, 91—; vol. Colby Sch. Dist., 1976—; music leader 4-H, Colby, 1981-88. Evangelical Christian.

MULLINS, JAMES LEE, library director; b. Perry, Iowa, Nov. 29, 1949; s. Kenneth Wiley and Lorene (Gift) M.; m. Kathleen Stiso, May 10, 1986; 1 stepchild, Michael Stiso. BA, U. Iowa, 1972, MA, 1973; PhD, Ind. U., 1984. Instr. Ga. So. U., Statesboro, 1973-74; assoc. law librarian Ind. U., Bloomington, 1974-78; dir. library Ind. U., South Bend, 1978-96; dir. Falvey Meml. Libr., Villanova U., 1996—. Contbr. articles to profl. publs. Mem. exec. com. South Bend Art Ctr., 1984-89; mem. Mayor's Task Force Redevel., South Bend, 1986; pres. Fischoff Nat. Chamber Music Assn., 1989-91, Gov. Conf. on Libr. Planning Com., 1989-91, Mich. Freenet bd., 1993—; pres. Ind. Coop. Libr. Svcs. Authority, 1993-94. Mem. ALA, Ind. Library Assn., Assn. Coll. and Research Libraries, Ind. Lib. Endowment Bd. (pres. 1988-91). Lodge: Rotary. Office: Falvey Meml Libr Villanova Univ 800 Lancaster Ave Villanova PA 19085-1699

MULLINS, MAIRE ELIZABETH, English language educator; b. Stamford, Conn., Dec. 17, 1960; d. Peter Francis and Harriet Bernice (Marsland) M.; m. Paul Joseph Contino, June 6, 1992. BA, U. Nev., 1983, MA, 1985; PhD, U. Notre Dame, 1990. Assoc. prof. St. Xavier U., Chgo., 1990—; Fulbright lectr. Tokyo Woman's Christian U., 1995-96, Tokyo Gakugei U., 1995-96. Editor: (jour.) Religion and Literature, 1989-90. Mem. MLA, AAUP, Nat. Coun. Tchrs. of English. Office: St Xavier U 3700 W 103d St Chicago IL 60655

MULLINS, RICHARD AUSTIN, chemical engineer; b. Seelyville, Ind., Apr. 22, 1918; s. Fred A. and Ethel (Zenor) M.; B.S. in Chem. Engring., Rose Poly. Inst., 1940; postgrad. Yale, 1942-43; m. Margaret Ann Dellacca, Nov. 27, 1946 (dec. Nov. 1982); children—Scott Alan, Mark Earl. Chemist, Ayrshire Collieries Corp., Brazil, Ind., 1940-49; chief chemist Fairview Collieries Corp., Danville, Ill., 1949-54; preparations mgr. Enos Coal Mining Co., Oakland City, Ind., 1954-72, Enoco Collieries, Inc., Bruceville, Ind., 1954-62; mining engr. Kings Station Coal Corp.; mgr. analytical procedures Old Ben Coal Corp., 1973-84; ret., 1984. Am. Mining Congress cons. to Am. Standards Assn. and Internat. Orgn. for Standards, 1960-74; mem. indsl. cons. com. Ind. Geol. Survey, 1958-72; mem. organizing com. 5th Internat. Coal Preparation Congress, Pittsburgh, 1966. Mem. exec. bd. Buffalo Trace council Boy Scouts Am., also mem. speakers bur. Bd. dirs. Princeton Boys Club. Served with AUS, 1942-46; ETO. Decorated Medaille de la France Liberee (France); recipient Eagle Scout award, Boy Scouts Am., 1935, Silver Beaver award, 1962, Wood Badge Beads award, 1960; Outstanding Community Svc. award Princeton Civitan Club, 1964; Engr. of Year award S.W. chpt. Ind. Soc. Profl. Engrs., 1965; Prince of Princeton award Princeton C. of C., 1981, Sagamore of the Wabash award Ind. gov. R.D. Orr, 1984. Registered profl. engr., Ind., Ill. Mem. AIME (life mem.), ASTM (sr. mem., R.A. Glenn award 1985), Am. Chem. Soc., Nat. Soc. Profl. Engrs. (life mem.), Ind., Ill. mining insts., Ind. Coal Soc. (pres. 1958-59), Am. Mining Congress (chmn. com. coal preparation 1964-68), Am. Legion (life, past county comdr.), VFW (life), 40 & 8 (life), Ind. Soc. Profl. Land Surveyors, Rose Tech. Alumni Assn. (pres. 1976-77, Honor Alumnus 1980), Order of Ring, Sigma Nu. Methodist (lay speaker). Mason, Elk. Contbr. articles to profl. jours. Home: RR 4 Box 310 Princeton IN 47670-9412

MULLINS, TERRI A., executive; b. Elgin, Ill., Apr. 28, 1965. BS in Psychology and Sociology, Regis U., 1987. V.p. Mullins and Assocs., Inc./ Syss. & Software Svcs., Inc./, Barrington, Ill., 1987—. Republican. Methodist. Office: Mullins and Assocs P O Box 887 Barrington IL 60011-0887

MULQUEEN, ROBERT EDWARD, public policy analyst; b. Council Bluffs, Iowa, Aug. 13, 1947; s. James Fearon and Kathryn (Moes) M. BA in History, Creighton U., Omaha, nebr., 1972; MPA, Iowa State U., 1982. VISTA vol. U.S. Office Econ. Opportunity, Duquesne, Pa., 1969-70; legis. corres. U.S. Senator Dick Clark, Washington, 1973-75; mem. legis. staff Iowa Senate, Des Moines, 1976; dist. field staff U.S. rep. Tom Harkin, Council Bluffs and Ames, Iowa, 1976-82; campaign mgr. Appel for Congress, Dubuque, Iowa, 1982; adminstrv. asst. to pres. Creighton Prep, Omaha, 1983; devel. officer Archdiocese of Omaha Schs., 1986-88; pub. policy analyst Iowa State Assn. of Counties, Des Moines, 1988—. Author mo. col. "Around the Statehouse" in The Iowa County, 1988—. Bd. dirs. Cath. Cmty. Credit Union, Council Bluffs, 1979-80; mem. Iowa Rural Devel. Coun., Des Moines, 1992—; del. Dem. Nat. Conv., Atlanta, 1988; county chair Pottowattamie County Dem. Party, Council Bluffs, 1988. Mem. Am. Planning Assn., Iowa Groundwater Assn., Cmty. Devel. Soc. Iowa (bd. dirs. 1995—). Roman Catholic. Office: Iowa State Assn of Counties 701 E Court Ave Des Moines IA 50309

MULQUEEN, SCOTT CHARLES, transportation executive; b. Cudahy, Wis., Nov. 28, 1956; s. Michael Thomas and Lois Jane (Detlaff) M.; m. Donna Janet Schulz, Jan. 15, 1977; children: David Joseph, Jennifer Janet. Logistics planner Tandem Transport, Inc., Milw.; terminal mgr. Packerland Transport, Milw.; v.p. ops. Flexible Transport, Inc., Cudahy, Wis.; sr. cons. SCM Cons., Ltd., Cudahy. Alderman City of Cudahy, 1986-90, chmn. Bd. Pub. Wks., 1988-90, chmn. traffic and safety com., 1986-90; dir., treas. Sch. Dist. of Cudahy, 1993—. Mem. Delta Nu Alpha.

MULROW, PATRICK JOSEPH, medical educator; s. Patrick J. and Delia (O'Keefe) M.; m. Jacquelyn Pinover, Aug. 8, 1953; children: Deborah, Nancy, Robert, Catherine. AB, Colgate U., 1947; MD, Cornell U., 1951; MSc (hon.), Yale U., 1969. Intern N.Y. Hosp., 1951-52, resident, 1952-54; instr. physiology Med. Coll. Cornell U., 1954-55; research fellow Stanford U., 1955-57; instr. medicine Yale U., 1957-60, asst. prof., 1960-66, assoc. prof., 1966-69, prof. medicine, 1969-75; chmn. dept. medicine Med. Coll. Ohio, Toledo, 1975-95, prof. medicine, 1975—; chmn. ednl. com. Council for high blood pressure rsch. Am. Heart Assn., 1968-70, mem. exec. com., 1986—, vice-chmn. of coun., 1990-92, chmn. 1992-94, past chmn., 1995—; mem. study sect. NIH, 1970-74. Editorial bd. Jour. Clin. Endocrinology and Metabolism, 1966-70, 75-79, Endocrine Rsch., 1974—, Jour. Exptl. Biology and Medicine, Hypertension, 1994—; contbr. articles to profl. jours. With USNR, 1944-46. Mem. ACP, Am. Soc. Clin. Investigation, Assn. Am. Physicians, Am. Physiol. Soc., Endocrine Soc., Am. Fedn. Clin. Rsch., Am. Clin. and Climatol. Assn., Am. Heart Assn. (nat. rsch. com., chmn. cardiovasc. regulation rsch. study com. 1986-91), Assn. Profs. Medicine, Assn. Program Dirs. in Internal Medicine, Cen. Soc. Clin. Rsch. (pres. 1988-89), Internat. Soc. Hypertension, World Hypertension League (sec.-gen. 1995—), Inter-Am. Soc. Hypertension, Sigma Xi (pres. Yale chpt. 1965-66), Alpha Omega Alpha. Home: 9526 Carnoustie Rd Perrysburg OH 43551-3501 Office: Med Coll of Ohio Dept of Medicine PO Box 10008 Toledo OH 43699-0008

MUNCEY, BARBARA DEANE, university official, consultant; b. Welch, W.Va., July 12, 1952; d. Juan Irvin and June Henryetta (Dowse) M. AB, Marshall U., Huntington, W.Va., 1974; postgrad., U. Ill., 1980; postgrad, U. Mich, 1984-85; postgrad., U. Oklahoma, 1987; MA, Western Mich. U., 1994. Asst. dir. Heartside Neighborhood Assn., Grand Rapids, Mich., 1979-80, Muncey Devel. Corp., Grand Rapids, Mich., 1979-80; coord. Northeast Mich. Econ. Devel. Assn., Gayland, Mich., 1980-81; dir. of econ. devel. Grand Rapids Internat Tribal Coun., Mich., 1984-86; dir. Sterling Indsl. Devel. Com., Ill., 1986-89; pres. Muncey Cons. Svcs., 1989-90; grad. asst. coord. Office Field Experiences, Western Mich. U., Kalamazoo, 1990-93; mem. grad. studies coun., grad. curriculum com. Western Mich. U., 1992-93, mem. com. to adviser pres. on acad. affairs, 1993; v.p. Sauk Valley Area Econ. Devel. Assn., 1989-90; mem. Whiteside County Regional Planning Commn., 1987-90. Mem. Rep. Women's Club. Mem. NAFE, Am. Econ. Devel. Coun., Ill. Devel. Coun., Mich. Indsl. Devel. Coun., Mid-Am. Econ. Devel. Coun., Phi Kappa Phi. Baptist. Office: Western Mich U The Grad Coll Grad Student Adv Com Kalamazoo MI 49008-5121

MUNCY, MARTHA ELIZABETH, retired newspaper publisher; b. Dodge City, Kans., Nov. 5, 1919; d. Jess C. and Juliet Mildred (Pettijohn) Denious.; m. Howard E. Muncy, June 5, 1943 (div. 1969); children: Martha Juliet, Suzanne M. Kerr, Howard E. Jr. Student, Lindenwood Coll. for Women, 1937-38; BA, U. Kans., 1941. Advt. mgr. Dodge City Broadcasting Co., 1942-43, copywriter, 1944-46, pres., 1973-88; saleswoman Boot Hill Mus., Inc., Dodge City, 1963; pub., pres. Dodge City Daily Globe, 1973-88. Mem. Kans. Cavalry, Topeka, 1976—; bd. dirs. Arrowhead West, Inc., Dodge City, 1976-90, Dodge City Roundup, Inc., 1976-89, Dodge City Crimestoppers, 1985—; bd. dirs., sec. Ford County Hist. R.R. Preservation and Found., Dodge City, 1984-90; trustee William Allen White Found., Lawrence, Kans., 1984—. Recipient Outstanding Service award Dodge City Lions, 1981; named Kans. Outstanding Rehab. vol. Kans. Rehab. Assn., 1985. Mem. AAUW, Kans. Press Women (Woman of Achievement award 1984), S.W. Kans. PressWomen, Dodge City Media Pros, Dodge City Women's C. of C. (Athena award 1989), Dodge City C. of C., The Philomaths, DAR, PEO, Salvation Army Aux., Sigma Delta Chi, Kappa Alpha Theta. Republican. Presbyterian. Home: 511 Annette St Dodge City KS 67801-2811

MUNDSCHAU, MICHAEL VICTOR, chemist; b. Milw., Mar. 15, 1955. BS in Chemistry, U. Wis., Milw., 1977, PhD in Chemistry, 1986. Rsch. assoc. Tech. U. Clausthal, Clausthal-Zellerfeld, Fed. Republic Germany, 1986-89; rsch. scientist Fritz Haber Inst., Berlin, 1989-91; asst. prof. Bowling Green State U., 1992—. Contbr. articles to profl. jours. Fellow Alexander von Humboldt Found., Bonn, Fed. Republic Germany, 1986. Mem. Am. Chem. Soc., Am. Phys. Soc., Am. Vacuum Soc., Materials Rsch. Soc., Metals Soc. Office: Bowling Green State U Crt Phorochem Sci Bowling Green OH 43403-0213

MUNGER, HAROLD HAWLEY, II, city engineer; b. Manila, Nov. 28, 1947; s. Elmer Lewis and Vivian Marie (Bloomfield) M.; m. Judith Ann Stacy, Aug. 27, 1977; children: Stacy J., Michelle A., Karrie R. Student, Norwich U., 1966-68; BSCE, Kans. State U., 1970. Registered profl. engr. Kans., Colo.; registered land surveyor Kans. Survey party instr. Vt. Hwy. Dept., Montpelier, 1968; design engr. Wilson & Co. Engrs., Salina, Kans., 1975-80; office mgr. Wilson & Co. Engrs., Hays, Kans., 1980-85; asst. city engr. City of Hutchinson (Kans.), 1985-87, city engr., 1987—. Mem. exec. bd. Pioneer Country Devel. Inc., Hill City, Kans., 1980-85, v.p., 1984-85; mem. exec. bd. Northwestern Kans. Planning and Devel., Hill City, 1984-85. Capt. U.S. Army, 1971-75. Mem. NSPE, Water Pollution Control Fedn., Am. Water Works Assn., Am. Pub. Works Assn., Kans. Engring. Soc. (membership chmn. 1987-88, bd. dirs. 1992—), Appaloosa Horse Club, Am. Quarter Horse Assn. Office: City of Hutchinson PO Box 1567 125 E Ave B Hutchinson KS 67501

MUNGER, WILLARD, state legislator; b. Jan. 11; m. Frances Munger; two children. Student, U. Minn. Motel owner; Dist. 7A rep. Minn. Ho. of Reps., St. Paul, 1955-65, 67—; former food sect. chief Off Price Stabilization; former mem. mkt. inspection svc. Dairy and Food Divsn. State of Minn.

Dept. Agr. and State Grain Inspection Svc.; former mem. Water Pollution Control Adv. Commn.; chmn. environ. and natural resources com., mem. appropriations, rules and legis. adminstrn., and energy coms., Minn. Ho. of Reps. Office: 479 State Office Bldg Saint Paul MN 55155*

MUNOZ, MARIO ALEJANDRO, civil engineer, consultant; b. Havana, Cuba, Feb. 27, 1928; s. Ramón and Concepción (Bermudo) M.; came to U.S., 1961, naturalized, 1968; M.Arch., U. Havana, 1954; postgrad. City Colls. Chgo., 1974, U. Wis., 1974; m. Julia Josephine Garrofe, Jan. 17, 1970. Owner, Muñoz Bermudo-Construcciones, Havana, 1954-61; designer various cos., Chgo., 1961-65; designer Chgo. Transit Authority, Mdse. Mart, Chgo., 1965-69; civil engr. Dept. Water and Sewers, City of Chgo., 1969-79, supervising engr. Dept. of Sewers, 1979-85, coordinating engr., 1985-88, asst. chief engr., 1988-93; mem. central area subway system utilities com. City of Chgo., 1974-93 , mem. computer graphics com., 1977-78. Mem. Am. Pub. Works Assn., Western Soc. Engrs., Chgo. Architecture Found., Theodore Thomas Soc. Chgo. Symphony, Chgo. Council Fgn. Rels., Am. Mgmt. Assn., Ground Hog Club, Execs. Club (mem. speaker's table com.), Polo and Equestrian Club of Oak Brook. Roman Catholic. Home: 5455 N Sheridan Rd Apt 1912 Chicago IL 60640-1933

MUÑOZ, ROMEO SOLANO, audio visual curator, educator; b. Daraga, Philippines, July 2, 1933; s. Maximo M. and Fe (Solano) M.; married, Jan. 2, 1964; children: Francis Vincent, Theresa Lourdes, Romualdo Romeo, Maria Cecilia, Anafe, Stephen Ignatius. BA in Psychology, Letran Coll., Manila, 1965; MS, Ea. Ill. U., 1968; MA, Gov.'s State U., 1989; EdD, No. Ill. U., 1995. Audio visual curator Ateneo U., Quezon City, Philippines, 1962-67; audio visual dir. Olive-Harvey Coll., Chgo., 1969—; assoc. prof. City Coll. Chgo., 1969—; cons. adminstrv. svcs., fin. City Coll. Bd. Trustees, Chgo., 1988—. Del. AFL/CIO, Chgo., 1989, 90; deacon Archdiocese Chgo. Roman Cath. Ch., 1976—, Professed Secular Franciscan; trustee Calumet City Libr., 1993. Recipient fellowship Ea. Ill. U., Charleston, 1967-68, So. Ill. U., Carbondale, 1968-70, Gov.'s State U., Univ. Park, Ill., 1981-84. Mem. ALA, Gov.'s State U. Alumni (bd. dirs.), Philippine Hist. Soc., Phi Delta Kappa (v.p. 1992—). Home: 383 Hoxie Ave Calumet City IL 60409-2330 Office: Olive-Harvey Coll 10001 S Woodlawn Ave Chicago IL 60628-1645

MUNRO, ROBERT ALLAN, lawyer; b. Kearney, Nebr., June 16, 1932; s. George Allan and Alta Susan (Corn) M.; m. Patricia Lee Purcell, Apr. 29, 1961; children: Michael Duncan, Diane Purcell. Student Harvard U., 1950-53; B.S., U. Nebr., 1957, J.D., 1957. Bar: Nebr. 1957, U.S. Dist. Ct. Nebr. 1957, U.S. Ct. Appeals (8th cir.) 1975, U.S. Tax Ct. 1967. Assoc. Munro & Parker, Kearney, 1957-60; county atty. Buffalo County, Kearney, 1959-63; ptnr. Munro & Munro (and predecessor firms), Kearney, 1960-75, sr. ptnr., 1975—; dir. The RAM Co., Kearney, 1982—, Husker Hostelries, Inc., Kearney, 1983—. Contbr. wildlife photos to jours. Sec., dir. Kearney Conv. Ctr. Inc., 1963—, pres., dir. 1983—; chmn. Buffalo County Young Reps., 1958-62; co-chmn. Gov.'s Adv. Com. on Drug and Alcohol Abuse, 1980-84; bd. dirs. Nebr. Art Collection Found., 1984—, mem. exec. com., 1986-95, sec. 1989-95; trustee Nebr. State Hist. Soc. Found., 1993—. Mem. ABA, ATLA, Nebr. Assn. Trial Attys., Buffalo County Bar Assn., (pres. 1964), Cen. Nebr. Bar Assn. (pres. 1970-71), Nat. Trust Hist. Preservation, Smithsonian Assocs., Friends of Music, Nebr. Bar Assn. (chmn. com. on ethics 1972-73), Am. Arbitration Assn. (panel arbitrators 1974—), Nebr. Diplomats, Kearney Country Club, Masons, Shriners, Knights of Malta. Presbyterian. Home: 2915 5th Ave Kearney NE 68847-3423 Office: Munro & Munro PC 220 W 15th St PO Box 2375 Kearney NE 68848

MUNRO, RODERICK ANTHONY, quality assurance professional, human performance technologist; b. Toronto, Ont., Can., Jan. 16, 1955; s. William George and Georgina Antoniette (Schembri) M.; m. Elizabeth J. Rice, 1993; came to U.S., 1956. BA, Adrian Coll., 1979, secondary provisional cert., 1981; MS, Eastern Mich. U., 1984; postgrad., Wayne State U. Instrnl. Tech., 1993—. Cert. quality engr., quality auditor, hypnotherapist, quality examiner, quality mgr. Tchr. Lincoln Park High Sch., Mich., 1980-82; mgmt. trainee Fabricon Automotive, River Rouge, Mich., 1982-84; statis. process control coord. ASC, Inc., Southgate, Mich., 1984-86; quality svcs. coord. container div. Johnson Controls, Inc., Manchester, Mich., 1987-88; program dir. Ford Motor Co., Dearborn, Mich., 1988—; cons. in field, 1986—; adj. faculty quality classes Henry Ford Community Coll. Served to sgt. USMCR, 1974-80. Fellow Am. Soc. Quality Control (cert., past chmn. Greater Detroit sect., past chair human resources div., Testimonial award 1988, Disting. Svc. award 1989); mem. ASTD, Internat. Assn. Counselors and Therapists (cert.), Aircraft Owners and Pilots Assn., Am. Statis. Assn., Internat. Soc. for Performance Improvement, Assn. Quality and Participation, Deming Study Group Greater Detroit. Home: 3966 Catalpa Dr Berkley MI 48072-1043

MUNSON, BRUCE N., state legislator. BS, Ball State U.; JD, Ind. U., Indpls. Bar: Ind. Atty. in pvt. practice; mem. from 35th dist. Ind. State Ho. of Reps., 1992—, mem. aged and aging com., commerce and econ. devel. com., mem. family, children and human affairs coms. Bd. dirs. Century Legal Svc. Program; mem. lega. adv. com. Habitat for Humanity. Mem. Century City Bus. Assn., Dalaware County Rep. Men's Club, Kiwanis, Century Ind. Old Car Club. Home: 2710 W Burgewood Dr Muncie IN 47304-2625*

MUNSON, DAVID ROY, state legislator; b. Sioux Falls, S.D., Apr. 16, 1942; s. Roy Elmer Munson and Theil Severson; m. Linda Marie Carlson, 1972; children: Steven David, Paul James, John Jeffrey. BA, Sioux Falls Coll.; postgrad., Augustana Coll. Mem. S.D. Ho. of Reps., 1979—, asst. majority whip, 1983-84, 89-90, mem. commerce and health and human svc. coms.; vice chmn. state affairs com., banker; mem. commerce, labor and regulation coms., state-fed. assembly Nat. Conf. State Legislators. Past mem. Sioux Vocat. Bd.; mem. Multiple Sclerosis Bd., Luth. Social Svc. Consumers Credit Adv. Bd. and Cmty. Disabilities Svc. Bd.; mem. S.D. Devel. Corp.; mem. Sioux Empire Fire Bd. Fellow Augustana Coll. Mem. NEA. Home: 1009 S Lyndale Ave Sioux Falls SD 57105-0233*

MUNSON, DONALD E., state legislator. Mem. S.D. Ho. of Reps.; mem. govt., oper. and audit, taxation and transp. coms., corp. mgr., acct. Home: 2012 Ross St Yankton SD 57078-1851*

MUNSON, NORMA FRANCES, biologist, ecologist, nutritionist, educator; b. Stockport, Iowa, Sept. 22, 1923; d. Glenn Edwards and Frances Emma (Wilson) M.; BA, Concordia Coll., 1946; MA, U. Mo., 1955; PhD (NSF fellow 1957-58, Chgo. Heart Assn. fellow 1959), Pa. State U., 1962; postgrad. Ind. U., 1957, Western Mich. U., 1967, Lake Forest Coll., 1971, 72, 78; student various fgn. univs., 1964-71. Tchr., Aitkin (Minn.) H.S., 1946-48, Detroit Lakes (Minn.) H.S., 1948-54, Libertyville (Ill.) H.S., 1955-79; rschr. Nutrition, Arthritis, Alzheimer's, Hypoglycemia and Multiple Sclerosis, Libertyville, 1965—; lectr. counseling and nutrition. Author biology lab. manual; contbr. articles to profl. jours. Ruling elder 1st Presbyn. Ch., Libertyville, 1971-77; pres. Lake County Audubon Soc., 1975-79, 82-86, 88-89, treas., 1990—; pres. Libertyville Edn. Assn., 1964-67, news editor Lake County Audubon Newsletter, 1972-96; active Rep. Party Ill., Citizens to Save Butler Lake, Citizens Choice, Defenders; mem. U.S. Congl. Adv. Bd., 1985—; bd. dirs. Holy Land Christian Mission Internat.; mem. Heritage Found., Citizens Lake County for Environ. Action Reform, Wilderness Soc. Recipient Hilda Mahling award, 1967, C. of C. award, 1971, Ill. Best Tchr. award, 1974; Biology Tchr. of Yr. award, 1971; NSF fellow, 1957, 58, 60-62, 70-71. Fellow Am. Biog. Inst. Rsch., Internat. Biog. Assn.; mem. Nat. Biology Tchrs. Assn. (rsch. in degenerate diseases, award 1971), AAAS, Am. Inst. Biol. Sci., Ill. Environ. Coun., Nat. Audubon Soc., Ill. Audubon Coun., Nat. Health Fedn., Internat. Platform Assn., Internat. Profl. and Bus. Women, Nat. Wildlife Fedn., N.Y. Acad. Scis., Chgo. Acad. Sci., Parks and Conservation Assn., Concerned Women for Am. Nature Conservation, Evanston North Shore Bird Club, Delta Kappa Gamma. Home and Office: 206 W Maple Ave Libertyville IL 60048-2174

MUNSON, ROBERT DEAN, agronomist, soil scientist; b. Stockport, Iowa, Mar. 14, 1927; s. Glenn Edward and Frances Emma (Wilson) M.; m. Mary Jane Miesen, Dec. 23, 1950; children: Anthony Kirby, Susan Lee, John Simpkin. BS, U. Minn., Mpls., 1951; MS, Iowa State U., 1954, PhD, 1957; postgrad., U. Minn., St. Paul, 1965. Cert. profl. agronomist, soil scientist. Agrl. economist TVA, Knoxville, 1957-58; agronomist Am. Potash Inst., St. Paul, 1958-64, Midwest dir., 1964-76; North Cen. dir. Potash and Phosphate Inst., St. Paul, 1976-86; cons. St. Paul, 1987-95; project assoc. Ctr. Internat. Food and Agrl. Policy U. Minn., St. Paul, 1990-91; v.p. rsch., edn. and mktg. devel. Nat. Fertilizer Solutions Assn. and Fluid Fertilizer Found., Manchester, Mo., 1991-92; adj. prof. soil, water and climate U. Minn., St. Paul, 1987—; project scientist Internat. Fertilzer Devel. Ctr., Muscle Shoals, Ala., 1979; lectr. on soil fertility and plant nutrition Acads. of Agrl. Sci., China, 1985, 91; hon. dir. Minn. Plant Food and Chems. Assn., 1991-93; bd. dirs. Soil and Plant Analysis Coun., 1991-93; cons. Internat. Fertilizer Devel. Ctr./Dhaka Bangladesh Project, 1993. Editor: Potassium in Agriculture, 1985; co-editor: Moving Off the Yield Plateau, 1971; editl. bd. Comms. in Soil Science and Plant Analysis, 1970-96, Soil Sci. Soc. Am. Jour., 1981-82, Jour. Potassium Rsch., 1985-90; assoc. editor Jour. Agronomic Edn., 1971-72; contbr. chpts. to books and articles to profl. jours. Mem. state cen. com. Minn. Rep. Orgn. Recipient Merit Cert. award Am. Forage and Grass Coun., 1983. Fellow AAAS, Am. Soc. Agronomy (Agronomy Svc. award, 1970, Werner L. Nelson award, 1990, bd. dirs., chair fertilizer tech. divsn.), Crop Sci. Soc. Am., Soil Sci. Soc. Am.; bd. dirs., chair extension agronomy divsn.; Minn. Forage and Grassland Coun. (organizing dir. vice pres, 1976, pres. 1977, Outstanding Svc. award), Minn. Fertilizer Industry Assn. (sec. 1959-62), Minn. Plant Food Assn. (sec. 1962-63, pres. 1963-65, prog. tech. advisor 1965-72, valuable and devoted svc. hon.), Minn. Agr.-Growth Coun. (organizing dir., initial sec. and bd. dirs.), Minn. Plant Food and Chems. Assn. (Dedicated Svc. award 1986), Wis. Fertilizer and Chem. Assn. (recognition for meritorious work related to soil fertility mgmt. 1986), U. Minn. Coll. of Agr. Alumni Soc. (Outstanding Alumnus award 1990), Wis. Fertilizer Assn. (organizing dir., v.p.1962-63), Internat. Soil Sci. Soc., Coun. Agrl. Sci. and Tech., Minn. Assn. Profl. Soil Scientists, FarmHouse, Sigma Xi, Gamma Sigma Delta, Alpha Zeta. Republican. United Methodist. Home: 2147 Doswell Ave Saint Paul MN 55108-1731

MUNSON, VIRGINIA ALDRICH, interior designer, decorator; b. Evanston, Ill., Oct. 10, 1932; d. Jefferson Elliott and Catherine (Stinson) Aldrich; m. John Chester Munson, Feb. 4, 1956; children: Catherine, John Jr., Laura. AA, Bennett Junior Coll., 1952. Owner, pres. Virginia Munson Interiors, Lake Forest, Ill., 1967—. Mem. Lake Forest Ctr. Infant Welfare Soc., 1957-93, pres., 1976-78; active com. candidates caucus, Lake Forest, 1984-87; mem. women's bd. Lake Forest Hosp., 1977—, Guild of Chgo. Hist. Soc., 1990—; bd. dirs. Infant Welfare Soc. Chgo., 1967-93; Ill. Regent Gunston Hall, 1988—. Mem. Am. Soc. Interior Designers (allied 1989—), Nat. Soc. Colonial Dames Am. (pres. State of Ill. br. 1982-84), Soc. Mayflower Descendants, Contemporary Club, Onwentsia Club, Winter Club. Republican. Episcopalian.

MUNZINGER, JUDITH MONTGOMERY, investment executive; b. Dayton, Ohio, June 16, 1944; d. Russell Eric and Margaret Lois (Weltzheimer) Montgomery; m. John Stephen Munzinger, May 28, 1977; children—Laurie Anne, Lisa Michelle. B.S. in Edn., Ohio State U., 1966, M.A., 1979, cert. remedial reading, 1980. Cert. tchr., Iowa. Tchr. elem. sch., Lafayette, Ind., 1966-69, Hilliard, Ohio, 1976-79; remedial reading tchr. Sioux City, Iowa, 1979-82; instr., dir. early childhood devel. Briar Cliff Coll.; talented and gifted coordinator, Sioux City, 1982-85; investment exec. Piper Jaffray, Sioux City, 1985—, asst. v.p., 1993; owner Elan Arabians, 1986—. Treas. Siouxlanders for Talented and Gifted; mem. Coalition for Children; judge for Iowa Future Problem Solving Bowl, 1982; sustainer Jr. League; mem. vestry, clk. St. Thomas Episcopal Ch., 1982-84; mem. Children's Hosp. support group, Columbus, Ohio, 1972-79; active Women's Assn. for Columbus Zoo, 1973-76, PTA; asst. Girl Scouts U.S.A., 1980-82.; co-chmn. Sioux City Symphony Debutante Ball, 1990, chmn., 1991. Recipient Service commendation Girl Scouts U.S.A., 1980. Mem. Internat. Arabian Horse Assn., Nat. Show Horse Assn., Ohio State U. Alumni Assn., Delta Zeta. Republican. Home: 3301 W 52nd St Sioux City IA 51108-9502 Office: Piper Jaffray 700 4th St Ste 100 Sioux City IA 51101

MURAD, TARIQ, surgical pathologist; b. Karbala'a, Iraq, July 28, 1936; came to U.S., 1962; s. Mohammed and Faida (Al-Soufi) M.; m. Nijood Al Sharif, Sept. 1, 1969; children: Faris, Laith, Nadia. MD, U. Baghdad, 1959; PhD, Ohio State U., 1967. Instr., pathology Ohio State U., Columbus, 1965-67; asst. prof. Ohio State U., 1967-71, assoc. prof., dir. cytopathology, 1971-72; prof. pathology, dir. surg. path. and cytology U. Ala., Birmingham, 1972-82; dir. surgical pathology Northwestern Meml. Hosp., Chgo., 1982-91; prof. pathology Northwestern U. Med. Sch., Chgo., 1982-91; dir. anatomic pathology St. John's Hosp., Springfield, Ill., 1991-96; pathologist Good Shepherd Hosp., Barrington, Ill., 1996—. Contbr. over 80 papers to scientific jours. Mem. Am. Assn. Pathologists Bacteriologists, Internat. Acad. Pathology, Internat. Acad. Cytology, Internat. Soc. Gynecology Pathology. Office: Good Shepherd Hospital 450 W Hwy 22 Barrington IL 60010-1901

MURARKA, NARAYAN P., electronics engineer, engineering executive; b. Calcutta, India, Oct. 7, 1938; s. Misri L. and Moni Bai (Khemka) M.; m. Usha Kanodia, Jan. 22, 1972; children: Monica, Naveen N. BS in Physics, U. Calcutta, India, 1959, B. Tech., 1961, M. Tech., 1962; PhD, U. Birmingham, Eng., 1968; MBA, U. Chgo., 1980. With ITT Rsch. Inst., Chgo., 1969-73, sr. engr., 1973-77, mgr., 1977-84, dir., 1984-88, v.p., 1988-93, sr. sci. adv., 1993-95; pres. Mutronix, Inc., Hoffman Estates, Ill., 1995—. Contbr. articles to profl. jours.; patentee for rugate optical filter sys. Mem. (sr.) IEEE (publicity chmn. Chgo. sect., 1995—), Am. Vacuum Soc., Assn. Old Crows, Soc. Photo Instrumentation Engrs., Optical Soc. Am. Home: 1485 Ashley Rd Hoffman Estates IL 60195 Office: Mutronix Inc 1485 Ashley Rd Hoffman Estates IL 60195

MURASKI, ANTHONY AUGUSTUS, lawyer; b. Cohoes, N.Y., July 28, 1946; s. Adam Joseph and Angeline Mary (Vozzy) M.; m. Janice Kay Selberg, Nov. 25, 1978; children: Adam Peter, Emily Jo. BA, MA in Speech/Hearing, Sacramento State Coll., 1970; PhD in Audiology/ Hearing Sci., U. Mich., 1977; JD, Detroit Coll. Law, 1979. Bar: Mich. 1980, U.S. Dist. Ct. (ea. dist.) Mich. 1981, U.S. Ct. Appeals (6th cir.) 1982, U.S. Claims Ct. 1989, U.S. Supreme Ct. 1990, Pa. 1990. Asst. Kresge Hearing Research Inst. U. Mich., Ann Arbor, 1971-77; asst. prof. Wayne State U. Med. Sch., Detroit, 1979-82; assoc. Kitch, Suhrheinrich, Saurbier & Drutchas, Detroit, 1982-83; assoc. prof. Detroit Coll. Law, 1983-85; mng. ptnr. Muraski & Sikorski, Ann Arbor, 1985—; cons. audiology Ministry of Environment, Ont., Can., 1980-81; trustee Deaf, Speech and Hearing Ctr., Detroit, 1981—; legal adv. on air WWJ Radio, Detroit, 1984—; mem. mental health adv. bd. on deafness Dept. Mental Health, 1984, vis. com. U. Mich. Sch. Edn., 1986—. Author: Legal Aspects of Audiological Practice, 1982, Hearing Conservation in Industry: Licensure, Liability and Forensics, 1985. Mem. ABA, Mich. Bar Assn., Washtenaw County Bar Assn., Am. Speech-Lang.-Hearing Assn. (sci. merit award, 1981), Ann Arbor C. of C. Home: 1603 Westminster Pl Ann Arbor MI 48104-4358 Office: Muraski & Sikorski 3300 Washtenaw Ave Ste 240 Ann Arbor MI 48104-4200

MURAT, WILLIAM M., state legislator; b. Stevens Point, Wis., Dec. 4, 1957; s. James L. and Rose (Hanson) M. BS, U. Wis., Stevens Point, 1980, MD, 1983; MBA, Columbia U. From asst. dist. atty. to dist. atty. Portage County, Wis., 1988-91; assemblyman Wis. State Dist. 71, 1995—; vice chmn. Portage County Dem. Com., 1976-80, chmn., 1985—; exec. dir. Wis. Young Dems., 1978-79, pres., 1982-83; mem. exec. com. Seventh Dist. Dems., Wis., 1978-80, 82—; adminstrv. com. Wis. Dem. Com., 1982—. Mem. Phi Delta Phi, Pi Kappa Delta. Address: 1540 Plover St Stevens Point WI 54481

MURCH, EVERETT LLOYD, manufacturing executive; b. Springfield, Vt., June 10, 1935; s. Harold Leslie and Cleone Christine (Lloyd) M.; m. Ann Marie Conlon (div. Aug. 1981); children: Robert, Richard, Amy, Kevin; m. Carol Jean Sloane, Oct. 23, 1981. BA in Journalism, Syracuse (N.Y.) U., 1957; MS in Journalism, Northwestern U., 1959. Rewrite man Phila. Inquirer, 1961; with GE, 1961-63, 66—; mgr. Ohio pub. affairs GE, Columbus, 1973-86, mgr. Ea. Great Lakes region state govt. rels., 1986—; employee communications specialist Gen. Electric Credit, N.Y.C., 1963-64; Asst. dir. pub. rels. AICPA, 1964-66. Author: chpt. Winning at the Grass Roots, 1988. Chmn. Unemployment Compensation adv. Commn., Columbus, 1991-93; chmn. Ohio Pub. Expenditure Coun., Columbus, 1988-90. Mem. Govt. Affairs Soc. Ind., Gt. Lakes Govtl. Affairs Coun., South Western Ohio Pub. Affairs Group, Ohio Mfrs. Assn. (com. chmn. 1985-87), Ohio C. of C. (exec. com.), Capital Club, Univ. Club, Little Turtle Country Club, Order of Ohio Commodores. Presbyterian. Home: 4764 Crazy Horse Ln Westerville OH 43081-4416

MURCKO, DONALD LEROY, architect; b. Warren, Ohio, Jan. 24, 1953; s. Joseph Mathew and Sophie May (Hidukawich) M. BArch, Kent State U., 1977. Registered architect, Ohio. Archtl. draftsman Angel Constrn. Co., Garrettsville, Ohio, 1977-80; apprentice architect E.S. Jakubick & Assoc.s, Warren, Ohio, 1980-82; assoc. architect Mosure & Assocs., Inc., Youngstown, Ohio, 1982-90; project architect MS Consultants, Inc., Youngstown, 1990-91, Buchanan Ricciuti Balog, Youngstown, Ohio, 1991—; cons. architect VA, Cleve., 1986—. Mem. Western Pa. Conservancy, Pitts., 1985—, Mahoning Valley Hist. Soc., Youngstown, 1989—, Butler Inst. Am. Art, Youngstown, 1991—. Recipient Cert. of Merit, Ohio Edison Co., 1976. Mem. AIA, Architects Soc. Ohio, Cath. Alumni Club Youngstown (pres.). Democrat. Roman Catholic. Office: Buchanan Ricciuti Balog 1500 Metropolitan Tower Youngstown OH 44503

MURDOCH, ARTHUR ROY, chemistry educator; b. Duboise, Nebr., Aug. 25, 1934; s. Albert Roy and Dorothy Enid (Johns) M.; m. Gail Reeves, July 28, 1957; children: Scott Kevin, Kristy Lynn. BA, Westmar Coll., 1956; MS, Yale U., 1958, PhD, 1964. Secondary teaching cert., Iowa. Asst. prof. chemistry Morningside Coll., Sioux City, Iowa, 1962-65, assoc. prof., 1965-68; assoc. prof. Mt. Union Coll., Alliance, Ohio, 1968-80, prof. chemistry, 1980—, chmn. chem. dept., 1968-84. Mem. AAUP, (pres. Ohio 1977-78), Am. Chem. Soc., Fedn. Am. Scientists, Union Concerned Scientists, Soc. Sigma Xi. Presbyterian. Avocations: boating, camping, water skiing. Home: 1457 Robinwood Rd Alliance OH 44601-3932 Office: Mt Union Coll Chemistry Dept Alliance OH 44601

MURDOCH, BRUCE THOMAS, health physicist; b. Prague, Okla., Mar. 15, 1940; s. Thomas J. and Mary E. (Waller) M.; m. Carol Ann Heggblom, June 28, 1968; children: Vanessa J., Robert W. BA in Physics, Carleton Coll., Northfield, Minn., 1962; MA in Physics, Rice U., 1966; PhD in Nuclear Physics, Utah State U., 1975. Devel. engr. Goodyear Aerospace Corp., Litchfield Park, Ariz., 1967-70; profl. assoc. physics dept. U. Manitoba, Winnipeg, Can., 1974-78; devel. project engr. Schlumberger Well Services, Houston, 1978-82; nuclear devel. mgr. NL McCullough, Houston, 1982-88; sr. rsch. scientist, engring. mgr. Atlas Wireline, Houston, 1988-93; health physicist Argonne (Ill.) Nat. Lab., 1994—. Contbr. articles to profl. jours. Mem. Soc. Profl. Well Log Analysts (calibration com. 1986-88), Health Physics Soc., Am. Phys. Soc., Am. Acad. Health Physics (assoc. mem.). Home: 181 Sparrow Ln Bolingbrook IL 60440 Office: Argonne Nat Lab 9600 S Cass Ave Argonne IL 60439-9999

MURDOCK, NANCI C., women's health nurse; b. Dearborn, Mich., July 18, 1946; d. John C. (dec.) and Mildred G. (Rogan) Talpos; m. Rogan C. Murdock, July 18, 1970; children: Brant A., Meigan L. ADN, Owens Tech. Coll., Perrysburg, Ohio, 1983; BS, Mary Manse Coll., Toledo, 1968; post-grad., Ea. Mich. U., 1970-72. Cert. sch. nurse. Tchr. life sci., earth sci. and health Otsego Jr. High Sch., Tontogany, Ohio, 1973-77; tchr. physics, life sci. and art St. Andrews High Sch., Detroit, 1971-72; staff nurse peripheral vascular dept. St. Vincent Med. Ctr., 1983-85; staff nurse labor and delivery St Vincent Med. Ctr., Toledo, 1985-88; sch. nurse Rossford (Ohio) Bd. Edn., 1988—; outpatient surgery staff nurse Riverside Hosp., Toledo, 1991-95, surgery staff nurse main oper. rm., 1995—; evaluator Nat. Sci. Tchrs. Assn. Conv., Washington. Mem. ANA, OHNA, Nat. Assn. Sch. Nurses, Ohio Edn. Assn., Rossford Assn. Classroom Tchrs. Home: 105 Lones Dr Perrysburg OH 43551-2331

MURDOCK, NORMAN ANTHONY, judge; b. Cin., Nov. 6, 1931; s. Charles and Anna Murdock; m. Patricia Higgins, Feb. 16, 1957; children: Norman, Louis, Patrick, Suzanne, Michael, John. BS, Xavier U., 1955; JD, U. Cin., 1968. Bar: Ohio 1968; PA, Ohio. Dist. scout exec. Boy Scouts of Am., Dodge City, Kans., 1956-59; acct., Cin., 1959-68; ptnr. Ahlrichs & Murdock, Cin., 1968-89. Clk., treas. Delhi Township, Cin., 1964-67; mem. Ohio Ho. of Reps., Cin., 1967-78; commr. Hamilton County, Cin., 1979-89; judge Hamilton County Common Pleas Ct., 1989-93; atty. at law, arbitrator, mediator, 1993—; vice chmn. Intergovtl. Adv. Coun. on Edn., Washington, 1982-85; trustee Coll. Mt. St. Joseph, Cin., 1975-81. Served to 2d lt. U.S. Army, 1956. Recipient Disting. Svc. award Arthritis Found., 1978; named Legislator of Yr., Ohio Pharm. Assn., 1972, Legislator of Yr., Ohio Assn. Trial Lawyers, 1976, Man of Yr., Ohio Pub. Transit Assn., 1975. Mem. ABA, Ohio Bar Assn., Cin. Bar Assn. Republican. Roman Catholic. Avocations: art and antiques, golf, reading, music appreciation. Home: 1220 Mercantile Ctr 120 E Fourth St Cincinnati OH 45202-4007 Office: 593 Hamilton County Ct House Cincinnati OH 45205

MURDOCK, PHELPS DUBOIS, JR., marketing consultant; b. Kansas City, Mo., May 5, 1944; s. Phelps Dubois and Betty Jane Murdock; BA, U. Mo., Kansas City, 1993; m. Cathy Ann Broadfoot, 1991; children: Susan, Kathleen, Phelps DuBois III, McKenna McCosh. Sales svc. mgr. Sta.-KCMO-TV, Kansas City, 1965-66; account exec. Fremerman-Papin Advt., Kansas City, 1966-71, TV prodn. mgr., 1966-70, v.p., 1970-71; mng. ptnr. New Slant Prodns., Kansas City, 1971-73; v.p., creative dir. Travis-Walz-Lane Advt., Kansas City, and Mission, Kans., 1973-76; pres., chief exec. officer Phelps Murdock Mktg. and Advt., Inc., Kansas City, Mo., 1977-91; CEO, strategic planning, pub. policy, mktg., comm., Phelps Murdock Strategic/Mktg. Planning, 1992—; exec. dir. Kansas City Indsl. Coun., 1991—; guest lectr. colls., univs. Active Heart of Am. United Way, 1966-80, mem. exec. bd., 1976-80, bd. dirs., 1976-80; active Help Educate Emotionally Disturbed, Inc., Kansas City, Mo., 1968-80, founder, pres., bd. dirs. HEED Found., 1979-80; active Heart of Am. coun. Boy Scouts Am., 1975-85, bd. govs. Bacchus Ednl. and Cultural Found., Kansas City, 1973-76, beneficiary selection chmn., 1974, found. chmn., 1975; mem. Kansas City Bicentennial Commn., 1975-76; founder, bd. dirs., sec. Kansas City Union Sta. Inc., 1988-96, sec., 1988-92, treas. 1992-96; mem. Union Sta. Commn., 1986-88; founder, bd. dirs., 1st v.p. Com. for Union Sta., 1987-93; pres. Friends of Union Sta., 1994—; bd. dirs., chmn. long-range planning Hist. Kansas City Found., 1989-92, bd. dirs. Hist. Garment Dist., 1991—; mem. Kansas City Consensus, 1988—, issues select. com., 1988-90, metro. area strategic planning focus group, 1989-90, bd. dirs., 1990-93, chmn. community rels. com., 1990-92, 1st v.p., 1991-93, Focus Kansas City Bus. & Urban Fabric Perspectives Groups, 1993-95; founder Kansas City Bus. Retention Roundtable, 1992—; mktg. legal com. MARC Regional Amentities Task Force, 1993-94; mem. steering com. COMPASS: Citizens Charting A Greater Kansas City Community, 1990-92; mem. Aligning for Action Conf., 1993; mem. adv. bd. Western Mo. Mental Health Ctr., 1990-92; chmn. Eco-Kansas City Steering Com., 1992-94; steering com. Main Link Study, 1990-91, Studies for Econ. and Environ. Devel. 1993-94, KU Sch. of Architecture and Urban Design; adv. bd. Mid-Am. Mfg. Tech. Ctr., 1992-95; mem. steering com. Capital Resources Network, 1992-95; chmn. Industrial Blight Comm. 1994-95; chmn. Blight Comm. Environ. Mgmt. Comm., 1995—; mem. Blight Task Force, 1995—, Steering Comm. Bi-State Brownfields Task Force, 1996—; Development Rev. Process Task Force, 1996—. vol. coach, local youth leagues, 1975-83; cons. Com. for County Progress Campaigns, 1966-70, Charter Campaign, Jackson County, Mo., 1970; Kansas City Magnet Schs., 1986-88, speaker internat. conf., 1988. Recipient various awards including United Way Nat. Comm. award, 1975; Effie citation N.Y. Mktg. Assn., 1975; 1st Place Print Ad award and 1st Place Poster award 9th Dist. Addy Awards, 1975, 1st Place Regional-Nat. TV Campaign award, 1976; Omni award, 1980-82, 86, 87; Silver award KCAD, 1981; 1st Place TV Campaign award KCAF Big One Show, 1976; Best-of-Show and Gold medal award Dallas Soc. Visual Communications, 1976; Gold medal Kansas City Litho Craftsmen, 1988, CUBE award, 1995; named Mic-O-Say hon. warrior, 1978. Democrat. Author numerous articles, TV, radio commls., film, TV and radio musical compositions; radio and TV programs; film with Walter Cronkite, Union Station is US, 1988. Home: 14150 Ode Rd Platte City MO 64079-8240 Office: PO Box 901670 Kansas City MO 64190-1670

MURNANE, EDWARD DAVID, state agency association administrator; b. Chgo., Mar. 2, 1944; s. Edward Francis and Dorothy Lucille (Vanosky) M.; m. Laurel Ann Steffes, Jan. 22, 1966; children: Michael, Teresa, Brian. BS, No. Ill. U., 1966. Polit. editor The Daily Herald, Arlington Heights, Ill., 1966-71; press sec. U.S. Rep. Philip Crane, Washington, 1971-73, adminstrv. asst., 1973-76; owner Ed Murnane & Assocs., Arlington Heights, 1976-83; pub. affairs dir. Regional Transp. Authority, Chgo., 1984-89; regional administr. U.S. SBA, Washington and Chgo., 1989-92; dep. asst. to Pres. The White House, Washington, 1992-93; pres. Ill. Civil Justice League, Chgo., 1993—; advance coord. The White House, Washington, 1981-90. Author: It's Not Such a Long Way to Tipperary, 1991. Campaign dir. George Bush for Pres., Washington and Chgo., 1987-88; alt. del. Rep. Nat. Conv., New Orleans, 1988; dep. dir. Reagan-Bush Campaign, Ill., 1984; communications dir. Reagan for Pres., Ill., 1980. Recipient Disting. Reporting of Pub. Affairs award Am. Polit. Sci. Assn., Congl. fellow, 1971. Republican. Roman Catholic. Office: Ill Civil Justice League Bldg 2902 200 W Adams St Chicago IL 60606-5234

MURNIK, JAMES MICHAEL, corporate executive; b. Fitchburg, Mass., Aug. 13, 1934; s. Michael and Alice (Goss) M.; m. Linda Smalley, Dec. 26, 1957 (div. June 1969); children: Michael, Peter; m. Mary Fae Rengo, July 30, 1970; 1 child, John Rengo. AB in English, Colby Coll., 1957; AM in English, U. Pa., 1962. Instr. Drexel Inst. Tech., Phila., 1963-65; owner, mgr. Murnik's Second Story, Fitchburg, 1965-69; food svc. dir. Graham Hosp. Corp., Canton, Ill., 1970-80; v.p. Rengo Oil Co., Manistee, Mich., 1980-85; pres. Rengo-Murnik Corp., Reed City, Mich., 1985—. Mayor City of Bushnell, Ill., 1977-80; pres. Fulton-McDonough County Mental Health Bd., 1974-78; projects coord. Osceola (Mich.) Dems., 1990-92; elected chmn. Reed City Charter Commn., 1992—. Roman Catholic. Home: 331 W Slosson Ave Reed City MI 49677-1167 Office: Rengo Murnik Inc Church & Chestnut Sts Reed City MI 49677

MURNIK, MARY RENGO, biology educator; b. Manistee, Mich., Aug. 30, 1942; d. John Everett and Lorraine P. (ReVolt) R.; m. James M. Murnik, July 30, 1970; 1 child, John. Student Marquette U., 1960-62; B.S., Mich. State U., 1964, Ph.D., 1969. Asst. prof. Fitchburg State Coll., Mass., 1968-70; from asst. prof. to prof. Western Ill. U., Macomb, 1970-80; prof., head biol. sci. dept. Ferris State U., Big Rapids, Mich., 1980-92, prof. 1992—. articles to profl. jours. Author two lab. manuals. NIH fellow HEW, Mich. State U., 1965-68; NIH grantee Western Ill. U., 1976; grantee Environ. Mutagen Soc., Edinburgh, Scotland, 1977, Western Ill. U., 1972-79. Mem. AAAS, Genetics Soc. Am., Behavior Genetics Soc., Mich. Acad. Sci., Arts and Letters, Sigma Xi. Roman Catholic. Home: 331 W Slosson Ave Reed City MI 49677-1167 Office: Ferris State U Dept Biol Scis Big Rapids MI 49307

MURPHY, ANDREW J., managing news editor. Now mng. editor, news editor Columbus (Ohio) Dispatch. Office: Columbus Dispatch 34 S 3rd St Columbus OH 43215-4201

MURPHY, CAMILLE SUZANNE, nurse; b. Ely/Winton, Minn., Feb. 2, 1957; d. Arthur Enrico and Jeanne KAtherine (Young) Tome; m. Kevin Patrick Murphy, June 5, 1982; children: Raymond, Monica, Brendan, Sean. Ba in Nursing, Coll. St. Catherine, 1979; MA in Health and Human Svcs., St. Mary's Coll., 1992. Staff nurse Fairview Hosp., Mpls., 1979-80; staff nurse, asst. head nurse St. Mary's Hosp., Rochester, Minn., 1980-83; staff nurse labor and delivery Olmsted Community Hosp., Rochester, Minn., 1983-88, Merritt-Peralta Med. Ctr., Oakland, Calif., 1989, Humana Hosp., San Leandro, Calif., 1989; staff nurse. float nurse maternal child health St. Mary's Med. Ctr., Duluth, Minn., 1991-95; parish nurse Cathedral of Our Lady of the Rosary, 1994—. Roman Catholic. Home: 439 Hartley Pl Duluth MN 55803-2473

MURPHY, D. EVAN, consulting psychologist; b. Ill., Jan. 3, 1950; s. Robert Francis and Barbara (Evans) M.; m. Celeste Murphy; children: Jacqueline, Colin, Graeme. BA in Psychology, San Francisco State U., 1974, MA in Psychology, 1977; PhD in Psychology, Ill. Inst. Tech., 1984. Cons. psychologist, Lake Forest, Ill., 1986—. Office: PO Box 770 Lake Forest IL 60045-0770

MURPHY, DANIEL PATRICK, database developer; b. St. Louis, July 9, 1966; s. Vincent John and Joanne Ernestine (Klein) M.; m. Christine M. Cusimano, Sept. 4, 1993; 1 child, Erin Kathleen. BS in Computer Sci., U. Mo., St. Louis, 1987; MS, U. Mo., Rolla, 1989, PhD, 1992. Software engr. Generic Mineral Tech. Ctr. for Pyrometallurgy, Rolla, 1987-89, Intelligent Systems Ctr., Rolla, 1989-91; software engr., cons. Precision Software Systems, Inc., Rolla, 1991-92, DemMaTec Found., Inc., Rolla, 1992-93; pres. Chrimex, Inc., Kansas City, Mo., 1993-94, Cerner Corp., Kansas City, 1994—. Contbr. articles to profl. jours. Univ. scholar U. Mo., St. Louis, 1985-87, Chancellor's fellow, Rolla, 1987-92. Mem. Assn. for Computing Machinery, IEEE, Assn. for Automated Reasoning, Assn. for Logic Programming. Roman Catholic.

MURPHY, DIANA E., federal judge; b. Faribault, Minn., Jan. 4, 1934; d. Albert W. and Adleyne (Heiker) Kuske; m. Joseph Murphy, July 24, 1958; children: Michael, John E. BA magna cum laude, U. Minn., 1954, JD magna cum laude, 1974; postgrad., Johannes Gutenberg U., Mainz, Germany, 1954-55, U. Minn., 1955-58. Bar: Minn. 1974, U.S. Supreme Ct. 1980. Assoc. Lindquist & Vennum, 1974-76; mcpl. judge Hennepin County, 1976-78, Minn. State dist. judge, 1978-80; judge U.S. Dist. Ct. for Minn., Mpls., 1980-94, chief judge, 1992-94; judge U.S. Ct. of Appeals (8th cir.), Minneapolis, 1994—. Bd. editors: Minn. Law Rev., Georgetown U. Jour. on Cts., Health Scis. and the Law, 1989-92. Bd. dirs. Spring Hill conf. Ctr., 1978-84, Mpls. United Way, 1985—, treas., 1990-94, vice chair, 1996—; bd. dirs. Bush Found., 1982—, chmn. bd. dirs., 1986-91; bd. dirs. Amicus, 1976-80, also organizer, 1st chmn. adv. coun.; mem. Mpls. Charter Commn., 1973-76, chmn., 1974-76; bd. dirs. Ops. De Novo, 1971-76, chmn. bd. dirs., 1974-75; mem. Minn. Constl. Study Commn., chmn. bill of rights com., 1971-73; regent St. Johns U., 1978-87, 88—, vice chmn. bd., 1985-87, chmn. bd. 1995—; mem. Minn. Bicentennial Commn., 1987-88; trustee Twin Cities Pub. TV, 1985-94, chmn. bd., 1990-92; trustee U. Minn. Found., 1990—, treas., 1992—; bd. dirs. Sci. Mus. Minn., 1988-94, vice chmn., 1991-94; trustee U. St. Thomas, 1991—; dir. Nat. Assn. Pub. Interest Law Fellowships for Equal Justice, 1992-95. Fulbright scholar; recipient Amicus Founders' award, Outstanding Achievement award U. Minn., Outstanding Achievement award YWCA. Fellow Am. Bar Found.; mem. ABA (mem. ethics and profl. responsibility judges adv. com. 1981-88, standing com. on jud. selection, tenure and compensation 1991-94, mem. standing com. on fed. jud. improvements, 1994—, Appelate Judges conf. 1996—), Minn. Bar Assn. (bd. govs. 1977-81), Hennepin County Bar Assn. (gov. coun. 1976-81), Am. Law Inst., Am. Judicature Soc. (bd. dirs. 1982-93, v.p. 1985-88, treas. 1988-89, chmn. bd. 1989-91), Nat. Assn. Women Judges, Minn. Women Lawyers (Myra Bradwell award), U. Minn. Alumni Assn. (bd. dirs. 1975-83, nat. pres. 1981-82), Fed. Judges Assn. (bd. dirs. 1982—, v.p. 1984-89, pres. 1989-91), Hist. Soc. for 8th Cir. (bd. dirs. 1988-91), Fed. Jud. Ctr. (bd. dirs. 1990-94, 8th cir. jud. coun. 1992-94, mem. U.S. jud. conf. com. on ct. adminstrn. and case mgmt. 1994—), Order of Coif, Phi Beta Kappa. Office: US Dist Ct 684 US Courthouse 110 S 4th St Minneapolis MN 55401

MURPHY, EUGENE F., aerospace, communications and electronics executive; b. Flushing, N.Y., Feb. 24, 1936; s. Eugene P. and Delia M.; m. Mary Margaret Cullen, Feb. 20, 1960. BA, Queens Coll., 1956; JD, Fordham U., 1959; LLM, Georgetown U., 1964. Bar: N.Y. With RCA Global Communications Inc., N.Y.C., 1964-81, v.p. and gen. counsel, 1969-71, exec. v.p. ops., 1972-75, pres., chief operating officer, 1975-76, pres., chief exec. officer, 1976-81; chmn., chief exec. officer RCA Communications Inc., N.Y.C., 1981-86; sr. v.p. communications and info. svcs. GE, N.Y.C., 1986-91; pres., chief exec. officer GE Aerospace, King of Prussia, Pa., 1992-93; pres., CEO GE Aircraft Engines, Cin., 1993—; bd. dirs. Lockheed Martin Corp.; mem. Pres. Reagan's Nat. Sec. Telecommunications Adv. Com.; bd. govs. Aerospace Industries Assn. Bd. Served with USMCR, 1959-60. Mem. Armed Forces Comm. and Electronics Assn. (past nat. chmn.). Clubs: Marco Polo, Plandome Country, Plandome Field and Marine. Office: GE Aircraft Engines Maildrop 101 1 Neumann Way Cincinnati OH 45215-1915

MURPHY, HAROLD, state legislator. Student, Northeastern Ill. U. Owner, operator King's Lake Resort, Ind.; mem. Ill. Ho. of Reps. from 30th dist. Supervising mgr. Charles Chew Facility, Sec. of State of Ill.; alderman Markham, Ill. Democrat. Home: PO Box 25 Markham IL 60426-0025*

MURPHY, JAMES C., rehabilitation services professional; b. Cedar Rapids, Iowa, Sept. 29, 1953; s. James J. Murphy and Eva J. (Vernon) Jones; m. Priscilla Kay Dennie, June 15, 1973; children: Joshua James, Elijah Curtis. Cert. substance abuse counselor; nat. cert. chem. dependency counselor. Psychiat. aide Iowa State Mental Health Inst., Independence, 1973-75, adolescent counselor, 1975-76, counselor trainee, 1975-76; outpatient substance abuse counselor Northeast Coun. on Substance Abuse, Waterloo, Iowa, 1976-77, supr. minority alcohol prog., 1978-79, case mgmt. cons., 1977-79, residential counselor, 1978-80, dir. residential facility, 1980-84; prog. dir. Adolescent Treatment Ctr. of Winnebago, Minn., 1984—; CEO Addiction Recovery Techs., Inc., 1991—; provider rep. Faribault/Martin County DHS Adv. Com., Fairmont, Minn., 1987—; cons. Pharm. Mgmt. Systems, St. Louis, 1988-92; CEO, pres. Addiction Recovery Techs., 1991—. Sect. leader 4-H, Winnebago, 1985-87. With USMC, 1970-72, Vietnam. Mem. So. Minn. Assn. Alcohol/Drug Abuse Counselors (pres.-elect 1990-92), So. Minn. Regional Coalition of C.D. Profls. (steering com. 1990-93), Nat. Assn. Alcohol/Drug Abuse Counselors (Minn. del. 1990), Minn. Chem. Dependency Assn. (region 10 bd. dirs.), Minn. Assn. Resources for Recovery (v.p. charter bd. 1995, gov. region 9 1995—). Mem. Christian Ch. Home: 31453 240th St Winnebago MN 56098-9748

MURPHY, JAMES LAWSON, music educator; b. Greenville, S.C., Jan. 30, 1951; s. Marion Wales and Clyde (Morgan) M.; m. Karen Joyce Antolick, May 29, 1973; 1 child, Bethany. MusB, Stetson U., 1973; MusM, Southwestern Sem., 1976; PhD, Tex. Tech U., 1980. Entertainer Walt Disney World, Orlando, Fla., 1973; choral dir. DeLand High Sch., Fla., 1973; asst. prof. music Wayland Bapt. U., Plainview, Tex., 1976-81; chmn. dept. music Temple Jr. Coll., Tex., 1981-87; Esther Becker Simplot prof., chmn. dept. music, chmn. Div. Performing and Fine Arts Coll. Idaho (name changed to Albertson Coll. Idaho), Caldwell, 1987-93; chair dept. music Fort Hays (Kans.) State U., 1993—; choral clinician, various sch. choirs, Tex., 1981-87, Idaho, 1987—, Kans., 1993—; chair music recert. com. Kansas State Bd. Edn., 1994—. Author: The Choral Music of Halsey Stevens, 1980; contbr. music rev. articles and commentaries to profl. jours. including Idaho Statesman, 1988—; composer various works for miscellaneous media, 1971—. Choir dir., various chs., U.S., 1970—; bd. dirs. Plainview Civic Theater, 1980, Central Tex. Orchestral Soc., Temple, 1981-83, Community Concert Assn., Temple, 1983-85, Caldwell Fine Arts Series, 1987-91; artistic dir., condr. Boise Master Chorale, 1990-93, Boise River Festival Grand Chorale, 1991-93; chair Idaho Alliance for Arts Edn., 1990-92,. Named one of Outstanding Young Men Am., U.S. Jaycees, 1980; named Best Actor 1980-81, Plainview Civic Theater, 1981; Tex. Gen. Bapt. Conv. fellow Tex. Tech U., 1977. Mem. Coll. Music Soc. (life), Nat. Assn. Tchrs. Singing, Music Edn. Nat. Conf., Am. Choral Dirs. Assn. (state chmn. com. for music in jr. colls., gen. chair N.W. honors choir 1990, chair Idaho chpt. com. cmty. choirs 1992-93, chair Kans. chpt. com. youth and student activities 1993—, chair com. advocacy 1996—), Tex. Music Educators Assn., Tex. Choral Dirs. Assn., Tex. Assn. Music Schs. (acad. standards commn. 1982-85, dir. 2-yr. schs. 1985-88), Idaho Alliance for Arts Edn. (bd. dirs., chair elect 1988-90, chmn. 1990-92), Idaho Music Educators Assn. (govt. rels. chair 1988-89, tech. chair 1989-93, bd. dirs.), N.W. Am. Guild Organists (conv. choir dir, clinician 1990), Music Educators Nat. Conf., Idaho Humanities Coun. Speakers Bur., Phi Mu Alpha Sinfonia (Province VII gov. 1995—), Omicron Delta Kappa. Presbyterian. Avocations: travel, photography, tennis, golf. Home: 304 W 40th St Hays KS 67601-1519 Office: Ft Hays State U Dept Music Hays KS 67601

MURPHY, JANET GORMAN, college president; b. Holyoke, Mass., Jan. 10, 1937; d. Edwin Daniel and Catherine Gertrude (Hennessey) Gorman. B.A., U. Mass., 1958, postgrad. 1960-61, Ed.D., 1974, LL.D. (hon.) 1984; M.Ed., Boston U., 1961. Tchr. English and history John J. Lynch Jr. High Sch., Holyoke, 1958-60; tchr. English, Chestnut Jr. High Sch., Springfield, Mass., 1961-63; instr. English and journalism Our Lady of Elms Coll., Chicopee, 1963-64; mem. staff Mass. State Coll., Lyndonville, Vt., 1977-83; pres. Mo. Western State Coll., St. Joseph, 1983—. Mem. campaign staff Robert F Kennedy Presdl. Campaign, 1967. Recipient John Gunther Tchr. award NEA, 1961, award Women's Opportunity Com., Boston Fed. Exec. Bd., 1963, Phi Delta Kappa Educator of Yr. award NAACP, 1992; named one of 10 Outstanding Young Leaders of Greater Boston Area, Boston Jr. C. of C., 1973. Office: Mo Western State Coll Office of the President 4525 Downs Dr Saint Joseph MO 64507-2246

MURPHY, JEANETTE CAROL, education educator; b. Hot Springs, S.D., June 6, 1931; d. George W. and Jessie S. (Whetstone) M.; A.B., U. S.D., 1960; M.S. in Edn. Adminstrn., Chadron State Coll., 1978, Ed.S. Ednl. Adminstrn., 1979, Ph.D in Ednl. Adminstrn., U. Mo., 1987. Mgr. cen. supply, operating rooms specialist Luth. Hosp., Hot Springs, 1957-58, 60-61; tchr. Spanish and French, Sidney (Nebr.) High Sch., 1962-64; reservations clk. Peninsula Hosp., Burlingame, Calif., 1964-65; tchr. San Lorenzo Valley Unified Schs., Felton, Calif., 1965-67; propr. Masters Career Inst., Salinas, Calif., 1969-70; tchr. English and Spanish Oglala Community High Sch., Pine Ridge, S.D., 1970-72; tchr. biology and substitute Hot Springs High Sch., 1971-73; clk. Fall River County (S.D.) Treas.'s Office, 1973-74; Title I adminstr. Loneman Day Sch., Ogala, S.D., 1974-75, adminstr., 1975-77; contract dir. and exec. officer bd. Unified Sch. Bd. Found., Inc., Pine Ridge, 1977-78; grad. asst. div. edn. and psychology Chadron (Nebr.) State Coll., 1978-79; supt. schs. Lyman (Nebr.) Pub. Schs., 1979-80, Kadoka (S.D.) Sch. Dist., 1981-83; registered rep. for IDS/Am. Express, 1983-84; grad. teaching asst. doctoral program in edn. adminstrn. with spl. emphasis in polit. sci. U. Mo., 1984-86 ; asst. state dir. for Mo. North Central Assn., 1984-86; assoc. prof. edn. U. Nebr. at Kearney, 1987—; rsch. assoc. joint effort U. Mo.-Columbia and Mo. House of Reps., 1985-86; pres. Faculty Senate U. Nebr., Kearney, 1994-95, bd. dirs. Kearney Fed. Credit Union, mem. grad. faculty. Author: The Missouri Career Development and Teacher Excellence Plan: An Initial Study of Missouri Career Ladder Program, 1987, My Plan Book: For The Student Teacher, 1990, Teaching Reflectively About Contemporary Issues in Education, 1993; contbr. articles to profl. publs. Chairperson Heart Fund Drive, Hot Springs, 1974-76; Bible sch. tchr. United Presbyn. Women, 1976-77; mem. choir Presbyn. Ch., 1970-76. Served with WAC, 1954-57. Rsch. grant for study of Brain Devel., 1990-92. Mem. Assn. Tchr. Educators, Nebr. Assn. Tchr. Educators, Mizzou Alumni Assn., Daus. of Nile, Internat. Order Job's Daus. of S.D. (past. grand guardian, grand sec.), Order Ea. Star (past matron), Phi Delta Kappa (historian, v.p. membership ctrl. Nebr. chpt.). Democrat.

MURPHY, JIM, state legislator; b. St. Louis, Feb. 4, 1925; s. William Francis and Jane Marie (Lavin) M.; m. Carol Pell Popovsky, 1961; children: Karen Ann, James William. BA, St. Louis U., 1948. Alderman Crestwood, Mo., 1981-83; mem. Mo. State Ho. of Reps. Dist. 95, 1983—. del. Mo. State Rep. Conv., 1984, 92. Recipient Globe-Dem. Meritorious Svc. award. Home: 9314 Cordoba Ln Saint Louis MO 63126-2708*

MURPHY, JO ANNE, data processing administrator; b. Chgo.; d. Joseph Francis and Elizabeth M. (Nowak) M. BS, Coll. St. Francis, 1970; MEd in Adminstrn. and Supervision, U. Ill., 1977. Cert. adminstr. and supr., Ill.; joined Sisters of St. Francis, Roman Cath. Ch., 1965. Tchr. St. Jude Sch., Joliet, Ill., 1969-70; math tchr. St. Raymond Sch., Joliet, 1970-75; prin. St. Matthew Day Sch., Champaign, Ill., 1976-78, St. John Sch., Joliet, 1978-82; math instr. Coll. St. Francis, Joliet, 1983-85; computer specialist Our Lady of Angels Retirement Home, Joliet, 1983-85; programmer/analyst Household Internat., Northbrook, Ill., 1985-88; ops. mgr. Coll. of St. Francis, Joliet, 1988-90; exec. office mgr. Sisters of St. Francis, Joliet, 1991-96; coord. Peoria Diocesan Prins., Champaign, 1976-78, Joliet Diocesan Prins., 1978-82; cons. Sisters of St. Francis, Joliet, 1972—, Vicar for Religious, Joliet, 1-90-95. Mem. NAFE, Assn. for Music and Imagery. Home: 424 Bethel # 1 S Joliet IL 60435-5381 Office: 520 N Plainfield Rd Joliet IL 60435-6162

MURPHY, MARY C., state legislator. BA, Coll. St. Scholastica; postgrad. U. Minn., Macalester Coll., U. Wis.-Superior, Am. U., Indiana U. H.s. tchr.; mem. Minn. Ho. of Reps., 1976—, mem. com. chair judiciary fin. com., tourism consumer affairs, labor-mgmt. relations coms.; active del. Duluth Central Labor Body AFL-CIO; mem., lector St. Raphael's Parish; dir. State Democratic Farmer-Labor Party, 1972-74, chmn. 8th Dist. credentials com., 1974—, chmn. St. Louis County Legis. Delegation, 1985-86. Mem. Duluth Fedn. Tchrs. (1st v.p. 1976-77, various coms.), Minn. Fedn. Tchrs. (legis. com. 1972-75), Am. Fedn. Tchrs. (del. nat. convs.), Minn. Hist. Soc., Alpha Delta Kappa. Office: State Office Bldg Saint Paul MN 55155-1201

MURPHY, MARY KATHRYN, industrial hygienist; b. Kansas City, Mo., Apr. 16, 1941; d. Arthur Charles and Mary Agnes (Fitzgerald) Wahlstedt; m. Thomas E. Murphy Jr., Aug. 26, 1963; children: Thomas E. III, David W. BA, Avila Coll., Kansas City, 1962; MS, Cen. Mo. State U., 1975. Cert. in comprehensive practice of indsl. hygiene. Indsl. hygienist Kansas City area office Occupational Safety and Health Adminstrn., 1975-78, regional indsl. hygienist, 1979-86; dir. indsl. hygiene Chart Svcs., Shawnee, Kans., 1986-87; dir. indsl. hygiene and hazardous substance control Hall-Kimbrell Environ. Mgmt. and Pollution Control, Lawrence, Kans., 1987-88, mgr. dept. indsl. hygiene div. environ. mgmt. and program control, 1988-89; dir. indsl. hygiene Hazardous Waste divsn. Burns & McDonnell, Engrs., Architects, Kansas City, Mo., 1989-93; mgr. health & safety dept. Burns & McDonnell Waste Cons., Inc., Overland Park, Kansas, 1990-93, dir. indsl. hygiene U.S. Army Corps Engrs., Kansas City, 1993; regional program mgr. environ. & safety ctrl. region FAA, Kansas City, 1993—; asst. dir. safety office U. Kans. Med. Ctr., 1978-79; adj. prof. continuing edn. divsn. U. Kans.; adj. lectr. Ctrl. Mo. State U. Summer talent fellow Kaw Valley Heart Assn., 1961. Mem. AAAS, Am. Indsl. Hygiene Assn. (sec.-treas. Mid-Am. sect. 1978-79, bd. dirs. 1981, mem. auditcom.), Am. Chem. Soc., Am. Conf. Govt. Indsl. Hygienists (mem. chem. agts. threshold limit value com.), Am. Acad. Indsl. Hygiene, Air and Waste Mgmt. Assn., Environ. Audit Roundtable, N.Y. Acad. Scis., Internat. Soc. Environ. Toxicology and Cancer, Am. Coll. Toxicology, Am. Conf. on Chem. Labeling. Home: 10616 W 123rd St Shawnee Mission KS 66213-1952 Office: FAA-ACE 473 601E 12th St Kansas City MO 64106

MURPHY, MAUREEN, state legislator. Student, Moraine Valley C.C. Twp. clk. Worth, Ill.; mem. Ill. Ho. of Reps. from 36th dist.; broker-assoc. R.B. Konie & Co. V.p., area leader Worth Twp. Regular Rep. Orgn.; pres. Evergreen Pk. Regular Rep. Orgn. Home: 10015 S Clifton Park Ave Evergreen Park IL 60642-3408 Office: Ill Ho of Reps State Capitol Springfield IL 62706*

MURPHY, MAX RAY, lawyer; b. Goshen, Ind., July 18, 1934; s. Loren A. and Lois (Mink) M.; m. Ruth Leslie Henricson, June 10, 1978; children: Michael Lee, Chad Woodrow. BA, DePauw U., 1956; JD, Yale U., 1959; postgrad., Mich. State U., 1960. Bar: Mich. 1960. Assoc. Glassen, Parr, Rhead & McLean, Lansing, Mich., 1960-67, Lokker, Boter & Dalman, Holland, Mich., 1967-69; ptnr. Dalman, Murphy, Bidol, & Bouwens, P.C., Holland, 1969-91; ptnr. Cunningham Dalman, P.C., Holland, 1991—; instr. Lansing Bus. U., 1963-67; asst. pros. atty. Ottawa County, Mich., 1967-69. Democratic candidate for Ingham County (Mich.) Pros. Atty., 1962, 1964. Mem. ABA, Ottawa County Bar Assn. (sec. 1970-71), Mich. Bar Assn. (mem. family law sect.), Ingham County Bar Assn. Clubs: Holland Country. Home: 363 Oak Harbor Ct Holland MI 49424-6632 Office: 321 Settlers Rd Holland MI 49423-3760

MURPHY, MICHAEL B., state legislator; m. Suzanne Thompson. BA, U. Notre Dame, 1979. TV, polit. reporter, 1979-87; dir. comm. Lt. Gov. John Mutz, 1987-89; pub. rels. mgr. Melvin Simons Assocs., 1989-92; dir. external affairs Anthem, Inc., 1992—; mem. Ind. State Ho. of Reps. Dist. 90, mem. families, children and human affairs com., mem. ways and means, rules com. Sec. Rep. 6th Dist. Com., 1993—.

MURPHY, MICHELE SUSAN, non-profit agency executive; b. Cleve., Aug. 11, 1949; d. Edward Jerry and Violet Agnes (Lozick) M. BS in Journalism, Ohio U., 1971; M Non-Profit Orgns., Case Western Res. U., 1993. Press rep. Cuyahoga Community Coll. West, Parma, Ohio, 1971-75; pub. info. specialist Cuyahoga Community Coll., Cleve., 1975-76, news bur. mgr., 1976-77, asst. dir. info. svcs., 1977-78, cons., 1979; coord. U.S. Senate Campaign, Cleve., 1981-82; communications liaison Cuyahoga County Bd. Elections, Cleve., 1982-94; exec. dir. Crime Stoppers of Cuyahoga County, Inc., Cleve., 1994; founder, exec. dir. Conflict Resolution Ctr. of the West Shore, Inc.; cons. in mktg. The City Club, Cleve., 1991. Mem. Leadership Cleve., Greater Cleve. Growth Assn., 1986; editor Rep. News, Cuyahoga County Rep. Orgn., 1983-84. Recipient Appreciation award Greater Cleve. Crime Prevention Com., 1992, Ohio State Chiefs of Police Assn., 1990, Vol. Achievement award CIVAC, Cleve., 1987, Cert. of Appreciation Community Rels. Bd., City of Cleve., 1987, Sports Promotion award Nat. Jr. Coll. Athletic Assn., 1973, 74, 75. Mem. Ohio Mediation Assn., Acad. Family Mediators, Cuyahoga County Police Chiefs Assn. (hon., named Citizen of Yr. 1995). Office: CRC West Shore Inc 24700 Center Ridge #6 Westlake OH 44145

MURPHY, PATRICK JOSEPH, state representative; b. Dubuque, Iowa, Aug. 24, 1959; s. Lawrence John and Eileen (Heitz) M.; m. Therese Ann Gulick, Dec. 27, 1980; children: Jacob, John, Joey, Natalie. BA, Loras Coll., 1980. Transporter, security and safety officer, mental health technician Mercy Health Ctr., Dubuque, Iowa, 1975-88; documentation specialist software systems Cycare Systems Inc., Dubuque, 1988-90; state representative State of Iowa, Des Moines, 1989—. Adv. com. Iowa Birth Defects, 1995. Recipient Robert Tyson award Cmty. Action Assn., 1993, Pub. Svc. award Coalition for Family and Children's Svcs., 1994; Henry Toll fellow, 1996. Mem. NAACP, YMCA, Dubuque Mental Health Assn. (bd. dirs., Legis. of Yr.), Loras Club, FDR Club. Democrat. Roman Catholic. Home: 1770 Hale St Dubuque IA 52001-6049 Office: Ho of Reps Des Moines IA 50319

MURPHY, RAYMOND, state legislator; b. St. Louis, Dec. 15, 1937; m. Lynette; eight children. Student, Detroit Inst. Tech. Rep. Mich. Dist. 17, 1983-94, Mich. Dist. 7, 1995—; spkr. pro tem Mich. Ho. Reps., chair labor com., mem bus. & fin. com., house oversight com., tourism & recreation coms. real estate broker. Mem. NAACP, Nat. Black Caucus State Legis., Elks, Masons, Lions, Optimist. Office: State Capitol PO Box 30014 Lansing MI 48913-7514*

MURPHY, ROBERT BRADY LAWRENCE, lawyer; b. Madison, Wis., Dec. 5, 1905; s. Lawrence B. Murphy and Elizabeth M. Brady; m. Arabel Zenobia Alcott, Oct. 11, 1947. AB, U. Wis., 1929, AM, 1930, LLB, 1932, LLD (hon.), 1994. Bar: Wis. 1932. Mem. Murphy & Desmond, S.C. and predecessors, Madison, 1932—; lectr. U. Wis. Law Sch.; mem. Supreme Ct. Wis. Bd. Bar Examiners, 1981-86. Mem. Madison Police and Fire Commn., 1947-52; curator State Hist. Soc. Wis., 1948-90, pres., 1958-61; bd. dirs. Wis. History Found., 1958—, pres., 1960-90; bd. advisors Nat. Trust Hist. Preservation, 1967-73; bd. dirs. or advisor several founds.; bd. visitors U. Wis. Law Sch., 1975-81. Lt. USNR, 1943-46. Fellow Am. Bar Found.; mem. ABA, State Bar Wis., Am. Law Inst., Selden Soc. (Eng.), Bascom Hill Soc. (Wis.), Phi Beta Kappa Assocs., Phi Kappa Phi, Chi Phi, Phi Delta Phi. Republican. Roman Catholic. Clubs: Madison, Blackhawk Country. Home: 3423 Valley Creek Cir Middleton WI 53562-1991 Office: Murphy & Desmond S C 2 E Mifflin St Madison WI 53703-2868

MURPHY, SHARON L., financial company executive; b. Milw., Wis., Feb. 13, 1953. BBA, U. Wis., 1979. Lic. enrolled agent. Pres. Murphy Fin. Svcs., Milw., 1980—. Mem. St. Catherine's Sch. Bd., Milw., 1994—; coach Notre Dame/Don Bosco Softball League, 1994—. Mem. Nat. Assn. of Enrolled Agents; bd. dirs. Sch. of Irish Dance.

MURPHY, STEVEN LESLIE, state senator, utilities company official; b. San Francisco, Sept. 9, 1957; s. Russell Jr. and Helen Glendora (Black) M.; m. Robin Estelle Stelling, Feb. 9, 1979; children: Nikolaas Russell, Matthew Steven. AS in Bus. Mgmt., Red Wing (Minn.) Tech. Coll., 1992. Operator No. States Power, Red Wing, 1981—; senator Minn. State Senate, St. Paul, 1992—; steward Unit 47 Local 949 Internat. Brotherhood Elec. Workers, Red Wing, 1987—. Bd.dirs. CSAP Open/Charity Golf Tournament, Frontenac, Minn.; co-chair Fireman Caucus, Minn. Legislature, 1992—; vice-chair Vets. Com., Minn. Senate, 1992—. Served with USMC, 1976-80. Mem. Am. Legion, Marine Corps League. Mem. Democratic-Farmer Labor Party. Methodist. Home: 28421 Highway 61 Blvd Red Wing MN 55066-5531 Office: Minn State Senate State Capital Building # 301 Saint Paul MN 55155-1606

MURPHY, WILLIAM HOST, sales executive; b. South Bend, Ind., June 7, 1926; s. Joseph Patrick and Edna Emma (Host) M.; m. Dorothy A. Dubala, Jan. 29, 1949 (div. 1968); m. Barbara Joan Mellinger, Sept. 11, 1987; children: Kent Alan, Thomas Aquinas, Catherine Ann, Molly Teresa. BS in Commerce, U. Notre Dame. Lic. English and Math tchr. Salesman Lyon Metal Products, Inc., Aurora, Ill., 1954; sales tng. dir. Lyon Metal Products, Inc., Aurora, 1987—. With US Navy, 1944-46. Mem. Mensa, South Bend Press Club. Christian. Home and Office: 1913 Stonehedge Ln South Bend IN 46614-6367

MURPHY, WILLIAM MICHAEL, literature educator, biographer; b. N.Y.C., Aug. 6, 1916; s. Timothy Francis and Florence Catherine (McDonald) M.; m. E. Harriet Doane, Sept. 2, 1939; children: David Timothy Michael, Susan Doane, Christopher Ten Broeck. B.A. magna cum laude, Harvard U., 1938, M.A., 1941, Ph.D., 1947. Instr. English Harvard U., 1938-40, 42-43, sec. univ. com. edni. relations, 1940-42; asst. prof. English Union Coll., Schenectady, 1946-48, assoc. prof., 1948-60, prof., 1960-78, Thomas Lamont prof. ancient and modern lit., 1978-83, rsch. prof., 1983-94, prof. emeritus, 1995—; mem. adv. bd. Cornell Yeats Series, Ithaca, N.Y., 1978—; resident fellow Rockefeller Found. Study and Conf. Ctr., Bellagio, Italy, 1991. Author: David Worcester (1907-1947): A Memorial, 1953, The Yeats Family and the Pollexfens of Sligo, 1971, Prodigal Father: The Life of John Butler Yeats (1839-1922), 1978, Family Secrets: William Butler Yeats and His Relatives, 1995. Mem. N.Y. State com. U.S. Commn. on Civil Rights, 1962-74. Served to lt. USNR, 1943-46. Recipient Meritorious Service award United Negro Coll. Fund, 1967; fellow Am. Council Learned Soc., 1968; grantee Am. Philos. Soc., 1968, 75. Mem. MLA, AAUP, Am. Com. on Irish Studies, Can. Assn. Irish Studies, N.S. Bird Soc., Phi Beta Kappa (pres. Alpha chpt. 1954-56). Clubs: Harvard of Eastern N.Y. (pres. 1960-62); Fortnightly (Schenectady) (pres. 1966-67). Office: Humanities Bldg Union Coll Schenectady NY 12308

MURPHY, WILLIAM MICHAEL, public relations executive; b. Beverly, Mass., July 1, 1947; s. Philip David and Claire Priscilla (McGlynn) M.; m. Mary Lamar Riley, Aug. 31, 1985. Student, Benedictine U., 1965-67; AB in History, U. Notre Dame, 1969; AM in British History, U. Chgo., 1970, PhD in Modern Irish History, 1981; postgrd., NYU, 1978. Editor Chronicle U. Chgo., 1981-82, assoc. dir. pubs., 1982-84, dir. Univ. Pubs. Office, 1984-88, acting dir. Univ. News & Info., 1988, asst. v.p. Univ. News & Pubs., 1988-95; assoc. chancellor pub. affairs U. Ill., Urbana-Champaign, 1995—; sec. Inst. Adminstrv. Mgmt. Am. Pub. Works Assn., 1978-81, dir. pub. affairs, 1978-79, dir. chpt. rels., 1979-80, dir. membership, 1980-81; mem. pub. issues task force Coun. Advancement & Support Edn., 1990-92; faculty mem. CASE workshop, 1992. Author: The Parnell Myth and Irish Politics, 1891-1956, 1986; co-editor: The Idea of the University of Chicago: Selections from the Papers of the First Eight Chief Executives of the University of Chicago from 1891 to 1975, 1976; contbr. articles to profl. jours. Mem. coord. com., chair promotions com. 125th Anniversary St. Thomas the Apostle Parish, Chgo., 1995. Ford Found. fellow, 1971-74; Ford Found. scholar, 1968-69. Mem. Assn. Am. Univs. (pub. affairs network 1989—, pub. affairs com. 1993—), Am. Conf. Irish Studies, Execs. Club Chgo. Roman Catholic. Home: 302 W Florida Ave Urbana IL 61801-4913 Office: Univ Ill 601 E John St Champaign IL 61820

MURPHY-BARSTOW, HOLLY ANN, financial consultant; b. St. Joseph, Mo., Jan. 16, 1960; d. Roy Edward and Kathryn Louise (Bachle) Murphy; m. Bruce William Barstow, Oct. 1, 1983; children: Brett Murphy, Taylor Lin. Student, U. Mo., 1978-79; BS, N.W. Mo. State U., 1981. Acct. exec. S.C. Johnson, Omaha, Nebr., 1982-83; dir. mktg. YMCA, Omaha, Nebr., 1983-85; fin. cons. Merrill Lynch, Omaha, Nebr., 1985-89, Smith Barney, Omaha, Nebr., 1989—; instr. fin. seminar Creighton U., Omaha, 1993—, Dana Coll., Blair, Nebr., 1993—; fin. corres. KMTV-3, KETV-7, WOWT-6, Omaha, 1993—. Pres. Am. Lung Assn. Nebr., Omaha, 1992-96; vice chair bd. trustees First Presbyn. Ch., Omaha, 1989-93; membership chair bd. mgrs. West YMCA, Omaha, 1991—; mem Columbian Sch. PTA; campaign chair Toys for Tots, 1994—; founding mem. Omaha Women's Fund. Named one of Ten Outstanding Young Omahans, Omaha Jaycees, 1994. Mem. Omaha Panhellenic Assn., Leadership Omaha (grad.), River City Roundup (trail boss 1989), Sigma Sigma Sigma. Office: Smith Barney 9394 W Dodge Rd # 250 Omaha NE 68114-3319

MURRAY, BETTY JEAN KAFKA, plant physiologist, researcher; b. Council Bluffs, Iowa, June 6, 1935; d. Adolph Joseph and Loretto Audrey (Hobel) Kafka; m. Brownson Murray, June, 14, 1958; 1 child, Michael Maxwell. BBA, U. Mich., 1957, Profl. Devel. Degree in Biology, 1979, MS in Biology, 1983, PhD in Botany, 1987. Exec. trainee Jordan Marsh, Boston, 1957-58; founder, owner, mgr. Marigold Marsh Tree Farm, Manchester, Mich., 1980—; adj. rsch. investigator U. Mich., Ann Arbor, 1987—. Contbr. articles to profl. publs. Mem. AAAS, Am. Soc. Plant Physiologists, Am. Soc. for Hort. Sci., Mich. Nursery and Landscape Assn., Scroll, Sigma Xi, Kappa Kappa Gamma. Republican. Roman Catholic. Office: Marigold Marsh Tree Farm 15490 Buss Rd Manchester MI 48158

MURRAY, CHARLES LEROY, medical oncologist; b. Mpls., Nov. 22, 1935; s. Ned Charles and Ruth Adelaide (McFarland) M.; m. Hilda Costa, June 8, 1957; children: Karen Lynn, Steven Charles, John Charles. BS in Quantitative Biology, MIT, 1957; MD, U. Minn., 1961. Diplomate in internal medicine and med. oncology Am. Bd. Internal Medicine. Resident, fellow Stanford U., Palo Alto, Calif., 1962-65; cons. Geisinger Med. Ctr., Danville, Pa., 1967-71, Park-Nicollet Clinic/Health Systems, Mpls., 1972—; clin. prof. medicine U. Minn. Med. Sch., Mpls., 1972—; med. dir. Upper Midwest Oncology Registry System, Mpls., 1974—; med. dir. oncology Meth. Hosp., Mpls., 1980-92. Contbr. more than 40 articles to med. jours. Trustee Park Nicollet Clinic, 1976-82, 87-95; pres. Minn. divsn. Am. Cancer Soc., 1986-87; co-prin. investigator Minn. Metro Clin. Oncology Program, Mpls., 1983—. Capt. USAF, 1965-67. Recipient St. George medal Minn. divsn. Am. Cancer Soc., 1990. Fellow ACP; mem. AMA (tech. assessment com. 1988-90), Am. Soc. Clin. Oncology, Am. med. Informatics Assn., Minn. Soc. Clin. Oncology (bd. dirs. 1994-96), Am. Cancer Registrars Assn., Sigma Xi, Alpha Omega Alpha. Presbyterian. Office: Park Nicollet Clinic Minneapolis MN 55416

MURRAY, CHRISTINE J., managing editor; b. Marlette, Mich., Apr. 7, 1966; d. Gerald Andrew and Wanetta Bessie (Cope) M. BS, Cen. Mich. U., 1994. Reporter Tuscola Co. Advertiser, Caro, Mich., 1988, South Lyon (Mich.) Herald, 1989, Brown City (Mich.) Banner, 1990-91, The County Press, Lapeer, Mich., 1991-94; mng. editor Isabella Co. Herald, Mt. Pleasant, Mich., 1994—; judge Pa. Press Assn., Harrisburg, 1996. Contbr. articles to profl. jours. Judge Lapeer Co. 4-H, 1989, 93-94. Recipient 1st pl. Feature Story award Mich. Press Assn., 1993, 2d pl. News Reporting award, 1993, 95, Paddle Your Own Canoe award Mich. Press Women, 1996. Mem. Nat. Fedn. Press Women (recruiter 1994-95, 3d pl. Feature Writing award 1995), Soc. Profl. Journalists. Roman Catholic. Office: Isabella Co Herald 300 E Broadway Mount Pleasant MI 48858

MURRAY, CONNIE WIBLE, state legislator; b. Tulsa, Oct. 13, 1943; d. Carl Prince Lattimore and Jimmie Bell Henry; m. Jarrett Holland Murray, May 4, 1995. Cert. of oral hygiene, Temple U., 1965; BA, Loyola Coll., 1975; JD, U. Md., 1980. Registered dental hygienist Bethlehem, Pa., 1965-66, Joppa, Md., 1966-77; law clk. Hon. Albert P. Close, Belair, Md., 1980-81; atty., 1981-85, realtor, 1985-90; mem. Mo. Ho. of Reps., Jefferson City, 1990—; house mgr. Articles ot Impeachment of Judith Moriarty, Mo. Sec. of State, 1994; mem. budget com. Mo. Ho. of Reps., also mem. appropriations social svcs. and corrections com., judiciary and ethics com., civil and criminal law and accounts, opers. and fin. com., interim com. for fed. funds and block grants, commn. on intergovtl. affairs, commn. on mgmt. and productivity, legis. oversight com. for ct. automation, ho. automation com. Bd. dirs. North Springfield Betterment Assn., 1989; vocat. adv. bd., dir. house intern programs Nat. Conf. State Legislators. Named Outstanding Freshman Legis. on Health Care Issues, Mo. Rep. Caucus, 1992; recipient Jud. Conf. Legis. award Mo. Jud. Conf., 1994, Outstanding Woman Legis. award Assn. Probate and Assoc. Cir. Judges, 1995. Mem. LWV (bd. dirs. Springfield 1989, treas.), Nat. Order Women Legis., Nat. Conf. State Legis., Nat. Women's Polit. Caucus, Women Legis. Mo., Mo. Bar Assn. (Adminstr. for Justice award), Am. Legis. Exch. Counsel, Ctr. for Am. Women in Politics, Greene County Bar Assn., Forum-A Women's Network, Women in Govt. Home: 2118 S Catalina Ave Springfield MO 65804-2829 Office: Mo Gen Assembly State Capitol Office Bldg Jefferson City MO 65101-6806

MURRAY, DAVID, pastor, social worker; b. Chicago, Ill., Mar. 4, 1953; s. Julius and Alberta (Tolbert) M. m. Debra McKnight, Oct. 7, 1989; 3 foster children. BS in Criminal Justice, Wayne State U., Detroit, 1982; DDiv, God's Divine Emancipation Tng., 1975; cert. mktg., Detroit Bus. Inst., 1978; MA in Teaching, Wayne State U., 1989; MA in Criminal Justice Studies, U. Detroit Mercy, 1994. Pastor First Holy Temple Ch., Detroit, 1975—; asst. payments worker Mich. Dept. of Social Svcs., Detroit, 1981-85, social svcs. specialist, 1985—. Inventor cardiovascular display system. Pres., bd. dirs. Project Care, Detroit, 1975; mem. Detroit Police Res., 1978-83; instr. CPR ARC, Detroit, 1979, advanced 1st aid, 1980—; instr., trainer Am. Heart Assn., Detroit, 1983—; active Big Bros/Big Sisters Am.; chaplain Detroit Receiving Hosp.; asst. chaplain Wayne County Youth Home, 1978—; chmn. David Murray Scholarship Fund; chmn. com. help handicapped student Mary Grove Coll. Recipient Cert. Appreciation, IRS, Acctg. Aid Soc., 1987, Detroit City Clk. Disting Citizen award, 1988, Wayne County Commrs. Cert. Appreciation, Mich. Senate Spl. tribute, 1988, U.S. Senate proclamation, 1988, TV 2 Jefferson award 1991 Cert. Nomination, Life award Met. Youth Found., 1991. Mem. NAACP, NASW, AACD, Internat. Conf. Police Chaplains, Detroit Fedn. Tchrs., Eighth Point Investigations, Detroit Police Chaplains Corps, Detroit Police Officers Assn., Wayne County Sheriff Dept. (sheriff chaplain), Masons, Golden Key. Home: 18994 Oak Dr Detroit MI 48221-2264

MURRAY, DELBERT MILTON, manufacturing engineer; b. Fordland, Mo., Aug. 22, 1941; s. Chester Augustus and Iris Morene (Hamilton) M.; m. Orilla Maxine Stoaks, Sept. 15, 1962; children: Cynthia Ann, Norman Lee, Orilla Mae, Delbert Lynn. BS, S.W. Mo. State U., 1963. Prodn. planner McDonnell Douglas Corp., St. Louis, 1963-65; tool planning engr. The Boeing Corp., Wichita, Kans., 1965-70; indsl. engr. NCR Corp., Wichita, 1972-77; sr. mfg. engr. Emerson Electric Co., Ava, Mo. Chmn. Mt. Zion Ch. of God., Mo., 1977—. Mem. NRA, N.Am. Hunting Club, Gideons. Republican. Home: RR 1 Box 305 Ava MO 65608-9720 Office: Emerson Electric Co 1400 NW 3D St Ava MO 65608

MURRAY, EDDIE CLARENCE, professional baseball player; b. L.A., Feb. 24, 1956. Student, Calif. State U., L.A. Player minor league teams Bluefield, Miami, Asheville, Charlotte, Rochester, 1973-76; player Balt. Orioles, 1973-88, L.A. Dodgers, 1988-91, N.Y. Mets, 1991-93, Cleveland Indians, 1993—. Named to All-Star Team, 1978, 81-86, 91; named Appalachian League Player of Yr., 1973, Am. League Rookie of Yr., Baseball Writers Assn. Am., 1977, First Baseman, Sporting News Am. League All-Star Team, 1983, 90, ; recipient Gold Glove award, 1982-84, Silver Slugger award, 1983-84, 90. Office: Cleve Indians 2401 Ontario St Cleveland OH 44115*

MURRAY, KENNETH MALCOLM, JR., physicist; b. Phila., July 17, 1925; s. Kenneth M. and Phyllis Murray; divorced; children: Leslie Maria, Kenneth M. III. MSc, U. Md., 1962; PhD, Georgetown U., 1969. Rsch. physicist U.S. Naval Rsch. Lab., Washington, 1952-81; cons. KM Scis., Indpls., 1981—. Contbr. articles to Nuclear Physics, Optical Instruments and Particle Beam Dosimetry. 2d lt. USAF, 1943-45. Recipient Presdl. Citation U.S. Govt., 1963. Mem. Am. Phys. Soc., Soc. Photo Optical Instrumentation Engrs. Office: KM Scis 80 S 11th Ave Beech Grove IL 46107

MURRAY, MICHAEL JOHN, psychiatrist; b. Fond du Lac, Wis., May 8, 1954. BS, U. Wis., Eau Claire, 1976; MPH in Epidemiology, U. Minn., 1981; MD, Med. Coll. Wis., 1982. Head divsn. mil. medicine U.S. Naval Hosp., Newport, R.I., 1983-85; gen. med. officer U.S. Naval Hosp., Groton, Conn., 1986; med. officer U.S.S. Coronado, San Francisco, 1986-88; resident in preventive medicine U. Hawaii, Honolulu, 1988-89; resident in psychiatry St. Elizabeth's Hosp., Boston, 1989-92; staff psychiatrist Midelfort Clinic, Eau Claire, Wis., 1992-93, Northwest Psychiat. Clinic (name changed to Sacred Heart Behavioral & Psychiat. Svcs. 1995), Eau Claire, 1993—; asst. clin. prof. dept. family medicine U.Wis., 1984—. Mem. Am. Psychiat. Assn., Mass. Med. Soc., Wis. Med. Soc., Wis. Psychiat. Assn., Tri-County Med. Assn. Office: Sacred Heart Behavioral & Psychiat Svcs 2125 Heights Dr Ste 3H Eau Claire WI 54701

MURRAY, PETER BRYANT, English language educator; b. N.Y.C., Oct. 6, 1927; s. Frederick James and Florence (Leech) M.; m. Frances N. Pearson, Apr. 24, 1954 (div. Apr. 1970); children: Jean P., Stephen F., Susan C., Christopher J.; m. Karen Louise Olson, Aug. 14, 1970. Student, Va. Mil. Inst., 1945-47; A.B., Swarthmore Coll., 1950; M.A., U. Pa., 1959, Ph.D., 1962. Research chemist Sun Oil Co., Marcus Hook, Pa., 1950-57; instr. English U. Pa., 1961-63, asst. prof., 1963-67; assoc. prof. English U. Del., 1967-68; prof. Macalester Coll., St. Paul, 1968—; chmn. dept. Macalester Coll., 1971-77; Vice pres. Spencer-Murray Corp., Swarthmore, Pa., 1961—. Author: A Study of Cyril Tourneur, 1964, A Study of John Webster, 1969, Thomas Kyd, 1969, Shakespeare's Imagined Persons: The Psychology of Role-Playing and Acting, 1996. Served with AUS, 1946-47. Mem. Modern Lang. Assn. Am., Modern Humanities Research Assn., Am. Assn. U. Profs. (past chpt. pres.), Shakespeare Assn. Am., Nat. Council Tchrs. English. Office: Macalester Coll Dept English Saint Paul MN 55105

MURRAY, RICHARD EDWARD, university administrator, career consultant; b. St. Paul, July 26, 1949; s. Robert Ernest and Dorothy Jane (Olson) M.; m. Susan Mrurray, Aug. 12, 1972 (div. 1984). BS, Mankato (Minn.) State U., 1971, MS in Counseling, 1976. Contract specialist Minn. Dept. Econ. Security, St. Cloud, 1976-80; residence hall dir. St. Cloud (Minn.) State U., 1973-76, assoc. dir. career svcs., 1980-92, dir. career svcs., 1992—; career cons. in pvt. practice, St. Cloud and Mpls., 1985—; mem. followup outcome com. Minn. State Colls. and Univs., St. Paul, 1992—. Inventor traction treads. Bd. dirs., vice chair Ctr. Minn. Sexual Assault Ctr., St. Cloud, 1992—; bd. dirs. WINGS, St. Cloud, 1990—, Unity Ch. of Christ, St. Cloud, 1994—; bd. dirs., vol. action com. United Way, St. Cloud, 1985-95. Direct Mail Advt. Assn. jr. scholar, 1970. Mem. Assn. Minn. Recruiter and Placement Dirs. (sec., treas., v.p., pres.), Nat. Career Devel. Assn. (state del. 1993-95), Minn. Career Devel. Assn. (v.p., pres. 1993-95), Minn. Assn. Counseling Devel. (trustee 1993-95), Minn. Coll. Univ. Placement Assn. (pres.). Home: 137 Riverside Dr NE Saint Cloud MN 56304 Office: St Cloud State U AS-101 720 S 4th Ave Saint Cloud MN 56301

MURRAY, ROBB, software educator; b. Lima, Ohio, Sept. 12, 1953; s. Emmett Jr. and Pauline (List) M. Student, Kalamazoo Coll., 1971-72, Ohio State U., 1974; BA cum laude, Bob Jones U., 1975; MA, U. Chgo., 1977. Reference librarian Chgo. Pub. Library, 1977-80; computer programmer Sears Roebuck & Co., Chgo., 1980-83; software product cons. Davka Corp., Chgo., 1983-84; bus. systems analyst Beatrice Foods, Chgo., 1984-86; software tng. specialist Beatrice U.S. Foods, Chgo., 1985-86; comml. voice-over talent Chgo., 1986—, devel. cons., 1987—; exec. distbr. Nu Skin Internat., Provo, Utah, 1990—; software instr., conf. presenter Project Micro Ideas, Glenview, Ill., 1982-84. Composer, producer (rec.) Classical Mosquito, 1982; co-inventor (computer adventure game) The Lion's Share, 1983; producer, talent: (comml. voice tape) The Refreshing Voice, 1987, (indsl. voice tape) The Credible Voice, 1987, nat. TV comml. O'Boises are O'Boisterous Keebler Products, 1988-89. Counselor Metrohelp Crisis Hotline, Chgo., 1979; adult edn. instr. Lincoln Park Cmty. Ctr., Chgo., 1989—; vol. Children's Meml. Hosp., 1994-96. Mem. The Social Network, Chgo. Area Internet Soc., Chgo. OD Network, Lincoln Park Pacers. Home and Office: 444 W St James Pl Apt 1203 Chicago IL 60614-2707

MURRAY, THOMAS VEATCH, lawyer; b. Phoenix, July 17, 1947; s. Robert Morrison and Jane Veatch (Murray) Barber; m. Cynthia Ann Burnett, June 2, 1971; children: Anne Caroline, Thomas Veatch Jr. BA, U. Kans., 1969; JD, U. Mich., 1972. Bar: Kans. 1972, U.S. Dist. Ct. Kans. 1972, U.S. Ct. Appeals (10th cir.) 1983, U.S. Supreme Ct. 1976. Assoc. Barber, Emerson, Six, Springer & Zinn, Lawrence, Kans., 1972-76; mem. Barber, Emerson, Springer, Zinn & Murray, L.C., Lawrence, Kans., 1976—; dir. The First Nat. Bank of Lawrence, 1980-91, Hall Ctr. for the Humanities, Lawrence, 1988—. Contbr. articles to profl. jours. Mem. Kans. Bd. Law Examiners, 1995—, Bd. Edn. Unified Sch. Dist. 497, Lawrence, 1991-95; dir. Lawrence C. of C., 1993-95. Mem. Fedn. Ins. and Corp. Counsel (regional v.p. 1994—), Kans. Assn. Def. Counsel (dir. 1993—), Univ. Club (Kansas City). Republican. Presbyterian. Office: Barber Emerson Springer Zinn & Murray LC 1211 Massachusetts St Lawrence KS 66044

MURRAY, WILLIAM J., marketing executive; b. Mt. Clair, N.J., May 3, 1949. Grad. in Electronic Engring., Valparaiso Tech. Inst., 1970. Sr. v.p. sales and mktg. Q.R. Inc., Chgo., 1984-90; v.p. sales Merchandise Mart, Chgo., 1991-92; v.p. LMB Mktg. Ltd., Flossmoor, Ill., 1992—. Bd. dirs. Valparaiso (Ind.) Bd. Pub. Works and Safety, 1982-84. Democrat. Roman Catholic. Office: LMB Mktg Ltd 18116 Riegel Rd Homewood IL 60430-2319

MURREY, DANA L., state legislator. Mem. dist. 69 Mo. Ho. of Reps. Office: 2422 Mary Rm 409 B Saint Louis MO 63136

MURRIE, HERBERT LEE, package design executive, consultant; b. Chgo., Sept. 4, 1935; s. Benjamin and Anne (Glazier) M.; m. Lisa Leisten Murrie, Mar. 18, 1961; children: Linda Ann, Karen Lynn, Jennifer Lee, Michael Benjamin. BA advanced design, U. Ill., Champaign, 1953-57. Art dir. Marvin Frank Adv., Chicago, 1960-61; designer/account exec. Robert Snyder & Assoc., Chicago, 1961-62; account exec. Ideographics, Inc., Northbrook, IL, 1962-63; ptnr. Sovereign Lee, Inc., Chicago, 1963-65; founder/pres. Murrie, White, Drummond Lienhart & Assoc., Inc., Chicago, 1965-89; princ./chairman California Dreamers, Inc., Chicago, 1981-88; prin./chairman CEO Murrie, Lienhart, Rysner, Chicago, 1989—; cons. Quaker Oats, Proctor & Gamble, Bristol-Myers, Nestle, Gerber Co., Kraft Foods, Lever Bros., Dow Brands, Coca Cola. Contbr. articles to various publications and newspapers. Sgt. Ft. Bragg, N.C., 1958-64. Recipient over 600 design awards Graphics, Comm. Arts, AIGA, PDC, and various publs. throughout the world, 1965—. Mem. Am. Inst. Graphic Arts, Package Design Coun., Am. Ctr. for Design. Office: Murrie Et Al & Assoc 58 W Huron St Chicago IL 60610

MURRIE, WILLIAM STEPHEN, science educator; b. Anna, Ill., Apr. 8, 1948; s. Daniel Monroe and Clare Elenore (Henehan) M.; m. Nancy Jean Murrie, June 10, 1972; children: Daniel, Matthew, Elizabeth. BA in Zoology, So. Ill. U., 1970; MS in Sci. Edn., Pa. State U., 1974. Tchr. sci. Perryville (Mo.) Pub. Sch., 1970-80, Union (Mo.) Sch. Dist., 1980-89, Rockwood Sch. Dist., Eureka, Mo., 1989—. Author: Creative Science Activities, 1992. Mem. Kiwanis of Union. Baptist. Home: 3 Graham Dr Union MO 63084-2049

MURRY, BARBARA R., social services administrator, public administrator; b. Grand Forks, N.D., Feb. 23, 1950; d. C. Emerson and Donna Dean (Kleve) M.; divorced; children: Angela Bushaw, Tom Bushaw. BA, BS in Edn., U. N.D., 1972; MSA, Cen. Mich. U., 1994. Lic. social worker. Coord. devel. disablities Area Social Svc. Ctr., Grand Forks, 1973-77, marriage and family therapist, 1977-81; marriage and family therapist N.E. Human Svc. Ctr., Grand Forks, 1981-87, intake specialist, 1987-89, dir. devel. disabilities dept., 1989-91; adminstr. day svcs. devel. disabilities div. Dept. Human Svcs., Bismarck, N.D., 1991-95; COO Pride Inc., Bismarck, 1995—. Assoc. mem. Conflict Resolution Ctr., Univ. of N.D. Mem. Am. Assn. Mental Retardation, Nat. Rehab. Assn. (adv. bd. ctr. for tech. assistance and tng.). Home: 156 E Independence Ave Bismarck ND 58501-0463 Office: Pride Inc 1929 N Washington St Bismarck ND 58501

MURSTEIN, DENIS, human services administrator; b. N.Y.C., July 29, 1952; s. Norman and Rosalyn (Gordon) M.; m. Deborah Ruth Granite, June 28, 1975; 1 child, Zachary. BA in Psychology, SUNY, Buffalo, 1974; MA in Social Svc. Adminstrn., U. Chgo., 1981. Cert. social worker, Ill. Child care worker Hillside Children's Ctr., Rochester, N.Y., 1974-77, group home supr., 1977-79; rsch. asst. U. Chgo., 1980-81; exec. dir. Crisis Homes, Park Ridge, Ill., 1981-83; adminstrv. dir. Youth Network Coun., Chgo., 1983—. Pres. 3550 Condominium Assn., Chgo., 1989-91. Mem. Assn. Child Care Workers (pres. Western chpt. 1978-79), Acad. Cert. Social Workers (cert.). Home: 3550 N Lake Shore Dr Apt 1601 Chicago IL 60657-1907 Office: Youth Network Coun 59 E Van Buren # 1610 Chicago IL 60605-1607

MUSA, MAHMOUD NIMIR, psychiatry educator; b. Arraba, Jenin, Palestine, Mar. 22, 1943; came to U.S., 1964; s. Nimir A. and Zarifa (Haseeb) M.; m. Wafaa M. Arafat, Mar. 24, 1991. BS, Am. U. Beirut, 1964; MS, U. Wis., 1966, PhD, 1972; MD, Med. Coll. Wis., 1979. Diplomate Am. Bd. Psychiatry. Rsch. assoc. U. Wis., Madison, 1972-75; asst. prof. Idaho State U., Pocatello, 1975-76; resident Ill. State Psychiat. Inst., Chgo., 1979-83; assoc. prof. psychiatry Chgo. Med. Sch., North Chicago, Ill., 1987-90; prof. psychiatry Loyola U., Maywood, Ill., 1990—; cons. Mus. Sci. & Industry, Chgo., 1985-90; editl. bd. Jour. Clin. Pharmacology. Editor: Pharmacikinetics and Monitoring Psychiatry Drugs, 1992; mem. editl. bd. Jour. Clin. Pharmacology. Cons. Kovler Ctr. for Treatment of Survivors of Torture, CHgo., 1989-92. Recipient Scientific Achievement award Ill. Psychiat. Soc., Chgo., 1982. Fellow Am. Coll. Clin. Pharmacology, Great Lakes Soc. Clin. Pharmacology (pres. 1991-92); mem. AAAS, Am. Psychiat. Assn. Home: 1115 S Plymouth Ct Apt 102 Chicago IL 60605-2027

MUSER, DANIEL DONALD, city official; b. St. Louis, Sept. 6, 1947; s. Robert A. and Arline (Davis) M.; m. Nancy S. March, June 7, 1969; children: Erik, Kelly. BS, U. Mo., 1970, MS, 1975. Hort. prodn. mgr. Neosho (Mo.) Nurseries, Inc., 1975-85; parks supt. City of Cape Girardeau, Mo., 1985-91; dir. parks and recreation City of Cape Girardeau, 1991—. Author: A Natural Area Survey of the Kaysinger Basin Area, 1975. Dir. S.E. Mo. Dist. Fair Assn., Cape Girardeau, 1992—. With U.S. Army, 1970-72. Recipient Award for paper to trees program Dept. Natural Resources, 1991. Mem. Nat. Parks and Recreation Assn., Mo. Parks and Recreation Assn., C. of C. (mem. beautification bd. 1992—). Office: Cape Girardeau Parks/Rec 410 Kiwanis Dr Cape Girardeau MO 63701

MUSEUS, ROBERT ALLEN, city manager; b. Mpls., Dec. 30, 1955; s. Jewel Melbourne Museus and Gladys Mercedes (Leipold) Johnson; m. Jutta Ziehmer, Oct. 29, 1982. BA in History, U. Minn., 1979; MA in Pub. Adminstrn., Hamline U., St. Paul, 1991. City adminstr. City of Rushford, Minn., 1984-92, City of Hugo, Minn., 1992—. Legis. policy com. League Minn. Cities, St. Paul, 1984-89. 1st lt. U.S. Army, 1979-83; maj. Minn. N.G., 1984—. Mem. Internat. City Mgmt. Assn. Republican. Lutheran. Home: 13550 Freeland Ave N Hugo MN 55038-9229 Office: City of Hugo 5524 Upper 146th St N Hugo MN 55038-9367

MUSGRAVE, CHARLES EDWARD, retired music director, correctional official; b. Alton, Ill., Nov. 17, 1932; s. Clay Everett and Fannie Adeline (Peek) M.; m. Barbara Jean Robertson, Aug. 11, 1952 (div. Feb. 1971); children: Michael David, Debra Ann; m. Toby Elaine Riley, Aug. 18, 1973. B in Mus. Edn., Shurtleff Coll., 1954; MS, U. Ill., 1957; postgrad., U. No. Colo., 1970. Cert. tchr., Ill., Ind. Tchr. music Alton (Ill.) Pub. Schs., 1953-67; v.p. Monticello Coll., Godfrey, Ill., 1967-69; asst. to v.p. U. No. Colo., Greeley, 1970; chmn. dept. music Duneland Sch. Corp., Chesterton, Ind., 1970-72; dir. devel. Interlochen (Mich.) Arts Acad., 1972-73; v.p. Musart Corp., Chgo., 1973-74; dir. music and coll. coord. Ind. State Prison, Michigan City, 1974-95; ret., 1995; asst. dir. music Willowbrook Meth. Ch., Sun City, Ariz., 1996—; vice chmn. La Porter Fed. Credit Union, Michigan City, 1975—; facility coordinator adult continuing edn. Ind. U. Author: Fussell's Individual Technique Guide, 1973, (music) Why Only on Christmas, 1981. Rep. committeeman, Chesterton, 1976-95, del. to state conv., Ind., 1978-89; mem. Porter County (Ind.) Planning Commn., 1984-85; chmn. govt. workers sect. United Way, Michigan City, 1981-90; mem. Ind. Gov.'s Adv. Com., 1983; minister of music 1st United Meth. Ch., Chesterton, 1978-91; bd. dirs. Five Lakes Conservation Club, Wolcottville, Ind., 1983-95; bd. dirs., v.p. Valparaiso Cmty. Concerts Assn., 1986-95. Grantee Systems Mgmt. U. W. Va., U. Chgo., 1979. Mem. Correctional Edn. Assn. (Internat. Tchr. of Yr. 1981), Ind. Soc. Chgo., LaGrange Country Club, Masons, Shriners, Scottish Rite, Phi Delta Kappa. Home: 750 Graham Dr Chesterton IN 46304-1620

MUSGRAVE, SCOTT ALLEN, mechanical engineer; b. Phila., Aug. 29, 1969. BSME, U. Mo., 1991. Engr.-in-tng., Mo. Product engr. Deere & Co., Dubuque, Iowa, 1991—. Adv. Jr. Achievement, Dubuque, 1994—. Mem. Soc. Automotive Engrs. Office: Deere & Co PO Box 538 Dubuque IA 52004

MUSICUS, RAPHAEL J., lawyer, accountant; b. N.Y.C., Oct. 20, 1920; s. Boris and Sofia (Dorfman) M.; m. Selma Gould, Apr. 6, 1952; children:

Bruce Ronald, Lonore Michelle. BS, CCNY, 1938, MBA, 1943; LLB summa cum laude, St. John's U., Queens, N.Y., 1946. Bar: N.Y. 1946, Ill. 1949; CPA, N.Y., Ill. Officer, dir. Englander Co., Inc., Chgo.; pres. Olson Rug Co., Chgo., 1974, Raphael J. Musicus, Ltd., Wilmette, Ill., 1974—; chmn. bd. Raphael J. Musicus, Ltd., Wilmette, 1976—. Editor St. John's U. Law Rev., 1945-46. Mem. Chgo. Bar Assn. Office: 530 Locust Rd Wilmette IL 60091-2268

MUSSEHL, ALLAN ARTHUR, program director; b. Edgerton, Wis., Aug. 12, 1942; s. Arthur John and Ruth Anna (Miller) M. BA, Milton Coll., 1965; MA, U. Wis., Madison, 1971, U. Wis., Milwaukee, 1973. Chairperson speech dept. Cumberland (Wis.) High Sch., 1965-71; asst. prof. mass communications Milton (Wis.) Coll., 1971-74; asst. prof. communications media Bemidji (Minn.) State U., 1974-79; assoc. prof. mass communications Middle Tenn. State U., Murfreesboro, 1979-85; dir. Learning Resources, assoc. prof. humanities Southeastern U., Washington, 1985-87; dean of instrn. Transitional Coll. & Learning Resources Nicolet Coll., Rhinelander, Wis., 1987—; vocat. tech. adult edn. rep. Coun. Wis. Librs., 1990—. Author: Man, Media and Society, 1976; also articles. Disting. Mellon fellow, Vanderbilt U., 1981; named Sch. of Libr. and Info. Sci. Notable Alumnus, U. Wis., Milw., 1993. Mem. ALA, ACLU, Coun. Wis. Librs. (elected). Democrat. Lutheran. Home: W 2148 Eagle Dr Neshkoro WI 54960-9729 Office: Nicolet Coll Learning Resource Ctr Rhinelander WI 54501

MUSSER, MARGARET MORRIS, marketing professional; b. N.Y.C., Nov. 1, 1962; d. John Daniel and Jean Bingham (MacCollom) M.; m. Gary E. Musser Jr., May 1, 1993. BA in English, Georgetown U., 1984. Mem. staff mktg. programs AT&T Nat. Fed. Mktg., Arlington, Va., 1985; mktg. tech. cons. AT&T Nat. Fed. Systems, Washington, 1985-87; tech. cons. computer mktg. Cin. Bell Tel. Co., 1987-89, mktg. tech. cons., 1989-95; sr. acct. exec.-strategic accts., 1995—; tutor (vol.) Ptnrs. in Edn. Editor: (newsletter) District Action Project RAP, 1981-82. Intern Citizen's Complaint Ctr., Washington, 1981-82. Mem. NAFE, Cin. Updowntowners, Soroptimist Internat., Telephone Pioneers Am. Office: Cin Bell Tel Co 201 E 4th St Rm 102-1180 Cincinnati OH 45202-4122

MUSSER, TERRY M., state legislator. Home: RR 1 Box 98 Black River Falls WI 54615-9731*

MUSTAFA, ALI SYED, structural engineer, consultant; b. Hyderabad, India, Oct. 21, 1935; came to U.S., 1962; s. Syed Inayat and Habib-Un-Nissa (Begum) Husain; m. Abida Meher Sultana, July 26, 1964; children: Rohina, Rubina, Sameena, Raabia, Arjumund. BCE, U. Peshawar, Pakistan, 1957; MS in Structural Engring., Okla. State U., 1963. Registered profl. structural engr., Ill. Asst. engr. Burlington R.R., Chgo., 1963-66; structural engr. Sargent & Lundy Engrs., Chgo., 1966-74; project mgr. Bur. Engring. Dept. Pub. Works, Chgo., 1974-91; project mgr. Divsn. Planning & Design Dept. of Aviation, Chgo., 1991-94; chief structural engr. Divsn. of Engring., Dept. of Aviation, Chgo., 1995—; bd. dirs. Delta Engring. Inc., Chgo. Bd. dirs. Muslim Community Ctr., Chgo., 1974-84. Fellow ASCE. Home: 6900 N Minnetonka Ave Chicago IL 60646-1518 Office: Dept Aviation O'Hare Internat Airport PO Box 66142 Chicago IL 60666

MUSTAIN, BRIAN CLARK, plant consultant; b. Dallas, Dec. 9, 1945; s. Rhoads and Carolee (Blackburn) M.; m. Elaine Carol Huddleston, June 10, 1969; children: Andrea Elaine, Nathan Hall, Patrick Lewis, Stefan John, Adrian Anna. BA in Anthropology, Rice U., 1967; MDiv in Old Testament, Harvard U., 1972; MS in Agronomy, Rutgers U., 1976; PhD in Plant Genetics, Tex. A&M U., 1981. Rsch. sta. mgr. Clyde Black and Son Inc., Lake Crystal, Minn., 1980-81, Zoecon Corp., Lincoln, Ill., 1981-83; dir. soybean rsch. United AgriSeed, Champaign, Ill., 1983-86; pres. Plant Breeding Cons., Urbana, Ill., 1986—, New Start Mktg., Inc., 1990—. Bd. dirs. Cons. Ctrl. Ill., Urbana, 1988-89, Men's Emergency Shelter, 1996—. Home: 407 W Illinois St Urbana IL 61801-3214 Office: New Start Mktg Inc PO Box 972 Urbana IL 61801-3257

MUSTARD, MARY CAROLYN, financial executive; b. North Bend, Nebr., Sept. 21, 1948; d. Joseph Louis and Rosalie Margaret (Emanuel) Smaus; m. Ronald L. Mustard, Apr. 19, 1969 (div. 1988); children: Joel Jonathan, Dana Marie. Student, Creighton U., 1966-67, C.E. Sch. Commerce, 1967-68, Coll. of St. Mary, 1983-84, Met. C.C., Omaha, 1988-90, Bellevue U., 1991-92. With Platte County Dept. Pub. Welfare, Columbus, Nebr., 1968-69; sec. to plant mgr. B.L. Montague Steel Co., Sumter, S.C., 1969-70; property disposal technician Property Disposal Office, Shaw AFB, S.C., 1970-71; libr. technician Hdqs. Strategic Air Command Librarian, Offutt AFB, Nebr., 1971-76; sec.-steno Hdqs. Strategic Air Command Communications/Frequency Mgmt., Offutt AFB, Nebr., 1976-79; security specialist/program analyst Hdqs. Strategic Air Command Security Police, Offutt AFB, Nebr., 1979-88; budget analyst Hdqs. Strategic Air Command Fin. Mgmt., Offutt AFB, 1988-92; funds control analyst Hdqs. Air Mobility Command, Scott AFB, Ill., 1992-93, chief hdqs. and comm. account, 1993-94, chief hdqs. relocation, transition assistance/comm. programs, 1994-95; chief base realignment and closure program Air Mobility Command, Scott AFB, Ill., 1995—. Mem. Am. Soc. Mil. Comptrollers (SAC Budget Analyst of Yr. 1990). Democrat. Roman Catholic. Office: AMCFSS/FMBO 402 Scott Dr Unit 1k1 Scott AFB IL 62225-5301

MUTCH, DUANE, state legislator; b. Grand Forks, N.D., May 13, 1925; m. Dolores, 1949; children: Martha, John, Paul. Mem. N.D. Senate, 1959—, chmn. indsl., bus. and labor com., mem. transp. com.; distbr. bulk oil and propane. Mem. Am. Legion, Farm Bur. Office: 711 Terry Ave Larimore ND 58251-4526*

MUTHUSWAMY, PETHAM PADAYATCHI, pulmonary medicine and critical care specialist; b. Salem, Tamil Nadu, India, June 12, 1945; came to U.S., 1970; s. Petham Padayatchi and Anjalam M.; m. Rajeswari Muthuswamy, Nov. 11, 1975; children: Sudha, Sathya, Senthil. MB, BS, Stanley Med. Sch., Madras, India, 1969. Diplomate Am. Bd. Internal Medicine, Am. Bd. Pulmonary Disease, Am. Bd. Critical Care Medicine, Can. Bd. Respiratory Medicine. Attending physician Cook County Hosp., Chgo., 1976-79; dir. respiratory therapy Hyde Park Hosp., Chgo., 1977-80; co-dir. ICU Jackson Park Hosp., Chgo., 1978-80; chmn. pulmonary medicine Cook County Hosp., Chgo., 1980—, program dir. pulmonary medicine/critical care, 1980—; assoc. prof. medicine U. Ill. Coll. Medicine, Chgo., 1989-94; dir. cardiopulmonary dept. Jackson Park Hosp., 1994—; consulting physician Mercy Hosp., Chgo., 1978—, Trinity Hosp., 1978—, Jackson Park Hosp., 1978—, Drs. Hosp. of Hyde Park, 1978—. Contbr. numerous articles to profl. jours. Life mem. Tamil Nadu Found., Balt., 1980—; mem. fin. com. Indo Am. Dem. Orgn., Chgo., 1984-86. Recipient Recognition award Statue of Liberty Ellis Island Centennial Commn., N.Y., 1986. Fellow ACP, Am. Coll. Chest Physicians, Royal Coll. Physicians and Surgeons of Can.; mem. AMA (Physician Recognition award 1980—), AAAS, Am. Sleep Disorders Assn., Am. Thoracic Soc., Soc. Critical Care Medicine, Am. Coll. Physician Execs., European Respiratory Soc., Assn. Am. Physicians of Indian Origin, India Med. Assn. of Ill. (life). Office: Cook County Hosp Div Pulmonary Medicine 1835 W Harrison St Chicago IL 60612-3701

MUTZENBERGER, MARV, state legislator; m. Barbara; 3 children. Student, Wartburg Coll., Wartburg Sem. Mem. N.D. Ho. of Reps., 1991—, mem. human svcs. com., mem. vet. affairs com., mem. fed. govt. com., mem. judiciary com., mem. nat. resources com.; prof.; minister. Mem. Social Svc. Bd. Bush fellow. Mem. AARP, Elks, Eagles. Home: 205 E Arbor Ave Apt 112 Bismarck ND 58504-5703*

MUZIC, RAYMOND FRANK, JR., radiology educator, biomedical engineering educator; b. Cleve., June 27, 1965; s. Raymond F. Sr. and Joan M. (Dannemiller) M.; m. Linda Lee Selby, Sept. 14, 1991. BS in Biomedical Engring., Case Western Res. U., 1987, MS in Biomedical Engring., 1988, PhD in Biomedical Engring., 1991. Asst. prof. radiology Case Western Reserve Univ., Cleve., asst. prof. biomedical engring.; with divsn. of nuclear medicine U. Hosps. of Cleve. Contbr. articles to profl. jours. Rsch. grant NSF, 1994-95, Rsch. grant Whitaker Found., 1994—. Mem. IEEE, Biomedical Engring. Soc. (meeting organizer, track chair). Roman Catholic. Office: Univ Hosps of Cleve 11100 Euclid Ave Cleveland OH 44106

MUZZILLO, RACHEL EVELYN SHEELEY, reporter; b. Richmond, Ind., Nov. 22, 1966; d. Lysle Leavitt and Alecia Eilene (Hindsley) S. BA, Franklin Coll. of Ind., 1989. Intern, writer weekend dept. Indpls. Star, 1988; intern, writer Brandon (Man., Can.) Sun, 1989; intern, writer Palladium-Item, Richmond, 1986-89, reporter, 1989—. Winner first prize Bulwer-Lytton Fiction Contest, San Jose State U., 1988, 3rd pl. spot news Best Gannett Corp. award. Mem. Women in Communications, Soc. Profl. Journalists, Phi Alpha Theta. Home: 516 Riley Rd New Castle IN 47362-1609 Office: Palladium-Item 1175 N A St Richmond IN 47374-3226

MWAKISUNGA, CHARLES G., mechanical engineer; b. Mbeya, Tanzania, Nov. 7, 1957. BSME, Marquette U., 1985; postgrad., Cardinal Stritch Coll. Design mech. engr. Milsco Mfg. Co., Milw., 1986—. Co-inventor garden tractor seat suspension. Home: 6154 W Port Ave Milwaukee WI 53223-4118 Office: Milsco Mfg Co 9009 N 51st St Milwaukee WI 53223-2403

MYATT, G., company executive; b. Cleve., Aug. 16, 1930. BS in Mech. Engring., Cleve. State Coll., 1964. Pres. Pearce Inc., Cleve., 1962—. Patentee: Paper feeding device, 1963. Office: Pearce Inc 12026 Zelis Rd Cleveland OH 44135-4660

MYER, PAUL JOSEPH, hotel company executive; b. Bad Constatt, Germany, Jan. 31, 1954; came to U.S., 1954; s. Anthony Phillip and Caroline Ann (Molter) M.; m. Michelle Lynne Jacoby, Sept. 25, 1982. BS in Hotel Adminstrn. with distng., Cornell U., 1976; MBA, Roosevelt Univ., 1994. Mgr. Hyatt Hotels, Chgo., 1976-79; asst. and gen. mgr. Henricis Restaurants, Chgo., 1979-81; gen. mgr. Midway Hotel, Elk Grove, Ill., 1981-83; pres. Paul J. Myer & Assocs., Buffalo Grove, Ill., 1983—; v.p. Chase Waterford, Schaumburg, Ill., 1986-91; instr., lectr. Northwestern Bus. Coll., 1987—. Mem. Coun. Hotel, Restaurants, Institutional Educators. Republican. Roman Catholic. Home and Office: 520 Burnt Ember Ln Buffalo Grove IL 60089-1614

MYERHOLTZ, RALPH W., JR., retired chemical company executive, research chemist; b. Bucyrus, Ohio, July 29, 1926; s. Ralph W.E. and Vera (Kirkland) M.; m. Lois Ellen Congram, June 24, 1951; children: Carl Alan, Lynne Elaine Myerholtz Patterson. BS, Purdue U., 1950; PhD in Organic Chemistry, Northwestern U., 1954. Project chemist Standard Oil Co. (Ind.), Whiting, Ind., 1954-58; group leader Amoco Chem. Corp., Whiting, 1958-66, rsch. assoc., 1966-69; dir. polymer physics divsn. Amoco Chem. Corp., Naperville, Ill., 1969-86. Contbr. articles to profl. jours.; holder 7 patents. Trustee Greenfield (Ind.) Pub. Libr., 1995—; radio officer CD, Naperville, 1971-81; scoutmaster Boy Scouts Am., Hammond, Ind., 1955-59. Sgt. U.S. Army, 1944-46, PTO. Mem. Am. Chem. Soc., Sigma Xi, Pi Kappa Phi, Phi Lambda Upsilon. Home: 1125 Cricket Reel Greenfield IN 46140

MYERS, CHRISTY COLWELL, historian, retail merchandiser; b. Toledo, Ohio, July 7, 1953; d. Richard E. and Joyce A. (Snyder) Colwell; m. Dennis D. Myers, June 5, 1971; 1 child, Damian D. Grad., high sch., 1971. CEO Myers Gen. Mdse., Deshler, Ohio, 1986-95; trustee Henry County Hist. Soc., Napoleon, Ohio, corr. sec., cons.; supr. events Henry County Hist. Soc., Napoleon; mem. Med. Mission Tour, Port-Au-Prince, Haiti, 1968, 73. Author poetry and newspaper articles. Mem. Henry County Hist. Soc. (trustee 1989-94, corr. sec. 1993-94). Home and Office: 330 W Maple Deshler OH 43516

MYERS, DON V., state legislator; m. Mary Myers. Rep. dist. 82 State of Kans., 1993—. Republican. Home: 613 Briarwood Rd Derby KS 67037-2112*

MYERS, EDDIE EARL, clinical psychologist; b. Ardmore, Okla., Nov. 24, 1937; s. Finis Weldon and Fern Durrell (Johnson) M.; m. Ineta June Moore, July 2, 1955 (div. Mar. 1988); children: Richard Weldon, Ronald Leland, Marilyn June, Rebecca Jean; m. Ann Clymer Taylor, July 15, 1988; Clark Clymer Taylor, Katy Ann Taylor. BSEd, Tex. Christian U., 1958; MEd, U. N. Tex., 1967, EdD, 1969. Lic. psychologist, Ohio; Nat. Drug Edn. Leadership Tng. Adlephi U., 1970. Machinist Chance Vaught Aircraft, Grand Prairie, Tex., 1957-58; 5th grade tchr., jr. high coach Ft. Worth Christian Schs., 1958-59; 6th grade tchr., jr. high coach Corpus Christi (Tex.) Ind. Sch. Dist., 1959-60; youth, music, ednl. min. Norton St. Ch. Christ, Corpus Christi, 1960-61, Procter St. Ch. Christ, Port Arthur, Tex., 1963-65; min. Cameron (Tex.) Ch. Christ, 1961-63; high sch. English tchr. Christian Schs., Inc., Dallas, 1965-66; psychology instr. Tex. Women's U., Denton, 1968-69; sr. rsch. assoc., dir. psychology dept. Ednl. Rsch. Coun. Am., Cleve., 1969-78; clin. psychologist pvt. practice Cleve., 1978—; faculty dept. guidance anc counseling U. Oreg. Workshop, Frankfurt, German, 1972; Ea. U.S. drug abuse task force Am. Soc. Health Assn., N.Y.C., 1971-73; chmn. drug abuse and alcoholism task force Fedn. Cmty. Planning, Cleve., 1970-71; adv. bd. Freedom House Rehab. Ctr., Cleve., 1993—; adj. assoc. prof. ednl. specialists Cleve. State U., 1970-74; mem. med. staff St. John Westshore Hosp., West Lake, Ohio, Fairview Hosp., Cleve. Author: Social Isolation and Personality, 1973, Handy Asks the Psychologist, 1974, (tchr. manual) Human Persons and Use of Psychoactive Agents, 1974; co-author: (tchr. manual) New Model Me: Operator's Guide to Coping with Aggression, 1974; contbr. articles to profl. jours. R & D grantee NIMH, Washington, 1974-78, Nat. Def. Edn. Rsch. Tng. grantee U.S. Dept. Edn., Washington, 1965-69. Mem. APA, Cleve. Psychol. Assn. (bd. trustees 1981-85), Cleve. Acad. Consulting Psychologists (pres. 1984-86), Ohio Psychol. Assn. (bd. trustees 1978—), Phi Delta Kappa. Home: 28602 W Oviatt Rd Bay Village OH 44140 Office: 3865 Rocky River Dr Ste 2 Cleveland OH 44111

MYERS, GLORIA J., elementary education educator; b. Atlantic, Iowa, Feb. 14, 1949; d. Louis E. Sr. and Jean M. (Horacek) M. BA in Elem. Edn., U. No. Iowa, 1971, MA in Spl. Edn., 1978. Cert. tchr., K-14 endorsements in behavioral disorders and mental disabilities, Iowa. Title I remedial reading tchr. Council Bluffs (Iowa) Pub. Schs., 1971-75; K-12 multicategorical resource tchr. Walnut (Iowa) Community Sch., 1975—. Mem. planning com. for annual transition fair for S.W. Iowa, Pottawattamie County, 1987—. Recipient Outstanding Achievement award Loess Hills Area Edn. Agy., 1989, Excellence in Edn. award, 1992. Mem. NEA, Iowa Edn. Assn. (local chpt. pres., v.p., sec., treas.), Walnut Edn. Assn. (pres. local chpt., cochmn.), Delta Kappa Gamma Soc. Internat. Home: PO Box 301 Walnut IA 51577-0301 Office: PO Box 528 Walnut IA 51577-0528

MYERS, JACK FREDRICK, artist, educator, author; b. Lima, Ohio, Feb. 17, 1927; s. Harold Frank and Lesta Arvilla (Ross) M.; m. Frances Dydek, Apr. 30, 1949; children: Steven Ross, David Gene, Kevin Douglas. Student, Cleve. Inst. Art, 1947-49; MFA, Kent State U., 1980. Staff artist Bill Ripley & Assocs., Cleve., 1951-57; art dir. Premier Indsl. Corp., Cleve., 1957-70; instr. Cooper Sch. Art, Cleve., 1970-80; assoc. prof. art U. Dayton, Ohio, 1982-87; ret., 1987. Author: The Language of Visual Art, 1989. With USNR, 1945-46, PTO. Recipient First prize in art Newsweek/Pallard S.A., 1969. Home and Office: 4420 Woodner Dr Dayton OH 45440-1223

MYERS, JOHN ELDRIDGE, quality assurance professional; b. Henderson, Ky., Aug. 26, 1917; s. Lancelot and Mae (Cox) M.; m. Mary Kathryn Burris, Sept. 3, 1949. Grad. high sch., Evansville, Ind. Lic. pub. acct. Receiving inspector Bucyrus-Erie Co., Evansville, Ind., 1946-49, inspector cranes, 1949-60, final inspector, 1960-80; pvt. practise Evansville, 1955—. With U.S. Army, 1943-46. Mem. Eagles, Am. Legion, Fire Siren, Ky. Cols. Democrat. Home and Office: 1511 Cole Ave Evansville IN 47712-4518

MYERS, JOHN MOORE, fraternal organization administrator; b. Urbana, Ohio, Jan. 24, 1946; s. Louis Walter and Dorothy Caroline (Vordermark) M.; m. Nancy Lee Huff, Dec. 30, 1971; children: David Lawrence, Edward Louis. BS in Edn., Bowling Green State U., 1968; postgrad., U. Kansas, 1968-71, Columbia Sch. Broadcasting, 1971-72. Pub. svc. dir. KAKE Radio, Wichita, Kans., 1972-79; pub. svc. dir. Morning Dr. KFH Radio, Wichita, Kans., 1979-81, community rels. dir., 1985-87; dir. devel. Kans. Masonic Home, Wichita, Kans., 1981-84; ops. mgr. Morning Dr KAKZ Radio, Wichita, Kans., 1984-85; sec.-treas. Scottish Rite Bodies of Wichita, 1987—; bd. dirs. Episcopal Social Svcs., 1990—; bd. dirs. Sta. KPTS-TV; sec./treas. Kans. Scottish Rite Found., 1987—; bd. dirs. Kans. Masonic Found., 1988—. Speakers Bur. United Way, Sedgwick County; co-host Children's Miracle Network Telethon, Wichita, 1985-87; bd. dirs. Sedgwick Co. Hist. Mus. Named Broadcaster of Yr., Kans. Assn. Broadcasters, 1979, Wichitan Mag., 1980-91; col. Confederate Air Force. Fellow Titanic Hist. Mus.; mem. Sir John Falstaff Lit. Soc., Rotary (sec. 1989, chmn. membership 1990-91), Kans. Aviation Mus. Episcopalian. Home: 2221 Bramblewood St Apt 501 Wichita KS 67226-1067 Office: Scottish Rite Bodies 332 E 1st St N Wichita KS 67202-2402

MYERS, JOLYNNE, cardiovascular nurse educator; b. Wichita, Kans., Apr. 26, 1957; d. Lynn Currier and Betty Jean (Arvin) M. Diploma, St. Luke's Hosp. Sch. Nursing, 1979; BSN, Webster Coll., 1981; MS in Edn., U. Kans., 1990; postgrad., U. Mo., 1995—. Staff nurse CCU Wesley Med. Ctr., Wichita, 1979-80; clin. nurse I, II MICU St. Luke's Hosp., Kansas City, Mo., 1980-86, staff devel. clin. educator, 1986-90, supr. Mid Am. Heart Inst., 1990-92; cardiac rehab. coord., critical care instr. Independence (Mo.) Regional Health Care Ctr., 1992—; vice-chair clin. practice com. St. Luke's Hosp., Kansas City, 1986-90, voting mem. clin. excellence com., chair ad hoc com., 1988-90; instr. ACLS affiliate faculty, 1986—, BLS affiliate faculty, 1991—, coord., 1987-90; lectr. to various orgns. Mem. heart ball com. fund raiser Am. Heart Assn., 1993-95. Mem. AACN, CCRN (coord. edn. fund-raising fashion show 1990, 91), ANA, Mo. Nurses Assn., Sigma Theta Tau Lambda Phi chpt. Republican. Baptist. Home: 5110 NE 44th St Kansas City MO 64117-1930

MYERS, JON D., state legislator; m. Cheryl Myers; children: Shon, Jerrod, Ashley. BS, Urbana U. City councilman Lancaster, Ohio; state rep. Dist. 78 Ohio State Congress, state rep. Dist. 6, 1993—; employee Am. Electric Power, Lancaster. Named Freshman Legislator of Yr., 1992. Mem. Lancaster Law Commn. (chmn.), Friends of Lancaster Parks, Cameo and Cmty. Concerts, C. of C. *

MYERS, KENNETH ELLIS, hospital administrator; b. Battle Creek, Mich., Jan. 1, 1932; s. Orlow J. and Kathryn (Brown) M.; m. Nancy Lee Lindgren, June 9, 1956; children—Cynthia Lynn, Anne Lisa, Thomas Scot, Susan Elaine. BBA, U. Mich., 1956, MBA, 1957. Research analyst Bur. Bus. Research, U. Mich., 1956-57; in financial mgmt. Burroughs Corp., Detroit, 1957-66; controller William Beaumont Hosp., Royal Oak, Mich., 1966-68; asso. dir. William Beaumont Hosp., 1968-69, hosp. dir., 1969-80, exec. v.p., 1976-80, pres., 1981—; pres. Trinity Loss Prevention Systems, 1980-81; bd. dirs. Chateau Properties, Inc. Elder Bloomfield Hills Christian Ch., 1979-82, Grace Chapel, 1988-92, 95—; bd. visitors Oakland Sch. Bus. Adminstrn., 1978-92; adv. bd. Salvation Army, 1985—; bd. dirs. William Tyndale Coll., 1992—, West Bloomfield Bldg. Authority, 1978—; trustee St. Mary's Hosp., 1992—. Mem. Mich. Hosp. Assn. (past chmn.), Vol. Hosps. Am. Enterprises (bd. dirs. 1984-87), Full Gospel Businessmen's Fellowship, Bloomfield Hills Country Club, Old Club, Phi Delta Theta, Beta Gamma Sigma. Home: 5085 Lakebluff Rd West Bloomfield MI 48323-2430 Office: William Beaumont Hosp Corp 3601 W 13 Mile Rd Royal Oak MI 48073-6712

MYERS, KENNETH L(EROY), secondary education educator; b. Auburn, Nebr., Oct. 5, 1954; s. Kenneth E. and Erma F. (Hardwick) M.; m. Willo Kay Dykstra, July 1, 1995. BS in Edn., Peru State Coll., 1985, mid. sch. endorsement, 1990, MS in Edn., 1992. Cert. tchr., Nebr., Mo., S.D. Tchr. math., coach Nodaway-Holt High Sch., Graham, Mo., 1985-87, Nebraska City (Nebr.) Lourdes High Sch., 1987-89; tchr. math., social studies, coach Newcastle (Nebr.) High Sch., 1989—; chair Newcastle Math. Curriculum Team, 1991—; master tchr. N.E. Nebr. Masters Tchrs. Project, 1991—; mem. N.E. Nebr. Math. Cadre. Mem. NEA, ASCD, Nat. Coun. Tchrs. Math., Nebr. Assn. Tchrs. Math., Nebr. Coaches Assn., Nebr. State Edn. Assn., Newcastle Faculty Orgn. (pres. 1992-95). Office: Newcastle Pub Schs PO Box 187 Newcastle NE 68757-0187

MYERS, LARRY STEVEN, senior designer; b. Lorain, Ohio, May 22, 1950. A in Elec. Tech., Lorain C.C., 1971. Sr. designer Nordson Corp., Amherst, Ohio, 1978—; cons. in field. Co-inventor of New Way of Applying Powder Paint. Coach South Amherst (Ohio) Recreation League, 1985-90. Republican. Office: Nordson Corp 1150 Nordson Dr Amherst OH 44001-2422

MYERS, MICHAEL CHARLES, marketing executive; b. Chgo., Oct. 15, 1949; s. Allen Jerome and Helen Emma (Schreiner) M.; m. Diana Jane Usalis, June 23, 1972; children: James Brandon, William Grant. BS in Biology, Northeastern Ill. U., 1974; MBA, Depaul U., 1982. Sales rep. Ortho Pharm., Raritan, N.J., 1974-76; midwest regional mgr. Gambro, Inc., Chgo., 1976-80, IDX Corp., Burlington, Vt., 1985-88, Candela Laser Corp., Wayland, Mass., 1988-90; mktg. mgr. Technicare, Inc., Solon, Ohio, 1980-82; mktg. exec. HBO & Co., Atlanta, 1982-85; v.p. Comdisco, Inc., Rosemont, Ill., 1990—; adj. asst. prof. Kellstadt Grad. Sch. Bus. Depaul U., 1983—; bd. dirs. Prism Data Systems, Inc, Lebanon, Ind., Check Six, Inc., Chgo. With USAF, 1969-72. Home: 5176 N Tamarack Dr Barrington IL 60010 Office: Comdisco Inc 6111 N River Rd Rosemont IL 60018

MYERS, MICHELE TOLELA, university president; b. Rabat, Morocco, Sept. 25, 1941; came to U.S., 1964; d. Albert and Lilie (Abecassis) Tolela; m. Pierre Vajda, Sept. 12, 1962 (div. Jan. 1965); m. Gail E. Myers, Dec. 20, 1968; children: Erika, David. Diploma, Inst. Polit. Studies, U. Paris, 1962; MA, U. Denver, 1966, PhD, 1967; MA, Trinity U., 1977; LHD, Wittenberg U., 1994. Asst. prof. speech Manchester Coll., North Manchester, Ind., 1967-68; asst. prof. speech and sociology Monticello Coll., Godfrey, Ill., 1968-71; asst. prof. communication Trinity U., San Antonio, 1975-80, assoc. prof., 1980-86, asst. v.p. for acad. affairs, 1982-85, assoc. v.p., 1985-86; assoc. prof. sociology, dean Undergrad. Coll. Bryn Mawr (Pa.) Coll., 1986-89; pres. Denison U., Granville, Ohio, 1989—; comm. analyst Psychology and Commn., San Antonio, 1974-83; bd. dirs. Am. Coun. on Edn., chair elect. Nat. Assn. Ind. Colls. and Univs., Sherman Fairchild Found.; mem. Fed. Res. Bank of Cleve., 1995—; pres.'s commn. Na. Collegiate Athletic Assn., 1993—. Author: (with Gail Myers) The Dynamics of Human Communication, 1973, 6th and internat. edits., 1992, transl. into French, 1984, Communicating When We Speak, 1975, 2d edit., 1978, Communication for the Urban Professional, 1977, Managing by Communication: An Organizational Approach, 1982, transl. into Spanish, 1983, internat. edit., 1982. Trustee Phila. Child Guidance Clinic, 1988-89; trustee assoc. The Bryn Mawr Sch., Balt., 1987-89; v.p., bd. dirs. San Antonio Cmty. Guidance Ctr., 1979-83. Am. Coun. Edn. fellow in acad. adminstrn., 1981-82, Bank One Columbus, 1990-94. Mem. Am. Coun. Edn. (commn. on women in higher edn. 1990-92, bd. dirs. 1993—, chmn.-elect 1996—). Home: 204 Broadway W Granville OH 43023-1120 Office: Denison U Office of the President Granville OH 43023

MYERS, MINOR, JR., academic administrator, political science educator; b. Akron, Ohio, Aug. 13, 1942; s. Minor and Ruth (Libby) M.; m. Ellen Achin, Mar. 21, 1970; children—Minor III, Joffre V.A. B.A., Carleton Coll., Northfield, Minn., 1964; M.A., Princeton U., 1967, Ph.D., 1972. From instr. to assoc. prof. Conn. Coll., New London, 1968-81, prof. govt., 1981-84; provost, dean of faculty, prof. polit. sci. Hobart and William Smith Colls., Geneva, N.Y., 1984-89; pres., prof. polit. sci. Ill. Wesleyan U., Bloomington, 1989—; adv. Numismatic Collection Yale U., 1975-84; chmn. adv. coun. Lyman Allyn Mus., 1976-81, 82-84, pres., 1982-84. Author: Liberty Without Anarchy: A History of the Society of the Cincinnati, 1983; (with others) New London County Furniture, 1974, (with others) The Princeton Graduate School: A History, 1978, (with others) American Interiors: A Documentary History from the Colonial Era to 1915, 1980. Asst. sec. gen. Soc. of the Cin., 1983-86, sec.-gen., 1986-89; trustee Inst. for European Study, 1992—. Mem. Princeton Club (N.Y.C.), University (Chgo.). Office: Ill Wesleyan U PO Box 2900 Bloomington IL 61702-2900

MYERS, PHILLIP FENTON, financial services and technology company executive; b. Cleve., June 24, 1935; s. Max I. and Rebecca (Rosenbloom) M.; m. Hope Gail Strum, Aug. 13, 1961. B in Indsl. Engring., Ohio State U., 1958, MBA, 1960; D in Bus. Adminstrn., Harvard U., 1966. Staff indsl. engr. Procter & Gamble Co., Cin., 1958; sr. cons. Cresap, McCormack & Paget, N.Y.C., 1960-61; staff assoc. Mitre Corp., Bedford, Mass., 1961; cons. Sys. Devel. Corp., Santa Monica, Calif., 1963-64; dir. long range planning Electronic Specialty Co., Los Angeles, 1966-68; chmn. Atek Industries, 1968-72; pres. Myers Fin. Corp., 1973-82; chmn. Amvid Comm. Svcs., Inc., 1975-79, Omni Resources Devel. Corp., 1979-83; chmn., pres. Am. Internat.

Mining Co., Inc., 1979-83; pres. Advent Internat. Mgmt. Co., Inc., 1982—; chmn. Global Bond Mktg. Svcs., Inc., 1987-90; pres., CEO Whitehall Container Mfg. Corp., 1988-91; pres. Whitehall Motors Co., 1989—, Allied Metamatter Tech. Corp., 1994—; chmn. U.S. Water Resources, Inc., 1994—; pres. Am. Tech. Venture Fund Mgmt., Inc., Advent Internat. Realty Corp., 1996—, First Internat. Capital Corp., 1996—; pres. Turbogon, Inc., 1995—, pres. Advent Internat. Realty Corp., 1996—, pres. First Internet Capital Corp., 1996—; founding dir. Warner Ctr. Bank, 1980-83; lectr. bus. adminstrn. U. So. Calif., L.A., 1967-74; prof. Grad. Sch. Bus. Adminstrn. Pepperdine U., 1974-81. Trustee, treas. Chamber Symphony Soc. Calif., 1971-78; mem. campaign issues com. Reagan for Pres., 1976, 80; pub. safety commr. City of Hidden Hills, Calif., 1977-83, chmn., 1982-83; co-chmn. budget adv. com. Las Virgenes Sch. Dist., 1983-86; mem. Mayor's Blue Ribbon Fin. Com., 1981-82; mem. dean's select adv. com. Coll. Engring., Ohio State U., 1984-94; mem. state exec. com. Calif. Libertarian Party, chmn. region 61, 1989-90, chmn. strategic planning com.; dep. chmn. Los Angeles County Libertarian Party, 1991-92; chairperson campaign sisues com. Marrou for Pres., 1991-92; chmn. bd. trustees WWII Hist. Soc., 1992—; pres. Harvard Bus. Club Columbus, 1996; dir. Ohio State Alumni Club, Franklin County, 1996—. Capt. USAF, 1958-60. Ford Found. fellow, 1961-64. Mem. Harvard Bus. Sch. Assn., Ohio State Alumni Assn., Harvard Club (bd. dirs. 1970-74, treas. 1971-73). Office: 682 Laurel Ridge Dr Gahanna OH 43230-2196

MYERS, RICHARD P., state legislator. Ill. state rep. Dist. 95, 1995—. Office: 331 N LaFayette Macomb IL 61455

MYERS, RONALD EUGENE, chemist, consultant; b. Hanover, Pa., Aug. 12, 1947; s. Ivan Elmer and Betty Jane (Gibbons) M.; m. Ewha Chun, June 18, 1972; children: Michele, Jennifer. BA in Chemistry, Gettysburg (Pa.) Coll., 1969; PhD in Inorganic Chemistry, Purdue U., 1977. Advanced R & D chemist B.F. Goodrich Co., Brecksville, Ohio, 1977-80, sr. R & D chemist, 1980-83, R & D assoc., 1983-88, sr. R & D assoc., 1988-94; pres. Myers Consulting, Cleve., 1994—; vis. scholar Ohio Acad. Sci., Brecksville, 1990-92. Instr. sci. Strongsville (Ohio) Assn. for Gifted and Talented Students, 1987-91. Sgt. U.S. Army, 1970-72, Korea. Fellow Am. Inst. Chemists; mem. AAAS, Am. Chem. Soc., Am. Ceramic Soc. (presdl. com. on pre-coll. edn. 1990—), Phi Lambda Upsilon, Sigma Xi. Office: Myers Consulting 18436 Rustic Hollow Cleveland OH 44136-7154

MYERS, TODD R., project engineer; b. Cochocton, Ohio, Oct. 23, 1968. BS magna cum laude, DeVry Inst. Tech., 1990. Wireman Control Sys. and Equipment, Columbus, Ohio, 1987-88; project engr. Hydraulic & Air Controls, Columbus, 1988-93, Pizza Sys., Pataskala, Ohio, 1994—; cons. in field. Prodr. ann. TV auction Cochocton C. of C., 1985—. Lutheran.

MYERS, VICTORIA CHRISTINA, state official; b. Indpls., Nov. 23, 1943; d. Stanley Louis and Victoria A. (Knox) Porter; m. Albert Louis Myers, Sept. 4, 1965; children: David Allen, John Anthony, Matthew Albert. BA, Ind. U., 1966; MA, Webster U., Webster Groves, Mo., 1975. Juvenile probation officer Marion County Juvenile Ct., Indpls., 1967-69; bond investigator Mo. Bd. Probation and Parole, St. Louis, 1970-71, probation and parole officer, 1971-73, unit supr., 1973-78, dist. supr., 1978-84; bd. mem. Mo. Bd. Probation and Parole, Jefferson City, 1984—; mem. Commn. on Accreditation for Corrections, Laurel, Md., 1982-94. Bd. dirs. Lincoln U. Found., Jefferson City, 1990—, United Way, 1994—; pres. PTA Jefferson City, 1993-94; sr. warden Grace Episcopal Ch., Jefferson City, 1993-94. Mem. Am. Correctional Assn. (chair program coun. 1994—, E.R. Cass Correctional Achievement award 1994), Am. Probation and Parole Assn. (bd. dirs. 1984-90), Mo. Corrections Assn. (pres. 1979), Nat. Assn. Blacks in Criminal Justice (nat. bd. dirs. 1982-88, nat. sec. 1985-88, nat. program chmn. 1988—, Chmn.'s award 1977), Assn. Paroling Authorities (coord. internat./nat. conf. 1994—), Alpha Kappa Alpha (treas. 1992-95, pres. 1996-97). Democrat. Home: 2408 Parkcrest Dr Jefferson City MO 65101-5152 Office: Mo Bd Probation and Parole 1511 Christy Blvd Jefferson City MO 65101

MYERS BLOOD, SUSAN KAY GUNNESS, marketing professional; b. Fargo, N.D., Sept. 17, 1949; d. Gordon William and Lois Mae Gunness. BS, S.D. State U., 1971; MS, Kans. State U., 1982. Dir. community rels. Fairview Hosps., Mpls., 1971-72; instr. U. Minn., Mpls., 1972-73, 77-78; dir. pub. rels. Kans. Coun. Econ. Edn., Manhattan, 1979-80, Pawnee Comprehensive Mental Health Ctr., Manhattan, 1980-81; instr. Kans. State U., Manhattan, 1982; community rels. dir. Weiner Meml. Med. Ctr., Marshall, Minn., 1982-86; exec. dir. Mainstay, Inc., Marshall, 1986-88; dir. community rels. North Hennepin C.C., Brooklyn Park, Minn., 1988—; vice chairperson bd. dirs. Minn. Job Skills Partnership, 1991—; chairperson bd. dirs. Direct Dialogue, U.S. West, Minn., 1989-96; cons. Search for Solutions, Pioneer Hybrid, Iowa, 1989-95; mem. nat. adv. bd. Heartland Ctr. Leadership, Nebr., 1988—. Founder, co-dir. Cmty. Quest, Minn., 1986—; mem. task force Citizens League Telecom., Mpls., 1988-90; mem. internat. adv. bd. Baiki, N.Am. Jour. of Sami Life; pres. Sami Assn. N.Am.; del. Sami Coun. of Pan-Nordic Countries; co-chairperson pub. awareness Success by Six N.W., Mpls., 1990-93; bd. dirs. Midwest Inst. for Telecommuting Edn. Recipient Communicator of Yr. award Nat. Coun. for Mktg. and Pub. Rels. Dist. V, 1993. Mem. Coun. Advancement and Support Edn., Minn. Women's Consortium, World Future Soc., Citizens League, Countryside Coun., Rotary (bd. dirs. 1990-91). Office: North Hennepin CC 7411 85th Ave N Brooklyn Park MN 55445-2231

MYHAND, WANDA RESHEL, paralegal, legal assistant; b. Detroit, Aug. 15, 1963; d. Ralph and Geraldine (Leavell) M. Office mgr./adminstrv. asst. Gregory Terrell & Co., CPA, Detroit, 1987-90; legal sec. Ford Motor Co., Detroit, 1990-91; office mgr. M.G. Christian Builders, Inc., Detroit, 1991; paralegal, legal asst. Law Office of Karri Mitchell, Detroit, 1991—. Vol. UNCF Telethon Detroit, 1988. Mem. NAFE.

MYLOD, ROBERT JOSEPH, banker; b. Bklyn., Nov. 21, 1939; s. Charles Joseph and Katherine (Normile) M.; m. Monica Manieri, July 11, 1964; children: Rosemary, Robert, Kevin, Paul, Monica, Megan. B.A., St. John's U., 1961. Vice pres. Citibank (N.A.), N.Y.C., 1965-70; V.p. Citicorp., N.Y.C., 1970-73; exec. v.p. residential loan div. Advance Mortgage Corp., Detroit, 1973-75; pres. Advance Mortgage Corp., 1975-83; pres., chief operating officer, dir. Fed. Nat. Mortgage, 1983-85; chmn., pres., chief exec. officer, dir. Mich. Nat. Corp., 1985—; chmn., CEO, dir. Mich. Nat. Bank, 1987—, chmn., dir., 1985—. Served to lt. (j.g.) USN, 1961-65. Office: Mich Nat Corp 27777 Inkster Rd Farmington Hills MI 48334*

MYNTTI, BILL W., electrical engineer; b. St. Paul, Oct. 13, 1966; s. Jon Nicholas and Gail (Bartelous) M.; m. Lisa Myntti, Dec. 19, 1992. BSEE, Purdue U., Indpls., 1992. Field technician Varityper, Addison, Ill., 1992-94; sys. support analyst PrePress Solutions, Parsippany, N.J., 1994-95; chief engr. Control Brain, Newark, Ohio, 1995—. Office: Control Brain 1510 W Church St Newark OH 43055

MYNTTI, JON NICHOLAS, software engineer; b. Virginia, Minn., Mar. 11, 1940; s. William and Irene Myntti; m. Gail Bartolas, July 10, 1965; children: William, Mike, Donald. AS, Virginia Jr. Coll., 1960; BSEE, N.D. State U., 1963, MSEE, 1966. Assoc. engr. Control Data Corp., Mpls., 1963-65; engr. Univac, St. Paul, 1966-68; sr. engr. Electro Magnetic Rsch., Bloomington, 1968-69; prodn. devel. mgr. Copycomposer, Rockville, Md., 1969-71, Standard Register Co., Dayton, Ohio, 1971-77; cons. analyst Nat. Cash Register Co., Wichita, Kans., 1977-78; dir. prodn. and engring. Reporter Times Inc., Martinsville, Ind., 1978—; divsn. chair engring. tech. COTC, Newark, Ohio, 1995—, exec. v.p. control brain, 1994—; instr. Ind. Vocat. Coll., Indpls., 1985-88; chmn. electronics Wright State U., Dayton, 1988-94, editor computer paper, 1988-92; chmn. bd. Newsmate Products, Martinsville, 1979—. Author: Automatic Control of A Manual Shift Transmission, 1966; contbr. articles to profl. jours. Mem. IEEE, Minutemen Assn. Inc., Mooresville, Ind. (pres. 1975—). Home: 899 Glen Evans Ct Newark OH 43055 Office: COTC 1179 University Dr Newark OH 43055-1979

MYRDAL, ROSEMARIE CARYLE, state official, former state legislator; b. Minot, N.D., May 20, 1929; d. Harry Dirk and Olga Jean (Dragge) Lohse; m. B. John Myrdal, June 21, 1952; children: Jan, Mark, Harold, Paul, Amy. BS, N.D. State U., 1951. Registered profl. first grade tchr., N.D. Tchr. N.D., 1951-71; bus. mgr. Edinburg Sch. Dist., 1974-81; mem. N.D. Ho. of Reps., Bismarck, 1984-92, mem. appropriations com., 1991-92; lt. gov., State of N.D., Bismarck, 1992—; sch. evaluator Walsh County Sch. Bds. Assn., Grafton, N.D., 1983-84; evaluator, work presenter N.D. Sch. Bds. Assn., Bismarck, 1983-84; mem. sch. bd. Edinburg Sch. Dist., 1981-90; adv. com. Red River Trade Corridor, Inc., 1989—. Co-editor: Heritage '76, 1976, Heritage '89, 1989. Precinct committeewoman Gardar Twp. Rep. Com., 1980-86; leader Hummingbirds 4-H Club, Edinburg, 1980-83; bd. dirs. Camp Sioux Diabetic Children, Grand Forks, N.D., 1980-90, N.D. affiliate Am. Diabetes Assn., Families First-Child Welfare Reform Initiative, Region IV, 1989-92; dir. N.D. Diabetes Assn., 1989-91; chmn. N.D. Ednl. TelecommunicationsCoun., 1989-90; vice chmn. N.D. Legis. Interim Jobs Devel. Commn., 1989-90. Mem. AAUW (pres. 1982-84 Pembina County area), Pembina County Hist. Soc. (historian 1976-84), Northeastern N.D. Heritage Assn. (pres. 1986-92), Red River Valley Heritage Soc. (bd. dirs. 1985-92). Lutheran. Club: Agassiz Garden (Park River) (pres. 1968-69). Home: 121 E Arikara Ave Apt 302 Bismarck ND 58501-2638 Office: 600 E Boulevard Ave Bismarck ND 58505

MYREN, DAVID JAMES, aeronautical engineer; b. Eau Claire, Wis., July 30, 1960; s. Gerald Vernon and Donna Mae (Stuber) M.; m. Beth Marjorie Olsen, May 25, 1985; children: Sarah Beth, Brent David. BS, U. Minn., 1984. Mgr. inventory control Sears Bus. Systems Ctr., Mpls., 1983-85; test engr. FluiDyne Engring. Corp., Mpls., 1985-89, project leader, aerotest mktg., 1989—. Mem. AIAA (coun. 1987-89, sect. treas. 1989, sect. sec. 1990, vice chmn. 1991, chmn. 1992, hons. and awards chmn. 1993—), U. Minn. Alumni Bd., Air Force Assn. Exptl. Aircraft Assn. Methodist. Office: Aero Systems Enging Inc FluiDyne Aerotest Group 358 Fillmore Ave E Saint Paul MN 55107-1204

MYRVIK, DONALD ARTHUR, college administrator; b. Mpls., June 13, 1936; s. Otto Arthur and Mildred Clenora (Monseth) M.; m. Rhoda Corrine Dahl, Aug. 17, 1957; children: Michael Jon, Peter Alan. BA, Augsburg Coll., 1958; MA, U. Minn., 1963, PhD, 1975. Exec. sec. Luth. Soc. Worship, Music and Arts, Mpls., 1961-69; coordinator U. Minn., Mpls., 1969-78; dean Suomi Coll., Hancock, Mich., 1978-87; devel. officer Concordia Coll., Moorhead, Minn., 1988—; founding pres. Minn. Assn. for Field Experience Learning, Mpls., 1977-78; cons.-evaluator North Cen. Assn., Chgo., 1983—, cmmr.-at-large, 1986-90. Author: Musical and Social Interaction, 1975. Mem. State Adv. Coun. for Vocat. Edn., Lansing, Mich., 1984-86; treas., Moorhead (Minn.) Healthy Cmty. Initiative, 1995—. Mem. Minn. Pub. Radio (bd. dirs. 1988-90), Rotary (pres. 1985-86). Lutheran. Office: Concordia Coll Devel Office 901 8th St S Moorhead MN 56562-0001

MYTINGER, GEOFFREY JAMES, writer, antiques and arts dealer; b. Wheeling, W. Va., June 3, 1960; s. Walter Henry and Nancy Jane M. AA in Human Svc. Tech., Ohio U., 1980. Joined Catholic Brothers of Christ United Evangelical Church, 1989. Social worker Chillicothe, Ohio, 1980-95; v.p. Scioto Office Svc., Inc., 1984-86; Cath. brother Damien Ministries, Order, Joliet, Ill., 1989-90; pres., bd. dirs. Once Upon a Time, Inc., Circleville, Ohio, 1990—; Author: (pen name Geoffrey Dillinger) Playing the Game, 1995. Vol. Home Between Homes, 1990-92, Crisis Ctr., 1980-95, AIDS Task Force, 1990-93, Chillicothe, Ohio; mem. Columbus AIDS Task Force, 1985-89, Civic Theatre, vol.; 1987—; mem. Christ Eccumenical Ch.; founding mem. Ross County AIDS Task Force, 1990—; founding treatment team mem. Floyd Semantal Clin. (formerly Adult Res. Ctr.). Mem. Xerox Tng., Boise Cascade Tng., YMCA Ctrl. Ohio, Drummers of Columbus, Scott Antique Assn. Democrat. Roman Catholic. Home: 164 N Mulberry St Chillicothe OH 45601 Office: Once Upon a Time Inc 130 W Main St Circleville OH 43113

NAADEN, PETE, state legislator; m. Mary Ellen; 12 children. City councilman; mem., N.D. Senate, 1973—, vice chmn. appropriations com. farmer, rancher. Mem. Lions Club, Farm Bur., N.D. Pork Producers, N.D. Stockman's Assn. Home: PO Box 53 Braddock ND 58524-0053*

NACLERIO, ROBERT M., otolaryngologist, educator; b. N.Y.C., Mar. 30, 1950; s. Albert Paul and Lee Ann (Rabinowitz) N.; m. Sharon Ann Silhan, Mar. 30, 1983; children: Jessica, Daniel. BA, Cornell U., 1972; MD with honors, Baylor U., 1976. Diplomate Am. Bd. Otolaryngology. Intern in surgery Johns Hopkins Hosp., Balt., 1976-77, resident in surgery, 1977-78; resident in otolaryngology Baylor Coll. Medicine, Houston, 1978-80, chief resident in otolaryngology, 1982-83; fellow in clin. immunology divsn. Johns Hopkins U. Sch. Medicine, Balt., 1980-82, asst. prof. medicine and otolaryngology, 1983-87, asst. prof. pediatrics, 1986-87, dir. divsn. pediatric otolaryngology, 1986-94, assoc. prof. otolargyngology, medicine and pediatrics, 1987-92, prof. otolaryngology, medicine and pediatrics, 1992-94; chief of otolaryngology, head and neck surgery U. Chgo., Chgo., 1994—; cons. Richardson-Vicks Inc., 1986-89, 90, NIH, 1987, Proctor & Gamble, 1987, 94, Sandoz Rsch. Inst., 1988, Schering Rsch., 1988, Wallace Labs., 1989, Joint Rhinologic Conf., 1989, Internat. Congress Rhinology, 1991, Norwich-Eaton Pharm. Inc., 1991-92, Ciba-Geigy Corp., 1991-92, Mktg. Corp. Am., 1993—, others; mem. med. bd. Children's Ctr., 1991-94, other local comms.; reviewer Am. Jour. Rhinology, others; lectr. in field. Editor: Rhinoconjunctivitis: New Perspectives in Topical Treatment, 1988; asst. editor: Am. Jour. Rhinology, 1986—, Rhinology, 1988—; mem. editorial bd. Otolaryngology-Head and Neck Surgery, 1990—, Laryngoscope, 1990—, Jour. Allergy and Clin. Immunology, 1992-97; contbr. numerous chpts. to books, papers and abstracts to profl. jours. and procs. Fellow ACS, Am. Acad. Otolaryngology-Head and Neck Surgery (mem. com. 1985-90, 90-92, subcom. 1987-92), Am. Laryngol., Rhinol. and Otol. Soc., Inc.; mem. Am. Acad. Allergy and Immunology (mem. com. 1983-88, 88-89, 88-95, chmn. com. 1990-91, 91—, Jerome Glazer Meml. lectureship), Am. Fedn. Clin. Rsch., Am. Soc. Pediatric Otolaryngology (rsch. com. 1990-94, chmn. subcom. 1990), Md. Soc. Otolaryngology-Head and Neck Surgery, Soc. Univ. Otolaryngologists-Head and Neck Surgeons, Pan-Am. Assn. Otorhinolaryngology, Internat. Symposium on Infection and Allergy of the Nose (v.p.). Office: U Chgo MC1035 5841 S Maryland Ave MC 1035 Chicago IL 60637

NACULICH, PAUL A., mechanical engineer; b. Erie, Pa., Feb. 22, 1958. BSME, Rensselaer Poly. Inst., Troy, N.Y., 1980. Engr. Gen. Dynamics, Groton, Conn., 1980-85; product devel. engr. Terry Corp., Groton, 1985-88; sr. project engr. Copeland Corp., Sidney, Ohio, 1989—. Mem. ASME. Office: Copeland Corp 1675 Campbell Rd Sidney OH 45365-2479

NADAS, JOHN ADALBERT, psychiatrist; b. Innsbruck, Austria, Mar. 14, 1949; came to U.S., 1950; s. Julius Zoltan and Ibolya Erzsebet (Szöllösy) N.; m. Gabriella Ilona Ormay, Apr. 11, 1981; children: János, Miklós, István. BA, Case Western Res. U., Cleve., 1970; MD, Duke U., Durham, N.C., 1974. Diplomate Am. Bd. Psychiatry and Neurology. Resident in psychiatry U. Chgo., 1974-77; pvt. practice Munster, Ind., 1977-84, Canton, 1984—; instr. psychiatry Northeastern Ohio U. Coll. Medicine, Rootstown, 1985-86; coord. psychiat. edn. Timken Mercy Med. Ctr., Canton, Ohio, 1985-87, clin. dir. psychiat. svcs., 1990-91; asst. prof. Northeast Ohio U. Coll. Medicine, Rootstown, 1986—; cons. Crisis Ctr., Canton, 1985-92. Author: Philosophical Basis of Depth Psychotherapy, 1983, Journey Toward Energy, 1995. Mem. AMA, Am. Psychiat. Assn. Roman Catholic. Office: 1330 Timken Mercy Dr NW Ste 320 Canton OH 44708-2624

NADATHUR, GOPALAN, computer science educator; b. Puni, India, Sept. 1, 1956; arrived in U.S., 1980; s. Narasimhan Nadathur and Lakshmi (Seshadri) Narasimhan; m. Ameeta Kelekar, May 18, 1982; 1 child, Prerna. B of Tech., Indian Inst. Tech., Kharagpur, India, 1977; M of Engring., Indian Inst. Tech., Bangalore, India, 1979; PhD, U. Pa., 1987. Asst. prof. Duke U., Durham, N.C., 1987-95; assoc. prof. U. Chgo., 1995—; vis. asst. prof. U. Chgo., 1991; vis. prof. Ludwig-Maximilians-U., Munich, 1995; mem. program com. Internat. Logic Programming Symposium, 1991, 93; co-organizer Internat. Workshop on Lambda Prolog Programming Lang., Phila., 1992; mem. U.S.-Japanese Workshop on Paralegal Knowledge Sys. and Logic Programming, Tokyo, 1990. Contbr. articles to profl. jours. Recipient Jawaharlal Nehru prize for acad. excellence Jawaharlal Nehru Trust, India, 1980; rsch. grantee NSF, 1988-89, 90-92, 93-97, Army Rsch. Orgn., 1988-91. Mem. Assn. for Computing Machinery, Assn. for Symbolic Logic, Assn. for Logic Programming. Office: U Chgo Computer Sci Dept 1100 E 58th St Ryerson Hall Chicago IL 60637

NADEL, ROGER, radio executive; b. Washington, Oct. 31, 1950; m. Debbie Nadel; children: Adam, Cory. BA in Psychology, U. Pacific, 1971. Newsgatherer AP Audio News Svc., Santa Barbara, Calif., 1974-76; news writer and editor KNX Newsradio, L.A., 1976-82, exec. news producer, 1982-89; dir. news and programming WWJ Newsradio, Detroit, 1989-92, v.p., gen. mgr., 1992—. Bd. trustees New Detroit, Inc., mem. media subcom.; bd. dirs. Media Partnership for Jobs, chair United Way Ann. Torch Dr. Campaign, 1993; mem. Greater Detroit Pride Enhancement Campaign. Mem. Radio-TV News Dirs. Assn., Soc. Profl. Journalists, Mich. Assn. Broadcasters (bd. dirs.), Detroit Press Club, Detroit Adcrafter Club, Detroit Econ. Club, Greater Detroit C. of C. (chair trade and procurement fair com., crime prevention/awareness com.), Sigma Alpha Epsilon. Office: WWJ/WYST Radio 16550 W 9 Mile Rd Southfield MI 48075-4705

NADEN, VERNON DEWITT, manufacturing executive; b. Waukegan, Ill., Feb. 5, 1947; s. Vernon D. and Beatrice (Gedvillas) N.; m. Linda Jean Edwards; children: Brian, Mike, Joseph, Annette. BS, Culver Stockton U., 1969. Dist. mgr. Johnson Outboards, Waukegan, 1970-77; nat. sales mgr. Coral Chem. Co., Waukegan, 1977-82; bus. dir. Desoto, Inc., Des Plaines, Ill., 1982-91; pres., chief exec. officer Kraiburg of Am., Inc., Chgo., 1991-95; pres., COO Pittinger & Cook Engring. Inc., Genoa, Ill., 1995—. Contbr. articles to profl. jour. Mem. Nat. Coil Coaters Assn., Archtl. Assn. Mfg. Am., Metal Constrn. Assn. Constrn. Specifiers Inst., am. Spray Coaters Assn. Republican. Home: 16571 W Apple Ln Gurnee IL 60031-2401 Office: Pittenger & Cook Engring 538 S Sycamore St Genoa IL 60135

NADIAN, BEHRDOOZ, mechanical engineer; b. Tehran, Iran, Mar. 24, 1961. BS in Mech. Engring., Tehran Poly. Inst., 1986, MS, 1988; PhD, Case Western Res. U., 1994. Project and rsch. engr. Parspazhoh Engring. Cons., Tehran, 1986-89; tchr. design Case Western Res. U., Cleve., 1994; project engr. Delco Electronics, Kokomo, Ind., 1994—; cons. BHN, 1993. Case Western Res. U. fellow, 1992. Office: Delco Electronics 1916 S Elizabeth St Kokomo IN 46902-2432

NADIG, GERALD GEORGE, manufacturing executive; b. Astoria, N.Y., May 9, 1945; s. Charles Edwin and Louise (Hahn) N.; m. Nancy Hanford Stewart, June 20, 1970; children: Sara Hanford, Jennifer Stewart. AB cum laude, Harvard Coll., 1967, MBA, 1974. Fin. mgr. Rockwell Internat., Hopedale, Mass., 1974-76; materials mgr. Rockwell Internat., Oshkosh, Wis., 1976-78, Marysville, Ohio, 1978-79; ops. mgr. Rockwell Internat., Marysville, 1979-80, plant mgr., 1980-82; regional mgr. Rockwell Internat., Atlanta, 1984-85; mng. dir. Rockwell Maudslay Ltd., Great Alne, Eng., 1982-84; dir. mfg. Toyoda Machinery USA, Arlington Heights, Ill., 1985-87; v.p., gen. mgr. Toyoda Machinery USA, Arlington Heights, 1987-88; v.p., gen. mgr. Littell div. Allied Products Corp., Chgo., 1988-89; exec. v.p. pre finish metals Material Scis. Corp., 1989-90; pres. Pre Finish Metals Materials Scis. Corp., 1990-91; pres., chief oper. officer Material Scis. Corp., Chgo., 1991—. Trustee Village of Lake Barrington, 1989-91. With U.S. Army, 1966-70. Mem. Soc. Mfg. Engrs. (sr.), Biltmore Country Club. Home: 24354 N Grandview Dr Barrington IL 60010-6218 Office: Material Scis Corp 2300 Pratt Blvd Elk Grove Village IL 60007-5919

NADLER, HENRY LOUIS, pediatrician, geneticist, medical educator; b. N.Y.C., Apr. 15, 1936; s. Herbert and Mary (Kartiganer) N.; m. Benita Weinhard, June 16, 1957; children: Karen, Gary, Debra, Amy. A.B., Colgate U., 1957; M.D., Northwestern U., 1961; M.S., U. Wis., 1965. Diplomate: Am. Bd. Pediatrics, Am. Bd. Med. Genetics. Intern NYU Med. Ctr., 1961-62, sr. resident pediatrics, 1962-63, chief resident, 1963-64; teaching asst. NYU Sch. Medicine, 1962-63, clin. instr., 1963-64; clin. instr. U. Wis. Sch. Medicine, 1964-65; practice medicine specializing in pediatrics Chgo., 1965—; fellow Children's Meml. Hosp. dept. pediatrics Northwestern U., 1964-65; assoc. in pediatrics Northwestern U. Med. Sch., 1965-66, asst. prof., 1967-68, assoc. prof., 1968-70, prof., 1970-81, chmn. dept. pediatrics, 1970-81; prof. Northwestern U. Med. Sch. (Grad. Sch.), 1971-80; mem. staff Children's Meml. Hosp., 1965-81, head div. genetics, 1969-81, chief of staff, 1970-81; dean, prof. pediatrics, ob-gyn Wayne State U. Med. Sch., Detroit, 1981-88; prof. U. Chgo., 1988-89, U. Ill., 1989—; pres. Michael Reese Hosp. and Med. Ctr., Chgo., 1988-91; market med. dir. Aetna Health Plans, Phoenix, 1993-94, mktg. v.p., CEO, 1994-95; v.p. managed care/physician integration, med. dir. Am. Healthcare Sys., San Diego, 1995; mem. vis. staff, div. medicine Northwestern Meml. Hosp., 1972-81; staff Children's Hosp. of Mich., 1981-88. Mem. editorial bd. Comprehensive Therapy, 1973-84, Am. Jour. Human Genetics, 1979-83, Pediatrics in Rev., 1980-83, Am. Jour. Diseases of Children, 1983-91; contbr. articles to profl. jours. Recipient E. Mead Johnson award for pediatric rsch., 1973, Meyer O. Cantor award for Disting. Svc. Internat. Coll. Surgeons, 1987; Irene Heinz Given and John La Porte Given rsch. prof. pediatrics, 1970-81. Fellow Am. Acad. Pediatrics; mem. Am. Soc. for Clin. Investigation, Am. Soc. Human Genetics, Am. Pediatric Soc., Soc. for Pediatric Rsch., Midwest Soc. for Pediatric Rsch., Pan Am. Med. Assn., Alpha Omega Alpha. Home & Office: 25150 N Windy Walk Dr # 23 Scottsdale AZ 85255

NAEGELE, EUGENE ALEXANDER, electronics company executive; b. Omaha, July 10, 1946; s. Eugene H. and Ruth M. (Schmick) N.; m. Susan J. Wheatley, Dec. 16, 1972; 1 child: Eugene J. Student, Lasalle U., Chgo., 1977. Operator cen. office equipment Gen. Telephone and Electronics, Downey, Calif., 1967-68; with toll transmission communications Pacific Tel. & Tel., L.A., 1968-72; mgr. Heath, Toledo, 1973-77; sr. tech. Gen. Dynamics Commn., Oak Park, Mich., 1977; mgr. AAMCO Transmission, Toledo, 1977-79; owner, operator N.Am. Van Lines, Ind., 1981; pres. Naegele Co. Enterprises, Maumee, Ohio, 1981-87, Olathe, Kans., 1987—. Author: Computer Software Packages; writer song lyrics. Sponsor Fraternal Order of Police, Maumee, 1986-87, Ohio Hwy. Patrol, 1985-87. With USMC, 1963-67, Vietnam. Decorated D.S.M., Cross of Gallantry (Vietnam).recipient Alumnus award LaSalle U., 1977, Outstanding Catch award State of Ohio Wildlife, 1986. Mem. Electronic Engrs. Designers, Internat. Brotherhood Elec. Workers, Internat. Brotherhood Teamsters, Vietnam Vets. of Am. Democrat. Roman Catholic. Office: Naegele Co Enterprises 1913 E Mohawk Cir Olathe KS 66062-2442

NAEGER, PATRICK A., state legislator. Mem. dist. 155 Mo. Ho. of Reps. Office: RR 2 Box 139 rm 103-BB Perryville MO 63775

NAFZGER, SAMUEL HENRY, pastor; b. Plainview, Tex., Jan. 28, 1939; s. Ralph Adolph and Esther Caroline (Gaertner) N.; m. Janis Elaine Schoppa, July 2, 1967; children: Heidi, Christian, Peter, Jonathan. BA, Concordia Sr. Coll., 1961; MDiv, Concordia Sem., 1965; postgrad., Ruprecht-Karl Universitat, Heidelberg, Germany, 1965-66; ThD, Harvard U., 1980. Ordained to ministry, Luth. Ch., 1967. Pastor St. Paul's Luth. Ch., Canyon, Tex., 1967-70; chaplain Norfolk County House of Correction, Dedham, Mass., 1972-73; asst. sec. Commn. on Theology and Ch. Rels. Mo. Synod Luth. Ch., St. Louis, 1973-75, exec. dir., 1975—; exec. sec. Internat. Luth. Coun., 1994—. Contbr. articles to The Luth. Witness, Concordia Theol. Jour., Concordia Theol. Quar., Christianity Today, others. Mem. N.Am. Acad. Ecumenists, Faith and Order commn. of Nat. Coun. Chs. Republican. Home: 4315 Green Briar Ct Washington MO 63090-5747 Office: The Luth Ch-Mo Synod 1333 S Kirkwood Rd Saint Louis MO 63122-7226

NAGARAJU, MARIGOWDA, gastroenterologist; b. Kayyambally, Karnataka, India, June 14, 1942; s. Marigowda and Marinanjamma Marigowda; m. Renuka Channagiri Rampappa, Oct. 5, 1965; children: Pradeep Nagaraju, Priya Muniyappa, Prameela Nagaraju. MBBS, Mysore (India) Med. Coll., 1964. Diplomate Am. Bd. Internal Medicine, Am. Bd. Gastroenterology. Cons. Hurley, McLaren, Genesys, Flint, Mich., 1973—; chief of gastroenterology Hurley Med. Ctr., Flint, 1974-84, McLaren Regional Med. Ctr., Flint, 1974-78; asst. clin. prof. Mich. State U., East Lansing, 1974-78, assoc. clin. prof., 1978—. Contbr. articles to profl. jours. Sec., founding mem. Kasi Temple, Flint, 1980, coord. free med. clinic, 1982-84; pres. Ganga Kaveri Bhagirathi Trust, Flint, 1989—; founder, pres. Genesee County Free Med. Clinic, Flint, 1990—; chmn., Maharastra (India) Earthquake Fundraising Com., Flint, 1993. Named Pub. Citizen of Yr., Am. Assn. Social Workers, 1994, Health Advocate of Yr., 1994, Am. Lung Assn.,

1995; recipient Paul Harris award Rotary Internat., 1994, Humanitarian award, 1996. Fellow ACP; mem. Royal Coll. Physicians, AMA, Am. Assn. Gastroenterology, Am. Coll. Gastroenterology, Am. Soc. Gastrointestinal Endoscopy, Mich. State Med. Soc. (Cmty. svc. award 1992), Genesee County Med. Soc. Office: 2425 Austins Pky Flint MI 48507

NAGEL, SHIRLEY ANN, executive secretary; b. Quincy, Ill., Aug. 22, 1944. Engring. sec. Gardner Denver Machine Inc., Quincy, 1972—. Christian Ch. Office: Gardner Denver Machine Inc 1800 Gardner Expy Quincy IL 62301-9464

NAGEL, STUART SAMUEL, political science educator, lawyer; b. Chgo., Aug. 29, 1934; s. Leo I. and Florence (Pritikin) N.; m. Joyce Golub, Sept. 1, 1957; children: Brenda Ellen, Robert Franklin. Student, U. Chgo., 1954-55; BS, Northwestern U., 1957, JD, 1958, PhD, 1961. Bar: Ill. 1958. Instr. Pa. State U., 1960-61; asst. prof. U. Ariz., 1961-62; prof. polit. sci. U. Ill., 1962—; law and social sci. vis. fellow Yale Law Sch., 1970-71; vis. fellow Nat. Inst. Law Enforcement and Criminal Justice, 1974-75; Sr. scholar East-West Center, Honolulu, 1965; fellow Behavioral Scis. Center, Palo Alto, Calif., 1964-65; dir. O.E.O. Legal Services Agy. of Champaign, 1966-69; vol. atty. Lawyers Constl. Def. Com., Miss., 1967; asst. counsel U.S. Senate Jud. Com., 1966. Author: The Legal Process from a Behavioral Perspective, 1969, Law and Social Change, 1970, New Trends in Law and Politics Research, 1971, Rights of the Accused, 1972, Comparing Elected and Appointed Judicial Systems, 1973, Minimizing Costs and Maximizing Benefits in Providing Legal Services to the Poor, 1973, Improving the Legal Process: Effects of Alternatives, 1975, Operations Research Methods: As Applied to Political Science and The Legal Process, 1976, The Application of Mixed Strategies: Civil Rights and Other Multiple Activity Policies, 1976, Legal Policy Analysis: Finding an Optimum Level or Mix, 1977, Too Much or Too Little Policy: The Example of Pretrial Release, 1977, The Legal Process: Modeling the System, 1977, Decision Theory and the Legal Process, 1979, Policy Analysis: In Social Science Research, 1979, Policy Studies Handbook, 1980, Policy Evaluation: Making Optimum Decisions, 1982, Public Policy: Goals, Means and Methods, 1984, Contemporary Policy Analysis, 1984, Prediction Causation and Legal Analysis, 1986, Law, Policy and Optimizing Analysis, 1986, Evaluation Analysis with Microcomputers, 1988, Policy Studies: Integration and Evaluation, 1988, Higher Goals for America, 1988, Decision-Aiding Software and Legal Decision-Making, 1988, Introducing Decision-Aiding Software, 1989, Multi-Criteria Dispute Resolution, 1989, Evaluative and Explanatory Reasoning, 1990, Legal Scholarship and Microcomputers, 1990, Decision-Aiding Software: Skills, Obstacles and Applications, 1990, Judicial Decision-Making and Decision-Aiding Software, 1991, Legal Process Controversies and Super-Optimum Solutions, 1991, Public Policy Substance and Super-Optimum Solutions, 1991, Teach Yourself Decision-Aiding Software, 1991, Social Science, Law, and Public Policy, 1991, Policy Analysis Methods and Super-Optimum Solutions, 1992, Professional Developments in Policy Studies, 1992, Developing Nations and Super-Optimum Policy Analysis, 1993, The Policy Process and Super-Optimum Solutions, 1994, Win-Win Policy: Basic Concepts and Principles, 1996, The Super-Optimum Society, 1996, Developmental Policy Studies, 1996, Creativity and Public Policy: Generating Super-Optimum Solutions, 1996, others; editor: Policy Studies Jour., The Policy Studies Directory, 1973, Environmental Politics, 1974, Policy Studies in America and Elsewhere, 1975, Policy Studies and the Social Sciences, 1975, Sage Yearbooks in Politics and Public Policy, 1975—, Lexington-Heath Policy Studies Orgn. Series, 1975—, Political Science Utilization Directory, 1975, Policy Studies Review Annual, 1977, Policy Grants Directory, 1977, Modeling the Criminal Justice System, 1977, Policy Research Centers Directory, 1978, Policy Studies Personnel Directory, 1979, Improving Policy Analysis, 1980, Policy Publishers and Associations Directory, 1980, Encyclopedia of Policy Studies, 1982, The Political Science of Criminal Justice, 1982, Productivity and Public Policy, 1983, The Policy Studies Field: It's Basic Literature, 1983, Public Policy Analysis and Management, 1986, Law and Policy Studies, 1987, Social Science and Computers, 1988, Decision-aiding Software and Decision Analysis, 1990, Decision-aiding Software and Public Administration, 1990, Global Policy Stdies, 1990, Law, Decision-making and Microcomputers, 1990, Policy Theory and Policy Studies, 1990, Advances in Developmental Policy Studies, 1991—, Applications of Decision-Aiding Software, 1991, Applications of Super-Optimum Solutions, 1991, Decision-Aiding Software and Decision Analysis, 1991, Law, Decision-Making, and Microcomputers, 1991, Policy Studies and Developing Nations: A Multi-Volume Treatise, 1991, Public Administration, Public Policy, and The People's Republic of China, 1991, Systematic Analysis in Dispute Resolution, 1991, Computer-Aided Decision Analysis, 1992, Resolving International Disputes Through Win-Win or SOS Solutions, 1992, Computer-Aided Judicial Analysis, 1992, Developing Nations and Super-Optimum Policy Analysis, 1992, Evaluative and Explanatory Reasoning, 1992, Developing Nations and Super-Optimum Policy Analysis, 1993, Legal Scholarship, Super-Optimizing, and Microcomputers, 1993, Encyclopedia of Policy Studies, 1993, African Development and Public Policy, 1994, Asian Development and Public Policy, 1994, East European Development and Public Policy, 1994, Latin American Development and Public Policy, 1994, Policy Studies in Developing Nations, 1994—, Political Reform and Developing Nations, 1995, Policy Studies in Developing Nations, 1994, India Development and Public Policy, 1995, Policy Studies Index, 2nd edit., 1995, Applications of Super-Optimizing Analysis, 1996, Resolving International Disputes through Super-Optimum Solutions, 1996, Creativity: Being Usefully Innovative, 1996, others; mem. editorial bd.: Law and Soc. Assn, 1966—, Law and Policy Studies, 1986—, Pub. Policy Analysis and Mgmt., 1986—. Grantee Social Sci. Research Council, 1959-60; Grantee Am. Council Learned Socs., 1964-65; Grantee NSF, 1970-73; Grantee Rockefeller Found., 1976; Grantee Dept. Transp., 1976; Grantee Ford Found., 1975—; Grantee ERDA, 1977; Grantee Dept. Agr., 1977; Grantee NIE, 1976; Grantee HUD, 1978; Grantee ILEC, 1978; Grantee Dept. Labor, 1978; Grantee NIJ, 1979; Grantee Am. Bar Assn., 1980. Fellow AAAS; mem. ABA, Am. Polit. Sci. Assn., Law and Soc. Assn. (trustee), Policy Studies Orgn. (sec.-treas.). Home: 1720 Park Haven Dr Champaign IL 61820-7153

NAGY, JOANNE ELIZABETH BERG, associate dean university; b. Green Bay, Wis., Jan. 28, 1956; d. Hubert Frederick and Dolores Elizabeth (Busch) Berg; m. Casey Abraham Nagy, Sept. 20, 1980; children: Erin Elizabeth, Nathan Abraham. BS, U. Wis., LaCrosse, 1978; student, Wash. State U., 1978-80. Admissions counselor U. Puget Sound, Tacoma, 1981-82, asst. dir. admissions, 1982-83, dir. admissions, 1983-87; student svc. coord. U. Wis., Madison, 1987-88, asst. dean admissions, 1988-89, asst. dean admissions and student svcs., 1989-94, assoc. dean admissions and student svcs., 1994—; admissions cons. coun. of grad. schs. U. North Tex., Denton, 1995. Contbr. articles to profl. jours. Recipient USA Today and Rochester Inst. Tech. Quality Crystal award, 1993. Mem. Am. Assn. Coll. Registrars and Admissions Officers, Nat. Assn. Grad. Admissions Prof. (rsch. chair 1994-96), Midwest Assn. Coun. Grad. Schs., Coun. Grad. Schs. Office: U Wis Grad Sch 500 Lincoln Dr Madison WI 53706

NAGY, LOUIS LEONARD, engineering executive, researcher; b. Detroit, Jan. 15, 1942; s. Alex and Helen (Marth) N.; m. Dianna M. Skarjune, Aug. 5, 1961; children: Tammy, Kimberly, Kristine, Amanda. BSEE, U. Mich., Dearborn, 1965; MSEE, U. Mich., Ann Arbor, 1969, PhDEE, 1974. Rsch. engr. U. Mich., Ann Arbor, 1962-69; staff rsch. engr. GM Rsch. Labs., Warren, Mich., 1969—. Contbr. articles to profl. jours.; patentee in field. Bd. dirs. Convergence Ednl. Found., Birmingham, Mich., 1990—, Convergence Transp. Electronics Assn., Birmingham, 1990—. Fellow IEEE; mem. Convergence Fellowship (bd. dirs. 1988—), Vehicular Tech. Soc. (Spl. Recognition award 1979, Avant Garde award 1986, Paper of Yr. 1975), Soc. Automotive Engrs., Tau Beta Pi, Eta Kappa Nu. Office: GM Rsch Labs Dept 3 Engineering Warren MI 48090

NAHAT, DENNIS F., artistic director, choreographer; b. Detroit, Feb. 20, 1946; s. Fred H. and Linda M. (Haddad) N. Hon. degree, Juilliard Sch. Music, 1965. Prin. dancer Joffrey Ballet, N.Y.C., 1965-66; prin. dancer Am. Ballet Theatre, N.Y.C., 1968-79; founder, artistic dir. Cleve. Ballet, 1976—; co-chair Artists Round Table Dance USA, 1991; mem. bd. trustees Cecchetti Council of Am., 1991; adv. bd. Ohio Dance Regional Dance Am. Pin. performer Broadway show Sweet Charity, 1966-67; choreographer Two Gentlemen of Verona (Tony award 1972), 1969-70; (ballet) Celebrations and Ode (resolution award 1985), 1985, Green Table, Three Virgins and a Devil (Isadora Duncan award 1985); co-founder Sch. of Cleve. Ballet, 1972, Cleve. Ballet, 1976; founder, artistic dir. San Jose Cleve. Ballet; choreographer, dir. Blue Suede Shoes, 1996. Grantee Nat. Endowment Arts, 1978, Andrew Mellow Found., 1985; recipient Outstanding Achievement award Am. Dance Guild, 1995. Office: Cleve Ballet 1375 Euclid Ave Cleveland OH 44115-1808 also: Cleve San Jose Ballet PO Box 1666 San Jose CA 95109-1666

NAHRSTEDT, KLARA, computer science educator; b. Bratislava, Czechoslovaki; came to U.S., 1990.; Bachelor's degree, Humbold U., Berlin, 1984, Master's degree, 1985; PhD, U. Pa., 1995. Sys. adminstr. Computer Ctr. for Agr. Ministry, Berlin, 1985-86; rschr. Inst. Informatik, Acad. of Sci., Berlin, 1986-89; rsch. asst. U. Pa., Phila., 1990-95; asst. prof. U. Ill., Urbana, 1995—. Co-author: Multimedia: Computing, Communications and Applications, 1995; contbr. articles to profl. jours. Recipient Weierstrass prize Weierstrasse Inst., Berlin, 1985. Mem. IEEE. Office: U Ill-Urbana 1304 Springfield Ave Urbana IL 61801

NAINEE, RAJAN, manufacturing engineer; b. Secunderabad, India, Apr. 22, 1951; came to U.S., 1987; BSME, Hyderabad, India, Hyderabud, India, 1976; postgrad., Ashland U., 1994—. Sales engr. HMT & Ltd., Hyderabad, India, 1977-87; mfg. engr. Stein Inc., Sandusky, Ohio, 1990—. Coach soccer Bay Area League, Sandusky, 1992. Home: 201 Marion Ave Huron OH 44839 Office: Stein Inc 1622 1st St Sandusky OH 44870-3902

NAIR, MADHAVAN PUTHIYA VEETHIL, immunologist, nutritionist, consultant; b. Kattachira, Kerala, India, Oct. 18, 1943; came to U.S., 1977; s. Narayanan Pillai and Kutyamma K. Nair; m. Rema Devi, Oct. 31, 1961; children: Narayanan, Harikrishnan. MS, U. Bombay, India, 1973, PhD, 1977. Research Cancer Inst., Bombay, 1973-77; postdoctoral scholar Sloan-Kettering Cancer Inst., N.Y.C., 1977-79; postdoctoral scholar U. Mich., Ann Arbor, 1979-82, rsch. immunologist, 1982-84, asst. rsch. scientist, 1984-89, dir. AIDS Rsch. Lab., 1988—, assoc. rsch. scientist, 1989—; rsch. prof., 1994; cons. Hoffman LaRoche Inc., Nutley, N.J., 1990—; rev. mem. Nat. Inst. Drug Abuse (NIDA), Bethesda, Md., 1988—, NIDA AIDS Tng. program, 1990—. Contbr. articles to profl. jours. Mem. PTA, Ann Arbor, 1991—. Recipient Disting. Rsch. Soc. award, U. Mich., 1990; grantee faculty rsch. U. Mich., 1986, Children's Leukemia Found., 1986, Hoffman LaRoche Inc., 1988—, NIMH, 1990—. Fellow Am. Acad. Allergy, Asthma, and Immunology, Am. Coll. Nutrition; mem. AAAS, Am. Assn. for Cancer Rsch., Am. Assn. Immunologists, N.Y. Acad. Scis., Rsch. Soc. Alcoholism. Office: SUNY-Buffalo Buffalo Gen Hosp 100 High St Buffalo NY 14203-1126

NAIRN, RODERICK, immunologist, biochemist, educator; b. Dumbarton, Scotland, Mar. 25, 1951; came to U.S., 1976; s. James Bell and Muriel Elizabeth (Hyde) N.; m. Morag Gilhooly, Dec. 29, 1971; 1 child, Carolyn Mhairi. BS, U. Strathclyde, Glasgow, Scotland, 1973; PhD, U. London, 1976. Postdoctoral fellow Albert Einstein Sch. Medicine, N.Y.C., 1976-81; asst. prof. U. Mich. Med. Sch., Ann Arbor, 1981-87, assoc. prof., 1987-95, dir. student biomed. rsch. programs, 1989-92, dir. med. scientist tng. program, 1992-95; prof., chair dept. med. microbiology and immunology Sch. Medicine, Creighton U., Omaha, 1995—. Contbr. chpts. to books, articles to profl. jours. Grantee NIH, Am. Cancer Soc. Mem. AAAS, Am. Che. Soc., Soc. for Microbiology, Am. Assn. Immunologists. Presbyterian. Office: Creighton U Sch Medicine Dept Med Microbiology & Immunology Omaha NE 68178

NAJAR, LEO MICHAEL, conductor, arranger, educator; b. Grand Rapids, Mich., Jan. 29, 1953; s. Ammiel George and Claire Elizabeth (Grant) N.; m. Tamara Sinkevich, Aug. 24, 1974; m. Jean Anne Van Winkle, May 10, 1986; children: John Andrew, Erik. MusB in Viola Performance, U. Mich., 1976, MusM in Viola Performance, 1977. Asst. condr. Flint (Mich.) Symphony Orch., 1975-80; dir. Flint Community Music Sch., 1976-80; music dir. Saginaw (Mich.) Symphony Orch., 1980—; conductor The Gazebo Orch., 1993—; lectr. music Wayne State U., Detroit, 1983-86; guest asst. prof. music U. Mich., Ann Arbor, 1986-87; artistic adviser Dearborn (Mich.) Symphony Orch., 1987-89, Traverse Symphony Orch., 1988-90; spl. artistic adviser Flint Inst. Music, 1991-92; asoc. prof. Ctrl. Mich. U., 1995—; artistic dir. Midland Symphony Orch., 1996—. Producer, host radio program Preludio: The String Thing, 1978-80; co-producer After Glow, 1994-96. Mem. adv. panel Mich. Coun. for Arts, 1989-91; rev. panel Mich. Coun. for Arts & Cultural Affairs, 1996—. Mem. Am. Symphony Orch. League (various coms. 1980—, Helen M. Thompson award 1982), Mich. Orch. Assn. (pres. 1985-88), Condrs. Guild Am. (bd. dirs. 1991-93), Asn. Can. Orchs. Home: 973 S Linwood Beach Rd Linwood MI 48634-9433 Office: Saginaw Symphony Orch 420 Symphony Ln # 415 Saginaw MI 48607-1211

NAKAMOTO, KAZUO, chemistry educator; b. Kobe, Hyogo, Japan, Mar. 1, 1922; came to U.S., 1957; s. Tsuneji N. and Ko (Nishikawa); m. Kimiko Hamano, Feb. 21, 1929; children: Takuya, Masaya, Mary. BS, Osaka U., 1945, DSc, 1953. Postdoctoral fellow Iowa State U., Ames, 1953-55; assoc. prof. Osaka U., Japan, 1955-57; asst. prof. Clark U., Worcester, Mass., 1959-61; assoc. prof. Ill. Inst. Tech., Chgo., 1961-67, prof., 1967-69; Wehr prof. chemistry Marquette U., Milw., 1969-91, prof. emeritus, 1991—; cons. Argonne Nat. Lab., Ill., 1965-73. Author: Infrared and Raman Spectra of Inorganic and Coordination Compounds, 1961, 4th edit., 1986; assoc. editor: Inorganica Chinica Acta, Internat. Jour., 1967-89. Recipient U.S. Sr. Scientist award Alexander von Humboldt Found., Germany, 1974; recipient award Japan Soc. for Promotion of Sci., 1977; named hon. prof. U. La Plata, Argentina, 1983; honoris causa Tech. U. Wroclaw, Poland, 1978. Mem. Am. Chem. Soc. (award Milw. sect. 1979), Japan Chem. Soc., Soc. for Applied Spectroscophy (hon. mem. 1990— , pres. Milw. sect. 1975-76), Sigma Xi (Disting. Sci. Research Achievement award 1988). Office: Marquette U Dept Chemistry PO Box 1881 Milwaukee WI 53201-1881

NAKER, MARY LESLIE, export transportation company executive; b. Elgin, Ill., July 6, 1954; d. Robert George and Marilyn Jane (Swain). BS in Edn., No. Ill. U., 1976, MS in Edn., 1978, postgrad., 1980; postgrad., Coll. Fin. Planning, 1990. Cert. tchr., Ill., fin. paraplanner. Retail sales clk. Fin'n Feather Farm, Dundee, Ill., 1972-75; self-employed tchr. South Elgin, Ill., 1974-78; teaching asst. Sch. Dist #13, Bloomingdale, Ill., 1976-78, substitute tchr.; office mgr. Tempo 21, Carol Stream, Ill., 1978-82, LaGrange, Ill., 1982-85; sales coord. K&R Delivery, Hinsdale, Ill., 1986-89; fin. planner coord. Elite Adv. Svcs., Inc., Schaumburg, Ill., 1989-90; adminstrv. coord. Export Transports, Inc., Elk Grove Village, Ill., 1990—. Leader Girl Scouts U.S.A., 1972-77, camp counselor, 1972-79. Recipient Music Scholarship PTA, U. Wis., 1967, PTA, U. Iowa, 1968-69. Mem. Nat. Geographic Soc., Smithsonian Assn. Lutheran. Home: 2020 Clearwater Way Elgin IL 60123-2588 Office: Export Transports Inc 1660 Carmen Dr Elk Grove Village IL 60007-6504

NALEPA, JIM, real estate investor; b. Ramsey AFB, P.R., Dec. 24, 1956; divorced; 1 child. BS, U.S. Mil. Acad., 1978. Mem. South Barrington Bd. Trustees, 1989-93; Dem. candidate for U.S. House, 1994, 96. With U.S. Army, 1978-84, USAR, 1984-91. Roman Catholic. Office: Nalepa 96 PO Box 57 La Grange IL 60525*

NAMDARI, BAHRAM, surgeon; b. Oct. 26, 1939; s. Rostam and Sarvar Namdari; M.D., 1966; m. Kathleen Diane Wilmore, Jan. 5, 1976. Resident in gen. surgery St. John's Mercy Med. Ctr., St. Louis, 1969-73; fellow in cardiovascular surgery with Michael DeBakey, Baylor Coll. Medicine, Houston, 1974-75; practice medicine specializing in gen. and vascular surgery and surg. treatment of obesity, Milw., 1976—; mem. staff St. Mary's, St. Luke's, St. Michael, St. Francis hosps. (all Milw.); founder, pres. Famous Mealwaukee Foods Enterprises. Diplomate Am. Bd. Surgery. Fellow ACS, Internat. Coll. Surgeons; mem. Med. Soc. Milw. County, Milw. Acad. Surgery, Wis. Med. Soc., Wis. Surg. Soc., Royal Soc. Medicine Eng. (affiliate), Am. Soc. for Bariatric Surgery, AMA, World Med. Assn., Internat. Acad. Bariatric Medicine (founding mem.), Michael DeBakey Internat. Cardiovascular Soc. Contbr. articles to med. jours.; patentee med. instruments and other devices. Office: Great Lakes Med and Surg Ctr 6000 S 27th St Milwaukee WI 53221-4805

NANCE, EARL EDWARD, JR., clergyman, educational administrator; b. St. Louis, Mar. 28, 1953; s. Earl Edward and Thelma Emelyn (Brown) N.; m. Cassandra Hicks, Dec. 21, 1974 (div. June 1983); 1 child, Candice Nicole; m. Viola Teressa Harvey, Oct. 19, 1985; 1 child, Evita Elaine. BA in Edn., Harris-Stowe Coll., St. Louis, 1974; MEd, Ga. State U., 1976; DD (hon.), Ark. Bapt. Coll., 1987. Ordained to ministry Bapt. Ch., 1975. Clk. G.A.D. Printing Co., St. Louis, 1970-74; tchr. St. Louis Bd. Edn., 1974-79; co-pastor Greater Mt. Carmel Bapt. Ch., 1979-94, pastor, 1994—; pres. Mo. Progressive Bapt. Conv., 1991—, Progressive Bapt. Midwest Congress, 1990-94, 91-93, 95-96. Pres. St. Louis Bd. Edn., 1987—; trustee Mo. Bot. Gardens, St. Louis, 1991—, Pub. Sch. Retirement System, St. Louis, 1987—; bd. dirs. Boys Club St. Louis, 1990—, Monsanto YMCA, St. Louis, 1991—, Walbridge Caring Communities, 1990—; cons., bd. dirs. Mathews-Dickey Boys Club, St. Louis, 1989—; mem. alumni bd. Harris-Stowe State coll., St. Louis Caring Communities. Recipient Govt. Achievement award East-West Gateway Coordinating Coun., 1987, Disting. Alumni award Mathews-Dickey Boy Club, 1989, Outstanding Young Religious Leader award St. Louis Jaycees, 1989, Disting. Svc. award St. Louis U. Black Alumni Assn., 1991, edn. award Walbridge Caring Communities, 1992. Mem. St. Louis Clergy Coalition (asst. sec. 1988-90, edn. award 1991), Sumner High Sch. Alumni Assn. (pres. 1991—, named to Hall of Fame 1992, Martin Luther King Holiday Comm. award 1996). Home: 4146 West Pine Blvd Saint Louis MO 63108 Office: Greater Mt Carmel Bapt Ch 1617 N Euclid Ave Saint Louis MO 63113-1716

NANCE, JAMES CLIFTON, company executive; b. Bryan, Tex., Sept. 2, 1957; s. Joseph Milton and Eleanor Glenn (Hanover) N.; m. Eileen Bonner, June 14, 1980; children: Jordan Eleanor, Robert Clifton, Kira Liane, Sarina Jenet. BS, U.S. Naval Acad., 1980. Registered quality sys. lead auditor Registrar Accreditation Bd. U.S.; cert. lead assessor Internat. Register of Cert. Auditors U.K.; cert. head auditor Internat. Register Cert. Auditors U.K. Quality assurance engr. Tex. Instruments, Inc., Dallas, 1985-86; people and asset effectiveness coord. Tex. Instruments, Inc., Plano, Tex., 1986-87; mgmt. cons. KPMG, Newport, R.I., 1987-88; sr. compliance auditor Litton Corp. Office, Beverly Hills, Calif., 1989; dir. continuous process improvement Litton Aero Products, Moorpark, Calif., 1989-93; v.p. P-E Handley-Walker, Inc., Independence, Ohio, 1993—; mem. Malcolm Baldridge Nat. Quality Award Bd. Examiners, 1993, 94. Troop com. chmn. Boy Scouts Am., Orlando, 1980-81, unit commr., Vallejo, Calif., 1984-85, varsity coach, McKinney, Tex., 1985-87, scouting coord., Newport, R.I., 1988, chmn. advancement com., Thousand Oaks, Calif., 1989-93, Medina, Ohio, 1994, asst. blazer leader, Medina, 1995—. Recipient Adult Varsity Letter, Boy Scouts Am., Circle Ten Coun., 1986, Scouter's Tng. award, 1987. Mem. Assn. for Quality and Participation (chpt. pres. 1992-93), Am. Soc. Quality Control (sr.), U.S. Naval Acad. Alumni Assn. (life), Sons of the Republic of Tex. (life). Home: PO Box 259 9103 Westfield Rd Westfield Center OH 44251-0259 Office: P-E Handley-Walker Inc 6000 Freedom Square Dr Ste 140 Independence OH 44131-2554

NANNEY, DAVID LEDBETTER, genetics educator; b. Abingdon, Va., Oct. 10, 1925; s. Thomas Grady and Pearl (Ledbetter) N.; m. Jean Kelly, June 15, 1951; children: Douglas Paul, Ruth Elizabeth Beshears. A.B., Okla. Bapt. U., 1946; Ph.D., Ind. U., 1951; Laurea honoris causa, U. Pisa, Italy, 1994. Asst. prof. zoology U. Mich., Ann Arbor, 1951-56; asso. prof. U. Mich., 1956-58; prof. zoology U. Ill., Urbana-Champaign, 1959-76; prof. genetics and devel. U. Ill., 1976-86, prof. ecology, ethology and evolution, 1987-91, prof. emeritus, 1991—; sr. postdoctoral fellow Calif. Inst. Tech., 1958-59; predoctoral fellow NIH, Ind. U., 1949-51. Author: (with Herbert Stern) The Biology of Cells, 1965, Experimental Ciliatology, 1980. Recipient Disting. Alumnus award Okla. Bapt. U., 1972; named Disting. Lectr. Sch. Life Scis., U. Ill., 1981; Preisträger, Alexander von Humboldt Stiftung, Fed. Republic Germany, 1984. Fellow AAAS, Am. Acad. Arts and Scis.; mem. Genetics Soc. Am., Am. Genetic Assn. (pres. 1982), Soc. Protozoologists. Home: 703 W Indiana Ave Urbana IL 61801-4835 Office: U Ill Dept Ecology Ethology and Evolution 505 S Gregory St Urbana IL 61801

NAPOLI, WILLIAM BILL, state legislator. Rep. S.D. State Dist. 35; taxation com. S.D. Ho. Reps., transp. com.; owner Car Mus. Address: 6180 S Hwy 79 Rapid City SD 57701-8467

NAPTON, DARRELL EUGENE, geography educator; b. Kansas City, Mo., Sept. 20, 1951; s. Clyde Edward and Eunice Maxine (Ketner) N.; m. Mary Luanne Redford, Aug. 5, 1988. BS in Edn., U. Mo., 1973, MA in Geography, 1975; PhD, U. Minn., 1987. Student advisor U. Mo., Columbia, 1975-78; instr. S.W. Tex. State U., San Marcos, 1985-87, asst. prof., 1987-92; assoc. prof. S.D. State U., Brookings, 1992—. Contbr. articles to profl. jours. and chpts. to books. Mem. Assn. Am. Geographers (dir. contemporary agriculture and rural land use group 1988—), Nat. Coun. Geographic Edn., Soil and Water Conservation Soc., Am. Geographical Soc., Omicron Delta Kappa. Home: 1234 42d St Brookings SD 57006 Office: SD State U Dept Geography Scobey Hall Brookings SD 57007

NAPUE, O'DELL CHRISTELL, small business owner; b. Bogue, Kans., Sept. 6, 1927; s. Causby Doyle and Ruby Dodo (Groves) N.; m. Lesceillea Marie Webb, June 16, 1957; children: Monique Christell, Michelle June, Rachael Junette. Student, Springhill Conf. Ctr., Mpls., 1972, Vocat. Tech. Schs., Mpls., 1973. Decorating, painting contractor, pvt. practice Mpls., 1957—; owner, pres. Moles Auto Sales, Elk River, Minn., 1965-70, Napue's Trucking, Elk River, 1970-74, Napue's Rental Property, Mpls., 1975—; ptnr., instr. profl. painting divsn. LORMCO Constrn., Inc., Mpls., 1977-79. Mem. Urban League, NAACP, Twin City Seventh Day Adventist Scholarship Assn. Recipient Cert. Appreciation Glendale 7th-Day Adventist Ch., Mpls., 1978, 87, 88, 89, 90, Silver Cup award Twin City Scholarship Assn., Mpls., 1983. Republican. Home and Office: 23810 Jarvis St NW Elk River MN 55330-9162

NARDI, MICHAEL ANGELO, public policy consultant; b. Chgo., May 30, 1957; s. Michael Guy and Rosalie Mary Nardi; m. Mary Lynn Patterson, Aug. 1982. BS in Physics, Rensselaer Poly. Inst., 1980; MS in Pub. Policy, Purdue U., 1985; MPA, U. So. Calif., 1993, DPA, 1995. Project engr. U.S. Naval Avionics Ctr., Indpls., 1981-83; rsch. asst. Purdue U., West Lafayette, Ind., 1983-85; legis. and congl. liaison N.J. Dept. Environ. Protection, Trenton, 1986-87, spl. asst. radiation program, 1987-88; pres. The Nardi Group, Carmel, Ind., 1988—. Contbr. articles to profl. jours. Mem. Carmel Parks Bd., 1990-91; mem. planning commn. Carmel-Clay Twp., 1991. Mem. ASPA, Assn. for Pub. Policy Analysis, Am. Chem. Soc., Air & Waste Mgmt. Assn. Office: The Nardi Group PO Box 219 Carmel IN 46032

NARDIN, TERRY, political science educator; b. N.Y.C., Jan. 19, 1942. BA, NYU, 1963; PhD, Northwestern U., 1967. Asst. prof. polit. sci. SUNY, Buffalo, 1967-73, assoc. prof., 1973-85; prof. polit. sci. U. Wis., Milw., 1985—. Author: Law, Morality and the Relations of States, 1983, Traditions of International Ethics, 1992, The Ethics of War and Peace, 1996; mem. editl. bd. Ethics and Internat. Affairs; gen. editor The Ethikon Series; mem. internat. adv. bd. European Jour. Internat. Rels.; contbr. articles to profl. pubs. Rockefeller Found. humanities fellow, 1978. Mem. Am. Polit. Sci. Assn., Am. Soc. for Polit. and Legal Philosophy, Conf. for Study of Polit. Thought, Am. Soc. of Internat. Law, Internat. Studies Assn. Office: U Wis PO Box 413 Milwaukee WI 53201-0413

NARULA, CHAITANYA KUMAR, research scientist; b. Etawah, India, Apr. 9, 1955; came to U.S., 1981; s. Suraj Parkash and Kanta Rani (Sudarshana) N. BS, Kanpur (India) U., 1973; MS, U. Roorkee, India, 1975; PG diploma, Panjab U., India, 1976; PhD, Rajasthan U., Jaipur, India, 1981. Postdoctoral fellow U. Del., Newark, 1982; Alexander von Humboldt fellow U. Munich, 1983-84; rsch. assoc. U. N.Mex., Albuquerque, 1985-88; sr. rsch. sci. Ford Motor Co., Dearborn, Mich., 1988-92, prin. rsch. sci., 1992—; vis. sci. MIT, Cambridge, Mass., 1993-94. Author book; contbr. articles to sci. publs.; patentee in field. Mem. Am. Chem. Soc., Am. Ceramic Soc., Materials Rsch. Soc., Sigma Xi. Home: 3471 Richmond Ct Ann Arbor MI 48105-1521 Office: Dept Chemistry Ford Motor Co PO Box 2053 Dearborn MI 48121-2053

NASH, J. FRANK, pharmacologist, toxicologist; b. Indpls., July 11, 1958; s. J. Frank and Arlene Jean (Kandel) N.; m. Patricia Marie Anselmo, June 15, 1991. BS, Purdue U., 1981, MS, 1984, PhD, 1986. Postdoctoral fellow Case Western Res. U., Cleve., 1986-88, asst. prof. psychiatry and neurosci., 1988-92; toxicologist Procter & Gamble Co., Cin., 1992—. Contbr. articles to profl. jours. Recipient Young Investigators award, Nat. Alliance for Rsch. on Schizophrenia and Depression, 1988, 90. Mem. Am. Soc. Pharmacology and Exptl. Therapeutics, Soc. for Neurosci., Sigma Xi, Rho Chi. Presbyterian. Office: Procter & Gamble Co Sharon Woods HB Bldg 11511 Reed Hartman Hwy Cincinnati OH 45241-2421

NASH, JANET RAE, geriatrics nurse; b. Taylorville, Ill., Aug. 12, 1953; d. Rayford C. and Dorothy L (Chlebus) Hurtte; m. James V. Nash, Sept. 17, 1976; children: Cherise, Brian, Brandon, Amanda. Diploma, Decatur Meml. Hosp. Sch. Nsg., 1975. RN, Ill. Staff nurse, charge nurse Decatur (Ill.) Meml. Hosp., 1976-81; clin. coord./head nurse long term care Decatur Meml. Hosp., 1985-91; dir. nursing Americana Healthcare Ctr., Decatur, 1981, Lincoln Manor Nursing Home, Decatur, 1991-92, Cedarwood Health-care Ctr., Decatur, 1993-94; nurse restorative nursing Ea. Star Home, Macon, Ill., 1992-93; dir. nursing Pershing Estates Psychiat. Facility, Decatur, 1994; supr. Friendship Manor, Mt. Zion, Ill., 1994-95; resident care coord. Fairhaven's Christian Home, Decatur, Ill., 1995—.

NASH, JESSIE MADELEINE, journalist, science writer; b. Elizabeth City, N.C., Sept. 11, 1943; d. John V. and Jessie (Douglas) B.; m. E. Thomas Nash, June 9, 1970. AB magna cum laude, Bryn Mawr Coll., 1965. Clip girl, sec. Time Mag., N.Y.C., 1965-66, reporter rschr., 1966-70; stringer Time Mag., Hamburg (Germany) and Chg, 1970-74; corr. Time Mag., Chgo., 1974-87, sr. corr., 1987—; mem. adv. com. on pub. infor. Am. Inst. of Physics, 1993-95. Contbr. articles to mags. Recipient Westinghouse Sci. Journalism award AAAS, 1987, 91, Page One award Newspaper Guild of N.Y., 1981, award Leukemia Soc. Am., 1994. Mem. Nat. Assn. Sci. Writers. Office: Time Mag 303 E Ohio St Chicago IL 60611

NASH, JOHN JOSEPH, secondary education educator; b. Des Moines, Aug. 25, 1970; s. Donald Harry and Dortha Darlene (Underwood) N. BA, Iowa State U., 1992. Cert. secondary tchr., Iowa. Office mgr. JDJ Investments, Ankeny, Iowa, 1988-94, resident mgr., 1994—; tchr. sci. Hubbard (Iowa) Cmty. Sch. Dist., 1992-93, Urbandale (Iowa) Cmty. Sch. Dist., 1994-95, Twin Cedars Comty. Sch. Dist., Bussey, Iowa, 1995-96. Author: (textbook) Simply Chemistry, 1993. Mem. U.S. Chess Fedn. (life; cert. local tournament dir. 1990—), Iowa State Chess Assn. (bd. dirs. 1994—, Svc. award 1990). Democrat. Methodist.

NASR, SUHAYL JOSEPH, psychiatrist; m. Norma Nasr; children: Joseph, Carla, Talia. BSc, Am. U., Beirut, Lebanon, 1970, MD, 1974. Diplomate Am. Bd. Psychiatry and Neurology. Intern U. Rochester (N.Y.), 1974-77, fellowship, 1977; from v.p. med. staff to med. dir. Kingwood Hosp., Michigan City, Ind., 1987-95; pvt. practice Michigan City, Ind., 1986—; v.p., dept. medicine, staff physician St. Anthony's Hosp., Michigan City, 1986—; staff physician Meml. Hosp., Michigan City, 1986—, behavioral medicine dir., 1995—; staff physician LaPorte Hosp., 1986—; cons. Notre Dame (Ind.) U. Counseling Ctr., 1987—; cons. Valpo U., 1992—. Contbr. articles to profl. jours. Mem. AMA, Am. Psychiat. Assn., Soc. Biol. Psychiatry, Am. Acad. Clin. Psychology, Internat. Psychgeriatric Assn., Obsessive Compulsive Found., Anxiety Disorders Assn. Am. Office: Nasr Psychiat Svcs 2814 S Franklin St Michigan City IN 46360

NASS, STEPHEN L., state legislator. Home: W8948 Willis Ray Rd Whitewater WI 53190-3752*

NASSER, WILLIAM KALEEL, cardiologist; b. Terre Haute, Ind., June 3, 1933; s. T.K. and Maude Nasser; m. Wanda Hurst, Dec. 23, 1958; children: Teresa, Tom, Tony. BS, Ind. State U., 1957; MD, Ind. U., Indpls., 1961. Intern Ind. U. Sch. Medicine, Indpls., 1962-63, resident, 1962-64, USPHS trainee in cardiology, 1964-66, from instr. to clin. assoc. prof. medicine, 1966-84, clin. prof. medicine, 1984—; dir. cardiac catheterization lab. St. Vincent Hosp., Indpls., 1973-79, also cons. cardiologist; cons. cardiologist Community Hosp., Indpls.; mem. Indpls. bd. assocs. Rose-Hulman Inst. Tech., 1986—. Contbr. chpts. to books, articles to profl. jours. Bd. dirs. Ind. Pub. Health Found., 1985-89, Ind. Heart Inst., 1986—; trustee Ind. State U., 1983-87. Cpl., U.S. Army, 1953-55, Korea. Recipient Vital award Marion County chpt. Am. Heart Assn., 1980, others. Fellow ACP, Am. Coll. Cardiology, Am. Heart Assn. (coun. on clin. cardiology); mem. AMA, Am. Soc. Echocardiography, Ind. State Med. Assn., Ind. Heart Assn. (bd. dirs.), Marion County Med. Soc., Marion County Heart Assn. Republican. Roman Catholic. Home: 10662 Winterwood Carmel IN 46032-9688 Office: Nasser Smith & Pinkerton 8333 Naab Rd Ste 400 Indianapolis IN 46260

NASSTROM, ROY RICHARD, education educator, academic administrator; b. Oakland, Calif., Oct. 28, 1930; s. Roy Richard and Edith Dolores (Spilman) N., m. Sally Louise Shaw, Aug. 29, 1964; children—Karen, Eric. BA, U. Calif.-Berkeley, 1956, MA, 1964, PhD, 1971. Asst. to supt. Ravenswood Sch. Dist., East Palo Alto, Calif., 1964-65; acting instr. edn. U. Calif.-Berkeley, 1965-68; asst. prof. ednl. adminstrn. U. Ky., Lexington, 1969-70; asst. prof. edn. Purdue U., West Lafayette, Ind., 1971-76; asst. grad. dean Winona State U., Minn., 1976-77, chmn. ednl. adminstrn. dept., 1976-88, prof., 1976—; cons., spkr. various orgns. and schs., 1969—. Mem. bd. abstractors Ednl. Administrn. Abstracts, 1976-83, mem. bd. editors, AASA Professor, 1979-82; manuscript reviewer Edn. Rechr., 1983-87; dir. postmasters studies, Winona State U., 1992—; coord. Inst. Ednl. Studies, 1995—. Contbr. articles to profl. jours. Served as cpl. U.S. Army, 1952-54. Recipient numerous grants, 1969—. Mem. Midwest Coun. Ednl. Administrn., Am. Ednl. Rsch. Assn. (paper reviewer 1983—), Am. Assn. Sch. Adminstrs., Nat. Coun. Profs. of Ednl. Administrn., Internat. Assn. of Mgmt., Phi Delta Kappa, Pi Sigma Alpha. Avocation: photography. Home: 1702 Edgewood Rd Winona MN 55987-2149 Office: Winona State U Dept Ednl Leadership Winona MN 55987

NATH, MAHENDRA, real estate investor; b. Lahore, W. Punjab, Pakistan, June 11, 1940; came to U.S. 1964; s. Chetan Dass and Ram Piari N.; m. Asha Nath, June 22, 1967; children: Shalini, Deepak. BSME, Delhi U., 1961; MS in Indsl. Engring., U. Minn., 1965. Group mgr. indsl. engring. Sperry Corp., Mpls., 1965-83; pres. Nath Mgmt., Inc., Mpls., 1983—; pres., CEO Nath. Franchise Group, several cities, also Fla., 1990—. Contbr. articles to profl. jours. Bd. dirs. North Hennepin Cmty. Coll. Found., Mpls., 1987—; trustee Hindu Soc. Minn., Mpls., 1988-90. Mem. Am. Inst. Indsl. Engring. (Twin City chpt. pres. 1984-85, exec. com. 1991—), Rotary. Office: Nath Cos 5775 Wayzata Blvd Ste 800 Saint Louis Park MN 55416-1234

NATHAN, CHARLES HAROLD, banking software executive; b. Kansas City, Mo., Jan. 27, 1958; s. James Ludwig and Virginia Lee (Snoddy) N.; m. Denise Sharon Daniels, Dec. 15, 1990; children: Bradley Ryan, Anna Elizabeth. Rockhurst Coll., 1981-85, S.W. Mo. State U., 1991-95. Customer support rep. CenterreBank, Kansas City, Mo., 1976-85; svc. rep. First Fin. Mgmt. Corp., Kansas City, Mo., 1985-87; dir. customer support BancTec Fin. Systems, Springfield, Mo., 1987—. Named Man of the Yr., Am. Biog. Inst., 1993. Mem. Compass Lodge #120, Scottish Rite, Ararat Shrine, Order of DeMolay. Republican. Methodist. Home: 2380 Old Prospect Rd Ozark MO 65721 Office: 3343 E Montclair Springfield MO 65804

NATHAN, PETER E., psychologist, educator; b. St. Louis, Apr. 18, 1935; s. Emil and Kathryn (Kline) N.; m. Florence I. Baker, Nov. 26, 1959; children: David Edward, Anne Miller, Laura Carol, Mark Andrew. A.B., Harvard U., 1957; Ph.D., Washington U., 1962. Research fellow psychology Harvard U., 1962-64, research asso., 1964-68, asst. prof. psychology, 1968-69; research psychologist Boston City Hosp., 1964-68, dir. alcohol study unit, 1967-70; prof. Rutgers U., New Brunswick, N.J., 1969-89; dir. clin. psychology tng. Rutgers U., 1969-87, dir. Alcohol Behavior Research Lab., 1970-87, chmn. dept. clin. psychology, 1976-87, dir. Ctr. Alcohol Studies, 1983-89, Henry and Anna Starr prof. psychology, 1983-89; sr. program officer, health program MacArthur Found., 1987-89; v.p. acad. affairs, found. disting. prof. psychology U. Iowa, 1990—, dean faculties, 1990-93, provost, 1993-95, acting pres., 1995; mem. advisory council VA, 1972-76; chmn. alcoholism com. Nat. Inst. on Alcohol Abuse and Alcoholism, 1973-76, co-chmn. spl. rev. com., 1985, mem. nat. adv. coun., 1990-94; mem. psychol. scis. fellowship rev. com. NIMH, 1977-79; chmn. N.J. State Community Mental Health Bd., 1981-84; mem. working group substance use disorders, DSM-IV. Author: Cues, Decisions, and Diagnoses, 1967, Psychopathology and Society, 1975, 2d edit., 1980, Experimental and Behavioral Approaches to Alcoholism, 1978, Alcoholism: New Directions in Behavioral Treatment and Research, 1978, Clinical Case Studies in the Behavioral Treatment of Alcoholism, 1982, Professionals in Distress, 1987, Neuropsychological Deficits in Alcoholism, 1987, Introduction to Psychology, 1987, 2d edit., 1990, Abnormal Psychology, 1992, 2d edit., 1996; exec. editor Jour. Studies Alcohol, 1983-90; assoc. editor Am. Psychologist, 1977-85, Contemporary Psychology, 1991—; mem. numerous editl. bds. including Jour. Clin. Psychology, 1969—, Jour. Cons. Clin. Psychology, 1973—, Profl. Psychology, 1976-89. Fellow Am. Psychol. Assn. (chmn. sect. 3 div. 12 1976-77, rep. to council 1976-79, 82-85, pres. div. 12 1984-85). Democrat. Jewish. Home: 248 Black Springs Cir Iowa City IA 52246-3800 Office: Univ Iowa E119 Seashore Hall Iowa City IA 52242-1316

NATHAN, ROBERT BURTON, life insurance agent; b. Chgo., Aug. 7, 1917; s. Louis and Della (Lustgarden) N.; m. Shirley Caplan, Dec. 24, 1939; children: Richard A., Jill S., Lisbeth M. BS, Northwestern U., 1939. Founder, chmn. bd. Presdl. Life Ins. Co., 1959-65; pres. Consolidated Funding Corp., Chgo., 1968-82, Consolidated Assocs. Inc., Chgo., 1968-82; agt. Equitable Life Assurance Soc., Chgo., 1940-63, 70—; nat. sales cons. Equitable Life Assurance Soc., N.Y.C., 1970-74; co-founder, pres. Robert B. Nathan Assocs. Inc., Chgo., 1966—; pres. NEFS, Inc., Chgo., 1980—, also chmn. bd. dirs.; pres. SCN Inc., Chgo., 1981—, also chmn. bd. dirs. Author: (with others) Encyclopedia of Tax Procedure, 1956; contbr. articles to profl. jours. 1st lt., MAC, 1943-46. Mem. NALU, Assn. Advanced Life Underwriters, Anti-defamation League, Chgo. Assn. Life Underwriters, Million Dollar Round Table, Northmoor Country Club, The Standard Club. Office: 600 Central Ave Ste 320 Highland Park IL 60035-3257

NAUERT, CHARLES GARFIELD, history educator; b. Quincy, Ill., July 26, 1928; s. Charles G. and Helen C. (Frazer) N.; m. Jean Grace Porter, June 21, 1964; children: Paul, Jonathan. AB, Quincy (Ill.) Coll., 1950; AM, U. Ill., 1951, PhD in History, 1955. Instr. Bowdoin Coll., Brunswick, Maine, 1955-56; asst. prof. Williams Coll., Williamstown, Mass., 1956-61; prof. history U. Mo., Columbia, 1961—, chair dept., 1965-68; exec. sec.-treas. Mo. Conf. on History, Columbia, 1980-93; hist. annotator Erasmus in English, Toronto, Ont., 1984—; sr. rsch. fellow Am. Coun. Learned Socs., London, 1975-76. Author: Agrippa and the Crisis of Renaissance Thought, 1965, Age of Renaissance and Reformation, 1977, rev. edit., 1992, Humanism and the Culture of Renaissance Europe, 1995; mem. editl. bd. Sixteenth Century Jour., 1972—; gen. editor 16th Century Essays and Studies, 1980—. Bd. dirs. Columbia Soccer Club, 1969-73. Recipient Middlebush Chair, U. Mo., Columbia, 1982-85, Thomas Jefferson award U. Mo. Ctrl. System, 1991. Mem. Am. Hist. Assn. (chair Adams prize 1978-81), Renaissance Soc. Am. (coun. 1991-94), 16th Century Studies Conf. (pres. 1978), Ctrl. Renaissance Conf. (pres. 1974, 91), Soc. Reformation Rsch. (coun. 1985-88). Democrat. Episcopalian. Home: 1009 Falcon Dr Columbia MO 65201-6235 Office: U Mo Dept History 101 Read Hall Columbia MO 65211

NAUGLE, ROBERT PAUL, dentist; b. Cleve., May 3, 1951; s. Paul Franklin Albert and Olga (Bigadza) N.; m. Nancy Elaine Baker, June 14, 1975; 1 child, Jennifer Elaine. BS, Heidelberg Coll., Tiffin, Ohio, 1973; DDS, Case Western Res. U., 1977. Pvt. practice Uniontown, Ohio, 1980—. Capt. USAF, 1977-80. Mem. ADA, Ohio Dental Assn., Acad. Gen. Dentistry, Stark County Dental Soc., Akron Dental Soc., Air Force Assn., Rotary (past program chmn. Uniontown, Student of Month chmn., past pres., past v.p., past treas., Paul Harris fellow, sgt.-at-arms). Republican. Mem. United Church of Christ. Office: 13027 Cleveland Ave NW Uniontown OH 44685

NAVARRE, ROBERT WARD, manufacturing company executive; b. Monroe, Mich., May 21, 1933; s. Joseph Alexander N.; m. Barbara Anne Navarre, June 26, 1953; children—Veo Anne, Robert Ward, Jan Louise. B.S. in Commerce, U. Notre Dame, 1955; grad., exec. program Stanford U., 1979. Sales mgr. Marben Corp., Jackson, Mich., 1958-64; mktg. adminstr. Simpson Industries, Litchfield, Mich., 1964-67; pres., CEO Simpson Industries, 1967-89, chmn., 1989—, also bd. dirs.; bd. dirs. Webster Industries, Kysor Insl. Corp., Cadillac, Mich., Libertyville Toyota, Ill. Chmn. Jackson/Hillsdale Mental Health Service Bd., 1972-78; mem. Hillsdale Schs. Bd. Edn., 1972-76. Mem. NAM (regional vice chmn. 1978-79, chmn. membership com. 1979-80, bd. dirs.), Mich. Mfg. Assn. (bd. dirs., chmn. 1991—). Roman Catholic. Office: Simpson Industries Inc 47603 Halyard Dr Plymouth MI 48170-2429

NAVIS, GLEN EDWARD, industrial engineer; b. Beaver Dam, Wis., Apr. 13, 1950; s. George Marian and Rachel (VanBuren) N.; m. LaVerne Lee Mischler; children: Jon Anthony, Steven Glen, Anne Laverne. A in Acctg., Moraine Park Tech. Coll., 1971; B in Liberal Studies, U. Wis., Oshkosh, 1986; BBA, Marian Coll., Fond du Lac, Wis., 1991. Acct. Mercury Marine/Brunswick, Fond du Lac, Wis., 1971-74, controller, 1987-96, sr. indsl. engr., 1989—; asst. controller 3F Inc., Waupun, Wis., 1975-76; cost acct. Deere & Co., Horicon, Wis., 1976-86, indst. engr., 1986-87. Song writer, vocalist cassettes You Are My Life, 1986, Heartbeats, 1990. Pres., founder Waupun (Wis.) Soccer Assn., 1978-88; acctg. instr. BlackCulture Group, Wis. State Prison, Waupun, 1986. Republican. Office: Mercury Marine/Brunswick 1939 Pioneer Rd Fond Du Lac WI 54935

NAWALANIEC, CHRISTOPHER JOSEPH, mechanical engineer; b. Cin., July 23, 1966; s. Robert and Margaret N. BSME, U. Cin., 1989. Cert. project engr. Engr. Champion Internat., Hamilton, Ohio, 1989-93; engring. mgr. Rotex Inc., Cin., 1993—. Inventor in field. Project bus. cons. Jr. Achievement, Hamilton, 1989-91; Eagle scout, asst. scoutmaster Boy Scouts Am., Cin., 1983-88; company chmn. United Way, Cin., 1994. Roman Catholic. Office: Rotex Inc 1230 Knowlton St Cincinnati OH 45223-1845

NAYLOR, JIM C., engine manufacturing company executive; b. Washington, Ind., July 9, 1933. AS, Lain Tech. Sch., Evansville, Ind., 1958. Designer John Deere Co., Waterloo, Iowa, 1958-81; tech. specialist Cummins Engine Co., Columbus, Ind., 1981—. Patentee on temperature control system. Past coach Little League. Staff sgt. U.S. Army, 1951-53. Mem. Toastmasters (pres.). Office: Cummins Engine Co METC 1532 14th St Columbus IN 47201-5613

NAYLOR, RUTH EILEEN BUNDY, clergyperson; b. Ohio, Sept. 3, 1934; m. Stanley F. Naylor, 1954; children: Kimberly Anne Naylor McCullough, Geoffrey Alan. BA, Bluffton (Ohio) Coll., 1971; MA, Bowling Green State U., 1976. Ordained to ministry, Mennonite Ch., 1987. Tchr. Perry Jr. High Sch., Lima, Ohio, 1972, Bluffton Exempted Village Schs., 1972-84; assoc. pastor 1st Mennonite Ch., Bluffton, 1984-90, visitation pastor, 1990-95; mem. integration exploration com. Gen. Conf. Mennonite Ch., 1989-95; Ctrl. Dist. Interim Conf. minister, 1995—; mem. East Ctrl. States Inter-Mennonite Coun., 1989—. Contbr. poems, articles to religious mags. Pres. Ctrl. Dist. Gen. Conf. Mennonite Ch., 1990-92; bd. dirs. Bluffton Child Devel. Ctr., 1993-95. Mem. Bluffton Ministerial Assn. (past pres.), Ecumenical Peer Group Spiritual Dirs., Mennonite Pastor-Peer Group, Bluffton Writers' Fellowship, Pi Delta (pres.). Democrat. Home and Office: 123 Villanova Dr Bluffton OH 45817-9529

NDENGA, LUCY VIOLA, librarian; b. Manning, Ark., Aug. 1, 1933; d. Samuel Peter and Naomi Tommie Lee Watson; 1 child, Peter Andrew Watson Ndenga. BS cum laude, Philander Smith Coll., 1957; MLS, U. Wash., 1962; postgrad., U. Minn., 1973-76. Faculty, head reference libr. Lewis & Clark Coll., Portland, Oreg., 1962-63; head reference libr. U. Wash., Seattle, 1963-67; head reference libr., instr. U. Minn., St. Paul, 1967-73; head libr., faculty, audio visual dir. Bishop Whipple Schs., Faribault, Minn., 1976-78; head libr., computer tape libr. Jud. Data Ctr. Mich. Supreme Ct., Detroit, 1978-80; asst. editor Gale Rsch. Publ. Co., Detroit, 1982-83; dir. McGregor Pub. Libr., Highland Park, Mich., 1983—. Bd. dirs. YWCA No. Br., Detroit, Detroit Unity Temple, sec. 1990-93; active Democrats. Mem. ALA (pub. rels. com.), AAUW (v.p. 1990-93), Mich. Libr. Assn. (continuing edn. and profl. stds. com.), Detroit Assn. Libr. Coop. (exec. staff), Mich. Libr. Consortium (trustee). Office: McGregor Pub Libr 12244 Woodward Ave Highland Park MI 48203

NEAD, KAREN L., university professor; b. Grayville, Ill., Sept. 25, 1944; d. Vernon M. and Imogene (Hamilton) Green; m. Morris James Nead, Dec. 22, 1960; children: Martin, Bryan, Morris James II, Serenity Dawn. AS, Wabash Valley Coll., Mt. Carmel, 1976; BA in English, Eastern Ill. U., Charleston, 1978, MA in English, 1979; PhD in higher edn., So. Ill. U., Carbondale, 1994. Prof. English Vincennes U., Vincennes, Ind., 1979—. Recipient Higher Edn. Adminstrn. Acad. Scholarship So. Ill. U., 1994. Mem. Am. Assn. of Univ. Prof. Republican. Methodist. Home: RR 1 Box 415 Lawrenceville IL 62439 Office: Vincennes Univ 1002 N 2nd St Vincennes IN

NEAD, THOMAS (EDWARD), electrical engineer. BSEE, U. Cin., 1964. Elec. engr. Milacron, Cin., 1964-95, Vickers Electronics Systesm, South Lebanon, Ohio, 1996—; tchr. engring. U. Cin., Ohio, 1970-80. Patentee in field. Office: Vickers Electronics Systems 1151 W Mason Morrow Rd South Lebanon OH 45036

NEAL, DENNIS R., manufacturing executive; b. Forbus, Tenn., May 16, 1929. Mgmt. positions Engleking Patterns, Inc., Columbus, Ind., 1959-83; pres. N & S Patterns, Inc., Columbus, Ind., 1983—. With USAF, 1946-49. Mem. Masons, Shriners. Office: N & S Patterns Inc 10957 E State Rd 7 Columbus IN 47203-9546

NEAL, JEFF, stage director. Exec. dir. Organic Theatre Co., Chgo., 1993—. Office: Organic Theatre Co 3319 N Clark St Chicago IL 60657-1603*

NEAL-VITTIGLIO, CYNTHIA KAREN, clinical psychologist; b. Detroit, Dec. 30, 1952; d. Gaston O. and Evelyn Jewel (Dunn) N.; m. Thomas Anthony Vittiglio, July 10, 1988; 1 child, Anthony. BA, Wayne State U., 1975, MA, 1977, PhD, 1983. Licensed psychologist. Clin. researcher Sinai Hosp., Detroit, 1977-78; clin. asst. Dept. Neuropsychology Lafayette Clinic, 1974-75; faculty mem. Inst. for Sex Rsch., Bloomington, Ind., 1975, 80; sch. psychologist Lakeshore Pub. Schs., St. Clair Shores, Mich., 1979-80; staff psychologist Evergreen Counseling Ctr., St. Clair Shores, 1979—; consulting psychologist St. John Hosp., Detroit, 1983—. Mem. Jr. Coun., Founders Soc., Detroit, 1985—, Cranbrook Women's Soc., Bloomfield Hills, Mich., 1987—, Am. Ballet Soc., N.Y.C., 1980—. Recipient Grad. Fellowship Wayne State U., 1988. Mem. APA, DAR (Louise St. Clair chpt.). Republican. Home: PO Box 250628 Franklin MI 48025-0628 Office: Evergreen Counseling Svcs 19900 Ten Mile Saint Clair Shores MI 48009

NEBENZAHL, PAUL, broadcast executive; b. Chgo., Nov. 1, 1954; s. Irving Arthur and Norma (Waggett) N.; m. Christina Marie Senese, Sept. 17, 1982; children: Ian, Aria. B of Philosophy, Thomas Jefferson Coll., 1979. Dir. devel. The Peace Mus., Chgo., 1982-83, The Acad. - Art, Music, Dance, Theatre, Chgo., 1983-84; co-dir. Chgo. Filmmakers Inc., Chgo., 1984-85; asst. dir. Gateway Found. Inc., Chgo., 1985-87; dir. corp./found. rels Field Mus. Nat. History, Chgo., 1987-89; asst. exec. dir. Boys and Girls Clubs of Chgo., 1989-90; assoc. dir. WTTW/Chgo., 1990-91, dir. devel., 1991-92, v.p. devel., 1992—; bd. com. Donors Forum Chgo., 1991-92. Composer, performer with Joseph Jarman, Leroy Jenkins, Carei Thomas, Big Walter Horton, Homesick James, Corky Siegal; composer soundtract Chicago Matters, Dread (nomination Emmy), A Man and His School, 1994. Bd. dirs. Circle Pines Ctr., Delton, Mich., 1987-90, chmn. 60th Anniversary Celebration com.; bd. dirs. Joseph Holmes Dance Theatre, Chgo., 1990-91; mem. fundraising com. Greater Chgo. Food Depository, 1990; mem. com. bd. Issues Com. Donors Forum, Chgo., 1993—, Bus. Vol. for Arts, 1993—; co-chair NSFRE Support Com., 1993—. Mem. Nat. Soc. Fund Raising Execs. (mem. Chgo. chpt. ethics com./membership com. 1990-92, long range planning com.), 410 Club. Home: 550 Barton Ave Evanston IL 60202-2109 Office: WTTW/Chgo 5400 N Saint Louis Ave Chicago IL 60625-4623

NEBERGALL, DONALD CHARLES, investment consultant; b. Davenport, Iowa, Aug. 12, 1928; s. Ellis W. and Hilda (Bruhn) N.; m. Shirley Elaine Williams, Apr. 12, 1952; children: Robert W., Nancy L. Nebergall Bosma. BS, Iowa State U., 1951. With Poweshiek County Nat. Bank, 1958-72, sr. v.p., to 1972; founding pres., CEO Brenton Bank and Trust Co., Cedar Rapids, Iowa, 1972-82, chmn. bd., 1982-86; v.p. Chapman Co., 1986-88; bd. dirs. Telephone & Data Systems, Inc., chmn. audit com., 1977—; bd. dirs. Guaranty Bank and Trust, Barlow Investment Co.; former vice chmn. bd. Iowa Transfer Svc. V.p., bd. dirs. Iowa 4-H Found., 1972-76; div. campaign chmn. United Way; former bd. dirs., past pres. Methwick Retirement Community; founding trustee Cedar Rapids Community Sch. Dist. Found.; past pres. Cedar Rapids Greater Downtown Assn. With AUS, 1946-48. Recipient Ptnr. in 4-H award Iowa 4-H, 1983, charter 4-H Found. Ct. of Honor, 1989. Mem. Rotary, Alpha Zeta, Gamma Sigma Delta, Delta Upsilon. Republican. Methodist. Office: 2919 Applewood Pl NE Cedar Rapids IA 52402-3323

NECKERMANN, PETER JOSEF, insurance company executive; b. Wuertzburg, Fed. Republic Germany, Oct. 26, 1935; came to U.S., 1977; s. Josef and Annemarie (Brueckner) N.; m. Jutta Voelk, Feb. 10, 1960; children: Susanne, Christian. Grad., J.W. Goethe U., Frankfurt, Fed. Republic Germany, MA, 1962; PhD, Ohio State U., 1990. Pres. Neckermann Versand KGaA, Frankfurt, 1962-77; dir. econ. analysis and systems Nationwide Ins. Cos., Columbus, Ohio, 1977-79, v.p. econ. and investment services, 1979—. CIV. Mem. Columbus Assn. Bus. Economists, Columbus Coun. on World Affairs (bd. dirs.), Rotary Club of Columbus, Univ. Club of Columbus (pres.). Home: 1261 Fountaine Dr Columbus OH 43221-1519 Office: Nationwide Ins Cos 1 Nationwide Plz Columbus OH 43215-2220

NECKERS, DOUGLAS CARLYLE, chemistry educator; b. Corry, Pa., Aug. 15, 1938; m. Suzanne Ames Evans, June 18, 1960; children: Pamela, Andrew. AB, Hope Coll., 1960; PhD, U. Kans., 1963. Fellow Harvard Corp., 1963-64; asst. prof. Hope Coll., Holland, Mich., 1964-67, assoc. prof., 1967-71; assoc. prof. chemistry U. N.Mex., Albuquerque, 1971-73; prof. and chmn. dept. chemistry Bowling Green (Ohio) State U., 1973—, Disting. rsch. prof., 1986—; McMaster Disting. rsch. prof., 1993; exec. dir. Ctr. for Photochem. Scis. Bowling Green (Ohio) State U., 1986—; vis. lectr. Ohio State U., Columbus, 1965, U. Ill., Urbana, 1970; vis. prof. U. Groningen, The Netherlands, 1968-69, U. Nijmegen, The Netherlands, 1975. Co-author: Organic Chemistry, 1977, Programmed Introduction to Organic Chemistry, 1977, Organic Chemistry: Structure, Mechanism and Synthesis, 1973; author: Mechanistic Organic Photochemistry, 1967. Recipient Paul R. Block Jr. award Toledo sect. Am. Chem. Soc., 1987, Paul and Ruth Olscamp Rsch. award, 1987, Leo Friend award for Chem. Tech., 1978, Honors Disting. Alumnus award U. Kans., 1982, Morley medal Cleve. sect. Am. Chem. Soc., 1994; named McMaster Prof. Photochem. Scis., 1993, hon. alumnus Bowling Green State U., 1995. Fellow AAAS. Office: Bowling Green State U/Ctr Photochem Scis/Dept Chem 141 Overman Hall Bowling Green OH 43403

NEDERLANDER, MARJORIE SMITH, retired interior designer and decorator; b. Springfield, Mo., Nov. 10, 1922; d. Laurence Jabe and Harriet George S.; m. William Howard Breech, Mar. 16, 1945 (div. Sept. 1971); children: William Kimball Breech, Kathryn Breech Raft; m. Harry Jay Nederlander, July 2, 1976. Student, Sullins Coll., 1938-40, U. Mo., 1940-41, Am. Acad. of Dramatic Art, 1941-42. Prin. Marjorie Breech Interiors, Bloomfield Hills, Mich., 1970-95; ret. Mem. Village Club. Episcopal.

NEEDHAM, DANIEL RYAN, marketing professional; b. Muskegon, Mich., Aug. 3, 1962; s. Virgil C. and Kathryn (Ryan) N.; m. Michaelene Marie Liecko, July 13, 1991; children: Daniel, Matthew. BA in Mktg. and Bus., Drake Univ., 1985. Salesperson Minolta, Chgo., 1986-87; mktg. dir. Communicom, Chgo., 1988-89; sales mgr. LPC Software, Lombard, Ill., 1990-91; mgr. govt. rels. SPS Payment Sys., Riverwoods, Ill., 1991—; bd. dirs. AIM, Des Moines; trustee Delta Found., Deerfield, Ill. 1994—. Bd. dirs. Chgo. Symphony Young Profl., 1989-92, Northwestern Hosp. Aux. Bd., Chgo., 1989—, Shedd Aquarium Aux. Bd., Chgo., 1994—, Lyric Opera Aux. Bd., Chgo., 1995; zone chmn. Ducks Unltd., Chgo., 1992-1994. Mem. The Tavern Club, The Adventurers Club, Kropp Duster Sailing Syndicate and others, English Speaking Union, Glen View Club. Republican. Home: 587 Melody Highland Park IL 60035 Office: SPS Payment Sys 2500 Lake Cook Rd Riverwoods IL 60015-3851

NEEDHAM, GEORGE, librarian. Libr. State of Mich., Lansing, 1996—. Office: State Libr 717 W Allegan St PO Box 30007 Lansing MI 48909*

NEEDHAM, JAMES ROBERT, television station executive, producer, telecommunications educator; b. New Albany, Ind., July 2, 1944; s. Frederick Homer and Jeannette Elizabeth (Cushman) N.; m. Judy Ann Grimes, Aug. 31, 1967 (div. Apr. 1974); m. Linda Lou Loats, Oct. 15, 1977; children: Kirsten, Steve, Brian. BS in Speech and Psychology, Ind. State U., 1967, MS in Speech, 1968. Prodn. engr. Sta. WTHI-TV, Terre Haute, Ind., 1968-69; asst. audio-visual coord. U. Guelph, Ont., Can., 1969; TV prodr. Ea. Ky. U., Richmond, 1969-72; dir. community affairs Sta. WISH-TV, Indpls., 1972-74, adminstrv. asst. to gen. mgr., 1974-76; gen. mgr. Sta. WIPB-TV Ball State U., Muncie, Ind., 1976-93, asst. prof. telecomms., 1993—; treas., bd. dirs. Ind. Pub. Broadcasting Stas., Indpls. Prodr. (TV programs) Conversation on Africa, 1969, Conversation on Russia, 1969, Family Planning in Rockcastle County, 1970, Fashion Close-up, 1970, Meat, Truth and Labeling, 1970, Jesse Owens: Today, 1971, Tangent: On Black Poetry, 1971, Tangent: Doc Looks at Music, 1972, Tangent: Joe's Beat, 1972 (Jazz Poll award); prodr., host (TV programs) Religion in the News, 1974-75, Teleconference, 1975-76, Bioethics, 1976-77; prodr. dir. numerous other programs on indsl. tech., agrl. sci. Com. mem. Young Life of Delaware County, Muncie, 1976—, pres., 1978-80. Mem. Small Sta. Assn. (midwest regional dir. 1986-92), Muncie Delaware County C. of C. (v.p. govt. rels. 1979-82). Home: 600 S Riviera Ln Yorktown IN 47396-9620 Office: Ball State Univ 2180 EF Ball Bldg Muncie IN 47306

NEELD, VAUGHN DELEATH, technical publications editor; b. Denison, Tex., June 15, 1943; d. Ernest Woodrow and Jewel Frances (Thomas) N.; m. David LeRoy Davis, Aug. 19, 1961 (div. Jan. 1974); children: Kerry Dawn, York David, Shan Michelle, Ryan Neeld. BA in Liberal Studies, St. Mary Coll., 1995. Phototypesetter The Estes Park (Colo.) Trail-Gazette, Estes Park, Ft. Collins, Colo., 1973-78; editorial asst. The Type House, Ft. Collins, Colo., 1978-84; tech. publ. editor The Triangle Rev., Ft. Bliss, Tex., 1975-78; editorial asst. U.S. Geol. Survey, Kans., Colo., 1984—; cons. U.S. Forest Svc., Ft. Collins, 1979-83; editorial asst. U.S. Army, Ft. Bliss, Tex., 1983-84, tech. publ. editor, 1984-86; tech. publ. editor U.S. Army, Ft. Leavenworth, Kans., 1986—. Author numerous poetry; artist (drawing, paintings) Grand Rapids, Larimer County Fair, Stone Lion Book Store, Gallmeyer and Livingston Mft. Co. Logo Contest; photographer one-woman show Rocky Mountain Forest and Range Experiment Sta., 1981, Western Camera Photography Contest, 1983 (1st place), Kans. Flower, Lawn and Garden Show, 1996 (hon. mention); singer Okla. Coll. for Women Chorus, 1961-62, Ft. Collins Lyric Opera "Carmen", 1982, Parkville, Mo. Philharm., 1988, Carnegie Choraliers, 1990, CAC Ladies' Chorus, Ft. Leavenworth, 1995—. Instr. water therapy for bioltd., Ft. Leavenworth, 1995—, 1986-88; photographer, artist, archivist, vol. Hueco Tanks State Park, El Paso, 193-84; vol. dirt mover Coe Lake Pueblo Archeol. Dig. Ft. Bliss, 1985; mem. City of Leavenworth Human Rels. Commn., 1989-92, Fed. Women's Mentor Program, Ft. Leavenworth, 1992, Mainstreet USA Mural Com., Leavenworth. Mem. Leavenworth County Artists' Assn., Leavenworth Vintage Home Soc. Mem. Ch. of Christ. Home: 622 Pawnee St Leavenworth KS 66048-1448 Office: US Command & Gen Staff Coll Doctrine Mgmt 2nd Prodn Div Bell Hall # 222 Fort Leavenworth KS 66027

NEELY, JOHN DOUGLAS, information services consultant; b. Cin., May 20, 1959; s. Edward Rex and Janet (Henchie) N.; 1 child, Kristin Michelle. BS in Computer Sci., Duke U., 1981, MA, 1984; MBA, U. Chgo., 1989. Computer programmer IBM Corp., Raleigh, N.C., 1981-84; systems engr. IBM Corp., Chgo., 1984-86, comm. industry specialist, 1987-89, specialist unit mgr., 1989-91, mgr. LAN cons. practice, 1992-94; dir. network cons. Entex Info. Svcs., Oak Brook, Ill., 1994—. Coach boys travelling soccer Wheeling (Ill.) Soccer Club, 1993-95, Lake Cook United Soccer Club, Long Grove, Ill., 1995—. Mem. Real F.C. Soccer Club (pres. 1992—, Player of Yr. 1990). Office: Entex Info Svcs 2100 S York Rd Oak Brook IL 60521

NEELY, MARK EDWARD, JR., writer; b. Amarillo, Tex., Nov. 10, 1944; s. Mark Edward and Lottie (Wright) N.; m. Sylvia Eakes, June 15, 1966. BA, Yale U., 1966, PhD, 1973; LHD (hon.), Lincoln Coll., 1981. Former dir. Louis A. Warren Lincoln Library and Museum, Ft. Wayne, Ind.; vis. instr. Iowa State U., Ames, 1971-72; editor Lincoln Lore, 1973—; mem. adv. bd. Ind. Historical Bureau, 1980—; mem. editorial adv. com. Ind. Mag. of History, 1981—; mem. editorial bd. Ulysses S. Grant Assn., 1981—. Author: The Abraham Lincoln Encyclopedia, 1981, The Lincoln Family Album: Photographs From The Personal Collection of a Historic American Family, 1990, The Fate of Liberty: Abraham Lincoln and Civil Liberties, 1991 (Pulitzer Prize for history 1992), The Last Best Hope on Earth: Abraham Lincoln and the Promise of America, 1993; (with Harold Holzer and Gabor S. Boritt) The Lincoln Image: Abraham Lincoln and the Popular Print, 1984, The Confederate Image: Prints of the Last Cause, 1987; (with R. Gerald McMurty) The Insanity File: The Case of Mary Todd Lincoln, 1986; (with Holzer) Mine Eyes Have Seen the Glory: The Civil War in American Art, 1993. Mem. Abraham Lincoln Assn., Soc. Ind. Archivists (pres. 1980-81), Ind. Assn. of Historians (pres. 1987-88).

NEENAN, THOMAS FRANCIS, association executive, consultant; b. Kansas City, Mo., Apr. 3, 1923; s. Emmet Joseph and Mary Helen (Liebst) N.; m. Eileen Margaret Vala, Aug. 4, 1951; children: Nancy, Tom Jr., Pamela, Kathleen, Maureen. BA, Iowa U., 1948; MA, Iowa State U., 1978. Trademark researcher Lampa Christopherson, Chgo., 1948-50; sales mgr. Cedar Rapids (Iowa) Block Co., 1950-53; owner Tywal Co., Center Point, Iowa, 1953-60; mem. sales staff Capp Homes, Center Point, Iowa, 1960-78; property mgr. Center Point, Iowa, 1978-86; exec. dir. Iowa Trails Coun., Center Point, Iowa, 1984—. Editor: (mag.) Trails Advocate, 1986—. Mayor City of Center Point, 1959-61, 65-69; chmn. City Planning an dzoning Com., Center Point, 1970—; active County Dem. Ctrl. Com., Linn County, Iowa, Linn County Conservation Bd., 1972-83; vice chair state legis. com. AARP, Des Moines, 1988-93; active leader Boy Scouts Am. Recipient Silver Beaver award Boy Scouts Am., 1961, St. George award Cath. Archdiocese Dubuque, 1973; named to Iowa's Vol. Hall of Fame, 1995. Mem. Am. Hiking Soc. (bd. dirs., Kern award 1986), Rails to Trails Conservancy, Am. Trails (treas., bd. dirs., award of excellence 1992). Democrat. Roman Catholic. Home: 1201 Central Ave Center Point IA 52213-9638 Office: Trails Coun Inc PO Box 131 Center Point IA 52213-0131

NEESON, PEG, broadcast executive; b. Dayton, Ohio, Aug. 12, 1954; d. John J. and Eloise (Whitmore) N. BA, Miami U., Oxford, Ohio, 1976. Dir. pub. info. WVIZ-TV, Cleve., 1979—. Recipient Oebie award Ohio Ednl. Broadcasting, 1988, 93, 95, Advt. and Promotion awards PBS, 1987, 90, Beryl Spector award, 1990, Ohio Ednl. TV award, 1996. Mem. NATAS, Soc. Profl. Journalists, Pub. Rels. Soc. Am.

NEFF, BONITA DOSTAL, communication developmental facilitator; b. Grinnell, Iowa, Aug. 16, 1942; d. Lester Ernest and Mary Margaret (Hudnut) Dostal; m. Gregory Pall Neff, Apr. 27, 1974; 1 child, Kristiana. BA, U. N. Iowa, 1964, MA, 1966; PhD, U. Mich., 1973; AA cum laude, Lansing (Mich.) C.C., 1980. Edn. leadership fellow George Washington U., Washington, 1976-77; specialist Mich. State U., East Lansing, 1977-80, co-investigator family and child inst. energy rsch. team, 1980-82; asst. prof. comm. Purdue U., Hammond, Ind., 1982-87; pres. Pub. Comm. Assocs., Munster, Ind., 1986—; asst. prof. comm. Valparaiso (Ind.) U., 1991—; presenter more than 80 rsch. papers to regional, nat. and internat. profl. confs.; cons. in field. Mem. adv. bd., reviewer Jour. Applied Comm. Rsch.; reviewer Mgmt. Comm. Quar.: An Internat. Jour.; editor procs. on accreditation for nat. conf.; contbr. chpts. to books, profl. articles and poetry to jours. Chancellor's rep. Calumet (Ind.) N.W. Forum Econ. Devel., 1982-84; mem. Lake County (Ind.) Community Devel. Com., 1984—; bd. dirs. Big Bros. and Big Sisters N.W. Ind., 1984, 87; pres., chmn. bd. dirs. N.W. Ind. Youth Chorus. Faculty rsch. grantee U. Mich., 1971, Consumer Product Safety Coun. grantee, 1976-77, Ind. Arts Commn./Nat. Endowment for Arts grantee, 1990-92; recipient top rsch. honors regional confs. Mem. Internat. Comm. Assn. (pub. rels. dir. Pub. Rels. Interest Group, chmn. task force on accreditation 1988), Internat. Pub. Rels. Assn., Speech Comm. Assn. (chmn. commn. for pub. rels. 1988, chmn. nat. Pub. Rels. Rsch. awards com. PRIDE 1988, nat. com. on convs. allied orgns., task force on nat. policy, nat. legis. coun. rep. 1993—), Ctrl. State Comm. Assn. (chmn. 1988-89, pub. rels. officer 1989-92), Internat. Assn. Bus. Comm., Women in Comm. (pres. Calumet chpt. 1985-90, advisor Valparaiso Student WICI, Inc., Outstanding Communicator 1990), Assn. Educators in Journalism Mass Comm. (chair internat. com. 1994—), World Comm. Assn. Democrat. Roman Catholic. Home: 8320 Greenwood Ave Hammond IN 46321-1813 Office: Pub Comm Assocs 8320 Greenwood Ave Hammond IN 46321-1813

NEFF, FRED LEONARD, lawyer; b. St. Paul, Nov. 1, 1948; s. Elliott Ira and Mollie (Poboisk) N.; m. Christa Ruth Powell, Sept. 10, 1989. BS with high distinction, U. Minn., 1970; JD, William Mitchell Coll. Law, 1976. Bar: Minn. 1976, N.D. 1994, U.S. Dist. Ct. Minn. 1977, U.S. Ct. Appeals (8th cir.) 1985, U.S. Supreme Ct. 1985, Wis. 1986, U.S. Dist. Ct. (ea. and we. dists.) Wis. 1992. Tchr. Hopkins (Minn.) Pub. Schs., 1970-72; instr. U. Minn., Mpls., 1974-76; pvt. practice law Mpls., 1976-79; asst. county atty. Sibley County, Gaylord, Minn., 1979-80; mng. atty. Hyatt Legal Svcs., St. Paul, 1981-83, regional ptnr., 1983-85, profl. devel. ptnr., 1985-86; pres. Neff Law Firm, P.A., Mpls., 1986—; CEO Profl. Devel. Inst. Inc., Edina, Minn., 1994—, also bd. dirs.; instr. Inver Hills Coll., 1973-77; counsel Am. Tool Supply Co., St. Paul, 1976-78; cons. Nat. Detective Agy., Inc., St. Paul, 1980-83; CEO A Basic Legal Svc., Bloomington, 1990—; CEO, bd. dirs. Profl. Devel. Inst., Inc., Edina, Minn., 1994—; lectr., guest instr. U. Wis., River Falls, 1976-77; spl. instr. Hamline U., St. Paul, 1977; vis. lectr. Coll. St. Scholastica, Duluth, Minn., 1977; program. faculty, cons. Employment Law Seminar for Colo., Fla., La., Oreg., Employment and Labor Law Seminar for Ala., Alaska, Calif., Conn., Ind., N.C., Ohio, Va., N.C. Safety and Health at the Workplace, S.C. Labor Law, Ohio Safety at the Workplace; bd. dirs. Acceptance Ins. Holdings, Inc., Omaha; active Internat. Confederation Jurists, 1993; mem. faculty sem. Ariz. Safety at Workplace, Hawaii Employment & Labor, Miss. Employment & Labor Law, Del. Employment & Labor, Alaska Employment and Labor Law, Ga. Employment & Labor Law, N.J. Employment & Labor, Wash. Employment Law, Mass. Employment & Labor Law, 1995—, Ark. Employment and Labor Law, Mo. Employment and Labor Law, Iowa Employment and Labor Law, Utah Employment and Labor Law. Author: Fred Neff's Self-Defense Library, 1976, Everybody's Self-Defense Book, 1978, Karate Is for Me, 1980, Running Is for Me, 1980, Lessons from the Samurai, 1986, Lessons from the Art of Kempo, 1986, Lessons from the Western Warriors, 1986, Lessons from the Fighting Commandos, 1990, Lessons from the Ancient Japanese Masters of Self-Defense, 1990, Lessons from the Eastern Warrors, 1990, Mysterious Persons of the Past, 1991, Great Mysteries of Crime, 1991; host TV series Great Puzzles In History; co-host TV series Great Unsolved Crimes, Minn.; asst. editor: Hennepic County Lawyer, 1992—. Advisor to bd. Sibley County Commrs., 1979-80; speaker civic groups, 1976-82; mem. Hennepin County Juvenile Justice Panel, 1980-82, Hennepin County (Minn.) Pub. Def. Conflict Panel, 1980-82, 86—, Hennepin County Bar Assn. Advice Panel Law Day, 1987, mem. dist. ethics com., 1990—; mem. Panel Union Privilege Legal Svcs. div. AFL-CIO, 1986—, Montgomery Wards Legal Svcs. Panel, 1986—, Edina Hist. Soc., Decathlon Athletic Club; charter mem. Commn. for the Battle of Normandy Mus.; founding sponsor Civil Justice Found., 1986—; mem. com. for publ. Hennepin County Lawyer, 1992. Recipient Outstanding Tchr. award Inver Hills Coll. Student Body, 1973, St. Paul Citizen of Month award Citizens Group, 1975, Kempo Club award U. Minn., 1975, U. Minn. Student Appreciation award Kempo Club, 1978, Sibley County Atty. Commendation award, 1980, Good Neighbor award WCCO Radio, 1985, Lamp of Knowledge award Twin Cities Lawyers Guild, 1986, N.W. Cmty. TV Commendation award, 1989-91, Presdl. Merit medal Pres. George Bush, 1990, N.W. Cmty. TV award, 1991, HLS Leadership award, 1984, Mng. Attys. Guidance award, 1985, Creative Thinker award Regional Staff, 1986, HLS Justice award, 1986, Honors cert. for Authors, Childrens Reading Round Table of Chgo., 1988. Fellow Roscoe Pound Found., Nat. Dist. Attys. Assn.; mem. ABA, ATLA, Minn. Bar Assn. (com. on ethics, 1994—, com. on alternative dispute resolution, 1994—), Minn. Trial Lawyers Assn., Hennepin County Bar Assn. (dist. ethics com. 1990—), Minn. Bar Assn. (co994, com. on alternative dispute resolution 1994), Wis. Bar. Assn., Ramsey County Bar Assn., Am. Judicature Soc., Internat. Platform Assn., Am. Arbitration Assn. (panel of arbitrators 1992), Minn. Martial Arts Assn. (pres. 1974-78, Outstanding Instr. award 1973), Nippon Kobudo Rengokai (bd. dirs. North Cen. States 1972-76, regional dir. 1972-76), Internat. Confederation Jurists, Edina C. of C., Southview Country Club, Masons, Kiwanis, Scottish Rite, Sigma Alpha Mu. Home: 4515 Andover Rd Minneapolis MN 55435-4031 also: 7250 France Ave S Ste 107 Edina MN 55435-4311 also: 5930 Brooklyn Blvd Ste 206 Brooklyn Center MN 55429-2518 also: 1711 W County Rd B Ste 340N Roseville MN 55113

NEFF, GREGORY PALL, manufacturing engineering educator, consultant; b. Detroit, Nov. 23, 1942; s. Jacob John and Bonnie Alice (Pall) N.; m. Bonita Jean Dostal, Apr. 27, 1974; 1 child, Kristiana Dostal Neff. BS in Physics, U. Mich., 1964, MA in Math., 1966, MS in Physics, 1967; MSME, Mich. State U., 1982. Registered profl. engr., Ind.; cert. mfg. engr.; cert. mfg. technologist; cert. sr. indsl. technologist. Rsch. asst. cyclotron lab U. Mich., Ann Arbor, 1968-72, teaching fellow physics dept., 1973; instr. sci. dept. Lansing (Mich.) C.C., 1976-82; guest lectr. Purdue U. Calumet, Hammond, Ind., 1982-83, asst. prof., 1984-91, assoc. prof. mech. engring. tech., 1991—; cons. Inland Steel Co., Indsl. Engring., East Chicago, Ind., 1984-86, Polyurethane div. Pinder Industries, East Chicago, 1990-92, Elevated div. Pitts. Tank & Tower, Henderson, Ky., 1990-91. Contbr. articles to profl. jours. County commr. Ingham County Bd. of Commr., Mason, Mich., 1977-80, Tri-County Regional Planning Commn., Lansing, 1978-80, chair, non-motorized adv. coun. Mich. Dept. Transp., Lansing, 1982-83. Mem. ASME, AAUP, Soc. Mfg. Engrs. (chpt. 112 bd. dirs. 1986—, Appreciation award 1990, 92, Outstanding Faculty Advisor award 1991,), Ind. Soc. Profl. Engrs., Am. Soc. for Engring. Edn. (Merl K. Miller award 1994), Nat. Assn. Indsl. Tech., Order of the Engr. Democrat. Roman Catholic. Office: Purdue U Calumet 2200 169th St Hammond IN 46323-2068

NEFF, KENNETH D., realtor; b. Montpelier, Ind., Oct. 19, 1929; s. Clyde A. and Cora I. N.; m. Nancy Stiffler, Dec. 26, 1951; children: David, Susan, Julie, Bradley. BS in Bus., Ball State U. Owner Neff Realty, Montpelier, 1983-95; mayor City of Montpelier, 1983-95. Mem. air pollution bd. Ind. Dept. Environ Mgmt., Indpls., 1991-95; mem. Purdue Hwy. Extension and Rsch. Project, Ind. Counties and Cities Bd., West Lafayette, 1991-95; chmn. adminstrv. coun. Montpelier United Meth. Ch. Lt. col. USAF, 1958-81. Mem. Ind. Dem. Editl. Assn., Ind. Assn. Cities and Towns (exec. bd., legis com. 1988-96), North Ctrl. Mayors' Roundtable (pres. 1991-92), Kiwanis (past state lt. gov.). Democrat. Home: 129 S Washington St Montpelier IN 47359-1331 Office: 109 W Huntington St Montpelier IN 47359-1123

NEFF, ROBERT CLARK, lawyer; b. St. Marys, Ohio, Feb. 11, 1921; s. Homer Armstrong and Irene (McCulloch) N.; m. Betty Baker, July 3, 1954 (dec.); children: Cynthia Lee Neff Schifer, Robert Clark, Abigail Lynn (dec.); m. Helen Picking, July 24, 1975. BA, Coll. Wooster, 1943; postgrad. U. Mich., 1946-47; LLB, Ohio No. U., 1950. Bar: Ohio 1950, U.S. Dist. Ct. (no. dist.) Ohio 1978. pvt. practice law, Bucyrus, Ohio, 1950—; law dir. City of Bucyrus, 1962-95. Chmn. blood program Crawford County (Ohio) unit ARC, 1955-89; life mem. adv. bd. Salvation Army, 1962—; clk. of session 1st Presbyterian Ch., Bucyrus, 1958—; bd. dirs. Bucyrus Area Cmty. Found, Crawford County Bd. Mental Retardation and Devel. Disabilities, 1977-82 . With USNR, World War II; comdr. Res. ret. Recipient "Others" plaque for 30 yrs. adv. bd. svc. Salvation Army, Ohio No. U. Coll. Law Alumni award for cmty. svc. Mem. Ohio Bar Assn., Crawford County Bar Assn., Naval Res. Assn., Ret. Officers Assn., Am. Legion, Bucyrus Area C. of C. (past bd. dirs., Outstanding Citizen award, 1973, Bucyrus Citizen of Yr., 1981). Republican. Clubs: Kiwanis (life mem., past pres.), Masons. Home: 1085 Mary Ann Ln # 406 Bucyrus OH 44820-0406 Office: 840 S Sandusky Ave Box 406 Bucyrus OH 44820-0406

NEGSTAD, RICHARD B., state legislator; m. Mary Negstad; 2 children. Student, S.D. State U. Mem. S.D. Ho. of Reps., mem. agr. and natural resources coms., mem. taxation and health and human resource coms.; mem S.D. Senate; elec. engr., farmer. Home: RR 1 Box 46 Volga SD 57071-9723*

NEHER, LESLIE IRWIN, engineer, former air force officer; b. Marion, Ind., Sept. 15, 1906; s. Irvin Warner and Lelia Myrtle (Irwin) N.; m. Lucy Marion Price; 1 child, David Price; m. Cecelia Marguerite Hayworth, June 14, 1956; BS in Elec. Engring., Purdue U., 1930. Registered profl. engr., Ind., N.Mex. Engr. high voltage rsch., 1930-32; engr. U.S. Army, Phila., 1933-37; heating engr. gas utility, 1937-40; commd. 2d lt. U.S. Army, 1929, advanced through grades to Col., 1947; dir. tng., Tng. Command, Heavy Bombardment, Amarillo (Tex.) AFB, 1942-44; dir. mgmt. tng., 15th AF, Colorado Springs, Colo., 1945-46; mgr. Korea Electric Power Co., Seoul, 1946-47, ret., 1960; engr. Neher Engring. Co., Gas City, Ind., 1960—; researcher volcanic materials, 1948-49. Chmn. Midwest Indsl. Gas Coun., 1969; historian Grant County, Ind., 1982-95. Named Outstanding Liaison Officer, Air Force Acad., 1959; Ambassador for Peace, Republic of Korea, 1977; recipient Republic of Korea Svc. medal, 1977. Mem. Ind. Soc. Profl. Engrs. (Outstanding Engr. 1982, Engr. of Yr. Ind. 1986), Nat. Soc. Profl. Engrs., Midwest Indsl. Gas Assn. (chmn. 1969), Am. Assn. of Retired Persons (pres. Grant County chpt. 1986, 87, 89, 90, dir. dist. 5 1992-93), NAUS (pres. Grissom chpt. 1992—). Republican. Methodist. Lodge: Kiwanis (Disting. sect. 1979-85, lt. gov. 1964; Disting. Svc. award 1962).

NEHRING, WENDY MARIE, pediatrics nurse; b. Waukegan, Ill., Aug. 17, 1957; d. Virgil M. and R. Allene (Nelson) Nehring. BSN, Ill. Wesleyan U., Bloomington, 1979; MS, U. Wis., Madison, 1983; PhD, U. Ill., Chgo., 1989. Primary nurse level III pediatrics Evanston (Ill.) Hosp., 1979-81; staff/charge nurse pediatrics Kishwaukee Community Hosp., DeKalb, Ill., 1981; staff/charge nurse geriatrics Madison (Wis.) Convalescent Ctr., 1982; instr. parent-child nursing Ill. Wesleyan U., Bloomington, 1983-85; clin. nurse specialist/rsch. asst. U. Ill. Chgo. and Peoria, Coll. Nursing, 1985-87; rsch. asst./nurse cons. U. Ill. at Chgo., Early Intervention Project, 1987-89; sr. rsch. specialist, project dir. U. Ill. Chgo. U. Affiliated Prog. in Devel. Disabilities, 1989-90; sr. rsch. specialist child and family studies U. Ill. at Chgo., Coll. Nursing, Ctr. for Narcolespsy Rsch., 1990-92; pediatric clin. instr. U. Ill., Chgo., 1992, asst. prof. maternal-child nursing, 1992—, coord. undergrad. pediatric nursing program, 1994-95, coord. undergrad. maternal-child nursing programs, 1995—; lectr. in field; conductor workshops in field; cons. in field. Cons. editor Mental Retardation, 1996—; contbr. articles to profl. jours. HEW traineeship, 1981-82, 82-83; Downs Syndrome Rsch. fund grantee, 1988, 93—; Nat. Rsch. Svc. awardee, Nat. Ctr. Nursing Rsch.-NIH, 1989, others. Mem. Ctrl. Ill. Down Syndrome Orgn., Nat. Down Syndrome Congress (profl. adv. com. 1988—), Nat. Assn. on Down Syndrome (adv. bd. 1990—, 2d v.p. 1991-94), Am. Assn. on Mental Retardation (prevention com. 1989-92, prs. nursing divsn. 1992-94), Midwest Nursing Rsch. Soc. (co-chmn. pediat. sect. 1995-96, chmn. 1996—), Soc. for Pediat. Nurses, Alpha Tau Delta, Sigma Theta Tau. Office: U Ill 845 S Damen Ave Rm 816 Chicago IL 60612-7350

NEIBEL, OLIVER JOSEPH, JR., medical services executive; b. Kansas City, Mo., Apr. 17, 1927; s. Oliver Joseph and Eula Lee (Durham) N.; m. Patricia Helen O'Keefe, June 24, 1950 (div. 1971); children: Oliver Joseph III, Deborah Sue; m. Diane Bachus Nelson, Apr. 11, 1981. BS U. Ariz., 1949; JD U. Va., 1952. Bar: Wash. 1952, Ill. 1961, Nebr. 1973. Instr., U. Washington, 1952-53; practiced in Seattle, 1953-57; asst. atty. gen. State of Wash., 1957-61; legislative atty. AMA, Chgo., 1961-63; exec. dir., gen. counsel Coll. Am. Pathologists, Chgo., 1963-72; v.p., gen. mgr. Physicians Lab., Omaha, 1973—. Justice of peace, Mountlake Terrace, Wash., 1955-57. Served with USNR, 1945. Mem. Wash. Bar Assn., Nebr. Bar Assn., Ill. Bar Assn., Nat. Health Lawyers Assn., Med. Group Mgmt. Assn., Phi Kappa Psi (chpt. pres. 1948-49), Delta Theta Phi, Alpha Kappa Psi, Delta Sigma Rho. Mason, Elk, Rotarian, Shriners. Clubs: Wash. Athletic (Seattle); Tavern (Chgo.); Omaha Press. Home: 7918 Potter Plz Omaha NE 68122-1449 Office: 4840 F St Omaha NE 68117-1407

NEIDHARDT, FREDERICK CARL, microbiologist; b. Phila., May 12, 1931; s. Adam Fred and Carrie (Fry) N.; m. Elizabeth Robinson, June 9, 1956 (div. Sept. 1977); children: Richard Frederick, Jane Elizabeth; m. Germaine Chipault, Dec. 3, 1977; 1 son, Marc Frederick. BA, Kenyon Coll., 1952, DSc (hon.), 1976; PhD, Harvard U., 1956; DSc (hon.), Purdue U., 1988, Umea U., 1994. Research fellow Pasteur Inst., Paris, 1956-57; H.C. Ernst research fellow Harvard Med. Sch., 1957-58, instr., then assoc., 1958-61; mem. faculty Purdue U., 1961-70, assoc. prof, then prof., assoc. head dept. biol. scis., 1965-70; mem. faculty U. Mich., Ann Arbor, 1970—, chmn. dept. microbiology and immunology, 1970-82, F.G. Novy disting. univ. prof., 1989—, assoc. dean faculty affairs, 1990-93, assoc. v.p. for rsch., 1993—; Found. for Microbiology lectr. Am. Soc. Microbiology, 1966-67; cons. Dept. Agr., 1964-65; mem. grant study panel NIH, 1965-69, 88-92; mem. commn. scholars Ill. Bd. Higher Edn., 1973-79; mem. test com. for microbiology Nat. Bd. Med. Examiners, 1975-79, chmn., 1979-83; mem. sci. adv. com. Neogen Corp., 1982-92; mem. basic energy scis. adv. com. U.S. Dept. Energy, 1994—; Wellcome vis. prof. in microbiology U. Ky., 1986. Author books and papers in field; mem. editorial bd. profl. jours. Recipient award bacteriology and immunology Eli Lilly and Co., 1966; Alexander von Humboldt Found. award for U.S. sr. scientist, 1979; NSF sr. fellow U. Copenhagen, 1968-69. Mem. Am. Soc. Microbiology (pres. 1981-82), Am. Acad. Arts and Scis., Am. Soc. Biochemistry and Molecular Biology, Am. Inst. Biol. Scis., Genetics Soc. Am., Soc. Gen. Physiology, Phi Beta Kappa, Sigma Xi. Office: U Mich Med Sch Dept Microbiology and Immunology Ann Arbor MI 48109-0620

NEIDORF, ROBIN MARA, writer, magazine; b. Chgo., May 17, 1969; d. Barry Michael and Louise Rae (Potek) N. BA, Williams Coll., 1991; MFA, Bennington Coll., 1996. Editl. asst. Graywolf Press, St. Paul, 1992-94; staff writer Environ. Info., Mpls., 1994—; founder Clio's Pen Custom Rsch., 1996—. Contbr. Minn. Women's Press, 1992—, Jour. of Women's Health, 1992—. Jewish.

NEIHARDT, HILDA, foundation administrator, writer; b. Bancroft, Nebr., Dec. 6, 1916; d. John Gneisenau and Mona (Martinsen) N.; m. Albert Joseph Petri, Apr. 18, 1942 (div. Oct. 1963); children; Gail Petri Toedebusch, Robin, Coralie Joyce Hughes. AB, U. Nebr., 1937; JD, U. Mo., 1963. Bar: Mo. 1963. Adminstrv. asst. Consulate of Switzerland, St. Louis, 1937-42; pvt. practice Columbia, Mo., 1963-85, Lake Ozark, Mo., 1985-88; pres. John G. Neihardt Found., Bancroft, 1987—. Author: Black Elk and Flaming Rainbow, 1995; editor: The Giving Earth, 1991, The End of The Dream, 1991, The Ancient Memory, 1991. Trustee John G. Neihardt Trust, Columbia and Tekamah, Nebr., 1973—. With USN, 1944-45. Mem. AAUW, Westerners, Internat. Home: Rt 1 Box 44A Tekamah NE 68061 Office: John G Neihardt Found Box 344 Bancroft NE 68004

NEIHEISEL, THOMAS HENRY, marketing research consultant; b. Cin., Dec. 1, 1953; s. Vincent John and Mary Jane (Haverkos) N.; m. Cynthia Lynn Dirk, Aug. 5, 1977; children: Matthew Thomas, Andrew John. BBA, U. Cin., 1977, MBA, 1981. Group project leader The Procter & Gamble Co., Cin., 1974-77; mgr. project svcs. Burgoyne, Inc., Cin., 1977-81; mgr. market rsch. Kenner Products, Cin., 1982-84; dir. mktg. rsch. Kenner Parker Toys, Inc., 1984-91; pres. Youth Mktg. Solutions, Inc., 1992—; speaker mktg. confs. Coach Pisgah Youth Orgn., West Chester, 1988—. John Burgoyne Rsch. scholar, 1976, U. Cin. Honor scholar, 1972, Alpha Kappa Psi scholar; recipient Eagle Scout award Boy Scouts Am., 1968. Mem. Am. Mktg. Assn., Assn. MBA Execs., Market Rsch. Assn., Wetherington Country Club. Roman Catholic. Home and Office: 7599 Legendary Ln West Chester OH 45069-4602

NEIMARK, VASSA, interior architect; b. Miami, Fla., Dec. 9, 1954; d. William Rolla and Bettijean (Davison) Meyer; m. Philip John Neimark, Oct. 29, 1982; children: Dashiel Charles, Darq-Amber. Student, Art Inst. Ft. Lauderdale, 1974, Art Inst. Chgo., 1980. Owner, prin. Vassa Inc., Chgo., 1979—. Contbr. articles to local mag. Bd. dirs. M.R.I.C. Michael Med. Found., Chgo., Expressways Mus., Chgo., Orchard Village Home for Retarded Adults, Park Ridge Youth Campus, Des Plaines, Ill. Recipient Star on Horizon award Chgo. Mdse. Mart-Chgo. Design Sources, 1985, Spl. Recognition in Design award, 1987. Mem. Internat. Soc. Interior Designers (bd. dirs. 1985-86), Women in Design Industry, IFA Found. N. Am. (v.p.), Internat. Inst. for Bau-Biologie and Ecology, Inc., Carlton Club, Club Internat.

NEIN, SCOTT R., state legislator; m. Janis Nein; children: Jason, Courtney, Beckett, Brody. BS, Bowling Green State U., 1974. State rep. Dist. 58 Ohio State Congress, state rep. Dist. 57, 1993—; agt. Miller Ins.; mem. Butler County Rep. exec. com. Recipient Congl. appt. 8th Congl. Dist. Awards Coun., 1987. Mem. Prol. Ins. Agts. Assn., Ohio Ind. Ins. Agts. Assn., Middletown Ind. Ins. Agts. Assn. (past pres.), Rotary (past pres., Paul Harris Fellow), Middletown C. of C. (bd. dirs.), Farm Bur. *

NEITZEL, LISA ANN, newscaster, reporter; b. Watertown, Wis., Jan. 5, 1970; d. Deane Allen and Ruth Emma (Johnson) N. BA in Broadcast Journalism, U. Wis., 1993, BA in Polit. Sci., 1993. News reporter, anchor WBKB-TV (CBS), Alpena, Mich., 1994-94; reporter, weathercaster WDIO-TV (ABC), Duluth, Minn., 1994-95. Mem. Soc. Profl. Journalists, Women in Comms, Inc.

NEKOLA, LOUIS WILLIAM, utility line clearance executive; b. Queens, N.Y., Mar. 8, 1954; s. Louis William and Helen Jean (Gillespie) N. Student, Nassau Community Coll., 1972. Cert. pesticide applicator. Owner Jal Tree Svc., Plainview, N.Y., 1972-79; foreman Tree Preservation Co. Inc., Briarcliff Manor, N.Y., 1979-83; gen. foreman Tree Preservation Co. Inc., Bergen County, N.J., 1983-85; div. mgr. Tree Preservation Co. Inc., Ohio, W.Va., Ind., Mich., Wisc., 1985-93; v.p. Nelson Tree Svc. Co. Inc, Dayton, Ohio, 1993—. Mem. Utility Arborist Assn., Int. Soc. Arboriculture, Am. Forestry Assn. (Ohio chpt.), Internat. Soc. Arboriculture, Ohio Pesticide Applicators for Responsible Regulation. Republican. Home: 10830 Meadow Trl Strongsville OH 44136-2118

NELMS, CHARLIE, academic administrator; b. Crawfordsville, Ark., Sept. 11, 1946. BS in Agronomy, U. Ark., Pine Bluff, 1968; MS, Ind. U., 1971, EdD, 1977. Various collegiate positions to lectr. and counselor Lehman Coll./CUNY, Pine Bluff, 1971-73; assoc. dean, asst. prof. edn. Earlham Coll., Richmond, Ind., 1973-77; assoc. dir. Ctr. Human Devel. and Edn. Svcs., asst. prof. U. Ark., Pine Bluff, 1977-78; assoc. dean for acad. affairs Ind. U., Northwest Gary, Ind., 1978-84; v.p. student svcs. Sinclair C.C., Dayton, Ohio, 1984-87; chancellor, prof. edn. Ind. Univ., 1987-94; chancellor and prof. edn., pub. adminstrn. Univ. Mich., Flint, 1994—; cons., evaluator N.Cen. Assn. Schs. & Colls., 1987—, Middle States Assn., 1994—. Contbr. articles to profl. jours. Recipient Outstanding Svc. award NASPA, 1990, I-MAEOPP, 1990, Disting. Svc. award Negro Edn. Review, 1990, Nat. Alliance Bus., 1984, Wall Street Joun. Student Achievement award, 1968, Rockefeller Student Leadership award, 1968. Office: U Mich Office of Chancellor 221 University Pavilion Flint MI 48502 Home: 915 Woodlawn Pk Dr Flint MI 48503

NELSON, BRENT LYNN, city auditor; b. Pocatello, Ind., June 25, 1951; s. Lynn and Freeda (Lowe) N.; m. Vicki Jean Morgan, Oct. 19, 1979 (div. Mar. 1995); children: Jessica, Melissa, Joshua. BS in acctg., bus. adminstrn., Ariz. State U., 1978. CPA, Okla., Mo. Sr. performance analyst Office Auditor Gen. State Ariz., Phoenix, 1979-84; performance audit supr. City Tulsa, 1984-86; city auditor City Independence, Mo., 1986—. Charter unit rep. Boy Scout Troop 646, Independence, 1991-94. Mem. Nat. Assn. Local Govt. Auditors (exec. bd. dirs. 1992-94), Am. Inst. CPAs, Intergovtl. Audit Forum (mem. exec. com. 1988—). Mormon. Home: 15718 E 40th Terr Independence MO 64055 Office: City Independence 111 E Maple St Independence MO 64050

NELSON, CARL VINCENT, secondary education educator; b. Highland, Ill., July 29, 1947; s. Charles Clarence and Marian Elizabeth (Williams) N.; divorced. BS in Secondary Edn., Southeast Mo. State U., 1970; MS in Edn., Ind. U., 1986. Cert. secondary tchr., Mo., Ind.; lic. secondary adminstrn. and supervision, Ind.; ordained min. Bapt. Ch., 1971. Tchr. Soldan High Sch., St. Louis, 1970-78; job placement coord. Arsenal Tech. High Sch., Indpls., 1978, ombudsman, 1978-82; home/sch. advisor Ben Davis High Sch., Indpls., 1982—; numerous positions within chs. and religious orgns. Contbr. articles to mags. Life mem. Amateur Bowlers Tour; cert. coach, instr. youth bowling, 1989—; judge Regional State Essay Contest U.S. Acad. Decathlon Program, Inc., 1990-94; wresting coach, 1970-71; founder, sponsor Youth Voices in Govt. Club, 1982—; high sch. coord. Project Leadership Svc., 1988-91. Home: 3539 Beluga Ln Apt 2D Indianapolis IN 46214-1326 Office: Ben Davis High Sch 1200 N Girls School Rd Indianapolis IN 46214-3403

NELSON, CAROLYN, state legislator; b. Madison, Wis., Oct. 8, 1937; m. Gilbert W. Nelson; children: Paul, John, Karla. BS, N.D. State U., 1959, MS, 1960. Lectr. in math. N.D. State U., 1968—; mem. N.D. Ho. of Reps., 1986-88, 92-94, N.D. Senate, 1994—; mem. N.D. State Investment Bd., 1989-92; mem. Judiciary com., Vet. Affairs com., N.D. Senate, Employee's Benefits Com. Mem. Bd. Edn., Fargo, N.D., 1985-91, pres., 1989-90; mem. bd. trustees N.D. Tchrs. Fund for Retirement, 1985-92, pres., 1990-92; mem. Nat. PTA, N.D. PTA, pres., 1978-81, League of Women Voters, N.D. Women's & Children's Caucus. Recipient Merit Svc. award Gamma Phi Beta, 1978, 90. Mem. Am. Guild English Handbell Ringers (area chmn. 1982-84, nat. bd. dirs. 1982-90), N.D. Fedn. Music Clubs (pres.-elect), Fargo C. of C., Gamma Phi Beta, Phi Kappa Phi, Sigma Alpha Iota, Phi Delta Kappa. Address: 1125 College St Fargo ND 58102-3433 Office: ND Senate State Capitol Bismarck ND 58505*

NELSON, DAVID ALDRICH, federal judge; b. Watertown, N.Y., Aug. 14, 1932; s. Carlton Low and Irene Demetria (Aldrich) N.; m. Mary Dickson, Aug. 25, 1956; 3 children. A.B., Hamilton Coll., 1954; postgrad., Cambridge U., Eng., 1954-55; LL.B., Harvard U., 1958. Bar: Ohio 1958, N.Y. 1982. Atty.-advisor Office of the Gen. Counsel, Dept. of the Air Force, 1959-62; assoc. Squire, Sanders & Dempsey, Cleve., 1958-67, ptnr., 1967-69, 72-85; cir. judge U.S. Ct. Appeals (6th cir.), Cin., 1985—; gen. counsel U.S. Post Office Dept., Washington, 1969-71; sr. asst. postmaster gen., gen. counsel U.S. Postal Svc., Washington, 1971; mem. nat. coun. Coll. Law, Ohio State U., 1988—. Trustee Hamilton Coll., 1984-88. Served to maj. USAFR, 1959-69. Fulbright scholar, 1954-55; recipient Benjamin Franklin award U.S. Post Office Dept., 1969. Fellow Am. Coll. Trial Lawyers; mem. Fed. Bar Assn., Ohio Bar Assn., Cleve. Bar Assn., Cin. Bar Assn., Emerson Lit. Soc., Ct. of Nisi Prius (sgt. emeritus), Phi Beta Kappa. Office: US Ct Appeals 6th Cir Potter Stewart US Ct House 5th and Walnut St Cincinnati OH 45202-3988

NELSON, E. BENJAMIN, governor; b. McCook, Nebr., May 17, 1941; s. Benjamin Earl and Birdella Ruby (Henderson) N.; B.A., U. Nebr., 1963, M.A., 1966, J.D., 1970; LLD (hon.) Creighton U., 1992, Peru State Coll., 1993; m. Diane C. Gleason, Feb. 22, 1980; children by previous marriage—Sarah Jane, Patrick James; stepchildren—Kevin Michael Gleason, Christine Marie Gleason. Bar: Nebr. 1970. Instr. dept. philosophy U. Nebr., 1963-65; supr. Dept. Ins., State of Nebr., Lincoln, 1965-72, dir. ins., 1975-76; asst. gen. counsel, gen. counsel, sec., v.p. The Central Nat. Ins. Group of Omaha, 1972-75, exec. v.p., 1976-77, pres., 1978-81, CEO, 1980-81, of counsel, Kennedy, Holland, DeLacy & Svoboda, Omaha, 1985-90; gov. State of Nebr., Lincoln, 1991—. Co-chmn. Carter/Mondale re-election campaign, Nebr., 1980; chair Nat. Edn. Goals Panel, 1992-94; co-founder Gov.'s Ethanol Coalition, chair 1991, 94; pres. Coun. of State Gov's., 1994. Recipient Disting. Eagle award Nat. Eagle Scout Assn., 1994; named Amb. Plenipotentiary, 1993. Mem. Consumer Credit Ins. Assn., Nat. Assn. Ind. Insurers, Nat. Assn. Ins. Commissioners (exec. v.p. 1982-85), Nebr. Bar Assn., Am. Bar Assn., Midwestern Gov's. Assn. (chair 1994), Western Gov.'s Assn. (vice chair 1994, chair 1995), Happy Hollow Club, Omaha Club, Hillcrest Country Club. Democrat. Methodist. Home: 1425 H St Lincoln NE 68508-3759 Office: State Capitol 2nd Floor Lincoln NE 68509

NELSON, FREDA NELL HEIN, librarian; b. Trenton, Mo., Dec. 16, 1929; d. Fred Albert and Mable Carman (Doan) Hein; m. Robert John Nelson, Nov. 1, 1957 (div. Apr. 1984); children: Thor, Hope. Nursing diploma, Trinity Luth. Hosp., Kansas City, Mo., 1950; B. Philosophy, Northwestern U., 1961; MS in Info. and Libr. Sci., U. Ill., 1986. RN. Operating rm. nurse Trinity Luth. Hosp., Kansas City, Mo., 1950-52, Johns Hopkins Hosp., Balt., 1952, Wesley Meml. Hosp., Chgo., 1952-58, Tacoma Gen. Hosp., 1958-59, Chgo. Wesley Hosp., 1959-61; libr. asst. Maple Woods Campus Met. Community Colls., Kansas City, 1987-89, libr., libr. mgr. Blue Springs Campus, 1989—; co-founder Coll. for Kids, Knox Coll., Galesburg, Ill., 1982. Nurses scholar Edgar Bergen Found., 1947; recipient Award of Merit, Chgo. Bd. Health, 1952. Home: 7000 N Elm St Pleasant Valley MO 64068 Office: Blue Springs Campus Libr 1501 W Jefferson St Blue Springs MO 64015-7242

NELSON, FREDERICK DICKSON, lawyer; b. Cleve., Oct. 19, 1958; s. David Aldrich and Mary Ellen (Dickson) N. AB, Hamilton Coll., 1980; JD, Harvard U., 1983. Bar: Ohio 1984, D.C. 1985. Majority counsel subcom. on criminal law U.S. Senate Judiciary Com., Washington, 1983-85; spl. asst. to asst. atty. gen., Office of Legal Policy U.S. Dept. Justice, Washington, 1985-86, dep. asst. atty. gen., Office of Legal Policy, 1986-87; assoc. Taft, Stettinius & Hollister, Cin., 1988-89, of counsel, 1991-93; assoc. counsel to Pres. of U.S. The White House, Washington, 1989-90; advisor to govts. of Ukraine and Russia, ABA Ctrl. and East European Legal Law Initiative, 1992-93; adj. prof. constl. law Salmon P. Chase Coll. Law, U. No. Ky., 1994; chief of staff U.S. Rep. Steve Chabot, 1995—. Exec. editor Harvard Jour. of Law and Pub. Policy, 1982-83. Dir. issues and rsch. Nahra for Congress campaign, Cleve., 1980; mem. Hamilton County Rep. Leadership Coun., 1992; cons. Chabot for Congress Campaign, Cin., 1994. Harry S. Truman Found. scholar, 1978-81. Mem. Federalist Soc., Harvard Club of Cin. (bd. dirs. 1989), Phi Beta Kappa. Republican. Home: 7900 Brill Rd Cincinnati OH 45243-3944

NELSON, GARY J., state legislator; m. Linda; 3 children. Degree, Concordia Coll. Mem. N.D. Senate, 1977—; minority whip, 1991, majority whip; past pres. Cent. Cass Sch. Bd.; farmer. Mem. Farm Bur., Crop Improvement Assn., Casselton Cmty. Club, Masons, N.D. Wildlife Fedn., Wildlife Club. Office: 2970 158th Ave SE Casselton ND 58012-9725 also: State Senate State Capital Bismarck ND 58505*

NELSON, GENE F., manufacturing executive; b. St. Paul, June 25, 1940. B, U. Miami, 1964; M, St. Paul U., 1989. Plant mgr. U.F.E., Inc., Stillwater, Wis., 1977-90; pres. Ideal Coating Inc., Amery, Wis., 1994—; v.p. Thompson Machine, Amery, Wis., 1990—. Mem. Lions. Office: 705 Keller Ave S Amery WI 54001-1420

NELSON, JANICE ELIZABETH, educator; b. Chgo., June 17, 1952; d. Arthur Eugene and Jessie (Cook) O'Neill; m. Garth Ralph Casteel, June 21, 1975 (div. Oct. 1985); children: Gabriel Garth, Callyann Elizabeth, Malena Jean; m. Robert Guy Nelson, Aug. 4, 1990. AA, Fullerton Coll., 1972; BA in Biology, Calif. State U., Fullerton, 1976. Lab. tech. Fullerton (Calif.) Coll., 1983-88; tchr. sci. Valle Lindo High Sch., El Monte, Calif., 1988-90, Alexis (Ill.) High Sch., 1990—. Mem. Planned Parenthood Assn., Calif. and Ill., 1978—. Chapman Coll. Grad. fellow, 1987; Calif. State scholar, 1970, U. Women's scholar Fullerton Coll., 1971. Mem. Nat. Sci. Tchrs. Assn., Sierra Club, Alpha Gamma Sigma. Democrat. Lutheran. Home: 2594 180th St Alexis IL 61412 Office: Alexis High Sch Holloway Ave Alexis IL 61412

NELSON, JEFFREY OWEN, manufacturing executive; b. Portage, Wis., Dec. 18, 1956; s. Raymond Gerhard and Norene Sue (Joppa) N.; m. Patricia Marie Norlander, Sept. 6, 1980; children: Jeanette, Jodi, Kristin. BS in Mining Engring. with honors, U. Wis., Platteville, 1979. Registered profl. engr., Wis. Assoc. application engr. Allis Chalmers Corp., Milw., 1979-80, application engr., 1980-81, sr. application engr., 1981-83, project mgr., 1984; area sales mgr. Trelleborg, Inc., Kenosha, Wis., 1984-85; regional sales mgr. Trelleborg, Inc., Chgo., 1986-88; mgr. engineered products divsn. Trelleborg, Inc., Solon, Ohio, 1988-89, v.p., gen. mgr., 1989-90; v.p. Viking Supply, Inc., 1989—; pres. Trellex, Inc., Solon, 1990-91; bus. mgr. Trellex, Inc., Appleton, Wis., 1992-94; product mgr. Svedala Industries, 1995—; v.p., treas. Automatic Belting Corp., Solon, 1989-90, v.p. Trellex Midwest, Inc., 1989-93; pres. P.E. Holdings Corp., Solon, 1990-92. Mem. AIME. Office: Trellex Inc 2600 N Roemer Rd Appleton WI 54911-8626

NELSON, KATHERINE MACTAGGART, educator; b. Mattoon, Ill., Aug. 27, 1953; d. Leonard John and Wandalee Mae (Clodfelder) Stabler; m. John Robert Nelson; children: Scott MacTaggart, Robert John, Matthew David. BS in Edn., Eastern Ill. U., 1973; postgrad., Carroll Coll., 1989—. Tchr. Owen Valley Schs., Spencer, Ind., 1974-76; acad. support coordinator Whitefish Bay Schs., Milw., 1976-80; dir. research Sullivan, Murphy Assoc., Milw., 1980-81; tng. specialist Northwestern Ins., Milw., 1981-84; tng. coordinator Cath. Knights Ins. Soc., Milw., 1984-87; tchr. Pewaukee (Wis.) High Sch., 1988-95, Arrowhead H.S., Hartland, Wis., 1995—. Pres., mem. bd. Cushing Elem. Sch. PTO, 1994—; mem. Milw. Zool. Soc., Women's Fellowship Bd.; founder Mgmt. Resources Exec. Sec. Roundtable, Milw., 1986; vol. com. mem. Wis. Make-A-Wish Found.; mem. Christian edn. com. Congl. Ch., 1990-93, chair women's fellowship com., 1993-96, Bible sch. dir., 1990, 91; vol. Cross for State Supt. campaign. Recipient Leadership award YMCA, 1986. Mem. NEA, ASTD (bd. dirs., chmn. pub. rels. 1984, vol. trainer 1982-89), Internat. Assn. Pers. Women (chmn. pub. rels. 1984-85, chmn. membership and registrar, nominating com., by-laws com., vol. trainer 1981-89), Arrowhead Union Edn. Assn. (exec. com. 1990-93), Law Wives Assn. (v.p. membership and soc. coms., PYC sidestays fin. com.), Pewaukee Yacht Club, Wis. Club, P.E.O. Sisterhood (guard, chaplain). Republican. Home: N23w28796 Louis Ave Pewaukee WI 53072-5029 Office: Arrowhead Union High School 700 North Ave Hartland WI 53029

NELSON, KAY ELLEN, speech and language pathologist; b. Milw., Apr. 14, 1947; d. John A. and Margaret B. (Janke) Strobel; m. Kuglitsch Dale, Mar. 2, 1974 (div. Dec. 1981); 1 child, Ashley Lara. BA with distinction, U. Wis., Madison, 1969; MA, U. Wis., Milw., 1972. Speech and lang. pathologist Sch. Dist. 146, Dolton, Ill., 1970-71, Waukesha County Handicapped Children's Edn. Bd., Waukesha, Wis., 1972-77, 79-80, Kettle Moraine Area Schs., Wales, Wis., 1980-94; dir. speech/lang. pathology MJ Care, Inc., Fond du Lac, Wis., 1994-96; speech-lang. pathologist NovaCare, Inc., New Berlin, Wis., 1996—; pvt. practice Dousman, Wis., summers 1991-93. Fellow Herb Kohl Found., 1993. Mem. Am. Speech, Lang. and Hearing Assn. (cert. of clin. competence, ACE awards 1990, 91, 92, 94, 95), Wis. Speech., Lang. and Hearing Assn. (sch. rep. dist VII 1991—, chmn. sch. svcs. com. 1992-94, v.p. sch. svcs. 1994-95, rep.-at-large 1995-96), Internat. Soc. for Augumentive and Alternative Comm., U.S. Soc. for Augumentive and Alternative Comm., Wis. Soc. for Augumentive and Alternative Comm. (sec. 1990-92, membership chmn. 1990-93, v.p. profl. affairs 1993). Unitarian. Office: NovaCare Inc 13700 W National Ave New Berlin WI 53151

NELSON, KIRK RICHARD, telecommunications executive; b. Portland, Oreg., Mar. 30, 1956; s. Richard John and Gloria Mae (Kraxberger) N.; m. Patricia Lee Zech, Aug. 6, 1983; children: Brandon Kirk, Kyle Patrick. BA magna cum laude, Pacific Luth. U., 1978; MBA, Seattle U., 1985; postgrad., U. So. Calif., 1991. Various managerial positions Pacific N.W. Bell, Seattle, 1979-85, dir. regulatory and fin. mgmt., 1985-87; dir. investor rels. US West, Inc., Denver, 1987-88; asst. v.p., exec. dir. external affairs US West Communications, Salt Lake City, 1988-92, exec. dir. rural strategy, 1992-94; v.p., gen. mgr. Exchange Carrier Svcs., US West, Mpls., 1994—. Chmn. United Way, Salt Lake City, 1987-90, People of Vision, 1990; bd. dirs. Pioneer Meml. Theatre, Salt Lake City, 1987-93, Nat. Soc. to Prevent Blindness, Salt Lake City, 1990-94, apptd. Salt Lake City-County Bd. Health, 1992-93. Mem. Utah Mfg. Assn. (bd. dirs. 1988-94, chmn. 1991), U.S. West Pres. Club, Coun. Leaders, Beta Gamma Sigma. Lutheran. Home: Eden Prairie MN Office: US West 150 S 5th St Ste 510 Minneapolis MN 55402-4200

NELSON, LOREN ELWAN, engineering administrator; b. Gillett, Wis., Nov. 14, 1946; m. Virginia, Sept. 20, 1969; children: Candice, Diana, Eric. A of Mech. Design, Northeastern Wis. Tech. coll., 1966. Chief draftsman Patz Sales, Inc., Pound, Wis., 1966-75, engring. svcs. mgr., 1975-89, dir. engring., 1989—; mem. engring. com., past chmn. Farmstead Equip. Assn. Coun. of Equip. Mfrs. Inst., 1991-93. mem. village bd. Village of Coleman (Wis.), 1977—. Home: 714 Hwy 141 N Coleman WI 54112-9535 Office: Patz Sales Inc Hwy 141 S Pound WI 54161

NELSON, LUCILLE BONEVIEVE LEWIS, journalist; b. St. Louis County, Mo., Apr. 19, 1993; d. Ben J. and Leonora Mathilda (Romsdahl) Pierson; m. Richard Stanley Lewis, June 2, 1956 (dec. Aug. 1989); children: Steven Richard, Jane Lewis Ucin; m. Alton Emmanuel Nelson, June 22, 1995. BA, Augustana Coll., Sioux Falls, S.D., 1954. Cert. tchr., Minn., S.D. Tchr. Mountain Lake (Minn.) Pub. Schs., 1955-57, Freeman (S.D.) Jr. Coll./Acad., 1962-65, Sanborn (Minn.) Pub. Sch., 1956-68; owner Lewis Sewing Ctr., Windom, Minn., 1971-78; writer Worthington (Minn.) Daily Globe, 1972—. Lay reader Ch. of Good Shpeherd, Windom, 1991-95; adminstr. Larry Buhler Statue Fund, Windom, 1994; v.p. Pioneerland Tourism, Mankato, Minn., 1971-83; bd. dirs. S.W. Minn. Arts and Humanities, 1991-94. Mem. Am. Legion (Meml. Day spkr. 1993-95), Windom C. of C. (cert. of appreciation 1995), Windom Concert Assn., Cottonwood County Hist. Soc. (2d v.p., life mem.). Home: 11051 Grover Ave NW Maple Lake MN 55358

NELSON, MARCUS THOMAS, playwright, producer; b. Elizabeth, Miss., Oct. 29, 1919; s. Benjamin Marshall and Maude Elizabeth (Threlkeld) N.; m. Vivian O. Walker, Dec. 5, 1942 (div. Mar. 1950); m. Susan Hill, Oct. 22, 1960 (div. May 1963); m. Sally Lou Spurgat Nelson, April 25, 1973 (div. Febr. 1983). Leader Civilian Conservation Corps., Aledo, Ill., 1937-39; spice grinder LaSalle Mfg. Co., Chgo., 1939-43; machinist journeyman Pearl Harbor Navy Yard, Honolulu, Hawaii, 1943-49; streetcar motorman Chgo. Transit Authority, 1949-51; machinist, journeyman Kodiak (Alaska) Naval Air Base, 1951-52; photo-journalist The Good Publishing Co., Paris, Tex., 1953; bus operator Chgo. Transit Authority, 1954-65; cab driver The Yellow Cab Co., Chgo., 1965-66; theatre mgr. Hull House Parkway Cmty. Theatre, Chgo., 1966-68; short order cook USAR-McNair Barracks, Berlin, Germany, 1968-69; specialist in theatre U. Wis.-Downer Campus, Milw., 1970-71; playwright prodr. The Village Church, Milw., 1971-73, New Concept Theatre, Chgo., 1973—. Adaptor: (plays) The Lord is Thy Passion, 1986, The Jogger Story, 1988, author over 42 plays; listed playwright Black Playwright, 1823-1977 Annotated Bibliography of Plays (James V. Hatch and Omanii Obdullah), 1977; contbg. poet: (anthologies) Beyond the Stars, 1995, 96, The Best Poems of the '90s, 1996. Mem., resource person Chgo. Theatre Coalition, 1974; mem. Chgo. Alliance for the Performing Arts, 1975; co-founder, mem. Black Theatre Alliance, Chgo., 1975; mem. South Shore Cultural Coun., Chgo., 1977. Recipient Playwright grantee Wis. Arts Coun., NEA, 1972, Ill. Arts Coun., 1976, 80, 81, 91, Playwright/Producer grantee Mayor's Office of Tng. and Employment, 1975, Chgo. Office of Fine Arts, 1977, Robert R. McCormick Found., 1978, Continental Bank Found., 1980, Chgo. Coun. on Fine Arts, 1980, 81, Midwest Playwrights Program, East Mpls., 1982, Chgo. Dept. Cultural Affairs and Ill. Arts Coun. Access Program, 1991. Democrat. Mem. Ch. of God. Office: New Concept Theatre PO Box 4456 Chicago IL 60680-4456

NELSON, MARGARET MOGENSEN, journalist; b. Eau Claire, Wis., May 13, 1947; d. Martin T. and Catherine (Burke) Mogensen; children: Elissa, Emily. BA, U. Wis., 1969; MSJ, Northwestern U., 1976. Reporter The Paper, Oshkosh, Wis., 1969; editor Marlennon Corp., Chgo., 1970-71; pub. rels. mgr. Michael Reese Med. Ctr., Chgo., 1971-73; editorial dir. Nat. Easter Seal Soc., Chgo., 1973-75; vis. instr. Northwestern U. Sch. Journalism, Evanston, Ill., 1976-79; upper Midwest corr. People Mag., N.Y.C., 1985—. Contbr. articles to nat. publs. including Newsweek, USA Today. Vol. editor Basilica mag., Basilica of St. Mary; vol. mentor U. Minn. Sch. Journalism. Mem. Soc. Profl. Journalists, Nat. Writers Union. Home: 201 Valleyview Pl Minneapolis MN 55419-1376

NELSON, MARK EDWARD, civil engineer; b. Omaha, Apr. 23, 1954; s. Norbert Edward and Ruth (Johnson) N.; m. Melanie Ann Noel, Aug. 27, 1983; children: Joel William, Carly Marie, David Jonathan. BCE, U. Nebr., Omaha, 1977; MS in Agrl. Engring., U. Nebr., Lincoln, 1978. Registered profl. engr., Nebr. Supr. stream gaging program Nebr. Dept. Water Resources, Lincoln, 1979-86; design engr. Nebr. Dept. Roads, Lincoln, 1986-87; hydraulic engr. U.S. Army C.E., Omaha, 1987—. Mem. ASCE. Home: 20008 Rondo Dr Gretna NE 68028-3622 Office: Omaha Dist Corps Engrs 215 N 17th St Omaha NE 68102-4910

NELSON, MARY BERTHA, public relations executive; b. Mpls., Aug. 26, 1921; d. Charles and Edna Eva (Wrabek) Ring; m. Roger Anton Nelson, Jan. 4, 1941 (dec. 1981); children: Barbara Leigh, Judith Ann, Ward Anton. BA in Pub. Rels. and Journalism, Columbia Pacific U., 1983, MA, 1984. Reporter East Mpls. Argus, 1949-57, Southtown Economist, Oak Lawn, Ill., 1958-59; columnist-reporter S.W. Messenger Press, Midlothian, Ill., 1959-68; pub. info. dir. Moraine Valley Coll., Palos Hills, Ill., 1968-82; pub. rels. officer Oak Lawn Pub. Libr., 1982-91; owner, pres. Promoplans, Evergreen Park, Ill., 1991—. Contbr. articles to profl. jours. Bd. dirs. Family/Mental Health Svcs., Worth, Ill., 1968-80, Children's Craniofacial Assn., Dallas, 1994—; exec. dir. Ch. Coun., Chgo., 1982-92; trustee Ednl. Found., Oak Lawn, 1993—, Cmty. Libr. Found., Oak Lawn, 1993. Mem. South Suburban Programmers, Publicity Club Chgo., Cmty. Coll. Annuitants, Oak Lawn C. of C. (bd. dirs. 1984—). Lutheran. Office: Promoplans 9940 S Spaulding Evergreen Park IL 60805-3441

NELSON, MARY ELLEN DICKSON, actuary; b. Mpls., Mar. 24, 1933; d. William Alexander and Laura Winona (Baxter) Dickson; m. David Aldrich Nelson, Aug. 25, 1956; children: Frederick Dickson, Claudia Baxter, Caleb Edward. BA, Vassar Coll., 1954; postgrad., Cambridge (Eng.) U., 1954-55. Enrolled actuary under program adminstr. by joint bd. Dept. Labor and Dept. Treas. Rsch. assoc. N.Am. Life & Casualty Co., Mpls., 1955-56; actuarial asst. John Hancock Mut. Life Ins. Co., Boston, 1956-58; actuary David R. Kass & Assocs., Cleve., 1973-74; pres. Nelson & Co., Cleve., 1975, Conrad, Nelson & Co., Cleve., 1975-81, Nelson & Co., Cleve./Cin., 1981—; bd. dirs. Blount Internat., Inc., Montgomery, Ala., Cin. Bell Inc., Union Ctrl. Life Ins. Co., Cin. Fulbright scholar, 1954-55. Fellow Soc. Actuaries, Phi Beta Kappa; mem. Am. Acad. Actuaries, Cin. Actuaries Club, Midwest Benefits Conf. (chair 1991). Republican. Office: 105 W 4th St Cincinnati OH 45202-2735

NELSON, MORTON, county health commissioner; b. Mpls., Jan. 29, 1930; s. Solomon and Sarah (Eren) N.; m. Lois Ney Miller, Dec. 29, 1950; 1 child, Steven. BS, UCLA, 1956; MD, U. Calif., Irvine, 1962; MPH, U. Calif., Berkeley, 1971. Internship Rio Hondo Meml. Hosp., Downey, Calif., 1961-62; pvt. practice Granada Hills, Calif., 1962-65; asst. health officer Alameda County, Oakland, Calif., 1965-71; pub. health tng. Alameda County Health Dept., 1968-70; health officer Alameda County, Oakland, Calif., 1971-75; assoc. clin. prof. U. Calif., Irvine, 1975-77; health officer Orange County, Santa Ana, Calif., 1977-79; assoc. dir. family practice program United Western Med. Ctrs., Santa Ana, 1979-83; health commr. Montgomery County, Dayton, Ohio, 1983—; adj. prof. Wright State U., Dayton, 1984—, prof. cmty. health, 1991. Contbr. articles to profl. jours. Active Task Force on Sch. Health, Columbus, Ohio, 1990-91; trustee Dayton Area Health Plan, 1985—. With U.S. Army, 1948-52; lt. col. USAR M.C., 1982-86. Recipient Cert. of Appreciation Ohio State Med. Soc., 1990, Cert. of Merit City of Dayton, 1989, Recognition award Dep. Community Medicine/Wright State U., 1987. Fellow Am. Acad. Family Physicians; mem. Pan Am. Med. Assn., Am. Coll. Preventive Medicine, Soc. Tchrs. Family Medicine, AMA, Ohio Med. Assn., Montgomery County Med. Soc., Am. Assn. Pub. Health Physicians (trustee 1990-92). Office: Combined Health Dist 451 W 3rd St Dayton OH 45422-0001

NELSON, PAUL RAYMOND, church executive, minister; b. Fargo, N.D., July 13, 1951; s. Ingvald and Inez Loreen (Cogdill) N.; m. Mary Ann Urbashich, June 7, 1980. BA, Concordia Coll., 1973; MDiv, Yale U., 1977; MA in Theology, Notre Dame U., 1985, PhD in Theology, 1987. Ordained to ministry Luth. Ch., 1978. Interim pastor St. John-St. Paul Luth. Parish, Marxville, Wis., 1977; assoc. pastor Immanuel Luth. Ch., Watertown, Wis., 1978-82; asst. pastor Gloria Dei Luth. Ch., South Bend, Ind., 1982-88; vis. asst. prof. U. Notre Dame, Ind., 1986-88; dir. Study of Ministry Evang. Luth. Ch. Am., Chgo., 1988-93, dir. for worship, 1993—. Speaker, lectr. various orgns.; contbr. articles to profl. jours. Recipient Rockefeller fellowship Fund for Theol. Edn., 1973-74, Zimmermann Lecture Luth. Theol. Sem., Gettysburg, 1990. Mem. N.Am. Acad. Liturgy (assoc.), Societas Liturgica, Luth. Hist. Soc., Liturgical Conf. Office: Evang Luth Ch Am 8765 W Higgins Rd Chicago IL 60631-4101

NELSON, RICHARD DAVID, lawyer; b. Chgo., Jan. 29, 1940; s. Irving E. and Dorothy (Apolsky) N.; m. Davida Distenfield, Dec. 17, 1960; children: Cheryl, Laurel. BS in Acctg., U. Ill., 1961, LLB, 1964. Bar: Ill. 1964. Ptnr. Defrees & Fiske Law Offices, Chgo., 1964-81; ptnr., counsel, CFO, chief adminstrv. officer Heidrick & Struggles, Inc., Chgo., 1981—; bd. dirs., exec. com. Heidrick & Struggles, Inc., Chgo., 1981—. Pres. Jewish Cmty. Ctrs. of Chgo., 1987-89; chmn. Sign Graphics Task Force, Highland Park, Ill., 1986-88, Bus. and Econ. Devel. Commn., Highland Park; chmn. Econ. Devel. Commn. Highland Park, 1993—. Mem. ABA, Ill. State Bar Assn., Chgo. Bar Assn., Standard Club, Northmoor Country Club. Office: Heidrick & Struggles Inc 125 S Wacker Dr Ste 2800 Chicago IL 60606-4501

NELSON, RICHARD LAWRENCE, public relations executive; b. Chgo., Nov. 13, 1953; s. Stanley Eric and Joan Carol (Greif) N. BS in Speech, Northwestern U., 1975. Dep. dir. radio/TV Dem. Nat. Com., Washington, 1975-76; press sec. U.S. Ho. of Reps., Washington, 1976-78; spl. asst. office of media liasion The White House, Washington, 1978-80, asst. press sec. office of media liasion, 1980-81; acct. supr. Hill & Knowlton, Inc., Chgo., Ill., 1981-82; dir. corp. pub. rels. Playboy Enterprises, Inc., Chgo., 1982-84; v.p. pub. rels. First Chgo. Corp., Chgo., 1984-87; prin. Richard Nelson Pub. Rels., Chgo., 1987-89; v.p. pub. rels. The NutraSweet Co., Deerfield, Ill., 1989-94, v.p. integrated mktg. comm., 1994-95; v.p. pub. affairs The NutraSweet Kelco Co., Deerfield, Ill., 1996—; mem. exec. com. Internat. Food Info. Coun., Washington, 1991—; dir. Calorie Control Coun., Atlanta, 1990—. Dir., past pres. Nat. Runaway Switchboard, Chgo., 1987—; dir. AIDS Found. Chgo., 1993—, treas., 1995—. Recipient Silver Trumpet award Publicity Club Chgo., 1991, 94. Trustee Arthur W. Page Soc.; mem. Chgo. Pub. Rels. Forum. Democrat. Home: 1220 Noyes St Evanston IL 60201-2636 Office: The NutraSweet Co 1751 Lake Cook Rd Deerfield IL 60015-5615

NELSON, RICKY EUGENE, financial executive; b. Newman Grove, Nebr., Jan. 26, 1956; s. Eugene Theodore and Lorraine Doris (Osterloh) N.; m. Roxanne Sich, Sept. 16, 1978. BS in Agrl. Econs./Fin., U. Nebr., 1977; MS in Wealth Mgmt., Coll. Fin. Planning, Denver, 1996; MS, Coll. Fin. Planning, 1996. Cert. fin. planner; registered investment advisor. Br. mgr./loan officer Fed. Land Bank, Beatrice, Nebr., 1976-82; reg. rep. Edward D. Jones & Co., Atlantic, Iowa, 1982-84; dir. investments Darryl D. Smith Co., Atlantic, 1984-87; reg. rep. Investment Mgmt. & Rsch. Inc., Atlantic, 1984-87; br. mgr. Investment Mgmt. & Rsch. Inc., Hastings, Nebr., 1987—; pres. Nelson Capital Mgmt. Inc., Hastings, 1989—. Mem. Rotary, Masons (32 deg.). Office: Nelson Capital Mgmt Inc PO Box 1385 747 N Burlington Ste 307 Hastings NE 68902-1385

NELSON, ROBERT EDDINGER, management and development consultant; b. Mentone, Ind., Mar. 2, 1928; s. Arthur Irven and Tural Cecile (Eddinger) N.; B.A., Northwestern U., 1949; L.H.D., Iowa Wesleyan Coll., 1969; LLD, North Cen. Coll., 1987; m. Carol J., Nov. 24, 1951; children—Janet K. Nelson Callighan, Eric P. Asst. dir. alumni relations Northwestern U., Evanston, Ill., 1950-51, 54-55; v.p. and dir. pub. relations Iowa Wesleyan Coll., Mt. Pleasant, 1955-58; vice chancellor for devel. U. Kansas City, 1959-61; v.p. instl. devel. Ill. Inst. Tech., Chgo., 1961-68; pres. Robert Johnston Corp., Oak Brook, Ill., 1968-69, Robert E. Nelson Assocs., Inc., Oak Brook, Ill., 1969—; bd. dirs. Chautauqua Workshop in Fund Raising and Instl. Relations, Continental Bank of Oak Brook Terr., The Sun Cos.; nat. conf. chmn. and program dir. Am. Coll. Pub. Relations Assn., 1961; trustee, Iowa Wesleyan Coll., 1962-68; faculty mem. Ind. U. Workshops on Coll. and Univ. Devel., 1963-65, Lorretto Heights Summer Inst. for Fund Raising and Pub. Relations, 1964-68; mem. Pub. Review Panel for Grants Programs, Lilly Endowment, Inc., 1975. Served with U.S. Army, 1951-54. Mem. Council on Fin. Aid to Edn. (bd. dirs. 1957-63), Public Relations Soc. Am., Nat. Soc. Fund Raisers, Nat. Small Bus. Assn., Chgo. Soc. Fund Raising Execs., Blue Key, Delta Tau Delta. Methodist. Clubs: Execs., Econ., Union League (Chgo.), DuPage; Masons. Author chpt. in Handbook of Coll. and Univ. Adminstrn., 1970. Home: 5 Oakbrook Club Dr # 101 Oak Brook IL 60521-1348 Office: 120 Oakbrook Ctr Ste 208 Hinsdale IL 60521-1825

NELSON, RONALD WILLIAM, journalist; b. Evanston, Ill., Nov. 15, 1940; s. William Waldemar and Ethel Helen (Swan) N. BBA, U. Cin., 1969. Mgr. Nelson Real Estate, Evanston, Ill., 1969-95; journalist Independent, Evanston, Ill., 1985—; hon. chmn. Roman Protestant, Evanston, Ill., 1981—. Dir. office svcs. United Citizens for Nixon-Agnew, Washington, 1968. With U.S. Army, 1965-67, Korea. Recipient George Washington Honor medal Freedoms Found., 1967. Mem. Am. Legion, VFW. Presbyterian. Home and Office: Nelson Pubs 860 Hinman Ave Apt 223 Evanston IL 60202

NELSON, STEVEN FRANK, social services administrator; b. Kansas City, Mo., Mar. 12, 1949; s. Vernon Rex and Verna Ruth (Martens) N.; m. Connie Lee Trammel, 1974 (div. 1979); children: Erica L., Crystal A.; m. Rebecca L. Boltin, Sept. 7, 1983; children: Steven F. Jr., James V. Student, Dodge City Community Coll., 1972-73, 75, Wichita State U., 1984, Butler County Community Coll., El Dorado, Kans., 1988. Outreach counselor outpatient program St. John's Hosp., Wichita, Kans., 1985-87; asst. dir. Keystone, Riverside Hosp., Wichita, 1987-89; exec. dir. Keystone, Geary Community Hosp., Junction City, Kans., 1989-90, dir. chem. dependency unit, 1990—; mem. Kans. Alcohol Safety Action Project; mem. task force alcohol and drug svcs. Kans. Hosp. Assn., 1988-90; cons. peer counseling Geary County Health Dept., Junction City; bd. dirs. Substance Abuse Among Youth Prevention, Junction City, 1989-92. With USN, 1968-70, Vietnam. Recipient Crossroads of Leadership award Junction City C. of C., 1990. Mem. Nat. Assn. Alcohol and Drug Abuse Counselors, Kans. Alcohol and Drug Abuse Counselors, Assn. U.S. Army, Amateur Trap Assn., Kans. trap Assn., Kiwanis. Office: Geary Community Hosp CDU 1102 St Mary's Rd PO Box 490 Junction City KS 66441

NELSON, TERI LYNN, social worker; b. Anderson, Ind., Jan. 22, 1956; d. Gordon Dey and Carolyn Jean (Hasler) N. BA, Anderson (Ind.) U., 1978; MSW, Ind. U., Indpls., 1985. Cert. clin. social worker, Ind.; cert. criminal justice specialist. Pub. liaison A Better Way, Inc., Muncie, Ind., 1979-80; substance abuse counselor Aquarius House, Inc., Muncie, 1980-85; staff therapist Community Mental Health Ctr., Inc., Lawrenceburg, Ind., 1985; program dir. Cmty. Mental Health Ctr., Inc., Lawrenceburg, Ind., 1985-95; pres., CEO New Directions, Inc., Lafayette, Ind., 1995—; mem. Ind. Substance Abuse Task Force, Indpls., 1985—, co-chair, 1991-94; co-chair Ind. State Ann. Addictions Conf., 1992—; mem. adv. bd. Gov.'s Commn. for a Drug-Free Ind., Jeffersonville, 1988-92; clin. supr. Cmty. Mental Health Ctr., Inc., Lawrenceburg, 1989-95; ad. faculty Union Inst., Cin., 1993—; tng. cons. Fairbanks Rsch. and Tng. Inst., Indpls., 1994—; mem. conf. faculty Midwest Inst., Kalamazoo, 1992—; mem. adv. bd. Addiction Counselor Tng. Partnership, Indpls., 1993—; v.p. Ind. Addictions Treatment Providers, Indpls., 1995—; v.p. Addications Resource Network of Ind., 1995—; presenter in field. Contbr. articles to profl. jours. Vol. Crisis Intervention Ctr., Muncie, 1979-84, bd. sec., 1979-82; bd. sec. Family Svcs. Delaware County, Muncie, 1980-84; chairperson Dearborn County Citizens Against Substance Abuse, Lawrenceburg, Ind., 1990. Recipient Citations, VA Med. Ctr., 1985, Am. Bus. Women's Assn., 1985. Mem. NASW, Acad. Cert. Social Workers, Nat. Forensic Counselor Assn., Native Am. Legal Def. Assn. Office: New Directions Inc 360 N 775E Lafayette IN 47905

NELSON, THOMAS GEORGE, consulting actuary; b. Mason City, Iowa, Mar. 27, 1949; s. George Burton and Bonny Sue (Sharp) N.; m. Beverlee Joan Trindl, Sept. 28, 1974; children: Kristen Elizabeth, Joseph Charles. BA in Math., U. Iowa, 1971; MA in Math., U. Mich., 1972. Actuary CNA, Chgo., 1972-80; consulting actuary William M. Mercer, Inc., Chgo., 1980-82, A.S. Hansen, Inc., Chgo., 1982-83; sr. consulting actuary, prin. Milliman & Robertson, Inc., Chgo., 1983—; mem. task force on acctg. for non-pension retiree benefits Fin. Acctg. Standards Bd., Norwalk, Conn., 1986-90. Contbr. articles to profl. jours. Fellow, 1972, teaching fellow, 1972, U. Mich. Fellow Soc. Actuaries; mem. Am. Acad. Actuaries (bd. dirs. 1989-92, chmn. com. on health and welfare plans 1984-89, com. on rels. with accts. 1987-89, budget and fin. com. 1987-89, chmn. audit subcom. 1991-92, task force on taxation employee benefits 1986), Conf. of Consulting Actuaries (bd. dirs. 1989-95, v.p. 1991-92, exec. com. 1991-95, treas. 1992-95, chmn. com. on recognition of continuing profls. 1989-92, com. on health issues 1985-91), Chgo. Actuar. Roman Catholic. Home: 820 N Waiola Ave La Grange Park IL 60525-1452 Office: Milliman & Robertson Inc 55 W Monroe St Ste 4000 Chicago IL 60603-5001

NELSON, THOMAS ROY, hotel executive; b. Deadwood, S.D., July 30, 1957; s. John Edward and Olga Marie (Girardi) N.; m. Melodee Sharlet Stell, Aug. 18, 1978; children: Abigayle Louise, Adam James, Benjamin Gerald. BS, S.D. State U., 1979. Pub. rels. writer S.D. State U., Brookings, 1975-79; dir. coll. rels. Yankton (S.D.) Coll., 1979-81; typography coord. Dakota Advt., Yankton, 1981-83; mgr. Yankton Elks Lodge, 1983-84; gen. mgr. Best Western Hickok House, Deadwood, 1984-91; acting pub., publ. mgr. Lawrence County Centennial, Deadwood, 1991-92; owner, operator Mineral Palace Hotel and Gaming, Deadwood, 1992—; bd. dirs. Black Hills Badlands & Lakes, Rapid City, S.D., Black Hills Visitor Ctr., Rapid City, Deadwood Jam, Deadwood Festivals. Lobbyist S.D. State Legislature, Pierre, 1993—; pub. affairs com. chmn. Black Hills, Badlands and Lakes Assn., Rapid City, 1995—; candidate S.D. Ho. of Reps., 1996. Mem. Deadwood-Lead C. of C. (bd. dirs. 1995), Elks (exalted ruler 1988-89, dist. dep. 1993-94, state officer 1993—). Republican. Roman Catholic. Office: Mineral Palace Hotel Gaming 601 Historic Main St Deadwood SD 57732

NELSON-WALKER, ROBERTA, company executive; b. N.Y.C., Sept. 1, 1936; d. Richard E. and Esther (McBride) Martin; m. Robert L. Nelson, July 20, 1957 (div.); children: Carol, Craig, Robert H.; m. Dan Walker, Nov. 1978 (div.). BA, DePaul U., 1976, MS in Mgmt. with distinction, 1977. Dir. devel. Ray Graham Assocs., Elmhurst, Ill., 1970-76; dir. human resources Nat. Easter Seal Soc., Chgo., 1979-81; v.p. Butler Walker Inc., Oak Brook, Ill., 1981-85; pres. CNR, Inc., Oak Brook, Ill., 1985-91; spl. agt. Prudential Ins., Oak Brook, Ill., 1991-95; mng. dir. Visimark L.L.C., Oak Brook, Ill. Author: Creating Acceptance for Handicapped People, 1975, Creating, Planning, and Financial Housing for Handicapped People, 1979. Founder, organizer Found. for Handicapped, 1970-76,; pres. DuPage County Pub. Health Coun., 1974; bd. dirs. DuPage County Mental Health Assocs., 1970, Forest Found. DuPage County, 1976-86, Shakespeare Globe, London and Chgo., 1982—; mem. DuPage County Bd. Health, 1975, Ill. Gov.'s Com. for Handicapped, 1976, women's coun. Chgo. Heart Assn., 1979—. Recipient Meritorious Svc. award, Chgo. Heart Assn., 1968, 70, Fond du Coer award AHA, 1968, Cursade of Mercy Achievement awards, 1974-76, State of Ill. procalmation by Gov. James Thompson, Ill. Epilepsy Assn., 1978. Office: Visimark LLC 2100 Clearwater Dr Oak Brook IL 60521

NEMEC, NICHOLAS, state legislator. Mem. S.D. Ho. of Reps.; mem. comm. and taxation coms.; mem. S.D. State Senate; farmer, rancher. Home: HC 63 Box 45 Holabird SD 57540-9611*

NEMETH, DIAN JEAN, secondary school educator; b. Lakewood, Ohio, Mar. 5, 1949; d. Alex Ray and Doris Jean (Sakach) N.; 1 child, Kymberlee Marie. BS, Kent State U., 1971, MEd, 1994. Cert. home econs. tchr., vocat. consumer-homemaking tchr., Ohio. Tchr. vocat. family and consumer scis. Cleve. Bd. Edn., 1972—; piloted modern design fine arts course Cleve. Bd. Edn., 1989-90; writer course of study for hospitality and facility care svcs. Active Tchrs.-Leader Inst., 1994—, Urban Task Force. Mem. Am. Vocat. Assn., Ohio Vocat. Assn., Greater Cleve. Assn. Family and Consumer Sci. (auditor 1994-95, treas. 1995—), Am. Assn. Family and Consumer Scis., Nat. Assn. Vocat. Edn. Spl. Needs Pers., Ohio Hotel and Motel Assn., Ohio Assn. Family and Consumer Scis., Kiwanis (bd. dirs. 1993-94, sec. 1994-95), Sigma Sigma Sigma (chpt. adv. bd. 1992, chpt. housing coord. 1992), Omicron Tau Theta. Democrat. Roman Catholic. Home: 8061 Greenwood View Dr Apt 1107 Parma OH 44129-5859

NEMIROW, JOEL ALAN, small business executive, psychotherapist; b. Chgo., Sept. 18, 1951; s. Albert Louis and Betty Lillian (Hyman) N.; m. Sherri Siess, Oct. 6, 1989. BS, Loyola U., Chgo., 1973, MA, 1982. Pres. A-N Parts & Svcs. Co. Inc., Chgo., 1974—. Pres 5455 Edgewater Condominium Assn., Chgo., 1979-86; mem. bd. dirs. 100 East Bellevue Place Condominium Assn. Mem. APA, ACA, Am. Mental Health Counselors Assn., Ill. Psychol. Assn., Ill. Counseling Assn., Ill. Mental Health Counselors Assn., Multi-Housing Laundry Assn., Coin Laundry Equipment Operators Midwest Assn., Mus. Sci. and Industry, Mus. Contemporary Art, U.S. Holocaust Meml. Mus., Chgo. Internat. Film Festival, Art Inst. Chgo., League Chgo. Theatres, Chgo. Athenaeum, WTTW Chgo. Home: 100 E Bellevue Pl Apt 20E Chicago IL 60611-1123 Office: A-N Parts & Svc Co Inc 4023 N Broadway St Chicago IL 60613-2110

NEMO, ANTHONY JAMES, lawyer; b. St. Paul, May 18, 1963; s. Joseph Marino Jr. and Dianne Marie (Wegner) N.; m. Mary Rose Mazzitello, July 17, 1987; children: Anne Marie, Katherine Mary, Anthony James Jr. BA in English Lit., U. St. Thomas, 1986; JD, William Mitchell Coll. Law, 1991. Bar: Minn. 1991, U.S. Dist. Ct. Minn., U.S. Dist. Ct. Ariz., U.S. Ct. Appeals (4th cir.). Account exec. div. info. svcs. TRW, Mpls., 1986-90; assoc. atty. Meshbesher & Spence, Ltd., St. Paul, 1990—. Assoc. editor William Mitchell Law Rev., 1988-90; author law rev. note. Recipient R. Ross Quaintance award, Douglas K. Amdahl-Mary O'Malley Lyons Trial Advocacy award. Mem. ABA, Assn. Trial Lawyers Am., Minn. State Bar Assn., Hennepin County Bar Assn., John P. Sheehy Legal History Soc. Roman Catholic. Home: 2125 Heath Ave N Oakdale MN 55128-5207 Office: Meshbesher & Spence Ltd 2600 World Trade Ctr Saint Paul MN 55101

NESS, GARY GENE, accountant; b. Fargo, N.D., Feb. 7, 1948; s. Gene Stanley and Myrtle (Lattimore) N.; m. Janet Lynn, Jan. 30, 1971; children: Jennifer Lynn, Kam Elizabeth. BA in Acctg., Moorhead State U., 1973. CPA. Supr. corp. taxes Nat. Rental Systems, Inc., Mpls., 1973-76; sr. tax specialist Maine LaFrentz and Co., Mpls., 1976-77; tax mgr. Mason Folkert and Co., Detroit Lakes, Minn., 1977-78; ptnr. in charge tax dept. Eide Helmeke and Co., Fargo, 1979—; pres. Acctg. Ctrs. Am., Inc., 1991—. Author: (pamphlet) Tax Guide for North Dakota Legislature, 1985. Treas. N.D. State U. Bison Hockey Club, Inc., Fargo, 1988; treas. Ea. N.D. Synod Evang. Luth. Ch. Am., Fargo, 1988; chmn., found. dir. Moorhead State U. Devel. Coun., 1993—. With U.S. Army, 1969-71. Mem. AICPA, N.D. Soc. CPAs, Minn. Soc. CPAs, Gateway Lions (pres. 1991), C. of C., Elks, Moose. Home: 86 Cedar Ave Fargo ND 58102-1638 Office: Eide Helmeke and Co 500 Dakota Bank Bldg Fargo ND 58102

NESS, ROBERT, state legislator, education consultant; b. 1935; m. Marianne Ness; four children. BS, Bemidji State U.; MA, U. Minn. Edn. cons., constrn. mgr.; Dist. 20A rep. Minn. Ho. of Reps., St. Paul, 1993—. Home: 24966 729th Ave Dassel MN 55325-3436*

NESTER, WILLIAM RAYMOND, JR., retired academic administrator and educator; b. Cin., Feb. 19, 1928; s. William Raymond and Evelyn (Blettner) N.; m. Mary Jane Grossman, Aug. 21, 1950; children: William Raymond, Mark Patrick, Brian Philip, Stephen Christopher. BS, U. Cin., 1950, EdM, 1953, EdD, 1965. Tchr. high sch. English and history Cin., 1950-52; dir. student union U. Cin., 1952-53, asst. dean of men, 1953-60, dean of men, 1960-67, assoc. prof. edn., 1965-70, dean of students, 1967-69, vice provost student and univ. affairs, 1969-76, prof. edn., 1970-78, assoc. sr. v.p., assoc. provost, 1976-78; v.p. student svcs. Ohio State U., Columbus, 1978-83, prof. edn., 1978-83; pres. Kearney State Coll., Nebr., 1983-91, prof. edn., 1983-93; chancellor U. Nebr., Kearney, 1991-93, prof. emeritus, chancellor emeritus, 1993—; pres. emeritus Mus. Nebr. Art, 1991—; cons. on edn., 1993—. Pres. Metro-Six Athletic Conf., 1975-76, Cen. States Intercollegiate Conf., 1986-89. Mem. AAUP, Am. Assn. State Colls. and Univs. (bd. dirs.), Nat. Assn. Intercollegiate Athletics (pres.), Nat. Assn. Student Pers. Adminstrs. (past regional v.p., mem. exec. com.), Am. Assn. Higher Edn., Ohio Assn. Student Pers. Adminstrs. (past pres.), Nat. Intrafrat. Conf. (pres. 1991-92), Frat. Scholarship Officers Assn. (past pres.), Mortar Bd., Pi Kappa Alpha (nat. pres. 1978-80, past pres. ednl. found.), Omicron Delta Kappa, Phi Delta Kappa, Phi Alpha Theta, Phi Eta Sigma, Sigma Sigma. Episcopalian. Home: 7674 Coldstream Dr Cincinnati OH 45255-3932

NETHING, DAVID E., state legislator; m. Marjorie; 3 children. Degree, Jamestown Coll., U. N.D. Attorney; mem. N.D. Senate, 1966—; majority whip, 1974-86, mem. appropriations com.; past pres. Nat. Conf. State Legislators, Found. State Legislators, Coun. State Govt.; past mem. adv. commn. Intergovt. Rels.; past adm. Conf. of U.S. Mem. ABA, Am. Legion, Masonic Bodies, Rotary (past pres.), Elks (past bd. dirs, past exalted ruler), N.D. Affiliate Diabetic Assn. Office: PO Box 1059 Jamestown ND 58402-1059 also: State Senate State Capital Bismarck ND 58505*

NETTLETON, MARYANNE, veterinarian; b. St. Paul, July 17, 1964; d. Floyd Lyman and Janice Mary (Bennett) N. BA magna cum laude, Bethel Coll., 1986; D in vet. medicine, U. Minn., 1990. Emergency veterinarian Profl. Vet. Hosp., Detroit, 1990-93; emergency veterinarian, hosp. dir. Animal Emergency Clinic Rockford, Ill., 1993—; consulting veterinarian Mulford Animal Hosp., Rockford, 1994-95. Contbr. poetry Rockford Rev., 1994. Mem. AVMA, Ill. Vet. Med. Assn., Minn. Vet. Med. Assn., Greater Rockford Vet. Med. Assn., Rockford Writer's Guild. Democrat. Baptist. Home: 1532 12th Ave Rockford IL 61104 Office: Animal Emergency Clinic 1211 11th St Rockford IL 61104

NETZLEY, ROBERT E., state legislator; b. Laura, Ohio, Dec. 7, 1922; s. Elmer and Mary (Ingle) N.; m. Marjorie Lyons; children: Kathleen, Carol Anne, Robert. Grad. Midshipman Sch., Cornell U., 1944; BS, Miami U., 1947. State rep. 7th Dist. Ohio State Congress, 1961-82, state rep. Dist. 68, 1982—; pres. Miami County Young Reps., Ohio, 1952-54; chmn. Miami County Rep. Ctrl. and Exec. com., 1958—; del. Rep. Nat. Conv., 1980, presdl. elector, 1980; sec.-treas., part owner Netzley Oil Co., 1947—; v.p. Romale Inc., 1961—. Recipient Purple Heart, Am. and Pacific Theaters. Mem. VFW, Miami County Heart Coun., Am. Legion, AmVets, Grange, Laura Lions; Phi Kappa Tau. *

NEU, SUZANNE MARIE, toxicologic pathologist; b. Green Bay, Wis., Sept. 7, 1951; d. Robert Joseph and Donna Marie (Tahlier) N.; m. John William Williams, Jan. 5, 1974 (div. June 1986); children: Elizabeth, Joseph; m. Harry Stephen Marsh, May 16, 1988. BS in Zoology and Microbiology, U. Minn., 1975, DVM, 1979; PhD in Exptl. Pathology, U. Ky., 1988. Cert. anatomic pathologist; diplomate Am. Coll. Vet. Pathologists. Vet. Lexington, Ky., 1979-82; resident in pathology U. Ky., Lexington, 1982-85, fellow, 1983-88; pathologist Breathitt Vet. Ctr./Murray State U., Hopkinsville, Ky., 1983-88; sr. pathologist Procter & Gamble Pharmaceuticals, Cin., 1993—. Contbr. articles to profl. jours. Fellow Knight Found., U. Ky., 1983-88. Mem. Am. Coll. Vet. Pathologists. Office: Miami Valley Labs Procter & Gamble Pharm Ross OH

NEUENSCHWANDER, THOMAS RAY, industrial automation company executive; b. Berne, Ind., Nov. 25, 1944; s. Edward Leon and Anna Marie (Amstutz) N.; m. Sharlene Marie Walley, Dec. 19, 1964 (div. Oct. 1990); m. Cheryl Sue Heller, 1996. Grad., Gen. Electric Apprentice Prog., 1968; student, Ind. U., Ft. Wayne, 1963-64, 68-70. Design engr. GE, Ft. Wayne, 1968-76; mgr. engring. LH Carbide Corp., Ft. Wayne, 1976-83; pres. Digitech Corp., Ft. Wayne, 1983-86; v.p. mktg. AMT Corp., Ft. Wayne, 1986-90; v.p. tech. LH Carbide Corp., 1990—; bd. dirs. LH Industries Corp., Ft. Wayne. Holder 11 patents. Pres. Gleneagles Assn., Ft. Wayne, 1995. Office: LH Industries Corp 4420 Clubview Dr Fort Wayne IN 46804

NEUFELD, MELVIN J., state legislator; m. Maxine Neufeld. Student, Tabor Coll. Rep. dist. 115 State of Kans. Mem. NRA, Lions Club, Nat. Railroaders Club. Republican. Address: RR 1 Box 13 Ingalls KS 67853-9706*

NEUGER, SANFORD, orthodontics educator; b. Cleve., Aug. 17, 1925; s. Samuel and Ethel (Manheim) N.; m. Marjorie Odess, Sept. 8, 1963; 1 child, Howard Michael. BS, Western Res. U., 1947, DDS, 1953; MS in Orthodontics, Ind. U., 1957. Diplomate Am. Bd. Orthodontics. Orthodontics demonstrator Western Res. U., Cleve., 1957-58; asst. prof., assoc. prof. orthodontics Western Res. U./Case Western Res. U., Cleve., 1958-75; clin. prof. orthodontics Case Western Res. U., Cleve., 1975—, acting chmn. Orthodontics Dept., 1969-71; asst. dental surgeon U. Hosp., Cleve., 1967—. Author: (syllabus) Contemporary Edgewise Mechanics-Sliding Mechanics, 1973, Limited Tooth Movement, 1970; author-presenter: (videotape) Orthodontics Soldering, 1970. Vol. United Way, 1988, Case Western Res. U. Alumni Assn., Jewish Nat. Fund. Comdr. USNR (ret. 1972). Named Man of Yr. Case Western Res. U. Orthodontics alumni, 1982. Fellow Am. Coll. Dentists; mem. Am. Dental Soc., Cleve. Dental Soc. (bd. dirs. 11965-90), Cleve. Soc. Orthodontists (pres. 1969)., Great Lakes Assn. Orthodontists Assn., Am. Assn. Orthodontists, Pierre Fauchard Soc., Alpha Omega (pres. Cleve. chpt. 1984-85), Omicron Kappa Upsilon. Jewish. Home: 24850 Hilltop Dr Cleveland OH 44122-1350 Office: 1500 S Green Rd Cleveland OH 44121-4040

NEUHOFF, KATHLEEN TOEPP, veterinarian, podiatrist; b. South Bend, Ind., Nov. 2, 1953; d. Frank Conrad and Rosemary (Williams) Toepp; m. Kenneth Leo Neuhoff, June 27, 1953; children: Carolyn, Patricia, Michael, Matthew. BS in Agr., Purdue U., 1976, DVM, 1979; D of Podiatric Medicine, Scholl Coll., 1993. Diplomate Am. Bd. Veterinary Practitioners, Am. Bd. Podiatric Surgery. Assoc. Magrane Animal Hosp., Mishawaka, Ind., 1979-83; dir. Magrane Animal Hosp., South Bend, Ind., 1983—; surg. residency Mich. Community Hosp., 1993-94; owner Family Foot Care Clinic, South Bend, 1994—; pres., bd. dirs. Animal Emergency Clinic, South Bend, 1988-92, St. Michael's Eme. Sch., 1989-91; cons. on animal control South Bend City Coun., 1987; mem. pres.'s coun. Purdue U., 1989—. Contbr. articles to profl. jours and book revs. to popular mags. Bd. dirs. St. Michael's Elem. Sch., Plymouth, Ind., 1989-92; bd. dirs. Holy Cross Sch., 1993—. Recipient Humanitarin Svc. award Humane Soc. St. Joseph County, 1985, Woman Veterinarian of Yr. award, also Pub. Rels. award Ind. Vet. Med. Assn., 1991. Mem. AVMA (alternative and complementary therapy com. 1995—), Am. Animal Hosp. Assn. (area dir. 1988-90, regional coord. 1990-93, regional bd. dirs. 1994—, chmn. student com. 1990-91), Am. Assn. Avian Vets., Ind. Vet Med. Assn. (pub. rels., ethics and animal welfare coms. 1984—), Michiana Vet. Med. Assn. (sec. 1986-87, treas. 1987-88, v.p. 1988-90, pres. 1990-91), Am. Horse Show Assn., Lake Michigan Hunter-Jumper Assn., Mishawaka C. of C. (Svc. award 1990), Am. Podiatric Med. Assn., Am. Bd. of Foot and Ankle Surgery, Stickle Soc., Scholl. Coll. of Podiatric Medicine. Republican. Roman Catholic. Office: Magrane Animal Hosp 2324 Grape Rd Mishawaka IN 46545-3006 also: Family Foot Care Clinic 727 E Jefferson Blvd South Bend IN 46617-2902

NEUMAN, LINDA KINNEY, state supreme court justice; b. Chgo., June 18, 1948; d. Harold S. and Mary E. Kinney; m. Henry G. Neuman; children: Emily, Lindsey. BA, U. Colo., 1970, JD, 1973. Lawyer Betty, Neuman, McMahon, Hellstrom & Bittner, 1973-79; v.p., trust officer Bettendorf Bank & Trust Co., 1979-80; dist. ct. judge, 1982-86; supreme ct. justice State of Iowa, 1986—; mem. adj. faculty U. Iowa Grad. Sch. of Social Work, 1981; part-time jud. magistrate Scott County, 1980-82; mem. Supreme Ct. continuing legal edn. commn.; chair Iowa Supreme Ct. commn. planning 21st Century; mem. bd. counselors Drake Law Sch., time on appeal adv. com. Nat. Ctr. State Cts. Dir. Nat. Assn. Women Judges. Recipient Regents scholarship. Fellow ABA (chair appellate judges conf., mem. appellate standards com., JAD exec. coun.); mem. Am. Judicature Soc., Iowa Bar Assn., Iowa Judges Assn., Scott County Bar Assn. Office: Iowa Supreme Ct State Capitol Des Moines IA 50319

NEUMANN, FREDERICK LLOYD, plant breeder; b. Waterloo, Iowa, Apr. 9, 1949; s. Lloyd Frederick and Leita Evangeline (Otto) N.; m. Diane Marie Brown, Aug. 18, 1973 (div. 1995); children: Bradley, Brian; m. Jamie Lynn Cox, June 22, 1996. BS, Iowa State U., 1972, MS, 1974. Research dir., plant breeder Ames Seed Farms Inc. (Iowa), producers hybrid popcorn seed, 1973-85; plant breeder Crow's Hybrid Corn Co., Milford, Ill., 1985-93; sales rep. Tri-State Foods, Springfield, Ill., 1993-94; meat packer Swissland Packing, Ashkum, Ill., 1994—; mem. research com. Popcorn Inst., Chgo., 1976-85, mem. prodn. and seed research subcom., 1982-85. Treas. Laurel Tree Nursery Sch., Inc., 1981-83; bishop's com. St. Paulinus Episcopal Ch., 1986-87; stephen Minister First Christian Ch., 1989—, deacon, 1989, elder, 1990-91, 93-94, 96—. Mem. Am. Soc. Agronomy, Iowa Crop Improvement Assn. (com. to recommend to bd. dirs. certification requirements for hybrid corn and hybrid sorghum 1979), Crop Sci. Soc. Am., Phi Kappa Phi, Gamma Sigma Delta. Republican. Mem. Disciples of Christ. Home and Office: 304 E Mulberry St Watseka IL 60970

NEUMANN, WILLIAM ALLEN, judge; b. Minot, N.D., Feb. 11, 1944; s. Albert W. and Opal Olive (Whitlock) N.; m. Jaqueline Denise Buechler, Aug. 9, 1980; children: Andrew, Emily. BSBA, U. N.D., 1965; JD, Stanford U., 1968. Bar: N.D. 1969, U.S. Dist. Ct. N.D. 1969. Pvt. practice law Williston, N.D., 1969-70, Bottineau, N.D., 1970-79; former judge N.D. Judicial Dist. Ct., N.E. Judicial Dist., Rugby, 1979-92; justice N.D. Supreme Ct., Bismarck, 1993—; chmn. elect N.D. Jud. Conf., 1985-87, chmn. 1987-89. Mem. ABA, State Bar Assn. N.D., Am. Judicature Soc. Lutheran. Office: ND Supreme Ct Judicial Wing 1st Fl 600 E Boulevard Ave Bismarck ND 58505-0530

NEUMEIER, LORRAINE, mechanical engineer; b. Rockville Center, N.Y., May 15, 1967; d. John and Barbara (Marcin) N. BS, N.Y. Inst. Tech., 1992. Sys. analyst/mgt. IT plastics divsn. GE, Mexico City, 1993; sys. analyst aircraft engines divsn. GE, Cin., 1992—. Home: 208 E Mechanic St Cincinnati OH 45215

NEUMEIER, MATTHEW MICHAEL, lawyer; b. Racine, Wis., Sept. 13, 1954; s. Frank Edward and Ruth Irene (Effenberger) N.; m. Lori Gerard Nantelle, Sept. 4, 1976 (div. 1985); m. Annmarie Prine, Jan. 31, 1987; children: Ruthann Marie, Emilie Irene. B in Gen. Studies with distinction, U. Mich., 1981; JD magna cum laude, Harvard U., 1984. Bar: N.Y. 1987, Mich. 1988, Ill. 1991, U.S. Dist. Ct. (ea. dist.) Mich. 1988, U.S. Dist. Ct. (ea. and no. dists.) Ill. 1991, U.S. Ct. Appeals (7th cir.) 1992, U.S. Supreme Ct. 1991. Sec.-treas. Ind. Roofing & Siding Co., Escanaba, Mich., 1973-78; mng. ptnr. Ind. Roofing Co., Menominee, Mich., 1977-78; law clk. to presiding justice U.S. Ct. Appeals (9th cir.), San Diego, 1984-85; law clk. to chief justice Warren E. Burger U.S. Supreme Ct., Washington, 1985-86; spl. asst. to chmn. U.S. Constn. Bicentennial Commn., Washington, 1986; assoc. Cravath, Swaine & Moore, N.Y.C., 1986-88; spl. counsel Burnham & Ritchie, Ann Arbor, Mich., 1988; assoc. Schlussel, Lifton, Simon, Rands, Galvin & Jackier, P.C., Ann Arbor, 1988-90, Skadden, Arps, Slate, Meagher & Flom, Chgo., 1990-96; ptnr. Jenner & Block, Chgo., 1996—. Editor Harvard Law Rev., 1982-84. Pres., bd. dirs. Univ. Cellar Inc., Ann Arbor, 1979-81; bd. dirs. Econ. Devel. Corp., Menominee, 1978-79, Midwestern divsn. Am. Suicide Foun., sec. 1992—. Mem. ABA, State Bar Mich., Assn. of Bar of City of N.Y., Ill. State Bar Assn., Chgo. Bar Assn. Republican. Office: Jenner & Block Ste 4100 One IBM Plz Chicago IL 60611

NEUSCHEL, ROBERT PERCY, educator, former management consultant; b. Hamburg, N.Y., Mar. 13, 1919; s. Percy J. and Anna (Becker) N.; m. Dorothy Virginia Maxwell, Oct. 20, 1944; children—Kerr Anne Ziprick, Carla Becker Neuschel Wyckoff, Robert Friedrich (Fritz). B.A., Denison U., 1941; M.B.A., Harvard U., 1947. Indsl. engr. Sylvania Elec. Products Co., Inc., 1947-49; with McKinsey & Co., Inc., 1950-79, sr. partner, dir., 1967-79; prof. corp. governance, assoc. dean J. L. Kellogg Grad. Sch. Mgmt.; former dir. Northwestern U., assoc. dean J.L. Kellogg Sch. Mgmt.; mem. exec. coun. Internat. Air Cargo Forum, 1988—; mem. com. study air passenger svc. and safety NRC, 1989—; bd. dirs. Butler Mfg. Co., Combined Ins. Co. Am., Templeton, Kenly & Co., TNT Freightways Co.; lectr. in field; mem. McKinsey Found. Mgmt. Research, Inc.; transp. task force Reagan transition team. Contbr. to profl. jours. Pres. Bd. Edn., Lake Forest, Ill., 1965-70; rep. Nat. council Boy Scouts Am., 1970—, mem. N.E. exec. coun., 1969—; chmn. bd. Lake Forest Symphony, 1973; bd. dirs. Loyola U., Chgo., Chgo. Boys' Club, Nat. Ctr. Voluntary Action, Inst. Mgmt. Consultants; trustee N. Suburban Mass Transit, 1972-73, Loyola Med. Ctr.; mem. adv. coun. Kellogg Grad. Sch. Mgmt., Northwestern U., White House conferee Drug Free Am.; mem. Nat. Petroleum Coun. Transp. and Supply Com. Served to capt. USAAF, World War II. Named Transporation Man of Yr. Chitransp. Assoc., 1994. Fellow Acad. Advancement Corp. Governance; mem. Transp. Assn. Am., Nat. Def. Transp. Assn. (mem. subcom. transp. tech. agenda 1990—). Presbyterian (ruling elder). Clubs: Harvard Bus. Sch. (pres. 1964-65), Economic, Executive, Chicago, Mid America, Mid-Day (Chgo.); Onwentsia (Lake Forest). Home: 101 Sunset Pl Lake Forest IL 60045-1834 Office: 1936 Sheridan Rd Evanston IL 60208-0849

NEUTZLING, VIRGINIA RUTH, healthcare company executive; b. Canton, Ohio, Dec. 10, 1942; d. James F. and Ruth E. (Swank) Roush; m. Homer S. Neutzling, Sept. 26, 1964 (dec. July 1976); children: Melanie L., Kimberly L., H. Lee. Grad., Mercy Profl. Sch. Nursing, 1963; BS, Walsh Coll., 1982; MEd, Kent State U., 1985. RN, Ohio. From staff nurse to head nurse Timken Mercy Med. Ctr., Canton, Ohio, 1963-77; staff nurse UpJohn Healthcare Svcs., Canton, 1979-83; health educator Stark County Health Dept., Canton, 1983-87; exec. dir. Stark County Health Care Coalition, Inc., Canton, 1987-94; pres., owner Health & Wellness Concepts, Inc., Canton, Ohio, 1994; trustee Drs. Hosp. Inc. of Stark County. Mem. adv. com. YMCA Big Bros.-Big Sisters Greater Canton, 1986—, Rotary, 1989—; chmn. Health Care for Uninsured, Canton, 1988—; chair steering com. Hall of Fame Regional Sr. Olympics, 1994—. Mem. Nat. Wellness Assn., Nat. Assn. for Female Execs., Ohio Pub. Health Assn., Northeastern Ohio Wellness Com. (chair 1987—). Avocations: family, reading, needlework, gardening, travel, music. Home and Office: 2223 45th St NE Canton OH 44705-2922

NEUZIL, MARK RILEY, journalism educator; b. Eldora, Iowa, Apr. 18, 1958; s. Jack Edward and Frances Cecilia (Gillette) N.; m. Deirdre Cox, June 2, 1979 (div. Aug. 1987); m. Amy Kuebelbeck, Sept. 1993; 1 child, Elena. BA, Iowa State U., 1980; MA, U. Minn., 1991, PhD, 1993. Reporter New Ulm (Minn.) Jour., 1980; asst. sports editor Ames (Iowa) Daily Tribune, 1980-82; reporter Quad City Times, Davenport, Iowa, 1982-87, Cedar Rapids (Iowa) Gazette, 1987-88, Associated Press, Mpls., 1990-93; asst. prof. U. St. Thomas, St. Paul, 1993—; pres. Sutliff Bridge Media Group, Mpls., 1989-93. Co-author: Green Crusades, 1996; contbr. articles to profl. jours. Page ways and means com. Iowa Ho. of Reps., Des Moines, 1976. Mem. Ducks Unltd., Kappa Tau Alpha. Roman Catholic. Office: U St Thomas 2115 Summit Ave Saint Paul MN 55105

NEVILLE, ROBERT P., executive; b. Rock Island, Ill., Apr. 2, 1995. BA in Polit. Sci., St. Joseph Coll., 1971. Dir. mktg. ops. D.A. Lubricant Co., Inc., Indpls., 1971-80; mktg. mgr. Mallore Controls, Indpls., 1980-92; v.p. client svcs. The Keenan Group, Inc., Indpls., 1992. Mem. St. Joseph Coll. Alumni (past bd. dirs. v.p. 1978-85), Adv. Club Indpls., Carmel Toastmasters Club. Roman Catholic. Home: 6126 Thrushwood Dr Indianapolis IN 46250 Office: The Keenan Group Inc 1690 E 80th St Indianapolis IN 46240-2708

NEW, ELOISE OPHELIA, special education educator; b. Jeffersonville, Ind., Jan. 14, 1942; d. Ivan Foster and Nellie Katherine (Harman) Baugh; m. Paul Eugene New, Nov. 23, 1961; children: Paula, Paul Jr. BS in Elem. Edn., Eastern Ky. U., 1963; MA in Edn., Coll. Mt. St. Joseph, 1987. Cert. elem. K-8, and developmentally handicapped tchr. K-12, Ohio. Tchr. Newport (Ky.) City Schs., 1963-69, Ross County and Chillicothe (Ohio) City Schs., 1977-78; developmentally handicapped tchr. Mt. Logan Middle Sch., Chillicothe, 1979—. Tchr. Sunday sch. Tabernacle Bapt. Ch., Chillicothe, 1987-93, chmn. elem. edn. com., 1988-93, Sunday sch. supt., 1994—, mem. christian Bd. Edn., 1988—; spokesperson for edn. selectin Chillicothe Edn. Found., 1989. Recipient Excellence in Edn. award Pllasco-Ross Adminstrn. Conf. for Spl. Educators, 1984, Ohio Jennings Scholar award, 1991-93. Mem. NEA, Ohio Edn. Assn., Chillicothe Edn. Assn. (rep. 1986-88). Baptist. Home: 828 Orange St Chillicothe OH 45601-1340 Office: Mt Logan Mid Sch 841 E Main St Chillicothe OH 45601-3509

NEW, ROSETTA HOLBROCK, home economics educator, nutrition consultant; b. Hamilton, Ohio, Aug. 26, 1921; d. Edward F. and Mabel (Kohler) Holbrock; m. John Lorton New, Sept. 3, 1943; 1 child, John Lorton Jr. BS, Miami U., Oxford, Ohio, 1943; MA, U. No. Colo., 1971; PhD, The Ohio State U., 1974; student Kantcentrum, Brugge, Belgium, 1992, Lesage Sch. Embroidery, Paris, 1995. Cert. tchr., Colo. Tchr. English and sci. Monahans (Tex.) H.S., 1943-45; emergency war food asst. U.S. Dept. Agr., College Station, Tex., 1945-46; dept. chmn. home econs., adult edn. Hamilton (Ohio) Pub. Schs., 1946-47; tchr., dept. chmn. home econs. East H.S., Denver, 1948-59, Thomas Jefferson H.S., Denver, 1959-83; mem. exec. bd. Denver Pub. Schs.; also lectr.; exec. dir. Ctr. Nutrition Info. U.S. Office of Edn. grantee Ohio State U., 1971-73. Mem. Cin. Art Mus., Nat. Trust for Historic Preservation. Mem. Am. Home Econs. Assn., Am. Vocat. Assn., Embroiders Guild Am., Hamilton Hist. Soc., Internat. Old Lacers, Ohio State U. Assn., Ohio State Home Econs. Alumni Assn., Fairfield (Ohio) Hist. Soc., Republican Club of Denver, Internat. Platform Assn., Phi Upsilon Omicron. Presbyterian. Lodges: Masons, Daughters of the Nile, Order of Eastern Star, Order White Shrine of Jerusalem. Home and Office: 615 Crescent Rd Hamilton OH 45013-3432

NEWBORG, GERALD GORDON, historical agency administrator; b. Ada, Minn., Dec. 13, 1942; s. George Harold and Olea (Halstad) N.; m. Jean Annette Gruhl, Aug. 14, 1964; children: Erica, Annette. BA, Concordia Coll., Moorhead, Minn., 1964; MA, U. N.D., 1969; MBA, Ohio State U., 1978. Cert. archivist. Tutor, preceptor Parsons Coll., Fairfield, Iowa, 1964-67; state archivist Ohio Hist. Soc., Columbus, 1968-76; v.p. Archival Systems Inc., Columbus, 1978-81; state archivist State Hist. Soc. of N.D., Bismarck, 1981—; instr. Franklin U., Columbus, 1974; adj. prof. Bismarck State Coll., 1985-86. Co-author: North Dakota: A Pictorial History, 1988. Recipient Resolution of Commendation Ohio Ho. of Reps., Columbus, 1976. Mem. Soc. Am. Archivists, Nat. Assn. Govt. Archives & Records Adminstrs. (bd. dirs. 1984-86, sec. 1994—), Midwest Archives Conf., N.D. Libr. Assn. (exec. bd. 1985-86). Home: 1327 N 18th St Bismarck ND 58501-2827 Office: State Hist Soc 612 E Boulevard Ave Bismarck ND 58505-0660

NEWBROUGH, STACEY ANN SNYDER, environmental educator; b. Iowa, Nov. 11, 1963; d. Phil Mark and Garnetta Ann (Nielsen) Snyder; m. Robert Joseph Newbrough, June 28, 1986; children: Erica Ann, Austin Joseph. BA in Biology Edn., Wartburg Coll., 1986; MA in Sci. Edn., U. No. Iowa, 1990. Tchr. sci. Underwood (Iowa) Community Sch., 1987; resident counselor Quakerdale Home, New Providence, Iowa, 1987-88; environ. educator Johnson County Conservation Bd., Iowa City, Iowa, 1990; interpretive naturalist Pocahontas County Conservation Bd., Pocahontas, Iowa, 1990-93; tchr. earth scis., biology and conservation Waverly-Shell Rock H.S., Waverly, Iowa, 1994—. Author: Seeds, Nuts and Fruits of Iowa Plants, 1994, Iowa Food Webs and Other Interrelationships, 1995. Mem. Nat. Assn. Interpretation, Iowa Assn. Naturalists, Iowa Conservation Edn. Coun. (pres. 1992-94), Iowa Acad. Sci., Iowa Wildlife Fedn., Delta Kappa Gamma Internat. Office: Waverly-Shell Rock HS 1405 4th Ave SW Waverly IA 50677

NEWBY, JOHN ROBERT, metallurgical engineer; b. Kansas City, Mo., Nov. 17, 1923; s. Merritt Owen and Gladys Mary (McCleery) N.; m. Audry Marie Loniker, Sept. 21, 1963 (div. 1980); children: Deborah A., Walter J., William F., Matthew O., Robert J. BA, U. Mo., Kansas City, 1947; BS in Metall. Engring., Colo. Sch. Mines, 1949; MS, U. Cin., 1963. Cert. profl. engr. Chemist Bar Rusto Plating Corp., Kansas City, 1949; supr. United Chromium, Ferndale, Mich., 1949-52; prin. rsch. metallurgist Armco Inc., Middletown, Ohio, 1952-85; prin. John Newby Cons., Middletown, 1985—; cons. Phoenix Cons., Inc., Cin., 1988—. Author, editor: Formability 2000, 1982, Metallic Materials, 1978, Sheet Metal Forming, 1976; editor: Mechanical Testing, Vol. 8, 9th edit., 1985. Scoutmaster Boy Scouts Am., Middletown, 1955-86; chmn. Safety Coun., Middletown, 1978-80. Staff sgt. USAF, 1943-46, PTO. Fellow ASTM (chmn. 1963—, Award of Merit 1984), ASM (chpt. chmn. 1970, Award of Merit 1980); mem. SAE (sect. chmn. 1984). Democrat. Home and Office: 100 Marymont Ct Middletown OH 45042-3735

NEWBY, THOMAS PAUL, accountant; b. Danville, Ill., Apr. 11, 1958; s. Max Ray and Arleen Florence (Shols) N.; m. Karen Ellen Smith, Dec. 24, 1981; 2 children. BA in Acctg. and Bus. Adminstrn., Augustana Coll., 1980; MBA, St. Xavier Coll., 1991. CPA, Ill. Staff acct. Fed. Signal Corp., University Park, Ill., 1980-86; acctg. mgr. Landis Plastics Inc., Chicago Ridge, Ill., 1986-95; contr. Mayfair Molded Products, Schiller Park, Ill., 1995—. Mem. publicity com. S.W. Cmty. Concert Band, Worth, Ill., 1984-91; mem. audit com. First United Meth. Ch., Evergreen Park, Ill., 1986-94, Chgo. So. Dist. bd. stewards, 1994—. Mem. Ill. CPA Soc. Home: 5045 Lamb Dr Oak Lawn IL 60453-3931 Office: Mayfair Molded Products 3700 N Rose St Schiller Park IL 60176

NEWCOM, H. LEE, communications consultant; b. Burbank, Calif., Feb. 15, 1951; s. Herbert Lloyd and Bessie June (Barnard) N.; m. Janice Elizabeth Nunemacher, July 28, 1990; children: Katherine Elaine, Sara Elizabeth, Matthew Lee. AA, Glendale (Calif.) C.C., 1976; BA, Calif. State U., L.A., 1986. Exec. dir. Ill. Christian Coalition, Bloomington, 1991-95; prin. cons. Lee Newcom Comm., 1995—. Mem. McLean County (Ill.) bd., 1994—; bd. dirs. United Rep. Fund, Chgo., 1993—, Citizens for Responsible Schs., Palos Heights, Ill., 1994—; precinct committeeman Rep. Party, McLean County, 1988—; pres., founder Found. Ill. Future, 1995—; Ill. State chmn. Nat. Coun. Rep. County Officials, 1995—. Mem. Pi Sigma Alpha.

NEWMAN, ANDREW EDISON, restaurant executive; b. St. Louis, Aug. 14, 1944; s. Eric Pfeiffer and Evelyn Frances (Edison) N.; m. Peggy Gregory, Feb. 14, 1984; children: Daniel Mark, Anthony Edison. BA, Harvard U., 1966, MBA, 1968. With Office of Sec. Def., Washington, 1968-70; with Edison Bros. Stores, Inc., St. Louis, 1970-95, v.p. ops. and adminstrn., 1975-80, dir., 1978—, exec. v.p., 1980-86, chmn., 1987-95; chmn., CEO Race Rock Internat., St. Louis, 1995—; bd. dirs. Edison Bros. Stores, St. Louis, Sigma-Aldrich Corp., St. Louis, Lee Enterprises, Davenport, Iowa, Dave and Buster's, Dallas. Trustee Washington U. Office: 501 N Broadway Saint Louis MO 63102-2196

NEWMAN, BARBARA MAE, retired special education educator; b. Rockford, Ill., July 16, 1932; d. Greene Adam and Emma Lorene (Fields) N. BS Edn., No. Ill. U., 1973. Cert. elem. edn. K-8 tchr., spl. edn. (blind and p.s.) K-12 tchr. Exec. sec. Rockford Art Assn., 1961-70; tchr. Title 1 Rockford Pub. Sch. Dist. #205, 1975-76, tchr. vision impaired, 1977-91. Feature editor (Rock Valley Coll. newpaper) The valley Forge, 1970; contbg. writer (Rockford Coll. history) A Retrospective Look, 1980. St. Bernadette adult choir, 1958-95, Cathedral Chorale, 1995—; holder 5 offices Am. Bus. Women's Assn., Forest City chpt., 1963-70; vol. Winnebago Ctr. for the Blind, Rockford, 1965-70; mem. Rockford Diocesan Chorale, 1969—. Named Woman of Yr., Am. Bus. Women's Assn., Forest City chpt., Rockford, 1966; scholar Ill. State Scholarship Commn., No. Ill. U., 1970-73. Mem. Ill. Ret. Tchrs. Assn. Roman Catholic.

NEWMAN, BARBARA MILLER, psychologist, educator; b. Chgo., Sept. 6, 1944; d. Irving George and Florence (Levy) Miller; student Bryn Mawr Coll.; AB with honors in Psychology, U. Mich., 1966, PhD in Devel. Psychology, 1971; m. Philip R. Newman, June 12, 1966; children: Samuel Asher, Abraham Levy, Rachel Florence. Undergrad. research asst. in psychology U. Mich., 1963-64, research asst. in psychology, 1964-69, teaching fellow, 1965-71, asst. project dir. Inst. for Social Research, 1971-72, univ. lectr. in psychology and research assoc., 1971-72; asst. prof. psychology Russell Sage Coll., 1972-76, assoc. prof., 1977-78; assoc. prof. dept. family relations and human devel., chmn. dept. family relations and human devel. Ohio State U., 1978-83, prof., 1983-86, assoc. provost for faculty recruitment and devel., 1987-92, prof., 1992—. Mem. Eastern Psychol. Assn., Soc. Research in Child Devel., AAAS, Am. Psychol. Assn., Nat. Council Family Relations, Groves Conf. on Marriage and Family, N.Y. Acad. Scis., Midwestern Psychol. Assn., Western Psychol. Assn., Am. Assn. Family and Consumer Scis. Author books including: (with P. Newman) Living: The Process of Adjustment, 1981; Development Through Life, 1995; Understanding Adulthood, 1983; Adolescent Development, 1986; When Kids Go to College, 1992; contbr. chpts., articles to profl. publs. Office: Ohio State U Dept Family Rels & Human Devel 151 Campbell Hall Columbus OH 43210

NEWMAN, BARRY MARC, pediatric surgeon; b. N.Y.C., Dec. 13, 1951; s. Sheldon and Miriam (Jasphy) N.; m. Jane Post, July 2, 1989; 1 child, Alexander Ross. BA, U. Pa., 1973; MD, SUNY, Stony Brook, 1976. Diplomate Nat. Bd. Med. Examiners, Am. Bd. Surgery, Am. Bd. Pediatric Surgery. Resident in surgery N.Y. Med. Coll., N.Y.C., 1976-78; sr. resident in surgery SUNY, Stony Brook, 1978-81; chief resident pediatric surgery Childrens Hosp. of Buffalo, 1981-83, fellow pediatric surgery and gastroenterology, 1983-84; asst. prof. surgery U. Va., Charlottesville, 1984-88, U. Ill., Chgo., 1988-93; dir. pediatric surgery Luth. Gen. Children's Hosp., Park Ridge, Ill., 1991-96; clin. assoc. prof. surgery U. Chgo., 1993-95; dir. pediatric surg. svcs. Loyola U. Med. Ctr., Maywood, Ill., 1996—, co-dir. surg. laparoscopy lab., 1996—, assoc. prof. surgery and pediatrics, 1996—; instr. Adv. Trauma and Life Support, ACS, Chgo., 1984—. Contbr. articles to profl. jours., chpts. to books. NIH grantee, 1982-83, 87-88. Fellow Am. Acad. Pediatrics, ACS; mem. Am. Gastroenterol. Assn., Am. Pediatric Surg. Assn. Democrat. Jewish. Office: Loyola U Med Ctr Dept Surgery 2160 S First Ave Maywood IL 60153

NEWMAN, DONALD JOHN, marketing executive; b. Chgo., Dec. 22, 1939; s. William Francis and Dorothy Isabel (Asay) N.; m. Arlene Louise Neustadt, Apr. 4, 1964; children: Nancy, Julie. BA in Polit. Sci., St. Ambrose U., 1961. Br. mgr. Dun & Bradstreet, Inc., Chgo., 1962-68; mktg. mgr. 3M Co., St. Paul, 1968-87; v.p. mktg. Oce Industries, Inc., Chgo., 1987-88; v.p. mktg. and product devel. Bell & Howell Document Mgmt. Products Co., Chgo., 1988-91; v.p. mktg. Bankers Systems, Inc., 1991-96; v.p. sales & mktg. Gen. Pump, Inc., Mendota Heights, Minn., 1996—; keynote speaker Info. and Image Mgmt. Congress conf. and exposition, Sydney, Astralia, 1990. Contbr. articles to profl. jours. Program chmn. Internat. Info. and Image Mgmt. Congress, Vienna, Austria, 1987. With U.S. Army Res. 1961-67. Recipient Smithsonian award for innovative use of technology. Mem. Assn. Info. and Image Mgmt. (bd. dirs. 1990-93), Internat. Image Mgmt. Congress (bd. dirs. 1989-92). Democrat. Roman Catholic. Home: 603 7th St N Sartell MN 56377-1517 Office: Gen Pump Inc PO Box 1457 1174 Northland Dr Mendota Heights MN 55120

NEWMAN, ELSIE LOUISE, mathematics educator; b. Bowling Green, Ohio, Mar. 25, 1943; d. Carroll E. and Grace G. (Underwood) Frank; m. Lawrence J. Newman, Sept. 15, 1962; children: Timothy, Jennifer. BS cum laude, Bowling Green (Ohio) State U., 1968; MEd, U. Toledo, 1992. Study supr. After Sch. Study Tutorial Program, Bowling Green, 1983-85; asst. prof. Owens C.C., Toledo, 1987—; office mgr. K.C. Ins. Co., Bowling Green, 1984; tutor in maths. Bowling Green City Schs., 1984-88, Bur. of Vocat. Rehab., Oregon, Ohio, 1988-91. Contbr. articles to profl. publs. Advisor 4H Club, Bowling Green, 1985—; asst. Christmas Clearing bur. Voluntary Action Ctr., United Way, Bowling Green, 1982-86, residential crusade chmn. Am. Cancer Soc., Bowling Green, 1981-82. Bowling Green U. scholar, 1966-68. Mem. Nat. Coun. Tchrs. of Math., Math. Assn. Am., Ohio Assn. Devel. Edn., Phi Kappa Phi, Kappa Delta Pi, Pi Lambda Theta. Home: 328 S Summit St Bowling Green OH 43402-3017

NEWMAN, LINNAEA ROSE, horticulturist; b. Milw., Sept. 23, 1953; d. Arthur Fred and Katherine Elnora (Cook) N. BS, U. Wis., 1977. Cert. interior horticulturist, cert. performax cons. Grower Shroeder's Flowerland, Green Bay, Wis., 1977-78; with installation Tropical Plant Rentals, Inc., Prarie View, Ill., 1978, with spl. svc., 1978-84, mgr. edn. and rsch., 1984-88; pres. Linnaea Newman & Assocs., Mundelein, Ill., 1989—; regional mgr. Income Builder's Internat., 1994—. Author: Interior Horticulture A Training Manual, 1990, (with others) Retail Store Planning and Design Manual, 1986; contbr. articles to profl. jours. Named one of Outstanding Young Women Am., 1985. Mem. Entomol. Soc. Am., Internat. Soc. Arboriculture, Nat. Assn. Women in Horticulture (v.p. 1986-87), Nat. Coun. Interior HortiCulture Cert. (bd. gov. 1982-88, vice chmn. 1985-86, chmn. 1986-88), Ohio Florists Assn. (mem. planning com. 1983, bd. dirs. 1990-93), Assoc. Landscape Contractors Am. (interior plantscape divsn., edn. com. 1987—). Home: 1051 N Midlothian Rd Mundelein IL 60060-1234 Office: Linnaea Newman Assocs 1051 N Midlothian Rd Mundelein IL 60060-1234

NEWMAN, MARY ALICE, academic administrator; b. Goshen, Ind., Nov. 11, 1940; d. Milton J. and Kathleen E. (Gibson) Brunk; m. William Cammock (divorced); 1 child, Julie Lee; m. Hale Newman. BA, Goshen Coll., 1962; MS, W.Va. U., 1965. Rsch. assoc. Case Western Res. U., Cleve., 1966-68; sci. tchr. West Geauga Jr. H.S., Chesterland, Ohio, 1968-70; owner book/antique/art shop Thought, Form & Function, Claridon, Ohio, 1977-80; tchg. assoc. Hiram (Ohio) Coll., 1980-82, dir. corp. found. rels., 1981-85, dir. spl. projects, 1984-85, exec. dir. East Ctrl. Consortium, 1983-85; sales mgr. Northland Engring., White Pigeon, Mich., 1985-92; dir. corp. found. rels. Alfred (N.Y.) U., 1993-95; asst. dir. devel. U. Cin. Found., 1995—. Treas., bd. dirs. League of Women Voters, Elkhart, Ind., 1985-93; bd. dirs. YWCA, Elkhart, 1986-93; v.p., sec. bd. edn. Goshen Comm. Schs., 1988-92. NSF scholar, 1961, 63-65. Mem. Coun. for Advancement and Support of Edn. Office: Univ Cin Found 425 Oak St Cincinnati OH 45219-2594

NEWMAN, MICHAEL J., linguistic educator; b. N.Y.C., Jan. 15, 1957; s. Robert and Ruth Ellen (Jackson) N. BA, Bates Coll., 1979; MA, U. Autonormale Barcenola, Spain, 1988; EdD, Columbia U. Adj. asst. prof. Hunter Coll., N.Y.C., 1990-93; asst. prof. applied linguistics William Paterson Coll., Wayne, N.J., 1993, Ohio State U., Columbus, 1994—; book reviewer Harper Collins, N.Y.C. Contbr. articles to profl. publs. Mem. Linguistic Soc. Am., Out in Linguistics, Am. Ednl. Rsch. Assn. Democrat. Office: Ohio State U Dept Theory & Practice 1945 N High St Rm 257 Columbus OH 43210

NEWMAN, PHILIP ROBERT, psychologist; b. Utica, N.Y., Dec. 17, 1942; s. Samuel M. and Sara Rose (Dumain) N.; A.B. with high distinction, U. Mich., 1964, Ph.D. (Woodrow Wilson fellow 1964, Univ. fellow 1964-66, Horace H. Rackham Research scholar 1969-71), 1971; m. Barbara Miller, June 12, 1966; children: Samuel Asher, Abraham Levy, Rachel Florence. Asst. prof. psychology U. Mich., Ann Arbor, 1971-72; asst. prof. psychology Union Coll., Schenectady, 1972-76; dir. human behavior curriculum project Am. Psychol. Assn., Washington, 1977-81; pvt. practice psychology, Columbus, Ohio, 1978—; adj. prof., sr. researcher young scholars program Ohio State U., 1990; cons. Agy. Instructional TV, 1979. Mem. APA, Internat. Assn. Applied Psychology, Internat. Sociol. Assn., Soc. Psychol. Study Social Issues, Am. Sociol. Assn., Nat. Council Family Relations, Groves Conf. Marriage and Family, Eastern Psychol. Assn., Midwestern Psychol. Assn., Western Psychol. Assn., Am. Pub. Health Assn., N.Y. Acad. Sci., Gerontol. Soc. Am., Am. Orthopsychiat. Assn., Am. Statis. Assn., Phi Beta Kappa, Sigma Xi, Phi Kappa Phi. Author: (with B. Newman) Development through Life: A Psychosocial Approach, 1975, 6th edit., 1995; Infancy and Childhood Development and Its Contexts, 1978; An Introduction to the Psychology of Adolescence, 1979; Personality Development through the Life Span, 1980; Living: The Process of Adjustment, 1981; Understanding Adulthood, 1983; Principles of Psychology, 1983; Adolescent Development, 1986, When Kids Go to College: A Parents Guide to Changing Relationships, 1992; editor: (with B. Newman) Development Through Life: A Case Study Approach, 1976. Home and Office: 1969 Chatfield Rd Columbus OH 43221-3703

NEWMAN, RAYMOND MELVIN, biologist, educator; b. New Castle, Pa., June 10, 1956; s. Raymond Melvin and Sarah L. (Lawton) N.; m. Patricia Ann Scott, Nov. 22, 1989. BS in Biology, Slippery Rock (Pa.) U., 1978; MS, U. Minn., 1982, PhD in Fisheries, 1985. Grad. asst. U. Minn., St. Paul, 1979-84, rsch. specialist forest resources, 1985-86, asst. prof. fisheries, 1986-94; assoc. prof. fisheries, 1995—; postdoctoral fellow natural resources U. Conn., Storrs, 1986-88; investigator U. Mich. Biol. Sta., Pellston, 1987-88; mem. exotics task force Nat. Sea Grant, Silver Spring, Md., 1991; mem. interagy. exotic species com. Minn. Dept. Natural Resources, St. Paul, 1992—. Assoc. editor Jour. N.Am. Biol. Soc., 1994—; mem. editorial bd. Ecology Freshwater Fish, 1992-95; contbr. articles to profl. jours. Bd. dirs. Twin Cities Trout Unltd., Mpls., 1982-87. Mem. Am. Fisheries Soc. (chair river com. Minn. chpt. 1989-91), Am. Inst. Fishery Rsch. Biologists, Ecol. Soc. Am., North Am. Benthological Soc. Office: U Minn Fisheries Wildlife 1980 Folwell Ave Saint Paul MN 55108-1037

NEWNAM, PHYLLIS SUE See SAND, PHYLLIS SUE NEWNAM

NEWPHER, JAMES ALFRED, JR., management consultant; b. New Brighton, Pa., Nov. 14, 1930; s. James Alfred and Olive Myrtle (Houlette) N.; BS, U. Pa., 1952; postgrad., Lebanon Valley Coll., 1956; MBA, Wharton Sch. U. Pa., 1957; m. Mildred Taylor, Aug. 23, 1953. Indsl. engr., Corning Glass Works (N.Y.), 1957-58, plant supr., 1958-60, prodn. supt., 1960-61, plant mgr., 1961-63, dept. mgr. advance products, 1963-64; assoc. Booz, Allen & Hamilton, Inc., Chgo., 1964-69; v.p., mng. officer Lamalie Assocs., Chgo., 1969-73; pres., chief exec. officer Newpher & Co., Inc., Chgo., 1973—; bd. dirs. Design Tech., Inc. With USN, 1951-56. Decorated Purple Heart. Mem. Naval Res. Assn., Nat. Assn. Corp. Profl. Recruiters, Inst. Mgmt. Cons., Retired Officers Assn., Met. Chgo. Club. Presbyterian. Home: 5210 Central Ave Western Springs IL 60558-1805 Office: Newpher & Co Inc 768 Burr Oak Dr Westmont IL 60559-1122

NEWTON, BILL EDWARD, electrical engineering executive; b. Carbondale, Ill., Nov. 13, 1942; s. Robert Ralls and F. Alieen (Henley) N.; m. Donna S. Perry, Sept. 26, 1964; children: Perry Todd, Eric Sean. BS in Applied Sci., So. Ill. U., 1964. Sys. engr. Motorola Comm. and Electronics, Inc., Chgo., 1964-66; distbn. engr. Ctrl. Ill. Pub. Svc. Co., Marion, 1966-79; distbn. engring. supr. Ctrl. Ill. Pub. Svc. Co., Springfield, Ill., 1979—; charter mem. indsl. adv. coun., So. Ill. U. Dept. Elec. Engring., Carbondale, 1994—; mem. engring. annex adv. com. So. Ill. U., Carbondale, 1995—. Mem. First United Meth. Ch., Springfield, Ill. Mem. IEEE (sr. mem.), Titanic Hist. Soc., Masons (3rd degree), Swarovski Collectors' Soc. Office: Ctrl Ill Pub Svc Co 607 E Adams St Springfield IL 62739

NEWTON, GEORGE ADDISON, investment banker, lawyer; b. Denver, Apr. 2, 1911; s. George Addison and Gertrude (Manderson) N.; m. Mary Virginia Powell, Sept. 18, 1937; children: George Addison IV, Nancy Ella

Newton Shaxer, Virginia Powell Newton Jacobi. AB, U. Colo., 1933; LLB, Harvard U., 1936. Bar: Ill. 1937, Mo. 1946. Asso. firm Scott, MacLeish & Falk, Chgo., 1936-42; partner G.H. Walker & Co., St. Louis, 1946-62; mng. partner G.H. Walker & Co., 1962-72; chmn. bd. Stifel Nicolaus & Co., Inc., St. Louis, 1972-82, chmn. emeritus, 1982—; chief exec. officer Stifel Nicolaus & Co., Inc., 1974-78. Bd. govs. Greater St. Louis Cmty. Chest; mem. Coun. on Civic Needs; bd. dirs. Goodwill Industries, 1963—, chmn., 1980-82; bd. dirs. U. Colo. Improvement Corp., U. Colo. Found., St. Louis Conservatory Music; dir. devel. fund U. Colo., 1954-55, chmn., 1955; trustee Fontbonne Coll., 1972-80, chmn., 1974-77; trustee Govtl. Rsch. Inst.; trustee Whitfield Sch., 1978—, chmn., 1986-88, 89-90. Served to maj., USAAF, 1942-45. Decorated Order of the Rising Sun, Gold Rays and Rosette, Emperor of Japan, 1991; recipient C. Fobb award U. Colo., 1955, alumni Recognition award, 1958, named to C Club Hall of Fame, 1968, Silver Ann. All Am. award Sports Illustrated, 1957, Norlin award U. Colo., 1968; U. Colo. medal, 1984. Mem. Investment Bankers Assn. Am. (pres. 1961), Nat. Assn. Securities Dealers (gov. 1954-56, vice chmn. 1956), Assn. Stock Exchange Firms (gov. 1969-72), Sales Execs. Assn. (dir. 1955-60), U. Colo. Assn. Alumni (dir. 1965-67), Japan-Am. Soc. St. Louis (dir. 1980—, pres. 1982-85), The Robert Burns Club of St. Louis (pres. 1993), Phi Beta Kappa, Phi Gamma Delta. Episcopalian (treas. diocese of Mo., 1958-69; sr. warden; trustee diocesan investment trust). Clubs: Racquet (St. Louis), Noonday (St. Louis), St. Louis (St. Louis), Bellerive Country (St. Louis). Home: 6428 Cecil Ave Saint Louis MO 63105-2225 Office: Stifel Nicolaus & Co Inc 500 N Broadway Saint Louis MO 63102-2110

NEWTON, PYNKERTON DION, chiropractor; b. Marion, Ind., Nov. 9, 1960; s. John Walter Newton and Olivia (Taylor) McNair. BA, Ball State U., 1983, MA, 1986; D of Chiropractic, Logan Coll., 1992. Substitute tchr. Marion (Ind.) Community Schs., 1983-86; group leader Ops. Crossroads Africa, Kenya, 1986; acting asst. dir. admissions Ball State U., Muncie, Ind., 1986; corp. analyst Marine Midland Bank, N.Y.C., 1986-87, ops. mgr., 1987-89; admissions coord. Logan Coll. Chiropractic, St. Louis, 1989-92; chiropractic physician Pynkerton Chiropractic Group, P.C., Indpls., 1992—; cons. Logan Coll. Chiropractic, 1993-95. Grad. fellow Ball State U., 1984, 85, 4 Yr. Football scholar, 1979-83. Mem. NAACP, Am. Chiropractic Assn., Nat. Assn. Med. Minority Educators (cons. 1990-91), Ind. State Chiropractic Assn., Am. Black Chiropractic Assn. (exec. dir. 1995—), Schomburg Ctr. Rsch. Black Culture, Ball State U. Alumni Assn., Pi Kappa Chi. Democrat. Baptist. Office: 2102 E 52nd St Ste E Indianapolis IN 46205-1408

NEWTON, ROBERT GEORGE, radio station executive; b. Tulsa, Mar. 26, 1948; s. George Robert and Dorothy (Clark) N.; m. Patricia Dressler, Dec. 27, 1969; children: William, Christina. BS in Journalism, U. Kans., 1970, postgrad., 1970-71. Announcer, reporter Sta. KLWN-AM-FM, Lawrence, Kans., 1969-70, program dir., 1971-72; mgr. ops. Stas. KLWN/KLZR, Lawrence, 1974-85, mgr., 1985—; prodr., engr. Kans. Jayhawk Network, Lawrence, 1984—; vol. tech. advisor Citizens Network for Fgn. Affairs in Washington, Ukraine, 1994; emergency mgmt. duty officer, Douglas County, 1996—. Mem. Douglas County Emergency Preparedness Bd., Lawrence, 1979—, chmn., 1979-94; mem. Leadership Lawrence, 1983, bd. dirs., 1983-88, chmn., 1987-88; mem. Leadership Kans., 1985, trustee, 1985-88; bd. dirs. Lawrence United Fund, 1983-84; mem. Lawrence Aviation Adv. Bd., 1985-90, 91—, chmn., 1989-90; mem. Lawrence Police Dept. Citizens Acad., 1992; mem. citizens adv. com. on transp. City of Lawrence, 1994-95. 1st lt. U.S. Army, 1972-74, capt. res. Recipient Friends of Edn. award Lawrence H.S., 1993. Mem. Nat. Assn. Broadcasters, Kans. Assn. Broadcasters (bd. dirs. 1989-93, pres. 1992), Lawrence C. of C. (bd. dirs. 1982-85). Republican. Mem. Plymouth Congl. Ch. (chmn., bd. trustees, 1981-83, moderator-elect 1996). Lodge: Kiwanis (pres. Lawrence chpt. 1981-82). Home: 2724 Lawrence Ave Lawrence KS 66047-3016 Office: Stas KLWN/KLZR PO Box 3007 Lawrence KS 66046-0007

NEWTON, SEAN RICHARD, electrical engineer; b. Pomona, Calif., Apr. 27, 1966; s. Ronald Richard and Shirley Jane (Scholten) N. BSEE, BS in Computer Sci., U. Nev., 1990. Cert. engr.-in-tng., Nev.; registered prof. engr. and land surveyor. Elec. engr. Electronic Data Systems, Anderson, Ind., 1990—, team leader, 1993—. Mem. IEEE, Engring. Soc., Soc. Mfg. Engrs. (cert. mfg. technologist, judge student robotics/automation contest 1994). Republican.

NEWTSON, RICHARD EVAN, stockbroker; b. Decatur, Ill., Aug. 17, 1950; s. Raymond Earl and Evelyn Lucille (Johnson) N.; m. Robyn Elaine Bock, Dec. 21, 1974; children: Rachel Elizabeth, Randall Eric. BS, Culver-Stockton Coll., 1973. Registered rep. Investors Diversified Svcs., Springfield, Ill., 1972-74; securities broker Reinholdt & Gardner, Springfield, 1975-78; securities broker A.G. Edwards & Sons, Inc., Springfield, 1978—, v.p. investments, 1981—. Fin. industry appointee Ill. Coal Devel. Bd., 1990—. With USAR, 1971-77. Melvin Jones fellow, 1994. Mem. Lions (pres. Springfield Noon club 1980, zone chmn. dist. 1-L 1981-82). Republican. Presbyterian. Home: 2400 Westchester Blvd Springfield IL 62704-5427 Office: AG Edwards & Sons Inc Ste 100 1 W Old State Capitol Plz Springfield IL 62701-1217

NEY, MICHAEL VINCENT, university administrator; b. Indpls., Nov. 19, 1947; s. Marshal M. and Delphine M (Deitrick) N.; m. Karen R. Beck, June 25, 1975 (div. 1978). Student, U. Hawaii, 1966; BS, Butler U., Indpls., 1972; MHA, Ind. U.-Purdue U., Indpls., 1990. EDP operator L.S. Ayres & Co., Indpls., 1963-65; city surveyor Indpls., 1969; with Am. Fletcher Nat. Bank, Indpls., 1970-74; credit adjuster Am. States Ins. Co., Indpls., 1974; adminstr. asst. to dean Sch. Medicine Ind. U., Indpls., 1974-80, asst. dir. fiscal affairs, 1980-83, asst. to chmn. opthalmology, 1983-85, adminstr. dept. surgery, 1985-95, dir. adminstrn. & info., 1995—; bd. dirs. Ind. U. Fed. Credit Union; adj. faculty Schs. Pub. and Environ. Affairs, 1991; pres., CEO Cyberhelp, Inc., 1996—. 2nd v.p. United Cerebral Palsy Cen. Ind., Indpls. 1983-85, bd. dirs., 1978-80; pres. United Cerebral Palsy Cen. Ind. Found. Inc., Indpls. 1987; v.p. United Cerebral Palsy Ind., Indpls., 1985-87; treas. Collaboration 2000, Inc., 1996—. With U.S. Army, 1965-69, Vietnam, capt. USAR, 1990. Decorated Vietnam Svc. medal, Vietnam Camp medal, Commendation medal USNG, 1981; recipient Mktg. cert. Ford Mktg. Corp., Dearborn, Mich., 1971, Samuel H. Hopper award for Acad. Achievement, Sch. Pub. and Environ. Affairs, 1990. Mem. ALA, Am. Coll. Healthcare Execs., Am. Med. Colls. Assn., Am. Med. Info. Assn., Assn. Acad. Surg. Adminstrs., Med. Group Mgmt. Assn., Group on Bus. Affairs, Am. Soc. for Info. Sci., Healthcare Info. Mgmt. Systems Soc., Libr. and Info. Tech. Assn., Ind. Fedn. Rsch. Adminstrs., Boston Computer Soc., U.S. Long Distance Learning Assn., Collaboration 2000, Ind. Health Sci. Librs. Assn., Am. Legion (comdr. 1980-85), Lions, Kiwanis. Republican. Methodist. Home: 2318 Golden Oaks N Indianapolis IN 46260-5076 Office: 545 Barnhill Dr # 245 Indianapolis IN 46202-5112

NEY, NEAL JOHN, library director; b. Dubuque, Iowa, Jan. 8, 1947; s. John J. and Marge (Lubbers) N.; m. Karen Smith (div.); m. Marie Dunlap, Feb. 20, 1983. Bachelor's degree, George Williams Coll., 1970; Master's degree, Rosary Coll., River Forest, Ill., 1974. Asst. reference libr. Chgo. Hist. Soc., 1971-76; br. libr. Chgo. Pub. Libr., 1976-78, adult materials selection specialist, 1978-79; libr. dir. Kankakee (Ill.) Pub. Libr., 1979-83, Park Forest (Ill.) Pub. Libr., 1983-92, Evanston (Ill.) Pub. Libr., 1992—. Contbr. articles to profl. jours. Mem. ALA, Ill. Libr. Assn. (bd. dirs. 1982-84). Office: Evanston Pub Libr 1703 Orrington Evanston IL 60201

NEYER, JIM V., product development manager; b. Cin., Jan. 6, 1937. B, Marquette U., 1961, Ill. Inst. Tech., 1970; M, Ill. Inst. Tech., 1972. Mgr. product devel. Rayovac Xorp., Madison, Wis., 1985—. With U.S. Army, 1957-59. Mem. ASME. Office: Rayovac Corp 601 Ray O Vac Dr Madison WI 53711-2460

NG, LEWIS YOK-HOI, civil engineer; b. Chaozhou, Guangdong, People's Republic of China, Aug. 28, 1955; came to U.S., 1976; s. Shing Yee and Sukyau Ng; m. Sandra Jane Moy, June 19, 1982; children: Andrea, Gabriel. BS, U. Wis., Platteville, 1980; MS, U. Minn., 1984. Cert. profl. engr., Minn., Ohio, Wis. Sr. engr. Twin City Testing Corp., St. Paul, 1980-86; project mgr. Walker Engrs., Mpls., 1986-88; chief engr., mgr. Twin City Testing Corp., 1988-91; mgr., prin. STS Cons., Mpls., 1992-94; pres. Bldgs. Cons. Group, Inc., Mpls., 1994—. Chmn. deacons bd. Twin City Chinese Christian Ch., 1992-93, 94-96; mem. Metro. Econ. Devel. Coun., Mpls., 1995—. Mem. ASCE, Am. Concrete Inst. (tech. com. 1985—, planning com. 1989-95), Constrn. Specifier Inst. Home: 3107 Evelyn St Saint Paul MN 55113-1214

NGAI, KA-LEUNG, biochemist, researcher; b. Kowloon, Hong Kong, Aug. 31, 1950; came to U.S., 1969; s. Chung-Yin and Wen-Yue (Sun) N. BSChemE, U. Wis., 1972; PhD, U. Pa., Phila., 1981. Rsch. fellow Yale U., New Haven, Conn., 1981-86; dir. biotech. facility Northwestern U., Evanston, Ill., 1986-92, Northwestern U. Med. Sch., Chgo., 1990-92; dir. genetic engring. facility U. Ill., Urbana, 1992—. Author: (with others) Methods in Enzymology, 1990; ad hoc reviewer Jour. Bacteriology, 1985—; mem. adv. bd. Who's Who in Technology, 6th edit., 1988; contbr. articles to sci. jours. Mem. AAAS, Am. Chem. Soc., Am. Soc. for Microbiology, Tau Beta Pi. Roman Catholic.

NGO, PAUL YEN LY, psychology educator; b. Ames, Iowa, Mar. 21, 1961; s. Peter D.T. and Cecilia T.L. (Pho) N. BA with distinction in Psychology, Rutgers U., 1983; MA in Exptl. Psychology, U. Notre Dame, 1986, PhD in Exptl. Psychology, 1988. Tchg. aide Douglass Coll. Rutgers U., New Brunswick, N.J., 1982-83; instr. freshman writing program U. Notre Dame (Ind.), 1984-88, tchg. asst. in psychology, 1987; adj. prof. psychology St. Mary's Coll., City of Notre Dame, 1988, Ind. U., South Bend, 1988-89; asst. prof. psychology U. Wis.-Stout, Menomonie, 1989-93, assoc. prof. psychology, 1993-96; assoc. prof. psychology St. Norbert Coll., De Pere, Wis., 1996—; reviewer Harcourt Brace Coll. Publs., Ft. Worth, 1994-96; instr. ergonomics dept. apparel textiles and design U. Wis.-Stout, 1995. Author (videotape) Advantages of Campus Diversity, 1991, (book chpts.) Torn Between Two Worlds, 1994, Resiliency in Ethnic Minority Families, 1995. U. Notre Dame fellow, 1983-84, Nakatani Ctr. Curriculum Devel. grantee, 1994. Mem. Midwestern Psychol. Assn. (Chgo. moderator 1993-96, local rep.), Internat. Assn. for Cross-Cultural Psychology. Roman Catholic. Home: 900 Liebman Ct #12 Green Bay WI 54302 Office: St Norbert Coll Dept Psychology JMS 204 De Pere WI 54415

NICE, PAMELA MICHELE, theatre director; b. Mpls., Apr. 24, 1949; d. Charles Monroe and Mary Ellen (Cranmer) N.; 1 child, Nicole Michele. BA, U. Minn., 1972, MA, 1980, PhD, 1984. Cert. in acting, London Acad. Music and Dramatic Art. Actress Rochester (N.Y.) Shakespeare Theatre, 1973-74, GEVA Repertory Theatre, Rochester, 1974-75; reporter Capitol Hill News Svc., Washington, 1975; theatre dir. Mpls., St. Paul, 1976—; artistic dir. Paul Bunyan Playhouse, Bemidji, Minn., 1987-90; asst. prof. theatre Gustavus Adolphus Coll., St. Peter, Minn., 1981-85; vis. instr. Macalester Coll., St. Paul, 1992, 95; assoc. dir. faculty devel. U. St. Thomas, St. Paul, 1990-95; artistic dir. Lagniappe Theatre, St. Paul, 1993—; mem. conf. planning com. Bush Regional Collaboration, St. Paul, 1992. Dir. including (opera) Flying Dutchman, 1992, (flamenco ballets) Flor, 1990, Sadja, 1996, (playsú Wild Honey, Romeo and Juliet, Good, As You Like It, 1986-92, Death and the Maiden, 1994, Love and Anger; video-dir., co-writer: Opening Doors. Recipient Best Dir. award Minn. One-Act Play Festival, 1991, 93; Fulbright fellow, 1972-73; grantee Paul Bunyan Playhouse, 1989, Lagniappe Theatre, 1994, MRAC, 1995. Mem. Actors' Equity Assn., Theatre Comm. Group, Profl. and Orgn. Devel. Network, Bush Regional Collaboration for Faculty Devel. Home: 2008 Brewster St Apt 301 Saint Paul MN 55108-2014 Office: U St Thomas 2115 Summit Ave Saint Paul MN 55105-1048

NICHOLAS, JOHN JEFFREY, physiatrist, educator; b. Murphysboro, Ill., Jan. 15, 1933; s. Charles Albert and Ethel Martha Elizabeth (Seaton) N.; m. Barbara Ann Knauff, Mar. 2, 1957; children: Sara Jeffrey, John Jeremiah, Matthew Calvin. AB, Harvard Coll., 1955; MD, Case Western Res. U., 1959. Intern SUNY, Syracuse, 1959-61, resident, 1963-65; instr. Syracuse Upstate N.Y. Med. Ctr., 1959-61, 63-69; from asst. to assoc. prof. Rehab. Inst. Chgo., 1969-72; from assoc. prof. to prof. U. Pitts., 1972-90; chmn., prof. Rush Presbyn. St. Luke's Med. Ctr., Chgo., 1990—. Capt. U.S. Army, 1961-63. Democrat. Episcopalian. Office: Rush Presbyn St Lukes Med Ctr 1725 W Harrison St Chicago IL 60612

NICHOLLS, THOMAS MAURICE, business owner; b. Hancock, Mich., June 22, 1960; s. David and Ericka (Weiss) N.; m. Mary Ann Erspamer, Apr. 30, 1983; 1 child, Michael. Owner Northland Svcs., Hurley, Wis., 1983—; gen. mgr. K & L Enterprises, Marquette, Mich., 1985-91; exec. mgr. S & S Inc., Sun Prairie, Wis., 1991-94; 1992—. Mem. Just Say No, Ironwood, Mich., 1992. With USN, 1979-83. Mem. Jaycees (v.p. 1986, Presdl. award of Honor 1986, Jaycee of Yr., Mich. 1986). Home and Office: Northern Venture 502 Poplar St Hurley WI 54534-1169

NICHOLS, GREG MARK, systems analyst; b. Elgin, Ill., Nov. 25, 1967; s. Grace (Ipema) N. A in Data Processing, Blackhawk Tech.; student, U. Wis., Whitewater. Cert. assoc. computer profl. Analyst Ameritech Svcs., Milw., 1988—, analyst, LAN adminstr., 1990—; pres. Nichols Consulting, Delavan, Wis., 1991—. Sunday sch. tchr. Delavan Christian Ch., 1990; cadet leader Ch. Boys Club, Delavan, 1990-91; speaker Boy Scouts Am., Milw., 1991—. Home: 518 E Washington St Delavan WI 53115-1820 Office: AmeriTech Svcs 2000 W Ameritech Center Dr Schaumburg IL 60196-5000

NICHOLS, HAROLD JAMES, theatre educator; b. Mitchell Field, N.Y., July 27, 1945; s. Harold J. and Ruth (McCain) N.; m. Mary Frances Lutes, Nov. 25, 1967 (div. 1992); children: Ruth, David, Debra; m. Anna Marie Douet, July 4, 1992. BS, Iowa State U., 1967; MA, Ind. U., 1969, PhD, 1971. Assoc. instr. Ind. U., Bloomington, 1970-71; asst. prof. Kans. State U., Manhattan, 1971-75, assoc. prof., 1975-81, prof., 1981-84, prof., head speech dept., 1985-93; dean coll. fine arts and humanities U. Nebr., Kearney, 1993—; guest scholar DePauw U. Undergrad. Honors Conf., Greencastle, Ind., 1988; cons. Commonwealth of Va. Dept. Edn., 1988, Nebr. Wesleyan U., Lincoln, 1989, So. Ill. U., 1989, U. Va., 1992, U. No. Iowa, 1992. Co-editor: Status of Theatre Research-1984, 1986; contbr. articles to profl. jours. Named Outstanding Coll. Tchr., Kans. Speech Communications Assn., 1985. Mem. Assn. Theatre in Higher Edn. (pres. 1987-88), Am. Coll. Theatre Festival (region chair 1987-88, Kennedy Ctr. medallion 1990), Mid-Am. Theatre Conf. (chief regional officer 1978-81). Home: 1418 8th Ave Kearney NE 68847-6637 Office: Univ Nebr at Kearney Coll Fine Arts Humanities Kearney NE 68849

NICHOLS, JERRY L., production engineer; b. Sigourney, Iowa, Oct. 16, 1948. B, Iowa State U., 1987. Registered profl. engr., Iowa. Machinist Engring. Rsch. Inst., Ames, Iowa, 1984-87; project engr. Gen. Filter Co., Ames, Iowa, 1987-91, supr. product engring., 1992—. Mem. com. Meth. Ch., Ames. With USNR, 1966-74, Vietnam, hon. disharge. Methodist. Home: 812 7th St Ames IA 50010-5914 Office: Gen Filter Co 600 Arrasmith Trl Ames IA 50010-9760

NICHOLS, JOHN ALDEN, history educator; b. Westerly, R.I., Feb. 28, 1919; s. Thomas Pitman and Jennie Althea (Howland) N.; m. Barbara Searles Tuttle, June 8, 1946 (dec. Dec., 1975); children: Catherine Tyler Nichols Thompson, David Alden, Margaret Foster. BA with high honors, high distinction, Wesleyan U., Middletown, Conn., 1941; MA, Columbia U., 1943, PhD, 1951. History instr. Wesleyan U., Middletown, Conn., 1948-50; asst. prof. history Wesleyan U., Middletown, 1959-61, Skidmore Coll., Saratoga Springs, N.Y., 1950-51; fellowship Ford Found., 1951-52; editor Ginn & Co., Boston, 1952-59; assoc. prof. history U. Ill., Champaign-Urbana, 1961-67, prof. history, 1967-89. Author: (books) Germany After Bismarck, 1958, The Year of the Three Kaisers, 1987; mng. editor Daedalus, 1959-61. Schiff fellow, Columbia U., N.Y.C., 1947, sr. rsch. fellow Fulbright Program, West Germany. Mem. AAUP, Am. Hist. Assn., Philosophy Club (U. Ill.). Democrat. Home: 505 W Pennsylvania Ave Urbana IL 61801

NICHOLS, JOHN DOANE, diversified manufacturing corporation executive; b. Shanghai, China, 1930; m. Alexandra M. Curran, Dec. 4, 1971; children: Kendra E., John D. III. BA, Harvard U., 1953, MBA, 1955. Various operating positions Ford Motor Corp., 1958-68; dir. fin. controls ITT Corp., 1968-69; exec. v.p., chief operating officer Aerojet-Gen. Corp., 1969-79; exec. v.p., COO Ill. Tool Works Inc., Chgo., 1980-81; chief exec. officer, dir. Ill. Tool Works Inc., 1982—, chmn., 1986—; bd. dirs. Household Internat., Philip Morris Cos., Inc., Rockwell Internat., Stone Container Corp.; overseer Harvard U. Trustee U. Chgo., 1987-93, Chgo. Symphony Orch., 1986-94, Lyric Opera Chgo., Mus. Sci. and Industry, Jr. Achievement Chgo., Chgo. Commerce Civic Com., Bus. Roundtable, Art Inst. Chgo.; bd. govs. Argonne (Ill.) Nat. Lab., 1988-93. Mem. Harvard Club (N.Y., Chgo.), Indian Hill Club (Winnetka, Ill.), Chgo. Club, Comml. Club, Econ. Club Chgo. Home: 900 Mount Pleasant Rd Winnetka IL 60093-3613 Office: Ill Tool Works Inc 3600 W Lake Ave Glenview IL 60025-1215

NICHOLS, MARCI LYNNE, gifted education coordinator, educator, consultant; b. Cin., July 7, 1948; m. James G. Nichols, June 19, 1970; children: Lisa, Jeannette. B in Arts & Sci., Miami U., 1970, MEd, 1990, postgrad. Cert. Secondary English, elem. gifted edn., computer edn., Ohio. Secondary English tchr. West Clermont Local Schs., Cin., 1970-71; coord. gifted edn. and tchr. Batavia (Ohio) Local Schs., 1981—; speaker, cons. Local Gifted Orgns., Cin., 1988—; vis. instr. dept. ednl. psychology Miami U., Oxford, Ohio, 1991—; presenter Nat. Rsch. Symposium on Talent Devel., 1991. Author, presenter: (videotape series) Parenting the Gifted Parts I and II, 1992; columnist, contbr. Resources for Everyday Living; contbr. articles to profl. jours. Speaker Christian Women's Club, Ohio, Ind., Ky., W.Va., 1981—; deacon First Presbyn. Ch. of Batavia, Ohio, 1986-88. Recipient Douglas Miller Rsch. award Miami U., 1991. Mem. ASCD, Am. Ednl. Rsch. Assn., Nat. Assn. for Gifted Children, Consortium Ohio Coords. of Gifted, Midwest Ednl. Rsch. Assn. (presenter), Internat. Platform Assn., Phi Kappa Phi. Home: 110 Wood St Batavia OH 45103-2923 Office: Batavia Local Schs 800 Bauer Ave Batavia OH 45103-2837

NICHOLS, RICHARD (ROCKY NICHOLS), state legislator; b. Topeka, Kans., Sept. 4, 1969; s. Kenneth Nichols and Rita (Spellman) N. BA, Washburn U., 1993. Database cons.; intern Kans. Ho. of Reps., Topeka, 1991; legis. aide for Spkr. of House Kans. Ho. of Reps., 1992, mem. from dist. 58, 1992—. Address: 2329 SE Virginia Topeka KS 66605

NICHOLS, RICHARD DALE, former congressman, banker; b. Ft. Scott, Kans., Apr. 29, 1926; s. Ralph Dale and Olive Marston (Kittell) N.; m. Constance Weinbrenner, Mar. 25, 1951; children: Philip William, Ronald Dale, Anita Jane Nichols Bomberger. BS in Agr. and BS in Journalism, Kans. State U., 1951. Info. counsel Kans. State Bd. Agr., Topeka, 1951-54; assoc. far, dir. Sta. WIBW, WIBW-TV, Topeka, 1954-57; agr. rep. to v.p. Hutchinson (Kans.) Nat. Bank and Trust, 1957-69; pres., CEO Home State Bank, McPherson, Kans., 1969-79, chmn., pres., CEO, 1979-91; chmn. Home State Bank & Trust, McPherson, Kans., 1985-91, 93—; mem. 102d Congress from 5th Kans. dist., 1991-92. Pres. Arts Coun., McPherson, 1979; 5th Dist. chmn. Kans. Rep. Party, 1986-89; bd. dirs. Camp Wood YMCA Camp, Elmdale, Kans., 1995; Meth. Ch. lay spkr., 1994—; bd. trustees Ctrl. Coll., McPherson. Ensign USNR, 1944-47; ATO. Named Hon. Citizen N.Y.C., 1988. Mem. VFW, Kans. Bankers Assn. (pres. 1985-86), Am. Bankers Assn. (advisor 1986-88), Kans. Assn. Banking Ag. Reps. (pres. 1965), Am. Legion, McPherson C. of C. (pres. 1977), Optimist (pres. Hutchinson club 1965), Rotary (pres. McPherson club 1978), Kans. Cavalry (cmdg. gen. 1986-89). Methodist. Home: 404 N Lakeside Dr Mc Pherson KS 67460-3600 Office: Home State Bank and Trust PO Box 1266 Mc Pherson KS 67460-1266

NICHOLS, ROCKY See NICHOLS, RICHARD

NICHOLS, ROGER SABIN, school counselor; b. Ames, Iowa, Oct. 21, 1938; s. Sabin Alfred and Margaret Pauline (Andrew) N.; m. Glendene Donna Greta, June 12, 1960; children: Margaret Emily, Charles Sabin II. BS, Iowa State U., 1960; MA in Edn., U. No. Iowa, 1965, EdS, 1976. Cert. tchr. sci., social studies, lang. arts, counselor K-12, dir. pupil svcs., Iowa. Tchr., counselor Bridgewater-Fontanelle (Iowa) Cmty. Sch. Dist., 1960-66; counselor, guidance dir. Sioux City (Iowa) Cmty. Sch. Dist., 1966—; human rels. cons. Western Hills Area Edn. Agy., Sioux City, 1979-82, mem. spl. edn. transition adv. com., 1987—, chair career devel. unit writing com., 1989-90; mem., chairperson spl. needs adv. com. Western Iowa Tech. Cmty. Coll., Sioux City, 1982-87, mem. area planning coun. for vocat. edn., 1986-90; active numerous coms. Sioux City Cmty. Sch. Dist., 1967-89; mem. evaluation team N. Ctrl. Assn. Colls. and Schs., 1983; mem. brief counseling rsch. project Iowa State U., 1989-90; mem. counselor's adv. com. office of admissions U. S.D., 1990-92; state conf. presenter Iowa Assn. Counseling and Devel., 1990, 94; local coord. Counseling for Higher Skills Rsch. Project, Kans. State U., 1994-95. Contbg. author: Critical Incidents in School Counseling, 1973, Simmerman Family Record, 1995; contbr. poetry to Lyrical Iowa, 1965, 67; contbr. articles to profl. jours. On-air friendraiser host Friends of FM-90, Sioux City, 1982—; mem. 4-H subcom. Woodbury County Extension Svc., Sioux City, 1984—; fair supt. Woodbury County Fair Assn., Moville, Iowa, 1984-89. Named Iowa Counselor of Yr., Iowa Assn. Coll. Admissions Counselors, 1995; recipient Nat. Def. Edn. Act Stipend, U. S.D., 1968. Mem. NEA (life), Iowa State Edn. Assn. (del. assembly 1965), Sioux City Edn. Assn. (chair profl. rights and responsibilities com. 1967-68, rep. assembly 1968-69), Am. Counseling Assn., Iowa Counseling Assn., Am. Sch. Counselors Assn., Iowa Sch. Counselors Assn., Nat. Career Devel. Assn. (career info. rev. svc. 1970-73), Iowa Career Devel. Assn. (state membership chair 1975-76), Iowa Specialists in Group Work, Iowa State Hist. Soc., Iowa State Geneal. Soc., Conn. Soc. Genealogists, N.Y. Historic Geneal. Soc., Derbyshire Family History Soc., Siouxland Master Chorale (pres. 1968-71, v.p. 1977-80, 88-90, treas. 1982-83), Sioux City Chamber Music Assn. (pres. 1980-81), Phi Delta Kappa. Republican. Methodist. Home: 3819 Peters Ave Sioux City IA 51106 Office: East High Sch 5011 Mayhew Ave Sioux City IA 51106

NICHOLS, RONALD, state legislator; m. Sue; 4 children. BS, N.D. State U., MS. Mem. N.D. Ho. of Reps., 1991—; past. mem. fin. and taxation com. N.D. Ho. Reps., Agr. com., edn.; agr. loan officer; farmer, rancher. Mem. Stanley Cmty. Hosp.; past pres. coun. Holy Rosary Cath. Ch. Recipient Outstanding Agriculturist award N.D. State U. Mem. KC, Stanley Am. Legion (past comdr.), N.D. Stockman's Assn., Vietman Vet. Am. Home: RR 1 Box 3 Palermo ND 58769*

NICHOLS, RYAN J., engineer; b. Crawfordsville, Ind., July 24, 1969. AD, Ivy Tech. U., Columbus, Ind., 1991. Electrician North Vernon Electric, Madison, Ind., 1990-92; drafting engr. Clifty Engring. & Tool Co., Madison, 1992—. Home: 1900 Vanburen Dr Madison IN 47250-1920 Office: Clifty Enging & Tool Co 2949 Clifty Dr Madison IN 47250-1640

NICHOLS, THOMAS BRITT, state legislator; m. Diane Conway. Atty.; mem. from dist. 22 Kans. State Ho. of Reps., Topeka. Address: 8330 Reinhardt Prairie Village KS 66206

NICHOLSEN, JAMES THERMAN, computer company executive; b. Omaha, Aug. 10, 1950; s. Therman James and Doris June (Modlin) N.; m. Kathryn Linnae Keeney, May 5, 1974; children: Darcy Linnae, Joren James. BA in Psychology, U. Nebr., Lincoln, 1974; BS in Computer Sci., U. Nebr., Omaha, 1984. Program analyst State of Nebr., Lincoln, 1978-80; mgmt. trainee Mark Anthony Co., Omaha, 1980-81; mgr. quality assurance Crown Products Co., Ralston, Nebr., 1981-84; systems analyst Sterling Software, Inc., Bellevue, Nebr., 1984-85; mgr. contracts adminstrn. Sterling Software, Inc., Bellevue, 1985—. Mem. Omaha Henry Doorly Zoo; pres. Krasova & Co. Midwest Youth Ballet, Omaha, 1984; past pres. Ralston After Sch. Youth Program, 1995. 1st lt. U.S. Army, 1973-77. Mem. Nat. Contract Mgmt. Assn., Assn. Computing Machinery, Spl. Interest Group Artificial Intelligence, Nat. Arbor Day Found. Lutheran. Home: 5105 S 93rd St Omaha NE 68127-2470 Office: 1404 Ft Crook Rd S Bellevue NE 68005-2969

NICHOLSON, GERALD LEE, medical facilities administrator; b. Belleville, Ill., Dec. 30, 1944; s. Chester Lee and Bette Joan (Tarr) N.; m. Cathy Ann Sammons, May 3, 1975; children: Laura, Brianna. BA in Sociology, So. Ill. U., 1974, BS in Math., 1976, MBA, 1976. Bus. mgr. Northland Orthopedic Group, St. Louis, 1976-78; cons. AMA, Chgo., 1978-80; cons. pvt. practice Evansville, Ind., 1981-85; adminstr. Mo. Eye Inst., St. Louis, 1985-91; regional v.p. Co-Care Eye Cts., St. Louis, 1985-91; adminstr. Orthopaedic Assoc., P.C., Cape Girardeau, Mo., 1992—; tax preparer Nicholson Cons., St. Louis, 1990-92. Mem. Citizen Interaction Com., Chesterfield, Mo., 1989, Leadership Cape, 1992. Capt. USMC, 1966-72, Vietnam.

Mem. Marine Corps Res. Officers Assn., Am. Coll. Med. Practice Execs., Med. Group Mgrs. Assn., S.E. Mo. Med. Mgrs. (pres.), Aircraft Owners and Pilots Assn., Rotary Internat. (pres. club). Home: 3010 Melrose St Cape Girardeau MO 63703-2200 Office: Orthopedic Assocs of SE Mo PC 48 Doctors Park Cape Girardeau MO 63703

NICHOLSON, JOYCE ELAINE, radio station official; b. Martins Ferry, Ohio, Mar. 2, 1956; d. Nick and Teresa Helen (Gazdik) Toth; m. W. Harry Nicholson; 1 child, Emily Erin. Grad. high sch., Tiltonsville, Ohio. Writer, prodr. Sta. WTOV-TV (formerly Sta. WSTV-TV), Steubenville, 1974-76; traffic dir. Sta. WSTV, Steubenville, 1977-84; continuity writer Stas. WRKY-FM and WSTV, Steubenville, 1976, on-air announcer, disc jockey, 1985; ops. and program mgr. WSTV/WOMP-Am and WRKY/WOMP-FM, Steubenville, 1985—. Bd. dirs., media rep. Jefferson County Emergency Planning Commn., 1987-92; vol. Media Day, ARC, Jefferson County, 1990-92; bd. dirs. Greater Steubenville-Jefferson County Conv. and Visitors Bur., 1988-89, Old Ft. Steuben Festival Com., 1990-92, Discoveries of Christopher Columbus, Jefferson County, 1992—, AmeriFlora '92 Com., Steubenville, 1992—; mem. cen. and exec. coms. Jefferson County Rep. Com., 1992—; v.p. Habitat for Humanity, 1992—; Rep. precinct committeeman, 1996—. Mem. Steubenville-Jefferson County C. of C. (bd. dirs., pride com. 1992, chmn. bus. at breakfast 1992, Amb. Club 1991-92), Nat. Honor Soc. Methodist. Office: Stas WSTV and WRKY-FM PO Box 1340 320 Market St Steubenville OH 43952

NICHOLSON, LAWRENCE ALVIN, university administrator; b. St. Paul, Dec. 1, 1947; s. Alvin Foster and Bernadine Eunice (Michaud) N.; m. Elizabeth Ann Mickelson, June 3, 1972 (dec. June 1988); children: Rebecca Ann, Michael Alan; m. Eldean Kay Kriedeman, Aug. 28, 1989; children: Shaun Eugene, Melissa Kay. Student, Moorhead (Minn.) State U., 1965. Warehouseman Simon's, Moorhead, 1970-78; bldg. svcs. foreman Moorhead State U., 1978—. Mem. Moorhead City Coun., 1991-95; cand. for Minn. Ho. of Reps., 1995; mem. chicano/Latino Task Force on Discrimination, Gov. of Minn., 1993-94. With USAF, 1965-68. Named Employer of the Yr., State of Minn., 1994. Mem. Minn. Sports Fedn. (dir. 1980), Middle Mgmt. Assn. (dir. 1983), Am. Fedn. State, County, Mcpl. Employees (bus. rep. 1981), VFW, Am. Legion, Amvets. DFL Party. Roman Catholic. Home: 1219 4th Ave S Moorhead MN 56560 Office: Moorhead State Univ 1104 7th Ave S Moorhead MN 56560

NICHOLSON, WILLIAM NOEL, clinical neuropsychologist; b. Detroit, Dec. 24, 1936; s. James Eardly and Hazel A. (Wagner) N.; A.B., Wittenberg U., 1959; M.Div., Luth. Theol. Sem., Phila., 1962; Ph.D. (HEW fellow), Mich. State U., 1972; m. Nancy Ann Marshall, June 15, 1957; children—Ann Marie, Kristin, Scott. Ordained to ministry Lutheran Ch., 1962; parish pastor Our Savior Luth. Ch., Saginaw, Mich., 1962-69; psychologist Ingham-Eaton-Clinton Mental Health Bd., 1971-72; psychologist Bay-Arenac Mental Health Bd., 1972-74; dir., psychologist Riverside Center, Bay City, Mich., 1974-75; pres. Bay Psychol. Assos., P.C., Bay City, 1975—; cons. Gov.'s Office of Drug Abuse, 1972-74. Cert., Nat. Register Health Care Providers in Psychology. Fellow Am. Bd. Med. Psychotherapists; mem. Am. Psychol. Assn., Midwest Psychol. Assn., Mich. Psychol. Assn., Mental Health Assn. (pres. Bay-Arenac Chpt. 1981), Bay city Yacht Club. Lutheran. Author: A Guttman Facet Analysis of Attitude-Behaviors Toward Drug Users by Heroin Addicts and Mental Health Therapists, 1972; contbr. articles to profl. jours. Office: Behavioral Med Ctr 3442 Wilder Rd Bay City MI 48706-2331

NICKEL, JANET MARLENE MILTON, geriatrics nurse; b. Manitowoc, Wis., June 9, 1940; d. Ashley and Pearl (Kerr) Milton; m. Curtis A. Nickel, July 29, 1961; children: Cassie, Debra, Susan. Diploma, Milw. Inst., 1961; ADN, N.D. State U., 1988. Nurse Milw. VA, Wood, Wis., 1961-62; supervising nurse Park Lawn Convalescent Hosp., Manitowoc, 1964-65; newsletter editor Fargo (N.D.) Model Cities Program, 1970-73; supervising night nurse Rosewood on Broadway, Luth. Hosps. and Homes, Fargo, 1973-92; assoc. dir. nursing Elim Nursing Home, Fargo, 1992-94, night supr., 1994—. Mem. Phi Eta Sigma. Home: 225 19th Ave N Fargo ND 58102-2352 Office: 3534 S University Dr Fargo ND 58104-6228

NICKEL, MELVIN EDWIN, metallurgical engineer; b. St. Louis, Aug. 24, 1915; s. Jacob William and Mary Anna (Madsen) N.; m. Mary Louise Breuer, Sept. 12, 1942; children: Elizabeth Ann Nickel Medve, Mary Patricia Nickel Hepburn, Sheila Breuer Nickel Stojak, William Louis. BS in Metall. Engring., U. Mo., Rolla, 1938, Profl. Degree of Metall. Engring., 1967. Mgmt. trainee Bethlehem (Pa.) Steel Corp., 1938-39; asst. to supt. blast furnaces Wis. Steel div. Internat. Harvester Co., Chgo., 1939-43, gen. foreman furnaces, blast furnaces, 1943-48, asst. supt. blast furnaces, 1948-49, supt. open hearths, 1949-61, supt. basic oxygen furnaces, mgr. steel prodn., 1961-68, mgr. primary ops., 1968-77; mgr. facilities planning and appropriations, works mgr. Envirodyne Industries, Inc., Wis. Steel Corp., 1977-80; pres. Melvin E. Nickel & Assocs., Inc., Chgo., 1980—. Contbr. articles to profl. jours.; developer early practices for prodn. of spl. bar quality and alloy steel in top blown basic oxygen furnace, 1962-64. Bd. trustees Iron and Steel Soc. Found., Warrensdale, Pa., 1980-91. Recipient Disting. Merit award U. Mo., Rolla, 1960; inducted Mo. Sch. Mines/U. Mo.-Rolla Athletic Hall of Fame U. Mo., Rolla, 1993. Mem. AIME (hon., nat. v.p., dir. 1974-76), Iron and Steel Soc. of AIME (nat. pres. 1974-75), Metall. Soc. of AIME (nat. chmn. iron and steel divsn. 1972-74), Assn. of Iron and Steel Engrs., Western States Blast Furnaces and Coke Assn., U. Mo., Rolla Alumni Assn. (pres. 1956-59, bd. dirs.), Triangle Fraternity, Jackson Hole Wildlife Soc., Ridge Country Club of Chgo., Beverly Hills Univ. Club. Republican. Roman Catholic. Home and Office: 10601 S Hamilton Ave Chicago IL 60643-3127

NICKELSON, WILLIS F., agricultural products executive; b. Freedom, Okla., Nov. 17, 1931. BS, Okla. State U., 1953, MS, 1957; PhD, U. Ill., 1960. Dir. nutrition tech. svcs. Standard Chem. Co., Omaha, 1965-81; pres. Livestock Nutrition and Mgmt. Svcs., Omaha, 1981—. 1st lt. U.S. Army, 1955-57, Korea. Mem. Am. Soc. Animal Sci., CAST Coun. Agriculture. Republican. Home: 2224 S 86th Ave Omaha NE 68124-2136

NICKERSON, GARY LEE, secondary education educator; b. Cleve., Nov. 7, 1942; s. Alto Lee and Louise Evelyn (Watson) N.; m. Barbara Marie Butler, Aug. 17, 1968; 1 child, L'Oreal. BS, Ohio U., 1966; MA, Atlanta U., 1971. Cert. secondary tchr., Ohio. With Cleve. Pub. Schs., 1966—; sci. dept. chmn. John F. Kennedy High Sch., Cleve., 1985—; physics instr. Case Western Res. U., Cleve., summer 1988; sci. instr. Std. Oil Elem. Teaching Retraining Program summer 1986; mem. adv. panel Ednl. Devel. Ctr., Inc., Newton, Mass., 1989—; sci. instr. Cleve. Ednl. Found. Elem. Teaching Retraining Program, 1990—, Baldwin Wallace U. Upward Bound Program, 1992; engring. project instr. MEIOP Summer Program Case Western Res. U., 1991; tchr. trainer Kent State U. Trivet program, 1991—; sci. tchr. Gov.'s Inst. for Gifted and Talented, Cleve. State U., 1992—. Co-author curriculum guides. Recipient Cert. of Excellence in Teaching Rotary, 1990. Mem. NAACP, Urban League, Cleve. Regional Coun. Sci. Tchrs. (bd. dirs. 1986-87), Metrocabse Assn., Nat. Sci. Tcrhrs. Assn., Sci. Edn. Coun. Ohio, Kappa Alpha Psi. Democrat. Baptist. Home: 5871 White Pine Dr Cleveland OH 44146-3075 Office: John F Kennedy High Sch 17100 Harvard Ave Cleveland OH 44128-2214

NICKISCH, WILLARD WAYNE, funeral director; b. Bismarck, N.D., July 23, 1939; s. Elmo and Frieda (Moser) N.; m. Eileen Lawlar, June 12, 1993; children: Daphne D., Dirk D. AA, Cin. Coll. of Mortuary Sci., 1959. Lic. mortician, N.D., S.D., Minn. Mortician, funeral dir. Nickisch Funeral Home, Wishek, N.D., 1960-72; funeral dir., pres. Nickisch-Ressler Funeral Home, Bismarck, N.D., 1972-91, Boelter Funeral Home, Bismarck, 1981-91; regional sales mgr. United Family Life Ins., St. Charles, Mo., 1991—. Mem. lay bd. St. Alexius Med. Ctr., Bismarck, 1976-91, pres. 1984; pres. S.W. region Luth. Social Svcs. N.D., 1987-91. Mem. N.D. Funeral Dirs. Assn. (pres. 1978-79), Nat. Funeral Dirs. Assn. (dist. gov. 1980-83), Nat. Selected Morticians, Luth. Brotherhood (publicity counselor Bismarck br. 1986-88), Bismarck State Coll. Found. Bd., Masons, Shriners (pres. Mo. orgn. 1988-89), Kiwanis. Republican. Lutheran. Home: 2840 La Brea Dr Saint Charles MO 63303-9008

NICKLAS, F. WILLIAM, city official; b. Pitts., Oct. 30, 1948; s. Floyd William and Janet Louise (Felker) N.; m. Karen Combs, Feb. 15, 1972 (div. 1976). BA, Bucknell U., 1970; MA, No. Ill. U., 1973, PhD, 1983. Counselor Ben Gordon Ctr., DeKalb, Ill., 1971-75; pvt. builder DeKalb, 1976-86; instr. No. Ill. U., DeKalb, 1985-86; dir. bldg. and cmty. svcs. City of DeKalb, 1986-91, city mgr., 1992—; plant mgr. resource mgmt. City of Plainfield, Ill., 1991-92; mem. exec. com. DeKalb (Ill.) County Econ. Devel. Corp., 1992—. Mem. exec. com. Bus. and Industry of No. Ill. U., DeKalb, 1993—; active No. Ill. U. Found., 1994—. Named Vol. of Yr., DeKalb Spl. Agys., 1990. Mem. Internat. City Mgmt. Assn., Ill. Mcpl. League, Internat. Brotherhood of Carpenters. Presbyterian. Home: 3 Meadow Trl De Kalb IL 60115 Office: City of DeKalb 200 S 4th St De Kalb IL 60115

NICKLAUS, MATT P., manufacturing engineer; b. St. Paul. BS in Mfg. Engring., St. Cloud State U., 1986. Mfg. engr. tech. Lee Data, Eden Prairie, Minn., 1987-89; mfg. engr. FSI Internat., Chaska, Minn., 1990—. Mem. SME. Republican. Office: FSI Internat MS2-1369 322 Lake Hazeltine Dr Chaska MN 55318-1034

NICOLAY, JANICE, state legislator; b. Watertown, S.D.; m. Jerry Nicolay. MEd, S.D. State U. Mem. S.D. Ho. of Reps., 1983—; chair appropriations com., pub. sch. adminstr.; bd. dirs. 1st Bank S.D. Mem. United Way. Recipient Leadership award YWCA. Mem. Nat. Edn. Assn., S.D. Edn. Assn. Republican. Home: 1401 S Suburban Dr Sioux Falls SD 57103-3762 Office: SD House of Reps Office of House Mems Pierre SD 57501

NIDETZ, MYRON PHILIP, health care delivery systems consultant, medical administrator ; b. Chgo., Dec. 29, 1935; s. David J. and Rose Y. (Yudell) N.; B.S., U. Ill., 1958; M.B.C., Hamilton Inst., Phila., 1972; M.P.A., Roosevelt U., 1981. Diplomate Am. Acad. Med. Adminstrs.; m. Linda Freeman, Dec. 18, 1960; children: Julia, Allison. Dir., Union Coop. Eye Care Ctr., Chgo., 1961-65; dir. med. adminstrv. svcs. Michael Reese Hosp. and Med. Ctr., Chgo., 1966-75; assoc. dir. program to improve med. care and health svcs. in correctional instns. AMA, 1975-79; exec. dir. North Cen. Dialysis Ctrs., Chgo., 1979-92; pres. Myron P. Nidetz & Assocs., Inc., 1992—; adj. prof. health care adminstrn. Roosevelt U., Chgo., Lewis U., Romeoville, Ill., 1987—; mem., bd. dirs. Renal Network of Ill.; NIC tech. cons. U.S. Dept. Justice, 1978—; bd. govs. Roosevelt Univ., pres. Pub. Adminstrn. Coun., mem. Curriculum Rev. com. Pub. Adminstrn. Active Health Planning Facilities Bd., Ill., Ill. Dept. Pub. Aid, Ill. Dept. Aging; mem. adv. bd. Am. Kidney Fund, chmn. Midwest Core Group, Nat. Kidney Found., Inst. of Medicine, Am. Assn. Retired Persons (Met. Area Satellite Group, State Legis. com., community coord.); sec. bd. dirs. Suburban Area Agy. on Aging. Served with U.S. Army, 1959-60. Fellow Am. Public Health Assn., Royal Soc. Health, Am. Acad. Med. Adminstrs.; mem. AMA, Assn. Hosp. Med. Edn., Nat. Dialysis Assn. (sec.), Am. Assn. Kidney Patients, Nat. Renal Adminstrs. Assn. (govt. affairs com.), Am. Acad. Polit. and Social Sci., Am. Geriatrics Soc., Am. Hosp. Assn., Am. Mgmt. Assn., Inst. of Soc. Ethics and Life Scis., Gerontol. Soc., Assn. Univ. Programs Health Adminstrn., Am. Mgmt. Assn. Home and Office: 14800 Minerva Ave Dolton IL 60419-2321

NIEDER, MICHAEL LOUIS, pediatrician; b. Chgo., May 30, 1956; s. Leonard and Mary Elaine (Shubin) N. BA in Biology, Johns Hopkins U., 1978; MD, U. Ill. Coll. Medicine, 1982. Diplomate Am. Bd. Pediatrics, Am Bd. Pediatrics-Hematology/Oncology. Pediatric resident Children's Meml. Hosp., Chgo., 1982-85, pediatric hematology-oncology fellow, 1985-88; asst. prof. pediatrics Case Western Res. Med. Sch., Cleve., 1988—, vice chmn. pediatrics, 1991—; dir. pediatric bone marrow transplantation Rainbow Babies & Children's Hosp., Cleve., 1990—, dir. residency program in pediatrics, 1995. Recipient Glenn Found. fellowship, 1979. Fellow Am. Acad. Pediatrics; mem. AMA, Ohio State Med. Assn. (del. 1990—), Cleve. Acad. Medicine, Ill. State Med. Soc. (del. 1980-81, 83-84), Alpha Omega Alpha. Office: Rainbow Babies Children's Hosp 2074 Abington Rd Cleveland OH 44106-2602

NIEDERJOHN, RUSSELL JAMES, electrical and computer engineering educator; b. Schenectady, June 13, 1944; s. Russell Kelly and Jeanette Ody (Burnison) N.; m. Susan A Swenson, June 7, 1969; children: Matthew Scott, Jeremy Michael. B.S. in Elec. Engring., U. Mass., Amherst, 1967, M.S. in Elec. Engring., 1968, Ph.D. in Elec. Engring., 1971. Registered profl. engr., Wis. Research asst. elec. engring. dept. U. Mass., Amherst, 1968-71; asst. prof. elec. engring. dept. Marquette U., Milw., 1971-75, assoc. prof., 1975-80, prof. elec. engring. and computer sci., dir. computer sci. and engring., 1980-87, prof., chmn. elec. and computer engring. dept., 1987-94; prof. elec. and computer engring. dept., 1994—; dir. speech and signal processing lab. Marquette U., Milw., 1973—, co-dir. signal processing rsch. ctr., 1991—; cons. William C. Brown Co. Pubs., Dubuque, Iowa, 1981-85, Eaton Corp., Milw., 1978-85, Seaman Nuclear Corp., Milw., 1979-81, 92-93, MacMillan Pubs., Encino, Calif., 1983-86. Contbr. articles to profl. jours. Mem. Milw. Ednl. TV Auction Com., 1978-81. Recipient Dow Outstanding Young Faculty award, 1977, award Western Electric Fund, 1981, Marquette U. Faculty award for teaching excellence, 1988. Fellow IEEE (mem. exec. com. Milw. sect. 1974-75, 76-79, 82-89, treas. 1982-83, sec. 1983-84, vice chmn. 1984-85, chmn. 1985-86, edn. chmn. 1977-80, chmn. nominating com. 1986-87, awards chmn. 1987-89, Meml. award 1979); mem. IEEE Signal Processing Soc., IEEE Computer Soc. (bd. dirs. Milw. chpt. 1981-85), IEEE Ind. Elec. Soc. (adminstrv. com. 1986—, edn. com. 1986-89, soc. chpt. coord. 1989-91, assoc. editor Trans. 1988—, v.p. for confs. 1992, v.p. for pubs. 1993, v.p. adminstrn. 1994-95, pres. 1996—, IEEE Systems, Man and Cybernetics Soc. (bd. dirs. Milw. chpt. 1975-79), Am. Soc. Engring. Edn. (exec. com. North Midwest sect. 1974-89), Acoustical Soc. Am., Milw. Symposium on Automatic Control (program chmn. 1975), Sigma Xi (pres. elect Marquette U. chpt. 1986-87, pres. 1987-88, sci. achievement award 1993), Eta Kappa Nu (C. Holmes MacDonald Outstanding Elec. Engring. Prof. in U.S. 1978, Marquette U. chpt. adv. 1986—, bd. dirs. 1993-95), Tau Beta Pi. Home: 2545 S Brookside Pky New Berlin WI 53151-2907 Office: 1515 W Wisconsin Ave Milwaukee WI 53233-2222

NIEDNER, KATHRYN ELLEN, commerical lender; b. St. Louis, Apr. 15, 1946; d. Frank Bartholdt and Kathryn Dell (Lyon) Niedner. Student, DePauw U., 1964-67; BA, Washington U., St. Louis, 1968; MBA, U. Chgo., 1981. Convention mgr. Internat. Franchise Assn., Washington, D.C., 1970-73; fin. counselor First Nat. Bank Chgo., 1974-76; asst. to officers First Nat. Bank, Chgo., 1976-79, loan officer to asst. v.p.; asst. v.p. Citicorp, (USA), Inc., Chgo., 1982-84; v.p. Citicorp. (USA), Inc., 1984-86; pres. owner Cardinal Cons Group, Inc., Chgo., 1986-92; mgr. acquisitions Capital Mgmt. Ptnrs., Ltd., Skokie, Ill., 1987-90; v.p. pvt. bus. group Continental Bank, Chgo., 1992-94; chief oper. officer Camins & Swarthchild, Inc., Chgo., 1995—; bd. dirs. Chicagoland Enterprise Ctr., 1993—; mem. entrepreneurial svcs. com. MIT Enterprise Forum of Chgo., 1993—. Mem. Budget and Fin. Com. Planned Parenthood, Chgo. 1986-88, dir. Recording for the Blind, Chgo., 1985-87, St. James Cathedral Counseling Ctr., Chgo. 1981-83. Office: Frain Camins & Swartchild 300 W Washington Chicago IL 60606

NIEHAUS, JAMES WILLIAM, accountant; b. Cin., Feb. 16, 1955; s. John William and Marilyn Marie (Burleigh) N.; m. Patricia Ann Walter, July 10, 1982; children: Sean P. Hayes, Kristen Marie, Jonathan William (Jay). BS in Math., Marshall U., 1977; MBA, U. Cin., 1979. CPA, Ohio, Ind. Acct. Arthur Andersen & Co., Cin., 1978-80; sr. tax acct. Coopers & Lybrand, Cin., 1980-84; tax acct. Sohn Dillenburger & Beyer CPA's Inc., Cin., 1984-87; tax supr. Blue & Co., Indpls., 1987-90, tax mgr., 1990—, dir. agribus. taxation, 1993—; sr. tax mgr. Blue & Co., Carmel, Ind., 1994—. Treas. Boy Scouts Am., Monfort Heights, Ohio, 1985. Mem. AICPA (tax com.), Ohio Soc. CPAs, Ind. CPAs Soc. (mem. agribus. com. 1990-93, chmn. 1992-93). Republican. Methodist. Office: Blue & Co LLC 11460 N Meridian St Carmel IN 46032-4530

NIELSEN, CARL HELGE, anesthesiologist; b. Lunde, Denmark, Nov. 5, 1948; came to U.S., 1976; s. Otto Henrik and Anna Marie (Pedersen) N.; m. Marianne Axboe, 1970; children: Christian, Benedicte. MD, U. Copenhagen, 1979. From asst. prof. to assoc. prof. Washington U., St. Louis, 1985—. Office: 660 S Euclid Ave #8054 Saint Louis MO 63110-1010

NIELSEN, GAIL ANN, radiologic technologist; b. Waterloo, Iowa, Mar. 30, 1947; d. Raymond Zack and Marlys Leota (Timmerman) Eikenberry; m. David Harry Nielsen, June 8, 1968; children: Jennifer Lyn, Kristen Michelle. BS Health Care Adminstrn., St. Joseph's Coll., Windham, Maine, 1989. Staff technologist Allen Meml. Hosp., Waterloo, 1967-69, 72-75, supr. vascular imaging, 1973-80, asst. dir. radiology, 1975-84, adminstrv. dir. radiology svcs., 1984-95, adminstrv. coord. radiology, adminstr. managed care, 1995—, mgr. health info. svcs., managed care & quality improvement, 1996—; vol. technologist U.S. Army Hosp., Bremerhaven, Fed. Republic Germany, 1970-71; instr. radiologic tech. edn., Waterloo, 1975—. Vol. ARC, Waterloo, 1986-88, United Way Black Hawk County, 1987-89, Cedar Valley Breast Cancer Awareness Task Force, Waterloo, 1988—. Recipient letter of commendation U.S. Army, 1971. Mem. Am. Soc. Radiologic Technologists (registeres AART 1967, Matt Keilley Meml. award 1990), Am. Healthcare Radiology Adminstrs. (sec. 1988-90, lectr. 1989, nat. stats. chmn. 1989-91, elected chmn. summit on manpower 1992-93, v.p. nat. and midwest region 1991-92, nat. pres. 1994-95, pres. edn. found. 1995-96, fellow 1991—), Health Professions Network (team leader 1995-96), Iowa Soc. Radiologic Technologists (sec. lectr. 1985, pres. N.E. dist. 1976-77, 81-82), Toastmasters (edn. com. Waterloo 1987-88). Lutheran. Office: Allen Meml Hosp 1825 Logan Ave Waterloo IA 50703-1916

NIELSON, JEFFREY D., mechanical engineer; b. Lincoln, Nebr., Oct. 11, 1960. BSME, U. Nebr., 1985, M Engring. Mechanics, 1992. Mech. engr. Martin Marietta Aerospace, Denver, 1986-88, AT&T Network Cable Sys., Omaha, 1988—. Patentee electronic wiring and cable material. Mem. Telephone Pioneers, Sierra Club. Office: AT&T Network Cable Sys PO Box 37000 Omaha NE 68137-9000

NIEMANN, BIRGIE ANN, college official; b. Ainsworth, Nebr., Aug. 28, 1951; d. Ralph Sidney and Norma June (Smith) Collins; m. Michael Victory Houston, Aug. 20, 1971 (div. Dec. 1992); children: John, Mark; m. Scott Thomas Niemann, Dec. 11, 1993. AA in Speech, York Coll., 1971; BA in Communication, Pepperdine U., 1975; MS in Counseling, Calif. State U., 1982. Sec., adminstrv. asst. Pepperdine U., Malibu, Calif., 1971-75; asst. dean of students Pepperdine U., Malibu, 1976; bus. mgr. Wayne-Ferrell, Inc., Iowa City, 1980-82; parent counselor Systems Unlimited Inc., Iowa City, 1982-84; adminstrv. asst. U. Iowa Found., Iowa City, 1984-87; assoc. dean of students Mich. Christian Coll., Rochester Hills, Mich., 1987-89, dean of students, 1989-91; asst. to pres., 21st century advance campaign dir. York (Nebr.) Coll., 1991-94, dir. devel. and pub. rels., 1995—. Contbr. articles to profl. jours. Vol. Drug Free Comty. Task Force, Oakland County, 1989; lectr., guest speaker Ch. of Christ, Calif., Iowa, Ohio, Mich., Nebr., Kans., Mo., Tex., 1976—; bd. dirs. United Way. Mem. York County Writers Guild. Mem. Ch. of Christ. Office: York Coll 9th And Kiplinger York NE 68467

NIEMANN, NICHOLAS KENT, lawyer; b. Quincy, Ill., May 2, 1956; s. Ferd E. and Rita M. (Jochem) N.; m. Ann Marie Forbes, June 14, 1980; children: Katie, Becky, Christine, David, Lisa, Trish. BSBA summa cum laude, Creighton U., 1978, JD magna cum laude, 1981. Bar: Nebr. 1981, U.S. Dist. Ct. Nebr. 1981, U.S. Ct. Appeals (8th cir) 1981, U.S Tax Ct. 1981, U.S. Claims Ct. 1985; CPA, Nebr. Assoc. McGill, Koley, Parsonage & Lanphier, P.C., Omaha, 1981-83; assoc. McGrath, North, Mullin & Kratz, P.C., Omaha, 1983-85, ptnr., 1985—; mem. Nebr. tax rsch. coun., Nebr. tax forum; adj. faculty Creighton Law Sch., Creighton U., 1993—. Mem. AICPA (taxation sect. 1984—), Nebr. Bar Assn., Omaha Bar Assn., (pub. svc. com. 1983-84, Nebr. Soc. CPAs (taxation com. 1983-90, vice chmn. 1987-88, chmn. 1988-89, small bus. com. 1989-92, vice chmn. 1989-90, chmn. 1990-91)), Omaha C. of C. (pres. club. 1986-90, exec. dialogue 1986-93, taxation com. 1988—), Nebr. Tax Forum, Nebr. C. of C. and Industry (taxation coun. 1989—), Kiwanis (membership com. Omaha club 1986), Optimists (bd. dirs. 1987-89), Alpha Sigma Nu (exec. com. 1985—, sec. 1986-87, treas. 1990, pres. 1992), Beta Gamma Sigma. Mem. AICPA (taxation sect. 1984—), ABA (taxation sect. 1984—, corp. banking and bus. law sect. 1986—), Nebr. Bar Assn., Omaha Bar Assn. (pub. svc. com. 1983-84, Nebr. Soc. CPAs (taxation com. 1983—, vice chmn. 1987-88, chmn. 1988-89, small bus. com. 1989—, vice chmn. 1989-90, chmn. 1990-91), Omaha C. of C. (pres. club. 1986-90, exec. dialogue 1986—, taxation com. 1988—), Nebr. Tax Forum, Am. Mgmt. Assn., Nebr. C. of C. and Industry (taxation coun. 1989—), Kiwanis (membership com. Omaha club 1986), Optimists (bd. dirs. 1987-89), Alpha Sigma Nu (exec. com. 1985—, sec. 1986-87, treas. 1990, pres. 1992), Beta Gamma Sigma. Roman Catholic. Home: 1537 N 131st Ave Omaha NE 68154-3619 Office: McGrath North Mullin & Kratz One Central Park Plz Ste 1400 Omaha NE 68102-1675

NIEMOLLER, ARTHUR B., electrical engineer; b. Wakefield, Kans., Oct. 4, 1912; s. Benjamin Henry and Minnie Christine (Carlson) N.; m. Ann Sochor, May 29, 1937 (dec. June 1982); children: Joanna Matteson, Arthur D. BSEE, Kans. State U., 1933. Registered profl. engr., N.Y., N.J., Pa., Ill., Ohio. Engr. Westinghouse, Newark, N.J., 1937-48, Hillside, N.J., 1948-59, Chgo., 1959-61, Pitts., 1961-65, Cin., 1965-77; pvt. practice engr. Montgomery, Ohio, 1977—. Patentee in field. Elder Presbyterian Church. Served with USN, 1933-37. Mem. AAAS, IEEE, NSPE, N.Y. Acad. Scis. Republican. Home and Office: 13 Arnold Dr Foxboro MA 02035-3014

NIENHOUSE, LAURENCE JAY, secondary education educator; b. Chgo., May 14, 1948; s. Clarence and Ruth Marie (Brinkman) N.; m. Caryn Ann Schmidt, July 23, 1983; children: Vanessa, Kyle. BS in Engring., U. Ill., Chgo., 1972, MS in Math., 1978. Math. instr. H.S. Dist. 211, Ill., 1972—.

NIENKE, STEVEN A., construction company executive; b. 1950. Carpenter Halsey Tevis, Wichita, Kans., 1970-72; pres. Midwest Drywall Co. Inc., Wichita, Kans., 1972—. Office: Midwest Drywall Co Inc 1351 S Reca St Wichita KS 67209*

NIERSTE, JOSEPH PAUL, software engineer; b. Marion, Ind., Feb. 20, 1952; s. Louis Lemuel and Mary Catherine (Dragstrem) N.; m. Deborah Mae Goble, Sept. 20, 1986. BA Applied Piano, Bob Jones U., 1975; MM in Musical Performance, Ball State U., 1977, MS in Computer Sci., 1984. Instr. Marion Coll., 1983-84, Ball State U., Muncie, Ind., 1983-84; software engr. Tokheim Corp., Ft. Wayne, Ind., 1984, Delco Electronics, Kokomo, Ind., 1984—. Mem. Pi Kappa Lambda. Republican. Baptist. Home: 3508 Melody Ln W Kokomo IN 46902-7514 Office: Delco Electronics Corp CT-40-C Kokomo IN 46902

NIEUWSMA, MILTON JOHN, newspaper syndicate executive; b. Sioux Falls, S.D., Sept. 5, 1941; s. John and Jean (Potter) N.; BA, Hope Coll., Holland, Mich., 1963; postgrad. Wayne State U., 1963-65; MA, Sangamon State U., 1978; m. Marilee Gordon, Feb. 1, 1964; children: Jonathan, Gregory, Elizabeth. Public info. officer Wayne State U., Detroit, 1963-69; pub. rels. dir. Sinai Hosp., Detroit, 1969-72; dir. div. officer svcs. Am. Hosp. Assn., Chgo., 1972-73; asst. prof. journalism Wayne State U., Detroit, 1974; dir. pub. rels. and devel. Meml. Med. Ctr., Springfield, Ill., 1975-79; v.p. for pub. affairs Grant Hosp., Chgo., 1979-87; v.p. devel., 1987-88; pres. Trans Am. Syndicate, Inc., Chgo., 1988—; vis. prof. Rutgers U., New Brunswick, N.J., 1990-95, St. Xavier U., Chgo., 1996—. Governing mem. Chgo. Zool. Soc., 1981—; bd. dirs. Springfield (Ill.) Boys Clubs, 1979-80, Sangamon County Heart Assn., 1978-80; campaign chmn. Riverside Community Fund (Ill.), 1986; pub. rels. chmn. Sangamon County Heart Fund Campaign, 1978; pres. Ford Com., 1975-76; bd. dirs. United Meth. Housing Corp., Detroit, 1968-70; pres. Riverside-Brookfield Edn. Found., 1987-90; chmn. Sch. Dist. 205 Caucus, 1983-89; mem. exec. com. Village Riverside, 1986-90. Mem. Pub. Rels. Soc. Am., Lincoln Park C. of C. (bd. dirs.). Contbr. articles in field to profl. jours. Home: 322 Scottswood Rd Riverside IL 60546-2226

NIGH, JAY JACKSON CASEY, investment analyst; b. Omaha, Jan. 21, 1965; s. Leon Jackson and Norma Jean (Proplesch) N. BS, U. Nebr., Kearney, 1987; MBA, U. Nebr., Omaha, 1991. Chartered fin. analyst; registered rep.; registered gen. prin.; registered options prin.; registered mcpl. prin. Mgmt. trainee, rep. First Investors Corp., Omaha, 1987-88; sr./investment analyst Securities Am., Inc., Omaha, 1989-95; chief portfolio mgr. Maestro Investment Mgmt., Omaha, 1994-95; CFO, treas. Calif. Med. Transport, Mountain View, Calif., 1994—; sr. fin. specialist No. Plains Natural Gas Co., Omaha, 1995—; reg. rep. Securities Am., Inc., Omaha, 1995—; rsch. coord. econs. dept. U. Nebr., Kearney, 1985-86; fin. advisor Omaha Cath. Archdiocese TSA Com., Omaha, 1992—. Mem. socially responsible investment task force Omaha Cath. Archdiocese, 1993-95. U. Nebr. at Kearney Coop. scholar, 1983-87; Beta Sigma Psi Edn. Found. scholar, 1986. Mem. Nat. Assn. Securities Dealers, Internat. Soc. Fin.

Analysts, Assn. for Investment Mgmt. and Rsch., Omaha/Lincoln Soc. Fin. Analysts, Inter Frat. Coun., Inst. Mgmt. Accts., Beta Sigma Psi (treas., pres. chpt.). Republican. Lutheran. Office: No Plains Natural Gas Co PO Box 3330 Omaha NE 68103-0330

NIGHORN, SHARON KAY, nurse educator, psychotherapist; b. Chgo., Mar. 21, 1956; d. Richard Louis and Catherine Nighorn. AA, AAS, Harper Coll., 1975; BS in Nursing, No. Ill. U., 1977; MS, U. Ill. Med. Ctr., 1980; Psy.D., Chgo. Sch. Profl. Psychology, 1995. Cert. clin. specialist in adult psychiat.-mental health; cert. substance abuse counselor. Staff nurse N.W. Community Hosp., Arlington Heights, Ill., 1975-77, Ill. State Psychiat. Inst., Chgo., 1977-80; supervising nurse Barclay Hosp., Chgo.; staff nurse Northwestern Meml. Hosp., Chgo., asst. head nurse, 1980-85; clin. mgr. Weiss Hosp. Lifeline Program, Chgo., 1985-86; instr., practitioner, tchr. Rush Presbyn. St. Luke's, Chgo., 1986-96; psychotherapist, group and ind. practice Evanston, 1987—; psychology intern Forest Hosp., Des Plaines, Ill., 1992-96; pres. bd. dirs. Ill. Peer Assistance Network for Nurses Found. Contbr. articles to profl. jours. Mem. ANA, Ill. Nurses Assn., Nat. Nurses Soc. on Addiction. Office: Forest Hosp 555 Wilson Ln Des Plaines IL 60016-4729

NIGHTINGALE, EDMUND JOSEPH, clinical psychologist, educator; b. St. Paul, Jan. 10, 1941; s. Edmund Anthony and Lauretta Alexandria (Horejs) N.; m. Marie Arcara, Apr. 9, 1978 (dec. April 1992); 1 child, Edmund Bernard. Student, Nazareth Hall Prep. Sem., 1959-61; AB, St. Paul Sem., 1963; AB magna cum laude, Catholic U. of Louvain (Belgium), 1965, MA, 1967, S.T.B. cum laude, 1967; postgrad. U. Minn., 1971; MA, Loyola U., Chgo., 1973, PhD in Clin. Psychology, 1975. Lic. clin. psychologist, Ill., Minn.; cert. Nat. Registry of Health Svc. Providers in Psychology. With Cath. Archdiocese of St. Paul and Mpls., 1967-73; intern in clin. psychology Michael Reese Hosp. and Med. Ctr., Chgo., 1973-74, W. Side VA Hosp., Chgo., 1974-75; staff psychologist, student counseling ctr., Loyola U., Chgo., 1975; staff psychologist and clin. coordinator of inpatient unit, drug dependency treatment ctr. Hines (Ill.) VA Hosp., 1975-79, acting chief drug dependency treatment ctr., 1979-80; chief psychology VA Med. Ctr., Danville, Ill., 1980-86; chief psychology VA Med. Ctr. Mpls., 1986—; mem. personnel bd. Archdiocese of St. Paul and Mpls., 1968-70; lectr. psychology, Loyola U., Chgo., 1975; asst. professorial lectr. psychology, St. Xavier Coll., Chgo., 1975-78; adj. asst. prof. psychology in psychiatry, Abraham Lincoln Sch. Medicine, Med. Ctr. U. Ill., Chgo., 1977-82; adj. prof. psychology Purdue U., 1981-87; asst. prof. psychiatry Med. Sch., U. Minn., 1987—, clin. assoc. prof. psycholgy Coll. Liberal Arts, 1986-90, adj. asst. prof., 1990—; clin. asst. prof. U. Ill. Sch. Medicine, Urbana/Champaign, 1982-87; mem. grad. faculty in counseling psychology Ind. State U., Terre Haute, 1983-86. Bd. dirs. Inst. Postgrad. Studies, Ill. Psychol. Assn. Mem. APA (clin. psychology, pub. svc., psychol. hypnosis, sec. treas. pub. svc. 1990-91), Ill. Psychol. Assn. (clin. psychology and acad. sects.; sec. 1982-83, pres.-elect 1983-84, pres. 1984-85), AAAS, Am. Group Psychotherapy Assn., Am. Soc. Clin. Hypnosis, Minn. Psychol. Assn., Am. Evaluation Assn., Am. Assn. Univ. Profs., Assn. VA chief Psychologists (sec., treas. 1987-90, pres.-elect 1990-91, pres. 1991-92, past pres. 1992-93). Founding editor: Louvain Studies, 1966; editor: VA Directory of Psychology Staffing and Services, 1982, 83, 84, 85, 87. Recipient Outstanding Leadership award Ass. VA Chief Psychologists, 1992. Home: 2281 Ocala Ct Mendota Hts MN 55120-1646 Office: VA Med Ctr Minneapolis MN 55417

NIKIFORUK, MICHAEL, product engineer, educator; b. Warren, Mich., June 17, 1970; s. Terry and Nadia (Pinczuk) N. BEE, U. Detroit, 1992, postgrad., 1993—. Plant engr. General Motors, Detroit, 1990-92; adj. prof. U. Detroit, Detroit, 1995—; product engr. Ford Motor Co., Dearborn, Mich., 1992—. Contbr. article to profl. jours. Named Nat. Dean's List Ednl. Communications Inc., 1992-93. Mem. IEEE. Office: Ford Motor Co MD 5034 Bldg 5 P O Box 2053 Dearborn MI 48121

NIKOLAI, CHRISTOPHER MARK, electronic engineer; b. Wausau, Wis., Sept. 17, 1958; s. Lawrence Leo and Gail Delois (Sillars) N.; m. Jill Ann Wagner, Apr. 8, 1978 (div. May 1988); children: Sarah Elizabeth, Stephanie Ann; m. Tina Lee Tetzlaff, Aug. 8, 1990; children: Chelsea Marie Clark, Christopher Lawrence Nikolai. AD in Electronics, NTC, Wausau, Wis., 1988; student, UWMC, Wausau, Wis., 1993-94. Asst. mgr. Angelos Pizza Villa, Wausau, Wis., 1975-87; engring. technician Marathon Elec. Mfg. Corp., Wausau, Wis., 1987-93; owner, operator CTA Video Transfer Svcs., Wausau, Wis., 1993—; assoc. engr. Marathon Elec. Mfg. Corp., Wausau, Wis., 1993—. Sch. bd. mem. Wausau Sch. Dist., 1994—, grade sch. restructuring com., 1993-94. Home: 1423 Cherry St Wausau WI 54401

NIKOLAI, ROBERT JOSEPH, dean, biomechanics in orthodontics educator; b. Rock Island, Ill., Apr. 6, 1937; s. Joseph Lawrence and Martha Marie (Holt) N.; m. Susan Eloise Shannon, June 10, 1961; children: Catherine, Teresa, Margaret, David, Philip. BSME, U. Ill., Urbana-Champaign, 1959; MS, U. Ill., 1961, PhD, 1964. Registered profl. engr., Mo. Teaching asst., instr., rsch. assoc. dept. theoretical and applied mechanics U. Ill., Urbana, 1959-64; asst. prof. engring. Saint Louis U., 1964-68, assoc. prof. dept. engring. mechanics, orthodontics, 1968-75, prof. biomechanics dept. orthodontics, 1975—, assoc. grad. dean, 1972-87, 88—, acting grad. dean, 1987-88, univ. marshal, 1989—; presenter in field at nat. and internat. meetings, 1975—. Author: Bioengineering Analysis of Orthodontic Mechanics; contbr. Am. Jour. Orthodontics and Dentofacial Orthopedics, Jour. Biomechanics, Jour. Dental Rsch., The Angle Orthodontist, Jour. Applied Mechanics, Dental Materials; manuscript referee various profl. jours., 1976—. Grantee Nat. Inst. Dental Rsch., 1984, 85, 87, grantee Am. Assn. Orthodontists Found., 1996. Mem. ADA (orthodontic wire com. 1983), Am. Acad. Mechanics, Internat. Assn. Dental Rsch., Orthodontic Edn. and Rsch. Found. (grantee 1980, 86, 91), Assn. Cath. Grad. Deans (sec.-treas. 1988—), Pi Tau Sigma, Sigma Xi (pres. Saint Louis U. chpt. 1993-95, past pres. 1995—). Roman Catholic. Home: 7134 Stanford Ave Saint Louis MO 63130-2335

NIKOLICH, MICHEL MIRO, retired secondary education educator; b. Gary, Ind., Mar. 16, 1938; s. Miroslav and Helen (Bicanic) N.; m. Jacie Kathryn Hedges, June 15, 1939; children: Kevin Lee, Rick Gene. BS in History, Ind. State U., 1960, MS in Phys. Edn., 1967. Life lic. in edn., Ind. Tchr., coach Switz City (Ind.) Sch. Dist., 1960-61, LaCrosse (Ind.) H.S., 1961-63, Knox (Ind.) H.S., 1963-65, Crown Point (Ind.) H.S., 1965-94; ret., 1994; sch. bd. mem. Crown Point (Ind.) Cmty. Schs., 1994—; operator, mgr. Michel's, Crown Point, 1965—; mem. devel. com. N.W. Career Ctr., Crown Point, 1971-94; seminar conductor in field; designer, initiator Crown Point H.S. Automotive and Welding work areas; tchr. welding classes Adult Night Sch., 1966-70. Contbr. articles to profl. jours. Pledge drive mem. St. Anthony's Med. Ctr., Crown Point; spearheaded dedication of Russ Keller Athletic Ctr., Crown Point, 1992; bd. dirs. Ind. State Sch. Bd. Assn., 1994—; mem. Rep. Club, Crown Point, 1995—. Mem. NEA, Ind. State Tchrs. Assn., Ind. Indsl. Edn. Assn., Nat. Antique Oldsmobile Club, Oldsmobile Club of Am.,, Ind. High Sch. Athletic Assn. (basketball ofcl. 1962-65). Republican. Baptist. Home: 10711 Porter St Crown Point IN 46307

NIKOUI, HOSSEIN REZA, quality assurance professional; b. Tehran, Iran, Feb. 4, 1949; came to U.S., 1977; s. Gholam Reza and Monireh (Jahanshahi) N.; m. Niki Forouzi, Oct. 25, 1983; children: Neda Lili, Amir Reza. BS in Chem. Engring., Arya-Mehr Univ., Tehran, 1971; Diploma in Ops. Rsch., U. Toronto, 1981; cert. in quality assurance, Ryerson Univ., Toronto, 1983. Registered profl. engr.; cert. quality engr., cert. quality auditor, cert. quality systems lead auditor, cert. quality mgr. Quality engr. Gen. Motors, Tehran, 1971-72, supt. supplier quality assurance, 1973-74, mgr. quality assurance, 1975-78; resident materials mgr. Gen. Motors, Oshawa, Ont., Can., 1978-79; mgr. quality control G.S. Woolley, Toronto, 1979-82, mgr. quality assurance, 1982-85; dir. corp. quality assurance The Progressive/Woolley Group, Toronto, 1985-88, Manchester Plastics, Troy, Mich., 1988—; instr. Centenial Coll., Toronto, 1984-88; cons. Can. Post Corp., Toronto, 1985-86. Author numerous manuals, guides and articles in field. Fellow Am. Soc. for Quality Control; mem. ASTM, Soc. Plastic Engrs., Am. Inst. Indsl. Engrs., Soc. Automotive Engrs., Engring. Soc. Detroit, Inst. of Quality Assurance. Home: 8275 Fawn Valley Dr Clarkston MI 48348-4545 Office: Manchester Plastics 201 W Big Beaver Rd Ste 1040 Troy MI 48084-4154

NIMS, DICK K., designer; b. Milw., May 19, 1936. Designer All States Design, Milw., 1965-73, Oligear Co., Milw., 1973—. Sgt. U.S. Army, 1958-50. Roman Catholic. Home: 5815 S 31st St Milwaukee WI 53221-4137 Office: Oligear Co 2300 S 51st St Milwaukee WI 53219-2340

NINDRA, BEANT SINGH, electrical engineer; b. La Hore, India, Dec. 25, 1938; came to U.S., 1974; B of Engring. with honors, Govt. Engring. coll., Jabalpur, India, 1962. Registered profl. engr., Ohio. Design engr., section head Bhel Ltd.,, Bhopal, India, 1962-74; mgr. of engring. Nat. Electric Coil, Columbus, Ohio, 1975—. Mem. IEEE (sr.). Sikh. Office: Nat Electric Coil 800 King Ave Columbus OH 43212-2644

NISSEL, MARK EDWARD, software engineer; b. Akron, Ohio, July 31, 1962; s. Floyd Dale and Patricia Lee (Michaels) N.; m. Julie Collett Heimlich, Feb. 5, 1984 (div. June 1988); children: Karyn Nancy, Kristine Patricia; m. Karen Ruth Johnson, May 25, 1990; children: Kenneth Jordan, Cheryl Lynn, Paige Alyson, Alexandra Ryan. BSEE, U. Akron, 1989. Software engr. Steelastic, Akron, 1989-92, Facts Inc., Cuyahoga Falls, Ohio, 1992-94; sr. software engr. Measurex, Cin., 1994—; artificial intelligence cons. RTAI, Cuyahoga Falls, 1991—. Author software, articles in field. With USN, 1984-88. Mem. IEEE. Home: 8275 Fox Knoll Ct West Chester OH 45069-2895 Office: Measurex 1280 Keamper Meadow Dr Cincinnati OH 45240

NISSEN, BART ALAN, systems analyst; b. Colorado Springs, Colo., June 8, 1960; s. Charles LaVern N. and Barbara Ann (Kirk) Poldervaart; m. Kathryn Jean Rosendahl, Dec. 22, 1979 (div. Jan. 1985); children: Erika Jean, Brett Alan, Sydney Rae; m. Jordana Lee Kurtzman, May 23, 1993; 1 child, Aaron Nathan. AA in Computer Sci., Coll. of Air Force, 1987; BS in Computer Info. Systems, Bellevue U., 1995. Tech. specialist Honeywell Fed. Systems, Omaha, 1988-95; computer cons. Bass & Assocs., Omaha, 1995-96; v.p. Exec. Consulting Group, Inc., 1996—; cons. Mutual of Omaha, 1995-96. Staff sgt. USAF, 1979-88. Republican. Office: Exec Consulting Group Inc 8031 W Center Rd Ste 203 Omaha NE 68124

NISWANDER, IRVIN F. (BUD), manufacturing engineer; b. Fostoria, Ohio, May 29, 1935. Mfg. engr. Cummins Engine Co., Jamestown, N.Y., 1983-85, Fostoria, Ohio, 1955-83; mgr. mfg. engring. Atlas Industries, Gibsonburg, Ohio, 1985—. Vol. YMCA, Fostoria, Ohio, 1972—. Mem. SME. Office: Atlas Industries Country Rd 42 Gibsonburg OH 43431

NITSCHE, JOHANNES CARL CHRISTIAN, mathematics educator; b. Olbernhau, Germany, Jan. 22, 1925; came to U.S., 1956; s. Ludwig Johannes and Irma (Raecke) N.; m. Carmen Dolores Mercado Delgado, July 1, 1959; children: Carmen Irma, Johannes Marcos and Ludwig Carlos (twins). Diplom für Mathematik, U. Göttingen, 1950; PhD, U. Leipzig, 1951; Privatdozent, Tech. U. Berlin, 1955. Asst. U. Göttingen, 1948-50; rsch. mathematician Max Planck Institut für Strömungsforschung Göttingen, 1950-52; asst. Privatdozent Tech. U., Berlin, 1952-56; vis. assoc. prof. U. Cin., 1956-57; assoc. prof. U. Minn., Mpls., 1957-60; prof. math. U. Minn., 1960—, head Sch. Math., 1971-78; vis. prof. U. P.R., 1960-61, U. Hamburg, 1965, Tech. Hochschule Vienna, 1968, U. Bonn, 1971, 75, 77, 80, 81, U. Heidelberg, 1979, 82, 83, U. Munich, 1983, U. Florence, 1983; keynote speaker Festive Colloquium, U. Ulm, 1986; co-organizer workshop statis. thermodynamics and differential geometry U. Minn., 1991; keynote speaker Meml. Colloquium Tech. U. Berlin, 1991, speaker Internat. Workshop on Geometry and Interfaces, Aussois, France, 1990. Author: Vorlesungen uber Minimalflachen, Springer-Verlag, 1975, Lectures on Minimal Surfaces, 1989; mem. editorial bd. Archive of Rational Mechanics and Analysis, 1967-91; editor: Analysis, 1980—; assoc. editor: Contemporary Math., 1980-88, Zeitschrift für Analysis und ihre Anwendungen, 1993—; contbr. articles to profl. jours. Mem. Am. del. joint Soviet-Am. Symposium on Partial Differential Equations, Novosibirsk, 1963, U.S.-Japan Seminar on Differential Geometry, Tokyo, 1977; speaker 750th Berlin Anniversary Colloquium, Free U. Berlin, 1987. Recipient Lester R. Ford award for outstanding expository writing, 1975, George Taylor Disting. Svc. award U. Minn. Found., 1980, Humboldt prize for sr. U.S. scientists Alexander von Humboldt Found., 1981; Fulbright rsch. fellow Stanford, 1955-56. Fellow AAAS; mem. Am. Math. Soc., Circolo Matematico di Palermo, Deutsche Mathematiker-Vereinigung, Edinburgh Math. Soc., Gesellschaft für Angewandte Mathematik und Mechanik, Math. Assn. Am., N.Y. Acad. Scis., Österreichische Mathematische Gesellschaft, Soc. Natural Philosophy. Home: 2765 Dean Pky Minneapolis MN 55416-4382

NITSCHKE, SHAUN MICHAEL, bank professional; b. Toledo, Aug. 29, 1966; s. Michael Walter Nitschke and Cynthia Alice (Tussing) Davis; m. Nicole Kathleen Huegel, Feb. 9, 1991. AA, U. Toledo, 1994. Mil. policeman U.S. Army, 1984-88; security supervisor Continental Security, Toledo, 1988-89; br. customer svc. rep. II Nat. City Bank, Toledo, 1989-95; br. customer svc. rep. III Nat. City Bank NW, Toledo, 1995-96, sr. platform, 1996—; student advisor U. Toledo Legal Assisting Adv. Com., 1993. Recipient achievement medals U.S. Army, 1985, 88, good conduct medal, 1988. Mem. Non-Commissioned Officers Assn., Am. Legion. Lutheran. Home: 1478 Sabra Rd Toledo OH 43612 Office: Nat City Bank 4210 Sylvania Ave Toledo OH 43623

NITTERHOUSE, DENISE, accountant, business educator, consultant; b. Chambersburg, Pa., Jan. 11, 1950; d. Theodore Karper and Nellie Elizabeth (Bent) N. BA, Duke U., 1971; MBA, Harvard U., 1977, D in Bus. Adminstrn., 1981. Staff acct. Haskins & Sells, CPA's, New Haven, 1971-74; acct. Planned Parenthood League Conn., New Haven, 1974-75; instr. Kennedy Sch. Govt. Harvard U., 1978; asst. prof. U. Ill., Champaign, 1981-85; asst. prof. DePaul U., Chgo., 1985-89, assoc. prof., 1989—, head MIS group, 1991-92; adj. faculty U. New Haven, 1974-75; cons., speaker, 1974—; sr. rsch. fellow Harvard U., 1990-91. Pub. book; contbr. articles and chpts. to book. Treas., bd. dirs. A Woman's Fund, Inc., Urbana, Ill., 1982-85. Doctoral fellow Haskins & Sells Found., 1977, Am. Acctg. Assn., 1979, thesis fellow Harvard U., 1980; named Celebration of Feminism honoree NOW, 1984. Mem. Am. Acctg. Assn. (acctg. behavior and orgns. sect., Midwest regional coord. 1985-86, working paper series coord. 1984-85, Midwest region steering com. 1989-91). Home: 2633 N Emmett St Chicago IL 60647-1511 Office: DePaul U Sch Accountancy 1 E Jackson Blvd Chicago IL 60604-2201

NIVEN, NORMA JEAN, artist; b. Silverwood, Mich., Oct. 31, 1924; d. Joseph and Mary (Mott) Sian; m. Robert N. Niven, Oct. 16, 1943; children: Robert W., Martha J., David M., Dennis A., Rosemary S. Student, Delta Coll. Instr. Saginaw (Mich.) Valley Rehab., 1970's-80's; entertainer Clown Ministry, Saginaw, 1980's-90's, Flint, Mich., 1988-94; asst. mgr. Action Thrift Store, Saginaw, 1988-89. Author: Gloria and Her Adventures, 1995. Libr. Our Saviour Ch., Saginaw, 1988-95; vol. Am. Legion Aux., Saginaw, 1989—, VFW Aux., Saginaw, 1980—, WWI Aux., Saginaw, 1994; vol. Bethesda Thrift Store, Saginaw, Mich. Lutheran. Home: 1600 N Center Rd Saginaw MI 48603

NIX, ROBERT ROYAL, II, lawyer; b. Detroit, Mar. 27, 1947; s. Robert R. and Betty Virginia (Karicofe) N.; m. Suzanne Martha Turner, July 11, 1970; children: Christian Michael, Heather Michele. BS, Ea. Mich. U., 1968; JD cum laude, Wayne State U., 1971. Bar: Mich. 1971, U.S. Dist. Ct. (ea. dist.) Mich. 1971, U.S. Ct. Appeals (6th cir.) 1976. Rsch. atty. Mich. Ct. Appeals, Lansing, 1971-72; law clk. to Hon. Charles L. Levin Mich. Ct. Appeals, 1971; law clk. to Hon S. Jerome Bronson Mich. Ct. Appeals, Detroit, 1972-73; ptnr. Kerr, Russell and Weber, Detroit, 1973—; lectr. in field. Contrb. articles to Michigan Real Property Law Review. Mem. ABA (partnership com. real property, probate and trust law sect., mortgages and secured financing com. corp., banking and bus. law sect., forum constrn. industry sect.), State Bar Mich. (chmn. real property law sect. 1994-95, coun. vice chmn. 1992-93, chmn. com. on mortgage related financing devices, 1984-87, mem. sect., 1973—, partnership com. 1982—), Oakland County Bar Assn., Detroit Bar Assn., Am. Coll. Real Estate Lawyers. Republican. Methodist. Office: Kerr Russell and Weber Detroit Ctr Ste 2500 Detroit MI 48226

NIX, TAMMY MICHELLE, medical records administrator; b. Hannibal, Mo., May 22, 1966; d. Samuel Nealy Latta and Mary Christine (Thompson) Harper; 1 child, Abbey Danielle Reed; m. David L. Nix, Sept. 10, 1994; 1 child, Haylee Noel. Asst. patient accounts mgr. Hannibal Clinic, 1986—. Fundraiser Am. Cancer Soc., 1990-95; chmn. Nat. Tom Sawyer Days Fireworks, 1991, 92. Named to Outstanding Young Women of Am., 1991. Mem. Palmyra Jaycees (treas. 1994-96). Lutheran. Home: 416 W Jefferson Palmyra MO 63461-9652 Office: Hannibal Clinic 711 Grand Ave Hannibal MO 63401-3179

NIXON, CURTIS D., marketing executive; b. Detroit, May 22, 1948. BS, Spring Arbor Coll., 1991. Sales engr. Tektronix, Farmington Hills, Mich., 1988-92; regional sales mgr. Kinetic Systems, Lockport, Ill., 1992-93; mktg. mgr. GM Hughes, Troy, Mich., 1993—. Vol. Farmington Area Philharmonic. With USN, 1969-73.

NIXON, DAVID W., financial services executive, business analyst; b. Pitts., Jan. 24, 1955; s. Donald Ellsworth and Elizabeth Joan (Hanley) N.; m. Kathryn Elizabeth Kirkman, June 26, 1976; children: Matthew David, Jonathan David. BA in Speech Comms., Calif. U. Pa., 1976. Asst. to pres. Pram, Inc., Wilmerding, Pa., 1976-79; svc. rep. Am. Funeral Computer Svc., Springfield, Ill., 1979-81; sr. sales rep. AM, Pitts., 1981-83; dir. field svcs. Am. Funeral Computer Svc., Springfield, Ill., 1983-87; v.p. mgmt. svcs. Funeral Mgmt. Svcs., Inc., Springfield, 1987—; mem. exhibit adv. com. Nat. Funeral Dirs. Assn., 1995—. Contbr. articles to profl. jours. Mem. Am. Mgmt. Assn. Office: Funeral Mgmt Svc Inc 107 W Cook Springfield IL 62704

NIXON, JEREMIAH W. (JAY NIXON), state attorney general; b. DeSoto, Mo., Feb. 13, 1956; s. Jeremiah and Betty (Lea) N.; m. Georganne Nixon; children: Jeremiah, Will. BS in Polit. Sci., U. Mo., 1978, JD, 1981. Ptnr. Nixon, Nixon, Breeze & Roberts, Jefferson County, Mo., 1981-86; mem. Mo. State Senate from Dist 22, 1986-93; atty. gen. State of Mo., 1993—; chmn. select com. ins. reform.; created video internat. devel. and edn. opportunity program. Honoree, Conservation Fedn. Mo., 1992; named Outstanding Young Missourian, Mo. Jaycees, 1994, Outstanding Young Lawyer, Barrister's Mag., 1993. Mem. Nat. Assn. Attys. Gen. (antitrust com., chair FTC working group, criminal law com., consumer protection com.), Midwest Assn. Attys. Gen. (chmn.), Mo. Assn. Trial Attys. Democrat. Methodist. Office: Atty Gen Office PO Box 899 Jefferson City MO 65102-0899

NOBLE, ALLEN GEORGE, geography and planning educator; b. Astoria, N.Y., Jan. 28, 1930; s. Chauncey Helmer and Mary Oliver (Van Allen) N.; m. Jane Sylvia Walter, June 27, 1959; children: Lisa, Matthew, Douglas. BA, Utica Coll., 1951; MA, U. Md., 1953; PhD, U. Ill., 1957. Joined Fgn. Svc., 1957, resigned, 1963; assoc. prof. geography California (Pa.) State Coll., 1963-64; prof. geography and planning U. Akron, Ohio, 1964—. Author: Wood Brick & Stone, 1984; co-author: The Old Barn Book, 1995; editor: To Build in a New Land, 1992 (Kniffen prize 1995); co-editor: Barns of the Midwest, 1995. Fulbright scholar U. Peradeniya, Sri Lanka, 1979. Mem. Am. Geog. Soc., Can. Geog. Assn., Assn. Am. Geographers (Honors award 1989), Ohio Acad. Sci. (pres. 1989-90, Centennial Honoree 1991), Pioneer Am. Soc. (exec. dir. 1977-86), Sigma Xi. Office: Dept Geography and Planning U Akron Akron OH 44325-5005

NOBLE, ROBERT B., advertising executive; b. 1945. BFA, Southwest Mo. State U. With Batz, Hodgson & Nevwoehner Advt. Agy., St. Louis, 1965-69; with Noble & Assocs., Springfield, Mo., 1969—, now pres., CEO. Office: Noble & Assocs 336 S Barnes Ave Springfield MO 65802*

NOBLES, JAMES L., marketing and sales executive; b. Savannah, Ga., Aug. 15, 1938; s. Lee A. and Adele M. (White) N.; m. Dolores Offutt, Feb. 15, 1976 (div. Jan. 1980); 1 child, Elizabeth Melissa; m. Cheri A. Nobles, Nov. 26, 1982; children: Michelle Kathleen, Julie Adele. BSBA, CUNY, 1963. Mgr. Medicare "B" ops. Group Health Ins., Inc., N.Y.C., 1967-70; asst. to adminstr. dist. coun. 37, health and security plan AFSCME AFL/CIO, N.Y.C., 1970-73; cons. Inter-Plan Svc. Benefit Bank Blue Cross Blue Shield Assn., Chgo., 1973-76, cons. specific assistance rev. team, 1976-77, sys. cons. nat. account performance rev. team, 1977-80, dir. midwest mktg. region, 1980-82; account exec. nat. accounts dept. Blue Cross Blue Shield Mich., Detroit, 1982-83, mgr. control plan accounts, 1983-89, mgr. nat. accounts sales rebion II, agt. cons. rels., 1989-95; v.p. cen. region sales Mida Dental Plans, Inc., Southfield, Mich., 1995—. Mem. consumer adv. bd. Citizens Ins. Co., Howell, Mich.; bd. dirs. Campfire Girls of Chgo., Met. Detroit Campfire Coun. With USN, 1956-59. Mem. Assn. Profls. in Risk-Related Disciplines (charter mem., bd. dirs.), Nat. Urban League (charter mem.), Lafayette Park Kiwanis Club Detroit. Democrat. Methodist. Home: 4474 Tanbark Dr Bloomfield Heights MI 48302 Office: Mida Dental Plans Ste 2200 2000 Town Center Southfield MI 48075

NOCHMAN, LOIS WOOD KIVI (MRS. MARVIN NOCHMAN), educator; b. Detroit, Nov. 5, 1924; d. Peter K. and Annetta Lois (Wood) Kivi; AB, U. Mich., 1946, AM, 1949; m. Harold I. Pitchford, Sept. 6, 1944 (div. May 1949); children: Jean Wood Pitchford Horiszny, Joyce Lynn Pitchford Undiano; m. Marvin A. Nochman, Aug. 15, 1953; 1 child, Joseph Asa. Tchr. adult edn., Honolulu, 1947, Ypsilanti (Mich.) H.S., 1951-52; spl. instr. English, Wayne State U., Detroit, 1953, 54; tchr. Highland Park (Mich.) Coll., 1950-51, instr. English, 1954-83. Mem. exec. bd. Highland Park Fedn. Tchrs., 1963-66, 71-72, mem. 1st bargaining team, 1965-66, 73, del. to Nat. Conv., 1964, 71-74, rep. higher edn. to Mich. Fedn. Tchrs. Exec. Com., 1972-76; mem. faculty adv. com. Gov.'s Commn. on Higher Edn., 1973—. Tchr. Baha'i schs., Davison, Mich., 1954-55, 58-59, 63-66, Beaulac, Que., Can., 1960, Greenacre, Maine, 1965; sec. local spiritual assembly Baha'is, Ann Arbor, 1953, sec., Detroit, 1954, chmn., 1955; mem. nat. com. Baha'is U.S., 1955-68; sec. Davison Bahai Sch. Com. and Council, 1956, 58, 63-68; Baha'i lectr. Subject of local TV show Senior Focus, 1992. Mem. NOW, Modern Lang. Assn., Nat. Coun. Tchrs. English, Mich. Coll. English Assn., Am. Fedn. Tchrs., Nat. Soc. Lit. and Arts, Women's Equity and Action League (sec. Mich. chpt. 1975-79), Alpha Lambda Delta, Alpha Gamma Delta. Contbr. poems to mags. Recipient Women's Movement plaque Women Lawyers Assn. Mich., 1975, Lawrence award Mich. Masters Swimming, 1991, 9 World Master Records In Age Group and short course meters, 1994 Long Course Meters, 1995, 23 Nat. Masters Records, 1994-96, 6 Nat. YMCA records, 1995, 2 U.S. Nat. Sr. Sports Classic Records, 1995, 2 World Sr. Games Records, 1993, All-Am. award, 1990-96, 2 U.S. Nat. Sr. Sports Classic Records, U.S. MS Long Distance All Star, 1995, U.S. MS Finals All Star, 1995; named one of 10 Best of 1995 Swim Mag. Avocation: U.S. Swimming Master Champion.

NOE, ELNORA (ELLIE NOE), retired chemical company executive; b. Evansville, Ind., Aug. 23, 1928; d. Thomas Noe and Evelyn (West) Dieter. Student Ind. U.-Purdue U., Indpls. Sec., Pitman Moore Co., Indpls., 1946; with Dow Chem. Co., Indpls., 1960-90, pub. rels. asst. then mgr. employee comm., 1970-87, mgr. cmty. rels., 1987-90, DowBrands Inc., 1986-90; vice chmn. corp. affairs discussion group, 1988-89, chmn., 1989-90; mem. steering com. Learn About Bus. Recipient 2d pl. award as Businesswoman of Yr., Indpls. Bus. and Profl. Women's Assn., 1980, Indpls. Profl. Woman of Yr. award Zonta, Altrusa, Soroptomist & Pilot Svc. Clubs, 1985, DowBrands Great Things Cmty. Svc. award, 1991. Mem. Am. Bus. Women Assn. (Woman of Yr. award 1965, past pres.), Ind. Assn. Bus. Communicators (hon., Communicator of Yr. 1977), Women in Comm. (Louise Eleanor Kleinhenz award 1984), Zonta (dist. pub. rels. chmn. 1978-80, area dir. 1980-82, pres. Indpls. 1977-79, bd. dirs. 1993-95), Dow Indpls. Retiree Club (pres. 1995—).

NOE, JAMES KIRBY, computer consultant; b. Denver, June 21, 1951; s. George F. and Fern D. (Wilterdink) N. BSBA in Mgmt. Info., U. No. Colo., 1983. Cert. data processor, systems profl. Systems supr. USN Tactical Support Ctr., Sigonella, Sicily, Italy, 1978-79; tech. mgr. Empire Dispatch of No. Colo., Greeley, 1979-80; cons. Greeley C. of C., 1983; project mgr. software devel. Microhealth Systems Corp., Denver, 1983-84; database analyst Manville Corp., Littleton, Colo., 1984; leader project devel. Citicorp Diners Club, Englewood, Colo., 1985; cons. Mountain Bell Telephone, Denver, 1985-86; computer programmer Colo. Dept. Revenue, Denver, 1986-87; cons. DST Systems, Inc., Kansas City, Mo., 1987-91, Broadcast Data Systems, Kansas City, Mo., 1991-92, U.S. Sprint, Kansas City, 1992—. Pres. Pine Tree Players, Brunswick, Maine, 1976-77, Sigonella Theatre Co., 1978; bd. dirs. Theatre Assocs. Group, Inc., Denver, 1985-86, v.p., 1987. Recipient 5-Yr. Svc. award Am. Cancer Soc., Brunswick, 1977; named Outstanding Vol. Theatre Assocs. Group, Inc., 1987. Mem. Assn. for Computing Machinery (com. mem. 1984—, chmn. Denver chpt. 1987), Data Processing Mgmt. Assn. (com. mem. 1984—). Republican. Presbyterian. Home: 600 E 8th St Apt 813 Kansas City MO 64106-1621

NOEBE, RONALD DEAN, materials research engineer; b. Canton, Ohio, July 17, 1961; s. Donald Richard and Ellen Marie (Makley) N.; m. Anita Diane Tenteris, June 8, 1985. BS, Case Western Reserve U., 1983, MS, 1986; MS in Materials Engring., U. Mich., 1986, PhD in Materials Sci. and Engring., 1994. Technician Rep. Steel, Ctrl. Alloy Div., Canton, Ohio, 1980; asst. turn metallurgist Ctrl. Alloy divsn. Republic Steel, Canton, Ohio, 1981; lab. mgr. Chase Brass & Copper, Solon, Ohio, 1982; materials rsch. engr. NASA Lewis Rsch. Ctr., Cleve., 1987—. Contbr. more than 120 papers to profl. publs.; mem. editl. bd. Metall. and Materials Transactions, Materials and Mfg. Processes. Mem. The Metall. Soc. (symposium organizer Cleve. conf. 1995, high temperature alloys com.), Materials Rsch. Soc. (symposium organizer Boston conf. 1994), ASM, Am. Welding Soc., Alpha Sigma Mu. Independent. Home: 2510 1/2 Medina Rd Medina OH 44256-8144 Office: NASA Lewis Rsch Ctr 21000 Brookpark Rd # Ms 49 3 Cleveland OH 44135-3127

NOEL, TALLULAH ANN, healthcare industry executive; b. Detroit, Oct. 21, 1945; d. Harry Carababas and Ruby Dimple (Gentry) Caruso; m. Vernon E. Noel (div. 1965); children: Cynthia L. Robbins, Kimberly J. Wise. AA in Nursing, Morton Coll., Cicero, Ill., 1976; BS, Coll. St. Francis, Joliet, Ill., 1983; MS in Mgmt., Nat.-Louis U., Evanston, Ill., 1990. RN. Staff nurse Mt. Sinai Hosp., Chgo., 1976-78, head nurse, 1978-79, critical care nurse, 1979-80, oncology clinician, 1980-82; head nurse McNeal Hosp., Berwyn, Ill., 1982-84; dir. nursing Nursefinders of Elmwood Park (Ill.), 1984-86; dir. profl. svcs. Nursefinders of Chgo., Elmwood Park, 1986-87, v.p. profl. svcs., 1987-88, v.p. ops., chief oper. officer, 1988-90; area v.p. Nursefinders, Inc., Hillside, Ill., 1990-91; v.p. Amserv Healthcare, Inc., Riverside, Ill., 1992-94; pres., owner Staffing Team Internat., Inc., Oak Brook, Ill., 1994—. Bd. dirs. Morton Coll. Found., 1987-88, Chgo. Heart Assn., 1985—, Grant Works Children's Ctr., Cicero, 1982-85. Mem. Women's Health Exec. Network, Nat. League Nursing, Oncology Nursing Soc., Am. Fedn. Home Health Agys., Assn. Critical Care Nurses, others. Democrat. Roman Catholic. Office: Staffing Team Internat Inc 1100 Jorie Blvd Ste 234 Oak Brook IL 60521-2244

NOETH, CAROLYN FRANCES, speech and language pathologist; b. Cleve., July 21, 1924; d. Sam Falco and Barbara Serafina (Loparo) Armaro; m. Lawrence Andrew Noeth Sr., June 29, 1946; children: Lawrence Andrew Jr. (dec.), Barbara Marie. AB magna cum laude, Case Western Res. U., 1963; MEd, U. Ill., 1972; postgrad., Nat. Coll. Edn., 1975—. Lic. speech and lang. pathologist, Ill. Speech therapist Chgo. Pub. Schs., 1965; speech, lang. and hearing clinician J. Sterling Morton High Schs., Cicero and Berwyn, Ill., 1965-82, tchr. learning disabilities/behavior disorders, 1982, dist. ednl. diagnostician, 1982-84; Title I Project tchr., summers 1966-67, lang. disabilities cons., summers 1968-69, in-service tng. cons., summer 1970, dir. Title I Project, summers 1973-74, learning disabilities tchr. W. Campus of Morton, 1971-75, chmn. Educable-Mentally Handicapped-Opportunities Tchrs. Com., 1967-68, spl. edn. area and in-sch. tchrs. workshops, 1967—. Precinct elections judge, 1953-55; block capt. Mothers March of Dimes and Heart Fund, 1949-60; St. Agatha's rep. Nat. Catholic Women's League, 1952-53; collector various charities, 1967, 93-94; mem. exec. bd. Morton Scholarship League, 1981-84, corr. sec., 1981-83; vol. Am. Cancer Soc., 1985—; vol. judge Ill. Acad. Decathlon, 1988—. First recipient Virda L. Stewart award for Speech, Western Res. U., 1963, recipient Outstanding Sr. award, 1963. Mem. Am. (life, cert.), Ill. Speech, Language, and Hearing Assns. (life mem.), Council Exceptional Children (divsn. for learning disabilities, pioneers divsn., chpt. spl. projects chmn., exec. bd. 1976-81, chpt. pres. 1979-80), Council for Learning Disabilities, Profls. in Learning Disabilities, Internat. Platform Assn., Kappa Delta Pi, Delta Kappa Gamma (chmn., co-chmn. chpt. music com. 1979—, mem. state program com. 1981-83, chpt. music rep. to state 1982—, chmn. chpt. promotion com. 1993-94, 96—). Roman Catholic. Clubs: St. Norbert's Women's (Northbrook, Ill.), Case-Western Res. U., U. Ill. Alumni Assns., Lions (vol. Northbrook, 1966—). Chmn. in compiling and publishing Student Handbook, Cleve. Coll., 1962; contbr. lyric parodies and musical programs J. Sterling Morton High Sch. West Retirement Teas, 1972-83. Home and Office: 1849 Walnut Cir Northbrook IL 60062-1245

NOETZEL, ARTHUR JEROME, business administration educator, management consultant; b. East Cleveland, Ohio, July 2, 1916; s. Arthur John and Margaret (Weinfurtner) N.; m. Dorothy Elizabeth McKeon, Oct. 23, 1945 (dec. March 1988); children: Catherine Ellen Noetzel Levitt, Gretchen Marie Noetzel Walsh. BSBA, John Carroll U., 1938; MBA, Northwestern U., 1940; PhD, U. Mich., 1955; LittD (hon.), John Carroll U., 1985. Instr. John Carroll U., Cleve., 1941-42, asst. prof., 1942-46, prof. bus. adminstrn., 1955—; asst. dean Sch. Bus. John Carroll U., Cleve., 1945-56, dean, 1956-70, academic v.p., 1970-84; bd. dirs. Ctr. for Family Bus., Cleve., Ohio Coll. Podiatric Medicine, Cleve. Contbr. articles and book reviews to profl. jours. Bd. dirs. St. Vincent Charity Hosp., Cleve., 1970-82, Borromeo Coll., Wickliffe, 1978-84; chmn. Communication and Devel. Commn., Univ. Heights, Ohio, 1980—. Named Citizen of Yr., City of Univ. Heights, Ohio, 1983; recipient Alumni award John Carroll U., 1984, Cert. of Merit, Minority Developers Council, Cleve., 1985; Danforth Found. fellow, 1956. Roman Catholic. Home: 2405 Fenwood Rd Cleveland OH 44118-3805 Office: John Carroll U University Hts Cleveland OH 44106

NOLAN, CAROLE RITA, broadcasting executive; b. Chgo., Jan. 28, 1932; d. Martin Francis and Caroline Rita (Alton) N.; B.A., De Paul U., 1954, M.A., 1961. Tchr. Chgo. public schs., 1954-61, sci. cons., 1961-66, dir. instructional TV, 1966-71; dir. bur. telecommunications and broadcasting, mgr. Sta. WBEZ-FM, Chgo., 1971-90; pres, CEO, 1990-96, pres. emeritus 1996—; mem. faculty Northeastern U., 1964-65, De Paul U., 1975—; cons. Comptons Ency., 1964-65, Chgo. Area Sch. TV, 1964-72, Ill. TV Adv. Council, 1969. Bd. dirs. Chicagoland Radio Info. Services, Pub. Radio Internat., Ill. Arts Alliance, Bright New Cities. Mem. Chgo. Network, Nat. Pub. Radio, DePaul Univ. Women's Alumni Assn. (bd. dirs., treas.), Delta Kappa Gamma. Office: Sta WBEZ-FM 848 E Grand Chicago IL 60611

NOLAND, GARY LLOYD, vocation educational administrator; b. Lindsborg, Kans., July 29, 1942; s. Willard L. and Florence L. (Waggoner) N.; m. Deborah L. Homan, Mar. 20, 1981; children: Krista L., Timothy L. BSBA, Cen. Mo. State U., 1971, MEd, 1974. Cert. vocat. dir., Mo. V.p. sales First Nat. Land Co., Scottsdale, Ariz., 1961-66; student grad. asst. Cen. Mo. State U., Warrensburg, 1968-72; instr. State Fair CC., Sedalia, Mo., 1972-74, dir. job placement, 1974-79; dir. Statewide Job Placement Svc., Sedalia, 1979-84, State Fair Area Vocat. Sch., Sedalia, 1984—; dir. State Fair C.C. Found., Sedalia, 1986—; mgr. State Fair Coll. Farm, Sedalia, 1987-92. Author: Help Yourself to Successful Employment, 1980; author instructional modules. mem., chmn. ctrl. Mo. chpt. March of Dimes, Sedalia, 1979; v.p. Pettis County Farm Bur., Sedalia, 1987-91, pres., 1991-95; bd. dirs. Mo. Farm Bur., 1995—, Am. Cancer Soc., Sedalia, 1989-92. Named Outstanding Young Man Am., 1979, Outstanding Placement Specialist, Mo. Guidance and Placement, 1980, Outstanding Vocat. Program Area VII, U.S. Dept. Edn., 1982. Mem. VFW (life), Am. Simmental Assn., Am. Legion, Mo. Coun. Local Adminstrs., Mo. Assn. Secondary Prins., Mo. Cattleman's Assn., Pettis County Cattleman's Assn., Lions (pres. Sedalia 1979-80), Masons, Sedalia Area C. of C. (amb. 1975-92). Baptist. Home: 19776 Ridge Crest Pl Sedalia MO 65301-2199 Office: State Fair Area Vocat Sch 3201 W 16th St Sedalia MO 65301-2188

NOLAND, MARIAM CHARL, foundation executive; b. Parkersburg, W.Va., Mar. 29, 1947; d. Lloyd Henry and Ethel May (Beare) N.; m. James Arthur Kelly, June 13, 1981. BS, Case Western Res. U., 1969; M in Edn., Harvard U., 1975. Asst. dir. admissions, fin. aid Baldwin-Wallace Coll., Berea, Ohio, 1969-72; asst. dir. admissions Davidson (N.C.) Coll., 1972-74; case writer Inst. Edn. Mgmt., Cambridge, Mass., 1975; sec., treas., program officer The Cleve. Found., 1975-81; v.p. The St. Paul Found., 1981-85; pres. Community Found. for S.E. Mich., 1985—; chair bd. trustees Coun. of Mich. Founds., Grand Haven, Mich., 1988—. Trustee Coun. on Founds., 1994—, Henry Ford Health System, 1994—, Alma Coll., 1994—. Mem. Detroit Com. Fgn. Rels., Detroit Econ. Club. Office: Community Found Southeastern Mich 333 W Fort St Bsmt 2010 Detroit MI 48226-3134

NOLAND, N. DUANE, state legislator; b. Blue Mound, Ill., Sept. 12, 1956; m. Tina L. Beckett; children: Grant, Blake. BS with high honors, U. Ill., 1978. V.p. Noland Farms, 1982—; mem. Ill. Ho. of Reps. from 102d dist., 1990—; minority vice spokesman Agr., Counties and Twps. Coms. Ill. Ho. of Reps., mem. Econ. and Urban Devel., Ins., Pub. Safety and Infrastructure Appropriations Coms. Recipient Award of Excellence Nat. Corn Growers Assn., Ill. Young Leader award Am. Soybean Assn.; named Outstanding Young Farmer, Decatur-Mason (Ill.) Jaycees. Mem. Ill. Corn Growers Assn. (bd. dirs., treas.), Macon County Farm Bur. (bd. dirs.), Corn-Soy Commodity Orgn. (chmn.), Masons, Aircraft Owners and Pilots Assn. Republican. Home: RR 2 Box 206 Blue Mound IL 62513-9557*

NOLD, CARL RICHARD, state historic parks and museums administrator; b. Mineola, N.Y., Nov. 26, 1955; s. Carl Frederick and Joan Catherine (Heine) N.; m. Mary Beth Krivoruchka (div.). BA in History magna cum laude, St. John's U., Jamaica, N.Y., 1977; MA in History Mus. Studies, SUNY, Oneonta, 1982. Pres. Gregory Mus., Hicksville, N.Y., 1977; registrar N.Y. State Hist. Assn., Cooperstown, 1978-80; dir., curator Gadsby's Tavern Mus., Alexandria, Va., 1980-84; dir. State Mus. Pa., Harrisburg, 1984-91; exec. dir. Mackinac State Hist. Parks, Lansing, Mackinac Island, Mich., 1992—; grant reviewer Inst. Mus. Svcs., Washington, 1982-90, 95—, mus. assessment prog. reviewer, 1985—, panelist, 1992-94; panelist mus. grant prog. Nat. Endowment for Humanities, 1990-93. Co-author: Gadsby's Tavern Mus. Interpretive Master Plan, 1984; contbr. articles to profl. jours. Mem. adv. bd. for Grad. History George Mason U., Fairfax, Va., 1982-84, adv. com. Susquehanna Mus. Art, Harrisburg, 189-91; bd. dirs. Harrisburg-Hershey-Carlisle Tourism and Visitor Bur., 1987-91, bd. sec., 1990-91; mem. mayor's adv. bd. city of Mackinac Island, 1993—. Mem. Midwest Mus. Assn., Mich. Mus. Assn. (bd. dirs. 1995—), Am. Assn. Mus. (vis. com. mus. accreditation 1989—), Am. Assn. for State and Local History (elections chmn. 1990), Cooperstown Grad. Assn. (bd. dirs. 1985-87).

NOLDE, SHARI ANN, pediatrics, critical care nurse; b. Bad Axe, Mich., Nov. 24, 1960; d. Kurt E. and Leona P. (Ruthkowski) Zinger; m. Bart David Nolde, May 22, 1982; children: Byron David, Bart William. BSN, Saginaw Valley State U., 1982. Cert. ACLS, PALS. Pediatric staff nurse Bay Medical Ctr., Bay City, Mich., 1982-83; medical/surgical nurse Sierra Vista Cmty., Sierra Vista, Ariz., 1983; pediatric nurse St. John's Hosp., Leavenworth, Kans., 1983-85; chief nurse ambulatory clinic U.S. Army Hosp., Fulda, Fed. Republic Germany, 1986-88; pediatric charge nurse Potomac Hosp., Woodbridge, Va.; staff nurse neonatal ICU Fairfax (Va.) Hosp., 1988-90; charge nurse NICU No. Mich. Hosp., Petroskey, Mich., 1990-94; staff nurse emergency rm. Tex. Children's Hosp., Houston, 1994; staff nurse Neonatal ICU Saginaw (Mich.) Gen. Hosp., 1994-95; emergency rm. nurse Bay Med. Ctr., 1995—; neonatal resusitation instr., 1992.

NOLTING, EARL, academic administrator; b. Columbus, Ind., July 24, 1937; s. Earl Seeger and Gladys Marie (Veale) N.; m. Judith Lynn Tegeler, June 18, 1961; children: Susan, Matthew, David. BSBA, Ind. U., 1959, MS in Edn., 1961; PhD in Psychology, U. Minn., 1967. Lic. psychologist, Wis., Minn. Counselor, asst. prof. U. Minn., Mpls., 1966-68; assoc. dir. U. Wis., Madison, 1968-72, assoc. dean, assoc. vice-chancellor, 1970-74; assoc. prof. edn. Kans. State U., Manhattan, 1974-86, dean of students, 1974-86; dir. dept. counseling, Univ. Coll. U. Minn., Mpls., 1986—; cons. psychologist Alberg and Assocs., Shoreview, Minn., 1989—. Contbr. articles to profl. publs. Exec. bd. Adult Learner Svcs. Network, St. Paul, 1989-90. 1st lt. U.S. Army, 1961-62. Mem. AACD, APA, Minn. Psychol. Assn., Am. Coll. Pers. Assn. (news editor 1977-82, sen. 1982-85, Presdl. award 1982), Am. Counseling Assn., Am. Coll. Counseling Assn., Acad. of Family Mediators. Home: 3336 Lake Johanna Blvd Saint Paul MN 55112-7942 Office: Univ Coll U Minn 315 Pillsbury Dr SE Minneapolis MN 55455-0139

NOLTING, FREDERICK WILLIAM, dentist; b. Mpls., Aug. 15, 1950; s. Robert William and Lorraine Marie (Ritten) N.; m. Norma Jean Anderson, Nov. 10, 1973; children: Erick William, Andrew Frederick. BS, U. Minn., 1972, DDS, 1974, MS, 1977. Asst. prof. Sch. Dentistry U. Louisville, 1976-78; gen. practice dentistry Byron, Minn., 1978—; mem. dental hygiene adv. com., dental assisting adv. com. Riverland Tech. Coll., 1991—; bd. dirs. Star of the North, Minn. State Games, 1992—. Contbr. articles to profl. jour. Mem. coun. Christ Luth. Ch., 1980-87, fin. dir., 1983-86, v.p., 1985-86, pres., 1986-87, mem. community edn. adv. bd., 1981-82; referee U.S. Tae Kwon Do Union, 1989—; dir. state tournament Minn. State Tae Kwon Do Assn., 1992; mem. U.S. Olympic Com., 1986—. Recipient Nat. Medal of Merit, Boy Scouts Am., 1993; named to Park Inst. Hall of Fame, 1988. Mem. ADA, Minn. Dental Assn. (dental edn. com. 1988-92, trustee SE dist. 1995—), Zumbro Valley Dental Soc. (sec. 1982-85), Acad. Gen. Dentistry, Am. Assn. Physics in Medicine, Upper Midwest Alpha Computer Consortium (pres. 1986—), Internat. Human Powered Vehicle Assn., NRA, Jaycees, Byron Sportsman and Conservation Club. Office: 111 Frontage Rd NE Byron MN 55920

NOME, WILLIAM ANDREAS, lawyer; b. Springfield, Ohio, May 21, 1951; s. Reidar Andreas and Nancy Louisa (Smith) N.; m. Carolyn Ruth Johnson, Feb. 7, 1981. BA, Akron U., 1973; JD, Cleve. State U., 1976. Bar: Ohio 1976, U.S. Dist. Ct. (no. dist.) Ohio 1977, U.S. Ct. Appeals (6th cir.) 1985, U.S. Supreme Ct. 1987. Asst. prosecutor Portage County Prosecutor's Office, Ravenna, Ohio, 1977; pvt. practice Ravenna, 1977-82; assoc. Arthur & Clegg, Kent, Ohio, 1982-85; ptnr. Arthur, Nome & Assocs., Kent, 1985--; legal advisor Portage Area Regional Transit Authority, Kent, 1986--. Chmn. Highland Home Health Care, Ravenna, 1980, Kent Bd. Bldg. Appeals, 1987, Portage County Mental Health Bd., 1988; trustee Kevin Coleman Mental Health Ctr., 1989-93, pres., 1991-93. Col. Ohio Mil. Res., 1986—. Recipient Cert. of Achievement, Emergency Mgmt. Inst., Fed. Emergency Mgmt. Agy., 1987, 93, 95. Mem. Ohio Bar Assn., Akron Bar Assn., Portage County Bar Assn. (sec.-treas. 1982-85), Portage County Estate Planning Coun., Delta Theta Phi. Republican. Lutheran. Office: Arthur Nome & Assocs 1325 S Water St Kent OH 44240-3845

NONDORF, JANICE KATHRYN, special education educator; b. Hoisington, Kans., Oct. 30, 1956; d. Francis Joseph and Evelyn Helen (Huschka) Behr; m. John Raymond Nondorf, Aug. 3, 1979; 1 child, AdreAnne Claire. BS in Edn., Ft. Hays State U., Hays, Kans., 1978; MS in Spl. Edn., Ft. Hays State U., 1982. Early childhood handicapped tchr. Early Childhood Developmental Ctr., Hays, 1979-82, Russell Child Devel. Ctr./ High Plains Ednl. Coop., Liberal, Kans., 1982-85, Russell Child Devel. Ctr., USD # 457, Garden City, Kans., 1985-91; family svcs. coord. Parents and Children Together, Inc., 1992—. Dem. precinct committeewoman, Liberal, 1988; active Rainbow Players Cmty. Theatre; Internat. Pancake Day Race contestant, 1989, 90; mem. Internat. Pancake Day bd. execs., 1990—; bd. dirs. Liberal Latchkey, 1996. Named an Outstanding Young Woman in Am., 1982. Mem. AAUW (pres. 1987-89, membership v.p. 1984-86, edn. rep. 1983-84, corr. sec. 1989-91), Coun. for Exceptional Children, Baker Arts Found./Liberal Arts Coun., Ft. Hays U. Alumni Assn., Delta Kappa Gamma. Roman Catholic.

NONTELL, STEVEN EARL, systems analyst; b. Indpls., Dec. 10, 1954; s. Lee J. Junior and Frances Kathryn (Stockwell) N.; m. Jhoni Jenee Pence, Oct. 26, 1980. BA magna cum laude, Ind. Ctrl. U., Indpls., 1977; MA in Speech Comm., Ball State U., 1979. Cert. wrestling coach. Sec., office asst. Employment and Tng. div. City Govt. of Indpls., 1980-83; office asst., data mgr. Equal Opportunity div. City Govt. of Indpls., 1983-92; svc. fee processor Pub. Works Dept., City Govt. of Indpls., 1992-96, geographic info. sys. analyst, 1996—; interscholastic pub. address announcer, youth wrestling coach Beech Grove (Ind.) H.S., 1971—. Contemporary Christian music reviewer Ind. Christian Advocate newspaper, 1996—. Youth wrestling coach Beech Grove Athletic Boosters Club, 1984—; ch. camp counselor United Meth. Ch., Bloomington, Ind., 1982—. Recipient Todd Goebel Meml. Citizen of Yr. award Beech Grove Promoters Club, 1993; named to Beech Grove H.S. Hall of Fame, 1994; Hoosier scholar, 1973. Mem. Friends of Cornerstone Festival, Children's Mus. of Indpls., Indpls. Zoo, Amateur Athletic Union of U.S.A. (life), USA Wrestling, U.S. Wrestling Ofcls. Assn., Ind. H.S. Wrestling Coaches Assn. Mem. United Methodist Ch. Office: Dept Pub Works/Solid Waste 2700 S Belmont Ave Indianapolis IN 46221-2009

NOONAN, JOHN ROBERT, electrical engineer, material science engineer; b. Springfield, Mo., Sept. 26, 1946; s. Robert F. and Elizabeth J. (Stewart) N.; m. Patricia Kwinn, Mar. 1, 1974. BSEE, Washington U., St. Louis, 1968, MSEE, 1970; PhD in Elec. Engring., U. Ill., 1974. Rsch. scientist Oak Ridge (Tenn.) Nat. Lab., 1974-91; group leader vacuum sys. Argonne (Ill.) Nat. Lab., 1991—. Pres. Westwood Homeowners Assn., Knoxville, Tenn., 1980. Recipient Pollution Prevention award U.S. Dept. Energy, 1994, Gov.'s Pollution Minimization award State of Ill., 1994. Mem. IEEE, Am. Vacuum Soc. (symposium program chair 1988, publs. com. chair 1984-86, b. dirs. 1989-90, pres. 1994), Sigma Xi. Office: Argonne Nat Lab 9700 S Cass Ave Argonne IL 60439

NOONAN, NORMA LINA CORIGLIANO, political science educator; b. Phila., May 19, 1937; d. Domenic and Amelia (Stendardo) Corigliano; m. Thomas Schaub Noonan, June 1, 1963; 1 child, Thomas Robert. BA, U. Pa., 1959; MA, Ind. U., 1962, PhD, 1965. Asst. prof. polit. sci. Western Ky. U., Bowling Green, 1965-66; asst. prof. polit. sci. Augsburg Coll., Mpls., 1966-68, assoc. prof., 1969-74, prof. polit. sci., 1974—, dir. MA in Leadership Program, 1996—; adj. prof. dept. ind. study U. Minn., Mpls., 1973-93; cons. evaluator North Ctrl. Assn., Chgo., 1973—; lectr. in field. Contbr. articles to profl. jours. Vol. DFL Party, Minn., 1972-80, St. Edward's Ch., Bloomington, Minn., 1977—. NDEA IV fellow, 1959-62; Evang. Luth. Ch. scholar, 1975, 83, 90. Mem. Am. Polit. Sci. Assn., Am. Assn. Advancement of Slavic Studies, Assn. Women in Slavic Studies (v.p. 1991-93, pres. 1993-95), Am. Hist. Assn., Minn. Polit. Sci. Assn. (pres. 1971-73, officer 1990-92), Internat. Studies Assn., Phi Beta Kappa, Alpha Chi, Pi Sigma Alpha, Omicron Delta Kappa, Pi Gamma Mu. Roman Catholic. Office: Augsburg Coll PO Box 107 2211 Riverside Minneapolis MN 55454

NORA, GERALD ERNEST, lawyer; b. Chgo., May 25, 1951; s. Gerald Edwin and Lois (Billingham) N.; m. Patricia Cunniff, June 19, 1976; children: Gerald Joseph, Thomas More, Mary Elizabeth, John Paul. Student, U. Ill., 1970-71; BA, Georgetown U., 1973, JD, 1978. Bar: Ill. 1978, U.S. Supreme Ct. 1983, U.S. Dist. Ct. (no. dist.) Ill. 1986, U.S. Dist. Ct. Ariz. 1993. Pvt. practice Chgo., 1986-87; assoc. Hofeld & Schaffner, Chgo., 1987-91; asst. state's atty. Cook County Office of State's Atty., Chgo., 1978-86, dep. state's atty., chief spl. prosecutions bur., 1991-93; ptnr. Davidson, Goldstein, Mandell & Menkes, Chgo., 1995—; instr. Loyola U. Sch. Law, 1988—; mem. Cook County Revenue Enhancement Com.; bd. dirs. Chgo. Legal Aid for Incarcerated Mothers. Mem. Ill. State Bar Assn., Nat. Dist. Attys. Assn., Chgo. Bar Assn., Fed. Bar Assn., Chgo. Crime Commn., High Tech. Crime Investigation Assn. Office: Davidson Goldstein Mandell & Menkes 303 W Madison Ste 1900 Chicago IL 60606

NORA, RICHARD ERNEST, hematologist, oncologist, educator; b. Chgo., July 18, 1953; s. Gerald Edwin and Lois (Billingham) N.; m. Lucille Ann Berger, Mar. 19, 1983; children: Daniel, Richard, Michael. BS, U. Notre Dame, 1974; MD, Royal Coll. Surgeons, Dublin, Ireland, 1980. Resident Good Samaritan Hosp., Balt., 1980-83; fellow hematology Johns Hopkins Hosp., Balt., 1983-84; fellow hematology, oncology U. Md. Cancer Ctr., Balt., 1984-87; hematologist, oncologist Rockford (Ill.) Clinic, 1988—; asst. prof. SUNY, Syracuse, 1987-88; clin. asst. prof. U. Ill. Coll. Medicine, Rockford, 1989—. Contbr. articles to profl. jours. Fellow ACP; mem. AMA, Am. Soc. Clin. Oncology, Am. Soc. Hematology, Am. Soc. Apheresis, Winnebago County Med. Soc. (bd. dirs., sec. 1994—). Office: Rockford Clinic 2300 N Rockton Rockford IL 61103

NORBECK, EDWIN, JR., physics educator; b. Seattle, June 10, 1930; s. Edwin and Rosella Ann (Wellington) N.; m. Betty Ann Samuelson, Sept. 1, 1956 (div. Nov. 1982); children: David Andrew, Sarah Margaret, Susan Diane, Martha Marie; m. Janet Sue Branson, June 3, 1984. BA, Reed Coll., 1952; MA, U. Chgo., 1956, Phd., 1956. Chem. physicist GE, Richland, Wash., 1951, 1952; rsch. assoc. U. Chgo., 1956-57, U. Minn., Mpls., 1957-60; from asst. prof. to assoc. prof. U. Iowa, Iowa City, 1960-67, prof., 1967—; vis. prof. Techniche Hochschule, Darmstadt, Fed. Republic Germany, summer 1990. Contbr. some 110 articles on nuclear physics to profl. jours.; patentee for Norbeck clarinet pad. Fulbright rsch. grantee, France, 1989-90. Fellow Am. Phys. Soc.; mem. IEEE (computer applications sci. award 1987), Am. Assn. Physics Tchrs., Phi Beta Kappa, Sigma Xi. Democrat. Methodist. Office: U Iowa Dept Physics And Astro Iowa City IA 52242

NORDBY, EUGENE JORGEN, orthopedic surgeon; b. Abbotsford, Wis., Apr. 30, 1918; s. Herman Preus and Lucille Violet (Korsrud) N.; m. Olive Marie Jensen, June 21, 1941; 1 child, Jon Jorgen. B.A., Luther Coll., Decorah, Iowa, 1939; M.D., U. Wis., 1943. Intern Madison Gen. Hosp., Wis., 1943-44, asst. in orthopedic surgery, 1944-48; practice medicine specializing in orthopedic surgery Madison, Wis., 1948—; pres. Bone and Joint Surgery Assocs., S.C. 1969-91; chief staff Madison Gen. Hosp., 1957-63; assoc. clin. prof. U. Wis. Med. Sch., 1961—; chmn. Wis. Physicians Svcs., 1979—; dir. Wis. Regional Med. Program, Chgo. Madison and No. RR; bd. govs. Wis. Health Care Liability Ins. Plan; chmn. trustees S.M.S. Realty Corp.; mem. bd. attys. Profl. Responsibility of Wis. Supreme Ct., 1992—. Assoc. editor Clin. Orthopaedics and Related Research, 1964—. Pres. Vesterheim Norwegian Am. Mus., Decorah, Iowa, 1968—. Served to capt. M.C., AUS, 1944-46. Decorated Knight 1st class Royal Norwegian Order St. Olav; named Notable Norwegian Dane County Norwegian-Am. Fest, 1995; recipient Disting. Svc. award Internat. Rotary,1 987, Den Hoyeste Aere award Vesterheim, 1993. Mem. Acad. Orthopaedic Surgeons (bd. dirs. 1972-73), Clin. Orthopaedic Soc., Assn. Bone and Joint Surgeons (pres. 1973), Internat. Soc. Study Lumbar Spine, State Med. Soc. Wis. (chmn. 1968-76, treas. 1976—, Coun. award 1976), Am. Orthopaedic Assn., N.Am. Spine Soc., Internat. Intradiscal Therapy Soc. (sec. 1987—), Wis. Orthopaedic Soc., Dane County Med. Soc. (pres. 1957), Nat. Exch. Club, Madison Torske Klubben (founder, pres. 1978—), Norwegian-Am. Orthopaedic Soc., Phi Chi. Lutheran. Home: 6234 S Highlands Ave Madison WI 53705-1115 Office: 2704 Marshall Ct Madison WI 53705-2256

NORDEN, LEO GEORGE, internist; b. Grinnell, Iowa, Jan. 31, 1942; s. George A. and Ruby A. Norden; m. Marilyn A. Pfaff, June 20, 1964; children: Jennifer, Mark. BS, Cornell Coll., 1963; MD, U. Iowa, 1967. Diplomate Am. Bd. Internal Medicine. Resident in internal medicine U. Hosps., Iowa City, 1970-73; intern Emanuel Hosp., Portland, Oreg., 1967-68; physician Rhinelander (Wis.) Med. Ctr., 1973—, pres., 1989—. Capt. USAF, 1968-70. Mem. AMA, Wis. State Med. Sop., Am. Coll. Physicians. Republican. Mem. United Ch. of Christ. Office: Rhinelander Med Ctr 1020 Kabel Ave Rhinelander WI 54501

NORDHEDEN, KAREN JEAN, electrical engineering educator, researcher; b. Champaign, Ill., Feb. 4, 1958; d. Albert Per-Eric and Angelene M.S. (Mitchem) N.; m. Michael Harlan Hoeflich, Sept. 13, 1986. BS in Physics, Mich. State U., 1980; MSEE, U. Ill., 1984, PhD in Elec. Engring., 1988. Sr. process engr. Gen. Electric, Syracuse, N.Y., 1988-93, Martin-Marietta, Syracuse, 1993-94; asst. prof. elec. engring. and computer sci. U. Kans., Lawrence, 1994—. Contbr. articles to profl. jours. Fellow IBM, 1983-84. Mem. IEEE, Soc. Women Engrs. (advisor local chpt., mem. adv. bd. engring. diversity program 1995—), Am. Vacuum Soc., Am. Phys. Soc., Golden Key, Tau Beta Pi, Phi Kappa Phi, Eta Kappa Nu. Office: U Kans Dept EECS 1013 Learned Hall Lawrence KS 66045

NORDLIE, PAUL EDWARD, physician, pathologist; b. Willmar, Minn., July 17, 1934; s. Peter Conrad and Myrtle Clare (Spindler) N.; m. Margaret Jean Fickes, June 9, 1963; children: Brian, Susan. BA, U. Minn., 1957, BS, 1961, MD, 1961. Diplomate Am. Bd. Pathology. Intern St. Luke's Hosp., Duluth, Minn., 1961-62; resident in internal medicine Mpls. VA Hosp./U. Minn., 1965-68, resident in anat. and clin. pathology, 1970-74; postdoctoral rsch. fellow U. Minn., 1962-63; staff pathologist VA Hosp., Mpls., 1974-75, St. Joseph's Hosp., St. Paul, 1975—. Trustee Ripon (Wis.) Coll., 1991—. Lt. comdr., surgeon USPHS, 1963-65. Fellow Coll. Am. Pathologists, Am. Soc. Clin. Pathologists; mem. Internat. Acad. Pathology, Minn. Soc. Clin. Pathology, Minn. Med. Assn. Home: 8280 Kentucky Ave S Bloomington MN 55438 Office: St Josephs Hosp Dept Pathology 69 W Exchange St Saint Paul MN 55102

NORDMAN, ERIC CHARLES, insurance regulatory specialist; b. Jackson, Mich., Feb. 19, 1949; s. Charles Edward and Ruth Joan (Penn) N.; m. Ann Frances Vanhecke, Aug. 28, 1970 (div. Oct. 1990); children: Aaron Eric,

Lauren Vanessa; m. Marsha Lee Garrett, May 16, 1993. AS, Jackson C.C., 1969; BA, Mich. State U., 1971. CPCU; cert. ins. examiner. Self-employed self-employed, Lansing, Mich., 1971-79; ins. analyst Mich. Ins. Bur., Lansing, 1979-88, dep. dir. comml. market standards div., 1988-91; sr. regulatory specialist Nat. Assn. Ins. Commrs., Kansas City, Mo., 1991—. Contbr. articles to profl. jours. Mem. Delhi Parks and Recreation Commn., Delhi Twp., Holt, Mich., 1986-88. Mem. Soc. CPCU (bd. dirs., legis. and regulatory interest sect. 1992—), Ins. Regulatory Examiners Soc. Office: Nat Assn Ins Commrs 120 W 12th St Ste 1100 Kansas City MO 64105-1925

NORDQUIST, SANDRALEE RAHN, lay worker; b. Chgo., Dec. 5, 1940; d. Herbert Henry and Elinor Gertrude (Duben) Rahn; m. George Leczewski, Oct. 13, 1962 (div. Dec. 1968); 1 child, Peter George (dec.); m. David Arthur Nordquist, July 19, 1969; children: Kerilinn D., Sharianne R. AA, Harper Coll., 1982; BS in English, Elmhurst (Ill.) Coll., 1985, BS in Theology, 1988; postgrad., Northestern Ill. U., Chgo., Drake U. Cert. tchr. English, history, learning disordered, behaviorally disordered, Ill. Tchr. English, gen. music and spl. edn. Foreman H.S., Chgo., 1990—; tchr. English summer sch. Luther H.S., Chgo., 1990, 92-94; feature writer Daily Herald, Paddock Publs., 1991—; tchr. sci. summer sch. Weber H.S., Chgo., 1995. Columnist (newspaper) Pulitzer Pubs. Notebook, 1986-90. Leader Girl Scouts U.S., Chgo. and Elk Grove, 1968-70, 77-81; v.p. Dist. 59 Orch. Assn., Elk Grove Village, Ill., 1985-87; pres. Sch. Dist. 59 Project 444, Elk Grove Village, 1981; confirmation tchr. Evang. Luth. Ch. of the Holy Spirit, Elk Grove, Ill., 1990-91, guild pres., adv. trinity preaching, 1990-91, leader adult Bible study, 1991-93; lector, greeter, actress Trinity Luth. Ch., Roselle, Ill., 1992—, also Drama Guild. Mem. Nat. Coun. Tchrs. of English, Ill. Assn. Tchrs. of English, Sigma Tau Delta. Home: 639 Sycamore Dr Elk Grove Village IL 60007-4624 Office: Foreman High Sch 3235 N Leclaire Ave Chicago IL 60641-4238

NORDSIECK, KAREN ANN, custom design company owner; b. Ft. Campbell, Ky., Nov. 2, 1955; d. Reuben James and Shirley Jean (Walters) Simpson; m. Kenneth M. Farber, Mar. 5, 1977 (div. July 1982); children: Carissa Ann, Laurie Jean; m. Derrell E. Hiett, May 10, 1985 (div. May 1989); m. Michael Louis Nordsieck, June 2, 1989. Student, El Paso Community Coll., 1976, 84. Sales clk. Busy B Gift Shop, El Paso, Tex., 1973; svc. rep. Bell System, El Paso and Seattle, 1974-85; substitute tchr. Cleburne County Elem. Sch., Heflin, Ala., 1986; credit clk. Wakefields, Anniston, Ala., 1986-87; svc. rep. Ala. Power, Anniston, 1986-88; beauty cons. May Kay Cosmetics, El Paso and Heflin, Ala., 1983-88; mgr. Rock's T-Shirts & Screen Printing, El Paso, 1988-92; owner Custom Designs and Promotions, Richmond, Mo., 1992-96; svc. rep. Southwestern Bell Telephone Co., Kansas City, Mo., 1993—; owner Kreations by Karen, Richmond, 1996—; liaison for ptnrs. in edn. El Paso Ind. Sch. Dist., Rock's T-Shirts and Screen Print, El Paso, 1990—; co-chairperson Quality of Work Life Com. Southwestern Bell, El Paso, 1984; union steward Communication Workers Am., El Paso, 1974-75; owner Custom Designs and Promotions, 1992—. Troop leaders Brownies, Girl Scouts U.S.A., troop # 126, Heflin, 1985-88, mag. chairperson, 1986; v.p. Clendenin Elem. PTA, El Paso, 1989-90, pres., 1990-92; family support leader Ft. Bliss Family Support, El Paso, 1990-91; mem. El Paso Ind. Sch. Dist. Strategic Planning Com., 1990-91; mem. campus improvement com. Clendenin Elem., 1991-92, vol. pub. schs., 1989-92; mem. parent adv. com. ctrl. area El Paso Ind. Sch. Dist., 1989-92; mem. Richmond PTA, 1992—; mem. com. Richmond At Sch. Planning, 1994-95; co-chairperson Jr. Class Parents After Prom/Project Graduation, 1995—; mem. Battlefield Piece Makers Quilt Guild, 1995—. Recipient Outstanding Troop Leader award Girl Scouts U.S.A., Anniston, 1987, cert. outstanding svc. Clendenin PTA, El Paso, 1990, 91, 92; cert. of honor Clendenin Elem. Sch., 1990, 91, 92, Cert. of Appreciation, 1991, 92; Cert. of Appreciation, Ft. Bliss Army Family Support, 1991, plaque Vols. in Pub. Sch., El Paso, 1991, 92, Ptnrs. in Edn., El Paso Ind. Sch. Dist., 1991, 92, Desert Storm vol. pin Ptnrs. in Edn., 1991. Mem. Battlefield Peacemakers Quilt Guild, Order Ea. Star. Mem. Assembly of God. Office: Kreations by Karen PO Box 187 Richmond MO 64085

NORDSTROM, GRACE IRENE, retired elementary educator; b. Walnut Grove, Minn., Nov. 21, 1916; d. Samuel and Bertha Sophie Louise (Kluck-ing) N.; m. Victor Wm. Nordstrom, June 6, 1939; children: Bill, Bruce, Karen Nordstrom Cruit. BS, Mankato State U., 1968. Cert. tchr., Minn. Tchr. Sun Sch., Walnut Grove, 1944-50; Author poems. Democrat. Methodist. Home: 630 Washington St Walnut Grove MN 56180

NORDSTROM, MARK ALLEN, journalist; b. Mpls., July 7, 1952; s. Stanley Gilbert and Martha Helen (Carr) N.; m. Mary Margaret Ralstin, Jan. 16, 1982; 1 child, Karin Rose. BA, Ohio State U., 1974, MA in Journalism, 1980. Artist WLWT, Cin., 1978-79; copy camera operator Suburban News, Columbus, Ohio, 1980-81; student instrn. asst. WOSU Radio, Columbus, 1980-81; news dir. WDLR Radio, Delaware, Ohio, 1981-87; news reporter WLOH Radio, Lancaster, Ohio, 1988, WMAN Radio, Mansfield, Ohio, 1987-94, WWCD Radio, Columbus, 1993-94; statehouse reporter Ohio News Network, Columbus, 1994—; prin. M-A-N, Canal Winchester, Ohio, 1992—, North Stream Pub., Canal Winchester, 1992—; lectr. broadcast journalism Ohio State U., 1996—. Office: Ohio News Network 175 S 3d St Columbus OH 43215

NORDVOLD, HOMER BLAINE, cattle ranch manager; b. Eagle Butte, S.D., Apr. 15, 1945; s. Sydney Olaf and Rose Alvira (Powell) N.; m. Linda Roan, Dec. 11, 1973; children: Lakota Sioux, Wendell Robert, Yura Lee, Sabrena Sioux. Student, Cheyenne River C.C., Eagle Butte, S.D., 1989-90. Cert. heavy equip. operator, N.Mex. Clk. Rissone Auto Parts, Reno, Nev., 1969-71; svc. sta. mgr. Cheyenne River Sioux Tribe, Eagle Butte, S.D., 1971-72; detention sgt. Cheyenne River Sioux Tribe, Eagle Butte, 1991-94; opticion Navajo Tribe, Window Rock, Ariz., 1976-77; water treatment opr. Tri County Water Assn., Eagle Butte, 1986-88; ranch mgr. Ridgiew Grazing Assn., Ridgeview, 1995—; bonding magistrate Cheyenne River Sioux Tribal Courts, Eagle Butte, 1996—. Author poem. Trail ride coord., 1987-92. Mem. Tri County Water Assn. (dist. dir. 1992), Suanne Big Crow Visions (bd. dirs. 1994—), Braves Booster Club (v.p. 1995—). Home: Box 32 Eagle Butte SD 57625

NORDWALD, CHARLES, state legislator; b. Aug. 25, 1955; m. Nina Hoelscher; 3 children. Mem. dist. 19 Mo. Ho. of Reps., 1992—; co-owner Allen & Nordwald Auction Svc., Warrenton, Mo. Mem. Warren County Fair Bd. Mem. NRA, Montgomery City C. of C., Elks Club. Office: 20 Hawthorne Warrenton MO 63383

NORDYKE, HARRY RANDALL, company president, business owner; b. Detroit, June 16, 1945; s. Ralph R. and Irene N.; m. Janet, May 24, 1969; 1 child, Andrea. BS in Econs., Oakland U., 1968; MBA, Wayne State U., 1972. Economist Comerica, Detroit, 1969-72; v.p. Kolar and Assocs., Troy, Mich., 1972-85; pres. Nordyke & Assocs., Troy, Mich., 1985—. Mem. Blue Lake Club (sec.-treas. 1992—, v.p. 1990-91, Distinction award 1990-91). Home: 4811 Riverchase Dr Troy MI 48098

NOREIKA, JOSEPH CASIMIR, ophthalmologist; b. Scranton, Pa., Aug. 21, 1950; s. Joseph C. and Joan (Stirna) N.; m. Joanne Elizabeth Keane, May 14, 1977; children: Sarah, Michael, Katya, Mathew. BS, U. Scranton, 1972; MD, Jefferson Med. Coll., 1976; MBA, Case Western Res. U., 1988. Diplomate Am. Bd. of Opthalmology. Intern Dartmouth Hosps., Hanover, N.H., 1976-77; resident in ophthalmology U. Pitts., 1977-80, assoc. clin. prof., 1981-83; fellow U. Calif., San Francisco, 1980-81; pvt. practice Medina, Ohio, 1983—; bd. dirs. Physician Resource Group; adj. clin. staff Cleve. Clinic Found., 1980-92. Editl. advisor The Argus; sect. contbr.: Ocular Surgery News, editl. bd., Adminstrv. Ophthalmology; contbr. articles to profl. jours. Bd. dirs. Physician Resource Group. Recipient Shoemaker award Pa. Acad. Ophthalmology, 1979; Heed Found. fellow, 1980. Mem. AMA (Physician Recognition award 1984-96), Am. Acad. Ophthalmology (chmn. computerized patient record task force, practice mgmt. com., managed care adv. com., Honor award 1996), Am. Soc. Cataract and Refractive Surgeons (scientific adv. bd. rep., rep. to AMA CPT adv. com., govt. rels. com.), Am. Soc. Ophthalmology Adminstrs. (editl. bd.), Ohio State Med. Assn., Ohio Ophthalmology Soc. (editor Managed Care-In Focus, chmn. managed care com.), Medina County Med. Soc. (past pres., program chmn.), Cleve. Ophthalmology Soc. (past pres.), Alpha Sigma Nu, Beta Gamma Sigma. Office: Eye Care Medina Inc 3637 Medina Rd Ste 70 Medina OH 44256-8154

NORLIN, ERL E., drafter; b. Boston, 1938. AS, Northeastern Coll., 1959. Designer, chief drafter Warner Elec., S. Beloit, Ill., 1961-78; chief drafter DEC Internat. Inc., Madison, Wis., 1978—; bd. dirs. High Sch. Drafting, Madison. Office: DEC Internat Inc PO Box 8050 Madison WI 53708-8050

NORLING, IRWIN DENISON, retired measurement specialist, photographer; b. Mpls., June 8, 1916; s. Carl Oscar and Harriet (Denison) N.; m. June Rose Mills, Aug. 28, 1943; children: Patricia June Erwin, Michael Carlos, David Irwin. Student, U. Minn., 1936. Machine operator Electric Machinery Co., Mpls., 1935-37; salesman Minn. Mut. Life Ins. Co., Mpls., 1938-39; draftsman No. Pump Co., Mpls., 1939; machine operator V.A. Boker & Sons, Mpls., 1939-40; measurement specialist Honeywell, Inc., Mpls., 1940-79; photographer Richfield (Minn.) Police Dept., Fire Dept., 1953-75, Bloomington (Minn.) Police and Fire Dept., 1953-75; staff photographer Bloomington Sun Weekly Newspaper, 1954-65; cons., designer of measuring devices for several mfrs., 1989—. Contbr. photographs to numerous publs. Dir. Emergency Mgmt. Communications Divsn., Bloomington, Minn., 1964-72, 79-86; mem. Bloomington Sch. Bd. Adv. Commn., 1973-79. Mem. Soc. Mfg. Engrs. (life), Am. Assn. Retired Persons (pres. Bloomington chpt. #1328 1989-90), Bloomington Citizens Crime Prevention Assn. (bd. dirs. 1983-90, sec. 1987-91, hon. bd. mem. 1992—), Bloomington Lions (pres. 1966-67). Republican. Episcopalian. Home: 101 E Old Shakopee Rd Bloomington MN 55420-4926

NORLING, RAYBURN, food service executive; b. 1934. Pres. Willmar (Minn) Poultry Co., Inc.; with Norling Farms, Inc., Svea, Minn., 1979—. Office: Willmar Poultry Co Inc 3735 County Rd 5 SW Willmar MN 56201*

NORMAN, CHARLES HENRY, broadcasting executive; b. St. Louis, June 13, 1920; s. Charles Henry and Grace Vincent (Francis) N. BS, U. So. Calif., L.A., 1942. Announcer WIL, KSTL Radio Stas., St. Louis, 1948-55; owner Norman Broadcasting Co., St. Louis, 1961—. Lt. USN, 1943-45. Mem. St. Louis Ambassadors, Phi Kappa Phi. Episcopalian. Office: Portland Towers 275 Union Blvd Ste 1315 Saint Louis MO 63108-1236

NORMAN, PETER MINERT, fundraising consulting company executive; b. Rochester, N.Y., Mar. 23, 1932; s. Jesse George and Doris (Colony) N.; m. Janet G. Wasson, Sept. 6, 1952; children: Susan Jane, Paula Lea, Christa MacLeod, Peter Minert II. BA, Trinity Coll., Hartford, Conn., 1954; MDiv, Yale U., 1957. Ordained priest Episcopal Ch., 1957; lic. nursing home adminstr. Curate St. Stephen's Episc. Ch., Rochester, 1957-60; rector Zion Episc. Ch., Avon, N.Y., 1960-68; cons. Health and housing programs, Rochester and Washington, 1968-73; dir. Ward, Dreshman, Reinhardt, Worthington, Ohio, 1973-77; v.p. Seabury Western Sem., Evanston, Ill., 1977-80; exec. dir. Cathedral Found., Jacksonville, Fla., 1980-82; chmn. CEO Ward, Dreshman & Reinhardt, Worthington, 1982-92, WDR Community Svcs., Worthington, 1990-92; exec. v.p. Goettler Assocs., Columbus, Ohio, 1992-93; corp. v.p. of devel. svcs. St. Francis Acad., Salina, Kans., 1993-94; exec. officer devel. Episcopal Retirement House, Cin., 1994—; pres. Clan MacLeod Soc. U.S.A., 1988-89; chmn. Dunvegan Fund, N.Y./Edinburgh, 1988; chmn. World Fundraising Counsel, Amsterdam, 1990-92. Author: How to Assure Successful Every Member Canvass, 1979, Hospital Prayer Book, 1958. Mem. Worthington Hills Country Club, Am. Assn. Fundraising Counsel (treas. 1989-90, vice-chmn. 1990-91), Phi Beta Kappa, Pi Gamma Mu. Republican. Home: 1308 Clubview Blvd S Columbus OH 43235-1643 Office: Episcopal Retirement Homes 3870 Virginia Ave Cincinnati OH 45227-3431

NORMAN, STEVE RONALD, librarian; b. San Diego, July 18, 1955; s. Ronald Victor and Anita Christine Louise (Redstrom) N.; m. Linda Jennifer Knohl, Sept. 20, 1986; 1 child, Siri Elizabeth Margaret. BA, Macalester Coll., 1983; AM, U. Chgo., 1987. Editl. asst. Libr. Quar., Chgo., 1985-86; head of reference River Bluffs Regional Libr., St. Joseph, Mo., 1986-90; dir. Waupun (Wis.) Pub. Libr., 1990—; adv. coun. Mid-Wis. Fed. Libr. System, 1992—. Author (column) Waupun Leader News, 1990—. Bd. dirs. Dodge County Concert Assn., 1991—; mem. Waupun Cmty. Edn. Coun., 1992—. Mem. ALA (new mems. round table 1990-92), Wis. Libr. Assn., Rotary Club of Waupun (sgt.-at-arms 1991-92, sec. 1994—). Congregationalist. Office: Waupun Pub Libr PO Box 391 120 S Mill St Waupun WI 53963

NORQUIST, JOHN OLOF, mayor; b. Princeton, N.J., Oct. 22, 1949; s. Ernest O. and Jeannette (Nelson) N.; m. Susan R. Mudd, Dec. 1986; 1 child, Benjamin Edward. Student, Augustana Coll., Rock Island, Ill., 1967-69; BS, U. Wis., 1971, MPA, 1988. Assemblyman Wis. State Assembly, Madison, 1974-82, co-chmn. state joint com. fin., 1980-81; mem. Wis. State Senate, 82-88, asst. majority leader, 1984-85, 87; mayor City of Milw., 1988—. Sgt. USAR, 1971-77. Mem. Nat. League of Cities, Wis. Alliance of Cities. Democrat. Presbyterian. Office: Office of Mayor City Hall Rm 201 200 E Wells St Milwaukee WI 53202-3515

NORRIS, ALAN EUGENE, federal judge; b. Columbus, Ohio, Aug. 15, 1935; s. J. Russell and Dorothy A. (Shrader) N.; m. Nancy Jean Myers, Apr. 15, 1962 (dec. Jan. 1986); children: Tom Edward Jackson, Tracy Elaine; m. Carol Lynn Spohn, Nov. 10, 1990. BA, Otterbein Coll., 1957, HLD (hon.), 1991; cert., U. Paris, 1956; LLB, NYU, 1960; LLM, U. Va., 1986. Bar: Ohio 1960, U.S. Dist. Ct. (so. dist) Ohio 1962, U.S. Dist. Ct. (no. dist) Ohio 1964. Law clk. to judge Ohio Supreme Ct., Columbus, 1960-61; assoc. Vorys, Sater, Seymour & Pease, Columbus, 1961-62; ptnr. Metz, Bailey, Norris & Spicer, Westerville, Ohio, 1962-80; judge Ohio Ct. Appeals (10th dist.), Columbus, 1981-86, U.S. Ct. Appeals (6th cir.), Columbus, 1986—. Contbr. articles to profl. jours. Mem. Ohio Ho. of Reps., Columbus, 1967-80. Named Outstanding Young Man, Westerville Jaycees, 1971; recipient Legislator of Yr. award Ohio Acad. Trial Lawyers, Columbus, 1972. Mem. ABA, Am. Judicature Soc., Inst. Jud. Adminstrn., Ohio Bar Assn., Columbus Bar Assn. Republican. Methodist. Lodge: Masons (master 1966-67). Office: US Ct Appeals 328 US Courthouse 85 Marconi Blvd Columbus OH 43215-2823

NORRIS, ANDREA SPAULDING, art museum director; b. Apr. 2, 1945; d. Edwin Baker and Mary Gretchen (Brendle) Spaulding. BA, Wellesley Coll., 1967; MA, NYU, 1969, PhD, 1977. Intern dept. western European arts Met. Mus. Art, N.Y.C., 1970, 72; rsch. and editorial asst. Inst. Fine Arts NYU, 1971, lectr. Washington Sq. Coll., 1976-77; lectr. Queens Coll. CUNY, 1973-74; asst. to dir. Art Gallery Yale U., New Haven, 1977-80, lectr. art history, 1979-80; chief curator Archer M. Huntington Art Gallery, Austin, Tex., 1980-88; lectr. art history Dept. Art U. Tex., Austin, 1984-88; dir. Spencer Mus. Art U. Kans., Lawrence, 1988—. Co-author: (catalogue) Medals and Plaquettes from the Molinari Collection at Bowdoin College, 1976; author: (exhbn. catalogues) Jackson Pollock: New-Found Works, 1978; exhbn. The Sforza Court: Milan in the Renaissance 1450-1535, 1988-89. Mem. Renaissance Soc. Am., Coll. Art Assn., Assn. Art Mus. Dirs., Phi Beta Kappa. Office: Spencer Mus Art U Kans Lawrence KS 66045

NORRIS, BLANCHE LEE, business consultant, educator; b. Washington, Dec. 30, 1958; d. Arthur Norman and Helen (Calos) Lee; m. Barry L. Norris, June 8, 1991. BA magna cum laude, No. Ill. U., 1982. Behavior counselor Nutri/Systems, Aurora, Ill., 1983-84, ctr. mgr., 1984-87, area mgr., 1987-89; employment and tng. officer KDK Tng. Employment and Bus. Svc., Geneva, Ill., 1989-91; trainer bus. programs office Bus. and Profl. Inst. Coll. of DuPage, Glen Ellyn, Ill., 1991—; seminar leader Coll. DuPage, Glen Ellyn, Ill., 1989—. Sponsor Compassion, Colorado Springs, 1989—. Home: 44W-36 Hazelcrest Dr Sugar Grove IL 60554

NORRIS, CHARLEY WILLIAM, otolaryngologist, educator; b. Morganville, Kans., Jan. 3, 1933; s. George P. and Mary (Kaiser) N.; m. Linda Larson, Nov. 30, 1963; children: Andrew William, Erik Christopher. BA, U. Kans., 1960, MD, 1964. Intern Latter Day Saints Hosp., Salt Lake City, 1964-65, resident gen. surgery, 1965-66; ear, nose and throat resident Tufts Univ., Boston, 1966-69; jr. mem. staff Tufts U. Med. Sch., Boston, 1968-69; attending staff physician Boston City Hosp., 1969-71; asst. prof. U. Kans., Kans. City, 1971-75; assoc. prof. U. Kans., 1975-81, prof., chmn., 1981-90; chief of staff U. Kans. Hosp., 1989-92; prof. otolaryngology U. Kans., 1992—; instr. Tufts U., Boston, 1969-71; cons. Vets. Hosp., Kans. City, Mo., 1971—. Contbr. chpt. to book and articles to profl. jours. With USN, 1951-56. Fellow ACS, Am. Soc. for Head and Neck Surgery, Am. Laryngol., Rhinological and Otological Soc., Am. Acad. Otolaryngic Allergy, Am. Soc. Head and Neck Surgery, Am. Acad. Otolaryngology, N.Y. Acad. Scis. Office: U Kans Med Ctr 39th and Rainbow Blvd Kansas City KS 66160-7380

NORRIS, DEBRA LYNN, physical therapist assistant; b. Detroit, Apr. 29, 1963; d. Donald Gene and Shirley Ann (Gurchiek) Carter; m. Kevin Eugene Norris, Sept. 3, 1988; 1 child, Sarah Jo. AAS in Phys. Therapy Asst., Macomb C.C., Clinton Twp., Mich., 1986. Lic. phys. therapist asst., Ind., Ill. Phys. therapy asst. St. John Hosp., Detroit, 1986-89, Saratoga Hosp., Detroit, 1987, ARN-Macomb Inst., Clinton Twp., Mich., 1989-94, Robert Ochmanski Phys. Therapists & Assocs., Clinton Twp., Mich., 1993—, Profl. Spectrum, Troy, Mich., 1994—. Fin. sec. Stony Creek Ch. Mem. Mich. Phys. Therapy Assn.

NORRIS, JAMES RUFUS, JR., chemist, educator; b. Anderson, S.C., Dec. 29, 1941; s. James Rufus and Julia Lee (Walker) N.; m. Carol Anne Poetzsch, Dec. 28, 1963; children: Sharon Adele, David James. BS, U. N.C., 1963; PhD, Washington U., St. Louis, 1968. Postdoctoral appointee Argonne (Ill.) Nat. Lab., 1968-71, asst. chemist, 1971-74, chemist, 1974-79, photosynthesis group leader, 1979-95, sr. chemist, 1991-95; prof. dept. chemistry U. Chgo., 1995—; prof. chemistry U. Chgo., 1984—; chmn. internat. organizing com. 7th Internat. Conf. on Photochemical Conversion and Storage of Solar Energy, Northwestern U., Evanston, Ill., 1988. Co-editor: Photochemical Energy Conversion, 1989; mem. editorial bd. Applied Magnetic Resonance Jour., 1989—. Recipient Disting. Peformance award U. Chgo., 1977, 2 R&D 100 awards R&D mag., 1988, E.O. Lawrence Meml. award Dept. of Energy, 1990, Rumford Premium AAAS, 1992, Humboldt Rsch. award for Sr. Scientists, 1992, Zavoisky award Am. Acad. Arts and Scis., 1994. Mem. Am. Chem. Soc., Biophysical Soc. Office: U Chgo Dept Chemistry 5735 S Ellis Ave Chicago IL 60637-1403

NORRIS, RUTH ANN, social worker; b. Leavenworth, Kans., Oct. 29, 1955; d. Ival Eugene and Maxine Barbara (Ripper) Scholtz; m. V.W. Rusty Norris, May 21, 1977. BA, Graceland Coll., 1978; MSW, U. Kans., 1988. Lic. clin. social worker. Social worker Okla. Dept. Human Svcs., Miami, 1979-82, Mo. Div. Family Svcs., Kansas City, Mo., 1982-87; clin. social worker Western Mo. Mental Health Ctr., Kansas City, 1988—; exec. dir., pres. Ctr. for Wholeness Concepts, Independence, Mo., 1992-93; with Norris Counseling Svcs., Independence, 1993—. Named one of Outstanding Young Women Am., 1991. Mem. NASW, Acad. Cert. Social Workers. Office: Norris Counseling Svcs 10704 E Westport Rd # 200 Independence MO 64052-3470

NORRIS, TRACY HOPKINS, retired public relations executive; b. Ainsworth, Iowa, Nov. 1, 1927; s. Lee E. and Ruth C. (Simpson) N.; m. Emilie Lathrop, Nov. 11, 1956; 1 child, Shawn Tracy. BA, Cornell Coll., Mt. Vernon, Iowa, 1952; MA, U. Iowa, 1957. Admissions counselor Cornell Coll., Mt. Vernon, 1952-54; dir. news bur. Wittenberg U., Springfield, Ohio, 1956-70; exec. dir. univ. relations and communications Ball State U., Muncie, Ind., 1970-88. Active United Way Springfield, Ohio, Muncie, 1965—. Served with USN, 1945-48. Recipient Silver Anvil award Pub. Relations Soc. Am., 1967. Mem. Council for Advancement and Support Edn., Exchange Club. Lutheran. Home: 3810 S Burlington Dr Muncie IN 47302-9679

NORRIS, WILLIAM C., retired computer systems executive; b. Inavale, Nebr., July 14, 1911; s. William H. and Mildred A. (McCall) N.; m. Jane Malley, Sept. 15, 1943; children: W. Charles, George, Daniel, Brian, Constance, Roger, Mary N., David. B.S., U. Nebr., 1932. Sales engr. Westinghouse Electric Mfg. Co., Chgo., 1935-41; v.p., gen. mgr. Engring. Research Assocs., 1946-55, Univac (div. Sperry Rand Corp.), 1955-57; pres. Control Data Corp., Mpls., 1957-77; now past chmn. Control Data Corp., also bd. dirs.; bd. dirs. N.W. Bank Corp., N.W. Growth Fund, Tronchemics, Inc. Trustee Hill Reference Library; adv. com. White House Conf. on Balanced Nat. Growth and Econ. Devel., 1978—. Served to comdr. USNR, 1941-46. Recipient Nat. Medal Tech., 1986.

NORTH, ANITA, secondary education educator; b. Chgo., Apr. 21, 1963; d. William Denson and Carol (Linden) N. BA, Ind. U., 1985; MS in Edn., Northwestern U., 1987. Cert. tchr., Ill. High sch. social studies and English tchr. Lake Park High Sch., Roselle, Ill., 1987-89; high sch. social studies tchr. West Leyden High Sch., Northlake, Ill., 1989—; exch. program coord. West Leyden High Sch., 1989—, head coach boys' tennis team, 1989—, asst. coach girls' tennis team, 1994—, asst. speech coach, 1992-93. Humanities fellow Nat. Coun. Humanities, 1995; recipient Fern Fine Tchg. award West Leyden H.S., 1992. Mem. AAUW, Nat. Coun. for Social Studies, Ill. Coun. for Social Studies, Orgn. Am. Historians, Ill. Tennis Coaches Assn., Phi Delta Kappa. Christian.

NORTH, CAROL SUE, psychiatrist, educator; b. Keokuk, Iowa, May 6, 1954; d. Ray Stemen and Doris Ethelyn (Wood) N. BS in Gen. Sci., U. Iowa, 1976; MD, Wash. U., St. Louis, 1983, M in Psychiatric Epidemiology, 1993. Resident in psychiatry Barnes Hosp., Washington U. Med. Sch., St. Louis, 1983-87; rsch. fellow dept psychiatry Washington U., St. Louis, 1987-90, instr. dept. psychiatry, 1987-89, asst. prof. dept. psychiatry, 1989—; staff psychiatrist Grace Hill Neighborhood Health Ctr., St. Louis, 1987—, Midwest Psychiatry, 1993-95, Adapt of Am., 1995—. Author: Welcome, Silence, 1987, Multiple Personalities, Multiple Disorders: Psychiatric Classification and Media Influence, 1993; contbr. articles to profl. jours. Bd. Dirs. St. Louis Met. Alliance for the Mentally Ill, 1992—; trustee Rosati Stblzn. Ctr. for Homeless and Mentally Ill, 1992-94. Nat. Inst. Alcoholism and Alcohol Abuse grantee, 1988-93, Nat. Hazards Rsch. Applications Info. Ctr. grantee, 1987-88, NIMH grantee, 1991-95. Mem. Am. Psychiat. Assn., Life History Rsch. Soc., Ea. Mo. Psychiat. Soc. (exec. coun. and pres. 1996—), Am. Psychopathol. Assn., Am. Acad. Clin. Psychiatrists, Nat. Alliance for Mentally Ill, Am. Assn. Cmty. Psychiatrists, St. Louis Track Club. Presbyterian. Office: Washington U Sch Medicine Dept Psychiatry 4940 Childrens Pl Saint Louis MO 63110-1002

NORTH, WALTER, state legislator; b. Jan. 31, 1933. Grad., Mich. State U. County commr.; senator Mich. State Dist. 37, 1995—; chmn. agriculture & forestry com. Mich. State Senate, edn. com., transp. com., tourism com., joint com. on adminstrv. rules. Address: PO Box 30036 Lansing MI 48909-7536

NORTHENOR, D(ORIS) JEAN, banker, senior vice president; b. Kosciusko County, Ind., Dec. 21, 1932; d. Merl and Ruth B. (Decker) Nelson; m. James W. Northenor, Feb. 26, 1961; children: Rick, Steve Reed. Student, Essential Bank Mktg., 1984, Sch. Banking, 1986. Packer, inspector Kimble Glass, 1956-60; owner, operator Northenor Orchard, 1961-68; admitting clk. Charleston (Ill.) Community Hosp., 1969-70; sec. Tucker Realty, 1971-72; dep. Kosciusko County Auditor, Warsaw, Ind., 1972-74; Kosciusko County auditor Warsaw, 1975-83; sr. v.p. Lake City Bank, Warsaw, 1984—; resource panelist Assn. Ind. Counties, Acad. Pub. Svc., Ind. Sate Bd. Accounts;mem. steering com. Grace Coll.; mem., chmn. criteria and endorsement com. Ind. Bus. for Responsive Govt. Past commr. Bur. Motor Vehicles, State of Ind.; past pres. bd. dirs. Warsaw Cmty. Devel. Corp.; past mem. mktg. and pub. rels. com. YMCA; mem. Kosciusko County Sheriff's Merit Bd.; mem. IBA Govt. Rels. Coun.; mem. Grace Coll. Prs. Cmty. Coun.; past treas. bd. trustees Atwood Aldersgate Ch.; past chmn. ctrl. com. Kosciusko County Rep. Party; past pres. bd. dirs. Acad. Pub. Svc., Kosciusko Leadership Acad.; past treas. Warsaw Cmty. Found. for Pub. Edn.; past bd. dirs. YMCA. Named Sagamore of the Wabash, Gov. Bowen Ind., 1980, Gov. Orr Ind., 1984, Gov. Bayh, 1989, Woman of Yr., Warsaw C. of C., 1983; hon. Sec. of State, hon. Lit. Gov.; recipient Ind. Tribute to Women, 1981. Mem. Assn. Ind. Counties (past bd. dirs., past pres. N.E. dist.), Nat. Assn. Bank Women, Fin. Women Internat., Kosciusko County Assn. Female Execs., Order Eastern Star. Republican.

NORTHROP, STUART JOHNSTON, manufacturing company executive; b. New Haven, Oct. 22, 1925; s. Filmer Stuart Cuchow and Christine (Johnston) N.; divorced; children: Christine Daniell, Richard Rockwell Stafford. B.A. in Physics, Yale U., 1948. Indsl. engr. U.S. Rubber Co., Naugatuck, Conn., 1948-51; head indsl. engring. dept. Am. Cyanamid Co., Wallingford, Conn., 1951-54; mfg. mgr. Linear, Inc., Phila., 1954-57; mgr. quality control and mfg. Westinghouse Electric Co., Pitts., 1957-58; mfg. supt. SKF Industries, Phila., 1958-61; v.p. mfg. Am. Meter Co., Phila., 1961-69; founder, v.p., gen. mgr. water resources div. Singer Co., Phila.; pres., dir. Buffalo Meter Co., Four Layne Cos.; dir. Gen. Filter Co., 1969-72; chmn., CEO Huffy Corp., Dayton, Ohio, 1972-85, chmn. exec. com., 1985-94; bd. dirs. Lukens, Inc., Coatesville, Pa., Union Corp., N.Y.C., DSLT, Inc., St. Clair, Mich., Elbit Sys. Am., Ft. Worth. County fin. chmn. George Bush Presdl. campaign, 1980; presdl. appointee Pres.'s Commn. on Ams. Outdoors, 1985-86; chmn. nat. hwy. safety adv. com. Dept. Transp., 1986—; founder, dir. emeritus Recreation Roundtable, Washington. Served with USAAF, 1944-45. Named Chief Exec. Officer of Yr. for leisure industry Wall Street Transcript, 1980. Mem. Del. Valley Investors (past pres.), Interlocutors, Elihu, Am. Bus. Conf. (founding), Fin. Commn. of Funds Am. Future, Boulders Club (Scottsdale), KOA Soc., Delta Kappa Epsilon. Home: 7474 E Boulders Pky Unit 4 Scottsdale AZ 85262-1247 Office: Huffy Corp 7701 Byers Rd Miamisburg OH 45342-3657

NORTHUP, BEVERLY A. BAKER, pricipal chief; b. Columbia, Mo., Feb. 14, 1938; d. Charles Clayton Rupard and Annie Cecil Barnes Rupard Collins; m. Erbie M. Baker, Sept. 10, 1955 (div. Sept. 1970); children: Sherry, Peggy, Erbie Jr., Phillip, Jason; m. Robert Lionel Northup, June 29, 1991. Oper. room sec. Ellis Fischel Cancer Hosp., Columbia, Mo., 1976-77; sec. Mo. Cancer Registry, Columbia, 1977-78, U. Mo. Dept. of Fisheries & Wildlife, Columbia, 1980-84; sec. sterile processing U. Mo. Hosp., Columbia, 1984-85; sec. Ctrl. Mo. Regional Ctr., Columbia, 1985-86; rsch. dir. No. Cherokee Nation, Columbia, 1986-88; propr. Physicians Eyewear & Hearing Aid Ctr., Columbia, 1989—; prin. chief No. Cherokee Nation, Columbia, 1984—; pres. bd. No. Cherokee Tribe, Inc., Columbia, 1984—; Indian task force to the gov. Mo. Dept. of Econ. Dev., Jefferson City, Mo., 1994; tribal historian, spokesperson, consulting geneologist, No. Cherokee Nation, Columbia, 1984—. Author: History of the Northern Cherokee Nation Part I, 1993, History of the Northern Cherokee Nation Part II, 1996. Del. Boone County Rep. Conv., Columbia, 1992, Ninth Dist. Mo. Rep. Conv., Columbia, 1992, Mo. Rep. Conv., 1992; bd. dirs. Boone County Elections Verification Bd., Columbia, 1992. Grantee Adminstrn. for Native Ams., 1986, 87, 88, United Meth. Ch., 1986, 87, 88. Mem. Nat. Am. Indian Coun. (tribal del. 1994—), Nat. Orgn. for the Unification of Native Ams. (tribal del. 1994—), White House Com. for the Recognition of all Indian People (tribal del. 1995—), No. Cherokee Cmty. Assn. (bd. dirs. 1983—). Republican. Baptist. Office: No Cherokee Nation Old LA Territory 1502 E Broadway Ste 201 Columbia MO 65201

NORTHWAY, DENNIS EDWARD, conductor; b. St. Louis, Nov. 5, 1958; s. Wayne Elfred and Dolores Helen (Gerichten) N. MusB, U. Mo. St. Louis, 1981; MusM, Concordia U., 1982; predoctoral, Northwestern U., 1986, MusD, 1993. Cert. choir master. Dir. music St. Paul Luth. Ch., Addison, Ill., 1981-94; cond. Chgo. Children's Choir, 1988-95, Grace Episcopal Ch., Oak Park, Ill., 1995—; cond. North Shore Musician's Club, Evanston, Ill., 1984-91, Luth. Choir Chgo., 1984-90, Park Forest (Ill.) Singers, 1994—; chorus master Light Opera Works, Evanston, 1986—; artistic dir. and cond. Fleur de Lys, Chgo., 1990-95; music dir. McCormick Theol. Sem., Chgo., 1990-92; parish musician Grace Episc. Ch., Oak Park, Ill., 1994—; subdean Am. Guild Organists, Chgo. Composer: Prelude on Erhalt Uns Herr, 1989, Prelude on Schmucke Dich, 1986, Passacaglia, 1995, Prelude on Herzliebster Jesu, 1994. Home: 2501 W Lunt Chicago IL 60645 Office: Grace Epsicopal Ch 924 Lake St Oak Park IL 60301

NORTON, JODY (JOHN DOUGLAS NORTON), English language educator; b. Princeton, N.J., Nov. 13, 1943; s. Paul Foote and Alison Edmunds (Stuart) N.; m. Alexandra Holt Morey, Aug. 20, 1977; children: Joselle, Jackson, Tayo. BA, U. Mass., Amherst, 1966; MA, U. Calif., Berkeley, 1981, PhD, 1988. Vis. asst. prof. Rice U., Houston, 1988-89, Albion (Mich.) Coll., 1989-94; lectr. Ea. Mich. U., Ypsilanti, 1994—. Contbr. articles to profl. jours. Fellow U. Calif., 1979-80, 80-81, 84-85, 87-88, Yale U., 1966-67; faculty rsch. grantee Albion Coll., 1992, 93, 94. Mem. MLA, Midwest MLA, Soc. for Critical Exch., Popular Culture Assn., Phi Beta Kappa, Phi Kappa Phi. Home: 415 Ventura Ct Ann Arbor MI 48103-4319 Office: Eastern Mich U Dept English Lang & Lit Ypsilanti MI 48197

NORTON, LLOYD DARRELL, research soil scientist; b. Batesville, Ind., Oct. 20, 1953; s. Milton Walker and Enamay (Doan) N.; children: Benjamin D., Amber J., Jon A. BS, Purdue U., 1975, MS, 1976; PhD, Ohio State U., 1981. Soil scientist Ind. Dept. Natural Resources, Indpls., 1974; rsch. assoc. Purdue U., West Lafayette, Ind., 1975-77, Ohio State U., Columbus, 1977-82; soil scientist Nat. Soil Erosion Rsch. Lab. USDA, West Lafayette, 1982—; prof. agronomy and earth and atmospheric scis. Purdue U., 1982—; cons. AID, Washington, 1986, 87, FAO, Rome, 1991; vis. scientist div. soils Commonwealth Sci. and Indsl. Rsch. Orgn., Canberra, Australia, 1990. Contbd. over 140 articles to profl. jours. Mem. Internat. Soc. Soil Sci. (cert. of appreciation 1988), Soil Sci. Soc. Am. (cert. of appreciation 1988), World Assn. Soil Water Cons. Office: Purdue U USDA Nat Soil Erosion Lab 1196 Soil Building West Lafayette IN 47907

NORTON, MARY LETA, educator; b. Butler County, Iowa, June 28, 1938; d. Martin P. and Hazel Leta (Garner) Holm; m. James Byron Norton, June 13, 1958; children: James Byron Jr., Jill Leta. BS in Elem. Edn. and Reading, U. Wis., Milw., 1972; MA in Elem. Sci. Edn., U. No. Iowa, Cedar Falls, 1987. Tchr. Multi-Cultural Ctr. Milw. Pub. Schs., 1968-74, Cedar Falls (Iowa) Cmty. Sch., 1974-96; instr. U. No. Iowa, 1996—; state bd. mem. Iowa Coun. Environ. Educators, Gov.'s Environ. Edn. Congress; mem. Butler County Coun. Environ. Educators, Cedar Falls MC/NS Coun., U.S. Fish and Wildlife Walnut Creek Prairie and Learning Ctr. Planning Group, North Cedar Quality Behavior Com., North Cedar Outdoor Ednl. Habitat Com.; mem. conf. planning com. Hearst Ctr. for Arts Edn. Adv. Panel, Cedar Valley Arboretum Edn. and Planning Com. and Bd.; edn. cons. land stewardshp environ. edn. program State of Mont., 1989. Free lance author environ. edn. articles and curriculum, 1983-96; author: North Cedar Elementary School Environmental Education Mentoring Program Handbook, 1985-96; author Project LS (Lifestyle and Land Stewardship, 1994; contbr. articles to profl. jours. Named Outstanding Conservation Educator of Yr. Iowa Wildlife Fedn., 1990; recipient Outstanding Achievement in Environ. Edn. award Sierra Club, 1990, Spl. award Iowa Dept. Edn., 1991, Gold Star award KWWL & McElroy Trust Fund, 1991, Grant Resource Enhancement and Protection Act, 1992, Nat. Bd. Profl. Tchg. Stds. award Pres. Clinton, 1995, Carver grant Devel. of Natural Habitat Reconstrn. Connections to Tech., 1995-96, Environ. Educator of Yr. award EPA, 1995. Mem. NEA, Nat. Sci. Tchrs. Assn., Nat. Reading Coun., Iowa Reading Coun., Nat. Math. Tchrs., Iowa Math. Tchrs., Tchrs. as Writers and Pubsl., Iowa State Edn. Assn., Cedar Falls Edn. Assn., Nat. Wildlife Found., Iowa Wildlife Found., Nat. Heritage Found., Wetland Preservations, World Wildlife Fund, Rails to Trails, Nat. Geog. Soc., Smithsonian Soc., Questers Antiques and Preservation Clubs, Citizens for Equal Rights, Nat. and Local Pub. Radio and TV Support Groups, U. Iowa and Theater Support Group, Chgo. Mus. Art.

NORTON, PETER BOWES, publishing company executive; b. London, May 4, 1929; came to U.S., 1969; s. James Peter and Margaret (Bowes) N.; m. Heather Pearch, Jan. 16, 1954; children: Jan Heather, Fiona Mary. Student, S.E. Essex Tech. Coll., 1942-45, Royal Naval Colls., 1949-54. Commd. officer Royal Navy, 1945, advanced through grades to lt., 1954, ret., 1960; pers. officer United Dominions Trust, London, 1960-63; jr. exec. to mng. dir. Ency. Britannica, London, 1963-68, mng. dir., 1968-69; v.p. internat. div. Ency. Britannica, Chgo., 1969-70; pres. Ency. Britannica Can., 1970-73, Ency. Britannica U.S.A., Chgo., 1974-85; pres. Ency. Britannica Inc., 1986-93, pres., CEO, 1993-95; also bd. dirs. Ency. Britannica Inc., Chgo.; bd. dirs. Ency. Universalis (Paris); chmn. bd. dirs. Ency. Britannica Edml. Corp., Chgo., 1988-95. Bd. dirs. William Benton Found., 1986-95. Fellow Chartered Inst. Secs. (Eng.), Chartered Inst. Adminstrs. U.K., Chartered Inst. Dirs. U.K.; mem. Japan Am. Soc. Chgo., Inc., Chgo. Club. Mem. Ch. of Eng. Clubs: Royal Automobile (London); Chgo., Carlton. Home: 180 E Pearson St Apt 3401 Chicago IL 60611-2125

NORWICH MCLENNAN, JAMIE LOU, clergywoman, writer; b. Cheyenne, Wyo., May 8, 1956; d. Ross Roosevelt Peery and Margo Frances (Price) Teague; m. Richard Lee Watkins, July 15, 1978 (div.); m. John Byron Norwich McLennan, Sept. 2, 1989. BA in French, U. Wyo., 1977; MBA, U. Phoenix, Denver, 1987; MDiv, Iliff Sch. Theology, Denver, 1992. Cert. tchr., Colo. Substitute tchr. Boulder County, Colo., 1979-81; purchasing agt. Brown Palace Hotel, Denver, 1981-84; fine paper buyer Butler Paper Co., Denver, 1984-87; cons. Cornerstone Libr., Westminster, Colo., 1985-87; assoc. pastor First United Meth. Ch., North Platte, Nebr., 1990-91; pastor Dakota City/Homer United Meth. Ch., Dakota City, Nebr., 1992-94, Pearl Meml./Asbury United Meth. Ch., Omaha, 1994—; cons. Creative Thoughts & Things, Westminster, 1987-88; retreat leader United Meth. Ch., 1985—; bd. dirs. ex officio United Ministries of N.E. Omaha, 1994—; bd. dirs., treas. United Meth. Ministries, Omaha, 1995—; leader workshops. Author: (poetry) Alive Now!, 1988, 89. Mem. clergy adv. bd. Mayor of Omaha, 1995—; active Omaha Together One Cmty., 1994—. Recipient Good Citizenship award DAR, 1974. Mem. Women in Ministry in Nebr. (adminstrv. coord. 1992—). Office: Pearl Meml United Meth Ch 2319 Ogden St Omaha NE 68110

NOSSETT, PAULA MARIE, English language educator; b. Oakland City, Ind., Nov. 14, 1937; d. William Paul and Genevieve (Scribner) Eskew; m. Jack Alan Nossett, June 7, 1957; 1 child, Nancy Maria. BS, Oakland City Coll., 1958; MS, Ind. State U., 1963. Tchr. English, Monroe City (Ind.) High Sch., 1958-59, Lawrenceville (Ill.) Twp. High Sch., 1959-67; tchr. English and journalism Rivet High Sch., Vincennes, Ind., 1975-79; prof. English, Vincennes U., 1979—, chmn. experience-based learning program, 1982-94. Author: Credit for Experience-Based Learning, 1983. Coord. fund drive Multiple Sclerosis Found., Vincennes, 1971, co-capt., 1972; capt. Cancer Drive, Vincennes, 1974; mem. book selection com. PTO, Vincennes, 1978; mem. Knox County Child Abuse Prevention Bd. Mem. Coun. for Adult and Experiential Learning, Nat. Coun. Instrnl. Adminstrs., AAUW (pres. Vincennes 1976-77), DAR, Delta Kappa Gamma, Phi Delta Kappa. Republican. Methodist. Office: Vincennes U 1002 N 1st St Vincennes IN 47591-1504

NOTESTEIN, BARBARA, state legislator. Address: 1724 E Geneva Pl Milwaukee WI 53211-3557 Office: Wis State Assembly State Capitol Madison WI 53702*

NOTTESTAD, DARRELL, state legislator; m. Ellen Nottestad; 2 children. Student, Mayville State Coll.; MEd, U. N.D.; postgrad., N.D. State U., Denver U., Ctrl. Mich. U. Sch. prin.; rep. Dist. 43 N.D. State U., mem. judiciary and natural resources com. Bd. dirs. Area Sch. Credit Union; mem. Grand Forks County Hist. Soc. Mem. Sons of Norway. Home: 2110 Westward Dr Grand Forks ND 58201

NOTTINGHAM, WILLIAM JESSE, church mission executive, minister; b. Sharon, Pa., Nov. 22, 1927; s. Jess William and Alice May (Green) N.; m. Patricia Clutts, Feb. 1, 1949; children: Theodore Jess, Deborah Joan Selke, Nancy Alice, Gregory Philip. BA, Bethany Coll., W.Va., 1949, DD (hon.), 1987; BD, Union Theol. Sem., N.Y.C., 1953; PhD, Columbia U., 1962; DD (hon.), Christian Theol. Sem., Indpls., 1984. Ordained to ministry Christian Ch. (Disciples of Christ), Oct. 21, 1945. Pastor Ch. of Christ, Canoe Camp and Covington, Pa., 1949-50; field worker Ch. of the Master, N.Y.C., 1950-53; assoc. min. Nat. City Christian Ch., Washington, 1954-58; fraternal worker Coun. on Christian Unity, France, 1958-65; with CIMADE and Centre de Glay; with youth dept. World Coun. of Chs., Geneva, 1965-68; exec. sec. for Latin Am. and Caribbean Divsn. Overseas Ministries, Christian Ch. (Disciples of Christ and United Ch. Christ), Indpls., 1968-76, exec. sec. East Asia and Pacific, 1976-83, pres., 1984-94; affiliate prof. mission Christian Theol. Sem., 1995—. Author: Chriatian Faith and Secular Action: An Introduction to the Life and Thought of Jacques Maritain, 1968, The Practice and Preaching of Liberation, 1986, The Social Ethics of Martin Bucer, 1491-1551; translator: God's Underground, 1970, Prayer at the Heart of Life, 1975, Materialist Approaches to the Bible, 1985, Madeleine Barot, 1991. Fulbright scholar, Strasbourg, France, 1953-54. Mem. Nat. Coun. Chs. of Christ in USA (gen. bd.), Assn. Disciples for Theol. Discussion, Christians Associated for Relations with Eastern Europe. Democrat.

NOVACKY, ANTON JAN, plant pathologist, educator; b. Bratislava, Czechoslovakia, June 3, 1933; came to U.S., 1968; s. Jan Martin and Katarina (Fischer) N.; m. Dorothy Edit Hyross, June 28, 1958; children: Andrea Novacky Congdon, Thomas Martin. Student, Charles U., Prague, Czechoslovakia; BS, Comenius U., Bratislava, 1955, MS, 1956; PhD, Czechoslovak Acad. Sci., Prague, 1965. Postgrad. fellow U. Moscow, Russia, 1964; postdoctoral fellow U. Ky., Lexington, 1966-69; postdoctoral rsch. assoc. U. Mo., Columbia, 1969-70, asst. prof., 1970-74, assoc. prof., 1974-82, prof., 1982—; rsch. phytopathologist Inst. Exptl. Phytopathology and Entomology, Bratislava, Czechoslovakia, 1962-68. Author: (with R.N. Goodman) The Hypersensitive Reaction in Plants to Pathogens, 1994; speaker various seminars and meeting presentations; contbr. articles to profl. jours. Grantee NSF, 1986-89, 1978-82, USDA, 1978-83, 93-95, MSMC, 1986-89; fellow Japanese Soc. for Promotion of Sci. Rsch., 1984; recipient German Academic Exch. award, 1976, Alexander von Humboldt Sr. U.S. Scientist, 1983. Mem. AAAS, Am. Phytopathol. Soc. (fellow 1986, chair 1984-85), Am. Soc. Plant Physiologists, Sigma Xi. Roman Catholic. Home: 311 Crown Pt Columbia MO 65203-2202 Office: U Mo Agriculture Bldg 3-18 Columbia MO 65211

NOVAK, DONALD F., physical therapist; b. Elgin, Ill., May 19, 1964; s. Donald Jr. and Elizabeth J. (Meyer) N.; m. Karin Sue Kaiser, May 18, 1991. BA in Biol. Scis., No. Ill. U., 1987, BA in Phys. Therapy, 1989. Lic. phys. therapist, Ill. Photolab technician Agri-Graphics, Cary, Ill., 1982-89; phys. therapist NIMC, McHenry, Ill., 1989—. Mem. Am. Phys. Therapy Assn.

NOVAK, FRANCIS ALPHONSUS, religious organization executive, priest; b. Dwight, Nebr., Feb. 4, 1923; s. Frank and Mary (Tomes) N. MA in Liturgical Studies, Cath. U. Am., 1980; D Ministry, St. Mary's Sem. and Univ., Balt., 1984. Ordained priest Roman Cath. Ch., 1949. Missionary, 1951-55, retreat dir., 1952-58; staff mem. Ligouri (Mo.) Publs., 1958-67; pastor St. Alphonsus Ch., Grand Rapids, Mich., 1967-71; dir. devel. and pastoral couns. Diocese of Grand Rapids, 1971-74; exec. dir. Nat. Cath. Stewardship Coun., Washington, 1974-80; pres. Nat. Cath. Conf. for Total Stewardship, Chgo., 1980—. Author: Homily Helps-Stewardship of Giftedness, 1993, Homily Helps Treasure, The Eucharist, 1993, Total Stewardship Manual, 1992. Home: 1633 N Cleveland Ave Chicago IL 60614-5601 Office: Nat Cath Conf Stewardship 5420 S Cornell Ave Unit 203 Chicago IL 60615-5646

NOVAK, HARRY R., manufacturing company executive; b. Chgo., Sept. 30, 1951; s. Edward M. and Rose (Loncar) N.; m. Shawn Sternquist, Sept. 7, 1975; children: Andrea, Jacob, Bethany. BS in Econs., MacMurray Coll., Jacksonville, Ill., 1973; MBA in Fin., DePaul U., 1977. Ops. mgr. to v.p., regional mgr. Heller Fin. Inc., Chgo., 1974-87; v.p. Golenberg & Assocs., Cleve., 1987-88; sr. v.p., CFO Gibson-Homans Co., Twinsburg, Ohio, 1988—. Congregation pres. First Luth. Ch., Strongsville, Ohio, 1987-92; founder Strongsville Area Youth Group, 1992; mem. Strongsville Choral Boosters, 1991-94. Mem. Cleve. Growth Assn. Office: Gibson-Homans Co 1755 Enterprise Pky Twinsburg OH 44087-2203

NOVAK, JOHN PHILIP, state legislator; b. Berwyn, Ill., Feb. 15, 1946; s. John Peter and Cordelia Ann (Moss) N.; (div.); 1 child, Todd Alexander. BS, Eastern Ill. U., Charleston, 1971, MA, 1973. Asst. pers. adminstr. Ill. Dept. Mental Health, 1973-76; pers. adminstr. Manville Corp., 1976-81; labor rels. adminstr. Am. Spring Wire, 1981-82; mem. Ill. Ho. of Reps. from 85th dist., 1987—; mem. Agr., Edn. Appropriations, Environ. & Energy, Vet. Affairs Com. Ill. Ho. of Reps., vice chmn. Mcpl. and Conservation Laws Coms. Trustee Village of Bradley, Ill., 1975-82; treas. Kankakee County, Ill., 1982-86, 86-87, chmn., 1986-87, precinct committeeman, 1974-80, 86—; bd. dirs. Am. Cancer Soc., 1985-88. Decorated Unit Campaign Clusters; recipient Good Conduct medal, Agr. award, Ill. Farm Bur., 1987, 1988, Major Legislation Sponsorship award Northeastern Ill. Waterfowlers Assn., 1990, Friend of Edn. award Ill. Edn. Assn., 1990; named Outstanding Freshman Legislator, Ind. Cmty. Banks, 1987, Legislator of Yr., Ill. Assn. County Treas. Mem. Lions (treas. Bradley County chpt. 1982-83), Am. Legion (bd. dirs. Post No. 702 1981—), Vietnam Vets. Am. (bd. dirs. 1984—, Cert. of Recognition 1988), Moose, Pi Sigma Alpha. Democrat. Home: 1317 Marla Ter Bradley IL 60915-2052*

NOVAK, STEVEN G., state legislator; b. May 26, 1949; m. Julie Novak; four children. BA, Hamline U.; postgrad., U. Minn., Duluth. Comm. coord. Minn. Mus. Art; v.p. devel. Ramsey Health Care, Inc., and Ramsey Found.; state rep. Minn. Ho. of Reps., St. Paul, 1975-82; Dist. 52 senator Minn. State Senate, St. Paul, 1982—; chmn. jobs, energy and cmty. devel. com., mem. environ. and natural resources, jobs, energy and cmty. devel. (fin. divsn.), rules and adminstrn., taxes and tax laws, transp. and pub. transit, and fin. divsn. coms., Minn. State Senate. Office: 747 Redwood Ln Saint Paul MN 55112-6620 also: State Senate State Capital Building Saint Paul MN 55155-1606*

NOVITSKI, CHARLES EDWARD, biology educator; b. Rochester, N.Y., Oct. 3, 1946; s. Edward and Esther Ellen (Rudkin) N.; m. Margaret Thornton Sime, June 15, 1968; children: Nancy Ellen, Linda Nicole, Elise Michelle. BA in Biology, Columbia Coll., 1969; PhD in Biophysics, Calif. Inst. Tech., 1979. Rsch. fellow and assoc. City of Hope Nat. Med. Ctr., Duarte, Calif., 1977-80; sr. tutor in biochemistry Monash U., Victoria, Australia, 1980-82, lectr. in biochemistry, 1982-84; program leader and rsch. scientist in nematode control Agrigenetics Advanced Sci. Co., Madison, Wis., 1985-88; assoc. prof. molecular biology Cen. Mich. U., Mt. Pleasant, 1989—. Assoc. editor Jour. Nematology, 1994—; contbr. articles to various profl. jours. Mem. Soc. of Nematologists, Internat. Soc. of Plant Molecular Biology. Home: 1208 E Preston Rd Mount Pleasant MI 48858-3927 Office: Cen Mich U Dept Biology Mount Pleasant MI 48859

NOVOTNEY, NORMAN EDWARD, electrical engineer; b. Cleve., July 10, 1960; s. Edward Louis and Loretta (Catullo) N. BSEE, Ohio State U., 1983. Missile guidance engr. Gen. Dynamics Corp., Pomona, Calif., 1983-84; avionics engr. Foster Airdata, Columbus, Ohio, 1984-86; devel. engr. Scriptel Corp., Columbus, 1986-87; sr. elec. engr. R & D electro-optics Spectra-Physics, Dayton, Ohio, 1988—. Home: 9420 Saddlebrook Ln Apt 1B Miamisburg OH 45342-5532 Office: Spectra-Physics Laserplane 5475 Kellenburger Rd Dayton OH 45424-1099

NOWAK, CHESTER JOSEPH, optometrist; b. Chgo., Jan. 30, 1923; s. Peter Joseph and Josephine (Starsiak) N.; OD, Ill. Coll. Optometry, 1945, B in Ocular Diagnostic Pharm. U. Mo., St. Louis, 1988; m. Florence J. Wardach, Feb. 14, 1943; children: Sandra Jane, Susan Michaline, Sharlene Joyce, Pamela Jo, Robert Chester, Jerome Cyril. Pvt. practice optometry, Chgo., 1946-91, Niles, Ill., 1956-92, Arlington Heights, Ill., 1992—; sch. lectr. children's visual problems; mem. Optometric Extension Program Found., 1947-93. Mem. Am. Optometric Assn. (Optometric Recognition award 1981-92), Ill. Optometric Assn. Nat. Eye Research Found. (cert. in contact lenses), Am. Pub. Health Assn., Ill. Pub. Health Assn., Coll. Optometrists in Vision Devel. (assoc.), Am. Acad. Optometry. Roman Catholic. Club: K.C. Author: What Parents Should Know About Their Children's Eye Vision, 1972, The Brain's Vision, 1981. Patentee devices for diagnosing and correcting eye fusion and neuro-reflex, 1973; registered trade name of contact lens called Power Blend, 1965.

NOWAK, JOHN E., law educator; b. Chgo., Jan. 2, 1947; s. George Edward and Evelyn (Bucci) N.; m. Judith Johnson, June 1, 1968; children: John Edwin, Jeffrey Edward. AB, Marquette U., 1968; JD, U. Ill., 1971. Law clk. Supreme Ct. of Ill., Chgo., 1971-72; asst. prof. U. Ill., Urbana, 1972-75, assoc. prof., 1975-87, law prof., 1978—, grad. coll. faculty, 1982—, Baum Prof. Law, 1993—; chmn. Constl. Law Sch. Sect.; faculty rep. Big Ten Intercollegiate Conf., Schaumburg, Ill., 1981—; vis. prof. law U. Mich., Ann Arbor, 1985; Lee Disting. vis. prof. Coll. William and Mary, 1993. Coauthor: Constitutional Law, 4th edit. 1991, Treatise on Constitutional Law, 1986, 2nd edit., 1992, Story's Commentaries on the Constitution, 1987. Scholar-in-Residence, U. of Ariz., Tucson, 1985, 87. Mem. Assn. of Am. Law Schs. (chm. constl. law sect., accreditation com. 1980-88), Nat. Collegiate Athletic Assn. (mem. infractions com. 1987—), Am. Law Inst., Am. Bar Assn., Ill. Bar Assn., Order of the Coif (Triennial Book award com.). Roman Catholic. Home: 1701 Mayfair Rd Champaign IL 61821-5522 Office: U Ill Coll Law 504 E Pennsylvania Ave Champaign IL 61820-6909

NOWAK, PATRICIA ROSE, advertising executive; b. Toledo, Nov. 29, 1946; d. Robert Joseph and Hedwig Rose (Rutkowski) Stack; m. Casimir Robert Nowak Jr., June 3, 1967 (dec.); children: Martin Robert, Laura Kristen. Student, Bowling Green State U., 1964-67. Events dir. Sta. WTTO, Toledo, 1967-68; dir. spl. events Tiedtke's, Toledo, 1968-72; dir. fashion and pub. rels. Lion Store, Toledo, 1980-86; owner, mgr. Pat Nowak & Assocs., Sylvania, Ohio, 1986-90; dir. pub. rels., consumer affairs Seaway Foodtown Stores, Maamee, Ohio, 1990—. Contbr. fashion articles to Toledo Blade, 1980-88. Auction chmn. Toleda Opera, 1978, 86-87; bridge chmn. Toledo Symphony, 1987; gifts chmn. St. Johns High Sch., Toledo, 1988-89; chmn. holiday parade Citifest, Toledo, 1988-89; dir. opening ceremonies World Cup, Toledo, 1988-90; bd. dirs. Am. Heart Assn., Toledo Repertoire Theatre, Pvt. Industry Coun. Mem. Toledo C. of C. (solicitation com., vol. award 1989), Jr. League Toledo (pub. rels. com. 1984-85). Roman Catholic. Home: 8130 Hidden Harbour W Holland OH 43528 Office: 1020 Ford St Maumee OH 43537-1820

NOWAK, THOMAS, engineering company executive; b. Mar. 13, 1955. Draftsman Butler Mfg., Salina, Kans., 1974-77, Wilson Constrn., Salina, 1978-83; mech. designer Coronado Engring., Salina, 1983—. Mem. KC. Office: Coronado Engring 431 N 13th St Salina KS 67401-2007

NOWICKI, DAVID MICHAEL, manufacturing engineer; b. Detroit, Feb. 7, 1968; s. Thomas Edward and Virginia Ann (Farr) N. BEE, U. Detroit, 1990. Mfg. engr. Ford Motor Co., Dearborn, Mich., 1989—. Home: 32160 Joy Rd Livonia MI 48150

NOYES, RICHARD FRANCIS, optometrist; b. Des Moines, May 8, 1952; s. Robert F. and Mary C. N.; m. Martha J. Noyes; children: Jennifer, Bethany, Marcus, Erica. BS in Gen. Sci., U. Iowa, 1975; BS in Visual Sci., Ill. Coll. Optometry, 1976, OD, 1978. Practice optometry specializing in ocular disease, Marion, Iowa, 1978—; adj. faculty Pacific U. Coll. Optometry, 1992-93, 93—; lectr. in ocular disease, advanced diagnostic and treatment techniques and practice mgmt. Contbr. articles to profl. jours. Dir. Haiti Med. Mission, 1978—. Named Outstanding Young Optometrist State Iowa, 1985, Outstanding Optemetrist of Yr., 1993. Fellow Am. Coll. Optometric Physicians; mem. Iowa Optometric Assn. (legis. com. 1984, bd. dirs. 1985—, sec.-treas. 1987-88, v.p. 1988-89, pres.-elect 1989-90, pres. 1990-91), Am. Optometric Assn. (chmn. primary care & ocular disease com. 1992-96, North Cen. State Optometric conf. cabinet 1989-92, chmn. OD edn. north cen. states optometric conf.), Lions (bd. dirs. 1979-89, Disting. Svc. award 1983, A. Melvin Jones fellow 1988), Sertoma (Outstanding Svc. to Mankind award 1987), Beta Sigma Kappa. Republican. Methodist. Home: 4196 Brookside Dr Marion IA 52302-9327 Office: 1065 E Post Rd Marion IA 52302-5214

NUCKLOS, SHIRLEY, medical administrator, consultant; b. Canton, Ohio, Aug. 30, 1949; d. Boyd Alexander and Julia Lillian (Hood) Curtis; m. William W. Nucklos, Mar. 11, 1972; children: Túere Tené, Tiombé Nigina, Khari Oji-Lee. BS in Edn., Cen. State U., Wilberforce, Ohio, 1970; MA, Ohio State U., 1971. Cert. elem. tchr., guidance counselor. Guidance counselor Scioto Village High Sch., Powell, Ohio, 1973-78; acad. advisor Franklin U., Columbus, Ohio, 1980-82, acting asst. dir. records, 1982-83, asst. registrar, 1983-90; registrar Ohio Dominican Coll., Columbus, 1990-93; dir. human resources Mid-Am. Phys. Medicine & Exec. Med., Inc., Columbus, Ohio, 1994—; adminstrv. advisor to Black Student Union, Franklin U., 1982-85; human resource cons. Mid-Am. Phys. Medicine, Exec. Med., Inc., Westerville, Ohio, 1989-93, dir. human resources/bus. mgr., 1993—. Vol. tchr. Umoja Sasa Shule, Columbus, 1971-74; booster Mid-west Gymnastic and Cheerleading, Dublin, Ohio, 1988-93; active various com. for minority concerns. Mem. Ohio Assn. Collegiate Registrars and Admissions Officers (sec. 1991-93, Cert. Appreciation 1985, 93), Am. Assn. Collegiate Registrars and Admissions Officers, Nat. Assn. Coll. Deans, Registrars and Admissions Officers, Ohio Assn. Women Deans, Adminstrs. and Counselors, Nat. Assn. Women Deans, Adminstrs. and Counselors, Am. Assn. Univ.

Adminstrn., Va. Admissions Counselors for Black Concerns, Ohio Health Info. Mgmt. Assn. Democrat. Mem. Church of God in Christ. Office: Mid Am Phys Medicine & Exec Med Inc 254 Woodland Ave Ste 105 Columbus OH 43203-1782

NUGENT, B.A., executive director, professor; b. Sept. 26, 1934; s. M.H. and Velma (Randolph) N.; m. Clara B. Nugent, July 8, 1983; 1 child, Natasha Nugent Kendall. MusB, So. Meth. U., 1956, MusM, 1957; PhD in musicology, U. North Texas, Denton, 1970. Head, music dept. Emporia State U., Emporia, Kans., 1961-71; dir., sch. of music U. Okla., Norman, Okla., 1971-74; dean, sciences and arts Wash. State U., Pullman, Wash., 1974-79; v.p., academic affairs W. Va. U., Morgantown, W.Va., 1979-81; chancellor, prof. (music) U. Ark., Fayetteville, Ark., 1981-86; exec. dir. U. Ill. Found., Urbana, Ill., 1986—. Editor: Collected Works of Antonius Divitis, 1993, In One Lifetime, 1984, Oklahoma Terror, 1974. Recipient Disting. Alumnus U. North Tex., 1993. Office: Univ Ill Found Harker Hall 1305 W Green St Urbana IL 61801

NUGENT, DANIEL EUGENE, business executive; b. Chgo., Dec. 18, 1927; s. Daniel Edward and Pearl A. (Trieger) N.; m. Bonnie Lynn Weidman, July 1, 1950; children: Cynthia Lynn, Mark Alan, Dale Alan. BSME, Northwestern U., 1951. With U.S. Gypsum Co., Chgo., 1951-71, dir. corp. devel., to 1971; pres. Am. Louver Co., Chgo., 1971-72; v.p. ops. ITT Corp., Cleve., 1972-74; exec. v.p. ITT Corp., St. Paul, 1974-75; v.p., ops. Pentair, Inc., St. Paul, 1974-75, pres., COO, 1975-81, pres., CEO, 1981-86, chmn., CEO, 1986-92, chmn. exec. com., 1992—; chmn. nominating com., dir. Pentair, Inc.; bd. dirs., audit, exec., compensation and corp. governance coms. Apogee Enterprises, Inc. Vice-chmn. local planning commn., 1968-72; co-chmn. Wellspring, 1989-92; trustee Harper Coll., Palatine, 1970-73; mem. adv. commn. McCormick Engring. and Kelloggg Schs. at Northwestern U., MBA Sch. of St. Thomas U., St. Paul; mem. exec. com. Indian Head coun. Boy Scouts Am. With AUS, 1946-47. Mem. North Oaks Golf Club, Mpls. Club. Republican. Presbyterian.

NUGENT, JOHNNY WESLEY, tractor company executive, state senator; b. Cleve., July 18, 1939; s. Carl Howard and Velma (Holland) N.; m. Nancy Carol Whiteford, Dec. 16, 1960; 1 child, Suzette. Grad. high sch., Aurora, Ind. Owner, mgr. Nugent Tractor Sales, Lawrenceburg, Ind., 1960—; mem. Ind. Senate, Indpls., 1978—; bd. dirs. 1st Nat. Bank Aurora. Commr. Dearborn County, Lawrenceburg, 1966-74. With USAR, 1957-64. Republican. Baptist. Office: State Senate State Capital Indianapolis IN 46204

NUGENT, ROBERT LEON, modern languages educator, librarian; b. L.A., Sept. 12, 1920; s. Robert W. and Audrey (Perry) N. BA, UCLA, 1942; student, U. Paris, 1949; PhD, Yale U., 1950; BLS, U. Calif., Berkeley, 1954. Teaching asst. Yale U., New Haven, 1946-48; instr. U. Calif., Santa Barbara, 1950-53; reference libr. Honnold Libr., Claremont (Calif.) Coll., 1954-56; prof. modern langs. Lake Erie Coll., Painesville, Ohio, 1956-83, coll. libr., 1960-78; libr. emeritus, 1978—, prof. emeritus, 1984—; vis. prof. We. Res. U., Cleve., 1960-61. Author: Paul Eluard, 1966; translator: Jean de Sponde, 1962, (with others) Giaovanni Pascoli, 1973, Ana Maria Matute, 1995. 1st lt. USMCR, 1943-45, PTO. Am. Field Svc. fellow U. Paris, 1948. Mem. Am. Assn. Tchrs. French, Am. Assn. Tchrs. Spanish and Portuguese, Am. Assn. Tchrs. Italian, Am. Assn. Tchrs. Japanese. Republican. Anglican. Office: Lake Erie Coll 391 W Washington St Painesville OH 44077-3309

NUGENT, SHANE VINCENT, lawyer; b. Bozeman, Mont., July 14, 1962; s. John Vincent Nugent and Marilyn Jean (Piotrowski) Cloven; m. Lori Sue Meyer, June 14, 1986; 1 child, Justine Nicole. BA, Knox Coll., 1984; JD, Northwestern U., 1987. Bar: Ill. 1987. Assoc. Lord, Bissell & Brook, Chgo., 1987-93; pvt. practice Barrington, Ill., 1993-94; counsel Blatt Hammestahr & Eaton, Chgo., 1994-96; pvt. practice Barrington, 1996—. Contbr. articles to profl. jours. Named one of Outstanding Young Men Am., 1987. Mem. Chgo. Bar Assn., Beta Theta Pi (Ray M. Arnold prize Xi chpt. 1984, chpt. advisor 1987-92, asst. gen. sec. 1992—), Xi Alumni (pres. 1992—).

NUMBERE, DAOPU THOMPSON, petroleum engineer, educator; b. Buguma, Nigeria, Mar. 30, 1951; came to the U.S., 1975; s. Thompson and Norah (West) N.; m. Tonye Eugenia Higgwe, Dec. 29, 1987. BS in Mech. Engring., U. Coll. Swansea, 1975; MS in Petroleum Engring., Stanford U., 1977; PhD, U. Okla., 1982. Asst. prof. U. Mo., Rolla, 1982-88, assoc. prof., 1988-96, prof., 1996—; cons. Sigma Cons., Mattoon, Ill., 1987—. Author: Petroleum Reservoir Class Manual, 1991, Notes on Water Flooding, 1994. Recipient Shell-BP award, 1971-75, Caswell Massey prize U. Coll. Seansea, 1975, Okla. Rsch. award Okla Rsch. Coun., 1981. Mem. ASME, Internat. Soc. for Computer Methods and Adv. in Geomechanics, Soc. Petroleum Engrs., Sigma Xi. Office: U Mo Rolla 119 Mcnutt Hall Rolla MO 65401

NUTT, AMBROSE BENJAMIN, aerospace engineer; b. Milw., Mar. 16, 1920; s. Ambrose Benjamin and Willette (Owens) N.; m. Viola Elaine Henderson, June 29, 1953; children: Jacqueline, Sandra. BSc in Aero. Engring., U. Mich., 1940; MSc in Aero. Engring., Ohio State U., 1950. Registered profl. engr., Ohio. Aerospace engr. USAF Aircraft Lab., Wright-Patterson AFB, Ohio, 1941-55; br. chief USAF Flight Dynamics Lab., Wright-Patterson AFB, 1956-64, staff engr., 1965-75, div. dir., 1976-81; dir. engring. and computer sci. Wilberforce (Ohio) U., 1981-88; sr. tech. staff engr. Tractell Corp., Dayton, Ohio, 1988—. Co-author: Planning for Technology Quantitative Methods, 1970, Quantitative Decision Aiding Techniques for Research and Development Managers, 1971; also articles. Mem. Yellow Springs (Ohio) Sch. Bd., pres. 1971-74. Mem. NSPE, AIAA, Nat. Tech. Assn. (chpt. pres. 1976-88), Tuskegee Airmen. Episcopalian. Home: 8379 Adams Rd Dayton OH 45424-4031

NUTTER, ZOE DELL LANTIS, retired public relations executive; b. Yamhill, Oreg., June 14, 1915; d. Arthur Lee Lantis and Olive Adelaide (Reed) Lantis-Hilton; m. Richard S. West, Apr. 30, 1941 (div. Nov. 1964); m. Ervin John Nutter, Dec. 30, 1965. Assoc. in Bus., Santa Ana Jr. Coll., 1944. Cert. gen. secondary sch. tchr., Calif.; FAA cert. lic. commercial, instrument, single/multi engine land airplanes pilot. Promoter World's Fair & Comml. Airlines Golden Gate Internat. Expn., San Francisco, 1937-39; pirate theme girl, official hostess Treasure Island's World Fair, San Francisco, 1939-40; prin. dancer San Francisco Ballet, 1937-41; artist, 1941-45; program dir. Glenn County High Sch., Willows, Calif., 1952-58; pub. rels. Monarch Piper Aviation Co., Monterey, Calif., 1963-65; pilot, pub. rels. Elano Corp., Xenia, Ohio, 1968-85; bd. dirs. Nat. Aviation Hall of Fame, Dayton, Ohio, pres., chmn., 1989-92, bd. trustees, 1976—, chmn. bd. nominations, 1992—; bd. trustees Ford's Theatre, Washington, Treasure Island Mus., San Francisco; charter mem. Friends of First Ladies, Smithsonian, Washington, 1990-93. Assoc. editor KYH mag. of Shikar Safari Internat., 1985-87; contbg. columnist Scripps Howard San Francisco News, 1938. Bd. dirs. Cin. May Festival, 1976-80; cen. com. Glenn County Rep. Party, Willows, 1960-64; state cen. com. Rep. Party, 1962-64; adv. bd. Women's Air & Space Mus., Dayton, 1987-94. Warrant officer, Civil Air Patrol, 1967-69. Recipient Civic Contbn. Honor award Big Brothers/Big Sisters, 1991, John Collier Nat. award Camp Fire Girls & Boys, 1988, Tambourine award Salvation Army, 1982, State of Ohio Gov.'s award for Volunteerism, 1992; named Most Photographed Girl in World, News Burs. & Clipping Svcs., 1938-39. Fellow Pres.'s Club U. Ky., Ohio State U., Wright State U.; mem. 99's Internat. Women Pilots Orgn. (life, hospitality chmn. 1968), Monterey Bay Chapter 99's (mem. chmn. 1964-65), Walnut Grove Country Club, Lost Tree Country Club, Windstar County Club (Naples, Fla.), Rotary (Paul Harris fellow 1987), Old Port Yacht Club, Shikar Safari Internat. (host com. 1976). Home: 986 Trebein Rd Xenia OH 45385-9534

NUZMAN, CARL EDWARD, hydrologist; b. Topeka, Aug. 5, 1930; s. Loren Manuel and Loraine Lillian (Bowler) N.; B.S. in Agrl. Engring., Kans. State U., 1953; M.S. in Water Resources Engring., U. Kans., 1966; m. Janet Ruth Steck, Aug. 23, 1952. Engr. div. water resources Kans. Bd. Agr., Topeka, 1957-65; hydrologist Kans. Water Resources Bd., Topeka, 1965-66; hydrology supr., sales engr. Layne-Western Co., Inc., Shawnee Mission, Kans., 1967-72, mgr. hydrology div., 1972-86; v.p., chief hydrologist, Groundwater Mgmt. Inc., 1986-88; chief hydrologist Layne Western Co. Inc., 1988-92; v.p., chief hydrologist Layne GeoSci., Inc., 1992-97. Treas. local sch. bd., 1958-59. Served to 1st lt. USAF, 1953-56. Registered profl. engr., Kans., Mo.; cert. hydrologist Am. Inst. Hydrology. Mem. Am. Soc. Agrl. Engrs., ASCE, Am. Geophys. Union, Kans. Engring. Soc. (sec.-treas. 1965-68, Outstanding Young Engr. award Topeka chpt. 1965), Nat. Soc. Profl. Engrs., Alpha Kappa Lambda, Sigma Tau, Steel Ring. Elk. Contbr. articles to profl. jours.; author, inventor. Home: 3314 NW Huxman Rd Silver Lake KS 66539-9243 Office: 1900 Shawnee Mission Pky Shawnee Mission KS 66205-2001

NUZZI, RONALD JAMES, priest, educator; b. Niles, Ohio, July 12, 1958; s. Paul Angelo and Ann Marie (DePasquale) N. BA in Philosophy, St. Gregory Sem., Cin., 1979; MA in Theology, Athenaeum of Ohio, Cin., 1984; MA in Adminstrn., Ursuline Coll., Cleve., 1991; PhD in Ednl. Leadership, U. Dayton, 1995. Ordained priest Roman Catholic Ch., 1984. Assoc. pastor St. Mary Ch., Massillon, Ohio, 1984-87; assoc. prin. St. John H.S., Ashtabula, Ohio, 1987-91; rsch. asst. U. Dayton, Ohio, 1991-94, adj. prof., 1995—; ednl. cons. Marianist Edn. Consortium, Dayton, 1992-95. Contbr. articles to profl. jours. Recipient Human Rels. award Ohio Assn. Coll. Admissions Counselors, Cleve., 1990. Mem. NEA, Nat. Cath. Ednl. Assn., Cath. Theol. Soc., Am. Acad. Religion, Soc. Bibl. Lit., Phi Delta Kappa. Democrat. Home: 2025 Woodman Dr Kettering OH 45420

NWA, WILLIA L., special education educator; b. Cleve., July 20; d. Thurman and Josephine (Deadwyler); m. Umoh U. Nwa, Sept. 4, 1971; children: Idara Umoh, Jakitoro Deadwyler, Ayama Nseabasi, Ifiok Odudu, Uko Obong. Student, Cleve. Inst. Music, 1965-66; BS, Ohio State U., 1971; MS, U. Akron, 1975, PhD, 1992. Cert. elem. and secondary edn. tchr., spl. edn. tchr., spl. edn. supr., Ohio. Pianist/organist 7th Ave Community Bapt. Ch., Columbus, Ohio, 1970-71; educator N.E. Local Schs., Springfield, Ohio, 1971-74; supr. U. Akron, Ohio, 1989; educator Canton (Ohio) City Schs., 1975—; presenter, instr. 13th, 14th, and 15th ann. internat. confs. critical thinking and ednl. reform Sonoma State U., Rohnert Park, Calif., 1993-95, 7th Internat. Conf. Career Devel. and Transition, Albuquerque, 1993, 41st Ann. Conf. Connecting Edn./Collaboration, Toledo, 1993, 8th Internat. Conf. Collaboration/Cooperation in Edn., Lewis & Clark Coll., Portland, Oreg., 1994, 4th Internat. Conf.: Mental Retardation and Devel. Disabilities, Arlington Heights, Ill., 1994. Co-author: (grant) Reading for Survival, 1988; author: The Extent of Participation in Extracurricular Activities with Exceptional Children, 1992. Mem. Bapt. Student Union, Ohio State U., Columbus, 1969-71, mem. choir, 1969-71; pianist, organist Freedom Bapt. Ch., Canton, 1994—. Recipient Impact 11 award Ohio Dept. Edn., 1995; named Outstanding Educator, Pi Lambda Theta, 1995; Charles S. Seelback scholar Forest City Foundaries, Cleve., 1966, Alice A. White scholar Ohio State U., 1970, univ. scholar U. Akron, 1989; Kurdziel Found. grantee, 1995. Mem. ASCD, NEA, Am. Edn. Rsch. Assn., Nat. Alliance of Black Sch. Educators, Coun. Exceptional Children (exec. com., Outstanding Contbn. in Edn. recognition 1993), Ohio Edn. Assn., East Ctrl. Ohio Edn. Assn., Canton Profl. Educators Assn., Leila Green Alliance of Black Sch. Educators, Deaconess Bd., Missionary Soc., Kappa Delta Pi (presenter 38th biennial convocation Memphis 1992), Pi Lambda Theta (presenter Great Lakes region II profl. conf. Beechwood, Ohio 1994). Office: Canton City Schs 521 Tuscarawas St W Canton OH 44702-2019

NWAGBARA, CHIBU ISAAC, industrial designer, consultant; b. Umuahia, Abia, Nigeria, Apr. 24, 1957; s. Marcus and Catherine (Onyemairo) N.; m. Audrey Denis Rainey, July 5, 1985; children: Obinna Alex, Amara Joy. BS, No. Ill. U., 1984, MS, 1986; MS, Purdue U., 1990, PhD, 1993. Cert. indsl. technologist. Tech. mgr. 3M Internat., Lagos, Nigeria, 1977-80; founder, pres. ChiMarc Assocs., DeKalb, Ill., 1981-84; rsch. asst. No. Ill. U., DeKalb, Ill., 1985-86; assoc. editor Purdue U., West Lafayette, Ind., 1987-89, rsch. assoc., 1990-91, grad. lectr., 1990-93; cons. Arthur Andersen & Co., St. Charles, Ill., 1993-95; program mgr. Allen-Bradley Co., Milw., 1995—; cons. Arnett Clinic, Lafayette, 1992—, Chimarc Assocs., DeKalb, 1986—, GoldMark Ltd., Lagos, 1985—. Coord. community outreach program Purdue U. Afro-Am. Studies and Rsch. Ctr., West Lafayette, 1990-91; coach Am. Youth Soccer Orgn., West Lafayette, 1987-90. Named one of Outstanding Young Men of Am., 1989, Men of Achievement, 1994. Mem. Inst. Indsl. Engrs., Am. Soc. for Quality Control, Am. Edn. Rsch. Assn., Nat. Assn. Indsl. Tech., Nat. Soc. for Performance and Instrn. Methodist. Home: 6826 W Obikoba Circle Mequon WI 53092 Office: Allen-Bradley Co Inc 1201 S Second St Milwaukee WI 53204

NYCKLEMOE, GLENN WINSTON, bishop; b. Fergus Falls, Minn., Dec. 8, 1936; s. Melvin and Bertha (Sumstad) N.; m. Ann Elizabeth Olson, May 28, 1960; children: Peter Glenn, John Winston, Daniel Thomas. BA, St. Olaf Coll., 1958; MDiv, Luther Theol. Sem., St. Paul, 1962; D of Ministry, Luth. Sch. Theology, Chgo., 1977. Ordained to ministry Am. Luth. Ch., 1962. Assoc. pastor Our Savior's Luth. Ch., Valley City, N.D., 1962-64; assoc. pastor Our Savior's Luth. Ch., Milw., 1964-67, co-pastor, 1967-73; sr. pastor Our Savior's Luth. Ch., Beloit, Wis., 1973-82, St. Olaf Luth. Ch., Austin, Minn., 1982-88; bishop Southeastern Minn. Synod, Evang. Luth. Ch. in Am., Rochester, 1988—; bd. dirs. Luth. Social Svcs. of Minn., Mpls., Bd. of Social Ministries, St. Paul, Minn. Coun. Chs., Mpls. Mem. bd. regents St. Olaf Coll., Northfield, Minn., 1988—. Office: SE Minn Synod Evang Luth Ch Am Assist Heights Box 4900 Rochester MN 55903

NYCZ, JOSEPH DONALD, engineer; b. Toledo, Jan. 16, 1951; s. Joseph Louis and Alice Elizabeth (Defore) N.; m. Nancy Lynne Olszanski, Jan. 5, 1973; children: Jonathan, Eric, Zachary. Student, U. Toledo, 1969-72. Asst. mechanic Sankewicz Union 76 Oil, Toledo, 1971-73; carton sealer Libby div. Owens Ill., Toledo, 1972-73; model designer glass container div. Owens Ill., Toledo, 1973-79, product designer closure div., mold designer closure div., 1982-84, sr. product designer closure div., 1984-87; sr. product design engr. Tri-Tech Systems Internat. Inc., Maumee, Ohio, 1987-90; design draftsman Applied Techs. Inc., 1991-93; engr. Diversified Capping Equipment, Toledo, 1993—; project engr., safety dir. Diversified Cappping Equipment, Perrysburg, Ohio, 1994—; chmn. Owens-Ill. Cadcam Steering Com., Toledo, 1982-84. Councilman Haskins Town Council, 1975. Democrat. Roman Catholic. Home: 109 Greenwood Dr Haskins OH 43525-9706 Office: Tri-Tech Systems Internat I 316 N Michigan St Ste 800 Toledo OH 43624-1627

NYE, ERIC, financial services company executive; b. Warren, July 30, 1962. BA in Polit. Sci., U. So. Fla., 1992. V.p. NYE Fin. Group Agy., Inc., Hudson, Ohio, 1987—; Chartered fin. cons., Pa. Republican. Methodist. Home: 1819 Akron Peninsula Rd Akron OH 44313-4807 Office: NYE Fin Group Agy Inc PO Box 307 Hudson OH 44236-0307

NYE, MICHAEL EARL, state legislator; b. Indpls., Aug. 3, 1946; s. Clair Zurmehly and Isabelle (Volk) N.; m. Marceline Leuzinger, 1974; children: Jessica E., Justin M. BS, Purdue U., 1968, JD, 1973. Rep. Mich. Dist. 58, Mich. Dist. 41; minority vice chmn. House Jud. Com. Mich. Ho. Reps., mem. conservation com., environ. com., recreation com., labor & tourism com., wildlife com., civil rights com., women's issues com. farmer; pvt. practice law; adv. bd. State Bar Mich. Named environ. legis. of yr. Mich. Environ. Def. Assn., 1990, legis. of yr. Mich. Assn. Chiefs of Police. Mem. ABA, Am. Legion, Hillsdale County Bar Assn., Masons, Scottish Rite, Litchfield Exch. Clubs, Hillsdale Exch. Clubs, Mich. Farm Bur., Alpha Gamma Rho. Home: 7111 Anderson Rd Litchfield MI 49252-9772 Address: State Capitol PO Box 30014 Lansing MI 48909-7514*

NYENHUIS, JACOB EUGENE, college official; b. Mille Lacs County, Minn., Mar. 25, 1935; s. Egbert Peter and Rosa (Walburg) N.; m. Leona Mae Van Duyn, June 6, 1956; children: Karen Joy, Kathy Jean, Lorna Jane, Sarah Van Duyn. AB in Greek, Calvin Coll., 1956; AM in Classics, Stanford U., 1961, PhD in Classics, 1963. Asst. in classical langs. Calvin Coll., Grand Rapids, Mich., 1957-59; acting instr. Stanford (Calif.) U., 1962; from asst. prof. to prof. Wayne State U., Detroit, 1962-75, dir. honors program, 1964-75, chmn. Greek and Latin dept., 1965-75; prof. classics, dean for humanities Hope Coll., Holland, Mich., 1975-78, dean for arts and humanities, 1978-84, provost, 1984—; cons. Mich. Dept. Edn., Lansing, 1971-72, Gustavus Adolphus Coll., St. Peter, Minn., 1974, Northwestern Coll., Orange City, Iowa, 1983, Whitworth Coll., Spokane, Wash., 1987, The Daedalus Project, 1988; reviewer NEH, Washington, 1986-87, Lilly Endowment, Indpls., 1987-89, U.S. Dept. Edn., 1993; vis. assoc. prof. U. Calif., Santa Barbara, 1967-68, Ohio State U., Columbus, 1972; vis. rsch. prof. Am. Sch. Classical Studies, Athens, Greece, 1973-74, also mem. mng. com.; panelist NEH, 1991; vis. scholar Green Coll. Oxford U., 1989. Co-author: Latin Via Ovid, 1977, rev. edit., 1982; editor: Petronius: Cena Trimalchionis, 1970, Plautus: Amphitruo, 1970; articles in field. Elder Christian Reformed Ch., Palo Alto, Calif., 1960-62; elder, clk. Christian Reformed Ch., Grosse Pointe, Mich., 1964-67; elder, clk. Christian Reformed Ch., Holland, Mich., 1976-85, v.p., 1988-91, mem. exec. com., 1994-95; chmn. human rels. coun. Open Housing Com., Grosse Pointe, 1971-73. Mem. Am. Philol. Assn., Danforth Assocs. (chmn. regional com. 1975-77), Mich. Coun. for Humanities (bd. dirs., 1976-84, 88-92, chmn. 1980-82, Disting. Svc. award 1984), Nat. Fedn. State Humanities Couns. (pres. 1979-84), Gt. Lakes Colls. Assn. (bd. dirs. 1991-93), Coun. on Undergrad. Rsch. (councilor-at-large 1993—). Democrat. Home: 51 E 8th St Ste 200 Holland MI 49423-3501 Office: Hope Coll Office of the Provost 141 E 12th St PO Box 9000 Holland MI 49422-9000

NYERGES, ALEXANDER LEE, museum director; b. Rochester, N.Y., Feb. 27, 1957; s. Sandor Elek and Lena (Angeline) N.; 1 child, Robert Angeline. BA, George Washington U., 1979, MA, 1981. Intern The Octagon, Washington, 1976-79; archeol. asst. Smithsonian Instn., Washington, 1977, curatorial intern Nat. Mus. Am. History, 1978-79; adminstrv. asst. George Washington U., Washington, 1979-81; exec. dir. DeLand Mus. Art, Fla., 1981-85, Miss. Mus. Art, Jackson, 1985-92; dir. Dayton (Ohio) Art Inst., 1992—; grants panel Nat. Endowment for the Arts, 1988—; field surveyor Inst. Mus. Svcs., Washington, 1985-88, nat. review panel, 1990-92; treas., bd. dirs. Volusia County Arts Coun., Daytona Beach, Fla., 1983-85. Contbr. articles to profl. jours. Bd. dirs. West Volusia Hist. Soc., 1984-85; pres. Miss. Inst. Arts and Letters, 1987-88; trustee Cultural Arts Ctr., DeLand, 1984-85, Miami Valley Cultural Alliance, 1993—, Intermus. Conservation Lab., 1993—, Montgomery county arts and culture district, 1994—. U.S. Dept. Edn. scholar, 1973. Mem. DeLand Area C. of C. (bd. dirs., tourist adv. com. 1984-85), Assn. Art Mus. Dirs., Am. Assn. Mus. (SE regional rep. to non-print media com. 1983-85, nat. legis. com. 1986-93), Miss. Mus. Assn., Assn. Art Mus. Dirs., Southeastern Mus. Conf. (bd. dirs. 1991-92), Fla. Mus. Assn., Fla. Art Mus. Dirs. Assn., Cultural Roundtable (pres. 1993—), Ohio Mus. Assn. (trustee 1993—), Phi Beta Kappa. Presbyterian. Avocations: restoring old houses, gardening, music, writing, sports. Home: 1719 Auburn Ave Dayton OH 45406 Office: Dayton Art Inst 456 Belmonte Park N Dayton OH 45405-4700

NYGAARD, LANCE COREY, nurse, data processing consultant; b. Casper, Wyo., June 21, 1952; s. Miles Adolph and Jenile Hansine (Mosman) N.; m. Susan Leigh Wilson, May 8, 1995; 1 child from previous marriage, Kari Melissa. AA in Nursing, U. S.D., 1980; BS in Chemistry, 1974; MLS, U. Ill., 1975. Libr. asst. Brookings Pub. Libr., S.D., 1971-75, asst. dir., 1975-77; emergency med. technician Brookings Hosp., 1976-78; sr. emergency med. technician Vermillion Ambulance, S.D., 1978-80; nurse McKennan Hosp., Sioux Falls, S.D., 1980-91, VA Hosp., 1991—; owner operator Data Processing Svcs., Sioux Falls, 1983—; applications cons. Computer Dimensions, Sioux Falls, 1984-85. Fin. sec., mem. ch. coun. Holy Cross Luth. Ch., Sioux Falls, S.D., 1986-91, info. resources coord., 1991-92; troop leader Minn-Ia-Kota coun. Girl Scouts U.S., 1989—, region troop supr., 1991—. Mem. Vermillion Chemistry Club (pres. 1973-74), Sioux Valley Rose Soc. (v.p. 1988-89, pres. 1989-90), Sons of Norway (guard 1976-77). Republican. Lutheran. Avocations: World War II military history, rose gardening, photography, amateur radio. Home: 3500 S Grace Cir Sioux Falls SD 57103-7226 Office: Royal C Johnson Vets Meml Hosp 2501 E 22nd St Sioux Falls SD 57117

NYGARD, ANDREW CHARLES, management consultant; b. Madison, Wis., Sept. 1, 1960; s. Charles H. and Arliss (Paulson) N.; m. Petra Marie Dietiker, Aug. 28, 1982; 1 child, Camille Marguaritte. BA, SUNY, Albany, 1991; MBA, Vanderbilt U., 1993. Enlisted U.S. Army, 1981, advanced through grades to staff sgt., 1990, voice intercept supr., 1981-90; mgr. Deloitte & Touche, LLP, Cleve., 1993—. Office: Deloitte & Touche LLP 127 Public Square Ste 2500 Cleveland OH 44114

NYGREN, E(LLIS) HERBERT, theology educator; b. Bklyn., June 27, 1928; s. Erik H. and Jenny (Walaas) N.; m. Louise Whitton, June 9, 1951; children: E. Herbert, Steven E. BA, Taylor U., 1951; STB, Biblical Sem., N.Y.C., 1954; MA, NYU, 1954, PhD, 1960. Ordained min. Meth. Ch., 1951. Min. United Meth. Ch., various locations, 1951-60; prof. Emory and Henry Coll., Emory, Va., 1960-69; prof. Taylor U., Upland, Ind., 1969-91, prof. emeritus, 1991—. Contbr. articles to profl. publs., chpts. to books. Mem. Evangelical Theol. Soc., Am. Soc. Ch. History. Republican.

NYHART, ELDON HOWARD, employee benefits consultant, lawyer; b. Lafayette, Ind., Jan. 17, 1927; s. Howard E. and Mabel (Keller) N.; m. Frieda Ernie, Apr. 12, 1971; children: Maria, Malott, Sallie, Eldon Jr. AB cum laude, Princeton U., 1948; JD, Ind. U., 1952. Exec. v.p. The Nyhart Co., Inc., Indpls., 1953-55, pres., chief exec. officer, 1955-60, chief exec. officer, 1960-91, chmn. bd. dirs., 1991—; lectr. Purdue U., Lafayette; tchr. Ind. U. Grad. Sch. Bus., Bloomington, dir. Midwest Pension Conf. Contbr. articles to profl. jour. Life trustee Indpls. Mus. Art, bd. govs., 1990—; bd. dirs. Ind. Swiss Found., pres. 1991—, Ind. State Symphony Soc., 1990—, Eiteljorg Mus., 1990, Contemporary Art Soc., 1991—, Friends of Herron Gallery, 1990—; del. White House Conf. on Aging. Mem. ABA, Internat. Bar Assn., Ind. Bar Assn., Assn. Pvt. Pension and Welfare Plans, trustee 1987-91, Am. Judicature Soc., Am. Pension Conf., Woodstock Club, Chgo. Racquet Club, Univ. Club (Indpls.), Princeton Club (N.Y.). Episcopalian. Home: 7468 Lions Head Dr Apt D Indianapolis IN 46260-3457 Office: Nyhart Co Inc 3515 N Washington Blvd Indianapolis IN 46205-3718

NYMANN, P. L., lawyer; b. Clermont, Iowa, May 18, 1924; s. Jens Christian and Minnie Amalia (Osmundson) N.; m. Charmaine Ann Petersen, Dec. 2, 1951 (div. 1979); children: Michel, Candace, Kimberly, Christopher, Jon (dec.); m. Anne Barrett McDermott, Feb. 15, 1992. BA, U. Iowa, 1949, JD, 1951. Bar: Iowa 1951. Assoc. Louis S. Goldberg, Sioux City, Iowa, 1951-57; ptnr. Goldberg, Nymann & Probasco, Sioux City, 1957-64; v.p., gen. counsel IBP, Inc., Dakota City, Nebr., 1964-72; pvt. practice Sioux City, 1972-74, 83-87; ptnr. Jacobs, Gaul, Nymann & Green, Sioux City, 1974-83, Nymann & Kohl, Sioux City, 1987—. Chmn., Civil Svc. Commn., 1977-79; bd. dirs. United Way Siouxland, 1979-85. With AUS, 1943-46. Mem. ABA, Iowa Bar Assn., Am. Arbitration Assn., Rotary Club. Republican. Home: PO Box 1760 Lake Ozark MO 65049-1760 Office: Nymann & Kohl 383390 Orpheum Electric Sioux City IA 51101

NYQUIST, GERALD WARREN, engineering consultant; b. Detroit, Dec. 28, 1940; s. Paul Gustave and Lucille Phyllis (Reiter) N. BS, Lawrence Tech. U., 1963; MS, Wayne State U., 1967; PhD, Mich. State U., 1970. Registered profl. engr., Mich. Product test engr. Ford Motor Co., Dearborn, Mich., 1963-65; rsch. asst. Wayne State U., Detroit, 1965-67, rsch. assoc., 1970-72; grad. asst. Mich. State U., East Lansing, 1968; sr. rsch. engr. GM, Warren, Mich., 1972-76, sr. project engr., 1976-80, staff analysis engr., 1980-82; prin. Gerald W. Nyquist, inc., Eastpointe, Mich., 1982-91; assoc. cons. Packer Engring., Inc., Troy, Mich., 1990—. Contbr. articles to profl. jours. Recipient Safety award Nat. Hwy. Traffic Adminstrn., 1980. Mem. Soc. Automotive Engrs., Sanilac County Hist. Soc. (life).

NYQUIST, RICHARD ALLEN, vibrational spectroscopist; b. Rockford, Ill., May 3, 1928; s. Harry William and Anna Svea (Nelson) N.; m. Irene Mae Cote, 1956; children: Richard H., Jean S., Kathryn A., Robert A. BA, Augustana Coll., 1951; MS, Okla. State U., 1953; PhD, Utrecht U., 1994. Chem. Dow Chem. Co., Midland, Mich., 1953-58; rsch. chemist Dow Chem. Co., Midland, 1959-65, assoc. scientist, 1966-84, sr. scientist, 1985-93, rsch. scientist, 1993—; pres. Nyquist Assocs., 1995. Author: The Interpretation of Vapor-Phase Infrared Spectra: Group Frequency Data, 1984, Infrared Spectra-Building Blocks of Polymers, 1989; co-author: Infrared Spectra of Inorganic Compounds and Organic Salts, 1996; contbr. articles to profl. jours. Recipient Williams-Wright award Coblentz Soc., 1985, Analytical Chemistry award Analytical Chemistry Soc., 1993. Mem. ASTM, Am. Chem. Soc., Soc. Applied Spectroscopy (chmn. Mich. sect. 1982, 83).

OAKES, FRANK LESLIE, JR., insurance agency executive; b. Springfield, Mass., Dec. 6, 1918; s. Frank Leslie and Isabel (Sanderson) O.; m. Helen Francis Smith, July 24, 1943 (dec. Oct. 1990); children: Lynne, Gerald. BA, Wesleyan U., 1941. CPCU. Underwriter Aetna Casualty Ins. Co., Hartford, Conn., 1941-47; acct. exec., asst. sec., v.p., exec. v.p. Picton-Cavanaugh Ins., Toledo, Ohio, 1948-70, pres., 1970-83, chmn. bd., 1983-93. Bd. dirs. Toledo

Safety Coun., 1970, Conlon Ctr. for Severely Handicapped, Toledo, 1960-80, Toledo Zool. Soc., 1981-89; ccomm. chmn. United Way Toledo, 1978-81. Recipient Hon. Dir. award Toledo Zoo, 1989. Mem. Toledo Rotary Club, Toledo Torch Club (pres. 1980), Toledo Country Club, Toledo Compass Club (pilot 1990), Toledo Assn. Ind. Ins. Agys. (dir., pres. 1960's), N.W. Ohio Soc. CPCU (dir. 1960's). Republican. Home: 3014 Plumbrook Maumee OH 43537

OAKLAND, CAROL JEAN, athletic development administrator; b. Canby, Minn., Sept. 23, 1949; d. Clarence Edwin and Phyllis Amy (Borgendale) Saltee; m. James Alan Oakland, May 28, 1971; children: Kristin Amy, Jeffrey Alan. BA summa cum laude, Augustana Coll., 1971; postgrad. in Sci. Edn., U. S.D., 1972-74. Tchr. Garretson (S.D.) H.S., 1971-72; mid. sch. tchr. Jefferson (S.D.) Schs., 1972-74; jr. high tchr. Robious Jr. High, Chesterfield County, Va., 1974-76; tchr. O'Gorman H.S., Sioux Falls, S.D., 1977; coll. instr. Augustana Coll., Sioux Falls, S.D., 1978, assoc. in devel., 1985-87, dir. athletic devel., 1987—; presenter in field of time mgmt. Mem. long range planning bd. Our Saviour's Luth., Sioux Falls, 1992-95, stewardship bd. dirs., 1988-92, edn. bd. dirs., 1980-84; bd. dirs., dinner chair Nordland Festival, Sioux Falls, 1980-83; rec. sec., bd. dirs., orientation chair, project chair Jr. League of Sioux Falls, 1980-86. Recipient Leader award for bus. YWCA, Sioux Falls, 1991. Mem. Nat. Assn. Athletic Devel. Dirs. (exec. bd. 1994—), Nat. Assn. Collegiate Dirs. of Athletics, Nat. Assn. Collegiate Marketers of Athletics, Sioux Falls C. of C. (sports and recreation com. 1990—). Office: Augustana Coll 2001 S Summit Sioux Falls SD 57197

OAKS, JOHN ADAMS, cell biologist, parasitologist; b. Alma, Mich., Apr. 8, 1942; s. L. Robert and Mathilda R. (Vaschak) O.; m. Rebecca Neese; children: Jeffrey, Timothy. BA, Colby Coll., 1964; MS, Tulane U., 1968, PhD, 1970. Asst. professor parasitology Sch. Pub. Health Tulane U., New Orleans, 1970-73; from asst. to assoc. prof. Sch. Medicine U. Iowa, Iowa City, 1973-82; assoc. prof. Sch. Vet. Medicine U. Wis., Madison, 1982—; coord. Ctr. Rsch. and Tng. in Parasitic Diseases, U. Wis., 1984-95; cons. Am. Med. Womens Hosp. Svc. com. Contbr. articles to profl. jours. Mem. Am. Soc. Parasitologists (coun. mem. 1990-93, v.p. 1995-96, pres-elect 1996—), Am. Soc. Cell Biologists, Southwestern Assn. Parasitologists, Am. Soc. Tropical Medicine Hygiene. Office: U Wis Dept Comp Biosci Sch Vet Medicine 2015 Linden Dr W Madison WI 53706-1102

OATHOUT, BRENDA HALM, auditor; b. Tecumseh, Nebr., Aug. 16, 1960; d. William W. and H. Lenore (Bentzinger) B.; m. Randall L. Oathout, Sept. 26, 1992. BSBA, U. Nebr., Omaha, 1983. Clk. Boardwalk Hardware, Omaha, 1976-81; claims auditor Physicians Mut. Ins. Co., Omaha, 1981-87; auditor LaHood & Assocs., Overland Park, Kans., 1987-89; advanced auditor Physicians Mut. Ins. Co., Omaha, 1989-92, sr. auditor, 1992—. Republican. Methodist.

OBAN, BILL, state legislator; b. Mpls., Jan. 30, 1947; s. Richard and Clarice (Lester) O.; m. Alice Kay Hay, 1969; children: Shawn, Chad, Heather. BA, U. N.D., 1969, BS, 1971, MS, 1979. Supr. residential facility Grafton (N.D.) State Sch., 1972-73; tchr. spl. edn. Grafton H.S., 1973-76, Bismarck (N.D.) H.S., 1976-81; spl. edn. coord. Bismarck pub. schs., 1981—; mem. N.D. Ho. of Reps., 1985—; minority whip; mem. indstl. bus. and labor com. N.D. Ho. of Reps., nat. resources com., joint construction rev. com.; pres. Bismarck Edn. Assn., 1980-81. Contbr. articles to profl. pubs. Mem. N.D. PTA, Riverside PTA, pres. 1983-84. Mem. Vietnam Vets. Am., Coun. Exceptional Children, Mental Health Assn., Legislators Forum. Home: 616 Meadow Ln Bismarck ND 58504-5365*

O'BANNON, FRANK LEWIS, state official, lawyer; b. Louisville, Jan. 30, 1930; s. Robert Pressley and Rosella Faith (Dropsey) O'B.; m. Judith Mae Asmus, Aug. 18, 1957; children: Polly, Jennifer, Jonathan. AB, Ind. U., 1952, JD, 1957. Ind. 1957. Pvt. practice Corydon; ptnr. Hays, O'Bannon & Funk, Corydon, 1966-80, O'Bannon, Funk & Simpson, Corydon, 1980-94, Funk, Simpson, Thompson & Byrd, Corydon, 1995—; mem. Ind. Senate, Corydon, 1970-89, minority floor leader, 1979-89, asst. minority floor leader, 1972-76; lt. gov. State of Ind., Corydon, 1989—; chmn., dir. O'Bannon Pub. Co., Inc. Served with USAF, 1952-54. Mem. Ind. Dem. Editorial Assn. (pres. 1961), Am. Judicature Soc., Am. Bar Assn., Ind. Bar Assn. Democrat. Methodist. Office: Lt Govs Office 333 State House Indianapolis IN 46204

OBERDANK, LAWRENCE MARK, lawyer, arbitrator; b. Cleve., Nov. 1, 1935; s. Leonard John and Mary (Pavelich) O.; m. Arlene C. Baldini, Aug. 25, 1962; 1 child, Karen A. BA, Western Res. U., 1958, JD, 1965. Bar: Ohio 1965, U.S. Dist. Ct. (no. dist.) Ohio 1966, U.S. Ct. Appeals (6th cir.) 1968, U.S. Supreme Ct. 1970. Assoc. Law Offices Mortimer Riemer, Cleve., 1965-69; ptnr. Riemer and Oberdank, Cleve., 1969-76; prin. Lawrence M. Oberdank Co., L.P.A., Cleve., 1976—; arbitrator Ohio Employment Rels. Bd., 1985-89, Cleve. Civil Svc. Commn., 1983—, FMHA, 1989—; chmn. mandatory arbitration panel Ct. Common Pleas; mem. Nat. Mediation Bd., 1986—; instr. indsl. rels. law Cleve. State U., 1982-85; instr. labor rels. Cuyahoga C.C., 1983; arbitrator/mediator U.S. Dist. Ct. (no. dist.) Ohio, ea. divsn. fee dispute panel Cleve. Bar Assn.; mem. securities arbitration panel Am. Stock Exch., N.Y. Stock Exch., 1995—. Lt. USNR, 1958-62. Mem. ABA (labor and employment sect., labor arbitration, law collective bargaining agreements, alternate dispute resolution sect., fed. ct. annexed/connected programs com.), Am. Arbitration Assn. (securities arbitrator, nat. labor panel 1973—, comml. arbitration panel, nat. panel of employment arbitrators), Nat. Assn. Securities Dealers, Inc., Bar Assn. Greater Cleve. (labor law com.), Cuyahoga County Bar Assn., Fed. Bar Assn., Am. Judicature Soc., Internat. Soc. Labor Law and Social Legislation, Ohio State Bar Assn. (chmn. labor law sect. 1970-73), Indsl. Rels. Rsch. Assn., Pub. Sector Labor Rels. Assn., Soc. Profls. in Dispute Resolution (bd. dirs. Southwest Ohio chpt.), Masons, Phi Gamma Delta. Roman Catholic. Home: 8051 Lakeview Ct N Royalton OH 44133-1214 Office: Corporate Plaza I Ste 100 6450 Rockside Woods Blvd S Cleveland OH 44131

OBERMANN, GEORGE, engineering executive; b. Grobla, Poland, Aug. 26, 1935; came to U.S. 1950; s. Hugo and Amanda (Merwitz) O.; m. Alice A. Volpel, Oct. 7, 1961; children: Mark George, James Joseph. BS, U. Mass., Lowell, 1959. Design engr. Controls Co. Am., Schiller Park, Ill., 1959-60; project engr. Oak Mfg. Co., Crystal Lake, Ill., 1960-62; project engr. Controls Co. Am., Shiller Park, 1962-67, engr. supr., 1967-72; prod. engr. mgr. controls div. Singer Co., Shiller Park, 1972-76, rsch. devel. engr. mgr. controls div., 1976-82, staff engr. Eaton controls div., 1982-88; engr. mgr. controls div. Eaton Corp., Carol Stream, Ill., 1988-94; project engr. Otto Engring., Carpentersville, Ill., 1995, ret., 1995; coms. mem. Nat. Elec. Mfrs. Assn., Washington, 1972-78, gen. engrs. com., 1978-93. Patentee in field; contbr. article to profl. jours. Lutheran. Home: 6713 W Forest View Ln Niles IL 60714-4405

OBERREUTER, JOHN EDWARD, police inspector; b. Mpls., Aug. 3, 1943; s. John Edward and Mary Jane (Woolsey) O.; m. June Elizabeth Rhodes, Aug. 5, 1973 (div. June 1984); children: Nicole Constance, Matthew John (dec.), Erin Liv. BA, Met. State U., 1974. Police officer New Hope (Minn.) Police Dept., 1967-69; social svcs. coord. Mpls. Head State Program, 1968-70; counselor Mpls. Age & Opportunity Ctr., 1970-72; police officer New Hope Police Dept., 1972-78, police sergeant, 1978-82, police inspector, 1982—; rep. Law Enforcement Labor Svc., Mpls., 1994—. Del. to state conv. Dem. Farmer Labor Party, St. Paul., Minn., 1994. Mem. Minn. Chiefs of Police Assn., Internat. Assn. Chiefs of Police, Minn. Police & Peace Officers Assn., Emerald Soc. Minn., Fraternal Order of Police. Roman Catholic. Home: 4625 Abbott Ave S Minneapolis MN 55410 Office: New Hope Police Dept 4401 Xylon Ave N New Hope MN 55428

OBERST, BYRON BAY, pediatrician, consultant; b. Omaha, Mar. 15, 1923; s. Byron Bay and Claire Matilda (Healy) O.; m. Mary Catherine Nadolny, Dec. 27, 1945; children: Byron Joseph, Terrence Martin, Matthew Robert. BA, U. Omaha, Omaha, 1944; MD, U. Nebr. Coll. Med., Omaha, 1946. Diplomate Am. Bd. Pediat. Pres. Omaha Children's Clinic, Omaha, 1951-88; med. advisor Med. Computer Mgmt., Inc., Omaha, 1988-95; med. dir. Omaha Branch Plasma Alliance, Omaha, 1993—; med. advisor CUSA Tech., Inc., Salt Lake City, 1995—; cons. Dept. Pediat. Univ. Nebr. Med. Ctr., Omaha, 1988—. Author: Practical Guidelines for General Pediatric & Adolescent Office Practice, 1973; co-author: Computer Applications to Private Practice, 1984, Computer Application to Private Practice - 2nd Edition, 1987; contbr. articles to profl. jours. Bd. dirs. Omaha Learning Skills, Learning Techniques, Acad, Ability and Remediation (STAAR) program for Sch. Learning Disabilities, Omaha, 1968-78; mem. Omaha-Douglas County Bd. of Health, Omaha, 1982-84, health planning com. Health Planning Coun. Midlands, Omaha, 1976-78; scoutmaster Boy Scouts Am., Omaha, 1960-67. Fellow Am. Acad. of Pediat. (rep. to nat. PTA con.). Republican. Roman Catholic. Home: 307 S 93rd St Omaha NE 68114

OBERSTAR, JAMES L., congressman; b. Chisholm, Minn., Sept. 10, 1934; s. Louis and Mary (Grillo) O.; m. Jo Garlick, Oct. 12, 1963 (dec. July 1991); children: Thomas Edward, Katherine Noelle, Anne-Therese, Monica Rose; m. Jean Kurth, Nov. 1993; stepchildren: Corinne Quinlan Kurth, Charles Burke Kurth, Jr. B.A. summa cum laude, St. Thomas Coll., 1956; postgrad. in French, Laval U., Que., Can.; M.S. in Govt. (scholar), Coll. Europe, Bruges, Belgium, 1957; postgrad. in govt, Georgetown U. Adminstrv. asst. Congressman John A. Blatnik, 1963-74; adminstr. Pub. Works Com. U.S. Ho. of Reps., 1971-74; mem. 94th-104th Congresses from 8th Minn. Dist., 1975—; ranking minority mem. transp. and infrastructure subcom. on aviation. Mem. Am. Polit. Sci. Assn. Office: US Ho of Reps 2366 Rayburn HOB Washington DC 20515-2308*

OBEY, DAVID ROSS, congressman; b. Okmulgee, Okla., Oct. 3, 1938; s. Orville John and Mary Jane (Chellis) O.; m. Joan Therese Lepinski, June 9, 1962; children: Craig David, Douglas David. BS in Polit. Sci, U. Wis., 1960, MA, 1962. Mem. Wis. Gen. Assembly, 1963-69, asst. minority leader, 1967-69; mem. 91st-104th Congresses from 7th Wis. dist., 1969—; ranking minority mem. appropriations com., ranking minority mem. labor, HHS and edn. subcom., mem. joint econ. com.; mem. adminstrv. com. Wis. Dem. Com., 1960-62. Named Edn. Legislator of Yr., Rural div. NEA, 1968; recipient Legislative Leadership award Eagelton Inst. Politics, 1964, award of merit Nat. Council Sr. Citizens, 1976, citation for legis. statesmanship Council Exceptional Children, 1976. Office: US Ho of Reps 2462 Rayburn HOB Washington DC 20515*

OBLIGATO, MARY F., electrical power executive; b. Beloit, Wis., June 19, 1947; d. John L. and Ada F. (Soulek) Baker; m. Charles A. Obligato, Aug. 5, 1967 (div. Aug. 1982); children: Rose Marie, John. BA, Beloit Coll., 1986. From acctg. clk. to small comml. rep. Wis. Power & Light, Beloit, 1967-94, comml. and indsl. rep., 1994—; mortar bd. Beloit Coll., 1986. V.p. Blackhawk Devel. Com., Rockton, Ill., 1994—; archeol. asst. Macktown Restoration, Rockton, 1993. Mem. Archeol. Inst. Am., Rockton Hist. Soc., Rotary (pres. No. Windebago County 1994, v.p. 1993, sec. 1992), Sunset Golf League (pres. 1990—). Office: Wis Power and Light 500 Public Ave Beloit WI 53511

OBRECHT, KENNETH WILLIAM, banker; b. Elmhurst, Ill., Mar. 2, 1933; s. John Matthew and Ida Elizabeth (Spears) O.; m. Nancy Marie Larimer, Oct. 10, 1958; children: Merry Kathleen, Michael Dorset, Gordon Alexander, Paul Andrew. BS in Commerce, N. Cen. Coll., 1959. Exec. v.p. York State Bank, Elmhurst, 1960-67; pres., chief exec. officer Louis Joliet (Ill.) Bank, 1967-70, Hawthorne Bank of Wheaton, Ill., 1970-81; v.p. Albany Bank & Trust Co., N.A., Chgo., 1981—; chmn. Coop. Computer Ctr., Naperville, Ill., 1977-79; apptd. by Gov. Ill. to chmn. bd. trustees State of Ill. Retirement System; also vice chmn. Ill. Investment Bd., 1985—. DuPage (Ill.) County coord. com. to re-elect the pres., Wheaton, 1972, mem. DuPage County Sch. Dist. Bd. Edn., Wheaton, 1975-81; treas. DuPage County Rep. Ctrl. Com., Wheaton, 1974-93. Cpl. U.S. Army, 1953-55, ETO. Republican. Office: Albany Bank & Trust Co NA 3400 W Lawrence Ave Chicago IL 60625-5104

O'BRIEN, BRIEN MICHAEL, investment firm executive; b. Waukesha, Wis., Jan. 21, 1957; s. John Francis and Nancy L. (Nugent) O'Br.; m. Mary Hasten, Nov. 15, 1985. BS cum laude, Boston Coll., 1980. V.p. Oppenheimer & Co., Chgo., 1980-84, Bear Stearns & Co., Chgo., 1984-86; pres. Marquette Assocs., Chgo., 1986—, Marquette Capital, Chgo., 1986—. Pres. Jobs for Youth, Chgo. Office: Marquette Assocs 321 N Clark St Chicago IL 60610-4714

O'BRIEN, CAROL JEAN, municipal parks administrator; b. Chgo., June 18, 1939; d. Charles August and Frances Carolyn (Reese) Boeck; m. Thomas Joseph McEvoy, Oct. 18, 1958 (div. Mar. 1982); 1 child, Corrine Marie McEvoy; John Patrick O'Brien, July 18, 1985 (div. Mar. 1988). Grad. high sch., Maywood, Ill., 1957. Cert. leisure profl. Mfrs. rep. Midwest Cen., Chgo., 1969-71; supt. recreation Wood Dale (Ill.) Park Dist., 1977-87, bus. mgr., 1988-89, exec. dir. parks and recreation, 1989—; commr. Medinah Park Dist., 1991-95. Mem. Nat. Parks and Recreation Assn., Suburban Parks and Recreation Assn. (chairperson 1983-85, sec. 1985-86, spl. projects com. 1986-87), Ill. Parks and Recreation Assn., Wood Dale C. of C. (dir. and sec. 1989-92). Lutheran. Office: Wood Dale Park Dist 533 N Wood Dale Rd Wood Dale IL 60191-1535

O'BRIEN, CHERYL ANN MARIE, educator; b. Sioux Falls, S.D., Jan. 23, 1955; d. Junior Corwin and Donna Mae (Eilertson) Christianson; m. Mark Everin O'Brien, Sept. 2, 1978; children: Patrick Mark, Lauren Ashley. BS in Home Econs. Edn., S.D. State U., 1977, MEd in Ednl. Adminstrn., 1992; EdS in Ednl. Adminstrn., U. S.D., 1994. Instr. home econs. Sioux Falls Pub. Schs./Lincoln H.S., 1977-78; grad. asst. textiles/clothing S.D. State U., Brookings, 1978-79; substitute tchr. Sioux Falls Pub. Schs., 1981-83, cmty. edn. svcs. instr., 1981-84; adult basic edn. instr. Turn About, Inc., Sioux Falls, 1983-85, employment/edn. coord., 1985-87, program dir., 1987-90; tchr. Whittier Mid. Sch., Sioux Falls, 1990-95, Meml. Mid. Sch., Sioux Falls, 1995—. Chmn., mem. Vol./Info. Ctr. Adv. Bd., Sioux Falls, 1987—; sec. Minnehaha County Ext. Bd., Sioux Falls, 1990-92; chmn. Sioux Falls Homeless Coalition, 1990; mem. Sioux Falls Literacy Coun., 1986-88; mem. com. Sioux Falls ARea Found., 1993—; vol. Sioux Falls Cmty. Playhouse, 1991—; exec. coun., nominating com., bd. mem. youth/parish life Gloria Dei Luth. Ch., Sioux Falls, 1990—. Recipient Award for Outstanding Program JTPA, S.D. Dept. Labor, 1989. Mem. ASCD, S.D. Assn. Supervision and Curriculum Devel., S.D. Mid. Sch. Assn., Nat. Mid. Sch. Assn., Phi Delta Kappa. Home: 4505 Southridge Dr Sioux Falls SD 57105

O'BRIEN, DANIEL JOSEPH, pharmacologist, toxicologist; b. Chgo., Aug. 23, 1931; s. Daniel Joseph and Mary Isabelle (Horan) O'B.; m. Ruth Marilyn Glass, May 4, 1957; children: Mary Kathleen, Kevin Daniel. BS, Loras Coll., 1953; MS, So. Ill. U., 1960; PhD, Ind. U., 1964. Cert. in regulatory affairs by Regulatory Affairs Certification Bd., forensic examiner, forensic medicine Am. Bd. Forensic Medicine. Assoc. dir. Gillette Co., Rockville, Md., 1963-70; dir. Lakeside Labs., Milw., 1970-75; corp. mgr. Mobay Chem. Corp., Stilwell, Kans., 1976-83; pres. D.J. O'Brien & Assocs. Inc., Olathe, Kans., 1983—. Sgt. U.S. Army, 1956-57. Fellow, So. Ill. U., 1958-59, NIH, 1962-63. Mem. Am. Soc. Pharm. and Exptl. Therapeutics, Soc. Toxicology, Regulatory Affairs Profls. Soc. (cert.), Internat. Soc. Occupl. Medicine and Toxicology, Am. Coll. Toxicology, Am. Coll. Forensic Examiners. Home and Office: 1953 E Frontier Ln Olathe KS 66062-2344

O'BRIEN, DONALD EUGENE, federal judge; b. Marcus, Iowa, Sept. 30, 1923; s. Michael John and Myrtle A. (Toomey) O'B.; m. Ruth Mahon, Apr. 15, 1950; children: Teresa, Brien, John, Shuivaun. LL.B., Creighton U., 1948. Bar: Iowa bar 1948, U.S. Supreme Ct. bar 1963. Asst. city atty. Sioux City, Iowa, 1949-53; county atty. Woodbury County, Iowa, 1955-58; mcpl. judge Sioux City, Iowa, 1959-60; U.S. atty. No. Iowa, 1961-67; pvt. practice law Sioux City, 1967-78, U.S. Dist. judge, 1978—; chief judge U.S. Dist. Ct. (no. dist.) Iowa, Sioux City, 1985-92, sr. judge, 1992—; rep. 8th cir. dist. ct. judges to Jud. Conf. U.S., 1990—. Served with USAAF, 1943-45. Decorated D.F.C., air medals. Mem. Woodbury County Bar Assn., Iowa State Bar Assn. Roman Catholic. Office: US Dist Ct PO Box 267 Sioux City IA 51102-0267

O'BRIEN, JEFF J., engineer; b. Chgo., Ill., Aug. 1, 1967. BSEE, U. Ill., Chgo., 1992. Engr. Scripfel Corp., Columbus, 1992—. Vol. Greater Chgo. Food Depository, 1991-92. Mem. IEEE. Office: Scripfel 4145 Arlingate Plz Columbus OH 43228-4115

O'BRIEN, KATHLEEN ANN, health association executive, educator; b. Ft. Dodge, Iowa, June 2, 1948; d. Lyal John and Denise Fahey (Bagan) O'Brien. BA, Webster U., 1969; MSW, Washington U., St. Louis, 1971. Tchr. Ferguson-Florissant Sch. Dist., St. Louis, 1969-71, 75-87; social worker St. Louis County Juvenile Ct., St. Louis, 1971-73; exec. dir., CEO Alzheimer's Assn., St. Louis, 1987—; adj. prof. U. Mo., St. Louis; faculty Washington U.; co-chair Mo. State Task Force on Alzheimer's Jefferson City, 1985-89; chair Alzheimer's Disease adv. bd. Washington U., 1986-90; cons. long-term care facilities; mem. Mo. Dept. Mental Health, 1988—; adj. prof. U. Mo.; faculty U. Mo., Washington U.; presenter at profl. confs. Contbr. articles to profl. publs. Chair blood bank United Way, St. Louis, 1987-89; active Mo. Leadership League, 1993—. Named Vol. of Yr. United Way, St. Louis, 1987; recipient Humanitarian award Gov. of Mo., 1988; named Outstanding Citizen Mo. Ho. of Reps., 1988. Mem. Nat. Soc. Fundraising Execs., Confluence, Leadership St. Louis. Home: 533 Warren St Saint Louis MO 63102 Office: Alzheimers Assn 9374 Olive Blvd Saint Louis MO 63132-3214

O'BRIEN, MARGARET ANN, obstetrics nurse, community health nurse; b. Cleve., Mar. 19, 1943; d. Joseph Andrew and Cecelia Marie (Gedeon) Kilburg; m. Francis Maurice O'Brien, Aug. 8, 1967; children: Christopher Alan, Scott Michael, Sean Martin. Student, St. John's Coll., Cleve., 1961-62; AS, Cuyahoga Community Coll., Cleve., 1967; student, Akron U., 1985-87, Denison U., 1986. Cert. inpatient obstetric nursing NAACOG Certification Corp. Staff nurse obstetrics Grace Hosp., Cleve., 1966-73; instr. Childbirth Educator's Inc., Cleve., 1975-78; staff nurse obstetrics Amherst (Ohio) Hosp., 1978-80, Lamaze childbirth educator, 1987-91; staff nurse labor and delivery St. Joseph Hosp., Lorain, Ohio, 1980-85; staff nurse obstetrics Amherst (Ohio) Hosp., 1985-91; nurse Vis. Nurse Assn. Cleve., 1991—; tchr. Cen. Cath. High Sch., Cleve., 1983—. Author: Prepared Childbirth, 1986, Early Pregnancy, 1990. Instr. Prolife Orgn., Lakewood, Ohio. Mem. NAACOG. Home: 1350 Columbia Rd Westlake OH 44145-2413 Office: 2500 E 22nd St Cleveland OH 44114

O'BRIEN, MARLYS CAROL HOWE, library director; b. St. Paul, Dec. 10, 1937; d. James Melvin and Emma Linda (Luthi) Howe; m. Gerald Thomas O'Brien, Mar. 29, 1970 (dec. Aug. 1993); stepchildren: Michael, David, Joseph, Kristine, Patrick, Colleen. Cert., U. Oslo, Norway, 1958; BA, U. Minn., 1960, MA, 1963. Libr. asst. St. Paul Pub. Libr., 1954-63; pub. libr. cons. Minn. Office of Libr. Devel. and Svc., St. Paul, 1963-65; librarian Cass County Libr., Pine River, Minn., 1965-69; dir. Kitchigami Regional Libr., Pine River, Minn., 1969—; bd. dirs. Minn. Libr. Found., St. Paul, 1983-86. Mem. ALA (pub. libr. assn. cmty. info. sect., pres. 1994), Minn. Libr. Assn. (councilor Minn. chpt. 1974-78, pres. 1982-83, Cert. of Merit award 1967, 91). Lutheran. Home: HC 78 Box 321 Pine River MN 56474-9547 Office: Kitchigami Regional Libr PO Box 84 403 Barclay Ave Pine River MN 56474

O'BRIEN, MICHAEL J., state legislator; b. Sept. 5, 1942; m. Patricia Shoals; children: Michael James, Kathleen Jamie. Student, Mich. State U. Sen. Mich. Dist. 5, 1974—; comm. & tech. com. Mich. State Senate, state affairs & mil./vet. affairs com., transp. & tourism com., joint adminstrv. rules com., legis. coun. com. Recipient Waymond C. Birdsong award for Svc. to Vets., 1981—, disting. svc. award Assn. Food Dealers, 1981—, Walter P. Patenge award Mich. State U. Coll. Osteopathic Medicine, 1983—; named humanitarian of yr. 1985 Mich. Fedn. Humane Socs. Office: 8248 Ashton Ave Detroit MI 48228-3160 Address: State Senate PO Box 30036 Lansing MI 48909-7536*

O'BRIEN, PATRICK AUGUSTINE, business executive; b. Methuen, Mass., Sept. 30, 1951; s. Augustine Joseph and Marie Frances (Pineau) O'B.; m. Cherryl S. O'Brien, July 12, 1992; children: Erin Christine, Kelly Nicole. BS in Aeronautical and Astro. Engring., Ohio State U., 1974; MS in Mgmt., U. So. Calif., 1978. Project mgr. Naval Air Test Ctr., Patuxent River, Md., 1974-77; engr. mgr. Ford Motor Co., Dearborn, Mich., 1978-79; regional sales mgr. Foster Air Data, Worthington, Ohio, 1980-81; regional sales mgr. GE Superabrasives, Worthington, 1982-86, sales mgr., 1989-91; mktg. mgr. Longyear Co., Sun Valley, Calif., 1987-88; pres. O'Brien Internat. Sales, Dublin, Ohio, 1992—; spkr. in field. Mem. Concrete Sawing and Drilling Assn. (exec. dir. 1991-95), Polycrystalline Products Assn. (exec. dir. 1992-95), Internat. Gooving and Grinding Assn. (exec. dir.), Bldg. Stone Inst. (bd. dirs. 1990-91). Roman Catholic. Office: O'Brien Internat Sales Inc Ste 101 6089 Frantz Rd Dublin OH 43017

O'BRIEN, WALTER JOSEPH, II, lawyer; b. Chgo., Apr. 22, 1939; s. Walter Joseph O'Brien and Lorayne (Stouffer) Steele; children: Kelly A., Patrick W., Kathleen; m. Sharon Ann Curling, July 8, 1978; 1 child, John Joseph. BBA, U. Notre Dame, 1961; JD, Northwestern U.-Chgo., 1964. Bar: Ill. 1965, U.S. Dist. Ct. (no. dist.) Ill. 1965, U.S. Supreme Ct. 1973. Assoc. Nicholson, Nisen, Elliott & Meier, Chgo., 1966-70; pres., Capstan Co., Chgo., 1970-73, Walter J. O'Brien II, Ltd., Oak Brook, Ill., 1973-78, O'Brien & Assocs., P.C., Oakbrook Terrace, Ill., 1978—; dir. Atty. Title Guaranty Fund, Inc., Champaign, Ill., 1979—. Contbr. articles to legal jours. Commr., Oak Brook Plan Commn., 1980-85 ; mem. Oak Brook Zoning Bd. Appeals, 1985-87, Bd. Edn. Elem. Dist. # 53, Oak Brook, Ill., 1991—; commr. Ill. and Mich. Canal, Nat. Heritage Corridor Commn.; v.p. Oak Brook Civic Assn., 1972; trustee St. Isaac Jogues Ch., Hinsdale, Ill., 1975-76. Served as capt. Q.M.C., U.S. Army, 1964-66. Fellow Ill. Bar Found.; mem. Ill. State Bar Assn. (mem. assembly), DuPage Bar Assn. (bd. dirs. 1987-88, elected Man of Yr. 1988), Am. Inn of Ct. (master DuPage chpt.). Roman Catholic. Club: Butterfield Country (bd. dirs. 1982-88) (Oak Brook). Office: O'Brien & Assocs PC 17w200 22nd St Oakbrook Terrace IL 60181

O'BRIEN, WAYNE EDWARD, planner; b. South Bend, Ind., Sept. 2, 1949; s. William Edward and Alice Phyllis (Sienkiewicz) O'B. m. Elizabeth Rozow, Feb. 19, 1972. Student, Purdue U., 1976. Program dir. WJVA AM/FM, South Bend, Ind., 1966-71; staff announcer WNDU AM/FM, South Bend, 1971-72; d.p. tech. staff City of Fort Wayne, Ind., 1972-77; asst. supr. City of Fort Wayne, Fort Wayne, 1977-79; permit co-ordinator Tech. Services City of Fort Wayne, 1979-82; Bd. dir. NEI PC Users Group, Ft. Wayne, IAM Local 2569, (Steward 1974-76, Dist. Del. 1975-76). Contbr. numerous articles to profl. jours. Mem. Ft Wayne Zool. Soc., Southwest Conservation Club. Dean's List, Purdue Univ., Corp. Suggestions Program, 1986, Employee of the Quarter, Community Devel. and Planning, City of Ft. Wayne, 1986. Mem. Mensa. Home: 2109 Lindenwood Ave Fort Wayne IN 46808-1860

O'BROCHTA-WOODWARD, RUBY CATHERINE, orthopedic nurse; b. Waynesburg, Pa., Aug. 9, 1953; d. Thomas Anthony and Betty Lou (Clark) O'Brochta; m. F. Kelley Woodward, July 6, 1985; 1 child, Jesse Thomas Woodward. BSN, U. Pitts., 1975. Cert. orthopaedic nurse. Staff/charge nurse, instr., head nurse Children's Hosp. Pitts., 1975-82; orthopaedic nurse clinician, nursing supr. Oakland Orthopaedic Assocs., 1982-84; orthopaedic nurse clinician John Winter, MD and Thomas Gasser, MD, Cheyenne, Wyo., 1984-90; orthopaedic nurse clinician, orthopaedic coding specialist Orthopaedic Assocs. Ltd., Edina, Minn., 1990-93; orthopaedic nurse clinician Minn. Orthopaedic Foot & Ankle Ctr., 1993—. Mem. Am. Soc. Orthopaedic Physician Assts., Am. Acad. Procedural Coders, Nat. Assn. Orthopaedic Nurses, Nat. Assn. Physicians Nurses, Am. Assn. Office Nurses, Minn. Soc. Orthopaedic Physician Assts. Home: 5797 Fulbright Circle SE Prior Lake MN 55372-1941

OBST, NORMAN PHILIP, economist, educator; b. Bklyn., May 25, 1944; s. Joseph J. and Pearl L. (Newmark) O.; m. Barbara E. Brudevold, Dec. 23, 1970; children: Lindora, Jannise, Laara, Benjamin. BA, SUNY, Binghamton, 1965; MS in Econs., Purdue U., 1967, PhD in Econs., 1970. Asst. prof. U. Wash., 1970-73; asst. prof. Mich. State U., East Lansing, 1973-77, assoc. prof., 1977-92, prof. econs., 1992—; cons. NSF, Social Scis. and Humanities Rsch. Coun. of Can., Mich. Bar Assn., Little, Brown & Co., Prentice-Hall, Scott-Foresman, Times-Mirror Mosby, D.C. Heath & Co., Allyn & Bacon, West Ednl. Pub., Dryden Press, John Wiley & Sons, Inc., BS&A Software, Law Offices of Joseph H. Speigel. Referee Am. Econ. Rev., Internat. Econ. Rev., Jour. of Money, Credit and Banking, Eastern Econ. Jour., Jour. of Econ. Issues, Jour. of Macroeconomics, Jour. of Econs. and Bus., Zentralblatt fur Mathematik; contbr. articles to profl. jours. Supr., assessor Williamstown Twp., 1988—, sec. bd. appeals, 1988—, planning commn. mem. 1974-88, vice chmn. 1985-88; chief adminstrv. officer, Williamstown Twp. Budget, 1989—; cen. adminstr. Williamstown Twp. Sewer System, 1988—; bd. determination Ingham County Drain Commn., 1989; co-chair govt. com. I-96 strategic econ. plan with Lansing area bus. leaders, 1990. Mem. Am. Econ. Assn., Am. Fin. Assn., Midwest Econ. Assn., Mich. Assessors Assn. Office: Mich State U Marshall Hall Dept Econs East Lansing MI 48824-1038 also: Williamstown Twp Hall 4990 Zimmer Rd Williamston MI 48895-9609

O'CALLAGHAN, PATTI LOUISE, court program administrator; b. Bklyn., Mar. 26, 1953; d. Cornelius Leo and Louise Patricia (Casey) O'C.; m. Mark A. Diekman, Dec. 17, 1977; children: Casey, Brian. BA in Biology, NYU, 1975; MS in Physiology, Colo. State U., 1983. Cert. in program adminstrn. Grad. asst. Colo. State U., Ft. Collins, 1975-78; rsch. technician Iowa State U., Ames, 1978-80; counselor trainer Tecumseh Planned Parenthood, Lafayette, Ind., 1985; program coord. Date-rape Awareness and Edn., Lafayette, 1986-89; dir. Tippecanoe Ct. Apptd. Spl. Advocates, Lafayette, 1989—; mem. adv. commn. Ind. State Supreme Ct., Indpls., 1992—, chair, 1995—; mem. Tippecanoe Child Abuse Prevention, 1992—, pres. 1996; mem. Tippecanoe County Child Protection Team, 1995—. Editor tng. manuals; contbr. articles to profl. jours. Mem. adv. com. Jour. and Courier, Lafayette, 1992-93; vol. adv. Urban Ministries Homeless Shelter, Lafayette, 1992-93; coach Tippecanoe Soccer Assn., West Lafayette, Ind., 1989—; coach girls soccer West Lafayette H.S., 1994—; sec., v.p., pres. West Lafayette Sch. Bd., 1988—; mem. Tippecanoe County Child Protection Team, 1994—; mentor Mothers Adv. Bd., 1994—. Named Ind. Child Adv. of Yr., 1992, Nat. CASA Dir. of Yr., 1995; D.A.T.E. grantee Ind. Bd. Health, 1988. Mem. Ind. Chpt. for Prevention of Child Abuse, Ind. Advs. for Children (program com. 1991-92), Ind. Sch. Bd. Assn. (legis. com. 1991-92), Ctrl. Ind. Assn. Vol. Adminstrs., Assn. of Women in Sci., Nat. Ct.Apptd. Spl. Adv. Assn., West Lafayette Swim Club (v.p. 1989-92). Democrat. Christian. Office: Tippecanoe CASA Tippecanoe Superior Ct 3 County Courthouse Lafayette IN 47901

OCHSNER, EDWARD CONNER, diagnostic radiologist; b. Indpls., Apr. 26, 1941; s. Harold Conrad and Julia Hannah (Conner) O.; m. Soili Aulikki Poutiainen, Sept. 5, 1964; children: Mark Conrad, Erik Eino. AB, Brown U., 1962; MD, Northwestern U., 1968. Diplomate Am. Bd. Radiology. Gen. med. officer U.S. Army, Wildflecken, Fed. Republic Germany, 1969-72; resident in radiology Meth. Hosp. Ind., Indpls., 1972-75; diagnostic radiologist, sec. Hendricks County Radiology, Inc., Danville, Ind., 1976—; chief of staff Hendricks County Hosp., Danville, 1987-88; v.p. med. staff Putnam County Hosp., Greencastle, Ind., 1985. Contbr. articles (with others) to profl. jours. Served as maj. U.S. Army, 1969-72. Named Intern of Yr., Evanston Hosp., 1969. Mem. AMA, Am. Roentgen Ray Soc., Radiol. Soc. N. Am., Soc. Nuc. Medicine, Am. Inst. Ultrasound in Medicine, Am. Coll. Radiology, Soc. Radiologists in Ultrasound. Home: 5154 E County Rd 200 South Danville IN 46122-8816 Office: Hendricks County Radiology Inc 998 E Main St Ste 100 Danville IN 46122-1900

OCHSNER, OTHON HENRY, II, importer, restaurant critic; b. Chgo., May 19, 1934; s. Othon Henry and Louise Catherine (Schlichenmaier) O. AA, Chgo. City Coll., 1961. Pub. relations staff Walgreen Co., Chgo., 1961-65; sales mgr. Porsche Car Imports, Northbrook, Ill., 1966-67; nat. sales mgr. Pirelli Tire Corp., N.Y.C., 1968-73; pres., chief exec. officer Ochsner Internat., Chgo., 1974—, also bd. dirs.; pres. Swiss-U.S.A. Racing Team, Chgo., 1976—. Author: Ochsner Pocket Guide to the Finest Restaurants in the World, 11th edit., 1994, Ochsner Restaurant Newsletter, 1986—. With U.S. Army, 1957-59. Mem. The Am. Inst. Wine and Food, Am. -Swiss C. of C., Swiss-Am. Hist. Soc., Swiss Gourmet Soc. (pres. U.S. chpt.), Swiss Travel Club, Swiss Club Chgo., The Bagatelle Club, Conf. de la Chaine des Rotisseurs, Ordre des Canardiers. Baptist. Avocation: visiting and reviewing world class French and Swiss restaurants worldwide. Home: 5885 N Forest Glen Ave Chicago IL 60646-6652 Office: The Ochsner Bldg 246 Marquardt Dr Wheeling IL 60090

O'CONNELL, DAVID PAUL, state legislator; b. Bottineau County, N.D., June 3, 1940; s. Basil and Dorothy (Zimny) O'C.; m. Anadine Picard, 1960; children: Russell, Patricia Hetland, Marlys. Student, N.D. U. Mem. N.D. Ho. of Reps., 1983-88; mem. N.D. Senate, 1989—, chmn. joint constrn. revision com., vice chmn. edn., transp. coms.; farmer. Mem. Lansford Fire & Ambulance Squad. Named Legislator of Yr., N.D. Vocat. Edn., 1990. Mem. KC, Farmers Union, Farm Bur., C. of C. Home: 2531 Country Rd 30 Lansford ND 58750*

O'CONNELL, EDWARD JOHN, pediatrician; b. Rochester, Minn., May 30, 1934; s. Edward J. and Celia M. (Schwartz) O'C.; m. Maureen D. Gallagher, June 9, 1958; children: Kathleen, Maureen, Colleen, Sheila, Edward. BS, U. St. Thomas, 1956; MD, St. Louis U., 1960. Diplomate Am. Bd. Pediatrics, Am. Bd. Pediatric Allergy, Am. Bd. Allergy and Immunology. Intern in pediatrics Cardinal Glennon Hosp., St. Louis, 1960-61; pediatric and allergy fellowship Mayo Clinic, Rochester, 1961-65; instr. Mayo Med. Sch., Rochester, 1968-73, asst. prof. pediatrics, 1973-76, assoc. prof. pediatrics, 1976-83, prof. pediatrics, 1983—; cons. in pediatrics Mayo Clinic and Found., 1965—, curricula-self study com., 1983-86, grad. edn. subcom. med. and lab. specialities, 1980-83, pediatric exec. com., 1979-87, dir. gen. pediatric tng. program, 1979-82, dir. cystic fibrosis ctr., 1976-89, co-dir. allergy/immunology tng. program, 1972-92; cons. Am. Med. Assn.'s Drug Evaluations, 1991-93. Editl. bd. Annals of Allergy, 1989-93, Immunology and Allergy Practice, 1987-92; contbr. chpts. to books and numerous articles to profl. publs. With USAF, 1966-68. Fellow Am. Coll. of Chest Physicians, Am. Coll. of Allergy and Immunology (family practice tng. programs com. 1995—, managed care com. 1994—, chair ethics com. 1994—, rep. ho. of delegates 1988-94, pres. 1990-91, pres.-elect 1989-90, v.p. 1988-89, chmn. allied health program, 1986-88, mem. fin. com. 1986-87, mem. annals of allergy coun. 1985, 86, 88-92, chmn. continuing med. edn. com., 1985-86, allergy/immunology tng. program dirs. com. 1985-87), Am. Acad. Pediatrics, Am. Acad. of Allergy and Immunology; mem. AMA, Internat. Assn. of Allergology and Clin. Immunology (exec. com. 1988-91), N.W. Pediatric Soc., Mid-West Soc. for Pediatric Rsch., Irish and Am. Paediatric Soc., North Ctrl. Allergy Soc., Am. Assn. of Cert. Allergists, Minn. Allergy Soc., Ambulatory Pediatric Soc., Am. Thoracic Soc, Minn. Med. Soc., Zumbro Valley Med. Soc., Am. Lung Assn. of Minn., Am. Pediatric Soc. for Rsch., Joint Coun. of Allergy and Immunology, Orton Soc., Sigma Xi. Roman Catholic. Office: Mayo Med Sch Dept Pediatrics 200 1st St SW Rochester MN 55905

O'CONNELL, HAROLD PATRICK, JR., banker; b. Chgo., Sept. 11, 1933; s. Harold P. and Charlotte Anne (Woodward) O'C.; m. Geraldine Taylor McLaughlin, 1979; children: Alexandra T. Close, Geraldine S. Kuchman, Peter B. McLaughlin Jr. AB, Dartmouth Coll., 1955; JD, U. Mich., 1958. V.p. Continental Ill. Nat. Bank and Trust Co., Chgo., 1958-83, No. Trust Co., Chgo., 1983-86; dir. Terra Mus. of Am. Art, Chgo., 1987-92; chmn. exec. com. Mid-Am. Nat. Bank, 1989-92, pres., CEO, dir., 1992-93, chmn. bd., 1993—. Trustee Better Govt. Assn. Chgo., 1974—, pres., 1979-83; governing mem. Chgo. Symphony Orchestra, 1979—; sustaining fellow Art Inst. Chgo., 1982—; bd. dirs. Rehab. Inst. Chgo., 1980—. Mem. Chgo. Club, Racquet Club, Econ. Club, Casino Club (pres. 1988-91), Onwentsia Club (Lake Forest, Ill.), Shoreacres (Lake Bluff, Ill.), Old Elm Club (Highland Park, Ill.), Cypress Point Club (Pebble Beach, Calif.). Home: 435 Thorne Ln Lake Forest IL 60045-2343 Office: Mid-Am Nat Bank of Chgo 130 E Randolph St Chicago IL 60601

O'CONNELL, JAMES JOSEPH, port official; b. Lockport, Ill., Feb. 7, 1933; m. Phyllis Ann Berard, Aug. 1, 1953; children: Lynn, Kathryn, Julie. BSBA, Lewis U., 1958. lic. pvt. pilot FAA. Recorder Will County, Joliet, Ill., 1976-88; dir., treas., corp. sec., v.p. Joliet Regional Port Dist., 1972-96; dir. Des Plaines Valley Enterprise Zone, Joliet. Precinct committeeman Will County, Joliet, 1962-72, exec. cen. committeeman, 1965-70, dir. Will County Young Reps., Joliet, 1984, sec. Will County Econ. Affairs Commn., Joliet; candidate for U.S. Congress, 1994. With U.S. Army, 1953-54, Korea. Mem. Ill. Assn. Port Dists. (sec., treas. 1982—), Ill. Jaycees (senate pres. 1972-73, named to Hall of Fame 1993), Joliet Flying Club (sec.), K.C., Joliet Exch. Club, Three Rivers Mfg. Assn. (pub. affairs com.), Joliet Columbian Club (pres.), Am. Legion (life, former post officer), VFW (life), others. Roman Catholic. Office: 1009 Western Ave Joliet IL 60435-6801

O'CONNELL, KATHLEEN LECLEAR, nursing educator; b. Steubenville, Ohio, Jan. 28, 1952; d. E. Robert and Irene (Ciancetta) LeClear; m. Thomas Barry O'Connell, July 1, 1970; children: Christopher Thomas, Ryan Thomas. ADN, Purdue U., 1978, BSN, 1986; MSN, Ind. U., 1988; post-grad., Ball State U., Ind. U. Staff and charge nurse critical care unit Parkview Meml. Hosp., Ft. Wayne, Ind., 1978-84, patient care mgr. critical care unit, 1984-86; assoc. faculty Ind. U.-Purdue U., Ft. Wayne, 1986-89, asst. prof. nursing, 1990-95, assoc. prof. nursing, 1996—; nurse cons. Assn. for Retarded Citizens, Ft. Wayne, 1988—; nurse reviewer Lincoln Nat. Corp., Ft. Wayne, 1989-90; cons. Assn. for Retarded Citizens, Ft. Wayne, 1998—; nurse reviewer Lincoln Nat. Corp., Ft. Wayne, 1989-90. Contbr. articles to profl. jours. Vol. nurse practitioner Matthew 25 Health Clinic, Ft. Wayne, 1988—; bd. dirs Whitley County chpt. Am. Cancer Soc., Columbia City, Ind., 1991—, pres., 1994—, mem. state bd., med. dir. Region 3, 1994—. Mem. ISNA (publs. com. 1994—), Sigma Theta Tau (Alpha chpt. 1988—). Roman Catholic. Office: Ind U Purdue U Ft Wayne 2101 E Coliseum Blvd Fort Wayne IN 46805-1445

O'CONNELL, KATHLEEN M., pediatric, medical-surgical, psychiatric nurse; b. Omaha, Aug. 5, 1941; d. Francis D. and Marie A. (Suchan) McPherson; children: John P. Neuhaus, Michael F., Kathleen E. Diploma, St. Catherine's Sch. Nursing, Omaha, 1962; BS in Profl. ARts, St. Joseph's Coll., Windham, Maine, 1988; MS in Counseling, Creighton U., 1991. RN, Nebr., Iowa; bd. eligible nat. cert. counselor. Staff nurse labor and delivery Bergan Mercy Hosp., Omaha, 1962-67, charge nurse labor and delivery, 1967-69, head nurse labor and delivery, 1969-72, staff nurse pediatrics and adult med./surg., 1973—; home health nurse, 1992-93; psychiat. nurse St. Joseph Ctr. for Mental Health, 1993—; ind. travel agent World Class Travel, 1996—. Mem. ACA, Parents United-Daughters and Sons United (co-facilitator for group of sexually abused adolescents 1991-95). Democrat. Roman Catholic. Home: 12417 Yates St Omaha NE 68164-3461 Office: Bergan Mercy Med Ctr 7500 Mercy Rd Omaha NE 68124-2319

O'CONNOR, EARL EUGENE, federal judge; b. Paola, Kans., Oct. 6, 1922; s. Nelson and Mayme (Scheetz) O'C.; m. Florence M. Landis, Nov. 3, 1951 (dec. May 1962); children: Nelson, Clayton; m. Jean A. Timmons, May 24, 1963; 1 dau., Gayle. B.S., U. Kans., 1947, LL.B., 1950. Bar: Kans. 1950. Practiced in Mission, Kans., 1950-51; asst. county atty. Johnson County, Kans., 1951-53; probate and juvenile judge, 1953-55; dist. judge 10th Jud. Dist., Olathe, Kans., 1955-65; justice Kans. Supreme Ct., 1965-71; judge U.S. Dist. Ct., Dist. of Kans., Kansas City, 1971—, chief judge, 1981-92; mem. Jud. Conf. U.S., 1988-91. Served with AUS, World War II, ETO. Mem. ABA, Nat. Conf. Fed. Trial Judges, Kans. Bar Assn., Phi Alpha Delta. Office: US Courthouse 500 State Ave Kansas City KS 66101-2403

O'CONNOR, FRANCINE MARIE, magazine editor; b. Springfield, Mass., Apr. 8, 1930; d. Wallace Harold and Celestine Margaret (Morrison) Provost; m. John Francis O'Connor, Dec. 27, 1951 (dec. Feb. 1992); children—Margaret Anne McGlynn, Kathryn Mary Boswell, Timothy John. Grad. high sch., Springfield. Editorial asst. Liguori Publs., Mo., 1975-76, assoc. editor, 1976-79, mng. editor, 1979-93; assoc. editor Parish Edn. Products, Mo., 1993—. Author: ABC's of Faith series, including The Stories of Jesus, 1982, The ABC's of the Rosary, 1984, The ABC's of the Mass, 1989, The ABC's of the Sacraments, 1989, The ABC's of the Old Testament, 1989, The ABC's of Prayer, 1989, Lessons of Love, 1991 (hon. mention Cath. Press Assn. 1992), God and You: Friends Forever, 1993, The ABC's of Christmas, 1994, The ABC's of Our Church, 1996, Forming Children in the Faith, 1996. Religious edn. coord. Sts. Peter and Paul Roman Cath. Ch., St. Louis, 1978—. Mem. Cath. Press. Assn. Home: 157 Crest Manor Dr House Springs MO 63051-1477 Office: Liguorian 1 Liguori Dr Liguori MO 63057-9998

O'CONNOR, FRANCIS GERALD, computer systems management executive; b. Yonkers, N.Y., Apr. 20, 1960; s. Francis Gerald O'Connorand Eileen Emma (Boyle) Cleary; m. Kim Marie Raphel O'Connor, Aug. 20, 1989; children: Lucas, Kellen, Evan. Student, Rochester Inst. Tech., 1978-79, N.Y. Inst. Tech., Old Westbury, 1980-82. Cert. data processor. Programmer/analyst Omega Sys., Plainview, N.Y., 1982-83; product support specialist Periphonics, Bohemia, N.Y., 1984-87; dir. MIS Jenny Craig Internat., San Diego, 1987-90; pres., CEO Cons. on Call, San Diego, 1990-92; v.p. ops. Profl.'s Choice, San Diego, 1992-94; mgr. ops. LeFebure, Cedar Rapids, Iowa, 1994-95, mgr. bus. systems group, 1996—; cons. telecomms., San Diego, 1990-94. Co-chair Jamul (Calif.) Action Com., 1993; active Little League. Mem. ICCA, LeTip. Republican. Roman Catholic. Office: LeFebure 308 29th St NE Cedar Rapids IA 52402

O'CONNOR, SISTER GERTRUDE THERESA, clinical nurse specialist in surgery and anesthesia; b. O'Fallon, Ill., Jan. 4, 1939; d. Edward Charles and Gertrude Beatrice (Gerardi) O'C. Diploma, St. John's Hosp. Sch. Nursing, Springfield, Ill., 1963; BSN, Marillac Coll., St. Louis, 1971; EdM, U. Ill., 1979; MSN, Rush U., Chgo., 1988. Cert. nurse oper. rm. Staff nurse St. Elizabeth's Hosp., Belleville, Ill., 1963-68; instr. perioperative nursing St. John's Hosp., Springfield, 1972-83; supr. nursing home St. Francis Convent, Springfield, 1983-87; clin. specialist St. John's Hosp., Springfield, 1988—. Mem. Assn. Oper. Rm. Nurses (nat. level, nat. com. edn., local sec., pres., bd. dirs., treas.). Office: St John's Hosp 800 E Carpenter St Springfield IL 62769

O'CONNOR, JACK, state legislator; m. Mari Kay O'Connor; children: John, Eileen, Patrick. Police officer City of Chgo., 1966-84; mgr. O'Connor Auto Group, Palos Heights, Ill., 1984—; mem. Ill. State Ho. of Reps., Springfield, 1995—, mem. jud.-criminal laws, aging, energy coms., 1995—, mem. environ. registration and regulation coms., 1995—. Basketball coach Incarnation Cath. Ch.; youth activity mgr. St. Clair Cath. Ch. Mem. Fraternal Order Police, St. Jude Police League. Address: 12307 S Harlem Ste 7 Palos Heights IL 60463

O'CONNOR, JAMES JOHN, utility company executive; b. Chgo., Mar. 15, 1937; s. Fred James and Helen Elizabeth O'Connor; m. Ellen Louise Lawlor, Nov. 24, 1960; children: Fred, John (dec.), James, Helen Elizabeth. BS, Holy Cross Coll., 1958; MBA, Harvard U., 1960; JD, Georgetown U., 1963. Bar: Ill. 1963. With Commonwealth Edison Co., Chgo., 1963—, asst. to chmn. exec. com., 1964-65, comml. mgr., 1966, asst. v.p., 1967-70, v.p., 1970-73, exec. v.p., 1973-77, pres., 1977-87, chmn., 1980—; CEO, also bd. dirs.; chmn., CEO Unicom Corp., 1994—; bd. dirs. Corning, Inc., Chgo. Bd. of Trade, Tribune Co., United Air Lines, Scotsman Industries, Am. Nat. Can., 1st Chgo. NBD Corp., 1st Nat. Bank Chgo.; past chmn. Nuc. Power Oversight Com., Edison Electric Inst., bd. dirs.; chmn. Advanced Reactor Corp. Mem. The Bus. Coun.; bd. dirs. Assocs. Harvard U. Grad. Sch. Bus. Adminstrn., Lyric Opera, Helen Brach Found.; bd. dirs., trustee Mus. Sci. and Industry; past chmn. Met. Savs. Bond Campaign; trustee Northwestern U.; bd. dirs., past chmn. Chgo. Urban League, Chicagoland C. of C.; past chmn. bd. trustees Field Mus. Natural History; life trustee Adler Planetarium; mem. exec. bd. Chgo. area Coun. Boy Scouts Am.; chmn. Cardinal Bernardin's Big Shoulders Fund; exec. v.p. The Hundred Club Cook County; dir., past pres. Cath. Charities; past chmn., hon. dir. Am. Cancer Soc., Chgo. Conv. and Tourism Bur. With USAF, 1960-63. Mem. ABA, Ill. Bar Assn., Chgo. Bar Assn., Chgo. Assn. Commerce and Industry (bd. dirs., chmn.), Ill. Bus. Roundtable, Chicagoland C. of C. (dir., past chmn.). Home: 1500 Lake Shore Dr 5C Chicago IL 60610 Office: Commonwealth Edison Co PO Box 767 1 1st Nat Plz Chicago IL 60690-0767

O'CONNOR, JOHN JOSEPH, insurance company executive; b. Worcester, Mass., Apr. 26, 1950; s. John J. and Alice M. (Grogan) O'C.; m. Mary Ellen Nyberg, July 10, 1976; children: Ryan J., Caitlin Mary, Kevin T. Assoc. Mech. Engring., Quinsigamond Community Coll., Worcester, 1971; BSBA cum laude, Worcester State Coll., 1988. Account rep. Wausau Ins. Cos., Worcester, 1975-81, field sales mgr., 1981-85; regional sales mgr. Wausau Ins. Cos., Boston, 1985-91; asst. v.p., corp. sales mgr. Wausau (Wis.) Ins. Cos., 1991-93, v.p. mktg. Mid Atlantic divsn., 1993—. Designer A to Z Strategic Planning Guide, Sales and Sales Management Fin. Planning Disk, 1991; creator Risk Mgmt. Audiocassette Tng. Tape. Exec. bd. Boy Scouts Am., Wausau, 1992—, den leader, 1987-91; pres. Holden (Mass.) Baseball, 1991, Everest Soccer Assn., Schofield, Wis., 1992—. Recipient Citizenship award Town of Holden/Holden Soccer, 1991, Outstanding Leadership award Boston Region, 1986. Mem. Exchange Club (bd. dirs. 1980-82, Merit award 1982). Home: 1066 Victory Dr Yardley PA 19067-4517 Office: Wausau Ins Co 1700 Market St Philadelphia PA 19103-3913

O'CONNOR, JOHN PAUL, judge; b. Evanston, Ill., Sept. 30, 1939; s. James C. and Alice (Daly) O'C.; m. Judith Byrne Dec. 27, 1961 (div. June 1976); children: John P., Kathleen A., James B.; m. Kathleen A. Ballinger, Nov. 29, 1985. BS Xavier Coll., Cin., 1963; JD, Chase Law Sch., 1967. Bar: Ohio 1967, U.S. Ct. Appeals (6th cir.) 1968, U.S. Dist. Ct. (so. dist.) Ohio 1968. Ptnr., Schuch, Grossmann & O'Connor, Cin., 1967-73; referee Juvenile Ct. Cin., 1967-73; judge Mcpl. Ct., Cin., 1973-79; judge juvenile divsn. Ct. of Common Pleas, 1979-93, gen. divsn. Ct. of Common Pleas, 1993—; adj. asst. prof. Xavier U. Grad. Sch., Cin., 1969-78; adj. asst. prof. Chase Law Sch., 1988—; lectr. Ohio Judicial Coll., 1989—. Author: Juvenile Offenders and the Law, 1971, Beyond the Star Chambers, 1986, Diseases of Children. Mem. ABA, Ohio Bar Assn., Am. Judges Assn., Cin. Bar Assn., Ohio Juvenile and Probate Judges. Republican. Roman Catholic. Office: Hamilton County Courthouse 1000 Main St Cincinnati OH 45202-1217

O'CONNOR, KAY, state legislator; b. Everett, Wash., Nov. 28, 1941; d. Ernest S. and Dena (Lampers) Wells; m. Arthur J. O'Connor, Sept. 1, 1959; 6 children. Diploma, Lathrop H.S., Fairbanks, Alaska, 1959. Office mgr. Blaylock Chemicals, Bucyrus, Kans., 1981-84; store mgr. Copies Plus, Olathe, Kans., 1984-86; acct. Advance Concrete Inc., Spring Hill, Kans., 1986-92; mem. Kansas Ho. of Reps., 1993—; bd. dirs. Hometel Ltd.; author sch. voucher legis. for State of Kans., 1994, 95, 96. Republican. Roman Catholic. Home: 1101 N Curtis St Olathe KS 66061-2709 Office: PO Box 2232 Olathe KS 66051-2232

O'CONNOR, PATRICK J., state legislator; m. Susan Reckert; children: Patrick, Michael, Meghan. Student, U. Mo., St. Louis. Mem. Mo. State Ho. of Reps. Dist. 79, 1993—, mem. labor, higher edn., pub. health and safety coms., 1993—, mem. children, youth and family com., 1993—. Mem. Woodson Terrace Lion's Club, North County Labor Legis. Club, Pipefitters Local 562, N.W. Twp. Dem. Club (v.p.). Home: 4413 Claremont Ct Bridgeton MO 63044-1716*

O'CONNOR, SARA ANDREWS, theater director; b. Syracuse, N.Y., Apr. 5, 1932; d. Harlan Francis and Ethel (Hoyt) Andrews; m. Boardman O'Connor, Aug. 23, 1955 (div. 1969); children: Ian, Douglas. BA with high honors, Swarthmore Coll., 1954; MA, Tufts U., 1955. Assoc. producer Theatre Co. of Boston, 1965-68, producer, 1969-71; pub. relations dir. Repertory Theatre of New Orleans, 1968-69; mng. dir. Cin. Playhouse, 1971-74, Milw. Repertory Theater, 1974-; dir. fundraising Milw. Reperatory Theater, 1995S; cons. Found. for Extension and Devel. Am. Profl. Theatre, N.Y.C., 1973-83. Translator; (plays) The Workroom, 1979, At Fifty, She Discovered The Sea, 1982, Them, 1985, A Flea In Her Ear, 1986, The Puppetmaster of Lodz; The Mizer, 1988, Gone Hunting, 1989. Mem. Schlitz Audubon Ctr., Milw., 1980—, Amnesty Internat., N.Y.C., 1981—, ACLU, 1981—, Milw. Art Mus.; bd. dirs. Woodland Pattern, Milw., 1985—. Recipient Sacajawea award Profl. Dimensions, 1985. Mem. Internat. Theatre Inst. (bd. dirs. 1980-83), Am. Arts Alliance (bd. dirs. 1981-87), Dramatists Guild, League Resident Theatres (pres. 1984-87, v.p. 1972-79), Theatre Communications Group (bd. dirs. 1978-82, pres. 1982-84), Wis. Citizens for the Arts, Theater Jocks (founder). Zen Buddhist. Office: Milw Repertory Theater 108 E Wells St Milwaukee WI 53202-3504*

O'CONNOR, TERRENCE PATRICK, engineering educator; b. Milw., Jan. 1, 1957; s. Donald Louis and Ellen Nadine (Smith) O'C.; m. Becky Elaine Barrington, July 11, 1987; children: Michael Patrick, Terrence Patrick II. BS, No. Ariz. U., 1982; MS, West Tex. State U., 1985. Assoc. engr. Martin Marietta Aerospace, Denver, 1980-81, engr., 1986-88; instr. Tex. State Tech. Inst., Amarillo, 1981-84, Amarillo Coll., 1984-86; asst. prof. U. So. Maine, Gorham, 1988-92, Purdue U., New Albany, Ind., 1992—; mem. adv. bd. electronics tech. program IVy Tech. Coll., Sellersburg, Ind., 1994—. Contbr. articles to Am. Soc. Engring. Edn. Conf., Jour. Sci. and Engring. Ethics. Mem. IEEE, Am. Soc. Engring. Edn. Republican. Baptist. Home: 633 Hunt Dr Borden IN 47106-8855 Office: Purdue U Statewide Tech 4201 Grant Line Rd New Albany IN 47150-2158

O'CONNOR, TIMOTHY LEWIS, health science association administrator; b. Evanston, Ill., July 30, 1953; s.. Francis Coyne and Roberta Maxine (Lewis) O'C.; m. Margaret Diane Stevenson, Sept. 13, 1975; children: Cassandra Elizabeth, Samuel Levi, Molly Suzanne. BS in Agrl., Western Ill. U., 1975. Sec., treas., sales mgr. Ill. Simmatel Assn., 1974-80; cons. breeder Monmouth, Ill., 1975-85; mgr. Brewer Farms, Leasburg, Mo., 1985-86; v.p. mem. svcs. Ill. Beef Assn., Springfield, 1987-88, exec. v.p., 1989—; mem. exec. com. Nat. Cattlemen's Assn., Denver, 1993-94, chmn. affiliate execs., 1993-94; mem. exec. com. Nat. Livestock & Meat Bd., Chgo., 1990-91, chmn. state beef execs., 1990-91. Editor/creator Ill. Beef Mag., 1987-89. Bd. dirs. South Winds Homeowners Assn., Chatham, Ill., 1995; mem. U.S. trade team U.S. Meat Export Fedn., Tokyo, 1991. Mem. Am. Soc. Assn. Execs., Ill. Soc. Assn. Execs., Jaycees. Office: Ill Beef Assn 993 Clock Tower Dr Springfield IL 62704

O'CONNOR, WILLIAM CODY, retired transportation executive, consultant; b. Port Jervis, N.Y., Mar. 4, 1927; s. Walter Charles and Anna Gunning (Cody) O'C.; m. Jeanne Audrey Kieselmann, Aug. 21, 1948; children: Kathleen Ann, Laurie Jeanne, William Cody Jr., Matthew Sean. BA, Alfred U., 1950; MA, U. Pa., 1951. Traffic analyst Western Elec., N.Y.C., 1950-53; dir. transp. and energy The Anaconda Co., N.Y.C., 1953-75; v.p. distbn. and purchasing Brown Co., Kalamazoo, Mich., 1975-80; v.p. corp. transp. Kimberly-Clark, Neenah, Wis., 1980-90, ret., 1990. Dir. regional bd. Boy Scouts Am., Neenah, 1983-85. With USMC, 1945-46. Fellow Am. Numismatic Soc.; mem. Svc. Corps. Retired Exec., Internat. Exec. Svc. Corp. Roman Catholic. Home: 507 Vassar Ln Neenah WI 54956-3532

O'DANIEL, WILLIAM L., state legislator; b. Union County, Ky., Dec. 4, 1923; m. Norma Norris; 5 children. Student, Agr. Ext. Svc. Farmer, businessman; mem. Ill. Ho. of Reps., 1974-77; exec. dir. Agr. Stabilization and Conservation Svc. U.S. Dept. Agr., 1977-81; mem. Ill. State Senate from 54th dist.; vice chmn. Agr. Com. Ill. State Senate, mem. Revenue, Transp., Elec., Joint Com. on Adminstrv. Rules Coms. Decorated Purple Heart, Bronze Star. Office: 2700 Broadway St Mount Vernon IL 62864-2342 Home: RR 4 Mount Vernon IL 62864-9804*

O'DAY, EDWARD JOSEPH, JR., history educator; b. West Brookfield, Mass., Sept. 13, 1932; s. Edward Joseph and Grace Mary (Dillon) O'D.; m. Patricia Anne Duncan, Apr. 3, 1961; children: Kathleen O'Day Pham, E. Michael, Stephen P., Anne C. BA, U. Mass., 1954; MA, Ind. U., 1956. Lectr. U. Mich., Ann Arbor, 1960-61; instr. DePauw U., Greencastle, Ind., 1961-62; asst. prof. So. Ill. U., Carbondale, Ill., 1962-95; assoc. prof., 1995—; dir. undergrad. studies history So. Ill. U., Carbondale, 1982-92; pres. Ill. State Geneal. Soc., Springfield, 1989-91; coord. off-campus programs So. Ill. U., 1974-76; cons. Ill. State Bd. Edn., Springfield, 1986-94. Contbr. articles to profl. jours. Chair Carbondale Human Rels. Commn., Carbondale, 1967-69. Recipient Amoco and Queen awards for Teaching Excellence, 1976, 81. Mem. Am. Hist. Assn., Am. Conf. for Irish Studies, Nat. Geneal. Soc., Geneal. Soc. So. Ill. (parliamentarian 1985-92, 1st v.p. 1993—), Ill. State Geneal. Soc. (v.p. 1987-89, pres. 1989-91, gov. bd. 1992-94). Democrat. Roman Catholic. Office: So Ill Univ History Dept Carbondale IL 62901

O'DAY, JOHN HERVEY, JR., broadcast journalist; b. Cleve., Mar. 5, 1953; s. John H. and Margaret (Thomas) O'D. Staff reporter Sta. WJMO, Cleve., 1971-74, Sta. WUSS, Atlantic City, 1974-75, Sta. WMID and WGRF, Atlantic City, 1975-77, Sta. WJLB, Detroit, 1978-79; staff announcer Sta. WAMM, Flint, Mich., 1977-78; dir. news and program Sta. WMML-AM-FM, Mobile, Ala., 1987-89; news dir. Sta. WKRG-AM-FM-TV, Mobile, 1990-91; news and pub. affairs reporter Sta. KATZ-AM-FM, St. Louis, 1979-87, dir. news and pub. affairs, 1991—; instr. radio Herbert Hoover Boys Club, St. Louis, 1991—, Saturday Acad., St. Louis, 1992—; dir. youth program Sta. WCH Radio, 1995—. Instr. karate Herbert Hoover Boys Club, 1991-92; active mentor program St. Louis Div. Youth Svcs., 1992—; bd. dirs. Gateway 70001, St. Louis, 1992—, Saturday Youth Acad.,

1992—; vol. Christ Ch. Homeless Shelter, St. Louis, 1992; dep. juvenile officer St. Louis County Juvenile Ct. Recipient Yes I Can award St. Louis Sentinal Newspaper, 1995, April Wind Beneath My Wings award Herbert Hoover Boys and Girls Club, 1996; named Vol. of Yr., Pagedale (Mo.) Police Dept., 1986. Democrat. Roman Catholic. Office: KATZ AM-FM 10155 Corporate Sq Saint Louis MO 63132

O'DAY, JOSEPH, state legislator; m. Nell O'Day. Clk. Vanderburgh Circuit Ct., 8 yrs.; mem. Ind. State Senate, 1974—; mem. ethics com., ins. and fin. instns. com., pub. policy com., transp. and interstate coop. com. Mem. City Coun., Evansville, 9 yrs. Mem. Masons, Scottish Rite Shriners. Home: 311 Van Dusen Ave Evansville IN 47711-3355 Also: State Senate State Capitol Indianapolis IN 46204*

ODDEN, ALLAN ROBERT, education educator; b. Duluth, Minn., Sept. 16, 1943; s. Robert Norman and Mabel Eleanor (Bjornnes) O.; m. Eleanor Ann Rubottom, May 28, 1966; children: Sarina, Robert. BS, Brown U., 1965; MDiv, Union Theol. Sem., 1969; MA, Columbia U., 1971, PhD, 1975. Tchr. N.Y.C. Pub. Schs., 1967-72; rsch. assoc. Teachers' Coll. Columbia U., N.Y.C., 1972-75; dir. policy Edn. Commn. of the States, Denver, 1975-84; prof. U. So. Calif., L.A., 1984-93, U. Wis., Madison, 1993—; rsch. dir. Sch. Fin. Commns. Conn., 1974-75, S.D., 1975-76, Mo. 1975-76, 93, 94, N.Y., 1978-81, N.J., 1991-92; dir. finance ctr. Consortium for Policy Rsch. in Edn.; cons. Nat. Govs. Assn., Nat. Conf. State Legislatures, U.S. Sec. Edn., U.S. Senate, U.S. Dept. Edn. and many state legislatures and govs. Author: Education Leadership for America's Schools, 1995; co-author: School Finance: A Policy Perspective, 1992; editor: Education Policy Implementation, 1991, Rethinking School Finance, 1992; contbr. articles to profl. jours., chpts. to books. Mem. L.A. Chamber Edn. and Human Resources Commn., 1986, Gov.'s Sch. Fin. Commn., Calif., 1987, Calif. Assessment Policy Com., Gov.'s Edn. Task Force, Wis., 1996, Carnegie Corp. Task Force on Edn. in the Early Years, 1994. Grantee Dept. Edn., Spencer Found., Ford Found., Mellon Found., Carnegie Corp., Pew Charitable Trusts. Mem. Am. Ednl. Rsch. Assn., Am. Ednl. Fin. Assn. (pres. 1979-80), Nat. Tax Assn., Politics of Edn. Assn., Nat. Soc. for Study of Edn. Democrat. Home: 3128 Oxford Rd Madison WI 53705-2224 Office: U Wis Sch Edn Wis Ctr Edn Rsch 1025 W Johnson St # 753E Madison WI 53706-1706

ODEGARD, DANIEL JAMES, publisher, bookselling and publishing consultant; b. Anoka, Minn., Dec. 1, 1945; s. Donald Reuben Odegard and Rosella (Dehn) Hansen; m. Michele Poire, June 17, 1957 (div. 1983); children: Peter Poire Odegard, Zoë Odegard; m. Wilma Venchi, Jan. 17, 1985. BA cum laude, U. St. Thomas, St. Paul, Minn., 1967. Brewer, teamster Schmidt Brewery, St. Paul, 1967-68; tchg. asst. Pa. State U., State University, 1968-69, 73-75; gen. mgr., buyer First Edition Bookstores, Harrisburg, Pa., 1974-78; owner Odegard Books, St. Paul, 1978-84, Mpls., 1984-92; cons. assoc. SLC Enterprises, Southwest Harbor, Maine, 1992—; pub. Hazeldon Pub. and Edn., Center City, Minn., 1995—; tchr. of pub. U. Minn., Mpls., U. Wis., River Falls, 1986-89, 88-90; adv. bd. Random House Pub., N.Y.C., 1989-90, Bantam Doubleday Dell, 1988-90. Bd. dirs. Minn. Ctr. for Book Arts, Mpls., 1990-91; lectr. Ch. of Incarnation Parish, Mpls., 1987-92; vol. non-custodial visitor Pillsbury House, Mpls., 1992—. With USAF, 1969-73. Recipient Best Bookstore award Twin Cities Reader, Mpls., 1988-90, City Pages, Mpls., 1985-91. Mem. Milkweed Edits. (bd. dirs., v.p. 1987-92), Am. Booksellers Assn. Democrat. Roman Catholic. Home: 1210 Scheffer Ave Saint Paul MN 55116 Office: Hazeldon Publishing Center City MN 55012

O'DELL, LYNN MARIE LUEGGE (MRS. NORMAN D. O'DELL), librarian; b. Berwyn, Ill., Feb. 24, 1938; d. George Emil and Helen Marie (Pesek) Luegge; student Lyons Twp. Jr. Coll., La Grange, Ill., 1957; student No. Ill. U., Elgin Community Coll., U. Ill., Coll. of DuPage; m. Norman D. O'Dell, Dec. 14, 1957; children—Jeffrey, Jerry. Sec., Martin Co., Chgo., 1957-59; dir. Carol Stream (Ill.) Pub. Library, 1964—; chmn. automation governing com. DuPage Library System, v.p., 1982-85, pres. exec. com. adminstrv. librarians, 1985-86, chair automation search com., 1991-92. Named Woman of Yr., Wheaton Bus. and Profl. Woman's Club, 1968. Mem. ALA, Ill. Library Assn., Library Adminstrs. Conf. No. Ill. Lutheran. Home: 182 Yuma Ln Carol Stream IL 60188-1917 Office: 616 Hiawatha Dr Carol Stream IL 60188-1616

ODEN, FAY GILES, author, educator; b. Nashville, Nov. 17, 1929; d. Charley Jr. and Phenizie (Hodge) Giles; m. Edward A. Oden, Apr. 16, 1961. BA, Tenn. A&I State U., Nashville, 1951. Cert. in cosmetology. Elem. tchr. Cin. Pub. Schs., 1954-84, substitute tchr., 1985-94; author, pub. Tennedo Pubs., Cin., 1992—; supervising tchr. Ctrl. State Coll./U. Cin., 1968-75; vol. tutor; storyteller at various schs. and day care ctrs., Cin., 1993—. Author: Calvin and His Video Camera, 1993, (inspirational poetry) Believe, 1995; author, illustrator: Where Is Calvin?, 1993; author, editor: (pamphlet) The Flying School, 1995. Fin. sec. New Hope Bapt. Ch. Credit Union, Cin., 1982; vol. Pres.'s Coun. for a Drug Free Am., Cin., 1986; pub. speaker and mistress of ceremonies; piano tchr. to talented children, 1994—. Recipient award for Dedicated Vol. Svc., Cin. Charter of Ohio Credit Union League, 1983, other awards. Mem. Silverton Neighborhood Club (sec. 1987), Zeta Phi Beta. Home: 6315 Elwynne Dr Cincinnati OH 45236

ODEN, JEAN PHIFER, special education educator; b. Chgo., May 2, 1936; d. Dillard James and Lena (Conner) Phifer; m. James Edward Oden, Apr. 26, 1959; 1 child, Eric James. BE, Chgo. Tchrs. Coll., 1958; MEd in Learning Disabilities, Chgo. State U., 1973; postgrad., Nat. Coll. Edn., Evanston, Ill., 1986—, cert. advance studies, 1987; EdD, Nat.-Louis U., 1995. Tchr. elem. schs. Chgo., 1958-73, tchr. learning disabilities elem. schs., 1973-81, cons. spl. edn., ind. edn. program facilitator, 1981; learning disability specialist Phillips High Sch., Chgo., 1982—, Englewood High Sch., Chgo., 1987-94; Harold Washington Elem. Sch., 1994—; mem. Ill. Guidelines for Learning Disabilities Devel. Com., Springfield, Ill., 1981—, Com. to Devel. State Test for Learning Disabilities Tchrs., Springfield, 1986—; speaker Who's Who Congress, Cambridge, Eng., 1992; mem. del. to Vietnam, 1993, mem. del. to China, 1994. Speaker Nat. Urban League N.Y.C. conf., 1980; mem. Congl. Victory Fund, Chgo., 1985, SCLC Met. Chgo., 1979-81, Mayoral Summit Parent-Community Coun. on Ednl. Reform, 1987—, Chgo. Mayor's Edn. Summit on Sch. Reform, 1988; charter mem. Rep. Presdl. Adv. Task Force, 1989, Rep. Inner Circle, 1991; mem. Coalition Black Trade Unionists, 1991—, cons. pool Nat. Juvenile Justice Resource Ctr., 1991—, NAACP; state chair African Am. Econ. Devel. Task Force, Ill. Legis. Black Caucus, 1992—. U.S. Dept. Edn. grantee, 1986; recipient Citizenship award Chgo. mayor, 1984, Cert. merit NAACP South Side Br., 1978; named state advisor U.S. Congl. Adv. Bd., 1985; speaker edn. seminar 19th Congress on Arts and Communicatiion, Cambridge, Eng. Mem. ASCD, LWV, Minority Mainstream, United Neighborhoods Intertwined for Total Equality (founder, exec. dir., rschr.), Assn. for Citizens with Learning Disabilities, Coun. for Exceptional Children (liaison to state bd. Ill. Divsn. for Citizens with Learning Disabilities 1980), Spl. Edn. Tchrs. Assn. (1st pres., founder), Black Parents United for Edn. and Related Svcs. (founder), Kappa Delta Pi, Lehigh (Fla.) Country Club, Thousand Trails Club (Ottawa, Ill.). Mem. Carter C.M.E. Ch.

ODGAARD, ANDERS JACOB, civil and environmental engineer, educator; b. Hvidbjerg, Denmark, Aug. 8, 1942; came to U.S., 1977; s. Peter Johannes and Margrethe (Jensen) O.; m. Anna Joyce Rogers, Feb. 18, 1978; children: Peter Jacob, Christel Margrethe. MS in Civil and Structural Engring., Tech. U. Denmark, Lyngby, 1966, PhD in Civil and Structural Engring., 1970. Registered profl. engr., Iowa. Lectr. Tech. U. Denmark, 1969-72; UN cons. U. Minas Gerais, Belo Horizonte, Brazil, 1972-73; postdoctoral scholar U. Cambridge, Eng., 1973-74; sr. rsch. engr. Danish Hydraulic Inst., Hørsholm, Denmark, 1974-77; adj. asst. prof. U. Iowa, Iowa City, 1977-80, from asst. prof. to assoc. prof., 1984-89, prof. civl and environ. engring., 1989—, assoc. dean engring., 1992—; assoc. rsch. scientist Iowa Inst. Hydraulic Rsch., Iowa City, 1977-80, rsch. engr., 1980—; cons. Bechtel, San Francisco, 1993—, DHV Cons. BV, Amersfoort, The Netherlands, 1993—, Minn. Dept. Transp., Mpls., 1993—. Editor Jour. Hydraulic Engring.; contbr. articles to Jour. Hydraulic Engring., Water Resources Rsch., Jour. Hydraulic Rsch. Achievements include patent for Iowa Vane: A Submerged Structure for Sediment Control in Rivers. Fellow ASCE (Karl Emil Hilgard Hydraulic prize 1991); mem. Am. Soc. Engring. Edn., Internat. Assn. for Hydraulic Rsch., Sigma Xi, Chi Epsilon. Home: 934 Estron St Iowa City IA 52246 Office: U Iowa Coll Engring Iowa City IA 52242

ODIM, JONAH, cardiac surgeon, educator; b. Kansas City, Mo., Dec. 10, 1955. BA in Neurosci. & English, Amherst Coll., 1977; MD, Yale U., 1981; PhD, McGill U., Can., 1995. Diplomate Nat. Bd. Med. Examiners, Am. Bd. Surgery, Am. Bd. Thoracic Surgery, Am. Bd. Surg. Critical Care. Intern in gen. surgery U. Chgo., 1981-82, resident in gen. surgery, 1982-87; chief resident in cardiovascular and thoracic surgery McGill U., Montreal, 1987-89, rsch. and clin. fellow Montreal Gen. Hosp., 1989-92; clin. fellow dept. surgery Harvard U. Med. Sch. The Children's Hosp., Boston, 1993-94; assoc. prof. surgery, pediats. & child health & physiology U. Man. Health Sci. Ctr., Winnipeg, Can., 1994—; instr. dept. exercise sci. Concordia U., Montreal, 1990, Advanced Cardiac Life Support, 1985—, Advanced Trauma Life Support, 1986—, Pediatric Advanced Life Support, 1992—; spkr., presenter in field. City desk reporter The Pitts. Press, 1975-76; mem. edilt. bd. Yale Jour. Biology and Medicine, 1977-81; author chpts. to books; contbr. articles to profl. jours. John Woodruff Simpson fellow in medicine Yale U., 1977, Rsch. fellow, 1979, Heart and Stroke Found. Can., 1990; Huber Found. grantee, 1975, Rsch. grantee Yale U., 1979; recipient Rsch. award Heart and Stroke Found. Can., 1990. Fellow Royal Coll. Surgeons, Royal Coll. Surgeons of Can., Am. Coll. Chest Physicians; mem. ACS, Am. Soc. Artificial Internal Organs (Fellowship award 1991), Royal Coll. Physicians and Surgeons, Can. Cardiovascular Soc., N.Y. Acad. Scis., Soc. Thoracic Surgeons, Soc. Critical Care Medicine, Can. Cardiovascular Soc., Assn. Acad. Surgery. Office: Children's Hosp Health Scis Ctr, 685 William Ave, Winnipeg, MB Canada R3E 0Z2

O'DONNELL, MARK JOSEPH, accountant; b. St. Louis, Mar. 28, 1954; s. William E. and Jeanne M. (Collins) O'D.; m. Jane E. Wismann, Sept. 29, 1973; children: Sean, Mark Jr., Kyle. BSBA magna cum laude, U. Mo., 1977. CPA, Mo. Cost acct. Hunter Engring., St. Louis, 1973-76; acct. Gen. Dynamics, St. Louis, 1976-77; acct. Lester Witte & Co., St. Louis, 1977-80, mgr., 1980-82; ptnr. Bounds, Poger & O'Donnell, St. Louis, 1982-86, mng. ptnr., 1986-94; mng. prin. O'Donnell, Bonebrake & Co., P.C., St. Louis, 1994—. Named one of Outstanding Young Men Am., U.S. Jaycees, 1978. Mem. Am. Inst. CPA's, Mo. Soc. CPA's, Am. Soc. Quality Control. Roman Catholic. Office: O'Donnell Bonebrake & Co PC 11457 Olde Cabin Rd Ste 310 Saint Louis MO 63141-7139

O'DONNELL, THOMAS MICHAEL, brokerage firm executive; b. Cleve., Apr. 9, 1936; s. John Michael and Mary L. (Hayes) O'D.; m. Nancy A. Dugan, Feb. 4, 1961; children—Christopher, Colleen, Julie. BBA, U. Notre Dame, 1959; MBA, U. Pa., 1960. Cert. Chartered Fin. Analyst. Fin. analyst Saunders Stiver & Co., Cleve., 1960-65; rsch. dir. McDonald & Co., Cleve., 1965-66, exec. v.p. corp. fin., 1967-83, gen. ptnr., 1968-83; pres. McDonald & Co. Investments, Inc./McDonald & Co. Securities, Cleve., 1984-88; chmn., chief exec. officer McDonald & Co. Securities, Cleve., 1988—; bd. dirs. Seaway Food Town; mem. regional firms adv. com. N.Y. Stock Exch., 1986-92, chmn., 1991-92; dir. C.I.D. Venture Funds. Author: The Why and How of Mergers, 1968. Trustee Cath. Charities, Cleve.; bd. dirs. Greater Cleve. Growth Assn., Inroads Northeast Ohio, PlayHouse Square Found.; adv. bd. Salvation Army; bd. regents St. Ignatius High Sch., Cleve.; steering com. Leadership Cleve. Mem. Cleve. Soc. Security Analysts (cert.), Securities Industry Assn. (dir. 1988-94, chmn. 1993), Union Club, Westwood Country Club, 50 Club Cleve., Pepper Pike Club, Double Eagle Club. Roman Catholic. Home: 1325 Timber Lea Ct Cleveland OH 44145-2648 Office: McDonald & Co Securities Inc 800 Superior Ave E Ste 2100 Cleveland OH 44114-2601

ODOR, DAVID LEE, utility official; b. Washington, Nov. 5, 1943; s. Hammond Leese and Virginia (Maloney) O.; m. Marilyn Elaine Hampton, June 8, 1968; children: David Lawrence, Christopher Lloyd. BS, W.Va. Wesleyan Coll., 1965; MS, U. Okla., 1967; PhD, Purdue U., 1972. Rsch. asst. USDA, Beltsville, Md., 1967; radiol. engr. Potomac Electric Power Co., Washington, 1972-74; supervisory environ. engr. Pub. Svc. Ind., Plainfield, 1974-8l, rsch. coord., l98l—; mem. renewable resource task force EPRI, 1985-87, solar power sys. program com., 1985—, on-line coal analysis adv. com., 1988—, by-product utilization adv. com., 1989—, tech. delivery com., 1994-95. Tech. reviewer Radiation Protection Mgmt. Bd. dirs. Plainfield Pub. Libr., pres., 1985, 86; applied econs. rep. Jr. Achievement Plainfield H.S., 1991-95. Lt. USN, 1967-70. Mem. Nat. Hon. Rsch. Soc., Ind. Libr. Trustee Assn. (bd. dirs. 1985-89, pres. 1987), Ind. Ctr. Innovative Superconductivity, Ind. Libr. Automation Task Force, Hoosier Health Physics Soc. (pres. 1980). Republican. Office: PSI Energy 1000 E Main St Plainfield IN 46168-1765

ODOR, RICHARD LANE, mental health administrator, psychologist; b. Oberlin, Ohio, Aug. 11, 1954; s. Frank and Marjorie Ann (Carpenter) O. Student, Moody Bible Inst., 1972-74; BA, Ohio State U., 1977, MA, 1978, PhD, 1986. Counselor children's group Gladden Community House, Columbus, Ohio, 1978-79; partial hospitalization counselor Columbus Area Community Mental Health Ctr., 1979-81, residential counselor, 1978-82; grad. rsch. assoc. dept. family rels. and human devel. Ohio State U., 1983-85; emergency svcs. counselor S.E. Community Mental Health Ctr., Columbus, 1983-86, dir. emergency svcs., 1986-87; program dir., psychologist Southeast Counseling Svcs., Columbus, 1987-92; psychologist Psychol. and Counseling Svcs., Reynoldsburg, Ohio, 1989—; psychologist, clin. supr. New Source Counseling Ctrs., Twinsburg, Ohio, 1990—; psychologist, owner Pschol. and Recovery Svcs., Columbus, 1991-94; employee assistance program affiliate McDonnell Douglas Corp., Columbus, 1992-95; staff Grant Med. Ctr., Columbus, 1995—. Profl. adv. bd. Ctrl. Ohio Chpt. Nat. Multiple Sclerosis Soc., 1995—. Mem. APA, Ohio Psychol. Assn., Ctrl. Ohio Psychol. Assn., U.S. Weightlifting Fedn., Ohio State U. Ski Club, Ohio State U. Water Ski Club, Ohio State U. Weightlifting Club (coach 1982-85, faculty advisor 1984-85), Rotary (bd. dirs. Reynoldsburg-Pickerington chpt. 1992-94), Phi Kappa Phi, Omicron Nu, Phi Upsilon Omicron. Republican. Office: Psychol & Counseling Svcs 7664 Slate Ridge Blvd Reynoldsburg OH 43068-3126

OELSLAGER, W. SCOTT, state legislator; b. Oct. 15, 1953; m. Holly Hill, 1976. BA, Mt. Union Coll., 1975. Aide to U.S. rep. Ralph Regula, 1973-78; asst. Sen. Thomas Walsh, 1981-84; state senate Ohio Dist. 29, 1985; chmn. Hwy. & Transp. com., mem. Health & Human Svcs. State Local Gov. & Vets Affairs, Edn. Retirement & Aging Com.; dir. pub. rels. Malone Coll., 1978-80; dir. svc. Ohio Auto Dealers Assn., 1984. Bd. dir. Akron & Canton Arthritis Found. Recipient Watchdog of Treas. award, 1986, 88, 90; Rep. Legis. of Yr. award Nat. Rep. Legis. Assn., 1986, Disting. Legis. award Assn. Ohio Health Commr., 1989, Lay Person of Yr. award Phi Delta Kappa, 1989, Pub. Officer of Yr. award Social Workers Assn., 1992, Legis. of Yr. award Common Cause of Ohio & Ohio Nurses Assn., 1993. Home: 318 22nd St NW Canton OH 44709 Office: State Senate State Capital Columbus OH 43215*

OESTERLING, JOSEPH EDWIN, urologic surgeon; b. Greensburg, Ind., May 28, 1956; s. Walter Bernard and Leona Martha (Muckerheide) O.; m. Carmen Teresa Noguera, June 9, 1984; children: Christopher Charles, Jennifer Marie. BA, Columbia Coll., 1978; MD, Columbia U., 1982. Diplomate Nat. Bd. Med. Examiners, Am. Bd. Urology; lic. in Md., Fla., Ariz., Minn., Mich. Intern, dept. gen. surgery Johns Hopkins U. Sch. of Med., Balt., 1982-83, resident, dept. gen. surgery, 1983-84, resident, dept. urology, 1984-87, chief resident, dept. urology, 1988, instr., dept. urology, 1988-89; cons. dept. urology Mayo Clinic, Rochester, Minn., 1989-94; asst. prof. urology Mayo Med. Sch., Rochester, 1989-93; assoc. prof. urology Mayo Clinic, Rochester, 1993-94; prof., urologist-in-chief, dir. Mich. Prostate Inst., U. Mich., Ann Arbor, 1994—; dir. Mich. Prostate Inst., U. Mich. Med. Ctr., Ann Arbor, 1994—; cons./researcher in field. Cons. The Jour. of Urology, Balt., 1988—, The Prostate, 1990, Cancer, 1990, Cancer Rsch., 1990; editor-in-chief Urology. Recipient Emil T. Hofman Chemistry award Univ. Notre Dame, 1975, Albert B. Schweitzer award for Acad. Excellence, Columbia Coll., 1978, Salutatorian, Columbia Coll., 1978, Samuel W. Rover and Lewis C. Rover Biochemistry award Coll. of Physicians and Surgeons of Columbia U., 1982, Valedictorian, 1982, Am. Soc. Clin. Oncology Rsch. award 1987, Devel. award Am. Cancer Soc., 1988, others in field. Fellow ACS; mem. AMA, Am. Urol. Assn. (voting mem., Grand Champion prize 1991 Western sect.), N.Y. Acad. Sci., Sci. Rsch. Soc., Nat. Assn. Residents and Interns, Minn. State Med. Assn., Minn. Urol. Soc., Zumbro Valley Med. Soc., So. Minn. Med. Assn., Mich. Urol. Soc., Am. Soc. Andrology, Am. Assn. Clin. Urologists, Am. Geriatrics Soc., Am. Soc. Clin. Oncology, Can. Urol. Assn., European Assn. Urology, Endourol. Soc., Pan-Pacific Surg. Assn., Soc. for Basic Urologic Rsch., Soc. Internat. Urology, Johns Hopkins Med. and Surg. Assn., Soc. Univ. Urologists, North Cen. Sect. Am. Urologic Assn. (1st prize Clin. Rsch. 1986, 87, 1st prize Lab. Rsch. 1987), Mayo Alumni Assn., Sigma Xi. Home: 3622 Lamplighter Dr Ann Arbor MI 48103-1713

OETTING, DAVID D., state legislator; b. Concordia, Mo., Mar. 19, 1951; m. Carol Oetting; children: Timothy, Jakelin. Student, Ctrl. Mo. U. Mem. Mo. State Ho. of Reps. Dist. 121, 1989-93; mem. Mo. State Ho. of Reps. Dist. 122, 1993—, mem. appropriations com., mem. agr.-bus., ins., pub. health and safety coms.; ins. agt. Mem. Lions Club, Concordia C. of C. Home: PO Box 734 Concordia MO 64020-0734*

OFENSTEIN, JOHN PATRICK, pediatrics educator; b. Tipperrary, Ireland, Mar. 17, 1950; came to the U.S., 1953; s. Robert Charles and Catherine Lois Ofenstein; m. Cathy Ann Groat, Feb. 13, 1987; children: Chelsea Ann, Stephanie Marie. BS, Western Mich. U., 1980, MS, 1982; PhD in Physiology/Endocrinology, Wayne State U., 1986. Asst. prof. pediat. Wayne State Med. Sch., Detroit. Roman Catholic. Office: Wayne State Univ 421 E Canfield Detroit MI 48201

OFFENGENDEN, ANATOLY A., manufacturing company executive; b. Donetsk, Ukraine, Apr. 22, 1947; came to U.S., 1990; s. Maria E. Oppengenden; m. Sophia L. Offengenden; children: Dimitri, Leonid. MS in Physics, Donetsk State U., 1970; PhD in Metallurg. Engring., Belorussia Politechnik Inst., Minsk, 1988. Engr. All-Union Inst of Non-ferrous Metals, Donetsk, 1971-72, scientific rschr., 1972-77, sr. scientific rschr., 1978-89; chief process engr. Western Res. Mfg. Co., Lorain, Ohio, 1990-91, v.p. metallurgical, 1991—. Inventor in field; contbr. numerous articles to profl. jours. Mem. ASM Internat. Home: 840 Deer Run Dr Amherst OH 44001 Office: Western Reserve Mfg Co 5311 W River Rd N Lorain OH 44055

OFFERDAHL, JACK ALBERT, respiratory therapy administrator; b. Northwood, N.D., July 31, 1950; s. Chester Earl and Olive Evangeline (Ovrid) O. AS, Lake Region Jr. Coll., Devils Lake, N.D., 1970, North Hennepin C.C., Brooklyn Park, Minn., 1976. Respiratory therapist Merit Care Med. Ctr., Fargo, N.D., 1976-80, respiratory care coord., 1980—. Bd. dirs. Big Bros. and Big Sisters, Fargo, 1977-79;l treas. Hoglum Luth. Ch., Lake Park, Minn., 1995—. Mem. Am. Assn. Respiratory Care. Home: RR 1 Box 49B Lake Park MN 56554

OFFERMAN, ANN GUDKESE, rehabilitation nurse; b. Monterey, Calif., Feb. 15, 1953; d. Vernon Wallace and LaVon Fay (Cartwright) Gudkese; m. J. Stephen Offerman, Aug. 16, 1980; children: Kristin Nicole, Heather Michelle, Ryan Elliott. BSN, U. Evansville, 1977, MSN, 1983. Staff nurse neonatal ICU St. Mary's Med. Ctr., Evansville, Ind., 1977-78, Vis. Nurse Assn., Evansville, 1978-81; coord., dir., clin. nurse specialist Ohio Valley Hospice, Evansville, 1981-89; coord. program evaluation and utilization mgmt. Novacare Tri-State Regional Rehab. Hosp., Evansville, 1990-95; utilization rev. coord. HealthSouth Tri-State Rehab. Hosp., Evansville, 1995—. Asst. treas. Washington Ave. Ch. Christ, Evansville, 1985-91; treas. bd. dirs. U. Evansville Sch. Nursing and Health Sci. Alumni Assn., 1988-91, bd. dirs., 1987-91; organizer, co-pres. Beat 4 Neighborhood Watch Assn., 1994—; mem. Newburgh C. of Christ; bd. dirs. Hebron Elem. Sch., 1994—, Plaza Mid. Sch., 1995—. Named one of Outstanding Young Women of Am., 1986. Mem. Sigma Theta Tau, Phi Kappa Phi. Office: Tri-State Regional Rehab 4100 Covert Ave Evansville IN 47714-5559

OGAARD, DONALD HARVEY, farmer; b. Fertile, Minn., Oct. 9, 1926; s. Selmer M. and Mathilda T. (Tuff) O.; m. Marlys Ann Fristrom, June 24, 1951; children: Steven D., Bruce D. (dec.), Catherine A., Patricia L. Grad. high sch. Owner, operator Ogaard Farms Inc., Ada, Minn., 1949-93, Ada Implement Co., 1973-78. Inventor Quik Jak, snowmobile jack, 1969; inventor numerous items in agrl. machinery related industries, 1970-94. Mem. Minn. Future Commn., 1973-74, Minn. Water Planning Bd., 1980-84; chmn. Minn. Bd. Water and Soil Resources, 1987-92; mem. Minn. Environ. Quality Bd., 1987-93; pres., v.p. Minn. Assn. Watershed Dists., 1971-86; pres., mem. Wild Rice Watershed Dist., Minn., 1971-86, adminstr., 1986-93; pres. Red River Watershed Mgmt. Bd., Minn., 1993—. Democratic Farmer Labor. Lutheran. Home: 705 Fifth St W Ada MN 56510

OGDEN, WILLIAM MICHAEL, school system administrator; b. Wooster, Ohio, Oct. 29, 1944; s. Raymond Job and Vinnie Lena (Ensminger) O.; m. Norena Faith Parker, June 4, 1966 (div. 1978); children: Michele Rae, John Michael; m. Mary Ann Pusey, Oct. 6, 1978; 1 stepchild, Jeffrey Clare Applegate. BA, Coll. Wooster, 1968; MEd, LaVerne (Calif.) Coll., 1975; postgrad., Akron U., Ashland (Ohio) Coll. Cert. elem. tchr., prin., spl. edn. tchr. Tchr. Mansfield (Ohio) City Schs., 1968-77, adminstr., 1977—, dist. energy officer, 1980-83, dir. elem. summer reinforcement program, 1986-88. Martha Holden Jennings Found. scholar, 1977. Mem. ASCD, Ohio Assn. Elem. Sch. Prins., Mansfield Adminstrs. Assn., Ashland-Richland-Morrow County Assn. Elem. Sch. Prins. (pres. 1990-91), Mohican Assn. Edn. of Young Children, Mansfield Univ. Club, Jaycees, Elks, Phi Delta Kappa (Mohican Area Ohio chpt., area chpt. 1231, divsn. V). Republican. Presbyterian. Home: 79 Redwood Rd Mansfield OH 44907-2430 Office: Mansfield City Schs 53 W 4th St Mansfield OH 44902-1205

OGESEN, ROBERT BRUCE, dentist; b. Council Bluffs, Iowa, Aug. 26, 1934; s. Ever Julius and Agnes Elizabeth (Treptow) O.; m. Suzanne Jones, June 19, 1954; children: Cindy Sue, Robert B. II, Ann Elizabeth. DDS, U. Iowa, 1958. Gen. practice dentistry Iowa City, Iowa, 1961-73; with Towncrest Dental Offices, PC, Iowa City, 1973—; adj. faculty dentistry U. Iowa, 1965-85; mem. adv. com. Lab Tech Program, Kirkwood Community Coll., Iowa, 1992—. Co-author: Hypnosis in Dentistry, 1985; contbr. articles to profl. jours. Mem. Iowa City Planning and Zoning Commn., 1971-81. Served to capt. USAF, 1958-61. Mem. ADA, Iowa Dental Assn. (coun. dental care programs 1976-80, coun. ethics, intraprofl. and pub. rels. 1985-91), Pierre Fauchard Acad., Univ. Dist. Dental Soc., Johnson County Dental Soc., Omicron Kappa Upsilon, Delta Sigma Delta. Presbyterian. Home: 305 Woodridge Ave Iowa City IA 52245-6055 Office: Towncrest Dental Offices PC 1039 Arthur St Iowa City IA 52240-6629

OGG, WILLIAM L., state legislator; m. Janice Ogg; children: Julie Lynne, William Kenneta, Shana Jo. Student, Ohio U. Commr. Scioto County, Ohio; vice mayor, mem. city coun. City of Portsmouth, Ohio; mayor City of Portsmouth; rep. dist. 92 Ohio Ho. Reps., Columbus; chmn. Ohio Valley Regulation Devel. Commn., 1986-91. Named to Dem. Hall of Fame, Scioto County, 1990. Mem. Portsmouth C. of C.

OGILVIE, BRUCE CAMPBELL, financial consultant; b. N.Y., Apr. 1, 1944; s. Bruce Crossan and Martha M. (Campbell) O.; m. Rebecca Jane Reedy, June 12, 1967; children: A Christy, Kathryn L. BA, Monmouth Coll., 1968; grad., Am. Coll., 1973, MS in Fin. Svcs., 1985. CLU, ChFC; registered rep., gen. securities broker. Salesman coll. div. Little, Brown & Co., Boston, 1968-70, devel. editor, 1970-71; editor Coll. Mktg. Group, Reading, Mass., 1971-72; field dir. Northwestern Mut. Life Ins. Co., Milw., 1972-95; pres. Ogilvie and Assocs. Ltd., Evanston, Ill., 1978-91; exec. v.p. One North State Street Corp., Chgo., 1979-81; sr. assoc. John O. Todd Orgn., Evanston, Ill., 1976-80; dir. training, edn., ins. agency John A. Myaard Agy., Grand Rapids, Mich., 1986-89; fin. and mktg. advisor not-for-profit corps. and founds., Arcadia, Mich., 1991—; ednl. chmn. Fin. Independence Week, Grand Rapids, Mich., 1987; active Chgo. Estate Planning Coun., Grand Traverse Estate Planning Coun., 1992—; advisor Rotary Charities of Traverse City, Inc., 1991-95, Grand Traverse Regional Cmty. Found., Inc., 1991—, Grand Traverse Regional Land Conservancy, Inc., 1991-92, Crystal Springs Children's Ctr., Inc., 1994, Blaine Twp. Bd. of Trustee, 1994—. Bd. dirs. Glenview (Ill.) Pu7. Libr., 1979, sec., 1980-81; sec. Monmouth Coll. Senate, 1982-90; chmn. Residential Living Com. Senate, 1986-89; trustee Kendall Coll., Evanston, 1981-82; long range planning commn. Diocese Western Mich., campus ministries commn., 1991, parish del. to 1990 and 1994 convs.; elected jr. warden St. Philip's Ch., Beulah, Mich., 1993-95, vestry mem., 1993-95; trustee Frankfort-Elberta Area Schs. Found., 1994—, treas., 1995—. Recipient Gardiner scholarship

Northwestern Mut. Life Ins. Co., 1985. Mem. Nat. Assn. Life Underwriters, Am. Soc. CLU and ChFC (edn. com. Chgo. chpt. 1984-86), Chgo. Assn. Life Underwriters (pres. north br. 1980-81), Frankfort Rotary Club (elected treas 1994—), Willoughby Rotary Found. (trustee 1992—, chmn. investment com. 1993-95, sec. 1994—), Sigma Alpha Epsilon. Republican. Episcopalian. Home: 1725 Love Ct Arcadia MI 49613-9617

O'HAIR, MICHAEL THOMAS, electrical engineering educator, administrator; b. Indpls., July 3, 1944; s. Gale Keyt and Dorothy Jane (Tonchoff) O'H.; m. Sharon Kay Seward, June 5, 1966; children: Scott David, Tiffany Ann. AAS in Elec. Engrng. Tech., Purdue U., 1964, BS in Indsl. Edn., 1967; MS in Tech., Western Mich. U., 1968; EdD in Higher Edn., Ind. U., 1982. Lectr. elec. engrng. tech. Purdue U., Hammond, Ind., 1968-70; prof. elec. engrng. tech., adminstr. Purdue U., Kokomo, Ind., 1970—; cons. in field. Editor: Engineering Technology: An ASEE History, 1995; contbr. articles to profl. jours. Bd. dirs. Kokomo/Howard County C. of C., 1985-88, North Ctrl. Ind. Pvt. Industry Coun., Peru, Ind., 1988-90; mem. adv. bd. Kokomo Ctr. Sch. Corp., 1991-93. Recipient Gratitude award Jour. Engrng. Tech., 1985, Svc. award, 1991. Mem. IEEE, Am. Soc. Engrng. Edn., Rotary (bd. dirs. 1992—), Kokomo Country Club. Republican. Methodist. Office: Purdue U 2300 S Washington St Kokomo IN 46904-9003

OHANIAN, LEE EDWARD, economist, consultant; b. L.A., Feb. 24, 1957; s. Edward and Martha Loraine (Taylor) O.; m. Nancy Frances Kane, May 28, 1988. BA, U. Calif., Santa Barbara, 1979, MA, 1982; postgrad., U. Rochester, 1988—. Sr. analyst Continental Airlines, L.A., 1981-82; v.p. Security Pacific Bank, L.A., 1982-88; PhD U. Rochester, N.Y., 1993; pvt. practice Rochester, 1990—; asst. prof. econs. U. Pa., Phila., 1992—. Contbr. articles to profl. jours. W. Allen Wallis fellow U. Rochester, 1988—; fellow Nat. Inst. on Aging, 1983-84; recipient Kaplan Prize, 1991. Office: U Minn Dept Econs 271 19th Ave S Minneapolis MN 55455

O'HARA, JOHN PAUL, III, orthopaedic surgeon; b. Detroit, June 10, 1946; m. Randy Baird, Mar. 11, 1987; children: Riley Anne, Nolan Baird, Evan John. BA, U. Mich., 1968, MD, 1972. Resident U. Va. Med. Ctr., Charlottesville, 1973-77; fellow Nuffield Orthopaedic Ctr., Oxford, Eng., 1977; practice medicine specializing in orthopaedic surgery Southfield, 1978—; staff Providence Hosp., Southfield, Mich., 1978—, pres. elect med. staff, 1990, pres. med. staff, 1991; sect. chief orthopedics; pres. Providence Hosp. Med. Staff Research Found., 1984-85, bd. dirs., 1982—; bd. dirs. Mich. Master Health Plan, Southfield, 1982. Contbr. articles to profl. jours. Recipient Disting. Alumni award Brother Rice High Sch., 1986. Fellow Am. Acad. Orthopaedic Surgery, Mid Am. Orthopaedic Soc.; mem. Detroit Orthopaedic Soc., Mich. Orthopaedic Soc., Detroit Acad. Orthopaedic Surgeons (past pres.), Oakland Hills Country Club (Birmingham, Mich.), Beverly Hills (Mich.) Club. Home: 627 Waddington St Bloomfield Hills MI 48301-2346 Office: Porretta & O'Hara Orthopaedic Surgeons PC 22250 Providence Dr Ste 401 Southfield MI 48075-6212

O'HARE, DANIEL JOHN, electrical engineer; b. Bay City, Mich., Dec. 17, 1955; s. John William and Vida Flo (Roberts) O'H.; m. Betty Joanne Luczak, May 23, 1979; children: Jennifer Louise, Meghan Elizabeth, Amanda Jayne. BSEE, Mich. Technol. U., 1978; postgrad., U. Minn., 1979-84, SUNY, Binghamton, 1985. Jr. engr. IBM, Rochester, Minn., 1978-79; assoc. engr. hard file integration IBM, Rochester, 1979-82, sr. assoc. engr. hardfile integration, 1982-85, project engr., mgr. subsystem serviceability, 1985-88, devel. engr., mgr. hardware devel., 1988-91, adv. engr. interdivsnl. project leader, 1991-95; program mgr. common I/O adapter all IBM server syss., 1995—. Referee Rochester Youth Baseball Assn., 1988, 89, coach, 1992, 93; line judge Rochester Youth Soccer, 1989; vol. tchr. for gifted and talented edn. at local pub. elem. sch., 1989-94; asst. youth competitive cheerleading squad, 1995—. Roman Catholic. Home: 2607 Westview Ln NW Rochester MN 55901-2362 Office: IBM Hwy 52 at 37th St NW Rochester MN 55901

OHEAREN, JOHN ROBERT, mechanical engineer; b. Cin., Oct. 1, 1929. A of Mfg. Tech., U. Ky. Engr. Avey Machine Tool Co., Covington, Ky., 1952-79; chief engr. U.S. Drill Head Co., Machine Tool Divsn., Cin., 1979—. Chmn. Boy Scouts Am., Ky., 1958. With U.S. Army, 1946-48. Mem. Assn. Mfg. Tech. Republican. Roman Catholic. Home: 1506 Linden Rd Hebron KY 41048-9610 Office: US Drill Head 5298 River Rd Cincinnati OH 45233-1643

OHLSON, SARA FAYE, real estate executive; b. Paris, Ark., Dec. 29, 1944; d. Clifford Andrew Odom and Nellie Beatrice (Love) Riedl; m. Glyn Dean Albertson, July 15, 1962 (div. 1977); children: Candace, Julia, Jeffrey, Jennifer; m. Bradley Kent Ohlson, June 14, 1980. Grad., Real Estate Inst., Wichita, 1989. Realtor Coldwell Banker Dinning Beard, Wichita, 1984-86; assoc. broker Plaza Del Sol Realtors, Inc., Wichita, 1986—. Mem. Realtors Polit. Action Com., Wichita, 1986—. Mem. Wichita Area Bd. Realtors, Kans. Assn. Realtors (mem. Honor Soc.), Nat. Assn. Realtors (mem. residential sales coun., mem. various coms.). Lutheran. Home: 3220 Elmwood St Wichita KS 67218-4815 Office: Plaza Del Sol Realtors 6100 E Central Ave Ste 215 Wichita KS 67208-4237

OJARD, BRUCE ALLEN, photographer, educator; b. Duluth, Minn., Dec. 20, 1951; s. Robert Nelson and Theresa Ann (Kurshoff) O.; m. Susan Kathleen van Druten, Aug. 20, 1983. BBA, U. Minn., 1974. Owner Bruce Ojard Photographics, Duluth, Minn., 1974-85; lab. coordinator Duluth Art Inst., 1975—; staff photographer St. Louis County Heritage & Arts Ctr., Duluth, 1975-83; photography instr. Duluth Art Inst., 1976—; staff photographer City Hall Info. Office, Duluth, 1976-78; photography instr. Duluth Sch. Dist. #709, 1979—; dir., writer, actor Colder by the Lake Theater Co., Duluth, 1983—; owner Digital Audio-Visual Co., Duluth, 1985—; video, performance artist, 1984—; tech. dir. Storymakers Theater Co., Duluth, 1983-84, Norshor Theatre in the State, Duluth, 1992-94; cons. Minn. Ballet Co., 1988-90, Duluth Playhouse, 1985—, photographer, 1983—. Writer, actor video prodn. Academy O'Comedy, 1985 (Silver Addy award 1986); actor movie Iron Will, 1993; photographs published in numerous jours. Advisor Duluth Community Schs., 1984; vol. The Depot Cultural Arts Ctr., 1976. Prodn. grantee Arrowhead Regional Arts Coun., 1985, 89, 91-96. Mem. Duluth Art Inst., Friends of Feathers, Scrabble Players. Home: 1729 E 8th St Duluth MN 55812-1224 Office: Duluth Art Inst 506 W Michigan St Duluth MN 55802-1505

O'KEEFE, GERALD FRANCIS, bishop, retired; b. St. Paul, Mar. 30, 1918; s. Francis Patrick and Lucille Mary (McDonald) O'K. Student, St. Paul Sem., 1938-44; B.A., Coll. St. Thomas, 1945; LLD (hon.), St. Ambrose Coll., 1967, Loras Coll., 1967; LHD, Marycrest Coll., 1967. Ordained priest Roman Cath. Ch., 1944. Asst. St. Paul Cathedral, 1944, rector, 1961-67; chancellor Archdiocese of St. Paul, 1945-61, aux. bishop, 1961-67, vicar gen., 1962-67; bishop Diocese of Davenport, Iowa, 1967-93; ret., 1993; instr. St. Thomas Acad., St. Paul, 1944-45. Home: 2706 Gaines St Davenport IA 52804-1914

O'KEEFE, PATRICIA RIGG, public relations professional; b. Gary, Ind., Sept. 6, 1926; d. Harry and Beulah May (Reynolds) Rigg; m. Raymond Charles O'Keefe, Apr. 26, 1952 (div. 1962); children: Kathleen O'Keefe Reed, Ann Elizabeth. BS, Ind. U., 1948. Copywriter Young & Rubicam, Chgo., 1948-53; writer Smith, Bucklin & Assocs., Chgo., 1963-70, dir. pub. rels., 1970-80; dir. communications Am. Assn. Affirmative Action, Chgo., 1985-93; dir. communications Nat. Assn. Perinatal Addiction Rsch. and Edn., Chgo., 1987-93, sec., newsletter editor, 1988-93; owner Assn. Comms., Evanston, Ill., 1985—; pub. rels. dir. Pers. Images, Ltd., 1983—. Mng. editor Kennedy's Career Strategist, 1985—; newsletter editor Bob Gordon & Assocs.; contbr. articles to various publs. Dir. vols. The Birth Project, Houston, 1980-83; dep. clk. New Trier Twp., 1995—. Mem. Women in Communications, Chgo. Soc. Assn. Execs. Office: Assn Comm 1918 Harrison St Evanston IL 60201-2296

OKESON, THOMAS L., financial company executive; b. Woodstock, Ill., Oct. 3, 1946; s. Robert Harold and June L. (Luplow) O.; m. Betty J. Stec, Oct. 25, 1975; 1 child, Lisa Lea. Student, George Wash. U., 1969-71, No. Ill. U., 1973-74. CLU, Am. Coll., 1980, ChFC Am. Coll., 1982, CFP Coll. for Fin. Planning, 1984. V.p. H. Parker Sharpe Inc., Barrington, Ill., 1976-80; pres. Eighties Fin. GroupLtd., Woodstock, Ill., 1980—. Contbr. articles to profl. jours. Ssgt. USMC, 1964-68. Mem. Am. Soc. CLU and ChFC, Internat. Assn. For Fin. Planning. Office: Eighties Fin Group Ltd PO Box 368 Crystal Lake IL 60039-0368

OKHAMAFE, IMAFEDIA, English literature and philosophy educator; b. Otuo, Nigeria; s. Obokhe and Olayemi (Bello) O. Double PhD, Purdue U., 1984. Prof. philosophy and English U. Nebr., Omaha, 1993—. Office: U Nebr Annex 39 Omaha NE 68182-0208 also: U Nebr English Dept Omaha NE 68182-0175

OKUNADE, SAMUEL ADEKUNLE, science educator; b. Awe, Nigeria, June 22, 1938; m. Christianah Togun; children: Lola, Bola, Kemi, Ayo, Wole. BA, Cen. State U., 1970; MS, U. Nebr., 1972; MA, U. Pa., 1976; PhD, Kent State U., 1986. Cert. in edn., Nigeria; permanent tchr. cert., N.Y. Acting chair earth sci., assoc. prof. earth sci. Cen. State U., Wilberforce, Ohio, 1989-93, prof. water resources, 1993—, asst. dir. water resources, 1995—; adj. prof. Urbana (Ohio) U., 1989-93; cons. to schs. Xenia (Ohio) Sch. Tchrs. of Earth Sci., 1990—; prin. investigator U.S. Geology Survey, Huntington, W.Va., 1992—; mem. African studies adv. com. Cen. State U., Wilberforce, 1994—; cons. Assuiti (Egypt) U., 1992; investigator, author Soil Analysis-U.S. Geol. Survey, 1995. Author: Traditional Oral Literature, 1992. Egyptian grantee USAID, 1991. Mem. AAUP, Assn. Am. Geographers, Ohio Acad. Sci. Democrat. Baptist. Home: 244 Kansas Dr Xenia OH 45385 Office: Cen State Univ Earth Sci Dept Wilberforce OH 45384

OLCOTT, THOMAS W., clergyman; b. Hartford, Conn., Apr. 16, 1941; s. Arthur W. and Priscilla (Manchester) O.; m. Lois Bennett, May 22, 1965; 1 child, Brenda B. BS, Clark U., 1964; B Divinity, Andover Newton, 1968; cert. advanced pastoral, Hartford Sem., 1986. Multiple ministry First Bapt. Ch., Holden, Mass., 1964-67; neighborhood ministry Calvary Bapt. Ch., Providence, 1967-71; dir. urban ministry R.I. State Coun. Chs., Providence, 1971-75; pastor First Bapt. Ch., Roselle, N.J., 1975-76; exec. dir. Coun. Chs., Springfield, Mass., 1976-83, Interch. Coun., Cleve., 1983—; guest pastor Seroe Colorado, Aruba, 1982; adj. faculty Notre Dame Coll., South Euclid, Ohio, 1995. Commr. Office Sch. Monitoring, Cleve., 1983-94; mem. coun. agy. execs. United Way of Cleve., 1983—; participant Leadership Cleve., 1989; bd. dirs. Greater Cleve. Com. on Hunger, 1992—. Recipient Ten Yr. Vol. award No. Ohio Live, 1990, Ecumenical award Ohio Coun. Chs., 1994, Vol. award No. Ohio Live, 1994, award for Week of Prayer for Unity Diocese Cleve., 1995. Mem. Nat. Assn. Ecumenical Staff. Home: 1010 Englewood Rd Cleveland Heights OH 44121 Office: Interchurch Coun Cleveland OH 44121

OLDANI, LOUIS JOSEPH, literature educator; b. St. Louis, Mar. 1, 1933; s. Louis Vincent and Angela Josephine (Ponciroli) O. AB, St. Louis U., 1957, MA, 1962; PhD, U. Pa., 1972. Clergyman, Soc. of Jesus, 1951—; ordained priest, 1964. Instr. Rockhurst Coll., Kansas City, Mo., 1971-73, asst. prof., 1973-77, assoc. prof., 1977-85, prof., 1985—; chmn. Rockhurst Libr. Bd., 1973-80, 93-95; mem. Rockhurst Rank and Tenure com., Kansas City, 1979-84, 87-91; pres. Rockhurst Faculty Demos, Kansas City, 1989-91, 93-95. Editor: (books) Introduction to Jesuit Theater, 1983, Jesuit Theater Englished, 1989; contbr. articles to profl. publs. Rsch. grantee Lilly Found., 1975-77, sabbatical grantee Rockhurst Coll., 1986-87; recipient Mellon Sr. fellowship U. Kans., Lawrence, 1979, Disting. Tchg. award Alpha Sigma Nu, 1995. Mem. MLA, Am. Lit. Sect. MLA, AAUP (pres. Rockhurst chpt. 1993-95), Nat. Coun. Tchrs. of English. Democrat. Roman Catholic. Office: Rockhurst Coll 1100 Rockhurst Rd Kansas City MO 64110

OLDENBURGER, NORMA JANE, medical surgical nurse; b. Carrington, N.D., Oct. 13, 1947; d. Joseph and Edna J. (Larson) Hoggarth; 1 child, Kristen Nicole. Diploma, St. Luke's Hosp. Sch. Nursing, Fargo, N.D., 1968; BSN, Mary Coll., Bismarck, N.D., 1978. RN, N.D.; CCRN; cert. pediatric advanced life support. Staff nurse ICU St. Luke's Hosp., Fargo, insvc. instr. ICU; flight staff nurse ICU St. Alexius Hosp., Bismarck, 1975—; instr. ACLS. 1st lt. USAR, 1975-77. Mem. ANA, AACN, Sigma Theta Tau. Home: 3100 Winnipeg Dr Bismarck ND 58501-0451

OLDENDORF, LAWRENCE EDWARD, engineering executive; b. Chgo., Aug. 20, 1934; s. Edward H. and Anna (Jaska) O.; m. Katherine A. Kenney, June 9, 1956; children: Karen, Mark, Paul, Kevin, Lynn, Susan, John, Peter, Steven. BS in Fire Protection/Safety Engring., Ill. Inst. Tech., 1956. Cert. safety profl.; registered fire protection engr., Calif. Fire ins. engr. Mo. Inspection Bur., St. Louis, 1956-59; safety and fire protection engr. Marsh & McLennan Inc., Chgo., 1959-62, Atomic Energy Commn. & Energy Rsch. & Devel. Adminstrn., Argonne, Ill., 1962-77; safety and fire protection engr. Dept. of Energy, Argonne, Ill., 1977-85, mgmt. analysis officer, 1985-93; v.p. engring. Kopp & Assocs., Rosemont, Ill., 1993—; safety and fire protection engr. cons. L.E. Oldendorf Consulting, Burbank, Ill., 1980—. Editor: AEC-Chgo. Safety News, 1969-79; contbr. articles to profl. jours. Named Safety Profl. of Yr., Midwest region Am. Soc. Safety Engrs., 1985, Engr. of Yr. for D.O.E., NSPE, 1982,. Mem. Am. Soc. Safety Engrs. (v.p. rsch. and stds. devel. 1989-93, 1st v.p. 1994, pres-elect 1995, pres. 1995-96). Roman Catholic. Home: 8253 Lorel Ave Burbank IL 60459-2151

OLDEWURTEL, F. KEITH, maintenance service company executive; b. Ontario, Oreg., Aug. 18, 1957; S. Fredrick E. and Virginia A. (Clowser) O; m. Kerry Laine Weber, May 22, 1982; children: Kathryn Lynn, Jackson Keith. AAS, Bay De Noc C.C., 1977. Oper. specialist WW Operation Svcs., Grand Rapids, Mich., 1985-87, dir. opers., 1987-90, exec. v.p., 1990-94; sr. v.p. Earth Tech Operation Svcs., Grand Rapids, Mich., 1994—. Mem. adv. bd. Bay De Noc C C., Escanaba, Mich., 1982-91; active Forest Hills Pub. Schs. Bus. Adv. Coun. Mem. Am. Water Works Assn., Internat. City Mgrs. Assn., Water Environ. Fedn. Home: 6616 Tanglewood Dr SE Grand Rapids MI 49546-7240 Office: Earth Tech Operation 5555 Glenwood Hills Pky SE Grand Rapids MI 49506

OLDFIELD, E. LAWRENCE, lawyer; b. Lake Forest, Ill., Dec. 21, 1944; s. W. Ernest and Evelyn Charlotte (Gyllenberg) O.; m. Kaaren Elaine Sabey, Aug. 24, 1974; 1 stepchild, Kimberly Jo; 1 child, Lauren Elizabeth. BA in Polit. Sci., No. Ill. U., 1969; JD, DePaul U., 1973. Bar: U.S. Dist. Ct. (no. dist.) Ill. 1973, U.S. Ct. Appeals (7th cir.) 1974, U.S. Supreme Ct. 1979, U.S. Ct. Appeals (3d cir.) 1985, U.S. Ct. Appeals (10th cir.) 1986, U.S. Ct. Appeals (8th cir.) 1990. Assoc. Ruff & Grotefeld Ltd., Chgo., 1973-77; gen. counsel livestock dept. Hartford Fire Ins. Co., Chgo., 1977-87; prin. E. Lawrence Oldfield & Assocs., Oak Brook, 1987—. Trustee Village of Glen Ellyn, 1981-85; committeeman Milton Twp., DuPage County Reps., Wheaton, Ill., 1985-88; publicity chmn. Milton Twp. Reps., Wheaton, 1986-88; mem. Dist. 41 Sch. Bd., 1991-95; elder Christ Ch. of Oak Brook, 1993—. Mem. ABA, Ill. Bar Assn., Chgo. Bar Assn., DuPage County Bar Assn., West Suburban Bar Assn., Fed. Trial Bar Assn., Ill. Trial Lawyers' Assn., Assn. Trial Lawyers Am., Safari Club Internat., Am. Legion, VFW, Kiwanis, Moose, Masons, Shriners. Home: 1050 Crescent Blvd Glen Ellyn IL 60137-4276 Office: 2021 Midwest Rd Ste 201 Oak Brook IL 60521-1338 also: 1 N La Salle St Ste 1721 Chicago IL 60602-3907

OLDHAM, LEA LEEVER, business owner, author; b. Cleve., Feb. 8, 1931; d. Harold G. and Virginia K. (Hubbard) Reed; m. John W. Leever, Apr. 16, 1949 (div. June 1977); children: Katherine Gavin, John, Lorraine Brooks, Pattie Buscema, Mary Ella Novotny, Christine Skrynecki; m. Jack R. Oldham (dec.); children: James, Naomi Uchnar. Grad. high sch., Cleve. Assoc. editor Diocese L.A., Garden City, N.Y., 1966-69; sr. writer L.I. Daily Rev., Syosset, N.Y., 1969-74; publs. editor Chemco Photoproducts, Glen Cove, N.Y., 1974-77; owner Images to Impress, Willoughby, Ohio, 1980—; instr., coord. Auburn Career Ctr., Painesville, Ohio, 1985-89; mem. part-time faculty Lakeland C.C., 1979—, Cuyahoga C.C., 1991-94; mem. Pvt.Industry Coun., Painesville, 1986—, mktg. com., 1986-91; founder, coord. Western Res. Writers and Freelance Conf., 1983, Western Res. Writers Mini-Conf., 1992—; Cleveland Heights-Univ. Heights Mini Writers Conf., 1992-94; mgmt. cons. various bus. and govt. agys., 1981—. Author: Non-Credit Instruction: A Guide for Continuing & Adult Education, 1995; co-author: Expand Horizons by Understanding Self and Others, 1985, Expand Your Time Use Potential, 1987; editor (newspaper) Mature View, 1993-94; contbr. articles to profl. mags. Sec. Hicksville (N.Y.) Coordinating Coun., 1961; v.p. Hicksville Dem. Club, 1960; advisor to newspaper Richmond Heights H.S., 1994-95; bd. dirs. Divsn. Lay Ministry, Diocese of Ohio, 1986-91. Recipient Bishop's Cross award Diocese of L.I., 1975, Outstanding Pacesetter award Greater Cleve. Women, 1985. Mem. Women Bus. Owners Western Res. (pres. 1984, achievement award 1988), Nat. League Am. Pen Women, Internat. Mgmt. Coun., Garden Writers Assn. Am., Press Club Cleve. Home and Office: 34200 Ridge Rd Apt 110 Willoughby OH 44094-2954

OLDHAM, PHYLLIS VIRGINIA KIDD, retired librarian; b. Lafayette, Ind., Mar. 19, 1926; d. Hulbert Haven and Grace Ellene (Doup) Kidd; BS, Purdue U., 1948, MS, Butler U., 1966; 1 child, Stephen Kidd. Tchr. English, Jefferson High Sch., Lafayette, 1950; tchr., librarian Tudor Hall Sch., Indpls., 1954-70; librarian Park Tudor Sch., 1970-91; ret. 1991; mem. exec. bd. Central Ind. Area Library Svcs. Authority, sec., 1983-85. Mem. People-to-People Internat., dist. dir. Student Ambassador Program, 1970-80; chmn. bd. Cen. Christian Ch., Indpls., 1979-81, 89-90, bd. trustees, 1991; mem. vol. council Indpls. Zool. Soc. Mem. ALA, Marion County Librarians Assn. (pres. 1969-72), Ind. Media Educators, Kappa Delta Pi, Delta Kappa Gamma (treas. Alpha Eta chpt. 1974-80), Pi Beta Phi. Home: 7015 Warwick Rd Indianapolis IN 46220-1050

O'LEARY, TIMOTHY FRANCIS, real estate developer; b. Chgo., Aug. 14, 1948; s. Timothy Joseph and Margret (Scully) O'L.; m. Mansie Baron, Oct. 9, 1988; children: Matthew, Meghan. Student in Engring., Marquette U., 1966. Mem. tech. support staff ITT, Greenland, 1967; owner, prin. Sicilian Bakery, 1978-81; pres., chief exec. officer Country Estate Developers, Gurnee, Ill., 1979—. Co-chmn. Polit. Legis. Action Com., Vernon Hills, Ill., 1988-89; chmn. fundraising St. Patrick's Ch., Wadsworth, Ill., 1988—, Alexis de Tocqueville Soc. United Way, 1993-94; bd. dirs. Lake County United Way, Gurnee, 1989. Recipient Bronze Club award United Way, 1986, Silver Club award United Way, 1987, Pacesetter award United Way, 1987, Outstanding Corp. Achievement award United Way, 1989, 90, 92. Mem. Home Builders Assn. Lake County (bd. dirs. 1988—, pres. 1991, bd. govs.), Home Builders Assn. Greater Chgo. (exec. com., bd. dirs., Silver Key award 1986, Gold Key award 1985, 86, 87), Downtown Businessmen's Assn. Waukegan, Natural History Soc. Republican. Roman Catholic. Home: 32191 River Rd Gurnee IL 60031

O'LEARY, TIMOTHY MICHAEL, real estate corporation officer; b. Savanna, Ill., Mar. 24, 1946; s. John Patrick and Hazel O'Leary; m. Patricia Ann Woosnam; children: Kevin, Kathleen, Maureen, Mary Margaret, Michael John. Student, Loras Coll., 1964-68; BS, No. Ill. U., 1970, MSBA, 1974. Systems programmer Newel Co., Freeport, Ill., 1970-71, acting mgr. accounts receivable, 1971-73; v.p., treas. HTO Real Estate Svcs., Northbrook, Ill., 1974-90; pres., treas. HTO Real Estate Svcs., Des Plaines, Schaumburg, Ill., 1990-94; sr. v.p. Anderson Schroud Group, Schaumburg, 1994—; chmn. profl. stds. com. Chgo. Bd. Realtors, 1984-85; treas. The Real Estate Consortium, 1993, v.p., 1994-95. Mem. sch. bd. St. Luke Sch., River Forest, Ill., 1985-88, chmn. 1987-88. Mem. Soc. Indsl. and Office Realtors (vice chmn. regional seminar edn. 1984-87, exec. com. Chgo. chpt. 1987-91, nat. bd. dirs. 1987-90, treas. 1988, sec. 1989, v.p. 1990, pres. 1991), Oak Park Jaycees (past pres.), Realtors Nat. Mktg. Inst. (bd. dirs. Ill. chpt. cert. comml. investment 1988-89), Ill. Assn. Realtors (chmn. comml. indsl. subcom. 1990-91, chmn. CI com. 1991-92, Presdl. award 1991), Am. Soc. Real Estate Counselors, Realtors 40 Club (clk. 1985-86, cashier 1989-90, chmn. 1992). Roman Catholic.

OLEEN-BURKEY, MERRIKAY ADELLE, research epidemiologist, educator, pharmacist; b. Princeton, Minn., Oct. 30, 1949; d. Walter Burdette and Virginia Emelia (Carlson) Oleen; m. Jeff Ray Burkey, July 7, 1990. BS in Pharmacy, N.D. State U., 1972, MS in Pharmacy, 1975; PhD in Social and Adminstrv. Pharmacy, U. Minn., 1985. Registered pharmacist, N.D., Minn. Pharmacist intern Mora (Minn.) Drug Co., 1972-73; pharmacy resident VA Med. Ctr., Fargo, N.D., 1973-75; asst. dir. clin. pharmacy svcs. Brokaw Hosp., Normal, Ill., 1976-79; dir. drug info. Wash. State U., Pullman, 1979-81; Kellogg Found. fellow U. Minn., Mpls., 1981-84; research epidemiologist Upjohn Co., Kalamazoo, 1985-90, health econs. scientist, 1990—; adj. prof. epidemiology Western Mich. U., Kalamazoo, 1988-91. Contbr. articles to profl. jours. Vol. CROP Walk, 1987-95, Planned Parenthood, 1986-90; chair adult edn. com. Prince of Peace Luth. Ch., Portage, Mich., 1992-93. Named Hosp. Pharmacist of Yr., Ill. Coun. Hosp. Pharmacists, 1979; Kellogg Found. fellow U. Minn., 1981-84; recipient Upjohn Mktg. Excellence award, 1994. Mem. APHA, LWV, Internat. Soc. Pharmacoepidemiology (membership chair 1995-96), Soc. Epidemiologic Rsch., Am. Pharm. Assn., Drug Info. Assn., Vasa. Home: 4441 Frontier Ave Kalamazoo MI 49024 Office: Pharmacia & Upjohn Inc 7000 Portage Rd Kalamazoo MI 49001-0102

OLEKSEY, VICKY JOYCE, business owner; b. Glasgow, Mont., Dec. 12, 1952; d. Frank Smith Jr. and Mary Helen (Smith) McIntyre; m. John Peter Oleksey, Jr., Aug. 7, 1976 (div. May 1984); 1 child, Kathryn Elizabeth. Student, U. Colo., 1973-76, U. Md., Fed. Republic Germany, 1977-81; BSBA, U. Phoenix, 1984; MBA, Boise State U., 1988. Cert. quality analyst, quality award examiner, Minn.; cert. MBTI and ISO 9000 lrsf auditor. Keytape operator lst Security Bank, Glasgow, 1968-71; programmer analyst Baldwin Data Svcs., Denver, 1973-76; acctg. technician dept. non-appropriated funds U.S. Govt., Ramstein, Fed. Republic Germany, 1977-79, systems operator dept. non-appropriated funds, 1979-80; programmer analyst II, United Banks Colo., Denver, 1982-85; programmer analyst Moore Fin. Group, Boise, Idaho, 1985-87, career developer, 1987-88; mgr. quality assurance West One Bancorp, Boise, 1988-90; mgr. quality assurance software products Bankers Systems, Inc., St. Cloud, Minn., 1991-93, sr. bus. analyst, 1993-95; owner Applied Bus. Strategies, St. Cloud, Minn., 1995—. Mem. pers. com., leader single parents group 1st Presbyn. Ch., Boise, 1988-89; bd. dirs. St. Cloud All-City H.S. Marching Band, 1995-96, Forum of Exec. Women, 1996. Recipient Outstanding Project Chmn. award, Jaycee of Month award U.S. Jaycees-Idaho, 1989, Staff Officer of Yr., 1991, Project Chmn. of Yr. 1991, Ambassador, 1993; named Statesman Minn. Jaycees, 1993, Single Parent of the Yr., 1994. Mem. Am. Bus. Women's Assn. (v.p. Boise chpt. 1987-88, Woman of Yr. award 1987), Capitol Jaycees (v.p. for mgmt. devel. 1989), Sartell Jaycees (pres. 1992-93, state del. 1993-94). Republican. Episcopalian. Home: 2808 21st Ave S Saint Cloud MN 56301-9063 Office: Applied Bus Strategies PO Box 7614 Saint Cloud MN 56302

OLEKSY, WALTER GEORGE, author; b. Chgo., June 24, 1930; s. John Joseph and Pauline Louise (Standacher) O. BJ, Mich. State U., 1955. Reporter City News Bur., Chgo., 1958; reporter, writer Chgo. Tribune, 1958-65; mag. editor Geyer, Morey, Ballard, Chgo., 1965-67; editor ChicagoLand mag., Chgo., 1967-68, Discovery mag., Northbrook, Ill., 1968-71. Works include Military Leaders of World War II, 1994, The Information Revolution, 1995; co-editor: Lincoln's Unknown Private Life, 1995. Pres. Evanston (Ill.) Alliance of Taxpayers, 1995, Stadium Neighbors, Evanston, 1995. With U.S. Army, 1955-57, Germany. Mem. Chgo. Children's Writers Roundtable, Midwest Writers Assn., Soc. Children's Book Writers. Home: 2656 Bryant Ave Evanston IL 60201

OLESKO, RON, engineering manager; b. Detroit, May 29, 1942. AD, Henry Ford C.C., 1963. Mgr. elec. engring. Summit Products, Brighton, Mich., 1976-88; elec. engr. K.J. Law Engrs., Farmington Hills, Mich., 1988-90; mgr. engring. Novi Precision, Brighton, 1990—. Coach Little League Baseball and Football. Office: Novi Precision 11777 Grand River Rd Brighton MI 48116-8505

OLIGER, YVONNE CHINN, librarian; b. Butte, Mont., Oct. 26, 1949; d. William Mun and Gene Letitia (Wu) Chinn; m. Stephen P. Benowitz, Feb. 3, 1973; m. Robert W. Oliger, July 21, 1991. BS in Edn., Mont. State U., 1971; MLS, Ind. U., 1982. Cert. libr., Inst. Tchr. Boulder (Mont.) Sch., 1976-79; children's libr. Bedford (Ind.) Pub. Libr., 1980-92; dir. Brown County Pub. Libr., Nashville, Ind., 1992—; chmn. Children's and Young People's Divsn. Ind. Libr. Fedn., 1985—. Pres. alumni bd. Ind. Univ. Sch. of Libr. and Info. Sci., 1994-96; mem. Dunn Meml. Hosp. Found., Bedford, 1990-92; chmn. March of Dimes Walkathon, Bedford, 1988; pres. Kappa Kappa Kappa Philanthropic, Nashville, Ind., 1995. Democrat. Episcopalian. Home: 3510 N Greasy Creek Rd Nashville IN 47448 Office: Brown County Pub Libr 246 E Main St Nashville IN 47448

OLINGER, WAYNE WILLIAM, insurance agent; b. Ferdinand, Ind., June 29, 1957; s. Wilfred Mathias and Josephine Johanna (Bickwermert) O.; divorced; 1 child, Jennifer; m. Kimberly Jo Duckworth, Sept. 27, 1986;

children: Winston, Nathan. BS in Acctg. with honors, Ind. U., 1979, MBA in Managerial Fin., 1980. CPA, Ind.; registered investment advisor affiliate, lic. life and health ins., Ind. Acct., credit mgr. Maxon Corp., Muncie, Ind., 1980-88; bus. broker Ind. Bus. Brokers, Indpls., 1988-90; ins. agt Comprehensive Fin. Group., Muncie, 1990—. Treas. Big Bros./Big Sisters, Muncie, 1993—. Home: 5200 Grass Way Muncie IN 47304 Office: Comprehensive Fin Group 3591 N Briarwood Ln Muncie IN 47304

OLIVER, EDWARD CARL, state senator, retired investment executive; b. St. Paul, May 31, 1930; s. Charles Edmund and Esther Marie (Bjugstad) O.; m. Charlotte Severson, Sept. 15, 1956; children—Charles E., Andrew T., Peter A. B.A., U. Minn., 1955. Sales rep. Armstrong Cork Co., N.Y.C., 1955; registered rep. Piper, Jaffray & Hopwood, Mpls., 1958; mgr. Mut. Funds, Inc. subs. Dayton's, Mpls., 1964; mgr. NWNL Mgmt. Corp. subs. Northwestern Nat. Life Ins. Co., Mpls., 1968-72, v.p., 1972-81, pres., dir., 1981-90; mem. Minn. Senate, 1992—; arbitrator, Nat. Assn. Securities Dealers, 1988—; bd. dirs. Minn. World Trade Ctr. Corp. Commr. Great Lakes Commn., 1993—. Served to sgt. USAF, 1951-52. Mem. Internat. Assn. Fin. Planners (past pres. Twin City chpt., mem. nat. governing com.), Psi Upsilon. Presbyterian (elder). Club: Mpls. Athletic. Home: 20230 Cottagewood Rd Deephaven MN 55331-9300 Office: Washington Sq Securities Inc 100 Washington Ave S Ste 1639 Minneapolis MN 55401-2154

OLIVER, G(EORGE) BENJAMIN, educational administrator, philosophy educator; b. Mpls., Sept. 17, 1938; s. Clarence P. and Cecile (Worley) O.; m. Paula Rae Foust, Sept. 15, 1963; children: Paul Benjamin, Rebecca Lee. B.A. with honors, U. Tex., 1960; M.Div., Union Theol. Sem., N.Y.C., 1963; M.A., Northwestern U., 1966, Ph.D., 1967. Lectr. Northwestern U., Evanston, Ill., 1966-67; asst. prof. Hobart & William Smith Coll., Geneva, N.Y., 1967-71, chmn. dept. philosphy, 1969-77, assoc. prof., 1971-77; prof., 1977; dean Southwestern U., Georgetown, Tex., 1977-89, provost, 1986-89; pres. Hiram (Ohio) Coll., 1989—; chmn. Coun. of Acad. Deans and V.P.s of Tex., 1987-88. Contbr. articles to profl. jours. Trustee John Cabot Univ., Rome, 1989—, Grand River Acad., Austinburg, Ohio, 1991—, Northeast Ohio Coun. Higher Edn., 1991—, Ohio Found. Ind. Colls., 1989—, Assn. Ind. Colls. and Univ. of Ohio, 1993—, Am. Coun. Edn. Commn. Govtl. Rels., 1994—; chmn., bd. trustees, East Central Coll. Consortium, 1993-95. Rockefeller Found. fellow, 1960-61, Internat. fellow Columbia U., 1962-63; research grantee NEH, 1973-74. Mem. AAUP, Am. Coun. Edn. (mem. comm. on govtl. rels.), Soc. for Values in Higher Edn., Assn. Indep. Coll. and Univ. of Ohio (treas. 1993-94), East Ctrl. Colls. Consortium (chair, bd. trustees, 1993-95), Ohio Found. Ind. Colls. (exec. com. 1994—), Am. Assn. Higher Edn., Interat. Assn. U. Pres. Episcopalian. Office: Hiram Coll Office of Pres Hiram OH 44234

OLIVER, MARGUERITE BERTONI, food service executive; b. Ann Arbor, Mich., June 5, 1929; d. Ralph Angelo and Margaret Amelia (Rovegno) Bertoni; m. William John Oliver, May 28, 1949; children: R. Scott, Catherine Oliver Allen, Susan M. Mgr. complaint dept. Sears Roebuck Co., Ann Arbor, 1949-50; dir. meals-on-wheels program U. Mich. Hosp., Ann Arbor, 1974-76; fund raiser U. Mich. Art Sch., Ann Arbor, 1976-80; founder Pastabilities (named outstanding pasta shop in U.S. by CNN TV), Ann Arbor, 1980—; participant, speaker Midwest Assn. State Depts. Agr., 1987; mem. adv. com. Gov.'s Conf. on Future of Mich. Agr., 1988; co-chmn. Gov.'s Conf. on Agr., 1989. Mem. com. on aging Ann Arbor Coun., 1970-74; bd. dirs. Hands-On-Mus., Ann Arbor, 1980-82; mem. market commn. Ann Arbor, 1982—; founded Internat. Neighbors; mem., adv. com. Mich. Future 2020 Team; trustee Washtenaw Community Coll., 1989—; mem. Mich. Dept. Agr. Industry Task Force, 1990; invited del. Moscow Bus. Conf., 1991; fundraiser Mott Children's Hosp. U. Mich., 1979-80. Recipient Washtenaw Community Service award Washtenaw Community Coll., 1985. Democrat. Roman Catholic. Club: Women's City. Home: 2892 Bay Ridge Dr Ann Arbor MI 48103-1704 Office: Pastabilities 708 State Circle Ann Arbor MI 48108

OLLAND, CHERIE WALLACE, marketing professional; b. Rochester, N.Y., June 28, 1950; d. Leroy Stephen and Ann Virginia (Tortora) Wallace; m. Paul Keith Thomas, Sept. 1, 1973 (div. June 1977); m. Timothy David Olland, July 25, 1981; children: Adam Gray, Alexandra Scott. BS, Ithaca (N.Y.) Coll., 1972; MS, Elmira (N.Y.) Coll., 1975. Secondary tchr. English Odessa (N.Y.)-Montour Schs., 1972-74, Corning (N.Y.) City Schs., 1974-80; proposal writer Richard Fleischman Architects, Cleve., 1980-81; legal asst. Jones, Day, Reavis & Pogue, Cleve., 1981-83; editor McKinsey & Co. Inc., Cleve., 1983-85; edn. program officer Greater Cleve. Roundtable, 1986-89; asst. adminstr. litigation Jones, Day, Reavis & Pogue, 1989-91, dir. bus. devel. and comm., 1991—. Bd. mem. Steuben Humane Soc., Steuben County, N.Y., 1979-80. Recipient Bronze Anvil/Commendation Pub. Rels. Soc. Am., 1994, Achievement in Comm. award Women in Comm., Inc., 1994. Mem. Internat. Assn. Bus. Communicators, Nat. Law Firm Mktg. Assn. Office: Jones Day Reavis & Pogue North Point 901 Lakeside Ave Cleveland OH 44114

OLLHOFF, BARBARA JEAN, marketing educator; b. Wausau, Wis., July 12, 1947; d. Franklin H. and Mrytle E. (Giese) O.; m. Halbert C. Heath, July 18, 1992. BS, U. Wis., Whitewater, 1969; MS, U. Wis., Madison, 1974; EdD, Va. Poly. and State U., 1991. Instr. mktg. and fashion mktg. Waukesha County Tech. Coll., Pewaukee, Wis., 1969—; fashion tng. cons. Tweeds, Inc., Salem, Va., 1990-91. Recipient Leavey award The Freedom Found., 1986; named Vocat. Tchr. of Yr., Wis. Edn. Assn. and Wis. Vocat. Assn., 1987. Mem. NEA, Am. Vocat. Assn. (Vocat. Tchr. of Yr. region 3, 1988), Am. Bus. Women's Assn. (pres. Waukesha chpt. 1987, 88, Bus. Woman of Yr. 1986), Mktd. Edn. Assn. (chairperson fashion profession interest category, Wis. Mktg. Educator of Yr. 1993), Wis. Edn. Assn., Wis. Vocat. Assn. Lutheran. Office: Waukesha County Tech Coll 800 Main St Pewaukee WI 53072-4601

OLMAN, LYNN, state legislator. Rep. dist. 51 Ohio Ho. of Reps., Columbus, 1995—.

OLMSTEAD, CLARENCE WALTER, geography educator, retired; b. Ludington, Mich., Nov. 4, 1912; s. Verne Lloyd and Anna Mary (Rinebolt) O.; m. Rhea Nancy Donnelly, Aug. 18, 1939; children: Clarence W., Jr., Nancy, John V. BA, Cen. Mich. U., 1937; MS, U. Mich., 1938, PhD, 1951. Tchr. Lincoln Valley Sch., Mason County, Mich., 1931-34; instr. Cen. Mich. Coll., Mt. Pleasant, Mich., 1938-40; grad. tchrs. asst. U. Calif., Berkeley, 1940-42; goegrapher, analyst Office Strategic Svc./Dept. State, Washington, 1942-46; asst. prof. geography and edn. U. Wis., Madison, 1946-50, asst. prof. to prof. geography, 1950-81, emeritus prof. geography, 1981—; vis. prof. geography, George Peabody Coll. Tchrs., Nashville, 1951, UCLA, 1959, Syracuse U., Greeley, Colo., 1964, U. Auckland, New Zealand, 1968; active various coms. including Commn. on Agrl. Typology, Internat. Geograph. Union, 1968-76, others. Collaborator: North America, A Regional Geography, 7th edit., 1984; contbr. articles and book chpts. to publs. in field. Lt. USN Res., 1943-46, ETO. Mem. Assn. Am. Geographers (various coms.), Nat. Coun. Geographic Edn., AAUP. Unitarian. Home: 602 N Segoe Rd Apt 606 Madison WI 53705-3118 Office: Univ Wis Dept Geography 413 Sci Hall 550 N Park St Madison WI 53706-1404

OLMSTED, ANN GARVER, lawyer; b. Ft. Dodge, Iowa, Dec. 11, 1924; d. H. Woodford and Florence Edna (Hoppe) Garver; m. Donald Warren Olmsted, Sept. 9, 1950; 1 child, Caroline Ellen. BA, U. No. Iowa, Cedar Falls, 1945; PhD, U. Minn., 1954; JD, Mich. State U., 1982. Bar: Mich. 1982. Tchr. pub. schs., Algona, Iowa, 1945-46; teaching asst. U. Minn., Mpls., 1946-49, asst. dir., instr., 1950-55; instr. W.Va. U., Morgantown, 1949-50; rsch. assoc. U. Wis., Madison, 1955-57; from rsch. assoc. to prof. Mich. State U., East Lansing, 1957—, interim dir. med. sch. admissions, 1992-93; workshop dir. Hunan Med. U., Changsha, Peoples Republic of China, 1991. Contbr. chpts. to books, articles to profl. jours. Bd. dirs., officer Mich. Dyslexia Inst., Lansing, 1980—; bd. dirs. Mich. Lung Assn., Lansing, 1986-92, Mich. Health Data Corp., Lansing, 1984-90, Mich. Peer Rev. Orgn., Plymouth, 1992—. Recipient Lester Evans Disting. Svc. award Coll. Human Medicine/Mich. State U., 1991. Mem. Mich. State Bar Assn., Ingham Bar Assn., Am. Sociol. Assn. Democrat. Congregationalist. Home: 1555 W Pond Dr # 24 Okemos MI 48864

OLOFSON, TOM WILLIAM, electronics executive; b. Oak Park, Ill., Oct. 10, 1941; s. Ragnar V. and Ingrid E. Olofson; BBA, U. Pitts., 1963; m. Jeanne Hamilton, Aug. 20, 1960; children: Christopher, Scott. Various mgmt. positions Bell Telephone Co. of Pa., Pitts., 1963-67; sales mgr. Xerox Corp., Detroit, 1967-68, nat. account mgr., Rochester, N.Y., 1968, mgr. govt. planning, Rochester, 1969, mgr. Kansas City (Mo.) br., 1969-74; corp. v.p. health products group Marion Labs., Inc., Kansas City, Mo., 1974-78, sr. v.p., mem. Office Pres., 1978-80; exec. v.p., dir. Electronic Realty Assocs., Inc., 1980-83; chmn. bd., CEO Emblem Graphic Systems, Inc., 1983-88, Electronic Processing, Inc., 1988—; dir. DemoGraFX, Wordenglass & Electricity, Inc., Elinco Internat., Access Industries, Inc., Saztec Internat., Capital Ptnrs. Bd. visitors U. Pitts. Joseph M. Katz Grad. Sch. Bus.; past trustee Barstow Sch.; past chmn. bd. trustees Village United Presbyn. Ch.; bd. dirs. Mid. Am. Immunotherapy and Surg. Research Found., Inc. Mem. Omicron Delta Kappa, Sigma Chi. Republican. Presbyterian. Club: Kansas City. Office: Electronic Processing Inc 501 Kansas Ave Kansas City KS 66105-1309

OLSCAMP, PAUL JAMES, academic administrator; b. Montreal, Que., Can., Aug. 29, 1937; s. James J. and Luella M. (Brush) O.; m. Ruth I. Pratt, Dec. 2, 1978; children by previous marriage: Rebecca Ann, Adam James. BA, U. Western Ont., 1958, MA, 1960; PhD, U. Rochester, 1962. Instr. Ohio State U., Columbus, 1962, asst. prof., 1963-66, assoc. prof., 1966-69, assoc. dean humanities, 1969; dean faculties, prof. philosophy Roosevelt U., Chgo., 1970-71, v.p. acad. affairs, 1971-72; prof. philosophy Syracuse (N.Y.) U., 1972-75, exec. asst. to chancellor, 1972, vice chancellor student programs, 1972-75; pres. Western Wash. U., Bellingham, 1975-82, Bowling Green (Ohio) State U., 1982—; Grad. fellow in humanities U. Western Ont., 1959. Author: Descartes: The Discourse, Optics, Geometry and Meteorology, 1965, The Moral Philosophy of George Berkeley, 1970, An Introduction to Philosophy, 1971, Malebranche: The Search After Truth, 1980; contbr. articles to profl. jours. Mem. Nat. Coun. on the Humanities, 1988-92, NCAA Pres.'s Commn., 1989-91; bd. dirs., treas. Inter-Am. Univ. Coun. for Econ. and Social Devel. 1991—. Recipient Mackintosh Pub. Speaking and Lecturing award U. Western Ont., 1959-60, Alfred J. Wright award Ohio State U., 1970; Grad. fellow in humanities U. Western Ont., 1959, Grad. Studies fellow U. Rochester, 1960, 61-62; Danforth Found. assoc., 1966—. Mem. Am. Assn. State Colls. and Univs. (mem. com. undergrad. edn. 1982-90, com. confs. and profl. devel. 1989-92), Am. Philos. Assn. Office: Bowling Green State U McFall Ctr Bowling Green OH 43403*

OLSCHESKE, THOMAS JOHN, information systems specialist, researcher; b. Mauston, Wis., Aug. 22, 1950; s. Arthur and Clara (Satorius) O. BA, U. Wis., 1977, MS, 1987, postgrad., 1987—. Computer systems analyst N. Ctrl. Computer Inst., Madison, Wis., 1981-86; mng. dir. Golden Sands, Hong Kong, 1988-91; computer programmer U. Wis., Madison, 1971-81; sr. info. analyst Med. Sch. U. Wis., 1986-88, project rschr., info analyst, product innovation mgmt., 1991-94; group leader flexible learning U. Wis., Madison, 1994—; internat. bus. cons. Komo Internat., Madison, 1983-88. Recipient Chinese Lang. Study grant Dept. of Defense, 1972. Mem. IEEE, Assn. for Computing Machinery, Chinese Lang. Computer Soc. Office: Engring Profl Devel U Wis 432 N Lake St Madison WI 53706-1415

OLSEN, GARY ALVIN, design engineer; b. Ypsilanti, Mich., Feb. 13, 1949; s. Reinhart Alvin and Marian (Losee) O. AS in Archtl. Drafting Tech., Washtenaw Community Coll., Ann Arbor, Mich., 1972. Draftsman, rodman Washtenaw Engring., Inc., Ann Arbor, 1969; archtl. draftsman Campbell Engring., Inc., Detroit, 1972-73, Garity Constrn. Co., Southfield, Mich., 1973; engring. draftsman Bechtel Power Corp., Ann Arbor, 1974; archtl. draftsman engring. dept. U. Mich., Ann Arbor, 1974-76; engring. detailer Ford Motor Co., Dearborn, Mich., 1977-90, engring. designer, 1990—. Republican. Lutheran. Home: 41445 Elsa Ct Canton MI 48187-3815

OLSEN, GEORGE EDWARD, retired insurance executive; b. Antigo, Wis., Sept. 16, 1924; s. Hjalmar and Clara Marcella (Kramer) O.; m. Mary Susan Rice, Oct. 8, 1958 (div. Nov. 1969); children: Thomas George, Elizabeth Alice, James Phillip. BA, U. Wis., 1949. From underwriter to underwriting mgr. Employers Ins. Wausau, Milw., Phila., N.Y.C. and San Francisco, 1949-59; dir. casualty underwriting dept. Mut. Service Ins. Co., St. Paul, 1959-62; underwriting mgr. Celina Ins. Group, Cleve., 1962-71; mgr. nat. accounts Nationwide Ins. Co., Columbus, Ohio, 1971-74; v.p., regional mgr. Reinsurance Facilities Corp., Columbus, 1974-78; pres., dir. Century Surety Co., Columbus, 1978-89; treas., dir. Latitude Premium Fin. Co., Columbus, 1987-90; prin. Ins. Mgmt. Advisors. With U.S. Army, 1943-45, ETO. Republican.

OLSEN, GERALD JAMES, art industry executive; b. Owatonna, Minn., Jan. 29, 1946; s. James Edward and Edna Elma (Brokl) J.; m. Barbara Ann Eck (div.); children: Forrest, Robin. BA, Macalester Coll., 1968; MA, St. Cloud State U., 1971; student, Ind. U., 1972-75, 77-78. Asst. dir. Minn. State Arts Bd., St. Paul, 1979-81, exec. dir., 1981-84; pres., CEO United Arts, St. Paul, 1984-87; chief advancement officer Crosier Fathers and Bros., Shoreview, Minn., 1987—; adv. bd. MA in theology program Coll. St. Catherine, St. Paul, 1993—. Contbr. articles to profl. jours., newsletters. Pres., bd. dirs. Affiliated State Agys. of Upper Midwest, Mpls., 1983-84, mem. 1981-84; commr. Human Rights Commn., Falcon Heights, Minn., 1988-91; pres., bd. dirs. Minn. Humane Soc., St. Paul, 1987-91; bd. dirs. Listening House, St. Paul, 1994—. Theatre and drama fellow Ind. U., Bloomington, 1972-74, 77-78. Mem. Nat. Soc. Fund Raising Execs. (chair pub. rels. Minn. chpt. 1992-93), Nat. Assembly Local Arts Agys., Nat. Assembly State Arts Agys., Pub. Rels. Soc. Am., Minn. Planned Giving Coun. Office: Crosier Fathers & Bros 3510 Vivian Ave Shoreview MN 55126

OLSEN, LUTHER S., state legislator; b. Feb. 26, 1951. BA, U. Wis. Assemblyman Wis. State Dist. 41, 1994—; owner (farm supply store) Omro. Mem. Berlin Area Bd. Edn., 1976-95. Address: 2021 Hwy 49 Berlin WI 54923

OLSEN, PAUL GARY, computer operator; b. Elkhorn, Wis., Dec. 31, 1963; s. Glenn F. and Dorothy Helen (Garity) O. AA, U. Wis., Rock County, 1985; BA in English Lit. and History, U. Wis., Whitewater, 1988; MA Creative Writing emphasis, U. Wis. Milw., 1993. Tel. operator Cross Country, Whitewater, Wis., 1989-90; computer operator Lakeland Med. Ctr., Inc., Elkhorn, Wis., 1990—; editl. asst. The Cream City Review, Milw., 1989. Roman Catholic.

OLSEN, STANLEY SEVERN, minister; b. Denver, Mar. 10, 1944; s. Olaf S. and Margaret Ruth (Hook) O.; m. Patricia Joy Wahlen, Sept. 17, 1966; children: Nathaniel S., Nisse J. BA, Bethel Coll., 1966; postgrad., U. Minn., 1968; MA in Christian Edn., Bethel Theol. Sem., 1969; postgrad., U. Mid. Am., 1975; Theol. Orientation, North Park Theol. Sem., 1984; D of Ministry, Trinity Divinity Sch., 1995. adj. prof. Bethel Theol. Sem., St. Paul, 1980-85; chmn. N.W. Covenant Conf. Bd. of Christian Edn., Mpls., 1980-84, Nat. Bd. of Christian Edn. and Discipleship, 1987-93; pres. Nat. Assn. Dirs. Christian Edn., 1981-85; vis. prof. AIM Pastors Conf., Nairobi, Kenya, 1995; ednl. cons. Greater Europe Mission, 1994—. Minister of Christian Edn. Aldrich Ave. Presbyn. Ch., Mpls., 1969-71; minister of children, dir. children's ctr. Grace Community Ch., Tempe, Ariz., 1972; minister of Christian Edn. Bethel Reformed Ch., Bellflower, Calif., 1973-77; assoc. pastor First Covenant Ch., Mpls., 1977-85; exec. pastor Hillcrest Covenant Ch., Prairie Village, Kans., 1985—; adj. prof. Bethel Theol. Sem., St. Paul, 1980-85; chmn. N.W. Covenant Conf. Bd. of Christian Edn., Mpls., 1980-84, Nat. Bd. of Christian Edn. and Discipleship, 1987-93; pres. Nat. Assn. Dirs. Christian Edn., 1981-85; vis. prof. AIM Pastors Conf., Nairobi, Kenya, 1995, Ecuadorisn Pastor's Seminar, Quito, 1996. Pub., editor (mag.) Infocus, 1981-85; author: (with others) Introduction to Christian Education, 1991, Adult Education in the Church, 1992; keynote speaker Christian Edn. Meeting of Seminarians, Dallas, 1992. Mem. Young Reps., Mpls., 1966-69; pres. Bellflower (Calif.) Ministerial Assn., 1974-77; sec. Downtown Pastors Ministerial Assn., Mpla., 1981-84; civics chmn. Mission Valley PTA, 1995—. Mem. Profl. Assn. Christian Educators (bd. dirs., v.p. 1986-93). Republican. Office: Hillcrest Covenant Ch 8801 Nall Ave Shawnee Mission KS 66207-2106

OLSEN, THERESA MARIE GRIMALDI, freelance writer, educator; b. Chgo., Aug. 1, 1960; d. Ignatius William and Geraldine Anne (Rudnick) Grimaldi; m. Dean R. Olsen, June 5, 1985; children: Crystal Maria, Kyle Dean. BS in Journalism, U. Ill., 1982; MA in Pub. Affairs Reporting, Sangamon State U., Springfield, Ill., 1983. Reporter Star Publs., Chicago Heights, Ill., 1983-84, Jour. and Courier, Lafayette, Ind., 1984-86; sci. and tech. editor Purdue U., West Lafayette, Ind., 1986-87; freelance writer Morton, Ill., 1987-91, 94—; instr. journalism Ill. State U., Normal, 1991-92, Bradley U., Peoria, Ill., 1992-94. Contbr. articles to Parade, Columbia Journalism Rev., Chgo. Tribune, others; writer newsletters and brochures. Sec. Bethel Luth. PTL, Morton, 1995-96. Recipient Vanguard award Women in Comms., 1986, 1st place award AP Mng. Editors, 1986; James E. Armstrong scholar, 1982. Mem. Pub. Rels. Assn. Peoria. Lutheran. Home: 219 E Lakewood St Morton IL 61550

OLSHOVE, DENNIS, state legislator; b. Detroit, Jan. 18, 1950; m. Fran, 1980; children: Steven, Michael, Marc, Ryan. BA, Mich. State U., 19736. Rep. Mich. Dist. 23; pub. utilities joint com. Mich. State Reps., adminstrv. rules com. Mem. Polish Am. Cong., Polish Caucus, Sylvester Usher's Club, Polish Century Club, Sterling Heights. Home: 29723 Roan Dr Warren MI 48093-3533 Address: 406 Roosevelt Bldg Lansing MI 48909*

OLSON, ALICE, state legislator; b. Winnipeg, Manitoba, May 24, 1928; d. Ames Carl and Olga (Lutz) Sandgren; m. Keith Cox Olson, 1948 (dec.); children: Linda Renee, Douglas Keith. Degree, Aaker's Bus. Coll., Grand Forks, N.D., 1946. Mem. N.D. Ho. of Reps., 1973—, chmn. nat. resources com., mem. fin. and taxation com.; farmer. V.p. Pembina County (N.D.) Rep. Women Dist. 10, 1968-70, pres., 1970-72; mem. platform com. N.D. Rep., 1972; del. Rep. Nat. Conv., 1980; sec. Pembina County Agent, 1946-47, Swift & Co., South St. Paul, Minn., 1947-48; dir. handbell choir, Peace Garden; mem. nat. resources com. NCSL, GarrisonDiversion Overview com., Capitol Grounds Planning Commn.; mem. Pembina County Hosp. Aux., Pembina County Hist. Soc., Cavalier Study Club. Mem. Bathgate Homemakers Club, Am. Legion Aux., Pioneer Daus. Address: PO Box 8 Cavalier ND 58220-0008 Office: ND Ho of Reps State Capitol Bismarck ND 58505*

OLSON, BARBARA FORD, physician; b. Iowa City, June 15, 1935; d. Leonard A. and Anne (Swanson) Ford; m. Robert Eric Olson, March 21, 1959 (div. 1973); children: Katherine Gee, Eric Ford, Julie Marie. BA, Gustavus Adolphus Coll., 1956; MD, U. Minn., 1960. Diplomate Am. Bd. Family Practice (cert. added qualifications geriatric medicine). Intern St. Paul-Ramsy Med. Ctr., 1960-61; resident in anesthesiology U. Hosp. Cleve., 1961-62, U. Minn. Hosp., Mpls., 1962-63; pvt. practice anesthesiology St. Johns Hosp. and Devine Redeemer Hosp., St. Paul, 1963-67, Mercy Hosp., Coon Rapids, Minn., 1967-74; staff physician Oak Terrace Nursing Home, Minnetonka, Minn., 1974-88; med. dir. nursing home care unit VA Med. Ctr., St. Cloud, Minn., 1988—. Pres., bd. dirs. Alpha Epsilon Iota Med. Found., Mpls., 1980-86. Mem. Minn. Med. Assn., Minn. Women Physicians (pres. 1981-82), Minn. Nursing Home Med. Dirs. Home: PO Box 7306 Saint Cloud MN 56302-7306 Office: VA Med Ctr 4801 8th St N Saint Cloud MN 56303-2014

OLSON, BARRY GAY, advertising executive, creative director; b. Glendale, Calif., July 3, 1933; s. Gay Frank and Dorothy Barry (Guay) O. Student, U. So. Calif., 1952-54, UCLA, 1953, Coll. of San Mateo, Calif., 1954. In prodn. Neiman-Marcus, Dallas, 1956; prodn. mgr. Grant Advt., San Francisco, 1957-60; copywriter D'Arcy, MacManus, Masius, San Francisco, 1960-62, Norman, Craig & Kummel, N.Y.C., 1965-67, W. B. Doner, Balt., 1967-68, Ted Bates, L.A., 1969; creative dir., v.p. McCann-Erickson, Melbourne, Australia, 1963-65, J. Walter Thompson, Detroit, 1972-75, Vickers & Benson, Montreal, Can., 1976-77, Meldrum & Fewsmith, Cleve., 1971-72, 77-79, Stockton West Burkhart, Cin., 1981-82; creative dir. Hitchcock Fleming, Akron, Ohio, 1982-83, Muller Jordan Weiss, St. Louis, 1984-85; creative dir., v.p., shareholder Innis-Maggiore-Olson, Canton, Ohio, 1985-91; exec. v.p., creative dir., ptnr. Olson and Gibbons, Cleve., 1991—, also bd. dirs.; instr. creative advt. part-time Dynamic Graphics Edn. Found., Peoria, Ill., 1989; bd. dirs. Meldrum & Fewsmith, Cleve. Contbr. to textbooks: American Corporate Identity 11 and 12, and to Contemporary Advertising. Bd. trustees Cleve. Signstage Theater, 1996—; trustee N.E. Ohio chpt. March of Dimes Birth Defects Found., 1991-93, Big Bros., San Francisco, 1962, Palace Theater Assn., Canton, 1987. With USAF. Recipient Spl. Jury Gold award Atlanta Film Festival, 1975, Clio, 1976, Silver and Bronze Lions Cannes Film Festival, 1977, Ace award B/PAA of N.Y.C., 1989, Best of Show award Columbus Advt. Club, 1981, Canton Advt. Club, 1988, 89, 90, Mktg. Mag. Silver award, Toronto, Can., 1976, Spl. Merit award Inst. Outdoor Advt., N.Y., 1986, Silver Microphone radio awards, Nat. Winner, 1987, 90, 86 Gold Addy awards Akron Advt. Club, Canton Club, Cleve. Advt. Club, Columbus Advt. Club, 1981, 85, 86, 87, 88, 90, 95, 5th Dist. Addy awrd, 1995-96, Gold Plaque award Chgo. Internat. Film Festival, 1992, Bronze Telly award, 1995, 96, Silver Telly award, 1996, 3 Gold Tower award BMA Cleve., 1994, Gold Tower award BMA Cleve., 1996; voted one of top 100 creative people in Am. Ad Daily mag., 1971. Mem. Cleve. Mus. Art. Home: 16305 Glynn Rd Cleveland Heights OH 44112-3549 Office: Olson and Gibbons 1501 Euclid Ave Ste 518 Cleveland OH 44115-2108

OLSON, CLIFFORD LARRY, management consultant, entrepreneur; b. Karlstad, Minn., Oct. 11, 1946; s. Wallace B. and Lucille I (Pederson) O.; m. B.A. Blue Blodgett, March 18, 1967; children: Derek, Erin. B in Chemical Engring., U. Minn., 1969, B in Physics, 1969; MBA, U. Chgo., 1972; Licence en Sciences Economiques, U. de Louvain, Brussels, 1972. CPA, Cert. mgmt. cons. Project engr. Procter & Gamble, Chgo., 1969-71; engagement mgr. McKinsey & Co., Chgo., 1972-75; ptnr., midwest regional dir. mgmt. consulting Peat, Marwick, Mitchell, St. Louis, 1976-87; chmn. Casson Industries Inc., Mpls., 1987—; bd. dirs. Castlerock Group, Inc., Chevron, Inc. Mem. AICPA, Inst. Mgmt. Cons., Union League Club Chgo., Tavern Club, Interlachen Country Club. Episcopalian. Office: 5804 Schaefer Rd Minneapolis MN 55436-1116

OLSON, DAVID WENDELL, bishop; b. St. Paul, Apr. 4, 1938; s. Wendell Edwin and Eva Victoria (Edstrom) O.; m. Nancy Grace Evans, July 9, 1961; children: Kathryn, Jonathan, Justin. BA, St. Olaf Coll., 1960; MDiv, Luther Sem., St. Paul, 1964. Ordained to ministry Am. Luth. Ch.,1964. Pastor St. Paul's Ch., Balt., 1964-69; co-pastor St. James Ch., Crystal, Minn., 1969-78; dir. North Mpls. Luth. Coalition, 1978-82; asst. prof. Luther N.W. Sem., St. Paul, 1982-84; asst. to bishop S.E. Minn. dist. Am. Luth. Ch., St. Paul, 1984-87; bishop Mpls. area synod Evang. Luth. Ch. in Am., Mpls., 1987—. Chair Robbinsdale (Minn.) Sch. Bd., 1976-82; trustee Fairview Hosp., Mpls. Bush Found. fellow, 1975. Office: Evang Luth Ch in Am 122 W Franklin Ave Ste 600 Minneapolis MN 55404-2455

OLSON, EDGAR, state legislator; b. Nov. 19, 1937; m. Phyllis Olson; 2 children. Degree, N.D. State U. Mem. Minn. Ho. of Reps. St. Paul, 1984—; mem. taxes, agr., local govt. and met. affairs coms., others; farmer. Democrat. Home: RR 3 Box 99 Fosston MN 56542-9546*

OLSON, EDWARD WARREN, county official; b. Red Bank, N.J., Dec. 24, 1946; s. John Theodore and Hulda Gertrude (Millington) O.; m. Linda Gay Gerhart, June 22, 1974 (div. Oct. 1994); children: Kurt Lars, Stephen Todd, Douglas Edward. BA, Ohio U., 1969; postgrad., Ohio No. U., 1972-74, 75, Ohio State U., 1991-92. Account rep. Investors Diversified Svcs., Inc., Lima, Ohio, 1974-75; communications cons. United Telephone Co. of Ohio, Lima, 1976-80; data communications product mgr. United Telephone Co. of Ohio, Mansfield, 1980-85; county commr. Richland County Ohio, Mansfield, 1985—. Bd. dirs. United Way of Richland County, Mansfield, 1987-94, Richland Econ. Devel. Corp., Mansfield, 1986-91; chmn. Richland County Records Commn., Mansfield, 1986-90; chmn. Dist. 16 Ohio Pub. Works Commn., 1988—; treas., exec. com. Richland County Rep. Party, Mansfield, 1988-94; adv. bd. Salvation Army, 1988—, chmn., 1994-95. Mem. County Commrs. Assn. Ohio (trustee 1986-88), Res. Officers Assn. (life) (state pres. 1980-81, nat. jr. v.p. for USN 1981-82). Republican. Home: 419 W 3rd St Mansfield OH 44903-1745 Office: Richland County Bd Commrs 50 Park Ave E Mansfield OH 44902-1850

OLSON, ERIK RICHARD, chemistry educator; b. Bellefonte, Pa., Sept. 8, 1964; s. Robert C. and Margaret L. (Strobel) O.; m. Renee M. Bauer, Oct. 24, 1992. BA, Juniata Coll., 1987; PhD, Dartmouth Coll., 1993. Postdoctoral rsch. assoc. U. Notre Dame, Ind., 1993-94; asst. prof. chemistry

Upper Iowa U., Fayette, 1994—. Contbr. articles to profl. jours. Recipient Wolfenden tching. award, Dartmouth Coll. Dept. Chemistry, Hanover, N.H., 1991. Mem. AAUP, Am. Chem. Soc. Democrat. Lutheran. Office: Upper Iowa U. 605 S Washington St Fayette IA 52142

OLSON, ERNESTINE LEE, nurse; b. Gregory, S.D., Oct. 14, 1952; d. Ervin E. and Nila Lee (Ritterbush) Neiman; divorced; children: Nathan, Candice. BSN, U. Nebr., 1974. RN, Nebr. Charge nurse Perkins County Hosp., Grant, Nebr.; mem. Gov.'s Rural Health Task Force, Region II Mental Health Adv. Com.; instr. CPR. Recipient Writing award Am. Jour. Nursing, 1984, Woman of Distinction award Girl Scouts Am., 1995. Mem. ANA, VFW, Nebr. Nurses Assn. (continuing edn. reviewer), Am. Heart Assn., Am. Legion Aux. (chmn. unit 40 Girls State), Am. Cancer Soc. S.W. Regional SIDS Coun. Mennonite. Home: 976 Garfield Box 312 Grant NE 69140 Office: 900 Lincoln Ave Grant NE 69140

OLSON, GARY DUANE, college administrator, history educator; b. Spring Grove, Minn., July 30, 1939; s. Raymond G. and Ethel N. (Storlie) O.; m. Rosaaen Marie Skifton, Sept. 4, 1960; children—Erik Lee, Timothy Karl, Lars Christian. B.A., Luther Coll., 1961; M.A., U. Nebr., 1965, Ph.D., 1968. Social studies tchr. Kerkhoven Pub. Schs., Minn., 1961-63; asst. prof. history Augustana Coll., Sioux Falls, S.D., 1968-73, assoc prof., 1973-79, prof., 1979—, dean academic services, 1981-87, v.p. acad. affairs, dean, 1987-95; cons., evaluator North Ctrl Assn., 1992—. Author: (with H. Krause) Prelude to Glory, 1974, (with E. L. Olson) Sioux Falls, South Dakota: A Pictorial History, 1985; contbr. articles to profl. jours. Mem. S.D. Hist. Soc., Vesterheim Mus. Assn., Norwegian-Am. Hist. Soc. Lutheran. Avocation: woodworking. Home: 2505 S Main Ave Sioux Falls SD 57105-4820 Office: Augustana Coll Augustana Coll Sioux Falls SD 57197

OLSON, GEN, state legislator; b. May 20, 1938. BS in Edn. with distinction, U. Minn., EdD. Mayor Minnetrista, Minn., 1981-82; mem. Minn. State Senate, 1983—. Former mem. Park and Recreation Commn., Planning and Zoning Commn., Police Commn., City Council. Republican. Office: Minn State Senate State Capitol Building Saint Paul MN 55155-1606

OLSON, JAMES ALLEN, biochemist, educator; b. Mpls., Oct. 10, 1924; s. Ralph William and Minnie Azalea (Holtin) O.; m. Giovanna F. Del Nero, Dec. 10, 1953; children: Daniel, Lisa, Eric. BS, Gustavus Adolphus Coll., 1946; PhD, Harvard U., 1952; Doctor Honoris Causa, U. Ghent, Belgium, 1988. Postdoctoral fellow NIH, Rome, 1952-54; rsch. assoc. Harvard U., Cambridge, Mass., 1954-56; from asst. prof. to prof. U. Fla. Coll. Medicine, Gainesville, 1956-66; prof., chmn. dept. biochemistry Mahidol U., Bangkok, 1966-74; prof. biomed. sci. dept. biochemistry U. Bahia, Salvador, Brazil, 1974-75; prof., chmn. dept. biochemistry Iowa State U., Ames, 1975-85, disting. prof. dept. biochemistry, 1984—; cons. NIH, Bethesda, Md., NSF, Washington, other agys. and industries; plenary lectr. FAOBMB, 1994, European Retinoid lectr., 1993. Editor: Modern Nutrition in Health and Disease, 1989—; contbr. over 350 articles and revs. to profl. jours. Lt. USN, 1942-44. Named Atwater Meml. Lectr., 1992, Wellcome Lectr. Burroughs-Wellcome Co., 1991, Kullavanijaya Lectr., U. Leeds, 1990; recipient Disting. Alumni Citation Gustavus Adolphus Coll., 1973, Disting. Svc. award Mahidol U., 1975. Fellow Am. Inst. Nutrition (pres. 1986-87, Borden award 1989); mem. Soc. Exptl. Biology (councilor 1989-92). Office: Iowa State U Dept Biochemistry Biophysics Ames IA 50011

OLSON, JOHN MICHAEL, lawyer; b. Grafton, N.D., Feb. 9, 1947; s. Clifford Inguold and Alice M. (Schwandt) O.; children: Dana Michel, Kirsten Lee. BA, Concordia Coll., Moorhead, Minn., 1969; JD, U. N.D., 1972. Bar: N.D. 1972. Asst. atty. gen. N.D. Atty. Gen.'s Office, Bismarck, 1972-74; state's atty. Burleigh County, Bismarck, 1974-82; pvt. practice Bismarck, 1983-91; mem. 49th dist. N.D. Senate, Bismarck, 1983-91, minority leader, 1987-91; ptnr. Olson Cichy Bismarck, Bismarck, 1994—, Olson Cichy Attys., Bismarck, 1994—. Recipient Disting. Svc. award N.D. Peace Officers Assn., 1981, Outstanding Bismarcker award Bismarck Jaycees, 1981. Mem. N.D. Bar Assn. Republican. Lutheran. Office: 115 N 4th St Bismarck ND 58501

OLSON, KEITH RAYMOND, clergyman; b. Peoria, Ill., Sept. 1, 1943; s. Raymond P. and Kathleen M. (Rodems) O.; m. Helen Mary Griffin; 1 child, Colleen M. MA in Theology, St. Louis U., 1969; MDiv, Kenrick Sem., 1969. Assoc. pastor St. Paul Ch., Danville, Ill., 1969-72, Grace United Meth. Ch., Decatur, Ill., 1972-73, First United Meth. ch., Monmouth, Ill., 1973-76; pastor Ellsworth (Ill.) United Meth. Ch. & Cooksville Union, 1976-84, Trinity United Meth. Ch., Crawfordsville, Ind., 1984-88, Amity United Meth. Ch., Greenfield, Ind., 1988-89, Centenary United Meth. Ch., New Albany, Ind., 1989-94; assoc. pastor Meridian St. United Meth. Ch., Indpls., 1994-95; pastor Forest Park United Meth. Ch., Ft. Wayne, Ind., 1995—. Home: 1827 Florida Dr Fort Wayne IN 46805 Office: Forest Park United Meth Ch 2100 Kentucky Ave Fort Wayne IN 46805

OLSON, LYNN, sculptor, painter, writer; b. Chgo., Mar. 23, 1952; s. Ellen (Nelson) Olson. instr. direct cement sculpture workshops Montoya Art Studios, West Palm Beach, Fla., 1988-89, Alta. Sculptors Assn., Edmonton, Can., 1990, Mendocino (Calif.) Art Ctr., 1992-93, Sierra Nev. Coll. at Lake Tahoe, Incline Village, 1993, Lighthouse Art Ctr., Crescent City, Calif., 1990-96, Elisabet Ney Sculpture Conservatory, Austin, Tex., 1995, Tarrant County Jr. Coll., Ft. Worth, 1995. Prin. works include Good Shepherd, Ch. Good Shepherd, Albion, Ind., Kneeling Figure, Manta Ray. World of Concrete, Addison, Ill., Rose, Carter Meml., Chesterton, Ind., Redwood Tree, Lighthouse Art Ctr., Crescent Cuty, Calif., George Bartholomew Meml., Bellefontaine, Ohio, Color Concerto, Purdue U., Hammond, Ind., Continuity III, Tower East, Shaker Heights, Ohio, Aluma Beam, Aluma Corp., Toronto; author, pub.: Sculpting with Cement, 1981-95; contbr. over 50 articles to mags. Mem. Am. Concrete Inst. (com. 124 concrete aesthetics). Home and Office: Steelstone 4607 Claussen Ln Valparaiso IN 46383

OLSON, LYNNETTE GAIL, personnel executive; b. Omaha, Oct. 9, 1945; d. Norman Lester and Harriet Grace (Carlson) Skillman; m. Gary Allen Olson, Aug. 1, 1964 (div. Oct. 1972); 1 child, Michael John. BA, Augustana Coll., 1980. Legal sec. May, Johnson, Doyle & Becker PC, Sioux Falls, S.D., 1963-76; benefits mgr. Raven Industries, Inc., Sioux Falls, 1980-87, Midcontinent Media, Inc., Mpls., 1987-95; dir. benefits, 1995—. Bd. dirs. Cornerstone Advocacy Svcs., Inc. (chair human resources com., benefits com., exec. com.). Mem. Soc. for Human Resource Mgmt., Midwest Pension Conf., Twin Cities Pers. Assn., Minn. C. of C. (comm. com.), Rotary (Bloomington, Minn.). Republican. Home: 8149 Curtis Ln Eden Prairie MN 55347-1117 Office: Midcontinent Media Inc 7900 Xerxes Ave S Ste 1100 Minneapolis MN 55431-1104

OLSON, MARK, state legislator; b. July 1955. Mem. Minn. Ho. of Reps. St. Paul, 1993—; carpenter. Republican. Home: 17085 142nd St SE Big Lake MN 55309-8925*

OLSON, MAURICE ALAN, state legislator; b. Pierpont, S.D., Apr. 8, 1926; s. Olen Enger Olson and Alice Marie Moe; m. Mildred Aileen Erickson, 1950; children: Debra Ann, Cynthia Ruth, Barbara Louise, Jerald Keith, Ronald Mark. Student, Augustana Coll., S.D., 1948-49. Precinct committeeman Egeland Precinct, S.D., 1960-64; pres. Day County Dem. Com., 1966-70; mem. S.D. Ho. of Reps., 1970-82, 93—, mem. comm. and transp. coms.; mem. exec. bd. S.D. Legis. Rsch. Coun., 1973-76; dir. Lake Area Hosp. Corp., 1984—; owner, operator Comml. Grain & Livestock Farm. Mem. Nat. Farmers Union, Nat. Farmers Orgn. Home: 610 E 3rd St Webster SD 57274-1503*

OLSON, MEL, state legislator. Mem. S.D. State Senate, mem. edn. and state affairs coms.; tchr. Home: 600 W 3rd Ave Mitchell SD 57301-2434*

OLSON, PAUL BUXTON, retired social studies, marketing, and business educator; b. Waterloo, Iowa, Feb. 5, 1937; s. Ethan Sidney and Esther May Olson; m. Jean Elaine Rinehart, Aug. 18, 1962 (div. 1993); children: Brent Sidney, Kimberly Jean, Julie Elaine. BA cum laude, Tarkio Coll., 1958; MEd, U. Mo., 1966; EdS, U. No. Iowa, 1975. Tchr. bus. edn. Riverton/Farragut Cmty. Schs., 1962-68; mktg. and distributive edn. tchr. Mason City (Iowa) Cmty. Schs., 1968-96, ret., 1996; adj. instr. mktg. No. Iowa Area C.C., Mason City, 1969-89. Bd. dirs. Jr. Achievement, 1970-88; layspkr. Meth. Ch. Served with U.S. Army, 1960-62. Named Outstanding Distributive Edn. Tchr., Iowa Distributive Edn. Tchrs. Assn., 1978, 89, to Mktg. Edn. Hall of Fame, 1985; recipient Leadership award Jr. Achievement, 1977, Writer's award Interstate Distributive Edn. Curriculum Consortium, 1975. Mem. NEA (life del. rep. 1963, 67, 93, 94), Am. Vocat. Assn. (life), Nat. Bus. Edn. Assn., Mktg. Edn. Assn. (life), Distributive Edn. Clubs Am., Iowa State Edn. Assn., Iowa Mktg. Educators (rep., 1967, 68, 93, sec./treas., pres.-elect 1986-87, pres. 1987-88, 20 yrs. svc. plague 1989), Iowa Bus. Edn. Assn. (rep.), Iowa Vocat. Assn. (rep.), Mason City Edn. Assn. (past treas., v.p., pres. elect 1992-93, pres. 1993-94, past pres. 1994-95), Delta Pi Epsilon (past treas.), Phi Delta Kappa (life, charter, past historian, pres. 1995-96). Republican. Methodist. Lodge: Sons of Norway (hist. 1994, 95). Home: 610 Briarstone Dr # 21 Mason City IA 50401

OLSON, RICHARD GOTTLIEB, nuclear engineer; b. Terre Haute, Ind., Dec. 17, 1922; s. Gottlieb William and Lucille Adella (Clifton) O.; m. Virginia Ann Abbinett, June 22, 1947; children: Stephen Philip, Mary Ann. BSEE, Rose-Hulman Inst., Terre Haute, 1947; MSE, U. Mich., 1955; postgrad., U. Mass., 1970. Control and kinetics mgr. Atomic Power Devel. Assn., Inc., Detroit, 1955-64; supr. computer facilities and tng. Power Reactor Devel. Co., Detroit, 1959-67; tech. work leader Detroit Edison, 1965-83, sr. nuclear fuel engr., 1982-89, ret., 1989; instr. electrical engring. and math Rose Hulman Inst., Terre Haute, 1946-49, Wayne State U., Detroit, 1949-76; instr. computer devel. Cass Tech. High Sch., Detroit, 1960-70. Author: Dynamics of Fast Breeder Reactor, 1956 (Nucleonics award 1957), Instrumentation and Control, 1962 (Am. Nuclear Soc. award 1962). Mem. citizen's adv. com. Dearborn Bd. Edn., 1956-70. Sgt. U.S. Army, 1942-46, ETO, PTO, Korea. U. Mich. fellow, 1954, NSF fellow, 1970. Mem. IEEE (Svc. award 1954), Am. Nuclear Soc. (Svc. award 1966), Assn. for Computing Machines (Svc. award 1968), Tau Beta Pi. Home: 3501 Hipp St Dearborn MI 48124-3815

OLSON, RONALD A., parks and recreation administrator; b. Mpls., Dec. 24, 1948; 1 child, Erika. BS, U. Minn.; MA, Ind. U. Dir. parks and recreation City of Ann Arbor, Mich. Mem. Nat. Recreation and Park Assn. (cert. leisure profl., bd. dirs. 1989, 91, program com.), Mich. Recreation and Park Assn. (pub. affairs com. 1989-94, Innovative Program award 1988, 89, Innovative Park Resource award 1988, 95), Mich. Mcpl. League, Nat. League of Cities. Office: Ann Arbor Parks & Recreation Dept 100 N Fifth Ave Ann Arbor MI 48107

OLSON, ROY ARTHUR, government official; b. Ashland, Wis., Dec. 8, 1938; s. Elof Herman and Beatrice Lorraine (Dolezal) O.; m. Elisabeth Rigge Behrens, June 24, 1967; children—Heather Elisabeth, Peter Roy. B.S., Northwestern U., 1960. Lic. real estate salesman, Ill. Writer, editor Chgo. Am., 1956-68; pres. Roy Olson Pub. Relations Co., Oak Park, Ill., 1968-70; asst. regional adminstr. SBA, Chgo., 1970-95; Chgo. spkesman Ill. Dept. Transp., 1995—; dir. Am. Food Industries, Chgo., Covenant Village Retirement Ctr., Northbrook, Ill., 1975-81, Brandel Care Ctr., Northbrook, 1975-81. Chmn. Northbrook Covenant Ch., 1980-81. Mem. Soc. Profl. Journalists, Art Inst. Chgo., City Club (media com.), Execs. Club, Chgo. Press Club, Chgo. Headline Club (past dir. 1964-66), Northwestern Club. Home: 2015 Prairie St Glenview IL 60025-2824 Office: Ameritech 310 S Michigan Chicago IL 60604

OLSON, RUE EILEEN, librarian; b. Chgo., Nov. 1, 1928; d. Paul H. and Martha M. (Fick) Meyers; m. Richard L. Olson, July 18, 1964; children: Catherine, Karen. Student Herzl Coll., 1946-48, Northwestern U., 1948-50, Ill. State U., 1960-64, Middle Mgmt. Inst. Spl. Librs. Assn., 1985-87. Acct. Ill. Farm Supply Co., Chgo., 1948-59; asst. libr. Ill. Agrl. Assn., Bloomington, 1960-66, libr., 1966-86, dir. libr. svcs., 1986—; bd. dirs. Corn Belt Libr. System, 1989-94, sec., 1991—. Mem. area Com. Nat. Libr. Week, 1971, area steering com., 1972; mem. steering com. Illinet/OCLC, 1985-87; mem. adv. council of librs. Grad. Sch. Libr. Sci. U. Ill., 1976-79; mem. Ill. State Libr. Adv. Com. for Interlibr. Cooperation, 1979-80; del. Ill. White House Conf. on Libr. and Info. Svcs., 1978; coordinator Vita Income Tax Assistance, Bloomington, Ill., 1986-89, preparer 1978—. Mem. Am., Ill., McLean County (pres. 1970-71) Libr. Assns., Spl. Librs. Assn. (pres. Ill. chpt. 1977-78, first to be named Disting. Mem. food, agr. and nutrition div. 1989), Ill. OCLC Users Group (treas. 1988-90, bd. dirs. 1991-92), Internat. Assn. Agrl. Librs. and Documentalists, Am. Soc. Info. Sci., Am. Mgmt. Assn., USAIN, Mended Hearts, Inc. (sec. Ill. chpt. 250 1994-95, v.p. 1995—, newsletter editor, 1994—), Zonta (pres. 1987-89), Bloomington Club. Office: Ill Agrl Assn 1701 N Towanda Ave Bloomington IL 61701

OLSON, SCOTT, company executive; b. St. Paul, Jan. 25, 1954. V.p. mktg. Dytec, St. Paul, 1976-93; pres. Edutec Inc., St. Paul, 1993—. Author: Barcode Master Plan, 1993; contbr. over 30 articles to profl. jours. Scout leader Cub Scouts, Lake Elmo, Minn., 1994—. Mem. Assn. for Mfg. Excellence (regional pres. 1991—, Outstanding Achievement award 1992), Automatic Identification Mfr. (com., vice chair 1989—, Top 10 Prodr. 1992). Lutheran. Home: 4150 Irish Ct N Lake Elmo MN 55042-9408 Office: Edutec Inc 1336 Energy Park Dr Saint Paul MN 55108-5202

OLSON, WALTER L., agricultural engineer; b. Junction City, Kans., June 10, 1920; s. Swen Daniel and Mary (Engstrom) O.; m. Martha Frances Shelton, Nov. 12, 1945 (div. Jan. 1981); 1 child, Daniel Lee; m. Gladys Lou Sexton Alexander, Nov. 22, 1981. BS in Agrl. Engring., Kans. State U., 1949. Agrl. engr. U.S. Soil Conservation Svc., Ft. Scott, Kans., 1949-55; equipment mgr. U.S. Soil Conservation Svc., Washington, 1955-62; landscape architect NASA, Beltsville, Md., 1962-70; engr. Schoff & Auchard, A&E, Council Grove, Kans., 1983-84; asst. city engr. City of Junction City, 1985—. 1st lt. U.S. Army, 1942-45, ETO. Home: 1922 Sunflower Dr Junction City KS 66441 Office: City Engr 702 N Jefferson St Junction City KS 66441

OLSON, WALTER STEVEN, psychologist, educator; b. Chgo., July 1, 1941; s. Walter and Ann (Ward) O. m. Susan Zigann, Aug. 1967 (div. 1977); children: James, David; m. Karen Rosenstein, Apr. 15, 1984 (div. 1993); m. Ivette Ramos, Aug. 22, 1993; 1 child, Andres. BS, No. Ill. U., 1965; MS, Chgo. State U., 1968; PhD, Calif. Western U., 1981. Lic. sch. psychologist, Ill.; nat. cert. sch. psychologist. Counselor Chgo. Bd. Edn., 1968-69, psychologist, 1969—; psychologist, therapist Family Counseling Svc., Chgo., 1969-91; adj. faculty U. Sarasota, Fla., 1991—; practicum supv. Gov. State U., 1991—; cons. Dept. Corrections and Criminal Justice, Chgo. State U., 1969-90; adv. bd. Chgo. Metro Wk. Release Program, 1988-89, Chgo. State U. Dept. Criminal Justice, 1988-90. Co-author: Children, Psychology and the Schools, 1970; author TV study guide for ednl. psychology, 1972; co-author internship guide for coorections and criminal justice, 1988. Mem. nat. Assn. Sch. Psychologists, Ill. Sch. Psychologists Assn., Chgo. Assn. Sch. Psychologists, Learning Disability Assn. Am., Coun. for Exceptional Children (mental retardation div.). Office: Piccolo Middle Sch 1040 N Keeler Ave Chicago IL 60651-3507

OLSON-HELLERUD, LINDA KATHRYN, elementary school educator; b. Wisconsin Rapids, Wis., Aug. 26, 1947; d. Samuel Ellsworth and Lillian (Dvorak) Olson; m. H. A. Hellerud, 1979; BS, U. Wis.-Stevens Point, 1969, teaching cert., 1970, MST, 1972; postgrad. U. Wis. at Madison, 1969-70; MS, U. Wis. Whitewater, 1975; EdS, U. Wis.-Stout, 1978; cert. k-12 reading tchr. and specialist. Clk., Univ. Counseling Ctr., U. Wis., Stevens Point, 1965-69; elementary sch. tchr., Wisconsin Rapids, 1970-76, sch. counselor, 1976-79, dist. elem. guidance dir., 1979-82, elem. and reading tchr., 1982—, also cons.; advocate Moravian Ch. Sunday sch. Mem. NEA, Wisconsin Rapids Edn. Assn., Internat. Reading Assn., Wis. Reading Assn., Ctrl. Wis. Reading Assn., Wis. State Hist. Soc., Wood County Hist. Soc., Wood County Literacy Coun. (cons.). Mem. United Ch. of Christ.Avocations: gardening, piano. Home: 120 11th St N Wisconsin Rapids WI 54494-4548 Office: Howe Elem Sch Wisconsin Rapids WI 54494

OLSTON, MARY KAY, school psychologist; b. Milw., Oct. 27, 1949; d. Gordon Rhodes and Mary Anne (Popp) O. BA, Carroll Coll., Waukesha, Wis., 1970; MS, U. Wis., 1971. Assoc. sch. psychologist Milw. Pub. Sch., 1971-74, sch. psychologist, 1974—; cons. U. Wis., 1973-76. Mem. APA, Milw. Area Psychol. Assoc. (treas. 1982-84), Alliance Française de Milw. (libr. 1980-82), Double Click, Milw. Webmasters. Home: 10541 W Wood-ward Ave Wauwatosa WI 53222-2365 Office: EESS Ctr 6620 W Capitol Dr Milwaukee WI 53216-2040

OLT, JOHN EDWARD, insurance agent; b. Dayton, Ohio, Aug. 13, 1913; s. Oscar Cleveland and Edna Victoria (Euchenhofer) O.; m. Jane Gray, Sept. 17, 1938; children: Nancy Jane Olt Healy, John Gray, Mary Lynn Olt Blake. BA, Denison U., 1935. Mem. staff Oscar C. Olt Co., Dayton, 1935-40; ptnr. Olt Ins. Co., Dayton, 1940—. Team capt. Community Chest, Dayton, 1938-39; fundraiser for local hosps., Dayton, 1940-50; sec. Dayton Assn. Ins. Agts., 1936-43, pres., 1948; nat. pres. Soc. of Alumni Denison U., Granville, Ohio, 1959. Mem. Kiwanis (bd. dirs. Dayton club 1955), Junto Club of Dayton (pres. 1943), Dayton Racquet Club, Phi Beta Kappa, Phi Gamma Delta. Republican. Episcopalian. Home: 121 E Schantz Ave Dayton OH 45409-2222 Office: Olt Ins Co 604 American Bldg Dayton OH 45402

OLVER, ELWOOD FORREST, retired agricultural engineering educator; b. Connelsville, Pa., Apr. 10, 1922; s. F. Emmett and Edith Mabel (Van Wert) O.; m. Miriam Jones, May 6, 1944; children: Deanne Elizabeth Braden, Thomas Wesley, Larry Scott. BS in agrl. engring., Pa. State U., 1943, MS, 1949; PhD, Iowa State U., 1957. Registered profl. engr., Ill., Pa. Rural engr. Pa. Power and Light Co., Williamsport, 1946-48; asst. prof. Pa. State U., Univ. Park, 1948-50, assoc. prof., 1952-57, dir. security, 1957-60; ednl. dir. Iowa Rural Elec. Coop. Assn., Des Moines, 1950-52; assoc. prof., prof. U. Ill., Urbana, 1960-82, group leader edn. team to India, 1967-69, head electric power & processing Divsn. Agrl. Engring., 1970-80, asst. dean, 1985-87; mgr. energy farms U.S. Dept. Energy, Washington, 1980-82; field advisor U.S. Dept. Energy, Urbana, 1982-84; cons. U.S. Dept. Agriculture, 1977-78; engring. cons., Urbana, 1984-85. Author: Agricultural Education in Developing Countries, 1977; co-author: Engineering Applications in Agriculture, 1964. 2d lt. USAAF, 1943-46. Recipient Merit award Ill. Farm Electrification Coun., Urbana, 1977. Fellow Agrl. Engring. Soc.; mem. Phi Kappa Phi, Gamma Sigma Delta, Sigma Xi. Republican. Methodist. Home: 402 Burkwood Ct Urbana IL 61801

O'MALLEY, PATRICIA, critical care nurse; b. Boston, May 13, 1955; d. Peter and Catherine (Dwyer) O'M. BSN, Coll. Mt. St. Joseph, Cin., 1977; MS, Ohio State U., 1984, postgrad., 1990—. Cert. critical care nurse. Primary nurse critical care unit Miami Valley Hosp., Dayton, Ohio, nurse educator, clin. nurse specialist, cons.; adj. faculty Wright State U., Dayton. Contbr. articles to profl. jours., textbooks. Recipient honors Dayton Area Heart Assn., Ohio Ho. of Reps., 1994, Ohio Dept. Health, 1996. Mem. AACN (bd. dirs. Dayton-Miami Valley), Soc. Critical Care Medicine, Sigma Theta Tau. Office: Miami Valley Hosp 1 Wyoming St Dayton OH 45409-2722

O'MALLEY, PATRICK J., state legislator. BS, Purdue U., MS; JD, John Marshall Law Sch. Mem. Ill. State Senate from 18th dist. Trustee Moraine Valley C.C.; pres. Palos Fire Protection Dist., Ill.; active Am. Cancer Soc., Vietnam Vets. Leadership Program, Coletta's of Ill. Found. Mem. Southwest Bar Assn., Chgo. Bar Assn. Republican. Home: 12744 S 87th Ave Palos Park IL 60464-1868*

O'MARA, JOHN ALOYSIUS, bishop; b. Buffalo, Nov. 17, 1924; s. John Aloysius and Anna Theresa (Schenck) O'M. Student, St. Augustine's Sem., Toronto, Ont., Can., 1944-51; J.C.L., St. Thomas U., Rome, 1953. Ordained priest Roman Catholic Ch., 1951; mem. chancery Archdiocese of Toronto, 1953-69; pres., rector St. Augustine's Sem., Toronto, 1969-75; pastor St. Lawrence Parish, Scarboro, Ont., 1975-76; bishop Diocese of Thunder Bay, Ont., 1976-94, Diocese of St. Catharines, Ont., 1994—; St. Catharines, 1994—; pres. Ont. Conf. Cath. Bishops, 1986-92. Bd. dirs. Ont. Hosp. Assn., 1961-65, Cath. Ch. Extension Soc. Can.; mem. Ont. Hosp. Services Commn., 1964-69. Named hon. prelate of Papal Household with title monsignor, 1954. Mem. Cath. Ch. Ext. Soc. (bd. dirs. 1992-96). Address: 122 Riverdale Rd, Saint Catharines, ON Canada L2R 4C2

O'MARA, MARILYN MAE, communications executive; b. Willoughby, Ohio, Nov. 15, 1942; d. Peter Milan and Mildred (Babic) Aleksic; m. Richard James O'Mara, Feb. 16, 1963 (div. Feb. 1982); children: Kimberly Ann, Richard James Jr. Student, Oakland Community Coll., 1974-81, Am. Inst. Banking, 1973-77, St. Mary's Coll., 1983-87. Finger print clk. U.S. Dept. Justice FBI, Washington, 1962; sales clk. Sears, Roebuck, & Co., Jacksonville, Fla., 1962-63; asst. mgr. Community Nat. Bank, Pontiac, Mich., 1969-78; office mgr. State Farm Ins. Co., Waterford, Mich., 1978-84; sales sec. Guardian Alarm Co., Detroit, 1984-85; office mgr. Jack McCarthy Restaurant, West Bloomfield, Mich., 1985-86; escrow sec. Conselyea Realtor, Royal Oak, Mich., 1986-87; ins. sec. Meemic Life Ins., Birmingham, Mich., 1987; telemarketing supr. Guest House Hosp., Lake Orion, Mich., 1987-90; field mgr. Internat. Edn. Forum, Clarkston, Mich., 1991-92; postal carrier U.S. Post Office, 1992-93; field mgr. Pace Internat., Independence, Mich., 1993-94; scheduling supt. Sr. Vision Care, Clawson, Mich., 1994-96; adminstrv. asst. Nissho Iwai, Southfield, 1996—. Trustee Waterform Dem. Group, 1985-88, del. fin. com., 1985-88, pres. Orchard Lake Ladies Aux., 1987-88, sec. nat. chpt., 1987-88; area coord. Internat. Edn. Forum, 1989-90; treas. chpt. Parents Without Ptnrs., Waterford, 1993-94, treas. ea. Mich. regional coun., 1994-95. also: PO Box 738 Royal Oak MI 48068

OMDAHL, BECKY LYNN, communications educator; b. Bismarck, N.D., July 17, 1958; d. Lloyd B. and Ruth E. (Jones) O. BS, Moorhead State U., 1980; MA, U. Wis., Milw., 1983; PhD, U. Wis., Madison, 1991. Info. officer Minn. State Coun. for Handicapped, St. Paul, 1981; teaching asst. U. Wis., Milw., 1982; start-up pub. rels. asst. Hamilton Test Systems, Milw., 1984; human resource asst. Milw. Med. Clinic, S.C., 1984; teaching asst. U. Wis., Madison, 1985-88, project asst., 1988-89, lectr. communication, 1989-90; lectr. SUNY, Buffalo, 1990-91, asst. prof., 1991-92; asst. prof. U. Minn., Mpls., 1992—. Author: Cognitive Appraisal, Emotion, and Empathy. Named one of Outstanding Young Women of Am., 1984. Mem. Internat. Communication Assn. (Outstanding Teaching award 1989, various awards for papers), Speech Communication Assn. (Outstanding Dissertation award 1992), Internat. Network on Personal Relationships. Democrat. Office: U Minn Dept Speech Communication 460 Folwell Hall 9 Pleasant St SE Minneapolis MN 55455-0194

O'MEARA, JOHN F., lawyer; b. Chgo., Apr. 14, 1936; s. John J. and Mary (Joyce) O'M.; children: Marcia A. Hiehle, John A., Timothy D. BS, Loyola U., 1959; JD, Northwestern U., 1960. Bar: Ill. 1961, U.S. Dist. Ct. (no. dist.) Ill. 1964, U.S. Ct. Appeals (7th cir.) 1992. Assoc., ptnr. Lord, Bissell & Brook, Chgo., 1961-74; atty. pvt. practice, Chgo. and Park Ridge, Ill, 1975—; instr. John Marshall Sch. Law, Chgo., 1966-71. Author: Tort Liability of Illinois Land Occupiers, 1968. Bd. dirs. St. Mary of Angels, 1987—; founder, officer Ind. Precinct Orgn., Chgo., 1969-71. With U.S. Army Res., 1960-66. Mem. Holy Name Soc. Roman Catholic. Office: 123 S Northwest Hwy Park Ridge IL 60068

O'MEARA, PATRICK O., political science educator; b. Cape Town, South Africa, Jan. 7, 1938; came to U.S., 1964; s. Daniel and Fiorina (Allorto) O'M. B.A., U. Capetown, 1960; M.A., Ind. U., 1966, Ph.D., 1970. Dep. dir. African studies program, asst. prof. polit. sci. Ind. U., Bloomington, 1970-72, dir. African studies program, 1972—, assoc. prof. polit. sci. and pub. and environ. affairs, 1972-81, prof. polit. sci. and pub. and environ. affairs, 1981—, dean office of internat. programs, 1993—; cons. in field. Author: Rhodesia: Racial Conflict or Coexistance?, 1975; editor: (with Gwendolen M. Carter) Southern Africa in Crisis, 1977, African Independence: The First Twenty-Five Years, 1985, Southern Africa: The Continuing Crisis, 1979, International Politics in Southern Africa, 1982 (with Phyllis M. Martin) Africa, 1977, 2d edit. 1986, 3d edit. 1995, (with C.R. Halisi and Brian Winchester) Revolutions of the Late Twentieth Century, 1991; contbr. articles to profl. jours., book chpts. Mem. African Studies Assn., Pi Alpha Alpha. Roman Catholic. Office: Ind U Woodburn Hall # 211 Bloomington IN 47405

OMMODT, DONALD HENRY, dairy company executive; b. Flom, Minn., July 7, 1931; s. Henry and Mabel B. (Kvidt) O.; m. Evelyn Mavis Blilie, June 15, 1957; children—Linette, Kevin, Lee, Jodi. Student, Interstate Bus. Coll., Fargo, N.D. Acct. Farmers State Bank, Waubun, Minn., 1950-53; chief acct.

Cass-Clay Creamery, Inc., Fargo, 1953-61, office mgr., 1961-65, gen. mgr., 1965-83, pres., 1983—. Pres. Messiah Luth. Ch., Fargo, 1976-78; mem. Minn. Dairy Task Force Com., 1988-90; bd. dirs. Communicating for Agr., Fergus Falls, Minn., 1977-80, Blue Cross of N.D., Fargo, 1971-88. Recipient Builder of the Valley award Minn. Red River Valley Devel. Assn., 1991, N.D. Milky Way award, 1993. Mem. N.D. Dairy Industries Assn. (bd. dirs., past pres.), Am. Dairy Assn. (bd. dirs. N.D. 1970-80), N.D. Dairy Product Promotion Commn. (bd. dirs. 1970-80), Messiah Found. Christian Communications (pres. 1987—), Moorhead C. of C. Office: Cass-Clay Creamery Inc 1220 Main Ave # 2947 Fargo ND 58103-8201

O'MORCHOE, CHARLES CHRISTOPHER CREAGH, administrator, anatomical sciences educator; b. Quetta, India, May 7, 1931; came to U.S., 1968; s. Nial Francis C. and Jessie Elizabeth (Joly) O'M.; m. Patricia Jean Richardson, Sept. 15, 1955; children: Charles Eric Creagh, David James Creagh. B.A., Trinity Coll., Dublin (Ireland) U., 1953, M.B., B.Ch., B.A.O., 1955, M.A., 1959, M.D., 1961, Ph.D., 1969, Sc.D., 1981. Resident Halifax Gen. Hosp., U.K., 1955-57; lectr. in anatomy Sch. Medicine Trinity Coll., Dublin (Ireland) U., 1957-61, 63-65, lectr. in physiology, 1966-67, assoc. prof. in physiology, 1967-68; instr. in anatomy Harvard Med. Sch., Boston, 1962-63; vis. prof. physiology U. Md. Sch. Medicine, Balt., 1961-62, assoc. prof. anatomy, 1968-71, prof. anatomy, 1971-74; chmn. anatomy bd. State of Md., 1971-73; prof., chmn. dept. anatomy Stritch Sch. Medicine Loyola U., Maywood, Ill., 1974-84; dean Coll. Medicine, U. Ill., Urbana-Champaign, 1984—, prof. anat. scis. and surgery, 1984—; WHO cons., vis. prof. physiology Jaipur, India, 1967, S.M.S. Med. Coll., U. Rajasthan, vis. prof. anatomy, 1971. Assoc. editor: Anatomical Record, 1978—, Am. Jour. Anatomy, 1987-91; contbr. articles to profl. jours. Elected fellow Trinity Coll., Dublin U., 1966; named faculty mem. of yr. Loyola U., Chgo., 1982. Mem. AMA, Am. Soc. Nephrology, N.Am. Soc. Lymphology (v.p. 1982-84, pres. 1984-86, sec. 1993—, Cecil K. Drinker award 1992), Am. Assn. Anatomy Chairmen (emeritus), Am. Assn. Anatomists (dir. placement svc. 1981-91), Internat. Soc. Lymphology (exec. com. 1987—, pres. 1993-95), Ill. State Med. Soc., Champaign County Med. Soc., Alpha Omega Alpha. Mem. Church of Ireland. Home: 2709 Holcomb Dr Urbana IL 61802 Office: U Ill Coll Medicine 190 Med Scis Bldg 506 S Mathews Ave Urbana IL 61802

OMTVEDT, IRVIN THOMAS, academic administrator, educator; b. Rice Lake, Wis., June 12, 1935; s. Thomas and Irene M. (Nelson) O.; m. Wanda Ruth Rank, Aug. 15, 1959; children: Mark, Penny. BS in Agr., U. Wis., Madison, 1957; MS in Animal Science, Okla. State U., Stillwater, 1959, PhD in Genetics and Animal Breeding, 1961. Fieldman livestock program, Meat and Animal Science Dept. U. Wis., 1956-57; grad. rsch. asst., Animal Science Dept. Okla. State U., 1958-61; extension livestock specialist U. Minn., 1962-64; assoc. prof. animal science Okla. State U., 1964-70, prof. animal science, 1970-73; asst. dean agr., assoc. dir. Ala. Agrl. Experiment Sta. Auburn U., 1973-75; grad. faculty fellow U. Nebr., Lincoln, 1975—, prof. animal science, 1975—, head animal science dept., 1975-82, dean agrl. rsch., dir. Nebr. Agrl. Experiment Sta., 1982-88, interim vice chancellor for agr. and natural resources, 1987-88, vice chancellor Inst. Agr. and Natural Resources, 1988—, v.p. agr. and natural resources, 1992—, interim sr. vice chancellor for acad. affairs, 1996—. Author: 1 textbook; contbr. numerous articles to profl. jours. Mem. bd. dirs. Kiwanis Club of Lincoln, Capital City, 1977-83, pres. 1982; mem. Lincoln Agribusiness Club, 1982—; mem. bd. dirs. St. Mark's United Methodist Ch. Found., 1989-95, Nebr. Human Resources Found., 1990-91. Recipient Appreciation award Nebr. SPF, 1981, Booster award Nat. Pork Producers, 1983, Agrl. Achievement award Ak-Sar-Ben, 1989. Fellow Am. Soc. Animal Science (editl. bd. Jour. Animal Sciencce 1970-73, intersociety coun. rep. 1984-86, mem. bd. dirs. 1980-86, sec.-treas. 1980-83, pres. 1984-85); mem. Am. Registry of Profl. Animal Scientists (gov. bd. 1985-88, pres. 1986-87), Coun. for Agrl. Science and Technology (bd. dirs. 1986-89, chair nat. concerns com. 1986-89), Innocents Soc. U. Nebr.-Lincoln (hon.), Sigma Xi, Alpha Zeta, Gamma Sigma Delta (Merit award 1993), Phi Beta Delta. Office: U Nebr Inst Agr & Natural Resources 202 Agrl Hall Lincoln NE 68583

ONCKEN, HAROLD W., machine service company executive; b. Hermann, mo., Dec. 16, 1925. Shop foreman LeBrell Co., Hermann, 1956-71, Stevens Mfg., Hermann, 1971-81; pres. Oncken Machine Svc. Co., Hermann, 1981—. Patentee drill press vise. Served with U.S. Army, 1945-46. Mem. Am. Lodge (comdr. 1985-95). Christian. Office: Oncken Machine Svc Inc 238 E 1st St Hermann MO 65041-1114

O'NEAL, MICHAEL RALPH, state legislator, lawyer; b. Kansas City, Mo., Jan. 16, 1951; s. Ralph D. and Margaret E. (McEuen) O'N.; m. Tammy E. Miller, Dec. 30, 1978 (div.); children: Haley Anne, Austin Michael. BA in English, U. Kans., 1973, JD, 1976. Bar: Kans. 1976, U.S. Dist. Ct. Kans. 1976, U.S. Ct. Appeals (10th cir.) 1979. Intern Legis. Counsel State of Kans., Topeka, 1975-76; assoc. Hodge, Reynolds, Smith, Peirce & Forker, Hutchinson, Kans., 1976-77; ptnr. Reynolds, Peirce, Forker, Suter, O'Neal & Myers, Hutchinson, 1980-88, Gilliland & Hayes, P.A., Hutchinson, 1988—; mem. Kans. Ho. of Reps.; chmn. jud. com., 1984, 93—; minority whip Kans. Ho. of Reps., 1991-92, majority whip, 1995—; instr. Hutchinson C.C., 1977-88. Vice chmn. Rep. Ctrl. Com., Reno County, Kans., 1982-86; bd. dirs. Rento County Mental Health Assn., Hutchinson, 1984-89, YMCA, 1984-86, Crime Stoppers (ex-officio), Hutchinson; chmn. adv. bd. dirs. Wesley Towers Retirement Cmty., 1984-96; mem. Kans. Travel and Tourism Commn., 1990-94; bd. govs. U. Kans. Law Sch., 1991—. Recipient Leadership award Kans. C. of C. and Industry, 1985; named one of Outstanding Young Men Am., 1986. Mem. ABA, ATLA, Nat. Conf. State Legislatures (criminal justice com.), Kans. Assn. Def. Counsel, Def. Rsch. Inst., Kans. Bar Assn. (prospective legis. com., Outstanding Svc. award), Hutchinson C. of C. (ex-officio bd. dirs., Leadership award 1984), Am. Coun. Young Polit. Leaders (del. to Atlantic conf. biennial assembly), Kans. Jud. Coun., Commn. on Uniform State Laws. Home: 8 Windemere Ct Hutchinson KS 67502-2020 Office: Gilliland & Hayes PA 335 N Washington St Ste 2977 Hutchinson KS 67501-4863

ONEIL, SUSAN JEAN, media specialist; b. Decatur, Ill., Nov. 19, 1952; d. Richard Greer and Patricia Jane (Miller) Schenk; m. Kevin E. Oneil, Feb. 10, 1952; children: Erin and Patrick. BA, Ill. Wesleyan U., Bloomington, 1974; MSEd, Northern Ill. U., Dekalb, 1978, Northern Ill. U., Dekalb, 1989. Cert. elem. tchr., secondary tchr., media specialist with supervisory endorsement. Tchr. Waldo Jr. High, Aurora, Ill., 1975-76; commercial loan cons. Control Data, Naperville, Ill., 1978-79; tchr. Braidwood Jr. High, Braidwood, Ill., 1979-80; librarian Forrestville Sch. Dir., Forreston, Ill.; media specialist Byron Middle Sch., Byran, Ill., 1982—; pres. Byron Fedn. Tchrs. Byron, 1984-86. Contbg. author: Teaching Electronic Information Skills: A Resource Guide for Grades K-5, 1995. Bd. dirs. Rockford (Ill.) Symphony Orch., 1994—. Recipient Electronic Reference Grant Franklin Computers Byron, 1989; grantee ISBE Profl. Devel., 1995. Mem. AAUW, NOW, Ill. Edn. Assn., Ill. Sch. Libr. Media Assn. (treas. 1993—), Northwestern Consortium of Media Dir., Rockford Symphony Orch. (bd. dirs.). Democrat. Methodist. Office: Byron Middle Sch Libr Tower Rd Byron IL 61010

O'NEILL, ANN RENEE, lawyer, metallurgical engineer; b. Grosse Pointe, Mich., Feb. 27, 1959. BS in Metallurgical Engring. high honors, Mich. Tech. U., 1981; AA in Metrology and Calibration Scis. summa cum laude, Macomb Community Coll., 1983; JD magna cum laude, Detroit Coll. Law, 1987. Bar: Mich. 1987, U.S. Patent Office 1992. Metallurgical tech. IBM, Rochester, Minn., 1980; quality engring asst. TRW Steering and Suspension Systems, Sterling Heights, Mich., 1981-82, assoc. quality engr., 1982-83, quality engr., 1983-84, supr. quality svcs., 1984-87, quality mgr., 1987-88, plant supt., 1988-89, mgr. quality engring., 1989-92; dir. quality Monroe (Mich.) Auto Equipment, 1992-94; dir. quality and continuous improvement United Technologies Motor Systems, Inc., 1994—; mem. pres.'s coun. Mich. Tech. U., Houghton, Mich., 1989-92; bd. dirs. Registrar Accreditation Bd., 1994—; bd. dirs. Am. Supplier Inst. Trustee Mich. Tech. Fund, Mich. Tech. U., 1993—. Mem. Am. Soc. for Quality Control (cert. quality engr., cert. reliability engr., sec. human resources divsn. 1984-86, treas. automotive divsn. 1990-91, chmn. automotive divsn. 1991-92, bd. dirs. 1992-94, Cecil Craig award 1988, William P. Koth award 1993), Soc. Automotive Engrs., State Bar Mich., Am. Soc. for Metals, Tau Beta Pi, Alpha Sigma Mu. Office: 5200 Auto Club Dr Dearborn MI 48126-4212

O'NEILL, ERIN LEIGH, physical therapist; b. Wadsworth, Ohio, May 12, 1960; d. William Harold and Vivian Mae (Rumburg) O'N. AA, Miami U., Oxford, Ohio, 1982; BS, Ohio State U., 1984. Lic. phys. therapist, Ohio. Staff phys. therapist Am. Phys. Rehab. Network, Toledo, Ohio, 1984-86; mgr. phys. therapy Henry County Hosp., Napoleon, Ohio, 1986; staff phys. therapist Wooster (Ohio) Cmty. Hosp., 1986-91, asst. mgr., mgr. phys. therapy, 1991-92; mgr. phys. therapy Wooster Clinic, Inc., 1992—; speaker at various coaches clinics, sports clubs and med. support group, 1985—. Mem. Am. Phys. Therapy Assn., Ohio Horsemen's Coun. Republican. Lutheran. Office: Wooster Clinic 1740 Cleveland Rd Wooster OH 44691

O'NEILL, KATHERINE TEMPLETON, journalist, museum administrator, former nursing educator; b. Moline, Ill., Jan. 13, 1949; d. Morris John and Patricia (Collins) Templeton; 1 child by previous marriage, Carolyn Patricia Coquillette; m. William James O'Neill Jr., July 18, 1987; children: Alec, Sara, Jessie, Laura O'Neill. BSN, U. Mich., 1971; postgrad., St. Clare's Hall, Oxford, Eng., 1971-72; MSN, Boston U., 1974. RN, Ohio, Mass. Instr. Mass. Gen. Hosp., Boston, 1974-76; assoc. prof. Ursuline Coll., Cleve., 1976-81; dir. devel. and pub. rels. Ohio Coll. Podiatric Medicine, Cleve., 1985-87; dir. Chisholm Halle Costume Wing We. Res. Hist. Soc., Cleve., 1989-90; fashion editor Chagrin Valley Times, 1989—; vice chmn. bd. dirs. Cleve. Health Edn. Mus., 1983—, Cleve. Music Sch. Settlement, 1983—. Corp. bd. dirs. Hathaway Brown Sch., 1981—, pres. alumnae bd. dirs., 1984-96; bd. dirs. Cleve. Ballet, 1987-95, Cleve. Inst. Music, 1994—, Cleve. Scholarship Programs, 1995—, Ursuline Coll., 1995—, Mus. Arts Assn. The Cleve. Orch., 1995—; mem. adv. bd. Francis Paine Bolton Sch. Nursing, Case We. Res. U., Cleve., 1990—, GAMUT, Cleve. State U., 1992-93, Cleve. Publs., 1993—. Mem. Vis. Nurse Assn. (bd. dirs. 1995—). Office: Clanco Mgmt Pepper Pike OH 44124

O'NEILL, KATHRYN J., librarian, educator; b. Flint, Mich., Oct. 28, 1942; d. Edward Robert and Mary Elizabeth (Day) Zahn; m. A. Michael O'Neill, June 1964 (div. 1984); children: Daniel Sean, Margaret Anne, Matthew M. (dec.). Student, Ctrl. Mich. U., 1960-62; BA in Edn., U. Mich., 1964, MLS, 1969. Tchr. English Ann Arbor (Mich.) Pub. Schs., 1964-69, libr., media specialist, 1970-71; libr., media specialist Ladue Sch. Dist., St. Louis, 1977—; cons. in field; ind. distbr. Dorling Kindersley Family Libr., Inc. Contbg. editor: Down-to-Earth Publs. Mem. Brentwood (Mo.) Planning and Zoning Commn., 1987-93; alt. mem. Brentwood Bd. Adjustment, 1990-95; bd. dirs. Brentwood Libr., 1995—; elder Richmond Heights Presbyn. Ch. Recipient Tchr.-Libr. Collaboration award Mo. Assn. Sch. Librs., 1995. Mem. NEA (pres. Ladue chpt. 1991-93), AAUW (bd. dirs. Ann Arbor and Kirkwood-Webster Groves chpts.), U.S. Orienteering Fedn. (level I coach U.S. Olympic Com. 1989—, 4th ranked U.S. woman in master's category U.S. championship 1991, Mo. state orienteering champion 1986, 91, 95), St. Louis Orienteering Club (v.p. 1985-87, editor 1990-92), Hosteling Internat.-Am. Youth Hostel (trip leader), Phi Kappa Phi, Beta Phi Mu, Alpha Chi Omega. Home: 1716 Blue Jay Cv Brentwood MO 63144-1604

O'NEILL, MATT, state legislator; b. St. Louis, Nov. 23, 1937; m. Maureen Concagh, 1962; children: Matt, Erin. Student, Harris Stowe State Coll., Forest Park C.C. Mem. Mo. State Ho. of Reps. Dist. 66, vice-chmn. mcpl. corp., appropriations gen. adminstrn., mem. govt. orgn. com., labor com. and social svc. com. Mem. Nat. Criminal Justice Assn., Legis. Equality Assn., Internat. Narcotics Enforcement Assn., St. Louis Hills Homeowners Assn., Ancient Order Hibernians. Home: 6414 Devonshire Ave Saint Louis MO 63109-2662*

ONG, JAMES SHAUJEN, mechanical engineer; b. Taipei, Republic of China, June 10, 1957; came to the U.S., 1980; s. Wai-Cham and Wai-Ching (Ho) O.; m. Diana W. Ou, Jan. 3, 1984. BS, Tamkang U., 1980; MS, Northwestern U., 1982, PhD, 1986. Registered profl. engr., Ind. Analytical method engr. Allison Engine Co. (formerly Allison Gas Turbine div. GM), Indpls., 1986—, sr. project engr., 1988-94; devel. engr., 1994—. Contbr. articles to profl. jours. Mem. ASME, ASCE, Am. Acad. Mechanics. Home: 13660 Thistlewood Dr W Carmel IN 46032-5135

ONG, JOHN DOYLE, lawyer; b. Uhrichsville, Ohio, Sept. 29, 1933; s. Louis Brosee and Mary Ellen (Liggett) O.; m. Mary Lee Schupp, July 20, 1957; children: John Francis Harlan, Richard Penn Blackburn, Mary Katherine Caine. BA, Ohio State U., 1954, MA, 1954; LLB, Harvard, 1957; LHD, Kent State U., 1982. Bar: Ohio 1958. Asst. counsel B.F. Goodrich Co., Akron, 1961-66, group v.p., 1972-73, exec. v.p., 1973-74, vice chmn., 1974-75, pres., dir., 1975-77, pres., chief operating officer, dir., 1978-79, chmn. bd., pres., chief exec. officer, 1979-84, chmn. bd., chief exec. officer, 1984—; asst. to pres. Internat. B.F. Goodrich Co., Akron, 1966-69, v.p., 1969-70, pres., 1970-72; bd. dirs. Cooper Industries, Ameritech Corp., The Kroger Co., Asarco, Inc., Geon Co., TRW, Inc. V.p. exploring Great Trail coun. Boy Scouts Am., 1974-77; bd.d irs. Nat. Alliance of Bus., 1981-84; trustee Mus. Arts Assn., Cleve., Bexley Hall Sem., 1974-81, Case Western Res. U., 1980-92, Kenyon Coll., 1983-85, Hudson (Ohio) Libr. and Hist. Soc., pres., 1971-72, Western Res. Acad., Hudson, 1975-95, pres. bd. trustees, 1977-95; nat. trustee Nat. Symphony Orch., 1975-83, John S. and James L. Knight Found., 1995—; mem. bus. adv. com. Transp. Ctr. Northwestern U., 1975-78, Carnegie-Mellon U. Grad. Sch. Indsl. Adminstrn., 1978-83; trustee U. Chgo., 1991—; chmn. Ohio Bus. Roundtable, 1994—. Mem. Ohio Bar Assn. (bd. govs. corp. counsel sect. 1962-74, chmn. 1970), Rubber Mfrs. Assn. (bd. dirs. 1974-84), Chem. Mfrs. Assn. (bd. dirs. 1988-91, 94—), Conf. Bd., Bus. Roundtable (chmn. 1992-94), Bus. Coun., Portage Country Club, Union Club, Links, Union League, Ottawa Shooting Club, Met. Club, Rolling Rock Club, Castalia Trout Club, Phi Beta Kappa, Phi Alpha Theta. Episcopalian. Home: 230 Aurora St Hudson OH 44236-2941 Office: The B F Goodrich Co 3925 Embassy Pky Akron OH 44333-1799

ONKEN, HENRY DRALLE, plastic surgeon; b. St.Louis, Feb. 22, 1932; s. John Werner and Clara Ruth (Dralle) O.; m. Deborah Dorsett Smith, June 3, 1961; children: John D., Michael D., Katherine Minna. AB, Princeton U., 1953; MD, Harvard U., 1957. Diplomate Am. Bd. Plastic Surgery. Resident in gen. and plastic surgery Barnes Hosp., St. Louis, 1957-66; practice medicine specializing in plastic surgery St. Louis, 1966—; pres. staff Deaconess Hosp., St. Louis, 1986-89. Bd. dirs. English Lang. Sch., 1987—; St. Louis Christmas Carolers, 1981—; co-chmn. Theater Factory of St. Louis, Webster Groves, Mo., 1984-88. Capt. USMC, 1962-64. Mem. AFTRA, Am. Soc. Plastic and Reconstructive Surgeons, Mo. State Med. Assn., Midwestern Assn. Plastic Surgeons (pres. 1996—), St. Louis Area Soc. Plastic Surgeons (treas. 1984—), St. Louis Med. Soc. (councilor 1996—), Univ. Club, Princeton Club, Aesculapian Club (Boston). Democrat. Office: 1034 S Brentwood Blvd Ste 750 Saint Louis MO 63117-1207

ONNEN, TONY, state legislator; b. July 5, 1938; m. JoAnn M. Thorland, 1970; 5 children. BS, U. Nebr. Hosp. adminstr., 1970-75; pub. acct. pvt. practice; mem. Minn. Ho. of Reps., 1977—; mem. health and human svc. com., local and met. affairs com., taxes com., others; controller Stitchcraft Corp; ins. salesman. Republican. Home: 277 State Office Bldg Saint Paul MN 55155*

ONO, CHERYL EIKO, senior controls engineer; b. Chgo., Feb. 26, 1965; d. Mitsuo and Sachiye (Ikeda) O. BS, Eastern Ill. U., 1987, MS, 1988. Grad. asst. Eastern Ill. U., Charleston, 1987-88; intern GE Co., Mattoon, Ill., 1988, mfg./quality engr., 1988-92; controls engr. GE Co., Ravenna, Ohio, 1992-94; advanced process engr. GE Co., Nela Park, Cleve., 1994-95, sr. controls engr., 1995—. Mem. Am. Soc. Quality Engrs., Epsilon Pi Tau. Office: GE Lighting 1975 Noble Rd Cleveland OH 44112-1719

OOMS, J(AMES) WESLEY, insurance company executive; b. Chgo., Nov. 1, 1929; s. Simon and Lena (Kros) O.; m. Audrey Rodgers, Sept. 11, 1953; children: Wesley, April, Roger, Gordon (dec.), Bradley. BS in Fire Protection-Safety Engring., Ill. Inst. Tech., 1951. Safety insp. U.S. Army, Pine Bluff, Ark., 1951-53; insp. Fire Underwriters Inspection Bur., Mpls., 1953-55; adminstrv. asst. Western Actuarial Bur., Chgo., 1955-61; supr. habitational risks Inter-Regional Ins. Conf., N.Y.C., 1961-63; mgr. Multi-Line Rating Bur., N.Y.C., 1963-70; exec. asst. State Farm Fire & Casualty Co., Bloomington, Ill., 1971, asst. v.p. R & D, 1971-79, asst. v.p. product planning and devel., 1979-91, asst. v.p., 1991—; trustee CPCU-Harry J. Loman Found., Malvern, Pa., 1987—; dir. Nat. Com. on Property Ins., Boston, 1991-93. Contbg. author: Dimensions in Corporate Stategy, 1983; also articles. Pres. Home Sweet Home Mission, Bloomington, 1990-92, dir., 1995—; chmn. Emergency Mgmt. Inst., Fed. Emergency Mgmt. Agy., Emmitsburg, Md., 1990; trustee Corn Belt Libr. Sys., Normal, Ill., 1991-93, Alliance Libr. Sys., Normal, 1993-96. Recipient Dir.'s award Fed. Emergency Mgmt. Agy., 1989. Mem. Soc. CPCUs (pres. 1993-94), Am. Soc. CLUs, Soc. Ins. Rsch. (pres. 1981-82), Am. Risk and Ins. Assn., Nat. Flood Insurers Assn. (exec. com. 1972-78), Kiwanis (bd. dirs. Bloomington 1984-86). Republican. Office: State Farm Fire & Casualty Co 112 E Washington St Bloomington IL 61701-1001

OPATZ, JOE, state legislator. BA, St. Cloud U.; MEd, Kent State U.; PhD in Edn., U. Minn. Mem. Minn. Ho. of Reps. St. Paul, 1993—; univ. adminstr. Democrat. Home: 402 Riverside Dr SE Saint Cloud MN 56304-1032*

OPELKA, GREGORY P., composer, lyricist, conductor; b. Chgo., June 11, 1956; s. Frank Gregory and Pauline Therese (Briody) O.; m. Tatiana Aleksandrovna Chaika, Dec. 17, 1993. BA in English Lit. and Classical Langs., Lawrence U., 1978; MA in Classical Langs., U. Mich., 1980. Music dir. New Tuners Theater, Chgo., 1990-92, Apple Tree Theater, Highland Park, Ill., 1990, Nat. Jewish Theater, Skokie, Ill., 1994—; conductor, composer Mus. Theater of Yekaterinburg (Russia), 1992-93; conductor Mus. Theater of Khabarovsk (Russia), 1993—; freelance musician, composer, 1990—. Composer, lyricist (mus.) Charlie's Oasis, 1990, The Three Musketeers, 1993, Hotel d'Amour, 1993, Monky Business, 1995. Recipient Hon. Citizen award (for song My Omsk) City of Omsk, Russia, 1992, H.P. Laser Printer award, 1995.

OPEM, JOHN DAVID, library manager; b. Rochester, Minn., Feb. 23, 1933; s. Palmer I. and Mary Elizabeth (Ulrich) O.; m. Joyce D. Stefan, Jan. 30, 1960; children: Jeffrey, Jennifer, Jonathan. BA in Chemistry, St. Olaf Coll., 1955; MA in Libr. Sci., U. Chgo., 1964. Analytical chemist Swift & Co., Chgo., 1955-56, devel. chemist, 1958-62, lit. chemist, 1962-65; head libr. Abbott Labs., North Chicago, Ill., 1965-78; mgr. Rsch. Info. Ctr. Abbott Labs., Abbott Park, Ill., 1978-85, mgr. libr./info. svcs., 1985—; mem. info. svcs. adv. coun. The Conf. Bd., N.Y.C., 1986—; mem. tech. info. adv. com. Nat. Security Indsl. Assn., Washington, 1968-73. Mem. editl. adv. bd. Unlisted Drugs, 1985—; patentee in field. Dir., trustee Waukegan (Ill.) Pub. Libr., 1982-84, Comty. Libr., Salem, Wis., 1992-95. With U.S. Army, 1956-58. Mem. ALA, Am. Chem. Soc., Indsl. Tech. Info. Mgr.'s Group, Drug Info. Assn., Spl. Librs. Assn. Republican. Lutheran. Home: 1432 NW Windermere Dr Tremont IL 61568

OPFER, DARRELL WILLIAMS, state representative, educator; b. Genoa, Ohio, June 17, 1941; s. Milton William and Iva Marie (Gleckler) O. BS in Edn., Bowling Green State U., 1963, MA, 1964. Cert. tchr., Ohio. Tchr. Peace Corps, Kenya, East Africa, 1965-68, Woodward High Sch., Toledo, 1969, Genoa High Sch., 1969-82; county commr. Ottawa County, Port Clinton, Ohio, 1983-92; state rep. State of Ohio, 1993—. Sec. Dem. Party, Ottawa County, 1974-80; pres. Ottawa County Dem. Club, 1976-80. Named Outstanding Pub. Ofcl., Ohio Dirs.-Pvt. Industry Coun., 1992. Mem. Commodore Perry Fed. Credit Union (pres. 1982-92), Moose, Kiwanis. Mem. United Ch. of Christ. Home: 12342 W State Route 105 Oak Harbor OH 43449-9410 Office: State Rep Office 77 S High St Columbus OH 43266-0603

OPPENHEIMER, CHARLES K(ENNETH), JR., financial executive, consultant; b. Hartford, Conn., Dec. 8, 1949; s. Charles Kenneth and Marjorie (Harlow) O.; m. Bonnie Ann Toriani, Jan. 22, 1972 (div. 1977); m. Janice Sue Eaves, June 26, 1993. Student Hartford Inst. Acctg., 1967-69. Pres., C & M Oppenheimer Notepaper Co., (now Park Nat. Industries), 1961—; newspaper exec. Hartford Times, 1967-75; founder, pres. Circulation Systems, Inc. (now div. Pacific Crest Communications Corp.), 1971—; exec. v.p. Gt. Northern Trust, 1974-79, also dir.; founder, pres. Plant City Corp., 1976-90; pres. Amvest Fin. Group, Inc., 1976—, mng. dir., 1993—; dir. Diversified Brokerage, Inc, 1995—; newspaper exec. Jour. Pub. Co., Manchester, Conn., 1978-79; newspaper fin. mgmt. exec. Kansas City (Mo.) Star Co., 1981-83; pres., CEO Paperchase Corp. (name changed to Amcrest Corp.), 1983-89, Crane & Co. Inc. subs. Amcrest Corp., 1985-89; pres. Westar Nat. Inc., 1986—; exec. officer Park Nat. Corp., Transrail Corp., Pacific Crest Communications Corp.; mgmt. and pub. cons.; condr. seminars. Mem. Inst. Newspaper Controllers and Fin. Officers, Printing Industries Am., Inst. Bus. Appraisers, Assn. Merger & Acquision Profls., N.Y. Fin. Execs. Assn., Ind. Merchants Assn. (bd. dirs. 1984-87, pres. 1984-86). Author: Expense Code Numbering System, Central Purchasing Mgrs. Manual, Retail Operations Manuel, Corporate Accounting Manuel. Address: PO Box 413036 Kansas City MO 64141-3036

OPPERMAN, DANNY GENE, packaging professional, consultant; b. Fostoria, Ohio, June 29, 1938; s. Roy and Iva Ann (Dotson) O.; m. Dorothy Rae Bugner, Dec. 30, 1957; children: Carrie Rae Opperman Hammond, Melissa Ann Opperman Lee, Jon Aaron, Christopher Douglas. Assoc., ICS, 1960. Tool engr. Ford Motor Co., Fostoria, 1957-68; packaging engr. Allied-Signal Corp., Fostoria, 1968-86; machine designer Interconnect, Inc., Toledo, 1987; prodn. engr. TRW, Elyria, Ohio, 1987-88; pres. packaging consulting firm Opperman/Assocs., Inc., Fostoria, 1988—. Pres. Fostoria Jaycees, 1970-71; advisor Fostoria Teen Ctr., Inc., 1960-66. Mem. ASTM (D-10 packaging com), Inst. Packaging Profls. (cert., chpt. bd. dirs. 1984-92), Packaging Cons. Coun., Elks (exalted ruler 1984-85), Masons.

OPPLIGER, PEARL LAVIOLETTE, alcohol and drug abuse services professional; b. Barre, Vt., Aug. 16, 1942; d. Roland Bernard Sr. and Mae C. (Bouley) Laviolette; m. William Gregory Wotschak, Sept. 8, 1962 (div. Feb. 1983); children: Robin Lee Hillier, Rene Beth Greff, Rana Mae Wotschak; m. Edward Lee Oppliger, Aug. 16, 1988. BSW, Bowling Green State U., 1986; MSW, Ohio State U., 1995, Ohio State U., 1995. Lic. social worker, Ohio, CCDC III, Ohio. Sec. Ohio State U., Columbus, 1964-66; hostess Welcome Wagon, Bowling Green, Ohio, 1975-76; owner, mgr. children's clothing store Rhymes 'n' Reasons, Bowling Green, 1976-84; bookkeeper Friendly Ice Cream Inc., Bowling Green, 1979-80; sales clk. Wilson's Shoe Store, Bowling Green, 1984-85; alcoholism counselor Wood County Coun. on Alcoholism and Drug Abuse, Inc., Bowling Green, 1985-86, family counselor, 1986, supr., 1986-90, dir. recovery svcs., 1990—; adj. instr. in social work Bowling Green State U., 1988—; co-facilitator Parents Helping Parents, Bowling Green, 1990-95. Coun. mem.-at-large City of Bowling Green, 1990-93, mem. planning commn., 1988-89, asst. chmn. Bowling Green Rep. Club, 1989-91, chmn. 1991-92; co-founder Downtown Bus. Assn., Bowling Green, 1980-82; sec. Bowling Green Housing Agy., 1994—. Am. Bus. Women's Assn. scholar. Mem. AAUW (v.p. mem. com. Bowling Green br. 1991-93, Outstanding Woman in Cmty. Work 1990, 96), NASW, Phi Kappa Phi. Roman Catholic. Home: 910 N Main St Bowling Green OH 43402-1819 Office: Wood County Coun Alcoholism 320 W Gypsy Lane Rd Bowling Green OH 43402-4506

ORCUTT, DANIEL C., airport terminal executive. Dir. Oklahoma Airport, 1965-1970; exec. dir. Indpls. Airport Authority, 1970—. Office: Indpls Ind Airport Authority PO Box 100 2500 S High School Rd Indianapolis IN 46241-4943

O'REILLY, HUGH JOSEPH, restaurant executive; b. Emporia, Kans., July 20, 1936; s. Henry Charles and Mary Esther (Rettiger) O'R.; m. Eileen Ellen Browne, Feb. 11, 1961; 1 child, Hugh Jr. Student, St. Benedicts Coll., Atchison, Kans., 1954-57, Kansas City Conservatory of Music, 1957-58. Banquet mgr. Stouffer Corp., N.Y.C., 1958-61; gen. mgr. Howard Johnsons, L.I., N.Y., 1961-65; regional mgr. Malt Village Corp., St. Louis, 1965-68; ops. cons. McDonald's Corp., Chgo., 1968-78; pres., chief exec. officer O'Reilly Mgmt. Corp., Emporia, Kans., 1978—; nat. advt. cons. McDonalds Operators Assn., Oak Brook, Ill., 1980-84. Republican. Roman Catholic. Lodge: Shriner. Office: 907 Commercial St Emporia KS 66801-2916

O'REILLY, KENNETH WILLIAM, military officer; b. N.Y.C., July 17, 1953; s. Thomas Michael and Dorothy Marie (Garvin) O'R.; m. Ginger Lee Jacobs, Apr. 22, 1978; children: Ryan, Erin. AAS, SUNY, Farmingdale, 1973; BS, Dowling Coll., 1975; MA, Webster U., 1982. Sales rep. N.W. Airlines, N.Y.C., 1976-78; commd. 2d lt. USAF, 1978—, advanced through grades to lt. col.; student navigator 452 Flight Tng. Squadron, Mather AFB, Calif., 1979-80; KC135 unit navigator 11th Air Refueling Squadron, Altus AFB, Okla., 1980-83; instr. navigator 11th Air Refueling Squadron, Altus AFB, 1984-85; wing exec. officer 340 Air Refueling Wing, Altus AFB, 1984-85; chief of navigation 34 Strategic Squadron, Zaragoza AB, Spain, 1985-88; strategic plans advisor 2 Airborne Command and Control Squadron, Offutt AFB, Nebr., 1988-91; action officer Hdqrs. SAC/Directorate of Strategic Plans, Offutt AFB, 1991-92; chief of tanker plans Hdqrs. Air Mobility Command/Dir. Ops. and Transp., 1992-93, chief personnel mgmt. br., 1993-96; chief opers. watch divsn., headqrs., dir. opers. and plans The Pentagon, 1996—. Committeeman Levittown South-North Wantagh, Rep. Club, N.Y.C., 1971-78. Decorated 2 Meritorious Svc. medal, 2 Commendation medals, others. Mem. Air Force Assn., Inst. of Navigation, Airlift Tanker Assn. Roman Catholic. Home: 7017 Petunia St Springfield VA 22152 Office: HQ USAF/X000 1480 Air Force Pentagon Washington DC 20330-1480

O'REILLY, MICHAEL JOSEPH, lawyer, real estate investor; b. Columbus, Ohio, May 19, 1958; s. John Joseph and Virginia Joyce (Bradley) O'R.; m. Angelique I. Gaal, Feb. 25, 1995. AB, Miami U., Oxford, Ohio, 1980; JD, Ohio State U., 1984. Bar: Ohio 1984. Lawyer The Galbreath Corp., Columbus, 1984-89; gen. counsel R.J. Solove & Assocs. Mgmt./Devel., Inc., Columbus, 1989-95; pvt. practice Law Offices of Michael J. O'Reilly, Columbus, 1995—; seminar speaker Ohio CLE Inst., Nat. Bus. Inst. Mem. Ohio State Bar Assn., Columbus Bar Assn., Univ. Club. Roman Catholic. Office: PO Box 340228 Columbus OH 43234

O'REILLY, ROSANN TAGLIAFERRO, computer educator; b. Bronx, N.Y., July 4, 1948; d. Neil F. and Antoinette C. (Odierno) Tagliaferro; children: Jean Marie, Ann Maureen. BA in French, Fordham U., 1970. Cert. tchr., N.Y., Ohio. Asst. supr. EDP audit Deloitte Haskins and Sells, N.Y.C., 1968-72; payroll clk. U. Va., Charlottesville, 1972-74, Great Am. Ins., Cin., 1974-76; computer coord. St. Mary Sch., Cin., 1986-96. Pres. Hyde Park Neighborhood Coun., Cin., 1985; founder, pres. Sitters Anonymous, 1978. Mem. Mensa. Roman Catholic.

OREL, HAROLD, literary critic, educator; b. Boston, Mar. 31, 1926; s. Saul and Sarah (Wicker) O.; m. Charlyn Hawkins, May 25, 1951; children: Sara Elinor, Timothy Ralston. BA cum laude, U. N.H., 1948; MA, U. Mich., 1949, PhD, 1952; postgrad., Harvard U., 1949. Teaching fellow U. Mich., 1948-52; instr. dept. English, U. Md., 1952-54, 55-56; overseas program U. Md., Germany, Austria, Eng., 1954-55; tech. editor Applied Physics Lab., Johns Hopkins U., Balt., 1953-56; flight propulsion lab. dept. Gen. Electric Co., Cin., 1957; asso. prof. U. Kans., Lawrence, 1957-63; prof. U. Kans., 1963-74, Disting. prof. English, 1974—, asst. dean faculties and research adminstrn., 1964-67; cons. to various univ. presses, scholarly jours., Can. Coun. Arts, Nat. Endowment of Humanities, Midwest Rsch. Inst., 1958—; lectr., Japan, 1974, 88, India, 1985. Author: Thomas Hardy's Epic-Drama: A Study of The Dynasts, 1963, The Development of William Butler Yeats, 1885-1900, 1968, English Romantic Poets and the Enlightenment: Nine Essays on a Literary Relationship in Studies in Voltaire and the Eighteenth Century, vol. CIII, 1973, The Final Years of Thomas Hardy, 1912-1928, 1976, Victorian Literary Critics, 1984, The Literary Achievement of Rebecca West, 1985, The Victorian Short Story: Development and Triumph of a Literary Genre, 1986, The Unknown Thomas Hardy: Lesser-Known Aspects of Hardy's Life and Career, 1987, A Kipling Chronology, 1990, Popular Fiction in England, 1914-1918, 1992, The Historical Novel from Scott to Sabatini, 1995; contbg. author: Thomas Hardy and the Modern World, 1974, The Genius of Thomas Hardy, 1976, Budmouth Essays on Thomas Hardy, 1976, Twilight of Dawn: Studies in English Literature in Transition, 1987; contbr. numerous articles on English lit. history and criticism to various mags.; editor: The World of Victorian Humor, 1961, Six Essays in Nineteenth-Century English Literature and Thought, 1962, Thomas Hardy's Personal Writings: Prefaces, Literary Opinions, Reminiscences, 1966, British Poetry 1880-1920: Edwardian Voices, 1969, The Nineteenth-Century Writer and his Audience, 1969, Irish History and Culture, 1976, The Dynasts (Thomas Hardy), 1978, The Scottish World, 1981, Rudyard Kipling: Interviews and Recollections, 2 vols., 1983, Victorian Short Stories: An Anthology, 1987, Critical Essays on Rudyard Kipling, 1989, Victorian Short Stories 2: The Trials of Love, 1990, Sir Arthur Conan Doyle: Interviews and Recollections, 1991, Critical Essays on Sir Arthur Conan Doyle, 1992, Gilbert and Sullivan: Interviews and Recollections, 1994, Critical Essays on Thomas Hardy's Poetry, 1995; delivered orations Thomas Hardy ceremonies, Westminster Abbey, 1978, 90. With USN, 1944-46. Recipient Higuchi Endowment Rsch. Achievement award, 1990; grantee Am. Coun. Learned Socs., 1966, NEH, 1975, Am. Philos. Soc., 1964, 80. Fellow Royal Soc. Literature; mem. Thomas Hardy Soc. (v.p. 1968—), Am. Com. on Irish Studies (v.p. 1967-70, pres. 1970-72). Unitarian. Home: 713 Schwarz Rd Lawrence KS 66049-4507 Office: U Kans Dept English Lawrence KS 66045

OREL, SARA ELINOR, art history educator, archaeologist; b. Lawrence, Kans., July 2, 1962; d. Harold and Charlyn (Hawkins) O. AB, Bryn Mawr Coll., 1984; MA, U. Toronto, Ont., Can., 1986, PhD, 1993. Asst. prof. art history Truman State U., Kirksville, Mo., 1991—. Editor, contbg. author: Death and Taxes in the Ancient Near East, 1992; contbr. articles to profl. jours. Mem. Am. Rsch. Ctr. in Egypt, Egypt Exploration Soc., Soc. for Study of Egyptian Antiquities, Coll. Art. Assn., Midwest Art History Soc., Can. Mediterranean Inst., Titanic Hist. Soc. Democrat. Unitarian. Office: Truman State U Divsn Fine Arts Kirksville MO 63501

ORENSTEIN, HOWARD, state legislator; b. Nov. 1955; m. Barbara Frey; 3 children. BA, Vanderbilt U.; JD, Northwestern U. Mem. Minn. Ho. of Reps. St. Paul, 1986—; mem. appropriations com., edn. com., met. affairs. com., others., vicechmn. judiciary com.; atty.; prof. Democrat. Home: 521 State Office Building Bldg Saint Paul MN 55155-1201*

ORFIELD, MYRON WILLARD, JR., state legislator, educator; b. Mpls., July 27, 1961. BA summa cum laude, U. Minn., 1983; grad., Princeton U., 1983-84; JD, U. Chgo., 1987. Bar: Minn. 1988. Law clk. Judge Gerald W. Heaney, U.S. Ct. Appeals, 8th Cir., 1987-88; rsch. assoc. Ctr. for Studies in Criminal Justice, U. Chgo., 1988-89; assoc. Faegre & Benson, 1989; asst. atty. gen. Minn. Atty. Gen.'s Office, 1989—; Bradley fellow Ctr. for Studies in Criminal Justice, U. Chgo., 1990-91; rep. Minn. Ho. of Reps. Dist. 60B, Mpls., 1991—; adj. prof. law U. Minn., 1991—, Hamline U., 1991—; prin. Met. Area Project, Mpls. Author: Metropolitics, 1996; contbr. articles to profl. jours. Office: 521 State Office Bldg Saint Paul MN 55155

ORIMENKO, MARTIN PAUL, chiropractor; b. Syracuse, N.Y., Mar. 25, 1956; s. Harry Paul and Phyllis Ann (Gibi) O. BA, Earlham Coll., 1978; D Chiropractic, Logan Coll. Chiropractic, 1989. Pvt. sch. tchr. Scattergood Friends Sch., West Branch, Iowa, 1978-80, Friends Select Sch., Phila., 1980-83, Maharishi Internat. U. Sch., Fairfield, Iowa, 1983-86; pvt. practice chiropractic medicine Healing Arts Ctr., St. Louis, 1990—; lectr., seminar leader in field. Fellow Internat. Acad. Clin. Acupuncture. Office: Healing Arts Ctr 734 De Mun Ave Clayton MO 63105-2219

ORLOFF, DEBORAH BETH, art educator, photography program director; b. N.Y.C., Feb. 11, 1964; d. Jay William and Bette Lynn (Becker) O.; m. Donald Eric Resnick, July 23, 1994. BFA in Photography, Clark U.; MFA in Art Photography, Syracuse U., 1992. Lab. asst., tchg. asst. dept. art media studies Syracuse (N.Y.) U., 1989-92; lectr. Sch. Art Coll. St. Rose, Albany, N.Y., 1992-94; asst. prof. art dept. U. Toledo, 1994—; lectr. various coll. and univs. One-woman shows include Soc. Contemporary Photography, Kansas City, Mo., 1996, Tilman Gallery, Toledo, 1996, Photo Gallery 2D Prarie State Coll., Chgo., 1993, The White Cube Gallery Syracuse U., 1990, numerous others; two-person shows include Stubnitz Gallery Adrian Coll., Adrian, Mich., 1995, Sch. of Art Gallery Munson-Williams-Proctor Inst., Utica, N.Y., 1993, Altered Space Gallery, Syracuse, 1992, numerous others; exhibited in group shows at McDonough Mus. of Art, Youngstown, Ohio, Ctr. for Fine and Performing Arts, Univ. W. Fla., Pensacola, Toledo Mus. of Art (first place), Anglewood Gallery, Grand Rapids, Mich. Anderson Arts Ctr. (Bussalachi award), Kenosha, Wis., Owens-Ill. Gallery, Toledo, Priebe Gallery (best of show), Oshkosh, Wis., Art Ctr. Gallery Ctrl. Mo. State Univ., Warrensburg, Mo., 1995, numerous others. Bd. dirs. Toledo Friends of Photography, 1994—. Mem. Soc. Photographic Edn., Coll. Art Assn. Office: Univ Toledo Dept of Art Ctr for the visual arts 620 Grove Place Toledo OH 43620

ORMS, HOWARD RAYMOND, drama educator; b. Keota, Iowa, Oct. 25, 1920; s. Emmett Hartwell and Anna Marie (Fry); m. Vivian MacDowell, Feb. 6, 1914; children: Vivian Evans, Russell H., Kenneth A. BA, Cornell Coll., Mt. Vernon, 1947; MFA, Yale Drama Sch., New Haven, 1950. Asst. prof. Howard Coll., Birmingham, 1950-51; mng. dir. Nashville Community Playhouse, 1951-53, Des Moines Community Playhouse, 1953-61; mng. dir. Tulsa Little Theatre, Tulsa, 1961-66, Springfield, 1966—; prof. Southwest Mo. State U., Springfield, 1966-93, prof. emeritus, 1993—, performance coach, 1993—; owner, mng. dir. Merry-Go-Round Summer Theatre, 1949-62; cons. St. Johns Regional Hosp. Springfield, 1988; voice cons. St. Johns Personel, Springfield, 1988, Pub. Defenders Office, Springfield, 1986-88. Guest dir. Cornell Coll. of Iowa, 1993. Staff sgt. AAA, 1942-45. Recipient S.W. Mo. State U. Found. Outstanding Tchr. award, 1987-88, Achievement award, 1995-96. Mem. Am. Assn. Cmty. Theatre (Founding fellow 1987), Nat. Theatre Conf., N.C. Inc. Drama League. Republican. Presbyterian. Home: 3363 S Winton Pl Springfield MO 65804-6415 Office: Southwest Mo State U Dept Theatre & Dance 901 S National Ave Springfield MO 65804-0027

ORNBURN, KRISTEE JEAN, accountant; b. Moberly, Mo., Feb. 24, 1956; d. Lloyd Edward and Ruth Maxine (Major) O. AA, Moberly Jr. Coll., 1976; BSBA magna cum laude, U. Mo., Columbia, 1978. CPA, Mo. Teller City Bank & Trust, Moberly, 1974-78; supr. gen. ledger Orscheln Farm & Home Supply, Moberly, 1978-80, supr. accounts payable, 1980, supr. sr. acctg., 1981-82, mgr. acctg., 1982-86; controller Orscheln Consumer Products Div., Moberly, 1986-93; v.p./controller Orschein Farm & Home Supply, 1993—. Youth worker Carpenter St. Bapt. Ch., Moberly; adv. coun. mem. Moberly Community Coll. Recipient Youth Leadership award Moberly C. of C., 1974. mem. AICPA, Am. Bus. Women's Assn. (pres.), Mo. Sco. CPAs, U. Mo. Alumni Assn., Bapt. Young Women's Club (Moberly) Phi Theta Kappa. Democrat. Office: Orscheln Farm & Home Supply 339 N Williams St Moberly MO 65270-1531

O'ROURKE, JOAN B. DOTY WERTHMAN, educational administrator; b. N.Y.C., June 7, 1933; d. George E. Doty and Lillian G. Bergen; 10 children, 8 stepchildren. BA summa cum laude, Marymount Coll., Manhattan, N.Y., 1953; MA, Columbia U., 1958; PhD, St. John's U., 1971. Tchr. History Marymount High Sch., N.Y.C., 1953-55; hist. instr. Marymount Manhattan Coll., 1957-59; acting chmn. hist. dept. Nassau Community Coll., Mineola, N.Y., 1959-60; prof. History Westchester Community Coll., Valhalla, N.Y., 1963-74; prin. Pius X Sch., Scarsdale, N.Y., 1974-77; assoc. dir. alumni relations Fordham U., N.Y.C., 1980-84; co-founder, dir. Assn. for Profl. Psychol. and Ednl. Counseling, Wilmette, Ill., 1987—; ptnr. O'Rourke and Assocs., 1993—; pres. O'Rourke and Assocs., mgmt. cons., 1993—; dir., writer Sta. WFAS Radio, White Plains, 1963-64; adj. prof. social sci. Fordham U., 1974-76. Teaching fellow St. John's U., Jamaica, N.Y., 1968; recipient Alumni award Marymount Coll., 1987-88. Mem. Soc. Mayflowers Descs. Ill., Michigan Shores Club. Democrat. Roman Catholic. Office: 78614 Blooming Ct Palm Desert CA 92211

OROZCO, RAYMOND E., fire protective services official; b. Chgo., Dec. 17, 1933; m. Patricia King; children: Linda Orozco Stinson, Raymond II, Maripat Orozco Lannin, Michael. Cert. in firefighting and fire instrn. State of Ill. Br. chief Chgo. Fire Dept., 1970-80, dep. dist. chief, 1980-81, exec. asst. to fire commr., 1981-82, dist. chief, 1982-86, asst. dep. fire commr., 1986-88, dep. fire commr., 1988-89, fire commr., 1989—. With USN, 1953-57. Office: Fire Department City Hall Rm 105 121 N La Salle St Chicago IL 60602-1202

ORR, SAMUEL JOSEPH, state agency administrator; b. Cairo, Ill., July 28, 1953; s. Noel Curtis and Rosemary (Rolwing) O.; m. Janice Mae Wankum, Apr. 5, 1986; children: Louisa Mae, Angela Rose. BS in Forestry, U. Mo., 1975, MPA, 1987. Soil conservationist USDA Natural Resources Conservation Svc., Mo., 1975-78; advisor soil and water conservation Mo. Dept. Natural Resources, Jefferson City, Mo., 1978-80, environ. specialist, 1980-83, mgr. soil survey, 1983-94, energy planner, 1994—; staff mem. Comm. Mgmt. Productivity, Jefferson City, 1994; mem. inaugural com. Dept. Nat. Resources Inst., Jefferson City, 1990-92; mem. adv. com. S.W. Mo. State U., Springfield, 1987-93. Recipient Spl. Recognition award Mo. Milk, Food & Environ. Health Assn., 1990; named Disting. Vol. leader March of Dimes, JEfferson City, 1986. Mem. Am. Soc. Pub. Adminstrn. (chpt. pres. 1988-89), Mo. Inst. Pub. Adminstrn. (v.p. 1994-96), Mo. Assn. Profl. Soil Scientists (chair constn. and by-laws 1988-89), Soil and Water Conservation Soc., KC, Lions (Jefferson City bd. dirs. 1991-92), Gamma Sigma Delta, Pi Alpha Alpha, Sigma Xi. Independent. Roman Catholic. Home: 1315 Dixon Dr Jefferson City MO 65101 Office: Mo Dept Natural Resources PO Box 176 Jefferson City MO 65102

ORSBON, BENJAMIN THOMAS, transportation planner; b. North Wilkesboro, N.C., Nov. 28, 1951; s. Richard Chapman and Ruby Estelle (Wyatt) O. BA, U. N.C., 1973, MRP, 1975. Regional planner Region D Coun. Govt., Pierre, S.D., 1976-77; policy aide State Planning Bur., Pierre, 1977-79, dep. commr., 1979-84; transp. planner S.D. Dept Transp., Pierre, 1985—; Bd. dirs. Western Planning Resources, Helena, Mont., pres., 1989. Contbr. articles to profl. jours. Backpacking instr. Boy Scouts Am. Mem. APA (pres. western ctrl. chpt. 1996), Am. Inst. Cert. Planners, Kiwanis. Baptist.

ORTH-AIKMUS, GAIL MARIE, police chief; b. Kansas City, Dec. 31, 1956; d. Ben Roy and Janet Ferrell (Buckner) O.; m. Frank Henry Aikmus Jr., Oct. 5, 1980 (div. Oct. 1990); 1 child, Brian Russell. Cert. law enforcement officer, Mo.; cert. drug canine handler; cert. vanner. Patrol officer Parkville (Mo.) Police Dept., 1977-78; deputy Platte County Sheriff, Platte City, Mo., 1978-79; patrol officer, sgt., lt. Pleasant Valley (Mo.) Police Dept., 1979-85, police chief, 1985-95; police chief Avondale (Mo) Police Dept., 1995-96; dep. sheriff Clay County Police Dept., Liberty, Mo., 1996—; bd. dirs. Clay County Investigative, pres. bd. dirs., 1991-93; guest spkr. Clay County Mcpl. Judges Conf.; testified before House Com. with Mo. Ho. of Reps., 1994. Appeared in fraud investigation on ABC 20/20 mag., 1980. Named Officer of Yr. Vets. Fgn. Wars Aux., Kansas City, 1991; recipient Key to Manor Pleasant Valley Manor, 1990, Puppy Trucker award Heart of Am. Van Club, 1994, Lifesaving award ribbon, 1996, Unit citation ribbon, 1996. Mem. Mo. Police Chief's Assn., Mo. Peace Officer's Assn., Kansas City Police Chief's Assn., Kansas City Major Case Squad, Kansas City Women in Law Enforcement, Nat. Assn. Chief's of Police, NRA, Weimaraner Club Am., Weimaraner Club Greater Kansas City (pres. 1991—), World Wide Race Fans. Home: 8405 Kaill Rd Pleasant Vly MO 64068-9007 Office: Clay County Sheriffs Liberty MO 64068

ORTIZ-BUTTON, OLGA, social worker; b. Chgo., July 12, 1953; d. Luis Antonio and Pura (Acevedo) Ortiz; m. Dennis Vesley, Aug. 11, 1973 (div. 1976); m. Randall Russell Button, Nov. 3, 1984 (div. Oct. 1993); children: Joshua, Jordan, Elijah. BA, U. Ill., 1975; MSW, Western Mich. U., 1981. Cert. social worker, sch. social worker. Social svcs. dir. Champaign County Nursing Home, Urbana, Ill., 1976; social svcs. and activity dir. Lawton (Mich.) Nursing Home, 1977; job developer Southwestern Mich. Indian Ctr., Watervliet, 1977-78; staff asst. New Directions Alcohol Treatment Ctr., Kalamazoo, 1978; counselor, instr. Alcohol Hwy. Safety, Kalamazoo, 1978-79; clin. social worker Mecosta County Community Mental Health, Big Rapids, Mich., 1981-84; program dir. substance abuse Sr. Svcs., Inc., Kalamazoo, 1984-85; sch. social worker Martin (Mich.) Pub. Schs., 1985-96; owner, therapist Plainwell (Mich.) Counseling Ctr., 1989—; S.W. cons. Med. Pers. Pool, 1993-94, G.L. Network Mktg., 1993—. Vol. social worker Hospice-Wings of Hope, Plainwell, 1984-85, mem. CQI bd., 1993—; supporter Students Against Aparteid South Africa, Kalamazoo, 1979-81; mem. World Vision and Countertop Ptnr., 1984—; sponsor, vol. People for Ethical Treatment of Animals, 1986-91; vol. helper Sparkies for Awana Club Ch., 1989-95; consortium mem. Mich. Post Adoption Svc. System, 1994—. NIMH Rural Mental Health grantee, 1979-81. Mem. NASW, Mich. Assn. Sch. Social Workers, Am. Assn. Christian Counselors. Office: Plainwell Counseling Ctr 211 E Bannister St Ste K Plainwell MI 49080-1372

ORTIZ-QUIÑONES, CARLOS RUBEN, electronics engineer, educator; b. Bayamon, P.R.; s. Gregorio and Andrea (Quiñones) O. BSEE, U. P.R., 1986; MSEE, U. Dayton, 1990, PhD in Electronic Engring., 1994. Computer tech. instr. U. P.R., Mayaguez, 1986; electronics engr. USAF Wright-Patterson AFB, Dayton, Ohio, 1987—. Contbr. articles to profl. jours. Mem. IEEE.

ORTMANN, JEFFREY, theater producer, director; b. Chgo., June 2, 1954; s. Robert Thomas and Lorraine Rose (Charpentier) O. BFA in Theatre Adminstrn., U. Ill., 1976. Mng. dir. Great Am. People Show, Petersburg, Ill., 1975-76; mgr. audience ops. U. Ill. Krannert Ctr. for Performing Arts, Urbana, 1976-77; dir. ops. St. Louis Symphony Orchestra, 1977-79; exec. dir. Wisdom Bridge Theatre, Chgo., 1979-88, producing dir., 1989—; part-time faculty Roosevelt U., Chgo., 1991—. Producer Hamlet, 1985 (Joseph Jefferson award), Kabuki Macbeth, 1982 (Joseph Jefferson award), Getting Out, 1980 (Joseph Jefferson award). Treas., chmn. Howard/Paulina Devel. Corp., Chgo., 1984—; mem. adv. bd. Artists Abroad, 1986-88; trustee, v.p., pres. Chgo. Theatre Found., 1983—; bd. dirs., pres. League of Chgo. Theatres, 1980-86; co-founder, pres. Centre East for the Arts, 1978—. Mem. Am. Arts Alliance, Ill. Arts Alliance, Theatre Communications Group. Democrat. Roman Catholic. *

ORTON, GEORGE FREDERICK, aerospace engineer; b. Flushing, N.Y., Aug. 8, 1941; s. Harry and Evelyn (Brostrom) O.; m. Susan K., Dec. 21, 1962; children: Karen, Kevin, Kristen. BS in Aeron. Engring., U. Md., 1964; MS in Engring. Mechanics, St. Louis U., 1971. Engr. propulsion McDonnell Douglas, St. Louis, 1964-73, sr. engr. propulsion, 1973-77, unit chief propulsion, 1977-81, sect. chief propulsion, 1981-86, br. chief nat. aerospace plane, 1986-90, staff dir. nat. aerospace plane, 1990-92, dir. space programs, 1992-93, program mgr. Hypersonics Ctr. Excellence, 1993—. Contbr. articles to profl. jours. Advisor Explorer Post 9005, St. Louis, 1980-87; sci. advisor University City (Mo.) Schs. Fellow AIAA (assoc., mem. liquid propulsion tech. com. 1980-84, 91-95, Best Paper award 1986), St. Louis Head Injury Assn. Methodist. Office: McDonnell Douglas Corp Mailcode 1067250 PO Box 516 Saint Louis MO 63166

ORWOLL, GREGG S. K., lawyer; b. Austin, Minn., Mar. 23, 1926; s. Gilbert M. and Kleonora (Kleven) O.; m. Laverne M. Flentie, Sept. 15, 1951; children: Kimball G., Kent A., Vikki A., Tristen A., Erik G. BS, Northwestern U., 1950; JD, U. Minn., 1953. Bar: Minn. 1953, U.S. Supreme Ct. 1973. Assoc. Dorsey & Whitney, Mpls., 1953-59, ptnr., 1959-60; assoc. counsel Mayo Clinic, Rochester, Minn., 1960-63, gen. counsel, 1963-87, sr. legal counsel, 1987-91, sr. counsel, 1991-92; gen. counsel, dir. Rochester Airport Co., 1962-84, v.p., 1981-84; gen. counsel Mayo Med. Svcs., Ltd., 1972-90; bd. dirs., sec. and gen. counsel Mayo Found. for Med. Edn. and Rsch., 1984-90; gen. counsel Mid-Am. Orthopaedic Assn., 1984—, Minn. Orthopaedic Soc., 1985—; asst. sec./sec. Mayo Found., Rochester, 1972-91; bd. dirs. Charter House, 1986-90; dir. Travelure Motel Corp., 1968-86, sec., 1968-83, v.p., 1983-86; dir., v.p. Echo Too Ent., Inc.; dir., v.p. Oberhamer Inc.; bd. dirs. Am. Decal and Mfg. Co., 1989-93, sec., 1992-93; adj. prof. William Mitchell Coll. Law, 1978-84. Contbr. articles and chpts. to legal and medico-legal publs.; bd. editors HealthSpan, 1984-93; editorial bd. Minn. Law Rev., 1952-53. Trustee Minn. Coun. on Founds., 1977-82, Mayo Found., 1982-86; trustee William Mitchell Coll. Law, 1982-88, 89—, mem. exec. com. 1990—; bd. visitors U. Minn. Law Sch., 1974-76, 85-91; mem. U. Minn. Regent Candidate Adv. Coun., 1988—, Minn. State Compensation Coun., 1991, 91-95. With USAF, 1944-45. Recipient Outstanding Svc. medal U.S. Govt., 1991. Mem. ABA, AMA (affiliate), Am. Corp. Counsel Assn., Minn. Soc. Hosp. Attys. (bd. dirs. 1981-86), Minn. State Bar Assn. (chmn. legal/med. com. 1977-81), Olmsted County Bar Assn. (v.p., pres. 1977-79), Rochester C. of C., U. Minn. Law Alumni Assn. (bd. dirs. 1973-76, 85-91), Rochester U. Club (pres. 1977), The Doctors Mayo Soc., Mid Am. Ortho. Assn. (hon.), Mayo Alumni Assn. (hon.), Phi Delta Phi, Phi Delta Theta. Republican. Home: 2233 Fifth Ave NE Rochester MN 55906-4017 Office: Mayo Clinic 200 1st St SW Rochester MN 55905-0001

ORYSHKEVICH, ROMAN SVIATOSLAV, physician, physiatrist, dentist, educator; b. Olesko, Ukraine, Aug. 5, 1928; came to U.S., 1955, naturalized, 1960; s. Simeon and Caroline (Deneszczuk) O.; m. Oksana Lishchynsky, June 16, 1962; children: Marta, Mark, Alexandra. DDS, Ruperto-Carola U., Heidelberg, Ger., 1952, MD, 1953, PhD cum laude, 1955. Cert. Am. Assn. Electromygraphy and Electrodiagnosis, 1964; diplomate Am. Bd. Phys. Medicine and Rehab., 1966, Am. Bd. Electrodiagnostic Medicine, 1989. Research fellow in cancer Esptl. Cancer Inst., Rupert-Charles U., 1953-55; rotating intern Coney Island Hosp., Bklyn., 1955-56; resident in diagnostic radiology NYU Bellevue Med. Ctr.-Univ. Hosp., 1956-57; resident, fellow in phys. medicine and rehab. Western Res. U. Highland View Hosp., Cleve., 1958-60; orthopedic surgery Met. Gen. Hosp., Cleve., 1959; asst. chief rehab. medicine service VA West Side Med. Ctr., Chgo., 1961-74, acting chief, 1974-75, chief, 1975—; dir., coord. edn. U. Ill. Integrated Residency Program, Phys. Medicine & Rehab, 1974-89; clin. instr. U. Ill., 1962-65, asst. clin. prof., 1965-70, asst. prof., 1970-75, assoc. clin. prof., 1975-94, clin. prof., 1994—. Author, editor: Who and What in U.W.M.M., 1978; contbr. articles to profl. jours; splty. cons. in phys. medicine and rehab. to editorial bd. Chgo. Med. Jours., 1978-89. Founder, pres. Ukrainian World Med. Mus., Chgo., 1977; founder, 1st pres. Am. Mus. Phys. Medicine and Rehab., 1980-91. Fellow AAUP, Am. Acad. Phys. Medicine and Rehab.; mem. Assn. Acad. Physiatrists, Am. Assn. Electromyography and Electrodiagnosis, Ill. Soc. Phys. Medicine and Rehab. (pres., dir. 1979-80), Ukrainian Med. Assn. N.Am. (dir., pres. chpt. 1977-79, fin. mgr. 17th med. conv. and congress Chgo. 1977, adminstr. and conv. chmn. 1979), World Fedn. Ukrainian Med. Assns. (co-founder and 1st exec. sec. research and sci. 1977-79), Internat. Rehab. Medicine Assn., Rehab. Internat. U.S.A., Nat. Assn. VA Physicians, AAAS, Assn. Med. Rehab. Dirs. and Coordinators, Nat. Rehab. Assn., Nat. Assn. Disability Examiners, Am. Med. Writers Assn., Biofeedback Research Soc. Am., Chgo. Soc. Phys. Medicine and Rehab. (pres., founder 1978-79), Ill. Rehab. Assn., Ukrainian Acad. Med. Scis. (founder, pres. 1979-80), Gerontol. Soc., Internat. Soc. Electrophysiol. Kinesiology, Internat. Soc. Prosthetics and Orthotics, Fedn. Am. Scientists. Ukrainian Catholic. Home: 1819 N 78th Ct Chicago IL 60635-3502 Office: 820 S Damen Ave Chicago IL 60612-3728

OSBORN, JANET LYNN, information systems executive; b. Berea, Ohio, Dec. 25, 1952; d. Walter Martin and Mary Alice O. BS in Systems Analysis, Miami U., Ohio, 1975; MBA, U. Mich., 1984; postgrad., Universidad de las Americas, Puebla, Mex., 1974. Cons. mgmt. info. systems Arthur Andersen and Co., Cinn., 1975-77; systems analyst Consumers Power Co., Jackson, Mich., 1977-79, sr. systems analyst, 1979-81, supr. analyst, 1982, mgr. corp. systems, 1983-85, mgr. litigation systems, 1985-87, mgr. quality assurance and data adminstrn., 1988-89, mgr. info. and tech. planning and quality assurance, 1989-90; project dir. customer info. systems Consumer Power Co., Jackson, Mich., 1991-93; mgr. large project planning and mgmt. Consumer Power Co., Jackson, 1993—. Solicitor United Way, Jackson, 1983-84; vol. LPGA Oldsmobile Classic Golf Tournament, 1994—, Jackson City Christmas Parade, 1994—; mem. Jackson Community Band, 1995—. Mem. Project Mgmt. Inst., Pi Mu Epsilon, Phi Kappa Phi, Delta Delta Delta. Office: Consumers Power Co 1945 W Parnall Rd Jackson MI 49201-8658

OSBORN, JOHN DAVID, credit union executive; b. Indpls., Feb. 29, 1948; s. John Isaac and Belva M. (Grubb) O.; m. Wanda Sue Hall, June 22, 1974; children: John David II, Heather Marie, James Michael. BBA, U. Ga., 1971. Office mgr. United Empire Life Ins. Co., Indpls., 1971-73, adminstrv. v.p., 1973-76; mgr. data and devel. Ind. Telco Fed. Credit Union, 1976-82; pres. Fin. Ctr. Fed. Credit Union, 1982-92, Anheuser-Busch Employees Credit Union, St. Louis, 1992—; past bd. dirs., vice chmn. Ind. Corp. Credit Union, Indpls., Fin. Ctr. Svc. Corp., Indpls.; past chmn. Def. Credit Union Coun., Washington; past bd. dirs. Teeter Found., Noblesville, Ind. Pres. Wellington North Civic Assn., Noblesville, Ind., 1985-86. Mem. Credit Union Execs. Soc., Nat. Exch. Club (pres. Lawrence 1985). Republican. Methodist. Office: Anheuser Busch Employees Credit Union 1001 Lynch St Saint Louis MO 63118-1818

OSBORN, KENNETH LOUIS, financial executive; b. Belleville, Ill., Jan. 9, 1946; s. William Arthur and Louise Mary (Bruegenn) O.; BBA, U. N.Mex., 1968; m. Roberta Marie Vodicka, Oct. 23, 1971; 1 son, David Anthony. Auditor, Ernst & Ernst, Albuquerque, 1968; budge mgr. Rockwell

Internat., Chgo., 1970-74; mgr. internat. acctg. Allied Van Lines, Chgo., 1974-76; fin. mgr. Sealy, Inc., Chgo., 1976-79; sr. fin. analyst Newark Electronics, Chgo., 1979-80, internat. dir. credit, 1980-82; bus. mgr. Prime Computer, 1982-90; acctg. mgr., CFO Flexonics, Inc., Chgo., 1990-96; contr. Jackson Industries, Chgo., 1996—; fin. cons. Am. European Expres. Mem. Rep. Nat. Com., presdl. task force. With AUS, 1968-70. Decorated Air medal. Mem. Mensa, Soc. Am. Baseball Rsch., Inst. Mgmt. Accts.

OSBORN, LARRY LEE, farmer, county official; b. Breckenridge, N.D., Oct. 2, 1943; s. Leonard Raymond and Clara Etta (Stelton) O.; m. Jeanne Eunyce Baird, Oct. 24, 1944; children: Steven, Mark. AS, N.D. State Sch. Sci., 1963; BS, Valley City State Coll., 1965. Tchr. Dickey (N.D.) Sch. Dist., 1966-67, Graceville (Minn.) Pub. Schs., 1967-69; quality control specialist Peavey Co., Chaska, Minn., 1969-72; quality control mgr. trainee Peavey Co., Hastings, Minn., 1972-76; ind. farmer LaMars Twp., N.D., 1976—; supr. tax and property County of Richland, Wahpeton, N.D., 1988—; instr. N.D. Farmland Appraisers, 1993—. Tax columnist several daily and weekly newspapers. NSF scholar, 1966; recipient Nat. award Nat. Assn. Counties, 1994. Mem. N.D. Farm Mgrs. and Appraisers, N.D. Farm Bur., N.D. Farmers Union, N.D. Assn. Assessing Officers (v.p., region pres. 1991-93, legis. com. 1992—). Democrat. Methodist. Office: County of Richland 418 2nd Ave N Wahpeton ND 58075-4400

OSBORN, MARK ELIOT, dentist; b. Buffalo, Apr. 22, 1950; s. Thomas Earl and Ruth Frances (Martin) O. BA, U. Mo., Columbia, 1972; DDS, U. Mo., Kansas City, 1977. Dir. Westport Free Health Clinic, Kansas City, Mo., 1974-76; clinician St. Louis Dept. Health, 1977-82; gen. practice dentistry Troy, Mo., 1978-92; pvt. practice St. Louis, 1993-94; mem. gen. practice staff Gravois-Gustine Dental Group, St. Louis, 1994—. Mem. ADA, Greater St. Louis Dental Soc., Am. Soc. Dentistry for Children, St. Louis Dental Rsch. Group, Delta Sigma Delta, Troy C. of C., Rotary (Troy chpt., dir. dental program 1985—, sec. 1988, pres. 1989, bd. dirs. 1989-91). Home: 360 W Point Ct Saint Louis MO 63130-4028 Office: 3921 Gravois Ave Saint Louis MO 63116

OSBORNE, GAYLA MARLENE, sales executive; b. Owenton, Ky., Aug. 9, 1956; d. Frederick Clay and Helen Beatrice (Mason) O. AAS, No. Ky. U., 1982, BS, 1986; cert. in Chinese Mandarin, Def. Lang. Inst., 1975. Pers. clk. Dept. Edn. State Ky., Frankfort, 1974; sec. Dept. Health, Edn., Welfare Nat. Inst. Occupational Safety Health, Cin., 1977-79; specialist sales promotion U.S. Postal Svc., Cin., 1980, coord. customer liaison, task force pub. image, account rep., 1986-87, with stamp distbn. task force, 1993—; reservation sale agt. Delta Airlines, 1987-89. Councilmember Florence City Coun., Ky. 1984-87; vol. Children's Home, Covington, 1982, 87. With USAF, 1974-76. Named to Hon. Order Ky. Cols. Mem. Disabled Am. Veterans, No. Ky. U. Alumni Assn., Nat. Assn. Postmasters U.S., Boone County Fraternal Order Police, Ky. Assn. Realtors, Nat. Bd. Realtors, Women in Mil. Svc. for Am. (charter). Democrat. Baptist. Club: Fraternal Order Police. Home: 8395 Juniper Ln Florence KY 41042-9279

OSBORNE, JOHN HAMPTON, publishing company executive; b. Harlan, Ky., Dec. 10, 1945; s. John and Onedia (Taylor) O.; m. Marie-Angela Mazzocco, Oct. 28, 1978; children: Domenique, Robert, John. BS in Econs. and Mgmt., Oakland U., Rochester, Mich., 1973. Thread gage insp. Alameda Gage Co., Oak Park, Mich., 1967-71; in prodn. Warren (Mich.) Truck Assembly, 1964-67, 71-73; pub. Auto Swapper Mag., Southfield, Mich., 1976-89; pres. Hampton Pubs., Inc., Southfield, 1978-89; cons. Landmark Communications, Norfolk, Va., 1989—; pub. Track & Tire, Southfield, 1991—; pres. CBET Pub. Co., Southfield, 1991—; founder, pres. Nationwide Searches, Inc., Southfield, 1996—, Nationwide Auto Search, Southfield, 1996—, Nationwide Machinery Search, Southfield, 1996—; ptnr. Sierra Mgmt. Co., Southfield, 1985—. Mem. Birmingham (Mich.) Hist. Soc., 1989—; mem. Founders Soc./Greenfield Village, Dearborn, Mich., 1985—; volleyball, basketball and softball coach Birmingham CYO, 1990—; bd. dirs. Hampton Humanities Coun., 1985—. Named to Hon. Order of Ky. Cols. Mem. Evarts Alumni Assn., Rotary Internat. Republican. Home: 583 Bloomfield Ct Birmingham MI 48009-3876 Office: Nationwide Searches Inc 29829 Greenfield Rd Ste 101 Southfield MI 48076-2201

OSBORNE, QUINTON ALBERT, psychiatric social worker; b. Hopkinsville, Ky., May 14, 1951; s. Willie Lee and Elizabeth (Talley) O.; m. Gwendolyn G. Flowers, Oct. 19, 1991; 1 adopted child, Quinton A. Jr.; children: Ashley Elain, Shelbie Elizabeth. BS in Sociology, Austin Peay State U., 1978; MS in Health Adminstrn., Calif. Coll. Health Sci., 1996. Lic. social worker, Ohio, Ky., D.C. Fin. specialist U.S. Army, Karlsruhe, Fed. Republic Germany, 1972-75; resident advisor Breckinridge Job Corps, Morganfield, Ky., 1978; clk., typist Govt. D.C., Washington, 1979; asst. worker's compensation Dept. Labor, Mt. Sterling, Ky., 1979-80; social svc. asst. U.S. Forest Svc., Mariba, Ky., 1980-85; mil. pay clk. Ky. N.G., Frankfort, 1985-86; social worker Cin. VA Med. Ctr., 1986-88; equal opportunity specialist US Dept. HUD, Columbus, Ohio, 1988-90; family tchr. Maryville Acad., 1991-93; mem. Victorian Eva Vet. Group, Cin., 1975—, task force for homeless U.S. Dept. HUD, Columbus, 1988-89; chair ptnrs. in edn. VA Med. Ctr., Cin., 1986-88, Op. Feed, Columbus, 1988-89; social worker Vets. Homeless Program, Cin., 1988—; sect. and employees asst. coord., chairperson Adopt-A-Sch. Program, 1991—. Mem. Ptnrs. in Edn. (chairperson 1986-88), Alpha Phi Alpha (pres. Clarksville, Tenn. chpt. 1977-78), Alpha Phi Alpha (Clarksville chpt.). Republican. Baptist. Home: 509 14th Avenue Middletown OH 45044 Office: Lebanon Correctional Instn Lebanon OH 45036

OSDOBY, PHILIP ARNOLD, biologist, educator; b. Monticello, N.Y.; s. Ben and Ida (Kapito) O.; m. Patricia Collin, Aug. 12, 1977; children: Megan, Lauren. BA, Hofstra U., 1971; MA, CUNY, 1974; PhD, Case Western Res. U., 1978. Arthritis Found. fellow, postdoctoral fellow Case Western Res. U., Cleve., 1978-81; asst. prof. dental sch. Washington U., St. Louis, 1981-87, assoc. prof., 1987-90, assoc. prof. dept. biology, 1990-94, prof., 1994—. Contbr. articles to profl. jours. and chpts. to books. Mem. AAAS, Endocrine Soc., Am. Soc. for Bone and Mineral Rsch., Am. Soc. Cell Biology. Office: Washington U Dept Biology Box 1229 Saint Louis MO 63130

OSERMAN, STUART, internist; b. Chgo., Aug. 5, 1953; s. Ben and Tess (Zemel) O.; m. Lanis Lynn Kuyzin, June 26, 1982. BA, Northwestern U., Evanston, Ill., 1974; MD, U. Ill., 1978. Diplomate Am. Bd. Internal Medicine; cert. added qualifications in geriatric medicine. Resident, internal medicine Luth. Gen. Hosp., Park Ridge, Ill., 1978-81, fellow ambulatory medicine, 1981-82, supervising internist, 1982—; clin. faculty U. Ill. Coll. Medicine, Chgo., 1979-92, lectr. in medicine, 1992—; clin. assoc. prof. U. Chgo.-Pritzker Sch. of Medicine, 1992—; pres. med. staff Parkside Luth. Hosp., Park Ridge, 1991-92; assoc. med. dir. Luth. Gen. Health Plan, Park Ridge, 1988-89. Trustee Morton Grove (Ill.) Pub. Libr., 1985-93, pres., 1992-93. Fellow ACP; mem. AMA (Physician Recognition awards 1981-96), Am. Coll. Physician Execs., Am. Geriatrics Soc., Am. Soc. Internal Medicine, Med. Amateur Radio Coun., Soc. for Gen. Internal Medicine. Home: 7729 Church St Morton Grove IL 60053-1623 Office: Advocate Med Group 1775 Ballard Rd Park Ridge IL 60068-1005

OSHEFSKY, CAROL ANN, retired elementary education educator; b. Kewaunee County, Wis., Apr. 28, 1931; d. William Edward and Mayme (Hostak) Lazansky; m. Norman Earl Oshefsky, June 20, 1953; children: Quin, Norman II, Cathleen. BS, U. Wis., Oshkosh, 1964; MS, U. Wis., Green Bay, 1980. Cert. tchr., Wis. Tchr. West Klondike Sch., Mountain, Wis., 1950-53, St. Mary Cath. Sch., De Pere, Wis., 1956-57, Howard-Suamico Sch. Dist., Green Bay, Wis., 1962-64, Ashwaubenon Sch. Dist., Green Bay, 1966-90; ret., 1990. Choralier Czech Choraliers, Wis., 1978—; bd. dirs. Wis. Czechs, Inc., Kewaunee County, 1987-89, Kewaunee County Hist. Soc., 1994—. Mem. NEA (life), Wis. Ret. Tchrs. Assn., Brown County Ret. Tchrs. Assn., Bay Area Geneal. Soc., Czechoslovak Geneal. Soc. Internat. Roman Catholic. Home: E4311 Hwy 54 Algoma WI 54201-9720

OSINIAK, RANDALL C., mechanical design engineer; b. Youngstown, Ohio, Jan. 4, 1961. BS in Applied Sci., Youngstown State U., 1988. Mech. design engr. Ajax Magnethermic Corp., Warren, Ohio, 1988—. Mem. Bethlehem United Ch., Youngstown, 1968—. Home: 74 Forest Garden Dr Youngstown OH 44512 Office: Ajax Magnethermic Corp PO Box 991 1745 Overland Ave NE Warren OH 44482-0991

OSIYOYE, ADEKUNLE, obstetrician, gynecologist, educator; b. Lagos, Nigeria, Jan. 5, 1951; came to U.S., 1972; s. Alfred and Grace (Apena) Oshiyoye; m. Toyin Osinowo Oshiyoye, Dec. 28, 1991; children: Adekunle Jr., Adedayo Justice. Student, Howard U., 1972-73; BS, U. State of N.Y., 1974; postgrad., Columbia U., 1974-78; MD, Am. U., Montserrat, West Indies, 1979. Intern South Chgo. Community Hosp., 1980-81; intern dept. obstetrics-gynecology Cook County Hosp., Chgo., 1981-82, resident physician, 1982-84, chief resident physician dept. obstetrics-gynecology, 1984-85; assoc. prof. dept. obstetrics-gynecology Chgo. Osteo. Coll. Medicine, 1986—; health physician, cons. physician City of Chgo. Dept. Health, 1989—; attending physician St. Bernard Hosp., Chgo., 1985—, Hyde Park Hosp., Chgo., 1986—, Mercy Hosp., Chgo., 1987—, Roseland Hosp., Chgo., 1985—, Columbus Hosp., Chgo., 1985—, Jackson Park Hosp., Chgo., 1985—; coord. emergency rm. Cook County Hosp., 1983-85. Med. editor African Connections, 1990—; med. columnist Newsbreed Mag., 1990—; founding mem. Ob-Gyn Video Jour. Am. Organizer Harold Washington Coalition, Chgo., 1983-87; operation mem. Operation P.U.S.H., Chgo., 1987—; active Chgo. Urban League, 1989—, Cook County Dem. Party, 1988—; mem. Mayor's Commn. on Human Rels., Chgo., 1990—, State of Ill. Inaugural Com., 1991. Shell scholar, 1965-69; recipient Fed. Govt. scholarship award, 1972, Howard Univ. scholarship award, 1973, Fed. Govt. Nigeria grad. med. scholarship award, 1975-79, Cerebral Palsy rsch. award, 1977, Ob-gyn. Video Jour. award, 1989, Role Model award Chgo. Police Dept., 1991, 92, Chgo. Bd. Edn., 1991, Chgo. 100 Black Men, 1991, Gov.'s Recognition award, 1992; named one of Best Dressed Men in Chgo., Chgo. Defender, 1990, 91. Fellow Am. Coll. Internat. Physicians, Am. Coll. Obstetricians & Gynecologists; mem. AMA (physician recognition award 1986), Am. Coll. Glegal Medicine (edn. com.), Am. Soc. Law Medicine, Am. Pub. Heart Assn., Nat. Med. Assn., Ill. Med. Soc., Chgo. Med. Assn., Chgo. Gynecol. Soc., Cook County Physician Assn., Nigerian Am. Forum (chmn. health com., chmn. election com.), Cook County Hosp. Surg. Alumni Assn., Howard U. Alumni Assn. (regent, chmn. scholarship com. Chgo. chpt.), Eureka Lodge (investigating com.), Masons, Shriners, Order of Eastern Star, Alpha Phi Alpha (life mem., mem. Labor Day com., dir. ednl. programs Xi Lambda chpt. 1990—, co-chmn. courtesy Black & Gold com. 1989, 90, Recognition award 1991), Pan Hellenic Action Coun. (chmn. pub. rels. com.), Ill. Maternal and Child Health Coalition, Beta Kappa Chi. Apostolic. Home: PO Box 15187 Lansing MI 48901-5187 Office: Dept Health 37 W 47th St Chicago IL 60609-4657

OSMYCKI, DANIEL A., commercial real estate broker, consultant; b. Detroit, Nov. 26, 1931; s. Henry Stanley and Mary Dorothy (Machowski) O.; m. Judith Marilyn Soltess, Aug. 31, 1963; children: Jennifer Marie, David Alan. BCS in Acctg., Detroit Bus. U., 1954; BBA in Acctg., Detroit Inst. of Tech., 1973; cert. in real estate, U. Mich., Ann Arbor, 1976. Exec. v.p., treas. Griswold Mortgage Co., Detroit, 1962-65; broker, ptnr. various mortgage cos., Detroit, 1965-75; broker, owner Daniel A. Osmycki, Realtor, Mt. Clemens, Mich., 1976—; pres. Grand Traverse Realty, Inc., 1994—. Contbr. article to local newspaper. With USN, 1948-52. Mem. Realtors Alumni of Mich., Am. Real Estate Soc., Am. Real Estate and Urban Econs. Assn., U.S. Coast Guard Aux. (vice commdr. 1977), Clinton River Boat Club (commodore 1978).

OSOWIEC, DARLENE ANN, clinical psychologist, educator, consultant; b. Chgo., Feb. 16, 1951; d. Stephen Raymond and Estelle Marie Osowiec; m. Barry A. Leska. BS, Loyola U., Chgo., 1973; MA with honors, Roosevelt U., 1980; postgrad. in psychology, Saybrook Inst., San Francisco, 1985-88; PhD in Clin. Psychology, Calif. Inst. Integral Studies, 1992. Lic. clin. psychologist, Mo., Ill. Mental health therapist Ridgeway Hosp., Chgo., 1978; mem. faculty psychology dept. Coll. Lake County, Grayslake, Ill., 1981; counselor, supr. MA-level interns, chmn. pub. rels. com. Integral Counseling Ctr., San Francisco, 1983-84; clin. psychology intern Chgo.-Read Mental Health Ctr. Ill. Dept. Mental Health, 1985-86; mem. faculty dept. psychology Moraine Valley C.C., Palos Hills, Ill., 1988-89; lectr. psychology Daley Coll., Chgo., 1988-90; cons. Gordon & Assocs., Oak Lawn, Ill., 1989—; adolescent, child and family therapist Orland Twp. Youth Svcs., Orland Park, Ill., 1993; psychology fellow Sch. Medicine, St. Louis U., 1994-95; clin. psychologist in pvt. practice Chgo., 1996—. Ill. State scholar, 1969-73; Calif. Inst. Integral Studies scholar, 1983. Mem. APA, Am. Psychol. Soc., Am. Women in Psychology, Am. Statis. Assn., Ill. Psychol. Assn., Calif. Psychol. Assn., Mo. Psychol. Assn., Gerontol. Soc. Am., Am. Soc. Clin. Hypnosis, Internat. Platform Assn., Chgo. Soc. Clin. Hypnosis, NOW (chair legal adv. corps, Chgo. 1974-76). Home: 6608 S Whipple St Chicago IL 60629-2916

OSSKOPP, MIKE, state legislator; b. Oct. 3, 1951; m. Monica Osskopp; 2 children. BA, Inst. Broadcast Arts; MA, Moody Bible Inst. Minn. state rep. Dist. 29B, 1994—; radio broadcast journalist. Address: 1024 Lilac Ln Lake City MN 55041

OSTER, LEWIS HENRY, manufacturing executive, engineering consultant; b. Mitchell, S.D., Jan. 18, 1923; s. Peter W. and Lucy (Goetsch) O.; m. Mary Mills, Aug. 17, 1948; children—David, Lewis, Nancy, Susan. B.S. in Engring., Iowa State U., 1948; M.B.A., Syracuse U., 1968. Registered profl. engr., Iowa. Mgr., Maytag Co., Newton, Iowa, 1953-59; sr. staff engr., mgr. Philco-Ford Corp., Phila., 1959-62; mgr. mech. and indsl. engring. Carrier Corp., Syracuse, N.Y., 1962-75; v.p. Superior Industries Internat., Van Nuys, Calif., 1981—; v.p., gen. mgr. Superior/Ideal, Inc., Oskaloosa, Iowa, 1975—; engring. cons., Louisville, 1951-53. Author: MTM Application Manual, 1957. Leader, Boy Scouts Am., Syracuse, 1965-73; fund chmn. United Fund, Syracuse, 1965-73. Served to lt. col. USAFR, 1942—; ETO. Mem. Am. Inst. Indsl. Engrs. (pres. 1951-53). Club: Oskaloosa Country. Lodge: Elks.

OSTERBERG, THOMAS KARL, construction company executive; b. Worthington, Minn., Sept. 20, 1953; s. Milton A. and Lucille I. (Pawek) O.; m. Pamela L. Adams, June 14, 1980; children: Emily L., Tucker S. AA, Worthington C.C., 1975; BA, Minn. State U., 1978. Football coach Worthington C.C., 1973-75, Mankato (Minn.) State U., 1975-78; carpenter Pepper Constrn., Mankato, 1976-78; prin. Osterberg Constrn., Mankato, 1978-82; project mgr. Constrn. 70, Inc., Roseville, Minn., 1982-83; gen. mgr., exec. v.p. Carlson-LaVine, Inc., Mpls., 1983—; v.p. Benson-Orth Assocs., Inc.; mem. Young Execs. Mpls., 1985; exec. Mgmt. Com., Mpls., 1988-91. Mem. Am. Swedish Inst., The Swedish Soc. Lutheran. Home: 17500 64th St SW Cokato MN 55321-4700 Office: 14300 Ridgedale Dr Ste 320 Minnetonka MN 55343

OSTERHOUDT, CORA LAVINE SHULTS, mental health and medical/surgical nurse; b. Maywood, Nebr., June 5, 1930; d. Glen E. and Berniece (Doudna) Shults; m. Howard A. Osterhoudt, Dec. 25, 1947; children: Marlin, Cheryl, Dwight, Leslie. AA, Dakota Wesleyan U., 1985; BSN, Clarkson Coll., Omaha, 1995. RN, Nebr. Pool nurse Great Plains Med. Ctr., North Platte, Nebr., 1985-86; staff nurse McCook (Nebr.) Community Hosp., 1986-88; psychiat. nurse, supr. Richard Young Hosp. (div. Good Samaritan System), Kearney, Nebr., 1988-92; nurse supr. divsn. Good Samaritan Homes, Inc. St. John's Ctr., Kearney, Nebr., 1992—. Mem. ANA, Nebr. Nurses Assn., DAV, NRA. Home: # 42 2701 Grande Ave Kearney NE 68847-4133

OSTERKAMP, LYNN BOWIE, gerontologist, consultant, social worker; b. Cambridge, Mass., June 6, 1941; d. Winton Stuart and Genevieve Rose (Spear) Bowie; m. Waite R. Osterkamp, June 15, 1963, (div. June 29, 1978); children: Jeffrey Mark Osterkamp, Laurel Alyce Osterkamp; m. Allan N. Press, Oct. 20, 1978. BA, U. Colo., 1963; MA, U. Ariz., 1970; PhD, U. Kans., 1979; MSW, 1995. Speech and hearing therapist Laradon Hall Sch., Denver, 1964-65, Colo. State Home and Tng. Sch., Wheatridge, Colo., 1965-66, Headstart Program, Helena, Mont., 1966-68; teaching asst. U. Ariz., Tucson, 1968-69; speech clinician Lawrence (Kans.) USD # 497, 1975-76; rsch. asst. U. Kans., Lawrence, 1977-79; cons., trainer pvt. practice, Lawrence, Kans., 1979-81; rsch. assoc. U. Kans., Lawrence, 1981-94; v.p. Preventive Measures, Inc., Lawrence, Kans., 1984—; social worker Horizon Splty. Hosp., Overland Park, Kans., 1995, Social Work P.R.N., 1996—; reviewer Adminstrn. on Aging Discretionary Grants, Washington, 1984-90; mem. adv. bd. Housing Options Made Easier, Lawrence, Kans., 1990-93; mem. Task Force for Older Kans., Topeka, 1991-92. Author: Stress? Find Your Balance, 1983, 88, How to Deal With Your Parents, 1992; editor: Parent Care, 1985-91; co-author: Computerized Stress Inventory, 1984. Vol. Douglas County Hospice, Lawrence, Kans., 1992—, Sr. Health Ins. Counseling for Kans., 1994—. AOA grantee, 1985-88; Mary Switzer Disting. Rehab. Rsch. fellow NIDRR, 1992-93. Mem. NASW, Gerontological Assn. Am., Speech Comm. Assn. Am. Home: 1115 W Campus Rd Lawrence KS 66044 Office: Preventive Measures Inc 1115 W Campus Rd Lawrence KS 66044-3115

OSTERLOH, EVERETT WILLIAM, county official; b. Luxemburg, Mo., June 7, 1919; s. Fred and Esther (Miller) O.; m. Eunice Gramann, Oct. 20, 1940 (dec. Apr. 1983); m. Herta Anna Emery, Oct. 25, 1987. BSME, Washington U., St. Louis, 1958. Registered profl. engr., Mo.; cert. code ofcl. Plant engr. Jasper-Blackburn Corp., St. Louis, 1958-60; equipment engr. Monsanto Chem. Co., St. Louis, 1960-68; pres. Caribean Beach Club, Antigua, West Indies, 1968-73; dep. dir. pub. works St. Louis County Govt., Clayton, Mo., 1973-93; assoc. dir. emergency preparedness pub. works St. Louis County Govt., St. Louis, 1993—; engring. instr. St. Louis Community Coll., 1986-91; exec. sec. Profl. Code Com. St. Louis, 1975—, Met. Area Code Com., St. Louis, 1982—. Staff sgt. USAF, 1942-53. Mem. Mo. Soc. Profl. Engrs. (emergency response task force 1990-92, pres. St. Louis chpt. 1991-92, chmn. disaster response com. 1992—, Outstanding Engr. in Govt. 1987). Lutheran. Home: 283 Spring Oaks Dr Ballwin MO 63011-3835 Office: St Louis County Govt Emergency Ops Ctr 14847 Olive St Saint Louis MO 63103

OSTERMAN, FREDERIC J., retail executive; b. Buffalo, N.Y., Aug. 18, 1952; s. Maurice and Ella (Kenyon) O.; m. Barbara Rogers, Aug. 21, 1977. BA in History, Canisius Coll., 1974. Sales Tandy Corp. (Radio Shack), Buffalo, N.Y., 1969-74; store mgr. Tandy Corp. (Radio Shack), Buffalo and Niagara Falls, N.Y., 1974-77; dist. mgr., Western Pa. Tandy Corp. (Radio Shack), Pitts., 1977-78; dist. mgr., N.E. Ohio Tandy Corp. (Radio Shack), Akron, Ohio, 1978; dist. mgr., Cen. Ohio Tandy Corp. (Radio Shack), Columbus, 1978-80; computer ctr. mgr. Tandy Corp. (Radio Shack), Louisville, 1980-81; regional computer mktg. mgr. Tandy Corp. (Radio Shack), Columbus, 1981-83; owner, pres. Universal Radio, Inc., Reynoldsburg, Ohio, 1983—, Universal Shortwave Radio Rsch., Reynoldsburg, Ohio, 1984—. Author: The DXer's Dictionary, 1985, 86, 88, The Shortwave Log, 1984, Shortwave Receivers Past and Present, 1987, Russian Maritime Radioteletype Dictionary, 1988; contbr. articles to profl. jours. Republican. Office: Universal Radio Inc 6830 Americana Parkway Dr Reynoldsburg OH 43068-4113

OSTHOFF, TOM, state legislator; b. 1936; m. Sandra Osthoff; 1 child. Student, U. Minn. Mem. Minn. Ho. of Reps. St. Paul, 1974—; asst. minority leader; former chmn. transp. and transit com., mem. appropriations com., gaming com., others. Mgr. county records divsn. Ramsey County, Minn. Democrat. Office: 591 State Office Bldg Saint Paul MN 55155-1201*

OSTLUND, RICHARD ALLEN, designer; b. Mpls., June 20, 1947. Designer Brown Boveri Turbo Machinery, Mpls., 1976-83; designer Frigidaire Co., St. Cloud, Minn., 1983-91, supr. design and drafting, 1991—. Chmn., March of Dimes, 1995; referee soccer and sports. With U.S. Army, 1967-68. Mem. Eagles. Democrat. Lutheran.

OSTMANN, CINDY, state legislator. BS, Lindenwood Coll. Tchr. Ft. Zumwalt Sch. Dist., 1958-62, 64-67, Fayetteville Sch. Sys., 1963-64; owner, mgr. residential property; mem. Mo. State Ho. of Reps. Dist. 14, 1992—, mem. children, youth and families com., mem. energy and environ. com., mem. local govt. and related matters com. Recipient Outstanding Contbr. to Edn. award Phi Delta Kappa, 1988. Mem. Coun. of Chambers Charter Govt. Com., St. Chalres County Arts Coun., Grand Order of Pachyderm, Friends of St. Louis Symphony, Mo. Fedn. Rep. Women, First Capitol Rep. Club. Home: 445 Knaust Rd Saint Peters MO 63376-1713 Office: Mo Ho of Reps State Capitol Building Jefferson City MO 65101-1556*

OSTREM, WALTER MARTIN, librarian, educator, consultant; b. Mpls., May 27, 1930; s. Oscar Martin and Helen Therese (Marcio) O.; m. Gertrud Franciska Tunkel, Aug. 6, 1956; children—Thomas, Paul, Francine. B.A., U. Minn., 1953, M.A., 1958; B.S., Mankato State U., 1962, M.S., 1964; postgrad. U. Mich., U. Iowa. Serials librarian Agr. Library U. Minn., 1958-59; acquisitions librarian Mankato State U., Minn., 1959-66, Eastern Mich. U., 1966-67; dir. media Iowa City Sch., 1967-69; librarian John F. Kennedy Sch., Berlin, W.Ger., 1969-73; dist. profl. librarian St. Paul Schs., 1973-90; librarian Open Sch. St. Pauls Schs., 1990-93; cons. in field. Served to 1st lt. U.S. Army, 1954-55. Recipient Ency. Brit. 1st place Sch. Library Media System award, 1969. Mem. Minn. Ednl. Media Orgn., Am. Fedn. Tchrs., M Club, Phi Delta Kappa. Contbr. articles in field. Home: 5536 Harriet Ave Minneapolis MN 55419-1830

OSTROM, DON, state legislator, political science educator; b. Chgo., Mar. 9, 1939; s. Irving and Margaret (Hedberg) O.; m. Florence Horan, Jan. 13, 1972; children: Erik, Rebecca, Katherine. BA, St. Olaf Coll., Northfield, Minn., 1960; MA, Washington U., 1970, PhD, 1972. Prof. polit. sci. Gustavus Adolphus Coll., St. Peter, Minn., 1972—; state rep. Minn. Ho. of Reps., St. Paul, 1988—. Democrat. Home: 405 N 4th St Saint Peter MN 56082-1921

O'SULLIVAN, CHRISTINE, executive director social service agency; b. Washington, July 5, 1947; d. George Albert and Mary Ruth (Stalcup) Markward; m. Donald Phillip O'Sullivan, June 27, 1985; 1 child: Kimberly Molly. Sec. Gas Distributors Info. Svc., Washington, 1966-70; adminstr. asst. Nat. Airlines, Washington, 1970-71; office mgr. Tire Industry Safety Coun., Washington, 1971-75; pres. Type-Right Exec. Sec. Svc., Washington, Pitts., 1976-91; exec. dir. Eastside Cmty. Ministry, Zanesville, Ohio, 1991—; pres. FEMA Emer. Bd., Muskingum, Morgan and Perry Counties, Ohio, 1994-96; chair United Way Exec. Dirs. Coun., 1994-96; v.p. Muskingum County Hunger Network, Zanesville, 1993-95. Author: Write a Good Resume, 1976. V.p. Muskingum County Women's Rep. Club, 1994, sec., 1995; bd. dirs. Muskingum County Women's Coalition, 1994-96; pres. Downtown Clergy Assn., 1992-96, pres., 1995-96; mem. bd. human care ministry, Ohio Dist., Lutheran Ch., Mo. Synod; task force mem. Literacy Coun., 1993-96, Pro-Muskingum, 1995-96; bd. dirs. Families and Children First Coun., 1995-96; commr. Mo. Synod Luths. to Commn. on Religion in Appalachia; mem. steering com. Muskingum County Operation Feed, 1992-96. Recipient Excellence in Cmty. Svc. Muskingum Coun. DAR, 1994, Excellence in Cmty. Svc. award Aid Assn. Luths., 1993, Cert. of Achievement for Mil. Family Support, U.S. Army, 1991. Mem. Kiwanis, Richvale Grange. Home: 509 Van Horn Ave Zanesville OH 43701 Office: Eastside Cmty Ministry 40 N 6th St Zanesville OH 43701

O'SULLIVAN, MARY COLETTE, chemistry educator; b. Orpington, Kent, U.K., Apr. 19, 1963; came to U.S., 1989; d. Desmond Gerard and Dorothy Mary (Wilson) O'S. BSc in Biochemistry, U. Warwick, U.K., 1985; PhD in Organic Chemistry, U. Newcastle Upon Tyne, U.K., 1989. Chartered chemist, chartered biologist. Postdoctoral rsch. assoc. Medicinal Chemistry Dept., Purdue U., West Lafayette, Ind., 1989-91; asst. prof. chemistry Chemistry Dept., Ind. State U., Terre Haute, 1991—. Contbr. articles to profl. publs. Mem. Am. Chem. Soc., Royal Soc. of Chemistry. Office: Chemistry Dept Ind State U Terre Haute IN 47809

O'SULLIVAN, MICHAEL DAVID, foundation executive; b. Pitts., Dec. 20, 1953; s. James C. and Gladys Vera (Erler) O'S.; m. Kathy Louise Lewis, Aug. 10, 1975; children: Caitlin Alaine, Kevin Patrick. BA, Ind. U. of Pa., 1975; MSW, MA in Pub. Policy, Ohio State U., 1980. Sr. div. dir. United Way, Columbus, Ohio, 1980-88; v.p. United Way, San Diego, 1988; assoc. dir. Riverside Meth. Hosps. Found., Columbus, 1989-90, dir. major gifts, 1991-92, dir. devel., 1993, v.p., COO, 1994—. Treas. Huckleberry House, Inc., Columbus, 1993—. Mem. Nat. Soc. Fund Raising Execs. (cert.), Ctrl. Ohio Planned Giving Coun. (v.p. 1992—), Estate Planning Group II. Office: 941 Chatham Ln Ste 215 Columbus OH 43221-2416

OSWALD, EVA SUE ADEN, insurance executive; b. Ft. Dodge, Iowa, Feb. 2, 1949; d. Warren Dale Aden and Alice Rae (Gingerich) Aspeslet; m. Bruce Elliott Oswald, Nov. 27, 1976. BBS, U. Iowa, 1972. With Great Am. Ins. Co., 1975—; v.p. mktg. div. Great Am. Ins. Co., Orange, Calif., 1987, v.p. profit ctr., 1988-90; pres. Garden of Eva, Inc., 1990—; mem. Snelling-Selby Bus. Coun. Mem. Nat. Assn. Ins. Women, State Guarantee Fund (bd. dirs.

1986-87), Exec. Women St. Paul, Midway C. of C., White Bear Lake C. of C. Methodist. Office: 1585 Marshall Ave Saint Paul MN 55104-6222

OSWALT, ARIA LUCINDA, real estate broker; b. Marion, Ind., July 11, 1953; d. Chester Von and Georgia Shoaff (Waltz) O. AB in French, Ind. U., 1975. Cert. residential specialist. Real estate broker Owens Bryan & Reed, Bloomington, Ind., 1977-89; real estate broker F.C. Tucker Co., Bloomington, Ind., 1989-96, v.p. residential divsn., 1994—. Bd. dirs. Bloomington YMCA, 1994—. Mem. Realtors Nat. Mktg. Inst., Ind. Assn. Realtors (bd. dirs. 1990-94, chmn. bd. leadership forum 1992-93), Bloomington Bd. Realtors (bd. dirs. 1990-94, pres. 1991-92, chmn. strategic planning com., 1993, v.p. multiple listing svc. 1994-95, pres. multiple listing svc., 1995-96, Realtor of Yr. 1995), Realtors Honor Soc., Greater Bloomington C. of C., Coalition for Positive Progress (bd. dirs. 1992-95, chmn. pub. rels. com. 1987-95), Friends of Art Ind. U., Friends of Music Ind. U., Ind. U. Alumni Assn., Pres. Club (life), Phi Beta Kappa. Office: F C Tucker 2670 E 2nd St Bloomington IN 47401-5371

OTHARSSON, HANS BERNHARD, software company executive; b. Reykjavik, Iceland, Oct. 19, 1962; came to U.S., 1968; s. Othar and Elin (Thorbjorndottir) Hansson; m. Sonia Maritza Chavarria, June 11, 1988; children: Kristin, Elin, Arndis. BS, Bryant Coll., 1985; D (hon.), U. Iceland, Reykjavik, 1990. Mng. dir. EDP Nat. Bank of Iceland, Reykjavik, 1985-91; dir. ops. NAO Consist Internat., Rolling Meadows, Ill., 1991—; op. rev. bd. Ctrl. Processing Ctr., Iceland, 1985-91; mem. internat. adv. panel Software AG, 1988-91; dir. tech. rev. bd. Swift Nat. Com., Scandanavia, 1989-91. Com. mem. Montessori Sch., Wilton, Conn., 1993—; vol. U.S. Spl. Olympics, Conn. Recipient cert. appreciation ARC, 1976. Mem. Internat. Tech. Assn., Tau Epsilon (pres. 1984). Office: Consist Internat 3701 Algonquin Rd Ste 390 Rolling Meadows IL 60008

O'TOOLE, JAMES, state legislator. Mem. Mo. State Ho. of Reps. Dist. 68. Home: 5445 Finkman St Saint Louis MO 63109-3540*

O'TOOLE, JOANNE ROSE, journalist; b. Cleve., Jan. 27, 1939; d. Anthony Thomas and Congettina Frances (Titolo) Cavoli; m. Thomas J. O'Toole, July 31, 1965. Student, Ursuline Coll., Cleve., 1960, John Carroll U. Mem. Soc. Am. Travel Writers, The Travel Journalists Guild, Midwest Travel Writers Assn. Office: Travel Journalist 4603 Wood St Willoughby OH 44094

OTREMBA, KEN, state legislator; b. Oct. 29, 1948; m. Mary Ellen Otremba; 4 children. Minn. state rep. Dist. 11B, 1994—; farmer. Address: Rte 2 Box 17 Long Prairie MN 56347

OTT, ALVIN R., state legislator. Home: PO Box 112 N8855 Church St Forest Junction WI 54123*

OTT, BELVA JOLEEN, state legislator; b. Wichita, Kans., June 5, 1940; d. Kenneth Theodore and Vera Esther (Harvey) Massey; m. Harold Arthur Ott, 1959; children: Teresa Dawn, Bruce Kenton. Mem. from dist. 92 Kans. State Ho. of Reps., 1977-82, 95—, chmn. ho. election com., 1979-82. Mem. Women's Polit. Caucus; med. sec. Mid-Am. Heart Assn., Pa., 1977-81; mem. Kans. Fedn. Rep. Women; precinct committeewoman Sedgwick County Rep. Party, 1972—, ward chmn., 1973—; del. 4th Dist. Rep. Party Conv., 1976—; alt. del. Kans. State Rep. Conv., 1976. Mem. LWV, Am. Coun. Young Polit. Leaders, Sedgwick County Rep. Women's Club. Address: 821 Litchfield Wichita KS 67203

OTTENHEIMER, HARRIET JOSEPH, anthropologist, educator; b. N.Y.C., June 11, 1941; m. Martin Ottenheimer, June 15, 1962. BA, Bennington Coll., 1962; PhD, Tulane U., 1973. Asst. prof. anthropology Kans. State U., Manhattan, 1969-80, assoc. prof., 1980-86, prof., 1986—, dir. Am. ethnic studies, 1988—. Book rev. editor Nat. Assn. for Ethnic Studies; coauthor: Cousin Joe: Blues From New Orleans, 1987; (recording) Music of the Comoro Islands, 1982, Historical Dictionary of the Comoro Islands, 1994; author: Shinzwani-English Dictionary (disk data set), 1986; contbr. articles to profl. jours. Office: AMETH Leasure Hall Kans State U Manhattan KS 66506

OTTENWESS, J. LEA, data processing executive; b. Kalamazoo, June 23, 1943. Programmer DBS, Kalamazoo, 1982-84; database analyst Eaton Corp., Marshall, Mich., 1984-87; mortgage broker AAA Mortgage, Grand Rapids, Mich., 1987-88; programmer analyst Merit Systems, Grand Rapids, Mich., 1988-89; pres. MacEnron & Assocs. Inc., Richland, Mich., 1989—. Libertarian. Methodist.

OTTI, ROBERT F., author, retired soldier; b. Chatham, Ill., June 4, 1930; s. Benjamin Frank and Edna Gladys (Bennett) O.; m. Juanita Ann Williams, Mar. 25, 1951 (dec. Oct. 1994); m. Eileen E. Backer, July 1, 1995; children: Bonnie J., David D., Robert Mark. BA, Park Coll., 1969; MA, Lael Coll., 1995. Advanced through ranks to capt. U.S. Army, 1948-68. Author: Let He Who Is Without Sin, 1980, The Master, The Miracle & Malchus, 1991, Loyality Deceived, 1992, Murder in the Temple, 1994. Cert. lay spkr. Sunrise Meth. Ch. Mem. Am. Legion. Republican. Home: 440 Sun Set O'Fallon MO 63366

OTTO, ALBERT DEAN, mathematics educator; b. Marshalltown, Iowa, Nov. 5, 1939; s. Albert Peter and Lorraine Anita (Sievers) O.; m. Judy Ann Jondahl, Aug. 25, 1962 (div. Nov. 1988); children: Denise Ann, Gregory Dean. BA in Math., U. Iowa, 1961, MS in Math., 1962, PhD of Math., 1965. Asst. prof. math. Lehigh U., Bethlehem, Pa., 1965-69; assoc. prof. Ill. State U., Normal, 1969-75, prof., 1975—, chairperson dept. math., 1976-85. Co-author: Discrete Mathematics, 1987; contbr. articles to profl. jours. Recipient James Armstrong award Ill. Math. Assn. C.C., 1988, Outstanding Tchr. award Ill. State U. Alumni Assn.; NSF grantee, 1992—. Mem. Math. Assn. Am. (mem. bd. govs. 1992-95, Disting. Svc. award Ill. sect.), Nat. Coun. Tchrs. of Math., Nat. Coun. Suprs. of Math., Group of Psychology of Math. Edn. Home: 10 Aspen Ct Bloomington IL 61704-2781 Office: Ill State U Dept Math Normal IL 61790-4520

OUIMET, BERNARD, programmer; b. Milw., May 6, 1952. Diploma, Greenfield H.S., 1970. CNC programmer George J. Meyer, Cudahy, Wis., 1978-82, Waukesha (Wis.) Engine/Dresser Industries, 1983-84; machinist Huth Mfg., Hartford, Wis., 1983-84. With USAR, 1972-78. Home: 4618 S 47th St Greenfield WI 53220-4110

OURADA, MARK, state legislator; b. Apr. 28, 1956; m. Christi Ourada. Student, St. John's U. Minn. state sen. Dist. 19, 1994—; former lab. technician. Address: 1110 Innsbrook Ln Buffalo MN 55313

OURADA, THOMAS D., state legislator. Home: 425 Dorr St Antigo WI 54409-1400*

OUSELEY, WILLIAM NORMAN, security services consultant; b. N.Y.C., May 26, 1935; s. Norman J. Ouseley and Helen (Accurso) Loffredo; m. Josephine B. Ouseley, Mar. 17, 1962; children: John W., Elizabeth A. BA, Coll. of William & Mary, 1957; LLB, Fordham U., 1960. Spl. agt., supervisory spl. agt. organized crime FBI, nationwide, 1960-85; security rep. NFL, Kansas City, Mo., 1985—. Adv. bd. YMCA, Kansas City, 1987-88. Mem. Soc. Former FBI Spl. Agents (chmn. Kansas City chpt. 1992-93).

OUTCALT, DAVID LEWIS, academic administrator, mathematician, educator; b. Los Angeles, Jan. 30, 1935; s. Earl Kinyon and Alberta Estes Ferguson O.; m. Marcia Lee Beach, July 1, 1956; children—Jeffrey David, Kevin Douglas, Gregory Mark, Eric Matthew. B.A. in Math., Pomona Coll., 1956; M.A. in Math., Claremont Grad. Sch., 1958; Ph.D. in Math., Ohio State U., 1963; D.Pub. Adminstrn. (hon.), Kyung Hee U., Korea, 1984. Asst. prof. math. Clarement McKenna Coll., 1962-64; asst. prof. to prof. math. U. Calif.-Santa Barbara, 1964-80, chmn. dept. math., 1969-72, dean instrnl. devel., 1977-80; vice chancellor acad. affairs U. Alaska, Anchorage, 1980-81, prof. math., 1980-86, chancellor, 1981-86; prof. natural and applied sci. U. Wis., Green Bay, 1986-93, chancellor, 1986-93, Hendrickson prof. econ. devel., 1994—; pres. Mid-Continent athletic conf., 1990-91. Author math. textbooks; contbr. articles on math. and higher edn. to profl. jours. Moderator bd. trustees Humana Hosp. Anchorage, 1982-83; mem. exec. bd. Western Alaska coun. Boy Scouts Am., 1982-86, Bay-Lakes coun., 1987—, v.p. exploring, 1988-92, v.p. ops., 1992-93, pres., 1993-94; mem. Anchorage Symphony bd., 1986, Green Bay Symphony Bd., 1988—, mem. Weidner Ctr. Presents Bd., 1994—. Grantee USAF Office Sci. Research, 1964-71, U. Calif., 1975-78, NSF, 1976-79. Mem. Math. Assn. Am., Internat. Assn. Univ. Pres.'s (exec. com. 1988—, vice chair N.Am. coun. 1988-94, newsletter editor 1994-95), Greater Green Bay C. of C. (advance bd. 1987—, bd. dirs. 1991-94, 95-96), Brown County Indsl. Devel. (pres. bd. dirs. 1994—), Rotary, Sigma Xi. Mem. Congregational Ch. Home: PO Box 89 Athelstane WI 54104-0089

OUTCALT, MERLIN BREWER, child care center administrator, consultant; b. Reedsburg, Wis., Aug. 26, 1928; s. Raymond Arthur and Ruby (Brewer) O.; m. Ruth Ann Auble, Sept. 22, 1950; children—Roger Lee, Dennis Alan, Steven Len. B.S., Ind. U., 1955, M.A. in Social Service, 1957; postgrad Ind. U. Cert. social worker. Probation officer Juvenile Court, Indpls., 1957-59; exec. dir. Travelers Aide Soc., Cin., 1959-65, Meth. Youth Service, Chgo., 1965-68; cons. United Meth. Ch., Evanston, Ill., 1968-74; exec. dir. Group Child Care Services, Chapel Hill, N.C., 1974-77; exec. dir., CEO Webster-Cantrell Hall, Decatur, Ill., 1977-94, dir. planned giving, 1994—; Contbr. articles to profl. jours. and mags. Lay leader Decatur Dist. United Meth., Ill., 1980-87; mem. Council Community Services, Decatur, 1980-84, United Meth. Global Ministries, N.Y.C., 1984-92. Cpl. U.S. Army, 1950-52. Mem. Acad. Cert. Social Workers, Ill. Child Care Assn., Rotary (sec., bd. dirs.). Avocations: camping, traveling. Office: Webster-Cantrell Hall 1942 E Cantrell St Decatur IL 62521-3214

OUZTS, DALE KEITH, broadcast executive; b. Miami, Fla., Aug. 26, 1941; s. Jacob C. and Edna P. (Sloan) O.; m. Judy Olcott, June 11, 1964 (div. Mar. 1980); children: Dale Keith Jr., Karen J. Frost; m. Kathleen Gross, Mar. 15, 1982 (div. Nov. 1991); m. Suzanne Kasavage, June 18, 1993; 1 child, Ryan Keith. BJ, U. Ga., 1965, MA, 1966; postgrad. advanced mgmt. seminar, Harvard U., 1977. Mgr. Sta. WSJK-TV, Knoxville, Tenn., 1966-69; exec. v.p., gen. mgr. Sta. KPTS-TV, Wichita, Kans., 1969-72; gen. mgr. Sta. WSSR-FM, Springfield, Ill., 1972-77; sr. v.p. Nat. Pub. Radio, Washington, 1977-79; gen. mgr. Sta. WOSU-AM-FM and Sta. WOSU-TV Ohio State U., Columbus, Ohio, 1979—; gen. mgr. WPBO-TV, Portsmouth, Ohio, 1979—, WOSV-FM, Mansfield, Ohio, 1988—, WOSP-FM, Portsmouth, 1993—; assoc. prof. communications Ohio State U., Columbus, Ohio, 1979—, assoc. prof. journalism, 1983—; adminstrv. dir. Ohio State Awards, 1979—; mem. Ohio Ednl. TV Stas., v.p., 1983-84, pres., 1988-90; pres. Ohio Pub. Radio, 1995-96; chmn. Nat. Pub. Radio, 1990-92; pres. Pub. Radio in Mid-Am., 1976-77, 85-87. Bd. dirs. Ctr. of Vocat. Alts. in Mental Health, 1985-93, sec.-treas., 1986-88, chmn., 1988-90, Pub. Radio Expansion Task Force, 1989-90; bd. dirs. Brule Conservation Trust, 1985-94, Columbus Zoo, 1984—, Mental Health Assn., Franklin County, 1987-93, Ohio China Coun., 1982-93, v.p., 1984-85, pres., 1987-89; advisor Chinese Student and Scholar Soc. at Ohio State U., 1987-91; program rev. panel Nat. Telecomms., 1988; mgmt. cons. Corp. for Pub. Broadcasting, 1975—. Recipient Disting. Service award Nat. Pub. Radio, 1986, Disting. Service award Nat. Black Program Consortium, 1985, Disting. Service award PRIMA, 1977, 87, award for fundraising and promotion Corp. Pub. Broadcasting, 1971, Outstanding Broadcaster award Wichita (Kans.) Chpt. of Kappa Mu Psi, 1970, OEBIE award Ohio Ednl. Broadcasting Network Commn., 1987, Emmy award nomination Acad. TV Arts and Scis., 1987. Mem. Nat. Assn. Broadcasters, Ohio Assn. Broadcasters, Nat. Assn. State Univs. and Land Grant Colls. (mem. telecomms. com. 1980-93), Columbus Ducks Unltd. (bd. dirs. 1982-93), Scioto Valley Skeet Club (bd. dirs. 1982-92), Grand Hotel Hunt Club, Sawmill Athletic Club, Ohio-Rocky Mountain Elk Found., Rotary (Dublin-Worthington, v.p. 1988-89, pres. 1990-91). Home: 2038 Michelle Dr Grove City OH 43123-4019 Office: Sta WOSU 2400 Olentangy River Rd Columbus OH 43210-1027

OVERBY, KENNETH WAYNE, design engineer; b. Marion, Ind., Dec. 4, 1961; s. Kenneth Paul and Karen Sue (Zirkle) O. AA in Drafting and Design, Tri-State U., Angola, Ind., 1983. Asst. plant mgr., product engr. LaMan Corp., Hamilton, Ind., 1984—. Patentee: Compressed Air Filters Indsl. Application, 1989-92. Office: LaMan Corp PO Box 487 Hamilton IN 46742-0487

OVERHAUSER, ALBERT WARNER, physicist; b. San Diego, Aug. 17, 1925; s. Clarence Albert and Gertrude Irene (Pehrson) O.; m. Margaret Mary Casey, Aug. 25, 1951; children—Teresa, Catherine, Joan, Paul, John, David, Susan, Steven. A.B., U. Calif. at Berkeley, 1948, Ph.D., 1951; D.Sc. (hon.), U. Chgo., 1979. Research asso. U. Ill., 1951-53; asst. prof. physics Cornell U., 1953-56, asso. prof., 1956-58; supr. solid state physics Ford Motor Co., Dearborn, Mich., 1958-62; mgr. theoret. scis. Ford Motor Co., 1962-69, asst. dir. phys. scis., 1969-72, dir. phys. scis., 1972-73; prof. physics Purdue U., West Lafayette, Ind., 1973-74; Stuart disting. prof. physics Purdue U., 1974—. With USNR, 1944-46. Recipient Alexander von Humboldt sr. U.S. scientist award, 1979, Nat. Medal of Sci., Pres. of U.S., 1994. Fellow Am. Phys. Soc. (Oliver E. Buckley Solid State Physics prize 1975), Am. Acad. Arts and Scis.; mem. NAS. Home: 236 Pawnee Dr West Lafayette IN 47906-2115 Office: Purdue U Dept Of Physics West Lafayette IN 47907

OVERSCHMIDT, FRANCIS S., state legislator. Mem. Mo. State Ho. of Reps. Dist. 110. Home: 151 N Outer Rd Union MO 63084-4400*

OVERTON, SARITA ROSA, psychologist; b. South Haven, Mich., June 7, 1954; d. Samuel Edward and Rosa Jane (McGuire) O. BA in Psychology with honors, Mich. State U., 1976, MA in Rehab. Counseling, 1978, MA in Counseling Psychology, 1987, PhD in Counseling Psychology, 1988. Lic. psychologist, Mich. Dir. Job Club, Capital Area Community Svcs., Lansing, Mich., 1978-84; instr. rehab. counseling master's program Mich. State U., East Lansing, 1981-82, program teaching asst., 1985-87, coord. career assistance project, 1984, 84-85, clin. trainee Counseling Ctr., 1986, rsch. asst. disability mgmt. project, 1985-87; clin. trainee St. Lawrence Hosp., Lansing, 1986-87, psychologist Psychol. Svcs. and Addictions Clinic, 1987-91; psychologist Comprehensive Psychol. Svcs., P.C., East Lansing, 1990-95; pvt. practice psychologist Meridian Health and Wellness Ctr., East Lansing, 1995—; conf. and clin. presenter in field. Contbr. articles to profl. publs. Recipient Presdl. recognition award Mich. Rehab. Assn., 1986; grantee Nat. Inst. Handicapped Rsch., 1985; dissertation rsch. fellow Mich. State U., 1985. Mem. APA. Democrat. Office: Meridian Health and Wellness 139 Lake Lansing Rd Ste 200 East Lansing MI 48823

OVITSKY, STEVEN ALAN, musician, symphony orchestra executive; b. Chgo., Oct. 12, 1947; s. Martin N. and Ruth (Katz) O.; m. Camille Levy; 1 child, David Isaac. MusB, U. Mich., 1968; MusM, No. Ill. U., 1975. Fine arts dir. Sta. WNIU-FM Pub. Radio, Dekalb, Ill., 1972-76; program mgr. Sta. WMHT-FM Pub. Radio, Schenectady, N.Y., 1976-79; gen. mgr., artistic dir. Grant Park Concerts, Chgo., 1979-90; v.p., gen. mgr. Minn. Orch., Mpls., 1990-95; exec. dir. Milw. Symphony Orch., 1995—; panelist Ill. Arts Coun., 1986, 87, 88, Chgo. Artists Abroad, 1987-91, Nat. Endowment for the Arts, 1987-89; bd. dirs. Ill. Arts Alliance, Chamber Music Chgo.; hon. dir. Chgo. Sinfonietta. With U.S. Army, 1968-71, Korea. Mem. NARAS, Am. Symphony Orch. League. Jewish. Office: Milw Symphony 330 E Kilbourn Ave Ste 900 Milwaukee WI 53202

OWEN, FERRIS SYDNEY, farmer, international development administrator; b. Newark, Ohio, Jan. 25, 1918; s. Wilfred Robert and Maria Emily (Nichol) O.; m. Helen Irene Cavins, Oct. 12, 1940; children: Gwendolyn Rae, Barbara, James, Sue. BS in Home Econs., Ohio State U., 1940, BS in agricultural engring., 1940. Pres., oper. mgr. Owen Potato Farm, Newark, Ohio, 1940-66; dir. internat. programs Coop. League U.S.A., 1966-83, v.p. internat. devel., 1980-83, internat. coop. cons., 1983—; organizer farm supply and mktg. assn. in western Ukraine for Internat. Exec. Svc. Corps., 1990; bd. dirs. Coop. Devel. Found. Democrat. Home: 965 Sharon Valley Rd Newark OH 43055

OWEN, KEITH LYNN, communications engineer; b. Ft. Collins, Colo., Apr. 25, 1963; s. Norris Virl and Helen Alice (Williams) O.; m. Cathy Sue Branham, Apr. 6, 1991; 1 child, Caitlin Erin. BAS, ITT Tech. Inst., Indpls., 1987. Asst. network engr., lab. technician Ind. Higher Edn. Telecomm. Sys., Indpls., 1985-88; network control engr. GTE Telecomm., Indpls., 1988—. Office: GTE Telecomm Inc 175 N College Ave Indianapolis IN 46202

OWEN, KENNETH ALAN, reporter; b. Chgo., Nov. 28, 1960; s. John Henry Jr. and Lois (Smisek) O. BS, DePauw U., 1982. News anchor, reporter Radio Sta. WIRE, Indpls., 1982, Radio Sta. WIBC, Indpls., 1983, TV Sta. WXIN, Indpls., 1984, TV Sta. WANE, Ft. Wayne, Ind., 1984-87, TV Sta. WLOS, Asheville, N.C., 1987-89, TV Sta. WISH, Indpls., 1989—. Bd. dirs. Big Bros./Big Sisters, Ft. Wayne, 1985-87, Asheville, 1987-89, Indpls., 1989—, Multiple Sclerosis Found., Indpls., 1990—, Make-a-Wish Found., Indpls., 1995—. Recipient Best Ind. Radio Documentary award UPI, 1982, Friend of Youth award N.C. Gov., 1989, Best Live Spot News Coverage award AP, 1994. Mem. Soc. Profl. Journalists, Indpls. Athletic Club. Office: WISH-TV 1950 N Meridian St Indianapolis IN 46202

OWEN, LYNN, state legislator; b. Lawrence County, Ala., Feb. 22, 1946; m. Diana; children: Amy, Andrew. Student, Washtenaw C.C., Cerritos Jr. Coll. Supervisor, assessor London Twp., Mich., 1978-84; rep. Mich. State 56, 1986—; house appropriations com. Mich. Ho. Reps. Gov. bd. dirs. Monroe County Opportunity Program; pres. Milan Area Fire Dept.; chmn. London-Maybee-Raisinville Fire Dept. Named pub. servant of yr. Mich. chpt. Paralyzed Vet. Am., state legis. yr. Vientam Vets. Am.; recipient star award Dep. Sheriff's Assn.. Mem. Am. Legion, Disabled Am. Vets., Purple Heart Assn., West County Ambulance Assn. (former vice chair). Home: 4826 Sycamore Rd Newport MI 48166-9014 Address: Olds Plz Bldg Rm 925 Lansing MI 48913*

OWEN, VIRGINIA LEE, economist educator; b. Harrisburg, Ill., Sept. 11, 1941; d. Wayne Lee and Lola Virginia (Randolph) Smith; m. Philip James Owen, Apr. 13, 1963 (div. 1973); children: Trefan Philip, Whityn James, Brynnen Randolph. BS in Edn., Ill. State Normal U., 1962; MS in Econs., U. Ill., 1963, PhD in Econs., 1969. Instr. econs. Ill. State U., Normal, 1964-65, asst. prof., 1965-72, assoc. prof. econs., 1972-80, chair dept. econs., 1978-81, prof. econs., 1980—, dean Coll. of Arts and Scis., 1982-93; dir. Ctr. for Econs. Edn., 1995—; cons. U.S. Office of Edn. Grant Project, Normal, 1972-74; judge Nat. Coun. on Econ. Edn. Nat. Teaching Award Contest, 1986—. Co-author: Economics: A Synergetic Approach, 1972; co-editor books, manuals and monographs; contbr. articles to profl. jours. Trustee, v.p. Cmty. Action Assocs., Bloomington; bd. dirs., program chair Stevenson Meml. Lecture Fund, Bloomington; trustee Ill. Coun. on Econ. Edn., DeKalb, 1984—; bd. dirs. Ctr. for Regulatory Studies, Normal, 1986-94; trustee Assn. for Cultural Econs. Internat., 1993—. U. Ill. fellow, 1962-63. Mem. Assn. for Cultural Econs. (Great Lakes regional dir. 1975-93), Am. Econ. Assn., Midwest Econ. Assn., Coun. for Colls. of Arts and Scis., Assn. Am. Colls., Soc. for Coll. and Univ. Planning. Baptist. Office: Ill State U Dept Econs Stevenson Hall 425 Normal IL 61790-4200

OWENS, BOYD ERDICE, manufacturing executive, educator; b. Olean, N.Y., Nov. 12, 1962; s. Donald F. and Judith A. (Trowbridge) O.; m. Doris L.B. Owens; children: Cameron Ryan, Keir Alec. BS in Mechanical Engring., Valparaiso U., Ind., 1985; MS in Bus. Adminstrn., Northwestern U., Evanston, 1992, PhD in Physics, 1994. Cert. quality engr., I.I.T., Ind. Quality engr. ITW Switches Divsn., Chgo., 1985-86, test lab supr., 1986, QC/QA mgr., 1986-88; reliability program mgr. C.P. Clare Corp., Chgo., 1988-89; product engr. Otto Engring. Inc., Carpentersville, Ill., 1990, asst. prodn. mgr., 1990-93, materials mgr., 1993-94, asst. ops. mgr., 1994—; mem. admissions bd. Chgo. Commons Assn., 1988. Author: (books) A New Way of Thought, 1994, I Know SPC, 1995. Mem. ASQC (controller 1988-89), ASTD, Am. Prodn. & Inventory Control Soc.

OWENS, CAROL, state legislator. Address: 144 County Road C Oshkosh WI 54904-9065*

OWENS, ELIZABETH D., environmentalist; b. Feb. 11, 1950. BS, U. Idaho, 1972; MS, Iowa State U., 1976; PhD, U. Mass., 1982. Supr. prodn. Proctor & Gamble, Iowa City, 1972-74; rsch. asst. Iowa State U., Ames, 1974-76, U. Mass., Amherst, 1977-81; scientist GTE Labs., Waltham, Mass., 1980-86; vis. scientist U. Mass, Boston, 1986; mgr. comml. devel. BioTechnica Internat., Cambridge, Mass., 1987-91; mgr. product registrations ISK Bioscis. Corp., Mentor, Ohio, 1991-95, mgr. govt. affairs, 1995—; study com. mem. NAS, Washington, 1993—; steering com. mem. Ohio State U., Columbus, 1994—; working group mem. Nat. Ctr. Food and Agrl. Policy, Washington, 1994—; task force sec. MAA Rsch. Task Force, Mentor, 1991—. Inventor ednl. games, Gene Rummy, 1988; contbr. articles to profl. jours. Spkr. Food Safety Ambs., Mentor, 1991—. Mem. AAAS, Entomol. Soc. Am., Phytopathology Soc., Biotech. Industries Orgn. (corp. rep.), Dahlia Soc. Ohio. Office: ISK Bioscis Corp 5966 Heisley Rd Mentor OH 44061

OWENS, LUVIE MOORE, association executive; b. Cleve., July 26, 1933; d. Dan Tyler and Elizabeth (Oakes) Moore; m. Lloyd Owens, Jan. 1, 1955; children: Luvie Owens Myers, Elizabeth, Lloyd H. Student, Smith Coll., Northampton, Mass., 1956. Tchr. Howard Jr. High Sch., Wilmette, Ill., 1971-75; U.S. ops. mgr. Frank T. Ross & Co., Evanston, Ill., 1976-86; dir. Internat. Platform Assn., Winnetka, Ill., 1972—, chief exec. officer, 1986—. Treas., mem. jr. coun. Cleve. Mus. Art, 1964-65; commr. Police and Fire Commn., Winnetka, 1980-86; chmn. bd. Lake Shore Unitarian Ch., Winnetka, 1986-87; mem. alumnae bd. Madeira Sch., Greenway, Va., 1984-88. Mem. Jr. League Club (Chgo.), Rotary. Office: Internat Platform Assn PO Box 250 Winnetka IL 60093-0250

OWENS, SCOTT ANDREW, sales executive; b. Waconia, Minn., Jan. 6, 1958; s. John Herbert and Amy Lou (Anderson) O.; m. Cheri Lynn Anderson, Sept. 22, 1988. BSBA magna cum laude, U. Nebr., Omaha, 1986. Adminstrv. asst. Hodne Stageberg Ptnrs., Mpls., 1978-80; pres. Orange Triangle Co., Mpls., 1980; asst. mgr. Wendy's, Mpls., 1980; pres. We Deliver, Mpls., 1980-81; asst. mgr. Color Tile, Roseville, Minn., 1982-83; v.p. mktg. 20/20 Minn., St. Louis Pk., 1983; account rep. Unisys Corp., Minnetonka, 1986-88; sr. account rep. Unisys Corp., Eagan, 1988-89, third party sales mgr., 1990-91; v.p. mktg. TEP Systems, Bloomington, 1991-93; v.p. Benchmark Comms. Svcs., Mpls., 1992—; strategic alliance regional mgr. Dataserv, a BellSouth Co., Eden Prairie, 1994-96. Classroom cons. Jr. Achievement, Bloomington, Minn., 1990. Mem. Am. Mktg. Assn., Am. Prdn. Inventory Control Soc., Profl. Sales Assn., Sales and Mktg. Execs. Home and Office: Benchmark Comm PO Box 580135W Minneapolis MN 55458

OWSIANY, DAVID J., lawyer, lobbyist; b. Livonia, Mich., Dec. 15, 1964; s. Thaddeus S. and Beatrice (DeBeul) O.; m. Kathryn Karoski, May 15, 1993. BA, U. Mich., 1987; JD, Washington U., St. Louis, 1991. Legal asst. U.S. Senate Jud. Com., Washington, 1991; jud. law clk. to Hon. Robert W. Cook Ill. Appellate Ct., Quincy, 1992-94; dir. legal and legis. affairs Ohio Dental Assn., Columbus, 1994—. Precinct del. Rep. Party, Redford, Mich., 1986-88; del. Mich. Rep. Convs., Lansing/Grand Rapids, 1986, 88; trustee Ohio Alliance for Civil Justice, Columbus, 1995—; mem. steering com. Phil Gramm for Pres., Columbus, 1995—; cons. Ohio Citizens Against Lawsuit Abuse, 1995—. Mem. Mich. Bar Assn., Ohio Lobbying Assn., U. Mich. Alumni Assn., Federalist Soc. (Columbus lawyers chpt.), Century Club (mem. Ohio dental polit. action com.). Home: 7856 Red Hill Ct Worthington OH 43085 Office: Ohio Dental Assn 1370 Dublin Rd Columbus OH 43215

OXENDER, GLENN S., state legislator; b. Three Rivers, Mich.e, Aug. 8, 1943; s. Harry Bryan and Myrtle (Sherck) O.; m. F. Dianne Ellis, 1966; children: Xanne, Katrina, Robert, Kalynn, Melinda. BS, Manchester Coll., 1965; MA, Western Mich. U., 1969; postgrad., U. Mo., 1971. Math. tchr. Livonia (Mich.) Pub. Schs., 1965-66, Sturgis (Mich.) Pub. Schs., 1966-69, Sturgis H.S., 1969-82; rep. Mich. State Dist. 42, Mich. State Dist. 59; farmer, 1974—; appropriations standing com. Mich. Ho. Reps., cmty. coll. subcom., mental health subcom., joint capital outlay subcom., state police subcom., mil. affairs subcom., ad hoc edn. com., chmn. K-12 Dept. Edn. subcom. Trustee Libr. Mich. Named outstanding legis. of yr., 1989, 94, Mich. Occupl. Edn. Assn.; recipient pres.'s award Mich. Assn. Sch. Bd., 1995. Mem. Sturgis Exch. Club, NEA, Mich. Edn. Assn., Sturgis Edn. Assn., Rotary,

Nat. Rep. Legis. Assn., Am. Legis. Exch. Coun., Ctrl. Regional Edn. Lab. Home: 27221 Wait Rd Sturgis MI 49091-9154 Address: Olds Plz Rm 48933 Lansing MI 48933*

OXLEY, ANN, television executive; b. Canton, Ohio, Aug. 3, 1924; d. Edward and Dorothy (Duffy) Adang. B.A. with distinction, Ind. U., 1974, M.P.A., 1982; m. Jack Raymond Oxley, Aug. 10, 1946; children: Kathleen Oxley Wiggins, Maureen Oxley Gaff, Joseph, Jeffrey, Christeen Oxley Rhodes, Daniel, Sister Julie Marie Oxley, Jamie, Kevin, Valerie Oxley Fouch, Amy. Advt. account salesperson Ft. Wayne (Ind.) Jour. Gazette, 1945-47; office mgr. Ind. Equestrian Assn., Ft. Wayne, 1971-73; rsch. dir. Taxpayers Rsch. Assn., Ft. Wayne, 1974-76; exec. dir. Ft. Wayne Pub. TV Inc., 1976-86; founder, owner Akin Assocs., 1987—. Active Bicentennial Com., 1976; adviser Media Arts Panel Ind. Arts Commn. Mem. AAUW, Svc. Corp Retired Execs. (publicity chair., 1986nat. mktg. dir. 1989-90), Mensa Internat., C. of C. (cultural com.), Phi Alpha Alpha. Roman Catholic. Home: 4305 Arlington Ave Fort Wayne IN 46807-2635 Office: SCORE 1300 S Harrison Federal Bldg Fort Wayne IN 46807

OXLEY, MARGARET CAROLYN STEWART, elementary education educator; b. Petaluma, Calif., Apr. 1, 1930; d. James Calhoun Stewart and Clara Thornton (Whiting) Bomboy; m. Joseph Hubbard Oxley, Aug. 25, 1951; children: Linda Margaret, Carolyn Blair Oxley Greiner, Joan Claire Oxley Willis, Joseph Stewart, James Harmon, Laura Marie Oxley Brechbill. Student, U. Calif., Berkeley, 1949-51; BS summa cum laude, Ohio State U., 1973, MA, 1984, postgrad., 1985, 88, 92. Cert. tchr., Ohio. 2d grade tchr. St. Paul Sch., Westerville, Ohio, 1973—; presenter in field. Editl. adv. bd. Reading Tchr., vol. 47-48, 1993—; editl. rev. bd. Children's Literature Jour., 1996—; co-author: Reading and Writing, Where it All Begins, 1991, Teaching with Children's Books: Path to Literature-Based Instruction, 1995. Active Akita Child Conservation League, Columbus, Ohio, 1968-70. Named Columbus Diocesan Tchr. of Yr., 1988; Phoebe A. Hearst scholar, 1951, Rose Sterheim Meml. scholar, 1951; recipient Mary Karrer award Ohio State U., 1994. Mem. Nat. Coun. Tchrs. English (Notable Trade Books in the Lang. Arts com. 1993-94, chair 1995-96), Internat. Reading Assn. (Exemplary Svc. in Promotion of Literacy award 1991), Literacy Connection (pres.), Children's Lit. Assembly, Ohio Coun. Tchrs. English Lang. Arts (Outstanding Educator 1990), Phi Kappa Phi, Pi Lambda Theta (hon.). Democrat. Roman Catholic. Home: 298 Brevoort Rd Columbus OH 43214-3826

OYAMA, JOSEPH HIKARU, internist, nephrologist; b. Stockton, Calif., Nov. 19, 1939; s. Andrew Yoshimatsu and Toshiko (Nakamura) O.; m. Pauline Sachiko Nagatani, Nov. 28, 1943; children: Jennifer, Mark, Kristen. BS, U. Ill., 1961; MD, U. Ill., Chgo., 1965. Diplomate Am. Bd. Internal Medicine. Intern Cook County Hosp., Chgo., 1965-66; resident internal medicine U. Ill. Hosp., Chgo., 1966-68; renal fellowship Rush-Presbyn. St. Luke's Hosp., Chgo., 1968-71; asst. prof. Rush Med. Coll., Chgo., 1975-96; pres. S.W. Nephrology Assocs., Oak Lawn, Ill., 1979—; v.p. North Cen. Dialysis Ctrs., Chgo., 1985-95; asst. prof. U. Ill., 1996—; chief nephrology sect. Christ Hosp., 1974—; pres. med. staff Christ Hosp./Med. Ctr., Oak Lawn, 1989-91; dir. Advocate Health Care Network, 1995—. Contbr. articles to profl. jours. Mem. med. adv. bd. Nat. Kidney Found. of Ill., Chgo., 1985—; med. rev. bd. Renal Network of Ill., Chgo., 1989-91; co-chair South Cook County Heart Assn., 1981. Kidney Found. of Ill. fellow, 1970, Schweppe-Sprague Found. fellow, 1971. Fellow ACP; mem. Internat. Soc. Nephrology, Am. Soc. Nephrology, N.Y. Acad. Scis. Office: Southwest Nephrology Assocs 9115 S Cicero Ave Oak Lawn IL 60453-1804

OYSTER, CAROL KATHLEEN, psychology educator; b. Arlington, Va., Dec. 10, 1948; d. Dale Eugene and Anna Katherine (Jennison) O. BA, UCLA, 1970; MA, Loyola-Marymount, 1978, U. Del., 1980; PhD, U. Del., 1982. Vis. asst. prof. dept. psychology U. Del., Newark, 1981-84; from. asst. prof. to assoc. prof. Goldey Beacom Coll., Wilmington, Del., 1984-89; assoc. prof. dept. psychology U. Wis., La Crosse, 1989-94, prof. dept. psychology, 1994—; cons., reviewer Acad. Press, West Pubs., John Wiley Pub., 1987-90; rsch. cons. J. B. Lippincott Pub., Phila., 1988, M & M Mars, Inc., 1983. Author: Introduction to Research, 1987; contbr. articles to profl. jours. Vol. counselor Coulee Region Family Planning, La Crosse, 1990; classroom vol. Emerson Elem. Sch., La Crosse, 1991-94. Rsch. grantee Soc. for Psychol. Study of Social Issues, 1979, U. Wis., La Crosse, 1989, U. Wis. System Inst. for Race and Ethnicity, 1991. Office: U Wis Psychology Dept 1725 State St La Crosse WI 54601-3742

OZAR, MILTON BERNARD, urologist; b. Kansas City, Mo., Sept. 14, 1924; s. Simon Jacob and Sadie (Friedman) O.; m. Marilyn Brand, June 29, 1947; children: Stuart, Judith, Donna. BS in Pharmacy, U. Mo., Kansas City, 1944; MD., U. Kans., 1949. Diplomate Am. Bd. Urology. Intern U. Kans. Med. Ctr., Kansas City, 1949-50; resident surgery Menorah Med. Ctr., Kansas City, 1950-51; resident urology U. Kans. Med. Ctr., Kansas City, 1951-54; staff Bapt. Med. Ctr., Kansas City, pres., 1969-70; staff Rsch. Med. Ctr., Kansas City, Menorah Med. Ctr., Kansas City; pvt. practice urology Kansas City, 1957-91; asst. clin. prof. U. Kans., Kans. City, 1962, U. Mo., Columbia, 1963; clin. prof. U. Mo., Kansas City, 1980—; mem. curriculum coun. U. Mo., Kansas City, 1973-75, selection coun., 1983-87; guest examiner Am. Bd. Urology, Kansas City, Mo., 1975-76. Contbr. articles to profl. jour. Mem. 16th Judicial Commn., Kansas City, Mo., 1969-74. Capt. USAF, 1955-57. Fellow Am. Coll. Surgeons, Internat. Coll. Surgeons; mem. AMA, So. Med. Assn., Am. Assn. Clin. Urologists, Am. Urol. Assn. (pres. s. cen. section 1989), Mo. Fedn. Urologists (pres. 1975), Kansas City Urol. Soc. (pres. 1959-60), Jackson County Med. Soc. (pres. 1979-80), Met. Med. Soc. Jewish. Home: 14745 SW 79th Ct Miami FL 33158-2023

OZBUN, JIM L., academic administrator. Dean agr. and home econs. Wash. State U., Pullman, until 1988; pres. N.D. State U., Fargo, 1988—. Office: ND State U Office of Pres PO Box 5167 Fargo ND 58105-5167*

OZINGA, CONNIE JO, library director; b. Zeeland, Mich., Sept. 3, 1955; d. Dr. Bernard J. and Carol Mae (Middel) O.; m. Thomas G. Elmore, Sept. 30, 1978; 1 child, Julie Ann. MA, U. Mich., Ann Arbor, 1978; BA, Mich. State Univ., East Lansing, 1976. Adult svcs. libr. Upper Arlington Pub. Libr., Columbus, OH, 1978-79; head, adult svcs. Herrick Pub. Libr., Holland, Mich., 1979-83; dir. Jackson County Pub. Libr., Seymour, Ind., 1983—; bd. dirs. Ind. Libr. Fedn., Indpls. Bd. dirs. Seymour Oktoberfest, Inc., Seymour, Ind. Recipient Lion of the Year award Seymour Noon Lions, 1990; Intellectual Freedom award Ind. Libr. Fedn., 1995. Mem. Seymour Noon Lions, Greater Seymour C. of C., Am. Libr. Assn., Ind. Libr. Assn. Office: Jackson County Pub Library 303 W 2nd Seymour IN 47274

OZKAN, UMIT SIVRIOGLU, chemical engineering educator; b. Manisa, Turkey, Apr. 11, 1954; came to U.S., 1980; d. Alim and Emine (Ilgaz) Sivrioglu; m. H. Erdal Ozkan, Aug. 13, 1983. BS, Mid. East Tech. U., Ankara, Turkey, 1978, MS, 1980; PhD, Iowa State U., 1984. Registered profl. engr., Ohio. Grad. rsch. assoc. Ames Lab. U.S. Dept. Energy, 1980-84; asst. prof. Ohio State U., Columbus, 1985-90, assoc. prof. chem. engring., 1990-94, prof., 1994—. Contbr. articles to profl. jours. French Ctr. NAt. Rsch. Sci. fellow, 1994-95; recipient Women of Achievement award YWCA, Columbus, 1991, Outstanding Engring. Educator Ohio award Soc. Profl. Engrs., 1991, Union Carbide Innovation Recognition award, 1991-92, NSF Woman Faculty award in sci. and engring., 1991, Engring. Tchg. Excellence award Keck Found., 1994—, Ctrl. Ohio Outstanding Woman in Sci. & Tech., 1996. Fellow Am. Inst. Chemists; mem. NSPE, Am. Inst. Chem. Engring., Am. Soc. Engring. Edn., Am. Chem. Soc., Combustion Inst., Sigma Xi. Office: Ohio State U Chem Engring 140 W 19th Ave Columbus OH 43210-1110

OZMENT, DENNIS DEAN, state legislator; b. Farmington, Minn., May 2, 1945; s. Clyde Lee and Dolores (Bell) O.; m. Gayle Farrior, 1967; children: Wanda Kaye, Dennis Eugene. Student, U. Minn., Met. Cmty. Coll., Minn. Mem. Minn. Ho. of Reps. St. Paul, 1984—; mem. edn. com., environ. and natural resources com., regulated industry com.; fire capt. Republican. Home: 3275 145th St E Rosemount MN 55068-5909*

PAANANEN, VICTOR NILES, English educator; b. Ashtabula, Ohio, Jan. 31, 1938; s. Niles Henry and Anni Margaret (Iloranta) P.; m. Donna Mae Jones, Aug. 15, 1964; children: Karl, Neil. AB magna cum laude, Harvard U., 1960; MA, U. Wis., 1964, PhD, 1967. Instr. English Wofford Coll., Spartanburg, S.C., 1962-63; asst. prof. Williams Coll., Williamstown, Mass., 1966-68; asst. prof. Mich. State U., East Lansing, 1968-73, assoc. prof., 1973-82, prof., 1982—, asst. dean Grad. Sch., 1977-82, chmn. dept. English, 1986-94; vis. prof. Roehampton Inst., London, 1982, 96, hon. fellow, 1992. Author: William Blake, 1982, 2d edit., 1996; contbr. articles to profl. and scholarly jours. Univ. fellow U. Wis., 1962, 63-64, Roehampton Inst. hon. fellow, London, 1992—; Harvard Nat. scholar, 1956-60. Mem. MLA, AAUP, Labor Party Advocates. Episcopalian. Home: 152 Orchard St East Lansing MI 48823-4536 Office: Mich State Univ Dept of English Morrill Hall East Lansing MI 48824-1036

PAARMANN, LARRY DEAN, electrical engineering educator; b. Maquoketa, Iowa, Feb. 3, 1941; s. Arthur Herman Paarmann and Blanche Caroline (Lozenzen) Earles. BS, No. Ill. U., 1970; MS, U. Ill., 1977; PhD, Ill. Inst. Technology, 1983. Instr. Kishwaukee Coll., Malta, Ill., 1970-75; rsch. asst. U. Ill., Urbana, 1975-76; engr. IIT Rsch. Inst., Chgo., 1977-78; instr. IIT, Chgo., 1978-83; asst. prof. Drexel U., Phila., 1983-90; assoc. prof. Wichita (Kans.) State U., 1990—; co-organizer IEEE ednl. seminar, Phila., 1988, session of 15th N.E. Bioengring. Conf., Boston, 1989, session of 34th Midwest Symposium on Cirs. and Systems, Monterey, Calif., 1991; reviewer IEEE Transactions on Signal Processing. Assoc. editor IEEE Signal Processing Mag.; contbr. articles to profl. jours. Rsch. grantee NSF, 1984, 85, AT&T Found., 1984, Am. Heart Assn., 1985, Kans. Electric Utilities Rsch., 1992. IEEE (sr., chpt. chmn. 1989-90, tech. program chmn. 1994 Wichita conf. on comm., networking and signal processing), European Assn. for Signal Processing. Home: 3224 N Longfellow Ct Wichita KS 67226-1200 Office: Wichita State U Dept Elec Engring Wichita KS 67260-0044

PAAU, ALAN SHIUKEE, industrial microbiologist, administrator; b. Macau, Dec. 16, 1951; came to U.S., 1971, naturalized, 1985; s. Lokfu and Ping (Li) P.; m. Florence Hau, Aug. 14, 1978. PhD, U. Houston, 1978; MBA, Cardinal Stritch Coll., 1990. Teaching coord. U. Houston, 1974-78; rsch. assoc. U. Wis., Madison, 1978-79, project scientist, 1979-81; scientist, project leader Cetus Madison Corp., Middleton, Wis., 1982-84; sr. scientist, project mgr. Agracetus Corp., Middleton, 1984-90; project mgr., assoc. W.R. Grace & Co., Columbia, 1991-92; assoc. dir. Biotech. Ctr. Ohio State U., Columbus, 1992-94; exec. dir. Iowa State U. Rsch. Found. Inc., Ames, 1994—; cons. in field; tech. advisor Chimertech Devel. Corp, 1990—; bd. dirs. PreComp, Inc. Recipient Outstanding Grad. Student award, Am. Soc. Plant Physiologists, 1974. Sigma Xi grantee, 1980. Mem. AAAS, Am. Soc. Microbiology, Am. Soc. Industrial Microbiology, Am. Phytopathol. Soc., Am. Soc. Agronomy, Licensing Execs. Soc., Assn. Univ. Tech. Mgrs., Sigma Xi. Roman Catholic. Contbr. articles to profl. jours. Patentee. Office: Iowa State U Rsch Found 214 O & L Iowa St U Ames IA 50011

PACH, CHESTER JOSEPH, JR., history educator; b. Schenectady, N.Y., July 31, 1949; s. Chester Joseph and Helen Jean (Kaminski) P.; m. Mary Jane Kelley, May 26, 1990; children: Gregory Frank, Lauren Elizabeth. AB, Brown U., 1971; MA, Northwestern U., 1975, PhD, 1981. Instr. Northwestern U., Evanston, Ill., 1981; historian airlift comm. div. USAF, Scott AFB, Ill., 1982; asst. prof. history Tex. Tech U., Lubbock, 1982-87; vis. asst. prof. history U. Kans., Lawrence, 1986-91, asst. dir. Hall Ctr. for Humanities, 1989-91; assoc. prof. history Ohio U., Athens, 1991—, acting dir. Contemporary History Inst., 1992-93, dir., 1993—; Fulbright vis. prof. U. Otago, Dunedin, New Zealand. Author: Arming the Free World, 1991, The Presidency of Dwight D. Eisenhower, rev. edit., 1991. Vis. rsch. fellow U.S. Army Ctr. Mil. History, 1976-77. Mem. Soc. for Historians of Am. Fgn. Rels. (coun. 1996—, Stuart L. Bernath prize 1983), Am. Hist. Assn., Orgn. Am. Historians, Phi Beta Kappa. Office: Ohio Univ Contemporary History Inst Brown House Athens OH 45701

PACKARD, SANDRA PODOLIN, education educator, consultant; b. Buffalo, Sept. 13, 1942; d. Mathew and Ethel (Zolte) P.; m. Martin Packard, Aug. 2, 1964; children: Dawn Esther, Shana Fanny. B.F.A., Syracuse U., 1964; M.S.Ed., Ind. U., 1966, Ed.D., 1973. Cert. tchr. art K-12, N.Y. Asst. prof. art SUNY-Buffalo, 1972-74; assoc. prof. art Miami U., Oxford, Ohio, 1974-81, spl. asst. to provost, 1979-80, assoc. provost, spl. programs, 1980-81; dean Coll. Edn. Bowling Green State U., Ohio, 1981-85; provost and vice chancellor for acad. affairs U. Tenn., Chattanooga, 1985-92; pres. Oakland U., Rochester, Mich., 1992-95; prof. edn., 1995—; sr. fellow, dir. tech. in edn. Am. Assn. State Colls. and Univs., 1995; prof. Oakland U., Rochester, Mich., 1995—; cons. Butler County Health Ctr., Hamilton, Ohio, 1976-78; vis. prof. art therapy Simmons Coll., 1979, Mary Mount Coll., Milw., 1981; bd. dirs. SE Ctr. for Arts in Edn., 1994—; mem. corp. adv. com. Corp. Detroit Mag., 1994-95. Sr. editor Studies in Art Edn. jour., 1979-81; editorial adv. bd. Jour. Aesthetic Edn., 1984-90; editor: The Leading Edge, 1986; contbr. articles to profl. jours., chpts. to conf. papers. Chmn. com. Commn. on Edn. Excellence, Ohio, 1982-83, Tenn. State Peformance Funding Task Force, 1988, Tenn. State Task Force on Minority Tchrs., 1988; reviewer art curriculum N.Y. Bd. Edn., 1985; mem. supt. search com. Chattanooga Pub. Schs., 1987-88; mem. Chattanooga Met. Coun., 1987-88, Chattanooga Ballet Bd., 1986-88, Fund for Excellence in Pub. Edn., 1986-90, Tenn. Aquarium Bd. Advisors, 1989-92, Team Evaluation Ctr. Bd., 1988-90; mem. Strategic Planning Action Team, Chattanooga City Schs., 1987-88, Siskin Hosp. Bd., 1989-92, Blue Ribbon Task Force Pontiac 2010: A New Reality, City of Pontiac Planning Divsn., 1992—; steering com., cultural action bd. Chattanooga, planning com United Way, 1987; Jewish Fedn. Bd., 1986-91; mem. coun. for policy studies Art Edn. Adv. Bd., 1982-91; ex-officio mem. Meadow Brook Theatre Guild, 1992-95; bd. chair Meadow Brook Performing Arts Co., 1992-95; chair World Cup Soccer Edn. Com./Mich. Host Com. 1993-95; bd. dirs. Ptnrs. for Preferred Future, Rochester Cmty. Schs., 1992-95, Traffic Improvement Assn. Oakland County, 1992-95, Oakland County Bus. Roundtable, 1993-95; Rochester C. of C. host com. chair on edn. World Cup, 1992-95; bd. dirs. United Way Southeastern Mich.: active United Way Oakland County, Pontiac 2010: A New Reality, mayor's transition team city/sch. rels. task force: team evaluation leader Dept. of State Am. Univ. Bulgaria, 1995; bd. trustees Cohn's & Colitis Found., 1996—. Am. Coun. on Edn. and Mellon fellow Miami U., 1978-79; recipient Cracking the Glass Ceiling award Pontiac Area Urban League, 1992. Fellow Nat. Art Edn. Assn. (disting.); mem. Am. Assn. Colls. for Tchr. Edn. (com. chair 1982-85), Am. Art Therapy Assn. (registered), Nat. Art Edn. Assn. Women's Caucus (founder, pres. 1976-78, McFee award 1986), Am. Assn. State Colls. and Univs. (com. profl. devel. 1993-95, state rep. 1994-95), Econ. Club Detroit (bd. dirs. 1992-95), Rotary Club, Phi Delta Kappa (Leadership award 1985). Home: 5192 Mirror Lake Ct West Bloomfield MI 48323 Office: Oakland U 503 O'Dowd Hall Rochester MI 48309

PACKER, DIANA, reference librarian; b. Cleve., Sept. 4; d. Herman and Sabina (Hochman) Reich; m. Herbert Packer, June 21, 1964 (dec.); children: Cynthia, Jeremy, Todd. BA, Case Western Res. U., 1951, MLS, 1952. Libr. Horizons Rsch. Inc., Cleve., 1952-64, Cleveland Heights (Ohio) University Heights Pub. Libr., 1969—. Officer Cleveland Heights PTA, 1971-84; bd. dirs. LWV, Cleveland Heights, 1974—; officer Spl. Librs. Assn., 1952-64. Mem. Ohio Libr. Assn. Home: 2201 Acacia Park Dr Apt 522 Lyndhurst OH 44124-3841

PACKER, GREG A., state legislator; m. Laurie Packer. Rep. dist. 51 State of Kans., 1993—. Republican. Home: 7200 SW Wattling Ct Topeka KS 66614-4683*

PACKER, JAMES EARNEST, classics educator; b. L.A., Dec. 25, 1937; s. James Bryant Claypoole and Lona (Mosk) Packer. AB, U. Calif., Berkeley, 1959, MA, 1960, PhD, 1964. Asst. prof. Calif. State U., Northridge, 1964-66; asst. prof. Northwestern U., Evanston, Ill., 1966-71, assoc. prof., 1971-90, prof., 1990—; cons. Getty Ctr. for the History and Art of the Humanities, Santa Monica, 1985-87, Time Life Books, Alexandria, Va., 1992-94. Author: The Insulae of Imperial Ostia, 1971. Recipient grant Am. Philos. Soc., 1965, 68, 82, 83, Am. Coun. of Learned Socs., 1965, 73, 75, Nat. Endowment for the Humanities, 1970, 72, Samuel H. Kress Found., 1989, 95, 96, Graham Found. for Advanced Studies in the Visual Arts, 1989, Getty Ctr. for History of Art and the Humanities, 1985-86, 86-87, 96. Fellow Am. Acad. in Rome (adv. coun.); mem. Archaeol. Inst. of Am., Soc. of Ancient Historians, Soc. for Classical Am., Soc. of Archl. Historians. Home: Apt 1424 3600 N Lake Shore Dr Chicago IL 60613-4620 Office: Dept Classics Northwestern Univ 1859 Sheridan Rd Evanston IL 60208

PADBERG, HELEN SWAN, violinist; b. Shawnee, Okla.; d. Frank P. and Birdie B. (Rudell) Swan; AA, Stephens Coll., 1938; Mus.B., U. Okla., 1940; Mus.M., Northwestern U., 1941; student Jacques Gordon; m. Frank Padberg, Feb. 6, 1943; children: Frank, Kristen. Solo performances and concerts, 1932—; mem. faculty string quartet and symphony soloist Stephens Coll., 1937-38; violinist Oklahoma City Symphony Summer Concerts, 1940; soloist Northwestern U. Symphony, 1941; USO performer, 1941-43; violinist Nat. Orchestral Assn. and Am. Youth Orch., N.Y.C., 1944-46; tchr. strings Maywood (Ill.), 1946-47; asst. concertmaster West Suburban Symphony, Chgo., 1947-48; mem. Chgo. Women's Symphony, Chgo. Civic Orch. and chamber music groups, 1947-51; violinist Ark. String Trio, 1952-58; concertmaster Ark. Symphony and Little Rock Philharmonic, 1953-57, Marjorie Lawrence TV Series, Ark., 1953-54; pvt. tchr. violin, Little Rock, 1953-66; accompanist and performer on piano, harp. Pres., Ark. Med. Soc. Aux., 1962-63, historian, 1963-94; co-founder Little Rock Chamber Music Soc., 1954; pres. bd. dirs. Vis. Nurse Assn. of Pulaski County, Ark., 1967-69; bd. dirs. Internat. Visitors Ctr., Chgo., 1988—, Stephens Coll. Alumna Assn. Bd.; elder, trustee Presbyn. ch. Mem. Am. Harp Soc., Chgo. Harp Soc. (sec. 1979-84), Am. Fedn. Musicians, Am. Opera Soc. (historian 1987—), Am. Opera Soc. of Chgo. (v.p. and program chmn. 1981-82, pres. 1984-87), Internat. Women Assocs. (pres. 1988-91), Pi Kappa Lambda, Mu Phi Epsilon, Pi Beta Phi (pres. Little Rock Alumnae Club). Clubs: Aesthetic (pres. Little Rock); Womens' Athletic of Chgo. Home: 175 E Delaware Pl Chicago IL 60611-1756

PADDOCK, JOHN, professional hockey team head coach; b. Oak River, Man., Can.; m. JIll Paddock; children: Jenny, Sally, Anna. Coach Maine Mariners, 1983-84, Hershey Bears, 1988-89; asst. gen. mgr. Phila. Flyers, 1989-90; coach Binghamton Rangers, 1990-91; head coach Winnipeg (Man.) Jets, 1991—, also gen. mgr. Twice named Am. League Coach of Yr. *

PADDOCK, STUART R., JR., publishing executive. Bd. chmn. Daily Herald/Sunday Herald, Arlington Heights, Ill. Office: Daily Herald/Sunday Herald Paddock Publs PO Box 280 Arlington Heights IL 60006-0280*

PADDON, ANNA RUTH OLSEN, journalist, educator; b. Fergus Falls, Minn., June 8, 1938; d. Olaf and Martha (Larsen) Olsen; m. Richard Wallace Paddon, Aug. 31, 1963; children: James Wallace, Jonathan Warren, Joel Bradford. BS, Wheaton (Ill.) Coll., 1961; MS, Columbia U., 1962; PhD, U. Tenn., Knoxville, 1985. Newspaper reporter World-Telegram & Sun, N.Y.C., 1962-64; pub. rels. profl. Ga. Dept. Edn., Atlanta, 1964-65; instr. U. Tenn., Knoxville, 1974-84; prof., chmn. dept. journalism Benedict Coll., Columbia, S.C., 1985-88; asst. prof. journalism So. Ill. U., Carbondale, 1988—. Contbr. articles to profl. jours. Mem. Assn. for Edn. in Journalism and Mass Comm., Soc. Profl. Journalists, Am. Journalism Historians Assn., Kappa Tau Alpha, Phi Kappa Phi. Presbyterian. Home: 2710 Sunset Dr Carbondale IL 62901 Office: So Ill U Sch Journalism Carbondale IL 62901

PADEN, CAROLYN EILEEN BELKNAP, dietitian; b. Takoma Park, Md., Dec. 10, 1953; d. Donald Julius and Lydian Allyne (Plyer) Belknap; m. Raymond Louis Paden, Dec. 29, 1985; children: Matthew Louis, Luke Andrew, Mark Anthony. BS in Home Econs. cum laude, Southern Coll., 1977; MS in Nutrition, Loma Linda (Calif.) U., 1983. Registered dietitian. Dietitic tech. Loma Linda U. Med. Ctr., 1978-82, nutritional support dietitian, 1982-84; clin. dietitian Mercy Meml. Med. Ctr., St. Joseph, Mich., 1984-86, mgr. clin. nutrition svcs., 1986-94; mem. adj. faculty Andrews U., Berrien Springs, Mich., 1994—; rschr. nutritional status of hospitalized patients Mercy Meml. Med. Ctr., St. Joseph, 1986, 87; cons. nutritional support various Berrien County hosps., 1984—; adj. prof. Andrews U., Berrien Springs, Mich., 1982—. Mem. Am. Dietetic Assn. Adventist. Home: 195 Knott Rd Niles MI 49120-9025 Office: Mercy Meml Med Ctr 1234 Napier Ave Saint Joseph MI 49085-2112

PADFIELD, JON R., state legislator. BS, Purdue U. Design engr. Delco Electronics; mem. Ind. State Ho. of Reps. Dist. 30, mem. aged and aging com., mem. commerce and econ. devel. com., mem. edn. com., vice chmn. elections and apportionment com. Active Citizens for Excellence in Edn., Boy Scouts Am. Mem. NRA, Kokomo Engring. Soc.

PADGETT, DAVID RAMON, manufacturing executive; b. Atlanta, Aug. 31, 1956; s. Fred Padgett and Mary Kate (Parker) Hicks; m. Barbara Jane Garvin, Oct. 1, 1974; children: David Ramon, Ashley Edward. Student, Yorktown Tng. Ctr., 1976, GM Tng. Ctr., 1980, Leavenworth (Kans.) Tng. Ctr., 1983. Machinery technician USCG, Yorktown, Va., 1974-77; svc. technician Dixie Engine Co., Atlanta, 1977-80, Trax Inc., Atlanta, 1980-82, Cen. Power Products, Liberty, Mo., 1982; svc. supr. Cen. Power Products, Emporia, Kans., 1984-86, re-mfg. mgr., 1986-87, ops. mgr., 1987-90; plant mgr. Ctrl. Power Products, Grandview, Mo., 1990—; quality control advisor Johnson County C.C., Kansas City, Kans., 1987—, mgmt. cons., 1988; cons. Quality Control Program Advisor, Kans., 1987—, Flint Hills Avts., Emporia, 1987—. Home: 517 Stacey Dr Belton MO 64012-1832 Office: 11100 W 58th St Shawnee KS 66203

PADGETT, GREGORY LEE, lawyer; b. Greenfield, Ind., May 9, 1959; s. William Joseph and Anna Katherine (Hyre) P.; m. Ruth Anne Dorworth, June 5, 1982; children: Joshua David, William Joel. BA summa cum laude, DePauw U., 1981; JD, Northwestern U., 1984. Bar: Ill., U.S. Dist. Ct. (no. dist.) Ill. 1984, U.S. Ct. Appeals (7th cir.) 1986, Ind. 1988, U.S. Dist. Ct. (no. & so. dists.) Ind. 1988. Assoc. Kirkland & Ellis, Chgo., 1984-88, Baker & Daniels, Indpls., 1988-92; ptnr. Johnson, Lawhead and Padgett P.C., Indpls., 1992—; adj. prof. Butler U., 1989-90; bd. dirs. Meridian St. Found. Mem. Marion County Prosecutor's Rev. Task Force, Indpls., 1991; pres., bd. dirs. Theatre on the Square, Indpls.; mem. coun. Hope Evang. Covenant Ch. Mem. Ind. State Bar Assn., Indpls. Bar Assn. (exec. com. alternative dispute resolution sect.), Christian Legal Soc., Phi Beta Kappa. Office: Johnson Lawhead and Padgett 8900 Keystone Crossing Ste 940 Indianapolis IN 46240-2162

PADGETT, JOY, state legislator; m. Don Padgett; 1 child, Walter. BS, Kent State U. Mem. Ohio Ho. of Reps.; owner Main Off Supply. Mem. YWCA. Recipient Don K. Wales award CORC Joint Policy Bd., 1990, Tchr. of Yr. award Southwestern Ohio, 1992. Mem. Coshocton, Holmes and Muskingum C. of C., Farm Bur., Coshocton Area Personnel Assn. Republican. Home: 871 Walnut St Coshocton OH 43812-1649 Office: OH Ho of Reps State House Columbus OH 43215

PADGITT, DOROTHY ANGELOS, library director; b. Oak Park, Ill., Feb. 18, 1951; d. Michael T. and Katherine (Kyriazopulos) Angelos; m. R. Scott Padgitt, Sept. 8, 1984. Student, U. Vienna, Austria, 1971-72; BA, Augustana Coll., 1974; MLS, Rosary Coll., River Forest, Ill., 1995. Libr. dir. River Grove (Ill.) Pub. Libr. Dist., 1991—. Mem. Leyden Twp. Mcpl. League, Harwood Heights, Ill., 1991—. Recipient Cert. of Appreciation, Rehab. Inst. Chgo., 1994. Mem. ALA, Libr. Admintrn. and Mgmt. Assn., Pub. Libr. Assn., Ill. Libr. Assn. Home: 8416 Center St River Grove IL 60171

PADILLA, SUE ANN, librarian; b. Horton, Kans., Dec. 11, 1950; d. Mouler and Elva Mae (Grimes) Oaks; m. John H. Padilla (div.); children: Elizabeth, Matthew. BS in Edn., Kans. State Tchrs. Coll., 1972; MLS, Emporia State U., 1988. Tchr. Our Lady of Guadalupe Sch., Topeka, Kans., 1973-75, Topeka Pub. Schs., 1975-88; libr. Ida Long Goodman Meml. Libr., St. John, Kans., 1988—. Contbg. author: Booktalk!3, Booktalk!4, Booktalk!5, The Booktalkers' Companion, Vol. 1. Bd. dirs. St. John Hosp. Dist., 1991-92; chair Community Arts Series, St. John, 1990—. Mem. ALA, Kans. Libr. Assn., Kans. Assn. Sch. Librs., Emporia State U. Alumni Assn. (bd. dirs. 1991-94), Lions Club (com. chair St. John's club 1990—), Delta Kappa Gamma (com. chair 1989-95). Office: Ida Long Goodman Meml Libr 406 N Monroe Saint John KS 67576

PAFFHAUSEN, FREDERICK JOHN, librarian; b. Highland Park, Ill., Mar. 11, 1947; s. James Anthony and Teresa Mary (Dirner) P.; m. Amy Cecelia Paffhausen, Dec. 6, 1976; children: Elisabeth Teresa, Frederick

Douglas. BA, U. Mich., 1971, MLS, 1972. Cert. libr., Mich. Libr. Wayne County (Mich.) Libr. Sys., 1974-86, 91-94; dist. adminstr. 16th Congrl. Dist., Dearborn, Mich., 1986-91; libr. dir. Redford (Mich.) Twp. Dist. Libr., 1995—; libr. bldg. cons. City of Westland, 1984. Campaign mgr. Chris Dingell for State Senate, Trenton, Mich., 1984; cmty. devel. v.p. Mich. Jaycees, Lansing, 1982; pres. Tenton Jaycees, 1980; mem. 16th Dist. Dem. Party, 1976. Recipient Dennis Hamilton Meml. award U.S. Jaycees, 1983, John H. Ambruster Keyman award, 1980. Mem. NRA, Mich. Libr. Assn., Alumni Soc. Univ. Mich. Roman Catholic. Home: 2890 Truwood Trenton MI 48183 Office: Redford Twp Dist Libr 15150 Norborne Redford MI 48239

PAGANO, JON ALAIN, data processing consultant; b. Kankakee, Ill., Dec. 26, 1958; s. Antoine and Agnes P.; m. Linda S. Gound, Dec. 22, 1983. BA in Philosophy, U. Ill., 1979; BA in Computer Sci., North Cen. Coll., 1989. Computer ops. staff Roper Inc., Kankakee, 1979-81; programmer Harris Bankcorp, Chgo., 1981-84; cons. Circle Cons., Kankakee, 1984; sr. programmer/analyst First Nat. Bank, Chgo., 1984-86; programmer/analyst Internet Systems Corp., Chgo., 1986-87; sr. systems analyst, mgr. Concord Computing Corp., Elk Grove, Ill., 1987-89; pres. Circle Cons., Naperville, Ill., 1989—. Ednl. lobbying U. Ill., Urbana, 1986—, alumni networking North Cen. Coll., 1991—. Mem. ACM, IEEE, U. Ill. Alumni Assn. (Pres.'s Coun. 1988—, Bronze Circle 1988), Pres. Club North Ctrl. Coll. Home: 344 Westbrook Cir Naperville IL 60565-3242 Office: Circle Cons 344 Westbrook Cir Naperville IL 60565-3242

PAGE, ALAN CEDRIC, judge; b. Canton, Ohio, Aug. 7, 1945; s. Howard F. and Georgianna (Umbles) P.; m. Diane Sims, June 5, 1973; children: Nina, Georgianna, Justin, Khamsin. BA, U. Notre Dame, 1967; JD, U. Minn., 1978; LLD, U. Notre Dame, 1993; LLD (hon.), St. John's U., 1994, Westfield State Coll., 1994, Luther Coll., 1995. Bar: Minn. 1979, U.S. Dist. Ct. Minn. 1979, U.S. Supreme Ct. 1988. Profl. athlete Minn. Vikings, Mpls., 1967-78, Chgo. Bears, 1978-81; assoc. Lindquist & Vennum, Mpls., 1979-85; former atty. Minn. Atty. Gen.'s Office, Mpls., 1985-92; assoc. justice Minn. Supreme Ct., St. Paul, 1993—; cons. NFL Players Assn., Washington, 1979-84. Commentator Nat. Pub. Radio, 1982-83. Founder Page Edn. Found., 1988. Named NFL's Most Valuable Player, 1971, one of 10 Outstanding Young Men Am., U.S. Jaycees, 1981; named to NFL Hall of Fame, 1988, Coll. Football Hall of Fame, 1993. Mem. ABA, Minn. Bar Assn., Hennepin County Bar Assn., Minn. Minority Lawyers Assn. Office: 427 Minnesota Judicial Ctr 25 Constitution Ave Saint Paul MN 55155-1500

PAGE, BENJAMIN INGRIM, political science educator, researcher; b. Los Angeles, Sept. 17, 1940; s. Benjamin Markham and Virginia Claire (Ingrim) P.; m. Mary Herbert Robertson, Dec. 30, 1964; children: Benjamin R., Alexandra C., Timothy M., Eleanor St. J. AB in History, Stanford U., 1961, PhD in Polit. Sci., 1973; LLB, Harvard U., 1965. Asst. prof. govt. Dartmouth Coll., 1971-73; asst. prof. polit. sci. U. Chgo., 1973-77, assoc. prof., 1978-82, prof., 1982-83; assoc. prof. U. Wis.-Madison, 1977-78; Frank C. Erwin Jr. Centennial chair in govt. U. Tex., Austin, 1983-88; Gordon Scott Fulcher prof. of decision making Northwestern U., 1988—; rsch. assoc. Nat. Opinion Rsch. Ctr., Chgo., 1978-82; bd. overseers Nat. Election Studies, Ann Arbor, Mich., 1975-81; cons. in field. Author: (with Sullivan, Pressman and Lyons) The Politics of Representation, 1974, Choices and Echoes in Presidential Elections, 1978, (with Petracca) The American Presidency, 1983, Who Gets What From Government, 1983, (with Shapiro) The Rational Public, 1992, (with Greenberg) The Struggle for Democracy, 1993, Who Deliberates?, 1996; contbr. articles to numerous jours. Recipient Law Week award Bur. of Nat. Affairs, 1965; fellow Social Sci. Research Council, 1972-73, Hoover Instn., 1981-82. Mem. AAAS, Am. Polit. Sci. Assn. (governing coun. 1984-86), Midwest Polit. Sci. Assn. (v.p. 1991-93), Pub. Choice Soc., Am. Assn. Pub. Opinion Rsch., Am. Econs. Assn., Phi Beta Kappa. Democrat. Episcopalian. Home: 1633 Asbury Ave Evanston IL 60201-4101 Office: Northwestern U Polit Sci Dept Evanston IL 60208

PAGE, JOHN ARTHUR, professional association executive, educator; b. New Rochelle, N.Y., Sept. 23, 1957; s. Arthur John and Yolanda Gloria (Malzone) P.; m. Patricia Alta Marsh, June 18, 1984; 1 child, Amy Jean. BA in Sci., Pa. State U., 1980, BS in Health Planning and Adminstrn., 1980; MS in Health Sys., Ga. Inst. Tech., 1982. Strategic planner Gnaden Huetten Meml. Hosp., Lehighton, Pa., 1980; grad. tchg. and rsch. asst. Ga. Inst. Tech. Sch. Health Sys., Atlanta, 1981-82; mgmt. sys. engr. Good Shepherd Med. Ctr., Longview, Tex., 1982-84; dir. mgmt. engring. U. Nebr. Med. Ctr., Omaha, 1984-88; dir. mgmt. svcs. Children's Hosp., Inc., Columbus, Ohio, 1988-90; pres., CEO, Innovative Healthcare Assocs., Inc., Columbus, 1990—; PAGE Techs., Inc., Columbus, 1990—; exec. dir., CEO, Healthcare Info. and Mgmt. Sys. Soc., Chgo., 1991—; mem. grad. program adv. bd. U. Ill., Chgo., 1991—, adj. asst. prof., 1994—; mem. grad. program adv. bd. U. Ala., Birmingham, 1991—; pres., chmn. bd. Healthcare Info. and Mgmt. Sys. Soc. Found., 1995—. Contbg. author: Patients and Purse Springs, 1987, Productivity and Performance Management in Healthcare Institutions, 1989, An Orientation for Management Engineers New to Health Care, 1992, The Emergency Department: A Guide to Operational Excellence, 1992, Clinical Administration of Audiology and Speech Language Pathology, 1994, Guide to Effective Health Care Informaton and Management Systems and the Role of the CIO, 1994; mem. editl. adv. bd. Report on Health Care Info. Mgmt., 1993—. Advisor Med. Explorers, 1988-90, Jr. Achievement, 1988-90; alumni admissions counselor Pa. State U., 1986—; campaign chmn. United Way, 1988, 89, 90; vol. Am. Heart Assn., 1991, March of Dimes, 1991-93, Am. Cancer Soc., 1990. Recipient Tech. Paper of Yr. award Healthcare Info. and Mgmt. Sys. Soc., 1989. Mem. Masons (chmn. blood drive 1990—). Home: 3123 N Orchard St Chicago IL 60657-4518 Office: Healthcare Info and Mgmt Sys Soc 230 E Ohio St Ste 600 Chicago IL 60611-3201

PAGE, LLOYD E., civil engineer; b. Galesburg, Ill., Nov. 1, 1944; s. Robert L. and Violet E. (Ekstrom) P.; m. Nancy J. Griffith, June 15, 1968; children: Scott L., John D. BSCE, Bradley U., 1966, MSCE, 1969. Registered engr. Ill., Ariz. Civil engr. Ill. Dept. Transp., Peoria, Ill., 1966-74; staff engr. Daily & Assocs. Engrs., Inc., Peoria, Ill., 1974; exec. v.p. Randolph & Assocs., Inc., Peoria, Ill., 1974-75; mem. adv. bd. Bradley U. Dept. Civil. Engring. & Constrn., Peoria, 1987—. Mem. ASCD, NSPE, Am. Pub. Worls Assn. Office: City of Galesburg 55 W Tompkins St Galesburg IL 61401

PAGE, SALLY JACQUELYN, university official; b. Saginaw, Mich., July, 1943; d. William Henry and Doris Effie (Knippel) P.; BA, U. Iowa, 1965; MBA, So. Ill. U., 1973. Copy editor, C.V. Mosby Co., St. Louis, 1965-69; edit. cons. Edit. Assos., Edwardsville, Ill., 1969-70; research adminstr. So. Ill. U., 1970-74, asst. to pres., affirmative action officer, 1974-77; officer of instn. U. N.D., Grand Forks, 1977—, lectr. mgmt., 1978—; polit. commentator Sta. KFJM, Nat. Public Radio affiliate, 1981-90; bd. dirs. Agassiz Enterprises, 1990-91, mayor's com. Employment of People With Disabilities, 1980—. Contbr. to profl. jours. Chairperson N.D. Equal Opportunity Affirmative Action Officers, 1987-96; pres., Pine to Prairie council Girl Scouts U.S., 1980-85; mem. employment com. Ill. Commn. on Status of Women, 1976-77; mem. Bicentennial Com. Edwardsville, 1976, Bikeway Task Force Edwardsville, 1975-77, Grand Forks Homes, 1986—, chair 1996—; mem. Civil Service Rev. Task Force, Grand Forks, 1982, civil service commr., 1983, chmn., 1984, 86, 88, 92, 96; ruling elder 1st Presbyn. Ch. Mem. AAUW (dir. Ill. 1975-77), PEO, Coll. and Univ. Personnel Assn. (research and publs. bd. 1982-84) Am. Assn. Affirmative Actiative Action, Soc. Research Adminstrs. Republican. Presbyterian. Home: 3121 Cherry St Grand Forks ND 58201-7461 Office: U ND Grand Forks ND 58202

PAGE, SCOTT LEE, medical association administrator; b. Sedalia, Mo., May 9, 1971; s. Jimmy Dean and Kathy Jean (Kruse) P.; m. Cynthia Lyn Sweaney, June 10, 1995. AA in Bus. Adminstrn., State Fair C.C., Sedalia, 1991; BS in Polit. Sci., Ctrl. Mo. State U., 1993. Mgr. Otterville (Mo.) Estates Ltd., 1987-89; assoc. J.C. Penney Co., Sedalia, Mo., 1989-91, Sears, Roebuck & Co., Sedalia, 1991-93; legis. asst. Mo. State Senate, Jefferson City, Mo., 1993-96; govtl. liaison Mo. Pharm. Assn., Jefferson City, 1996—; rsch. cons. Mo. C. of C., Jefferson City, 1993. Mem. Tipton United Meth. Ch.; sec. 6th senatorial dist. Rep. Com., 1992-94, chmn. Cooper County Rep. Ctrl. Com., Booneville, Mo., 1992-94; pres. Capital Aea Young Reps., 1994—; grad. Jefferson City Citizen Police Acad., 1994; campaign mgr. Rohrbach for Senate, Jefferson City, 1994; state sec. Mo. Fedn. Young Reps., 1995-96. Mem. Mo. Aso. Assn. Execs., Pi Sigma Alpha (sec.-treas. 1992-93). Home: 401 Prospect Tipton MO 65081 Office: Mo Pharm Assn 213 Capital Ave Jefferson City MO 65101

PAGE, TERRY, publishing executive; b. Chgo., July 16, 1953; s. Milton Jr. and Ruth (Davis) P.; m. Debra Ann McNeil, Oct. 4, 1995. Pres. Boo Books, Inc., Chgo., 1994—. Author: The Captain's Coins, 1993, Horse-n-Around, 1993, The Case of the Missing Blue, 1993, My Wings, 1995. Office: Boo Books Inc PO Box 201128 Chicago IL 60620

PAGE, THOMAS LESLIE, poet, writer; b. Wichita, Kans., Sept. 28, 1937; s. Thomas F. Page and Mary L. (O'Hara) Turner; m. Leslie Ellen Fox, Sept. 2, 1971; children: Thomas O., Mary C.E., Will A. BA, Wichita U., 1960; MA, Vanderbilt U., 1963; MFA, Wichita State U., 1985. Asst. prof. Latin Am. studies U. Fla., Gainesville, 1966-73; high sch. tchr. various, 1974-81; officer Wichita Police Dept., 1981-82; instr. Wichita State U., 1982-87; writer Wichita, 1987—. Author: ERA Vet, 1988, Name of the Place, 1989, The Fort Scott Poems, 1994. Com. mem. Fla. State McGovern Com., Orlando, 1970-72; organizer Vanderbilt Students for Kennedy, Nashville, 1960-63; ctrl. committeeman Dem. Party, 1984-86; sec., treas. The Forum, Wichita, 1973-78; dir. Mother Jones Found., 1988-91. With U.S. Army, 1964-65. NDEA fellowship Vanderbilt U., 1960-63, Ford Found. grant, 1961. Mem. Sons of Union Vets. of the Civil War, Soc. for the Study of Midwestern Lit., Associated Writing Programs, Sir John Falstaff Soc.

PAGE-CARAHER, DENISE, mediator, arbitrator; b. Indpls., Aug. 27, 1952; d. Russell W. and Deronda M. (Bird) Page; m. James H. Caraher; children: Paige Meredith, Patrick James. BA, Ind. U., Bloomington, 1974; JD, U. Notre Dame, South Bend, 1977. Atty., assoc. Hilgedag, Johnson, Secrest & Murphy, Indpls., 1977-81; atty., ptnr. Meils, Zink, Thompson, Dietz & Page, Indpls., 1981-87, Sheeks, Ittenbach & Page, Indpls., 1987-91; mediator, arbitrator pvt. practice, Indpls., 1991—; nat. jud. adv. bd., panelist Resolute Sys., Inc., Brookfield, Wis., 1994—; panelist Resolution Resources, Inc., Atlanta, 1995—, Arbitration Forums, Inc., Atlanta, 1994—; exec. com. alternative dispute resolution com. Indpls. Bar Assn., 1994—, bd. mgrs., 1985-87. Author, composer, lyricist, performer Play It Safe, 1994; lyricist, author, composer, performer Peace Is For Everyone, 1995; author, lyricist Carmenella, 1995, Goldilocks and the 3 Bears-A Space Fantasy, 1994, Jack and the Beanstalk, 1993. Mem., superior ct. rep. Marion County Jud. Nominating Comn., 1990-94; children's choir dir. North United Meth. Ch., Indpls., 1979—; parent vol., musical dir. Orchard Country Day Sch., Indpls., 1991—; performer, chorus mem. Indpls. Opera, 1980—. Methodist. Home: 4348 Central Ave Indianapolis IN 46205

PAIGE, DIANE LOUISE, physical therapist; b. Lorain, Ohio, June 7, 1967; d. John Harvey and Beverly Larue (Hertlein) P. BS in Allied Med. Professions, Ohio State U., 1989; MEd in Sports Mgmt. and Exercise Sci., Cleve. State U., 1995. Lic. phys. therapist, athletic trainer, Ohio. Staff phys. therapist Lorain Cmty. Hosp., 1989-94; clin. specialist, coord. clin. edn. Lorain Cmty./St. Joseph's Regional Health Ctr., 1994—. Mem. Am. Phys. Therapy Assn., Nat. Strength and Conditioning Assn., Nat. Athletic Tng. Assn. Home: 699 Lincoln St Amherst OH 44001 Office: Lorain Cmty Saint Josephs Regional Health Ctr 3700 Kolbe Rd Lorain OH 44053

PAIGE, NORMA, lawyer, corporate executive; b. Lomza, Poland, Oct. 11, 1922; came to U.S., 1927; d. Morris and Edith (Kachourek) Zelaso; children: Holly Paige Russek, Madelyn Paige Givant. BA, NYU, 1944, JD, 1946; postgrad. in bus. adminstrn., CCNY, 1953, NYU, 1969. Bar: N.Y. 1946, U.S. Supreme Ct. 1951. Ptnr. Paige and Paige, N.Y.C., 1948—; v.p., bd. dirs. Astronautics Corp. Am., Milw., 1959—, chmn. bd., 1984—; exec. v.p., bd. dirs. Kearfott Guidance & Navigation Corp., Wayne, N.J., 1988—; bd. dirs. Astronautics C.A., Ltd., Israel. Recipient Jabotinsky Centennial medal Prime Minister of Israel, 1980, Tribute to Women in Indsl. Industry Twin II award YWCA, 1981, NYU Sch. Law Outstanding Alumnus of Yr. award, 1991, Judge Edward Weinfeld award, 1996. Mem. N.Y. Women's Bar Assn. (pres. 1958-59). Office: Astronautics Corp Am 4115 N Teutonia Ave Milwaukee WI 53209-6731

PAIGE, PHILIP HAROLD, publishing executive, newspaper; b. Eau Claire, Wis., Sept. 24, 1956; s. Edmund Wakefield and Viola Helen (Hendrickson) P.; m. Jane Brekke, Aug. 9, 1986; children: Connor Edmund, Hailey Jane. B in Journalism, U. Wis. Madison, 1980, B in History, 1980; MBA, Cardinal Stritch Coll., 1993. Reporter Courier Hub, Stoughton, Wis., 1980; reporter, editor The Bee, Phillips, Wis., 1981-85; editor The Guide, Grafton, Wis., 1985-88; publ. Lakeshore Newspapers, Inc., Cedarburg, Wis., 1988—; editor: Northshore Lifestyle Mag., Cedarburg, 1993—. Home: N106 W7077 Dayton St Cedarburg WI 53012 Office: Lakeshore Newspapers Inc N19 W6733 Commerce Ct Cedarburg WI 53012

PAINE, RICHARD EARL, communication educator; b. Springfield, Vt., July 18, 1953; s. Lester Earl and Madalene Edna (Lacillade) P. BA, Harding U., 1976; MA, Western Ky. U., 1979; PhD, U. Okla., 1989. Asst. forensics coach Harding U., Searcy, Ark., 1976-77; dir. forensics U. Okla., Norman, 1979-82, North Cen. Coll., Naperville, Ill., 1983—; assoc. prof. North Cen. Coll., Naperville, 1989—, chair dept. speech comm. & theatre, 1994—. Recipient Dissinger Outstanding Teaching award, 1993. Mem. Ill. Intercollegiate Forensics Assn. (bd. dirs. 1991—), So. States Comm. Assn. (vice chair 1987, intercultural comm. divsn.), Speech Comm. Assn., Mid-Am. Forensics League, Pi Kappa Delta (nat. std. debate champion 1975), Nat. Forensics Assn. (constn. com. 1990-92, impromptu topics com. 1993—). Democrat.

PAINTER, MARK PHILIP, judge; b. Cin., Apr. 6, 1947; s. John Philip and Marjorie (West) P.; m. Sue Ann Painter. BA, U. Cin., 1970; JD, 1973. Bar: Ohio 1973, U.S. Dist. Ct. (so. dist.) Ohio 1973, U.S. Supreme Ct. 1980. Assoc. Smith & Schnacke (and predecesor firm, now part of Thompson, Hines & Flory), 1973-78; sole practice, Cin., 1978-82; judge Hamilton County Mcpl. Ct., Cin., 1982-95, Ohio 1st Dist. Ct. Appeals, 1995—; adj. prof. law U. Cin., 1990—. Co-author: Ohio DUI Law, 1988, 4th edit., 1995; mem. editorial bd. Criminal Law Jour. Ohio, 1989-92; contbr. articles to profl. jours. Bd. dirs. Citizens Sch. Com., Cin., 1974-76; trustee Freestore Foodbank, Cin., 1984-90, Mary Jo Brueggeman Meml. Found., Cin., 1981-92; bd. commrs. on grievances and discipline Ohio Supreme Ct., 1993-95; mem. Rep. Cen. Com., Cin., 1972-82. Recipient Superior Jud. Service award Ohio Supreme Ct., 1982, 84, 85. Mem. ABA, Ohio State Bar Assn., Cin. Bar Assn. (trustee 1988-90), Am. Judges Assn., Am. Judicature Soc., Potter Stewart Inn of Ct. (master of bench emeritus), Bankers Club. Home: 2449 Fairview Ave Cincinnati OH 45219-1170 Office: Ct of Appeals 1000 Main St Ste 300 Cincinnati OH 45202-1217

PAISLEY, KEITH WATKINS, state senator, small business owner; b. Mpls., Dec. 29, 1928; s. Manley G. and Maxine Alice (Watkins) P.; m. Jean Clare Robson, Sept. 23, 1950; children: Mark, Susan, Julie, Jeanne. BA, Hamline U., 1950. Rep. State of S.D., Pierre, 1981-84, senator, 1985—; owner Robson Hardware, Sioux Falls, S.D., 1972-93. Lutheran. Home: 2409 S Elmwood Ave Sioux Falls SD 57105-3315 Office: Robson Hardware 2322 W 12th St Sioux Falls SD 57104-3811

PAIVA, JOSEPH VINCENT ROSHAN, software integration company executive; b. Colombo, Sri Lanka, Oct. 27, 1948; came to U.S., 1963; s. Joseph Francis Xavier and Mano (Pereira) P.; m. Dorothea Luise Leach, May 25, 1974 (div. Aug. 1990); children: Mikel Sherhan, Menola Melantha, Gavin Carson. BS in Civil Engring., U. Mo., 1973, MS in Civil Engring., 1976, PhD in Civil Engring., 1982. Registered profl. engr., Mo.; registered land surveyor, Mo. Staff engr. J.C. Stevens & Assocs., Columbia, Mo., 1971-76; cons. Columbia, 1975-86; ptnr. Schoech & Assocs., Columbia, 1978-83; grad. asst., lectr., instr. civil engring. U. Mo., Columbia, 1975-82, ast. prof., 1982-86; tech. and rsch. advisor Sokkisha Co. Ltd., Overland Park, Kans., 1986-89; v.p. R&D The Lietz Co., Overland Park, 1989-91; v.p. Sokkia Tech. Inc., Overland Park, 1991-94, v.p., gen. mgr., 1994—; Contbr. exam. questions Nat. Coun. Engring. Examiners, Clemson, S.C., 1977-86. Contbr. articles to profl. jours. Mem. parish coun. and fin. com. Newman Ctr., Columbia, 1975-78; mem. liturgical commn. Cure of Ars Parish, Leawood, Kans., 1993-95. Mem. NSPE, ASCE, Am. Congress Surveying and Mapping (chmn. procs. papers rev. subcom. 1986-89), Mo. Soc. Profl. Engrs., Inst. Navigation, Mo. Assn. Registered Land Surveyors (chmn. edn. com. 1976-86). Home: 6125 Monrovia Shawnee KS 66216 Office: Sokkia Tech Inc 9102 Barton Overland Park KS 66214

PAK, HENRY H., biomedical engineer, researcher; b. Hinsdale, Ill., Oct. 7, 1961; s. Chan I. and Verna M. (Lyu) P.; m. Helen E. Moon, Sept. 6, 1992. BS, Northwestern U., 1984, MEM, 1996; MS, U. Ill., 1987. Biomed. engr. Northwestern Med. Ctr., Chgo., 1987-89; sr. devel. engr. Abbott Labs., Abbott Park, Ill., 1989—. Active Northwestern U. Alumni Bd., Evanston, Ill., 1991-95. Mem. IEEE, Am. Soc. Quality Control (cert. quality engr., cert. quality auditor, cert. reliability engr.), Assn. for Advancement of Med. Instrumentation, Parenteral Drug Assn. Mem. Seventh Day Adventist Ch. Office: Abbott Labs 100 Abbott Park 976/AP4 Abbott Park IL 60064

PAK, WILLIAM LOUIS, biologist, researcher, educator; b. Suwon, Korea, Sept. 27, 1932; came to U.S., 1948; m. Marion Whitehouse, June 21, 1958; children: William L. Jr., Dorothy K. AB summa cum laude, Boston U., 1955; PhD, Cornell U., 1960. Inst. physics Stevens Inst. Tech., Hoboken, N.J., 1960-61, asst. prof. physics, 1961-65; asst. prof. biology Purdue U., West Lafayette, Ind., 1965-67, assoc. prof. biology, 1967-72, prof. biology, 1972-87, Oreffice disting. prof. biol. sci., 1987—; panel mem. Visual Scis. B Study Sect. NIH, 1972-75; mem. Vision Rsch. Rev. Com. Nat. Eye Inst., 1986-90; Roche Rsch. Found. vis. prof., Basel, Switzerland, 1984. Author: (with others) The Molecular Biology of the Retina, 1991, Molecular Genetics of Inherited Eye Disorders, 1994, Degenerative Diseases of the Retina, 1995; mem. editl. bd. Jour. Neurogenetics, 1982-88, mem. adv. bd., 1988—; contbr. articles to Cell, Procs. NAS U.S.A., Jour. Biol. Chemistry, Jour. Gen. Physiology, European Molecular Biology Orgn. Jour. Recipient rsch. career devel. award USPHS, McCoy award for rsch. Purdue U., 1982, merit award NIH, 1989, Friedenwald award Assn. for Rsch. in Vision and Ophthalmology, 1995. Mem. AAAS, Am. Physiol. Soc., Assn. Rsch. in Vision and Ophthalmology (Friedenwald award 1995), Biophys. Soc., Collegium of Disting. Alumni Boston U., Nat. Alumni Coun. Boston U., Phi Beta Kappa. Office: Purdue U Biol Sci Lilly Hall West Lafayette IN 47907-1392

PALACE, THOMAS MICHAEL, trade association executive; b. Bayshore, N.Y., Apr. 20, 1956; s. John Thomas and Elizabeth (Power) P.; m. Leslie Janet Warner, Mar. 18, 1978; children: Adam Cristofer, Justin Warner. BEd, Washburn U., 1978. Law officer State Savs., Topeka, 1978-80, Peoples Savs., Topeka, 1980-82; exec. v.p. Savs. League Svcs. Inc., Topeka, 1982-96; with Kans. Oil Marketers Assn., Topeka, 1996—. Republican. Roman Catholic. Home: 4945 NW Rochester Rd Topeka KS 66617-1359 Office: Kans Oil Mktg Assn 201 NW Hwy 24 Ste 320 Topeka KS 66608

PALADINO, LYN A, retired English educator; b. New Rochelle, N.Y., Mar. 2, 1926; s. Joseph John and Janet Elizabeth (Avallone) P.; m. Marcia Joan Montie, Dec. 28, 1966; children: Lance Robert, Kyle Dylan. BA, Champlain Coll., 1952; MA, Columbia U., 1954. Cert. tchr., N.Y., Ohio. Tchr. English Clarkstown Ctrl. Sch., N.Y.C., 1955-56; tchr. English and history Leonard Jr. H.S., New Rochelle, N.Y., 1957-73; asst. prof. English W.Va. Tech, Montgomery, 1957-62, Jersey City State Coll., 1964; instr. English Clark Coll., Atlanta, 1964-65; assoc. prof., English chair Mayville (N.D.) State Coll., 1966-69; asst. prof. English Ctrl. Mich. U., Mount Pleasant, 1969-73; tchr. college English Black River H.S., Sullivan, Ohio, 1973-89; ret., 1989. Author: (book of poems) The Horological Tree, 1979, Paean to Freedom, 1995, (two-page poem) Defenders of Wildlife, 1975, (essay) Black River Review, 1986 (First Place). Vol. Medina (Ohio) United Neighbors Challenging Hunger, 1991—, Operation: Homes. Coxswain USNR, 1943-46. Home: # 11 1038 N Jefferson Medina OH 44256

PALAGI, ROBERT GENE, college administrator; b. Chgo., Aug. 20, 1948; s. Gene and Stella (Vasick) P.; m. Diane Joyce Sanderson, July 31, 1971; children: Melissa, Jason. AS, So. Ill. U., 1969, BS, 1972; MEd, DePaul U., 1975; MS, No. Ill. U., 1994. Cert. secondary tchr., cert. counselor. Educator Dept. Mental Health, Tinley Park, Ill., 1972-75; mental health specialist Dept. Mental Health, Tinley Park, 1975-77, grant coord., 1977-80; vocat. therapist Our Lady of Mercy Hosp., Dyer, Ind., 1980-81, mgr. edn. and tng., 1981-84; edn. cons. devel. St. Mary of Nazareth Hosp.; instr., counselor Chgo. City Colls., 1986-89, assoc. dir., 1989-90, coord. career devel., 1990-91, dir. acad. support, 1991-94; indsl. arts. specialist Ingalls Hosp., 1994—; cons. Chgo. Merc. Exch., Chgo., 1985-86; faculty Ind. U. N.W., Gary, Ind., 1981-82; mgr. evening svcs. Ind. Vocat. Tech. Coll., Hammond, Ind., 1990—. Chairperson pub. rels. Pullman Civic Orgn., Chgo., 1983, bd. dirs., 1993. Mem. Am. Vocat. Assn., Coop. Edn. Assn., Midwest Coop. Edn. Assn., Ill. Vocat. Assn., Ill. Coop. Edn. Assn. Home: 11316 S Langley Ave Chicago IL 60628-5126 Office: Ingalls Ctr for Otpt Rehab Dawson Tech Inst 1551 Huntington Dr Calumet City IL 60409

PALAGYI, JAMES J., electrical engineer; b. Cleve., Jan. 29, 1948. A.Elec. Tech., Lakeland C.C., Kirtland, Ohio, 1971; BSEE, Cleve. State U., 1980. Jr. engr. Life Systems, Beachwood, Ohio, 1071-77; sr. design engr. Technicare, divsn. Johnson & Johnson, Solan, Ohio, 1977-87; sr. project engr. Valtronic Tech., Cleve., 1987—. Sgt. U.S. Army, 1967-70. Roman Catholic. Office: Valtronic Tech 6168 Cochran Rd Cleveland OH 44139-3306

PALAMARA, JOSEPH, state legislator; s. Sam and Eleanor P.; m. Aline; children: Lauren Grace, Lance Joseph. BA, Mich. State U., 1975; JD, Detroit Coll. Law, 1985. Rep. Mich. State Dist. 30, 1985-94, Mich. State Dist. 24, 1995—; majority whip Mich. Ho. Reps., chmn. election com., mem. corp. & fin. com., pub. health com., ins. com., jud. com.; pvt. practice law, Mich., 1986—. Home: 2315 20th St Wyandotte MI 48192-4127 Address: PO Box 30014 Lansing MI 48909-7514*

PALAZZOLO, DANIEL P., mechanical engineer; b. Cin., Feb. 20, 1968. BSME, Rose Hallman Inst. Tech., 1990. Project engr. Dwyer Instrument, Michigan City, Ind., 1990-92, Ellis and Watts, Batavia, Ohio, 1992—. Patentee in field. Mem. ASME, Am. Nuclear Soc. Office: Ellis & Watts 4400 Glen Willow Lake Ln Batavia OH 45105-2320

PALECEK, SANDRA MARIE, reading education specialist; b. Ashland, Wis., Oct. 31, 1940; d. Francis Joseph and Martha Evelyn (Verville) Bonneville; m. John Allan Palecek, Oct. 3, 1964; children: Stephanie Lynn, Michael John. BS in Elem. Edn., U. River Falls, 1971; MS in Reading, U. Superior, 1981. Tchr. grades 2 and 3 Spring Valley (Wis.) Sch., 1959-62; tchr. grade 2 Pleasant Hill Sch., Waukesha, Wis., 1962-64; tchr. grades 2 and 3 Glidden (Wis.) Sch., 1964-65; Chpt. I tchr. Butternut (Wis.) Sch., 1966-68; Chpt. I reading specialist Glidden Schs., 1968—; amb. of reading People to People to China, 1993. Pres. Chequmegon Reading Coun., Park Falls, Wis., 1981. Herb Kohl fellow, 1994; recipient Outstanding Svc. award Title I Program, Glidden, 1980, Significant Contbns. award Chpt. I Program, Madison, Wis., 1990; named Dist. Tchr. of Yr., Dept. Pub. Instrn., Madison, 1980, 94, Exemplary Remedial Reading award, 1989, 30 Yr. Svc. award Chpt. I, New Orleans, 1996. Mem. Internat. Reading Assn., Wis. State Reading Assn., Glidden Fedn. Tchrs. Union (v.p., then pres.). Home: N15517 Town Hall Rd Park Falls WI 54552-8069 Office: Glidden Sch Glidden WI 54527

PALEKAR, INDIRA S., psychologist, physical therapist; b. Madras, India, Mar. 31, 1954; came to U.S., 1976; d. Kasturi K. and Saroja Krishnawsamy (Srinivasachari); m. Sanjay S. Palekar; children: Rakhee, Sunita, Nikhil. BSc in Phys. Therapy, U. Bombay, 1973; MA in Audiology and Speech Pathology, Cleve. State U., 1987; PhD of Counseling Psychology, U. Akron, 1994. Diplomate Am. Acad. Pain Mgmt.; lic. phys. therapist, Ohio, N.C.; cert. biofeedback therapist. Clin. instr., staff phys. therapist K.E.M. Hosp., Bombay, India, 1973-75; phys. therapist Murray Ridge Ctr., Elyria, Ohio, 1980-81, Elyria Meml. Hosp., 1983-85, Jaworski Phys. Therapy, Inc., 1986-90; pvt. practice, 1990-92; predoctoral intern Massillon (Ohio) Psychiatric Ctr., 1992; intern in psychology Northeast Ohio U., 1992-93; predoctoral intern Edwin Shaw Rehab. Hosp., 1993; postdoctoral fellow in counseling psychology Dr. Kenneth A. DeLuca & Assocs., 1994-95, psychologist, 1995—; adj. faculty U. Akron, 1995; clin. instr. Bombay U.; guest lectr. Cleve. State U. Mem. APA, Am. Phys. Therapy Assn., Assn. Applied

Psychophysiology and Biofeedback, Ohio Psychol. Assn., Ohio Phys. Therapy Assn. Hinduism. Home: 10700 Deer Run Grafton OH 44044

PALENICK, JAMES MICHAEL, city manager; b. Allegan, Mich., Oct. 2, 1959; s. John Andrew and Anne Louise (Grudecki) P.; m. Suzanne Jandasek, Oct. 5, 1991; 1 child, Austin James. AAS, Kalamazoo (Mich.) Valley C.C., 1979; BS summa cum laude, Western Mich. U., Kalamazoo, 1981, MPA, 1987. Mgr., harbormaster Moorings Marine Condos, New Buffalo, Mich., 1986-87; village mgr. Village of Dexter, Mich., 1987-92; city mgr. City of Dowagiac, Mich., 1992—; v.p. Washtenaw Devel. Coun., Ann Arbor, 1990-92; exec. dir. Dowagiac Downtown Devel. Authority, 1992—; bd. mem. Cass County Planning Commn., Cassopolis, Mich., 1992—, Cass County Ctrl. Dispatch, Cassopolis, 1992—. Named to Alumni Wall of Distinction Western Mich. U., Kalamazoo, 1987; recipient Overall Econ. Excellence award Mich. Gov. J. Blanchard, Lansing, 1989. Mem. Internat. City Mgrs. Assn., Mich. City Mgrs. Assn., Rotary Club Dowagiac (bd. mem. 1994—). Democrat. Roman Catholic. Home: 502 Bauer Dowagiac MI 49047 Office: City of Dowagiac 231 S Front St Dowagiac MI 49047

PALEY, HIRAM, mathematician; b. Rochester, N.Y., Sept. 9, 1933; s. Lesser (Eliezer) and Zelda (Fine) P.; m. Jean Lorraine Passovoy, June 11, 1961; children: Joshua, Elizabeth, Nina. AB, U. Rochester, 1955; MA, U. Wis., 1956, PhD, 1959. Teaching asst. math. U. Wis., Madison, 1958-59; asst. prof. math. U. Ill., Urbana, 1959-66, assoc. prof., 1966—; vis. assoc. prof. Ind. Coop. Program Shah Alam, Selangor, Malaysia, 1989-91. Co-author: (with Paul M. Weichsel) A First Course in Abstract Algebra, 1967, Elements of Abstract and Linear Algebra, 1971. Alderman City of Urbana, 1967-73, Mayor, 1973-77; many other civic activities. Mem. Math. Assn. Am. (chmn. Ill. sect. 1969-70), Am. Math. Soc., Photog. Soc. Am., Champaign County Camera Club (pres. 1982-85). Democrat. Home: 706 W California Ave Urbana IL 61801-3912 Office: U Ill Dept Math 1409 W Green St Urbana IL 61801-2917

PALIGANOFF, DAVID JAMES, insurance executive, consultant; b. Ft. Wayne, Ind., Apr. 16, 1941; s. James Thomas and Alice Mary (Roloff) P.; m. Mary Jean Blotcky, July 10, 1965; children: Christopher, Timothy, Melissa. BA, U. Notre Dame, 1963; postgrad., St. Francis Coll., 1964. Cert. ins. counselor; registered rep. and ltd. securities prin. Nat. Assn. Securities Dealers. Group rep. Lincoln Nat. Ins. Corp., Ft. Wayne, 1964-65; mgr. devel. underwriting Allstate Ins. Co., Indpls., 1965-69; adminstrn., sales mgr. Reserve Ins. Co., Chgo., 1969-72; asst. v.p. Northland Ins. Group, St. Paul, 1972-73; v.p., corp. sec. Home and Auto Ins. Co., Chgo., 1973-77; pres. Telegraph Ins. Agy., Inc., Chgo., 1977-80; pvt. practice ins. and investments Elk Grove, Ill., 1980-84; pres. Pathway Ins. Agy., Inc. subs. Pathway Fin., Tinley Park, Ill., 1984-90, also bd. dirs.; mgr. Charter Point Investment Ctrs., NBD Illinois, Inc., Mt. Prospect, Ill., 1992-96; v.p. First Chgo. NBD Investment Svcs., Inc., 1996—; conf. speaker Quality Ins. Agy., 1990-93; cons. on govtl. deferred compensaton, TSA annuity, bank ins. programs. Contbr. articles to profl. jours. Sec. EGV Basketball Pk. Bd. Recipient Bank Investment Rep. Mgmt. Leadership award, 1994. Mem. Profl. Ins. Agts. Assn., Cert. Ins. Counselors, Fin. Instn. Ins. Assn., Nat. Tax Sheltered Annuity Assn., Am. Assn. Ins. Mgmt. Cons., Am. Soc. Quality Control, Ill. CISR Faculty. Republican. Home: 100 Essex Rd Elk Grove Village IL 60007-3937

PALLASCH, B. MICHAEL, lawyer; b. Chgo., Mar. 30, 1933; s. Bernhard Michael and Magdalena Helena (Fixari) P.; m. Josephine Catherine O'Leary, Aug. 15, 1981; children: Bernhard Michael III and Madeleine Josephine (twins). B.S.S., Georgetown U., 1954; J.D., Harvard U., 1957; postgrad., John Marshall Law Sch., 1974. Bar: Ill. 1957, U.S. Dist. Ct. (no. dist.) Ill. 1958, U.S. Tax Ct. 1961, U.S. Ct. Claims 1961, U.S. Ct. Appeals (7th cir.) 1962. Assoc. Winston & Strawn, Chgo., 1958-66; resident mgr. br. office Winston & Strawn, Paris, 1963-65; ptnr. Winston & Strawn, Chgo., 1966-70, sr. capital ptnr., 1971-91; sr. ptnr. B. Michael Pallasch & Assocs., 1991—; dir., corp. sec. Tanis, Inc., Calumet, Mich., 1972—, Greenbank Engring. Corp., Dover, Del., 1976-91, C.B.P. Engring. Corp., Chgo., 1976-91, Chgo. Cutting Svcs. Corp., 1977-88; corp. sec. Arthur Andersen Assocs., Inc., Chgo., 1976—, L'hotel de France of Ill., Inc., Chgo., 1980-85, Water & Effluent Screening Co., Chgo., 1988-91; dir. Bosch Devel. Co., Longview, Tex., 1977-87, Lor Inc., Houghton, Mich., 1977-87, Rana Inc., Madison, Wis., 1978-87, Woodlak Co., Houghton, 1977-87, Zipatone, Inc., Hillside, Ill., 1975-82, Keco Inc., Madison, 1977-81. Bd. dirs. Martin D'Arcy Mus. Medieval and Renaissance Art, Chgo., 1975—; bd. dirs. Katherine M. Bosch Found., 1978—; asst. sec. Hundred Club of Cook County, Chgo., 1966-73, bd. dirs., sec., 1974—. Served with USAFR, 1957-63. Knight of Merit Sacred Mil. Constantinian Order of St. George of Royal House of Bourbon of two Sicilies, knight Sovereign Mil. Order of temple of Jerusalem; named youth mayor City of chgo., 1950; recipient Outstanding Woodland Mgmt. Forestry award Monroe County (Wis.) Soil and Water Conservation Dist., 1975. Mem. Ill. Bar Assn. (tax lectr. 1961), Advs. Soc., Field Mus. Natural History (life), Max McGraw Wildlife Found., English Speaking Union. Roman Catholic. Clubs: Travellers (Paris); Saddle and Cycle (Chgo.). Home: 737 W Hutchinson St Chicago IL 60613-1519 Office: 35 W Wacker Dr Ste 4700 Chicago IL 60601-1614

PALM, RANDY B., mechanical engineer; b. North Fairfield, Ohio, Feb. 2, 1968. BSME, U. Toledo, 1990. Project engr. Armstrong Air Conditioning, Bellevue, Ohio, 1990—. Mem. eagles. Republican. Office: Armstrong Air Conditioning 421 Monroe St Bellevue OH 44811-1730

PALMER, ANN THERESE DARIN, lawyer; b. Detroit, Apr. 25, 1951; d. Americo and Theresa (Del Favero) Darin; m. Robert Towne Palmer, Nov. 9, 1974; children: Justin Darin, Christian Darin. BA, U. Notre Dame, 1973, MBA, 1975; JD, Loyola U., Chgo., 1978. Bar: Ill. 1978, U.S. Supreme Ct. 1981. Reporter Wall Street Jour., Detroit, 1974; freelancer Time Inc. Fin. Publs., Chgo., 1975-77, extern, Midwest regional solicitor U.S. Dept. Labor, 1976-78; tax atty. Esmark Inc., 1978; counsel Chgo. United, 1978-81; ind. contractor Legal Tax Rsch., 1981-89; fin. and legal news contbr. The Chgo. Tribune, 1991—, Bus. Week Chgo. Bur., 1991—, Automotive News, 1993—, Crain's Chgo. Bus., 1994—. Mem. Saddle and Cycle Club of Chgo., Detroit Golf Club. Roman Catholic. Home: 873 Forest Hill Rd Lake Forest IL 60045-3905

PALMER, ARTHUR EUGENE, nursing home administrator; b. Newark, Nov. 23, 1923; s. Frederick A. and Grace (Miller) P.; m. Rosemary Louise Pierce, June 11, 1949; children: Christine, David. BA in Econs., Coll. Wooster, 1947; MBA, NYU, 1955. Traffic engr. N.J. Bell Telephone, Newark, 1947-57; bus. mgr. Coll. Wooster (Ohio), 1958-78, dir. gen. svcs., 1978-79; adminstr. Lima (Ohio) Convalscent Home, 1979-87, Allen County Health Care Ctr., Lima, 1988, Nursing Home Cons., West Ctrl., Ohio, 1988—; pres. Ohio Assn. Coll. Univ. Bus. Officers, 1971, Ohio Assn. Ednl. Buyers, 1973-74; com. chmn. Planning Sabbatical Leaves, 1975-78, Ea. Assn. Coll. and Univ. Bus. Officers. Health facility coord. United Way, Lima, 1975-78; fundraiser Lima Symphony Orch., 1974-85; elder Presbyn. Ch., 1949—, Sunday sch. tchr. and dept. supt., 1953-59, head usher, 1982-87; bd. dirs. Marimor Industries for MRDD, 1985—; mem. advising bd. Wooster Outdoor Ctr., 1970-79. With U.S. Army, 1943-45, ETO. Decorated Bronze Star. Mem. Allen County Diabetes League (pres. 1985-88), Kiwanis (sec. 1980—, Disting. sec. 1989, 92, 93, Kiwanian of Yr. 1995), Lima Men's Garden Club. Republican. Home: 2815 Lowell Ave Lima OH 45805-3032

PALMER, CURTIS RAY, video company executive; b. Evansville, Ind.; s. August Van and Wanda Jeanetta (Davis); m. Elizabeth Ann Crawford, May 17, 1966; children: Michael, Mark, Matthew. BS, BA, Roosevelt U., 1975. Commd. ensign USN, 1966, advanced through grades to sr. petty officer, 1983; sales acctg. analyst Gold Bond Stamp Co., 1965-66; fire control technician USN, 1966-72; instr. svc. schs. USN, Great Lakes, Ill., 1972-76; counselor Area Indsl. Inst., Evansville, 1976-80; dept. head indsl. maintenance Ind. Voc. Tech. Coll., Evansville, 1980-87; owner, pres. Palmer Enterprises, 1983—; with Budjet Video Warehouse, Huntingburg, Ind., 1989—; owner U.S. Auto, Huntingburg, Ind., 1993—, Am. Auction & Liquidators; pres. Victory Films, 1995—; cons. So. Ind. Gas and Electric Co. Evansville, 1982; agt. Contel Cellular, 1994. Author: Workbook for MK152 Computer, 1975. Mem. Internat. Assn. Bus., Soc. Mfg. Engring., Robotics Internat., Instrument Soc. Am., Machine Vision, Huntingburg C. of C., Nat. Fedn. Ind. Bus. Republican. Methodist. Home: PO Box 253 Elberfeld IN 47613-0253 Office: Budget Video Warehouse 1103 N Main St Huntingburg IN 47542-1051

PALMER, GARY CHARLES, university lecturer; b. Balt., Oct. 17, 1950; s. Charles Wesley and Doris Leona (Hall) P.; m. Independence Kae Bradbery, June 23, 1972. BS in Edn., Concord Coll., Athens, W.Va., 1972; MDiv, Ctrl. Bapt. Theol. Sem., Kansas City, Kans., 1986; MA, U. Mo., Kansas City, 1990; MLA, Baker U., 1995. Ordained to ministry Bapt. Ch., 1986. Social studies tchr. Wood County Schs., Parkersburg, W.Va., 1972-83; divinity student Ctrl. Bapt. Theol. Sem., Kansas City, Kans., 1983-86; grad. asst. Ctrl. Bapt. Theol. Sem., Kansas City, 1985-86; grad. teaching asst. U. Mo., Kansas City, 1986; min. State Line Bapt. Ch., Kansas City, Kans., 1986-90, First Bapt. Ch. of Greenwood, Shawnee, Kans., 1990-94; univ. lectr. U. Mo., Kansas City, 1995—; bd. dirs. Ctrl. Bapt. Sem. Fed. Credit Union, 1991-94. Local and dist. officer Toastmasters Internat., Parkersburg, 1975-86, The Gideons Internat., Parkersburg, 1974-83; Key Club sponsor, Kiwanis, Parkersburg, 1976-78. Named Toastmaster Yr. Toastmasters Internat. Dist. 40, 1979. Mem. Orgn. Am. Historians, U.S. Capitol Hist. Soc., Phi Alpha Theta. Democrat. Home: 15020 W 124th St Olathe KS 66062-5907 Office: U Mo Dept History 203 Cockefair Hall Kansas City MO 64110

PALMER, JOCELYN BETH, civic worker; b. Salina, Kans., Dec. 19, 1927; d. Paul Franklin and Josie Murtle (Schultz) Swartz; m. Gerald Keith Palmer, Dec. 28, 1952; children: David, Paula, Brian, April. AA, Christian Coll., Columbia, Mo., 1947; BS, Kans. State U., 1949; MA, U. Iowa, 1951. Grad. asst. presch. U. Iowa, Iowa City, 1949-51; instr. U. Ill., Urbana, 1951-52; co-dir. child devel. ctr. Long Beach (Calif.) City Coll., 1954-56. Tchr. trainer, presch. tchr., cons., chmn. nursery com., elder, deacon Presbyn. Ch.; mem. Com. to Develop Stds. for Presch. Handicapped, Salina, 1981-83; pres., bd. dirs. # 305 Salina Sch. Dist., 1975-87; com. chair, bd. dirs. St. Francis Boyd Home, Salina, Ellsworth, 1984-87; bd. dirs. YWCA, 1993—; bd. dirs. Asburg Hosp. Aux., 1993-96, sec. 1994-96. Mem. Clippership Mariners (chaplain 1991-93, logkeeper 1994-95), Saline County Med. Alliance (bd. dirs. 1992-96), Twentieth Century Forum (courtesy chmn. 1989-93), PEO (pres. 1989-91, 94-95, treas. 1993-95), Salina Downtown Lioness (bd. dirs. 1988-89, 91-93). Republican.

PALMER, MARCIA ANN, healthcare management consultant, pharmacist; b. Hammond, Ind., Aug. 26, 1951; d. John J. and Millee (Ivan) P. BS in Pharmacy, Purdue U., 1974; MBA, Loyola U., 1984. Lic. pharmacist, Ind., Ill., Ariz., Fla. Staff pharmacist St. Margaret Hosp., Hammond, Ind., 1974-75; drug info. pharmacist to clin. coord. Ingalls Meml. Hosp., Harvey, Ill., 1975-77; dir. pharmacy Ingalls Meml. Hosp., Harvey, 1977-89; pres. Palmer Assocs., Healthcare Mgmt. Cons., Munster, Ind., 1989—; asst. prof. Purdue U., West Lafayette, Ind., 1972-89; tchg. assoc. U. Ill., Chgo., 1979-89; mem. adj. faculty pharmacy technician program South Suburban Coll., South Holland, Ill. Named Pharmacist Yr., Ill. Coun. Health-System Pharmacists, 1988. Mem. Am. Soc. Health-System Pharmacists, Am. Pharm. Assn., Am. Soc. Cons. Pharmacists, Acad. Managed Care Pharmacy, Am. Soc. Parenteral and Enteral Nutrition. Home: 1514 Cardinal Ct Munster IN 46321-3801 Office: Palmer Assocs 9245 Calumet Ave Ste 202 Munster IN 46321-2807

PALMER, RICHARD JOSEPH, communications director; b. Mpls., June 23, 1929; s. Charles Henry and Josephine (Shimek) P.; m. Bernice Arvilla Schumacher, Sept. 18, 1954; children: Howard, Penny Rae, Pamela, Randall, Roger. Diploma in Journalism, U. Minn., 1957. Reporter/photographer Fairmont Daily Sentinel, Minn., 1953-54, 57-59; newsman, capitol corrs. AP, Mpls., Fargo and Bismarck, N.D., 1959-67; comms. dir. N.D. Education Assn., Bismarck, 1967-93; comms. cons. NEA, Washington, 1993—; pres., State Edn. Editors of NEA, 1974, sec./treas. Pub. Rels. Coun., 1977-79, chmn. Sml. States Printing Consortium, 1977-88. Editor/photographer: (video) Come In, Please, To My World, 1990 (Best of Show in NEA Pub. Rels. Coun. 1991); contbr. publs. in field. Coun. mem. Trinity Luth. Ch., Bismarck, 1994-96. Ssgt. U.S. Army, 1950-52, Korea. Named Outstanding Male Grad. in Journalism, Sigma Delta Chi, 1957; recipient Friend of Edn. award N.D. Edn. Assn., Bismarck, 1993. Mem. N.D. Wildlife Fedn. (Conservation Comms. award 1971), Soc. for Profl. Journsalists, Lions (3d to 1st v.p. Bismarck club, 1994-96). Home: 1801 Marian Dr Bismarck ND 58501 Office: Palmer Comms 1801 Marian Dr Bismarck ND 58501

PALMER, ROBERT TOWNE, lawyer; b. Chgo., May 25, 1947; s. Adrian Bernhardt and Gladys (Towne) P.; m. Ann Therese Darin, Nov. 9, 1974; children: Justin Darin, Christian Darin. BA, Colgate U., 1969; JD, U. Notre Dame, 1974. Bar: Ill. 1974, D.C. 1978, U.S. Supreme Ct. 1978. Law clk. Hon. Walter V. Schaefer, Ill. Supreme Ct., 1974-75; assoc. McDermott, Will & Emery, Chgo., 1975-81, ptnr., 1982-86; ptnr. Chadwell & Kayser, Ltd., 1987-88, Connelly, Mustes, Palmer & Schroeder, 1988-89; of counsel Garfield & Merel Ltd., 1990—; mem. adj. faculty Chgo. Kent Law Sch., 1975-77, Loyola U., 1976-78; mem. adv. com. Fed. Home Loan Mortgage Corp., 1988-89; bd. dir. Lincoln Legal Found., Cen. Fed. Savs. & Loan Assn. of Chgo.; mem. Chgo. Ctr. Adv. Bd. Voyageur Outward Bound Sch., 1988-91. Mem. ABA, Ill. State Bar Assn. (Lincoln award 1983), Chgo. Bar Assn., Internat. Assn. Def. Counsel, Chgo. Club, Dairymen's Country Club, Lambda Alpha. Contbr. articles to legal jours. and textbooks. Office: Garfield & Merel Ltd 211 W Wacker Dr Ste 1500 Chicago IL 60606-1217

PALMER, THOMAS WATSON, mechanical engineer; b. Aurora, Ill., Sept. 9, 1927; s. Kenneth and Janet (Watson) P.; m. Martha McGowan, Sept. 15, 1956; children: Jane E. Palmer Aloi, Julia A., James T. ME, U. Ill., Champaign, 1949. Owner, operator Irrigation Spltys. Mfg. Co. Inc., Gering, Nebr., 1974-95, Palmer Engring., Gering, 1978-95, Safe Knight, Gering, 1995—. Mem. Scottsbluff Bldg. and Planning, Twin Cities Devel. With USN, 1949-54. Mem. Scottsbluff Aging Soc., Elks, Scottsbluff Country Club. Home: 1019 E 38th St Scottsbluff NE 69361

PALMERI, SHARON ELIZABETH, freelance writer, community educator; b. Gary, Ind., July 23, 1948; d. Theodore and Eugena (Bias) Wozniak; m. John James Palmeri, Apr. 9, 1969: 1 child, Renee Suzanne. BS in Edn. English/Journalism with honor, Ind. U. NW, 1991. Health columnist Lake County Star, Crown Point, Ind., 1989-92; corr. Post Tribune, Gary, 1992-93; feature corr. The Munster (Ind.) Times, 1993—; educator creative and news writing Merrillville (Ind.) Adult Edn., 1989—; educator writer's workshop Purdue U. Calumet, Hammond, Ind., 1990—; educator creative writing Purdue U. N. Ctrl., Westville, Ind., 1995—; bd. dirs. N.W. Ind. Arts and Humaniteis Consortium, Gary, 1994; dir. Write-On Hoosiers, Inc., Crown Point, 1989—. Exec. editor: Hoosier Horizon, 1991—; co-editor: Hoosier Horizon Children's Mag., 1993—; contbr. short stories and essays to Spirits Mag., 1990, 91. Recipient Best of Show award Southlake Camera Club, Crown Point, 1975, Focal Point Camera Club, Portage, 1982. Mem. Nat. Coun. Tchrs. English, Soc. Profl. Journalists, N.W. Ind. Arts Assn., Communicators N.W. Ind., Ind. U. Alumni Assn., Kappa Delta Pi (newsletter editor 1991-94). Home and Office: 3605 Kingsway Dr Crown Point IN 46307

PALMIERI, GUY JOSEPH, manufacturing executive, retired military officer; b. Lawrence, Mass., Jan. 15, 1936; s. Domenic and Jennie (Archetti) P.; m. Susan Mary Anthony, June 5, 1957; children: David, Ann, Carol, Leslie. BS, U.S. Mil. Acad., 1957; MS in Adminstrn., George Washington U., 1972. Commd. 2nd lt. U.S. Army, 1957, advanced through grades to col., 1978; battery comdr. 3rd armored div. U.S. Army, Fed. Republic of Germany, 1962-63; ops. officer 23rd artillery group U.S. Army, Republic of Vietnam, 1969-72; comdr. 3rd battalion, 6th field artillery, 1st div. U.S. Army, 1973-75, chmn. joint task force, 1977-78; attache Def. Intelligence Agy., Ottawa, Ont., Can., 1978-82, Canberra, Australia, 1982-85, Wellington, New Zealand, 1982-85, Port Moresby, Papua, New Guinea, 1982-85; ret. U.S. Army, 1987; tech. dir. Day & Zimmermann, Inc., Parsons, Kans., 1988—; asst. prof. mil. sci. U. Okla., 1965-68. Decorated Bronze Star with two bronze oak leaf clusters, Air medal, Legion of Merit (twice), Def. Meritorious Svc. award (twice). Mem. Nat. Mgmt. Assn., Assn. Grads. of U.S. Mil. Acad., Assn. of U.S. Army, Ret. Officers Assn., Am. Def. Preparedness Assn., Assn. Indsl. Coll. of Armed Forces. Republican. Roman Catholic. Home: 3829 Rustwood Rd Joplin MO 64801-1580 Office: Day & Zimmermann Inc Kans Army Ammunition P Parsons KS 67357

PALOMBO, JOSEPH, clinical social worker; b. Cairo, July 18, 1928; came to U.S., 1949; s. Albert H. and Regina (Costi) P.; m. Dorothy D. Denton, Aug. 4, 1957. PhB, New Sch. Social Rsch., N.Y.C., 1954; MA in Philosophy, Yale U., 1958; MSW, U. Chgo., 1959; cert. in child therapy, Inst. Psychoanalysis, Chgo., 1964. Cert. social worker, Ill. Pvt. practice Chgo., 1970—; dean Inst. Clin. Social Work, Chgo., 1981-92, founding dean, 1992—; assoc. dir. Rush Neurobehavioral Ctr. dept. pediats. Rush-Presbyn.-St. Luke's Med. Ctr., 1995—; adminstrv. dir. child therapy program Inst. Psychoanalysis, 1970-78, mem. faculty, 1970—; adminstrv. dir. Barr-Harris Ctr. Inst. Psychoanalysis, Chgo., 1976-78; mem. faculty advanced cert. program Smith Coll. Sch. Social Work, 1985-87. Contbr. articles to profl. jours. Mem. NASW, Acad. Cert. Social Workers, Assn. Child Psychotherapists (pres. 1976), Nat. Acads. Practice in Social Work (founding), Ill. Soc. Clin. Social Workers, Chgo. Psycoanalytic Soc. (affiliate). Democrat.

PALS, TIMOTHY RAY, transportation and marketing executive; b. Harvey, Ill., Feb. 13, 1964; s. Charles Ray and Violet Faye (DeMick) P.; m. Tina Genine Eitel, May 6, 1984; children: Mallory, Lindsey, Andrew, Blake. Cert., Coll. Advanced Traffic, 1984; cert. completion, Northwestern U., 1994. Dispatcher Pals Cartage Co., South Holland, Ill., 1978-82; terminal mgr. Pals Cartage Co., Bridgeview, Ill., 1983-84; sales mgr. Pals Cartage Co., Calumet City, Ill., 1985-90; asst. gen. mgr. Transcanada Truck Lines, Mississauga, Ont., 1990; v.p. mktg. and sales Pals Express, Inc., Calumet City, 1991-96; pres. Easle Express Lines, Inc., South Holland, Ill., 1996—; pres. Sys. Leasing Co., South Holland, 1983—; cons. Reimer Internat. Express Ltd., Winnipeg, 1994—. Republican. Office: Easle Express Lines Inc. 1579 Valancia Ct Calumet City IL 60409

PAN, YI, computer science educator; b. Wujiang, Jiangsu, China, May 12, 1960; came to U.S., 1987; s. Jun and Xiuzhen (Fei) P.; m. Hong Miao, AUg. 4, 1986; 1 child, Marissa. BEng, Tsinghua U., Beijing, 1982, MEng, 1984; MSc, U. Pitts., 1988, PhD, 1991. Rsch. asst. Tsinghua U., 1982-86; teaching asst. U. Pitts., 1987-89, teaching fellow, 1989-91; asst. prof. computer sci. U. Dayton, Ohio, 1991-96, assoc. prof., 1996—. Contbr. articles to profl. jours. Recipient Rsch. Opportunity award NSF, 1995, Investment Competition Fund award Ohio Bd. Regents, 1996; Mellon Found. fellow 1990, Summer Rsch. fellow U. Dayton Rsch. Coun. Mem. IEEE Computer Soc. chmn. student task force region 2, 1992), Assn. for Computing Machinery. Home: 2285 Springmill Rd Kettering OH 45440-2563 Office: U Dayton Computer Sci Dept 300 College Park Ave Dayton OH 45469-0001

PANASY, CRAIG W., sales and marketing professional; b. Stamford, Conn., Oct. 17, 1960. AD in Mktg., Norwalk (Conn.) Tech. Coll., 1981; BS in Mfg. Engring., Rochester Inst. Tech., 1985. Metall. technologist Am. Machine & Foundry, Stamford, 1981-83; engr. Am. Cyanamid, Stamford, 1983-88; project mgr. Lodige U.S. A., Westport, Conn., 1988-90; mfg. mgr. Advanced Tech. Materials, Danbury, Conn., 1990-91; sr.sys. engr. Ultrasonics, Danbury, 1991-94; sales and mktg. mgr. FMF Inc., Findlay, Ohio, 1994—. Mem. Soc. Mfg. Engrs. Office: Findlay Machine & Tool 1950 Industrial Dr Findlay OH 45840-5441

PANAYIRCI, SHARON LORRAINE, textiles executive, design engineer; b. San Diego, Nov. 11, 1957; d. Robert Vernon and Edna Ruth (Bayless) Reed; m. Mehmet Vefki Panayirci, Mar. 1, 1985; 1 child, Ruth Naile. AAS cum laude, Sinclair Coll., 1981; B in Tech. cum laude, U. Dayton, 1984. Designer Dayton (Ohio) Progress Corp., 1981-85; design engr. Hartzell Propeller Inc., Piqua, Ohio, 1987-88; v.p. Patex Exim Inc., Dayton, 1986-93, Aegean Apparel, Dayton, 1993—; cons. Cepateks A.S. Indsl. Engr., Denizli, Turkey, 1985-86; fin. cons. Aegean Apparel Inc., Dayton, 1991-93. Mem. NAFE, AAUW. Democrat. Office: Aegean Apparel Inc 4365 Lisa Dr Tipp City OH 45371

PANCERO, JACK BLOCHER, restaurant executive; b. Cin., Dec. 27, 1923; s. Howard and Hazel Mae (Blocher) P.; m. Loraine Fielman, Aug. 4, 1944; children: Gregg Edward, Vicki Lee. Student, Ohio State U., 1941-44. Ptnr. Howard Pancero & Co., Cin., 1948-66; stockbroker Gradison & Co., Cin., 1966-70; real estate assoc. Parchman & Oyler, Cin., 1972-87; v.p. Gregg Pancero, Inc., Kings Mills, Ohio, 1972—. Mem. Vineyards C. of C., Western Hills Country Club, Cin. Engrs. Table, Pelican Bay Club, Vineyard Country Club, Royal Poinciana Golf Club, Met. Club., Collier Athletic Club, Masons, Shriners. Methodist. Home and Office: 806 Rue De Ville Pelican Bay Naples FL 33963-8531 Office: Kings Island Kenwood Ctr Bldg 7565 Kenwood Rd Cincinnati OH 45236-2835

PANCHERI, EUGENE JOSEPH, chemical engineer; b. South Bend, Ind., Jan. 23, 1947; s. Raymond Albert and Dora Lugenia (Martin) P.; m. Janice Edwina Sutton, Mar. 9, 1986; children: Brent Jason, Ayrie Ann, Joseph Sutton. BSChE, Purdue U., 1969. Staff mem. Procter & Gamble, Cin., 1969-74, group leader, 1974-92, prin. engr., 1993-95, rsch. fellow, 1995—. Mem. AIChE, Am. Oil Chemists Soc., Nat. Geneal. Soc., Trentini nel Mondo, Phi Eta Sigma, Alpha Tau Omega. Office: Procter & Gamble ITC 5299 Spring Grove Ave Cincinnati OH 45217-1025

PANDE, RONALD G., realtor; b. Chgo., Jan. 11, 1939; s. Lawrence Anton and Alice (Jacobsen) P.; m. Marilyn Louise Andersen, Sept. 28, 1960; children: Donald Scott, Debra Lee, Robin Lynn, Cynthia Lynn. Auditor Beckley Cardy Co., Chgo., 1960-63; sales adminstr. Jewels By Park Lane, Inc., Chgo., 1963-69; territory mgr. Victor Compicmetor Corp., Chgo., 1969-71; dir. sales & svc. Master, Inc., Arlington, Tex., 1971-74; dir. food & beverage Abisterat Inns Am., Chgo., 1974-79; mfrs. agt. Barry Midwest, Inc., Arlington Heights, Ill., 1979-85; ptnr. Biker Island Distbrs., Chgo., 1985-87; sales agt. Starek Relators, Schaumburg, Ill., 1987-91, Nat. Real Estate, Schaumburg, Ill., 1991—. Trustee Village of Schaumburg, 1993—, chmn. engring., 1995—, mem. adv. bd. Cook County Crime Commn., 1996—; mem. Kasper policy bd. Schaumburg Twp., 1993—. Mem. Nat. Assn. Realtors, Nat. League Cities, Ill. Assn. Realtors, Ill. Mcpl. League, Northwest Assn. Realtors (dir. 1990-94, mem. grievance com. 1994—, mem. pub. rels. 1989-90, membership com. 1988-89), Northwest Mcpl. Conf. Republican. Lutheran. Home: 501 Cottonwood Ln Schaumburg IL 60193 Office: Nat Real Estate Svc 33 S Roselle Rd Schaumburg IL 60193

PANDEYA, NIRMALENDU KUMAR, plastic surgeon, flight surgeon, military officer; b. Bihar, India, Feb. 9, 1940; came to U.S., 1958, naturalized, 1965; s. Balbhadra and Ramasawari (Tewari) P.; children: by previous wife Alok, Kiran; m. Haripriya Pradhan, June 15, 1988; 1 stepchild, Bibek. BSc, MS Coll., Bihar U.-Motihari, 1958; MS, U. Nebr., 1962; postgrad. U. Minn., 1959, Ft. Hays State Coll., 1961, D.O., Coll. Osteo. Medicine and Surgery, Des Moines, 1969, Hamilton Co. Pub. Hosp.; grad. Sch. Aerospace Medicine, U.S. Air Force, 1979. Diplomate Nat. Bd. Osteo. Med. Examiners. USPHS fellow dept. ob-gyn Coll. Medicine, U. Nebr., Omaha, 1963-65; intern Doctors Hosp., Columbus, Ohio, 1969-70; resident in gen. surgery Des Moines Gen. Hosp., 1970-72, Richmond Heights Gen. Hosp. (Ohio), 1972-73; fellow in plastic surgery Umea U. Hosp. (Sweden), 1973, Karolinska Hosp., Stockholm, 1974-75; mil. cons. in plastic surgery, USAF surgeon gen.; clin. prof. scis. Coll. Osteo. Medicine and Surgery, Des Moines, 1975-76, also adj. clin. prof. plastic and reconstructive surgery; chief flight surgeon Iowa Air Nat. Guard; practice in reconstructive and plastic surgery, Des Moines, 1975—; mem. staff Des Moines Gen. Hosp., Mercy Hosp. Med. Ctr., Charter Cmty. Hosp., Davenport Osteo. Hosp., Franklin Gen. Hosp., Ringgold County Hosp., Madison County Meml. Hosp., Winterset, Iowa, Mt. Ayr Surgery Ctr. of Des Moines, Hamilton County Hosp., Webster City Decatur County Hosp., Leon, Story County Hosp., Nev., Kirksville Osteopathic Med. Ctr., Grim Smith Hosp., Kirksville, St. Anthony's Hosp., Carroll, Iowa Meth. Hosp., Des Moines. Served to col. M.C., USAF; chief flight surgeon Iowa Air N.G. Regents fellow U. Nebr., Lincoln, 1961-62. Fellow Internat. Coll. Surgeons, Assn. Surgeons of India (life), Interam. Coll. Surgeons, Assn. Physicians India; mem. Assn. Plastic Surgeons of India (life), Assn. Mil. Surgeons of U.S. (life), Assn. Mil. Plastic Surgeons, AMA, Am. Osteo. Assn., Polk County Med. Soc., Iowa Soc. Osteo. Physicians and Surgeons, Polk County Soc. Osteo. Physicians and Surgeons (pres. 1978), Soc. U.S. Air Force Clin. Surgeons, Aerospace Med. Assn., Air N.G. Alliance of Flight Surgeons, AAUP, Am. Coll. Osteo. Surgeons, Am. Acad. Osteo. Surgeons (cert.), Soc. U.S. Air Force Flight surgeons. Hindu. Club: Army Navy. Contbr. numerous articles to profl. jours. Home: 4405 Mary Ann Cir West Des Moines IA 50265-5328 Office: Midwest Plas Surg Ctr 411 Laurel St Ste 1300 Des Moines IA 50314

PANENKA, JAMES BRIAN JOSEPH, financial company executive; b. Milw., July 13, 1942; s. Alois J. and Jeanette (Buettner) P.; m. Kimberly A., Kerry A., Kristine A. BA, Marquette U., 1965. Sales rep. Pillsbury Corp., Milw., 1965-71; investment broker Marshall Co., Milw., 1971-72, E.F. Hutton, Milw., 1972-77; v.p. investments Dean Witter Inc., Milw., 1977-81; sr. v.p. investments Blunt Ellis & Loewi Inc./Kemper Securities, Inc./ Everen Securities, Inc., Milw., 1981—; mem. Pres.'s Coun., Kemper Securities Group, Inc., 1981—. Bd. dirs. Mental Health Assn. of Wis., Milw., 1981-91, Sherri Steinhauer LPGA Mental Health Golf Tournament, Madison, Wis., 1991—; life mem. Marquette U. Pres.'s Coun., Milw., 1985—. Mem. Western Racquet Club (Elm Grove, Wis.), Geneva Nat. Golf Club (Lake Geneva, Wis.), Milw. Yacht Club. Roman Catholic. Office: Blunt Ellis & Loewi Kemper Securities Everen Securities 815 N Water St Milwaukee WI 53202-3526

PANG, JOSHUA KEUN-UK, trade company executive; b. Chinnampo, Korea, Sept. 17, 1924; s. Ne-Too and Soon-Hei (Kim) P.; came to U.S., 1951, naturalized, 1968; m. He-Young Yoon, May 30, 1963; children: Ruth, Pauline, Grace. BS, Roosevelt U., 1959. Chemist, Realemon Co. Am., Chgo., 1957-61; chief-chemist chem. div. Bell & Gossett Co., Chgo., 1961-63, Fatty Acid Inc., div. Ziegler Chem. & Mineral Corp., Chgo., 1963-64; sr. chemist-supr. Gen. Mills Chems. Inc., Kankakee, Ill., 1964-70; pres., owner UJU Industries Inc., Broadview, Ill., 1971—, also dir. Bd. dirs. Dist. 92, Lindop Sch., Broadview, 1976-87; chmn. Proviso Area Sch. Bd. Assn., Proviso Twp., Cook County, Ill., 1976-77; bd. dirs. Korean Am. Community Svcs., Chgo., 1979-80; mem. governing bd. Proviso Area Exceptional Children, Spl. Edn. Joint Agreement, 1981-84, 85-87; alumni bd. govs. Roosevelt U., 1983-89; pres. Korean Am. Sr. Ctr., 1991-92; pres. Korean Am. Srs. Assn. Chicagoland, 1992—. Mem. Am. Chem. Soc., Am. Assn. Arts and Science, Am. Inst. Parliamentarians (region 2 treas. 1979-81, region 2 gov. 1981-82), Internat. Platform Assn., Ill. Sch. Bd. Assn., Nat. Assn. Sch. Bds., Chgo. Area Parliamentarians, Parliamentary Leaders in Action (pres. 1980-81), Nat. Speakers Assn. (dir. Ill. chpt. 1981-82, nat. parliamentarian 1982-84, 2d v.p. chpt. 1983-84), Toastmasters (dist. gov. 1969-1970), DADS Assn. U. Ill. (chmn. Cook County 1985—, bd. dirs. 1987-95, treas. 1990-91, v.p. 1991-92), Korean Am. Assn. of Chgo. (exec. dir. 1990), World Future Soc. (Chgo. area chpt. coord. 1988—, pres. Greater Chicagoland Futurists 1991-95), Chicagoland C. of C. (ednl., environ. and Pacific-Rim coms., internat. divsn.). Home: 2532 S 9th Ave Broadview IL 60153-4804 Office: UJU Industries Inc PO Box 6351 Broadview IL 60153-6351

PANKAU, CAROLE, state legislator; b. Aug. 13, 1947; m. Anthony John Pankau Jr., 1967; 4 children. BS, U. Ill., 1981. Mem. Ill. Ho. of Reps. from 49th dist., 1993—. Mem. DuPage County (Ill.) Bd., 1984-92; committeeman Bloomingdale Twp. Rep. Precinct 51; mem. Keeneyville (Ill.) Sch. Dist. 20; vice chair Bloomingdale Twp. Rep. Orgn. Mem. Bartlett, Roselle, Bloomingdale and Hanover C. of C. Home: 1250 Waterbury Ln Roselle IL 60172-2655 Office: Ill Ho of Reps State Capitol Springfield IL 62706*

PANNKE, PEGGY M., insurance agency executive; b. Chgo., Oct. 26; d. Victor E. and Leona (O'Leary) Stich; children: Thomas Scott, David Savonne, Heidi Mireille, Peter Helmut. Office mgr. DeHaan & Richter P.C., Chgo. and Des Plaines, Ill., 1983-86; v.p. long term care ins. Sales & Seminars, Des Plaines, 1986-90; pres., founder. Nat. Consumer Oriented Agy., Des Plaines, 1990—; cons. on long-term care ins. The Travelers, Tchrs. Ins. & Annuity Assocs., and numerous other ins. cos., N.Y.C., Hartford, Conn. and throughout U.S.; speaker Exec. Enterprises, N.Y.C., 1988-93. Contbr. articles on long-term care ins. to profl. jours.; columnist Senior News. Sponsor Ill. Alliance for Aging, Chgo., 1990—, Ill. Assn. Homes for Aging, 1990-91; bd. govs. St. Matthew Luth. Home, Park Ridge, Ill., 1993-95. Recipient Speakers awards Health Ins. Assn. Am., Washington, 1990, Retired Officers Assn., Glenview, Ill., 1991, 93, Nat. Assn. Sr. Living Industries, Denver, 1992, Exec. Enterprises, N.Y.C., 1993. Mem. Nat. Assn. Sr. Living Industries, Nat. Assn. Long Term Care Profls. (charter), Ctr. for Applied Gerontology, Nat. Coun. on Aging, Mature Ams. (ad hoc com.), Am. Mensa of Ill. (program dir. 1983-85), Kiwanis (bd. dirs. Park Ridge 1992—, pres. 1996—), Am. Soc. on Aging, Internat. Soc. for Retirement Planning. Office: Nat Consumer Oriented Agy 2200 E Devon Ste 356 Des Plaines IL 60018-4503

PANTSCHAK, VERA, public relations executive; b. Farnworth, Eng.; came to U.S., 1956; BA, Bowling Green State U., 1971. Adminstrv. asst. Sta. WVIZ-TV, Cleve., 1972; pub. info. specialist US EPA, Chgo., 1972-73, USDA, Chgo., 1974; pub. rels. writer-dir. Planned Parenthood/Chgo. Area, 1974-77; from account exec. to v.p. Bernard Ury Assocs., Chgo., 1977-81; sr. account supr. HLB Pub. Rels., Chgo., 1981-82; news editor Nat. Home Furnishings Assn., Chgo., 1982-83; account exec. Bernard Ury Assocs., Chgo., 1983-84, v.p., 1984-90; sr. communication specialist R.R. Donnelley & Sons Co., Chgo., 1990-95, comm. mgr., 1996—. Mem. Alumni Bd. Trustees, Bowling Green (Ohio) State U., 1985-88, sec., 1986-87, v.p., 1987-88. Mem. Pub. Rels. Soc. Am., Women in Comm. (sec. Chgo. chpt. 1982-84, Disting. Svc. award 1985), Publicity Club Chgo. Home: 100 W Chestnut St Apt 2204 Chicago IL 60610-3232

PANZER, MARY E., state legislator; b. Waupun, Wis., Sept. 19, 1951; d. Frank E. and Verna L. P.; 1 adopted child, Melissa. BA, U. Wis., 1974; mem., Wis. State Ho. Reps. from 53rd dist. Rep. State of Wis., Madison, 1980-93, senator, 1993—. Home: 635 W Tamarack Dr West Bend WI 53095-3653 Office: Wis State Senate State Capital Madison WI 53702

PAO, LUCY YA, electrical engineering and computer science educat; b. Washington, Apr. 27, 1968; d. Hsien Ping and Chia Ming (Chen) P.; m. Leo Robert Radzihovsky, Sept. 7, 1991. BS, Stanford U., 1987, MS, 1988, PhD, 1992. Engrng. technician Naval Surface Warfare Ctr., Silver Spring, Md., 1983-86; tech. intern Pacific Gas & Elec. Co., San Francisco, 1986; mem. tech. staff Hughes Aircraft Co., El Segundo, Calif., 1987, AT&T Bell Labs., Holmdel, N.J., 1988; rsch. asst. Stanford (Calif.) U., 1988-91; mem. tech. staff The MITRE Corp., Bedford, Mass., 1991-93; prof. Northwestern U., Evanston, Ill., 1993—; mem. program com. Am. Control Conf., Seattle, 1994-95; mem. proposal review panel NSF, Washington, 1994. Contbr. articles to profl. jours. Recipient Grad. Fellowship award NSF, 1988-91, Control Rsch. Equipment grant Northwestern U., 1994-95. Mem. IEEE, AIAA, Northwestern U. Chinese-Am. Faculty Assn. (sec./treas. 1994-95), Soc. Women Engrs. (v.p. Stanford chpt. 1986-88, scholarship 1985-87, Tech. Presentation award 1986), Tau Beta Pi, Phi Beta Kappa. Office: Northwestern Univ EECS Dept 2145 Sheridan Rd Evanston IL 60208-3118

PAPAELIOU, LOUIS, occupational medicine physician; b. Chgo., Nov. 9, 1953; s. Demosthenes Stavros and Helen (Spiniolas) P.; children: Daniel, Matthew, Alexander, Emily. BS, Loyola U., Chgo., 1977; DO, Chgo. Osteopathic Coll., 1984; MPH, U. Ill., Chgo., 1990. Diplomate Am. Osteopathic Bd. of Preventive Medicine. Intern West Suburban Hosp. Med. Ctr., Oak Park, Ill., 1984-85; med. dir. Workcare St. Francis Cabrini Hosp., Chgo., 1985-88; med. dir. Copley Health Wks. Copley Meml. Hosp., Aurora, Ill., 1988-89; med. dir. occupational svcs. Delnor-Community Hosp., Geneva, Ill., 1990-93; med. dir. occupational health svcs. Mercy Ctr. for Health Care Svcs., Aurora, 1993; pres. Corp. Med. Specialists, 1993—; lectr. in field. Mem. AMA, Ill. Med. Soc. Kane County Med. Soc., Am. Osteo. Coll. of Preventive Medicine, Am. Osteo. Assn., Am. Coll. Occupl./Environ. Medicine. Office: Mercy Ctr for Health Care Svcs 2410 Unit C Sycamore Rd De Kalb IL 60115

PAPANIKOLOPOULOS, NIKOLAOS PANAGIOTIS, computer science educator; b. Piraeus, Greece, July 23, 1964; came to U.S., 1987; s. Panagiotis Nikolaos and Vasiliki Vasiliou (Polymenakos) P.; m. Tasoulla Zacharias Hadjiyanni, June 13, 1992; 1 child, Vasiliki. BS in Elec. and Computer Engrng., Nat. Tech. U. of Athens, Greece, 1987; MS in Elec. and Computer Engrng., Carnegie Mellon U., 1988, PhD in Elec and Computer Engrng., 1992. Software retail store owner Piraeus (Greece) Svc. Bur., 1982-87; grad. rsch. asst. Carnegie Mellon U., Pitts., 1987-92; asst. prof. computer sci. U. Minn., Mpls., 1992-94, McKnight land grant asst. prof., 1995-96, McKnight land grant assoc. prof., 1996—; cons. Sportex, Inc., Piraeus, 1985-86. Contbr. articles to profl. jours. Recipient NSF Initiation and Career awards, 1994. Mem. IEEE (reviewer sci. jours. 1991—, local arrangements chmn. for 1996 Internat. Conf. Robotics & Automation), Tech. Chamber of Greece, Carnegie-Mellon U. Hellenic Assn. Home: 4125 Garfield Ave S Minneapolis MN 55409 Office: U Minn 200 Union St Minneapolis MN 55455

PAPARELLA, MICHAEL M., otolaryngologist; b. Detroit, Feb. 13, 1933; s. Vincent Paparella and Angela Creat; m. Treva Buzard, Oct. 2, 1992; children: Mark, Steven, Lisa. BS, U. Mich., 1953, MD, 1957. Diplomate Am. Bd. Otolaryngology (guest examiner 1967-75, bd. dirs. 1976, mem. standards and residencies com. 1976, fgn. med. grads. com. 1978, credentials com. 1984-85, examiner 1976—); lic. physician, Mich., Mass., Ohio, Minn. Rotating intern Emanuel Hosp., Portland, Oreg., 1957-58; resident in otolaryngology Henry Ford Hosp., Detroit, 1958-61, jr. mem. staff, 1960-61; mem. geographic staff, asst. Mass. Eye and Ear Infirmary, Boston, 1963-64; instr. Harvard U. Med. Sch., Boston, 1963-64; asst. prof. otolaryngology, dir. otological research lab. Ohio State U., Columbus, 1964-67; mem. staff dept. otolaryngology Ohio State U. Hosps., 1964-67; prof., chmn. dept. otolaryngology U. Minn., Mpls., 1967-84, dir. otopathology lab., 1967—, clin. prof., 1984—; mem. staff U. Minn. Hosps., 1967-84; pres. Minn. Ear, Head and Neck Clinic, Mpls., 1984—; dir. Nat. Temporal Bone Bank Program Midwestern Ctr., Mpls., 1979—; cons. VA Hosp., Dayton, Ohio, 1964-67. Mem. editl. bd. Minn. Med. Assn. Medicine, The Laryngoscope, Modern Medicine, Am. Jour. Clin. Rsch, Am. Jour. Otolaryngology, Annals Otology, Rhinology & Larynology, Acta Oto-Laryngologica; editor: (films) Surgical Techniques and Auditory Rsch., Surgical Treatment for Intractable External Otitis, Tympanoplasty, parts 1 and 2, Endolymphatic Sac, Canalplasty; (books) Atlas of Ear Surgery, 1968, 2d ed., 1971, 3d ed., 1980, Biochemical Mechanisms in Hearing and Deafness, 1970, Clinical Otology: An International Symposium, 1971, Year Book of the Ear, Nose and Throat, 1972-75, Otolarynology: Basic Sciences and Related Disciplines, 1973, 2d ed. vol I, 1980, Otolarynology: Ear, vol. II, 1973, 2d ed., 1980, Otolayrnology: Head and Neck, vol. III, 1973, 2d ed., 1980, Year Book of Otolarynology, 1976—, Boies's Fundamentals of Otolarynology: A Textbook of Ear, Nose and Throat Diseases, 5th ed., 1978, Ear Clinics International, vols. I-III. 1982, Medicassette Otolarynolgy, 1986; also contbr. numerous article to profl. pubs. Founder, sec., bd. dirs. Internat. Hearing Found., 1984—; mem. Presch. Med. Survey Vision and Hearing. Grantee NIH, Am. Otological Soc., Deafness Research Found., Hartford Found., Guggenheim Found., Bodman Found.; recipient Kobrak Research award, 1960, Amicitiae Sacrum honor Collegium Oto-Rhino-Laryngologicum, 1976; named Brinkman lectr. U. Nijmegen, Holland, 1986, Guest of Honor 5th Asia-Oceanic Meeting, Korea, 1983. Fellow ACS, Am. Acad. Ophthalmology and Otolaryngology (assoc. sec. continuing edn., assoc. sec., chmn. undergrad. edn. subcom., chmn. otorhinolaryngology self-improvement com., chmn. subcom. on evaluation new info. and edn. of hearing and equilibrium com., head and neck surgery equilibrium subcom. 1984-86, Merit award 1975); mem. Acad. Medicine Columbus County, Acad. Medicine Franklin County, Am. Assn. for Lab. Animal Scis., AMA, Am. Neurotology Soc. (audiology study com. 1976), Am. Otological Soc. (trustee research fund, pres.), Assn. Acad. Depts. Otolaryngology (pres. pro tem, organizer 1971-72, sec.-treas. 1972-74, pres. elect 1974-76, pres. 1976-78), Barany Soc., Better Hearing Inst. (adv. bd.), Deafness Research Found. (trustee, Centurion Club), Collegium Oto-Rhino-Laryngologicum Amicitiae Sacrum, Columbus Ophthalmology and Otolaryngological Soc., Hennepin County Med. Soc., Mpls. Hearing Soc. (bd. dirs.), Minn. Acad. Medicine, Minn. Acad. Ophthalmology and Otolaryngology (council), Minn. Coll. Surgeons, New England Otolaryngological Soc., Ohio State Med. Soc., Pan Am. Med. Assn., Soc. Univ. Otolaryngologists (exec. council 1969-71), Triological Soc. (v.p. middle sect. 1976, council mem. 1976, asst. editor), Alpha Kappa Kappa, Sigma Xi. Lodge: Lions (dir. hearing ctr., adv. council hearing ctr.). Office: 701 25th Ave S # 200 Minneapolis MN 55454-1443

PAPAS, GEORGE NICK, bakery company executive; b. Milw., Sept. 21, 1961; s. Nicholas Peter and Angeline (Petropoulos) P. B of Fin., U. Wis. Milw., 1986, MBA, 1988. Baker Nick Papas & Son Bakery, Milw., 1975-81, ptnr., 1982-89; pres. Papas Bakery, Inc., Milw., 1989—; owner, mgr. various investment properties, Milw., 1985—. Mem. Phi-Hellenic Profl. Soc., Beta Gamma Sigma. Office: Papas Bakery Inc 6055 S Howell Ave Milwaukee WI 53207-6233

PAPAS, ROBERT FELTON, fraternal organization administrator; b. Mpls., Feb. 11, 1939; s. Alfred Charles and Beatrice Hazel (Anderson) P.; m. Donita Genevieve Beguhn, June 21, 1959; children: Susan, Jeffrey, Amy, Jennifer. BS, U. Wis.-Stout, 1961; postgrad., Mankato State Coll., U. Minn. Cert. tchr. indsl. arts. math., chemistry, physics; cert. vocat. program dir., supr. trade and indsl. edn.; cert. in graphic arts. Printer, print and prodn. mgr., pressman and foreman in printing industry, Mpls.; graphic arts cons. AP Art Studio; owner, mgr. Mentor Press; tchr. high sch. Mpls. Pub. Schs., 1961-72; graphic arts instr. Hennepin Tech. Coll., Plymouth, Minn., 1972-95, various adminstrv. positions, 1984—; exec. dir. Masons, St. Paul, Minn., 1995—. Mem. St. Louis Park (Minn.) Charter Commn.; mem. St. Louis Park Religion in the Schs. Com.; mem. Minnetonka Charter Commn.; active Boy Scouts Am.; mem. Hopkins Vocat. Edn. Adv. Com.; mem. Osseo Vocat. Edn. Adv. Com.; mem. Robbinsdale Vocat. Edn. Adv. Com.; mem. Clearing House and Tng. Ctr. Adv. Com. Recipient Elmer G. Voight award Graphic Arts Industries Am., 1981, Good Neighbor award Sta. WCCO, 1991. Mem. Am. Indsl. Arts Assn. (life, past pres. local chpt.), Am. Vocat. Assn., Minn. Vocat. Assn., Internat. Assn. Printing House Craftsman (past local, dist., internat. pres., Internat. Craftsman of Yr., 1987) Minn. Assn. Secondary Vocat. Administrs., Masons (Grand Master Minn. 1990-91), Optimists (past pres.) Scottish Rite (past master, 33d Degree), Shriners, Sigma Tau Gamma, Epsilon Pi Tau. Republican. Lutheran. Home: 10214 Mildred Ter Minnetonka MN 55305-3131 Office: Grand Lodge AF&AM of Minn Hennepin Tech Coll 200 E Plato Blvd Saint Paul MN 55107

PAPAY, LILLIAN D., state legislator; m. Emit L. Papay. Senator dist. 33 State of Kans., 1993—. Republican. Home: 1416 Coolidge St Great Bend KS 67530-3308 Office: Kans State Senate State Capitol Topeka KS 66612*

PAPAZIAN, DENNIS RICHARD, history educator, political commentator; b. Augusta, Ga., Dec. 15, 1931; s. Nahabed Charles and Armanouhe Marie (Pehlevanian) P.; m. Mary Arshagouni. BA, Wayne State U., 1954; MA, U. Mich., 1958; NDG, Moscow State U., 1962; PhD, U. Mich., 1966. Head dept. social and behavioral scis. U. Mich., Dearborn, 1966-69, head div. lit., sci. and the arts, 1969-73, assoc. dean acad. affairs, 1973-74; dir. Armenian Assembly Am., Washington, 1975-79; dir. grad. studies U. Mich., Dearborn, 1979-85, prof. history, dir. Armenian Rsch. Ctr., 1985—; fellow Ctr. for Russian and East-European Studies, U. Mich., Ann Arbor, 1982-92; chmn. bd. dirs. Mich. Ethnic Heritage Studies Ctr., U. Mich., 1987-92. Author: St. John's Armenian Church, 1974; editor: The Armenian Church, 1983, Out of Turkey, 1994; editor Jour. of Soc. Armenian Studies, 1995—. Bd. dirs. Armenian Apostolic Soc., Southfield, Mich., 1968-78; chmn. bd. dirs. Alex Manoogian Found., Taylor, Mich., 1969-77; mem. evaluation team Ind. Schs. Assn. Ctrl. States, Chgo., 1985; polit. commentator WXYZ-TV, ABC, Detroit, Southfield, 1984—, WWJ-Radio, Detroit, 1984—; bd. dirs. Southeastern Mich. chpt. ARC, 1988—, chmn. internat. svcs. com., 1988—, disaster and mil. family svcs. com., 1988—. Scholar/diplomat U.S. Dept. State, Washington, 1976; grantee NEH, Washington, 1977, AID, Washington, 1978, Knights of Vartan, 1984; recipient Dadian Armenian Heritage award, 1993. Mem. AAUP (chpt. pres. 1962-65), Nat. Assn. Armenian Studies and Rsch. (bd. dirs. 1961-91), Nat. Ethnic Studies Assn. (bd. dirs. 1976-85), Am. Hist. Assn., Soc. Armenian Studies (pres. exec. com. 1988-91, sec./treas. exec. com. 1991-95), Am. Assn. Advancement of Slavic Studies, Am. Acad. Polit. Sci., Armenian Students Assn. (Arthur S. Dadian Armenian Heritage award 1993), Knights of Vartan. Armenian Orthodox. Home: 1935 Bluff Ct Troy MI 48098-6616 Office: U Mich 4901 Evergreen Rd Southfield MI 48075

PAPAZIAN, ROSALIE MARIE, elementary education educator; b. Augusta, Ga., Aug. 27, 1927; d. Nahabed Charles and Armanouhe Marie (Pehlivanian) P.; m. Diran Garo Papazian, Aug. 21, 1957; children: Garo Dennis, Elise Priscilla. MEd, Wayne State U., 1956. Tchr. elem. edn. Dearborn (Mich.) Pub. Schs., 1956-86; supt. Sunday sch. St. John's, Detroit, 1946-50, St. Joachim & Anne Armenian Ch., Palos Heights, Ill., 1990-94; coord. worship svc. St. John's Armenian Ch., Southfield, Mich., 1994—; religion tchr. St. Vartan Camp & Midwest Diocesan Camp, Conn. and Wis.; midwest coord. of Sunday schs. Dept. Religious Edn. of the Diocese of Armenian Ch., N.Y.C., 1991-93. Author: (9th grade text) We Believe, 1986; editor: (monthly pub.) Torchbearer, 1946; contbr.: Mirror Spectator, Armenian Reporter. Seminar presenter Manoogian Manor, Livonia, Mich., 1993—, Armenian Chs. in U.S. and Can., N.J., Fla., Ill., Wis., Mich., N.Y., Toronto, Ont., Can. Mem. Daus. of Vartan (matron 1986-88, grand matron 1988-90, chaplain 1951), Mich. Assn. Ret. Sch. Pers., Detroit Inst. Arts Founders Soc. Armenian Apostolic Orthodox.

PAPE, JERRY LEE, public relations specialist, retired naval officer; b. Gonzales, Tex., Sept. 17, 1934; s. Max William and Fay (Helms) P.; m. Carolyn Lee Hornbeek, Oct. 20, 1962; 1 child, Gretchen Marie Pape Crigler. BS, S.W. Tex. State U., 1955; postgrad., U. Minn., 1956-57. Instr. journalism, dir. publicity San Marcos (Tex.) Acad., 1955-56; various naval assignments as pub. affairs specialist worldwide, 1957-70; officer in charge Navy Office of Info., Chgo., 1971-75; dir. field activites Navy Office of Info., Pentagon, Washington, 1975-77; dep. pub. affairs hdqrs. Atlantic Command, Atlantic Fleet, Norfolk, Va., 1977-79; pub. affairs officer hdqrs. U.S. Naval Forces Europe, London, 1980-82; dir. pub. rels. ARC, Cin., 1983—. Decorated Bronze Star with Combat "V" Device, Legion of Merit. Mem. Pub. Rels. Soc. Am., Am. Mktg. Assn., Ret. Officers Assn. (life). Home: RR 2 Box 246A Butler KY 41006-9674 Office: ARC 720 Sycamore St Cincinnati OH 45202-2115

PAPPAGEORGE, JOHN, state official; b. Detroit, July 19, 1931; widowed; 2 children. BS, U.S. Mil. Acad., 1954; MA, U. Md., 1971; postgrad., U.S. Army War Coll., 1972-73. Active Oakland County Bd. Commrs., 1989-93; Rep. candidate U.S. House, 1992, 96. With U.S. Army, 1954-84. Greek Orthodox. Office: 33138 Dequindre Sterling Heights MI 48310*

PAPPAS, BARBARA E., Biblical studies educator, author; b. Chgo., July 26, 1941; m. George G. Pappas, Sept. 20, 1964; children: Dheanna Pappas Fikaris, Michele Pappas Glavanovics, Laina. Lay asst. Holy Apostles Ch., Westchester, Ill., 1976—; sec., lectr. Diocese of Chgo. Religious Edn. Commn., 1982—; founder, dir. Holy Apostles Resource Ctr., Westchester, 1984—. Author: Are You Saved?, The Orthodox Christian Process of Salvation, 1984, 3d edit., 1995, The Christian Life in the Early Church and Today, Vol. I, 1989, Vol. II, 1996. Mem. ASCD. Greek Orthodox. Home: 379 Arboretum Cir Wheaton IL 60187

PAPPAS, DAVID CHRISTOPHER, lawyer; b. Kenosha, Wis., Mar. 18, 1936; s. Theros and Marion Lucille (Piperas) P.; m. Laurie Jean Lacaskey, Nov. 26, 1956 (div. 1969); children— Christopher David, Andrea Lynn; m. Nancy Marie Pratt, June 11, 1983. B.S., U. Wis., 1959, S.J.D., 1961. Licensed master mariner. Bar: Wis. 1961, U.S. Dist. Ct. (ea. and we. dists.) Wis. 1965, U.S. Supreme Ct. 1971. Asst. corp. counsel Racine County, Wis., 1961; atty., adviser U.S. Dept. Labor, Washington, 1961-62; staff atty. U.S. Commn. Civil Rights, Washington, 1962-63; asst. city atty. City of Madison, Wis., 1963-65; sole practice, Madison, 1965—. Chmn. Madison Mayor's Citizen Adv. Com., 1964-65; pres. Wis. Cup Assn., Madison, 1965; co-chmn. 2d Congl. Dist. Humphrey for Pres., Madison, 1972. Recipient commendation for Supreme Ct. work Madison City Coun., 1965, commendation resolution City of Madison, 1965. Mem. Wis. Bar Assn., Dane County Bar Assn., Wis. Acad. Trial Lawyers, Am. Assn. Trial Lawyers, Lawyer-Pilot Bar Assn. (master mariner), Gt. Lakes Hist. Soc. Republican. Clubs: Madison; South Shore Yacht (Milw.). Home and Office: 1787 Strawberry Rd Deerfield WI 53531-9779

PAPPAS, EDWARD HARVEY, lawyer; b. Midland, Mich., Nov. 24, 1947; s. Charles and Sydell (Sheinberg) P.; m. Laurie Weston, Aug. 6, 1972; children: Gregory Alan, Steven Michael. BBA, U. Mich., 1969, JD, 1973. Bar: Mich. 1973, U.S. Dist. Ct. (ea. dist.) Mich. 1973, U.S. Dist. Ct. (we. dist.) Mich. 1980, U.S. Ct. Appeals (6th cir.) 1983, U.S. Supreme Ct. 1983. Ptnr. firm Dickinson, Wright, Moon, Van Dusen & Freeman, Detroit and Bloomfield Hills, Mich., 1973—; mediator Oakland County Cir. Ct., Pontiac, Mich., 1983—; hearing panelist Mich. Atty. Discipline Bd., Detroit, 1983—, chmn., 1987—; mem. bus. tort subcom. Mich. Supreme Ct. Com. Standard Jury Instructions, 1992-94. Trustee Oakland Community Coll., Mich., 1982-90, Oakland-Livingston Legal Aid, 1982-90, v.p., 1982-85, pres., 1985-87; trustee, adv. bd. Mich. Regional Anti-Defamation League of B'nai B'rith, Detroit, 1983-90; mem. nat. and community rels. agy. div. Jewish Welfare Fedn.; planning commr. Village of Franklin, Mich., 1987-91, chmn. 1989-91, councilman, 1991-92, chmn. charter com., 1993-94; bd. dirs. Franklin Found., 1989-92; trustee The Settlement Ctr., 1992—. Fellow Mich. State Bar Found., Oakland Bar-Adams Pratt Found., ABA Found.; mem. ABA, Fed. Bar Assn., State Bar Mich. (co-chmn. nat. moot ct. competition com. 1974, 76, com. on legal aid, chmn. standing com. on atty. grievances 1989-92, comml. litigation com., civil procedure com. 1992-94), Oakland County Bar Assn. (vice-chmn. continuing legal edn. com., chmn. continuing legal edn. com. 1985-86, mediation com. 1989-90, chmn. mediation com. 1990-91, bd. dirs. 1990—, chmn. select com. Oakland County cir. ct. settlement week 1991, chmn. strategic planning com. 1992-93, editor Laches monthly mag. 1986-88, co-chair task force to improve justice systems in Oakland County 1993—, pres.-elect, bd. dirs. 1996—), Am. Judicature Soc., Mich. Def. Trial Lawyers, Def. Rsch. and Trial Lawyers Assn., (com. practice and procedure), B'nai B'rith Barristers. Home: 32223 Scenic Ln Franklin MI 48025-1702 Office: Dickinson Wright Moon Van Dusen & Freeman 525 N Woodward Ave Bloomfield Hills MI 48304-2971

PAPPAS, PHILIP JAMES, real estate company executive; b. Chgo., Sept. 29, 1954; s. Nicholas James and Ann (Nicholson) P.; m. Ana Lucia Sant'Anna; children: Tiago, Marcelo, Amanda. BA, Shimer Coll., 1975. Mgr. Cook County Hosp., Chgo., 1975-77, purchasing agt., 1977-81; pres. L.G. Properties, Chgo., 1980—, Tiamar Real Estate, 1990—; docent Chgo. Archictecture Found., 1976-78. Life mem. OSA Boy Scouts Am.; v.p. Lincoln Park Builders Assn., Lake View Developers, pres., 1988-89. Recipient 1st pl. award for best interior restoration Nat. Hist. Trust for Preservation, 1991, Good Neighbor award for exceptional property restoration Northwide Real Estate Bd. Chgo. and Nat. Assn. Realtors, 1992, 95. Mem. Oxford Union Soc. (life), Chgo. Assn. Realtors. Greek Orthodox. Office: L G Properties 3654 N Lincoln Chicago IL 60613

PAPPAS, SHARON K., investment company executive; b. 1959. With Stinson, Mag & Fizzell, Kansas City, Mo., 1984-89; with Waddell & Reed Inc., Shawnee Mission, Kans., 1989—, sr. v.p., sec., gen. counsel. Office: Waddell & Reed Inc 6300 Lamar Ave Shawnee Mission KS 66202*

PAPPAS, WILLIAM JOHN, principal, educator; b. Grand Rapids, Mich., Oct. 23, 1937; s. John Basil and Sadie (Kurlas) P.; m. Susan Kay Payne, Aug. 18, 1962; 1 child Laurie Ann. BA, Western Mich. U., 1962; MA, Eastern Mich. U., 1966; cert. in edn. spl., Wayne State U., 1971. Tchr. Mt. Clemens (Mich.) High Sch., 1962-67, asst. prin., 1967-71; prin., co-dir. system-wide curriculum Northview High Sch., Grand Rapids, Mich., 1971—, co-dir. curriculum, 1989—; adj. prof. grad. sch. Ctrl. Mich. U., Mt. Pleasant, 1974—; regional rep. North Ctrl. Assn. Mich., 1995-96; spl. cons. Charter Schs. Ctrl. Mich. U., 1995-96. Contbr. articles to profl. jours. Recipient Northview High Sch. Exemplary Sch. Recognition award U.S. Dept. Edn., 1985, 89, 93; I/D/E/A fellow, 1974-76, 78-84, 86-89, 90-92. Mem. NASSP (Mich. state coord. 1990-93), Mich. Assn. Secondary Sch. Prins. (exec. bd. 1975-86, 91-94, pres. 1981-82, Outstanding Secondary Prin. Yr. 1985-86), Lions (pres. Grand Rapids chpt. 1976), Elks, Phi Delta Kappa. Greek Orthodox. Home: 3237 Woodberry Dr SE Kentwood MI 49512

PAPPENFUS, MABEL LOUISE, retired educator; b. Porter, Minn., Sept. 21, 1926; d. Clarence Nels and Sadie Elizabeth (Gillespie) Rasmussen; m. Ben Pappenfus, June 13, 1957 (dec. Sept. 1989); 1 child, Bettyann. BS, St. Cloud (Minn.) State U., 1956. Elem. tchr. pub. schs., Aurora, Minn., 19544-56, Hutchinson, Minn., 1956-57; elem. tchr. Benton County Rurala Schs., Foley, Minn., 1957-62, Sch. Dist. 742, St. Cloud, 1968-85; supt. schs. Benton County, 1962-68; dir. Sch. Bd. Dist. 51, Foley, 1985-93; ret., 1993. Mem. coun. Gethsemane Luth. Ch., Oak Park, Minn., 1975—, also treas. Ch. Women and other offices; dir. Benton County Dem.-Farmer-Labor Party, 1983-94. Recipient Friend of Edn. award Ea. Minn. Uniserv, 1992, Dem.-Farmer Labor award for dedicated svc., 1995. Mem. NEA (life), Minn. Edn. Assn. (life), Future Farmers Am. (hon. mem. Foley chpt.), Benton County 4-H Leaders Assn. (Pioneer award 1989), Kiwanis. Home: 1128 Laurel Ave Saint Paul MN 55104-6921

PARCELLS, FREDERICK R., product management; b. Chgo., May 14, 1957; s. Charles Hubbard and Winifred Elaine (Summer) P. AA, Barton County C.C., Great Bend, Kans., 1977; BA in Fin., U. Ill., 1980; MBA, Ind. U., 1985. CFP, CPCU; assoc. in risk mgmt., assoc. in reinsurance/Ins. Inst. Am. Actuarial trainee CNA Ins., Chgo., 1980-81; actuarial technician Sentry Ins., Stevens Point, Wis., 1982-83; scouting intern The Buffalo Bills, Orchard Park, Fredonia, N.Y., 1984; underwriting trainee Kemper Group, Chgo., 1986-87; casualty underwriter Kemper Group, Chgo. and St. Louis, 1987-88; acct. underwriter Northbrook P&C Ins. (subs. Allstate), Chgo., 1988-91; sr. account underwriter Northbrook Property and Casualty Ins., Chgo./Rolling Meadows, 1991; sr. underwriter Allstate Ins., South Barrington, Ill., 1991-95; product analyst CNA Ins. Cos., Chgo., 1995—. Asst. chmn. civic affairs com., Cambridge Forest Assn., Lincolnshire, Ill., 1980-81; treas. Santa Claus Anonymous, Chgo., 1990-91, 91-92, pres., 1992-93; vol. duplex constrn. Habitat for Humanity, Chgo., 1988, 89. Mem. CPCU Soc. (sec. Chgo. chpt. 1994-95, bd. dirs./pub. rels. chmn. 1993-94, mem. nat. underwriting sect. com. 1994—, treas. Chgo. chpt. 1995-96, v.p. Chgo. chpt. 1996—). Presbyterian. Home: 512 Inverrary Ln Deerfield IL 60015-3605 Office: CNA Ins Cos CNA Plz 38 South Chicago IL 60685

PARCH, GRACE DOLORES, librarian; b. Cleve., May ; d. Joseph Charles and Josephine Dorothy (Kumel) P. B.A., Case Western Res. U., 1946, postgrad., 1947-50; B.L.S., McGill U., 1951; M.L.S., Kent State U., 1983; postgrad., Newspaper Library Workshop, Kent State U., 1970, Cooper Sch. Art, 1971-72, API Newspaper Library Seminar, Columbia U., 1971, Coll. Librarianship, U. Wales, 1984, 85. Cert. literacy instr., Ohio. Publicity librarian Spl. Services U.S. Army, Germany, 1951; post librarian Spl. Services U.S. Army, Italy, 1952; USAF base librarian, 1953-54; br. librarian Cleveland Heights (Ohio) Pub. Library, 1954-63; asst. head reference div. Va. State Library, Richmond, 1964; dir. Twinsburg (Ohio) Pub. Library, 1965-70; dir. newspaper library Cleve. Plain Dealer, 1970-83; county librarian N.C., 1987-92; cons. Cath. Library Assn., 1961-64; mem. home econs. adv. com., Summit County, 1969, books/job com., 1968; mem. adv. com. Guide to Ohio Newspapers, 1793-1973, 1971-74; appointed to del. spl. librs. for People-to-People Program in Russia, 1995. Contbr. articles to Plain Dealer, N. Summit Times, Twinsburg Bull., Sun Press; author: Where In the World But in the Plain Dealer Library, 1971; Editor: Directory of Newspaper Libraries in the U.S. and Canada, 1976. Recipient MacArthur Found. award, 1988, Libr. of Am. award, 1988. Mem. McGill U. Alumnae Assn. (sec. 1973), Kent State U. Alumni Assn., ALA (rep. on joint com. with Cath. Library Assn. 1967-70), John Cotton Dana award 1967, Library Pub. Rels. Coun. award 1972), Cath. Library Assn. (co-chmn. 1960-63), Spl. Libraries Assn. (chmn. newspaper library directory com. 1974-76, chmn. pub. relations Cleve. chpt. 1973, chmn. edn. com. newspaper div. 1982-83, mem. edn. com. nominating com. 1984), Ohio Library Assn., Western Res. Hist. Soc., Am. Soc. Indexers, Cleve. Mus. Art Assn., Coll. and Research Librarians, Nat. Micrographic Assn., Women Space, Women's Nat. Book Com., Nat. Trust Hist. Preservation. Roman Catholic. Clubs: Cleve. Athletic, Cleve. Women's City. Home: 688 Jefferson St Bedford OH 44146-3711

PARDO, ROBERT EDWARD, software marketing and development executive; b. Chgo., Apr. 26, 1951; s. Edward Edwin and Marion (Brent) P.; m. Nora Kay Okerholm, July 14, 1979; children: Kathryn Elizabeth, Christopher Robert. BA, Northwestern U., 1972. Pres. R.E. Pardo & Co., Chgo., 1978; ops. supr. Bache & Co., Chgo., 1978-79; asst. ops. mgr. Conti Commodities, Chgo., 1979-80; internat. monetary market floor ops. mgr. Salomon Bros., Chgo., 1980; pres., chmn. Pardo Corp., Evanston, Ill., 1980—; pres. Pardo Capital Ltd. Author: Design, Testing and Optimization of Trading Systems; author, designer numerous fin. software programs; contbr. several articles to profl. jours. Mem. Assn. Data Processing Service Orgns.

PARFET, JOHN RICHARD, business development specialist; b. Ft. Collins, Colo., Jan. 23, 1957; s. A. James and Barbara (Geiser) P.; m. Kristie Ann Rohde, Oct. 4, 1987; children: Erin Nicole, Alyson Rose. BS, Colo. State U., 1980; MS, Purdue U., 1984; MBA, William Woods U., 1995. Rsch. technician Colo. State U., Ft. Collins, 1977-81; lab. mgr. Purdue U., West Lafayette, Ind., 1981-84; tech. cons. Monsanto Co., St. Louis, 1985-87; rsch. assoc. U. Mo., Columbia, 1985-90; diagnostic sales rep. ICN Pharm., Costa Mesa, Calif., 1990; client svcs. rep. ABC Labs., Columbia, 1990-93, bus. devel. specialist, 1993—. Contbr. numerous articles to profl. publs. Mem. exec. com. Meml. Day Corp., Columbia, 1991—; coord. for sci. program Ptnrs.-in-Edn., Columbia, 1993. Named Vol. of Yr., Meml. Day Corp., 1993. Mem. Rotary (chmn. youth exch. 1996—, bd. dirs. 1996—). Home: 1810 Garden Dr Columbia MO 65202-1251

PARGOFF, ROBERT MICHAEL, small business owner; b. Garden City, Mich., May 22, 1961; s. Andrew Stephen and Virginia (Dimanin) P.; m. Diane Elizabeth Bailey, Feb. 25, 1985; children: Andrew Stephen III, Patrick Robert. BA in Indsl. Mgmt., Lawrence Inst. Tech., 1988. Beverage mgr. Hilton Hotels, Plymouth, Mich., 1980-82; food and beverage dir. Holiday Inn, Inc., Farmington Hills, Mich., 1982-83; v.p., sec. Mich. Info. Systems, Plymouth, 1983-84; group ops. John Hancock Ins., Farmington Hills, Mich., 1986-88; chmn., pres. B. Bear Industries, Inc., Farmington Hills, 1985—; sales mgr. Tng. Express, Southfield, Mich., 1995—. Assoc. Presdl. Re-election Campaign, Detroit, 1984; mem. Young Macedonian Polit. Orgn., past pres., 1979-80, 83-85, Rep. Nat. Com. Mem. Am. Mgmt. Assn., Ind. Mgmt. Soc., Highland Club. Orthodox. Office: 33117 Hamilton Ct Ste 200 Farmington Hills MI 48334-3355

PARHI, KESHAB KUMAR, electrical engineering educator; b. Balasore, Orissa, India, June 15, 1959; came to U.S., 1983; s. Budhiram and Kamalini Parhi; m. Jagruti Mahapatra, Dec. 11, 1988; 1 child, Megha. B of Tech., Indian Inst. Tech., Kharagpur, 1982; MSEE, U. Pa., 1984; PhD, U. Calif., Berkeley, 1988. Teaching and rsch. asst. U. Pa., Phila., 1983-84; postgrad. researcher U. Calif., Berkeley, 1984-88; mem. tech. staff T.J. Watson Rsch. Ctrs. IBM, Yorktown Heights, N.Y., 1986, AT&T Bell Labs., Holmdel, N.J., 1987; asst. prof. U. Minn., Mpls., 1988-92; assoc. prof. U. Minn., 1992-95; prof., 1995—; vis. researcher NEC Computer Comm. Lab., Kawasaki, Japan, 1992; cons. AT&T Bell Labs., 1987, U.S. West Sci. and Techs., Boulder, Colo., 1989. Editor Jour. VLSI Signal Processing, 1993—; contbr. numerous articles to profl. jours. Recipient NSF Young Investigator award, 1992, Eliahu Jury award U. Calif., Berkeley, 1987, Demetri Angelakos award U. Calif., Berkeley, 1987; IBM grad. fellow, 1987-88, Regents fellow U. Calif., 1986-87. Fellow IEEE (assoc. editor transactions on cirs. and sys. 1990-91, assoc. editor transactions on signal processing 1993-95, assoc. editor transactions on cirs. and sys. part II 1995—, signal processing soc. paper award 1991, Browder J. Thompson Meml. Prize Paper award 1991), Cirs. and Sys. Soc. (Guillemin-Cauere award 1993, Darlington award 1994, Disting. lectr. 1994—, Design Automation Conf. Best Paper award 1996). Office: U Minn Dept Elec Engring 200 Union St SE Minneapolis MN 55455-0154

PARINS, ROBERT JAMES, professional football team executive, judge; b. Green Bay, Wis., Aug. 23, 1918; s. Frank and Nettie (Denissen) P.; m. Elizabeth L. Carroll, Feb. 8, 1941; children: Claire, Andrée, Richard, Teresa, Lu Ann. B.A., U. Wis., 1940, LL.B., 1942. Bar: Wis. Supreme Ct. 1942. Pvt. practice Green Bay, Wis., 1942-68; dist. atty. Brown County, Wis., 1949-50, cir. judge, 1968-82, res. judge, 1982—; pres. Green Bay Packers, Inc., 1982-90, chmn. bd., 1990-92; hon. chmn. bd., 1992-94. Mem. Wis. State Bar Assn. Roman Catholic. Office: Green Bay Packers PO Box 10628 Green Bay WI 54307-0628

PARIS, DAVID ANDREW, dentist; b. Milw., Jan. 16, 1962; s. John Baptistia and Geraldine Louella (Grosso) P. BA, UCLA, 1985, DDS, 1989. Oral surgery extern VA, Phoenix, 1989; primary practitioner Aids Project L.A. Dental Clinic, 1990-94; assoc. M. Marchese D.D.S., Sun Valley, Calif., 1990-92, D. Pickrell DMD, West Hollywood, Calif., 1992-94, Dental Arts Assocs., Milw., 1994—, Family Dental Ctr., Milw., 1994—. Mem. ADA, Wis. Dental Assn., Calif. Dental Assn., Acad. Gen. Dentistry, Delta Sigma Delta.

PARIS, KATHLEEN ANNE, educational consultant; b. Phillips, Wis., June 26, 1948; d. Vincent L. and Elaine S. (Andrus) P; m. Matthew J. Cullen, Sr., Aug. 28, 1993; 1 child, Meaghan M. Sass; stepchildren (Cullen): Catherine J., Julia M., William P., Matthew J. Jr. BS in Secondary Edn. magna cum laude, U. Wis., Oshkosh, 1971; MS in Ednl. Adminstrn., U. Wis., Madison, 1975, PhD in Ednl. Adminstrn., 1981. Lic. adminstr. Wis. Bd. Vocat., Tech. and Adult Edn. Tchr. Woodstock (Ill.) High Sch., 1971-74; asst. prin. Columbus (Wis.) High Sch., 1975-76; supr. Wis. Dept. Pub. Instrn., 1976-78; pub. info. mgr. Fox Valley Tech. Coll., Appleton, Wis., 1979-83, v.p. rsch., planning and mktg., 1983-85; adj. faculty Cardinal Stritch Coll., Milw., 1986-90; lectr. dept. continuing and adult edn. U. Wis., Madison, 1991—; dir. Leadership Inst. for Sch. to Work Transition Ctr. on Edn. and Work, U. Wis., Madison, 1993—; cons. Nat. Assn. State Dirs. Vocat. Edn., 1987, Am. Assn. Sch. Pers. Adminstrs., 1989, Wis. Gov.'s Trade Mission to Hong Kong, 1986, 87. Editor Wis. Vocat. Educator, 1990-91; author monographs. Bd. dirs. Wis.-Chiba Sister State Corp., Milw., 1990—. Recipient Export Achievement award Gov. of Wis., 1990, Resolution of Appreciation, Wis. Bd. Vocat., Tech. and Adult Edn., 1985. Mem. Am. Vocat. Assn., Wis. Vocat. Assn. (Disting. Leadership award 1979), Greenpeace, Phi Delta Kappa. Office: U Wis Office Quality Improv 195 Bascom Hall 500 Lincoln Dr Madison WI 53706-1706

PARIS, MICHAEL ANTHONY, mathematics educator; b. Watseka, Ill., Feb. 11, 1970; s. Douglas Charles and Julie Ann Paris. BA, Ill. State U., 1992. Teaching asst. Ill. State U., Normal, 1990-91, grad. asst., 1992-93; math. tchr. Princeton (Ill.) H.S., 1993-94, Red Hill H.S., Bridgeport, Ill., 1994—. Mem. Ill. Coun. Tchrs. Math. Home: PO Box 239 Crescent City IL 60928-0239

PARISH, CHARLES THERON, guidance counselor; b. Keokuk, Iowa, July 8, 1935; s. Charles Thadius and Cora L. (Refior) P.; m. Marjorie Ann Klingaman, Jan. 21, 1961 (div. Jan. 1985); children: Kelly, Jennifer Parish Stevens, Derek; m. Joanne T. Horvath, Feb. 10, 1985. BSBA, U. Denver, 1956; MA in Secondary Adminstrn., N.E. Mo. State U., 1970; postgrad., LaSalle U., 1994—. Cert. tchr., sch. adminstr., guidance counselor, ins. agt., securities agt. Counselor, tchr., coach Morning Sun (Iowa) Schs., 1970-72; prin., vocat. dir. Schuyler County H.S., Rushville, Ill., 1973-76; sales, owner Morning Sun Industries, Inc., Memphis, Mo., 1965-74; supr., agt. Aetna Life and Casualty, Hartford, Conn., 1976-81, Farmland Ins. Svc., Des Moines, 1981-94; cons. Mount Morris, Ill., 1985—; ins. agt. Parish Ins. Agy., Inc., Mount Morris, 1965—; dir. guidance Aquin Cath. Jr. and Sr. H.S., Freeport, Ill., 1990—; estate planning and bus. ins. seminar presenter Farmland & Aetna, Iowa, Ill., Mo., 1976-94; cons. in field; diplaced farmer counseling Ogle County, Ill., Mount Morris, 1987—. Contbr. articles to profl. jours. Precinct chmn. Rep. Party, Mount Morris, 1994—, Lee County, Iowa, 1967-70, Appanoose County, Iowa, 1963-66; various planning, zoning and indsl. devel. com., 1986-92. Recipient Journalism award Santa Fe R.R., 1961. Mem. NEA (life), Lions (past pres. 1956—), NASD, Life Underwriters, Phi Delta Kappa, NASSP. Republican. Presbyterian.

PARISH, THOMAS SCANLAN, human development educator; b. Oak Park, Ill., Jan. 24, 1944; s. Robert S. and Florence Catherine (Fleming) P.; m. Joycelyn Pingel, Oct. 2, 1964; children: Robert V., Kimberly E., David G., Thomas P., Kathryn E. BA, No. Ill. U., 1968; MA, Ill. State U., 1969; PhD, U. Ill., 1972. Instr. psychology Parkland Coll., Champaign, Ill., 1971-72; asst. prof. Okla. State U., Stillwater, 1972-76; assoc. prof. Kans. State U., Manhattan, 1976-80, prof., 1980—, asst. to dean of edn., 1992—; assoc. dir. ARIOS-Kan., 1994—; rsch. coord. for Midwest Desegration Asst. Ct., 1994—. Assoc. editor: Jour. of Social Studies Rsch., 1994—; cons. editor Jour. Genetic Psychology, 1984—, Jour. Reality Therapy, 1992—, The Genetic, Social and General Psychology Monographs, 1984—; contbr. articles to profl. jours. Bd. dirs. Friendship Tutoring Program, Manhattan, 1982-91, Stillwater Awareness Coun., 1973-74; co-founder, bd. dirs. Youth Alternatives, Inc., Champaign, 1971-72. Fellow Am. Psychol. Soc.; mem. Am. Ednl. Rsch. Assn., APA, Assn. Reality Therapists, Soc. for Rsch. in Child Devel., Phi Delta Kappa, Phi Kappa Phi. Home: 3313 Germann Dr Manhattan KS 66503-8446 Office: Kans State U Coll of Edn Bluemont Hall Manhattan KS 66506

PARK, CHUNG IL, librarian; b. Chang-won, Korea, Aug. 25, 1938; s. Zung S. and Bong-y (Choo) P.; m. Jung Yoo, Aug. 30, 1969; children: Charlotte, Sue, Andrew. BA, Yonsei U., 1961; MLS, U. So. Calif., L.A., 1971; postgrad., U. Ill., 1975. Libr., mem. faculty Malcolm X Coll., Chgo., 1972—. Compiler, editor: (books) Best Sellers and Best Choices 1980-83, Best Books by Consensus 1984-88, Advertisement Digest: Library and Information Services, 1979; editor COINT, 1980-88; contbr. articles to profl. jours. Mem. ALA, Am. Fedn. Tchrs. Home: 9302 Parkside Ave Morton Grove IL 60053-1570 Office: Malcolm X Coll 1900 W Van Buren Chicago IL 60612

PARK, JOHN THORNTON, academic administrator; b. Phillipsburg, N.J., Jan. 3, 1935; s. Dawson J. and Margaret M. (Thornton) P.; m. Dorcas M Marshall; June 1, 1956; children: Janet Ernst, Karen Daily. BA in Physics with distinction, Nebr. Wesleyan U., 1956; PhD, U. Nebr., 1963. NSF postdoctoral fellow Univ. Coll., London, 1963-64; asst. prof. physics U. Mo., Rolla, 1964-68, assoc. prof. physics, 1968-71, prof., 1971—, chmn. dept. physics, 1977-83, vice chancellor acad. affairs, 1983-85, 86-91, interim chancellor, 1985-86, 91-92, chancellor, 1992—; vis. assoc. prof. NYU, 1970-71; pres. Talema Electronics, Inc., St. James, Mo., 1983—; prin. investigator NSF Rsch. Grants, 1966—; bd. dirs. Mo. Tech. Corp., Jefferson City, Mo., 1994—. Contbr. articles to profl. jours. Recipient Most Disting. Scientist award Mo. Acad. Sci., 1994. Fellow Am. Phys. Soc. (mem. divsn. elec. and atomic physics); mem. Am. Assn. Physics Tchrs., Rotary. Methodist.

PARK, JOON BU, biomedical engineer, researcher, educator; b. Pusan, Korea, June 20, 1944; came to U.S., 1964; s. Sung Sub and Jung Ju (Kim) P.; m. Bea Young Kim, Sept. 11, 1963; children: Misun, Yoon Ho, Yoon Ji. Student, Seoul Nat. U., Korea, 1962-64; BS, Boston U., 1967; MS, MIT, 1969; PhD, U. Utah, 1972. NIH postdoctoral fellow U. Wash., Seattle, 1972-73; vis. asst. prof. U. Ill., Urbana, 1973-76; asst./assoc. prof. Clemson (S.C.), 1976-81; prof. Tulane U., New Orleans, 1981-83; prof. biomed. engring. U. Iowa, Iowa City, 1983—; adv. bd. Space Tech., 1994—; advisor/cons. FDA, Rockville, Md., 1980—. Author: Biomaterials: An Introduction, 1979, 2d edit., 1992, Biomaterials Science and Engineering, 1984, also more than 80 jour. articles, more than 100 abstracts. Recipient McQueen Quattlebaum award Clemson U., 1980. Fellow Am. Inst. Med. and Biol. Engring.; mem. Soc. for Biomaterials (founding mem.), Biomed. Engring. Soc., Orthopaedic Rsch. Soc., N.Y. Acad. Scis. Home: 1810 Country Club Dr Coralville IA 52241 Office: Univ of Iowa Dept Biomedical Engring Iowa City IA 52242

PARK, JUNE SUNG, information systems educator; b. Seoul, Korea, Nov. 10, 1954; came to U.S., 1983; s. Moon Soo and Gyl Bok (Kim) P.; m. Hyun Sook Woo, Apr. 23, 1977; children: Sohon April, Joonghun David. BBA, Seoul Nat. U., 1979, MBA, 1983; PhD in Info. Systems, Ohio State U., 1988. Mem. planning staff Korea Devel. Fin. Corp., Seoul, 1978-80; mem. rsch. staff Korea Inst. Indsl. Econs. and Tech., Seoul, 1980-82; rsch. fellow Hanyang U., Seoul, 1982-83; grad. rsch. assoc. Ohio State U., Columbus, 1984-87; asst. prof. La. State U., Baton Rouge, 1987-89; asst. prof. info. systems U. Iowa, Iowa City, 1989-95, dir. grad. program mgmt. sci., 1990-93, assoc. prof. info. systems, 1995—; project analysis cons. Hyundai Engring., Seoul, 1981-83; software engring. cons. Samsung Data Systems, Seoul, 1992. Assoc. editor Telecom. Systems jour.; contbr. articles to profl. publs. Mem. IEEE Computer soc., Assn. for Computing Machinery, Inst. Mgmt. Scis. and Ops. Rsch. (vice chair/chair elect tech. sect. on telecom.). Office: Univ Iowa Dept Mgmt Scis Iowa City IA 52242

PARK, STEVEN LYNN, architect; b. Fort Wayne, Ind., Sept. 30, 1957; s. Paul Eugene and Verla Jane (McFadden) P.; m. Kimberly Lynn Bowling, Apr. 4, 1982; children: Ashton Nichole, Paul Tanner. BS, Ball State U., 1981, BArch, 1981. Registered architect. Intern Schenkel & Shultz, Fort Wayne, Ind., 1978; architect MSKTD & Assocs., Fort Wayne, 1981-88; prin. Moake Park & Assocs. Inc., Fort Wayne, 1988-92, Able Ringham Moake Park, Inc., Fort Wayne, Indpls., 1992-95; Moake Park Group Inc., Ft. Wayne, 1995—; bd. dirs. Allen County Bldg. Dept., Fort Wayne. Mem. AIA (bd. dirs. Fort Wayne chpt.), Am. Correctional Assn., Builders Contractors Assn. Office: Moake Park Group Inc 202 W Berry St Ste 630 Fort Wayne IN 46802-2242

PARKE, TERRY R., state legislator; b. Pittsfield, Ill., Feb. 21, 1944; m. Joanne Parke; 2 children. BS, 1970. Ins. agt.; mem. Ill. Ho. of Reps. from 53d dist., 1985—; mem. Consumer Protection, Ins. Pensions and Pers., Energy and Environ. Coms. Ill. Ho. of Reps., Minority Spokesman, mem. Labor and Commerce and Econ. and Fiscal Commn.; past pres. Elgin Area Life Underwriters. Chmn. Bus. and Labor Am. Legis. Exch. Coun. Workers Compensation and Nat. Coun. of Ins. Legis.; past pres. N.W. Suburban Assn. Commerce and Industry; bd. dirs. Girl Scouts Crossroads Coun. Mem. Rotary (past pres. Schaumburg chpt.). Republican. Home: 1572 Rosedale Ln Hoffman Estates IL 60195-2653*

PARKER, ALAN LESLIE, II (CHIP PARKER), architect; b. Aberdeen Proving Ground, Md., July 8, 1952; s. Alan Leslie and Joanne Marie (McDonnel) P.; m. Rebbeca Ann Zerger, Nov. 15, 1974; children: Kristofer, Timothy. BS in Architecture, U. So. Calif., 1982. Registered architect, Kans., Tex., Colo.; lic. interior designer, Tex. Med. photographer and illustrator VA Hosp., Lexington, Ky., 1972-74; owner, operator heavy equipment contracting co. heavy equipment contracting co., Lexington, 1974-78; cartographer GRW Aerial Surveys, Lexington, 1978-80; project mgr. real estate and constrn. div. IBM, L.A., 1980-82; facility planner rsch. div. IBM, San Jose, Calif., 1982-84, staff rschr., scientist, 1984-85, staff architect, 1985-86; archtl. project mgr. real estate and constrn. div. IBM, Dallas, 1986-88; prin., owner Prairie Works Designs, P.A., Moundridge, Kans., 1988—. Merit badge counselor Boy Scouts Am., McPherson, Kans., 1988—, den leader, 1988-89, Webelos leader, 1989-91, pack cubmaster, Moundridge, 1991-95, asst. scoutmaster, 1995—; bd. dirs. McPherson County Habitat for Humanity, 1992-95. Alumni scholar U. Ky. Sch. Architecture, 1980. Mem. AIA. Democrat. Mennonite. Office: Prairie Works Designs PA Box 141 RR 2 1678 Cheyenne Rd Moundridge KS 67107

PARKER, ALLAN LESLIE, marketing executive; b. Bronx, N.Y., Aug. 31, 1938; s. Henry S. and Sylvia G. (Gross) P.; m. Vicky Ann Williams, Aug. 25, 1965; 1 child, David Henry. BSBA, Syracuse U., 1960; MBA, Creighton U., 1966. Cert. data processor. Acct. Hertz Corp., N.Y.C., 1960-62; systems analyst J.C. Penney Co., N.Y.C., 1966-67; mktg. mgr. Xerox Corp., Rochester, N.Y., 1967-78; nat. mktg. mgr. Cheshire div. Xerox Corp., Mundelein, Ill., 1978-82; v.p., chief oper. officer Internat. Software Enterprises, Arlington Heights, Ill., 1982-83; v.p. sales and mktg. First Computer Corp., Westmont, Ill., 1983-85; mktg. mgr. Wang Labs., Rosemont, Ill., 1985-87; mgr. ea. region Odesta Corp., Northbrook, Ill., 1987-88; nat. sales mgr. Zenith Electronics Corp., Glenview, Ill., 1988-94; dir. mktg. and sales Oryx Power Products, Mt. Prospect, Ill., 1994—; pres. A&V Assocs., Hoffman Estates, Ill., 1987-90; co-owner A&V Printing, Hoffman Estates, 1987-90; instr. bus. Rochester Inst. Tech., 1968-78, Keller Grad. Sch. Mgmt., Lincolnshire, Ill., 1986—. 1st lt. USAF, 1962-66. Mem. Am. Philatelic Soc., Creighton U. Alumni Assn. (coll. recruiting coordinator 1987—), Beta Gamma Sigma. Republican. Jewish. Home: 997 Commonwealth Ct Barrington IL 60010-3154 Office: Oryx Power Products Ste 300 1601 Feehanville Dr Mount Prospect IL 60056

PARKER, ANN E., writer, astrologer; b. Evanston, Ill., Nov. 18, 1927; d. Woodruff J. and Ruth (Ballantyne) P. BA in English, Brown U. Editor Chgo. Tribune; nat. lectr. in field. Author: (book) Astrology and Alcoholism, 1982, Earthquakes in the 1990's, 1990, Arabic Parts in Relationships, 1992, Earthquakes, 1994, Arabic Parts, 1995, Galactic Astrology. Mem. Am. Fedn. Astrologers, Nat. Coun. Geocosmic Rsch. (mem. sec. 1976—), Internat. Soc. Astrological Rsch., Soc. of Women Geographers (pres. 1960—). Home: 8836 N Lavergne Skokie IL 60077

PARKER, CHARLES WALTER, JR., consultant, retired equipment company executive; b. nr. Ahoskie, N.C., Nov. 22, 1922; s. Charles Walter and Minnie Louise (Williamson) P.; m. Sophie Nash Riddick, Nov. 26, 1949; children: Mary Parker Hutto, Caroline Parker Robertson, Charles Walter III, Thomas Williamson. B.S. in Elec. Engring, Va. Mil. Inst., 1947; Dr. Engring. (hon.), Milw. Sch. Engring., 1980. With Allis-Chalmers Corp., 1947-87; dist. mgr. Allis-Chalmers Corp., Richmond, Va., 1955-57, Phila., 1957-58; dir. sales promotion industries group Allis-Chalmers Corp., Milw., 1958-61; gen. mktg. mgr. new products Allis-Chalmers Corp., 1961-62, mgr. mktg. services, 1962-66, v.p. mktg. and public relations services, 1966-70, v.p., dep. group exec., 1970-72, staff group exec. communications and public affairs, 1972-87, ret., 1987; prin. Charles Parker & Assocs., Ltd., Milw., 1987—; retired chmn. bd. dirs. Associated Dental Svc. Inc., Milw., 1989-93; founding mem. World Mktg. Contact Group, London; bd. dirs. Internat. Gen. Ins. Corp., Dinermite Corp. Gen. chmn. United Fund Greater Milw. Area, 1975; trustee Boy Scouts Am. Trust Fund, Milw.; bd. dirs. Jr. Achievement; pres. bd. trustees Univ. Sch. Milw., 1978-80; trustee Carroll Coll., Waukesha, Wis.; bd. dirs. Milw. Children's Hosp.; bd. regents Milw. Sch. Engring.; mem. Greater Milw. Com.; chmn. bd. dirs. Milw. Found., 1987-89. Served to capt. AUS, 1943-46, ETO. Decorated Bronze Star. Mem. NAM (dir.), IEEE (assoc.), Wis. C. of C. (pres. 1974-76), Sales and Mktg. Execs. Internat. (pres., CEO 1974, 75, Eduardo Rihan Internat. Mktg. Exec. of Yr. award 1979), Wis. Mfrs. and Commerce Assn. (exec. com.), Pi Sigma Epsilon (pres. 1976-77, trustee and chmn. nat. edn. found. 1979-86), Kappa Alpha. Home: 4973 N Newhall St Milwaukee WI 53217-6049 Office: PO Box 92398 828 N Broadway Milwaukee WI 53202-3611

PARKER, DENNIS GENE, former sheriff, karate instructor; b. Kansas City, Kans., Jan. 5, 1956; s. Billy Gene and Lola Ruth (Martens) P.; m. Rebecca Shepherd, Nov. 1, 1994; children: Heatheryn Ruth, Jessica Elise. Student, U. Kans., 1984. Martial arts instr. Northland Tai-Ryuku, Kansas City, Mo., 1974-84; police cpl. Atchison (Kans.) Dept. Police, 1984-90; estate investigator Am. Rsch. Bur., L.A., 1990; sheriff Atchison County, Kans., 1990-94; bd. dirs. Atchison County Community Corrections; team mem. Atchison County Multidisciplinary Child Protection Team, 1992—; bd. dirs. N.E. Kans. Drug Task Force, Oskaloosa, 1990-91. Bd. dirs. N.E. Kans. Community Action Program, Atchison, 1991—, Atchison Area Drug Task Force, 1993—. Recipient Silver Star for Bravery Am. Police Hall of Fame, 1992, Honor award, 1992, John Edgar Hoover Meml. award Nat. Assn. Chiefs of Police and Police Hall of Fame, 1993, State of Kans. medals of valor, 1992, 93, Pres.'s Nat. medal of patriotism, 1993. Mem. World Black Belt Bur., Sandan-3d Level Black Shito-Ryo Okinawa Te. Baptist. Home and Office: 5125 NW Parkdale Kansas City MO 64151

PARKER, EUGENE NEWMAN, retired physicist, educator; b. Houghton, Mich., June 10, 1927; s. Glenn H. and Helen (MacNair) P.; m. Niesje Meuter, 1954; children—Joyce, Eric. BS, Mich. State U., 1948; PhD, Calif. Inst. Tech., 1951; DSc, Mich. State U., 1975; Doctor Honoris Causa in Physics and Math., Univ. Utrecht, The Netherlands, 1986; Doctor of Philosophy Honoris Causa in Theoretical Physics, U. Oslo, 1991. Instr. math. and astronomy U. Utah, 1951-53, asst. prof. physics, 1953-55; mem. faculty physics U. Chgo., 1955-95, prof. dept. physics, 1962-95, prof. dept. astronomy and astrophysics, 1967-95, prof. emeritus, 1995—. Author: Interplanetary Dynamical Processes, 1963, Cosmical Magnetic Fields, 1979, Spontaneous Current Sheets in Magnetic Fields, 1994. Recipient Space Sci. award AIAA, 1964, Chapman medal Royal Astron. Soc., 1979, Gold medal, 1992, Disting. Alumni award Calif. Inst. Tech., 1980, Karl Schwarzschild award Astronomische Gesselschaft, 1990; named James Arthur Prize Lectr. Harvard-Smithsonian Ctr. Astrophysics, 1986. Mem. NAS (H. K. Arctowski award 1969, U.S. Nat. Medal of Sci. award 1989), Am. Astron. Soc. (Henry Norris Russell lectr. 1969, George Ellery Hale award 1978), Am. Geophys. Union (John Adam Fleming award 1968, William Bowie medal 1990), Am. Acad. Arts and Scis., Norwegian Acad. Sci. and Letters. Home: 1323 Evergreen Rd Homewood IL 60430-3410

PARKER, JAMES JOHN, engineering and marketing manager; b. Oak Park, Ill., June 16, 1947; s. John J. and Marjorie (Grohmann) P.; m. Mary P. Nash, Oct. 21, 1972; children: Elizabeth Ann, John James, Patricia Mary. BS in Elec. Engring., Marquette U., 1971; BSBA, Elmhurst Coll., 1981; MBA, U. Chgo., 1987. Student engr. Motorola Consumer Products, Franklin Park, Ill., 1968-70, engring. assoc., 1972-74; co-op engr. Warwick Electronics, Niles, Ill., 1971-72; sr. engr. rsch. and devel. Quasar Electronics, Inc., Franklin Park, 1974-76; sr. project engr. Motorola Data Products, Carol Stream, Ill., 1976-79; sr. project engr. Zenith Electronics Co., Glenview, Ill., 1979-82, market rsch. mgr., 1982-85, sect. mgr., 1985-88, program mgr., 1988-95; mgr. displays Zenith Data Sys./Groupe Bull, Buffalo Grove, Ill., 1995—; part-time faculty Wright Jr. Coll., Chgo., 1975-80. Editorial adv. bd. Electronic Products Mag., 1976-77. Adviser Jr. Achievement, Chgo., 72-78; treas. I.C. Christian Svc. Commn.; vol. Public Action to

Deliver Shelter, 1987—. Mem. IEEE Midcon. (vice-chmn. pub. rels., 1979, chmn. spec. exhibits, 1981, vice-chmn. spec. exhibits, 1983), Delta Mu Delta, Alderman 5th ward Elmhurst 1993—; vice-chmn. fin. com. City of Elmhurst, 1995—. Home: 421 Berkley Ave Elmhurst IL 60126-3706 Office: Zenith Data Sys/Groupe Bull 2150 E Lake Cook Rd Buffalo Grove IL 60089

PARKER, JERRY L., mechanical engineer; b. Mt. Clemens, Mich., May 5, 1959; s. Leon Frederick and Shirley Ann (Jackson) P. Assoc. Degree, Ferris State Coll., 1982; postgrad., Macomb C.C. Field mechanic Fraza Equipment, Roseville, Mich., 1986-88; pattern maker Braum Pattern Co., Fraser, Mich., 1988-90; pres., mech. engr. Parker Pattern Inc., Sterling Heights, Mich., 1990—. Lutheran. Office: Parker Pattern Inc 202142 Carlo Dr Clinton Township MI 48038

PARKER, KATHLEEN K., state legislator; m. Keith Parker; 2 children. BA, U. Miami. Tax assessor Northfield Twp., 1979-83; mem. Regional Transp. Authority Bd., 1983-95; del. Ill. and Nat. Rep. Convs., 1988; Northfield Twp. coord. George Bush's Presdl. Campaign, 1988; mem. U.S. Archtl. and Transp. Barriers Compliance Bd., 1991-94; Ill. state sen., 1995—, m; mem. Fin. Inst. and Pub. Health and Welfare Coms., vice chair Transp. Com., 1995—; co-owner Keith Parker and Assocs., 1985—; pres., bd. dirs. Chgo. divsn. Busch Jewelry Co., 1988-93. Mem. Northeastern Ill. Planning Coun., Met. Planning Coun. Office: 191 Waukegan Rd Northbrook IL 60093

PARKER, LEE FISCHER, sales executive; b. Chgo., Nov. 28, 1932; d. Meyer Louis and Lena (Raphael) Fischer; m. Joseph Schwartz, Mar. 18, 1950 (div. Jan. 1986); 1 child, Steven Darryl; m. Robert K. Parker, Jan. 13, 1991. Student, Mallinkroudt Coll., Wilmette, Ill., 1976. Freelance fashion model Chgo., 1958-78; sales assoc. Neiman-Marcus, Northbrook, Ill., 1978-79; owner Keystone Svcs., Woodale, Ill., 1969-82; sales assoc. Marshall Field's, Skokie, Ill., 1986-94; fashion coord. Arnie's Restaurant, Chgo., 1964-68, Blackhawk Restaurant, Chgo., 1964-66, Jim Conway TV Show, Chgo., 1968-70. Mem. Brandeis Women's Aux., Holocaust Mus. Democrat. Jewish.

PARKER, MICHAEL GEORGE, plastic surgeon; b. Prophetstown, Ill., Dec. 8, 1951; s. Donald George and Melva Arlene P.; m. Marie Ann, Oct. 11, 1980; children: Brittany, Taylor, Colin. BA, Millikin U., 1973; MD, U. Ill., 1978. MD, Ohio; diplomate Am. Bd. Gen. Surgery, Am. Bd. Plastic Surgery, Nat. Bd. Med. Examiners. Intern gen. surlgery Albany (N.Y.) Med. Sch., 1978-79, resident gen. surgery, 1979-82, chief resident gen. surger, 1982-83; resident plastic/reconstrv. surgery/chief resident Cleve. Clinic Found., 1983-85; fellow in surgery of head and neck Canniesburn Hosp., Berasden, Glasgow, Scotland, 1985; pvt. practice plastics and reconstrv. surgery Akron, Ohio, 1985—; assoc. p[rof. plastic surgery N.E. Ohio U., Rootstown; lectr. in field; active staff Akron Gen. Med. Ctr., Akron City Hosp., Children's Hosp. Med. Ctr., Akron, St. Thomas Hosp. Med. Ctr., Akron, Barberton (Ohio) Citizens Hosp., Cuyahoga Falls (Ohio) Gen. Hosp., Medina (Ohio) Gen. Hosp., Robinson Meml. Hosp., Ravenna, Ohio; vis. prof. Ethicon Rsch. Inst., Edinburgh, Scotland, 1985, Interplast: Ecuador, 1985, Operation Rainbow, Philipines Treatment of Cleft Lip and Palate Deformities, 1989, 90. Contbr. articles to profl. jours. Fellow ACS; mem. AMA, Am. Cleft Palate Assn., Phio Med. Assn., N.E. Ohio Soc. Plastic and Reconstructive Surgeons (v.p. 1989-92, pres. 1995-96), Cleve. Acad. Medicine, Summit County Med. Soc., Am. Soc. Maxillofacial Surgeons, Am. Soc. Plastic and Reconstructive Surgeons, Brit. Microsurg. Soc., Am. Acad. Pediatrics, Am. Assn. Pediatric Plastic Surgeons, Am. Soc. for Laser Medicine and Surgery. Office: Plastic & Reconstrv Surgeon 300 Locust St Ste 590 Akron OH 44302-1809

PARKER, NORMAN W., chief corporate scientist; b. Brewster, Ohio, Nov. 3, 1922; s. Norman W. Sr. and Blanche (Rexford) P.; m. Margaret Marsh Parker, Mar. 15, 1947; children: Norman William Parker III, Margaret Ann Cooper. Cert. profl. engr. Ill. Engr. Brush Devel. Co., Cleve., AVCO, Cin.; v.p. Motorola, Inc., Schaumberg, Ill. Inventor, over 50 U.S. patents. Mem. bd. dirs. Erie Neighborhood House, Chgo. With U.S. Navy, 1941-45. Recipient Inventor of the Yr. award Chgo. Bar Assn. Sr. mem. IEEE (life). Office: Motorola Inc 1303 E Algonquin Rd Schaumburg IL 60196

PARKER, PATRICK STREETER, manufacturing executive; b. Cleve., 1929. BA, Williams Coll., 1951; MBA, Harvard U., 1953. With Parker-Hannifin Corp. and predecessor, Cleve., 1953—, sales mgr. fittings div., 1957-63, mgr. aerospace products div., 1963-65, pres. Parker Seal Co. div., 1965-67, corp. v.p., 1967-69, pres., 1969-71, pres. and chief exec. officer, 1971-77, chmn. bd. and chief exec. officer, 1977-84, chmn. bd., 1984—, pres., 1982-84, also bd. dirs., 1982—. Bd. trustees Case Western Res. U.; With USN, 1954-57. Mem. Union Club, Country Club, Pepper Pike Club. Office: Parker Hannifin Corp 17325 Euclid Ave Cleveland OH 44112-1209

PARKER, ROBERT CHAUNCEY HUMPHREY, clergyman, publishing executive, psychic; b. N.Y.C., Apr. 6, 1941; s. Robert Humphrey and Edith Louise (Corya) P. Student, U. Va., 1960-61, 62-63; diploma, Inst. Psychorientology, Laredo, Tex., 1973. Ordained to ministry Ch. of Antioch-Malabar Rite, 1975. Law clk. Shearman & Sterling, N.Y.C., 1961-62; owner Parker's Pronto-Pups Inc., N.Y.C., 1962-64; asst. to pres. U.S. Packaging, N.Y.C., 1964-66; asst. nat. sales mgr. Elliott Svc. Co. Inc., Mt. Vernon, N.Y., 1966-67; pres., cons. Lenfield Assocs. & Cons., N.Y.C. and Washington, 1967-71; founder, pres. Occult Comm. Corp., N.Y.C., Washington, and Danbury, Conn., 1971-76, New Awareness Corp., London and Mpls., 1973-81; dir., resident minister The Healing Ctr. at St. Patricia's, Inver Grove Heights, Minn., 1975; lectr., minister Ch. of Antioch-Malabar Rite, 1975—; editor New Awareness News, 1975—; founder, pres. Parker/Tofte Comm., Robert Parker Assocs., Minnetonka, Minn., 1977—; pres., CEO Am. Energy & Alcohol Corp., Mpls., 1981-84; cons. Boat Owners Assn. U.S., Washington, 1967-70, Durance Co., 1994-95; rschr., cons. Am. Marine Corp., Marblehead, Mass.; new product devel., venture capital and cons. investment, banking houses, N.Y.C. and Washington, 1967-71; dir., cons. to regional and nat. healing orgns. and publs., 1973-81; pres. Field Harmonics Rsch. Group Inc., 1993—; spkr., tchr. numerous orgns. Author: Watergate Flight 553, 1974, Reabsorption Energy, 1975, Finding Your Own Four-Leaf Clover, 1993; author Telsa Newsletter, 1979; editor New Awareness Mag., 1973-75 (newsletter) Sunbeams; editor, pub. New Awareness News and Book News, 1977—, psychic/parapsychology internat. trade jours., 1971-75; designer, pub.: Henry's Hilarious One Liners, 1991, Henry's Just a Chuckle, 1992, Henry's Just a Laugh, 1992, Henry's Just a Witticism, 1992; contbr. articles to profl. jours.; guest spkr. various radio and TV programs, including Dimension, Sta. WCCO-AM-FM, featured on Dimension, 1991, 93; host cable TV program Astrology and Mind, Etc., 1994-96. Bd. dirs. Toutorsky Ednl. Found., Washington, 1988-91. Mem. Nat. Press Club (Washington), Internat. Telsa Soc. Inc., Knickerbocker Greys Vet. Corps (N.Y.C.), N.W. Racquet Club, Browning Sch. Alumni Assn. (N.Y.C.), Lenox (Mass.) Sch. Alumni Assn. Home and Office: 5208 Woodhill Rd Minnetonka MN 55345-4751

PARKER, ROBERT RUDOLPH, podiatrist; b. Carthage, Ill., Nov. 10, 1927; s. Elmer B. and Lena Amelia (Rudolphi) P.; m. Beverly Elaine Phillipi, June 11, 1951; children: Mary Elizabeth, Robert Mitchell. DPM, Ill. Coll. Podiatric Medicine, 1951. Diplomate Am. Bd. Podiatric Surgery. Pvt. practice podiatric medicine Springfield, Ill., 1951—. Served with USN, 1945-46. Fellow Am. Coll. Foot Surgeons; mem. Am. Podiatric Med. Assn., Ill. Podiatric Med. Assn. Clubs: Sangamo, Island Bay Yacht (Springfield), Springfield Motor Boat. Lodge: Elks. Office: 1200 S Fifth St Springfield IL 62703-2316

PARKER, RONALD BRUCE, telecommunications executive; b. L.A., Mar. 21, 1932; s. Ralph and Anita Madeline (Chapman) P.; m. Teresa Kay Garrison, July 6, 1971; 1 child, Joshua Aaron. AB, U. Calif., Berkeley, 1953, PhD, 1959. Instr. U. Calif., Berkeley, 1959; from asst. prof. to prof. U. Wyo., Laramie, 1959-76; cons. Henning, Minn., 1976—. Editor: Contbns. to Geology, 1960-76; author: The Sheep Book, 1983, Inscrutable Earth, 1984, The Tenth Muse, 1986. Supr. Elmo Twp., Minn., 1986-95. With U.S. Army, 1954-56. Postdoctoral fellow NSF, 1957-59, NATO, 1965-66. Fellow AAAS, Geol. Soc. Am. Home and Office: Rt 1 Box 153 Henning MN 56551

PARKES, WRIGHT C., corporate lawyer; b. N.Y.C., Aug. 2, 1942; s. Walter C. and Mary Wright (Aber) P.; m. Linda A. Delappa, June 12, 1969; children: Rachel L., Rebecca A. BA, Wilmington Coll., 1965; MA, Ohio U., 1969; JD, Cleve. Marshall Coll. Law, 1983. Bar: Ohio. Editor Solon (Ohio) Free Press, 1971-73; tech. editor HNTB, Cleve., 1973-76; adminstr. legal contract Davy-McKee Corp., Cleve., 1976-83; pvt. practice Cleve., 1983-85; mgr. contract Picker Internat. Inc., Cleve., 1985-86; counsel, mgr. contract Sharon Cos., Medina, Ohio, 1986-90; adminstr. sr. contract Regional Transit Authority, Cleve., 1990—. Mem. Adminstv. Svcs. Commn., Cleveland Heights, Ohio, 1994—, Charter Rev. Commn., Solon, 1972-73. Mem. Nat. Contract Mgmt. Assn., Tri-State Purchasing Assn., Ohio State Bar Assn. (govt. contracts com.), Phi Alpha Theta (del. nat. conv. 1963-64), Alpha Phi Gamma (chpt. pres. 1964-65). Office: Regional Transit Authority 615 Superior Ave W Cleveland OH 44113

PARKHILL, MIRIAM MAY, retired librarian; b. Ada, Ohio, July 8, 1913; d. Thomas Jefferson Jr. and Cora Anita (Kemp) Smull; m. Edwin Hamilton Parkhill, Oct. 4, 1935 (div. July 1966); children: Diane Paget Parkhill Seils, Thomas Hamilton. AB, Ohio No. U., 1934; MA, Ohio State U., 1935; MA in Libr. Sci., U. Mich., 1963; student, Detroit Bus. Inst., 1937. Staff mem. Nat. Youth Adminstrn., Ada, 1937-38; asst. supr. Nat. Youth Adminstrn., Lima, Ohio, 1939-40; libr. staff mem. Ohio No. U., Ada, 1959-62, asst. libr., instr., 1963-68, catalog dept. head, asst. prof., 1969-72, catalog dept. head, assoc. prof., 1973-78, assoc. prof. emerita, 1980—. Vol. Ada Pub. Libr., 1980—. Mem. AAUW, DAR, Ohio Libr. Coun., Acad. Libr. Assn. of Ohio, Colonial Dames XVII Century, Hardin County Mus., Inc., Alpha Phi Gamma, Zeta Tau Alpha. Republican. Presbyterian. Home: 301 S Main St Ada OH 45810-1415

PARKINSON, DWIGHT CLARENCE, electrical engineer; b. Prairie Du Chien, Wis., Dec. 25, 1968. BSEE, Mich. Tech. U., 1992. Design engr. Cooper Power Sys., Waukesha, Wis., 1992—. Office: Cooper Power Sys 1900 E North St Waukesha WI 53188-3844

PARKINSON, GREG THOMAS, museum director; b. Decatur, Ill., Aug. 1, 1950; s. Robert Lewis and Marilyn Jane (Laws) P.; children: Julie, Emily, Scott, John. BA, Millikin U., 1972. Area office engr. Com-Plex, U.S. Industries, Jackson, Miss., 1976-77; rsch. ctr. asst. dir. Circus World Mus., Baraboo, Wis., 1978-82, program dir., 1983-84, exec. dir., 1985—; cons. Circus records for The Guinness Book of Records, 1992—. Pres. Bd. Edn., Baraboo, 1985-86. Mem. Circus Hist. Soc. (v.p. 1987-90). Office: Circus World Mus 426 Water St Baraboo WI 53913-2560

PARKINSON, MARK VINCENT, state legislator, lawyer; b. Wichita, Kans., June 24, 1957; s. Henry Filson and Barbara Ann (Gilbert) Horton; m. Stacy Abbott, Mar. 7, 1983; children: Alex Atticus, Sam Filson, Kit Harlan. BA in Edn., Wichita State U., 1980; JD, Kans. U., 1984. Assoc. Payne and Jones Law Firm, Olathe, Kans., 1984-86; ptnr. Parkinson, Foth & Reynolds, Lenexa, Kans., 1986—; mem. Kans. Ho. Reps., 1990-92, Kans. Senate, 1993—. Mem. ABA, Johnson County Bar Found. (pres. 1993—), Kans. Bar Assn. Republican. Office: Parkinson Foth & Reynolds 13628 W 95th St Lenexa KS 66215-3304

PARKS, CORRINE FRANCES, insurance agency owner; b. Pulaski, Ill., May 23, 1934; d. Elizabeth (Stanfield) Daniels; m. Charles Robert Parks, July 6, 1957; children: Reginald, Pierre. BA, Chgo. State U., 1976; student, Columbia Coll., 1986-87; MA, Gov.'s State U., 1981; postgrad., Chgo. U. Sem., 1990—. Exec. rep. Marsh & McLennon, Inc., Chgo., 1970-74; account exec. Internat. Ins. Cons., Chgo., 1974-77; mktg. rep. Alexander & Alexander, Chgo., 1977-79; v.p. AABACA Ins. Agy., Chgo., 1981; pres. AA& A Ins. Agy., Chgo., 1981—; radio show host Sta. WBEE, Chgo., 1985—; bd. dirs. Unity Chgo., Chgo. Urban Day Sch. Sec. Englewood Redevel. Group, Chgo., Butter's Career Acad., Chgo., 1987; rep. State Sun. Sch., N.I. Juris. Mem. Ind. Ins. Agts. Ill., Women in Radio and TV, Chgo. Bd. Underwriters, Chgo. Mus. Sci. and Industry, Group V Video Club (dir. 1986), Order of Eastern Star (treas. 1983). Democrat. Home: 100 Park Ave Calumet City IL 60409-5065 Office: AA & A Ins Agy 10615 S Halsted St Chicago IL 60628-2309

PARKS, MARY, state legislator. Student, Wayne State U. Rep. Mich. State Dist. 3, 1995—; house oversight & ethics com. Mich. Ho. Reps., local govt. com., transp. com. Address: PO Box 30014 Lansing MI 48909-7514

PARKYN, JOHN DUWANE, nuclear engineer; b. La Crosse, Wis., Feb. 20, 1944; s. Lionel Eric and Florence Katrina (Klum) P.; m. Betty Christine Tarnutzer, Aug. 13, 1966; children: Christine Peggy, Sarah Katherine, John Martin. Student Wis. State U., 1962-64, U. N.Mex., 1968-69; BS in Nuclear Engring. and Physics, U. Wis., 1972. Cert. assessor, Wis.; registered profl. nuclear engr., Calif.; registered profl. engr., Wis.; lic. sr. reactor operator; lic. min. United Ch. of Christ. Asst. plant engr. Ohio Med. Products Co., 1966-67; party chief U.S. Geol. Survey, Madison, Wis., 1971-72; asst. ops. group Point Beach Nuclear Plant, Two Rivers, Wis., 1972-74; asst. supt. La Crosse Boiling Water Reactor, Genoa, Wis., 1974-82, supt., 1982—; mem. industry rev. bd. Inst. Nuclear Power Ops.; past chmn. bd. dirs. Bank Stoodard, Bank Ferryville; chmn. bd. dirs. Wis. Masonic Home; dir. River Bank; chmn. bd. Mescalero Fuel Storage LLC; v.p. Genoa Fuel Tech Co. Mem. Two Rivers City Coun., 1974; mem. Vernon County Bd. Suprs., 1976—, now vice chmn. county bd., mem. fin. com., chmn. human svcs. rev. bd., chmn. community options program; assessor Bergen Twp. (Wis.), 1976-77, Sterling Twp. (Wis.), 1977-79; chmn. Vernon County Libr. Com., 1976—; chmn. pers. com. Vernon County Bd. Equalized Values; chmn. Vernon County Com. for Programs of Aging; pres. Winding Rivers Libr. System, v.p.; treas. Sch. Dist. of La Crosse, pres.; pres. Riverland coun. Girl Scouts U.S.A.; mem. exec. bd. Gateway Area coun. Boy Scouts Am.; advisor, mem. Wis. staff Order of DeMolay; chmn. Wis. Masonic Home; pres. St. Johns United Ch. Christ; pres. River Rails Inc.. Served with U.S. Army, 1967-69. Mem. Am. Nuclear Soc. (chmn. Wis. sect., mem. nat. planning com.), Nat. Assn. of Former Youth Govs., Nat. Assn. R.R. Passengers (nat. bd. dirs.), Wis. Assn. R.R. Passengers (state pres.), Am. Legion, Wis. Legis. Coun., Masons, Frontier Lodge 45 F.A.M. (past worshipful master). Home: Pleasant Vly Stoddard WI 54658 Office: La Crosse Boiling Water Reactor RR 1 Genoa WI 54632-9801

PARLOR, KAREN WETTLIN, microbiologist; b. Saginaw, Mich., May 12, 1961; d. Lawrence and Muriel Elaine (Banks) Wettlin; m. Randy Eugene Parlor, Sept. 15, 1990. BS in Med. Tech., Mich. State U., 1983. Lab. technologist I Mich. State U. Vet. Clinic, East Lansing, 1983-89, lab. technologist II, 1989—. Author: Grace Trilogy, 1994; wedding floral designer The Parlor, 1993—. Co-dir. youth program New Grace Tabernacle Ch., Lansing, 1994—. Home: 5808 LaPorte Lansing MI 48911

PARMELEE, WALKER MICHAEL, psychologist; b. Grand Haven, Mich., Apr. 26, 1952; s. Walker Michael and Evelyn Mae (Essengerg) P.; m. Gayle Ann Klempel, Jan. 11, 1975; children: Morgan Christine, Kathryn Ann, Elizabeth Mae. BS, Ctrl. Mich. U., 1974, MA, cert. specialist in psychology, 1977; D in Counseling Psychology, Western Mich. U., 1986. Lic. psychologist, Mich. Sch. psychologist Oakridge Pub. Schs., Muskegon, Mich., 1977-82, Ravenna (Mich.) Schs., Muskegon Heights (Mich.) Schs., 1982-84; sr. staff therapist Steelcase Counseling Svcs., Grand Rapids, Mich., 1984-90; prin., psychologist Parmelee Psychology Ctr., Grand Haven, 1989—; consulting psychologist Chem. Dependency Clinic, Grand Haven, 1989—. Contbr. articles to profl. jours. Bd. dirs. Planned Parenthood, Muskegon, 1979-82, Harbinger Inc., Grand Rapids, 1986-90; elder 2d Ref. Ch., Grand Haven, 1989-92; mem. women and families adv. group Allegan, Muskegon, Ottawa Substance Abuse Agy., 1992—. Mem. Am. Psychol. Assn., Am. Group Psychotherapy Assn., Nat. Assn. Child Alcoholics, Mich. Psychol. Assn., Mich. Sch. Psychologists. Home: 215 Howard St Grand Haven MI 49417-1806 Office: Parmelee Psychology Ctr 321 Fulton Ave Grand Haven MI 49417-1231

PARMENTER, LONNIE LEROY, dairy products executive; b. Solo, Mo., Nov. 16, 1944; s. Roy and Anna O. (Medlock) P.; m. Jane M. Phillips, Nov. 30, 1963; children: James L., Lisa L. AS, Sch. of the Ozarks, 1964; student, Mo. Inst. Tech., 1969, 87. Auditor Hiland Dairy, Springfield, Mo., 1965-67, purchasing mgr., 1967-74, asst. plant mgr., 1974-79, plant mgr., 1979—. Mem. Ozarks Purchasing Assn. (sec. 1969-73), Internat. Mgmt. Coun., Springfield C. of C., Quality Check Quality Assurance Com. (charter spl svc. 1988), Mo. State Milk Bd. (adv. com. 1988—), Masons, Abou Ben Adheim Shrine. Office: Hiland Dairy Co 1133 E Kearney St Springfield MO 65803-3435

PARNELL, CHARLES L., speechwriter; b. Myrtis, La., Feb. 13, 1938; s. Forrest L. and Dorothy D. (Jones) P. BA, Rice U., 1960; M Bus. and Pub. Adminstrn., Southeastern U., 1977. Commd. ens. USN, 1960, advanced through grades to comdr., 1975, ret., 1987; speechwriter Mead Data Cen., Dayton, Ohio, 1987-89, Nationwide Ins. Co., Columbus, Ohio, 1989-90; exec. speechwriter Miller Brewing Co., Milw., 1990—. Contbr. articles to profl. publs. Mem. U.S. Naval Inst., Ret. Officers Assn., World Future Soc. Office: Miller Brewing Co 3939 W Highland Blvd Milwaukee WI 53208-2816

PARRIGIN, ELIZABETH ELLINGTON, lawyer; b. Colon, Panama, May 23, 1932; d. Jesse Cox and Elizabeth (Roark) Ellington; m. Perry G. Parrigin, Oct. 8, 1975. BA, Agnes Scott Coll., 1954; JD, U. Va., 1959. Bar: Tex. 1959, Mo. 1980. Atty. San Antonio, 1960-69; law libr. U. Mo., Columbia, 1969-77, rsch. assoc., 1977-82; atty. pvt. practice, Columbia, 1982—. Elder, clk. of session First Presbyn. Ch., Columbia; mem. permanent jud. commn. Presbyn. Ch. U.S., 1977-83, mem. advisory com. on constitution, 1983-90. Mem. ABA, Mo. Bar Assn. (chmn. sub-com. revision of Mo. trsut law 1988-92). Democrat. Presbyterian. Home: 400 Conley Ave Columbia MO 65201-4219 Office: 224 N 8th St Columbia MO 65201-4844

PARRISH, MAURICE DRUE, museum executive; b. Chgo., Mar. 5, 1950; s. Maurice and Ione Yvonne (Culumns) P.; m. Gail Marie Sims, Sept. 2, 1978; children: Theodore, Andrew, Brandon, Cara. BA in Arch., U. Pa., 1972; MArch, Yale U., 1975. City planner City of Chgo., 1975-81; architect John Hiltscher & Assocs., Chgo., 1981-83, Barnett, Jones & Smith, Chgo., 1983-84; zoning adminstr. City of Chgo., 1984-87, bldg. commr., 1987-89; dep. dir. Detroit Inst. of Arts, 1989—. Bd. dirs. Arts League of Mich., Detroit, 1994—; co-chmn. Mayor's Affordable Housing Task Force, Chgo., 1984-89; chmn. Chgo. Elec. Commn., 1988-89; mem. Chgo. Econ. devel. Commn., 1987-89; pres. St. Philip Neri Sch. Bd., Chgo., 1981-85, South Shore Commn., Chgo., 1982-84. King Chavez Parks fellow U. Mich., 1991, H.I. Feldman fellow Yale U., 1972; Franklin W. Gregory scholar Yale U., 1974, Nat. Achievement scholar U. Pa., 1968. Mem. Am. Assn. Mus., Am. Assn. Mus. Adminstrs., Constrn. Specifications Inst., Lambda Alpha. Office: Detroit Inst of Arts 5200 Woodward Detroit MI 48202

PARSH, PHILLIP J., manufacturing executive; b. Grand Rapids, Mich., Oct. 15, 1958. Tool and die apprentice Major Tool & Die, Grand Rapids, Mich., 1976-80; pres. Robb Machine Tool Co., Grand Rapids, Mich., 1980—. Office: Robb Machine Tool Co 4301 Clyde Park Ave SW Grand Rapids MI 49509-4036

PARSONS, DANIEL CHARLES, accountant; b. St. Louis, Dec. 17, 1948; s. Robert Hopkins and Helen (Scannell) P.; m. Joyce Roschnafsky, Oct. 24, 1981. AB, St. Louis U., 1971, MA, 1972, MBA, 1976. Lab. technician Bristol-Myers Co., St. Louis, 1971-76, v.p. Credit Union,, 1976-83; fin. officer EE-Jay Motors Transport, East St. Louis, Ill., 1977; asst. contr. Barad and Co., St. Louis, 1977-86, Nat. Garment Co., St. Louis, 1986-87; auditor to treasury City of St. Louis, 1988—. Mem. Augustinian Acad. Alumni Assn. (treas. 1987-89), Nat. Honor Soc., Phi Alpha Theta, Alpha Sigma Nu. Republican. Roman Catholic. Home: 1215 Cheshire Ln Saint Louis MO 63119-4815

PARSONS, DONALD, JR., critical care nurse; b. Warren, Ohio, Jan. 17, 1952; s. Donald and Arlow M. (Plott) P.; married, Oct. 11, 1980; children: Douglas C., Devon A., Daniel J. Student, U. Akron, 1978, Kent State U., Champion, 1989. RN, Ohio, Ga.; cert. instr. BLS, provider ACLS, ACLS instr., CEN. TNCC provider, basic trauma life provider, basic trauma provider, basic emergency med. technician instr., instr. cardiac life support. Staff and charge nurse Warren Gen. Hosp., 1980-81, Trumbull Meml. Hosp., Warren, 1981-83, Med. Coll. Ga., Augusta, 1984; staff nurse CCU, ICU, air-land mobile intensive care, emergency rm. St. Vincent Charity Hosp., Cleve., 1985-92; First Am. Home Care, 1992-94, Cleve. Clinic Found./U. Hosp. Cleve. Emergency Dept., 1995—. Mem. AMA, Am. Nurses Assn., Ohio Nurses Assn.

PARSONS, MARK FREDERICK, fundraiser; b. Mpls., Nov. 18, 1950; s. Frederick A. and Margaret C. (Anderson) P. BA, U. Minn., 1972; MDiv, United Theol. Sem., New Brighton, Minn., 1976; JD magna cum laude, William Mitchell Coll. Law, St. Paul, 1987; PhD, U. Minn., 1993. Bar: Minn. 1987; ordained deacon Meth. Ch., 1975, elder, 1978. Assoc. min. First United Meth. Ch., Worthington, Minn., 1976-77; min. Fairfax (Minn.) United Meth. Ch., 1977-78, Gethsemane United Meth. Ch., Lino Lakes, Minn., 1979-83; sr. min. Edgewater Emmanuel United Meth. Ch., Mpls., 1983-92; dir. gift planning Hamline U., St. Paul, 1992—; assoc. atty. Lange & Anderson, P.A., Bloomington, Minn., 1988-91. Merrill fellow Harvard Div. Sch., Cambridge, Mass., 1992. Mem. Minn. State Bar, Minn. Planned Giving Coun., Phi Kappa Phi. Office: Hamline U 1536 Hewitt Ave Saint Paul MN 55104

PARTRIDGE, ERNEST DEALTON, environmental philosopher, educator; b. N.Y.C., May 14, 1935; s. Ernest DeAlton and Nell (Clark) P.; m. Elinore Helen Hughes, Dec. 21, 1957 (div. Mar. 1990). BS with honors, U. Utah, 1957, MS, 1961, PhD, 1976. Instr. Weber State Coll., Ogden, Utah, 1968-70, assoc. prof. philosophy, 1976-79; assoc. prof. environ. studies U. Calif., Santa Barbara, 1980-82; rsch. assoc. U. Colo., Boulder, 1982-86; assoc. prof. philosophy Calif. State U., Fullerton, 1989-92, U. Calif., Riverside, 1984-93; Hulings prof. humanities and environ. ethics Northland Coll., Ashland, Wis., 1993—; advisor Lake Superior Binat. Forum, U.S. Forest Svc., Ont. Ministry of Natural Resources; mem. internat. adv. bd. Ctr. for Ecol. Protection of Baikal Region, Ulan-Ulde, Buryat Republic, SSR; advisor Comprehensive Land Use Policy and Allocation program Lake Baikal Watershed, Davis Assocs., Ctr. for U.S.-USSR Initiatives, Russian Acad. Scis., 1991; symposium dir. "Environ. Ethics: Now and Into the 21st Century," Calif. State U., Fullerton, 1991; lectr. in field of environ. and applied ethics. Editor: (anthology) Responsibilities to Future Generations: Environmental Ethics, 1981; mem. editl. bd.: Environ. Ethics, Jour. Environ. Edn.; co-editor: (with Anton Struchkov) On the Other Hand: News from the Russian Environment; contbr. numerous scholarly papers and book revs. to profl. jours. and publs. Mem. pub. adv. panel Chem. Mfrs. Assn., Washington, 1994—. Recipient Interdisciplinary award NSF, 1984-86; Rockefeller Found. fellow in environ. affairs, 1978, rsch. fellow Calif. State U., Fullerton, 1991. Mem. AAAS, Internat. Soc. Environ. Ethics, Am. Philos. Assn., Am. Soc. for Polit. and Legal Philosophy, Am. Soc. for Value Inquiry, Soc. for Philosophy and Pub. Affairs, The Wilderness Soc., Inst. for Global Comms., Union of Concerned Scientists, Concerned Philosophers for Peace, Sierra Club. Office: Northland Coll Humanities Dept Ashland WI 54806

PASALA, KRISHNA MURTHY, electrical engineering educator; b. Eluru, Andhra, India, Feb. 14, 1949; came to U.S., 1980; s. Krishna K. and Tayaramma (Madhyannapu) P.; m. Usha Rani Madhyannapu, Oct. 10, 1979; children: Swapna, Prasanthi, Kavitha. B in Engring., Govt. Coll. Engring., Kakinada, Andhra, 1970; PhD, Indian Inst. Sch., Bangalore, Karnataka, 1974. Sr. sci. officer Indian Inst. Sci., 1974-79; scientist, head atmospheric sci. divsn. Ctr. for Earth Sci. Studies, Trivandrum, Kerala, India, 1979-80; rsch. engr. Rsch. Inst. U. Dayton, Ohio, 1980-87, prof. elec. engring., 1988—; cons. Spectra * Rsch., Dayton, 1990—. Contbr. rsch. articles to profl. publs. Mem. IEEE (sr.), Signal Processing Soc. of IEEE (officer local chpt.). Home: 1021 Millerton Dr Centerville OH 45459 Office: Univ Dayton 300 College Park Dayton OH 45469

PASCOE, E(DWARD) RUDY, insurance sales executive; b. Sioux Falls, S.D., Oct. 13, 1948; s. Marvin E. Pascoe and Celesta M. (Heaton) Hymore; m. Janice A. Kistler, Sept. 2, 1967; children: Jennifer L., Matthew R., Stephan J. BE, U. S.D., 1972; postgrad., U. Iowa, 1972-74. CIC; cert. life underwriter. Tchr. Jo-Daviess Area Vocat. Ctr., Elizabeth, Ill., 1972-74; pvt. practice ins. sales Elizabeth, 1974—; personal line mgr. Herrling & Schmitt, Inc. Multi Line Ins. Agy., Freeport, Ill., 1981—. Vice coordinator Elizabeth

Ambulance Corp., 1981—; fin. sec. Elizabeth United Meth. Ch., 1977—, others. Named one of Outstanding Young Men Am., Jaycees Am., 1969. Mem. Life Underwriters Assn. (sec./treas. 1976-77). Republican. Lodges: Lions (pres., v.p., sec./treas. 1973-81), Masons. Office: Herrling & Schmitt Inc PO Box 300 Freeport IL 61032-0300

PASHLEY, EUGENE W., JR., financial services company executive; b. Somers Point, N.J., Oct. 21, 1954; s. Eugene W. and Ruth E. (Stahler) P.; m. Laureen J. Smith, Feb. 4, 1978; children: Jenna, Christopher, Anna, Ellen, Lauren. BS in Systems/Polit. Sci., Taylor U., Upland, Ind., 1977. Systems analyst Basic Am. Industries, Indpls., 1977-79; mgmt. cons. Price Waterhouse & Co., Indpls., 1979-81; ind. cons. Greenwood, Ind., 1981—; pres. Pashley Fin. Svcs., Spencer, Ind., 1988—; sec. Hyden Shore Inc., Spencer, 1986—; bd. dirs. Pashley Ins. Agy., Marmora, N.J. Bd. dirs. Overseas Coun. U.S.A., Greenwood, 1989—, U.S. rep., 1989—; bd. dirs. Kellie Plumbina and Johnson County Distbrs., 1994—; elder 1st Christian Ch., Spencer, 1990. Mem. Nat. Assn. Security Dealers, Mcpl. Securities Rule Making Bd., Nat. Rifle Assn., Taylor Presidents Club. Republican. Office: Pashley Fin 8 W Market St Spencer IN 47460-1736

PASHOLK, PAUL DOUGLAS, retail executive; b. Columbus, Ohio, Mar. 24, 1968; s. Jerome Joseph and Norma Anne (Weigand) P.; m. Rebecca Jean Eaton, June 10, 1995. BA in History, Ohio State U., 1990, BA in Polit. Sci. 1990. Dept. supr. Kohl's Dept. Stores, Columbus, 1991—. Author: The Columbus Public Schools and 75 Years of School Board Elections, 1990, King of the Hill - U.S. Presidential Elections, 1992. Vol., rschr. Bill Moss for Columbus Sch. Bd., 1985, 89, 91, Bill Buckel for Columbus Sch. Bd., 1987, treas. 1989, 91, 93; presdl. elector cand. Eugene McCarthy for Pres., Columbus, 1988; vol. Bruce Babbit for Pres., Cedar Rapids, Iowa, 1988, Jesse Jackson for Pres., Columbus, 1988, Richard Letts for Judge, Columbus, 1989, Jerry Brown for Pres., Columbus, 1992; local organizer Hands Across Am., Columbus, 1986; vol. recruiter AFL-CIO suport group Frontlash, Columbus, 1988-90; mem. Indsl. Workers of the World, San Francisco/Ypsilanti, 1992—; organizer, chmn. West H.S. Class Reunion, Columbus, 1991; Ohio state campaign chmn. Ray Rollinson for Pres., Columbus, 1992; non-voting del. Libertarian Nat. Conv., Salt Lake City, 1993; contbr. Kirtland (Ohio) Reorganized LDS Ch. Temple Restoration, 1996. Democrat. Home: 948 Kirkwood Dr West Jefferson OH 43162 Office: 317 S Burgess Ave Columbus OH 43204

PASTERNAK, JAN, chief engineer; b. Poland, Nov. 17, 1945. BS, Poland, 1968. Chief engr. Littlefuse Inc., Des Plaines, Ill., 1983—. Office: Littlefuse Inc 800 E Northwest Hwy Des Plaines IL 60016-3049

PATE, CHARLIE D., electrical engineer; b. Mount Clemons, Mich., Mar. 28, 1947. BEE, Univ. Calif. Berkeley, 1972; MBA, UPI Perdue, Indpls., 1978. Gen. mgr., chief engr. Garden Metal Fabricators Inc., Ferndale, Mich., 1979—. Mem. Assn. Metal Fabricators and Engrs. Office: Carden Metal Fabricators Inc 981 E Saratoga St Ferndale MI 48220-1913

PATE, CLARA HAIRSTON, education director; b. Clemmons, N.C., Apr. 10, 1936; d. Paul Alexander and Eva (Brown) Hairston; m. Edward Collins Pate, Nov. 23, 1958; children; Paula Carlene, Paul Collins. BS, N.C. Ctrl. U., 1958; M, Ill. Tchrs. Coll., Chgo., 1965. Tchr. phys. edn. Chgo. Bd. of Edn., 1958-63; tchr. phys. edn. Evanston (Ill.)-Skokie Bd. of Edn., 1963-69, adminstrv. intern, 1969-70, prin. elem., 1971-94; dir. edn. Exec. Svc. Corp., Chgo., 1994—. Recipient Instrnl. Leadership award Ill. Prin. Assn., 1991, Leadership award Nat. Elem. Prin. Assn., 1994. Mem. Zonta Internat (chmn. 1992-96, bd. dirs., author mag. 1994, Woman of Yr. award 1993), Phi Delta Kappa. Democrat. Baptist. Home: 6033 N Sheridan Rd Apt 5A Chicago IL 60660

PATE, PAUL DANNY, state senator, business executive, entrepreneur; b. Ottumwa, Iowa, May 1, 1958; s. Paul Devern and Velma Marie (McConnell) P.; m. Jane Ann Wacker, July 15, 1978; children: Jennifer Ann, Paul Daniel III, Amber Lynn. AA in Bus., Kirkwood Coll., 1978; grad. in fin. mgmt., U. Pa., 1990. Exec. dir. Jr. Achievement, Cedar Rapids, Iowa, 1978-82; pres. PM Systems Corp., Cedar Rapids, 1982—; pres., pub. DAVCO Inc., Cedar Rapids, 1985—; senator Iowa State Senate, Des Moines, 1989—; Sec. of State State of Iowa. Chmn. Iowa Young Reps., Des Moines, 1989—, Rep. Senate Campaign Com., 1990; co-chmn. Young Rep. Nat. Platform Com., Miami, Fla., 1991; bd. dirs. Iowa Right to Work Com., Linn County Hist. Soc. Recipient Guardian Small Bus. award Nat. Fedn. Independent Bus., 1990; named Young Entrepreneur of Yr. U.S. Small Bus. Adminstrn., Iowa, 1988, Alumnus of Yr. Kirkwood Coll., Cedar Rapids, 1990. Methodist. Home: 2670 27th Ave Marion IA 52302-1240 Office: Off of State Senate Capitol Bldg Des Moines IA 50319

PATEL, MALINI, psychiatrist; b. Perak, Malaysia, July 17, 1954; d. N.S. and Poovayee (Navaratnam) Selvamany; m. Pankaj H. Patel, July 13, 1980; children: Sangeeta, Vikram. MD, U. Mysore, India, 1980. Lic. psychiatrist, Ill. Resident psychiatry Chgo. Med. Sch., 1988; med. dir., psychiatrist Drug Dependency Treatment Unit North Chgo. VA Hosp., 1990—; clin. asst., prof. psychiatry Chgo. Med. Sch., 1990—; cons. DuPage County Health Dept., Wheaton, Ill., 1991—; chief resident Jackson Park Hosp., Chgo., 1987-88, St. Mary of Nazareth Hosp., Chgo., 1986-87. Mem. Am. Psychiat. Assn., Ill. Psychiat. Soc.

PATEL, MINNIE HARIPRASAD, educator; b. Navasari, India, Oct. 17, 1956; arrived in U.S., 1978; d. Hariprasad H. and Kamu H. Patel. BSc, Maharaja Sayajirao U., Baroda, India, 1976, MS in Stats., 1978; MS in Sys. Engring., U. Ill., 1981; MS in Ops. Rsch., Ga. Inst. Tech., 1984, PhD in Indsl. and Sys. Engring., 1988. Ins. rater U.S. Fidelity & Guarantee Co., Houston, 1979-80; teaching asst. U. Ill., Chgo., 1980-81; ops. rsch. analyst World Book, Inc., Chgo., 1981-82; teaching asst. Ga. Inst. Tech., Atlanta, 1982-87; asst. prof. U. Tenn., Knoxville, 1987-90, U. Wis., Milw., 1990—; faculty advisor Soc. Women Engrs., Milw., 1993-94. Contbr. articles to profl. jours. Mem. IEEE (sr.), Inst. Ops. Rsch. and Mgmt. Sci., IEEE Engr. Mgmt. Soc. Office: U Wis 3200 N Cramer St Milwaukee WI 53201

PATEL, NARESH J., management consultant; b. Ahmedabad, India, June 16, 1962; came to U.S., 1986; BS, 1978. Program mgr. Circuit System Inc., Elk Grove Village, Ill., 1986—. Home: PO Box 55 Antioch IL 60002-0055

PATEL, PRAVIN, manufacturing executive; b. Broda, India, Dec. 20, 1935; came to U.S., 1974; B, London U., 1952. Chmn. Advance Systems, Inc., Green Bay, Wis., 1990—. Vol. local schs., Green Bay, 1980—.

PATEL, RAJ-RAJENDRA AMBALAL, dentist, clinical geneticist; b. Kitale, Kenya, Feb. 19, 1949; came to U.S., 1976; s. Ambalal Vaheribhai and Shardaben Ambalal (Kalidas) P.; m. Shobhna Rajendra Dahyabhai, Dec. 27, 1976; children: Risheet, Reisha. DDS, U. Bombay, 1973; MS in Clin. Genetics, Ind. U., 1990. Diplomate Am. Bd. Med. Genetics. Fellow in dental surgery Royal Coll. Surgeons, London, 1973-76; pvt. practice Indpls., 1976-85; postdoctoral fellow dept. med. and oral-facial genetics Ind. U. Med. Ctr., Indpls., 1985-90, clin. geneticist, rsch. assoc. dept. oral-facial genetics, 1990—; clin. geneticist, cons. Ind. U. Med. Ctr., Indpls., 1990—, St. Vincent Hosp., Indpls., 1990—. Contbr. articles to profl. jours. Boy scout leader St. Richards Sch., Indpls., 1987; vol. Republican Party, Indpls., 1988, 92; soccer coach Youth Soccer League, Indpls., 1990. Recipient Pub. Svc. award Colgate-Palmolive Co., 1985, Superior Genetic Rsch. award Jackson Lab., 1988, Individual Nat. Rsch. Svc. award U.S.A. Pub. Health Svc., NIH, 1987-90, Appreciation cert. Hamilton Southeastern H.S., 1996. Fellow Am. Coll. Med. Genetics; mem. ADA, Internat. Genetics Fedn., Am. Assn. Dental Rsch., Acad. Gen. Dentistry, Am. Cleft Palate and Craniofacial Assn., Am. Soc. Human Genetics, Soc. Craniofacial Genetics. Address: 10999 Windjammer Ter Indianapolis IN 46256-9676

PATRICK, GEORGE MILTON, dentist; b. Accoville, W.Va., Sept. 27, 1920; s. Milton Michael and Martha Mary (Mullins) P.; m. Shirley Ann Rutherford, Mar. 22, 1952 (div. June 1966); 1 child, Geoffrey Milton (dec.); m. Jane Lee Austin, Oct. 1, 1971; stepchildren: Duke Anthony-Spencer Austin, T.L.C. Hughes. BS, Capital U., 1950; DDS, Ohio State U., 1955; postgrad., U. N.C., 1972. Gen. practice dentistry Columbus, Ohio, 1956-67; dir. mktg. and rsch. Kirkman Labs., Portland, Oreg., 1968; gen. practice dentistry specializing in orthodontics Columbus, 1968; pub. health dentist Ohio Dept. Health, Bowling Green, Ohio, 1968-80; practice dentistry specializing in pedodontics, 1980-82; pvt. practice computer cons. Columbus, 1982-87, mgmt. cons., 1987—; pres. Shamrock Patrick Cons., 1991—. Prodn. mgr. Vaud-Vilities, Columbus, 1979-86; singer First Community Ch., Columbus, 1972-90, Opera/Columbus Chorus, 1984-86. 2d lt. U.S. Army, 1942-46, ETO. Decorated Soldier's Medal Bronze Star, Purple Heart with Oak Leaf Cluster. Mem. ADA, Ohio Dental Assn., Columbus Dental Soc. (chmn. children's dental health week), Columbus Coun. World Affairs, Pub. Rels. Soc. (membership com. 1986), Career Execs. of Columbus (pres. 1987-91). Home and Office: 2610 Love Dr Columbus OH 43221-2645

PATRICK, JANE AUSTIN, association executive; b. Memphis, May 27, 1930; d. Wilfred Jack and Evelyn Eudora (Branch) Austin; m. William Thomas Spencer, Sept. 11, 1952 (dec Apr. 1970); children: Duke Anthony-Spencer Austin, ToniLee Candice Spencer Hughes; m. George Milton Patrick, Oct. 1, 1971. Student Memphis State U., 1946-47; BSBA, Ohio State U., 1979. Svc. rep. So. Bell Tel. and Tel., Memphis, 1947-52; placement dir. Mgmt. Pers., Memphis, 1965-66; pers. asst. to exec. v.p. E & E Ins. Co., Columbus, Ohio, 1966-69; Ohio exec. dir. Nat. Soc. for Prevention of Blindness, Columbus, 1969-73; regional dir. Ohio and Ky. CARE and MEDICO, Columbus, 1979-87; v.p. Career Execs. of Columbus, 1987-91; owner, pres. Patrick Distribution, 1987—; lectr., cons. in field. Mem. choir 1st Cmty. Ch., Columbus, Ohio State Univ. Svc. Bd.; bd. dirs. Columbus Coun. on World Affairs, 1980-92, sec., 1983-91, chmn. devel. com.; chmn. pers. com. Ohio Hunger Task Force, 1989-90. Recipient commendations Nat. Soc. Prevention Blindness and Ctrl. Ohio Lions Eye Bank, 1973. Plaques for Svc. award Upper Arlington Pub. Schs., 1986. Mem. Non-Profit Orgn. Mgmt. Inst. (pres.), Nat. Soc. Fund-Raising Execs. (cert., nat. dir.), Pub. Rels. Soc. Am. (cert., membership com. chairperson), Ins. Inst. Am. (cert.), Mensa Internat., Columbus Dental Soc. Aux. (historian and publicity chair), Alpha Gamma Delta, Epsilon Sigma Alpha (pres.). Home: 2620 Love Dr Columbus OH 43221-2645

PATRICK, WILLIAM BRADSHAW, lawyer; b. Indpls., Nov. 29, 1923; s. Fae William and Mary (Bradshaw) P.; m. Ursula Lantzsch, Dec. 28, 1956; children: William Bradshaw, Ursula, Nancy. AB, The Principia, 1947; LLB, Harvard U., 1950. Bar: Ind. Supreme ct. 1950, U.S. Dist. Ct. (so. dist.) Ind. 1950, U.S. Ct. Apls. (7th cir.) 1961. Ptnr., Patrick & Patrick, Indpls., 1950-53; sole practice, Indpls., 1953—; gen. counsel Met. Planning Commn. Marion County and Indpls., 1955-66; dep. prosecutor Marion County, Ind., 1960-62; past pres., dir. The Cemetery Co., operating Meml. Park Cemetery, Indpls.; sec., dir. Rogers Typesetting Co., Indpls., 1966-85. Pres. Indpls. Legal Aid Soc., 1963. Served to lt. (j.g.) USNR, 1942-46. Recipient DeMolay Legion of Honor. Mem. ABA, Ind. Bar Assn., Indpls. Bar Assn., Lawyers Assn. Indpls., Indpls. Estate Planning Coun., Am. Legion, SAR (sec. Ind. Soc. 1953-59), Svc. Club Indpls., U.S. Navy League, Mil. Order Loyal Legion, Mason (33 deg.), Shriner. Address: 7 N Meridian St Indianapolis IN 46204

PATRICKS, EDWARD J, elementary education educator; b. Chgo., Jan. 19, 1958; s. John Anthony and Marion Nora (Kinnavy) P. Ed, Ill. Benedictine, Lisle, Ill., 1981. Cert. tchr., Ill. Sci. tchr. St. Pius X, Stickney, Ill., 1981-84; dept. chair, sci. tchr. St. Giles Junior High, Oak Park, Ill., 1984—. Commr. City of Berwyn, 1991—, North Berwyn Pk. Dist., 1995—; past commr. St. Mary of Celle Little League; sponsor Berwyn Playground and Recreation Commn., Berwyn Blazers Taveling Soccer; bd. dirs. Dem. Orgn. Berwyn, St. Mary of Celle, St. Vincent De Paul Conf. Mem. ASCD, NSTA, Nat. Cath. Educators Assn., Ill. Assn. Pk. Dists., Ill. Sheriffs Assn., Suburban Pks. and Recreation Divsn., Nat. Recreation and Pk. Assn., Berwyn Devel. Corp., KC (4 degree). Home: 1809 Euclid Ave Berwyn IL 60402-1845 Office: Saint Giles 1030 Linden Ave Oak Park IL 60302-1351

PATRIZIO, FRANK, JR., city manager; b. Phila., July 19, 1933; m. Arlene Storey, June 2, 1962; children: Carolyn, Diane, Frank, Thomas, William, Daniel. BS, U. Pa., 1955, MGA, 1959. Adminstrv. asst. City of Fort Lauderdale, Fla., 1959-60; adminstrv. asst. to city mgr. City of Portland, Maine, 1962; borough mgr. Bristol Borough, Pa., 1962-67; city mgr. City of Canandaigua, N.Y., 1967-74, City of Zanesville, Ohio, 1974-79, City of Piqua, Ohio, 1979—. With U.S. Army, 1955-57. Mem. Internat. City Mgrs. Assn. (midwest v.p. 1990-91), Ohio City Mgmt. Assn. (pres. 1987-88), Ohio Mcpl. League, Ohio Health Commr. Assn., Elks, KC. Office: City of Piqua 219 W Water St Piqua OH 45356-2235

PATRONE, JOSEPH S., project engineer; b. Warren, Ohio, Aug. 6, 1935. Student, ATES, Niles, Ohio, 1956-58. Designer Taylor-Winfield, Warren, 1966-76; project engr. Fairfield Machine, Columbiana, Ohio, 1976-92, JB Industries, Warren, 1992—. Democrat. Roman Catholic. Office: JB Industries 1098 Harvard Dr SE Warren OH 44484-4815

PATROW, KRISTINE LYDAL, television news anchor, reporter, producer; b. Camp LeJuene, N.C., Oct. 1, 1963; d. Lelon LaVerne and Marjorie Lucille (Peterson) Patrow. BA magna cum laude, Lawrence U., 1986. Intern, reporter Sta. WQOW-TV, Eau Claire, Wis., 1987; reporter, prodr. Sta. KTTC-TV, Rochester, Minn., 1987-88; freelance field prodr. Cable News Network, Chgo., 1988-89; anchor, prodr., writer, reporter Orbis Broadcast Group/CNBC, Chgo., 1989-95; on-camera reporter, anchor Sta. KARE-TV, Mpls., 1995—. Recipient Harriet Averill music scholarship, 1982, Miss Wis. Pageant scholarship, 1982, Miss Chippewa Valley scholarship, 1982, Good Citizenship award DAR, 1982, U.S. Constitution award, 1982, voice performance award Wis. State competition, 1977-83. Mem. Athena Women's Group, Kappa Kappa Gamma (marshall 1984-85), Phi Beta Kappa. Lutheran. Office: KARE-11 News 8811 Olson Memorial Hwy Minneapolis MN 55427

PATT, YALE NANCE, computer science educator; b. Medford, Mass., June 29, 1939; s. Abraham Walter and Sarah Clara (Tankel) P. BSEE, Northeastern U., 1962; MS, Stanford U., 1963, PhD, 1966. Asst. prof. elec. engring. Cornell U., Ithaca, N.Y., 1966-67; assoc. prof. computer sci., elec. engring/N.C. State U., Raleigh, 1969-76; prof. San Francisco State U., 1976—, U. Mich., Ann Arbor, 1988—; vis. prof. U. Calif., Berkeley, 1979-88; co-dir. Aquarius High Performance Computer Rsch. Group, Berkeley; cons. numerous cos., orgns. including Digital Equipment Corp., Frankford Arsenal, 1973-77, EPA, 1975-76, NCR Corp.; frequent lectr.; seminar and conf. coord. numerous computer sci. orgns. Contbr. articles to profl. jours. Served to capt. U.S. Army, 1967-69. Mem. IEEE Computer Soc. (chmn. curriculum assistance com. 1978-81, bd. govs. 1989—, jour. and conf. reviewer, assoc. editor Computer jour. 1988—), Assn. for Computing Machinery (5 time nat. lectr. 1975-87), Sigma Xi, Tau Beta Pi, Eta Kappa Nu. Office: Univ Mich 148 Atl Bldg Ann Arbor MI 48109

PATTEN, MAURINE DIANE, psychologist; b. Peoria, Ill., Aug. 30, 1940; d. Maurice H. and Esther Ann (Wilkenson) Foote; m. C. Alfred Patten, Aug. 26, 1961; children: Paul A., Bethany M. BS, Bradley U., 1961; MS, Chgo. State U., 1971; EdD, No. Ill. U., 1977. Lic. psychologist, Ill. Tchr. Elementary Schs., Skokie and Manhattan, Ill., 1961-63; dir. Southwest Coop Presch., Chgo., 1970-74; tchr. spl. edn. Dekalb County (Ill.) Spl. Edn. Assn., 1974-76, asst. dir., 1978-80; resource tchr. Sycamore (Ill.) Sch. Dist., 1976-78; asst. prof. Chgo. State U., 1980-81; pvt. practice as clin. psychologist Sycamore, 1981—; cons. Arthur Andersen & Co., St. Charles, Ill., 1981—; pvt. practice, 1981—. Fellow APA, Ill. Psychol. Assn. Methodist. Office: 964 W State St Sycamore IL 60178-1335

PATTEN, RONALD JAMES, university dean; b. Iron Mountain, Mich., July 17, 1935; s. Rudolph Joseph and Cecelia (Fuse) Pataconi; m. Shirley Ann Bierman, Sept. 5, 1959; children: Christine Marie, Cheryl Ann, Charlene Denise. BA, Mich. State U., 1957, MA, 1959; PhD, U. Ala., 1963. Acct. Price Waterhouse & Co., Detroit, 1958; instr. No. Ill. U., 1959-60; asst. prof. U. Colo., 1963-65; assoc. prof. Va. Poly. Inst. and State U., 1965-67, prof., 1967-73, head dept. accounting, 1966-73; dir. research Financial Accounting Standards Bd., Conn., 1973-74; dean Sch. Bus. Adminstrn., U. Conn., Storrs, 1974-88; chief of party-Eastern Caribbean Arthur D. Little Internat., 1988-89; dean Coll. Commerce and Kellstadt Grad. Sch. Bus. De Paul U., Chgo., 1989—; cons. to industry; bd. dirs. Transco Inc.; mem. individual investors adv. com. N.Y. Stock Exch., 1993—. Contbr. articles to profl. jours., chpts. to books. Bd. dirs. U.S. com. UNICEF, Chgo. 2d lt. F.A. AUS, 1958. Recipient Nat. Quartermaster award Nat. Quartermaster, Assn., 1956. Mem. AICPA, Am. Acctg. Assn., Inst. Mgmt. Accts., Acad. Internat. Bus. (Dean of Yr. award 1987), Internat. Assn. for Acctg. Edn. and Rsch., Chgo. Coun. Fgn. Rels., Ill. Coun. Econ. Edn. (Chgo., trustee 1989—), Execs. Club Chgo., Econ. Club Chgo., Pacioli Soc., Scabbard and Blade, Golden Key, Beta Gamma Sigma (mem. bd. govs. 1975-90, nat. sec.-treas. 1980-82, nat. v.p. 1982-84, nat. pres. 1984-86), Beta Alpha Psi (bd. dirs. 1992-94), Delta Sigma Pi, Phi Kappa Phi, Delta Mu Delta. Home: 334 N Montclair Ave Glen Ellyn IL 60137-5253

PATTERSON, DEBORAH MAE, educator, researcher; b. Mt. Pleasant, Mich., Dec. 14, 1956; d. Harold Edward Schmaltz and Virginia Mae (Carlson) Van Note; 1 child, Elissa Mae. Hair stylist St. Johns, Mich., 1975-80, Cheboygan, Mich., 1986-87; restaurant hostess Mackinaw City, Mich., 1987; hair stylist Cheboygan, 1987-89; cashier, deliverer Indian River, Mich., 1988-89; self-employed Cheboygan, 1989-95. Tchr. 1st Ch. of God, St. Johns, 1981-86. Methodist. Home: 1327 Mackinaw Ave #217 Cheboygan MI 49721

PATTERSON, DOUG J., printing company executive; b. Grand Haven, Mich., May 22, 1955. BA, Western Mich. U., 1977. With sales dept. Dana Printing, Grand Haven, Mich., 1977-90; v.p. Maple Leaf Press Inc., Grand Haven, 1989—. Co-coach Odyssey of the Mind Griffin Elem. Sch., Grand Haven, 1991—. Office: Maple Leaf Press Inc 1215 S Beechtree St Grand Haven MI 49417-2839

PATTERSON, HARLAN RAY, finance educator; b. Camden, Ohio, June 27, 1931; s. Ernest Newton and Beulah Irene (Hedrick) P.; children by previous marriage: Kristan Lee, Elizabeth Jane, Nolan Gene. BS cum laude, Miami U., Oxford, Ohio, 1953, MBA, 1959; PhD, Mich. State U., 1963. Asst. prof. fin. U. Ill., Champaign-Urbana, 1962-66; mem. faculty Ohio U., Athens, 1966—; prof. fin. Ohio U., 1977-94, prof. emeritus fin., 1994—; vis. prof., fellow Chgo. Merc. Exc., 1971; fin. cons., researcher projects for industry. Contbr. articles to acad. and profl. jours. Chmn. City of Athens Rainbow Adv. Bd., 1972-77; state chmn. scholarship com. for Ohio Rainbow Girls, 1975-87. Commd. officer USN, 1953-56. Recipient Fred Astaire Bronze I Achievement level; named Congressional Alternate to West Point, 1949; won competitive appointment U.S. Naval Acad., 1950; NROTC scholar, 1950; Stonier fellow, 1961, Mortgage Banking fellow, 1974, Found. Econ. Edn. fellow, 1965, 67, 69, 71. Mem. Internat. Platform Assn., Rotary Internat., Masons, Shriners, Order Eastern Star (worthy patron 1989, 92), Phi Beta Kappa (pres. faculty chpt. 1975), Beta Gamma Sigma (faculty adviser), Phi Eta Sigma, Alpha Kappa Psi, Delta Sigma Pi, Sigma Tau Alpha (adviser), Omicron Delta Epsilon, Pi Kappa Alpha. Republican. Home: 9B Station St Athens OH 45701-2758

PATTERSON, JANICE LAVELLE, academic administrator; b. Wichita, Kans., Sept. 6, 1938; d. Harvey Clayton and Audine Mae (Clark) Bates; m. Lewis E. Patterson, Sept. 6, 1964; 1 child, Elizabeth Anne. BS in Home Econs. and Journalism, Kans. State U., 1960; MEd, Pa. State U., 1965. Asst. women's editor The Salina (Kans.) Jour., 1960; women's editor The Norman (Okla.) Transcript, 1960-63; sr. residnt Pa. State U., University Park, 1963-64, asst. area coord., 1964-65; instrnl. developer Cleve. State U., 1975-79, asst. dean adminstrn., 1985—; tng. mgr. Lake Erie Girl Scout Coun., Cleve., 1979-83, bus. ops. dir., 1983-85. Mem. LWV (dir. Ohio chpt. 1995—), Cleve. Restoration Soc., Mat. Trust Historic Preservation, Citizens League.

PATTERSON, JANICE PAULINE, community and geriatrics health nurse; b. Riobamba, Ecuador, Oct. 7, 1941; d. Michael James and Ella Catherine (Patzsch) Ficke; m. Michael Milton Patterson, June 11, 1966; children: Michael Shane, Shad Milton. Diploma, West Suburban Hosp., Oak Park, Ill., 1963; BSN, U. Iowa, 1968. Emergency rm., ICU staff nurse Bloomington (Ind.) Hosp.; operating rm. staff nurse VA Hosp., Iowa City; operating rm. supr. Kirksville (Mo.) Osteopathic Hosp., 1973-77; clinic coord. Cancer Screening Clinic County Health Dept., Athens, Ohio, 1987-94; supr. Hickory Creek Nursing Ctr., The Plains, Ohio, 1989-90; dir. nursing Arcadia Nursing Ctr., Coolville, Ohio, 1990-93; staff nurse Med. Splty. Unit of Kansas City at Alpine North, Riverside, Mo., 1993—. Mem. Ohio Dir. Nursing Assn., Sigma Theta Tau (Lambda Omega chpt. 1990—). Home: 4837 NW 57th Ct Kansas City MO 64151-4632

PATTERSON, MARTHA ELLEN, artist, art educator; b. Anderson, Ind., Mar. 12, 1914; d. Clarence and Corrine Ringwald; m. John Downey, Nov. 27, 1935 (div. 1946); 1 child, Linda Carol; m. Raymond George Patterson, May 6, 1947. Student, Dayton (Ohio) Art Inst., Bendell Art Sch., Bradenton, Fla. Beauty operator WRENS, Springfield, Ohio, 1932-40; co-owner Park Ave. Gallery, Dayton; window decorator, art tchr.; tchr. art; judge art shows. One-woman shows include N.C.R. Country Club, Bill Turner Interiors, U. Dayton, High Street Gallery, Trails End Club, The Designerie, Riverbend Park, Statesman Club, State Fidelity Bank, Wegerzyn Horticultural Ctr., Pebble Springs, Backstreet, First City Fed. Bank, Bradenton, Fla., Alley Gallery, Merrill Lynch, Miami U., Gem. City Bank, Dayton, Ohio, Winters Bank, Dayton, Sherwin Williams, Howard Johnsons, Dayton Woman's Club, Bergamo, Dayton Meml. Hall, Bob and Arts, Del Park Med. Soc., The Dayton Country Club, Christ Methodist Ch., Unitarian Ch., The Metropolitan, Rikes, Dr. Pavey's, Dr. Chaney's, Dayton Convention Ctr., The Yum Yum, Jan Strunk Interiors, Park Avenue Gallery; artist: (water colors, oils, acylics, inks and pastels) group exhbns. include: Dayton Art Inst., Meml. Hall of Dayton, Dayton Country Club, Bergamo, Women's Club of Dayton, Am. Watercolor Soc., Riverbend Park, First City Fed., NCR Country Club, Springfield (Ohio) Mus., Longboat Key Art Ctr., others; in private collections of Mr. and Mrs. Richard Nixon, Virginia Graham, Les Brown, Paul Lynde, Air Force Mus. at Wright Patterson, Mr. and Mrs. Charles Lange of NCR, U. Dayton-Ohio, Stephen House, Doug Yeager and others. Vol. Christian Woman's Soc. of Am., Twig Children's Hosp., Dayton, The Utopians; mem. Tri Art Dayton, Long Boat Key Art Ctr., Fla. Recipient first prize Dayton Soc. Painters and Sculptors Show Rikes, First Prize, 1976, 77, First Prize, Best in Show, 1978, Beavercreek Art Assn. First Place, Best in Show, Artist and Sculpture Yearly Show, 1966, 68 2d place, Dayton Art Inst. 2d prize, Tri County Hon. Mention, Walker Motor Sales 2d place, Bendell Art Gallery 2d and 3d, Montgomery County Fair Best in Show. Mem. Art League of Manatee County (Fla.), Nat. Mus. Women in Art, Am. Watercolor Soc., Springfield Mus. Art, Dayton Soc. Painters, N.Y. Watercolor Soc., Long Boat Key Art League, Tri Art. Republican. Methodist. Home: 3853 Lawrenceville Dr Springfield OH 45504-4459 Winter Address: 5920 7th Ave W Bradenton FL 34209-3519

PATTERSON, RUSSELL, conductor, opera executive; b. Greenville, Miss., Aug. 31, 1930; s. Dudley Russell and Elizabeth (Taylor) P.; m. Teresa Gutierrez de Celis, Aug. 28, 1979; children: Richard Russell, Christopher Leonard. B.A., B.Mus., S.E. La. U., 1950; M.Mus., Kansas City Conservatory of Music, 1952; D.M.A., U. Mo. at Kansas City. Prof. music Kansas City Conservatory of Music, 1960-68; mem. profl. com. Met. Opera, 1962—; condr. Kansas City Symphony, 1982-83, artistic dir., 1982-86, condr. emeritus, 1986—; cons. Ford Found. Musician with Baton Rouge Symphony, 1948-50, Brevard Music Festival, 1947-49, Kansas City Philharmonic Orch., 1951-59, Bayrische Staatsoper, Munich, Germany, 1952-53; condr. Kansas City Philharmonic Orch., 1965-66, Point Lookout (Mo.) Festival, 1967—, Kansas City Ballet, 1965-66, Am. Ballet Co., European tour, 1958; gen. dir., Lyric Opera of Kansas City, 1958—, artistic dir., Missouri River Festival, 1976—; dir. Sunflower Music Festival, 1978—. Mem. opera com. Mo. Council Arts, 1965-69; mem. music panel Nat. Endowment Arts, 1970-72; mem. Univ. Assocs. U. Mo. at Kansas City, 1970—. Recipient Alice M. Ditson condrs. award Columbia U., 1982, W.F. Yates medalion William Jewell Coll.; named Disting. Alumni Southeast La. U. Mem. Friends of Art, Opera America (v.p. 1971-73), Phi Mu Alpha Sinfonia, Pi Kappa Lambda, Mensa. Home: 4618 Warwick Blvd Apt 1A Kansas City MO 64112-1751 Office: Lyric Opera Lyric Theater 1029 Central St Kansas City MO 64105-1619*

PATTERSON, WILLIAM GLENN, II, military officer; b. Jefferson City, Mo., Jan. 31, 1954; s. William Glenn and Marceline Ann (Bacon) P.; m. Debbie Kay Pirner, Feb. 23, 1974; children: William Glenn III, Nathan Andrew, Morgan B. BA in Bus. Adminstrn., Columbia (Mo.) Coll., 1983. Commd. 2d lt. Mo. Nat. Guard, advanced through grades to maj., 1990;

ops. officer Mo. Nat. Guard, Jefferson City, 1979-81, chief SIDPERS br., 1981-88; logistics officer Mo. Nat. Guard, St. Louis, 1988-91; recruiting officer, chief drug demand reduction program Mo. Nat. Guard, Jefferson City, Mo., 1991—. Ambassador U.S. Jr. C. of C., 1990; senator Jr. Chamber Internat., 1990. Mem. SAR, Mo. Nat. Guard Assn., Mil. Order World Wars, Jefferson City Jaycees (membership v.p. 1984), Mo. Jaycees (state editor), Rotary Internat. Roman Catholic. Home: 1700 Delta Pl Jefferson City MO 65109-1287

PATTIS, S. WILLIAM, publisher; b. Chgo., July 3, 1925; s. William Robert and Rose (Quint) P.; m. Bette Z. Levin, July 16, 1950; children: Mark Robert, Robin Quint Himovitz. BS, U. Ill., 1949; postgrad., Northwestern U., 1949-50. Exec. v.p., pub. United Bus. Publs., 1949-59; chmn., CEO 3M/Pattis, 1959-88; pres. NTC Pub. Group, Lincolnwood, Ill., 1961-96; dir. P-B Comm., Winnetka, Ill., 1978—; bd. dirs. 1st Colonial/Highwood; mem. book and libr. com. USIA, Washington, 1986-89, chmn., 1989-93; mem. exec. com. Pub. Hall of Fame, 1987—; chmn. U.S.-USSR Bilateral Info. Talks, Moscow, 1990. Mem. Pres.'s Coun. Youth Opportunity, 1968-70; bd. dirs. Photography Youth Found., 1970-73, Expt. in Internat. Living, 1970, Inst. Human Creativity, 1983—, Annenberg Ctr. for Health Scis., 1991—; trustee Eisenhower Med. Ctr., Rancho Mirage, Calif., 1989—; trustee Am. Coun. Tchrs. Russian, 1992—; bd. dirs. Nat. Security Edn. Act, Washington, 1993-94; lord of manor, Kirkbride, Eng., 1989—. Recipient Human Rels. award Am. Jewish Com., 1971, Paul Simon award Cen. States Conf. on Tchg. Fgn. Langs., 1992. Mem. Standard Club (Chgo.), Northmoor Country Club (Highland Park, Ill.), Tamarisk Country Club (Rancho Mirage). Home: 195 Elder Ln Highland Park IL 60035-5368 Office: NTC Pub Group 4255 W Touhy Ave Lincolnwood IL 60646

PATTISHALL, BEVERLY WYCKLIFFE, lawyer; b. Atlanta, May 23, 1916; s. Leon Jackson and Margaret Simkins (Woodfin) P.; children by previous marriage: Margaret Ann Arthur, Leslie Hansen, Beverly Wyckliffe, Paige Terhune Pattishall Watt, Woodfin Underwood; m. Dorothy Daniels Mashek, June 24, 1977; 1 stepchild, Lyssa Mashek Piette. BS, Northwestern U., 1938; JD, U. Va., 1941. Bar: Ill. 1941, D.C. 1971. Pvt. practice law Chgo., 1946—; ptnr. Pattishall, McAuliffe, Newbury, Hilliard & Geraldson and predecessor firms, Chgo.; dir. Juvenile Protective Assn. Chgo., 1946-79, pres., 1961-63, hon. dir., 1979—; dir. Vol. Interagy. Assn., 1975-78, sec., 1977-78; U.S. del. Diplomatic Confs. on Internat. Trademark Registration Treaty, Geneva, Vienna, 1970-73, Diplomatic Conf. on Revision of Paris Conv., Nairobi, 1981; mem. U.S. del. Geneva Conf. on Indsl. Property and Consumer Protection, 1978; adj. prof. trademark, trade identity and unfair trade practices law Northwestern U. Sch. Law, Chgo. Author: (with David C. Hilliard) Trademarks, Trade Identity and Unfair Trade Practices, 1974, Unfair Competition and Unfair Trade Practices, 1985, Trademarks, 1987, Trademarks and Unfair Competition, 1994, 2d edit., 1996; contbr. articles to profl. jours. Lt. comdr. USNR, WWII, ETO, PTO, ATO, ret. comdr. Fellow Am. Coll. Trial Lawyers (bd. regents 1979-83); mem. ABA (chmn. sect. patent, trademark copyright law 1963-64), Internat. Patent and Trademark Assn. (pres. 1955-57, exec. com. 1955—), Assn. Internat. Pour La Protection Propriete Indsl. (mem. of honor), Ill. Bar Assn., Chgo. Bar Assn., D.C. Bar Assn., Chgo. Bar Found. (dir. 1977-83), U.S. Trademark Assn. (dir. 1963-65), Legal Club, Law Club (pres. 1982-83), Econ. Club, Chikaming Country Club, Univ. Club, Mid-Am. Club, U. Va. Lile Law Soc. (sr. counselor), Selden Soc. (London, Ill. rep.). Office: Pattishall McAuliffe Newbury Hilliard & Geraldson 311 S Wacker Dr Ste 5000 Chicago IL 60606-6618

PATTISON, ROBERT MAYNICKE, architect; b. Colonia, N.J., Feb. 22, 1923; s. Maynicke Munn Pattison and Lillian Cornelia (Garretson) Pattison Fox; divorced; children: Jeannine (Mrs. D. Harper), Darrel Keith, Michael Shaun. Lic. architect, Ohio. Project coord. Walker & Weeks, Cleve., 1948-60; project architect Shaefer, Flynn & Williams, Cleve., 1960-62; v.p. Williams-Pattison Assoc., Inc., Cleve., 1962-74; prin. Robert M. Pattison, Architect, Berea, Ohio, 1974-85, 90—; architect, plan examiner City of Cleve. Bldg Dept., 1985-90; project architect Dalton-Dalton-Newport A/E, Shaker Heights, Ohio, 1977-78; asst. supr. Turner Constrn., Inc., Cleve., 1980; architect Lawson Co., Cuyahoga Falls, Ohio, 1980-81. Co-author: IEEE White Book, 1979. With USN, 1943-45. Mem. Kiwanis (pres. Middleburg Heights club 1991-92). Republican. Home and Office: 444 Woodlawn Cir Berea OH 44017-1231

PATTON, JAMES ELLIOTT, architectural technology educator; b. Cleve., Apr. 17, 1956; s. John Wesley and Ruby Delores (Hill) P.; children: Jessica M., James S., Jonathan A. B in Environ. Design, Miami U., 1978; MArch, Ohio State U., 1980. Historic bldg inventory Columbus (Ohio) Landmarks Found., 1979-80; grad. teaching assoc. Ohio State U., Columbus, 1979-80; grad. architect The LOM Corp., Indpls., 1980-81, Archonics Design Partnership, Indpls., 1981-84; head specifications James Architects & Engrs., Indpls., 1984-86, Cole Assocs., Indpls., 1986-87; asst. prof. archtl. tech. Purdue U., Indpls., 1987-95, dir. minority affairs, 1992-95; tech. coord. Schmidt Assocs. Architects and Engrs., 1996—; faculty instr. Grad. Home Builders Inst., Indpls., 1987, 90, Inroads/Indpls., 1992. Asst. home group leader Jesus Is the Word Ch., Indpls., 1990; vol. troop 1040 Pike Twp. coun. Girl Scouts U.S.A., 1990-91; bd. dirs. Pike Twp. Found., 1993; mem. Pike Twp. Sch. Bd., 1994—; asst. cubmaster pack 400 Boy Scouts Am., 1994—. Ensign USNR, 1994—. Mem. AIA (assoc.), U.S. Tennis Assn. (umpire), Kappa Sigma (grand master of ceremonies 1976-77). Democrat. Office: Purdue U 799 W Michigan St Indianapolis IN 46202-5160

PATTON, JON MICHAEL, research consultant, decision science educator; b. North Canton, Ohio, Sept. 10, 1942; s. David and Lela Virginia (Mast) P. BSCE, Ohio State U., 1965; MA in Math., U. Ala., Huntsville, 1968; MSc in Indsl. Engring., Purdue U., 1976, PhD in Math., 1981. Assoc. engr. Boeing Co., Huntsville, 1965-67; instr. math. U. Ala., Huntsville, 1968; teaching asst. Purdue U., West Lafayette, Ind., 1969-79; systems engr. Pritsker & Assocs., West Lafayette, 1979-81; systems analyst Computer Task Group, Independence, Ohio, 1981-82; asst. prof. systems analysis Miami U., Oxford, Ohio, 1983-89, applications cons., 1989—, adj. asst. prof. decision sci. dept., 1989—. Contbr. articles to profl. jours. Mem. Inst. Ops. Rsch. and Mgmt. Sci., Am. Statis. Assn., Math. Assn. Am., Omega Rho (faculty advisor 1985-89). Home: 80 Charleston Dr Oxford OH 45056-2063

PATTON, MARK EDWARD, consultant, educator; b. Detroit, June 6, 1966; s. Edward Wilson and Carol Ann (Segler) P.; m. SonHi Han, Aug.6, 1988; children: Michelle JinHi and David Jiseong. BA, Mich. State U., 1990, MBA, 1992. Rsch. asst. Mich. State U., East Lansing, 1989-92; exam. coord. Ednl. Inst. Am. Hotel and Motel Assn., Washington, 1992-94; asst. dir. MBA Advising Eli Broad Grad. Sch. Mgmt. Mich. State U., 1995; adj. faculty Lansing C.C., 1991-92, Davenport Coll. Bus., 1993-96; cons. Lifestyle Rsch., Lansing, 1989—; prin. Patton Cons., 1992—; vis. lectr. dept. tourism mgmt. Keimyung U., Taegu, South Korea, 1996—. Missionary Ch. of Jesus Christ LDS, Seoul, 1986-88. Mem. Asia Pacific Tourism Assn., Coun. on Hotel, Restaurant, and Instnl. Edn. Republican.

PATTON, RAY BAKER, financial consultant, real estate broker; b. Enid, Okla., Jan. 24, 1932; s. Dwight Lyman Moody and Opal (Hembre) P.; BA, U. Okla., 1955, MRCP, 1960, MAPA, 1969. Chartered fin. cons.; m. Gloria Ruth Chambers, June 6, 1954; children: David Baker, Dayna Erin. Asst. dir. planning San Joaquin, Calif., 1959-61; dir. planning City of Norman (Okla.) and planning cons. U. Okla., Norman, 1961-65; dir. planning Oklahoma City, 1965-67; dir. planning St. Louis County, Mo., 1967-71; pres. Creative Environs., Inc., Clayton, Mo., 1972-74; chmn. Creative Cons., Inc., Clayton, 1972-75; v.p. Land Dynamics, Inc., 1973-74; pres. Patton Real Estate, Inc., Success Power, Inc., St. Louis; prin. Raymond B. Patton & Assocs., Ballwin, Mo., 1975-81; dir. pub. works and planning, health commr., zoning enforcement officer City of Des Peres, Mo., 1977-79; zone mgr. Investors Diversified Svc.s, Chesterfield, Mo., 1980-81; investment broker, fin. planner A.G. Edwards & Sons, Inc., Clayton, 1981-83; fin. planning coord., dir. seminars E.F. Hutton & Co., Inc., St. Louis, 1983-84; securities prin. The Patton Fin. Group, Inc., Westport Fin. Group, Inc., St. Louis, 1984-86; securities products coord., agy. edn. coord., fin. planner, chmn. compliance com., asst. agy. mgr. Equitable Fin. Cos., St. Louis, 1986-91; also motivational speaker; chmn. bd., CEO Success Power, Body Works, St. Louis, 1989-93; bus. and fin. cons. Mo. Automotive Svc. Assn., St. Louis, 1991-93; broker, sales assoc. Coldwell Banker Real Estate, Chesterfield, Mo., 1994—; mem. faculty Nat. Inst. Farm and Land Brokers, 1971-76. Scoutmaster, St. Louis Area coun. Boy Scouts Am., 1976-80, vice chmn. adult tng., 1977-83; mem. Christian Bus. Men's Com., Chesterfield, Mo. Served with USMC, 1955-58. Named Outstanding Mcpl. Employee, State of Okla., 1963; recipient IDS Mercury award, 1980; A.G. Edwards & sons Crest award, 1982; Outstanding Exec. award E.F. Hutton, 1983, Blue Chip award, 1983; designated profl. fin. advisor 1984. Mem. Am. Inst. Cert. Planners, Am. Inst. Planners (pres. elect Mo., Kans., Okla. chpt. 1967, co-founder St. Louis Metro sect. 1969), Inst. Cert. Fin. Planners, Internat. Platform Assn., Internat. Assn. Fin. Planners, Eagle Scout Assn. (life), Fellowship Christian Fin. Advisors, Lambda Chi Alpha (pres. 1953-54). Methodist (minister of music, Ballwin 1978-83, choir dir. E. Free Ch., Ladue, Mo. 1986-87). Contbr. articles to profl. jours. Home: 146 Carmel Woods Dr Ballwin MO 63021-4220 Office: Mason Ridge Sch Parkway Sch Dist Des Peres MO 63131

PATTON, ROBERT LEE, sales executive; b. Highland Park, Mich., Nov. 1, 1949; s. George Kenneth Patton and Phyllis Stella (Fenn) Bewick; m. Kathy E. Williams, Nov. 2, 1949; children: Gregory Robert, Amy Kathryn. Student, Wayne State U., 1969, Miss. State U., 1967-70; BA in Polit. Sci., Millsaps Coll., 1974; MBA in Mktg., U. Houston, 1988. Supr. shear room Keystone Mfg., Detroit, 1971-72; quality control engr. Consol. Packaging, Clinton, Miss., 1972-73, cost estimator, 1973-75, mgr. customer svc., 1975-76; sales rep. Consol. Packaging, Houston, 1976-82; sales rep. Malnove, Inc., Omaha, 1982-87, nat. account sales rep., 1987-90; regional sales mgr. Old Dominion Box Co., Lynchburg, Va., 1990-92; nat. sales mgr. Old Dominion Box Co., 1992-94; gen. sales mgr. Riverwood Internat. USA, Inc., Lombard, Ill., 1994—; bd. dirs. Harris County Mcpl. Utility Dist. # 81, 1977-91, pres., 1983-91; bd. dirs. Cinco Ranch Mcpl. Utility Dist. # 3, 1991—. Pres. Living Word Luth. Ch., Katy, Tex., 1980, SCS supt., 1977-86; commr. for parish svcs. Tex.-La. Synod, Austin, 1979-83; mem. outreach commn. SETSLA Synold ELCA, 1988-92. With U.S. Army, 1970-72. Mem. Inst. Packaging Profls. (chmn. advt. 1986-90), Tex. Food Processors Assn., Nat. Paperbox and Packaging Assn., Assn. Water Bd. Dirs. Lutheran. Home: 21222 Lochmere Ln Katy TX 77450-5235 Office: Riverwood Internat USA Inc Packaging Divsn 288 South-Tec Dr Kankakee IL 60901

PATTON, THOMAS JAMES, sales and marketing executive; b. Cleve., Nov. 2, 1948; s. Michael Anthony and Delores (Bammerlin) P.; m. Thomasina Bernadette Cavallaro, Aug. 9, 1969; children: Thomasina, Thera V. A in Transp., Cleve. State U., 1971, BA in Mktg., 1973; BA, SUNY, Empire State, 1994. CLU; ChFC. Ins. salesman Manulife, Cleve., 1972-75, Mass. Mut., Cleve., 1976-80, Patton Ins. Assn., Inc., Avon Lake, Ohio, 1976—; ins. cons. Diversified Benefit Plans, Inc., Avon Lake, 1978-93, dir. sales and mktg., 1993—; pres. commerce Benefits Group, Inc. and Ins. Mktg. Group, Inc., 1995; prin. Cmty. Health Ptnrs., Ltd., Ill., 1994; pres. Commerce Benefits Group, Inc.; cons. Regional Sch. Consortium, Lorain County, Ohio, 1986—, County of Lorain, 1984—, City of Lorain, 1986—, County of Lorain, 1984—, City of Lorain, 1985—; prin. Comty. Health Ptnrs. Ltd.; bd. Italian Cultural Found. Pres. Lake Erie Rate Coun., Cleve., 1970-71; mem. Lorain County Dem. Ctrl. Com., Avon Lake, Ohio, 1986—; mem. com. Cleve. Leukemia Soc., 1985; bd. dirs. Villa Serena Sr. Housing, St. Francis Soc., Italian Cultural Found. Mem. Nat. Assn. Life Underwriters, Profl. Ins. Agts. Assn., Cert. Profl. Ins. Agts. Soc., Soc. Benefit Plan Adminstrn., Lorain County Life Underwriters, Irish Heritage, Order Italian Sons and Daus., Profl. Assn. Dive Instrs./Nat. Assn. Underwater Instrs. (SCUBA diving instr.). Roman Catholic. Office: Diversified Benefit Plan Inc PO Box 900 Elyria OH 44036-0900

PATTON, WILLIAM E., designer; b. Chgo., Ill., Aug. 26, 1950. A in Arts & Scis., Elgin (Ill.) C. C., 1970, A in Plastic Tech., 1977. Sr. designer Battelle Meml. Inst., Columbus, 1991—. Achievements include devel. of cardio-vascular valve, 1989. Roman Catholic. Office: Battelle Meml Inst 505 King Ave Columbus OH 43201-2696

PATZKE, FRANK THOMAS, investment advisor; b. Chgo., Dec. 14, 1950; s. John Leo and Alice Josephine (O'Donnell) P., m. Susan Carsello, Aug. 26, 1989; children: Steven John, Kevin Francis. BA in Pre-Law and Polit. Sci., U. Ill., 1973, MBA in Fin., 1978. Cert. fin. planner. Investment advisor, v.p. Burton J. Vincent, Chesley & Co., Chgo., 1978-83, Prescott, Ball & Turben, Chgo., 1984-88, The Chgo. Corp., 1988-93; co-founder Responsible Investment Group, Chgo., 1993-95; instr. Harper Coll., Palatine, Ill., 1982-85; commentator cable TV and radio program Dollars and Sense, 1984, 86. With USNR, 1973-78. Mem. Social Investment Forum, Bus. Execs. for Econ. Justice, Union League Club, Rotary. Roman Catholic. Office: Linsco Pvt Ledger Ste 2153 135 S La Salle St Chicago IL 60603-4109

PAUGH, C(HARLES) MICHAEL, political activist; b. Valparaiso, Ind., July 25, 1967; s. Charles William and Judy Ann (Gunter) P. AS in History, Tomlinson Coll., 1985-87; BS in Edn., Lee Coll., 1987-89; PhD in Polit. Sci., U. Leiden, 1992. Phys. edn. tchr. Portage (Ind.) Twp. Sch. Corp., 1989-90; import/export cons. Am. Nursery Products, Inc., Tallequah, Okla., 1990-92; pres./CEO Internat. Assocs., Inc., Gervais, Oreg., 1991—; pres. Am. Nat. Socialist Workers Party, Inc., Portage, 1993—; pres. adv. bd. Aryan Nat. Skinheads, Inc., Portage, 1993-96; cons. Russian Nationalist Party, Tomsk, Russia, 1994—, German People's Union, Bremen, Germany, 1994—; nat. socialist adv. bd. Bundesamt fur Verfasungsschutz, Berlin, 1995—. Author: Counsels for the Life of a Young National Socialist: An Offering to Contemporary National Socialism, 1994 (Vanguard award 1994); editor: National Socialist Primer, 1994; editor/pub. Aryan Voices, 1993-96. Mem. Federated Russian Orthodox Clubs, Gary, Ind., 1990—; mem. Russian Relief Fund, Syosset, N.Y., 1990—. Fellow Nat. Socialist Vanguard, Theta Kappa Alpha; mem. Nat. Forensic League (Double Ruby 1985), Collegiate Forensic League (Ruby 1989), Valparaiso Rubgy Club, N.W. Ind. Soccer Assn. Home: 922 N 200 W Valparaiso IN 46383 Office: Am Nat Socialist Workers Party Inc PO Box 542 Portage IN 46368

PAUL, JACK DAVIS, retired state official, addictions consultant; b. Bismarck, N.D., Mar. 16, 1927; s. Harry Ernest and Bernice Ambert (Davis) P.; m. Mary Ann Langness, Aug. 23, 1955; children: Steven, William. BSc in Law, U. N.D., 1956, LLB, 1957, JD, 1969. Bar: N.D. 1957; cert. master addiction counselor, addictions clin. supr., profl. educator; lic. social worker, N.D. Pvt. practice law Bismarck, 1957-71; exec. sec., gen. counsel N.D. Trade Commn., 1965-69; master addiction counselor N.D. Corrections Dept., Bismarck, 1972-79, dir. programs, 1980-89; ret., 1989; instr. alcohol and drug edn. St. Mary's Ctrl. High Sch., Bismarck, 1977-87; lectr. psychology Bismarck State Coll., 1992—; cons. additions, sex therapist and sex offender rehab. programs, Mandan, N.D., 1974—; lectr. on addictions, 1974—; mem. faculty N.D. Internat. Alcohol Studies, Grand Forks, 1980-83; cons. Internat. Orgn. for Treatment of Sex Offenders and Violence, 1979—. Mem. Mandan City Citizens Planning Com. for Law Enforcement, 1984; del. Nat. Conf. on Corrections Policy, Washington, 1986. With USN, 1945-46, PTO; capt. U.S. Army, 1949-53. Recipient citation for nat. flood relief Govt. of Netherlands, 1953. Mem. N.D. Social Workers Assn., N.D. Lic. Addiction Counselors (v.p. 1980). Democrat. Congregationalist. Home: 701 3rd Ave NW Mandan ND 58554-2810

PAUL, JAMES FRANCIS, humanities and social science educator; b. Evansville, Ind., Jan. 10, 1946; s. Philip Francis and Leona Mary (Schenk) P.; m. Patricia Maxine Rodgers, Mar. 21, 1970; 1 child, Christina. BA, St. Meinrad Coll., 1968; MA, So. Ill. U., 1972; ArtsD, Ill. State U., 1986. Ins. adjuster Gen. Adjustment Bur., Kankakee, Ill., 1970-72; instr. Kankakee C.C., 1972—; chairperson social studies evalution team North Ctrl. Assn., Kankakee, 1988; travel cons. tour leader Kankakee C.C., 1979—, advisor history/social sci. club, 1985—; faculty rep. Ill. Bd. Higher Edn., Springfield, 1987-90, chairperson acad. affairs, 1989-90; keynote spkr./presenter slide lecture topics in social sci. and humanities, 1975—; impersonator hist. inds. for question-answer presentations. Recipient Excellence in Tchg. award dept. ednl. psychology Ea. Ill. U., Charleston, 1988, Most Inspirational Tchr. award Western Ill. U., 1995. Mem. Kankakee C.C. Faculty Assn. (pres. 1988-92, editor newletter 1990—), Kankakee Area Fedn. Tchrs. (pres. 1991—ú, Ill. Hist. Soc., Kankakee County Hist. Soc. (life), KC, United Way Allocation Com., Phi Alpha Theta, Phi Theta Kappa (hon. Alpha Delta Eta chpt.). Democrat. Roman Catholic. Home: 764 Woodstock Ln Bourbonnais IL 60914-1714 Office: Kankakee Comm Coll PO Box 888 River Rd Kankakee IL 60901

PAUL, JOHN JOSEPH, bishop; b. La Crosse, Wis., Aug. 17, 1918; s. Roland Philip and Louise (Gilles) P. B.A., Loras Coll., Dubuque, Iowa, 1939; S.T.B., St. Mary's Sem., Balt., 1943; M.Ed., Marquette U., 1956. Ordained priest Roman Catholic Ch., 1943; prin. Regis High Sch., Eau Claire, Wis., 1948-55; rector Holy Cross Sem., La Crosse, 1955-66, St. Joseph's Cathedral, La Crosse, 1966-77; aux. bishop Diocese of La Crosse, 1977-83, bishop, 1983—. Office: PO Box 4004 La Crosse WI 54602-4004

PAUL, PETER VINCENT, special education educator; b. Newark, N.J., Dec. 29, 1952; s. Joseph Lawrence and Rose Marie (Curchy) P.; m. Mary Elizabeth Pilewski, Oct. 29, 1983; 1 child, Peter Benedict. BA, U. South Fla., 1974, MS, 1976; PhD, U. Ill., 1984. Cert. hearing impaired tchr., Fla. Tchr. deaf students Cross Bayou Elem. Sch., Pinellas Park, Fla., 1975-76, Lakeland (Fla.) Sr. High Sch., 1976-79, Oscar Pope Elem. Sch., Eaton Park, Fla., 1979-80; grad. asst. U. Ill., Champaign, 1981-83; asst. prof. Ohio State U., Columbus, 1984-89, assoc. prof. spl. edn., 1989-95, prof. spl. edn., 1995—. Author: Language and Deafness, 1984, 2d edit., 1994, Education and Deafness, 1990, Toward a Psychology of Deafness, 1993; contbr. articles to profl. jours. Recipient Outstanding Svc. award Ohio Assn. of the Deaf, 1988; Stephen Quigley fellow, 1980-84. Mem. AAUP, Alexander Graham Bell Assn. for the Deaf, Conv. Am. Instrs. of Deaf, Coun. Exceptional Children, Phi Kappa Phi, Kappa Delta Pi. Office: Ohio State U 1945 N High St Columbus OH 43210-1120

PAUL, RHONDA ELIZABETH, university program director, career development counselor; d. John and Vivian (Griffin) P. BA, Mich. State U., 1977; MA, Atlanta U., 1979; postgrad., Wayne State U., 1982—. Cert. counselor, Mich.; nat. cert. career counelor; lic. profl. counselor. Counselor, student affairs dept. Spelman Coll., Atlanta, 1978-79; life/career devel. specialist Wayne State U., Detroit, 1979-81, minority devel. counselor, 1981-83; prog. dir. recruitment dept. Wayne State Sch. of Medicine, Detroit, 1983—; cons./proprietor RP Career Assocs., Detroit, 1990—. Recipient Award of Pride, Mich. State U., Lansing, 1977, Spl. Recognition award Nat. Bd. for Cert. Counselors, 1993. Mem. NAACP, Am. Counseling Assn., Mich. Counseling Assn., Assn. Multicultural Counseling and Devel. (nat. stds. and cert. com.), Nat. Career Devel. Assn., Nat. Coalition of 100 Black Women (bd. dirs.), Alpha Kappa Alpha. Home: 4068 Cortland St Detroit MI 48204-1506 Office: Wayne State U H N J 1-East Detroit MI 48202

PAULEY, JIM G., state legislator; b. Ashland, Mo., June 16, 1932; m. Adele Windsor; three children. Student, U. Mo. Mem. Mo. State Ho. of Reps. Dist. 24, 1983—. Mem. Masons. Home: PO Box 138 500 Tandy St Ashland MO 65010-9525*

PAULS, JANICE L., state legislator; m. Ron Pauls. Rep. dist. 102 State of Kans. Democrat. Home: 1634 N Baker St Hutchinson KS 67501-5621 Office: Kans Ho of Reps State Capitol Topeka KS 66612*

PAULSEN, ELIZABETH ROBERTSON, public relations manager; b. Joplin, Mo., July 29, 1954; d. Henry W. and Elizabeth (Pate) Robertson; m. James R. Paulsen, June 27, 1981 (div. Jan. 1988); children: John Wilson, Hannah Elizabeth. AA, Sullins Coll., 1974; BJ, U. Mo., 1976. Staff writer Am. Acad. Family Physicians, Kansas City, Mo., 1976-78, pub. rels. mgr., 1978-83, pub. rels. dept. mgr., 1988—; cons. in field. Active numerous community based coms. Jr. League Kansas City, 1984-90. Mem. Pub. Rels. Soc. Am. (publicity com. 1991, accreditation chair 1993-94, v.p. membership 1994-95, pres.-elect 1996), Phi Beta Kappa. Republican. Presbyterian. Office: Am Acad Family Physicians 8880 Ward Pky Kansas City MO 64114-2756

PAULSEN, ERIK, state legislator; b. Bakersfield, Calif., May 14, 1965; s. Gerald and Janet (Lindfors) P.; m. Kelly Spowls, 1989; 1 child, Cassandra. BA, Olaf Coll., Norfield, Minn., 1987. Mktg. mgr. CVN Co., 1987-89; field dir. U.S. Sen. Rudy Baschwitz, 1989-90; legis. asst. U.S. Congressman Jim Ramstad, 1991-92, dist. dir., 1994; Minn. state rep. Dist. 42B, 1995—. Mem. C. of C. Address: 9158 E Staring Ln Eden Prairie MN 55347

PAULSON, SUZANNE MORROW, English educator; b. Elgin, Ill., Apr. 19, 1949; d. Forrest Louis and Louise Gayle (Ladwig) Morrow; m. James Mitchell Paulson, Aug. 20, 1969; children: Mark Forrest Paulson, Craig Alan Paulson. MA, U. Minn., 1978, PhD, 1984. Tchg. assoc. U. Minn., Mpls., 1977-84; lectr., dir. writing lab. Calif. State U., Fresno, 1987-88; assoc. prof. Minot (N.D.) State U., 1988—; vis. asst. prof. U. St. Thomas, St. Paul, Minn., 1984-85, U. Minn., Morris, 1985-86, U. Ill., Urbana, 1986-87. Author: (books) Flannery O'Connor, 1988, William Trevor, 1993; contbg. author: Flannery O'Connor in the Eighties, 1994, Carson McCullers, 1995. Bush Found. grantee, 1989, NEH grantee, Cornell U., 1990. Mem. Flannery O'Connor Soc., MLA, Midwest Modern Lang. Assn., Nat. Conf. of Tchrs. of English, Soc. for Study of Narrative Lit. Office: Divsn Humanities Minot State Univ Minot ND 58707

PAULU, FRANCES BROWN, international center administrator; b. Hastings, Minn., June 22, 1920; d. Thomas Andrew and Florence Ida (Tuttle) Brown; m. Burton Paulu, June 29, 1942; children: Sarah Leith Paulu Boittin, Nancy Jean Paulu Hyde, Thomas Scott. BA magna cum laude, U. Minn., 1940. Case worker Family Welfare Assn. Mpls., 1943-45; interviewer Community Health and Welfare Council, Mpls., 1963; sch. social worker Project Head Start, Mpls., 1966; program dir. Minn. Internat. Ctr., Mpls., 1970-72, exec. dir., 1972-89; mem. tourism adv. com. City of Mpls., 1976-83; mem. adv. council Minn. World Trade Ctr., 1984-86. Pres. UN Rally, 1970-72; chmn. Mpls. Charter Commn., 1972-74; bd. dirs. Urban Coalition of Mpls., 1967-70; dir. Minn. World Trade Week, 1977-81; participant Intercultural Communication Project, Japan, 1974; mem. mgmt. team Minn. Awareness Project, 1982-89—; dir. Elder Learning, 1995—. DeWitt Jennings Payne scholar, 1939-40; Sch. Social Work fellow U. Minn., 1942-44; recipient Nat. People to People Disting. Membership award, 1987, Schmoker award YMCA Internat. Program Svcs., 1991. Mem. Nat. Council for Internat. Visitors (officer and/or exec. com. mem. 1975-81, leader fact-finding team North Africa, Middle East, India 1978, conf. chair 1989), Nat. Assn. for Fgn. Student Affairs, People to People Internat., LWV (pres. Mpls. 1967-69), UN Assn. Minn. (adv. coun. 1979-92, sec. 1994-96), Mpls.-St. Paul Com. on Fgn. Rels., Nat. Coun. World Affairs Orgns. (participant Taipei-Manila Study Tour 1988), Alliance FranÇaise (dir. 1991-94), U. Minn. Women's Club (pres. 1992-94), Phi Beta Kappa, Alpha Omicron Pi, Lambda Alpha Psi. Home: 5005 Wentworth Ave Minneapolis MN 55419-1302

PAULY, SANFORD DICKSON, sales professional; b. Cin., July 9, 1963; s. Charles Pauly and Jean (Schmidlapp) Clapson; m. Bridgitt Ann Cassidy, June 14, 1996. AA, U. Cin., 1989; BSBA in Econs., Xavier U., 1991. Sales assoc. The Limited, Cin., 1989-90; sales rep. Winn Art Group, Cin., 1990-92, Scott Bus. Sys., Cin., 1992-93; indsl. sales engr. Vulcan Oil & Chem. Products, Cin., 1993-94, distbr. sales mgr., 1994—. Bd. mem. Summer Fair Inc., Cin., 1992—, Mt. Lookout Civic Club, Cin., 1995—. Mem. Soc. Tribologist & Lubrication Engrs., Automation News Network. Republican. Home: 2713 Erie Ave #36 Cincinnati OH 45208 Office: Vulcan Oil & Chem Products 5353 Spring Grove Ave Cincinnati OH 45217

PAVALON, EUGENE IRVING, lawyer; b. Chgo., Jan. 5, 1933; m. Lois M. Frenzel, Jan. 15, 1961; children: Betsy, Bruce, Lynn. BSL, Northwestern U., 1954, JD, 1956. Bar: Ill. 1956. Sr. ptnr. Pavalon & Gifford, Chgo., 1970—; mem. com. on discovery rules Ill. Supreme Ct., 1981—; lectr., mem. faculty various law schs.; bd. dirs. ATLA Mut. Ins. Co. Former mem. state bd. dirs. Ind. Voters Ill; bd. overseers Inst. Civil Justice, Rand Corp., 1993—; mem. vis. com. Northwestern U. Law Sch., 1990-96. Capt., USAF, 1956-59. Fellow Am. Coll. Trial Lawyers, Internat. Soc. Barristers, Internat. Acad. Trial Lawyers, Roscoe Pound Found. (life fellow, pres. 1988-90); mem. ABA, Chgo. Bar Assn. (bd. mgrs. 1978-79), Ill. Bar Assn., Ill. Trial Lawyers Assn. (pres. 1980-81), Trial Lawyers for Pub. Justice (founding mem., v.p. 1991-92, pres.-elect 1992-93, pres. 1993-94), Assn. Trial Lawyers Am. (parlimentarian 1983-84, sec. 1984-85, v.p. 1985-86, pres. elect 1986-87, pres. 1987-88), Am. Bd. of Profl. Liability Attys. (diplomate), Chgo. Athletic Assn., Standard Club. Author: Human Rights and Health Care Law, 1980, Your Medical Rights, 1990; contbr. articles to profl. jours., chpts. in books. Home: 1540 N Lake Shore Dr Chicago IL 60610-1623 Office: Pavalon & Gifford 2 N La Salle St Chicago IL 60602-3702

PAVELKA, ELAINE BLANCHE, mathematics educator; b. Chgo.; d. Frank Joseph and Mildred Bohumila (Seidl) P.; B.A., M.S., Northwestern U.; Ph.D., U. Ill. With Northwestern U. Aerial Measurements Lab., Evanston, Ill.; tchr. Leyden Community High Sch., Franklin Park, Ill.; prof. math. Morton Coll., Cicero, Ill.; invited speaker 3d Internat. Congress Math. Edn., Karlsruhe, Germany, 1976. Recipient sci. talent award Westinghouse Elec. Co. Mem. Am. Edn. Research Assn., Am. Math. Assn. 2-Year Colls., Am. Math. Soc., Assn. Women in Math., Can. Soc. History and Philosophy of Math., Ill. Council Tchr. of Math., Ill. Math. Assn. Community Colls., Math. Assn. Am., Math. Action Group, Ga. Center Study and Teaching and Learning Math., Nat. Council Tchrs. of Math., Sch. Sci. and Math. Assn., Soc. Indsl. and Applied Math., Northwestern U. Alumni Assn., U. Ill. Alumni Assn., Am. Mensa Ltd., Intertel, Sigma Delta Epsilon, Pi Mu Epsilon. Home: PO Box 7312 Westchester IL 60154-7312

PAVLOVICH, DONALD, technical writer; b. Euclid, Ohio, Mar. 25, 1957; s. Paul George and Carroll Rose (McDonald) P. BS, Cleve. State Univ., 1981. Tech. writer, instr. Cleve. (Ohio) Inst. Electronics, 1982-85; instr. Lorain (Ohio) County Community Coll., 1985-86; tech. writer Picker Internat.-Gov. systems, Highland Heights, Ohio, 1986-87; sr. tech. writer Picker Internat.-MRI, Highland Heights, Ohio, 1987-94; part-time regulatory specialist Picker Internat., 1994-95; part-time instr. Sawyer Coll. Bus. Author (lesson books): ROMS, PROMs, and PLAs, 1983; co-author (lesson books): Karnaugh Maps, 1984, One-Shots, Astables and Schmitt Triggers, 1983; editor: Microprocessor Course, 1985; book reviewer. Vol. Cleve. Mus. of Art, 1991. Named Jr. Tech. Student of Yr. Cleve. State Engring. Alumni Assn., 1980. Mem. IEEE (reviewer Microprocessor and Microcomputer stds. subcom., 1990—), Alpha Beta Kappa. Home: 19015 Van Aken Blvd Apt 404 Shaker Heights OH 44122

PAWLENTY, TIM, state legislator; b. Nov. 1960; m. Mary Pawlenty; 1 child. BA, U. Minn., JD. Chmn. Eagan Planning Commn., 1988-89; mem. Minn. Ho. of Reps. St. Paul, 1993—; atty. Active Eagan city coun., 1990-92. Fannie Gilbertson Coll. scholar. Republican. Office: 4117 Countryview Dr Eagan MN 55123-3948*

PAWLEY, RAY LYNN, zoological park herpetology curator; b. Midland, Mich., Nov. 7, 1935; s. Lynn Richard and Alice Marie (Skelton) P.; m. Ethel Marie Condon, Feb. 19, 1955 (div. 1974); children: Ray Allyn, Shanna Sue, Cynthia Ann, Dawn Marie, Brandon Earl, Dareen Joy. Student in zoo adminstrn., Mich. State U., 1954-57. Asst. curator/lectr. Black Hills Reptile Gardens, Rapid City, S.D., summers 1952-53; owner, adminstr. Reptile Exhibit, St. Ignace, Mich., 1957-59; animal coord. Marlin Perkin's Wild Kingdom (Don Meier Prodns.), Chgo., 1961-62; zoologist Lincoln Park Zool. Gardens, Chgo., 1961-64; curator Brookfield (Ill.) Zoo, 1964—; assoc. dept. zoology Field Mus. Natural History, Chgo.; internat. zoo and conservation cons., Russia, Latvia, Mex., Kenya, China, Ecuador, Czechoslovakia; past instr. herpetology Field Mus., Coll. of DuPage, Triton Coll.; info. resource for fed. and state wildlife agys.; lectr., cons. in field. Contbr. oer 50 articles to profl. jours. and popular mags.; co-creator money bench Chgo. Children's Mus. Immediate past v.p. Ill. Endangered Species Protection Bd., Springfield; liaison Endangered Species Tech. Adv. Com., Springfield. Mem. Am. Zoo Assn. (3d Outstanding Svc. awards), Internat. Herpetological Alliance (officer), Chgo. Acad. Scis. (life), Chgo. Herpetological Soc. (life, cons.), Mensa. Home: PO Box 218 Hinsdale IL 60522-0218 Office: Chicago Zool Park Brookfield IL 60513

PAWLICKI, ELEANOR GENEVIEVE, information specialist; b. Ashtabula, Ohio, July 29, 1929; d. Olli and Hilma Maria Immonen; m. Clarence Francis Pawlicki, Feb. 23, 1957; 1 child, Dana Clarence. BS, Kent State U., 1970, MEd, 1975, MLS, 1988; student, U. Bus. and Econs., Beijing, China. Cert. tchr. Ohio. Tutor K-12 Trumbull Bd. Edn., Warren, Ohio, 1965-70; substitute tchr. K-8 Summit County Bd. Edn., Hudson, Ohio, 1979-81; fgn. lang. tchr. Kent (Ohio) State U., 1984-88; fin. com. Hudson Local Schs., 1979—. Steering com. Summit County, 1994—, poll worker, 1994. Episcopalian. Home: PO Box 312 Hudson OH 44236

PAWLIK, JAMES DAVID, lawyer, historian; b. Cleve., May 26, 1958; s. Eugene Joseph and Eleanor Therese Marie (Gorzelanczyk) P. BA cum laude, Ohio State U., 1980, MA, 1991; JD cum laude, Harvard U., 1983. Bar: Calif. 1984, U.S. Ct. Appeals (9th cir.), 1985, U.S. Dist. Ct. (no. dist.) Calif. 1984, U.S. Dist. Ct. (ctrl. and ea dists.), Calif. 1986, Ohio 1980. Intern Dept. Def., Washington, 1980; assoc. Chandler, Wood, Harrington & Maffly, San Francisco, 1983-87, ptnr., 1988-89; teaching assoc. Ohio State U., 1990-91; pvt. practice Law Offices of James D. Pawlik, Cleve., 1991-93; ind. contractor Gallagher, Sharp, Fulton & Norman, Cleve., Ohio, 1992-93; jud. law clk. to Hon. Robert J. Krupansky U.S. Ct. Appeals (6th cir.), Cleve., 1993—; instr. dept. history Cuyahoga C.C., Parma, Ohio, 1993—; instr. dept. polit. sci. Lourdes Coll., Sylvania, Ohio, 1993. Mem. staff Harvard Internat. Law Jour., 1981-83. Campaign mgr. for city coun. candidate, Westerville, Ohio, 1977. William Green Meml. scholar 1979, Kosciuszko scholar 1989-91; Ohio State U. fellow, 1989-90. Mem. ABA, State Bar Ohio, Cleve. Bar Assn., Mensa, Ohio U. Alumni Assn., Harvard Alumni Assn., Phi Beta Kappa, Phi Kappa Phi, Phi Alpha Theta.

PAWLITSCHEK, DONALD PAUL, business consultant; b. Heron Lake, Minn., Aug. 5, 1941; s. Paul P. and Marion (Erickson) P.; student Southwest Tech. Inst., 1960, Mankato State Coll., 1965-66; m. Korrine Kunerth, Oct. 9, 1965; children: Andrew, Jennifer, Heidi, Sarah, Benjamin. Farmer, Heron Lake, 1967-73; pres. Dundee Steel Inc., 1973-75, Alpha Prime Inc., Heron Lake, 1975-80, Prime Ventures, Inc., 1980—; dir. Am. Search and Referral Co. Served with AUS, 1960. Mem. Nat. Assn. Fin. Cons., Am. Entrepreneurs Assn., Am. Legion. Conservative. Roman Catholic. Club: Elks. Patentee livestock flooring. Home and Office: Prime Ventures Inc RR 1 Box 144A Lake Crystal MN 56055-9700

PAXTON, JOAN SUSAN, vocalist; b. Lake Forest, Ill., Aug. 11, 1963; d. Ervin F. and Alice Martha Wojciechowski. BA, Columbia Coll., 1986; vocal/choral masterclass, Margaret Hillis. owner Paxton Prodns., Grayslake, Ill., 1982—. Vocal performances include 1991 Norge Winter Ski Festival, 1990 U.S. Summer Nat. Ski Jumping, Hist. Franklin Hotel & Casino, Village Cay, Caribbean, Aladdin hotel, Las Vegas, Nev., Caesar's Palace hotel, Las Vegas, Marriott-Linconshire-Park Ave. hotel, Exceptions, USO shows; performer films including: Ground Hog Day, Last Day in Chicago; (commls.) Piggly Wiggly, Oscar Mayer, Sea World, KDSR; (indsl. prodns.) President's Shoot McDonalds; (TV) Inside the NFL, Legs; spokesperson Microsoft, Shiva, Jessica McClintock, Elizabeth Arden, Nekoosa. Recipient Internat. TV award for Best Health Care Video, 1986, 87, Chgo. Emmy award for Best Children's Spl., 1987. Mem. AFTRA, NARAS (Chgo. bd. govs. 1994-98, co-chair spl. events com., edn. com.), NATAS. Office: Paxton Prodns PO Box 486 Grayslake IL 60030-0486

PAYNE, CRAIG WILLIAM, information scientist, educator; b. Aurora, Ill., Aug. 23, 1943; s. Richard Allan P. and Jeanne Marie (Blake) Van Bebber; m. Deborah Kay Watson, Sept. 28, 1969; children: Christine Laree, Clayton Allen. AA, Waubonsee C.C., 1973; BA, Aurora Coll., 1976; MS, Aurora U., 1989. Cert. Inventory and Prodn. Mgr. Test equipment tech. AT&T Montgomery (Ill.) Works, 1965-89; mem. tech. staff AT&T Network Systems, Lisle, Ill., 1989-96, Lucent Techs., Inc., Lisle, 1996—; v.p. I.B.E.W. Local, 1942, Montgomery, 1977-80, chmn. exec. bd., 1983-86; ownerPayne Builders, Aurora, 1986—; part-time faculty Aurora U., 1991-95. Dep. registrar Aurora Election Commn., 1984-89. With USMC, 1962-65. Mem. IEEE, Exptl. Aviation Assn. (v.p. 1983-86), Aurora Sportsmens Club. Home: 2311 Independence Dr Aurora IL 60506-3269 Office: Lucent Techs Inc 2443 Warrenville Rd Lisle IL 60532-1098

PAYNE, DAVID MICHAEL, public policy group executive; b. Kansas City, Mo., Sept. 25, 1952; s. William Richard and Patricia Ruth (Folley) P.; m. Katherine Ann Marland, Aug. 10, 1974; children: Paul, Daniel, Janelle, Jonathan. BS in Edn., U. Kans., 1975, MS in Edn., 1984. Tchr. Maranatha Acad., Kansas City, Kans., 1975-77, prin., 1977-80; adminstr. Maranatha Acad., Shawnee, Kans., 1980-92; exec. dir. Kans. Family Rsch. Inst., Wichita, 1992—; dist. rep. Assn. Christian Schs. Internat., Colorado Springs, Colo., 1978-80; bd. dirs. Trinity Acad., Wichita, 1994—, Assn. State Policy Couns., 1995—. Editor, columnist Kansas Citizen, 1992—. Recipient Dove award Wellspring Found., Prairie Village, Kans., 1990. Republican. Office: Kans Family Rsch Inst Ste 160 8080 E Central Wichita KS 67226

PAYNE, FLORA FERN, retired social service administrator; b. Carrollton, Mo., Sept. 25, 1932; d. George Earnest and Bernadine Alice (Schaefer) Chrisman; m. H.D. Matticks, Oct. 20, 1950 (div. Oct. 1959); children: Dennis Don, Kathi D.; m. S.L. Freeman, Nov. 25, 1960 (div. Jan. 1973); 1 child, Gary Mark; m. Vernon Ray Payne, Mar. 18, 1988. Student, S.E. C.C., Burlington, Iowa, 1976-77; cert. stenographer, Corr. Sch., Chgo., 1960-61. Social svc. designee Mo. League Nursing, 1991. Sec. to v.p. Moore Co., Marceline, Mo., 1973-75; steno to trainmaster A.T. & S.F. Rlwy. Co., Fort Madison, Iowa, 1975-88; with social svc. Brookfield (Mo.) Nursing Ctr., 1990-95; candidate for Linn County Pub. Adminstr., 1996. Mem. NAFE, Mo. Orgn. Social Svcs. Republican. Home: 205 W 6th St Bucklin MO 64631-9097

PAYNE, HOMER LEMUEL, retired religious institution administrator; b. Wayzata, Minn., Nov. 27, 1910; s. Wilbur Newton and Charlotte (Beebe) P.; m. Margaret Monson, Aug. 9, 1940; children: Laurel Janet Payne Gutmann, David Douglas, Pierre Daniel. BS, Wheaton (Ill.) Coll., 1933; ThM, Dallas Theol. Sem., 1947, ThD, 1948; cert. French lit., U. Lausanne (Switzerland), 1951. Cert. chaplaincy. Asst. to dir. Inst. Emmaüs, Lausanne, 1950-63; pres. France Mission, Paris, 1960-63, 75-83; dir. Belgian Gospel Mission, Brussels, 1963-69; prof. Inst. Biblique Béthel, Sherbrook, Que., Can., 1969-70; dir. program of study Operation Mobilization, Paris, 1970-84; dir. Inst. Biblique Béthel, Sherbrooke, 1984-90; cons. l'Inst. Biblique de Genève, Switzerland, 1991—. Editor: (songbook) Worldwide Praise, 1982; co-author: (with C.A. Ryrie, treatise) Mille Ans de Paix, 1982; translator, editor: (biography) Tison Ardente des Flandrës, 1973; editor documentary; contbr. articles to Action Missionaire (Paris). Grad. sponsor Inter-Varsity Fellowship, Lausanne, 1953-63; coord.-liaison Billy Graham Crusades, Lausanne, 1960, Brussels, 1975, Montreal, Can., 1990; com. mem. Internat. Fellowship Evang. Students, Switzerland, 1950-53; mem. Nat. Taxpayers' Union, Pres.'s Senatorial Adv. Com. Capt. Ordnance Chaplain, U.S. Army, 1943-45, ETO. Mem. VFW, DAV, Greater Minn. Assn. Evangs., Conservative Caucus, Christian Coalition Ctr. for Am. Values, Nat. Rep. Senatorial Com., Lincoln Inst., Paralyzed Vets. Am., Am. Indian Relief Coun., Nat. Right to Life, Heritage Found., USS Constitution Mus., Am. Air Mus. (Britain). Republican. Plymouth Brethren. Home: Maranatha Pl 5415 69th Ave N Brooklyn Center MN 55429

PAYNE, HOWARD JAMES, insurance company executive; b. Des Moines, Iowa, Oct. 22, 1940; s. James W. and Wilma F. (Kever) P.; m. Mary J. Kellam, June 8, 1963; children: Scott D., Steven M. MBA, U. Iowa, 1986. CPCU; assoc. in underwriting, assoc. in mgmt. Underwiter Allied Ins. Co., Des Moines, 1963-70; br. underwriting mgr. Allied Ins. Co., Phoenix, 1973-75; asst. br. mgr. Allied Ins. Co., Santa Rosa, Calif., 1975-77; casualty underwriting mgr. Am. States Ins. Co., Indpls., 1970-73; asst. v.p. underwriting Lumberman's Mut. Ins. Co., Mansfield, Ohio, 1977-80; asst. v.p., underwriting mgr. Hastings (Mich.) Mutual Ins. Co., 1980-82; v.p. underwriting John Deere Ins. Co., Moline, Ill., 1982-86, v.p., regional mgr., 1986-90; v.p. credit ins. mgr. John Deere Ins. Co, Des Moines, 1990-93; v.p., spl. program mgr. John Deere Transp., Brookfield, Wis., 1993—; ins. instr. Am. States Ins. Co., Indpls., 1971-73, CPCU chpt., Phoenix, 1973-75; ins. instr. and adviser C.C. Mansfield, Ohio, 1978-80; pres. Am. States Credit Union, Indpls., 1973. Mem. CPCU Soc., West Des Moines C. of C. Republican. Home: 1641A S Coachlight Dr New Berlin WI 53151 Office: John Deere Transp 350 N Sunny Slope Rd Brookfield WI 53005-4846

PAYNE, JOHN B(URTON), lawyer; b. Chgo., Dec. 26, 1944; s. John Burton and Shirley Marcella P.; m. Roberta Lelis Mau; children: Andrew, Marcella, Piper, Pauli. BS, Grand Valley State U., 1976; JD, Detroit Coll. of Law, 1983; LLM in Taxation, Wayne State U., 1988. Bar: Mich. 1983, Pa. 1985, U.S. Tax Ct. 1986, U.S. Ct. Appeals (6th cir.) 1986, U.S. Supreme Ct. 1989. Pvt. practice Dearborn, Mich., 1983—; lectr. on estate planning. Contbr. articles to legal jours. Bd. dirs., chair, Fairlane Behavioral Svcs., Dearborn Pub. Schs. Edn. Mem. ABA, State Bar Mich. (chair law day com.), Mich. Bar Assn., Pa. Bar Assn. Home: 411 Ft Dearborn St Dearborn MI 48124-1032 Office: 22374 Garrison St Dearborn MI 48124-2228

PAYNTER, MARY, English literature educator; b. Madison, Wis., May 23, 1931; d. Arthur John and Jennie Mary (O'Neill) P. BA, Rosary Coll., 1952; MA, U. Wis., 1953, PhD, 1965. Instr. Rosary Coll., River Forest, Ill., 1955-61, assoc. prof., 1964-66, acad. dean, 1965-70; prof. Edgewood Coll., Madison, Wis., 1970-74, 89—; gen. councillor Sinsinawa (Wis.) Dominican Sisters, 1973-82; prof. Rosary Coll., River Forest, 1982-89. Local organizer United Way, Madison, 1992-93; mem. local bd. dirs. Urban League. Fellow Sorbonne, U. Paris, 1953-54. Mem. MLA, Amnesty Internat., Nat. Coun. Tchrs. English, Sinsinawa Dominican Sisters. Roman Catholic. Home: 2011 Jefferson St Madison WI 53711-2115 Office: Edgewood Coll 855 Woodrow St Madison WI 53711-1958

PAYUK, EDWARD WILLIAM, elementary education educator; b. St. Louis, July 19, 1948; s. Stanley Eli and Lillian (Bluestein) P.; m. Pamela Karen Miller, Sept. 5, 1970 (div. Oct. 1986); children: Stacy Lynne, Lori Michelle; m. Judith Ann Cohen, Dec. 4, 1986; stepchildren: Jeffrey Alan Kieffer, Kimberly Beth Kieffer. AA, Meramec C.C., St. Louis, 1969; BS, U. Mo., St. Louis, 1971; MA, Webster U., 1973, postgrad., 1976. Educator Ferguson (Mo.) Florissant Sch. Dist., 1971—; tutor, St. Louis, 1984-91; tchr. mentor Ferguson-Florissant Sch. Dist., St. Louis, 1986—, mem. sci. Cadre, 1988—. Contbr. articles to profl. jours. Sci. literacy com. St. Louis Sci. Acad., 1991—; rep. Tchrs., Industry & Environment Conf., Jefferson City, Mo., 1995. With U.S. Army, 1969-70. Mem. NEA, Mo. Edn. Assn., Ferguson-Florissant Edn. Assn. Jewish. Home: 13660 Amiot Dr Saint Louis MO 63146-3608 Office: Ferguson-Florissant Sch Dist 1005 Waterford Dr Florissant MO 63033-3649

PAZIRANDEH, MAHMOOD, rheumatologist, consultant; b. Hamadan, Iran, Jan. 1, 1932; came to U.S., 1966; naturalized U.S. Citizen, 1977; s. Rahim and Zahra (Shoushtar) P.; m. Parvin Danesh, Apr. 19, 1961; children: Bruce, Justin, Navid. MD, U. Tehran, 1958; postgrad., Eng., 1959-64, Pitts. U., 1967-68. Diplomate Am. Bd. Internal Medicine and Rheumatology. Asst. prof. Tehran U., Iran, 1964-67; clin. assoc. Cleve. Clinic Found., 1969-70; clin. instr. Case Western Res. U., Cleve., 1970-72, sr. clin. instr., 1972-78, clin. asst. prof., 1979-93, clin. assoc. prof., 1993—; dir. med. edn. Lake Hosp., Cleve., 1984-96, pres. med. staff, 1990-93; mem. CME com. Case Western Res. U. Sch. Medicine, 1994-96; dir. med. edn. Euclid Hosp., Cleve., 1971-73, dir. quality assurance, 1989-93. Contbr. articles to profl. jours. Speaker pub. edn. radio, TV and seminars, Cleve., 1984—; chmn. pub. forums Arthritis Found., Cleve., 1985—, trustee, 1986-96, chmn. pub. edn. com., 1987—. Recipient recognition svc. award Arthritis Found., 1976, Robert Stecher Vol. award, 1988, Nat. Vols. Svc. citation, 1989; Eng. and Iranian Govt. scholar, 1959-63. Fellow ACP, Am. Coll. Rheumatology; mem. Am. Soc. Internal Medicine, Ohio State Med. Assn. (del. 1989-96), Lake County Med. Soc. (pres. 1988—), Cleve. Rheumatism Soc. (pres. 1974), N.Y. Acad. Scis. Republican. Home: 124 Pheasant Ln Hunting Valley OH 44022-4043 Office: Case Western Res U 36100 Euclid Ave Willoughby OH 44094-4456

PEACOCK, INEZ W., physical therapist; b. Kindersley, Sask., Can., Oct. 18, 1919; came to U.S., 1925; d. Milton and Muriel Inez (Carroll) Schroeder; m. Thomas Arthur Peacock, Sept. 11, 1942 (dec. June 1948); 1 child, Christine Carroll Peacock Powers. BS in Phys. Edn., Wash. State U., 1942; postgrad., U. Wash., 1943, secondary teaching cert., 1944; grad. cert. phys. therapy, Harvard U., 1944. Physical therapist Detroit Curative Workshop, 1945-46, Detroit Vis. Nurse Assn., 1946-48, Swedish Hosp., Seattle, Wash., 1949, Children's Orthopaedic Hosp., 1950-51, Dearborn Pub. Schs., 1952-82; Huntington's Disease phys. therapist, cons., 1982—. Contbr. articles to profl. jours. Founder Huntingtons Disease Camp, 1988, Huntingtons Disease Fun Olympics, 1995. Mem. Am. Phys. Therapy Assn. (life, past del., active pediatrics sect., licensure and regulation sect., geratrics sect., and neurology sect., Special Svc. award sect. on licensure and regulation 1978, Lucy Blair Svc. award 1978), Mich. chpt. Am. Phys. Therapy Assn. (active 1945-48, pres. 1953-55, archivist and historian 1990—, active ea. dist., Past Pres. award 1962, Outstanding Svc. award 1976), Am. Phys. Therapy Assn. Prime Timers (founder, chmn. 1987—), World Confdn. Phys. Therapy (speaker 1978, 87, 91, planner and chair program on internat. licensure and cert. Montreal 1974, chair special interest meeting 1995 Congress Washington, Appreciation award 10th Congress 1987), Huntingtons Disease Soc. Am. (cons. to S.E. Mich. chpt. 1983—, Svc. award 1987, Ruby and Joseph Horansky award for exemplary patient care 1993). Home: 1631 North Vernon Dearborn MI 48128-2508

PEAKE, CANDICE K. LOPER, data processing professional; b. Sublette, Kans., Oct. 29, 1953; d. Robert Franklin and Marion Joyce (Sooby) L.; m. Eugene E. Peake, Aug. 12, 1993. Student, McPherson (Kans.) Coll., 1971-72; lic. in cosmetology, Crums Beauty Sch., Manhattan, Kans., 1974; student, Garden City (Kans.) Community Coll., 1975-76, Diablo Valley Coll., 1988-89. ICCP cert. data processor. Owner, operator Candi's For Beautiful Hair, Garden City, 1974-78; systems project librarian Bank of Am., San Francisco, 1980, analyst, 1981, systems analyst, 1981-82, sr. systems analyst, 1982-83, cons., 1983-84, systems cons., team leader, 1984; project mgr. Wells Fargo Bank, Concord, Calif., 1984-86; systems analyst 1st Nationwide Bank, San Francisco, 1986-88; adv. systems engr. Bank Am., Concord, Calif., 1988-89; owner Candi's Visions, Independence, Mo., 1988—; sys. svcs. mgr. Continuum Co., Kansas City, Mo., 1989—. Home: 3419 S Home Ave Independence MO 64052-1239 Office: Continuum Co 2d Fl 301 W 11th St Kansas City MO 64105-1634

PEAK-HOFFMANN, CYNTHIA SUE, academic administrator; b. Brigham City, Utah, Dec. 19, 1963; d. James Matthew and Julia Jeanette (Lord) Peak; m. Izzet Rifat Guney, Feb. 14, 1986 (div. Aug. 1991); m. Mark Joseph Hoffmann, Nov. 26, 1994; 1 stepchild, Terrin Abigail. BBA, U. Tex., El Paso, 1985. Alumni/devel. coord. U. Tex., El Paso, 1986-89; asst. to gen. dir. St. Louis Ballet, 1991-92; assoc. dir. spl. gifts & projects Webster U., St. Louis, 1992-94; assoc. dir. devel. Maryville U., St. Louis, 1994—; head instr. St. Charles County YMCA, St. Peters, Mo., 1993—. Docent Bravo! Dance St. Louis, 1991—. Mem. Nat. Soc. Fund Raising Execs., Coun. for Advancement and Support of Edn. Republican. Roman Catholic. Home: 2536 Hidden Meadow Ballwin MO 63021 Office: Maryville U 13550 Conway Rd Saint Louis MO 63141

PEAL, CHRISTOPHER JOHN, educational administrator; b. Moline, Ill., Dec. 17, 1963; s. Gerald J. and Annette M. Peal. BA, Olivet Nazarene U., 1986; MA, U. Mich., 1989; PhD, Loyola U., 1996. Cert. supt., adminstr., tchr., Ill., Mich., Wis. English, lang. arts, speech, journalism tchr., newspaper advisor Plymouth-Canton High Sch., Mich., 1986-90; asst. prin. Muskegon Catholic Ctrl. Jr./High Sch., Mich., 1990-91; dean students Canton Mid. Sch., Streamwood, Ill., 1991-94; prin. North Elem. Sch., Watervliet, Mich., 1994—; ins. agt. Mich. Educators Ins. Agy., Coloma, Mich., 1995—; mem. Watervliet Sch. Improvement Team; mem. Elgin (Ill.) Sch. Dist. U-46 Mid. Sch. Task Force, 1991-94. Mem. Watervliet PTO, 1994—. Recipient Spl. Tribute award State of Mich., 1987, Gold Apple Teaching Excellence award Wayne County (Mich.) Intermediate Sch. Dist., 1987, 88, 89; dean's merit fellow U. Mich., 1987, 88, Dow Jones Newspaper Fund fellow, 1988. Mem. ASCD, Mich. Elem. and Mid. Sch. Prins. Assn., Nat. Assn. Elem. Sch. Prins., Mich. Interscholastic Press Assn. (judge 1988-90), Columbia Scholastic Press Assn. (bd. judges 1987-90, conv. speaker), Gt. Lakes Interscholastic Press Assn. (judge 1988-90), Journalism Edn. Assn. Office: North Sch 287 Baldwin Ave Watervliet MI 49098

PEARLMAN, SAMUEL SEGEL, lawyer; b. Pitts., May 28, 1942; s. Merle Maurice and Bernice Florence (Segel) P.; m. Cathy Schwartz, Aug. 16, 1964; children: Linda P. Kraner, Caren E. AB, U. Pa., 1963, LLB magna cum laude, 1966. Bar: Pa. 1966, Ohio, 1967, U.S. Ct. Appeals (3d cir.) 1967. Law clk. U.S. Dist. Ct. (Ea. dist.) Pa., 1966-67; assoc. Burke, Haber & Berick, Cleve., 1967-72, prin., 1973-86, prin. Berick, Pearlman & Mills, 1986—; lectr. law Case Western Res. U. Sch. Law, 1978-82; mem. registration com. Ohio Div. Securities, 1979-89; adv. dir. Midland Title Security, Inc. Trustee Realty ReFund Trust (NYSE). Mem. ABA, Ohio State Bar Assn., Greater Cleve. Bar Assn. (chmn. securities law sect. 1985-86), Order of Coif. Republican. Jewish. Author: Cases, Forms and Materials for Modern Real Estate Transactions, 1978, 82. Office: 1111 Superior Ave 1350 Eaton Ctr Cleveland OH 44114

PEARSALL, HARRY JAMES, dentist; b. Bay City, Mich., Apr. 12, 1916; s. Roy August and Gladys Agnes (Tierney) P.; m. Betty Almina Dahlke, Oct. 5, 1946 (dec. Nov. 1982); 1 child, Paul Roy. BS, Marquette U., 1937, DDS, 1939. Gen. practice dentistry Bay City, 1939—; cons. Delta Dental Ins., Lansing, Mich., 1975-86. Mem. Bay City chpt. Revision Com., 1965-66; bd. dirs. Downtown Bay City, 1962-73. Served to maj. U.S. Army, MC, 1940-46. Mem. ADA, Am. Coll. Dentists, Internat. Coll. Dentists, Mich. Dental Assn. (pres. 1972-73, spl. com. on life mems.), Saginaw Valley Dental Soc. (pres. 1955-56), Bay County Dental Soc. (pres. 1950-51), Am. Legion. Lodge: Elks. Home: 1820 E Worfolk Dr Apt 1 Essexville MI 48732 Office: 404 Shearer Bldg Bay City MI 48708

PEARSALL, LUCILLE J., company executive; b. Denver, Dec. 24, 1937. BFA, U. Akron, 1987. Tchr. USAF, Laon, France, 1960-62; assoc. dir. devel. Akron (Ohio) City Hosp., 1977-84; v.p. James Duncan Assoc. Inc., Akron, 1984—; ad hoc cons. Akron Blind Ctr. and Workshop, 1992—. Mem. Womens Network. Republican. Congregationalist. Office: James Duncan Assoc Inc 611 W Market St Akron OH 44303-1406

PEARSON, BARBARA LEE, social worker; b. Detroit, July 21, 1951; d. Lee and Muriel (Paddy) Gauchey; m. Arthur Reed Pearson, Oct. 14, 1972 (div. 1987); children: Christopher R., Nicholas A. BS, Oakland U., 1984; MSW, U. Mich., 1986. Cert. social worker. Psychiat. social worker Community Mental Health, Pontiac, Mich., 1986-87, Woodside Hosp., Pontiac, 1987-88, Pontiac Gen. Hosp., 1988-89, Oakland County Sheriff's Dept., 1989-90. Mem. Nat. Assn. Social Workers, Assn. Cert. Social Workers. Lutheran.

PEARSON, CRAIG ALAN, academic administrator, educator, author; b. Berwyn, Ill., Apr. 17, 1950; s. Algrid J. and Betty K. Pearson; m. Melissa Holly Sinder, July 8, 1978; 1 child, Soren. BA, Duke U., 1971; M in Sci. of Creative Intelligence, Maharishi European Rsch. U., Seelisberg, Switzerland, 1979; MA, Maharishi Internat. U., Fairfield, Iowa, 1979, U. Iowa, 1983. From dir. undergrad. composition to dean students Maharishi Internat. U., Fairfield, 1977-87, assoc. prof. profl. writing, 1983—; assoc. dir. MA program in profl. writing Maharishi Internat. U., Fairfield, 1985—, chmn. press coun., 1987-95, dean of faculty, chief acad. officer, 1995—; trustee Radio Sta. KHOE, Fairfield, 1991—. Recipient Enlightened Educator award Maharishi Internat. U., 1990. Home and Office: 1600 Badgett Dr #5 Fairfield IA 52556

PEARSON, DAVID J., electronic design manager; b. Detroit, Nov. 19, 1954. B, Lawrence Tech. Sch., 1994. Elec. engr. Ford Motor Co., Dearborn, Mich., 1977-85, Volkswagon of Am., Troy, Mich., 1985-86; elec. design mgr. Electro-Wire, Troy, Mich., 1986—. Patentee in field.

PEARSON, LOUIS W., architect; b. Hot Springs, S.D., May 28, 1935; s. William Ernst and Anna Christine (Goos) P. BFA, U. N.Mex., 1959. Registered profl. arch., Colo., S.D. Designer Ewing & Forrette, Rapid City, S.D., 1959-62, Flahart, Dittman & Hengel, Rapid City, 1962-67; job capt. Rysdale Assocs., Phoenix, 1967-68, Carlisle Guy & Assocs., Colorado Springs, Colo., 1968-78; assoc. Hengel Assocs. P.C., Rapid City, 1982-95; design cons. Divine Shepherd Luth. Ch., Black Hawk, S.D., 1994—. Mem. Am. Alpine Club (life mem.), Colo. Mountain Club (life mem.), Parks and Monuments Assn. (life mem.), Cold Spring Hist. Soc. (life mem.), Nat. Cathedral Assn., Mammoth Site. Lutheran. Home: 4549 Candlewood Pl # 205 Rapid City SD 57701

PEARSON, LOUISE MARY, retired manufacturing company executive; b. Inverness, Scotland, Dec. 14, 1919 (parents Am. citizens); d. Louis Houston and Jessie M. (McKenzie) Lenox; grad. high sch.; m. Nels Kenneth Pearson, June 28, 1941; children: Lorine Pearson Walters, Karla. Dir. Wauconda Tool & Engring. Co., Inc., Algonquin, Ill., 1950-86; reporter Oak Leaflet, Crystal Lake, Ill., 1944-47, Sidelights, Wilmette, Ill., 1969-72, 79-82. Active Girl Scouts U.S.A., 1955-65. Recipient award for appreciation work with Girl Scouts U.S., 1965. Clubs: Antique Automobile of Am. (Hershey, Pa.), Vet.

Motor Car (Boston), Classic Car of Am. (Madison, N.J.), Hoseless Carriage Club. Home: 125 Dole Ave Crystal Lake IL 60014-5837

PEARSON, NELS KENNETH, retired manufacturing executive; b. Algonquin, Ill., May 2, 1918; s. Nels Pehr and Anna (Fyre) P.; grad. high sch.; m. Louise Mary Houston Lenox, June 28, 1941; children—Lorine Marie Pearson Walters, Karla Jean. Assembler, Oak Mfg. Co., Crystal Lake, Ill., 1936-38, machine operator, assembly line foreman, 1938-43, apprentice tool and die maker, 1946-50; co-founder, pres. Wauconda Tool & Engring. Co., Inc., Algonquin, 1950-86; owner, founder Kar-Lor Enterprises, 1987—; co-founder, treas. Kenmode Tool & Engring. Co., Inc., Algonquin, 1960-72. Mem. McHenry County Edn. and Tng. Com., 1961-86, treas., 1961-86. With AUS, 1943-46. Mem. Am. Soc. Tool and Mfg. Engrs., Am. Legion. Clubs: Antique Auto, Classic Car, Vet. Motor Car, Horseless Carriage. Lodge: Moose. Home: 125 Dole Ave Crystal Lake IL 60014-5837 Office: Pyott Rd Crystal Lake IL 60014

PEARSON, NORMAN, urban and regional planner, administrator, academic and planning consultant, writer; b. Stanley, County Durham, Eng., Oct. 24, 1928; arrived in Can., 1954; s. Joseph and Mary (Pearson) P.; m. Gerda Maria Josefine Riedl, July 25, 1972. BA in Fine Arts with honors in Town and Country Planning, U. Durham (Eng.), 1951; PhD in Land Economy and Ecol. Planning, Internat. Inst. Advanced Studies, 1979; MBA, Pacific Western U., Colo., 1980, DBA, 1982; PhD In Mgmt., Calif. U. for Advanced Studies, 1986. Cons. Stanley Urban Dist. Coun., U.K., 1946-47; planning asst. Accrington Town Plan and Bedford County Planning Survey, U. Durham Planning Team, U.K., 1947-49, Allen and Mattocks, cons. planners and landscape designers, Newcastle upon Tyne, U.K., 1949-51; adminstrv. asst. Scottish Div., Nat. Coal Bd., Edinburgh, Scotland, 1951-52; planning asst. London County Coun., Westminster, U.K., 1953-54; planner Ctrl. Mortgage and Housing Corp., Ottawa, Ont., Can., 1954-55; planning analyst City of Toronto (Ont.) Planning Bd., 1955-56; dir. planning Hamilton Wentworth Planning Area Bd., Hamilton, Ont., 1956-59, Burlington (Ont.) and Suburban Area Planning Bd., Can., 1959-62; commr. planning City of Burlington, Ont., 1959-62; pres. Tanfield Enterprises Ltd., London, Ont., Can., 1962—, Norman Pearson & Assocs. Ltd., London, Ont., Can., 1962—, Internat. Planning Mgmt. Cons., London, Ont., Can., 1962—, Leahy, Pearson, Toll & Assocs. Ltd., London, Ont., Can., 1993-95; cons. in urban, rural and regional planning, 1962—; life mem. U.S. Com. for Monetary Research and Edn., 1976—; spl. lectr. in planning McMaster U., Hamilton, 1956-64, Waterloo (Ont.) Luth. U., 1961-63; asst. prof. geography and planning U. Waterloo (Ont.), 1963-67; assoc. prof. geography U. Guelph (Ont.), 1967-72, chmn., dir. Ctr. for Resource Devel.; prof. polit. sci. U. Western Ont., London, 1972-78; chmn. bd. dirs. Alma Coll., St. Thomas, Ont., 1990—; adj. prof. of ecological planning and land econs. Internat. Inst. for Advanced Studies, Clayton, Mo., 1980-89; core faculty Doctoral Program in Adminstrn/Mgmt. Walden U., Mpls., 1986—, chair adminstrn.-mgmt., 1989—; mem. acad. coun. Walden U., 1992—; mem. bd. regents Calif. U. for Advanced Studies, Petaluma, 1987-94; mem. Social Scis., Econ. and Legal Aspects Com. of Rsch. Adv. Bd. Internat. Joint Commn., 1972-76; cons. to City of Waterloo, 1973-76, Province of Ont., 1969-70; advisor to Georgian Bay Regional Devel. Coun., 1968-72; real estate appraiser, province of Ont., 1976—; pres., chmn. bd. govs. Pacific Western U., Canada, 1983-84. Author: Franchise & Partnership: A New Concept of Urban Development, 1995, Pipelines & Farming, 1995, Resources Development Policies in Canada, 1995, Planning for Eastern Georgian Bay, 1996; (with others) An Inventory of Joint Programmes and Agreements Affecting Canada's Renewable Resources, 1964, An Emerald Light, 1994, Light Beyond the Craft in Canada, 1994; editor, co-author: Regional and Resource Planning in Canda, 1963, rev. edit., 1970; editor (with others): The Pollution Reader, 1968; contbr. numerous articles on town planning to profl. jours., chpts. to books. Pres. Unitarian Ch. of Hamilton, 1960-61. With RAF, 1951-53, RAFVR, 1953-68. Decorated knight of grace Sovereign Order St. John of Jerusalem, 1979, knight Order St. Lazarus of Jerusalem, 1991, Internat. Order of Merit, 1991, Order Internat. Fellowship, 1995. Fellow Royal Town Planning Inst. (Bronze medal 1957), Royal Econ. Soc., Lambda Alpha Internat.; mem. Am. Inst. Planners, Can. Inst. Planners, Can. Polit. Sci. Assn., Internat. Soc. City and Regional Planners, Internat. Assn. Engrs. and Drs. Indsl. pplied Scis., Empire Club, Univ. Club (London), Baconian Club. Office: PO Box 5362, Station A, London, ON Canada N6A 4L6

PEARSON, PAUL GUY, academic administrator emeritus; b. Lake Worth, Fla., Dec. 5, 1926; s. Eric Conrad and Dora Wilma (Capen) P.; m. Winifred Clowe, June 30, 1951; children: Thomas, Jean, Andrew. Student, Palm Beach Jr. Coll., 1946-47; B.S. with honors, U. Fla., 1949, M.S., 1951, Ph.D., 1954; Litt.D. (hon.), Rutgers U., 1982; LL.D. (hon.), Juniata Coll., 1983; commandeu de L'ordre de merite, Grand Duchy of Luxembourg, 1988. Asst. prof. U. Tulsa, 1954-55; asst. prof. Rutgers U., New Brunswick, N.J., 1955-60; assoc. prof. Rutgers U., 1960-64, prof., 1964-81, assoc. provost, 1972-77, exec. v.p., 1977-81, acting pres., 1978; pres., prof. Miami U., Oxford, Ohio, 1981-92; bd. dirs. Union Ctrl. Life Ins., Cin., S.W. Ohio Sr. Svcs., Cin., Nat. Conservancy, Ohio. Mem. U.S. Army Sci. Bd., 1984-86. Served with USNR, 1944-46. Fellow AAAS; mem. Am. Inst. Biol. Scis. (governing bd. 1968-79, v.p. 1977, pres. 1978), Rotary Internat. (Paul Harris fellow), Phi Beta Kappa (assoc.). Home: 5110 Bonham Rd Oxford OH 45056-3606

PEARSON, WILLIAM HARDY, chemistry educator; b. Raleigh, N.C., Sept. 8, 1956; s. James R. Jr. and Elizabeth (Warwick) P.; m. Lorna I. Gall, July 24, 1978 (div. 1985); 1 child, Andrew E.; m. Victoria L. Schroeder, May 19, 1989 (div. 1994). BS in Chemistry with honors, U. N.C., 1978; PhD in Chemistry, U. Wis., 1982. NIH postdoctoral fellow Yale U., New Haven, Conn., 1982-84; asst. prof. chemistry U. Mich., Ann Arbor, 1984-90; assoc. prof., 1990-96; prof. U. Mich., Ann Arbor, 1996—; vis. prof. Emory U., Atlanta, 1991; cons. Warner-Lambert/Parke-Davis, Ann Arbor and Holland, Mich., 1986—. Editor: Advances in Heterocyclic Natural Product Synthesis, 1991—; contbr. articles to profl. jours. Mem. adv. bd. Am. Cancer Soc., Atlanta, 1990-93. Lilly grantee, 1988; recipient Camille and Henry Dreyfus award, 1984. Mem. Am. Chem. Soc., Internat. soc. Heterocyclic Chemistry. Home: 12 Northwick Ct Ann Arbor MI 48105 Office: U Mich Dept Chemistry 930 N University Ave Ann Arbor MI 48109-1055

PEASE, EDWARD ALLAN, lawyer, former state senator, university official; b. Terre Haute, Ind., May 22, 1951; s. Robert Richard and Joanna Rose (Pilant) P.; A.B. with distinction (Wendell Willkie scholar), Ind. U., Bloomington, 1973, J.D. cum laude, Indpls., 1977; postgrad. Memphis State U., 1975-76, Ind. State U., 1978-85. Gen. law clk. appellate and contracts div. Office Ind. Atty. Gen., Indpls., 1974-75; nat. dir. alumni affairs Pi Kappa Alpha Frat., Memphis, 1975-76; admitted to Ind. bar, 1977; partner firm Thomas, Thomas & Pease, Brazil, Ind., 1977-84; of counsel firm Thomas & Thomas, Brazil, 1984—; v.p. Ind. State U., 1993; mem. Ind. Senate, 1980-92, chmn. Judiciary Com.; chmn. Ind. Commn. Trial Cts., 1987-89; mem. adv. bd. 1st Bank & Trust Co. Clay County; mem. exec. bd. Wabash Valley council Boy Scouts Am., 1972—, exec. bd. east cen. region, 1986-88, v.p., 1977-84, pres., 1984-88, mem. nat. Order of Arrow com., 1984—, nat. vice chmn., 1990-93, nat. chmn., 1993—; Rep. candidate 7th dist. Mo. U.S. House of Reps., 1996; mem. Ind. Senate, 1980-92. Recipient Silver Beaver award Boy Scouts Am., 1975, Silver Antelope, 1992, Disting. Eagle Scout award, 1995. Mem. Ind. Bar Assn., Phi Beta Kappa, Pi Kappa Alpha (nat. pres. 1988-90). Republican. Methodist. Club: Columbia (Indpls.). Office: PO Box 511 Seelyville IN 47878*

PEASE, ELLA LOUISE, elementary education educator; b. Kokomo, Ind., May 31, 1928; d. James E. and Carrie Alice (Ringer) Earnest; m. Harold Edwin Pease, Aug. 10, 1985; children: Charles Miller, James Miller, Ricky Ensley, Wanda Cisna. BS, Ball State U., 1956, MA, 1959; postgrad., Ind. U., Ft. Wayne. Tchr. 1st grade Union Twp. (Ind.) Pub. Schs., 1953-56, Wells City (Ind.) Pub. Schs., Forest Park Sch., Ft. Wayne, Ind., 1956-93. Docent Ft. Wayne Art Mus.; libr. Simpson United Meth. Ch., Ft. Wayne, bd. dirs., mem. child care bd. Mem. NEA-Ret., Internat. Reading Assn., Ret. Ind. Tchrs. Assn., Ft. Wayne Ret. Tchrs. Assn. Home: 5108 E State Blvd Fort Wayne IN 46815-7467

PEASLEY, LOUIS CARL, lawyer, law educator; b. Bloomington, Ill., July 24, 1956; s. Clarence Edward Sr. and Ada Marie 9Oesch) P.; m. Katherine A. Kobs, June 6, 1976; children: Seth, Naomi, Esther, Isaac. BS, Pa. State U., 1992; MA, U. Ill., 1996, JD, 1996. Bar: Ill.; U.S. Dist. Ct. Ill., U.S. Dist. Ct. N.D. Missionary Ch. of the Nazarene, Pierre, S.D., 1985-88; instr., rschr. Pa. State U., University Park, 1991-93; law clk. Krukowski & Costello, Milw., 1995; student rep. West Pub. Co., Champaign, Ill., 1994-96; instr. U. Ill., Champaign, 1994-96; atty. Fraternal Order of Police, Springfield, Ill., 1996—. Mem. Phi Kappa Phi. Office: U Ill Coll of Commerce 350 Commerce West 6345 W Joliet Rd Countryside IL 60625

PEAT, WANDA JEAN, critical care nurse; b. Sioux Center, Iowa, July 6, 1956; d. Ralph and Arlene (Rozeboom) Punt; m, Alex Peat, June 11, 1976; children: Jennifer, Daniel, Bethany, Michael. Student, Buena Vista Coll., Storm Lake, Iowa, 1974-75; RN with distinction, Laramie County Community Coll., Cheyenne, Wyo., 1988. Cert. advanced cardiac life support. Staff nurse med./surg. unit DePaul Hosp., Cheyenne, 1988; staff nurse emergency rm. Home Hosp., Lafayette, Ind., 1988-89; high tech. pediatric home health nurse Hosp. Home Health Care of Midlands, Omaha, 1989-91; charge nurse, pvt. duty nurse Nursefinders, Inc., Omaha, 1989-91; pub. health nurse Sioux County Pub. Health, Orange City, Iowa, 1991-92. Mem. Am. Nurses Assn., Student Nurses Assn. (treas., fundraiser chmn.).

PEAVY, HOMER LOUIS, JR., real estate executive, accountant; b. Okmulgee, Okla., Sept. 4, 1924; s. Homer Louis and Hattie Lee (Walker) P.; children: Homer Martin, Daryl Mark. Student Kent State U., 1944-49; grad. Hammel-Actual Coll., 1962. Sales supr. Kirby Sales, Akron, Ohio, 1948-49; sales mgr. Williams-Kirby Co., Detroit, 1949-50; area distributor Peavy-Kirby Co., Phila., 1953-54; salesman James L. Peavy Realty Co., Akron, 1954-65; owner Homer Louis Peavy, Jr., Real Estate Broker, Akron, 1965—; pvt. practice acctg., Akron, 1962—; fin. aid officer Buckeye Coll., Akron, 1982. Author: Watt Watts, 1969; poet: Magic of the Muse, 1978, P.S. I Love You, 1982; contbr. poetry to Am. Poetry Anthology, 1983, New Worlds Unlimited, 1984, Treasures of the Precious Moments, 1985, Our World's Most Cherished Poems, 1985; songs: Sh...Sh, Sheree, Sheree, 1976, In Akron O, 1979; teleplay: Revenge, 1980. Bd. dirs. Internat. Elvis Gold Soc., 1978—; charter mem. Statue of Liberty-Ellis Island Found., 1984, Nat. Mus. of Women in Arts, 1986, Nat. Mus. Am. Indian, U.S. Holocaust Meml. Mus.; mem. Nat. Trust for Hist. Preservation, Ohio Hist. Soc., Preservation/N.C., Japanese Am. Nat. Mus.; charter mem. USS Constn., Libr. Congress Nat. Assocs. Mus. Recipient Am. Film Inst. Cert. Recognition, 1982, Award of Merit cert. World of Poetry 10th ann. contest, 1985, Golden Poet award World of Poetry, 1985, 87, 88, 89. Mem. NAACP (mem.-at-large), Ohioana Library Assn., Internat. Black Writers Conf., Acad. Am. Poets, Poetry Soc. Am., Smithsonian Nat. Assocs., Manuscript Club Akron, Internat. Platform Assn., Ohio Theatre Alliance, Kent State U. Alumni Assn. Democrat. Home and Office: 1160 Cadillac Blvd Akron OH 44320-2858

PECENKA, CRAIG D., engineer; b. Waterloo, Iowa, Apr. 28, 1960. BS in Agrl. Engring., Iowa State U., 1983. Product engr. Hay & Forage Industries, Hesston, Kans., 1984—. Patentee in field. Mem. Am. Soc. Engrs. Republican. Office: Hay & Forage Industries 420 W Lincoln Blvd Hesston KS 67062

PECK, CHARLES N., mechanical engineer; b. Hamilton, Ohio, July 15, 1954. A.Mech. Engring., Miami U., Oxford, Ohio, 1985. Quality engr. Glenmoore, Harrison, Ohio, 1986-90; process and quality engr. Sealtron Corp., Cin., 1990-92; quality engr. Rapid Design, Dayton, Ohio, 1992—. Mem. Am. Soc. for Quality Control. Office: Rapid Design Interpoint Blvd Dayton OH 45424

PECK, CURTISS STEVEN, organization development consultant; b. Kenosha, Wis., May 3, 1947; s. Curtiss Wesley and Frances Helen (Kowalkowski) P.; m. Susan Carol Kostritza, Nov. 3, 1973; children: Stephanie Jean, Curtiss Wesley II, Stacey Marie. BS, U. Wis., Milw., 1976, MS, 1980. Investigator, officer Greendale (Wis.) Police Dept., 1971-80; cons. Nat. Cons. and Tng. Inst., Milw., 1980-83, pres., 1983-92; exec. v.p. Team Mgmt. Sys. (U.S.A.) Inc., Reston, Va., 1994; pres. Assessment Sys. Internat. Inc., Milw., 1992—; instr. Cardinal Stritch Coll., Milw., 1982-89; advisor Booth-Wright, Inc., Boulder, Colo., 1983-87; cons. Howard & Assocs., Chgo., 1985-91, Mgmt. Resources Assn., Brookfield, 1985-91; coord. Trainer's Roundtable Inst. Fin. Edn., 1985-89; mem. adv. com. Milw. Area Tech. Coll., 1988-91; mem. adv. bd. Inst. Team Mgmt. Studies, Queensland, Australia. Author: Guide to Management and Leadership, 1990, Management and Leadership Profile, 1990, Team Effectiveness Profile, 1993, Guide to Linking Within and Between Teams, 1990, Management and Leadership Systems, 1992. Bd. dirs. Multiple Sclerosis Soc., Milw., 1983-89, pres., 1985, 86; bd. dirs. Muskego Scholastic Found., 1993-95; coord. Assn. Adult Educators, Milw., 1984; advisor Goodwill Industries, Milw., 1985, 86. With USAF, 1966-67, USANG, 1970-80. Mem. Nat. Orgnl. Devel. Network, Chgo. Orgnl. Devel. Network, Nat. Soc. for Performance and Instrn., Internat. Pers. Mgmt. Assn. (assessment coun.), Soc. for Human Resource Mgmt., Pers. and Indsl. Rels. Assn., Orgnl. Devel. Inst. (cert.). Lutheran. Home: S68w17924 East Dr Muskego WI 53150-9603 Office: ASI 15350 W National Ave New Berlin WI 53151-5158

PECK, ERNEST JAMES, JR., academic administrator; b. Port Arthur, Tex., July 26, 1941; s. Ernest James and Karlton Maudean (Luttrell) P.; children from previous marriage: David Karl, John Walter; m. Frances R. Taylor; 1 stepchild, Michael R. Taylor. BA in Biology with honors, Rice U., 1963, PhD in Biochemistry, 1966. Rsch. assoc. Purdue U., West Lafayette, Ind., 1966-68, asst. prof., 1968-73; asst. prof. Baylor Coll. Medicine, Houston, 1973-74, assoc. prof., 1974-80, prof., 1980-82; prof., chmn. biochemistry Sch. Med. Sci., U. Ark., Little Rock, 1982-89; dean sci. and math. U. Nev., Las Vegas, 1989-95; vice chancellor acad. affairs U. Nebr., Omaha, 1995—; adj. prof. U. Ark., Pine Bluff, 1986-88; program dir. NSF, Washington, 1988-89; mem. edit. bd. Jour. Neurosci. Rsch., N.Y.C., 1982-92. Co-author: Female Sex Steroids, 1979, Brain Peptides, 1979. Recipient Rsch. Career award NIH, Nat. Inst. of Child Health and Human Devel., 1975-80; NIH fellow, 1964-66. Fellow AAAS; mem. Am. Chem. Soc., Am. Soc. Biochemistry and Molecular Biology, Am. Soc. Neurochemistry, Endocrine Soc., Sigma Xi. Office: U Nebr-Omaha Vice Chancellor Acad Affair 60th and Dodge Sts Omaha NE 68182-0001

PECK, JULIE ELLEN WALSH, consultant; b. Charleston, Ill., Oct. 9, 1947. M in Vocat. Edn., U. Ill., 1976. Vocat. tchr. Oakwood Twp. H.S., Fithian, Ill., 1968-73, Elmhurst (Ill.) Sch. Dist., 1973-78; recruiter Mgmt. Recruiters, Milw., 1978-81; ptnr., cons. exec. search Peck and Assoc. Ltd., Milw., 1981—; bd. dirs. Coun. Small Bus. Execs., Milw., Next Door Found., Milw. Methodist. Office: Peck and Assocs Ltd 4555 W Schroeder Ltd Milwaukee WI 53223-1400

PECK, WILLIAM ARNO, physician, educator; b. New Britain, Conn., Sept. 28, 1933; s. Bernard Carl and Molla (Nair) P.; m. Patricia Hearn, July 10, 1982; children by previous marriage: Catherine, Edward Pershall, David Nathaniel; stepchildren: Andrea, Elizabeth, Katherine. A.B., Harvard U., 1955; M.D., U. Rochester, N.Y., 1960. Intern, then resident in internal medicine Barnes Hosp., St. Louis, 1960-62; fellow in metabolism Washington U. Sch. Medicine, St. Louis, 1963; mem. faculty U. Rochester Med. Sch., 1965-76, prof. medicine and biochemistry, 1973-76, head div. endocrinology and metabolism, 1969-76; John E. and Adaline Simon prof. medicine, co-chmn. dept. medicine Washington U. Sch. Medicine, St. Louis, 1976-89; physician in chief Jewish Hosp., St. Louis, 1976-89; prof. medicine and exec. vice chancellor med. affairs, dean sch. medicine, pres. univ. med. ctr. Washington U., St. Louis, 1989—; chmn. endocrinology and metabolism adv. com. FDA, 1976-78; chmn. gen. medicine study sect. NIH, 1979-81; chmn. Gordon Conf. Chemistry, PHysiology and Structure of Bones and Teeth, 1977; chmn. Consensus Devel. Conf. on Osteoporosis, NIH, 1984; co-chmn. Workshop on Future Directions in Osteoporosis, 1987; chmn. Spl. Topic Conf. on Osteoporosis, U.S. FDA, 1987; dir. Angelica Corp., Boatman's Trust Co., Allied Healthcare Products, Hologic, Reinsurance Group of Am. Editor Bone and Mineral Rsch. Anns., 1982-88; mem. editorial adv. bd. Osteoporosis Internat., other jours.; contbr. to med. jours. Pres. Nat. Osteoporosis Found., 1985-90. Served as med. officer USPHS, 1963-65. Recipient Mosby Book award Alpha Omega Alpha, 1960, Doran J. Stephens award U. Rochester Sch. Medicine, 1960, Lederle Med. Faculty award, 1967, NIH Career Program award, 1970-75, Commr.'s Spl. citation FDA, 1988, Humanitarian award Arthritis Found. Ea. Mo., 1995. Fellow ACP, AAAS; mem. Am. Assn. Clin. Endocrinologists, Am. Geriatric Soc., Am. Soc. for Biochemistry and Molecular Biology, Am. Soc. Clin. Investigation, Am. Fedn. Clin. Rsch., Am. Diabetes Assn., Internat. Bone and Mineral Soc., Assn. Am. Physicians, Am. Soc. Bone and Mineral Rsch. (pres. 1983-84), Endocrine Soc., Orthopedic Rsch. Soc., Nat. Inst. Arthritis, Musculoskeletal and Skin Diseases (adv. coun. 1986-89), Assn. Am. Med. Colls. (adminstrv. bd. Coun. of Deans 1993—, chmn. elect 1991-97, group on bus. affairs rsch. task force), Sigma Xi, Alpha Omega Alpha (bd. dirs. 1992-95). Home: 2 Apple Tree Ln Saint Louis MO 63124-1601 Office: Washington U Sch Medicine 600 S Euclid Ave Saint Louis MO 63110-1093

PECKERMAN, BRUCE MARTIN, lawyer; b. Milw., Sept. 28, 1949; s. Joseph and Doris (Kassel) P.; m. Jeanette Chrustowski, Aug. 19, 1973. BA, U. Wis., 1971; JD, Washington U., St. Louis, 1973. Bar: Wis. 1974, U.S. Dist. Ct. (we. dist.) Wis. 1974, U.S. Ct. Appeals (7th cir.) 1977. Ptnr. Samster, Aiken, Peckerman & Mawicke, Milw., 1974-85; sole practice Milw., 1985—. Recipient young leadership award Milw. Jewish Fedn., 1985. Mem. ABA, Wis. Bar Assn. (chmn. elect-family law sect.), Milw. Bar Assn. (bench/bar com. 1987-88), Am. Acad. Matrimonial Lawyers (pres.). Democrat. Office: Ste 133 5150 N Port Washington Rd Milwaukee WI 53217-5470

PEDDICORD, ROLAND DALE, lawyer; b. Van Meter, Iowa, Mar. 29, 1936; s. Clifford Elwood and Juanitas Irene (Brittain) P.; m. Teri Linn O'Dell; children: Erin Sue, Robert Sean. BSBA with honors, Drake U., 1961, JD with honors, 1962. Bar: Iowa 1962; cert. civil trial specialist Nat. Bd. Trial Advs. Asst. atty. gen. State of Iowa, 1962-63; assoc. Steward, Crouch & Hopkins, Des Moines, 1962-65; ptnr. Peddicord, Wharton, Thune & Spencer, Des Moines, 1968—; lectr. in law Drake U., 1962-68; lectr. law Coll. Osteo. Medicine, Des Moines, 1965-72. Editor and chief Drake Law Rev., 1961-62. Past mem. nat. bd. dirs., nat. coun. YMCA of U.S.A., past vice chmn. nat. bd.; bd. dirs., past chmn. Greater Des Moines YMCA, 1968-89. With USMC, 1954-57. Mem. ABA, ATLA, Iowa Bar Assn., Polk County Bar Assn., Iowa Trial Lawyers Assn., Iowa Acad. Trial Lawyers, Am. Bd. Trial Advs. (pres. Iowa chpt., cert. civil trial specialist). Republican. Methodist. Office: 405 6th Ave Ste 700 Des Moines IA 50309-2412 Office: Peddicord Wharton Thune Spencer PO Box 9130 Des Moines IA 50306-9130

PEDERSEN, BERNARD EDWIN, state legislator; b. Grinnell, Iowa, Nov. 24, 1925; s. Edwin Bernard and Hattie (Jantzen) P.; m. Patricia Jean O'Brien, 1950; children: Christina Pedersen Tinning, Edwin, Andrew. BA, Grinnell Coll., 1949. Ins. broker Palatine and Chgo., Ill., 1949—; mem. Ill. Ho. of Reps. from 54th dist., 1983—; mem. Ins. Com. Ill. Ho. of Reps., Minority Spokesman Consumer Protection, Labor & Commerce, Small Bus., Aging, Vet. Affairs, Citizen Coun on Pub. Aid Coms.; co-chmn. Day Care Task Force; Ill. Chmn. Am. Legis. Exch. Coun.; chmn. Children and Family Svc. Assessor Palatine Twp., Ill., 1966-83, committeeman, 1969—; chmn. Crane for Congress, 1969; sec. Cook County Suburban Rep. Orgn., 1974-82; Cook County coord. Crane for Pres. Com., 1979; chmn. Palatine Twp. Reagan for Pres. Com., 1980. Decorated Purple Heart; recipient Disting. Unit Citation. Mem. KC (4th degree), Am. Coll. Life Underwriters, Chgo. Bd. Underwriters, Jesuit Retreat League of Chgo., Am. Legion. Home: 220 S Hale St Palatine IL 60067-6214*

PEDERSON, GORDON ROY, state legislator, retired military officer; b. Gayville, S.D, Aug. 8, 1927; s. Roy E. and Gladys F. (Masker) P.; m. Betty L. Ballard, Mar. 8, 1955; children: James D., Carol A. Pederson Niemann, Nancy G. Pederson Holub, Gary W. Student, Yankton Coll., 1948-50, Fla. State U., 1963; advanced course, Infantry Sch., 1958-59. Drafted U.S. Army, 1945-47, commd. 2d lt., 1952, advanced through grades to lt. col., 1967, served Korean War, 1950-54; served CONUS World War II, platoon leader 17th infantry regiment, 7th infantry divsn. U.S. Army, Korea, 1953-54; rifle co. commdr. 10th mountain divsn. U.S. Army, Germany, 1955-58; instr., dir. instrn. U.S. Army Jungle Warfare Tng. Ctr. U.S. Army, Ft. Sherman, Canal Zone, 1961-63, comdr. post, 1963-64; 1st bri., 1st infantry divsn. U.S. Army, Vietnam, 1965-66; dir. tng. hdqs. U.S. Army, Ft. Leonard Wood, 1966-68; advisor Ministry of Nat. Def., Rep. China on Taiwan, Rep. China on Taiwan, 1969-70; retired U.S. Army, 1970; rep. S.D. Ho. Reps., Pierre, 1977—; operator Dairy Queen, Wall, S.D., 1990-95; chmn. transp. com. S.D. Ho. Reps., 1979-93. Del. S.D. Rep. Conv., 1974-78, 80, 82, 84, 86, 88, 90, 92, Rep. Conv. S.D., 1994, Nat. Rep. Conv., 1976, 80, 84, 88, 92; bd. dirs. Legis. Rsch. Coun., 1988, 90, 92. Decorated Bronze Star, Medal of Merit, U.S. Presdl. Unit Citation, Rep. Korea Presdl. Unit Citation, Rep. Vietnam Presdl. Unit Citation, Combat Infantry Badge with Star, Legion of Merit, Air Medal with 2 Oak Leaf Clusters, Army Accomodation medal with 2 oak leaf clusters, Cross of Gallantry with Palm, Republic Vietnam. Mem. VFW, DAV, Am. Legion, Retired Officers Assn., Wall C. of C., Internat. Lions Club. Lutheran. Home: PO Box 312 116 W 7th St Wall SD 57790 Office: SD Ho of Reps State Capitol Bldg Pierre SD 57501

PEDERSON, JAY PORTER, editor, writer; b. Springfield, Minn., June 18, 1961; s. Charles Kenneth and Faith Lorene (Seymour) P.; m. Linda Margaret Plotz, June 2, 1984; children: Kyle, Mark, John. BA in English and Religion, St. Olaf Coll., 1983. Cert. secondary English tchr., Mich. Sr. asst. editor Gale Rsch., Inc., Detroit, 1984-87; owner, editor The Write One, Maple Grove, Minn., 1988—. Editor: (reference book) African American Almanac, 1994, African American Breaktrhoughs, 1995, St. James Guied to Science Fiction Writers, 1995, St. James Guide to Crime and Mystery Writers, 1996. Roman Catholic. Office: The Write One 7131 Maplewood Dr Maple Grove MN 55311-3314

PEDERSON, JON RUSSELL, construction equipment company owner; b. Willmar, Minn., July 5, 1950; s. Russell Gordon and Mildred Hazel (Wagner) P.; m. Sophie Cropsal, May 15, 1978; children: Celine-Marie, Adele Mildred, Joseph Cropsal. BA, Concordia Coll., Moorhead, Minn., 1974; MS, N.D. State U., 1976. With Pederson & Clough, Raymond, Minn., 1976-77, Duininck, Prinsburg, Minn., 1977-78; with Ruffridge-Johnson Equipment, Mpls., 1978-83, owner, 1983—; pres. Equipment Distributors Assn. Minn., 1988, Associated Egipment Distributors, Minn. Transp. Alliance. Scoutmaster Troop 579 Boy Scouts Am., Boy Scouts Am., Osseo, Minn., World Jamboree Scoutmaster, Holland, 1995. With USMC, 1970-72. Mem. Minn. Waterfowl Assn., Ducks Unltd., Pheasants Forever, Norske Torske Klubben, Sons of Norway, Marine Corps Hist. Found. Methodist. Office: Ruffridge-Johnson Equip Co 3024 4th St SE Minneapolis MN 55414-3302

PEDERSON, KATHRYN MARIE, college administrator; b. Minot, N.D., Apr. 28, 1958; d. Clifford Artine and Leona (Schlecht) Lang; m. Robert Norman Pederson, Oct. 11, 1986. BA, Minot State U., 1984; MA, U. Mary, 1989. Mgr. Answer Dakota Answering Svc., Minot, 1980-82; legal sec. Teevens, Johnson, Montgomery, Minot, 1982-86; acctg. clk. Interstate Brands Corp., Minot, 1986; data input operator N.D. Legis. Coun., Bismarck, N.D., 1986-87; asst. Bismarck Pub. Schs./Tech. Enabling Disabled Individuals, Bismarck, 1987-89; state tech. dir. Dept. Pub. Instrn., Bismarck, 1989-92; instructional tech. adminstr. Prairie Pub. Broadcasting, Fargo, 1992-95; ctr. dir. N. D. State Coll. of Sci., 1995—. Editor: (newsletter) CEC Newsletter, 1987-89, TEDIgram, 1987-89, Superintendent's Report, 1990-92; author: (newsletter) TecTalk, 1990-95. Fin. com. Faith United Meth. Ch., Minot, 1986. Mem. N.D. Edn. Assn., N.D. Libr. Assn., Assn. Instrnl. Tech., N.D. Ednl. Telecommunications Coun. (exec. dir. 1989-92), Okla. State U. Satellite Program (adv. coun. 1989-92), Satellite Ednl. Resources Consortium (adv. coun. 1989-92), Jaycees (Outstanding Fundraiser 1989, Jaycee of Month 1989, Outstanding Com. chmn. 1989, Project of Yr. 1989, Top Mem. Recruiter 1990). Methodist. Office: NDSCS 5M55Q/DPE 210 Missile Ave Unit 2 Minot AFB ND 58705

PEDICINI, LOUIS JAMES, manufacturing company executive; b. Detroit, June 29, 1926; s. Louis I. and Myra Ann (Bergan) P.; m. Ellen Sylvia Mulden, June 5, 1948; 1 child, Eric Louis. B.S.E.E., Wayne U., 1955. Dept. head Gen. Motors Corp., 1948-58; exec. v.p. Lester B. Knight & Assos., Inc., Chgo., 1959-76; exec. v.p. ops. Pullman Trailmobile, Chgo., 1976-81; mng. dir. Ingersoll Engrs. Inc., Rockford, Ill., 1981-82; pres. George Fischer Foundry Systems Inc., Holly, Mich., 1982-93; also bd. dirs.; chmn. George Fischer Corp., Bloomingdale, Ill., 1994—. Served with U.S. Army, 1944-46. Fellow Inst. Brit. Foundrymen; mem. Am. Foundrymen's Soc. (past bd.

dirs., William H. McFadden gold medal 1994), Skokie Country Club, Plaza Club. Republican. Office: 230 Covington Dr Bloomingdale IL 60108-3106

PEDLER, SUZANNE PHYLLIS, sales professional, recruiter; b. South Bend, Ind., Jan. 16, 1935; d. H. Melvin and Elizabeth (Gyorgyi) Williams; m. Russell E. Snyder, Aug. 30, 1953 (div. 1979); children: Bradford, Rodney; m. Richard A. Pedler, May 16, 1980 (div. 1991). BS in Sociology, Western Mich. U., 1977. Interior decorator MAB Paints, Elkhart, Ind., 1965-75; sales, recruiter Mgmt. Svcs., Elkhart, 1977-82; pres. Employment Recruiters, Elkhart, 1982—. Mem. Soc. Mfg. Engrs. (chairwoman 1995). Methodist. Home: 3118 Cherry Tree Ln Elkhart IN 46514 Office: Employment Recruiters Inc PO Box 1624 Elkhart IN 46515

PEDOTO, GERALD JOSEPH, supplier quality engineer; b. Jersey City, Jan. 5, 1948; s. Salvatore Joseph and Rosalie (Benigno) P.; m. Karen Sue Knutty, June 28, 1975; children: Deborah Louise, Donald Lee, Timothy Scott. BS, Bowling Green (Ohio) State U., 1970; MBA, U. Akron, 1976. Cert. mgr., quality engr. Trainee indsl. engring. Timken Co., Canton, Ohio, 1970, asso. indsl. engr., 1972-73, supervisory candidate, 1973-74, foreman product inspection, 1974-75, supr. indirect labor, 1975-80, supr. heat treatment, 1980-82, sr. product acceptance engr., 1982-96; sr. supplier quality engr., 1996—. Active United Way, YMCA fund drs.; region & automotive divsn. councilor. With U.S. Army, 1970-72. Mem. Nat. Mgmt. Assn., Assn. MBA Execs., Am. Soc. for Quality Control (bd. dirs. 1992—), Alpha Tau Omega, Beta Gamma Sigma, Omicron Delta Kappa. Republican. Mem. United Ch. of Christ. Home: 5596 Brookstone St NW Canton OH 44718-1280 Office: The Timken Co GNW-35 1835 Dueber Ave SW Canton OH 44706-2728

PEDRAM, MARILYN BETH, reference librarian; b. Brewster, Kans., Apr. 3, 1937; d. Edgar Roy and Elizabeth Catherine (Doubt) Crist; m. Manouchehr Pedram, Jan. 27, 1962 (Oct. 28, 1984); children: Jaleh Denise, Cyrus Andre. BS in Edn., Kans. State U., 1958; MLS, U. Denver, 1961. Cert secondary educator, Mo. 7th grade tchr. Clay Ctr. (Kans.) Pub. Schs., 1958-59, Colby (Kans.) Pub. Sch. System, 1959-60; reference libr. Topeka (Kans.) Pub. Libr., 1961-62, extension dept. head, 1963-64, reference libr., 1964-65; br. libr. asst. Denver Pub. Libr., 1965-67; reference libr. Kansas City (Mo.) Pub. Libr., Plaza Br., 1974-79, Kansas City (Mo.) Main Libr., 1979—. Mem. AARP, ALA, NAFE, Mo. Libr. Assn., Pub. Libr. Assn., Kansas City Assn. Law Librs., Gluten Intolerance Group N.Am., Celiac Sprue Assn., Kans. State U. Alumni Assn., Kansas City Online Users Group, Nat. Parks and Conservation Assn. Office: Kansas City Pub Libr 311 E 12th St Kansas City MO 64106-2412

PEEBLES, ALLENE KAY, manufactured housing company executive; b. Waukegan, Ill., Feb. 9, 1938; d. Allan Laverne and Kathryn Bernice (McGill) Sedlmayr; m. William Ross Peebles, July 9, 1960; children: Ross William, Robb Allan, Raymond John, Renda Kay. BS with high honors, U. Wis., 1960, MS, 1967; grad., Realtors Inst., 1968. Cert. home economist. Tchr. Horicon (Wis.) High Sch., 1960-61, Oconomowoc (Wis.) High Sch., 1961-67; freelance writer, 1967-70; v.p. Luxury Homes, Inc., Watertown, Wis., 1970-93, Plus Devel. Inc., Watertown, 1970—; co-developer Hidden Meadows Condominium Community, Watertown, 1976-96; gen. ptnr. W and A Elderly Housing Ltd. Partnership, Watertown, 1988—; pres. Housing Am., Inc., 1991—; gen. ptnr. Sunrise Housing Ltd. Ptnrship., 1990—; builder new and rehab low-income housing, 1983—. Mem. Wis. Gov.'s Conf. on Family, 1980; chmn. adminstrv. bd. United Meth. Ch., Oconomowoc, 1974-77, 96—; chmn. family ministry Wis. Conf., United Meth. Ch.; membership chmn. Boy Scouts Am., 1984-90; chmn. Ams. abroad Am. Field Svc., Oconomowoc, 1982-87. Recipient Dist. award of Merit Potawatomi Area coun. Boy Scouts Am., 1986. Mem. NAFE, AAUW (pres. Oconomowoc 1983-85), Am. Home Econs. Assn., Wis. Home Econs. Assn. (parliamentarian 1988—), Nat. Home Economists in Bus. (internat. com. 1985-87, regional U.S. advisor 1990-92), Nat. Assn. Home Builders, Internat. Profl. and Bus. Women, Wis. Home Economists in Bus. (state chmn. 1987-88, Home Economist in Bus. of Yr. 1987), Nat. Assn. Realtors, Wis. Assn. Realtors, Waukesha Bd. Realtors, Wis. Builders Assn., Wis. Manufactured Housing Assn. (bd. dirs. 1979-90, chmn. bd. 1985-88, Mem. of Yr. award 1986), Internat. Fedn. of Home Ecoms., Met. Builders Assn. Greater Milw., Phi Kappa Phi, Phi Upsilon Omicron, Omicron Nu, Phi Lambda Theta. Republican. Home: 37788 Mapleton Rd Oconomowoc WI 53066 Office: Housing Am Inc Hidden Meadows Pky Watertown WI 53094

PEEK, GARY EDWIN, computer consultant, skydiving instructor, author; b. St. Louis, Mo., Dec. 31, 1953; s. Lloyd Elva and Elizabeth Gene (Conner) P. Grad., H.S., Berkeley, Mo. Computer and electronic cons. St. Louis, 1974—; skydiving instr. St. Louis area skydiving ctrs., 1985—, pilot for jump aircraft, 1989—; cons. to safety and tng. com. U.S. Parachute Assn., Alexandria, Va., 1995—. Author: (book) Test and Repair Your Own Avionics Accessories, 1994; (computer software) Equipment Color Programs for Skydivers, 1990-95 (Author of Yr. 1993); contbr. articles to Parachutist Mag. Mem U.S. Parachute Assn. (instr., examiner 1990—). Home: 3201 Highgate Ln Saint Charles MO 63301

PEENO, LARRY NOYLE, state agency administrator, consultant; b. Evansville, Ind., Dec. 24, 1941; s. Paul Albert and Marcella (Imogene) Franz; m. Margaret Marie Graf, June 8, 1973. AB, Western Ky. U., 1968, MA, 1969; EdD, U. Mo., 1977. Cert. tchr. Mo. Art tchr. Normandy Sr. High Sch., St. Louis, 1974-90, chmn. art dept., 1976-89; dist. art coord. Normandy Sch. Dist., St. Louis, 1983-88; fine arts supr. Dept. Elem. and Secondary Edn., Jefferson City, Mo., 1990—; mem. adv. bd. St. Louis Art Mus., 1988—. Contbg. author: Supervision and Administration: Programs, Positions, Perspectives, 1991, Nat. Standards For Arts Edn.: What Every Young American SHould Know and Be Able To Do in The Arts, 1994, Nat. Visual Arts Standards, 1994; editor Show-Me-Art newsletter, 1983-84. With USAF, 1959-62. Mem. ASCD, Nat. Art Edn. Assn. (nat. program coord. 1993, bd. dirs. 1995-97, Nat. Newsletter award 1983-84, Award of Excellence 1983-84), Nat. Assn. State Dirs. Art Edn., Mo. Art Edn. Assn. (Secondary Art Tchr. of Yr. 1987-88, Outstanding Art Educator award 1983-84), Music Educators Nat. Conf., Mo. Music Educators Assn. Office: Dept Elem and Secondary Edn 205 Jefferson State Ofc Jefferson City MO 65102

PEET, HOWARD DAVID, English language and literature educator; b. Fargo, N.D., Oct. 7, 1930; s. Howard Morrison and Beatrice Katherine (Gunness) P.; m. Jacquelyn Marie Hegge, June 20, 1953; children: Terry H., Pamela Peet Astrup. BA, Macalaster Coll., St. Paul, 1956; BS, Moorhead State U., 1965, MS, 1965; postgrad., U. Minn., 1970. Ride trumpet Ray Palmer Orch., Chgo., 1950-52; lead trumpet Kliff Riggs Orch., Omaha, 1954-55; ins. investigator Retail Credit Assn., St. Paul, 1955-60; prof. English N.D. State U., Fargo, 1965-86, prof. emeritus, 1986—, dir. concentrated approach program, 1970. Author and co-author 65 books including The English Book: A Complete Course, 1980, Wordskill for The Micro Computer, 1982, MacMillan Spelling, 1983, Vocabulary for College Reading and Writing, 1984, Linguistics For Teachers, 1993, Wordskills, 1993. Pres. Young Reps., Wilkin county, Minn., 1970's, PTA, Barnesville, Minn., 1970's; treas. Presbyn. Ch., Deerhorn, Minn., 1970's. With USN, 1952-54, Korea. Named Red River Valley Educator, Red River Valley Heritage Soc., 1992. Mem. Nat. Coun. Tchrs. English, Writers of the Purple Sage, Am. Legion, La. Soc. Des 40 Hommes Et 8 Chevauk. Home: 25 Prairiewood Crossing Fargo ND 58103

PEISNER, DAVID BALFOUR, medical educator; b. Detroit, Mar. 25, 1952; s. Balfour and Nora P.; m. Bonnie Levy, June 9, 1996. BS, Calif. Tech. U., 1974; MD, Wayne State U., 1978. Resident Wayne State U., Detroit, 1982; asst. prof. divsn. maternal-fetal medicine dept. ob.-gyn. Case Western Res. U., Cleve., 1982-87, Columbia U., N.Y.C., 1987-95; asst. clin. prof. dept. ob.-gyn. Mich. State U., East Lansing, 1995—; staff perinatologist Bronson Hosp., Kalamazoo, Mich., 1995—. Contbr. articles to profl. jours. Fellow Case Western Res. U., 1984, Am. Coll. Ob-Gyn., Washington, 1986. Fellow Am. Coll. Ob-Gyn.; mem. IEEE, Am. Med. Info. Assn., Am. Inst. Ultrasound Medicine, Soc. Perinatal Obstetricians, Assn. Computing Machinery. Office: Bronson Hosp Dept Perinatology 252 E Lovell Kalamazoo MI 49007

PEITHMAN, MARVIN H., retired farmer, income tax practitioner; b. Richview, Ill., Aug. 8, 1919; s. William George and Mary Alma (Haun) P.; m. Ruth Mary Rumig, Aug. 11, 1944; 1 child, Janet Ruth Peithman McCleary. BS, U. Ill., 1941. Farmer, Richview, 1941-89; tchr. vocat. agr. Ashley (Ill.) Twp. High Sch., 1947-48; tax practitioner, Nashville, Ill., 1966—; bd. dirs. Washington County Svc. Co., Nashville, 1971-83, also past pres.; mem. adv. com. Agrl. Ext. Svc., Urbana, Ill., 1954-56; mem. adv. com. agrl. econs. dept. U. Ill., Urbana, 1956-58. Pres. bd. trustees Washington County Sch. Bd., Nashville, 1952-61; bd. dirs. Nashville Community High Sch., 1961-83, also past pres., sec.; bd. dirs. Ill. Health Improvement Assn., Springfield, 1977-80. Recipient Outstanding Conservation Farmer award Washington County Soil and Water Conservation Dist., 1973, recognition of svc. Ill. Assn. Sch. Adminstrs., 1982. Methodist. Home and Office: 1115 S Community Ave Nashville IL 62263-2058

PELANT, BARNEY FRANK, international business consulting executive; b. L.A., Mar. 4, 1942; s. Barney William and Marie Bohumila (Riha) P.; m. Judith Ann Proctor, May 23, 1970; 1 child, Nicole Marie; 1 step-child, Dalina Lynn DuBois. AA, El Camino Coll., 1962; BS, U. So. Calif., L.A., 1969, MBA, 1970. Cert. disaster recovery planner. Engr., scientist McDonnell Douglas Corp., Culver City, Calif., 1963-70; sect. mgr., officer Continental Bank, Chgo., 1970-84; dir. contingency svcs. SunGard Recovery Svcs., Northbrook, Ill., 1984-89; dir. cons. Harris Devlin Assocs., Northbrook, 1989-90; sr. mgr. Ernst & Young, Chgo., 1990-91; owner, prin. Barney F. Pelant & Assocs., Bloomingdale, Ill., 1991—; exec. bd. dirs. Disaster Recovery Inst., St. Louis, 1992-93, 95—, certification bd. dirs., 1991—, chmn., 1995—; bd. dirs. Can. Ctr. Emergency Preparedness, Hamilton, Ont., 1993—. Contbr. articles to profl. jours. chmn. Plan Commn., Bloomingdale, 1984—, Zoning Bd. Appeals, Bloomingdale, 1984—, Sesquicentennial Landmark Com., Bloomingdale, 1983-86. With U.S. Army NG, 1964-70. Mem. U. So. Calif. Midwest Alumni Club, U.S. Hang Gliding Assn., Beta Gamma Sigma. Office: Barney F Pelant & Assocs 243 Harvard Ln Bloomingdale IL 60108-2141

PELC, KAROL I., engineering management educator, researcher; b. Czestochowa, Poland, July 29, 1935; came to U.S., 1985; s. Stanislaw Pelc and Kamilla (Hecko) Pelc-Kosna; m. Ryszarda Lidia Ryglewicz, Sept. 24, 1959; 1 child, Dariusz. MScEE, Tech. U. Wroclaw, Poland, 1958, PhD in Econs., 1976; PhD in Electronics, U. Uppsala, Sweden, 1968. Electronic design engr. Rsch. Inst. Tech. U. Wroclaw, Poland, 1957-60; prodn. & engring. mgr. Energopomiar Co., Wroclaw, 1960-65; rsch. asst. dept. electronics U. Uppsala, 1961-62; assoc. dir. div. Inst. Electric Power Industry, Wroclaw, 1966-68; rsch. dir. Tech. U. Wroclaw, 1968-77; founder, dir. Forecasting Rsch. Ctr., Wroclaw, 1971-81; lectr., dir. Jelenia Gora Coll. br. Tech. U. Wroclaw, 1982-85; prof. Mich. Technol. U., Houghton, 1985—; vis. prof. Indian Inst. Tech., Bombay, 1981, Stevens Inst. Tech., Hoboken, N.J., 1993; vis. scholar Japan Ctr. for Mich. Univs., Hikone, 1992; mem. innovation task force Internat. Inst. for Applied Systems Analysis, Laxenburg, Austria, 1983-84; chmn. forecasting seminar Polish Acad. Scis., Warsaw, 1974-81; v.p. div. Soc. Mgmt. and Orgn., Wroclaw, 1979-80. Author: Planning of Research and Development, 1981; mem. editl. bd. Technol. Forecasting and Social Change, U.S. R&D Mgmt., Eng., Transformations, Poland; contbr. more than 80 articles to scholarly jours.; patentee in field. Mem. Internat. Assn. Mgmt. Tech., Internat. Assn. for Rsch. and Devel. Mgmt., Am. Soc. Engring. Mgmt. Soc. of IEEE, Acad. Mgmt. Roman Catholic. Office: Mich Technol Univ Sch Bus & Engring Adminstrn Houghton MI 49931

PELL, WILBUR FRANK, JR., federal judge; b. Shelbyville, Ind., Dec. 6, 1915; s. Wilbur Frank and Nelle (Dickerson) P.; m. Mary Lane Chase, Sept. 14, 1940; children: Wilbur Frank III, Charles Chase. A.B., Ind. U., 1937, LL.D. (hon.), 1981; LL.B. cum laude, Harvard U., 1940; LL.D., Yonsei U., Seoul, Korea, 1972, John Marshall Sch. Law, 1973. Bar: Ind. 1940. Pvt. practice Shelbyville, 1940-42, 45-70; spl. agt. FBI, 1942-45; sr. ptnr. Pell & Good, 1949-56, Pell & Matchett, 1956-70; judge U.S. Ct. Appeals (7th cir.), 1970—, now sr. judge; mem. 3 judge spl. divsn. U.S. Ct. Appeals (D.C. cir.), appointing ind. counsel, 1987-92; dep. atty. gen., Ind., 1953-55; dir., chmn. Shelby Nat. Bank, 1947-70. Bd. dirs. Shelbyville Community Chest, 1947-49, Shelby County Fair Assn., 1951-53; dir. Shelby County Tb Assn., 1948-70, pres., 1965-66; dist. chmn. Boy Scouts Am., 1956-57; mem. pres.'s council Nat. Coll. Edn., 1972-87; dir. Westminster Found., Ind. U.; hon. dir. Korean Legal Center. Fellow Am. Coll. Probate Counsel, Am. Bar Found.; mem. ABA (judge Edward R. Finch Law Day USA Speech award 1973), Ind. Bar Assn. (pres. 1962-63, chmn. ho. of dels. 1968-69), Fed. Bar Assn., Ill. Bar Assn., Shelby County Bar Assn. (pres. 1957-58), 7th Fed. Cir. Bar Assn., Am. Judicature Soc., Am. Coun. Assn., Shelby County C. of C., Nat. Conf. Bar Pres.'s, Riley Meml. Assn., Ind. Soc. Chgo. (pres. 1978-79), Harvard Law Soc. Ill. (pres. 1980-81), Rotary (dist. gov. 1952-53, internat. dir 1959-61), Union League, Legal Club (pres. Chgo. 1976-77), Law Club (pres. Chgo. 1984-85), Kappa Sigma, Alpha Phi Omega, Theta Alpha Phi, Tau Kappa Alpha, Phi Alpha Delta (hon.). Republican. Presbyterian (elder, deacon). Office: US Ct Appeals 7th Cir 219 S Dearborn St Ste 2760 Chicago IL 60604-1803

PELLEGRENE, THOMAS JAMES, JR., editor, researcher; b. Wilmington, Del., Dec. 26, 1959; s. Thomas J. and MaryBelle (McGowan) P.; m. Pamela Heinecke, Apr. 5, 1986. BS in Journalism, Northwestern U., 1981, MS in Journalism, 1982. Staff writer Ft. Wayne (Ind.) Journal-Gazette, 1982-87, bus. editor, 1987-95, asst. metro editor, 1995—. Mem. Am. Assn. Pub. Opinion Rsch., Soc. Profl. Journalists. Office: Fort Wayne Journal-Gazette 600 W Main St Fort Wayne IN 46802-1408

PELLOW, DICK, state legislator; b. 1931; m. Jean Pellow; 5 children. G-rad. h.s. Minn. state rep. Dist. 52B, 1988-92, 95—; former mem. Commerce, Econ. Devel., Edn., Transp. Coms.; currently self-employed. Address: 1471 18th St NW New Brighton MN 55112-5451

PELOWSKI, GENE P., JR., state legislator; b. Feb. 1952; m. Deborah Pelowski; 2 children. BS, Winona State U. Mem. Minn. Ho. of Reps. St. Paul, 1986—; mem. econ. devel. com., gen. legis. com., gaming com., edn. com., others, vicechmn. vet affairs and elec. coms.; educator; golf profl. Democrat. Home: 257 Wilson St Winona MN 55987-5238*

PELTON, RUSSELL MEREDITH, JR., lawyer; b. Chgo., May 14, 1938; s. Russell Meredith and Mildred Helen (Baumrucker) P.; m. Patty Jane Rader, Aug. 12, 1961; children: James, Thomas, Michael, Margaret. BA, DePauw U., 1960; JD, U. Chgo., 1963. Bar: Ill. 1963, U.S. Supreme Ct. 1979. Assoc., Peterson, Ross, Schloerb & Seidel, Chgo., 1966-72, ptnr., 1972-90; ptnr. Oppenheimer, Wolff & Donnelly, 1990—, Chgo. mng. ptnr., 1992-95; co-founder, gen. counsel Chgo. Opportunities Industrialization Ctr., 1969-83; gen. counsel Delta Dental Plan Ill., 1979—; bd. dirs. First United Life Ins. Co., 1979-82. Pres. Wilmette Jaycees, 1970; chmn. Wilmette Sch. Bd. Caucus, 1970-71; Wilmette Dist. 39 Bd. Edn., 1972-80; gen. counsel Am. Assn. Neurol. Surgeons, 1981—; bd. dirs. Wilmette United Way, 1980-86, campaign chmn., 1983-85, pres., 1985-86; Wilmette Zoning Bd. Appeals, 1989—, chmn., 1990—. Served to capt. USAF, 1963-66. Mem. Chgo. Bar Assn., Ill. Bar Assn., ABA, Ill. Trial Lawyers Assn., Soc. Trial Lawyers. Office: Oppenheimer Wolff & Donnelly Two Prudential Plz 45th Fl 180 N Stetson Ave Chicago IL 60601-6710

PELZER, CHARLES FRANCIS, molecular geneticist, biology educator, cancer researcher; b. Detroit, June 5, 1935; s. Francis Joseph and Edna Dorothy (Ladach) P.; m. Veronica Ann Killeen, July 7, 1972; 1 child, Mary Elizabeth. BS in Biology, U. Detroit, 1957; PhD in Human Genetics, U. Mich., 1965. Postdoctoral fellow Wabash Coll., Crawfordsville, Ind., 1965-66; instr. U. Detroit, 1966-68; asst. prof. Saginaw Valley State U., University Center, Mich., 1969-74, assoc. prof., 1974-79, prof., 1979—; rsch. assoc. Mich. State U., East Lansing, 1976-77; rsch. fellow Henry Ford Hosp., Detroit, 1982-83, 88-92; v.p. Saginaw Valley Retinitis Pigmentosa Found., Mich., 1979-81; vis. scientist Am. Inst. Biol. Scis., Washington, 1975-78; grant reviewer U.S. Dept. Edn., Washington, 1984-87, 91. Contbr. articles to profl. jours. Recipient Alumni award Saginaw Valley State U. Alumni Assn., 1971, Outstanding Svc. award Mich. Assoc. Biology Tchrs, 1995; grantee Fund for Ford Hosp., 1983, Mich. State U., 1977, Saginaw Valley State U. Found., 1979-82, 83-85, 86-89, Mich. Rsch. Excellence Fund, 1993, Kettering Found., 1965-66, Kellogg Found., 1961, NIH, 1961-64, Monsanto Co. rsch. grant, 1987, Dow Chem., 1988, 89, Dow Corning, 1988, 89. Fellow Human Biology Coun.; mem. Am. Soc. Human Genetics, Genetics Soc. Am., N.Y. Acad. Sci., Internat. Electrophorisis Soc., Nat. Assn. Biology Tchrs. (dir. for Mich. Outstanding Biology Tchrs. award), others. Home: 4900 Schneider St Saginaw MI 48603-4513 Office: Saginaw Valley State U Dept Biology 7400 Bay Rd University Center MI 48710-0001

PEMBERTON, BRADLEY POWELL, lawyer; b. Ft. Scott, Kans., June 15, 1952; s. Howard Duane and Juanita Lucille (Powell) P.; m. Kathleen Frances Querrey, May 22, 1976 (div. Feb. 1984); m. Lori Scott, June 18, 1994. BSBA, U. Mo., Columbia, 1974; JD, U. Mo., Kansas City, 1977. Bar: Mo. 1977, U.S. Dist. Ct. (we. dist.) Mo. 1981, U.S. Tax Ct. 1981; CPA, Mo. Tax acct. Alexander Grant & Co., Kansas City, Mo., 1977-79; shareholder Polsinelli, White, Vardeman & Shalton, Kansas City, 1979—, also bd. dirs. Active Vol. Atty. Project, Kansas City, 1984—; bd. dirs. Synergy House Inc., Kansas City, 1985-88, Youth Vol. Corps of Am., 1991—, March of Dimes, 1995—. Mem. ABA, Internat. Entrepreneurs Coun. (bd. dirs.), Mo. Bar Assn., Kansas City Bar Assn., AICPAs, Mo. Soc. CPAs, Kansas City C. of C., Entrepreneurs Club of Kansas City (bd. dirs.), KC. Home: 10222 Briar St Shawnee Mission KS 66207-3418 Office: Polsinelli White Vardeman & Shalton 700 W 47th St Ste 1000 Kansas City MO 64112-1805

PEMBERTON, WILLIAM ERWIN, historian, educator; b. Duncan, Okla., Mar. 26, 1940; s. Kermit and Coy Bernice (Erwin) P.; m. Barbara Lucinda Eppard, May 1, 1960; m. Martha Elsie Wallace, Nov. 15, 1967; children: David Gregory, Gregory Alan, Sage Tsou, Sophia El. BA, U. Okla., 1963; MA, U. Mo., 1965, PhD, 1974. Asst. prof. U. Wis., LaCrosse, 1966-69, assoc. prof., 1970-73, prof., 1974—. Author: Bureaucratic Politics, 1979, Harry S Truman, 1988, George Bush, 1993; contbr. articles to profl. jours. Mem. Orgn. Am. Historians, Am. Hist. Assn., Econ. History Assn. Home: 20163 W Ridge Ave Galesville WI 54630-8035 Office: U Wis Dept History La Crosse WI 54601

PEÑAS-BERMEJO, FRANCISCO JAVIER, Spanish language educator; b. Segovia, Spain, Mar. 13, 1961; came to U.S., 1984; s. Francisco Javier Peñas and Maria Del Carmen Bermejo. BA in English Philology, U. Complutense, Madrid, 1984; MA in Spanish, U. Ga., 1986, PhD in Romance Langs., 1991. Teaching asst. U. Ga., Athens, 1984-91, preceptor in Spanish, 1986-89; asst. prof. U. Dayton, Ohio, 1991—. Author: Julia Uceda. Poesía, 1991, Poesía existencial española del siglo XX, 1993; editor: Ulula, 1986-91; also articles. Recipient outstanding teaching asst. award U. Ga., 1986, outstanding performance award, 1985, 88, excellence in teaching award, 1989; scholar Southland Corp. Dallas, 1988-89, Dolores E. Artau scholar U. Ga., 1988-89. Mem. MLA, Am. Assn. Tchrs. Spanish and Portuguese, Assn. Licenciados y Doctores Españoles en Estados Unidos, Instituto Literario y Cultural Hispanico, Asociación Internacional de Hispanistas. Phi Beta Kappa, Sigma Delta Pi. Home: 4294 Bellemeade Dr Bellbrook OH 45305 Office: U Dayton 300 College Park Ave Dayton OH 45469-0001

PENCE, JOHN THOMAS, dietitian; b. Lafayette, Ind., June 21, 1941; s. M.O. and Florence (Lindley) P.; m. Karen Sue Turner, June 19, 1976. BS, Purdue U., 1963; MS, Kans. State U., 1970. Registered dietitian. Asst. dir. residence hall food service Kans. State U., Manhattan, 1973-82, head residence hall food service, 1982-87, assoc. dir., housing head residence hall food service, 1987—, instr. hotel, restaurant, instn. mgmt. dietetics, 1987—. Author: (with others) Recipes From the Heartland '80, 1980, Recipes From the Land of Ah's, 1982. Mem. Kans. Travel and Tourism Commn., 1987—; chmn. bd. dirs. Manhattan Community Sr. Svc. Ctr., 1990—. Recipient Silver Plate award Internat. Food Service Mfrs. Assn., 1987; named Kans. Employer Yr. Kans. Rehab. Assn., 1980. Mem. Am. Dietetic Assn., Am. Sch. Food Service Assn., Soc. For Advancement of Food Service Research, Nat. Assn. Coll. and Univ. Food Service (nat. treas. 1979-85, nat. pres. 1986-87, Meritorious Service award 1981, 83, 85). Republican. Methodist. Lodge: Kiwanis. Home: 2361 Grandview Ter Manhattan KS 66502-3729 Office: Kans State U Pittman Bldg Manhattan KS 66506

PENCE, LELAND HADLEY, organic chemist; b. Kearney, Mo., Oct. 1, 1911; s. Samuel Anderson and Rosa Louise (Reid) P.; m. Mary Ellen Elliott, Aug. 6, 1938; children: Jean, Daniel, Elizabeth. BS, U. Fla., 1932; MS, U. Mich., 1933, PhD, 1937. Teaching fellow U. Mich. Dept. Chemistry, Ann Arbor, 1933-37; organic rsch. chemist Biochem. Rsch. Found. of Franklin Inst., Phila., 1937-39; instr. Reed Coll., Portland, Oreg., 1939-42, asst. prof., 1942-45; sr. scientist Difco Labs., Inc., Detroit, 1945-83; organic rsch. chemist Mayo Clinic, Rochester, Minn., summer 1940; rsch. fellow Calif. Inst. Tech., Pasadena, 1943. Author: Phytohemagglutinin Preparations, 1962; co-contbr. articles to jour. Am. Chem. Soc. Active Tax Rev. Bd., Ferndale, Mich., 1990—; trustee Presbyn. Ch., 1969-75, 1978-81. Fellow AAAS; mem. Am. Chem. Soc. (emeritus, Detroit exec. bd. 1950-52, cert.), Tissue Culture Assn., Audubon Soc., Sierra Club, Nature Conservancy, Wilderness Soc., World Wildlife Fund, Nat. Wildlife Fedn., Circumnavigators Club, Detroit Econs. Club, Sigma Xi, Kappa Kappa Psi. Home: 972 Alberta St Ferndale MI 48220-1627

PENCHANSKY, DAVID, religious studies educator; b. Bklyn., Dec. 3, 1951; s. Charles and Mimi (Black) P.; children: Simon Graham, Maia Lucy. BA cum laude, Queens Coll., 1974; MA, Assemblies of God Grad. Sch., 1980; PhD, Vanderbilt U., 1988. Assoc. prof. U. St. Thomas, St. Paul, 1989—. Author: The Betrayal of God, 1990, Storyteller's Companion, vol. 2, 1992, The Politics of Biblical Theology, 1995, "Proverbs," Mercer Bible Commentary, 1995; contbr. articles to profl. jours. Mem. Soc. Bibl. Lit., Cath. Bibl. Assn., Phi Beta Kappa, Phi Alpha Theta. Home: 1743 LaFond Saint Paul MN 55104 Office: U St Thomas Mail # 4328 2115 Summit Ave Saint Paul MN 55105-1048

PENDLETON, BARBARA JEAN, retired banker; b. Independence, Mo., Aug. 14, 1924; d. Elmer Dean and Martha Lucille (Friess) P. Student, Cen. Mo. State Coll., 1942; D of Bus. Adminstrn. (hon.), Avila Coll., 1986. V.p. Grand Ave. Bank, Kansas City, Mo., 1962-76, exec. v.p., 1976-79; vice chmn. City Bank & Trust Co., Kansas City, 1979-82, chmn., 1982-83; exec. v.p. United Mo. Bank of Kansas City, 1983-93, United Mo. Bancshares, Inc., 1990-93; bd. dirs. Shepherd Ctrs. of Am., Inc., 1992—. Vice chmn., mem. Dept. Def. adv. com. Women in Svc., Washington, 1967-69; chmn. City of Kansas City Employee Retirement Fund, 1985—; mem. bd. dirs. YMCA USA, 1996—. Recipient Matrix award Press Women, 1963, Wohelo award Campfire, Inc., 1979. Mem. Fin. Women Internat. (nat. pres. 1972-73), Am. Humanics, Inc. (chmn. 1987-88). Club: Cen. Exchange (Kansas City) (pres. 1983-84).

PENDLETON, BRIAN FRANKLIN, sociology educator, former college dean; b. Kansas City, Mo., Nov. 3, 1950; s. Frank Schilling and Arline (Hendrickson) P.; m. Marcile ELaine Frank, May 27, 1979; children: Michelle Annette, Jennifer Christine. BA, U. Minn., Duluth, 1972; MA, U. N.D., 1974; PhD, Iowa State U., 1977. Postdoctoral research assoc. Iowa State U., Ames, 1977-78; asst. prof. sociology U. Akron, Ohio, 1978-82, assoc. prof., 1982-90, assoc. dean grad. studies and research, 1986-87; prof. sociology U. Akron, 1990—; pres. Pendleton Cons., Silver Lake, Ohio, 1984—; dir. rsch. and evaluation, mgr. Decker Family Devel. Ctr., 1990—; assoc. dir. Inst. for Motivatior and Attention Tng., Children's Hosp. Med. Ctr. of Akron. Contbr. numerous articles to profl. jours. Recipient Outstanding Citizen cert. Ohio Senate, 1984, '88, '90, Appreciation plaque City of Akron, 1982, Cuyahoga Falls Kiwanis, 1982, Appreciation cert. Multiple Schlerosis Soc., 1982, Recognition Citizen Achievements cert. Ohio Ho. Reps., 1987. Mem. APHA, Soc. Study of Biology, Am. Sociol. Assn. (Demography cert. 1987), Internat. Rural Sociol. Assn., Midwest Sociol. Soc., Multiple Linear Regression Group, North Ctrl. Sociol. Assn., Population Assn. Am., Population Ref. Bur., Rural Sociol. Soc., Soc. for Applied Sociology, World Population Soc., U.S. Karate Assn., U.S. Karate Fedn. (life, bd. dirs., chmn. laws and regulation com.), U.S. Judo Assn. (life), U.S. Jujitsu Assn. (nat. treas.), Ctrl. Tae Kwon Do Assn. Lutheran. Clubs: U. Akron Karate/Judo (faculty advisor 1978—); Ctr. for Martial Arts (Kenmore, Ohio) (bd. dirs.). Home: 3032 Englewood Dr Cuyahoga Falls OH 44224-3808 Office: U Akron Sociology Olin 247 Akron OH 44325-1905

PENKA, ELOISE MARIE, physical therapist; b. Scott City, Kans., Oct. 18, 1960; d. Victor Eugene and Eleanor Lucy (Birzer) P. AA, Dodge City

(Kans.) Coll., 1980; student, Ft. Hays State U., 1980-82; BS in Phys. Therapy magna cum laude, Wichita State U., 1984. Registered phys. therapist, Kans., Nebr., Colo., S.D., N.D., Minn., Iowa, Mo., Wyo., Okla., Mich. With Penka Farms/Ranch, Healy, Kans., 1974-84; phys. therapy technician St. Anthony Hosp., Hays, Kans., 1981-82, Agy. for Home Health Care, Wichita, Kans., 1983-84; staff phys. therapist Humana Hosp., Dodge City, Kans., 1984-87; field mgr. Rehab. Visions, Omaha, 1987—; pvt. contractor Mobile Agy. for SW Health, Garden City, Kans., 1984-87. Scholar Wichita State U., 1983-84. Mem. Am. Phys. Therapy Assn., Kans. Phys. Therapy Assn., World Confederation Phys. Therapy, Mortar Bd., Phi Kappa Phi. Democrat. Roman Catholic. Home: Draggin S Ranch Healy KS 67850-9720 Office: Rehab Visions 11623 Arbor St Omaha NE 68144-2934

PENKE, CYNTHIA MARIE, critical care nurse; b. Omaha, Jan. 8, 1963; d. Gary and Barbara K. (Ulrich) Toman; children: Jason, Stephanie Jo. ASN, U. Nebr. Med. Ctr., 1984. Charge nurse rehab. unit Irving (Tex.) Community Hosp., 1984-87; BCLS instr., home health nurse Health Force, Dallas, 1987-88; staff nurse med./surg. unit Baylor U., Dallas, 1987-88; nurse ICU, ethics com. St. Joseph Hosp., Omaha, 1988-92; home health nurse Tabitha Home Health Agy., 1990-92; home health resource nurse We Care Nursing Svcs., Milw., 1992-93, asst. dir. nursing, 1993-95; ICU staff nurse St. Joseph Hosp., Omaha, 1995—; clin. supr. NurseFinders, Omaha, 1996—.

PENKOFF, DIANE WITMER, communication educator; b. Pasadena, Jan. 20, 1945; d. Stanley Lamar and Mary Evelyn Witmer; m. Robert D. Joyce (div. 1987); 1 child, David William Penkoff. AA, Golden West Coll., Huntington Beach, Calif., 1977; BS in BA, U. LaVerne (Calif.), 1980; MS in Sys. Mgmt., U. So. Calif., L.A., 1989; MA in Communication Arts, U. So. Calif., 1993, PhD in Orgnl. Comm., 1994. Dir. pub. rels. Weight Watchers, Santa Ana, Calif., 1980-84; dir. comm. March of Dimes, Costa Mesa, Calif., 1986-90; prin. Penkoff Comm. Resources, L.A., 1990-92; instr. Calif. State U., Fullerton, 1990-94; asst. lectr. comm. arts and scis. U. So. Calif., University Park, 1991-94; asst. prof. Purdue U., West Lafayette, Ind., 1994—. Editor, The Paper Weight, 1981-84. Chmn. award com. March of Dimes, Costa Mesa, nat. vol., 1980—, also chair speakers bur. Sagemore divsn., mem. exec. com. Mem. Pub. Rels. Soc. Am. (accredited mem.), U. So. Calif. Alumni Assn., Indpls. Symphony Chorus.

PENN, RONALD HULEN, manufacturing executive; b. Pocahontas, Ark., Dec. 31, 1951; s. Hulen and Isabell (Smith) P.; m. Janieca Ann Thielemier, May 31, 1975; children: Alicia, Candace, Dustin. BS in Mktg., Ark. State U., 1973. Office mgr. Brown Shoe Co., Houston, Mo., 1973-76; overseas technician Brown Shoe Co., South America, 1976-77; asst. plant mgr. Brown Shoe Co., Pittsfield, Ill., 1978-79, plant mgr., 1979-84, mgr. tech. svcs., 1984-88, dir. tech. svcs., 1989-93, dir. tech. svc. sourcing, coord. internat. ops., 1994—. Advisor Pikeland Cmty. Unit Sch., Pittsfield, 1980; coach Little League Baseball, Union, Mo., 1986-92, sec., 1987-91; coach Little Basketball, 1987-93, pres., 1991-93; bd. dirs. Union Pks., 1992-93, treas., 1990-91, pres., 1991-94, co-chmn. aquatic/civic ctr. project; v.p. RII Athletic Booster Club, 1995-96. Named All-Conf. and Regional Football Player N.E. Ark. Athletic Assn., 1969. Mem. Alpha Kappa Psi. Republican. Mem. Ch. of Christ. Office: Meramec Group Sullivan MO 63080

PENNA, NANCY SUE, dean, registrar; b. Omaha, May 11, 1956; d. Roy E. and Helen L. (Lund) Bauermeister; m. Gary Penna, Jan. 8, 1977; children: Christopher, Tara. BSBA, Midland Luth. Coll., 1985; MS, U. Nebr., Omaha, 1991. Asst. dir. career resource ctr. Midland Luth. Coll., Fremont, Nebr., 1985-87, dir. career resource ctr., 1987-88; asst. dean, registrar Dana Coll., Blair, Nebr., 1988—. Bd. dirs. Domestic Abuse/Sexual Assault Crisis Ctr., Fremont, 1987-90, chair bd. devel. com., 1988-90; mem. Arlington Pub. Sch. Bd., 1993-97. Named Young Profl. Woman, Bus. and Profl. Women, Fremont, 1986; Edn. grantee Evang. Luth. Ch. Am., 1988, 90. Mem. Am. Assn. Collegiate Registrars and Admissions Officers, Nebr. Assn. Collegiate Registrars and Admissions Officers (sec., bd. dirs., 1990-91), Coun. Adult Experiential Learning. Lutheran. Home: 1240 W Dodge Ave Arlington NE 68002-3039 Office: Dana Coll 2848 College Dr Blair NE 68008-1041

PENNEL, MARIE LUCILLE HUNZIGER, elementary education educator; b. Oregon, Mo., Jan. 16, 1934; d. William Henry and Milree (Huff) Hunziger; m. Berres H. Pennel, Mar. 6, 1955; children: Patricia Lu Pennel Wolfe, Pamela Cille Pennel Ginther. BS, Northwest Mo. State U., 1954; MS, Kans. U., 1959; postgrad., Kans. State U. Cert. elem. tchr., Kans. 1st grade tchr. Lawrence, Kans.; kindergarten tchr. Atchison, Kans., Unified Sch. Dist. 415, Hiawatha, Kans., 1972-94. Recipient Outstanding Svc. award, Lawrence Jaycees, 1958, 59. Mem. NEA, Kans. Edn. Assn., ASCD, Assn. for Childhood Edn. Internat., Kappa Delta Pi, Delta Kappa Gamma. Home: 403 Woodbury Ln Hiawatha KS 66434-1525

PENNIMAN, NICHOLAS GRIFFITH, IV, newspaper publisher; b. Balt., Mar. 7, 1938; s. Nicholas Griffith Penniman III and Esther Cox Lony (Wight) Keeney; m. Linda Jane Simmons, Feb. 4, 1967; children: Rebecca Helmle, Nicholas G. V. AB, Princeton U., 1960. Asst. bus. mgr. Ill. State Jour. Register, Springfield, 1964-69, bus. mgr., 1969-75; asst. gen. mgr. St. Louis Post-Dispatch, 1975-84, gen. mgr., 1984-86, pub., 1986—. Chmn. Downtown St. Louis, Inc., 1988-90, Mo. Health and Ednl. Facilities Adminstrn., 1982-85, Ill. State Fair Bd., Springfield, 1973-75, St. Louis Sports Com., 1992-93; trustee St. Louis Country Day Sch., 1983-86; bd. dirs. St. Louis Arts and Edn. Coun., 1987—, St. Louis area Boy Scouts Am., 1987-96, Mercantile Libr., 1995—, Regional Commerce Assn., 1995—; v.p. Fair Found., Gateway Arch Park Extension; chmn. Forest Park Forever, 1991-93, Caring Found. for Children, 1988-91. With U.S. Army, 1962-67. Clubs: St. Louis Country, Noonday (pres. 1994). Home: 7540 Maryland Ave Saint Louis MO 63105 Office: Pulitzer Pub Co 900 N Tucker Blvd Saint Louis MO 63101-1069

PENNINGER, WILLIAM HOLT, JR., lawyer; b. Springfield, Mo., May 4, 1954; s. William Holt Sr. and Marjorie Marie (Emanuel) P.; m. Una Lee McLeer, Aug. 8, 1981; children: Una Lee, William Holt III. BS, MIT, 1976; JD, MBA, Tulane U., 1981; LLM, Tulane, 1983. Bar: La. 1981, N.Y. 1984, Mo. 1987. Customer service rep. CIT Fin. Services, Inc., Springfield, Mo., 1976-77; lexis rep. Mead Data Cen., New Orleans, 1981-83; assoc. Hill, Betts & Nash, N.Y.C., 1983-85, Cole & Deitz, N.Y.C., 1985-86; fin. planner IDS Fin. Services Inc., Springfield, Mo., 1986-87; assoc. Farrington & Curtis, Springfield, 1987-90; legal counsel Med. Def. Assocs., Springfield, 1990—; bd. dirs. Med. Def. Ins. Co., Med. Def. Assoc. Composer, performer: The Accessible Penninger, 1991, Man/Machine/Music, 1991, Fdt=mdv, 1992, The Coyote, The Scorpion & The Goat, 1993. Mem. Greene County Estate Planning Coun., 1987-91; bd. dirs. Springfield Regional Opera, 1989-93. Mem. ABA, Mo. Bar Assn. (ins. law com.), Springfield Met. Bar Assn., Nat. Assn. Securities Dealers (lic. 1986-89). Republican. Presbyterian. Home: 2705 S Patterson Ave Springfield MO 65804-3913 Office: Legal Counsel Med Def Assoc 1311 E Woodhurst Dr Springfield MO 65804-4282

PENNINGTON, BEVERLY MELCHER, financial services company executive; b. Vermillion, SD, Feb. 8, 1931; d. Cecil Lloyd and Phyllis Cecelia (Walz) M.; m. Glen D., Sept. 1, 1965 (dec. Aug. 1986); 1 child, Terri Lynn. BS, U. S.D., Vermillion, 1952. Enrolled agt. cert. IRS 1989. Sec. budget dept. Bur. of Indian Affairs, Aberdeen, S.D., 1952-53, pvt. sec., 1953-54; pvt. sec. U.S. P.H.S. Indian Health, Aberdeen, 1954-55; adminstr. asst. U.S. Pub. Health Svc., Anchorage, 1955-58, U.S. Pub. Health, Dental Pub. Health, Washington, 1958-61; grant adminstr. Dental Pub. Health, Washington, 1961-65; co-owner Penn Mel Marina, Platte, S.D, 1965-74; co-owner Pennington Tax Service, Platte, 1974-86, owner, 1986-93; pres., CEO, White Tiger Fin. Svc., Inc., Platte, 1994—. Contbr. articles to profl. jours. Mem. Platte Women's Club, sec., 1965-68, pres., 1968-70, 89-91; mem. Libr. Bd., sec., 1982-85, treas., 1995—. Fellow Am. Soc. Tax Profls. (sec. 1989-91, 2d v.p. 1995); mem. NAFE, Platte C. of C. (v.p. 1989, pres. 1990), Lyric Theatre Mus. Soc. (pres. 1988-92), U.S. C. of C., Washington Dakota Cen. Com. Republican. Presbyterian. Office: White Tiger Fin Svc Inc 420 Main Platte SD 57369

PENSIS, HENRI BRAM, music educator, conductor; b. Luxembourg, Mar. 18, 1927; came to U.S., 1940; s. Henri Paul and Marielouise (Deltgen) P.; m. Patricia Adams Robinson, June 14, 1951; children: Henri Paul, Claude Norris. Student, Morningside Coll., 1944-45; MusB, Northwestern U., 1950, MusM, 1951, postgrad., 1952. Conductor Chamber Orch., Evanston, Ill., 1947-51; prof., chair music dept. Salem (W.Va.) Coll., 1952-55; asst. prof., conductor orch. Cen. Meth. Coll., Fayette, Mo., 1955-65; prof., conductor emeritus U. Wis., Oshkosh, 1965-95; music dir., conductor, mem. exec. com. Oshkosh Symphony Orch., 1967-96; guest conductor Radio Luxembourg Symphony Orch., 1964, 72, 76, 78, 82, 84, 88;. Recipient Key to City of Oshkosh, 1976, cert. of appreciation U.S. Ambassador to Luxembourg, 1976, cert. of commendation Gov. of Wis., 1988: Henri B. Pensis Day declared in his honor, 1988, Maestro Pensis Week declared in his honor, 1996; selected as an influential citizen The Oshkosh Northwestern, 1993; Maestro. Mem. Assn. Wis. Symphony Orchs. (exec. com. 1976—, past pres.), Am. Symphony Orch. League, Conductors Guild, Phi Mu Alpha Sinfonia (life), Pi Kappa Lambda. Office: Oshkosh Symphony Orch PO Box 522 Oshkosh WI 54902-0522

PEPER, CHRISTIAN BAIRD, lawyer; b. St. Louis, Dec. 5, 1910; s. Clarence F. and Christine (Baird) P.; m. Ethel C. Kingsland, June 5, 1935 (dec. Sept. 1995); children: Catherine K. Peper Larson, Anne Peper Sale, Christian B.; m. Barbara C. Pleiter, Jan. 25, 1996. AB cum laude, Harvard U., 1932; LLB, Washington U., 1935; LLM, Yale U., 1937. Bar: Mo. 1934. Since practiced in St. Louis; of counsel Peper, Martin, Jensen, Maichel & Hetlage.; lectr. various subjects Washington U. Law Sch., St. Louis, 1943-61; ptnr. A.G. Edwards & Sons, 1945-67; pres. St. Charles Gas Corp., 1953-72; bd. dirs. St. Louis Steel Casting Inc., Hydraulic Press Brick Co., El Dorado Paper Bag Mfg. Co., Inc. Editor: An Historian's Conscience: The Correspondence of Arnold J. Toynbee and Columba Cary-Elwes, 1986. Contbr. articles to profl. jours. Mem. vis. com. Harvard Div. Sch., 1964-70; counsel St. Louis Art Mus. Sterling fellow Yale U., 1937. Mem. ABA, Mo. Bar Assn., St. Louis Bar Assn., Noonday Club, Harvard Club, East India Club (London), Order of Coif, Phi Delta Phi. Roman Catholic. Home: 1454 Mason Rd Saint Louis MO 63131-1211 Office: 720 Olive St Saint Louis MO 63101-2338

PEPITONE, VITO C., design engineer; b. Beloit, Wis., Dec. 27, 1961. AAS, Dunwoody Indsl. Inst., Mpls., 1990. Mech. drafter Beloit Corp., 1988-90; design engr. May Coating Tech., Inc., St. Paul, 1990—. Mem. Democratic Farm-Labor Party. Roman Catholic. Home: 5716 Boone Pl N New Hope MN 55428-3101 Office: May Coating Techs Inc 1825 Buerkle Rd Saint Paul MN 55110-5246

PEPONIS, HAROLD ARTHUR, insurance agent, broker; b. Chgo., Dec. 12, 1928; s. Arthur Harold and Ethel (Karambis) P.; m. Toula H. Preketes, Mar. 1, 1952 (dec. Dec. 1984); 1 child, Arthur Harold II; m. Aphrodite E. Stavros, May 26, 1990. BS, Loyola U., Chgo., 1950, postgrad., 1991—. Treas. Plaza Cleaners & Dyers, Inc., Chgo., 1950-58; owner Exch. Cleaners, Chgo., 1958-63, Park West Plaza Cleaners, Chgo., 1963-69; ins. agt. Aetna Life & Casualty, Lisle, Ill., 1969—; ptnr. lecture series/pub. co. Images of Orthodoxy; pres. Tesera Assoc., Evanston, Ill., 1973—. Pres. parish coun. United Greek Orthodox Chs. of Chgo., 1963-64, Annunciation Cathedral, 1991-92, 94; archon Order of St. Andrew, Greek Orthodox Ch., state comdr., 1994; mem. diocesan coun. Diocese of Chgo. Greek Orthodox Ch., 1994, mem. archdiocesan coun., 1996. Mem. Pan Arcadian Fedn. Am. (nat. pres. Chgo. 1963-64), Du Page Life Underwriters Assn.. Home: 715 Sheridan Rd Wilmette IL 60091-1959 Office: Aetna Life & Casualty 2956 Central St Evanston IL 60201-1246

PEPPE, KATHRYN KLUSS, pediatrics nurse, educator; b. Akron, Ohio, Mar. 4, 1947; m. Michael G. Peppe, May 15, 1976. BSN, Ohio State U., 1969, MS in Pediatric Nursing Edn., 1971. RN, Ohio. From nurse gen. surgery to burn unit nurse Ohio State U. Hosps., Columbus, 1969-70; instr. Orient (Ohio) State Inst., 1971, Ohio State U., Columbus, 1971-75; asst. nursing dir. Div. Maternal and Child Health Ohio Dept. Health, Columbus, 1975-77, adminstrv. staff nurse cons. Divsn. Maternal and Child Health, 1977-89, asst. chief Divsn. Maternal and Child Health, 1989-93, acting chief Divsn. Maternal and Child Health, 1993-94, chief Divsn. Maternal and Child Health, 1994-95; chief div. Family and Cmty. Health Svcs. Ohio Dept. Health, 1995—; mem. Ohio Devel. Disabilities Planning Coun., 1980-94. Co-author numerous publs.; editorial bd. mem. Infants and Young Children, 1991—. Grantee Ohio Dept. Health 1980, 83-86, 85-86. Fellow Am. Acad. Nursing; mem. ANA (Coun. on Maternal-Child Nursing nominating com. 1989-91), Am. Assn. on Mental Retardation (fellow 1982, chair Nat. Task Force 1973-75, chair nursing div. Ohio chpt. 1972-75), Ohio Nurses Assn. (liaison com. with Ohio State Med. Assn. and Ohio Osteopathic Assn. 1988—, selection com. March of Dimes, 1982, 85, 89—, Maternal-Child Nurse of Yr. 1981), Mid-Ohio Dist. Nurses Assn. (bd. dirs. 1980-84, bylaws com. 1973, 84, 88, nominating com. 1976, scholarship com. 1983—, methods/resources com. Office: Ohio Dept Health Div Family & Cmty Health Svcs PO Box 118 Columbus OH 43266-0118

PERDREAU, CORNELIA RUTH WHITENER (CONNIE PERDREAU), English as a second language educator, international exchange specialist; b. Beacon, N.Y.; d. Henry Kato Whitener and Mazie Althea (Martin) Whitener-Johnson; m. Michel Serge Yves Perdreau, June 14, 1969; 1 child, Maurice Laurence Henri. BA, SUNY, Potsdam, 1969; MA, Ohio U., 1971, 72. French/Latin tchr. Walt Whitman Jr. High Sch., Yonkers, N.Y., 1969-70; French teaching asst. Ohio U., Athens, 1970-71, ESL tchr., 1976—; English/French tchr. Lycee de Chambery, France, 1972; English tchr. Acad. de Paris, France, 1984; study abroad coord. Ohio U., Athens. Contbr. articles to profl. jours. Chair Tri-County Community Action Agy., Sugarcreek, Ohio, 1982; mem. bd. Dairy Barn Arts Ctr., Athens, 1985-91; trustee Ohioana Bd. Trustees, Columbus, 1987—. Mem. NAFSA Assn. Internat. Educators (pres.-elect 1995-96, pres. 1996—), TESOL (chair rules and resolutions com. 1993-95), Internat. Assn. Black Profls. in Internat. Affairs (founder), Adminstrs. and Tchrs. in ESL (chair 1992-93), Internat. Black Profls. in TESOL (founder, chair 1992-95), Ohio TESOL (pres. 1986-87), Assn. Internat. Educators (pres.-elect 1995). Office: Ohio U Study Abroad Office 243 Scott Quadrangle Athens OH 45701

PERERA, VICUMPRIYA SRIYANTHA, mathematics educator; b. Colombo, Sri Lanka, Feb. 19, 1961; came to U.S., 1986; s. George Paul and Chandrawathi (Perera) P.; m. Lilani Devika Silva, June 21, 1986; children: Vidushani Sriyanka, Vindya Sumedhika. BSc in Math. with honors, U. Colombo, 1984; MS in Math., Purdue U., Indpls., 1988; PhD in Pure Math, Purdue U., West Lafayette, 1993. Postdoctoral fellow in math. Purdue U., Indpls., 1986-94; lectr. Ohio State U., Newark, 1994—. Mem. Am. Math. Soc. Roman Catholic. Home: 64E S Westmoor Ave Newark OH 43055-1818 Office: Ohio State U Dept Math 1179 University Dr Newark OH 43055-1766

PERETTI, MARILYN GAY WOERNER, human services professional; b. Indpls., July 30, 1935; d. Philip E. and Harriet E. (Meyer) Woerner; children: Thomas A., Christopher P. BS, Purdue U., 1957; postgrad., Coll. DuPage, 1980—, U. Wis., 1981—. Nursery sch. lab. asst. Mary Baldwin Coll., Staunton, Va., 1957-58; tchr. 1st grade, nursery sch. No. Ill. area schs., 1958-61; asst. tchr. of blind Glenbard E. H.S., Lombard, Ill., 1978-80; adminstrv. asst. Elmhurst Coll., 1980-81; dir. vol. svcs. DuPage Convalescent Ctr., Wheaton, 1981-95; dir. cmty. outreach Sr. Home Sharing, Inc., Lombard, Ill., 1996—; developer new vol. pos. for vis. the non-verbal handicapped, 1994; prodr. 4 ednl. slide programs on devel. countries, 1988-91; initiator used book collection for library project U. Zululand, S. Africa, 1993-94. Editor, designer newsletter Our Developing World's Voices, 1994—. Bd. dirs. Lombard YMCA, 1977-83, pres., 1980; vol. Chgo. Uptown Ministry, 1979; participant fact finding trips El Salvador, 1988, Honduras, 1989, Nicaragua, 1989, Republic of South Africa, 1991; mem. Nature Artists Guild of Morton Arboretum; vol. PADS, 1994—. Mem. Nature Artists Guild of Morton Arboretum. Office: Sr Home Sharing Inc 837 Westmore-Meyers Rd Lombard IL 60148

PEREZ, GERARD VINCENT, art publishing company executive; b. LeMans, France, Oct. 5, 1946; came to U.S., 1971; s. Georges and Marie-Laurence (Anziani) P.; m. Nancy J. Rudin, Apr. 23, 1976; children: Samantha, Amanda. BA, B. Franklin Coll., Orleans, France, 1966; MBA, ESCAE Marseille, France, 1970; postgrad., Am. Grad. Sch. Internat. Mgmt., Glendale, Ariz., 1973. Owner, mgr. Mariettes Unltd., St. Tropez, France, 1967-69; sales engr. Paper Converting Machine Co., Inc., Green Bay, Wis., 1973-75; mgr. sales J.D. Marshall Internat., Skokie, Ill., 1975-77; pres. Fine Art Resources, Inc., Chgo., 1977-86, London Contemporary Art, Prospect Heights, Ill., 1986-91, Art Emotion Corp., Prospect Heights, 1991—. Served with French Armed Forces, 1970-71. Home: 1758 S Edgar St Palatine IL 60067-7435

PERKINS, CATHERINE ANN, corporate executive; b. Syracuse, N.Y., Oct. 13, 1946. Degree in jr. acctg., Bliss Bus. Coll., 1966. With dept. dairy tech. Ohio St. U., Columbus, 1967-68; v.p. Roger Perkins & Assocs., Belmont, Ohio, 1989—. Active Barnesville (Ohio) Hosp. Aux., 1983—; advisor 4-H, Bellsville, Ohio, 1980-90. Office: Roger Perkins & Assocs 41601 Dunlap Dr Belmont OH 43718-9600

PERKINS, MERLE LESTER, French language educator; b. West Lebanon, N.H., Apr. 16, 1919; s. Charles Elisha and Ethel (Armstrong) P.; m. Barbara Marion Cunningham, June 16, 1951; children: Elizabeth Cunningham, Janet Blair. AB, Dartmouth Coll., 1941; AM, Brown U., 1942, PhD in French, 1950. Instr. French Brown U., 1948-50, U. Chgo., 1950-53; mem. faculty U. Calif., Davis, 1953-67; prof. French U. Calif., 1963-67, chmn. dept. fgn. langs., 1962-65, chmn. dept. Italian and French, 1965-67; prof. French U. Wis., 1967—, chmn. grad. studies French, 1967-74, 77-89, Pickard Bascom prof. French, 1983—; dir. univs. Mich. and Wis. Year in France, Aix-en-Provence, 1976-77, chmn. admissions, 1979-89. Author: The Moral and Political Philosophy of the Abbè de Saint-Pierre, 1959, Voltaire's Concept of International Order, 1965, J.-J. Rousseau on History, Liberty, and National Survival, 1968, Jean-Jacques Rousseau on the Individual and Society, 1974, Diderot on the Time-Space Continuum, 1982, Montesquieu on National Power and International Rivalry, 1986, Six French Philosophes on International Rivalry and War, 1989, Marquis de Sade, His Ethics and Rhetoric: Suspense in Sade, 1989, Diderot: A Study Guide, 1990, Enlightenment Writers, Their Contributions to Two Revolutions, 1993, Ordeal of Arms, Air Combat, Europe and the Balkans, 1993, Recollections of Air Combat, World War II, 1996; also anthology, articles, reviews. Served with USAAF, 1942-45. Decorated Air medal with 3 oak leaf clusters.; Parker fellow Dartmouth Coll., 1941-42; Edwards fellow Brown U., 1948-49; Penrose Fund grantee Am. Philos. Soc., 1956-57, 72-73, 74-75; Fulbright research grantee France, 1960-61, 67-68. Mem. Am. Assn. Tchrs. French, Philol. Assn. Pacific Coast, Modern Lang. Assn. (grantee 1956-57), Internat. Assn. for 18th Century Studies, Modern Humanities Research Assn., Phi Beta Kappa. Episcopalian. Office: U Wis Dept French 1220 Linden Dr Madison WI 53706-1525

PERKINS, NORRIS LYNWOOD, III, newspaper columnist and writer; b. Smithfield, N.C., Nov. 3, 1947; s. Norris Lynwood Jr. and Mildred Mary (Brate) P.; m. Zoe Katherine Annis, May 1, 1982; children: Molly, Drew. Student, U. N.C., 1965-68; AB in English Lit., So. Ill. U., Edwardsville, 1970, postgrad., 1971-75. Store mgr. Streetside Records, St. Louis, 1975-81, mgr. retail ops., 1981-83; music columnist Riverfront Times, St. Louis, 1983--; music reviewer, feature writer St. Louis Post-Dispatch, 1984--; freelance bus. and tech. writer, producer bus. meetings and promotional events, St. Louis, 1988--; producer Busch Creative Svcs., St. Louis, 1985-87; tech. writer McDonnell Douglas Fed. Health Systems Co., St. Louis, 1987-88. Editor Sou'wester, 1972-76; contbr. articles to Post, Riverfront Times, others under name of Terry Perkins. Mem. Jazz St. Louis (bd. dirs. 1988—). Episcopalian. Home and Office: 32 Orchard Ln Saint Louis MO 63122-6945

PERKINS, WILLIAM CLYDE, business educator; b. Lebanon, Ind., Aug. 2, 1938; s. Clyde Philip and Dorothy May (Finch) P.; m. Phyllis Louise Swinford, June 18, 1960; children: Bonnie Michele, Betsy Ann Hawkins, Jeffrey William. BS in Civil Engring., Rose Polytech. Inst., 1960; MBA, Ind. U., 1962, D of Bus. Adminstrn., 1966. Instr. U.S. Mil. Acad., West Point, N.Y., 1964-65, asst. prof., 1965-66; asst. prof. Ind. U., Bloomington, 1966-69, assoc. prof., 1969-74, prof., 1974—. Author: Managing Information Technology, 1991, 94, FORTRAN for Business Students, 1981, Computers and Information Systems, 1973. Capt. U.S. Army, 1964-66. Fellow Decision Scis. Inst. (treas. 1984-86, v.p. 1982-84, pres. 1992-93, disting. svc. award 1988); mem. Midwest Decision Scis. Inst. (pres. 1984-85, 25 yr. disting. svc. award 1994), Assn. for Info. Sys., Soc. for Info. Mgmt. Mem. United Ch. of Christ. Home: 4308 Cambridge Dr Bloomington IN 47408 Office: Ind U Sch Bus Bloomington IN 47405

PERKINS, WILLIAM H., JR., finance company executive; b. Rushville, Ill., Aug. 4, 1921; s. William H. and Sarah Elizabeth (Logsdon) P.; m. Eileen Nelson, Jan. 14, 1949; 1 child, Gary Douglas. Ed., Ill. Coll. Pres. Howlett-Perkins Assos., Chgo.; mem. Ill. AEC, 1963-84, sec., 1970-84; mem. adv. bd. Nat. Armed Forces Mus., Smithsonian Instn., 1964-82. Sgt.-at-arms Democratic Nat. Conv., 1952, 56, del.-at-large, 1964, 68, 72; spl. asst. to chmn. Dem. Nat. Com., 1960; mem. Presdl. Inaugural Com., 1961, 65, 69, 73. Served with U.S. Army, 1944-46. Mem. Ill. Ins. Fedn. (pres. 1965-84), Ill. C. of C. (chmn. legis. com. 1971), Chgo. Assn. Commerce and Industry (legis. com., Raoul Wallenberg Humanitarian award 1993), Sangamo Club, Masons, Shriners. Methodist. Home: 52 N Cowley Rd Riverside IL 60546-2042 Office: 19 Riverside Rd Ste 6 Riverside IL 60546-2263

PERKINSON, ROBERT RONALD, psychologist; b. Richmond, Va., Aug. 8, 1945; s. Gordon Archibald and Sarah (Haskins) P.; m. Elizabeth Godfrey Fly, July 27, 1968 (div. 1984); children: Robert Reps, Nyshie Page, Shane William; m. Angela Kaufman, Sept. 20, 1991. BS, Colo. State U., 1968; MS, Eastern Wash. State U., 1970; PhD, Utah State U., 1974. Lic. psychologist, Wyo., S.D. Juvenile ct. psychologist, Cedar City, Utah, 1971-72; cert. chem. dependency counselor level III, S.D.; nat. cert. gambling counselor; nat. cert. alcohol and drug counselor; psychologist in pvt. practice, Jackson, Wyo., 1974-83; dir. psychol. services Western Wyo. Mental Health Assn., Jackson, 1977-78, psychologist, 1983—; psychologist, clin. dir. Keystone Treatment Ctr., 1988—; cons. in field; chief psychologist Grand Teton Nat. Pk., Teton County Sheriff's Office and Police Dept. Copyrights: The Yellowstone Park Game, The Good Health Game, The Grizzly Control Team, Communication from God, Chemical Dependency Counseling, The Mystics. Contbr. articles to profl. jours. Mem. Am. Psychol. Assn., Wyo. Psychol. Assn., S.D. Psychol. Assn., S.D. Chem. Dependency Assn., Biofeedback Soc. Am. (bd. dirs. Wyo. br.), Wyo. Bd. Psychologist Examiners (sec.-treas., bd. dirs. S.D. coun. problem gambling), Nat. Register of Health Service Providers in Psychology. Address: PO Box 159 Canton SD 57013-0159

PERLES, GEORGE JULIUS, coach, educator; b. Detroit, July 16, 1934; s. Julius George and Nellie (Romain) P.; m. Sally Ann Bradford; children: Kathleen, Terrance, John, Patrick. BS, Mich. State U., 1960, MA, 1961. Tchr., coach St. Rita H.S., Chgo., 1961-62, St. Ambrose Sch., Detroit, 1962-65; asst. coach U. Dayton, Ohio, 1965-67, Mich. State U., East Lansing, 1967-72, Pitts. Steelers, 1972-82; head coach Phila. Stars, 1982; head coach Mich. State U., East Lansing, 1983-94, athletic dir., 1990-92. Author: Ride of Lifetime, 1995. Cpl. U.S. Army, 1954-56. Named to Hall of Fame, Detroit Western H.S., 1987; named Coach of Yr., Am. football Coaches Assn., 1987, Man of Yr., Detroit News, 1988. Mem. Rotary of East Lansing, KC. Roman Catholic. Home: 6153 W Longview East Lansing MI 48823

PERLMAN, LAWRENCE, business executive; b. St. Paul, Apr. 8, 1938; s. Irving and Ruth (Mirsky) P.; children: David, Sara. BA, Carleton Coll., 1960; JD, Harvard U., 1963. Bar: Minn. 1963. Law clk. for fed. judge, 1963; assoc., ptnr. Fredrikson & Byron, Mpls., 1964-75; gen. counsel, exec. v.p. U.S. pacing ops. Medtronic, Inc., Mpls., 1975-78; sr. ptnr. Oppenheimer, Wolff & Donnelly, Mpls., 1978-80; sec., gen. counsel, v.p. corp. svcs. Control Data Corp., Mpls., 1980-82; pres. Comml. Credit Co., 1983-85, Imprimis Technology, 1985-88; pres., chief oper. officer Control Data Corp., Mpls., 1989; pres., chief exec. officer Control Data Corp. (now Ceridian Corp.), 1990-92; chmn., pres., CEO Ceridian Corp., Mpls., 1992—; bd. dirs. Ceridian Corp., Kmart Corp.,Inter-Regional Fin. Group, Inc., Seagate Tech., Inc., The Valspar Corp., Computer Network Tech.; mem. nat. adv. bd. Chem. Banking Corp. Chmn., bd. dirs. Walker Art Ctr.; regent Univ. of Minn., 1993-95. Mem. Bus. Roundtable (mem. policy com.). Office: Ceridian Corp 8100 34th Ave S Minneapolis MN 55425-1640

PERLMUTTER, NORMAN, finance company executive; b. 1934. BS, U. Ill., 1956. With Greenbawm Mortgage Co., Chgo., 1959-66; with Heitman Fin. Svcs. Ltd., Chgo., 1966—, chmn., CEO. With USN, 1956-59. Office: Heitman Fin Ltd 180 N La Salle St Ste 3600 Chicago IL 60601-2804*

PERLOZZI, DARLA RAE, musician, composer; b. Youngstown, Ohio, June 20, 1967; d. Raymond Joseph and Palma Mary (Kennedy) P. MA, Dana Sch. Music, Youngstown. Tech. WYTV Broadcasting, Youngstown, 1985-86; producer, dir., engr. WKBN Broadcasting, Youngstown, 1986-94; producer, writer, sales rep. The Image Producers, Canfield, Ohio, 1995—; internat. rep. Maxtone, Taiwan, Asia, Europe, 1994-95; tchr. Music Gallery, Canfield, 1993-95; drummer Cloverleaf Band, Youngstown, 1980—; pres. Raydar Recording Prodns., Poland, Ohio, 1988-95, The Darper Agy., Poland, 1995; adv. bd. WKTL Govt. Funding, Struthers, Ohio, 1992. Mem. IBEW, Am. Fedn. Musicians, Songwriters Assn. Home and Office: RayDar Prodns 130 Massachusetts Ave Poland OH 44514

PERLT, WALTER E., state legislator; m. Louise M. Swan; 2 children. BA, Hamline U., 1951. Mem. Minn. Ho. of Reps. St. Paul, 1992-96; mem. commerce and econ. devel. com., judiciary and labor-mgmt. rels. com. Democrat. Home: 6116 Linden Rd Saint Paul MN 55125-2052*

PEROTTI, ROSE NORMA, lawyer; b. St. Louis, Aug. 10, 1930; d. Joseph and Dorothy Mary (Roleski) Perotti. BA, Fontbonne Coll., St. Louis, 1952; JD, St. Louis U., 1957. Bar: Mo. 1958. Trademark atty. Sutherland, Polster & Taylor, St. Louis, 1958-63, Sutherland Law Office, 1964-70; trademark atty. Monsanto Co., St. Louis, 1971-85, sr. trademark atty., 1985-91, assoc. trademark counsel, 1991-94, trademark counsel, 1994-96; trademark counsel, Polster, Lieder, Woodruff & Lucchesi, 1996—. Honored with dedication of faculty office in her name, St. Louis U. Sch. Law, 1980. Mem. Mo. Bar, Bar Assn. Met. St. Louis, ABA, Am. Judicature Soc., Smithsonian Assocs., Friends St. Louis Art Museum, Mo. Bot. Garden. Office: Polster, Lieder, Woodruff & Lucchesi 80763 S New Ballas Rd Saint Louis MO 63141

PERREAULT, LAURA CECILE, retired educator, volunteer; b. Detroit, Aug. 28, 1925; d. Joseph Hector and Cecile (St. Jacques) P.; m. Marvin Andrew Carlson, Nov. 29, 1947 (div. Dec. 1966); children: Lisa Marie Carlson Van Houzen, Kirk Andrew Carlson; m. Frank Longo, Dec. 19, 1968 (div. Sept. 1972). BS, Wayne State U., 1947, MEd, 1969. Cert. elem. tchr., Mich. Sch. tchr. Allen Park (Mich.) Bd. Edn., 1948-53, Detroit Bd. Edn., 1953-87; reading tutor Christ Child Soc., Detroit, 1988-90, St. Vincent de Paul & Sarah Fisher Home for Children, 1995—; co-chair adult edn. St. Ives Ch., Southfield, Mich., 1990-91; moderator nat. issues forum Southfield Libr., 1991-94. Bd. dirs. The Friends of Southfield Pub. Libr., 1994-95; vol. catechist St. Ives Ch., 1993-94; beautification chair San Marino Villas Improvement Assn., Southfield, 1985-87, 94-95, pres., 1988-91; active Cranbrook Peace Found., Bllomfield Hills, Mich., 1991-95. Mem. AAUW (co-chair internat. affairs study group 1990-91, bd. dirs. Birmingham br. 1991—, v.p., program chair 1991-93), LWV (Oakland County dep. registrar 1993—, precinct del. Southfield City 1994), Womens Internat. League for Peace and Freedom (environ. com. 1994—), Womens Action for New Directions, Peace Action (telephone com. 1993-95), Mich. Coalition for Safe Energy, ERAm. Roman Catholic.

PERRICONE, CHARLES, state legislator; b. Oct. 10, 1960. Student, Kalamazoo Coll., Western Mich. U. Rep. Mich. State Dist. 61, 1995—; higher edn. com. Mich. Ho. Reps., human resources com., labor com., vice chair tax policy com. Address: PO Box 30014 Lansing MI 48909-7514

PERROTTO, LARRY J., newspaper executive; married; 3 children. Degree, Edinboro U., 1959. Pres., CEO Am. Pub. Co.; mem. bd. dirs. Am. Pub. Co., West Frankfort, Ill., Argus Corp., Toronto, Ont., Barber Mine Timber Co., DuQuoin, Ill., Hollinger, Inc., Toronto, Shawnee Bancorp, Harrisburg, Ill., Western Dominion Investments, Vancouver, B.C. Recipient Disting. Alumni award U. Edinboro, 1991. Mem. Delta Sigma Chi. Home: 47 Frankfort Dr West Frankfort IL 62896 Office: President/CEO Chicago Sun Times 401 N Wabash Ave Chicago IL 60611

PERRY, CHRIS NICHOLAS, advertising executive; b. Pitts., Dec. 25, 1945; s. Nicholas and Georgia (Demas) P.; Kathleen Clarke, June 19, 1971; children: Damien, Adam, Dana. BA, U. Pitts., 1968. With Youngstown (Ohio) Steel, 1968-70; creative supr. Ketchum Communications, Pitts., 1970-74; pres., creative dir. Hedding, Perry, Davis Inc., Charlotte, N.C., 1974-76; v.p., creative dir. Fahlgren & Swink Advt., Marion, Ohio, 1976-79; v.p., creative dir. Meldrum and Fewsmith Communications, Inc., Cleve., 1979-82, sr. v.p. creative services, 1982-85, exec. v.p. creative services, 1985-86, pres., chief operating officer, 1986-87, chmn., chief exec. officer, creative dir., 1987—, also bd. dirs. Mem. bd. disting. judges and advisors The N.Y. Festivals, 1988—. Recipient numerous awards for creative excellence. Mem. Am. Assn. Advt. Agys. (sec.-treas. cen. region 1990-91, chmn. 1992-93), Cleve. Advt. Club, Cleve. Soc. Communicating Arts (pres. 1985-87, Disting. Communicator award 1991), The Hermit Club, Columbia Hills Country Club, The Union Club, Firestone Country Club. Office: Meldrum & Fewsmith Comm Inc 1350 Euclid Ave Cleveland OH 44115-1815*

PERRY, DEBORAH VEY, senior clinical research associate; b. Waynesboro, Va., May 18, 1966; d. Donald Paul Vey and Judith Louise (Tremel) Daniels. BS in Biology, James Madison U., 1988; cert. nuclear medicine tech., U. Va., 1989. Cert. nuc. medicine technologist. Nuclear medicine tech. asst. dept. nuclear medicine U. Va. Health Scis. Ctr., Charlottesville, 1988, gastrointestinal rsch. tech., 1989, radiology tech. asst., 1989; staff nuclear medicine tech. divsn. nuclear medicine Mallinckrodt Inst. Radiology, St. Louis, 1989-92, sr. staff nuclear medicine tech., 1992; sr. clin. rsch. coord. Mallinckrodt Med., Inc., St. Louis, 1992-93, clin. rsch. assoc., 1993-95, sr. clin. rsch. assoc., 1995—; nuclear medicine student coord. Mallinckrodt Inst. Radiology, 1989-92; clin. faculty mem. sch. allied health professions St. Louis U. Med. Ctr., 1991-92. Contbr. articles to profl. jours. Active CAP, 1987-88. Mem. Nat. Soc. Nuclear Medicine, Mo. Vall Chpt. Soc. Nuclear Medicine, Greater St. Louis Soc. Nuclear Medicine. Office: Mallinckrodt Med Inc PO Box 5840 675 McDonnell Blvd Saint Louis MO 63134

PERRY, ESTON LEE, real estate and equipment leasing company executive; b. Wartburg, Tenn., June 16, 1936; s. Eston Lee and Willimae (Heidle) P.; m. Alice Anne Schmidt, Oct. 21, 1961; children: Julie Anne, Jeffrey John, Jennifer Lee. B.S., Ind. State U., 1961. With Oakley Corp., 1961—, dir., 1965—, v.p., 1981-86, pres., 1986—; corp. officer Ind. State Bank, Terre Haute, 1975-80; pres. One Twenty Four Madison Corp., Terre Haute, 1979—, also bd. dirs., chmn. bd., 1981—. Bd. dirs. Aviation Commn., Terre Haute, pres., 1970; bd. dirs. Salvation Army, Terre Haute, 1975-91, mem. exec. adv. bd., 1979-87; bd. dirs. Vigo County Dept. Pub. Welfare, 1979-82, Jr. Achievement Wabash Valley, 1980-86; bd. dirs. United Way of Wabash Valley, 1984-89, chmn. fund campaign, 1984, bd. dirs. United Way of Ind., 1984-90, v.p., 1986, pres. 1988-89; trustee Oakley Found., 1970—; bd. dirs. Terre Haute Symphony Orch., 1984-87, Ind. State U. Found., 1988—, Goodwill Industries of Terre Haute, 1984—, Leadership Terre Haute, 1984-88, Cen. Eastside Assocs., 1984-88, pres., 1984-85; mem. exec. com. Ind. State U. Found., 1990-94; bd. dirs. City of Terre Haute Hulman Links Commn., pres., 1986-91; mem. President's Assocs., Ind. State U., adv. bd. Ctr. Econ. Devel., 1984—; bd. overseers Sheldon Swope Art Gallery of Terre Haute, 1984-87; nat. mem. Council on Founds.; mem. adv. com. comml. air service study Ind. Dept. Commerce; bd. assocs. Rose Hulman Inst. Tech., 1986—. Served with U.S. Army, 1955-57. Mem. Jaycees Terre Haute (v.p. 1967-69), C. of C. Terre Haute (bd. dirs. 1984-93, vice chmn. 1986-88, chmn. 1990), Wabash Valley Pilots Assn., Aircraft Owners and Pilots Assn., Air Safety Found., Aviation Trades Assn., Lambda Chi Alpha. Clubs: Country of Terre Haute (bd. dirs.), Aero of Terre Haute; Sycamore Varsity (Ind. State U.). Lodges: Lions (pres. Terre Haute 1983-84), Elks. Home: 25 Bogart Dr Terre Haute IN 47803-2401 Office: 8 S 16th St Terre Haute IN 47807-4102

PERRY, GEORGE, neuroscience researcher; b. Lompoc, Calif., Apr. 12, 1953; s. George Richard and Mary Arlene (George) P.; m. Paloma Aguilar, May 21, 1983; children: Anne A., Elizabeth A. BA, U. Calif., Santa Barbara, 1974; PhD, U. Calif., Scripps Inst. of Oceanography, San Diego, 1979. Postdoctoral fellow Baylor Coll. Medicine, Houston, 1979-82; from asst. prof. to prof. pathology, neurosci. Case Western Res. U., Cleve., 1982—, chmn. med. sch. faculty coun., chmn. faculty senate, 1996—; chmn. study sect. NIH, Bethesda, Md., 1988-93. Editor: Alterations in the Neuronal Cytoskeleton in Alzheimer Disease, Clin. Neurosci.; assoc. editor Am. Jour. Pathology, 1994—; mem. 1992—; mem. editl. bd. Am. Jour. Pathology, 1992—, African Jour. Neuroscis., Alzheimer Assoc. Disorder, Alzehimer's Disease Review; contbr. papers to profl. publs. Fellow Muscular Dystrophy Assn., 1980; recipient Career Devel. award NIH, 1988; grantee NIH, 1988—. Mem. AAAS, Microscopy Soc. N.E. Ohio (treas. 1986-88, trustee 1988-90, pres. 1990-91), Am. Soc. Cell Biology, Soc. Neurosci., Am. Assn. Investigative Pathologists, Am. Assn. Neuropathologists (awards com. 1992-96, coun. 1995—). Democrat. Roman Catholic. Home: 2500 Eaton Rd University Ht OH 44118-4339 Office: Case Western Res U 2085 Adelbert Rd Cleveland OH 44106-2622

PERRY, GLENN EARL, political science educator; b. Barbourville, Ky., Jan. 28, 1940; s. Tollie and Pearl (Taylor) P.; m. Eleanor Rose Hypes, Aug. 13, 1963; children: Barbara, Glenn E. Jr., Cathy, Lucy, Alex. AB summa cum laude, Union Coll., Barbourville, Ky., 1960; PhD, U. Va., 1964; postgrad., Princeton U., 1967-68. assoc. mem. Ctr. for Mid. Ea. Studies, U. Chgo. Instr. Union Coll., 1960; asst. prof. U. Southwestern La., Lafayette, 1963-66, Am. U. in Cairo, 1968-70; asst. prof. polit. sci. Ind. State U., Terre Haute, 1966-68, assoc. prof., 1970-77, prof., 1977—. Author: The Middle East: Fourteen Islamic Centuries, 1983, 3d edit., 1996, The Palestine Question: An Annotated Bibliography, 1990; editor: The Palestinians: Exile and Occupation, 1985, Palestine: Continuing Dispossession, 1986; mem. adv. editorial bd. Internat. Jour. Islamic and Arabic Studies, 1984-85, assoc. editor, 1985—; contbr. articles, chpts. to books. Woodrow Wilson fellow, 1960-61, NDEA fellow, 1960-63, Nat. Def. Fgn. Lang. fellow, 1967-68; Fulbright scholar, 1965. Mem. Am. Polit. Sci. Assn., Mid East Studies Assn. N.Am. (com. on images 1971-75, com. on precollegiate edn. 1975-79), Mid. East Inst., Assn. Arab-Am. Univ. Grads. Home: 2913 Crawford St Terre Haute IN 47803 Office: Ind State U Dept Political Science Terre Haute IN 47809

PERRY, GLORIA BURGESS, retired nursing educator; b. St. Louis, Sept. 30, 1936; d. John Henry and Elizabeth Amanda (Holtmann) Kruse; m. Albert T. Perry, Aug. 14, 1981; children: (previous to current marriage) Mark, John, Joe, Chris. BSN, U. Mo., St. Louis, 1960; MSN, St. Louis U., 1971, PhD, 1974; postdoctoral studies, U. Ill., Peoria, 1981-82. Clin. instr. Luth. Hosp. Sch. Nursing, St. Louis, 1960-61; staff nurse Mo. Bapt. Hosp., St. Louis, 1963-65; instr. Mo. Bapt. Sch. Nursing, St. Louis, 1965-69; supr. newborn ICU Jewish Hosp., St. Louis, 1971-72; from asst. to assoc. prof. sch. nursing So. Ill. U., Edwardsville, 1975-87, prof. then prof. emeritus, 1987—, prof. emeritus, 1992; asst. dean rsch. and planning So. Ill. U., 1976-82, project dir. nurse traineeship grants, 1985-92. Mem. merit badge counselor Boy Scouts Am., St. Louis, 1976—. Mem. Nat. League for Nursing (coun. baccalaureate and higher degree programs, accreditation site vis. 1990-92), Mo. League for Nursing (pres. 1988-90, chair fin. com. 1990-92), Phi Kappa Phi, Sigma Phi Omega, Sigma Theta Tau. Presbyterian. Home: 3323 Haas Ave Bridgeton MO 63044-3320

PERRY, JAMES ALFRED, environmental scientist, consultant, educator, administrator; b. Dallas, Sept. 27, 1945. BA in Fisheries, Colo. State U., 1968; MA, Western State Coll., 1973; PhD, Idaho State U., 1981. Sr. water quality specialist Idaho Div. Environ., Pocatello, 1974-82; area mgr. Centrac Assocs., Salt Lake City, 1982; prof. forest water quality U. Minn., St. Paul, 1982—, dir. natural resources policy and mgmt., 1985—, dir. grad. studies in water resources, 1988-92; dep. dir. AID-funded Environ. Tng. Project for Ctrl. and Ea. Europe, 1992-96; spl. asst. to dean grad. sch. U. Minn., St. Paul, 1996—; vis. scholar Oxford U., Green College, Eng., 1990-91; internat. cons. in water quality. Charter mem. Leadership Devel. Acad., Lakewood, Minn., 1988. ACOP/ESCOP nat. leadership fellow, 1995—. Mem. Minn. Acad. Scis. (bd. dirs. 1987-90), Am. Water Resources Assn., Internat. Water Resources Assn., Internat. Soc. Theoretica and Applied Limnology, N.Am. Benthol Soc. (exec. bd. Albuquerque 190-91), Sigma Xi, Xi Sigma Pi, Gamma Sigma Delta. Office: U Minn Dept Forest Resource 115 Green Hall 1530 Cleveland Ave N Saint Paul MN 55108-1027

PERRY, MICHAEL DEAN, professional football player; b. Aiken, S.C., Aug. 27, 1965. Student, Clemson. Defensive tackle Cleveland Browns, 1988-94, Denver Broncos, 1994—. Voted to Pro Bowl, 1989-91, 93; named defensive tackle The Sporting News All-Pro team, 1989-93. Office: Denver Broncos 13655 Broncos Pkwy Englewood CO 80112*

PERRY, MICHAEL MOORE, electrical engineer; b. Carthage, Mo., July 24, 1951; s. Michael M. and Margaret E. (Mink) P.; m. Janice Nell Hazlett, Nov. 15, 1975; children: Darlene, Heather, Michelle. BEE, U. Mo., Rolla, 1975. Design engr. Beech Aircraft Corp., Wichita, Kans., 1975-77, Rockwell Internat., Richardson, Tex., 1977-80; product design engr. King Radio Corp., Olathe, Kans., 1980-83; quality assurance engr. DCASR, St. Louis, 1983-85; test equipment design engr. Zenith Electronics Corp., Springfield, Mo., 1985-92; test engr. Display Techs., Carthage, Mo., 1992-93; engr. Eagle Picker, Joplin, Mo., 1995—. Republican. Baptist. Home: 210 N Fountain Carterville MO 64835

PERRY, RICHARD JOEL, information systems professional; b. Detroit, Mar. 23, 1943. BS in Math. and Computer Sci., Mich. State U., 1969. Regional sales dir. CAE Systems, Sunnyvale, Calif., 1981-86; regional dir. Test Systems Strategies, Beaverton, Oreg., 1986-91; CEO Teknowledgy Inc., Eden Prairie, Minn., 1991—; mem. adv. bd. Inter Active Multi Media, Mpls., 1991—; advisor Hennepin Tech. Coll., Eden Prairie, 1994—. With U.S. Army, 1961-65. Mem. Norex CEO Club. Roman Catholic.

PERSHING, ROBERT GEORGE, telecommunications company executive; b. Battle Creek, Mich., Aug. 10, 1941; s. James Arthur and Beulah Francis P.; BS in Elec. Engring., Tri-State Coll., Angola, Inc., 1961; m. Diana Kay Prill, Sept. 16, 1961, (div. Jan. 1989); children: Carolyn, Robert; m. Charlene Jean Reed Wallis, Mar. 18, 1989 (div. Dec. 1995). Comm. engr. Am. Elec. Power, Ind., N.Y. and Ohio, 1961-69; design supr. Wescom, Inc., Ill., 1969-74; dir. engring. Tellabs, Inc., Lisle, Ill., 1974-78; pres., CEO, bd. dirs. Teltrend, Inc., St. Charles, Ill., 1979-89, chmn. bd., 1979-88; CEO DKP Prodns. Inc., St. Charles, Ill., 1986-89; exec. cons. Teltrend, 1979-93, bd. dirs., 1988-93; asst. treas. Magnekopy Inc., Villa Park, Ill, chmn. bd.; bd. dirs. TI Investors, Inc.; advisor entrepreneurial studies U. Ill.; engring. cons. Recipient Chgo. Area Small Bus. award, 1986, INC 500 awards, 1987, 88. Mem. IEEE. Office: 1519 Kirkwood Dr Geneva IL 60134-1659

PERSICO, VINCENT ANTHONY, state legislator; b. Oak Pk., Ill., Dec. 9, 1948; s. Vincent Michael and Lavergne (Gehrke) P.; (div.); 1 child, Derek. BA, U. Ill., 1971; MA, No. Ill. U., 1986. Tchr.; mem. Ill. Ho. of Reps. from 39th dist., 1991—; mem. Edn. Appropriations, Elem. and Secondary Edn., Energy & Environ., Transp. & Motor Vehicles Coms. Ill. Ho. of Reps., vice spokesman Edn. Fin. Com. Trustee Milton Twp., Ill., 1988-91. Mem. Ill. Edn. Assn. Republican. Home: 650 Lenox Rd Glen Ellyn IL 60137-4270*

PERSKY, SEYMOUR HOWARD, real estate development and management executive; b. Chgo., May 22, 1922; s. Joseph E. and Bertha (Solomon) P.; divorced; children: Abby Joan, Jonathan Edward. AA magna cum laude, City Coll., Chgo., 1949; BA, Roosevelt U., 1952; JD, DePaul U., 1952; postgrad., Northwestern U., 1962. Ptnr. Persky, Phillips & Berzock, Chgo., 1961-63; resident counsel Mid-West Loan Co., Chgo., 1963; pub. defender narcotics ct. Mcpl. Ct. of Chgo., 1964; chmn. bd. dirs. Parliament Enterprises, Ltd., Chgo., 1964—. Bd. dirs. arch. com. Art Inst. Chgo.; mem. bd. overseers Sch. Arch., Ill. Inst. Tech., Chgo.; bd. advisors Chgo. Musical Coll.; trustee Roosevelt U., Chgo.; bd. dirs. Jewish United Fund/Jewish Fedn. Met. Chgo., Inst. for Psychoanalysis, Chgo.; mem. Commn. on Chgo. Landmarks. Recipient Resolution, City Coun. of Chgo., 1986, Disting. Svc. award AIA, 1993, I Will award Ctrl. Mich. Ave Assn., 1995; named to Sr. Citizens Hall of Fame, City of Chgo., 1992, Entrepreneurship Hall of Fame, U. Ill.-Chgo., 1994. Mem. Soc. Archtl. Historians (bd. dirs.), Cliff Dwellers Club Chgo., Union League Club of Chgo., Standard Club of Chgo., Carlton Club of Chgo., Chgo. Mercantile Club Exch. Club, Univ. Club. Jewish. Office: Parliament Enterprises Ltd 123 W Madison St 20th Fl Chicago IL 60602

PERSON, GARY CHARLES, economic development administrator; b. Banner County, Nebr., Nov. 24, 1954; s. Charles and Viola P.; m. Joyce Person, Oct. 30, 1976; children: Crystal, Cassandra. AA, Nebr. Western Coll., 1975; BS in Journalism, U. Nebr., Kearney, 1977. Mng. editor Clay County Sun, Clay Center, Nebr., 1977-78, Clay County News, Sutton, Nebr., 1977-78; news editor Sidney (Nebr.) Telegraph, 1978-79; in news and pub. rels. So. Panhandle bur. Scottsbluff (Nebr.) Star-Herald, 1979-85; mgr. Employee of High Plains Devel. Group Cheyenne County C. of C., 1985-88; dir. Scottsbluff and Sidney offices Western Office of Gov., 1988-91; project coord. Person to Person Pub. Rels. Firm, 1991; econ. devel. dir. City of Sidney/Cheyenne County, 1991—. Bd. dirs. Meml. Health Ctr., 1995—; bd. dirs. Nebr. Jaycee Found., 1989—, state v.p., 1994-95; mem. Nebr. Devel. Network; mem. betterment in edn. com. Chadron State Coll.; mem. Mid-Am. Econ. Devel. Coun., Am. Econ. Devel. Coun.; cmty. bd. rep. Sidney Head Start. Recipient Enda Anderson award C. of C., 1994, Disting. Cmty.Svc. award, 1993, Cmty. Svc. to Humanity award, 1987, Nebr. Daily Newspaper Columnist of Yr. award, 1982, Sidney's Outstanding Young Man of Yr. award, 1981, numerous others; named Outstanding Young Nebraskan of Yr., 1988, Alumnus of Yr., Nebr. C.C., 1996. Mem. Nebr. Econ. Developers Assn. (bd. dirs. 1992-93, state treas. 1993-94, state v.p. 1994-95, state pres. 1995-96), Nebr. C. of C. and Industry (bd. dirs. 1990-91, econ. devel. com. 1991-95), Cheyenne County C. of C. Address: PO Box 79 Sidney NE 69162

PERSON, PAULA (MRS. P. BARRY PERSON), social skills organization executive, entrepreneur; b. Worcester, Mass., Feb. 19, 1935; d. Leo Joseph and Imelda Mary (Elmore) Barry; married; children: Suzanne Elizabeth Person Tapley, John Lloyd III, Christian Barry. BA in Edn. and Spanish, Marymount Coll., 1957; postgrad., Harrington Inst. Interior Design, 1974-75. Cert. elem. tchr., N.Y. Founder, tchr. Post Nursery Sch. U.S. Forces, Aschaffenbrug, Fed. Republic Germany, 1958, Post Kindergarten Sch. U.S. Forces, Aschaffenbrug, 1959-62; tchr. King Solver Sch., Ft. Knox, 1963-64, Model Sch., Louisville, 1964-66; free lance interior designer Chgo., 1974-79; pres., founder The Children's Spoon, Winnetka, Ill., 1979—, London, 1985—; co-founder Aschaffenburg Players, 1960-90, creater of cultural events for children U.S./Eng., 1980—. Author, designer The Children's Spoon Coloring Book of Manners for Boys and Girls, 1985; creater 9 musical ditties for program and cassete tape. Active presdl. campaigns, 1972, 80; swimming instr. ARC, Milton, Vt. Marymount Coll.; fundraiser UNICEF Children with AIDS, 1992, 93, 94, 95; organizer Mothers United for Manners Soc., 1995. Named Showcase House Designer, Park Ridge Youth Campus Fundraiser, 1982, 84, 85. Mem. Internat. Platform Assn., Internat. Women Assocs. Internat. Visitor's Ctr., The English Speaking Union (Chgo. chpt.), Marymount Coll. Alumnae Assn. (pres. 1977-80). Office: The Children's Spoon PO Box 148 Winnetka IL 60093-0148

PERUSEK, WESLEY, educational program developer, administrator; b. Lorain, Ohio, Nov. 2, 1930; s. Rudolph and Edna Mae (Bowditch) P.; m. Patricia Ann Ellison, Aug. 25, 1956; children: Glenn W., Dawn K. Perusek Stang, Gail P. BS in Edn. with honors, Kent (Ohio) State U., 1959, MA, 1964; EdD, Rutgers U., 1979. Lic. tchr., supr., Ohio, N.J. Tchr. Twinsburg (Ohio) Schs., 1959-61; instr., asst. prof. Kent State U. Sch. Coll. Edn., 1961-67; supr., state rsch. assoc. N.J. Dept. Edn., Trenton, 1967-75; state assoc. dir. Ford Found. Tech. for Children program, Trenton, 1975-81; initiator, team mem. devel. N.J. Statewide Inventive thinking Program MIIT/SITE, 1978-81; assoc. prof. Ohio No. U., Ada, 1981-85; cons. Sarasota (Fla.) County Schs., 1985-86; asst. prof. Lima br. Ohio State U., 1988; cons. Ohio schs., Ohio Dept. Edn., Wright State U., Toledo, Marion, Lorain, Allen & Putnam Co., Ohio; coord. diversified indsl. edn. Apollo Career Ctr., Lima, 1993-95; cons. Texaco Corp. R&D, Create S.E. Tex. Project, Port Arthur, 1993—, schs. and programs in Mass., N.C., Tex., Vt., Pa., Conn., Ohio, N.H., Fla., 1970-80, Ohio Dept. Edn., New Am. Schs. Devel. Corp., Am. Coals 2000, U.S. Dept. Edn., design teams, Columbus, Ohio, 1991; mem. Edn. Roundtable Project XL, U.S. Patent and Trademark Office, Washington, 1988-95; nat. judge edn. Donald Quigg award for excellence in edn. Project XL, 1990-92; state judge Ohio Sci. Day, Ohio Jr. Acad. Sci., 1993-96. Coord. vols. habitat for Humanity, Sarasota, Fla., 1985-86; Boy Scouts Am., Trenton, 1970—. With USAF, 1951-55. Mem. ASCD, Internat. Tech. Edn. Assn., Am. Creativity Assn., Am. Vocat. Assn., Nat. Inventive Thinking Assn., Assn. Childhood Edn. Internat. (standing com. on later, childhood and early adolescence 1989-95), Optimists, Phi Delta Kappa (v.p. programs Findlay Millstream chpt. 1992-95). Home and Office: 215 Willeke Ave Ada OH 45810-1641

PERUZZO, ALBERT LOUIS, actuary, accountant; b. Chgo., Dec. 27, 1951; s. Anthony L. and Annette (Gentile) P. BS in Math., No. Ill. U., 1973, BS in Accountancy, 1974, MBA, 1975. CPA, Ill. Auditor Deloitte, Haskins & Sells, CPA's, Chgo., 1976-79; valuation analyst IV CNA Ins., Chgo., 1979-89, mgr. valuation compliance, 1989-92, valuation analyst, actuarial asst., 1992—. Treas., bd. dirs. Dignity/Chgo., 1982-84, Integrity/Chgo., 1988-93; dep. vol. Voter's Registrar Bd. Elections, Chgo., 1984-86; bd. dirs. Colonial Condo, 1990—. Mem. AICPA, Am. Acad. Actuaries, Soc. Actuaries (assoc.), Ill. CPA Soc. (Silver medal 1975), Chgo. Actuarial Assn. Democrat. Roman Catholic.

PERZ, SALLY, state legislator; m. Joseph Perz; children: Allison, Julie, Melanie, Andrea, Brian. BA, Siena Heights. Ohio State rep. Dist. 52, 1993; mgmt. cons. Perz, Inc., 1996—. Active Boy Scouts Am. Recipient Carlson Counyt Mktg. award, 1984-93, Women of Achievement award, 1993. Mem. Toledo Club, Toledo C. of C., Toledo Rotary, Toledo Sisters Cities (exec. bd.). Home: 3205 River Rd Toledo OH 43614 Office: Ohio Ho of Reps State House Columbus OH 43215*

PESAVENTO, MARI JO, physical therapist; b. Chgo., Dec. 12, 1950; d. Joseph R. and Mary Jo (Samelack) Q.; m. Robert J. Pesavento, Mar. 16, 1974; children: Michael, Lynne, Bobby, Lisa. BS in Phys. Therapy, U. Health Sci./Chgo. Med. Sch., 1972. Clin. faculty Northwestern U., Chgo., 1975-77; pediat. phys. therapist Cook County Hosp., Chgo., 1972-74, Med. Pers., Oak Lawn, 1984—; phys. therapist Brandecker Easter Seal, Chgo., 1974-83; specialist Kids in Motion, Midlothian, Ill., 1990-94; cons. St. Francis Hosp., Blue Island, Ill., 1986-89; pvt. practice Pediatric Phys. Therapy, Chgo., 1985—; bd. dirs. Oak Lawn Hosp. Health Care, 1976-78. Contbr. articles to profl. jours. Com. chmn. Boy Scouts Am. Troop 617, Chgo., 1993-94; profl. assistance mem. Winners for Wheels, Orland Park, 1994; cheerleading moderator St. Christina Grammar Sch., Chgo., 1988—. Mem. Am. Phys. Therapy Assn., Neurodevelopmental Treatment Assn., Nat. Spina Bifieda Assn. Roman Catholic. Office: Pediatric Phys Therapy 3417 W 115th Pl Chicago IL 60655

PESEC, DAVID JOHN, data systems executive; b. Cleve., Apr. 19, 1956; s. Rudolph J. and Martha C. (Kessler) P. BS, Cleve. State U., 1988. Cons. in pvt. practice Cleve., 1976-78; programmer Champion Svc. Corp., Cleve., 1978; sr. systems programmer United Telephone of Ohio, Mansfield, 1978-89; dir. devel. Broderick Data Systems, Mansfield, 1989—. Bd. dirs. ARC, Mansfield, 1989—, Mansfield Emergency Svc., 1996; assoc. pastor Cornerstone Grace Bapt. Ch., 1995—; life mem. Rep. Nat. com., 1991—, Rep. Senatorial Inner Circle, 1991—. Mem. Am. Mgmt. Assn., Assn. Computing Machinery, Intercity Radio Club (pres. 1987-90), NRA, Gideons (v.p. 1992), Profl. Photographers. Republican. Mem. Grace Brethren Ch. Home: 1633 Hickory Ln Mansfield OH 44905-2945 Office: Broderick Data Systems 777 Laver Rd Mansfield OH 44905-2307

PESKILUOMA See PESKLO, CHRISTOPHER RICHARD

PESKLO, CHRISTOPHER RICHARD (PESKILUOMA), history educator; b. N.Y.C., Dec. 27, 1959; s. Joseph Richard and Violet (Andersen) P. BA in History, U. Minn., 1992. Cert. paralegal; cert. tchr., Minn. Case asst. Dorsey & Whitney, Mpls., 1993—; sr. page Minn. Ho. of Reps., St. Paul, 1995—; genealogist Scandinavian Genealogy Svcs., Mpls., 1985—. Editor: Original Documents: Vital Documents of Margit Christiansen, 1992; author: Technology and Innovation: The U.S. Chain Mesh. Industry from 1860 to 1930, 1992. Vol. Bosnia War Crime tribunal, 1993, Mpls. Neighborhood Svcs., 1996; rsch. intern DFL caucus rschr. Minn. Ho. of Reps., 1994. Mem. Sami Siida N. Am. (corr. sec. 1994—), Sami Assn. N.Am., Reindeer Owners and Breeders Assn., Nordlandslag. Home: 727 14 Ave SE Minneapolis MN 55414 Office: Scandinavian Geneal Svcs PO Box 13031 Minneapolis MN 55414

PESOLA, WILLIAM ERNEST, restaurant management executive; b. Marquette, Mich., May 2, 1945; s. Ernest Ensio and Janice Mary (LeDuc) P.; m. Kathleen Mary Deschaine, July 9, 1966; children: Christie Lynn,

Laurie Anne. BS, No. Mich. U., 1968, MS, 1971. Route driver Coca Cola Co., Marquette, 1963-68; tchr. Gwinn (Mich.) Schs., 1968-78; pub. Sch. News, 1969; pres. Pesola Mgmt., Marquette, 1974—; pres. Humboldt Ridge, Marquette, 1977—; treas. Elite Bar, Inc., Marquette, 1978—; pres. Upper Peninsula Big Boy, 1990—; v.p. Marquette Cablevision, 1981-85, also dir.; cons. cable TV, 1985—, Bresnan Communications, 1984—. Pres. Gwinn Edn. Assn., 1975-77; regional pres. Upper Peninsula Edn. Assn., 1977-78; mem. Marquette City Commn., 1977-81. Mem. NEA, Marquette Econ. Club, Mich. Edn. Assn. C. of C. (named Exemplary Citizen 1990). Roman Catholic. Lodge: Rotary. Home: 1026 N Front St Marquette MI 49855-3514

PESTUREAU, PIERRE GILBERT, literature educator, literary critic, editor; b. Civray, Vienne, France, Feb. 8, 1933; came to U.S., 1991; s. Pierre and Madeleine (Bernard) P.; divorced; children: Veronique, Christophe, Charlotte; m. Ann Shepstone Wakefield, July 12, 1980. MA in Lit., U. Poitiers, France, 1955; profl. degree, Paris, 1956; PhD, Sorbonne U., Paris, 1975, SD in Lit., 1981. Prof. Nat. Edn., France, 1956-65, Tahiti, 1966-70; prof. The French Embassy, Madagascar, 1971-73, U. Natal, Durban, South Africa, 1974-80, U. Ocean Indien, La Reunion, France, 1981-83, U. Nantes, France, 1986-91, Loyola U., Chgo., 1991—; lectr. Alliance Francaise, South Africa, U.S., 1976-96; vis. prof. San Diego State U., spring 1990. Author: Boris Vian, 1978, Dictionnaire Vian, 1985, 93; editor: Boris Vian Oeuvres Choisies, 1991, Romans, 1992, 93, 94, Andrè Brink, 1992, Raymond Queneau, 1993, 94, 95, 96. Rep. Prof.'s Union, France, 1956-70. Sgt. Svc. Corps French Mil., 1960-62. Decorated chevalier Palmes Académiques. Office: Loyola U 6525 N Sheridan Rd Chicago IL 60626-5311

PETACQUE, ARTHUR M., journalist; b. Chgo., July 20, 1924; s. Ralph David and Fay Nora (Brauner) P.; m. Regina Battinus, Dec. 10, 1944; children: Susan Wendy Petacque Leshin, William Scott. Student, U. Ill., 1940-42; PhD (hon.), So. Ill. U., 1987. With Chgo. Sun, 1942-47; with Chgo. Sun-Times, 1947—, investigative reporter, 1957—, columnist, 1974—; crime editor World Book Ency., 1970-75; lectr. various univs. and civic orgns. Recipient Page One awards for outstanding journalism Chgo. Newspaper Guild, 1949, 57, 59, 62, 63, 65, 68; Joseph M. Fay Meml. award Chgo. Newspaper Reporters Assn., 1960; Prof. Jacob Scher-Theta Sigma Phi Daily Newswriting award Chgo. chpt. Theta Sigma Phi, 1964; John Baptist Scalabrini award for leadership Am. Community Italian Ancestry, 1966; awards for investigative reporting and spot news AP, 1963, 66, 68, (2) 74, 76; Marshall Field award for outstanding editorial contbn. in behalf of Chgo. Sun-Times, 1968; Pulitzer Prize for gen. reporting, 1974; State of Israel Prime Minister's medal, 1976; Dante award Civic Com. Italian Americans, 1980; UPI award for best spot news coverage Ill., 1980; Emmy award for ABC-TV local news spot reporting, 1984; Award for Long and Dedicated Newspaper Reporting on Crime and the Criminal Justice System, Ill. Acad. Criminology, 1985; named to Chgo. Journalism Hall of Fame Chgo Headline Club, 1990. Mem. Chgo. Newspaper Guild, Jewish War Vets. (hon.), Sigma Delta Chi, Sigma Alpha Mu. Jewish. Club: B'nai B'rith. Office: 401 N Wabash Ave Chicago IL 60611-3532

PETAK, GEORGE, state legislator; b. Nov. 6, 1949. BA, Kent State U. Wis. state sen. Dist. 21, 1990—; mem. Wis. Housing and Econ. Devel. Authority Bd.; vice-chmn. housing com. Govt. Ops. and Cultural Affairs Coms.; chmn. Bus., Econ. Devel. and Urban Affairs Com. Address: 1626 Thurston Ave Racine WI 53405*

PETERS, ANN LOUISE, accounting manager; b. Knoxville, Tenn., Jan. 26, 1954; d. William Brown and Louise (Emerson) Nixon; m. Raymond Peters, July 11, 1975. BBA, Miami U., Oxford, Ohio, 1976; MBA, Xavier U., 1985. Cert. internal auditor. Acctg. officer Soc. Bank (formerly Citizens Bank), Hamilton, Ohio, 1977-85; internal auditor Procter & Gamble Co., Cin., 1985-86, audit sect. mgr., 1986-88, sr. cost analyst, beauty care, 1988-90; plant fin. mgr. Procter & Gamble Mfg. Co., Phoenix, 1990-92; sr. fin. analyst, beauty care Procter & Gamble Co., Cin., 1992-93, group mgr., gen. acctg., 1993-96, group mgr. R&D fin., 1996—. Mem. Inst. Internal Auditors, Inst. Mgmt. Accts. Republican. Congregationalist. Home: 7889 Ironwood Way West Chester OH 45069-1623 Office: Procter & Gamble Co Sharon Woods Tech Ctr Box 221 HB2J14A 11511 Reed Hartman Hwy Cincinnati OH 45241

PETERS, BOYD LEON, agricultural engineer; b. Seymour, Ind., May 2, 1951; s. Ralph Edward and Wilma (Nieman) P.; m. Janice Eileen Simpson, Nov. 9, 1985; children: Nathan Robert, Joshua Ryan, Jacob Tyler. BS in Agrl. Engring., Purdue U., 1973; postgrad., U. Ill., Hinsdale, 1978, Moody Bible Inst., 1982, Coll. of DuPage, 1987-88, North Cen. Coll., 1989-92. Registered profl. engr., Ill. Engr. in tng. Soil Conservation Svc., Greencastle, Ind., 1972, White Farm Equipment Co., South Bend, Ind., 1973; design engr. II, Internat. Harvester Co., Hinsdale, 1974-79, design engr. I, 1979, engr., 1989-92; engr. Case IH-Tenneco Inc., Hinsdale, 1985, sr. engr., 1985-88; design engr. Caterpillar Inc., Aurora, Ill., 1988-94, sr. design engr., 1994—. Author: American Society of Agricultural Engineers Paper Tractor Weight Transfer Analysis, 1983. Mem. Soc. Automotive Engrs., Am. Soc. Agrl. Engrs., Computer Soc., Profl. Assn. Diving Instrs., Alpha Epsilon, Gamma Epsilon Delta. Republican. Home: 1219 Andria Ct Naperville IL 60540-0982

PETERS, CARL H., insurance physician; b. St. Cloud, Minn., Nov. 13, 1946; s. Carl H. and Gladys Aileen (White) P.; m. Renae Doris Anderson, Mar. 18, 1972. BA, St. Cloud State U., 1969; MD, U. Minn., 1974. Diplomate Am. Bd. Ins. Medicine; CLU. Psychology aide VA Hosp., St. Cloud, 1969-70; assoc. med. dir. Prin. Fin. Group, Des Moines, 1974—; reviewer Jour. Ins. Medicine, 1992. Fellow Life Mgmt. Inst.; mem. AMA, Am. Acad. Ins. Medicine, U.S. Chess Fedn. Lutheran. Office: Prin Fin Group 711 High St Des Moines IA 50392-0001

PETERS, CAROL ANN DUDYCHA, counselor; b. Ripon, Wis., Dec. 23, 1938; d. George John and Martha (Malek) Dudycha; m. Milton Eugene Peters, Aug. 27, 1960. AB, Wittenberg U., 1960, MEd, 1963; leadership devel. cert., Ctr. for Creative Leadership, Greensboro, N.C., 1986; postgrad., U. Toledo, 1973—. Lic. profl. counselor, Ohio; nat. cert. counselor, nat. cert. career counselor Nat. Bd. Cert. Counselors, Inc. Tchr. Springfield (Ohio) City Schs., 1960-62, Mad River-Green Local Schs., Springfield, 1962-63; counselor Napoleon (Ohio) Area Schs., 1963-70, Findlay (Ohio) City Schs., 1970—; field counselor Career Relocation Corp. Am., Armonk, N.Y., 1992-95; cons., prin. Peters and Peters, Findlay, 1979—; leader Creative Edn. Found., Buffalo, 1980-91, colleague, 1985—; founder ednl. corp. Career Info. Bur. Hancock County, 1974. Pres. Big Bros./Big Sisters Hancock County, 1982-83; bd. dirs. Citizens Opposing Drug Abuse (C.O.D.A.), Findlay, 1982—; advisor, leader Hancock Addictions Prevention for Youth (H.A.P.P.Y.), 1985-91; mem. Hancock County Community Devel. Found. Edn. Com., 1990-93, Findlay/Hancock County Am. 2000 New Sch. Design Team, 1991-92; mem. Hancock County Crisis Response Team, 1991—. Named One of Outstanding Young Women of Am., 1967; named Outstanding Woman in Edn., Bus. and Profl. Women, 1983; recipient Outstanding Citizenship award The Lincoln Ctr., Findlay, 1989, Meritorious Svc. award Big Bros./Big Sisters Hancock County, 1988. Mem. ACA, AAUW (Findlay br.), NEA (life), Am. Sch. Counselor Assn., Nat. Career Devel. Assn., Ohio Edn. Assn., Ohio Counseling Assn., Ohio Sch. Counselor Assn., Findlay-Hancock County C. of C. (sec. edn. com. 1984-90). Lutheran. Office: Findlay City Schs 227 S West St Findlay OH 45840-3324

PETERS, CONNIE JANE, secondary education media specialist; b. Decatur, Ill., Oct. 21, 1949; d. Sylvester Thomas and Kathryn Harriett (Wittig) P. BA in History, Millikin U., 1971; MA in History, Sangamon State U., 1972; MS in LS, Ea. Ill. U., 1973, Edn. Specialist degree in Inst. Media, 1985. Cert. elem. and secondary tchr., Ill. Grad. asst. Ea. Ill. U., Charleston, Ill., 1972-73; media ctr. cons. Decatur Pub. Schs., Decatur, 1974-76; libr. St. Teresa H.S., Decatur, 1976-77; media specialist Thomas Jefferson Mid. Schs., Decatur, 1978, Cerro Gordo (Ill.) Unit Schs., 1980-81, St. Teresa H.S., Decatur, 1982-92; instrnl. media specialist Stephen Decatur H.S., Decatur, 1995—. Mem. Ill. Assn. for Ednl. Comms. and Tech., Ill. Sch. Libr. and Media Assn. Mem. Foursquare Gospel (Pentecostal). Office: Stephen Decatur HS #1 Educational Park Decatur IL 62526

PETERS, DANIEL J., manufacturing executive; b. Quincy, Ill., Oct. 28, 1959. Drafting Cert., Quincy Tech. Sch., 1980; AAS, John Woods C.C., Quincy, 1986. Detailer Basler Electric, Highland, Ill., 1980-84; CAD mech. designer Broadcash Electronics, Quincy, 1984-88, Knapheide Mfg. Co., Quincy, 1988-94, Quincy Design & Mfg. Co., 1994—. Coach Girls and Boys Soccer Team, Quincy, 1991—. Mem. Quail Unltd. Roman Catholic.

PETERS, DEBORAH LYNN, management consultant; b. Wabasha, Minn., Mar. 24, 1954; d. Harold Peter and Sophia Madeline (Loechler) P.; m. Lawrence Richard Splett, Aug. 23, 1985; children: Jamison Lawrence, Katelynn Sophia, McKenna Rebecca. BS, Winona State U., 1976; MBA, U. St. Thomas, St. Paul, 1986. Cert. to administr. Myers-Briggs Type Indicators. Tchr. Minn. Schs., Faribault, 1977-81; mgmt. devel. specialist NCR Corp., St. Paul, 1982-87, mktg. edn. analyst, 1987-90; sr. ptnr. and pres. Morgan McGuire Cons., St. Paul, 1990—; bd. dirs. Minn. Quality Conf. Steering Com., Bloomington, 1991-92; examiner Minn. Quality award, Bloomington, 1992-93. Writer, editor On-Line, 1986-87. Bd. mem. N.E. Coun. for Quality, St. Paul, 1991-92, Econ. Devel. Corp., Vadnais Heights, Minn., 1991-94. Mem. ASTD (chair profl. devel. group 1988-89, recognition award 1988), Women in Transition (bd. mem. 1987-89), Human Resource Profls. Minn. Address: Morgan McGuire Cons 2214 5th St Ste 1 Saint Paul MN 55110-3205

PETERS, GARY CHARLES, state senator, lawyer, educator; b. Pontiac, Mich., Dec. 1, 1958; s. Herbert Garrett and Madeleine (Vignier) P.; m. Colleen Ochoa; children: Gary Jr., Madeleine. BA, Alma Coll., 1980; MBA, U. Detroit, 1984; JD, Wayne State U., 1989. Bar: Mich. 1990. Fin. cons., resident mgr., asst. v.p. Merrill Lynch, Pierce, Fenner & Smith, Inc., Rochester, Mich., 1980-89; br. mgr., v.p. Paine Webber, Inc., Rochester, Mich., 1989—; state senator Mich., Lansing, 1994—; securities arbitrator, Nat. Assn. Securities Dealers, N.Y. Stock Exchange, Am. Arbitration Assn., 1990—; adj. prof. Oakland U., Rochester, 1991—, instr. Wayne State U., 1992-94; vice chair Mich. Senate fin. com.; mem. edn. com., judiciary com., families, mental health and svcs. com., law revision com. Del State Ctrl. Com., 1991; membership chair Oakland County Dem. Party, 1991; officer-at-large Mich. Dem. Party, 1996. Officer USNR. Mem. Mich. State Bar Assn., Sierra Club. Home: 2645 Bloomfield Crossing Bloomfield Hills MI 48304-1710 Office: PaineWebber Inc PO Box 80730 Rochester MI 48308-0730

PETERS, MILTON EUGENE, educational psychologist; b. Anderson, Ind., July 22, 1938; s. Olen A. and Dorothy LaVerne (Lambert) P.; m. Carol Ann Dudycha, Aug. 27, 1960. BA, Wittenberg U., 1960; M in Div., Hamma Sch. Theology, 1963; MA, Bowling Green State U., 1965; PhD, U. Toledo, 1975. Lic. psychologist, Ohio. Pastor Luth. Ch. Am., 1966-69; instr. psychology Defiance (Ohio) Coll., 1969-70, Bluffton (Ohio) Coll., 1970-72; tchr., research asst. U. Toledo, 1973-75; vis. asst. prof., 1975-76; dir. instl. research, asst. prof. psychology U. Findlay, Ohio, 1976-85, assoc. prof. psychology, 1985-89, prof., 1989—; past pres. Am. Assn. Univ. Profs. U. Findlay; cons., lectr. in field; ednl. rschr. Contbr. articles to profl. and religious jours. Mem. APA, Midwestern Psychol. Assn., Creative Edn. Found. (colleague). Clubs: Findlay Beacon, Fostoria Power Squadron. Home: 1130 Country Club Dr Findlay OH 45840-6342 Office: 1000 N Main St Findlay OH 45840-3653

PETERS, R. JONATHAN, lawyer, chemical company executive; b. Janesville, Wis., Sept. 6, 1927; m. Ingrid H. Varvayn, 1953; 1 dau., Christina. B.S. in Chemistry, U. Ill., 1951; J.D., Northwestern U., 1954. Bar: Ill. 1954. Chief patent counsel Englehard Industries, 1972-82, Kimberly-Clark Corp., Neenah, Wis., 1982-85; gen. counsel Lanxide Corp., Newark, Del., 1985-87; pvt. practice Chgo., 1985—. Served with CIC, U.S. Army, 1955-57. Patentee in field. Mem. ABA, Am. Intellectual Property Law Assn., Lic. Execs. Soc., Assn. Corp. Patent Counsel. Clubs: North Shore Golf (Menasha, Wis.), Masons, Scottish Rite, Shriners.

PETERS, ROBERT ALLEN, retired drug company executive; b. Aurora, Ill., Dec. 13, 1927; s. Frank Albert and Amalia Cecelia (Harter) P.; m. Mary Jeanne Galos, June 23, 1962 (dec. May 1979); children: Robert Allen, Thomas Allen, Mary Ann. BS in Pharmacy, U. Ill., Chgo., 1951. Pharmacist Plache Drug Co., Aurora, 1951-61; co-owner, pharmacist Town & Country Drugs, Aurora, 1961-82, owner, 1982-94; ret., 1994; bd. dirs. Merchants Nat. Bank, Aurora. Bd. dirs., treas. Aurora C. of C. Served ti U.S. Army, 1946-47, Korea. Mem. Am. Pharm. Assn., Ill. Pharm. Assn., Aurora Area Pharm. Assn. Republican. Roman Catholic. Lodges: K.C., Moose.

PETERS, RONNIE D., steel executive, labor analyst; b. Cape Girardeau, Mo., Mar. 6, 1949; s. Paul Anthony Peters and LaWanda Druscilla (Allen) Peters-Bartels; m. Betty Jean Henry Hunter, June 4, 1989. Staff St. Louis ship Pott Industries, St. Louis, Mo., 1969-72; staff St. Louis refrigerator car Anheuser Busch Transp., St. Louis, Mo., 1972—. Author: (books) Times, Thoughts...Words, 1993, Auserstetten, 1990, Freighters, 1990, (mag.) Things Less Than Human, 1995. Office: Iron Pyramid Publs PO Box 160232 Saint Louis MO 63116

PETERS, THOMAS ROBERT, English language educator, writer; b. Detroit, Nov. 14, 1929; s. Norman Addison and Eleanor H. (Schneider) P.; m. Lillian J. Tremonti, Aug. 21, 1954; children: Jennifer Leigh Hartman, Thomas R. Jr., Sarah Jeanne. BA, Hillsdale Coll., 1954; MA, Wayne State U., 1963. Screen writer Jam Handy Film Prodns., Detroit, 1956-59; secondary tchr. English, Detroit Pub. Schs., 1960-69; edn. coord. Detroit Free Press, 1969-72; mgr. pub. rels. Blue Cross, Blue Shield Mich., Detroit, 1972-86; prof. English Macomb C.C, Warren, Mich., 1986-95; guest speaker Mich. Schs. and Colls., 1970—. Author: (novels) Education of Tom Webber, 1977, Two Weeks in the Forties, 1988, Selected Works, 1995, (play) Mensa Meeting, 1987; contbr. numerous stories, articles and poems to nat. mags., anthologies; writer several published speeches. Bd. dirs. Friends of Grosse Pointe Librs., 1978-84. With U.S. Army, 1948-49; U.S. Army Res. 1950-55. Recipient Alumni Achievement award in Literature Hillsdale Coll., 1993; grantee: Grosse Pointe Found., 1978, Utica Community Schs., 1989. Mem. Fine Arts Soc. Detroit (pres. 1978-79). Roman Catholic. Home: 350 Moselle Pl Grosse Pointe MI 48236-3307

PETERSEN, DOUGLAS ARNDT, financial development consultant; b. Albert Lea, Minn., Sept. 18, 1944; s. Arndt H. and Helen L. (Slater) P.; m. Winnifred K. Taylor, Aug. 14, 1964 (div. July 1970); children: Scott, Jennifer; m. Cynthia L. Schnabel, June 14, 1975; 1 child, Christopher. BS in Edn., Mankato State U., 1966, postgrad., 1966-68. Youth dir. Mankato (Minn.) YMCA, 1965-68; tchr. Mankato State U., 1965-68; exec. dir. YMCA Camp Christmas Tree, Mound, Minn., 1968-72; asst. exec. dir. West Suburban YMCA, Minnetonka, Minn., 1968-72; exec. dir. Eastside YMCA, Mpls., 1972-75; program/fin. devel. dir. Eastside Neighborhood Svc., Mpls., 1975-79; asst. exec. dir. Mpls. Red Cross, 1979-89; dir. major/planned gifts ARC Nat. Staff, Mpls., 1989-91; pres./chief exec. officer/cons. D.A. Petersen Assocs., Mpls., 1992—. Mem. St. Anthony/New Brighton Found. (chair 1988-92), YMCA Am. (pres. APD 1974), ARC (pres. MFDDC 1988-89). Lutheran. Home: 3216 Skycroft Dr Minneapolis MN 55418-2552 Office: PO Box 18411 Minneapolis MN 55418-0411

PETERSEN, GEORGE JAMES, education educator; b. L.A., Nov. 11, 1957; s. George James Sr. and Mabel Marie (Crabtree) P.; m. Jennifer Lynn Faue, Dec. 22, 1984; children: Elijah F., Jacob Warren. BA in Philosophy, Angelicum U., Rome, 1981; BA in Anthropology, U. Calif., Santa Barbara, 1986, MA in Ednl. Adminstrn., 1991, PhD in Ednl. Adminstrn., 1993. Cert. social studies tchr., Calif. Tchr. social studies Bishop Garcia Diego High Sch., Santa Barbara, 1981-82, Hollister (Calif.) High Sch., 1987-89; lectr. Grad. Sch. Edn., U. Calif., Santa Barbara, 1990—; asst. prof. ednl. adminstrn. Bowling Green State U.; cons. Bishop Diego High Sch., 1991-92, Calif. Dairy Coun., Santa Barbara, summer 1992. Named Sallie Mae Outstanding Tchr., Sallie Mae Mktg. Assn., 1988; U. Calif. regents fellow, U. Calif. gen. affiliates grad. fellow. Mem. ASCD, Am. Ednl. Rsch. Assn., Mid-Western Ednl. Rsch. Assn., Assn. of Tchr. Educators, Nat. Coun. of States Inservice Educators, Ea. Ednl. Rsch. Assn., Phi Delta Kappa, Phi Beta Kappa. Office: Bowling Green State U Dept Ednl Admin & Super Bowling Green OH 43403-0250

PETERSEN, JOAN MARIE, talented and gifted education coordinator, educator, florist; b. Sioux City, Iowa, Nov. 19, 1942; d. John B. and Helen Marie (Runge) Belfrage; m. Charles Louis Petersen, June 5, 1964; children: Ruth Anne, Sarah Rosamond. BS, U. S.D., 1964. Cert. tchr., tchr. gifted, Iowa. Elem. tchr. Maple Valley Community Sch., Mapleton, Iowa, 1964-68, substitute tchr., 1968-71; mgr., owner Mapleton Greenhouse, Inc., 1971-79; co-mgr., owner Onawa (Iowa) Florist, Inc., 1971—; talented and gifted coord., tchr. West Monona Community Sch., Onawa, 1981—. Mem. Burgess Meml. Hosp. Aux., Onawa, 1975—, ticket chmn., 1980-83; bd. dirs. Onawa United Meth. Ch., Sunday sch. tchr. Mem. Nat. Assn. Gifted, Iowa Talented and Gifted (mem. speakers bur. 1990—), West Monona Edn. Assn., Order Ea. Star (Worthy Matron 1971, 85), PEO (chpt. EF, officer). Home: 904 12th St Onawa IA 51040-1308 Office: West Monona Community Sch 1314 15th St Onawa IA 51040-1738

PETERSEN, MAUREEN JEANETTE MILLER, management information consultant, former nurse; b. Evanston, Ill., Sept. 4, 1956; d. Maurice James and M. Joyce (Mielke) Miller; m. Gregory Eugene Petersen, July 7, 1984; 1 child, Trevor James. BS in Nursing cum laude, Vanderbilt U., 1978; MS in Biometry and Health Info. Systems, U. Minn., 1984. Nurse U. Iowa Hosps. and Clinics, Iowa City, 1978-82; research asst. Sch. Nursing, U. Minn., Mpls., 1982-83; mgr. Arthur Andersen/Andersen Cons., Mpls., 1984—. Mem. Minn. 100. Mem. Minn. 100, Women in Biocomputing, Mensa. Methodist. Home: 1050 County Rd C2 W Saint Paul MN 55113-1945 Office: Andersen Cons 45 S 7th St Minneapolis MN 55402-1614

PETERSON, BRADLEY EUGENE, insurance agent; b. Princeton, Minn., Mar. 26, 1961; s. Graydon Kedrick and Helen Virginia (Dawson) P. Cert., Reisch Coll. Auctioneering, Mason City, Iowa, 1983. Mgr., shoe buyer Johnson's Dept. Store, Elk River, Minn., 1979-87; ins. agt. John Hancock, Bloomington, Minn., 1987-90, Minn. Ins. Svc., New Brighton, Minn., 1990-92, Bradley Peterson Agy., Monticello, Minn., 1992—. Treas. United Way Elk River, 1987, Oakview Cemetery, St. Francis, Minn., 1988-94. Republican. Mem. Ch. of God of Prophecy. Home: 16311 127th St Becker MN 55308-8731 Office: PO Box 1583 Monticello MN 55362-1583

PETERSON, DAVID CHARLES, photojournalist; b. Kansas City, Mo., Oct. 22, 1949; s. John Edward and Florence Athene (Hobbs) P.; m. Adele Mae Johnson, Dec. 31, 1952; children: Brian David, Scott Ryun, Anna Victoria. BS in Edn., Kansas State U., 1971; BS in Journalism, U. Kans., 1973, U. Kans., 1974. Staff photographer Topeka Capital-Jour., 1975-77, Des Moines Register, 1977—. Photographer (photo essay) Shattered Dreams-Iowa's Rural Crisis, 1986 (Pulitzer prize 1987); exhibited at Creative Ctr. Photography, Tucson, 1989. Mem. Nat. Press Photographers Assn. (Nikon sabbatical 1986). Democrat. Home: 2024 35th St Des Moines IA 50310-4438 Office: Des Moines Register News Dept 715 Locust St Des Moines IA 50309-3724

PETERSON, DAVID GLENN, service center mangager communicatons company; b. Burlington, Iowa, Sept. 11, 1943; s. Glenn Albert and Helen May (Kint) P.; m. Dianne Carol Tady, Sept. 28, 1963; children: JoAnn Carol, Stephaie Lynn, Peggy Sue, Ann Kirsten. AS in Data Processing, U. Akron, 1972, BS in Education, 1976. Data processor, programmer supr. Eagle Signal Corps., Davenport, Iowa, 1961-69; from supr. data processing to mgr. svc. ctr. AllTEL, Hudson, Ohio, 1969—; part-time tchr. U. Akron, Ohio, 1975-76. Chmn., project mgr., Our Lady of Victory Expanson Com., Tallmadge, 1993-94; softball coach, 1979-96. Mem. Nat. Woodcarvers Assn., Tallmadge, Ohio Jaycees (pres. 1979-80). Roman Catholic. Home: 278 Dunbar Rd Tallmadge OH 44728

PETERSON, DONN NEAL, forensic engineer; b. Northwood, N.D., Jan. 1, 1942; s. Emil H. and Dorothy (Neal) P.; m. Lorna Jean Kappedal, July 8, 1962 (div. July 1966); m. Donna Sue Butts Daiker, Aug. 26, 1967; children: Barbara Daiker, Elizabeth Plamondon, Phoebe, Phaedra, Rosalind Peterson. BSME, U. N.D., 1963; MSME, U. Minn., 1972. Registered profl. engr. Advanced engrng. courses student GE, Evendale, Ohio, 1963-66; systems engr. GE Aircraft Engine Group, Evendale, Ohio, 1963-70; prin. Donn N. Peterson & Assocs., Mpls., 1971-74; pres. Donn N. Peterson & Assocs., Inc., Mpls., 1974-85, Peterson Engring., Inc., Mpls., 1985—; instr. GE Edn. Program, 1968-69; seminar presenter State Bd. of Registration, Mpls., 1980; seminar leader Minn. Fedn. Engring. Socs., Mpls., 1990-91; speaker in field; expert witness 100 ct. trials and 100 depositions. Del. Minn. 6th Dist. Rep. Conv., Brooklyn Park, Minn., 1982. Fellow Am. Acad. Forensic Scis. (sect. chmn. 1989-90, Founders award 1991), Nat. Acad. Forensic Engrs. (v.p. 1996); mem. ASME (Young Engr. of Yr. 1976, state chmn. 1979-80), NSPE, Profl. Engrs. in Pvt. Practice (state pres. 1987-88, Svc. award 1988), Soc. of Automotive Engrs., Rotary Club (sec. Brooklyn Park chpt. 1990-93, v.p. 1993-94, pres.-elect 1994-95, pres. 1995-96, Svc. award 1992), Brooklyn Park C. of C. (city hwy. 610 corridor com. 1992-94). Lutheran. Home: 15720 15th Pl N Plymouth MN 55447-2405 Office: 4455 Hwy 169N Plymouth MN 55442-2856

PETERSON, DOUG, state legislator; b. 1948; m. Elly Peterson; 2 children. BS, Augustana Coll., Sioux Falls, S.D. Mem. Minn. Ho. of Reps. St Paul, 1990—; mem. agrl. com., environ. and natural resources com., met. affairs com., others; tchr., farmer. Democrat. Home: RR 3 Box 90 Madison MN 56256-9452*

PETERSON, DOUGLAS ARTHUR, physician; b. Princeton, N.Y., Sept. 13, 1945; s. Arthur Roy William and Marie Hilma (Anderson) P.; m. Virginia Kay Eng., June 24, 1967; children: Rachel, Daniel, Rebecca. BA, St. Olaf, 1966; PhD, U. Minn., 1971, MD, 1975. Postdoctoral fellow U. Pitts., 1971-72; intern Hennepin County Med. Ctr., Mpls., 1975-76, resident in medicine, 1976-78; physician Bloomington Lake Clinic, Mpls., 1978-82; staff physician Mpls. VA Med. Ctr., Mpls., 1992—, chief compensation and pension, 1992—; asst. prof. U. Minn., 1985—. Bd. dirs. Rolling Acres Home, Victoria, Minn., 1985—. Lt. Col. M.C., USAR. Mem. AAAS, Am. Assn. Pathologists, N.Y. Acad. Scis. Home: 5008 Queen Ave S Minneapolis MN 55410 Office: VA Med Ctr One Veterans Dr Minneapolis MN 55417

PETERSON, DOUGLAS EUGENE, sales executive; b. Ft. Leavenworth, Kans., Mar. 10, 1955; s. Bob Hubert and Helen Christine (Palmer) P.; m. Kathy Lynn Coorts Peterson, Sept. 1, 1979; children: Ashley, Kaitlyn. BS in Biology, Northeast Mo. State U., Kirksville, 1977. Sales rep. Marion Labs., Fargo, N.D., 1979-83; instnl. rep. Des Moines, 1983-86; instnl. dist. mgr. Northville, Mich.; product mgr. Marion Merrell Dow Inc., Kansas City, Mo., 1989-91; sales dir. Instnl., 1991-93, area sales dir., 1993—; ctrl. region leadership team, USBR-Contracting, Marion Merrell Dow Inc., Kansas City, 1993—. Named Sales Rep. of Yr., Fargo, N.D., 1983, Top Ten Roundtable, Des Moines, 1986, Marion Labs.; recipient Sales Excellence, Des Moines, 1986, Mgrs. Award, Northville, Maine, 1988, Marion Labs. Republican. Presbyterian. Home: 13808 Hayes Overland Park KS 66221 Office: Marion Merrell Dow Kansas City MO 66221

PETERSON, ELAINE GRACE, technology director; b. Chgo., Feb. 6, 1943; d. Lincoln and Martha (Guthmiller) Wyman; m. Robert J. Peterson, June 5, 1965; children: Wesley, Christian. Certificate in computer programming, Moraine Valley Coll., Palos Hills, 1975; BA in Edn., Governors State U., 1981, MA in Comm. Sci. and Adminstrn., 1981. Computer coord. Dist. 144, Hazel Crest, Ill., 1984-86; adj. prof. Governors State U., University Park, Ill., 1986-87; program coord. ISBE - Ednl. Svc. Ctr., Flossmoor, Ill., 1986-92; rsch. assoc. Argonne Nat. Lab., Argonne, Ill., 1991-93; dist. tech. dir. Lombard Dist. 44, Lombard, Ill., 1991-92; dir. tech./media svcs. DuPage H.S. Dist. 88, Villa Park, Ill., 1992—; dir. tech./Media Svcs. DuPage H.S. Dist. 88, Addison, Ill., 1992—; grant writer Layne Cons., Addison, Ill., 1993-94; bd. dirs. Audio-Visual Inst. of DuPage, Lombard, 1991—; mem. Bus. Profl. of Am., Flossmoor, 1990-92, Reg. Ofc. Edn./Profl. Dev. Ctr., Lombard, 1993—; tech. mem. Addison 2000 Cmty. Org. of Village and Schs., Addison, 1993—; tech. com. adv. Dist. 45 - Feeder Sch., Villa Park, 1994—; grant reader Ednl. Svc. Ctrl. Ill. Math Sci. Acad., Aurora, Ill., 1992-94, Ill. State Bd. of Edn., Springfield, Ill., 1995—; mem. adv. bd. ISBE Area # 1 tech. hub. 1996. Contbr. articles to profl. jours. Mem. Internat. Soc. for Tchr. Edn., Ill. Computing Educators, Tech 2000, Ill. Sch. Libr. Media Assn., Argonne Cmty. of Tchrs., Ill. Assn. for Sch. Curriculum Devel., Phi Delta Kappa of DuPage County (treas.). Home: 567 Crystal

Springs Ct Lake Zurich IL 60047 Office: DuPage HS Dist 88 101 W Highridge Rd Villa Park IL 60181

PETERSON, GALE EUGENE, historian; b. Sioux Rapids, Iowa, May 23, 1944; s. George Edmund and Vergene Elizabeth (Wilson) P. B.S., Iowa State U., 1965; M.A., U. Md., 1968, Ph.D., 1973. Instr. dept. history U. Md., College Park, 1971-72, Cath. U. Am., Washington, 1972-73; prin. investigator Gregory Directory project Orgn. Am. Historians, Bloomington, Ind., 1973-75; instr. dept. history Purdue U., West Lafayette, Ind., 1975-76; dir. U.S. Newspaper Project, Orgn. Am. Historians, Bloomington, Ind., 1976-78; exec. dir. Cin. Hist. Soc., 1978—. Author: (with John T. Schlebecker) Living Historical Farms Handbook, 1970, Harry S Truman and the Independent Regulatory Commissions 1945-52, 1985. Mem. Cin. Bicentennial Commn., 1983-88. Mem. Orgn. Am. Historians (treas. 1993—), Am. Assn. State and Local History, Am. Hist. Assn., Am. Assn. Mus., Midwestern Mus. Conf. (v.p.-at-large 1993-95, exec. v.p. 1996—), Cincinnatus Assn., Nat. Coun. on Pub. History (bd. dirs. 1992-95). Home: 3767 Middleton Ave Cincinnati OH 45220-1143 Office: Cin Hist Soc Cin Mus Ctr Cin Union Terminal Cincinnati OH 45203

PETERSON, GIL, university director; b. Warren, Ohio, Oct. 29, 1937; s. Gilbert and Garnet (Miller) P.; m. Lorraine Wooke, May 13, 1956; children: Gil, Cristin, Laurine, Julie. BS, Youngstown State U., 1966; M Urban Planning, U. Wash., 1969, PhD, 1974. Regional planner Puget Sound Govtl. Conf., Seattle, 1970-72; prof. environ. planning and geography Western Wash. U., Bellingham, 1972-83; regional mgr. Environ. Sci. and Engring., Anchorage, Alaska, 1983-88; dir. Pub. Svc. Inst., dir. Ctr. for Urban Studies Youngstown (Ohio) State U., 1988—; pres. GPA Cons. Svcs., Bellingham, 1979-83, Team I Cons. Svc., Bellingham, 1974-79. Contbr. numerous articles and reports to profl. publs. With USAR, 1955-59. Named Disting. Alumni, Phi Kappa Phi, 1995. Democrat. Lutheran. Home: 1650 5th Ave Youngstown OH 44504 Office: Youngstown State U Pub Svc Inst Youngstown OH 44555

PETERSON, HANS C., business executive; b. Detroit, June 13, 1959. BS in Mktg., Western Mich. U., 1986. Pres. Epic Enterprises, Inc., Ferndale, Mich., 1986—, Peterson Window Corp., Northville, Mich., 1986—. Mem. USA Cycling team U.S. Cycling Fedn., Colorado Springs, 1980-85. Episcopalian. Office: 42975 Mill St Northville MI 48167

PETERSON, HARRY LEROY, academic administrator; b. Duluth, Minn., Feb. 22, 1940; s. Harry Leonard and Pearl Vivian (Rhode) P.; m. Sylvia K. Brinkley, Sept. 1, 1963; 1 child, Aaron B. BA in Sociology, San Diego State U., 1963; MSW, U. Calif., Berkeley, 1966; PhD in Ednl. Policy Studies, U. Wis., 1977. Psychiat. social worker Brown County Guidance Clinic, Green Bay, Wis., 1966-68; dir. student life programs U. Wis., Green Bay, 1969-75; exec. asst. to sec. Wis. Dept. of Transp., Madison, 1975-77, Wis. Dept. of Industry Labor & Human Rels., Madison, 1977-78; sr. spl. asst. U. Wis., Madison, 1978-87, exec. asst. to chancellor, 1988-90; v.p. Univ. Rels. and Devel. U. Idaho, Moscow, 1990-94; dep. chancellor Minn. Colls. and Univs., St. Paul, 1994—. Contbr. articles to profl. jours. Home: 313 Laurel Ave Saint Paul MN 55102-2105 Office: Minn State Colls and Univs 550 Cedar St Ste 203 Saint Paul MN 55101

PETERSON, JAMES BURDELL, management consultant; b. Spokane, Wash., Apr. 11, 1931; s. Eugene Herman and Bernice Genevive (Beil) P.; m. Patricia Marie McKeogh, Dec. 11, 1954. BS, U. Wash., 1953; MBA, Washington U., St. Louis, 1962. Adminstr. Union Elec., St. Louis, 1957-62; v.p. internat. Booz Allen Hamilton, London, 1962-75; pres. Mid. West Svc. Co., Chgo., 1975-79, L.B. Knight and Assoc., Chgo., 1979-83, James B. Peterson and Assoc., Inc., Chgo., 1983—; vice chmn. bd. dirs. Swedish Covenant Hosp., Chgo., 1991—; dir. Libr. of Internat. Rels., Chgo., 1992. Served with USAF, 1954-57. Recipient Am. Spirit Honor medal USAF, 1953. Mem. Inst. Mgmt. Cons. (pres. 1991-92). Republican. Methodist. Home: 1448 N Lake Shore Dr # 4A Chicago IL 60610 Office: James B Peterson & Assoc 70 W Madison St # 1400 Chicago IL 60602

PETERSON, JAMES LINCOLN, museum executive; b. Kewanee, Ill., Nov. 12, 1942; s. Reinold Gustav and Florence Josephine (Kjellgren) P.; m. M. Susan Pepin, Aug. 15, 1964; children: Hans C., Erika C. BA, Gustavus Adolphus Coll., 1964; PhD, U. Nebr., 1972. Sci. tchr. pub. schs. Ill. and Minn., 1964-68; research asst. U. Nebr., Lincoln, 1968-72; research assoc. U. Wis., Madison, 1972-74; staff ecologist Nat. Commn. Water Quality, Washington, 1974-75; v.p. research Acad. Nat. Scis., Phila., 1976-84, v.p. devel., 1982-84; pres. Sci. Mus. Minn., St. Paul, 1984—. Bd. dirs. Ea. Pa. chpt. Nature Conservancy, Phila., 1982-84, Downtown Coun., St. Paul, 1986-93, Keystone (Colo.) Ctr., 1989-93; mem. St. Paul Riverfront Commn., 1987-91; mem. adv. com. U. Minn. Coll. Biol. Scis., 1989-95. Mem. Assn. Sci. Mus. Dirs., Assn. Sci. and Tech. Ctrs. (pres. 1993-95), Sci. Mus. Exhibit Collaborative (pres. 1986-89), St. Paul C. of C. (bd. dirs. 1985-89), Informal Club. Office: Sci Mus Minn 30 10th St E Saint Paul MN 55101-2205

PETERSON, JOHN EDWARD, minister; b. Seattle, Aug. 12, 1953; s. Wilbur Glen and Donna Jean (Nielsen) P.; m. Judith Arlene Coleman, Dec. 19, 1975; children: Bjorn Karl, Christine Anna, Joel Thomas. BA in Polit. Sci., Bethel Coll., 1976; MDiv. in Ch. History, Bethel Theol. Sem., 1980, D of Ministry, 1993. Ordained min. Bapt. Ch., 1982. Pastor Bethel Bapt. Ch., Hartford, Conn., 1980-83, Ord, Nebr., 1983—; chmn. bd. trustees Great Plains Bapt. Conf., Omaha, 1990-92; bd. regents Bethel Coll. and Sem., St. Paul, 1990-95. Unit commr. Boy Scouts Am., Ord, 1988—; pres. Ord Twp. Libr. Found., 1995—; moderator, Great Plains Bapt. Conf., Omaha, 1995-96. Mem. Am. Soc. Ch. History. Republican. Home: 1819 N St Ord NE 68862 Office: Bethel Bapt Ch 212 N 21st St # 144 Ord NE 68862-1322

PETERSON, LEVI K., machine shop owner; b. Ogaallala, Nebr., Jan. 31, 1951. Owner Peterson Machine Shop, Ogallala, Nebr., 1969—. Episcopalian.

PETERSON, MARILYN ANN WHITNEY, journalism educator; b. Holdrege, Nebr., July 22, 1933; d. Claude Francis and Esther (Soderholm) Whitney; m. Richard Fay Peterson, June 17, 1956. BA, U. Nebr., Kearney, 1955; MA, U. No. Colo., 1963. Tchr. Gothenburg (Nebr.) N.H., 1955-56, Kearney Jr. H.S., 1956-57, Cozad (Nebr.) H.S., 1957-60, Wheatridge H.S., Denver, 1960-62, Eustis (Nebr.) H.S., 1962-64; prof. Journalism Midland Luth. Coll., Fremont, Nebr., 1964-94; faculty pres. Midland Luth. Coll., 1992-94. Author (book) The Mimeographed Newspaper, 1972; co-author (book) Transformational Grammar, 1964; contbr. articles and poetry to profl. jours., mags. and newspapers. Recipient Zimmerman Disting. professorship Midland Luth. Coll., 1993-94. Mem. Coll. Media Advisers Inc. (nat. sec. 1986-92, Nat. Disting. Newspaper Adviser 1975, Nat. Disting. Yearbook Adviser 1980, Nat. Disting. Multi-Media Adviser 1991), Assoc. Collegiate Press (Hall of Fame 1988), Columbia Scholastic Press Assn. (Gold Key 1993), Nebr. Collegiate Media Assn. (charter), Am. Scholastic Press Assn., Nat. Journalism Hall of Fame (charter coll./univ. advisers 1994), Soc. Collegiate Journalists (nat. 2nd v.p. 1992-94), PEO, Delta Kappa Gamma. Republican. Methodist. Home: 76325 Rd 420 Cozad NE 69130-4300

PETERSON, OSCAR EMMANUEL, pianist; b. Montreal, Que., Can., Aug. 15, 1925; s. Daniel and Olivia (John) P. Studied with, Paul deMarky; LL.D. (hon.), Carleton U., 1973, Queen's U., 1976, Concordia U., 1979, McMaster U., 1981, U. of Victoria, 1981, U. Toronto, 1985; D.Mus. (hon.), Sackville U., 1980, U. Laval, 1985; Litt.D. (hon.), York U., 1982; D.F.A. (hon.), Northwestern U., Evanston, Ill., 1983; LLD (hon.), U. Toronto, 1985; MusD (hon.), U. Laval, 1985. Founder Advanced Sch. Contemporary Music, Toronto; former chancellor York U., 1991-94; chancellor York U., 1991. Began music career on weekly radio show, then with Johny Holmes Orchestra, Can., 1944-49; recorded with RCA Victor Records; appeared with Jazz at the Philharmonic, Carnegie Hall, 1949; toured the U.S. and Europe, 1950—; leader trio with Ray Brown, Irving Ashby, later Barney Kessel, Herb Ellis, Ed Thigpen, Sam Jones, Louie Hayes, concert appearances with Ella Fitzgerald, Eng., Scotland, 1955; appeared Stratford (Ont.) Shakespeare Festival, Newport Jazz Festival; recorded and performed solo piano works, 1972—; toured USSR, 1974, recordings with Billie Holiday, Fred Astaire, Benny Carter, Count Basie, Roy Eldridge, Lester Young, Ella Fitzgerald, Niels-Henning, Joe Pass, Orsted Pederson, Dizzy Gillespie, Harry Edison, Clark Terry ; composer: Canadiana Suite, Hymn to Freedom, Fields of Endless Day, City Lights, Begone Dull Care, (with Norman McLaren) salute to Johann Sebastian Bach, music for films Big North and Silent Partner; author: Jazz Exercises and Pieces: Oscar Peterson New Piano Solos; numerous TV specials. Decorated officer Order of Canada, 1972, companion, 1984; recipient award for piano Down Beat mag. 13 times, Metronome mag. award, 1953-54, Edison award, 1962, Award of merit City of Toronto, (1st mention) 1973 (2d mention 1983), Diplome d'honneur Can. Conf. of the Arts, 1975, Grammy award 7 times, Olympic Key to Montreal, The Queen's medal, 1977, Genie Film award for film score The Silent Partner, 1978, Grand-Prix du Disques for Night Child album, 1981, Canadian Band Festival Award, 1982, Juno Hall of Fame award, 1982, George Peabody medal Peabody Conservatory of Music, Balt., 1987, Volunteer award Roy Thompson Hall, Toronto, 1987, Can. Club Arts and Letters award, N.Y.C., 1987, Officer in Order of Arts and Letters, France, 1989, Chevalier Order of Que., 1991, Lifetime Achievement Toronto Arts Award, 1991, appointed Order of Ontario, 1992, Lifetime Achievement Gov. Gens. award, 1992, Glenn Gould prize, 1993, Carnegie Hall Anniversary medal, Charlie Parker bronze medal, Ville de Salon de Provence medal, Award of Thanks, Mexico City; 12-time jazz poll winner Playboy mag.; named number one (piano) Jazz and Pop, Readers Poll 1968, 85; named to U. Calif. at Berkeley Hall of Fame, 1983, Contemporary Keyboard Hall of Fame, 1983; Oscar Peterson Day proclaimed by Baltimore, Oreg., 1981, 83; Oscar Peterson Scholarship founded in his honor Berklee Sch. of Music, Boston, 1982. Office: Regal Recordings Ltd, 2421 Hammond Rd, Mississauga, ON Canada L5K 1T3

PETERSON, PATRICIA ELIZABETH, library network administrator, educator; b. Iowa City, July 25, 1942; d. Gregory Raymond and Ruth Elizabeth (Green) Patterson; m. Sylvan Johnathan Peterson, June 14, 1964; children: Deborah Lynn, Christine Elizabeth. BS, Mayville State Coll., 1963; MS, St. Cloud State U., 1979. Tchr., libr. Nekoma (N.D.) High Sch., 1963-67, Gackle (N.D.) High Sch., 1967-70; tchr. Lester Prairie (Minn.) High Sch., 1971-73; dir. media Kimball (Minn.) High Sch., 1978-83; dir. Cen. Minn. Librs. Exch., St. Cloud, 1983—; pres. Coun. Coop. Librs., St. Paul, 1987-88, 94-95. mem. ALA, AAUW, Assn. for Ednl. Comm. and Tech., Forum of Exec. Women, Friends of the Libr. Devel. and Svcs. Libr., Friends of the Great River Regional Libr., Minn. Libr. Assn., Minn. Ednl. Media Orgn. (v.p. 1992-94), Minn. Assn. Libr. Friends, Cold Spring Lioness Club, Phi Delta Kappa. Home: 591 Central Ave SE Richmond MN 56368-8117 Office: Ctrl Minn Librs Exch Bldg Ch 61 St Cloud State U Saint Cloud MN 56301

PETERSON, PAUL EDWARD, sales executive; b. Albert Lea, Minn., Mar. 19, 1935; s. Chester Donald and Matie A. (Boland) P.; m. Jeanette Florence Cashman, July 14, 1956; children: Diana J., Thomas J., Gerald E. Sales agt. Minn. Mut. Life Ins., St. Paul, 1964-67; with sales RJR/Nabisco, St. Paul, 1967-87; regional sales mgr. southwest states Tremco divsn B.F. Goodrich, Dewey, Ariz., 1987-92, ter. mgr. for Ariz. and So. Nev., 1992—. Trustee Lea Coll., Albert Lea, 1972-75; past trustee, treas. First Bapt. Ch., Albert Lea; chmn. Freeborn County Safety Coun., Albert Lea, 1970-77; trail adminstr. Freeborn County Snowmobile Trails, Albert Lea, 1976-84; assoc. mem., choir United Meth Ch., Prescott Valley, Ariz., v.p. trustees, 1993; bd. dirs., vol. dep. Yavapai County Sheriffs Vol. Protection. Mem. Prescott Country Club P.O.A. (bd. dirs. 1991—, v.p. 1993, pres. property owners assn. 1994-95, bd. dirs. 1996), Elks, Kiwanis (membership chmn. Bradshaw Mountain 1988-90, v.p. 1993, pres. 1994-95, Kiwanian of Yr. award Daybreakers 1987, Exemplary Svc. award). Republican. Home: 11433 Concho Cyn Dewey AZ 86327-5705 Office: Tremco 2040 Heiserman Dr Brighton MI 48116

PETERSON, PAUL EDWARD, economist; b. Sycamore, Ill., Apr. 18, 1954; s. Herbert Francis and Alice Mae Gronbeck (Neklasson) P.; m. Peggy Ann Kolberer, Mar. 31, 1984; children: Amy Michelle, Lisa Aileen. BS, U. Ill., 1976, MS, 1978, PhD, 1983. Mgr. market analysis Am. Farm Bur. Fedn., Park Ridge, Ill., 1983-86; mktg. mgr. Chgo. Bd. Trade, 1986-88; v.p. rsch. Brock Assocs., Milw., 1988-89; economist Chgo. Merc. Exch., 1989-92, dir. commodity rsch., 1992-93, sr. dir. commodity rsch., 1993-95, v.p. commodity rsch., 1996—; mem. state adv. com., dept. agrl. and consumer econs. U. Ill., Urbana-Champaign, 1994—. Contbr. articles to profl. jours. Mem. Chgo. Agrl. Economists Club (sec.-treas. 1988-89, v.p. 1989-90, pres. 1990-91), Chgo. Assn. Bus. Economists. Lutheran. Home: 977 Stephen Ave Elgin IL 60123 Office: Chgo Merc Exch 30 S Wacker Dr Chicago IL 60606

PETERSON, RICHARD ELTON, publisher; b. Spokane, Wash., Apr. 26, 1941; s. Darrel Emil and Katherine (Millar) P.; m. Ruthanne Hawkins, Aug. 12, 1977; children—Scott Edward, Andrew Richard; stepchildren—Troy Donald Slocum, Sean James Slocum. B.S. in Edn., U. Mo., 1963; M.B.A., U. Chgo., 1975; postgrad., Stanford U. Tchr. high sch. math. Brunswick, Mo.; tchr. Park Ridge, Ill., 1963-65; profl. baseball player N.Y. Mets., 1963-65; with Scott, Foresman & Co., 1965-93, sales rep., 1965-70, market rsch. profl., 1970-73; mktg. coord. Scott, Foresman & Co., Calif., 1973-77; regional v.p., mgr. ea. region Scott, Foresman & Co., Oakland, N.J., 1977-78; sr. v.p. mktg. Scott, Foresman & Co., Glenview, Ill., 1978-84, sr. v.p., gen. mgr. sch. div., 1984-88, pres., CEO, 1988-93, also bd. dirs.; group v.p. Harper/Collins Pub., N.Y.C., 1992-93. Bd. dirs. Evanston Hosp. Corp., 1991—; bd. govs. Northwestern U. Libr., Evanston, Ill., 1993—; bd. dirs. The Youth Campass, Park Ridge, Ill., 1995—. Mem. Assn. Am. Pubs. (chmn. Calif. com. 1980-86, exec. com. sch. divsn. 1985-88, 90-93, chmn. exec. com. 1986-88), Western Golf Assn. (bd. dirs. 1987—). Home: 707 Edgemont Ln Park Ridge IL 60068-2652

PETERSON, ROBERT L., meat processing executive; b. Nebr., July 14, 1932; married; children: Mark R., Susan P. Student, U. Nebr., 1950. With Wilson & Co., Jim Boyle Order Buying Co.; cattle buyer R&C Packing Co., 1956-61; cattle buyer, plant mgr., v.p. carcass prodn. Iowa Beef Processors, 1961-69; exec. v.p. ops. Spencer Foods, 1969-71; founder, pres., chmn., chief exec. officer Madison (Nebr.) Foods, 1971-76; group v.p. carcass div. Iowa Beef Processors, Inc. (name now IBP, Inc.) div. Occidental Petroleum Corp., Dakota City, Nebr., 1976-77, pres., chief operating officer, 1977-80, chief exec. officer, 1980-81, co-chmn. bd. dirs., 1981-82, chmn., chief exec. officer, pres., 1981—, also dir.; exec. v.p., dir. Occidental Petroleum Corp., Los Angeles, 1982-87. Served with Q.M.C. U.S. Army, 1952-54. Mem. Sioux City Country Club. Office: IBP Inc IBP Ave PO Box 515 Dakota City NE 68731-0515*

PETERSON, ROGER ANDREW, marketing educator; b. Niagara Falls, N.Y., Aug. 29, 1934; s. Walter Octave and Mary Luvance Peterson; m. Barbara L. Scott, Oct. 25, 1960 (div. Apr. 1966); m. Takako Grace Shinya, Dec. 30, 1967; children: Kristina, Reiko. BBA in Acctg. with distinction, U. Hawaii, 1972; MS in Transp., U. B.C., Can., 1974; D of Bus. Adminstrn. in Transp. and Logistics, U. Tenn., 1980. Dir. traffic and supply Channel Air Lift, Honolulu, 1967-69; gen. mgr., mgr. airline services Air Service Internat., Air Service Corp., Honolulu Internat. Airport, 1969-70; mgr. night maintenance Aero Services Inc. Honolulu Internat. Airport, 1970-71; project coordinator Hawaii environ. area rapid transit study SEAGRANT and Dept. Marine Affairs U. Hawaii, Honolulu, 1972; grad. asst. sch. travel industry mgmt. coll. bus. adminstrn. U. Hawaii, Honolulu, 1972-73; research asst. dept. transp. faculty commerce and bus. U. B.C., Vancouver, 1973-74; sr. analyst transp. and distbn. Burns Foods Ltd., Calgary, Alta., Can., 1974; dir. maintenance Day and Ross Trucking Ltd., Hartland, N.B., Can., 1974-76; asst. prof. div. adminstrn. U. N.B., Saint John, 1976-78; grad. teaching, research asst. dept. mktg. and transp. U. Tenn., Knoxville, 1978-80; prof. dept. mktg. and bus. law coll. bus. Ea. Mich. U., Ypsilanti, 1985—; pres. Peterson and Assocs. Inc., Ypsilanti, 1985-95, Augusta Industries, Willis, Mich., 1995—; vis. assoc. prof. transp. dept. purchasing, transp. and ops., coll. bus. Ariz. State U., Tempe, 1985; project dir. grant to further internat. edn. Ea. Mich. U. and U.S. Dept. Edn., 1985-86; following coms. all at Ea. Mich. U., chmn. com. rev. appointment, promotion and tenure procedures dept. mktg. and bus. law 1982-83, chmn. com. student skills 1981-86, chmn. screening com. disting. faculty awards Office V.p. Acad. Affairs 1984, chmn. research com. Coll. Bus. 1983-84, 85—, coordinator internat. bus. activities and programs Coll. Bus. 1982-95, editor research activities newsletter Coll. Bus. 1983-84, 85-86, editor research interests newsletter dept. mktg. and bus. law 1986-87, mem. adv. com. gen. aviation mgmt. program Coll. Tech. 1981—, mem. curriculum internationalization com. Coll. Bus. 1984-85, mem. dean's adv. com. space allocation Coll. Bus. 1984, mem. faculty council com. hon. degrees 1981-84, faculty council com. scholarly awards 1986-87, faculty adv. council Coll. Bus. 1981-84, chmn. sub-com. elections Coll. Bus. 1982-83, mem. personnel com. dept. mktg. and bus. law 1981-83, program rev. com. grad. programs in physics 1981-82, world bus. com. joint com. Coll. Bus. and Coll. Arts and Scis. 1984—, vis. prof. dept. fng. langs. 1981-84; cons. in field; mem. bd. & pres. Augusta Indus., Ypsilanti; vis. scholar dept. naval architecture and marine engring. U. Mich., Ann Arbor, 1981-82. Contbr. articles to profl. jours. Gt. Sgt. Select USMC, 1966-68. Grantee Eastern Mich. U., 1981, 83. Mem. Am. Soc. Transp. and Logistics (cert.), Nautical Inst. (U.K.), Royal Inst. Navigation (U.K.), Warehouse Edn. and Rsch. Coun., Nat. Def. Transp. Assn., Transp. and Utilities Group of Am. Econs. Assn., Internat. Coun. (exec. com. 1983-90, vice chmn. 1983-85), Mich. Intertribal Assn., Marine Corps League, Yankee Air Mus., Kalamazoo Aviation Mus., Southwind Am. Indian Assn., Masons, Shriners, Beta Gamma Sigma. Home: 1211 Whittier Rd Ypsilanti MI 48197-2151 Office: Eastern Mich U Dept Mktg Ypsilanti MI 48197

PETERSON, ROGER LYMAN, insurance company executive; b. Cumberland, Wis., Apr. 14, 1938; s. Oscar Adolph and Myrtle (Nelson) P.; children: Jeffrey, Scott, Robert Michael. BS in Econs., Ill. Inst. Tech., 1960. CPCU, CLU; cert. assoc. in risk mgmt.; cert. ins. counselor. Field rep. Sun Atlas, Chgo., 1961-64, Western Casualty & Surety, Champaign, 1964-67, Am. States Ins. Co., Champaign, 1967-73; field rep., v.p. Tyler, Fletcher, Fink, Peterson, Champaign, 1973-83; v.p. Ins. Risk Mgrs., Champaign, 1983-94, sr. v.p., 1994—; chmn. Arm Internat., Austin, Tex., 1980-95. Bd. dirs. YMCA, Champaign, 1979—. With USCG, 1960-68. Mem. CPCU Soc., CLU Soc., Champaign County Ind. Ins. Agts. Assn. (past pres.), Lincolnshire Fields Country Club (past pres.), Cert. Ins. Counselors Soc., Chgo. Dist. Golf Assn. (bd. dirs.). Republican. Lutheran. Home: 2308 Briar Hill Dr Champaign IL 61821 Office: Ins Risk Mgrs Ltd 2507 S Neil St Champaign IL 61824-4016

PETERSON, ROLF OLIN, ecology educator; b. Mpls., Apr. 5, 1949; s. Gerhard Clifford and Ruth Josephine (Streed) P.; m. Carolyn Louise Clarke, Sept. 5, 1970; children: Jeremy David, Trevor Scott. BA, U. Minn., Duluth, 1970; PhD, Purdue U., 1974. Asst. prof. Mich. Tech. U., Houghton, 1975-83, assoc. prof., 1983-87, prof. ecology, 1987—; dir. Wolf-Moose Rsch. Program, Isle Royale Nat. Park, Houghton, 1975—. Author: The Wolves of Isle Royale—A Broken Balance, 1995. Recipient Conservation award Gulf Oil Corp., 1981, Ann. Publ. award The Wildlife Soc., Bethesda, Md., 1981, Disting. Moose Biologist N.Am. Moose Conf., Saskatoon, Sask., 1991. Mem. AAAS, Am. Soc. Mammalogists, The Wildlife Soc. Office: Mich Tech U 1400 Townsend Dr Houghton MI 49931-1200

PETERSON, SALLY LU, communications executive; b. Waukegan, Ill., July 23, 1942; d. George C. and Luella Alice (Flood) P. BA, Govs. State U., Park Forest, Ill., 1983; MA, Calif. Grad. Sch. Theology, 1994; grad., United Christian Bible Inst.; ThD, Internat. Seminary, 1995. Ordained to ministry United Christian Ch. Ministerial Assn., 1990. V.p. Cabac TV, Gurnee, Ill., pres.; producer, dir. WHKE Channel 55, Wis.; outreach to Moscow, Jerusalem, Europe and Africa; founder, organizer, pres. radio ministry Trumpet Ministries, 1991—. Evangelist, founder, organizer TV ministry Calling Revival, 1977—, producer, dir. TV programming for Northern Ill., 1983—; co-founder, co-organizer TV ministry Interfaith Community Svc. Prayer for Peace. Mem. Cabac Cable TV Producers of Lake County Ill. (pres. 1984, 88—), Order Ea. Star (Worthy Matron of Waukegan 209, 1968), Warren-Newport Woman's Afternoon Club of Gurnee (pres. 1982-84, 86-80). Home and Office: 33712 S Oplaine Rd Gurnee IL 60031-3416

PETERSON, SCOTT BRIAN, journalist; b. Milw., Oct. 31, 1957; s. Tyrand Bruce and Bette Lou (Diel) P.; m. Nancy Joy Mehring, July 31, 1982; children: Kyle, Nathan. BA, U. Wis., Milw., 1980. Reporter, stringer Wauwatosa (Wis.) Post, 1979, Milw. Sentinel, 1979-80, Lake Country Reporter, Hartland, Wis., 1980-82; editor Lake Country Reporter, 1985-86, Hartford (Wis.) Times-Press, 1982-85; mng. editor Lake Country Publs., Hartland, 1986—; mem. steering com. Diversity Network, Add, Inc., Waupaca, Wis., 1995—. Mem. Soc. Profl. Journalists, Rotary. Episcopalian. Office: Lake Country Publs PO Box 200 440 Cardinal Ln Hartland WI 53029

PETERSON, THOMAS HULL, physician; b. Madison, Wis., June 18, 1929; s. Alfred Walter and Irene Lillian (Hull) P.; m. Lucille Ruth Schultz, June 14, 1951; children: Christian, Lorinda, Jane, Mark, David, Rebecca. BA, Cornell U., 1951; MD, U. Wis., 1958. Internship St. Mary's Hosp., Madison, Wis., 1959; family physician Freeman Med. Group, Wausau, Wis., 1959-62, Wausau Clinic, 1962-77, Wausau Med. Ctr., 1977-78; dir. family practice residency program U. Wis. Med. Sch., Wausau, 1978-84, faculty family practice residency program, 1984-94, assoc. prof. family medicine, 1980-94, assoc. prof. emeritus, 1994—. Contbr. articles to profl. jours., newspapers, mags. Mem. Wausau Health Found., 1984—. Lt. (j.g.) USN, 1951-54. Named Wis. Family Physician Educator of the Yr., 1986. Mem. Wis. Acad. Family Physicians (bd. dirs. 1968-86, chmn. bd. dirs. 1985-86, pres. 1984-85), Marathon County Med. Soc. (pres. 1991-93), Soc. Tchrs. Family Medicine, U. Wis. Med. Alumni Assn. (pres. 1993-94). Lutheran.

PETERSON, VIRGINIA BETH, counselor; b. Oak Park, Ill., July 19, 1946; d. Edward Henry and Lorraine Minnie (Hermann) Schmidtke; m. Roger Alan Peterson, Aug. 20, 1966; children: Mark Alan, Ross Edward, Ryan David. BS, U. Wis., Stevens Point, 1972, M in Edn. Profl. Devel., 1984; cert. in Guidance and Counseling, U. Wis., Stout Menomonie, 1987, EdS in Guidance and Counseling, 1993. Cert. K-8 tchr., K-12 counselor, Wis. Tchr. elem. sch. Deerfield (Wis.) Community Schs., 1966-68; tchr. elem. sch. Nekoosa (Wis.) Pub. Schs., 1972-86, tchr. elem. sch., dir. alcohol and drug program, 1986-90, dir. dist. alcohol and drug program, elem. sch. counselor, 1990-91; dist. counselor for at risk dist. alcohol and drug dir., elem. sch. counselor Wausau (Wis.) Pub. Schs., 1991—; apptd. mem. Citizens Coun. on Alcohol and Other Drugs, Madison, Wis., 1989-94; trainer, cons The Wood Group, Port Edwards, Wis., 1990—; apptd. mem. State Coun. on Alcohol and Other Drugs Prevention Com., 1994—. Contbg. author: SOS (Study on Suicide), 1989. Chmn., vice-chmn., mem. Reaching Others on Alcohol and Drugs, Nekoosa, 1986-91; bd. dirs. Wood County Partnership, Wisconsin Rapids, Wis., 1988-91, Family Counseling Svcs., Wausau, 1992—, U. Wis. Clearinghouse, Madison, 1987—, reviser pamphlets and booklets, 1987—. Recipient Drug Buster for Wis. award USA Today, 1989, Dirs. Community Leaders award FBI, 1990, Gov's. award for outstanding work in alcohol and other drug prevention, 1996, Resolution of Commendation award Wausau Sch. Dist. Bd. Edn., 1996. Mem. Wis. Sch. Counselor Assn., Wisconsin Rapids Area C. of C. (drug free task force 1989-91). Lutheran. Home: 802 E Lakeshore Dr Wausau WI 54401-6708 Office: GD Jones Elem Sch 1018 S 12th Ave Wausau WI 54401-5873

PETERSON, WALLACE CARROLL, SR., economics educator; b. Omaha, Mar. 28, 1921; s. Fred Nels and Grace (Brown) P.; m. Eunice V. Peterson, Aug. 16, 1944 (dec. Nov. 24, 1985); children: Wallace Carroll Jr., Shelley Lorraine; m. Bonnie B. Watson, Nov. 11, 1988. Student, U. Omaha, 1939-40, U. Mo., 1940-42; BA in Econs. and European History, U. Nebr., 1947, MA in Econs. and European History, 1948, PhD in Econs. and European History, 1953; postgrad., Handelshochschule, St. Gallen, Switzerland, 1948-49, U. Minn., 1951, London Sch. Econs. and Polit. Sci., 1952. Reporter Lincoln (Nebr.) Jour., 1946; instr. econs. U. Nebr., Lincoln, 1951-54, asst. prof., 1954-57, assoc. prof., 1957-61, prof., 1962—, chmn. dept. econs., 1965-75, George Holmes prof. econs., 1966-92; George Holmes prof. econs. emeritus, 1992—; v.p. faculty senate U. Nebr., Lincoln, 1972-73, pres. faculty senate, 1973-74; S.J. Hall disting. vis. prof. U. Nev., Las Vegas, 1983-84. Author: The Welfare State in France, 1960, Elements of Economics, 1973, Our Overloaded Economy: Inflation, Unemployment and the Crisis in American Capitalism, 1982, Market Power and the Economy, 1988, Transfer Spending, Taxes and the American Welfare State, 1991, Income, Employment and Economic Growth, 8th edit., 1996, Silent Depression: The Fate of the American Dream, 1994; contbr. articles to profl. jours. and columns to newspapers. Mem. Nebr. Dem. Cen. Com., 1968-74, vice-chmn., chmn. Nebr. Polit. Accountability and Disclosure Commn., 1977-80; chmn. Nebr. Coun. Econ. Edn., 1976-77. Capt. USAAF, 1942-46. Recipient Champion Media award for Econ. Understanding, 1981; Fulbright fellow, 1957-58, 64-65; Mid-Am. State Univs. honor scholar, 1982-83. Mem. ACLU, AAUP (pres. Nebr. 1963-64, nat. coun.), Assn. for Evolutionary Econs. (pres. 1976, Veblen-Commons award 1991), Am. Econs. Assn., Midwest Econs. Assn.

(pres. 1968-69), Mo. Valley Econ. Assn. (pres. 1989), Assn. Social Econs. (pres. 1992, Thomas F. Devine award 1995), Fedn. Am. Scientists. Home: 4549 South St Lincoln NE 68506-1253 Office: U Nebr Dept Econs CBA Lincoln NE 68588-0489

PETERSON, WALTER FRITIOF, academic administrator; b. Idaho Falls, Idaho, July 15, 1920; s. Walter Fritiof and Florence (Danielson) P.; m. Barbara Mae Kempe, Jan. 13, 1946; children: Walter Fritiof III, Daniel John. BA, State U. Iowa, 1942, MA, 1948, PhD, 1951; HHD (hon.), Loras Coll., 1983; LHD (hon.), Clarke Coll., 1991. Asst. prof. history, chmn. dept. history Milw. Downer Coll., 1952-57, assoc. prof. history, chmn. social sci. div., 1957-64; assoc. prof. history Lawrence U., Appleton, Wis., 1964-67; prof. history, Alice G. Chapman libr. Lawrence U., 1967-70; pres. U. Dubuque, 1970-90, chancellor, 1990—; regional tng. officer Peace Corps, 1965-68; cons. history Allis-Chalmers Mfg. Co., 1959-75, Secura Ins. Group, 1968-92, Wm. C. Brown Pub. Co., 1981-92, bd. dirs. Editor: Transactions of Wis. Acad. Scis., Arts and Letters, 1965-72, The Allis-Chalmers Corporation: An Industrial History, 1977, A History of Wm. C. Brown Cos., 1994, A History of Haukeye Bancorporation, 1996. Advisor Templeton Prize for Progress in Religion, 1986-91; bd. dirs. Finley Hosp., pres., 1983-84; chmn. Finley Health Found., 1986-95; bd. dirs. Dubuque Symphony Orch., Dubuque Art Assn., Jr. Achievement, Nat. River Hall of Fame, 1984; chmn. Iowa Assn. Coll. and Univ. Pres., 1975-76; chmn. Iowa Coll. Found., 1982-83. With USAAF, 1942-45, PTO. Recipient Dubuque Citizen award, 1990, Disting. Civic Svc. award, 1991, Benjamin Franklin award Nat. Soc. Fundraising Execs., 1994, Paul Harris fellowship, 1993; named to Dubuque Bus. Hall of Fame, 1990. Mem. Iowa Assn. Ind. Colls. and Univs. (chmn. 1988-89), Dubuque County Hist. Soc. (bd. dirs.), Phi Alpha Theta, Kappa Delta Pi, Phi Delta Kappa. Office: U Dubuque Office of Chancellor 2000 University Ave Dubuque IA 52001-5050

PETERSON, WILLIAM ALLEN, lawyer; b. Marshall, Mo., Oct. 1, 1934; s. R.O. and Marjorie E. (Mallot) P.; m. Mary Kay Moore, July 26, 1958; children: Laura, Clayton, Mary M., Sarah. BS, Drury Coll., Springfield, Mo., 1958; JD, Washington U., 1963. Bar: Mo. 1963, U.S. Dist. Ct. (ea. dist.) Mo. 1964, U.S. Dist. Ct. (we. dist.) Mo. 1965, U.S. Supreme Ct. 1967. Assoc. Riddle, O'Herin & Newberry, Malden, Mo., 1963-65; asst. atty. gen. State of Mo., Jefferson City, 1965-70; legislator Mo. Ho. Reps., Jefferson City, 1970-74; pvt. practice Marshall, 1974—; atty. City of Marshall, 1976-78, City of Slater, Mo., 1988-89; judge mcpl. divsn. State Cir. Ct., Marshall, 1979-80, Slater, 1990-94; pros. atty. County of Saline, Marshall, 1979-80, 84-88. With USN, 1954-56. Mem. ABA, Mo. Bar Assn., Assn. Trial Lawyers Am., Mo. Assn. Trial Attys., Mo. Orgn. Def. Attys., Am. Legion, VFW. Methodist. Home: 503 E Eastwood St Marshall MO 65340-1535 Office: PO Box 9 54 W Arrow Marshall MO 65340-0009

PETERSON, WILLIAM E., state legislator; b. Chgo., Feb. 2, 1936; m. Patricia Guiffre; 3 children. BA, North Pk. Coll.; MS, No. Ill. U.; postgrad., Loyola U., Chgo. Tchr., prin.; mem. Ill. Ho. of Reps. from 60th dist., 1983-93, Ill. State Senate from 26th dist., 1993—; mem. Consumer Protection, Aging, Aeronauticsm, Counties and Twps. Coms. Ill. Ho. of Reps., Minority Spokesman, mem. Energy, Environ and Natural Resources, Ins. and Revenue Coms. Trustee, supr. Vernon Twp. (Ill.); active Lake County (Ill.) United Way. With U.S. Army Reserve. Mem. LWV, Lions. Republican. Home: 1480 Meadowlark Dr Long Grove IL 60047*

PETERSON, WILLIAM GENE, public affairs executive; b. Vermillion, S.D., Dec. 15, 1950; s. William Henry and Opal Irene (Johnson) P.; m. Sue Kathryn Lucas, June 15,1991; children: Lucas William, Robert William. BA, U. S.D., 1974. With Nat. Bank S.D., Vermillion, 1973-79; dir. legislation and rsch. Sioux Falls C. of C., 1979-83; v.p. pub. affairs S.D. C. of C., Pierre, 1983-84; adminstrv. asst. Lt. Gov. Lowell Hansen, Sioux Falls, 1984-86; v.p. mktg. Jack Rabbit Bus Lines, Sioux Falls, 1984-86; account exec. Colle McVoy Advt., Sioux Falls, 1987-88; asst. v.p. pub. affairs Western Surety Co., Sioux Falls, 1988—; dir. legis. com. Nat. Assn. Ind. Sureties; prof. Kilian C.C., Sioux Falls, 1982-83, 86-89. Mem. Vermillion Planning Commn., 1975-78, chair, 1977-78; bd. dirs. Clay-Union Health Found., 1979, Kilian C.C., 1989-95, chair, 1991-93; bd. dirs. Family Svc., Inc., Sioux Falls, 1989-95, chair, 1993-94; chmn. Minnehaha County Lincoln Day, 1985; co-chairCitizens for Modern City Govt., Sioux Falls, 1994; chair Minnehaha County Republican Party, 1995—, other civic activities. Named to Outstanding Young Men of Am., 1983. Mem. Pub. Rels. Network of Sioux Falls (pres. 1988, Pub. Rels. Person of Yr. 1994), Sioux Falls C. of C. (chair tax coun. 1988-90, chair pub. affairs com. 1988-90), Masons, Shriners. Republican. Lutheran. Home: 3808 E Marson Dr Sioux Falls SD 57103

PETHLEY, LOWELL SHERMAN, management consultant; b. Tacoma, Nov. 14, 1928; s. Sherman and Faye Maude (Newton) P.; m. Agnes Lenore Hudgins, Feb. 21, 1953; children: Lynn Louise, Curtis Sherman, Christopher Lowell, Suzanne Elizabeth. BS, U. Wash., 1956, MBA, 1957. Cert. mgmt. cons., CPA. Sr. acct., consulting prin. Deloitte & Touche, Seattle, 1957-65, San Francisco, 1965-67; ptnr. in charge, Midwest consulting Deloitte & Touche, Chgo., 1967-86; ptnr., 1986—. Author, editor: Bank Costing for Planning and Control, 1973. Mem. AICPA (cons.), Inst. Mgmt. Cons., Ill. Soc. CPA, Wash. Soc. CPA, Inverness Golf Club (treas. 1971-73), PGA, Nat. Golf Club, PGA West Club, Phi Beta Kappa. Home: 111 S Baybrook Dr Unit 610 Palatine IL 60067 Office: Deloitte & Touche 10 Westport Rd Wilton CT 06897

PETINGA, CHARLES MICHAEL, business executive; b. Atlantic City, July 9, 1946; s. Thomas Joseph and Rose Marie (Merindino) P.; m. Velna Mae McVicker, June 7, 1969; children: Scott, Jeffery. BS in Geology, Geography, U. Wis., Superior, 1969. Ops. supr. Schneider Transport, Inc., Green Bay, Wis., 1973-74, prodn. mgr., 1974-76, safety dir., 1976-79; dir. safety Schneider Nat., Inc., Green Bay, 1979-82, dir. risk mgmt., 1982-87; gen. mgr. Petinga Candy Co., Atlantic City, 1987-89; mgr. bus. devel., sr. v.p. Marsh and McLennan, Appleton, Wis., 1989—; cons. local charitable groups, Green Bay, 1985-88; adviser, cons. Small Bus. Execs., Green Bay, 1989; mem. worker compensation task force Wis. Motor Carriers, Madison, 1991; speaker at vocat. schs. and high schs.; speaker to motor carrier assns. and industry mgmt. goups. Co. liaison Green Bay United Way, 1985, 86. With U.S. Army, 1971-73. Mem. Wis. Coun. Safety Suprs., Nat. Safety Mgmt. Soc., Wis. Motor Carriers Assn., Risk and Ins. Mgmt. Soc., Nat. Safety Coun., Am. Trucking Assn. Office: Marsh and McLennan Inc 2631 N Meade St Appleton WI 54911-2203

PETITAN, DEBRA ANN BURKE, educator, education counselor, design engineer, writer, author; b. Chgo., Mar. 12, 1932; d. James Marcellus and Susan Florence (Hines) Burke; m. Kenneth Charles Petitan, Aug. 9, 1952; 1 child, Susan Florence. AA, Wilson Jr. Coll., Chgo., 1951, N.Y. Inst. Photography, 1952; BS in Primary Edn., Chgo. State U., 1956, MS in Indsl. Edn., 1967; DSc in Applied Sci. and Tech., London Inst. Tech., 1971; postgrad., U. Wis., Bradley U., U. Calif., U. Ill.; grad., Inst. Children's Lit., West Redding, Conn., 1991. Tchr. Chgo. Bd. Edn., 1958-71, guidance counselor, 1976-84, now tchr., cons.; nat. dir. edn. Nation of Islam, 1971-75; design engr. Fed. Sign and Signal Corp., Chgo., 1975-76; mem. nat. adv. bd. Nat. Right to Work Orgn., 1976-85; cons. ednl. devel., 1978; computer libr. cons.; owner, CEO, Fayzah's Fin. Svcs., Fayzah's Creative Prodns., Inc.; participant summer writing festival U. Iowa, 1991. Photographer VISTA News, 1969-70; writer children's lit. Dir. Christian Edn. Trinity United Ch. Christ, Chgo., 1978-81, family counselor, 1978-81, organizer, leader family counseling ministry, lic. lay Eucharistic minister Episcopal Ch. St. Edmund, 1989; chmn. Career Women for Johnson/Humphrey, Chgo., 1965; navigator, pub. rels. officer 1L Wing, Squadron 8, capt. Civil Air Patrol, 1953-56. Named Woman of Yr. Iota Phi Lambda, 1978; recipient 250 Hr. medal Ground Observer Corps, 1952, 25 Yr. Service medallion Chgo. Bd. Edn., 1987. Mem. Off-Campus Writer's Workshop (editor newsletter Green River Writers), Soc. of Children's Book Writers, Children's Reading Roundtable, Green River, Ky. Writers, Epsilon Pi Tau. Office: Chgo Bd Edn 1839 W Pershing Rd Chicago IL 60609-2317

PETKA, ED, state legislator; b. Chgo., Mar. 10, 1943; m. Phyllis Petka; children: Jennifer, Edward, Tanya, Melinda. AB, So. Ill. U., 1966; JD, John Marshall Law Sch., 1971. Atty.; mem. Ill. Ho. of Reps. from 82d dist., 1986-93, Ill. State Senate from 42d dist., 1993—; mem. Judiciary II, Exec. and Vet. Affairs, Cities and Villages, Election Law, Consumer Protection Coms, Ill. Ho. of Reps.; mem. Aging, Election Law, Judiciary II, Labor, Registration and Regulations Coms. Ill. State Senate. Mem. Ill. State Attys. Assn. (past pres.). Republican. Home: 27 Lake Dr Plainfield IL 60544-8945*

PETKUS, ALAN FRANCIS, microbiologist; b. Chgo., Feb. 4, 1956; s. Frank Anthony and Valeria (Shimkus) P.; m. Karan Elaine Blakely, Apr. 21, 1990; children: Sabrina Marie, Alexandra Louise. BS, Ill. Benedictine Coll., Lisle, 1979; PhD, Chgo. Med. Sch., North Chicago, 1986. Technologist Palos Community Hosp., Palos Heights, Ill., 1973-79, med. technologist, 1979-86; microbiologist South Bend (Ind.) Med. Found., 1986-91; microbiology dir. Met. Hosp., Grand Rapids, Mich., 1991—. Mem. AAAS, Am. Soc. Clin. Pathologists, Am. Soc. Microbiology, N.Y. Acad. Sci., Ill. Soc. Microbiology, South Ctrl. Assn. Microbiology. Roman Catholic. Office: Met Hosp 1919 Boston St SE Grand Rapids MI 49506-4160

PETRAMALE, DONALD LESLIE, insurance company executive; b. Chgo., May 1, 1935; s. Domenico and Serafina (Martino) P.; m. Diana Mae Silvestri, Aug. 3, 1980. Student, Harper Coll., 1990. Lic. real estate broker. Sec. Chgo., 1988; owner, pres., CEO D & D Ventures Inc. & D & D Office Machines Inc., Barrington, Ill., 1967—; dir. Am. Heritage S & C Assn., Bloomingdale, Ill. 1975-77. Chmn. Addison Lake Manor Park Assn., Addison, Ill., 1961; Dem. twp. chmn. Bloomingdale Twp., 1971; com. mem. Holy Family Ch., Inverness, Ill., 1990. Recipient leading ins. agent awards, Am. Natl. Ins. Co., Chgo., 1953-67. Mem. Bus. Tech. Assn. Democrat. Roman Catholic. Home: 1518 Guthrie Dr Barrington IL 60010 Office: D & D Ofc Mailings 1518 Guthrie Dr Barrington IL 60010

PETRI, THOMAS EVERT, congressman; b. Marinette, Wis., May 28, 1940; s. Robert and Marian (Humleker) P.; m. Anne Neal, Mar. 26, 1983; 1 child, Alexandra. BA in Govt., Harvard U., 1962, JD, 1965. Bar: Wis. 1965. Law clk. to presiding justice U.S. Dist. (we. dist.) Wis., Madison, 1965-66; vol. Peace Corps, Somalia, 1966-67; aide White House, Washington, 1969-70; dir. crime and drug studies Pres.'s Nat. Adv. Coun. on Exec. Orgn., 1969; pvt. practice Fond du Lac, Wis., 1970-79; mem. Wis. State Senate, Madison, 1973-79, 96th-104th Congress from 6th Wis. Dist., Washington, 1979—. Editor: National Industrial Policy: Solution or Illusion, 1984. Republican. Lutheran. Office: US Ho of Reps 2262 Rayburn Bldg Washington DC 20515-0005

PETRO, DAVID W., electronics product manager; b. Cleve., Mar. 30, 1959; s. William Frank Petro and Carolyn Ann (Dynes) Stacks.; m. Debora Christine Voss,July 28, 1984 (div. Nov. 1991); 1 child, Alec Willliam. B in Engring., Youngstown State U., 1981; MBA, Cleve. State U., 1991. Sales engr. Eaton Corp., Cleve., 1981-84, 89-90, Cin., 1984-1989; mktg specialist Reliance Electric, Cleve., 1990-93, product mgr., 1993—. Contbr. articles to profl jours. Mem. IEEE (chmn. rubber and plastics com. 1993-95). Lutheran. Home: 32285 Franklin Dr # 108 Solon OH 44139 Office: Reliance Electric 24701 Euclid Ave Cleveland OH 44117-1714

PETRO, JAMES MICHAEL, lawyer, politician; b. Cleve., Oct. 25, 1948; s. William John and Lila Helen (Janca) P.; m. Nancy Ellen Bero, Dec. 16, 1972; children: John Bero, Corbin Marie. BA, Denison U., 1970; JD, Case Western Res., 1973. Bar: Ohio 1973, U.S. Dist. Ct. (no. dist.) Ohio 1974, U.S. Ct. Appeals (6th cir.) 1981. Spl. asst. U.S. senator W.B. Saxbe, Cleve., 1972-73; asst. pros. atty. Franklin County, Ohio, 1973-74; asst. dir. law City of Cleve., 1974; ptnr. Petro & Troia, Cleve., 1974-84; dir. govt. affairs Standard Oil Co., Cleve., 1984-86; ptnr. Petro, Rademaker, Matty & McClelland, Cleve., 1986-93, Buckingham, Doolittle & Burroughs, Cleve., 1993-95. Mem. city coun. Rocky River, Ohio, 1977-79, dir. law, 1980; mem. Ohio Ho. of Reps., Columbus, 1981-84, 86-90; commr. Cuyahoga County, Ohio, 1991-95; Auditor of State of Ohio, 1995—. Mem. ABA, Ohio State Bar Assn., Cleve. Bar Assn. Republican. Methodist. Home: 315 Falmouth Dr Cleveland OH 44116-1326 Office: 88 E Broad St Columbus OH 43216-1140

PETRU, SUZANNE MITTON, health care finance executive; b. Shawano, Wis., Sept. 26, 1947; d. William Wallace and Gertrude Priscilla (Humphrey) Mitton; m. W. James Petru, Jan. 2, 1987. BSBA, Northwestern U., 1970, MBA, 1971. Diplomate Am. Coll. Healthcare Execs. Sr. acct. Arthur Andersen & Co., Chgo., 1971-77; v.p. fin. Thorek Hosp. and Med. Ctr., Chgo., 1977-82; sec./treas. La Grange (Ill.) Meml. Health Sys., 1982-85; v.p. fin. La Grange Meml. Hosp., 1982-85; audit prin. Deloitte & Touche (formerly Touche Ross & Co.), Chgo., 1985-88; sr. v.p. fin., treas. SSM Health Care Sys., St. Louis, 1988-95; pres. healthcare divsn. Am. Home Assurance Co. (subs. Am. Internat. Group, Inc.), 1995—. Mem. investment com. Sisters of Charity Healthcare Sys., Cin., 1993—, mem. fin. com., 1994—; mem. assoc. bd. La Grange Meml. Hosp., 1988—; advisor Jr. Achievement, 1971-76. Fellow Healthcare Fin. Mgmt. Assn. (bd. dirs. 1989-91), principles and practices bd. 1992-95, nat. matrix 1985-86, 88-89, pres., pres.-elect, sec., bd. First Ill. chpt. 1979-86, Follmer Bronze award 1982, Reeves Silver award 1985, Muncie Gold ward 1988, Alice V. Runyan chpt. 1988); mem. Fin. Execs. Inst., Country Club at Legends (adv. bd. 1991-93), St. Louis Club (house com. 1991-95). Republican. Presbyterian. Home: 12033 Tindall Dr Saint Louis MO 63131-3135 Office: Am Home Assurance Co 70 Pine St New York NY 10270

PETRY, CARL FORBES, history educator; b. Camden, N.J., June 29, 1943; s. Eduard Carl Petry and Jean Forbes (Hamill) Klauder. BA, Carleton Coll., 1965; MA, U. Mich., 1966, PhD, 1974. Asst. prof. history Northwestern U., Evanston, Ill., 1975-80; assoc. prof. Northwestern U., Evanston, 1980-92, prof., 1992—; mem. exec. bd. Am. Rsch. Ctr. in Egypt, N.Y.C., 1987-91. Author: The Civilian Elite of Cairo, 1982, Twilight of Majesty, The Reigns of al-Ashraf Qaytbay and Qansuh al-Ghawri in Egypt, 1993, Protectors or Practorians, the Last Mamluk Sultans and Egypt's Waning as a Great Power, 1994. Recipient NEH fellowship, 1980-81, U.S. Info. Agy. fellowship, 1985, Guggenheim Found. fellowship, 1987, Inst. for Advanced Study fellowship, 1996. Fellow Middle East Study Assn., Medieval Acad. Am., Am. Rsch. Ctr. in Egypt. Office: Northwestern U Dept History 1881 Sheridan Rd Evanston IL 60208-2220

PETRY, DAVID P., mechanical engineer; b. Fairmont, W.Va., Apr. 13, 1955. BSME, Cleve. State U., 1994. Chief controls engr. Bardons & Oliver, Cleve., 1974-90; mgr. design engr. Kent Corp., Cleve., 1990—. Patentee method to facilitate material handling within accumulators; contbr. articles to profl. publs. Mem. NSPE, Tau Beta Pi. Democrat. Home: 16141 W River Rd Columbia Station OH 44028-9435 Office: Kent Corp 9941 York Theta Dr Cleveland OH 44133-3512

PETTES, ROBERT CARLTON, artist; b. Mpls., May 16, 1922; s. Robert Oscar and Mertez Jennie (Swartwood) P.; m. Gladys Arlene Pettes, July 27, 1922 (div. Feb. 1976); children: Jo Anne, Roberta Gay, Douglas Kent; m. Phyllis Gwen Browne, Apr. 3, 1976. Grad. high sch., Mpls.; student, Oberlin Coll., 1944-45, Mpls. Sch. Art, 1945-48. Artist Brown and Bigelow, St. Paul, 1946-56; illustrator Creative Group, Mpls., 1956-60; studio mgr. Bob Pettes Art For Advt., Mpls., 1960-67; builder, architect Bob Pettes Rustique Homes, Mpls.; illustrator Design Studios Inc., St. Paul, 1969-70; artist Hallmark Cards, 1972-80, Nostalgic Impressions, Prairie Village, Kans., 1980—. Group precinct leader Rep. Group, Edina 1961-64. With Coast Guard Navy, 1942-45. Mem. Soc. Artists and Art Dirs. (treas. 1962). Home and Studio: 7403 NW Oak Dr Parkville MO 64152-1947

PETTEY, PATRICIA HIGGINS, state legislator; m. John M. Pettey. Rep. dist. 31 State of Kans., 1993—. Democrat. Home: 3500 Gibbs Rd Kansas City KS 66106-3810 Office: Kans Ho of Reps State Capitol Topeka KS 66612*

PETTIGREW, FRANK EDWIN, JR., assistant dean, physical education educator; b. Ravenna, Ohio, Mar. 6, 1950; s. Frank Edwin Sr. and Darlene Marie (Carver) P.; m. Amy Allen Atkinson, Nov. 4, 1978; children: Emily Erin, Hallie Allyn. BS in Edn., Ashland Coll., 1972; MA in Phys. Edn., Kent State U., 1977; PhD in Edn., U. Idaho, 1984. Tchr. phys. edn. Canton (Ohio) City Schs., 1972-74, Lake Placid (Fla.) Schs., 1974-76; grad. asst. Kent (Ohio) State U., 1976-77, asst. prof., 1985-90, assoc. prof., 1990—, asst. dean Sch. Phys. Edn., Recreation and Dance, 1992—, dir. Sch. Exercise, Leisure and Sport, 1995—; instr. phys. edn. Northwestern U., Evanston, Ill., 1977-81; asst. prof. U. Idaho, Moscow, 1981-85. Author: Secondary Physical Education, 1993; contbr. chpt. to: Preventing Catastrophic Injuries in Recreation, 1985; contbr. articles to profl. jours. Softball coach Lake Youth Sport Programs, Hartville, Ohio, 1992-93. Recipient Outstanding Alumni award Ashland Coll., 1987. Mem. AAHPERD (fellow Rsch. Consortium 1990), Ohio Assn. Health, Phys. Edn., Recreation and Dance (v.p. 1989-91, chairperson rsch. grants 1991—). Republican. Mem. Brethren Ch. Home: 3396 Smith Kramer St NE Hartville OH 44632-9157

PETTIJOHN, WILLIAM LEE, singer, poet; b. Cleve., July 4, 1956; s. Lee Halsted and Mary Jane (Sinclair) H.; 1 child, William Lee II, July 8, 1979. Student, Cleve. State U., 1975-77; diploma, Ohio Sch. Broadcasting, 1978. Lead singer Dragonwyck rock band, Cleve., 1973-77, Moonlight Drive band, Cleve., 1981—. Author: (poetry) The Gift Given Twice, 1996; recorded album Moonlight Drive, 1982; writer, performer, soundtrack for film Strangers in Paradise, 1983, When I Come to L.A., The Ties That Bind: appeared in film Devonshire Terror, on Jerry Springer Tribute Artists show, 1995. Congregational. Home: 9855 Memphis # 12 Cleveland OH 44144-2024

PETTIT, SUE, artist; b. Bellville, Ill., Jan. 2, 1951; d. Jacob Howard and Alice (Richardson) V.; m. Kenneth Lloyd Jackson, April 1, 1995. Grad. high sch., Warsaw, Mo., 1968. Sec. Shelter Ins., Columbia, Mo., 1981—; owner, operator Pettit Originals, Columbia, 1993—. Author: I am Soft Breeze, 1993; author, artist, narrator The Drug Monster (video), 1994 (Best of Show award 1994, MidMo ADDY Charleston Worldfest Gold award 1994); executed mural The World Is Your Playground, battered women's safehouse, 1993. Mem. Ctrl. Reg. Adv. Bd. Drug and Alcohol Div. Mo. Dept. of Mental Health, Jefferson City, 1995. Recipient 1st place Jazz Art Festival, Mo. Arts Coun., Jefferson City, 1993, 1st place Jefferson City Adult Art Exhibit, Jefferson City Art League, 1994, Columbia Conv. and Visitors Bur./C. of C. Purchase award, 1994. Mem. Show Me Cosmopolitan Club, Columbia Art League (bd. dirs. 1992, 2nd place 35th Ann. Boone County Art Show, 1994).

PETTYJOHN, SHIRLEY ELLIS, lawyer, real estate executive; b. Liberty, Ky., Aug. 16, 1935; d. Wesley Barker and Ada Lou (Bryant) Ellis; m. Flem D. Pettyjohn, Sept. 24, 1955; children: Deena Renee, Ellisa Denise. BS in Commerce, U. Louisville, 1974, JD, 1977. Bar: Ky. 1978, Ind. 1988; lic. real estate broker, Ky., Ind.; cert. mediator. Pres. Universal Devel. Corp., Ky. and Fla., 1984—, Pettyjohn Inc., Ky. and Ind., 1967—, Ind. Mediation Svcs., Inc., 1990—, Ky. Mediation Svcs., Inc., 1991—; v.p. Continental Investments Corp., 1986—; sr. ptnr. Pettyjohn & Assocs., Attys., 1987—. Editor Law-Hers Jour. Vice chmn. Louisville and Jefferson County Planning Commn., 1971-75; mem. Gov.'s Conf. on Edn., 1977, jud. nominee, 1981, Met. Louisville Women's Polit. Caucus, Bluegrass State Skills Corp., 1992—, Ky. Opera Assn. Guild; elected mem. Ky. State Dem. Exec. Com., 1988-92; del. Nat. Dem. Conv. and Dem. Nat. Platform Com., 1988; bd. dirs. Ky. Dem. Hdqs., Inc., 1988-92, Pegasus Rising, Inc.; chmn. Okolona Libr. Task Force; mem. Clinton-Gore Nat. Steering Com., 1995. Recipient Mayor's Cert. Recognition, 1974, Mayor's Fleur de lis award, 1969-73, Excellence in Writing award Arts Club Louisville, 1986, 87, 93. Mem. ABA, NAFE, Nat. Assn. Adminstrv. Law Judges, Ky. Bar Assn., Louisville Bar Assn., Women Lawyers Assn. of Jefferson County, Am. Judicature Soc., Clark County Bar Assn., Ind. Bar Assn., Ind. Assn. Mediators, Am. Inst. Planners, Women's C. of C. of Ky. (past bd. dirs., chmn. legis. com.), Am. Legion (aux.), Fraternal Order Police Assn. (award 1982), Louisville Legal Secs. (past pres., editor Law-Hers Jour.), Coun. of Women Pres. (past pres., Woman of Achievement award 1974), Louisville Visual Arts Assn. (former bd. dirs.), Louisville Ballet Guild (chair audience devel. 1989-91), Dem. Leadership Coun., Jefferson County Dem. Women's Club (past v.p.), Nat. Fedn. Dem. Women's Clubs, Spirit of 46th Club, Mose Green Club, North End Club, 12th Ward Club, S. End Club, 3rd Ward Club, Highland Pk. Club, Grass Roots Club, Harry S. Truman Club, Beargrass Club, Arts Club of Louisville (past pres.), Sigma Delta Kappa, Chi Thi Theta, Century 2000 Democrat Club. Home: 6924 Norlynn Dr Louisville KY 40228-1471 Office: PO Box 787 600 E Court Ave Ste 102 Jeffersonville IN 47131-0787

PETUCHOWSKI, ELIZABETH RITA, German language and literature educator; b. Bochum, Germany; came to U.S., 1948; d. Alfred and Martha Caroline Mayer; m. Jakob Josef Petuchowski (dec. Nov. 1991); children: Samuel, Aaron, Jonathan. BA (honors), U. Coll. London, 1946; PhD, U. Cin., 1975. Adj. assoc. prof. German U. Cin., 1983—. Translator Jewish German History, 1992; contbr. articles to profl. publs. Republican. Jewish.

PETYO, MICHAEL EDWARD, construction company owner; b. East Chicago, Ind., Mar. 29, 1949; m. Janet Lynn; 2 children. Candidate for Lake County Sheriff, 1994; Rep. candidate for U.S. House, 1st Dist., Ind., 1996. Office: PO Box 599 Chesterton IN 46304*

PETZ, THOMAS JOSEPH, internist; b. Detroit, Feb. 10, 1930; s. Arthur J. and Marie (McCarthy) P.; m. Catherine Crowe, June 13, 1959; children: Thomas Jr., William, David, John, Catherine. BS, U. Detroit, 1951; MD, Wayne State U., 1955. Diplomate Am. Bd. Internal Medicine and Pulmonary Disease. Intern Harper Hosp., Detroit, 1955-56, resident, 1958-59, 60-62; resident U. Calif., San Francisco, 1959-60; clin. instr. Wayne State U., Detroit, 1962-72, assoc. prof., 1972-76, clin. assoc. prof., 1976—; pvt. practice pulmonary disease and internal medicine Detroit, 1962-72, St. Clair Shores, Mich., 1977—; chief pulmonary Wayne State U., Detroit, 1974-76, Harper Hosp., Detroit, 1972-79; dir. med. intensive care unit Harper Hosp., Detroit, 1977-83; chmn. dept. medicine Bon Secours Hosp., Grosse Pointe, Mich., 1984-86; chmn. Gen. Motors human rsch. com., 1995. Bd. govs. Wayne State Sch. of Medicine Alumni Assn., Detroit, 1981-85. Fellow Detroit Acad. Medicine (pres. 1982-83), Am. Coll. Chest Physicians; mem. Am. Coll. Physicians, Detroit Med. Club. Republican. Roman Catholic. Office: 23201 Jefferson Ave Saint Clair Shores MI 48080-1903

PEURYE-HISSONG, CELENE NAN, foundation executive; b. Chgo., Feb. 9, 1953; d. Albert and Rose (Salpeter) Peurye; m. Roland Dean Peurye-Hissong, Sept. 21, 1975; children: Justin, Alex, David. BA in Polit. Sci., U. Ill., 1974, M in Social Work, 1976. Cert. clin. social worker. Program auditor City Chgo. Dept. Personnel, 1976-77; clin. therapist City Chgo. Alcoholism Treatment Ctr., 1977-78; pvt. practice therapy Chgo. Women's Counseling Collective, 1977-80; therapist Family Svc. Bur. United Charities of Chgo., 1978-80; adminstrv. assoc. United Charities of Chgo., 1980-81; cons. to non profit orgnrs., employee assistance programs pvt. practice, Chgo., 1981-84; exec. dir. S. Suburban Family Shelter, Homewood, Ill., 1982-83; acting exec. dir. Chgo. Abused Women Coalition, 1983-84; cons., therapist Employee Consultation Svcs., Wilmette, Ill., 1983-84; dir. corp. contributions, programs Fel-Pro Mecklenburger Found., Skokie, Ill., 1984—; cons. LifeSpan, Des Plaines, Ill., 1981, Minority Econ. Resources Program, Des Plaines, 1981-82. Bd. dirs. Chgo. Abused Women Coalition, 1976-84, Chgo. Met. Battered Women Network, 1980-84, LWV of Wilmette, 1987-89, 92-95, Ctrl. Sch. PTA, Wilmette, 1990-94, 95—, Chgo. Found. for Women, 1992—, sec., 1995—. Recipient Fellowship NIMH, Bethesda, Md., 1975-76. Mem. Donors Forum of Chgo (bd. dirs. 1989-92, chmn. libr. com.), Chgo. Women in Philanthropy (bd. dirs. 1989-92, chmn. 1990-91). Jewish. Office: Fel/Pro Mecklenburger Found 7450 Mccormick Blvd Skokie IL 60076-4046

PEWICK, HAROLD EUGENE, social worker; b. Des Moines, Mar. 31, 1925; s. Charles M. P.; children: Roger Edward, Tammera Anne. BS, Jackson Coll., 1962. Enlisted USAF, 1943, advanced through grades to master sgt.; ret. U.S. Army, 1970. Dist. scout exec. Boy Scouts Am., Ft. Dodge, Iowa, 1970-72, leader, 1946—. Recipient Silver Beaver award Boy Scouts Am., Vigil Honor Order of Avvoce, 1957, Touch and Flame award United Meth. Ch., 1984. Mem. Masons, Shriners. Home: 1575 Oak Ave #GF Evanston IL 60201-4274

PEZL, JOHN JOSEPH, engineer; b. Marshfield, Wis., Nov. 15, 1949; s. John F. and Agnes B. (France) P; m. Dawn G. Scroggins, June 12, 1976; children: Ryan F., Christopher J., Ross A. BS in Civil Engring., U. Wis., 1972; postgrad., IIT, Chgo., 1974. Cert. engr. Ill., Ind., Wis., Mich., Ky., Ohio, Pa. Staff engr. EPA, Chgo., 1972; asst. engr. Village of Buffalo Grove, Ill., 1972-76; project engr. Applied Engring. Co., Rolling Meadows, Ill., 1976-78, Balsamo/Olson Group, Oakbrook Terrace, Ill., 1978-80; dir. enging. Village of Arlington Heights, Ill., 1980-87; pres. NW Engr. Assoc., Ltd.,

1987-89; prin. Triton Cons. Engrs., Schaumburg, Ill., 1989-90; pres. CE Design, Ltd., Rolling Meadows, 1990—. Leader Boy Scouts Am. Arlington Heights, 1988. Fellow ASCE (chmn. urban planning and devel. divsn. 1985-86, bd. dirs.); mem. Cellular Telephone Industry Assn., Am. Pub. Works Assn. Office: CE Design Ltd 1875D Rohlwing Rd Rolling Meadows IL 60008

PFAU, NANCY ANN, secondary education educator; b. Albany, N.Y., Oct. 18, 1942; d. Vito Anthony Di Pace and Helen Nancy (Madison) Bowmaker; m. Richard Anthony Pfau, Sept. 12, 1964; children: Bradley, Aleksandra. BA, Syracuse U., 1964; MA, Columbia U., 1966. Tchr. social studies Stimson Jr. High Sch., Huntington, N.Y., 1965-66; tchr. English Pass Christian (Miss.) High Sch., 1966-67, Eureka Union Sch., Roseville, Calif., 1967-69, Iranzamin Internat. Sch., Tehran, Iran, 1969-71; tchr. Greensbrier Elem. Sch., Charlottesville, Va., 1971-72; tchr. social studies St. Thomas Sch., Miami, 1980-85, Patrick Henry High Sch., Glade Spring, Va., 1987-93; mentor Emory & Henry Coll., 1989-93; coord. S.W. Va. Tchrs. Network, 1991-93; instr. edn. dept. Ill. Coll., 1995—; bd. dirs. Coun. on World Affairs. Mem. McGaw Fine Arts Bd., 1993—, Jacksonville Symphony Bd. Named Outstanding Social Studies Tchr. of S.W. Va., Va. Coun. for the Social Studies, 1991. Mem. Nat. Coun. for Social Studies, S.W. Va. Coun. for Social Studies (pres.-elect 1991-92, pres. 1992-93), AAUW. Democrat. Episcopalian. Home: 310 Lockwood Pl Jacksonville IL 62650-2225

PFEFFER, SCOTT M., communications archtiect; b. N.Y.C., Nov. 20, 1963; s. Richard Lawrence and Roslyn (Ziegler) P. BS in Info. and Computer Sci., Ga. Inst. Tech., 1986, MS in Info. and Computer Sci., 1988. Sys. engr. Compaq Computer, Houston, 1989-91; computer cons. Digital Cons., St. Louis, 1992-93; distributed sys. architect Southwestern Bell Telephone, St. Louis, 1993—; ind. contractor Distibute Comm. Tech., Atalnta, Houston and St. Louis, 1983—. Designer computer software and network. fund raising capt. Leukemia Soc., Atlanta, 1985; vol. coord. Jewish Cmty. Ctr., St. Louis, 1993-95. Mem. IEEE Computer Soc., SIG, Assn. Computing Machinery, St. Louis Jugglinc Club. Jewish.

PFEFFER, WALTER LOUIS, II, sales executive, columnist; b. St. Louis, Mar. 8, 1955; s. Robert Niver and Suzanne (Chappuis) P.; m. Beverely Gail Hillebrand, Nov. 7, 1987; 1 child, Hillary Taylor Pfeffer. B in Gen. Studies, U. Mo., 1989. Sr. sales and svc. rep. The Mut. of Omaha Cos., Columbia, 1978—; columnist Columbia (Mo.) Daily Tribune, 1989-92; course moderator Life Underwriters Tng. Coun., Columbia, 1990-93. Nominee for sec. of state Rep. party Mo., 1980; committeeman, treas. Boone County Rep. Ctrl. Com., 1984-91; Century Club donor Life Underwriters Polit. Action Com., 1987—; mem. risk mgmt. adv. com. City of Columbia, 1989-91, Housing Stds. and Appeals Bd., 1979-81, 89-91; mem. Bldg. Code Bd. Appeals County of Boone, 1986-87; mem. community devel. com. City of Columbia, 1979-81, 89-91. Recipient Evans Scholars Found. scholarship, 1973-77, Health Ins. Quality award Nat. Assn. Life Underwriters, 1984-91, Nat. Sales Achievement award Nat. Assn. Life Underwriters, 1986-90, Nat. Quality award Nat. Assn. Life Underwriters, 1990-92; named fellow Life Underwriters Tng. Coun., 1993—. Mem. Columbia Assn. Life Underwriters (pres. 1987-88), Mo. Assn. Life Underwriters (vice-chmn. state law and legis. com. 1995—), DeSmet Jesuit High Alumni Assn. (pres. 1984-85), U. Mo. Alumni Assn. (chmn. Boone County chpt. 1990-91, nat. mem. com. 1993—, mem. exec. com. 1994—, pres. Leaders/Coll. of Arts and Sci. Alumni 1995—, Jefferson Club 1983—), Travelers Protective Assn. Am. State Hist. Soc. Mo. (life), Conservation Fedn. Mo. Columbia C. of C. (com. chair 1990-91, Amb. of Yr. 1991), Katy Trail Friends, Columbia Pacyderms, Ducks Unltd., Southside Optimists Club (bd. dirs. 1987-88). Republican. Roman Catholic. Office: The Mut of Omaha Cos PO Box 1706 Columbia MO 65205-1706

PFEFFERKORN, MICHAEL GENE, SR., secondary school educator, writer; b. Delano, Calif., July 19, 1939; s. E. Michael and N. Ruth (Ervin) P.; m. Sandra J. Carter, June 15, 1963; children: Michael Jr., Patricia. AB, S.E. Mo. State, 1961, BS in Secondary Edn., 1961; MEd, U. Mo., 1963. Cert. Eng., life Social Studies tchr., Mo. Tchr. De Soto (Mo.) Pub. Schs., 1961-62, Cleveland High Sch., St. Louis, 1963-84; tchr. S.W. High Sch., St. Louis, 1984-86, tchr., history dept. head, 1987-92; tchr. Gateway Inst. of Tech. High Sch., St. Louis, 1992—; cons. Internat. Edn. Consortium, St. Louis, 1989-92. Co-author: Chits, Chiselers, and Funny Money, 1976; editor Mo. Jour. Numismatics; contbr. articles to numis. jours. Pres. Carondelet Hist. Soc., 1977-78, mem., 1970—; mem. Landmarks and Urban Design Com., St. Louis, 1976-80. Mem. ASCD, Am. Fedn. Tchrs., Nat. Coun. Social Studies Tchrs., State Hist. Soc. Mo., Am. Numis. Assn., Mo. Numis Soc., Numis. Lit. Guild, World Coin Club Mo. Roman Catholic. Home: 6803 Leona St Saint Louis MO 63116-2833 Office: Gateway Inst of Tech 5101 McRee Ave Saint Louis MO 63110-2019

PFEIFER, EUGENE, clinical pharmacist, nursing home consultant; b. Melrose Park, Ill., Apr. 16, 1945; s. Eugene Paul and Leota Agnus (Dreher) P.; 1 child, Jennifer Lynn; m. Virginia A. Perun. BS in Zoology, No. Ill. U., 1967; BS in Pharmacy, U. Ill., Chgo., 1970; MBA, Keller Grad. Sch. Mgmt., 1983; PharmD, Purdue U., 1995. Registered pharmacist, Ill., Va. Dir. pharmacy Westlake Cmty. Hosp., Melrose Park, 1970-71; staff pharmacist Northwestern Meml. Hosp., Chgo., 1975-77; pharmacist in charge Whitehall Convalescent and Nursing Home, Chgo., 1975-76; asst. dir. pharmacy/metabolic support svc. St. Mary of Nazareth Hosp. Ctr., Chgo., 1977-85; pharmacy mgr./cons. pharmacist Conva-Care, Inc., Glenview, Ill., 1985-87; cons., pharmacist-in-charge Healthcare Pharmacy, Chgo., 1987-88; pharmacist VA Med. Ctr., Danville, Ill., 1988-89, Covenant Med. Ctr., Urbana, Ill., 1989-93; staff clin. pharmacist USMC, Danville, Ill., 1990—; off-site preceptor pharmacy residency program Rush Presbyn. St. Luke's Med. Ctr., Chgo., 1978-83. Mem. exec. coun. Boy Scouts Am. With USN, 1971-75. Mem. Am. Soc. Health Sys. Pharmacy, Am. Coll. Clin. Pharmacy, Kappa Psi. Roman Catholic. Contbr. articles to profl. jours. Home: 2402 Cedar Ct Danville IL 61832 Office: USMC Pharmacy Dept 812 N Logan Ave Danville IL 61832-3716

PFEIFER, PAUL E., state supreme court justice; b. Bucyrus, Ohio, Oct. 15, 1942; m. Julia Pfeifer; children: Lisa, Beth, Kurt. BA, Ohio State U., 1963, JD, 1966. Asst. atty. gen. State of Ohio, 1967-70; mem. Ohio Ho. of Reps., 1971-72; asst. prosecuting atty. Crawford County, 1973-76; mem. Ohio Senate, 1976-92, minority floor leader, 1983-84, asst. pres. pro-tempore, 1985-86; ptnr. Cory, Brown & Pfeifer, 1973-92; justice Ohio Supreme Ct., 1992—; chmn. jud. com. Ohio Senate, 10 yrs. Mem. Grace United Meth. Ch., Bucyrus. Mem. Bucyrus Rotary Club. Office: 30 E Broad St Fl 3 Columbus OH 43215-3414

PFENDER, EMIL, mechanical engineering educator; b. Stuttgart, Germany, May 25, 1925; came to U.S., 1964, naturalized, 1969; s. Vinzenz and Anna Maria (Dreher) P.; m. Maria Katharina Staiger, Oct. 22, 1954; children: Roland, Norbert, Corinne. Student U. Tuebingen, Germany, 1947-49; Diploma in Physics, U. Stuttgart, 1953, D. Ing. in Elec. Enging., 1959. Assoc. prof. mech. engring. U. Minn., Mpls., 1964-67, prof., 1967—. Contbr. articles to profl. jours. Patentee in field. Fellow ASME, ASM; mem. IEEE (assoc.), NAE, ASM Internat. Home: 1947 Bidwell St Saint Paul MN 55118-4417 Office: U Minn Dept of Mech Engrg 111 Church St SE Minneapolis MN 55455-0150

PFISTER, KARL ANTON, industrial company executive; b. Ernetschwil St. Gallen, Switzerland, Oct. 17, 1941; came to U.S., 1966; s. Josef Anton and Paula (Hobi) P.; m. Karen Antonie Sievers; children: Kirsten, Marc, Theodore, Alexandra. Student trade sch., Rapperswil, Switzerland, 1957-61; student bus. sch., Zuerich, Switzerland, 1964-65. Tool and die maker H. Schmid, Rapperswil, Switzerland, 1957-61, Neher AG, Ebnat-Kappel, Switzerland, 1962-63; process engr. NCR, Buelach, Switzerland, 1964-66, Gretag, Regensdorf, Switzerland, 1966; tool and die maker Stoffel Fineflow Corp., White Plains, N.Y., 1966-67; mgr. mfg. Finetool Corp., Detroit, 1968; pres. Mich. Precision Ind., Inc., Detroit, 1969—; chmn. bd., pres. Kautex N.Am., Inc., 1994; pres. Kloeckner Automotive, Inc., Rochester Hills, Mich., 1996; dir. Kloeckner Capital Corp., Gordonsville, Va., MPI Internat., Inc., Kautex N.Am., Inc., Kloeckner Automotive, Inc. Consul, consulate Switzerland, Detroit, 1984—. Mem. Plum Hollow Club, Fairlane Club. Republican. Roman Catholic. Office: MPI Internat Inc 2129 Austin Ave Rochester Hills MI 48309

PFLUEGER, M(ELBA) LEE, academic administrator; b. St. Louis, Sept. 2, 1942; d. Pless and Edna Mae (Russell) Counts; m. Raymond Allen Pflueger, Sept. 14, 1963 (div. June 1972); children: Salem Allen, Russell Counts. BS in Home Econs., Univ. Mo., 1969; MEd in Guidance and Counseling, Washington Univ., St. Louis, 1973. Ednl. psychologist Ozark Regional Mental Health Ctr., Harrison, Ark., 1974-75; from account mgr. to mgr. pers. Enterprise Leasing Co., St. Louis, 1977-79; mgr. employee rels. Eaton Corp., Houston, 1979-80; owner Nature's Nuggets Fresh Granola, St. Louis, 1980-83; dir. corp. ednl. svcs. Maryville Coll., St. Louis, 1983-84; adminstr. mgmt. skills devel. McDonnell Douglas, St. Louis, 1984-85, mgr. employee involvement, 1985-86, prin. specialist human resources mgmt., 1988-89; mgr. human resources McDonnell Douglas, Houston, 1986-88; dir. devel. sch. engring. U. Mo., Rolla, 1989-93, dir. devel., corp. and found. rels., 1992-93; regional dir. devel., assoc. dir. maj. gifts and capital projects Washington U., St. Louis, 1994—; part-time leader trainer Maritz Motivation, St. Louis, 1984-89. Chair United Fund Campaign for U. Mo., Rolla, 1991. Mem. PEO. Office: Washington U Office Maj Gifts and Capital Projects Campus Box 1228 One Brookings Dr Saint Louis MO 63130-4899

PHELAN, PHYLLIS WHITE, psychologist; b. Harrisonburg, Va., Aug. 12, 1951; d. Shirley Lewis and Jean Elwood (Driver) White; m. Kenneth Edward Phelan, May 21, 1983. BA with honors, Coll. William and Mary, 1973, MA, 1977; PhD, U. Minn., 1984. Lic. cons. psychologist. Intern Ramsey Mental Health Ctr., St. Paul, 1983-84; psychologist Mental Health Clinics of Minn. P.A., St. Paul, 1983-84, Harley Clinics, Mpls., 1983-84; psychologist, dir. eating disorders program Primary Health Care, Bloomington, Minn., 1984-87; pvt. practice psychology St. Paul, 1987—; exec. dir. Eating Disorders Inst. for Edn. and Research, St. Paul, 1987—; instr. Continuing Edn. program, U. Minn., 1983-84, clin. asst. prof. dept. psychiatry, 1986—, clin. asst. prof. dept. psychology, 1989—. Author: Trust the Hungers; contbr. articles to profl. jours. Coll. of William and Mary scholar, 1975-77; U. Minn. fellow 1981, 82-83. Mem. Am. Psychol. Assn., Minn. Psychol. Assn., Minn. Psychologists in Pvt. Practice, Minn. Women Psychologists. Home: 942 Summit Ave Saint Paul MN 55105-3031 Office: 570 Asbury St Saint Paul MN 55104-1849

PHELPS, BRADY JUSTIN, psychology educator, editor, author; b. Soda Springs, Idaho, May 1, 1959; s. Justin and Beverly (Arnell) P. BS, Utah State U., 1983, PhD in Behavioral Psychology, 1992. Psychol. examiner, behavior specialist Logan (Utah) Bd. Edn., 1988-90, 91-92; vis. lectr. U. Md. Asian Divsn., Republic of Korea, 1990-91; asst. prof. psychology S.D. State U., Brookings, 1992—. Contbr. chpt. to book, articles to profl. jours. Recipient New Instrnl. Idea award S.D. State U., 1995. Mem. APA, Assn. for Behavior Analysis, Internat. Behaviorology Assn. (affiliate, New Rschr. award 1994), Sigma Xi. Office: SD State U Dept Psychology Scobey Hall Brookings SD 57007

PHELPS, CARRIE LYNN, public relations executive; b. Ft. Wayne, Ind., June 18, 1964; d. Richard Clair and Judith Elaine (Potts) P. BA in Journalism/Criminal Justice, Ind. U., 1986. Dir. communications Ind. Mfrs. Assn., Indpls., 1987-89, Ind. Dept. Commerce, Indpls., 1989-90; dir. Gray, Miller & Mitsch, P.R., Indpls., 1990-91; dir. comm. and devel. Wapehani coun. Girl Scouts U.S., Daleville, Ind., 1991-94; account exec. Caldwell VanRiper Advt./Pub. Rels., Indpls., 1994—. Contbr. articles to profl. jours., mags., and newspapers. Recipient Addy award, 6th dist. Addy award, Epic award of merit Internat. Assn. Bus. Communicators, Comm. Arts Design Ann. # 36 award of excellence. Mem. Pub. Rels. Soc. Am. (Keystone award). Home: 12139 Suffolk Ln Indianapolis IN 46260-9999 Office: Caldwell VanRiper Advt/Pub Rels 1314 N Meridian St Indianapolis IN 46202-2303

PHELPS, DAVID D., state legislator; b. Eldorado, Ill., Oct. 26, 1947; m. Leslie Phelps; 4 children. BS, So. Ill. U. Mem. Ill. Ho. of Reps. from 118th dist., 1985—; mem. Transp. and Motor Vehicles, Appropriations I, Energy, Environ. and Natural Resources, Edn. Appropriations, Human Svcs., Elem. and Secondary Edn., Counties and Twp., Econ. Devel. Coms. Ill. Ho. of Reps., vice chmn. Coal Devel. and Mktg., Econ. and Urban Devel. Coms., chmn. Health Care Com. Democrat. Home: RR 1 Box 114 Eldorado IL 62930-9727*

PHELPS, G. ROBERT, retired architect; b. Cleve., Mar. 18, 1918; s. Merle W. and Reva A. (Loeffler) P.; m. Margaret F. Zink, May 17, 1947; children: Beverly, Elaine. BArch, Western Res. U., 1940, MArch, 1941. Registered architect, Ohio. Architect The Austin Co., Cleve., 1941-42, 46-81. Lt. USN, 1942-46. Republican. Home: 13927 Sweetbriar Novelty OH 44072

PHELPS, PAUL MICHAEL, lawyer; b. Lake Forest, Ill., Sept. 19, 1933; s. Paul and Elizabeth Anne (Wilson) P.; m. Laura Elaine Pepe, Dec. 26, 1966; stepchildren: Kimberly A. Springer, Wendy L. Field, Gregory L. Field. BA, Wesleyan U., Middletown, Conn., 1955; LLB, Harvard U., 1958. Bar: Ill. 1958, U.S. Ct. Mil. Appeals 1959. Assoc. atty. Keck Mahin & Cate, Chgo., 1958, 63-65; atty. Ekco Products Co., Chgo., 1965-67, E. J. Brach & Sons, Chgo., 1967-69; asst. corp. sec. R. R. Donnelley & Sons Co., Chgo., 1969-73; asst. counsel Marsh & McLennan, Chgo., 1973-74; corp. sec. Morton-Norwich Products, Inc. (name changed to Morton Thiokol Inc., 1982, and to Thiokol Corp., 1989), Chgo., 1974-89; v.p., corp. sec. Morton Internat. Inc., Chgo., 1989—. Trustee Wanger Advisors Trust, 1994—. Served to capt. JAGC, U.S. Army, 1959-63. Mem. Am. Soc. Corp. Secs. (bd. dirs. 1987-93, chmn. 1991-92), Univ. Club, Chikaming Club (Lakeside, Mich.), Phi Beta Kappa, Psi Upsilon. Home: 222 E Chestnut St Apt 10B Chicago IL 60611-2351 Office: Morton Internat Inc 100 N Riverside Plz Chicago IL 60606-1596

PHENIX, GLORIA GAYLE, educational association administrator; b. Dallas, Mar. 4, 1956; m. Douglas William Phenix, Aug. 8, 1987; children: David William, Duncan Kenneth. BA, U. North Tex., 1979, postgrad., 1979-81; PhD, ABD, U. Minn., 1981-89. Dean Jordan Coll., Benton Harbor, Mich., 1990; pres. Phenix & Assocs. Tng. Cons., St. Joseph, Mich., 1991—, Topeka, Kans., 1993—; bd. dirs. Cornerstone, Inc. Mem. allocation com. United Way, 1990-92, Literacy Coun., 1991-93; mem. Topeka Race Rels. Task Force, 1994; mayor's commn. status women, 1996—; bd. dirs. Cmty. Youth Homes, 1996—, Cornerstone, Inc. Fulbright-Hayes fellow Africa, 1990; Hewlett Mellon Found. grantee, 1987, Benton Found. grantee, 1988. Mem. Am. Polit. Sci. Assn., Minn. Polit. Sci. Assn. (bd. dirs. 1989-90), Midwest Polit. Sci. Assn., Am. Assn. Trainers and Developers, Am. Soc. for Quality Control. Presbyterian. Office: Phenix & Assocs 505 Pleasant St # 200 Saint Joseph MI 49085-1269 also: Phenix Assocs 530 S Kansas Topeka KS 66604

PHIBBS, CLIFFORD MATTHEW, surgeon, educator; b. Bemidji, Minn., Feb. 20, 1930; s. Clifford Matthew and Dorothy Jean (Wright) P.; m. Patricia Jean Palmer, June 27, 1953; children—Wayne Robert, Marc Stuart, Nancy Louise. B.S., Wash. State U., 1952; M.D., U. Wash., 1955; M.S., U. Minn., 1960. Diplomate Am. Bd. Surgery. Intern Ancker Hosp., St. Paul, 1955-56; resident in surgery U. Minn. Hosps., 1956-60; practice medicine specializing in surgery Oxboro Clinic, Mpls., 1962—, pres., 1985—; cons. to health risk mgmt. corps., 1994—; mem. Children's Hosp. Ctr., Northwestern-Abbott Hosp., Fairview-Southdale Hosp., Fairview Ridges Hosp.; clin. asst. prof. U. Minn., Mpls., 1975-78, clin. assoc. prof. surgery, 1978—; med. dir. Minn. Protective Life Ins. Co. Contbr. articles to med. jours. Bd. dirs. Bloomington Bd. Edn., Minn., 1974—, treas., 1976, sec., 1977-78, chmn., 1981-83; mem. adv. com. jr. coll. study City of Bloomington, 1964-66, mem. community facilities com., 1966-67, advisor youth study commn., 1966-68; vice chmn. bd. Hillcrest Meth. Ch., 1970-71; mem. Bloomington Adv. and Rsch. Coun., 1969-71; bd. dirs. Bloomington Symphony Orch., 1976—, Wash. State U. Found., trustee, 1990—; dir. bd. mgmt. Minnesota Valley YMCA, 1970-75; bd. govs. Mpls. Met. YMCA, 1970—; bd. dirs. Bloomington Heart-Health Found., 1989—, Martin Luther Manor, 1989; pres. Oxboro Clinics, 1985—; bd. dirs. Bloomington History Clock Tower Assn., 1990—; bd. dirs. Fairview Hosp. Clinic, 1994—. Capt. M.C., U.S. Army, 1960-62. Mem. ACS, AMA (Physician Recognition awards 1969, 73, 76, 79, 82, 85, 88, 91, 94), Assn. Surg. Edn., Royal Soc. Medicine, Am. Coll. Sports Medicine, Minn. Med. Assn. (del. 1991-94), Minn. Surg. Soc., Mpls. Surg. Soc., Hennepin County Med. Soc., Pan-Pacific Surg. Assn., Jaycees, Bloomington C. of C. (chmn. bd. 1984, chmn. 1985-86). Home: 9613 Upton Rd Minneapolis MN 55431-2454 Office: 600 W 98th St Minneapolis MN 55420-4773

PHILIP, JAMES (PATE PHILIP), state senator; b. May 26, 1930; married; 4 children. Student, Kansas City Jr. Coll., Kans. State Coll. Ret. dist. sales mgr. Pepperidge Farm, Inc.; rep. State of Ill., 1967-74, senator, 1975—; asst. senate minority leader, 1979, senate minority leader, 1981-93, senate pres., 1993—; chmn. DuPage County Rep. Ctrl. Com.; committeeman Addison Twp. Precinct 52; past Jr. Nat. Rep. Committeeman. Past dir. Nat. Found. March of Dimes; past gen. chmn. Elmhurst March of Dimes; spl. events chmn. DuPage Heart Assn.; mem. DuPage Meml. Hosp. Century Club; dir. Ray Graham Assn. Handicapped Children; mem. bd. sponsors Easter Seal Treatment Ctr.; active Lombard YMCA; bd. dirs. Danada Sculpture Garden. With USMC, 1950-53. Recipient Ill. Coun. on Aging award, 1989, Leaders of 90's award Downers Grove Twp., 1989, Man of Yr. award United Hellenic Voters Am., 1989, Legis. of Yr. award Ill. County Treas.'s Assn., 1990, Tax$avers award Ill. Assn. County Auditors, 1990, Statesman of Yr. award Internat. Union of Operating Engrs. Local 150, 1991, Friend of Youth award Assn. Ill. Twp. Com. on Youth, 1991, Spl. Svc. award Serenity House, 1991, Recognition award DuPage Ctr. Independent Living, 1991. Mem. Am. Legion, Ill. Young Reps. (past pres.), DuPage County Young Rep. Fedn. (past chmn.), DuPage County Marine Corps League (life), DuPage Indsl. and Mfg. Assn. (past dir.), Suburban Bus. Mgmt. Coun. (past v.p.), Mil. Order Devil Dogs, Gocery Mgmt. and Sales Exec. Club Chgo., Exec. Club DuPage County, Shriners, Elks, Masons, Order of DeMolay (life), Moose. Office: Ill State Senate 327 State Capitol Bldg Springfield IL 62706

PHILLIPS, ALICE ELIZABETH, government relations professional; b. Taylorville, Ill., Dec. 12, 1939; d. Ralph Chester and Anna Mable (Curtis) Fulsom; m. Lewis V. Morgan Jr., May 8, 1971 (div. 1977); children: Lee Ann, Sandra, Pamela. Student, Coll. of DuPage, 1972-74, DePaul U., 1977-78. Adminstrv. asst. Ill. Gen. Assembly, Springfield, 1967-71; office mgr. Morgan and Assocs., Wheaton, Ill., 1971-78; 2d v.p. Continental Bank, Chgo., 1978-87; dir. govt. rels. Chgo. Title Ins. Co., 1988—; spkr. Ill. Third House, 1996; pres. Ill. Women in Govt., Springfield, 1990-92; chair Prairie State 2000 Authority, Chgo., 1991-96; adv. com. Civic Fedn., Chgo., 1991—; adv. bd. Leadership Ill., Chgo., 1992—; founder, v.p. Ill. Lincoln Excellence in Pub. Svc. Series. Bd. dirs., treas. DuPage Art League, 1989-92; bd. dirs. Chgo. Women in Govt. Rels., 1990; bd. dirs. Nat. Women's Polit. Caucus Greater Chgo., 1992, pres., 1994-95; mem. Ill. Rep. Committeewoman's Roundtable, 1992, pres., 1995—. Mem. Chgo. Real Estate Exec. Women, Bus. and Industry Fedn. Econ. Concern, Chgo. Area Pub. Affairs Group. Methodist. Office: Chgo Title Ins Co 171 N Clark St Chicago IL 60601-3203

PHILLIPS, DAVID LEE, data processing executive; b. Emporia, Kans., Jan. 28, 1948; s. Otis Orville and Norma Jean (Marlar) P.; m. Charlotte Patrice Setness, Feb. 2, 1972; children: Jeannine Kay, Suzanne Patrice, David Lee Jr., Sean Patrick. BS in Bus., Emporia State U., 1974. Clk. Santa Fe Railroad, Emporia, Kans., 1967-75; computer programmer Santa Fe Railroad, Topeka, 1976-82, system analyst, 1982-87, sr. system analyst, 1988—. Served with USAF, 1968-72, Vietnam. Named Eagle Scout Boy Scouts Am., 1965. Home: 5607 SW 15th Topeka KS 66604-2230 Office: Santa Fe RR 920 Quincy Topeka KS 66608-1221

PHILLIPS, DOROTHY ORMES, elementary education educator; b. Denver, July 26, 1922; d. Jesse Edward and Belle (Noisette) Ormes; m. James Kermit Phillips, Apr. 28, 1945; children: William K., Dorothy E., Valerie A. BBA, Case Western Res. U., 1946, MA, 1959; PhD, U. Akron, 1989. Cert. tchr., adminstr., Ohio. Tchr. Cleve. Pub. Schs., 1955-68, math. cons., 1968-83, adminstrv. intern, 1970-73; grad. asst. U. Akron, Ohio, 1983-85, lectr. elem. edn., supr. student tchrs., 1985—; math. workshop presenter Norton (Ohio) Pub. Schs., 1986. Presenter Career Day, Cleve., 1992; chmn. bd. Centerville Mills YMCA Camp, Chagrin Falls, Ohio, 1996—. Grantee NDEA, 1960, NSF, 1966. Mem. ASCD, Nat. Coun. Tchrs. Math., Ednl. Computer Consortium Ohio, Cleve. Pub. Schs. Math. Cons. (assoc.), Alpha Kappa Alpha, Pi Lambda Theta. Home: 8746 Crackel Rd Chagrin Falls OH 44023-1807

PHILLIPS, FREDERICK FALLEY, architect; b. Evanston, Ill., June 18, 1946; s. David Cook and Katharine Edith (Falley) P.; m. Gay Fraker, Feb. 26, 1983 (div. Dec. 1993). BA, Lake Forest Coll., 1969; MArch, U. Pa., 1973. Registered architect, Ill., Wis. Draftsman, Harry Weese & Assocs., 1974, 75; pvt. practice architecture Frederick F. Phillips, Architect, Chgo., 1976-81; pres. Frederick Phillips and Assocs., Chgo., 1981—. Bd. dirs. Landmarks Preservation Coun., 1981-85, Chgo. Acad. Sci., 1988—, Friends of Ceuros de Escazu, Costa Rica, 1992—; mem. aux. bd. Chgo. Architecture Found., 1975-89; chmn. Task Group on Manufactured Housing, AIA Nat. Com. on Design, 1994—. Recipient award Townhouse for Logan Square Competition, AIA and Econ. Redevel. Corp. Logan Square, 1980, Gold medal award Willow St. Houses, Ill. Ind. Masonry Coun., 1981, Silver award for pvt. residence, 1989, Gold medal award for private residence Archtl. Record, 1994, Three Record Houses awards Archtl. Record, 1990, 95, award 2d Compact House Design Competition, 1990, award of exellence for pvt. residence AIA/Nat. Concrete Masonry Assn., 1992, award for pvt. residence Am. Wood Coun., 1993, Honorable mention-Best in Am. Living award Profl. Builders Mag., 1995, Jury's Choice award for pvt. residence Chgo. Athenaeum, 1996 . Fellow AIA (Disting. Bldg. award for Willow St. Houses, Chgo. chpt. 1982, for Pinewood Farm 1983, for Pvt. Residences 1990, 92); mem. Chgo. Archtl. Club, Racquet Club (bd. govs. 1983-89), Arts Club, Cliff Dwellers Club (bd. govs. 1985-88). Office: Frederick F Phillips & Assocs 53 W Jackson Blvd Ste 1752 Chicago IL 60604-3705

PHILLIPS, GARY L., rehabilitation specialist; b. S.D., Feb. 19, 1951; s. Robert L. P. and Lorraine B. Phillips; m. Linda L. Phillips, Aug. 15, 1970; children: Niki Renae, Brent Alan. BS, U. S.D., 1974; MA, Goddard Coll., 1978; PhD, Clayton U., 1987. Rehab./mktg. specialist IRA, Rapid City, S.D., 1984-86; rehab. specialist Rehab. Mgmt., Rapid City, 1987-89; exec. dir., rehab. specialist Garlin Rehab. Svc., Rapid City, 1989—. Author manual: Rehab: Design, Implementation and Operation, 1987. Mem. Nat. Assn. Rehab. Profls. in Pvt. Sector, Black Hills Pers. Assn. (assoc.). Office: Garlin Rehab Svc PO Box 5746 Rapid City SD 57709-5746

PHILLIPS, HOWARD R., adult education educator, director; b. Davenport, Iowa, Aug. 31, 1938; s. Howard Watson and Pauline Esther (Bell) P.; m. Laura Jane Irvine, June 5, 1962; children: Jon Eric, Janis Rae. BS, Greenville (Ill.) Coll., 1960; MS, U. Ill., Springfield, 1984; PhD, So. Ill. U., 1992. Cert. in education, education adminstr., Ill. Tchr. Greenfield (Ill.) Sch. Dist. #10, 1960-86; principal Bluffs (Ill.) Sch. Dist., 1986-88; adult edn. dir. Calhoun-Greene-Jersey-Macoupin Regional Office of Edn., Jerseyville, Ill., 1992—; grad. asst., tchng. asst. So. Ill. U., Carbondale, Ill., 1988-91. Bd. dirs. Greenfield Dist. #10 sch. bd., 1991—; treas. bd. dirs. Tri-County Counseling, Jerseyvill, 1992-95. Home: 607 Sycamore Greenfield IL 62044 Office: Regional Office of Edn PO Box 409 100 Lincoln Jerseyville IL 62052

PHILLIPS, JOHN ROBERT, college dean, political scientist; b. Henderson, Ky., Dec. 16, 1942; s. Leander Armstead and Ann Reid (Brown) P. Diploma, Lang. Inst., Chateauroux, France, 1966; BA, Centre Coll., Danville, Ky., 1969; MA, Western Ky. U., Bowling Green, 1973. Instr. Drury Coll., Springfield, Mo., 1971-73, Western Ky. U., Bowling Green, 1975-79; asst. prof. Thiel Coll., Greenville, Pa., 1979-83, scholar-in-residence, 1983-85; pvt. cons. Henderson, Ky., 1985-87; adj. prof. Lockyear Coll., Evansville, Ind., 1987-88, acad. dean, 1988-90, v.p. acad. affairs, dean coll., 1990-91; exec. dir. human rels. commn. Henderson (Ky.) Mcpl. Ctr., 1991-93; dean acad. affairs, prof. political studies/govt. Springfield (Ill.) Coll., 1993—; adj. prof. pub. adminstrn. Ind. State U., Terre Haute; field investigator on religion and culture in ancient city of Taxila, 1968, on indsl. pollution of hist. bldgs. and monuments, France, Italy, Austria, 1969; rschr. on nationalism, Scotland, 1972, on local govt. and urban deves., 1993; participant in internat. confs. on The Future of a United Germany, 1991; mem. adv. coun. St. John's Hosp. Sch. respiratory Therapy, 1993, Ursuline Acad Sch. Bd., v.p., 1995-96, fin. com., 1993-96, Cen. Ill. Fgn. Lang. and Internat. Studies Consortium, 1993—, chmn., 1994-95. Mem. editorial bd. Jour. Urban Affairs, 1985-89; manuscript referee Pub. Adminstrn. Rev., 1985-87;

contbr. chpts. to multi-vol. reference series The Small City and Regional Cmty. 1981, 85, 87, 95; contbr. articles on urban affairs, policy planning and federalism/intergovtl. rels. to profl. jours. Policy advisor Lt. Gov.'s Office, Frankfort, Ky., 1985-86; cons. Commn. on Ky.'s Future, Frankfort, 1985-87; mem. Bd. Cath. Edn., Diocese of Springfield, 1994—. With USAF, 1963-68. Mem. Am. Polit. Sci. Assn. (Leon Weaver Disting. Rsch. Award com. 1990-93), Am. Soc. Pub. Adminstrn. (publs. com. 1984-88, 92-95), Urban Affairs Assn. (publs. com. 1985-89, nominating com. 1984-85, 88-89), Am. Philatelic Soc., Am. Guild Organists, Pi Sigma Alpha. Democrat. Episcopalian. Home: 2605 Delaware Dr Springfield IL 62702-1213

PHILLIPS, LEO D., business executive; b. Phila., May 7, 1936. BS in Econs., Georgetown U., 1959; M in Fin., U. Detroit, 1962. Methods engr. GM/Chevrolet Divsn., Detroit, 1959-64; pres. LDP Inc., Birmingham, Mich., 1974—. With USMC, 1956-62. Roman Catholic.

PHILLIPS, RONALD C., personnel company executive; b. Tulsa, Okla., Jan. 24, 1942. BA in Biology, Phillips U., 1964; BDiv, U. Chgo., 1967. V.p. Pers. Adminstn. Svcs., Saline, Mich., 1979—. Editor Contractor Compensation Quar., 1992. Mem. Saline Area C. of C. Republican. Office: Pers Adminstrn Svcs 75 E Henry St Saline MI 48176-1536

PHILLIPS, RONDA JO, non-commissioned military officer; b. Colville, Wash., Nov. 3, 1958; d. Ronald Eugene and Joan (Ginnan) Addington; married; 1 child. Student, Malone Coll., 1984, Stark Tech. Coll., 1994, Army Inst. Profl. Devel., 1996. Keypunch operator Haines & Co., North Canton, Ohio, 1977-79; computer operator Superior's Brand Meats, Massillon, Ohio, 1979-81, Arnold Corp., Uniontown, Ohio, 1981-84; unit adminstrv. sgt. 1485th Transp. Co. Ohio Army Nat. Guard, Dover, 1984-88, unit supply sgt., 1988-89, unit trainer, 1989-94; detachment readiness noncommd. officer Ohio Army Nat. Guard, Steubenville, 1995—; cook Ohio Army Nat. Guard, Canton, 1976-79, vehicle driver, Dover, 1982-84, unit fund coun., 1984—, energy conservation sgt., 1987—, equal opporunity coun., 1985—, unit drug/alcohol coord., 1992—; nuclear, biol., chem. warfare specialist Operation Desert Storm, Saudi Arabia, 1990-91. Mem. VFW, Ohio Nat. Guard Enlisted Assn., Canton Lincoln High Sch. Alumni Assn. Democrat. Office: 1485th Transp Co Det 1 1629 Pershing Ave Steubenville OH 43952-1437

PHILLIPS, SCOTT ALLEN, public relations professional; b. Indpls., Dec. 1, 1957; s. Norman Rex and Mary Eleanor (Davis) P. BS, Purdue U., 1980. Editor Publs. Internat., Skokie, Ill., 1980-83; sr. group supr. Richardson Pub. Rels., Chgo., 1983-85; v.p. Janet Diederichs & Assocs., Inc., Chgo., 1985-90; pres. Phillips & Assocs. Inc., Chgo., 1990—; cons. Svc. Club of Chgo., 1992-93. Mem. Pub. Rels. Soc. Am., Publicity Club of Chgo., Econ. Club of Chgo., Lambda Chi Alpha. Home: 2836 N Burling St Chicago IL 60657-5216 Office: Phillips & Assocs Inc 730 N Franklin St Ste 220 Chicago IL 60610-3526

PHILLIPS, SPENCER KLECKNER, retired surgeon; b. Freeport, Ill., Nov. 6, 1914; s. Nelson Chancellor and Bertha Diana (Kleckner) P.; m. Marjorie Ann Figi, July 19, 1948; children: Julia Mae, Spencer Frederick. BA, Colgate U., 1935; MB, Northwestern U., 1939, MD, 1940; MS in Surgery, U. of Minn., 1947. Diplomate Am. Bd. Gen. Surgery. Surg. fellow Mayo Found., Rochester, Minn., 1941, 46-47; 1st asst. surgery Mayo Clinic, Rochester, 1947-48; practice medicine specializing in surgery Freeport, Ill., 1948-85; dir. of surgery Freeport Meml. Hosp., Freeport, 1983-85; asst. sec., bd. dirs. Scientific Safety Tech., Inc., Wood Dale, Ill., 1987-88; bd. dirs. Cartel, Inc., Woodstock, Ill. Contbr. articles to profl. jours. Commr. Freeport Drug and Alcohol Commn., 1988-95. Comdr. USNR, 1941-45, PTO. Decorated Legion of Merit. Fellow ACS; Phi Beta Kappa, Alpha Omega Alpha. Home: 1769 Highland Dr Freeport IL 61032-4605

PHILLIPS, TERRY LEMOINE, electrical engineer; b. Washington, July 27, 1938; s. Clifford LeMoin and Dorothy Louise (Schuman) P.; m. Lynne Ann Bruce, Aug. 12, 1962; children: Susan Rae, Stephen Kirk. BS, Purdue U., 1964, MS, 1966. Assoc. program leader, data processing Purdue U. Lab. Applications of Remote Sensing, West Lafayette, Ind., 1966-71, program leader, 1971-74, dep. dir., 1974-85; mgr. personal computer services Purdue U. Computing Ctr., 1986-92, admin. continuing edn. ctr., 1992— ; cons. AID, Computer Scis. Corp. Scoutmaster, explorer adviser Boy Scouts Am., bd. dirs. Sagamore council; sports coord., youth sports, Battleground, Ind.; elder, deacon, trustee Presbyn. Ch.; bd. dirs. Tippecanoe chpt. Am. Diabetes Assn. With USN, 1956-59. Recipient Most Innovative Idea award Am. Diabetes Assn., 1987. Mem. IEEE (sr.), Assn. Inst. for Certification of Computer Profls. (cert. in data processing 1986), Assn. Computing Machinery, Data Processing Mgmt. Assn. (internat. dir., co-founder, v.p., pres., treas. Sagamore chpt., Individual Performance award 1983, 85, 88), Tau Beta Pi, Eta Kappa Nu. Lodge: Rotary (bd. dir., treas.). Home: 1522 E 600 N West Lafayette IN 47906-8625 Office: Purdue U CEA 1588 Stew West Lafayette IN 47907

PHILLIPS, WILLIAM ROBERT, fluid dynamics educator; b. Adelaide, Australia, Apr. 14, 1948; came to U.S., 1986; s. Robert Ray and Eileen Marjorie (Richter) P. BE with honours, Adelaide U., 1970; MEng, McGill U., Montreal, Que., Can., 1974; PhD, Cambridge (Eng.) U., 1978. Rsch. engr. Mt. Isa Mines Ltd., Queensland, Australia, 1971-73; rsch. assoc. McGill U., 1975; lectr. Nat. U. Singapore, 1979-81, sr. lectr., 1981-84; sr. rsch. fellow U. Melbourne, Australia, 1984-85; vis. scientist Cornell U., Ithaca, N.Y., 1986, assoc. vis. prof., 1987-89; assoc. prof. fluid dynamics Clarkson U., Potsdam, N.Y., 1989-96; vis. prof. U. Ill., Urbana-Champaign, 1996—. Co-editor: Nonlinear Instability of Nonparallel Flows, 1994; contbr. numerous articles to sci. jours. Commonwealth U. scholar Govt. of Australia, 1966-70, scholar Nat. Coun. Can., 1974-75; Rolls Royce rsch. fellow Churchill Coll., Cambridge, 1975-78; grantee NSF, 1990-93, 95—. Mem. Soc. for Indsl. and Applies Math., Am. Phys. Soc., N.Y. Acad. Sci., Sigma Xi. Home: Riggs Dr Box 133 Hannawa Falls NY 13647 Office: U Ill Theoretical and Applied Mechanics Urbana IL 61801-2935

PHINAZEE, HENRY CHARLES, systems analyst, educator; b. Birdnest, Va., Oct. 26, 1956; s. Charlie Phinazee and Johnnie Belle (Harris) Brice. BEd, Fort Hays State U., 1978, B of Psychology, 1979, M of Psychology, 1980; MEd, Wichita State U., 1985. Cert. tchr., Kans., Tex. Minority advisor Fort Hays State U., 1978-80; tchr. Wichita Pub. Schs., 1980—; tchr. Wichita State U., 1988-92, dorm coord. coll. of health profession, 1986-92, work coord. coll. of health profession, 1988-91; computer analyst Beech Aircraft Corp., Wichita, 1992—. Author: (software) Dayreq, 1989. Mentor Grow Your Own Tchrs., Wichita Pub. Schs., 1990; liaison Com. on Polit. Edn., Wichita, 1988—. Recipient Svc. award Big Bros./Big Sisters, 1987. Mem. Am. Amature Racquetball, Wichita Assn. of Black Educators (treas. 1991-92), Wichita Fedn. of Tchrs. (2d v.p. 1988-92, Svc. award 1991), Kans. Assn. of Black Educators (com. head 1991-92), Phi Delta Kappa, Kappa Alpha Psi (polemark 1988-92, Svc. award). Democrat. Baptist. Home: 4400 Horizon Hill # 4807 San Antonio TX 78229 Office: Brackenridge HS 400 Eagleland Dr San Antonio TX 78210

PHINNEY, NATHAN, college administrator; b. Oklahoma City, Mar. 29, 1968; s. David Lucian Phinney and Carol Jo (Meland) Schumacher. BA, Taylor U., Upland, Ind., 1990. Admissions counselor Taylor U., Upland, 1990-91; dir. admissions Taylor U., Ft. Wayne, Ind., 1992—. Asst. tchr. Blackhawk Bapt. Ch., Ft. Wayne, 1995. Mem. Nat. Assn. Coll. Admissions Counselors, Nat. Assn. Christian Coll. Admissions Personnel, Inter Coll. Adult Network, U.S. Figure Skating Assn., Ice Skating Inst. Am. Office: Taylor U Ft Wayne 1025 W Rudisill Blvd Fort Wayne IN 46807

PHIPPS, MARK, technical illustrator; b. San Diego, Apr. 23. AAS, St. Louis C.C., Flourissint, Mo., 1986. Tech. illustrator Butler Svcs. Group, St. Louis, 1986-90, TWA, Bridgeton, Mo., 1990-91; tech. pubs. specialist Crane Nat. Vendors, Bridgeton, 1991—. Mem. Nat. Assn. Desktop Pubs., Corel Coop. Republican. Baptist. Office: Crane National Vendors 12955 Enterprise Way Bridgeton MO 63044-1206

PHIPPS, WILMA J., nursing educator, author; b. Detroit, Jan. 24, 1925; d. Walter and Inez M. (Steele) P. Diploma, Harper Hosp. Sch. Nursing, 1946; BSN, Wayne U., 1954; AM, U. Chgo., 1956, PhD, 1977. Assoc. prof. med./surg. nursing Case Western Res. U., Cleve., 1970-76, prof. med./surg. nursing, 1976-87, prof. emeritus, 1987—. Editor: Medical-Surgical Nursing, Concepts and Clinical Practice, 1995, Medical-Surgical Nursing, A Nursing Process Approach, 1993. Mem. ANA, APHA, Am. Acad. Nursing, Nat. League Nursing, Sigma Theta Tau, Pi Lambda Theta. Home: 3701 Mayfield Rd Apt 302 Cleveland OH 44121-1750

PIANKI, FRANCIS OWEN, manufacturing executive educator; b. Flushing, N.Y., Dec. 28, 1953; s. Helen Teresa (Fitzpatrick) P.; m. Kathleen Marie Moran, Jan. 5, 1974; children: Francis Robert, Jonathan Owen, Christopher Matthew, Kathryn Rachael. BSChemE, U. Conn., 1977; MSChemE, U. Ariz., 1981; MBA, Pepperdine U., 1990. Rsch. engr. Phillips Petroleum, Bartlesville, Okla., 1979-80; sr. process engr. Getty Oil/Texaco, Bakersfield, Calif., 1980-85; sales engr. Petrolite Corp., Brea, Calif., 1985-86; plant engr. Phila. Quartz Corp., Southgate, Calif., 1986-88, unit mgr., 1988-89; plant mgr. Phila. Quartz Corp., Anderson, Ind., 1989-91; COO First Benefit Corp., Anderson, 1991-94; v.p. ops. Barber Mfg., Anderson, 1994-95; asst. prof. bus. and environ. mgmt. Taylor U., Upland, Ind., 1995—; ptnr., sr. mgmt. cons. Marcon Corp., Anderson, 1993-95; adj. prof. Ind. Wesleyan U., Marion, 1993-95. Mem. adv. bd. March of Dimes, Anderson, 1992—; deacon North Anderson Ch. of God, Anderson, 1993-94; bd. dirs. Jr. Achievement, Anderson, 1993—; chmn. bd. dirs. Air Mgmt. Bd., Anderson, 1993—. Mem. Am. Soc. Quality Control. Republican. Home: 315 Edgewood Pl W Anderson IN 46011 Office: Barber Mfg 1824 Brown St Anderson IN 46018

PICCIRILLI, ROBERT JAMES, JR., small business owner; b. Balt., Dec. 2, 1943; s. Robert J. Sr. and Frances Rita (Mazel) P.; m. Joyce Marie Cole, Nov. 21, 1964 (dec. Sept. 1991); children: Angela Thompson, Christina Dahlberg, Gina. BSEE, GM Inst., Flint, Mich., 1966; cert., Dale Carnegie, Detroit, 1986; exec. tng. cert., U. Mich., 1988. Asst. supt. and supt. mfg. engring. Volkswagen of Am., Westmoreland, Pa., 1976-78; supt. mfg. planning corp. hdqrs. Volkswagen of Am., Detroit, 1978-79, mgr. mfg. planning, 1979-80; dir. engring. and quality products Chrysler Corp., 1980-81, plant mgr. Belvidere Assembly Plant, 1981-83; plant mgr. assembly plant Chrysler Corp., Sterling Heights, Mich., 1983-84; dir. quality and product engring. mfg. ops. div. hdqrs. Chrysler Corp., Detroit, 1984-85, dir. mfg. engring., 1985-86, gen. mgr. advance mfg. ops., gen. mgr. stamping ops., 1986-89; chmn. bd., pres. Performance Innovations Corp., Chgo., 1990—. Author: Practical Production Manual, 1991, Launch Manual, 1991. Century mem. Boy Scouts Am., Detroit, 1989. Mem. GM Inst. Alumni Assn. (bd. dirs. 1991—). Home and Office: Performance Innovations Corp 77 W Huron St Apt 214 Chicago IL 60610-5307

PICHLER, JAMES MICHAEL, computer engineer; b. St. Paul, Minn., Dec. 14, 1968; s. Walter James and Judith Mary (Sarfoleon) P. BS in Computer Engring., U. Minn., Duluth, 1992. MIS dir. Mac USA, Inc, Edina, Minn., 1992—; cons. Ind. Aves., St. Louis Park, Minn., 1992—. Mem. IEEE, U Minn Alumni, Minn. Sci. Mus. Roman Catholic. Home: 2625 Alabama Ave Saint Louis Park MN 55416 Office: MacUSA Inc 5198 W 76th St Edina MN 55439

PICHLER, JOSEPH ANTON, food products executive; b. St. Louis, Oct. 3, 1939; s. Anton Dominick and Anita Marie (Hughes) P.; m. Susan Ellen Eyerly, Dec. 27, 1962; children: Gretchen, Christopher, Rebecca, Josh. BBA, U. Notre Dame, 1961; MBA, U. Chgo., 1963, PhD, 1966. Asst. prof. bus. U. Kans., 1964-68, assoc. prof., 1968-73, prof., 1973-80; dean U. Kans. (Sch. Bus.), 1974-80; exec. v.p. Dillon Cos. Inc., 1980-82, pres., 1982-86; exec. v.p. Kroger Co., 1985-86, pres., COO, 1986—, also bd. dirs., 1986-90, pres., CEO, 1990, chmn., CEO, 1990—, also dir.; spl. asst. to asst. sec. for manpower U.S. Dept. Labor, 1968-70; chmn. Kans. Manpower Svcs. Coun., 1974-78; bd. dirs. B.F. Goodrich Co.; indsl. cons. Author: (with Joseph McGuire) Inequality: The Poor and the Rich in America, 1969; contbg. author: Creativity and Innovation in Manpower Research and Action Programs, 1970, Contemporary Management: Issues and Viewpoints, 1973, Institutional Issues in Public Accounting, 1974, Co-Creation and Capitalism: John Paul II's Laborem Exercens, 1983; Co-editor, contbg. author: Ethics, Free Enterprise, and Public Policy, 1978; Contbr. articles to profl. jours. Bd. dirs. Kans. Charities, 1973-75, Benedictine Coll., Atchison, Kans., 1979-83, Cin. Opera; nat. bd. dirs. Boys Hope, 1983—, Tougaloo Coll., 1986—; chmn. nat. bd. Nat. Alliance of Bus. Recipient Performance award U.S. Dept. Labor Manpower Adminstrn., 1969, Disting. Svc. citation U. Kans., 1992; Woodrow Wilson fellow, Ford Found. fellow, Standard Oil Indsl. Rels. fellow, 1966, Woodrow Wilson fellow adv. com., 1990-93; named Disting. Alumnus U. Chgo., 1994. Mem. Bus. Roundtable, Queen City Club, Comml. Club of Cin. Office: Kroger Co 1014 Vine St Cincinnati OH 45202-1100

PICKARD, MARY JEAN, education educator; b. Tampa, Fla., Feb. 2, 1946; d. Glen Fred and Ruby Rose (Kleinjan) Ritterbusch; m. Ronald D. Pickard, Sept. 8, 1967; children: Murray Ryan, Laura Suzanne. BS, S.D. State U., 1968, MS, 1983; PhD, Kans. State U., 1995. Cert. family and consumer scientist, family life educator; cert. tchr., S.D., Iowa, Nebr. Middle sch. tchr. West Sioux Community Schs., Hawarden, Iowa, 1968-69; high sch. tchr. Jefferson (S.D.) Schs., 1969-71, South Sioux City (Nebr.) Schs., 1971-73, Estelline (S.D.) Schs, 1979-84; coll. prof. Fort Hays State U., Hays, Kans., 1984-96; asst. dir. Adult Student Svcs., Kans. State U., Manhattan, 1992-93; Carson-Newman Coll., Jefferson City, Tenn., 1996—; chair Kans. Family and Consumers Tchr. Educators, Hays, 1989-90; cons. County 4-H Fairs, Kans., 1988-96, Hays Mall Assn., 1989-94. Mem. Kans. Assn. Family and Consumer Scientists (exec. dir. 1990-93), Kans. Vocat. Assn., Am. Vocat. Assn., Delta Kappa Gamma (Maude I. Gorham scholar 1994, sec., treas., v.p. 1988-92), Kappa Omicron Nu (Mitstifier fellow 1992), Phi Kappa Phi, Phi Delta Kappa. Office: Carson Newman Coll 316 Baker Hall Jefferson TN 33333

PICKERING, ED RICHARD, biology educator; b. Cin., Dec. 15, 1934; s. Carl Everet and Bonnie Lynn (Sollars) P.; m. Evalind Ellis, Aug. 18, 1962; children: Sarah Katherine, Mark Edward. BS in Agr., Ohio State U., 1956, MS in Botany, 1958; PhD in Botany, U. Calif., Davis, 1964. Std. life cert. tchr. h.s. sci., agr., and c.c., Calif. Instr. botany U. South Fla., Tampa, 1962-63; asst. prof. botany Rutgers-The State U. of N.J., Newark, 1964-66; from asst. to assoc. prof. biology Adrian (Mich.) Coll., 1966-74; instr. in horticulture Rhodes Career Ctr., Springfield, Ohio, 1974-77; assoc. prof. biology Cen. State U., Wilberforce, Ohio, 1977-78; spl. agt. Northwestern Mut. Life, Springfield, Ohio, 1978-91; asst. prof. biology Wilberforce (Ohio) U., 1992—; horticultural cons., mem. Comty. Beautification Com., City of Springfield, 1992—. Contbr. rsch. papers to profl. publs. Chair ch. and soc. work area Grace United Meth. Ch., Springfield, 1980-88, 94—, peace advocate, 1988—; local coord. Grace United Meth. Ch., Interfaith Hospitality Network, Springfield, 1990—. Recipient Acad. Recognition award Sigma Xi, 1960, Applied Environ. Problem-Solving Practicum award NSF, SUNY, 1994; postdoctoral faculty rsch. grantee NSF, Adrian Coll., 1969-71. Mem. AAUP (mem. Wilberforce U. chpt., sec. Wilberforce U. chpt. 1992—), Am. Soc. Plant Physiologists (emeritus mem.), Ohio Acad. Sci. Home: 2399 Versailles Ct Springfield OH 45502 Office: Wilberforce U Biology Dept Wilberforce OH 45384

PICKERT, ROBERT WALTER, accountant; b. Aurora, Ill., Sept. 4, 1936; s. Conrad Bonifas and Margaret Catherine (Brummel) P.; m. Tonda Ruth Sloane, Sept. 14, 1963 (div. Nov. 1966); children: Kelly, Christopher, Katherine, Mary Ellen, Scott; m. Patricia Ann Petersen, Aug. 16, 1986. BS in Bus. Adminstrn., U. Montana, 1964. CPA, Wis. Supr. Ernst and Young, CPAs, Chgo., 1964-68, Milw., 1968-73; v.p. fin., ops. Republic Bank, Milw., 1973-76; prin. Robert W. Pickert, CPA, Minocqua, Wis., 1976—; bd. dirs., treas. Howard Young Med. Ctr., Inc., Woodruff, Wis., Howard Young Health Care, Inc., Woodruff, 1985-95; pres. PIC-WEL, Inc., Minocqua, 1991—; chmn. bd. dirs. Howard Young Health Care, Inc., 1995—. Fellow AICPA, Wis. Inst. CPAs; mem. Rotary (treas. 1978-83). Republican. Roman Catholic. Office: 113 Front St Minocqua WI 54548-0680

PICKETT, ARTHUR WILLIAM, JR., minister; b. Detroit, Aug. 30, 1925; s. Arthur William Sr. and Florence Caroline (Erickson) P.; m. Donna Fredia Prince, Jan. 4, 1964; children: Thomas, Gerald, Susan, Winston. BS in Chemistry, Wayne State U., 1949; BTh, Concordia Sem., Ft. Wayne, Ind., 1962. Ordained min. Luth. Ch., 1962. Writer Brooke, Smith, French & Dorance, Detroit, 1950-53; TV writer D.P. Brother Inc., Detroit, 1954-57; vicar St. Paul's of Tremont, Bronx, N.Y., 1961-62; pastor Our Saviour Luth. Ch., Topsfield, Mass., 1962-63, Outer Drive Faith Luth. Ch., Detroit, 1963-66, Valley Luth. Ch., Chagrin Falls, Ohio, 1966-92; ret., 1993. Author: The Christian Seeker and the Contrary Church, 1994. Home: 3841 Wiltshire Rd Chagrin Falls OH 44022

PICKETT, STEVEN HAROLD, elementary education educator; b. Danville, Ill., Sept. 15, 1946; s. Harold George and Mary Margaret (Watson) P.; m. Marlene Mae Brumleve, June 23, 1973; children: Vincent Steven, Ryan Stephen, Alexander Maurice (dec.). AS, Danville Jr. Coll., 1966; BS, U. Ill., 1968, MEd, 1970. Cert. secondary tchr., Ill. Self-contained 8th grade classroom tchr. Gifford (Ill.) Grade Sch., 1968-70; 8th grade tchr. lang. arts, reading Effingham (Ill.) Ctr. Sch., 1970—; coach various basketball and track teams Effingham Cen. Sch., 1970-83. Mem. Effingham Pk. Dist. Bd., 1973—, v.p., 1978, pres., 1979-80; basketball coach Effingham County Youth Commn., 1972-73; coach Small Fry Baseball Team, 1985-89, 93—, Effingham Pony League, 1971-73, Effingham Bambino Little League, 1990-91, Effingham Babe Ruth Prep League, 1992; coach track team Effingham Flyers, AAU, 1977-78. Mem. NEA, Nat. Assn. English Tchrs. (life), Ill. Edn. Assn., Effingham Classroom Tchrs. Assn., Elks. Home: 703 N Cardinal St Effingham IL 62401-3210 Office: Effingham Cen Sch RR 1 Box 9 Effingham IL 62401-9702

PICKTON, THOMAS EMIL, psychologist; b. Akron, Ohio, Oct. 11, 1949; s. Robert James and Carolyn Jane (Schweitzer) P.; m. Kimberly Ann, Aug. 26, 1995; children: Elizabeth Jane, Patrick Thomas. BEd, Miami U., Oxford, Ohio, 1972; MEd, Xavier U., Cin., 1975; MS, U. Nebr., Kearney, 1981, EdS, 1982; PhD, U. Miss., 1986. Lic. psychologist, Ohio. Speech pathologist Hamilton Local Schs., Columbus, Ohio, 1972-74; cons. supr. Ednl. Svc. Unit #9, Hastings, Nebr., 1974-79; assoc. psychologist South Ctrl. Community Mental Health Ctr., Hastings, 1979-82; instr. U. Miss., Oxford, 1982-84; psychology intern Wichita (Kans.) Guidance Ctr., 1984-85; psychologist Child and Adolescent Svc. Ctr., Canton, Ohio, 1985-88, Kunstel, Grzegorek and Assocs., Stow, Ohio, 1988-94, Thomas Pickton & Assocs., Stow, Ohio, 1994—. Mem. Am. Psychol. Assn., Ohio Psychol. Assn., Phi Gamma Delta. Democrat. Presbyterian. Office: Thomas Pickton & Assocs 4301 Darrow Rd Ste 4400 Stow OH 44224

PICOTTE, SUSAN GAYNEL, geriatrics nurse, nursing educator, rehabilitation nurse; b. Omaha, Nov. 15, 1948; d. Gordon Pierre and Gaynel Ruth (Voris) Picotte; m. Kurt C. Foley, May 25, 1978 (div. 1995); children: Alicia Kate, Betsy Lyn. AA in Respiratory Therapy, Wichita State U., 1971, BSN, 1976, MN, 1988. RN, Kans.; cert. clin. nurse specialist, ARNP/clin. nurse specialist gerontology. Staff devel. coord. Cherry Creek Village Nursing Home and Retirement, Wichita, 1987-88; pulmonary nurse specialist Pulmonary Clinic of Wichita, 1981-86; outpatient pulmonary coord. Wesley Med. Ctr., Wichita, 1988—; lectr. in field; stress mgmt. coord., 1994, smoking cessation coord., 1993. Mem. AACN (v.p. local chpt. 1980-81), Am. Assn. Cardiovascular and Pulmonary Rehab., Wichita State U. Nursing Alumni Assn. (pro-tem officer 1991, nominating com. 1992, chair nominating com. 1992—), Sigma Theta Tau (chair by-laws com. 1987-89, treas. 1989-91, Upjohn adv. com. 1983-85). Home: 3410 S 231st St W Goddard KS 67052-9260

PIDERIT, JOHN J., university educator; b. N.Y.C., Feb. 26, 1944. BA in Math. and Philosophy magna cum laude, Fordham U., 1967; Lic. in Sacred Theology cum laude, Philosophische und Theologische Hochschule Sankt Georgen, Frankfurt, West Germany, 1971; MPhil, Oxford U., 1974; MA, PhD in Econ., Princeton U., 1979. Ordained Jesuit priest Roman Cath. Ch., 1971. Tchr. math. Regis H.S., N.Y.C., 1967-68; asst. campus minister Fordham U., 1971-72; asst. campus minister Princeton U., 1975-78, preceptor, 1976-77; asst. chairperson grad. studies Fordham U., 1984-88, dir. program internat. polit. econ. and devel., 1981-83, 87-88, asst. chairperson dept. econs., 1979-82, 88-89, asst. prof. econs., 1978-89, assoc. prof. econs., 1989-90; corp. v.p. Marquette U., 1990-93; pres. Loyola U. Chgo., 1993—; vis. fellow Woodstock Theol. Ctr., Washington, summer 1982; sabbatical Santa Clara U., 1989-90; master Queen's Ct. Residential Coll., 1987-90; chmn. responsible investment com. N.Y. province SJ, 1986-88, mem. fin. com., 1986-88; mem. joint commn. govtl. rels. of Am. Coun. Edn., 1994—; mem. exec. com. Nat. Planning Com. Jesuit Assembly '89, 1988-90. Contbr. articles to profl. jours. Founder, moderator Friends of Loyola, 1987-90; pres. Univ. Neighborhood Housing Corp., 1986-90, Maroon Enterprises, Inc., 1986-90; trustee Canisius Coll., Buffalo, 1983-88, 89-94; bd. dirs. Corp. Cmty. Schs. of Am., 1993—; promoter PIVOT H.S. and Middle Sch. with Milw. Pub. Schs., 1990-93; mem. Greater Milw. Edn. Trust, 1990-93; mem. steering com. Libr. Literacy Soc. Milw., 1991-93; mem. scholarship com. Knitworkers Union Local 155, N.Y.C., 1982-90; mem. Princeton Schs. Com. N.Y. Region, 1985-88. Mellon grantee Fordham U., summer 1983, summer grantee Fordham U., 1979, Princeton U. fellow, 1974-78. Office: Loyola U Chgo 820 N Michigan Ave Chicago IL 60611-2103

PIEPER, JEFFREY ROBERT, sales executive; b. Decatur, Ill., Aug. 10, 1964; s. Grantley Harold and Barbara Ann (Reed) P.; m. Lisa Ann Ernst, Aug. 30, 1986; children: Delaney, Keaton. BA, Benedictine Coll., 1986; MS, Baker U., 1992. Buyer, traffic mgr. Varn Products Co., Inc., Oakland, N.J., 1986-87, regional sales mgr., 1988—; pres. Raven Investment Group, Kansas City, Mo., 1994—. Mem. Am. Mensa Ltd. Roman Catholic.

PIEPER, MARTHA HEINEMAN, psychotherapist; b. Chgo., May 31, 1941; d. Ben W. and Natalie (Goldstein) Heineman; m. William F. Pieper, July 31, 1981; children: Joseph, Victoria, Jessica, Johanna; 1 child by previous marriage, Thalia Field. BA, Harvard U., 1962; MA, U. Chgo., 1974, PhD, 1979. Lic. cert. social worker, Ill. Assoc. clin. dir. Child Psychiatry Assocs., Chgo., 1974-78; pres. Martha H. Pieper, Chgo., 1976—; cons. Child & Family Svcs., Chgo., 1985-89. Co-author: Intrapsychic Humanism, 1990; mem. editl. bd. Smith Coll. Studies, 1989-92, Social Work, 1991-94; contbr. articles to profl. jours. Mem. Nat. Assn. Social Workers, Ill. Soc. Clin. Social Work.

PIEPKORN, EVONNE A., farming operation administrator; b. Stanley, N.D., July 4, 1939; d. Bennie C. and Bertina (Gilbertson) Thorvig; m. LeRoy Piepkorn, June 29, 1958; children: Craig, Lorie, Clark. BA in Psychology, U. N.D., 1994. Sec. Mountrail County Extension Office, Stanley, 1957-59; adminstrv. clk. Mountrail County ASCS, Stanley, 1960-62; Selective Svc. clk. Mountrail and Divide Counties of N.D., Stanley, 1971-73; income tax cons., sec. Mell & Jones Acctg., Stanley, 1979-88; ptnr. farming operation, Stanley, 1958—; bd. dirs. Piepkorn's, Inc., Grand Forks, N.D., 1990—. Producer, dir., script writer film Hidden Foundations of Prairie Women, 1994. Active Republican Party. Mem. Conflict Resolution Ctr. Grand Forks, Phi Beta Kappa, Psi Chi. Lutheran. Home: RR 1 Box 84 Stanley ND 58784-9768

PIERCE, ACQUANETTA, business executive; b. Columbus, Ga., July 13, 1952. BS in Comm., Ea. Mich. U., 1973; postgrad., Wayne State U. V.p. P.R. Networks, Inc., Detroit, 1989—. Recipient Silver Anvil Pub. Rels. Soc. Am., 1991. Mem. NAACP, Nat. Assn. of Black Journalists. Baptist. Office: 100 Renaissance Ctr Ste 2180 Detroit MI 48243-1102

PIERCE, LISA MARGARET, lecturer, product and market development manager; b. Nyack, N.Y., June 2, 1957; d. William Twining and Elizabeth P. BA with honors, Gordon Coll., Wenham, Mass., 1978; MBA, Atkinson Sch., Salem, Oreg., 1982. Campaign mgr. Carter/Mondale, Manchester, Mass., 1976; investigator Dept. Social Svcs., Nyack, 1977-78; paralegal Beverly, Mass., 1978-79; campaign mgr. Reagan Presdl. Primary, Rockland County, N.Y., 1980; cons. Sidereal, Portland, Oreg., 1981-82; performance analyst Dept. Social Svcs., Pomona, N.Y., 1982; market analyst Momentum Techs., Parsippany, N.J., 1983; cons. Booz Allen & Hamilton, Florham Park, N.J., 1984, Deloitte-Touche, Morristown, N.J., 1985; market researcher, forecaster AT&T, Bedminster, N.J., 1985-87, asst. pvt. line product mgr., 1987-89, Integrated Svcs. Digital Network product mgr., 1989-93; dir. Telecomms. Rsch. Assocs., St. Marys, Kans., 1993—; panelist, contbr. TeleComms. Assn., San Diego, 1992, Internat. Comm. Assn., Atlanta, Ea. Comm. Forum, N.Y., Nat. Engring. Consortium, Chgo.; contbr. N.Y.C. ISDN/Internat User's Group. Tutor Literacy Vols. Am., Somerville, N.J., 1989-91; mem. Jr. League Am., Morristown, N.J., 1987-90; mem. Internat. Oceanographic Found., Washington. Grantee in field. Mem. Am. Mgmt.

Assn. (profl.), Humane Soc. U.S., Internat. Platform Assn., W. Wilson Internat. Ctr. for Scholars, Environ. Def. Fund, Nat. Audubon Soc., Wilderness Soc., Nature Conservancy. Republican.

PIERCE, LORI J., physician, educator; b. Washington, Aug. 11, 1957; d. Melvin H. and Amy (Martin) Pierce; m. Anthony Denton, June 3, 1994. B of Sci. and Engring., U. Pa., 1979; MD, Duke U., 1985. Diplomate in radiation oncology Am. Bd. Radiology; lic. physician, Mich. Intern Thomas Jefferson U. Hosp., Phila., 1985-86; resident dept. radiation oncology Hosp. of U. Pa., Phila., 1986-88, chief resident, 1988-89; asst. prof. radiation oncology U. Pa., Phila., 1989-90; sr. investigator Nat. Cancer Inst., Bethesda, Md., 1990-92; asst. prof. radiation oncology U. Mich., Ann Arbor, 1992—; cons. Rohm and Haas Chem. Co. Cancer Registry, Bristol, Pa., 1993-94. Contbr. articles to profl. jours.; presenter in field. Recipient Clin. Oncology Career Devel. award Am. Cancer Svcs., 1995—, ESTRO Travel award, 1995, others; grantee in field. Mem. Am. Soc. Clin. Oncology, Nat. Med. Assn., Am. Soc. for Therapeutic Radiology and Oncology, Radiation Therapy Oncology Group, Southwestern Oncology Group. Office: U Mich Dept Rad Oncology UH-B2C490 Box 0010 1500 E Medical Center Dr Ann Arbor MI 48109

PIERCE, PATRICIA ANN, software engineer, consultant; b. Cin., Dec. 15, 1960; d. Ronald Eugene and Mary Ann (Enghouser) Purdon; m. Joseph Allyn Pierce, Nov. 28, 1986; children: David Allyn, Mark Andrew. BS in Computer Sci. and Math., Xavier U., 1983; MB MIS, Ga. Coll., 1995. Sys. analyst NCR, Corp., Dayton, Ohio, 1983-88; sys. engr. Cin. Bell Telephone, 1988-90, GE, Cin., 1990-92, Brown & Williamson, Macon, Ga., 1992-94; pvt. cons. Cin., 1993—. Mem. IEEE, Delta Mu Delta. Home: 7024 Monongahela Dr Cincinnati OH 45244

PIERCE, RICKY CHARLES, professional basketball player; b. Dallas, Aug. 19, 1959; m. Joyce Wright. Student, Walla Walla (Wash.) Community Coll., 1978-79, Rice U., 1979-82. Player Detroit Pistons, 1982-83, San Diego (now L.A.) Clippers, 1983-84, Milw. Bucks, 1984-91, Seattle Super Sonics, 1991-94, Golden State Warriors, 1994—; player NBA All-Star Game, 1991. Recipient Sixth Man award NBA, 1987, 90. *

PIERCE, ROBERT RAYMOND, materials engineer, consultant; b. Helena, Mont., Feb. 17, 1914; s. Raymond Everett and Daisy Mae (Brown) P.; m. Stella Florence Kankos, June 12, 1938; children: Keith R., Patricia L., Diana L. BS in Chem. Engring., Oreg. State U., 1937. Process supr. Pennwalt Corp., Portland, Oreg., 1941-45, asst. tech. svc. mgr., Tacoma, 1945-47, gen. mgr., Phila., 1947-58, Natrona, Pa., 1958-65, tech. mgr., Phila., 1965-78, sr. tech. cons., Phila., 1978-80; self-employed cons., also Ohio State U., 1980—; former pres. Pierce CorMat Svcs., Inc. Contbr. articles to prof. jours. Patentee in field. Vice chmn. Phila. Air Pollution Control Bd., Phila., 1969-79, chmn. Ad Hoc # 1, 1974-79; Ky. Colonel, Louisville 1975—; mem. People to People del. on corrosion, People's Republic China, 1986. Recipient Phila. award City of Phila., 1973, Resolution award, City of Phila., 1979, World Decoration of Excellence for Exceptional Contributions to World Communities award, 1980-90. Mem. AIChE (Spl. Half-Century Membership and Contbrns. to the Advancement of Chem. Engring. award 1992), Nat. Assn. of Corrosion Engr. (bd. dirs.), Inter Soc. Corrosion Com. (world chmn. 1960-61), Internat. Com. for Industrial Chimneys (recipient best paper award Dusseldorf, Germany 1970), Rotary (Paul Harris fellow 1988). Lutheran.

PIERCE, SHELBY CRAWFORD, oil consultant; b. Port Arthur, Tex., May 26, 1932; s. William Shelby and Iris Mae (Smith) P.; BSEE, Lamar U., Beaumont, Tex., 1956; student MIT Program for Sr. Execs., 1980; m. Marguerite Ann Grado, Apr. 2, 1954; children: Cynthia Dawn, Melissa Carol. With Amoco Oil Co., 1956—, zone supr., gen. foreman, maintenance, 1961-67, operating supt., 1967-69, coordinator results mgmt., Texas City (Tex.) refinery, 1969-72, dir. results mgmt., corp. hdqrs., Chgo., 1972-75, ops. mgr. refinery, Whiting, Ind., 1975-77, asst. refinery mgr., 1977-79, dir. crude replacement program, Chgo., 1979-81, mgr. refining and transp. engring., 1981-92, gen. mgr. engring. & constrn., 1992, v.p. internat. bus. devel., 1993-94, ret., 1994; pres. dir. Amoco Eurasia Oil Co., Amoco Mex. Oil Co., Amoco India, Inc., Amoco Tech. Assistance Co, Trinidad; chmn., dir. Amoco Orient Oil Co.; v.p. Amoco Corp. Devel. Co., Latin Am.; pres. Pierce Consulting Svc., 1995—; CEO, pres. Environ. Construction Co., 1996—. Fin. chmn. Bay Area coun. Boy Scouts Am., 1974; dir. Jr. Engring. Tech. Soc.; chmn. bd., chmn. fin. com. Meth. Ch., 1967-72; bd. dirs. Waste Tech. Svcs.; mem. steering com. Contractor Safety U.S. Dept. of Labor; mem. exec. bd. Nat. Ctr. Constrn. Edn. and Rsch. Mem. AICE (chmn. engring. constrn. contracting divsn., ann. divsn. award engring. constrn. contracting industry 1995), Constrn. Industry Inst. (chmn. bus. roundtable coun., mem. strategic planning com.), The Bus. Roundtable (constrn. com., CII adv. bd., chmn. constrn. industry cost effectiveness task force, exec. com., N.W. Ind. local user coun.), Flossmoor Country Club, Sigma Tau. Republican. Home and Office: 18840 Loomis Ave Homewood IL 60430-4047

PIERCEY, JAMES W., tool manufacturing company executive; b. Dayton, Ohio, Apr. 29, 1933. Student, Parker Trade Sch., Dayton, 1954. Apprentice Tietzman Tool, Englewood, Ohio, 1951-52; tool and die apprentice Frigidare, Dayton, 1952-55; journeyman Tool Craft Products, Dayton, 1955-60, Universal Tool & Die, Dayton, 1960; ptnr. Kemp Tool, Dayton, 1960-73; journeyman Oaks Industries, Vandalia, Ohio, 1973-74; from journeyman to pres. Metro Tool & Die Co., Inc., Englewood, 1974—. Office: Metro Tool & Die Co Inc PO Box 216 Englewood OH 45322-0216

PIERSANTE, DENISE, marketing executive; b. Detroit, Jan. 9, 1954; d. Joseph Lawrence and Virginia (Grunwald) P.; m. Wilfred Lewis Was II, June 7, 1975 (div. 1981). BA in Communications, Mich. State U., 1978. Tchr. Northwestern Ohio Community Action Comm., Defiance, 1979-80, counselor, 1980-82, job developer, 1982-83, Pvt. Industry Coun., Defiance, 1983, job developer coord., 1983-84, dir. pub. rels. and job devel., 1984-86; market master North Market, Columbus, Ohio, 1986-87; dir. mktg. Richard S. Zimmerman Jr., Columbus, 1987—; CEO Full Moon Lunatics, Columbus, 1992—; cons. Small Bus. Mgmt., Archbold, Ohio, 1985-87; promotion dir. Miss N.W. Ohio Pageant, Defiance, 1985-87, Uptowners Rib Fest, 1989; promotion dir. Gallery Jazz Series, 1988, organizer, Prism Awards Competition, 1987; scholarship auction, 1988; pub. relations coordinator Defiance County Social Svc. Agys., 1981-86. Author of various grants. Editor Job Tng. Partnership Act newsletter, 1984-86, (newsletter) North Market Soc., 1986-87. Defiance County Social Service Agys. newsletter, 1981-86; Value/Style Community News, 1987-96. Organizer Auglaize River Race, Defiance, 1985. Nat. Merit scholar, 1972; recipient Am. Legion Citizenship award, 1969, 72. Mem. NAFE, Pub. Rels. Soc. Am., Am. Mktg. Assn., Jaycees (Jaycee of Month 1985), Columbus C. of C. (amb. level II 1989-96, vol. of month 1991, bd. dirs., chmn. com. 1991-96), Bus. and Profl. Women (Defiance), Corps de Ballet (Columbus), Conductors (Columbus), Operation Operatics (Columbus). Home: 1010 Annagladys Dr Columbus OH 43085-4848 Office: 100 S 3rd St Ste 414 Columbus OH 43215-4236

PIERSON, EDWARD SAMUEL, engineering educator, consultant; b. Syracuse, N.Y., June 27, 1937; s. Theodore and Marjorie O. (Bronner) P.; m. Elaine M. Grauer, June 6, 1971; 1 child, Alan. BS in Elec. Engring., Syracuse U., 1958; SM, MIT, 1960, ScD, 1964. Asst. prof., fellow MIT, 1965-66; assoc. prof., assoc. dept. head U. Ill., Chgo., 1966-75; program mgr. Argonne Nat. Labs., Ill., 1975-82; head dept. engring. Purdue U. Calumet, Hammond, Ind., 1982-95, spl. asst to chancellor for environ. programs, 1995—; cons. Argonne Nat. Lab., 1972-75, 82—, Solmecs Corp., 1982-88, HMJ Corp., Washington, 1983-88, LM Mfg., 1994—. Contbr. numerous articles to profl. jours. NSF fellow, 1958-60. Mem. IEEE, Am. Soc. Engring. Edn., Am. Soc. Mech. Engrs. Office: Purdue U Calumet Hammond IN 46323

PIERSON, MARGARET ROSALIND, dance educator, choreographer; b. Salt Lake City, Jan. 10, 1941; Recipient Ohio State U. Coll. of Arts grant, 1985, 89, 93, 94; recognized Greater Colls. Arts Coun., 1985, Ohio Arts Coun., 1986.; d. George Arthur and Eily (McKey) P. BA, Bennington (Vt.) Coll., 1963. Dancer Ruth Currier Co., N.Y.C., 1964, Charles Weidman Co., N.Y.C., 1965, Dancer's Theatre Co., N.Y.C., 1964-66; dancer, choreographer Valerie Bettis Dancer's Studio, N.Y.C., 1964-69; soloist Ballet Concepts, N.Y.C., 1966-71, Garden State Ballet, Newark, 1969-71; asst. prof. Mt. Holyoke Coll., South Hadley, Mass., 1971-75; assoc. prof. Ohio State U., Columbus, 1975—; dir. Ohio State U. Dance Co., Columbus, 1983—, Summer Inst. in the Arts, Columbus, 1990, dance coord., 1987—, inst. dir., 1990—. choreographer of numerous works, 1963—. Recognized Greater Colls. Arts Coun., 1985, Ohio Arts Coun., 1986. Mem. Ohio Dance, Congress on Rsch. in Dance (bd.dirs. 1995—), Alliance for Dance and Movement Arts (media chairperson 1986-87), Ohio Alliance for Arts in Edn. Office: Ohio State U Dept Dance 1813 N High St Columbus OH 43210-1307

PIERSON, MARILYN EHLE, financial planner; b. Cleve., Feb. 27, 1931; d. Ernest John and Helen Irene (Steudel) Ehle; m. Edward G. Pierson, May 17, 1954; children: Melanie K., Edward G. III. BSBA, Miami U., 1953. Paralegal Kyte, Conlan, Wulsin & Vogeler, Cin., 1974-79; adminstr. United Way Svcs., Cleve., 1982-87; CFP, sr. fin. advisor Advanced Planner Group Am. Express Fin. Advisors, Cleve., 1987—; corp. presenter, fin. educator East Ohio Gas, AT&T, Cleve., Master Builders, Cleve., Preformed Line Products, Cleve., others; guest lectr. Chagrin Valley C. of C., Chagrin Falls, Ohio; lectr. adult edn. Shaker Heights (Ohio) H.S., 1993-96. Fin. columnist Bainbridge Banter newspaper. Chair stewardship and resources Valley Presbyn. Ch., Bainbridge, Ohio, elder, 1991-93, planned giving chmn., 1991-95; chmn., developer Meals on Wheels, Oil City, Pa., 1971-73. Mem. Internat. Assn. Fin. Planning (treas. exec. com. NE Ohio chpt. 1994—), Exec. Women Internat. (pres., bd. dirs. 1996), Estate Planning Coun. Cleve. Home: 8178 Chagrin Mills Rd Chagrin Falls OH 44022 Office: Am Express Fin Advisors 28601 Chagrin Blvd #200 Cleveland OH 44122

PIETROFESA, JOHN JOSEPH, education educator; b. N.Y.C., Sept. 12, 1940; s. Louis John and Margaret (Proietti) P.; BE cum laude, U. Miami, 1961, MEd, 1963, Ed.D., 1967; lic. psychologist; lic. social worker; m. Cathy Marks, June 22, 1985; children: John, Paul, Maria, Dolores. Counselor, Dade County (Fla.) pub. schs., 1965-67; prof. edn. Wayne State U., Detroit, 1967—, div. head theoretical and behavioral founds., 1977-83; cons. to various schs., hosps. and univs. Served to 1st lt. Mil. Police Corps, AUS, 1963-65. Mem. Am. Psychol. Assn., Am., Mich. personnel and guidance assns., Assn. Counselor Edn. and Supervision, Phi Delta Kappa. Author: The Authentic Counselor, 1971, 2d edit., 1980; School Counselor as Professional, 1971; Counseling and Guidance in the Twentieth Century, 1971; Elementary School Guidance and Counseling, 1973; Career Development, 1975; Career Education, 1976; College Student Development, 1977; Counseling: Theory Research and Practice, 1978; Guidance: An Introduction, 1980; Counseling: An Introduction, 1984; mem. editorial bd. Counseling and Values, 1972-75. Home: 121 Linda Knoll Bloomfield Hills MI 48304-2817 Office: Wayne State U 321 Education Detroit MI 48202

PIETRUS, CAROL LYNN, corporation executive; b. Chgo., Sept. 15, 1948; d. Alfred E. and Nellie V. (Komperda) Cregier; m. Walter Nmn, May 4, 1968; 1 child, Tracey Aileen. High sch. grad., Chgo. Adminstrv. asst. Spector Freight System, Inc., Bensenville, Ill., 1969-80; pres.'s asst. Kidco, Inc., Bensenville, Ill., 1980-82, Lauer Sbarbaro Assocs., Chgo., 1982-83, Cas Co., Lisle, Ill., 1984; pres. The Office Extension, Inc., Chgo., 1985-89, Originals Only, Inc., Ill., 1985-89, Money Mailer Greater Woodfield, Willowbrook, Ill., 1990-94, The Mktg. Coaches, Elk Grove Village, Ill., 1995—; town planner of Greater Woodfield Wheaton, Ill., 1994—; spkr. on direct mail mktg., networking, word of mouth mktg. for cos., chambers and convs. Author: (office info. series) "If You Asked Me About..."; co-author of 5 cassette series: Bullseye Marketing. Mem. North Suburban Assn. Commerce and Industry (mem. mktg. com.), Hoffman Estates C. of C., Palatine C. of C., Profl. Spkrs. of Ill., Nat. Spkrs. Assn. Home: 26w471 Grand Ave Wheaton IL 60187-2963 Office: Town Planner 26w471 Grand Ave Wheaton IL 60187-2963

PIETTE, EDWARD JAMES, television executive; b. Detroit, Mar. 25, 1947; s. William Henry and Bernice Marie (Teeters) P.; m. Janet Lynn Aube, Feb. 5, 1977 (div. July 1980); 1 child, Kathryn; m. Eva Diane Carraway, Dec. 31, 1983; children: Jacquelyn, Marissa. BA, Mich. State U., 1969. Camera operator, dir. Sta. WXDN-TV, Detroit, 1969-71; producer, dir. Sta. WKBO-TV, Detroit, 1971-74; exec. producer Sta. WJXT-TV, Jacksonville, Fla., 1974-75, Sta. WFSB-TV, Hartford, Conn., 1975-79, Sta. WDIV-TV, Detroit, 1979-81; program dir. Sta. KWWL-TV, Waterloo, Iowa, 1981-83; gen. mgr. Sta. KTIV-TV, Sioux City, Iowa, 1983-84; dir. broadcast ops. Sta. KSDX-TV, St. Louis, 1984—. Served with U.S. Army, 1969. Roman Catholic. Office: KSDX-TV 3030 Summit Kansas City MO 64108*

PIGNATELLI, ERMENIA R., retired physical therapist; b. San Lorenzo, Italy, Oct. 29, 1906; came to U.S., 1911; d. Peter Romano and Josephine (Zoratti) Baruzini; m. John C. Pignatelli, July 11, 1942; children: Regina, Maria. BS in Phys. Edn., U. Iowa, 1932; BS in Tchg., Drake U. Physiotherapist U. Iowa Hosp., Iowa City, 1930-37; with USPHS, New Orleans, S.I., N.Y., 1937-41; tchr. phys. edn. Newman H.S., Sterling, Ill. Sec. Am.-Italian Civic League, various states, 1929-30. Mem. Am. Physiotherapy Assn. Roman Catholic. Home: 211 W 14th St Sterling IL 61081-2350

PIGNOLET, KEITH GLENN, executive; b. Painsville, Ohio, Jan. 27, 1956; s. Victor Glenn and Mary Alice (Hall) P.; m. Margaret Kuchler; 1 child, Chelsea N.; 1 stepson, Aaron M. Bell. AS in Bus. Mgmt., Community Coll. R.I., 1980; BA in Managerial Econs., R.I. Coll., 1982. Cert. community coll. instr., Calif. Project supr., sales rep. Inryco, Inc., Fremont, Calif., 1982-84; regional sales mgr. Sencon Systems, Inc., Northbrook, Ill., 1984-85; nat. sales mgr. Wildeck, Inc., Waukesha, Wis., 1986-93; v.p. dealer sales Wildeck, Inc., 1993-96; v.p. Atlas Iron Works, Mezzanine divsn., St. Louis, 1996—. Co-editor: (mezzanine mfrs. guide) Competitor Analysis, 1990. V.p. Fremont Renters Assn., 1984; assoc. project bus. Jr. Achievement, Milw., 1990; mem. Zool. Soc., Milw., 1986—. Mem. Assn. Mezzanine Mfrs. (chmn. 1995—, chmn. membership com. 1990—), Cosntrn. Specification Inst. (chmn. program com. 1984). Republican. Roman Catholic. Office: Atlas Mezzanines Inc 4020 Geraldine Ave Saint Louis MO 63115

PIGOZZI, ROBERT J., marketing executive; b. Chgo., Ill., Mar. 7, 1959. BS in Econs., U. Ill., Champaign, 1977-81; MBA, DePaul U., 1982-85. Dir. mktg. Sooline-C.P. Rail Sys., Mpls., 1985-88; dir. corp. mktg. Dart Transit, St. Paul, 1988-90; v.p. Archo, Inc., Mpls., 1990—. Bd. dirs., Washburn Youth Hockey, Mpls., 1994-95, coach, 1990-95. Mem. Twin Cities Traffic Club. Roman Catholic. Office: Archo Inc 7101 York Ave S Ste 320 Minneapolis MN 55435-4408

PIIRTO, JANE MARIE, education educator, creativity educator; b. Negaunee, Mich., Dec. 19, 1941; d. George Isaac and Helmi Helena (Eskelinen) P.; m. Paul Edward Navarre, Aug. 29, 1963 (div. June 1980); children: Steven David, Denise Ruth. BA, No. Mich. U., 1963; MA, Kent State U., 1966; MEd, S.D. State U., 1974; PhD, Bowling Green State U., 1977. Tchr. Atwater (Ohio) H.S., 1965-66; instr. No. Mich. U., Marquette, 1966-71; tchr. Florence (S.D.) Schs., 1972-73; counselor Brookings (S.D.) H.S., 1973-74; cons. Hardin County (Ohio) Schs., 1977-79, Monroe County Interm. Sch. Dist., Monroe, Mich., 1979-83; prin. Hunter Coll. Campus Schs., N.Y.C., 1983-88; prof. Ashland (Ohio) U., 1988—; vis. prof. U. Ga., Athens, 1996; cons. and spkr. in field, U.S. and Europe. Author: (novel) The Three-Week Trance Diet, 1985 (award 1985), (nonfiction) Understanding Those Who Create, 1992, (collected works) A Location in the Upper Peninsula, 1995, (textbook) Talented Children & Adults, 1994. Individual Artist fellow Ohio Arts Coun., 1982, 93, Fulbright fellow, 1990. Home: 233 W Walnut St Ashland OH 44805 Office: Ashland U Ashland OH 44805

PIKLO, CHARLENE LORRAINE, retail professional; b. Camden, N.J., Sept. 21, 1954; d. John Alfred and Loretta H. (Vogt) P. BS, U. Tampa, 1975. Mgr. trainee Roses Stores Inc., Macon, Ga., 1975-76; asst. mgr. Roses Stores Inc., Onley, Va., 1976; sr. asst. mgr. Roses Stores Inc., Burlington, N.C., 1976-77; merchandiser Roses Stores Inc., Henderson, N.C., 1977-78; asst. buyer Roses Stores Inc., N.Y.C., 1978-79; buyer Roses Stores Inc., Henderson, 1979-83, div. mgr. mdse., 1983-86; gen. mdse. mgr. Conston Corp., Phila., 1986-90; gen. mdse. mgr., v.p. Crystal Brands Retail, Reading, Pa., 1990-93; pres. Creative Giftworks, Reading, 1993-95; v.p. Totes Inc., Loveland, Ohio, 1995—; dir. retail merchandising Disney Direct Mktg. Svcs., Inc., Edison, N.J., 1994-95. Recipient Torch of Liberty, Anti-Defamation League, 1988—. Mem. NAFE, Profl. Bus. Sorority, Phi Gamma Nu. Roman Catholic. Office: Totes Inc 10078 E Kemper Rd Loveland OH 45140

PILAND, DONALD SPENCER, internist; b. Austin, Tex., Aug. 19, 1954; s. Dudley Craton and Mary Frances (Spencer) P.; m. April Ann Dean, July 2, 1983; children: Spencer, Rachel, Rebecca. BA in Biology, U. Tex., 1976; MD, U. Tex. Med. Br., Galveston, 1980. Intern in anesthesiology U. Kans., Kansas City, 1980-81, intern in internal medicine, 1981-82, resident, 1982-84; staff physician Lucy Lee Hosp., Poplar Bluff, Mo., 1984—; chief med. staff Lucy Lee Hosp., 1989-90, chief med. svc., 1986-91, exec. com., 1986—, bd. dirs., 1987-91. Mem. Rep. Senatorial Policy Com., 1994-95; mem. adv. bd. 1st United Meth. Ch., 1990—. Recipient Spl. Recognition award Am. Cancer Soc., 1991. Office: NW Med Ctr 2210 Barron Rd Poplar Bluff MO 65901

PILARCZYK, DANIEL EDWARD, archbishop; b. Dayton, Ohio, Aug. 12, 1934; s. Daniel Joseph and Frieda S. (Hilgefort) P. Student, St. Gregory Sem., Cin., 1948-53; PhB, Pontifical Urban U., Rome, 1955, PhL, 1956, STB, 1958, STL, 1960, STD, 1961; MA, Xavier U., 1965; PhD, U. Cin., 1969; LLD (hon.), Xavier U., 1975, Calumet Coll., 1982, U. Dayton, 1990, Marquette U., 1990, Thomas More Coll., 1991. Ordained priest Roman Catholic Ch., 1959; asst. chancellor Archdiocese of Cin., 1961-63; synodal judge Archdiocesan Tribunal, 1971-82; mem. faculty Athenaeum of Ohio, St. Gregory Sem., 1963-74; v.p. Athenaeum of Ohio, 1968-74, trustee, 1974—; also rector St. Gregory Sem., 1968-74; archdiocesan dir. ednl. services, 1974-82, aux. bishop of Cin., 1974-82, vicar gen., 1974-82, archbishop of Cin., 1982—; bd. dirs. Pope John Ctr., 1978-85; trustee Cath. Health Assn., 1982-85, Cath. U. Am., 1983-91, Pontifical Coll. Josephinum, 1983-92; v.p. Nat. Conf. Cath. Bishops, 1986-89, pres., 1989-92; U.S. rep. Episc. Bd. Internat. Commn. on English in Liturgy 1987-97; chmn., 1991-97. Author: Praepositini Cancellarii de Sacramentis et de Novissimis, 1964-65, Twelve Tough Issues, 1988, We Believe, 1989, Living in the Lord, 1990, The Parish: Where God's People Live, 1991, Forgiveness, 1992, What Must I Do?, 1993, Out Priests: Who They Are and What They Do, 1994, Sacraments, 1994, Lenten Lunches, 1995, Bringing Forth Justice, 1996. Ohio Classical Conf. scholar to Athens, 1966. Mem. Am. Philol. Assn. Home and Office: 100 E 8th St Cincinnati OH 45202-2129

PILLATH, RICHARD JAMES, purchasing consultant; b. Pound, Wis., Dec. 19, 1954; s. Fred Jr. and Mildred P.; m. Karen Marie, June 20, 1986; 1 child, Daniel James. B, Northeast Wis. Tech. Inst., 1974. Purchasing cons. Graetz Mfg., Inc., Pound, Wis., 1975—. Office: Graetz Mfg Inc W11094 Hwy 64 Pound WI 54161

PILLING, PATRICIA LESLIE, oral historian, anthropologist; b. Manchester, Lancashire, Eng., Apr. 2, 1926; d. Norman Leslie and Leah Sarah (Sheldon) Marks; m. Arnold R. Pilling, June 30, 1956 (div. 1981); children: Laurie Asmus, Leslie, David, Daniel; m. Robert J. Halbeisen, Jan. 6, 1990; stepchildren: Johanna, Eric, Margaret. AB, U. Calif., Berkeley, 1950, MA, 1952; specialist cert. in gerontology, Wayne State U., 1977, PhD, 1987. Instr. Oakland County Community Coll., Farmington, Mich., 1971, Mercy Coll., Detroit, 1972, Macomb County Community Coll., Warren, Mich., 1974-75; instr. Wayne State U., Detroit, 1972-77, 79-80, program coord. oral history W.P. Reuther Libr., 1978; cons. oral historian Mich. Dept. Natural Resources, Lansing, 1978; pres. Share Your Memories, Birmingham, Mich., 1988—; vis. lectr. U. Windsor, Ont., Can., 1981, Shenyang Poly. U., China, 1987, UNESCO English Lang. Project, Ptock, Poland, 1988; cons. early childhood edn. Wayne State U., 1986, Ctr. for Advancement Family, Birmingham, 1990-93; evaluator oral history Oral History Assn., midwest states, 1977-79. Author: Oral History: Interviewing the Elderly, 1985, Manual for Shenyang Teachers, 1988; contbr. articles to profl. jours.; reviewer Mich. Coun. for Humanities, 1980-81, Nat. Coun. for Humanities, 1978-82. Chmn. recreation Midtown Community Action Coun., Detroit, 1960-63; founding mem. Birmingham Sr. Citizen Coun., 1977—; com. mem. on civil rights, human rights Open Hearts, Open Housing, 1967-75; mem. vol. coun. Detroit Symphony Orch. Hall. Grantee AAUW, 1971, Birmingham Hist. Soc., 1971-75, Madonna Coll., 1977. Mem. AAUW, NAFE, Nat. Assn. Career Women, Oral History Assn., Mich. Oral History Assn. (founding pres. 1979-80), Women's Internat. League for Peace and Freedom, Daus of Brit. Empire (Earl of Scarborough chpt. vice regent 1991-93). Home and Office: Share Your Memories 31115 Huntley Sq E Birmingham MI 48025-5335

PILON, DANIEL HENRY, academic administrator; b. Flint, Mich., Oct. 15, 1942; s. George Jerry and Rita Margaret (McPhillips) P.; m. Janice Maureen Alumbaugh, June 17, 1967; children: Mark Daniel, Christopher Jon, Margot Ann. AB, Sacred Heart Sem., 1964; MEd, Marygrove Coll., 1968; EdD, U. Mich., 1976. Tchr. Shrine High Sch., Royal Oak, Mich., 1965-68; asst. pres. Aquinas Coll., Grand Rapids, Mich., 1968-76; v.p. Council of Ind. Colls., Washington, 1976-81; pres. Coll. of St. Scholastica, Duluth, Minn., 1981—; bd. dirs. Minn. Pvt. Coll. Council Fund, St. Paul; cons.-evaluator North Cen. Assn. of Colls., Chgo. Author: Consultation in Higher Education, 1980; editor: Outcomes: Curriculum-Based Performances, 1981; Emerging Needs for Consultants in Higher Education, 1991. Pres. United Way of Greater Duluth, 1986-88; bd. trustees Miller-Dwan Hosp. Found., Duluth, 1982-95; bd. dirs. Pub. Radio, St. Paul, 1981-91. Pres. United Way of Greater Duluth, 1986-88; bd. trustees Miller-Dwan Hosp. Found., Duluth, 1982-95. Home: 3501 E 1st St Duluth MN 55804-1806 Office: Coll St Scholastica 1200 Kenwood Ave Duluth MN 55811-4199

PIMENTAL, PATRICIA ANN, neuropsychologist, consulting company executive, author; b. Warwick, R.I., Feb. 2, 1956; d. Thomas Robert and Veronica Madeleine (Costa) P.; m. John V. O'Hara, Dec. 16, 1989; children: John Bernard, Padraic James. BS in Pre-Med, Speech Pathology, Northwestern U., 1978, MA in Speech Pathology with honors, 1980; PsyD in Clin. Psychology with honors, Chgo. Sch. Profl. Psychology, 1987. Lic. psychologist, speech pathologist, Ill.; diplomate Am. Bd. Vocat. Neuropsychology, Am. Acad. Pain Mgmt., Am. Bd. Prof. Disability Cons., Am. Bd. Profl. Neuropsychology. Clin. psychology extern child psychology clinic U. Ill., Chgo., 1984-85, dir. psychol. svcs. dept. phys. medicine and rehab., 1987-91, asst. prof. dept. phys. medicine and rehab., 1987-91; clin. psychology extern Filmore Mental Health Ctr., Berwyn-Cicero (Ill.) Sr. Svcs., 1985-86; clin. psychology intern St. Elizabeth's Hosp., Chgo., 1986-87; mem. faculty Chgo. Sch. Profl. Psychology, 1991—; pres. Neurobehavioral Medicine Cons., Ltd., Oak Brook, Ill., 1991—. Sr. author: Neuropsychological Aspects of Right Brain Injury, 1989, The Mini Inventory of Right Brain Injury, 1989; contbr. articles and revs. to profl. jours., chpts. to books; manuscript reviewer Archives Phys. Medicine and Rehab., 1990; book reviewer Contemporary Psychology, 1991. Vol. trainer ARC Disaster Stress Relief Program, 1991—; leader U. Ill. Stroke Club, 1988-91; bd. dirs. Older Adult Rehab. Svcs., Cicero, 1987-90; active Chgo. Anti-Cruelty Soc., Lincoln Park Zool. Soc. Named one of Outstanding Young Women Am., 1984, 92; Am. Cancer Soc. scholar, 1979; recipient Outstanding Manuscript of Yr. award Am. Jour. of Pain Mgmt., 1993. Fellow Am. Coll. Profl. Neuropsychology; mem. APA, Am. Pain Soc., Ill. Psychol. Assn. (adv. bd. 1989-93, chair-elect, chair health and rehab. sect. 1991-92, 92-93, chair prescription privilege task force 1992-95, continuing edn. chair/clin. practice sect. 1993-95, pres.-elect 1995-96, pres. 1996—), Nat. Brain Injury Rsch. Found. (med. adv. coun. 1992—), Internat. Neuropsychol. Soc., Nat. Acad. Neuropsychology, Am. Congress Rehab. Medicine, Soc. Clin. and Exptl. Hypnosis, Midwest Neuropsychology Group, Am. Speech and Hearing Assn. Roman Catholic. Office: Glen Oaks Hosp Med Ctr Neurobehavioral Medicine 701 Winthrop Ave Glendale Heights IL 60139

PIMLEY, KIM JENSEN, financial training consultant; b. Abington, Pa., Apr. 29, 1960; d. Alvin Christian Jensen and Helen Marie (Kairis) Meinken; m. Michael St. John Pimley, Nov. 10, 1988; 1 child, Oliver Jensen Pimley. BA, Emory U., 1982, MA magna cum laude, 1982; postgrad., U. Chgo., 1985—. Mgr. tng. ops. Continental Bank, Chgo., 1986-88, mgr. coll. rels., 1988-90; mgr. client svcs. The Globecon Group, N.Y.C., 1990-92; prin. Pimley & Pimley, Inc., Glencoe, Ill., 1992-93; pres. P&P Tng. Resources, Inc., Glencoe, 1993—. Contbr. poetry to various jours. Mem. Chgo. Coun. on Fgn. Affairs, 1990—. Scholarship U. Chgo., 1984. Mem. ACLU, NOW, Oxford and Cambridge Club, Poetry Soc. Am. Office: P&P Tng Resources Inc 543 Grove St Glencoe IL 60022-1843

PINCHOK, NICHOLAS CHRISTOPHER, sales representative; b. Kettering, Ohio, Apr. 16, 1965; s. Nicholas and Judith Helen (Trebac) P. BS, Purdue U., 1987; postgrad. studies in creative writing, Columbia Coll.,

1994—. Sales rep. IBM Corp., Dayton, Ohio, 1987-89, Santa Monica, Calif., 1989-91; acct. mgr. Lexmark Internat., Rosemont, Ill., 1991-93; sales rep. Reed Elsevier, Des Plaines, Ill., 1994—. Vol. Chgo. Cares, 1994-95, United Way, Dayton and Santa Monica, 1987-91; mem. Purdue Pres. Coun., West Lafayette, Ind., 1988-95. Home: 936 Pleasant St Apt P3 Oak Park IL 60302 Office: Cahners Publ 1350 E Touhy Rd Des Plaines IL 60018

PINCHOT, SISTER MIRIAM FIDELIS, elementary education educator; b. Shamrock, Pa., Apr. 6, 1942; d. Joseph Kenneth and Mary Jane (Vernarsky) P. BSE, Ursuline/St. John Coll., Cleve., 1964; MSE, St. John Coll., Cleve., 1974. Pastoral Psychology, Religious Edn. for deaf/mentally handicapped, Order of St. Ursula. 4th grade tchr. St. Charles Sch., Parma, Ohio, 1964-66; 5th,6th grade tchr. Immaculate Conception Sch., Willoughby, Ohio, 1966-70; 4th,5th grade tchr. Holy Cross Sch., Euclid, Ohio, 1970-74; 6th grade tchr. and prin. of deaf religion schs. St. Timothy's Sch., Cleve., 1974-76; 6th grad tchr., prin. deaf religious schs. St. Mary Magdelene's Sch., Willowick, Ohio, 1976-79; program dir. Martin de Porres Ctr., Cleve., 1979-83; vol. Ursuline Ednl. Ctr., Pepper Pike, Ohio, 1983-85; 4th grade tchr. St. Joseph Sch., Avon Lk, Ohio, 1986-88; 3rd grade tchr. St. Charles Sch., Parma, Ohio, 1988-90, St. Ann Sch., Cleveland Heights, Ohio, 1990—; affiliate sponsor Ursuline Congregation, Pepper Pike, Ohio; Christian Life Community Retreat Directress, St. Charles CLC, Parma, Ohio; West Side Mental Health Bd. Mem., Cleve.; East Side Mental Health Bd. Mem. Author: Jephthath's Daughter, 1989, (poems) Red is the Color, Spring, To Sir Jesus: From the Woman of Samaria, 1991; artist St. Ursulas Companions, Cleve. Sky Front (watercolor). Bd. mem. Glenco Housing Group, Cleve., vol. staff Drop in Drug Ctr./Adv. Ctr., mem. of Parent and Tchr. Orgn. St. Charles Sch. Bicentennial Multi-Cultural Arts Program grantee Ursuline Ministry Fund, 1995-96, Touch Life grantee; recipient fund for creation of Habitat for Hamster, Art Therapy Program, Martha Holden Jennings Found., Many are the Sunbeams Program, St. Ann and Archibishop Lyke Elem. Schs., 1993-94. Mem. Ursuline Nuns of Cleve., Parent-Tchr. Orgn. (religion com.), Rainbows for All God's Children (counselor), Rite for Christian Initiation for Children (mem. global-interdependence com.). Christian Catholic. Home: Saint William Convent 321 E 260 Euclid OH 44132 Office: St Ann Sch 2160 Stillman Rd Cleveland OH 44118-2830

PINGATORE, SAM ROBERT, systems analyst, consultant, business executive; b. Chgo., Sept. 14, 1948; s. Samuel and Theresa (Kirchue) P.; m. Alicia Mae Morales, Aug. 16, 1969; 1 child, Joshua S.E. BA in Polit. Sci., Miami U., Oxford, Ohio, 1970; student, Baldwin Wallace Coll., Berea, Ohio, 1980, Ohio State U., 1985, Kent State U., 1973. Buyer, materials analyst FECO-Bangor Punta, Cleve., 1974-76; inventory analyst Van Dorn Co., Strongsville, Ohio, 1976-78; systems analyst Def. Logistics Agy., Dept. Def., Cleve., 1978-85, tng. officer, 1985-86, systems analyst-contracts, 1986-87, program analyst-budget, 1987-90; bus. mgr. ARVIN/CALSPAN NASA Lewis Operation, Cleve., 1990-95; v.p. ops. Morales Svcs., North Olmsted, Ohio, 1995—; bus. mgr., dir. H.R. Medina Co. Bd. MR/DD, Medina, Ohio, 1996—; mem. total quality mgmt. steering com. ARVIN/CALSPAN Corp., Cleve., 1991—; mem. curriculum com. Polaris Vocat. Sch., Middleburg Heights, Ohio, 1991—; mem. tng. and devel. com. Greater Cleve. Urban League; cons. Calspan Corp. Space Inds. Internat., North Olmsted, 1978—. Writer speeches, curriculum, position papers. Advisor St. Brendan Youth Group, North Olmsted, 1986; co-chair Pre-Cana, Marriage Preparation Com., North Olmsted, 1981—; co-chair Adult Edn. Commn., North Olmsted, 1979; mem. Human Rels. Coun., Darmstadt, Germany, 1972. With U.S. Army, 1970-73. Deocrated Army Commendation medal (2), Army Achievement medal. Mem. BBB, Nat. Contract Mgmt. Assn., Rampant Lion Found., Delta Kappa Epsilon. Republican. Roman Catholic. Home: 4547 Vernon Dr North Olmsted OH 44070-3457 Office: Morales Services 4547 Vernon Dr North Olmsted OH 44070 Other Office: Medina Co Achievement Ctr 4091 Windfall Rd Medina OH 44256

PINGLE, RICHARD C., project manager; b. Deerborn, Mich., Nov. 10, 1966. AD, Nat. Inst. Tech., 1988. Installer Guardian Alarm, Southfield, Mich., 1989-90; mgr. inside sales Burke Sales & Engring., Belleville, Mich., 1990-94; sr. project mgr. Ferro Tech. Inc., Wyandotte, Mich., 1994—. Patentee in field. Republican.

PINNEY, JON D., manufacturing engineer; b. Huntington, Ind., June 7, 1957. Ptnr. Computer Control Systems, Nashville, 1982-84; engr. Dressler Mfg., Bargersville, Ind., 1984—. Coach High Sch. baseball, 1985-88, Little League Baseball, 1988—. Mem. S.A.E. Republican. Office: Dressler Mfg PO Box 635 Bargersville IN 46106-0635

PINTER, DIANN, business executive; b. Milw., May 14, 1950. V.p. East Controls, Inc., Pleasant Prairie, Wis., 1983—. Adult Sunday sch. tchr. Kenosha Ch. of God, 1986—, childrens Sunday sch. tchr., 1986—, tchr., 1986—. Mem. Women's AGLOW (recording sec. 1988-90). Republican. Pentecostal. Office: East Controls Inc PO Box 90 Pleasant Prairie WI 53158-0090

PINTO, JOHN SALVADORE, real estate broker; b. Mangalore, Karnataka, India, Jan. 24, 1949; came to U.S., 1971; s. Basil Michael and Aileen (Saldanha) P.; m. Carolyn Gobin, Oct. 7, 1978. BS, Madras (India) U., 1968; MBA, U. Wis., Whitewater, 1988. Owner Pinto Real Estate, Madison, Wis., 1975—, Delta Vending Svcs., Madison, 1991—; investment salesman FPC Securities Corp., Madison, 1975-79. Columnist The Capital Times, 1989-94. Treas. Rep. Party of Dane County, 1979-81, chmn., 1985-89; 3d vice chmn. Rep. Party of Wis., 1987-93; Heritage Groups chmn. Rep. Party of Wis., 1993—; pres. Wexford Village Condominium Assn., Madison, 1992-96; mem. Dane County Solid Waste Adv. Commn., 1989—; chmn. equal opportunity com. Madison Bd., 1988-89; pres. Wis. chpt. Assn. Industry in Am., 1989-91; mem. bd. Combat Blindness Found., 1988—. Recipient Lifetime Achievement award Rep. Party of Dane County, Madison, 1986, Bovay award Rep. Party of Wis., 1988. Mem. Nat. Assn. Realtors, Wis. Realtors Assn., Greater Madison Bd. Realtors, Dane County Pub. Affairs Coun. Roman Catholic. Office: Pinto Real Estate PO Box 5554 Madison WI 53705-0554

PIPER, ADDISON LEWIS, securities executive; b. Mpls., Oct. 10, 1946; s. Harry Cushing and Virginia (Lewis) P.; m. Louise Wakefield (div.); children: Gretchen, Tad, William; m. Cynthia Schuneman, Nov. 14, 1979; children: Elisabeth LaBelle, Richard LaBelle. BA in Econs., Williams Coll., 1968; MBA, Stanford U., 1972. Mktg. cons. Earl Savage and Co., Mpls., 1968-69; mem. capital market dept. Piper and Jaffray, Mpls., 1969-70; asst. syndicate mgr. Piper, Jaffray and Hopwood, Mpls., 1972-73, v.p., 1973-79, dir. trading, 1973-77, dir. sales, 1977-79, exec. v.p., dir. mktg., 1979-83, chief exec. officer, chmn. mgmt. com., 1983—, chmn. bd. dirs., 1988—; adv. com. N.Y. Stock Exch., 1966-90; bd. dirs. Allina Health Systems, Greenspring Corp., Mpls., Minn. Bus. Partnership, Mpls.; vice chair Abbott Northwestern Hosp., Mpls.; trustee CARE Found., Mpls. Fin. chmn. Senator Durenberger Fin. Com., Mpls., 1980-88; chmn. Minn. Pub. Radio, 1985-95. Mem. Securities Industry Assn. (bd. govs. 1986-90, tax policy com.), Country Club of the Rockies (Colo.), Mpls. Club. Republican. Episcopalian. Clubs: Woodhill Country (Wayzata); Minneapolis. Office: Piper Jaffray Cos. PO Box 28 222 S 9th St Minneapolis MN 55440

PIPER, ANNETTE CLEONE, social services administrator, researcher; b. St. Paul, July 13, 1936; d. Frank Robert Zimmerman; m. Aaron Cleaves Piper, Apr. 17, 1958 (div. 1974); children: Michelle, Renee. BA, Wayne State U., 1960, MSW, 1965, postdoctoral, 1985—. Inst. rsch. Wayne State U., Detroit, 1965-69; program mgr. Ariz. Dept. Econ. Security, Bisbee, 1976-79; tng. and personnel coordinator Mich. Dept. Social Svcs., Detroit, 1971-73, mgr. svcs. sect., 1973-74; program mgr. Mich. Dept. Social Svcs., Pontiac, 1974-76; dep. dir. Sta. WCCYS Mich. Dept. Social Svcs., Detroit, 1979-88; dist. dir.r. Mich. Dept. Social Svcs., Westland, 1988—; ret., 1988; instr., cons. Cochise Community Coll., Douglas, Ariz., 1979. Mem. Nat. Assn. Child Welfare Adminstrs., Nat. Child Welfare Leadership Ctr., Am. Pub. Welfare Assn., Wayne State U. Alumni Assn, Psi Chi. Home: 23010 Webster Oak Park MI 48237-2119

PIPER, CAROL ADELINE, councilman; b. Chgo., Jan. 28, 1924; d. John and Myra May (Hughett) Preston; m. Robert Donald Piper, Dec. 18, 1945; children: Stephen, Barbara, Bruce, Diane. BA, North Cen. Coll., Naperville, Ill., 1945. Asst. rsch. chemist Quaker Oats Co., Chgo., 1945; office mgr. H. & R. Block, Ridgewood, N.J., 1977-82; councilman City of Naperville, 1987-91; re-elected to Naperville City Council, 1991-95; appointed to Electric Adv. Bd. of Naperville, 1987-91; bd. dirs. Naperville Settlement Mus. Bd., 1991-95. Precinct committeewoman Naperville Rep. Com., 1956-70; mem. Glen Rock (N.J.) Pub. Libr. Bd., 1975, Glen Rock City Coun., 1977-82, 91—; apptd. bd. Naperville City TV, 1991—. Mem. LWV (pres. Glen Rock 1972-74). Home: 104 Devon Ln Naperville IL 60540-5840 Office: City of Naperville 175 W Jackson Ave 400 S Eagle St Naperville IL 60540-5279

PIPER, DOUGLAS, manufacturing company executive; b. Milw., Aug. 19, 1951. Metal trade journeyman Butters-Fetting Inc., Milw., 1977-80; mem. staff fabrication dept. Aqua-Doc Ltd., Big Bend, Wis., 1980-87; plant mgr. Lange Lift Co., Inc., Pewaukee, wis., 1987—; bd. dirs. Lift Products, Inc., New Berlin, Wis. Office: Lange Lift Co Inc PO Box 28 Pewaukee WI 53072-0028

PIPER, JONATHAN BICKNELL, lawyer; b. Pasadena, Calif., Feb. 5, 1960; s. Henry Dan and Roberta Leslie (Bicknell) P.; m. Cecelia R., Apr. 18, 1992. AB, Princeton U., 1981; JD, Yale U., 1987. Assoc. Sonnenschein Nath & Rosenthal, Chgo., 1987-95, of counsel, 1995—. Co-author: Race for Justice, 1995. Mem. ABA, Nat. Lawyers Guild, Am. Birding Assn., Phi Beta Kappa. Office: Sonnenschein Nath Rosenthal 8000 Sears Tower Chicago IL 60606

PIPER, PAUL JOSEPH, municipal administrator; b. Detroit, Mar. 6, 1961; s. Paul Johnson and Mary Kay (Harris) P. BA in Bus. Adminstrn. and French, Capital U., Columbus, Ohio, 1983; student, U. Paris, 1982. Mgr. corp. devel. Rosenbluth Internat., Phila., 1985-93; asst. to mayor for econ. devel. City of Detroit, 1993—; mem. exec. bd. 15th Congl. Dist., Detroit, 1995—, Think Twice Found., Southfield, Mich., 1993—. Author articles. Trustee Franklin Wright Settlement, Detroit, 1994. Recipient Leadership award Mexican Town Devel. Corp., Detroit, 1994. Mem. N.E. Mfrs. Assn., Mich. Econ. Devel. Assn. Democrat. Roman Catholic. Office: City of Detroit Exec Office 1126 City County Bldg Detroit MI 48226

PIPITONE, PHYLLIS L., psychologist, educator, author; b. Chgo.; m. S. Joseph Pipitone, Aug. 28, 1948 (dec.); children: Guy, Daniel, Paul; m. Thomas A. Cox, Jan. 3, 1980. Student Chgo. Conservatory Music, 1941-44, Peabody Conservatory Music, 1945, Chgo. Tchrs. Coll., 1946-47, So. Meth. U., 1951-52; MA, U. Akron (Ohio), 1967; PhD, Kent (Ohio) State U., 1974. With B.S. & H. Advt. Agy., Chgo., 1941-43; instr. piano and theory Music Acad. Chgo.; psychologist, instr. U. Akron and Kent State U., 1970-79; pvt. practice psychology, Akron, 1967—; lectr. in field in U.S and abroad. Served with WAC, AUS, 1944-46. NIMH grantee, 1974, HEW Child Devel. fellow, 1974. Mem. Am. Psychol. Assn., Nat. Assn. Sch. Psychologists, Mensa, Council Exceptional Children, Am. Hypnosis Soc., Kent Psi Research Group, Assn. Study/Dreams, Am. Soc. Psychical Research, Phi Delta Kappa. Clubs: Tuesday Musical, Weathervane Theatre Women's Bd., Akron Women's City, Wadsworth Women's. Home: 224 Pheasant Run Wadsworth OH 44281-2344

PIPPEN, SCOTTIE, professional basketball player; b. Hamburg, Ark., Sept. 25, 1965. Student, U. Cen. Ark., 1983-87. With Seattle Super Sonics, 1987; guard/forward Chgo. Bulls, 1987—; player NBA Championship Team, 1991, 92, 93, U.S. Olympic Basketball Team, 1992. Named to All-Star team, 1990, 92-93, NBA All-Defensive First team, 1992, 93, 94, All-Defensive second team, 1991, NBA All-Star Team, 1992-94, NBA All-Star MVP, 1994, All-NBA First Team, 1994; mem. NBA championship team, 1991-93, 96. Office: Chgo Bulls United Ctr 1901 W Madison St Chicago IL 60612*

PIPPIN, JAMES REX, health care company executive, educator; b. Clovis, N.Mex., Apr. 3, 1949; s. C.A. and J. (Davis) P.; m. Annette Jacqueline Charsha, Feb. 6, 1971; children: Ken, Matthew, Sabrina. BS, Ea. N.Mex. U., 1971; MPA, U. Ariz., 1973. Cert. health care adminstr., Ill. Adminstr. The Mayflower, Grinnell, Iowa, 1973-78; exec. dir. Mayflower Homes, Inc., Grinnell, 1978-80; pres., CEO, Lifelink Corp., Bensenville, Ill., 1980—; preceptor, adj. prof. George Washington U., Washington, 1985—. Contbr. articles to profl. jours. Mem. Am. Coll. Health Care Adminstrs., Am. Assn. Homes for Aging (treas. 1988-90, Profl. of Yr. award 1979), Coun. for Health and Human Svcs. (pres. 1990-92, Exec. of Yr. award 1985), Ill. Assn. Homes for Aging (pres. 1986-88), Ill. Child Care Assn. (bd. dirs.). Republican. Mem. United Ch. of Christ. Office: Lifelink Corp 331 S York Rd Bensenville IL 60106-2673

PIROOZ, SAEED, chemical engineer, researcher; b. Isfahan, Iran, Nov. 20, 1959; came to U.S., 1977; s. Houshang and Parirokh (Housaini) P.; m. Sauedah Abdolahi Sabet, Oct. 26, 1990. BS, Washington U., St. Louis, 1982, MS, 1983, DSc, 1991. Rsch. asst. Washington U., 1984-89; cons. metallurgist Brian and Assocs., St. Louis, 1989-90; rsch. scientist on cleaning of silicon surfaces. MEMC Electronic Materials, Inc., St. Peters, Mo., 1990—. Contbr. articles to sci. jours. Mem. AIChE, Electrochem. Soc., Inst. Environ. Scis., IEEE Plasma Transactions Soc. Office: MEMC Electronic Materials Inc 501 Pearl Dr Saint Peters MO 63376

PIROS, MICHAEL GEORGE, adult education director; b. Warren, Ohio, Oct. 31, 1942; s. Michael George and Mamie (Berta) P.; m. Patricia Szabo, Apr. 5, 1944; children: Kevin, Keith, Shawn, Todd. BS in edn., Kent State U., 1987, postgrad., 1995—. Owner, mgr. Auto Repair, Cortland, Ohio, 1967-78; tchr. Auto Tech. TCJVS, Warren, Ohio, 1978-85; adult edn. supr. Trumbull County JVS, Warren, Ohio, 1985-94, adult edn. dir., 1994—; cons., tchr., Kent State U., 1978-85. Trustee Bazetta Twp., 1989—; chmn. Bazetta Twp. trustee, 1993-94, v.p., 1994—. Recipient Outstanding Tchr. award Trumbull County JVS, 1979, Youth Leadership award, 1983. Mem. Ohio Vocat. Assn., Postsecondary Adult Voc. Edn., Trumbull County JVS (pres. 1979-82), Ohio Industrial Training Program (chmn. 1991-92), Am. Voct. Assn., Iota Lambda Sigma, Youngstown-Warren Regional Chamber. Democrat. Roman Catholic. Home: 3246 Circle Dr Cortland OH 44410

PIRSCH, CAROL MCBRIDE, state senator, community relations administrator; b. Omaha, Dec. 27, 1936; d. Lyle Erwin and Hilfrie Louise (Lebeck) McBride; student U. Miami, Oxford, Ohio, U. Nebr., Omaha; m. Allen I. Pirsch, Mar. 28, 1954; children: Pennie Elizabeth, Pamela Elaine, Patrice Eileen, Phyllis Erika, Peter Allen, Perry Andrew. Former mem. data processing staff Omaha Public Schs.; former mem. wage practices dept. Western Electric Co., Omaha; former legal sec., Omaha; former office mgr. Pirsch Food Brokerage Co., Inc., Omaha; former employment supr. U.S. West Communications, Omaha, now mgr. pub. policy; mem. Nebr. Senate, 1979—. mem. Omaha Pers. Bd.; founder, past pres., bd. dirs. Nebr. Coalition for Victims of Crime. Recipient Golden Elephant award; Outstanding Legis. Efforts award YWCA, Breaking the Rule of Thumb award Nebr. Domestic Violence Sexual Assault Coalition, Cert. of Appreciation award U.S. Dept. Justice, Partnership award NE Credit Union League, 1995, Wings award League of Women Voters of Greater Omaha, 1995, NE VFW Spl. Recognition award for Exceptional Svc., 1995. Mem. VASA, Nat. Orgn. Victim Assistance (Outstanding Legis. Leadership award), Freedom Found., Orgn. U.S. West Women, Nat. Order Women Legislators, Tangier Women's Aux., Footprinters Internat., Nebr. Hist. Soc., Nebr. Taxpayers Assn., Gretna Optimists, Springfield Boosters, Keystone Citizen Patrol (Keystoner of the Month award), Audubon Soc., Rotary Internat., N.W. Community Club, Benson Rep. Women's Club, Bus. and Profl. Rep. Women Club. Office: State Capitol Lincoln NE 68509

PISANESCHI, FRED W., project engineer; b. Cleve., Mar. 4, 1944. Project engr. Teledyne Efficient Industries, Cleve., 1978—. Vol. City of Macedonia (Ohio) Fire Dept., 1969-76. Office: Teledyne Efficient Ind Die Plant # 2 5514 Old Brecksville Rd Cleveland OH 44131-1508

PISANO, CYNTHIA KAY, clinical therapist; b. Fayetteville, N.C., Oct. 31, 1963; d. Doan Bryce Moore and Janis Ann (Brandeberry) Below; m. Anthony Girard Pisano Jr., Jan. 9, 1982; children: Anthony G. III, Michael A., Jennifer M. AS, Lourdes Coll., 1982, B of Individualized Studies, 1985. Lic. social worker. Coord. AD/HD Ctr. Unison Behavioral Health Group, Toledo, 1985—; lifelong learning instr. Lourdes Coll., Sylvania, Ohio, 1988—; tchr. inservicing on ADHD, Lourdes Coll., 1993—, active parenting instr., 1992. Sunday presch. tchr. Little Flower Ch., Toledo, 1987—, co-organizer, 1990-91; mem. Children and Adults with Attention Deficit Disorder, Attention Deficit Disorder Active Parent Tng. Fellow Parents of Hyperactive Children; mem. Phi Theta Kappa (pres. 1983-84). Roman Catholic. Home: 3142 Westchester Rd Toledo OH 43615-1630

PISCHL, JOHN PAUL, electrical engineer; b. Chgo., Mar. 12, 1953. BSEE, Rose Poly. Inst., 1975. Project engr. Northrop, Rolling Meadows, Ill., 1977-81; mem. tech. staff GTE, Chgo., 1982-85; chief engr. AT Sys., Lombard, Ill., 1990—. Patentee in field. 1st lt. U.S. Army, 1975-77. Mem. IEEE. Office: AT Sys 920 N Ridge Ave Unit A4 Lombard IL 60148-1226

PISCIOTTA, VIVIAN VIRGINIA, psychotherapist; b. Chgo., Dec. 7; d. Vito and Mary Lamia; m. Vincent Diago Pisciotta, Apr. 1, 1951; children: E. Christopher, Vittorio, V. Charles, Mary A. Pisciotta Higley, Thomas Sansone. BA in Clin. Psychology, Antioch U., 1974; MSW, George Williams Coll., 1984; postgrad., Erickson Inst. of No. Ill., 1990. Lic. clin. social worker; diplomate in clin. social work. Short-term therapist Woman Line, Dayton, Ohio, 1976-79; psychotherapist Cicero (Ill.) Family Svcs., 1982-83, Maywood (Ill.) - Proviso Family Svcs., 1983-84, Maple Ave. Med. Ctr., Brookfield, Ill., 1985-88, Met. Med. Clinic, Naperville, Ill., 1986-88; allied staff Riveredge Psychiat. Hosp., Forest Park, Ill., 1986—, Linden Oaks Hosp., Naperville, Ill., 1990—; psychotherapist, pvt. practice Oakbrook, Ill., 1988—; psychotherapist, co-founder Archer Austin Counseling Ctr., Chgo., 1988-89; psychotherapist, founder Archer Counseling Ctr., Chgo., 1989—; allied staff Linden Oaks Psychiat. Hosp., Naperville, 1990—; substitute tchr. Chgo. Pub. High Sch., 1981. Author treatment prog., workshops in field. Co-founder Co-op Nursery Sch., Rockford, Ill., 1956; leader Great Books of the Western World series, Piqua, Ohio, 1977, Rockford, 1960-65; leader Girl Scouts U.S., St. Bridget Sch., Rockford, 1968-71. Mem. Assn. Labor-Mgmt. and Cons. on Alcoholism, Soc. Clin. Exptl. Hypnosis, Nat. Assn. Social Workers, Acad. Cert. Social Workers, Nat. social Wk. Register, Antioch Univ. Alumnus Assn. Rockford Coll. Alumnae Orgn. (newsletter contbr. 1972-73), Soc. for Clin. and Exptl. Hypnosis (assoc. mem.), Internat. Soc. for Clin. and Exptl. Hypnosis (assoc. mem.). Republican. Roman Catholic. Office: Archer Counseling Ctr 7002 W Archer Ave Ste 2B Chicago IL 60638-2202

PITONIAK, GREGORY EDWARD, state representative; b. Detroit, Mich., Aug. 12, 1954; s. Anthony Edward and Constance Elizabeth (Matuszak) P.; m. Denise Ruth Kadi, Apr. 21, 1979; children: Gregory, Mallory. BA, U. Mich., 1976; Masters, U. N.C., 1980. Adminstrv. asst. Taylor (Mich.) Neighborhood Devel. Com., 1977-78; pers. analyst Downriver Community Conf., Southgate, Mich., 1978-79; dir. client svcs. Econ. Devel. Corp. Wayne County, Dearborn, Mich., 1979-84; exec. dir. Econ. Devel. Corp. Wayne County, Livonia, Mich., 1984-88; dir. econ. dev. Downriver Community Conf., Southgate, Mich., 1988; state rep. Mich. Ho. Reps., Lansing, 1989—. Councilman Taylor City Coun., 1981-88, chmn., 1983-85, 87-88; pres. Mich. Young Dems., 1982-84; treas. 15th Congl. Dist. Dem. Orgn., Taylor, 1988-90. Named Outstanding Young Person, Taylor Jaycees, 1987, State Legislator of Yr., Mich. Credit Union League, 1993. Mem. Am. Econ. Devel. Coun. (cert. econ. developer 1984), Am. Soc. Pub. Adminstrn., Polish Am. Congress, Dem. Club Taylor, KC. Roman Catholic. Home: 9686 Rose St Taylor MI 48180-3046 Office: Mich Ho Rep PO Box 30014 Lansing MI 48909-7514

PITT, BERTRAM, cardiologist, educator, consultant; b. Kew Gardens, N.Y., Apr. 27, 1932; s. David and Shirley (Blum) P., m. Elaine Liberstein, Aug. 10, 1962; children—Geoffrey, Jessica, Jillian. BA, Cornell U., 1953; MD, U. Basel, Switzerland, 1959. Diplomate Am. Bd. Internal Medicine, Am. Bd. Cardiology. Intern Beth Israel Hosp., N.Y.C., 1959-60; resident Beth Israel Hosp., Boston, 1960-63; fellow in cardiology Johns Hopkins U., Balt., 1966-67; from instr. to prof. Johns Hopkins U., 1967-77; prof. medicine, dir. div. cardiology U. Mich., Ann Arbor, 1977-91, assoc. chmn. dept. medicine, 1991—. Author: Atlas of Cardiovascular Nuclear Medicine, 1977; editor: Cardiovascular Nuclear Medicine, 1974. Served to capt. U.S. Army, 1963-65. Mem. ACP, Am. Coll. Cardiology, Am. Soc. Clin. Investigation, Assn. Am. Physicians, Am. Physiol. Soc., Am. Heart Assn., Assn. Univ. Cardiologists, Am. Coll. Chest Physicians, Royal Soc. Mich. Home: 24 Ridgeway St Ann Arbor MI 48104-1739 Office: U Mich Divsn Cardiology 1500 E Medical Center Dr Ann Arbor MI 48109-0999

PITT, GAVIN ALEXANDER, management consultant, publishing executive; b. Berkeley, Calif., Aug. 4, 1915; s. David Alexander and Maude Elizabeth (Hanna) P.; m. Eleanore Whiting, Sept. 2, 1939; children: Gavin Alexander, Gaele Whiting, Judson Hamilton. AB, Brown U., 1938; MEd, Johns Hopkins U., 1959. Asst. dean Brown U., Providence, 1938-42; mgr. exec. tng. Macy's, N.Y.C., 1942-43; dir. personnel Hazeltine Electronics Corp., N.Y.C., 1943-45; asst. indsl. adminstr. AMF, Inc., N.Y.C., 1945-49; assoc. Booz, Allen & Hamilton, N.Y.C., 1949-55; dir. personnel services Gen. Dynamics Corp., N.Y.C., 1955-57; v.p. Johns Hopkins U. and Hosp., Balt., 1957-60; pres. Presbyn.-St. Lukes Hosp., Chgo., 1960-63; pvt. practice cons., 1963-66, 70-74; pres. St. John's Mil. Acad., Delafield, Wis., 1966-70; adminstrv. officer Antioch Coll. and U. Yellow Springs, Ohio, 1974-79; devel. officer Wright State U., Dayton, Ohio, 1981-87; pres. Gavin Pitt Assocs., Inc., Chgo., 1986—, Water Tower Pub. House Ltd., Chgo., 1990—; lectr. CCNY, 1948-57; exec. dir. Inst. Medicine of Chgo., 1963-66; bd. dirs. Balt. Life Ins. Co. Author: The Twenty Minute Lifetime, 1959. Sec., bd. dirs. Am. Assn. Gifted Children, N.Y.C, 1985-86, v.p. Chgo. area council Boy Scouts Am., 1961-66, mem. nat. and regional councils, 1966-68; trustee Latin Sch. Chgo., 1962-64; bd. corporators The Peddie Sch., Hightstown, N.J. Mem. Am. Mgmt. Assn. (pers. div. adv. coun.), Assn. Mil. Schs. and Colls., Nat. Coun. Chs. (gen. pers. com.), Brown U. Alumni Assn. (Brown Bear Disting. Alumnus 1961), Saddle and Cycle Club (Chgo.), Newcomen Soc., Omicron Delta Kappa.

PITT, GEORGE, lawyer; b. Chgo., July 21, 1938; s. Cornelius George and Anastasia (Geocaris) P.; m. Barbara Lynn Goodrich, Dec. 21, 1963 (div. Apr. 1990); children: Elizabeth Nanette, Margaret Leigh; m. Pamela Ann Pittsford, May 19,1990. BA, Northwestern U., 1960, JD, 1963. Bar: Ill. 1963. Assoc. Chapman and Cutler, Chgo., 1963-67; ptnr. Borge and Pitt, and predecessor, 1968-87; ptnr. Katten Muchin & Zavis, Chgo., 1987—. Notes and Comments editor Northwestern U. Law Rev., 1962-63. Served to 1st lt. AUS, 1964. Fellow Am. Coll. of Bond Counsel; mem. Ill. State Bar Assn., The Monroe Club, Univ. Club Chgo., Michigan City Yacht Club, Ind. Soc. of Chgo., Eta Sigma Phi, Phi Delta Phi, Phi Gamma Delta. Home: 600 N McClurg Ct Chicago IL 60611-3044 Office: Katten Muchin & Zavis 525 W Monroe St Ste 1600 Chicago IL 60661-3693

PITT, JUDSON HAMILTON, publisher; b. Glen Cove, N.Y., June 7, 1953; s. Gavin Alexander and Eleanore Gaehler (Whiting) P.; m. Elena U. Tokaeva, Dec. 16, 1995. BS in Communications, Ariz. State U., 1977. Resident advisor fraternity Ohio State U., Columbus, 1977-79; supr. student svcs. Loyola U., Chgo., 1979-81; asst. to CEO Flair Communications Agy., Inc., Chgo., 1981—; v.p. Gavin Pitt Assocs., Inc., Chgo., 1986—; pub. Water Tower Pub. House, Chgo., 1989—; dir. ops. Chgo. Marathon, 1984-93. Mem. Am. Mktg. Assn., Newcomen Soc. U.S., Chgo. Soc. Assn. Execs., Saddle & Cycle Club, Pi Kappa Alpha. Republican. Presbyterian. Home: 5510 N Sheridan Rd Chicago IL 60640-1633 Office: 214 W Erie St Chicago IL 60610-3611

PITTAWAY, KENNETH STANLEY, physician; b. Detroit, Jan. 17, 1941; s. Arthur Allen and Lottie (Goraji) P.; m. Diane Argelsinger, Nov. 7, 1968 (div.); children: Joel Arthur, Lydia Ruth. Doctorate, Mo. Coll., St. Louis, 1980; PhD, Natural Health Inst., St. Louis, 1985. Cert. hypnotherapist. Chief instr. Acad. Natural Arts, Detroit, 1962-68; pres. Pittaway Bus. Products, Detroit, 1968-86, Inst. Natural Health Scis., Novi, Mich., 1968—, Nat. Inst. Natural Health Scis., DePere, Wis., 1968—; physician Homeopathic medicine, Livonia, Mich., 1982—; co-chmn. Health Care Round Table, Taylor, Mich., 1990—; chief investor rsch., Compre Clinics, Houston; panel mem. Nat. Inst. of Health Alternative Medicine, Bethesda, Md., 1993. Author: Homeopathic First Aid, 1992. Home: Court C 20940 E Glen Haven Northville MI 48167 Office: Inst Natural Health Sci 20270 Middleblet Livonia MI 48152

PITTELKO, ROGER DEAN, clergyman; b. Elk Reno, Okla., Aug. 18, 1932; s. Elmer Henry and Lydia Caroline (Nieman) P.; A.A., Concordia Coll., 1952; B.A., Concordia Sem., St. Louis, 1954, M.Div., 1957, S.T.M., 1958; postgrad. Chgo. Luth. Theol. Sem., 1959-61; Th.D., Am. Div. Sch., Pineland, Fla., 1968; D.Min., Faith Evang. Luth. Sem., Tacoma, 1983; m. Beverly A. Moellendorf, July 6, 1957; children—Dean, Susan. Ordained to ministry, Lutheran Ch.-Mo. Synod, 1958; vicar St. John Luth. Ch., S.I., N.Y., 1955-56; asst. pastor St. John Luth. Ch., New Orleans, 1958-59; pastor Concordia Luth. Ch., Berwyn, Ill., 1959-63; pastor Luth. Ch. of the Holy Spirit, Elk Grove Village, Ill., 1963-87; chmn. Commn. on Worship, Luth. Ch.-Mo. Synod; asst. bishop Midwest region English dist., 1983; pres. and bishop English dist., 1987—. Mem. Luth. Acad. for Scholarship, Concordia Hist. Inst. Republican. Clubs: Maywood (Ill.) Sportsman; Itasca (Ill.) Country. Author: Guide to Introducing Lutheran Worship. Contbr. articles to jours. Home: 19405 Stamford Dr Livonia MI 48152-1240 Office: 23001 Grand River Ave Detroit MI 48219-3130

PITTELKOW, MARK ROBERT, physician, dermatology educator, researcher; b. Milw., Dec. 16, 1952; s. Robert Bernard and Barbara Jean (Thomas) P.; m. Gail L. Gamble, Nov. 26, 1977; children: Thomas, Cameron, Robert. BA, Northwestern U., 1975; MD, Mayo Med. Sch., 1979. Intern then resident Mayo Grad. Sch., 1979-84, post-doctoral exptl. pathology, 1981-83; from asst. to assoc. prof. dermatology Mayo Med. Sch., Rochester, Minn., 1984-95, prof. dermatology, 1995—, assoc. prof. biochemistry and molecular biology, 1992—; cons. Mayo Clinic/Found., Rochester, 1984—. Fellow Am. Acad. Dermatology; mem. AAAS, Am. Dermatol. Assn., Soc. Investigative Dermatology, Am. Burn Assn., Am. Soc. Cell Biology, N.Y. Acad. Scis., Chi Psi. Home: 721 12th Ave SW Rochester MN 55902-2027 Office: Mayo Clinic 200 1st St SW Rochester MN 55905-0001

PITTMAN, ANN BROAD, physical therapist; b. Canton, Ohio, Nov. 15, 1931; d. Fred Harding and Ida Elizabeth (Rogers) P.; m. Jesse James Pittman, Nov. 26, 1955; children: Vicki, Steven, Annette. BA, De Pauw U., 1953; cert. in phys. therapy, U.S. Army, San Antonio, 1954; cert. in manual therapy, Inst. Grad. Health Scis. (now Inst. Phys. Therapy), St. Augustine, Fla., 1981. Staff phys. therapist N.W. Hosp., Mpls., 1959-64, Luth. Gen. Hosp., Des Plaines, Ill., 1965-70, Akron (Ohio) City Hosp., 1970-80; sr. phys. therapist Summa Health, Akron, 1980—. Home: 1440 Chatham Ave North Canton OH 44720

PITTMAN, DAVID JOSHUA, sociologist, educator, researcher, consultant; b. Rocky Mount, N.C., Sept. 18, 1927; s. Jay Washington and Laura Frances (Edwards) P. BA, U. N.C., 1949, MA, 1950; postgrad., Columbia U., 1953; PhD, U. Chgo., 1956. Asst. prof. sociology Washington U., St. Louis, 1958-60, assoc. prof., 1960-64, prof., 1964-91, prof. sociology in psychology, 1991-92, prof. psychology, 1992-93, prof. emeritus, 1993—, chmn. dept. sociology, 1976-86, dir. Social Sci. Inst., 1963-76; cons. Jellinek Clinic, Amsterdam, The Netherlands, 1965-68, HEW, Washington, 1977-85, Wine Inst., 1985-94; mem. sci. adv. com. Distilled Spirits Coun., Washington, 1976-86; field editor social scis. Jour. Study Alcoholism, 1985-92, mem. editorial bd., 1992—; Dent Meml. lectr. U. London, 1989. Author: Revolving Door: A Study of Chronic Police Case Inebriates, 1958, The Drug Scene in Great Britain, 1967, Primary Prevention of Alcoholism, 1980; editor: Society, Culture and Drinking Patterns, 1962, Alcoholism, 1967, Society, Culture and Drinking Patterns Reexamined, 1991; mem. editl. bd. Internat. Jour. Advt., 1990—. Bd. dirs. Nat. Gay and Lesbian Task Force, 1993—; pres. N.Am. Assn. Alcoholism Programs, 1965-67; chmn. 28th Internat. Congress on Alcohol and Alcoholism, Washington, 1968, Mo. Adv. Coun. on Alcoholism and Drug Abuse, Jefferson City, 1972-75, 87-91; mem. Mo. Mental Health Commn., Jefferson City, 1975-78. Recipient Page One Civic award St. Louis Newspaper Guild, 1967, Bronze Key St. Louis Coun. on Alcoholism, 1976, Silver Key Nat. Coun. on Alcoholism, N.Y.C., 1978, Biennal Rsch. award Soc. of the Med. Friends of Wine, 1992; spl. fellow NIMH, 1966. Fellow Am. Sociol. Soc.; mem. Soc. Study Social Problems (chmn. alcoholism com. 1957-59, Disting. Sr. Scholar award 1993), Internat. Coun. on Alcohol and Addictions (exec. com. 1968-84), Am. Sociol. Assn. (chmn. alcohol and drugs sect. 1992), Phi Beta Kappa, Sigma Xi, Omicron Delta Kappa. Episcopalian. Office: Washington U Psychol Dept Box 1125 One Brookings Dr Saint Louis MO 63130

PITTMAN, PHILIP MCMILLAN, historian; b. Detroit, Apr. 6, 1941; s. Lansing Mizner and Sally Clotilde (Book) P.; m. Julie M. Ducharme, June 22, 1963 (div. 1975); children: Philip McMillan III, Mary Christine Steuart, Noel Ducharme; m. Adele Smith, June 26, 1976 (div. 1989); m. Margaret D. Schlueter, Aug. 26, 1990. AB, Kenyon Coll., 1963; MA, Vanderbilt U., 1964, PhD, 1967. Instr. Vanderbilt U., Nashville, 1966-67; asst. prof. U. Victoria, B.C., Can., 1967-68; assoc. prof. Marshall U., Huntington, W.Va., 1968-80; pres. W.Va. Assn. Coll. English Tchrs., 1978-79; author, historian Cedarville, Mich., 1980—; pub., salesman, v.p., sec., chmn. bd. Les Cheneaux Ventures Inc., 1985—. Author: The Les Cheneaux Chronicles: Anatomy of a Community, 1984, Ripples from the Breezes: A Les Cheneaux Anthology, 1988, North Shore Chinook: Lake Huron Salmon on Light Tackle, 1993, Don't Blame the Treaties: Native American Rights and the Michigan Indian Treaties, 1992; editor, compiler: The Portrayal of Life Stages in English Literature, 1500-1800, 1989. Active Les Cheaux Cmty. Action Com., 1985—, Mich. Nature Conservancy, 1994—; active Little Traverse Conservancy, 1990—, bd. dirs., 1994—. NEH fellow, 1971. Mem. Les Cheneaux Hist. Assn. (pres. 1987-89), Les Cheneaux Islands Assn. (pres. 1982-84), Les Cheneaux Club (sec. 1972-87), Delta Kappa Epsilon. Republican. Episcopalian. Home: PO Box 187 Cedarville MI 49719-0187 Office: Les Cheneaux Ventures Inc RR 1 Box 15 Cedarville MI 49719-9706

PITTS, KENNETH ERNEST, psychiatrist, educator; b. St. Louis, Mar. 2, 1924; s. Ernest J. and Nancy (Hopkins) P.; m. Jacqueline M. Brookes, June 25, 1949; children: David, Daniel, Gregory. MD, Washington U., St. Louis, 1951. Cert. Am. Bd. Psychiatry and Neurology. Med. dir. Detroit Psychiat. Inst., 1963-70; clin. assoc. prof. Wayne State U. Sch. Medicine, Detroit, 1970—; med. dir. Orchard Hills Psychiat. Ctr., Novi, Mich., 1975—, Oakwood Hosp. Merriman Ctr., Westland, 1991—; psychiat. dir. Rosehill Ctr. Holly, Mich., 1991—. Served with U.S. Army, 1942-45. Fellow Am. Psychiat. Assn. (rep. to assembly 1974-86, life fellow); mem. AMA, Mich. Psychiat. Soc. (pres. 1973-74). Home: 4610 Treasure Lake Dr Howell MI 48843-9473 Office: Orchard Hills Psychiat Ctr Pc 42450 W 12 Mile Rd # 305 Novi MI 48377-3011

PITZER, MARTHA SEARES, nursing educator; b. Pasadena, Calif., June 29, 1938; d. Richard Urmy and Doris Ann (Dunton) Seares; m. Russell Mosher, Sept. 2, 1959; children: Susan Merle, Kenneth Richard, David Seares. RN, Bishop Johnson Coll. Nursing, L.A., 1959; BSN, Ohio State U., 1974, MS, 1976, PhD in Family Rels. and Human Devel., 1984. Adj. asst. prof. Ohio State U., Columbus, 1990—; lactation educator specialist Riverside Meth. Hosp., Columbus, 1993—; perinatal clin. nurse specialist Ohio State U. Hosps., Columbus, 1990-91; educator Lamaze Childbirth Assn., 1991—; asst. prof. Coll. Nursing Ohio State U., Columbus, 1985-90; asst. prof. Otterbein Coll., Westerville, Ohio, 1978-79. Contbr. articles to profl. jours. NRSA predoctoral fellow. Mem. Assn. Women's Health, Obstetric and Neonatal Nurses, Am. Soc. Prophylaxis in Obstet. (cert. childbirth educator), Internat. Lactation Cons. Assn. (cert. lactation educator, cert. lactation cons.), Sigma Theta Tau. Home: 1308 Castleton Rd N Columbus OH 43220-3808

PIVERONUS, PETER JOHN, JR., education educator; b. Boston, Nov. 29, 1941; s. Peter John Sr. and Rose Camella (Pasciuto) P.; m. Bonnie Jean Kennedy, June 7, 1969 (div. 1981); children: Elizabeth Schaeffler, William Schaeffler, Michelle Montesano; m. Eliabeth Doris Roth, Nov. 21, 1988; children: Shannon Roth, Sara Roth. BA, Boston U., 1964, MA, 1966; PhD, Mich. State U., 1972. Asst. prof. SUNY, Buffalo, 1967-69, Claflin Coll., Orangeburg, S.C., 1969-70; adj. prof. Lansing (Mich.) Community Coll., 1972—, Montcalm Community Coll., Sidney, Mich., 1973—, Jackson (Mich.) Community Coll., 1979—; prof. humanities extended degree programs Cen. Mich. U., 1991—; vis. prof. Mich. State U., East Lansing, 1986, Alma (Mich.) Coll., 1987. Editor, contbr.: Conflict in Ireland, 1976; contbr. articles to profl. jours. Precinct del. Ingham County Dems., Lansing, 1980-81; trustee Southland Complex Condo Assn., Lansing, 1987-90; pres. Gaelic League of Lansing, 1981-82. HEW fellow Claflin Coll., 1969-70; U. Mich. grantee, 1985. Mem. Am. Com. for Irish Studies, Irish-Am. Cultural Inst., Soc. for History of Discoveries, Mich. Assn. Higher Edn. (faculty senator 1978-79), Mich. Edn. Assn. Unitarian. Home: 321 Brynford Ave Lansing MI 48917-2925 Office: Lansing Community Coll 419 N Capitol Ave Lansing MI 48933-1207

PIZOR, RAYMOND FRANCIS, secondary educator, guidance counselor, school psy. Tchr. H.S., secondary guidance counselor, sch. psychologist. Home: 5905 Jefferson Ave Ashtabula OH 44004-7507

PLACEK-ZIMMERMAN, ELLYN CLARE, school systems administrator, educator, consultant; b. Chgo., Sept. 3, 1951; d. Clarence Joseph and Jerrine LaMarr (Ruhlow) Placek; m. Allan John Zimmerman, Aug. 10, 1974; 1 child, Alissa Jan. BS, No. Ill., 1973, MS, 1977, CAS, 1978, EdD, 1982. Tchr. Arlington Heights Pub. Sch., Ill., 1973-75, 75-76, dir. libr. and learning ctr., 1976-81, tchr. lang. arts and reading jr. high sch., 1981-84, tchr. kindergarten, 1984-86; prin. Orchard St. Sch., Fox River Grove, Ill., 1988-89, Pritchett Sch., Buffalo Grove, Ill., 1989-90, Round Lake Ill., 1992-93, asst. supt. curriculum and instrn., 1993—; dir. Ill. State grant "At Risk Program" for pre-sch. children, Cary Pub. Schs., 1986-87; mem. part-time faculty Coll. of Edn., Roosevelt U., Chgo., 1983-84, 88-89; tchr. jr. high social, reading & lang. arts studies, 1988; cons. in field; mem. steering com. Curriculum 2000 Conf., De Kalb, Ill., 1985; lectr. in field; mem. registration com. Fall conf. IASCD, 1987; supr. student tchrs. Ill. State U., Normal, 1986, Roosevelt U., Chgo., 1988-89, Elmhurst Coll., 1992; freelance writer Daily Herald newspaper. Contbg. author: Feeling Good About Food. Sec. Scarsdale Estates Homeowners Assn., Arlington Heights, 1983; hon. life mem. PTA; bd. dirs. ABC/25 Found., 1991-92. Mem. Ill. Assn. for Supervision and Curriculum Devel. (triple I arrangements com. 1988, registration com. for fall conf. 1987), Ill. Assn. Tchrs. of English (cons., speaker conf. 1984), Ill. Women Adminstrs. (publicity com. conf. 1985), Phi Delta Kappa (bd. mem. 1992—). Avocation: playing guitar, calligraphy. Home: 402 E Orchard St Arlington Heights IL 60005-2660

PLACHE, KIMBERLY MARIE, state legislator; b. Racine, Wis., Jan. 4, 1961. Student, U. Wis., Whitewater, 1978-81; BS, U. Wis., Parkside-Kenosha, 1984. Legis. asst. to state rep. Jeff Neubauer, 1984-88; Wis. state assemblywoman Dist. 62, 1988—. Mem. NOW, AAUW, Wis. Action Coalition. Address: 2614 17th St Racine WI 53405 Office: Wis State Assembly State Capital Madison WI 53702*

PLACHTA, LEONARD E., academic administrator. Pres. Ctrl. Mich. U., Mt. Pleasant, Mich. Office: Ctrl Mich U Office of Pres Mount Pleasant MI 48859

PLANK, WILLIAM BRANDT, minister; b. Fond du Lac, Wis., Apr. 17, 1941; s. Lloyd Thomsen Plank and Helen Frances (Brandt) Plank Moersch; m. Susan Jane Hawthorne, June 29, 1963; children: David Hawthorne, Stephen Brandt, Elizabeth Anne. BA, Carleton Coll., 1963; MDiv, McCormick Theol. Seminary, Chgo., 1966; DMin, McCormick Theol. Seminary, 1986. Ordained minister Presbyn. Ch. Assoc. pastor Glen Avon Presbyn. Ch., Duluth, Minn., 1966-71, Highland Park (Ill.) Presbyterian Ch., 1971-76; pastor First Presbyn. Ch., Kankakee, Ill., 1976-81, Manitowoc, Wis., 1981—; staffing, nominating, evangelism coms., Winnebago Presbytery, N.E. Wis., 1994—, coun. mem., 1994—, moderator, 1986-87. Bd. dirs. Family Svc. Assn., Manitowoc, 1994—; sec./treas. Fairweather Lodge for Mentally Ill, Manitowoc, Wis., 1981—; founding bd. dirs. Peter's Pantry, Manitowoc, 1987-93. Mem. Rotary, Manitowoc County Clergy Assn. Home: 715 New York Ave Manitowoc WI 54220 Office: First Presbyterian Ch 502 N 8th St Manitowoc WI 54220

PLANTZ, CHRISTINE MARIE, librarian, union officer; b. Moscow, Idaho, July 28, 1946; d. John Albert and Marian Florence (Malm) Holmes; m. Charles Walter Plantz, May 19, 1973. BA, Shimer Coll., 1968; postgrad., U. Chgo. GLS, 1968-72; BS, Chadron State Coll., 1977. Children's libr. Chgo. Pub. Libr., 1969-73; libr. Rushville (Nebr.) Pub. Schs., 1974-77; tchr. Sheridan County Dist. 126, Rushville, 1979; libr. Bur. Indian Affairs, Pine Ridge, S.D., 1980—; tchr. Oglala Lakota Coll., 1994—; pres. local 150 Nat. Fedn. Fed. Employees, Pine Ridge, S.D., 1987-89, 91-92, 95—, sec. BIA coun., 1988—; owner LaserPress Desktop Pub., Rushville, 1992—; computer instr. Oglala Lakota Coll., Pine Ridge, S.D. Mem. Rushville City Coun., 1986-90, Rushville Pub. Libr. Bd., 1974-82; bd. dirs. Family Rescue Shelter, Gordon, Nebr., 1982-88, Black Hills Girl Scout Coun., Rapid City, S.D., bd. dirs. 1984—, pres. 1995—. Episcopalian. Home: PO Box 219 Rushville NE 69360-0219 Office: Laser Press PO Box 219 133 Main St Rushville NE 69360

PLASSMEYER, SUSAN ANNE, public policy analyst; b. Akron, Ohio, Oct. 9, 1963; d. Norbert Bernard and Eileen K. (Wade) P. BA, BS, N.E. Mo. State U., 1986; MBA in Fin., U. Chgo., 1990. First scholar, 1986-89; staff officer First Nat. Bank of Chgo., 1990-92, asst. v.p., 1992-93; dir. mktg. and ops. Environ. Law and Policy Ctr., Chgo., 1993—. Bd. dirs. Am. Cancer Soc. CanSurmount Program, Chgo., 1989-93; founder, tutor CHESS Tutor Program, Chgo., 1991—; treas. ACCION Chgo., 1994—. White House Fellowship Nat. finalist, Washington, 1993. Home: 1622 W Cornelia Ave Apt 1 Chicago IL 60657-1223

PLASTER, GEORGE FRANCIS, Roman Catholic priest; b. Lafayette, Ind., Dec. 6, 1950; s. Robert Lee and Ann Elizabeth (Klinker) P. BS in Econs. and Fin., St. Joseph's Coll., Rensselaer, Ind., 1973; MDiv, Sacred Heart Sch. of Theology, Hales Corners, Wis., 1980. Ordained Roman Cath. Priest, 1980. Bank examiner dept. fin. instns. State of Ind., Indpls., 1973-76; deacon, assoc. pastor St. Patrick Ch., Kokomo, Ind., 1979-82; assoc. pastor Our Lady Mt. Carmel (Ind.), 1982-86, St. Charles Ch., Peru, Ind., 1986-88, St. Joan of Arc Ch., Kokomo, 1988-89; hosp. chaplain St. Vincent's Hosp., Indpls., 1989—; spiritual counselor Jonah Ctr., Wabash, Ind., 1987-88; clin. pastoral educator Ctrl. State Hosp., Indpls., 1989-90, 91-92, 94-95. Mem. Nat. Right to Life, Washington, 1973—. Mem. Nat. Assn. Cath. Chaplains, KC (chaplain 1980-82, 84-85), Indpls. Cursillo (chaplain 1984, 89, 92). Office: St Vincent Hosp 2001 W 86th St Indianapolis IN 46240

PLATIS, CHRIS STEVEN, educator; b. East Chicago, Ind., May 21, 1926; s. Sam and Myra (Theodore) P.; m. Jeanette Brown. BS in Phys. Edn., Ind. U., 1955, MS in Edn., 1964, postgrad., 1965-68. Gen. foreman Cast Armor, Inc., East Chicago, 1951-53; tchr. East Chgo. and Ind. Pub. Schs., 1955—; asst. sports editor East Chgo. Calumet News, 1973-78; asst. dir. No. Ind. State Sports Mus., 1984-95. Author: Teaching Kids of Tomorrow, 1978. Master Boy Scouts Am., East Chicago, 1965-87; asst. recreational dir. North Twp., Northern Ind., 1993. With U.S. Army, 1944-46. Named to East Chgo. Hall of Fame All Am. Amateur Baseball Congress, 1955, 56, 57, Ind. Amateur Baseball Hall of Fame, 1962, U.S. Masters Track and Field All Am., 1995, 90 Yr. Greatest Athletes in East Chgo.'s History; recipient 12 league batting titles, 11 MVP awards, 16 times Ind. All State in Baseball, 21 times League Mgr. of Yr., Nat./European Tchr. of Yr., 1984; mem. team won 52 league championships, 53 playoff championships, 39 Ind. State baseball championships, 7 world regional titles, 5 world finalists, 2 runner-up world championships, Nat. C.I.O. baseball championship. Fellow VFW, Am. Legion, Normandy Invasion Club, Nat. Assn. of Basketball Coaches, Nat. Wildlife Assn. Republican. Home: 427 Fisher St Munster IN 46321

PLATIS, JAMES G., secondary school educator; b. Detroit, Mar. 23, 1927; s. Sam and Myra (Theodore) P.; m. Mary Lou Campbell, Aug. 16, 1974. BS in Physical Edn., Ind. U., 1955, MS in Edn., 1965; postgrad., Ind. State U., 1967. Cert. physical edn. tchr., Ind. Foreman Cast Armor, Inc., East Chicago, Ind., 1951-53, Youngstown Sheet & Tube, East Chicago, 1953-54; dir., tchr. East Chicago Pub. Schs., 1955—; sports editor East Chicago Globe/Calumet News, 1973-78, Herald Newspapers, Merrillville, Ind., 1973-78. Contbr. articles to newspapers, jours. Founder East Chicago Hall of Fame, 1975, Little Olympics, East Chicago, 1956; pres. Ind. Am. Amateur Baseball Congress, 1954-57, commr., 1984-96; dir. No. Ind. State Sports Mus., 1988-96. Cpl. AUS, 1945-47, ETO. Named to Ind. Amateur Baseball Hall of Fame, 1962, East Chicago Hall of Fame, 1976, All-Am. Amateur Baseball Congress, 1955, 56, The Athletic Congress Masters All-Am., 1986, 87, 88, 89, 90, 91, 92, 93, 94, 95, 96; selected to 90 Yr. Greatest Athletes in East Chicago History, Nat. Athletic Congress, 1990; named Amateur Coach of Yr., U.S. Baseball Fedn. Ind., 1990, Amateur Runner-up Coach of Yr., 1988; recipient 19 World and 27 Nat. No. 1 track rankings, Athletic Congress Masters, 1989, 90, 91, 92, 93, 94, 95, 96, 14 League Batting Titles, 12 MV League Players awards; 18 times Ind. all-state team; mem. team won 52 League Championships, 53 Playoff championships, 39 Ind. State Baseball Championships, 7 World Regional Titles, 5 World Finalists, 2 runner-up World Champions, Nat. C.I.O. Baseball Championship. Fellow Nat. Assn. Basketball Coaches, Am. Assn. Health, Phys. Edn. and Recreation; mem. Athletic Dirs. Assn. Sportswriters Guild, VFW, Am. Legion. Republican. Home: 427 Fisher St Munster IN 46321-2330 Office: E Chgo Pub Schs 2700 Cardinal Dr East Chicago IN 46312-3150

PLATT, ANN, animal care company executive. Owner, pres. Pets Are Inn, Mpls. Office: Pets Are Inn PO Box 27485 Minneapolis MN 55427*

PLATT, DWIGHT RICH, biology educator; b. Chgo., Aug. 4, 1931; s. Ferry Luther Platt and Selma Ione (Rich) Johnson; m. Edyth LaVonne Godwin, June 21, 1956; children: Kamala Joyce, Richard Dwight. B.S., Bethel Coll., 1952; M.A., U. Kans., 1954, Ph.D., 1966. Asst. instr. zoology U. Kans., Lawrence, 1952-54; edn. tech. Am. Friends Service Com., Barpali, Orissa, India, 1954-57; prof. biology Bethel Coll., North Newton, Kans., 1957-96, prof. emeritus, 1996—; vis. prof. biology Sambalpur U., Orissa, India, 1970-71; Contbr. articles on herpetology and prairie biology to profl. jours. Curator natural history Kauffman Mus., North Newton, Kans., 1982-92. Mem. Kans. Nongame Wildlife Adv. Council to Kans. Fish and Game Commn., 1980-87 , chmn. 1982-84. Coop. grad. fellow NSF, 1960-62. Mem. Kans. Acad. Sci. (pres. 1985), Kans. Ornithological Soc. (pres. 1969-70, 72-74), Kans. Herpetological Soc. (pres. 1992), Ecol. Soc. Am., Soc. Study Amphibians and Reptiles, Am. Ornithologists Union, Phi Beta Kappa. Avocations: birdwatching; gardening. Home: 702 NE 24th St Newton KS 67114-9275 Office: Bethel Coll North Dept Biology Newton KS 67117

PLATT, GEORGE MILO, university administrator; b. Rapid City, S.D., Jan. 1, 1931; s. George Lee and Josephine M. (Paulson) P.; B.S., S.D. State U., 1953; M.A., Syracuse U., 1955, Ph.D., 1962. Asst. prof. U. S.D., 1962-65, U. Iowa, 1965-69; dir. planning and instl. research Wichita (Kans.) State U., 1969-75, asso. v.p., 1979—; Ford Found. adv. to secs. of local govt., East and West Pakistan, 1963, 65-66, 68. Served with AUS, 1955-57. Mem. Am. Soc. for Public Adminstrn., Am. Polit. Sci. Assn., Midwest Polit. Sci. Assn., Western History Assn., Soc. for Coll. and Univ. Planning. Author: (with Richard O. Niehoff) Local Government in East Pakistan, 1964; (with Alan L. Clem) A Bibliography of South Dakota Government and Politics, 1965, (with others) Administrative Problems in Pakistan, 1966. Office: Wichita State Univ Off of VP Wichita KS 67208

PLATTHY, JENO, cultural association executive; b. Dunapataj, Hungary, Aug. 13, 1920; s. Joseph K. and Maria (Dobor) P.; m. Carol Louise Abell, Sept. 25, 1976. Diploma, Peter Pazmany U., Budapest, Hungary, 1942; PhD, Ferencz J. U., Kolozsvar, Hungary, 1944; MS, Cath. U., 1965; PhD (hon.), Yangmingshan U., Taiwan, 1975; DLitt (hon.), U. Libre Asie, Philippines, 1977. Lectr. various univs., 1956-59; sec. Internat. Inst. Boston, 1959-62; adminstrv. asst. Trustees of Harvard U., Washington, 1962-85; exec. dir. Fedn. Internat. Poetry Assns., UNESCO, 1976—; pub. New Muses Quar., 1976—. Author: Winter Tunes, 1974, Ch'u Yuan, His Life and Works, 1975, Springtide (opera), 1976, Bamboo, Collected Poems, 1981, The Poems of Jesus, 1982, Holiness in a Worldly Garment, 1984, Ut Pictures Poeta, 1984, European Odes, 1985, The Mythical Poets of Greece, 1985, Book of Dithyrambs, 1986, Asian Elegies, 1987, Space Ecologues, 1988, Cosmograms, 1988, Nova Comoedia, 1988, vols. II-III, 1992, Bartok: A Critical Biography, 1988, Plato: A Critical Biography, 1990, Near-Death Experiences in Antiquity, 1992, Celebration of Life, 1992, Idylls, 1992, Elegies Asiatiques, 1992, Paeans, 1993, Rhapsodies, 1994, Prosodia, 1994, Visions, 1994, Prophecies, 1994, Epyllia, 1994, Budapesttol Tokyoig, 1994, 2d edit., 1995, Walking Two Feet Above the Earth, 1995, Dictionarium Cumanico Hungaricum, 1996, Emblems, 1996, Epodes, 1996, Aeolian Lilts, 1996, Transformations, 1996, Inexpressions, 1996, Songs of the Soul, 1996, Sacrifices, 1996, numerous others, also translations; editor-in-chief Monumenta Classica Perennia, 1967-84. Named Poet Laureate 2d World Congress of Poets, 1973; recipient Confucius award Chinese Poetry Soc., 1974, Yunus Emre award 12th Internat. Congress of Poets, Istanbul, Turkey, 1991, Jacques Raphael-Leygues prize Société des Poètes Français, 1992, French Ordre des Arts et des Lettres (officer), 1992. Mem. PEN, ASCAP, Internat. Soc. Lit., Die Literarische Union, Internat. Poetry Soc., Acad. Am. Poets, Assn. Lit. Scholars and Critics, 3d Internat. Congress Poets (pres. 1976, poet laureate 1976). Office: UNESCO Fedn Internat Poetry Assns PO Box 579 Santa Claus IN 47579-0579

PLATTHY, TERRANCE LEE, accountant; b. Warren, Ohio, Apr. 15, 1950; s. Alexander B. and Vera M. (Vesey) P.; m. Sandra Jean Geltch, Oct. 22, 1968; children: Kerry L., Christina M., Amanda E. BSBA, Youngstown State U., 1973. CPA. Asst. project acct. Carter Green Joint Venture, Lordstown, Ohio, 1969-71; asst. mgr. Allied Constrn. Equip, Youngstown, Ohio, 1971-72; asst. controller United Svc. Corp., Youngstown, 1972-74; acctg. mgr. Anthony C. Davanzo, CPA, Youngstown, 1973-83; ops. mgr., v.p. sec. Davanzo, Platthy and Co., Inc., Youngstown, 1983-86; pres. Platthy, Sheffler and Co., Inc., Youngstown, 1986-90; Platthy & Assocs. Platthy, Clark & Assocs., 1990—; bd. dirs Dick Adlate Florist, Inc. Advisor Ursuline H.S. Devel. Comm., Youngstown, 1987; fin. com. advisor St. Joseph Ch. Mem. Youngstown C. of C., AICPA, Ohio Soc. CPAs., Sysop Youngstown Freenet Chess Club. Republican. Roman Catholic. Home: 4227 Claridge Dr Youngstown OH 44511-1011 Office: Platthy & Associates 103 W Market St #201 Warren OH 44481

PLEGGENKUHLE, LAVERN ROSS, business educator; b. Sumner, Iowa, Dec. 13, 1942; s. Ross Otto and Esther Selma (Bergman) P. BA, Wartburg Coll., 1965; MS in Teaching, U. Wis., Eau Claire, 1976. Tchr. bus. edn. Lancaster (Wis.) Sch. Dist., 1965-69, Campbellsport (Wis.) Schs., 1969-70, West Allis (Wis.) West Milw. Schs., 1970—; mem. adv. com. Project TYPIST U. Wis., Whitewater, 1979-82. Mem. NEA, Wis. Bus. Edn. Assn. (treas. 1986-90), Wis. Assn. Adults and Children with Learning Disabilities, Nat. Bus. Edn. Assn., Wis. Edn. Assn. Coun. Lutheran. Office: Cen High Sch 8516 W Lincoln Ave Milwaukee WI 53227-2543

PLIOPLYS, AUDRIUS VACLOVAS, neurologist, researcher; b. Toronto, Ont., Can., Sept. 14, 1951; Can. citizen; came to U.S., naturalized; MD, U. Chgo., 1975. Diplomate Am. Bd. Psychiatry and Neurology with Spl. Competence in Child Neurology, Royal Coll. Physicians and Surgeons Can.; cert. med. dir. Intern in adult internal medicine U. Wis. Hosps., Madison, 1975-76; resident in adult neurology Mayo Clinic, Rochester, Minn., 1979-80, 81-82, resident in gen. pediatrics, 1980-81, resident in electromyography, 1982; resident in gen. pediatrics Hosp. for Sick Children, Toronto, 1982-83, resident in pediatric neurology, 1983-84; Med. Rsch. Coun. Can. rsch. fellow in neuroimmunology Laval U., Quebec City, Que., Can., 1984-86; staff neurologist Hosp. for Sick Children and Surrey Place Ctr., 1986-89; project dir. Hosp. for Sick Children Inst., 1986-89; asst. prof. U. Toronto, U. Ill., Chgo.; mem. neurology staff, dir. Alzheimer's Disease Ctr., Mercy Hosp. and Med. Ctr., Chgo.; med. dir. Marklund Children's Home, Bloomingdale, Ill., Little Angels Nursing Home, Elgin, Ill., Philip J. Rock Sch. and Ctr., Glen Ellyn, Ill., Chronic Fatigue Syndrome Ctr., Mercy Hosp., Med. Ctr., Chgo., Alden Village Nursing Home, Bloomingdale, Ill.; mem. neurology staff Michael Reese Hosp., Chgo.; peer review cons. NIH, Bethesda, Md.; teaching asst. in neuroanatomy U. Chgo., Spring 1975; lectr. Chgo. Med. Soc., 1982, Rsch. Conf. on Autism, Goteborg, Sweden, 1989; vis. prof. neurology and neurosci. U. Vilnius, Lithuania, 1989. One man shows include Galerija, Stickney, Ill., 1980, 87, Washington Project for Arts, 1978, Dolly Fiterman Gallery, Mpls., 1980, 82, Contemporary Art Ctr. of Vilnius, Lithuania, 1995, Artemisia, Chgo., 1996; exhibited in group shows at Ciurlionis Gallery, Chgo., 1975, 90, 92, 93, Rockville (Md.) Civic Ctr., 1978, Visual Studies Workshop, Rochester, N.Y., 1979, Tweed Mus., Duluth, Minn., 1980, Lithuanian Mus. Art, Lemont, Ill., 1993, Art Gallery, Chgo., 1995, Art Ctr. of Douglas County, Colo., 1995, Berkeley (Calif.) Art Ctr., 1995, Chgo. Cultural Ctr., 1996, Mongerson Wunderlich Gallery, Chgo., 1996; contbr. 30 articles and 31 abstracts to med. jours. Recipient award for best rsch. and presentation Northwestern Pediatric Soc., 1981; rsch. fellow NIH, summers, 1971, 72, Parkinson's Disease Found., 1972-73, Mayo Clinic, summer, 1974; grantee Mayo Clinic Found., 1981-92, Physician Svcs. Inc. Found., 1987-88, Ont. Mental Health Found., 1989, Ill. Dept. Pub. Health,

1990-91, Michael Reese Hosp. Med. Rsch. Inst. Coun., 1990-91, Hoechst-Rousse Pharm. Co., 1991, CFS Assocs. Minn., 1994-95, Sigma-Tau Pharm. Co., 1993-95. Fellow Royal Coll. Physicians Can., Am. Acad. Pediatrics; mem. Am. Acad. Neurology, Child Neurology Sco., Soc. for Neurosci. Office: Mercy Hosp and Med Ctr Divsn Neurology Stevenson Expy at King Dr Chicago IL 60616

PLISEK, DON, design engineer; b. Enid, Okla., Mar. 21, 1950. AD in Mech. Tech., Coffeyville Jr. Coll., Coffey, Kans., 1970. Tech. engr. Pruest Industries, Independence, Kans., 1970; draftsman M-E-C Co., Independence, 1970-73; layout engr. Guaranteed Performance, Independence, 1973-74; process design engr. M-E-C, Neodesha, Kans., 1974—; cons. to cement plant in Fredonia, Kans., 1995. Bd. dirs. Rural Water Dist., Sycamore, Kans., 1995—; mem. Fire Dept., Sycamore, 1995—. Office: M-E-C PO Box 330 Neodesha KS 66757-0330

PLOGER, ROBERT RIIS, retired military officer, engineer; b. Mackay, Idaho, Aug. 12, 1915; s. Robert and Elfrieda (Riis) P.; m. Marguerite Anne Fiehrer, June 13, 1939 (dec. Feb. 1982); children: Wayne David, Robert Riis III, Daniel Bruce, Marguerite Anne, Marianne Ploger Hill, Gregory Fiehrer; m. Jeanne Allys Pray, Nov. 20, 1982. BS, U.S. Mil. Acad., 1939; MS in Engring., Cornell U., 1947; MBA, George Washington U., 1963. Registered civil engr., D.C. Commd. 2d lt. U.S. Army, 1939; served in corps of engrs. U.S. Army, ETO, Okinawa, 1939-65; advanced through grades to maj. gen. U.S. Army, 1966, div. engr. New England div., 1965, comdg. gen. 18th engr. brigade, 1965-66, comdg. gen. engr. command, Vietnam, 1966-67; dir. topography and mil. engring., Office Chief Engrs. U.S. Army, Washington, 1967-70; comdg. gen. Ft. Belvoir and commandant U.S. Army Engr. Sch. Va., 1970-73; ret. U.S. Army, 1973; engr. specialist Bechtel Power Corp., Ann Arbor, 1974-80, mgr. adminstrv. services, 1980-81; counselor SCORE, Ann Arbor, Mich., 1984—; lectr. Indsl. Coll. Armed Forces, 1962-65. Author: Vietnam Studies, U.S. Army Engineers 1965-70; contbr. numerous articles on war and mil. engring. to profl. jours. Chmn. gift com. Class of 1939 50th Reunion of U.S. Mil. Acad., 1985-89. Decorated DSM with oak leaf cluster, Legion of Merit, Silver Star with oak leaf cluster, Bronze Star with oak leaf cluster, Air medal, Purple Heart, Korean Order Mil. Merit Chung Mu, Nat. Order 5th Class Republic of Vietnam; recipient George Washington medal ICAF, 1965, Wheeler medal Soc. Am. Mil. Engrs., 1966, Silver Beaver award Boy Scouts Am., 1973, Médaille du Jubilé, Vire, France, 1994. Fellow Soc. Am. Mil. Engrs.; mem. NSPE (priviliged; chpt. pres. 1979-80), 29th Inf. Divsn. Assn. (Phila. award 1985), West Point Soc. Mich. (pres. 1981-84), SCORE (at-large exec. com. 1991, counselor chpt. 18), Ann Arbor C. of C. (counselor svc. corps ret. execs.), Army Engr. Assn. (life, Silver Order de Fleury medal 1995), SHAPE Officers Assn. (life). Baptist. Home: 2475 Adare Rd Ann Arbor MI 48104-4021

PLOMDON, DAVID S., state legislator; b. Stanley, Wis., May 27, 1961; s. William V. and Betty A. (Bernklau) P.; children: Mitchell S., Elizabeth N. AS, Milw. Area Tech. Coll., 1983. Assemblyman Wis. State Dist. 68, 1993—; agriculture, forestry & rural affairs com. Wis. State Assembly, 1993-94, sm. bus. and econ. devel. com., 1993—, edn., mandates & rural affairs com., 1995—, joint legis. coun. select com. child care econs., 1994—; funeral dir. Ryan Funeral Home, Madison, 1983-93, Plombon Funeral Home, Stanley, 1993—. Mem. Funeral Dirs. Assn. Address: PO Box 8953 Madison WI 53708

PLOTINSKY, ANITA H., research organization executive; b. N.Y.C., July 7, 1948; m. Melvin L. Plotinsky, Dec. 30, 1973; children: David, Benjamin, Miriam. MusB, Ind. U., 1970; MA, CUNY, 1972, PhD, 1978. Asst. dir. Ind. U. Ctr. Philanthropy, Indpls., 1989-94; exec. dir. Assn. for Rsch. on Nonprofit Orgns. and Voluntary Action, Indpls., 1994—; adj. asst. prof. Ind. U., Indpls., 1992—; spkr. and presenter on philanthropy. Contbr. articles and papers to profl. jours. Office: Ind U Ctr Philanthropy Ste 301 550 W North St Indianapolis IN 46202

PLUMMER, KENNETH ALEXANDER, communications executive; b. Chgo., Mar. 24, 1928; s. Alexander Oliver and Estella Marie (Koziol) P.; m. Marie M. Ricci, Oct. 10, 1943; children: Pamela, Diane, Kenneth, Stacy. Student North Cen. Coll., 1940-41, The Citadel, 1941-42, Far Eastern U. (Philippines), 1946-48. Commd. 2d lt. U.S. Army, 1943, advanced through grades to col., 1966, ret., 1973; dir. Ancilla Domini Health Svcs., Inc., Des Plaines, Ill., 1973-82; dir. Oak Park Hosp. (Ill.), 1982-85; pres., chmn. Cable TV Communications, Inc., Oak Park, 1985-90, ret.; chmn. Travel Adventures. Chmn. Vets. Adv. Commn. City of Chgo., 1986-87, Village Oak Park Bd. Health; cons. Cambodian Refugee Program for Cath. Relief Svs.; installed med. relief teams in Cambodian refugee camps; bd. dirs. USO of Ill.; chmn. WWII Commemorative and D-Day Reenactment com. City of Chgo. Decorated Silver Star, Bronze Star, Combat Infantry badge, Meritorious Svc. medal, Army Commendation medal; recipient Assn. of U.S. Army citation, 1961, Res. Officers Assn. award, 1964, Cath. Relief Svc. award, 1980; Ancilla Domini Sisters award, 1980. Mem. Mil. Order World Wars (comdr. 1962-63), Ret. Officers Assn., USO of Ill. (bd. dir.), Vets. of Am. (vice chmn. Vaughn Chpt. Paralyze D). Roman Catholic. Home: 415 N Elmwood Ave Oak Park IL 60302-2225 Office: Cable TV Commmunications Inc 715 Lake St Ste 275A Oak Park IL 60301-1411

PLUSQUELLIC, DONALD L., mayor; b. Akron, Ohio, July 3, 1949; m. Mary Plusquellic; children: Dave, Michelle. BS, Bowling Green State U., 1972; JD, U. Akron, 1981. Councilman Akron City Council, 1973-81, councilman-at-large, 1982-86, council pres., 1984-86; mayor City of Akron, 1987—. Home: 2785 Nesmith Lake Blvd Akron OH 44314-3427 Office: Office of the Mayor 200 Municipal Bldg 166 S High St Akron OH 44308

PLYLER, CONRAD A., military officer; b. Columbia, S.C., May 15, 1946; s. Conrad A. and Louisa B. (Banks) P.; m. Candida C. Crane, July 8, 1972. BSME with merit, U.S. Naval Acad., 1968. Commd. ensign USN, 1968, advanced through grades to capt., 1989; engring. divsn. officer USS James Madison, USS James K. Polk, Charleston, S.C., 1969-74; asst. material officer Submarine Squadron IV, Charleston, S.C., 1974-77; chief engr. USS Gato, New London, Conn., 1977-80; exec. officer USS Daniel Boone, Charleston, 1980-83; comdg. officer USS Casimir Pulaski, Charleston, 1983-87; chief of naval ops. fellow Ctr. for Naval Analyses, Alexandria, Va., 1987-89; head, analysis br. Office of the Chief of Naval Ops., Pentagon, Washington, 1989-91; comdg. officer USS Nevada, Bangor, Wash., 1991-93; exec. ast. to dep. C-in-C U.S. Strategic Command, Offutt AFB, Nebr., 1993-96; dir. doctrine devel. Naval Doctrine Command, Norfolk, Va., 1996—. Mem. Mil. Ops. Rsch. Soc., Am. Soc. of Naval Engrs., U.S. Naval Inst., Am. Legion, Submarine Vets. of WWII (assoc.), U.S. Naval Submarine League. Republican. Episcopalian. Office: US Strategic Command 901 Sac Blvd Offutt AFB NE 68113-6000

POAGE, ROY L., animal breeder; b. 1932. BS, Tex. Tech. U. Exec. v.p. Lubbock (Tex.) Swine Breeders, 1961-72; with DeKalb (Ill.) Swine Breeders, Inc., 1972—, pres., 1980—. Office: DeKalb Swine Breeders Inc 3100 Sycamore Rd De Kalb IL 60115*

POCZOS, GARY MICHAEL (A.B. SEYMORE), author, illustrator; b. Melrose Park, Ill., Dec. 5, 1963; s. Anton Joseph Poczos and Delores Lynn (Harlan) Seyfried; m. Kimberly Marie Jacobsen, Apr. 29, 1989. Student, William Rainey Harper Coll., Palatine, Ill., U. Wis., Milw. Pres. ABC's & More Co., Milw. Author, illustrator: (children's books) I Can Top That!, 1992, There Ought To Be a Law!, 1993, Would You Holler for a Dollar?, 1993, School Is Cool!, 1993, How the Snoots Almost Got Snuffed, 1993, Nursery Rhymes and Other Tales, 1994, The Thoughts In My Head..., 1995, The Sleeplessness Book, 1996. Recipient Arrow of Light award Boy Scouts Am., St. Paul Fed. grant, Wis. Higher Edn. grant. Mem. Zool. Soc. Am., Nat. Wildlife Fed., Nat. Geographic Soc., Wis. Arts Bd., Soc. Children's Book Writers and Illlustrators, Nat. Writers Assn., Puppeteers Am., Inc. Roman Catholic. Home and Office: 4850 S 69th St Ste 3 Milwaukee WI 53220-4454

PODBOY, ALVIN MICHAEL, JR., lawyer, law library director; b. Cleve., Feb. 10, 1947; s. Alvin Michael and Josephine Esther (Nagode) P.; m. Mary Ann Gloria Esposito, Aug. 21, 1971; children: Allison Marie, Melissa Ann. AB cum laude, Ohio U., 1969; JD, Case Western Res. U., 1972, MLS, 1977. Bar: Ohio 1972, U.S. Dist. Ct. (no. dist.) Ohio 1973, U.S. Supreme Ct. 1992. Assoc. Joseph T. Svete Co. LPA, Chardon, Ohio, 1972-76; dir. pub. services Case Western Res. Sch. Law Libr., Cleve., 1974-77, assoc. law libr., 1977-78; libr. Baker & Hostetler, Cleve., 1978-88, dir. librs., 1988—; instr. Notre Dame Coll. of Ohio, Cleve., 1991—, Am. Inst. Paralegal Studies, Cleve., 1991-96. Bd. overseers Case Western Res. U., 1981-87, mem. vis. com. sch. libr. sci., 1980-86, mem. Westlaw adv. bd., 1987-92, bd. govs. law sch. alumni assn., 1992-95, West's Legal Directory Ohio Adv. Panel, 1990-91; mem. adv. com. West's Info. Innovators Inst., 1995—; chmn. Case Western Res. Libr. Sch. Alumni Fund, 1979-80. Rep. precinct committeeman Cuyahoga County, Cleve., 1981-95, mem. exec. com., 1984-87. 1st lt. USAF, 1972. Mem. ABA, Ohio State Bar Assn. (chmn. libraries com. 1989-91), Cleve. Bar Assn., Am. Assn. Law Librs. (cert., chmn. pvt. law librs. spl. interest sect. 1994-95), Ohio Regional Assn. Law Librs. (pres. 1985), Case Western Res. U. Libr. Sch. Alumni Assn. (pres. 1981), Arnold Air Soc., Am. Legion, Pi Gamma Mu, Phi Alpha Theta. Roman Catholic. Lodge: K.C. Avocations: alpine skiing, boating. Home: 5705 Deercreek Dr Willoughby OH 44094 Office: Baker & Hostetler 3200 National City Ctr Cleveland OH 44114-3485

PODGORSKI, ROBERT PAUL, human resources executive; b. Chgo., July 18, 1943; s. Joseph Paul and Lillian Violet (Zahara) P.; m. Constance Francis Moore, Sep. 4, 1965; children: Debra Lynn, Katherine Ann, David Joseph. Student, Wright Community Col., Chicago, 1966-75; Roosevelt U., 1975-78. Personnel specialist Teletype Corp., Skokie, Ill., 1961-75; mgr. human res. North Am. Philips Corp. subs., Skokie, Alliance, Ill., Oh., 1975-79; dir. empl. and staffing Northrop Corp., Rolling Meadows, Ill., 1979-89, 90—; v.p. human res. Gen. Datacom Ind., Inc., Middlebury, Conn., 1989-90, Benton Schneider & Assoc., Inc., Lisle, Ill., 1990; pres. Corporate Relocation Coun., Chgo., 1986-88; cons. princ. RPP Ent., Chgo., 1982-91; chmn. Human Resources North Bus. and Ind. Coun., Chgo., 1975-76. Contbr. articles to profl. jours. Co-chmn., dir. Chicagoland Proj. with Ind., 1980—. Recipient Decade of Leadership award, Electronics Ind. Found., 1990. Mem. Electronics Personnel Assn. (editor 1982-90, pres. 1984), Human Resources Assn. (editor 1990, bd. dirs. Oakbrook chpt.), Employment Mgmt. Assn. (regional dir. 1989—, Pericles award 1987), Soc. Human Res. Mgmt. Republican. Roman Catholic. Office: Northrop Grumman Corp Elec Sys & Integration Div 600 Hicks Rd Rolling Meadows IL 60008-1015

PODLESNY, LAURA ANN, public relations executive; b. Chgo., Feb. 26, 1962; d. John Jerome and Rose (Szczesny) P. BA in Journalism/Pub. Rels., No. Ill. U., 1984. Accredited pub. rels. profl. Media specialist Mid-Am. chpt. ARC, Chgo., 1984-86; dir. pub. rels. Lifeline-Cocaine Treatment Program, Skokie, Ill., 1986-88; pub. rels. cons. Frankel & Co., Chgo., 1988-89; mgr. pub. rels. Midway Airlines, Chgo., 1989-91; pres. Visible Results Pub. Rels., Chgo., 1992—; acct. supr. Edelman Worldwide Pub. Rels., 1992-94, Ameritech Corp., 1994—; media cons. Colvin Communications; pub. rels. cons. Arthur Andersen & Co. Vol. Chgo. Starlight Found., 1989—, Multiple Sclerosis Soc., Chgo., 1988—, Juvenile Diabetes Found., Chgo., 1986—, Ill. Spl. Olympics, 1990-91; bd. dirs. Theatre Bldg. Mem. Pub. Rels. Soc. Am., Am. Soc. Profl. Exec. Women. Roman Catholic. Office: 23D 225 W Randolph St Chicago IL 60606

PODMOKLY, PATRICIA GAYLE, typesetting company professional; b. Chgo., May 15, 1940; d. Edwin Paul Baker and Frances (Williams) Popiela. Grad., Jones Comml. Sch., Chgo. Bookkeeper, sec. William C. Douglas & Ralph Falk II, Lake Forest, Ill., 1958—; owner Global Graphics, Inc., Elmhurst, Ill., 1987—. Roman Catholic. Home: 50 Lindy Blvd Elk Grove Village IL 60007

PODOLSKE, DIANE LYNNE, management consultant; b. Madison, Wis., Jan. 13, 1966; d. Wesley Robert and Marilyn Elvina (Schoess) P. BA in Psychology, S.W. State U., 1988; MA in Counseling, U. Nebr., 1990, post-grad., 1990—. Adminstrv. asst. S.W. State U., Marshall, Minn., 1985-87, peer adviser, 1987-88; rsch. asst. Bethesda Med. Ctr., St. Paul, 1986; adminstrv. asst. New Ulm (Minn.) Pub. Utilities, 1986-87, Countryside Coun., Marshall, 1987-88; grad. asst. for edn. rsch. U. Nebr., Lincoln, 1989-90, grad. asst. for leadership devel., campus activities, 1990-93; leadership cons., 1993-94, multi-cultural edn. cons., 1995—; presenter in field. Contbr. chpt. to: Evaluation in Student Housing, 1993. Adv. S.W. Minn. Sexual Assault Program, Marshall, 1987-88; bd. dirs. Women's Resource Ctr., Lincoln, 1990-92; mem. Chancellor's Commn. on Status of Women, 1992-93. Recipient Gerald Saddlemire Outstanding Grad. Student award, 1992, John A. Glover Meml. Rsch. award, 1993, Rising Star award NASPA, 1994. Mem. Am. Coll. Pers. Assn., Nebr. Coll. Pers. Assn., Psi Chi, Pi Gamma Mu. Home: 34 N Highland Ave New Ulm MN 56073-2032 Office: U Nebr-Lincoln 220 Adminstrn Bldg Lincoln NE 68588

PODZIMEK-KOTYSAN, JANA, surgeon; b. Prague, Czechoslovakia, Dec. 30, 1956; came to U.S., 1970; d. Josef and Miroslava (Curinová) P. BS, U. Mo., Rolla, 1978; MS, S.W. Mo. State U., 1980; DO, Kirksville Coll. Osteo. Med., 1984. Intern Garden City (Mich.) Osteo. Hosp., 1984-85, resident, 1985-86; resident Flint (Mich.) Osteop. Hosp., 1986-89; joint practice specializing in ENT/head and neck surgery Pekin, Ill., 1989-92; solo pvt. practice specializing in otorhinolaryngology/head and neck surgery, Pekin, 1992—. Mem. AMA, Am. Osteo. Assn., Am. Acad. Osteopathy, Tazewell County Med. Assn., Am. Osteo. Colls. of Ophthal. and Otolaryngology, Head and Neck Surgery, Am. Acad. Facial Plastic and Reconstructive Surgery (assoc.), Ill. Assn. Osteo. Physicians and Surgeons. Office: 1503 Valle Vista Blvd Pekin IL 61554-6239

POE, RAYMOND, state legislator; m. Carol Poe; children: Collette, Cherrilyn, Lance. Mem. Ill. State Ho. of Reps. Dist. 99, 1995—. Bd. mem. Williamsvill Cmty. H.S.; farm bur. rep. State Coun. on Bus. Edn. Partnership; exec. bd. mem. Farm Bur.

POE-JACKSON, GERTIE LAVERNE, sales executive; b. Chgo., Feb. 7, 1949; d. L.C. and Gertrude (Winfrey) Poe. BSBA, Roosevelt U., 1978, MBA, 1984. Policy analyst Continental Bank, Chgo., 1971-87; fin. planner IDS/Am. Express, Merrillville, Ind., 1987-89; sales rep. Valic, Chgo., 1990-94, Invest Fin. Svcs., Bridgeview, IL, 1994—. Mem. Sigma Gamma Rho. Baptist. Home: PO Box 19201 Chicago IL 60619-0201 Office: Invest Fin Svcs Bridgeview Bank & Trust 7940 S Harlem Ave Bridgeview IL 60455-1500

POETTER, BRUCE E., real estate executive; b. Berwyn, Ill., May 28, 1951; s. Robert K. and Nancy Marie (Classen) P.; m. Barbara Jo Nylander, Oct. 11, 1975; children: Brian E., Bradley J. BA, Hope Coll., 1974. Real estate appraiser Thorsen Realtors, Oak Brook, Ill., 1974-77, chief appraiser, 1977-81; asst. v.p. Coldwell Banker, Oak Brook, 1981-83, v.p., regional mgr., 1983-88; pres. Real Estate Valuation Svcs., La Grange, Ill., 1988-89; dir. real estate valuation svcs. Ernst & Young, Chgo., 1990-91; pres. Real Estate Valuation Svcs., La Grange, Ill., 1992—; real estate instr. Ill. Dept. Edn., Springfield, 1977—; sr. instr. U.S. League of Savs. Instns., 1985—. Mem. Appraisal Inst. (bd. dirs., chmn. Chgo. chpt. edn. com., pub. rels. com. 1976-84, life mem. young adv. coun. 1981, sr. instr. 1979—). Republican. Presbyterian.

POFELSKI, MARK A., city purchasing manager, computer service owner; b. Chgo., Jan. 14, 1951; s. William Joseph Pofelski and Annette May (Spreitzer) Powell; m. Patricia Santa Cruz, Aug. 21, 1993. Student Mgmt. and Mktg., Coll. of Du Page, 1979. Custom designer pvt. practice, Chgo., 1971-75; ops. mgr. F.C. Prodns., Crete, Ill., 1975-77; svc. mgr. Camp-Land, Inc., Merrillville, Ind., 1977-79; asst. ops. mgr. Wilco Food Ctr., Lowell, Ind., 1979-81; pruchasing agt. Carson, Pirie Scott & Co., Chgo., 1981-87; purchasing mgr. City of Chgo., 1987—; proprietor Fair Elms Data Svc., Chgo., 1994—. Mem. Nat. Inst. Govtl. Purchasing (cert. pub. purchasing officer). Home: 10400 S Avenue H Chicago IL 60617 Office: Fair Elms Data Sve 3647 E 106th St Ste 175 Chicago IL 60617

POFFENBERGER, DAVID JOHN, plant manager; b. Auburn, Ind., Sept. 12, 1959; s. John Phillip and Barbara Lou (Rice) P.; m. Lori Lynn Burger, Nov. 28, 1981; children: Ryan, Kelsie. AS, Ind. U., Ft. Wayne, 1981, 82; BS, Purdue U., 1984. Salesman Edison Bros., Ft. Wayne, Ind., 1978-81; warehouse shipping clk. Dana Corp., Ft. Wayne, 1978-81; product engr. Dana Corp., Churubusco, Ind., 1981-84, catalog mgr., 1984-87; product mgr. Dana Corp., Toledo, Ohio, 1987-89, mktg. mgr., 1990-91; mktg. mgr. Brown Bros. Ltd.-Dana Corp., Swindon, Eng., 1990-91; mgr. Dana Corp., Manteca, Calif., 1991-94; distbn. svcs. mgr. Copeland Corp., Fishers, Ind., 1994—. Office: Copeland Corp 9901 Kincaid Dr Fishers IN 46038

POGEMILLER, LAWRENCE J., state legislator; b. Sept. 18, 1951; 010. BS, U. Minn.; MPA, Harvard U. Mem. Minn. Ho. of Reps. St. Paul, 1981-82; U.S. senator from Minn., 1983—; chmn. edn. funding divsn. com., co-chmn. edn. com., mem. higher edn. divsn. com., tax laws com., others.; system project analyst. Democrat. Address: 201 University Ave NE Minneapolis MN 55413-2250 also: State Senate State Capital Building Saint Paul MN 55155-1606*

POGUE, RICHARD WELCH, lawyer; b. Cambridge, Mass., Apr. 26, 1928; s. Lloyd Welch and Mary Ellen (Edgerton) P.; m. Patricia Ruth Raney, July 10, 1954; children: Mark, Tracy, David. B.A., Cornell U., 1950; J.D., Mich. Law Sch., 1953. Bar: Mich. 1953, Ohio 1957, U.S. Dist. Ct. (no. dist.) Ohio 1960, U.S. Ct. Appeals (6th cir.) 1972, U.S. Ct. Appeals (D.C. and 9th cirs.) 1979. Assoc. Jones, Day, Reavis & Pogue, Cleve., 1957-60, ptnr., 1961—, mng. ptnr., 1984-92, sr. ptnr., 1993-94; sr. advisor Dix & Eaton, Cleve., 1994—; vis. prof. Mich. Law Sch., 1993-95; bd. dirs. Derlan Industries, Toronto, Continental Airlines, Inc., Houston, OHM Corp., Findlay, Ohio, M.A. Hanna Co., Cleve., Redland PLC, Reigate, Eng., Rotek Inc., Aurora, Ohio, Key Corp., Cleve, TRW Inc. Cleve. Chmn. Cleve. Found, 1985-89, Greater Cleve. Roundtable, 1986-89, Greater Cleve. Growth Assn., 1991-93, Univ. Hosps., 1994—, truste 1975—, Cleve. Ballet, 1983-85, United Negro Coll. Fund, Cleve., 1979. Mem. Adminstrv. Conf. U.S., 1974-80; vice chmn. Cleve. Tomorrow, 1988-93, 50 Club Cleve., 1988-89; United Way Cleve., 1989; trustee Case Western Res. U.; active Coun. Fgn. Rels., 1989—, Am./EC Assn. Bus. Adv. Coun., 1988-93; toun., 1988-93; trustee Rock and Roll Hall of Fame and Mus., 1986—; co-chmn 1996 Cleve. Bicentennial Commn., interim chmn. Cleve. Inst. Music, 1994. Army, 1954-57. Recipient Outstanding Alumnus award U. Mich. Club., Cleve., 1983, Torch of Liberty award Anti-Defamation League, 1989, Leadership Cleve. Vol. of Yr. award, 1990, 1st Econ. Devel. Workshop award Nat. Coun. on Urban Econ. Devel., 1992, Humanitarian award Nat. Conf. Christians and Jews, 1992. Mem. ABA (chmn. antitrust sect. 1983-84), Ohio State Bar Assn. (chmn. antitrust sect. 1969-73). Republican. Mem. United Ch. of Christ. Clubs: Bohemian (San Francisco), Soc., Union (Cleve.), Metropolitan (Washington), Links (N.Y.C.).

POGUE, THOMAS FRANKLIN, economics educator, consultant; b. Roswell, N.Mex., Dec. 28, 1935; s. Talmadge Franklin and Lela (Cox) P.; m. Colette Marie LaFortune, June 3, 1961; children: Michael Frederick, Robert Franklin. BS, N.Mex. State U., 1957; MS, Okla. State U., 1962; PhD, Yale U., 1968. Asst. prof. econs. U. Iowa, Iowa City, 1965-69, assoc. prof., 1970-75, prof., 1975—, chmn. dept., 1983-84; vis. prof. Tex. Tech. U., Lubbock, 1975-76, U. Adelaide, Australia, 1985, 89. Author: Government and Economic Choice, 1978; editor: State Taxation of Business, 1992; contbr. articles to profl. jours.; cons. on tax policy, welfare reform, pub. sch. fin., and econ. devel. in Iowa, 1992, Minn., 1984, Ariz., 1989, and local govts. Commd. officer with USAF, 1957-60. Grantee Nat. Inst. Justice, Washington, 1979, U.S. Dept. Transp., 1994. Mem. Am. Econ. Assn., Nat. Tax Assn. Democrat. Avocation: tennis. Home: 3 Wellesley Way Iowa City IA 52245-3830 Office: U Iowa Dept Econs 108 Pappajohn Bus Adminstrn Bldg Iowa City IA 52242

POHL, DANIEL MARTIN, college administrator; b. Syracuse, N.Y., Jan. 9, 1959; s. Raymond Alan Pohl and Ann (Baule) Bottrill; m. Kimberly Dawn Younkin, June 30, 1990. BA, Otterbein Coll., 1981; MA, Miami U., Oxford, Ohio, 1988. Admission counselor Otterbein Coll., Westerville, Ohio, 1982-86, asst. dir. admissions, 1986-89; dir. alumni rels. Wilmington (Ohio) Coll., 1989—. Advisor Wilmington Coll. Student Found., 1989—, Wilmington Coll. Sr. Class, 1991—; mem. Coun. for Advancement and Support of Edn., 1989—, Ind. Coll. Advancement Assocs., 1989—, Good Shepherd United Meth. Ch., Circleville, Ohio, 1990—; youth counselor, mem. Ch. of the Messiah, Westerville, 1984-90. Home: 720 N Pickaway St Circleville OH 43113-1449 Office: Wilmington Coll PO Box 1313 Wilmington OH 45177

POHL, DAVID L., diagnostic radiologist; b. Greenville, Ohio, June 11, 1954; s. Lavern F. and Rita A. (Dapore) P.; m. Kathleen E. Burke, Oct. 1, 1993; 1 child, Megan M. BA, Miami U., Oxford, Ohio, 1976; MA, U. N.C., 1979; MD, Washington U., St. Louis, 1985. Diplomate Am. Bd. of Radiology. Resident in radiology St. Louis U., 1985-89; diagnostic radiologist Ctrl Radiology Group, St. Louis, 1989—. Mem. AMA, Am. Coll. Radiology, Mo. Radiol. Soc., Mo. State Med. Assn., Greater St. Louis Radiol. Soc., St. Louis Met. Med. Soc. Office: Ctrl Radiology Group 6150 Oakland Ave Saint Louis MO 63139

POHL, KATHLEEN SHARON, editor; b. Sandusky, Mich., Apr. 7, 1951; d. Gerald Arthur and Elizabeth Louise (Neukamm) P.; m. Bruce Mark Allen Reynolds, June 11, 1982. BA in Spanish, Valparaiso U., 1973; MA in English, No. Mich. U., 1975. Producer, dir. fine arts Sta. WNMU-FM, Marquette, Mich., 1981-82; instr. communications Waukesha County (Wis.) Tech. Inst., 1983; editor Ideals mag., Milw., 1983-85; editor, mng. editor Raintree Pubs., Milw., 1985-87; mng. editor Country Woman mag., Greendale, Wis., 1987—; exec. editor Country Handcrafts mag., Greendale, 1990-93, Taste of Home Mag., Greendale, Wis., 1993—; editor Talk About Pets, Greendale, 1994-95. Author nature book series, 1985-87; sr. editor: Country Woman Christmas Book, 1996; mng. editor: Irwin the Sock (Chgo. Book Clinic award 1988). Mem. Internat. Platform Assn., Nat. Mus. of Women in Arts, Alpha Lambda Delta (hon.). Home: N54w26326 Lisbon Rd Sussex WI 53089-4249 Office: Country Woman Mag 5400 S 60th St Greendale WI 53129-1404

POHLAD, CARL R., professional baseball team executive, bottling company executive; b. West Des Moines, Iowa. Ed., Gonzaga U. With MEI Diversified, Inc., Mpls., 1959—, chmn. bd., 1976—; pres. Marquette Bank Mpls., N.A., pres., dir.; pres., dir. Bank Shares, Inc.; owner Minn. Twins, 1985—; dir. Meth. Hosp. Adminstrv. Group, T.G.I. Friday's, Tex. Air Corp., Ea. Airlines, Continental Air Lines, Inc., Carlson Cos. Inc. Address: Minnesota Twins 501 Chicago Ave S Minneapolis MN 55415*

POHLMAN, CARLYLE GEORGE, retired accountant; b. Lakefield, Minn., Aug. 31, 1931; s. George Reinhold and Lillian (Burmeister) P.; m. Marion Milbrath, Aug. 10, 1952; children: Scott, Laurie Sue, Lisa. BBA, U. Minn., 1953. Mem. staff Touche Ross & Co., Mpls., 1955-65, adm. ptnr., 1965-75, dir. audit ops., 1975-80, assoc. ptnr. in charge, 1980-82, ptnr. in charge, 1982-88, sr. ptnr., 1988-90; ret., 1991. Commodore Mpls. Aquatennial Assn., 1984; bd. dirs., v.p. devel. United Arts Coun., St. Paul, 1985-87; bd. dirs. Minn. Orchestral Assn., 1987-90. 1st lt. USAF, 1953-55. Mem. Nat. Assn. Accts. (pres. Mpls. chpt. 1966-67, nat. bd. dirs. 1967-68), Minn. Soc. CPAs (bd. dirs. 1982-85), Mpls. C. of C., Mpls. Club, Interlachen Country Club. Lutheran. Home: PO Box 370 11657 Gulden Ave NW Maple Lake MN 55358-2323

POHLMAN, WILLIAM JOHN, advertising executive; b. Berwyn, Ill., June 27, 1954; s. Alfred H. and Doris M. (Faust) P.; m. Loretta Z. Pohlman, Aug. 25, 1984; 1 child, Caroline M. AA, Morton Coll., Cicero, Ill., 1974; BS, No. Ill. U., DeKalb, 1976. Cert. bus. communicator. Asst. product promotion mgr. Motorola, Inc., Schaumburg, Ill., 1976-80; account exec. Rylander Co., Chgo., 1980; v.p., account supr., co-owner Anderson Perlstein Ltd., Buffalo Grove, Ill., 1981—. Mem. Bus./Profl. Advt. Assn. (pres. 1994-95, New Mem. of Yr. 1988), Palatine Jr. C. of C. Office: Anderson Perlstein Ltd 1330 Busch Pkwy Buffalo Grove IL 60089-4501

POHLMANN, PATTY LOU, college official; b. Duluth, Minn., Nov. 11, 1939; d. Lewis A. and Josephine (Mainella) Gooler; m. William Albert Pohlmann, June 9, 1962; children: William Andrew, Barry Alan. BS, U. Wis., Milw., 1961, MS, 1972. Cert. secondary English and speech tchr., Wis. Tchr. English Brookfield (Wis.) East High Sch., 1961-66; substitute tchr. Manitowoc (Wis.) Pub. Schs., 1981-86; lectr. U. Wis., Sheboygan, 1984; instr. Doctor's Clinic, Two Rivers, Wis., 1985; lectr. Silver Lake Coll., Manitowoc, 1983-86, asst. dir. devel., 1986-87, dir. devel., 1988-90, v.p.

devel., 1990—, mem. Speakers' Bur., 1983—. Mem. bd. edn., v.p. coun., chair bd. pers., coun. pres. 1st Luth. Ch., Manitowoc, 1972—, pres. coun. 1993-94; merit badge counselor Boy Scouts Am., Manitowoc, 1984—; assoc. mem. Jr. Svc. League, chmn. charity ball, 1980-82; vol. solicitor Wis. Found. Ind. Colls. Recipient Rahr award Jr. Svc. League, 1984, Ariel award Silver Lake Coll., 1987; Newcomer scholar Coun. Advancement and Support Edn., 1988. Mem. PEO (chpt. CD), Wis. Assn. Ind. Colls. and Univs., Bus. Profl. Women (Bus. Woman of Yr. 1992), Manitowoc-Two Rivers Area C. of C., Rotary (past v.p., pres. 1995-96, Paul Harris fellow). Republican. Office: Silver Lake Coll 2406 S Alverno Rd Manitowoc WI 54220-9340

POINDEXTER, BEVERLY KAY, media and communications professional; b. Noblesville, Ind., Nov. 12, 1949; d. Wayne Francis and Rosalie Christine (Nightenhelser) Hunter; m. Jerry Roger Poindexter, Dec. 7, 1969; children: Nick Ashley, Tracy Lynne, Wendy Dawn, Cory Matthew. Student, Purdue U. Editor Tri Town Topics Newspaper, 1965-69; reporter, photographer Noblesville Daily Ledger, 1969-70; asst. mgr., sales mgr., sports dir. Sta. WHYT Radio, Noblesville, Ind., 1973-79; sales mgr., music dir., DJ, news Sta. WBMP Radio, Elwood, Ind., 1979-88; acct. exec. Stas. WAXT-WHBU Radio, Anderson, Ind., 1988-89; gen. mgr., sales mgr. Sta. WEWZ, Elwood, Ind., 1989-90; now news stringer Sta. WRTV-6, Indpls., Sta. WTHR TV-13, Indpls.; acct. exec. Sta. WLHN Radio, Elwood, Ind.; real estate broker Booker Realty, Cicero, Ind., 1990—. Area rep. Am. Field Svc.. Hamilton County, Ind.; pres. bd. dirs. Hamilton Heights Elem. Football, Arcadia, Ind., 1981-83; founder, chmn. Hamilton Heights Elem. Cheerleaders, Arcadia, 1981-87; youth leader, counselor Ch. of the Brethren, Arcadia, 1991-94; active Ch. of Brethren Women's Fellowship. Mem. Nat. Assn. Realtors, Ind. Assn. Realtors, Met. Indpls. Bd. Realtors. Republican. Home: 14645 E 281st St Atlanta IN 46031-9722 Office: Booker Realty PO Box 437 99 S Peru Cicero IN 46034

POINDEXTER, KATHLEEN A. KRAUSE, nursing educator, critical care nurse; b. Platteville, Wis., Aug. 30, 1956; d. Gene A. and Catherine E. (Boyle) Gilbertson; m. David L. Poindexter, July 20, 1990; children: Nicholas, Brendon, Ashley, Anna, Steve. BA in Nursing, Coll. of St. Scholastica, Duluth, Minn., 1978; MSN, No. Mich. U., Marquette, 1990. RN, Minn., Mich.; cert. ACLS, BCLS instr.; PALS. Staff nurse pediatrics ICU St. Mary's Med. Ctr., Duluth, 1978-83, head nurse pediatrics/pediatric ICU, 1983-85; clin. III staff nurse ICU/critical care unit Marquette Gen. Hosp., 1985-88; staff nurse critical care unit Bell Meml. Hosp., Ishpeming, Mich., 19909—; assoc. prof. No. Mich. U. Sch. Nursing, Marquette, 1988-96, 1996—; researcher in field. Mem. coll. adv. coun., mem. faculty grante com. No. Mich. U.; advisor, founder No. Mich. U. Practical Nurses Assn. Recipient Excellence in Edn. award; Exemplary Citizen award, 1995. Mem. AACN (edn. advisor), AAUP (staff coun.), ANA, Am. Heart Assn., Hursing Honor Soc. (sec.), Sigma Theta Tau. Home: 1806 Gray St Marquette MI 49855-1546

POINTER, PETER LEON, investment executive; b. Erie, Pa., Aug. 3, 1934; s. Leon Royce and Katherine (Hermen) P.; m. Linda Milla Jensen, Sept. 21, 1957; children: Philip Leon, David Andrew. BS in Econs., U. Pa., 1956; MBA, U. Mo., 1968. V.p. Roose-Wade & Co. Inc., Toledo, 1976-78; br. mgr. Wm. C. Roney & Co., Detroit, 1978-79; v.p. Lowe & Assocs., Columbus, Ohio, 1979-88; pres. Pointer Investment Co., Columbus, 1988—; arbitrator Nat. Assn. Security Dealers, Washington, 1987—; adv. com. mem. Dept. Commerce Div. of Securities, Columbus, 1988—. Trustee, sec.-treas. Univ. Urology Ednl. and Rsch. Found., 1993—. Lt. col. USAF, 1956-76. Mem. Brookside Golf and Country Club (treas., trustee 1991-94), Sigma Nu (treas. 1955-56). Republican. Methodist. Home: 2290 Haverford Rd Columbus OH 43220-4320 Office: Pointer Investment Co 1550 Old Henderson Rd Ste N 152 Columbus OH 43220-3626

POINTS, ROY WILSON, municipal official; b. Quincy, Ill., Oct. 21, 1940; s. Jess C. and Gladys (Wilson) P.; m. Karen Lee Olsen, July 23, 1966; children: Eric, Holly. BBA, Culver Stockton Coll., 1968. Tchr., coach Lewis County C-1, Ewing, Mo., 1968-69, Community Unit 3, Camp Point, Ill., 1969-78; real estate salesman Landmark, Quincy, 1978-80; supr. of assessment County of Adams, Quincy, 1980-90; assessor City Twp. of Quincy, 1990—; mem., chmn. Adams County Bd. Rev., 1977-80. Bd. dirs., 1st v.p., sec. Quincy Jaycees, 1970-76, Quincy Rotary East, 1980. Mem. Cert. Ill. Assessing Officers, Internat. Assn. Assessing Officers (cert. ednl. recognition 1988), Ill. Assessors Assn. (bd. dirs. 1992—), Tri-Twp. Ofcls. Ill. Democrat. Office: Quincy Twp Assessor City Hall Annex 706 Maine St Quincy IL 62301-4042

POKORNI, ORYSIA, musician; b. Ternopil, Ukraine, Aug. 4, 1938; came to U.S., 1951; d. Gregory and Olha (Moroz) Danylkiw; m. Paul Pokorni, Jan. 25, 1958; children: Daniel, Mark. Student, Cosmopolitan Sch. Music, 1962; AA, Truman Coll., 1984; BA, Northeastern Ill. U., 1989. Mgr. Internat. Theatre of Chgo., 1963—; asst. office mgr. Ravenswood Hosp., Chgo., 1980-83; radio announcer Sta. WEDC, Chgo., 1965-66; tchr. Sch. Ukrainian Studies, Chgo., 1966—, Chgo. Pub. Schs., 1990—; choir dir. Moloda Dumka Children's Choir, Chgo., 1981-85. Accompanist various choirs and soloists, 1960—, All City Youth Chorus of Chgo., 1992—; composer songs; music arranger for children's plays. Active Ukrainian Women's League, Chgo., 1985. Mem. Ukrainian Congress Com. (chmn. spl. events com. 1984—). Home and Office: 4520 N Richmond St Chicago IL 60625-3826

POKORNOWSKI, RONALD FELIX, internist; b. Chgo., July 8, 1933; s. Felix Florian and Isabella Helen (Mrazek) P.; m. Joan Barbara Krygier, Feb. 8, 1958; children: Barbara Karen, John Ronald. Grad. pre-med., Marquette U., 1953, MD, 1957; MD (hon.), Med. Coll. Wis., 1977. Resident internal medicine Northwestern U., Evanston and Chgo., Ill., 1961-64; gen. practice internal medicine Wheaton, Ill., 1964-72; pres. Ctrl. DuPage Internist Assocs., S.C., Carol Stream, Ill., 1972—, also bd. dirs.; v.p. Cen. DuPage Hosp. Med. Staff, 1968-69, pres., 1969-70, mem. bd. govs.; chief med. cons. DuPage Convalescent Ctr., 1980-83; bd. dirs. Allmed Inc., Libertyville, Ill., Fun 'N Travel, Wheaton. Mem. DuPage County Bd. Health, 1993—. Capt. U.S. Army, 1958-61. Mem. AMA, Am. Soc. Addiction Medicine, Ill. Med. Soc., DuPage County Med. Soc. (bd. dirs., alt. del. to Ill. State Med. Soc.), Nat. Assn. Children of Alcoholics. Republican. Roman Catholic. Home: 26w260 Blair St Winfield IL 60190-1104 Office: Cen DuPage Internist Assocs SC 381 S Main Pl Carol Stream IL 60188-2452

POLACHEK-LIPTAK, MICHELLE, agency executive; b. Cleve., Sept. 21, 1954; d. Mike and Amelia (Giuliano) Polachek; m. George Louis Liptak, Apr. 3, 1976. Grad., Television Workshop, 1984; student, Cuyahoga Community Coll., 1985-86. EMT Ohio, 1990. Co-founder Television Workshop, Beachwood, Ohio, 1982-84; exec. dir. Cleve. Ballet Coun., 1982-86; dir. instrn. John Casablancas, Beachwood, Ohio, 1984-85; pres., chief exec. officer Liptak, Oshaben & Assocs., Inc., Garfield Heights, 1986—; dir. devel. Cleve. Sports Legend Found., 1987-88; soc. editor The Leader Newspaper, Garfield Heights, Ohio, 1988-89; pres., CEO, chairperson of bd. Health Exams, Inc., Garfield Heights, Ohio, 1993; co-founder, co-pres. Prime Life Care Ctr., Inc., Cleve., 1993; dir. pub. rels. Providence House, Cleve., 1987-88, OASIS, Cleve., 1987-88; mem. adv. bd. Harper's Bazaar. Dir. pub. rels. City Club of Cleve., 1983-88 (Pub. Rels. Svc. award 1988); mem. Nat. Mus. Women in Arts; trustee Leukemia Soc. Am. Named One of Most Interested People in Ohio, No. Ohio Live Mag., 1987; proclaimed Michelle A. Liptak Day City of Garfield Heights, 1988. Mem. NAFE, Nordonia Hills C. of C. (dir. pub. rels. 1991-92), Garfield Heights C. of C., 1995, City Club of Cleveland, Am. Heart Assn. Duck Race (chairperson 1995). Home and Office: 10712 Wadsworth Ave Garfield Heights OH 44125-2255

POLANIN, W. RICHARD, engineering educator; b. Chgo., Apr. 14, 1952; s. Walter R. and Marie F. (Zents) P.; m. Terryl Ann Bush, July 22, 1978; children: Joshua R., Bradley J., Krista A. BS, Ill. State U., 1974, MS, 1977; EdD, U. Ill., 1990. Cert. tchr., Ill.; cert. welding insp.; cert. mfg. engr. Classroom tchr. Ill. Valley Cen. High Sch., Chillicothe, 1974-79; prof. mfg. Ill. Cen. Coll., East Peoria, 1979—; v.p. precision labor mfg.; pres. WRP Assocs., Metamora, Ill., 1978—; presenter nat. and internat. confs.; lectr. Lakeview Mus., Peoria, Ill., 1985-88; mem. adj. faculty Bradley U. Contbr. articles to profl. jours.; tech. reviewer. Mem. citizens adv. bd. Germantown Hills (Ill.) Sch., 1991—. Mem. Am. Welding Soc.-Peoria (chmn. 1987-89), Soc. Mfg. Engrs. (v.p. Peoria sect. 1994—), Am. Soc. for Metals, Ill. Indsl. Edn. Assn. Home: 702 W Bayside Dr Metamora IL 61548-9051 Office: Ill Cen Coll 1 College Dr Peoria IL 61635-0001

POLASCIK, MARY ANN, ophthalmologist; b. Elkhorn, W.Va., Dec. 28, 1940; d. Michael and Elizabeth (Halko) Polascik; BA, Rutgers U., 1967; MD, Pritzker Sch. Medicine, 1971; m. Joseph Elie, Oct. 2, 1973; 1 dau., Laura Elizabeth Polascik. Jr. pharmacologist Ciba Pharm. Co., Summit, N.J., 1961-67; intern Billings Hosp., Chgo., 1971-72; resident in ophthalmology U. Chgo. Hosp., 1972-75; practice medicine specializing in ophthalmology, Dixon, Ill., 1975—; pres. McNichols Clinic, Ltd.; cons. ophthalmology, Jack Mabley Devel. Ctr., 1976-93; mem. staff Katherine Shaw Bethea Hosp. Bd. dirs. Sinnossippi Mental Healh Ctr., 1977-82, Dixon Cmty. Trust Mental Health Ctr., 1989—. Mem. AMA, Ill. Med. Soc., Ill. Assn. Ophthalmology, Am. Assn. Ophthalmology, Alpha Sigma Lambda. Roman Catholic. Club: Galena Territory. Office: 1700 S Galena Ave Dixon IL 61021-9600

POLAY, BRUCE, music director, music eductor; b. Bklyn., Mar. 22, 1949; s. Benjamin and Joan Polay; m. Louise Phillips, Dec. 17, 1983; children: Elizabeth Louise, Bruce Adam, Rachel Joanne, Jacob Benjamin, Julia Christine. MusB, U. So. Calif., 1971; MA, Calif. State U., 1977; DMA, Ariz. State U., 1989. Music dir. So. Calif. Philharm., Long Beach, 1971-81; grad. asst. in theory and orch., asst. condr. univ. symphony Ariz. State U., Tempe, 1981-83; condr. Phoenix Symphony Guild Youth Orch., 1981-83; music dir. Knox-Galesburg (Ill.) Symphony, 1983—; assoc. prof. music Knox Coll., Galesburg, 1983—; guest condr. in Romania, Russia, Ukraine; mem. music panel for symphonies and ensembles Ill. Arts Coun., Chgo., 1986-88; bd. dirs. Ill. Coun. of Orchs., 1992—; mem. adv. bd. Found. for New Music, 1996—. Orchestral compositions include Enconium, 1986, perspectives, 1989, Con. for Tenor Trombone, 1990, Tranquil Cycle for Tenor and Orch., 1992, Cathedral Images, 1993, Bondi's Journey: An Orchestral Rhapsody on Jewish Themes, 1994; orchestrator Poulenc Oboe Sonata, 1985, Lyric Pieces for Piano, 1990, Sound Images for Piano, 1995. Mem. ASCAP, Condrs. Guild, Am. Fedn. Musicians, Am. Music Ctr., N.Y. Artists Bur., Phi Kappa Phi. Democrat. Home: 1577 N Cherry St Galesburg IL 61401-1820 Office: Knox Coll PO Box 5 Galesburg IL 61402-0005

POLING, DOUGLAS EMMETT, small business owner; b. Harrisburg, Pa., Feb. 13, 1964; s. Harry Paul and Regina Florence (Hartley) P.; m. Linda Ann Marker, Dec. 3, 1994; children: Robert Alan, Andrew Trey, Terrie Deborah, Lucas Emmett, Daren Ray, Conor Eugene. Cert. in archtl. drafting, Montgomery County Joint Vocat., Dayton, Ohio, 1982; elec. cert., HVACR cert., ITT Tech. Inst., Dayton, 1990. Cert. fed. refrigerant specialist. Kitchen mgr. L&K Restaurant, Huber Heights, Ohio, 1984-86, Sommerfelds, Vandelia, Ohio, 1987-88; mgr. Church's Chicken, Dayton, 1988-89; machinist RW Screw Products, Dayton, 1989-90; HVACR maintenance specialist ITT Ednl. Svcs. Inc., Dayton, 1990-95; owner Poling Lawnscaping, Huber Heights, 1990—; HVAC svc. technician Elder-Beerman Stores Corp., Cin.-Dayton area, 1995; HVACR svc. and repair specialist Refrigeration Equipment Co., Dayton, 1995—; cons., sch. news columnist ITT Tech. Inst., Dayton, 1990, chmn. picnic com., 1994—. Mem. N.Am. Fishing Club, N.Am. Hunting Club. Home: 116 Brownstone Dr Englewood OH 45322 Office: Refrigeration Equipment Co 132 S Ludlow St Dayton OH 45402-2688

POLIS, MICHAEL PHILIP, university dean; b. N.Y.C., Oct. 24, 1943; s. Max and Sylvia (Goldner) P.; m. Claudette Martin, May 28, 1966; children: Melanie Bobby, Martin Pascal, Karine Melissa. BSEE, U. Fla., 1966; MSEE, Purdue U., West Lafayette, Ind., 1968, PhD, 1972. Grad. instr. elec. engring. Purdue U., West Lafayette, 1966-71; postdoctoral fellow Ecole Polytechnique, Montreal, 1972-73, asst. prof. elec. engring., 1973-74, assoc. prof., 1974-82, prof., 1982-83; program dir. sys. theory NSF, Washington, 1983-87; chmn. dept. elec. and computer engring. Wayne State U., Detroit, 1987-93; dean Sch. Engring. and Computer Sci. Oakland U., Rochester, Mich., 1993—; expert witness various law firms, 1989—; cons. Mich. Bell-Ameritech, Detroit, 1989-95, ICAM Technologies, Inc., Montreal, 1981-83; vis. rsch. assoc. LAAS, Toulouse, France, 1978. Contbr. articles to profl. jours. Mem. IEEE (sr.), IEEE Control Sys. Soc. (bd. govs. 1993-95, Best Paper Trans. on Automatic Control 1974-75, Disting. Mem. 1993, v.p. mem. activities 1990-91, assoc. editor 1981-82). Office: Oakland Univ Sch Engring & Computer Sci Rochester MI 48309

POLITOFF, ALBERTO LIFSCHITZ, neurologist, neurobiologist; b. Santiago, Chile, July 31, 1935; came to U.S., 1964; s. Leonidas and Emilia (Lifschitz) P.; m. Ida Marticorena, June 2, 1979; 1 child, Violeta. MD, U. Chile, 1960. Asst. prof. physiology Boston U. Med. Sch., 1973-78, assoc. prof., 1978-81; assoc. prof. neurology SUNY L.I. Hosp., New Hyde Park, 1985-89; assoc. prof. U. N.D. Med. Sch., Fargo, 1989—. Author: Introduccion a la Neurologia; contbr. articles to profl. jours. Recipient NIH grants, 1974, Muscular Dystrohpy grants, 1978. Office: U ND Med Sch 1919 Elm St Fargo ND 58102-2416

POLKOWSKI, DELPHINE THERESA, elementary education educator, speech therapist; b. Chgo., Dec. 13, 1930; d. Harry and Rosalie Eleanor (Swiatkowski) P. BS, U. Ill., 1952; MA, Northwestern U., 1957. Speech therapist Community Unit Sch. Dist. 300, Dundee, Ill., 1952-53, S.W. Cook County Co-op Spl. Edn., Tinley Park, Ill., 1960-61; caseworker IV, intake interviewer, caseworker III, case mgr. Ill. Dept. Pub. Aid, Chgo., 1969-87; tchr. Chgo. pub. schs., 1953-88; proctor City Chgo., 1973—. Republican. Roman Catholic. Home: 1320 Carlson Dr Streamwood IL 60107-3020

POLL, HEINZ, choreographer, artistic director; b. Oberhausen, Germany, Mar. 18, 1926; came to U.S., 1964, naturalized, 1975; s. Heinrich and Anna Margareta (Winkels) P. Co-founder, dir. The Dance Inst., U. Akron, 1967-77; founder, artistic dir., choreographer Ohio Ballet, Akron, 1968—; tchr. Chilean Instituto de Extension Musical, 1951-61, N.Y. Nat. Acad., 1965-66. Dancer Göttingen Mcpl. Theatre, 1947-49, Deutsches Theatre Konstanz, 1949-50, East Berlin State Opera, 1950-51, Nat. Ballet Chile, 1951-62, Ballet de la Jeunesse Musicales de France, 1963-64; guest appearances with Nat. Ballet Chile, 1964, Am. Dance Festival, 1965; choreographer works for Nat. Ballet Chile, Paris Festival Ballet, Ballet Jeunesse de la Musicales de France, Nat. Ballet Can., Pa. Ballet, Ohio Ballet, Limon Dance Co. Recipient Ohio Dance award, 1983, 88-89, Achievement Dance award No. Ohio Live Mag., 1985-86, 88-89, 93-94, 94-95, Cleve. Arts prize, 1995; Nat. Endowment for Arts grantee, 1974-75. Mem. NEA (dance panelist 1987-89, 92-93). Office: Ohio Ballet U Akron Akron OH 44325-2501

POLLACK, ERWIN WILBURT, adult education educator, reseacher, writer; b. Chgo., Jan. 8, 1935; s. Morris and Bluma Edith (Lipson) P.; m. Eunice Sue Berger, July 1969. BS, Roosevelt U., 1956; MEd, Loyola U., Chgo., 1963, PhD, 1989. Cert. tchr., Ill. Tchr. Chgo. Pub. Schs., 1958-68; dir. Dist. 14 Learning Ctr., Chgo., 1968-81, Dist. 14 Gifted Ctr., Chgo., 1981-89; tng. specialist Kennedy-King Coll., Chgo., 1974—; vis. assoc. prof. U. Ill., Chgo., 1975-79, edn. ext. Chgo. Circle Campus; cons. Unesco's Edn. Jour. Prospects., 1992-95. Sr. author: Spanish-Speaking Students and Guidance, 1971; co-editor: (textbook) Emerging Educational Issues: Conflicts and Contrasts, 1974; contbr. articles to profl. jours. Mem. Comparative Edn. Soc., Nat. Soc. for the Study of Edn., Ill. Coun. for the Gifted, AERA-Spl. Interest Group on Internat. Studies, Phi Delta Kappa. Office: Kennedy-King Coll ALSP 6800 S Wentworth Ave Chicago IL 60621-3733

POLLACK, JOE, retired newspaper critic and columnist, writer; b. Bklyn., Feb. 3, 1931; s. Samuel H. and Anna (Weisman) P.; m. Joan S., Mar. 6, 1952 (div. 1964); children: Wendy, Dara, Sharon; m. Carol Atchison, Dec. 1, 1964 (dec. 1993); m. Ann Lemons, Nov. 20, 1994. BJ, U. Mo., 1952. Sports writer St. Louis Globe-Democrat, 1955-61; dir. pub. rels. St. Louis Football Cardinals, 1961-72; critic, columnist St. Louis Post-Dispatch, 1972-95; critic Sta. KSDK-TV, St. Louis, 1973-88, Sta. KMOV-TV, St. Louis, 1988-92; commentator Sta. KMOX, St. Louis, 1960-85, Sta. KWMU, St. Louis, 1994—. Author: Joe Pollack's Guide to St. Louis Restaurants, 1988, updated, 1992; contbr. numerous articles to mags. Mem. Am. Theatre Critics Assn., Profl. Football Writers Assn., Am. Soc. Profl. Journalists, Internat. Writers Ctr. (adv. bd. St. Louis). Home: 7417 Oxford Dr Saint Louis MO 63105

POLLAK, OLIVER BURT, lawyer, educator, writer; b. London, Nov. 10, 1943; came to U.S., 1953; s. William and Ruth (Bachmann) P.; m. Karen Pollak, May 8, 1966; children: Noah, Aaron. BA, Calif. State U., 1964; MA, UCLA, 1965, PhD, 1973; JD, Creighton U., 1982. Bar: Nebr. 1982, Iowa 1992; cert. in consumer bankruptcy law, Am. Bankruptcy Bd. Cert. Asst. prof. U. Nebr., Omaha, 1974-76, assoc. prof., 1976-84, prof., 1984—, chmn. dept. of history, 1979-82; ptnr. Pollak & Hicks, P.C., Omaha, 1982—; lectr. U. Rhodesia, Zimbabwe, 1971-74, UCLA, 1974. Author 4 books; contbr. articles to profl. jours. Treas. Nebr. Humanities Coun., Lincoln, 1984; pres. Omaha Jewish Press, 1989-90, Nebr. Jewish Hist. Soc., Omaha, 1991; bd. dirs. Art Omaha, 1991-92. Home: 1315 S 155th St Omaha NE 68144-5105 Office: Pollak & Hicks PC 1823 Harney St Omaha NE 68102-1908

POLLARD, PHIL EARL, electrical engineer; b. Shelbyville, Ky., July 13, 1946. BSEE, Tri-State Coll., 1969. Project engr. spl. projects Berne (Ind.) divsn. CTS Corp., 1969—. Elder Calvary Chapel, Decatur, Ind., 1985—. Mem. Am. Soc. Quality Control (cert. quality engr., quality auditor). Home: 318 E Franklin St Berne IN 46711-2206

POLLEI, DANE F., historical society executive; b. Fond du Lac, Wis., Oct. 28, 1964; s. Gerald E. and Barbara May (Bassett) P.; m. Jean M. Grabowski, July 15, 1994; 1 child, Marley; stepchildren: Bonny, Daniel, Catherine. BA in Anthrop., Mus. Studies, Beloit (Wis.) Coll., 1986; cert. in Non-Profit Mgmt., U. Wis., Parkside, 1990; cert. in Archival Adminstr., U. Wis. Mus. asst. Logan Mus. of Anthrop., Beloit, Wis., 1983-85; asst. to dir. Beloit Coll. Museums, 1985-86; dir., curator Freeport (Ill.) Art Mus., 1987-89; exec. dir. Kenosha (Wis.) County Hist. Soc., 1989—; instr. Highland C.C., Freeport, IL, 1988-89; adv. com. Wis. Fedn. Museums, 1990-92; cons. Font Bank On-Line, Evanston, IL, 1994. Author, editor: W.E.S.T. Word Traveller, 1992—. Pres. bd. dirs. Kenosha (Wis.) Unified Sch. Dist., 1993—; mem. Hist. Preservation Commn., Kenosha. Mem. Am. Assn. Museums. Populist Progressive. Home: 909 72nd St Kenosha WI 53143-5419 Office: Kenosha County Hist Soc 6300 3rd Ave Kenosha WI 53143-5102

POLLIN, PIERRE LOUIS, executive chef; b. St. Pierre, Normandy, France, Mar. 7, 1947; came to U.S., 1974; s. Emile and Denise Juliette (Broc) P.; m. Judith Lynn Simonsen, June 27, 1977; children: Patric Alexandre, Cynthia Nicole. Student, Tregaro, Gace, France, 1956-65, Lycee Robillard, St. Pierre Sur Dives, France, 1965-67. Apprentice Le Table Du Roi, Paris, 1967-68; comis Westbury Hotel, London, 1969-70; chef de partie Hotel Royal Monceau, Paris, 1970, Lucas Carton, Paris, 1970, Maxim's, Paris, 1971-73, Cafe De La Paix, Paris, 1973-74; exec. chef Le Titi de Paris, Arlington Heights, Ill., 1974—. Mem. Vatel Club, Am. Culinary Fedn., Heartland Food Soc., Chefs of Cuisine Assn., Societe Mutualiste des Cuisiniers de Paris, Academie Culinaire de France, Maitres Cuisiniers de France, Chaine des Rotisseurs, Am. Inst. Food and Wine. Roman Catholic. Office: Le TiTi de Paris 1015 W Dundee Rd Arlington Heights IL 60004-1419

POLLOCK, KAREN ANNE, computer analyst; b. Elmhurst, Ill., Sept. 6, 1961; d. Michael Paul and Dorothy Rosella (Foskett) P. BS, Elmhurst Coll., 1984; MS, North Cen. Coll., 1993. Formatter Nat. Data Corp., Lombard, Ill., 1985; computer specialist Dept. VA, Hines, Ill., 1985—. Lutheran.

POLLOCK, LESLIE STUART, city planning consultant; b. Chgo., Mar. 25, 1942; s. Reuben and Nettie (Brickman) P.; m. Sharon Iris Levine, Jan. 30, 1965; children: Elizabeth, Barbra. BArch, U. Ill., Urbana, 1966, M in Urban Planning, 1968. Lectr. dept. planning U. Ill., Urbana, 1968; sr. assoc. Barton-Aschman Assocs., Chgo., 1968-76; prin. cons. and co-founder Camiros Ltd., Chgo., Indpls., Mpls., 1977—; Madison (Wis), Orlando; adj. prof. Loyola U., Chgo., 1974-86, U. Ill., Chgo., 1989—; vis. prof. U. Ill., Urbana, 1987-88. Contbr. articles to profl. jours. Chmn. planning commn. Village of Wilmette, Ill., 1973-81, trustee, 1981-89; mem. Wilmette Coun. Comml. Renewal, 1973-76, Chgo. Park Dist. task force, 1987-90. Mem. Am. Inst. Cert. Planners, Am. Planning Assn. (chair dept. transp. 1976-77, Student award 1968), Urban Land Inst., Land Econs. Soc., Lambda Alpha, Beth Hillel Men's Club (v.p. Wilmette 1980-82, 86-88). Office: Camiros Ltd 411 S Wells St Chicago IL 60607-3924

POLLOCK, SANDRA ANN, physical therapist; b. Pitts., Nov. 21, 1962; d. Maurice Pierre and Stella Marie (Campolo) Schulte; m. James Allen Pollock, Oct. 22, 1988; children: Emily Marie, Samantha Nicole. BS in Phys. Therapy, Fla. A&M U., Tallahassee, 1986. Cert. phys. therapist, Pa., Ohio, W.Va.; cert. in neurodevel. treatment of adult hemiplegia. Staff phys. therapist Ohio Valley Hosp., McKees Rocks, Pa., 1986-87, Montefiore Hosp., Pitts., 1987, Ohio Valley Hosp./Harmarville Satellite, Steubenville, Ohio, 1988-92, Wheeling (W.Va.) Hosp., 1992; staff/contract phys. therapist CMS Therapies, Steubenville, 1993-95, N.W. Rehab., Pitts., 1994—; contract phys. therapist Valley Hospice, Steubenville, 1988—, Carriage Inn Home Health, Steubenville, 1993—. Mem. Gold Key Circle, Richmond (Ohio) United Meth. Ch., 1988—. Mem. Am. Phys. Therapy Assn. (geriatric sect.), Ohio Phys. Therapy Assn., Countryside Garden Club (pres. 1992-94). Democrat. Roman Catholic. Home: PO Box 682B Sunset Lake Rd RD 1 Richmond OH 43944

POLLOCK, TONY JOE, nurse consultant; b. St. Mary's, Ohio, Apr. 10, 1961; s. Gary D. and Loretta J. (Lowe) P. BSN, U. Minn., 1983. CCRN, CEN. Staff nurse ICU VA Med. Ctr., Martinez, Calif., 1986-88; charge nurse emergency room Mad River Community Hosp., Arcata, Calif., 1988-90; staff emergency med. technician, paramedic Hupa Health Assn. EMS, Hoopa, Calif., 1989-91; charge nurse emergency svcs. Health One Unit Hosp., Fridley, Minn., 1991-93; mgr. NurseLine United Healthcare, Golden Valley, Minn., 1993-95; sr. ptnr. Midwest Legal Nurse Cons., Inc., Edina, Minn., 1995—; staff nurse Park Nicollet Clinic Phone Care, Wayzota, Minn., 1995—. Capt. Nurse Corps, U.S. Army, 1983-86. Home: # 2 601 S 9th St Minneapolis MN 55404-1179 Office: PO Box 39155 Edina MN 55439

POLSFUSS, CRAIG LYLE, management consultant, psychologist, social worker; b. Mpls., Nov. 16, 1950; s. Lyle Henry Polsfuss and Ethel Geneva (Langert) Cannon; m. Mary Louise Davenport, June 10, 1972; children: Zachary Abel, Samuel David, Benjamin James. BA with honors, Macalester Coll., 1972; MA with honors, U.S.I.U., 1976; MSW, U. Minn., 1979. Lic. ind. clin. social worker, psychologist, Minn.; diplomate NASW. Pvt. practice counselor, psychotherapist Mpls., 1972—, pvt. practice mgmt. cons., 1983—; instr. Augsburg Coll., U. Minn., Mpls. Cmty. Coll., Lakewood Cmty. Coll., Nat. Coll. Bus., 1976-86; dir. Heartland Counseling and Edn. Ctrs., Twin Cities met. area, 1991; founder Perpetual Prosperity Enterprises, 1994. Mem. NASW (diplomate), Minn. Psychol. Assn. (cert. POM/Health realization practitioner). Office: Vantage Place Cons 121 W Franklin Ave Minneapolis MN 55404-2434

POLSINELLI, ANTHONY RENATO, manufacturing company executive; b. Canton, Ohio, Feb. 2, 1944; s. Placid John and Mary Ann (Primavera) P.; m. Allison Light, Feb. 16, 1991; children: Michael, Tedd Petruna, Jason Petruna. BS in Engring. Mgmt., Case Inst. Tech., 1968. Registered profl. engr., Calif. Prodn. supr. Gen Motors, Hudson, Ohio, 1967-69; mgr. indsl. engring. Bailey Meter Co., Wickliffe, Ohio, 1969-72; asst. ops. mgr. Bailey Japan Ltd., Tokyo, 1972-74; sr. engr. Anvil Industries, Brecksville, Ohio, 1975, Technicare Corp., Solon, Ohio, 1976-78; dir. corp. prodn. engring. Eaton Corp., Cleve., 1978—; indsl. adv. com. Case Inst. Tech., 1982-84. Contbr. articles to profl. mags. Mem. Soc. Mfg. Engrs. (pres. local chpt. 1982), Am. Mgmt. Assn., Inst. Indsl. Engrs., Boston U. Mfg. Roundtable. Home: 32297 Pinehurst Dr Avon Lake OH 44012-2530 Office: Eaton Corp 32500 Chardon Rd Willoughby OH 44094-8446

POLSINELLI, JERRY, osteopathic obstetrician and gynecologist; b. Detroit, May 21, 1928; s. Pietro and Louisa (Romanelli) P.; m. Virginia Mary Pompilius, June 25, 1949; children: Michael, Stephan, Janet, Patti-Jo. BA, Wayne State U., 1948; DO, U. Health Scis., Kansas City, Mo., 1953. Diplomate Am. Bd. Ob-Gyn. Intern Detroit Osteo. Hosp., 1953-54, resident in ob/gyn, 1954-56, fellow in gynecology, 1957-58; pvt. practice Detroit, 1957-64; med. administr. Detroit Osteo. Hosp. Corp., 1964-70; asst. dean Chgo. Coll. Osteo. Medicine, 1964-67; pvt. practice Warren, 1970-93; clin. prof. ob-gyn. Mich. State U. Coll. Medicine, Lansing, 1971—; exec. dir. Am.

Coll. Osteo. Ob-Gyn, Pontiac, Mich., 1980-82, 1984—; med. dir. Bicounty Cmty. Hosp., Warren, 1984-93. Fellow Am. Coll. Osteo. Ob-Gyn. (pres. 1983-84, Disting. Svc. award 1988); mem. Detroit Curling Club (pres. 1974), Edgewood Golf and Country Club (pres. 1984), KC. Roman Catholic.

POLSKY, MICHAEL PETER, mechanical engineer; b. Kiev, Ukraine, Aug. 5, 1949; s. Peter and Basheva P.; m. Maya, June 28, 1975; children: Alan, Gabriel. BSME, Kiev Poly. Inst., 1973; MBA, U. Chgo., 1987. Registered profl. engr., Ill., Mich. Sr. devel. engr. Indsl. Power Corp., Kiev, Ukraine, 1973-76; mech. engr. Bechtel Power Corp., Ann Arbor, Mich., 1976-78; sr. application engr. Brown Boveri Corp., St. Cloud, Minn., 1978-80; product mgr. congeneration Fluor/Daniel, Chgo., 1980-85; pres. Indeck Energy Svcs., Wheeling, Ill., 1985-90, Polsky Energy Corp., Northbrook, Ill., 1990—; bd. dirs. Ind. Power Producers of N.Y., Albany, 1988-89. Author: Public Utilities Fortnightly, 1985, Power, 1984, 83, Hydrocarbon Processing, 1981, 82; author: (book chpt.) Handbook of Power Plant Engineering, 1991. Mem. ASME, Soc. Energy Engrs. Office: Polsky Energy Corp 650 Dundee Rd Ste 150 Northbrook IL 60062-2753

POLUCHOWICZ, ROXOLANA SOFIA, information systems executive; b. Hamburg, Germany, June 12, 1947; came to the U.S., 1951; d. Stefan and Maria (Baranowsky) Skrobach; m. Jan Poluchowicz, Nov. 1, 1969; children: Andrei, Alexander, Larissa. BS, U. Ill., Chgo., 1969; MBA, Roosevelt U., 1980. Programmer Rust-Oleum Corp., Evanston, Ill., 1969-71; sr. programmer Rust-Oleum Corp., Evanston, 1972-74, project leader, 1975-77; mgr. applications programming Rust-Oleum Corp., Vernon Hills, Ill., 1978-80; mgr. computer ops. Rust-Oleum Corp., Vernon Hills, 1981-83; data ctr. mgr. Stone Container Corp., Chgo., 1983-84, mgr. computer resources, 1985-86, mgr. computing facilities, 1987-91, mgr. MIS adminstrn., 1992—; spkr. 10th plenary conf. Diebold Group, N.Y.C., 1982. Mem. editl. bd. Computerworld, 1988. V.p. bd. dirs. Ela Area Pub. Libr., Lake Zurich, 1990—. Mem. Chgo. Resource & Planning Group (tng. com.). Office: Stone Container Corp 150 N Michigan Ave Chicago IL 60601

POLYAK, STEPHEN T., systems consultant; b. Joliet, Ill., July 28, 1969; s. Thomas V. and Elizabeth (Jaworski) P; m. Amy K. Sunderman, Oct. 9, 1993. BS in psychology, U. Iowa, 1991; MS in computer sci., DePaul U., 1995. Rehab. specialist The Center (Schwab), Chgo., 1991; cmty. liaison/employment cons. Cornestone Svcs., Inc., Joliet, 1991-92; systems cons., sr. cons. Access Health, Arlington Heights, Ill., 1992-94; staff cons. CSC Consulting, Oak Brook, Ill., 1994-95; cons. Ameritech, Hoffman Estates, Ill., 1995. Mem. IEEE-Computer Soc. Home: 2010N Howe Chicago IL 60614 Office: CSC Consulting 2051 N Mohawk St Chicago IL 60614

POLYDORIS, NICHOLAS GEORGE, electronics executive; b. Evanston, Ill., July 7, 1930; s. George and Annetta (Karas) P.; m. Gloria Ann Lucas, Dec. 28, 1952; children: Steven, Janet, Lynn, Susan, Nancy. BSEE, Northwestern U., 1954. Trainee Fairbanks Morris Co., 1954-55; dist. mgr. Fasco Industries, Rochester, N.Y., 1955-57; founder, pres. ENM Co., Chgo., 1957—, also bd. dirs.; bd. dirs. Universal Clay Products, Inc., Sandusky, Ohio, Gladston-Norwood Bank, Chgo., Grt. Hellenic Found., Chgo., North Shore Mental Health Assn., Chgo. Patentee in field. Recipient Svc. award Northwestern U., Evanston, Ill., 1965. Mem. Soc. Automotive Engrs., Aircraft Owners and Pilots Assn., Ill. Soc. Profl. Engrs., Mich. Shores Club, Old Willow Club, Kenilworth Club, John Evans Club (pres.), Tau Beta Pi. Republican. Home: 1630 Sheridan Rd Wilmette IL 60091 Office: ENM Co 5617 N Northwest Hwy Chicago IL 60646-6135

POLZIN, JOHN THEODORE, lawyer; b. Rock Island, Ill., Dec. 23, 1919; s. Max August and Charlotte Barbara (Trenkenschuh) P.; m. Helen Louise Hosford, Nov. 27, 1969. A.B., U. Ill., 1941, J.D., 1943. Bar: Ill. 1943. Sole practice, Galva, Ill., 1946-55, Chgo., 1975—; city atty., Galva, 1950-54; assoc. Langner, Parry, Card & Langner, Chgo., 1955-75; lectr. Ill. Inst. for Continuing Legal Edn., 1978. Served to lt. USNR, 1943-46. Mem. ABA, Ill. State Bar Assn. (chmn. patent, trademark and copyright law sect. 1981-82), Patent Law Assn. Chgo. (chmn. fgn. trademark com. 1972, 74). Republican. Home and Office: 1503 Oak Ave Evanston IL 60201-4260

POMERANZ, JEROME RAPHAEL, dermatologist; b. Newark, Dec. 29, 1930; s. Raphael and Zina (Rubinow) P.; m. Jacqueline R. Goldenberg, June 15, 1953 (div. 1973); m. Barbara P. Barna, May 5, 1978; children: Russell Carl, William Eric, Emily Suzanne. BS, George Washington U., 1952; MD, Boston U., 1956. Diplomate Am. Bd. Dermatology, Am. Bd. Pathology. Intern, then resident Johns Hopkins Hosp., Balt., 1957-58, resident in dermatology, 1960-63, fellow in allergy, 1963-65, mem. staff; assoc. prof. dermatology Case Western Res. U., Cleve., 1965—, assoc. prof. pathology, 1967—; dir. dermatology Metro Health Med. Ctr., 1965-92, mem. staff, 1992—. Contbr. articles to profl. jours. Served to capt. M.C., U.S. Army, 1958-60. Fellow ACP, Am. Am. Acad. Dermatology; mem. AAAS, NAS (drug efficacy studyjpanel 1967-69, com. to rev. use of ionizing radiation for treatment of benign diseases 1975-78), Am. Dermatol. Assn., FDA Bur. Drugs (dermatology adv. com. 1981-85, 92-94), Cleve. Dermatol. Soc. (pres. 1973-75), Am. Soc. Dermatopathology, Soc. Investigative Dermatology (membership com. 1975, 76, 77, chmn. 1977, audit com. 1993—), Assn. Profs. Dermatology, N.Y. Acad. Scis., Cleve. Acad. Medicine. Home: 490 Merrimak Dr Berea OH 44017-2241 Office: Cleve Skin Pathology Lab 2475 E 22d St Rm 611 Cleveland OH 44115

POMEROY, BRUCE MARCEL, critical care nurse, educator; b. East St. Louis, Ill., July 11, 1959; s. Martin Bruce and Loretta Emma (Klasing) P. ADN, Kaskaskia Jr. Coll., Centralia, Ill., 1979; BSN, McKendree Coll., Lebanon, Ill., 1981; MSN, St. Louis U., 1992. RN, Ill., Mo.; cert. ACLS provider, BLS instr. Staff and charge nurse Washington County Hosp., Nashville, Ill., 1979-81; staff nurse ICU-telemetry-orthopedic units St. Elizabeth Hosp., Belleville, Ill., 1981-83; staff nurse/ preceptor ICU, critical care nursing edn. instr. Meml. Hosp., Belleville, 1983—; house supr. Deaconess Hosp., St. Louis, 1995—; clinical nursing instr. Belleville Area Coll., 1992-93, Kaskaskia Coll, Centralia, Ill., 1993—; clinical nursing instr., Sch. Nursing. Luth. Med. Ctr., St. Louis, Mo., 1995—; clin. nursing instr. Sch. Nursing, Deaconess Coll. Nursing, St. Louis, 1996—. Mem. sr. choir St. Peter's United Ch. of Christ; v.p. ch. coun. St. Paul's United Ch. Christ, Okawville, Ill. Mem. AACN (co-founder Metro East chpt.), nat. League Nursing, N.Am. Nursing Diagnosis Assn., McKendree Coll. Nursing Hon. Soc. (charter), Sigma Theta Tau, Sigma Zeta, Phi Theta Kappa. Home: PO Box 66 316 W Elm St Okawville IL 62271-0066

POMEROY, EARL R., congressman, former state insurance commissioner; b. Valley City, N.D., Sept. 2, 1952; s. Ralph and Myrtle Pomeroy; m. Laurie Kirby, Dec. 26, 1986. BA, U. N.D., 1974, JD, 1979. Atty. Sproul, Lenaburg, Fitzner and Walker, Valley City, 1979-84; commr. of ins. State of N.D., Valley City, 1984-92; mem. 103rd Congress from N.D. (at large), Washington, D.C., 1993—; mem. coms.: budget, agriculture. State rep. N.D. Legis. Assembly, 1980-84. Recipient Found. award Rotary, 1975; named Outstanding Young North Dakotan N.D. Jaycees, 1982. Mem. Nat. Assn. of Ins. Commrs. (chmn. midwest zone 1987-88, exec. com. 1987-88), Phi Beta Kappa. Democrat. Presbyterian. Office: US Ho Rep 1533 Longworth Washington DC 20515-3401*

POMEROY, GLENN, state insurance commissioner; m. Jean; 3 children. Grad., U. N.D., 1978, U. N.D., 1983. Pvt. practice N.D.; asst. states atty. Barnes County, N.D.; state rep. dist. 42 N.D. Ho. of Reps.; asst. atty. gen. State of N.D. Govt., 1986-88, securities commr., 1988-92, ins. commr., 1992—, chmn. sr. issues task force, vice chmn. accident and health ins., mem. exec. com. Mem. Nat. Assn. Ins. Commrs. Address: 600 East Blvd Bismarck ND 58505*

PONCAR, PATRICIA JANE, nursing educator; b. Hamilton, Ont., Canada, Mar. 7, 1944; d. Lloyd Russel and Sara LaRue (Bloom) Schaffer; m. Jan Edward Poncar, Apr. 6, 1968; children: Jeffrey Eric, Rebecca Elise. Diploma, Trumbull Meml. Hosp., 1964; BSN, Case Western Res. U., 1968; MSN, Kent State U., 1988. RN, Ohio. Instr. Trumbull Meml. Hosp. Sch. Nursing, Warren, Ohio, 1968-70, asst. dir. nursing, 1972-79, staff nurse coronary care, 1979-81; nursing supr. Health Maintenance Plan, Cortland, Ohio, 1981-83, dir. of nursing, 1983-86; staff nurse Visiting Nurse Assn., Warren, Ohio, 1986-94; asst. prof. nursing Kent State U., Ashtabula, Ohio, 1989—, faculty chair, 1994—. Contbr. articles to profl. jours. Vol. Hospice, Warren, 1983-89; active Lakeview Band Boosters, Cortland, 1991-96; sec. Warren Jr. Crafts, 1971-76. Mem. ANA, Ohio Nurses Assn. (conv. del. 1993), Ashtabula Dist. Nurses Assn. (sec. 1992-94, v.p. 1991-92), Kent State U. Nursing Alumni Assn. (bd. dirs. 1994—), NLN, Sigma Theta Tau. Methodist. Home: 100 Dennis Dr Cortland OH 44410 Office: Kent State U Ashtabula 3325 W 13th St Ashtabula OH 44004

POND, PHYLLIS JOAN, state legislator; b. Warren, Ind., Oct. 25, 1930; d. Clifford E. and Rosa E. (Hunnicutt) Ruble; m. George W. Pond, June 10, 1951; children: William, Douglas, Jean Ann. BS, Ball State U., Muncie, Ind., 1951; MS, Ind. U., 1963. Tchr. home econs., 1951-54; kindergarten tchr., 1961—; mem. Ind. Ho. of Reps. from 15th dist., 1978-82, from 20th dist., 1982-92, from 85th dist., 1992—, majority asst. caucus chmn., vice chmn. ways and means com., 1995. Del. Ind. State Rep. Conv., 1976, 80, 84, del., 1986, 88; alt. del. Rep. Nat. Conv., 1980. Mem. AAUW, New Haven Woman's Club. Lutheran.

PONITZ, DAVID H., academic administrator; b. Royal Oak, Mich., Jan. 21, 1931; s. Henry John and Jeanette (Bouwman) P.; m. Doris Jean Humes, Aug. 5, 1956; children: Catherine Anne, David Robinson. BA, U. Mich., 1952, MA, 1954; EdD, Harvard U., 1964. Prin. Waldron (Mich.) Area Schs., 1956-58, supt., 1958-60; cons. Harvard U., Boston Sch. Survey, 1961-63; supt. Freeport (Ill.) Pub. Schs., 1962-65; pres. Freeport C.C., 1962-65, Washtenaw C.C., 1965-75, Sinclair C.C., 1975—; cons. to community colls.; chmn., pres. Ohi Advanced Tech. Ctr. Mem. editorial adv. bd. Nations Schs, 1963-70; chmn. adv. bd. Community Coll. Rev, 1978-89. Past chmn. Dayton Mayor's Coun. on Econ. Devel., 1977-85; mem. Nat. Adv. Coun. on Nursing; former co-chair Performing Arts Edn. Task Force; bd. dirs. Alliance for Edn.; former campaign chmn. Ann Arbor and Dayton United Way; past vice chmn. Dayton Citizens Adv. Coun. for Desegregation Implementation; v.p. Miami Valley Rsch. Park; mem., past chmn. Area Progress Coun., Dayton; bd. dirs. Dayton Devel. Coun.; mem. F.S.B. bd. Citizens Fed. Banks, Universal Energy Systems Bd.; past chmn. Miami Valley Joint Labor/Mgmt. Profls., Area Progress Coun.; bd. dirs Ctr. Occupational R & D; chmn. Human Svcs. Levy, Tech-Prep Coll. H.S. Consortium; vice chair Miami Valley Rsch. Found.; bd. dirs. League Innovation C.C., Miami Valley Regional Planning Commn. Served with U.S. Army, 1954-56. Named Outstanding Alumnus U. Mich., One of Top 100 Pres. in U.S. Council for Advancement and Support of Edn., Exec. of Yr., Bd. Realtors, Presdl. medallion Patron emeritus Horry-Georgetown Tech. Coll.; recipient Bogie Buster Red Jacket award, 1987, Thomas J. Peters award for Excellence Assn. Community and Jr. Colls. 1988, Marie N. Martin Chief Exec. Officer award, ACCT, 1989, The Living Legend award Martin Luther King Jr. Holiday Celebration Com., 1991, Sinclair Hon. Alumnus award, 1991, India Found. Honor, 1992, Disting. Eagle Scout award Nat. Eagle Scout Assn., 1993. Mem. Am. Assn. Community and Jr. Colls. (nat. future commn., bd. dirs., chmn. 1988-89), Ohio Tech. and Community Coll. Assn. (pres. 1979-80), Rotary. Methodist. Office: Sinclair Community Coll 4444 W 3rd St Dayton OH 45417

PONKA, LAWRENCE JOHN, automotive executive; b. Detroit, Sept. 1, 1949; s. Maximillian John and Leona May (Knobloch) P.; m. Nancy Kathleen McNamara, Feb. 20, 1988. AA, Macomb County Community Coll., 1974; BS in Indsl. Mgmt., Lawrence Tech. U., 1978; MA in Indsl. Mgmt., Cen. Mich. U., 1983. Cert. internat. cons. Engr.'s asst. Army Tank Automotive Command, 1967-68; with Sperry & Hutchinson Co., Southfield, Mich., 1973, Chrysler Corp., Detroit, 1973; with GM Corp., Warren, Mich., 1973-82, engring. systems coord. engring. staff, 1976-82, current product engring. until 1982; mfg. engr. Buick-Oldsmobile-Cadillac Group, GM Assembly Div.-Orion Pontiac, Mich., 1982-84, sr. analyst advanced vehicle engring. Chevrolet-Pontiac-Can. group Engring. Ctr., Warren, 1985-86; mfg. planning adminstr. Detroit-Hamtramck Assembly Ctr., Cadillac luxury car divsn., Allanté, 1986-92, ops. mgr., 1992—; mgr. Cadillac Allanté Assembly Ops., 1992—; mfg. planning adminstr./human resource advisor; acting mgr. Allanté Cadillac Allanté Assembly Ctr., 1992—; plant planning adminstr. Cadillac luxury car divsn. Detroit/Hamtramck Assembly Ctr., Cadillac El Dorado, Seville, Deville, Concours, 1993—, sr. mfg. project engr. N.Am. Ops., 1994, Flint, Mich., 1996, advanced mfg. engr., N.Am. ops. mfg. process liaison Cadillac luxury car divsn., 1996—; mem. people strategy team on environment Cadillac Motor Car Co., until 1992. Elected del. Dem. County Convention. Served with USAF, 1968-72. Decorated Air Force Commendation medal. Mem. Disabled Am. Vets. Assn. (life), Vietnam Vets. Assn. (life), Am. Diabetes Assn., Salvation Army (bed and bread club), Am. Legion. Roman Catholic. Home: 35537 Oakdale St Livonia MI 48154-2237 Office: NAm Ops Gen Assembly Ctr Vehicle Devel & Tech Ops Group Warren MI 48090-9025

PONTYNEN, ARTHUR JOHN, art historian, educator; b. Bklyn., Mar. 23, 1950; s. Eino Adolf and Aili Ilona (Lassi) P.; m. Alison Louise Tripp, Aug. 7, 1982; children: Alina, Abigail, Anson. BA, Western Wash. U., 1973; MA, U. Iowa, 1977, PhD, 1983. Lectr. Lewis and Clark Coll., Portland, Oreg., 1980-82; asst. prof. U. No. Iowa, Cedar Falls, 1982-83, Stephen F. Austin U., Nacogdoches, Tex., 1985-89; assoc. prof. U. Wis., Oshkosh, 1989—. Contbr. chpts. in books and articles to profl. jours. Fellow Heritage Found., 1991-93. Fellow Smithsonian Instn.; mem. Nat. Assn. Scholars (chair fine arts 1994—), Wis. Assn. Scholars (bd. dirs.), Winnebago County Hist. and Archaeol. Soc. (bd. dirs.). Republican. Home: 619 Franklin St Oshkosh WI 54901 Office: Dept Art Univ Wisconsin Oshkosh WI 54901

POOLE, BRENDA LYNNE, post-anesthesia nurse; b. Uniontown, Pa., Dec. 13, 1952; d. Lawrence Anderson Tomb and Oweda Jane (Furry) Osolin; m. Donald Kevin Poole, Aug. 20, 1977; children: Bryan Kevin, Chandra Janay. BA in Biology, Greenville Coll., 1975; BSN, Rush U., 1980. RN, Ill. Staff RN Ctrl. Dupage Hosp., Winfield, Ill., 1980-91; same day surgery, endoscopy, post anesthesia care unit mgr. Edward Hosp., Naperville, Ill., 1991—. Mem. Am. Soc. Post Anesthesia Nurses, Assn. Ops. Room Nurses, Soc. Gastroenterology Nurses and Assocs., Sigma Theta Tau, Beta Beta Beta. Lutheran. Home: 5707 Essex Rd Lisle IL 60532-2642 Office: Edward Hosp 801 S Washington St Naperville IL 60540-7430

POOLE, DAVID LARUE, management consultant; b. Kansas City, Mo., Jan. 29, 1938; s. LaRue Masten and Opal Mae (Harsh) P.; children: Jeffrey, Steven, Eric; m. Barbara Ann Roberts, June 18, 1983. BS in Bus., U. Mo., 1960; postgrad., U. Mo., Kansas City, 1961-63. Quality control tech. Ford Motor co., Kansas City, 1960-63; human resources specialist AT&T, Kansas City, 1963-66; human resources mgr. Rexall Drug & Chems., Kansas City, 1966-70; dir. employment, mgr., mgr. internat. human resources The Vendo Co., Kansas City; divsn. human resources mgr. Butler Mfg., Kansas City, 1970-75; exec. dir. human resources Farmland Industries, Kansas City, 1975-85; dir./practice leader career svcs. DeFrain Mayer Lee & Burgess, Kansas City, 1985—; adj. prof. U. Mo.-Kansas City, 1992-94. Bd. dirs. Better Bus. Bur., Kansas City, 1972-73, DREAM Ctr. Urban Svcs., 1993—; bd. dirs., mem. human resource com., outreach com., new mem. host, deacon Country Club Christian Ch., Kansas City, 1985-95. Mem. Human Resource Mgmt. Assn. (life, pres. 1971-72, 93, 94, bd. dirs. 1995—), U. Mo. Alumni Assn. (bd. dirs. 1995—). Home: 5656 Riley Overland Park KS 66202

POOLMAN, JIM, state legislator; b. Fargo, N.D., May 15, 1970; s. Robert Francis and Susan Faye (Brown) P. BBA, U. N.D., 1992, postgrad., 1994—. Sales cons. Straus Co., Grand Forks, N.D., 1987-95; state representative N.D. State Ho. of Reps., 1992—; trust officer First Am. Bank, 1995—. Task force State of N.D., Grand Forks, 1992; mem. United Hosp. Corp. United Health, Grand Forks, 1992—, Presdl. Search Com., U. N.D., 1992; bd. dirs. Red River Red Cross, 1995—. Mem. Toastmasters Internat. (sec.), Phi Delta Theta Alumni (varsity bachelors club scholarship ednl. found. 1992). Republican. Lutheran. Home: 529 Oxford St # 4 Grand Forks ND 58203-2846

POPE, ANNIE, health association administrator, planning consultant; b. Toledo, Ohio, Mar. 23, 1949; d. John James and Myra Jean (Tate) Fojtik; m. Michael Jay Pope, Feb. 4, 1969 (div. 1973); m. Robert Warren Hazel, Apr. 8, 1988; stepchildren: Elizabeth Alice, Peter Robert. Student, U. Mo., 1967-71. Patient svcs. rep. Nat. Multiple Sclerosis Soc., Columbia, Mo., 1978-79; field rep. Am. Cancer Soc., Jefferson City, Mo., 1979-81; field svcs. dir. Am. Cancer Soc., St. Louis, 1981-83; planning cons. St. Louis and Orlando, Fla., 1983—; exec. dir. Arthritis Found., St. Louis, 1986-89; dir. ARC, St. Louis, 1989—; mem. Mo. Arthritis Adv. Bd., Jefferson City, 1986-89, Mo. Medicaid Oversight Com, Jefferson City, 1987—, Mo. Long Term Care Planning Com., Jefferson City, 1991—, Mo. Alternative Care Coalition, Jefferson City, 1990—. Mem. Women's Polit. Caucus, St. Louis, 1991—, Aging Task Force, Jefferson City, 1990—. Recipient Patient Svcs. awards Am. Cancer Soc., 1982, Arthritis Found., 1987, Healthy Innovations award ARC, 1990. Mem. LWV, Nat. Soc. Fund Raising Execs., Women in Health Adminstrn., Mo. Adult Day Care Assn. (exec. com. 1989—). Office: ARC 5615 Pershing Ave Saint Louis MO 63112-1757

POPE, CHRISTIE FARNHAM, historian; b. Bristol, Va., Apr. 8, 1937; d. Floyd Royce and Christine (Sutton) F.; m. Whitney Pope, July 15, 1961; children: Dulany Lucetta, Delanie Penrose, Whitney Bancroft, Norwood Braxton. AB (highest honors), U. N.C., 1959; AM, U. Chgo., 1962, PhD, 1977. Vis. asst. prof. history Ind. U., Bloomington, 1977-79, U. Oregon, Eugene, 1980-81, U. Ky., Lexington, 1982; dir. Women's Studies Ind. U., Bloomington, 1982-85, asst. prof. Afro-Am. Studies, 1982-90; assoc. prof. history Iowa State U., Ames, 1990—; chmn. women's study panel Consortium for Instrnl. Cooperation, 1983-84; membership chmn. Coordinating Com. for Women in History Profession, 1986-87. Author: The Education of the Southern Belle; editor: The Impact of Feminist Research in the Academy, 1987; founder, editor Jour. Women's History, 1988—; contbr. articles to profl. jours. Grantee Am. Coun. of Learned Soc., 1977. Mem. Orgn. Am. Historians, Am. Hist. Assn., So. Hist. Assn., World History Assn., Alpha Gamma Delta. Democrat. Episcopalian. Home: 2994 N Bankers Dr Bloomington IN 47408-1020 Office: Iowa State Univ History Dept Ross Hall Ames IA 50011

POPE, DURAND L., opera manager; b. Akron, Ohio, Aug. 15, 1946; s. Doyle Chester and M. Jo Ann (Barlow) P.; m. Nancy Newman, Sept. 26, 1970. AB in English Lit., Brown U., 1968; postgrad., U. Akron, 1969-72; MA in Theatre, Case Western Res. U., 1974; postgrad., Ind. U., 1974-79. Tchr. Sagamore Hills Children's Hosp., Cleve., 1968-73; adminstv. dir. dept. theatre, lectr. Ind. U., Bloomington, 1975-87; gen. mgr. Indpls. Opera, 1987-1993; adminstrv. dir. Brown County Playhouse, Nashville, Ind., 1985-87; mng. dir. Peninsula (Ohio) Playhouse, 1968-73. Dir. over 25 plays and musicals, 1968—.

POPE, LAWRENCE S., lawyer; b. Cleve., Nov. 2, 1945; s. Jack and Ida Mae Pope; m. Reina Bellotti, July 21, 1968; children: Thaddeus, Nedra, Lessandra, Neil, Matthias, Cameron, Clay, Tucker. BS, Case Western Res. U., 1968; JD, Duquesne U., 1973. Rsch. engr. Jones Laughlin Steel, Pitts., 1968-72; patent atty. ALCOA, Pitts., 1972-74; div. counsel MOBAY Corp., Pitts., 1974-87; of counsel Venable, Baetjer, Howard, Washington, 1987-90; assoc. div. counsel Abbott Labs., Abbott Park, Ill., 1990—. Mem. ABA, Am. Intellectual Property Lawyers Assn. (chmn. subcom.). Republican. Roman Catholic. Office: Abbott Labs 100 Abbott Park Rd Abbott Park IL 60064-3500

POPE, SARAH ANN, elementary education educator; b. Granite City, Ill., Dec. 4, 1938; d. Vance Guy and Lily Lovinia (Fischer) Morgan; m. Thomas E. Pope; children: Robert, Susan, James, John, William. BS in Edn., So. Ill. U., Edwardsville, 1970, MS in Edn., 1976. Lang. arts, humanities, sci., English, reading, math. tchr. Madison (Ill.) Community Sch. Dist., 1970—. Co-founder libr. Harris Elem. Sch., 1990. Fellow Old Six Mile Hist. Soc.; mem. Am. Hemerocallis Soc. Office: Madison Community Unit Sch 1707 4th St Madison IL 62060-1505

POPOFF, FRANK PETER, chemical company executive; b. Sofia, Bulgaria, Oct. 27, 1935; came to U.S., 1940; s. Eftim and Stoyanka (Kossoroff) P.; m. Jean Urse; children: John V., Thomas F., Steven M. B.S. in Chemistry, Ind. U., 1957, M.B.A., 1959. With The Dow Chem. Co., Midland, Mich., 1959—, exec. v.p., 1985-87, dir., pres., chief executive officer, 1987-92; chmn., CEO, dir. Dow Chemical Corp., Midland, Mich., 1992—; exec. v.p., then pres. Dow Chem. Europe subs., Horgen, Switzerland, 1976-85; bd. dirs. Dow Corning Corp., Am. Express, Chem. Bank & Trust Co., Chem. Fin. Corp., Midland. Mem. dean's adv. coun. Ind. U.; mem. vis. com. U. Mich. Sch. Bus.; mem. Pres.' Commn. Environ. Quality. Recipient Internat. Palladium medal, 1994, Société de Chimie Industrielle (Am. Section). Mem. Chem. Mfrs. Assn. (bd. dirs.), U.S. Coun. for Internat. Bus., Bus. Roundtable, Conf. Bd., Am. Chem. Soc. Office: Dow Chem Co 2030 Dow Ctr Midland MI 48674*

POPOVICH, PETER STEPHEN, lawyer, former state supreme court chief justice; b. Crosby, Minn., Nov. 27, 1920; s. Peter and Rose Mary (Mehelich) P.; children: Victoria, Dorothy, Stephen, Susan Jane; stepchildren: Michelle, Paul, Stephen; m. Gail Prince Javorina, July 5, 1985. AA, Hibbing (Minn.) Jr. Coll., 1940; BA, U. Minn., 1942; LLB, St. Paul Coll. of Law, 1947; LLD (hon.), William Mitchell Coll. Law, 1991. Bar: Minn. 1947, U.S. Dist. Ct. Minn. 1947, U.S. Supreme Ct. 1956, U.S. Ct. Appeals (8th cir.) 1975. Sr. ptnr. Peterson & Popovich, St. Paul, 1947-83; chief judge Minn. Ct. Appeals, St. Paul, 1983-87; assoc. justice Minn. Supreme Ct., St. Paul, 1987-89, chief justice, 1989-90; ptnr. Briggs & Morgan, St. Paul, 1991—. Chmn. Minn. Statehood Centennial Com., 1955-59; rep. Minn. State Legis., St. Paul, 1953-63. Named Outstanding Minnesotan, Minn. Broadcasters Assn., 1983; recipient Dist. Svc. to Journalism award Minn. Newspaper Assn., 1991, John Finnegan Freedom of Info. award, 1991. Mem. ABA, Minn. Bar Assn. Minn. Hist. Soc. (hon. council). Roman Catholic. Home: 2301 River Rd S Lakeland MN 55043-9777 Office: Briggs & Morgan 2200 1st Nat Bank Bldg Saint Paul MN 55101

POPP, NATHANIEL, bishop; b. Aurora, Ill., June 12, 1940; s. Joseph and Vera (Boytor) P. BA, Ill. Benedictine U., 1962; ThM, Pontifical Gregorian U., 1966. Ordained priest, 1966, bishop, 1980. Asst. priest St. Michael Byz Cath. Ch., Aurora, Ill., 1967; parish priest Holy Cross Romanian Orthodox Ch., Hermitage, Pa., 1975-80; aux. bishop Romanian Orthodox Episcopate of Am., Orthodox Ch. in Am., Jackson, Mich., 1980-84, ruling bishop, 1984—; mem. Holy Synod, Orthodox Ch. in Am., Syosset, N.Y., 1980—; participant Monastic Consultation World Coun. Chs., Cairo, 1979, 7th Assembly, Vancouver, Can., 1983. Author: Holy Icons, 1969; working editor: (monthly newspaper) Solia. Trustee Romanian-Am. Heritage Ctr., Grass Lake, Mich.; chmn. bd. dirs. Congress of Romanian Ams., 1990. Mem. Mineral and Rock Soc. Mich. Home: 2522 Grey Tower Rd Jackson MI 49201-9120 Address: PO Box 309 Grass Lake MI 49240-0309

POPRICK, MARY ANN, psychologist; b. Chgo., June 25, 1939; d. Michael and Mary (Mihalcik) Poprick; B.A., De Paul U., 1960, M.A., 1964; Ph.D., Loyola U., Chgo., 1968. Intern in psychology Elgin (Ill.) State Hosp., 1961-62; staff psychologist, 1962; staff psychologist Ill. State Tng. Sch. for Girls, Geneva, 1962-63, Mt. Sinai Hosp., Chgo., 1963-64; lectr. psychology Loyola U. at Chgo., 1964-67; asst. prof. Lewis U., Lockport, 1967-70, assoc. prof., 1970-75, chmn. dept., 1968-72 (on leave 1972-73); postdoctoral intern in clin. psychology Ill. State Psychiat. Inst., Chgo., 1972-73; pvt. clin. practice David Psychiat. Clinic, Ltd., South Holland Ill., 1973-87; pvt. practice, South Holland, Ill., 1987—; assoc. sci. staff Riveredge Hosp., Forest Park, Ill., 1975-76; ltd. lic. practitioner dept. psychiatry Christ Hosp., Oak Lawn, Ill., 1983—; ancillary staff dept. psychiatry Ingalls Meml. Hosp., Harvey, Ill., 1994—. Co-chmn. commn. on personal growth and devel. Congregation of 3d Order St. Francis of Mary Immaculate, Joliet, 1970-71; clin. resource person Cath. Archdiocese of Chgo., 1977—. Mem. Am. Psychol. Assn. (rep. from Ill. 1985-88)), Ill. (sec.-treas. acad. sect. 1975-77, mem. student devel. com. 1975-77, chmn. acad. sect. 1977-78, 78-79, mem. program com. 1977-78, sec. 1979-81, pres.-elect 1981-82, pres. 1982-83, past pres. 1983-84, chmn. program com. 1981-82, awards com. 1983-86, rep. Com. of ET and Minority Affairs 1988-89, rep. Cook County 1989-91)), Anxiety Disorders Assn. Am., Midwestern Psychol. Assn. (Cook County rep. 1989-91), Soc. for Sci. Study Religion, AAAS, Chgo. Assn. Psychoanalytical Psychology (rsch. com. 1988), Kappa Gamma Pi, Psi Chi (sec. 1964-65, pres. 1965-66). Home: 547 Marquette Ave Calumet City IL 60409-3316 Office: 16284 Prince Dr South Holland IL 60473-3233

PORCH, ROGER A., state legislator; m. Lois Porch; 2 children. Grad., U. S.D. Mem. S.D. Ho. of Reps., 1985-90; mem. agr. and natural resources com., edn. com.; mem. S.D. State Senate, 1990—, mem. agr. and natural resources coms., mem. edn., legis. procedure and state affairs coms.; rancher. Address: HC 1 Box 25 Wanblee SD 57577-9605*

PORCHIA, JOSEPH, chemical engineer, researcher; b. Pogos de Caldas, Brazil, Nov. 15, 1954; came to U.S., 1971; s. Leonardo and Raffaela (Lattari) P.; m. Joan Kapouralis, June 13, 1982; children: Leonardo Elias, Eliana Rafaela. BSCE, U. Cin., 1981. Packaging scientist Drackett, Cinn., 1976-78; hydraulics engr. Caterpilar, Peoria, Ill., 1978-80; rsch. leader Dow Chem., Midland, Mich., 1988—; pres. Unoteck, Midland, 1989—. Inventor, patentee in field. V.p. Midland Soccer Club, 1994—. Recipient Spl. Achievement award Dow Chem., 1991, Teck Ctr. award, 1992, 94. Mem. AIChE, Instrument Soc. Am., TAPPI. Home: 3614 Windsor Midland MI 48640

PORILE, NORBERT THOMAS, chemistry educator; b. Vienna, Austria, May 18, 1932; came to U.S., 1947, naturalized, 1952; s. Irving and Emma (Intrator) P.; m. Miriam Eisen, June 16, 1957; 1 son, James. B.A., U. Chgo., 1952, M.S., 1954, Ph.D., 1957. Rsch. assoc. Brookhaven Nat. Lab., Upton, N.Y., 1957-59; assoc. chemist Brookhaven Nat. Lab., 1959-63, chemist, 1963-64; vis. prof. chemistry McGill U., 1963-65; assoc. prof. chemistry Purdue U., West Lafayette, Ind., 1965-69; prof. chemistry Purdue U., 1969—; rsch. collaborator Brookhaven Nat. Lab., Argonne Nat. Lab., Los Alamos Sci. Lab., Lawrence Berkeley Lab.; vis. prof. Facultes des Scis., Orsay, France; fellow Soc. Promotion of Sci. in Japan, Inst. Nuclear Study, U. Kyoto, 1961. Editor: Radiochemistry of the Elements and Radiochemical Techniques, 1986-90. John Simon Guggenheim meml. fellow Institut de Physique Nucleaire Orsay, 1971-72; recipient F.D. Martin Undergrad. Teaching award, 1977; Von Humboldt Sr. U.S. Scientist award Philipps U., Marburg, W. Ger., 1982. Mem. Am. Chem. Soc., Am. Phys. Soc. Office: Purdue U Dept Chemistry Chemistry Bldg Lafayette IN 47907

PORRECA, VINCENT JOE, state legislator; b. Greensburg, Pa., Oct. 17, 1941; m. Renee, 1966; children: Victor, Vincent. Student, Wayne County C.C. Supervisor chem. div. Chrysler Corp., Trenton, Mich.; mayor pro tem Trenton; state rep. Mich. Dist. 23, Mich. Dist. 27; mem. Trenton City Coun., 1978-83, precinct del.; mem. appropriations com. Mich. Ho. Reps., co-chair transp. com., 1993—; mem. ins. com., local govt. com., tourism & recreation com., pub. health com. Mem. Am. Legion, K. of C., Elks, Police Officers Assn., Motor City Traffic Club. Home: 3571 Edison St Trenton MI 48183-3683 Address: PO Box 30014 Lansing MI 48909-7514*

PORRETTA, LOUIS PAUL, education educator; b. Malvern, Ohio, Sept. 24, 1926; s. Peter A. and Rosa (Tersigne) P.; B.A., Eastern Mich. U., 1950; Ed.M., Wayne State U., 1959, Ed.D., 1967; m. Elizabeth M. Murphy, Oct. 13, 1951; children—Leslie Elizabeth, Paul Louis, Jeffrey Mark. Tchr. elem. sch. Mason Consol. Sch., Erie, Mich., 1952-53, tchr., prin., 1953-54; prin. Mason Jr. High Sch., Erie, Mich., 1954-59; asst. prof. edn. Eastern Mich. U., Ypsilanti, 1959-62, assoc. prof., 1962-66, prof. edn., 1967-71, prof. dept. curriculum and instruction, 1974-83, prof. emeritus, 1983—, dir. Office Internat. Projects, 1979-81; dir., owner Sylvan Learning Ctr., Ann Arbor, Mich., 1984—; chief-of-party Nat. Tchr. Edn. Center, Somalia, 1967-70; mem. edn. survey team AID, Botswana, Lesotho and Swaziland, 1970, sr. adv. U. Botswana, Lesotho and Swaziland, 1972-74; campus coordinator Swaziland Primary Curriculum Devel. Project, AID, 1978; chief-of-party projects AID, Swaziland, 1975-78, Yemen, 1981-83. Chmn. March of Dimes, Westenaw County, Mich., 1956. Mem. Assn. Tchr. Educators, Inst. Internat. Edn., AAUP, ASCD, Phi Delta Kappa, Pi Gamma Mu. Club: Ypsilanti Rotary. Home: 1273 Laurel View Dr Ann Arbor MI 48105-9765 Office: Sylvan Learning Ctr Concord Ctr 2900 S State St Ann Arbor MI 48104

PORTER, CLOYD ALLEN, state representative; b. Huntley, Ill., May 22, 1935; s. Cecil and Myrtle (Fischer) P.; m. Joan Hawkins, July 25, 1959; children: Ellen, LeeAnn, Jay, Joli. Grad. high sch., Burlington, Wis. Ptnr. Cecil W. Porter & Son Trucking, 1955-70; treas. Burlington Sand and Gravel, 1964-70; owner Cloyd A. Porter Trucking, Burlington, 1970-72; state rep. 43d dist. Wis. State Assembly, Madison, 1972-82; state rep. 66th dist. Wis. State Assembly, 1982—; mem. coun. on recycling, Wis., 1991-94, fire svc. legis. adv. com., 1987-94, legis. coun. com. on fire inspections and fire dues, 1991, legis. coun. spl. com. on emergency med. svcs., 1992-93, mem. joint com. fins., 1995-96. Contbr. articles to profl. jours. Chmn. Town of Burlington, 1971-75; state and met. affairs chmn. Jaycees, Wis., 1963, state v.p., 1969, adminstrv. asst., 1970, exec. v.p., 1971; mem. Wis. Conservation Congress for Natural Resources Leadership and Support in the State Assembly, 1994. Recipient many awards and honors including being named hon. mem. State Fire Chiefs Assn., Wis., 1992, Guardian of Small Bus., NFIB, Wis., 1991, Friend of Agr., Farm Bur. of Wis., 1992, 94, Friend of Edn. Fair Aid Coalition, 1995, Cert. of Appreciation, Wis. Counties Assn., 1993, award Wis. Sate Fire Chiefs Assn., 1995, Oustanding Legislator Wis. Counties Assn., 1996; named to Vietnam Vets. Am. Legis. All-Star Team Wis. Coun. Vietnam Vets. Am., 1995-97. Mem. Wis. Alliance for Fire Safety. Republican. Roman Catholic. Home: 28322 Durand Ave Burlington WI 53105-9408 Office: State Capitol PO Box 8953 309 North Madison WI 53708

PORTER, DARRELL CARTER, evangelist; b. Chgo., Apr. 18, 1952; s. Charles and Constance C. (Dunigan) P.; m. Janis Goodman, Feb. 11, 1980 (div. Apr. 1982); 1 child, Serena; m. Wanda A. Odeneal, May 28, 1994; children: Zachary, Chase, Wrazsanié. BA in Theatre and English, Regis U., Denver, 1974; MA in Christian Edn., Internat. Bible Coll. and Sem., Independence, Mo., 1995. Cert. substance abuse preventionist, Ill. Itinerant evangelist Darrell C. Porter Evangelistic Assocs., Inc., Pasadena, Calif., 1984—; prevention specialist Decatur (Ill.) Mental Health Ctr., 1992-95; pastor Christians in Fellowship, Decatur, 1992—; prevention coord. DeWitt County Human Resource Ctr., Clinton, Ill., 1995—; exec. producer African Am. Cmty. Arts Theatre, Decatur, 1995—; mem. adv. bd. Ill. 4-H, Champaign, 1993-95. Author: Past and Present Day Attacks on the Holy Bible, 1993, (booklet) Spiritual Warfare Prayer, 1988; writer, dir.: (stage play) No Tears in My Eyes, 1995; editor quar. Prayerline Newsletter, 1988-95. Mem. Concerned Citizens Com., Decatur, 1994—; chmn. Macon County Youth Violence and Gang Task Force, Decatur, 1993—. Recipient Arts in the Cmty. award Decatur Area Arts Coun., 1995. Mem. Ctrl. Ill. Theatre Network, Ill. Assn. for Prevention, Ill. Coun. for Prevention of Violence. Office: PO Box 528 Decatur IL 62525

PORTER, DONALD RICHARD, training specialist, teacher; b. Pitts., Aug. 31, 1944; s. Walter Thomas and Mary Rebecca (Brookes) P.; m. Patricia Helen Brown, June 8, 1968 (div. Jan. 1984); children: Jennifer Jo, Vicki Jo, Gerald Matthew; m. Mary Beth Wisniewski, Sept. 21, 1985. Student, Le Tourneau Coll., 1962-64; BEd, No. Ill. U., 1968. Cert. tchr., Ill., Fla. Tchr. Homewood (Ill.) Pub. Sch., 1968-71, St. Lucie County Schs., Ft. Pierce, Fla., 1971-72, Pasco County Schs., Port Richey, Fla., 1972-73, Crete (Ill.) Monee High Sch., 1973-74; application engr. Pullman-Standard, Chgo., 1975-81; mgr. tng. Urban Engring., Johnson Controls World Svcs., Inc., Oakbrook, Ill., 1981—. Patentee sliding baggage door. Mem. Am. Soc. Tng. and Devel., Ill. Tng. and Devel. Assn. Republican. Roman Catholic. Home: 1511 Ceres Dr Crown Point IN 46307-9673 Office: Urban Engring Johnson Controls World Svcs Inc 2000 Spring Rd Oak Brook IL 60521-1804

PORTER, GREGORY W., state legislator; m. Yvette Brewster. BA, Earlham Coll. Property mgr. Cmty. Action of Greater Indpls.; mem. from 96th dist. Ind. State Ho. of Reps., 1992—; mem. cts. and criminal code com., edn. com., pub. safety com., vice chmn. urban affairs com. Bd. dirs., pres. Near Eastside Fed. Credit Union, Friends of Urban League; bd. dirs. Indpls. Urban League; mem. Ch. Fedn. Greater Indpls.; mem. United N.W. Area Devel. Corp.; bd. dirs. Martin Ctr. Home: 3614 N Pennsylvania St Indianapolis IN 46205-3436*

PORTER, HERSCHEL DONOVAN, organic chemist; b. Silverton, Ohio, Aug. 9, 1924; s. Walter Henry and Jennie Bonita (Hadley) P.; m. Margaret Susan Ross, Jan. 23, 1965 (div. 1983); 1 child, Jon Michael Bruce; m. Angela Elizabeth Gorman, Nov. 12, 1988. BS in Chemistry, Wilmington (Ohio) Coll., 1944; PhDin Organic Chemistry, U. Ill., 1947. Instr. chemistry lab. Wilmington Coll., 1942-44; asst. tchr. U. Ill., Urbana, 1944-46; organic chemist Monsanto, Anniston, Ala., summer 1946; organic chemist Eli Lilly & Co., Indpls., 1947-90, ret., 1990; tchr. chemistry Ind. Cen. Coll., Indpls., 1960-64, 66-67, Purdue U. Extension, Indpls., 1963. Contbr. articles to Jour. Am. Chem. Soc., Jour. Organic Chemistry. Mem. Am. Chem. Soc. (editor local sect. publ. 1951, treas. Ind. chpt. 1982-84, chmn. 1985, Outstanding Contbn. award 1991). Mem. Soc. of Friends. Home: 5911 Central Ave Indianapolis IN 46220-2511

PORTER, JOHN EDWARD, congressman; b. Evanston, Ill., June 1, 1935; s. Harry H. and Beatrice V. P.; m. Kathryn Cameron; 5 children. Attended, MIT; BSBA, Northwestern U., 1958; JD with distinction, U. Mich., 1961; DHL, Barat Coll., 1988; LLD (hon.), Kendall Coll., 1992. Bar: Ill. 1961, U.S. Supreme Ct. 1968. Former honor law grad. atty., appellate div. Dept. Justice, Washington; mem. Ill. Ho. of Reps., 1973-79; mem. house appropriations com., subcoms. on labor, health & human svcs., edn., fgn. ops. 96-103rd Congresses from 10th Ill. Dist., Ill., 1980—; mem. legis. select com. on aging, 1980-92; founder, co-chmn. Congl. Human Rights Caucus; founder Congl. Coalition on Population and Devel. Past editor: Mich. Law Rev. Recipient Best Legislator award League of Conservation Voters, 1973, Ind. Voters Ill., 1974, Chgo. Crime Commn., 1976, Lorax award Global Tomorrow Coalition, 1989, Spirit of Enterprise award U.S. C. of C., 1988, 89, 90, Golden Bulldog award Watchdogs of the Treasury, 12 times, Taxpayer's Friend award Nat. Taxpayers Union, Taxpayer Superhero award Grace Commn.'s Citizens Against Government Waste. Republican. Office: US Ho of Reps 2373 Rayburn House Bldg Washington DC 20515-1310

PORTER, JOHN WILSON, education executive; b. Ft. Wayne, Ind., Aug. 13, 1931; s. James Richard and Ola (Phillips) P.; m. Lois Helen French, May 27, 1961; children: Stephen James, Donna Agnes. BA, Albion Coll., 1953; MA, Mich. State U., 1957, PhD, 1962; D in Pub. Adminstrn. (hon.), Albion Coll., 1973; LLD (hon.), Mich. State U., 1977, Cleary Coll., 1987; LHD, Adrian Coll., 1970, U. Detroit, 1979; LLD, Western Mich. U., 1971, Eastern Mich. U., 1975; HHD, Kalamazoo Coll., 1973, Detroit Coll. Bus., 1975, Madonna Coll., Livonia, Mich., 1977; DEd, Detroit Inst. Tech., 1978; AA, Schoolcraft Coll., Livonia, Mich., 1979; DBA, Lawrence Inst. Tech., 1988; LLD, Cleary Coll., 1989. Counselor Lansing (Mich.) Pub. Schs., 1953-58; cons. Mich. Dept. Pub. Instrn., 1958-61; dir. Mich. Higher Edn. Assistance Authority, 1961-65; assoc. supt. for higher edn. Mich. Dept. Edn., 1966-69, state supt. schs., 1969-79; pres. Ea. Mich. U., Ypsilanti, 1979-89; CEO Urban Edn. Alliance Inc., Ann Arbor, Mich., 1988—; v.p. Nat. Bd. for Profl. Teaching Standards, 1989; gen. supt. Detroit Pub. Schs., 1989-91; CEO Urban Edn. Alliance, Inc., Ypsilanti, Mich., 1991—; mem. numerous profl. commns. and bds., 1959—, including; Commn. on Financing Post-secondary Edn., 1972-74, Commn. for Reform Secondary Edn., Kettering Found., 1972-75, Edn. Commn. of States, 1973-79, Nat. Commn. on Performance-Based Edn., 1974-76, Nat. Commn. on Manpower Policy, 1974-79, Mich. Employment and Tng. Svcs. Coun., 1976-79, Nat. Adv. Coun. on Social Security, 1977-79, Commn. on Ednl. Credit, Am. Coun. on Edn., 1977-80; task panel on mental health of family Commn. on Mental Health, 1977-80; mem. Nat. Coun. for Career Edn. (HEW), 1974-76; pres. bd. dirs. Chief State Sch. Officers, 1974-79; pres. Coun. Chief State Sch. Officers, 1977-78; bd. dirs. Comerica Bank; former chmn. bd. Coll. Entrance Exam. Bd., 1984-86. Trustee Nat. Urban League, 1973-79, Charles Stewart Mott Found., 1981—, Albion Coll., 1989—; bd. dirs. Mich. Internat. Council, 1977—, Mich. Congress Parents and Tchrs.; mem. bd. overseers com. for Grad. Sch., Harvard U., 1980-88; mem. edn. com. NAACP; convener goal 6 Nat. Edn. Goals Panel, 1990—; mem. East Lansing Human Relations Commn.; chmn. Am. Assn. State Colls. and U.'s Task Force on Excellence in Edn.; mem. Mich. Martin Luther King, Jr. Holiday Commn., Gov.'s Blue Ribbon Commn. on Welfare Reform; trustee East Lansing Edgewood United Ch.; mem. Catherine McAuley Health Systems Bd., 1990—. Recipient numerous awards including Disting. Svc. award Mich. Congress Parents and Tchrs., 1963, Disting. Svc. award NAACP, Lansing, 1968; cert. of outstanding achievement Delta Kappa chpt. Phi Beta Sigma, 1970; award for disting. svc. Assn. Ind. Colls. and Univs. Mich., 1974; Disting. Alumni award Coll. Edn., Mich. State U., 1974; award for disting. svc. to edn Mich. State U., 1974; Disting. Alumni award, 1979; award for disting. svc. to edn. in Mich. Mich. Assn. Secondary Sch. Prins., 1974; President's award as disting. educator Nat. Alliance Black Sch. Educators, 1977; Marcus Foster Disting. Educator award, 1979; recognition award Mich. Ednl. Rsch. Assn., 1978; recognition award Mich. Assn. Secondary Sch. Prins., 1978; recognition award Mich. Assn. Intermediate Sch. Adminstrs., 1979; recognition award Mich. Assn. Sch. Adminstrs., 1979; Mich. Sch. Bus. Ofcls., 1979; resolution Mich. State Legislature, 1978; Anthony Wayne award Coll. Edn., Wayne State U., 1979; Educator of Decade award Mich. Assn. State and Fed. Program Specialists, 1979; Spirit of Detroit award Detroit City Coun., 1981; Disting. Svc. award Ypsilanti Area C. of C., 1988; Philip A. Hart award Mich. Women's Hall of Fame, 1988; Summit award Greater Detroit C. of C., 1991; Mich. State C. of C. award 1991; inducted Mich. Edn. Hall of Fame, 1992. Mem. Am. Assn. Sch. Adminstrs., Am. Assn. State Colls. and Univs. (president's council, chmn. task force on excellence in edn.), Nat. Measurement Council, NAACP (life), Greater Detroit C. of C. (Summit 1991), Mich. State C. of C. (Disting. Svc. and Leadership award 1991), Tuskeegee Airmen (Disting. Svc. award 1991), Mich. PTA (hon. life), Econ. Club (dir. 1979), Sigma Pi Phi, Phi Delta Kappa. Office: Urban Edn Alliance Inc 900 Victors Way Ste 210 Ann Arbor MI 48108-1779

PORTER, KAREN COLLINS, non-profit organization administrator, counselor; b. Detroit, Dec. 3, 1953; d. Cecil Allen and Mary Louise (Grzena) Collins; m. Frederick James Porter, Aug. 16, 1975; children: Suzanne Catherine, Kirstin Maureen. Student, Albion Coll., 1971-74, U. Mich., 1975; BA, U. Colo., Boulder, 1976; MA, U. Colo., Denver, 1979. Co-dir. Loveland (Colo.) Resource Ctr., 1982-84; asst. dir. Interim House-YWCA, Detroit, 1985; assoc. dir. First Step, Canton, Mich., 1985—; bd. dirs., sec. Loveland Childbirth Edn. Assn., 1980-82; bd. dirs., chairperson Thompson Valley Presch., Loveland, 1980-84; advocate Larimer County Sexual Assault Team, Loveland, 1982-84; mem. bd. dirs. Samaritan Counseling Ctr., Farmington Hills, Mich., 1985-89, mem. program com., 1985-91. Leader Girl Scouts Am., Farmington Hills, 1985-90; ch. leader Sunday Sch., various ch. and soc. coms. Home: 29113 Forest Hl Farmington MI 48331-2445 Office: Ste 5 5820 Lilley Rd Canton MI 48187-3674

PORTER, RUSSELL DENNIS, marine and railroad artist and historian; b. Chgo., Nov. 5, 1918; s. Robert James Porter and Mary Kasson; m. Florence Margaret Thompson, Sept. 25, 1943; children: Robert James, Susan Dee. Grad. high sch., Chgo. Draftsman GE X-Ray Corp., Chgo. and Milw., 1937-51; assoc. editor, artist Kalmbach Pub. Co., Milw., 1951-56; tech. illustrator Ken Cook Pub. Co., Milw., 1956-89; midwest editor Carstens Publs., Ramsey, N.J., 1958-68. Contbr. articles to r.r. mags. and books. With AUS, 1941-42. Mem. Nat. R.R. Hist. Soc. (photog. award 1969), Internat. Soc. Marine Painters, Manitowoc Maritime Mus. Home and Studio: 2228 S 81st St West Allis WI 53219-1724

PORTER, WARREN M(ATTHEW), electrical engineer; b. Orange, Calif., July 3, 1965; s. James L. and Julia N. (McGregor) P. BA in Physics, Carleton Coll., 1987; BS in Elec. Engring., Kansas State U., 1989, MS in Elec. Engring., 1991. Rsch. asst. Mayo Clinic, Rochester, Minn., 1987, USDA Wind Erosion Lab., Manhattan, Kans., 1988-89; grad. rsch., tchg. asst. Dept. Elec. and Computer Engring., Kansas State U., Manhattan, 1989-91; analyst Sprint Corp., Overland Park, Kans., 1991-92; computer applications specialist Kelly Temporary Svcs., Mpls., St. Paul, Minn., 1992-94; document control Sanofi Diagnostics Pasteur, Chaska, Minn., 1992-93; personal computer technician Electronic Data Systems Corp., Bloomington, Minn., 1993; electronic hardware engring. Shadin Co., Inc., Saint Louis Park, Minn., 1994—. Activities coord. Hennepin Ave. United Meth. Ch., Mpls., 1993-96. Mem. IEEE, Engring. in Medicine and Biology Soc., (chair Twin Cities chpt., 1994-96).

PORTER, WILLIAM L., electrical engineer; b. Leeds, N.D., July 2, 1929; s. Ernest Cecil and Dena Grace (Thompson) P.; m. Mary Lynn Lindsey, Oct. 9, 1948; children: Belinda Joyce, William Harry, Terry Jane, Derek Lewis, Michael Ronald. AA, Springfield Coll., 1960; BSEE, U. Ill., 1963. Registered profl. engr., Ill., Minn., Iowa, N.D., S.D., Ohio, Mich., Wis., Ind., Nebr. Lineman City Water, Light and Power, Springfield, Ill., 1947-54, troubleshooter, 1954-62, gen. supt. elec. divsn., 1962-76; prin. engr. R.W. Beck and Assocs., Columbus, Nebr., 1976-77; engring. mgr. R.W. Beck and Assocs., Mpls., 1977-80, ptnr., mgr., 1980-90, sr. cons., 1990—; speaker on engring. and utilities; cons. to electric utilities. Author numerous engring. reports and engring. and utilities papers. Street light com. chair City of Springfield, 1964, mem. CATV com., 1966; mem. Planning Commn. Spring Park (Minn.), 1978-79; chair environ. quality com. region IV Ill. Soc. Profl. Engrs., chair ethics and practices com. Capital chpt.; mem. tech. adv. com. Fed. Power Commn's Nat. Power Survey; chair engring. and ops. com. Am. Pub. Power Assn., 1967-70, chair power supply planning com., 1973-74. Named Engr. of Yr., Capital chpt. Ill. Soc. Profl. Engrs., 1975. Mem. NSPE, IEEE (chmn. Cen. Ill. sect. 1974-75), Minn. Soc. Profl. Engrs., Cons. Engrs. Coun., Am. Bus. Club, Eta Kappa Nu. Republican. Home: 4349 Channel Rd Spring Park MN 55384-9734 Office: R W Beck and Assocs 8300 Norman Center Dr Ste 860 Minneapolis MN 55437-1030

PORTER, WILLIAM ROBERT, chemist; b. Cleve., May 10, 1946; s. William Harvey and Arlene Louise (Howe) P.; m. Rita Bhagwan Gulrajani, June 29, 1974; 1 child, Meaghan Elizabeth. BS, U. Calif., Berkeley, 1968; PhD, U. Wash., 1976. Rsch. assoc. Vanderbilt U., Nashville, Tenn., 1976-78; asst. prof. U. Wis., Madison, 1978-84; rsch. pharmacist Abbott Labs., North Chgo., Ill., 1984-87, sr. pharm. scientist, 1987-88, assoc. rsch. fellow, 1988—; lectr. Ctr. for Profl. Advancement, East Brunswick, N.J., 1988—. Contbr. articles to profl. jours. Am. Found. for Pharm. Edn. fellow, 1974-76. Mem. AAAS, Am. Assn. Pharm. Scientists, Am. Chem. Soc., Am. Stat. Assn., N.Y. Acad. Scis., Phi Beta Kappa, Rho Chi. Office: Abbott Labs 100 Abbott Park Rd Abbott Park IL 60064-3500

PORTERFIELD, NOLAN, English language educator, writer; b. Milliken, Colo., Feb. 26, 1936; s. Afton Arthur and Ora Oneda (Beattie) P.; m. Peggy Pearce, Dec. 21, 1956 (div. 1980); 1 child, Kelly Lynn; m. Erika Brady, Sept. 20, 1981. BA, Tex. Tech. U., 1962, MA, 1964; PhD, U. Iowa, 1970. Reporter Gallup (N.Mex.) Daily Ind., 1955; advt. mgr. Lamesa (Tex.) Daily Reporter, 1955-56, pub., 1956-58; instr. English S.E. Mo. State U., Cape Girardeau, 1964-70, asst. prof. English, 1970-74, assoc. prof. English, 1974-78, prof. English, writer-in-residence, 1978—; cons. Smithsonian Press, Washington, 1981-86. Author: A Way of Knowing, 1971 (Best Novel of Tex. Inst. of Letters 1971), Jimmie Rodgers, 1979 (ASCAP award 1979), Last Cavalier: The Life and Times of John A. Lomax, 1996; editor: Trail to Marked Tree, 1968; contbr. short stories to nat. mags. With U.S. Army, 1958-60. Mem. Am. Folklore Soc., Assn. for Recorded Sound Collections. Home: 564 Boyce Fairview Rd Alvaton KY 42122-9648

PORTMAN, ROB, congressman; b. Cin., Dec. 19, 1955; m. Jane Portman; children: Jed, Will. BA, Dartmouth Coll., 1979; JD, U. Mich., 1984. Ptnr. Head & Ritchey, Cin., 1986-89; assoc. counsel to President of U.S., then dep. asst. to President, dir. Office Legis. Affairs White House, Washington, 1989-92; mem. U.S. Del. to UN Subcom. on Human Rights, 1992, 103d-104th Congresses from 2nd Ohio dist., 1993—; mem. ways and means com., mem. Leaders' Econ. Task Force; asst. whip U.S. Ho. of Reps. Bd. trustees Springer Sch., The United Way, Hyde Park Community United Meth. Ch.; founding trustee Cin.-China Sister City Com.; former bd. dirs. United Home Care; vice chmn. Hamilton County George Bush for Pres. Campaign, 1988, 92; chmn. Rep. Early Bird Campaign com., 1992; del. Rep. Nat. Conv., 1988, 92; active Hamilton County Rep. Party Exec. com., Hamilton County Rep. Party Fin. Com. Mem. Cin. World Trade Assn. Office: US Ho of Reps 238 Cannon HOB Washington DC 20515-0509*

POSADAS, BARBARA MERCEDES, history educator; b. Chgo., Oct. 2, 1945; d. Alipio Gutierrez and Estelle Frances (Hazack) P.; m. Roland Lincoln Guyotte III, July 10, 1982. BA, DePaul U., 1967; MA, Northwestern U., 1971, PhD, 1976. Instr. No. Ill. U., DeKalb, 1974-76, asst. prof., 1976-82, assoc. prof. History, 1982—; dir. Ill. State Hist. Soc., Springfield, 1992-95. mem. editl. adv. bd. Ill. Hist. Jour., 1982-93, AMERASIA Jour., 1985—, Jour. Women's History, 1988—; contbr. articles to profl. jours. Mem. Ill. Hist. Sites Adv. Coun., 1984-86; mem. City of DeKalb (Ill.) Landmark Commn., 1988-96. Recipient Sr. Fulbright Rsch. award Fulbright Found., Philippines, 1982, Postdoctoral Rsch. U. Calif., L.A., 1987. Mem. Am. Hist. Assn., Orgn. Am. Historians, Chgo. Hist. Soc., Filipino Am. Nat. Hist. Soc., Immigration History Soc., Ill. State Hist. Soc., Assn. for Asian Am. Studies. Office: No Ill U Dept History De Kalb IL 60115

POSHA, D. RICHARD, real estate developer, home builder, designer; b. Indpls., Jan. 23, 1951; s. Octavian Dan and June (Kendall) P.; m. Tina Louise Kissel, May 27, 1977; children: Dan Richard, Benjiman William. Student, Ind. U., 1971. Constrn. mgr. Stuart Constrn., Indpls., 1970-72, Nelson Constrn., Indpls., 1972-74; pres. D.R. Posha, Inc., Indpls., 1974-86; v.p. Weston Devel. Inc., Indpls., 1986-88; pres. D.R. Posha and Assocs., Inc., Indpls., 1988—, Posha Realty Inc., Fishers, Ind., 1994—. Contbr. articles to profl. jours. Mem. Nat. Assn. Home Builders, Builders Assn. Indpls. (Best Interior Indpls. Home Show award), Metro. Indpsl. Bd. Realtors, Ind. State Builders Assn., Am. Motorcycle Assn., NRA. Republican. Office: D R Posha and Assoc Inc 10089 Allisonville Rd Ste 300 Fishers IN 46038-2071

POSHARD, GLENN W., congressman; b. Herald, Ill., Oct. 31, 1945. BA, So. Ill. U., 1970, MS, 1974, PhD, 1984. Tchr. high sch.; asst. dir. then dir. Ill. State Regional Edn. Svc. Ctr.; mem. Ill. State Senate, 1984-88, 101st-104th Congresses from 22nd (now 19th) Ill. Dist., 1989—; ranking minority mem. small bus. subcom. on govt. programs, mem. transp. and infrastructure com. Served with U.S. Army. Democrat. Office: US Ho of Reps 2334 Rayburn HOB Washington DC 20515*

POSKANZER, STEVEN GARY, university administrator, lawyer; b. Cortland, N.Y., Sept. 1, 1958; s. Charles Newton and Joan Rae (Mamolen) P.; m. Jane Anne Nofer; children: Jill Madeline, Craig Robert. BA, Princeton U., 1980; JD, Harvard U., 1983. Assoc. Arent, Fox, Kintner, Plotkin & Kahn, Washington, 1983-85; assoc. gen. counsel U. Penn., 1985-93; exec. asst. to pres. U. Chgo., 1993—. Mem. Phi Beta Kappa. Home: 5505 South Kenwood Ave Chicago IL 60637 Office: U Chicago 5801 South Ellis Ave Chicago IL 60637

POSNER, KATHY ROBIN, communications executive; b. Oceanside, N.Y., Nov. 3, 1952; d. Melvyn and Davonne Hope (Hansen) P. BA in Journalism, Econs., Manhattanville Coll., 1974. Fin. planner John Dreyfus Corp., Purchase, N.Y., 1974-80; corp. liaison Gulf States Mortgage, Atlanta, 1980-82; dir. promotion Gammon's of Chgo., 1982-83; coordinator trade show mktg. Destron, Chgo., 1983-84; pres. Postronics, Chgo., 1984-87; v.p. Martin E. Janis & Co., Inc., Chgo., 1987-90; exec. v.p., CEO Comm. 2000, Chgo., 1990—. Editor: How to Maximize Your Profits, 1983; contbg. editor Internat. Backgammon Guide, 1974-84, Backgammon Times, 1981-84, Chgo. Advt. and Media; columnist Food Industry News. Bd. dirs. Chgo. Beautification Com., 1987, Concerned Citizens for Action, Chgo., 1987; mem. steering com. Better Boys Found.; campaign mgr. Brown for Alderman, Chgo., 1987; mem. bd. dirs. Little City Found. Mem. NATAS, NOW, Women in Comm., Am. Soc. Profl. and Exec. Women, Women in Film-Chgo. (bd. dirs.), Mensa, Acad. Arts (v.p.), Ill. Restaurant Assn. (mem. adv. bd.), Chgo. Area Pub. Affairs Group, Baderbrau Beer Drinking Soc. (v.p. pub. rels.), Gammon's Chgo. (bd. dirs. 1980-83, editor newsletter 1982-83), Little City Found. (bd. dirs.), City Club Chgo. (bd. dirs.), Cavendish North Club (bd. dirs. 1984-87), Met. Club, Plaza Club, Monroe Club, 410 Club. Republican. Jewish. Office: Comm. 2000 921 W Van Buren St Ste 240 Chicago IL 60607

POSNER, LINDA ROSANNE, charity volunteer, educator; b. Rockford, Ill., Sept. 24, 1940; d. Lawrence George and Genevieve Annette (Reecher) Turnquist; m. Christian John Posner, Oct. 14, 1972; children: Katrina E., Christian L. BA, Rockford Coll., 1962; MEd, U. Md., 1970. Elem. sch. tchr. Elmhurst and Villa Park, Ill., 1962, 68; spl. edn. tchr. Christ Ch. Child Ctr., Bethesda, Md., 1970-72. Chmn. Heart Ball, 1988—, Golden Thimble IX, Hosp. of Good Samaritan, L.A., 1986-87, Heart of Gold recognition dinner; chmn. Am. Heart Assn. Greater L.A., 1983, now bd. dirs.; pres. St. Vincent Med. Ctr. Auxiliary, L.A., 1983-84; trustee St. Alban's Episc. Ch., L.A., 1985-87; bd. dirs. Claremont Young Musicians Orch., Claremont Heritage, home tour 1991-93, Los Angeles County Med. Assn., pres. aux. dist. 14, 1992-93; co-chair Charity Ball Mercy Hosp., Janesville, 1996, AAUW conv., Janesville; pres. Janesville Symphony Guild, 1995—; bd. dirs. Beloit Janesville Orch., 1996. Mem. U. So. Calif. Med. Faculty Wives (pres. 1986-87). Home: 3455 N Spring Hill Dr Janesville WI 53545-9022

POSPISIL, FREDERICK JOHN, financial services; b. Hinsdale, Ill., Feb. 25, 1954; s. Charles Edward and Marie Barbara (Maruska) P. BA, U. St. Thomas, St. Paul, 1976; MBA, Loyola U. Chgo., 1980. With St. Paul Fed. Bank for Savings, Chgo., 1976-94; dir. Branch Sales and Ops., 1994—; pres. Loyola U. Chgo. Grad. Sch. Bus. Alumni Assn., 1987-88. Trustee Village of Oak Park, Ill., 1994-99. Recipient Outstanding Contbn. Oak Park (Ill.) Festival Theatre, 1994. Mem. Bank Mktg. Assn. Office: St Paul Fed Bank for Saving 10035 W Grand Ave Franklin Park IL 60131

POSTHUMA, ALBERT ELWOOD, surgeon; b. Grand Rapids, Mich., Apr. 25, 1919; s. Gerrit Pylman and Alice (Mandemaker) P.; A.B., Calvin Coll., 1940; M.D., U. Mich., 1943, M.S. 1949; m. Jean L. Swann, Aug. 17, 1974; children by previous marriage: Beth Alicia Posthuma Jenkins, Ann Maureen Posthuma Eizyk, Jane Marie Robertson, Susan Swann Gregory. Intern, St. Mary's Hosp., Grand Rapids, 1943-44, resident, 1944-46, 48-50; practice medicine specializing in surgery, 1950-86; cons. surgeon St. Mary's Hosp., 1972—, chief of staff, 1972-78; cons. surgeon Ferguson-Droste-Ferguson hosps. Pres., Kent County Med. Found., 1979. Served from 1st lt. to capt. AUS, 1946-48. Recipient citation U. Mich., 1949. Diplomate Am. Bd. Surgery. Fellow A.C.S.; mem. Pan-Pacific Surg. Assn., Kent County Med. Soc. (pres. 1978-79). Club: Blythefield Country. Home: 6025 Belinda Dr NE Rockford MI 49341-9444

POSTHUMUS, RICHARD EARL, state senator, farmer; b. Hastings, Mich., July 19, 1950; s. Earl Martin and Lola Marie (Wieland) P.; m. Pamela Ann Bartz, June 23, 1972; children—Krista, Lisa, Heather, Bryan. B.S. in Agrl. Econs. and Pub. Affairs Mgmt., Mich. State U., 1972. Exec. v.p. Farmers and Mfrs. Beet Sugar Assn., Saginaw, Mich., 1972-74, Mich. Beef Commn., Lansing, 1974-78; dir. constituent relations Republican Caucus, Mich. Ho. of Reps., 1979-82; self-employed farmer, 1974—. Third vice chmn. Mich. Republican Com., 1971-73; mem. Hope Ch. of the Brethren. Mem. Alpha Gamma Rho. Office: State Senate State Capitol Lansing MI 48909

POTAMIANOS, PETER G., editor, educator; b. Chgo., July 14, 1940; s. George P. and Beatrice (Economos) P.; m. Mary Georgacopulos, Nov. 1, 1964; children: George, Madelene. BA, Northwestern U., 1962; MATE, Northeastern U., 1968; PhD, U. Ill., 1971. Cert. tchr. & adminstr., Ill. English prof. Va. State U., Petersburg, 1971-72; curriculum devel. cons. Ill. Dept. Edn., Chgo., 1972-74; mgr. instrn. tech. Bell Sys. Ctr./ AT&T, Lisle, Ill., 1974-83; mgr. extension svcs. Bellcore TEC, Lisle, Ill., 1984-88; staff mgr. univ. rels. Ill. Bell, Chgo., 1988-91; dir. cmty. rels. Ameritech, Hoffman Estates, Ill., 1991-95; mng. editor Soc. Actuaries, Schaumburg, Ill., 1995—; v.p., bd. dirs. NSACI, Schaumburg, 1992-95; pres.-elect, bd.dirs. Hoffman Estates C.C., 1991-95. V.p., bd. trustees Glen Ellyn (Ill.) Pub. Libr.; bd. trustees DuPage Libr. Sys., Geneva, Ill., Carol Stream (Ill.) Pub. Libr., 1972-74. U. Ill. fellow, 1969-71. Mem. Phi Delta Kappa (pres.), Lambda Iota Tau (pres. 1967-68). Mem. Eastern Orthodox Ch.

POTENTE, EUGENE, JR., interior designer; b. Kenosha. Wis., July 24, 1921; s. Eugene and Suzanne Marie (Schmit) P.; Ph.B., Marquette U., 1943; postgrad. Stanford U., 1943, N.Y. Sch. Interior Design, 1947; m. Joan Ciroffe, Jan. 29, 1946; children: Eugene J., Peter Michael, John Francis, Suzanne Marie. Founder, pres. Studios of Potente, Inc., Kenosha, Wis., 1949—; pres., founder Archtl. Services Assos., Kenosha, 1978—, Bus. Leasing Services of Wis. Inc., 1978—; past nat. pres. Inter-Faith Forum on Religion, Art and Architecture; vice chmn. Wis. State Capitol and Exec. Residence Bd., 1981—. Sec., Kenosha Symphony Assn., 1968-74. Bd. dirs. Ctr. for Religion and the Arts, Wesley Theol. Sem., Washington, 1983-84. Served with AUS, 1943-46. Mem. Am. Soc. Interior Designers (treas., pres. Wis. chpt. 1985-86, 94-95, chmn. nat. pub. svc. 1986), Illuminating Engring. Soc. N.Am., Internat. Inst. Interior Designers, Sigma Delta Chi. Roman Catholic. Lodge: Elks. Home: 8609 2nd Ave Kenosha WI 53143-6511 Office: 914 60th St Kenosha WI 53140-4041

POTRA, FLORIAN ALEXANDER, mathematics educator; b. Cluj, Romania, Dec. 7, 1950; came to the U.S., 1982; s. Ioan and Ana (Popa) P.; m. ELena Lavric, Nov. 15, 1973; 1 child, Valentin. MS, Babes-Bolyai U., Cluj, 1973; PhD, U. Bucharest, 1980. Analyst IPGGH, Bucharest, Romania, 1974-78; researcher INCREST, Bucharest, 1978-82; postdoctoral researcher U. Pitts., 1982-83, asst. prof., 1983-84; assoc. prof. U. Iowa, Iowa City, 1984-90, prof., 1990—; vis. rschr. Lawrence Livermore Nat. Lab., Rice U., U. Catania, Italy, Konrad Zuse Zentrum, Berlin, U. Darmstadt, Germany, 1990, U. Karlsruhe, Germany, 1987-91, Argonne Nat. Lab., 1991, U. Geneva, 1993, U. NSW, Sydney, 1995. Assoc. editor: SIAM Jour. on Optimization, 1991—, Jour. Optimization Theory and Applications, 1991—; co-author: Research Notes in Mathematics 103, 1984; contbr. articles to profl. jours. Andrew Mellon fellow, 1982, Old Gold fellow, 1984, James Van Allen fellow in natural scis., 1991; NSF grantee, 1985-87., 94—. Home: 4029 W Overlook Rd NE Iowa City IA 52240-7942 Office: U Iowa Mathematics Iowa City IA 52242

POTT, SANDRA KAY, finance company executive; b. Denver, Apr. 1, 1946; d. Sanford N. and Mary Helen (Davis) Groendyke; m. Joel Frederic Pott, Mar. 7, 1970; children: Eric Christopher, Jessica Elizabeth. BA in English, Ea. Mich. U., 1969. CFP, Mich. Account exec. Dean Witter Reynolds, Troy, Mich., 1984-93, assoc. v.p., 1993—. Mem. AAUW (bd. dirs. 1977-83), Nat. Assn. Women Bus. Owners (bd. dirs. 1994—), Royal Oak C. of C. (edn. com. 1991—, econ. devel. com. 1991—), Royal Oak League Women Voters (bd. dirs. 1977-83). Office: Dean Witter Reynolds 100 W Big Beaver Ste 500 Troy MI 48099

POTTER, CALVIN J., state legislator; b. Sheboygan, Wis., Nov. 3, 1945; married. Student, U. Wis., Sheboygan; BA, Lakeland Coll., 1968; postgrad., U. Wis. Past Wis. state assemblyman dist. 26; with dist. 9 Wis. State Senate, 1990—, chmn. edn. com.; former tchr. Mem. Sheboygan County Hist. Soc. Mem. NEA, Wis. Edn. Assn., Izaak Walton League. Address: 808 Green Tree Rd Kohler WI 53044*

POTTER, DAVID LYNN, retail executive; b. Vincennes, Ind., Sept. 1, 1938; s. Lynn David and Margaret Francis (Gould) P.; m. Katherine Bonner Harris, Feb. 18, 1961; children: Michael, Bradley, Gregory. BS in Bus. with honors, Eastern Ill. U., 1971. Supr. data processing Golden Rule Ins. Co., Lawrenceville, Ill., 1961-67; instr. data processing Vincennes (Ind.) U., 1967-69; adminstr. Weber Med. Clinic, Olney, Ill., 1971-77; v.p. Harris Supply Co., Inc., Olney, 1977-87, pres., 1987—. Bd. dirs. Weber Med. Found., Olney, 1992—; mem. Richland County Bd., Olney, 1989-90; mem. governing bd. Richland Meml. Hosp., Olney, 1989-90; mem. citizens adv. com. East Richland Sch. Dist., Olney, 1982-83. With U.S. Navy, 1956-59. Mem. Petroleum Club, Elks, Delta Mu Delta. Home: 3 Watergate Olney IL 62450-8996 Office: Harris Supply Co Inc PO Box 244 Olney IL 62450-0244

POTTER, JACK ARTHUR, optometrist; b. Peoria, Ill., Sept. 7, 1917; s. John Bernard Potter and Mary Bernadot Purcell; m. Charlotte Helen Brubaker, Apr. 5, 1941 (dec. Jan 1974); children: Jack Allen, Lynn Ann; m. Dorothy Grantz Styx, July 24, 1975. OD, Ill. Coll. Optometry, 1938; postgrad., Purdue U., 1946. Pvt. practice optometry East Peoria, Ill., 1938—; coordinator optometry St. Francis Hosp., Peoria, 1975-82; lectr. Bradley U., Peoria, 1949-72. Contbr. articles on reading and vision problems to profl. jours. Served with U.S. Army, 1941-45. Fellow Am. Acad. Optometry; mem. Am. Optometric Assn. (bd. trustees 1967-73, sec., treas. 1973-75), Ill. Optometric Assn. (pres. 1965-67, Optometrist of Yr. 1967, Disting. Svc. award 1975, del. for life), Ill. Valley Optometric Soc. (pres.). Republican. Mem. Christian Ch. Lodges: Masons, Shriners. Home: 609 Hilldale Ave Washington IL 61571-1607 Office: 2400 N Main St East Peoria IL 61611-1735

POTTER, JOHN WILLIAM, federal judge; b. Toledo, Ohio, Oct. 25, 1918; s. Charles and Mary Elizabeth (Baker) P.; m. Phyllis May Bihn, Apr. 14, 1944; children: John William, Carolyn Diane, Kathryn Susan. PhB cum laude, U. Toledo, 1940; JD, U. Mich., 1946. Bar: Ohio 1947. Assoc. Zachman, Boxell, Schroeder & Torbet, Toledo, 1946-51; ptnr. Boxell, Bebout, Torbet & Potter, Toledo, 1951-69; mayor City of Toledo, 1961-67; asst. atty. gen. State of Ohio, 1968-69; judge 6th Dist. Ct. Appeals, 1969-82; judge U.S. Dist. Ct., Toledo, 1982—, sr. judge, 1992—; presenter in field. Sr. editor U. Mich. Law Rev., 1946. Pres. Ohio Mcpl. League, 1965; past assoc. pub. mem. Toledo Labor Mgmt. Commn.; past pres., bd. dirs. Commn. on Rels. with Toledo (Spain); past bd. dirs. Cummings Sch. Toledo Opera Assn., Conlon Ctr.; past trustee Epworth United Meth. Ch.; hon. chmn. Toledo Festival Arts, 1980. Capt. F.A., U.S. Army, 1942-46. Decorated Bronze Star; recipient Leadership award Toledo Bldg. Congress, 1965, Merit award Toledo Bd. Realtors, 1967, Resolution of Recognition award Ohio Ho. of Reps., 1982, award for outstanding rsch. or svc. in law or govt. Ohio State Bar Found., 1995. Fellow Am. Bar Found., Am. Judicature Soc., 6th Jud. Cir. Dist. Judges Assn., Fed. Judges Assn.; mem. ABA, Ohio Bar Assn. (Ouststanding Rsch. award 1995), Toledo Bar Assn. (exec. com. 1962-64, award 1992), Lucas County Bar Assn., Toledo Area C. of C. (v.p. 1973-74), U. Toledo Alumni Assn. (past pres.), Toledo Zool. Soc. (past bd. dirs.), Old Newsboys Club, Toledo Club, Kiwanis (past pres.), Phi Kappa Phi. Home: 2418 Middlesex Dr Toledo OH 43606-3114 Office: US Dist Ct 210 US Courthouse 1716 Spielbusch Ave Toledo OH 43624-1347

POTTER, ROSEMARY, state legislator; b. Apr. 15, 1952; m. Steve Nichols, 1994. BA, U. Wis., Milw., 1974, MA, 1983. Former dist. dir. Combined Health Appeal Wis. Ho. of Reps.; chairwoman Dem. Caucus; Wis. state assemblywoman Dist. 20, 1989—; former tchr. Address: 3113 S Pennsylvania Ave Milwaukee WI 53207-2913*

POTTER, VAN RENSSELAER, cancer researcher, author; b. Day County, S.D., Aug. 27, 1911; s. Arthur Howard and Eva (Herpel) P.; m. Vivian Pearl Christensen, Aug. 3, 1935; children: Karin, John, Carl. BS, S.D. State U., 1933, DSc, 1959; MS, U. Wis., 1936, PhD, 1938. Jonathan Bowman fellow U. Wis., Madison, 1940-42, asst. prof. oncology, 1942-45, assoc. prof., 1945-47, prof., 1947-80, Leonardo scholar, 1973, Hilldale prof. oncology, 1980-82, emeritus prof., 1982—; asst. dir. McArdle Lab., Madison, 1958-72; vis. prof. Andean biology U. San Marcos, Lima, Peru, 1952-53; mem. com. on growth NIH, Bethesda, Md.; mem. com. on analysis and projection Am. Cancer Soc., N.Y.C. Author: Enzymes, Growth and Cancer, 1950, Nucleic Acid Outlines, 1960, Bioethics, Bridge to the Future, 1971, Global Bioethics, 1988. Pres. Citizens for Monona Terr., Madison, 1961; mem. Mayor's Auditorium Com., Madison, 1964. Recipient Paul-Lewis award Am. Cancer Soc., 1947, Bertner award M.D. Anderson Hosp., 1961, Bristol-Myers award, 1981, Basic Sci. award Am. Cancer Soc., 1986. Mem. Am. Acad. Arts and Scis., Nat. Acad. Scis., Am. Assn. Cancer Rsch. (pres. 1974, Clowes award 1964), Am. Soc. Cell Biology (pres. 1965). Democrat. Unitarian. Home: 163 N Prospect Ave Madison WI 53705 Office: McArdle Lab U Wis 1400 University Ave Madison WI 53706

POTTERTON, JOHN PAUL, financial executive; b. Wantagh, N.Y., June 12, 1951; s. James Edward and Marie Dolores (Sheridan) P.; m. Dolores Bopp, June 5, 1976; children: Kristen, Erin, Kieran. BA in Sociology, Fairfield U., 1973, MA in Counseling, 1986. Mgr. Appalachian Vols., Inc., Darien, Conn., 1973-84; tchr. Fairfield Coll. Prep., Conn., 1979-84; adminstr. Diocese of Rockville Center (N.Y.), 1984-86; dir. KPMG's Ctr. for Leadership Devel. Conf. Ctr., Chgo., 1986—; cons. Internat. Assn. Conf. Ctrs., St. Louis, 1991—. Tchr. St. Thomas the Apostle High Sch. Program, Naperville, Ill., 1986-92; counselor Covenant House, N.Y.C., 1987-88. Mem. Meeting Profls. Internat. (cert. meeting profl., pres. Chgo. chpt. 1992—, Rising Star award 1991, The Kathy Osterman award 1995), Internat. Assn. Conf. Ctrs. (study tour leader 1991-92, bd. dirs. 1995—). Roman Catholic. Office: KPMG Peat Marwick 205 N Michigan Ave Chicago IL 60601-5925

POTTORFF, JO ANN, state legislator; b. Wichita, Kans., Mar. 7, 1936; d. John Edward McCluggage and Helen Elizabeth (Alexander) Ryan; m. Gary Nial Pottorff; children: Michael Lee, Gregory Nial. BA, Kansas State U., 1957; MA, St. Louis U., 1969. Elem. tchr. Pub. Sch., Keats and St. George, 1957-59; cons., elem. specialist Mid Continent Regional Edn. Lab., Kansas City, Mo., 1971-73; cons. Poindexter Assocs., Wichita, 1975; campaign mgr. Garner Shriver Congl. Camp, Wichita, 1976; interim dir. Wichita Area Rape Ctr., 1977; conf. coord. Biomedical Synergistics Inst., Wichita, 1977-79; real estate sales asst. Chester Kappelman Group, Wichita, 1979—; state rep. State of Kans., Topeka, 1985—. Mem. sch. bd. Wichita Pub. Schs., 1977-85; bd. dirs. Edn. Consol. and Improvement Act Adv. com., Kans. Found. for the Handicapped; mem. Children and Youth Adv. com. (bd. dirs.); active Leadership Kans.; chairperson women's network Nat. Conf., State Legislators; mem. Wichita Children's Home Bd. Recipient Disting. Svc. award Kans. Assn. Sch. Bds., 1983, Outstanding Svc. to Sch. Children of Nation award Coun. Urban Bds., 1984, awards Gov.'s Conf. for Prevention of Child Abuse and Neglect, Kans. Assn. Reading. Mem. Leadership Am. Alumnae (bd. dirs., sec.), Found. for Agr. in Classroom (bd. dirs.), Jr. League, Vet. Aux. (pres.), Bd. Nat. State Art Agys., Rotary, Ky. Assn. Rehab. Facilities (Ann. award), Nat. Order Women in Legislature (past bd. dirs.), Rotary, Chi Omega (pres.). Office: Chester Kappelman Group PO Box 8036 Wichita KS 67208-0036

POTTS, ANTHONY VINCENT, optometrist, orthokeratologist; b. Detroit, Aug. 10, 1945; m. Susan Claire, July 1, 1967; 1 child, Anthony Christian. Student, Henry Ford Community Coll., 1964-65, Eastern Mich. U., 1965-66; OD, So. Coll. Optometry, 1970; MS in Health Svcs. Mgmt., LaSalle U., 1995. Practice orthokeratology and contact lenses Troy, Mich., 1975—; adj. prof. optometry Ill. Coll. Optometry; lectr., author orthokeratology, contact lenses and astigmatism. Lt. USNR, 1971-73, lt. MSC USNR, 1992—. Fellow Internat. Orthokeratology Soc. (membership chmn. 1976-83, bd. dirs. local chpt. 1976-83, chmn. Internat. Eye Rsch. Found. sect. 1981-83, bd. dirs. nat. chpt. 1985—, adminstrv. dir. nat. chpt. 1985—, chmn. nat. chpt. 1987—), Am. Acad. Optometry; mem. Am. Optometric Assn., Armed Forces Optometric Soc., Nat. Eye Rsch. Found., Naval Order Am. Roman Catholic. Office: Med Sq Troy 1575 W Big Beaver Rd # 11C Troy MI 48084-3525

POTTS, BARBARA JOYCE, historical society executive; b. L.A., Feb. 18, 1932; d. Theodore Thomas and Helen Mae (Kelley) Elledge; m. Donald A. Potts, Dec. 27, 1953; children: Tedd, Douglas, Dwight, Laura. AA, Graceland Coll., 1951; grad., Radiol. Tech. Sch., 1953; grad. program for sr. execs. in state and local govt., Harvard U., 1989. Radiol. technician Independence (Mo.) Sanitarium and Hosp., 1953, 58-59, Mercy Hosp., Balt., 1954-55; city coun. mem.-at-large City of Independence, 1978-82, mayor, 1982-90; exec. dir. Jackson County Hist. Soc., 1991—; chmn. Mid-Am. Regional Coun., Kansas City, Mo., 1984-85; bd. dirs. Mo. Mcpl. League, Jefferson City, 1982-90, v.p., 1986-87, pres., 1987, 88; chmn. Mo. Commn. on Local Govt. Cooperation, 1985-90. Author: Independence, 1985. Mem. Mo. Gov.'s Conf. Edn., 1976, Independence Charter Rev. Bd., 1977; bd. dirs. Hope House Shelter Abused Women, Independence, 1982—, Vis. Nurses Assn., 1990-93, Mid-Continent Coun. U.S. Girl Scouts, 1991-95; pres. Child Placement Svcs., Independence, 1972-89, Greater Kansas City region NCCJ, 1990—; trustee Independence Regional Health Ctr., 1982-90, 94—, Park Coll., 1989—, chmn. bd. trustees, 1995—; mem. Nat. Women's Polit. Caucus, 1978—; mem. adv. bd. Greater Mo. Focus on Leadership, mem. steering com., 1989—; bd. mem. Independence Cmty. Found., 1990—; bd. mem. Harry S. Truman Libr. Inst., 1995—. Recipient George Lehr Meml. award for community svc., 1989, Woman of Achievement award Mid-Continent coun. Girl Scouts U.S.A., 1983, 75th Anniversary Women of Achievement award Mid-Continent coun. Girl Scouts, 1987, Jane Adams award Hope House, 1984, Community Leadership award Comprehensive Mental Health Svcs., Inc., 1984, 90, Graceland Coll. Alumni Disting. Svc. award 1991, Disting. Citizen award Independence C. of C., 1993, Outstanding Community Svc. award Jackson County Inter-Agy. Coun., 1994; named Friend of Edn. Indpendence NEA, 1990. Mem. LWV (Community Svc. award 1990), Am. Inst. Pub. Svc. (mem. bd. nominators), Nat. Trust for Hist. Preservation. Mem. Reorganized LDS Ch. Home: 18508 E 30th Ter S Independence MO 64057-1904

POTTS, CAROL JEAN FOX, geriatrics nurse, quality assurance coordinator; b. Plainwell, Mich., Jan. 26, 1954; d. Edward Iman and Grace (Dendel) Fox.; m. Stephen Potts, Dec. 1, 1978; children: Michael, Jonathan. BSN, U. N.Mex. Coll. Nursing, 1983. Clin. specialist, substance abuse instr. Pine Rest Christian Hosp., 1983-85; nursing quality assurance coord. Mich. Vets. Facility, Grand Rapids, 1985-91; innovations panel presenter Nat. Quality Assurance Forum, Milw., 1990. Contbr. articles to profl. jours. Mem. APHA, Am. Soc. on Aging. Home: PO Box 423 Wayland MI 49348-0423

POUCHE, FREDRICK, JR., state legislator; b. Independence, Mo., Aug. 3, 1945; m. Martha M. Pouche; children: Sean R. Scobee, Ash Thomas. BA in Bus. Adminstrn. summa cum laude, Park Coll., Parkville, Mo.; MA in Bus. Adminstrn. and Mgmt. magna cum laude, Webster U. Prin. Pouche Corp.; adminstr. labor rels., sr. fin. analyst Trans World Airlines, 1965-84; fee agt. Mo. Dept. Revenue, 1985-89; auditor Platte County, 1989-91; state rep. 30th dist. Mo. Ho. of Reps., 1995-96; candidate Mo. Ho. of Reps., 1982, 86, 88, 94; committeeman Platte County Rep. Com., 1983-84; staff rep. Ashcroft for Gov. Com., 1984; fin. chmn. Platte Rep. Com., 1984-85; dist. chmn. Dole for Pres. Com., 1987-88; Mo. del. Rep. Nat. Conv., 1988; Platte County coord. Roy Blunt for Gov. Com., 1994. Decorated Army Commendation medal with oak leaf cluster (2), others. Mem. KC (# 3430), Northland C. of C., South Platte Rotary Club (Paul Harris fellow), Platte Rep. Assn. Roman Catholic. Office: Mo Ho of Reps Rm 116-5 State Capitol Jefferson City MO 65101

POULSEN, FERN SUE, special events and public relations consultant; b. Chgo., Sept. 29, 1959; d. Herman and Renne (Greenberg) Bass; m. Gregory Carl Poulsen; children: Michael Carl, Michelle Jennifer. Ba, N. Ill. U., 1981. Corporate communications staff coordinator Centel Corp., Chgo., 1981-86; mgr. special events Network Mktg. Group, Oak Brook, Ill., 1986-88; pres. Poulsen Promotions, Chgo., 1988—; cons. spl. events and pub. rels. Vol. Easter Seal Soc. and March of Dimes, Chgo., 1987-88, Penny Pullen Campaign Com., Park Ridge, Ill., 1981-83, Am. Cancer Soc., Des Plaines, Ill., 1983; exec. advisor Jr. Achievement, Chgo., 1982-83; active Lincoln Park Cen. Assn., Chgo., 1988. Named Outstanding Woman Student Leader N. Ill. U. Women's Faculty, 1980. Mem. Internat. Assn. Bus. Communicators, Women's Am., ORT, Ad-Net Chgo., Parents and Child Edn. Soc., Nat. Coun. Jewish Women, Omicron Delta Kappa, Phi Kappa Phi.

POURKERMANI, MAHMOOD, electrical engineer, consultant; b. Tehran, Iran, Oct. 15, 1944; came to U.S., 1990; s. Abolghassem and Aghdas (Pahlevan) P.; m. Mina Naghshineh, Nov. 15, 1975; children: Peyman, Saman. MSc, Hanover (Germany) U., 1969, PhD, 1971. Asst. prof. elec. engring. Sharif U., Tehran, 1971-75, assoc. prof., 1981-90, vice chmn. dept., 1975-78, chmn., 1978-81; rsch. assoc. Ill. Inst. Tech., Chgo., 1990-91; staff scientist C.E. Niehoff & Co., Evanston, Ill., 1991—. Contrb. articles to profl. jours. Office: CE Niehoff & Co 2021 Lee St Evanston IL 60202-1557

POVISH, KENNETH JOSEPH, retired bishop; b. Alpena, Mich., Apr. 19, 1924; s. Joseph Francis and Elizabeth (Jachcik) P. A.B., Sacred Heart Sem., Detroit, 1946; M.A., Cath. U. Am., 1950; postgrad., No. Mich. U., 1961, 63. Ordained priest Roman Catholic Ch., 1950; asst. pastorships, 1950-56; pastor in Port Sanilac Mich., 1956-57, Munger, Mich., 1957-60, Bay City, Mich., 1966-70; dean St. Paul Sem., Saginaw, Mich., 1960-66; vice rector St. Paul Sem., 1962-66; bishop of Crookston Minn., 1970-75; bishop of Lansing Mich., 1975-95; bd. consultors Diocese of Saginaw, 1966-70; instr. Latin and U.S. history St. Paul Sem., 1960-66. Weekly columnist Saginaw and Lansing diocesan newspapers. Bd. dirs. Cath. Charities Diocese Saginaw, 1969-70. Mem. Mich. Hist. Soc., Bay County Hist. Soc., Lions Club, KC (pres. Mich. Cath. Conf. 1985-95), Kiwanis.

POWDRILL, GARY LEO, production operations manager; b. Butte, Mont., Nov. 26, 1945; s. Harold Holmes and Genevieve Marie (Tansey) P.; BS, Gonzaga U., 1969; MBA, U. Detroit, 1973; MPA in Environ. Policy, Ind. U., 1984; m. Marsha A. McKeon, Oct. 6, 1979 (div.); 1 child, Amy Marie. Plant design engr. Ford Motor Co., Sterling Heights, Mich., 1969-73, div. plant engr. Chassis div., 1973-74, supr. plant engring. sect., Indpls. plant, 1974-78, mgr. plant engring., 1978-80, mgr. engring. and facilities, 1980-87, mgr. mfg., plant engring. dept., 1987-88, pres., mgr. prodn. ops. area A, 1988-95; mgr. plant engring. and tech. svcs., 1996—. Chmn. Ind. State Water Pollution Control Bd., 1986-91; mem. Indpls. Mayor's Tech. Adv. Com., 1975—. Mem. labor and mgmt. del. to U.S.-USSR Emerging Leaders Summit Conf., USSR, 1990; bd. dirs., chmn. Ruth Lilly Health Edn. Ctr.; chmn. environ. com. Ind. State C. of C. Lic. profl. engr., Ind.; cert. plant engr. Mem. Ind. Soc. Profl. Engrs, Elks.. Roman Catholic. Home: 6 Forest Ct Greenfield IN 46140-8739 Office: 6900 English Ave Indianapolis IN 46219-7416

POWELL, ANTHONY J., state legislator, lawyer; m. Betty Powell. Atty. Wichita, Kans.; mem. from dist. 85 Kans. State Ho. of Reps., Topeka. Address: 7313 Winterberry Wichita KS 67226

POWELL, CAROL CHRISTINE, restaurant owner; b. Seattle, Feb. 15, 1941; d. Benjamin Olaf and Lois Carol (Smith) Michel; m. William Fred Roth, Apr. 8, 1961 (div. Dec. 1972); children: Christine Roth Elliott, Fred Roth, Traci Roth Bailey; m. George Benjamin Powell, Dec. 22, 1972 (dec. 1993); children: Kathy Powell Nickles, George Benjamin. Grad. high sch., Seattle. Dishwasher Happy Chef, Cherokee, Iowa, 1978; dishwasher, waitress Randall's Cafe, Cherokee, 1978-79, mgr., 1979-82; owner, operator The FoodBroker, Cherokee, 1983-92; with Amway Network Mktg., 1988—; health aide Cherokee (Iowa) County Home, 1994—. Mem. Cherokee C. of C. Democrat. Home and Office: Cherokee County Home 418 N 6th St Cherokee IA 51012-1306

POWELL, CHRISTOPHER ROBERT, systems programmer, computer scientist; b. Summit, N.J., Feb. 2, 1963; s. Robin Powell and Nancy Mae (Spurling) Gould; m. Bonnie Jean Manning, June 10, 1989. BS in Math. and Computer Sci., Clarkson U., 1984; postgrad. in Computer Sci., Syracuse U., 1988; postgrad. in Philosophy, SUNY, Binghamton, 1990. Sr. assoc. program IBM Corp., Endicott, N.Y., 1984-90; sr. systems analyst/ programmer Supercomputer Systems, Inc., Eau Claire, Wis., 1990-93; prin. systems programmer Network Systems Corp./Central Networking Strategic Bus. Unit, Brooklyn Park, Minn., 1993—. Appt. City of Spring Lake Park Energy Commn., 1995; vice chmn. Energy Commn., 1996. Mem. Assn. for Computing Machinery, Nat. Systems Programmers Assn., NSC Leadership Forum, Alpha Phi Omega (torchbearer 1987-95), Pi Mu Epsilon, Pi Delta Epsilon. Democrat. Home: 8220 6th St NE Spring Lake Park MN 55432

POWELL, DELMER HENRY, JR., county official; b. Danville, Ill., Aug. 2, 1954; s. Delmer Henry and Margaret Ella (Reik) P.; children: Meghan Elizabeth, Jonathan Patrick. BA, Ea. Ill. U., 1976; postgrad., U. Miss., 1976-77; M. Urban Planning, U. Ill., 1979. Project coord. City of Pontotoc, Miss., 1977-78; planning adminstr. City of Tuscola, Ill., 1978-79; comprehensive planning City of Burlington, Iowa, 1979-81; coun. liaison Chgo. Area Transp. Study, 1981-83; sect. chief planning Kane County Hwy. Dept., St. Charles, Ill., 1983-85; dir. planning and programming Lake County Divsn. of Transp., Libertyville, Ill., 1985—. Chmn. Cary (Ill.) Planning Commn., 1984-87; trustee Cary Village Bd., 1987-88; vice chmn. Wauconda (Ill.) Plan Commn., 1990-93; student rep. coun. acad. affairs Ea. Ill. U., Charleston, 1974-76. Recipient Achievement award Nat. Assn. Counties, 1991. Mem. Am. Inst. Cert. Planners (cert.), Am. Planning Assn., Am. Pub. Wks. Assn. (program chmn. Lake br. 1993), Nat. Soc. of SAR, Alpha Kappa Delta, Phi Alpha Theta. Lutheran. Office: Lake County Divsn Transp 600 W Winchester Rd Libertyville IL 60048

POWELL, EDWARD LEE, broadcasting company executive; b. Columbus, Ohio, July 3, 1958; s. Louis Andrew and Margaret Letitia (Steen) P.; m. Denise Noel Harlow, July 11, 1981; children: Edward Lee II, Sarah Elizabeth. BS in Bus. Mgmt. and Mktg., Franklin U., 1988. Freelance square dance caller, rec. artist Reynoldsburg, Ohio, 1976—; columnist Columbus Dispatch Newspaper, 1976-79; disc jockey, salesperson Sta. WWWJ, Johnstown, Ohio, 1978-79; disc jockey, ops. dir. Sta. WLGN-AM-FM, Logan, Ohio, 1980-81; disc jockey Sta. WMNI, Columbus, 1980-89, creative dir., disc jockey, 1987-89; disc jockey Sta. WMGG-FM, Columbus, 1986-87; sales assoc. Tom Yontz and Assocs., Eagle Realty, Westerville, Ohio, 1987—; gen. mgr. Radio Sound Network, Columbus, Ohio, 1989-90; prin. Group X, Reynoldsburg, Ohio, 1990—, Radio Cafe Hour/Cafe Prodns. Inc., Branson, Mo., 1993-95; Cons. mktg. and advt. programs, 1984-95, Central Ohio Corp. of Dance Clubs, Columbus, 1982—, direct mail; spokeman, guest on TV; bd. dirs. Y.E.S. (wheelchair) Dancers, Inc., 1986-89, nat. and state square dance conventions, 1976—. Creative dir. advt. campaigns: Levi's, Cavalier; producer, talent advt. campaign Suzuki Motorcycles, 1981 (award of excellence), (record) Phoenix on Her Mind, 1978; author, pub.: So You Want to Be a Caller, 1979; speaker BMI. Active Ctrl. Ohio Muscular Dystrophy Assn., 1990-92; co-host, organizer

Muscular Dystrophy Local Telethon, Beulah Park, Grove City, 1987-89, Reynoldsburg, 1977-80; asst. scoutmaster Boy Scouts Am., 1975-80; hon. dep. sheriff Franklin County, 1988-92. Recipient Eagle Scout award, 1971; Ohio State Life Ins. scholar, 1987, Farmer's Ins. Group scholar, 1986, Honda of Am. Found. scholar, 1986; named one of nation's Top 10 Square Dance Callers, 1979. Mem. Franklin U. Alumni Assn., Columbus Bd. Realtors, Ohio Bd. Realtors, Nat. Bd. Reators, Cen. Ohio Sq. Dancers, Reynoldsburg Promenaders, Muscular Dystrophy Assn.-Cen. Ohio (past bd. dirs.) Franklin U. Top Execs. Club. Home: PO Box 40 Reynoldsburg OH 43068-0040 Office: Group X Inc Radiowriters PO Box 65 Reynoldsburg OH 43068-0065 also: Tom Yontz & Assocs/Eagle Realty 180 Allview Rd Westerville OH 43081-2909

POWELL, ERNESTINE BREISCH, retired lawyer; b. Moundsville, W.Va., Feb. 16, 1906; d. Ernest Elmer and Belle (Wallace) Breisch; student Dayton YMCA Law Sch., 1929; m. Roger K. Powell, Nov. 15, 1935; children—R. Keith (dec.), Diane L.D., Bruce W. Admitted to Ohio bar, 1929; tax analyst tax dept. Wall, Cassell & Groneweg, Dayton, Ohio, 1929-31; practiced law, 1931-42; gen. counsel for Dayton Jobbers and Mfrs. Assn., 1931-41; mem. firm Powell, Powell & Powell, Columbus, Ohio, 1944-86, ret. Ohio chmn. Nat. Woman's Party, Washington, 1950-51, nat. chmn., 1953, hon. nat. chmn. Pres. vol. activities com. Columbus State Sch., 1960-61, mem. bd. trustees, 1957-59. Mem. Nat. Assn. Women Lawyers, Am., Ohio, Columbus bar assns., Nat. Soc. Arts and Letters (pres. Columbus chpt. 1963-64), Nat. Lawyers Club (charter mem.) . Co-author: Tax Ideas, 1955; Estate Tax Techniques, 1956-90. Editor-in-chief: Women Lawyers Jour., 1943-45. Office: 6000 Riverside Dr Apt B308 Dublin OH 43017-2058

POWELL, JOHN WILMER, retired broadcast consultant; b. Kansas City, Mo., July 29, 1920; s. Wilmer Elvis and Georgia Dell (Watkins) P.; m. Rosemary Freimuth, Jan. 15, 1946 (div. Apr. 1986); children: Diane (dec. 1950), Rosanne, JoAnn, Colleen, Kara. AB, Kent State U., 1942. Announcer Radio Sta. WCED, DuBois, Pa., 1941, Radio Sta. WJW, Akron, Ohio, 1942; program dir. Radio Sta. KLBM, LaGrande, Oreg., 1942, 46; comml. mgr., announcer Radio Sta. KSRV, Ontario, Oreg., 1946-52; salesman Radio Sta. WVLK, Lexingotn, Ky., 1952-53; gen. mgr. Radio Sta. KRES, St. Joseph, Mo., 1953-54, Radio Sta. KWBW, Hutchinson, Kans., 1954-55; sta. mgr. Radio Sta. KSMN, Mason City, Iowa, 1956-57; exec. v.p., gen. mgr. Radio STa. KHAS, Hastings, Nebr., 1957-85; pvt. cons. Hastings, Nebr., 1985-91, ret., 1991. Bd. dirs. Hastings C. of C., 1963-65; adv. bd. Adams County Sr. Svcs., Hastings, 1974—, Midlands Agy. on Aging, 1980—; gov.'s adv. bd. Nebr. Dept. of Aging, Lincoln, Nebr., 1992—. 2d sgt. USAF, 1942-46. Nedm to Nebr. Broadcasters Hall of Fame, 1986, Broadcasters Hall of Fame, 1988. Fellow Nebr. Broadcasters (bd. dirs. 1964-66, ret.); mem. Am. Legion, Elks, Kiwanis, Kent State U. Alumni Assn. Republican. Home: 1022 W 11th St Hastings NE 68901

POWELL, JOYCE KING, administrative assistant; b. Chgo., Jan. 12, 1948; d. Charlie McCauley and Louise (Moss) Davis; m. Sylvester V. Powell Sr., Aug. 27, 1977; children: Allison Lanee, Alicia Lanee, Christopher Curtis. BS, Harold Washington Coll., 1994. Office mgr. Ctrs. for New Horizons, Inc., Chgo., 1973-80; cons. Ambassador, Chgo., 1980-82; adminstrv. asst. Soft Sheen Products, Inc., Chgo., 1982-94; pres. Powell Industries, South Holland, Ill., 1994. Author, editor (newsletter) Cathedral Connection, 1992; contbr. articles to newspaper for srs. Voter registration/edn. vol. Project V.O.T.E., Chgo., 1982—; sr. typist Prison Outreach Ministries, Chgo., 1984—; chmn. of the bd. Mau-Glo Sch., Chgo., 1984—; pub. rels. dir. Cathedral Bapt. Ch., 1991—; bd. dirs. Marvin Yancy Found., Chgo., 1994—. Named one of Outstanding Young Women in Am., 1984; recipient Svc. award Black On Black Love Campaign, 1990, Meritorious Svc. award United Negro Coll. Fund, 1992. Mem. Nat. Exec. Housekeepers (corr. sec. 1982-95, pres. 1995—, registered exec. housekeeper). Baptist. Home: 15510 Champlain St South Holland IL 60473-1350

POWELL, KENNETH ALGER, physician; b. El Dorado, Kans., May 27, 1925; s. Frank Berlin and Alice Belle (Davis) P.; m. Carol Ruth Wineinger, Nov. 22, 1950; children: Gail Lynn, Leigh Ann. BA, U. Kans., 1950, MD, 1953. Intern U. Kans. Hosp., Kansas City, 1953-54, resident internal medicine, 1954-57; pvt. practice Leavenworth, Kans., 1957-65; v.p., med. dir. Kans. Life Ins. Co., Kansas City, Mo., 1965-85; med. dir. Employers Reassurance Corp., Overland Park, Kans., 1985-95, Centennial Life Ins. Co., Mission, Kans., 1986-90, Exec. Life Assurance Co., Overland Park, Kans., 1985-88, Individual Assurance Corp., Kansas City, Mo., 1986—, Nat. Fidelity Life Ins., Overland Park, 1987-88, Old Am. Ins. Co., Kansas City, Mo., 1987-92, State Sys., Inc., Overland Park, 1992-95, State Life Inst. co., Overland Park, 1988-95; med. dir. Fidelity Security Ins. Co., Kansas City, 1992—, Pyramid Life Ins. Co., 1992—. With USN, 1946. Fellow ACP; mem. AMA, Kans. Med. Soc., Greater Kansas City Soc. Internists.

POWELL, KENNETH GRANT, aerospace engineering educator; b. Euclid, Ohio, July 3, 1960; s. Thomas Edward and Mary Catherine (Byrum) P.; m. Susanne Maria Krummel, Aug. 31, 1991; 1 child, Jasmine Tara. SB in Math., MIT, 1982, SB in Aeronautics, 1984, SM in Aeronautics, 1984, ScD in Aeronautics, 1987. Asst. prof. dept. aerospace engring. U. Mich., Ann Arbor, 1987-93, assoc. prof. dept. aerospace engring., 1993—; lectr. Von Karman Inst. for Fluid Dynamics, Bursseis, 1990, 96; cons. Ford Motors, Dearborn, Mich., 1992—. Named Presdl. Young investigator NSF, 1988; recipient Tchg. Excellence award U. Mich. Coll. Engring., 1992, Outstanding Tchg. award Tau Beta Pi, 1988, Tchg. Excellence award Sigma Gamma Tau, 1989, 95. Mem. AIAA (sr. mem.), Tau Beta Pi, Sigma Xi, Sigma Gamma Tau. Home: 5531 Spring Hill Dr Ann Arbor MI 48105 Office: U Mich Dept of Aerospace Engring Ann Arbor MI 48109

POWELL, NANCY EGAN, elementary education educator; b. Galesburg, Ill., Nov. 5, 1944; d. Robert Matthew and Eva (Fullerton) Egan; m. Dennis Lynn Powell, May 26, 1973; children: Matthew, Susan. BE, Washburn U., 1968; postgrad., Emporia State U., 1973-78, Ottawa U., 1979-85, Avilia U., 1985-89, Portland State U., 1987-88. Cert. K-8, Kans. Tchr. grade 2, permanent substitute tchr. Kansas City Dist. 500, Kans., 1968-69; kindergarten tchr. Kansas City (Kans.) Dist. 500, 1969-91, collaborative kindergarten tchr., 1991—; instr. Math Learning Ctr., Portland State U., 1989—; tchr.'s adv. bd. Kans. Children's Mus., Kansas City, 1988—; presenter S.W. Regional Conf. Kans. Assn. Tchrs. Math., 1989, 90, 92, mem. Kindergarten Curriculum Guide Com., 1988, Math Curriculum Guide Com., 1990, U.S. Russian Joint Conf. Math. Edn., Moscow, 1993, Scope Sequence Writing Team, 1993, Kansas City Math Cadre; mem. Hartcourt Brace Math Tchrs. Adv. Bd., 1995. Mem. Harcourt Brace Math. Tchrs. Adv. Bd., 1995. Troop leader, trainer Santa Fe Trail coun. Girl Scouts U.S., 1982—; troop leader Mid Am. coun. Boy Scouts Am., 1983-90. Grantee Kansas City, Kans. Profl. Devel. Coun. Spl. Edn. Dept., 1990, N.E. Kans. Elem. Sch. Math. Dissemination Project, 1993, 94. Mem. NEA, Internat. Reading Assn., Assn. Childhood Edn. Internat., Nat. Coun. PTA, Nat. Assn. Tchrs. Math., Nat. Assn. Edn. Young Children, Profl. Devel. Coun. Kansas City, Alpha Delta Kappa (v.p. 1986-88, pres. 1988-90, state courtesy chmn. 1992-94). Republican. Methodist. Home: 7924 Armstrong Ave Kansas City KS 66112-2547 also: Kansas City Pub Schs Libr Bldg 625 Minnesota Ave Kansas City KS 66101-2805

POWELL, RALPH EDWIN, manufacturing company executive; b. Ross, Calif., Sept. 22, 1946; s. Ralph Edwin and Essie (Harris) P.; m. Wendy Kovac, Dec. 29, 1969; children: Elizabeth, Ralph Edwin III, Jonathan Edwin, Eleanor, David Edwin, Emily. BS, USAF Acad., 1969; MBA, U. Colo., 1978. Meteorologist USAF, Big Spring, Tex., 1970-74; engr. Joy Mfg. Co., Colorado Springs, 1974-75, project mgr., 1975-76, ops. mgr., 1975-78, product mgr., 1978-79, mktg. and sales mgr., 1979-84; pres., CEO, CAIRE, Inc., Bloomington, 1984—; vp. mktg. and sales Worldwide Cryogenics, Bloomington, Minn., 1988-93; pres. Cryogenic Assocs. med. div. Worldwide Cryogenics, Bloomington, Minn., 1993—; pres., CEO, CAIRE, Inc., Bloomington, 1993—; bd. dirs. Med. Ally. Bd. dirs. The Navigators. Mem. Health Industry Distbrs. Assn. (bd. dirs.), Minn. Health Orgns. Assn. Presbyterian. Office: CAIRE Inc 8011 34th Ave S Bloomington MN 55425-1637

POWELL, ROBERT CHARLES, marriage and family counselor; b. Champaign, Ill., Sept. 19, 1958; s. William York and Betty (Holt) P.; m. Trudy Suedell Graham, May 5, 1986; children: Emily, Amy. BS, We. Ill. U., 1981, MS, 1985. Pvt. practice LaSalle, Ill., 1990—; counselor Luth. Social Svcs., Dixon, Ill., 1994—; founder, leader support group for parents, Peru, Ill., 1990—; co-founder Human Resource Network. Chmn. steering com. Ill. Valley Christian Ch., Peru, 1989-90; bd. dirs. LaSalle County Habitat for Humanity. Mem. AACD, Internat. Assn. Marriage and Family Counselors. Office: 2513 5th St Peru IL 61354-2401

POWELL, ROBERT EUGENE, computer operator; b. Fairmont, W.V., Mar. 31, 1955; s. Grover E. and Mary Jo (Hart) P. BS, Kent State U., 1980. Clk. Premier Screening, 1987-89; computer operator Sage Computer Svcs., 1989-95. Found mem., treas. Alliance for Mentally Ill; active Pres.'s Com. on Employment People with Disabilities Pres.'s Trophy Candidate for Ohio, 1992. Recipient award of Excellence Ohio Rehab. Assn., 1989, 90, named Internat. Man of Yr., 1992-93. Mem. KC. Democrat. Roman Catholic. Home: 1052 Welton Ave Apt 2 Akron OH 44306-2818

POWELL, RONALD ROWE, library science educator; b. Columbia, Mo., May 24, 1944; s. Hampstead Rowe and Elizabeth Floris (Sapp) P.; m. Jeanne Ann Branstetter, Jan. 28, 1967; children: Rebecca Lynn, Angela Leigh. AB, U. Mo., 1967; MS, Western Mich. U., 1968; PhD, U. Ill., 1976. Bibliographer U. Ill., Urbana, 1968-69, asst. circulation libr., 1969-71, rsch. asst., 1971-74, rsch. assoc., 1974-75; libr. dir. U. Charleston, W.Va., 1976-79; asst. prof. U. Mich., Ann Arbor, 1979-86; assoc. prof. U. Mo., Columbia, 1986-92, dir. grad. studies, 1987-90, chmn. Dept. Libr. Sci., 1990-92; prof. Wayne State U., Detroit, 1993—; editl. bd. Assn. Libr. & Info. Sci. Edn., Raleigh, 1984-88, dir., 1989-91; vis. prof. Universidade de Brasilia, Brazil, 1985; sec. Coll. Libr. Sect., Assn. for Coll. and Rsch. Libr., Chgo., 1982; sr. fellow Coun. Libr. Resources, Wash., 1982; guest lectr. Moscow State U. of Culture, 1996. Author: Basic Research Methods for Librarians, 1991; co-author: Success in Answering Reference Questions, 1987, Basic Reference Sources, 1990; co-editor: Topics in Library and Information Studies, 1989—, Qualitive Research in Information Management, 1992; co-editor Jour. Edn. for Libr. and Info. Sci., 1995—. Recipient Curator's scholarship U. Mo., Columbia, 1962. Mem. ALA (chmn. standing com. libr. edn. 1992-93), Assn. Coll. and Rsch. Libr., Assn. for Libr. and Info. Sci. Edn., Mich. Libr. Assn., Beta Phi Mu. Home: 22741 Alexandrine Dearborn MI 48124 Office: Wayne State Univ Libr and Info Sci Program 106 Kresge Detroit MI 48202

POWELL-BROWN, ANN, special education educator, public relations executive; b. Boonville, Mo., Mar. 19, 1947; d. Edward Marsh and Ethel M. (Benton) Powell; m. Richard Lee Brown, Dec. 29, 1978. BS, Cen. Mo. State U., 1969, MSE, 1975; PhD U. Mo., Kansas City, 1989. Tchr. Gulfport and Biloxi (Miss.) Schs., 1969-70; mem. adj. staff Providence Coll., Taichung, Taiwan, 1971-72; mem. reading and learning disabilities staff, Kansas City (Mo.) Sch. Dist., 1973-78, mem. spl. edn. identification team, 1978-79, mem. spl. edn. placement com., 1979-83; co-founder, co-owner Am. Media Enterprises, 1983—; learning disabilities cons., 1984—; v.p., bd. dirs. Nat. Tutoring Inst., 1976; adj. faculty Ottawa Coll., 1980, U. Mo., Kansas City, 1981—, instr. English as 2d lang., 1976-77; adj. faculty Cen. Mo. State U., 1990—; editorial bd. Exceptional Children and Teaching Exceptional Children; bi-weekly columnist Kansas City Bus. Jour., 1985-86; speaker various orgns. Mem. public affairs com. Jewish Community Center, 1978; v.p. Com. for Indochinese Devel., 1977; mem. edn. council Episcopal Diocese Western Mo., 1977; mem. selection com. Paul Harris Fellowship; founder, bd. dirs. Friends of St. Mary's; mem. Kansas City Jazz Festival Com., 1983; mem. adv. com. CASE Program, 1988; sub-com. chmn. IRA State Conf.; mem. Inter Dist. Coop. Task Force, 1989—, Leon Jordan Scholarship Com., 1989—; bd. dirs. Kans. Accessible Arts. Recipient Rsch. award, 1990. Mem. Coun. Exceptional Children , Assn. Children with Learning Disabilities, Internat. Reading Assn. (state publicity com. 1983, Mo. intellectual freedom rep.), Nat. Reading Council, Gt. Alkali Plainsmen, St. David's Welsh Soc., Eggs and Issues Breakfast, Kansas City Blues Soc., Phi Delta Kappa. Democrat. Episcopalian. Home and Office: Am Media Enterprises 137 W 61st Ter Kansas City MO 64113-1455

POWER, THOMAS EDWARD, insurance brokers, consultant; b. Barton, Vt., May 27, 1946; s. Richard Bertrand and Dorothy Hectorine (Currier) P.; m. Sheila Ann Pitt, Sept. 17, 1966; children: Thomas E., James R., Emily M. BS, U. Hartford, 1974. Analyst new. bus. Conn. Gen. Life, Bloomfield, 1967-71, underwriter group ins., 1971-77; sr. account exec. Conn. Gen. Life, Springfield, N.J., 1977-84; v.p. sales CIGNA Employee Benefits, Atlanta, 1984-92; v.p. Willis Carroon, Dublin, Ohio, 1992-94; pres. T.E. Power and Co., Inc., Dublin, 1995%. Republican. Roman Catholic. Home: 7703 Worsley Pl Dublin OH 43017-9661 Office: TE Power & Co Inc PO Box 1510 Dublin OH 43017-6510

POWERS, ANTHONY RICHARD, JR., educational sales professional; b. Chgo., June 14, 1942; s. Anthony Richard and Bernadine Rene (Schwenke) P.; m. Marianne Fugiel, Mar. 15, 1980; children: Kathleen Mary, Anthony Richard III. BA, Quincy Coll., 1964; MS, U. Notre Dame, 1974. Cert. tchr., Ill. Sci. tchr. St. Rene Sch., Chgo., 1964-70; sci. coord. Queen of All Saints Sch., Chgo., 1970-76; sci. and math. product mgr. Ideal Sch. Supply Co., Oak Lawn, Ill., 1976-79, customer svc. mgr., 1980-83, Midwest sales mgr., 1983-85; nat. sales mgr. Ednl. Teaching Aids, Vernon Hills, Ill., 1985-89, v.p., 1989—; lectr., De Lourdes Coll., Des Plaines, Ill., 1970-78; sci. adviser, Archdiocese of Chgo., 1969-76. Author sci. edn. materials. Pres. Orchard Estates Condominium Assn., 1986-87; mem. Vernon Hills Fire and Police Commn., 1995—. Mem. Northeastern Ill. Sci. Assn. (pres. 1970-75), U.S. Golf Assn., Internat. Brotherhood Magicians, K.C. Roman Catholic. Home: 241 Tally Ho Dr Vernon Hills IL 60061-2900 Office: Ednl Tchg Aids 620 Lakeview Pky Vernon Hills IL 60061-1828

POWERS, BRUCE THEODORE, state legislator; b. Plymouth, Ind., June 24, 1934; s. Theodore Roosevelt and Mary (McKee) P.; m. Betty Mae Wehling; children: Cindy Jo (Mrs. John G.K. Kennedy), Shari Lynn (Mrs. Peter Bonneson), Charles Theodore. BMF, Phillips U., 1956; MME, Wichita State U., 1960; postgrad., Kans. U., 1963. Music tchr. Unified Sch. Dist. 263, 1956-92; band and vocal tchr. Mulvane, Kans., 1992—; mem. from dist. 81 Kans. State Ho. of Reps., 1993—. Mem. NRA, AARP, Numismatic Assn., Optimists, Lions, Phi Mu Alpha. Office: Capitol Bldg Rm 115E Topeka KS 67110

POWERS, DAVID RICHARD, educational administrator; b. Cambridge Springs, Pa., Apr. 5, 1939; s. William Herman and Elouise Fancheon (Fink) P.; m. Mary Julia Ferguson, June 11, 1960. Student, Pa. State U., 1957-60; BA, U. Pitts., 1963, MA, 1965, PhD, 1971. Dir. CAS advising ctr. U. Pitts., 1966-68, asst. dean faculty, 1968-70, asst. to chancellor, 1970-76, assoc. provost, 1976-78, vice provost, 1978-79; v.p. for acad. affairs George Mason U., Fairfax, Va., 1979-82; vice chancellor for acad. affairs W.Va. Bd. Regents, Charleston, 1982-88; exec. dir. Minn. Higher Edn. Coord. Bd., St. Paul, 1989-94, Nebr. Coord. Commn. Post-secondary Edn., Lincoln, 1994—. Prin. author: Making Participatory Management Work, 1983, Higher Education in Partnership with Industry, 1988; contbr. articles to Ednl. Record, Adult Learning, Forum for Applied Rsch. on Pub. Policy. Grantee USOE Faculty Seminar, Taiwan, 1967, ARC Ctr. for Edn. & Rsch. with Industry Appalachian Regional Commn., 1983, Republic of China Sino-Am. Seminar, 1985; recipient Award for Acad. Quality W.Va. Coun. Faculty, 1986. Mem. Am. Assn. for Higher Edn., Am. Soc. for Pub. Adminstrn., State Higher Edn. Exec. Officers, Civil Air Patrol, Pi Sigma Alpha. Home: 1928 High St Lincoln NE 68502-4825 Office: Nebr Coord Comm Post secondary Edn PO Box 95005 Lincoln NE 68509-5005

POWERS, DENNIS NORBERT, lawyer; b. Detroit, Aug. 5, 1942; s. William Paul and Theresa Powers; m. Patricia Ann Donovan, June 1, 1962; children: Michael Dennis, Kathryn Ann, Scott William. BA, U. Detroit, 1964, MA, 1968; JD, Detroit Coll. Law, 1974. Bar: Mich.; lic. profl. counselor. Atty. Powers, Hallowell, Nickolai, Highland, Mich., 1975—; sch. adminstr. Royal Oak (Mich.) Pub. Schs., 1971-79; trouble shooter Gen. Motors Corp., Flint, Mich., 1968-71; tchr. Gate of Heaven Sch., Detroit, 1966-68, St. Theresa H.S., Detroit, 1964-66; production foreman Chrysler Corp., Detroit, 1964; Oakland County commn. Oakland County, Pontiac, Mich., 1993—; instr. in problem solving, Detroit, 1969-74. Author: Supervision, Problem Solving, 1970. Trustee Highland Twp. (Mich.) Libr., 1981-92, Highland Twp. Bd., 1987-92; commr. Oakland County, 1993—; vice chair Oakland County Solid Waste Bd., 1993—; chair Highland Twp. Solid Waste Bd., 1988—; chair Oakland County Pers. Appeal Bd., 1995—; vice chair Oakland County Airports Commn., 1995—, Oakland County Pub. Svcs. Com., 1995—; chair Oakland County Strategic Planning Com. With USMCR, 1961-63. Recipient Keep Mich. Beautiful award State of Mich., 1992. Mem. Highland Bus. Assn. (dir. 1981), Huron Valley C. of C., Oakland County Bar Assn. (chmn. dist. ct. com. 1995—). Republican. Office: Powers Hallowell & Nickolai 2254 E Highland Highland MI 48356

POWERS, JAMES STEVENSON, state adjutant; b. Pitts., May 6, 1938; s. Jack Allen and Mary Josphein (Stevenson) P.; m. Violet Anne Woodage, Jan. 31, 1959; children: Lynne Angela, Julie Mary, Mark William. Assoc., Cin. Tech. Coll., 1977. Enlisted U.S. Army, 1956, retired, 1986; svc. officer Am. Legion, Indpls., 1986-89; dept. adjutant DAV, Indpls., 1989—; bd. dirs. Vietnam Meml., Indpls. Mem. VFW, Masons, Am. Legion, Scottish Rite, Shrine Temple. Home: 910 Buck Creek Rd Greenfield IN 46241 Office: DAV 2439 W 16th St Indianapolis IN 46222

POWERS, JUANITA CARPENTER, mental retardation and developmental disability nurse; b. Williamsburg, Ky., July 21, 1951; d. Dillard Lee and Litha (McKiddy) Carpenter; m. David Lee Powers, Jan. 17, 1968; children: Jamie R., Daniel Lee. AD, Sinclair Sch. Nursing, Dayton, Ohio, 1987. Cert. qualified mental retardation profl. Med.-surg. nurse Grandview Hosp., Dayton, 1987-88; nurse Am. Nursing Care, Dayton, 1988; supr. King Tree Nursing Ctr., Dayton, 1988; floor nurse in young adult unit Children's Med. Ctr., Dayton, 1989; nurse Montgomery County Bd. Mental Retardation, Dayton, 1989—; rep. Ohio Ind. Options Waiver, Dayton, 1991—; cons., educator Bd. Mental Retardation, Transp. Dept., Dayton, 1989—; cons. Individual Habilitation Plans, Dayton, 1989—. Active United Way, Dayton, 1991, Arthritis Found., Dayton, 1992; mem. NADD, Dayton, 1991. Republican. Baptist. Home: 2403 Ottello Ave Dayton OH 45414-4713

POWERS, KATHRYN DOLORES, social services administrator; b. Chgo., Dec. 17, 1929; BMTS, Colgate-Rochester U., 1951; MSW, Smith Coll., 1964. Diplomate Am. Bd. Clin. Social Work; lic. social worker, Ill. Child welfare worker, supr. Cook County Dept. Pub. Aid Children's Divsn., Chgo., 1953-68; dir. program Ctrl. Bapt. Children's Home/Family Svcs., Lake Villa, Ill., 1968-82, asst. exec. dir., 1983-90, assoc. exec. dir., 1990-92, sr. v.p., 1993—; assoc. Realty World, Dale Shea & Co, 1987-88, Realty World-Tiffany, 1988-93; pres. bd. dirs. Cmty. Residential Network, Inc., 1978-79; instr. field work U. Wis., 1975-76; mem. habilitation/rehab. task force Health Sys. Agy., Kane, Lake and McHenry counties, Ill., 1979. Recipient Spl. Merit citation Am. Bapt. Homes and Hosps. Assn., 1979, Women of Achievement Bus. award Lake County YWCA, 1990. Mem. Nat. Assn. Social Workers, Acad. Cert. Social Workers. Office: PO Box 1128 Lake Villa IL 60046-1128

POWERS, MIKE, state legislator; b. Mar. 31, 1962. BA, U. Wis., Platteville. Assemblyman Wis. State Dist. 80, 1994—; conservationist Green County Dept. Land Conservation. Address: N6842 Attica Rd Albany WI 53502

POWERS, PAUL J., manufacturing company executive; b. Boston, Feb. 5, 1935; s. Joseph W. and Mary T. Powers; m. Barbara Ross, June 3, 1961; children: Briana, Gregory, Jeffrey. BA in Econs., Merrimack Coll., 1956; MBA, George Washington U., 1962. Various mfg. and fin. positions with Chrysler Corp., Detroit and overseas, 1963-69; v.p., gen. mgr. Am. Standard, Dearborn, Mich., 1970-78; pres. Abex-Dennison, Columbus, Ohio, 1978-82; group v.p. Comml. Intertech Corp., Youngstown, Ohio, 1982-84, pres., chief ops. officer, 1984-87, chmn., pres., CEO, 1987—; bd. dirs. Acme-Cleve. Corp., Ohio Edison Co., Twin Disc, Inc., Global Marine Inc. Bd. dirs. Youngstown Symphony, 1984-88. Lt. USNR, 1957-63. Mem. NAM (bd. dirs. 1986-93, 95—), Nat. Fluid Power Assn. (bd. dirs. 1984-87), Mfrs. Alliance (bd. dirs. 1995—), Youngstown Area C. of C. (bd. dirs. 1990—). Office: Comml Intertech Corp 1775 Logan Ave # 239 Youngstown OH 44505-2622

POWERS, PIERCE WILLIAM, JR., insurance specialist; b. St. Louis, Oct. 22, 1946; s. Pierce William and Estelle (Brabant) P.; m. Susan Purcell, Apr. 5, 1975; children: Elizabeth K., Pierce W. III, Dorothy L., Henry P., John D., Mary Estelle. AB, Rockhurst Coll., 1968; MBA, St. Louis U., 1973. Ind ins. agt. and broker Charles L. Crane Agy., St. Louis, 1969-91; founder, pres. Powers Group, Inc., St. Louis, 1991—. Chmn. fin. com. St. Joseph's Ch., Clayton, Mo., 1983; bd. dirs. Fontbonne Coll., St. Louis, 1988—, Christians in Commerce, St. Louis, 1987—; bd. AMC Cancer Rsch. Ctr., St. Louis, 1986—, pres., 1989-91.; past mem. futures com., mem. non-uniformed employees retirement bd. City of Clayton. Mem. Ind. Ins. Agts. (bd. dirs. 1982-84), The Tenn. Soc. of St. Louis (pres. 1988-89), Mo. Athltic Club (chmn. jr. com. 1973). Republican. Roman Catholic. Office: Powers Group Inc 7745 Carondelet Ave Ste 200 Saint Louis MO 63105-3316

POWERS, RICHARD DANIEL, bank executive; b. Albuquerque, July 11, 1956; s. Richard James and Laura Love (Daniel) P.; m. Savanna Lee Anderson, Aug. 27, 1988; 1 child, Sara Elizabeth. BA, U. State of N.Y., Albany, 1993; MBA, U. Chgo., 1995. Account rep. Covington Knox, Inc., Houston, 1976-78; sales mgr. Morse Realty, Inc., Houston, 1979-86; asst. v.p. Dollar Dry Dock Savs. Bank, White Plains, N.Y., 1986-87; cons. Deloitte & Touche, N.Y.C., 1987; sr. v.p. Gt. Western Mortgage Co., Chatsworth, Calif., 1987-94, Charter One Bank, Cleve., 1994—. With USAF, 1973-75. Mem. Am.'s Cmty. Bankers (mortgage fin. com., secondary market subcom.), Mortgage Bankers Assn., Bank Adminstrn. Inst., Cleve. Athletic Club, Pine Lake Trout Club. Home: 3108 Royal Oak Ct Westlake OH 44145 Office: Charter One Bank 1215 Superior Ave Cleveland OH 44114

POWERS, RUTH EILEEN, library director; b. Pomeroy, Ohio, Jan. 24, 1930; d. Robert Edgar and Grace Ann (Ebersbach) Pratt; m. Franklin Forrest Powers, July 12, 1958; children: Deborah Jones, Pamela Marshall, Robert. Student, Mountain State Coll., 1950. Bookkeeper Royal Crown Bottling Co., Middleport, Ohio, 1950-51; mgr. Home Restaurant, Middleport, Ohio, 1951-58; libr. clk./bldg. supr. Meigs County Pub. Libr., Pomeroy, Ohio, 1976-82, libr. dir., 1982—; chair Librs. Adv. Com., Wellston, Ohio, 1995; mem. Friends of Libr., Middleport, 1980—. Ctrl. committeeman Rep. Party, Pomeroy, 1985—, presiding judge, 1980—; mem. Meigs Cmty. Edn., Pomeroy, 1992-93. Recipient Pinnacle award Ohio Sec. of State, 1995. Mem. Ohio Libr. Coun. (libr. action coun. 1992-95), Pomeroy C. of C. Office: Meigs County Pub Libr 216 W Main St Pomeroy OH 45769

POWLESS, DAVID GRIFFIN, accountant; b. Marion, Ill., June 16, 1953; s. Kenneth Barnett and Emily Mary (Cygnar) P.; m. Patricia Kay Walker, Aug. 23, 1975; children: Nathaniel Ryan, Nicholas Andrew. BS in Accountancy, U. Ill., 1975. CPA, Ill. Mgr. Gray Hunter Stenn, CPA's, Marion, 1974-81; pvt. practice acctg. Marion, 1981-87; ptnr. Powless, Bragee & Hudgens, Marion, 1988—. Bd. dirs. John A. Logan Coll. Found., 1993—. Mem. AICPA, Ill. CPA Soc., Marion C. of C. (mem. com. 1992-94), U. Ill. Alumni Assn. (bd. dirs. 1985-91, Loyalty award 1992), Champaign-Urbana Alumni Coun. (bd. dirs. 1983-89), Egyptian Illini (pres. 1981-87, 89), Elks, Phi Sigma Kappa (alumni bd. dirs., treas. 1980-87, Outstanding Alumnus award 1984). Republican. Roman Catholic.

POWLESS, KENNETH BARNETT, lawyer; b. Marion, Ill., Aug. 11, 1917; s. George Newton and Sarah Maud (Barnett) P.; m. Emily Mary Cygnar, July 17, 1943; children: Linda Carol, James Kenneth, David Griffin, Catherine Celeste. B.S., U. Ill., 1938, J.D., 1940. Bar: Ill. 1940. Ptnr. Powless and Winters, Marion, Ill., 1946-52, Winters, Powless & Morgan, Marion, 1958-63; sole practice, Marion, 1940-41, 52-58, 63-74; ptnr. Powless Law Office, Marion, 1974-82; arbitrator Indsl. Commn. Ill., 1983-90; ret. counsel, dir. 1st Bank & Trust Co. of Williamson County. Chmn. bd. Marion Meml. Hosp., 1956-76, bd. dirs. emeritus, 1976—; spl. asst. atty. gen. State of Ill., 1954-58, 73-82; state's atty. Williamson County, 1968-72, former arbitrator Indl. Commn., 1980-89. Capt. U.S. Army, 1941-46; ETO. Mem. Ill. State Bar Assn., Williamson County Bar Assn., Am. Soc. Hosp. Attys. Republican. Methodist. Clubs: Egyptian Illini, Marion Kiwanis (dist. lt. gov. 1971), Elks (exalted ruler 1951), Masons, Shriners. Home: 905 N Van Buren St Marion IL 62959-2255 Office: Indsl Commn Ill 905 N Van Buren St Marion IL 62959-2255

PRACHT, DRENDA KAY, psychologist; b. Carrollton, Mo., Jan. 15, 1952; d. Ethan Lyle Pracht and Wilma Esteleen (Henderson) Lucas; 1 child,

Matthew Kent. BA in Psychology, William Jewell Coll., 1974; MS in Clinical Psychology, Cen. Mo. State U., 1976; postgrad. in clin. psychology, Fielding Inst., Santa Barbara, Calif., 1987—. Lic. psychologist, marriage and family therapist, Minn., Kans.; lic. psychologist, Mo., Minn. Therapist Briscoe Carr Cons., Kansas City, Mo., 1978-79; psychologist Crittenton Ctr., Kansas City, 1979-81, Cen. Minn. Mental Health Ctr., St. Cloud, 1981-85, St. Cloud Hosp., 1985-87; gen. practice psychology St. Cloud, 1985-92, Kansas City, 1992—; cons. St. Benedicts Ctr., Country Manor, 1986-92. Mem. Cen. Minn. Child Abuse Team, St. Cloud, 1981-85; bd. dirs. Cen. Minn. Child Care Assn., St. Cloud, 1982-83. Mem. Am. Psychol. Assn., Cen. Minn. Psychol. Assn. (pres. 1984-85), Minn. Lic. Psychologists, Minn. Psychol. Assn., Alpha Delta Pi Aumni Assn. Presbyterian. Office: Ste 110 4500 College Blvd Overland Park KS 66211

PRADY, NORMAN, journalist, advertising executive, writer, marketing consultant; b. Detroit, Sept. 19, 1933; s. Calvin and Mildred Prady; m. Susan Frank, July 5, 1959 (div. Nov. 1991); children: William Scott, Anne Elizabeth Prady Sheehan. Student, Wayne State U., 1951-53, Fordham U., 1952. Reporter, feature writer Detroit Times, 1955-60; writer various advt. agys. Detroit, 1960-65, creative dir. various advt. agys., 1965-80; exec. v.p., creative dir., prin. Stone, August & Co., Birmingham, Mich., 1980-84; pres. The Norman Prady Co., Farmington Hills, 1985—; editor, pub. The Riverside Journal, Farmington Hills, 1995—. Contbr. features various newspapers. Bd. dirs. ARC, Detroit, 1983—, exec. com., 1987—, vice-chmn. pub. affairs com., 1986—, fin. devel. com., 1987—.

PRAEGER, SANDY, state legislator; b. Oct. 21, 1944; m. Mark A. Praeger. Student, U. Kans., 1966. V.p. Douglas County Bank; mem. Kans. Ho. of Reps. Vice chmn. Douglas County Rep. Cent. Com.; chmn. Leadership Kans.; pres. bd. dirs. United Way. Home: 3601 Quail Creek Ct Lawrence KS 66047-2134 Office: Kans State Senate State Capitol Topeka KS 66612

PRANGE, CEDRIC WILLIAM, management consultant; b. Mankato, Minn., Dec. 10, 1941; s. Arthur L. and Helen C. (Shirk) P.; m. Sandra Kay Kruse Prange, June 17, 1967; children: Kristi M., Kraig A. BS, Gustavus Addphus Coll., St. Peter, Minn., 1963; MBA, U. Nebr.-Omaha, 1969. Acct. Western Electric, Omaha, 1965-66; sys. analyst Omaha Steel Workers, 1966-67; floor supr. Continental Can Co., Omaha, 1967-69; mgmt. cons. pvt. practice, 1969—; bd. mem. Prof. Mgmt. Cons. Assn., Lansing, Mich., 1990—, Nat. Assn. Health Care Cons., Washington, 1990-97; pres. Inst. Cert. Prof. Bus. Cons., Chgo., 1994-95. Contbr. articles to profl. jours. Pres. Bethany Luth Ch., Elkhorn, Nebr., 1994-95. 1st lt. U.S. Army, 1963-66. Republican. Lutheran. Office: Cedric Prange Assn Inc 11120 Fort St Omaha NE 68164

PRASAD, RAM A., communications systems engineer; b. Coimbatore, India, Aug. 23, 1954; came to U.S., 1982; s. Vytheeswaran and Jayalakshmi (Mahadevan) Anathanarayanan; m. Sabitha Veeramani Prasad, Feb. 2, 1987; 1 child, Rohan Vignesh. BME, Coll. Engring., Guindy, Madras, India, 1976; MBA, U. Houston, 1986, PhD, 1988. Comml. engr. exports BHEL, Tiruchirapalli, 1976-80; sr. project engr. BHEL Piping Ctr., Madras, 1980-82; systems engr. AT&T Bell Labs., Holmdel, N.J., 1988-91, Naperville, Ill., 1991—. Home: 1126 Crimson Ct Naperville IL 60564 Office: AT&T 1000 E Warrenville Rd Naperville IL 60566

PRASIL, LINDA ANN, lawyer, writer; b. Chgo., July 27, 1947; d. Joseph J. and Helen Marie (Palucki) P.; m. John T. Rank, July 25, 1970; 1 child, Sean Patrick Prasil Rank. BA in Interdisciplinary Studies, Am. U., Washington, 1974, JD, 1977; MALS, Mundelein Coll., Chgo., 1992. Bar: Ill. 1977. Ind. contractor Baker & McKenzie, Chgo., 1977-78; atty. Pretzel, Stouffer, Nolan & Rooney, Chgo., 1978-79; sole practitioner Lincolnshire, Ill., 1979—; atty. Leonard M. Ring, Chgo., 1982; grader Ill. State Bar Examiners, Chgo., 1978-90; organizer Kennedy for Pres., Chgo., 1979-80, NOW-ERA Ill., Chgo., 1980, Ill. Polit. Action Com., Chgo., 1981. Legal advisor Holy Cross Talk of Town, Deerfield, Ill., 1992-96; tchr. Holy Cross Drug Awareness Program, Deerfield, 1993-94; religious tchr. Holy Cross, Deerfield, 1983-86. Mem. Ill. State Bar Assn., Internat. Alliance of Holistic Lawyers. Office: 35 Keswick Ct Lincolnshire IL 60069-3425

PRATER, WILLIS RICHARD, county government agency official; b. Hueysville, Ky., Apr. 6, 1942; s. Elmer and Zella (Allen) P.; m. Peggy Sue Reed, 1962 (div. 1966); children: Richard Bradley, Christopher Lee; m. Margaret Louise Price, Dec. 8, 1967; 1 child, Allison Marie. Grad. high sch., Plymouth, Ohio. Proofreader R.R. Donnelly Co., Willard, Ohio, 1960-63; announcer, news dir. Sta. WCLW-AM/FM, Mansfield, Ohio, 1963-65; news dir. Sta. WNCO-AM/FM, Ashland, Ohio, 1965-69, Sta. WVNO-FM, Mansfield, 1969-72; dir. devel. City of Mansfield, 1972-82; comml. real estate sales agt. Chuck Warner & Assocs., Mansfield, 1982-87; exec. dir. Richland County Child Support Enforcement Agy., Mansfield, 1987—. Active local Rep. campaigns, 1970—; funds chmn. Richland County Bicentennial Commn., 1975-76; head govt. div. Mansfield United Way, 1979-80; mem. City Schs. Reorgn. Com., Mansfield, 1984-85. Sgt. U.S. Army, 1967-68. Mem. Ohio Family Support Assn., Ohio Support Enforcement Assn. (trustee 1988—, pres. 1989-90), Ohio Child Support Enforcement Agy. Dirs. Assn. (1st v.p. 1990-91, pres. 1992, pres. Canton dist. 1995, 96), Nat. Child Support Enforcement Assn. (bd. dirs. 1993—, 1st v.p. 1995-96, pres.-elect 1996-97). Lutheran. Office: Richland County CSEA PO Box 547 Mansfield OH 44901-0547

PRATHER, R. WILLIAM, III, banking executive; b. Kansas City, Mo., Feb. 11, 1962; s. Roy William Jr. and Margaret (Humphreys) P.; m. Priscilla Higgins; children: Katherine, Alexandra, Benjamin. BA in Chemistry, William Jewell Coll., 1984; MBA, Rockhurst Coll., 1987. Comml. banking officer Boatmen's First Nat. Bank Kansas City, 1984-94; mktg. rep. Unger Acctg., Liberty, Mo., 1994-95; mem. Habitat for Humanity com. for Boatmen's Bank, Kansas City, 1991. Leader, coord. Boatmen's Bank campaign for United Way, 1987-88; fundraising vol. Boy Scouts Am., Kansas City, 1991-92; vol. Habitat for Humanity, Kansas City, 1990-91, March of Dimes, Kansas City, 1991-92; mem. Second Bapt. Ch., Liberty, Mo., 1970—, chmn. major fin. needs com., 1991-92; treas. Clay Platte Bapt. Assn., 1994-95; mem. alumni bd. govs. Rockhurst Coll. Named one of Outstanding Young Men of Am., 1987. Mem. Clay County Econ. Devel. Coun., Liberty Rotary Club, Liberty Area C. of C. Home: 22 Camelot Pl Liberty MO 64068-1103 Office: Platte Valley Bank of Missouri 102 S 291 Hwy Liberty MO 64068

PRATT, DIANE ADELE, elementary education educator; b. Battle Creek, Mich., Oct. 24, 1951; d. John Robert and Kathleen Adele (Cooper) Dickert; m. Stephen Howard Pratt, Apr. 29, 1972; children: Eric Stephen, Elizabeth Adele. BS, Western Mich. U., 1972. Cert. elem. tchr., Ohio, Iowa, Mich. Elem. tchr. Berea (Ohio) Cmty. Schs., 1973-76; ednl. cons. Kolbe Products, Inc., Phoenix and Scottsdale, Ariz., 1982-84; tchr. Lemon Tree Nursery Sch., Battle Creek, 1985-88; instr. Jr. Great Books, 1984-87; elem. tchr. Ft. Dodge (Iowa) Cmty. Schs., 1976-78, 90, substitute tchr., 1988-90, middle sch. tchr., 1990—, team leader, 1994—; exec. sec. Born Free Safari Club, Dodgen Industries, Humboldt, Iowa, 1988; advt. exec. Ft. Dodge Today mag., 1989-92; ednl. tutor, Battle Creek, Ft. Dodge, 1986-96; mem. adv. bd. Inst. for Instrn. Svcs., Battle Creek, 1984-88; dir., instr. Battle Creek Presch. Enrichment Program, 1984; chmn. Ft. Dodge Supr.'s Comty. Com. to Study K-8 Curriculum, 1988-89, facilitator K-3 human growth and devel. curriculum, 1989-92; mem. standing com. early childhood needs assessment com. Ft. Dodge Comty. Schs., 1989-95; mem. adv. bd., instr. Kids on Kampus Iowa Cen. C.C., Ft. Dodge, 1990-95; speaker State Conv. Childbirth Educators, Lansing, Mich., 1982; trustee Ft. Dodge Comty. Sch. Found. Bd., 1992—, mem. talented and gifted selection com. Ft. Dodge Comty. Schs., 1993—; mem. pub. rels. com. Ft. Dodge Comty Sch. Dist., 1992-94, mem. ednl. outcomes standing com., 1993-94. Author, editor various newsletters. Mem., past chmn. bd. Christian edn. 1st Bapt. Ch., Ft. Dodge, 1978-79, 89—, music com., 1992-94, dir. children's choirs, 1988-90, mem. bell choir, 1990-91, ch. sch. supt. 1993—; membership chmn. Battle Creek Parents, 1981-83; neighborhood coord. mothers' march March of Dimes, Battle Creek, 1981-83; troop leader Lakota coun. Girl Scouts U.S., 1988-90; pres. La Mora Park PTA, 1985-87, Phillips Mid Sch. PTA, Ft. Dodge, 1990-91; bd. dirs. Main Stage Players, jr. theater, Ft. Dodge, 1990-91; sec., pres. Jr. Women's Club, Ft. Dodge, 1977-80; mem. kickoff com. United Way, 1991; membership co-chair Ft. Dodge Athletic Booster Club, 1994—. Recipient Mem. of Yr. award La Mora Park PTA, 1987. Mem. NEA, AAUW (sec., pres. Battle Creek br. 1986-88), PEO (N.J. chpt., Ft. Dodge chpt. 1990—), Iowa Edn. Assn., Ft. Dodge Edn. Assn., Iowa Assn. Middle Level Educators, Iowa Coun. Tchrs. English. Home: 1851 9th Ave N Fort Dodge IA 50501

PRATT, GEORGE BYINGTON, III, pediatric radiologist; b. Goshen, Ind., Sept. 6, 1936; s. George Byington and Estelle (Hudson) P.; m. Patricia Mae Hammer, June 22, 1957 (div. 1970); children: George B. IV, Pamela; m. Susan Pettijohn, June 23, 1972; 1 child, Lisa Susan. BA, DePauw U., 1958; MD, Northwestern U., 1962; JD, Ind. U., 1978. Diplomate Am. Bd. Radiology. Pediatric radiologist Radiologic Specialists of Ind., Indpls., 1968-93; pvt. practice radiologist, 1993—; cons. Cook Imaging, Bloomington, Ind., 1996—. Contbr. articles to profl. jours. Pres. Marion City Child Abuse and Neglect Coun., Indpls., 1984-86; bd. dirs. Family Support Ctr., Indpls., 1984-93, adv. com., 1993—; bd. dirs. Boone County Found., 1991—; v.p. Zionsville (Ind.) Pk. and Recreation Bd., 1978-93, pres., 1994-95, Zionville Little League, 1985-93; mem. bd. dirs. ULEN C.C. Served to capt. USAF, 1963-65. Fellow Am. Coll. Legal Medicine; mem. AMA, Am. Coll. Radiology, Radiol. Soc. N.Am., Ind. State Med. Assn. (3d place award Med. Exhibit 1970), Am. Acad. Pediatrics (3d place award Med. Exhibit 1984), Ind. U. Alumni Club Boone County (bd. dirs.), Masons, Rotary (treas. 1994-95, sec. 1995-96, pres.-elect 1996—). Avocations: snow and water skiing, sailing.

PRATT, MICHAEL ANTHONY, SR., manufacturing executive; b. Council Bluffs, Iowa, Oct. 30, 1949. Owner Sound of Am., Omaha, 1971-73; regional distbr. Masterguard of Midwest, Omaha, 1973-77; pres., CEO Mike Pratt & Sons Inc., Omaha, 1977—; owner Pratt Protection Sys., Omaha, 1977-87, Pratt Prodns., Omaha, 1982-87, Collector's Display Case Co.; owner Pratt Performance, Omaha, 1976-87. Office: Collectors Display Case Co RR 2 Box 73 Fremont NE 68025-9635

PRATT, RICHARD ALAN, newspaper editor; b. Cedar Rapids, Iowa, May 5, 1965; s. Alan LeRoy and J. Jean (Begley) P. BA, U. Iowa, 1988. Assoc. editor Daily Standard, Excelsior Springs, Mo., 1988-90; staff writer, editor trainee Pilot-Tribune, Storm Lake, Iowa, 1990-92; editor Journal Express, Knoxville, Iowa, 1992-94; assoc. editor The Messenger, Clemson, S.C., 1994; editor News Republic, Baraboo, Wis., 1994—; editl. panelist Iowa Newspaper Assocs., Iowa and Wis., 1993, 94; newspaper contest judge Wis. Newspaper Assn., 1994. Recipient Best Editl. Writing, Feature Story, Feature Photo award Iowa Newspaper Assn., Des Moines, 1994. Mem. Knoxville Kiwanis Club (charter), Baraboo Rotary Club. Democrat. Lutheran.

PRATT, SUSAN G., architect; b. Kansas City, Mo., Sept. 24, 1951; d. John Bohman and Alice Marguerite (Harris) Grow; m. W. Scott Pratt; children: David, Alice; stepchildren: David, Laura. BArch, Kans. State U., 1973. Registered architect, Mich., Wis. Project arch. Skidmore Owings & Merrill, Chgo., 1973-78, 83-85; project arch. Murphy/Jahn, Inc., Chgo., 1978-82, 86—, now v.p.; sr. project arch. Froelich & Marik, L.A., 1982-83, Marshall & Brown, Kansas City, 1985-86. Prin. works include New World Ctr., Hong Kong, Group Repertory Theatre, North Hollywood, Calif., Bi State Indsl. Park, Kansas City, Mo., State of Ill. Ctr., Chgo., John Deere Harvester Works Office Facility, Moline, Ill., Two Liberty Pl., Phila., Livingston Pla., Bklyn., North Loop Block 37, Chgo., 1st and Broadway, L.A., Kudamm 119, Berlin, Cologne/Bonn Airport, Cologne, Jeddah Airport, Saudi Arabia, Sony European Hdqs., Berlin, Munich Airport Ctr., 21st Century Tower, Shanghai, China. Mem. AIA (corp. mem.). Office: Murphy/Jahn 35 E Wacker Dr Chicago IL 60601

PRAY, MERLE EVELYN, nurse psychotherapist, educator; b. Washington, Vt., Apr. 19, 1931; d. Clifton Clough and Dorothy (Wadleigh) P. Diploma in nursing, N.H. Sch. Nursing, Concord, 1952; BSN, Loyola U., Chgo., 1977; MS, U. Ill., Chgo., 1983. RN, Ill.; cert. in addictions nursing Nat. Nurses Soc. on Addictions; cert. clin. specialist in adult psychiat. and mental health nursing ANA. Community placement coord. Ill. Dept. Mental Health and Devel. Disability, Chgo., 1977, mental health adminstr., planning area coord., 1978-81; head nurse VA West Side Med. Ctr., Chgo., 1984, clin. specialist, 1985—; adj. clin. instr. psychiat. nursing U. Ill., 1986—. Mem. ANA, Nat. Nurses Soc. on Addictions, Am. Psychiat. Nurses Assn., Ill. Nurses Assn. Home: 175 E Delaware Pl Chicago IL 60611-1756 Office: VA West Side Med Ctr 820 S Damen Ave Chicago IL 60612-3728

PREBLE, ROBERT CURTIS, JR., insurance executive; b. Oak Park, Ill., Dec. 19, 1922; s. Robert Curtis and Dorothy (Seidel) P.; m. Lidia Blazik, May 29, 1963. BA, Amherst Coll., 1947; MBA, Harvard U., 1949, postgrad., 1971. Registered Am. Coll. of Life Underwriters, 1955; CLU, 1983, Chartered Fin. Cons. Asst. to gen. supt., asst. buyer Carson Pirie Scott & Co., Chgo., 1949-52; with sales dept. Northwestern Mut. Life Ins. Co., Chgo., 1952-53, Nat. Life Ins. Co., Chgo., 1953-59; prin. Preble Assocs., Chgo., 1959—; pres., treas. Savs. Plans Inc., 1980—; cons. Iowa Savs. & Loan League, 1959-82; consul of Colombia, 1981-86, Bolivia, 1965-70; bd. dirs., chm. fin. com. Guardsman Life Ins. Co., 1962-74; chmn. exec. com. World Book Life Ins. Co., 1974-83; mem. Gov.'s Adv. Bd., Ill. Dept. Ins., 1965-70; bd. dirs. Scandia Savings & Loan Assn. Dep. regional chmn. Dem. Nat. Fin. Com., 1952; bd. dirs. McCormick Theol Sem., 1977-83, Sr. Ctrs. Met. Chgo., 1974-77; deacon 4th Presbyn. Ch. of Chgo., 1967-70. Recipient svc. award Chgo. coun. Boy Scouts Am., 1962. Mem. Am. Soc. of CLU (past pres. Chgo. chpt., Huebner scholar 1991), Million Dollar Roundtable, Nat. Assn. Life Underwriters, Assn. Advanced Life Underwriting (founding pres.), Harvard Bus. Sch. Assn. (alumni coun. 1977-82), Harvard Alumni Assn. (dir. 1980-82), Inst. Internat. Edn. (midwest adv. bd.), Found. Study Cycles (internat. adv. bd.), Soc. Colonial Wars (coun.), Mil. Order World Wars, Univ. Club, Chgo. Club, Harvard Bus. Sch. Club (past pres.), Amherst Club (past pres.), Oak Park Country Club, Chi Psi (past chmn. ednl. trust pres. 1992-95, Svc. award 1986). Home: 300 N State St Apt 5406 Chicago IL 60610-4804 Office: Savs Plans Inc 300 N State St #5005 Chicago IL 60610-4803

PREECE, NANCY ANN, quality professional; b. Wyandotte, Mich., Sept. 3, 1960; d. Duncan William and Theresa Marie (Schlaff) P. BBA, U. Mich., 1982, BS, 1984; MBA, So. Meth. U., 1988. Programmer Gen. Dynamics, Sterling Heights, Mich., 1984-85; programmer analyst Ford Motor Co., Dearborn, Mich., 1985-90; fin. analyst Gen. Motors, Detroit, 1990-91; cons./analyst Process Devel. Corp., Rochester, Mich., 1991-92; cons. Decision Cons., Inc., Southfield, Mich., 1992-93, Renaissance Systems Techs., Southfield, Mich., 1993-94; divsn. quality mgr. Johnson Controls, Plymouth, Mich., 1994—. Recipient Human Rels. award Dale Carnegie Assn., 1985. Mem. U. Mich. Alumni Assn. (life), Martha Cook Alumnae Assn. (bd. dirs. 1982-86), So. Meth. U. MBA Assn., So. Meth. U. Alumni Assn. (life), Jr. League. Home: Apt 5 9461 Marguerite Plymouth MI 48170

PREES, PAT T., industrial designer; b. Sidney, Ohio, June 8, 1968. Grad., high sch., 1986. Designer SMT Industries Inc., Sidney, Ohio, 1987—.

PREHM, JOHN THOMAS, JR., retired retail executive; b. Columbus, Ohio, Mar. 11, 1922; s. John Thomas and Myrtle Florence (Webb) P.; m. Kora Louise Davis, Apr. 26, 1947; children: John III, Joy, Douglas, Cindy, Matthew. Student, Ohio Wesleyan U., Delaware, 1941-42. Personnel rsch. F&R Lazarus, Columbus, 1946-47, head of stock draperies, 1947-49; floor supr. home furnishings Stock Drapery Products, Columbus, 1947-49; asst. buyer children's products F&R Lazarus, Columbus, 1949-51, buyer men's products, 1952-54, buyer draperies, fabrics, drapery hardware, bedspreads, 1954-58, buyer main store, 1958-65, buyer sheets products, 1965-75; ret., 1975. With U.S. Army, 1942-46, ETO. Mem. Draperies Assocs. Mdse. Assn. (corp. steering com. for bedding 1967-75, chmn. 1970-75), Lazarus 20 Yr. Club. Democrat. Lutheran. Home: 5614 Ramblewood Ct Columbus OH 43235-7346

PREHN, DONALD FREDERICK, dentist; b. Wausau, Wis., June 19, 1927; s. Delos Carl and Anita Ida (Mueller) P.; m. Patricia Lee Booth, Aug. 9, 1952; children: Ronald, Constance, Frederick, Robert. BS, U. Wis., 1949; DDS, Marquette U., 1953. Gen. practice dentistry, Wausau, 1953—; mem. dental staff Wausau Hosps., 1953—, chief dental staff, 1957-58; pres. Bear-Superior Corp., Wausau, 1981-83, 87—. Pres., mem. bd. Wausau Dist. Sch. Bd., 1966-78; pres., v.p. exec. bd. Samoset council Boy Scouts of Am., 1973—; jr. and sr. warden, vestryman St. John the Bapt. Episcopal Ch., Wausau, 1963-85; mem. exec. bd., fin. com. Episcopal Diocese Fond du Lac, Wis., 1976—; mem. Birch Trails council Girl Scouts of Am., 1972—. Served as 2d lt. inf., U.S. Army, 1946-47, PTO. Recipient Merit award Rib Mountain dist. Samoset council Boy Scouts of Am., 1977, Silver Beaver award, 1978. Mem. ADA, Wis. Dental Assn. (hosp. accreditation com. 1964-65), Cen. Wis. Dental Soc., Marathon County Dental Soc. (pres. 1958-59, cert. appreciation 1982), Marathon County Hist. Soc. (bd. dirs. 1995—), Wausau Area C. of C., Downtown Wausau Assn., Downtown Action Coun., Ctrl. Wausau Progress (exec. bd.), Mar County Geneal. Soc., Am. Legion. Republican. Club: Wausau. Avocations: fishing, hunting, boating, skiing, traveling. Home: 1010 Adams St Wausau WI 54403-5056

PREISLER, HARVEY D., medical facility administrator, medical educator; b. N.Y., Feb. 5, 1941; s. Leonard and Estelle Preisler; m. Angela Preisler; children: Sarah, Mark, Vanessa; m. Arza Raza; 1 child, Sheharzad. BA, Bklyn. Coll., 1961; MD, U. Rochester, 1965. Assoc. prof. medicine SUNY, Buffalo, 1974-88; assoc. chief dept. med. oncology Roswell Park Meml. Inst., Buffalo, 1975-82, chief leukemia svcs., 1982-86, acting chief BMT, 1985-87, chief dept. hematology and oncology, 1986-88; head, sec. cell biology and myeloproliferative Buffalo, 1979-82; founder, chmn. Leukemia Intergroup, 1980-89; dir., prof. medicine, chief divsn. hematology Charles M. Barrett C.C., 1989-91; prof. medicine divsn. hematology U. Cin. Med. Ctr., 1989-92; dir. Rush Cancer Inst., chief hematology/oncology, prof. Rush-Presbyn.-St. Luke's Med. Ctr., Chgo., 1992—; founder, chmn. Buffalo Coop. Group of Cmty. Hematologists for Rx Myeloid Diseases, 1977-84, Leukemia Intergroup, 1980-89; chmn. teaching session on acute leukemia Am. Soc. Hematology, 1982-84, co-chmn. session XVIII leukemia and myeloid disorders, 1985. Contbr. articles to profl. jours. Mem. med. adv. bd. Lincoln Park Zoo, Chgo., 1994. Grantee NIH, 1988-89, 89-90, 90-91, 92—. Mem. Internat. Soc. Experimental Hematology, Am. Cancer Soc., Am. Assn. Cancer Rsch., Am. Soc. Clin. Oncology, Cell Kinetics Soc., Soc. Internal Medicine. Office: Rush Cancer Inst 1725 W Harrison Ste 809 Chicago IL 60612

PREISS, JACK, biochemistry educator; b. Bklyn., June 2, 1932; s. Erool and Gilda (Friedman) P.; m. Judith Weil Rosen, June 10, 1959; children: Jennifer Ellen, Jeremy Oscar, Jessica Michelle. BS in Chemistry, CCNY, 1953; PhD in Biochemistry, Duke U., 1957. Scientist NIH, Bethesda, 1960-62; asst. prof. dept. biochemistry, biophysics U. Calif., Davis, 1962-65, assoc. prof., 1965-68, prof., 1968-85, chair dept. biochemistry, 1971-74, 77-81; prof. dept. biochemistry Mich. State U., East Lansing, 1985—, chair dept., 1985-89; Mem. editorial bd. Jour. Bacteriology, 1969-74, Arch. Biochem. Biophysics, 1969—; mem. editorial bd. Plant Physiology, 1969-74, 77-80, assoc. editor, 1980-92, editor, 1993-95; editor Jour. Biol. Chemistry, 1971-76, 78-83, 94—. Recipient Camille and Henry Dreyfus Disting. scholar award Calif. State U., 1983, Alexander von Humboldt Stiftung Sr. U.S. Scientist award, 1984, Alsberg-Schoch Meml. Lectr. award Am. Assn. Cereal Chemists, 1990, Nat. Sci. Coun. lectr. Republic of China, 1988, award of merit Japanese Soc. Starch Sci., 1992; Guggenheim Meml. fellow, 1969-70, Japan Soc. for Promotion of Sci. fellow, 1992-93; grantee NIH, 1963—, NSF, 1978-89, Dept. of Energy, 1993—, USDA, 1988—. Mem. AAAS, Am. Chem. Soc. (Charles Pfizer award in enzyme chemistry 1971), Biochem. Soc., Am. Soc. Biol. Chemists and Molecular Biology, Am. Soc. Microbiologists, Am. Soc. Plant Physiologists, Soc. for Complex Carbohydrates, Protein Soc. Office: Mich State Univ Dept Of Biochemistry East Lansing MI 48824

PREISTER, DONALD GEORGE, greeting card manufacturer, state senator; b. Columbus, Nebr., Dec. 23, 1946; s. Maurice J. Preister and Leona T. (Dusel) Chereck. BS in Edn., U. Nebr., 1977. Unit dir. Boys' Clubs of Omaha, 1973-83; dep. city clk. City of Omaha, 1984-85; tchr. The Great Peace March, U.S., 1986; founder, owner Joy Creations, Co., Omaha, 1988—; instr. Metro C.C., Omaha, 1979-80. Author: (sect.) Drug Abuse Prevention, 1977. Troop leader Boy Scouts Am., Omaha, 1973-83. Served with U.S. Army, 1966-68, Vietnam. Decorated Bronze Star. Mem. Vets. for Peace, Nebr. Sustainable Agr. Soc., Optimist. Democrat. Roman Catholic. Home: 3937 W St Omaha NE 68107-3152 Office: State Capitol Dist # 5 Lincoln NE 68509

PRELLWITZ, GRANT ALAN, software developer; b. Chgo., Mar. 8, 1966; s. LeRoy Raymond Prellwitz and Carol Lillian Goerne; m. Leslie Whitted, May 20, 1989. BA in Chemistry, U. Chgo., 1990. Prin. Prellwitz Computing Svcs., Lincolnshire, Chgo., 1982—; software developer Follett Campus Resources, Chgo., River Grove, 1988-94, CCC Info. Svcs., Chgo., 1994—. Editor, author Jour. Southside Computer People, 1989-91. Nat. Merit scholar, 1984. Mem. IEEE Computer Soc., Assn. Computing Machinery. Home: 3449 N Troy St Fl 2 Chicago IL 60618 Office: CCC Info Svcs 444 Merchandise Mart Chicago IL 60654

PREM, GREGORY A., mechanical designer; b. Madison, Wis., May 8, 1969. Assoc. Mech. Design Tech., Milw. Area Tech. Coll., 1992. Mech. designer Key Products Inc., Milw., 1992—. Office: Key Products Inc 10600 W Glenbrook Ct Milwaukee WI 53224-1116

PRENTICE, ROBERT CRAIG, cardiologist; b. Chgo., Sept. 2, 1951; s. Robert Lee and Helen (Virginia) P.; m. Mary Ellen Toomey, Oct. 3, 1981; children: Ryan, Laura, Sarah. BA, Wabash Coll., Crawfordsville, Ind., 1973; MA, So. Ill. U., 1978; DO, Chgo. Coll. Osteo. Medicine, Chgo., 1982; PhD, U. Ill., 1982. Faculty asst. So. Ill. U., Carbondale, 1974-78; med. scientist Chgo. Osteo. Hosp., 1978-82; resident in medicine Hines (Ill.) VA Hosp., 1982-85; fellow in cardiology Loyola U., Maywood, Ill., 1985-87; staff asst. prof. medicine Loyola U., 1987-88; cardiologist Olympia Fields (Ill.) Med. Ctr., 1988-90; cardiologist, dir. cardiac lab. Michael Reese Hosp., Chgo., 1990-92; pvt. practice interventional cardiology Blue Island, Ill., 1992—; rsch. asst. U. Ill., 1980-82; dir. cardiac lab. Michael Reese Hosp., 1990-92. Grantee Chgo. Heart Assn., 1985. Fellow ACP, SCAI, Am. Coll. Cardiology; mem. AMA, Chgo. Med. Soc. Office: 3611 W 183rd St Hazel Crest IL 60429-2029

PRENTISS, C.J., state legislator. BA in Edn., Cleve. State U., 1969, MEd, 1975; cert., Kent State U., 1976; grad. Weatherhead Sch. Mgmt., Case Western Res. U., 1978. Mem. Ohio Ho. of Reps., Columbus, 1991—; chair edn. policy Ohio legislative Black Caucus and Black elected Democrats of Cleve., vice-chair edn. com. Nat. Conf. State Legislatures; past vice-chair HouseEdn. com., ways and means, ins.; mem. State Bd. Edn., 1984-90, chair lit. and youth-at-risk com., legis. stds. com., past chair joint select com. on infant health and family support. Past Vice-chair Black Leadership Cleve. Alumni; past mem. gov.'s com. Socially Disadvantaged Black Males. Office: 77 S High St Columbus OH 43266

PRENZLOW, ELMER JOHN-CHARLES, JR., minister; b. Norfolk, Nebr., Apr. 4, 1929; s. Elmer Edward and Alvina C. (Henning) P.; m. Karen McHarg DeMoss, July 4, 1980; 1 child, Elmer Carl III. BA, Northwestern Coll., Watertown, Wis., 1950; BD in Theology, WELS Luth. Sem., Mequon, Wis., 1953; MA in English and Philosophy, U. Minn., 1961; MS in Edn. Psychology, U. Wis., 1969; PhD in Psychology and Criminal Justice, Walden U., 1975. Pastor St Paul's Lutheran Ch., Bloomer, Wis., 1953-62; chaplain, instr. U. Wis., Milw., 1962-79; dir. devel. and pub. relations Luth. Ch.-Mo. Synod, Southern Wis. Dist., Milw., 1979-82; major gifts counselor Luth. Ch.-Mo. Synod Internat. Hdqrs., St. Louis, 1982-88; dir. devel. and fin. resources Adult Christian Edn. Found. Bethel Series, Madison, Wis., 1988-89; world relief devel. counselor Luth. Ch.-Mo. Synod Internat. Hdqrs., St. Louis, 1989-94; v.p. major gifts Luth. Ch.-Mo. Synod Found., St. Louis, 1994—; vice chmn. Standing Com. Dept. Campus Ministry Luth. Coun. U.S.A., N.Y., 1964-83; chmn. Milw. Religious Counselors, 1965-72, dept. humanities Spencerian Bus. Coll., 1967-77; v.p. Patricia Stevens Career Coll., bd. dirs. 1978-91; spkr., lectr. in field. Contbr. articles to profl. jours. Mem. Wis. State Legis. Com for Kerner Report, Madison, 1968-69, Nat. Adv. Commn.U.S. Justice Dept. on Law Enforcement standards and goals, Washington, 1971-73, ad hoc com. for establishing U.S. Bur. Prisons Nat. Inst. for Corrections, Washington, 1973-75, 19th congr. dist. Wis. svc. acad. review bd., Milw., 1975-82. Named Outstanding Prof. Spencerian Bus. Coll., Milw., 1972. Mem. Assn. of Luth. Devel. Execs., Optimists, Wis. Club.

Republican. Home: 715 Windy Ridge Dr Ballwin MO 63021-7707 Office: LCMS Internat Ctr 1333 S Kirkwood Rd Saint Louis MO 63122-7226

PRESCOTT, RICHARD PAUL, JR., computer company consultant; b. Bloomington, Ill., Apr. 20, 1939; s. Richard Paul Sr. and Kathern Grace (Rhodus) P.; m. Winifred Luce Rockefeller, June 15, 1962 (dec. 1966); children: Paul Luce and Peter Grace (dec.). Bus., Ill. Wesleyan U., 1960; MBA, U. Chgo., 1963; PhD, London Sch. Econ., 1966; lic. real estate sales, Ill. State U., 1992. Systems analyst Honeywell EDP, Chgo., 1963-67; info. specialist IBM, White Plains, N.Y., 1967-68; sr. project dir. United Artists, N.Y.C., 1969-70; info. mgr. Blue Cross Assn., Chgo., 1971-72; software cons. Bloomington, Ill., 1973-92, Referral Co. of McLean County, 1992; founding mem., owner Software Info. Svc. Bd., 1993; cons. Gen. Acct. Office, Washington, Sec. of State, Washington, Econ. Devel. Peru, Lima, 1990—. Author: SSA and Blue Cross Instruction Manual, 1970, (software) Easy Tran-sort, 1971, Operating System, 1974. Mem. Rep. Nat. Com., Pres.'s Conf. Econ. Advisors, 1990—. Comdr. USN, 1963—. Decorated Navy Cross, Silver Star, Purple Heart. Mem. DAV, Chgo. Econ. Coun., Am. Legion, Smithsonian Inst., Chgo. Art Inst., Bloomington Symphony, Libr. of Congress Assocs. (charter mem.), Mensa, Theta Chi (chpt. pres.). Methodist. Home and Office: 1128 N Colton Ave Bloomington IL 61701-1922

PRESKA, MARGARET LOUISE ROBINSON, education educator, district service professional; b. Parma, N.Y., Jan. 23, 1938; d. Ralph Craven and Ellen Elvira (Niemi) Robinson; m. Daniel C. Preska, Jan. 24, 1959; children: Robert, William, Ellen Preska Steck. B.S. summa cum laude, SUNY, 1957; M.A., Pa. State U., 1961; Ph.D., Claremont Grad. Sch., 1969; postgrad., Manchester Coll., Oxford U., 1973. Instr. LaVerne (Calif.) Coll., 1968-75, asst. prof., asso. prof., acad. dean, 1972-75; instr. Starr King Sch. for Ministry, Berkeley, Calif., summer, 1975; v.p. acad. affairs, equal opportunity officer Mankato (Minn.) State U., 1975-79, pres., 1979-92; project dir. Kaliningrad (Russia) Mil. Re-Tng., 1992—; Disting. svc. prof. Minn. State U., Winona, 1993—, pres. Inst. for Effective Tchg., 1993—; bd. dirs. No. States Power Co., Norwest Corp., Mankato, Minn. Pres. Pomona Valley chpt. UN Assn., 1968-69, Unitarian Soc. Pomona Valley, 1968-69, PTA Lincoln Elem. Sch., Pomona, 1973-74, Campfire Boys and Girls, 1986-88; mem. Pomona City Charter Revision Commn., 1972; chmn. The Fielding Inst., Santa Barbara, 1983-86; bd. dirs. Elderhostel Internat., 1983-87, Minn. Agrl. Interpretive Ctr. (Farmam.), 1983-92, Am. Assn. State Colls. and Univs., Moscow on the Mississippi - Minn. Meets the Soviet Union; nat. pres. Campfire, Inc., 1985-87; chmn. Gov.'s Coun. on Youth, Minn., 1983-86, Minn. Edn. Forum, 1984; mem. Gov.'s Commn. on Econ. Future of Minn., 1985—, NCAA Pres. Commn., 1986-92, NCAA Cost Cutting Commn., Minn. Brainpower Compact, 1985-92; commr. Great Lakes Govs.' Econ. Devel. Coun., 1986, Minn Gov.'s Commn. on Forestry. Carnegie Found. grantee Am. Coun. Edn. Deans Inst., 1974; recipient Outstanding Alumni award Pa. State, Outstanding Alumni award Claremont Grad. Sch., YWCA Leader award 1982, Exch. Club Book of Golden Deeds award, 1987; named one of top 100 alumni, SUNY, 1985, Hall of Heritage award, 1988, Wohelo Camp Fire award, 1989. Mem. AAUW (pres. Mankato 1990-92), LWV, Women's Econ. Roundtable, St. Paul/Mpls. Com. on Fgn. Rels., Am. Coun. on Edn., Am. Assn. Univ. Adminstrs., Zonta, Rotary, Benedicts Dance Club. Unitarian. Home: 476 W Broadway St Winona MN 55987-5218 Office: Minn State Univ Inst for Effective Teaching 1125 W Wabasha St Winona MN 55987-2452

PRESSLER, LARRY, senator; b. Humboldt, S.D., Mar. 29, 1942; s. Antone Lewis and Loretta Geneive (Claussen) P.; m. Harriet Dent, 1982. B.A., U. S.D., 1964; diploma (Rhodes scholar), Oxford U., Eng., 1965; M.A., Kennedy Sch. Govt., Harvard U., 1971; J.D., Harvard U., 1971. Mem. 94th-95th Congresses from 1st S.D. Dist.; mem. U.S. Senate from S.D., 1979—; U.S. del. Inter-Parliamentary Union for 97th Congress; mem. bd. visitors all mil. svc. academies; now chmn. Commerce Com. U.S. Senate; U.S. Senate com. chmn. commerce, sci. and transp. subcoms.; chmn. comm., aviation, ocieans and fisheries, sci., tech. and space; fin. com. mem.; small bus. com. mem.; mem. spl. com. on aging; congl. del. to UN Gen. Assembly, 1986, 92; mem. U.S. Commn. on Improving the Effectiveness of UN, 1993. Author: U.S. Senators from the Prairie, 1982, Star Wars: The SDI Debates in Congress, 1986. All-Am. del. 4-H agrl. fair, Cairo, 1961, U.S. Rep. (appointed by Vice Pres.) to UN Fall Gen. Assembly, 1986. Served to 1st lt. AUS, 1966-68, Vietnam. Recipient Nat. 4-H Citizenship award, 1962, Report to the Pres. 4-H award, 1962. Mem. Am. Assn. Rhodes Scholars, VFW, ABA Phi Beta Kappa. Office: US Senate 243 Russell Senate Bldg Washington DC 20510

PRESSMAN, THANE ANDREW, consumer products executive; b. San Diego, June 6, 1945; s. Harold Andrew and Audre Ethelyn (Negus) P.; m. Caroline Hannah Hood Snyder, Nov. 23, 1966; children: Sean, Steven. BS, Springfield (Mass.) Coll., 1967; MS, Syracuse U., 1969. Various to brand mgr. Procter & Gamble Co., Cin., 1968-76, assoc. mgr. advt., 1976-79; v.p. Lamalie Assocs., Inc. Chgo., 1979-81; dir. new products Alberto Culver Co., Melrose Park, Ill., 1981-84; group staff, v.p. Sara Lee Corp., Northbrook, Ill., 1984-85; pres., COO Kitchens of Sara Lee Can., Bramalee, Ont., 1986-88; exec. v.p. Sara Lee Bakery Co., Bramalee and Deerfield, Ill., 1988-90; pres., CEO Crestar Food Products, Inc. (affiliate of H.J. Heinz Co.), Eugene, Oreg., 1991-92, Crestar Food Products Inc. & Crestar Food Products Can. Ltd., Nashville and Mississauga, Ont., Can., 1992-93; pres. Labatt Ont. Breweries, Etobicoke, 1993-95; pres., CEO Labatt U.S.A. LLC., Darien, Conn., 1995—; guest lectr. U. Mich. Grad. Sch. Bus., Ann Arbor, 1977-79; bd. dirs. Brewers Retail Inc., Toronto; bd. dirs. Brewers of Ont., 1994-95, chmn., 1995. Bd. dirs. Am. Field Svc. U.S.A., N.Y.C., 1986-91, trustee AFS Intercultural Programs, N.Y.C., 1988-93; trustee Springfield Coll., 1988—; campaign co-chmn. United Way Cin., Chgo., Bramalea, Deerfield, 19876-94. Mem. Assn. Governing Bds. Univs. and Colls., David Allen Reed Soc., Grocery Product Mfrs. Can., Internat. Dairy Deli Assn., Dixie Curling Club, Eugene Country Club, Richland Country Club, Mississaugua Country Club.

PRESTASH, RANDY JOHN, optometrist; b. Milw., Jan. 27, 1955; s. George and Anna (Stachelski) P.; m. Patricia Ann Lohman, Aug. 26, 1978. BS, Ill. Coll. Optometry, 1978, OD, 1980, therapeutic lic., 1985. Assoc. intern Ill. Coll. Optometry, Chgo., 1979-80, Chgo. Lighthouse for the Blind, 1979-80; pvt. practice optometry Oconomowoc, Wis., 1980—; clin. dir. Operation Kapawa Rotary Internat. Eye Health Mission to Phillipines, 1983, 84, 86; pres. cons., corp. pres. Fishdoctors Fishing Specialists, Oconomowoc; corp. pres. Nat. Optical Services Corp., Oconomowoc, 1980—. Contbr. to mags.; featured on TV show PM Magazine, 1984. Named one of Outstanding Young Men Am. Jaycees, Chgo., 1979; recipient Albert H. Rodriquez Research award Ill. Coll. Optometry, 1980. Mem. Am. Optometric Assn., Wis. Optometric Assn., Kettle Moraine Optometric Assn., Vols. of Optometric Services to Humanity. Club: Fishers of Men (Oconomowoc) (v.p. 1985—). Lodge: Rotary (bd. Oconomowoc club dirs. 1985—). Home: 6028 Mary Ln Oconomowoc WI 53066-2110 Office: 508 E Summit Ave Oconomowoc WI 53066-3892

PRESTON, KIM K., electrical-mechanical designer; b. Dennison, Iowa, Sept. 24, 1954. AAS, Albuquerque Tech. Sch., 1983, AD in Elec.-Mech. Design, 1984. Design svcs. supr. Reach Electronics, Lexington, Nebr., 1988-89, J-TEC Assocs., Cedar Rapids, Iowa, 1989-91; sr. product designer Norand Corp., Cedar Rapids, 1991-92; elec.-mech. designer Cedar Rapids Inc., 1992—; v.p., co-owner Preston Bus. Svcs., Cedar Rapids, 1990—. Mem. Visitors and Conf. Bur. of Cedar Rapids, 1995—. Sgt. U.S. Army, 1973-80, Europe. Mem. Nat. Mgmt. Assn. (v.p., program dir. 1991—), Coun. Indsl. and Profl. Socs. (pres. 1995), Cedar Rapids C. of C. Democrat. Presbyterian. Office: Cedar Rapids Inc 916 16th St NE Cedar Rapids IA 52402

PRETLOW, THERESA PACE, biomedical educator, researcher; b. Rochester, N.Y., July 8, 1939; d. Peter and Mary (Stefano) Pace; m. Thomas Garrett Pretlow II, June 29, 1963; children: James Michael, Joseph Peter, David Mark. BS, Le Moyne Coll., 1961; PhD, U. Rochester, N.Y., 1966. Postdoctoral fellow in bacteriology U. Wis., Madison, 1965-67; rsch. assoc. dept. pathology U. Ala., Birmingham, 1974-77, from rsch. instr. to asst. prof. dept. pathology, 1978-83; asst. prof. Inst. Pathology Case Western Res. U., Cleve., 1983-89, assoc. prof. Inst. Pathology, 1989-96; prof. Inst. Pathology Case Western Res. U., Cleve., 1996—; mem. spl. study sects., ad hoc mem. study sect. on metabolic pathology NIH. Assoc. editor Cancer Rsch.; ad hoc reviewer Am. Gastroent. Assn., NAS, Carcinogenesis, VA Merit Rsch.; contbr. over 80 articles to profl. jours. Vol. leader Boy Scouts Am., Birmingham and Cleve., 1976-94. Grantee Nat. Cancer Inst., Am. Inst. Cancer Rsch., Am. Cancer Soc., Wendy Will Case Cancer Fund; recipient Silver Beaver and St. George awards Boy Scouts Am. Mem. Am. Assn. for Cancer Rschrs. (ad hoc reviewer, assoc. editor Cancer Rsch. 1996), Am. Soc. Investigative Pathology, Am. Soc. Cell Biologists, Histochem Soc. (councilor 1992-96, pres. elect 1995, pres. 1996, ad hoc reviewer), Women in Cancer Rsch. (sec.-elect 1995, sec., 1996-98). Roman Catholic. Office: Case Western Res U Inst Pathology 2085 Adelbert Rd Cleveland OH 44106-2622

PRETTYMAN, PAULA MARIE, critical care nurse, home infusion nurse; b. Dayton, Ohio, Dec. 20, 1964; d. Gene Clifton and Betty Jean (Rasnick) P. AAS, Sinclair Community Coll., Dayton, 1987; BSN, U. Cin., 1992. RN, Ohio; CRNI. Staff nurse Bethany Luth. Village, Centerville, Ohio, 1987-89, shift supr., 1988-89; staff nurse CCU Grandview Hosp., Dayton, 1988-89; staff nurse ICU and relief charge Southview Hosp., Dayton, 1989; staff nurse burn unit U. Cin. Hosp., 1990-92; burn life support instr. Am. Nursing Care/Amerimed, Cin., 1991-92; home infusion nurse Am. Nursing Care/Ameremed., Cin., 1992-95; home infusion liaison The Alliance Home Health Svcs., Cin., 1995—; homecare nurse Am. Nursing, Dayton, 1989-91. Office: The Alliance Home Health 2415 Auburn Ave Cincinnati OH 45219

PRETTYMAN-BAKER, SHEILA, pediatrics, neonatal nurse; b. Dayton, Ohio, May 22, 1957; d. Gene Clifton and Betty Jean (Rasnick) Prettyman; m. Stephen Ray Baker, Feb. 4, 1989. AS, Kettering Coll. Med. Arts, 1978, AD in Emergency Med. Tech., 1985. Cert. emergency med. technician-paramedic. Nursing supr. Bethany Luth. Village, Centerville, Ohio; neonatal nursery nurse St. Elizabeth Hosp., Dayton; charge nurse Mercy Hosp., Fairfield, Ohio; office nurse Kettering; IV nurse educator St. Elizabeth Hosp., Dayton.

PREUSS, ROGER E(MIL), artist; b. Waterville, Minn., Jan. 29, 1922; s. Emil W. and Edna (Rosenau) P.; m. MarDee Ann Germundson, Dec. 31, 1954 (dec. Mar. 1981). Student, Mankato Comml. Coll., Mpls. Sch. Art. instr. seminar Mpls. Coll. Art and Design, Mpls. Inst. Arts Speakers Bur.; former judge ann. Goodyear Nat. Conservation Awards Program. Painter of nature art; one-man shows include: St. Paul Fine Art Galleries, 1959, Albert Lea Art Center, 1963, Hist. Soc. Mont., Helena, 1964, Bicentennial exhbn., Le Sueur County Hist. Soc. Mus., Elysian, Minn., 1976, Merrill's Gallery of Fine Art, Taos, N.Mex., 1980; exhbns. include: Midwest Wildlife Conf. Exhbn., Kerr's Beverly Hills, Calif., 1947, Laguna Art Mus., Calif., 1947, Joslyn Meml. Mus., Omaha, 1948, Hollywood Fine Arts Center, 1948, Minn. Centennial, 1949, Federated Chaparral Authors, 1951, Nat. Wildlife Art, 1951, 52, N.Am. Wildlife Art, 1952, Ducks Unltd. Waterfowl exhibit, 1953, 54, St. Paul Winter Carnival, 1954, St. Paul Gallery Art Mart, 1954, Harris Fine Arts Center, Provo, Utah, 1969, Galerie Internationale, N.Y.C., 1972, Holy Land Conservation Fund, N.Y.C., 1976, Faribault Art Ctr., 1981, Wildlife Artists of the World Exhbn., Bend, Oreg., 1984, U. Art Mus., U. Minn., Mpls., 1990, Rochester Art Ctr., 1991, Minn. Hist. Soc.-Hill House, 1992, Bemidji Art Ctr., 1992, Jack London Ctr., Dawson City, Yukon Territory, Can., 1992, Weyerhaeuser Meml. Mus., Little Falls, Minn., 1995, Minn. Valley Nat. Wildlife Refuge Ctr., Bloomington, 1995, Sagebrush Artists Exhbn., Klamath Falls, Oreg., 1995; represented in permanent collections: Demarest Meml. Mus., Hackensack, N.J., Smithsonian Instn., N.Y. Jour. Commerce, Mont. Hist. Soc., Inland Bird Banding Assn., Minn. Capitol Bldg., Mont. State U., Wildlife Am. Collection, LeSueur Hist. Soc., Voyageurs Nat. Park Interpretive Ctr., Krause-Hartig VFW Post, Mpls., Nat. Wildlife Fedn. Collection, Minn. Ceremonial House, U.S. Wildlife Svc. Fed. Bldg., Fort Snelling, Minn., Crater Lake Nat. Park Visitors Ctr., VA Hosp., Mpls., Luxton Collection, Banff, Alta., Can., Internat. Inst. Arts, Geneva, Mont. Capitol Bldg., People of Century-Goldblatt Collection, Lyons, Ill., Harlem Savings Collection, N.Y.C., Weisman Art Mus., Mpls., Minn. Vets. Home, Mpls., Blauvelt Art Mus., Oradell, N.J., Roger Preuss Art Collection, Augustana Ctr. for Western Studies, Sioux Falls, S.D., Minn. Mus. Am. Art, St. Paul, U. Minn. Art Mus., C.M. Russell Mus., Great Falls, Mont., others, numerous galleries and pvt. collections; designer: Fed. Duck Stamp, U.S. Dept. Interior, 1949, Commemorative Centennial Pheasant Stamp, 1981, Gold Waterfowl medallion Franklin Mint, 1983, Gold Stamp medallion Wildlife Mint, 1983, 40th Anniversary Commemorative Fed. Duck Stamp etching, 1989; panelist: Sportsman's Roundtable, Sta. WTCN-TV, Mpls. (emeritus), from 1953; author: Is Wildlife Art Recognized Fine Art?, 1986; contbr.: Christmas Echos, 1955, Wing Shooting, Trap & Skeet, 1955, Along the Trout Stream, 1979; contbr. Art Impressions mag., Can., Wildlife Art, U.S.; also illustrations and articles in Nat. Wildlife and over 300 essays on North American animals, others.; assoc. editor: Out-of-Doors mag.; compiler and artist: Outdoor Horizons, 1957, Twilight over the Wilderness, 1972, 60 limited edition prints Wildlife of America, from 1970; contbr. paintings and text Minnesota Today; creator paintings and text Preuss Wildlife Calendar; inventor: paintings and text Wildlife Am. Calendar; featured artist Art West, 1980-84, Wildlife Art; featured in films Your BFA- Care and Maintenance, Black Ducks Along the Border. Del. Nat. Wildlife Conf.; bd. dirs. emeritus Voyageurs Nat. Park Assn., Deep-Portage Conservation Found., 1977—; bd. dirs. Wetlands for Wildlife U.S.A.; active Wildlife Am.; co-organizer, v.p., bd. dirs. Minn. Conservation Fedn., 1952-54; mem. U.S. Hospitalized Vets. Venison Program, 1957—; trustee Liberty Bell Edn. Found.; Waseca Arts Coun.; founder, dir. Roger Preuss Conservation Preserve for Sty of Nature, 1990—. With USNR, World War II. Recipient Stamp Design award U.S. Fish and Wildlife Svc., 1994, Minn. Outdoor award, 1956, Patron of Conservation award, 1956, award for contbns. conservation Minn. Statehood Centennial Commn., 1958, 1st award Am. Indsl. Devel. Coun., citation of merit VFW, award of merit Mil. Order Cootie, 1963, merit award Minn. Waterfowl Assn., 1976, silver medal Nat. SAR, 1978, Svcs. to Arts and Environ. award Faribault Art Ctr., 1981, Ptnrs. for Wildlife award U.S. Fish and Wildlife Svc., 1994; named Wildlife Conservationist of the Yr., Sears Fund.-Nat. Wildlife Fedn. program, 1966, Am. Bicentennial Wildlife Artist, Am. Heritage Assn., 1976; hon. mem. Ont. Chippewa Nation of Can., 1957; named Knight of Mark Twain for contbns. to Am. art Mark Twain Soc., 1978; named to Water, Woods and Wildlife Hall of Fame, named Dean of Wildfowl Artists, 1981, Hon. Ky. Col.; recipient hon. degree U.S. Vets. Venison program, 1980, Western Am. award significant contbns. to preservation arts and history No. Prairie Plains, Augustana Coll. Ctr. for Western Studies, Sioux Falls, S.D., 1992, Pub. Svc. award for outstanding contbns. to Am. conservation and environ. U.S. Dept. Interior, 1996; named creator first signed, numbered photolithographic print pub. in N.Am., 1959; documented Colorado Springs Fine Arts Ctr., 1993, colleague of Frederick R. Weisman Mus., Mpls., 1994; grantee NEH, 1995. Fellow Internat. Inst. Arts (life), Soc. Animal Artists (emeritus), N.Am. Mycol. Assn., Nat. Wildlife Fedn. (nat. wildlife week chmn. Minn.), Minn. Ducks Unltd. (bd. dirs. emeritus), Minn. Artists Assn. (v.p., bd. dirs. 1953-59), Soc. Artists and Art Dirs., Outdoor Writers Am. (emeritus), Soc. Artists and Art Dirs. (emeritus), Am. Artists Profl. League (emeritus), Mpls. Soc. Fine Arts, Wildlife Soc., Minn. Mycol. Soc. (pres. emeritus, hon. life mem.), Le Sueur County Hist. Soc. (hon. life mem.), Minn. Conservation Fedn. (hon. life), Wildlife Artists World (charter mem., internat. v.p. 1986—, chmn. fine arts bd.), Internat. Platform Assn. (emeritus), Great Lakes Outdoor Writers (emeritus), The Prairie Chicken Soc. (patron), The Sharp-tailed Grouse Soc. (patron), Mission Oceanic Arctic, 1992, Beaverbrook Club (hon. life), Minn. Press Club (emeritus), Explorers Club (N.Y.C., emeritus). Office: care Wildlife Am PO Box 580004-a Minneapolis MN 55458-0004 Studio: 2224 Grand Ave Minneapolis MN 55405-3412

PREUSS, RONALD STEPHEN, lawyer, educator; b. Flint, Mich., Dec. 1, 1935; s. Edward Joseph and Harriette Beckwith (Pease) P.; 1 child, William Stephen. AB, U. Mo., 1958, MA, 1963; JD, St. Louis U., 1973; postdoctoral, Worcester Coll., Oxford, Eng., 1979, U. Calif., Berkeley, 1979, U. Paris, 1984. Bar: Mo. 1973, U.S. Dist. Ct. (ea. and we. dists.) Mo. 1973, U.S. Tax Ct. 1979. From instr. to assoc. prof. English St. Louis Jr. Coll. Dist., 1965—; ptnr. Anderson & Preuss, Clayton, Mo., 1973—. Author: Laudamus Te, 1962, The St. Louis Gourmet. 1979, 86, English Elegies, 1983, Melville: A Psychic Biography, 1984, Theater I, 1987, Letting Go, 1988; editor St. Louis Gourmet Newsletter, 1981-88; co-editor Criterion mag. 1961-62; columnist Capital Courier newspaper 1962-64. Mem. Eisenhower Commn., 1995. Mem. Mo. Bar Assn., Phi Alpha Delta (John L. Sullivan chpt. vice justice 1971-72, justice 1972-73), Eisenhower Commn. Home: 32 Conway Cove Dr Chesterfield MO 63017-2069 Office: Anderson & Preuss 230 S Bemiston Ave Ste 410 Saint Louis MO 63105-1907

PREUSSER, JOSEPH WILLIAM, academic administrator; b. Petersburg, Nebr., June 18, 1941; s. Louis Henry and Elizabeth Sophia (Oberbrocking) P.; m. Therese Marie Mahoney, Aug. 12, 1967; children: Scott, Michelle, Denise. BA in Social Scis., Wayne State Coll., 1965; MA in Geography, U. Nebr., Omaha, 1971; PhD in Adminstrn., U. Nebr., 1978. Coord. social studies Lewis Cen. Community Sch. Dist., Council bluffs, Iowa, 1967-71; chmn. social sci. div., instr. Platte Jr. Coll., Columbus, Nebr., 1972-73; dean instrn./Platte campus Cen. Community Coll., Columbus, 1973-82, v.p. ednl. planning community edn., pres. Platte campus, 1982-84; pres. Cen. Community Coll., Grand Island, Nebr., 1984—; mem. edit com. devel. Nebr. Tech. Community Coll., 1973-75, sec., , dean instrn., 1974-76, chmn. coun. pres's., 1990-91,; mem. Archdiocese Omaha Bd. Edn., 1980-84; chmn. bd. St. Bonaventure Bd. Edn., 1976-80; pub. speaker in field. Contbr. articles to profl. jours. Bd. dirs. Ctrl. Nebr. Goodwill Industries, Gand island, 1987-95, treas., 1990-91, chmn. 1992; chmn. sustaining membership enrollment campaign Overland Trails Boys Scouts Am., 1990; worker YMCA Fund Drive, Columbus, 1980; mem. Columbus City Planning Commn., 1979-84, chmn., 1981, 82; coach boys baseball and girls softball, Council Bluffs, Columbus and Grand Island, 1968-95. With U.S. Army, 1959-61. Named one Outstanding Young Mem of Am., 1976; recipient Nat. Leadership award U. Tex., 1988-89, Pres. of Yr. award Am. Assn. Women i Comm., 1996. Mem. Am. Assn. Cmty. and Jr. Colls., Am. Voct. Assn., Nebr. Vocat. Assn. (Outstanding Svc. award 1986), Am. Assn. Ret. People, Nat. Coun. Instructional Officers, Nat. Coun. Instructional Adminstrs., Am. Assn. for Women in Cmty. Colls. (Pres. of Yr. 1996), Saddle Club, Rotary, KC, Greater Columbus Area C. of C., Phi Delta Kappa. Democrat. Roman Catholic.

PREVOST, GARY FRANCIS, government educator, researcher, writer; b. Glens Falls, N.Y., Apr. 15, 1947; s. Henry J. and Dorothy M. (Craw) P.; m. Catherine Ann Kocy, June 8, 1985. BA, Union Coll., 1969; MA, U. Minn., 1972, PhD, 1977. Prof. govt. St. John's U., Collegeville, Minn., 1977—. Author: Democracy and Socialism in Sandinista Nicaragua, 1993; editor: Political Change in Spain, 1985, Cuba--A Different America, 1992. Mem. nat. exec. com. Nicaragua Network, Washington, 1985-90; bd. dirs. Middle East Outreach Consortium, Mpls., 1986—; treas. Faculty-Student Cuban Youth Lecture Ctr., Mpls., 1993-95. Recipient NEH summer stipend, 1978, 80; Fulbright fellow, 1990-91. Mem. AAUP (pres. St. John's U. chpt. 1991—), Latin Am. Studies Assn., Coun. European Studies, Am. Polit. Sci. Assn., Internat. Polit. Sci. Assn. Office: St John's U Dept Govt Collegeville MN 56321

PREY, YVONNE MARY, real estate broker; b. Milw., Mar. 14, 1945; d. Irvin Raymond Reindl and Viola Rose Schneider Maresh; m. John V. Prey, Sept. 2, 1967 (div. Dec. 1984); children: James Carter, Jacquelyn Rue. BS in Sociology, U. Wis., Oshkosh, 1967, postgrad., 1967-69. Lic. real estate broker, Wis.; cert. residential specialist, relocation profl. Social worker Winnebago State Hosp., Oshkosh, 1967-69; social worker Div. Family Svcs., State of Wis., Fond du Lac, 1969-72, Green Bay, 1972-75; real estate broker Action Realty, Inc., Wausau, Wis., 1975-81, Williams Realty, Inc., Wausau, 1982-92, RE/MAX of Wausau, 1992—. Active Habitat for Humanity, Friends of Wausau Hist. Landmarks; sponsor Wis. River Valley Jour. Mem. NAFE, LWV, Wausau Area C. of C. (bd. dirs. Coun. Women Bus. Owners 1990—, Amb. 1975-89, edn. com.), Marathon County Hist. Soc., Wausau Bd. Realtors, Wis. Realtors Assn., Realtors Nat. Mktg. Inst. Roman Catholic. Home: 811 Becher Dr Wausau WI 54401-2177 Office: RE/MAX of Wausau 1314 Grand Ave Wausau WI 54403-6672

PRICE, BRIDGETTE DENISE, industrial engineer; b. Pensacola, Fla., Oct. 3, 1965; d. William Lamar and Doris Jean (George) P. BS in Indsl. Engring., U. Fla., 1990; MA in Profl. Studies, DePaul U., 1993. Engr. Frito-Lay, Inc., Orlando, Fla., 1990-92; gen. bus. mgr. Taco Bell, 1993, Pepsico, Inc., Chgo., 1993; with United Parcel Svc., Chgo., 1994—; owner, founder Career Planning and Ednl. Devel., 1993—. Mem. profl. aux. bd. Chgo. Youth Success Found.. Mem. ASPA, NAFE, Am. Inst. Indsl. Engrs., Assn. Supervision and Curriculum Devel., Toastmasters (pres.), Alpha Kappa Alpha. Democrat. Baptist. Home: 4347 N Keeler Ave # 1W Chicago IL 60641-2119

PRICE, CHARLES H., II, former ambassador; b. Kansas City, Mo., Apr. 1, 1931; s. Charles Harry and Virginia (Ogden) P.; m. Carol Ann Swanson, Jan. 10, 1969; children: Caroline Lee, Melissa Marie, Charles H., C. B., Pickette. Student, U. Mo., 1951-53; LLD (hon.), Westminster Coll., 1984; LLD (honoris causa), U. Mo., 1988; LHD, Baker U., 1991; DSc (hon.), U. Buckingham, Eng., 1993. Chmn. bd., dir. Price Candy Co., Kansas City, 1969-81, Am. Bancorp., Kansas City, 1973-81; chmn., chief exec. officer Am. Bank & Trust Co., Kansas City, 1973-81; Am. ambassador to Belgium Brussels, 1981-83; Am. ambassador to U.K. London, 1983-89; chmn. bd. Americanc, Inc., St. Joseph, Mo., 1989-92, pres., CEO, 1990-92; chmn. bd. Mercantile Bank Kansas City, Mo., 1992-96, bd. dirs., 1996—; bd. dirs. US Industries, Inc., Hanson PLC, London, N.Y. Times Co., Texaco, Inc., 360 Degree Comm., Inc., Kansas City, Mercantile Bancorp, Inc. Bd. dirs. St. Luke's Hosp., Kansas City, 1970-81, hon. dir., 1989—, advisor Heart Inst. com.; bd. dirs. Midwest Rsch. Inst., Kansas City, chmn., 1990-93. Hon. fellow Regent's Coll., London, 1986; recipient William Booth award Salvation Army, 1985, World Citizen of Yr. award Mayor of Kansas City, 1985, Trustee Citation award Midwest Rsch. Inst., 1987, Disting. Svc. award Internat. Rels. Coun., 1989, Mankind award Cystic Fibrosis Found., 1990, Gold Good Citizenship award SAR, 1991, Chancellor's medal U. Mo. Kansas City, 1992. Mem. Brook Club, Cypress Point Club, Eldorado Country Club, Castle Pines Country Club, Kansas City Country Club, River Club, Swinley Forest Golf Club, White's Club. Republican. Episcopalian. Office: 1 W Armour Blvd Ste 300 Kansas City MO 64111-2087

PRICE, CHARLTON REED, management consultant; b. Morristown, N.J., Aug. 14, 1927; s. Harold Archibald and Elizabeth (Reed) P.; m. Virginia Jones, Aug. 16, 1952 (div. June 1965); m. Greta Emilie Meyer, June 8, 1980. AB, Princeton U., 1949. Cert. mgmt. cons. Rsch. assoc. Bur. Applied Social Rsch. Columbia U., N.Y.C., 1952-56; staff sociologist The Menninger Found., Topeka, 1956-64, Stanford Rsch. Inst., Menlo Park, Calif., 1965-70; assoc. prof. Grad. Sch. Bus. Columbia U., N.Y.C., 1970-71; prof. Grad. Sch. Bus. U. Puget Sound, Tacoma, 1979-80; ind. mgmt. cons. and educator various locations, 1971—. Author: Global Cooperation and Productivity, 1990; co-author: Men, Management and Mental Health, 1962; contbr. numerous articles to profl. jours. Vol. in Internat. Exec. Svc. Corps. Sgt. U.S. Army, 1946-47. Mem. Inst. Mgmt. Cons. (cert.). Home and Office: 10242 Cedarbrooke Ln Kansas City MO 64131-4210

PRICE, CLARA SUE, state legislator; b. Sept. 10, 1953; m. Gary Price; 1 child. BA in Bus. Adminstrn., Minot State U., 1977. Mem. N.D. Ho. of Reps., 1991—, chmn. Rep. caucaus, 1993-94, vice chmn. human svcs. com., mem. transp. com.; employee benefit specialist BCBS of N.D., 1982-87; stockbroker INVEST, 1988-90; sec. Cal-Dak Cabinets, 1975—; owner, operator Dakota Gardens & Herbs, 1993—. Past mem. Minot Commn. Status of Women. Mem. Eureka Homemakers, Internat. Peace Garden, Kiwanis, C. of C. Home: RR 6 Box 363 Minot ND 58703-9265 Office: ND Ho of Reps State Capitol Bismarck ND 58505*

PRICE, EDWARD FRANCIS, civil engineer; b. L.A., Oct. 3, 1934; s. Francis Edward and Carol Evelyn (Cole) P.; m. Bonnie Mae Buol, Oct. 2, 1972 (div. June 1973). BSCE, Chgo. Tech. Coll., 1967, BS, 1970; PhD (hon.), U. Mo., 1986. Registered profl. engr., Ill. Loftsman Douglas Aircraft Co., El Segundo, Calif., 1953-57; tool designer Chgo. Allis Mfg. Co., 1963-67; civil engr. Met. Water Reclamation Dist., Chgo., 1967—; pollution control programmer Albert Einstein Peace Orgn., Malta, 1986-91, Outstanding Civil Servant, 1985. Clk. of vestry St. David's Episc. Ch., 1990. With U.S. Army, 1957-61. Mem. ASCE (chpt. com. chmn. 1987, cert. 1993), Am. Inst. Design and Drafting (pres Chgo. chpt. 1983, cert. 1988), Instrument Soc. Am. (program dir. 1982, cert. 1989), Ill. Soc. Profl. Engrs. (sec. 1992). Republican. Home: 6011 N Winthrop Ave Chicago IL 60660 Office: Met Water Reclamation Dist 111 E Erie St Chicago IL 60611

PRICE, FOREST WALTER, clinical social worker; b. Vandalia, Mo., Oct. 17, 1930; s. James and Velma Marie (Anderson) P.; m. Marjorie Partridge,

Dec. 11, 1955; children: Karen Marie Grant (dec.), Forest Walter II. BA, Lincoln U., 1955; MSW, Denver U., 1958. Lic. Ill. Clin. social worker Denver Gen. Hosp., 1958-61, Winnebago M.H. Soc., Rockford, Ill., 1961-65, Psychiatric Evaluation Ctr., Rockford, 1965-77; sr. clin. social worker Glenwood Ctr., Rockford, 1977—; cons. Floberg Ctr. for Children, Rockford, 1985-88; assoc. prof. North Eastern Ill. U., Chgo., 1975-79; mem. Gov's. Child Death Review Team, Ill., 1995—; mem. ethics com. NASW, Ill., 1993—. Commr. Rockford Police and Fire Commn., 1986—. Sgt. 1st class USAF, 1950-54. Mem. Nat. Parks & Conservation Soc., Al Waris Shrine Temple, Alpha Phi ALpha Fraternity, Welcome Star Lodge, Balthasar Consistory. Home: 5848 Old Millstone Rd Rockford IL 61114 Office: Glenwood Ctr 2823 Glenwood Ave Rockford IL 61101

PRICE, GARY ROBERT, postal worker, broadcaster; b. Peoria, Ill., Sept. 20, 1948; s. Robert Rex and Elsie Jean (Miller) P.; m. Judy Talma Hutson, June 30, 1969 (div. Apr. 30, 1978); m. Judy Catherine Johnson, June 26, 1981; children: Edward Douglas, Angela Kaye, Julie Rene. Student, Florissant Valley C.C., Florissant, Mo., 1978-79, St. Louis U., 1980-82. Cameraman Lithocraft Studios, St. Louis, 1971-74; owner Great River Records, Alton, Ill., 1974-78; mgr. Village Music, St. Louis, 1980-82; automation clk. U.S. Postal Svc., St. Louis, 1982—; bluegrass music dir. KCLC/Lindenwood Coll., St. Charles, Mo., 1976—; vice-chmn. Mo. Area Bluegrass Com., St. Louis, 1974-76; mem. FCC, 1976—. Producer/broadcaster: Society for the Preservation of Bluegrass Music in America, 1988, 92; contbr. articles to profl. jours. Vol. Rep. Party, Alton, 1974-76; mem. Nat. Wildlife Fedn., Mt. Morris, Ill., 1994—, Humane Soc. of U.S., Washington, 1994—. Recipient Best Sta. Programming Bluegrass award Soc. for Preservation of Bluegrass Music in Am., Kirksville, Mo., 1988, 92. Mem. Internat. Bluegrass Music Assn. (media/broadcast mem.), Am. Postal Workers Union, Disabled Vets. Home: 4302 Sun Lake Dr Saint Charles MO 63301

PRICE, HENRY ESCOE, broadcast executive; b. Jackson, Miss., Oct. 13, 1947; s. Henry E. Price Sr. and Alma Kate (Merrill) Noto; m. Maria Diane Harper, Apr. 8, 1972; children: Henry E. III, Norman Harper. BS in Radio, TV, Film, Journalism, U. So. Miss., 1972. Announcer, news dir. Sta. WROA Radio, Gulfport, Miss., 1967-69; comml. producer Sta. WJTV-TV, Jackson, Miss., 1969-73; prodn. mgr. Sta. WAAY-TV, Huntsville, Ala., 1973-77, Sta. WPEC-TV, West Palm Beach, Fla., 1977-79; dir. promotion Sta. WPTV-TV, Palm Beach, Fla., 1979-81; TV cons. Frank Magid Assoc., Marion, Iowa, 1981-83; dir. advt. and promotion Sta. WJLA-TV, Washington, 1983-84; v.p., dir. programming Sta. WUSA-TV, Gannett TV, Washington, 1984-88; pres., gen. mgr. Sta. WFMY-TV, Gannett TV, Greensboro, N.C., 1988-91, Sta. KARE-TV, Mpls., 1991—; pres. Carolina News Network, 1988-91. Vice chair, bd. dirs. The Courage Ctr., Mpls.; regional dir. Nat. Conf.; mem. exec. com., bd. dirs. The Minn. Orch.; Pacesetter program chair Mpls. United Way Campaign; active Twin Cities Dunkers, Twin Cities Comm. Coun., 11 Who Care. Mem. Minn. Broadcasters Assn. (bd. dirs.), Greater Mpls. C. of C. (bd. dirs.). Office: KARE-TV 8811 Olson Memorial Hwy Minneapolis MN 55427-4762

PRICE, HUBERT, state legislator. Rep. Mich. State Dist. 43, 1995—. Mem. Dem. Nat. Conv. 1983—. Address: PO Box 30014 Lansing MI 48909-7514

PRICE, JAMES GORDON, physician; b. Brush, Colo., June 20, 1926; s. John Hoover and Rachel Laurette (Dodds) P.; m. Janet Alice McSween, June 19, 1949; children: James Gordon II, Richard Christian, Mary Laurette, Janet Lynn. B.A., U. Colo., 1948, M.D., 1951. Diplomate: Charter diplomate Am. Bd. Family Practice (dir., pres. 1979). Intern Denver Gen. Hosp., 1951-52; practice medicine specializing in family medicine Brush, 1952-78; prof. family practice U. Kans. Med. Ctr., 1978-93; chmn. dept. U. Kans. Med. Center, 1982-90, exec. dean, 1990-93, prof. emeritus in family practice, 1993—; mem. Inst. Medicine, Nat. Acad. Scis., 1973—; med. editor Gen. Learning Corp., 1973-92. Editorial bd.: Med. World News, 1969-79; editor: Am. Acad. Family Physician Home Study Self Assessment Program, 1978-83; contbr.: (column) Your Family Physician, 1973-90. Trustee Family Health Found. Am., 1970-82. Served with USNR, 1943-46. Charter fellow Am. Acad. Family Physicians (pres. 1973); mem. Phi Beta Kappa, Alpha Omega Alpha. Home: 12205 Mohawk Rd Shawnee Mission KS 66209-2137

PRICE, JANIS, medical center administrator; b. N.Y.C.; d. Marvin Howard and Helen (Saks) Davidson; m. H. Laurence Price, May 28, 1972; children: Sarah Lynn, David Matthew. BA, SUNY, Brockport, 1972. Cert. healthcare access mgr. Admissions clk. U. Mich. Med. Ctr., Ann Arbor, 1972-74, patient rep., 1974-76, admissions supr., 1976-82, asst. admitting mgr., 1982-85, admissions mgr.-psychiatry, 1985-89, asst. dir. psychiatry, 1989—; speaker in field. Contbr. articles to profl. jours. and chpts. to books. Tutor Washtenaw Literacy program, 1994—. Recipient JFK Good Citizenship award Reader's Digest, 1968. Mem. Nat. Assn. Healthcare Access Mgmt. (nomination chmn. 1989-92, strategic planning chairperson 1992-93, Doris Gleason Publ. award 1989), Hosp. Admitting Mgrs. S.E. Mich. (pres. 1985-89, editor newsletter 1989-93, Pres.'s award 1993), Med. Group Mgmt. Assn., Acad. Practice Assembly, Adminstrs. in Acad. Psychiatry (mem.-at-large 1993-94, assoc. editor newsletter 1989-94, editor newsletter 1994—). Jewish.

PRICE, JOHN RICHARD, lawyer; b. Indpls., Feb. 2, 1941; s. Cecil Ralph and Dorothy Elizabeth (Imbler) P.; m. Suzanne Cathy Lammert, June 8, 1961; children: Andrea, John II, Heather, Adam. BA, Wabash Coll., 1963; JD, Ind. U., Indpls., 1968. Bar: Ind. 1968. Chmn. bd. Carmel (Ind.) Bank and Trust Co., 1974-76; assoc. John Price and Assocs., Indpls., 1968—; chmn. bd. Equal Justice Under Law Inst., Indpls., 1993—. Author: America at the Crossroads, 1979; contbr. (book) The Rebirth of America, 1986. Pres. Hamilton County Hosp. Authority, Carmel, 1987—. Recipient Angel award Execllence in Media, 1990, Clean Cmty. award Indpls. Bapt. Schs., 1989-90. Republican. Office: John Price & Assocs 9000 Keystone Crossing #150 Indianapolis IN 46240

PRICE, LAWRENCE EDWARD, physicist; b. Altadena, Calif., July 25, 1943; s. Edward Thomas and Margaret Christian (Muckleston) P.; m. Sandra Jeanne Wheat, Nov. 29, 1968; children: Matthew Edward, Jeffrey Yarnall. BA, Pomona Coll., 1965; MA, Harvard U., 1966, PhD, 1970. From rsch. assoc. to asst. prof. Columbia U., N.Y.C., 1970-78; from asst. physicist to dir. HEP div. Argonne (Ill.) Nat. Lab., 1978—; HEPNET review com. U.S. Dept. Energy, 1987-88, ESNET steering com., 1988—; mem. organizing com. Future Directions for HEP, Snowmass, 1996. Fellow Am. Phys. Soc.; mem. AAAS. Office: Argonne Nat Lab Bldg 362 9700 S Cass Ave Argonne IL 60439

PRICE, LEONARD RUSSELL (LEN PRICE), state legislator; b. Sept. 21, 1942; m. Stephanie Wright; 3 children. BS, MS, U. Wis., River Falls. Mem. Minn. Ho. of Reps. St. Paul, 1982-90; vicechmn. gen. legis. com., vet. affairs com., gaming com., mem. appropriations com., environ. and natural resource com., U.S. senator from Minn., 1990—; co-vice chmn. edn. com., mem. commerce and consumer protection com., taxes com., others; tchr. Mem. NEA (life), Minn. Edn. Assn. Democrat. Home: 6264 Applewood Ct Woodbury MN 55125-1105*

PRICE, (WILLIAM) MARK, professional basketball player; b. Bartlesville, Okla., Feb. 15, 1964. Student, Ga. Tech. With Dallas Mavericks, 1986; guard Cleve. Cavaliers, 1986—. Winner NBA Long Distance Shootout, 1993, 94; named to NBA All-Star team, 1989, 92, 93, 94, NBA First Team, 1993, Dream Team II, 1994. *

PRICE, (JOHN) NELSON, journalist; b. Augusta, Ga., May 7, 1957; s. John Paul and Joy Gertrude (Scheck) P. BA in Journalism and Psychology, Ind. U., 1978. City hall reporter Lawrence (Kans.) Journal-World, 1978-79; fed. cts. reporter, social issues writer Fort Wayne (Ind.) Journal-Gazette, 1979-80; edn. writer Indpls. News, 1981-85; columnist, feature writer Indpls. Star-News, 1985—; bd. dirs. The Sagamore, Indpls. Contbr. articles to profl. jours. Bd. dirs. Riley Area Revitalization Program, Indpls. Recipient Sagamore of the Wabash award Gov. Ind., 1995, Martin Luther King Jr. award Indpls. Edn. Assn., 1986, Best Sports Writing award Hoosier State Press Assn., 1994, Best Column award, 1994, Best Feature Story award, 1994, Best Personality Profile award, 1994. Mem. Soc. Profl. Journalists (awards), Mental Health Assn. Marion County (awards). Office: Indianapolis Star-News 307 N Pennsylvania Indianapolis IN 46204

PRICE, PAUL S., insurance agency executive; b. Milw., June 18, 1951; s. William J. and Helen E. (Emanuelson) P.; m. Christine June Cuiray, Apr. 30, 1977; children: Eric Paul, Mark Christopher. BA, Carthage Coll., 1973. CPCU. Comml. underwriter Travelers Ins. Co., Milw., 1973-78; v.p. Frank F. Haack & Assoc., Milw., 1978-94; pres. BenePac, Inc., Milw., 1994—. Pres. Lake County Sch. Bd., Nashotah, Wis., 1991-94. Mem. Am. Coll. Property, Liability Underwriters. Republican. Lutheran. Home: 1833 Price Rd Hartland WI 53029-8830

PRICE, THEODORA HADZISTELIOU, individual and family therapist; b. Athens, Greece, Oct. 1, 1938; came to U.S. 1967; d. Ioannis and Evangelia (Emmanuel) Hadzisteliou; m. David C. Long Price, Dec. 26, 1966 (div. 1989); children: Morgan N., Alkes D.L. BA in History/Archaeology, U. Athens, 1961; DPhil, U. Oxford, Eng., 1966; MA in Clin. Social Work, U. Chgo., 1988; Diploma in Piano Teaching, Nat. Conservatory, Athens, 1958. Lic. clin. social worker. Mus. asst. and resident tutor U. Sydney, Australia, 1966-67; instr. anthropology Adelphi U., N.Y.C., 1967-68; archaeologist Hebrew Union Coll., Gezer, Israel, 1968; asst. prof. classical archaeology/art U. Chgo., 1968-70; jr. rsch. fellow Harvard Ctr. Hellenic Studies, Washington, 1970-71; clin. social worker Harbor Light Ctr., Salvation Army, Chgo., 1988-89; therapist Inst. Motivational Devel., Lombard, Ill., 1989-90; caseworker Jewish Family & Community Svc., Chgo., 1989-90; staff therapist Family Svc. Ctrs. of South Cook County, Chicago Heights, 1990-91; pvt. practice child, adolescent, family therapy Bolingbrook, Ill., 1991—; dir. counseling svcs., clin. supr., psychotherapist The Family Link, Inc., Chgo., 1993; therapist children, adolescents and families dept. foster care Catholic Charities, Chgo., 1993-94; individual and family therapist South Ctrl. Cmty. Svcs. Individual-Family Counseling Svcs., Chgo., 1994—; staff therapist Cen. Bapt. Family Svcs., Chgo., 1991, Gracell Rehab., Chgo., 1991-92; casework supr., counselor Epilepsy Found. Greater Chgo., 1992-93; lectr. in field; bd. mem., counselor Naperville Sch. for Gifted and Talented, 1982-84. Author: (monograph) Kourotrophos, Cults and Representations of the Greek Nursing Deities, 1978; contbr. articles to profl. jours. Meyerstein Traveling awardee, Oxford, Eng., 1963, 64; Sophocles venizelos scholar, 1962-65; nominated Internat. Woman of Yr. for 1995-96 Internat. Biog. Ctr., 20th Century Achievement award, 1996. Mem. NASW, Nat. Acad. Clin. Social Workers, Ill. Clin. Social Workers. Home and Office: 10 Pebble Ct Bolingbrook IL 60440-1557

PRICE, THOMAS ALLAN, entrepreneur; b. Rhinelander, Wis., Dec. 1, 1944; s. Lawrence Frederick and Myrtle Lee (Sparks) P.; m. Camilla Davis, June 15, 1968; children: Jeffery, Leslie Ann. BA, Northland Coll., Ashland, Wis., 1967; postgrad., Drake U., 1967-69. Asst. mgr. Res Man, Hammond, Ind., 1972, mgr., 1972-73, supr., 1973-74, dir. ops., 1974-76; dir. ops. Chart House, Inc., Oakbrook, Ill., 1976-77, sr. dir. ops., 1977-79, v.p., midwest mktg., 1979-81; regional mgr. Pizza Hut Am., Dallas, Tx., 1981-82; pres. Omni Restaurants, Inc., Indpls., 1982-84; also bd. dirs. Omni Restaurant, Inc., Indpls.; bd. dirs. Bloomington (Ind.) Mgmt. Inc., Mgmt. Internat. Devel., Rockville, Ind., Devel., Inc., Wilson Mgmt., Inc., Johnson Mgmt. Inc., FTD Partnership, Lafayette Devel. Co., Inc. Sgt. U.S. Army, 1968-72. Sgt. U.S. Army, 1968-72. Home: 1624 Beech Dr N Plainfield IN 46168-2129 Office: Internat Devel Ltd 4374 W 52nd St Indianapolis IN 46254-3705

PRICE, THOMAS EMILE, investment company executive; b. Cin., Nov. 4, 1921; s. Edwin Charles and Lillian Elizabeth (Werk) P.; BBA, U. Tex., 1943; postgrad. Harvard U., 1944; m. Lois Margaret Gahr Matthews, Dec. 21, 1970 (dec. Nov. 26, 1988); 1 child by previous marriage, Dorothy Elizabeth Wood Price; stepchildren: Bruce Albert, Mark Frederic, Scott Herbert, Eric William Matthews. Co-founder Price Y Cia, Inc., Cin., 1946—, sec., 1946-75, treas., 1946—, pres., 1975—, also dir.; co-founder Price Paper Products Corp. (merger Price Y Cia, Inc.), Cin., 1956, treas., 1956-75, pres., 1975-90, sec., 1956-75, also dir.; mem. Cin. Regional Export Expansion Com., 1961-63; dir. Cen. Acceptance Corp., 1954-55; founding mem. and dir. Cin. Royals Basketball Club Co., 1959-73. Referee Tri-State Tennis Championships, 1963-68, Western Tennis Championships, 1969-70, Nat. Father-Son Clay Court Championships, 1974—, Tennis Grand Masters Championships, 1975-77, 80; vol. coach Walnut Hills High Sch. Boys Team, Cin., 1970-81; chmn. and coach Greater Cin. Jr. Davis Cup, 1968-78; co-founder Tennis Patrons of Cin., Inc., 1951, trustee, 1951-79, pres., 1958-63, 68; co-founder Greater Cin. Tennis Assn., 1979. Participant in fund raising drives Cin. Boys Amateur Baseball Fund; chmn. Greater Cin. YMCA World Svc. Fund Drive, 1962-64; trustee Cin. World Affairs Inst., 1957-60, gen. chmn., 1959. 1st lt. USAAF, 1943-46; ETO. Elected to Western Hills High Sch. Sport Hall of Honor; named hon. Almaden Grand Master, 1980. Cin. Met. Tennis Tournament renamed Thomas E. Price Cin. Met. Tennis Torunament, 1991. Mem. Cin. World Trade Club (pres. 1959), U.S. Trotting Assn., Cin. Hist. Soc., U.S. Lawn Tennis Assn. (trustee 1959-60, 62-64, chmn. Jr. Davis Cup com. 1960-62, founder of Col. James H. Bishop award 1962), Ohio Valley Tennis Assn. (trustee 1948—, Gillespie award 1957, Dredge award 1973, pres. 1952-53, Tom Price award named in his honor at Jr. Davis Cup 1988), Western Tennis Assn. (trustee 1951—, mem. championships adv. com. 1969-78, pres. 1959-60, Hall of Fame, 1994, Melvin R. Bergman Disting. Svc. award 1979), Greater Cin. Tennis Assn. (named after and recipient of Tom Price award 1989), Assn. Tennis Profls. (nat. championship adv. 1979—), Cin. Country CLub, Univ. Club, Cin. Tennis Club (hon. life, pres. 1957-58, adv. com. 1959—, Founders and Guardians award 1983), Indoor Tennis CLub, Ea. Hills Indoor Tennis Club, Cin. Rotary, Phi Gamma Delta. Republican. Presbyterian. Nationally ranked boys 15, 1936, jr. tennis player, 1939. History columnist Tennis Talk Greater Cin., 1978-80. Home: 3249 Epworth Ave Cincinnati OH 45211-7037 Office: Dixie Terminal Buildin Ste 216 Cincinnati OH 45202

PRICER, WAYNE FRANCIS, counseling administrator; b. Bogue, Kans., Feb. 11, 1935; s. William C. and Lena I. (Hecke) P.; m. Alice M. Fitzpatrick, July 25, 1964; children: Wayne F. Jr., Elizabeth Anne. AB, Ft. Hays State U., 1957; MEd, U. N.D., 1963; postgrad., Wayne State U. Nat. cert. counselor; nat. cert. career counselor; nat. cert. sch. counselor; lic. prof. counselor Mich. Counselor Lamphere High Sch., 1963-64, 69-75; asst. prin. Page Jr. High, Madison Heights, Mich., 1964-68; prin. Page Jr. High, Madison Heights, 1968-69; adj. counselor Oakland Community Coll., Bloomfield Hills, Mich., 1969—; dir. guidance Lamphere Schs., Madison Heights, Mich., 1975—. Contbr. articles to prof. jours. Mem. ACA, Nat. Assn. Collegiate Registrars and Admission Officers, Assn. for Counselor Edn. and Supervision, Am. Coll. Pers. Assn., Am. Fedn. Tchrs., Am. Sch. Coun. Assn., Am. Vocat. Assn., Assn. for Adult Devel. and Aging, Assn. for Assessment in Counseling, Lamphere Fedn. Tchrs., Mich. Assn. for Adult Devel. and Aging, Mich. Assn. Coll. Admission Counselors, Mich. Counseling Assn., Mich. Assn. for Counselor Edn. and Supervision, Mich. Assn. for Measurement and Evaluation in Guidance (pres.), Mich. Assn. Specialists in Group Work, Mich. Career Devel. Assn. (treas. 1994—), Mich. Coll. Pers. Assn., Mich. Sch. Counselors Assn., Mich. Assn. for Humanistic Edn. and Develop., Mich. Assn. for Multi-Cultural Develop., Nat. Assn. Coll. Admission Counselors, Nat. Career Devel. Assn., Oakland Assn. for Counseling and Devel. (former pres.), Phi Delta Kappa. Office: 610 W 13 Mile Rd Madison Heights MI 48071-1858

PRICKETT, GORDON ODIN, mining, mineral and energy engineer; b. Morris, Minn., Nov. 26, 1935; s. Glenn Irvin and Edna Margaret (Erickson) P.; m. Jean Carolyn Strobush, Oct. 8, 1958; children: Karen Joan Keating, Laura Jean, Glenn Thomas. B Mining Engring., U. Minn., 1958, MS in Mineral Engring. and Econs., 1965. Registered profl. engr., Mo., Ill. U.S. Steel fellow U. Minn., Mpls., 1963-65; rsch. mineral engr. Internat. Minerals & Chem. Corp., Skokie, Ill., 1965-68; mgmt. sci. cons. Computer Mgmt. Cons., Northfield, Ill., 1968-71; mgr. tech. systems Duval Corp., Tucson, Ariz., 1971-77; dir. mgmt. info. systems Arch Mineral Corp., St. Louis, 1977-78; supr. mine planning projects Peabody Coal Co., St. Louis, 1978-82; mgr. elec. tech. transfer, nuclear plant simulator, rsch. Union Electric Co., St. Louis, 1983-95; tech. network advisor GordMett, Ltd., Aitkin, Minn., 1995—; presenter papers at industry confs. Contbr. articles to profl. jours. Co-founder, chmn. Lake Forest-Lake Bluff (Ill.) Com. for Equal Opportunity, 1968-71; com. Confluence St. Louis, 1987-95; bd. dirs., officer ch. bds., polit. twp. orgn. Lake Forest, Tucson, St. Louis, Aitkin, Minn., 1968—. Lt. USN, 1958-63, naval aviator, Cuba; to comdr. USNR, 1963-79. Mem. AIME (chair program com. 1958—), Assn. Quality and Participation (chair programs 1986-90), Norwegian Soc. St. Louis, LWV (charter mem. Brainerd Lakes uint, 1996—), Engrs. Club St. Louis (chair affiliated socs. and pub. affairs. 1987-88, 93-95). Home and Office: Nord Lake HC 5 Box 16 CC Aitkin MN 56431

PRIDDY, ROBERT ALLEN (BOB), news director; b. Decatur, Ill., July 16, 1941; s. Robert Milton Jr. and Lota Lucille (Motes) P.; m. Nancy Lee Hanson, Nov. 23, 1967; children: Sara Elizabeth, Robert Allen Jr. BJ, U. Mo., 1963. Asst. news dir. KFRU Radio, Columbia, Mo., 1963-66; news dir. KLIK/KJFF Radio, Jefferson City, Mo., 1967-74, Missourinet, Jefferson City, 1974—; mem. accrediting team Accrediting Coun. on Edn. in Journalism and Mass Comm., 1995—; media coord. Supreme Ct. Mo., 1995—; seminar leader on devel. of ind. radio news depts. in Poland and Romania for Internat. Media Fund, 1991. Author: Across Our Wide Missouri, Vol. 1, 1982, Vol. 2, 1984, Vol. 3, 1994, Only the Rivers Are Peaceful: The Missouri Mural of Thomas Hart Benton, 1985; contbr.: Thomas Hart Benton: Artist, Writer, Intellectual, 1989. Trustee State Hist. Soc. Mo., Columbia, 1985—; pres. Jefferson City Libr. Bd., 1976-77, 87-89; founder, chmn. Mo. Elections Consortium, Jefferson City, 1987—; dir. Mo. Inst. for Justice, 1990—; trustee Friends of State Archives, Jefferson City, 1993—; trustee, exec. com. Radio and TV News Dirs. Found., 1989—. Named Boss of Yr. Am. Bus. Women's Assn., Jefferson City, 1988; recipient Citation of Merit Am. Assn. State and Local History, 1989, Outstanding Achievement in Cmty. Svc. DAR, Mo., 1994. Mem. Radio-TV News Dirs Assn. (regional dir. 1984-87, chmn. bd. 1988-89, Rob Downey award 1993). Mem. Disciples of Christ Ch. Home: 218 Landwehr Hills Rd Jefferson City MO 65101 Office: Missourinet 505 Hobbs Rd Jefferson City MO 65109

PRIDE, MURRAY FRANKLIN, school system administrator; b. Morganfield, Ky., Nov. 30, 1941; s. Charles Tinsley and Mary Charlotte (Morgan) P.; m. Sara Anne Albright, Dec. 28, 1964; children: Susan Paige, Charles Howell. BS in health, physical edn., Austin Peay State U., 1964; MA in edn., Western Ky. U., 1970; EdS in edn. adminstrn., Ind. State U., 1983. Tchr., coach Union County H.S., Morganfield, 1965-69; tchr., coach Tell City (Ind.) H.S., 1969-76, athletic dir., 1976, asst. prin., 1977-83, prin., 1983-86; asst. supt. Tell City-Troy Twp. Sch. Corp., 1986-91, supt., 1992-92; child svcs. coord. Ind. Divsn. Spl. Edn., Indpls., 1992-94; supt. N. Putnam Cmty. Sch. Corp., Bainbridge, Ind., 1994—; bd. dirs. Old Nat. Trail Spl Edn. Corp., Greencastle, Ind., 1994—, Area 30 Vocat. Co-op, Greencastle, 1994—, Bus. Edn. Partnership, Tell City, 1991-92; mem. Ind. Spl. Edn. Fin. Stockholder Com., Indpls., 1994-95. Contbr. articles to profl. jours. Recipient Disting. Lt. Gov. award Optimist Internat., 1987. Mem. Ind. Assn. Pub. Sch. Supts. (selected to Ednl. Leadership Acad. 1995), Ind. Coun. Adminstrs. Spl. Edn., Phi Delta Kappa (del. internat. conv.). Roman Catholic. Home: 292 Patriots Landing Coatesville IN 46121 Office: N Putnam Cmty Sch Corp PO Box 169 Bainbridge IN 46105

PRIDONOFF, EUGENE ALEXANDER, music educator; b. L.A., Sept. 15, 1942; s. George Artemi and Frances Evelyn (Lieberman) P.; m. Bonnie Arlene Wolfgang, July 3, 1965 (div. 1977); children: George Randall, Anton Alexander, Stephan Eugene; m. Elizabeth Anne Cox, Nov. 22, 1979; children: Weldon Alexander, Eric Michael, Nicholas Artemi. MusB, Curtis Inst. Music, 1965; MusM, Temple U., 1966. Lectr. in piano Temple U., Phila., 1965-68; assoc. prof. Iowa State U., Ames, 1968-71; prof. Ariz. State U., Tempe, 1971-80, U. Cin., 1980—; head. divsn. performance U. Cin., 1982-87, head divsn. keyboard, 1987-89; cons. Nat. Endowment Arts, Washington, 1980; adjudicator numerous major U.S. piano competitions. Recipient prize Edgar M. leventritt Piano Competition, N.Y.C., 1965, Montreal Internat. Piano Competition, 1965, Brazil Internat. Piano Competition, 1965, Cert. of Honor Tchaikowsky Piano Competition, Moscow, 1966. Office: U Cin Coll Conservatory of Music Keyboard Divsn Cincinnati OH 45221

PRIEST, RUTH EMILY, music minister, choir director, composer arranger; b. Detroit, Nov. 7, 1933; d. William and Gertrude Hilda (Stockley) P. Student, Keyboard Studios, Detroit, 1949-52, Wayne State U., Detroit, 1953, 57, Ea. Pentecostal Bible Coll., Peterborough, Ont., Can., 1954-55, Art Ctr. Music Sch., Detroit Inst. Mus. Arts, 1953-54. Legal sec., 1951-90; organist, pianist, vocalist Berea Tabernacle, Detroit, 1943-61; organist Bethany Presbyn. Ch., Ft. Lauderdale, Fla., 1961-67, 69-72; choir dir., organist Bethany Drive-in Ch., Ft. Lauderdale, Fla.; organist First Bapt. Ch., Pompano Beach, Fla., 1967-68, St. Ambrose Episcopal Ch., Ft. Lauderdale, 1969-72; music dir., organist Grace Brethren Ch., Ft. Lauderdale, 1972-75; organist Boca Raton (Fla.) Community Ch., Bibletown, 1975-85; min. music, organist Warrendale Community Ch., Dearborn, Mich., 1985—; ptnr. Miracle Music Enterprises; concert and ch. organist/pianist; organist numerous weddings, city-wide rallies of Detroit and Miami Youth for Christ, Christ for Labor and Mgmt., Holiness Youth Crusade, numerous other civic and religious events; featured weekly as piano soloist and accompanist on Crusade for Christ Telecast, Detroit, 1950-60, CBC-TV, Windsor, Ont., Can.; staff organist Enquire Hotel, Galt Ocean Mile, Ft. Lauderdale, Fla., 1962-67; tchr. piano adult edn. evening sch. program Southfield (Mich.) Pub. Sch. System, 1991—. Ongoing educator in pvt. piano, organ, music theory; Recording artist: Ruth Priest at the Organ, Love Notes from the Heart, Christmas with Ruth. Mem. Am. Guild Organists (past mem. exec. bd. Detroit chpt.). Office: Miracle Music Enterprises care Warrendale Cmty Ch 19700 Ford Rd Dearborn MI 48128

PRIESTMAN, BRIAN, classical musician; b. Birmingham, England, Feb. 10, 1927; Came to the U.S., 1962; s. Miles and Margaret Ellen (Messer) P.; m. Mary-Ford McClave, Mar. 2, 1972; 1 child, Catherine Kelly. BMus., Birmingham U., 1950, MA, 1952; DFA (hon.), Regis Coll., 1973; DHL (hon.), U. Colo., 1974. Music dir. Royal Shakespeare Co., 1960-64, Edmonton Symphony, 1964-68; prin. conductor Balt. Symphony, 1968-70; music dir. Denver Symphony, 1970-78, Fla. Philharmonic, 1978-80; dean Sch. Music U. Cape Town, 1980-86; prin. conductor Malmö (Sweden) Symphony, 1988-90; artist-in-residence U. Kans., 1992—. Home: 3700 Clinton Pky Lawrence KS 66047 Office: U Kans 220 Murphy Hall Lawrence KS 66045

PRIEVE, E. ARTHUR, arts administration educator. BBA in Adminstrn. and Art History, U. of Wis., 1959, MBA in Mgmt. and Orgn. Behavior, 1961; DBA in Mgmt. and Psych., George Washington U., Washington, 1965. Asst. dean adminstrv. affairs Sch. Bus. U. Wis., Madison, 1966-69, prof. mgmt. Grad. Sch. Bus., 1969—, dir. exec. MBA program, 1993—; dir. Ctr. For Arts Adminstrn., Madison, 1969—; curriculum cons. for arts adminstrn.; cons. visual, performing and arts svc. orgns.; workshops and presentations on planning, bd. dirs. Mem. Assn. of Arts Adminstrn. Educators (chmn. U.S., Can.). Office: U Wis Ctr Arts Adminstrn 4171 Grainger Hall 975 University Ave Madison WI 53706-1324

PRIGGE, GLENN RUSSELL, educator; b. Drayton, N.D., Nov. 18, 1941; s. John D. and Inga Alice (Abrahamson) P.; m. Lila Lou, June 6, 1959; children: Glenn Randall, Traci Kay. PhB, U. N.D., 1963, MEd, 1967; PhD, U. Minn., 1974; postgrad., Rutgers U., Utah State U., 1967, 68. Teaching asst., instr. undergrad., grad. math. U. Minn., Mpls., 1971-74; asst. prof. math. U. N.D., Grand Forks, 1974-78; assoc. prof. math. U. N.D., 1978-81, prof. math., 1981—. Contbr. articles to profl. jours. Recipient numerous grants. Mem. NEA, Nat. Coun. Tchrs. Math., Minn. Coun. Tchrs. Math., N.D. Coun. Tchrs. Math., Nat. Coun. Suprs. Math., N.D. Edn. Assn., Phi Delta Kappa. Office: Dept Math U ND PO Box 8376 Grand Forks ND 58202-8376

PRIMO, JOAN ERWINA, retail and real estate consulting business owner; b. Detroit, Aug. 28, 1959; d. Joseph Carmen and Marie Ann (Nash) P. BA, Wellesley Coll., 1981; MBA, Harvard U., 1985. Acct. exec. Michigan Bell, Detroit, 1981-82, AT&T Info. Sys., Southfield, Mich., 1983; planning analyst Gen. Motors, Detroit, 1984; v.p. Howard L. Green & Assocs., Troy, Mich., 1985-89; prin., founder The Strategic Edge, Inc., Southfield, 1989—. Contbr. articles to profl. jours. Founders soc. mem. Detroit Inst. Arts, 1989—. Mem. Internat. Coun. Shpping Ctrs. (faculty, seminar leader 1987-), Wellesley Club Southeastern Mich. (pres. 1994—), Harvard Bus. Sch. Club Detroit (bd. dirs. 1994—, v.p. 1995—, exec. v.p. 1996), Ivy Club Detroit (bd. dirs. 1994—, sec. 1995—). Republican. Roman Catholic. Home: 1185

Stonecrest Dr Bloomfield Hills MI 48302-2841 Office: The Strategic Edge 24333 Southfield Rd Ste 211 Southfield MI 48075-2849

PRIMUS, MARY JANE DAVIS, social worker, author; b. Marion, Iowa, May 31, 1924; d. Lawrence Henry and Verna Leona (Suman) Davis; m. Paul C. Primus, Aug. 23, 1955; children: Kenneth Roy, Donald Karl. BS, Iowa State U., 1950. Asst. cashier First State Bank, Greene, Iowa, 1942-46; tchr. Oskaloosa (Iowa) pub. schs., 1950-52; extension home economist Iowa State U., Oskaloosa-Eldora, 1952-57; homemaker, dist. supr. Iowa Dept. Social Svc., Webster City, 1970-77; substitute tchr. Eldora Pub. Schs., 1966-68; homemaker health aide supr. Mid-Iowa Community Action OEO, Iowa Dept. Social Svc., 1968-69; ptnr. LMAJ Herbs and Spices, Unltd. Author: Through the Window, 1973; Through the Window Twice, 1974; Tracery Windows, 1975; Shuttered Windows, 1977; Wings, 1979; Wings II, 1980; area news corr., 4 newspapers; columnist Iowa Wildlife Fedn.; murals in Steamboat Rock, Iowa H.S. Bldg., Iowa City Hall, Kiwanis Bldg., 1983-94; contbr. poems to various publs. Den mother Boy Scouts Am., Steamboat Rock, Iowa, 1966-71; leader Girl Scouts Am., Steamboat Rock, 1969-72; mem. Iowa State U. Extension Family Living Coun., Hardin County, 1961-65, 82-86, chmn. 1984-86, 90-94; outreach chmn. Iowa Family and Children Svcs., 1966-72; chmn. Hardin County Coun. on Aging, 1989-91; field days women's program chmn. Iowa Soil Conservation, 1968; pres. United Ch. of Christ, 1963-65. Mem. LWV, AAUW, AARP, Nat League Am. Pen Women, Am. Home Econs. Assn., Nat. Council Homemaker-Home Health Aide Services, Nat. Soc. Lit. and the Arts, Soil Conservation Soc. Am., Am. Legion, Internat. Platform Assn., Herb Soc. Am., Hardin County Hist. Soc., Federated Women's Club, PEO, Order Eastern Star.

PRINCE, FRANCES ANNE KIELY, civic worker; b. Toledo, Dec. 20, 1923; d. John Thomas and Frances (Pusteoska) Kiely; m. Richard Edward Prince, Jr., Aug. 27, 1951; children: Anne, Richard III (dec.). Student U. Louisville, 1947-49; AB, Berea Coll., 1951; postgrad., Kent Sch. Social Work, 1951, Creighton U., 1969; MPA, U. Nebr., Omaha, 1978. Instr. flower arranging Western Wyo. Jr. Coll., 1965, 66; editor Nebr. Garden News, 1979-81, 83-90, emeritus, 1990. Author poems. Chmn. Lone Troop coun. Girl Scouts U.S.A., 1954-57, trainer leaders, 1954-68, mem. state camping com., 1959-61, bd. dirs. Wyo. state coun., 1966-69; chmn. Cmty. Improvement, Green River, Wyo., 1959, 63-65, Wyo. Fedn. Women's Clubs State Libr. Svcs., 1966-69; mem. Wyo. State Adv. Bd. on Libr. Inter-Co-op., 1965-69, state libr. bd., 1965-69, Nat. sub com. Commn. on the Bicentennial of the U.S. Constitution, 1986-91; bd. dirs. Sweetwater County Libr. System, 1962-69, pres. bd., 1967-68; adv. coun. Sch. Dist. 66, 1970-79; bd. dirs. Opera Angels, 1971, fund raising chmn., 1971-72, v.p., 1974-80; bd. dirs. Morning Musicale, 1971-82; bazaar com. Children's Hosp., 1970-75; docent Joslyn Art Mus., 1970—; mem. Nebr. Forestry Adv. Bd., 1976—; citizens adv. bd. Met. Area Planning Agy., 1979—; mem. Nebr. Tree-Planting Commn., 1980—; bd. dirs. U.S. Constn. Bicentennial Commn. Nebr., 1986-92, Omaha Commn. on the Bicentennial, 1987-92, Nat. commn. on Bicentennial of U.S. Constitution, 1986-92; bd. dirs. United Ch. Christ, Intermountain, 1963-69, mem. exec. com., 1966-69. Recipient Libr. Svc. award Sweetwater County Library, 1968; Girl Scout Svcs. award, 1967; Conservation award U.S. Forest Service, 1981; Plant Two Trees award, 1981; Nat. Arbor Day award, 1982; Pres. award Nat. coun. of State Garden Clubs, 1986, 87, 89, Joyce Kilmer award Nat. Arbor Day Found., 1990; awards U.S. Constn. Bicentennial Commn. Nebr., 1987, 91, Omaha Commn. on the Bicentennial, 1987, Nat. Bicentennial Leadership award Coun. for Advancement of Citizenship, 1989, Nat. Conservation medal DAR, 1991, George Washington silver award Nat. commn. on Bicentennial of U.S. Constitution, 1992, Mighty Oak award Garden Clubs of Nebr., 1992. Mem. ALA, AAUW (Vol. of Yr. Omaha br. 1989), New Neighbors League (dir. 1969-71), Ikebana Internat., Symphony Guild, Assistance League Omaha, Omaha Playhouse Guild, Nebr. Libr. Assn., Omaha Coun. Garden Clubs (1st v.p. 1972, pres. 1973-75, state bd. dirs. 1979—, mem. nat. council bd. dirs. 1979—, pres. award 1988, 89, 90), Internat. Platform Assn., Internat. Soc. Poets (Disting. mem. 1996), Nat. Trust for Hist. Preservation, Nebr. Flower Show Judges Coun. (chmn. 1995—), Nat. Coun. State Garden Clubs (chmn. arboriculture 1985-90, 93—, chmn. nature conservancy 1991-93), Nebr. Fedn. Garden Clubs (pres. 1978-81), Garden Club (dir. 1970-72, pres. 1972-75). Home: 8909 Broadmoor Dr Omaha NE 68114-4248

PRINGLE, BARBARA CARROLL, state legislator; b. N.Y.C., Apr. 4, 1939; d. Nicholas Robert and Anna Joan (Woloshinovich) Terlesky; m. Richard D. Pringle, Nov. 28, 1959; children: Christopher, Rhonda. Student, Cuyahoga C.C. With Dunn & Bradstreet, 1957-60; precinct committeewoman City of Cleve., 1976-77; elected mem. Cleve. City Coun., 1977-81; mem. Ohio Ho. of Reps., Columbus, 1982—; 20th dist. state ctrl. commeteewoman, 1982-92; mem. family svcs. com., ranking mem. children and youth subcom., pub. utilities com.; mem. Ohio Children's Trust Fund, Supreme Ct. Domesticc Violence Task Force. Vol. Cleve. Lupus Steering Com., various community orgns.; charter mem. Statue of Liberty Ellis Island Found. Recipient cert. of appreciation Cleve. Mcpl. Ct., 1977, Exch. Club Bklyn., 1978, Cmty. Recreation Appreciation award City of Cleve., 1978, Key to City of Cleve., 1979, Cleve. Area Soapbox Derby cert., 1976, 77, 81, cert. of appreciation Ward 9 Youth League, 1979-82, No. Ohio Patrolman's Benevolent Assn. award, 1983, Cuyahoga County Firefighters award, 1983, Outstanding Pub. Servant award for Outstanding Svc. to Hispanic Cmty., 1985, Nat. Sr. Citizen Hall of Fame award, 1987, cert. of appreciation Cleve. Coun. Unemployed Workers, 1987, Ohio Farmers Union award, 1990, award of appreciation United Labor Agy., 1993, Susan B. Anthony award, 1995. Mem. Nat. Order Women Legislators, Fedn. Dem. Women of Ohio, Nat. Alliance Czech Catholics, St. Michael Ch. Altar and Rosary Soc., Ward 15 Dem. Club, Polish Falcons. Democrat. Home: 708 Timothy Ln Cleveland OH 44109-3733

PRIOR, JOSEPH LAFAYETTE, counseling administrator; b. Cin., May 4, 1935; s. Martin Willis and Bernice Elsie (Young) P.; m. Ann Ballantyne Atkins, June 22, 1963; children: Julie Ann, Martin Robert, Fredrick Joseph. BS in Edn., U. Cin., 1957; MA in Guidance Counseling, U. Colo., 1963; MA, U. Cin., 1979. Head football mgr. U. Cin., 1955-57; tchr. social studies Cin Pub. Schs., 1958-68, jr. high sch. counselor, 1968-73, high sch. counselor, 1973-78, head counselor, 1978-94; ret., 1994; active Prostate Cancer Support Group, Wellness Ctr. Officer Juvenile Ct. Hamilton County, Ohio, 1975-78; head usher Montgomery Presbyn. Ch., 1981-83; mem. Cin. Schs. Guidance Svcs. Revision, 1986. Mem. Southwestern Ohio Coun. Social Studies, Ohio Coun. Social Studies, Cin. Nat. Edn. Assn., Nat. Sch. Counselors Assn., Cin. Fed. Tchrs. Marking, Nat. Coun. Accrediation Tchrs. Coll., Cin. Pub. Sch. Coun. Assn., Phi Delta Kappa, Mason. Republican. Home: 6980 Stonehenge Dr Cincinnati OH 45242-6204 also: 4168 Long Point Dr Cheboygan MI 49721

PRITCHARD, MICHAEL GREGG, legal services director, lawyer; b. Fayetteville, Ark., Feb. 13, 1949; s. Ross Joseph Pritchard and Emily Gregg; m. Deborah Hoffman Jan. 31, 1971 (div. Mar. 1977); 1 child, Kerri-Anne; m. Lynn Olsen, Sept. 5, 1987, 1 child, Irene Marie. BA, U. Ark., 1971; JD, Yale U., 1974. Bar: Wis. 1974, U.S. Dist. Ct. (we. dist.) Wis. 1978, Trust Ters. of Pacific Islands 1979, Ark. 1981, U.S. Dist. Ct. (we. dist.) Ark. 1981, S.C. 1986, U.S. Dist. Ct. S.C. 1986, U.S. Ct. Appeals (4th cir.) 1990. Staff atty. Ctr. for Pub. Representation, Madison, Wis., 1975-77, Wis. Indian Legal Services, Madison, 1977-78, Micronesia Legal Services, Majuro, Marshall Islands, 1979-80; from staff atty. to dep. dir., then exec. dir. Ozark Legal Services, Fayetteville, 1981-85; exec. dir. Palmetto Legal Services, Columbia, S.C., 1985-92, Ctr. for Pub. Representation, Madison, 1992—; adj. prof. U. Wis., Milw., 1977, lectr. 1993—; adj. prof. U. S.C. Law Scho., 1992; chmn. Ark. Legal Svcs. Project Dirs. Group, 1982-84. Mem. Wis. Gov.'s Study Com. on Solar Rights, Madison, 1977, Wis. Legis. Metallic Mining Reclamation Act Revision Com., Madison, 1977, Wis. Pub. Svc. Commn. Privacy Coun., Young Dems. of Washington County, Fayette, Ark., 1982-85; pres. Ctrl. Madison Housing Corp., 1977-79; bd. dirs. Southeast Tng. Ctr., Little Rock, 1982-85, 87-92. Mem. ABA, ACLU (bd. dirs. Ark. chpt. 1983-85), S.C. Bar Assn. (ethics adv. com. 1986-92), Ark. Bar Assn., Wis. Bar Assn., Leadership Columbia, Phi Beta Kappa. Home: 2922 Lakeland Ave Madison WI 53704-5831 Office: Ctr for Pub Representation 121 S Pinckney St Ste 320 Madison WI 53703-3338

PRITCHARD, PETER HUGH ANSON, banker; b. Bulawayo, Zimbabwe, May 31, 1949; came to U.S., 1989; s. Francis Hugh and Hilda Beatrice Pritchard; m. Randi Magni Nielsen, Apr. 11, 1978; children: A. Christine, P. David, Emily R., P. Nicholas. BS in Civil Engring., U. Cape Town, South Africa, 1971, MBA, 1979; Higher Diploma in Co. Law, U. Witwatersrand, Johannesburg, South Africa, 1983. Asst. civil engr. Rhodesia Rys., Bulawayo, 1972-76; resident engr. Iran-Kampsax, Bandar Shahpour, Iran, 1977-79; asst. v.p. Citibank, Johannesburg, 1980-85; v.p. Citibank, Tokyo, 1985-88, London, 1988-89; v.p. Mitsubishi Bank, N.Y.C., 1989-93, ABN AMRO Bank, Chgo., 1994—. Recipient Internat. Fin. award Grad. Sch. Bus., Cape Town, 1979. Lutheran. Office: ABN AMRO Bank 135 S La Salle St Chicago IL 60603-4105

PRITCHETT, ALLEN MONROE, healthcare administrator; b. St. Louis, June 29, 1949; s. Allen M. Jr. and Jane (Baird) P.; m. Linda Jasper (div. Apr. 1980); 1 child, Brett A. (dec.). AA, Meramec Coll., 1969; BS, U. Mo., 1971; MA, Webster U., 1978. Tchr. social studies Union (Mo.) High Sch., 1971-77; mgr. edn. and tng. Luth. Med. Ctr., St. Louis, 1977-78, asst. dir. human resources, 1978-81; dir. pers. Grandpa John's, Inc., Murphysboro, Ill., 1981-82; mgmt. instr. So. Ill. U., Carbondale, 1982-84; dir. human resources Meml. Hosp., Carbondale, 1984-93; v.p. So. Ill. Hosp. Svcs., Carbondale, 1993-95; pres. Pritchett/Baird Assocs., 1995—; mem. coun. on healthcare human resources Ill. Hosp. Assn., 1991-93; bd. dirs. So. Ill. Regional Social Svcs., Inc., 1994—, sec./treas., 1996—; So. Ill. U. Coll. Bus. Ctr. for Mgmt. and Exec. Devel., 1987-93. Mem. bus. adv. com. Carbondale Cmty. H.S., 1984-95; mem. So. Ill. Bus./Employer Advisors, Carbondale, 1984—; mem. Carbondale Postal Customer Adv. Coun., 1995-96; mem. human resources adv. bd. Commerce Clearing House, 1995-96. Mem. So. Ill. Healthcare Human Resources Assn. (pres. 1987-88, 90-91, exec. com. 1986—, sec. 1986-87), Am. Soc. Healthcare Human Resources Adminstrn. (pres. So. Ill. chpt. 1987-88, 90-91), Soc. for Human Resource Mgmt., Am. Coll. Healthcare Execs. (diplomate), Carbondale C. of C. (bd. dirs. 1995-96).

PRITIKIN, JAMES B., lawyer, employee benefits consultant; b. Chgo., Feb. 18, 1939; s. Stan and Anne (Schwartz) P.; m. Barbara Cheryl Demovsky, Apr. 20, 1968 (dec. 1988); children: Gregory, David, Randi; m. Mary Szatkowski, July 7, 1990; 1 child, Peyton. BS, U. Ill., 1961; JD, DePaul U., 1965. Bar: Ill. 1965, U.S. Dist. Ct. (no. dist.) Ill. 1965, U.S. Supreme Ct. 1985; cert. matrimonial arbitrator. Pvt. practice, Chgo., 1965-68, 1984—; ptnr. Sudak, Grubman, Pritikin, Rosenthal & Feldman, Chgo., 1969-80, Pritikin & Sohn, Chgo., 1980-84; pres. Prepaid Benefits Plans Inc., Chgo., 1978—; exec. dir. The Ctr. for Divorce Mediation Ltd. Fellow Internat. Acad. Matrimonial Lawyers, Am. Acad. Matrimonial Lawyers; mem. ABA, Ill. Bar Assn., Chgo. Bar Assn. (cir. ct. Cook County liaison com.), Chgo. Pub. Schs. Alumni Assn. (v.p. 1984—). Office: 221 N La Salle St Chicago IL 60601-1206

PRITT, JUDITH KAY, service executive, nurse; b. Arthurdale, W.Va., Aug. 14, 1945; d. Ralph Norman and Eleanor Collins B.; m. Jimmie Martin Pritt, June 12, 1965; children: James Scott, Tammyra Renee. BS in Nursing, W. Va. U., 1967; MA in Counseling, Ball State U., 1973; Postgrad., Ga. State U., 1978. Cert. Nurse Adminstr. Advanced, Am. Nursing Assn. 1988. Insvc. instr./supr. Singing River Hosp., Pascagoula, Miss., 1968; staff nurse in neurosurg. W. Va. U. Med. Ctr., Morgantown, W.Va., 1971-72; curriculum coord./instr. Darmstadt (Germany) Career Ctr., 1972-73; sch. nurse Aukamn Elem. Sch., Weisbaden, Germany, 1973-75; dir. of Edn. Svcs. Med. Ctr. of Cen. Ga., Macon, Ga., 1976-78; dir. of Clinical Nursing Marysvale Samaritan, Phoenix, 1979-80; patient care coord. Albert Einstein Med. Ctr., Phila., 1981-82; asst. dir. nursing Fox Chase Cancer Ctr., Phila., 1983-84; coord. of Edn. Mercy Med. Ctr., Springfield, Ohio, 1984—; v.p. Madison County Hosp., London, Ohio, 1985—; Instr. trainer, CPR, Am. Heart Assn., Ga. and Ariz., Am. Red Cross, Ohio; cons. speaker and organizer for various orgns. including counseling employees and patients, crisis intervention, the nursing process; presenter Oncology Nurse's Soc., San Diego 1982. Tchr. Ch. of Christ, Springfield, Ohio, 1988-87. Recipient Faculty Award, Convocation, W. Va. U., Morgantown, W.Va., 1967. Fellow Am. Acad. Med. Adminstrs. (pres. 1989-91, Disting. Svc. award 1991, diplomate in health care 1992, state dir. 1992-95, region IV dir. 1995—); mem. Ohio Nurse Exec. Assn., Sigma Theta Tau. Democrat. Office: Madison County Hosp Inc 210 N Main St London OH 43140-1115

PRITTS, BRADLEY ARTHUR, JR., management systems consultant; b. Cleve., July 8, 1955; s. Bradley A. and Nannette (Roehm) P.; m. Susan A. Pritts, May 22, 1976. BS, Ohio State U., 1975; MBA, U. Mich., 1982. Cert. quality systems provisional auditor, quality systems auditor, quality systems lead auditor. Acct. mgr. Automatic Data Processing, Ann Arbor, Mich., 1976-79, product trainer, 1979-82; mtkg. rep. Automatic Data Processing, Dearborn, Mich., 1982-83, project mgmt. specialist, 1983-84; tech. mgr. Automatic Data Processing, Southfield, Mich., 1984-85, sr. tech. mgr., 1985-87, sr. product mgr., 1987-88; pvt. practice Ann Arbor, Mich., 1988. Pres. Saline Area Players. Mem. Project Mgmt. Inst., Soc. Mfg. Engrs., U. Mus. Soc. Am., Am. Soc. Quality Control (cert. quality engr., cert. quality control auditor, cert. quality mgr.), Automotive Industry Action Group. Republican. Roman Catholic. Home and Office: 3030 Lexington Dr Ann Arbor MI 48105-1460

PRIZ, EDWARD JOHN, worker's compensation consultant; b. Chgo., Aug. 3, 1952; s. Edward J. Sr. and Margaret A. (Nalon) P.; m. June A. Novalich, June 14, 1975 (div. Nov. 1982); children: James K., Scott M.; m. Marirose Brown, Aug. 31, 1990. BA, Roosevelt U., 1974. CPCU; assoc. in premium auditing. Dist. exec. Calumet coun. Boy Scouts Am., Munster, Ind., 1975-76; ins. agt. Equitable Life Ins. Co., Calumet City, Ind., 1976-78, Am. Mut. Ins. Co., Hillside, Ill., 1978-80, Vanguard Ins., Hillside, 1980-81; ins. cons. Auditrate, Inc., Chgo., 1981-86, Corp. Policyholders Counsel, Park Ridge, Ill., 1987; cons., pres. Advanced Ins. Mgmt., Addison, Ill., 1987—. Author: Comp Control Secrets of Reducing Workers Compensation Costs, 1995. Mem. Soc. CPCU (bd. dirs. West Suburban Chgo. chpt. 1991-92). Office: Advanced Ins Mgmt 33 N Addison Rd Ste 100 Addison IL 60101-3843

PROCHNOW, HERBERT VICTOR, JR., lawyer; b. Evanston, Ill., May 26, 1931; s. Herbert V. and Laura (Stinson) P.; m. Lucia Boyden, Aug. 6, 1966; children: Thomas Herbert, Laura. A.B., Harvard U., 1953, J.D., 1956; A.M., U. Chgo., 1958. Bar: Ill. 1957, U.S. Dist. Ct. (no. dist.) Ill. 1961. With 1st Nat. Bank Chgo., 1958-91, atty., 1961-70, sr. atty., 1971-73, counsel, 1973-91, adminstrv. asst. to chmn. bd., 1978-81; pvt. practice, 1991—. Author: (with Herbert V. Prochnow) A Treasury of Humorous Quotations, 1969, The Changing World of Banking, 1974, The Public Speaker's Treasure Chest, 1986, The Toastmaster's Treasure Chest, 1988; also articles in legal publs. Mem. ABA, Ill. Bar Assn., Chgo. Bar Assn. (chmn. com. internat. law 1970-71), Am. Soc. Internat. Law, Phi Beta Kappa. Clubs: Harvard (N.Y.C.); Chicago (Chgo.), Legal (Chgo.), Law (Chgo.), Onwentsia, Economic (Chgo.), University (Chgo.). Home: 949 Woodbine Pl Lake Forest IL 60045-2275 Office: 155 N Michigan Ave Chicago IL 60601-7511

PROCTOR, EDWARD GEORGE, lawyer; b. Chgo., July 16, 1929; s. Harold Proctor and Catherine Elliott; m. Kathleen Friend, Apr. 4, 1959; children: Brian, Diana, Edward, Laurel, Abigail, John. BS, Loyola U., Chgo., 1951; JD, Loyola U., 1953. Bar: Ill. 1953. From assoc. to ptnr. Kirkland & Ellis, Chgo., 1953-78; ptnr. Reuben & Proctor, Chgo., 1978-87, Isham, Lincoln, Beale (merger with Reuben & Proctor), Chgo., 1987-88, Hinshaw & Culbertson, Chgo., 1988—; adj. prof. Loyola U. Sch. of Law; trustee Loyola U.; chmn. bus. dept. Hinshaw & Culbertson. Co-chmn. Com. to Elect Mary Ann McMorrow to Ill. Supreme Ct., 1991-92; mem. Legal Assistance Found. Friends Com. Chgo.; former tchr. CCD classes St. Barnabas Ch., Chgo.; former fundraiser Mt. Carmel H.S., Morgan Park Acad., St. Ignatius Coll. Prep. Recipient Medal of Excellence Loyola U. Sch. Law, 1989, plaque of Appreciation Cath. Charities, 2 plaques of Appreciation Loyola Alumni Assn. Fellow ABA (life); mem. Ill. Bar Assn., Chgo. Bar Assn. (comml. fin. and transactions coms.), Bankruptcy Inst., Loyola Law Alumni Assn. (past pres.), Olympia Fields Country Club (past pres.), Lambda Alpha Internat. Roman Catholic. Office: Hinshaw & Culbertson 222 N La Salle St Chicago IL 60601-1003

PROCTOR, NICK HOBERT, toxicologist, pharmacologist; b. Moscow, Idaho, Nov. 1, 1941; s. Hobert Basle and Cleo Evelyn (Rothwell) P.; m. Terry Ladd Whiting, June 27, 1964; children: Ken Lawrence, John David. B Pharmacy, Wash. State U., 1965; PhD in Comparative Pharmacology, U. Calif., San Francisco, 1973. Diplomate Am. Bd. Toxicology; registered pharmacist Wash., Calif. Toxicologist Kaiser Found. Internat., Oakland, Calif., 1975-76; toxicologist, dir. health Kaiser Aluminum & Chem. Corp., Oakland, Calif., 1976-84; dir. product safety Kimberly-Clark Corp., Neenah, Wis., 1984—. Co-author: Chemical Hazards of the Workplace, 1978, 2d edit., 1987, 3d edit., 1991. Lt. USPHS, 1966-68. Recipient Jean Spencer Felton award Western Occupational Med. Assn., 1978. Mem. Soc. Toxicology, Am. Coll. Toxicology. Home: 53 N Parkview Dr Appleton WI 54915-9509 Office: Kimberly-Clark Corp Box 999 2100 Winchester Rd Neenah WI 54957-0999

PROCTOR, STANLEY MATTHEW, business owner; b. Cambridge, Mass., Dec. 13, 1920; s. Matthew and Harriet Proctor; m. Lois Stern, Feb. 23, 1947; 1 child, John D. SB, MIT, 1943. Registered profl. engr., Ohio. Lighting specialist GE, various, 1946-48; br. mgr. B.W. Rogers Co., Akron, Ohio, 1948-55; founder, pres., chmn. Stanley M. Proctor Co. Inc., Twinsburg, Ohio, 1955—; bd. dirs. Johnson Rubber Co., Inc., Middlefield, Ohio, Europro, Luxemburg, Duramax Corp., Middlefield, Ohio, Duramax Corp., Middlefield; lectr. Case Western Res. U., Cleve., 1955-65; mem. vis. com. mech. engring. dept. MIT, life mem. corp. devel. com., vice chmn. capital campaign com. Bd. dirs., vice chmn. Hiram (Ohio) Coll., 1974-92, mem. fin. com., 1974—, life trustee; trustee John Cabot Internat. U., Rome, 1987—, MIT, 1978-83, Cleve. Engring. Found. Soc.; chmn. Reves adv. coun. on internat. studies Coll. William and Mary. Mem. Fluid Power Distbrs. (bd. dirs., treas. 1975-80), Cleve. Engring. Soc. (bd. dirs., treas. 1950—). Republican. Office: 2016 Midway Dr PO Box 446 Twinsburg OH 44087-0446

PROCTOR, VALERIE FLOYD, educational administrator; b. Detroit, Dec. 27, 1932; d. Wallace Walker and Dorcelle (Wingfield) Floyd; m. Louis Anderson Proctor, Nov. 7, 1953; children: Diane Proctor Reeder, Rosemarie Doris Proctor. BS in Edn., Wayne State U., Detroit, 1956; MS in Edn., 1963. Tchr., libr. Highland Park & Detroit Pub. Schs., 1956-64; guidance counselor Detroit Jr. High Pub. Schs., 1964-68, Detroit Sr. High Pub. Schs., 1968-80; career counselor, 1980-84, adult edn. tchr., counselor, 1974-88, guidance dept head, adminstr., 1984—; mem. Delta Sigma Theta, Inc., Detroit Alumnae, 1952—; archivist, historian Links, Inc., Great Lakes Chpt., Detroitm 1989-95; past pres. Wayne County Counselors Assn. 1964—; diaconate bd. Plymouth United Ch. of Christ, Detroitm 1995—; bd. dirs. Minerva Edn. and Devel. Found., Detroit, 1993—. Vol. fund raiser Likns, Inc. Detroit, 1992—; mem. Rep. Nat. Com., Washington, 1990-94; scholarship chairperson NAUW, Detroit, 1993—, Delta Sigma Theta, Arts and Letters, Detroit, 1990—. Named Counselor of Yr. Mich. Personnel and Guidance Assn.-Detroit Assn. of Non-White Concerns. Republican. Home: 8421 Marygrove Dr Detroit MI 48221 Office: Mumford High School 17525 Wyoming Ave Detroit MI 48221

PROECHEL, GLEN FRED, foreign language educator, minister; b. Janesville, Minn., Jan. 3, 1938; s. Chester Ernest Julius and Irene Elizabeth (Van Slyke) P.; m. Helen Huber, Jan. 15, 1964 (div. 1970); children: Lisa, Sarah; m. Maryse Chenier, Apr. 27, 1991. AA, Concordia, St. Paul, 1958; BA, U. Minn., 1962; MS, Mankato State U., 1973; BS, Bemidji State U., 1978; MDiv, Luth. Brethren Seminary, 1996. Cert. fgn. lang. edn. Social worker Hennepin County Welfare, Mpls., 1964-72; tchr. German, Archbishop Brady High Sch., West St. Paul, Minn., 1974-75; tchr. French, Bjorkdale High Sch., Sask., Can., 1975-76; instr. lang. Bemidji (Minn.) State U., 1977-78; instr. English, Mid. East East Tech. U., Gaziantep, Turkey, 1979-80; tchr. German and Spanish, Frankfurt (Germany) Am. High Sch., 1980-81; tchr. English, Moscow Spl. Sch. 29 Moscow Spl. Sch. #29, 1981; Russian and German trainer U.S. Mil., Frankfurt, 1982-90; dir. N.W. Minn. Global Studies Inst., Red Lake Falls, 1990-92; instr. Spanish, U. Minn., Crookston, 1992-94; dir. Interstellar Lang. Sch. Klingon Lang. Sch., 1993—; organizer Klingon Lang. Camp., 1993—; curriculum developer Concordia Lang. Village, Moorhead, Minn., 1975-85; conf. interpreter Internat. Correspondence Chess Fedn., Kelkheim, Germany, 1988-90; coord. Computer-Augmented German Instrn., St. Paul, 1978-79; Russian interpreter, tour guide Eurotours, Frankfurt, 1982-89. Author: (textbook series) Read Russian I, II, III, 1982-84, (textbook) On the Black Sea, 1984, Alien Language Primer, 1994, Good News for Warrior Race, 1995, Homlet: Prince of Kronos, 1995, Missionary to Russia, 1996. Recipient stipend Victor Gollancz Found., Frankfurt, 1971, Key to the Village, Condordia Lang. Village, 1984; Nat. Endowment for Humanities fellow Arabic Inst., Ohio State U., 1991-92. Mem. Fgn. Lang. Tchrs. (bd. dirs. 1991), Luth. Bible Translators (rep. 1992), U.S. Chess Fedn. (expert 1963—), Iowa State Chess Assn. (state champion). Home: PO Box 281 Red Lake Falls MN 56750-0281

PROFIO, JANICE CAROL, critical care nurse; b. Ravenna, Ohio, July 28, 1957; d. Anthony J. and Shirley J. (Detwiler) Bytnar; m. Joseph A. Profio, June 20, 1987; children: Andrew Joseph, David Campbell. BSN, Kent State U., 1980. RN, Ohio. Charge nurse surg. ICU VA Med. Ctr., Tucson, 1984-86; clin. mgr. ICU Robinson Meml. Hosp., Ravenna, 1988—. Mem. AACN, CCRN (cert.). Home: 3211 Summit Rd Ravenna OH 44266-9018

PROFIT, KIRK A., state legislator; b. Mt. Pleasant, Mich., Sept. 12, 1952; s. Lewis Edwin and Maxine (Merritt) P.; m. Sharon Grace Langen; children: Jennifer, Kristine, Kirk. BS, Ea. Mich. U.; JD, U. Detroit; DSc (hon.), Cleary Coll. Bar: Mich. Pvt. practice law, 1979-80; legal adv., undersheriff Washington County Sheriff's Dept., Mich., 1981-84; res. Mich. Dist. 54, 1989—; chmn. higher edn. com. Mich. Ho. Reps., ethics & oversight com., judiciary com., taxation com., bus. com., fin. com. Mem. Dem. Leadership Coun. Named legis. of yr. Police Officers Assn. Mich., 1991, Mich. Assn. Chiefs of Police, 1993; recipient disting. svc. award Ind. Colls. and Univs. Mich., 1994. Mem. Sierra Club, Optimists Internat. Home: 205 Valley Dr Ypsilanti MI 48197-4460*

PROFT CINK, CECILIA JO, animal scientist; b. Tulsa, Jan. 16, 1963; d. B.W. and Beverly Jo (Bryson) Proft; m. James Henry Cink, Nov. 28, 1987; 1 child, Christopher James. BS in Agr., Okla. State U., 1985; postgrad., U. Minn., St. Paul, 1988, Iowa State U., 1990. Bursar teller Okla. State U., Stillwater, 1986-87; data technician Minn. Dairy Records Processing Ctr., U. Minn., St. Paul, 1987-89; systems support specialist Mid-States Dairy Records Processing Ctr., Ames, Iowa, 1989-95. Author, editor: (manual) Electronic Barnsheet and Management Option Reports, 1990, 91, 92, 93, 94, 95, Dairy Talk Manual, 1991, 92, 95; contbg. author: A Little Extra, A Dairy Records Processing Center.

PROKOPOFF, STEPHEN STEPHEN, art museum director, educator; b. Chgo., Dec. 24, 1929; s. Stephen George and Jadwiga M. (Borejszo) P.; m. Paula M. Delle Donne, Oct. 26, 1957 (div. 1981); children—Alexander, Ilya; m. Lois A. Craig, June 21, 1982. B.A., U. Calif.-Berkeley, 1951, M.A., 1952; Ph.D., NYU, 1962. Dir. Hathorn Gallery, Skidmore Coll., Saratoga Springs, NY, 1966-67; dir. Inst. Contemporary Art, U. Pa., Phila., 1967-71, Mus. Contemporary Art, Chgo., 1971-78, Inst. Contemporary Art, Boston, 1978-82, Krannert Art Mus., U. Ill., Champaign, 1982-92, Univ. Art Mus., U. Iowa, Iowa City, 1992—. Co-author and co-designer (with Joan Siegfried): 19th Century Architecture of Saratoga Springs, New York, 1972 (named 1 of 50 Best Designed Books of Yr.); co-author (with text by Marcel Franciscono) The Modern Dutch Poster: The First Fifty Years, 1986; contbr. articles to art periodicals. Grantee Fulbright, 1956-57, German Govt., 1958, U.S. State Dept., 1974, Am. Council on Germany, 1980, 82. Mem. Coll. Art Assn., Assn. Art Mus., Assn. Art Mus. Dirs. Home: 200 Ferson Ave Iowa City IA 52246-3507 Office: U Iowa U Art Mus 150 N Riverside Dr Iowa City IA 52246-3536

PROMINSKI, EILEEN ALICE, school nurse, educator; b. Winona, Minn., Oct. 11, 1938; d. Donald W. and Florence (Berzinski) Anderson; m. James Prominski, Sept. 22, 1962; children: Geneane, Maria Lynn. BSN, Coll. Saint Teresa, 1960; postgrad., U. Ill., Champaign, 1982-83, Northern Ill. U., 1969-70, 82; MEd, Nat. Coll. Edn., 1983; postgrad., St. Xavier Coll., Chgo., 1992, Nat. Louis U., 1995, No. Ill. U., 1995, Aurora U., 1996. RN, Ill., Minn., Iowa; cert. sch. nurse, Ill.; tchr., Ill. Nursing instr. Mercy Hosp. Sch. Nursing, Cedar Rapids, Iowa, 1960-61; nurse ob-gyn. St. Mary's Hosp., Duluth, Minn., 1961-62; nursing instr. West Suburban Hosp. Sch. Nursing, Oak Park, Ill., 1963-65; health educator Proviso West High Sch., Hillside, Ill., 1965-73; tchr. nursery sch. TreeView Sch., 1980-82; sch. nurse Dist.

#41, Glen Ellyn, Ill., 1982—. P.E.P. grantee, 1995. Mem. Glen Ellyn Edn. Assn., Coun. of Cath. Women (pres. 1986-87, 87-88, v.p. 1982-83, 85-86).

PROSEN, MICHAEL A., company executive; b. Cleve., Nov. 27, 1955; s. John Ward and Lois Ann (Adams) Prosen. Student, U. Akron, 1976. Exec. chef Mariott Hotel, Bethesda, Md., 1984-89; pres., CFO, Barons Inc., Bedford Heights, Ohio, 1990—. Mem. Northfield Growth Assn., 1983—. Mem. Am. Culinary Fedn., Cleve. Zool. Assn. Office: Barons Inc 6000 Robertdale Rd Bedford OH 44146-2554

PROSPERI, DAVID PHILIP, public relations executive; b. Chgo., June 20, 1953. BSBA, U. Ill., 1975; MBA in Internat. Bus., George Washington U., 1983. Moving cons. Fed. Safety Moving & Storage, Elmhurst, Ill., 1975-79; press aide 1980 Reagan for Pres. campaign, Los Angeles, 1979-80, Reagan-Bush Campaign, Alexandria, Va., 1980-81; asst. press sec. to the Pres. White House, Washington, 1981-82; mgr. govt. affairs The Superior Oil Co., Washington, 1982-84; press. sec. U.S. Dept. Energy, Washington, 1985; asst. to sec. dir. pub. affairs U.S. Dept. Interior, Washington, 1985-88; asst. sec. transp. U.S. Dept. Transp., Washington, 1989-90; sr. v.p. Chgo. Bd. Trade, 1990-95, 1995—; prin. Coun. on Excellence in Govt. Bd. dirs. Corp. Pub. Broadcasting, 1992-93. Republican. Roman Catholic. Office: Chgo Bd Trade 141 W Jackson Blvd Ste 1740A Chicago IL 60604-3001

PROSSER, FRANCIS WARE, JR., physics educator; b. Wichita, Kans., June 30, 1927; s. Francis Ware and Harriet (Corinne (Osborne) P.; m. Nancy Lou Baugh, Aug. 10, 1952; children: David Francis, Rebecca Ann, Martha Lou. BS, U. Kans., 1950, MS, 1954, PhD, 1955. Rsch. assoc. Rice U., Houston, 1955-57; asst. prof. U. Kans., Lawrence, 1957-62, assoc. prof., 1962-67, prof. physics, 1967—; sr. postdoctoral assoc. Aerospace Rsch. Lab., Dayton, Ohio, 1969-70; vis. scientist Argonne Nat. Lab., Chgo., 1975-76. Contbr. articles to profl. jours. Served with USNR, 1945-46. Fellow Am. Phys. Soc.; mem. Kans. Acad. Sci., N.Y. Acad. Scis., Am. Assn. Physics Tchrs., Sigma Xi, Sigma Pi Sigma, Tau Beta Pi. Home: 1622 Cambridge Rd Lawrence KS 66044-2508 Office: U Kans Dept Physics & Astronomy Lawrence KS 66045

PROST, DONALD, state legislator. Mem. Mo. State Ho. of Reps. Dist. 162. Home: 1801 Marilyn Dr Caruthersville MO 63830-2349*

PROUD, RICHARD FRENCH, lawyer, teacher, writer; b. Des Moines, Jan. 19, 1922; s. George C. and Florence (French) P.; m. Jean Hancock, July 16, 1950; children: Carol, John, George. AB, U. Neb., 1947; JD, U. Colo., 1949. Bar: Nebr. 1950. Pvt. practice Arapahoe, Neb., 1950-55; corp. atty. Mut. of Omaha, Omaha, 1955-77; asst. prof. U. Neb., Omaha, 1977-79; dep. dir. welfare State Neb., Lincoln, 1979-84; writer, part-time tchr. Omaha, 1984—. Neb. State Sen., 1965-74; speaker to Neb. Legis., 1973-74. Fellow Neb. Bar Assn.; mem. Am. Legion. Republican. Home: 8306 Martha St Omaha NE 68124-2253

PROUTY, BUTCH H., maintenance supervisor; b. Zanesville, Ohio, Oct. 7, 1953. Machinist, welder Cambridge (Ohio) Machine & Supply, 1968-78; maintenance supr. Jeffrey Mining, Cambridge, 1978-83, Detroit Diesel RMFT East, Cambridge, 1983—. Softball coach. Mem. Masons. Office: Detroit Diesel RMFT E Rte 209 S PO Box 687 Cambridge OH 43725-0687

PROUTY, CHILTON EATON, geologist, educator; b. Tuscaloosa, Ala., Sept. 8, 1914; s. William Frederick and Lucille Winifred (Thorington) P.; m. Norma Victoria Fruvog, Sept. 3, 1942; children: William Eaton, John Fruvog. B.S., U. N.C., 1936; M.S., Mo. Sch. Mines, 1938; Ph.D., Columbia, 1944. With Va. Geol. Survey, 1939, N.Y. Geol. Survey, 1940; geologist TVA, 1942-44, U.S. Geol. Survey, 1944-46; asst. prof. geology U. Pitts., 1946-48, asso. prof., 1948-51, prof., head dept., 1951-57; prof., head dept. Mich. State U., 1957-69, prof., 1969-85, prof. emeritus, 1985—; cons. geologist, 1946—; cooperating geologist Pa. Topog. and Geol. Survey, 1947—; pres. Geo-Research & Indsl. Devel. Corp., 1956; Cons.-examiner commn. on colls. and univs. N. Central Assn. of Colls. and Secondary Schs., 1967—. Contbr. articles to profl. publs. Fellow Geol. Soc. Am.; mem. Assn. Geology Tchrs. (pres. Eastern sect. 1952, nat. pres. 1958), Pitts. Geol. Soc. (pres. 1950), Paleontological Soc. Am., A.A.A.S., Am. Assn. Petroleum Geologists, Soc. Econ. Paleontologists and Mineralogists, Am. Inst. Profl. Geologists (editor 1977-78), Sigma Xi. Home and Office: Geo-Dynamics Corp 4690 Kingswood Dr Okemos MI 48864-2139

PROVANCE, TERRANCE LESTER, administrator; b. Washington, Pa., Feb. 27, 1953; s. Franklin Joseph and Bertha (Willhoft) P.; m. Beverly Anne Hampson, Aug. 2, 1975 (div. Jan. 1985); m. Nancy Ann Drake, Nov. 1, 1985; 1 child, Adam Drake. BA cum laude, Ind. U. Pa., 1975. Dir. dormitory Zanesville (Ohio) Welfare Orgn. and Goodwill Industries, 1976-78; social worker Muskingum County Children Svcs. Bd., Zanesville, 1978-80; mgr. pub. housing Zanesville Met. Housing Authority, 1980-87; dist. agt., registered rep. Prudential Ins. & Fin. Svcs., 1987-88; mgr. ops., sect. 8 Cambridge Met. Housing Authority, Cambridge, Ohio, 1988—; pres. Guernsey Homeless Coalition, Cambridge, 1992—; mgr. master money Noble County Coop. Extension, Caldwell, Ohio, 1992—; bd. dirs. GMN Tri-County Cmty. Action, Caldwell. Facility chmn.Jail N' Bail Am. Cancer Soc., Cambridge, 1990; mem. adv. bd. Zanesville Litter Control Dept., 1982-89; bd. dirs. Zanesville Cmty. Theatre, 1983-85; mem. Zanesville Amateur Radio Club, 1989-91. Recipient Vol. award Muskingum County Head Start, 1985, 87. Mem. N.Am. Shortwave Assn., Assn. Clandestine Radio Enthusiasts, Alpha Kappa Delta, Pi Gamma Mu, Psi Chi. Methodist. Home: 2530 Oakwood Ave Zanesville OH 43701-1948

PRUD'HOMME, CINDY JO, controller; b. Milw., June 3, 1959; d. James Frederick and Patricia Sharon (Kennedy) P.; m. William Lee Clifton, May 17, 1978 (div. 1982); 1 child, Erica Laine Clifton. Student in bus. mgmt., Santa Monica (Calif.) Coll., 1976, West LA Coll., 1977-80. Acctg. coord. Mega Ins. Agy./Midland Ins., Menlo Park, Calif., 1980-82; prodn. mgr. Corp. Graphics, L.A., 1982-84; acct., adminstv. mgr. Thomson Consumer Products Corp., Culver City, Calif., 1984-87; mgr. acctg. and pers. Hogg Robinson, Inc., L.A., 1987-90; contr. Hogg Robinson, Inc., Saginaw, Mich., 1990-94, Acordia, Inc., Saginaw, 1995—. Contbr. articles to profl. jours. Site leader Clinic Def. Alliance/L.A., 1989-90; active Calif. Abortion Rights Action League, L.A., 1989-90, Amnesty Internat., 1989-90; bd. dirs. Underground Railroad, Inc., Saginaw, Mich., 1995—. Named Young Careerist, Glendale (Calif.) Bus. and Profl. Women, 1989. Mem. Calif. Fedn. Bus. and Profl. Women (cert., instr.; Wilshire Bus. and Profl. Women treas.-fin. chair 1988, rec. sec.-treas. 1989); L.A. Sunset Dist. chair PEP/PAC 1989 (rec. sec. 1990, Dist. Individual Devel. winner 1988), Saginaw Bus. and Profl. Women (2d v.p., chair issues mgmt. Dist. II Mich. Fedn. 1991). Democrat. Lutheran. Office: Acordia Inc 5090 State St Bldg C Saginaw MI 48603-7705

PRUETT, HELEN GORHAM, home economist; b. Cardwell, Mo., Nov. 9, 1919; d. Zeron T. Gorham and Beckie Lou (Warren) Gorham Hart; m. Finis Q. Pruett, May 4, 1945; 1 child, Beckie Ann. BS in Edn., S.W. Mo. State U., 1941; cert., Mo. U., Columbia, 1941. Voc. home economics tchr. Ava (Mo.) High Sch., 1941-43; home economist, supr. Chr. Hansen's Lab., St. Louis, 1943-46; home economist, dem. Brown Supply Co., St. Louis, 1949-57; home economist & mgr. consumer affairs Milnot Co., St. Louis, cons., 1958-88; ret., 1990. Author: Tested and Tasted Economical Recipes, 1961, 2nd Editon, 1963, New and Favorite, 1965, Great Food Ideas and 2nd Edition, 1983-88. Mem. Mo. Vocat. Adv. Bd., Pkwy. Dist. Adv. Bd. Mem. Am. Home Econs. Assn., Mo. Home Economists Assn. (Table Honors award 1981, pres. 1983-84), St. Louis Home Economist Bus. (chmn. 2 terms). Democrat. So. Baptist. Home: 1468 Surrey Ln Saint Charles MO 63304

PRUIM, FRED JAMES, food service consultant; b. Chgo., Dec. 18, 1938; s. Frederick J. and Loretta J. (McLaughlin) P.; m. Ruth J. DeYoung, Feb.28, 1959; children: Peter, Glenn. In engring. Albert Pick, Chgo., 1957-65, Leitner Co., Franklin Park, Ill., 1965-66; in mktg. and engring. So.Equip-McGraw Edison, Elk Grove Village, Ill., 1966-77; owner, CEO Sys. Planning, Inc., Wood Dale, Ill., 1977—; mem. adv. coun. Joliet (Ill.) Jr. Coll., 1986-95, FoodSvc. Cons. Soc., Louisville, 1992-95. Office: Sys Planning Ltd 1527 Jarvis Ave Elk Grove Village IL 60007

PRUITT, RUSSELL CLYDE, industrial and interment foundries executive; b. Damascus, Va., Aug. 31, 1927; s. R. Martin and Pearl K. (Osborne) P.; BA, Fenn Coll., 1954; MBA Western Res. U., 1957-62; lic. realtor, investor. m. Clarice Furchess, Apr. 5, 1947; children: Phyllis , Russell C., Mark, Daniel. Auditor, Standard Oil Co., Cleve., 1948-53; contr. Nelson Worldwide TRW, Cleve., 1953-83; pres., treas., dir. Oreg. Brass Works, Portland, 1983—; dir. Sheidow Bronze Co., Williamsburg Bronze Co. Notary pub., Lorain County, 1958—; pres. Endura Memls., Miami, Fla.; mgr. mfg. Matthews Internat.; cons. income tax and investment. Mem. Sheffield Lake (Ohio) Charter Commn., 1960-62; chmn. finance com. Sheffield Lake City Council, 1964-66; pres. bd. edn. Black River, Medina County, Ohio, 1973—. Bd. dirs., treas. Lorain YMCA. Served with USNR, 1944-46, 50-51; PTO, Korea. Mem. U.S. Judo Fedn., Smithsonian Inst., Ohio Sch. Bds. Assn., Nat. Assn. Accountants, Am. Inst. Corp. Controllers, Am. Accounting Assn., Am. Quarter Horse Assn., Appaloosa Horse Club. Home: RR 58 Wellington OH 44090

PRUSI, MICHAEL, state legislator. Attended, No. Mich. C.C., Lansing. Rep. Mich. State Dist. 109, 1995—. Address: PO Box 30014 Lansing MI 48909

PRUSSING, LAUREL LUNT, state official, economist; b. N.Y.C., Feb. 21, 1941; d. Richard Valentine and Maria (Rinaldi) Lunt; m. John Edward Prussing, May 29, 1965; children: Heidi Elizabeth, Erica Stephanie, Victoria Nicole Johanna. AB, Wellesley Coll., 1962; MA, Boston U., 1964; postgrad., U. Calif., San Diego, 1968-69, U. Ill., 1970-76. Economist Arthur D. Little, Cambridge, Mass., 1963-67, U. Ill., Urbana, 1971-72; mem. county bd. Champaign County, Urbana, 1972-76, county auditor, 1976-92; mem. local audit adv. bd. Office Ill. Compt., Chgo., 1984-92. Contbr. to Illinois Local Government: A Handbook, 1990. Founder Com. for Intelligent Tax Reform, Urbana, 1982—, Com. for Elected County Exec., Urbana, 1986—; state rep. 103d dist. Ill. Gen. Assembly, 1993-95; dem. cand. Ill. 15th dist. U.S. Congress, 1996. Named Best Freshman Legislator Ind. Voters Ill., 1994; recipient Friend of Agriculture award Ill. Farm Bur., 1994; named to Legis. Honor Roll Ill. Environ. Coun., 1994. Mem. LWV, Govt. Fin. Officers Assn., U.S. and Can. (com. on acctg., auditing and fin. reporting 1980-88, Fin. Reporting award 1981-91, Disting. Budget award 1986), Nat. Assn. Local Govt. Auditors (charter), Ill. Assn. County Auditors (pres. 1984-85). Democrat. Home: 2106 Grange Dr Urbana IL 61801-6609

PRUTER, MARGARET FRANSON, encyclopedia editor; b. Oak Park, Ill., Jan. 16; d. Frederick G. and Margaret K. (Svoboda) Franson; m. Robert D. Pruter, July 22, 1972; 1 child, Robin. AB, Rosary Coll., 1961; MA, Northwestern U., 1965. Asst. editor Am. People's Ency., Chgo., 1961-62; rsch. assoc. AMA, Chgo., 1962-63; asst. editor New Standard Ency., Chgo., 1964-66, assoc. editor, 1966-75, sr. editor, 1975—; exec. dir.Militaria Archives, Elmhurst, Ill., 1972—. Co-author: DuPage Roots, 1985 (Ill. State Hist. Publ. award 1986). Mem. Elmhurst Hist. Commn., 1981—, v.p., 1995—; bd. dirs. DuPage County Hist. Soc., Wheaton, Ill., 1982—, Dupage County Sesquicentennial Com., 1988-89; mem. Friends of Elmhurst Pub. Libr., Elmhurst Art Mus. Found.; bd. dirs. North Ctrl. Coll. Parents Assn., 1995—. Mem. AAUW (bd. dirs. Elmhurst br. 1995—), Orgn. Am. Historians, Nat. Trust Historic Preservation, Am. Studies Assn., Ill. Hist. Soc., Elmhurst Hist. Soc., Chgo. Hist. Soc., Chgo. Architecture Found., Byrd's Nest Chapel Questers (pres. 1992-94), Sisters in Crime, Pi Gamma Mu. Office: Standard Ednl Corp 200 W Madison St Chicago IL 60606-5015

PRUTER, ROBERT DOUGLAS, editor; b. Phila., July 1, 1944; s. Hugo Rehling and Nancy Lee (Taylor) P.; m. Margaret Franson; 1 child, Robin Franson. BA, Roosevelt U., 1967, MA, 1976. Asst. editor New Std. Ency., Chgo., 1969-74, assoc. editor, 1974-79, sr. editor, 1979—. Author: Chicago Soul, 1991, Doowop: The Chicago Scene, 1996; editor: Blackwell Guide to Soul Recordings, 1993; adv. editor Popular Music and Society, 1995—. Mem. adv. com. Chgo. Blues Festival, 1992—. Served U.S. Army, 1967-69, Vietnam. Mem. NARAS, N.Am. Soc. for Sport History, Chgo. Hist. Soc. Democrat. Office: Std Ednl Corp 200 W Madison Chicago IL 60606

PRUZAN, IRENE, arts administrator, music educator, flutist, marketing and public relations specialist; b. Watertown, N.Y., Jan. 3, 1949; d. John Edward and Esther (Coahn) P.; m. Charles G. Ullery, Jan. 30, 1972 (div. 1978); m. Charles Robert Freeman, May 20, 1988. Student, U. Ariz., 1966-68; MusB, U. So. Calif., 1971; postgrad., San Francisco State U., 1972-74, U. Minn., 1976-80. Tchr. flute, coach chamber music MacPhail Ctr. for Arts, U. Minn., Mpls., 1976-85, coordinator instrumental music, 1978-81, program dir. instrumental music, 1982-85, div. head of programs, 1985-86; regional dir. Music On The Move, Inc., Valley Cottage, N.Y., 1986-87; pres. Music On the Move Minn., Inc., St. Paul, 1987—; founding mem. Crocus Hill Trio, 1976—; pub. rels. cons. Sch. of Music, U. Minn., 1991; faculty Nat. Music Camp, Interlochen, Mich., 1983, 84; cons. edn. and festival Ordway Music Theatre, St. Paul, 1985-87; mgr. Sartory String Quartet, Mpls., 1986-93; developer numerous master classes. Writer teaching materials for flute. Mem. Ariz. Chamber Orch., Tucson, 1967, San Gabriel (Calif.) Symphony, 1968-71; extra player St. Paul Chamber Orch., 1977-91; bd. dirs. Twin Cities Friends of Chamber Music, 1982-89; organizer German jazz residency USIA, Minn. and Wis., 1986; cons., program dir. Young Audiences Minn., Mpls., 1986-88. Mem. Nat. Flute Assn. (dir. mktg. 1987-90), Minn. Alliance for Arts in Edn., Twin Cities Musicians Union. Office: Music On The Move Minn Inc PO Box 4125 Saint Paul MN 55104-0125

PRYCE, DEBORAH D., congresswoman; b. Warren, Ohio, July 29, 1951. BA cum laude, Ohio State U., 1973; JD with honors, Capital U., 1976. Bar: Ohio 1976. Former asst. city prosecutor, asst. city atty., first asst. city prosecutor Columbus, Ohio; former judge Franklin County Mcpl. Ct., Columbus; mem. 103rd Congress from 15th Ohio dist., Washington, D.C., 1993—; mem. coms. rules. Republican. Presbyterian.

PRYOR, CHUCK, state legislator. Rep. dist. 116 State of Mo., Versailles. Office: 410 Newton Rm 109-H Versailles MO 65084

PRZYBYLOWSKI, THAD M., engineering manager; b. Chgo., June 4, 1963. Engring. mgr. WPC Machinery Corp., Downers Grove, Ill., 1986—. Patentee in field.

PRZYBYLSKI, DIANE JOAN, women's health nurse; b. South Bend, Ind., Nov. 22, 1953; d. Robert Eugene and Genevieve Anne (Mroczkiewicz) Rathwick; children: Scott, Bryan, Mary. BS in Law Enforcement, U. Evansville, 1975; BS in Nursing, Ind. U., South Bend, 1990. Cert. profl. childbirth educator. Tng. supr., mgr. mentally retarded & devel. disabled adults Logan Industries, South Bend, 1975-81; sibling instr. Meml. Hosp., South Bend, 1988-90, childbirth educator, 1990-92, clin. assoc., 1989-91, nurse labor and delivery/high risk antepartum, 1991-92, sec. unit practice coun., 1991-92; nurse family practice residency program obstetrics clinic St. Joseph's Med. Ctr., South Bend, 1992-93; staff nurse homecare Vis. Nurse Assn., Mishawaka, Ind., 1993-95; clin. mgr. for pvt. duty program House Calls Home Care, Mishawaka, 1995—; guest speaker Ind. U., South Bend, 1991—. Developer sibling edn. program at Meml. Hosp., 1989. Mem. Sigma Theta Tau (Alpha chpt.). Home: 608 S Summit Dr Apt 3 South Bend IN 46619-2436

PRZYBYLSKI, SANDRA MARIE, speech pathologist; b. Berwyn, Ill.; d. Raymond and Julie Marie (Vocelka) Hammers; m. James Przybylski; children: Eric, Sara. BS, U. Iowa, 1968; MA, U. Ill., 1971. Cert. clin. speech pathologist; speech/lang., educable mentally retarded education, learning disabilites and elem. tchr., life, Mo. Speech, lang. pathologist LaPlata (Mo.) Sch. Dist., 1974-87, Maysville (Mo.) Sch. Dist., 1990-92, Bucklin (Mo.) Sch. Dist., 1992—. Named one of Outstanding Young Women of Am., 1980, to Disting. Svc. Registry-Speech and Hearing, 1990. Mem. Am. Speech, Lang., Hearing Assn., Autism Soc. Am., Mo. Edn. Assn., Mo. Speech Language Hearing Assn.

PSIHARIS, JOHN PETER, community services executive; b. Chgo., July 31, 1964; s. Peter and Barbara (Langacker) P. BA in Human Svcs., Nat. Louis U., 1986; postgrad., Roosevelt U. Program coord. Hellenic Found., Chgo.; coord. comty. svcs. Comty. Advocacy Network Luth. Social Svcs. of Ill., Chgo.; exec. dir., CEO Greek-Am. Comty. Svcs., Chgo., 1986—; pres. Alpha Internat., Chgo., 1994—; cons. to various orgns., Chgo., 1990—. Contbg. author: Organizing a Volunteer Program to Serve the Elderly, 1987. Mem. local sch. coun. Taft H.S., Chgo., 1993—; mem. Mayor's Comty. Developing Adv. Com., Chgo., 1986—; chmn. Chgo. Office Fine Arts City Arts Grants Com., 1988-92; founder, bd. dirs. Greek-am. Nursing Home, Chgo., 1986—. Mem. Coalition for Ltd. English Speaking Elderly (v.p., pres. 1988—), Hellenic Profl. Soc. Ill., Chgo. Coun. Justice for Cyprus (bd. dirs. 1995—), Krikos. Democrat. Greek Orthodox. Office: Greek-Am Comty Svcs 3940 N Pulaski Rd Chicago IL 60641

PTASHKIN, BARRY IRWIN, management consultant; b. Chgo., May 6, 1944; s. Fred and Pearl (Geneles) P.; m. Roxanne Schwartz, Aug. 21, 1966; children: Jill Sheri, Joy Sandra. BA in History, U. Ill., Champaign, 1966; MBA, Loyola U., Chgo., 1969. Cert. mgmt. cons. Tchr. Chgo. Bd. Edn., 1967-68; staff officer labor rels. Chgo. and Northwestern Transp. Co., 1968-70; dist. supr. labor rels. Chgo. and Northwestern Transp. Co., Mpls., 1970-72; trainmaster Chgo. and Northwestern Transp. Co., Chgo., 1972-73, mgr. cost effectiveness, 1973-74; cons. ops. improvement Coopers & Lybrand, Chgo., 1974-76; mgr. transp. cons. group Coopers & Lybrand, Phila., 1976-77, human resources nat. dir. mgmt. cons. svcs., 1977-79, nat. dir. transp. cons. group, 1979-81; group dir. profit imprvement cons. services Coopers & Lybrand, Chgo., 1981-83; regional dir. mgmt. cons. services KMG, Chgo., 1983-84; ptnr.-in-charge mgmt. adv. services FER&S, Chgo., 1984-87; ptnr.-in-charge mgmt. cons. svcs. BDO Seidman, Milw. and Chgo., 1987-90; mng. ptnr. RPB Assocs., Chgo., 1990-92; mng. assoc. performance improvement svcs. and dir. transp. cons. Coopers & Lybrand, Chgo., 1992-95; mng. ptnr. RPB Assocs., Chgo., 1995—. Contbg. editor profl. and bus. jours; contbr. articles to profl. jours. Mem. Inst. Mgmt. Cons. (v.p. 1980-86, 89-92, bd. dirs. 1988-95, pres. Chgo. chpt. 1992-95), Inst. Indsl. Engrs. (sr. mem.), Soc. for Human Resources Mgmt.

PUCKETT, CARLISSA ROSEANN, non-profit association executive; b. Effingham, Ill., Jan. 21, 1951; d. Carl Winston and Flora Pauline (Cox) Browning; m. Steve Dawson Puckett, Oct. 27, 1973; children: Heather Nicole, Adam Dawson, Christopher Alex. AS, Lake Land Jr. Coll., Mattoon, Ill., 1972; BA, Ea. Ill. U., 1976; MS, So. Ill. U., 1986. Child care aide Assn. Retarded Citizens Effingham County, Effingham, 1972-74, asst. supr. devel. work activities, 1975-77, residential coord., 1981-84, residential dir., case coord. dir. family support, 1984-88; owner, mgr. Denim's Inn, Effingham, 1977-81; coord. housing Ill. Dept. Mental Health and Devel. Disabilities, Springfield, 1988-89, coord. Community Integrated Living Arrangements, 1989-90; bur. chief Bur. Resource Design, Springfield, 1990-91, Bur. Devel. Field Svcs., 1991-93; exec. dir. Springfield Assn. for Retarded Citizens Inc., 1993—. Named Bus. and Profl. Woman of Yr., Effingham County Jr. Women's Club, 1986. Mem. Am. Assn. on Mental Retardation (membership com. Ill. chpt. 1992—, bd. dirs. 1995—), Assn. for Retarded Citizens, Sons and Daus. of Pearl Harbor Survivors (charter, pres. Ill. chpt.), Rotary (fellowship dir. 1995-96), Women in Mgmt. Women of Achievement-Not-for-Profit, Phi Kappa Phi. Home: 2516 Kipling Dr Springfield IL 62707 Office: Springfield Assn Retarded Citizens Inc One SPARCenter Plz 232 Bruns Ln Springfield IL 62702

PUCKORIUS, PHILIP MICHAEL, editor; b. Springfield, Ill., Sept. 11, 1956; s. Theodore Donald and Joyce Carolyn (Bormuth) P.; m. Kay Lynn Ertman, July 31, 1982 (div. Jan. 21, 1987); m. Lisé Ann Misiewicz, Sept. 12, 1992; 1 child, Hannah Lisbeth. BS, Carroll Coll., 1978. Sales rep. Xerox Corp., Milw., 1978-79, sr. sales rep., 1980, sales exec., 1981, sr. sales exec., 1982; sales rep. Sunstrand Solar Products, Richfield, Wis., 1983; med. sales rep. Alcon Pharm. Co., Ft. Worth, 1983-85; assoc. editor Kendall/Hunt Publ. Co., Dubuque, Iowa, 1985-89, editor, 1989-92, sr. cons. editor, 1992-94, mng. editor assoc. bus. program, 1994—. Mem. NRA (life), Amateur Trapshooting Assn., Nat. Sporting Clays Assn., Waukesha Gun Club (life), Harley Owner's Group, Ruffed Grouse Soc. (sponsor and com. mem. T. Stanton Armor chpt.). Office: Kendall Hunt Publ Co 500 N Dearborn #1300 Chicago IL 60610

PUDLES, LYNNE, art historian; b. Pitts., July 30, 1951; d. Saul B. and Claire (Marcus) P.; m. Martin Davis, July, 1974 (div. 1978); m. R.B. Duncan, June 10, 1989. BA summa cum laude, U. Pitts., 1973; MA, U. Calif., Berkeley, 1977, PhD, 1987. Vis. instr. art history Humboldt State U., Arcata, Calif., 1977-78, U. Chgo., 1985-86; instr. art history Cleve. State U., 1986-87, asst. prof. art history, 1987; asst. prof. art history Lake Forest (Ill.) Coll., 1987-93, assoc. prof. art history, 1993—; exec. adv. com. Interdisciplinary Nineteenth Century Studies, 1988-91; commr. Winnetka (Ill.) Archtl. Landmarks Preservation, 1992—; advisor Ill. Acad. Fine Arts; cons. in field. Author: (exhbn. catalogue) Roger Snakkers Retrospective Exhbn., 1991, Michael Croydon, "The Love Poems" Exhbn., 1988; contbr. articles to profl. jours. Founder The Pitts. Women's Ctr., 1970-73, Pitts. Rape Crisis Ctr., 1970-73; coord. Letter Drive to Support Reauthorization of NEA, Lake Forest, 1990. Fellow Samuel Kress Found., 1975, U. Calif., Berkeley, Found. and Alumni Assn., 1979-80, Danforth Found., 1974-79, 1981-82, Theodore Rousseau Met. Mus. Art, 1981-82, Belgian Ministry of Edn. and Culture, 1981-82, U. Calif., Berkeley, Grad. Humanities Rsch., 1981-82. Mem. AAUP, Am. Assn. Museums, Soc. for Values in Higher Edn., Midwest Art History Soc., Coll. Art Assn. Am., Phi Beta Kappa (U. Calif. Berkeley fellow 1985, No. Calif. Assn. fellow 1985), Mortar Board Nat. Hon. Soc. Home & Office: Lake Forest Coll Art Dept 555 N Sheridan Rd Lake Forest IL 60045-2338

PUEPPKE, DARRELL E., design draftsman; b. Mount Clemons, Mich., Dec. 6, 1946. Design draftsman Fasco Ind. Inc., Cassville, Mo., 1966—. Baptist. Office: Fasco Ind Inc PO Box 548 Cassville MO 65625-0548

PUGH, COY, state legislator; b. Chgo., Feb. 27, 1952; s. Willie James and Martha (Nelson) P.; m. Laura L. Williams; children: Courtney, Leshawn. BA, Northeastern Ill. U., 1992. Adminstrv. asst. to State Rep. Ill. Ho. of Reps., 1984-86; owner Wescor Contracting, 1991-93; mem. Ill. Ho. of Reps., 1993—. Democrat. Home: 1748 N Mason Ave # 2 Chicago IL 60639-4011*

PUGH, EDWARD W., state legislator. Atty.; mem. from dist. 61 Kans. State Ho. of Reps., Topeka. Address: 16705 Mil Trail Rd Wamego KS 66547

PUGH, MARGARET JEANNE, nurse practitioner; b. St. Louis, June 3, 1931; d. Marion George and Marian Margaret (Morrison) Cornet; m. J. Thomas Pugh, Apr. 5, 1952; children: Martha Jane Pugh Bergien, David Michael. Diploma, Meth. Sch. Nursing, Peoria, Ill., 1952; cert. in nurse practice, Planned Parenthood of Wis., 1974. RN, Ill.; cert. nurse practitioner NAACOG. Staff nurse Meth. Hosp., Peoria, 1952-65; labor and delivery nurse U.S. Army Hosp., Camp Atterbury, Ind., 1953, Highland Park (Ill.) Hosp., 1954; staff nurse Planned Parenthood, Peoria, 1965-69, clin. coord., 1969-74, family planning nurse practitioner, 1974-79, dir. patient svcs., 1976-79, mgr. Women's Health Advantage Ctr., 1988—; women's health practitioner Med. and Surg. Clinic, Peoria, 1979-87; mem. nursing adv. bd. Ill. Ctrl. Coll., Peoria, 1983-90. Pres. Columbia Sch. Mothers' Club, Peoria, 1970; women's adv. bd. YWCA, Peoria, 1984-85; troop leader Girl Scouts U.S., Peoria, 1962-68; vol. clinic dir. nurse Planned Parenthood, 1965-69, bd. dirs., 1965-69, mem. regional com. Gt. Lakes chpt., 1974-91; vol. tchr. U. Ill. Sch. Medicine, Peoria, 1975-90; lectr. sex edn.for teens, 1965—. Recipient cert. of excellence ANA and NAACOG, 1976, Svc. awards Planned Parenthood, 1979, 93, Women's Health award NOW, 1990. Methodist. Home: 500 W Melbourne Peoria IL 61604 Office: Women's Health Advantage 300 E War Memorial Dr Peoria IL 61614

PUGH, MICHAEL A., mechanical engineering associate; b. Columbus, Ohio, Jan. 17, 1956. A in Mech. Engring., Columbus Tech. Inst., 1986. Design draftsman Wearever Proctor Sylex, Chilicothe, Ohio, 1983-85; supr. assembly/welding Nestle Dairy Systems, Columbus, Ohio, 1985—. Religious edn. tchr. St. Phillips Cath. Ch., Columbus, 1987-95. With USN, 1975-79. Republican. Roman Catholic. Office: Nestle Dairy Systems PO Box 1869 Columbus OH 43216-1869

PUGH, THOMAS WILFRED, lawyer; b. St. Paul, Minn., Aug. 3, 1949; s. Thomas Leslie and Joann Marie (Tauer) P.; m. Susan Elizabeth Beattie, Sept.

12, 1971; children: Aimee Elizabeth, Douglas Thomas. AB cum laude, Dartmouth Coll., 1971; JD cum laude, U. Minn., 1976. Assoc. Thuet & Lynch, South St. Paul, 1976-79; ptnr. Thuet, Lynch & Pugh, South St. Paul, 1980-85; atty., pres. Thuet, Pugh & Rogosheske, Ltd., South St. Paul, 1986—; mem. Minn. Ho. of Reps., St. Paul, 1989—; mem. Supreme Ct. Task Force Conciliation Ct., St. Paul, 1992, Dakota County Tech. Coll. Adv. Bd., 1991—. Bd. dirs. Wakota Arena, South St. Paul, 1984-87; pres. Luther Meml. Ch., South St. Paul, 1983-84. Daniel Webster scholar Dartmouth Coll., 1970, Rufus Choate scholar, 1971. Mem. Minn. State Bar Assn., 1st Dist. Bar Assn., Ducks Unltd., Pheasants Forever, South St. Paul C. of C. (local issues chair 1982, Dedicated Svc. award 1983), South St. Paul Jaycees (pres. 1978-79, Key award 1979), Lions. Lutheran. Office: Thuet Pugh & Rogosheske 833 Southview Blvd South Saint Paul MN 55075-2237

PUGLISI, PHILIP JAMES, electrical engineer; b. Paterson, N.J., Feb. 26, 1943; s. Philip James and Josephine Theresa (Guido) P.; children: Brent, Tara. BEE, Poly. U., 1971; MEE, Stanford U., 1972. Researcher, mem. staff Bell Telephone Labs., Whippanny, N.J., 1967-77; chief engr. Dionex Corp., Sunnyvale, Calif., 1977-80; engring. supr. AT&T Microelectronics, Lees Summit, Mo., 1980-83, with semiconductor design dept., 1983-86, mktg. mgr., 1986-91; dir. engring. PPG Biomed. Systems, Lenexa, Kans., 1991-93; product mgr.- optics AT&T, Lee's Summit, Mo., 1993—, global product mgr. optical connectors, 1995—; mem. exec. com. Optical Data Link Forum, Murry Hill, N.J., 1987-91; cons. for optical interconnection. Contbr. articles to profl. jours. Organizing parent Dist. and State Music Festival, Springfield & Columbia, Mo., 1984-88; bd. dirs. Dist. Water Com., Groves-pring, Mo., 1987-88; scoutmaster Boy Scouts Am., Bonny Doon, Calif., 1976-79. With USN, 1960-64. Mem. ISHM, Electronic Industries Assn. (mem. optical comm. com. 1987-91). Home: 405 Cline St Pleasant Hill MO 64080-1805 Office: Lucent Techs CS & CT 777 NW Blue Pky Lees Summit MO 64086-5712

PULFREY, ROY ALLAN, environmental engineer; b. Britton, S.D., Dec. 19, 1953; s. Ralph Lincoln and Virginia Reel (Buffington) P.; m. Carrie Suzanne Guhin, May 25, 1985; children: James Lincoln, Laura Eileen. BS in Civil Engring., S.D. Sch. Mines & Tech., 1976. Registered profl. engr., S.D. Student trainee Soil Conservation Svc., Pierre, S.D., 1976; civil engr. Soil Conservation Svc., Rapid City, S.D., 1977-78, Lake Andes, S.D., 1978-79; agrl. engr. Soil Conservation Svc., Aberdeen, S.D., 1979-83; hwy. engr. Bur. Indian Affairs, Aberdeen, 1983-88, supr. hwy. engr., 1988-89, civil engr., 1989-95, environ. engr., 1995—. Sports official high sch., coll. basketball & football, S.D., 1982—. Mem. ASCE, Nat. Soc. Profl. Engrs. (pres. N.E. S.D. chpt. 1987). Home: PO Box 256 Claremont SD 57432-0256 Office: Bur Indian Affairs 115 4th Ave SE Aberdeen SD 57401-4360

PULITZER, MICHAEL EDGAR, publishing executive; b. St. Louis, Feb. 23, 1930; s. Joseph and Elizabeth (Edgar) P.; m. Cecille Stell Eisenbeis, Apr. 28, 1970; children: Michael Edgar, Elizabeth E. Voges, Robert S., Frederick D., Catherine D. Culver, Christina H. Eisenbeis, Mark C. Eisenbeis, William H. Eisenbeis. Grad., St. Mark's Sch., Southborough, Mass., 1947; AB, Harvard U., 1951, LLB, 1954. Bar: Mass. 1954. Assoc. Warner, Stackpole, Stetson & Bradlee, Boston, 1954-56; reporter Louisville Courier Jour., 1956-60; reporter, news editor, asst. mng. editor St. Louis Post-Dispatch, 1960-71, assoc. editor, 1978-79; pub. Ariz. Daily Star, Tucson, 1971—; pres. chief operating officer Pulitzer Pub. Co. (and subs.), 1979-84, vice chmn., 1984-86, pres., chmn., 1986—, also bd. dirs., chief exec. officer, 1988—. Trustee St. Louis U., 1989—. Clubs: St. Louis Country; Mountain Oyster (Tucson). Office: Pulitzer Pub Co 900 N Tucker Blvd Saint Louis MO 63101-1069

PULLIAM, EUGENE SMITH, newspaper publisher; b. Atchison, Kans., Sept. 7, 1914; s. Eugene Collins and Myrta (Smith) P.; m. Jane Bleecker, May 29, 1943; children: Myrta, Russell, Deborah. A.B., DePauw U., 1935, LL.D., 1973. Reporter, UP, Chgo., Detroit, Buffalo, 1935-36; news editor Radio Sta. WIRE, Indpls., 1937-41; city editor Indpls. Star, 1947-48; mng. editor Indpls. News, 1948-62; asst. publisher Indpls. Star and News, 1962-76; pres. Phoenix Newspapers, 1979—; exec. v.p. Central Newspapers, Indpls., 1979—. With USNR, 1942-46. Mem. Am. Soc. Newspaper Editors, Am. Newspaper Pubs. Assn. Found. (past pres.), Soc. Profl. Journalists, Delta Kappa Epsilon. Club: Crooked Stick Golf. Office: Indpls Star Indpls Newspapers Inc 307 N Pennsylvania St Indianapolis IN 46204-1811 also: Phoenix Newspapers Inc 120 E Van Buren St Phoenix AZ 85004-2227

PULLIAM, FREDERICK CAMERON, educational administrator; b. Mesa, Ariz., Jan. 5, 1936; s. Fredrick Posy and Nathana Laura (Cameron) P.; AA., Hannibal LaGrange Coll., 1955; AB, Grand Canyon Coll., 1958; M.Ed., U. Mo., Columbia, 1966, Ed.S., 1976, EdD, 1981; m. Deborah Jean Botts, June 1, 1979; 1 child, Sarah Elizabeth; children by previous marriage: Cameron Dale, Joy Renee. tchr., Centerview (Mo.) Public Schs., 1958-59; ordained to ministry So. Baptist Conv., 1955; minister Bethel Bapt. Ch., Kansas City, Mo., 1959-61; adminstr. Fiti'uta, Manu'a sch., Am. Samoa, 1966-69; cons. in fin. Mo. State Tchrs. Assn., Columbia, 1969-79; supt. schs. Midway Heights C-VII, Columbia, 1979-83; dir. elem. edn. Brentwood Pub. Schs. (Mo.), 1983-90; founder, coordinator Mo. Computer-Using Educators Conf., 1982-84; contbg. writer St. Louis Computing News, 1984—; adj. asst. prof. ednl. studies U. Mo., St. Louis, 1986-90; assoc. prof. edn. Mo. So. State Coll., 1990—, dir. clinical and field experiences in tchr. edu., Mo. So. Stae Coll., 1994—; adj. assoc. prof. grad. studies Southwest Baptist Univ., 1991-95; cons. sch. fin., curriculum improvement. Mem. Columbia Am. Revolution Bicentennial Commn. Inst. Devel. Ednl. Activity fellow, 1969, 78-84. Mem. Am. Assn. of Colls. for Tchr. Edn., Assn. Childhood Edn. Internat. Nat. Assn. Supervision and Curriculum Devel. (bd. dirs. 1984-90),Mo. Gov's. Transition Team (edn. adv. com. 1992-93), Phi Delta Kappa (chpt. pres.). Contbr. articles to profl. jours. Home: 2140 Kayla Ln Mount Vernon MO 65712-1243 Office: Mo So State Coll 224 Taylor Hall Joplin MO 64801-1595

PULSIFER, EDGAR DARLING, leasing service and sales executive; b. Natick, Mass., Jan. 11, 1934; s. Howard George and Elvie Marion (Morris) P.; m. Alice Minarik, Feb. 16, 1957 (div. Oct. 1979); children: Mark Edgar, Audrey Carol, Lee Howard; m. Barbara Ann Chuhak, Apr. 19, 1980. BSEE, MIT, 1955. With sales and service dept. Beckman Instruments, Fullerton, Calif., 1956-59; regional sales mgr. Hewlett Packard, Palo Alto, Calif., 1959-72, Gen. Automation, Anaheim, Calif., 1973-74; exec. v.p. Systems Mktg., Elk Grove Vlg., Ill., 1975-79; pres. Consol. Funding, Mt. Prospect, Ill., 1979—. Served as 1st lt. U.S. Army, 1956. Mem. MENSA, Coast Guard Auxiliary. Republican. Episcopalian. Clubs: North Shore Country (Glenview, Ill.), Itasca (Ill.) Country. Home: 370 Dulles Rd Des Plaines IL 60016-2755 Office: Consol Funding Corp P O Box 801 Mount Prospect IL 60056-0801

PULTZ, JOHN FRANCISCO, art historian, curator; b. Columbus, Ohio, Sept. 9, 1952; s. Frederick Dickinson and Frances Lynn (Ross) P.; m. Susan Elizabeth Earle, Nov. 12, 1988. BA cum laude, Amherst (Mass.) Coll., 1974; MA in Art History, Williams Coll., Williamstown, Mass., 1981; PhD in Art History, Inst. Fine Arts NYU, 1993. Newhall fellow Dept. Photography Mus. Modern Art, N.Y., 1981-84; instr. Tyler Sch. of Art, Elkins Park, Pa., 1986; vis. asst. prof. Bard Coll., Annandale-on-Hudson, N.Y., 1986; instr. Dept. Art Kean Coll., Union, N.J., 1991; instr. Dept. Fine Arts NYU, 1992; curator of photography Spencer Mus. Art U. Kans., Lawrence, 1993—, asst. prof. Kress Found. Dept. Art History, 1993—; cons. Dept. Photographs J. Paul Getty Mus., Santa Monica, Calif., 1985. Author: (books) Harry Callahan: Early Street Photography, 1990, The Body and the Lens, 1995; co-dir.: (exhbn.) Big Pictures by Contemporary Photographers, 1983, (exhbn. catalogue) Cubism and American Photography, 1910-1930, 1981. Recipient Summer Stipend award NEA, 1995. Mem. Coll. Art Assn. Office: U Kans 209 Spencer Mus of Art Lawrence KS 66045

PUND, MARVIN LOUIS, optical engineering consultant; b. Ferdinand, Ind., Jan. 14, 1950; s. Alvin Bernard and Florentine Elizabeth (Denning) P; m. Joyce Elizabeth Salih, Apr. 2, 1977; children: Elizabeth Katherine Salih, Richard Salih. BS in Physics, Purdue U., 1972. Engr. Bendix Aerospace Systems Divsn., Mishawaka, Ind., 1972-73; sr. engr. McDonnell Douglas Corp., St. Louis, 1973-82; pres. Perspective Displays Inc., Chesterfield, Mo., 1983—. Inventor projection system and process, 1979, wide angle projection system, 1984, stereoscopic display, 1987, automated lensometer, 1994. Alfred P. Sloan Found scholarship, 1968-72. Mem. IEEE, Internat. Soc. Optical Engring., Optical Soc. Am., Phi Beta Kappa, Sigma Pi Sigma. Office: Perspective Displays Inc 14529 Amstell Ct Chesterfield MO 63017

PUNDMANN, ED JOHN, JR., automotive company executive; b. St. Charles, Mo., Feb. 24, 1939; s. Ed J. Sr. and Ruth O. (Brehme) P.; m. Dolores Anne Lienau, June 15, 1963; children: Mary Anne, Steven A., Susan K. BA, Westminster Coll., 1961. Jr. accountant Peat, Marwick & Mitchell, St. Louis, 1961-62; salesman Pundmann Ford, St. Charles, 1962-82, gen. mgr., 1982-92, pres., 1992—; bd. dirs., vice chmn. First State Bank; bd. dirs. Mut. Fire Ins., St. Charles; vice chmn. St. Charles City Tax Incremental Financing Commn.; mem. Ford Motor Dispute Settlement Bd., 1993-94. Treas. St. Charles City Charter Commn., 1981; chmn. St. Charles City Econ. Devel. Commn.; mem. St. Charles City Park Found. Bd.; St. Louis Regional Commerce and Growth Assn.; adv. bd. St. Charles County; mem., past pres. Handicapped Facilities Bd. St. Charles County; past pres. St. John United Ch. of Christ; bd. dirs. Emmaus Homes, 1981-91, Parkside Meadows Retirement Facility. Recipient Gov. of Mo. award, 1989, Mo. Time Quality Dealer award, 1995. Mem. Mo. Auto Dealers Assn. (bd. dirs. 1983—), Greater St. Louis Ford Dealers Assn. (past pres.), St. Charles C. of C. (past bd. dirs., past pres., Citizen of Yr. award 1986). Lodge: Rotary. Home: 3304 Lennox Dr Saint Charles MO 63301-0632 Office: Pundmann Ford 2727 W Clay St Saint Charles MO 63301-2539

PUNT, LEONARD CORNELIS, educational services company executive; b. Bongondza, Zaire, Nov. 16, 1940; came to U.S., 1954, naturalized, 1960; s. Harry Marius and Clara (VandeGevel) P.; m. Sarah Elizabeth Walton, Dec. 18, 1966; children: John, Amy, Brian. B.A., Wheaton Coll., 1964, M.A., 1967; M.Ed., Loyola U., 1981. Owner, dir. The Reading Tree Inc., Downers Grove, Ill., 1976—, v.p. Am. Bus. Communications, Downers Grove, 1978—. Contbr. articles to profl. jours. Mem. Naperville C. of C. Office: Reading Tree Inc 5117 Main St Ste D Downers Grove IL 60515-4654

PURAVS, JOHN ANDRIS, journalist; b. Ruckersdorf, Germany, Feb. 23, 1945; s. Janis Alfreds and Alma Otilija (Grundulis) P.; m. Trudi Ann Tiedeman, July 2, 1966 (div. Feb. 1982). BA, U. Mich., 1966. Reporter Saginaw (Mich.) News, 1966-78, suburban editor, 1978-79, editorial editor, 1979—, chmn. editorial bd., 1981—; commentator Sta. WUCM-TV, Univ. Ctr., Mich. Contbr. articles to profl. jours. Mem. adv. bd. Saginaw State Valley State U. Coll. Edn., 1991—. 1st lt. U.S. Army, 1967-69, Vietnam. Medill fellow Northwestern U., 1970; Regents-Alumni scholar U. Mich., 1962-66, Chgo. House Coun., 1963-64; numerous journalism awards. Mem. Soc. Profl. Journalists, Am. Coun. on Germany (McCloy fellow 1980, Haus Rissen fellow 1982, del. German-Am. Biennial Conf. 1989), Saginaw Valley Press Club (pres. 1976), Nat. Conf. Editl. Writers (group chmn. 1991), Latvian Club Saginaw. Home: 3925 Cabaret Trl W Apt 4 Saginaw MI 48603-2205 Office: Saginaw News 203 S Washington Ave Saginaw MI 48607-1244

PURCELL, KEVIN JOHN, business executive; b. Omaha, June 21, 1955. BSBA, U. Nebr., 1979, MBA. Asst. to pres. Milder Oil Co., Omaha, 1976-84; dir. acctg. svcs. Douglas County Ct., Omaha, 1985-89; gen. mgr. Fun Plex, Omaha, 1989-90; site mgr. Computer Scis. Corp., Omaha, 1990-92; pres. KePur Inc., Omaha, 1992—. Commr. baseball league Prairie Lane Sports Assn., Omaha, 1993-95; money counting team leader Mary Our Queen Cath. Ch., Omaha, 1989-95. Roman Catholic. Home: 3345 S 115th Ave Omaha NE 68144-4505 Office: KePur Inc 4428 S 108th St Omaha NE 68137-1203

PURDES, ALICE MARIE, adult education educator; b. St. Louis, Jan. 8, 1931; d. Joseph Louis and Angeline Cecilia (Mozier) P. AA, Belleville Area Coll., 1951; BS, Ill. State U., Normal, 1953, MS, 1954; cert., Sorbonne U., Paris, 1964; PhD, Fla. State U., Tallahassee, 1976. Cert. in music edn., elem. edn., secondary edn., adult edn. Teaching/grad. asst. Ill. State U., 1953-54; music supr. Princeton (Ill.) Pub. Schs., 1954-55; music dir. Venice (Ill.) Pub. Schs., 1955-72, secondary vocal music dir., 1955-72; coord. literacy program Venice-Lincoln Tech. Ctr., 1983-86, chair lang. arts dept., 1983—; tchr. in space candidate, 1985. Mem. St. Louis chpt. World Affairs Coun., UN Assn., Nat. Mus. of Women in the Arts, Humane Soc. of Am.; charter mem. St. Louis Sci. Ctr., Harry S. Truman Inst.; contbr. Old Six Mile Mus., 1981, Midland Repertory Players, Alton, Ill., 1991; chair Cystic Fibrosis Spring Bike-A-Thon, Madison, Ill., 1981, Granite City, Ill., 1985. Recipient gold medal Nat Senior Olympics, 1989, Senior World Games, 1992, several scholarships. Mem. AAUW, Music Educators Nat. Conf., Ill. Music Educators Assn., Am. Choral Dirs. Assn., Fla. State Alumni Assn., Ill. Adult and Continuing Educators Assn., Am. Fedn. Tchrs. (pres. 1957-58), Western Cath. Union, Croation Fraternal Union, Nat. Space Soc., Travelers Abroad (pres. 1966-68, 89—), Internat. Platform Assn., Archaeol. Inst. Am., Friends St. Louis Art Mus., St. Louis Numis. Assn. Madison Rotary Club (internat. amb., Humanitarian award 1975), Slavic and East European Friends (life), Lovejoy Libr. Friends, Ill. State U. Alumnia Assn. Roman Catholic. Home: PO Box 274 Madison IL 62060-0274 Office: Venice-Lincoln Tech Ctr S 4th St Venice IL 62090-1063

PURDY, MICHAEL WAITE, speech and communications educator; b. New Berlin, N.Y., Oct. 21, 1945; s. Rex Wilson and Marion Elizabeth (Emhof) P.; m. Deborah Claire Vartanian, May 24, 1975; children: Nathanael, Jessica. BS in Math., SUNY, Albany, 1967; MS in Rhetoric and Pub. Address, Kans. State U., 1969; PhD in Interpersonal Communications, Ohio U., 1973. Instr. No. Ill. U., DeKalb, 1968-70; asst. prof. U. R.I., Kingston, 1972-80; prof., chair dept. communication Governors State U., University Park, Ill., 1980—. Mem. editl. bd. Jour. Internat. Listening Assn., 1988—, Speech Communication Ann., 1991—; mng. editor Integrative Explorations: Jour of Culture and Consciousness, 1983—; author: (with Borisoff) Listening in the Everyday Life: A Personal and Professional Approach, 1991, 2d rev. edit., 1996. Mem. Internat. Communication Assn., Internat. Listening Assn., Speech Communication Assn., Jean Gebser Soc. Office: Governors State Univ Stunkel Rd University Park IL 60466

PURI, MADAN LAL, mathematics educator; b. Sialkot, Feb. 20, 1929; came to U.S., 1957, naturalized, 1973; s. Ganesh Das and S. V. P.; m. Uma Kapur, Aug. 24, 1962; 3 children. B.A., Punjab U., India, 1948, M.A., 1950, D.Sc., 1975; Ph.D., U. Calif. at Berkeley, 1962. Head dept. math. D.A.V. Coll., Punjab U., 1955-57; instr. U. Colo., 1957-58; teaching asst., research asst., jr. research statistician U. Calif. at Berkeley, 1958-62; asst. prof., asso. prof. math. Courant Inst., N.Y. U., 1962-68; vis. asso. prof. U. N.C., summers 1966-67; prof. math. Ind. U., Bloomington, 1968—; guest prof. stats. U. Gottingen, West Germany, 1972, Alexander von Humboldt guest prof., 1974-75; guest prof. U. Dortmund, West Germany, 1972, Technische Hochschule Aachen, West Germany, 1973, U. Goteborg, Chalmers U. Tech., both Sweden, 1974; vis. prof. U. Auckland, N.Z., 1977, U. Calif., Irvine, 1978, U. Wash., Seattle, 1978-79, U. Bern (Switzerland), 1982, Va. Poly. Inst., 1988; disting. visitor London Sch. Econs. and Polit. Sci., 1991; vis. prof. U. Göttingen, Germany, 1991, June-July 1992; rsch. fellow Katholieke U., Nijmegen, The Netherlands, 1992; vis. prof. U. Des Scis. et Tech. de Lille, France, 1994, U. Basel, Switzerland, 1995—. Coauthor: Non Parametric Methods in Multivariate Analysis, 1971, Non Parametric Methods in General Linear Models, 1985. Editor Statochastic Process and Related Topics, 1975, Statistical Inference and Related Topics, 1975, Non Parametric Techniques in Statistical Inference, 1970; co-editor: Nonparametric Statistical Inference, Vols. I and II, 1982, New Perspectives in Theoretical and Applied Statistics, 1987, Mathematical Statistics and Probability Theory, Vol. A, 1987, Statistical Sciences and Data Analysis, 1993, Recent Advances in Statistics and Probability, 1994. Recipient Sr. U.S. Scientist award, Humboldt Preis, 1974-75, 83. Fellow Royal Statis. Soc., Inst. Math. Statistics, Am. Statis. Assn.; mem. Math. Assn. Am., Internat. Statis. Inst., Bernoulli Soc. Math. Stats. and Probability. Office: Ind U Dept Math Rawles Hall Bloomington IN 47405

PUSTOVAR, PAUL THOMAS, insurance agency owner; b. Chisholm, Minn., Dec. 17, 1951; s. John Anton and Perena Esther (Martini) P. AS, Hibbing Jr. Coll., 1971; BS, U. Minn., 1973; M in Curriculum and Instrn., Mankato (Minn.) State U., 1976; grad., Life Underwriting Tng. Coun., 1984. CLU. Tchr. sci. Nicollet Jr. H.S., Burnsville, Minn., 1973-74; sci. prof. Hibbing (Minn.) C.C., 1974-80; owner, agt. MSI Ins. Agy., Hibbing, 1980—; Nat. leader Am. Youth Hostels, Washington, 1979—; announcer World Curling Championships, 1983-84. Mem. Nat. Assn. Life Underwriters, U.S. Men's Curling Assn. (U.S. curling champion 1977, 80, 84, 91, Minn. champion 1977, 80, 82, 84, Wis. champion 1991, 92, 94, 96, Bronze medal at World Championships 1991), Minn. Curling Assn. (bd. dirs. 1980-82), Minn. Soc. Ins. Agts., Hibbing Jaycees, U.S. Curling Media Assn., Hibbing Curling Club (sec.-treas. 1980-82, bd. dirs. 1982-84). Democrat. Roman Catholic. Home: 2809 1st Ave Hibbing MN 55746-2561 Office: MSI Ins 2509 1st Ave Hibbing MN 55746-1904

PUTATUNDA, SUSIL KUMAR, metallurgy educator; b. Santipur, W. Bengal, India, Jan. 31, 1948; came to U.S., 1983; s. Provat Chandra and Santi Kana Putatunda; m. Ivy M. George, June 7, 1984; children: Sujata, Shibani. BS, Instn. Engrs., Calcutta, 1975; MS, U. Mysore (India), 1979; PhD, Indian Inst. Tech., Bombay, 1983. Metallurgist Hindustan Copper Ltd., Khetri, Rajsthan, 1973-77; grad. rsch. asst. U. Mysore, Mangalore, India, 1977-79; rsch. and devel. engr. Hindustan Electrographites, Bhopal, India, 1979-80; grad. rsch. asst. Indian Inst. Tech., Bombay, 1980-83; Fulbright scholar U. Ill., Urbana, 1983-84; assoc. prof. metallurgy Wayne State U., Detroit, 1985—. Recipient Scholarships, Govt. India, New Delhi, 1977, 80; Fulbright fellow USIA, Washington, 1982. Mem. Am. Soc. Metals, The Metall. Soc., ASTM (editor spl. tech. pub. on fractography 1989), Iron and Steel Soc., Engring. Soc. Detroit. Home: 2732 Brady Dr Bloomfield Hills MI 48304 Office: Wayne State U Coll Engring 5050 Anthony Wayne Dr Detroit MI 48202-3902

PUTCHAKAYALA, HARI BABU, engineering company executive; b. Maddirala, India, July 15, 1949; came to the U.S., 1978; s. Seshadri Chowdary and Sambrajyam (Penubothu) P.; m. Vijay Lakshmi, Aug. 9, 1976; children: Sashi Manohar, Gopi Krishna. BS in Chem. Engring., REC, Warangal, India, 1971; MS, BITS, Pilani, India, 1974; PhD, IIT, New Delhi, 1978. Registerd profl. engr., Mich., Md., Calif., Pa., Mo. Trainee Fertilizer Corp., Bombay, 1971; environ. engr. Madison Madison Internat., Detroit, 1978-81, project coord., 1981-84, project mgr., 1984-89, v.p., 1990-95, total quality officer, 1995—, also bd. dirs.; bd. dirs. Spack Inc., Brownstown, Mich., 1990—. Contbr. articles to Canadian Jour. Chem. Engring. Rsch. fellow Univ. Grants Commn., 1974-78; recipient Cert. Boiler Efficiency Inst., 1981, U. Wis., 1986, 1992, Mich. State U., 1989, Ctr. for Hazardous Materials Rsch., 1990. Mem. AICE, NSPE, Am. Soc. for Quality Control, Am. Cons. Engrs. Coun. Home: 654 Fox River Dr Bloomfield Hills MI 48304-1012 Office: Madison Internat 1420 Washington Blvd Detroit MI 48226-1716

PUTHOFF, FRANCIS URBAN, insurance salesman; b. Minster, Ohio, Mar. 2, 1922; s. Bernard Leo and Bertha Eliz (Menker) P.; m. Freda Althea Foster, Sept. 20, 1947; children: Francis C., Patricia J., Mary L., Donna M., Frederick U., Teresa A. BS in Health and Phys. Edn., Ohio State U., 1949, MA, 1952; postgrad., Bryn Mawr (Pa.) Coll., 1974, Sinclair Coll., Dayton, Ohio, 1976, U. Dayton, 1960. CLU. Tchr. Vandalia-Butler High Sch., Vandalia, Ohio, 1949-56, St. Christopher's Cath. Sch., Vandalia, 1958-61; salesman Ohio Nat. Life Ins. Co., Cin., 1953-91; gen. agt. Ohio Nat. Life Ins. Co., Dayton, Ohio, 1985-91. Editor: Career Counseling in a Horse Stable, 1984, Paths of Heritage, 1986; author: My Homeland, 1996. Rep. to sister city Ft. Loramie H.S. of 1940, Germany; pres. Ft. Loromie Future Farmers of Am., 1940, St. Christopher Ch. Soc., Vandalia, 1959. Lt. col. USAR; ret. Decorated Bronze Star, Arrowhead. Mem. Nat. Assn. Life Underwriters, Dayton Assn. Life Underwriters, 1Million Dollar Round Table (assoc.), St. Christopher Holy Name Club (pres.), St. Christopher Bldg. Club (pres.). Republican. Roman Catholic. Home: 8725 Haloran Ln Dayton OH 45414-2407 Office: Ohio Nat Life Ins Co 237 Williams St Cincinnati OH 45215-4603

PUTNAM, J. E. (JIM), state legislator. Grad. high sch., Armour, S.D. Mem. S.D. Ho. of Reps., 1993—; mem. appropriations and legis. procedure coms., farmer. Home: RR 1 Box 98 Armour SD 57313-9801*

PUTNEY, MARK WILLIAM, lawyer, utility executive; b. Marshalltown, Iowa, Jan. 25, 1929; s. Lawrence Charles and Geneva (Eldridge) P.; m. Ray Ann Bartnek, May 25, 1962; children: Andi Bartnek, William Bradford, Blake Reinhart. BA, U. Iowa, 1951, JD, 1957. Bar: Iowa 1957, U.S. Supreme Ct. 1960. Ptnr. Bradshaw, Fowler, Proctor & Fairgrave, Des Moines, 1961-72, of counsel, 1992-94; chmn., CEO. Bradford & Blake Ltd., Des Moines, 1992—; pres., chmn., chief exec. officer Iowa Resources, Inc., 1984-90; chmn., chief exec. officer Iowa Power & Light Co., 1984-90, Iowa Gas Co.,, 1984-85, Midwest Resources Inc., 1990-92. Civilian aide to Sec. Army for Iowa, 1975-77; bd. dirs. Greater Des Moines YMCA, 1976-86, Boys' Home Iowa, 1982-86, Hoover Presdl. Libr. Assn., 1983—, U. Iowa Found., 1984—, Edison Electric Inst., 1986-89; bd. dirs. Greater Des Moines Com., 1984—, pres. 1988; bd. dirs. Assoc. Edison Illuminating Cos., 1988-93, pres., 1991-92; chmn. Iowa Com. Employer Support of Guard and Res., 1979-86; bd. dirs. Des Moines Devel. Corp., 1984-92, chmn., 1989-90. With USAF, 1951-53. Mem. Iowa Utility Assn. (chmn. 1989, dir.), Des Moines Club (pres. 1977), Desert Forest Golf Club (Carefree, Ariz.), Masons, Shriners, Delta Chi, Phi Delta Phi. Republican. Episcopalian. Home: 600 Stevens Port Dr Dakota Dunes SD 57049-5188 Office: # 101 600 Stevens Point Dr Dakota Dunes SD 57049

PYATT, LEO ANTHONY, real estate broker; b. Key Port, N.J., Oct. 20, 1925; s. Ralph James and Anna Regina (Kussmaul) P.; m. Geraldine Genevive Gibb, May 31, 1947; children: Steven Lee, Rebecca Lynn. Student, Franklin U., 1947-49. Salesperson Standard Oil Co., Columbus, Ohio, 1947-49, Borden Dairy Co., Columbus, 1950-57, Frito-Lay, Inc., Columbus, 1958-74; sec., treas. Snack Time, Inc., Columbus, 1974-75; agt. N. NE Realty Co., Columbus, 1976-86; owner-broker Pyatt's Rose Realty Co., Columbus, 1986—. Presiding judge County Rep. Party, Franklin County, 1991; mem. Citizens for an Alternative Tax System. With USN, 1943-46, PTO. Decorated Air medal, Philippine Liberation award. Republican. Roman Catholic. Home: 4400 Wanda Lane Rd Columbus OH 43224-1026 Office: Pyatts Rose Realty Co 4400 Wanda Lane Rd Columbus OH 43224-1026

PYLE, ANTHONY L., sales executive; b. Lexington, Mo., Nov. 24, 1954; s. Louis E. and Clara Louise (Nance) P.; m. Patricia L. Wares, June 6, 1977 (div. Nov. 1987); children: Trisha D., Toni E. BS, N.E. Mo. State U., 1977. Tchr., coach Otterville (Mo.) H.S., 1977-80; from sales agt. to sales tng. mgr. Am. Family Ins., Madison, Wis., 1980-94; dist. sales mgr. Farmers Ins. Group, Des Moines, Iowa, 1994—. Home: 3329 Forest Run Ct Madison WI 53704-7723 Office: Farmers Ins Group 950 Office Park Rd #110 West Des Moines IA 50265

PYLE, DENNIS LEE, city administrator; b. Albia, Iowa, Aug. 11, 1963; s. Raymond Patricius and Betty Lou (Cooper) P.; m. Karen Ann Kauzlarich, June 30, 1984 (div. Aug. 1988); 1 child, Jacqueline Lea; m. Tammy Renee Courter, Aug. 25, 1989; 1 child, Joseph Christian. BA, Truman State U., Kirksville, Mo., 1986. Cert. mcpl. clk. Store mgr. Place's Discount Stores, various locations, 1986-89; co-mgr. Sernett Dept. Stores, Algona, Iowa, 1989-91; city adminstr./clk. City of Nora Springs, Iowa, 1991-93, City of Humboldt, Iowa, 1993—. Mem. Pi Sigma Alpha. Home: 1 Rainbow Dr Humboldt IA 50548 Office: City of Humboldt 29 S 5th St Humboldt IA 50548

PYLE, GEORGE BOWER, newspaper editor, columnist; b. Kansas City, Mo., Sept. 10, 1956; s. George Walter and Donna May (Bower) P.; m. Rebecca L. Brown, Dec. 29, 1995. BA magna cum laude, Wichita State U., 1978. Reporter Garden City (Kans.) Telegram, 1978-80, Ottawa (Kans.) Herald, 1980-82; reporter, news editor Olathe (Kans.) Daily News, 1982-88; mng. editor Chanute (Kans.) Tribune, 1988-90; editor, sec.-treas. Salina (Kans.) Jour., 1990—; mem. adv. bd. Sta. KRPS, pub. radio, Pittsburg, Kans., 1989-90. Mem. Kans. Press Assn. (awards of excellence 1990, 91, 94). Office: Salina Jour 333 S 4th St Salina KS 67401-3903

PYLE, PAUL WILLIAM, religious studies educator; b. Denton, Tex., July 4, 1956; s. William Eads and Pacheco Jane (Umphress) P.; m. Nanette Louise Smart, July 15, 1977; children: Sarah Elizabeth, Nathan William, Gabriel Clinton, Benjamin Christian. BS, Evangel Coll., 1977; MA, Dallas Theol. Sem., 1993. Tchr., head Bible dept. Dayton (Ohio) Christian Schs.,

1977—; editor (newspaper) The Christian Citizen, Dayton, 1991—. Office: Dayton Christian Schs Inc 325 Homewood Dayton OH 45420

PYNN, KATHLEEN ANN, accounting manager; b. Sioux City, Iowa, Mar. 28, 1950; d. Clarence John and Yvette Ida (DeMers) Backer; m. Gordon Edwin Pynn Jr., Mar. 15, 1969; children: Teresa, Marce. Student, Augustana Coll., Sioux Falls, S.D., 1979-80, C.C. Sioux Falls, 1982, Wayne State Coll., South Sioux City, Nebr., 1989-91, Morningside Coll., Sioux City, Idaho, 1991-94. Acct. Fiscal Control Office, Karamursel AFB, Turkey, 1970-72, Williams & Co., Sioux City, 1976-78, Jerald B. Davis Co., Sioux Falls, 1981-82; contr. Warren Supply Co., Sioux Falls, S.D., 1982-84; ops. mgr. Designers Ltd., Sioux Falls, 1984-85; co-owner, operator LaVentura Ltd., Sioux City, 1986-89; customer acctg. mgr. Gateway 2000, North Sioux City, S.D., 1989-90; contr. Network Comm., Sioux City, 1990; acct. Terry Lockie, CPA, Sioux City, 1991-93; acctg. mgr. Mid Bell Music Inc., Sioux City, 1993—; v.p. comm. Inst. Mgmt. Accts., 1996—; cons. Minnikota Girl Scouts, Sioux Falls, 1986, fin. chair, 1985; presenter in field. Bd. dirs. Women Aware, Sioux City, 1989-91. Mem. Nat. Assn. for Women in Careers (advisor, pres. 1986-89, treas. 1986-87, Woman of Achievement 1988, Woman of Yr. 1984), Women of Excellence Program (nomination com. 1989, co-chair 1990, 91), Tri-State Women Bus. Conf. (planning com. 1987-88), Sioux City C of C, PEO, Quota. Roman Catholic. Home: 3813 Douglas Ct Sioux City IA 51104-1405 Office: Mid Bell Music Inc Sioux City IA 51106

PYSH, JOSEPH JOHN, neurologist; b. Olyphant, Pa., Nov. 14, 1935; s. John Andrew and Anna Mary (Marusin) P.; m. Deborah Ann Prass, Dec. 15, 1991. BA in Biology, Wayne State U., 1958; DO, Chgo. Coll. Osteo. Medicine, 1962; PhD in Neuroanatomy, Northwestern U., Chgo., 1967. From instr. to assoc. prof. anatomy Northwestern U., Chgo., 1966-86, acting chmn. cell biology and anatomy, 1978-81, resident physician in neurology, 1983-86; assoc. prof. neurology Mich. State U., East Lansing, 1986-95, prof. neurology, 1995—; grant referee NSF, Washington, 1974—; frequent CME neurology speaker in field. Contbr. numerous articles to profl. jours; manuscript reviewer various orgns., Washington and N.Y.C. NIH grantee, 1969-82. Mem. AAAS (life), NIH (mem. rsch. grant neurology study sect. 1976-77), Am. Acad. Neurology, Am. Coll. Neuropsychiatrists, Am. Soc. Cell Biology, Am. Assn. Anatomists, Soc. Neurosci., Sigma Xi. Republican. Office: Mich State U Coll Osteo Medicine Dept Internal Medicine B305 W Fee East Lansing MI 48824

PYTTE, AGNAR, academic administrator; b. Kongsberg, Norway, Dec. 23, 1932; came to U.S., 1949, naturalized, 1965; s. Ole and Edith (Christiansen) P.; m. Anah Currie Loeb, June 18, 1955; children: Anders H., Anthony M., Alyson C. A.B., Princeton U., 1953; A.M., Harvard U., 1954, Ph.D., 1958. Mem. faculty Dartmouth Coll., 1958-87, prof. physics, 1967-87, chmn. dept. physics and astronomy, 1971-75, assoc. dean faculty, 1975-78, dean grad. studies, 1975-78, provost, 1982-87; pres. Case Western Res. U., Cleve., 1987—; researcher in plasma physics; mem. Project Matterhorn, Princeton, 1959-60, U. Brussels, 1966-67, Princeton U., 1978-79; bd. dirs. Goodyear Tire & Rubber Co.; A.O. Smith Corp. Bd. dirs. Sherman Fairchild Found. Inc., 1987—; bd. trustees Univs. Rsch. Assn., Ohio Aerospace Inst., Cleve. Inst. Music, Cleve. Orch. Mem. Am. Phys. Soc., Ohio Sci. and Tech. Coun., Cleve. Roundtable, Cleve. Tech. Leadership Coun., Phi Beta Kappa, Sigma Xi. Office: Case Western Res U Office of Pres Cleveland OH 44106

QUAAL, WARD LOUIS, broadcast executive; b. Ishpeming, Mich., Apr. 7, 1919; s. Sigfred Emil and Alma Charlotte (Larson) Q.; m. Dorothy J. Graham, Mar. 9, 1944; children: Graham Ward, Jennifer Anne. A.B., U. Mich., 1941; LL.D. (hon.), Mundelein Coll., 1962, No. Mich. U., 1967; D.Pub. Service, Elmhurst Coll., 1967; D.H.L. (hon.), Lincoln Coll., 1968, DePaul U., 1974. Announcer-writer Sta. WBEO (now sta. WDMJ), Marquette, Mich., 1936-37; announcer, writer, producer Sta. WJR, Detroit, 1937-41; spl. events announcer-producer WGN, Chgo., 1941-42, asst. to gen. mgr., 1945-49; exec. dir. Clear Channel Broadcasting Service, Washington, 1949-52, pres., chief exec. officer, 1964-74; v.p., asst. gen. mgr. Crosley Broadcasting Corp., Cin., 1952-56; v.p., gen. mgr., mem. bd. WGN Inc., Chgo., 1956; exec. v.p., then pres. WGN Continental Broadcasting Co. (now Tribune Broadcasting Co.), 1960-75; pres. Ward L. Quaal Co., 1975—; dir. Tribune Co., 1961-75; dir., mem. exec. com. U.S. Satellite Broadcasting Co., 1982—; bd. dirs. Christine Valmy Inc., Nat. Press Found., chmn. exec. com., dir. WLW Radio Inc., Cin., 1975-81; co-founder, dir. Universal Resources Inc., 1961-86; mem. FCC Adv. Com. on Advanced TV Sys., 1988-96. Author: (with others) Broadcast Management, 1968, rev. edit., 1996; coprodr. (Broadway play) Teddy and Alice, 1988. Mem., Hoover Commn. Exec. Br. Task Force, 1949-59; mem. U.S.-Japan Cultural Exchange Commn., 1960-70; mem. Pres.'s Council Phys. Fitness and Sports, 1983-93; bd. dirs. Farm Found., 1963-73; bd. trustees Hollywood (Calif.) Mus., 1964-78, MacCormac Jr. Coll., Chgo., 1974-80; chmn. exec. com. Council for TV Devel., 1969-72; mem. bus. adv. coun. Chgo. Urban League, 1964-74; bd. dirs. Broadcasters Found., Internat. Radio and TV Found., Sears Roebuck Found., 1970-73; trustee Mundelein Coll., 1962-72, Hillsdale Coll., 1966-72. Served as lt. USNR, 1942-45. Recipient Disting. Bd. Gov.'s award Nat. Acad. TV Arts and Scis., 1966, 87, Freedoms Found. award, Valley Forge, 1966, 68, 70, Disting. Alumnus award U. Mich., 1967, Loyola U. Key, 1970, Advt. Man of Yr. Gold medallion, Chgo. Advt. Club, 1968, Disting. Svc. award Nat. Assn. Broadcasters, 1973, Ill. Broadcaster of Yr. award, 1973, Press Vet. of Yr. award, 1973, Comm.award of distinction Brandeis U., 1973, Founder & Leadership award Broadcast Pioneers Libr., 1991; first recipient Sterling Medal, Barren Found., 1985, Lifetime Achievement award in broadcasting Ill. Broadcasters Assn., 1989; 1st person named to Better Bus. Bur. Hall of Fame, Council of Better Bus. Burs. Inc., 1975; named Radio Man of Yr. Am. Coll. Radio, Arts, Crafts & Scis., 1961, Laureate in Order of Lincoln, Lincoln Acad. Ill., 1965, Communicator of Yr., Jewish United Fund, 1969, Advt. Club Man of Yr., 1973; named to Broadcasting mag. Hall Fame, 1991, Delta Tau Delta Disting. Svc. Chpt., 1970. Mem. NATAS (bd. govs. 1966-76, Silver Circle award 1993), Nat. Press Found. (bd. dirs. 1991—), Nat. Assn. Broadcasters (bd. dirs. 1952-56), Fed. Comm. Bar Assn., Broadcast Music Inc. (bd. dirs. 1953-70), Assn. Maximum Svc. Telecasters Inc. (bd. dirs. 1952-72), Broadcast Pioneers (pres., bd. dirs. 1962-73), Broadcast Pioneers Libr. (pres. 1981-84), Broadcast Pioneers Ednl. Fund Inc., Am. Advt. Fedn. (ethics com.), Delta Tau Delta (Alumni Achievement award 1990, disting. svc. chpt.), The George Town Club (Washington), Mid-Am. Club, Exmoor Country Club (Chgo.). Office: Ward L Quaal Co 401 N Michigan Ave Ste 3140 Chicago IL 60611-4207

QUADHAMER, BETTEE COLLEEN, oncological nurse, educator; b. Kearney, Nebr., Sept. 22, 1953; d. Alvin Lynn and Marjorie Bertha (Bishop) Burchell; m. Steven R. Quadhamer, Feb. 26, 1972; children: Chad Lynn, Lindsay Leigh, Colt Thomas. Diploma, St. Francis Sch. of Nursing, 1976; BS in Biology, U. of Nebr., Kearney, 1976; MSN, Bishop Clarkson Coll., 1992. Charge nurse obstetrics Good Samaritan Hosp., Kearney, Nebr., 1976-78; instr. nursing, program coord. Cen. C.C., Kearney, Nebr., 1978—, program coord., 1995—; cons. health Zion Luth. Sch., Kearney, 1982-89; mem. Oncology Workshop Planning Com., 1992—; adv. bd. mem., sec. St. Lukes Good Samaritan Village, 1993—, adv. bd. mem. Health Adv. Coun. for Mid-Nebr. Cmty. Svcs., Inc. Counselor health merit badge Boy Scouts Am., Kearney, 1983-90, dep. leader, 1980-82, mem. scout com., 1983-90; mem., sec. ch. bd. dirs. 1st Christian Ch., Minden, Nebr., 1987-90, 92—, deacon, 1980-94, elder 1995—; sec., v.p., pres. Kearney Swim Assn., 1984-91. Mem. ANA, Oncology Nursing Soc. Office: Cen C C 3203 8th Ave Kearney NE 68847-7336

QUATMAN, ROBERT J., manufacturing engineer; b. Dayton, Ohio, Sept. 17, 1945; s. John I. and Dorothy E. (Hummert) Q.; m. Patricia A. Kelley, Oct. 19, 1968; children: Victoria, Michelle. B, Marquette U., 1968. Mgr. divsn. Square D Co., Mesquite, Tex., 1976-86; pres. Patnry Foods, Inc., Dallas, 1986-88; mgr. engrng. Elkay Mfg. Co., Lanark, Ill., 1988—. Patentee in field. Bd. dirs. Dallas Sch. Bd., 1984-86; vol. tchr. high sch. jazz bands; cert. judge musical activities. Recipient New Product of Yr. award Popular Sci. mag., 1993. Office: Elkay Mfg Co 105 N Rochester St Lanark IL 61046-1149

QUAY, JOYCE CROSBY, writer; b. Dayton, Ohio, Aug. 8, 1928; d. Wilson Hill and Marianne (Mitchell) Crosby; m. John Grier Quay, Nov. 12, 1952; children: Peter Crosby, John Paul, Leslie Quay McMillan. Student, Simmons Coll., 1951, NYU, 1959-60. Ptnr. Quay Assocs., 1961-84. Author: Early Promise, Late Reward, 1995; contbr. articles to popular publs. Mem. Rep. Nat. Com., 1990, 94-95. Presbyn.

QUAYLE, J(AMES) DANFORTH, former vice president United States, entrepreneur; b. Indpls., Feb. 4, 1947; s. James C. and Corinne (Pulliam) Q.; m. Marilyn Tucker, Nov. 18, 1972; children: Tucker Danforth, Benjamin Eugene, Mary Corinne. BS in Polit. Sci., DePauw U., Greencastle, Ind., 1969; JD, Ind. U., 1974. Bar: Ind. 1974. Ct. reporter, pressman Huntington (Ind.) Herald-Press, 1965-69, assoc. pub., gen. mgr., 1974-76; mem. consumer protection div. Office Atty. Gen., State of Ind., 1970-71; adminstrv. asst. to gov. State of Ind., 1971-73; dir. Ind. Inheritance Tax Div., 1973-74; mem. 95th-96th Congresses from 4th Dist. Ind.; U.S. Senator from Ind., 1981-89, V.P. of U.S., 1989-93; author, speaker, columnist, corp. bds. $D; $D; tchr. bus. law Huntington Coll., 1975, author, speaker, columnist, corp. bds. Author: Standing Firm, 1994. Capt. Ind. Army N.G., 1970-76. Mem. Huntington Bar Assn., Hoosier State Press Assn., Huntington C. of C. Club: Rotary. Office: 11711 N Pennsylvania St 100 Carmel IN 46032

QUAYLE, MARILYN TUCKER, lawyer, wife of former vice president of United States; b. 1949; d. Warren and Mary Alice Tucker; m. J. Danforth Quayle, Nov. 18, 1972; children: Tucker, Benjamin, Corinne. BA in Polit. Sci., Purdue U., 1971; JD, Ind. U., 1974. Pvt. practice atty. Huntington, Ind., 1974-77; ptnr. Krieg, DeVault, Alexander & Capehart, Indpls., 1993—. Author: (with Nancy T. Northcott) Embrace the Serpent, 1992, The Campaign, 1996. Office: Krieg DeVault Alexander & Capehart 1 Indiana Sq Ste 2800 Indianapolis IN 46204-2017

QUDEIMAT, ISAM A., mechanical engineer; b. Nablus, Jordan, Feb. 15, 1962. BSME, Milw. Sch. Engrng., 1986, BS in Engrng. Mgmt., 1992. Design engr. Filtration Sys. Inc., Waukesha, wis., 1986—; cons. Jansen Controls, Milw., 1994. Mem. ASME, Soc. Automotive Engrs. (vice chmn. 1994—). Office: Filtration Sys Inc W 229 N 591 Foster Ct Waukesha WI 53186

QUELLA, DANIEL C., manufacturing company executive; b. Racine, Wis., Sept. 1, 1962. Assoc. Mech. Design, Gateway Tech. Coll., 1982. Products designer Racine R.R. Products, 1984-87, Andis Co., Racine, 1987-94; spl. products designer Ruud Lighting, Racine, 1994—; mem. adv. com. mech. design Gateway Tech. Coll., Racine, 1989-92. Patentee for hair clipping devices, railroad maintenance equipment. Office: Ruud Lighting 9201 Washington Ave Racine WI 53406-3750

QUELLMALZ, FREDERICK, foundation executive, editor; b. N.Y.C., May 24, 1912; s. Frederick and Edith (Grant) Q.; m. Jayne Elizabeth Osten, May 29, 1942; children: Barbara Jayne Coffin, Carol Grant Arran, Patricia Ellen, Sandra Lee Erchinger, Tracy Louise Koziel. AB, Princeton U., 1934; grad., Woodrow Wilson Sch. Pub. & Internat. Affairs, 1934; B of Profl. Arts (hon.), Brooks Inst., 1968. Statis. asst. Pepperell Mfg. Co., 1934-40; dir. photographic activities N.Y. World's Fair, 1940; editor PSA Jour., 1939-52; exec. sec. Photographic Soc. Am., Phila., 1940-42; asst. to chief engr. U.S. Naval Ordinance Plant, York, Pa., 1942-45; exec. v.p. Profl. Photographers Am., Des Plaines, Ill., 1952-74; editor, pub. Profl. Photographer mag., 1953-74; exec. dir. Photog. Art and Sci. Found., Oklahoma City, 1965-94, pres., 1988—; pres. Internat. Photog. Hall of Fame and Mus., Kirkpatrick Ctr., Oklahoma City, 1988—. Trustee Winona Sch. Profl. Photography, 1953-75; amb. Oakton Community Coll. Named to Hon. Order Ky. Cols.; recipient Father Smyth Humanitarian award City of Des Plaines, Ill., 1991. Fellow Royal Soc. Arts (London); mem. Photo Soc. Am. (hon. mem., assoc.), Profl. Photographers Am. (hon. master of photography, photo craftsman), Cert. Assn. Execs., Am. Soc. Assn. Execs. (bd. dirs. 1963-66), Chgo. Soc. Assn. Execs. (life mem.), Internat. Assn. Exposition Mgrs. (life mem., cert. exposition mgr., bd. dirs. 1959-61), Wis. Soc. Assn. Execs. (sec. 1963, pres. 1965), Am. Soc. Photographers (hon. assoc.), Nat. Press Photographers Assn. (life), Royal Photographic Soc., Am. Society Medalists, Am. Assn. Retired Persons (treas. Des Plaines chpt. 1982, 83, 90, pres. 1984-85, tax-aide coord. 1980—), Sister Cities Internat. (treas. local chpt. 1980-88, pres. 1989—, treas. Ill. state chpt. 1986—), Elks, Princeton Club, York Camera Club, Bella Vista Country Club, Kappa Alpha Mu. Office: 111 Stratford Rd Des Plaines IL 60016-2105

QUERESHI, MOHAMMED YOUNUS, psychology educator, consultant; b. Haripur Hazara, Pakistan, Dec. 12, 1929; came to U.S., 1953; s. Mohammed Noor and Meryam Khatoon Q.; m. Nora Jane Knapp, May 27, 1958 (div. Nov. 1979); children—Ahmed, Amna, Shukria, Shawn; m. Farzana Kaukab, May 17, 1980; children—Ajmel, Sabeeha, Azem. Ph.D., U. Ill., 1958. Lic. psychologist, Wis. Asst. prof. psychology U. Minn., Duluth, 1960-62, U. N.D., Grand Forks, 1962-64; assoc. prof. psychology Marquette U., Milw., 1964-70, prof., 1970—, chmn. dept. psychology, 1971-77; cons. psychologist. Pres. 81st Street Sch. PTA, 1968-70; merit badge counselor Milw. County council Boy Scouts Am., 1973-88; pres. Islamic Assn. Greater Milw., 1978-83. NIH grantee, 1962-69; Office of Edn. grantee, 1970-71; TOPS Club grantee, 1969-76. Mem. Am. Psychol. Assn., Psychometric Soc., AAAS, Sigma Xi. Author: Statistics and Behavior: An Introduction, 1980, 2nd edit., 1991; contbr. articles to sci. and profl. jours. Home: 2759 N 68th St Milwaukee WI 53210-1204 Office: Marquette U Schroeder Health Complex PO Box 1881 Milwaukee WI 53201

QUICK, EDWARD E., state legislator; b. Rich Hill, Mo., Feb. 16, 1935. City councilman Kansas City, Mo., 1975-85; mem. Mo. State Senate Dist. 17, 1985—. Office: 2212 NE 38th St Kansas City MO 64116-2511 also: State Senate State Capitol Building Jefferson City MO 65101-1556*

QUICK, EDWARD RAYMOND, museum director, educator; b. L.A., Mar. 22, 1943; s. Donald Russell Quick and Gertrude Ruth (Albin) Thornbrough; m. Ruth Ann Lessig; children: Jeannette Lee, Russell Raymond. BA, U. Calif., Santa Barbara, 1970, MA, 1977. Adminstr. supr. Civil Service, Santa Ana, Calif., 1971-75; sr. computer operator Santa Barbara Rsch. Ctr., 1975-77; asst. collections curator Santa Barbara Mus. Art, 1977-78; registrar Montgomery (Ala.) Mus. Fine Arts, 1978-80; head dept. registration and preparation Joslyn Art Mus., Omaha, 1980-85; dir. Sheldon Swope Art Mus., Terre Haute, Ind., 1985-95, Berman Mus., Anniston, Ala., 1995—; adv. Ind. Arts Commn., Indpls., 1986-91; mem. Arts in Pub. Places Commn., Terre Haute, Ind., 1986-93; bd. dirs. Arts Illiana, Terre Haute, 1986-91; pres. Friends Vigo County Pub. Libr., 1988-95, treas., 1990-93. Author: Code of Practice for Couriering Museum Objects, 1985, Gilbert Brown Wilson and Herman Melville's "Moby Dick", 1993, The American West in the Berman Collections, 1996; co-author: Registrars in Record, 1987. Bd. dirs. Vol. Action Ctr., Terre Haute, 1987-90; Terre Haute Cmty. Relief Effort for Environ. and Civic Spirit, 1989. With USAF, 1961-65, Air N.G., 1979-96. Mem. Am. Assn. Mus., Assn. Ind. Mus., Am. Assn. State and Local History, Internat. Coun. Mus., Rotary Internat., Alpha Gamma Sigma. Republican. Office: Berman Mus 840 Museum Dr PO Box 2245 Anniston AL 36202-6261

QUIE, PAUL GERHARDT, physician, educator; b. Dennison, Minn., Feb. 3, 1925; s. Albert Knute and Nettie Marie (Jacobson) Q.; m. Elizabeth Holmes, Aug. 10, 1951; children: Katie, Bill, Paul, David. B.A., St. Olaf Coll., 1949; M.D., Yale U., 1953; PhD (hon.), U. Lund, 1993. Diplomate Am. Bd. Pediatrics, Nat. Bd. Med. Examiners (mem.). Intern Hennepin County Hosp., 1953-54; pediatric resident U. Minn. Hosps., 1957-59; mem. faculty U. Minn. Med. Sch., 1959—, prof. pediatrics, 1968—, prof. microbiology, 1974—; assoc. dean of students, 1992—; Am. Legion meml. heart research prof. U. Minn. Med. Sch., 1974-91, Regents prof., 1991, interim dir. Ctr. for Biomed. Ethics, 1985-86; attending physician Hennepin County Hosp., 1959-91; cons. U. Minn. Nursery Sch., 1959-91; chief of staff U. Minn. Hosp., 1979-84; vis. physician Radcliffe Infirmary, Oxford, Eng., 1971-72; mem. Adv. Allergy and Infectious Disease Coun., 1976-80; mem. pediat. com. NRC, 1978; mem. bd. sci. counselors Gamble Inst., 1985-90; vis. prof. U. Bergen, 1991; hon. prof. U. Hong Kong Med. Sch., 1995; vis. prof. pediat. Chubu Hosp., Nagasaki, Japan, 1996. Mem. editorial bd. Pediatrics, 1970-76, Rev. Infectious Diseases, 1989-92. Served with USNR, 1954-57; med. officer. Recipient E. Mead-Johnson award Am. Acad. Pediatrics, 1971; Guggenheim fellow, 1971-72; John and Mary R. Markle scholar, 1960-65; Alexander Von Humbolt fellow, 1986. Mem. Inst. Medicine of NAS, N.W. Pediatrics Soc., Minn. Med. Found. (pres. 1986-88), Am. Fedn. Clin. Rsch., Am. Soc. Microbiology, Infectious Diseases Soc. Am. (coun. 1977-82, pres. 1985, Bristol award 1994), Soc. Pediatric Rsch., Am. Pediatric Soc. (coun. 1976-83, pres. 1987-88), Am. Soc. Clin. Investigation, Minn. Acad. Pediatrics, Am. Acad. Pediatrics, Assn. Am. Physicians, Minn. Acad. Medicine (pres. 1993-94). Home: 2154 Commonwealth Ave Saint Paul MN 55108-1717 Office: U Minn Hosp PO Box 483 Minneapolis MN 55440-0483

QUIEL, DAVID EARL, information management professional; b. Mpls., Feb. 7, 1947. Student, Concordia Coll., 1967-93. Adminstr. No. States Power, Mpls., 1993—; pres. Precyent Corp., Mpls., 1980—; cons. in field. Author: Information Management and Technology Business Plan, 1995. Office: Precyent Corp 7714 Brooklyn Blvd Minneapolis MN 55443-2965

QUIGLEY, SAMANTHA LEIGH, journalist, photographer; b. Adrian, Mich., Sept. 30, 1972; d. Terrence and Teresa (Gobba) Q. Degree in journalism, Ball State U., 1994. Staff writer, photographer Daily Telegram, Adrian, Mich., 1990-95; freelance writer, photographer, 1994—; sales assoc. photographic equipment Huron Camera Svc., Inc., Saline, Mich., 1995; editl. intern Am. Soc. Mag. Editors, 1993. Contbr. articles, photograph to mags. Reader's Digest mag. travel/rsch. grantee, 1993. Mem. Tri Sigma (Photographer, historian 1992-93). Home: 3422 Spielman Rd Adrian MI 49221

QUIKO, EDUARD, political science educator, consultant; b. Jakarta, Indonesia, Sept. 15, 1941; s. Jozef and Juliana (Tjiong) Q.; m. Lily Santo, June 21, 1976; children: Albin, Anjelica. BA, Bethel Coll., 1965; MS, Fort Hays State U., 1967; PhD, So. Ill. U., 1970. Asst. prof. Sch. of the Ozarks, Point Lookout, Mo., 1970-72, assoc. prof., 1972-75; vis. assoc. prof. World Campus Afloat, Orange, Calif., 1975; prof. dept. polit. sci., dir. pro-law program Coll. of Ozarks, Point Lookout, Mo., 1975—. Washington field trip program dir., 1972—, small city/county mgmt. dir., 1975-76; cons., pres. Am. Bus. Edn. Service, Inc., Springfield, Mo., 1983—. Author: The ABC's of State and Local Government in America, 1981. Editor: Firman Hidup, 1981. Contbr. articles to profl. jours. Title I grantee HEW and Mo. Dept. Community Affairs, Jefferson City, 1975-76. Mem. Am. Soc. Internat. Law, Mo. Polit. Sci. Assn. Avocation: Sports. Office: Coll of Ozarks Coll of Ozarks Point Lookout MO 65726

QUIMBY, ROBERT SHERMAN, retired humanities educator; b. St. Albans, Vt., Feb. 20, 1916; s. Christopher Sherman and Lura Mae (Wills) Q.; m. Shirley Lenore Lay, Oct. 19, 1957. B.S. in Edn, U. Vt., 1937, M.A., 1938; Ph.D., Columbia U., 1952; postgrad., Am. Sch. Classical Studies, Athens, Greece, 1958. Teaching asst. in history U. Vt., Burlington, 1938-39, 41-42; instr. history U. Vt., 1942-44, Cornell U., Ithaca, N.Y., 1944-45; instr. history of civilization Mich. State U., East Lansing, 1945-52; asst. prof. humanities Mich. State U., 1952-59, asso. prof., 1959-68, prof., 1968-81, prof. emeritus of humanities, 1981—; Mem. Mich. Commn. of United Ministries in Higher Edn., 1970-87, sec., 1975-77. Author: The Background of Napoleonic Warfare; contbr. articles to profl. jours. and encys. George Ellis fellow Columbia U., 1939-41. Mem. Mich. Hist. Soc., U.S. Naval Inst., Rwy. and Locomotive Hist. Soc. Republican. Episcopalian. Club: University. Address: 145 Columbia Ave Apt 207 Holland MI 49423-2983 Address (winter): 3400 S Ironwood Dr Lot 379 Apache Junction AZ 85220-7114

QUINN, JACK J., professional hockey team executive; b. Boston; s. John Quinn; m. Connie Quinn; children: Beth, Kay, Connie, John. Exec. v.p. St. Louis Blues, 1983-86, pres., 1986-95, chrm., ceo, 1995—. Office: St Louis Blues Kiel Ctr 1401 Clark Saint Louis MO 63103*

QUINN, RICHARD KENDALL, environmental engineer; b. Cleve., July 15, 1957; s. William Jerome and Nancy Drysdale (Kendall) Q.; m. Ann Marie (Beebe), Jan. 28, 1984; children: Ryan K., Eric E., Margaret A., Emily E. BS in Civil Engrng., U. Mich., 1979; BS in Geology, Colo. Sch. Mines, 1981; M Environ. Engrng., Iowa State U., 1989. Registered profl. engr., Colo., Nebr., Mich., Ill., Minn., Ind., N.C. Geophysic surveyor Shell Oil Co., Denver, 1980-84; profl. engr., environ. engr. Camp Dresser & McKee Engrng., Denver, 1985-91; engr. Harco Tech. Corp., Schaumburg, Ill., 1991-92, Walker divsn. Chgo. Bridge & Iron, Aurora, Ill., 1992-94; sr. v.p. Tonka Equipment Co., Plymouth, Minn., 1994—; sec./treas. Minn. sect. Water Pollution Control Agy., 1995, pres. elect, 1996-97. Cons. Iowa Community Devel. Block Grants, Des Moines, 1988—; active Big Bros. Assn. Grantee Iowa Engrng. Soc., 1989. Mem. ASCE (chpt. sec. 1986-87), NSPE (edn. and coll. rels. com.), Am. Pub. Works Assn. (chpt. sect. 1987—), Am. Water Works Assn., Water Pollution Control Fedn., Am. Soc. Mil. Engrs., Iowa Engrng. Soc., Ill. Engrng. Soc., N.C. Engrng. Soc., Mich. Engrng. Soc., Nat. Assn. Corrosion Engrs., CSWEA Minn. sect. (pres. 1996—), Ctrl. State Water Pollution Control Assn. (sec.-treas.). Republican. Roman Catholic. Home: 9176 Yates Bay Ct Brooklyn Park MN 55443-1629 Office: Tonka Equipment Co 13305 Water Tower Cir Plymouth MN 55441-3803

QUINN, THOMAS, advertising executive; b. 1935. V.p. sales and mktg. Spartan Foods, Inc., 1957-76; gen. mgr., pres. Family Foods, Inc., 1976-80; pres. JW Messner Inc., Grand Rapids, Mich., 1980—. Office: JW Messner Inc 161 Ottawa Ave NW Ste 403 Grand Rapids MI 49503*

QUINTANILLA, ANTONIO PAULET, physician, educator; b. Peru, Feb. 8, 1927; came to U.S., 1963, naturalized, 1974; s. Leandro Marino and Edel Paulet Q.; m. Mary Parker Rodriguez, May 2, 1958; children: Antonio Paulet, Angela, Francis, Cecilia, John. PhD, San Marcos U., 1948, MD, 1957. Assoc. prof. physiology U. Arequipa, Peru, 1960-63; assoc. in physiology Cornell U., N.Y., 1963-64; prof. physiology U. Arequipa, 1964-68; assoc. prof. medicine Northwestern U., 1969-80, prof., 1980—; chief renal sect. VA Lakeside Hosp., 1976-90; cons. nephrologist Northwestern Meml. Hosp., Evanston Hosp., 1990—; lectr. nat. Ctr. Advanced Med. Edn., Chgo.; mem. adv. bd. Kidney Found. Ill., Am. Fedn. Clin. Rssch. Fellow ACP; mem. Chgo. Heart Assn. (hypertension council), Central Soc. Clin. Rsch., Am. Soc. Clin. Pharmacology and Therapeutics, Am., Internat. socs. nephrology, Chgo. Soc. Internal Medicine, Am. Physiol. Soc. Contbr. articles on renal disease to med. jours.; author books, poetry, short stories. Home: 9352 Karlov Ave Skokie IL 60076-1415 Office: 2650 Ridge Ave Evanston IL 60201-1718

QUIOGUE, HONESTO D., mechanical engineer; b. The Philippines, Nov. 2, 1942. BA in Mech. Engrng., Nat. U., 1965. Mktg. rsch. Proctor & Gamble, Manila, Philippines, 1966-68; structural design engr. Boeing, Seattle, 1968-70; mgr. product design Hobbuel Lighting, Christiansburg, Va., 1970-88; engrng. and design Spaulding Lighting, Inc., Cin., 1989—. Patentee in field. Recipient Nat. Plastic awards, 1982, Lighting Design award North Am. Phillips Corp., 1982. Mem. Soc. of Mfg. Engrs., Illuminating Soc., Am. Testing Material. Office: Spaulding Lighting Inc 1736 Dremen Ave Cincinnati OH 45223-2435

QUIRING, FRANK STANLEY, chemist, educator; b. Goessel, Kans., Sept. 2, 1927; s. Henry and Helen (Lehrman) Q.; m. Evelyn Ruth Wiebe, Aug. 16, 1950; children: Samuel, Sherwood, Natalie, Powell. BA, Bethel Coll., 1950; MA, U. Kans., 1957. Cert. tchr. Kans., Mo. Tchr. sci. Coldwater (Kans.) High Sch., 1950-51, Pretty Prairie (Kans.) High Sch., 1952-55; tchr. chem. Wyandotte High Sch., Kansas City, Kans., 1955-59, Clayton (Mo.) High Sch., 1959-91; lab. dir. NSF Summer Insts. Hope Coll., Holland, Mich., 1964-92; rsch. assoc. Washington U., St. Louis, 1967-68; rsch. chemist Monsanto U., St. Louis, 1976-77, 84-85; cons. Coll. Bd. Adv. Placement Divsn., Princeton, N.J., 1966—, Ohaus Corp., Florham Park, N.J., 1986-90. Contbr. articles to profl. jours. With USN, 1945-46. Recipient Presdl. award NSF, 1984, Catalyst award Chem. Mfgs. Assn., 1973; Tandy Corp. Tech. scholar, 1990. Mem. NEA (pres. Clayton chpt. 1965-66), Am. Chem. Assn. (pres. St. Louis chpt. 1970-71), Am. Chem. Soc. (Conant award 1969), Nat. Sci. Tchrs. Assn. Mennonite. Home: 32 Regal Crescent St North Newton KS 67117-8039

QUIRING, PATTI LEE, human resource consulting company executive; b. Indpls.; d. Harold Woodrow and Flora Lee (Hoffman) Dulin; m. David Allen Niederhaus, June 1972; (div. May 1974); m. David Jonathon Quiring, Dec. 7, 1976; 1 child: Erin Ashley. AA, Ball State U., Muncie, 1972, BS, 1975; MBA, Ind. Wesleyan U., 1990. Profl. Sec. Summer employee P. R. Mallory and Co., Inc., Indpls., 1970, 1971; student asst. Ball State U.,

Muncie, Ind., 1970-72; adminstrv. asst. Ball Corp., Muncie, 1972-74; student asst. Ball State U., Muncie, 1975; adminstrv. asst. P. R. Mallory and Co., Inc., 1975-76; various mgmt. level positions Blue Cross and Blue Shield of Ind., Indpls., 1976-87; exec. recruiter Tech. Resource Group, Indpls., 1988-91; pres. Quiring Assocs., Inc., Indpls., 1991—; co-facilitator Corp. Bd. Task Force, 1993—; bd. dirs. Mega Sys, Inc. Co-chmn. venture com. United Way, 1991-93, mem. adv. com. women's divsn., 1991—, bd. dirs., mem. exec. com., 1993—, mem. goals and priorities com., 1993, vice chmn. agy. rels. cabinet 1993-94, chmn., 1995—, co-chmn. campaign cluster, 1994-95, mem. campaign cabinet, 1995, N.E. area team leader, 1995; vol. Pan. Am. Games, Indpls., 1987; dir. alumni rels. Ball State U. Coll. Bus., Muncie, 1988—, mem. alumni coun., 1994—; bd. dirs. Heritage Place Sr. Citizens Ctr., Indpls., 1988-90, Indpls. YWCA, 1988-90, Feathercove Homeowners Assn., 1990—, Geist Harbors Property Owner's Assn., 1994—; corp. capt. Humane Soc., 1990-91; mem. mktg. com. Children's Mus., 1992—, mem. bd. advisors, 1995—; mem. Equal Opportunity Adv. Bd., 1992-95, Indpls. BBB. Recipient Blue Cross award of Excellence, Indpls., 1985, City Ctr Vol. award, Indpls., 1985, Salute to Women of Achievement Individual award YWCA, 1993, Network of Women in Business Networker of Yr. award, 1993; named Blue Cross Bus. Women of Yr., Indpls. 1982, 86, Humane Soc. Outstanding Vol., Indpls., 1985. Mem. Ind. Assn. Pers. Svc. Bd., Network Women in Bus. (pres. 1993), Ind. C. of C. (small bus. coun. bd.), Ind. Med. Group Mgmt. Assn., Nat. Assn. Pers. Svcs. (mem. bd.), Indpls. and Ind. C. of C. (bd. dirs.), Better Bus. Bur. Office: Quiring Assocs Inc 7321 Shadeland Sta # 150 Indianapolis IN 46256

QUIRMBACH, HERMAN CHARLES, economics educator; b. St. Paul, Minn., Oct. 6, 1950; s. William Herman and Elizabeth Lou (Ziegler) Q. AB in Govt. cum laude, Harvard U., 1972; AM in Econs., Princeton U., 1980, PhD in Econs., 1983. Assoc. economist, cons. Rand Corp., Santa Monica, Calif., 1981—; assoc. prof. econs. Iowa State U., Ames, 1990—. Contbr. articles to profl. jours. Treas. Story County Dem. Party, Ames, 1992-94; councilman 4th ward Ames City Coun., 1995—; mem. bd. dirs. Iowa Civil Liberties Union, 1996—. Mem. AAUP, ACLU, Am. Econ. Assn., Econometric Soc., Ames C. of C. Office: Iowa State Univ Econs Dept Heady Hall Ames IA 50011

QUIROZ, PETER B., marketing executive; b. Quito, Equador, July 24, 1950; came to the U.S., 1953; BS in Psychology, U. Mich., 1977. V.p. mktg. Preferred Labs., Auburn Hills, Mich., 1980-93; pres. MedCon Corp., Ann Arbor, 1994—; mktg. cons. Midwest Diagnostic Imaging, Waterford, Mich., 1994—. Co-author: Clinical Laboratory Improvement Amendments, 1993. Pres. Interfaith Hospitality Network, Ann Arbor, 1994—; bd. dirs. Westminster Presbyn. Ch., Ann Arbor, 1990-93. Office: Med Con Corp 5340 Plymouth Rd Ann Arbor MI 48105-9341

QUIST, GORDON JAY, federal judge; b. Grand Rapids, Mich., Nov. 12, 1937; s. George J. and Ida F. (Hoekstra) Q.; m. Jane Capito, Mar. 10, 1962; children: Scot D., George J., Susan E., Martha J., Peter K. BA, Mich. State U., 1959; JD with honors, George Washington U., 1962. Bar: D.C. 1962, Ill. 1964, U.S. Dist. Ct. (no. dist.) Ill. 1964, U.S. Supreme Ct. 1965, Mich. 1967, U.S. Dist. Ct. (we. dist.) Mich. 1967, U.S. Ct. Appeals (6th cir.) 1967. Assoc. Hollabaugh & Jacobs, Washington, 1962-64, Sonnenschein, Carlin, Nath & Rosenthal, Chgo., 1964-66; assoc. Miller, Johnson, Snell & Cummiskey, Grand Rapids, 1967-72, ptnr., 1972-92, mng. ptnr., 1986-92; judge U.S. Dist. Ct. (we. dist.) Mich., Grand Rapids, 1992—. Bd. dirs. Wedgewood Acres-Ch. Youth Home, 1968-74, Mary Free Bed Hosp., 1979-88, Christian Ref. Publs., 1968-78, 82-88, Opera Grand Rapids, 1986-92, Mary Free Bed Brace Shop, 1988-92, Better Bus. Bur., 1972-80, Calvin Theol. Sem., 1992-93; bd. dirs. Indian Trails Camp, 1970-78, 82-88, pres., 1978, 88. Mem. Am. Indicature Soc., Mich. State Bar Assn., Univ. Club Grand Rapids, Order of Coif. Office: 482 Ford Fed Courthouse 110 Michigan St NW Grand Rapids MI 49503-2313

QURESHI, SHAMIM, psychiatrist; b. Hyderabad, India, Oct. 30, 1942; came to U.S., 1978; s. Mohadded and Iqbal Q.; m. Feb. 12, 1972 (div. Apr. 1988; 1 child, Abrar Qureshi. Pre-medicine, Saifabad Coll., Hyberbad, India, 1959-62; MD, Gandhi Med. Coll., Hyberbad, India, 1962-67. Med. officer Illante Kunta-Husnabad, India, 1969-71, Family Planning Bur., India, 1971-73; sr. house officer High Royds Hosp., Yorkshire, U.K., 1974-75; registrar psychiatry Hellesdon Hosp., Norfolk, U.K., 1975-76; clin. asst. Stone House Hosp., Kent, U.K., 1976-77; registrar psychiatry Hellingly Hosp., Eng., 1977-78; resident psychiatry Loyola U., Maywood, Ill., 1978-82; psychiatrist Hinsdale (Ill.) Hosp. and Good Sam, 1983-92; pvt. practice Willowbrook, Ill., 1983-92; faculty mem. Layola U., Maywood, Ill., 1992—. Gov. Ameer Khusno Soc., mem. Am. Profl. Mgmt. Assn. Mem. Greater Centralia C. of C. Office: 1050 M L King Dr Ste 110 Centralia IL 62801-3060

RAASH, KATHLEEN FORECKI, artist; b. Milw., Sept. 12, 1950; d. Harry and Marion Matilda (Schwabe) Forecki; m. Gary John Raash, June 13, 1987. BS, U. Wis., Eau Claire, 1972; MFA, U. Wis., Milw., 1978. One-, two- and three-person shows include Sight 225 Gallery, Milw., 1979, 81, Nicolet Coll., Phinelander, Wis., 1981, Messing Gallery, St. Louis, 1982, Arts Consortium, Cin., 1982, Ctr. Gallery, Madiwon, Wis., 1982, Otteson Theatre Gallery, Waukesha, Wis., 1982, Foster Gallery, Eau Claire, 1984, Duluth (Minn.) Art Inst., 1984, West Bend (Wis.) Gallery of Fine Arts, 1987, U. Wis.-Waukesha Fine Arts Gallery, 1988, Marion Art Gallery, Milw., 1990, Layton Honor Gallery, Milw., 1991, West Bend Art Mus., 1995, Gwenda Jay Gallery, Chgo., 1995, Wis. Acad., Madison, 1996; exhibited in group shows at River Edge Galleries, Wis., 1990, 91, 94, 95, Peltz Gallery, Milw., 1990, 91, 92, 93, 94, 95, Minnetonka Ctr. Arts, Wazata, Minn., 1996; represented in permanent collections United Bank and trust of Madison, Fine Arts Gallery U. Wis., Miller Brewing Co., Independence Bank Waukesha, U. Wis. Home and Studio: W 1630 Bear Trail Rd Gleason WI 54435

RABB, GEORGE BERNARD, zoologist; b. Charleston, S.C., Jan. 2, 1930; s. Joseph and Teresa C. (Redmond) R.; m. Mary Sughrue, June 10, 1953. BS, Coll. Charleston, 1951, LHD (hon.), 1995; MA, U. Mich., 1952, PhD, 1957. Teaching fellow zoology U. Mich., 1954-56; curator, coord. rsch. Chgo. Zool. Park, Brookfield., Ill., 1956-64; assoc. dir. rsch. and edn. Chgo. Zool. Park, 1964-75, dep. dir., 1969-75, dir., 1976—; rsch. assoc. Field Mus. Natural History, 1965—; lectr. dept. biology U. Chgo., 1965-89; mem. Com. on Evolution Biology, 1969—; pres. Chgo. Zool. Soc., 1976—; mem. steering com. Species Survival Commn., Internat. Union Conservation of Nature, 1983—, vice chmn. for N.Am., 1986-88, dep. chmn., 1987-89, chmn., 1989—; chmn. policy adv. group Internat. Species Info. System, 1974-89, chmn. bd., 1989-92; mem. bd. dirs. Ill. State Mus., 1994—. Fellow AAAS; mem. Am. Soc. Ichthyologists and Herpetologists (pres. 1978), Herpetologists League, Soc. Systematic Zoology, Soc. Mammalogists, Soc. Study Evolution, Ecol. Soc. Am., Soc. Conservation Biology (council mem. 1986), Am. Soc. Zoologists, Soc. Study Animal Behavior, Am. Assn. Museums, Am. Soc. Naturalists, Am. Assn. Zool. Parks and Aquariums (dir. 1979-80), Internat. Union Dirs. Zool. Gardens, Am. Com. Internat. Conservation (chmn. 1987—), Chgo. Coun. Fgn. Relations (Chgo. com.), Sigma Xi. Club: Economic (Chgo.), Tavern. Office: Brookfield Zoo 3300 Golf Rd Brookfield IL 60513-1060

RABIG, ANTHONY JOHN, librarian; b. Chgo., Nov. 8, 1949; s. John H. and Margaret (McNamara) R.; m. Carol Ann Powers, Mar. 17, 1972; children: Stephanie A., Devin J. BA, Blackburn Coll., 1971; MLS, Emporia Kans. State Coll., 1975. Libr. asst. Bridgeview (Ill.) Pub. Libr., 1971-73, libr. adult svcs., 1974-76; bookseller Kroch's & Brentano's, Chgo., 1976-85; programmer Labette C.C., Parsons, Kans., 1985-91, libr., 1991—. Office: Labette Cmty Coll 200 S 14th St Parsons KS 67357

RABIN, JOSEPH HARRY, marketing research company executive; b. Chgo., Dec. 12, 1927; s. Morris and Libby (Broder) Rabinovitz; m. Barbara E. Leader, Oct. 31, 1954; children: Marc Jay, Michelle Ann, Deborah Susan. BSc, Roosevelt U., 1950; MBA, DePaul U., 1951. Account exec. Gould, Gleiss & Benn, 1951-56; asst. dir. mktg. rsch. Paper Mate Co., Chgo., 1956-63; pres. Rabin Rsch. Co., Chgo., 1963—. Pres. Mather H.S. Coun., 1972-74; mem. adv. coun. U. Toledo, 1976-77, Kellstadt Ctr. DePaul U., 1986-93; mem. adv. com. Bur. of the Census, 1978-83; bd. dirs. Market Rsch. Inst., 1973-75, Ner Tamid Synagogue, 1976—, Jewish Vocat. Svc., 1977-80. With AUS, 1946-47. Mem. Am. Mktg. Assn. (pres. Chgo. chpt. 1961-62, nat. dir. 1973-75, nat. v.p. mktg. rsch. 1978-79, nat. pres. 1981-82), Assn. Consumer Rsch., Am. Statis. Assn. (pres. Chgo. chpt. 1962-63), Am. Assn. Pub. Opinion Rsch. Home: 7061 N Kedzie Ave Chicago IL 60645-2846 Office: Rabin Rsch Co 150 E Huron St Chicago IL 60611-2912

RACHOW, SHARON DIANNE, realtor; b. St. Joseph, Mo., Apr. 12, 1939; d. Norman DeLos Zancker and Sylvia Lavina (Hawkins) Trouel; m. Thomas Eugene Rachow, Oct. 22, 1968. Student, So. Ill. U., 1969-72. Cert. residential specialist, Grad. Realtor Inst. Sec. Westab, Inc. (now Mead), St. Joseph, 1957-60, Seitz Packing Co., St. Joseph, 1960-66; exec. asst. Kansas City (Mo.) Chiefs, 1972; co-owner, mgr. Pool 'N Patio Plus, St. Joseph, 1973-84; realtor Coldwell Banker Gen. Realtors, St. Joseph, 1984-93, RE/MAX, 1993—. Trustee Nat. Multiple Sclerosis Soc., Mid Am. chpt., Midland M.S. Express Br., 1993-96. Mem. St. Joseph Regional Bd. Realtors (polit. action com. task force, membership com. 1985-86, pub. rels. and events task force, resdl. sales coun. 1987, Top Residential Sales award 1986, MLS com., vice chmn. forms com., new svcs. task force com. 1993, chmn. MLS com. 1994), Million Dollar Club (life), Re/Max 100% Club (referrral and relocations cert.), St. Joseph Regional Bd. Realtors-Chmn.'s Club, Real Estate Buyer's Agt. Coun. Republican. Lutheran. Home: 4211 Country Ln Saint Joseph MO 64506-2454 Office: RE/MAX of St Joseph Inc 1119 N Woodbine Rd Saint Joseph MO 64506-2434

RACINE, MARK ALLEN, insurance claims representative; b. Ft. Wayne, Ind., Feb. 11, 1951; s. Raymond Edward and Theresa (Rathgeber) R.; m. Elizabeth Kay Schaefer, Feb. 28, 1981; 1 child, Adam Drew. Student, Ind. State U., 1969-70. Assoc. in claims. Claims adjuster M.M. Johnson Claims, Ft. Wayne, 1974-84, Home Mut. Ins. Co., Ft. Wayne, 1984-85; sr. claims rep. Cin. Ins. Co., Ft. Wayne, 1985—; instr. Cin. Ins. Co., 1990—. Author: Insurance Settlement Handbook, 1992. Mem. Ft. Wayne Adjusters Assn. (pres. 1987-88, Adjuster of Yr. 1990). Roman Catholic. Office: Cin Ins Co PO Box 5742 Fort Wayne IN 46895

RACZKOWSKI, WALDEMAR TADEUSZ, medical research biochemist, analyst, consultant; b. Detroit, Aug. 10, 1964; s. Bogdan Mieczyslaw and Zenona Jozefa (Stojek) R.; m. Annette T. Szczepanik, June 27, 1992. Cert., Marie Curie Fgn. Lang. Sch., 1982; BS in Chemistry, Wayne State U., 1986. Rsch. asst. Wayne State U. Radiation Oncolocy Ctr., Detroit, 1983-86; rsch. assoc. and lab. mgr. C.S. Mott Ctr., Hutzel Hosp., Detroit, 1986—; cons. Subway Film Ptnrs., L.A., 1987—. Contbr. articles to med. jours. Mem. Am. Heart Assn., Polish Nat. Alliance, Cog., 1972—; leader Polish Scouting Orgn., Detroit, 1972—; treas. Polish 2d Army Corps Found., Orchard Lake, Mich., 1986-95; nat. bd. dirs. Polish-Am. Congress, Chgo., 1990—. Recipient Outstanding Young Ethnic award Polish 2d Army Corps Found., 1991; rsch. fellow Sinai Hosp. Detroit, 1985, Wayne State U. Sch. Medicine, 1986. Mem. AAAS, Am. Assn. Individual Investors, N.Y. Acad. Scis. Republican. Home: 28619 Herndonwood Dr Farmington Hills MI 48334-5234

RADCLIFFE, GERALD EUGENE, judge, lawyer; b. Chillicothe, Ohio, Feb. 19, 1923; s. Maurice Gerald and Mary Ellen (Wills) R.; children: Jerilynn K. Radcliffe Ross, Pamela J. Radcliffe Dunn. BA, Ohio U., 1948; JD, U. Cin., 1950. Bar: Ohio 1950, U.S. Dist. Ct. 1951, U.S. Supreme Ct. 1957. Sole practice, Chillicothe, 1950-66; asst. pros. atty. Ross County, Ohio, 1966-70; acting mcpl. judge Chillicothe Mcpl. Ct., 1970-72; judge probate, juvenile divs. Ross County Ct., Chillicothe, 1973—; mem. rules adv. com. Ohio Supreme Ct., 1984; mem. Ohio Legis. Oversite com., 1974-81; trustee Ohio Jud. Coll., 1980-87. Editor Cin. Law Rev., 1949-50. Co-author: Constitutional Law, 1979. Contbr. articles to profl. jours. Project dir. South Central Ohio Regional Juvenile Detention Ctr., 1971-72; co-founder, developer Roweton Family Complex; co-chmn. Chillicothe United Way Fund Campaign, 1972; mem., chmn. Adv. Coun. of Gov. Dept. Youth Svcs., 1983-89; mem. N.W. Ordinance and U.S. Constn. Bicentennial Com., 1993-96. Recipient Superior Jud. award Ohio Supreme Ct., 1976-82, Meritorious Service award Probate Ct. Judges Ohio, 1984-89, Commendation 118th Ohio Senate, 1990, Gov's. Spl. Recognition Svc. and Leadership to Youth Svcs. Adv. Coun., 1990, Nat. Commendation Ohio Conf. Nat. Assn. Blacks in Criminal Justice; Dirs. award Ohio Dept. Youth Svcs., 1984, Silver Helmet award for Americanism Nat. Amvets, 1992; named Outstanding Citizen Chillicothe Edn. Assn., 1987, Outstanding Citizen of Yr. Jr. C. of C., 1972. Mem. Ohio Juvenile Judges Assn., (pres. 1983-84), Nat. Coun. Juvenile and Family Ct. Judges (trustee 1982-84, 93-95, chmn. govtl. rels. com., recipient Meritorious Svc. award 1988), Nat. Ctr. Juvenile Justice (bd. fellows 1995—), Ohio Jud. Conf., Ohio State Bar Assn. Democrat. Lodges: Kiwanis (lt. gov. 1983-84, Ohio Statehood Achievement award 1979), Ohio State Bar Assn., Masons. Avocation: golf. Office: Common Pleas Ct Probate Div Ross County Courthouse Chillicothe OH 45601

RADCLIFFE, JEFFERY ELLIS, insurance agent; b. Normal, Ill., June 1, 1955; s. Paul Eugene and Phyllis (Trower) R.; m. Hilda Miller, Dec. 29, 1975; children:Abigail, Margaret, Elizabeth. BA, Ill. Coll., Jacksonville, 1977. Budget analyst Ill. State Senate, Springfield, 1977-85; bus. adminstr. Ill. Sch. for the Deaf., Jacksonville, 1985-93; ins. agt. Northwestern Mut. Life, Jacksonville, 1993—. Councilman City of Jacksonville, 1983-85; pres. Jacksonville Hist. Preservation Commn., 1983-91; bd. dirs. United Way, 1985-87, Alvin Eades Ctr., 1991—, sec.; vestryman, treas. Trinity Episc. Ch., Jacksonville, 1986—; mem. Morgan County Hist. Soc. Mem. Nat. Assn. Life Underwriters, Jacksonville Lit. Union (sec. 1991—). Republican. Home: 1302 W State Jacksonville IL 62650

RADDATZ, JOHN D., manufacturing executive; b. Alexandria, Va., Aug. 26, 1943. BS, Western Mich. U., 1966; MS, Ctrl. Mich. U., 1971. V.p. Tri City Tool & Die Co., Bay City, Mich., 1973-79; pres. Tri City Tool & Die Co., Bay City, 1979—. Lt. col. U.S. Army, 1967-70. Office: Tri City Tool & Die Co 3515 N Euclid Ave Bay City MI 48706-2042

RADEL, WILLIAM HAROLD, design engineer; b. Marion, Ohio, Dec. 9, 1932; s. William Carl and Ethel G. (Firtch) R. AS in Mech. Engring. summa cum laude, Marion Tech. Coll., 1981. Design engr. Komatsu Am. Internat. Co. (formerly Komatsu Dresser Co.), Galion, Ohio, 1965—. Republican. Baptist. Home: 870 Belleflower Pl Galion OH 44833-2358 Office: Komatsu Am Internat Co 850 South St Galion OH 44833-3363

RADELL, KAREN MARGUERITE, educator; b. Binghamton, N.Y., Feb. 1, 1949; d. Daniel and Marguerite Anne (Murray) R. BA, Binghamton U., 1971, MA, 1980; PhD, Kent State U., 1985. Instr. English Kent State U., Kent, Ohio, 1985-87; asst. prof. English Ctrl. Mich. U., Mt. Pleasant, Mich., 1987-92; assoc. prof. English Ctrl. Mich. U., Mt. Pleasant, 1992—. Author: Affirmation in a Moral Wasteland: A Comparison of Ford Madox Ford & Graham Greene, 1987; co-author: Season of the Eel, 1996; contbr. articles to profl. jours; author, poem (finalist 1995 poetry competition). Portraiture grantee Nat. Endowment for the Humanities, Harvard U. 1990. Mem. Soc. for Study of Narrative Literature, Joseph Conrad Soc., Soc. for Inter-Disciplinary Study of the Arts, Assn. Lit. Scholars & Critics. Democrat. Roman Catholic. Home: 1030 1/2 S Fancher St Mount Pleasant MI 48858 Office: Ctrl Mich Univ English Dept Washington St Mount Pleasant MI 48859

RADEMACHER, GARY EDWARD, secondary school educator; b. Washington, Mo., Jan. 17, 1954; s. Henry Ralph and Gloria Ann (Hellweg) R.; m. Janna Rae Hall, Nov. 23, 1985; children: Jared Hall, Andrew James. BS in Edn., S.W. Mo. State U., 1977, MS in Edn., 1980, EdS, 1984; EdD, Vanderbilt U., 1996. Dept. chair Springfield (Mo.) Pub. Schs., 1995. Maj. USAR, 1977-95. Mem. ASCD, Nat. Coun. for Social Studies, Springfield Edn. Assn. (pres. 1991-93), Mo. Tchrs. Assn. Home: 1006 E Linwood Dr Springfield MO 65807-1850

RADEMACHER, RICHARD JOSEPH, librarian; b. Kaukauna, Wis., Aug. 20, 1937; s. Joseph Benjamin and Anna (Wyuts) R.; m. Mary Jane Liethen, Feb. 12, 1966; children: Alicia Mary, Ann Marie, Amy Rose. A.B., Ripon Coll., 1959; M.S., Library Sch. U. Wis., 1961. Dir. Kaukauna Public Library, 1964-66, Eau Claire (Wis.) Public Library, 1966-69; librarian Salt Lake City Public Library, 1969-76; dir. Wichita (Kans.) Public Library, 1976—. Bd. dirs. Salt Lake Art Center, Reading Room for the Blind.; mem. Kans. Com. for the Humanities, 1977-82; mem. exec. bd. Wichita Girl Scouts, 1977—. Served with AUS, 1962-64. Mem. ALA; Mem. Mountain Plains Library Assn. (sect. chmn.); mem. Kans. Library Assn. (pres. 1982-83); Mem. Wichita Library Assn. Office: Wichita Pub Libr 223 S Main St Wichita KS 67202-3715

RADEN, LOUIS, tape and label corporation executive; b. Detroit, June 17, 1929; s. Harry M. and Joan (Morris) R.; m. Mary K. Knowlton, June 18, 1949; children: Louis III, Pamela (Mrs. T.W. Rea III), Jacqueline. BA, Trinity Coll., 1951; postgrad. NYU, 1952. With Time, Inc., 1951-52; with Quaker Chem. Corp., 1952-63, sales mgr., 1957-63; exec. v.p. Gen. Tape & Supply, Inc., Detroit, 1963-68, pres., chmn. bd., 1969—; pres. Mich. Gun Clubs, 1973-77. Fifth reunion chmn. Trinity Coll., 1956, pres. Mich. alumni, 1965-72, sec. Class of 1951, 81-86, pres. 1986-91, The McCook Fellow Soc.; trustee, v.p. Mich. Diocese Episcopal Ch., 1980-82, mem. urban evaluation com., 1975-78, chmn. urban evaluation com., 1978, chmn. urban affairs com., 1977-79; vice chmn., bd. dirs. Robert H. Whitaker Sch. Theology, 1983-85; vice chmn. Mich. Diocese Econ. Justice Commn., 1989—, bd. dirs. Poverty and Social Reform Inst., 1992—; founding sponsor World Golf Hall of Fame; mem. Founders Soc. Detroit Inst. Arts; trustee Mich. Housing Trust Fund, 1993—; soccer coach Detroit County Day Sch., 1975-78. Recipient Person of Yr. award Mich. Diocese Econ. Justice Commn., 1994; inductee Hall of Fame Robert H. Whitaker Sch. Theology, 1996. Mem. NRA (life), Nat. Skeet Shooting Assn. (life, nat. dir. 1977-79, 5 Man Team World Champion award 1977, pres. coun.), Mich. Skeet Assn. (all state team 1975-80, inductee Hall of Fame 1994), Greater Detroit Bd. Commerce, Automotive Industry Action Group, Mich. C. of C., U.S. C. of C., Greater Hartford Jaycees (exec. v.p. 1955-57, Key Man award 1957), Theta Xi (life, Disting. Service award 1957, alumni pres. 1952-57, regional dir. 1954-57). Republican. Clubs: Detroit Golf, Detroit Gun (bd. dirs., 1996—), Katke-Cousins Golf, Midland Country, Black Hawk Indians, Pinehurst Country; Oakland U. Pres.'s, Round Table, Detroit Sportsmen's Congress. Home: 1133 Ivyglen Cir Bloomfield Hills MI 48304-1236 Office: Gen Tape & Supply Inc 7451 W 8 Mile Rd Detroit MI 48221-1262

RADER, CHARLES PHILLIP, chemist; b. Greeneville, Tenn., Apr. 9, 1935; s. Fred Henry and Mary (Lowe) R.; m. Clarita Anne Morgan, June 6, 1958; children: Clarita Marie, Charles Andrew. BS in Chemistry, U. Tenn., 1957, MS in Chemistry, 1960, PhD in Chemistry, 1961. Sr. rsch. chemist Monsanto Co., St. Louis, 1961-65, rsch. specialist, 1966-69; rsch. group leader Monsanto Co., Akron, Ohio, 1969-74; sr. rsch. group leader Monsanto Indl. Chem. Co., Akron, 1975-82; sr. mktg. tech. svc. specialist Monsanto Chem. Co., Akron, 1983-87, mktg. tech. svc. prin., 1988-90; mktg. tech. svc. prin. Advanced Elastomer Systems, L.P., Akron, 1991—. Editor: Handbook of Thermoplastic Elastomers, 1988, Plastics, Rubber and Paper Recycling: A Pragmatic Approach, 1995; assoc. editor: Rubber Chemistry and Tech., 1978—; contbr. over 175 papers, articles to profl. publs. Chmn. spl. study group Copley-Fairlawn Sch. System, Akron, 1981; elder, clk. of session local Presbyn. Ch. 1st lt. U.S. Army, 1961-63. Recipient Disting. award of Coun., Akron Coun. Engring. and Sci. Socs., 1984. Mem. ASTM, Am. Chem. Soc. (chmn. Akron sect. 1975, councilor 1976—, chmn. rubber divsn. 1986, Disting. Svc. award 1981), Soc. Plastic Engrs., Soc. Automotive Engrs., N.Y. Acad. Scis. Home: 2457 Greenhaven Dr Akron OH 44333-2753 Office: Advanced Elastomer Systems 388 S Main St Akron OH 44311-1058

RADKE, DALE LEE, religious organization administrator, deacon, editor, pastor; b. Sheboygan, Wis., July 9, 1933; s. Alfred and Viola (Aschenbach) R.; m. Diane Jean Simon, Aug. 16, 1958; children: Laura Lee, Jay Ryan. AA, Concordia Wis., 1954. Store mgr. Badger Paint Stores, Milw., 1958-65; with sales dept. Hilton Co., Butler, 1965-67; with sales and customer service depts. Century Hardware, Milw., 1967-72; exec. dir. Greater Milw. Fedn. Luth. Chs. Mo. Synod, Milw., 1973-87, 90-92; exec. dir. Luth. of Wis., Milw., 1982-89; Wis. affiliate Am. Heart Assn., Milw., 1989; editor Badger Luth. newspaper, Milw., 1990-92; pastor Savior Luth. Ch.-AFLC; CEO Creative Concepts Comm. and Servant of the Savior; voice of God-Love Prayer Telephone, 1973—. Editor The Milw. Luth., 1982-89, South Wis. Dist. News, 1992-93; contbr. articles to clown mags. Pastor Lith. Free Ch.; chaplain Milw. Fire Dept.; mem. Milw. Citizenship Commn., 1960-63; mem. religious leaders divsn. Nat. Safety Coun., Chgo., 1980-91, bd. dirs., 1987-89; mem. Milw. Safety Commn., 1970—, chair., 1983-89; chair Park Watch; mem., comty. svc. dir. Nat. Safety Coun., 1990—; pres. Capital W. Neighborhood Assn. Mem. Milw. Advt. Club, Milw. Press Club, Milw. Jaycees (Outstanding Young Man of Yr. 1962), Variety Club, Kiwanis, various clown orgns. Lutheran. Home: 6410 W Melvina St Milwaukee WI 53216-2129 Office: PO Box 18024 Milwaukee WI 53218-0024

RADKE, LINDA KAYE, foreign language educator; b. Beloit, Wash., Sept. 1, 1961; d. Edwin J. and Vera Rose (Ghormley) Harper; m. Carl R. Radke, May 28, 1983; 1 child, Keith M. Radke. BA in Spanish and Child Devel., Rockford (Ill.) Coll., 1983; MA in Edn. and Spanish, U. Wis., Madison, 1989. Elem. tchr. Kinnikinnick Schs., Roscoe, Ill., 1985-88; tchr. Spanish Hononegah H.S., Rockton, Ill., 1988—. Mem. sch. bd. Kinnikinnick Schs., Roscoe, 1989—. Recipient Quest For Excellence grantee Ecolab, Roscoe, 1993, 96, Fulbright Tchr. Exchange award Fulbright Commn., Santiago, Chile, 1994-95. Mem. VFW (post 9555, chair youth activities), Bruce Samlan Soccer League (bd. sec. 1995—), Phi Beta Kappa. Office: Hononegah HS 307 Salem Roscoe IL 61073

RADMER, MICHAEL JOHN, lawyer, educator; b. Wisconsin Rapids, Wis., Apr. 28, 1945; s. Donald Richard and Thelma Loretta (Donahue) R.; children from previous marriage: Christina Nicole, Ryan Michael; m. Laurie J. Anshus, Dec. 22, 1983; 1 child, Michael John. B.S., Northwestern U., Evanston, Ill., 1967; J.D., Harvard U., 1970. Bar: Minn. 1970. Assoc. Dorsey & Whitney, Mpls., 1970-75, ptnr., 1976—; lectr. law Hamline U. Law Sch., St. Paul, 1981-84; gen. counsel, rep., sec. 150 federally registered investment cos., Mpls. and St. Paul, 1977—. Contbr. articles to legal jours. Active legal work Hennepin County Legal Advice Clinic, Mpls., 1971—. Mem. ABA, Minn. Bar Assn., Hennepin County Bar Assn. Club: Mpls. Athletic. Home: 4329 E Lake Harriet Pky Minneapolis MN 55409-1725 Office: Dorsey & Whitney Pillsbury Ctr S 220 S 6th St Minneapolis MN 55402-4502

RADWICK, MELISSA JANE, elementary counselor; b. Memphis, Nov. 26, 1954; d. Nelson Arthur and Mary Jane (Loss) Haas; m. Douglas Martin, Oct. 23, 1976; children: Nathan, Eric. BA in Elem. Edn., Mich. State U., 1975; MA in Health Edn., U. Mich., 1981; counseling endorsement, Ctrl. Mich. U. 6th grade tchr. North Branch (Mich.) Schs., 1976-93, elem. counselor, 1993—; student asst. coord. North Br. Schs., 1991-93, Ruth Fox. Mid. Sch., 1996, coord. parent class, 1991—, chmn. cmty. teen, 1993—; county schs. rep. Continuum Care Com., Lapeer, Mich., 1992-93. Active Lapeer County Strong Family/ Safe Children com., 1996—. Grantee Genesee Intermediate Dist., 1991, 93—. Mem. AAUW, PEO. Republican. Lutheran. Home: 8635 Gera Rd Birch Run MI 48415-9717

RAE, JUDITH, individual, couple and family therapist; b. Cin., July 24, 1946; d. Jess Palfrey Giles and Betty Jane (Zastrow) Kenyon; widowed; children: Robert David Rogers, Michael David Rogers; m. Earl W. Hoppert, Nov. 12, 1994. BA, Emory U., 1967; MS, Butler U., 1976, MA, 1986. Cert. marriage and family therapist, clin. social worker, Ind.; cert. Rational Recovery Sys. Tchr. social studies Franklin Ctrl. H.S., Acton, Ind., 1968; cataloger, subs. libr. Carmel (Ind.) Clay Schs., 1975-76; supr. resource ctr. Grad. Sch. Sao Paulo, Brazil, 1977-78; libr., counselor Clark Jr. Coll. Bus., Indpls., 1978-89; pvt. practice individual, couple and family therapy, Indpls., 1989—; clin. assoc. Marion County Crisis and Suicide Intervention, Indpls., 1980-82; trainer crisis and suicide intervention Marion county Mental Health Assn., Indpls., 1981-83, mem. spkrs. bur., 1993—; profl. advisor Rational Recovery Self-Help Network, 1991-95. Contbr. author: Rational Recovery Self-Help Network, 1992, 101 Interventions in Family Therapy, 1993; contbr. articles to profl. jours. Commentator local Nat. Pub. Radio sta., Indpls., 1983-87. Recipient non-fiction and juvenile award Ill. Wesleyan U. Writers Conf., 1979. Mem. Am. Assn. for Marriage and Family Therapy (clin.), Ind. Assn. for Marriage and Family Therapy (clin., sec. 1992-95), Nat. League Am. Pen Women, Mensa (columnist Mind newsletter Indpls. 1984—), Pi Sigma Alpha, Kappa Delta Epsilon, Kappa Delta Pi. Office: 819 E 64th St Ste D-4 Indianapolis IN 46220

RAETH, PETER GEORGE, computer engineer, research scientist, consultant; b. Jackson, Mich., July 10, 1951; s. Nicholas Conrad and Theresa Elizabeth (Roehm) R.; m. Marilyn Laverne Schumann, Jan. 8, 1983; 1 child, Daniel Nicholas. AS in Elec. Engring. Tech., Trident Tech. Coll., 1975; BSEE, U. S.C., 1979; MS in Computer Engring., Air Force Inst. Tech., 1980; cert. in Info. Systems, U. So. Calif., 1984. Cons. software applications Columbia, S.C., 1973-79; computer performance analyst Fed. Computer Performance Ctr., Alexandria, Va., 1980-83; info. systems project officer Headquarters Air Force Systems Command, Laurel, Md., 1983-85; chief tech. support branch 3246th Test Wing, Fort Walton Beach, Fla., 1985-88; artificial intelligence program mgr. USAF Wright Lab., Dayton, Ohio, 1988-92; ind. rsch. and devel., dep. mgr. Hdqs. Air Force Material Command, Dayton, 1992; chief, pilot/vehicle integration USAF Wright Lab., Dayton, 1992—. Editor, author: Expert Systems: A Software Methodology for Modern Applications, 1990; author: Trade Journal Index, 1989; mem. peer review staff IEEE Computer mag., 1989-93, Acad. Press, 1992—, Neural Ware, Inc., 1989-93. Lector St. Luke Parish, Beavercreek, Ohio, 1988—, Sun. sch. tchr., 1992-94; sci. fair judge Ohio Acad. Sci., Columbus, 1989—; choir mem., 1980-88. Major USAF, 1990—. Recipient Nat. Gold medal Armed Forces Comm. and Electronics Assn.; named one of Outstanding Young Men of Am., 1981, one of Top 20 Tech. Leaders in Dayton Ohio Region, Dayton Affiliate Socs. Coun., 1994, 95. Mem. IEEE (computer soc.), Dayton Spl. Interest Group in Artificial Intelligence, Tau Beta Pi, Omicron Delta Kappa, Eta Kappa Nu. Roman Catholic. Home: 2435 Flyway Ct Beavercreek OH 45431-4115 Office: USAF Wright Lab WL/FIGP-1 Wright Patterson AFB OH 45433-7511

RAETHER, EDWARD W., appraising company executive, valuation consultant; b. Lebanon, Wis., Feb. 22, 1936; s. Edward W. and Verena (Braunschweig) R.; m. Arlene J. Creydt, Dec. 27, 1957; children: Renee Ann, Scott Edward, Jay James. AS in Bus. Mgmt., Milw. Sch. Engring., 1968; BA in Valuation Scis., Lindenwood Coll., St. Charles, Mo., 1990. Various positions to plant supr. Automatic Welding Co., Waukesha, Wis., 1957-68; staff and sr. appraiser Am. Appraisal Assocs., Inc., Milw., 1968-73, asst. mgr. indsl. valuation group, 1973-78, mgr. indsl. valuation group, 1978-83, regional mgr. Cen. Nat. Practice Office, 1983-87, v.p. Nat. Practice Office, 1987-90; v.p. Am. Appraisal Assocs., Inc., Budapest, Hungary, 1990-91; v.p., dir. ops. cen. Europe Am. Appraisal Hungary Co. Ltd., Budapest, 1991—. Various offices St. Luke's Luth. Ch., Waukesha; bd. regents Milw. Sch. Engring., 1983—. With USN, 1956-57. Recipient Master Key of Success award Milw. Sch. Engring., 1988. Mem. Am. Soc. Appraisers (sr.), Nat. Assn. Real Estate Appraisers, Internat. Real Estate Inst. (sr. cert. valuer), Robotics Internat. Republican.

RAEUCHLE, JOHN STEVEN, computer analyst; b. Washington, Sept. 21, 1955; s. Richard Frank and Ruth Darlene (Fulton) R. BS, Tex. Christian, 1978. Programmer Tex. Christian U., Fort Worth, 1976-78, Warrex Computer Systems, Fort Worth, 1978-79; systems programmer Tandy Data Processing, Fort Worth, 1979-84; sr. programmer, analyst Commodity News Svcs., Leawood, Kans., 1984-86, Logica Data Architects, St. Louis, 1986-89; computer analyst Credit Systems, Inc., St. Louis, 1989-95; software engr. Master Card Internat., St. Louis, 1995—. Mem. St. Louis Ambassadors, 1989—; active Boy Scouts Am., 1964—. Recipient awrd of merit Boy Scouts Am., Commrs. Key, 1982. Mem. St. Louis Jaycees Found. (treas. 1990-94, sec. 1994-96, pres. 1996—), Mo. Jaycees (state officer 1989-94), Kansas City Jaycees (bd. dirs. 1985-87), Kansas City Jaycees Found., St. Louis Jr. C. of C. (pres. 1988-89). Democrat. Methodist. Home: 52 Country Creek Dr Saint Peters MO 63376-3041 Office: Master Card Internat 12115 Lackland Rd Saint Louis MO 63146

RAFFENSPERGER, HELEN ELIZABETH, writer; b. Marion, Ind., Apr. 21, 1904; d. Oliver Wilbert and Isabelle M. (Pulaski) Gould; widowed; 1 child, John. Student, Purdue U., 1922-24. Libr. asst. Marion Pub. Libr., 1924-26, Elkhart (Ind.) Libr., 1926-28; libr. Henry (Ill.) Pub. Libr., 1943-71; v.p. Henry Hist. and Geneal. Soc., 1990—; columnist Henry News Rep., 1935—. Author: Henry, Best Town in Illinois by a Dam Site, 1976; author, illustrator: Henry Homes in History, 1993; co-author Marshall County Census for 1860, 1870, 1880. Recipient Outstanding Svc. award Henry C. of C., 1931, 58; named Citizen of Yr., Rotary Club, 1987. Mem. Soc. Mayflower Descs., Ill. State Geneal. Soc., Purdue Alumni Assn. (life), Ill. State Hist. Soc., Presbyn. Women, Kappa Alpha Theta. Home: 1022 Green St Henry IL 61537

RAGER, KATHLEEN BYRNE, academic administrator; b. Port Chester, N.Y., Oct. 5, 1943; d. Lawrence Sylvester Jr. and Mary Josephine (Matthews) Byrne; m. James J. DeFilippo, July 16, 1966 (div.); children: Elizabeth Anne, Sharon Marie, Kristen Leigh; m. Ira S. Rager, July 2, 1994. BA in English, Coll. Mt. St. Vincent, 1965; MS in Edn., SUNY, New Paltz, 1976. Tchr., television instr. Wappingers Ctrl. Sch. Dist., Wappingers Falls, N.Y., 1965-68; owner, mgr. Silver Apple, Inc., Hopewell Junction, N.Y., 1980-83; freelance comm. cons., 1983-88; dir. corp. and profl. edn. Marist Coll., Poughkeepsie, N.Y., 1988-93; dir. Downtown Ctr. and contract tng. svcs. Wichita (Kans.) State U., 1993—; cons. leadership tng. edn. com. So. Dutchess C. of C., Wappingers Falls, 1988-93, Poughkeepsie C. of C., 1991-93. Sunday sch. tchr. Hopewell Reform Ch., 1974-85, youth adviser, 1985-88; bd. dirs. Poughkeepsie YWCA, 1992-93. Mem. N.Y. State Assn. Women in Higher Edn., Am. Coun. Edn., N.Y. Assn. Continuing Community Edn. Republican. Home: 818 Whippoorwill Rd Derby KS 67037 Office: Wichita State U Downtown Ctr 127 N Market Wichita KS 67202-1801

RAGHAVAN, SRIKANT, educator, operations management specialist; b. Nagercoil, Tamilnadu, India, Mar. 4, 1950; came to U.S., 1982; naturalized citizen, 1992; s. Vetangaraikavu Ramiyer and Lakshmi (Krishnaiyer) R.; m. Devika Krishnamurthi, July 12, 1978; children: Minnie, Preethi. BS in Physics, U. Madras, 1969; MS in Ops. Rsch., U. Delhi, India, 1971, Case Inst. Tech., 1972; PhD in Bus. Adminstrn., U. Houston, 1978. Cert. operational researcher. Instr. U. Houston, 1972-76; asst. prof. Tex. So. U., Houston, 1976-78, Ill. State U., Normal, 1978; assoc. cons. Tata Cons. Svcs., Bombay, 1979-82; sr. rsch. engr. Gen. Motor Rsch. Labs., Warren, Mich., 1982-86; asst. prof. quantitative methods and ops. mgmt. Lawrence Tech. U., Southfield, Mich., 1987-91, assoc. prof., 1991—; vis. prof. U. Detroit (Mich.), 1987. Co-author: Cost of Energy and a Clean Environment, 1978, Large Scale Energy Models, 1982, Master of Science in Engineering Management: An Innovative Approach, 1993. Life mem., pres. Tamil Sangam, Mich., 1994. Mem. Ops. Rsch. Soc. India (life, founder Greater Bombay chpt., sec. treas. 1981-82), Inst. of Ops. Rsch. and Mgmt. Sci. (founder Southeastern Mich. Joint chpt., sec. treas. 1985-87, nat. meetings com., 1994), Am. Prodn. & Inventory Control Soc., Sigma Xi. Office: Lawrence Tech U 21000 W 10 Mile Rd Southfield MI 48075-1051

RAGLAND, ANNA MAE, educator; b. Cin., Jan. 25, 1935; d. Jessie James and Maggie (Givens) Anderson; m. Marshall Ragland, Fev. 19, 1962 (div. Mar. 1980); children: Camilla Seenaught, Johnny Dale Young, Charles M., MAxanne M., Lateefah J. Grad. high sch., Cin. Soda founrain worker Frische's Big Boys, Cin., 1955-60; clk. Sears & Roebuck, Cin., 1960-70, Newberry Dept. Store, Cin., 1970-73; jewerly clk. Kinks Dept. Store, Cin., 1973-76; instr. asst. Bd. Edn., Cin., 1976-95. Author and illustrator: Bits & Pieces, 1989; author of poems. Fellow Givens Found. Methodist. Home: 33 Juergens Ave Cincinnati OH 45220

RAGLE, GEORGE ANN, accountant; b. Detroit, Dec. 21, 1946; d. Joseph Theodore and Josephine Theresa (Mastrogiovanni) Gibson; m. James Albert, Sept. 3, 1976; children: Gina Ann, Jeffrey Allen. Assoc. Bus., Oakland C.C., Farmington Hills, Mich., 1974; B Accountancy, Walsh Coll., Troy, Mich., 1975; MBA, Ctrl. Mich. U., 1981. Cert. sch. bus. adminstr., Mich. Tax analyst Burroughs Corp., Detroit, 1976, Robillard & Joyce, St. Clair Shores, Mich., 1977-78; acctg. mgr. Baker Driveaway, Bloomfield Hills, Mich., 1978-79; staff acct. Macomb County Contr., Mt. Clemens, Mich., 1979-80; sr. acct. Macomb Intermediate Sch. Dist., Mt. Clemens, 1980-86; dir. bus. Mt. Clemens Community Schs., 1986-88, Pinconning (Mich.) Area Sch., 1988-90; dir. bus. and pers. St. Clair Intermediate Sch. Dist., Port Huron, Mich., 1990—. Bd. officer, treas. Fraser (Mich.) Pub. Schs. Bd. Edn., 1984-88; mem. Anchor Bay Schs. Bd. Edn., New Baltimore, Mich., 1991-95, treas., 1991-92, 94-95. Mem. Assn. Sch. Bus. Ofcls., Mich. Sch. Bus. Ofcls., Mich. Assn. Sch. Pers. Adminstrs., Macomb/St. Clair Sch. Bus. Ofcls. Home: 52134 Charleston Ln New Baltimore MI 48047-1191 Office: St Clair Intermediate Sch Dist 499 Range Rd Port Huron MI 48061

RAGSDALE, REX H., health facility administrator, physician; b. Henderson, Ky., July 31, 1957; s. Carl Wilkes and Sue Ann (Hart) R.; m. Sally E.; children: Leslie D'Anne, Kellen Edward. BSBA, U. Evansville, 1978; MD, St. Louis U., 1982. Diplomate Am. Bd. Family Practice. Resident St. Mary's Med. Ctr., Evansville, Ind., 1982-85; pvt. practice Newburgh, Ind., 1985-89; v.p. med. affairs Deaconess Hosp., Evansville, 1989—; bd. dirs. Ohio Valley Hospice, Evansville, 1990—, Impact Ministries Healthcare Ctr., Evansville, 1991—; mem. VHA Nat. Physician Leadership Coun., 1993—. Pres. 1st Dist. Med. Soc., Evansville, 1993-94; state del. Ind. State Med. Assn., Indpls., 1992—; med. advisor United Parents Support for Downs Syndrome, Newburgh, 1990, 91, 92; med. dir. Arts coun. Fun Run, Evansville, 1988. Mem. AMA, Am. Coll. Physician Execs., Am. Acad. Family Practice, Aircraft Owners and Pilots Assn., Phi Mu Alpha. Office: Deaconess Hosp Inc 600 Mary St Evansville IN 47747-0002

RAHMAN, AHMED ASSEM, principal engineer, staff stress analyst; b. Cairo, May 26, 1940; came to U.S., 1967; s. Abdel Fathalla and Wagida (Shorbagy) R.; m. Zinab Mostafa, Oct. 5, 1975 (div. Jan. 1980); 1 child, Mona. B of Aeronautical Engring., U. Cairo, 1962; M of Aerospace Engring., U. Toronto, 1971, PhD, 1976. Registered profl. engr., Mich. Aerodynamicist, aeroelectrician Egyptian Aero-Orgn., Cairo, 1962-67; liaison engr. Douglas Aircraft Can., Ltd., Malton, Ont., 1967-71; prof. mech. engring. Oakland U., Rochester, Mich., 1977-79, U. Mich., Dearborn, 1979-81; prin. engr., stress analyst AM Gen. divsn. LTV Corp., Livonia, Mich., 1981—. Contbr. articles on heat transfer and energy conversions to profl. jours.; invented modification of rotary engine at Oakland U., 1977. NSF fellow, 1974-75. Mem. ASME, IEEE, Am. Soc. for Metals, Soc. Automotive Engrs. Democrat. Home: 12156 Cavell St Livonia MI 48150-5315 Office: AM Gen Corp 32744 Enterprise Dr Livonia MI 48150-1960

RAHMAN, DESIRÉE, healthcare administrator; b. Cherokee, Okla., Jan. 15, 1959; d. Robert Leroy and Ruth Ann (Ackley) Kirby; m. S. Mark Rahman; 1 child, Ryan S. BA in Clin. Psychology, Purdue U., 1981; MS in Health Systems Mgmt., Rush U., Chgo., 1986. Mgr. product devel. U. Chgo., 1987-89, program mgr. neuroscis., 1989-91, mgr. fin. dept. nursing, 1991-93, adminstrv. mgr. obstetrics, 1993-94; adminstr. neurology Northwestern U., Chgo., 1994—. Mem. Health Care Fin. Mgmt. Assn., Med. Group Mgmt. Assn. Democrat. Home: 1296 Brookline Ct Naperville IL 60563 Office: 645 N Michigan Ave Chicago IL 60611

RAHMAN, SAMI UR, environmental engineer; b. Karachi, Pakistan, Jan. 25, 1962; came to U.S., 1972; s. Mohammad H. and Anis F. (Hakim) R.; m. Sabahat Siddiqui, Aug. 10, 1991. AA in Engring., St. Louis C.C. Forest Park, 1986. Assoc. engr., environ. scientist D. W. Ryckmann & Assocs., Inc., St. Louis, 1986-88; site survey and monitoring sect. supr., health and safety specialist Versar, Inc., Alameda, Calif., 1988-90; sr. staff engr., project mgr. Converse Environ. West, San Francisco, 1990-91; sr. staff environ. specialist, project mgr., acting health and safety officer Environ. Geotech. Cons., Inc., Hayward, Calif., 1991; pres. SUR Environ., St. Louis, 1992—. Mem. Am. Indsl. Hygiene Assn., Pakistani Engrs. and Scientists Assn.

RAHN, DONALD L., accountant; b. Horicon, Wis., Oct. 5, 1952; s. Leonard Adolph and Mildred Erna (Pribnow) R. BBA, U. Wis., 1974, MBA, 1975. CPA, Wis. With Virchow Krause, Madison, Wis., 1975-86, ptnr., 1986—. Contbr. various tech. articles and presentations in govtl. acctg. Mem. Friends of 21, Madison, Wis., 1978; bd. dirs. Wis. Chamber Orch. Mem. Am. Inst. CPA's, Wis. Inst. CPA's (chmn. various coms.), Govt. Fin. Officers Assn. (rev. com.). Office: Virchow Krause & Co PO Box 7398 Madison WI 53707-7398

RAHN, NOEL P., investment company executive; b. 1939. CEO Investment Advisers, Inc., Mpls. Office: Investment Advisers Inc 3700 First Bank Pl Minneapolis MN 55402*

RAIBLEY, PARVIN RUDOLPH, dentist; b. Boonville, Ind., Nov. 19, 1926; s. Otto Sr. and Hallie Marie (Hedges) R.; m. Mary Helen Holder, Aug. 31, 1946; children: Bruce D., Brian L., Brent A. Student, Purdue U., 1945, U. Evansville, 1946-50; BS in Dentistry, Ind. U., 1951, DDS, 1954. Practice gen. dentistry Evansville, Ind., 1954—; pres. Parvin Raibley Profl. Dental Corp.; bd. dirs. Health Resources Inc., Evansville, 1986-94; dir. Health Resources, Inc. of Ky., 1988-94; dir. Ill. Dental Plans, 1993-94. Served with U.S. Army, 1944-45. Named Dentist of Yr. Ind. Acad. Gen. Dentistry, 1992. Fellow Acad. Gen. Dentistry, Am. Soc. Dentistry, Internat. Coll. Dentists, Pierre Fauchard Acad.; mem. ADA, First Dist. Dental Soc., Ind. Dental Assn., Ind. Acad. Gen. Dentistry, Am. Soc. Dentistry for Children. Republican. Methodist. Lodge: Masons. Home: 7100 Olive St Evansville IN 47715-3625 Office: 207 S Green River Rd Evansville IN 47715-3199

RAICA, ROBERT M., state legislator; b. Mar. 13, 1954; m. Karen Raica; 3 children. Student, City Wide Coll., Chgo. Ill. state sen. Dist. 24, 1987—; mem. Pub. Health, Welfare, and Corrections, Local Govts. Appropriations I Coms., Fin. and Credit Regulations Com., Minority Spokesman, Consumer Affairs Com. Paramedic Chgo. Fire Dept. Address: 1040 La Grange Rd N C La Grange IL 60525*

RAICH, SUSAN ELIZABETH, kinesiotherapist, educator; b. Chgo., Aug. 18, 1961; d. John Frederick and Lydia Wiera (Eckhardt) R. BS in Phys. Edn., U. Ill., Chgo., 1983. Cert. phys. edn. K-10 tchr., Ill.; cert. kinesiotherapist. Corrective therapist, adapted phys. edn. tchr. Children's Habilitation Ctr., Harvey, Ill., 1983-85; tchr. spl. edn. and adapted phys. edn. Chgo. Assn. for Retarded Citizens--La Paz Sch., Chgo., 1985-87; corrective therapist, tchr. Potential Sch. for Exceptional Children, Chgo., 1987-88; kinesiotherapist Westside VA Med. Ctr., Chgo., 1988—; asst./acting chair patient edn. com. VA Westside Cardiac Rehab., Chgo., 1991-96. Editor: (profl. newsletter) Midwest Courier, 1991-94. Mem. AAPHERD, Am. Kinesiotherapy Assn. (pub. rels. chair 1993-94, v.p. Midwest chpt. 1991-93, proxy del. Midwest chpt. 1991, 93, del. Midwest chpt. 1993-95, presdl. citation 1995). New Apostolic. Office: VA Westside Med Ctr MC117 820 S Damen Chicago IL 60612

RAINEY, CHRISTINE ROSE, pharmacist, company executive; b. Detroit, Dec. 23, 1952; d. Percy Elmer and Nadine M. (Papke) R. BS, Wayne State U., 1977. Reg. pharmacist, preceptor. Chief pharmacist Community Pharmacy, Inc., Whitmore Lake, Mich., 1977-78; staff pharmacist Perry Drug Stores, Troy, Mich., 1978; pharmacy dept. mgr. Perry Drug Stores, Waterford, Mich., 1978-79; asst. store mgr. Perry Drug Stores, Troy, 1979-81; pharmacist, store mgr. Perry Drug Stores, Novi, Mich., 1981-84, pharm. buyer, 1984-90; pharm. buyer Nat. Wholesale Drug Co., Taylor, Mich., 1990-91; dir. purchasing Nat. Wholesale Drug. Co., Taylor, Mich., 1991-92; pharm. buyer Frank W. Kerr Co., Novi, Mich., 1992, v.p. purchasing, 1992-94; clin. pharmacist VA Med. Ctr., Allen Park, Mich., 1994—; bd. dirs. Whitmore Lake Health Clinic, 1977-78. Vol. faculty Wayne State U. Coll. of Pharmacy. Mem. Am. Pharm. Assn., Can. Pharmacy Assn., Mich. Pharmacists Assn., Oakland County Pharmacists Assn., Wayne State U. Pharmacy Alumni Assn. Office: VA Med Ctr Dept 119B Allen Park MI 48101

RAIRDIN, CRAIG ALLEN, software company executive, software developer; b. Cedar Rapids, Iowa, Oct. 23, 1959; s. Ernie W. and Sherryl E. (Asklund) R.; m. Johnna L. Miller, Jan. 9, 1982. BS in Computer Sci. with distinction, U. Iowa, 1981. Software engr. Rockwell Internat., Cedar Rapids, 1982-88; div. dir. Parsons Tech., Cedar Rapids, 1988-90, v.p., 1990—; cons. Creative Computer Systems, Cedar Rapids, 1987-90. Author: (software) Juliet, 1987, Quick Verse, 1988, Bible Illustrator, 1990. Chmn. Area Liaison Com., Campus Bible Fellowship, Iowa City, 1983-90; precinct chmn. Linn. County Rep. Party, Cedar Rapids, 1986-90. Mem. Iowa Home Educators Assn. Republican. Baptist.

RAISS, SARAH ELIZABETH, consulting firm executive; b. Flint, Mich., June 21, 1957; d. Carl F. and Jean Raiss. BS in applied math., U. Mich., 1975, MBA, 1987. Engr. Mich. Bell, Southfield, Mich., 1979-83, divestiture planning, 1983, mgr. tech. planning, 1984-86, product mgr., 1986-87; sr. cons. Richard Metzler & Assn., Deerfield, Ill., 1988-89; dir. corp. strategy Am. Publs., Troy, Mich., 1989-93; v.p. ops. Ameritech, Chgo., 1993-94; mng. ptnr. SE Raiss Group, Chgo., 1995—; adv. bd. Am. Bibliographic Inst., 1993—; alumni adv. bd. Leadership Am., 1994—. Bd. trustees Glenkirk, Northbrook, Ill., 1995; bd. dirs. pers. com., 1995; vol. Am. Cancer, Alzheimer's Assn., 1994-95; vol. Salvation Army, Debra's Place, Young Life, YMCA, Spl. Olympics, 1989-93, Leadership Am., 1994. Recipient Disting. Leadership award Am. Bibliographic Inst., 1988, Outstanding Young Women of Am. award, 1985-86, Cert. Appreciation Alzheimer's Assn., 1991. Mem. Strategic Planning Forum, Engring. Soc. Detroit (Young Engrs. com. 1985-87), Detroit Inst. Arts (Jr. Founders Coun. 1989-95), Leadership Am., Chi Omega (v.p. rush 1973-95). Office: SE Raiss Group 142 S Gary Ste 1310 Bloomingdale IL 60108

RAKES, GANAS KAYE, finance and banking educator; b. Floyd, Va., May 2, 1938; s. Samuel D. and Ocie J. (Peters) R.; m. Mary Ann Simmons, Oct. 1, 1961; 1 child, Sabrina Darrow. BS, Va. Tech., 1960, MS, 1964; D of Bus. Adminstrn., Washington U., St. Louis, 1971. Assoc. prof. commerce U. Va., Charlottesville, 1968-80; O'Bleness prof. fin. and banking Ohio U., Athens, 1980—; chmn. fin. dept. Coll. of Bus. Adminstrn., 1983—; bd. dirs. Caldwell Savs. and Loan Co.; pres. bd. dirs. Enterprise Devel. Corp. Contbr. articles to profl. jours. Served to 1st lt. U.S. Army, 1961-63. Mem. Fin. Mgmt. Assn., Midwestern Bus. Adminstrs. Assn., Eastern Fin. Assn., Rotary, Reynolds Nat. Club. Republican. Episcopalian. Avocation: sailing. Office: Ohio U Dept of Fin Athens OH 45701

RAKOCZY, JACOB DAVID, steel machining and fabricating executive; b. East Chicago, Ind., Apr. 16, 1955; s. John Joseph and Josephine Elizabeth (Huss) R.; m. Gwynne Ruth Rakoczy, Aug. 21, 1975 (div. May 1984); children: Jacob John, Jillian Christine; m. Sandra Sperka, May 14, 1988 (div. July 1995). Student, Calumet Coll., 1974, St. Joseph's Coll., 1975. Machinist, foreman Euclid Machine & Tool, Gary, Ind., 1976-78, supt., 1978-80; from v.p. to pres. Euclid Machine & Tool, East Chicago, Ind., 1980—, gen. mgr., 1985—. Pres. St. John (Ind.) Fire Dept., 1983, treas., 1982, capt., 1982, bd. dirs., 1981-83; active Boy Scouts Am. Mem. Ducks Unlimited, Waterfowl USA, Masons. Roman Catholic. Office: Euclid Machine & Tool PO Box 150 East Chicago IN 46312-0150

RAKOWSKI, MAREK, mathematician, engineer, educator; b. Gliwice, Poland, July 29, 1956; came to U.S., 1985; s. Alfred and Waleria (Szadurska) R.; m. Malgorzata Gabrys, Oct. 10, 1981; children: Maciek, Mateusz. MS, Silesian Tech. U., Gliwice, Poland, 1979; PhD, Va. Tech., 1989. Rschr. Inst. Electron Tech. CEMI, Warszawa, Poland, 1979-85; grad. teaching asst. Va. Tech., Blacksburg, 1985-90; asst. prof. N.C. State U., Raleigh, 1990-91, Southwestern Okla. State U., Weatherford, 1991-92; lectr. Ohio State U., Columbus, 1992-94; assoc. prof. U. Autónoma Metropolitana, Mexico City, 1994; vis. assoc. prof. Ohio State U., 1994—; cons. Axia Sys., Inc., 1995—; internat. spkr., presenter seminars in field. Contbr. articles to profl. jours. Mem. Am. Math. Soc., Polish Inst. Arts and Scis. Am., N.Y. Acad. Scis. Office: The Ohio State U Dept Math 231 W 18th Ave Columbus OH 43210-1174

RAKSAKULTHAI, VINAI, obstetrician, gynecologist; b. Rayong, Thailand, Mar. 20, 1942; came to U.S., 1968; s. Choosak and Ngo (Koo) R.; m. Vullapa Raksakulthai, Sept. 20, 1968; children: Vipavull, Vivian, Vipat. MD, ChiengMai Med. Sch., Thailand, 1966. Diplomate Am. Bd. Ob-Gyn. Intern New Britain (Conn.) Gen. Hosp., 1969; resident St. Joseph Mercy Hosp., Pontiac, Mich., 1970-72; practice medicine specializing in ob-gyn. Fredericktown, Mo., 1973—. Mem. Mo. Med. Assn., Mineral Area Med. Soc. Buddhist. Home: 201 Williams St Fredericktown MO 63645-1317 Office: 703 N Main Fredericktown MO 63645

RALPH, DAVID CLINTON, communications educator; b. Muskogee, Okla., Jan. 12, 1922; s. Earl Clinton and Rea Jane (Potter) R.; m. Kathryn Juanita Wicklund, Nov. 29, 1947; children: David Randall, Steven Wicklund. AA, Muskogee Jr. Coll., 1941; BS in Theatre, Northwestern U., 1947, MA in Theatre, 1948, PhD in Speech, 1953. Lectr. Ind. U., Hammond, 1947-48; instr. speech U. Mo., Columbia, 1948-53; tchr. debate-forensics summer program for high sch. students Northwestern U., Evanston, Ill., 1949-51; asst. prof. speech Mich. State U., East Lansing, 1953-57, assoc. prof., 1957-64, prof. speech and theatre, 1964-68, prof. communication, 1968—, dir. communication undergrad. program, 1968-88; cons. on pub. speaking, 1948—. Co-author: Group Discussion, 1954, 2d edit., 1956, Principles of Speaking, 1962, 3d edit., 1975; contbr. articles to profl. jours., chpts. to books. Coach Jr. League Boys' Baseball, Lansing, Mich., 1958-74; mem. civilian aux. to Lansing Fire Dept., 1987—. Lt. USNR, 1942-46, PTO, ETO. Named Hon. State Farmer, Future Farmers Am., 1965; recipient Community Svc. award Mich. State U. Sr. Class Coun., 1979, Outstanding Faculty award, 1987, 91; Teaching Excellence award State of Mich., 1990. Mem. AAUP, Speech Communication Assn., Internat. Communication Assn., Cen. States Communication Assn., Golden Key (hon., faculty advisor), Omicron Delta Kappa. Democrat. Methodist. Office: Mich State U Dept Communication East Lansing MI 48824

RAMADHYANI, SATISH, mechanical engineering educator; b. Bangalore, Karnataka, India, Aug. 1, 1949; came to U.S., 1975; s. K. R. Keshavachar and Padma (Iyengar) R.; m. Rachel B. Sparrow, June 17, 1979. B of Tech., Indian Inst. of Tech., Madras, India, 1971; MS, U. Minn., 1977, PhD, 1979. Asst. engr. devel. Motor Industries Co., Bangalore, 1971-75; asst. prof. Dept. Mech. Engring., Tufts U., Medford, Mass., 1979-83; asst. prof. Sch. of Mech. Engring., Purdue U., West Lafayette, Ind., 1983-86, assoc. prof., 1986-91, prof., 1991—; expert cons. Teltech, Inc., Mpls., 1990—; expert reviewer numerous profl. jours. and funding agys., 1979—. Assoc. tech editor ASME Jour. of Heat Transfer; contbr. over 60 articles to profl. jours. Recipient Pres. of India Gold Medal Govt. India, 1971. Mem. AIAA, ASME (mem. heat transfer div. K-6), Am. Soc. of Engring. Educators, Phi Kappa Phi, Tau Beta Pi, Sigma Xi. Office: Purdue U Sch Of Mech Engring West Lafayette IN 47907

RAMAKRISHNAN, VENKATASWAMY, civil engineer, educator; b. Coimbatore, India, Feb. 27, 1929; came to U.S., 1969, naturalized, 1981; s. Venkataswamy and Kondammal (Krishnaswamy) R.; m. Vijayalakshmi Unnava, Nov. 7, 1962; children: Aravind, Anand. B.Engring., U. Madras, 1952, D.S.S., 1953; D.I.C. in Hydropower and Concrete Tech, Imperial Coll., London, 1957; Ph.D., Univ. Coll., U. London, 1960. From lectr. to prof. civil engring., head dept. P.S.G. Coll. Tech., U. Madras, 1952-69; vis. prof. S.D. Sch. Mines and Tech., Rapid City, 1969-70, prof. civil engring., 1970—, dir. concrete tech. research, 1970-71, head grad. div. structural mechanic and concrete tech., 1971—; program coordinator materials engring. and sci. Ph.D. program S.D. Sch. Mines and Tech., —, 1985-86; disting. prof. S.D. Sch. Mines and Tech., Rapid City, 1996—. Author: Ultimate Strength Design for Structural Concrete, 1969; also over 200 articles. Recipient Outstanding Prof. award S.D. Sch. Mines and Tech., 1980, 1st Rsch. award, 1994; Colombo Plan fellow, 1955-60. Mem. Internat. Assn. Bridge and Structural Engring., ASCE (vice chmn. constrn. div. publs. com. 1974), Am. Concrete Inst. (chmn. subcom. gen. considerations for founds., chmn. com. 214 on evaluation of strength test results, sec.-treas. Dakota chpt. 1974-79, v.p. 1980, pres. 1981), Instn. Hwy. Engrs., Transp. Rsch. Bd. (chmn. com. on admixtures and curing, chmn. com. on mech. properties concrete), Am. Soc. Engring. Edn., NSPE, Internat. Coun. Gap-Graded Concrete Rsch. and Application, Sigma Xi. Address: 1809 Sheridan Lake Rd Rapid City SD 57702-4219

RAMASWAMI, DEVABHAKTUNI, chemical engineer; b. Pedapudi, India, Apr. 4, 1933; came to U.S., 1958, s. Veeriah and Rangamma Devabhaktuni; m. Vijayalakshmi, June 30, 1967; 1 child, Srikrishna. B.Sc., Andhra U., 1953, M.Sc., 1954, D.Sc., 1958; Ph.D., U. Wis., 1961. Research scholar Andhra U., Waltair, India, 1954-56, Indian Inst. Tech., Kharagpur, 1956-57; asst. prof. Benaras Hindu U., Varanasi, India, 1957-58; research asst. U. Wis., Madison, 1958-61; research engr. IBM Corp., San Jose, Calif., 1961-62; chem. engr. Argonne Nat. Lab., Ill., 1962—. Contbr. numerous articles to profl. jours. Patentee in field. Am. Chem. Soc. Disting. and Promising Asian in U.S. award Asia Found., 1960. Fellow Am. Inst. Chem. Engrs. Avocation: photography.

RAMEY, KAREN MARIE, political organization consultant; b. Chgo., June 20, 1956; d. Edward and Marjorie Estelle (Hansen) Masterson; m. Joseph Craig Ramey, June 20, 1981; 1 child, Brian Joseph. BS magna cum laude, Aquinas Coll., 1978. Educator Jefferson Jr. H.S., Woodridge, Ill., 1978-85; coach volleyball 13-15 Midwest Nat. Jrs., Hinsdale, Ill., 1976-80; legis. aide, dir. Kane County Constituent Svc., Aurora, Ill., 1992-94; exec. dir. Kane County Rep. Ctrl. Com., Geneva, Ill., 1994—; pres., political consultant, lobbyist Bricor, Inc., Geneva & Springfield, Ill., 1994—. Campaign com. Kane County Bd. Chmn., 1989—; county coord. Mayor Geneva County Bd. Atty. Gen., Ill., 1994; local coord. State Sen. Chris Lauzen, 1992-94; dep. com. mem. Ill. Rep. Ctrl. Com., 1995—. Mem. Ill. Rep. Womens Roundtable, Ill. Rep. Women. Home: 515 Oakwood Dr Geneva IL 60134 Office: Brycor Consulting Inc 2339 S 10th Ave Springfield IL 66666

RAMEY, REBECCA ANN, elementary education educator; b. Dayton, Ohio, Jan. 27, 1948; d. Donald Smith and Margaret Jeanne (Cross) Ingabrand; divorced; 1 child, Joshua David. BS, Miami U., Oxford, Ohio, 1970, MEd in Adminstrn., 1978. Cert. permanent tchr., prin., Ohio. Tchr. social studies and lang. arts Springboro (Ohio) Community Schs., 1970—; dept. head Clearcreek Elem. Sch., Springboro, 1991—. Choir dir. 1st Bapt. Ch., Franklin, Ohio, 1985—, chmn. bd. Christian edn., 1991-96; sec. exec. bd. Tamarack Swim Club, Springboro, 1990-96, Springboro Band Boosters Assn., 1992. Named Worker of Yr., 1st Bapt. Ch., 1992. Mem. NEA, Ohio Edn. Assn., Springboro Edn. Assn., Order Ea. Star (past matron 1973, 84), Ladies Oriental Shrine N.Am. Republican. Home: 205 Foliage Ln Springboro OH 45066-9312 Office: Clearcreek Elem Sch 750 S Main St Springboro OH 45066-1424

RAMIREZ, ALFRED, state legislator; m. Cathy Ramirez. Rep. dist. 40 State of Kans., 1983-92, senator dist. 5, 1993—; supr. AT&T. Republican. Address: 13848 Harbor Dr Bonner Springs KS 66012-9690*

RAMIREZ, SUSAN ELIZABETH, Latin-American history educator; b. Toledo, Ohio, Oct. 11, 1946; d. Eduardo Salvador and Helen Elizabeth (McCartney) R. BA, U. Ill., 1968; MA, U. Wis., 1973, PhD, 1977. Asst. prof. Ohio U., Athens, 1977-82; asst. prof. DePaul U., Chgo., 1982-84, assoc. prof., 1984-89, dir. Latin-Am. studies, 1988-95, prof., 1989—. Author: Provincial Patriarchs: Land Tenure...Peru, 1986, The World Upside Down, 1996; editor: Indian-Religious Relations in Colonial Spanish America, 1989. Named Fulbright-Hayes fellow, 1978-79, NEH fellow 1987, 92, Ford Found. fellow 1987-88; grantee De Paul U. 1992—; recipient Fulbright fellowship, 1993-94. Mem. Am. Hist. Assn. (coms.), Am. Cath. Hist. Assn. (program com. 1986, exec. com. 1992—), Conf. on Latin-Am. History (sec. colonial studies com. 1987-88, gen. com. 1987-90, chair program com. 1989-90), Ill. Congress Latin-Ams. (pres., 1988-89). Office: DePaul Univ Dept History Dept History 2320 N Kenmore Ave Chicago IL 60614-3210

RAMMING, MICHAEL ALEXANDER, school system administrator; b. St. Louis, Feb. 4, 1940; s. William Alexander and Emily Louise (Reingruber) R.; m. Susan Ray Oliver, July 9, 1962; children: Michael Murray, Todd Alexander. BS, Centenary Coll., 1963; MA, Washington U., St. Louis, 1968. Cert. adminstr. secondary schs., Mo. Teacher and coach Ladue Sch. Dist., St. Louis, 1963-88, adminstr., 1988—. Vol. Sr. Olympics, St. Louis, 1992, 93. Mem. Nat. Assn. Secondary Sch. Prins., Mo. Assn. Secondary Sch. Prins., Nat. Interscholastic Athletic Adminstrs. Assn., Mo. Interscholastic Athletic Adminstrs. Assn. (25 Yr. Svc. award). Home: 13309 Kings Glen Dr Saint Louis MO 63131-1022 Office: Ladue Horton Watkins High Sch 1201 S Warson Rd Saint Louis MO 63124-1266

RAMOS, FREDERICK, lawyer; b. Bklyn., Aug. 4, 1964; s. Felix and Minerva (LaSalle) R.; m. Julia Drits. BA, Columbia U., 1986; JD, U. Mich., 1989. Bar: Minn. 1990, U.S. Dist. Ct. Minn. 1992, U.S. Ct. Appeals (8th cir.) 1994, U.S. Supreme Ct. 1995. Jud. clk. to hon. Lawrence Bilder Appellate divsn. State Ct., Jersey City, 1989-90; asst. pub. defender Ramsey County Pub. Defender's Office, St. Paul, 1990-94; staff atty. Candlin & Wright, Bloomington, Minn., 1994—; bd. dirs. Bd. Lawyers Profl. Responsibility, St. Paul, 1995—. Contbr. articles to profl. jours. Sec. Teatro Latino de Minn., Mpls., 1993-95. Mem. ABA, Minn. State Bar Assn. (bd. govs.), Hennepin County Bar Assn. (co-chair governance com.), Hispanic Nat. Bar Assn. (pres. Minn. chpt. 1993-95), Columbia U. Club of Minn. Office: Candlin & Wright 3800 W 80th St Ste 1500 Bloomington MN 55431

RAMOS, VIVIAN ELEANOR, development and administrative consultant; b. St. Louis, Oct. 19, 1946; d. John Dominic and Aurea Genevieve (Schottel) Baron; m. John Paul Hargis, Aug. 21, 1964 (div. Mar. 1968); m. Filomeno Mariano Ramos, June 30, 1973 (dec.); children: William S., Kiersten E., Leilani A. Student, St. Louis U., 1968-69, U. Hawaii, 1986-87; BA in Mgmt., Nat. Louis U., 1991. Co-founder, co-owner, v.p. Batts Ramos and Assocs., Inc., St. Louis, 1991—; cons. Hawaii Govtl. Affairs Com., Honolulu, 1975-76, Brokers Adv. Com., Honolulu, 1984-85. V.p. Mo. Orthopedically Disabled, bd. dirs., 1993—; active Assoc. Pres.'s Youth Opportunity Program, St. Louis, 1968; vol. literacy coun., rschr. Vols. in Probation and Parole. Mem. Nat. Assn. Realtors (mem. com. on pub. rels. 1987), St. Louis Real Estate Bd., Mililani Mchts. Assn. (pres. 1985). Democrat. Roman Catholic. Home: 70 Willow Dr PO Box 474 Eureka MO 63025

RAMP, MARJORIE JEAN SUMERWELL, civic worker; b. Kansas City, Mo., July 20, 1924; d. Walter Francis and Helen Louise (Nichols) Sumerwell; m. Floyd Lester Ramp, Sept. 4, 1948; children: David L., Sandra Jean, Paul F., Cheryl Louise. BS in Nursing Edn., U. Minn., 1948. RN, Minn. Instr. nursing edn. U. Minn., Mpls., 1948-50; adminstrv. asst. to assn. minister Western Res. Assn. of Ohio Conf. United Ch. of Christ, Cleve., 1983-85. Former chmn. hunger task force Ohio Conf. of United Ch. of christ, moderator, 1981-82, moderator West. Res. Assn., 1976-77, mem. nat. exec. coun., N.Y.C., 1983-89, mem. nat. bd. for world ministries, 1971-82; past bd. dirs. Western Res. coun. Girl Scouts U.S.; nat. sec. Campaign for UN Reform, Washington, 1987-92; pres. Cleve.-Volgograd Ptnr. Cities, 1988—; coord., co-founder Richfield-Wolfach Twin City Program, 1970, bd. dirs., 1970-92; mem. numerous local and nat. peace groups; nongovtl. orgn. rep. Earth Summit, Rio de Janeiro, 1992, del. to UN commn. for sustainable development. Recipient Golden Trefoil award We. Res. Coun. Girl Scouts U.S., 1972; named Outstanding Woman of Ohio Conf., Gen. Synod United Ch. of Christ, 1985. Mem. AAUW, LWV, World Federalist Assn. (chmn. Ohio 1985—), Delta Kappa Gamma (hon.). Home: 225 Hollywood St Oberlin OH 44074-1011

RAMPERSAD, PEGGY A. SNELLINGS, sociologist; b. Fredericksburg, Va., Jan. 12, 1933; d. George Daniel and Virginia Riley (Bowler) Snellings; m. Oliver Ronald Rampersad, Mar. 19, 1955; 1 child, Gita. BA, Mary Washington Coll., Fredericksburg, 1953; student, Sch. of Art Inst. of Chgo., 1953-55; MA, U. Chgo., 1965, PhD, 1978. Grad. admissions counselor U. Chgo., 1954-57, adviser to fgn. students, 1958, dir. admissions Grad. Sch. Bus., 1959-63, rsch. project specialist Grad. Sch. Bus., 1970-78, pers. mgr. Grad. Sch. Bus., 1979-80, mgr. organizational devel. Grad. Sch. Bus., 1980-82, adminstr. dept. econs., 1983-95; cons. PSR Consulting, Chgo., 1995—; cons. North Ctrl. Assn. Colls. and Secondary Schs., Chgo.,1964-70, Orchestral Assn. of Chgo. Symphony Orch., 1982, Chgo. Ctr. for Decision Rsch., 1982, Harvard U., 1993—. Exhibited paintings in juried shows at Va. Mus. Fine Arts, Art Inst. Chgo., others; editor North Cen. Assn. Quar., 1972; contbr. articles to profl. jours. U. Chgo. grad. fellow, 1963-67. Mem. AAUW, Am. Econ. Assn., Am. Acad. Polit. and Social Sci., Art Inst. Chgo. (museum assoc.), Pi Lambda Theta (past pres.). Episcopalian. Home and Office: 5531 S Kenwood Ave Chicago IL 60637-1755

RAMSAY, KARIN KINSEY, publisher, educator; b. Brownwood, Tex., Aug. 10, 1930; d. Kirby Luther and Ina Rebecca (Wood) Kinsey; m. Jack Cummins Ramsay Jr., Aug. 31, 1951; children: Annetta Jean, Robin Andrew. BA, Trinity U., 1951. Cert. assoc. ch. edn., 1980. Youth coord. Covenant Presbyn. Ch., Carrollton, Tex., 1961-76; dir. ch. edn. Northminster Presbyn. Ch., Dallas, 1976-80, Univ. Presbyn. Ch., Chapel Hill, N.C., 1987-90, Oak Grove Presbyn. Ch., Bloomington, Minn., 1990-93; coord. ecum. ministry Flood Relief for Iowa, Des Moines, 1993; program coord. 1st Presbyn. Ch., Green Bay, Wis., 1994-95; publicity & tour dir. Hist. Resources Press, Green Bay, 1994—; mem. Presbytery Candidates Com., Dallas, 1977-82, Presbytery Exams. Com. Dallas, 1979-81; clk. coun. New Hope Presbytery, Rocky Mount, N.C., 1989-90; creator, dir. Thee Holy Fools and This Is Me retreats. Author: Ramsay's Resources, 1983—; contbr. articles to jours. in field. Design cons. Brookhaven Hosp. Chapel, Dallas, 1977-78; elder Presbyn. Ch. U.S.A., 1982—; coord. Lifeline Emergency Response, Dallas, 1982-84. Mem. Internat. Platform Assn., Assn. Presbyn. Ch. Educators.

RAMSDEN, MARY CATHERINE, substance abuse specialist. Diploma, St. Joseph Mercy Hosp., 1966; postgrad., Mason City Jr. Coll., Kirkwood Community Coll. RN, Iowa; cert. chem. dependency nurse. Nursing supr. children's unit State Mental Health Inst., Cherokee, Iowa, 1966-69, Iowa Security Med. Facility, Oakdale, 1969; staff nurse psychiatry St. Luke's Meth. Hosp., Cedar Rapids, Iowa, 1969-74, asst. psychiat. nursing instr., 1970-74; mem. staff Sedlacek Treatment Ctr. Mercy Hosp., Cedar Rapids, 1974-85; cons. drug and alcohol CareUnit, Jacksonville Beach, Fla., 1985-86; nursing mgr. adolescent chem. dependency unit Broadlawns Med. Ctr., Des Moines, 1987-88; tng. mgr. Div. Substance Abuse and Heath Promotion Iowa Dept. Pub. Health, 1988-91; clin. program dir. Forest City (Iowa) Treatment Ctr., 1991-92; intervention specialist employee and family resources Iowa Correctional Instn. for Women, Mitchellville, 1992—. Author: (with others) Nurses Quick Reference, 1989. Lt. Cmdr. Nurse Corps USNR. Named Nurse Expert Coll. Nursing U. Iowa., 1985. Mem. Nat. Consortium Chem. Dependence Nurses, Iowa Corrections Assn., Res. Officers Assn. Home: 400 E Division St Colfax IA 50054-1118

RAMSEY, ALLEN R., educator; b. Missouri Valley, Iowa, May 1, 1935; s. Carl William and Mildred Ettie Ramsey; m. Margaret Ellen, Mar. 18, 1967; 1 child, David Randall. BA, U. Iowa, 1957; MA, John Carroll U., 1967; PhD, Tulane U., 1972. Instr. Cleve. State U., 1966-67; prof. Ctrl. Mo. State U., Wareensburg, 1972—. Mem. AAUP. Home: 104 Broad St Warrensburg MO 64093 Office: Ctrl Mo State U Dept of Ed Warrensburg MO 64093

RAMSEY, SANDRA LYNN, psychotherapist; b. Camp LeJeune, N.C., Feb. 7, 1951; d. Robert A. and Lola J. (Hann) R.; m. Edward G. Schmidt, July 9, 1988; children: Seth, Sarah, Anna, Rachel. Student, U. Calif., Long Beach, 1969-70, Orange Coast Coll., Costa Mesa, Calif., 1971-72; BA in Psychology with distinction, U. Nebr., 1987, MA in Counseling Psychology, 1989. Vol. coord., client adv. Rape/Spouse Abuse Crisis Ctr., Lincoln, 1989-90; mental health therapist Health Am., HMO, Lincoln, 1991-94; pvt. practice, Lincoln, 1994—; adj. faculty S.E. Cmty. Coll; contract therapist Lincoln Pediatric Group, 1990-91, Family Svc. Assn., Lincoln, 1990-91, Cmty. Preservation Assocs., Lincoln, 1991-94. Mem. Nebr. Domestic Violence Sexual Assault Coalition; vol. ARC Disaster Mental Health Svcs.; mem. Nebr. Critical Incident Stress Debriefing team. Portenier scholar U. Nebr., 1986-87. Mem. APA (assoc., divsn. 50 addictions), Am. Assn. Sex Educators, Counselors, and Therapists, Assn. Pvt. Practice Therapists, Nebr. Assn. for Counseling and Devel., Am. Mental Health Counselors Assn. (clin.), Sex Info. and Edn. Coun. of the U.S., Golden Key, Psi Chi.

RAMSEY-RODRIGUEZ, SUSAN KAY, language educator, librarian; b. Terre Haute, Ind., Mar. 13, 1951; d. James H. and Frances E. (Erxleben) Anderson; m. John P. Ramsey, Aug. 8, 1978 (div. May 1987); children: Jamie Sue, Jessica Leora; m. John Omar Rodriguez, Nov. 21, 1990. Student, Cambridge (Eng.) U., spring 1972; BA in Latin, English and Psychology cum laude, Valparaiso U., 1973; MA with distinction in English, Ind. State U., 1976, MA in Libr. Sci., 1985; gifted/talented edn. endorsement, Purdue U., 1990. Lic. lifetime tchr.; cert. tchr. secondary English, Latin and psychology, Ind.; cert. in elem. and secondary gifted and talented edn., Ind.; lic. lifetime elem. and secondary libr. Tchr. English and Latin Clinton (Ind.) H.S., 1973-77, Austin (Ind.) H.S., 1977-78; tchr. Latin, English and psychology South Putnam H.S., Greencastle, Ind., 1978-85, tchr., libr. head dept., 1995—; past drama coach, yearbook instr. South Putnam H.S., acad. team coord., 1985—; adj. instr. libr. sci. Ind. State U., Terree Haute, summers 1986, 87; Fulbright exch. tchr. Southwood Secondary Sch., Cambridge, Ont., Can., 1994-95; adj. tchr. gifted and talented edn., libr. cons. Sacred Heart Sch., Terre Haute, 1994-95; cons. Dist. III Ind. Classical Conf., 1975-77. Contbr. articles to profl. publs. Mem. VFW aux.; past participant Habitat for Humanity. Named Creative Latin Tchr. of Yr., Ind. Classical Conf., 1976, 77; recipient Exch. cert. Fulbright Assn., Washington, 1995. Mem. NEA, INCOLSA (South Putnam Sch. Corp. rep. 1989—, mem. exec. com. 1989-95), Stone Hills Area Libr. Svcs. Authority (bd. dirs. Bloomington, Ind. br. 1989-95, treas., bd. dirs. 1993, 94, cons., mem. com. for cons./dir. rev. 1992, Dedicated Svc. award 1995), Acad. Coaches Assn. (Ind. br.), Ont. Libr. Assn. Episcopalian. Office: Ind Collection Libr Svcs 3784 W Highway 40 Greencastle IN 46135

RAMSTAD, JIM, congressman, lawyer; b. Jamestown, N.D., May 6, 1946; s. Marvin Joseph and Della Mae (Fode) R. BA, U. Minn., 1968; JD with honors, George Washington U., 1973. Bar: N.D. 1973, D.C. 1973, U.S. Supreme Ct. 1976, Minn., 1979. Adminstrv. asst. to speaker Minn. Ho. Reps., 1969; spl. asst. to Congressman Tom Kleppe, 1970; pvt. practice law, Jamestown, 1973, Washington, 1974-1978, Mpls., 1978-90; mem. Minn. Senate, 1981-90, asst. minority leader, 1983-87; mem. 102nd-103rd Congresses from 3rd Minn. dist., 1990—; adj. prof. Am. U., Washington, 1975-78. Bd. dirs. Children's Heart Fund, Lake Country Food Bank. Served as 1st lt. U.S. Army Res., 1968-74. Mem. Minn. Bar Assn., D.C. Bar Assn., N.D. Bar Assn., Hennepin County Bar Assn., U. Minn. Alumni Assn. (nat. dir.), Am. Legion, Wayzata C. of C., TwinWest C. of C., U. Minn. Alumni Club (past pres. Washington), Lions, Phi Beta Kappa, Phi Delta Theta. Republican. Office: 103 Cannon House Office Bldg Washington DC 20515

RAMUNNO, THOMAS PAUL, financial consultant; b. Chgo., Sept. 13, 1952; s. Anthony Michael and Dorothy (Buriak) R.; m. Deborah G. Pauline Benton, Jan. 31, 1976 (div. 1991); 1 child, Michael Thomas. BBA, U. Ga., 1974, MBA, 1978. Treas., Concept, Inc., Atlanta, 1974-77; product mgr. Johnson-Johnson, Inc., Atlanta, 1978-80; dir. Rollins, Inc., Atlanta, 1979-80; cons. Chase Econometrics, Atlanta, 1980-83; v.p. comml. svcs., dir. corp. product mgmt./mktg. Union Trust Co. Md., 1983-84; prin., exec. v.p. Mktg. Scis. Group, Inc., Hunt Valley, Md., 1984-85; v.p., dir. Citicorp, Chgo., 1985-86; sr. mgr. fin. instns. consulting group Deloitte & Touche, Chgo, 1987-90; dir. cons. svcs. FSA, Inc., 1990—; CEO Adv. Scis. Group, 1991—; pres. IASG, 1990—; ptnr. Info. Scis. Inc., 1996—; Home: 2023 Garden Ter Hoffman Estates IL 60195-2514

RAN, SHULAMIT, composer; b. Tel Aviv, Oct. 21, 1949; came to U.S., 1963; m. Abraham Lotan, 1986. Studied composition with, Paul Ben-Haim, Norman Dello, Joio, Ralph Shapey; student, Mannes Coll. Music, N.Y.C., 1963-67. With dept. music U. Chgo., 1973—, William H. Colvin prof. music; composer-in-residence Chgo. Symphony Orch., 1990—, Lyric Opera of Chgo., 1994—. Compositions include 10 Children's Scenes, 1967, Structures,1 968, 7 Japanese Love Poems, 1968, Hatzvi Israel Eulogy, 1969, O the Chimneys, 1969, Concert Piece for piano and orch., 1970, 3 Fantasy Pieces for Cello and Piano, 1972, Ensembles for 17, 1975, Double Vision, 1976, Hyperbolae for Piano, 1976, For an Actor: Monologue for Clarinet, 1978, Apprehensions, 1979, Private Game, 1979, Fantasy-Variations for Cello, 1980, A Prayer, 1982, Verticals for piano, 1982, String Quartet No. 1, 1984, (for woodwind quintet) Concerto da Camera I, 1985, Amichai Songs, 1985, Amichai Songs, 1985, Concerto for Orchestra, 1986, (for clarinet, string quartet and piano) Concerto da Camera II, 1987, East Wind, 1987, String Quartet No. 2, 1988-89, Symphony, 1989-90, Mirage, 1990, Inscriptions for solo violin, 1991, Chicago Skyline for brass and percussion, 1991, Legends for Orch., 1992-93, Invocation, 1994, Yearning for violin and string orch.; commd. pieces include for Am. Composers Orch., Phila. Orch., Chgo. Symphony, Chamber Soc. of Lincoln Ctr., Mendelssohn String quartet, Da Capo Chamber Players, Sta. WFMT; composer and soloist for 1st performances Capriccio, 1963, Symphonic Poem, 1967, Concert Piece, 1971. Recipient Acad. Inst. Arts and Letters award, 1989, Pulitzer prize for music, 1991, Friedheim award for orchestral music Kennedy Ctr., 1992; Guggenheim fellow, 1977, 90. Office: U Chgo Dept Music 1010 E 59th St Chicago IL 60637-1404

RANCK, SANDRA ANN, nurse; b. Ashtabula, Ohio, Apr. 16, 1962; d. Robert Jay Sr. and Sarah Alice (Hakala) Halman; m. Charles Thomas Ranck II, Sept. 26, 1987. BSN, Kent State U., 1985; postgrad., Gannon U., 1993—. RN, Ohio; cert. EMT. Nurse Huron Rd. Hosp., East Cleveland, Ohio, 1985-87, St. Joseph Riverside Hosp., Warren, Ohio, 1987-88; head nurse emergency svcs. Ashtabula (Ohio) County Med. Ctr., 1988—; co-chair critical incident stress mgmt. steering com. Ashtabula County, 1994-95. Mem. Local Emergency Planning Com., Ashtabula County, 1990—, Sexual Assault Team Ashtabula County, 1990—, chairperson, 1992-95. Recipient AMA award Explorers/Boy Scouts Am., Cleve., 1980. Mem. AAUW (sec. 1990-92), Emergency Nurses Assn. (pres. North Coast chpt. 1990-91, 92-93, 96—, legis. chair 1988—, treas. 1994-95), Women's Evening Fellowship (chmn. core com. 1989-91), Order Ea. Star, Ali Baba Caldron, Sigma Theta Tau (Eta Xi chpt. scholar 1995). Mem. United Church of Christ. Home: 4207 Lake Rd W Ashtabula OH 44004-2105 Office: Ashtabula County Med Ctr 2420 Lake Ave Ashtabula OH 44004-4954

RAND, LEON, academic administrator; b. Boston, Oct. 8, 1930; s. Max B. and Ricka (Muscanto) Rakisky; m. Marian L. Newton, Aug. 29, 1959; children: Debra Ruth, Paul Martin, Marta Leah. B.S., Northeastern U., 1953; M.A., U. Tex., 1956, Ph.D., 1958. Postdoctoral fellow Purdue U., 1958-59; asst. prof. to prof. U. Detroit, 1959-68; prof., chmn. dept. chemistry Youngstown (Ohio) State U., 1968-74, dean grad. studies and research, 1974-81, acting acad. v.p., 1980; vice chancellor acad. affairs Pembroke (N.C.) State U., 1981-85; chancellor Ind. U.-S.E., New Albany, 1986-96; bd. dirs. INB Banking Co., Jeffersonville, Ind, Jewish Hosp., Louisville, Ky., 1991—. Bd. dirs., mem. exec. com. Louisville (Ind.) Area chpt. ARC; bd. dirs. Floyd Meml. Hosp., New Albany, 1987-90. Mem. Am. Chem. Soc., Am. Inst. Chemists, Metroversity (bd. dirs.), Sigma Xi, Phi Kappa Phi. Home: 3119 Brazil Lake Pky Georgetown IN 47122-8605 Office: Office of Chancellor Ind U SE New Albany IN 47150

RANDA, RUDOLPH THOMAS, judge; b. Milw., July 25, 1940; s. Rudolph Frank and Clara Paula (Kojis) R.; m. Melinda Nancy Matera, Jan. 15, 1977; children—Rudolph Daniel, Daniel Anthony. B.S., U. Wis.-Milw., 1963; J.D., U. Wis.-Madison, 1966. Bar: Wis. 1966, U.S. Dist. Ct. (ea. and we. dists.) Wis., 1966, U.S. Ct. Appeals (7th cir.) 1973, U.S. Supreme Ct. 1973. Sole practice, Milw., 1966-67; prin. city atty. Office Milw. City Atty., 1970-75; judge Milw. Mcpl. Ct., 1975-79, Milwaukee County Circuit Ct., 1979-81, 1982-92, Appellate Ct., Madison, Wis., 1981-82; federal judge U.S. Dist. Ct. (ea. dist.) Wis., 1992—; chmn. Wis. Impact, Milw., 1980—; lectr. Marquette U. Law Sch., Milw., 1980—. Served to capt. U.S. Army, 1967-69, Vietnam. Decorated Bronze Star medal. Mem. Milw. Bar Assn., Wis. Bar Assn., Trial Judges Wis., Am. Legion (adjutant Milw. 1980), Thomas More Lawyers Soc. (former pres. Milw.), Milw. Hist. Soc., Phi Alpha Theta. Roman Catholic. Office: US Courthouse 517 E Wisconsin Ave Rm 247 Milwaukee WI 53202-4504

RANDALL, ELIZABETH ELLEN, press clippings company executive; b. Maple Hill, Kans., Mar. 21, 1915; d. Edwin and Ann (Scott) Sage; m. George Albert Randall, May 29, 1941; children: Cheryl Ann, Rebecca Lynn. Student, Kans. State U., 1932-34. Tchr. elem. sch Maple Hill, Kans., 1932-34, Dover, Kans., 1934-46; reader Luce Press Clippings, Topeka, 1959-63, supr., 1964, office mgr., 1964—. Tchr. Jr. High Ch. Sch., 1949-61; mem. pastoral com. Dover Federated Ch., 1991—. Mem. Dover 4-H Club (leader 1960-62), Dover Rebekah Lodge, Eastern Star, Am. Leg. Aux., Disabled Am. Vets. Aux., 14th Armored Divsn. Aux. Democrat. Home: 5731 SW 22nd Ter Topeka KS 66614-1831 Office: Luce Press Clippings 912 S Kansas Ave Topeka KS 66612-1211

RANDALL, GARY LEE, state legislator; b. Ithaca, Mich., June 18, 1943; s. Clifton Peet and Elsie Mae (Martyn) R.; m. Brenda Faye Martin, 1973; children: Amy Kathryn, Clifton Lee. BA, Mich. State U., 1970; MA, Ctrl. Mich. U., 1972. Program dir. WFYC Radio, Alma, Mich., 1965-70; dir. pub. affairs WCMU TV/WCML TV, Mt. Pleasant, Mich., 1970-79; rep. Mich. Dist. 89, Mich. Dist. 93; asst. Rep. leader Mich. Ho. Reps., former chair bus. & fin. com., mem. agriculture com., fin. com., edn. com., adminstrn. rules & capitol restoration coms. Trustee Libr. Mich. Mem. Assn. Edn. Broadcasters, Mich. Farm Bur., Lions, Jaycees, Elks, Sigma Delta Chi. Home: 11149 Pingree Rd Elwell MI 48832-9750 Address: PO Box 30014 Lansing MI 48909-7514*

RANDALL, ROBERT QUENTIN, nursery executive; b. Jacksonville, Ill., May 1, 1945; s. William Orlando and Agnes Johanna (Bruins) R.; m. Catherine Horn, Dec. 27, 1969. BS in Biology, Ill. Coll., 1967. Lab. technician Passavant Meml. Hosp., Jacksonville, 1966-68; sect. head in viral prodn. Beecham Labs., Whitehall, Ill., 1968-79, safety dir., 1970-79; prin. Jacksonville Landscape Nursery, 1979-89, nurseryman, 1989-95; ret., 1995. Contbr. articles on birding to topical publs. Sec. Jacksonville Theatre Guild; elder, deacon, trustee 1st Presbyn. Ch., Jacksonville, Ill. Coll. Jacksonville area Alumni Assoc., 1989; bd. dirs. Friends of the Libr., 1991-95; mem. Ill. Blue Ribbon Task Force, 1995-96. Mem. Jacksonville Kiwanis (bd. dirs. 1986-87), Morgan County Audubon Soc. (treas. 1989-91, pres. 1991-94), Ill. Audubon Soc. (bd. dirs.), Jacksonville Symphony Soc. (bd. dirs. 1994—). Home: 11 Pitner Pl Jacksonville IL 62650-2266 Office: Jacksonville Landscape Nursery RR 5 Jacksonville IL 62650-9805

RANDALL, SHARON ANN, mechanical engineer; b. Cleve., Feb. 19, 1967; d. Peter and Janet Randall. BS in Mech. Engring., U. Akron, Ohio, 1991. Application engr. Karbate Vicarb Inc., Strongsville, Ohio, 1992-93; sys. engr. Bailey Control Co., Wickliffe, Ohio, 1992-94; product engr. Delco Chassis Div., Sandusky, Ohio, 1994—. Office: Delco Chassis Div 2509 Hayes Ave Sandusky OH 44870-5359

RANDALL, WILLIAM LOUIS, banker; b. Milw., Dec. 20, 1930; s. Clifford A. and Renate (Zimmers) R.; m. Wendy Shea, June 18, 1955; children: Cynthia, Rebecca, Clifford W., Kevin. BA, Dartmouth Coll., 1952; LLB, U. Mich., 1956; Dr.Bus. Econs. (hon.), Milw. Sch. Engring., 1990. Bar: Wis. 1956. Atty., ptnr. Shea, Hoyt, Greene, Randall & Meissner, Milw., 1956-73; exec. v.p. First Bank Milw., 1973-90, pres., 1990-91, chmn. bd., 1991-93; chmn. emeritus, 1993—. Trustee Boys & Girls Club of Greater Milw.; bd. dirs. Pvt. Industry Coun.; past mem. Salvation Army Adv. Bd.; past dir. Family Svcs. of Milw., Music for Youth, Milw. Artists Found.; chmn. War Meml. Devel. Com.; founder, 1st chmn. United Performing Arts Fund; mem. ad hoc com. for study on the arts in Wis.; mem. Gov.'s Commn. on Univ. System Compensation; trustee Med. Coll. Wis., Alverno Coll., Bank Rep. Trustees Com. of the Milw. Found., Faye McBeath Found.; mem. Donor's Forum and many others in past. Recipient "Others" award Salvation Army, Alumni award Dartmouth Coll., Pro Urbe award Mt. Mary Coll., Citizen of the Yr. Milw. chpt. UNICO, Father of the Yr. award Am. legion, Gold Baton award Milw. Symphony Orch., Alumnus of the Yr. award U. Sch. Milw., Disting. Svc. award Milw., Jr. C. of C., UPAF Steimke award Support of the Arts, Mulw. Found. Frye award for Cmty. Svc. Home: 6122 N Berkeley Blvd Milwaukee WI 53217-4315 Office: First Bank Milw 201 W Wisconsin Ave Milwaukee WI 53203-2303

RANDOLPH, JOE WAYNE, machine manufacturing executive; b. Madisonville, Ky., Aug. 5, 1938; s. Albert Clay and Helen (Brown) R.; m. Mary Ann Rabenau, July 20, 1963; children: Ann E., Charles J. BS, Murray State U., 1962, MS, 1964; MBA, Washington U./Lindenwood Coll., 1978. High sch. tchr. Benton (Ky.) Sch. System, 1962-64, St. Charles (Mo.) Sch. System, 1964-65; mfg. mgr. Sunnen Products Co., St. Louis, 1967—. 1st lt. U.S. Army, 1965. Named Col., Hon. Order of Ky. Cols., 1990. Mem. AAIM Mgmt. Assn. (prodn. exec. round table, leader 1984—), Elks. Home: 5700 Highway 2 Augusta MO 63332-1419 Office: Sunnen Products Co 7910 Manchester Rd Saint Louis MO 63143-2712

RANDOLPH, LILLIAN LARSON, medical association executive; b. Spokane, Wash., May 3, 1932; d. Charles P. and Juanita S. (Parrish) Larson; m. Philip L. Randolph, Nov. 12, 1952; children: Marcus, Andrew. BA, U. Wash., 1954, MA, 1956; PhD, U. Calif., Berkeley, 1966; EdD, N.Mex. State U., 1979. Researcher U. Wash., Seattle, 1954-59; asst. prof. Calif. State U., Hayward, 1964-68, U. Tex., El Paso, 1972-74; dir. S.W. Conservatory of Music, El Paso, 1972-74; adj. prof. Loyola U. and DePaul U., Chgo., 1974-78; asst. prof. DeVry Inst. Tech., Lombard, Ill., 1982-84; mgr. AMA, Chgo., 1985—; cons. Weber Co., Chgo., 1979-85. Author: Fundamentals of Government Organizations, 1971, Third Party Settlement of Disputes, 1973. Mem. AAUP, Phi Beta Kappa. Home: 408 W Wilshire Dr Wilmette IL 60091-3154

RANDOLPH, WARREN EDWIN, small business owner; b. Denver, Nov. 23, 1950. With Farmers Coop., Lorenzo, Nebr., 1974-87, asst. mgr., 1981-87; owner, mgr. Goodwin Machine Shop, Sidney, Nebr., 1987—. With U.S. Army, 1970-72. Mem. Elks. Office: Goodwin Machine Shop 1112 Grant St Sidney NE 69162-1358

RANEY, CHARLES C., electrical engineer; b. Kansas City, Kans., Oct. 12, 1942. BS in Elec. Engring., Findlay Engring. Sch., Kansas City, Mo., 1972. Mgr. engring. Milbank, Kansas City, Mo., 1966-77; owner Rancy Tool & Die, Kansas City, Kans., 1976-81; pres. Preco Industries Inc., Shawnee Mission, Kans., 1982—. Patentee in field. Mem. Soc. Mfg. Engrs. Roman Catholic. Office: Preco 9501 Dice Ln Shawnee Mission KS 66215-1158

RANEY, DAVID ELLIOT, data processing consultant; b. Fairhope, Ala., Mar. 4, 1951; s. James Edward and Zoie Louise (Hastings) R.; m. Marian Stark Scovill, June 21, 1975; children: Brian Jesse, Sarah Ann. Student, Northwestern U., 1968-72, U. Va., 1983. Police cadet Bloomingdale (Ill.) Police Dept., 1971-72, police officer, 1972-76, sgt., 1976-83, comdr. adminstrv. svcs., 1983-88; pres. PC-Lab Svcs., Glen Ellyn, Ill., 1987—; cons. DevTech Assocs., Naperville, ILL., 1991-92, Ameritech Properties Corp., Chgo., 1991—, Motorola, Inc., Schaumburg, Ill., 1991-92; sr. programmer-analyst Liquid Carbonic Industries Corp., Oak Brook, Ill., 1992—; cons. Lundblad, Baker & Martier, Chgo., 1988—; promotion assessor, Hanover Park (Ill.) Police Dept., 1987; selected to attend 134th Session, FBI Nat. Acad. Contbr. articles to profl. jours. Pres., bd. trustees Church of the Cross, Hoffman Estates, Ill., 1986-87; mgr. Glen Ellyn (Ill.) Baseball, Inc., 1989-93. Mem. FBI Nat. Acad. Assocs., Shriners, Masons (master 1983-84, jr. warden 1982-83). Republican. Presbyterian. Home: 441 Geneva Rd Glen Ellyn IL 60137-3771 Office: 810 Jorie Blvd Hinsdale IL 60521-2216

RANGAN, RAVI MANGALAM, mechanical engineer; b. Bombay, India, Nov. 23, 1962; came to U.S. 1984; s. Mangalam Vaidyanathan and Vijayalakshmi (Narasimhan) B.; m. Yamini Gourishankar, Nov. 1, 1989; 1 child, Kamna Shastri. BE, M.S. U. Baroda, India, 1984; MS, U. Wyo., 1986; PhD, Ga. Inst. Tech., 1990. Grad. rsch. asst. U. Wyo., Laramie, 1984-86, Ga. Inst. Tech., Atlanta, 1986-90; doctoral intern N.C.R. Corp., Wichita, Kans., 1988-90; project engr., tech. advisor in engring. data mgmt. S.D.R.C. (Structural Dynamics Rsch. Corp.), Cin., 1990-95, tech. program dir., 1995—; cons. IBM, Germany, 1990-91, T.D.W., Inc., Tulsa, 1991-92, USAF Wright Labs., Dayton, 1992-93, Xerox Corp., 1993-94, Chrysler Corp., 1993-94, Goodyear Tire & Rubber Co., 1994, The Boeing Co.-DCAC/MRM, 1994—. Mem. readers com. Internat. Jour. Systems Automation: Rsch. & Applications, 1991—; mem. editl. rev. bd. Jour. Concurrent Engring.: Rsch. & Applications, 1993—; editor ASME Engring. Database Symposium Proceedings, 1995, co-editor, 1991, 92, 93, 94; contbr. articles to profl. jours. Mem. ASME (steering com. engring. database program 1990—, conf. chair 1995, conf. session chmn. Internat. Computers Engring. Conf. 1991, 92, 93, 94, Best Paper award 1990), IEEE, Assn. for Computing Machinery, Tau Beta Pi, Pi Tau Sigma. Office: SDRC 2000 Eastman Dr Milford OH 45150-2712

RANGER, DEE BRUCE, engineering manager; b. Kalamazoo, Mich., Sept. 1, 1937. AS, Western Mich. U., 1959, BA in Mech. Engring., 1984; AS, Lake Michigan Coll., Benton Harbor, Mich., 1992. Project engr. Striker Corp., Kalamazoo, Mich., 1977-86, Auto Specialties, St. Joseph, Mo., 1986-89; engring. mgr. State Tool & Mfg. Co., Benton Harbor, Mich., 1989—. Inventor: holds 2 patents for medical and commercial packaging. Mem. Soc. Mfg. Engrs. (registered engr.), Lions Club. Home: 7040 Ryno Rd Coloma MI 49038-9704 Office: State Tool & Mfg Co 1650 E Empire Ave Benton Harbor MI 49022-2024

RANKIN, ALFRED MARSHALL, JR., business executive; b. Cleve., Oct. 8, 1941; s. Alfred Marshall and Clara Louise (Taplin) R.; m. Victoire Conley Griffin, June 3, 1967; children: Helen P., Clara T. BA in Econs. magna cum laude, Yale U., 1963, JD, 1966. Mgmt. cons. McKinsey & Co., Inc., Cleve., 1970-73; with Eaton Corp., Cleve., 1974-81, pres. materials handling group, 1981-83, pres. indsl. group, 1984-86, exec. v.p., 1986, vice chmn., chief oper. officer, 1986-89; pres., COO NACCO Industries, Inc., Cleve., 1989-91, pres., CEO, 1991-94, also bd. dirs., chmn., pres., CEO, 1994—, chmn., 1994—; bd. dirs. B.F. Goodrich Co., The Std. Products Co., Vanguard Group. Former pres., trustee Hathaway Brown Sch.; trustee Univ. Hosps. Cleve., Mus. Arts Assn., Univ. Ctr., Inc., Cleve. Mus. Art, Greater Cleve. Growth Assn., John Huntington Art and Poly. Inst., Cleve. Tomorrow, The Cleve. Found. Mem. Ohio Bar Assn. Republican. Clubs: Chagrin Valley Hunt, Union, Tavern, Pepper Pike, Kirtland Country (Cleve.); Rolling Rock (Ligonier, Pa.); Met. (Washington). Home: 5875 Landerbrook Dr Ste 300 Mayfield Heights OH 44124 Office: NACCO Industries Inc 5875 Landerbrook Dr Mayfield Heights OH 44124

RANKIN, ARTHUR DAVID, paper company executive; b. Bklyn., July 5, 1936; s. David Emerson and Elizabeth Howe (Smart) R.; m. Judith Ann Clark, Sept. 6, 1958; children: Debi Lynn Murlowski, Kristen Lori. B-SChemE, 5-Yr. Cert. Pulp and Paper, U. Maine, Orono, 1960, MS in Pulp and Paper, 1960. Tech. svc. engr. Mead Corp., Chillicothe, Ohio, 1960-65; product engr. Jones div. Beloit Corp., Dalton, Mass., 1965-69; tech. asst. paper supt. Crown Zellerbach St. Francisville, La., 1969-71; stock prep. supr. Crown Zellerbach, St. Francisville, La., 1971-74; paper machine supt. Appleton Papers, Inc., Combined Locks, Wis., 1974-84, steps project coord., 1984-85, sr. paper machine supt., 1986-88, sr. prodn. assoc., 1988-90, edn. and mill planning mgr., 1991-95, tech. and devel. mgr. Coated Free Sheet divsn., 1995—; instr. video U. Wis., Stevens Point, 1988, 89. Officer Jaycees, Waverly, Ohio, 1960-63, Chillicothe, Ohio, 1963-65, Pittsfield, Mass., 1965-69; bd. dirs. acad. adv. coun. U. Minn. Paper Sci. Sch., Mpls., 1988—; bd. dirs. U. Minn. Paper, 1988—; acad. adv. coun. paper sci. U. Wis., Stevens Point, 1987—, bd. dirs., 1990—. Mem. ASTM, TAPPI, Nat. Paper Indsl. Mgmt. Assn. (bd. dirs. 1988, pres. 1993, treas. 1994—, Del Boutin award 1995), North Ctrl. Paper Indsl. Mgmt. Assn. (bd. dirs. 1977—). Republican. Congregationalist. Home: 1408 S Lee St Appleton WI 54915-3824

RANKIN, JOHN CARTER, consulting chemist; b. Knoxville, Tenn., Dec. 21, 1919; s. Nelson Henry and Rosine Bonna (Carter) R.; m. Ruth Elizabeth Kirk, Aug. 8, 1943; children—Christine, Mark, Ellen. B.S., Bradley U., 1942, M.S., 1955. Project leader derivatives and polymers, exploration research cereal products No. Regional Research Center, U.S. Dept. Agr., Peoria, Ill., 1946-79; cons. in starch chemistry, 1980—. Served with U.S. Army, 1944-46. Recipient Disting. Service award U.S. Dept. Agr., 1955, 64; Fed. Inventors award U.S. Dept. Commerce, 1980. Mem. Am. Chem. Soc., Am. Assn. Cereal Chemists, TAPPI, AAAS, Sigma Xi. Republican. Contbr. chpts. to sci. textbooks, numerous articles to profl. jours.; patentee. Home: 1734 E Maple Ridge Dr Peoria IL 61614-7914

RANKIN, JOSEPH WALTER, lawyer; b. Muncie, Ind., Sept. 6, 1941; s. Wilbert Franklin and Vera (Strickler) R.; m. Lena Kay Shelby, Aug. 24, 1968; children: Jolene, Justin Randall. AB, U. Indpls., 1963; JD, Ind. U., 1970. Bar: Ind. 1970, U.S. Dist. Ct. (so. dist.) Ind. 1970. Pvt. practice Muncie, 1970—; judge Muncie City Ct., 1972-76; atty. Ctr. Twp. Delaware County, Muncie, 1986—; bd. atty. Liberty Regional Waste Dist., Selma, 1986-90; dep. pros. Delaware County, 1987-91; bd. dirs. Ind. Jud. Ctr., Indpls., 1975-76; atty. Town of Selma, 1986-90. Past pres. Meals on Wheels, Muncie, 1972, bd. dirs., 1972-75; past pres. Big Bros./Big Sisters of Delaware County, 1976, bd. dirs., 1974-77; treas. Muncie PAL Club, Inc., 1992—; bd. dirs. Christian Ministries of Delaware County, 1994—. With U.S. Army, 1964-70. Mem. ABA, Ind. State Bar Assn. (fair trial free press com. 1977—), Delaware County Bar Assn., Ind. Mcpl. Judges Assn. (pres. 1975-76), Rooster Boosters, Chanticleer Club (trustee 1977-89), Optimist (pres. Muncie Noon chpt. 1991-92). Democrat. Methodist. Office: Chi-apppetta Rankin Winters 2810 W Ethel Ave Ste 1 Muncie IN 47304

RANKIN, SCOTT DAVID, artist, educator; b. Newark, Mar. 21, 1954; s. Clymont J. and Jean L. (Lane) R.; m. Linda K. Piemonte, Sept. 3, 1989. BFA, Tyler Sch. of Art, Phila., 1976; MFA, UCLA, 1980. Asst. prof. U. Iowa, Iowa City, 1985-86, U. Chgo., 1986-94; assoc. prof. Ill. State U., Normal, 1994—; video documentation cons. Math. Edn. Rsch. Project, L.A., 1991-93, 3d ann. math. and sci. study UCLA dept. psychology, 1994-95. Prodr., dir.: (videotapes) Fugue, 1985, This and that (version 1), 1987, (version 2), 1990, The Pure, 1993, Flow, 1996. Regional media arts fellow Nat. Endowment for Arts, 1984, visual artist's fellow Ill. Arts Coun., 1989, 90, visual artist's fellow Nat. Endowment for Arts, 1990, 93.

RANNEY, RICHARD WILLIAM, electronic data systems company official; b. Davenport, Iowa, Nov. 2, 1944; s. Robert Lee and June Rose (Holzhausen) R.; m. Geraldine Faith Cotten, Jan. 28, 1967 (div. Sept. 1976); m. Milda Maria Dargis, Mar. 28, 1981; children: Brianna Dargis, Robert Liutauras. BS in Mktg., Okla. State U., 1967; MBA, So. Meth. U., 1968. Systems engr. Electronic Data Systems Corp., Dallas, 1971-77, account mgr., 1977-80; mktg. rep. Electronic Data Systems Corp., Chgo., 1980-82, account mgr., 1982-88, strategic bus. planning mgr., 1988-91; quality advisor to strategic bus. unit pres. automotive Electronic Data Sys. Corp., Troy, Mich., 1991-94, enterprise reengring. project mgr., 1994—; instr., author course syllabus Computer Career Program De Paul U., Chgo., 1982-84. 1st lt. USAR, 1968-71. Fellow Life Mgmt. Inst., Life Office Mgmt. Assn.; mem. Am. Prodn. and Inventory Control Soc. (cert. in prodn. and inventory mgmt.), Sierra Club (outing chmn. Chgo. group 1979-81), Chgo. Mountaineering Club (sec. 1988-89). Home: 2808 Birch Harbor Ln West Bloomfield MI 48324-1908 Office: Electronic Data Systems Corp 5555 New King Dr Troy MI 48098-2616

RANSEL, DAVID LORIMER, history educator; b. Gary, Ind., Feb. 20, 1939; s. Joseph A. and Patricia (Lorimer) R.; m. Therese Holma; children: Shairstin, Annaliisa. BA, Coe Coll., 1961; MA, Northwestern U., 1962; PhD, Yale U., 1969. Instr. Tollare Folkhogskola, Boo, Sweden, 1959-60; asst. instr. Yale U., New Haven, 1966-67; instr. U. Ill., Urbana, 1967-69, asst. prof., 1969-73, assoc. prof., 1973-81, prof., 1981-85; prof. Ind. U., Bloomington, 1985—, dir. Russian and East European Inst., 1995—. Author: The Politics of Catherinian Russia, 1975, Mothers of Misery, 1988; editor: The Family in Imperial Russia, 1978; editor/translator: Village Life in Late Tsarist Russia, 1993; editor Slavic Rev., Urbana, 1980-85, Am. Hist. Rev., Bloomington, 1985-95. Guggenheim fellow, 1989-90, Wilson fellow, 1989-90; Fulbright-Hays grantee, 1979, 90, Irex grantee, 1990, 93. Mem. Am. Hist. Assn. (mem. gov. coun. 1985-95, mem. fin. com. 1989-95), Am. Assn. for Advancement of Slavic Studies (bd. dirs. 1979-85, mem. fin. com. 1980-85, chmn. com. on status of women 1991-93, mem. Irex program com. 1995—). Office: Ind Univ Russian/East European Inst Ballantine Hall 565 Bloomington IN 47401-3600

RANSHAW, JANE ELLEN, training consultant; b. Greencastle, Ind., Aug. 30, 1944; d. William C. and Rosella (Cantwell) R.; m. Louis Sorkin, Jan. 21, 1978. BS, Ind. U., 1966; MBA, U. Chgo., 1972. Account exec. Golin Harris, Chgo., 1974-76; assoc. dir. Nat. Affiliation of Concerned Bus. Students, Chgo., 1972-74; tng. coord. CNA Ins., Chgo., 1969-72; pres. Jane Ranshaw & Assocs., Inc., Chgo., 1976—. Author: 101 Tips for Marketing Your Services. Mem. ASTD, Am. Mgmt. Assn., Soc. for Human Resource Mgmt., Ind. Writers Chgo. (pres. 1990-91), Internat. Soc. for Performance Improvement (v.p. Chgo. chpt. 1995-96), Soc. for Tech. Comm., U. Chgo. Women's Bus. Group (v.p. 1985).

RANSOM, KEVIN RENARD DORTCH, investment banker; b. Detroit, Sept. 24, 1964; s. Donald Lewis and Etta Mae (Dortch) R. B in Econs., Morehouse Coll., 1988. Fin. analyst Goldman Sachs & Co., N.Y.C., 1987-88, Merrill Lynch & Co., N.Y.C., 1988-89; freelance journalist KDR & Assocs., N.Y.C., 1989-90; fiscal analyst Mich. State Legislature, Lansing, 1990-92; dir. fiscal analysis Detroit City Coun., 1992-95; asst. v.p. First of Mich. Investment Bank, Detroit, 1995—; cons. Lansing C.C., 1990—. Editor: Neighborhood Economic Development Strategies, 1990. Bd. dirs. Hollywood Fashion Clothes, Detroit. Mem. Investors Alliance, Nat. Smithsonian Found., Morehouse Nat. Alumni Assn., Kappa Alpha Psi. Democrat. Baptist. Home: 100 Riverfront Park # 1507 Detroit MI 48226

RANSOM, MARGARET PALMQUIST, public relations executive; b. Davenport, Iowa, Aug. 13, 1935; d. Herman Philip and Margaret (Burchell) Palmquist; m. David Duane Ransom, July 16, 1960; 1 child, David Burke. BA in Speech and English, Augustana Coll., 1957. Tchr. speech and English Beloit (Wis.) High Sch., 1957-59; tchr. English Lake Forest (Ill.) High Sch., 1959-60, Warren High Sch., Gurnee, Ill., 1960-62, 64-66; asst. to dean Grad. Sch. Bowling Green (Ohio) State U., 1963; freelance writer Coll. Bd. Examinations, 1966; market rsch. analyst Kitchens of Sara Lee, Deerfield, Ill., 1972-74; pub. affairs mgr. Sara Lee Bakery, Deerfield, 1975-89; sr. cons. Ransom Pub. Svc. Cons., Libertyville, Ill., 1990-94; cons. Olsten Staffing Svcs., Chgo., 1994—; judge nat. competitions Pub. Rels. Soc. Am., 1986-89; spkr. on motivation and orgn.; chmn. Ill. Dept. Employment Security's Job Security Employers Com., 1995—. Bd. dirs. Early Childhood Adv. Coun., Northeastern Ill. State U., 1989-91; mem. Main St. Libertyville com., 1990-92; creator Job Market Place '96, Lake County. Recipient Ill. Citizens Svc. medal, 1993. Mem. AAUW, Bus. and Profl. Women Lake County, Mortar Bd. Office: 1037 Mayfair Dr Libertyville IL 60048-3548

RANSON, PAT, state legislator; m. Jack Ranson. Senator dist. 25 State of Kans., 1993—. Republican. *

RANTA AHO, MARTHA HELEN, retired elementary education educator; b. Poplar, Wis., July 12, 1923; d. John and Aurora (Aho) Ranta; m. Wayne August Aho, Dec. 19, 1942 (dec. June 1978); children: Dennis Wayne, Marla Jane Thibodeau. BS in Elem. Edn. with honors, U. Wis., Superior, 1968, MS in Teaching, Elem. Edn., 1977, postgrad., 1979-86; postgrad., U. Minn., Superior, 1980-91, Coll. of St. Scholastica, 1978, Coll. St. Scholastica, Duluth, Minn, 1991. Cert. elem. tchr., Minn. Tchr. kindergarten Ind. Sch. Dist. #709, Duluth, 1968-75; tchr. first grade ISD #709, Duluth, 1975-89, master tchr., 1978-89, ret., 1989. Mem. St. Luke's Vol. Svc. Guild, tchr. leader insvc. sessions, 1972-80; docent St. Louis County Hist. Soc.-Depot Mus., Duluth, 1989—; mentor tchr. Kenwood Elem. Sch., 1987-89, vol. storyteller, 1989—, Chester Park Elem. Sch., 1993—; storyteller Rockridge Elem. Sch., 1995—, Congdon Park Elem. Sch., 1995—. Recipient trophy and award Wis. Indianhead Dist. of Garden Club, Superior, 1964. Mem. AAUW, Minn. Reading Assn., Arrowhead Reading Coun., Duluth Area Ret. Educators Assn., Am. Assn. Ret. Persons, Minn. Hist. Soc, Univ. for Srs. (vol. tchr. leader 1991), Parent Tchr. Student Assn. (hon. life), Finnish Am. Hist. Soc., Nat. Storytelling Assn., Minn. Gen. Fedn. Women's Clubs, Twentieth Century Club, Delta Kappa Gamma. Democrat. Lutheran. Home: 2722 E 1st St Duluth MN 55812-1907

RANUM, JANE BARNHARDT, lawyer; b. Charlotte, N.C., Aug. 21, 1947; d. John Robert and Gladys Rose (Swift) B.; m. James Harry Ranum, Mar. 29, 1972; 1 child, Elizabeth McBride. B.S., East Carolina U., 1969; J.D., Hamline U., 1979. Bar: Minn. 1979, U.S. Dist. Ct. Minn. 1979. Tchr. elem. sch. Durham County, Durham, N.C., 1969-70; tchr. Dept. Def., Baumholder, W.Ger., 1970-72, Dist. 196, Rosemount, Minn., 1972-76; law clk. Hennepin County Dist. Ct., Mpls., 1982; asst. county atty. Hennepin County, Mpls., 1982—. Mem. exec. com., lobbying coordinator DFL Feminist Caucus, St. Paul, 1980-84; bd. dirs. Project 13 for Reproductive Rights, Mpls., 1981-82; state del. Minn. Democratic Farmer Labor Party Conv., 1982, 84, precinct del., 1974—; mem. Minn. Sen., 1991—, chair legislature commn. on children, youth and their families, 1993—; senate rep. chemical abuse and prevention resource coun., 1993. Named Feminist of the Yr. Minn. NOW, 1994, Legis. of the Yr. Minn. Assn. for Retarded Citizens, 1994. Mem. Minn. Women's Lawyers, Minn. Family Support and Recovery Council, Hennepin County Bar Assn., Minn. Bar Assn. Democrat. Home: 5045 Aldrich Ave S Minneapolis MN 55419-1207 Office: County Govt Ctr A-2000 Hennepin Minneapolis MN 55487

RAO, SUBBANARASIMHIAH, management educator; b. Gargeswari, India, Dec. 19, 1937; came to U.S. 1968.; s. Subbanarasimhiah G.S. and Subbamma; m. Manorama Murthy, June 6, 1971; children: Dinesh, Suma. BS with honors, Maharaja's Coll., Mysore, India, 1958; MS, Mysore U., 1959; PhD, Delhi (India) U., 1967. Rsch. scientist Dept. Def., Delhi, 1960-68; asst. vis. prof. U. Rochester, N.Y., 1968-69; from asst. to assoc. prof. Case Western Res. U., Cleve., 1969-74; prof., dean, interim dir. Indian Inst. Mgmt., Bangalore, 1974-79, 81-85; prof., dir. PhD programs U. Toledo, 1986—; vis. prof. So. Meth. U., Dallas, 1979-80, Wash. State U., Pullman, 1985-86; cons. in field, India, 1974-85, Toledo, 1986—; bd. govs. Indian Inst. Mgmt., Bangalore, 1976-78. Contbr. articles to scholarly publs. Chmn. religious activities com. Hindu Temple, Toledo, 1996—; mem. organizing com. Bharati Assn., Cleve., 1969-74. Mem. Operational Rsch. Soc. India (life, past pres.), Inst. for Ops. Rsch. and Mgmt. Scis., Midwest Bus. Adminstrn. Assn. (track chair), Decision Scis. Inst. (session chair). Home: 6046 Peppermill Dr Sylvania OH 43560 Office: U Toledo Dept Info Sys and Ops Mgmt Toledo OH 43606

RAPAPORT, ROSS JAY, counseling administrator, educator; b. Lansing, Mich., Jan. 30, 1950; s. Ramond Harvey and A. Geraldine (Gauss) R.; m. Shelly Sue Becker, July 2, 1977; children: Lauren, Allison. BA, Mich. State U., 1972; MA, Ohio State U., 1975, PhD, 1979. Nat. cert. counselor; lic. profl. counselor. Sr. staff psychologist Univ. Counseling Service U. Iowa, Iowa City, 1979-82; assoc. prof., coord. alcohol and drug abuse intervention and prevention program Counseling Ctr. Ctrl. Mich. U., Mt. Pleasant, Mich., 1983-90; prof. counseling Counseling Ctr. Cen. Mich. U., Mt. Pleasant, Mich., 1990—; asst. to dean of students Ctrl. Mich. U., Mt. Pleasant, 1995—; mem. U.S. Dept. Edn. Planning Group for the Network of Colls. and Univs. Committed to the Elimination of Drug and Alcohol Abuse, 1988-93. Co-author over 20 articles to profl. jours. Bd. mem. Mt. Pleasant Counseling Service, 1984-90; mem. adv. council Mid-state Substance Abuse Commn., Clare, Mich., 1984-90. Recipient Profl. Service award Mid-State Substance Abuse Commn., 1987. Mem. ACA, Am. Coll. Pers. Assn. (chair, Disting. Svc. award com. XVIII 1990-92), Am. Coll. Counselors Assn., Mich. Counseling Assn., Mich. Coll. Pers. Assn. (Rsch. award 1988, Pub. award 1990, bd. dir. 1994-96), Phi Kappa Phi. Home: 1413 Crosslanes St Mount Pleasant MI 48858-1941 Office: Counseling Ctr Cen Mich U 102 Foust Hall Mount Pleasant MI 48859

RAPHTIS, ATHENA ELLEN, elementary school teacher; b. Warren, Ohio, Nov. 20, 1968; d. Thomas E. and Aliki C. (Collins) R. BS in Elem. Edn., Kent State U., 1991. Cert. elem. sch. tchr. Substitute tchr. Trumbull City Schs., Warren, 1991-93; head tchr., adminstr. Dublin Montessori Acad., Powell, Ohio, 1993-94; phys. edn. tchr. Warren City Schs., 1994-95, kindergarten tchr., 1995—. Active Am. Heart Assn., Warren. Mem. NEA, Internat. Reading Assn. (Trumbull Area Reading Coun.), Ohio Edn. Assn., Warren Edn. Assn., Delta Gamma. Greek Orthodox.

RAPP, LARRY P., financial advisor; b. Ravenna, Ohio, Feb. 20, 1948; s. George P. and Marie A. (Kormos) R.; m. Francine M. Koneval. BS, U. Dayton (Ohio), 1970. CPA. Sr. mgr. Price Waterhouse, Cleve. and N.Y., 1970-83; v.p. fin. Rotek Inc., Cleve., 1983-84; contr. Omnicare Inc., Cin., 1984-87; v.p. fin., chief fin. officer Animed Inc., Roslyn, N.Y., 1987-89; CFO Hawk Group/Weinberg Capital Corp., Cleve., 1989-93; pres. Sanctuary Fin. Group, Akron, 1993-96; CFO LCA-Vision Inc., Cin., 1996—; assoc. editor Ohio CPA Jour., 1987-88, manuscript rev. com., 1995—; mem. nat. com. Career Svcs., FEI. Mem. Am. Inst. CPAs, Ohio Soc. CPAs, Fin Execs. Inst. Home and Office: Sanctuary Fin Group 3596 Sanctuary Dr Akron OH 44333-1748

RAPPAPORT, CYRIL M., personnel administrator; b. N.Y.C., July 12, 1921; s. David M. and Saide (Newmark) R.; B.S., CCNY, 1942; M.A., Columbia U., 1943; postgrad. N.Y.U., 1943-44; m. Dorothy Pevsner, June 19, 1957 (dec. 1966); children—Stuart N., David M. Personnel cons., The Psychol. Corp., N.Y.C., 1943-44; indsl. relations asst. Emerson Radio Corp., N.Y.C., 1944-45; adminstrv. asst. A. Hollander & Son, Long Branch, N.J., 1946-52; prin. C.M. Rappaport, retailer, Hackensack, N.J., 1952-54; mem. exec. staff Martin E. Segal & Co., N.Y.C., 1954-56, Chgo., 1956-57; sec. Midcontinent Tube Service, Evanston, Ill., 1957-58; distbr. Investor's Diversified Services, Chgo., 1959-60; systems analyst Goldblatt Bros. Store, Chgo., 1960-64; personnel officer Ill. State Dept. Mental Health, 1964-69; dir. personnel Children's Meml. Hosp., Chgo., 1969-74, St. Joseph's Hosp., 1974-75, Edgewater Hosp., Chgo., 1975-76; dir. mgmt. and personnel svcs. Jewish Vocat. Svc., Chgo., 1976-88; human resources specialist Cyborg Systems Inc., 1988— ; dir. Paket, Inc., 1960-61. Bd. dirs. Bernard Horwich Community Center, 1971-73; mem. personnel planning and cons. com. United Way, 1978-79; mem. Age Discrimination Sub. Com. Mayor's Coordinating Com. Old Age, 1979—; mem. rehab. com. Chgo. Hosp. Council, 1979—, bd. health Village of Skokie. Master Mason; mem. AAHA, APHA, Am. Soc. Hosp. Personnel Adminstrn. (dir. 1971-72), Am. Soc. Mental Hosp. Bus. Adminstrn., Assn. of Mental Health Adminstrn., Indsl. Relations Research Assn., Chgo. Hosp. Personnel Mgmt. Assn., Chgo. Assn. Commerce and Industry (manpower devel. and tng. com.). Home: 4939 Coyle Ave Skokie IL 60077-3515 Office: 2 N Riverside Plz Chicago IL 60606

RARIDEN, ROBERT LEE, information scientist, educator; b. Flint, Mich., Mar. 7, 1949; s. Robert Cahill and Christine (Darby) R.; m. Lorraine Marie Larson, Aug. 19, 1970; children: Shannon, Robert, Madeline, John. BA, Ctrl. Mich. U., 1971; MA, U. Miami, 1979, PhD, 1983. Asst. prof. Grambling (La.) State U., 1982-88; assoc. prof. Ill. State U., Normal, 1988—; cons. State Farm Ins. Cos., Bloomington, Ill., 1989-90, Nat. Assn. Brad Repair Tele, Bloomington, 1990—, U.S. Army Corps of Engrs., Washington, 1992—; pres. Logical Sys. Solutions Inc., Normal, Ill., 1993—. Contbr. articles to profl. jours. Mem. IEEE, Data Processing Mgmt. Assn., Assn. Computer Mfrs. Roman Catholic. Office: Ill State Univ Applied Computer Sci Dept Normal IL 61791-5151

RASCHE, J. DAVID, retired architect; b. Dover, Ohio, May 31, 1929; s. George and Charlotte I. (Romig) R.; m. Doris Jean Hieber, Apr. 19, 1959; children: Brian, Tom. BArch, U. Mich., 1952; MArch, U. Pa., 1956. Registered architect, Minn., Ill., Ind., Wis., Mich., S.D., N.D., Tex., Ohio. Project mgr. Ganster & Hennighausen, Architects, Waukegan, Ill., 1956-64; inspector Waukegan Housing Authority, 1964-65; assoc. Kantola-Mizera, Architects, Chgo., 1965-66; asst. to dept. head U. Ill. Chgo. Cir., 1966-69; architect Dept. Store Div. Dayton Hudson Corp., Mpls., 1969-95; ret., 1995. Arch.: Dayton's Southdale, 1990, Dayton's Rosedale, 1991, Dayton's Mpls., 1991, Hudson's Traverse City, Mich., 1992, Marshall Field's Northbrook Court, 1994. With U.S. Army, 1952-54. Mem. AIA (Minn. Hist. Resources com.), Nat. Trust for Hist. Preservation, Soc. Archtl. Hist. Home: 13611 McGinty Rd E Minnetonka MN 55305-3648

RASCO, KAY FRANCES, antique dealer; b. Rienzi, Miss., Nov. 13, 1925; d. Robert Franklin and Sophia Agnes (Kinningham) Dilworth; m. H. Manfred Ray, July 9, 1943 (div. 1950); 1 child, Manfred Ray; m. Lavon Rasco, Mar. 22, 1951; children: Francine, Karen. BA, U. Miss., 1948, MA, 1953; PhD, Northwestern U., 1966. Instr. English Western Ill. U., 1953-54, 56-60, Northwestern U., 1960-61; lectr. De Paul U., Chgo., 1969, 71-74; master tchr. English Yale U., New Haven, Conn., summers 1963,64, 66,67; tchr. English New Trier High Sch., Winnetka, Ill., 1961-69, 71-73; assoc. prof. English Am. U., Cairo, 1969-71; prof. drama Al Azhar U., Cairo, 1976-77; sales assoc. Merrill Lynch Realty, Evanston, Ill., 1973-76, 78-83, mgr. area sales, 1983-89; owner Sarah Bustle Antiques, Evanston, Ill., 1989—. Mem. Rotary Internat. (dir. internat. svc. Evanston Lighthouse Rotary). Home: 1211 Hinman Ave Evanston IL 60202-1312 Office: 821 Dempster St Evanston IL 60201-4303

RASHID, HARUN UR, philosopher, educational administrator; b. Bakshimul, Comilla, Bangladesp, Oct. 6, 1954; came to U.S., 1984; s. Ali Akber and Zohra Begum; m. Jaha Afroz Sayeeda, June 10, 1979; children: Mashiyat, Anira. BA with honors, U. Dacca, Bangladesh, 1977, MA, 1978; MA, U. Waterloo, Ontario, Can., 1984; PhD, Wayne State U., 1993. Adminstrv. cert., Mich. Grad. teaching asst. U. Waterloo, Ontario, 1983-84; adj. prof. Wayne State U., Detroit, 1990—; asst. prof. philosophy Marygrove Coll., 1993—; asst. dir. Master in the Art of Tchg. Marygrove Coll., Detroit, 1995—; philosophy lectr. U. Dacca, 1980-83, U. Chittagong, Bangladesh, 1978-80; cons. on critical thinking Wayne State U. Sch. Edn., Detroit, 1986—. Author: (with others) Effective Secondary Teaching, 1989. U. Waterloo scholar, Ontario, 1983-84, Merit scholar U. Dacca, 1973-77, Residential scholar Bd. Edn., Comilla, 1971-73. Mem. Am. Philos. Assn., Philosophy Edn. Soc. Home: 20462 Glenmore Ave Redford MI 48240-1040 Office: Marygrove Coll Master in the Art Tchg 8425 W McNichols Rd Detroit MI 48221

RASINS, JAMES WILLIAM, auditor; b. Chgo., Oct. 10, 1950; s. William L. and Janice C. Rasins; m. Barbara L. Pfursich, Oct. 6, 1979; stepchildren: Kimberly, Suzanne. BS in Bus. cum laude, No. Ill. U., 1972, MS in Acctg., 1974. CPA, Ill.; cert. fraud examiner. Staff acct. Mueller, Sieracki & Kaun, Elgin, Ill., 1974-75; chief dep., auditor County of DuPage, Wheaton, Ill., 1975—; adj. faculty Coll. DuPage, Glen Ellyn, Ill., 1975—. Precinct committeeman DuPage County Reps., 1983—; parade chmn., com. chmn. Glen Ellyn 4th of July Celebration, 1985—; pres., treas. Luth. Brotherhood Br., DuPage County, 1986—; dir., chmn., budget and allocation com. United Way of Glen Ellyn; dir. Athletics Ofcls. Assn.; mem. Cen. Ofcls. Assn., Chgo., Grace Luth. Ch., Glen Ellyn, 1979—. Recipient Disting. Svc. award Glen Ellyn Jaycees, 1995, V.I.P. award Glen Ellyn Jr. Woman's Club, 1990. Mem. Inst. Internal Auditors, Assn. Cert. Fraud Examiners, Govt. Fin. Officers Assn., Nat. Assn. Local Govt. Auditors, Ill. Govt. Fin. Officers Assn., Kiwanis Club Ctrl. DuPage County (dir., charter). Home: 589 Maiden Ln Glen Ellyn IL 60137

RASMUSSEN, DONNA ILENE LEWIS, instructional technologist; b. Ferndale, Ill., Feb. 20, 1943; d. Frank Frederick and Anna Martha (Mills) Lewis; divorced; 1 child, Sharon Cristine Ann. BA, Wayne State U., 1964, MEd, 1975, BS, 1982, EdS, 1995. Cert. vocat. data processing. Tchr. Am. Career Acad., Oak Park, Mich., 1990; instrnl. and curriculum designer Van Buren Adult Edn., Belleville, Mich., 1990-92; tech. writer Frank's Nursery & Crafts, Detroit, 1992-93; computer cons. Process Devel. Corp., Livonia and Lincoln Park, Mich., 1993-94; trainer Profl. Data Resources, Livonia, 1994; instrnl. developer Mika Sys., Inc., Livonia, 1995; tech. writer EDP Contract Svcs., Southfield, Mich., 1995-96. Author: Lotus 1.2.3 for the Inexperienced PC User, Wordperfect. Mem. ASTD, Grosse Pointe Cinema League (pres. 1990-91, co-pres. 1991-96, co-sec. 1991-96), Sailing Singles. Episcopalian.

RASMUSSEN, JERRY WILLIAM, secondary school educator; b. Sioux City, Iowa, June 9, 1965; s. John William and Norene Kay (Schott) R.; m. Jean Rachel Richardson, June 6, 1992. BS in Hist. Edn., U. S.D., 1987. Cert. tchr., S.D. Instr. social sci. Dakota Valley H.S. (formerly Jefferson H.S.), North Sioux City, S.D., 1987—. Recipient Outstanding Young Educator award S.D. Jaycees, 1993. Mem. NEA, Nat. Strength and Conditioning Assn., Am. Football Coaches Assn., S.D. Football Coaches Assn. (regional dir. 1992-94), Phi Delta Kappa (Taft fellow 1993), Jefferson Alumni Assn. (pres. 1985). Home: PO Box 354 Elk Point SD 57025-0354 Office: Dakota HS PO Box 1960 North Sioux City SD 57049-1960

RATAJ, ELIZABETH ANN, artist; b. Flint, Mich., Oct. 3, 1943; d. Lloyd Milton Clem and Mildred (Lamrock) Clem-Taylor; m. David Henry Rataj, Oct. 17, 1970. BA, Bob Jones U., 1966; BFA, U. Iowa, 1987. Educator Oscoda (Mich.) Area Schs., 1966-71, 73-83, Ft. Wayne (Ind.) Pub. Schs., 1971-72, St. Louis Pub. Schs., 1983-85. Represented in permanent collections Mich. Edn. Assn., Lansing, 1978, Munson Williams Proctor Mus., Utica, N.Y., 1989, Jesse Besser Mus., Alpena, Mich., 1993; two-person shows include The Art Ctr., Mount Clemens, Mich., 1996; group shows include Mus. Modern Art Miami, 1995, San Bernardino County Mus., Redlands, Calif., 1995, Austin Pedy State U., Clarksville, Tenn., 1995, The Art Ctr., Mount Clemens, Mich., 1996. Mem. Delta Kappa Gamma (1978-82, 86-87, 76-87), Nat. Mus. of Women in the Arts (charter).

RATCLIFFE, JAMES MAXWELL, corporate relations executive; b. Kewanee, Ill., May 26, 1925; s. James Maxwell and Madeleine Elizabeth (Hoffrichter) R.; m. Hildegund Elisabeth Weide, Aug. 24, 1969; 1 child, James Maxwell III. BA, U. Chgo., 1946, JD, 1950. Bar: Ill. 1950. Exec. sec. Ill. Com. Constl. Revision, Chgo., 1950; field sec. U. Chgo., 1951, asst. dean Law Sch., 1952-68; dir. pub. affairs R.R. Donnelley & Sons Co., Chgo., 1968-88, v.p. corp. rels., 1989-94; cons. on pub. affairs, 1994—. Editor: The Good Samaritan and the Law, 1962. Bd. dirs., mem. exec. com. Better Govt. Assn., 1978—, Ill. Coun. Econ. Edn., 1981—; bd. dirs. Printing Industries Ill., Harper Ct. Fedn., Citizens' Bd., Loyola U., 1988—; trustee Met. Planning Coun., 1980—. Staff Sgt. U.S. Army, 1943-46. Mem. ABA, Nat. Assn. Mfrs. (chmn. pub. affairs com. 1991-93), Printing Industries Am. (v.p. 1974-80), Chgo. Bar Assn., Univ. Club, Quadrangle Club, Capitol Hill Club. Republican. Roman Catholic. Home: 5536 S Dorchester Ave Chicago IL 60637-1700 Office: RR Donnelley & Sons Co 77 W Wacker Dr Chicago IL 60601-1629

RATHER, MARSHA LEE, nurse educator; b. Freeport, Ill., Jan. 30, 1949; d. Vernon Leslie and Pauline Gransden (Wagner) Hill; m. Mark Douglas Thompson, Aug. 25, 1971 (div. Aug. 29, 1979); m. Jerome William Rather, Sept. 5, 1981. BS, U. Wis., 1971, MS in Med. Surg. Nursing, 1983, PhD in Curriculum and Instrn., 1990. RN, Wis. Staff nurse, nurse clinician U. Wis. Hosp. and Clinics, Madison, 1971-77, head nurse med. ICU, 1977-80; project asst. Wis. Clin. Cancer Ctr., Madison, 1982; teaching asst. U. Wis. Madison Sch. of Nursing, 1983, 85-90, lectr., assoc. lectr., 1983-85, 91, outreach faculty asst. Inst. for Heideggerian Studies, 1990, 91; clin. asst., prof. U. Wis. Madison Hosp. and Clinics, Madison, 1991-94; clin. asst. prof. Sch. Nursing U. Wis., Madison, 1991-94, clin. assoc. prof., 1994—; presenter in field. Mem. editl. bd. Nat. League for Nursing Press, 1991—; reviewer: (jour.) Rsch. in Nursing and Health (RINAH) & Image; contbr. articles to profl. jours. Chair adult Bible study program St. Thomas Aquinas Cath. Ch., 1990—, group leader Bible study, 1986—, Eucharistic minister; vol. Oakwood Village, Hebron Hall, 1986—. Vilas fellow, 1982. Mem. ANA, Wis. Nurses Assn., Nat. League for Nursing (coun. for Soc. for Rsch. in Nursing Edn.), Midwest Nursing Rsch. Soc., Am. Heart Assn. (edn. com. 1977-79), U. Wis.-Madison Sch. Nursing Alumni Orgn. (pres.-elect 1991-92, pres. 1992—), Sigma Theta Tau (Beta Eta chpt. faculty liaison 1990-91, treas. 1991-93). Roman Catholic. Home: 2524 Karakul Ct Madison WI 53711-5481 Office: U of Wis Madison Sch of Nursing 600 Highland Ave Madison WI 53792-2455

RATHER, SHARI ANNE, social worker; b. Neenah, Wis., Oct. 13, 1948; d. Michael Eugene and Gloria Margaret (Hubert) Curran; m. Richard J. Rather, July 10, 1971; children: Michael, Shannon, Kimberly, Ashley. BS, U. Wis., 1973. Dir. social svc. Appleton (Wis) Meml. Hosp., 1973-75, Marshfield (Wis.) Convalscent Ctr., 1975-76; social worker, cons. Colonial House, Colby, Wis., 1975-76; social worker S.D. Perinatal Assn., Sioux Falls, 1977-80; merchandiser Dayton Hudson Corp., Sioux Falls, S.D., 1984-86; patient svc. coord. Muscular Dystrophy Assn., Sioux Falls, S.D., 1987-88; social worker Waukesha County (Wis.) Dept. Human Svcs., 1988—, Wis. Assn. Nursing Home, Milw., 1988-92; cons. Muscular Dystrophy Assn. ALS Support Group, Sioux Falls, 1987-88. Team mgr. Spring City Soccer Club, 1994—; v.p. City Coun., 1989-90, pres., 1990-91; chmn. Jr. League, Sioux Falls, 1982-88, Milw., 1988-91; mem. Pewaukee chpt. PTO, Wis. Juvenile Ct. Intake Assn., 1991—; treas. Horrace Mann PTA, 1987-88, Pewaukee Parent for Soccer Registrar, 1990-92; mem. Pewaukee Friends and Neighbors, 1991—; child advocacy com. Scan, 1994-95; active Prevention Network, 1995—; sec. Pewaukee Select Soccer Club, 1991-95, pres., 1996, team mgr., 1996, select bd. dirs., 1996. Named One of the Outstanding Women in Am., Sioux Falls, 1985. Mem. NASW, Nat. Perinatal Social Worker Assn., Beta Sigma Phi (pres. local chpt. 1985-87, pres. Xi Beta Xi chpt. 1989-90), Alpha Xi Delta. Republican. Roman Catholic. Home: N29w22051 Kathryn Ct Waukesha WI 53186-8856 Office: 500 Riverview Ave Waukesha WI 53188-3632

RATHI, MANOHAR LAL, pediatrician, neonatologist; b. Beawar, Rajasthan, India, Dec. 25, 1933; came to U.S. 1969; s. Bagtawarmal and Sitadevi (Laddha) R.; m. Kamla Jajoo, Feb. 21, 1960; children: Sanjeev A., Rajeev. M.B.B.S., Rajasthan U., 1961. Diplomate Am. Bd. Pediats., sub-bd. Neonatal Perinatal Medicine; lic. physician, N.Y., Ill., Calif. Resident house physician internal medicine Meml. Hosp., Darlington, U.K., 1963-64; resident sr. house physician pediatrics Gen. Hosp., Oldham, U.K., 1964-65; dir. perinatal medicine, attending pediatrician Christ Hosp. Perinatal Ctr., Oak Lawn, Ill., 1974—; assoc. prof. pediatrics Rush Med. Coll., Chgo., 1979—; cons. obstetrician Christ Hosp., Oak Lawn, 1976—; cons. neonatologist Little Co. of Mary Hosp., Evergreen Park, Ill., 1972—, Palos Community Hosp., Palos Heights, Ill., 1978—, Silver Cross Hosp., Joliet, Ill., 1989—; cons./lectr. in field. Contbr. articles to profl. jours.; editor: Clinical Aspects of Perinatal Medicine, 1984, Vol. I, 1985, Vol. II, 1986, Current Perinatology, 1989, Vol. II, 1990; editor with others: Perinatal Medicine Vol. I, 1978, Vol. I, 1980, Vol. II, 1982. Hummell Found. grantee, 1976-77, WyethLab grantee, 1977-78; recipient Physicians Recognition award AMA, 1971-74, 91-92, Outstanding New Citizen's award State of Ill., 1978, Asian Human Svcs. of Chgo., 1988, Nitric Oxide Study by Ohmeda, 1994-95. Fellow Am. Acad. Pediats. (perinatal sect., Ill. chpt. treas. 1994-96); mem. AMA, Chgo. Med. Soc., Ill. Med. Soc., Chgo. Pediat. Soc., Med. Soc. County of Kings Bklyn., N.Y. Acad. Scis., Am. Thoracic Soc., Soc. Critical Care Medicine. Republican. Hindu. Office: Christ Hosp & Med Ctr 4440 W 95th St Ste N232 Oak Lawn IL 60453-2600

RATI, ROBERT DEAN, data processing executive; b. Pittsburg, Kans., Jan. 8, 1939; s. Steve Julius Rati and Dorothy Bill (Rodebush) McWilliams; m. Margaret Fort Henry, June 7, 1969; children: Susan Margaret, Robert Henry. BA, U. Kans., 1961; MA, Northeastern U., Boston, 1970; MBA, Columbia U., 1973. Systems engr. IBM Corp., Boston, 1965-72; mgr. mgmt. services Arthur Young and Co., N.Y.C., 1973-75; mgr. client systems Touche Ross and Co., N.Y.C., 1975-76; mgr. systems and programs Walker Mfg. div. Tenneco, Racine, Wis., 1976-78; mgr. data processing Schwitzer div. Household Internat., Indpls., 1979-87; mgr. mgmt. info. systems Nat. Machinery Co., Tiffin, Ohio, 1988-90; pres. Dunhill Profl. Search of Carmel (Ind.), 1990—; mgr. Muncie MIS Power Transformer div. Asea Brown Boveri, Muncie, Ind., 1991-94; dir. info. svcs. State Lottery Commn. Ind., Indpls., 1995—. Contbr. articles to fraternal orgs. newsletters. Mem. Rep. Com., Ramsey, N.J., 1972-74; treas. Rep. Club Ramsey, 1972-75; vice chmn. Swimming Pool Commn., Ramsey, 1972-74; bd. dirs., exec. com. Near Eastside Multi-Svc. Ctr., Indpls., 1984-87; fin. com. Carmel (Ind.) United Meth. Ch., 1984-87, adminstrv. bd., 1987-90. Lt. (j.g.) USN, 1961-64. Recipient Regional Mgrs. award, IBM Corp., 1967. Mem. Soc. Ind. Pioneers (bd. govs. 1985-91, v.p. 1994—), Huguenot Soc. Ind. (pres. 1985-89, S.R. (Ill. pres. 1980-82, chmn. awards com. 1983-91), Ind. Soc. Colonial Wars (gov. 1995—), Pi Mu Epsilon. Republican. Home: 4919 Regency Pl Carmel IN 46033-5959 Office: State Lottery Commn Ind 201 S Capitol Ave Indianapolis IN 46225

RATNASAMY, D.M. DANIEL, physician; b. Sankarankovil, India, Aug. 9, 1930; came to the U.S., 1967; s. P. David and Hilda D. (Dharmaraj) Muthiah; m. Jebakani Ratnasamy, Aug. 27, 1958; 1 child, Nathaniel. BS, U. Madras, India, 1954. Med. diplomate; cert. Am. Bd. Pediatrics. Intern Bergen Pines County Hosp., Paramus, N.J., 1967-68; resident in radiology and pediatrics Monmouth Med. Ctr., Long Branch, N.J., 1968-71; physician Neighborhood Med. Ctr., New Orleans, 1972-73; pediatrician Dakota Clinic, Jamestown, N.D., 1973-76, 80-84; pvt. practice pediatrician Rajapalayam, India, 1976-80; physician State Hosp., Jamestown, N.D., 1984-94; physician immediate care Meritcare Med. Group, Fargo, N.D., 1995—; chmn. infection control com. State Hosp., Jamestown, 1985-93. Mem. vestry Grace Episcopal Ch., Jamestown, 1989-93. Fellow Am. Acad. Pediatrics, Am. Coll. Allergy and Immunology; mem. N.D. Med. Assn. Home: 2315 Victoria Rose Dr Fargo ND 58104 Office: Meritcare Med Group 737 Broadway Fargo ND 58123

RATNER, HARVEY, health club owner, operator; m. Barbara Ratner; children: Mark, Edward, David, Rachel. Co-founder Northwest Racquet Swim and Health Clubs, Minn., 1963—; co-owner Minn. Timberwolves (NBA), Mpls., 1989-95; owner, operator Northwest Racquet Club, St. Louis Park, Minn., 1995—. Supporter numerous Mpls.-St. Paul charities including Crisis Nursery Ctr., Groves Learning Ctr., Mpls. Children's Med. Ctr., Intervarsity Christian Fellowship, Mpls. Fedn., also arts orgns. Office: Minn Timberwolves Northwest Racquet Club 5525 Cedar Lake Rd Saint Louis Park MN 55416

RATNER, LEAH W., mechanical engineer, researcher; b. Moscow, Jan. 10, 1933; came to U.S., 1979; d. Wolf A. and Fanya M. (Levyant) Marinberg; m. Michael Ratner, Jan. 31, 1957 (div. Nov. 1977); children: Jacob, Ilya. MS in Mech. Engring., Moscow Automech. Inst., 1956; MSME, U. Ill., Chgo. Design engr. Moscow Automation Lines Co., 1956-58; tchr. engring. mechanics Moscow Machine-Tool Coll., 1962-65; sr. engring. specialist in ednl. methods Dept. Engring. Edn., Moscow, 1966-67; rsch. engr. Moscow Machine-Tool Constrn. Plant, 1967-70; sr. engr. of tech. analyses Moscow Inst. Med. Equipment, 1970-78; design engr. several small companies, Chgo., 1979-87. Contbr. articles to profl. jours.; patentee in field, rschr. in new theory of strength and elastic stability of structures. Jewish. Home: 820 W Belle Plaine Apt 804 Chicago IL 60613

RAUSCH, JOAN MARY, art historian; b. Calmar, Iowa, Dec. 25, 1937; d. Bernard Joseph and Irene Sophia (Wieling) Menne; m. Gerald William Rausch, Sept. 3, 1960; children: John Thomas, Jennifer Nicole Rausch Goodhart. BS, Coll. St. Teresa, Winona, Minn., 1959; postgrad., U. Wis., LaCrosse, 1974-79; MA, U. Wis., Milw., 1982. Instr. nursing Mercy Hosp., Iowa City, Iowa, 1960-63, St. Francis Hosp./Viterbo Coll., LaCrosse, 1966-71; rsch. asst. dept. art U. Wis., LaCrosse, 1977-79; asst. dept. art history U. Wis., Milw., 1979-81; historic planner Southwest Regional Planning Commn., Platteville, Wis., 1982-83; pres. Archtl. Researches, Inc., LaCrosse, 1983—; cons. historic preservation divsn. State Hist. Soc. Wis., 1983—, Wis. Dept. of Transp., Dist. 5, 1991—. Author: A Catalog of the Oyen Collection, 1979, Historic LaCrosse Architectural and Historic Record, 1984, Chippewa Falls, 1985, Watertown, A Guide to Its Historic Architecture, 1987; (with Joyce Mckay) Richland Center Wisconsin, Architectural and Historical Survey Report, 1988; (with Carol Cartwright) City of Mineral Point, Architectural and Historic Survey Report, 1992, LaCrosse Wisconsin: Architectural and Historical Survey Report, 1996. Pres. Women's Polit. Caucus, 1972-78, coord., 1974-75. Recipience Scholarship award Victorian Soc. in Am., 1981, Workshop award Ctr. for Art Criticism, Mpls., 1986. Mem. Soc. Archtl. Historians (pres. Wis. chpt. 1982-84), Nat. Trust Hist. Preservation (Preservation Forum(, Wis. Trust Hist. Preservation (charter, task force mem. 1986), Preservation Alliance of LaCrosse (bd. dirs. 1982-88, Heritage award 1989), LaCrosse County Hist. Soc. (hist. preservation com. 1992—, bd. dirs. 1994—). Home and Office: Archtl Researches Inc W5722 Sherwood Dr La Crosse WI 54601

RAUSCHENBERGER, STEVEN J., state legislator. BBA, Coll. of William and Mary. Mem. Ill. State Senate, Dist. 33, Elgin Downtown Adv. Commn.; owner Rauschenberger Furniture Co.; gen. mgr. Ackerman Bros. Corp., Elgin, Ill. Active Boy Scouts Am. Home: 750 Jay St Elgin IL 60120-8240*

RAUSCHER, ELIZABETH ANN, physics educator, researcher; b. Berkeley, Calif., Mar. 18, 1943; d. Philip Jenkins and Claire Elsa (Soderblom) Webster; m. Warren Carleton Rauscher, Oct. 5, 1962 (div. June 1965); 1 child, Brent Allen; m. William Lloyd Van Bise, Mar. 1, 1995. BS in Chemistry and Physics, U. Calif., Berkeley, 1962, MS in Nuclear Engring., 1964, PhD in Nuclear Sci., 1979. Staff rschr. Lawrence Berkeley Lab. U. Calif., 1963-79; staff rschr. Lawrence Livermore Nat. Lab., Livermore, Calif., 1966-69; prof., instr. U. Calif., 1971-74; instr., rschr. Stanford (Calif.) Linear Accelerator Ctr., 1971-72; rschr. SRI Internat., Menlo Park, Calif., 1974-76; dir. Tecnic Rsch. Labs., San Leandro, Calif., 1979—; v.p. Magtek Labs, Inc., Reno, 1988-94; prof. physics U. Nev., Stanford, 1990—; cons. McDonnell-Douglass, L.A., 1978, 80, Learned Soc. Can., Montreal, 1981, USN, Silver Spring, Md., 1983, NASA, Martin-Marietta, New Orleans, 1988-89; adviser Engring. Inst., Provo, Utah, 1979. Patentee in field. Del. UN, N.Y.C., 1979, mem. UN com., 1989; adviser Congress Office Tech. Assessment, Washington, 1979-81; adviser, cons. City Coun., Reno, 1993. Recipient Outstanding Contbn. award Am. Astron. Soc., 1978, Honor award Rosebridge Grad. Sch., 1988; grantee USN, 1970-74, 82-83, PF Found., 1978, 79, 81; Delta Delta Delta scholar, 1960; Iota Sigma Pi Woman's fellow, 1961. Mem. IEEE, Am. Phys. Soc. (chair), Am. Chem. Soc. (v.p.), Lawrence Berkeley Lab. Fundametal Physics (chair, pres.), Psychology Rsch. Group San Franciso (bd. dirs., pres.).

RAUTH, JOHN FRANCIS, construction executive; b. Farm-Wabash, Nebr., Jan. 15, 1921; s. Aaron Francis and Anna Theresa (Stander) R.; m. Elizabeth Bridget Cobb, Aug. 5, 1944; children: Joyce Ann Rauth Fears, Eileen Marie Strider, Mary Kay Farley, Patricia Hayes, Michael G., Jeanne F. sheehan, Reine Seiler. Student, St. Louis U., 1945-51, Mo. Western State Coll., 1986-91. Founder, owner John Rauth Constrn., St. Joseph, Mo., 1953-86, semi-retired, chmn. bd., 1986—; founder, pres. St. Josephs Home Builders, 1957-61. 1st lt. U.S. Army Air Corps, 1940-45, ret. lt. col. USAF, 1969. Mem. KC, Soc. of Precious Blood. Independent. Roman Catholic. Home: 3403 Doniphan Ave Saint Joseph MO 64507-1918

RAVA, SUSAN ROUDEBUSH, French language and literature educator; b. St. Louis, June 6, 1939; d. George Shotwell and Dorothy Jean (Coleman) Roudebush; m. John A. Rava, Feb. 20, 1965; children: Ellen D'Arcy, William Cheever, Carol Elisa. BA, Vassar Coll., 1961; MA, Washington U., St. Louis, 1971, PhD, 1977. Mem. staff Am. Field Svc., N.Y.C., 1961-63; tchr. ESL Washington U., 1966-68, lectr. French, 1978-88, sr. lectr. French, 1988—, dept. dir. teaching asst. tng., 1990—; tchr. French U. Mo., St. Louis, 1977-78. Author: (short stories) Prairie Schooner, Crescent Rev.; asst. editor Pedagogy French Rev.; contbr. articles to profl. jours., bulls. and revs. Vol. coord. St. Louis Vis. Ctr., 1964-66; bd. dirs., sec. ACLU East Mo., St. Louis, 1967-72; bd. dirs. New City Sch., St. Louis, 1973-75, John Burroughs Sch., St. Louis, 1982-85, Alliance Française Sch., St. Louis, 1991-93; bd. dirs. Gateway Found., St. Louis, 1992—; mem. bd. deacons Trinity Presbyn. Ch., 1993-96. Recipient Excellence in Teaching award Emerson Electric, 1994. Mem. AAUP, MLA, Midwest MLA, Am. Assn. Higher Edn., Am. Assn. Tchrs. of French, Women in French. Democrat. Home: 7129 Washington Ave Saint Louis MO 63130-4313 Office: Washington U PO Box 1077 Saint Louis MO 63130-4899

RAVANI, KIRIT T., environmental engineering company executive; b. Bombay, Nov. 23, 1945; came to U.S., 1964; s. Trambak and Shanta (Domadia) R.; m. Alice F. Seip, Oct. 5, 1974; children: Jenna, Maya, Jay. BCE, Wayne State U., 1968, MCE, 1970; M Mgmt., U. Mich., 1978. Registered profl. engr., Mich., N.J. Project engr. Wade Trim Group, also other cos., Detroit, 1968-73.; group leader Giffels Assocs., Inc., Southfield, Mich., 1973-83; sr. project mgr. Argonaut AEC group GM, Detroit, 1983-89; v.p. City Mgmt. Corp., Detroit, 1989-93; founder, pres., chmn. bd. dirs. Enviro Matrix, Inc., Detroit, 1993—; bd. dirs. Ctrl. Coast Analytical Svc., Inc., San Luis Obispo, Calif.; vice chmn. Novi (Mich.) Hazardous Waste and Chems. Bd., 1988-89; seminar presenter in field. Contbr. articles to profl. jours. Mem. Soc. Environ. Sci. (chmn.), Water Pollution Control Fedn., Water Environ. Fedn., Inst. Hazardous Materials Mgmt., Engring. Soc. Detroit. Home: 26093 Hidden Valley Dr Farmington Hills MI 48331-4115

RAVEN, FRANCIS HARVEY, mechanical engineering educator; b. Erie, Pa., July 29, 1928; s. Frederick James and Eleanor Elizabeth (Sopp) R.; m. Therese Mary Strobel, June 21, 1952; children: Betty, Ann, Paul, John, Mary, Cathy, Linda. BS in Math., Gannon Univ., 1948; BSME, Pa. State U., 1950, MSME, 1951; PhD, Cornell U., 1958. Design engr. Hamilton Standard div. United Techs., Hartford, Conn., 1951-54; instr. Cornell U., Ithaca, N.Y., 1954-58; asst. prof. mech. engring. U. Notre Dame, 1958-62, assoc. prof., 1962-66, prof., 1966—; cons. McCauley Accessory div. Cessna Aircraft Co., Dayton, Ohio, 1980—, South Bend (Ind.) Lathe, 1987—; devel. "The Method of Ind. Position Equations" (first analytical method for kinematic analysis). Author: Automatic Control Engineering, 1961, 5th edit., 1995, Mathematics of Engineering Systems, 1966, Engineering Mechanics, 1973; pub. McGraw-Hill Book Co. Mem. ASME, Am. Soc. for Engring. Edn. (AT&T Teaching award 1968-69), Sigma Xi. Roman Catholic. Home: 52740 Brandel Ave South Bend IN 46635-1248 Office: U Notre Dame Dept Aerospace-Mech Engring Notre Dame IN 46556

RAVENS, ROBERT ALLEN, financial services company executive; b. Kankakee, Ill., Apr. 19, 1963. Lic. ins. prodr., Ill.; cert. securities rep., Ill., Ind. Gen. mgr. The Chgo. Dough Co., Chicago Heights, Ill., 1983-88, Bakers Sq., Matteson, Ill., 1988-93; regional mgr. Primerica Fin. Svcs., Homewood, Ill., 1990—. Treas. Brookwood PTA, Glenwood, Ill., 1992-95; chairperson picnic Glenwood Thunderbirds Softball, 1994-95.

RAWAL, DARSHAN LAL, civil, structural engineer, consultant; b. India, Nov. 12, 1934; came to U.S., 1966; s. Saudagar Mal and Kaushalya Devi R.; m. Raj Kumari, Dec. 5, 1956; children: Upma, Bela, Neeru. BSCE, M.U. Aligarh, U.P. India, 1957; MSCE, Utah State U., 1967. Registered profl. engr., Ill.; registered structural engr., Ill. Sr. civil engr. Ill. Dept. Transp., 1967-73; sr. structural engr. Sargent & Lundy, Chgo., 1974-86, Brown & Root, Lombard, Ill., 1979-81; sr. engr. Ambitech Engring. Corp., Downers Grove, Ill., 1988—, John Brown Engrs. & Constructor's, Chgo., 1991-93. Pres. Hindu Soc., Chgo., 1971-72; chmn. bd. trustees Hindu Soc., Medinah, Ill., 1993-96. Fellow ASCE. Hindu. Home: 2078 Audubon Dr Glendale Heights IL 60139-1808 Office: Ambitech Eng Corp Contractors 1333 Butterfield Rd Downers Grove IL 60515

RAWLES, EDWARD HUGH, lawyer; b. Chgo., May 7, 1945; s. Fred Wilson and Nancy (Hughes) R.; m. Margaret Mary O'Donoghue, Oct. 20, 1979; children: Lee Kathryn, Jacklyn Ann. BA, U. Ill., 1967; JD summa cum laude, Ill. Inst. Tech., 1970. Bar: Ill., 1970, Colo. 1984, U.S. Dist. Ct. (cen. dist.) Ill. 1970, U.S. Ct. Appeals (7th cir.) 1983, U.S. Supreme Ct. 1973. Assoc. Reno, O'Byrne & Kepley, Champaign, Ill., 1970-73, ptnr., 1973-84; pres. Rawles, O'Byrne, Stanko & Kepley P.C., Champaign, 1984—, pres., 1990—; mem. student legal svc. adv. bd. U. Ill., Urbana, 1982—; hearing officer Ill. Fair Employment Practice Commn., Springfield, 1972-74. Diplomate Nat. Bd. Trial Advocacy. Fellow Ill. State Bar Found., 1984. Mem. Ill. Bar Assn., Bar Assn. 7th Fed. Cir., Assn. Trial Lawyers Am., Ill. Trial Lawyers Assn., Colo. Trial Lawyers Assn.,, Kent Soc. Honor Men, Phi Delta Theta. Roman Catholic. Home: 6 Alice Dr White Heath IL 61884-9747 Office: Rawles O'Byrne Stanko & Kepley PC 501 W Church St Champaign IL 61820-3412

RAWLEY, ANN KEYSER, small business owner, picture framer; b. N.Y.C., July 11, 1923; d. Ernest Wise and Beatrice (Oberndorf) Keyser; m. James Albert Rawley, Apr. 7, 1945; children: John Franklin, James Albert. BA, Smith Coll., 1944. Owner Ann Rawley Custom Framing, Lincoln, Nebr., 1969—. Pres. Friends of Fairview, Lincoln, 1976, Lincoln City Ballet Co., 1983-84; bd. dirs. Lincoln Community Playhouse; mem. adv. bd. Nebr. Repertory Theatre. Mem. Nebr. Art Assn. (sec. 1976-77, life trustee). Republican. Episcopalian. Home and Office: 2300 Bretigne Dr Lincoln NE 68512-1910

RAWLINGS, HUNTER RIPLEY, III, university president; b. Norfolk, Va., Dec. 14, 1944; married; 4 children. BA, Haverford Coll., 1966; PhD in Classics, Princeton U., 1970. Asst. prof. U. Colo., Boulder, 1970-75, assoc. prof., 1975-80, prof. classics, 1980-88, v.p. acad. affairs, rsch., dean System Grad. Sch., 1984-88; pres. U. Iowa, 1988-95; pres., prof. classics Cornell U., Ithaca, N.Y., 1995—; chair Iowa Commn. on Fgn. Lang. Studies and Internat. Edn., 1988-91; bd. dirs. Tompkins County Trust Co. Author: The Structure of Thucydides' History, 1981; editor-in-chief: Classical Jour., 1977-83; contbr. articles to jours. Bd. dirs. Norwest Bank Iowa, N.A., 1988-95, Am. Coun. Edn., 1994, Tompkins County Trust Co., 1996—. Jr. fellow Ctr. Hellenic Studies, 1975-76. Fellow Am. Acad. Arts and Scis.; mem. Assn. Am. Univs. (exec. com. 1990-92), Am. Coun. on Edn. (bd. dirs. 1994—), Nat. Fgn. Lang. Ctr. (mem. nat. adv. bd. 1995—). Office: Cornell U Office of Pres Ithaca NY 14853

RAWLINS, DAVID D., automotive engineer; b. Lincoln, Ill., Feb. 17, 1965. A.Engring. Power, Ill. Ctrl. Coll., Peoria, 1985; BS in Indsl. Tech., Ill. State U., 1987. Project test engr. Tech. Devel. Inc., Dayton, Ohio, 1988—. Mem. ASME, Soc. Automotive Engrs. Office: Tech Devel Inc 6800 Poe Ave Dayton OH 45414-2530

RAWSKI, CONRAD H(ENRY), humanities educator, medievalist; b. Vienna, Austria, May 25, 1914; came to U.S., 1939, naturalized, 1944; s. Stanislaus and Johanna (Buberl-Maffei) R.; m. Helen Orr, July 5, 1957; children: Thomas George, Judith Ellen Rawski Kleen. M.A., U. Vienna, 1936, Ph.D., 1937; postgrad., Péter Pázmány Egyetem, Budapest, 1938-39, Harvard U., 1939-40; M.S. in L.S, Western Res. U., 1957. Lectr. in music U. Louisville, 1940; asst. prof., assoc. prof., prof. music Ithaca (N.Y.) Coll., 1940-56; dir. grad. studies, dean Ithaca (N.Y.) Coll. (Sch. Music), 1951-56; head fine arts dept. Cleve. Public Library, 1957-62; assoc. prof., prof. library sci., coordinator Ph.D. program in info. sci. M.A. Baxter Sch. Info. and Libr. Sci., Case Western Res. U., Cleve., 1957-80; prof., sr. research scholar M.A. Baxter Sch. Info. and Libr. Sci., Case Western Res. U., 1980-85, prof. emeritus for life, dean emeritus, 1985; music columnist Boston Evening Transcript, 1939-40, Ithaca Jour., 1943-50; lectr. in musicology, medieval studies, info. sci. Fellow Fund for the Advancement of Edn., Ford Found., 1952-53, Nat. Endowment for Humanities, 1979. Author: Petrarch: Four Dialogues for Scholars, 1967, Toward a Theory of Librarianship, 1973, Petrarch's Latin Prose Works and the Modern Translator, 1977, Introduction to Research in Information Sciane, 1982; translator, editor: Petrarch's Remedies for Fortune Fair and Foul, 5 vols., 1991, Petrarch to Boccaccio: The Griseldis Letters, 1994, Francisci Petrarchae lectoris Adminiculum: Late Antique and Medieval Latin Words in the Works of Petrarch, 1996; contbr. papers on

Petrarch's Latin prose works, Petrarch's Latinity, medieval music, info. sci. and theory to profl. jours. and encys. Mem. Renaissance Soc. Am., Medieval Acad. Am., Soc. for Medieval Latin, ALA (nat. Beta Phi Mu award 1979), Am. Musicol. Soc., Wembley Club. Club: Rowfant of Cleve. Address: 17877 Lost Trl Chagrin Falls OH 44023-5835

RAY, ANNETTE D., business executive; b. Decatur, Ind., Mar. 24, 1950; d. Gilbert O. and Florence L. Hoffman; m. Richard M. Ray, Nov. 28, 1975; children: Michelle Ann, Ellen Marie, Laura Leigh, David Richard, Ruth Anne. AA, Concordia Jr. Coll., Ann Arbor, Mich., 1970; BS, Concordia Tchrs. Coll., Seward, Nebr., 1972; attended, Ctrl. Fla. C.C., Ocala, 1974. Lic. real estate, Ind.; lic. tchr., Ind., Fla. Elem. tchr. St. John's Luth., Ocala, 1972-74; mgr. apt. complex Victoria Sq. Apts., Ft. Wayne, Ind., 1974-75; substitute tchr. East Allen County Schs., Allen County, Ind., 1976-79, Circut A Luth. Schs., Adams and Allen County, Ind., 1977-81; corp. sec., treas., office mgr. Heritage Wire Die, Monroeville, Ind., 1987—. Co-author, co-editor: 1928-1988 A Rememberance, 1988. Vol. Monroeville C. of C., 1987—, Concerned Area Residents Quality Edn., Allen County, 1990—, Am. Cancer Soc., Allen County, 1991—, chairperson Celebrity Bagger Day, 1995, 96; bd. dirs. Hoagland (Ind.) Hist. Soc., 1985—. Lutheran. Home: 16901 Berning Rd Hoagland IN 46745-9753 Office: Heritage Wire Die Inc 19819 Monroeville Rd Monroeville IN 46773-9113

RAY, CHARLES JOSEPH, dentist; b. South Sioux City, Nebr., June 4, 1911; s. Charles Joseph and Katherine Frances (Bridgeford) R.; m. Cecilia Estelle Radlinger, Nov. 22, 1933; children: Carole, Margie, Kathy, Jeane, Rita, Charles, Chrystal. EE, S.D. Sch. of Mines, 1932; DDS, U. Minn., 1936; postgrad. Forsythe Dental Infirmary, Boston, 1936-37, Eastman Dental Dispensary, 1937-38. Pvt. practice dentistry, 1938—, with Ray Dental Group, Rapid City, S.D., 1953—; mem. S.D. Med. Adv. Bd., 1958-65, S.D. Dental Legis. Com., 1985—, chmn. 1985-86. Active USO, 1959, pres. Rapid City chpt. 1952-60; pres. S.D. Crippled Children's Assn. Mem. ADA (life), S.D. Dental Assn. (Gold Tooth award 1980, pres. 1964), Am. Prosthodontic Soc. (pres. 1980-81, exec. coun. 1981-82, life mem.), Fedn. Prosthodontic Orgn. (sec. 1976-80), Am. Assn. Hosp. Dentists, Am. Soc. Psychosomatic Dentistry and Medicine, Pierre-Fauchard Acad. (award 1980), Am. Acad. Periodontology, Acad. Internat. Dentistry and Medicine, Internat. Coll. Dentistry, Am. Acad. Practice Adminstrn., Am. Acad. Gen. Dentistry, Am. Acad. Dental Group Practice, Colo. Prosthodontic Soc., Rapid City Dental Soc., Black Hills Dist. Dental Soc., Dental Group Mgmt. Assn., Chgo. Dental Soc. (assoc.), Internat. Coll. Dentists, Rapid City C. of C., Omicron Kappa Upsilon. Roman Catholic. Clubs: International Cosmopolitan (pres. 1972), Rapid City Cosmopolitan (pres. 1962; Disting. Service award 1977), Sioux Land Study, KC, Elks. Home: 250 Timberline Ct Rapid City SD 57702-2708 Office: Ray Dental Group PO Box 9625 Rapid City SD 57709-9625

RAY, DARRELL W., psychologist; b. Wichita, Aug. 24, 1950; s. Curtis E. and Anise B. (Parker) R.; m. Kathleen D. Ray, Nov. 21, 1970 (div. Feb. 15, 1989); children: Adrienne, Aaron. BA, Friends U., 1972; MA, Scarritt Coll., 1974; EdD, Vanderbilt U. Counselor State of Tenn., Nashville, 1974-76; supr. of tng. Tenn. Corrections Inst., Nashville, 1977-78; clin. psychologist State of Kans., Atchison, 1978-80, dir. staff devel., 1980-86; pvt. practice orgnl. devel. Mgrs. Cons. Svcs., Shawnee, 1983—; expert self directed work teams; bd. dirs. ODT, Inc., Amherst, Mass. Author: Teaming Up, 1995; contbr. articles to profl. jours. Mem. APA, ASTD, Assn. for Quality and Participation. Quaker. Office: Managers Cons Svcs 22612 W 53d Shawnee KS 66226

RAY, DOUGLAS, newspaper editor. Now editor, v.p. Daily Herald/ Sunday Herald, Arlington Heights, Ill. Office: Daily Herald/Sunday Herald Paddock Publs PO Box 280 Arlington Heights IL 60006-0280*

RAY, FRANK ALLEN, lawyer; b. Lafayette, Ind., Jan. 30, 1949; s. Dale Allen and Merry Ann (Fleming) R.; m. Carol Ann Olmutz, Oct. 1, 1982; children: Erica Fleming, Robert Allen. BA, Ohio State U., 1970, JD, 1973. Bar: Ohio 1973, U.S. Dist. Ct. (so. dist.) Ohio 1975, U.S. Supreme Ct. 1976, U.S. Tax Ct. 1977, U.S. Ct. Appeals (6th cir.) 1977, U.S. Dist Ct. (no. dist.) Ohio 1980, Pa. 1983, U.S. Dist. Ct. (ea. dist.) Mich. 1983, U.S. Ct. Appeals (1st cir.) 1986; cert. civil trial adv. Nat. Bd. Trial Advocacy. Asst. pros. atty. Franklin County, Ohio, 1973-75, chief civil counsel, 1976-78; dir. econ. crime project Nat. Dist. Attys. Assn., Washington, 1975-76; assoc. Brownfield, Kosydar, Bowen, Bally & Sturtz, Columbus, Ohio, 1978, Michael F. Colley Co., L.P.A., Columbus, 1979-83; pres. Frank A. Ray Co., L.P.A., Columbus, 1983-93, Ray & Todaro Co., LPA, Columbus, 1993-94, Ray, Todaro & Alton Co., L.P.A., 1994-96, Columbus, Ray, Todaro, Alton & Kirstein Co., L.P.A., 1996—; mem. seminar faculty Nat. Coll. Dist. Attys., Houston, 1975-77; mem. nat. conf. faculty Fed. Jud. Ctr., Washington, 1976-77; bd. mem. bar examiners Ohio Supreme Ct., 1992-95, Rules Adv. Com., 1995—. Editor: Economic Crime Digest, 1975-76; co-author: Personal Injury Litigation Practice in Ohio, 1988, 91. Mem. fin. com. Franklin County Rep. Orgn., Columbus, 1979-84; trustee Ohio State U. Coll. Humanities Alumni Soc., 1991-93. 1st lt. inf. U.S. Army, 1973. Named to Ten Outstanding Young Citizens of Columbus, Columbus Jaycees, 1976; recipient Nat. award of Distinctive Svc., Nat. Dist. Attys. Assn., 1977. Fellow Internat. Soc. Barristers, Columbus Bar Found., Roscoe Pound Found., Ohio Acad. Trial Lawyers; mem. ABA, Am. Bd. Trial Advocates, Columbus Bar Assn. (com. profl. ethics and grievances 1990-93, chmn. professionalism com. 1994-96, bd. govs. 1996—), Ohio State Bar Assn. (com. negligence law 1990—), Assn. Trial Lawyers Am. (state del. 1990-92), Ohio Acad. Trial Lawyers (trustee 1984-87, sec. 1987-88, pres.-elect 1988-89, pres. 1989-90, legis. coord. 1986-88, Pres.' award 1986), Franklin County Trial Lawyers Assn. (trustee 1982-83, treas. 1984-85, chmn. com. negligence law 1983-87, sec. 1985-86, v.p. 1986-87, pres. 1987-88, Pres's. award 1990), Inns of Ct. (sec. Judge Robert M. Duncan chpt. 1991-93, pres. 1993-94). Presbyterian. Home: 2030 Tremont Rd Columbus OH 43221-4330 Office: 175 S 3rd St Ste 350 Columbus OH 43215-5134

RAY, FRANK DAVID, government agency official; b. Mt. Vernon, Ohio, Dec. 1, 1940; s. John Paul and Lola Mae (Miller) R.; children: Susan M., Frank D. II; BS in Edn., Ohio State U., 1964, JD, 1967. Bar: Ohio 1967, U.S. Dist. Ct. 1969, U.S. Cir. Ct. Appeals (6th cir.) 1970, U.S. Supreme Ct. 1971. Legal aide to atty. gen. Ohio, 1965-66; bailiff probate ct., Franklin County, Ohio, 1966-67, gen. referee, 1967-68; with firm Stouffer, Wait and Ashbrook, Columbus, Ohio, 1967-71; jour. clk. Ohio Ho. of Reps., 1969-71; dist. dir. SBA, 1971—; mem. Ohio Pub. Defender Commn., 1983-91; mem. U.S. Dept. Commerce So. Ohio Dist. Export Council, 1988—; mem. Ohio Export Promotion and Trade Coun., 1992—, Ohio Rural Devel. Coun., 1993—; mem. vocat. edn. adv. com. Columbus Pub. Schs., 1993-95; mem. Columbus Mayor's Econ. Devel. Council, 1983-84; mem. Small Bus. and High Tech. adv. com. Ohio Div. Securities, 1983-84; mem. tech. alliance Central Ohio Adv. Bd., 1983-89; mem. Ohio Small Bus. and Entrepreneurship Coun., 1994-95. Editl. adv. bd. Columbus CEO Mag., 1995—. Mem. Upper Arlington (Ohio) Bd. Health, 1970-75; pres. Buckeye Republican Club, 1970, Franklin County Forum, 1970; chmn. Central Ohio chpt. Nat. Found.-March of Dimes, 1974-77; trustee Columbus Acad. Contemporary Art, 1976. Recipient Service award Nat. Found.-March of Dimes, 1974, 75, 76, 77; Am. Jurisprudence award for Excellence, 1967, In Search of Excellence award SBA, 1985; named Ohio Commodore, 1973. Mem. Leadership Columbus (grad. 1976), Delta Upsilon, Alpha Epsilon Delta. Clubs: Ohio Press, Ohio State U. Pres. Home: 4200 Dublin Rd Columbus OH 43221-5005

RAY, JOHN WALKER, otolaryngologist, educator, broadcast commentator; b. Columbus, Ohio, Jan. 12, 1936; s. Kenneth Clark and Hope (Walker) Ray; m. Susanne Gettings, July 15, 1961; children: Nancy Ann, Susan Christy. AB magna cum laude, Marietta Coll., 1956; MD cum laude, Ohio State U., 1960; postgrad. Temple U., 1964, Mt. Sinai Hosp. and Columbia U., 1964, 66, Northwestern U., 1967, 71, U. Ill., 1968, U. Ind., 1969, Tulane U., 1969. Intern, Ohio State U. Hosps., Columbus, 1960-61, clin. rsch. trainee NIH, 1963-65, resident dept. otolaryngology, 1963-65, 1966-67, resident dept. surgery 1965-66, instr. dept. otolaryngology, 1966-67, 70-75, clin. asst. prof., 1975-82, clin. assoc. prof., 1982-92, clin. prof., 1992—; active staff, past chief of staff Bethesda Hosp.; active staff, past chief of staff Good Samaritan Hosp., Zanesville, Ohio, 1967—; courtesy staff Ohio State U. Hosps., Columbus, 1970—; hon. active staff Meml. Hosp., Marietta, Ohio, 1992—; radio-TV health commentator, 1982—. Past pres. Muskingum chpt. Am. Cancer Soc.; trustee Ohio Med. Polit. Action Com.; bd. dirs. Zanesville Art Ctr. Capt. USAF, 1961-63. Recipient Barraquer Meml. award, 1965; named to Order of Ky. Col., 1966, Muskingum County Country Music Hall of Fame. Diplomate Am. Bd. Otolaryngology. Fellow ACS, Am. Soc. Otolaryn. Allergy, Am. Acad. Otolaryngology-Head and Neck Surgery (gov.), Am. Acad. Facial Plastic and Reconstructive Surgery; mem. Nat. Assn. Physician Broadcasters, Muskingum County Acad. Medicine (past pres.), AMA (del. hosp. med. Staff sect.), Ohio Med. Assn. (del.), Columbus Ophthalmol. and Otolaryngol. Soc. (past pres.), Ohio Soc. Otolaryngology (past pres.), Pan-Am. Assn. Otolaryngology and Bronchoesophagology, Pan-Am. Allergy Soc., Am. Acad. Invitro Allergy, Am. Auditory Soc., Am. Soc. Contemporary Medicine and Surgery, Acad. Radio and TV Health Communicators, Fraternal Order Police Assocs., Phi Beta Kappa, Alpha Tau Omega, Alpha Kappa Kappa, Alpha Omega Alpha, Beta Beta Beta. Presbyterian. Contbr. articles to sci., med. jours; collaborator with surg. motion picture: Laryngectomy and Neck Dissection, 1964. Office: 2945 Maple Ave Zanesville OH 43701-1753

RAY, MICHAEL D., design engineer; b. Decatur, Ill., Apr. 20, 1950. Design engr. Technicare, Denver, 1976-78; tooling engr. Grigoletit Co., Decatur, 1979—; project engr. Airfloat Systems, Decatur, 1991—; cons., pres. Design Inc., Decatur, 1995—. Patentee in field. Pres., coach Boys and Girls Softball, Decatur, 1991—; v.p. Maverick Adult Recreation/Sinawk Park Club, Decatur, 1992—. With USAF, 1968-72. Mem. ASME. Home: 1745 S Baltimore Ave Decatur IL 62521-5017 Office: Airfloat Systems 1550 E Mcbride Ave Decatur IL 62526-5082

RAY, R. GLENN, education and business director; b. Bowling Green, Ky., Oct. 18, 1953; s. William Brown Ray and Audrey Mabel (Benedict) Rinehart; divorced; children: Betsy Susannah, Elijah Everret. BA in Psychology, Ohio U., 1980, MEd in Student Personnel Svcs., 1982, PhD in Interpersonal Comm., 1988. Machine operator N.Am. Coal Co., Beallsville, Ohio, 1972-73; laborer, carpenter's helper R.E. Blevins Constrn. Co., Campbellsville, Ky., 1973-74; sect. foreman Youghiogheny & Ohio Coal Co., Beallsville, 1974-79, So. Ohio Coal Co., Wilkesville, Ohio, 1979-82; tchg. assoc. Ohio U., Athens, 1983-85; mgr. human resources devel. Borg Warner Chems., Washington, W.Va., 1985-89; mgr. tng. and devel. GE Plastics (formerly Borg Warner), Washington, 1989; tng. dir. Scot Fetzer Co., Westlake, Ohio, 1989-90; dir. inst. of edn. and tng. for bus. Marietta (Ohio) Coll., 1990—. Contbr. articles to profl. jours. Mem. ASTD (pres. 1988, jour. rev. bd. 1987—), Marietta C. of C. (presenter, facilitator telesis leadership devel., 1994, 95), Parkersburg W.Va. C. of C. (presenter, facilitator leadership devel. series 1994, 95). Democrat. Home: 58 Terri Ln Little Hocking OH 45742 Office: McDonough Ctr Leadership & Business Marietta Coll Marietta OH 45750

RAY, TUHIN, computer engineer; b. London, Aug. 28, 1963; came to U.S., 1987; s. Natabar and Rekha (Bhattacharya) R. B of Engring., Delhi (India) U., 1985; MSEE, Mich. State U., 1989; MBA, Ind. U., 1995. Project engr. Allen Bradley Ltd., Sahibabad, India, 1985-87; grad. rsch. asst. elec. engring. dept. Mich. State U., East Lansing, 1987-89; mgr. applied engring. Total Control Products Inc., Melrose Park, Ill., 1989-92; advanced software engr. Delco Electronics, Kokomo, Ind., 1992-95, software project mgr., 1995—; cons. Motorola Inc., Northbrook, Ill., 1988; teaching asst. De Paul U., Chgo., 1990-92. Capt. sch. and coll. field hockey, Delhi, 1981-84. Recipient Merit cert. Math. Olympiad, New Delhi, 1981, Appreciation award Monsanto Chemical, Sauget, Ill., 1990. Mem. IEEE, Engring. Soc. Detroit. Home: 3010 Courthouse Dr E Apt 2C West Lafayette IN 47906-1006 Office: Delco Electronics MS CT-60-I One Corporate Ctr Kokomo IN 46904-9005

RAYNOR, DENISE MARIE, educational consultant; b. Easton, Pa., Mar. 6, 1953; d. John Melvin and Josephine Barbara (Zadie) Oliver; m. Gregory L. Park, May 27, 1978 (dec. Sept. 1987); children: Emelia Lynn Park, Katherine Rose Park; m. Michael Lee Raynor, Mar. 11, 1989. BA, Bloomsburg (Pa.) U., 1975. Eligibility worker II State Dept. of Human Resources, Louisville, 1977-78; customer svc. agt. Piedmont Airlines, Louisville, 1978-85, customer svc. supr., 1985-87, regional mgr. pers., 1987-89; shift supr. USAir, Inc., Dayton, 1989-90; parent cons. Miami Valley Spl. Edn. Regional Resource Ctr., Dayton, 1994—; founder, trustee Aicardi Syndrome Newsletter, Inc., Casstown, Ohio, 1984—. Editor Aicardi Syndrome Newsletter, 1984—. Officer Miami County Bd. of Mental Retardation and Developmental Disabilities, 1990-94; mem. Miami East Strategic Planning Team, Casstown, 1993-94. Home: 5115 Troy Urbana Rd Casstown OH 45312 Office: Miami Valley Spl Edn Regional Resource Ctr 1831 Harshman Rd Dayton OH 45424

RAYNOR, JOHN PATRICK, university administrator; b. Omaha, Oct. 1, 1923; s. Walter V. and Mary Clare (May) R. AB, St. Louis U., 1947, MA, 1948, Licentiate in Philosophy, 1949, Licentiate in Theology, 1956; PhD, U. Chgo., 1959. Ordained priest Roman Cath. Ch., 1954. Joined Soc. of Jesus, 1941; instr. St. Louis U. High Sch., 1948-51, asst. prin., 1951; asst. to dean Coll. Liberal Arts, Marquette U., 1960, asst. to v.p. acad. affairs, 1961-62, v.p. acad. affairs, 1962-65, pres., 1965-90, ret., 1990; now, chancellor Marquette Univ., Milwaukee, Wis.; dir. Kimberly-Clark Corp. Mem. Greater Milw. Com.; Pub. Policy Forum; corp. mem. United Community Services Greater Milw.; hon. bd. dirs. Goethe House; mem. Froedtert Meml. Luth. Hosp. Corp.; hon. com. mem. Endowment Fund Metro Milw. Luth. Campus Ministry; trustee Milw. Heart Research Found., Inc.; bd. dirs. Greater Milw. Edn. Trust, Mus. Sci., Econs. & Tech., Inc. Discovery World. Recipient Disting. Service award Edn. Commn. of States, 1977. Mem. Nat. Cath. Edn. Assn., North Central Assn. (examiner, cons.), Am. Council Edn., Wis. Assn. Ind. Colls. and Univs. (past pres., exec. com.), Wis. Found. Ind. Colls. (past pres.), Assn. Jesuit Colls. and Univs. (past chmn., dir., mem. exec. com.), Internat. Fedn. Cath. Colls. and Univs., Met. Milw. Assn. Commerce, Phi Beta Kappa, Phi Delta Kappa, Alpha Sigma Nu. Office: Marquette U 615 N 11th St Milwaukee WI 53233-2305

REA, JAMES F., state senator; b. Mulkeytown, Ill., Sept. 7, 1937; s. Marion Allen and Lucy Melissa (Swisher) R.; m. Josephine Toigo, 1964; children: James Allen, Jo Ellen Brayfield. BS, So. Ill. U., 1960, MS, 1962. Mem. city coun., 1963-67, mem. zoning bd., 1964-67; dir. Gov.'s Office, 1973-76; Ill. state rep. Dist. 117, 1979-89; mem. Ill. State Senate, Dist. 59, 1989—, minority spokesman, fin. inst. com., pub. health, welfare and corrections, joint com. on adminstrv. rules coms., co-chmn. coal caucus, mem. SFA agrl., food policy and rural devel. com. Ill. Energy Coun., mine subsidence ins. program task force, adv. coun. on alcoholism and drug dependencies; chmn. Franklin County Dem. Com., 59th Senate Dist. of County chmn.; mem. faculty So. Ill. U., 1962-73; pub. info. dir. Ill. Dept. Conservation, 1976-79. precinct committeeman Tyrone 2 Precinct, Franklin County. Named Legislator of Yr. Ill. Assn. Pub. Health Adminstrn., 1993, Cert. of Appreciation Franklin County Civil Air Patrol, 1993, Sponsor's award Ill. Credit Union League, 1993, Plaque of Appreciation for Supporting SB956 Ill. Dept. Corrections, 1993, Cert. of Appreciation ABATE Franklin County chpt. 1994; named Friend of Rural Transit Rides Mass Transit Dist., 1993, Friend of Agrl. Gold award Ill. Farm Bur., 1994. Mem. Lions, Masons (32 degree) Am. Legion, Eagles, Shriners, Farm Bur. Democrat. Home: 602 W Ray Ave Christopher IL 62822-1248*

READ, C(ARLYLE) DEAN, JR., consultant; b. Colton, Calif., Jan. 7, 1931; s. C.D. and Martha Read; m. Sheila Ross, Mar. 14, 1981. BS, U. Ill., 1952, MS, 1957. Dir., mgr. Continental Can Co., Chgo., N.Y.C., Houston, 1960-78; gen. mgr. tech. and quality assurance Continental Can Co., Chgo., 1978-90; mng. ptnr. Purple S Enterprises, Fontana, Wis., 1990—. Contbr. articles to profl. jours. Mem. Fontana K-8 Sch. Bd., 1994—. Lt. in submarine force USN, 1952-60. Mem. Inst. Food Techs., Am. Soc. Brewing Chemists, Master Brewers Assn. of the Ams., Internat. Soc. Beverage Technologists, Naval Submarine League, Sports Car Club Am. Home and Office: Purple S Enterprises 880 Brickley Dr Fontana WI 53125

READ, SISTER JOEL, academic administrator. BS in Edn., Alverno Coll., 1948; MA in History, Fordham U., 1951; hon. degrees, Lakeland Coll., 1972, Wittenburg U., 1976, Marymount Manhattan Coll., 1978, DePaul U., 1985, Northland Coll., 1986, SUNY, 1986. Former prof., dept. chmn. history dept. Alverno Coll., Milw., pres., 1968—; pres. Am. Assn. for Higher Edn., 1976-77; mem. coun. NEH, 1977-83; bd. dirs. Ednl. Testing Svc., 1987-93, Neylan Commn., 1985-90; past pres. Wis. Assn. Ind. Colls. and Univs.; mem. Commn. on Status of Edn. for Women, 1971-76, Am. Assn. Colls., 1971-77; mem. exec. com. Greater Milw. com. GMC Edn. Trust. Mem. exec. bd. Milw. YMCA. First recipient Anne Roe award Harvard U. Grad. Sch. Edn., 1980. Fellow Am. Acad. Arts and Scis.; mem. Found. for Higher Edn. Office: Alverno Coll Office of the President PO Box 343922 Milwaukee WI 53234-3922

READEY, B(ARTLEY) JOHN, III, lawyer; b. Kansas City, Mo., Nov. 17, 1943; s. Bartley J. and Virginia T. (Crain) R.; m. Ann Parker North, Apr. 28, 1973; children: Katherine, Gordon, Ann Louise, Nathan. BA, Yale U., 1965; JD, U. Mo., Kansas City, 1968, LLM in Taxation, 1979. Bar: Mo. 1968, U.S. Dist. Ct. Mo. 1969. Assoc. Deacy and Deacy, Kansas City, Mo., 1969-74; ptnr. Hentzen, Haitbrink & Moore, Kansas City, 1974-77, Spradley, Wirken & Readey, Kansas City, 1977-79; shareholder Smith, Gill, Fisher & Butts, P.C., Kansas City, 1979-95; partner Bryan Cave LLP, Kansas City, 1995—. Pres., founder Kansas City Trolley Corp., 1982-83; co-chmn. Kansas City Spirit Festival, 1987; pres. Folly Theater, Performing Arts, Kansas City, 1989-90; mem. exec. com. Pembroke Hill Sch., Kansas City, 1990—, pres. 1994-96; co-chmn. Friends of YouthNet, Kansas City, 1991—. Fellow Am. Coll. Trust and Estate Counsel; mem. Lawyers Assn. Kansas City (pres. 1988), Kansas City Met. Bar Assn. (chmn. probate com. 1988), Mo. Bar (probate and trust com. 1988—), Kansas City Club, Kansas City Country Club. Office: Bryan Cave LLP 1200 Main St Ste 3500 Kansas City MO 64105-2100

REAMSNYDER, MARGARET ELIZABETH, nurse; b. Ottawa, Ohio, Dec. 5, 1923; d. Louis Henry and Minnie Mary (Mershman) Borgelt; m. Ross Allan Reamsnyder, July 4, 1948; children: Richard, Dennis, Thomas, Linda. Diploma, Toledo Hosp. Sch. Nursing, 1945; postgrad., Bowling Green State U., 1979. RN, Ohio. Operating room nurse Blanchard Valley Hosp., Findlay, Ohio, 1945-46, operating room supr., 1946-48, gen. duty nurse, 1965-66; sch. nurse Findlay City Schs., 1966—; advisor med. careers club Findlay High Sch., 1966-86, com. mem. student affairs, behavior screening, 1985-87. Vol. ARC, Findlay, 1984—. Mem. Nat. Assn. Sch. Nurses, Ohio Assn. Sch. Nurses (edn. com., chmn. 1974, cert.), N.W. Ohio Assn. Sch. Nurses (v.p. 1980-81), NEA, Ohio Edn. Assn., Findlay Edn. Assn. Lutheran. Home: 328 Warrington Ave Findlay OH 45840-6333 Office: Findlay High Sch 1200 Broad Ave Findlay OH 45840-2653

REARDON, PATRICK THOMAS, newspaper reporter; b. Chgo., Nov. 22, 1949; s. David Joseph and Audrey Joanne (Thomas) R.; m. Catherine Shiel, Oct. 30, 1982; children: David Joseph Shiel, Sarah Catherine Shiel. BA in English, St. Louis U., 1971. Reporter, photographer Austinite/N.W. Passage, Chgo., 1972-73; reporter, editor City News Bur. Chgo., 1973-76, Suburban Trib, Chgo., 1976-81; reporter, editor Chgo. Tribune, 1981-91, book reviewer, 1985—, columnist, 1990-92, urban affairs writer, 1991—. Author: Daily Meditations (with scripture) for Busy Dads, 1995; co-author: The American Millstone, 1986, Chicago Schools: "Worst in America," 1988. Recipient Lisagor award Headline Club, Chgo., 1988, 91, 92. Mem. Soc. Profl. Journalists. Roman Catholic. Home: 6220 N Paulina St Chicago IL 60660-1119 Office: Chgo Tribune 435 N Michigan Ave Ste 400 Chicago IL 60611-4001

REBBECK, LESTER JAMES, JR., artist; b. Chgo., June 25, 1929; s. Lester J. and Marie L. Rebbeck; B.A.E., Art Inst. Chgo., 1953, M.A.E., Art Inst. Chgo. and U. Chgo., 1959; m. Paula B., July 7, 1951; 1 child, Lester J. Asst. prof. art William Rainey Harper Coll., Pallatine, Ill., 1967-72; dir. Countryside Art Gallery (Ill.), 1967-73; gallery dir. Chgo. Soc. Artists, 1967-68; now artist, tchr.; one man exhbns. include Harper Jr. Coll.; group exhbns. include Univ. Club, Chgo., 1980, Art Inst., Chgo., 1953, Peace Mus., Chgo., 1985, Ill. State Mus., Springfield, 1985, Mus. Sci. and Industry Gallery, Chgo., 1985, Fort Wayne (Ind.) Mus. Art, 1990, Mus. Art South Bend, Ind., 1993, Purdue U. Galleries, 1994. Served with U.S. Army, 1951-52. Mem. NEA, Ill. Edn. Assn., Ill. Art Educators Assn., Chgo. Soc. Artists, Coll. Art Assn., Art Inst. Chgo. Alumni Assn. Republican. Presbyterian. Home: 2041 Vermont St Rolling Meadows IL 60008-2010

RECHTZIGEL, SUE MARIE (SUZANNE RECHTZIGEL), child care center executive; b. St. Paul, May 27, 1947; d. Carl Stinson and Muriel Agnes (Oestrich) Miller; m. Gary Elmer Rechtzigel, Aug. 20, 1968 (div. Feb. 1982); children: Brian Carl, Lori Ann. BA in Psychology, Sociology, Mankato (Minn.) State U., 1969. Lic. in child care, Minn. Rep. ins. State Farm Ins. Co., Albert Lea, Minn., 1969-73; free-lance child caretaker Albert Lea, Minn., 1973-78; owner, dir. Lakeside Day Care, Albert Lea, Minn., 1983—; asst. Hawthorne Sch. Learning Ctr., Albert Lea, 1978-83. Mem. New Residents and Newcomers Orgn., Albert Lea, 1970—, past. pres.; asst. pre-sch. United Meth. Ch., Albert Lea, 1975-78, tchr. Sunday sch., 1976-80, tchr. Bible sch., 1980-85; active Ascension Luth. Ch., 1976-80. Mem. Freeborn Lic. Day Care Assn. (v.p. 1986, pres. 1987), AAUW (home tour 1977, treas. 1980-81), Bus. and Profl. Women, YMCA, Albert Lea Art Ctr. Republican. Club: 3M Families. Home and Office: 1919 Brookside Dr Albert Lea MN 56007-2142

RECKER, DENNIS L., school superintendent; b. Lima, Ohio, Nov. 26, 1946; s. Joseph Herman and Laura Veronica (Vennekotter) R.; m. Irene Adeline Heitmeyer; children: Kimberly, Allison, Angela, Marci, Amber, Matthew, Anthony, Derek. BS, Bowling Green (Ohio) State U., 1968, MS, 1974. Basketball coach Miller City, Patrick Henry, Bluffton Coll., 1967-79; tchr., guidance counselor Cleveland Schs., Miller City, Ohio, 1969-83; staff devel./curriculum coord. Putnam County Schs., Ottawa, Ohio, 1983-90; supt. schs. Liberty-Benton Local Schs., Findlay, Ohio, 1990—; adv. bd. Regional Tchr. Tng. Ctr., Findlay, 1992—. Bd. dirs. MRDD of Putnam County, Ottawa, 1989-92; pres. Putnam County United Way, 1990-91. Recipient Outstanding Svc. award Putnam County United Way, 1991; recipient SPC in Edn., Ohio Bd. Regents, 1989. Mem. Ohio Assn. Sec. Sch. Adminstrs., Ohio Assn. Sch. Suprs., N.W. Ohio Assn. Supervision and Curriculum Devel. (pres. 1989), Findlay-Hancock County C. of C. (edn. com. 1990—), Buckeye Assn. Sch. Adminstrs., Ohio Assn. Local Sch. Supts. Office: Liberty-Benton Local Schs 9050 SR 12 W Findlay OH 45840

RECKLEIN, LINDA SUE, library administrator; b. St. Louis, Feb. 19; d. Clifford H. and Billie M. (Bader) Lincks; m. Dan S. Recklein, Sept. 4 1993; 1 stepchild, Allison Faith. BA in Psychology cum laude, U. Mo., St. Louis, 1972; MLS, U. Mo., 1977. Supr., para-profl. St. Louis County Libr., 1972-80; mgr. info. ctr., info. specialist Ralston Purina Co., St. Louis, 1980—; mem. bus. adv. bd. cons. group Gale Rsch., Detroit, 1990—; team mem. spl. librs. delegation Citizen Ambassador Program of People to People Internat., Russia and Czech Republic, 1995. Distbr. campaign lit. for Dem. and Rep. parties; vol. phone support at campaign hdqs.; vol. solicitor ARC Corp. Assocs. Ann. Fund, 1994. Recipient Cert. of Leadership, YWCA, 1991; named Outstanding Young Woman of Am., 1981. Mem. NAFE, AAUW, Soc. Competitive Intelligence Profls., Spl. Librs. Assn. (chpt. bd. dirs. 1983-84), Women in Bus. Network (treas. 1982-83), Am. Mgmt. Assn., St. Louis Regional Library Network (edn. com., info-lib lunchtime topics task force 1984-86). Roman Catholic. Home: 637 Laven Del Ln Saint Louis MO 63122-1115 Office: Ralston Purina Co Checkerboard Sq Saint Louis MO 63164

RECKNER, JERALD, marketing executive; b. Colby, Wis., May 12, 1932. A in Criminology, U. Wis., 1960, A in Bus. Mgmt., 1964. Chmn. bd. dirs. M.J. Group, Brookfield, Wis., 1978—, M.J. Mktg. Cons. Inc., Brookfield, Wis., 1978—, Mktg. Affiliates Inc., Brookfield, Wis., 1989—, Associated Speakers, Inc., Brookfield, Wis., 1988—, Reckner and Co., Inc., Brookfield, Wis., 1984—. Author: The Real Secrets of Life Fulfillment, 1994; co-author: The Power Within, 1978. Coach Little League Football and Baseball, Milw., 1975-79; scout master Boy Scouts Am., Milw., 1975-79. Served to sgt. U.S. Army, 1953-54. Mem. Nat. Speakers Assn. (events chair 1986—), Sales and Mktg. Execs. (com. chair 1986—), Toastmasters (pres., v.p., treas. 1984—), Elm Brook Rotary (com. mem. 1994—). Republican. Lutheran. Office: MJ Group 2525 N 124th St Ste 103 Brookfield WI 53005-4613

RECKTENWALD, FRED WILLIAM, financial executive; b. Fremont, Ohio, Dec. 24, 1946; s. Harold Louis and Geraldine Fern (Worthington) R.; m. Elaine Marie Denman, July 3, 1982. Acct. Henry Packing Co., Perrysburg, Ohio, 1969-70, Edward R. Moyer, CPA, Bellevue, Ohio, 1970-71; ptnr. Singer and Recktenwald Acctg., Fremont, Ohio, 1971-79; compt. Shortway Bus Lines, Inc., Toledo, 1979-80; city auditor City of Fremont, 1980—; mem. Coastal Resources Adv. Coun., 1992-93. Pres. Sandusky County Improvement Bd., Fremont, 1988-89, sec., 1990-95; chmn. Fremont Revolving Loan Fund Bd., 1989—; adv. bd. Terra Tech. Coll., Fremont, 1985—, Vanguard Vocat. Sch., Fremont, 1988—; fin. com. St. Joseph's Parish, Fremont, 1986-88. Mem. North Ctrl. Ohio Fin. Officers (pres. 1985), Ohio Govt. Fin. Officers Assn., Govt. Fin. Officers Assn. U.S. and Can. (Fin. Reporting Achievement award 1989, 90, 91, 92) Mcpl. Treas. Am., Ctrl. Cath. Boosters (trustee 1977-78), KC, Elks, Moose. Democrat. Roman Catholic. Office: City of Fremont 323 S Front St Fremont OH 43420-3037

RECTOR, WILLIAM DAVID, civil engineer; b. Terre Haute, Ind., Sept. 19, 1953; s. Charles Marshall and Sharon Lynn (Reeve) R.; m. Phyllis Ann Trefry, Feb. 23, 1974; children: Matthew David, Jennifer Layne. AS, Ind. State U., 1973, BS, 1981. Illustrator Hyster Co., Danville, Ill., 1974-76; draftsman Teepak, Inc., Danville, 1976-79; sr. designer Bristol-Myers, Evansville, Ind., 1979-86; sr. civil engr. Aluminum Co. of Am., Newburgh, Ind., 1986-90; sr. project mgr. John Brown Engring. & Constructors, Newburgh, 1990; plant mgr. Ameriqual Foods, Inc., Evansville, 1991—. Councilman Warrick County, Ind., 1989-92, precinct committeeman, 1984—, commr., 1996—; pres. Newburgh Storm Water Mgmt. Bd., 1988—; bd. dirs. Warrick Pub. Edn. Found., 1990—, Warrick County Park, 1993—, Warrick County Sheriff Merit, 1993—; mem. Bd. of Zoning Appeals, Warrick County, 1988-89; asst. scoutmaster Boy Scouts Am., 1985-89. Named Outstanding Young Man in Am., 1989, 92. Mem. ASCE, Assn. Ind. Counties, Hist. Newburgh, Newburgh Jaycees. Democrat. Lutheran.

REDDIG, WALTER EDUARD, architect, master cabinet maker; b. Meldorf, Holstein, Fed. Republic Germany, Apr. 3, 1936; came to U.S., 1960; s. Ernst and Frieda (Probst) R.; m. Irma Andresen, May 6, 1961; children: Sara Birgit, Ralph Edward. Student, Trade Sch., Meldorf, 1953-56; cert. design technician, Masters Sch., Flensburg, Fed. Republic Germany, 1959, cert. interior architect, 1960. Registered architect, Mich., Va., Md., Tex., Ill., Pa., N.H., Fla. Interior designer J. Holleman Assocs., Birmingham, Mich., 1963-66; project coordinator Levine-Alpern Assocs., Detroit, 1966-69; design and project dir. F. Stickel Assocs., Troy, Mich., 1969-73; project designer Greimel, Malcomson & James, Detroit, 1973; pvt. practice architecture Farmington Hills, Mich., 1973—; instr. Lawrence Tech. U. Coll. of Architecture and Design, Southfield, Mich., 1992—. Contbr. articles to mags.; artist water colors. Appointed to Ad Hoc Hist. Dist. Com., Farmington Hills, 1979-81; vice chmn. Hist. Dist. Commn., Farmington Hills, 1981-91; artist in residence Farmington Area Arts Commn., 1984. Mem. AIA, Mich. Soc. Architects, Nat. Council Archtl. Registration Bd. (cert.). Lutheran. Club: Farmington Artist (pres. 1983-85). Home and Office: 24003 Inkster Rd Farmington MI 48336-3855

REDDING, BARBARA J., nursing administrator, occupational health nurse; b. Youngstown, Ohio, Jan. 5, 1938; d. Richard Howard and Helen N. (Price) Sterling; m. Philip L. Redding, Nov. 7, 1957; children: Cheryl L., Jeffrey A., Scott P. Diploma in nursing, Miami Valley Hosp., Dayton, Ohio, 1959; AA in Sociology, Miami U., Oxford, Ohio, 1984; postgrad., U. Cin. RN, Ohio; cert. EMT, CPR, BLS. Office nurse Dr. Stewart Adam, Dayton; primary nurse Miami Valley Hosp; adminstr. employee health Armco Steel Co., L.P., Middletown, Ohio; v.p. Redding Ins. Agy., Inc., Middletown, Ohio, 1993—. Instr. CPR, ARC. Mem. NAFE, Am. Assn. Occupational Health Nurses, Ind. Ins. Agts. Am., Inc. Home: 4501 Riverview Ave Middletown OH 45042-2938

REDEL, THOMAS GREGORY, insurance regulatory executive, state official; b. Sullivan, Mo., Oct. 7, 1964; s. James Eugene and Jeannette Frances (Fechtel) R.; m. Denise Elaine Harker, Nov. 19, 1988; 1 child, Parker Thomas. BSBA in Econs., Lincoln U., 1988. CPCU, Am. Inst. Property and Casualty Underwriters. Worker's compensation supr. Mo. Dept. Ins., Jefferson, Mo., 1988-92, supr. property and casualty sect., 1992—; ex officio bd. dirs. Mo. Property Ins. Placement Facility, St. Louis, 1992—, Mo. Auto Joint Underwriting Assn., Chgo., 1992—. Mem. Soc. CPCU. Democrat.

REDFERN, RICHARD ROBERT, management consultant, geologist; b. Detroit, Sept. 8, 1951; s. Robert Clarence and Paula A. (Asam) Redfern Wenwieser; m. Joy Ann Reichmann, Sept. 2, 1983; children: Clayton Elliott, Christopher Dean. BS in Geology, Calif. State U., Northridge, 1973; MS in Geology, UCLA, 1977. Project geologist Urangesellschaft (USA), Inc., Denver, 1976-79; exploration geologist Homestake Mining Co., Lead, S.D., 1979-85; geol. cons. Spearfish, S.D., 1985—; chief geologist Goldstake Explorations, Inc., Toronto, Ont., Can., 1986-92; v.p. Goldstake Explorations (SD), Inc., Spearfish, 1986-92; pres. Redfern Mgmt. and Investments Co., Spearfish, 1988—; geol. cons. Republic of Congo, 1995—. Fellow Geol. Assn. Can., Soc. Econ. Geologists; mem. Internat. Assn. Genesis of Ore Deposits, Geol. Soc. Am., Soc. Mining Engrs., Spearfish Canyon Country Club, Sigma Xi. Republican. Presbyterian. Home: 1407 N 5th St Spearfish SD 57783-1412

REDLIN, ROLLAND W., state legislator; b. Lambert, Mont., Feb. 29, 1920; m. Christine Nesje; children: Ilene, Jeannette, Lisa, Daniel, Steven. Student, U. Wash., N.D. State Coll. Mem. N.D. Senate, 1958-64, mem. appropriations com.; mem. Congress, 1965-66; agr. cons. U.S. Dept. State, 1967; mem. N.D. Ho. of Reps.; cons. Bank of Agr. and Pub. Rels.; owner farm, past operator. Dem. candidate from N.D., Ho. of Reps., 1966, 68; pres. Minot Vocat. Workshop. Recipient Friend of Edn. award Minot Edn. Assn., 1988, Laura award for Dising. Svc. to Edn., 1991, Legis. award Libr. Assn. Mem. N.D. Bankers Assn., Farmers Union, Minot C. of C. Office: 1005 21st St NW Minot ND 58703-1724 also: State Senate State Capitol Bismarck ND 58505*

REDLINGER, SAMUEL EDWARD, chemical engineering consultant; b. Pitts., July 30, 1949; s. William Albert and Teresa Marie (Dobbins) R.; m. Rita D. Riley, Aug. 8, 1970 (dec. 1975); children: Timothy J., Thomas M., Daniel P.; m. Linda Jane Barkley, Dec. 16, 1978; 1 child, Aaron J. BAChemE, U. Dayton, 1971, MS in Analytical Instrumentation, 1974; MA in Mgmt., Pacific Western U., 1984. Cert. firefighter, hazardous material response, Ohio. Lead designer U.S. Steel Corp., Pitts., 1967-68; instrumental analyst Miami Conservancy Dist., Dayton, Ohio, 1968-73; prodn. engr. Delco-Moraine GMC, Dayton, 1973-74; sr. project engr. A. M. Kinney, Inc., Cin., 1974-76; plant engr. Sherwin-Williams Chem., Cin., 1976-78; mgr. engring. Midwest Tech. Inc., Cin., 1978-82; engring. mgr. Hilton/Davis Chems., Cin., 1982-86; pres. RsCo Innovative Solutions, Cin., 1986—; cons. Butler Co. (Ohio) FCA, 1986—. Inventor reverse osmosis, solidification, anionic membranes. Former bd. dirs. Presbyns. Pro-Life, Cin., 1989; chmn. com. Lakota Sch. Dist. Adv. Bd., Cin., 1986; vol. firefighter Union Twp. Fire Dept., 1985. Mem. Am. Inst. Chem. Engring., Gideons Internat., Masons (32d degree), K.T. Republican. Home: 9978 Boxwood Ct Cincinnati OH 45241-1032 Office: RsCo Innovative Solutions 9978 Boxwood Ct Cincinnati OH 45241-1032

REDMOND, PATRICK MICHAEL, graphic designer, art director, author, poet; b. Milw., Mar. 14, 1950; s. Gerald Francis and Carmella Marie (Gianquinto) R.; m. Barbara Jean McArdell, May 30, 1970 (div. June 1983); children: Katrina and Anna. Student, Mpls. Coll. Art and Design, 1968-70; BS, U. Minn., 1973, MA, 1990. Owner, prin. Patrick Redmond: Freelance Graphic Design and Illustration, West Allis, Wis., various locations, Minn., 1966-75, Redmond Design, Grand Rapids, Mpls., Minn., 1975-78, Barbara & Patrick Redmond Design, Mpls., 1978-82, Patrick Redmond Design, St. Paul, 1982—; graphic designer, illustrator De brey Design, Mpls., 1969; designer, prodn. asst. InterDesign, Inc., Mpls., 1970; artist-in-residence Eagle Bend (Minn.) Sch. Dist. and Community, 1971-74; designer-in-residence Grand Rapids (Minn.) Sch. Dist. and Cmty., 1974-76; sr. layout artist Gamble-Skogmo, Inc., Mpls., 1976-78; co-founder, v.p. Comcept Computer Graphics, Mpls. and St Paul, Minn., 1983-85; art dir. Norwest Corp., Mpls, 1988-89; sr. art dir. Carlson Frequency Mktg. Co. subs. Carlson Mktg. Group, Mpls., 1990-92; tchg. specialist U. Minn., St. Paul, 1983-84; instr. Coll. Associated Arts, St. Paul, 1984-89, Augsburg Weekend Coll., Mpls., 1989, 91; lectr. Mpls. Coll. Art and Design, 1992-93, U. Minn., St. Paul, 1992—. Author: I Thought a Loft Was For Hay: Accounts of My Experiences as an Artist-in-Residence in the Small, Rural Community of Eagle Bend, Minnesota, 1973; author, editor: Self-Portrait: Eagle Bend, a Book By and About a Rural Community, 1972; designer, illustrator numerous logos, books, book covers, publications, and packages; contbr. numerous articles to profl. and popular jours.; exhibitor numerous trade and profl. shows. Del. Minn. Small Bus. Conf., Mpls., 1981; active Mayor's Small Bus. Task Force, Mpls., 1978-79, State Minn. Art Edn. Task Force, St. Paul, 1975-76; parishioner Cathedral of St. Paul. Recipient awards from numerous entities including N.Y. Art Dirs., Soc. Publ. Designers, Creativity and Design N.Y., Soc. Typographic Arts, Nat. Endowment Arts/Minn. State Arts Bd., Waterford Crystal, Gilbert Paper; scholar Mpls. Sch. Art, 1968-69. Mem. U. Minn. Alumni Assn., Coll. Human Ecology Alumni Soc. (bd. dirs. 1992-95), Havurah Sivan (St. Paul). Roman Catholic. Office: Patrick Redmond Design PO Box 75430 Saint Paul MN 55175-0430

REECE, BETH PAULEY, commodities broker; b. Warsaw, Ind., June 4, 1945; d. Lester Elden and Genevene (Walter) Pifer; m. Gyle Barry Reece, June 20, 1987. BA, Grace Coll., 1967; interior design degree, Harrington Inst. Design, Chgo., 1995. Grain trader, hedger Cen. Soya Inc., Ft. Wayne, Ind., 1973-82; account exec. ACLI Internat. Inc., Chgo., 1982-83; account exec., hedger Cen. States Enterprises, Ft.Wayne, 1983-84; account exec. Stotler & Co., Chgo., 1984-89, LaSalle Brokerage Inc., Chgo., 1989—. Mem. Nat. Futures Assn., Art Inst. of Chgo., Met. Club. Republican. Presbyterian. Home: 227 E Delaware Pl Apt 5C Chicago IL 60611-1713

REECE, MARSHALL PHILIP, state official; b. Kansas City, Mo., Jan. 21, 1954; s. Jack and Frances (Pagano) R. BSBA summa cum laude, Rockhurst Coll., 1978; MPA, U. Kans., 1991. Reimbursement officer, bus. mgr. Rainbow Unit of Osawatomie State Hosp., Kansas City, Kans., 1974-78; acctg. supr. Park Lane Med. Ctr., Kansas City, Mo., 1978; cen. acct. II div. accounts and reports mcpl. acctg. Kans. Dept. Adminstrn., Topeka, 1978-81, cen. acct. III acctg. systems and procedures, 1981-86, cen. acct. IV, supr. agy. assistance and tng., 1986-94; state social security adminstr., 1990-95; instr. U. Kans., 1993—; bus. adminstr. Larned (Kans.) State Hosp., 1995—; adj. prof. acctg. Rockhurst Coll., Kansas City, 1980-81; cons. acctg. and data processing Tecumseh, Kans., 1987—. Author: The Kansas Legislative Process. Mem. Assn. Govt. Accts., Am. Soc. for Pub. Adminstrn. (sect. on budgeting and fin. mgmt., sect. crisis and emergency mgmt.), Am. Radio Relay League (sect. emergency coord. 1983-90, state govt. liaison 1986-90, 93—), Menninger Found. (contbg.), Austin (Tex.) Amateur Radio Club, Nat. Conf. of State Social Security Adminstrs., Internat. Platform Assn., Acad. Polit. Sci., Kaw Valley Amateur Radio Club (pres.-bd. dirs. 1982-85), Pi Alpha Alpha. Home: 303 Hillcrest Dr Larned KS 67550 Office: Larned State Hosp Office Bus Adminstrn Box 89 RR 3 Larned KS 67550

REED, CONSTANCE LOUISE, materials management and purchasing consultant; b. Point Pleasant, W.Va.; d. John Melvin Supple and Garnet L. Tooley; m. James Wesley Reed Jr., Sept. 20, 1985. Student, Ohio State U., 1974-76, Capital U., 1984-85. Buyer Abex Corp., Columbus, Ohio, 1971-79; maj. component buyer Grumman Corp., Delaware, Ohio, 1979-81; purchasing mgr. Atlantic Richfield (ANATEC), Dublin, Ohio, 1981-85; purchasing agt. Columbus Lodging, Inc., 1986-87, Monitronix Corp., Westerville, Ohio, 1988-89; contracts adminstr. Cellular Communications Inc., Worthington, Ohio, 1989-90; dir. materials mgmt. Fibrebond Corp., Minden, La., 1991-92; v.p. C&P Mgmt. Cons., Powell, Ohio, 1985—. Mem. NAFE, Am. Mgmt. Assn., Nat. Assn. Purchasing Mgmt., Bus. and Profl. Women's Club. Republican. Roman Catholic. Home: 1166 Highland Dr Columbus OH 43220-4940 Office: C&P Mgmt PO Box 158 Powell OH 43065-0158

REED, GERALD WILFRED, protective services official; b. Gary, Ind., Nov. 7, 1945; s. Lloyd Wilfred and Gertrude Ann (Nielsen) R. Student, N.E. Mo. State Tchrs. Coll., 1963-66; diploma, Control Data Inst., 1973. Cert. communications dispatcher Ind. State Police; cert. auto theft investigator, 1983. Incentive clk. U.S. Steel Corp., Gary, Ind., 1966; clk. dept. U.S. Steel Corp., Gary, 1967-73; telecommunicator Ind. State Police, Lowell, 1974—. Asst. scoutmaster troop 25 Boy Scouts Am., Kirksville, Mo., 1964-66, troop 620, Wichita, Kans., 1966-67, troop 91, Hobart, Ind., 1967-74, scoutmaster, 1974-75. Served with USAF, 1966-67. Recipient Scouters Training award Calumet Council Boy Scouts Am., 1970. Mem. Am. Numismatic Assn., Can. Numismatic Assn., Radio Comms. Monitoring Assn., Michigan City Model R.R. Workshop, Ohio Geneal. Soc. (Carroll County chpt.), Am. Philatelic Soc., Nat. Model R.R. Assn., Santa Fe Rwy. Hist. and Modeling Soc., Fraternal Order of Police, Ind. Police Radio Operators Club. Republican. Presbyterian. Lodge: Order of DeMolay (dist. gov. Franklin Ind. 1970-79, Cross of Honor 1973, Legion of Honor 1978, life mem., master councilor Hobart Ind., 1962-63), Masons. Office: Ind State Police Lowell Post 1550 E 181st Ave Lowell IN 46356-9526 also: PO Box 28 Hobart IN 46342-0028

REED, JAMES WESLEY, sales and marketing executive; b. Columbus, Ohio, Nov. 5, 1952; s. James Wesley and Donna Jean (Cavender) R.; m. Constance Louise Supple, Sept. 25, 1985. Student, Ohio State U., 1971-75; BS in Fin., Franklin U., Columbus, Ohio, 1983. In sales Clow Corp., Columbus, 1975-77; in materials specification Harvard Swan, Columbus, 1977-80; in purchasing/expediting Grumman Corp., Delaware, Ohio, 1980-83; account exec. A.G. Edwards, Columbus, 1983-85, Dean Witter Reynolds, Columbus, 1985-87; sr. tech. rep. Lucas Control Systems, Mellville, N.J., 1987-93; v.p. sales and mktg. NAL/Audipac, Grove City, Ohio, 1994—; cons. sales and mktg. JWR Cons., Columbus, 1993—. Pres. 40 Plus of Ctrl. Ohio, Columbus, 1995. Mem. Am. Mgmt. Assn., Am. Mktg. Assn. Republican. Presbyterian. Home: 1166 Highland Dr Columbus OH 43220 Office: PO Box 158 Powell OH 43065

REED, JANE GARSON, accounting educator, consultant; b. Cleve., Jan. 11, 1948; d. Joseph John Guzowski and Irene Sophie (Dominic) Garson; m. Wayne Ellis Reed, May 17, 1969; children: Craig Michael, Kevin Matthew. BBA magna cum laude, Baldwin Wallace Coll., 1977; MBA in Mgmt., Case Western Res. U., 1983; postgrad., Cleve. State U., 1991-96. CPA, Ohio. Letter carrier U.S. Postal Svc., Brecksville, Ohio, 1966-76; sr. asst. acct. Deloitte, Haskins & Sells, Cleve., 1977-78; sr. corp. auditor White Motor Corp., Beachwood, Ohio, 1979-81; instr. acctg. Cuyahoga C.C., Parma, Ohio, 1981-82; ind. contractor State of Wash., Olympia, 1982-84; dir. fin. The Montefiore Home, Cleveland Heights, Ohio, 1985-86; contr., bus. mgr. Western Res. Human Svcs., Inc., Akron, Ohio, 1986-87; lectr. mgmt. acctg. U. Akron, 1987-88; asst. prof. Baldwin-Wallace Coll., Berea, Ohio, 1989-94. Chairperson Trinity (Marymount) H.S. Reunion Com., 1990-91; mem. com. for Advanced Edn. in Brunswick, 1995—; mem. acctg. curriculum adv. com. Lorain County C.C. Mem. AICPA, AAUP, Am. Women's Soc. CPA, Ohio Soc. CPA (editl. bd. jour. com. 1992-95, task force on implementing quality edn. 1992-94), Inst. Mgmg. Accts. (faculty advisor to Baldwin-Wallace student chpt. 1990-94), Am. Soc. Women Accts. (pres. 1993-94), Am. Acctg. Assn. Methodist. Home and Office: 1254 Hadcock Rd Brunswick OH 44212-3018

REED, JOHN SHEDD, former railway executive; b. Chgo., June 9, 1917; s. Kersey Coates and Helen May (Shedd) R.; m. Marjorie Lindsay, May 4, 1946; children: Ginevra, Keith, Helen, Peter, John Shedd. Student, Chgo. Latin Sch., Hotchkiss Sch.; BS in Indsl. Adminstrn., Yale U., 1939; grad., Advanced Mgmt. Program, Harvard U., 1955. With A.T. & S.F. Ry., 1939-83; test dept. asst., successively spl. rep. to gen. supt. transp. Chgo.; transp. insp. Amarillo, Tex.; trainmaster Slaton, Tex., Pueblo, Colo.; supt. Mo. div., Marceline, Mo.; asst. to v.p. Chgo., 1957-59, exec. asst. to pres., 1957-59, v.p. finance, 1959-64, v.p. exec. dept., 1964-67, pres., 1967-78, chief exec. officer, 1968-82, chmn. bd., 1973-83; pres. Santa Fe Industries, Inc., 1968-78, chmn. bd. dirs., CEO Santa Fe So. Pacific Corp., 1987, chmn., 1987-88. Dir. Nat. Merit Scholarship Corp., 1996, past chmn.; trustee Shedd Aquarium, Chgo., 1996, past pres. With USNR, 1940-45. Mem. Chgo. Club, Old Elm Club, Shoreacres Club, Onwentsia Club (Lake Forest). Home: 301 W Laurel Ave # 112 Lake Forest IL 60045-1180 Office: 224 S Michigan Ave Rm 200 Chicago IL 60604-2507

REED, ROBERT PHILLIP, lawyer; b. Springfield, Ill., June 14, 1952; s. Robert Edward and Rita Anne (Kane) R.; m. Janice Leigh Kloppenburg, Oct. 8, 1976; children: Kevin Michael, Matthew Carl, Jennifer Leigh, Rebecca Ann. AB, St. Louis U., 1974; JD, U. Ill., 1977. Bar: Ill. 1977, U.S. Dist. Ct. (ctrl. dist.) Ill. 1979, U.S.Ct. Appeals (7th cir.) 1983, U.S. Dist. Ct. (so. dist.) Ill. 1992, Colo. 1993. Intern Ill. Legislature, Springfield, 1977-78; assoc. Traynor & Hendricks, Springfield, 1979-80; ptnr. Traynor, Hendricks & Reed, Springfield, 1981-88; pvt. practice Springfield, 1988—; pub. defender Sangamon County, Ill., Springfield, 1979-81; hearing examiner Ill. State Bd. Elections, Springfield, 1981-88; spl. asst. atty. gen. State of Ill., Springfield, 1983—; instr. Lincoln Land Community Coll., Springfield, 1988. Trustee Springfield Pk. Dist., 1985-89. Mem. Assn. Trial Lawyers Am., Comml. Law League Am., Ill. State Bar Assn., Colo. Bar Assn., Attys. Title Guaranty Fund, Inc., Phi Beta Kappa. Roman Catholic. Office: 1129 S 7th St Springfield IL 62703-2418

REED, SCOTT E., civil engineer; b. Crowley, La., Oct. 8, 1951; s. Frederick Hamilton and Beatrice (Curley) R.; m. Sheila Kara Turner, Oct. 18, 1975; 1 child, Scott Allen. BS in Civil Engring., U. Colo., 1974; MBA, U. Mo., St. Louis, 1981. Civil engr. Sverdrud & Parcel, St. Louis, 1974-83; site devel. engr. Anheuser-Busch Co., St. Louis, 1983—. Mem. Am. Soc. Civil Engrs., Internat. Devel. Rsch. Coun.

REED, SHEILA KAYE, program coordinator; b. East Prairie, Mo., Apr. 9, 1950; d. George Allen and Corine Laverne (Tyner) Turner; m. Scott Earl Reed, Oct. 18, 1975; 1 child, Scott Allen Hamilton. BS in Edn., S.E. Mo. State U., 1972; postgrad., N.E. Mo. State U., 1979; MBA, Lindenwood Coll., 1986; cert. adult edn., Ctrl. Mo. State U., 1991. Cert. coord. adult edn., cert. tchr. Tchr. Potosi (Mo.) Elem. Sch., 1972-74, Hazelwood (Mo.) Armstrong Sch., 1974-80; foster care worker Div. Family Svcs., St. Charles, Mo., 1987-89; coord. adult edn. Washington (Mo.) Sch. Dist., 1989-93; coord. admissions and fin. aid Sch. Nursing Mo. Bapt. Med. Ctr., St. Louis, 1993—; mem. adv. bd. Non-Traditional Careers, Union, Mo., 1991-93; mem. Franklin County Svc. Providers, 1992-93, Practical Nursing Program Adv. Bd., Washington, 1989-93. Bd. mem. Acad. Sacred Heart, St. Charles, Mo., 1989-91; chair Mktg. Com. for centennial celebration Mo. Bapt. Med. Ctr. Sch. Nursing, 1994-95. Recipient Certs. of Appreciation Enactment Com., Washington Sch. Dist./East Ctrl. Coll., 1991, Speaker for Todays Women Seminar, East Ctrl. Coll., 1991. Mem. Am. Vocat. Assn., Mo. Assn. Cmty. and Continuing Educators (bd. mem. for bus. and industry 1991-94, planning com.), Mo. Assn. Customized Trainers, Mo. Vocat. Assn. Office: Mo Bapt Med Ctr Sch Nursing 3015 N Ballas Rd Saint Louis MO 63131-2329

REED, VASTINA KATHRYN (TINA REED), child psychotherapist; b. Chgo., Mar. 5, 1960; d. Alvin Hillard and Ruth Gwendolyn (Thomas) R.; 1 child, Alvin J. BA in Human Svcs. magna cum laude, Nat.-Louis U., Chgo., 1988; MA, Ill. Sch. Profl. Psychology, 1991. Tchr. early childhood edn. Kendall Coll. Lab. Sch., Evanston, Ill., 1983-85, Rogers Park Children's Learning Ctr., Chgo., 1983-85; child life therapist Mt. Sinai Hosp., Chgo., 1988; child psychotherapist Nicholas Barnes Therapeutic Day Sch., Chgo., 1989-90. Den leader Boy Scouts Am., Chgo., 1989-92, scoutmaster troop 267, 1992—. Recipient Cub Scouter award Boy Scouts Am., 1990, Scoutmaster award of merit, 1993, 94, Scouters Vet. award, 1994, Scouters Key Tng. award, 1995, Scoutmasters Key award, 1996, Okpik Cold Weather Camping cert., 1994-95. Mem. APA, Nat. Orgn. for Human Svc. Edn., Order of the Arrow, Phi Theta Kappa, Kappa Delta Pi. Democrat. Roman Catholic. Home: 1872 S Millard Ave Chicago IL 60623-2542

REED, WILLIAM T., broadcasting executive; b. 1938. With Pub. TV, Reading, Calif., 1967-74, Pub. Broadcasting Sys., Washington, 1974-92; pres., gen. mgr. Sta. KCPT-TV, Kansas City, Mo., 1992—. Office: Sta KCPT-TV 125 E 31st St Kansas City MO 64108*

REEDER, ROBERT HARRY, retired lawyer; b. Topeka, Dec. 3, 1930; s. William Harry and Florence Mae (Cochran) R. AB Washburn U., 1952, JD, 1960. Bar: U.S. Dist. Ct. Kans. 1960, Kans. 1960, U.S. Supreme Ct. 1968. Rsch. asst. Kans. Legis. Council Rsch. Dept., Topeka, 1955-60; asst. counsel Traffic Inst., Northwestern U., Evanston, Ill., 1960-67, gen. counsel, 1967-92; exec. dir. Nat. Com. on Uniform Traffic Laws and Ordinances, Evanston, 1982-90. Co-author: Vehicle Traffic Law, 1974; The Evidence Handbook, 1980. Author: Interpretation of Implied Consent by the Courts, 1972. Served with U.S. Army, 1952-54. Mem. Com. Alcohol and Other Drugs (chmn. 1973-75). Republican. Methodist.

REEDY, JOHN J. (JOE), state legislator; b. Midland, S.D., Aug. 23, 1927. Grad. high sch., Vermillion, S.D. Mem. S.D. Ho. of Reps.; mem. agr. and natural resources and edn. coms.; owner Our Own Hardware, 1960-85; ins. salesman Mutual of Omaha, 1985—. Home: 948 Eastgate Dr Vermillion SD 57069-3618*

REEN, TERRY PETER, social worker; b. Grand Rapids, Mich., Jan. 21, 1951; s. Peter and Frances (Boersma) R.; m. Joanne Martha Byloff, May 21, 1983; children: Peter Nicholas, Marc Forrest. AB, Hope Coll., 1973; MSW, Mich. State U., 1979. Cert. social worker, school social worker, Mich. Psychiatric aide Pine Rest Christian Hosp., Grand Rapids, 1973-79; activities dir. Birchwood Manor Nursing Home, Holland, Mich., 1976-77; sr. therapist Project Recovery, Kalamazoo, 1979-81; therapist Ennis and Assocs., Flint, Mich., 1981-83; outpatient therapist Ucer's Psychiatric Clinic, Flint, 1981-84, Oakland Psychol. Clinic, Flint, 1984—; sch. social worker Birch Run (Mich.) Area Schs., 1984-85, Grand Blanc (Mich.) Area Schs., 1986—; instr. Mott C.C., Flint, 1989—; cons. Mott Middle Coll. High Sch., Flint, Our Community Cares, Grand Blanc, 1986-88. Vol. probation officer, Ottawa County Probate Ct., Grand Haven, Mich., 1975-76; speaker, John Anderson for Pres. Campaign, Kalamazoo, 1979-80. Recipient scholarship, NIMH, Washington, 1977. Mem. NASW, Acad. Cert. Social Workers, Mich. Sch. Social Workers Assn. Presbyterian. Home: 2237 Rollins St Grand Blanc MI 48439-4352 Office: Grand Blanc Community Schs 11920 S Saginaw St Grand Blanc MI 48439-1402

REENTS, RAY EDWARD, banking and stock consultant; b. Litchfield, Ill., Jan. 9, 1922; d. Lupke Henry Reents and Ruby May (Lant) Reents Glasscock; m. Irma Hazel Frey, Apr. 7, 1942; children: Donna, Ray T. (dec.), Cynthia, Steven. Attended, Rubicam Bus. Coll., St. Louis, 1941. Registered real estate broker, Ill. Jr. chemist Western Cartridge Co., East Alton, Ill., 1942-47; bank teller Marine Bank (now Bank One), Springfield, Ill., 1947-52; bank examiner State of Ill., Springfield, 1952-55; bank trust officer First Nat. Bank, Danville, Ill., 1956-57; cashier, COO Cmty. State Bank, Salem, Ill., 1957-58; banking and stock cons. Ray E. Reents, Inc., Springfield, 1958—. Mem. Masons (life). Home and Office: 2030 Clubview Dr Springfield IL 62704-3261

REES, ERICA SUE, insurance company executive; b. Muncie, Ind., Oct. 28, 1956; d. Richard E. and Henriette F. (Randt) Shinnock; m. Christopher Goens, July 6, 1976 (div. 1979); 1 child Gabriel Richard; m. Ken A. Rees, July 2, 1983; 1 child Derick Joseph. Student, Ball State U., 1977; grad., The Life Underwriters Tng. Coun., 1982. Registered Health Underwriter, 1988. Sales, bookeeper Wolf Bros. Inc., Bradenton, Fla., 1978; ins. agent, mgr. National Life and Accident Insurance Co., Muncie, Ind., 1979-81; prin. E. S. Goens Ins. Cntr., Hartford City, Ind., 1981-83; mgr. Bankers Life & Casualty Co., Muncie, Ind., 1983-85; br. sales mgr. Bankers Life & Casualty Co., Bridgeport, Ohio, 1985-90, Bankers Life and Casualty Co., Toledo, 1990—; instr. Life Underwriters Tng. Coun., 1991-92. Mem. Nat. Assn. Life Underwriters, Nat. Assn. Health Underwriters, Women's Life Underwriters (pres.), Exec. Women's Golf. Home: 5371 Co Rd F Delta OH 43515 Office: 135 Chesterfield Ln Ste 201 Maumee OH 43537-2299

REES, MICHAEL JOSEPH, real estate agency executive; b. Stockholm, May 22, 1954; came to U.S., 1960; s. Joseph R. and Phyllis A. (Snow) R.; m. Sue Griffith, Feb. 2, 1980, (div. Oct. 1984); 1 child, Kristoffer. BS in Bus. Fin., Ind. U., 1977; postgrad. in banking, U. Wis., 1986. Student co-op worker FDIC, Madison, Wis., 1975, 76; asst. bank examiner FDIC, San Francisco, 1977-79, bank examiner, 1979-84; bank examiner FDIC, Littleton, Colo., 1984-85; rev. examiner FDIC, Chgo., 1985-86; bank examiner FDIC, Indpls., 1986-87; ptnr. Rees Realty, Indpls., 1986—; exec., franchisee Holiday Inn, 1988—, Ponderosa Steakhouse, 1989—; co-founder SR9 Devel., L.P., Greenfield, Ind., 1994—. Active Planetary Soc., Pasadena, Calif., 1988, Nat. Space Soc., 1990. Mem. Delta Tau Delta. Republican. Office: PO Box 50735 Indianapolis IN 46250-0735

REESE, ALFERD GEORGE, retired army civilian logistics specialist; b. Granville, N.D., Apr. 5, 1934; s. Ferdinand Emil and lola May (Boulds) R.; m. Donna Mae Berger, 1955 (div. 1972); children: Rick, Denise, Roxanna; m. Nelda Cecilia Pena, May 31, 1985; children: Nancy, Joyce, Alfred, Jeffrey, Jessica, James, Alicia. AS, Humphreys Coll., 1963; BS, U. State of N.Y., Albany, 1983; MPA, U. Colo., Colorado Springs, 1985; postgrad., Ga. State U., 1987-88; PhD, Columbia Pacific U., 1994. Inspector, mechanic Sharp Army Depot, Lathrop, Calif., 1958-66; equipment specialist various stations U.S. Army Aviation Systems Command, 1966-84; supervisory equipment specialist U.S. Army Aviation Systems Command, Atlanta, 1984-88; supervisory logistics specialist U.S. Army Aviation Systems Command, St. Louis, 1988-93. Mem. com. Boy Scouts Am., Fed. Republic Germany, 1979-81. With USAF, 1953-57. Mem. Army Aviation Assn. Assn. (USAEUR Dept. Army Civilian of Yr. 1980, 81), Ctr. for the Study of the Presidency, Acad. Polit. Sci., Am. Soc. for Pub. Adminstrn., Nat. Rifle Assn. Home: 1590 Fairmount Dr Florissant MO 63033-2645

REESE, DOUGLAS WAYNE, geologist; b. Omaha, June 27, 1963; s. Larry Wayne and Sandra Kay (Bullerdick) R. BA in Geology, Case Western Res. U., 1987. Geologist, technician Mason de Verteuil Geotech. Svcs., Columbus, Ohio, 1987—, lab. supr., 1990—; owner D.R. Info. Sys., Reynoldsburg, Ohio. Mem. ASTM, ACLU, Am. Assn. Petroleum Geologists, Amnesty Internat., Electronic Frontier Found. Home: 1650 Hallworth Ct Columbus OH 43232-7400 Office: DLZ Corp 6121 Huntley Rd Columbus OH 43229 also: DR Info Sys 6326 E Livingston Ave # 199 Reynoldsburg OH 43068-2795

REESE, EDWARD W., medical products executive; b. Phila., May 21, 1943. BA, Metro State U., 1987; MS in Mgmt., Cardinal Stritch Coll., 1989; PhD, Union U., 1993. Cert. mfg. engr., Minn.; cert. forensic examiner. Dir. tech. svcs. Medtronic, Fridley, Minn., 1971-80; mgr. documentation and mfg. Daig Corp., Eden Prairie, Minn., 1980-81; mgr. mfg. and ops. AstroMed, Warrick, R.I., 1982-83; v.p. mfg. Angiomedics, Plymouth, Minn., 1983-86; founder Genesis Med. Inc., Prior Lake, Minn., 1986—; adj. prof. Bethel Coll., St. Paul, 1990—; cons. in field, Prior Lake, 1986—. Patentee catheter soft deformidable tip. Mem. Am. Bd. Forensic Examiners, Regulatory Affairs Profl. Soc., Am. Soc. Quality Control, Pub. Citizen Health Resource Group. Office: Genesis Med Inc 6520 Harborview Cir NE Prior Lake MN 55372-1445

REESE, JAMES W., orthodontist; b. Detroit, July 2, 1928; s. Ralph W. and Clarice M. (Turner) R.; m. Antonia L. Frazer, June 26, 1964; children: Matthew W., Gregory F., Elizabeth G. DDS, U. Mich., 1953, MS, 1959. Diplomate Am. Bd. Orthodontics. Dentist USNR, Calif., Korea, Japan, 1953-55; instr. U. Mich., Ann Arbor, 1955-59, asst. prof. grad. orthodontics Sch. Dentistry, 1964-85; pvt. practice San Francisco, 1959-64, Ann Arbor, Mich., 1964—; prof. emeritus, bd. regents, U. Mich., 1985; chmn. State Peer Review Panel, 1995—. Dental chmn. United Way, Ann Arbor, Mich., 1984-86. Lt. USNR, 1953-55. Fellow Internat. Coll. Dentists; mem. Am. Dental Assn., Am. Assn. Orthodontists, Mich. Dental Assn. (trustee 1976-81), Washtenaw Dist. Dental Soc. (pres. 1987), Mich. Assn. Orthodontists (pres. 1980). Home: 2009 Vinewood Blvd Ann Arbor MI 48104 Office: James W Reese DDS MS 3250 Plymouth Rd Ste 102 Ann Arbor MI 48105

REESE, NANCY IRENE ZANDER, journalist; b. Portland, Oreg., Oct. 8, 1950; d. Willard Earle and Margaret Amee (Hodges) Zander; m. Jon Harry Reese, Aug. 28, 1971. Student, Ind. State U., 1968-71; B degree, U. Ill., Chgo., 1978. Reporter, editor Des Plaines (Ill.) Pub., 1972-74; copy editor Daily Herald, Arlington Heights, Ill., 1974-79, Flint (Mich.) Jour., 1979-80; copy editor Chgo. Tribune, 1980-82, graphics coord., 1983-87, assoc. graphics editor, 1987—. Nat. editor The Phoenix Alpha Sigma Alpha, 1984—. Mem. Soc. Newspaper Design (contbg. editor 1993-95), Nat. Panhellenic Editors Conf. (chmn. 1995-97), Coll. Frat. Editors Assn. (pres. 1992-93), Alpha Sigma Alpha (Helen Corey award 1994). Home: 1312 E Kensington Mount Prospect IL 60056 Office: Chgo Tribune 435 N Michigan Ave Chicago IL 60611

REESE, NORMA CAROL, psychologist; b. Biloxi, Miss., Oct. 26, 1946; d. Virgil Stephen and Lila Mae (Shelton) Tatom; m. John Jay Reese, June 5, 1965 (div. Mar. 1983); children: Cher LeAnne, James Steven. AA in Psychology, Dade County Jr. Coll., Kendall, Fla., 1971; BS in Psychology, U. Miami, 1973; MS and PhD in Psychology, U. So. Miss., 1976. Lic. psychologist, Minn., N.D. Rsch. asst. NASA Lang. Rsch. Lab., Coral Gables, Fla., 1971-73; psychology instr. U. So. Miss., Hattiesburg, 1975-76, Grambling (La.) State U., 1976-78; clin. psychologist II Lake Charles (La.) Mental Health Ctr., 1979-83; tng. cons. Human Rels. Cons., Lake Charles, 1983-86; clin. dir. Grafton (N.D.) State Sch., 1986-89; dir. psychol. svcs. State Devel. Ctr., Grafton, 1989-95; ind. contractor, cons. psychol. svcs. Harley Residential Svcs. (name changed to Applied Behavioral Cons., Inc. 1990), Roseville, Minn., 1990-91; pvt. practice MYNDAK Moblie Cons., Minn. and N.D., 1990-95; program dir. for spl. needs Saint Coletta Sch., Jefferson, Wis., 1995—, mem. human rights and sexual health curriculum coms., 1995—; dir. sexual health project for devel. disabled and mentally retarded N.D. Dept. Human Svcs., Grafton, 1989-95, dir. sex offender and treatment program devel. disabled offenders, 1986-87; mem. adj. faculty grad. clin. psychology dept. U. N.D., Grand Forks, 1994—. Author: The Bulletin of the Psychonomic Soc., 1975-76; author/cartoonist The Worm Runner's Digest, 1975-80. Freedom writer Amnesty Internat., Midwest, 1989; founding mem. Sexual Health Coalition Steel of N.D., 1990; nat. disaster mental health technician, chpt. family svc. worker Red River Valley chpt. ARC, 1993—; mentor Am. Assn. Mental Retardation, 1992—; vol. Red Cross Nat. Disaster Mental Health Team, 1993, Emilys List, 1993. Named Silver Knight candidate, art, Miami (Fla.) Herald News, 1965; nominated Profl. of the Yr., La. Assn. Retarded Citizens, Lake Charles, 1983. Mem. APA (Div. 10), N.D. Psychol. Assn. (legis. action com. 1990-91, mem. disaster action com. 1993-94, mem. women in psychology 1995), Am. Assn. Mental Retardation (sec.-treas. N.D. chpt. 1991), Women in Networking, Assn. for Advancement of Psychology, Assn. for Sexual Abuse Prevention, Assn. for Play Therapy, Century Club. Republican. Methodist. Office: St Coletta Sch Hwy 18 Jefferson WI 53719-2428

REESE, ROBERT J., engineer; b. Milw., July 5, 1942. Project engr. Allis-Chalmers, Milw., 1961-66; asst. chief engr. Hydraulic Machinery Co., Milw., 1966-72, Unit Crane & Shovel, Milw., 1972-78; sr. project engr. Ctrl. Engring., Milw., 1978-87, Simon Aerials, Milw., 1987—; cons. Progressive Equipment Co., Heartland, Wis., 1989-92. Co-inventor engine streetsweeper. Mem. Soc. Automotive Engrs. Lutheran. Office: Simon Aerials 10600 W Brown Deer Rd Milwaukee WI 53224-1519

REESE, WINA HARNER, speech pathologist, consultant; b. Greensburg, Pa., Jan. 27, 1940; d. Clarence N. Harner and Gladys (Kell) Jaros; m. Richard F. Reese, Aug. 3, 1989; 1 child, Brian Olmsted. BS in Edn., Bowling Green (Ohio) State U., 1961. Speech pathologist La Grange (Ill.) Highlands, 1961-69, Richland Co., Mansfield, Ohio, 1970, Rehab. Svcs. N.C. Ohio, Mansfield, 1970-77; pvt. practice Lexington, Ohio, 1977-89; speech pathologist Mansfield City Schs., 1977—; cons., tutor Bur. Vocat. Rehab., Mansfield, 1980—; adj. prof. N. CT. C., 1995-96. Mem. Learning Disabilities Assn., Ohio Speech-Lang.-Hearing Assn. (dist. rep. 1975-76), N.C. Ohio Speech-Hearing Assn. (pres. 1975-76), Orton Dyslexia Soc. Home: 95 Otterbein Dr Mansfield OH 44904-9341 Office: Mansfield City/St Peters 67 Mulberry St S Mansfield OH 44902-1909

REEVE, LEE M., farmer; married; 3 children. BS in Agr. Econs., Kans. State U. Group mgr. Reeve Cattle Co., Garden City, Kans.; bd. dirs. Fidelity State Bank, Garden City, Garden City C. of C., Beef Empire Days, Garden City Fed. Land Bank. Mem. Agr. Value Added Processing Leadership Coun.; bd. dirs. Agrl. non-Food Use Task Force; mem. Kans. Coun. Vocat. Edn., Alt. Agr. Rsch. & Commercialization bd. Recipient Innovator of Yr. award State Bd. Agr., Environ. Achievement award Nat. Environ. Awards Coun., Wheeler McMillan award New Uses Coun., Disting. Agrl. Econs. Alumnus Kans. State U. Office: Reeve Cattle Co PO Box 1036 Garden City KS 67846*

REEVE, LORRAINE ELLEN, biochemist, researcher; b. Cato, Wis., Aug. 12, 1951; d. Robert K. and Lila M. (Breneman) R.; m. Dennis L. Kiesling, July 21, 1990. BS, U. Wis., 1973, MS, 1978, PhD, 1981. Postdoctoral scholar U. Mich., Ann Arbor, 1981-86; project scientist Cleve. Clinic Found., 1986-88; sr. rsch. scientist R.P. Scherer Corp., Troy, Mich., 1988-89, Mediventures, Inc., Dearborn, Mich., 1989-92; prin. investigator Mediventures, Inc., Dearborn, 1992-94; project mgr. MDV Technologies, Inc. (formerly Mediventures, Inc.), Dearborn, 1994—. Contbr. articles to profl. jours. Mem. Founders Soc. Detroit Inst. Art, 1989—, Nat. Trust for Historic Preservation, 1991—. Mem. AAAS, N.Y. Acad. Sci. Home: PO Box 2962 Ann Arbor MI 48106-2962 Office: MDV Techs Inc 15250 Mercantile Dr Dearborn MI 48120-1207

REEVES, ANN HOLT, conservationist; b. Mpls., Mar. 3, 1961; d. Robert Theodore and Shirley Jane (Russell) Holt; m. Randy L. Reeves, Oct. 5, 1991. BA, U. Minn., 1985. Dir. devel. ops. Hamline U., St. Paul, 1991-94; chief mgr., pres. River Valley Preservation, LLC, St. Paul, 1994—; cons., 1989-93; pres. Am. Prospect Rsch. Assn., 1991-93. Mem. Seward Neighborhood Group, Mpls., 1991—. Office: River Valley Preservation Pier One Harriet Island Saint Paul MN

REEVES, JUDITH ANN, critical care nurse; b. St. Louis, July 29, 1955; d. Charles David Reeves and Patricia Ann (Westerhold) Tutin. Student, U. Mo., St. Louis, 1973-76; ADN, Meramec C.C., 1978; BSN, St. Louis U., 1981. RN, Mo.; cert. BLS instr., ACLS instr. Staff nurse, team leader Firmin Desloge Hosp., St. Louis, 1978; relief nurse Staff Builders, St. Louis, 1978-79; paramed. examiner Meditest, St. Louis, 1979-80; relief nurse Kimberly Nurses, St. Louis, 1978-80; asst. head nurse surg. ICU Barnes Hosp., St. Louis, 1980-81; clin. instr., asst. head nurse surg. and cardiovascular ICU, staff nurse, charge nurse Jewish Hosp., St. Louis, 1981—. Vacation Bible sch. tchr. St. John's Luth. Ch., St. Louis, 1969-74, Sunday sch. tchr., 1972-78; vol. Mo. Hist. Soc., 1979-80; judge regional competitions Mo. Speed Skating Assn., 1978-84; beginners coach Clayton Speed Skating Club, 1977-84. Mem. AACN (past pres. St. Louis chpt., mem. symposium com., program com., pub. rels. com., membership com., symposium com. chair), Am. Heart Assn., St. Louis Soc. Critical Care Medicine (bylaws com. 1981), Mid Am. Transplant Assn (adv. coun. 1989-91). Office: Jewish Hosp St Louis 216 S Kings Hwy Saint Louis MO 63110

REEVES-DUDLEY, BEVERLY JAYNE, nurse anesthetist; b. New Orleans, Nov. 26, 1956; d. Clarence Thomas and Roberta Lilian (Preston) Reeves; m. Thomas Harris Dudley, Aug. 23, 1986. BSN, U. Iowa, 1979; MA in Biology, U. Mo., Kansas City, 1984. Cert. RN anesthetist, Kans., ACLS. Staff nurse neurology U. Iowa Hosp., Iowa City, 1979-80; staff nurse ICU and CCU Broadlawns Med. Ctr., Des Moines, 1980-82; instr. anesthesia U. Kans., Kansas City, 1985; free-lance anesthetist Anesthesia Svc., Inc., Leavenworth, Kans., 1986; staff nurse anesthetist Humana Hosp., Overland Park, Kans., 1987-94; self-employed Overland Park, 1994—; del. People to People Citizen Amb., People's Republic of China, 1989; mem. Kansas State Bd. of Nursing Adv. RN pracitioner adv. com. 1996. Contbr. articles to profl. jours. County del. Jimmy Carter Re-Election, Iowa City, 1980; vol. Com. for State ERA Amendment, Des Moines, 1980. Des Moines Women's Club scholar, 1982. Mem. ANA, Am. Assn. Nurse Anesthetists, Sigma Theta Tau, Phi Eta Sigma. Home and Office: 8118 Goodman St Overland Park KS 66204-3502

REGGIO, VITO ANTHONY, management consultant; b. Rochester, N.Y., Dec. 17, 1929; s. Salvatore and Carrie Angela (LoRe) R.; m. Mary Ann Dolores Pippie, Sept. 28, 1957; children: Salvatore, Angela. BS, Purdue U., 1952; postgrad. sch. modern langs., Middlebury Coll., 1948; postgrad. fellowship, U. Ky., U. Tenn. and U. Ala., 1952-53. Jr. engr. Rochester (N.Y.) Gas and Electric Co., 1950; designer/drafter Globe Constrn. Co., Rochester, 1951; rsch. analyst Commonwealth of Ky., Frankfort, 1952; orgn. & methods analyst, then wage adminstrn. specialist USN Dept. Indsl. Rels., Indpls., 1955-56; cons. mgmt. engr. to project mgr. to account exec. Bus. Rsch. Corp., Chgo., 1956-60; sr. cons. econ. feasibilities Ebasco Svcs., Inc., Chgo., 1960-63, dir. pers. mgmt. cons. dept., 1970-77; regional mgr., orgn. and pers. mgmt. svcs. EBS Mgmt. Cons., Chgo., 1963-65, nat. dir. orgn. and pers. mgmt. svcs., 1965-70; pres., bd. dirs. Reggio and Assocs., Inc., Chgo., 1977—; mng. dir. Pay Data Svc., 1977—; bd. dirs. Pay Data Svcs., Chgo. Contbr. papers to profl. publs. With U.S. Army, 1953-55. Named Solco Cultural Soc. fellow, Rochester, N.Y., 1948. Mem. Am. Compensation Assn., Am. Mgmt. Assn., Chgo. Compensation Assn., Soc. Human Resources Profls., Soc. Human Resources Mgmt., Human Resources Mgmt. Assn. Chgo., Western Soc. Engrs. Office: Reggio and Assocs Inc 550 W Jackson Blvd Chicago IL 60661-5716

REGIS, ROBERT STEPHEN, geology educator; b. Calumet, Mich., May 5, 1956; s. George Louis and Rebecca May (Bellaire) R.; m. Monica Elizabeth Gunderson, Aug. 7, 1982; children: Brent Louis, Stephanie Mae. BS in Earth Sci., No. Mich. U., 1986; MA in Geology, Ind. State U., 1989; postgrad., Mich. Tech. U., 1989—. Asst. coord. Groundwater Edn. Mich., Houghton, 1990-92; asst. prof. No. Mich. U., Marquette, 1992—; mem. adv. com. Groundwater Edn. Mich., 1992—; mem. steering com. Regional Gen. Ctr., Houghton, 1989-92; cons. in field. Deputy drain commr. Marquette County, 1993—. With USN, 1974-76. Mem. Am. Soc. Photogrammetry and Remote Sensing, Am. Geophys. Union, Sigma Xi, Gamma Theta Upsilon. Home: 1913 Clark St Marquette MI 49855 Office: No Mich U West Sci 233-C Marquette MI 49855

REGNELL, BARBARA CARAMELLA, media educator; b. Paterson, N.J., May 5, 1935; d. William Joseph and Mafalda Erminia (Benedetto) Caramella; m. Joseph C. Tirre, July 12, 1958 (div. June 1977); children: Conrad J., William C.; m. John Albin Regnell, Apr. 2, 1983. BS, Syracuse U., 1957, MA, 1966; postgrad., Washington U., St. Louis, 1972. Editor, continuity dir. Sta. WWBZ-AM, Vineland, N.J., 1958; dir. publicity Conti Adv., Ridgewood, N.J., 1958; copywriter Sta. KCNY, San Marcos, Tex., 1959; tchr. Henninger High Sch., Syracuse, N.Y., 1966-67; instr. Belleville (Ill.) Area Jr. Coll., 1968; from instr. to assoc. prof. So. Ill. U., Edwardsville, 1967—, chmn. mass communications, 1985-95; trainer Nat. Iranian Radio, TV, Tehran, Iran, 1974-75. Mem. NATAS (mem. bd. govs. St. Louis chpt. Syracuse unit regional coun.), BEA, Internat. Radio and TV Soc., Delta Sigma Rho, Alpha Chi Omega. Republican. Home: 6 Hawthorne Ct Saint Louis MO 63122-4512 Office: So Ill U Dept Mass Communications PO Box 1775 Edwardsville IL 62026

REGULA, RALPH, congressman, lawyer; b. Beach City, Ohio, Dec. 3, 1924; s. O.F. and Orpha (Walter) R.; m. Mary Rogusky, Aug. 5, 1950; children: Martha, David, Richard. B.A., Mt. Union Coll., 1948, LL.D., 1981; LL.B., William McKinley Sch. Law, 1952; LL.D., Malone Coll., 1976. Bar: Ohio 1952. Sch. adminstr. Stark County Bd. Edn., 1948-55; practiced law Navarre, from 1952; mem. Ohio Ho. of Reps., 1965-66, Ohio Senate, 1967-72, 93rd-104th Congresses from 16th Ohio dist., 1973—; chmn. appropriations subcom. on the interior; ptnr. Regula Bros.; Mem. Pres.'s Commn. on Fin. Structures and Regulation, 1970-71. Mem. Ohio Bd. Edn., 1960-64; hon. mem. adv. bd. Walsh Coll., Canton, Ohio; Trustee Mt. Union Coll., Alliance, Ohio, Stark County Hist. Soc., Stark County Wilderness Soc. Served with USNR, 1944-46. Recipient Community Service award Navarre Kiwanis Club, 1963; Meritorious Service in Conservation award Canton Audubon Soc., 1965; Ohio Conservation award Gov. James Rhodes, 1969; named Outstanding Young Man of Yr. Canton Jr. C. of C., 1957, Legis. Conservationist of Yr. Ohio League Sportsmen, 1969. Republican. Episcopalian. Office: US Ho of Reps 2309 Rayburn HOB Washington DC 20515*

REH, THOMAS EDWARD, radiologist, educator; b. St. Louis, Sept. 12, 1943; s. Edward Paul and Ceil Anne (Golden) R.; m. Benedette Texada Gieselman, June 22, 1968; children: Matthew J., Benedette T., Elizabeth W. BA, St. Louis U., 1965, MD, 1969. Diplomate Am. Bd. Radiology, Nat. Bd. Med. Examiners. Intern St. John's Mercy Med. Ctr., St. Louis, 1969-70; resident St. Louis VA Hosp., 1970-73; fellow in vascular radiology Beth Israel Hosp., Boston, 1973-74; radiologist St. Mary's Health Ctr., St. Louis, 1974—, chmn. dept. radiology, 1986—; clin. asst. prof. radiology St. Louis U. Sch. Medicine, 1978—; clin. assoc. prof. radiology, 1989—. Mem. Am. Coll. Radiology, AMA, Radiol. Soc. N.Am., St. Louis Met. Med. Soc., Alpha Omega Alpha, Alpha Sigma Nu, Delta Sigma Phi. Republican. Roman Catholic. Clubs: St. Louis, Confrerie des Chevaliers du Tastevin. Home: 9850 Waterbury Dr Saint Louis MO 63124-1046 Office: Bellevue Radiology Inc 1699 S Hanley Rd Saint Louis MO 63144-2913

REHA, ROSE KRIVISKY, retired business educator; b. N.Y.C., Dec. 17, 1920; d. Boris and Freda (Gerstein) Krivisky; m. Rudolph John Reha, Apr. 11, 1941; children: Irene Gale, Phyllis. BS in Bus. and Music Edn., Ind. State U., 1965; MA in Bus. and Psychology, U. Minn., 1967, PhD in Ednl. Psychology, 1971. With U.S. and State Civil Service, 1941-63; tchr. pub. schs., Minn., 1965-66; teaching assoc., instr. U. Minn., Mpls., 1966-68, 1975-85; prof. Coll. Bus., St. Cloud (Minn.) State U., 1968-85, prof. emeritus, 1985—, chmn. bus. edn. and office adminstrn. dept., 1982-83; court advocate for women in distress St. Cloud Women's Shelter, 1986-89; adj. prof. profl. and bus. communication Fla. Atlantic U., Boca Raton, Fla., 1989-90; substitute tchr. Broward County, 1990—; tutor (reading) Lauderdale, Fla., 1990-92; cons., lectr. in field; small business cons. Small Business Inst. Coll. Business. St. Cloud St. U. Minn. Reviewer of bus. communications and consumer edn. textbooks; contbr. articles to profl. jours. Camp dir. Girl Scouts U.S., 1960-62; active various community fund drives; sec., mem. relicensure rev. Com. Minn. Bd. Teaching Continuing Edn., 1984-85. Recipient Achievement award St. Cloud State U., 1985, St. Cloud State U. Rsch. and Faculty Improvement grantee, 1973, 78, 83. Mem. Am. Vocat. Assn., Minn. Econ. Assn., Minn. Women of Higher Edn., NEA, Minn. Edn. Assn. (pres. women's caucus 1981-83, award 1983), St. Cloud U. Faculty Assembly (pres. 1975-76), St. Cloud State U. Grad. Coun. (chmn. 1983-85), Parents Without Ptnrs. (moderator North Broward, Ft. Lauderdale chpts. 1994—), Pi Omega Pi (sponsor St. Cloud State U. chpt. 1982-85), Phi Chi Theta, Delta Pi Epsilon, Delta Kappa Gamma. Jewish. Home: 3671 Environ Blvd Fort Lauderdale FL 33319-4221 Office: St Cloud State U Coll Bus Saint Cloud MN 56301

REHM, JOHN EDWIN, manufacturing company executive; b. Bucyrus, Ohio, Oct. 20, 1924; s. Lester Carl and Mary C'Dale (Myers) R.; student Heidelberg U., 1942; U. Ala., 1943-44; Ohio State U., 1946-49. Asst. plant engr. Shunk Mfg. Co., Inc., Bucyrus, 1949-53, prodn. mgr., 1951-61, plant mgr., 1961-65, mgr. prodn. services, 1965-68, mgr. customer service dept., 1968-69, ops. mgr., 1969-70, v.p. ops., 1970-71; materials mgr. Oury Engring. Co., Marion, Ohio, 1971-73, W.W. Sly Mfg. Co., Cleve., 1973-79, 84—; v.p., gen. mgr. Moody Mfg. Co., Inc., Maben, Miss., 1979-84. Bd. dirs. Bucyrus United Community Fund, 1969-70. Served with AUS, 1943-46, PTO. Decorated Bronze Star with oak leaf cluster. Mem. Am. Soc. Personnel Adminstrn., Bucyrus Area C. of C. (v.p. 1966, pres. 1967). Republican. Lodges: Elks, Rotary. Home: 5246 Manchester Cir Elyria OH 44039-1336

REICHARD, CHRYSTAL JEAN, physical therapist; b. Chambersburg, Pa., Aug. 23, 1963; d. Gerald Willis and Jean Louise (Waite) R. BS, U. Scranton, 1985; MAR, Luth. Theol. Sem., Gettysburg, 1994. Cert. clin. specialist in geriatric phys. therapy. Staff phys. therapist Mercy Hosp. of Johnstown, Pa., 1985-87, Chambersburg (Pa.) Hosp., 1988-91; contract phys. therapist Borromeo & Assocs., Littlestown, Pa., 1991-92; staff. phys. therapist Lancaster (Pa.) Gen. Hosp., 1992-94; dir. phys. thearpy Omro (Wis.) Care Ctr. Hillhaven Corp., 1994-95; phys. therapist Sundance Rehab., Appleton, Wis., 1995-96; dir. rehab. svc. Americana Healthcare Ctr., Appleton, Wis., 1996—. Mem. Am. Phys. Therapy Assn., Wis. Phys. Therapy Assn. Home: 927 W Taylor St Appleton WI 54914-2610 Office: Americana Healthcare Ctr 1355 S Oneida St Appleton WI 54915

REICHERT, JACK FRANK, manufacturing company executive; b. West Allis, Wis., Sept. 27, 1930; s. Arthur Andrew and Emily Bertha (Wallinger) R.; m. Corrine Violet Helf, Apr. 5, 1952; children: Susan Marie, John Arthur. Cert. mktg., U. Wis., Milw., 1957; AMP, Harvard U., 1970; LLD (hon.), Marian Coll., 1994. Various mktg. positions GE, 1948-57; with Brunswick Corp., Lake Forest, Ill., 1957-95; pres. Mercury Marine div. Brunswick Corp., 1972-77; corp. v.p. Brunswick Corp., Lake Forest, 1974-77, group v.p. Marine Power Group, 1974-77, pres., COO, 1977-93; CEO Brunswick Corp., 1982-95; chmn. bd. dirs. Brunswick Corp., Lake Forest, Ill., 1983-95; dir. Brunswick Corp., 1977—; bd. dirs. The Dial Corp., Phoenix. Trustee Carroll Coll., Waukesha, Wis., 1972; indsl. chmn. Fond du Lac United Fund, 1977. With C.E. U.S. Army, 1951-53. Named Disting. Alumnus of the Yr., U. Wis., Milw. 1979, Top Chief Exec. Officer in Multi-Industry Group, Fin. World Mag., 1984; recipient Gold award in leisure industry Wall St. Transcript, 1983, 86, Bronze award in multi-industry category Wall St. Transcript, 1985, Leisure Industry Silver award, 1988. Mem. Am. Mgmt. Assn., U. Wis.-Milw. Alumni Assn., Knollwood Club, Harvard Club, Mid-Am. Club, Beta Gamma Sigma (hon.). Presbyterian. Home: 580 Douglas Dr Lake Forest IL 60045-3342 Office: Brunswick Corp 1 N Field Ct Lake Forest IL 60045-4810

REICHGOTT JUNGE, EMBER D., state legislator, lawyer; b. Detroit, Aug. 22, 1953; d. Norbert Arnold and Diane (Pincich) R.; m. Michael Junge. BA summa cum laude, St. Olaf Coll., Minn., 1974; JD, Duke U., 1977; MBA, U. of St. Thomas, 1991. Bar: Minn. 1977, D.C. 1978. Assoc., Larkin, Hoffman, Daly & Lindgren, Bloomington, Minn., 1977-84; counsel Control Data Corp., Bloomington, Minn., 1984-86; atty. The Gen. Counsel, Ltd., 1987—; mem. Minn. State Senate, 1983—, chmn. legis. com. on econ. status of women, 1984-86, vice chmn. senate edn. com., 1987-88, senate majority whip, 1990-94, chmn. property tax div. senate tax com., 1991-92, chmn. senate judiciary com., 1993-94; senate asst. majority leader, 1995—, chmn. spl. subcom. on Ethical Conduct; instr. polit. sci. St. Olaf. Coll., Northfield, Minn., 1993; dir. Citizens Ind. Bank, St. Louis Park, Minn., 1993—. Host (cable TV monthly series) Legis. Report, 1985-92. Trustee, bd. dirs. N.W. YMCA, New Hope, Minn., 1983-88; Greater Mpls. Red Cross, 1988—, United Way Mpls., 1989—. Youngest woman ever elected to Minn. State Senate, 1983; recipient Woman of Yr. award North Hennepin Bus. and Prof. Women, 1983, Award for Contbn. to Human Svcs., Minn. Social Svcs. Assn., 1983, Clean Air award Minn. Lung Assn., 1988, Disting. Svc. award Mpls. Jaycees, 1984, Minn. Dept. Human Rights award, 1989, Myra Bradwell award Minn. Women Lawyers, 1993, Disting. Alumnae award Lake Conf. Schs., 1993; named One of Ten Outstanding Young Minnesotans, Minn. Jaycees, 1984, Policy Advocate of Yr. NAWBO, 1988, Woman of Achievement Twin West C. of C., 1989, Marvelous Minn. Woman, 1993. Mem. Minn. Bar Assn. (bd. govs. 1992—, Pro Bono Publico Atty. award 1990), Hennepin County Bar Assn., Corporate Counsel Assn. (v.p. 1989—), Minn. Dem. Farmer-Labor Party (state co-chair Clinton/Gore Presdl. Campaign 1992, 96, del. nat. Dem. conv. 1984, 92). Home: 7701 48th Ave N Minneapolis MN 55428-4515

REICHLE, PAUL D., tool designer; b. Hamilton, Ohio, Sept. 6, 1955. Student, ITT Tech. Inst., Dayton, Ohio, 1973-75. In tool engring. McDonnell Douglas, St. Louis, 1976-87; contract engr. mech. tooling Aerospace Industry, St. Louis, 1987-91, Baldor Electric, St. Louis, 1991-94; tool deisgner Hoffman Tool Co., O'Fallon, Mo., 1994—. Republican. Office: Hoffman Tool Co 1029 E Terra Ln O'Fallon MO 63366-2750

REICKERT, ERICK ARTHUR, automotive executive; b. Newport, Tenn., Aug. 30, 1935; s. Frederick Arthur and Reva M. (Irish) R.; m. Diane Lois Comens, June 10, 1961 (div. Jan. 1979); children: Craig A., Laura L.; m. Heather Kathleen Ross, Sept. 1, 1982. BSEE, Northwestern U., 1958; MBA, Harvard U., 1965. Various positions Ford Motor Co., Dearborn, Mich., 1965-73, exec. dir. small car planning, 1979-84; v.p. export ops. Ford Motor Co., Brentwood, Eng., 1973-79; v.p. advance product devel. Chrysler Motors, Detroit, 1984-86, v.p. program mgmt., 1986-87; chmn., mng. dir. Chrysler Mexico, 1987-89; chmn., CEO Acustar Inc., Troy, Mich., 1990-91; v.p. power train ops. Chrysler Corp., Auburn Hills, Mich., 1991-92; pres., CEO New Venture Gear Inc., Troy, 1992—; bd. dirs. Truck Components Inc., Rockford, Ill., 1994-95. Bd. dirs. Jr. Achievement of S.E. Mich., Detroit, 1992—, Children's Ctr., Detroit, 1993—; regent for S.E. Mich., Northwestern U., Evanston, Ill., 1994—. Mem. Soc. Automotive Engrs., Engring. Soc. Detroit, Harvard Bus. Sch. Club of Detroit. Office: New Venture Gear Inc 1650 Research Dr Ste 300 Troy MI 48083-2100

REID, BAXTER ELLIS, JR., labor union representative; b. Peoria, Ill., Feb. 10, 1943; s. Baxter Ellis and Ardeane Mary (Braunagel) R.; m. Debra Kay Bowers, May 20, 1977 (div. Nov. 1983); children: Mary Linn, Baxter Ellis III; m. Charlene Teresa Badaukis, Oct. 20, 1984; 1 child, Charles Austin. Factory worker Caterpillar Tractor, Peoria, 1963-75; local rep. UAW, Peoria, 1963-75; internat. rep. v.p. staff UAW, Detroit, 1975-85, internat. rep. pres. staff, 1985-86, asst. dir. arbitration dept., 1986-93, dir. arbitration, 1993—. Contbr. articles to union jours. Mem.-at-large NAACP; Dem. precinct committeeman Peoria County, 1973-75, Dem. vice chmn., 1974-75; Dem. precinct del. Wayne County, Mich., 1986—, Dem. conv. del., 1986—. Served as cpl. USMC, 1962-64. Mem. Internat. Platform Assn., Am. Arbitration Assn. (cons. 1987—), Indsl. Relations Research Assn. Home: 3241 Stuart Ln Dearborn MI 48120-1334 Office: UAW-Internat Union 8000 E Jefferson Ave Detroit MI 48214-3963

REID, BRUCE EUGENE, video executive; b. Circleville, Ohio, June 24, 1950; s. Lawrence Welden and Joan Del (Davis) R.; m. Mildred Jeanne Reid, July 21, 1972; children: Nathan Lawrence, Bethany Shannon. BA, Ohio State U., 1972. Stage mgr. Avco Broadcasting, Columbus, Ohio, 1969-72, asst. dir. pub. affairs, 1972-76; account exec. Avco Broadcasting, Columbus, 1976-77, prodr., 1977-78, asst. dir. broadcast prodn., 1978-79; dir. broadcast prodn. Byer and Bowman Advt., Columbus, 1979-80, prodr., dir., editor, 1980-81; prodn. mgr. Prodrs. Video Corp., Kansas City, Mo., 1981-82; prodn. mgr., exec. prodr., 1982-83; v.p., gen. mgr. Laclede Comm. Svcs., St. Louis, 1983-84; comml. prodn. mgr. Pappas Telecasting of the Carolinas, Greenville, S.C., 1984; pres., gen. mgr. Prodrs. Video Corp., Balt., 1984-88; gen. mgr., ptnr. Prodn. Masters, Inc., Phoenix, 1988-91; exec. producer Mills/James Prodns., Columbus, Ohio, 1991—. Author: (booklet) What Every Account Executive Should Know About TV Production, 1979. Recipient Emmy award Nat. Asst. TV Arts and Scis., 1974, 95, best TV campaign design award Retail Advt. Burs., 1978, best TV comml. award, 1979. Mem. Internat. TV Assn. (Golden Slate award 1993), Columbus Ad Club, Sigma Nu. Office: Mills/James Prodns 3545 Fishinger Blvd Hilliard OH 43026-9550

REID, GERALDINE WOLD (GERALDINE REID SKJERVOLD), artist; b. Portland, Oreg., Apr. 11, 1944; d. Alden Elroy and Verna (Kocinski) Wold; B.A. in Fine Art, Calif. State U., Sacramento, 1972, M.F.A., 1975; postgrad. Ind. U.-Purdue U. Instr. dental aux. edn. U. Minn., 1966-70; anthrop. research asst., 1975-76; asst. prof. dental aux. edn. Ind. U.-Purdue U., 1976-78; mng. editor Nat. Arts Guide, Chgo., 1978-80; freelance artist, Chgo., 1981-94; pres. Chgo. Art Emerging Inc., 1983-85; graphic artist Reid Design & Illustration, Chgo., 1981-94; dir. show coordination Circle Fine Art, Chgo., 1981; instr. comm. art and design Alexandria Tech. Coll., Minn., 1994—; seminar lectr., 1977, 86; lectr. art and math. Dept. Math. U. Ill., 1987-88. One-woman shows include Artists' Coop. Gallery, Santa Fe, 1976, Artlink, Ft. Wayne, Ind., 1979, 84—, D.E.O. Fine Arts, Inc., Chgo., 1982-83, Union League Gallery, Chgo., 1989, Brodsky Gallery, 1993; group exhbns. include Crocker Art Mus., Sacramento, 1975, Ft. Wayne Mus. Art, 1978, Artists Guild Chgo., 1981, Charles A. Wustum Mus., Racine, Wis., 1983, Limelight, Chgo., 1986, 87, 88, Neville-Sargent Gallery, 1986, 87, Beacon Street Hull House Gallery, 1988, McDonalds Corp., Chgo., 1988, Prairie Ave. Gallery, Chgo., 1990, Peace Mus., Chgo., 1990, Hyde Park Art Ctr., Chgo., 1990, Lettuce Entertain You Enterprises, Inc., 1990. Olive Tree Gallery, Daley Coll., Chgo., 1991, Crown Ctr. Gallery, Loyola U., Chgo., 1992, Agora Syndicate, Inc., 1992, Kieffer-Nolde/TIC, 1992, Flora '92, 1992, Chgo. Botanic Garden, 1992, Open Spectrum, David Adler Cultural Ctr., 1994, August House Studio, Chgo., 1994—, Upper West Gallery, Alexandria Tech. Coll., Min., 1995; contbr. artwork to 2 ann. 1994 calendars. Mem. Artists Guild Chgo., Chgo. Artists' Coalition.

REID, JAMES SIMS, JR., automobile parts manufacturer; b. Cleve., Jan. 15, 1926; s. James Sims and Felice (Crowl) R.; m. Donna Smith, Sept. 2, 1950; children: Sally, Susan, Anne (dec.), Jeanne. AB cum laude, Harvard U., 1948, JD, 1951. Bar: Mich., Ohio 1951. Pvt. practice law Detroit, 1951-52, Cleve., 1953-56; with Standard Products Co., Cleve., 1956—, dir., 1959, pres., 1962-89, chmn., chief exec. officer, 1989—. Trustee John Carroll U., 1967—, chmn., 1987-91, Musical Arts Assn. of Cleve. Orch., 1973—. Office: Standard Products Co 2130 W 110th St Cleveland OH 44102-3510

REID, MARILYN JOANNE, state legislator, lawyer; b. Chgo., Aug. 14, 1941; d. Kermit and Newell Azile (Hahn) N.; m. M. David Reid, Nov. 26, 1966 (div. Mar. 1983); children: David, Nelson. Student, Miami U., 1959-61; BA, U. Ill, 1963; JD, Ohio No. U., 1966. Bar: Ohio 1966, Ark. 1967, U.S. Dist. Ct. 1967. Trust adminstr. First Nat. Bank, Dayton, Ohio, 1966-67; assoc. Sloan & Ragsdale, Little Rock, Ohio, 1967-69; ptnr. Reid and Reid, Dayton, 1969-76, Reid & Buckwalter, Dayton, 1975—; mem. Ohio Ho. of Reps., 1993—; mem. Judiciary and Criminal Justice com., vice chmn. ins. com., Vets. com., Pub. utilities com. Mem. Ohio adv. bd. U.S. Commn. Civil Rights; chmn., treas. various polit. campaigns, 1975—; trustee Friends Libr. Beavercreek (Ohio); bd. dirs. Beavercreek YMCA, 1985-88; active Mt. Zion United Ch. of Christ. Mem. ABA, Ohio Bar Assn., Greene County Bar Assn., Beavercreek C. of C. (pres. 1986-87), Dayton Panhellenic Assn. (pres. 1982), Altrusa (v.p. Greene County 1978-79, pres. 1979-80), Lioness (pres. Beavercreek 1975), Rotary, Kappa Beta Pi, Gamma Phi Beta (v.p. 1974-75). Republican. Mem. Ch. Christ. Office: Reid & Buckwalter 3866 Indian Ripple Rd Dayton OH 45440-3448

REID, SCOTT ALLEN, chemistry educator; b. Santa Maria, Calif., Sept. 20, 1963; s. Thomas James and Ruby Faye (Barfield) R. BS in Chemistry, Union U., 1985; PhD in Chemistry, U. Ill., 1990. Postdoctoral fellow U. So. Calif., L.A., 1990-94; asst. prof. Marquette U., Milw., 1994—; cons. Petrolaser, Inc., Las Cruces, N.Mex., 1991—, Phillips Petroleum, Tulsa, 1991-92. Contbr. articles to profl. jours. Mem. AAUP, Am. Chem. Soc. (type G rsch. grant 1995), Optical Soc. of Am., Internat. Assn. of Electronic and Elec. Engrs. Home: 2400 E Bradford #201 Milwaukee WI 53211 Office: Marquette Univ 535 N 14th St Milwaukee WI 53233

REIFENRATH, TODD FRANCIS, software developer; b. Cherokee, Iowa, Mar. 14, 1970; s. Quentin F. and Diana R. (Bowers) R.; m. Stephanie R. Coghlan, May 15, 1993. BA in Computer Sci., U. No. Iowa, 1993. Programmer Control-O-Fax, Waterloo, Iowa, 1992-93; sr. application developer Arthur Andersen & Co., Chgo., 1993-95; software engr. Sys. Software Assocs., Chgo., 1995; sr. software engr. Micro Mgmt., Inc., Chgo., 1995—. Tutor Cabrini-Green Tutoring, Chgo., 1993. Home: 4315 N Kenmore Ave Ste 1S Chicago IL 60613

REIFF, JAMES STANLEY, addictions physician, psychiatric physician, osteopathic physician, surgeon; b. Chgo., Mar. 17, 1935; s. Nathan Edgar and Freda Matilda (Imhoff) R.; m. Sharon Ann Kraybill, June 9, 1956 (div. Apr. 1970); children: Gregory James, James Stanley II, Cynthia Diane, Jeffery Cameron. B.A. in Chemistry, Goshen Coll., 1957; D.O., Chgo. Coll. Osteo. Medicine, 1961. Biochemist Miles/Ames Pharm. Co., Elkhart, Ind., 1955-57; gen. practice medicine, Michigan City, Ind., 1962-69; addictions physician Oaklawn Psychiat. Ctr., Elkhart, Ind. 1974-84; clin. team leader, addictions team Oaklawn Ctr., Elkhart, 1980-83. Alcohol Anonymous Cen. Service Area Inc., 1984-87; med. dir., Life Recovery Cen., Elkhart, 1987-90; med. dir., Substance Abuse Coun. St. Joe County, Mich., 1990-95; med. dir. Am. Plasma Mgmt., Inc., Kalamazoo and East Lansing, Mich., 1991—; staff psychiatrist Community Mental Health Svcs. St. Joe County, 1993—; bd. dirs. Home for Runaway Kids - Victory House, Elkhart, Ind., 1974-76, 12 Step House Meth. Ch.-Halfway House, Elkhart, 1974-77; bd. dirs., treas. Caldwell Home Corp.-Social Rehab. Ctr. for Alcoholism, Elkhart, 1984-87; bd. dirs. Hope House, Jonesville, Mich.; organist First Presbyn. Ch., Sturgis, Mich., 1993—. Mem. AMA, Am. Osteopathic Assn., Am. Soc. Addiction Medicine (com. on addiction medicine in correctional facilities 1993—), Am. Med. Soc. on Alcoholism, Soc. Correctional Physicians, Nat. Coun. on Alcoholism and Drug Dependence in Mich., Mich. State Med. Soc., St. Joe County Med. Soc., Am. Osteopathic Assn. Avocations: organ and piano playing. Home: 1301 E Congress St Sturgis MI 49091-2326 Office: Cmty Mental Health St Joe County 210 S Main St Three Rivers MI 49093

REIGEL, JAMES L., manufacturing executive; b. Marshfield, Wis., Feb. 11, 1950. A, Mid State Tech. Coll., 1970. Sales & engring. JBL Internat. Inc., Marshfield, Wis., 1971-85; pres. Paget Equipment Co./JBL Internat. Inc., Marshfield, Wis., 1985—; vice chmn. 3-A Stds. Com., Milw., 1995—. Comdr. Am. Legion, Marshfield, 1991-92; pres. Marshfield Jaycees, 1974. Capt. U.S. Army Guard, 1970-90. Mem. IMI. Roman Catholic. Office: JBL Internat Inc PO Box 369 Marshfield WI 54449-0369

REILING, CAROLYN RAE, library director; b. Lake City, Iowa, May 31, 1934; d. Carol Clifford and Aletha Henretta (Zierke) Youngdahl; m. Ralph Edward Reiling, Aug. 3, 1933; children: Stephen, Rodney, Carol, Debra, Glenda, Wendy. Grad. h.s., Storm Lake, Iowa. Cert. pub. libr. level III. Dir. Rembrandt (Iowa) Pub. Libr., 1985—; bookkeeper Moodie Refrigeration, Storm Lake, 1989—, Loew Custom Carpet, Storm Lake, 1990—; program presenter NAESP, Orlando, Fla., 1993. Pres. Rembrandt PTA, 1975; mem. Helping Hands, Rembrandt, 1985-94. Buena Vista Hosp. Aux., 1983—; mem., officer St. Joseph's Altar Guild, 1965—. Mem. Buena Vista Librs. (past pres.), Rembrandt Woman's Club (pres. 1986). Roman Catholic. Office: Rembrandt Pub Libr Box 186 Rembrandt IA 50576

REILLY, BRIAN J., executive; b. Newark, N.J., May 17, 1940. BS in Social Studies, Villanova U., 1962; M in Internat. Rels., Am. Grad. Sch. of Internat. Bus., 1966. Mgr. Armco, Inc., Middletown, Ohio, 1966-82; v.p. Jostens Learning, Inc., Mpls., 1982-87, Internat. Jostens, Inc., Mpls., 1982-87; pres. Paneltech, Mpls., 1987-88, The Reilly Co., Mpls., 1988—; adj. prof. U. St. Thomas, St. Paul, 1987—. 1st Lt. USMC, 1962-65. Mem. French Am. C. of C. (bd. dirs. 1987—). Office: The Reilly Co 1550 E 79th St Ste 680 Minneapolis MN 55425-3100

REILLY, FRANK KELLY, business educator; b. Chgo., Dec. 30, 1935; s. Clarence Raymond and Mary Josephine (Ruckrigel) R.; m. Therese Adele Bourke, Aug. 2, 1958; children: Frank Kelly III, Clarence Raymond II, Therese B., Edgar B. BBA, U. Notre Dame, 1957; MBA, Northwestern U., 1961, U. Chgo., 1964; PhD, U. Chgo., 1968; LLD (hon.), St. Michael's Coll., 1991. CFA. Trader Goldman Sachs & Co., Chgo., 1958-59; security analyst Tech. Fund, Chgo., 1959-62; asst. prof. U. Kans., Lawrence, 1965-68, assoc. prof., 1968-72; prof. bus., assoc. dir. divsn. bus. and econ. rsch. U. Wyo., Laramie, 1972-75; prof. fin. U. Ill., Champaign-Urbana, 1975-81; Bernard J. Hank prof. U. Notre Dame, Ind., 1981—, dean Coll. Bus. Adminstrn., 1981-87; bd. dirs. First Interstate Bank No. Ind., Brinson Global Fund Inc. (also chmn.), Assn. Investment Mgmt. and Rsch., Inst. Chartered Fin. Analysts (also chmn.), NIBCO Corp., Internat. Bd. CFPs, Greenwood Trust Corp., Ft. Dearborn Income Securities. Author: Investment Analysis and Portfolio Management, 1979, 4th edit., 1996, Investments, 1982, 4th edit., 1995; co-editor: Ethics and the Investment Industry, 1989; editor: Readings and Issues in Investments, 1975, High Yield Bonds: Analysis and Risk Assessment, 1990; assoc. editor Fin. Mgmt., 1977-82, Quar. Rev. Econs. and Bus, 1979-87, Fin. Rev., 1979-87, 92—, Jour. Fin. Edn., 1981—, Jour. Applied Bus. Rsch., 1986—, Fin. Svcs. Rev., 1989-96, Internat. Rev. Econs. and Fin., 1992—, European Jour. Fin., 1994—. Arthur J. Schmidt Found. fellow, 1962-65; U. Chgo. fellow, 1963-65. Mem. Midwest Bus. Adminstrn. Assn. (pres. 1974-75), Am. Fin. Assn., Western Fin. Assn. (exec. com. 1973-75), Ea. Fin. Assn. (exec. com. 1979-84, pres. 1982-83), Midwest Fin. Assn. (pres. 1993-94), Fin. Analysts Fedn., Fin. Mgmt. Assn. (pres. 1983-84, chmn. 1985-91, bd. dirs.), Acad. Fin. Svcs. (pres. 1990-91), Inst. Chartered Fin. Analysts (coun. of examiners, rsch. and edn. com., edn. steering com., C. Stewart Sheppard award 1991), Internat. Assoc. Fin. Planners (ednl. resource com., bd. dirs.), Assn. of Investment Mgmt. and Rsch., Investments Analysts Soc. Chgo. (bd. dirs. 1988-89), Beta Gamma Sigma. Roman Catholic. Office: U Notre Dame Coll Bus Adminstrn Notre Dame IN 46556

REILLY, JOAN RITA, nurse practitioner, educator, school nurse; b. Evanston, Ill., Apr. 3, 1947; d. Thomas A. and Elmira E. (McCauley) R. BSN, U. Mich., 1969; MSN, U. Colo., Denver, 1972, postgrad., 1974, 85. Pediatric nurse cons. U. Colo. John F. Kennedy Child Devel. Ctr., Boulder, 1972-74; pediatric nurse practitioner U. Chgo., Wyler Hosp., 1975-77; sch. nurse spl. edn. Chgo. Pub. Schs., 1977-86, sch. nurse coord. spl. svcs., 1986-89; sch. nurse, nurse practitioner Chgo. (Ill.) Pub. Schs., 1989—; adj. prof. U. Ill., 1981—; seminar dir., Chgo., 1981—. Contbr. articles to profl. jours.; contbr. to profl. books. Bd. dirs. Family and Children's AIDS Network. Angel scholar, 1969; recipient Shirley Titus award, 1972; named Sch. Nurse of Yr., Chgo. Pub. Schs., 1995-96. Mem. ANA, Ill. Nurses Assn., Sch. Nurses Assn., Interdivisional Coun. Nurse Practitioners, Sigma Theta Tau. Home: 2020 N Lincoln Park W Apt 5J Chicago IL 60614-4736 Office: Citywide Med Ctr North 2021 N Burling Chicago IL 60614

REILLY, PETER C., chemical company executive; b. Indpls., Jan. 19, 1907; s. Peter C. and Ineva (Gash) R.; AB, U. Colo., 1929; MBA, Harvard U., 1931; DSc (hon.), Butler U; m. Jeanette Parker, Sept. 15, 1932; children: Marie (Mrs. Jack H. Heed), Sara Jean (Mrs. Clarke Wilhelm), Patricia Ann (Mrs. Michael Davis). With accounting dept. Republic Creosoting Co., Indpls., 1931-32; sales dept. Reilly Tar & Chem. Corp. (became Reilly Industries, Inc. 1989), N.Y.C., 1932-36, v.p., Eastern mgr., 1936-52; v.p. sales, treas. both cos., Indpls., 1952-59, pres., 1959-73, chmn. bd., 1973-75, vice chmn., 1975-82, chmn., 1982-90, chmn. exec. com. 1990—; dir. Environ. Quality Control Inc. Dir. Goodwill Industries Found.; past bd. dirs. United Fund Greater Indpls., Indpls. Symphony Orch., Jr. Achievement Indpls., bd. govs.; mem. adv. council U. Notre Dame Sch. Bus. Adminstrn., 1947—; mem. adv. coun., past bd. dirs. Winona Meml. Hosp.; life mem. Boy Scouts Am., Crossroads of Am. Coun.; mem. adv. coun. Walther Cancer Inst.; Recipient Sagamore of Wabash award; named Disting. Eagle Scout Boy Scouts Am. Mem. Chem. Spltys. Mfg. Assn. (life; treas. 1950-60, past bd. dirs.), Chem. Mfrs. Assn. (past bd. dirs.), Am. Chem. Soc., Soc. Chem. Industry (past dir. Am. sect.). Clubs: Union League, Harvard, Chemist (N.Y.C.); Larchmont (N.Y.) Yacht; Indianapolis Athletic, Pine Valley Golf (N.J.), Meridian Hills Country (past bd. dirs.), Columbia (Indpls.); Rotary (Paul Harris award), One Hundred (past bd. dirs.); Crooked Stick Golf. Home: 3777 Bay Rd N Dr Indianapolis IN 46240 Office: Reilly Industries Inc 300 N Meridian St Ste 300 Indianapolis IN 46204-1763

REILLY, ROBERT FREDERICK, valuation consultant; b. N.Y.C., Oct. 3, 1952; s. James J. and Marie (Griebel) K.; m. Janet H. Steiner, Apr. 16, 1975; children: Ashley Lauren, Brandon Christopher, Cameron Courtney. BA in Econs., Columbia U., 1974, MBA in Fin., 1975. CPA, Ohio, Ill.; cert. mgmt. acct., CFA; cert. real estate appraiser; cert. gen. appraiser Ill., Va., Utah; accredited sr. appraiser, cert. rev. appraiser. Sr. cons. Booz, Allen & Hamilton, Cin., 1975-76; dir. corp. planning Huffy Corp., Dayton, Ohio, 1976-81; v.p. Arthur D. Little Valuation, Inc., Chgo., 1981-85; ptnr., nat. dir. of valution svcs. Deloitte & Touche, Chgo., 1985-91; mng. dir. Willamette Mgmt. Assocs., Chgo., 1991—; adj. prof. accounting U. Dayton Grad. Sch. Bus., 1977-81; adj. prof. fin. econs., Elmhurst (Ill.) Coll., 1982-87; adj. prof. fin. Ill. Inst. Tech. Grad. Sch. Bus., Chgo., 1985—; adj. prof. taxation U. Chgo. Grad. Sch. Bus., 1985-87. Co-author: Valuing Small Businesses and Professional Practices, 1993, Business Valuation Video Course, 1993, Valuing a Business, 1995; editor, columnist Small Bus. Taxation, 1989-90, Bus. Valuation Rev., 1989-90, Jour. of Real Estate Acctg. and Taxation, 1991-93, Ohio CPA Jour., 1984-86, 91—, Jour. Property Taxation Mgmt., 1993—, Jour. Am. Bankruptcy Inst., 1993—; contbr. more than 200 articles to profl. jours. Mem. AICPA, Nat. Assn. Real Estate Appraisers (cert.), Am. Soc. Appraisers (mem. bd. examiners 1985-89), Nat. Assn. Accts. (chpt. dir. 1976—), Inst. Property Taxation, Soc. Mfg. Engrs., Ill. Soc. CPAs, Ohio Soc. CPAs (chpt. dir. 1978-81), Accreditation Coun. Accountancy (accredited in fed. income tax), Bus. Valuation Assn., Chgo. Soc. Investment Analysts, Inst. CFAs, Am. Bankruptcy Inst., Am. Econ. Assn., Nat. Assn. Bus. Economists. Home: 310 Algonquin Rd Barrington IL 60010-6109 Office: 8600 W Bryn Mawr Ave Chicago IL 60631-3505

REINDL, RHINEHART, applications engineer; b. Milw., Oct. 6, 1936. Sales mgr. assembly sys. Acro Automations Sys., Milw., 1955-87; sr. applications engr. Giddings & Lewis, Janesville, Wis., 1987—; cons. R.T.E., Waukesha, Wis., 1986. Roman Catholic. Office: Giddings & Lewis 305 W Delavan Dr Janesville WI 53546-2547

REINECK, HENRY A., drafting engineer. Co-owner Park Ohio Electric, Inc., Gibsonburg, Ohio, 1973—. With USAF, 1957-61. Mem. KC (fin. sec. 1994-95). Democrat. Roman Catholic. Office: Park Ohio Electric 4390 State Route 600 Gibsonburg OH 43431-9702

REINHARD, NORMAN ARTHUR, accountant; b. Dayton, Ohio, Feb. 6, 1939; s. Aloys J. and Rita B. (Eifert) R.; m. Edith A. Sarver, July 12, 1969; children: Pamela A., Brian J. BS in Acctg., U. Dayton, 1963. Acct. Timken Co., Canton, Ohio, 1963-69; data processing mgr. Nordson Corp., Amherst, Ohio, 1969-71; acct., ptnr. Main-Hurdman, Canton, 1971-85, Reinhard & Co., Canton, 1985—. Treas. Am. Heart Assn., Canton, 1981-86, Ohio affiliate Am. Heart Assn., Columbus, 1989—. Served with U.S. Army, 1957-59. Mem. Am. Inst. CPA's, Nat. Assn. Accts., Ohio Soc. CPA's (pres. Akron-Canton chpt. 1982-83), Planning Forum (v.p. communications 1986-87). Roman Catholic. Clubs: Canton; Congress Lake (Hartville, Ohio).

REINHARDT, KENNETH G(ERALD), manufacturer's representative; b. Indpls., Sept. 18, 1951; s. Kenneth George and Hazel Louise (Stewart) R.; m. Peggy Ann Halsema, Sept. 3, 1977; children: Kristy, Holly, Sandy, Max. BS in Indsl. Mgmt., Gen. Mgmt., Purdue U., 1974. Sales rep. Monroe Div Litton Industries, Evansville, Ind., 1974-75; sub-br. mgr. Monroe Div Litton Industries, Paducah, Ky., 1975-76; acct. rep. Burroughs Corp., Indpls., 1976-79; mfrs. rep. Jack Harvey Assocs., Indpls., 1979-82; ptnr. Midstates Mktg., Inc., Indpls., 1982—, pres. Mem. Warren Twp. Planning Com., Indpls., 1991, Warren Twp. Schs. Strategic Planning, Indpls., 1992, yr.-round sch. com., 1994-95, redistricting com., 1995; Cub Scout leader, 1993—. Mem. Electronic Reps. Assn., Mfrs. Agts. Nat. Assn. Conservative. Office: Midstates Mktg Inc 1122 E Washington St Ste 100 Indianapolis IN 46202-3955

REINHARDT, RICHARD R., state legislator; b. Feb. 8, 1934; m. Linda Reinhardt. BS, Kans. State U. Rep. dist. 8 State of Kans. Mem. Alpha Gamma Rho. Democrat. Home: RR 1 Box 118 Erie KS 66733-9755*

REINKE, DORIS MARIE, retired elementary education educator; b. Racine, Wis., Jan. 12, 1922; d. Otto William Reinke and Louise Amelia Goehring. BS, U. Wis., Milw., 1943; MS, U. Wis., Whitewater, 1967. Tchr. kindergarten Elkhorn (Wis.) Area Sch. Sys., 1943-69, bldg. prin., 1968-70, summer sch. dir., 1974-75, grade 2 tchr., 1970-84, primary dept. chmn., 1971-84, administrv. asst., supervising tchr., 1957-83, student tchr., 1984, ret., 1984; oriented experience tchr. Program Area Sch. Sys., Elkhorn, 1966; pres. Elkhorn Edn. Assn., 1949-50; rep. dist. State Kindergarten Conf., Oshkosh, Wis., 1966; participant early edn. conf. State Early Edn. Conf., Eagle River, Wis., 1968. Columnist Mature Life Styles newspaper; monthly columnist Beacon, 1994—; contbr. weekly newspaper column Webster Notes, 1989; Walworth County Diary Monthly column in The Week, 1991—; author Doris' Corner newsletter Walworth County Geneal. Soc., 1992—. Bd. dirs. Food Pantry, Elkhorn, 1985-88, 95—, RSVP Vol. Food Pantry, Elkhorn, 1985-95; del. dist. constn. conv. Evang. Luth. Ch. Am., Beloit, Wis., 1987; com. mem. Luth. Ch., Elkhorn, 1987; chmn. sch. centennial, Elkhorn, 1987; mem. Elkhorn Hist. Preservation Com., 1991—: archivist Sugar Creek Luth. Ch., 1992—, choir mem., 1995—; dir. Webster House Mus., 1991—. Recipient Wis. Edn. Research, West Bend, Wis., 1966, Outstanding Elem. Tchrs., Wash., 1973, Wis. Dept. Edn., Madison, 1980, Local History award State Hist. Soc. Wis., 1993. Mem. Nat. Ret. Tchrs. Assn., Walworth County Ret. Tchrs. Assn. (v.p. 1988, pres . 1991), Walworth County Hist. Soc. (treas. 1985-89, v.p. 1990-91, pres. 1991-96), Walworth County Geneal. Soc. (bd. dirs. 1991-92), Alpha Delta Kappa (state pres. 1968-70, 76-78). Home: 516 N Wisconsin St Elkhorn WI 53121-1119

REINKE, WILLIAM JOHN, lawyer; b. South Bend, Ind., Aug. 7, 1930; s. William August and Eva Marie (Hein) R.; m. Sue Carol Colvin, 1951 (div. 1988); children: Sally Sue Taelman, William A., Andrew J.; m. Elizabeth Beck Lockwood, 1991. A.B. cum laude, Wabash Coll., 1952; J.D., U. Chgo., 1955. Bar: Ind. 1955. Assoc. Barnes & Thornburg and predecessors, South Bend, Ind., 1957-61, ptnr., 1961—, former chmn. compensation com., former mem. mgmt. com.; chmn. Constrn. Law Practice Group; trustee Stanley Clark Sch., 1969-80, pres. 1977-80; mem. adv. bd. Salvation Army, 1973—, pres., 1990-92; bd. dirs. NABE Mich. chpt., 1990-94, pres. 1993-94, Isaac Walton League, 1970-81, United Way 1978-81; pres. South Bend Round Table, 1963-65; trustee First Meth. Ch., 1967-70. Served with U.S. Army, 1955-57. Recipient Outstanding Local Pres. award Ind. Jaycees, 1960-61, Boss of Yr. award, 1969, South Bend Outstanding Young Man award, 1961. Mem. ABA, Ind. State Bar Assn., St. Joseph County Bar Assn., Ind. Bar Found. (patron fellow), Am. Judicature Soc., Def. Rsch. Inst., Ind. Soc. Chgo., Summit Club (past gov., founders com.), Rotary (bd. dirs. 1970-73, 94—). Home: 51795 Waterton Square Cir Granger IN 46530-8317 Office: Barnes & Thornburg 600 1st Source Bank Ctr 100 N Michigan St South Bend IN 46601-1630

REINOEHL, RICHARD LOUIS, artist; b. Omaha, Oct. 11, 1944; s. Louis Lawrence and Frances Margaret (Robinson) R.; m. Linda Dale Iroff, Feb. 28, 1982; 1 child, Joy Margaret Iroff-Reinoehl. BS in Sociology, Portland State U., 1970; MSW, U. Minn., Duluth, 1977; postgrad., Cornell U., 1984-88. Acting dir. Vanguard Group Homes, Virginia, Minn., 1976-77; dir. Minn. Chippewa Tribe Group Home, Duluth, 1978, Human Devel. Consortium, Minn., N.Y., Ohio, 1978—; faculty Social Work Program U. Wis., Superior, 1981-84; adv. bd. Computers in Social Svcs. Network, 1982-85; mem. Com. on Internat. Social Welfare Edn., 1982-86, Am. Evaluation Assn., 1986-89; affiliate scholar Oberlin Coll., 1991—. Editor: Computer Literacy in Human Services Education, 1990, Computer Literacy in Human Services, 1990, Men of Achievement, 16th edit., 1993; mem. editorial bd. Computers in Human Svcs., 1983—, assoc. editor, 1996; contbr. numerous articles to profl. jours. Mem. Legis. Task Force Regional Alcoholism Bd., 1972-73, Assn. Drug Abuse, Prevention and Treatment, 1973-74, Minn. Pub. Health Assn., 1976-78, Minn. Social Svc. Assn., 1976-83, Wis. Coun. Social Work Edn., 1983-84, N.Y. State Coun. Family Rels., 1986-89, Nat. Coun. Family Rels., 1986-89; exec. bd. Duluth Community Action Program, 1982-83; Dem. precinct chair, Portland, Oreg., 1972-74; precinct vice-chair Dem. Farmer-Labor Party, Duluth, 1979-81, chair, 1981-83, 2d vice-chair exec. bd., 1981-83. Mem. NASW (exec. com., chair program com. Arrowhead Region Minn. chpt., 1980-81, co-chair task force on computers in social work, 1981-82), Acad. Cert. Social Workers, Cornell U. Sailing Club (pres. 1990). Office: Human Devel Consortium Inc 46180 Butternut Ridge Rd Oberlin OH 44074-9778

REINS, RALPH ERICH, automated service company executive; b. Detroit, Sept. 18, 1940; s. Erich John and Florence (Franz) R.; m. Victoria Louise Kolts, Sept. 14, 1963; children—Ann Marie, Christine Louise. B.S.I.E., U. Mich., 1963. Asst. supt. Chevrolet Motor div., Gen. Motors Corp., Detroit, 1963-72; v.p., pres. hwy. product ops. Rockwell Internat., Troy, Mich., 1972-85; sr. v.p. ITT Corp., Bloomfield Hills, Mich., 1985-89; chmn. of the bd., pres., chief exec. officer Mack Trucks, Inc., Allentown, Pa., 1989-90; pres. United Tech. Automotive, Dearborn, Mich., 1990-91; exec. v.p., pres. automotive sector Allied Signal Corp., 1991-94; pres., CEO Envirotest Sys. Corp., Phoenix, 1995-96, A.P. Parts Internat., Toledo, 1996—. Mem. Roeper Sch. Bd. Trustees; mem. found. bd. Oakland U. Mem. Soc. Automotive Engrs., Bloomfield Hills Country Club. Republican. Home: 29612 Durham Dr Perrysburg OH 43551 Office: A P Parts Internat 543 Matzinger Rd PO Box 965 Toledo OH 43697-0965

REINSDORF, JERRY MICHAEL, professional sports teams executive, real estate executive, lawyer, accountant; b. Bklyn., Feb. 25, 1936; s. Max and Marion (Smith) R.; m. Martyl F. Rifkin, Dec. 29, 1956; children: David Jason, Susan Janeen, Michael Andrew, Jonathan Milton. BA, George Washington U., 1957; JD, Northwestern U., 1960. Bar: D.C., Ill. 1960; CPA, Ill.; cert. specialist real estate securities, rev. appraiser; registered mortgage underwriter. Atty. staff regional counsel IRS, Chgo., 1960-64; assoc. law firm Chapman & Cutler, 1964-68; ptnr. Altman, Kurlander & Weiss, 1968-74; of counsel firm Katten, Muchin, Gitles, Zavis, Pearl & Galler, 1974-79; gen. ptnr. Carlyle Real Estate Ltd. Partnerships, 1971, 72; chmn. bd. Balcor Co., 1973-87; mng. ptnr. TBC Films, 1975-83; chmn. Chgo. White Sox, 1981—, Chgo. Bulls Basketball Team, 1985—; ptnr. Bojer Fin., 1987—; lectr. John Marshall Law Sch., 1966-68; former bd. dirs. Shearson Lehman Bros., Inc., Project Academus of DePaul U., Chgo., Sports Immortals Mus., 1987-89, Com. Commemorate U.S. Constn., 1987; bd. dirs. La Salle Nat. Bank, La Salle Nat. Corp.; bd. overseers Inst. for Civil Justice, 1996—; lectr. in real estate, sports and taxation. Author: (with L. Herbert Schneider) Uses of Life Insurance in Qualified Employee Benefit Plans, 1970. Co-chmn. Ill. Profls. for Senator Ralph Smith, 1970; mem. Chgo. region bd. Anti-Defamation League, 1986—; trustee Ill. Inst. Tech., 1991—; mem. Ill. Commn. on African-Am. Males, 1992—; bd. dirs. Chgo. Youth Success Found., 1992—, Corp. for Supportive Housing, 1995—; nat. trustee Northwestern U., 1993—; bd. govs. Hugh O'Brian Youth Found.; mem. internat. adv. bd. Barrow Neurol. Found., 1996—. Recipient Hallmark award Chgo. Baseball Cancer Charities, 1986, Corp. Superstar award Ill. chpt. Cystic Fibrosis Found., 1988, Sportsman of Yr. award, 1994, Chicagoan of Yr. award Chgo. Park Dist., 1990, Kellogg Excellence award, 1991, Cmty. Hero award Interfaith Organizing Project, 1991, Operation Push Bridgebuilder award, 1992, Alumni Merit award Northwestern U., 1992, Ellis Island Medal of Honor award Nat. Ethnic Coalition of Orgns., 1993, Lifetime Achievement award March of Dimes, 1994, Hallmark Hall of Fame Civic award Ind. Sports Charities, 1994, Am. Spirit award USAF,

1995, Alpha Epsilon Pi Arthur and Simiteich Outstanding Alumnus award, 1995; inductee B'nai B'rith Nat. Jewish Am. Sports Hall of Fame, 1994. Mem. ABA, FBA, Ill. Bar Assn., Chgo. Bar Assn., Nat. Sports Lawyers Assn., Nat. Assn. Rev. Appraisers and Mortgage Underwriters, Northwestern U. Law Sch. Alumni Assn. (bd. dirs.), Comml. Club Chgo., Order of Coif, Omega Tau Rho. Office: Chgo White Sox 333 W 35th St Chicago IL 60616

REINSMA, HAROLD LAWRENCE, design consultant, engineer; b. Slayton, Minn., Sept. 6, 1928; s. Frank and Ida M. (Zabel) R.; m. Julia A. Tusek, Oct. 18, 1958; children: Frank, Michael, Diane. Student, Macalester Coll., 1948-50; BCE, U. Minn., 1953. Registered profl. engr., Ill. Cons. engr. GM Orr Engring. Co., Mpls., 1953-54; research test engr. Caterpillar Tractor Co., Peoria, Ill., 1955-58, research design engr., 1958-71, research project engr., 1971-73, research supervising engr., 1973-76, research staff engr., 1976-91; design cons. Dunlap, Ill., 1991—. Holder 44 patents including 1st viable sealed and lubricated track, sealed maintenance-free linkage and long life radial seal, both for use in abrasive environments. Home and Office: 13600 Lucerne Dr Dunlap IL 61525-9619

REIS, DONALD C., manufacturing executive; b. Mt. Sterling, Ky., July 14, 1948. AA in Applied Arts, Nebr. Tech. Vocat. Sch., Milford, 1968. Draftsmen Swine Svcs. Specialist, Lyons, Nebr., 1979-81; v.p. Ops. Jones Mfg. Co., Beemer, Nebr., 1981—. Office: Jones Mfg Co PO Box 38 Beemer NE 68716-0038

REISERT, CHARLES EDWARD, JR., real estate executive; b. New Albany, Ind., Apr. 5, 1941; s. Charles Edward Sr. and Jane. W. (Willcox) R.; m. Mary Lynn Nunemacher, Nov. 9, 1963; children: Perry G., Heidi L. BS in Edn., Ind. U., 1963, MA, 1968. Cert. residential specialist, residential broker. Tchr. Ind. Pub. Schs., 1963-67; mgr. Ind. Bell Tel. Co., Indpls., 1967-70; trust officer Ind. Nat. Bank, Indpls., 1970-72; ptnr. R.F.R. Prodns. Inc., Zionsville; dir. Wichita (Kans.) Art Assn., 1972-73; realtor Century 21 Reisert, Baker, Walker & Assocs., Jeffersonville, Ind., 1973—. Mem. Ind. Real Estate Commn., 1982-90, chmn., 1990; pres. bd. dirs. Clark County Youth Shelter, 1987—; bd. dirs., past pres. United Way Clark County; bd. dirs. New Hope, Inc., Sagamore of Wabash; mem. Leadership So. Ind., Leadership Louisville; trustee Jeffersonville Twp. Pub. Libr. Mem. So. Ind. Realtors Assn., (past pres. Realtor of Yr.) Nat. Assn. Realtors, Ind. Assn. Realtor (bd. dirs.), Realtors Nat. Mktg. Inst., So. Ind. C. of C. (past bd. dirs., Profl. of Yr.), Rotary (past pres., Paul Harris fellow). Roman Catholic. Home: 2005 Utica Pike Jeffersonville IN 47130-5003 Office: Century 21 Reisert Baker Walker & Assocs 1302 E 10th St Jeffersonville IN 47130-4231

REISINGER, JAMES JOHN, psychologist, educator; b. Allentown, Pa., June 14, 1944; s. Rudolph and Anna (Sharkazy) R.; m. Francene I. Fritz, Aug. 13, 1966; children: Deborah Ann, Stephanie Christine, James Michael. BA, U. Dayton, 1967; MA, Bucknell U., 1970; PhD, Peabody Coll., 1972. Dir. early intervention Holy Spirit Hosp., Camp Hill, Pa., 1972-75; med. rsch. scientist E.P. Psychiat. Inst., Phila., 1975-76; asst. Children and Youth Office of Mental Health, Harrisburg, Pa., 1976-77; chief psychologist, child psychiatry Children's Meml. Hosp., Chgo., 1977-85; exec. dir. Orchard Mental Health Ctr., Skokie, Ill., 1985—; cons. in field; mem. grad. faculty Northwestern U., 1979-86; grants reviewer Office Human Devel. Svcs. HHS, Washington, 1982-90. Contbr. articles to profl. jours. Grantee NIMH, 1970-73, U.S. Office Edn., 1973-76, Bur. Edn. for Handicapped , 1980-83. Mem. Am. Psychol. Assn., Assn. Advancement Behavior Therapy, Ea. Psychol. Assn., Soc. Pediatric Psychology. Home: 608 Bonnie Brae River Forest IL 60305-1929 Office: Turning Point Behavioral Health Care Ctr 8324 Skokie Blvd Skokie IL 60077-2545

REISINGER, JOY ANN, genealogist; b. Durand, Wis., Aug. 30, 1934; d. Alvin John and Adeline Mercedes (Latew) Deters; m. James Anthony Reisinger, Apr. 27, 1954; children: Barbara Ann, Mary Frances, Martha Leone, Jane Louise. Cert. in x-ray tech., Coll. of Med. Tech., 1952. Cert. Geneal. record searcher. X-ray technician Sparta (Wis.) Clinic, 1953-60, St. Mary's Hosp., Sparta, 1960-80; pvt. practice genealogist Sparta, 1980—. Author: The King's Daughters, 1988; co-author: Pioneer Settlers of Dane County, 1986; editor (periodical) Lost in Canada?, 1975-94. Mem. Wis. Task Force on Ct. & Local Govt. Records, Madison, 1990-91; pres. Sparta Jaycettes, 1968; bd. dirs. Monroe County Hist. Soc., liason to Monroe County Local Hist. Rm. Bd. Recipient Citation and Recognition of Outstanding Leadership, Sparta Jaycettes, 1969, Badger Jaycette Cert. of Merit, Nat. Geneal. Soc., 1989, Minn. Geneal. Soc., 1989, Presdl. Citation Fedn. Geneal. Socs., 1993, award of merit Fedn. Geneal. Socs., 1996. Mem. Wis. State Geneal. Soc. (1st, 2d v.p. 1977-82), Wis. Geneal. Coun. (bd. dirs. 1986-88, 93), Assn. Profl. Genealogists (v.p. 1994-95, Grahams T. Smallwood award 1996), Bd. for Certification Genealogists (v.p.). Republican. Roman Catholic. Home: 1020 Central Ave Sparta WI 54656-1513

REISS, KENNETH WILLIAM, computer services company executive, educator; b. St. Louis, Oct. 21, 1959; s. Kenneth Mason Reiss and Ruth Claudine (Colter) Atkins. Student, U. Winnipeg, Man., Can., 1978-79, U. N.D., 1981-84; BA, Webster U., St. Louis, 1987, MBA, 1990. Claims examiner Gen. Am. Life Ins. Co., St. Louis, 1976-77; adminstrv. asst. Atkins Underground, Winnipeg, 1978-80; freelance cons., Grand Forks, N.D., 1981-84; pres. Armadillo Computer Svcs., St. Louis, 1985—; adj. prof. Webster U., 1988—. Mem. Gateway Area Macintosh Users Group (pres. 1988-89), Am. Radio Relay League, Alpha Kappa Psi. Office: Armadillo Computer Svcs 301 Sovereign Ct Ste 209A Ballwin MO 63011-4435

REISTER, RAYMOND ALEX, retired lawyer; b. Sioux City, Iowa, Dec. 22, 1929; s. Harold William and Anne (Eberhardt) R.; m. Ruth Elizabeth Alkema, Oct. 7, 1967. AB, Harvard U., 1952, LLB, 1955. Bar: N.Y. 1956, Minn. 1960. Assoc. Paul, Weiss, Rifkind, Wharton & Garrison, N.Y.C., 1955-56; ptnr. Dorsey & Whitney, Mpls., 1959-92; ret., 1993; instr. U. Minn. Extension Divsn., 1964-66. Editor (with Larry W. Johnson): Minnesota Probate Administration, 1968. Trustee Mpls. Soc. Fine Arts, 1981-87; v.p. Minn. Hist. Soc., 1994—. 1st lt. U.S. Army, 1956-59. Mem. Am. Coll. Trust and Estate Counsel (regent 1980-86), ABA, Minn. Bar Assn., Hennepin County Bar Assn., Mpls. Club, Harvard Club Minn. (pres. 1969-70). Home: 93 Groveland Ter Minneapolis MN 55403-1142 Office: Dorsey & Whitney 220 S 6th St Minneapolis MN 55402-4502

REITEMEIER, JOSEPH RICHARD, municipal association executive; b. Rochester, Minn., Sept. 9, 1954; s. Richard Joseph and Patricia Claire (Mulligan) R.; m. Patricia Ruth Smiley, Aug. 11, 1979; children: Michele, Brent, Christopher, Stephanie. Student, Coll. St. Thomas, 1972-76. Intern U.S. C. of C., Mpls., 1976; exec. asst. Fort Dodge (Iowa) C. of C., 1976-77; exec. v.p. Northfield (Minn.) C. of C., 1977-79, Albert Lea (Minn.) C. of C., 1979-86, JOBS Inc., Albert Lea, 1979-86; pres., CEO Fond du Lac (Wis.) Area Assn. Commerce, 1986—; cons. Waukesha (Wis.) Chamber, 1990, Rhinelander (Wis.) Chamber, 1989, 92, 93, 94, Tomahawk (Wis.) Chamber, 1989, Mendota (Ill.) Chamber, 1989. Bd. dirs. Fond du Lac Festivals, treas., 1986—; bd. dirs. St. Francis Nursing Home, 1993—; Rep. del., Freeborn County, Minn., 1984-85. Recipient Cert. Spl. Recognition award Southeastern Minn. REACT, Inc., Outstanding Svc. award Nat. Mgmt. Assn., Albert Lea Cert. of Appreciation, Mayor's Office, Superior Leadership award Ft. Dodge Dragoons, Cert. Chamber Exec. award Am. C. of C. Execs., 1989. Mem. Nat. Assn. Membership Dirs., Wis. Econ. Devel. Assn., Wis. Chamber Execs. (bd. dirs., pres. 1991—), Wis. Mfrs. Commerce, Transp. Devel. Assn., Wis. Transp. Assn. (bd. dirs. 1992—), Mid-States Aluminum, Elks, Rotary (bd. dirs.). Roman Catholic. Home: 584 Ledgeview Blvd Fond Du Lac WI 54935-3727

REITER, BONNIE JEAN, training and development educator; b. Eau Claire, Wis., Dec. 16, 1948; d. Paul Francis and Beverly Jean (Steinmetz) Spallees; m. James Frederick Reiter, May 21, 1983; 1 child, Jason Edward. AD in Data Processing, Chippewa Valley Tech. Coll., Eau Claire, 1981, AD in Supervisory Mgmt., 1990; BS in Vocat. Adult Edn. magna cum laude, U. Wis.-Stout, 1992, postgrad., 1995—. Office mgr. KDI, Ltd., 1974-75; typist State of Wis., Eau Claire, 1977-78; mktg. coord. Profl. Edn. Systems, Eau Claire, 1982; data entry clk. Erickson Appraisal, Eau Claire, 1983; documentation clk. Cray Rsch., Inc., Chippewa Falls, Wis., 1985-86, asst. adminstr., 1986-88, assoc. adminstr., 1988-90; tchr. continuing edn. courses Chippewa Valley Tech. Coll., 1992, employment specialist, devel. and tng. ctr., 1993-95; grad. asst. dept. tng. and devel. U. Wis.-Stout, 1995—; vol. tutor English U. Wis.-Stout, 1991-92, South Mid. Sch., Eau Claire, 1992; mem. tng. and devel. program adv. bd. U. Wis.-Stout, 1995—; trustee on Bethesda Lutheran bd. trustees. Host parent to fgn. exch. students, 1987—; internat. exch. coord. EF Found., 1993-95; den leader St. Olaf's Cub Scout Troop, Eau Claire, 1984-85. Oasis scholar, 1991, Leo Buscaglia scholar, 1996. Mem. NAFE, Am. Soc. Tng. & Devel., Am. Vocat. Assn., Wis. Vocat. Assn., Cray Toastmasters (ednl. v.p. 1986). Lutheran. Home: 2709 Sherman St Eau Claire WI 54701-6655

REITER, ELAINE MARY, state agency administrator; b. Ellsworth, Minn., July 21, 1928; d. Jacob Nicholas and Esther Suzanne (Kappes) R.; BS in Bus. Adminstrn., Marquette U., Milw., 1953; MEd in Counseling, U. Mo., Columbia, 1967, MPA, 1976. Personnel asst. Square D Co., Milw., 1953-56; exec. asst. Psychol. Svc. Ctr., St. Louis, 1957-63; svcs. mgr. Psychol. Assos., St. Louis, 1963-64; counselor Mo. Employment Svc., St. Louis, 1964-68; dep. dir. Mo. Office Aging, Jefferson City, 1968-72; cons. adult svcs. to State of Mo., 1973-76; regional adminstr. Mo. Div. Family Svcs. and Aging, 1977-81, alternative svcs. adminstr. Mo. Div. Aging, 1981—; bd. dirs. Nat. Com. for the Prevention of Elder Abuse, 1981-94; aging cons., 1995—; gov. com. assistive tech., 1994—; del. White House Conf. Aging, 1971. Recipient various svcs. awards. Mem. AAUW, Am. Public Welfare Assn. (chmn. membership Mo. chpt. 1976-77), Mo. Assn. Social Welfare (bd. dirs. 1975-82, exec. com. 1976-79, chmn. aging task force 1975-80, chmn. Kansas City div. 1981-82), Nat. Coun. on Aging, Geront. Soc., Am. Soc. on Aging, Mid-Am. Congress Aging, Nat. Assn. Adult Protective Svc. Adminstrs., Lakewood Club, Zonta. Roman Catholic. Home: 1310 Swifts Hwy A101 Jefferson City MO 65109-2519

REITINGER, THOMAS ANTHONY, hospital administrator; b. Freeport, Ill., July 12, 1944; married. BA, U. Wis., 1967; MA, Washington U., 1971. Adm. resident Jewish Hosp. St. Louis, 1970-71; asst. admin. St. John's Regional Health Ctr., Springfield, Mo., 1971-73, assoc. dir., 1973-75; exec. dir. Waupun (Wis.) Meml. Hosp., 1975-77, Fort Atkinson (Wis.) Meml. Hosp., 1977-83; v.p. St. Joseph's Hosp., Milw., 1983-84, sr. v.p., 1984-86, exec. v.p., COO, 1986-90, pres., CEO, 1990-93; pres., CEO Mercy Hosp. Med. Ctr., Des Moines, 1993—. Home: 5554 Beechwood Ter West Des Moines IA 50266-6620 Office: Mercy Hosp Med Ctr 400 University Des Moines IA 50313

REITMEISTER, NOEL WILLIAM, financial planner, investment and insurance broker, author, consultant, columnist, television host and producer, educator; b. Bklyn., Aug. 12, 1938; s. Morris G. and Anna (Miller) R.; BA in Econs. and Fin., Queens Coll., CUNY, 1960; MBA in Indsl. Psychology and Bus., Baruch Coll., CUNY, 1969; diploma N.Y. Inst. Fin., 1969; cert. fin. planner, Coll. Fin. Planning, Denver; m. Elaine Schendelman, Sept. 16, 1961; children: Gregg Allen, Stephen Michael. Asst. merchandise mgr. Bloomingdales, 1962-63; sales and mktg. exec. Cosmair div. L'Oreal, Paris, 1963-67; project dir. advt. rsch. Toni Div. Gillette Co., 1967-68; account exec. duPont Walston, Chgo., Gary and Merrillville, Ind., 1969-71, br. coord., 1971-74; sr. investment broker A.G. Edwards & Sons Inc., Merrillville, 1974-79, v.p.-investments, 1979—, trust specialist 1992—; ptnr. Ind. Investors, 1980-88, Nat. Property Investors, 1980-84, Petro Lewis, 1979-84. Can. Am. Oil, 1980—, Rollingbrook Properties, 1983—, Nora Assocs., 1981—; vice chmn. bd. Menorah Credit Union, 1979-81, chmn., 1981-82, chmn., CEO, pres., 1982-83; owner Le Baron Communications; dir., prin. Arctic Exploration, Inc.; mng. ptnr. Filthy Rich Enterprises, 1980-90; conducted Roundtable at Advanced Conf. on Retirement Planning, Washington, 1986, also attended White House Briefing; lectr. in econs. Purdue U., Calumet, 1976-94, adj. prof. mgmt., 1995—; adj. prof. U. North Cen., Roosevelt U., Calumet Coll.; adj. faculty Coll. for Fin. Planning, Denver, 1974-92; columnist The Star, 1984-86, Am. Med. News Jour., Mute Weekly Column, The Times, 1989—. Author: Portfolios, Inc. "Key Objectives in Investments"; co-author text "Retirement Planning" for Coll. Fin. Planning; producer, host cable TV show Money Doctor, 1985-94, PBS spl. "Market Crisis of October 1987"; contbr. articles on fin. planning and retirement to profl. jours. including Jour. Inst. Cert. Fin. Planning, Fin. Planning and Nursing mags., Post Tribune, Times, Vidette Messenger, The Star, The Economist, Financial Services Weekly, N.Y. Times, Registered Rep. Mag., Merrillville Herald, Financial Planning News (reg. rep.). Decorated Order William Tell, Switzerland, 1986; appointed col. staff Gov. Ky., 1988, Disting Grad. Coll. for Fin. Planning, 1984, Man of the Yr. B'nai B'rith, 1986; recipient Excellence award Nat. Assn. Accts., 1985. Mem. exec. com., sec., Ill. Theatre Ctr., 1985-88; bd. dirs. South Suburban HELP, 1968-69, N.W. Ind. Pub. Broadcasting, 1986-90; trustee Temple Anshe Sholom, 1975-82, chmn. adult edn., 1977-82, chmn. house and grounds, 1977-78, co-chmn. social action com., 1979-82, Temple's Endowment Fund, 1992-95, Rabbinical Selection Com., 1981-82; dir. Visiting Nurse Assn. NW Ind., 1992— (mem. fin. com., devel. com., chmn. by-laws com.); dir. Drug and Alcohol Edn. Sheriff's Dept. Cook County, Ill., 1989-91; v.p., sec. S. Suburban Acad. Jewish Studies, 1979-82; local troop coordinator Boy Scouts Am., 1977-78, vol. Richton Crossing Nursing Home; mem. Anti-Defamation League Cabinet, 1978-82; pres. Young Rep. Club of Queens County, 1958-60; v.p. Chgo. B'nai B'rith Council; co-founder, treas. SESSA; life mem. Volunteered Optometrists Serving Humanity. With USAR, 1960-66. Fin. planning and retirement cons. Amoco, 1974—, LTV, 1982—, Inland Steel, 1983—, Ford Motor Co., 1987—, C.B. Geigy Pharm., 1991—; examiner in fin. planning, 1974-78; exec. com. Bd. Cert. Fin. Planners; lic. in investments, commodities and ins.; registered rep. N.Y. Stock Exchange, Am. Stock Exchange, Midwest Stock Exchange, Pacific Stock Exchange, Boston Stock Exchange, PBW Exchange, Chgo. Bd. Trade, Chgo. Merc. Exchange, Comex, NASD, Chgo. Options Exchange; lic. investment broker, N.Y., N.J., Mass., Fla., Ariz., Calif., Tex., Pa., Mich., Wis., Ill., Mich. Ind., Tenn., Hawaii, Kans., Wis.. La., Va. Mem. Inst. Cert. Fin. Planners (charter mem., pres. Illiana Soc., 1985-86, 87-93, chmn. 1993—, Dist. Service award 1987), Internat. Assn. Registered Fin. Planners, C. Planners (pres. 1975, charter 1973-78), Michigana Assn. Fin. Planners (charter), Internat. Assn. Fin. Planners (v.p. Chgo. South chpt.), Internat. Soc. Registered Reps. (charter), Registry Fin. Planning Practitioners (charter 1983—), Am. Arbitration Assn. (div. fin. planning, investments and ins., arbitrator), Am. Psychol. Assn., Midwest Psychol. Assn., Ill. Psychol. Assn., Weisenthal Inst., Chgo. Council on Fgn. Rels., Ind. TV producers Assn. (chmn.'s coun.), Pres.'s Council, Million Dollar Coun., Crest Club, Three Million Dollar Council, Alfred U. Alumni Assn., Queens Coll. Alumni Assn., Baruch Coll. Alumni Assn., Art Inst. Chgo., Ill. Philharm. Assn., Chgo. Coun. Foreign Affairs, Goodman Theater Prodn., Lyric Opera League, Grant Park Soc., Tau Delta Phi (chpt. v.p., pres., asst. nat. v.p.), Zeta Beta Tau, Alpha Epsilon Pi (chpt. pres.), Delta Omega Kappa (v.p. Alpha chpt. 1953, pres. Beta chpt. 1954-56, nat. pres. 1955-60). Clubs: Crest, Century, Convenent, Idlewild Country, Homewood Flossmoor Racquet and Tennis. Lodges: Masons (32d degree), Lions, Shriners (v.p. south suburban club), B'nai B'rith (pres. lodge), Soc. of Fellows Anti-Defamation League). Home: 2246 Flossmoor Rd Flossmoor IL 60422-1612 Office: AG Edwards & Sons Inc 8300 Mississippi St Merrillville IN 46410-6300

REITZ, BARBARA MAURER, poet, freelance writer; b. Teaneck, N.J., Dec. 26, 1931; d. William Ritschy and Ruth Gunhill (Noren) Maurer; m. William Stanley Reitz, Jr., Sept. 15, 1956; children: William Stanley III, David Stewart. BA in English, Bucknell U., 1953. Sec. UN, N.Y.C., 1953-54; sec. to pres. Charles Scribner's Sons, N.Y.C., 1954-56; freelance writer Chillicothe, Ohio, 1987—, poet, 1949—. Contbr. articles to local newspapers. Campaign mgr., creative dir. William S. Reitz, Jr. , Chillicothe City Coun. pres.; patron Bucknell Assn. for Arts, Columbus Symphony, Area Artist Series, Majestic Theatre; mem. Friends of WOSU-PBS, Pump House Art Gallery, Civic Theatre. Mem. AAUW (Chillicothe br. pres. 1988-90, v.p. Rockville, Md. br. 1961-62), Acad. Am. Poets, Bucknell Alumni Assn. (sec.-treas. Chillicothe-Ross county chpt. 1973-82), Sigma Tau Delta (pres. 1952-53), Pi Delta Epsilon, Alpha Lambda Delta, Pi Beta Phi (treas. 1952-53). Republican. Presbyterian (elder 1981—). Home: 675 Hilltop Ct Chillicothe OH 45601-2928

REITZ, CHARLES EDWARD, philosophy educator; b. Buffalo, N.Y., Mar. 10, 1946; s. Herman Gerard and Diana Maude (Henrich) R.; m. Roena Lindquist Haynie, Oct. 7, 1978; stepchildren: Aeron Haynie, Deirdre Haynie. BA, Canisius Coll., 1968; postgrad., Freiburg U., 1969-71; PhD, SUNY, Buffalo, 1983. Prof. Erie C.C., Buffalo, 1984-87, Kans. City (Kans.) C.C., 1987-96. Contbr. articles to profl. jours. Travel grantee SUNY, Freiburg, Germany, 1974, Univ. fellow, 1972-74; Regents Coll. scholar, Canisius Coll., Buffalo, 1964-68. Mem. Am. Philos. Assn., Am. Assn. Tchrs. of German (Wiesneck Inst. grantee 1990), German Studies Assn., Kans. NEA (pres. faculty assoc. 1991-96), Kansas City Area Philosophy Assn. (pres. 1991-92). Marxist. Socratic. Home: 2 E 58th St Kansas City MO 64113-2108 Office: Kansas City Kans C C 7250 State Ave Kansas City KS 66112-3003

RELLE, ATTILA TIBOR, dentist, geriodontist; b. Columbus, Ohio, Aug. 31, 1959; s. Ferenc Matyas and Trudi (Tubach) R.; m. Kim Ann McDonald, Apr. 26, 1986; 1 dau., Ilona. DDS, Case Western Reserve U., 1985; BS, Ohio State U., 1985, postgrad., 1985-88, 93; postgrad., Wright State U., 1988-93. Dentist Mobile Care Corp., Dublin, Ohio, 1985; assoc. dentist Richard P. Deed, D.D.S. and Assocs., Columbus, 1985-86; dentist Family Dental and Denture Ctr. II, Dayton, Ohio, 1986-87; geriodontist Midwest Mobile Dental Care, Inc., Hamilton, Ohio, 1988-91, Mobile Dental Care, Inc., Hamilton, Ohio, 1991-92; dentist/owner Attila T. Relle, DDS and Assocs., Columbus, 1985—; dentist, owner Attila T. Relle, DDS & Assocs., Hilliard, 1995—; dentist Jerry Owens, D.D.S. and Assocs., Lancaster, Ohio, 1989-92; state dir. Ohio residentcare dental geriatric program Meridian Svc. Care Corp. of Ohio, 1992-94, dentist/geriodontist, 1992-94; co-chmn. Ohio Dental Careers Day, Columbus, 1980-81; regional dir. Midwest Mobile Dental Care, Inc., 1988-89; mem. adv. com. N.Am. Health Corp., 1989-92; sci. judge Ohio Acad. Sci., Delaware, 1985—. Mem. Civitan Internat. (pres. Ea. Columbus Club 1986-87). Presbyterian. Home: 5203 Carifa Ct Hilliard OH 43026-9589 Office: Attila T Relle DDS & Assocs 5203 Carifa Ct Hilliard OH 43026-9589 also: Ste 100 4984-A Scioto Darby Rd Hilliard OH 43026-1550

RELLE, FERENC MATYAS, chemist; b. Gyor, Hungary, June 13, 1922; came to U.S., 1951, naturalized, 1956; s. Ferenc and Elizabeth (Netratics) R.; m. Gertrud B. Tubach, Oct. 9, 1946; children: Ferenc, Ava, Attila. B-SChemE, Jozsef Nador Poly. U., Budapest, 1944, MS, 1944. Lab. mgr. Karl Kohn Ltd. Co., Landshut, W.Ger., 1947-48; resettlement officer IRO, Munich, 1948-51; chemist Farm Bur. Coop. Assn., Columbus, Ohio, 1951-56; indsl. engr. N.Am. Aviation, Inc., Columbus, 1956-57; rsch. chemist Keever Starch Co., Columbus, 1957-65; rsch. chemist Ross Labs. div. Abbott Labs., Columbus, 1965-70, rsch. scientist, 1970-89; cons. in field. Chmn. Columbus and Central Ohio UN Week, 1963; pres. Berwick Manor Civic Assn., 1968; trustee Stelios Stelson Found., 1968-69; deacon Brookwood Presbyn. Ch., 1963-65, 92-93, trustee, 1990-91. Mem. Am. Chem. Soc. (alt. councilor 1973, chmn. long range planning com. Columbus sect. 1972-76, 78-80), Am. Assn. Cereal Chemists (chmn. Cin. sect. 1974-75), Ohio Acad. Sci., Arpad Acad., Internat. Tech. Inst. (adv. dir. 1977-82), Nat. Intercollegiate Soccer Ofcls. Assn., Am. Hungarian Assn., Hungarian Cultural Assn. (pres. 1978-81), Ohio Soccer Ofcls. Assn., Columbus Männerchor, Germania Singing and Sport Soc., Civitan (gov. Ohio dist. 1970-71, dist. treas. 1982-83, pres. Eastern Columbus 1963-64, 72-73, gen. sec. for Hungary 1991-92, Eastern European Growth Mgr., 1993-94, amb. at large, 1994—, established 1st Civitan club in Hungary 1991, Ukraine 1992, Slovakia 1994, Internat. Gov. of Yr. award 1971, Internat. Honor Key 1992, master club builder award 1992, various other awards), World Fedn. of Hungarian Engrs. Home and Office: 3487 Roswell Dr Columbus OH 43227-3560

RELWANI, NIRMALKUMAR MURLIDHAR (NICK RELWANI), mechanical engineer; b. Aug. 9, 1954; married. BS in Mech. Engring., U. Baroda, 1976; student, U. Nebr., 1977-78; MS in Mech. Engring., U. Wis., Milw., 1980. Registered profl engr., Wis., Ill. Rsch. asst. dept. mech. engring. U. Nebr., Lincoln, 1978; design engr. Allis Chalmers Corp., Milw., 1978-80; engring. cons. Bombay, 1980-86; assoc. engr. IIT Rsch. Inst., Chgo., 1986; mech. engr. Gen. Energy Corp., Oak Park, Ill., 1987-89, Arrowhead Environ. Control, Chgo., 1989-90; environ. engr. Ill. Dept. Pub. Health, Bellwood, 1990-92; environ. protection engr. field ops. sect. bur. air Ill. EPA, Maywood, 1992—. Recipient Cert. of appreciation Ill. EPA, 1993. Mem. ASME, ASHRAE (energy conservation award 1991), Assn. Energy Engrs. (sr.). Home: 413 Home Ave Apt 2B Oak Park IL 60302-3720

REMINGER, RICHARD THOMAS, lawyer; b. Cleve., Apr. 3, 1931; s. Edwin Carl and Theresa Henrietta (Bookmyer) R.; m. Billie Carmen Greer, June 26, 1954; children: Susan Greer, Patricia Allison, Richard Thomas. A.B., Case-Western Res. U., 1953; J.D., Cleve.-Marshall Law Sch., 1957. Bar: Ohio 1957, Pa. 1978, U.S. Supreme Ct. 1961. Personnel and safety dir. Motor Express, Inc., Cleve., 1954-58; mng. ptnr. Reminger & Reminger Co., L.P.A., Cleve., 1958-90; mem. nat. claims couns. adv. bd. Comml. Union Assurance Co., 1980-90; lectr. transp. law Fenn Coll., 1960-62; lectr. bus. law Case Western Res. U., 1962-64; lectr. products liability U. Wirtschaft at Schloss Gracht, Erfstadt-Liblar, Germany, 1990-91, Bar Assn. City of Hamburg, Germany, 1990; mem. faculty Nat. Inst. for Trial Advocacy, 1992. Mem. joint com. Cleve. Acad. Medicine-Greater Cleve. Bar Assn.; trustee Cleve. Zool. Soc., mem. exec. com., 1984-89, v.p., 1987-89; trustee Andrew Sch., 1984-96, Huron Road Hosp., Meridia Huron Hosp., Cleve., Cleve. Sch. for Blind, 1987-88, Cerebral Palsy Assn., 1984-87; trustee Good Samaritan Hosp., Palm Beach, Fla., 1992—, bd. govs., 1992—. With AC, USNR, 1950-58. Named Man of Yr. Cleve.-Marshall Law Sch., 1989. Mem. ABA (com. on law and medicine, profl. responsibility com. 1977-90), FBA, ATLA, Fedn. Ins. and Corp. Counsel, Internat. Ins. Law Soc., Internat. Bar Assn., Ohio Bar Assn. (coun. dels. 1987-90, internat. law com. 1990-91), Pa. Bar Assn., Cleve. Bar Assn. (chmn. med.-legal com. 1978-79, prof. liability com. 1977-90), Transp. Lawyers Assn., Cleve. Assn. Civil Trial Attys., Am. Soc. Hosp. Attys., Soc. Ohio Hosp. Attys., Ohio Assn. Civil Trial Attys., Am. Judicature Soc., Def. Rsch. Inst., Maritime Law Assn. U.S., Am. Coll. Law and Medicine, 8th Jud. Bar Assn. (life Ohio dist.), Internat. Ins. Law Soc., Oil Painters Am. (assoc.), Internat. Soc. Marine Painters (profl. mem.), Lost Tree Property Owners Assn., Mayfield Country Club (pres. 1980-82), Union Club, Hermit Club (pres. 1973-75), Lost Tree Club (bd. govs. 1991-94), Everglades Club (Fla.), Kirtland Counry Club, Rolling Rock Club (Pa.), The Bohemian Club (Calif.).

REMIS, STEVEN JOSEPH, robotics engineer; b. Kittanning, Pa., July 24, 1963; s. Albert Michael and Vera Jean (Douglass) R.; m. Patti Marie Ness, Oct. 22, 1988. BSEE, Carnegie-Mellon U., 1985; MSME, U. Notre Dame, 1993, PhD in Mech. Engring., 1994. Cert. competent overseer for asbestos abatement. Bioenviron. engr. USAF, Colorado Springs, Colo., 1986-88; biomed. rsch. engr. USAF, Dayton, Ohio, 1989-90; robotics engr. Yoder Software, Inc., South Bend, Ind., 1994-95; pres., robotics engr. Paragon Robotics, Inc., South Bend, Ind., 1995—; computer cons., South Bend, 1991—; instr. U. Notre Dame Office of Univ. Computing, 1992-94, asst. curriculum software developer accountancy dept., 1994-95. Author: Advances in Robot Kinematics and Computational Geometry, 1994; author IEEE Transactions on Robotics and Automation, 1993. Adult literacy tutor Right to Read, Colorado Springs, 1987-88; tutor Minority Engring. Program, Notre Dame, 1991-92; youth leader, Sunday sch. tchr. Northside Assembly of God, South Bend, 1994—. Decorated Air Force Commendation medals; recipient Allegheny Singer award for Biomed. Rsch., 1984. Mem. IEEE, The Health Physics Soc. Assembly of God. Office: Paragon Robotics Inc 3702 W Sample St Ste A-20 South Bend IN 46619

REMMEL, RORY PATRICK, pharmacy educator; b. Colorado Springs, Colo., Nov. 26, 1954; s. Urban Charles and Regina V. (Bojarski) R.; m. Cheryl L. Zimmerman, June 25, 1983. BS in Biochemistry, U. Wyo., 1976, BS in Pharmacy, 1977; PhD in Medicinal Chemistry, U. Wash., 1982. Lic. pharmacist, Colo., Wash. Pharmacy intern Target Pharmacy # 6, Glendale, Colo., 1977-78; rsch. fellow pharmacology Harvard Med. Sch., Boston, 1982-83; rsch. assoc. U. Minn., Mpls., 1983-84, asst. prof., 1984-91, assoc. prof., 1991—; vis. scientist U. Dundee, Scotland, 1992; mem. pharmacology com. NIH AIDS clin. trials Group, 1994—; mem. adv. panel natural products U.S. Pharmacopeia, Bethesda, Md., 1995. Fogarty Sr. Internat. fellow, 1992. Mem. Am. Assn. Colls. Pharmacy, Am. Assn. Pharm. Scientists, Internat. Soc. for Study Xenobiotics, Kappa Psi (grand coun. dep.). Home: 2374 Bourne Ave Saint Paul MN 55108 Office: U Minn Coll Pharmacy 308 Harvard St SE Minneapolis MN 55455

REMUS, DENISE RAE, nurse researcher; b. Worthington, Minn., Apr. 15, 1959; d. Derald Dean and Barbara Jean (Wasmund) Jones; m. Patrick Lance

Remus, Sept. 5, 1981; 1 child, Michael Scott. BA, Coll. of St. Scholastica, Duluth, Minn., 1981; MS, U. Minn., Mpls., 1990; PhD, U. Minn., 1994. RN, Minn., Wis. Staff nurse critical care, med./surg. units Fairview Ridges Hosp., Burnsville, Minn., 1986-88; rsch. and adminstrv. asst. Sch. Nursing, U. Minn., Mpls., 1987-89; sr. care nurse Hennepin County Med. Ctr., Mpls., 1989-90; ind. nursing cons., 1991—; adj. faculty Coll. St. Scholastica, Duluth, 1990-92; clin. rschr. St. Michael's Hosp., Stevens Point, Wis., 1993-95; v.p. R&D Weston Med. Data Sys., Inc., Stevens Point, 1995—. 1st lt. USAF, 1982-85. Mem. Gerontol. Soc. Am., Sigma Theta Tau, Phi Kappa Phi. Home: 1331 Chippewa Trail Mosinee WI 54455-9416

RENARD, PAUL STEVEN, music educator; b. N.Y.C., May 5, 1934; s. Joseph Maurice and Elsie (Wolpow) R. Student, Miami (Fla.) Conservatory, 1947-48, Sch. of Am. Music, 1950-51; cert., Ida Elkan Sch. of Music, 1958. Staff concert organist Hammond Organ Co., N.Y.C., 1950-74; staff organist various TV stas. N.Y.C., 1952-61; staff organist King Records and Riverside Records, N.Y.C., 1955-64; staff organist, ednl. dir. Lyon-Healy Music Co., Chgo., 1962-72; founder, dir. Paul Renard's Music Dynamics, Chgo., 1972—; cons. in field. Co-inventor first electric piano, Wurlitzer Mus. Instruments Co., 1953-54; author numerous piano and organ texts; contbr. articles tor profl. jours. Office: 320 N Michigan Ave Ste 602 Chicago IL 60601-3710

RENDLEMAN, DANNY LEE, English language educator; b. Flint, Mich., Nov. 25, 1945; s. William Franklin and Beatrice Jenny (Winn) R.; m. Alice Mae Sanford, Jan. 27, 1970 (div. 1984); 1 child, Eliot Franklin; m. Janice Marlene Worth, May 17, 1986. B Gen. Studies, U. Mich., Flint, 1974; MFA, Goddard Coll., 1978. Asst. Right to Read project U. Mich., Flint, 1974-75, instrnl. assoc., 1975-86, lectr. English dept., 1986—. Author: (poetry) Asylum, 1977, Skilled Trades, 1989, Victrola, 1994, The Middle West, 1995. Mem., bd. dirs. Friends of Modern Art, Flint, 1990-93; sec., artist-mem. Buckham Fine Arts Project, Flint, 1993—. Grantee Mich. Coun. Arts, 1986, 89, 94, U. Mich., Flint, 1995. Mem. Sigma Chi. Home: 942 E Seventh St Flint MI 48503 Office: U Mich English Dept 326 CROB Flint MI 48502

RENICK, PAUL RODNEY, library media director, educator; b. Elgin, N.D., Apr. 4, 1946; s. Elbert Joseph and Martha (Kurle) R.; m. Catherine Louise Patrick, Aug. 30, 1969; children: Kirsten Sue, Kimberly Annette, Kari Lynn. BS, Dickinson State Coll., 1968; MLS, Peabody Coll. for Tchrs., 1969. Cert. tchr., media dir., N.D. Circulation, reference libr. Dickinson (N.D.) State Coll., 1968; asst. prof. libr. sci. U. N.D., Grand Forks, 1969-73; media dir. Valley Jr. H.S., Grand Forks, N.D., 1973-94, Cen. H.S., Grand Forks, N.D., 1994—; part-time asst. prof. libr. sci. U. N.D., 1974-95. Named H.S. Swimming Ofcl. of Yr., N.D. H.S. Swim Coaches Assn., 1993-94; recipient Phillips 66 Meritorious Svc. to Swimming award, 1995. Mem. NEA, U.S. Swimming, N.D. Swimming (gen. chmn. 1989-93), N.D. Libr. Media Assn. (pres. 1979). Home: 2302 S 20th St Grand Forks ND 58201 Office: Grand Forks Central HS 115 N 4th Grand Forks ND 58201

RENNER, PAUL ERIC, systems analyst, consultant; b. Louisiana, Mo., Dec. 5, 1966; s. James Howard and Rita Anne (Chambers) R.; m. Amy M. Vanden Berghe, Oct. 26, 1991. BA in Computer Sci., U. Mo., 1989. Cert. netware engr. Programmer analyst Show-Me State Games, Columbia, Mo., 1989-91; systems analyst City of Columbia, 1991—; CEO After 5 Computer Svcs., Columbia, 1993—. Mem. IEEE. Roman Catholic. Office: City of Columbia 701 E Broadway Columbia MO 65201-4470

RENNER, ROBERT GEORGE, federal judge; b. Nevis, Minn., Apr. 2, 1923; s. Henry J. and Beatrice M. (Fuller) R.; m. Catherine L. Clark, Nov. 12, 1949; children: Robert, Anne, Richard, David. BA, St. John's U., Collegeville, Minn., 1947; JD, Georgetown U., 1949. Bar: Minn. 1949. Pvt. practice Walker, 1949-69; U.S. atty. Dist. of Minn., 1969-77, U.S. magistrate, 1977-80, U.S. dist. judge, 1980—. Mem. Minn. Ho. of Reps., 1957-69. Served with AUS, 1943-46. Mem. ABA, Fed. Bar Assn. Roman Catholic. Office: US Dist Ct 748 US Courthouse 316 Robert St N Saint Paul MN 55101-1423

RENNERFELDT, EARL RONALD, farmer, rancher; b. Epping, N.D., July 10, 1938; s. Carl John and Margaret E. (Long) R.; m. Lois Ann Thune, Sept. 12, 1959; children: Charysse Renee, Carter Ryan. Student, NDSSS, Wahpeton, N.D., 1958. Farmer/rancher Williston, N.D. Mem. N.D. Ho. of Reps., Bismarck, 1991—; mem. Lake Sacajawea Planning Bd., Williston, N.D., 1992; mem. Am. Legis. Exch. Coun., 1991-92; adv. bd. N.D. State U. Exptl. Sta.; bd. dirs. Mercy Med. Found. With U.S. Army, 1962-64. Recipient Harvest Bowl award N.D. State U., 1988; named Outstanding Young Farmer C. of C., 1972. Mem. Am. Legion, N.D. Grain growers, N.D. Durum Growers, Williston C. of C., N.D. Stockmen's Assn., Elks. Republican. Evangelical Free Ch. Home and Office: 1704 Rose Ln Williston ND 58801-4362

RENO, OTTIE WAYNE, former judge; b. Pike County, Ohio, Apr. 7, 1929; s. Eli Enos and Arbannah Belle (Jones) R.; A in Bus. Adminstrn., Franklin U., 1949; LLB, Franklin Law Sch., 1953; JD, Capital U., 1966; grad. Coll. Juvenile Justice, U. Nev., 1973; m. Janet Gay McCann, May 22, 1947; children: Ottie Wayne II, Jennifer Lynn, Lorna Victoria. Admitted to Ohio bar, 1953; practiced in Pike County; recorder Pike County, 1957-73; common pleas judge Probate and Juvenile divs. Pike County, 1973-79. Mem. adv. bd. Ohio Youth Services, 1972-74. Mem. Dem. Central Com. Camp Creek precinct, 1956-72, 83-90; sec. Pike County Central Com., 1960-70, 83-87; chmn. Pike County Dem. Exec. Com., 1971-72, 1988-90; del. Dem. Nat. Conv., 1972, 96; mem. Ohio Dem. Central Com., 1969-70; Dem. candidate 6th Ohio dist. U.S. Ho. of Reps., 1966, 88th Dist. Ohio Ho. of Reps., 1992; pres. Scioto Valley Local Sch. Dist., 1962-66. Recipient Distinguished Service award Ohio Youth Commn., 1974; 6 Outstanding Jud. Service awards Ohio Supreme Ct.; 15 times Ala. horseshoe pitching champion; named to Nat. Horseshoe Pitchers Hall of Fame, 1978; mem. internat. sports exchange, U.S. and Republic South Africa, 1972, 80, 82. Mem. Ohio, Pike County (pres. 1964) Bar Assns., Nat. Council Juvenile Ct. Judges, Am. Legion. Mem. Ch. of Christ in Christian Union. Author: Story of Horseshoes, 1963; Pitching Championship Horseshoes, 1971, 2d rev. edit., 1975; The American Directory of Horseshoe Pitching, 1983, Ohio vs. Smith, Murder, 1990, Reno and Apsaalooka Survive Custer, 1996. Home: 148 Reno Rd Lucasville OH 45648-9580

RENSING, ROBERT FRANCIS, independent investor, consultant; b. Cin., Dec. 8, 1946; s. Francis R. and Mary G. (Donnelon) R.; m. Marion L. Hartz, Oct. 11, 1974; children: Jennifer, Michael, Matthew, Patricia. BS in Elec. Engring., U. Cin., 1970, MBA, 1974. With Cin. Bell Telephone, 1966—, mgr. translations, 1985-87, dir. long range planning, 1988-90, dir. planning and engring., 1990-91, br. mgr., 1991-92, dir. network ops., 1992-93, dir. bus. reengring., 1994-95, v.p. net planning, 1995; ind. investor, cons., Cin., 1995—. Contbr. articles to profl. jours. Mem. IEEE, Vintage Thunderbird Club Internat., LEAD Clermont. Republican. Roman Catholic. Home and Office: 4150 Mclean Dr Cincinnati OH 45255-3325

RENTER, LOIS IRENE HUTSON, librarian; b. Lowden, Iowa, Oct. 23, 1929; d. Thomas E. and Lulu Mae (Barlean) Hutson; m. Karl A. Renter, Jan. 3, 1948; children: Susan Elizabeth, Rebecca Jean, Karl Geoffrey. BA cum laude, Cornell Coll., 1965; MA, U. Iowa, 1968. Tchr. Spanish Mt. Vernon High Sch., 1965-67; head libr. Am. Coll. Testing Program, Iowa City, Iowa, 1968-89, ret., 1989; vis. instr. U. Iowa Sch. Library Sci., 1972-82. Mem. Phi Beta Kappa. Methodist. Home: 1125 29th St Marion IA 52302-1529

RENTSCHLER, ALVIN EUGENE, mechanical engineer; b. Havre, Mont., Oct. 24, 1940; s. Alvin Joseph and Pauline Elizabeth (Browning) R.; m. Edna A. Sassen, Dec. 27, 1963; children: Elizabeth Louise, Richard Eugene; m. Marilyn Joan Bostrom, Dec. 7, 1974; 1 child, Alison Lynn. BS, Mont. State U., 1964. Sci. and math. instr. Helena (Mont.) Pub. Schs., 1964-66; dist. mgr. Woodmen Accident and Life Co., Helena, 1966-69; profl. med. rep. Abbott Labs., Great Falls, Mont., 1969-72; sales engr. Agribest, Inc., Great Falls, 1973; design engr. Anaconda Co., Mont., 1974-77; ops. and maintenance engr. Rochester Meth. Hosp., Minn., 1977-85; maintenance supr., 1985-89, ops. asst., 1989-92; facilities ops. and maintenance supr. Mayo Clinic, Rochester, Minn., 1993—; mem. engring. coordinating com. Franklin Heating Sta., 1977-85. Bd. dirs. Mont. affiliate Am. Diabetes Assn., 1975-78, pres. Butte-Anaconda chpt., 1974-77, mem.; mem. citizens adv. com. Minnesota Riverland Tech. Coll. (name formerly Rochester Tech. Inst.), 1977—, chmn. 1987-89; del. Mont. Edn. Assn. Conv., 1966. Recipient Greatest Achievement award Combined Tng., Inc., 1977, Pres.' Club award Woodmen Accident & Life Co., 1968. Mem. ASME, Am. Soc. Hosp. Engring., Internat. Congress Hosp. Engring., So. Minn. Health Care Engrs. Assn. Mem. Covenant Ch. Home: 2215 17th Ave NW Rochester MN 55901-7738

REPLOGLE, ARTHUR SEEDS, community development executive; b. Altoona, Pa., May 30, 1922; s. Arthur M. and Mary E. (Seeds) R.; m. Ruth E. Heiges, Sept. 7, 1946; children: Scott, Mark, Susan. BA, Washington & Jefferson Coll., 1943. Lic. real estate sales assoc., Ill. With Replogle Globes, Inc., Chgo., 1946-73; pres. Oak Park (Ill.) Devel. Corp., 1974—. V.p., dir. Downtown Oak Park Corp., 1985—; dir. Civic Arts Coun., Oak Park, 1987-92; life trustee Frank Lloyd Wright Home & Studio Found., Oak Park; sec., dir. West Suburban Coll. of Nursing, Oak Park, 1982—; mem., sec., pres. Bd. Edn. Oak Park/River Forest H.S., 1973-79; dir., past chmn. West Suburban Hosp. Med. Ctr., Oak Park, 1971-93; pres. Thatcher Woods Area Coun. Boy Scouts Am., Oak Park, 1970-72; mem. pres.'s coun. Rosary Coll., River Forest. Lt. USNR, 1944-46. Recipient Silver Antelope, Silver Beaver Boy Scouts Am., 1975, 76, Disting. Citizen award, 1976, Pres.'s award Concordia U., 1991. Mem. Geog. Soc. Chgo. (dir., past pres.), River Forest Tennis Club (pres. 1976), Econ. Club of Chgo., Oak Park Country Club, Rotary (pres. 1966, Community Merity award 1991). Republican. Home: 203 N Kenilworth Ave Apt 2H Oak Park IL 60302-2054 Office: Oak Park Devel Corp 104 N Oak Park Ave # 203 Oak Park IL 60301-1304

RESCORLA, CHARLES LAVERNE, manufacturing executive; b. York, Pa., Apr. 16, 1951; s. Charles L. and Charlotte (Mulder) R.; m. Sharon Brinks, Feb. 2, 1974; children: Susan, Laurie, Deborah. BSME, U. Mich., 1973; BS, Calvin Coll., 1973; M of Mgmt., Northwestern U., Evanston, Ill., 1977. Registered profl. engr. Minn. From design engr. to test lab supr. Internat Harvester, Hinsdale, Ill., 1974-83; mgr. engring. ARO Corp., Bryan, Ohio, 1983-88; dir. engring. Graco, Inc., Mpls., 1988-94, dir. mfg., 1994-95, v.p. mfg. ops., 1995—.

RESER, ELIZABETH MAY, bookkeeper; b. Le Roy, Kans., Sept. 4, 1939; d. William David II and Vera Hazel (Dreyer) Meats; m. William Joseph Reser, Sept. 26, 1958; children: Dee Anna, Eichinger, Donna Sue Reser Wessel. Diploma in computer programming, Control Data Inst., St. Louis, 1980; student, Washburn U., 1991. Cert. computer programmer, Mo. Computer programmer Regional Justice Info. Sys., St. Louis, 1980; sec. Shawnee Heights H.S., Tecumseh, Kans., 1973-78, bookkeeper, 1984-90. Treas. secs. Shawnee Heights Unified Sch. Dist. 450, 1975-76, 86-87; vol. March of Dimes, Topeka, 1995; mem. bd. trustees Susanna Wesley United Meth. Ch., Topeka, 1992-94, mem. prayer chain, 1993-94. Republican. Home: 2849 SW Dukeries Rd Topeka KS 66614

RESKA-HADDEN, MARCIA ANN, special education educator; b. LacKawanna, N.Y., Mar. 16, 1952; d. Edward Walter and Harriet Theresa (Kozlowski) Reska; m. Dennis Lynn Hadden; 1 child, Dennis Edward. BA in History, Canisius Coll., 1974, MS in Edn., 1979; MAT in History, Niagara U., 1974-76; mentally impaired student, Eastern Mich. U., 1988-90. Tchr. Spl. Edn., N.Y., Mich. Jr. high sch. tchr. St. Barbara's Sch., Lackawanna, N.Y., 1974-75; 5th grade tchr. St. Ambrose Sch., Buffalo, N.Y., 1975-76; jr. high sch. tchr. The Cathedral Sch., Buffalo, N.Y., 1976-79, St. Mary's of the Lake Sch., Hamburg, N.Y., 1979-83, Our Lady of Victory Sch., Lackawanna, N.Y., 1983-85; substitute tchr. Lakeville (Mich.) Sch. Dist., 1986-87; substitute tchr. Genesee Intermediate Sch. Dist., Flint, Mich., 1986-88, spl. edn. tchr., 1988—; mem. Coun. for Exceptional Children, Reston, Va., 1988—; speaker, presentor Functional Curriculum for a SMI Student, 1991. Co-author: Functional Curriculum GISD Secondary Functional Curriculum, 1989-90. Mem. Polish Union Am., Canisus Coll. Alumnae Assn., Genesee County Hist. Soc., Mich. Edn. Assn., Genesee Intermediate Ednl. Assn., Beta Sigma Phi. Home: 7211 Timberwood Dr Davison MI 48423-9522 Office: Genesee Intermediate Sch Dist 2413 W Maple Ave Flint MI 48507-3429

RESNICK, ALICE ROBIE, state supreme court justice; b. Erie, Pa., Aug. 21, 1939; d. Adam Joseph and Alice Suzanne (Spizarny) Robie; m. Melvin L. Resnick, Mar. 20, 1970. PhB, Siena Heights Coll., 1961; JD, U. Detroit, 1964. Bar: Ohio 1964, Mich. 1965, U.S. Supreme Ct. 1970. Asst. county prosecutor Lucas County Prosecutor's Office, Toledo, 1964-75, trial atty., 1965-75; judge Toledo Mcpl. Ct., 1976-83, 6th Dist. Ct. Appeals, State of Ohio, Toledo, 1983-88; instr. U. Toledo, 1968-69; justice Ohio Supreme Ct., 1989—; co-chairperson Ohio State Gender Fairness Task Force. Trustee Siena Heights Coll., Adrian, Mich., 1982—; organizer Crime Stopper Inc., Toledo, 1981—; mem. Mayor's Drug Coun.; bd. dirs. Guest House Inc. Mem. ABA, Toledo Bar Assn., Lucas County Bar Assn., Nat. Assn. Women Judges, Am. Judicature Soc., Toledo Women's Bar Assn., Ohio State Women's Bar Assn. (organizer), Toledo Mus. Art, Internat. Inst. Toledo. Roman Catholic. Home: 2407 Edgehill Rd Toledo OH 43615-2321 Office: Supreme Ct Office 30 E Broad St Fl 3 Columbus OH 43215-3414

RESS, CHARLES WILLIAM, management consultant; b. Columbus, Ohio, Aug. 6, 1933; s. George Leonard and Martha (Lake) R.; m. Virginia M. Beck, Aug. 28, 1954; children: Beverly Beck, Suzanne E., Charles W. Jr., Linda Perrins, Jennifer Laurel. BS, Miami U., 1955; MA in Psychology, Rutgers U., 1969. Buyer The Higbee Co., Cleve., 1956-59; asst. to gen. mdse. mgr. The Halle Bros. Co., Cleve., 1959-64; research dir. The Associated Mdse. Corp., N.Y.C., 1964-73; v.p. Mgmt. Horizons, Columbus, 1973-76; founder, chmn. bd. C.W. Ress & Assoc., Inc., Columbus, 1976-90; gen. mgr. Levi Strauss & Co., Columbus, 1990-94, mgmt. cons., 1994—; lectr. in field. Author: Future Trends in Retailing, 1983, Trans National Retailing, 1988, Retailing 2000, 1991; contbr. articles to profl. jours. Republican. Office: 123 Old Field Bend North Chatham MA 02650

REST, ANN H., state legislator; b. 1942; 1 child. BA, Northwestern U.; MA, U. Chgo.; MAT, MPA, Harvard U.; MBT, U. Minn. Mem. Minn. Ho. of Reps. St. Paul, 1985—; chmn. taxes com., rules and legis. adminstrv. com., mem. ways and means com.; CPA. Recipient Women of Achievment award North Hennepin Bus. and Profl. Women, 1988; named Legislator of Yr., Politics in Minn., 1990. Mem. Resources for Adoptive Parents, Libr. Found. of Hennepin County, YMCA. Democrat. Home: 7611 36th Ave N Apt 322 Minneapolis MN 55427-2085 Office: Minn State Senate 439 State Off Bldg Saint Paul MN 55155*

RETISH, ESTHER SHIFRA, elementary educator; b. Kingston, N.Y., Sept. 21, 1942; d. Zev William and Helen (Wohl) Chazanof; m. Paul Michael Retish, June 13, 1964; children: Joshua, Marc, Aaron. BS, Pa. State U., 1964; MA, Ind. U., 1966; PhD, U. Iowa, 1996. Speech clinician Iowa City Cmty. Schs., 1967-68; speech clinician-title I presch. Iowa City Schs., 1971-79, tchr. ESL (K-6), 1981-91, 92—, tchr. ESL (K-8), 1991-92; cons. Iowa State U., Ames, spring 1986, U. No. Iowa, Cedar Falls, spring 1988, State of Miss., 1990, State Dept. of Iowa, 1991. Author (newsletter) TESOL Matters, 1992, Elem. ESOL Edn. News, 1993. Mem. sisterhood Agudas Achim Congregation, Iowa City, 1968—; orientation chair person New Pioneer Coop. Grocery Store, 1980—. Kodak grant Kodak Co., 1983, Svc. Learning grant State of Iowa, 1993, 94. Mem. NEA, Mid TESOL (Iowa rep. at large 1990-92, 2nd v.p. 1992-94), TESOL (bd. dirs. 1991-95, co-chair literacy com. 1992—), Iowa City Edn. Assn., Am. Speech and Hearning Assn. Home: 66 Penfro Dr Iowa City IA 52246 Office: Iowa City Cmty Sch Dist Roosevelt Sch 911 Greenwood Dr Iowa City IA 52246

RETTON, SANDRA JO, physical education educator, coach; b. Fairmont, W.Va., June 1, 1956; d. Frank Richard and Shirley Jean (Martin) R. BA in Edn., Fairmont State Coll., 1978; AS in Data Processing, North Ctrl. Tech. Coll., Mansfield, Ohio, 1985; MS in Phys. Edn., Ohio U., 1991. Cert. profl. tchr., Ohio. Tchr. W.Va. Career Coll., Fairmont, 1979-80; tchr., coach Crestview High Sch., Ashland, Ohio, 1980-81; coal miner Consol. Coal Co., Mannington, W.Va., 1982-83; tchr., coach Morgan High Sch., McConnelsville, Ohio, 1986—. Named Muskingum Valley League Track Coach of Yr., 1993, 95, Ea. Dist. Divsn. I Girls Track Coach of Yr. Ohio, 1993, 95, Dist. # 8 Girls Track Coach of Yr. Mem. NEA, Ohio Edn. Assn., AAHPERD, Ohio Assn. Health, Phys. Edn., Recreation and Dance, Nat. Fedn. Interscholastic Coaches and Officials Assn., Ohio Assn. Track and Cross Country Coaches. Home: 60 N 9th St Mc Connelsville OH 43756-1106 Office: Morgan High Sch 800 Raider Dr Mc Connelsville OH 43756-9299

RETZER, ELMER R., state legislator; b. Feb. 5, 1931; m. Mary Lou Nelson, 1982; children: Troy Nelson, Kayleen, Kelsey. Farmer; rep. Dist. 29 N.D. Ho. of reps., formerly, 1995—, mem. indsl. bus. and labor and polit. subdivsns. com. Pres. Franklin Sch. Bd.; pres. Gideon Camp. Mem. Gideons Internat. Home: 6520 R St SE Cleveland ND 58424

REUBEN, DON HAROLD, lawyer; b. Chgo., Sept. 1, 1928; s. Michael B. and Sally (Chapman) R.; m. Evelyn Long, Aug. 27, 1948 (div.); children: Hope Reuben Paul, Michael Barrett, Timothy Don, Jeffrey Long, Howard Ellis; m. Jeannette Hurley Haywood, Dec. 13, 1971; stepchildren: Harris Hurley Haywood, Edward Gregory Haywood. BS, Northwestern U., 1949, JD, 1952. Bar: Ill. 1952. With firm Kirkland & Ellis, Chgo., 1952-78, sr. ptnr., until 1978; sr. ptnr. Reuben & Proctor, Chgo., 1978-86, Isham, Lincoln & Beale, Chgo., 1986-88; sr. counsel Winston & Strawn, 1988-94; of counsel Altheimer & Gray, Chgo., 1994—; spl. asst. atty. gen. State of Ill., 1963-64, 69, 84; counsel spl. session Ill. Ho. of Reps., 1964, for Ill. treas. for congl., state legis. and jud. reapportionment, 1963; spl. fed. ct. master, 1968-70; dir. Lake Shore Nat. Bank., 1973-93, Heitman Fin., 1993—; mem. citizens adv. bd. to sheriff County of Cook, 1962-66, mem. jury instrns. com., 1963-68; rules com. Ill. Supreme Ct., 1963-73; mem. pub. rels. com. Nat. Conf. State Trial Judges; mem. com. study caseflow mgmt. in law div. Cook County Cir. Ct., 1979-88; mem. adv. implementation com. U.S. Dist. Ct. for No. Dist. Ill., 1981-82; mem. Chgo. Better Schs. Com., 1968-69, Chgo. Crime Commn., 1970-80; mem. supervisory panel Fed. Defender Program.; lectr. on libel, slander, privacy and freedom of press; gen. counsel Tribune Co., 1965-88, Chgo. Bears Football Club, 1965-88, Catholic Archdiocese of Chgo., 1975-86. Bd. dirs. Lincoln Park Zool. Soc., 1972-84 ; trustee Northwestern U., 1977—; mem. vis. com. U. Chgo. Law Sch., 1976-79. Mem. Ill. Bar Assn., Chgo. Bar Assn. (chmn. subcom. on propriety and regulation of contingent fees com. devel. law 1966-69, subcom. on media liaison 1980-82, mem. com. on profl. info. 1980-82), ABA (standing com. on fed. judiciary 1973-79, standing com. on jud. selection, tenure and compensation 1982-85), Am. Law Inst., Am. Judicature Soc., Fellows Am. Bar Found., Am. Coll. Trial Lawyers (Rule 23 com. 1975-82, judiciary com. 1987-91), Am. Arbitration Assn. (nat. panel arbitrators), Internat. Acad. Trial Lawyers, Union League Club (Chgo.), Tavern Club, Mid-Am. Club, Law Club, Casino Club, The Springs Club, Desert Riders of Palm Springs, The Chgo. Club, Phi Eta Sigma, Beta Alpha Psi, Beta Gamma Sigma, Order of Coif. Home: 20 Jill Ter Rancho Mirage CA 92270-2635

REUBER, GRANT LOUIS, banking insurance company executive; b. Mildmay, Ont., Can., Nov. 23, 1927; s. Jacob Daniel and Gertrude Catherine (Wahl) R.; m. Margaret Louise Julia Summerhayes, Oct. 21, 1951; children: Rebecca, Barbara, Mary. BA, U. Western Ont., 1950; AM, Harvard U., 1954, PhD, 1957; LLD (hon.), Wilfred Laurier U., 1983, Simon Fraser U., 1985; U. Western Ont., 1985, McMaster U., 1994; postgrad., Cambridge U., 1954-55. Mem. research dept. Bank Can., Ottawa, 1950-52; mem. Can. Dept. Finance, Ottawa, 1955-57; asst. prof. econ. U. Western Ont., London, 1957-59, assoc. prof., 1959-62, prof., head dept., 1963-69; prof., head dept., 1963-69; mem. bd. govs. U. Western Ont., London, 1974-78, acad. v.p., provost, 1975-78, chancellor, 1988-92; sr. v.p., chief economist Bank of Montreal, Que., Can., 1978-79; exec. v.p. Bank of Montreal, 1980-81, dep. chmn., dep. chief exec. officer, 1981-83, dir., mem. exec. com., 1981-89, pres., chief operating officer, 1983-87, dep. chmn., 1987-89; dep. minister fin. Can., 1979-80; chmn. Can. Deposit Ins. Corp., 1993—; mem. Royal Commn. Banking and Fin., Toronto, 1962-63; chmn. Ont. Econ. Coun., 1973-78; cons. Can. Internat. Devel. Agy., 1968-69; hon. rsch. assoc. in econs. Harvard U., 1968-69; cons. devel. ctr. OECD, 1969-73; bd. dirs. Opinac Energy Corp.; mem. adv. com. U. Western Ont. Sch. Bus.; lectr. U. Chgo. Sch. Bus., 1992-93; econ. advisor to prime min. of Lithuania, 1991-92. Author: Private Foreign Investment in Development, 1973, Canada's Political Economy, 1980; contbr. articles to profl. jours. Pres. Can. Ditchley Found., 1991—; vice chmn. Can. Merit Scholarship Found., 1994—. Decorated officer Order of Can. Fellow Royal Soc. Can.

REUM, JAMES MICHAEL, lawyer; b. Oak Park, Ill., Nov. 1, 1946; s. Walter John and Lucy (Bellegay) R. BA cum laude, Harvard U., 1968, JD cum laude, 1972. Bar: N.Y. 1973, D.C. 1974, U.S. Dist. Ct. (so. dist.) N.Y. 1974, Ill. 1979, U.S. Dist. Ct. (no. dist.) Ill. 1982. Assoc. Davis Polk & Wardwell, N.Y.C., 1973-78; assoc. Minority Counsel Com. on Judiciary U.S. Ho. of Reps., Washington, 1974; ptnr. Hopkins & Sutter, Chgo., 1979-93, Winston & Strawn, Chgo., 1994—. Midwest advance rep. Nat. Reagan Bush Com., 1980; nominee commr. Securities and Exchange Comm., Pres. Bush, 1992. Served to SP4 USAR, 1969-75. Recipient Harvard U. Honorary Nat. Scholarship, 1964-72. Mem. ABA, Monte Carlo Country Club (Monaco), Chgo. Club, Univ. Club (N.Y.C.). Republican. Home: 12 E Scott St Chicago IL 60610 Office: Winston & Strawn 35 W Wacker Dr Chicago IL 60601-1614

REUMANN, VELMA ROSE, mathematician; b. Fairfax, Mo., Jan. 7, 1933; d. Earl Harold and Arlene Isobel (Inbody) V.; m. Richard Edward Reumann, Feb. 21, 1969; 1 child, Rhoda Arlou. BA, Tarkio Coll., 1954; MA, Roosevelt U., 1976. Math tchr. Fairfax R-1 Schs., 1978-82; satelite tchr. Adult Basic Edn., Maryville, Mo., 1985-93; math instr. Upward Bound, Maryville, 1987-95. Lt. USN, 1956-69. Lutheran.

REUSCHLEIN, ROBERT WILLIAM, accountant, researcher; b. Madison, Wis., Jan. 8, 1950; s. Earl Vincent and Rosemary Markham R. BSEE, U. Wis., 1972; MBA, Oregon State U., 1977. Surveyor and draftsman Ctrl. Wis. Builders, Madison, 1971-72; estimator Dyson Constrn., Madison, 1972; pub. acct. Earl V. Reuschlein & Assocs., Madison, 1973-74; mgmt. intern Portland (Oreg.) Gen. Elec., 1976; controller Doorcraft, Inc., Harrisburg, Oreg., 1977-79; pub. acct. C.F. Rogers CPA, Eugene, Oreg., 1980; lobbyist Dem. Party of Oregon, Salem, 1981-85; rschr. Earlwal, Ltd., Eugene, 1986-93; acct., pres. Earlwal, Ltd., Madison, Wis., 1993—; mem. Citizen Involvement Com., City of Springfield, Oreg., 1979; founding dir. Neighborhood Econ. Devel. Corp., Eugene, 1979-81; dir. Eugene Peace Works, 1991-93; gen. mgr. Jomblee, Inc., Madison, 1995—; instr. peace econs. U. Oreg., 1987, 89; lectr. Econ. Conversion Conf., Miami, Fla., 1990. Author: Peace Economics, 1986, Strength Through Peace, 1989; columnist Peace Economics in Oreg. Peace Worker, 1989— (columns also played on Radio for Peace Internat., Costa Rica, 1993); developer Natural Global Warming Theory, 1991. Mem. Dem. Exec. Com., Oreg., 1981-87; del. Dem. Nat. Conv., San Francisco, 1984; chmn. 4th Congl. Dist. Dems., Oreg., 1982-87, Eugene Peace Works, 1992-93; program dir. Prairie Soc. Unitarian Ch., 1995—. Mem. AICPA, Wis. Inst. CPAs, Madison Progressive Inst., World Federalists (bd. dirs. local chpt.). Office: Earlwal Ltd 6515 Grand Teton Plz Ste 120 Madison WI 53719

REUTER, JOHN ROBERT, JR., investment company executive; b. Indpls., Oct. 19, 1957; s. John Robert Sr. and Catherine Laura (White) R.; m. Alicia Ann Noppenberger, Aug. 31, 1986; children: Morgan, John Robert III, William, James. Student, Wabash Coll. Sales rep. Continental Corp., St. Louis, 1981-83, Hamilton Arnet, Carmel, Ind., 1983-85; mtkg./sales rep. M.C.S., Indpls., 1985-87; account exec. The Ohio Co., Indpls., 1987-90; v.p. investments A.G. Edwards and Sons Inc., Indpls., 1990—. Mem. parish coun. St. Matthew Parish, 1993—. Mem. Sertoma Club of East Indpls., Phi Delta Theta. Republican. Roman Catholic. Home: 5420 Roxbury Rd Indianapolis IN 46226 Office: AG Edwards & Sons Inc Ste 1200 251 N Illinois St Indianapolis IN 46204

REUTER, KEN, systems engineer; b. Columbus, Nebr., July 8, 1948. Student, U. Nebr. Quality control engr. Square D Co., Lincoln, Nebr., 1974-84; field svc. engr. Notifier Co., Lincoln, 1984-90; sys. engr. Spectronics Corp., Lincoln, 1990—. Contbr. articles to profl. jours. With U.S. Army, 1969-72. Mem. Nat. Fire Protection Assn. Office: Spectronics Corp 4645 Hartley St Lincoln NE 68504-1652

REUTIMAN, ROBERT WILLIAM, JR., lawyer; b. Mpls., June 4, 1944; s. Robert William and Elsbeth Bertha (Doering) R.; m. Virginia Lee Traxler, June 25, 1983; children: Robert James, Joseph Lee. BA magna cum laude, U. Minn., 1966, JD, 1969. Bar: Minn. 1969, U.S. Ct. Mil. Appeals 1969,

U.S. Dist. Ct. Minn. 1973, U.S. Ct. Appeals (8th cir.) 1976, U.S. Tax. Ct. 1979. Mem. Armstrong, Phleger, Reutiman & Vinokour, Ltd., Wayzata, Minn., 1973-76; ptnr. Phleger & Reutiman, Wayzata, 1976-81; pvt. practice Wayzata, 1981—. Chmn. Spring Pk. Planning Commn., 1978. Capt. U.S. Army, 1969-73. Decorated Army Commendation medal. Mem. ABA, Minn. Bar Assn., Hennepin County Bar Assn., Am. Arbitration Assn. (panel of arbitrators), Phi Beta Kappa. Lutheran. Home: 11610 3rd Ave N Plymouth MN 55441-5919 Office: 305 Rice St E Wayzata MN 55391-1615

REVELL, DOROTHY EVANGELINE TOMPKINS, dietitian; b. Rugby, N.D., Dec. 22, 1911; d. Clarence Herbert and Regina Andrea (Bergh) Tompkins; m. Eugene Allen Revell, Sept 17, 1935; children: Eugene Allen II, Dorothy Ann. BS in Food and Nutrition, U. N.D., Grand Forks, 1933. Lic. registered dietitian, N.D. Dietetic intern Harper Hosp., Detroit, 1933-34, staff dietitian, 1934-35; nutrition instr. student nurses Mercy Hosp., Valley City, N.D., 1958; dietitian Dakota Clinic, Fargo, N.D., 1958-76; pvt. practice Revell's Diet Svc., Fargo, 1977—; home nursing chmn. ARC, Fargo, 1952-54; participant at internat. dietetic meetings. Author 8 books; contbr. articles to profl. jours. Invitee Dietetic Assn. South Africa, Cape Town, 1974, Nutrition and Health Care Study, China, 1984; del. People to People, China, 1987; mem. nutrition study to former USSR, 1974. Recipient Sioux Award to Alumni U. of N.D., named Outstanding Alumni of U. N.D. Mem. Am. Dietetic Assn. (registered dietitian), N.D. Affiliate of Am. Dietetic Assn. (pres. 1950-59), Daughters Am. Colonists, Pi Beta Phi. Republican. Episcopalian. Home: 2407 E Country Club Dr Fargo ND 58103-5730 Office: Revell's Diet Svc 2407 E Country Club Dr Fargo ND 58103-5730

REVOR, BARBARA KAY, secondary school educator; b. Mt. Vernon, Ill., June 16, 1948; d. Russell Harold and Mary Alice (Byars) Page; m. Bryan J. Revor, Dec. 19, 1981; children: Rachel, Joshua, Jacob. BA, Okla. Bapt. U., 1971; MS in Edn., Nat. Louis U., 1991. Tchr. North Palos Sch. Dist. 117, Hickory Hills, Ill., 1971—. Mem. Nat. Coun. Tchrs. of English, Ill. Assn. Tchrs. of English, Nat. Writing Project.

REVZEN, JOEL, conductor. BS, MS, The Juilliard Sch. Music; studies with Jorge Master, Jean Martinon,Margaret Hills, Abraham Kaplan. Music dir., condr. Prince William Symphony Orch., Lake Ridge, Va.; mem. Fargo-Moorhead Symphony, Fargo, N.D., Berkshire Opera Co.; former dean St. Louis Conservatory Music. Recipient Grammy award for recording with Soprano Arleen Anger, 1993; named guest conductor of Kirov Opera, St. Petersburg, Russia, 1994, 95. Office: Fargo Moorhead Symphony 810 4th Ave S Moorhead MN 56560-2800

REXROAT, DEE ANN, publicist; b. Ames, Iowa, Feb. 6, 1960; d. William Estill Rexroat and Shirley May (Graessle) Taradash; m. James Lewis Martin, July 12, 1986 (div. Aug. 1991). BSS in Philosophy/Politics, Cornell Coll., 1982; MS in Journalism, Northwestern U., 1983; BSS in Music, Cornell Coll., 1990. Arts/entertainment writer and asst. editor. The Cedar Rapids (Iowa) Gazette, 1983-93; media rels. dir. Cornell Coll., Mt. Vernon, Iowa, 1994—; journalism instr. Kirkwood Community Coll., Cedar Rapids, 1990—. Mem. LWV (Mt. Vernon, Iowa v.p./publicist 1989-91), Kappa Tau Alpha, Phi Beta Kappa. Democrat. Office: Cornell Coll 600 1st St W Mount Vernon IA 52314-1006

REYDMAN, MELVIN MAXWELL, thoracic surgeon; b. Milw., Nov. 30, 1920; s. Saul and Rose Rebecca (Grossman) R.; m. Gladys Berger; children: Sally, Laurie. BA, U. Wis., 1941, MD, 1944. Diplomate Am. Bd. Surgery, am. Bd. Thoracic Surgery. Resident tng. surgeon Mt. Sinai Med. Ctr., Cleve., 1945-50; resident tng. thoracic surgery Met. Gen. Hosp., Cleve., 1950-52, traveling fellowship, 1952-53; fellow in cardiac surgery Univ. Hosp./Mt. Sinai Med. Ctr., Cleve., 1955-56; instr. surgery Case Western Res. Sch. Medicine, Cleve., 1953, sr. instr. surgery, 1954-60, asst. clin. prof., 1960—; pro tem chief dept. surgery Mt. Sinai Med. Ctr., 1980-81; surgeon-in-charge outpatient dept. surgery, 1993—. Achievements include patent for instruments for closed aortic valve surgery, movie-open heart surgery, mitral valve replacement. Mem. Shaker Heights Indoor Theatre, Cleve. Recipient Disting. Svc. award 50 Yrs. Svc. Ohio State Med. Assn., 1994. Mem. Cleve. Surg. Soc., Cleve. Vascular Soc. Democrat. Jewish. Home: 2950 Weybridge Rd Cleveland OH 44120 Office: Mount Sinai Med Ctr Dept Surgery One Mount Sinai Dr Cleveland OH 44120

REYES, JESUS EMMANUEL, university dean; b. Monterrey, Nuevo Leon, Mex., Nov. 24, 1952; came to U.S., 1964; s. Raul and Concepcion (Martinez) R.; 1 child, Jesus Daniel. BA in Sociology, Purdue U., 1980; MA, U. Chgo., 1985. Lic. clin. social worker, Ill.; cert. clin. social worker, Ind. Cmty. worker Ada S. McKinley Intervention Svcs., Chgo., 1982-83; family therapist, supr. vocat. awareness program Youth Guidance, Chgo., 1985-86; sr. therapist, clin. supr. child and family svcs. program Tri-City Mental Health Ctr., East Chicago, Ind., 1986-88; med. social worker St. Margaret Mercy Healthcare Ctrs., Hammond, Ind., 1988-93; asst. dean enrollment and placement Sch. Social Svc. Adminstrn., U. Chgo., 1993—; contractual home care social worker St. Margaret Mercy Healthcare Ctrs., 1989-90, on-call emergency social worker, 1989-93. Mem. NASW (cert., mem. com. on inquiry Ind. chpt. 1992—, Region I rep. to nominations and leadershp com. 1995—, Region I Social Worker of Yr. 1995). Office: Univ Chgo Sch Social Svc Adminstrn 969 E 60th St Chicago IL 60637

REYNOLDS, A. WILLIAM, manufacturing company executive; b. Columbus, Ohio, June 21, 1933; s. William Morgan and Helen Hibbard (McCray) R.; m. Joanne D. McCormick, June 12, 1953; children: Timothy M., Morgan Reynolds Brigham, Mary Reynolds Miller. AB in Econs., Harvard U., 1955; MBA, Stanford U., 1957. Pres. Crawford Door Co., Detroit, 1959-66; staff asst. to treas TRW Inc., Cleve., 1957-59, asst. to exec. v.p. automotive group, 1966-67, v.p. automotive aftermarket group, 1967-70, exec. v.p. indsl. and replacement sector, 1971-81, exec. v.p. automotive worldwide sector, 1981-84; pres. GenCorp, Akron, Ohio, 1984-85, pres., chief exec. officer, 1985-87, chmn., CEO, 1987-94, chmn., 1994-95; bd. dirs. Eaton Corp., Cleve., Boise (Idaho) Cascade Corp., Boise Cascade Office Products Corp., Itasca, Ill., Stant Corp., Richmond, Ind., Fed. Res. Bank Cleve., now chmn.; mem. dean's adv. coun. Stanford (Calif.) U. Grad. Sch. Bus., 1981-88. Chmn. United Way-Red Cross of Summit County, Ohio, 1987; trustee Univ. Hosps. of Cleve., 1984—, chmn., 1987-94. Mem. SAE, Bus. Roundtable (policy com.), Coun. on Fgn. Rels., Kirtland Country Club, Union Club, Rolling Rock Club, John's Island Club, Pepper Pike Club. Episcopalian. Office: GenCorp Inc 175 Ghent Rd Akron OH 44333-3330*

REYNOLDS, DAVID L., state legislator. Rep. dist. 77 State of Mo., Florissant. Office: State Capitol Rm 201 BA Jefferson City MO 65101

REYNOLDS, JACK W., retired utility company executive; b. Magazine, Ark., Feb. 28, 1923; s. Robert H. and Effie (Files) R.; m. Alberta Barkett, Nov. 13, 1949; children: John, David, Steven, Thomas, Laurie. B.S. in Phys. Sci., Okla. State U., 1943, B.S. in Indsl. Engring., 1947. With B.F. Goodrich Co., Akron, Ohio, 1947-75, dir. union relations, 1969-70, dir. indsl. rels., 1970-75; v.p. pers. Consumers Power Co., Jackson, Mich., 1975-78, sr. v.p. pers. and pub. affairs, 1978-81, exec. v.p. energy supply, 1981-88; pres. Mich. Gas Storage Co., Jackson, 1981-88, Plateau Resources, Ltd., Jackson, 1988; now ret. Served to 1st lt. C.E. U.S. Army, 1943-46, CBI. Republican. Methodist. Clubs: Jackson Country.

REYNOLDS, JOHN FRANCIS, insurance company executive; b. Escanaba, Mich., Mar. 29, 1921; s. Edward Peter and Lillian (Harris) R.; m. Dorothy Gustafson, May 1, 1946; children—Lois, Margaret, Michael. B.S., Mich. State U., 1942. Claims and assoc. surety mgr. Hartford Ins. Co., Escanaba, Mich. and Chgo., 1946-55; asst. v.p., bond mgr. Wolverine Ins. Co., Battle Creek, Mich., 1955-64, v.p. underwriting, 1964-69; Midwest zone underwriting mgr. Transamerica Ins. Co. (Wolverine Ins. Co.), Battle Creek, Mich., 1969-74; pres., gen. mgr. Can. Surety Co. subs. Transamerica Ins. Co., Toronto, Ont., Canada, 1974-75; v.p. midwestern zone mgr. Transamerica Ins. Group, Battle Creek, Mich., 1975-83; pres., chief operating officer Transamerica Ins. Group, Los Angeles, 1983-84, chmn., chief exec. officer, 1984-85; apptd. spl. dep. ins. commr., dep. conservator Cadillac Ins. Co., 1989; pres. Underwriting Exec. Council Midwest, 1967; dir. Underwriters Adjustment Bur., Toronto, 1974, Underwriters Labs. of Canada, Montreal, 1974; chmn. Mich. Assn. Ins. Cos., Lansing, 1976, Mich. Basic Property Ins. Assn., Detroit, 1973. Commr. City of Battle Creek, 1967-69; dir. Urban League, Battle Creek, 1969, 70, dir. Mich. Ins. Fedn., Lansing, 1975-83. Served to sgt. U.S. Army, 1942-45; New Guinea. Roman Catholic.

REYNOLDS, MARIAN K., state legislator. Senator dist. 38 State of Kans., 1993—; mgmt. analyst. in field. Republican. Home: 1300 Bristol Ave Dodge City KS 67801-3307 Office: Kans State Senate State Capitol Topeka KS 66612*

REYNOLDS, MARTIN L., state legislator; b. Feb. 8, 1950. Mayor Ladysmith, Wis., 1986-92; Wis. state assemblyman Dist. 87, 1990—; plumbing and heating contractor. Mem. VFW, NRA, Am. Legion. Address: 219 W 2d St N Ladysmith WI 54848*

REYNOLDS, NANCY HUBBARD, sociology educator; b. Norfolk, Va., Aug. 1, 1923; d. Francis Marion and Nancy Augustine (Bell) Jones; m. Lawrence James Hubbard, May 16, 1955 (dec. Nov. 1968); m. George Allen Reynolds, Feb. 19, 1970 (dec. Feb. 1971). AA, Longview Community Coll., 1974; BA, U. Mo., 1976, MA, 1979; PhD, Kans. State U., 1985. Clerical asst. U.S. Govt., 1942-67; rsch. asst., lectr. U. Mo., Kansas City, 1978-79; aging cons. North Cen.. Flint Hills Area Agy. on Aging, Manhattan, Kans., 1982-84; instr. Kans. State U., Manhattan, 1979-86, Emporia (Kans.) State U., 1986-92. Author: Older Volunteer Leaders in a Rural Community; contbr. articles to profl. jours. Bd. dirs. Hospice, 1989; hon. mem. Sr. Citizens of Marion County. Mem. Mental Health Assn. (bd. dirs. 1989), Am. Sociol. Assn., Midwest Sociol. Soc., Midwest Coun. for Social Rsch. in Aging, Nat. Assn. Retired Fed. Employees, Phi Kappa Phi, Mortar Bd.

REYNOLDS, ROBERT HUGH, lawyer; b. St. Louis, Jan. 3, 1937; s. Leslie A. and Rebecca (McWaters) R.; m. Carol Jemison, Apr. 8, 1961; children: Stephen H., Cynthia C., Laura M. BA, Yale U., 1958; JD, Harvard U., 1964. Assoc. Barnes & Thornburg, Indpls., 1964-70, ptnr., 1970—, chmn. bus. dept., 1983-91; chmn. internat. practice group, 1992—. Co-chmn., editor Comml. Real Estate Financing for Ind. Attys., 1968; vice-chmn., co-editor Advising Ind. Businesses, 1974; chmn., editor Counseling Ind. Businesses, 1981, The Purchase and Sale of a Business, 1987. Bd. dirs. Crossroads Am. Coun. Boy Scouts Am., 1970—, v.p., 1971-75, pres., 1987-89; v.p. Area 4 Ctrl. Region Boy Scouts Am., 1989-92, pres., 1992-93, pres. Ctrl. Region, 1993-96, Nat. Exec. Bd., 1993—; bd. dirs. Family Svc. Assn. Indpls., 1974-81, pres., 1978-80; bd. dirs. Family Svc. Am., 1979-88, Greater Indpls. Fgn. Trade Zone, 1987—, Indpls. Conv. and Visitors Assn., 1989—, Indpls. Econ. Devel. Corp., 1983—, exec. com., sec.; mem. Greater Indpls. Progress Com., 1986—, exec. com., vice chmn. (Charles L. Whistler award); disting. adviser, trustee Children's Mus. Indpls., 1988-96, chmn., 1992-94; mem. Indpls. Downtown Inc., 1993—; bd. gov. Legacy Fund, 1992—; bd. dirs. Noyes Mem. Found., 1986—, Japan-Am. Soc. Ind., 1988—, pres., 1994—, Terralex, co-chmn. N.Am., 1996—. Fellow Ind. Bar Found., Indpls. Bar Found.; mem. ABA, Ind. Bar Assn. (chmn. corp., banking and bus. law sect. 1981-82, chmn. internat. sect. 1994—), Internat. Bar Assn., Indpls. Bar Assn., Greater Indpls. C. of C. (bd. dirs. 1987—), Econ. Club Indpls. (bd. dirs. 1995—). Republican. Clubs: Univ., Skyline (Indpls.). Lodge: Kiwanis. Office: Barnes & Thornburg 1313 Merchants Bank Bldg 11 S Meridian St Indianapolis IN 46204-3506

REYNOLDS, RUTH CARMEN, school administrator, secondary school educator; b. Dec. 30; d. Jim and Beulah Eliza (Woods) R. BS in Math., Chgo. State U., 1973, BS in Acctg., 1983, MS in Edn., 1986; MA in Math. Edn., DePaul U., 1991. Cert. tchr., high sch. math., gen. adminstrv. Tchr. Chgo. Pub. Schs., 1973—; adminstrv. asst. South Shore Cmty. Acad., Chgo., 1995—, registrar, 1995—, dir. scheduling, grade coord., 1995—; adj. prof. Columbia Coll., Chgo., 1988-89; program officer Lindblom Tech. H.S., Chgo., 1985-95; chmn. pub. com. student sci. fair Chgo. Pub. Schs. Contbr. articles to profl. jours. Treas. Chgo. Chpt. NAAF, 1988, nat. phone contact. Frye Found. Math. fellow U. Chgo., 1991. Mem. ASCD, Nat. Coun. Tchrs. Math., Internat. Study Group Ethnomath., Ill. Coun. Tchrs. Math. (del. to Japan 1988), Nat. Coun. Suprs. Math., Notaries Assn. Ill., Benjamin Banneker Assn., Andover-Dartmouth Urban Tchr. Inst., Exeter Math. Inst., Nat. Afro-Am. Hist. and Geneal. Soc., Patricia Liddell Rschrs., Afro-Am. Geneal. and Hist. Soc. Chgo., Afro-Am. Hist. & Geneal. Soc. Washington, Nat. Coun. Negro Women, Math. Club Chgo., Phi Delta Kappa. Home: 2901 S King Dr Apt 1802 Chicago IL 60616-3315 Office: South Shore Community Acad 7529 S Constance Ave Chicago IL 60649

REYNOLDS, SALLIE BLACKBURN, artist, civic volunteer; b. Kansas City, Mo., Feb. 9, 1940; d. Anton and Sallie Churchill (Blackburn) Zajic; m. Jeffrey Calhoun Loker, Mar. 25, 1959 (div. May 1965); children: Toni Lynne, Michael David, Kathryn Lee Loker Simpson; m. Everett Lee Reynolds, Mar. 29, 1969 (dec. Sept. 1992). Student, William Jewell Coll., 1959, BA magna cum laude, 1977; student, U. Mo., Kansas City, 1966-67, Kansas City Art Inst., 1966-70; Cert., Famous Artists Sch., 1965. Cert. tchr., Mo. From clk. to sec. Hdqrs. Strategic Air Command, Offutt AFB, Omaha, 1960-62; sec., wage and hr. law enforcement asst. wage hr. div. U.S. Dept. of Labor, Kansas City, 1963-68, exec. sec. to regional manpower adminstr., 1968-71, spl. asst. to regional exec. com., 1971-72, mgmt. asst. Office of Regional Dir., 1972-73; from. clk. to sec. air carrier dist. office FAA, Kansas City, 1978-81; from clk. typist to sec. regional personnel officer Bur. of Reclamation, U.S. Dept. of Interior, Boulder City, Nev., 1982-84; editorial asst. div. of planning Bur. of Reclamation, Boulder City, 1984-86; owner, operator B-Bar-L Farms, 1990—. Editor newsletter Laurie Fine Art, 1989-90. Ofcl. commr., sec., corr. Clay County (Mo.) Bicentennial Commn., 1974-76; mem. Ozark Brush and Palette, Inc., Camdenton, Mo., 1987—, editor newsletter, 1988-89; v.p., sec. Clay County Hist. Soc., 1972—, active Nat. Wildlife Fedn. Recipient 1st Pl. award Nat. Soc. DAR Am. Heritage Contest in oil/acrylic painting, 1990, 3d pl., 1991, 1st pl. gold award 1992, 1st pl. award profl. photography Laurie Fine Art Show, 1991, miscellaneous local art show awards, 1988—. Mem. DAR (pub. rels. chmn., rec. sec., archives chmn., corr. sec. Niangua chpt. Camdenton 1987—), Nat. Oil and Acrylic Painters Soc., Phi Epsilon of Phi Beta Kappa, Versailles Saddle Club. Presbyterian. Home and Office: RR 1 Box 95A Versailles MO 65084-9724

REYNOLDS, WILLIAM JAMES, writer; b. Omaha, Dec. 17, 1956; s. William James and Rose Angela (Caliendo) R.; m. Peggy Blankenfeld, Sept. 5, 1981; children: Meredith Abbie, William Alexander. BA, Creighton U., 1979. Mng. editor TWA Ambassador mag., St. Paul, Minn., 1979-84; freelance writer St. Paul and Sioux Falls, S.D., 1984-85; v.p., creative dir. Stafford Advt., Sioux Falls, 1985-87; freelance writer Sioux Falls, 1987—. Author: (novels) The Nebraska Quotient, 1985, Moving Targets, 1987, Money Trouble, 1987, Things Invisible, 1989, The Naked Eye, 1990, Drive-By, 1995, (nonfiction) Sioux Falls: The City and the People, 1994. Named Author of the Yr., S.D. Coun. Tchrs. of English, 1987; recipient journalism award Aviation/Space Writers Assn., 1985, Gavel awards ABA, 1981-83. Mem. Author's Guild, Pvt. Eye Writers of Am., Mystery Writers of Am. (bd. dirs. 1990-94). Democrat. Roman Catholic. Home: 917 S Second Ave Sioux Falls SD 57104 Office: Ste 105-118 2601 S Minnesota Ave Sioux Falls SD 57105

REZA, ALI M., electrical engineering educator; b. Tehran, Iran, Mar. 16, 1953; s. Hossein and Huri Mogdhaddamjoo; m. Sohaila, July 15, 1977; 1 child, Salman. BS, Tehran U., 1976; MS, MIT, 1978; PhD, U. Wyo., 1986. Engr. Nuclear Rsch. Ctr., Tehran, 1978-83; instr. U. Wyo., Laramie, 1986; prof. elec. engring. U. Wis., Milw., 1986—; cons. Amoco Oil Co., Tulsa, 1986, Unical Oil Co., L.A., 1986, Rush Med. Sch., Chgo., 1987. Contbr. articles to profl. jours. Rsch. grad. scholar U. Wyo., Laramie, 1985. Office: U Wis Milw PO Box 784 Milwaukee WI 53201-0784

RHAME, FRANK SCORGIE, physician, educator; b. Pitts., Sept. 11, 1942; s. William Thomas and Thelma Grace (Scorgie) R.; m. Betsey Clark Ingraham, May 30, 1966; children: Lara, Caroline. BS, Calif. Inst. Tech., 1964; MD, Columbia U., 1968. Diplomate Am. Bd. Internal Medicine, Am. Bd. Infectious Diseases. Staff physician Palo Alto VA Med. Ctr., Calif., 1975-78; asst. prof. U. Minn., Mpls., 1979-92, assoc. prof., 1992—; physician Abbott Northwestern Hosp., 1995—. Gov.'s task force on AIDS, 1986-91, on gay and lesbian Minnesotans, 1990—. Served as asst. surgeon USPHS, 1970-72. Recipient Alex Langmuir award Epidemic Intelligence Service, 1972. Fellow Am. Coll. Epidemiologists; mem. Soc. Hosp. Epidemiologists Am. (treas. 1983-85), Infectious Diseases Soc. Am., Am. Soc. Microbiology, Am. Soc. Internal Medicine. Mem. Democratic Farm Labor Party. Avocation: running. Home: 401 S 1st St Apt # 702 Minneapolis MN 55401-2565 Office: U Minn Hosp Ctr PO Box 421 Minneapolis MN 55455

RHEE, HEASOON ARZBERGER, research chemist; b. Seoul, Korea, Mar. 6, 1958; came to U.S., 1980; d. Okyun and Kumyoung (Song) Rhee; m. Peter Arzberger, Dec. 20, 1986. BS, Sookmyung Womens' U., Seoul, 1980; MS, U. Wis., 1984, PhD, 1989. Teaching asst. U. Wis., Madison, 1984-86, instr., 1986-87, rsch. asst., 1987-90; sr. rsch. chemist Internat. Fabricare Inst., Silver Spring, Md., 1990-94; dir. tech. info. R.R. St. & Co. Inc., Naperville, Ill., 1994—; cons. Smithsonian Mus., Suitland, Md., 1990—. Vol. Internat. Visitors Info. Svc., Washington, 1989. Mem. ASTM, Am. Assn. Textile Colorists and Chemists (chaur tech. com. 1993—), Am. Chem. Soc. Home: 11551 Petenwell Rd San Diego CA 92131

RHEE, YANG HO, radiologist; b. Kunsan, Republic of Korea, Mar. 22, 1943; came to U.S., 1973; s. Young Whan and Ae Wol (Rah) R.; m. Shin Ae Kang; children: Hoyeon, Thomas, Karen. MD, Chonnam Med. Sch., Kwangju, Republic of Korea, 1968. Diplomate Am. Bd. Radiology. Intern Seoul Adventist Hosp., Republic of Korea, 1972-73, Cook County Hosp., Chgo., 1973-74; resident Hines (Ill.) VA Hosp., 1974-77; staff physician Illini Hosp., Silvis, Ill., 1977—. Chmn. bd. trustees Quad City Korean Assn., Ill. and Iowa, 1986-88, v.p., 1980-81; mem. adv. coun. on peaceful unification policy Republic of Korea, 1984-93; chmn. dept. radiology Ilini Hosp., Silvis, Ill., 1988—. Capt. Korean Army, 1968-72, Korea and Vietnam. Mem. AMA, Am. Coll. Radiology, Radiol. Soc. N.Am., Soc. Nuclear Medicine, Am. Inst. Ultasound in Medicine, Am. Roentgen Ray Soc. Office: 801 Hospital Rd Silvis IL 61282-1804

RHEM, LAUNY FREDERIQUE, marketing communication executive; b. Chgo., Mar. 11, 1957; s. Launy Sr. and Marine (McCloud) R. BA, DePaul U., 1982; postgrad., Columbia Coll., 1983-84. Account mgr. Xerox Corp., Chgo., 1988-90; pres., dir. mktg. and promotions Urban Entertainment Mktg., Chgo., 1990—; pres., CEO RHEM Comm. Group. Recipient Profl. Achievement award Young Men's Orgn., 1981. Mem. Chgo. Adv. Club (Excellence award 1981), Am. Mktg. Assn., U.S. Jaycees (pres. South End chpg. 1990, Outstanding Leadership Ability).

RHEW, PERRY JAMES, judge; b. Kennett, Mo., Jan. 15, 1959; s. James Atlas and Nina Louise (Breedon) R. BS in Psychology/Biology, Southeast Mo. State U., Cape Girardeau, 1980; JD, UMKC Sch. Law, Kansas City, 1983. Lic. Mo., 1983. Pub. defender State of Mo., Kennett, 1983-84; asst. prosecuting atty. Dunklin County, Kennett, Mo., 1985-86; prosecuting atty., 1986-90; adjunct prof. Bus. Law Southeast Mo. State U., Cape Girardeau, 1987-89; assoc. circuit judge 35th Judicial Circuit, Kennett, Mo., 1990—; bd. dirs. Family Counseling Ctr., Kennett, Mo., 1986-90, Stapleton Detoxification Ctr., Kennett, Mo., 1986-90, Ctr. for Family Resources, Malden, Mo., 1986-90, Cmty. Caring Counsel, Kennett, Mo., 1993—. Author: eight published plays. Elected prosecuting atty., 1986, elected assoc. circuit judge, Dunklin Co. Mo., Kennett, 1990, 94. Recipient Young Alumni Merit award Southeast Mo. State U., Cape Girardeau, Mo., 1993, Denman Dist. Evangelism award United Meth. Ch., 1993. Mem. Mo. Bar Assn., Dunklin County Bar, Lions Club Internat. Mem. United Meth. Ch. Office: Circuit Ct Divsn III PO Box 466 Kennett MO 63857

RHOAD, RICHARD ARTHUR, secondary school educator, writer; b. Tiffin, Ohio, May 7, 1935; s. Cecil Feree and Iva Grace (Spitler) R. BA, Heidelberg U., 1956; MEd, Ohio U., 1957; postgrad., Bowling Green (Ohio) State U., 1958, U. N.Mex., Albuquerque, 1960-63, Rhode Island State U., 1964, DePauw U., 1966, Ohio State, 1991, Roosevelt U., 1991. Tchr. Avon Lake (Ohio) High Sch., 1957-60; thcr. Homewood-Flossmoor (Ill.) High Sch., 1960-66, New Trier High Sch., Winnetka, Ill., 1966—; chmn. math. contest Ill. Coun. Tchrs. of Math., 1978-84. Writer and singer several original math. songs; contbr. articles to profl. jours. Mem. NEA (life), Ill. Edn. Assn., Nat. Coun. Tchrs. of Math. (life), Ill. Coun. Tchrs. of Math., Ohio Coun. Tchrs. of Math. (life), Sch. Sci. and Maths. (life), Phi Delta Kappa (life). Home: 1517 Elmwood Ave Wilmette IL 60091-1652 Office: New Trier H S 385 Winnetka Ave Winnetka IL 60093-4238

RHOADES, GENE J., software engineering director; b. New Castle, Ind., Apr. 30, 1949. B, Purdue U., 1971; M in Applied Mechanics, U. Bridgeport, 1975. Software programmer S.D.R.C., Milford, Ohio, 1976-82; software project mgr. Applicon Inc., Cin., 1982-85; dir. engring. software I.T.I., Milford, 1985—. Basketball coord. C.N.E.A.A., Owensville, Ohio, 1992—.

RHOADS, HARVEY DONALD, chiropractor; b. California, Mo., Sept. 19, 1951; s. D.R. and Edrie Y. (Schweer) R.; m. Patricia M. Gruenewald, Nov. 3, 1990; children Grant A., Kevin Gruenewald. BSBA, Washington U., 1980, MBA, 1980; D of Chiropractic, Logan Coll. Chiropractic, 1989. Employee, foreman, quality control analyst Chrysler Corp., Fenton, Mo., 1973-79; registered sales rep. Edward D. Jones & Co., Maryland Heights, Mo., 1980-81, mgmt. trainee, 1981-82, mgr. margin dept., 1982-85, mgr. ctrl. svcs., 1982-85; chiropractor Troy, Mo., 1990—. Mem. Troy C. of C. (pres. 1995), Rotary (immediate past pres. Troy chpt. 1994). Office: 103 Tyme Sq Troy MO 63379

RHOADS, PATRICIA MARY (GRUENEWALD), securities consultant; b. St. Louis, Mar. 17, 1953; m. Harvey D. Rhoads; children: Kevin G. Gruenewald, Grant A. BSBA, U. Mo., St. Louis, 1975; MA in Computer Data Mgmt., Webster U., 1985. Mgr. estates and legal securities Edward D. Jones & Co., St. Louis, 1978-80, mgr. money market fund processing, 1980-84, mgr. mut. fund processing, 1983-84, mgr., gen. prin. funds processing and daily passport cash trust, 1984-88, mgr. trade processing, 1989-93; ind. contractor Bridgeton, Mo., 1994—; mem. broker/dealer adv. com. Investment Co. Inst., Washington, 1987-88; mem. retail adv. bd. Chgo. Stock Exch., 1990-93; ind. contractor Coopers and Lybrand Internat., Rep. of Latvia, 1994. Bd. dirs. CORO, St. Louis, 1990-91; mem. day care svcs. panel United Way, 1990-94, mem. admissions com., 1993—; candidate for Bridgeton City Coun., 1995. Mem. NAFE, Bus. and Profl. Women of Troy.

RHODES, BETTY FLEMING, rehabilitation services professional, nurse; b. Franklin, Pa., Nov. 28, 1920; d. John and Twyla Odella (Callen) Fleming; m. Donald Muir Cain, Dec. 31, 1952 (div.); m. Lee Chester Rhodes, June 23, 1962. RN, Allegheny Gen. Hosp., Pitts., 1942. Lic. phys. therapist, Pa. Phys. therapist Ky. Soc. for Crippled Children, Louisville, 1947-51, St. Anthony Hosp., Louisville, 1953-78. Nurse U.S. Army, 1943-45; capt. Army Nurse Corps, 1951-52. Decorated Bronze Star. Mem. Am. Phys Therapy Assn. (pres. Ky. chpt.). Roman Catholic. Home: 5 Woodland Road Oak Pk Jeffersonville IN 47130

RHODES, HELEN MARY, real estate broker, educator; b. Ft. Branch, Ind., Jan. 12, 1921; d. Henry A. and Anna J. (Herr) Wirth; m. David A. I, May 3, 1952; children: David A. II and Brooke Anthony. Grad., Lockyear Coll., 1939, Real Estate Inst., 1981. Grad. Realtors Inst. Clk. War Dept., Washington, 1942-44; stenographer OSS, Washington (D.C.), 1944-45; clk. Dept. of Fgn. Svc., London, 1945-46; asst. sales mgr. printing and advt. Keller Crescent Co., Evansville, Ind., 1946-52; stenographer Indpls. Air Procurement, Evansville, 1952-53; asst. media dir. Grant Advt., 1953-56; freelance writer, 1955-70; prin. real estate Columbus, Ohio, 1970—; real estate instr. Columbus State Community Coll., 1977—. Author: Josie's Bedtime Stories, 1966; writer Chicago Heights Star, Ill., 1961-61; contbr. articles to profl. jours. Pub. rels. officer Sauk Village, Ill., 1962. Mem. Nat. Assn. Realtors, Ohio Assn. Realtors, Columbus Bd. Realtors, Nat. Real Estate Educators Assn. (charter), Ohio Real Estate Educators Assn.

RHODES, JACQUELINE YVONNE, marketing executive; b. Fairfield, Ala., Mar. 3, 1949; d. Lee Oliver and Jimmye Lucille (Warren) Rhodes. Student pub. schs., Cleve. Bus. services rep. Ohio Bell Telephone Co., Cleve., 1969-73, bus. officer instr., 1973-74, spl. communications cons., 1974-76, account exec. II, 1976-80, personnel mgr., 1980-82; account exec. American Bell, Cleve., 1983; dir. sales and mktg. Psychassess, Inc., Cleve., 1983-84 ; telecommunications analyst Clev. Clinic Found., 1985—; sec. Turner & Knight, Inc., Cleve., 1981-83. Vice pres. Harambee: Services to Black Families, Cleve., 1983. Mem. Nat. Assn. Female Execs., Citizens' League,

Women's City Club. Baptist. Home: 17722 Tarkington Ave Cleveland OH 44128-3961

RHODES, JIM, state legislator; b. Apr. 1942; m. Judy Rhodes. AA, U. Minn. Minn. state rep. Dist. 44B, 1993—; retail gen. mgr. Address: Rm 313 State Office Bldg Saint Paul MN 55155

RHODES, MARLENE RUTHERFORD, counseling educator, educational consultant; b. St. Louis; d. Odie Douglas and Helen (Ward) Rutherford; m. David L. Rhodes, Nob. 18, 1961; children: Jay David, Michael Stanford, John David, Mark Stanford. BS in Psychology cum laude, Washington U., St. Louis, 1973, MA in Counseling Edn., 1975; postgrad., St. Louis U., 1987—. Registered med. record libr. Caseworker I and II, Mo. Div. Family Svcs., St. Louis, 1961-65, supr. caseworker II's, 1965-70; personal effectiveness trainer women's program U. Mo., St. Louis, 1974-77; assoc. prof. counseling, chair counseling St. Louis C.C. at Forest Park, 1975—, chmn. dept., 1993—, dir. step up coll. program, 1990-93; developer, coord. crisis intervention facilitation tng. St. Louis Pub. Schs., 1987-88; ednl. project cons. Project Achievement, Ralston Purina Co., 1993-94; developer, presenter over 80 ednl. project consultations for area colls., profl. orgns. and bus. groups, 1975—. Author: Crisis Intervention Facilitation Training Manual, 1988. Chmn. Ft. Louis Friends of Arts, 1984—; coord. for coun. of elders for Better Family Life Orgn., 1995—; com. co-chmn. for black dance and unity ball Better Family Inc., St. Louis, 1990—; panelist for counseling support svcs. for families United Way Greater St. Louis, 1993—; mem. fin. com. St. Thomas Archdiocese, 1995—; bd. dirs. Bishop Hearly Cath. Sch. Recipient Disting. Svc. as Am. Educator award Alpha Zeta chpt. Iota Phi Lambda, 1990, role model award St. Louis Pub. Schs., 1993, cert. of achievement Nat. Orgn. for Victim Assistance, 1993. Mem. NEA (co-coord. polit. action com. St. Louis 1985-90, bargaining negotiator 1987—), ACA (nat. chair orgn., adminstrn. and mgmt. com. 1994-95), Assn. Multicultural Counseling and Devel. (nat. pres. 1994-95), Nat. Assn. for Multicultural Counseling and Devel. (rep. for 13 states 1990-92, pres. 1994-95, Exemplary Svc. award 1992, 94), Mo. Assn. Multicultural Counseling and Devel. (chpt. pres. 1977-78). Democrat. Roman Catholic. Home: 5935 Pershing Ave Saint Louis MO 63112-1513 Office: St Louis CC at Forest Park 5600 Oakland Ave Saint Louis MO 63110-1316

RHODES, ORAN WAYNE, religious educator; b. Santa Anna, Tex., July 21, 1942; s. Oran Doyal and Mertie Leota (Jones) R.; m. Sandra Lavern Trussell, Apr. 8, 1966; children: Renee, Kevin, Tracey Lee, Mark. BS, McMurry Coll., 1964; MEd, Hardin-Simmons U., 1967. Cert. tchr. secondary edn., sch. administrn., Tex. Tchr., coach Clyde (Tex.) Ind. Schs., 1964-66; tchr., sch. adminstr. Moffat County Schs., Craig, Colo., 1966-70; minister Ch. of Christ, Craig, Clyde, N.C., Sayre, Okla., West Plains & Sugar Creek, Mo., 1966—; tchr. Sayre Jr. Coll., 1977-78; dir., instr. Midwestern Sch. of Preaching, Sugar Creek, 1993—; speaker ann. Denton (Tex.) Lectrs., 1984, 85, 87, 92, 95; speaker, dir. El Paso (Tex.) Lectrs., 1984-92, Killeen (Tex.) Lectrs., 1986; speaker Ch. of Christ nationwide, 1972—. Editor Back to Basics jour., 1982, Sound Words jour., 1983-96; author: (books) God's Way for the Home, 1979, Beatitudes for Living, 1995. Campaign worker Rep. Party, Eastland, Tex., 1964; officer Jaycees, Eastland, Tex., 1962-65. Home: 17523 East RD Mize Rd Independence MO 64054 Office: Midwestern Sch Preaching 10800 Kentucky Sugar Creek MO 64054

RHODES, ROBERT CHARLES, cable company executive, consultant; b. Hannibal, Mo., Apr. 8, 1926; s. William Cleveland and Callie Lee (DeLaporte) R.; m. Doris Marie Priest, Oct. 12, 1947; children: Martha Rhodes Figley, Carol Rhodes Tempel, Robert Charles Jr. BA, Drury Coll., 1962. Communications engr. Southwestern Bell Telephone, Springfield, Mo., 1949-65; regional mgr. United Telephone, Pa., 1966-70; dir. mktg. United Transmission, Kansas City, Mo., 1970-72; pres. Met. Cable TV Mgmt., Kansas City, 1972-76, Higginsville, Mo., 1976-82; pres. R.C. Rhodes Investments, Higginsville, 1982—. Del. Nat. Republican Conv., New Orleans, 1988. With Mo. N.G., 1943-44. Mem. Springfield Jr. C. of C. (pres. 1962-67), Mo. Jr. C. of C. (Young Man of Yr. 1963), Nat. Pachyderms (v.p. 1986—), Pachyderm Club (pres. Lafayette County, Mo. chpt. 1981), Shriners. Republican. Methodist. Home and Office: PO Box 504 Higginsville MO 64037-0504

RHODES, ROYAL WILLIAM, religion educator; b. Brookline, Mass., Aug. 19, 1946; s. Royal Herbert and Rita Louise (Welch) R. AB, Fairfield (Conn.) U., 1968; BD, Yale U., 1971; PhD, Harvard U., 1979. From asst. to assoc. prof. religion Kenyon Coll., Gambier, Ohio, 1979-94, prof., 1994—. Author: The Lion and the Cross, 1995; co-author: The Faith of Christians, 1984, Eclipse of Justice, 1992. Chair ethics com. Knox County Hospice, Mt. Vernon, Ohio, 1990—; mem. ethics com. Knox Community Hosp., Mt. Vernon, 1991—. Mem. Coll. Theology Soc., Liturgical Arts Guild, Ohio Acad. Religion. Roman Catholic. Home: 106 W Woodside Dr Gambier OH 43022 Office: Kenyon Coll College Park St Gambier OH 43022

RHODES, STEVE NEIL, journalist; b. Mpls., Jan. 26, 1965; s. Sheldon Gene and Frances (Tanick) R. BA, U. Minn., 1989; MA, Northwestern U., 1993, masters cert. in telecomm., 1993. Mng. editor The Minn. Daily, Mpls., 1986-89; reporter, intern New Haven (Conn.) Register, 1989; reporter The Ledger, Lakeland, Fla., 1989-91, The Courier, Waterloo, Iowa, 1991-92; editor Pure Mag., Chgo., 1993—; reporter Chgo. Tribune, 1993-94; stringer Newsweek, Chgo., 1994—; editor/newsletter Midwest Human Resources Group, Chgo, 1993—; staff asst. Newspaper Mgmt. Ctr., Evanston, 1992—. Contbr. articles to profl. publs. Recipient Best Coll. Daily, Soc. Profl. Journalists, Best Spot News, 1988; Mpls. Star Tribune scholar U. Minn., 1987, Scottish Rite Journalism scholar, 1986, Bloomington scholar Bloomington Jefferson H.S., 1983. Mem. Minn. Daily Alumni Assn., Franklin Soc. Jewish.

RHODES, SUZANNE RUTH, computer specialist, property administrator; b. Mason City, Iowa, Mar. 28, 1945; d. Maynard Westly and Alice Ruth (Jacobson) Olson; m. Laurence D. Rhodes Jr., Apr. 15, 1965; children: Laurie Sue, Lynda Michelle. AA in Liberal Arts, Inver Hills C.C., 1989; BSBA, U. Wis., River Falls, 1992. Clk. Coope, Eau Claire, Wis., 1969; mgr., owner Sue's Day Care, Kent, Wash., 1971-88; dairy lab. technicion Dairy Head Improvement Assn., Menomonie, Wis., 1978-88; asst. database adminstr. Nat. Computer Systems, Eagan, Minn., 1993-94; mgr., acct. Rhodes Rental, Roseville, Minn., 1988—; computer specialist U. Minn., Mpls., 1994-95; coord. computer help desk Reli Star, Mpls., 1995—. Leader 4-H, Menomonie, 1963-68, Kent, Wash., 1976-78; mem. Nat. Day Care Orgn., Kent, 1971-78. Mem. Acad. Computing. Lutheran. Home: 2020 Asbury St Roseville MN 55113

RHODES ROWLEY, MARY LOUISE, school psychologist; b. Indpls., Oct. 11, 1943; d. Thomas Sr. and Julia Ann (Hutchins) R.; m. Virgil C. Rowley, Feb. 19, 1968; 1 child, Ayana Kai. BA, Purdue U., 1972; MS, Chgo. State U., 1975. Reading tchr. Deer Creek Jr. H.S., Park Forest, Ill., 1973-75; sch. psychologist Indpls. Pub. Schs., 1975-91; founder, exec. dir. Rhodes Rowley Corp., Indpls., 1992—; counselor Marion County Jail, Indpls.; publicist Brebuef Girls Swimming & Diving, Indpls. Fund raiser Sec. State Pam Carter. Mem. Toastmasters Internat., Jack & Jill, Black Psychologists Assn. Methodist. Office: Rhodes Rowley Corp PO Box 68371 Indianapolis IN 46268

RHONE, DOUGLAS PIERCE, pathologist, educator; b. Bloomsburg, Pa., Mar. 27, 1940; s. Wilbur Clayton and Marian Faye (Shaffer) R.; m. Leta Daiva Budelskis, Sept. 27, 1969; children: Jennifer Ann, Todd Brader. BS, Ill. Benedictine U., 1965; MD, MS in Pathology, U. Ill., 1969. Diplomate Am. Bd. Pathology. Attending pathologist Ill. Masonic Med. Ctr., Chgo., 1976, chmn. dept. pathology, 1976—; asst. prof. pathology U. Ill. Coll. Medicine, Chgo., 1976-80, assoc. prof. pathology, 1980—; dir. residency pathology Ill. Masonic Med. Ctr., Chgo., 1976-90, U. Ill. Metro. Hosps., Chgo., 1990—; assoc. dir. med. affairs, 1992-95, Ill. Masonic Med. Ctr. Pathologists, S.C., Chgo., 1977—, Lab. Cons., Ltd., Chgo., 1977—. Contbr. articles to profl. jours. Maj. U.S. Army, 1974-76. Recipient Raymond B. Allen award U. Ill. Coll. Medicine, 1979, 80, 95, C. Thomas Bombeck award, 1991. Fellow Am. Soc. Clin. Pathologists (Sheard-Sanford Rsch. award 1969), Coll. Am. Pathologists; mem. Chgo. Pathology Soc., Ill. Soc. Pathologists. Roman Catholic. Home: 222 S Spring Ave La Grange IL 60525-2243 Office: Ill Masonic Med Ctr Dept Pathology 836 W Wellington Ave Chicago IL 60657

RHUETAN, CHARLES W., mechanical engineer; b. Salem, Ohio, May 14, 1945. BS in Mech. Engring., Tri-State U., 1969. Student Electric Furnace Co., Salem, Ohio, 1963-69; field svc. engr. Electric Furnace Co. Salem, 1969-73; chief engr. Topco Sewage Treatment Equipment, Salem, 1972-77; sr. project engr. Indsl. Furnace Svcs. Inc., Streetsboro, Ohio, 1985-91; project engr. Electric Furnace Co., Salem, 1991—. Coach Little League Baseball Boys, Salem, 1993—. Home: 33871 Hoopes Rd Salem OH 44460-9440 Office: Electric Furnace Co 435 W Wilson St Salem OH 44460-2767

RIAHI, DANIEL NOUROLLAH, mathematics educator, researcher; b. Shahrekord, Chahar, Iran, Oct. 30, 1943; came to U.S., 1968; s. Ali Mohammed and Gohar Taj (Ale-ebrahim) R.; m. Eglantina Perez, May 24, 1984. MS, Fla. State U., 1970, PhD, 1974. Rsch. assoc. Fla. State U., Tallahassee, 1974-77; instr. Winthrop Coll., Rock Hills, S.C., 1977-78; sr. researcher U. Calif., L.A., 1978-80; vis. asst. prof. U. Ill., Urbana, 1980-82, asst. prof., 1982-85, assoc. prof., 1985-95, prof., 1995—; invited lectr. in field. Contbr. over 155 articles to profl. jours. Grantee NSF, NCSA, UIUC-CRB. Fellow AIAA (assoc.); mem. Am. Acad. Mechanics, Am. Phys. Soc., Soc. Indsl. and Applied Math., Sigma Xi. Office: U Ill Dept Applied Mechanics 104 S Wright St Urbana IL 61801-2935

RIBAR, DIXIE LEE, nursing administrator; b. Albia, Iowa, June 22, 1938; d. Eugene Guy Clark and Margaret Ellen (Edwards) De Joode; m. John David Ribar, Aug. 22, 1959 (div. 1981); children: Michael, Christopher, Patrick. Diploma, St. Joseph Hosp. Sch. Nursing, Ottumwa, Iowa, 1959; BSN, U. Dubuque, 1987, MSN, 1991. RN, Iowa; cert. emergency room nurse; cert. emergency med. technician, Iowa. Staff nurse Ottumwa Hosp., 1959-60; surg. staff nurse Jane Lamb Hosp., Clinton, Iowa, 1960-67; dir. nursing ICU-CCU Jane Lamb Health Ctr., Clinton, Iowa, 1967-79, dir. cardiac rehab., 1980-86; instr. edn. Samaritan Health Ctr., Clinton, 1986-91; nurse mgr. Asbury-Salina (Kans.) Regional Med. Ctr., 1991-92; assoc. chief nursing svc. ambulatory care VA Med. Ctr., Knoxville, Iowa, 1992-93, chief ambulatory care svcs., 1993—; internat. edn. cons. Am.-Mideast Ednl. and Tng. Svcs., 1989-90; contractual instr. med. svcs. Emergency Learning Resources Ctr., Univ. Iowa Hosp., Iowa City, 1976-90, Ea. Iowa Community Coll., Davenport, Iowa, 1978-90, Marycrest Coll., Davenport, 1986-90; parmedic River Cities Ambulance Co., Clinton, 1987-90; presenter in field. Contbr. articles to profl. jours. Bd. dirs. Clinton County Heart Assn., 1976-90; coord. emergency med. tech. program Clinton Fire Dept., 1980-88; med. missionary 1st Congl. Ch. Clinton, Ghana, 1983. Mem. ANA, Emergency Nurses Assn., Kans. Emergency Nurses Assn., Iowa Nurses Assn. Republican. Roman Catholic. Home: 905 W Robinson St Knoxville IA 50138-2822 Office: VA Med Ctr 1515 W Pleasant St Knoxville IA 50138-3354

RIBAUDO, ANTHONY D., state legislator; b. St. Louis, Nov. 21, 1941; m. Tina Mancuso, 1969; 1 child, Tony. Student, Wash. U. Mem. and majority leader Mo. State Ho. of Reps. Dist. 65; committeeman, former chmn. 24th Ward Dem. City Ctrl. Com., St. Louis; mem. 15th, 23rd and 28th coms. Mo. State Ho. of Reps. Recipient Outstanding Legis. award St. Louis Globe-Dem., 1981; Danforth Found. fellow Program for Sr. Exec. in State and Local Govt., Harvard's John F. Kennedy Sch. Govt., 1985. Mem. Am. Legion, Profl. and Businessman's Club of the Hill, Hill 2000, KC. Home: 5440 Daggett Ave Saint Louis MO 63110-2714*

RIBBY, ALICE MARIE, nurse; b. Lowell, Mich., Oct. 16, 1943; d. Merle Levi and Merleen Maude (Gooden) Bickford; children: Bobette Morgan, Mylie Wasylewski, Joseph R. Ribby, Barbara A. Cupp. AD in Gen. Edn. cum laude, Lansing (Mich.) Community Coll., 1975, AS in Nursing cum laude, 1976; BA in Family Life Edn., Spring Arbor Coll., 1990. Nurse ICU Ingham Med. Ctr., Lansing, Mich., 1976-81; nurse acute and chronic hemo and peritoneal dialysis Sparrow Hosp., Lansing, Mich., 1983-84; head nurse, alternate CEO Community Dialysis Ctr., Jackson, Mich., 1984-87, dir. Continuous Ambulatory Peritoneal Dialysis Program; dialysis cons. Cmty. Dialysis Ctr.; nurse adolescent in-patient psychiatry unit and geriatric psychiatry St. Lawrence Hosp., Diamondale and Lansing, Mich., 1990-95; co-founder, co-owner, nurse therapist Ptnrs. Psychol. Svcs., Lansing, 1994—; nurse cons., mental health therapist OBRA program Cmty. Mental Health-Older Adults Svcs., Lansing, 1996—; lectr. in field, preenter workshops and seminars on childhood sexual abuse; founder One Another's Support Group. Mem. Am. Assn. Christian Counselors, Profl. Staff Devel. Orgn. Republican. Address: 301 Ann St Mason MI 48854-1203

RICE, CHARLES DALE, labor relations specialist, writer; b. Coulterville, Ill., Sept. 6, 1934; s. Eugene Frank and Mildred Elizabeth (Patton) R.; m. Donna JoAnn Schnoeker, Feb. 8, 1958; children: Scott Alan, Stacy Lynn, Sherri Renee. AS, So. Ill. U., 1963. Spray painter Empire Stove Works, Belleville, Ill., 1952-53; top assembler Fisher Body Corp., St. Louis, 1953-62; coal miner Midland Coal Co., Marissa, Ill., 1962-64; surface coal miner Southwestern Ill. Coal Corp., Percy, Ill., 1964-74; pres. United Mine Workers Am., Percy, 1974-80; supr. human resources Arch of Ill. Coal Corp., Percy, 1980-85, mgr. labor rels., 1985-94; labor rels. cons. Arch of Ill. Coal Corp., Percy, Ill., 1994-96; ret. Arch of Ill. Coal Corp., Percy, 1996. Ret. capt. Steeleville (Ill.) Vol. Fire Dept., 1970-89. Cpl. U.S. Army, 1957-63. Mem. Am. Arbitration Assn., Ill. Labor Reps. Group. Lutheran. Office: Puxico Rd Box 167 Percy IL 62272

RICE, CINDY G., foundation development director; b. Kansas City, Mo., Mar. 13, 1951; d. Victor Eugene and Treva Irene (Glancy) Hutchison; m. Rex Dale Rice, May 22, 1971; children: Ami Rae, Lori Janelle. BS in English and Psychology cum laude, S.W. Bapt. U., Bolivar, Mo., 1973, Teaching Cert., 1976. Receptionist, office worker S.W. Bapt. U., Bolivar, Mo., 1970-77, libr. asst., 1971-73, student pers. sec., 1973-77, career placement sec., 1981-90, estate planning sec., 1990-92, dir. found. devel., 1992—; newsletter com. S.W. Bapt. U., Bolivar, 1993-95, homecoming com., 1993—. Mem. Nat. Soc. Fundraising Execs., Alpha Chi. Republican. Baptist. Office: SW Bapt U 1600 University Ave Bolivar MO 65613

RICE, DAVID LEE, university president emeritus; b. New Market, Ind., Apr. 1, 1929; s. Elmer J. and Katie (Tate) R.; m. Betty Jane Fordice, Sept. 10, 1950; children: Patricia Denise Rice Dawson, Michael Alan. B.S., Purdue U., 1951, M.S., 1956, Ph.D., 1958; degree (hon.), U. Evansville, 1994, U. So. Ind., 1995; LHD, U. Evansville, 1994; LLD, U. So. Ind., 1995. Dir. prof. research Ball State U., Muncie, Ind., 1958-66; v.p. Coop. Ednl. Research Lab., Inc., Indpls., 1965-67; research coordinator, bur. research HEW, Washington; dean campus Ind. State U., Evansville, 1967-71, pres. campus, 1971-85; pres. U. So. Ind., Evansville, 1985-94, pres. emeritus, 1994—; adminstrv. asst. Gov.'s Com. on Post High Sch. Orgn. Contbr. articles to profl. jours. Past mem. State Citizens Adv. Bd. Title XX Social Securtity Act; bd. dirs., past pres. bd. commrs. Evansville Houseing Auth.; pres. Leadership Evansville, 1978-79; bd. dirs., past pres. S.W. Ind. Pub. TV, 1972—; chair Indian Pub. Broadcasting Sts., 1990-93; bd. dirs. Villages Inc.; mem. Buffalo Trace Coun. Boy Scouts Am., 1963ú, New Harmony Commn., 1989-94; chair So. Ind. Rural Devel. Project., Inc.; bd. trustees Owen-Maclure Found. and RappGranary-Owen Found.; bd. dirs. So. Ind. Higher Edn. Inc., U. So. Ind. Found. With inf. U.S. Army, 1951-53. Decorated Bronze Star, Combat Infantryman's Badge; recipient Svc. to Others award Salvation Army, 1974, Citizen of Yr. award Westside Civitan Club, 1972, Boss of Yr. award Am. Bus. Women's Assn., 1976, Disting. Citizen of Yr. award Ivy Tech State Coll., 1994; David L. Rice Libr./U. So. Ind. named in his honor, 1994. Mem. Am. Assn. Higher Edn., Am. Ednl. Rsch. Assn., Am. Assn. State Colls. and Univs., Nat. Soc. Study Edn., Met. Evansville C. of C. (dir.), Evansville Kennel Club, Petroleum Club, Columbia Club, Rotary (civic award Evansville club 1985, life), Alpha Kappa Psi, Alpha Zeta, Phi Delta Kappa. Methodist. Home: 1223 S Main St New Harmony IN 47631 Office: Neef Lesueur House 404 Church St New Harmony IN 47631

RICE, DOUGLAS CHAPMAN, management consultant; b. Weymouth, Mass., May 5, 1954; s. Emery Kenniston and Doris Vaughn (Chapman) R.; m. Melanie Sue Carter, Sept. 3, 1989. AB, Dartmouth Coll., 1976; MBA, Harvard U., 1984. Economist Data Resources Inc., Lexington, Mass., 1977-80; cons. Strategic Info., Burlington, Mass., 1980-82; mgr. product devel. United Airlines Inc., Elk Grove, Ill., 1984-88; v.p. Graycon Group Inc., Schaumburg, Ill., 1988-95; pres. Stratus Mgmt. Group, Inc., Inverness, Ill., 1995—. George F. Baker scholar Harvard U., 1984. Mem. Dartmouth Club Chgo. (bd. dirs. 1994—).

RICE, FERILL JEANE, writer, civic worker; b. Hemingford, Nebr., July 4, 1926; d. Derrick and Helen Agnes (Moffatt) Dalton; m. Otis LaVerne Rice, Mar. 7, 1946; children: LaVeria June McMichael, Larry L. Student, U. Omaha, 1961. Dir. jr. and sr. choir Congl. Ch., Tabor, Iowa, 1952-66; tchr. Fox Valley Tech. Inst., Appleton, Wis., 1970-77; activity dir. Family Heritage Nursing Home, Appleton, Wis., 1972-75; dir. activity Peabody Manor, Appleton, Wis., 1975-76. Editor: Moffatt and Related Families, 1981; asst. editor (mag.) Yester-Year, 1975-76; contbr. articles to profl jours. Chmn. edn. Am. Cancer Soc., Fremont County, 1962, 63, 64; founder, 1st pres. Mothers Club Nishna Valley chpt. Demolay for Boys. Mem. DAR, Internat. Carnival Glass Assn., Heart Am. Carnival Glass Assn., Nat. Cambridge Collectors, Heisey Collectors Am., Iowa Fedn. Women's Clubs (Fremont county chmn. 1964, 65, 66, 67, 7th dist. chmn. libr. svcs. 1966-67), Tabor Women's Club (pres. 1962, 63, 64), Jr. Legion Aux. (founder, 1st dir. 1951-52), Fenton Art Glass Collectors Am. (co-founder 1977, sec., editor newsletter 1976-86, editor/sec. 1988-93, pres./editor 1993-95, treas. 1995—), Mayflower Soc., John Howland Soc., Ross County Ohio Geneal. Soc., Iowa Geneal. Soc., Dallas County Mo. Geneal. Soc., Imperial Collectors Am., Clay County (Ind.) Geneal. Soc., Owen County (Ind.) Geneal. Soc., Fenton Finders of Wis. (chpt. #1 pres. 1988-90). Republican. Methodist: Lodges: Order Ea. Star (worthy matron 1956, 64), Rainbow for Girls (bd. dirs. 1964), Internat. Order Job's Daus. (honored queen 1945). Home: 302 Pheasant Run Kaukauna WI 54130-1802 Office: Rice Enterprises & Rice & Rice 1665 Lamers Dr # 305 Little Chute WI 54140-2519

RICE, JAMES I., state legislator; b. Oct. 1925; m. Jill Rice; 8 children. SLA, U. Minn. Mem. Minn. Ho. of Reps. St. Paul, 1971—; mem. labor mgmt. rels. com., ways and means com., econ. devel. com., chmn. econ. devel. com., infrastructure com., regulation fin. com., mem. other coms.; fin. writer. Democrat. Home: 381 State Office Building Bldg Saint Paul MN 55155-1201*

RICE, JOHN ROBIN, music educator, singer; b. Longview, Tex., July 12, 1958; s. William Yngve and Rachel (Gallenkamp) R. BM, Baylor U., Waco, Tex., 1981; MM, U. Cin., 1984, DMA, 1993. Tchg. asst. U. Cin., Ohio, 1985-87; lectr. No. Ky. U., Cold Spring, 1986-87; assoc. prof. Ohio State U., Columbus, 1987—; guest vocal coach Fla. Grand Opera, Miami, 1994—, Utah Opera, Salt Lake City, 1994; guest artist, tchr. Assoc. Tchrs. of Singing, Cardiff, Wales, 1996; judge N.A.T.S., 1987—. Recipient Alumni Series award Baylor U., Waco, 1991, Nat. Semi-Finalist award NATSAA, Tampa, 1994; Outstanding Tchr. award Sphynx-Mortar Bd., 1994. Mem. Nat. Opera Assn., Nat. Assn. Tchrs. of Singing, Coll. Music Soc. Republican. Episcopalian. Home: 5107 Dalmeny Ct Columbus OH 43220

RICE, KENNETH LLOYD, environmental services executive, educator; b. St. Paul, June 17, 1937; m. Eliza Beth Lyman VanKat, May 11, 1963 (dec. 1992); children: Anne Louise, Kenneth L. Jr., Elizabeth Ellen, Stephen James. BBA, U. Wis., 1959; postgrad., N.Y. Inst. Finance, 1960-64; completed 71st Advanced Mgmt. Program, Harvard U., 1975. Trainee corp. finance Irving J. Rice & Co., St. Paul, 1959-64; asst. branch mgr. DB Marron & Co. Inc., St. Paul, 1964-65; mgr. corp. finance JW Sparks & Co. Inc., St. Paul, 1965-69, The Milw. Co., St. Paul, 1969-70; dir. finance Cedar Riverside Assocs. Inc., Mpls., 1970-71; prin. Kenneth L. Rice & Assocs., St. Paul, 1971-88; chmn., CEO investment banking Allegro Tech. Corp., St. Paul, 1988-92; prof. mgmt. and environ. econs. Budapest (Hungary) U. Econs. Scis., 1992—; chmn., edtl. bd. New Horizons Magazine, Hungary, 1995—; Minn. del. World Trade Ctrs. Assn., Budapest, Hungary, 1987; dir. Hungarian U.S. Fulbright Commn., 1995—. Founder Chimera Theatre, St. Paul, 1969; pres. Liberty Pla. Non-Profit Housing Project, St. Paul, 1975-77; judge Leadership Fellows Bush Found., St. Paul, 1985-90; co-chmn. Parents Fund, Macalester Coll., St. Paul, 1985-87; Hungary hon. rep. State of Minn. Trade Office. Bush Leadership fellow, 1974. Mem. Environ. Mgmt. and Law Assn. Hungary, Harvard Bus. Club (local bd. dirs. 1978-83), Harvard Club of Hungary (v.p. 1994—), Am. C. of C. in Hungary (dir. 1995—, chmn. edn. com. 1993—), Masons, KT, Shriners. Presbyterian.

RICE, LES J., company executive; b. Cleve., Dec. 18, 1924. BSME, Case Applied Scis., 1950. Project mgr. The Yoder Co., Cleve., 1958-65; proposal svcs. mgr. Wean Industries, Youngstown, Ohio, 1965—; owner Rice Tech. Inc., Youngstown, Ohio, 1988—. Patentee in field of traveling tube cutoff measureing system, overarm separating device. Served with U.S. Army, 1943-46, ETO. Decorated Bronze Star; recipient Belgian Croix DeGuerre, Belgium Govt., 1944. Home and Office: 789 Teakwood Dr Youngstown OH 44512-5017

RICE, RICHARD CAMPBELL, retired state official, retired army officer; b. Atchison, Kans., Dec. 11, 1933; s. Olive Campbell and Ruby Thelma (Rose) R.; m. Donna Marie Lincoln, Aug. 4, 1956; children: Robert Alden, Holly Elizabeth. BS in History, Kans. State U., 1955; MA in Social Studies, Eastern Mich. U., 1965; grad. U.S. Army Command and Gen. Staff Coll., 1968, U.S. Army War Coll., 1977, FBI Nat. Exec. Inst., 1990, grad. program for sr. execs. in state and local govt., Harvard U., 1985. Commd. 2d lt. U.S. Army, 1955; advanced through grades to col., 1976; with Joint Chiefs of Staff, Washington, 1975-76; faculty U.S. Army War Coll., Carlisle Barracks, Pa., 1977-79; chief of staff Hdqrs. 3d ROTC Region, Ft. Riley, Kans., 1982-83; ret. 1983; dir. Mo. State Emergency Mgmt. Agy., Jefferson City, 1983-85, dir. Mo. Dept. Pub. Safety, Jefferson City, 1985-93; trustee Mo. State Employees Retirement System, 1990-93; bd. visitors Nat. Emergency Mgmt. Inst., 1991-92. Grad. Leadership, Mo., 1991; mem. Coordinating Coun. Health Edn., Mo.'s Children and Adolescents., Mo. Jail and Prison Overcrowding Task Force, Gov.'s Domestic Violence Task Force, Gov.'s Conf. Health Needs Children, Gov.'s Commn. on Crime, Gov.'s Adv. Coun. on Driving While Intoxicated, Mo. Children's Svcs. Commn., Blue Ribbon Commn. on Svcs. to Youth, Campaign to Protect Our Children; mem. policy com. Mo. Youth Initiative; chmn. Gov.'s Cabinet Coun. for Justice Administrn., Mo. Statistical Analysis Ctr. adv. bd., adv. bd. Mo. Criminal Hist. Records; bd. dirs. Mo. Law Enforcement Meml. Found, Gt. Rivers coun. Boy Scouts Am., 1993—; peer rev. cons. Nat. Inst. of Justice; chmn. Alliance for Uniform Hazmat Transp. Procedures, 1991-93. Decorated Legion of Merit, Bronze Star (3), Meritorious Service medal (4), Air medal (2), Joint Service Commendation medal, Army Commendation medal (2); Republic of Vietnam Cross of Gallantry with Silver Star; recipient Conspicuous Svc. medal State of Mo. Mem. Nat. Eagle Scout Assn., Assn. U.S. Army, Soc. First Div., Am. Legion, VFW, Disabled Am. Vets., AMVETS, Mil. Order of World Wars, Nat. Soc. Sons Am. Revolution, The Retired Officers Assn., Nat. Criminal Justice Assn. (bd. dirs. 1987-93), Rotary (Paul Harris fellow), St. Andrews Soc., Theta Xi. Republican. Avocation: sailing.

RICE, WILLIAM ROSS, media specialist; b. Chillicothe, Ohio, Nov. 26, 1939; s. Daniel Oscar and Mildred Alice (McGee) R.; m. Mary Jane Middleton, Aug. 3, 1962; children: Ann Elizabeth, Judith Middleton, Richard Daniel. BA, Ohio State U., 1962; MS in Journalism, Northwestern U., 1966. Cert. Bus. Appraiser. Various positions Sta. WLS-AM-FM, Chgo., 1965-70; gen. mgr. Sta. WDXB, Chattanooga, 1971; v.p., gen. mgr. Sta. KXOL-AM-FM, Dallas, 1972-73, Sta. WLCY-AM-FM, Tampa, Fla., 1973-74; owner, mgr. Stas. KVOP/KATX, Plainview, Tex., 1975-82; ptnr. Jamar-Rice Co., Austin, Tex., 1983-87; v.p. Thoben-Van Huss, Inc., Indpls., 1988-90; owner William R. Rice Co., Indpls., 1991—; guest lectr. Ohio U., Athens, 1988—. Col. USMCR, 1957-92. Mem. Nat. Assn. Broadcasters, Nat. Assn. Media Brokers, Ohio Assn. Broadcasters, Marine Corps Res. Officers Assn. (bd. dirs. 1985-90), Inst. Bus. Appraisers, Am. Soc. Appraisers, Plainview C. of C. (pres. 1978), Rotary (pres. Plainview chpt. 1977), Sphinx Honorary, Phi Kappa Sigma, Sigma Delta Chi. Presbyterian. Office: William R Rice Co 9102 N Meridian St Ste 500 Indianapolis IN 46260-1809

RICH, CRAIG ROBERT, marketing professional, city councilman; b. Holland, Mich., Oct. 18, 1954; s. Charles Edward and Grace Virginia (Lehigh) R.; m. Vickie Lynn Nyhof, June 3, 1975; children: Allison Elizabeth, Catherine Elyse. AS, Davenport Coll., 1988. Program dir. West State Broadcasters, Zeeland, Mich., 1971-87; sales and mktg. mgr. Gemini Publ., Grand Rapids, Mich., 1987-95, sr. sales cons., 1995—. City coun. mem. Holland, 1982—, mayor pro tem, 1985—; pres. Zeeland Jaycees, 1973, 78; v.p. Mich. Jaycees, 1980-81, sec., 1979-80, dist. dir., 1977-78. Mem. Grand

Rapids C. of C. (chair small bus. coun. 1995—). Republican. Office: Gemini Publications 549 Ottawa Ave NW Grand Rapids MI 49503-1424

RICH, J. DENNIS, performing arts educator; b. Chgo., May 30, 1945; s. Max F. and Adele (Stipek) R.; m. Elizabeth Craig, June 1, 1968; children: Aaron Craig, Anna Katherine. BA, Grinnell Coll., 1967; MA, San Francisco State U., 1969; PhD, U. Wis., 1976. Mgr. Circle Theater U. Ill., Chgo., 1976-80; v.p. John Iltis Assocs., Chgo., 1980-82; mktg. dir. Studio Arena Theater, Buffalo, N.Y., 1982-84, The Atlanta Ballet, 1984-86; mng. dir. Ballet Met., Columbus, Ohio, 1986-89; dir. external affairs The Columbus Symphony Orch., 1989-91; chmn. arts, entertainment, media mgmt. dept. Columbia Coll., Chgo., 1991—; dir. Ohio Dance, 1986-91, Bus. Vols. for Arts, Corp. Cultural Reinvestment, 1991-93, The Theatre Bldg., Chgo.; cons.; exec. producer Oak Park (Ill.) Festival Theater, 1979-82. Author: (articles in books) Eugene O'Neill a World View, 1980, Women in American Theater, 1981. Pres. Friends of the Chgo. Cultural Ctr. Wis. Alumni Research fellow, 1975-76. Mem. Nat. Soc. Fundraising Execs. Home: 533 N Taylor Ave Oak Park IL 60302-2421 Office: Columbia Coll Chgo Arts Entertainment & Media Mgmt Dept 600 S Michigan Ave Chicago IL 60605-1901

RICH, JOSEPH JOHN, accountant; b. Detroit, Sept. 5, 1944; s. John H. and Edna R. (Swallow) R.; m. Carolyn A. Atkinson, Nov. 3, 1962 (div. Dec. 19, 1983); children: Marcella, Loren; m. Darlene E. Kornfehl, Aug. 2, 1985. A of Commerce, Alpena Community Coll.; A in Ins. Law, Am. Edn. Inst. Pres. Tax Svcs., Inc., Portland, Mich., 1965—; claim specialist State Farm Ins., Marshall, Mich., 1966-80; owner Someplace Else Travel Ctr., Portland, 1990—, The Expresso Experience, 1995—; Accredited bus. acct. Author: Insurance Guide for Theatres, 1977, Accounting for Non-Profit Theatres, 1976. Chmn. Ionia (Mich.) County Commn., 1986-90; mem. Ionia Social Svcs. Bd., 1992, Ionia Planning Commn., 1986, Portland Area Mcpl. Authority, 1992. Named one of Outstanding Young Men in Am., 1981. Mem. Portland Kiwanis Club, Ind. Accts. Assn. of Mich. Republican. Office: Tax Svcs Inc 200 W Bridge St Portland MI 48875-1153

RICH, JOSEPH WILLIAM, engineering educator, consultant; b. New Orleans, Aug. 6, 1937; s. William Edward and Hortense Maud (Martinez) R.; m. Beatrice Mae Jewell, July 9, 1960; children: Grant Jewell, Anne Elizabeth. BSME, Carnegie Inst. Tech., 1959; MAE, U. Va., 1961; M.A., Princeton U., 1963, PhD, 1965. Aero. engr. Calspan Corp., Buffalo, 1965-71, prin. engr., 1971-82, mgr. laser physics and chemistry program, 1982-86; adj. prof. elec. engring. SUNY-Buffalo, 1983-86; vis. prof. mech. engring. Carnegie-Mellon U., Pitts., 1985; prof. mech. engring. Ohio State U., 1986—, Ralph W. Kurtz prof. mech. engring, 1996—. Contbr. articles to profl. jours. Patentee in field. Mem. Com. on Ednl. Goals, East Aurora (N.Y.) pub. schs., 1982-83. Panelist Joint U.S.-Japan Seminar on Molecular Energy Transfer, U.S. Nat. Acad. Scis., 1976; Guggenheim Found. fellow, 1961-65, Fulbright sr. fellow Ecole Centrale Paris, 1988. Fellow AIAA (assoc.); mem. Am. Phys. soc., AAAS, Sigma Xi. Democrat. Office: Ohio State U Dept Mech Engring 206 W 18th Ave Columbus OH 43210

RICH, PATRICIA, non-profit executive; b. Detroit; m. Leslie Rich, 1966; children: Barbara, Kathryn. BA, U. Mich., 1964, MA, 1966. Dir. planning and devel. Mo. Botan. Garden, St. Louis, 1981-87; pres. Patricia Rich Assocs., St. Louis, 1987—, Arts and Edn. Coun. Greater St. Louis, 1990—; dir. nonprofit adv. bd. Mark Twain Bank, St. Louis, 1994—; dir. adv. bd. nonprofit mgmt. program Washington U., St. Louis. Commr. St. Louis County Police, 1990-93. Mem. Nat. Soc. Fund Raising Execs. (nat. bd., pres. St. Louis chpt. 1991-92, Fundraiser of Yr. award 1994), Univ. Club, St. Louis Women's Forum (past pres. 1988, Trailblazer award 1994). Office: Arts & Edn Coun 3526 Washington Ave Saint Louis MO 63103

RICH, PAUL MARTIN, environmental studies educator, biologist; b. Berkeley, Calif., Feb. 23, 1956; s. Marvin and Jeannette Alice (Holmes) R. BA in Biology with highest honors, U. Calif., Santa Cruz, 1979; MA in Biology, Harvard U., 1981, PhD in Biology, 1985. Teaching asst. Harvard U., Cambridge, Mass., 1979-83, rsch. assoc. Harvard Forest, 1985-86; rsch. asst. Rocky Mountain Biol. Lab., 1981; rsch. asst. Los Alamos Nat. Lab., 1983-85, postdoctoral fellow, 1988-90; asst. prof. environ. studies, systematics and ecology U. Kans., Lawrence, 1991—; sr. remote sensing/geographical info. systems specialist Kans. Biol. Survey, Lawrence, 1991—; rsch. cons. NASA, 1985, 86-92; NSF postdoctoral fellow U. Calif., Davis and Forest Rsch. Inst., New Zealand, 1990-92; editorial reviewer Am. Jour. Botany, Biotropica, Ecology, Evolution, Tree Physiology, Pears; reviewer Jessie Noyes Found., Nat. Geographic Pew Charitable Trust; seminars presented Carnegie Instn. Washington, Costa Rica Inst. Tech., Dept. Energy, Orgn. for Tropical Studies La Selva Biol. Field Sta., Costa Rica, Pa. State U., Smithsonian Tropical Rsch. Inst., Panama, Stanford U., U. Calif., Berkeley, Davis and Santa Cruz, Harvard U., U. Wash. Contbr. papers and abstracts to Remote Sensing Revs., Conservation Biology, IEEE Trans. on Geosci. and Remote Sensing, Plant and Soil, Bot. Gazette, Am. Jour. Botany, Ecology, Principes, Bull. Torrey Bot. Club, also others. Piedra Blanca scholar, 1974-75; Chancellor's rsch. grantee U. Calif., Santa Cruz, 1978-79, Atkins grantee Harvard U., 1982-83, grantee Orgn. for Tropical Studies, 1983, NSF, 1984-85, Smithsonian Tropical Rsch. Inst., 1985-86; President's undergrad. fellow U. Calif., Santa Cruz, 1978-79, Fulbright fellow, 1983-85, Jessie Noyes fellow, 1984-87, Los Alamos fellow, 1986-88, fellow Stanford U., 1988-90, NSF, 1990-92. Mem. AAAS, Am. Soc. Photogrammetry and Remote Sensing, Assn. for Tropical Biology, Bot. Soc. Am., Ecol. Soc. Am., Palm Soc., Soc. for Study Evolution, Sigma Xi (grantee 1981-82). Office: GIS & Environ Modeling Lab Nichols Hall Lawrence KS 66045

RICH, ROBERT F., political sciences educator, academic administrator; married; 3 children. BA in Govt. with high honors, Oberlin Coll., 1971; student, Free U. of Berlin, 1971-72; MA in Polit. Scis., U. Chgo., 1973, PhD in Polit. Scis., 1975. Project dir., asst. rsch. scientist Ctr. for Rsch. on Utilization Sci. Knowledge, Inst. Social Rsch., U. Mich., lectr. dept. polit. sci., 1975-76; asst. prof. politics and pub. affairs Princeton U., 1976-82, coord. domestic and urban policy field Woodrow Wilson Sch., 1979-81; assoc. prof. polit. sci., pub. policy and mgmt. Sch. Urban and Pub. Affairs, Carnegie-Mellon U., 1982-86; prof. polit. sci. Coll. of Law, health resources mgmt., medical humanities and social svcs., community health, prof. Inst. Environ. Studies U. Ill., Urbana, 1986—, dir. Inst. Govt. and Publ. Affairs; acting head med. humanities and social scis. program U. Ill., Urbana-Champaign, 1988-90, prof. Inst. for Environ. Studies; fellow Johns Hopkins U. Ctr. for Study of Am. Govt., Washington, 1993-95; cons. Carnegie-Mellon U., 1986—, MacArthur Found., NIMH, 1988-89, Food, Drug and Law Inst., HHS, 1989, others. Author: Social Science Information and Public Policy Making: The Interaction Between Bureaucratic Politics and the Use of Survey Data, 1981; co-author: Government Information Management: A Counter-Report of the Commission on Federal Paperwork, 1980; editor: Translating Evaluation into Policy, 1979, The Knowledge Cycle, 1981, Knowledge, Creation, Diffusion, Utilization, 1979-88, 88-91; co-editor: Competitive Approaches to Health Policy Reform, 1993, Health Care Policy, Federalism and the Role of the States, 1996; assoc. editor Society, 1984-88, Evaluation Rev., 1985-89; mem. editorial adv. rev. bd. Policy Studies Rev. Series, 1980-83; mem. editorial bd. Evaluation and Change, 1979-82; mem. editorial adv. bd. Law and Human Behavior, 1983-87; contbr. numerous articles to profl. jours., book chpts. Recipient Emil Limbach Teaching award Carnegie-Mellon U., Sch. Urban and Pub. Affairs, 1985; fellow German Acad. Exch. Program, Fed. Republic Germany, 1971-72, Nat. Opinion Rsch. Ctr. fellow, 1972-73, German Govt. fellow, 1974, Russel Sage Found. Rsch. fellow, 1974-75; vis. scholar Hastings Ctr. for Society, Ethics and Life Scis., 1982. Mem. APA (task force on victims of crime and violence 1982-84), Soc. for Traumatic Stress Studies (bd. dirs. 1980—), World Fedn. for Mental Health (chmn. com. on mental health needs of victims 1985—, vice chmn. 1981-83, Robert F. Rich rsch. ann. award established in his honor, sci. com. on mental health needs of victims 1983), Howard R. Davis Soc. for Knowledge Utilization and Planned Change (pres. 1986-89), Polit. Sci. 400, Policy Studies Assn. (Aaron Wildnusky award 1994), Phi Beta Kappa, Sigma Xi, Phi Kappa Phi. Office: U Ill Inst Govt & Pub Affairs 1007 W Nevada St # 204 Urbana IL 61801-3812 also: 921 W Van Buren St # C 191 Chicago IL 60607-3542

RICHARD, DAVID A., engineering manager; b. Opelousas, La., Sept. 12, 1960. Drafter Aurora (Ill.) Bearing, 1976-80, engring. mgr., 1980—. Republican. Lutheran. Office: Aurora Bearing 970 S Lake St Aurora IL 60506-5901

RICHARD, JOHN C., design engineer; b. Aurora, Ill., Apr. 7, 1964. AA in Mech. Design, Morrison Inst. Tech., Ill., 1986. Desinger Simula Inc., Phoenix, 1986-89; mech. designer Carlson Tool and Machinery, Geneva, Ill., 1989—. Republican. Roman Catholic. Office: Carlson Tool and Machine 2300 Gary Ln Geneva IL 60134-2521

RICHARD, LYLE ELMORE, retired school social worker, consultant; b. Lansing, Mich., Aug. 15, 1939; s. Lloyd M. and Ruth (Rider) R.; m. Karen Ann Gustafson, June 1963 (div. 1980); children: Deborah Ann, David Lyle; m. Julia Ann Quake, Sept. 19, 1981. BA, Albion (Mich.) Coll., 1961; MSW, U. Mich., 1963. cert. social worker, Mich. Psychiat. soc. worker Wayne County Gen. Hosp., Eloise, Mich., 1963-64; sr. social worker Los Guilocos Sch. for Girls Calif. Youth Authority, Santa Rosa, 1964-65; social worker Family Resource Ctr. Marin County Probation Dept., San Rafael, Calif., 1965-67, Sunny Hills Children Svcs., San Anselmo, Calif., 1967-68; sch. social worker Jackson (Mich.) Pub. Schs., 1968-92, ret., 1992; behavior mgmt. cons. Cline/Fay Inst., Golden, Colo., 1985—. Mem. ASCD, Acad. Behaviour Cons. (pres.), Coun. Exceptional Children (v.p. 1990-91, pres. 1991-92), Clowns Am.-Internat., Midwest Sch. Social Work Coun. (bd. dirs. 1971-84), Mich. Assn. Sch. Social Workers (state offices, Sch. Social Worker of Yr. 1989), Elks. Home: 3106 Faith Dr Spring Arbor MI 49283-9739

RICHARDS, DIANA LYN, psychologist; b. Baton Rouge, Dec. 8, 1944; d. William Allen Richards and Julia Viola (Hamilton) Richards Hamilton. AA, Stephens Coll., 1964; BA, U. Colo., 1966; MA, Miami U., Oxford, Ohio, 1969, PhD, 1974. Lic. psychologist, Mo. Dir. community psychol. svcs. Malcolm Bliss Mental Health Ctr., St. Louis, 1975-77; mem. staff Women's Counseling Ctr., St. Louis, 1976-78; mem. faculty Gestalt Inst., St. Louis, 1977-80; instr. Washington U., St. Louis, 1977; dir. psychology Lindenwood Coll. for Individualized Edn., St. Louis, 1978-80, core faculty in psychology, 1984-94; psychologist in pvt. practice St. Louis, 1977—; career cons. Stephens Coll., Columbia, Mo., 1994—; mem. Psychoanalytic Study Group, St. Louis, 1980—; supr. psychology clinic, clin. doctoral program U. Mo., St. Louis, 1994—; facilitator Coun. of All Beings Workshops, 1995—; presenter in field. Contbr. articles to profl. jours. and conf. presentations. Mem. Operation Food Search, Defenders of Wildlife, Humane Soc., People for Ethical Treatment of Animals, Arts and Edn. Fund, Mo. Bot. Garden, Digit Fund, Earth Island Inst., World Wildlife Fund, Nature Conservancy, Audubon Soc., Humane Farming Assn.;founding mem. The Pleiades; vol. food ministry, chair fellowship dinners edn. com. Trinity Episcopal Ch., Wildbird Rehab. Ctr.; vol. Wildbird Rehab. Ctr. Mem. APA, Mo. Psychol. Assn., St. Louis Psychol. Assn. (program chair 1988-89, pres.-elect 1995-96, pres. 1996—), Network of Women Psychologists (program chair 1986), St. Louis Psychoanalytic Inst. Democrat. Home: 2014 S Mason Rd Saint Louis MO 63131-1619 Office: 7396 Pershing Ave Saint Louis MO 63130-4206

RICHARDS, DONALD LEE, custodian; b. Newark, Ohio, Aug. 31, 1935; s. Walter Earl and Mary K. Richards; children: Don, Dale, David, Dennis, Pat. Tchr. creative writing Licking County Aging Progam, Newark, 1994—; tchr. Ben Franklin Elem. Sch., Newark, Ohio, 1996—. Author: (poetry) Whispers in the Wind, 1994, East of the Sun, 1995, Best Poets of '95, Best Poems of '95, 1996. Mem. Internat. Soc. Poets (honorable mention 1996, nominated for Poet of Yr. award 1994, 95, 96), Moose. Home: 20 Carey Ln Heath OH 43056

RICHARDS, HILDA, academic administrator; b. St. Joseph, Mo., Feb. 7, 1936; d. Togar and Rose Avalynne (Williams) Young-Ballard. Diploma nursing St. John's Sch. Nursing, St. Louis, 1956; BS cum laude, CUNY, 1961; MEd, Columbia U., 1965, EdD, 1976; MPA, NYU, 1971. Dep. chief dept. psychiatry Harlem Rehab. Ctr., N.Y.C., 1969-71; prof., dir. nursing Medgar Evers Coll., CUNY, N.Y.C., 1971-76, prof., assoc. dean, 1976-79; dean Coll. Health and Human Service, Ohio U., Athens, 1979-86; provost, v.p. for acad. affairs Indiana U., Pa., 1986-93; chancellor Ind. U. N.W., Gary, 1993—; bd. dirs. Sta. 56-TV; active N.W. Satir Inst., Execs. Coun. N.W. Ind., ACE Commn. on Minorities in Higher Edn., AASCU Com. on Diversity and Social Change. Author: (with others) Curriculum Development and People of Color: Strategies and Change, 1983; editor Black Conf. on Higher Edn. Jour., 1989-93. Bd. dirs. Avanta Network, 1984—, Urban League N.W. Ind., 1993, N.W. Ind. Forum, 1993, Bank One Regional Bd., Merrillville, Ind., 1994, The Meth. Hosps., Inc., Gary.Merrillville, 1994, Lake Area United Way, 1994, Boys and Girls Clubs N.W. Ind.; life mem. Gary chpt. NAACP; exec. com. Pa. Black Conf. on Higher Edn., 1988-93. Recipient Rockefeller Found. award Am. Council Edn., Washington, 1976-77, Black Achiever award Black Opinion Mag., 1989, Athena award Bus. and Profl. Women's Club Ind., 1991; Martin Luther King grantee NYU, N.Y.C., 1969-70, Gunt Found. grantee Harvard Inst. Ednl. Mgmt., Cambridge, Mass., 1981. Fellow Am. Acad. Nursing; mem. ANA (Outstanding Woman of Color award 1990), AAHE, AAUW, APHA, Am. Assn. State Colls. and Univs., Nat. Assn. Allied Health Profls., Am. Assn. Univ. Administrs., Assn. Black Nursing Faculty in Higher Edn. (bd. dirs. 1989—), Pa. Nurses Assn., Assn. Black Women in Higher Edn., Inc., Nat. Black Nurses Assn. (bd. dirs., 1st v.p. 1984—, editor jour. 1985—, Spl. Recognition award 1991, Disting. African-Am. Nurse Educator award Queens County chpt., 1991), Nat. Assn. Women in Edn., Am. Coun. Edn. (exec. com. coun. fellows), Internat. Assn. Univ. Pres., N.W. Rotary, N.W. Kiwanis, Phi Delta Kappa, Sigma Theta Tau, Zonta Club of Ind. County. Democrat. Avocations: needlepoint, travel. Home: 7807 Hemlock Ave Gary IN 46403-2164 Office: Ind U NW Office of Chancellor 3400 Broadway Gary IN 46408-1197

RICHARDS, JON FREDERICK, physician; b. Hays, Kans., May 1, 1950; s. Robert Clare and Jean G. (Fuller) R.; m. Kate Haines, July 31, 1973; children: Robert C. II, Travis Walker, Frederick Dinsmore, Jon Charles. BA in Psychology, U. Kans., 1972, MD, 1975. Intern internal medicine Brown U.-Miriam Hosp., Providence, 1976; resident internal medicine U. Kans. Sch. Medicine, Kansas City, 1981; physician pvt. practice, Phillipsburg, Kans., 1976-79, 81-85; attending physician Salina (Kans.) Regional Health Ctr., 1985—; ptnr. Salina Clinic, 1985—; bd. trustees Kans. Found. Med. Care, Topeka, 1983—, chmn., 1984—; clin. asst. prof. Smoky Hill Family Practice Residency, Wichita, 1989—; pres. Smoky Hill Ednl. Found., 1992—. Cubmaster Boy Scouts Am., Salina, 1987-91; asst. scoutmaster, 1990—. Summerfield scholar U. Kans., Lawrence, 1968-72. Mem. AMA, Am. Coll. Physicians, Kans. Med. Soc., Saline County Med. Soc. (pres. 1994), Phi Beta Kappa. Home: 2404 N Halstead Rd Salina KS 67401 Office: Salina Clinic 501 S Santa Fe Salina KS 67401

RICHARDS, KAREN KIRK, association executive; b. Hutchinson, Kans., Aug. 31, 1940; d. Earl Leroy and Mary Ann (Haines) Kirk; m. Gary Walter Richards, May 28, 1964 (div. Jan. 1980); children: Kirk Dawson, Kevin Patrick. BA, U. Kans., 1962. Pres. Classroom Cons., Prairie Village, Kans., 1990-94; co-founder Attention Deficit Disorder/Attention Deficit Hyperactivity Disorder Edn. and Resource Ctr., Prairie Village, Kans., 1990-94; v.p. ADD/ADHD Edn. and Resource Ctr., Prairie Village, Kans., 1994-95; dir. Prairie State Bank, Augusta, Kans., 1995—; staff cons. on attention deficit disorder Maur Hill Prep. Sch., 1994-97; mem. attention deficit disorder adv. com. Kans. State Bd. Edn., Topeka, 1995-96. Author: Turning the Tide: How to Be an Advocate for the ADD/ADHD Child, 1989; contbr. article to mag., 1994. Active in securing ADD/ADHD Public Awareness Week declaration by Kans. Gov. Bill Graves, Sept. 6-12, 1996. Mem. Coalition for Positive Family Relationships, Attention Deficit Disorder Assn., Children and Adults with Attention Deficit Disorder, Kappa Alpha Theta (Theta of the Yr. 1992). Republican. Presbyterian. Office: ADD/ADHD Edn Resource Assn 2110 W 75th St Prairie Village KS 66208

RICHARDS, LACLAIRE LISSETTA JONES (MRS. GEORGE A. RICHARDS), social worker; b. Pine Bluff, Ark.; d. Artie William and Geraldine (Adams) Jones; m. George Alvarez Richards, July 26, 1958; children: Leslie Rosario, Lia Mercedes, Jorge Ferguson. BA, Nat. Coll. Christian Workers, 1953; MSW, U. Kans., 1956; postgrad. Columbia U., 1960. Diplomate Clin. Social Work, Am. Bd. of Examiners in Clin. Social Work, Nat. Assn. Social Workers; cert. gerontologist. Psychiat. supervisory, teaching, community orgn., adminstrv. and consultative duties Hastings Regional Ctr., Ingleside, Nebr., 1956-60; supervisory, consultative and adminstrv. responsibilities for psychiat. and geriatric patients VA Hosp., Knoxville, Iowa, 1960-74, field instr. for grad. students from U. Mo., EEO counselor, 1969-74, 78-90, com. chmn., 1969-70, Fed. women's program coordinator, 1972-74; sr. social worker Mental Health Inst., Cherokee, Iowa, 1974-77; adj. asst. prof. dept. social behavior U. S.D.; instr. Dept. of Psychiatry U. S.D Sch. of Medicine, 1988-96, Augustana Coll., 1981-86; outpatient social worker VA Med. and Regional Office Center, Sioux Falls, S.D., 1978-96; med., surg. & intensive care social worker, 1990-92, surg. & intermediate care social worker, 1992-96; EEO counselor. Mem. Knoxville Juvenile Adv. Com., 1963-65, 68-70, sec., 1965-66, chmn., 1966-68; sec. Urban Renewal Citizens' Adv. Com., Knoxville, 1966-68; mem. United Methodist Ch. Task Force Exptl. Styles Ministry and Leadership, 1973-74, mem. adult choir, mem. ch. and society com.; counselor Knoxville Youth Line program; sec. exec. com. Vis. Nurse Assn., 1979-80; canvasser community fund drs., Knoxville; mem. Cherokee Civil Rights Commn.; bd. dirs., pub. relations, membership devel. and program devel. cons. YWCA, 1983-85; bd. dirs. Family Svc. Agy., 1989-90, Food Svcs. Ctr. Inc., 1992-96; mem. S.D. Symphonic Choir, 1991—; mem. Youth-At-Risk Task Force and Multicultural Ctr. Advocate. Named S.D. Social Worker of Yr., 1983. Mem. NAACP (chmn. edn. com. 1983-85), AAUW (sec. Hastings chpt. 1958-60), Nat. Assn. Social Workers (co-chmn. Nebr. chpt. profl. standards com. 1958-59), Acad. Cert. Social Workers, S.D. Assn. Social Workers (chmn. minority affairs com., v.p. S.E. region 1980, pres. 1980-82 exec. com. 1982-84, mem. social policy and action com.), Nebr. Assn. Social Workers (chmn. 1958-59), Seventh Dist. S.D. Med. Soc. Aux., Coalition on Aging., Nat. Assn. Social Workers (qualified clin. social worker 1991—), Methodist (Sunday sch. tchr. adult div.; mem. commn. on edn.; mem. Core com. for adult edn.; mem. Adult Choir; mem. Social Concerns Work Area); mem. 1st Evangelical Free Ch., 1995—. Home: 1701 E Ponderosa Dr Sioux Falls SD 57103-5019

RICHARDS, MICHAEL S., programmer; b. Ft. Wayne, Ind., Nov. 17, 1947; s. Roland Ray and Sharon Ann (Shive) R.; m. Cheryl June Siebert, June 1, 1967; children: Michelle J., David C. BS, Purdue U., West Lafayette, Ind., 1971. Dir. co. stores Orange Julius Am., Santa Monica, Calif., 1980-87; lead programmer Blue Cross/Blue Shield, Chgo., 1992—. Sec., Dem. Club, Hobart, Ind., 1993-96. Home: 628 S Ash St Hobart IN 46342

RICHARDS, NEIL STEPHEN, real estate executive; b. Indpls., Oct. 16, 1948; s. Neilon Morris and Anna Leona (Wohler) R.; m. Donna Jill Roach, Dec. 31, 1969 (div. 1977); children: Jennifer Lynne, Joshua Lee. BA, Ind. U., Indpls.; Grad. of Theology, Tenn. Temple Bible Sch., Chattanooga. Author: (play) The Last Walloon, 1995. Republican. Baptist. Home: 2319 S Sherman Dr Indianapolis IN 46203

RICHARDS, RICK A., newswriter; b. Muncie, Ind., Aug. 8, 1953; s. Mary Ann Chelminiak, Aug. 13, 1977; 1 child, Erika Theresa. BS, Bell State U., 1975. Reporter Nat. Rd. Traveler, Cambridge City, Ind., 1975-77, editor, 1977-79; editor Michiana Farmers Jour., Michigan City, Ind., 1979-80; bus. editor The News-Dispatch, Michigan City, Ind., 1980-86; bus. reporter Post-Tribune, Gary, Ind., 1986-89, asst. met. editor, 1989-91; Porter County bur. chief Post-Tribune, Valparaiso, Ind., 1989-91; asst. met. editor Post-Tribune, Gary, 1992-95, editorial writer, columnist, 1995—. Mem. Soc. Profl. Journalists. Office: Post-Tribune 1065 Broadway Gary IN 46402

RICHARDS, ROY CLARK, insurance company executive; b. Phila., Dec. 14, 1942; s. Riley Harry and Eloise (Smith) R.; m. Gloria Kay Wallis, Feb. 13, 1971; children: Kristen Leigh, Geoffrey Stephen. BA magna cum laude, Carleton Coll., 1965; MBA, U. Chgo., 1967. CPCU. Fin. analyst Ford Motor Co., Dearborn, Mich., 1970-73; sr. fin. analyst Rockwell Internat., Pitts., 1973-75; mgr. ops. Comml. Union Ins., Camp Hill, Pa., 1975-79; asst. corp. controller Booz, Allen & Hamilton, N.Y.C., 1979-80; dir. ins. strategy Continental Group, Inc., Stamford, Conn., 1980-84; sr. v.p., CFO, treas. Western Employers Ins. Co., Santa Ana, Calif., 1984-86; v.p. Atlantic Mgmt. Svcs., San Antonio, 1987-88; mgmt. cons. self-employed Des Moines, 1988-91; pres. RDS Group, Des Moines, 1991—, 1991-93; exec. v.p. M.J. Kelly Co., Des Moines, 1993—. Recipient Scholarship Recognition, Soc. Property-Casualty Underwriters, 1977. Mem. Soc. Property Casualty Underwriters. Republican. Presbyterian. Home and Office: 1740 Cedarwood Cir Des Moines IA 50325-8827

RICHARDSON, BARBARA CONNELL, transportation research scientist, consultant; b. N.Y.C., Dec. 29, 1947; d. John Joseph and Joan Marie (Tobin) Connell; m. Rudy James Richardson, Aug. 23, 1970 (div. Dec. 1984); 1 child, Anne Elizabeth. BA, SUNY, 1969; SM, MIT, 1973; PhD, U. Mich., Ann Arbor, 1982. Programmer/analyst The Phys. Review, Upton, N.Y., 1969-70; transp. planner Mass. Exec. Office of Transp. and Constrn., Boston, 1973-74; transp. research officer Greater London Council, 1974-75; assoc. research scientist and dir. transp. planning and policy U. Mich., Ann Arbor, 1975-86, rsch. scientist, 1994—; pres. Richardson Assocs., Inc., Ann Arbor, 1983—. Contbr. numerous articles on transp. to profl. jours. Mem. Transp. Rsch. Bd., Soc. Automotive Engrs., Intelligent Transp. Soc. Am., Sigma Xi, Kappa Mu Epsilon, Signum Laudis. Office: U Mich Transp Rsch Inst 2901 Baxter Rd Ann Arbor MI 48109

RICHARDSON, DEANNA RUTH, microbiologist; b. Columbus, Ohio, Jan. 7, 1956; d. Raymond and Anna Mary (Underwood) R. BS, Ohio State U., 1978. Lab tech. Ohio Dept. Agr., Reynoldsburg, Ohio, 1978-81, lab technologist, 1981-86, microbiologist, 1986—. Active East Columbus Christian Ch.; mem. Neighborhood Civic Assn., 1983-87. Mem. Ohio Valley Inst. Food Technologists, Vet. Microbiologists Assn., Ohio State U. Alumni Assn., Franklin County Alumni Club, Smithsonian Instn., Nat. Wildlife Fedn., Internat. Wildlife Fedn., World Wildlife Fund, African Wildlife Found., Columbus Zoo, Ohio State U. Century Club, Ohio State U. Friend of the Wexner Art Ctr. Home: 6267 Barberry Holw Columbus OH 43213-3308 Office: Ohio Dept Agr Labs 8995 E Main St Reynoldsburg OH 43068-3398

RICHARDSON, JOHN THOMAS, academic administrator, clergyman; b. Dallas, Dec. 20, 1923; s. Patrick and Mary (Walsh) R. B.A., St. Mary's Sem., Perryville, Mo., 1946; S.T.D., Angelicum U., Rome, Italy, 1951; M.A., St. Louis U., 1954. Prof. theology, dean studies Kenrick Sem., St. Louis, 1951-54; lectr. Webster Coll., 1954; dean Grad. Sch. DePaul U., Chgo., 1954-60, exec. v.p., dean faculties, 1960-81, pres., 1981-93; prof. DePaul U. Coll. Law, Chgo., 1955; chancellor DePaul U., Chgo., 1993—. Trustee DePaul U., Chgo., 1954—. Home: 2233 N Kenmore Ave Chicago IL 60614-3504 Office: De Paul U 1 E Jackson Blvd Chicago IL 60604-2201

RICHARDSON, JOSEPH HILL, physician, medical educator; b. Rensselaer, Ind., June 16, 1928; s. William Clark and Vera (Hill) R.; m. Joan Grace Meininger, July 8, 1950; children: Lois N., Ellen M., James K. MS in Medicine Northwestern U., 1950, MD, 1953. Intern, U.S. Naval Hosp., Great Lakes, Ill., 1953-54; fellow in medicine Cleve. Clinic, 1956-59; individual practice medicine specializing in internal medicine and hematology, Marion, Ind., 1959-67, Ft. Wayne, Ind., 1967—; assoc. clin. prof. medicine, Ind. U. Sch. Medicine, 1993—; med. dir. emeritus The Med. Protective Co., Ft. Wayne, 1995—. Served to lt. MC USNR, 1953-56. Diplomate Am. Bd. Internal Medicine. Fellow ACP, AAAS; mem. AMA, Masons. Contbr. articles to med. jours. Home and Office: 8726 Fortuna Way Fort Wayne IN 46815-5725

RICHARDSON, KATHY KREAG, state legislator. Ed., Purdue U. Clk. Hamilton County Circuit Ct., 1984-91; mem. from 29th dist. Ind. State Ho. of Reps., 1992—; mem. cts. and criminal code com., judiciary com., local govt., cityies and towns, county and twp. com., election and apportionment com., family and children com. Mem. Hamilton County Bd. Election Surps. Mem. Assn. Clks. Circuit Cts., Assn. Ind. Counties, Noblesville C. of C. (bd. dirs.), Noblesville H.S. Alumni Assn. (sec.), Kiwanis, Soroptimist, Republican Woman. Home: 1427 Harrison St Noblesville IN 46060-2122 Office: Ind Ho of Reps State Capitol Indianapolis IN 46204*

RICHARDSON, MARK, state legislator; b. Poplar Bluff, Mar. 19, 1952; married; children: Todd, Chris, Megan. BA in Polit. Sci. and History, S.E. Mo. State U., MA in Psychology; JD, Memphis State U., 1980. City atty.

City of Poplar Bluff, 1984-86; asst. prosecuting atty. City of Butler County, 1980-86; sr. ptnr. Richardson and Duncan; rep. Mo. Ho. of Reps., 1990—; minority fl. leader Mo. Ho. of Reps., 1994; mem. follow ho. coms. accounts, ops. and fin., join com. on wetlands, judiciary and ethics, rules, join rules, bill perfected and printed, workers compensation; mem. govs. standing com. on job tng. and work force readiness, 1993—, mem. Rep. caucus com. for higher edn., policy devel. com. Rep. campaign com., mem. statewide bldg. code com., 1994—; bd. dirs. Mo. First Vote Program; del. Am. Coun. of Young Polit. Leaders to Austria and Hungary, 1992; ACYPL task force to the Pacific Mantle Countries of Sinapore, Thailand and South Korea. Scoutmaster Boy Scout Troop #166; elder, bd. dirs. First Christian Ch., Poplar Bluff; former pres. bd. Local Shelter Workshop, March of Dimes, Poplar Bluff H.S. task force on drug abuse. Recipient Award of Merit Boy Scouts Am., 1990; named Outstanding Young Men, 1981. Office: Minority Fl Leader House of Reps Rm 204 Jefferson MO 65101

RICHARDSON, MICHAEL BARRETT, history educator; b. Ft. Monmouth, N.J., Jan. 19, 1964; s. Roy Victor and Luanne Frances (Jenkins) R.; m. Lisa Estelle Sofranko, July 14, 1984; children: Jonathan Barrett, Madeleine Lee. AAS personnel mgmt., C.C. of Air Force, 1991; BA in polit. sci., So. Ill. U., 1992, MA in hist. studies, 1995. Enlisted USAF, Clark AFB, The Philippines, 1984; rose through ranks to staff sgt. USAF, Scott AFB, Ill., 1987; resigned USAF, 1994; personnel technician USAF, Clark AFB, 1984-88; assignments mgr. Scott AFB, 1988-94; history instr. So. Ill. U., Edwardsville, 1995—. Mem. Phi Alpha Theta. Roman Catholic.

RICHARDSON, MICHAEL TYLER, small business owner, engineer; b. Akron, Ohio, June 26, 1957. Student, Bowling Green State U., 1975-77. Technician, supr. Danmar Inc., Huron, Ohio, 1978-86; owner, engr. Entratech Sys., Sandusky, Ohio, 1982—. Patent in Water and Fuel Sensor Engines. Mem. Erie City Conservations League. Republican.

RICHARDSON, MILDRED TOURTILLOTT, psychologist; b. North Hampton, N.H., May 8, 1907; d. Herbert Shaw and Sarah Louise (Fife) Tourtillott; m. Harold Wellington Richardson, June 25, 1932; children: Elizabeth Fern Ruben, Constance Joy Van Valer, Carol Louise Dennis. AB, Bates Coll., 1930; MA, U. Mich., 1948; EdS, Butler U., 1961; PhD, Ind. U., 1965. Diplomate Am. Bd. Profl. Psychology, Nat. Register Health Svc. Providers in Psychology, hosp. staff mem.; cert. clin. and sch. psychologist, Ind. Tchr. math. and sci. Norwich (Conn.) Free Acad., 1930-32, Port Huron (Mich.) High Sch., 1943-45; dir. intermediate girls Interlochen Nat. Music Camp, Mich., 1953, asst. dean univ. women, 1954; tchr., guidance counselor Community Sch. Corp., Franklin, Ind., 1956-64; supr. tng. Devereux Found., Devon, Pa., 1965-78, cons. clin. tng. in sch. and clin. psychology, 1975-78; tchr. psychology of spl. edn. Pa. State U.ext., King of Prussia, 1966-68; sch. psychologist Johnson County (Ind.) Spl. Svcs., 1979-82; head clin. psychology Community Psychiat. Ctrs. Valle Vista Hosp., Greenwood, Ind., 1983-88; pvt. practice psychol. health svc. Greenwood, 1985-95; clin. psychologist St. Francis Hosp., Indpls., 1988-95; clin. assoc. prof. Hahnemann Med. Coll., Phila., 1973-78; part-time dir. psychodiagnostics seminar; assoc. prof. sch. psychology, condr. grad. seminar, practicum Ind. U., Bloomington, 1982, lectr., 1987; mem. bd. examiners Midwest Regional Bd. Am. Bd. Profl. Psychology, 1988-95, Ind.Tchrs. Assn., Ind. Psychol. Assn.; cons. Valle Vista Guidance Ctr., 1991-94; adj. prof. psychology Ind. U., 1992-94, U. Indpls., 1992-94; cons. clin. psychologist Am. Stress Ctr., Inc., 1993-95; pvt. practice, Pa., 1970-78. Contbr. articles to profl. jours. Active Johnson County Commn. on Child Abuse, 1988-89, Gov.'s Drug-Free Ind. Coun. on Alcoholism; bd. dirs. Greater Johnson County Cmty. Found., 1990-95. Recipient Headliner award Theta Sigma Phi, 1964, Disting. Svc. award Bates Coll. Alumni Assn., 1990. Mem. APA (fellow sch. psychology, clin. psychology), Inst. Clin. Tng. Devereux Found. (hon.), Internat. Coun. Psychologists, Internat. Sch. Psychology Com., Exec. Svc. Corps (mem. mentor program), Franklin Coll. Alumnae (hon., assoc. 1988), Ben Franklin Soc., Phi Kappa Phi. Republican. Baptist. Address: Marquette Manor Apt 5302 8140 Township Line Rd Indianapolis IN 46260

RICHARDSON, RALPH HERMAN, lawyer; b. Detroit, Oct. 12, 1935; s. Ralph Onazime and Lucinda Ollie (Fluence) R.; m. Arvie Y., June 1, 1956 (div. 1961); children: Cassandra, Tanya, Arvie Lynn; m. Julia A., Sept. 16, 1962 (div. 1982); children: Traci, Theron. BA, Wayne State U., 1964, JD, 1970. Bar: Mich., U.S. Ct. Appeals (6th cir.), Supreme Ct. U.S. Ct., 1970. Postal transp. clk. U.S. P. O., Detroit, 1954-56; clk. pub. aid worker City Detroit, 1956-65; sr. labor relations rep. Ford Motor Co., Ypsilanti, Mich., 1965-70, wage admins., 1966, labor relations rep., 1967; atty. Brown Grier, Richardson P.C., Detroit, 1970-71; atty Richardson, Grier P.C., Detroit, 1971-73; ptnr. Stone, Richardson P.C., Detroit, 1973—; bd. dirs. Legal Aid, Defender Assn. Detroit, 1985-86. Mem. bd. dirs. YMCA Fisher Branch; Boy Scouts Am.; apptd. to Bd. Appeals for Hosp. Bed Reduction by Gov. State of Mich., 1982, apptd. Spl. Asst. Atty. Gen., by Frank J. Kelley, Atty Gen. for the State Mich., May 23, 1984, apptd. to Task Oriented Com. to review the issue in-home child care by Detroit City Council Mem., Maryann Mahaffey. With U.S. Army, 1964. Mem. NAACP (life), Am. Arbitration Assn., Legal Aid Defender Assn., Mich. State Bar Fellows, Optimists, Masons, Shriners (imperial legal advisor, gen. counsel 1994-96), Phi Alpha Delta, Kappa Alpha Psi. Democrat. Office: Stone Richardson PC 2910 E Jefferson Ave Detroit MI 48207-4208

RICHARDSON, ROBERT EDWARD, data processing analyst; b. Ann Arbor, Mich., Dec. 13, 1955; s. Stanley G. and Frances A. (Raes) R.; m. Pamela Lee Blewer. BBA, U. Iowa, 1978. Res. group mgr. Sears, Roebuck & Co., Des Moines, 1978-79; data processing mgmt. trainee Armstrong Dept. Store, Cedar Rapids, Iowa, 1979-81; level II programmer analyst City of Cedar Rapids, 1981-84; sr. programmer analyst Life Investors, Cedar Rapids, 1984-88; systems software programmer II, Wang system adminstr. AEGON USA Inc. (formerly Life Investors), Cedar Rapids, 1988-91; Wang system adminstr. Aegon USA, Inc., Cedar Rapids, 1991-92, tech. analyst, 1992—, sys. software programmer II, 1994—. Mem. Hawkeye PC Users Group, Alpha Kappa Psi (pres. Hawkeye State Alumni chpt. 1987-88, editor pub. directory 1989-95, Alumni Disting. Svc. award 1981, bd. dirs. north ctrl. region 1988-90). Home: 669 Staub Ct NE Cedar Rapids IA 52402-4330 Office: AEGON USA Inc 4333 Edgewood Rd NE Cedar Rapids IA 52499-0001

RICHARDSON, RUDY JAMES, toxicology and neurosciences educator; b. May 13, 1945. B.S. magna cum laude, Wichita State U., 1967; Sc.M., Harvard U., 1973, Sc.D., 1974. Diplomate Am. Bd. Toxicology. Research geochemist Columbia U., N.Y.C., summer 1966; NASA trainee SUNY, Stony Brook, 1967-70; research biochemist Med. Research Council, Carshalton, Eng., 1974-75; asst. prof. U. Mich., Ann Arbor, 1975-79, assoc. prof., 1979-84, prof. toxicology 1984—, assoc. prof. neurotoxicology neurology dept., 1987—, acting dir. dept. Toxicology, 1993; dir., 1994—; vis. scientist Warner-Lambert Co., Ann Arbor, 1982-83; vis. prof. U. Padua, Italy, 1991; cons. NAS, Washington, 1978-79, 84, Office Tech. Assessment U.S. Congress, 1988-90, Nat. Toxic Substance Disease Registry, 1990—; mem. sci. adv. panel on neurotoxicology EPA, 1987-89; chmn. work group on neurotoxicity guidelines Orgn. for Econ. Coop. and Devel., 1990, Nat. Inst. Orgnl. Safety and Health, 1990, 94. Contbr. articles to profl. jours., chpts. to books; mem. editorial bd. Neurotoxicology, 1980—, Toxicology and Indsl. Health, 1986—, Toxicology and Applied Pharmacology, 1989—. Mem. Mich. Lupus Found., Ann Arbor, 1979—. Grantee NIH, 1977-86, EPA, 1977-86; invited speaker Gordon Conf., Meriden, N.H., 1984, Cholinesterase Congress, Bled, Yugoslavia, 1983. Mem. AAAS, Soc. Toxicology (pres. neurotoxicology sect. 1987-88, councillor 1988-89), Soc. for Neurosci., Am. Diabetes Assn., Am. Chem. Soc., Internat. Soc. Neurochemistry, Internat. Brain Rsch. Orgn. Office: U Mich Toxicology Program M 7525 Sph # 2 Ann Arbor MI 48109

RICHARDSON, THOMAS HAMPTON, design consulting engineer; b. St. Louis, Nov. 25, 1941; s. Claude Hampton and Pearl Lily (Burks) R.; m. Lois Louise Atteberry June 8, 1963; children: Shelley Ann, David Hampton, Stephanie Lynn. BTEE, Wash. U., St. Louis, 1974. Registered profl. engr., Mo., Ill., Ind., Kans., Iowa, Fla., Ky., Miss. Elec. project designer Fruco Engrs. Inc., St. Louis, 1967-68; mgr., mech./elec. engr. MBA Engrs. Inc., St. Louis, 1968-74, Kenneth Balk and Assoc., St. Louis, 1974-76; instr. elec. engring. Wash. U., St. Louis, 1976; v.p., chief engr. John F. Steffen Assoc., St. Louis, 1976-79; prin. ptnr. Keeler, Webb and Richardson, St. Louis, 1979-94; pres./owner The Richardson Engring. Group, St. Louis, 1979—. Contbr. articles to profl. jours. Recipient Internat. Lgt. Des. award Illuminating Engr. Soc. St. Louis 1985, Edwin F. Guth award of Merit Illuminating Engr. Soc. N.Am. 1986. Mem. NSPE, ASHRAE, Am. Cons. Engr. Coun., Illuminating Engring. Soc. Past pres.), Soc. for Mkt. Profl. Svcs. (v.p.), Profl. Svcs. Mgmt. Assn. (bd. dirs.), Mo. Soc. Profl. Engrs. (govt. rels. com.), Nat. Fire Protection Assn., Green Turtle Bay Yacht Club, Grand Lake Yacht Club, Ky. Lake Club. Office: The Richardson Engring 7227 Devonshire Saint Louis MO 63119

RICHARDSON, TOD DAVID, financial planner, educator; b. Cedar Falls, Iowa, Mar. 18, 1962; s. David Joe and Judith Kay (Tott) R.; m. Lori Ann Stockton, Mar. 1, 1986; children: Alexander Tyler, Tanar Jace. BBA, Coe Coll., 1984; MA in Bus. Fin., Webster U., 1988. Registered rep. Nat. Assn. Securities Dealers. Auditor Rockwell Internat., Cedar Rapids, Iowa, 1986-87; prof. Ariz. Western Coll., Yuma, 1987-89; fin. planner IDS Fin. Svcs., Newton, Iowa, 1989-91, Interstate Ins. Svcs., Newton, 1991—; prof. Des Moines Area C.C. mem. Jasper County Estate and Fin. Planning Coun., 1990—, v.p., 1992-93, pres. 1993-94. With U.S. Army, 1986-89. Mem. Internat. Assn. for Fin. Planning, Jaycees. Republican. Office: Interstate Ins Svcs Ltd 215 N 2nd Ave W Newton IA 50208-3033

RICHERSON, HAL BATES, physician, internist, allergist, immunologist, educator; b. Phoenix, Feb. 16, 1929; s. George Edward and Eva Louise (Steere) R.; m. Julia Suzanne Bradley, Sept. 5, 1953; children: Anne, George, Miriam, Julia, Susan. BS with distinction, U. Ariz., 1950; MD, Northwestern U., 1954. Diplomate Am. Bd. Internal Medicine, Am. Bd. Allergy and Immunology, Bd. Diagnostic Lab. Immunology; lic. physician, Ariz., Iowa. Intern Kansas City (Mo.) Gen. Hosp., 1954-55; resident in pathology St. Luke's Hosp., Kansas City, 1955-56; trainee in neuropsychiatry Brooke Army Hosp., San Antonio, 1956; resident in medicine U. Iowa Hosps., Iowa City, 1961-64, fellow in allergy and immunology, 1964-66; fellow in immunology Mass. Gen. Hosp., Boston, 1968-69, instr. internal medicine, 1964-66, asst. prof., 1966-70, assoc. prof., 1970-74, prof., 1974—, acting dir. divsn. allergy/applied immunology, 1970-72, dir. allergy and clin. immunology sect., 1972-78, dir. divsn. allergy and immunology, 1978-91; gen. practice, asst. to Gen. Surgeon Ukiah, Calif., 1958; gen. practice medicine Holbrook, Ariz., 1958-61; vis. lectr. medicine Harvard U. Sch. Medicine, Boston, 1968-69; vis. prof., rsch. scientist U. London and Brompton Hosp., 1984; prin. investigator Nat. Heart, Lung and Blood Inst., 1971—, mem. pulmonary diseases adv. com., 1983-87; prin. investigator Nat. Inst. Allergy and Infectious Diseases, 1983-94; dir. Nat. Inst. Allergy and Infectious Diseases' Asthma and Allergic Diseases Ctr., U. Iowa, 1983-94; mem. VA Merit Rev. Bd. in Respiration, 1981-84; mem. com. NIH Gen. Clin. Rsch. Ctrs., 1989-93; mem. rev. reserve NIH, 1993—; mem. bd. sci. advisors Merck Inst., 1990-94; presenter lectures, seminars, continuing edn. courses; mem. numerous univ., coll. and hosp. coms., 1970—; cons. Merck Manual, 1982, 87, 92. Contbr. numerous articles and revs. to profl. jours., chpts. to books; reviewer Sci., Jour. Immunology, Jour. Allergy and Clin. Immunology, Am. Rev. Respiratory Disease, New Eng. Jour. Medicine, Ann. Internal Medicine. Served to capt. U.S. Army, 1956-58. NIH fellow 1968-69. Fellow ACP, Am. Acad. Allergy; mem. AMA (mem. residency and rev. com. for allergy and immunology; mem. accreditation coun. for grad. med. edn. 1980-85, vice-chmn. 1984-85), AAAS, Iowa Med. Soc., Iowa Thoracic Soc. (chmn. program com. 1964-65, 69-71, pres. 1972-73, mem. exec. com. 1972-74), Am. Thoracic Soc. (bd. dirs. 1981-82, councilor assembly on allergy and immunology 1980-81, mem. nominating com. 1988-90), Iowa Clin. Med. Soc., Am. Fedn. Clin. Rsch., Am. Assn. Immunologists, Ctrl. Soc. Clin. Rsch. (chmn. sect. on allergy-immunology 1980-81, mem. coun. 1981-84), Alpha Omega Alpha. Home: 331 Lucon Dr Iowa City IA 52246-3300 Office: U Iowa Hosps and Clinics Dept Internal Medicine SE 630 Gen Hosp Iowa City IA 52242

RICHERSON, PAULA KAY, hospice nurse, school nurse; b. Rosiclare, Ill., Sept. 18, 1939; d. Paul Enoch and Golda Arvetta (Reid) Turley; m. Jack Edward Richerson, Apr. 6, 1963; children: Brent Alan, Kevin Dale. Diploma in nursing, Protestant Deaconess Hosp., Evansville, Ind., 1960; BS in Profl. Arts, Health Care, St. Joseph's Coll., 1987; BSN, So. Ill. U., Edwardsville, 1990. Cert. hospice nurse. Staff nurse, supr. Hardin County Gen. Hosp., Rosiclare, 1960-62; staff nurse Peninsula Hosp., Burlingame, Calif., 1962; instr. Southeastern Ill. Coll. Sch. Practical Nursing, Harrisburg, 1963-69; sch. nurse Golconda, Golconda, Ill., 1970-78; sub. sch. nurse Pope County Unit Dist. I, Golconda, Ill., 1979-91; staff nurse Hospice of Ill., Belleville, 1991—; bd. dirs. So. Seven Health Dept., Ullin, Ill., Rural Health, Golconda; preceptor Zeta Delta. Chmn. blood program ARC, Pope County, 1980—; mem. Selective Svc. Bd., 1981—. Mem. Hospice Nurse Assn., Beta Sigma Phi (past officer). Home: RR 1 Box 10 Golconda IL 62938-9703 Office: Hospice So Ill 305 South St Belleville IL 62220 also: Hospice So Ill PO Box 338 Vienna IL 62995-0338

RICHMAN, JEFFERY ALAN, veterinarian; b. Cleve., Apr. 6, 1956; s. Samuel B. and Ruth Ann (Schneider) R.; m. Mary Ann Kozich, Feb. 15, 1991; 3 children. BS with distinction, Ohio State U., 1978, DVM, 1982. Assoc. Randall Vet. Hosp., Warrensville Heights, Ohio, 1982-84; owner, vet. Richman Animal Clinic, Willoughby Hills, Ohio, 1984-92, Richmond Hts, Ohio, 1992—; speaker at schs., librs., breeder clubs, 1984—. Developer (surgical technique) Char-Pet Lid Procedure, 1987. Mem. Am. Animal Hosp. Assn. (Excel award 1987), Feline Health Ctr. Cornell, Ohio Vet. Medicine Assn., Am. Med. and Vet. Rsch. Inst., United Martial Arts and Black Belt Assn. Office: Richman Animal Clinic Inc 26909 Chardon Rd Richmond Heights OH 44143-1111

RICHMAN, JOHN EMMETT, architect; b. East Liverpool, Ohio, June 8, 1951; s. Ethel M. (Thompson) R.; m. Susan E. Nusser, May 29, 1971; children: Stephen T., Sarah J. BArch, BS, Kent State U., 1982. Registered arch., Ohio, W.Va., Pa., Iowa, Ind., N.Y.; ordained elder Evang. Presbyn. Ch., 1978. Draftsman Fairfield Machine Co., Columbiana, Ohio; archtl. draftsman Robert F. Beatty, Architect, East Liverpool, 1973-80; archtl. draftsman Smiths & and Assocs., Architects, Columbiana, 1981-84, architect, 1984-85, architect, v.p., 1985-89, pres., 1989—. Bd. dirs. Beaver Local High Sch. Alumni Assn., 1990—; pres. Beaver Local High Sch. Alumni Band, 1991—; chmn. Youth Camp com. First Evang. Presbyn. Ch., 1983-93, asst. dir. Youth Camp, 1982-88, chmn. worship com., 1985-86, supt. Sunday sch., 1986-89, mem. choir; co-founder Tri-State Teen World, East Liverpool, 1978, chmn. bd. dirs., 1981—, Bible quiz dir., 1982-90, coach all-star quiz team, 1985, 1987. With U.S. Army, 1971-73. Mem. AIA (bd. dirs. Ea. Ohio chpt. 1985-90, sec. 1986-87, v.p. 1988, pres. 1989), Architects Soc. Ohio (alt. dir. 1986-87, trustee polit. action com. 1988), Nat. Inst. Bldg. Scis. (mem. Ohio consultive coun.), Youth Evangelism Assn. (mem. Bible quiz com. 1985—, bd. dirs. 1989—, treas. 1994), Columbiana C. of C. (bd. dirs. 1987-89), Rotary (sec. 1988-90, v.p. 1992-93, pres. 1993-94). Home: 47995 Calcutta Smith Ferry Rd East Liverpool OH 43920-9647 Office: Smith and Associated Architects 330 N Main St Columbiana OH 44408-1064

RICHMAN, JOHN MARSHALL, lawyer, business executive; b. N.Y.C., Nov. 9, 1927; s. Arthur and Madeleine (Marshall) R.; m. Priscilla Frary, Sept. 3, 1951; children: Catherine Richman Wallace, Diana H. BA, Yale U., 1949; LLB, Harvard U., 1952. Bar: N.Y. 1953, Ill. 1973. Assoc. Leve, Hecht, Hadfield & McAlpin, N.Y.C., 1952-54; mem. law dept. Kraft, Inc., Glenview, Ill., 1954-63; gen. counsel Sealtest Foods div. Kraft, Inc., Glenview, 1963-67, asst. gen. counsel, 1967-70, v.p., gen. counsel, 1970-73, sr. v.p., gen. counsel, 1973-75, sr. v.p. adminstrn., gen. counsel, 1975-79, chmn. bd., chief exec. officer, 1979; chmn. bd., chief exec. officer Dart & Kraft, Inc. (name changed to Kraft, Inc. 1986), Glenview, 1980; chmn. Kraft Gen. Foods, Glenview, Ill., 1988-89; counsel Wachtell, Lipton, Rosen & Katz, Chgo., 1990—; bd. dirs. BankAm. Corp. and Bank of Am. Nat. Trust and Savs. Assn., R.R. Donnelley & Sons. Co., USX Corp.; mem. Bus. Coun. Trustee Chgo. Symphony Orch.; trustee Northwestern U.; trustee Johnson Found.; bd. dirs. Evanston Hosp. Corp., Chgo. Coun. on Fgn. Rels., Lyric Opera Chgo. Mem. Comml. Club, Econ. Club, Chgo. Club, Casino Club (Chgo.); Union League Club (N.Y.C.); Westmoreland Country Club (Wilmette, Ill.); Old Elm Club (Ft. Sheridan, Ill.); Lost Tree Club (N. Palm Beach, Fla.), Shoreacres, Lake Bluff, Ill. Congregationalist. Office: Wachtell Lipton et al 227 W Monroe St Ste 4825 Chicago IL 60606-5018

RICHMOND, DEWAYNE, secondary school educator; b. Muncie, Ind., Dec. 15, 1963; s. Charles and Zola (Johnson) R. AA, Ball State U., 1986, BS, 1990. Substitute tchr. Burris Sch., Muncie, 1990-94; tchr. Tri High Sch., Straughn, Ind., 1994-95; residence counselor Ind. Acad., Muncie, 1990-92; communications specialist Del. County Emergency 911, Muncie, 1992-95; residence coord. Briarcliff Coll., Sioux City, Iowa, 1995. With U.S. Army, 1983-89. Decorated Army Achievement medal, Good Conduct medal. Mem. Ind. Tchrs. Assn., Indsl. Tchrs. Assn., Ctr. for Tech. Tchr. Educators, Masons. Republican. Home: 1712 E Royerton Rd Muncie IN 47303

RICHMOND, MARSHA LEIGH, science historian; b. Muskogee, Okla., Oct. 1, 1950; d. William Eugene and Eldora Pearl (Hyde) R.; m. Joe Harris Lunn, Oct. 4, 1980; children: Sarah Elizabeth Lunn, Laura Patricia Lunn. BS, U. Okla., 1972; PhD, Ind. U., 1986. Editor Charles Darwin Corr., Cambridge, Eng., 1987-93; asst. prof. Wayne State U., Detroit, 1994—; editl. advisor Corr. of Charles Darwin, Cambridge, 1993—. Mem. editl. bd. NTM, Internat. Jour. History and Ethics of Natural Scis., Tech. and Medicine, 1993—; contbr. articles to profl. jours. Grantee NSF, 1992-95. Mem. Internat. Soc. for History, Philosophy and Social Studies of Biology, Brit. Soc. for History of Sci., History of Sci. Soc. Home: 1950 Coronada Dr Ann Arbor MI 48103 Office: Wayne State U Interdisciplinary Studies 5700 Cass Ave Detroit MI 48202

RICHMOND, RICHARD THOMAS, journalist; b. Parma, Ohio, May 16, 1933; s. Arthur James and Frances Marie (Visosky) R.; m. Charlotte Jean Schwoebel, Dec. 19, 1933; children: Kris Elaine, Leigh Alison, Paul Evan. AB, Washington U., St. Louis, 1961. Bur. mgr. UPI News Pictures, St. Louis, 1957-62; asst. picture editor Post-Dispatch, St. Louis, 1962-64, editor color sect., 1964-80, columnist, 1971—, editor calendar sect., 1983-94; asst. entertainment editor, 1995; v.p. Golden Royal Enterprises, St. Louis, 1976-78; pres. Oroquest Press, St. Louis, 1977-80; dir. U.S. Mortgage & Investment Corp., Hilton Head Island, N.C., 1977-81; pres. Magalar Mining, Texarkana, Ark., 1979-83. Co-author: Treasure Under Your Feet, 1974, In the Wake of the Golden Galleons, 1976, Diabetes: The Facts That Will Let You Regain Control of Your Life, 1986. Home: 307 Lebanon Ave Belleville IL 62220-4126 Office: St Louis Post-Dispatch 900 N Tucker Blvd Saint Louis MO 63101-1099

RICHTER, ELIZABETH DUNLOP, television executive; b. Pitts., Sept. 21, 1944; d. Charles Langton and Katherine Sargent (Mills) Dunlop; m. Tobin Marais Richter, July 11, 1970; children: Ian McNeil Mills, Lauren Elizabeth Dunlop. BA in History, Wellesley (Mass.) Coll., 1966. Assoc. producer Altman Prodns., Washington, 1967-71; writer, traffic and continuity WCHV Radio, Charlottesville, Va., 1971-72; women's editor Charlottesville Daily Progress, 1972-73; newswriter, assoc. producer WLS-TV Channel 7, Chgo., 1973-78, producer, 1978-81, exec. producer, 1981-84; assoc. dir. pub. affairs WTTW-TV Channel 11, Chgo., 1984-86, dir. prodn., 1986-89, v.p. prodn., 1989-94; v.p. nat. devel., 1994—. Producer TV series Eyewitness Chgo. (Emmy award 1979), 1977-79. Bd. dirs. Archeworks, 1996—, Chapin Hall Ctr. for Children, U. Chgo., 1987—, Jr. League of Chgo., 1987-89, Aux. Bd. Lincoln Park Zoo, 1988-93; mem. women's bd. dirs. Rush-Presbyn. St. Luke's Hosp., Chgo., 1990—; vestry St. Chrysostom's Episcopal Ch., 1993—. Mem. The Chgo. Network, Women's Forum of Chgo., Nat. Acad. TV Arts and Scis. (bd. govs. 1991-92), Econ. Club of Chgo. (bd. dirs.), Wellesley Coll. Alumnae Assn. (class pres. 1996—). Home: 2034 N Clifton Ave Chicago IL 60614-4120 Office: Ste 1401 33 N Dearborn Chicago IL 60602

RICHTER, EWALD ARTHUR, public relations counselor; b. Washington, Mo., July 22, 1920; s. Edward Richter and Adele (Struebbe) Willenbrink; m. Ruth L. Jacquin, July 22, 1927. B in Journalism, U. Mo., Columbia, 1948. Advt. sales person Radio Sta. KFRU, Columbia, Mo., 1945-48; advt. sales mgr. Lebanon (Mo.) Daily Record, 1948-49; sta. mgr. Radio Sta. KWRE, Warrenton and Washington, Mo., 1949-50; advt. sales mgr. Radio Sta. KWOS, Jefferson City, Mo., 1950-57; dir. info. The Mo. Bar, Jefferson City, 1958-85; pub. rels. counselor Richter Pub. Rels., Jefferson City, 1986—; sec. Mo. Broadcasters Assn., Jefferson City, 1956-57, exec. sec. 1957-58; cons. Mo. Press Bar Commn., Jefferson City, 1970-95. Editor: Mo. Bar Prentice Hall Survey, 1961. Mem. legis. com. AARP, Jefferson City, 1987-94. Mem. Nat. Assn. Bar Execs. (hon., chair pub. rels. sect. 1977-78, Bolton award for profl. excellence 1985, Leadership award comm. and pub. rels. sect. 1983), Pub. Rels. Soc. Am. (accredited; fellow, past pres. Mid-Mo. chpt.), Am. Lung Assn. Ea. Mo. (life; bd. dirs. 1958-91, pres. 1972-75, chair task force on Tb 1977), Host Lions Club (pres. 1965-66), KC. Democrat. Roman Catholic. Home: 3101 Bess Hill Jefferson City MO 65101 Office: Richter Pub Rels PO Box 481 217 E McCarty Jefferson City MO 65102

RICHTER, MARY KAYE, foundation director; b. Belleville, Ill., Apr. 20, 1945; d. Henry Charles and Lillian Frieda (Wittlich) Heberer; m. Norman George Richter, Nov. 21, 1964; children: Michael, Sharon, Charles. Student, U. Ill., 1962-63. Instr., florist Belleville Area Coll., 1970-81; exec. dir. Nat. Found. for Ectodermal Dysplasias, Mascoutah, Ill., 1981—. Dir. Nat. Orgn. Rare Disorders, New Fairfield, Conn., 1988—; mem. coun. Nat. Inst. Dental Rsch., Bethesda, Md., 1989—; chair Nat. Alliance Oral Health, Washington, 1989—; mem. Nat. Adv. Dental Rsch. Coun., Coalition Patient Advisers for Skin Disease Rsch.; commr. Horner Pk. Dist., Lebanon, Ill., 1976-80; bd. dirs. Lebanon Unit Sch. Dist. #9; past leader 4-H; active United Ch. of Christ, past tchr. Sunday sch. Recipient Woman of Achievement award Nat. Synod United Ch. Christ, 1985, Belleville Zonta Orgn., 1989, Outstanding Achievement award St. Clair County YWCA, 1991, Exceptional Achievement award USPHS, 1993, Kimmel Svc. award, 1995, Humanitarian award ISMSA, 1995, Mascoutah Schs. Achievement award, 1996. Office: Nat Found for Ectodermal Dysplasias 219 E Main St # 114 Mascoutah IL 62258-2136

RICHTER, MITCH, state legislator. Rep. S.D. State Dist. 11; appropriations com. S.D. Ho. Reps. Address: 6608 W 51st St Sioux Falls SD 57106-1676

RICHTER, NAOMI BERNICE, mental health nurse; b. Chgo., Mar. 26, 1936; d. Otto Paul and Bernice Katherine (Plumbeck) R. BSN, U. Ill., Chgo., 1958; M of Religious Edn., No. Bapt. Sem., 1963; MS, No. Ill. U., 1977. Staff, H.N., instr. Cook County Hosp., Chgo., 1958-63; asst. dir. staff edn. Sherman Hosp., Elgin, Ill., 1963-64; instr. Bacone Coll., Muskogee, Okla., 1964-66; teaching asst. U. Ill. Coll. Nursing, Chgo., 1967; instr. South Chgo. Community Hosp., 1969-76; asst. prof. Nazareth Coll., Kalamazoo, Mich., 1977-80; asst. dir. South Chgo. Community Hosp. Sch. Nursing, 1980-82; dir., staff, patient edn. Borgess Med. Ctr., Kalamazoo, 1982-87; asst. prof. Nazareth Coll., Kalamazoo, 1987-92; psychiat. home health nurse Allegan (Mich.) Gen. Hosp. and Allegan County Health Dept., 1992-95; adjunct faculty Grand Valley State Univ., 1992-94. Bd. dirs. Allegan County Prevention of Child Abuse/Neglect Coun. Mem. ANA, Sigma Theta Tau. Baptist. Home: 47245 Hillcrest Dr Bloomingdale MI 49026

RICKE, DAVID LOUIS, agricultural and environmental consultant; b. Greensburg, Ind., Aug. 21, 1942; s. Louis Vincent and Lois (Malone) R.; m. Susan Jane Spenceman, July 20, 1968; children: Stephanie, Elizabeth, Sarah, Emily. BS in Agrl. Econs., Purdue U., 1964. Cert. to registry of environ. and agrl. profls., Nat. Alliance Profl. Crop Cons. Pres. R & R Farms, Inc., Greensburg, Ind., 1967-81; prin. David L. Ricke Cons. Svcs., Greensburg, Ind., 1981—. 1st lt. U.S. Army, 1965-67. Mem. Am. Soc. Agronomy, Ind. Assn. Profl. Crop Cons. (pres. 1991-92), Am. Soc. Agrl. Cons. (cert. mem.), Nat. Alliance of Ind. Crop Cons., Optimists. Home and Office: 601 E Hendricks St Greensburg IN 47240-1763

RICKEL, ANNETTE URSO, psychology educator; b. Phila.; d. Ralph Francis and Marguerite (Calcaterra) Urso; m. Peter Rupert Fink, July 21, 1989; 1 child, John Ralph. BA, Mich. State U., 1963; MA, U. Mich., 1965, PhD, 1972. Lic. psychologist, Mich. Faculty early childhood edn. Merrill-Palmer Inst., Detroit, 1967-69; adj. faculty U. Mich., Ann Arbor, 1969-75; asst. dir. N.E. Guidance Ctr., Detroit, 1972-75; asst. prof. psychology Wayne State U., Detroit, 1975-81; vis. assoc. prof. Columbia U., N.Y.C., 1982-83; assoc. prof. psychology Wayne State U., 1981-87, asst. provost, 1989-91, prof. psychology, 1987—; Am. Coun. on Edn. fellow Princeton and Rutgers Univs., 1990-91; dir. mental health and devel. Nat. Com. for Quality Assurance, Washington, 1995-96; clin. prof. dept. Psychiatry Georgetown U.,

Washington, 1995—; AAAS and APA Congl. Sci. fellow on Senate Fin. Subcom. on Health and Pres.'s Nat. Health Care Reform Task Force, 1992-93. Cons. editor Jour. of Cmty. Psychology, Jour. Primary Prevention; co-author: Social and Psychological Problems of Women, 1984, Preventing Maladjustment..., 1987; author: Teenage Pregnancy and Parenting, 1989; contbr. articles to profl. jours. Mem. Pres.'s Task Force on Nat. Health Care Reform, 1993; bd. dirs. Children's Ctr. of Wayne County, Mich., The Epilepsy Ctr. of Mich., Planned Parenthood League, Inc. Grantee NIMH, 1976-86, Eloise and Richard Webber Found., 1977-80, McGregor Fund, 1977-78, 82, David M. Whitney Fund, 1982, Katherine Tuck Fund, 1985-90; recipient Career Devel. Chair award, 1985-86; Congl. Sci. fellow AAAS, 1992-93. Fellow APA (div. pres. 1984-85); mem. Midwestern Psychol. Assn., Mich. Psychol. Assn., Soc. for Rsch. in Child Devel., Soc. for Rsch. in Child and Adolescent Psychopathology, Internat. Assn. of Applied Psychologists, Sigma Xi, Psi Chi. Roman Catholic.

RICKERL, SUSAN MARIE, writer; b. Pitts., Dec. 22, 1958; d. Kenneth L. and Betty Lee (Weisburg) Garver; m. Stephen M. Hammill, Dec. 10, 1983 (div. Oct. 1985); m. Richard D. Rickerl, Mar. 14, 1987; 1 child, Paul J. BA, Carlow Coll., 1983; dental asst., Boyce C.C., Pitts., 1984; writing degree, Inst. Children's Lit., West Redding, Conn., 1991. Staff, receptionist Magee Women's Hosp., Pitts., 1978-83, 85; dental asst., office mgr. Dr. Wm. Garver DDS, Pitts., 1985; tchr. Pflugerville Sch. Dist., Austin, Tex., 1986-87; tchr. pre-K, sci. Round Rock (Tex.) Sch. Dist., 1987-89; writer Reynoldsburg, Ohio, 1989—. Author: (anthology) Our Western World's Greatest Poems, 1983, Our Beloved Poets, 1984, Poetic Voices of America, 1992. Recipient Merit award World of Poetry, 1983-89, Oriental Martial Arts Coll., 1991, Best Poems of 1996 award Nat. Libr. Poetry. Democrat. Roman Catholic.

RICKETTS, SONDRA LOU, librarian; b. McFall, Mo., Aug. 4, 1941; d. Jewell E. and Daisie Glenn (Weller) Rainey; m. Rex Errol Ricketts, June 14, 1964; children: Chad Errol, Trina Rae, Neysa Carrie. BS, U. Mo., 1963—. Cert. tchr., Mo. Libr. East Ladue Jr. High Sch., Ladue, Mo., 1963-65; adminstrv. asst. Jacksonville (Ill.) Pub. Libr., 1965; reference libr. Ill. Coll., Jacksonville, 1965-66; cataloger Stephens Coll., Columbia, Mo., 1966-69; libr. Clark (Mo.) Elem. Sch., 1981-95. Sun. sch. tchr. Presbyn. Ch., Columbia, 1977-84; mem. Hallsville (Mo.) Sch. bond com., 1980; cmty. leader Hallsville 4-H, 1980-82, mem. state com., Columbia, 1985, project leader Hallsville 4-H, 1980-85, 94—; bd. dirs. 4-H Found., Columbia, 1991—; mem. Boone County 4-H Auction com., 1994—. Conf. honoree AIJCA, 1991. Mem. Am. Internat. Charolais Assn., Mo. Assn. of Sch. Librs., Mo. Univ. Alumnae Assn., Boone County Alumnae Assn., Alpha Chi Omega Alumnae Assn., Pi Lambda Theta.

RICKLEFS, KAREN LEE, quality assurance consultant; b. Elmore, Minn., Feb. 12, 1937; d. Ole Andrew and Florence Dorothy (Peterson) Anderson; m. Merlin John Ricklefs, Sept. 28, 1958; children: Linda Lee Ricklefs Baudry, Lowell John, Kristin Kay Ricklefs Bennett. Student, St. Olaf Coll., 1955-57; BS in Math., Iowa State U., 1957-60; postgrad., U. Minn., 1962, 70, 80, Pace U., 1976-78, Manhattanville Coll. Officer asst. NAS, Ames, 1959-60; tchr. math. various schs., Minn. and N.Y., 1960-69; dir., founder Coll. and Career Resource Ctr. Mayo H. S., Rochester, Minn., 1985-90; realtor K & K Realty, Rochester, 1987-90; exec. asst. U. Minn., Duluth, 1991-92; sr. cons., co-founder Quality Assocs. Internat., Rochester, 1991—; cons. Minn. Acad. Excellence Found., St. Paul, 1992—, Minn. Ptnrs. for Quality, St. Paul. 1992—; presenter in field. Treas., v.p., pres., chmn. bd. dirs. Rochester Bd. Edn., 1970-76; mem. exec. bd. Minn. Environ. Edn. Coun., St. Paul, 1972-76; commr. adv. coun. Minn. State Bd. Edn., 1973-76; pres., founder Rochester Area Intergovtl. Coun., 1973-76; v.p., founder S.E. Minn. Ednl. Computer Consortium Governance Bd., 1973-76; Minn. rep. Nat. Energy Conf., Washington, 1974; bd. dirs., pres. Olmsted Cmty. Hosp., Rochester, 1979-85; pres., founder Rochester Found. Ednl. Excellence, 1987-94. Named Outstanding Young Women of Am., 1970, Friend of Edn., Rochester Principals Assn., 1989; recipient Good Citizenship award City of Rochester, 1974, Outstanding Sch. Bd. Mem., Rochester Sch. Bd., 1975. Mem. AAUW (pres. 1963, Edn. Found. Fellowship award 1974), Am. Soc. Quality Control, Minn. Symphony Orch. Womens' Assn., Rochester C. of C., Sons of Norway. Pepublican. Lutheran. Office: Quality Assocs Internat 1535 Woodland Dr SW Rochester MN 55902

RICKLEFS, MERLIN JOHN, quality and performance improvement consultant; b. Ft. Dodge, Iowa, Aug. 27, 1936; s. John G. and Myrtle C. (Bendixon) R.; m. Karen Lee Anderson, Sept. 28, 1958; children: Linda, Lowell, Kristin. BS in Mech. Engring., Iowa State U., 1960, MS in Theoretical and Applied Mechanics, 1963. With Advanced Sys. Devel. divsn. IBM, Ossining, N.Y., 1960-61; in new product devel. Sys. Devel. divsn. IBM, Rochester, Minn., 1961-76; corp. program dir. storage products IBM, Armonk, N.Y., 1976-78; sr. level mgmt. and staff Gen. Sys. divsn. IBM, Rochester, Minn., 1978-87; bus. and sys. evaluation mgr. IBM Application Bus. Sys., Rochester, 1987-89, site quality mgr., 1989-91; internat. cons. and lectr. Quality Assocs. Internat., Rochester, 1991—; 3M McKnight disting. vis. prof. U. Minn., Duluth, 1991-92; mem. adv. com. for quality leadership ctr. Carlson Sch. Mgmt., U. Minn., Mpls., 1994—; mem. tech. adv. comm. ctr. for quality Dunwoody Tech. Inst., Mpls., 1995—; mem. bd. examiners Malcolm Baldridge Nat. Quality Award, Gaithersburg, Md., 1994, Minn. Quality Award, 1992. Contbr. chpt. to book, articles to profl. jours.; holder 5 patents. Pres., co-chair guarantee fund Minn. Orch. Assn., Rochester, 1980; chmn. pers. com. Rochester Civic Theatre, 1980; chmn. profl. unit United Way Guarantee Fund, Rochester, 1973; pres., chair trustees com. Gloria Dei Congregation, Rochester, 1968. Mem. Am. Soc. for Quality Control (sr.), Am. Assn. for Higher Edn., Rochester Quality Coun., Rochester C. of C., Rotary, Pi Tau Sigma. Office: Quality Assocs Internat 1535 Woodland Dr SW Rochester MN 55902

RIDDER, PETER B., publishing executive. Pub. St. Paul Pioneer Press. Office: St Paul Pioneer Press 345 Cedar St Saint Paul MN 55101-1014*

RIDGEWAY, LUANN, state legislator. Mem. Mo. State Ho. of Reps. Dist. 35. Home: 19405 Platte County Line Rd Smithville MO 64089-8798 Office: Mo Ho of Reps State Capitol Building Jefferson City MO 65101-1556*

RIDGWAY, MARCELLA DAVIES, veterinarian; b. Sewickley, Pa., Dec. 24, 1957; d. Willis Eugene and Martha Ann (Davies) R. BS, Pa. State U., 1979; VMD, U. Pa., 1983. Intern Univ. Ill., Urbana, 1983-84, resident in small animal internal medicine, 1984-87; small animal vet. Vet. Cons. Svcs., Savoy, Ill., 1987—. Contbr. articles to profl. jours. Mem. Am. Vet. Med. Assn., Am. Animal Hosp. Assn., Acad. Vet. Clinicians, Ednl. Resources in Environ. Sci. (bd. dirs.), Savoy Prairie Soc. (pres. 1989—), Grand Prairie Friends (bd. dirs. 1993-96). Home and Office: Vet Cons Svcs 194 Paddock Dr E Savoy IL 61874-9663

RIDLEN, SAMUEL FRANKLIN, agriculture educator; b. Marion, Ill., Apr. 24, 1916; s. Will and Leoma Josephine (Sneed) R.; m. Helen Louise Camp, Apr. 17, 1946; children: Judith Elaine, Barbara Jo, Mark Ellis. BS, U. Ill., 1940; MS, Mich. State U., 1957. Agr. instr. Westville (Ill.) Twp. High Sch., 1940-43; gen. mgr. Honegger Breeder Hatchery, Forrest, Ill., 1953-56; assoc. prof. poultry sci. U. Conn., Storrs, 1957-58; from asst. prof. to prof. poultry extension U. Ill., Urbana-Champaign, 1946-86, prof. emeritus poultry extension, 1986—, asst. head dept. animal scis., 1978-86. Author: An Idea and An Ideal-Nabor House Fraternity 1939-1989, 1989; poultry editorial cons. Successful Farming, Wonderful World Ency., 1960; poultry editor Am. Farm Youth, 1949-53, Ill. Feed Folks, 1949-53. Founding mem., charter mem. Nabor House Frat. Recipient Superior Svc. award U.S. Dept. Agr., 1982, Paul A. Funk Recognition award Coll. Agr., U. Ill., 1983, numerous others. Fellow Poultry Sci. Assn.; mem. World's Poultry Sci. Assn., Ill. State Turkey Growers Assn., Ill. Poultry Industry Coun., Ill Egg Market Devel. Coun. (adv. mem.), Ill. Animal Industry Coun., Coun. for Agr. Sci. and Tech., Ill. Alumni Assn. (life), DAV (life), Alpha Tau Alpha, Epsilon Sigma Phi, Gamma Sigma Delta (pres. 1982-83). Home: 1901 Lakeside Dr # C Champaign IL 61821-5967

RIECK, JAMES DEAN, copywriter, creative consultant; b. New Martinsville, W.Va., Aug. 13, 1962; s. James Nelson and Billie Jo (Daugherty) R.; m. Antoinette Julia Ventresca, Dec. 22, 1990. BA in English and Gen. Sci., West Liberty State Coll., 1984; postgrad., Western Ill. U., 1984. Cert. secondary educator, W.Va., Ohio. Writing tutor West Liberty (W.Va.) State Coll., 1982-83; writing instr. Western Ill. U., Macomb, 1984; acct. exec. Sta. WKWK-FM, Wheeling, W.Va., 1985; copywriter, producer Sta. WTOV-TV, Steubenville, Ohio, 1985-90; freelance copywriter Paul/Jay Assocs., Bellaire, Ohio, 1990-91; freelance editor Learning Design Assocs., Columbus, Ohio, 1991-92; pres. Dean Rieck Copywriting, Columbus, 1992—; guest spkr. Ohio State U., Columbus, 1994—; Columbus Writers Conf., 1994—. Rschr., writer (textbook) Marketing in a Global Economy, 1992; editor (textbook) Professional Selling, 1993; author, editor (newsletter) Direct Response Communication, 1993—; contbg. author DM News, 1994—, Target Marketing mag., 1995—, Direct Marketing mag., 1995—. Mem. Mid-Ohio Direct Mktg. Assn. (v.p. 1994—), Midwest Direct Mktg. Assn., Direct Mktg. Assn. Detroit, Dayton Direct Mktg. Club, Cin. Direct Mktg. Assn., Columbus Advt. Fedn. Home and Office: 2102 Brookhurst Ave Columbus OH 43229

RIECK, JANET RAE, special education educator; b. Atchison, Kans., Oct. 24, 1948; d. Clinton Everett and Bernice Marie (Schreurs) Wendland; m. Arthur Wyman Hand, Mar. 1970 (div. Feb. 1977); m. Doyle Elmer Rieck, Sept. 21, 1986. B in Music Edn., Otterbein Coll., 1970; MA, U. No. Colo., 1980; MS, No. Ill. U., 1989. Cert. tchr. Nebr. Music tchr. Blanchester (Ohio) Schs., 1970-74; tchr. aide N.Mex. Sch. for Visually Handicapped, Alamogordo, 1976-78; tchr. visually impaired Edn. Svc. Unit 7, Columbus, Nebr., 1979—; piano tchr., Cin., 1975-76, Alamogordo, 1976-78. Mem. NEA, Coun. Exceptional Children, Assn. for Edn. and Rehab. of Blind and Visually Impaired (Nebr. pres. elect 1990-92, pres. 1992-94, cert. orientation and mobility specialist). Lutheran. Home: RR 2 Box 148 Albion NE 68620-9323 Office: Ednl Svc Unit 7 2657 44th Ave Columbus NE 68601-8537

RIEDE, RONALD FREDERICK, JR., business professional; b. Oil City, Pa., July 12, 1957; s. Ronald Frederick and Phyllis Elaine (Jennings) R.; m. Cynthia Marie Primovic, Aug. 6, 1984. BS in Chemistry, Grove City Coll., 1979; MBA, Ind. U., South Bend, 1986. Raw material chemist B.F. Goodrich, Akron, Ohio, 1979; chemist B.F. Goodrich, Union, W.Va., 1979-82; process chemist Uniroyal Chem., Mishawaka, Ind., 1982-83, sr. process chemist, 1983-85, sr. devel. chemist, 1985-86, quality mgr., 1986-87, mkt. devel. mgr., 1987-88; product mgr. Nalco Chem. Co., Naperville, Ill., 1988-95, dir. quality, 1995-96, mktg. mgr., 1996—. Patentee in field. Mem. Am. Chem. Soc., Chem. Mfrs. Assn., Am. Soc. Quality Control. Republican. Home: 841 S River Rd Naperville IL 60540-6384 Office: Nalco Chem Co One Nalco Ctr Naperville IL 60563

RIEDINGER, EDWARD ANTHONY, international educator, Brazilianist; b. Cin., Mar. 26, 1944; s. Charles Anthony and Ida Gertrude (Winter) R. Student, Latin Sch. Indpls., 1962; BA cum laude, Butler U., 1967; MA, U. Chgo., 1969, PhD, 1978; MLIS, U. Calif., Berkeley, 1989; postgrad., Harvard U., 1969, U. Oxford, 1970, U. Cambridge, 1986. Pvt. sec. to ex-pres. Brazil Juscelino Kubitschek, 1972-76; asst. prof. Pontifical Cath. U., Rio de Janeiro, 1976-77, U. Ams., Puebla, Mex., 1978; ednl. adv. officer Fulbright Commn. U.S. Consulate, Rio de Janeiro, 1979-88; founder Overseas Ednl. Advisers Profl. Edn. Group Nat. Assn. for Fgn. Student Affairs, 1985, Latin Am. rep., 1988; acting bibliographer L.Am., Spain, Portugal U. Calif., Berkeley, 1990; lectr. Brazilian history San Francisco State U., 1990; bibliographer Latin Am., adj. assoc. prof. history Ohio State U., 1991—; mem. organizing exec. com. Brazilian Studies Assn., 1993, sec., 1994-96; founder, adminstr. OSEASNet, 1992-95. Author: Brief View of American Literature, 1976, Como Se Faz Um Presidente, a Campanha de J.K., 1988, Proceedings of 1st BRASA conf., 1994, Proceedings of 2d BRASA conf., 1995, Turned on Advising, 1995, Where in the World to Learn, 1995; contbr. numerous articles to profl. and scholarly jours. and reference books; mem. editl. bd. Phi Beta Delta Internat. Rev., 1992—, Manguinhos, 1994—. Ford Found. fellow, 1968-72; travel grantee NEH, 1992, OSU/Tinker Found. field rsch. grantee 1992, 96; Fulbright-Hays scholar, 1996; recipient commendations Brazilian Army Corps of Engrs., 1982, U.S. Info. Svc., 1984, Brazilian War Coll., 1985, Fulbright Commn., 1988, U.S. amb. to Brazil, 1988, Berkeley City Commons, 1990, Instituto Brasil-Estados Unidos, Rio de Janeiro, 1995. Office: Ohio State U Librs Office Lat Am Bibliography 1858 Neil Ave Rm 312 Columbus OH 43210-1225

RIEDL, JOHN ORTH, university dean; b. Milw., Dec. 9, 1937; s. John O. and Clare C. (Quirk) R.; m. Mary Lucille Priestap, Feb. 4, 1961; children: John T., Ann E., James W., Steven E., Daniel J. BS in Math. magna cum laude, Marquette U., Milw., 1958; MS in Math., U. Notre Dame, 1960, PhD in Math., 1963; postgrad., Northwestern U., 1963. Asst. prof. math. Ohio State U., Columbus, 1966-70, assoc. prof., 1970—, asst. dean Coll. Math. and Phys. Sci., 1969-74, assoc. dean, 1974-87, acting dean, 1984-86, spl. asst. to provost, 1987, dean, dir. Mansfield (Ohio) Campus, 1987—, coord. dean regional campus, 1988—; panelist sci. edn. NSF, 1980-91; cons. Ohio Dept. Edn., 1989, Ohio bd. regents subsidy cons., 1991, 95. Pres., v.p. exec. com. U. Cmty. Assn., Columbus, 1970-78; mem. edn. commn. St. Peter's Schs., Mansfield, 1989-95; trustee Rehab. Svc. N. Ctrl. Ohio, Mansfield, 1990—, v.p. 1993-94, pres. 1995—; pres. Ohio Assn. Regional Campuses, 1993-94. NSF grad. fellow, 1960, 61, 62; recipient Faculty Svc. award Nat. U. Continuing Edn. Assn., 1988, Creative Programming award, 1988. Mem. Math. Assn. Am. (chair com. on minicourse 1981-87), Rotary Internat. Democrat. Roman Catholic. Home: 745 Clifton Blvd Mansfield OH 44907-2284 Office: Ohio State U 1680 University Dr Mansfield OH 44906-1547

RIEDY, VIRGINIA KATHLEEN, nursing educator; b. Columbus, Ohio, Apr. 21, 1952; d. Oliver and Barbara A. Sheets; children: Elizabeth, Matthew, Andrew. Student, Bowling Green State U., 1976. RN, Ohio; cert. emergency nurse, ACLS provider, instr.; EMT, Ohio; paramedic, Ohio. Staff nurse emergency dept. Children's Hosp., Columbus, Ohio, 1973-74, Good Samaritan Hosp., Sandusky, Ohio, 1974-78, Providence Hosp., Sandusky, Ohio, 1978-86; site evaluator Ohio Bd. Regents, Paramedic Tng. Programs, State of Ohio, 1984—; paramedic coord. ER-DOC Providence Hosp., Sandusky, 1984—; continuing edn. cons. Lucas County/REMSNO, 1990—; program dir. N.W. Paramedic Program Med. Coll. Ohio, Toledo, 1993—; internat. EMS lectr. video game induced seizures; affiliate faculty State of Ohio Basic Trauma Life Support, 1986—; asthma camp nurse supr. Timberlane South Shore Lung Assn., 1984; EMS delegate People to People, Soviet Union and Germany, 1991. Contbr. articles to profl. jours. Trustee Erie County chpt. Am. Heart Assn., 1976—; REMSNO ednl. adv. com., 1986—; Erie County EMS Coun. rep., 1986—. Mem. Nat. Assn. EMT, Am. Trauma Soc. (N.W. Ohio unit affiliate), Ohio Instr. Coords. Soc. (charter mem.), Emergency Nurses Assn. (state coun. rep.). Roman Catholic. Home: 358 Portside Cr Apt 3 Perrysburg OH 43551 Office: Paramedic Tng Program 1912 Hayes Ave Sandusky OH 44870-4736

RIEGER, DONNA MARIE, critical care nurse, educator, consultant; b. St. Louis, May 5, 1957; d. Elvern E. and Eleanore E. (Zimmerer) R. BSN, St. Louis U., 1979. Cert. BLS affiliate faculty, Mo., ACLS affiliate faculty, Mo., BLS, ACLS Am. Heart Assn. Critical care nurse St. Anthony's Med. Ctr., St. Louis, 1979-86; critical care nurse Barnes Hosp., St. Louis, 1986-88, nursing edn. specialist, 1988—; mem. ACLS regional com., BCLS regional com. Am. Heart Assn., St. Louis, 1988—, chair ACLS regional com., 1991-95, mem. ACLS state com., 1993—, del. to bd., 1991—; adj. faculty Barnes Coll.; chair devel. critical care curriculum devel. BJC Health Sys. merger, 1994—. Mem. AACN, Greater St. Louis Chpt. of Critical Care Nurses (mem. edn. com. 1991-93), Barnes Coll. Nursing Honor Soc., Sigma Theta Tau (Internat. Nu Chi chpt. U. Mo.). Roman Catholic. Home: 418 Autumn Peak Dr Fenton MO 63026-3962 Office: Barnes Hosp One Barnes Hosp Plz Saint Louis MO 63110

RIEGER, MITCHELL SHERIDAN, lawyer; b. Chgo., Sept. 5, 1922; s. Louis and Evelyn (Sampson) R.; m. Rena White Abelmann, May 17, 1949 (div. 1957); 1 child, Karen Gross Cooper; m. Nancy Horner, May 30, 1961 (div. 1972); stepchildren: Jill Levi, Linda Hanan, Susan Perlstein, James Geoffrey Felsenthal; m. Pearl Handelsman, June 10, 1973; stepchildren: Steven Newman, Mary Ann Malarkey, Nancy Halbeck. A.B., Northwestern U., 1944; J.D., Harvard U., 1949. Bar: Ill. 1950, U.S. Dist. Ct. (no. dist.) Ill. 1950, U.S. Supreme Ct. 1953, U.S. Ct. Mil. Appeals 1953, U.S. Ct. Appeals (7th cir.) 1954. Legal asst. Rieger & Rieger, Chgo., 1949-50, assoc., 1950-54; asst. U.S. atty. No. Dist Ill., Chgo., 1954-60; 1st asst. No. Dist Ill., 1958-60; assoc. gen. counsel SEC, Washington, 1960-61; ptnr. Schiff Hardin & Waite, Chgo., 1961—; instr. John Marshall Law Sch. Chgo., 1952-54. Contbr. articles to profl. jours. Mem. Chgo. Crime Commn., 1964-94, life mem., 1995—; pres. Park View Home for Aged, 1969-71; Rep. precinct committeeman, Highland Park, Ill., 1964-68; bd. dirs. Spertus Mus. Judaica, 1987-91, vis. com., 1991—. Fellow Am. Coll. Trial Lawyers; mem. ABA, FBA (pres. Chgo. chpt. 1959-60, nat. v.p. 1960-61), Chgo. Bar Assn., Ill. Bar Assn., Am. Judicature Soc., 7th Circuit Bar Assn., Standard Club, Law Club Chgo., Vail Racquet Club, Phi Beta Kappa. Jewish. Home: 4950 S Chicago Beach Dr Chicago IL 60615-3207 Office: Schiff Hardin & Waite 7200 Sears Towers Chicago IL 60606

RIEGSECKER, MARVIN DEAN, pharmacist, state senator; b. Goshen, Ind., July 5, 1937; s. Levi and Mayme (Kauffman) R.; m. Norma Jane Shrock, Aug. 3, 1958; children: Steven Scott, Michael Dean. BA in Pharmacy, U. Colo., 1967. Pharmacist Parkside Pharmacy, Goshen, Ind., 1967-73; pharmacist, mgr. Hooks Drugs, Inc., Goshen, 1973-94; coroner Elkhart County, Goshen, 1977-84; mem. Ind. Senate, Indpls., 1988—; pharmacist Walgreens, Goshen, 1994—; bd. dirs. Goshen Gen. Hosp., 1985-94. Rep. commr. Elkhart County, 1985-88; bd. commrs. pres., 1987-88; past adv. bd. dirs. Oaklawn Hosp.; past chmn. Michiana Area Coun. of Govts. Mem. Ind. Pharm. Assn., Elkhart County Pharm. Assn., Exch. Club. Republican. Mennonite. Home: 1814 Kentfield Way Goshen IN 46526-4010 Office: Ind Senate Statehouse 4-D N 200 W Washington St Indianapolis IN 46204-2728

RIEKE, TOM JAMES, mechanical draftsman; b. Sleepy-eye, Minn., July 23, 1950. BS in Mech. Drafting, Vocat. Hutchinson Tech. Coll., 1992. Registered profl. engr., Minn. Heavy equipment operator Komatz Constrn., St. Peter, Minn., 1972-85, Fischer, Sand & Agrate, Apple Valley, Minn., 1985-89; mech. drafter Marv Nelson II Distbn. Inc., Hector, Minn., 1992—. Democrat. Roman Catholic. Office: Nelson Marv Distbg II Inc Hwy 4S Hector MN 55342

RIEKENBERG, WARREN GLENN, civil engineer; b. Topeka, Aug. 3, 1936; s. Lorenz J. and Vergie Weese (Ingraham) R.; m. Carol Lee Alberts, May 15, 1971; children: Eric Karl, Lee Ann Marie. BSCE, U. Kans., Lawrence, 1959. Registered profl. engr., Ill., Kans., Iowa. Civil engr. State Hwy. Commn. Kans., Topeka, 1959, 61-63, Consoer, Townsend and Assocs., Chgo., 1970-78, Clark, Dietz and Assocs., Chgo., 1978-82, Metcalf and Eddy, Inc., Arlington Heights, Ill. and Des Moines, 1982-92, Iowa Dept. Natural Resources, Des Moines, 1992-95, City of Des Moines, 1995—. Maj. U.S. Army, 1959-61, 63-70, Vietnam. Decorated Bronze Star. Mem. ASCE, NRA. Home: 3209 Melanie Dr Des Moines IA 50322-6851 Office: City Des Moines Wastewater Reclamation Fac 3000 Vandalia Rd Des Moines IA 50317

RIEPE, MARK WILLIAM, economic consultant; b. Lynwood, Calif., Apr. 7, 1964; s. William Joseph and Dolores Catherine (Klesener) R.; m. Tina Weatherbee, Dec. 5, 1992. BA, U.Chgo., 1986, MBA, 1991. Rsch. assoc. GNP Commodities, Chgo., 1986-90; v.p. Ibbotson Assocs., Chgo., 1990—. Editor: Pension Investment Handbook, 1996. Mem. Econ. History Assn., Econ. History Soc., Am. Real Estate and Urban Econs. Assn. Home: 100 E Walton St Unit 36C Chicago IL 60611 Office: Ibbotson Assocs 225 N Michigan Ave Chicago IL 60601-7601

RIES, DONALD, industrial designer; b. Cin., Oct. 6, 1950. Grad. H.S., Cin. CAD tng. cert., Cin. Designer Senco Products Inc., Cin., 1978—; tng. geometric tolerancing Senco, 1990.

RIES, THOMAS G. (TORCHY), state legislator; m. Janet Ries; 7 children. Student, U. S.D. Cir. ct. judge; mem. S.D. Ho. Reps., 1984-88, 93—, mem. judiciary com. and local govt. com.; mem. judiciary and transp. coms. Home: 420 S Lake Dr Watertown SD 57201-5433*

RIESENBERGER, JOHN RICHARD, pharmaceutical company executive; b. N.Y.C., Sept. 25, 1948; s. Richard Raymond and Marie Teresa (Long) R.; m. Patricia Ann Casey, Nov. 23, 1974; children: Christine, Jennifer. BS in Econs. and Bus., Hofstra U., 1970, MBA in Mgmt., 1975; cert. internat. sr. mgmt. program, Harvard U., 1989. Customer svc. supr. Chase Manhattan Bank, 1970-72; gen. sales rep. various regions Upjohn Co., Bklyn., 1972-75; sales rep., sales mgr. Upjohn Co., various locations, N.Y., 1976-81; profl. tng. and devel. officer Upjohn Co., Kalamazoo, Mich., 1981-83; dir. Chgo. sales area Upjohn Co., 1983-87; v.p., group mgr. Upjohn Co. of Can., Toronto, Ont., 1987-89; exec. dir., worldwide med. scis. liaison Upjohn Co., Kalamazoo, 1989-92, exec. dir. worldwide strategic mktg., 1992-95; exec. dir. corp. info. tech. Pharmacia & Upjohn, Inc., Kalamazoo, 1995, v.p. bus. info., 1996—; chmn. industry adv. bd. dirs. SEI Ctr. Advanced Studies in Mgmt., Wharton Sch., U. Pa.. Author: (with Robert T. Moran) The Global Challenge: Building the New Worldwide Enterprise, 1994, Global Business Management in the 1990's, 1995. Mem. Am. Mgmt. Assn., Am. Mktg. Assn., Midwest Healthcare Mktg. Assn., World Future Soc., Soc. for Competitive Intelligence Profls., Strategic Mgmt. Soc., Healthcare Mktg. and Comm. Coun., Pharm. Rsch. Mfrs. Am. (chmn. mktg. practices com.), Nat. Pharm. Coun., Am. Med. Informatics Assn., The Planning Forum, Internat. Soc. for Strategic Planning and Mgmt., Harvard Bus. Sch. Club, Pharm. Bus. Intelligence and Rsch. Group. Home: 7398 Oak Shore Dr Portage MI 49002-7858

RIESTER, BECKY J., orthopedics and neurology nurse; b. Tyndall AFB, Fla., July 1, 1962; d. Harlan Frederick and Natalie Naomi (Malacarne) Mueller; m. Matthew K. Riester, June 10, 1987. ADN, Belleville (Ill.) Area Coll., 1987. RN, Ill. Staff nurse/charge nurse orthopedic-neurosurgery ward St. Elizabeth's Hosp., Belleville, 1987—.

RIETOW, DOTTIE MILLER, government and public relations consultant; b. Mpls., July 11, 1937; d. Wesley Templeton and Sadie Amanda (Tegland) Miller; m. Robert George Rietow, Sept. 12, 1958; children: Cari Lynn, Gregory Thomas, Richard William. BA, U. Minn., 1958, cert. legal asst., 1976. Exec. sec. 1st Nat. Bank, Mpls., 1955-60; exec. sec. to bishop Episcopal Ch., Mpls., 1960-62; legal asst. Popham, Haik, Schobrich, Doty, Mpls., 1976-82; govt. rels. dir. Rogers Cable Sys., Mpls., 1982-85; pres. Consensus, Mpls., 1985-91, 95—; dir. Office of Waste Mgmt., St. Paul, 1991-92; acting chair Met. Waste Control Commn., St. Paul, 1992; chair Met. Coun., St. Paul, 1992-95; mem. state adv. coun. major transp. projects, Minn. Legis., 1994-95, mem. environ. quality bd., 1991-92, chair aggragate resources com., 1984-85; v.p. Mpls. Synod ELCA, 1995—; mem. policy adv. com. H.H. Humphrey Inst. U. Minn., 1992—. Commr. Miss. River Coord. Commn., St. Paul, 1990-91; mem. task force Mpls. St. Paul Planning Commn., 1991; mem. Met. Coun., St. Paul, 1984-91; bd. dirs. Hamline U. Women Govt., 1993—. Recipient Outstanding Achievement award Lt. Gov. Jonell Dyrstad, 1995; Dottie Rietow Day in State of Minn., Gov. Arne Carlson, 1995. Mem. Minn. Women's Polit. Caucus, GOP Feminist Caucus (state chair 1980-84), Horizon 100, World Future Soc., St. Louis Park Rotary (Paul Harris fellow 1989). Lutheran. Home: 1317 Kilmer Ave Minneapolis MN 55426

RIEW, CHANGKIU KEITH, materials scientist, polymer chemist; b. Seoul, Korea, May 25, 1928; came to U.S., 1961; s. Chanhee and Youngjun (Lee) R.; m. Hyunsoo Kim, Nov. 18, 1951; children: Claire Riew Choi, Elisa Riew Chung, K. Daniel. BS, Seoul Nat. U., 1959; MS, Wayne State U., 1965, PhD, 1967. Tchr. Kyunggi High Sch., Seoul, 1957-61; rsch. assoc. Wayne State U., Detroit, 1962-66; sr. R & D chemist B.F. Goodrich Co., Brecksville, Ohio, 1967-72, R & D assoc., 1973-76, R & D group leader, 1977, R & D mgr., 1977-80, R & D fellow, 1981-93; rsch. prof. coll. engring. U. Akron, Ohio, 1993-94; presenter at profl. meetings; speaker, lectr. in field. Co-editor: Rubber Modified Thermoset Resins, 1984; editor: Rubber-Toughened Plastics, 1989, Toughened Plastics I: Science and Engineering, 1993, Toughened Plastics II: Science and Engineering, 1995; contbr. articles to profl. jours.; patentee in field. Capt. C.E., Korean Army, 1950-56. Mem. AAAS, ASTM, AIChE, Am. Ceramic Soc., Am. Chem. Soc. (div. polymer chemistry, div. polymeric materials, div. rubber, Akron sect.), Soc. for Advancement of Material and Process Engring., Soc. Plastics Engrs., Soc. Plastics Industry, Korean Scientists and Engrs. Assn. Am., Sigma Xi.

RIFF, EMMANUEL RAPHAEL, internist; b. Chgo., Sept. 9, 1924; s. Chaim and Diana (Grobstein) R.; m. Rhoda June Gershen, June 29, 1947 (dec. July 1991); children: Kenneth Mark, Lawrence Paul. Student, Ill. Inst.

Tech., U. Ill., Ohio State U.; MD, Duke U., 1949. Diplomate Nat. Bd. Med. Examiners, diplomate Am. Bd. Internal Medicine. Intern, resident Cook County Hosp., Chgo., 1951-53; pres. med. staff Marymount Hosp., Garfield Heights, Ohio, 1980-82; dir. dept. internal medicine Marymount Hosp., Garfield Heights, 1983-90; internist pvt. practice Maple Heights, Ohio, 1990-95; ret.; tech. cons. Marymount Hosp. Heart Sta., Garfield Heights, 1987-92; active staff Marymount Hosp. Contbr. articles to profl. jours. With U.S. Army, 1943-45, WWII, capt. USAF, 1951-53. Decorated Bronze star USAF, Japan, 1952. Fellow ACP; mem. Am. Soc. Internal Medicine, Royal Soc. Medicine, Ohio State Med. Soc., Cleve. Acad. Medicine, Lakeside Yacht Club (fleet surgeon 1985). Republican. Jewish. Home: 3608 Norwood Rd Shaker Heights OH 44122

RIFFEL, TERESA LYNN, systems analyst, consultant; b. Wichita, Kans., Apr. 6, 1962; d. Keith Laverne and Patricia Ann (Biehler) R.; m. Michael Shae Kennedy, Nov. 29, 1980 (div. Apr. 1988); children: Jason Michael, Jocelyn Michelle. AAS in Bus. Adminstrn., Butler County C.C., El Dorado, Kans., 1992; BS in Bus. Mgmt., Kans. Newman Coll., 1993; postgrad. in Mgmt. Info. Sys., Friends U., 1994—. Tech. publs. operator Boeing Aircraft Co., Wichita, 1984-85; engring. asst. Beech Aircraft Corp., Wichita, 1985-94; cons. Midwest Consulting Group, Kansas City, Mo., 1994-95; sys. analyst Cessna Aircraft, Wichita, Kans., 1995—. Mem. NAFE, Music Tchrs. Nat. Assn., Kans. Music Tchrs. Assn., Phi Theta Kappa. Lutheran. Home: 2309 N Grant Rd Andover KS 67002 Office: Cessna Aircraft One Cessna Blvd Wichita KS 67215

RIGDON, GLENN JOSEPH, real estate appraiser, real estate broker; b. Phila., Dec. 28, 1950; s. Glenn Marvin and Anna Mae (Cassalia) R.; m. Judy Marie Perry, Dec. 28, 1971; children: Jennifer Alison, Melissa Ann. BS in Econs./Stats., No. Mich. U., 1976, MA in Adminstrv. Svc., 1992. Cert. real estate appraiser, Mich., Wis. Broker, owner Estate Agts. Real Estate, Marquette, Mich., 1977-81; rsch. analyst Ariz. Dept. Health Svcs., Phoenix, 1981-84; broker, owner G. Rigdon & Assocs., Inc. Comml. Real Estate Sales, Phoenix, 1987; economist Ariz. State Land Dept., Phoenix, 1984-86; broker, co-owner E.R.A. Racine's Realty, Marquette, Mich., 1988-93; mng. ptrn. Wellington Partnership, Phoenix, 1987-90, Cornerstone Gen. Partnership, Phoenix, 1986-90; cert. developer Apple Macintosh computers G. Rigdon & Assocs., Inc., Phoenix, 1985-88. Editor, pub. (newsletter) Marquette Bus. and Real Estate Report, 1988-90; pub. Realty Register, 1987-88. Sgt. USAF, 1971-75. Recognized for disting. svc. Ariz. State Land Dept., 1986. Mem. Upper Peninsula Assn. Realtors, Nat. Assn. Realtors, Am. Soc. Appraisers (accredited sr. appraiser), Multiple Listing Svc. Exec. Com. (exec. officer 1989-90), Nat. Assn. Real Estate Appraisers, Comml./Indsl. Broker Network, Mich. Assn. Realtors. Republican. Roman Catholic. Home: 1213 Nakomis St Negaunee MI 49866-1126 Office: G Rigdon Appraisal Svcs 1213 Nakomis St Negaunee MI 49866

RIGGLEMAN, JAMES DAVID, professional baseball team manager; b. Ft. Dix, N.J., Dec. 9, 1952. Degree in Physical Edn., Frostburg State U. Minor league baseball player, 1974-81, minor league baseball mgr., 1982-88, 91-92; dir. player devel., then coach St. Louis Cardinals, 1988-90; mgr. San Diego Padres, 1993-94, Chicago Cubs, 1995—. Office: Wrigley Field 1060 W Addison St Chicago IL 60613-4397

RIGGS, ANNA CLAIRE, metals service company executive; b. Danville, Ind., Jan. 22, 1944; d. Leland Wesley and Mary Alice (Miller) Cox; m. Michael Ross Riggs, Dec. 10, 1983; 1 child, Matthew. B.S. in Edn., Ind. U., 1966. Credit tng. and promotion mgr. L.S. Ayres, Indpls., 1966-74, cons., credit dept., 1984; credit ops. mgr. Burdine's, Miami, Fla., 1974-77; br. mgr. Centaur Metals, Indpls., 1977-85; regional mgr. Copper & Brass Sales, Indpls., 1985—, Louisville, 1989—, Dayton, 1995—, Mansfield, 1995—; sec. Ind. Jersey Cattle Club. Children's choir dir. and Sun sch. tchr. United Meth. Ch., Danville, Ind., chair noms. and personnel, chair vision com.; editor Ind. Jersey News. Mem. Nat. Assn. Female Execs., Am. Jersey Cattle Club (exec. com., all Am. 1991, 95). Avocations: traveling, sewing, reading. Home: 576 N 200 W Danville IN 46122 Office: Copper & Brass Sales 8084 Woodland Dr Indianapolis IN 46278-1349

RIGGS, BYRON LAWRENCE, JR., physician, educator; b. Hot Springs, Ark., Mar. 24, 1931; s. Byron Lawrence and Elizabeth Ann (Patching) R.; m. Janet Templeton Brewer, June 24, 1955; children: Byron Kent, Ann Templeton. B.S., U. Ark., 1953, B.S. in Medicine, 1955, M.D., 1955; M.S. in Medicine, U. Minn., 1962. Diplomate: Am. Bd. Internal Medicine. Intern Letterman Army Hosp., San Francisco, 1955-56; resident in internal medicine Mayo Grad. Sch. Medicine Hosp., Rochester, Minn., 1958-61; asst. to staff Mayo Clinic and Found., Rochester, 1961, mem. staff internal medicine and metabolism, 1962—; mem. faculty U. Minn. Med. Sch., Rochester, 1962—, assoc. prof., 1970-72, prof., 1972—; Purvis and Roberta Tabor prof. med. rsch. Mayo Clinic and Med. Sch., Rochester, 1974—, chmn. divsn. endocrinology and metabolism, 1974-84; mem. gen. medicine B study sect. NIH, 1979-82; nat. adv. bd. NIAMS/NIH, 1987-91, disting. investigator Mayo Found., 1991—. Contbr. articles to med. jours. Dist. investigator Mayo Found., 1991—. Served with M.C. AUS, 1956-58. Recipient Mayo Found. postgrad. travel award, 1961; Kappa Delta award Am. Acad. Orthopedic Surgery, 1972; traveling fellow Royal Soc. Medicine, 1973. Fellow ACP; mem. AMA, AAAS, Assn. Am. Physicians, Am. Soc. Clin. Investigation, Endocrine Soc. (Rorer Clin. Investigator award 1989), Am. Fedn. Clin. Rsch. (councillor Midwest sect. 1969-71), Am. Soc. for Bone and Mineral Rsch. (pres. 1985-86, Bartter Clin. Investigation award 1990, Career Recognition award, 9th Workshop on Vitamin D rsch.), Ctrl. Soc. Clin. Rsch. (councillor). Home: 432 10th Ave SW Rochester MN 55902-2911 Office: Mayo Clinic 200 1st St SW Rochester MN 55905-0001

RIGLING, RICHARD VAUGHN, sales engineer; b. Hamilton, Ohio, Feb. 19, 1950; s. Richard Vincent and Louise Catherine (Vereker) R.; m. Joyce Ann Hartmann, Aug. 21, 1971; children: Victoria Lynn, Brian David. BS in Physics, Xavier U., 1972, MBA, 1992. Product devel. engr. Kornylak Corp., Hamilton, 1972-74; indsl. designer Donner Design, Hamilton, 1976-79; product devel. engr. Hamilton Tool, 1980-81, Nestier/Buckhorn, Cin., 1981-83; v.p. engring. Esscorp., Cin., 1983-86; mgr. engring., product devel. Stanley-Vidmar Automated Systems, Cin., 1986-94; sales engr. Yorktown (Ohio) Tool & Die, 1994—; vice chmn. indsl. adv. bd. Material Handling Rsch. Ctr., 1990-91. Mem. Engrs. and Scientists of Cin., Jaycees, Sigma Pi Sigma. Home: 22 Weymouth Pl Fairfield OH 45014-5332 Office: Yorktown Tool and Die 2101 West St Yorktown OH 47396-0218

RIIPI, LINDA RUTH, biology educator; b. Hancock, Mich., June 19, 1952; d. Jacob and Linda Edna Maria (Lindgren) Karinen; m. Matthew William Riipi, Oct. 4, 1975; 1 child, Erin Elizabeth. BS in Med. Technology with honors, Mich. State U., 1974; MA in Biology, No. Mich. U., 1983; PhD in Biol. Scis., Mich. Technol. U., 1991. Cert. clin. lab. scientist. Med. technologist William Beaumont Hosp., Royal Oak, Mich., 1975; med. technologist, supr. E.W. Sparrow Hosp., Lansing, Mich., 1976-78; med. technologist Marquette (Mich.) Gen. Hosp., 1979; instr. No. Mich. U., Marquette, 1979-83, asst. prof. biology, 1983-88, assoc. prof., 1988-92; prof. No. Mich. U., 1992—; bd. dirs. Med. Tech. Internship Matching Program, East Lansing, Mich., 1985-87. Doctoral fellow Mich. Technol. U., Houghton, 1989-91; No. Mich. U. rsch. grantee, 1992; recipient Merit award No. Mich. U., 1985, 86, 92, Disting. Faculty award Mich. Assn. Governing Bds., 1993. Mem. AAAS, Am. Soc. Clin. Pathology (cert.), Am. Soc. Microbiology, Am. soc. Med. Technologists (coord 1980-81, pres.-elect 1983-84, pres. 1984-85, past pres. 1985-86), Am. Soc. for Clin. Lab Sci. (bd. dirs. 1985-89, 92-93, 95-96), Mich. Soc. for Clin. Lab. Scis. (bd. dirs. 1995—), Marquette Pub. Schs. Edn. Found. (bd. dirs. 1996-99), Phi Kappa Phi, Beta Beta Beta, Sigma Xi. Lutheran. Office: No Mich U Coll Nursing and Allied Health Scis Marquette MI 49855

RIKOSKI, RICHARD ANTHONY, engineering executive, electrical engineer; b. Kingston, Pa., Aug. 13, 1941; s. Stanley George and Nellie (Gober) R.; m. Giannina Batchelor Petrullo, Dec. 18, 1971 (div. 1979); children: Richard James, Jennifer Anne. BEE, U. Detroit, 1964; MSEE, Carnegie Inst. Tech., 1965; PhD, Carnegie-Mellon U., 1968; postdoctoral student, Case-Western Res. U./NASA, 1971. Registered profl. engr., Ill., Mass., Pa. Engr. 1st communication satellite systems Internat. Tel. & Tel., Nutley, N.J., 1961-64; engr. Titan II ICBM program Gen. Motors, Milw., 1964; trainee NASA, 1964-67; instr. Carnegie-Mellon U., Pitts., 1966-68; asst. prof. U. Pa., Phila., 1968-74; assoc. prof., dir. hybrid microelectronics lab., chmn. ednl. TV com. IIT, Chgo., 1974-80, chmn. ednl. TV com., 1974-80; rsch. engr. nuclear effects ITT Rsch. Inst., Chgo., 1974-75; pres. Tech. Analysis Corp., Chgo., 1980—; engr. color TV colorimetry Hazeltine Rsch., Chgo., 1969; engr. Metroliner rail car/roadbed ride quality dynamics analysis U.S. Dept. Transp., ENSCO, Inc., Springfield, Va., 1970; pres. Tech. Analysis Corp., Chgo., 1978-91; contractor analysis of color TV receiver safety hazards U.S. Consumer Product Safety Commn., 1977, analysis heating effect in aluminum wire Beverly Hills Supper Club Fire, Covington, Ky., 1978; engr. GFCI patent infringement study 3M Corp., St. Paul, 1979-81; elec. systems analyst Coca-Cola Corp., Atlanta, 1983-91; fire investigator McDonald's Corp., Oak Brook, Ill., 1987-90; engring. analyst telephone switching ctrs. ATT, Chgo., 1990-91; expert witness numerous other govtl. and corp. procs. Author: Hybrid Microelectronic Circuits, 1973; editor: Hybrid Microelectronic Technology, 1973; contbr. articles to profl. jours. Officer Planning Commn., Beverly Shores, Ind., 1987-93, trustee town coun., 1992—, police liason 1993—; mem. Chgo. Coun. Fgn. Rels., USAF SAC Comdrs. Disting. Vis. Program; adv. coun. Nat. Park Svc. Ind. Dunes Nat. Lake Shore, 1993—. NASA fellow, 1964-67, 70. Mem. IEEE (sr. ednl. activities bd. N.Y.C. 1970-74, USAB career devel. com. 1972-74, editor Soundings 1973-75, Cassette Colloquia 1973-74, del. Popov Soc. Tech. Exch. USSR, mgr. Dial Access Tech. Edn. program 1972), Assn. for Media Based Continuing Engring. Edn. (bd. dirs.), Nat. Fire Protection Assn., Sigma Xi, Tau Beta Pi, Eta Kappa Nu. Republican. Home: One E Lakefront Dr Beverly Shores IN 46301-0444 Office: Tech Analysis Corp 3600 N Lake Shore Dr Chicago IL 60613-4656

RILEY, ANTONIO, state legislator; b. Aug. 22, 1963. BA, Carroll Coll. Former staff asst. to Milw. mayor; Wis. state assemblyman Dist. 18, 1992—. Mem. Midtown Neighborhood Assn. Address: 3013 W Mount Vernon Ave Milwaukee WI 53208*

RILEY, DAVID RAY, aeronautical engineer; b. Avon, Ill., Feb. 12, 1955; s. Leroy Franklin and Alice Ilene (Orwig) R.; m. Ann Alice Campion, Aug. 26, 1978; 3 children. BS in Aero. and Astronautical Engring., U. Ill., 1977; M of Engring. Mgmt., Washington U., 1990, MS in Mgmt. of Tech., 1993. Assoc. engr. McDonnell Aircraft Co., St. Louis, 1977-78, engr., 1978-80, sr. engr., 1980-83, lead engr., 1983-88, unit chief, 1988-92, sect. chief, 1992-94, sr. prin. engr., 1994—; participant X-29 flight test team NASA Ames-Dryden Flight Rsch. Ctr., Lancaster, Calif., 1985-86; v.p. constituency bd. dept. aero. and astronautical engring. U. Ill., 1988—. Contbr. articles to profl. jours. Recipient Disting. Alumnus award Dept. Aero. and Astronautical Engring., U. Ill., 1995. AIAA (assoc. fellow, chairperson atmospheric and flight mechanics tech. com. 1993-95, bd. dirs., dir-at-large 1995—), Elks, Alpha Chi Rho (Phi Kappa chpt., pres. grad. bd. 1978-85). Roman Catholic. Office: McDonnell Douglas Aerospace Mail Code 0642808 PO Box 516 Saint Louis MO 63166

RILEY, DAVID RICHARD, management consultant, retired military officer; b. Spokane, Wash., Mar. 28, 1940; s. Lee James and Louise Elizabeth (Duncan) R.; m. Anna Maria Formigoni, July 6, 1963; children: David Scott, Michelle Andrea. BS in Naval Sci., USN Acad., 1963; MS in Applied Math., USN Post Grad. Sch., 1972; postgrad., Armed Forces Staff Coll., 1975. Navy ops. mgmt. specialist, Navy aerospace engring. specialist, Navy material specialist. Ensign USN, 1963, advanced through grades to capt., 1984; antisubmarine warfare/antisubmarine rocket officer USN, Mayport, Fla., 1963-65; pilot trainee USN, Pensacola, Fla., 1965-67; designated naval pilot USN, San Diego, 1967, with antisubmarine/antiair warfare, 1967-74, maintenace officer, 1976-78; officer in charge USN, Nerra Naples, Italy, 1978-81; exec. officer Naval Aviation Depot, Alameda, Calif., 1981-84; comdg. officer Naval Aviation Depot, Pensacola, 1987-90; aviation depot program mgr. Navairsyscom Hdqrs., Washington, 1984-87; ret., 1990; cons. bus. planning and organizational devel., internat. commerce Chula Vista, Calif., 1990-94; pres., COO Speco Corp., Springfield, Ohio, 1994-95. Mem. Assn. Naval Aviation, Ret. Officers Assn., Am. Legion, Naval Helicopter Assn. Republican. Presbyterian. Home & Office: David Riley Assocs. 115 Eastwick Ct Beaver Creek OH 45440-3647

RILEY, JOHN RICHARD, travel agency owner; b. Kansas City, Mo., Jan. 9, 1937; s. John Howard and Della Cora (Grooms) R.; m. Shirley Joan Smith, June 28, 1959; children: John Howard II, Catherine Sue, David Alan. BSBA, Kans. State U., 1959. Sales rep. Scott Paper Co., Phila., 1960-62; ptnr. Riley Feed Co., Shawnee Mission, Kans., 1962-66; sales mgr. Feed Flavors, Inc., Chgo., 1966-67, dir. mktg., 1967-68, v.p., 1968-72; exec. v.p. Feed Flavors, Inc., Wheeling, Ill., 1972-86; pres., CEO Feed Flavors, Inc., Wheeling, 1986-89, chmn., pres., CEO, 1989-94, chmn., pres., cons., 1994-95; owner CruiseOne, Glenview, Ill., 1994—. Capt. U.S. Army Res., 1959-67. Mem. Forge Club, Gaslight Club. Republican. Methodist. Home and Office: 612 Huber Ln Glenview IL 60025-4064

RILEY, MARGARET, academic administrator; b. Honolulu, Oct. 29, 1951; d. Richard and Elizabeth Kathleen (Callan) R. BA, U. No. Iowa, 1973; MA, Ohio U., 1987, PhD, 1991. Cert. ESL tchr. Vol. U.S. Peace Corps, Colombia, South Am., 1973-75; compliance specialist U.S. Dept. of Labor, Omaha, 1977-85; exec. Nat. Coun. RPCVs, Omaha; Peace Corps recruiter Ohio U., Athens, 1986-87, mgr. computer lab., 1987-91, teaching asst., 1987-90, internat. student vol. coord., 1990; dir. internat. edn. St. Norbert Coll., De Pere, Wis., 1991—. Author: (with others) Constructing and Re.Gender, 1992. Mem. Nat. Assn. Fgn. Student Affairs, Nat. Peace Corps. Assn. (sec. 1980-83, pres. 1983-86), Phi Beta Delta. Roman Catholic. Home: 3100 S Clay St Green Bay WI 54301-1579 Office: St Norbert Coll 100 Grant St De Pere WI 54115-2002

RILEY, NANCY MAE, retired vocational home economics educator; b. Grand Forks, N.D., May 1, 1939; d. Kenneth Wesley and Jeanne Margaret Olive (Hill) R. BS in Edn., Miami U., 1961; postgrad., Ohio U., 1964-69; MA, Marietta Coll., 1989. Cert. high sch. tchr. Tchr. home econs. Malta-McConnelsville (Ohio) High Sch., 1961-67; tchr. home econs. Waterford (Ohio) High Sch., 1968-92; advisor Malta-McConnelsville Future Homemakers, 1961-66, Waterford Future Homemakers Am., 1968-92; advisor to state officer Ohio Future Homemakers Am., McConnelsville, 1963, Waterford, 1976. Leader Girl Scouts Am., McConnelsville, 1962-66, camp counselor, 1962-76; fair judge Waterford Cmty. Fair, Waterford, 1970-85. Mem. NEA, Am. Vocat. Assn. (life), Ohio Edn. Assn. (life, del. 1979), Ohio Vocat. Assn. (life), DAR, Daus. Union Vets. (del. 1992—, tent pres. 1993-94, dist. pres. 1996), Daus. of War of 1812 (pres. 1991—, state sec. 1995—), Ohio Geneal. Soc., Order Ea. Star (worthy matron 1967-68, dep. grand matron 1978), White Shrine Jerusalem (worth high priestess 1979-81, 83). Republican. Baptist. Home: PO Box 137 Waterford OH 45786-0137

RILEY, THOMAS M., engineer; b. Wayne County, Mich., Feb. 7, 1942. AS, U. Mich., 1980. Mgr. ECAD Unisys, Plymouth, Mich., 1960—. Vol. local ch. With U.S. Army, 1966-68. Mem. Engring. Soc. Unisys.

RILEY, WILLIAM JAY, lawyer; b. Lincoln, Nebr., Mar. 11, 1947; s. Don Paul and Marian Frances (Munn) R.; m. Norma Jean Mason, Dec. 27, 1965; children: Brian, Kevin, Erin. BA, U. Nebr., 1969, JD, 1972. Bar: Nebr. 1972, U.S. Dist. Ct. Nebr. 1972, U.S. Ct. Appeals (8th cir.) 1974; cert. civil trial specialist Nat. Bd. Trial Advocacy. Law clk. U.S. Ct. Appeals (8th cir.), Omaha, 1972-73; assoc. Fitzgerald, Schorr Law Firm, Omaha, 1973-79, ptnr., 1979—; adj. prof. trial practice Creighton U. Coll. Law, Omaha, 1991—; chmn. fed. practice com. Fed. Ct., 1992-94. Scoutmaster Boy Scouts Am., Omaha, 1979-89. Recipient Silver Beaver award Boy Scouts Am., 1991. Fellow Am. Coll. Trial Lawyers, Nebr. State Bar Found.; mem. Am. Bd. Trial Advs., Nebr. State Bar Assn. (chmn. ethics com. 1996—). Republican. Methodist. Office: Fitzgerald Schorr Law Firm 1000 Woodmen Tower Omaha NE 68102

RILEY-DAVIS, SHIRLEY MERLE, advertising agency executive, marketing consultant, writer; b. Pitts., Feb. 4, 1935; d. William Riley and Beatrice Estelle (Whittaker) Byrd; m. Louis Davis; 1 child, Terri Judith. Student U. Pitts., 1952. Copywriter, Pitts. Mercantile Co., 1954-60; exec. sec. U. Mich., Ann Arbor, 1962-67; copy supr. N.W. Ayer, N.Y.C., 1968-76, assoc. creative dir., Chgo., 1977-81; copy supr. Leo Burnett, Chgo., 1981-86; freelance advt. and mktg. cons., 1986—; advt. and mktg. coord. Child and Family Svc., Ypsilanti, Mich., 1992—; vis. prof. Urban League Black Exec. Exch. Program; print, radio, and TV commercials; bd. dirs. Sr. Housing Bur., Ann Arbor; mem. adv. bd. Cmty. Diabetes, past bd. mem. People's Hope for Housing, Ypsilanti, Mich. Recipient Grand and First prize N.Y. Film Festival, 1973, Gold and Silver medal Atlanta Film Festival, 1973, Gold medal V.I. Film Festival, 1974, 50 Best Creatives award Am. Inst. Graphic Arts, 1972, Clio award, 1973, 74, 75, Andy Award of Merit, 1981, Silver medal Internat. Film Festival, 1982, Corp. Mgmt. Assistance Program award, 1986, Good Sam award 1981, Svc. Advt. Creativity of Distinction cert., 1981; Senatorial scholar. Bd. dirs. Housing bur. for Srs. of the U. Mich. Med. Ctr., 1995—. Mem. Women in Film, Facets Multimedia Film Theatre Orgn. (bd. dirs.), Greater Chgo. Coun. for Prevention of Child Abuse (past bd. dirs.), Internat. Platform Assn. Democrat. Roman Catholic. Avocations: dance, poetry, design, writing, volunteering. Office: 118 S Washington St Ypsilanti MI 48197-5427

RIMMEREIDE, ARNE M., engineering executive; b. Fitjar, Norway, Mar. 31, 1963; came to U.S., 1987; s. Torvald and Borghild R. BSME, S.D. Mines and Tech., 1989. Engring. mgr. Vikron Tech., Inc., St. Croix, Wis., 1990—. With Norwegian Navy, 1984-85. Mem. Am. Soc. Quality Control, Norwegian Am. Tech. Soc. Home: 5037 Drew Ave Minneapolis MN 55410 Office: Vikron 520 Blanding Woods Rd Saint Croix Falls WI 54024-9001

RINCK, JAMES RICHARD, lawyer; b. Grand Rapids, Mich., Mar. 6, 1958; s. Richard John and Ann Louise (Weening) R; m. Lorelei Landheer, Apr. 30, 1988. BA, Calvin Coll., 1975-79; JD, U. Ill., 1979-82. Bar: Mich. 1982, U.S. Dist. Ct. (we. dist.) Mich. 1982. Asst. prosecutor Muskegon County, Muskegon, Mich., 1983-84; sole practice Grand Rapids, 1984—. Deacon Westminster Presbyn. Ch., 1985-89, mem. pastoral search com., 1989-90; mem. exec bd. Kent County Dems., 1984—; mem. exec. bd. Mich. Young Dems., 1986-88, candidate Mich. State Senate, 1990; state asst. atty. gen., 1990—; mem. Bd. Edn. of Grand Rapids, 1993—; bd. dirs. Grand Rapids Downtown Devel., 1995—. Mem. Mich. Bar Assn. (workers' compensation and negligence sects. 1987—, criminal law sect. 1983—), Grand Rapids Bar Assn. Home: 2353 Swensberg Ave NE Grand Rapids MI 49505-4066 Office: 1108 McKay Twr 146 Monroe Center St NW Grand Rapids MI 49503-2820

RINEFORT, FOSTER CHRISTIAN, JR., business management educator; b. Flushing, N.Y., June 30, 1932; s. Foster C. Rinefort and Helen (Dart) Mahin; m. Jean Fildes, June 10, 1994; children: Anne E. Varns, Scott C. BA, Grinnell Coll., 1956; postgrad., U. Chgo., 1962; MBA, Calif. State U., San Francisco, 1972; PhD, Tex. A&M U., 1976. Registered profl. engr.; cert. safety profl., sr. profl. human resources. Asst. pers. mgr. Procter & Gamble Mfgr., St. Louis, 1956-58; corp. mgr. loss prevention IMCERA, Northbrook, Ill., 1958-68; sr. cons. Kemper Group, Chgo., 1968-70; pres. Foster C. Rinefort & Assocs., 1970—; lectr. Tex. A&M U., College Sta., Tex., 1972-75; assoc. prof. Ind. State U., Terre Haute, 1975-81; dir. grad. studies, prof. Eastern Ill. U., Charleston, Ill., 1981—; dir. Fire Sixteen, Inc., San Francisco, 1990—. Author one book; contbr. chpts. to books and over 60 publs. to profl. jours. and procs. Chairperson Safety Commn., Northbrook, 1965-70; trustee Wesley United Meth. Ch., Charleston, Ill., 1983-88. With U.S. Army, 1953-55. Recipient Cameron award Nat. Safety Coun., 1970, numerous awards in field of safety and health. Mem. Midwest Soc. for Human Resources (pres. 1982-83), Midwest Case Rsch. Assn. (v.p. dir. 1984-89), Midwest Bus. Adminstrn. Assn. (dir. 1989—), Acad. Mgmt., Am. Soc. Safety Engrs., Nat. Safety Coun., Vets. of Safety, Soc. Human Resource Mgmt., Safety & Health Hall of Fame, Assn. for Global Bus. Home: 1023 Colony Ln Charleston IL 61920-4264 Office: Eastern Ill U Lumpkin Coll of Business Charleston IL 61920

RINEHART, I. LYNN, clinical counselor; b. Parkersburg, W.Va., July 4, 1936; s. Robert Oliver and Loma Istrene (MacPherson) R.; m. Joy Marie Rinehart; children: Steven Robert, Scott Richard, Christopher Berry. BS in Group Work Edn., George Williams Coll., 1958; MA in Human Rels., Ohio U., 1962, postgrad.; PhD in Leadership and Human Behavior, U.S. Internat. U., 1977; MEd in Community Counseling, Ohio U., 1993. Lic. profl. clin. counselor. Exec. dir. East Whittier YMCA, Whittier, Calif., 1964-70; dep. dir. Neighborhood House Assn., San Diego, 1972-79; assoc. mng. dir. YMCA, San Diego, 1979-80; cons. Rinehart and Assocs., San Diego, 1980-89, Columbus, Ohio, 1989—; counselor CentrePoint Counseling Assocs., Worthington, Ohio, 1992—; adj. prof. Nat. U., San Diego, 1978-89, U. San Diego, 1985-89, State C.C., 1990—; cons. Met. Human Svcs. Commn., Columbus, 1990-93; creator human svcs. planning process; coord. Healthy People on the Hill/Health Coalition of Franklin County, 1994—. John R. Mott fellow Nat. Bd. YMCA, 1970-71, 71-72. Mem. ACA, Am. Bd. Hypnotherapy (cert.), Assn. for Pre- and Perinatal Psychology and Health, Ohio Counseling Assn., Chi Sigma Iota. Address: 7864 Leaview Dr Columbus OH 43235-7007 Office: CentrePoint Counseling Assocs 6797 N High St Ste 155 Worthington OH 43085-2533

RINEHART, KATHRYN ANN, principal; b. Eaton, Ohio, Nov. 15, 1948; d. Eugene Warner and Alice Kathryn (Eagle) Donson; m. Charles Edward Rinehart, Dec. 26, 1969. BS in Edn., Miami U., 1969, MEd, 1982, postgrad., 1982-85. Cert. local supt., high, middle, and elem. sch. prin., elem. tchr., vocat. home econs. tchr. Vocat. home econs. tchr Twin Valley Local Schs., West Alexandria, Ohio, 1969-85; community edn. supr. Twin Valley Local Schs., West Alexandria, 1983-90, middle sch. prin., 1985-90; vocat. prin. Ohio Vets. Children's Home, 1991-95; prin. Broadmoor Acad. Trotwood-Madison City Schs., Ohio, 1995—. Author: (manual) Community Education, 1983; (curriculum guide) Career Education, 1985; editor, writer: Entrepreneurship, 1982. Active Preble County Lit. Coun., Eaton, Ohio, 1989. Mem. NAFE, ASCD, Nat. Assn. Elem. Sch. Adminstrs., Nat. Assn. Secondary Sch. Adminstrs., Ohio Assn. Elem. Sch. Adminstrs., Ohio Assn. Secondary Sch. Adminstrs., Ohio Community Edn. Assn. (Gold award 1987, v.p. 1989-92), Ohio Elem. Prins. (county rep. 1987-89). Home: 4496 Sharpsburg Rd Eaton OH 45320-9433

RINES, JOHN RANDOLPH, automotive company executive; b. Balt., Aug. 3, 1947; s. John William and Betty (Singer) R.; m. Peggy J. Daugaard, Sept. 19, 1969 (dec. 1978); m. Katherine M. Duff, Nov. 29, 1980; children: Jacqueline D., Eleanor W. BS in Econs., Colo. State U., 1970; MBA, U. Va., 1977. With GM, 1970-75, 77—; fin. analyst GM, Detroit, 1977-78, dir. product programs, 1978-80, asst. to pres., 1980-81, gen. dir. fin., 1981-82; exec. dir. GM, Sao Paulo, Brazil, 1982-84; dir. fin. Buick/Oldsmobile/Cadillac group GM, Flint, Mich., 1984-85; gen. mgr. motors holding div. and GM auction GM, Detroit, 1985-91, gen. mgr. parts ops., 1991—; pres. GM Acceptance Corp., Detroit, 1992—. Trustee Arts Found. Mich., Detroit. Mem. Grosse Pointe (Mich.) Club, Old Club (Harsen's Island), Birmingham Athletic Club. Office: GM 3044 W Grand Blvd Detroit MI 48202-3091

RINESS, CLAY MORGAN, fishing guide, educator; b. Prairie du Chien, Wis., Oct. 15, 1958; s. Jerry Leigh and Charlotte JoAnn (Kolter) R.; m. Vicki Lynn Tippett-Riness, Mar. 30, 1984; children: Cole Clayton, Grace Victoria. Ind. singer, songwriter, performer, prodr., pub., 1978—; fly fishing guide, instr. Coon Valley, Wis., 1988—. Singer, songwriter, pub., prodr.: (albums) Rollin' in My Changes, 1982, Down to the Cellar, 1984, Live Bait, 1986, Walk Along John, 1989, One Season, 1992. Republican. Lutheran. Home and Office: PO Box 166 Coon Valley WI 54623

RING, DANIEL F(RANK), reference librarian; b. Milw., Feb. 26, 1945; s. Francis Alan and Dorothy (Lichtenberg) R.; m. Mary Dowling, Aug. 22, 1970; children: Benjamin, Katherine, Amy. BS in History, U. Wis., Milw., 1968, MS in History, 1971; MLS, U. Wis., Madison, 1973. History bibliographer, reference libr. Cleve. Pub. Libr., 1974-75; reference libr. Oakland U., Rochester, Mich., 1975—. Editor: Studies in Creativer Partnership, 1980; contbr. articles to profl. jours. Lance cpl. USMCR, 1962-70. Rsch. grantee Oakland U., 1989, 91, 93, 95. Lutheran. Home: 2950 Heidelberg Dr Rochester Hills MI 48309 Office: Oakland U Kresge Libr Rochester MI 48309

RING, HERBERT EVERETT, management executive; b. Norwich, Conn., Dec. 19, 1925; s. Herbert Everett and Catherine (Riordan) R.; m. Marilyn Elizabeth Dursin, May 21, 1955 (dec. Jan. 1994); children: Nancy Marie, Herbert Everett. BA, Ind. No. U., 1971, MBA, 1973; AMP, Harvard U., 1981. V.p. ops. Ogden Foods, Inc., Toledo, 1963-74; sr. v.p. Ogden Foods,

Inc., Boston, 1974-75; v.p. concessions SportSvc. Corp., Buffalo, 1976-78, sr. v.p., 1978-80, pres., 1980-83, bd. dir.; pres. Universal Mgmt. Concept Counseling, Sylvania, Ohio, 1983—; prin. Hysen Group II, Livonia, Mich., 1991-95; counselor L.A. Olympic Concessions Food Svc., 1984, Phila. Meml. Stadium, 1985, Del. North Cos. Internat. London Eng., 1985-86, Chgo. Stadium Corp., 1989-92, Buffalo Sabres N.Y., 1992, Fine Host Inc. Greenwich Ct., 1993, Delaware North of Australia Ltd., 1994, Temp DNC Health Support Ltd., Wellington, New Zealand, 1995; bd. dirs. Greenfield Restaurant Co., Inc., Letheby and Christopher Ltd., Reading, Berkshire, Eng., Air Terminal Svcs., Inc., The Aud Club, Inc., Bluegrass Turf Svc., Inc., Concession Suppliers, Inc., Cosel Drive-In Theatre, Inc., G&H Sports Concessions, Inc., Hazel Park Parking, Inc. Mem. Toledo Mus. Art., 1985-92. Sgt. Air Corps U.S. Army, 1944-46, ETO, USAF, 1950-51. Mem. Internat. Assn. of Auditorium Mgrs., N.W. Ohio Restaurant Assn. (bd. dirs. 1990-93), Am. Culinary Fedn. Inc., Harvard Bus. Club (Detroit). Roman Catholic. Home and Office: 5540 Radcliffe Rd Sylvania OH 43560-3740

RING, VICTORIA A., small business owner; b. Columbus, Ohio, July 5, 1958; d. James H. and Barbara C. (Wise) R. BA, East Tenn. State U., 1984; MA, Columbus Bus. U., 1986. Owner Tri-Angle Supreme Pizza, Sun, Va., 1981-86; typesetter, designer Battelle Meml. Inst., Columbus, Ohio, 1986-88; owner Graphico Pub., Columbus, Ohio, 1988—; instr. Ohio State U., Columbus, 1990-91; creator, designer GrapeVine News, 1992-94, Pizazz Network Mktg. Mag. 1996—; spkr. at seminars and workshops in field. Author: Be "In The Know" With Adsheet Publishing, 1989, Word Perfect Just For Fun. 1991, Something From Nothing, 1993; contbr. articles to profl. publs.

RINGEL, ROBERT LEWIS, university administrator; b. N.Y.C., Jan. 27, 1937; s. Benjamin Seymour and Beatrice (Salis) R.; m. Estelle Neuman, Jan. 18, 1959; children—Stuart Alan, Mark Joseph. B.A., Bklyn. Coll., 1959; M.S., Purdue U., 1960, Ph.D., 1962. cert. speech pathologist. Rsch. scientist, laryngeal rsch. lab. Ctr. Health Scis., UCLA, 1962-64; asst. prof. communication disorders U. Wis., 1964-66; mem. faculty Purdue U., 1966—, prof., head dept. audiology and speech sci., 1970-73, dean Sch. Humanities, Social Sci. and Edn. (Sch. Liberal Arts), 1973-86, v.p., dean Grad. Sch., 1986-90, exec. v.p. for acad. affairs, 1991—; vis. prof. Inst. Neurology and Nat. Hosps. Coll. Speech Scis., U. London, 1985; cons. NIH, NEH, Bur. Edn. Handicapped of U.S. Office Edn.; bd. dirs. Indpls. Ctr. for Advanced Rsch., 1988-92. Author sci. articles; contbr. to monographs and textbooks. Bd. dirs. Lafayette Home Hosp., 1978-87, Lafayette Symphony Orch., 1983-85. Recipient Research Career Devel. award Nat. Inst. Dental Research, 1967-70, Award for highest merit for sci. article Jour. Speech and Hearing Research, 1979, Disting. Alumnus award Bklyn. Coll., 1985. Fellow Am. Speech and Hearing Assn. (v.p. Found. 1990—); mem. AAUP, Nat. Assn. State Univs. and Land Grant Colls. (exec. com. 1988-91, rsch. policy and grad. edn., exec. com. coun. on acad. affairs 1991—, com. on instnl. coop., exec. com. provosts instn. coop. com. 1991—), Sigma Xi (v.p. 1986—). Office: Purdue Univ Off Exec VP for Acad Affairs West Lafayette IN 47907-1073

RINGQUIST, LYNN ANNE, micrographics company executive; b. Panama City, Fla., June 12, 1952; d. George Willard and Juanita Anne (Vinson) Thomas; m. Ronald Scott Nelson, Sept. 5, 1970 (div. Mar. 1978); children: Faith Nichole, Jason Jay; m. Eric James Ringquist, Sept. 19, 1993. Student, Fullerton (Calif.) Jr. Coll., 1970-71, Mpls. Coll. Art & Design, 1987-93. Microfilm technician Microfilming Services, Corona, Calif., 1970-71; microfilm technician Blue Cross/Blue Shield, Eagan, Minn., 1972-73, customer service rep., 1973-76; regional sales rep. MicroD Internat., Burnsville, Minn., 1974-83, gen. sales mgr., 1983-85, v.p., 1985—; bd. dirs. Neoteric Arts, Inc., Burnsville, 1983—; creator LA Beeds, 1994; distbr. Rexall Showcase Internat., 1995. Mem. Am. Soc. for Non-Destructive Testing, Assn. Info. and Image Mgmt. Home: 14901 Judicial Rd Burnsville MN 55306-4866 Office: MicroD Internat 3308 134th St W Burnsville MN 55337

RINGS, RANDALL EUGENE, lawyer; b. Colusa, Ill., June 9, 1962; s. Donald Eugene and Beverly Elaine (Schuster) R.; m. Danielle Rae Nutting, May 24, 1986. Student, Carl Sandberg Coll., Galesburg, Ill., 1979-80; BS with honors, U. Iowa, 1984, JD with high distinction, 1987. Bar: Kans., U.S. Dist. Ct. Kans., U.S. Dist. Ct. (we. dist.) Mo., U.S. Dist. Ct. (ctrl. dist.) Ill. Assoc. Watson, Ess, Marshall & Enggas, Olathe, Kans., 1987-88; corp. counsel Assn. Ill. Electric Coops., Springfield, 1988-92; assoc. March and McMillan, P.C., Macomb, Ill., 1992-96; gen. counsel Telecom*USA Pub. Co., Cedar Rapids, Iowa, 1996—. Vol. Am. Lung Assn. Ill., Springfield, 1989—; mem. Ill. 4-H Found., Champaign, 1989—. Mem. ABA, Ill. Bar Assn., The Mo. Bar, Ill. Trial Lawyers Assn., County Bar Assn., U. Iowa AlumniAssn., Rotary Internat. Presbyterian. Home: 3711 Terrace Hill Dr NE Cedar Rapids IA 52402 Office: Telecom*USA Pub Co PO Box 3162 201 3d Ave SE Cedar Rapids IA 52406

RINGS, ROY WILSON, entomologist, consultant; b. Columbus, Ohio, Aug. 15, 1916; s. John Jacob and Blanche Elizabeth (Tipton) R.; m. Virginia Mae Thalgott, Nov. 26, 1942 (dec. Oct. 1994); children: Gary Wayne, Steven Edward, Cynthia Marie; m. Lorraine F. Stone, Feb. 11, 1995. BSc, Ohio State U., 1938, MSc, 1939, PhD, 1946. Specialist Ohio Dept. Agr., Columbus, 1946-47; asst. entomologist Ohio Agr. Expt. Sta., Wooster, 1947-51, assoc. prof., 1951-63; assoc. chmn. dept. entomology Ohio State U., Columbus, 1963-77; prof. Ohio State U., Wooster, 1977, prof. emeritus, 1977—; cons. entomology Toledo Area Mosquito Abatement, 1966—. Sr. author: Owlet Moths of Ohio, 1992. 1st lt. AUS, 1941-46. NSF travel grantee, 1964. Fellow AAAS, Ohio Acad. Sci. (Centennial honoree 1991); mem. Entomol. Soc. Am. (pres. North Cen. br. 1962-63), Ohio Mosquito Control Assn., Ohio Lepidopterists Soc. (pres. 1984-88), The Lepidopterists Soc., Sigma Xi (pres. chpt. 1974-75). Home: 1840 Christmas Run Blvd Wooster OH 44691-1308 Office: Ohio State U 1680 Madison Ave Wooster OH 44691-4114

RINGSRED, JOHN NORMAN, electronics educator; b. Duluth, Minn., Sept. 2, 1924; s. Arthur Christian and Esther Theadora (Ness) R.; m. Mila Mae Matheson, Sept. 27, 1947 (div. Apr. 1978); children: Eric J., Karen J., Leif N., Chris P., Ted K.; m. Patricia Louise Quigley, Feb. 21, 1981; children: Margaret Scarcella, Pamala Peterson, Frank Rohde III. BA in Physics, U. Minn., 1962, BS in Physics, 1963; MS in Physics, U. Wis., 1972. Indsl. engr. Am. Steel and Wire Co., Duluth, 1948-51; pres. Ringsred TV & Engring., Duluth, 1951-63; prof. electronics U. Minn., Duluth, 1965—; cons. engr. DSI Inc., Superior, Wis., 1970-75. Inventor mercury bath tester, diaelectric strength tester, modulab teaching system, modublox teaching system. Pres. Duluth Ctrl. Little League, Duluth Amature Hockey Assn.; active Return Old Fog Horn, Duluth. Sgt. U.S. Army, 1943-45. Named Tchr. of Yr. U. Minn. Student Assn., 1982, Little League field named in honor of John Norman Ringsred, 1970. Mem. IEEE, Am. Inst. Physics, Duluth Radio and TV Assn. (pres. 1950-62), Delta Tau Delta. Lutheran. Home: 111 Marion St Duluth MN 55803 Office: Univ of Minn 10 University Dr Duluth MN 55812

RINK, JIM, editor, columnist; b. Traverse City, Mich., June 24, 1957; s. Bernard C. and Suzanne V. (Peplinski) R.; m. Traci L. Woodard, Dec. 28, 1991. AA summa cum laude, Oakland C.C., Royal Oak, Mich., 1985; AB in Comms. with high distinction, U. Mich., 1987. Assoc. editor The Reporter, Troy, Mich., 1985; asst. publs. editor NASCO, Ann Arbor, Mich., 1985-87; staff writer Gaylord (Mich.) Herald Times, 1987-88, Assoc. Newspapers, Wayne, Mich., 1988-89; contbg. editor Am. Wine Soc., Rochester, Mich., 1983—; sr. contbg. editor AAA Mich., Dearborn, 1989—. Bd. dirs. Ridgedale Players, 1983-95. Recipient awards Pub. Rels. Soc. Am., 1994, 95. Mem. Internat. Assn. Bus. Comms. (student rels. com. 1994, gallery editorial bd. 1993-95, awards 1989, 91, 92, 94, 95), Soc. Profl. Journalists. Home: 3174 Bacon Berkley MI 48072 Office: AAA Mich 1 Auto Club Dr Dearborn MI 48126

RINN, VICTORIA SUE, telecommunications industry executive; b. Dade County, Fla., June 28, 1966; d. James Thomas and Mildred Ellen (Heffernan) Owens; m. Danial Charles Rinn, Nov. 24, 1995; children: Rachel, Kristen. BS, Purdue U., 1988; MS, Stanford U., 1989. Customer support engr. AT&T, Naperville, Ill., 1989-95, project mgr., 1995—.

RIPP, BRYAN JEROME, geological engineer; b. Tucson, Dec. 22, 1959; s. Jerome Peter and Helen Marie (Bussmuss) R.; m. Susan Sorensen, Nov. 7, 1987; 1 child, Aaron. BS in Geol. Engring., S.D. Sch. Mines, 1982; MS in Geol. Engring., U. Mo., Rolla, 1984. Registered profl. engr., Ill., Mo., profl. geologist, Ark., Am. Inst. Profl. Geologists. Roustabout Shell Oil Co., Yorba Linda, Calif., 1980; geol. engr. Tenneco Oil Co., Lafayette, La., 1981; staff engr. Shannon and Wilson, Inc., St. Louis, 1984-88; prin. engr. Geotechnology, Inc., St. Louis, 1988-94; sr. geol. engr. Weir Internat. Mining Cons., Des Plaines, Ill., 1994—; cons. Consolidation Coal Co., St. Louis, 1986—, Union Pacific RR, Omaha, 1985-88, Mallinckrodt Chem., Inc., St. Louis, 1992-94. MWRD of Greater Chgo, 1994—; Robbins, Kaplan, Miller and Ciresi, 1994. Author: Underground Storage Tank Closure Manual, 1992; author, editor: Hydrocarbon Assessment Manual, 1992; reviewer WASTECH Innovative Site Remediation Tech. monographs; author reports. Mem. ASCE, Soc. Mining Engrs. (chmn. 1992-93), Assn. Engring. Geologists (treas. 1990-94), Ill. Soc. Profl. Engrs., Order of Engr., Ill. Mining Inst., Sigma Xi. Home: 1280 W New Britton Dr Hoffman Estates IL 60195-1732 Office: Weir Internat Mining Cons 2340 River Rd Ste 203 Des Plaines IL 60018

RIPP, DON J., mortgage banker; b. Sturgeon Bay, Wis., Dec. 28, 1933; m. Mary Jean Styza, Sept. 66, 1952; children: Michael B., Susan Ripp Heule, R.J. Ripp. Student, U. Wis., Milw., 1955-56. Pres. Fair Fin. Corp., Hales Corners, Wis., 1965—; v.p., sec. Fin. Svc. Corp., Manitowoc, Wis., 1972—; field auditor Beneficial Corp., Morristown, N.J., 1965; br. mgr. West Allis, Wis., 1955-64. Mem. Wis. Mortgage Bankers Assn. Roman Catholic. Home: Univ Park Comm Coll 8041 Hampton Ct University Park FL 34201 Office: Fair Fin Corp 10575 W Forest Home Ave Hales Corners WI 53130

RIPPERGER, KATHRYN LODAL, real estate broker; b. Lubbock, Tex., Oct. 20, 1942. BA in History, Tex. Tech. U., 1965; MA in Polit. Sci., Northwestern U., 1967. Lic. real estate broker, Mich. V.p. JHR Enterprises Inc., Grand Rapids, Mich., 1985—. Office: JHR Enterprises Inc PO Box 6347 Grand Rapids MI 49516-6347

RIPPLE, KENNETH FRANCIS, federal judge; b. Pitts., May 19, 1943; s. Raymond John and Rita (Holden) R.; m. Mary Andrea DeWeese, July 27, 1968; children: Gregory, Raymond, Christopher. AB, Fordham U., 1965; JD, U. Va., 1968; LLM, George Washington U., 1972, LLD (hon.), 1992. Bar: Va. 1968, N.Y. 1969, U.S. Supreme Ct. 1972, D.C. 1976, Ind. 1984, U.S. Ct. Appeals (7th cir.), U.S. Ct. Mil. Appeals, U.S. Dist. Ct. (no. dist.) Ind. Atty. IBM Corp., Armonk, N.Y., 1968; legal officer U.S. Supreme Ct., Washington, 1972-73, spl. asst. to chief justice Warren E. Burger, 1973-77; prof. law U. Notre Dame, 1977—; judge U.S. Ct. Appeals (7th cir.), South Bend, 1985—; reporter Appellate Rules Com., Washington, 1978-85; commn. on mil. justice U.S. Dept. Def., Washington, 1984-85; cons. Supreme Ct. Ala., 1983, Calif. Bd. Bar Examiners, 1981; cons. Anglo-Am. Jud. Exch., 1977, mem., 1980; adv. com. Bill of Rights to Bicentennial Constn. Commn., 1989; mem. adv. com. on appellate rules Jud. Conf. U.S., 1985-90, chmn., 1990-93; chmn. adv. com. on appellate judge edn. Fed. Jud. Ctr., 1996—. Author: Constitutional Litigation, 1984. Mem. bd. visitors Sch. Law, Brigham Young U., 1989-92. Served with JAGC, USN, 1968-72. Mem. ABA, Am. Law Inst., Phi Beta Kappa. Office: US Ct of Appeals 208 US Courthouse 204 S Main St South Bend IN 46601-2122 also: Fed Bldg 219 S Dearborn St Ste 2660 Chicago IL 60604-1803

RIS, HANS, zoologist, educator; b. Bern, Switzerland, June 15, 1914; came to U.S., 1938, naturalized, 1945; s. August and Martha (Egger) R.; m. Hania Wislicka, Dec. 26, 1947 (div. 1971); children: Christopher Robert, Annette Margo; m. Theron Caldwell, July 14, 1980. Diploma high sch. teaching, U. Bern, 1936; Ph.D., Columbia, 1942. Lectr. zoology Columbia U., 1942; Seessel fellow in zoology Yale U., 1942; instr. biology Johns Hopkins U., 1942-44; asst. Rockefeller Inst., N.Y.C., 1944-46; assoc. Rockefeller Inst., 1946-49; assoc. prof. zoology U. Wis., Madison, 1949-53; prof. U. Wis., 1953-84, prof. emeritus, 1984—; hon. prof. Peking U., Beijing, 1995—. Fellow AAAS; mem. Am. Acad. Arts and Scis., Nat. Acad. Scis., Electron Microscopy Soc. Am. (Disting. Investigator award 1983), Am. Soc. for Cell Biology (E.B. Wilson award 1993). Office: U Wis Zoology Rsch 1117 W Johnson St Madison WI 53706-1705

RISCH, RICHARD WILLIAM, horticultural manager; b. Milw., Jan. 8, 1941; s. Frederick William and Sophia (Banker) R. BS, U. Wis., Milw., 1965. Asst. floriculturist Mitchell Park Conservatory, Milw., 1968-72, asst. hort. dir., 1972-81, conservatory dir., 1981—. Editor, photographer: Mitchell Park Conservatory Souvenir Booklet, 1975, 81. Mem. Am. Assn. Bot. Gardens and Arborea (chmn. conservatory com. 1984-86), Milw. Bonsai Soc. (June Kelley award 1982). Office: Mitchell Pk Conservatory 524 S Layton Blvd Milwaukee WI 53215-1236

RISCHAR, CHARLES M., electrical engineer; b. Youngstown, Ohio, Mar. 24, 1958. BSEE, Case Western Res. U., 1980; postgrad. Sr. project engr. Allen Bradley AG-CL, Cleve., 1980—. Patentee on programable controls, 1985. Zoning commr. Manson Twp., Ohio, 1988—; advisor 4-H, Jeauga County, Ohio, 1989—; den leader Boy Scouts Am., Jeauga County, 1991—; mem. bus. adv. coun. Chardon Local Sch. Sys., 1995. Mem. Instrument Soc. Am. (mem. SP-84 subcom. 1992-94). Roman Catholic. Home: 10580 Wilson Mills Rd Chardon OH 44024-9783 Office: Allen Bradley AG-CL 747 Alpha Dr Cleveland OH 44143-2124

RISDON, MICHAEL PAUL, manufacturing executive; b. Hamburg, Iowa, Feb. 24, 1946; s. Paul A. and Vesta Mae (Melton) R.; m. Ann Lorraine Grandowski, June 4, 1966; children: Anita Ann, Carter Paul. BS, Iowa State U., 1967, U. Ky., 1968; MBA, U. Pitts., 1971. Sr. acct. Ernst & Ernst, Indpls., 1971-75; audit supr. Ashland (Ky.) Oil, Inc., 1975-77; v.p. fin. and sys. Diesel ReCon Co., Memphis, 1982-86; budget analyst Cummins Engine Co., Columbus, Ind., 1969-70, mgr. corp. audit, 1977-78, dir. corp. and EDP audit, 1978-82, dir. fin. and planning power sys. group, 1987-88; v.p. Metal Powder Products Co., Columbus, 1989; v.p. fin., CFO Metal Powder Products Co., Inc., Indpls., 1989—. V.p. Columbus Child Care Ctr., 1981-82; vol. Big Sisters Ctrl. Ind., 1994—. Mem. AICPA, Ind. CPA Soc., Metal Powder Industry Fedn. (fin. com. 1991—, chmn. 1994—), Fin. Execs. Inst., Treas. Mgmt. Assn., Nat. Assn. Accts. (nat. bd. dirs. 1981-87, v.p. 1985), Pitt Club of Ind. (steering com. 1992—, v.p. 1993—), Kiwanis (v.p. Columbus 1981). Roman Catholic. Office: Metal Powder Products Inc 10333 N Meridian St Ste 280 Indianapolis IN 46290-1081

RISELEY, MARTHA SUZANNAH HEATER (MRS. CHARLES RISELEY), psychologist, educator; b. Middletown, Ohio, Apr. 25, 1916; d. Elsor and Mary (Henderson) Heater; BEd, U. Toledo, 1943, MA, 1958; PhD, Toledo Bible Coll., 1977; student Columbia U., summers 1943, 57; m. Lester Seiple, Aug. 27, 1944 (div. Feb. 1953); 1 child, L. Rolland, III; m. Charles Riseley, July 30, 1960. Tchr. kindergarten Maumee Valley Country Day Sch., Maumee, Ohio, 1942-44; dir. recreation Toledo Soc. for Crippled Children, 1950-51; tchr. trainable children Lott Day Sch., Toledo, 1951-57; psychologist, asst. dir. Sheltered Workshop Found., Lucas County, Ohio, 1957-62; psychologist Lucas County Child Welfare Bd., Toledo, 1956-62; tchr. educable retarded, head dept. spl. edn. Maumee City Schs., 1962-69; pvt. practice clin. psychology, 1956—; instr. spl. edn. Bowling Green State U., 1962-65; instr. Owens Tech. Coll., 1973-78; interim dir. rehab. services Toledo Goodwill Industries, summer 1967, clin. psychologist Rehab. Center, 1967—; staff psychologist Toledo Mental Health Center, 1979-84. Dir. camping activities for retarded girls and women Camp Libbey, Defiance, Ohio, summers 1951-62; group worker for retarded women Toledo YWCA, 1957-62; guest lectr. Ohio State U., 1957. Health care profl. mem. Nat. Osteoporosis Found., 1988—. Mem. Ohio Assn. Tchrs. Trainable Youth (pres. 1956-57), NW Ohio Rehab. Assn. (pres. 1961-62), Toledo Council for Exceptional Children (pres. 1965), Greater Toledo Assn. Mental Health, Nat. Assn. for Retarded Children, Ohio Assn. Tchrs. Slow Learners, Am. Assn. Mental Deficiency, Am. Soc. Psychologists in Marital and Family Counseling, Psychology and Law Soc. Am. (assoc.), Ohio, NW Ohio (sec.-treas. 1974-77, pres. 1978-79), Am. Theater Orgn. Soc., Ohio Psychol. Assn. (continuing edn. com. 1978—), NEA, AAUW, Am. Soc. Psychologists in Pvt. Practice (nat. dir. 1976—), State Assn. Psychologists and Psychol. Assts., Bus. and Profl. Women's Club, (pres. 1970-72), Ohio Fedn. Bus. and Profl. Women's Clubs (dist. sec. 1970-71, dist. legis. chmn. 1972-74), Toledo Art Mus., Women's Aux. Toledo Bar Assn., League Women Voters (pres. Toledo Lucas County 1991-93), Y Matrons (pres. 1993—), Toledo Area Theater Orgn. Soc. (sec. 1991—), Zonta Internat. (local pres. 1973-74, 78-79, area dir. 1976-78, Maumee River Valley Woman of Yr. for svc. to community and Zonta, 1992), Maumee Valley Hist. Soc., MBLS PEO (chpt. pres. 1950-51), Toledo Council on World Affairs, Internat. Platform Assn. Baptist. Home and Office: 2816 Wicklow Rd Toledo OH 43606-2833

RISHEL, JAMES BURTON, manufacturing executive; b. Omaha, Apr. 27, 1920; s. James Blaine and Elizabeth Helen (Kerr) R.; m. Alice Jane Snyder, June 30, 1945; children: James Richard, Sara Jane Rishel Fields. BSME, U. Nebr., 1946. Profl. engr., Ohio. Pres. Corp. Equipment Co., Cin., 1962-82; chmn. bd. Systecon Inc., Cin., 1982—. Author: The Water Management Manual, HVAC Pump Handbook, 1996; patentee hydraulic systems; contbr. numerous articles to profl. jours. Capt. USAF, 1942-46, 51-52. Fellow ASHRAE; mem. Am. Water Works Assn., Water Environment Fedn. Home: 7570 Thumbelina Ln Cincinnati OH 45242-4937 Office: Systecon Inc 9750 Crescent Park Dr West Chester OH 45069

RISHER, STEPHAN OLAF, investment officer; b. Santa Ana, Calif., Jan. 12, 1951; s. Joseph Leo and Catherine Minnie (Selle) R.; m. Kimberly Jo Hought, May 10, 1984 (div. 1992); 1 child, Jordan Stephan; m. Susan Ekberg, 1995. Miles C.C., Miles City, Mont., 1970, U. Mont., Missoula, 1972. Tech. asst. Polizbohn Farms, Kermanshah, Iran, 1972-73; sales mgr. B & B Signs, Missoula, 1973-75; asst. mgr. and sales Northwest Indsl., Billings, Mont., 1975-79; dist. mgr. Power River Explosives, Williston, N.D., 1979-83; investment officer Dain Bosworth, Inc., Fargo, N.D., 1983—. Mem. Cass County Commn., Fargo, 1991-95; pres. Hospice Red River Valley, Fargo, 1992; vice chair Lake Agassiz Regional Solid Waste, Fargo, 1992; mem. steering com. Nat. Assn. Counties, Washington, 1991; bd. dirs. Cass County Social Svcs., Fargo, 1991. Mem. Cass County Econ. Devel., Williston Petroleum Club, Masons, Shriners, Toastmasters. Lutheran. Office: Dain Bosworth Inc 74 Broadway Fargo ND 58102-4934

RISKEN, JARED CLEVELAND, physician; b. Oakland, Calif., Dec. 13, 1947; s. Maurice Forrest and Virginia (Cleveland) R.; m. Gloria Leona Hanger, Jan. 11, 1969; children: Douglas Jared, Sarah Julianne. BA in Anthropology and Biology, Loma Linda U., 1973; MD, Am. U., 1979. Resident in family practice Luth. Med. Ctr., St. Louis, 1980-81; med. dir. Alpha Therapeutics, St. Louis, 1981-85; indsl. medicine-safety engr. Torno America, Cortez, Colo., 1989-91, OJB Engring., Apple Valley, Calif., 1990-92; with U. Ill. Sch. Medicine, Champaign, 1992—. Active cmty. and ch. activities. Mem. Am. Profl. Practice Assn., Nat. Assn. Residents and Interns, Physicians for Social Responsibility, Christian Med. Dental Soc. Office: 2604 Willoughby Rd Champaign IL 61821-7578

RISLEY, GREGORY BYRON, furniture company executive, interior designer; b. Vincennes, Ind., Feb. 2, 1949; s. Jack Byron and Elizabeth Louise (Rockwell) R.; children: Christopher Byron, Timothy Neal. BS, Oakland City (Ind.) Coll., 1973; postgrad., Butler U., 1973-74. Pres. Risley Furniture & Design, Bicknell, Ind., 1974—, Risley Enterprises Inc., Bicknell, Ind., 1979—. Co-author: Preview IV The Home Furnishings Store. Pres. Better Bicknell Club, 1971; coach Pee Wee League, Bicknell, 1975-77; leader cub pack Boy Scouts Am., Bicknell, 1977; chmn. Queen Pageant, Bicknell, 1978-85. Mem. Nat. Home Furnishings Assn. (chmn. nat. execs. 1978-80), Am. Contract Bridge League (life master, unit sec. 1986-88, v.p. 1989, pres. 1991-92, bd. dirs. unit 193, 1993-95), Bicknell Mchts. Assn., Interior Design Soc. (outstanding rm. design award 1980), Knox County Assn. Retarded Citizens, French Club, Masons, Scottish Rite, Old Town Players (charter), Elks (past exalted ruler Bicknell 1976-77). Office: 114-120 S Main St Bicknell IN 47512

RISSER, FRED A., state senator; b. Madison, Wis., May 5, 1927; married; 3 children. B.A., U. Wis.; LL.B., U. Oreg., 1952. Bar: Wis. Sole practice Madison, 1952—; mem. Wis. State Senate, 1962—, asst. minority leader, 1965-67, minority leader, 1967-75, pres. pro tem, 1975-79, pres., 1979-93, asst. minority leader, 1993—. Mem. Wis. State Assembley, 1956-62; del. Democratic Conv., 1960, 64; presdl. elector-chmn. Wis. Electoral Coll., 1964; vice chmn. Bldg. Commn., Wis. Office: State Capitol Rm 206 S Madison WI 53702 also: 5008 Risser Rd Madison WI 53705-1365

RISSER, PAUL GILLAN, botanist, academic administrator; b. Blackwell, Okla., Sept. 14, 1939; s. Paul Crane and Jean (McCluskey) R.; children: David, Mark, Stephen, Scott. BA, Grinnell Coll.; MS in Botany, U. Wis., PhD in Botany and Soils. From asst. prof. to prof. botany U. Okla., 1967-81, also asst. dir. biol. sta., chmn. dept. botany and microbiology, 1977-81; dir. Okla. Biol. Survey, 1971-77; chief Ill. Natural History Survey, 1981-86; program dir., ecosystem studies NSF; provost and v.p. acad. affairs U. N.Mex., 1989-92; pres. Miami U., Oxford, Ohio, 1993—. Author: (with Kathy Cornelison) Man and the Biosphere, 1979, (with others) The True Prairie Ecosystem, 1981; research, numerous publs. in field. Trustee Pioneer Multi-County Library Bd. Mem. Am. Acad. Arts and Scis., Ecol. Soc. Am. (pres.), Brit. Ecol. Soc., Soc. Range Mgmt., Southwestern Assn. Naturalists (pres.), Am. Inst. Biol. Sci. (pres.), Torrey Bot. Club. Presbyterian. Office: Miami U Roudebush Hall Oxford OH 45056*

RITCHEY, PAUL ANDREW, accountant; b. Zanesville, Ohio, July 24, 1950; s. Leonard E. and Emma Elizabeth (Geolz) R.; m. Molly McGee. Student, Ohio U., 1970; BS, Ohio State U., 1972; postgrad., Leadership Acad., Ohio U., 1988; Y. CPA, Ohio. Dir. fin. Mt. St. Mary Hosp., Nelsonville, Ohio, 1972-74; acct. Good Samaritan Med. Ctr., Zanesville, Ohio, 1974-76; staff assoc. Lynch, Tucker & Assocs., CPAs, Zanesville, 1976-80; mng. ptnr. Ritchey and Assocs., CPAs, Zanesville, 1980-90; ptnr. Norman Jones Enlow & Co., CPA's, Zanesville, 1990—. Mem. acct. curriculum com. Muskingum Area Tech. Coll; mem. various coms.; mem. fin. com. Bishop Rosecrans High Sch.; coach Little League Baseball; past pres. St. Nicholas Elem. Sch. Bd.; Eucharistic minister St. Nicholas Ch. Mem. AICPA, Ohio Soc. CPAs, Sml. Bus. Devel. Ctr., Zanesville Area C. of C., Aircraft Owners Pilots Assn., Zanesville Country Club, Rotary, KC. Republican.

RITLAND, DONALD MARVIN, environmental engineer; b. Mauston, Wis., Aug. 11, 1939; s. Oscar and Gertrude Corrine (Nelson) R.; m. Joanne Faye Wolseth, Mar. 24, 1973; children: Marc, Paul, Eric, Todd. BSCE, Wis. State U., Platteville, 1967; MS in Mgmt., Cardinal Stritch Coll., Madison, Wis., 1990. Civil engr. U.S. Forest Svc., Rhinelander, Wis., 1967-68; transp. engr. Wis. Dept. Transp., Superior, 1968-80; environ. engr. (constrn. mgmt.) Wis. Dept. Natural Resources, Fitchburg, 1980—. With USAF, 1960-63. Home: 157 Kierstead Ln Oregon WI 53575

RITSCHEL, JAMES ALLAN, computer research specialist; b. St. Paul, June 25, 1930; s. Florian Peter and Doris (Miller) R.; m. Dorothy Kvapil, Apr. 15, 1952. BA, Globe Coll., 1962. Cert. data processor, systems and office automation profl. Jr. underwriter St. Paul Cos., 1948-51; acct. Burlington North, St. Paul, 1951-66; bus. systems specialist 3M, Maplewood, Minn., 1966-85, micro rsch. specialist, 1985-92; cons. Mgmt. Assistance Project, Mpls., 1983—; co-founder Minn. Emerging Techs. Coun., 1988, 3M rep., 1989-92, advisor, 1993—; mem. professionalism adv. bd. Minn. Computer/Industry Coalition, 1990. Mem. Office Automation Soc. Internat. (exec. officer 1984-86, session chmn. and conf. speaker 1985), Assn. Inst. Cert. Computer Profls. (regional bd. dirs. 1987-88, internat. bd. dirs. 1989-92), Minn. Soc. Cert. Computer Profls. Home: 6059 48th St N Saint Paul MN 55128-1935

RITTENHOUSE, NANCY CAROL, elementary education educator; b. Humeston, Iowa, May 26, 1941; d. Myrl Matthews and Opal L. (McCartney) Hixson; m. J. Kent Rittenhouse, Dec. 18, 1960 (div. Mar. 1984); children: Brenda L. Carroll, J. Aaron, Timothy K. Student, St. Mary of the Plains Coll., 1984-87; degree in elem. edn., Ft. Hays State Coll., 1989. Cert. tchr., Kans. Reading instr. Sacred Heart Sch., Dodge City, Kans., 1984; elem. tchr. Miller Sch., Dodge City, Kans., 1985-86, Washington Sch., Hays, 1987; city-county recreation dir. Sherman County, Goodland, 1988; elem. tchr. Northside Sch., Larned, 1989-90; with Great Bend (Kans.) Tribune. Artist numerous paintings; author poetry. Mem. Menninger Found., Topeka, 1984—; hon. mem. Boy Scouts Am., 1978; camp instr. Spl. Olympics Blind Found., Junction City, Kans., 1985-90, Dodge City, 1984;

leader Girl Scouts USA, 1975-77. Recipient Hon. award Spl. Olympics, 1984, 1st pl. poetry award, 1990, watercolor award, 1990, oils award, 1988, pen and ink award, 1984. Mem. AAAS, Nat. Trust for Hist. Preservation, Nat. Geog. Soc., Planetary Soc., Smithsonian Assn., MIT. Republican. Home: Box 1872 Great Bend KS 67530 Office: Great Bend Tribune 2012 Forest St Great Bend KS 67530

RITTER, DAVID ALLEN, computer science consultant; b. West Reading, Pa., Oct. 14, 1954; s. David Franklin and Marjorie A. (Long) R. BS, No. Ill. U., 1976. Programmer, analyst Continental Ill. Nat. Bank, Chgo., 1976-79; sr. cons. SRZ Services, Chgo., 1979; sr. systems analyst United Airlines, Elk Grove Village, Ill., 1979-81; pres. Progressive Mgmt. Info. Systems, Schaumburg, Ill., 1981-82; sr. planner United Airlines, Elk Grove Village, 1982-86, computer systems engr., 1986-87; computer systems engr. Covia Corp., Rosemont, Ill., 1988-90; sr. cons. Computer and Engring. Cons., Ltd., Southfield, Mich., 1990-92; dir. consulting KnowledgeWare, Rosemont, Ill., 1992-94; dir. Proforma, Hoffman Estates, Ill., 1994—. Author: Preparing for AD/Cycle, 1990, Information Engineering and Strategic Planning, 1991; co-author: Systems Prototyping, 1986, Developer Workstation, 1988. Fellow Pi Mu Epsilon; mem. Chgo. Area Devel. Ctr. Round Table (founder, coord. 1984-89), GUIDE User Group (project mgr. 1986-88), Internat. CASE User Group (conf. chmn. 1990, v.p. 1991). Office: 2500 W Higgins Rd Ste 530 Hoffman Estates IL 60195

RITTER, DORIS STANDRING, human resources professional; b. Lakewood, Ohio, Apr. 11, 1926; d. James Allers and Anne Marie (Willms) Standring; m. Wayne L. Ritter, May 14, 1949; children: Gary W., Keith S., Sharon J., Curt P., Nancy R. Knightly. BS, Ohio U., 1948; MS, George Williams Coll., 1978. With retail sales dept. Kaufmann's, Pitts., 1948-50; hostess Pitts. Gas Co., 1955-56; head tchr. Head Start CEDA, Sandusky, Ohio, 1969-71; dir. head start CEDA, Norwalk, Ohio, 1971-73; parent coord. Des Plaines Valley Community Ctr., Summit, Ill., 1973-74; career devel. coord. Community and Econ. Devel. Assn. Cook County, Chgo., 1974-75; placement dir. Thornton Community Coll., South Holland, Ill., 1975-80; tng. specialist AT&T, Chgo., 1980-89; v.p. Tuggle Cons. Group, Chgo., 1990—; cons. Head Start, Summit, LaGrange, Ill., 1990-92. Bd. dirs., chmn. strategic planning com. and personnel com. Seguin Retarded Citizens Assn., Cicero, Ill.; chmn. mem. com. and mem. personnel com. Seguin Svcs. Inc.; mem. tng. and vol. devel. com., cons. United Way Suburban Chgo., 1987—, mem. diversity subcom., 1992—; vol. Spl. Olympics, Cicero and Berwyn, Ill., 1990—; elder 1st Presbyn. Ch., La Grange, 1991-94, moderator mem. com., stretagic planning com., nominating com., choir mem. 1991—, amateur play performance, 1995, youth com. mem. 1994—; mem. Community Diversity Group of LaGrange, 1992—, Kids at Work Program, 1994—; participant Summer Inst. Intercultural Comm., 1993. Mem. ASTD (spl. interest group Chgo. chpt. 1990-91), Bus. and Profl. Women (past membership chmn., program chmn. 1991—, network chmn. 1992-93, cert. highest honors outstanding programs 1991-92, young careerist chmn. 1993, 94), Toastmasters (sec., v.p. pres. 1982-85, Able Toastmaster award). Home: 234 S Brainard Ave La Grange IL 60525-2115 Office: Tuggle Cons Group 7744 S Michigan Ave Chicago IL 60619-2315

RITTER, MARY CATHERINE, research scientist; b. Mpls., May 10, 1943; d. George Michael and Lorraine Marie (Schwappach) R. BS, Coll. St. Francis, Joliet, Ill., 1965; MS, U. Minn., 1969, PhD, 1971. Postdoctoral rsch. fellow U. Chgo., 1971-75, rsch. assoc., 1975-77, rsch. assoc., instr., 1977-79, rsch. assoc., asst. prof., 1980; instr. endocrinology Rush-Presbyn.-St. Luke's Med. Ctr., Chgo., 1985—. Home: 1700 # 56th St Unit 3007 Chicago IL 60637-1935 Office: Rush Presbyn-St Lukes Md Ct Sect Digestive Diseases 1653 W Congress Pky Chicago IL 60612-3833

RITTINGER, CAROLYNE JUNE, newspaper editor; b. Swift Current, Sask., July 19, 1942; d. George Kelly Gaetz and Eva Evelyn (Hiebert) Olson; m. Robert Edward Rittinger, Aug. 16, 1958; children: Robert Wade, Angela Alison, Lisa Michelle. Women's editor Swift Current Sun, 1967-68; city editor Medicine Hat (Alta.) News, 1969-70; reporter Kitchener-Waterloo Record, Kitchener, Ont., 1972-75, copy editor, 1976, women's editor, then dist. editor, entertainment editor, wire editor, 1976-85, city editor, 1985-86, asst. mng. editor, 1986-89, mng. editor, 1989-92, editor, 1992—. Recipient News Story of Yr. award Calgary Women's Press Club, 1969, Best Feature Story on Fine Art award, 1970, Honorable Mention for A.R. McKenzie award for Info. Story, 1970; named Oktoberfest Woman of Yr., 1992. Office: Kitchener-Waterloo Record, 225 Fairway Rd, Kitchener, ON Canada N2G 4E5

RITTMER, ELAINE HENEKE, library media specialist; b. Maquoketa, Iowa, Feb. 4, 1931; d. Herman John and Clara (Luett) Heneke; m. Sheldon Lowell Rittmer, June 11, 1950; children: Kenneth, Lynnette, Robyn (dec.), infant son (dec.). BA, Marycrest Coll., 1973; MS, Western Ill. U., 1980. Permanent teaching cert. K-14, Iowa; cert. libr. media specialist K-14, Iowa. Sch. libr. Calamus-Wheatland (Iowa) Community Schs., 1970-74; high sch. libr. media specialist, libr. coord. Camanche (Iowa) Community Sch., 1974—; ind. tech. cons., 1988—. Mem. Iowa Edn. Media Assn., Iowa State Edn. Assn., Camanche Edn. Assn., Camanche Cmty. Schs. Tech. Com., Media Tech. Cons. Republican. Home: 3539 230th St De Witt IA 52742-9208 Office: Camanche High Sch PO Box 160 937 9th St Camanche IA 52730

RITTMER, SHELDON, senator, farmer; b. DeWitt, Iowa, Sept. 5, 1928; s. Elmer and Lois (Hass) R.; m. Elaine Heneke, June 11, 1950; children: Kenneth S., Lynnette Rittmer Jones, Robyn Jon (dec.), infant son (dec.). County supr. Clinton (Iowa) Conty Bd. Suprs., 1978-90; chmn. Clinton County Title III Com., 1987-90; v.p. Iowa Assn. County Suprs., Des Moines, 1989-90; senator dist. 19 State of Iowa, 1990—; mem. local govt. com., state govt. com., human svcs. appropriations subcom., 1990—; ranking mem. transp. com., 1994—, Dept. Elder Affairs Commn., 1990-94; adminstrv. rules rev. com. Iowa Legis., 1992—; mem. Iowa Coun. Human Investment, 1994—, Iowa Adv. Com. on Intergovtl. Rels., 1994—, Iowa Pub. Employees Retirement Sytem Bd., 1994—. Chmn. 1st Luth. Ch., Maquoketa, Iowa, 1964-68; active Clinton County Hist. Soc., 1980—. Recipient Spl. Recognition award Nat. Fedn. Ind. Bus., 1991-92, Spl. Recognition Iowa Soil Conservation award, 1994. Mem. Izaak Walton League Iowa, DeWitt Lions, Ducks Unlimited U.S.A, Clinton County Pork Prodr's. Assn., Clinton County Cattlemen's Assn., Pheasants Forever, City of Clinton C. of C., DeWitt C. of C., Bettendorf C. of C. Republican. Home: 3539 230th St De Witt IA 52742-9208 Office: State Senate of Iowa State Capital Des Moines IA 50319

RITZ, EUGENE FREDERICK, therapist; b. Watertown, S.D., Jan. 4, 1962; s. Donald Eugene and Darlene Margaret (Jacobs) R. BS in History and Math., S.D. State U., 1986, MS in Counseling and Human Resources, 1988. Lic. grad. social worker; lic. profl. counselor. In-home therapist Luth. Social Svc., Moorhead, Minn., 1989—. Mem. Minn. Family Base Svc. Assn., N.D. Family Base Svc. Assn., N.D. Counselors Assn., N.D. Mental Health Counselors Assn. Office: Lutheran Social Svc 715 11th St N Ste 401 Moorhead MN 56560

RITZER, KAREN RAE, executive secretary, office administrator; b. Sioux City, Iowa, Nov. 26, 1946; d. Robert Leland and Wanda Lily (Kirby) Taylor; m. Thomas Arthur Ritzer, Nov. 23, 1963; children: Robert Arthur, Kristina Marie, Teresa Lynn Ritzer Jones, Carl Robert White. Grad., Arnolds Park (Iowa) High Sch., 1968. Office mgr., sec. Tom's Plumbing and Heating, Arnolds Park, 1964—; sec./treas., bd. dirs. Ritz Closet Seat Corp., Arnolds Park, 1985—. Sec./treas. Concerned Citizens Com., Arnolds Park, 1985, 86, 87; chairperson Centennial Bd. for Arnolds Park 100th Birthday Celebration. Mem. Nat. Trust for Hist. Preservation, The Smithsonian Assn., Am. Mus. Natural History (assoc.), United We Stand Am. (founding), Friends of Iowa Pub. TV, Ladies Aus. VFW. Address: PO Box 496 Arnolds Park IA 51331-0496

RITZLIN, GEORGE, rare book and map dealer; b. Chgo., May 21, 1942; s. Philip and Pauline (Moskowitz) R.; m. Mary Eileen McMichael, Jan. 6, 1979; 1 child, David Michael. BSME, Ill. Inst. Tech., 1964; MBA, Ind. U., 1966. CPA, Ill. Asst. to v.p. fin. Chgo and North Western Ry. Co., Chgo., 1969-70; fin. analyst TransUnion Corp., Chgo., 1971; Adcock-Ingram Ltd., Johannesburg, South Africa, 1971-72; mgr. fin. analysis Blue Cross Assn., Chgo., 1973-77; controller G. W. Hoffman and Co., Chgo., 1978-79; pvt. practice C.P.A., Chgo., 1979-83, rare book and map dealer, Chgo., 1977—. Editor: Directory of Dealers in Antiquarian Maps, 1980. Contbr. articles to profl. jours. Treas. Sheffield Neighborhood Assn., Chgo., 1981-82; pres. 43d Ward Young Reps., Chgo., 1969-70; arbitrator Better Bus. Bur., Chgo., 1978-92; active Newberry Libr. Assocs., Chgo., 1980—, Clements Libr. Assocs., Ann Arbor, 1993, Friends of the Lilly Libr., Bloomington, Ind., 1993. Served with U.S. Army, 1967-69. Mem. Chgo. Map Soc., (pres., co-founder 1976-78, 1982, bd. dirs. 1976-83), Mich. Map Soc., Wash. Map Soc., Antiquarian Booksellers Assn. Am., Inc. (bd. govs. 1986-89), Ravinia Bus. Assn. (treas. 1992—). Office: George Ritzlin Maps & Books 469 Roger Williams Ave Highland Park IL 60035-4704

RIVENESS, PHILLIP J., state legislator; b. Karlstad, Minn., Dec. 14, 1947; s. John Anders and Ruth (Olson) R.; m. Gail Elaine Coffin, 1968; 3 children. BA, U. Minn., 1969. Former mem. Minn. Ho. of Reps. St. Paul; U.S. senator from Minn., 1991—; vicechmn. govt. ops. and reform com., mem. environ. and natural resources com., health care com., others.; exec dir. South Hennyson Svc. Coun., 1974-78; health care adminstr. Chmn. Bloomington Dem-Farmer-Labor Club, 1979-80. Democrat. Home: 2209 E Old Shakopee Rd Bloomington MN 55425-2172*

RIVER, GEORGE LAMBERT, hematologist, oncologist; b. Oak Park, Ill., June 5, 1932; s. Louis Philip and Mary Elizabeth (Lambert) R.; m. Renee DeVere Kaplan, Sept. 5, 1953 (div. May 1972); children: Gregory, Geoffrey, Catherine, Linda, Robert (dec.), David; m. Judith Ann Stav, Sept. 30, 1973; 1 child, John Thomas Wendorf. BS, U. Chgo., 1952; MD, Loyola U. Med. Sch., 1956. Intern, resident Cook County Hosp., Chgo., 1956-60; capt. USAF, San Antonio, 1960-62; staff Marshfield (Wis.) Clinic, 1962-71; head hematology St. Elizabeth's Hosp., Youngstown, Ohio, 1971-74; internal medicine Dr. William Stone, Atlanta, 1974-76; physician Internal Medicine Assocs., Davenport, Iowa, 1976-92, Dubuque (Iowa) Internal Medicine, 1992-96; dir. Cancer Ctr. Freeman Hsop., Joplin, Mo., 1996—; dir. cancer ctr. St. Luke's Hosp., Davenport, 1989-92, Finley Hosp., Dubuque, 1992—. Fellow Am. Coll. Physicians; mem. Am. Soc. Hematology, Am. Soc. Clin. Oncology. Republican. Roman Catholic. Home: 1527 Point Kirby Ave Las Vegas NV 89123 Office: Freeman Hosp Cancer Ctr 3201 McClelland Blvd Joplin MO 64803

RIVERS, DONALD LEE, marketing professional; b. Sioux City, Iowa, Feb. 10, 1943; s. Thomas Harvey and Helen Catherine (Brtenner) R.; m. Robin Dee Magee, Jan. 7, 1968 (div.); m. Beverly Doss, Oct. 13, 1979 (div.); m. Diane Dankenbring, Oct. 1, 1994. BS, Drake U., 1966; MA, U. Iowa, 1968. Sales rep. Holt, Rinehart & Winston, Inc., Mpls., 1969-72; editor Holt, Rinehart & Winston, Inc., N.Y.C., 1973-76; sales rep. Rand McNally & Co., Tampa, Fla., 1972-73; editor William C. Brown Co., Dubuque, Iowa, 1976-78; sales mgr. nat. accounts Better Homes & Gardens Books, Meredith Corp., Des Moines, 1978-85, dir. nat. accounts, 1985-87; dir. of nat. accounts XLM Co., 1988-89; v.p. sales Steelworks, Des Moines, 1989-94; v.p. sales and mktg. Enviro Industries, 1994-95; mktg. cons. Rivers & Assocs., Ankeny, Iowa, 1995—. Mem. Kappa Delta Pi. Republican. Home and Office: 2918 NW 5th St Ankeny IA 50021-1048

RIVERS, JESSIE MAE, writer; b. Chgo., Aug. 31, 1933; d. Charlie Hill and Eula (White) Cunningham; m. Willie Rivers,. Student, Palmer Writers Sch., 1974. Writer Palmer Writers Sch., Mpls., 1972-74; mgr. Jackson Pk. Hotel, Chgo., 1957-62, Herman Roberts Motel, Chgo., 1962-68; private duty Chgo., 1984-88. Home: 640 W Briar Pl Chicago IL 60657-4545

RIVERS, LAWRENCE ALAN, marketing professional; b. Sulphur, La., Mar. 26, 1956; s. Lawrence Harrison Jr. and Lois (Miller) R.; m. Roberta Choat, Oct. 7, 1978. B in Law Enforcement, La. State U., 1978; MS, Troy State U., 1982; JD, Tulane U., 1985. Bar: Colo. 1990, Calif. 1988, Tex. 1985, Ind. 1993. Assoc. Orgain, Bell & Tucker, Beaumont, Tex., 1985-87, Benton, Orr, Duval & Buckingham, Ventura, Calif., 1987-88; mktg. mgr. Santa Barbara Rsch. Ctr./Hughes Aircraft, Goleta, Calif., 1988-93; mgr. bus. devel. Delco Electronics Corp., 1993—; instr. U. LaVerne, 1992-93. Mem. Gen. Plan Adv. Com., Lompoc, Calif., 1991-92, Cable TV Com., Lompoc, 1991-92. With U.S. Army, 1978-82; maj. USAR, 1982—. Named one of Outstanding Young Men of Am., 1987. Mem. Calif. State Bar, Tex. State Bar, Colo. State Bar, Ind. State Bar. Republican. Baptist. Home: 3082 Hazel Foster Dr Carmel IN 46033-8700 Office: 1800 E Lincoln Kokomo IN 46902

RIVES, STANLEY GENE, university president emeritus; b. Decatur, Ill., Sept. 27, 1930; s. James A. and Frances (Bunker) R.; m. Sandra Lou Belt, Dec. 28, 1957; children: Jacqueline Ann, Joseph Alan. B.S., Ill. State U., 1952, M.S., 1955; Ph.D., Northwestern U., 1963. Instr. W. Va. U., 1955-56, Northwestern U., 1956-58; asst. prof. Ill. State U., Normal, 1958-63; assoc. prof. Ill. State U., 1963-67; prof. Ill. State U., Normal, 1967-80, asst. dean Coll. Arts and Scis., 1968-69, Am. Council on Edn. Fellows Program, 1969-70, assoc. dean faculties, 1970-72, dean undergrad. instrn., 1972-80, dir. W.K. Kellogg Faculty and Instructional Devel. Program, 1977-80, assoc. provost, 1976-80, acting provost, 1979-80; provost, v.p. acad. affairs, prof. Eastern Ill. U., Charleston, 1981-83, pres., 1983-92, pres. emeritus, 1992—; vis. prof. U. Hawaii, 1963-64. Author: (with Donald Klopf) Individual Speaking Contests: Preparation for Participation, 1967, (with Gene Budig) Academic Quicksand. Trends and Issues in Higher Education, 1973, (with others) Academic Innovation: Faculty and Instructional Development at Illinois State University, 1979, The Fundamentals of Oral Interpretation, 1981; contbr. articles to profl. jours. Bd. dirs. Ill. State Univs. Retirement System, 1992—, treas., 1995—, Ea. Ill. Univ. Found., 1993—, East Ctrl. Ill. Devel. Corp., 1983-92, Charleston Area Econ. Devel. Found., 1986-92, Coles Together, 1988-92; mem. pres. commn. NCAA, 1986-91; trustee Nat. Debate Tournament, 1967-75. With U.S. Army, 1952-54. Mem. Am. Assn. State Colls. and Univs., Ill. State C. of C. (bd. dirs. 1990-92), Charleston C. of C. (bd. dirs. 1985-88), Rotary, Theta Alpha Phi, Phi Kappa Delta, Pu Gamma Mu. Home: 2231 Andover Pl Charleston IL 61920-3807

RIZER, FRANKLIN MORRIS, physician, otolarynogologist; b. Gallipolis, Ohio, Aug. 13, 1953; s. Franklin Morris and Wanda Mae (Potts) R.; m. Maria Nicolette Guglielmi, Feb. 8, 1986. BS cum laude, Ohio State U., 1975; MD, U. Cin., 1979. Diplomate Am. Bd. Otolaryngology. Intern U. Calif., Davis, 1979-80; resident U. Wash., Seattle, 1980-81, Ea. Va. U. Coll. of Medicine, Norfolk, 1981-84; fellow House Ear Inst., 1984-87; chief otology St. Joseph's Riverside Hosp., Warren, Ohio, 1989—; assoc. prof. Ea. Va. Coll. of Medicine, Norfolk, 1987—, Northeastern Ohio U. Coll. of Medicine, Rootstown, 1987—, Ohio State U., Columbus, 1995—; fellowship dir. Warren Otologic Group, Warren, 1991—. Contbr. articles to profl. jours. Trustee Makoning Valley Macintosh Users Group, Warren, 1989-92; active Leadership Warren, 1989; bd. dirs. Humility of Mary Integrated Delivery Network, 1995—. With USAF, 1971-73. Fellow Am. Acad. Otolaryngology; mem. Am. Acad. Facial Plastics, Soc. of Wilderness Medicine, Undersea and Hyperbaric Med. Soc. United Methodist. Home: 469 Country Club Dr NE Warren OH 44484-4616 Office: Warren Otologic Group 3893 E Market St Warren OH 44484-4706

RIZZO, GERALDINE JOSEPHINE, private investigations company official; b. Chgo., Apr. 14, 1942; d. Joseph Esau and Teresa Marie (Biancalana) Bacci; m. Ernest Dominic Rizzo, July 6, 1963; children: Scott Matthew, Tracy Marie. Security cert., Triton Coll., River Grove, Ill., 1989. Cert. pvt. detective, pvt. security, Ill. Instr. Franklin Park (Ill.) Park Dist., 1984-85; early childhood devel. aide Dist. 84 Schs., Franklin Park, 1988-89; advisor Bur. Spl. Investigations, Franklin Park, 1980—; chiropractor asst., mktg. dir. Franklin Park Chiropractic Ctr., 1989—. Area coord. C.L.O.W.N. drug prevention program, 1987, Talkline Crisis Prevention, Franklin Park, 1987—; sec. Sch. Dist. 84 Sch. Bd., Franklin Park, 1989—; bd. dirs. United Way, Franklin Park, 1990—, v.p., 1994-95, pres., 1996; hon. life mem. Ill. Congress Parents and Tchrs., 1988—; mem. Comty. Svc. Coun., Leyden Twp., Ill., 1987—; past vice chmn.; adviser, chmn. Centennial Corp., Franklin Park, 1991; mem. Franklin Park PTA, 1973—, pres., 1986-88; chmn. dist. 28 Ill. PTA, 1988-91; mem. Leyden Hist. Soc. Named Individual of Yr., Franklin Park Chamber of Commerce and Industry, 1989; honored for leadership and devel. Ill. Assn. Sch. Bds., 1991, 92, 93, 94, 95 (master statis). Mem. Kiwanis (pres. Franklin Park Noon chpt. 1990-91, sec. 1991-92), Leyden High Schs. Alumni Assn. (bd. dirs. 1992—). Roman Catholic. Office: Bur Spl Investigations PO Box 1145 Franklin Park IL 60131-8145 Office: Franklin Park Chiropractic Ctr 3545 Rose St Franklin Park IL 60131

RIZZO, HENRY, state legislator. Mem. Mo. State Ho. of Reps. Dist. 40. Home: 575 Harrison St Kansas City MO 64106-1265*

RIZZO, RONALD STEPHEN, lawyer; b. Kenosha, Wis., July 15, 1941; s. Frank Emmanuel and Rosalie (Lo Cicero); children: Ronald Stephen Jr., Michael Robert. BA, St. Norbert Coll., 1963; JD, Georgetown U., 1965, LLM in Taxation, 1966. Bar: Wis. 1965, Calif. 1967. Assoc. Kindel & Anderson, L.A., 1966-71, ptnr., 1971-86; ptnr. Jones, Day, Reavis & Pogue, L.A., 1986-93, Chgo., 1993—; bd. dirs. Guy LoCicero & Son Inc., Kenosha, Wis. Contbg. editor: ERISA Litigation Reporter. Schulte zur Hausen fellow Inst. Internat. and Fgn. Trade Law, Washington, 1966. Fellow Am. Coll. Tax Counsel; mem. ABA (chmn. com. on employee benefits sect. on taxation 1988-89, vice chair com. on govt. submissions 1995—), Los Angeles County Bar Assn. (chmn. com. on employee benefits sect. on taxation 1977-79, exec. com. 1977-78, 90-92), State Bar Calif. (co-chmn. com. on employee benefits sect. on taxation 1980), Nat. Ctr. Employee Ownership, West Pension Conf. (steering com. L.A. chpt. 1980-83). Home: # 19C 1040 N Lakeshore Dr Chicago IL 60611 Office: Jones Day Reavis & Pogue 77 W Wacker Dr Chicago IL 60601-1629

RIZZOLO, LOUIS B. M., artist, educator; b. Ferndale, Mich., Oct. 8, 1933; s. Louis and Bella Lonita (Bronson) R.; m. Patricia Ann, June 30, 1956 (div. 1982); children; Connie Lucille, Louis Matthew, Marc Angelo; m. Linda Talbot, Dec. 3, 1982; stepchildren: Heather MacIntyre, Cameron Smith, Jennifer Talbot, Meghan Smith. BS in Art, Western Mich. U., 1956; MA in Fine Art, U. Iowa, 1960; postgrad., U. Ga., 1969. Tchr. art Petoskey (Mich.) Pub. Schs., 1956-64; tchr. history, art studio North Ctrl. Mich. Coll., Petoskey, 1959-64; grad. teaching asst. U. Iowa, Iowa CIty, 1958-60; tchr. painting Kalamazoo Inst. Art, 1970-85; prof. art Western Mich. U., Kalamazoo, 1964—; tchr. painting, drawing, interdisciplinary/multi media, installation/performance/exhbn. juror, lectr. and tchr. internat. workshops, Switzerlan, Austria, Can., France, Scotland, Hawaii, 1989—; artistic and gen. dir. Rizzolo and Assocs.: Inflatale Light Workshop, Kalamazoo, 1980-92; co-dir. rsch. Creative Learning Program, Kalamazoo, 1986-92; R.W.S. London Watercolor del. Rep. of China (Best of Watercolor Book 1995). Contbr.: Best of Watercolor Book, 1995. Capt. AUS, 1958-68. Grantee Ford Found., Dow Corning, Du Pont, Upjohn, Mich. Coun. Arts, Mich. Millenium Project, 1995-2000, Mich. Found. Arts, Edn. for the Arts, W.K. Kellogg, Kalamazoo Arts Coun., Nat. Exhbn./Collections: Western Mich. U. fellow. Mem. Internat. Soc. Art & Tech., Mich. Watercolor Soc., World Forum of Acoustic Ecology, Laser Inst. Am. Independent. Home: PO Box 62 Glenn MI 49416-0062

ROACH, JOHN ROBERT, retired archbishop; b. Prior Lake, Minn., July 31, 1921; s. Simon J. and Mary (Regan) R. B.A., St. Paul Sem., 1946; M.A., U. Minn., 1957; L.H.D. (hon.), Gustavus Adolphus Coll., St. Mary's Coll., St. Xavier U., Villanova U., U. St. Thomas, Coll. of St. Catherine. Ordained priest Roman Catholic Ch., 1946; instr. St. Thomas Acad., 1946-50, headmaster, 1951-68; named domestic prelate, 1966; rector St. John Vianney Sem., 1968-71; aux. bishop St. Paul and Mpls., 1971; consecrated bishop, 1971; pastor St. Charles Borromeo Ch., Mpls., 1971-73, St. Cecilia Ch., St. Paul, 1973-75; archbishop of St. Paul, 1975-95; appointed vicar for parishes, 1971, vicar for clergy, 1972—; Episc. moderator Nat. Apostolate for Mentally Retarded, 1974; Mem. Priests Senate, 1968-72; pres. Priests Senate and Presbytery, 1970; chmn. Com. on Accreditation Pvt. Schs. in Minn., 1952-57; mem. adv. com. Coll. Entrance Exam. Bd., 1964; Episc. mem. Bishops and Pres.'s Com.; chmn. Bishops Com. to Oversee Implementation of the Call to Action Program, 1979-80; chmn. priestly formation com.; mem. Cath. Charity Bd. Trustee St. Paul Sem. Sch. Div., 1971—, now chmn.; trustee Cath. U. Am., 1978-81, Coll. St. Catherine, 1975-95; chmn. bd. trustees St. Thomas Acad., U. St. Thomas, St. John Vianney Sem.; v.p. Nat. Conf. Cath. Bishops, 1977-80, pres., 1980-83, chmn. ad hoc com. on call to action, 1977; chair internat. policy com. U.S. Catholic Conf., 1990-93. Mem. Am. Coun. Edn. (del. 1963-65), Minn. Cath. Edn. Assn. (past pres.), Assn. Mil. Colls. and Schs. U.S. (past pres.), North Cen. Assn. Colls. and Secondary Schs., Nat. Conf. Cath. Bishops (adminstrv. com., priestly formation com., chmn. vocations com., priorities and plans com., com. on sexual abuse), U.S. Cath. Conf. (com. on social devel. and world peace 1990-93, priorities and plans com.), Nat. Cath. Edn. Assn. (chmn. bd. dirs.), Nat. Cath. Rural Life Conf. (past chmn. task force on food and agr. 1987-89). Address: Chancery Office 226 Summit Ave Saint Paul MN 55102-2121

ROARK, BARBARA ANN, librarian; b. Evanston, Ill., July 24, 1958; d. Edward B. and Ann H. Rowe; m. Paul E. Roark, Sept. 18, 1982; children: Sarah, John. BA in History, U. Ky., 1981, MLS, 1982. Libr. dir. Hopkins County Madisonville (Ky.) Pub. Libr., 1983-85; ops. mgr. Wurzburg Inc., Nashville, 1985-91; libr. dir. Spies Pub. Libr., Menominee, Mich., 1991—; v.p. adv. coun. Mid-Peninsula Libr. Coop., Mich., 1993-95, sec. adv. coun., 1991-93. Grant writer Title II, 1994, Title I, 1995. Recipient Cert. of Excellence Libr. of Mich., 1995. Mem. ALA, Mich. Libr. Assn., Spies Pub. Libr. Found., PEO Chpt. BK, Order Ea. Star, U. Ky. Alumni Assn., Zeta Tau Alpha. Methodist. Office: Spies Public Library 940 1st St Menominee MI 49858

ROATH, WILLIAM WESLEY, retired research agronomist; b. Torrington, Wyo., Dec. 7, 1934; s. Charles Wesley and Elisabeth Victoria (Speer) R.; m. Mary Catherine Phillips, July 2, 1955; children: Paul D., William W., Patricia L., Craig E., David J., Michelle G., Beverly R. BS, Montana State U., 1957, PhD, 1969. Cert. agronomy, crops and soils profl. Grad. rsch. asst. Montana State U., Bozeman, 1965-69; rsch. agronomist Dekalb AgResearch, Inc., Fargo, N.D., 1969-76; cons. agronomist Peavey Co., Fargo, 1976-77; rsch. geneticist USDA Agrl. Rsch. Svc., Fargo, 1977-82; rsch. agronomist USDA Agrl. Rsch. Svc., Ames, Iowa, 1984-95; agronomist U. Ill., Lusaka, Zambia, 1982-84; retired, 1995; bd. dirs. (ex offica) Sunflower Assn. Am., Fargo, 1978; plant breeder U. Ill. Oilseeds Project Planning Team, Cairo, 1980; crops subboard Am. Registry Cert. Profls. in Agronomy, Crops and Soils, Fargo, 1980-82; presenter in field. Author: Seed Science & Technology, 1988; co-author: Plant Breeding Review, 1989; contbr. over 70 articles to profl. pubis. Mem. Boarch Ch. and Soc. United Meth. Ch. N.D. Conf., 1979-82, Iowa Conf., 1986, Ann. Iowa Conf., 1987-94. Capt. USAF, 1957-65. Home: 506 Easy St Box 472 West Union IA 52175

ROBAK, JENNIE, state legislator; b. Surprise, Nebr., May 4, 1932; m. Cleo F. Robak, 1952; children: Karen, Kim, Frank, Kurt, Tony, Andrea. Mem. from 22d dist. Nebr. State Senate, Lincoln, 1988—, mem. transp. com., govt., mil. and vet. affairs com., past mem. banking com., ins., intervot. coop., jud. coms.; chmn. Nebr. Retirement Sysm. Com. Disaster chmn. ARC, Platte, Nebr.; mem. Columbus Hosp. Aux., Fed. Emergency Mgmt. Agy. Mem. VFW Aux., Nat. Orgn. Vol. Leaders, Eagles Aux., Kiwanis. Home: 2006 28th St Columbus NE 68601-2646 Office: Nebr State Senate State Capitol Rm 2715 Lincoln NE 68509*

ROBAK, KIM M., state official; b. Columbus, Nebr., Oct. 4, 1955; m. William J. Mueller; children: Katherine, Claire. BA with distinction, U. Nebr., 1977, JD with high distinction, 1985. Tchr. Lincoln (Nebr.) Pub. Schs., 1978-82; clerk Cline Williams Wright Johnson & Oldfather, Lincoln, 1983; summer assoc. Cooley Godward Castro Huddleson & Tatum, San Francisco, 1984, Steptoe & Johnson, Washington, 1985; ptnr. Rembolt Ludtke Parker & Berger, Lincoln, 1985-91; legal counsel Gov. E. Benjamin Nelson/State of Nebr., Lincoln, 1991-92, chief of staff, 1992-93; lt. gov. State of Nebr., Lincoln, 1993—; chair Prairie Fire Internat. Symposium on Edn., 1986. Fellow Leadership Lincoln, 1986-87, program com., 1987-90; chair program com. Leadership Lincoln Alumni Assn., 1987, selection com., 1990; chair Landfill Alternatives and Ops. Task Force, 1986-87; chair Gladys Forsyth award subcom. YWCA Tribute! to Women, 1987, chair nominations, 1991; mem. adv. com. U.S. Constn. Bicentennial Competition, 1987; gen. Dem. counsel, Nebr., 1985-92; mem. bd. women's ministries First Plymouth Congl. Ch., 1988-91, trustee, 1991-94; mem. Toll Fellowship Program, 1995; chair Nat. Conf. Lt. Govs., 1996; hon. chair Daffodil Day campaign Am. Cancer Soc.; hon. chair Walktoberfest, Am. Diabetes Assn.; hon. chair Nebr.'s campaign Prevent Blindness; hon. mem. Red Ribbon campaign Mothers Against Drunk Driving, 1994-95. Mem. Nat. Conf. Lt. Govs. (fed. practice com. 1986-92), Nat. Inst. Trial Advocacy, Nebr. State

Bar Assn. (ethics com. 1987-92, vice chair com. on pub. rels. 1988-92, chair com. on yellow pages advt. 1988, ho. of dels. 1988-95), Lincoln Bar Assn., U. Nebr. Coll. Alumni Assn. (bd. dirs. 1986-89), Updowntowners, Order of Coif.

ROBARDS, BOURNE ROGERS, elementary education educator; b. Milw., Jan. 5, 1950; s. William Simpson and Janet (Cross) R.; m. Martha Jane Snider, Oct. 29, 1977; children: Jonathan Matthew, Sara Elizabeth. BS, U. Mo., 1971; MAT, Webster U., St. Louis, 1989. Cert. elem. tchr., Mo. Classroom tchr. 4th and 6th grades Hazelwood Sch. Dist., Florissant, Mo., 1971-73; classroom tchr. 4th grade Jennings (Mo.) Sch. Dist., 1986—. Troop leader Boy Scouts Am., St. Louis, 1972-73; ch. leader St. Mark's Episcopal Ch., St. Louis, 1977—. Mem. Omicron Delta Kappa. Home: 6320 Monterey Dr Saint Louis MO 63123-1510 Office: Northview Elem Sch Jennings Sch Dist 8920 Cozens Ave Jennings MO 63136-3921

ROBB, KIMBERLY KAY, critical care nurse, medical/surgical nurse, infant immunization nurse, nursing administrator; b. Princeton, Ind., Nov. 18, 1963; d. Carl Eugene and Cherry Johnetta (Lewis) R. AD, Ind. Vocat. Tech. Sch., 1990. Cert. IV and TB nurs; cert. CPR; cert. ACLS; cert. advanced trauma mgmt. Staff nurse Holiday Manor Nursing Home, Princeton, Ind., 1990-91, Gibson Gen. Hosp., Princeton, 1991—; staff nurse Gibson County Health Dept., 1994—, relief supv. Mem. Nat. League for Nursing, Am. Assn. Critical Care Nurses. Baptist. Home: 611 N Hart St Princeton IN 47670-1449

ROBBINS, DOROTHY ANN, foreign language educator; b. Little Rock, Mar. 17, 1947; d. W.E. and Ina (Spencer) R. BA in Sociology, U. Ark., 1971; MS, U. Heidelberg, Germany, 1975; PhD, U. Frankfurt, Germany, 1981; postgrad., U. Hamburg, Germany, 1994—. Cert. state translato, Germany. Lectr. U. Heidelberg, 1977; head English dept. European Bus. Sch., Germany, 1978-80; dir. Inst. German Studies, Minn., 1985-87; asst. prof., then assoc. prof. fgn. lang. Ctrl. Mo. State U., Warrensburg, 1988—; Am. liaison Tolstoy Inst. Fgn. Langs., Moscow. Contbr. articles to profl. publs. Mem. Am. Assn. Applied Linguistics, Deutsch als Fremdsprache, Phi Beta Delta (pres. 1994-95). Office: Ctrl Mo State U Martin 236 Warrensburg MO 64093

ROBBINS, FRANCES ELAINE, educational administrator; b. Prescott, Mich., Oct. 27, 1928; d. Arlington Clifford and Anna Maria (Melrose) Osborne; m. Robert Allen Robbins, July 29, 1950 (dec. Feb. 1992); children: Gloria Jean, Reginald David, Eric Lynn. Student, Cen. Mich. U., 1948; BS, No. Mich. U., 1967, MA, 1974. Cert. elem. tchr., prin., Mich. Tchr. kindergarten Rose City (Mich.) Elem. Sch., 1948-51; tchr. Rudyard (Mich.) Elem. Sch., 1961-62, Pickford (Mich.) Elem. Sch., 1962-64, Skandia (Mich.) Elem. Sch., 1964-66; tchr. kindergarten Brimley (Mich.) Elem. Sch., 1966-69, tchr., coord., 1969-70, prin., 1970-95; mem. Ea. Upper Peninsula Substance Abuse Adv. Bd., Sault Ste. Marie, Mich., 1975-77; owner Robbins Refinishing and Repair, Brimley, 1985-95. Dir. choir, Sunday sch. tchr. Brimley Congl. Ch., 1970—; vol. Superior Twp. Ambulance Corp., Brimley, 1972-91. Recipient Celebrate Literacy award Internat. Reading Assn., 1986. Mem. NAESP, MARSP (life), Mich. Elem. and Mid. Sch. Prins. Assn., Ea. Upper Peninsula Reading Assn., Ea. Upper Peninsula Elem. Prins. Assn. (pres. 1990-91), Brimley Hist. Soc., Delta Kappa Gamma (state rec. sec. 1989-91, Woman of Distinction award Alpha Tau chpt. 1988), Chippewa Mackinaw Area Ret. Sch. Pers.

ROBBINS, FREDERICK CHAPMAN, physician, medical school dean emeritus; b. Auburn, Ala., Aug. 25, 1916; s. William J. and Christine (Chapman) R.; m. Alice Havemeyer Northrop, June 19, 1948; children: Alice, Louise. AB, U. Mo., 1936, BS, 1938; MD, Harvard U., 1940; DSc (hon.), John Carroll U., 1955, U. Mo., 1958, U. N.C., 1979, Tufts U., 1983, Med. Coll. Ohio, 1983; LLD, U. N.Mex., 1968. Diplomate Am. Bd. Pediatrics. Intern Children's Hosp., Boston, 1941-42, resident, 1940-41, resident pediatrican, 1946-48; sr. fellow virus disease Nat. Rsch. Coun., 1948-50; staff rsch. div. infectious diseases Children's Hosp., Boston, 1948-50, assoc. physician, assoc. dir. isolation svc., asso. rsch. div. infectious diseases, 1950-52; instr., assoc. in pediatrics Harvard Med. Sch., 1950-52; dir. dept. pediatrics and contagious diseases Cleve. Met. Gen. Hosp., 1952-66; prof. pediatrics Case Western Res. U., 1950-80, dean Sch. Medicine, 1966-80, univ. prof., dean emeritus, 1980—, univ. prof. emeritus, 1987—; pres. Inst. Medicine, NAS, 1980-85; vis. scientist Donner Lab., U. Calif., 1963-64. Served as maj. AUS, 1942-46; chief virus and rickettsial disease sect. 15th Med. Gen. Lab. investigations infectious hepatitis, typhus fever and Q fever. Decorated Bronze Star, 1945; recipient 1st Mead Johnson prize application tissue culture methods to study of viral infections, 1953; co-recipient Nobel prize in physiology and medicine, 1954; Med. Mut. Honor Award for, 1969; Ohio Gov.'s award, 1971. Mem. Assn. Am. Med. Colls. (Abraham Flexner award 1987), Nat. Acad. Scis., Am. Acad. Arts and Scis., Am. Soc. Clin. Investigation (emeritus mem.), Am. Acad. Pediatrics, Soc. Pediatric Research (pres. 1961-62, emeritus mem.), Am. Pediatric Soc., Am. Philos. Soc., Phi Beta Kappa, Sigma Xi, Phi Gamma Delta. Office: Case Western Res U Sch Med 10900 Euclid Ave Cleveland OH 44106-1712*

ROBBINS, KENNETH CARL, biochemist; b. Chgo., Sept. 1, 1917; s. Samuel and Mary (Silberbrandt) R.; m. Pearl Podorowsky, Mar. 31, 1946; children: Paula Lange, Shelley R. BS, U. Ill., 1939, MS, 1940, PhD, 1944. Asst. prof. pathology Western Res. U. Sch. Medicine, Cleve., 1947-51; head protein sec. biochemistry rsch. The Armour Labs., Chgo., 1951-58; dir. biochemistry rsch., scientific dir. Michael Reese Rsch. Found., Chgo., 1958-84; prof. medicine and pathology Pritzker Sch. Med./Univ. Chgo., 1970-87, prof. emeritus, 1987—; dir. exptl. pathology Michael Reese Hosp. and Med. Ctr., Chgo., 1984-86; rsch. scientist, prof. hematology and oncology medicine Northwestern Univ. Sch. Medicine, Chgo., 1989-95, ret., 1995; mem. hematol. study sect. NIH, Bethesda, Md., 1971-75, 76-80, blood diseases & resources adv. com. Nat. Heart, Lung, and Blood Inst., NIH, 1976-80; chmn. Gordon Conf. Hemostasis, N.H., 1975; mem. Internat. Com. on Thrombosis and Haemostasis, 1980-86, chmn. subcom. on Fibrinolysis, 1980-82; lectr. in field. Mem. editorial bd. Jour. Biol. Chemistry, 1975-80; contbr. articles to profl. jours. Recipient fouth Elwood A. Sharp award Wayne State U. Sch. Medicine, Detroit, 1971, Prix Servier Medal and Prize, Fifth Internal Congress Fibrinolysis, Malmo, Sweden, 1980; grantee NIH, Bethesda, 1960-95. Mem. Am. Assn. Immunologists, Am. Soc. Biochemistry and Molecular Biology, Am. Soc. Hematology, Soc. Exptl. Biology and Medicine. Home: 6101 N Sheridan Rd Ste 36C Chicago IL 60660-2801

ROBBINS, KENNETH E., manufacturing company executive; b. Perry, Okla., Oct. 19, 1939. BA in Bus. Adminstrn., Ctrl. State U., Edmond, Okla., 1968. Shop foreman Fergus Cart & Wheel Co., Edmond, 1957-80; gen. mgr. Fergus Cart & Wheel Co., Independence, Mo., 1980-82; pres. Circle K Mfg. Co., Blue Springs, Mo., 1982—. Lutheran. Office: Circle K Mfg Co 3700 W 40 Hwy Blue Springs MO 64015

ROBBINS, ROBERT MARVIN, accountant; b. Warren, Ohio, Aug. 2, 1924; s. Edward and May (Rubenson) R.; m. Phyllis Ann Dillon, Sept. 29, 1951; children: Michael C., Pat D., Robert J., Susan Jo Burkey. BSBA, Ohio State U., 1948; postgrad., NYU, 1972, 76, 79. CPA, Ohio. Sr. acct. Albert F. Turrell & Assocs. CPAs, Warren, Ohio, 1948-52; comptroller Harts Jewelry Stores, Ohio, 1952-54; pvt. practice Warren, 1954-59; mng. ptnr. Griffith & Robbins, CPAs, Warren, 1959-65; owner R.M. Robbins & Assocs., CPAs, Warren, 1966-82; pres., mgr. R.M. Robbins & Assocs., Inc., Warren, 1982—; sec. and acctg. cons. Ohio-Ont. Clean Fuels, Inc., Warren, 1986-90; area owner, franchisee Red Barn Restaurants, Omaha, 1968-72. Treas. Planned Parenthood, Youngstown, Ohio, 1970s; acct. Sisters of Humility of Mary, Villa Maria, Pa., 1978-83. Sgt. U.S. Army armored div., 1943-45, ETO. Mem. Am. Inst. CPAs, (mem. tax div. subcoms.), ACUTE, Ohio Soc. CPAs, Rotary, Exchange Club (treas. Warren chpt. 1968-73), Squaw Creek Country Club (past bd. dirs.), BPOE. Home: 376 Wainwood Dr SE Warren OH 44484-4650 Office: RM Robbins & Assocs Inc 2921 Youngstown Rd SE PO Box 671 Warren OH 44482

ROBBINS, STEPHEN A., state legislator; b. Connersville, Ind.; m. Julia L. Jeffries; children: Kyle, Jeffrey, Andrea. Ed., Ball State U., Cin. Coll. Mortuary Sci.; grad., Xavier U. Funeral dir. Miller Funeral Home; coroner Fayette County, 1984-90; mem. from 55th dist. Ind. State Ho. of Reps., 1990—; mem. com. pub. policy, ethics com., ways and means com., rds. and transp. com., vice chmn. vet. affairs com. Mem. Ind. Coroner Assn., Connersville C. of C., Connersville Lions Club (pres.), KC. Home: 926 Vine St Connersville IN 47331-3232*

ROBEL, ROBERT JOSEPH, environmental biology educator; b. Lansing, Mich., May 21, 1933; s. Joseph John and Loretta Rose (Pung) R.; m. Anice Marie Blanc, Aug. 27, 1960. BS, Mich. State U., 1956; MS, U. Idaho, 1958; PhD, Utah State U., 1961. cert. wildlife biologist. Rsch. fellow U. Idaho, Moscow, 1956-57; biologist aide Idaho Fish and Game Dept., Kooskia, 1957-58; rsch. asst. Utah State U., Logan, 1958-60, univ. fellow, 1960-61; asst. prof. zoology Kans. State U., Manhattan, 1961-66, assoc. prof., 1966-70; project mgr. U.S. Congress, Office Tech., 1976-77; prof. environ. biology Kans. State U., Manhattan, 1971—; vis. prof. Univ. Aberdeen (Scotland), 1967-68, Fulbright rsch. fellow to U.K., 1967-68; sci. advisor to Honorable Robert Docking, Gov. Kans., 1968-74, Honorable Robert Bennett, Gov. Kans., 1975-79; ecol. cons. Midwest Rsch. Inst., 1969—; mem. Kans. Nuclear Energy Coun., 1972-77; bd. mem. Midwest Nuclear Compact, 1972-80; vis. lectr. Sterling Univ., Scotland, 1981, Edinburg Univ., Scotland, 1983, Northwest Sch., Eng., 1984-90, Polytech. East London, Eng., 1990. Named Conservationist of the Yr. Gov. Kans., 1966, Hon. Lectr., Mid-Am. State Univs. Assn., 1979-80, Centennial Disting. Alumnus award U. of Idaho, 1989. Fellow AAAS; mem. Am. Ornithologists Union, Kans. Wildlife Fedn. (hon. life), Kans. Acad. Sci. (pres.), Boone and Crockett Club, Sigma Xi (coun. rep.). Office: Kans State U Div Biology Ackert Hal Manhattan KS 66506-4901

ROBERSON, LINDA, lawyer; b. Omaha, July 15, 1947; d. Harlan Oliver and Elizabeth Aileen (Good) R.; m. Gary M. Young, Aug. 20, 1970; children: Elizabeth, Katherine, Christopher. BA, Oberlin Coll., 1969; MS, U. Wis., 1970, JD, 1974. Bar: Wis. 1974, U.S. Dist. Ct. (we. dist.) Wis. 1974. Legis. atty. Wis. Legis. Reference Bur., Madison, 1974-76, sr. legis. atty., 1976-78; assoc. Rikkers, Koritzinsky & Rikkers, Madison, 1978-79; ptnr. Koritzinsky, Neider, Langer & Roberson, Madison, 1979-85, Stolper, Koritzinsky, Brewster & Neider, Madison, 1985-93, Balisle & Roberson, Madison, 1993—; lectr. U. Wis. Law Sch., Madison, 1978—. Co-author: Real Women, Real Lives, 1981, Wisconsin's Marital Property Reform Act, 1984, Understanding Wisconsin's Marital Property Law, 1985, A Guide to Property Classification Under Wisconsin's Marital Property Act, 1986, 2d edit. 1996, Workbook for Wisconsin Estate Planners, 2d edit., 1993, Look Before You Leap, 1996, Family Estate Planning in Wis., 1992, rev. edit. 1996. Fellow Am. Acad. Matrimonial Lawyers; mem. ABA, Wis. Bar Assn., Dane County Bar Assn., Legal Assn. Women, Nat. Assn. Elder Law Attys. Office: Balisle and Roberson 217 S Hamilton # 302 PO Box 870 Madison WI 53701-0870

ROBERTI, MARY TERESA, retired English language educator; b. St. Mary's, Pa., Oct. 21, 1933; d. Alfonso and Antonietta (Irace) R.; m. Milan Anton Bradac, Aug. 29, 1977 (dec. Sept. 25, 1991). BA magna cum laude, Marygrove Coll., Detroit, 1958; cert., U. Rome, 1961; MA, U. Mich., 1964, PhD, 1972. English tchr. Cantrick Jr. High Sch., Monroe, Mich., 1958-70, Monroe High Sch., 1970-88; humanities chair Monroe County Community Coll., 1988-92, English prof., 1992-95; Italian tchr. Italian/Am. Soc., Monroe. Mem. Internat. Platform Assn., St. Mary Acad. Alumnae, Marygrove Coll. Alumnae, U. Mich. Alumni. Republican. Roman Catholic. Home: 5710 W Dunbar Rd Monroe MI 48161-3786 also: 4555 E Rhonda Dr Phoenix AZ 85018

ROBERTS, BEVERLY RANDOLPH, accountant; b. Alexandria, La., Jan. 28, 1948; d. William Cullen and Elizabeth Rose (Madden) R.; 1 child, Gavin. BA, Lawrence U., 1969; postgrad., Drake U., 1975; M Bus. Taxation, U. Minn., 1990; JD cum laude, William Mitchell Coll. Law, 1995. CPA, Iowa, Colo., Minn. Bar: Minn., 1995. Staff acct. McGladrey & Hendrickson, Des Moines, 1975-77; sr. auditor Deloitte, Haskins & Sells, Des Moines, 1977-79; audit mgr. Coopers & Lybrand, Denver, 1979-84; dir. corp. acctg. Tennant Co., Mpls., 1985-88, asst. treas. corp. taxation, 1988—. Staff mem. William Mitchell Law Rev., 1992-93. Mem. AICPA, Minn. Soc. CPAs, Tax Exec. Inst., Minn. State Bar Assn., Hennepin County Bar Assn., Beta Gamma Sigma. Home: 3365 Shavers Lake Rd Wayzata MN 55391-3340 Office: Tennant Co PO Box 1452 Minneapolis MN 55440-1452

ROBERTS, BILL GLEN, retired fire chief, investor, consultant; b. Deport, Tex., June 2, 1938; s. Samuel Westbrook and Ann Lee (Rhodes) R.; m. Ramona Ryall, June 1, 1963 (dec. Nov. 1988); 1 child, Renee Ann. Student, So. Meth. U., 1968, North Tex. State U., 1974; grad. paramedic course, U. Tex. Southwestern Med. Sch., 1974; grad. Exec. Program for Fire Service, Tex. A&M U., 1978; AAS, El Centro Jr. Coll., Dallas, 1980; grad. exec. fire officer program, Nat. Fire Acad., 1989. With Dallas Fire Dept., 1958-82, lt., 1964-67, capt., 1967-71, div. fire chief, 1971-79, asst. fire chief, 1979-83; fire chief Austin (Tex.) Fire Dept., 1983-94; tech. bd. dirs. Found. Fire Safety, Washington, 1982-85; adj. faculty Nat. Fire Acad., 1981-86; aft. State Life of Indpls., Dallas, 1962; owner Personnel Testing Lab., Dallas, 1963; real estate salesman Dale Copus Realtor, Dallas, 1963-66; salesman intercommunications equipment Chandler Sound, Dallas, 1966-67; field engr. IBM Corp., Dallas, 1968; cons. U. Tenn., 1974, Ga. Inst. Tech., 1974, Tex. Dept. Health Resources, 1973-78, Rand Corp., Washington, Mission Rsch., Santa Barbara, Calif., Macro. Author: EMS Dallas, 1978; (with others) Anesthesia for Surgery Trauma, 1976, EMS Measures to Improve Care, 1980; contbr. articles to periodicals. Com. chmn. Dallas Jaycees, 1962-65; mem. task force Am. Heart Assn., Austin, 1973-83; bd. dirs. Brackenridge Hosp., 1989, Rehab. Hosp. Austin, 1992-94, Austin Police Pensions Bd., 1989, Capitol Area coun. Boy Scouts Am., 1989-92. Recipient John Stemmons Service award Dallas Fire Dept., 1979; Internat. Assn. Fire Chiefs scholar, 1967. Mem. Internat. Assn. Fire Chiefs, Nat. Fire Protection Assn., Nat. Critical Care Inst., Am. Heart Assn., Am. Trauma Soc. (founder), Am. Assn. Trauma Specialists, Nat. Assn. Emergency Med. Technicians, Tex. Assn. Emergency Med. Technicians, ACS, North Tex. Coun. of Govts. (regional emergency svc. adv. coun. 1973-79), Internat. Rescue and First Aid Assn., Found. Fire Safety (tech. bd. dirs. 1982-85), Tex. Assn. Realtors, Austin World Affairs Coun., People to People Internat., Rotary Internat. Methodist. Home: 3 Highlander Rd Asheville NC 28804-1112

ROBERTS, CHARLES PATRICK, congressman; b. Topeka, Kans., Apr. 20, 1936; m. Franki Fann, 1970; children: David, Ashleigh, Anne-Wesley. B.A., Kans. State U., 1958. Pub. Litchfield Park, Ariz., 1962-67; adminstrv. asst. U.S. Senator Frank Carlson, 1967-68, U.S. Congressman Keith Sebelius, 1968-80; mem. 97th to 104th Congresses from 1st Kans. Dist., 1980—. Served with USMC, 1958-62. Office: 1126 Longworth HOB Washington DC 20515-1601

ROBERTS, DALE BURTON, systems analyst; b. Phila., May 25, 1960; s. Burtona nd Ferne Garnet (Morris) R.; m. Michele Suzanne Roberts, Feb. 29, 1986; children: Charles, Christopher, Chelsea, Chad. BS in Computer Engrng., Purdue U., 1984; MS in Computer Sci., Purdue U., Indpls., 1988; MBA, Ind. Wesleyan U., 1995. Pres. Software Devel. Corp., Indpls., 1985-89; sr. computer sys. analyst Ameritech, Indpls., 1989—. Contbr. articles to profl. jours. Named Outstanding Grad. Student, Dept. Computer Sci., Purdue U., 1989. Mem. Delta Upsilon (v.p. 1980-81), Phi Eta Sigma. Republican. Presbyterian. Office: Ameritech 220 N Meridian Rm 1500 Indianapolis IN 46204

ROBERTS, DAVID, airport executive. Dir. Indpls. Internat. Airport. Office: Indpls Internat Airport Indpls Airport Authority Box 100 2500 S High School Rd Indianapolis IN 46241*

ROBERTS, DIANA KAYE, accountant; b. Independence, Mo., Mar. 14, 1959; d. Charles Mitchell Villines and Betty Jane (Mead) Crandall; m. Robert Lee Roberts Jr., May 16, 1980; children: Valerie Marie, Rosemary Kaye. Cert. tax preparer, Mr. Tax. of Am., 1979, Nat. Tax Tng. Sch., 1981, H&R Block, 1986; enrolled agt., IRS. Ins. agt. Mutual of Omaha, Kansas City, Mo., 1979; pres. Roberts Acctg. and Tax Svc., Independence, 1979—; enrolled agent IRS, 1988—; dir. Dream Weaver Branch Petra Fashions Inc., 1994-95. Editor Internat. Quill and Scroll, Independence, 1973-76. Mem. Bicentennial Liaison Com., Independence, 1975-76; cons. Pentecostal Ch. of God in Christ, Kansas City, 1986—. Mem. NAFE, Nat. Soc. Pub. Accts., Ind. Accts. Soc. Mo. (sec. 1987-88), Concept Therapy Inst. (navigator 1989—), Mo. Assn. Tax Practitioners, Independence C. of C. (creative referral network team capt. 1995-96, del.-at-large to Rep. Party Planning com.). Office: Roberts SMART TAX 17601 E 40 Hwy Ste I Independence MO 64055

ROBERTS, DOUGLAS B., state official. Treas. State of Michigan, Lansing, 1991—. Office: Michigan Dept Treasury PO Box 15128 Lansing MI 48901-5128

ROBERTS, JAMES ALLEN, gynecologic oncologist; b. Milw., May 6, 1947; s. John A. and Florence E. (Heil) R.; m. Rosemary Frankow. BA, UCLA, 1969; MD, Med. Coll. Wis., 1973; MS, U. Mich., 1993. Diplomate Am. Bd. Ob-Gyn. Resident in ob.-gyn. UCLA, 1973-77, fellow, 1977-79, acting asst. prof. ob-gyn, 1977-79; asst. prof. U. Iowa, Iowa City, 1979-80; asst. prof. U. Mich., Ann Arbor, 1980-86, assoc. prof., 1986-93, dir. gynecol. oncology, 1986-94, prof. ob.-gyn., 1993—; dir. gynecol. oncology Oakwood Hosp., 1987—; cons. Ann Arbor VA Hosp., 1981—, Oakwood Hosp., Dearborn, Mich., 1982—, St. Joseph Hosp., Ann Arbor, 1982—, Chelsea (Mich.) Hosp., 1983—. Contbr. articles to profl. jours.; chpts. to books. Fellow Am. Cancer Soc., 1977-79, 82-84. Fellow ACS, Am. Coll. Ob-Gyn.; mem. AMA, Soc. Gynecol. Oncologists (mng. editor newsletter 1992-95), Western Assn. Gynecologic Oncologists (pres. 1992-93, sec.-treas. 1986-91), Ctrl. Assn. Ob-Gyns., N.Y. Acad. Scis., Washtenaw Ob-Gyn. Soc. (pres. 1985-86), Mich. Med. Soc., Internat. Gynecol. Cancer Soc., Am. Soc. Colp and Cervical Pathology, Am. Soc. Clin. Oncology, Soc. Surg. Oncoloyg, Gynecol. Laser Soc., European Soc. Gynecol. Oncology, Assn. Profl. Ob-Gyns., Travis Pointe Country Club (Ann Arbor). Office: Univ Mich Dept Ob-Gyn 1500 E Medical Center Dr Ann Arbor MI 48109-0999

ROBERTS, JAMES ARNOLD, JR., engineering educator, electrical engineer; b. Vandalia, Ill., Mar. 11, 1944; s. James Arnold and Marjorie Alice (White) R.; m. Carol Diane Helton, June 6, 1965; children: John Michael, Sally Ann. BSEE, U. Kans., 1966; MSEE, MIT, 1968; PhD in Elect. Engrng., Santa Clara U., 1979. Registered profl. engr., Kans. Tech. staff RCA, Burlington, Mass., 1966-69; from tech. staff to lab. mgr. ESL, Inc., Sunnyvale, Calif., 1969-83; from program mgr. to mgr. Denver ops. TRW, Inc., Aurora, Colo., 1983-90; prof., chmn. elect. engring. and computer sci. U. Kans., Lawrence, 1990—; bd. dirs. Kantronics, Inc., Lawrence; trustee Ctr. for Rsch., Inc., Lawrence, 1991—; rsch. program tech. com. Kans. Electric Utilities, Topeka, 1991—; lectr. Santa Clara U., 1978-83. Bd. dirs. Big Bros. Denver, 1987-90. Summerfield scholar U. Kans., 1964-66, RCA scholar, 1966-68; NSF grantee, 1993-95. Mem. IEEE, Kiwanis (bd. dirs. 1993—), Tau Beta Pi, Eta Kappa Nu, Sigma Xi, Sigma Nu (bd. dirs. 1994—). Home: 1251 E 1900th Rd Lawrence KS 66046 Office: U Kans Dept Elec Engring & Computer Sci 415 Snow Hall Lawrence KS 66045

ROBERTS, JOETTA KAREN, nursing administrator; b. Columbus, Ohio, Jan. 12, 1949; m. Gilbert J. Moore (div.). LPN, Columbus Sch. Practical, 1971; AAS in Nursing, Columbus State C.C., 1989. RN, Ohio. Nurse's aide Grant Med. Ctr., Columbus, 1967-69, practical nurse, 1971-89; nurse Columbus Area Community Mental Health Ctr., 1989-95, nurse, case mgr., 1989-92, supr., 1992-94; cons. to exec. dir. Columbus Area Cmty. Mental Health Ctr., 1994-95; managed care coord. mental health Alcohol, Drug Addiction and Mental Health Svcs. Bd., Franklin County, Ohio, 1995—. Office: Franklin County Alcohol Drug Addiction and MH Svcs 447 E Broad St Columbus OH 43215

ROBERTS, JUDITH VIRGINIA, social worker; b. Phoenix, Mar. 31, 1940; d. George Merle and Edith Virginia (Sevitz) Nycum; m. Kenneth Richard Dragoo, Dec. 28, 1958 (div. 1976); children: Kathryn Virginia Dragoo Lewis, Charles Allen, Kenson Michael; m. Ronald William Roberts, July 12, 1979; stepchildren: Shane Kugler, Noelle Brooke. AA, Mid Plains Community Coll., 1983; BSW, Kearney State Coll., 1986; MSW, U. N.D., Omaha, 1993. Cert. social worker, Nebr. Bookkeeping, payroll clk. Dragon Enterprise, North Platte, Nebr., 1972-76, City of North Platte, 1976-83; social worker Nebr. Dept. Social Svcs., North Platte, 1987-91, Ctrl. Plains Home Health & Hospice, Corad, Nebr., 1995—. Bassist, Omaha Symphony Orch., 1965-72, Lincoln (Nebr.) Symphony Orch., 1965-72; Lincoln County Republican del., North Platte, 1988. Mem. Nat. Assn. Social Workers, Nebr. Assn. Social Workers, Nebr. Cattlewomen (publicity chair 1980-88). Office: Ctrl Plains Home Health & Hospice 300 E 12th Cozad NE 69130

ROBERTS, KEITH EDWARD, SR., lawyer; b. White Hall, Ill., Apr. 27, 1928; s. Victor Harold and Ruby Harriet (Kelsey) R.; m. Marthan Dusch, Sept. 4, 1954; 1 child, Keith Edward. Student, Western Ill. U., 1946-47, George Washington U., 1947-48; BS, U. Ill., 1951, JD, 1953. Bar: Ill. 1953, U.S. Dist. Ct. (no. dist.) Ill. 1957, U.S. Dist. Ct. (so. dist.) Ill. 1961, U.S. Dist. Ct. (no. dist.) Ohio 1960, U.S. Ct. Mil. Appeals 1954, U.S. Ct. Appeals (7th cir.) 1968. Assoc. J.D. Quarant, Elizabethtown, Ill., 1953-56; staff atty. Pa. R.R. Co., Chgo., 1957-60; assoc. Henslee, Monek & Henslee, Chgo., 1960-67; sole practice, Naperville, Ill., 1967-68; ptnr. Donovan, Atten, Mountcastle, Roberts & DaRosa, Wheaton, Ill., 1968-77; pres. Donovan & Roberts, P.C., Wheaton, 1977—. Served to capt. U.S. Army, 1954-57. Mem. ABA, Internat. Soc. Barristers, Assn. Trial Lawyers Am., Ill. Bar Assn., DuPage County Bar Assn. (gen. counsel 1976-86). Presbyterian. Office: Donovan & Roberts PC PO Box 417 Wheaton IL 60189-0417

ROBERTS, KYNA R., lobbyist; b. Marceline, Mo., Oct. 30, 1963; d. Walter Cleveland and Ruth Josephine (Green) Iman; m. Perry A. Roberts, July 10, 1993. BA, William Woods Coll., 1986. Asst. dir. govtl. affairs Home Builders Assn. Greater St. Louis, 1986-89; exec. dir. Mo. Citizens for Arts, St. Louis, 1989-94; govtl. cons. Kyna Iman-Roberts, St. Louis, 1994—; outside sales agt. Apex Travel, St. Louis, 1995. Mem. State Arts Advocacy League Am. (sec. 1992-94), Leadership Mo. (charter). Baptist. Home and Office: 411 Conway Meadows Dr Chesterfield MO 63017

ROBERTS, MARY LYNN, pediatrics mental health nurse; b. Rosiclare, Ill., Sept. 26, 1948; d. W.F. and Mary Imogene (Scott) Beavers; 1 child, Todd Wayne; m. David L. Roberts, June 7, 1975; children: David Brian Roberts, Sonya Gale Roberts Tenison. ADN, U. Evansville, 1986. Clin. nurse II chem. dependency unit Welborn Bapt. Hosp., Evansville, Ind., 1986-89, asst. nurse mgr., 1989-91, clin. nurse III, 1991-92; nurse mgr. children's unit Arbor Hosp. of Evansville, 1992-94; acting dir. nursing Charter Behavioral Health Sys., Evansville, 1994, utilization mgmt. RN, needs assessment and referral ctr., 1995—; dir. devel. and child svcs. Koala Hosp., Columbus, Ind., 1995; instr. Smokeless, Evansville, 1990-92. Bd. dirs. Am. Cancer Soc., Warrick County, Ind., 1990-92. Mem. ANA (mem. peer rev. and assistance program 1991-93), Am. Psychiat. Nurses Assn., Parent to Parent Welborn. Baptist. Home: 8511 Greywing Dr Newburgh IN 47630-9339

ROBERTS, NANCY LEE, journalism educator; b. Utica, N.Y., Feb. 12, 1954; d. Arthur William and Doris Jean (Pelletier) R. BA, Swarthmore Coll., 1976; MA, Brown U., 1977, U. Minn., 1979; PhD, U. Minn., 1982. Asst. prof. U. R.I., Kingston, 1982-83; asst. prof. U. Minn., Mpls., 1983-88, assoc. prof., 1988—. Contbg. editor, contbr. U.S. Art mag., 1986—; author: American Peace Writers, Editors, and Periodicals: A Dictionary, 1991, Dorothy Day and the "Catholic Worker,", 1984; co-author: The Press and America, 8th edit., 1995; co-editor: "As Ever, Gene": The Letters of Eugene O'Neill to George Jean Nathan, 1987, American Catholic Pacifism: The Influence of Dorothy Day and the Catholic Worker Movement, 1996. Rsch. grantee Am. Philos. Soc., 1989. Mem. Am. Journalism Historians Assn. (pres.-elect 1990-91, pres. 1991-92, book rev. editor Am. Journalism 1989-92, head history divsn. 1995-96), Assn. for Edn. in Journalism and Mass Commn., Orgn. Am. Historians, Am. Studies Assn., Soc. Profl. Journalists, Peace History Soc., Alumni Coun. Swarthmore Coll.

ROBERTS, NORA RUTH, English educator; b. L.A., Apr. 19, 1942; d. Daniel Robert Zhitlowsky and Frances Mary (James) Nicklas; m. (div. June 1975); children: Kit Adam Wainer, Robben Andrew Wainer. BA in English, CCNY, 1973, MA in Creative Writing, 1975; postgrad., Yale U., 1975-76; PhD in English, CUNY, 1995. Asst. fiction editor Good Housekeeping, N.Y.C., 1961-63; rsch. editor Voque Mag., N.Y.C., 1964-67; assoc. editor Daw Books, Inc., N.Y.C., 1976-85; English lectr. St. Peter's Coll., Jersey City, N.J., 1989-95, Medgar Evers Coll., Bklyn., 1993-95. Author: Three Radical Women Writers; Waterway Journey published fiction and poetry, 1996, American Thought and Language, 1995; contbr. articles to profl. jours.

Election chair Parents Assn., N.Y.C., 1970. Election chair Parents Assn., N.Y.C., 1970. Danforth fellow, 1973-75; grantee Theodore Goodman, 1971, Helena Rubinstein, 1992, Carolyn Heilbrun Dissertation award, 1995. Mem. MLA, N.J. Coll. English Assn., N.Y. Coll. English Assn., Popular Culture Assn. Home: 705-104 Cherry Lane East Lansing MI 48823

ROBERTS, PATRICK KENT, lawyer; b. Waynesville, Mo., Feb. 9, 1948; s. J. Kent and Winona (Clark) R.; m. Jeanne Billings, April 17, 1976; children: Christopher, Kimberly, Courtney. Student, U. Ill., Urbana, 1970; AB, U. Mo., 1970, JD, 1973. Bar: Mo. 1974, U.S. Dist. Ct. (we. dist.) Mo. 1974, U.S. Ct. Appeals (8th cir.) 1979. Lawyer U.S. Senator Stuart Symington, Columbia, Mo., 1973-76; ptnr. Daniel, Clampett, Powell & Cunningham, Springfield, Mo., 1976—. Mem. cen. com. Greene County Dems., Springfield, 1982-84, 88-90. Mem. Def. Res. Inst., Mo. Orgn. Def. Lawyers, Mo. Bar Assn., Greene County Bar Assn. Democrat. Methodist. Lodge: Rotary. Office: Daniel Clampett Powell & Cunningham PO Box 10306 3171 E Sunshine Springfield MO 65808

ROBERTS, PETER ALLEN, physical education educator; b. Buffalo, Feb. 20, 1943; s. Hobart Vosburgh and Bertha Jane (Ash) R.; m. Sherri Ann Olson, Sept. 12, 1986; 1 child, Sarah Jane. BS, Mich. State U., 1966, MA, 1970. Cert. tchr., Mich.; cert. water safety instr. trainer, lifeguard instr. trainer, CPR instr. trainer, standard first aid instr.-trainer. Educator Alpena (Mich.) Pub. Sch., 1966-69; prof. Wayne State U., Detroit, 1970—; head coach swimming Wayne State U., Detroit, 1969-84; cons. in field. Bd. dirs. ARC, Detroit, chair aquatic com., 1972—, mem. aquatic enhancement adv. com., 1993; staff mem. Mich. Aquatic Sch., 1968—. Recipient Outstanding Svc. medal ARC, 1981, Fifteen Yrs. Outstanding Svc. award, 1985, Joan B. Warren award ARC, 1986, 30 Yr. Svc. Pin, ARC, 1992. Mem. AAHPERD, Mich. AHPERD, Coll. Swimming Coaches Assn., Phi Epsilon Kappa. Democrat. Methodist. Home: 23055 Beck Rd Novi MI 48374-3622 Office: Wayne State U 264 Matthaei Bldg Detroit MI 48202

ROBERTS, THEODORE HARRIS, banker; b. Gillett, Ark., May 14, 1929; s. D. Edward and Gertrude (Harris) R.; m. Elisabeth Law, July 17, 1953; children: Susan, William (dec.), Julia, John. BA in Govt., Northwestern State U., 1949; MA in Polit. Sci., Okla. State U., 1950; attended, U. Chgo. Grad. Sch. Bus., 1956. With Harris Trust and Savs. Bank, Chgo., 1953-82; exec. v.p., sec., treas. Harris Bank and Harris Bankcorp Inc., 1971-82, dir., exec. com., 1975-82; pres. Fed. Res. Bank St. Louis, 1983-85; chmn. bd., chief exec. officer Talman Home Fed. Savs. & Loan, Chgo., 1985-92; pres. LaSalle Nat. Corp., 1992-95 retired. Mem. Chgo. Club, Comml. Club Chgo., Econ. Club Chgo., Exmoor Country Club (Highland Park, Ill.). Office: 135 S La Salle St Ste 1162 Chicago IL 60603-4105

ROBERTS, THOMAS MICHAEL, state legislator; b. Mar. 3, 1952; s. Harold Leonard and Susie (Williams) R.; m. Regina Michele Walker; children: Edward, Erienne.; Student, Sinclair Cmty. Coll.; BA, Univ. Dayton, 1977. Clerk Montgomery County Clerk's Civil Divsn., 1972-77; supr. Montgomery County Auto Title Divsn., 1977; bailiff Montgomery County Common Pleas Ct., 1977-86; mem. Montgomery County Dem. Com., 1984; mem. congress adv. coun. U.S. Rep. Tony Hall, 1985; Ohio State rep. Dist. 37, 1986-92, Dist. 39, 1993; mem. adv com. Dayton Job Corp., 1993—; chmn. Aging & Housing Com., mem. agrl. & Natural resources, Children & Youth, Energy & Environ. com., Zone oversights & Policy adv. group Dept. Youth Svc., chmn. Select Com. Homeless & Affordable Housing, mem. Judiciary & Criminal Justice Com., Child Abuse and Juvenile Justice. Active Boy Scouts, 1986; co-chmn. pub. affairs com. Montgomery County Mental Health Assn., 1979-84, pres., 1986-87. Recipient Outstanding Young Man of Yr. award Montgomery Coun. Young Dem., 1982, Outstanding Achievement award, 1986, Ohio Homeless Coalition award, Spl. Contbr. award Ohio Housing Coalition, Pres.'s award Ohio Youth Svc., Men & Women Courage award Cmty. Outreach. Mem. Dem. Voters League, Black Dem. of Ohio. Home: 1739 Catalpa Dr Dayton OH 45406*

ROBERTS, WILBUR EUGENE, dental educator, research scientist; b. Lubbock, Tex., Nov. 16, 1942; s. Wilbur Eugene Roberts and Elva Etna (Chance) Turnwall; m. Cheryl Ann Jones, June 6, 1967; children: Jeffery Alan, Carrie Jean. DDS, Creighton U., 1967; PhD in Anatomy, U. Utah, 1969; cert. in orthodontics, U. Conn., 1974; DHC (hon.), Lille (France) U., 1994. Diplomate Am. Bd. Orthodontics. Rsch. fellow U. Utah, Salt Lake City, 1967-69; postdoctoral fellow U. Conn., Farmington, 1971-74; from asst. prof. to prof. dentistry U. Pacific, San Francisco, 1974-88; prof. chmn. dept. orthodontics Ind. U., Indpls., 1988-93, chmn. dept. oral and facial devel., 1993—, prof. physiology and biophysics Sch. Medicine, 1988—; mem. steering com. Biomechs. and Biomaterials Rsch. Ctr. Ind. U.-Purdue U., Indpls., 1990—; NRC sr. rsch. assoc. NASA Ames Rsch. Ctr., Moffett Field, Calif., 1982-83; dir. Bone Rsch. Lab., U. Pacific, 1980-88, Oral Devel. Clinic, 1980-86; rsch. cons. Neodontics Corp., Laguna Nigel, Calif., 1982-85, Denar Corp., Anaheim, Calif., 1985-87, Nobelpharma AG, Goteborg, Sweden, 1988, Dental Implant Clin. Rsch. Group, Ann Arbor, Mich., 1991—, Oral Medicine and Biology Study sect. NIH, 1992—, Rsch. Coun. ADA, 1992; adj. prof. mech. engring. Purdue U., Indpls., 1990—; assoc. prof. implantology, maxillofacial surgery U. Lille, France, 1987—; guest prof. U. Western Ont., Can., 1987; Dr. Fred West Meml. lectr. U. Pacific, 1989, Dr. George Grieve Meml. lectr. Can. Dental Assn., 1993; ptnr. Vintner for Zuperb Zinfandel, Ltd. Contbr. sci. articles to profl. jours. Rep. campaign worker, Contra Costa County, Calif., 1980-82; ch. sch. supt. San Ramon Valley Meth. Ch., Alamo, Calif., 1979-81; adult ministries council San Ramon Valley Meth. Ch., Danville, Calif., 1984-86; sci. cons. St. Isadore Sch. and San Ramon Valley High Sch., Danville, 1978-86; chmn. bldg. com. Sunrise at Geist United Meth. Ch., Indpls. Served to lt. comdr. USN, 1969-71, Vietnam. Recipient Cosmos Achievement award NASA, 1981, 88, 92, medal City of Paris, 1989, City of Rouen, France, 1991, Rsch. award Ind. U. Sch. Dentistry, 1993. Fellow Internat. Coll. Dentists, Am. Coll. Dentists; mem. Med. Dental Guild Calif. (pres. 1982-83, Gold Key award 1985), Am. Assn. Dental Rsch., Pacific Dental Rsch. Found. (pres. 1976-80), Conf. of the Company of Wine Tasters of Normandy (pres. Ind. med. chpt. 1992—), Omicron Kappa Upsilon. Home: 8260 Skipjack Dr Indianapolis IN 46236-8429 Office: Ind U Sch Dentistry Sch Dentistry Dept Orthodontics 1121 W Michigan St Indianapolis IN 46202-5211

ROBERTSON, ALVIN CYRRALE, professional basketball player; b. Barberton, Ohio, July 22, 1962; m. Jackie Robertson; 1 child, Alvin Jr. Student, Crowder Jr. Coll., Mo., U Ark., 1981-84. With San Antonio Spurs, 1984-89; player Milw. Bucks, 1989-93, Detroit Pistons, 1993, Denver Nuggets, 1993—; mem. NBA All-Star team, 1986-88, 91. Recipient Gold medal Olympics, L.A., 1984; ranked 1st in NBA for steals, 1985-87, 91; named NBA Defensive Player of Yr., 1986, Most Improved Player, 1986; named to NBA All-Defense First Team, 1987, 91. Office: Detroit Pistons Palace Alburn Hills Two Championship Dr Auburn Hills MI 48326*

ROBERTSON, EDWARD NEIL, dentist; b. Rumford, Maine, Mar. 3, 1950; s. Edward Norris and Edith Louis (Kirk) R.; m. Rosalind Siegel, May 10, 1969 (div.); children: Christie Portia, Juliet Melissa (dec.), Jenni Celia, Edward Noah, Jessica Edith. BS in Biology, Antioch Coll., Yellow Springs, Ohio, 1973; MS in Epidemiology, Ohio State U., 1977; DDS, Case Western Res. U., 1983. Faculty adv. to med. students Ohio State U., Columbus, 1975-77; rsch. cons. Ohio Dept. Health, Columbus, 1976-77; rsch. assoc. UCLA, 1977; epidemiologic/statis. cons. L.A., 1977; medic J & L Steel Corp., Cleve., 1979-84; pvt. practice Cleveland Heights, Ohio, 1983—; mem. adj. faculty Cuyahoga C.C., Cleve., 1986-88; assoc. prof. Sch. Dentistry Case Western Res. U., 1991—. Pres. Robertson Family Assn. of N.Am., 1986-88. Recipient numerous rsch. grants. Mem. Acad. Gen. Dentistry, Am. Assn. Functional Orthodontists, U.S. Dental Inst., Acad. Laser Surgery, Alpha Omega. Office: 5031 Mayfield Rd # 105 Cleveland OH 44124

ROBERTSON, FLORENCE WINKLER, advertising and public relations agency executive; b. Hampton, Va., Sept. 11, 1945; d. Fred Felty Jr. and Florence Bernice (Shamo) Schnopp; m. John Park Winkler Jr., June 24, 1967 (div. 1977); m. James Milton Robertson, Oct. 21, 1982. AA, Palm Beach Jr. Coll., 1965; BA, U. South Fla., 1967. Reporter, Lexington (Ky.) Leader, 1967-70; freelance writer, 1971-76; TV and radio news reporter Sta. KCRG, Cedar Rapids, Iowa, 1972-73; asst. dir. pub. relations Coe Coll., Cedar Rapids, 1973-78; info. specialist Cedar Rapids (Iowa) Pub. Schs., 1979-83; adv. mgr. Smulekoff's Fine Home Furnishings, 1984-93; owner Fox Ridge Adv., Cedar Rapids, 1993—; mem. bd. dirs. Linn County Farm Bur., 1994—. Pres. Home Fire Safety Task Force of Ea. Iowa, 1983-86; chmn. Cedar Rapids Promotion Com., 1986-87; bd. dirs. Grant Wood Area chpt. ARC; organizer, bd. dirs., Cedar Rapids Christmas Parade, 1985—. Recipient Regional award Council Advancement and Support Edn., 1975, 77, 78, nat. award CASE, 1977; Gov.'s award for Volunteerism, 1986; Pub. Service awards Nat. Police Officers Assn., City of Shively (Ky.) and Am. Legion, 1970; Nat. award Nat. Sch. Pub. Relations Assn., 1981, 83, Gov.'s Award for Volunteerism, 1987. Mem. Nat. Mgnt. Assn. (v.p. 1993-94, local mgr. of yr. 1995). Home: 3794 Toddville Rd Toddville IA 52341-9773 Office: Fox Ridge Adv PO Box 134 Hiawatha IA 52233-0134

ROBERTSON, JOHN BERNARD, real estate professional; b. St. Joseph, Mo., Mar. 8, 1940; s. James Leo and Laura Elizabeth (Rupp) R.; m. Carolyn Lee Robertson, Aug. 11, 1962; children: John Leo, Margaret, Sally, Emily, Sam. Co-owner Leo Robertson Tire & Motor Supply, Inc., St. Joseph, 1962-85; realtor Summers Realtors, St. Joseph, 1985—. Bd. dirs. St. Joseph YMCA, 1980—; chmn. fund drive Bishop LeBlond H.S., St. Joseph, 1987—; chmn. bd. dirs. Andrew Buchanan County chpt. Am. Cancer Soc.; bd. dirs., fin. dir. LaVerna Village of Sisters of St. Francis, Savannah, Mo. Mem. Nat. Assn. Realtors (cert.), Mo. Assn. Realtors (mem. Million Dollar Club 1987-92), St. Joseph Regional Bd. Realtors (chmn. projects and events com. 1988, past pres., Newcomer of Yr., 1985, Realtor Agt. of Yr. 1988), St. Joseph C. of C. (diplomat 1989-92), Multi-Million Dollar Club, Sertoma, KC (state sec. 1986-88, Achievement award 1988). Roman Catholic. Home: 2510 Lovers Ln Saint Joseph MO 64506-1621 Office: Summers Realtors 1007 E Saint Maartens Dr Saint Joseph MO 64506-2993

ROBERTSON, JOSEPH EDMOND, grain processing company executive; b. Brownstown, Ind., Feb. 16, 1918; s. Roscoe Melvin and Edith Penina (Shields) R.; m. Virginia Faye Baxter, Nov. 23, 1941; 1 son, Joseph Edmond. BS, Kans. State U., 1940, postgrad., 1940. Cereal chemist Ewing Mill Co., 1940-43, flour milling engr., 1946-50, feed nutritionist, 1951-59; v.p., sec. Robertson Corp., Brownstown, Ind., 1960-80, pres., 1980—. Mem. Kans. State U. Varsity Basketball Team, 1937-40; pres. Jackson County (Ind.) Welfare Bd., 1948-52; mem. Ind. Port Commn., 1986-91; mem. Ind. Gov.'s Coun. of Sagamores of the Wabash. Forest products tech. writer Forest Prodn. Jour., 1973-78. Served with USAAF, 1943-45. Named to Hon. Order Ky. Cols. Mem. Hardwood Plywood Mfrs. Assn. (v.p. affiliate div. 1971-73, 87-88, internat. lectr. forest prodn. industry 1973-94), Am. Assn. Cereal Chemists, Assn. Operative Millers, Am. Legion, Brownstown C. of C. (dir. All Am. city program 1955), Kans. State U. Alumni Assn. (life), Blue Key, Phi Delta Theta, Phi Kappa Phi, Alpha Mu. Presbyterian. Clubs: Harrison Lakes Country Club, Internat. Travelers Century (Los Angeles), Circumnavigators Club (N.Y.C.). Lodge: Elks. Home: Lake and Forest Club 1268 E Lake Shore Dr PO Box A Brownstown IN 47220 Office: 200 N Front St Brownstown IN 47220-1040

ROBERTSON, MARTHA RAPPAPORT, state senator, consultant; b. Boston, Sept. 14, 1952; d. Jerome Lyle and Nancy (Vahey) Rappaport; m. T.L. Robertson, Nov. 22, 1980; 1 child, Colby. BA, Franklin & Marshall Coll., 1974; MBA, U. Pa., 1976. Mktg. and new bus. devel. exec. Gen. Mills, Inc., Mpls., 1976-91; state senator State of Minn., 1993—. Republican. Office: State of Minn 125 State Office Bldg Saint Paul MN 55155-1201

ROBERTSON, MARY VIRGINIA, retired elementary education educator; b. Lincoln, Nebr., Oct. 1, 1925; d. Dean Leroy and Anna Charlotte (Boge) R. AB in Philosophy and Psychology, U. Nebr., Lincoln, 1949, BS in Elem. Edn., 1953; postgrad., U. Toronto, Ont., Can., 1949. Cert. elem. tchr., Nebr. Country sch. tchr. Lancaster County schs., Nebr., 1943-44, Otoe County schs., Palmyra, Nebr., 1944-45; 3d-5th grade tchr. Palmyra Schs., 1945-46; 3d grade tchr. Valley (Nebr.) Schs., 1953-57, Lincoln Pub. Schs., 1957-81; ret.; leader workshop in field; math. coord. Riley Elem. Sch., Lincoln, 1970-71. Author pamphlet A Letter for You, 1954. Mem. NEA, AAUW, Nebr. State Edn. Assn., Nat. Coun. Math. Tchrs., Am. Child Edn. Internat., Belmont PTA (life), Eastern Star, Lincoln Women's Club. Methodist.

ROBERTSON, MELVINA, construction company executive; b. Guilford, Mo., June 3, 1934; d. Charlie Gale and Christina Gertrude (Nelson) Turner; m. Ponnie Leonard Robertson, June 3, 1955; children: Raymond Edward, Richard Leonard. Student, Cen. Mo. State Coll., 1966. Mgr. Knowles Restaurant, Kansas City, Mo., 1954-55; v.p. P.L. Robertson Concrete Found. Co., Inc., Ozark, Mo., 1972-90; pres. P.L. Robertson Concrete Found. Co., Inc., 1990—. Mem. Rose Soc. of Ozark, Nat. Audubon Soc. Mem. Reorganized LDS Ch.

ROBERTSON, PAUL JOSEPH, state legislator; b. Depauw, Ind., Apr. 25, 1946; s. William Edward and Mary Rita (Sieg) R.; m. Jill Ann Moss, 1971; children: Jennifer Lynn, Chad Alan, Heather Leigh, Jessica Moss. Student, Vincennes U., 1964-66; BS, Ind. State U., 1968, MS, 1970. Tchr., coach North Ctrl. H.S., 1968-69, Eng H.S., 1969-71, Vincennes H.S., 1971-73, Corydon H.S., 1973-85; mem. from 70th dist. Ind. State Ho. of Reps., 1978—. Del. Ind. State Dem. Conv., 1976-78; mem. Dem. Youth for Hamilton Campaign, 1974. Recipient Legis. award Ind. Alliance for Better Child Care, Legis. award UnitedWay. Mem. NEA, Ind. Tchrs. Assn., Lions, KC. Home: RR 1 Box 77A Depauw IN 47115-9801*

ROBERTSON, RUTH ANN, systems analyst, engineer; b. Oak Ridge, Tenn., Nov. 20, 1959; d. Arnold Powell and Beatrice (Lazaroff) L. BME, Ga. Inst. Tech., 1982; postgrad., U. Redlands, Calif., 1991. Engring. intern IBM, Gaithersburg, Md., 1980-81; packaging engr. Hughes Aircraft Co., El Segundo, Calif., 1982-85; field engr. Spectrum Control, Inc., Valencia, Calif., 1985-86; pres. Precision Jaunt, El Segundo, 1986-87; sr. systems analyst Marquardt Co., Van Nuys, Calif., 1987-91, Axcom Computer Cons., Springfield, Mo., 1991-92; open systems product mgr. DataTrade, Inc., Springfield, 1992-96; mgr.product realization Dayco Products, Inc., Springfield, 1996—. Mem. Whitehead Leadership Soc., Tau Beta Pi, Phi Tau Sigma. Office: Dayco Products Inc Tech Ctr 2601 W Battlefield Rd Springfield MO 65807

ROBERTSON, WILLIAM RICHARD, banker, holding company executive; b. Schenectady, N.Y., July 26, 1941; s. Bruce Manson and Mary Jo (Gillam) R.; m. Sarah Reed Parker, June 20, 1964; children: Deborah Graham, John William, Julie Elizabeth. AB, Colgate U., 1964; MBA, Case Western Res. U., 1967. Nat. City Bank/Nat. City Corp., 1964—; Exec. v.p., chief fin. officer Nat. City Corp., Cleve., 1982-89, dep. chmn. bd. dirs., 1986-95; pres., 1995—; bd. dirs. Nat. City Corp., Capitol Am. Fin. Corp., Kirtland Capital Corp. Trustee Coll. of Wooster, Ohio, 1982-91, Fairmount Presbyn. Ch., Cleve., 1983-86, St. Luke's Hosp., Cleve., 1984—, Cleve. Ballet, 1985-89, United Way, 1986-97, Karamu House, 1988—, Western Res. Hist. Soc., 1990—, Cleve. Mus. Art, 1991—, Salvation Army, 1985—, chmn. adv. bd., 1991-93; pres., trustee Big Bros. and Big Sisters, Cleve., 1973-80; chmn., bd. trustees United Way of Cleve., 1995—, trustee Musical Arts Assn., 1994—, chmn. vis. com. of Case Western Res. U. Weatherhead Sch. Mgmt., 1995—. Mem. Fin. Execs. Inst., Bankers Roundtable, Am. Bankers Assn., Cleve. Skating Club (pres. 1980-82), Union Club, Country Club, Pepper Pike Club, Ottawa Club, Desert Mountain Club. Republican. Home: 2700 Chesterton Rd Shaker Hts OH 44122-1805 Office: Nat City Corp Nat City Ctr 1900 E 9th St Cleveland OH 44114-3401

ROBESON, SCOTT MICHAEL, climatologist; b. Wilmington, Del., Sept. 7, 1962; s. James Ray and Beatrice Adelaide (Donovan) R.; m. Teresa Maria Ho, Aug. 19, 1989. BA, U. Del., 1984, PhD, 1992; MS, U. B.C., 1987. Rsch. asst. U. Del., Newark, 1984, grad. fellow, 1988-92; meteorol. trainee Nat. Climatic Data Ctr., Asheville, N.C., 1983-84; grad. fellow U. B.C., Vancouver, 1985-87; asst. prof. Ind. U., Bloomington, 1992—; reviewer jours. in field.; bd. dirs. Climate Specialty Group, AAG, Washington. Contbr. articles to profl. jours. Rsch. grantee NSF, 1996; summer faculty fellow Ind. U., 1993, 96. Mem. Am. Meteorol. Soc., Assn. Am. Geographers, Am. Geophys. Union, Phi Beta Kappa. Office: Ind U Dept Geography 120 Student Bldg Bloomington IN 47405

ROBIE, MICHAEL HENRY, airport services executive; b. Erie, Pa., Apr. 4, 1960; s. Henry Joseph and Agnes Isabel (Brown) R.; m. Jane MacLaren, Apr. 13, 1985; children: Kathryn, Joseph. BSEE, U. Mich., 1983. Elec. engr. Northrop Grumman DSD, Rolling Meadows, Ill., 1983-85; rsch. engr. Mark Controls, Skokie, Ill., 1985-86; design engr. United Airlines, Elk Grove, Ill., 1986-88; design engr. Covia Partnership, Rosemont, Ill., 1988, systems engr., 1988-89, section mgr. airport mktg., 1989-91; head airport profl. svcs. Covia Techs., Rosemont, Ill., 1991—; mem. Dist. 54 Sci. Adv. Bd., Schaumburg, Ill., 1994—. Cantor St. Marcelline Catholic Ch., Schaumburg, 1989—. Mem. IEEE, Aiport Cons. Coun. (tech. com. 1992-93, planning/design com. 1995—), Airport Coun. Internat., Audio Engring. Soc. Office: Siemens Nixdorf Trans Techs 6400 Shafer Ct Rosemont IL 60018

ROBINS, ARTHUR JOSEPH, social work and psychiatry educator; b. N.Y.C., July 21, 1921; s. Meyer and Marie Deborah (Kupferberg) R.; m. Betty Lucille Dashew, Sept. 26, 1948; children: Lisa Dale Robins-Pauze, Michael Lee. BS, CCNY, 1943; MSW, Carnegie Inst. of Technology, 1948; PhD, U. Minn., 1953. Cons. UN Tech. Assistance Bur., Dacca, E. Pakistan, 1961-62, UN, Teheran, 1968-69; 1st lt. mil. psychiatric social worker NP Clinic/Walter Reed Hosp., Washington, 1948-49; dir. social svcs. Clarinda (Iowa) State Hosp., 1949-51; prof. of social work and dir. Sch. of Social Work U. Mo. Columbia, 1953-70; prof. psychiatry Sch. of Medicine U. Mo., Columbia, 1975-91, prof. Honors Coll., 1995—; prof. psychology/dir. Ctr. for Advanced Study Mental Health Vanderbilt U., Nashville, 1970-75; reviewer hosp. and community psychiatry, Washington; mem. South Asian studies com., U. Mo., 1966—. Author: (book) Alcohol Detoxification Manual: A Guide to Administering Comprehensive Services, 1988; contbg. author numerous books including Social Administration, 1978, Mental Health Boards: Directive and Advsory in Community Mental Health, 1981, others; contbr. articles to profl. jours., reviewer in field. Rifle platoon sgt. U.S. Army, 1943-46, PTO, Asia; 1st lt. U.S. Army, 1948-49. Fulbright lectr. India, 1956-57, 81-82, Malaysia, 1988-89; Centennial fellow Vanderbilt U., Nashville, 1974; sr. rsch. fellow NSF, India, 1979; Arthur J. RobinsAnn. scholarship for grad. social work named for him established by Crandall Found., 1992—.

ROBINS, H(ENRY) IAN, medical oncologist; b. N.Y.C., Feb. 17, 1945; s. Edwin and Matilda (Morgenstern) R. AB in Biology, Boston U., 1966, AM in Biochemistry, 1968, PhD in Molecular Biology, 1971, MD, 1976. Diplomate Am. Bd. Internal Medicine, Am. Bd. Med. Oncology, Am. Bd. Forensic Medicine, Am. Bd. Forensic Examiners. Intern in internal medicine Univ. Hosps., Madison, Wis., 1976-77, resident in internal medicine, 1977-79; fellow in clin. oncology Wis. Clin. Cancer Ctr., Madison, 1979-81, fellow in rsch. oncology, 1981-82; instr. dept. human oncology, dept. medicine Dept. Human Oncology, Dept. Medicine U. Wis. Sch. Medicine, Madison, 1982-83, asst. prof., 1983-86, assoc. prof., 1986—; chief sect. med. oncology, dir. U. Wis. Sch. Medicine, Madison, 1990-95, prof. dept. human oncology, medicine and neurology, 1992—. Contbr. numerous articles to profl. jours.; reviewer numerous sci. jours. including Biochem. Pharmacology, Internat. Jour. Radiation Biology, Jour. Clin. Oncology, New Eng. Jour. Medicine, others. Mem. N.Y. Acad. Scis., AAAS, ACP, Internat. Clin. Hyperthermia Soc. , Radiation Rsch. Soc., N.am. Hyperthermia Group, Oncology Group, Am. Fedn. clin. Rsch., Ea. Coop. Oncology Group, European Soc. Hyperthermic Oncology, Vet. Cancer Soc., Transplantation Soc., Collaborative Ocular Melanoma Study Group, Am. Soc. Clin. Hypnosis, Minn. Soc. Clin. Hypnosis, Sigma Xi. Office: Clin Sci Ctr K4/662 600 Highland Ave Madison WI 53792-0001

ROBINS, MARJORIE MCCARTHY (MRS. GEORGE KENNETH ROBINS), civic worker; b. St. Louis, Oct. 4, 1914; d. Eugene Ross and Louise (Roblee) McCarthy; AB, Vassar Coll., 1936; diploma St. Louis Sch. Occupational Therapy, 1940; m. George Kenneth Robins, Nov. 9, 1940; children: Carol Robins Von Arx, G. Stephen, Barbara A. Robins Foorman. Mem. Mo. Libr. Commn., 1937-38; mem. bd. St. Louis Jr. League, 1945, 46; mem. bd. Occupational Therapy Workshop of St. Louis, 1941-46, pres., 1945, 46; mem. bd. Ladue Chapel Nursery Sch., 1957-60, 61-64, pres. bd., 1963, 64; past regional chmn. United Fund; past mem. St. Louis Met. Youth Commn., St. Louis Health and Welfare Coun.; bd. dirs. Internat. Inst. of St. Louis, 1966-72, 76-82, 83-92, sec., 1968, v.p., 1981; bd. dirs. Mental Health Assn. St. Louis, 1963-70, Washington U. Child Guidance and Evaluation Clinic, 1968-78; bd. dirs. Cen. Inst. for Deaf, 1970—, v.p., 1975-76, pres., 1976-78; bd. dirs. Met. St. Louis YWCA, 1954-63, 64-74, pres. bd., 1960-63, trustee, 1977—; mem. nat. bd. YWCA, 1967-79, nat. v.p., 1973-76; vol. tchr. remedial reading clinic St. Louis City Schs., 1968-71; trustee John Burroughs Sch., 1960-63, John Burroughs Found., 1965-80, Roblee Found., 1972—, Nat. YWCA Retirement Fund, 1979-88; bd. dirs. Gambrill Gardens United Meth. Retirement Home, 1979-85, Thompson Retreat and Conf. Center, 1981-87; bd. dirs. Springboard to Learning Inc., 1980—, v.p., 1980-90; tutor I Have A Dream Found., 1995—. Mem. Archeol. Inst. Am. (bd. dirs. 1993—, treas. St. Louis chpt. 1985-87, 93-95), Vassar Club (sec. and pres. 1939-40), Wednesday Club (dir. 1968-70, 77-79, 80-81, 93-95), St. Louis. Home: 45 Loren Woods Saint Louis MO 63124-1903

ROBINSON, ALEXANDER JACOB, clinical psychologist; b. St. John, Kans., Nov. 7, 1920; s. Oscar Frank and Lydia May (Beitler) R.; m. Elsie Louise Riggs, July 29, 1942; children: Madelyn K., Alicia A., David J., Charles A., Paul S., Marietta J., Stephen N. BA in Psychology, Ft. Hays (Kans.) State U., 1942, MS in Clin. Psychology, 1942; postgrad., U. Ill., 1942-44. Cert. psychologist, sch. psychologist. Chief psychologist Larned (Kans.) State Hosp., 1948-53, with employee selection, outpatient services, 1953-55; sch. psychologist County Schs., Modesto, Calif., 1955-61, Pratt (Kans.) Jr. Coll., 1961-66; fed. grantee, writer assoc. dir. Exemplary Federally Funded Program for Spl. Edn., Pratt, 1966-70; dir. spl. edn., researcher Stafford County Schs., St. John, 1970-81, ret., 1981; supr. testing and data Incidence of Exceptional Children in Kansas, Kans. State U., Ft. Hays, 1946; writer, asst. dir. Best Exemplary Federally Funded Program on Spl. Edn., Pratt, 1966-70; fed. grantee, researcher, writer, study dir. Edn. for the High-Performance Child, St. John, 1970—, Psychogenesis of the Sociopathic Personality, a longitudinal study. Minister, The Ch. of Jesus Christ. Served to 2d lt. U.S. Army, 1944-46, PTO. Mem. N.Y. Acad. Scis. Lodge: Lions (program chmn. St. John 1974-76). Home and Office: RR 1 Box 121A Saint John KS 67576-9801

ROBINSON, C.N. (BUD), state legislator; b. Blair, Nebr., Sept. 13, 1928; m. Janice Vaage, 1953; children: Kristen, Thomas, Richard, David, Stephen. BA, Dana Coll., 1950; MS, U. Omaha, 1957; PhD, U. Nebr., Lincoln, 1960. Mem. from dist. 16 Nebr. State Senate, Lincoln, 1990—, mem. appropriations and rules coms., vice chmn. com. on coms., urban affairs com., mem. gen. affairs com., govt., mil. and vet. affairs com., mem. intergovt. coop. com. Mem. Nebr. Coun. Sch. Adminstrs., Optimists Club. Office: Nebr State Senate State Capitol Rm 1202 Lincoln NE 68509*

ROBINSON, CELIA SUE, physical therapist; b. Memphis, Mo., Feb. 23, 1936; d. Andrew Ray and Celia Cecil (Drake) Keethler; m. Gayle Edward Robinson, June 24, 1938; children: Rebecca, Heather, Laural, Ross, Randall. BS in Edn., Truman U., 1961; cert. in phys. therapy, Mayo Found. Sch. of Allied Health Scis., 1964; postgrad., St. Mary's U. Cert. hand therapist. Staff phys. therapist Mayo Found., Rochester, Minn., 1964-73, 83—; phys. therapist Olmsted County Health Dept., Rochester, 1973-75; dir. phys. therapy Stewartville (Minn.) Nursing Home, 1975-82; mem. patient edn. com. Mayo Found., Rochester, 1992, arthritis com., 1992. Mem. 4-H Adult Vols. Leaders Assn., Minn. 4-H, Rochester, 1995, Republicans of Minn., Rochester, 1995. Mem. Am. Soc. Hand Therapists (com. mem. 1992), Am. Phys. Therapy Assn. (legis.- contact person (1992-95), Am. Assn. Hand Surgery (assoc. 1993). Lutheran. Home: 7600 80th Ave SW Stewartville MN 55976 Office: Mayo Found 2nd St SW Rochester MN 55905

ROBINSON, CHRISTOPHER SEAN, counselor, educator; b. Portsmouth, Va., July 17, 1967; s. Gary R. Robinson and Martha A. (Coleman) Smith. BA, U. Va., 1989, postgrad., 1992-94; MEd in Counseling Psychology, Coll. William and Mary, 1991. Lic. profl. counselor. Case mgr. Hampton (Va.) Cmty. Svc. Bd., 1991-92; counselor U. Va., Charlottesville, 1993-94, Madison (Wis.) Area Tech. Coll., 1994—. Vol. Madison AIDS Support Network, 1994—; mem. Madison Symphony Chorus, 1995—. Lincoln-Lane fellow, 1992-94. Mem. ACA, Am. Coll. Pers. Assn., Wis. Coll. Pers. Assn. Office: Madison Area Tech Coll 3550 Anderson St Madison WI 53704

ROBINSON, CHUCK FRANK, dairy company executive; b. Reno, Nev., May 13, 1956; s. Clifford Frank and Gracia Eva (Lancey) R.; m. Rebecca Sue Swafford, July 24, 1976; children: Timothy Charles, Jennifer Rebecca. Grad., Shasta High Sch., Redding, Calif., 1974. Machine operator Zarda Bros. Dairy, Shawnee, Kans., 1976-80, head operator, 1980-84, blow mold supr., 1984-89; blow mold mgr., prodn. supr. Fairmont Zarda Dairy, Kansas City, Mo., 1989—. Republican. Home: 6617 W 72nd Ter Shawnee Mission KS 66204-2018 Office: Fairmont Zarda Dairy 3805 Van Brunt Blvd Kansas City MO 64128-2356

ROBINSON, DIXIE FAYE, school system administrator; b. Lexington, Ky., Feb. 7, 1944; d. John David and Betty Lou (Taylor) Moore; m. Jim Darrell Robinson, June 25, 1978. BA, Georgetown (Ky.) Coll., 1966; MA in Edn., Ball State U., 1972; postgrad., Miami U., Oxford, Ohio, 1989—, Ind. U., 1990-92. Cert. tchr., Ind. Tchr. Richmond (Ind.) Community Schs., 1966-91, adminstr., 1991—; team leader Richmond Community schs., 1983-90, mentor tchr., 1989-91, coop. learning staff devel. mem., 1989-91, coord. ptnrship in edn., 1990-91, site-base convenor, 1990-91; v.p. Richmond Area Reading Coun., 1984. Pres. Historic Richmond, Inc., 1982; tour guide Richmond-Wayne County Tourism Bur., 1986-87; vice-chmn. Richmond Area Rose Festival, 1988-89; adv. bd. Palladium Item, Richmond, 1990. Recipient Hoosier Meritorious award Ind. Sec. of State, 1986, Nat. Energy Edn. Devel. award, Washington, 1991; grantee Newspapers in Edn., 1986. Mem. NEA, NAFE, ASCD, Nat. Middle Sch. Assn., Assn. Tchr. Educators, Nat. Coun. Tchrs. English (Ctr. of Excellence award 1988-91), Ind. Coun. Tchrs. of English (Hoosier Tchr. English 1991), Richmond Area Reading Coun., Kappa Delta Gamma, Phi Delta Kappa. Home: 100 NW 8th St Richmond IN 47374-4055

ROBINSON, DONALD PETER, musician, retired electrical engineer; b. Phila., Jan. 27, 1928; s. Warren Frederick and Marcella Theresa (Derry) R.; m. Beatrice Graves, Sept. 22, 1951 (dec.); children: Donald, Stephen, Sharon Robinson-Byrd, Michael; m. Mary Katherine Robertson, June 9, 1990. A.A., Temple U. Sch. Tech., 1956. Sr. engr./technician Gen. Electric Co., Utica, N.Y., 1956-89, ret., 1989; organist emeritus St. Joseph-St. Patrick's Ch., Utica, 1983—; minister music/organist St. Paul's Baptist Ch., Utica, 1961-88; organist Utica Council K.C., 1969—; organist/choir dir. 4th degree assembly Central N.Y. dist. K.C., 1985—; producer, host Organ Loft radio program WLFH, Little Falls, N.Y., 1962-90; pipe organ cons. Served with AUS, 1948-54. Mem. Am. Guild Organists (past dean central N.Y. chpt.), Am. Theatre Organ Soc., Nat. Assn. R.R. Passengers (bd. dirs.), K.C. (past faithful navigator 4th degree assembly). Roman Catholic. Home: 715 Garfield Ave Rockford IL 61103-6023

ROBINSON, GARY RAY, sales professional; b. Centralia, Ill., Dec. 12, 1952; s. Farrell Leslie and Betty Jane (Besant) R.; m. Cindy Jo Geilhausen, Oct. 15, 1976; children: Jonathan Farrell, Casey Lynn. BSBA, U. Tenn., 1975. Sr. cons. sales Searle Pharms. Divsn. Monsanto Chem., Chgo. and St. Louis, 1976—; bd. dirs. North Star Cable Industries, Knoxville. Pres. Centralia (Ill.) H.S. #200 Bd. Edn., 1989—; elder Trinity Luth. Ch., 1992—. Mem. Elks, U. Tenn. Alumni Assn., U. Tenn. Lettermans Club, Meadow Woods C. of C. (pres., bd. dirs. 1988-93). Home: 2053 Meadow Ln Centralia IL 62801

ROBINSON, GEORGIA MAY, education educator; b. Detroit, Sept. 6, 1926; d. George J. and Lena C. (Behrendt) Levin; m. Ralph M. Robinson, Apr. 15, 1956; children: Aron David, Stephen Mark. BS, Elmhurst (Ill.) Coll., 1950; MAT, Nat. Coll. of Edn., Evanston, 1978. Tchr. Am. Echod Congregation, Waukegan, Ill., 1966-74, AAUW Nursery Sch., Waukegan, 1965-76, Nat. Coll. Edn., Evanston, 1977-87; instr. childhood edn. Nat. Louis U., Evanston, 1977—; cons. Am. Sch. of Lima, Peru, 1979, Ill. State Bd. of Edn., Springfield, 1986—; scrip cons. Coronet Ednl. Films, Chgo., 1981-82; adv. coun. Mus. of Sci. and Industry, Chgo., 1980-81; chmn. for Ferguson lecture series Nat. Coll. Edn., 1984-85; presenter in field. Mem. cmty. adv. coun. Waukegan Sch. Dist. 60, 1977-78; mem. scholarship selection com. Altrusa, Waukegan, 1984-90; bd. dirs. Waukegan Sch. Found., 1991—; chmn. sch. bd. Am. Echod Congregation, 1994-96. Mem. Nat. Assn. for Edn. of Young Children (validator for accredidation process 1987—), Ill. Assn. for the Edn. of Young Children, Chgo. Assn. for the Edn. of Young Children, Midwest Assn. for the Edn. of Young Children, Ill. Soc. Early Childhood Profls. (membership chair 1992-96), Assn. for the Advancement of Therapeutic Edn. (founder, co-pres. 1987-92). Avocations: mixed media painting, sewing, golf. Home: 705 Colville Pl Waukegan IL 60087-5026

ROBINSON, JACK ALBERT, retail drug stores executive; b. Detroit, Feb. 26, 1930; s. Julius and Fannie (Aizkowitz) R.; m. Aviva Freedman, Dec. 21, 1952; children: Shelby, Beth, Abigail. B in Pharmacy, Wayne State U., 1952. Founder, chief exec. officer, chmn. bd. Perry Drug Stores, Inc., Pontiac, Mich., 1957-95; founder, chmn., pres. JAR Group LLC, Bloomfield, Mich., 1996; bd. dirs. Riser Foods, Inc.; corp. dir. R & B, Inc. Chmn. Wayne State U. Fund, Detroit, 1986, Concerned Citizens for the Arts in Mich., 1990, 91—; chmn. ann. fund Detroit Symphony Orch.; bd. dirs. United Way of Pontiac, Mich., 1986, United Found. of Detroit, 1986, Pontiac Area Urban League, Cmty. Found., S.E. Mich., Detroit Svc. Group, Save Orch. Hall, Inc., Cranbrook Inst. Sci., Jewish Fedn. Apts., Wetzman Inst. Sci., Holocaust Meml. Ctr., Harper-Grace Hosp., Detroit; past dir. Pontiac Symphony Boys Club, Detroit Osteo. Hosp.; pres. United Jewish Found. Met. Detroit, 1992, Greater Detroit Interfaith Round Table NCCJ, 1994-95, co-chmn., 1992; pres. Jewish Fedn. Met. Detroit, 1992-94. Recipient Disting. Alumni award Wayne State U. Coll. Pharmacy, 1975, Eleanor Roosevelt Humanities award from State of Israel, 1978, B'nai B'rith Youth Svcs. Am. Tradition award, 1982, Wayne State U. Disting. Alumni award, 1985, Tree of Life award Jewish Nat. Fund, 1985, Disting. Citizen award Pontiac Boy Scouts Am., 1985, Corp. Leadership award Wayne State U., 1985, Booker T. Washington Bus. Assn. Brotherhood award, 1986, Humanitarian award March of Dimes, 1987, award Weizmann Rsch. Inst., 1987, Humanitarian award Variety Club, 1988, Fred M. Butzel award Jewish Fedn. Met. Detroit, 1991, B'nai B'rith Great Am. Traditions award, 1991, Cmty. Svc. award Am. Arabic and Jewish Friends, 1995; named Entrepreneur of Yr. Harvard U. Bus. Sch., Detroit, 1982. Mem. Nat. Assn. Chain Drug Stores (chmn. 1987, Lifetime Achievement award 1995, Robert B. Begley award 1995), Am. Pharm. Assn., Am. Found. for Pharm. Edn. (bd. dirs.), Econ. Club (bd. dirs. Detroit chpt.). Office: JAR Group LLC 500 North Woodward Ste 220 Bloomfield Hills MI 48304

ROBINSON, JACK F(AY), clergyman; b. Wilmington, Mass., Mar. 7, 1914; s. Thomas P. and Ethel Lincoln (Fay) R.; A.B., Mont. State U., 1936; D.B., Crozer Theol. Sem., 1939; A.M., U. Chgo., 1949, postgrad., 1950-52; m. Eleanor Jean Smith, Sept. 1, 1937 (dec. 1966); 1 dau., Alice Virginia Dungey; m. Lois Henze, July 16, 1968. Ordained to ministry Bapt. Ch., 1939; minister Bethany Ch., American Falls, Idaho, 1939-41, 1st Ch., Coun. Grove, Kans., 1944-49; ordained (transfer) to ministry Congregational Ch., 1945; minister United Ch., Chebanse, Ill., 1949-52, 1st Ch., Argo, Ill., 1954-58, Congl. Ch., St. Charles, Ill., 1958-64; assoc. minister Plymouth Congregational Ch., Lansing, Mich., 1964-66; tchr. Chgo. Pub. Schs., 1966-68; minister Waveland Ave. Congl. Ch., Chgo., 1967-79, interim pastor Chgo. Met. Assn., 1979—, First Congl. Ch., Des Plaines, Ill., 1979, Bethany United Ch., Chgo., 1980, Eden United Ch. of Christ, Chgo., 1983-84, St. Nicolai Ch., Chgo., 1984, Grace United Ch. of Christ, Chgo., 1985-86, Christ Ch. of Chgo., 1987-87, First Congl., Evanston, Ill., 1987-88, First Congl. Ch., Brookfield, Ill., 1988-89, First Congl. Ch., Steger, Il., 1990-91, First Congl. Ch., Berwyn, Ill., 1992, Immanuel V.C.P. Ch., Streamwood, Ill., 1993—, Immanuel United Ch. of Christ, Bartlett, 1994; assoc. pastor, calling, min. of visitation People's Ch., Chgo., 1990-93; hist. cons. Bell & Howell Co., Chgo., 1981-82. Assoc. Hyde Park dept. Chgo. YMCA, 1942-44. U. Chgo. Libr. 1952-54; chmn. com. evangelism Kans. Congl. Christian Conf., 1947-48; city chmn. Layman's Missionary Movement, 1946-51; trustee Congl. and Christian Conf. Ill., v.p., 1963-64; mem. exec. coun. Chgo. Met. Assn. United Ch. of Christ, 1968-70, sec. ch. and ministry com., 1982-88 ; mem. gen. bd. Ch. Fedn. Greater Chgo., 1969-71; mem. Libr. Bd. Coun. Grove, 1945-49; city chmn. NCCJ, 1945-49; dean Northside Mission Coun. United Ch. of Christ, 1975-77, sec. personnel com. Ill. Conf. United Ch. of Christ, 1986-88. Recipient Pres'. award Congl. Christian Hist. Soc. Mem. Am. Soc. Ch. History, Am. Acad. Polit. Sci., Am. Hist. Assn., C. of C. (past dir.), Internat. Platform Assn. Author: The Growth of the Bible, 1969; From A Mission to a Church, 1976; Bell & Howell Company: A 75 Year History, 1982, (co-author) Harza: 65 Years, 1986, History of the Illinois Conference, United Church of Christ, 1990. Home: 321 E Morse Ave Bartlett IL 60103

ROBINSON, JOEL MARTIN, library director; b. Independence, Mo., July 19, 1947; s. Stewart Harold and Roslouise Kitty (Yancey) R.; m. Barbara Annette Denham Loven, Aug. 12, 1967 (div. May 1984); children: Cabot Joel, Amy Cheri; m. Deborah Lynn Williamson, Aug. 8, 1991. BS in Edn., Southwest Mo. State U., 1969; MLS, Ind. U., 1973. Cert. libr. I, Ind. Libr. & Hist. Bd. Dir. Westchester Pub. Libr., Chesterton, Ind., 1972-78; spl. projects coord. Broward County Libr., Ft. Lauderdale, Fla., 1978-81; asst. dir. Springfield (Mo.) Greene County Libr., 1981-85; dir. Chickasaw Libr. Sys., Ardmore, Okla., 1986-91, Tippecanoe County Pub. Libr., Lafayette, Ind., 1991—; del. Gov.'s Conf. Librs. & Info. Sci., Okla., 1985; pres. Mo. Libr. Assn., 1985; cons. Tempe (Ariz.) Pub. Libr., 1988; pres. Okla. Libr. Assn., 1990-91. Contbr. articles to profl. jours. Lay reader/eucharist min. St. John's Episcopal Ch., Lafayette, Ind., 1994—, mem. vestry. 1996—; pres. West Ctrl. Ind. Cmty. Network, 1995—; mem. Ind. Coun. on Libr. Automation, 1993-96. Recipient Intellectual Freedom award Ind. Libr. Fedn., 1996; named Rotarian of Yr., Chesterton-Porter Rotary Club, 1977-78; Paul Harris fellow Lafayette Daybreak Rotary, 1994. Home: 663 Perrin Ave Lafayette IN 47904 Office: Tippecanoe County Pub Libr 627 South St Lafayette IN 47901

ROBINSON, JOHN PAUL, engineering educator, consultant; b. Providence, Jan. 1, 1939. BSEE, Iowa State U., 1960; MS, Princeton U., 1962, PhD, 1966. Registered profl. engr., Iowa. Mem. tech. staff RCA Labs., Princeton, N.J., 1960-62, IBM T.J. Watson Labs., Yorktown Heights, N.Y., 1963-64; prof. elec. engring. U. Iowa, Iowa City, 1965—; expert witness various law firms, 1976-96; cons. several corps., 1968-94. Contbr. articles to profl. jours. Mem. bd. elec. examiners City of Iowa City, 1974-79, chair, 1992-94; mem. parish coun. St. Mary's Ch., Iowa City, 1984-86. Rsch. grantee Office Naval Rsch., 1968-73, NSF, 1968-71, 75-76, NASA, 1981-82, Rockwell Internat., 1991-95. Mem. IEEE (sr., student br. counselor 1958-96), Soc. for Computer Simulation (sr.), Soc. of Women Engrs., Sigma Xi, Tau Beta Pi (student br. advisor 1992-96). Office: U Iowa 3100 Engineering Bldg Iowa City IA 52242

ROBINSON, JOHN WILLIAM, broadcasting professional; b. Paterson, N.J., Feb. 13, 1951; s. William Bernard and Lorena Rose (Warner) R.; m. Cathy Noreen Cronkright, Nov. 18, 1970 (div. July 1975); 1 child, Jason Michael;m. Susan Elizabeth Sharp, June 30, 1990. On-air personality, copywriter WVIC-FM/WVGO-AM, Lansing, Mich., 1981-84; on-air personality K92-FM, St. Johns, Mich., 1983, WIBM-FM/AM, Jackson, Mich., 1984-88; morning show prodr., comedy writer, personality, copywriter WVIC-FM, Lansing, 1988-92; promotions dir., on-air personality WJXQ-FM/WIBM-FM, Lansing, 1992-95; talk show prodr., polit. and current event satirist WWWE-AM, Cleve., 1995—; isntr. Rock & Roll History class, 1988-89. Prodr. radio spls. The Beatles in America, British Rock '64, British Rock '65, Best of Summer Drag, Best of Michigan Rock Part 1, Best of Michigan Rock Part 2; creator, prodr. The Friday Night Flicks, 1990-95; bassist rock band The Concussions, 1966-70; prodr. spl. version of Joe Walsh's Vote for Me, 1992. Office: WWWE Radio 1468 W 9th St Cleveland OH 44113

ROBINSON, KRISTINE DANELLE, small business owner; b. Mexico, Mo., May 3, 1969. Cert. cosmotologist, Mo. Hair stylist Guys & Gals Hair Tanning Salon, Centralia, Mo., 1988-90; owner, sec. Robinson Heating & Air Conditioning, Mexico, 1991—. Mem. Centralia Country Club. Office: Robinson Heating & Air Conditioning 107 E Monroe St Mexico MO 65265-2811

ROBINSON, LARRY J., state legislator; m. Mary Lee; 2 children. BS, Valley City State U.; MS, N.D. State U. Mem. N.D. Senate, 1989—, mem. appropriations com.; mem. Gov.'s Coun. on Human Resources, Com. on Status of Women; aux. svc. dir. Valley City State U. Bd. dirs., adv. com. Mercy Hosp.; mem. adv. com. Barnes County, Extension Adv. Coun., Hi Soaring Eagle Ranch. Mem. KC, Elks, Eagles, Kiwanis, C. of C. (past pres.), Masons, Phi Delta Kappa. Office: State Senate State Capitol Bismarck ND 58505 Home: 3584 Sheyenne Cir Valley City ND 58072-9545*

ROBINSON, LOIS HART, retired public relations executive; b. Freeport, Ill., Aug. 9, 1927; d. Seril N. and Cora (Stabenow) Hart; m. Noel M. Henze, Nov. 15, 1947 (div. 1964); m. Jack Fay Robinson, July 16, 1968; children: Susan Henze Bentley, Cynthia Henze Berkeley, Charles Henze. Student Oakton Community Coll., 1976-77, Northwestern U., 1977-81. Med. sec. Freeport Meml. Hosp., 1945-47; sec. No. Ill. Corp., 1947-49; adminstrv. asst. to supt. schs. Community Sch. Dist. 303, St. Charles, Ill., 1962-68; exec. sec. Bell & Howell Co., Chgo., 1969-73, supr. corp. rels., 1973-79, mgr. corp. communications, 1979-85, mgr. corp. communication svcs., 1985-88; pres., dir. Bell & Howell Found., 1983-88; free-lance writer, Evanston, Ill., 1989-91. Recipient Effie award Am. Mktg. Assn., 1983. Bd. dirs. Evanston Ecumenical Action Coun., 1991-93. Congregationalist. Home: 321 E Morse Ave Bartlett IL 60103-4168

ROBINSON, LOUIS HILL, international sales manager; b. Chgo., June 26, 1954; s. Irwin B. and Charlene S. (Lasky) R.; m. Irene Geifman Robinson, Mar. 20, 1980 (div. Feb. 1995); children: Yoav, Maya, Daniel. BA in Econs. and Internat. Rels., Hebrew U., Jerusalem, 1976, MBA, 1982. Dir. student svcs. Hebrew U., 1975-76; diplomat Israeli Fgn. Ministry, Jerusalem, 1980-84; mng. dir. Ravit Irrigation Sys., Israel, 1984-92; internat. sales mgr. Eshed-Robotec Robotics, Tel Aviv, 1992-95, ARPAC L.P., Chgo., 1995-96, Lantech Inc., Louisville, 1996—; cons. in field. Mem. Childrens Welfare Fund, Jerusalem, 1981-84. Capt. Inf., 1976-79. Mem. Am. C. of C., Packaging Machinary Mfrs. Inst. Home: 1207 S Old Wilke # 202 Arlington Heights IL 60005 Office: Lantech Inc 11000 Bluegrass Pkwy Louisville KY 40299

ROBINSON, MARTIN, television and radio broadcaster, media consultant; b. Chgo., Sept. 7, 1932; s. Edward Emmanuel Robinson and Florence Ruth (Cohen) Mayer; m. Mary Alice Wellingham, May 31, 1959; children: Paul Edward, Jill Marie. Broadcaster, host WAAF, WGN and WNIB, Chgo., 1956-58, WFMT, Chgo., 1958-93, WTTW-TV, Chgo., 1971—; media cons. J. Walter Thompson, 1973-75, Hill & Knowlton, 1982-90, Burson Marsteller, 1990-94; freelance media cons., 1975—; speaker, concert narrator. Served with USN, 1950-53. Office: WTTW-TV 5400 N St Louis Chicago IL 60625

ROBINSON, MICHAEL A., mechanical engineer; b. Montpelier, Ohio, Mar. 2, 1965. A in Mech. Engring., Owens Tech. Coll., 1987; BSME, Tri-State U., Angola, Ind., 1993. Design engr. Aro-Corp., Bryan, Ohio, 1986-93, Leader Engr.-Fabrication Inc., Napoleon, Ohio, 1993-94; project engr. Richmond Machine Co., Montpelier, Ohio, 1994—. Home: 310 W Catherine W Unity OH 43570 Office: Richmond Machine Co 15828 Travis Dr Montpelier OH 43543

ROBINSON, PATRICIA ELAINE, women's health nurse practitioner; b. St. Louis, June 30, 1955; d. Harold Winford and Robbie LaVeal (Ferguson) Hammett; m. Kenneth M. Robinson, Nov. 18, 1978 (div.); children: Barry Christopher, Emily Vanessa; m. C. gilbert, Nov. 20, 1990. ADN, St. Louis Community Coll., 1987; student, Webster U., 1990—; cert. in forensic pathology, St. Louis U., 1975; cert. in pharmacology, St. Louis Coll. Health, 1984; womens health nurse practioner, U. Mo., 1995. Per diem float nurse St. Louis U. Hosp.; coord. ob-gyn. unit Group Health Plan, St. Louis; staff nurse Barnes Hosp., St. Louis; staff nurse dept. ob-gyn. Washington U. Sch. Medicine, St. Louis, 1990-93; chief exec. study coord. women's health rsch. Obstetric & Gynecologic Diagnosis & Consultation, Florissant, Mo., 1992—; acting dir. Nurses for Reproductive Health Svcs., St. Louis, 1990-93. Mem. NAFE, Nurse Assn. Am. Coll. Obstetrics and Gynecologists, Med. Group Mgmt. Assn., Nat. Assn. Nurse Practitioners Reproductive Health, Phi Theta Kappa. Office: OBG Diagnosis & Consultation 1150 Graham Rd Ste 105 Florissant MO 63031-8013

ROBINSON, PETER ELIOT, cable television executive; b. Detroit, July 5, 1950; s. Eliot F. and Sarah (Winston) R.; m. Corinne Mailliard, May 27, 1985 (dec.). BA, Trinity Coll., Hartford, Conn., 1972; MBA, U. Mich., 1975. System gen. mgr. Am. TV & Communications, Albany, N.Y., 1979, reg. gen. mgr., 1980; div. mgr. Am. TV & Communications, Denver, 1981, v.p., 1981-82; sr. v.p. Manhattan Cable, N.Y.C., 1982-84; pres. Am. Cablevision of Queens (N.Y.), 1984-85; sr. v.p. McCaw Communications, Kirkland, Wash., 1985-86; pres. Robinson Jeffrey Assocs., Inc., Birmingham, Mich., 1987—; chmn. Comm One Inc., 1992—; bd. dirs. Televista Comm., Inc., Comm One, Inc., Global Ins. Bd. dirs., mem. exec. com. Birmingham/Bloomfield Art Assn.; bd. dirs. Gilda Club Cancer Ctr.; bd. govs., mem. exec. com. Cranbrook Schs.; trustee Founders Soc., Detroit Inst. Art, 1990—. Trinity Coll. George F. Baker scholar, 1968. Mem. Cranbrook Sch. Tennis Club (v.p. 1990), Detroit Artists Market, Birmingham Athletic Club. Office: Robinson Jeffrey Assocs 400 W Maple Rd Ste 300 Birmingham MI 48009-3351

ROBINSON, SPENCER, JR., retired service club executive, accountant; b. Bridgeport, Conn., Apr. 16, 1942; s. Spencer Robinson and Helen (Diesinger) McNeill; m. Sally Emptage, June 21, 1963; children: David Spencer, Todd Wallace, John Marshall, Sarah Ann. BSIM, Ga. Tech. U., 1963; BS in Acctg., Jacksonville U., 1969; MSHA, U. Ala., Birmingham, 1989. Mng. ptnr. Deloitte Haskins & Sells, N.Y.C., 1963-85; exec. v.p., chief operating officer U. Ala. Health Svcs. Found., Birmingham, 1985-90; gen. sec., chief adminstrv. officer Rotary Internat., Evanston, Ill., 1990-94; adj. prof. Montreat Coll. Sch. Profl. and Adult Studies, 1995-96. Contbr. articles to profl. jours. Gen. sec. Rotary Found., Evanston, 1990-94; mem. Gov's. Com. of 100, La., 1985; trustee Nat. Multiple Sclerosis Soc., La., 1984; sec., treas. Crimestoppers, Inc., New Orleans, 1983. Recipient Razzberry award Birmingham Press Club, 1989, Disting. Alumni award Jacksonville U., 1993. Republican. Presbyterian. Home: PO Box 280 Montreat NC 28757-0280

ROBINSON, SPENCER T. (HERK ROBINSON), professional baseball team executive; b. June 25, 1940; m. Kathy Robinson; children: Ashley, Amanda. Student, U. Miami, Washington U., St. Louis. With Cin. Reds., 1962-67; asst. Baltimore Orioles, 1968; asst. scouting dir. Kansas City Royals, 1969-72, dir. stadium ops., 1973-74, v.p., 1975-85, exec. v.p. adminstrn., 1985-90, v.p., 1975-85, exec. v.p., gen. mgr., 1990—, former mem. bd. dirs. Office: Kans City Royals PO Box 419969 Kansas City MO 64141-6969*

ROBINSON, SUMNER MARTIN, college administrator; b. Boston, Dec. 7, 1928; s. Eli and Fannie (Solov) R.; m. Leanore Reiss, Dec. 20, 1953; children: Andrew, Eric, Evan. A.B., U. Maine, 1949; B.S., Mass. Coll. Pharmacy, 1954, M.S., 1956, Ph.D., 1961. Asst. prof. pharmacology Mass. Coll. Pharmacy, Boston, 1961-65; research biologist-pharmacologist U.S. Army Research Inst. Environ. Medicine, Natick, Mass., 1965-76, cons., 1976—; dean Mass. Coll. Pharmacy, Boston, 1976-83; pres. St. Louis Coll. Pharmacy, 1983-93, Mass. Coll. Pharmacy & Applied Health Sci., Boston, 1993—. Recipient Coll. medal Mass. Coll. Pharmacy, 1983. Mem. Am. Assn. Colls. Pharmacy, Am. Pharm. Assn., Nat. Assn. Retail Druggists. Democrat. Home: 59 Whitewood Rd Westwood MA 02090-2146 Office: Mass Coll Pharmacy & Allied Health Sci 179 Longwood Ave Boston MA 02115-5804

ROBINSON, TERRY EARL, neuroscience and psychology educator; b. Rochester, N.Y., May 22, 1949; s. Earl Leslie Robinson and Jean (Hanson) Fraser. BA, U. Lethbridge, 1972; MA, U. Sask., 1974; PhD, U. Western Ont., 1978. Postdoctoral fellow U. Calif., Irvine, 1977-78; asst. prof. then assoc. prof. U. Mich., Ann Arbor, 1978-89, prof., 1989—. Editor: Behavioral Approaches to Brain Research, 1983, Microdialysis in the Neurosciences, 1991; editor-in-chief: Behavioral Brain Research, 1996—; contbr. articles to profl. jours. Fellow AAAS, Am. Psychol. Soc. Office: Univ Mich Dept Psychology 525 E University St Ann Arbor MI 48109-1109

ROBINSON, THEODORE CURTIS, JR., lawyer; b. Chgo., Jan. 22, 1916; s. Theodore Curtis and Edna Alice (Willard) R.; m. Marynel Werner, Dec. 28, 1940; children: Theodore Curtis III, Peter S. BA, Western Res. U., 1938, LLB, 1940. Bar: Ohio 1940, U.S. Dist. Ct. (no. dist.) Ohio 1946, U.S. Ct. Appeals (8th cir.) 1948, U.S. Dist. Ct. (we. dist.) Wis. 1950, U.S. Dist. Ct. (we. dist.) N.Y. 1950, U.S. Ct. Appeals (6th cir.) 1950, Ill. 1957, U.S. Dist. Ct. (no. dist.) Ill. 1957, U.S. Ct. Appeals (7th cir.) 1964, U.S. Supreme Ct. 1972. Assoc. Davis & Young, Cleve., 1940; law clk. no. dist. ea. div. U.S. Dist. Ct., Cleve., 1940-42; assoc. Leckie, McCreary, et al, Cleve., 1945-52; ptnr. McCreary, Hinslea & Ray, Cleve., 1953-57, McCreary, Hinslea, Ray & Robinson, Chgo., 1957-90; counsel Ray, Robinson, Hannin & Carle, Chgo., 1990-91, Ray, Robinson, Carle, Davies & Snyder, Chgo., 1991—; mem. exec. com. Maritime Law Assn. of U.S., N.Y.C., 1981-83; pres. Propellor Club of U.S., Chgo., 1966-67; sec., treas. Internat. Shipmasters Assn., Chgo., 1958-91. Lt. USCG, 1943-45. Fellow Am. Coll. Trial Lawyers; mem. ABA, Chgo. Bar Assn. (com. chmn. 1973), Internat. Assn. Def. Counsel, Order of Coif, Traffic Club Chgo. (dir. 1986, 87), Whitehall Club (N.Y.), Nat. Eagle Scout Assn. Republican. Office: Ray Robinson Carle Davies & Snyder 850 W Jackson Blvd Chicago IL 60607-3025

ROBIRDS, ESTEL, state legislator. Mem. Mo. State Ho. of Reps. Dist. 143, 1993—. Home: RR 2 Box 2919 Theodosia MO 65761 Office: Mo Ho of Reps State Capitol Building Jefferson City MO 65101-1556*

ROBISON, BARBARA JANE, tax accountant; b. Bkln., Oct. 17, 1924; d. Matthews and Sara (Birnbaum) Brilliant; m. Morris Moses Robison, Aug. 30, 1945; 1 child, Susan Kay. BS, Ohio State U., 1945; MBA, Xavier U., 1976. CPA. Acct. Antenna Research Lab. Inc., Columbus, Ohio, 1948-51; office mgr. Master Distributors, Inc., Columbus, 1951-57; treas. Antlab Inc., Columbus, 1957-69; tax acct. AccuRay Corp., Columbus, 1969-76, tax mgr., 1976-92; pvt. practice Powell, Ohio, 1992—. Mem. AICPA, Ohio Soc. CPA's, Am. soc. Women Accts. (pres. 1978-79). Home: 1888 Jewett Rd Powell OH 43065-8988 Office: Ohio 04-1-16510 1888 Jewett Rd Powell OH 43065-8988

ROBSON, JUDITH BIROS, state legislator; b. Cleve., Nov. 21, 1939; d. George John and Mary Grace (Millen) Biros; m. Arthur Robson, Sept. 2, 1961; children: Marybeth, Marc, Matthew. BSN, St. John Coll., Cleve., 1961; MS, U. Wis., 1976. RN. Staff nurse Beloit (Wis.) Hosp., 1967-73; nurse practitioner Dr. Ken Gold, Beloit, 1976-78; instr. Blackhawk Tech. Coll., Jonesville, Wis., 1978-87; mem. Wis. Assembly, 1987—. Mem. bd. Bedcore, Beloit, 1990, YWCA, Beloit, 1992; sec. Majority Party Caucus, 1990—. Recipient Clean 16 award Environ. Decade. Office: State Legislature State Capital Box 8953 Madison WI 53708

ROBYN, RICHARD COURTNEY, political scientist; b. St. Louis, Nov. 17, 1949; s. Clarence K. and Mary Ellen (Nash) R.; m. Sylviane Collette Cretenet, Aug. 25, 1980; 1 child, Peggy. BS, U. Tenn., 1972; MA, Ohio U., 1980; postgrad., Kent State U., 1994—. Lectr. Peace Corps, Paknam, Thailand, 1972-74, Songkhla, Thailand, 1974-75; lectr. English Lang. Study Group, Paris, France, 1975-76, U. Besancon, France, 1976-77; dir. internat. student svcs. Ashland (Ohio) Coll., 1980-86; assoc. dean of admissions and dir. off-campus programs Albion (Mich.) Coll., 1986-94; grad. asst. in polit. sci. and internat. rels. Kent (Ohio) State U., 1994—. Contbr. articles to profl. jours. Mem. Nat. Fng. Student Affairs Assn. (grantee 1982), Region VI, Ohio Tesol, Phi Kappa Phi. Home: 3886 Lake Run Blvd Stow OH 44224-4358 Office: Kent State U Ctr for Internat-Comparative Progs 124 Bowman Hall Kent OH 44242

ROCCA, SUE, state legislator; b. May 12, 1949. AS, Ctrl. Mich. Coll. Commr. Macomb County, Mich.; rep. Mich. Dist. 30, 1995—; vice chmn. health policy com. Mich. Ho. Reps., joint com. on adminstrv. rules & regulatory affairs. Office: Office Bd Commrs Macomb County Court Bldg 2nd Fl 40 Gratiot Ct Mount Clemens MI 48043-5719 Address: PO Box 30014 Lansing MI 48909-7514*

ROCHE, MARK WILLIAM, German language educator; b. Weymouth, Mass., Aug. 29, 1956; s. Jason Bernard and Joan (Murphy) R.; m. Barbara Hampshire, June 13, 1981. BA, Williams Coll., 1978; MA, U. Tübingen, Germany, 1980, Princeton (N.J.) U., 1982; PhD, Princeton (N.J.) U., 1984. Asst. prof. German Ohio State U., Columbus, 1984-90, assoc. prof., 1990-96, chair dept. German, 1991-96; prof. German lang. and lit. U. Notre Dame, South Bend, Ind., 1996—. Author: Dynamic Stillness, 1987, Gottfried

Benn's Static Poetry, 1991. Fulbright fellow Germany, 1978-80, Whiting fellow, 1983-84, ACLS fellow, 1985; NEH Summer Stipend grantee, 1991, DAAD Study Visit Rsch. grantee, 1991. Mem. Soc. for Philosophic Study of contemporary Visual Arts (vice pres. 1990-92). Home: 2019 Surrey Dr Blacklick OH 43004-9758 Office: Ohio State U 312 Cunz Hall Columbus OH 43210

ROCHEFORT, JACK LEELAND, engineering executive; b. Bad Axe, Mich., Nov. 20, 1932. Pres. Thumb Tool Engineering Co., Bax Axe, 1952—. Home: 519 W Irwin St Bad Axe MI 48413-1022 Office: Tom Thumb Engring Co 354 Liberty St Bad Axe MI 48413-9302

ROCHELLE, ROBERT EDWIN, product manager; b. Albany, N.Y., Apr. 1, 1957; s. Robert & Gene R.; married Amy Brandt, June 18, 1983; children: Eric, Ryan. B, Va. Tech., 1979, M, 1983. Project engr. Hussmann Corp., Elgin, Ill., 1988-90; engring. mgr. Prototype Equipment, Lake Forest, Ill., 1990-93; project mgr. Elopak Inc., New Hudson, Mich., 1993—; stds. com. BISSC, Elgin, 1988-90. Patentee in field. Office: Elopak Inc PO Box S 30000 S Hill Rd New Hudson MI 48165-0247

ROCHEN, DONALD MICHAEL, osteopathic physician; b. Buffalo, Apr. 15, 1943; s. Leo Kant and Phoebe (Elkan) R.; m. Phyllis Helene Been, Aug. 15, 1971; children: Steven, Douglas, Deborah, Andrew. B.A., Northwestern U., 1964; D.O., Coll. Osteo. Medicine and Surgery, Des Moines, 1968. Intern, Detroit Osteo./Bi County Cmty. Hosps., 1968-69, resident in otorhinolaryngology, 1969-73; practice otorhinolaryngology otolaryngic allergy oro-facial plastic surgery, Madison Heights, Warren, Farmington Hills and Mt. Clemens, Mich., 1973—; program dir. residency and chmn. dept. otolaryngology and orofacial plastic surgery Bi County Cmty. Hosp., Warren, Mich.; past chmn. dept. otolaryngology Mt. Clemens Gen. Hosp.; mem. staff Mt. Clemens Gen. Hosp. (Mich.), Oakland Gen. Hosp., Botsford Gen. Hosp., Bi County Community Hosp.; assoc. prof. Mich. State U. Coll. Osteo. Medicine and Surgery, 1975—; adj. prof. Coll. Osteo. Medicine and Surgery, Des Moines, 1981—. Fellow Osteo. Coll. Ophthalmology and Otorhinolaryngology (diplomate), Am. Acad. Otolaryngology, Head and Neck Surgery, Am. Acad. Otolaryngic Allergy; mem. Am. Osteo. Assn., Mich. Assn. Osteo. Physicians and Surgeons, Am. Acad. Otolaryngic Allergy, N.Y. Acad. Scis., Mich. Otolaryngol. Soc., Oakland County Osteo. Assn., Macomb County Osteo. Assn. Home: 4808 Tyndale Ct West Bloomfield MI 48323-3351 Office: 27483 Dequindre Rd Madison Heights MI 48071-3491

ROCK, RICHARD RAND, lawyer, former state senator; b. Wichita Falls, Tex., Sept. 27, 1924; s. Parker Francis and Ruth Ann (Phillips) R.; m. Rosalee Deardorff, Aug. 23, 1947; children: Richard R. II, Darci Lee, Devon Ray, Robert Regan. BA, Washburn U., 1948, LLB, 1950, JD, 1970. Bar: Kans., U.S. Dist. Ct. Kans., U.S. Ct. Appeals (4th and 10th cirs.). Dir. indsl. rels. Maurer-Neuer Packers, Arkansas City, Kans., 1950-52, plant supt., 1952-54; atty. Rock, Smith & Mason, Arkansas City, Kans., 1955-95; pres., owner Shreveport (La.) Packing Co., 1972-83, Amarillo (Tex.) Beef Processors, 1977-82, Lubbock (Tex.) Beef Processors, 1978-81, Montgomery (Ala.) Food Processors, 1978-91, Humboldt (Iowa) Sausage Co., 1985-92, Great Bend (Kans.) Packing Co., 1984-95; state senator, asst. minority leader State of Kans., 1988—; chmn. bd. dirs. Rockgate Mgmt. Co., Overland Park, Kans. Judge Cowley County, Kans., 1952-56; state rep. State of Kans., 1957-61; authority mem. Kans. Turnpike Authority, 1980-83, chmn., 1993—; commr. Children with Spl. Health Care Needs, Kans., 1993-95. Served USN Air Corps, 1943-45. Mem. Kans. Bar Assn., Nat. Counsel State Legislatures, Kans. C. of C., VFW. Democrat. Mem. Disciples of Christ.

ROCKEY, DAWN E., state treasurer; b. Des Moines, Nov. 12, 1961; m. Brian Rockey. BA, U. Nebr. Formerly rsch. technician MX Missile Planning Project Gov.'s Policy Rsch. Office; legis. aide to sen. Jerry Miller, adminstrv. asst. to sen. Ron Withem; state treas. State of Nebr., 1991—. Mem. Nat. Mgmt. Assn., nat. Assn. State Treas. (Midwest regional v.p. 1993—), Assn. Govt. Accts., Nebr. Assn. Pub. Employees, Women Execs. in State Govt., Nat. Assn. Auditors, Comptrollers and Treas. Office: State Treas PO Box 94788 Lincoln NE 68509-4788*

RODDAN, RAY GENE, chiropractor; b. Springfield, S.D., Dec. 9, 1947; s. Glendon William and Marvel Grace (Brown) R.; m. Sheleth Lee, June 1, 1969; children—Erik, Kelene, Daniel. Student Oholone Coll., 1968-71, U. S.D., 1966-68, U. Calif., 1971-74; Dr. Chiropractic Medicine, Palmer Coll. of Chiropractic, 1978. Material control mgr. Guardian Packaging Corp., Newark, Calif., 1968-75; mid-states sales mgr. Agridustrial Electronic Co., Davenport, Iowa, 1975-78; gen. practice chiropractic medicine, Green Bay, Wis., 1978—; pres., clinic dir. J&R Chiropractic Office, S.C., Green Bay, 1978-85, ProCare Chiropractic Clinic, Ltd., Green Bay, Howard, Denmark, Milw. and Pulaski, 1985—; pres. ProCare Mgmt. Corp., 1995—, Talon Enterprises, 1995—; indsl. cons.; software developer Healthcare Office Mgmt. Active Green Bay Cmty. Ch. Mem. Profl. Chiropractic Soc. Am. (Chiropractor of Yr. 1983), Am. Chiropractic Assn., Wis. Chiropractic Assn., Christian Chiropractic Assn., Green Bay C. of C., Fellowship Cos. for Christ, Internat. Acad. Chiropractic Cons., Christian Athletes Outreach, Pi Tau Delta. Republican. Clubs: Businessmen's (Green Bay) (v.p. 1979-80). Home: 1414 Longtail Beach Rd Suamico WI 54173

RODEEN, JOHN K., business executive; b. Sioux City, Iowa, Mar. 13, 1937. BS in Sociology, Westmar Coll., 1960; BSBA, U. Iowa, 1960. Pub. rels. dir. Marion Health Ctr., Sioux City, 1975-85; pres. Storm Lake (Iowa) Indsl. Corp., 1985—. Home: Storm Lake Indsl Corp PO Box 224 Storm Lake IA 50588-0224

RODEMAN, FREDERICK ERNEST, accountant; b. Chgo., Jan. 29, 1938; s. Ernest August and Elizabeth Mae (Penrod) R.; m. Marilyn Kay Paul, June 17, 1967. BBA, Ind. U., 1959; cert. bank controllership, U. Wis., 1975; MBA, De Paul U., 1976. CPA, Ind., Wis. Auditor Arthur Andersen & Co., Chgo., 1959-67; acct. mgr. A.B. Dick & Co., Chgo., 1967-72; controller Beloit (Wis.) State Bank, 1972-77; pvt. practice acctg. Beloit, 1977—. Mem. Am. Inst. CPA's. Republican. Baptist. Home and Office: 2372 Tara Ct Beloit WI 53511-1938

RODENBERG-ROBERTS, MARY PATRICIA, advocacy services administrator; b. New Ulm, Minn., July 13, 1963; d. Richard Theodore and Patricia Rae (Malone) Rodenberg; m. Richard Lee Roberts, Oct. 28, 1989; 5 children. BS in Corrections, Law Enforcement, Mankato State U., 1985; JD, Hamline U., 1989. Bar: Wis. 1991. Shift supr. Reentry Svcs., Inc., St. Paul, 1986-87; coord. REM Lyndale, Inc., Mpls., 1987-89; dir. advocacy REM Minn., Inc., Edina, 1989—; case mgr. REM Consulting and Svcs., Edina, 1991—. Mem. ABA, Am. Assn. Mental Retardation, Coalition on Sexuality and Disability, Minn. Social Svcs. Assn., Wis. Bar Assn., Assn. Residential Resources Minn. Republican. Lutheran.

RODENBURG, CLIFTON GLENN, lawyer; b. Jamestown, N.D., Apr. 5, 1949; s. Clarence and Dorothy Irene (Peterman) R.; m. Donna Michele Stockman, Mar. 1, 1980. B.S., N.D. State U., 1971; J.D., U. N.D., 1974; M.L.I.R., Mich. State U., 1976. Bar: N.D. 1974, U.S. Dist. Ct. (N.D.) 1974, U.S. Ct. Appeals (8th cir.) 1974, Minn. 1980, U.S. Supreme Ct. 1980, S.D. 1983, Nebr. 1984, U.S. Dist. Ct. (Minn.) 1984, U.S. Dist. Ct. (Nebr.) 1984, Wis. 1985, U.S. Dist. Ct. Wis. 1985, Mont. 1986, U.S. Dist. Ct. (Mont.) 1986. Ptnr., Johnson & Rodenburg, Fargo, N.D., 1976—; pres., gen. counsel Rodenburg Group, Inc., Fargo, 1980—. Contbg. editor: The Developing Labor Law, 1976-80; drafter N.D. garnishment statutes, 1982. Mem. Acad. Comml. and Bankruptcy Law Specialists.

RODENKIRK, ROBERT FRANCIS, JR., journalist; b. Evanston, Ill., Apr. 28, 1952; s. Robert Francis and Joan Marie (Wolter) R. BA in History and Journalism, Ind. U., 1974; postgrad., Northwestern U., 1976. Program dir., pub. affairs dir. WIUS Radio, Bloomington, Ind., 1972-74; reporter City News Bur. of Chgo., 1974-77; news dir. WNUR Radio, Evanston, Ill., 1977; announcer WDHF Radio, Chgo., 1977; news dir. WMET Radio, Chgo., 1977-78; Chgo. corr. AP Radio Network, 1978-79; reporter, anchor WINS Radio, N.Y.C., 1984-88, WMAQ Radio, Chgo., 1979-84, 88—. Recipient Nat. Broadcast awards UPI, 1979, 81, 83, 90, Nat. award Sigma Delta Chi, 1996, others. Mem. Ill. News Broadcasters Assn. (bd. dirs. 1988—, v.p. 1994-96, pres. 1996—), Soc. Profl. Journalists, Radio-TV News Dirs. Assn., Chgo. Headline Club (bd. dirs. 1993—, pres.-elect 1995-96, pres. 1996—, Peter Lisagor award 1988, 96), Branford Electric Ry. Assn., Ill. Ry. Mus., Fox River Trolley Mus. (publicity dir.). Roman Catholic. Office: WMAQ Radio News 455 N Cityfront Plaza Dr Chicago IL 60611-5503

RODENSCHMIT, HELEN JULIANA, elementary education educator; b. Cross Plains, Wis., Jan. 8, 1932; d. Frank William and Juliana Helen (Schmelzer) R. BS in Edn., Alverno Coll., 1962; MS in Edn., U. Wis., Whitewater, 1988. Cert. elem. tchr., reading tchr., bilingual tchr., Wis., elem. tchr., Costa Rica; lifetime elem. tchr., N.Y. Tchr. primary St. Bernardine Sch., Forest Pk., Ill., 1951-58, St. Cyprian Sch., River Grove, Ill., 1958-59; tchr. elem. St. Monical Sch., N.Y.C., 1959-64, Holy Spirit Sch., Milw., 1964-66, St. Joseph Sch., Phlox, Wis., 1966-67; tchr. sci. and art St. Clare Collegio, Moravia, Costa Rica, 1968; tchr. elem. St. Joseph Primary, Moravia, Costa Rica, 1969-80; tchr. Kindergarten St. Francis Colegio, Moravia, Costa Rica, 1981-84; elem. libr. Lincoln Colegio, Moravia, Costa Rica, 1985-86; tchr. migrant and bilingual Marshall (Wis.) Pub. Sch., 1988-94; ESL tchr. Westside Elem. Sch., Sun Prairie, Wis., 1994-95, Mauston (Wis.) Elem. Sch., 1995—; rsch. project tchr. U. Minn., 1964-66; tchr. tng. ESL, St. Joseph Pirmary, St. Francis Colegio, Moravia, Costa Rica, elem. coord. ESL, 1981-84; home tutor, Costa Rica, 1975-86. Mem. St. Vincent DePaul Project, Barrio Corazon de Jesus, Moravia, Costa Rica, 1970-73. Mem. Assn. Childhood Internat., Tchrs. English as Second Lang., Nat. Assn. Bilingual Edn., Sch. Sisters of St. Francis. Home: 4517 County Trunk Hwy P Cross Plains WI 53528

RODERICK, WILLIAM RODNEY, academic administrator; b. Chgo., Aug. 6, 1933; s. William Forrest and June Hazel (Kurtz) R.; m. Dorothy Jean Paetel, Oct. 21, 1965. BS in Chemistry, Northwestern U., 1954; SM in Chemistry, U. Chgo., 1955, PhD in Chemistry, 1957. Prof. chemistry U. Fla., Gainesville, 1958-62; rsch. chemist Abbott Labs., North Chicago, Ill., 1962-71; prof. chemistry Roosevelt U., Chgo., 1972—; assoc. dean acad. affairs Roosevelt U., Arlington Heights, Ill., 1993—. Mem. AAAS, Am. Chem. Soc. (Tour Speaker of Yr. award 1969, 71), Sigma Xi, Phi Beta Kappa. Home: 15193 W Redwood Ln Libertyville IL 60048-1447 Office: Roosevelt U 1651 McConnor Pkwy Schaumburg IL 60173-4344

RODEWALD, JAMES MICHAEL, real estate company executive; b. Waco, Tex., Apr. 20, 1942; s. Howard Fred and Dorothy Mae (Faust) R.; m. Evelynn Brown, Dec. 19, 1965; children—Kara Lynn, Kevin James. BA, William Jewell Coll., 1964; MA, U. Wis., 1967; postgrad. Central Mo. U., 1970. Lic. real estate broker, Mo., Kans. Vol., Peace Corps, Malawi, Cen. Africa, 1967-68; property mgr. William C. Haas Co., Kansas City, Mo., 1970-72; exec. v.p., co-owner Roger L. Cohen Co., Kansas, City, 1972-81; pres. James M. Rodewald Co., Kansas City, 1981-86; pres. Investment Realty Advisors, Inc.; project ptnr. Elsenberg Co., 1986-91; sr. v.p. Cohen-Esrey Co., Kansas City, Mo., 1991-92; pres. James M. Rodewald Co., 1992—. Mem. Nat. Rep. Com.; mem. pres.'s adv. coun. William Jewell Coll.; bd. dirs. Downtown Inc., Kansas City. With U.S. Army, 1968-70, Vietnam. GM scholar, 1960-64; Phi Gamma Delta scholar, 1965. Mem. Kansas City Real Estate Bd. (Comml. Realtor Assoc. of Yr.), Urban Land Inst., Nat. Assn. Office and Indsl. Parks, Real Estate Syndication Inst., Nat. Assn. Realtors, Mo. Assn. Realtors. Republican. Presbyterian. Club: Carriage. Home: 6516 State Line Rd Mission Hills KS 66208-1948 Office: 3550 Rainbow Blvd Kansas City KS 66103

RODGERS, JOHNATHAN, broadcast executive; b. San Antonio, Jan. 18, 1946; s. Marion Alford and Barbara (Merriwether) R.; m. Royal Graves Kennedy, Sept. 27, 1976; children: David, Jamie. BA, U. Calif., Berkeley, 1967; MA, Stanford U., 1972; PhD (hon.), Columbia Coll., Chgo., 1991. Writer-reporter Sports Illustrated, N.Y.C., 1966-68; assoc. editor Newsweek, N.Y.C., 1968-72; producer WNBC-TV, N.Y.C., 1972-73; reporter WKYC-TV (NBC), Cleve., 1973-74; sta. mgr., news dir. KCBS-TV, L.A., 1978-83; exec. producer CBS News, N.Y.C., 1983-86; v.p., gen. mgr. WBBM-TV (CBS), Chgo., 1986-90; pres. CBS TV Stas., Chgo., 1990—. Bd. dirs. Jr. Achievement, Chgo., Sickle Cell Anemia Found., Chgo., 1986-90, Harold Washington Found., Chgo., 1988-90; advisor Make-A-Wish Found., Chgo. With U.S. Army, 1969-71, Korea. mem. Nat. Assn. Black Journalists. Home: 843 W Chalmers Pl Chicago IL 60614-3233 Office: CBS-TV 630 N Mcclurg Ct Chicago IL 60611-3007

RODGERS, LOUIS DEAN, surgeon; b. Centerville, Iowa, Nov. 24, 1930; s. John James and Anna Alice (Spraguer) R.; m. Gretchen Lynn Hendershot, Feb. 19, 1954; children—Cynthia Ann, Elizabeth Dee. M.D., U. Iowa, 1960. Diplomate Am. Bd. Surgery. Intern, Broadlawns Hosp., Iowa, 1960-61; resident Meth-Hosp., Des Moines, 1961-65; practice medicine specializing in gen. surgery, Des Moines, 1965—; chmn. dept. surgery Iowa Methodist Ctr., Des Moines, 1980-84, chief gen. surgery, 1982—; clin. assoc. prof. surgery U. Iowa, Iowa City, 1983—. Mem. steering com. Gov.'s Campaign, Republican Party, Iowa, 1982; bd. dirs. Iowa Meth. Med. Found., Des Moines, 1983, Des Moines Symphony, 1984—, Des Moines Children's Home, 1987. Served to staff sgt. U.S. Army, 1951-54. Named Surg. Tchr. of Yr., Iowa Meth. Med. Ctr. Dept. Surgery, 1978, 84. Fellow ACS (liaison to cancer com. 1973); mem. Western Surg. Assn. (mem. Iowa trauma com. 1983), Iowa Acad. Surgery (pres. 1982-83), Throckmorton Surg. Soc. (pres. 1986). Republican. Club: Des Moines Golf and Country. Home: 715 53rd St Des Moines IA 50312-1820 Office: Surgery PC 715 53rd St Des Moines IA 50312

RODGERS, ROBERT ALLEN, computer company executive, consultant; b. Montgomery, W.Va., Aug. 7, 1939; s. Boyd Benton and Mary Frances (Elliot) R.; m. Rhonda Lee Music, June 5, 1960 (dec. Nov. 1992); children: Tammy Sue, Tina Ann, Toni Lynn, Terry Allen; m. Bonne Holcomb Dickens, Oct. 14, 1994; stepchildren: Cathy Linda. Teresa Lynn, Ronald Edward. AB in Secondary Edn., Glenville State Coll., 1962; MS, Va. Commonwealth U., 1974; postgrad., Del Tech, 1989-91; grad., Profl. Career Inst., 1995. Head math dept. Queen Anne County Dept. Edn., Suddlersville, Md., 1962-63; surveyor Nuttel Co., Chestertown, Md., 1963; spl. edn. tchr. Del. State Hosp., Farnhurst, 1963-65; counselor, rehab. counselor, then sr. rehab. counselor Del. Div. Vocat. Rehab., Wilmington, 1965-87, rehab. engr., 1987-91; v.p., gen. mgr. R&T Enterprises, Unltd., Wilmington, 1991-94; computer cons., technician, owner Aardvark Industries, Wellston, Ohio, 1994—; cons. in living with cancer Wilmington Med. Ctr., Wilmington VA Hosp., 1977-82; rehab. cons. to Del. Curative Workshop, Wilmington, 1982-87; honorarium lectr., spkr. on epilepsy and cancer Coppin State Coll., Balt., 1978-79; frequent spkr. on Native Am. culture, rock and mineral collecting and gem stone collecting Jackson County Schs.; frequent lectr., presenter seminars U. Del. Grad. Nursing Sch., Lincoln U. Grad. Sch. Vocat. Rehab. Counseling. Designer devices for disabled persons. Active Boy Scouts Am., 1947—; apptd. emergency coord., Jackson County, 1995; coord. radio comm. for Ohilco parade and other county activities. Recipient Award of Merit Lenape Dist. Boy Scouts Am., Newark, Del., 1986, numerous awards for youth svcs.; named Man of the Yr. Am. Biog. Inst., 1991. Mem. NEA, NRA (life), Md. Tchrs. Assn., Nat. Rehab. Assn. (region 3 sec. 1969-71), Del. Rehab. Assn., First State Rehab. Counselors Assn. (co-founder, pres. 1972), Am. Radio Relay League, N.Am. Hunting Assn. (life), N.Am. Fishing Assn. (life), Airplane Pilot and Owners Assn., First State Amateur Radio Club (pres. 1994), Jackson County Amateur Radio Club (pres 1996—), Kiwanis, Moose. Baptist. Office: 120 Twin Oaks Dr Jackson OH 45640

RODMAN, DAVID LAWRENCE, investment counselor; b. Alliance, Ohio, Sept. 5, 1956; s. James Purcell and Margaret (Kinsey) R.; m. Sandra Moyer, June 19, 1982; children: Molly Elizabeth, Sam. BA cum laude, Mt. Union Coll., 1979; MBA, Washington U., St. Louis, 1981. Mgmt. trainee United Nat. Bank & Trust Co., Canton, Ohio, 1982; investment broker, fin. planner Butler Wick & Co., Inc., Alliance, 1982-88; investment counselor Rodman Capital Mgmt., Alliance, 1988—. Investment counsel, mem. First Presbyn. Ch., Alliance, 1984—. Mem. Assn. for Investment Mgmt. and Rsch., Cleve. Soc. Security Analysts, Alliance Rotary. Republican. Home: 643 Vincent Blvd Alliance OH 44601-3955 Office: Rodman Capital Mgmt 1630 S Union Ave Alliance OH 44601-4349

RODNE, KJELL JOHN, healthcare administrator; b. Haugesund, Norway, July 6, 1948; came to U.S., 1959; s. Johannes and Margit (Gautun) R.; m. Kathleen Anne Gordon, Sept. 21, 1966; children: Jay Robert, Lee Eric. BS, U. Minn., Duluth, 1971, MSW, 1985; cert. Univ. Assoc. Human Resources program, 1995; PMA sci. of success diploma, 1996, personal computer tng. program diploma, 1996. Asst. youth dir. YMCA, Duluth, 1967-68; counselor Northwood, Duluth, 1968-71, team leader, 1971-76, social worker, 1976-77, program dir., 1977-85; pers. dir. City of Duluth, 1985-86, adminstrv. asst. City of Duluth, 1986-92; mgmt. cons., 1992-93; adminstr. Northwood West, 1993-95, dir. quality assurance, 1995—; bd. dirs. Minn. Coun. Residential Treatment Ctrs., St. Paul, 1977-85, 93—. Mem. Duluth City Coun., 1978-85, pres., 1981; bd. dirs. United Devel. Achievement Ctr., Duluth, 1978-85, Arrowhead Regional Devel. Commn., Duluth, 1981-85, United Way of Duluth, 1981-89, Duluth Econ. Devel. Authority, 1989-92, Arrowhead Growth Alliance, 1990-92, Northspan, 1991-92. Mem. Lake Superior Assn. Labor Mgmt. (bd. dirs. 1989-92), Internat. City Mgrs. Assn. (pub. policy com. 1991—), Nat. Assn. Homes for Children. Democrat. Lutheran. Home: 1731 Kenwood Ave Duluth MN 55811

RODNITZKY, DONNA JOY, author; b. Chgo., Dec. 10, 1943; d. Leo Clarence and Dorothy (Gottlieb) Pliner; m. Robert Lee Rodnitzky, May 14, 1967; children: David, Adam, Laura. BA with honors, U. Iowa, 1970. Owner DJR Catering, Iowa City, Iowa, 1986-91. Author: The Prune Gourmet, 1990, 101 Great Lowfat Desserts, 1995 (Book Club selection 1995), The Lowfat Grill, 1996 (Book Club selection 1996). Chair Project Green, Iowa City, 1980-90. Mem. Mortar Board, Pi Lambda Theta. Home: 303 Lexington Ave Iowa City IA 52246

RODOS, JOSEPH JERRY, osteopathic physician, educator; b. Phila., July 7, 1933; s. Harry and Lisa (Perlman) R.; m. Bobbi Golden, Apr. 6, 1957; (div. 1974); m. Joyce L. Pennington, Sept. 26, 1981; children: Adam Justin, Nicole Ann. BS, Franklin & Marshall Coll., 1955; DO, Kirksville Coll. Medicine, Mo., 1959; DSc Pub. Health, Somerset Univ., 1993. Diplomate Am. Bd. Family Medicine, Am. Bd. Osteo, Am. Osteo. Bd. Pub., Health and Preventive Medicine, Bd. Neuro Psychiatry, Am. Bd. of Pain Mgmt, Am. Bd. Correctional Health Care, Am. Bd. Forensic Medicine. NIMH fellow in psychiatry, Brown U./Butler Hos., Providence, 1966-68; intern Grandview Hosp., Dayton, Ohio, 1959-60; gen. practice medicine, Cranston, R.I., 1960-78; exec. sec. R.I. Soc. Osteo. P/S, Cranston, 1960-78; assoc. exec. dir. Am. Osteo. Assn., 1978-79; dean New Eng. Coll. Osteo. Medicine, Biddleford, Maine, 1979-82; acting dean Chgo. Coll. Osteo. Medicine, 1982-88; spec. asst. to pres. Chgo. Osteop. Health Systems, 1987-95; chair dept. psychiatry Midwestern U.; prof. family medicine and psychiatry; adj. prof. U. Ill. Sch. Medicine; cons. to dir. Nat. Health Svc. Corps HHS; Disting. Practitioner Nat. Acad. Practitioners, 1990; fellow Inst. of Medicine, Chgo., 1990; clin. dir. Dept. Mental Health, Providence, R.I., 1973-78; med. dir. Dept. Corrections, Providence, 1976-78; sr. cons. medicine Pub. Sector Cons., Lansing, Mich., 1980—; prin. Health Cons. Rhodes Group, 1989—; lectr. in field. Editor, Jour. Osteo. Annals, 1982. Bd. dirs. Cranston Red Cross, R.I. Camps, Inc., Dial Dictation, Inc., Cranston Mental Health Clinic; mem. Internat. Platform Assn., ACLU; lectr. Premarital Confs., Catholic Diocese Providence. Fellow Am. Coll. Gen. Practice, Acad. Psychosomatic Medicine, Royal Soc. Health; mem. Am. Assn. Osteo. Specialists (cert.), Am. Coll. Osteo. and Obstetrics and Gynecology, Acad. Clin. and Exptl. Hypnosis. Avocations: breeding, showing Saint Bernards and Scottish Terriers. Licenced Am. Kennel Club judge. Home: 5204 Lawn Ave Western Springs IL 60558-1844 Office: Chgo Coll Osteopathic Medicine 5200 S Ellis Ave Chicago IL 60615-4314

RODRIGUES, DANIEL A., electronics company executive; b. Waterbury, Conn., Aug. 30, 1955; s. Frank and Phyllis (Amador) R.; m. Dolores Ann Elam, Nov. 25, 1978; children: Amy, Rebecca. BS in Aeronautics, Parks Coll. of St. Louis U., 1977. cert. cost estimator. Various cost estimating pos. E&S Corp., St. Louis, 1977-87, mgr. cost acctg., 1987-88, dir. cost control, 1988-90, asst. v.p. contracts, 1980-94, v.p. program mgmt. & contracts, 1990-94, v.p. program adminstrn., 1995—. Mem. Nat. Estimating Soc. (v.p.). Roman Catholic. Home: 766 Seven Hills Ln Saint Charles MO 63304

RODRIGUES-PAVAO, ANTONIO, vocal music teacher; b. Fall River, Mass., Dec. 13, 1943; s. Joseph Rodrigues and Maria Teresa (Braga) Pavao; children: Aaron, Stephen; m. Nora Macins, July 7, 1984. BMusic, U. Mass., 1970, MMusic, 1970; MMusic, U. Ill., 1974. Cert. secondary music tchr., Mass., Ill., Wis. Vocal music tchr. William Horlick H.S., Racine, Wis., 1977—; voice tchr. self-employed; artistic dir. Elizabethan High Renaissance Feaste, Racine, 1977—. Composer various choral pieces, pieces for voice and piano; bass-baritone solo profl. performances; dir. numerous profl. and amateur musicals; dir. choirs touring U.K., Denmark, Czech Republic, Austria, Slovakia. Served with USAF, 1961-65. Mem. Nat. Assn. Tchrs. of Singing (chpt. corr. sec. 1992—), Am. Choral Dirs. Assn. Home: 1239 N Osborne Blvd Racine WI 53405

RODRIGUEZ, JILL HOLOPIGIAN, library director; b. Hackensack, N.J., Apr. 26, 1952; d. Chares Nubar and Anita (Rosenthal) Holopigian; m. Russ A. Rodriguez, Sept 1, 1985; children: Maxxwel, Tylar, Carsyn. BA, St. Lawrence U., 1974; MLS, Rutgers U., 1977. Cmty. svc. libr. Bensenville (Ill.) Pub. Libr., 1977-80, asst. dir., 1980-81, dir., 1981—; adv. com. Ill. State Libr., Springfield, 1992—, DuPage Libr. Sys., Geneva, Ill., 1993—; presenter nat. confs. Lifelong Learning, Am. Libr. Assn. Chairperson Bensenville Youth Svcs. Coalition., 1979—, Bensenville Hist. Commn., 1986—; exec. bd. Bensenville Intergovtl. Group, 1988—; treas. Bensenville Hist. Soc., 1991—; bd. dirs. Bensenville 2000 Edn. Coalition Found., 1992—. Recipient Hometown award, Ill. 2000 award State of Ill., 1986, New Am. Sch. award New Am. Sch. Devel. Corp., 1986, Millennium Svc. award DuPage Libr. Sys., 1995. Mem. Am. Libr. Assn., Ill. Lib. Assn., Pub. Libr. Assn., Bensenville C. of C. Office: Bensenville Pub Libr 200 S Church Rd Bensenville IL 60106

ROE, ROBERT A., state legislator; b. Hayti, S.D., Mar. 3, 1954. BS, S.D. State U., 1976; postgrad., Northwestern U., 1979. Mem. S.D. Ho. of Reps., mem. judiciary and state affairs coms.; stockbroker Piper, Jeffrey & Hopwood, 1984—. Home: 1820 Skyview Ln Brookings SD 57006-3535*

ROEDER, GEORGE HOLZSHU, history educator, writer; b. Balt., Jan. 22, 1944; s. George Holzshu Sr. and Dorothy Virginia (Elmer) R.; m. Virginia Eleanor Ormsby, Aug. 23, 1963 (div. Sept. 26, 1989); children: Rebecca Virginia, George Holzshu III, Ethan Virgil Ormsby; m. Marie Gabrielle Basso, Oct. 28, 1989. BA, U. Md., 1965, MA, 1972; PhD, U. Wis., 1977. With Md. Book Exch., College Park, Md., 1962-68; rsch. assoc. State Hist. Soc. Wis., Madison, Wis., 1968-77; from asst. prof. to prof. liberal arts Sch. of the Art Inst., Chgo., 1981—, chair Undergrad. divsn., 1993—; lectr. in history Northwestern U., Evanston, Ill., 1981—; mem. adv. bd. Annenberg/Corp. for Pub. Broadcasting World of Art Project, Portland, 1994—; mem. selection com. Corp. for Pub. Broadcasting Annenberg Project, Washington, 1988, 94, NEH, 1985-87, 95; vis. asst. prof. history U. Mo., Columbia, 1977-79, Northwestern U., Evanston, Ill., 1979-81; prin. hist. cons. for filmstrip on Vietnam that won gold medal Internat. Film and Video Festival of N.Y., 1986 and for video on WWII that won 2d pl. award, 1986; appeared on CNN, Chgo. Pub. TV, and various radio programs to discuss visual presentation of war, 1991-95; keynote spkr. 10th Ann. Margaret Demorest Humanities Festival, Casper (Wyo.) Coll., 1995; lectr. Royal

Coll. Art, London, 1993; presenter Baxter Gallery, Maine Sch. of Art, 1992, Northwestern U., 1989, Stanford U., 1988, U. Mich., 1988, Smithsonian Instn./Wilson Ctr., 1987, U. Göttingen, 1985, State Hist. Soc. Wis., 1985, Chgo. Hist. Soc., 1985, among others, Am. Hist. Assn., Orgn. Am. Historians, Am. Popular Cultural Assn., and other profl. orgns.; participant Coun. for Internat. Ednl. Exch. faculty seminar, Univs. of Ho Chi Minh City and Hanoi, Vietnam, 1991. Author: Forum of Uncertainty, 1981, The Censored War, 1993; contbr. articles to profl. jours. and encys. Fellow NEH, 1987-88; grantee NEH, 1982. Mem. Orgn. Am. Historians, Am. Hist. Assn. Episcopalian. Office: Sch Art Inst Chgo 37 S Wabash Chicago IL 60603

ROEDER, REBECCA EMILY, software engineer; b. Findlay, Ohio, Nov. 2, 1959; d. Brian Eldon and Barbara Lee (Melton) R.; m. Stephen William Bigley, May 28, 1983. BS in Edn. and Computer Sci., Bowling Green State U., 1983, MS in Computer Sci., 1993. Systems analyst NCR Corp., Dayton, Ohio, 1983-84; sr. systems analyst Unisys (Burroughs) Corp., Detroit, 1984-88; asst. dir. St. Vincent Med. Ctr., Toledo, 1988-95; sr. cons. Advanced Programming Resources, Inc., Columbus, Ohio, 1996—. Active Sta. WGTE/WGLE Pub. Radio, Toledo, 1984-96, Sta. WOSU Pub. Radio, Columbus, 1996—, Sta. WCBE Pub. Radio, Columbus, 1996—, Toledo Mus. Art, 1988-96, Toledo Zoo, 1993-96; presenter Women in Sci. Career Day, Lourde's Coll., 1992. Marathon scholar Marathon Oil Co., Findlay, 1978, Hancock scholar Findlay Area C. of C., 1978. Mem. AAUW, Assn. for Computing Machinery, Columbus Computer Soc. Republican. Episcopalian. Home: 4964 Vicksburg Ln Hilliard OH 43026 Office: Advanced Programming Resources Inc 2929 Kenny Rd Columbus OH 43221

ROEDERER, SILVIA, concert pianist, educator; b. Buenos Aires, Argentina, Dec. 9, 1958; Came to the U.S., 1967; d. Juan Gualterio and Beatriz Susanna (Cougnet) R.; m. Leslie Thomas Tung, Dec. 23, 1983; children: Nicholas, Monica, Anita. BM, Eastman Sch. Music, Rochester, N.Y., 1980; MM, U. So. Calif., L.A., 1982, DMA, 1987. Asst. lectr. U. So. Calif., L.A., 1980-83; part-time faculty Irvine Valley Coll., Calif., 1985-86, Kalamazoo Coll., Mich., 1987-89; assoc. prof. We. Mich. U., Kalamazoo, 1989—; concert pianist Classical Music Series, Mich., Ill., Calif., Alaska, N.D., S.D., Iowa, Ind., Pa., Ohio, China, Europe, 1982—; music adjudicator Regional Festivals and Competitions, Mich., Ind., 1989—; artistic dir. Kalamazoo Chamber Music Soc., 1989—; lecture-recital presenter Music Tchr. Orgns., Mich., Ohio, 1990—. Author, performer: (lecture-recital) Rythmic Playing as Experienced in Music of Hispanic Composers, 1995; co-author, performer: (lecture-recital) The Enigma in Beethovens F Minor Sonatas, 1995. Co-pres. Parkwyn Neighborhood Assn., Kalamazoo, Mich., 1994-95. Recipient 1st prize and concerto appearance First Coast Piano Competition, Jacksonville, Fla., 1994. Mem. AAUP, Music Tchrs. Nat. Assn., Pi Kappa Lambda. Office: Western Mich U Sch Music Dalton Ctr Kalamazoo MI 49008

ROEHL, KATHLEEN ANN, financial executive; b. Chgo., June 1, 1948; d. Walter Steven and Catherine (Puss) Kalchbrenner; m. Eric C. Roehl, June 28, 1969; children: Aaron C., Marc E. BA with honors, U. Ill., 1969. Registered investment advisor. Tchr. Ft. Huachuca (Ariz.) Accomodation Schs., 1969-70; interior designer Key Kitchens, Dearborn Heights, Mich., 1979-80; stockbroker, fin. cons. Merrill Lynch, Dearborn, Mich., 1980-81; v.p., registered investment advisor Merrill Lynch, Northbrook, Ill., 1982—; bd. dirs. ATA Info. Systems. Mem. Ill. Govt. Fin. Officers Assn., Internat. Assn. for Fin. Planning (bd. dirs. 1987-88), Northbrook C. of C. (bd. dirs. 1991-93), Northbrook Early Risers Rotary (charter mem.). Office: Merrill Lynch 400 Skokie Blvd Northbrook IL 60062-2816

ROEHNER, PHIL G., engineer; b. Milw., Wis., Aug. 13, 1966. BSME, U. Miami, 1991. Engr. Glassfloss Industries, Inc., Millersport, Ohio, 1993—. Republican. Roman Catholic. Office: Glassfloss Industries Inc P O Box 427 Millersport OH 43046-0427

ROELS, SHIRLEY JEAN, academic administrator; b. Kalamazoo, Mich., July 22, 1950; d. Herbert John and Gertrude (Ditmar) Wolthius; m. John Michael Roels, June 10, 1972; children: Daniel, Steven. BA, Calvin Coll., 1971; MBA, U. Mich., 1977; PhD, Mich. State U., 1993. Cert. managerial acct. Inst. Mgmt. Acctg. Dir. instrnl. resources Calvin Coll., Grand Rapids, Mich., 1971-72; career counselor U. Mich., Ann Arbor, 1973-75; from asst. budget dir. to dir. cost analysis U. Detroit, 1977-79; from bus. prof. to dir. degree completion programs Calvin Coll., 1979—. Co-author: Business Through the Eye of Faith, 1990; co-editor: On Moral Business, 1995. Mem. Christian Bus. Faculty Assn. (chair 1985-89). Office: Calvin Coll 3201 Burton St SE Grand Rapids MI 49546

ROEMER, TIMOTHY J., congressman; b. South Bend, Ind., Oct. 30, 1956; m. Sarah Lee Johnston, 1989. BA in pol. sci, U. Calif., San Diego, 1979; MA, PhD in internat. rels., U. Notre Dame, 1986. Staff asst. to congressman John Brademas U.S. Congress; def., trade and fgn. policy advisor to senator Dennis DeConcini; mem. prof. 102nd-103rd Congresses from 3rd Ind. dist., 1991—; mem. economic and ednl. opportunity com., mem. sci. com.; adj. prof. Am. U. Office: 407 Cannon House Office Bu Washington DC 20515 also: 217 N Main St South Bend IN 46601-1216*

ROESCH, MARK ALAN, design engineer; b. Cleve., Aug. 5, 1951. BS in Mech. Engring., Cleve. State U., 1973. Sr. project engr. Automatic Sprinkler, Broadview Heights, Ohio, 1974-93; product design engr. Lamson & Sessions, Cleve., 1993—. Patentee: Electrical Fittings. Mem. Soc. Mfg. Engrs. Office: Lamson & Sessions New Products 25701 Science Park Dr Cleveland OH 44122-7313

ROESCH, ROBERT EUGENE, dentist; b. Falls City, Nebr., July 10, 1951; s. Wilber H. and Vivian (Reese) R.; m. Susan M. Tuttle, Aug. 25, 1973. BA, Midland Luth. Coll., 1973; DDS, U. Nebr., 1976. Pvt. practice dentistry, Fremont, Nebr., 1979—; dental cons. Dodge County Am. Cancer Soc., Fremont, Nebr. 1984—; cons. Nebr. Dental Assn., Dodge County, 1979—, third party dental care com. 1984-88, del., 1991—, dental care com. 1993-95; v.p. region 10 Acad. of Gen. Dentistry, 1990-91, dir., 1991-93, trustee, 1993—, budget & fin. com., 1994—. Campaign chmn. Fremont United Way, 1987, v.p., 1988; pres. Sinai Luth. Ch. Coun., Fremont, 1983-84, bd. dirs. 1987-90; mem. endowment com. Sinai Luth. Ch., 1990-95; bd. dirs. Gannett Found., Ascertainment Com., Fremont, 1981-88, Dodge County Reps., Fremont, 1981-88; bd. dirs. Dodge County Hist. Soc., 1989-92. Fellow Internat. Acad. Dentistry, Internat. Coll. Dentistry; mem. ADA, Acad. Operative Denistry, Nebr. Acad. of Gen. Dentistry (pub. info. officer 1983-85, sec., treas. 1985-88, pres. elect 1988-89, pres. 1990-92, exec. dir. 1992-94, continuing edn. chmn., 1994—), Am. Orthodontic Soc., Am. Assn. Functional Orthodontists, Am. Equilibration Soc., Omaha Dist. Dental Soc. (bd. dirs., pres.-elect 1996—), Salmon Soc., Dodge County Hist. Soc., Midland Coll. Alumni (bd. dirs. 1981-87, pres. 1983-84), Fremont Wellness Coun. (bd. dirs. 1996—), Fremont C. of C. (diplomat 1985-94, bd. dirs. 1991-94, vice-chmn. memberships and membership svcs. 1989-90, vice-chmn. pub. affairs 1992-94), Optimists (bd. dirs. 1981-83, 84-88, pres. 1987, bd. dirs. Fremont club 1991-93), Fremont Indsl. Found., Main St. Fremont (org. com. 1995—), Main St. Ambs. (co-chmn. 1996—), Fremont Tennis Assn., Am. Legion, Fremont Community Players, Midland Luth. Coll. Boosters Club (bd. dirs. 1988-94), Tri Valley Dental Study Club (sec.-treas. 1983, v.p. 1984, pres. 1985, v.p. 1989), Ak-Sar-Ben Dental Study Club. Republican. Avocations: tennis, racquetball, traveling. Home: 750 N Clarkson St Fremont NE 68025-5172 Office: 553 N Broad St Fremont NE 68025-4930

ROESSLER, DAVID A., manufacturing executive; b. Eauclaire, Wis., July 23, 1949. Product devel. engr. Trico mfg., Pewaukee, Wis., 1973-94; with Bryant Products, Oconomowoc, Wis., 1994—. Patentee: Micro Dispensing Tool and Die, 1990, 93. Office: Bryant Products 300 Chaffee Rd Oconomowoc WI 53066-2678

ROGALA, RICHARD EDWARD, psychologist; b. Chgo., Mar. 15, 1937. BA, DePaul U., 1959, MS, 1963; PhD in Psychology, Ill. Inst. of Tech., 1968. Cert. psychologist, Ill. Pres. Rogala & Assocs., Inc., LaGrange, Ill., 1987—. Contbr. articles to profl. jours. Mem. Am. Psychol. Assn., Ill. Psychol. Assn. Office: Rogala & Assocs Inc 1220 Carriage Ln La Grange IL 60525-2631

ROGALSKI, CAROL JEAN, clinical psychologist, educator; b. Chgo., Sept. 25, 1937; d. Casimir Joseph and Lillian Valentine Rogalski. BS, Loyola U., Chgo., 1961; PhD, NYU, 1968; cert. in psychoanalysis, Postgrad. Ctr. Mental Health, 1973. Lic. clin. psychologist, N.Y., Ill. Rsch. assoc. William Alanson White Inst., N.Y.C., 1961-66; rsch. asst., intern Hillside Hosp., Glen Oaks, N.Y., 1966-68; cons. Mt. Sinai Hosp., N.Y.C., 1968-73; staff psychologist Westside VA Hosp., Chgo., 1974—; clin. asst. prof. psychiatry Med. Sch. U. Ill., 1996—. Mem. editorial bd. Internat. Jour. Addictions, 1994—; contbr. articles to profl. publs. Mem. APA, Communal Studies Assn., Chgo. Soc. for Psychotherapy Rsch. (chair 1988-91). Office: Westside VA Hosp 820 S Damen Ave Chicago IL 60612-3728

ROGEN, MARK ENDRE, state senator, farmer; b. Sioux Falls, S.D., Dec. 29, 1956; s. E. Ordell and Ruth Alice (Hess) R.; m. Kristen M. Halvorson, Aug. 30, 1985; children: Ariana, Melysa, Zachary. BS in Animal Sci., S.D. State U., 1979. Farmer Sherman, S.D., 1979—; state senator State of S.D., Pierre, 1992—. Bd. dirs. Hermanson (S.D.) Sch. Bd., S.D. Cattleman's Assn., 1985-88; pres. S.D. Corn Growers Assn., 1986-88; sec. Nat. Corn Growers Assn., St. Louis, 1987-89. Democrat. Lutheran. Home and Office: 48790 246th St Sherman SD 57030-5519

ROGERS, AL R., design and development administrator; b. Madison, Wis., May 26, 1952. AD, Madison Area Tech., 1971. Mgr. design & devel. Bock Corp., Madison, Wis., 1977—. Mem. Soc. Mfg. Engrs. Office: Bock Corp. 110 S Dickinson St Madison WI 53703-3021

ROGERS, DOUGLAS GORDON, design engineer; b. Glasgow, Scotland, Sept. 4, 1961; came to U.S., 1988; s. William and Janeta G. R. BS, Glasgow Poly., 1983; MS, Cranfield (Eng.) Inst. Tech., 1986. Sr. designer Rolls Royce Plc, Derby, Eng., 1986-88; design engr. GE Aircraft Engines, Cin., 1988-91; sr. engr. Cummins Engine Co., COlumbus, Ind., 1991—. Recipient Caterpillar award Caterpillar Tractor Co., Kone-Marriott award. Mem. Lions Club.

ROGERS, FREDERICK CARL, network engineer; b. Dodge City, Kans., Jan. 19, 1966; s. Thomas Vernon and Mildred Ann (Reimer) R.; m. LeAnn Reneé Isaac, Oct. 7, 1968. AS, Dodge City (Kans.) C.C., 1987; BSEE, Kans. State U., 1993. Registered engr.-in-tng., Kans. Machinest Harry's Crankshaft, Dodge City, Kans., 1979-92; electronic technician I.C.E., Inc., Manhattan, Kans., 1993; network engr. Houston Assocs., Inc., Leavenworth, Kans., 1993—. Mem. IEEE. Republican. Home: 921 S Main # 7 Lansing KS 66043 Office: Houston Assocs Inc 213 Delaware Ste C-5 Leavenworth KS 66048

ROGERS, GARY C., educational administrator; b. Charleston, Ill., Dec. 18, 1935; s. Clarence O. and Zelpha Mary (DeCello) R.; m. Phyllis J. Reffeitt, Aug. 11, 1956; children: Kelly, Sidley Austin, Kara Rogers Dowell. BS in Edn., Ea. Ill. U., Charleston, 1961, MS in Ednl. Adminstrn., 1965. Cert. K-12 tchr., adminstrn. and supervision, Ill. Tchr. Franklin Sch., Danville, Ill., 1961-63; asst. prin. Liberty Sch., Danville, 1963-66, Tilton Sch., Danville, 1966-70; dean men East Park Jr. H.S., Danville, 1970-76; head prin. Daniel Sch., Danville, 1976-81, East Park Mid. Sch., Danville, 1981-85, Douglas Sch., Danville, 1986—; tchr. recruiter and trainer Ea. Ill. U., 1976—. Contbr. articles to various newspapers. Pres. Danville YMCA, 1981-82; leader edn. commn. St. James United Meth. Ch., Danvielle, 1979-87, youth vol., 1975-93, lay leader, 1983-87, mem. adminstrv. bd., 1985—; mem. Danville Zoning Commn., 1992—; pres. Vermilion County br. Am. Heart Assn., Danville, 1992-93; pres. alumni bd. Ea. Ill. U., Danville, 1991-92. Named 1st Citizen of Danville, Am. Bus. Club, 1982, Ky. col. Order of Ky. Cols., 1986; recipient Disting. Svc. award Ea. Ill. U., 1991, Outstanding Pres. award, 1992, Outstanding Youth Vol. award St. James United Meth. Ch., 1992. Mem. Ea. Ill. U. Alumni Assn. (state bd. dirs. 1886—, pres. Danville br. 1987-89, Outstanding Svc. award), Kiwanis (bd. dirs. Danville 1989—, pres. 1981-83, Outstanding Kiwanian award 1984). Home: 1314 N Gilbert St Danville IL 61832

ROGERS, GEORGE, III, college dean, athletic director, educator; b. Chgo., Jan. 8, 1947; s. George Jr. and Gertrude (Ellington) R.; m. Rita Faye Guhr, Aug. 14, 1976; children: Tara M., Bret Z. AA, Wilson City Coll., 1967; BS, Bethel Coll., 1969; MS, Wichita State U., 1972; postgrad., U. Ark., 1979-80. Dir. athletics, assoc. prof. phys. edn. Bethel Coll., North Newton, Kans., 1969—, also dean of students; instr. Educator Professions Devel. Act, McPherson, Kans., summer 1973; bd. dirs. Whitewing Constrn. Co. Pres. Newton Unified Sch. Dist. Sch. Bd., 1988, 94; bd. dirs. Mirror Inc. Alcohol and Drug Rehab. Svcs., Meadowlark-Homestead Psychol. Rehab. Svcs. Named State and Area Track Coach of Yr., Nat. Assn. Intercollegiate Athletics, 1975, Dist. 10 Athletics Adminstr. of Yr., Nat. Assn. Intercollegiate Athletics, 1989-90. Mem. Am. Alliance Health Phys. Edn., Nat. Assn. Collegiate Dirs. Athletics, U.S. Track Coaches Assn., Kappa Alpha Psi. Democrat. Baptist. Home: 3219 Royer West Dr Newton KS 67114-9639 Office: Bethel Coll 300 E 27th St North Newton KS 67117

ROGERS, JAMES EUGENE, electric and gas utility executive; b. Birmingham, Ala., Sept. 20, 1947; s. James E. and Margaret (Whatley) R.; m. Robyn McGill (div.); children: Chrissi, Kara, Ben; m. Mary Anne Boldrick, Oct. 28, 1977. BBA, U. Ky., 1970, JD, 1974. Asst. atty. gen. Commonwealth Ky., Louisville; asst. chief trial atty. Fed. Energy Regulation Commn., Washington, dep. gen. counsel litigation and enforcement; law clk. to presiding justice Supreme Ct Ky., Louisville; ptnr. Akin, Gump, Strauss, Hauer & Feld, Dallas, Akin Gump Strauss Hauer & Feld, Houston, 1985-86; formerly pres. Transwestern Pipeline, Houston; now with CINergy Corp. (formerly PSI Resources, Inc.), Cin.; bd. dirs. CINergy Corp., A O Irkutsk Energo, Fifth Third Bank, Bankers Life Holding, Inc., Edison Electric Inst., Duke Realty Investments, Inc. Trustee Nat. Symphony Orch.; bd. dirs. Cin. Mus. Assn., The Nature Conservancy-Ind. chpt., Butler U., Indpls., U. Ky. Bus. Partnership Found. Mem. FBA, Young Pres.' Orgn., Ky. Bar Assn., D.C. Bar Assn., Skyline Club, Meridian Hills Country Club, Crooked Stick Golf Club, Queen City Club, Bankers Club, Met. Club. Baptist. Office: CINergy Corp PO Box 960 Cincinnati OH 45201

ROGERS, JOHN RUSSELL, manufacturing company executive, engineer; b. St. Louis, May 12, 1929; s. John Flint and Faye (Russell) R.; m. Lorraine Esther Klockenbrink, Sept. 15, 1951; children: John Oliver, Gail Joanne. AB in Econs., Washington U., St. Louis, 1951. Registered profl. engr., Mo., Ill. Mfg. engr. Day Brite Lighting Inc., St. Louis, 1957-59; plant supt. Day Brite Lighting Inc., Tuptlo, Miss., 1959-64; plant mgr. White Rodgers Ltd., Markham, Ont., Can., 1964-66; ops. mgr. Metal Goods Corp., St. Louis, 1966-71; v.p., prin. Ross & Baruzzini, Inc., Cons. Engrs., St. Louis, 1971-84; pres. John R. Rogers Assocs., Inc., Cons. Engrs., St. Louis, 1984—. Bd. dirs. Grace Hill Settlement House, St. Louis, Grace Hill Child Devel. Bd.; pres. Thompson Ctr., St. Louis, 1984. Capt. U.S. Army, 1951-54. Mem. NSPE, Inst. Indsl. Engrs. (sr.), Am. Cons. Engrs. Coun., Assn. Profl. Materials Handling Cons. (pres. 1986-88, bd. dirs.), Materials Handling & Mgmt. Soc. (v.p. 1983—, bd. dirs.), Soc. Mfg. Engrs. (sr.), Rotary. Home and Office: John Rogers Assocs Inc 10332 Richview Dr Saint Louis MO 63127-1433

ROGERS, JUSTIN TOWNER, JR., retired utility company executive; b. Sandusky, Ohio, Aug. 4, 1929; s. Justin Towner and Barbara Eloise (Larkin) R. AB cum laude, Princeton U., 1951; JD, U. Mich., 1954. Bar: Ohio 1954. Assoc. Wright, Harlor, Purpus, Morris & Arnold, Columbus, 1956-58; with Ohio Edison Co., Akron, 1958-93, v.p., then exec. v.p., 1970-79, pres., 1980-91, chmn. bd., 1991-93; ret., 1993; bd. dirs. 1st Nat. Bank Ohio, 1st Merit Corp; past mem. coal adv. bd. Internat. Energy Agy. Past pres., trustee Akron Cmty. Trusts, Akron Child Guidance Ctr.; past chmn. Akron Assoc. Health Agys., U. Akron Assocs.; past chmn., trustee, mem. exec. com. trustees Akron Gen. Med. Ctr., Health Network Ohio; trustee Sisler McFawn Found., VNS-Hospice Found.; mem. Gt. Trail Coun. Boys Scouts Am. Mem. Portage Country Club, Mayflower Club, Rockwell Springs Trout Club (Castalia, Ohio), Princeton Club (N.Y.C.), Phi Delta Phi, Beta Gamma Sigma.

ROGERS, LAURA SUSAN, nursing case management; b. Lincoln Park, Mich., Dec. 7, 1958; d. Michael and Helen (Zakar) Szopo. BSN cum laude, U. Mich., 1981. Staff nurse gynecol., ENT and thoracic St. Joseph Mercy Hosp., Ann Arbor, Mich., 1981-84, staff nurse, clin. ladder IV, case mgr., 1986—, level IV case mgr., pre-op gynecol. class coord., women's health, 1989—; staff nurse gynecol. oncology U. Mich. Hosp., Ann Arbor, 1984-86; home care nurse Mich. Cancer Found., Detroit, 1986; presenter in field. Mem. U. Mich. Alumni Assn., Sigma Theta Tau. Democrat. Presbyterian. Home: 571 Liberty Pointe Dr Ann Arbor MI 48103-2087 Office: St Joseph Mercy Hosp Catherine McAuley Health System 5301 E Huron River Dr PO Box 992 Ann Arbor MI 48106

ROGERS, MIKE, state legislator; b. June 2, 1963. BA, Adrian Coll. Spl. agt. FBI; small bus. owner; senator Dist. 26 Mich. State Senate, 1995—, vice chmn. judiciary com., mem. fin. svc., human resources, labor and vet affairs coms.

ROGERS, MILLARD FOSTER, JR., retired art museum director; b. Texarkana, Tex., Aug. 27, 1932; s. Millard Foster and Jessie Bell (Hubbell) R.; m. Nina Olds, Aug. 3, 1963; 1 son, Seth Olds. BA with honors, Mich. State U., 1954; MA, U. Mich., 1958; studied with, John Pope-Hennessy; LHD, Xavier U., 1987. Gosline fellow Victoria and Albert Mus., London, Eng., 1959; curator Am. art Toledo Mus. Art, 1959-67; coord. Ford Found. intern program; dir. Elvehjem Art Ctr., prof. art history U. Wis.-Madison, 1967-74; dir. Cin. Art Mus., 1974-94, dir. emeritus, 1994—; vis. scholar Principia Coll., Elsah, Ill., 1982, 94; pres. Mariemont Preservation Found., Ohio, 1982-91, 95—; adj. prof. U. Cin., 1987-91. Author: Randolph Rogers, American Sculptor in Rome, 1971, Spanish Paintings in the Cincinnati Art Museum, 1978, Favorite Paintings from The Cincinnati Art Museum, 1980, Sketches and Bozzetti by American Sculptors, 1800-1950, 1988. Served with AUS, 1954-56. Named Outstanding Citizen of Mariemont, 1991. Mem. Assn. Art Mus. Dirs. (hon.), Am. Assn. Mus., Ohio Mus. Assn., Phi Beta Kappa. Office: Cin Art Mus Eden Park Cincinnati OH 45202-1596

ROGERS, PATRICIA G., nursing administrator; b. East St. Louis, Ill., Feb. 4, 1948; d. Edward and Helen Elizabeth (Leonard) Baker; m. William Lee Rogers, Dec. 18, 1982; children: Guy, Christina, Ronald, Dawn, Dana, Michelle. Student, Lewis and Clark Community Coll, 1981. Dir. nursing Sunshine Manor, Carlinville, Ill., 1984-87, D'Adrian Convalescent Ctr., Godfrey, Ill., 1988-89; nurse emergency rm. St. Joseph's Hosp., Alton, Ill., 1982; staff nurse multiple trauma and spl. surgery unit St. Elizabeth's Hosp., Granite City, Ill., 1981-82; owner, operator LTC Cons., Gillespie, Ill., 1991—; mgr. Pvt. Duty Program family Svcs./Vis. Nurses Assn., Alton, Ill, 1994—. Mem. Am. Coll. Health Care Adminstrs. Home and Office: 1 Circle Dr Gillespie IL 62033-2218

ROGERS, PAULA ANN, secondary school educator; b. Springfield, Ill., July 21, 1954; d. Paul I. and Pearl L. (Montgomery) R. BS in Math. Edn., Ill. State U., 1976; postgrad., Murray State, 1977; MS in Animal Sci., U. Ill., 1981. Cert. math. tchr., Ill. Math. tchr. Griffin High Sch., Springfield, Ill., 1976-78; adult educator Urbana, Ill., 1981-83; math. tchr. Danville (Ill.) High Sch., 1983-85, Urbana High Sch., 1985—; tutor Urbana Sch. Dist., 1985-93; Job Tng. Partnership Act summer youth worksite coord. Urbana Adult Edn., 1983—; coach math. team competitions Urbana H.S., 1985—, booster pal participant, 1992-93. Contbr. articles to profl. jours. Mem. Math. Assn. Am., Ill. Coun. Tchrs. Math., Delta Kappa Gamma. Methodist. Office: Urbana High Sch 1002 S Race St Urbana IL 61801-4957

ROGERS, RICHARD DEAN, federal judge; b. Oberlin, Kans., Dec. 29, 1921; s. William Clark and Evelyn May (Christian) R.; m. Helen Elizabeth Stewart, June 6, 1947; children—Letitia Ann, Cappi Christian, Richard Kurt. B.S., Kans. State U., 1943; J.D., Kans. U., 1947. Bar: Kans. 1947. Ptnr. firm Springer and Rogers (Attys.), Manhattan, Kans., 1947-58; instr. bus. law Kans. State U., 1948-52; partner firm Rogers, Stites & Hill, Manhattan, 1959-75; gen. counsel Kans. Farm Bur. & Service Cos., Manhattan, 1960-75; judge U.S. Dist. Ct., Topeka, Kans., 1975—. City commr., Manhattan, 1950-52, 60-64, mayor, 1952, 64, county atty., Riley County, Kans., 1954-58, state rep., 1964-68, state senator, 1968-75; pres. Kans. Senate, 1975. Served with USAAF, 1943-45. Decorated Air medal, Dfc. Mem. Kans., Am. bar assns., Beta Theta Pi. Republican. Presbyterian. Club: Masons. Office: US Dist Ct 444 SE Quincy St Topeka KS 66683

ROGERS, RICHARD LEE, educator; b. N.Y.C., Sept. 17, 1949; s. Leonard J. and Beverly (Simon) R.; m. Susan Jane Thornton, Aug. 14, 1976; children: Caroline, Meredith. BA, Yale U., 1971, MA in Religion, 1973; postgrad., U. Chgo., 1977-80; MS in Edn., Bank St. Coll. Edn., N.Y.C., 1989. Tchr. Foote Sch., New Haven, 1974-77; devel. assoc. U. Chgo., 1980-81, spl. asst. to v.p. planning, 1981-82; spl. asst. to pres. New Sch. Social Rsch., N.Y.C., 1982-83, sec. of corp., then v.p., sec., 1983-94; pres. Ctr. for Creative Studies, Detroit, 1994—. Mem. Univ. Cultural Ctr. Assn. (v.p., bd. dirs.). Office: Ctr Creative Studies 201 E Kirby Detroit MI 48202

ROGERS, ROY STEELE, III, dermatology educator, dean; b. Hillsboro, Ohio, Mar. 3, 1940; s. Roy S. Jr. and Anna Mary (Murray) R.; m. Susan Camille Hudson, Aug. 22, 1964; children: Roy Steele IV, Katherine Hudson. BA, Denison U., 1962; MD, Ohio State U., 1966; MS, U. Minn., 1974. Cert. dermatologist, dermatopathologist and immunodermatologist. Intern Strong meml. Hosp., Rochester, N.Y., 1966-67; resident Duke U. Med. Ctr., Durham, N.C., 1969-71; resident Mayo Clinic, Rochester, Minn., 1972-73, cons., 1973—, prof. dermatology, 1983—, dean Sch. Health Related Scis., 1991—; adv. coun. Rochester Community Coll., 1991—. Contbr. over 170 sci. articles to publs. Capt. USAF, 1967-69. Recipient Alumni Achievement award Ohio State U. Coll. of Medicine, 1991, Alumni citation Denison U., 1993, Faculty Svc. award Mayo Med. Sch., 1993. Mem. Am. Acad. Dermatology (bd. dirs. 1988-91), Am. Soc. Dermatologic Allergy and Immunology (sec.-treas. 1988—), Am. Dermatologic Assn., Soc. Investigative Dermatology, Assn. Schs. Allied Health Professions, Dermatology Found. Home: 1101 7th Ave SW Rochester MN 55902-6333 Office: Mayo Clinic 200 1st St SW Rochester MN 55905-0001

ROGERS, VIVIAN KOMMEDAHL, writer, homemaker; b. Mpls., Nov. 22, 1928; d. Thorbjorn and Martha (Blegen) Kommedahl; m. Rupert Valbert Coffey, July 7, 1951 (div. Oct. 1967); children: James Rupert, John Robert, Thomas Olaf; m. Philp Wiley Rogers, Oct. 4, 1986. Student, Denver U., 1948; shorthand cert., Barnes Sch. Bus., Denver, 1948. Clk.-typist St. Paul Fire and Marine Ins., 1946-47; sec. Denver Post, 1948-50, Pub. Svc. Co. Colo., Denver, 1950-53, Western Electric Co., Lee's Summit, Mo., 1967-73, Bapt. Meml. Hosp., Kansas City, Mo., 1974-77; exec. sec. Bott Broadcasting, Independence, Mo., 1977-80, Century Savs. Assn., Roeland Park, Kans., 1982-85, Hiawatha Savs., Fariway, Kans., 1985-86. Author: A Place Called Home, 1994. Republican. Mem. Covenant Ch. Home and Office: 13130 S Topeka Ave Carbondale KS 66414

ROGGE, MARY ELLEN, pharmacist; b. Pilger, Nebr., Apr. 28, 1942; d. Alfred Robert and Helen Josephine (Klima) Grenz; m. Robert Ralph Rogge, May 31, 1964; children: Robert Daniel, Ronald David. BS in Pharmacy, U. Nebr., 1965. Registered pharmacist, Nebr. Staff pharmacist Wagey Drug, Lincoln, Nebr., 1965-70, Bradfield Drug, Lincoln, Nebr., 1970-75; staff pharmacist Walgreens, Lincoln, Nebr., 1976-88, pharmacy mgr., 1988—. Bd. dirs. Lower Platte South Natural Resources, Lincoln, 1980—. Mem. Audubon Soc. Democrat. Lutheran. Home: 7321 Walker Ave Lincoln NE 68507-2771 Office: Walgreens 4780 Leighton Ave Lincoln NE 68504-3688

ROGGELIN, JOEL M., business owner; b. Monroe, Mich., May 4, 1957. Prin. Hullhorst Tools, Toledo, Ohio, 1992—.

ROGINA, JOSEPH FRANK, city assessor, zoning administrator; b. Calumet, Mich., Sept. 20, 1949; s. Joseph and Catherine (Severenski); m. Susan E. Limback, Jan. 17, 1975; 1 child, Joel Joseph. Student Property Tax Adminstr., Mich. Tech. U., 1971-72. City assessor City of Ishpeming, Mich., 1973-75; tax dir. Keweenaw County, Eagle River, Mich., 1976-79; quality control engr. Grede Foundry, Kingsford, Mich., 1979-84; dep. tax dir. Dickinson County, Iron Mountain, Mich., 1985-89; city assessor City of Iron Mountain, 1990—; owner Upper Penninsula Assessing Svcs., Iron Mountain, 1985—; instr. U. Mich. Extension, Marquette, 1970's; mem. bd. Dickinson Area Constrn. Code Commn. With U.S. Army, 1969-70, Viet Nam. Mem. Upper Penninsula of Mich. Assessors' Assn. (sec. 1986-88, v.p. 1989-90, prs. 1991-94, instr. 1980's, 90's), Mich. Assessors' Assn., U.P. Health Coalition,

Dickinson County Builders Exch. Office: City of Iron Mountain 501 S Stephenson Ave Iron Mountain MI 49801

ROGO, KATHLEEN, safety engineer; b. Carrollton, Ohio, Sept. 28, 1952; d. Silvio and Mary (Siragusano) R. Grad. high sch., Carrollton; PhD in Med. Sci. (hon.), Ohio Valley Pathologists, Inc., 1992. Cert. histotechnologist, emergency med. technologist, safety engr. Rsch. pathology trainee Aultman Hosp., Canton, Ohio, 1970-75, supr. anatomic pathology, 1974-75; lab. mgr. W. Morgan Lab., Canton, 1973-74; supr. anatomic pathology Dr.'s Hosp., Massillon, Ohio, 1975-78; emergency med. technician Canton Fire Dept., 1976-81; safety engr. Ashland Oil Co., Canton, 1980-82; rsch. pathologist assoc., med. cons, v.p. Ohio Valley Pathologists, Inc., Wheeling, W.Va., 1990—. Mem. Am. Soc. Clin. Pathology (cert. histotechnician), Am. Soc. Safety Engrs. (cert.), Am. Soc. Emergency Med. Technicians (cert.), Ohio State Med. Soc., Internat. Platform Assn. Democrat. Roman Catholic.

ROHLF, PAUL LEON, urologist; b. Davenport, Iowa, June 15, 1937; s. Lester Charles and Vera Bernice (Fisher) R.; m. Karen Kay Schnede, Aug. 8, 1959; children: David P., Gregory C., Elizabeth K., Kathryn A. BA, U. Iowa, 1959, MD, 1962. Diplomate Am. Bd. Urology. Intern Phila. Gen. Hosp., 1962-63; resident surgery VA Hosp., Iowa City, Iowa, 1963; resident urology U. Iowa Hosp., Iowa City, 1966-69; physician, urologist Urol. Assocs., Davenport, 1969—; dir., sec. UroSurgery Ctr., Inc., Davenport, 1986—; peer rev. com. Iowa Found. Med. Care, Des Moines, 1982-88; founder, dir. Urosurgery Ctr., Inc., 1986; cons. Vis. Nurse Assn., Davenport, 1976-79, Com. for Affordable Healthcare, Des Moines, 1985-87; chmn. dept. surgery Mercy Hosp., Davenport, 1978, utilization rev. chair Mercy and St. Lukes Hosp., Davenport, 1978-85, surg. appraisal chair, 1983-89, chmn. dept. surgery, 1993—. Bd. dirs. Maternal Health Ctr., Davenport, 1979—; peer rev. com. Heritage Nat. Health Plan, Davenport, 1991—. Capt. USAF, 1964-66. Fellow ACS; mem. AMA, Am. Urologic Assn., Am. Fertility Soc., Am. Soc. Outpatient Surgery, Iowa Med. Soc., Scott County Med. Soc. (pres. 1980-81), Iowa Urologic Soc. (pres. 1981-82). Republican. Lutheran. Home: 2412 E River Dr Davenport IA 52803-3702 Office: Urol Assocs PC 3319 Spring St Davenport IA 52807-2125

ROHLIK, HAROLD EDWARD, engineer; b. Cleve., Nov. 14, 1926; s. Arthur Anton and Mary Rose (Becka) R.; m. Eve Rose Kuzila, Feb. 11, 1950; children: James L., Lynne Herrle, Alice Tyrpak. BS, Purdue U., 1948. Aerospace engr. NASA Turbine Sect., Cleve., 1948-62, head, 1962-72; chief NASA, Turbine Br., 1972-85; trustee Brunswick Hills Twp., Brunswick Hills, Ohio, 1972-94; chief engr. NASA Propulsion Systems, Cleve., 1985-86; retired NASA, Cleve., 1986—; mem. space shuttle study com. NASA, Washington, 1971-77; chmn. gas turbine com. Soc. Automotive Engrs., Detroit, 1981-82; lectr. in field. Co-author: Turbine Design and Applications, 1972; contbr. articles to profl. jours. Trustee Brunswick Hills Twp., 1972-94; pres. Medina County Twp. Assn., 1988-89; chmn., bd. dirs. Ohio Twp. Assn. Risk Mgmt. Authority, 1991-92. With USN, 1944-46. Recipient Amos Alonzo Stagg medal YMCA, Medina, 1964. Mem. Am. Humanist Assn., Nat. Space Soc., Medina County Land Conservancy, Common Cause, NASA Alumni League. Republican. Home: 1960 Substation Rd Brunswick OH 44212

ROHRBACH, LARRY, state legislator; b. California, Mo., Nov. 12, 1946; s. Emmet H. and Ruth (Bieri) R.; m. Beth Ann Connell, 1974; 1 child, Eva Beth. BS, Ctrl. Mo. State U., 1968. Mem. Mo. State Ho. of Reps. Dist. 115, 1982-93, former asst. minority floor leader; mem. Mo. State Senate Dist. 6, 1993—. Pres. Ctrl. Mo. State Rep. Club, 1968, Moniteau County Rep. Club, Mo., 1974-76; chmn. Moniteau County Rep. Com., 23rd Senate Dist. Rep. Com. Recipient Taxpayers Watchdog award, 1988. Mem. Mo. Farmers Assn., Moniteau County Farm Bur., Moniteau County Pork Prodrs. (pres. 1973). Office: HC 60 Box 12 California MO 65018-9005*

ROHRBOUGH, LINDA JANDECKA, computer center administrator; b. Akron, Ohio, Dec. 7, 1947; d. Clyde William and Dorothy Jean (Nine) Jandecka; m. Gene L. Rohrbough; 1 child, Zachary William. AAS, U. Akron, 1967, BSBA, 1971. With info. svcs. U. Akron (Ohio) Computer Ctr., 1970-72, sec. to dir., 1972-75, computer svcs. coord., 1975—. Bd. dirs. Firestone Pk. Citizens Council, Akron, 1980—, newsletter editor Akron, 1984-87. Mem. NOW. Republican. Baptist. Home: 217 N Firestone Blvd Akron OH 44301-2060 Office: U Akron Computer Ctr 185 Carroll St Akron OH 44304-1713

ROHRER, SUSAN JANE, principal; b. Springfield, Ill., Apr. 30, 1945; d. Russell Shriver and Margaret (Shumaker) Rohrer. AB, MacMurray Coll., 1967; MS, U. Ill., 1971, PhD, 1973. Cert. tchr. spl. K-14, H.S., Gen. Adminstr. K-12, Ill. Instr., Virden Jr. H.S., Ill., 1967-69; asst. to dean U. Ill. Coll. Medicine-Urbana, 1974-75, adminstrv. assoc., 1975-80; asst. prin. Virden Jr. and Sr. H.S., 1983-84, prin., 1984-87; sports writer News Gazette Newspaper, Champaign, Ill., 1973-74; owner Home Care Svcs., Inc., 1990—. Dir. Dana Thomas Found., Springfield, Ill., 1989, Virden Unit 4 Sch. Bd.; sec. Virden Sch. Bd., 1992-93, v.p., 1993-94; mayor Virden. Ill., 1993—. Methodist. Home: 121 W Hill St Virden IL 62690-1232

ROIZMAN, BERNARD, virologist, educator; b. Chisinau, Rumania, Apr. 17, 1929; came to U.S., 1947, naturalized, 1954; s. Abram and Liudmilla (Seinberg) R.; m. Betty Cohen, Aug. 26, 1950; children: Arthur, Niels. B.A., Temple U., 1952, M.S., 1954; Sc.D. in Microbiology, Johns Hopkins, 1956; D.H.L. (hon.), Gov.'s State U., 1984; MD (hon.), U. Ferrara (Italy), 1991. From instr. microbiology to asst. prof. Johns Hopkins Med. Sch., 1956-65; mem. faculty div. biol. scis. U. Chgo., 1965—, prof. microbiology, 1969-84, prof. biophysics, 1970—, chmn. com. virology, 1969-85, 88—, Joseph Regenstein prof., 1981-83, Joseph Regenstein Disting. Svc. prof., 1984—, chmn. dept. molecular genetics and cell biology, 1985-88; convener herpes virus workshop, Cold Spring Harbor, N.Y., 1972; lectr. Am. Found. for Microbiology, 1974-75; mem. spl. virus cancer program, devel. rsch. working group Nat. Cancer Inst., 1967-71, cons. inst., 1967-73; mem. steering com. human cell biology program NSF, 1971-74, cons. found., 1972-74; mem. adv. com. cell biology and virology Am. Cancer Soc., 1970-74; chmn. herpes virus study group Internat. Commn. Taxonomy of Viruses, 1971-93; mem. Internat. Microbiol. Genetics Commn. Internat. Assn. Microbiol. Scis., 1974-81; mem. sci. adv. coun. N.Y. Cancer Inst., 1971-88; med. adv. bd. Leukemia Rsch. Found., 1972-77; mem. herpes-virus working team WHO/FOA, 1978-81; mem. bd. sci. cons. Sloan Kettering Inst., N.Y.C., 1975-81; mem. study sect. exptl. virology NIH, 1976-80; mem. task force on virology Nat. Inst. Allergy and Infectious Disease, 1976-77; mem. external adv. com. Emory U. Cancer Ctr., 1973-81, Northwestern U. Cancer Ctr., 1979-89; cons. Inst. Merieux, Lyon, France, 1979-91; mem. com. to establish vaccine priorities Nat. Inst. Medicine, 1983-85; chmn. sci. adv. bd. Teiky-Showa Univs. Ctr., Tampa Bay Rsch. Inst., 1983—, chmn. bd. trustees, 1991—. Author sci. papers, chpts. in books; editor: Herpes Viruses, Vol. 1, 1982, Vol. 2, 1983, Vols. 3 and 4, 1985, The Human Herpesviruses, 1993, Infectious Diseases in an Age of Change, 1995; adv. editor Progress in Surface Membrane Science, 1972; editor-in-chief Jour. Infectious Agts. and and Disease, 1992—; mem. editl. bd. Jour. Hygiene, 1985-61, Infectious Diseases, 1965-69, Jour. Virology, 1970—, Jour. Intervirology, 1972-85, Archives of Virology, 1975-81, Virology, 1976-78, 83—, Microbiologica, 1978—, Cell, 1979-80, Gene Therapy, 1994. Trustee Goodwin Inst. for Cancer Rsch., 1977—. Recipient Lederle Med. Faculty award, 1960-61, Career Devel. award USPHS, 1963-65, Pasteur award Ill. Soc. Microbiology, 1972, Esther Langer award for achievement in cancer research, 1974, Outstanding Alumnus in Pub. Health award Johns Hopkins U., 1984; named hon. prof. Shandong Acad. Med. Scis., People's Republic of China, 1985; Am. Cancer Soc. scholar cancer research at Pasteur Inst. Paris, 1961-62; ICN Internat. prize in virology, 1988; faculty research assoc., 1966-71; traveling fellow Internat. Agy. Research Against Cancer, Karolinska Inst., Stockholm, Sweden, 1970; grantee USPHS/NIH, 1958—, Am. Cancer Soc., 1962-90, NSF, 1962-79, Whitehall Found., 1966-74. Fellow Japanese Soc. for Promotion of Sci., Pan Am. Cancer Soc. (hon.); mem. Nat. Acad. Scis., Hungarian Acad. of Scis. (hon.), Am. Acad. Arts and Scis., Am. Acad. Microbiology, Am. Assn. Immunologists, Am. Soc. Microbiology, Am. Soc. Virology, Am. Soc. Biol. Chemists, Brit. Soc. Gen. Microbiology, Johns Hopkins U. Soc. Scholars, Quadrangle Club (Chgo.). Home: 5555 S Everett Ave Chicago IL 60637-1968 Office: U Chgo MB Kouler Viral Oncology Labs 910 E 58th St Chicago IL 60637-1432

ROLAN, BRET ROBERT, electrical engineer; b. Lincoln, Nebr., July 22, 1963. BSEE, Cleve. State U., 1989. Cert. profl. engr., Ohio. Sr. syss. engr. Reliance Elec. Co., Cleve., 1989—. Amish. Office: Reliance Electric Co 24703 Euclid Ave Cleveland OH 44117-1786

ROLELLI, CAM C., business executive; b. Perryapolis, Pa., Mar. 9, 1930. BS in Edn., California (Pa.) State U., 1953. Rsch. chemist Republic Steel Corp., Cleve., 1955-63, Diamond Shamrock Corp., Cleve., 1963-76; pres. Colelli & Assoc., Inc., New Philadelphia, Ohio, 1991—; cons. P.V.S. Chems., Copley, Ohio, 1992—. Co-inventor oil field remediation; contbr. articles to profl. jours. Roman Catholic. Home and Office: Colelli & Assocs Inc 417 Hillcrest Dr NE New Philadelphia OH 44663-2766

ROLEWICZ, ROBERT JOHN, estimating engineer; b. Chgo., Sept. 16, 1954; s. Frank Joseph and Margaret Mary (Ahlbach) R.; m. Vicki Lynn Heggeland, Sept. 1, 1985; children: Heather Margaret, Jeremy Robert. Diploma, Washburne Trade Sch., 1977. Level II inspector Kropp Forge Co., Chgo., 1974-77, chief cost estimator, 1978-88, mgr. estimating, chief estimating engr., 1989—; bd. dirs. Kropp Employees Fed. Credit Union, 1983-89, pres., 1986-88. Committeeman Citizens to Reelect Jack Kubik, Cicero, Ill., 1984—, Citizens to Reelect Judy Baar Topinka, Cicero, 1984—. Recipient Hold My Hand award Children's Ctr. Cicero, 1982. Mem. Vets. of Vietnam War Inc, Vietnam Vets. Am. Inc., Czechoslovak Soc. Am, Vietnow, Sacred Heart League, Cicero Hist. Soc., Broofield Zoo, St. Jude League, St. Patrick H.S. Alumni Club, Kropp Key Club (pres. 1984—, Golden Anvil award 1989), Elks (exalted ruler 1981-82, 94-95, v.p. N.E. dist., P.E.R. plaque 1982, Elk of Yr. award Cicero-Berwyn 1989, 93, Govt. Rels. award 1989). Republican. Roman Catholic.

ROLFE, GARY LAVELLE, forestry educator; b. Paducah, Ky., Sept. 5, 1946; s. George Washington and Inez (Holt) R.; m. Judy A. Moller, June 22, 1968 (div. Sept. 1982); 1 foster son, Terry Edwards: 1 son, Cory. B.S, U. Ill., 1968, M.S., 1969, Ph.D., 1972. With U. Ill., Urbana, 1968—, asst. prof. forestry, 1972-75, dir., prin. investigator, 1973-77, assoc. prof., 1975-80; asst. dir. Ill. Agrl. Expt. Sta., Urbana, 1977-81, prof., 1980—, head dept. forestry, 1981-95; interim assoc. dir. Ill. Agrl. Expt. Sta., 1992-95; assoc. dir. Ill. Agrl. Expt. Sta., Urbana, 1995—, head dept. natural resources and environ. sci., 1995—; cons. Soil and Land Use Tech., Inc., 1980—, EPA Rsch. Triangle Pk. Lead in the Environ., 1981-82, Ill. EPA, 1976-77; cons. environ. edn., Urbana, 1976-81, Rossville, Ill., 1978; del. Conservation Congress, 1993—. Author: Intergrating Ecology Education in Elementary Curricula, 1978, Field Activities in Ecology Education, 1981, Forests and Forestry, 4th edit., 1990; contbr. numerous articles to profl. jours. Mem. Ecol. Soc. Am., Am. Soc. Agronomy, Assn. Watershed Scientists, Soc. Am. Foresters, Sigma Xi, Gamma Sigma Delta, Xi Sigma Pi. Home: 2340 County Road 1150 N Sidney IL 61877-9758 Office: Univ of Ill 1102 S Goodwin Ave Urbana IL 61801-4730

ROLFE, MICHAEL N., management consulting firm executive; b. Chgo., Sept. 9, 1937; s. Mark Alexander and Antoinette (Wittgenstein) R.; m. Judith Mary Lewis, June 16, 1959; children—Andrew, Lisa, James. A.B. in Econs., U. Mich., 1959; MBA, U. Chgo., 1996. Sales staff Lewis Co., Northbrook, Ill., 1961-62; systems mgmt. staff Brunswick Corp., Chgo., 1962-68; v.p. Kearney Mgmt. Cons., Chgo., 1968-81; ptnr. KPMG/Peat Marwick, Chgo., 1981-92; dir. Keystone Group, Evanston, Ill., 1992—. Author: AMA Management Handbook, 1969. Bd. dirs. Common, Chgo., 1972-75, U. Chgo. Cancer Rsch., 1985-88, Am. Cancer Soc., Chgo., 1985—; trustee Michael Reese Med. Ctr., 1986-91; pres. Sch. Bd. Dist. 113, Highland Park, Ill., 1977-83, Sch.Dist. 113 Found., 1993—; mem. Am. Jewish Com., 1996—. Lt. (j.g.) USNR, 1959-61. Clubs: Northmoor Country (Highland Park); Standard (Chgo.). Home: 800 Deerfield Rd Apt 109 Highland Park IL 60035-3531 Office: Keystone Group 1560 Sherman Ave Evanston IL 60201-3624

ROLLAND, IAN MCKENZIE, insurance executive; b. Fort Wayne, Ind., June 3, 1933; s. David and Florence (Hunte) R.; m. Miriam V. Flickinger, July 3, 1955; children: Cheri L., Lawrence D., Robert A., Carol Ann, Sara K. B.A., DePauw U., 1955; M.A. in Actuarial Sci., U. Mich., 1956. With Lincoln Nat. Life Ins. Co., Ft. Wayne, 1956—, sr. v.p., 1973-75, pres., 1977-81, chief exec. officer, 1977-91, chmn., pres., 1981-92, chmn., chief exec. officer, 1992—; pres. Lincoln Nat. Corp., 1975-91, CEO, 1977-91, chmn., CEO, 1992—; bd. dirs. K&K Ins. Cos., No. Ind. Pub. Svc., Lincoln Fin. Corp., GTE North, Inc., Tokheim Corp., Am. States Ins. Cos., 1st Penn-Pacific Ins. Co., The Richard Leahy Corp., Vantage Global Advisors, Inc.; past chmn. Am. Coun. Life Ins.; mem. exec. com. Assn. Ind. Life Ins. Cos. Mem. adv. bd. Ind. U.-Purdue U., 1977, Fort Wayne Leadership, Fort Wayne Community Found., Corp. Innovation Devel. Ventures; bd. dirs. Associated Colls. Ind., Corp. Innovation Devel.; chmn. Ind. Fiscal Policy Com.; trustee Hudson Inst.; mem. Indiana Acad. Mem. Soc. Actuaries, Acad. Actuaries, Health Ins. Assn. Am., Am. Council Life Ins. (past chmn. bd. dirs.), Assoc. Ind. Life Ins. Cos. (exec. com.), Ind. Ins. Soc. (bd. dirs.), Internat. Ins. Soc. (bd. dirs.), Ind. C. of C. (mem. exec. com.). Office: Lincoln Nat Corp 200 E Berry St Fort Wayne IN 46802-2706

ROLOFF, KAREN MARIE, communication educator; b. Chgo., Sept. 16, 1946; d. Reid A. and Mabel A. (Tresemer) Olson; m. Michael E. Roloff, Sept. 7, 1974; children: Erika B., Katrina L., Carlissa F. BA, Augustana Coll., Rock Island, Ill., 1968; MA, U. Ill., 1969; postgrad., Ohio State U., 1970, Ind. U., 1973. Instr., asst. dir. forensics U. Toledo, 1969-71; dir. forensics Ind. State U., Terre Haute, 1971-74; rsch. asst. Mich. State U., East Lansing, 1974-75; mem. faculty U. Ky., Lexington, 1975-78; instr. Northwestern U., Evanston, Ill., 1978-90; instr., internship dir. comm. dept. DePaul U., Chgo., 1990—. Pres. bd. dirs. Northbrook (Ill.) Comty. Nursery Sch., 1984-89; mem. Sch. Dist. 30 Bd. Edn., Northbrook, 1989—, pres., 1993—; mem. selection com. Golden Apple Found., Chgo., 1991—. Title IV fellow NDEA, 1968-69. Mem. Nat. Sch. Bd. Assn., Speech Comm. Assn., Cen. State Comm. Assn., Ill. Assn. Sch. Bds. (Level I Leadership award 1991, Level II Leadership award 1992, Level III Leadership award 1993, mem. Master Sch. Bd.). Lutheran. Home: 2271 Asbury Rd Northbrook IL 60062-6001

ROLSHOVEN, ROSS WILLIAM, legal investigator, art photographer; b. Mandan, N.D., Oct. 20, 1954; s. Raymond Paul and Bernice June (Mastel) R.; divorced; 1 child, Ashley Anna. BA in Bus. Adminstrn., U. N.D., 1976. Lic. pvt. investigator, N.D., Minn. Claims adjuster, investigator Border Area Adjustments, Grand Forks, N.D., 1976-84; owner, mgr. Great Plains Claims, Inc., Grand Forks, N.D., 1984—; chmn. N.D. Claims Seminar, Grand Forks, 1988; guest lectr. U. N.D. Law Sch., 1993-96. Photographic exhibits include Artifacts, 1992 (1st pl. award 1992), Spirit of the Buffalo, 1992 (1st pl. award 1992), Grey Morn' on the Red, 1991 (Merit award 1991); featured artist Custer County Art Show, Miles City, Mont., 1995; sculpture How the West Was Won, 1992 (2d pl. award 1992). Mem. N.D. Mus. Art; patron Grand Forks Fire Hall Theater, 1988-92; mem. Fargo/Moorhead Art Assn., 1992; mem. bldg. restoration com. North Valley Arts Coun. Recipient Svc. Recognition award United Way, 1984, Hist. Preservation award N.D. Hist. Soc., 1990, Buckskinner award Roughrider Internat. Art Show Com., 1994, 2d Pl. award Fargo Regional Art Show, 1994-95. Mem. Nat. Assn. Legal Investigators, Minn. Assn. Detectives, Red River Valley Claims Assn. (pres. 1986-87), Upper Red River Valley Claims Assn. (pres. 1988-89), Dakota Masters Club Swim Club. Office: Great Plains Claims Inc 220 S 3rd St Grand Forks ND 58201-4732

ROMAGUERA, ENRIQUE, foreign language educator, corporate interpreter; b. Mayaguez, P.R., June 2, 1942; s. José Mariano Jr. and Aminta Marina (Martinez) R. BA, U. Dayton, Ohio, 1965; MA, Ohio U., 1966; cert., McGill U., Montreal, 1966, U. Leningrad, USSR, 1967; postgrad., U. Ariz., 1970. Cert. oral proficiency tester in French for Am. Coun. for Teaching of Fgn. Lang. and Ednl. Testing Svcs., 1988-90. Instr. in langs. U. Dayton, 1969-73, asst. prof. langs., 1973-85, tenured prof. langs., 1976, assoc. prof. langs., 1985—; acad. assoc. Avraham Y. Goldratt Inst., 1991—; part-time instr. Wilberforce (Ohio) U., summer 1971; interpreter, Nat. Cash Register, Dayton, 1973, Reynolds & Reynolds, Dayton, 1986; translator Delco Moraine/GM, Dayton, 1974, Congress of Astrol. Orgns., N.Y.C., 1978, Philips Industries, Dayton, 1980, WAMCO Products, Centerville, Ohio, 1991, Internat. Marian Rsch. Inst., Dayton, 1991, PMI Food Equipment Group, Troy, Ohio, 1993; translator, voice recorder in French and Spanish, Dayco Corp., Dayton, 1979, L/E/O Systems, Dayton, 1982, 83, AV Tech, Dayton, 1982, 94, Monarch Marking, Dayton, 1990, Bergamo Ctr., Dayton, 1991; translator, cons. Oracle Corp., Dayton, 1990; cert. yoga therapist Phoenix Rising, Housatonic, Mass., 1993—. Mem., composer, dir., tenor, percussion sect. Queen of Apostles Community Choir, Dayton, 1970—; vol. Yoga tchr. Greenewood Manor, Xenia, Ohio, 1978-88; marianist Assisted Living Ctr., Dayton, Ohio, 1989; workshop leader wellness program U. Dayton, 1986—; bd. dirs. Yoga Fellowship of Dayton, 1978—; Midwest regional coord. Kripalu Internat. Network, Kripalu Ctr. for Yoga and Health, Lenox, Mass., 1988—; cert. yoga therapist Phoenix Rising Housatonic, Mass., 1993—. Mem. Am. Assn. Tchrs. of French, Modern Lang. Assn., Internat. Soc. for Astrological Rsch., Ohio Fgn. Lang. Assn., Midwest Modern Lang. Assn. Roman Catholic. Office: U Dayton Dept Langs 300 College Park Ave Dayton OH 45469-0001

ROMAN, ALAN MARSHALL, general and peripheral vascular surgeon; b. Chgo., Dec. 1, 1949; s. Sol and Betty Jayne (Silverman) R.; m. Linda Helen Liberman, May 8, 1974; children: Justin Blair, Lindsay Megan. BA, Northwestern U., 1971; MD, Chgo. Med. Sch., 1975; advanced degree, Mayo Clinic/Mayo Found., 1980. Ptnr. Pronger Smith Med. Assn., Blue Island, Ill., 1980—; dir. Ill. State Med. Ins. Svcs. Chmn. Flossmoor (Ill.) Zoning Bd. Appeals, 1985—; co-chmn. Flossmoor Planning Com., 1985—; exec. com., bd. dirs. Ill. Polit. Action Com., Chgo., 1989—, Am. Cancer Soc., 1989; bd. dirs. Sch. Dist. #161 Edn. Found., Flossmoor, 1995. Recipient Med. Staff Apreciation award St. Francis Hosp., Blue Island, 1995. Mem. AMA, Soc. Am. Gastro Intestinal Endoscopic Surgeons, Ill. State Med. Soc. (pres. 1994-95), Chgo. Med. Soc. (pres. 1992-93), Soc. Laparoscopic Surgeons. Office: Pronger Smith Med Assocs 2320 W High St Blue Island IL 60406

ROMAN, JOHN CHARLES, retired publishing company executive; b. Gallatin, Pa., Dec. 25, 1920; s. John Sr. and Mary (Baka) R.; m. Elizabeth Ann Chesmar, Aug. 25, 1951; 1 child, John Chesmar II. BS in Bus. Edn., U. Pitts., 1949, MEd in Supervision and Adminstrn., 1951; postgrad., Mich. State U., 1957, U. Cin., 1958-63. Tchr. Butler (Pa.) Pub. Schs., 1949-50; tchr. Cin. Pub. Schs., 1950-57, supr. bus. and distributive edn., 1958-67; curriculum coord. Cen. Vocat. High Sch., Cin., 1955-56, evening prin., 1957-58; spl. projects dir., asst. secondary sch. mgr., asst. editor South-Western Pub. Co., Cin., 1967-90; vis. summer prof. U. Pitts., Mich. State U., East Lansing; evening lectr. econs. U. Cin., 1958-75, curriculum coord., 1966-67; sales rep. Nationwide Ins. and Heritage Securities, 1957-66; commentator profl. soccer Sta. WLYK-FM, 1973-75; mem. adv. bd. Cin. Tech. Coll., 1970-75, Cin. Pub. Schs., 1975. Author: Curriculum Guide in Business Education, 1965, Family Financial Management, 1972 (Golden Book award 1985); author monographs in field; contbr. articles to profl. jours. Audirot Forward Twp., Allegheny County, Gallatin, Pa., 1947-48; soccer referee U.S. Soccer Football Assn. and Mid.-m. Xoll. Assn., 1950-72; mem. soccer champions U.S. Open, Gallatin, 1942; vice comdr. Howard Trechter Post 638 Am Legion, Cin., 1988-95. With USN, 1943-46. Recipient Disting. Lectureship in Office Adminstrn. award Cath. U., Washington, 1979. Mem. Adminstrv. Mgmt. Soc. (pres. Cin. chpt. 1969-70, functional dir. internat. edn. com. 1970-71, 300 Club award 1969), Nat. Bus. Edn. Assn. (pres. suprs., tchrs. and adminstrs. sect. 1967-68), Ohio Bus. Tchrs. Assn. (pres. 1966), Am. Legion (Howard Trechter Post 638), Delta Pi Epsilon (pres. 1967). Democrat. Roman Catholic. Home: 904 Timber Trl Cincinnati OH 45224-1654

ROMANO, DAVID, company executive; b. Canton, Ohio, Aug. 21, 1948. BA in Acctg., Walsh Coll., 1978. Sr. acct. Coopers and Lybrand, Akron, Ohio, 1981—; CFO Summit Benefits Agy., Barberton, Ohio, 1987—. Treas., trustee Lake Cable Recreation Assn., Canton, Ohio, 1991—; mem. St. Michaels Sch. Bd., Canton, 1994—. Mem. Iowa Soc. CPAs. Roman Catholic. Office: Summit Benefits Agy 1403 Wooster Rd W Barberton OH 44203-7374

ROMANOFF, MARJORIE REINWALD, education educator; b. Chgo., Sept. 29, 1923; d. David Edward and Gertrude (Rosenfield) Reinwald; m. Milford M. Romanoff, Nov. 6, 1945; children: Bennett Sanford, Lawrence Michael, Janet Beth (dec.). Student, Northwestern U., 1941-42, 43-45, Chgo. Coll. Jewish Studies, 1942-43; BEd, U. Toledo, 1947, MEd, 1968, EdD, 1976. Tchr., Old Orchard Elem. Sch., Toledo, 1946-47, McKinley Sch., Toledo, 1964-65; substitute tchr., Toledo, 1964-68; instr. Mary Manse Coll., Toledo, 1974; instr. children's lit. Sylvania (Ohio) Bd. Edn., 1977; supr. student tchrs. U. Toledo, 1968-73, 85—, instr. advanced communications, 1977, researcher, 1973-74, instr. Am. Lang. Inst., 1978—; part-time asst. prof. elem. edn. Bowling Green (Ohio) State U., 1978-88; presenter numerous workshops and demonstrations in children lit. and analysis of tchr. behavior, 1976—; chairperson rsch. com. Am. Language Inst. U. Toledo, 1985-94, asst. prof. elem. edn. in lang. arts 1985-87; part time asst. prof. Elem. Edn., instr. U. Toledo, Am. Lang. Inst. 1978—. Author: Language and Study Skills: For Learners of English, Prentice Hall Regents, 1991. Trustee Children's Svcs. Bd., 1974-76; pres. bd. Cummings Treatment Ctr. for Adolescents, 1978-80; mem. Crosby Gardens Adv. Bd., 1976-82, Community Planning Coun., 1980-84, Citizens Rev. Bd. of Juvenile Ct., 1979—; mem. allocations com. Mental Health and Retardation Bd., 1980-81; mem. Bd. Jewish Edn., 1976-94, pres., 1982-84; mem. Jewish Family Svc., 1978-85, v.p., 1980-85; mem. allocations com. Jewish Welfare Fedn., 1980, 89-91; bd. dirs. Family Life Edn. Coun., 1984-90, sec., 1988-90; mem. budget and allocations com. Jewish Fedn., 1989-93; bd. dirs. Friends Toledo-Lucas County Librs., 1991—, bd. pres., 1991-93; program chair U. Toledo Women's Commn., 1991-93; bd. dirs. Ohio Friends of Pub. Librs., 1992-94; presenter ann. conf. N.W. Ohio Libr. Assn., 1993. Named One of Ten Women of Yr., St. Vincent's Hosp. Guild, 1984, Outstanding Instructional Staff Woman, U. Toledo, 1990. Mem. ASCD, Tchrs. English to Speakers Other Langs. (presenter 1986, presenter Internat. TESOL Atlanta 1993), Nat. Soc. for Study Edn., Toledo Libr. Legacy Found., Orgn. Rehab. and Tng. (named Outstanding Woman in Community Svc. 1987), Hadassah (chpt. pres. regional bd. 1961-64), Northwestern U. Alumni Assn., Phi Kappa Phi, Phi Delta Kappa, Kappa Delta Pi (pres./faculty adv. 1971-75, Point of Excellence award 1992), Pi Lambda Theta (chpt. pres. 1978-80, nat. com. 1979-84). Democrat. Home: 2514 Bexford Pl Toledo OH 43606-2414 Office: U Toledo SSAC # 2006B Toledo OH 43606

ROMANOFF, STANLEY M., JR., human resource specialist; b. Toledo, Feb. 3, 1948; s. Stanley M. and Helen (Feinberg) R.; children: Erika Lee, Jennifer Lyn, Tara Marie, Erin Michele. BBA, U. Cin., 1970. Pers. supr. assembly div. GM, Norwood, Ohio, 1969-72; pers. mgr. Diamond Internat. Corp., Norwood, 1972-73; property mgr., investment counselor Romanoff Enterprises, Toledo, 1973-77; pers. adminstr. wage and salary United Telephone Co. Ohio, Mansfield, 1977-79; compensation and benefits mgr. United Inter-Mountain Telephone Co., Bristol, 1979-84, employee rels. mgr., 1984-86; human resources cons. Romanoff Enterprises, Bristol, Tenn., 1986-87; bus. mgr. Magna Internat., Livonia & Southfield, Mich., 1987-94, dir. human resources and bus. systems, 1994—. Mem. Am. Compensation Assn., Am. Mgmt. Assn., Soc. for Human Resource Mgmt., Am. Soc. of Employers, Human Resources Assn. of Greater Detroit. Office: Magna Internat 26200 Lahser Rd Ste 300 Southfield MI 48034-7157

ROMANOWSKI, WILLIAM DAVID, cultural historian, writer; b. Edwardsville, Pa., Aug. 2, 1954; s. William Anthony and Mary (Sawchak) R.; m. Donna Lynn Buxton, June 11, 1977; children: Michael James, Tara Lynn. BA in English, Indiana U. of Pa., 1976; MA in English, Youngstown (Ohio) State U., 1981; PhD in Am. Culture, Bowling Green State U., 1990. With Coalition for Christian Outreach, Youngstown, 1976-88, resource specialist, 1982-88; grad. asst. Bowling Green (Ohio) State U., 1986-88; vis. faculty fellow Calvin Coll., Grand Rapids, Mich., 1988-89, assoc. prof. communication arts and scis., 1989—; prof., 1996—; manuscript reviewer; adv. editor Popular Music and Society, Bowling Green, 1988—. Author: Pop Culture Wars: Religion and the Role of Entertainment in American Life, 1996; co-author: Risky Business: Rock in Film, 1991; contbg. author: Dancing in the Dark, 1991; contbr. chpts. to books, essays and articles to mags. Billy Graham Ctr. Archives rsch. grantee, 1992; Calvin Coll. Alumni Assn. rsch. grantee, 1991-92; Calvin Ctr. for Christian Scholarship rsch. fellow, 1988-89. Mem. Am. Culture Assn., Popular Culture Assn. Mem. Christian Reformed Ch. Office: CAS Calvin Coll 3201 Burton St SE Grand Rapids MI 49546

ROMBS, VINCENT JOSEPH, retired accountant, lawyer; b. Newport, Ky., Mar. 8, 1918; s. John Thomas and Mathilda (Fromhold) R.; m. Ruth Burns, Aug. 15, 1942; 1 child, Ellen (Mrs. James P. Herman). Student Xavier U., 1936-37; BS with honors, Southeastern U., 1941; JD, Loyola U., Chgo., 1952. Bar: Ill. 1952; CPA, Ill. Tax ptnr. with local and nat. pub. acctg. firms, Chgo., 1952-89; assoc. Nat. Firm, Chgo., 1970-75; of counsel Edelman Chartered, 1975-89; Ostrow Reisin Berk & Abrams, Ltd., 1977-89; pres. Vincent J. Rombs, Ltd., 1982-88. Bd. dirs. Miller Found. Lt. comdr., USNR, 1941-46. Recipient Scholarship Key award Delta Theta Phi, 1953. Mem. Ill. Soc. CPA's. Home: 10370 W Plum Tree Cir # 202 Hales Corners WI 53130-2636

ROMERO, JOSEFINO TABERNILLA, nurse anesthetist; b. Lucena, Quezon, Philippines; came to the U.S., 1963; s. Melanio Merca and Teodorica (Tabernilla) R. Diploma, Quezon Meml. Hosp., 1961; cert. nurse anesthetist, Mt. Carmel Hosp., Detroit, 1968; D in Art, U. Found., Malta, 1986. RN, Mich. Psychiat. nurse Nat. Mental Hosp., Manila, 1961-63; operating room nurse St. Vincent Hosp., Worcester, Mass., 1963-64, Michael Reese Hosp., Chgo., 1964-65, Sarnia (Canada) Gen. Hosp., 1965-66; operating room nurse, nurse anesthetist Quezon Meml. Hosp., 1971-72; nurse anesthetist Mt. Carmel Hosp., 1973-74, Brent Hosp., Detroit, 1974-86, Straith Hosp., Southfield, Mich., 1986—. Exhibited paintings in numerous one-man shows including Beijing Internat. Conv. Ctr., 1991, Pontiac Art Ctr., 1989, Troy Libr. and Gallery, 1989, Scarab Club Detroit, 1989, Lawrence St. Gallery, Pontiac, Mich., 1989, Acad. Art Gallery, Paris, 1988, Gallert in the Grove, Canada, 1987, Southfield Civic Ctr., 1986, Electric Fantasy Gallery, 1986, Philippine Orgn. and Filipino Artists, Chgo., 1978, others; exhibited in several group shows including Detroit Press Club, 1989, Mich. Design Ctr., 1988, Philippine Cultural Ctr., Ayala Mus. Named one of Outstanding Men. Mich., City of Detroit, 1976; recipient Albert Einstein award Internat. Acad. Found., 1991, Merit award Mich. Ann. Art Festival, 1975, Cert. of Appreciation Gov. of Mich., 1986. Mem. Am. Assn. Nurse Anesthetists, Mich. Assn. Nurse Anesthetists, Filipino Nurse Assn., Beijing Watercolor Soc., Scarab Club Detroit (bd. dirs. 1988—), Knights of Rizal. Roman Catholic. Home: 6414 Wood Pond Rd West Bloomfield MI 48323-2270

ROMEYN, RICHARD LOREN, orthopedic surgeon; b. Detroit, Nov. 3, 1953; s. Richard J. and Frances (Gillette) R.; married. BA, Davidson Coll.; MD, Wayne State U. Bd. cert. orthopaedic surgeon, recert. Resident William Beaumont Hosp., Royal Oak, Mich., 1979-84; sports medicine fellow U. Pa., Phila., 1984-85; surgeon orthopedics Luth. Hosp., LaCrosse, Wis., 1985—; clin. adj. prof. U. Wis., LaCrosse, 1985—; dir. Western Wis. Sports Medicine, 1985-91; orthopedic cons. New Orleans Saints Football Team, 1989—, LaCrosse Catbirds Basketball Team, 1985-91. Fellow Am. Acad. Orthopedic Surgeons (diplomate), Am. Orthopedic Soc. Sports Medicine (state rep. 1990—). Office: Western Wis Sports Mediicne 505 King St Ste 001 La Crosse WI 54601-4062

RONALD, PAULINE CAROL, school system administrator; b. York, Yorkshire, Eng., Feb. 28, 1945; came to U.S., 1966; d. Peter Vincent Leonard and Doris Annie (Clark) Hume-Shotton; m. James Douglas Ronald, July 16, 1966 (div. 1986); 1 child, Alexia Denise; m. James Donald Wadsworth, Feb. 15, 1991 (div. July 1994). Diploma, Harrogate Sch. Art, Yorkshire, 1965, U. New Castle, Upon Tyne, 1966; MA, Ball State U., 1977. Cert. art tchr., Ind. Art tchr. Knightstown (Ind.) Schs., 1966-67, Dunkirk (Ind.) Schs., 1967-68, Richmond (Ind.) High Sch., 1968—; part time tchr. Ind. U., Earlham Coll., Richmond 1974-84; set painter Richmond Civic Theatre. Exhibited in numerous group shows; illustrator History of Wayne County, History of Centerville, 1996. Coach State Acad. Fine Arts State Team Champions, 1988, 96, 2d Pl. for the state, 1989, 95; bd. dirs., mem. permanent collection com. Richmond Art Mus. Recipient Best Set Painting awards, also numerous awards for drawing and painting. Mem. NEA, Ind. State Tchrs. Assn., Art Assn. Richmond, Indpls. Mus. Art. Home: 417 S 20th St Richmond IN 47374-5729

RONDEAU-BASSETT, CHERYL MARYANN, publisher, editor; b. Ortonville, Minn., Oct. 21, 1952; d. Walter T. and Martha Evelyn (King) Quade; m. Mark J. Rondeau, Oct. 21, 1971 (div. 1985); children: Christopher, Samuel, Daniel, Sally, Joseph, Patrick; m. Scott D. Bassett, Feb. 26, 1994. BA, Mount Marty Coll., Yankton, S.D., 1988; postgrad., S.D. State U., 1992. Proprietor Wilmot (S.D.) Cafe, 1972-73; from salesperson to dist. mgr. Beeline Fashions Inc., Wilmot, 1973-79; salesperson Century 21 - Accent Realty, Lebanon, Oreg., 1978-79; sales and mktg. dir. Hercules Metal, Corona, S.D., 1983-86; sales cons. Mary Kay Cosmetics, Wilmot, 1986-87; pub., editor Wilmot Enterprise, 1988—; Internat. Soc. Weekly Newspaper Editors grad. asst., dept. journalism S.D. State U., 1992-94; presenter in field. Dir., producer: Welcome Home Jennifer, 1990; dir., creator: After the Storm, 1991; dir. Just A Little Bit Country, 1995. Organizer Citizens for Edn., Wilmot, 1986-89; organizer, 1st pres. student body orgn. Harmony Hill Ctr., Watertown, S.D., 1986-88; chmn. Wilmot Summer Recreation, 1989-91; vice chmn. Roberts County Dems., Sisseton, 1989-93; cons., advisor Roberts County Econ. Devel. Com., 1991-93; dir. Ground Hog Day in Branson, 1994; people to people citizen amb. to U.S./China Joint Conf. on Women's Issues, 1995. Recipient Community Svc. award Mount Marty Coll., 1988, scholar. Mem. NAFE, AAUW, Soc. Profl. Journalists, Nat. Fedn. Press Women, Nat. Newspaper Assn., S.D. Newspaper Assn., S.D. Press Women's Assn., Mo. Valley Adult Edn. Assn. Nat. Fedn. Ind. Bus., Am. Legion Aux., Wilmot Alumni Assn. (pres., com. chair), Wilmot Community Club, Kappa Delta Pi. Lutheran. Home: PO Box 296 Wilmot SD 57279-0296 Office: The Wilmot Enterprise PO Box 37 Wilmot SD 57279-0037

RONEN, CAROL, state legislator. BS, Bradley U.; MA, Roosevelt U. Dir. legis. and cmty. affairs Chgo. Dept. Human Svcs., 1985-89; exec. dir. Chgo. Commn. on Women, 1989-90; dir. planning and rsch. Chgo.-Cook County Criminal Justice Commn.; asst. commn. Chgo. Dept. Planning, 1991, Chgo. Dept. Housing; mem. Ill. Ho. of Reps., 1993—. Former pres. Ill. Task Force on Child Support; bd. dirs. Cook County Dem. Women, St. Martin De Porres Shelter for Women and Children. Democrat. Home: 6033 N Sheridan Rd Chicago IL 60660-3003 Office: Ill Ho of Reps State Capitol Springfield IL 62706

RONEY DRENNAN, BETH HORTON, lawyer; b. Winston-Salem, N.C., Aug. 22, 1953; d. Harry Hubert and Barbara (Thomas) Horton; children from previous marriage: Sarah Teresa, John Paul; m. William R. Drennan, June 4, 1988. BFA, Fla. Internat. U., 1975; postgrad. study, The Juilliard Sch., N.Y.C., 1977-78; JD, U. Wis., 1991. Bar: Wis. Actress TV/radio commls. N.Y., Fla., Calif., 1976-85; assoc. editor Sailor's Gazette, St. Petersburg, Fla., 1978-83; atty. Cross, Jenks, Mercer & Maffei, Baraboo, Wis., 1991-94; found., dir., atty. People's Legal Assistance Ctr., Baraboo, 1994—; exec. dir., pres., founder Teresa House, Inc., Baraboo, 1993—. Family commn. St. Joseph Ch., Baraboo, 1995; vol. Hospice, Inc., Ft. Lauderdale, 1980-85, Meals on Wheels, Baraboo. Mem. Christian Legal Soc., Feminists for Life of Wis., Nat. Right to Life., Wis. Right to Life, St. James Soc. Ecumenical Orthodoxy (sec. 1993—), State Bar Assn., Sauk County Bar Assn., Kiwanis. Office: People Legal Assistance Ctr PO Box 192 Baraboo WI 53913

ROOD, JUDITH MENDELSOHN, historian; b. Pitts., Mar. 11, 1958; d. Herbert Mendelsohn and Miriam Laby Vinicur; m. Paul William Rood, July 10, 1983; children: Samuel Mendelsohn, Joshua Mendelsohn. BA, New Coll., 1980; MA, Georgetown U., 1982; PhD, U. Chgo., 1993. Elem. and spl. edn. art tchr., 1975-80; intern Rep. Gilbert Gude, Washington, 1975, State Dept., 1980, Ernst & Whinney, Chgo., 1982-83; curriculum writer secondary schs. Montgomery County, Md., 1976; asst. to v.p. devel. YMCA Met. Chgo., 1983-85; instr. U. Chgo., 1984-85; lectr. Ottoman history Ben Zvi Inst., Israel, 1985-86; spl. lectr. Oakland U., Rochester, Mich., 1994-95; lectr. Wayne State U., Detroit, 1994-95; spkr. at confs.; presenter in field. Contbr. articles to profl. jours. Vol. Walled Lake (Mich.) Sch. Dist., 1994—. Grantee Am. Coun. Learned Socs., 1994; Lady Davis Dissertation fellow Hebrew U., 1985-87, Title VI fellow U. Chgo., 1983-85, Fuerstenberg and McNair fellow, 1982-84. Mem. Am. Hist. Assn., Mid. East Studies Assn. Republican. Home: 3129 Linda Marie Way Walled Lake MI 48390

ROONEY, CAROL BRUNS, dietitian; b. Milw., Dec. 20, 1940; d. Edward G. and Elizabeth C. (Lemke) Bruns; m. George Eugene Rooney Jr., July 1, 1967; children: Steven, Sean. BS, U. Wis., 1962; MS, U. Iowa, 1965. Registered dietitian; cert. nutrition specialist; disting. health care food svc. adminstr. Intern VA Med. Ctr., Hines, Ill., 1962-63; resident in nutrition and food svc. VA Med. Ctr., Iowa City, 1963-65; dietitian nutrition clinic VA Med. Ctr., Hines, 1965-67, 69-70, chief clin. dietetics, 1970-71, chief adminstrv. dietetics, 1971-73; clin. dietitian VA Med. Ctr., Memphis, 1967-68; asst. chief nutrition and food svc. Zablocki VA Med. Ctr., Milw., 1974-85, chief nutrition and food svc., 1985-96, divsn. mgr., cons. care, 1996—, cons. nutrition and food svc. mgmt., 1995—; adj. lectr. Loyola U. Coll. Dentistry, Maywood, Ill., 1969-72; investigator nutrition VA/Med. Coll. Wis., Milw., 1975—, co-dir. ann. clin. nutrition symposium, Milw., 1979—; chmn. task force on ration allowance VA, Washington, 1977-84, mem. nutrition and food svc. spl. interest users group Washington, 1983-85, chmn. tech. adv. group region IV, 1986; mem. Dept. Vets. Affairs Mktg. Ctr. Subsistence Task Force, 1991—, dietetic internship adv. bd. St. Luke's Hosp., Milw., 1983-87; mem. Dept. Vets. Affairs Nat. Cost Containment Ctr. Nutrition & Food Svc. Benchmarking Tech. Adv., 1995—; lectr. in field, 1965—; mem. Dept. Vets. Affairs, Nutrition and Food Svc. Policy Manual Rev. Task Force, 1992-96, Dept. Vets. Chiefs, Food and Nutrition Svc. Mentor Group, 1992—. Author: (videocassette) VA Ration Allowance as a Management Tool 1976; editor: Nutrition Principles and Dietary Guidelines for Patients Receiving Chemotherapy and Radiation Therapy, 1980; contbr. articles to profl. jours., 1978—. Mem. profl. edn. com. Milw. South unit Am. Cancer Soc., 1976-86, bd. dirs. Milw. South unit, 1984-86, Milw. div., 1986-87, Wis. div., 1987-91, media spokesperson, 1983-91, del. to Milw. div., 1984-85, mem. organizational and expansion com. Milw. div., 1986-87, profl. edn. com. Milw. div., 1986-87, Wis. div., 1987-91, mem. taking control Wis. div., 1987-91, chmn. nutrition Wis. div., 1989-91; mem. med. adv. com. YMCA Met. Milw., 1985—; mem. Marquette U. High Sch. Mothers Guild, 1990-94. Recipient Disting. Svc. award Am. Cancer Soc. Milw. South unit, 1980, Women of Achievement award Girl Scouts USA Milw. area, 1987, Leadership award VA, 1989, Dept. Vets. Affairs Dietitian of Yr., 1994, Dept. Vets. Affairs Fed. Women's Program cert. merit for outstanding profl. leadership, 1994, Paralyzed Vets. Am. rsch. grantee, 1981-83. Fellow Am. Dietetic Assn. (registered, practice groups in mgmt. responsibilities in health care delivery, gerontology nutrition 1980—, dietetics in phys. medicine and rehab. 1983—, clin. nutrition mgmt. 1987—, amb. nat. media spokesperson 1983-89, Resource Amb. 1991—, Outstanding Svc. award 1983-89), FADA; mem. Am. Soc. Health Care Food Svc. Adminstrs. (dir.-at-large Wis. chpt. 1993-95, pres.-elect Wis. chpt. 1995-96, pres. 1996-97, Disting. Health Care Food Svc. Adminstr. 1995—), Wis. Dietetic Assn. (co-chmn. divsn. mgmt. practice 1976-77, chmn. 1977-78, bd. dirs. 1981-83, coord. cabinet 1984-91, pres. 1988-89, chmn. nominating com. 1989-90, chmn. long-range planning com. 1989-90, legis. com. 1988—, Wis. Medallion award 1986), Milw. Dietetic Assn. (cmty. nutrition and clin. dietetics and rsch. coms. 1975-76, chair ad hoc com. for nutrition and oncology patients 1976-79, clin. dietetics and rsch. study group 1981-90, chair 1983-85, pres. 1982-83, by-laws com. 1983-84, chair policies and procedures com. 1983-87, pub. rels. com. 1983-87, chair nominating com. 1984-85), Fed. Execs. Assn., Leadership Vets. Affairs Alumni Assn. (charter, life), Phi Upsilon Omicron, Kappa Delta. Home: 18230 Le Chateau Dr Brookfield WI 53045-4922 Office: Zablocki VA Med Ctr 5000 W National Ave Milwaukee WI 53295-0001

ROONEY, JOHN PHILIP, law educator; b. Evanston, Ill., May 1, 1932; s. John McCaffery and Bernadette Marie (O'Brien) R.; m. Jean Marie Kliss, Feb. 16, 1974 (div. Oct. 1988); 1 child, Caitlin Mairin. BA, U. Ill., 1953; JD, Harvard U., 1958. Bar: Ill. 1958, Calif. 1961, Mich. 1975, U.S. Tax Ct. 1973. Assoc. lawyer Chapman & Cutler, Chgo., 1958-60, Wilson, Morton, San Mateo, Calif., 1961-63; pvt. practice San Francisco, 1963-74; prof. law Cooley Law Sch., Lansing, Mich., 1975—. Author: Selected Cases (Property), 1985; contbr. articles to profl. jours. Pres. San Francisco coun. Dem. Clubs, 1970. 1st lt. U.S. Army, 1953-55. Recipient Beattie Teaching award Cooley Law Sch. Grads., 1979, 90, 92. Mem. ABA (real estate fed. tax problems com. 1986—, title ins. com.), Mich. Bar Title Stds. Com., Ingham County Bar Assn., Univ. Club. Democrat. Unitarian. Office: Cooley Law Sch 217 S Capitol Ave Lansing MI 48933-1503

ROONEY, SCOTT WILLIAM, lawyer; b. Suffern, N.Y., Sept. 25, 1961; s. Joseph William and Shirley Dorothy (Morris) R.; m. Linda Marie Miencier, July 24, 1987; children: Brendan Kenneth, Katy Lynn. BA, U. Mich., Dearborn, 1984; JD, Detroit Coll., 1989. Bar: Mich. 1989, U.S. Dist. Ct. Mich. 1989. Assoc. Charfoos & Christensen, P.C., Detroit, 1989—; founder Inst. Injury Reduction, Washington, 1988—, SAFE-Consumer Rights Group, Washington, 1992—; atty. pro-bono activity Legal Aid Clinic, 1990—. Bd. dirs. Bouy 13 High Sch. Scholarship Found.; adv. com. Detroit Cath. Pastoral Alliance, 1994—; com. mem. S.E. Mich. Bus. Consortium Alliance, 1994—. Mem. Ctr. Automotive Safety, Mich. Trial Lawyers Assn., Am. Trial Lawyers Assn., Fed. Bar Assn. (atty. pro bono activity 1990—), Cath. Lawyers Assn., Irish Am. Lawyers Assn., Mich. Bar Assn., Detroit Athletic Club. Roman Catholic. Office: Charfoos & Christensen PC 5510 Woodward Ave Detroit MI 48202-3804

ROOP, JAMES JOHN, public relations executive; b. Parkersburg, W.Va., Oct. 29, 1949; s. J. Vaun and Mary Louise (McGinnis) R.; m. Margaret Mary Kuneck (div. 1982); m. Susan Lynn Hoell (div. 1989); m. Daisy P. Billue, 1990. BS in Journalism, W. Va. U., 1971. Various account mgmt. postions Ketchum Pub. Rels., Pitts., 1972-77, v.p., 1977-79; v.p. Burson-Marsteller, Chgo., 1979-81; sr. v.p. Hesselbart & Mitten/Watt, Cleve., 1981-84, exec. v.p., 1984-86, pres., 1986-87; pres. Watt, Roop & Co. (formerly Hesselbart & Mitten/Watt), Cleve., 1987—. Contbr. articles to profl. jours. Bd. dirs. Ctr. for Families and Children. Fellow Pub. Rels. Soc. Am. (chmn. investor rels. sect. 1984-85, chmn. honors and awards com. 1995); mem. Nat. Investor Rels. Inst. (charter pres. Cleve./Akron chpt., sr. investor rels. roundtable), Boys Hope, Police Athletic League, Econs. Am., Leadership Cleve., Cleve. Skating Club, Mayfield Country Club. Republican. Home: 2574 Fairmount Blvd Cleveland Hts OH 44106-3241 Office: Watt Roop & Co 1100 Superior Ave E Ste 1350 Cleveland OH 44114-2518

ROOS, KATHLEEN MARIE, special education educator; b. Kansas City, Mo., Feb. 1, 1962; d. Edward Joseph Jr. and Teresa Angela (Houlihan) R. BS in Edn., Avila Coll., 1984, MS in Edn. Exceptionalities, 1987. Tchr. behavior disorder and learning disabled Ctr. Sch. Dist. 58, Kansas City, 1985—. Mem. Richards-Gebaur Cmty. Coun., Kansas City, 1985—, mem. scholarship com., 1989-92, mem. airshow com., 1988-92, corr. sec., 1991-92, v.p., 1993-94, pres., 1994-95, chmn. 31st ann. awards banquet, co-chair 4 Las Vegas Nights. Mo. State Dept. grantee, 1988. Mem. Mo. Nat. Edn. Assn., Coun. Exceptional Children (bldg. rep. 1986-89), Ctr. Edn. Assn. (bldg. rep. 1986-89), Ctr. Elem. PTA (treas. 1990-91). Roman Catholic. Home: 401 Sandra Ln Belton MO 64012 Office: Ctr Elem Sch 8401 Euclid Ave Kansas City MO 64132-2207

ROOS, MARIANNE LOUISE, library director; b. Ft. Belvoir, Va., Nov. 27, 1955; d. William Fredrick and Miriam (Kelley) R.; m. David Wayne Bland, Aug. 23, 1980; children: Elizabeth, Gregory. BA, UCLA, 1976, MLS, 1978. Maunuscript librarian Library of Congress, Washington, 1978-83; v.p. Bland, Roos & Assocs., Inc., Winchester, Va., 1983-89; pres., owner Morgan's Choice Restaurant, Winchester, 1986-88; dir. Handley Regional Libr., Winchester, 1988—. Presbyterian. Office: Ramsey County Libr 4570 N Victoria St Shoreview MN 55126

ROOSA, JAN BERTOROTTA, clinical psychologist; b. Champaign, Ill., Apr. 19, 1927; s. Walter Laidlaw and Giannina (Bertorotta) R. BS, U. Ill., 1950; MA, U. Denver, 1951, Ph.D., 1957. Coord., clin. psychologist Child Rsch. Coun., Kansas City, Mo., 1954-57; supr., psychologist State Hosp., Fulton, Mo., 1957-59; chief of psychotherapy VA Hosp., Kansas City, 1959-63; clinical psychologist in pvt. practice, Kansas City area, 1963—; dir., cofounder Learning Resource Ctr., Kansas City, 1969-79; dir. Gestalt, Social Competence Inst., Kansas City, 1969-89. Active Conflict Resolution of Met. Kansas City. Served with USNR, 1945-47, 1951-52. Mem. APA, Greater Kansas City Psychol. Assn., Mo. Psychol. Assn., Kansas Assn. Profl. Psychologists, Mental Health Profls. Author: Situation-Options-Consequences-Simulation: A Technique for Teaching Social Skills, 1973; Psychological and Social Competence Model and Skills, 1975, 88, 92. Office: 4551 W 107th St Ste 239 Shawnee Mission KS 66207-4037

ROOT, JONATHAN BURCH, environmental specialist; b. Deerfield, Ill., Oct. 4, 1963; s. Allen Louis and Katherine Fay (Cobb) R.; m. Marguerite Therese Ivers, July 20, 1991. Foreman, carpenter Recommended Builders Inc., Evanston, Ill., 1983-87; owner Root Constrns., Chgo., 1987-90; environ. site supt. Luse Co., Melrose Park, Ill., 1990—. Mem. Citizens Commn. on Human Rights of Chgo., 1989-93, dep. exec. dir., 1993-95, exec. dir., 1995—. Named Commr. of Yr., Citizens Commn. on Human Rights, 1994. Mem. Ch. of Scientology.

ROOT, WILLIAM KEITH, lawyer; b. Mt. Vernon, Ohio, Oct. 4, 1948; s. William and June (Ezzo) R.; m. Christina Marie Cantlon, Sept. 4, 1971; children: Lisa Michelle, Erin Elizabeth. BA in Polit. Sci., Ohio State U., 1971, MBA, 1972; JD, Capital U., 1978. Bar: Ohio 1978. Ptnr. Resch & Root, Dublin, Ohio, 1978—. Mem. Nat. Network Estate Planning Attys. (founding mem.), Dublin C. of C. (dir., officer 1990—, pres.-elect 1995—). Home: 5968 Macewen Ct Dublin OH 43017 Office: Resch & Root 2715 Tuller Pkwy Dublin OH 43017

ROOZEN, MARY LOUISE, public relations executive; b. Milw., Mar. 31, 1921; d. Edward E. and Margaret (May) Silverman; m. Edwin Cramer Roozen, Sept. 18, 1943; children: Mary Katrina Roozen Hass, Joanna Roozen Satorius, Margaret Roozen Monahan. BA in Speech, U. Wis., 1942. With Met. Milw. Assn. Commerce, 1942-43; adminstrv. asst. Curative Workshop of Milw., 1968-69; adminstrv. asst. mktg. Marine Corp., Milw., 1969-70, mktg. officer, 1970-73, asst. v.p., 1973-76, v.p. pub. relations, 1976-84, v.p. pvt. banking, 1984-87; dir. Germantown Marine Bank, 1977-83v.p. Marine Bank, N.A., Milw., 1977-87, cons. corp. pub. relations, 1987-93; devel. dir. VNA Milw., 1989-90; curator Marine Collection of Wis. Art, 1969-87, v.p. Marine Found., 1980-87; bd. dirs. Plaza Bldg. Mgmt., 1980-87. Bd. dirs. Neighborhood House, Milw., 1963-78, co-chair capital fund drive, 1984; pres. Tempo, 1980-81; chair 440th Tactical Air Wing Community Council, USAFR, 1988, dir. 1985-90; bd. dirs. Curative Workshop, Milw., 1970-78, Wis. Humane Soc., 1976-85, Friends of Art, Milw., 1980-84, Ozaukee Humane Soc., 1983-86, Vol. Ctr. Greater Milw., Friends of PBS Channel 10/36, bd. dirs. Red Bus. Corp., 1993—, docent Milw. Art Mus., 1991—. Recipient Recognition award Nat. Ctr. for Voluntary Action, 1977. Mem. Pub. Relations Soc. Am. (chair fin. insts. sect. 1983-85, exec. com. 1980-84), Am. Heritage Soc., Wis. Sr. Pub. Relations Forum, Nat. Assn. Bank Women (chmn. Milw. group 1976-77), Women's Club of Wis. (mem. fin. com. 1983-85, mem. art com., 1993-94, mem. house com., 1994-95), Fine Arts Soc., River Tennis Club (Milw.). Episcopalian. Home and Office: 7716 N Boyd Way Milwaukee WI 53217-3209

ROPER, CHRIS L., public safety director; b. Columbus, Kans., Mar. 12, 1956; s. Donald L. and Shirley R. (McKenzie) R. Student of basic law enforcement, State of Kans., Lansing, 1978, Police Acad. State, Oklahoma City, 1983. Correctional officer Kans. State Penitentiary, Lansing, 1977-78; police officer City of Picher, Okla., 1980-82; dep. sheriff Ottawa County, Miami, Okla., 1982-83; area security mgr. Wells Fargo Security, Joplin, Mo., 1988-92; pub. safety dir. Gen. Growth Inc., Joplin, Mo., 1992—. Presbyterian. Office: Gen Growth Inc 101 N Rangeline Joplin MO 64801

ROPER, DONNA LOUISE, ambulatory services director; b. Lebanon, Mo., Dec. 17, 1946; d. William James and Elsie Lois (Magee) Morgan; m. H. James Roper, June 18, 1970; 1 child, Patrick Neil. Diploma, Burge Sch. of Nursing, 1967; BSN, Drury Coll., 1973, MEd, 1982. Staff nurse Cox Med. Ctr., Springfield, Mo., 1967-69, head nurse med.-surg., 1969-71, head nurse recovery, 1971-74; faculty Burge Sch. of Nursing, Springfield, Mo., 1974-85; nurse mgr. post anesthesia care unit, same day surg., endoscopy, and pre admission Cox Med. Ctr., Springfield, Mo., 1985-94; dir. ambulatory svcs. Cox Health Systems, Springfield, Mo., 1994—; item writer AORN Cert. Exam, Denver, 1986, 87; nurse mgr. rep. exec. coun. nursing Cox Med. Ctr., Springfield, 1990-92. Com. mem. Boy Scouts Am., Springfield, 1982—, mem. explorer team, 1993—. Mem. Am. Soc. Post Anesthesia Nurses (cert.), Soc. Gastrointestinal Nurses and Assts., Mo. Coun. Nurse Mgrs. (bd. dirs. 1991-92), Mo. Orgn. Nurse Execs., Burge Sch. Nursing Alumni, Kappa Delta Pi. Methodist. Office: Cox Med Ctr South 3801 S National Ave Springfield MO 65807-5210

ROSCOE, CHARLOTTE MARIE, accountant; b. Tilden, Nebr., Aug. 28, 1954; d. Robert Charles and Marjorie Bernice (Fleming) Willard; m. Robert Milton Roscoe, May 24, 1975; children: Marie Marjorie, Paula Ellen, Rhonda Lynn. BS in Acctg., Wayne (Nebr.) State Coll., 1975. Tax auditor IRS, Omaha, 1975-76, internal revenue agt., 1976—, mgr. fed. women's program, 1979-84; mem. joint quality coun. for human resources-servicewide IRS, Washington, 1988-93. Leader Gt. Plains coun. Girl Scouts U.S.A., 1976-83, 90-92, dir. resident camp, summer, 1995, 96; foster parent Nebr. Dept. Social Svcs., Omaha, 1989-92. Mem. Am. Soc. Women Accts., Nat. Treasury Employees Union (pres. chpt. 3 1986—, chair nominations and election com. 1989, 91). Methodist. Office: IRS 7215 Ontario St Omaha NE 68124

ROSDAHL, CAROLINE BUNKER, nurse, educator, author; b. Sauk Centre, Minn., May 15, 1937; d. Frank Everett and Pearl Louella (Gaalaas) Bunker; m. Ronald LeRoy Christensen, Dec. 19, 1981; 1 son by previous marriage, Keith Bunker Rosdahl. Assoc. in Liberal Arts, U. Minn., 1957, BSN, 1960, M.A. in Counseling and Guidance, 1968, also postgrad. R.N., Minn.; ANCC, cert. public health nurse, tchr., adminstr., tchr. educator, vocat. edn. dir.; cert. psych-mental health nurse. Dir., Wright County Pub. Health Service, Buffalo, Minn., 1960-62; sch. nurse, counselor Hopkins (Minn.) Ind. Sch. Dist. 274, 1962-66; staff nurse Hennepin County Med. Ctr., Mpls., 1964-66, 91—; instr. Northwestern Hosp. Sch. Nursing, Mpls., 1966-67; instr. U. Minn., Mpls., 1971-91, assoc. edn. specialist, 1994—; asst. dir. Anoka Area Vocat.-Tech. Inst., Minn., 1967-89; exec. dir. Minn. Lion's Eye Bank, U. Minn., 1990-91; site visitor Nat. League for Nursing, N.Y., 1982—; cons. McGraw-Hill, 1970-80; mem. nat. adv. com. in high sch. health careers Nat. Health Council, N.Y., 1970-73; mem. curriculum adv. com. Dist. 877, Buffalo, Minn., 1972-76; mem. U. Minn. Alumni Band, 1970—; ednl. cons. Gen. Coll. U. Minn., 1975-76. Named Woman of Distinction, 1982; EPDA fellow, 1975-76; Vocat. Rehab. trainee, 1966-67; Delta Kappa Gamma scholar, 1975-76. Mem. Minn. Vocat. Assn. (named Outstanding Vocat. Educator 1976), Am. Vocat. Assn., Nat. League for Nursing, Minn. Vocat. Asst. Dirs. Assn., Am. Nurses Assn., Minn. Nurses Assn., U. Minn. Alumni Assn., Mensa, Delta Kappa Gamma, Phi Mu, Sigma Theta Tau. Lodge: Order Eastern Star. Author: Textbook of Basic Nursing, 6th edit., 1995; editor and cons. Nursing and Allied Health Series, 1976-80; contbr. articles on nursing edn. to profl. jours. Home: PO Box 417 Mound MN 55364-0417

ROSE, DAVID JAMES, electrical engineer; b. Evansville, Ind., Apr. 26, 1964; s. James M. and Eva Joyce (Day) R.; m. LeAnn Young, Mar. 18, 1988; 1 child, Kristen Joyce. AS, John A. Logan Jr. Coll., 1984; BS in Elec. Engring. Tech., So. Ill. U., 1987. Project mgr. Nutherm Internat., Mt. Vernon, Ill., 1988-91; project mgr., elec. engr. Ctrl. Elec. Co., Fulton, Mo., 1991—. Republican. Baptist. Home: 1109 Ashton Cir W Fulton MO 65251 Office: Ctrl Elec Co Rte BB at Hwy 54 S Fulton MO 65251

ROSE, DEREK J., mechanical engineer; b. Long Beach, Calif., Mar. 15, 1963. BS in Applied Sci., M.E., Youngstown (Ohio) State U., 1987. Product engr. Therm-O-Disc Inc., Mansfield, Ohio, 1988—. Patentee in field. Christian. Office: Therm-O-Disc Inc 1320 S Main St Mansfield OH 44907-2516

ROSE, ERNST, dentist; b. Oldenburg, Germany, July 22, 1932; s. William and Elsie (Lowenbach) R.; came to U.S., 1940, naturalized, 1946; m. Shirley Mae Glassman, Dec. 24, 1960; children: Ruth Ellen, Michele Ann, Daniel Scot, Seth Joseph. BS, Georgetown U., 1955; DDS, Western Res. U., 1963. Intern, Waterbury (Conn.) Hosp., 1964; pvt. practice dentistry, Hubbard, Ohio, 1964—; pres., treas. Dr. Ernst Rose, Inc. Lab. instr. Ohio State U., Columbus, 1956-57; dental adviser Assoc. Neighborhood Ctr. Mem. Liberty Twp. Zoning Commn., 1967-74, 1988-92, vice chmn.; chmn., 1970-74, chmn., 1990; chmn. Hubbard (Ohio) Urban Renewal Com., 1968-74. Mem. brotherhood bd., 1967—, treas. 1971-73, 88-90, pres. 1975-77, 90-92, temple bd. dirs. 1975-84, 89-95. Served with AUS, 1957-59. Mem. ADA, Ohio Dental Assn., Corydon Palmer Dental Soc. (mem. coun. 1983-87), Warren Dental Soc., Hubbard C. of C. (bd. dirs. 1967—, v.p. 1995—), Jewish

Chatauqua Soc. (life), Alpha Omega (council mem. 1968—, sec. 1970-71, v.p. 1971-72, pres. 1972-73, pres. 1989-90). Lodges: B'nai B'rith (pres. 1970-71, trustee 1971—), Rotary (vice chmn. Kashrut com. 1983-85, chmn. Kashrut com. 1985—, vice chmn. Mikvah com. 1983-93). Home: 418 Arbor Cir Youngstown OH 44505-1916 Office: 30 N Main St Hubbard OH 44425-1653

ROSE, HOMER CAMERON, JR., dean; b. Omaha, Nebr., Nov. 29, 1947; s. Homer Cameron and Julia Lola (Smead) R.; m. Kathleen Elizabeth Kirk, Aug. 23, 1969; children: Renee Catherine, Rachel Lore. BA, U. Denver, 1972; MA, U. Colo., 1976; PhD, U. Mich., 1980. Adminstrv. officer U. Colo. Med. Ctr., Denver, 1975; grad. counselor sch. edn. U. Denver, 1976-77; asst. ot vice chancellor U. Mich., Dearborn, 1978-80; rsch. fellow, adj. asst. prof. Mont. State U., Bozeman, 1980-81; sr. rsch. assoc. U. Mich., Ann Arbor, 1981-86, asst. dean Rackham Grad. Sch., 1986—. With U.S. Army, 1966-69. Office: Univ Mich Horace Rackham Sch Grad Std Ann Arbor MI 48109

ROSE, JAMES SCOTT, audiologist, hearing technology consultant; b. Warren, Ohio, June 25, 1966; s. Robert Lee and Nancy Eileen (Pritchard) R.; m. Amy Jo Altobelli, May 24, 1995; 1 child, Chase Pritchard. BS, U. Akron, 1991. Hearing specialist Audio Hearing Systems, Youngstown, Ohio, 1991-94; hearing specialist, owner Ear Care Ctr., Girard, Ohio, 1994—; co-owner, pres. Wine & Roses, Niles, Ohio, 1995—; cons. Ear Care Ctr., 1994—; v.p. Akron chpt. OSHA, 1990. Contbr. to World of Poetry Anthology, 1991. Vol. ARC, 1988-91. Mem. Nat. Fedn. Ind. Bus., Girard C. of C., Niles Alumni Assn. (pres. 1995—), Masons, Phi Gamma Delta. Republican. Methodist. Office: Ear Care Ctr 325 N State St Girard OH 44420

ROSE, MICHAEL R., consulting company executive; b. Herrin, Ill., Dec. 26, 1948; m. Georgia Rose, 1976; children: Derrick, Darrenn. Student, U. Cin., 1966-67. Machinist apprentice Fuside Corp., Cin., 1967-76; real estate broker Barnhorn Realtors, Cin., 1982-85; v.p. Homeowner Conss., Cin., 1985—. Host talk show 550 WCKY, Cin., 1993—. Mem. Cin. Bd. Realtors (Million Dollar Club). Episcopalian. Office: Homeowner Conss Inc 6171 Colerain Ave Cincinnati OH 45239-6417

ROSE, NELSON HENRY, state government administrator; b. Washington, Aug. 11, 1945; s. Nelson Peabody and Elizabeth N. (Hitchcock) R.; m. Janis L. Russell, Aug. 24, 1973 (div. Feb. 1981); children: Elizabeth Liva, Averell Stewart. BA, Princeton U., 1967; MSSA, Case Western Res. U., 1970; MPA, Cornell U., 1974; AAS, Ill. Ctrl. Coll., 1996. Analyst Ill. Bur. of Budget, Springfield, 1974-77, chief capital budget sect., 1977-78; chief fiscal officer Ill. Emergency Mgmt. Agy., Springfield, 1978-83; mgr. med. distributive budget sect. Ill. Dept. Pub. Aid, Springfield, 1984-86; chief div. fin. svcs. Ill. Dept. Pub. Health, Springfield, 1986-94. Mem. Am. Soc. for Pub. Adminstrn. (treas. ctrl. Ill. chpt. 1984-95). Democrat. Home: 2067 Hill Meadows Dr # 2 Springfield IL 62702-4683

ROSE, ROBERT JOHN, bishop; b. Grand Rapids, Mich., Feb. 28, 1930; s. Urban H. and Maida A. (Glerum) R. Student, St. Joseph Sem., 1944-50; B.A., Seminaire de Philosophie, Montreal, Que., Can., 1952; S.T.L., Pontifical Urban U., Rome, 1956; M.A., U. Mich., 1962. Ordained priest Roman Catholic Ch., 1955; dean St. Joseph Sem., Grand Rapids, 1966-69; dir. Christopher House, Grand Rapids, 1969-71; rector St. John's Sem., Plymouth, Mich., 1971-77; pastor Sacred Heart Parish, Muskegon Heights, Mich., 1977-81; bishop Diocese of Gaylord, Mich., 1981-89, Diocese of Grand Rapids, Mich., 1989—. Mem. Nat. Conf. Cath. Bishops.

ROSE, TERRI KAYE, obstetrical gynecological nurse practitioner, nurse midwife; b. Joplin, Mo., June 9, 1954; d. Leonard Roscoe and Lenora Pearl (Everitt) R.; children: Meghan, Kaisley. Lic. vocat. nurse cert., Rancho Santiago Coll., 1979, ADN, 1982; nurse practitioner cert., Harbor-UCLA Med. Ctr., 1984; BSN, Calif. State U., Dominguez Hills, 1992; postgrad., U Ala, Birmingham, 1992-95; nurse midwife cert., Calif. State U., San Jose, 1997. Cert. nurse practitioner, Calif., advanced practice nurse, Mo., pub. health nurse, Calif., nurse midwife. Staff nurse Coastal Communities Hosp., Santa Ana, Calif., 1979-82, charge nurse obs., 1982-85; ob.-gyn. nurse practitioner Huntington Beach (Calif.) Community Clinic, 1984-87; charge nurse labor and delivery Western Med. Ctr., Santa Ana, 1985; ob.-gyn. nurse practitioner with pvt. practice physician Huntington Beach, 1987-89; patient educator Healthdyne Perinatal Svcs., Smyrna, Ga., 1989-95; staff nurse labor and delivery Citizen's Hosp., Talladega, Ala., 1991; family planning nurse practitioner OACAC, Springfield, Mo., 1992-93; prenatal nurse practitioner, clin. coord. S.W. Regional Prenatal Clinic, Springfield, Mo., 1993-94; women's health care nurse practitioner Family Health Care Clinic, Springfield, Mo., 1994-96; clin. instr. U. Mo., St. Louis, 1995—. Mem. ANA (cert. high risk perinatal nurse 1984-89, elected to Nat. Registry Cert. Nurses in Advanced Practice 1988), Am. Coll. Nurse Practitioners, Am. Coll. Nurse Midwives, Mo. Nurses Assn., Mo. Coalition Nurses in Advanced Practice, Nat. Assn. Nurse Practitioners in Reproductive Health, Assn. Reproductive Health Profls., Assn. Women's Health, Obstetrics, and Neonatal Nursing (cert. obstetrics and gynecolog. nurse practitioner, co-chairperson planning com. Dist. VII Mo. sect. conf.). Home: PO Box 255 Riverton KS 66770

ROSE, WILLIAM, retired business executive; b. Waukegan, Ill., Nov. 7, 1919; s. Louis and Bertha Rose; m. Vivian May Gulledge, July 15, 1951; children: Whyland, Calvin, Marcia. LittD (hon.), Shimer Coll. Pres. Jobs Temporaries, Waukegan, 1951-86; ret. Jobs Temporaries, 1986. Fin. chmn. Boy Scouts Am., 1959-60, bd. dirs., 1966-71; mem. Lake County (Ill.) Mental Healt Adv. Com., 1971-80, bd. auditors Shields Twp., Ill., 1957-61; justice of peace Lake County, 1956-61, police magistrate, 1959-61; bd. dirs. Shimer Coll., Lake County Mental Health Clinic, 1957-68, United Community Services, 1964-71, Lake County Crime Commn., 1969-75; treas. Lake County Econ. Devel. Corp., 1982-83; bd. dirs., v.p. Lake County Welfare Council, 1963; bd. dirs. Pvt. Industry Council, 1977-83. Served with Signal Corps, AUS, 1944-46. Mem. Ind. Office Svcs. Inst. (pres. 1971-73), Nat. Assn. Temporary Svcs. (dir. 1975-78), Lake County Mental Health Soc. (pres. 1951), Waukegan-North Chgo. C. of C. (bd. dirs. 1968-74, pres. 1976), Am. Legion (comdr. 1951), VFW. Jewish (treas. congregation 1968-74, pres. 1976). Lodge: B'nai B'rith. Clubs: Waukegan Exchange (pres. 1963-64), North Shore Craftsman (pres. 1965). Home: 2439 Dunlay Ct Waukegan IL 60085-4537

ROSEL, CAROL ANN, artist; b. Dodge City, Kans., June 12, 1944; d. John Elbert and Mary Claire (Wetmore) Frazier; m. Herbert Carey Zortman, Aug. 21, 1960 (div. Jan. 1989); children: Elaine Marie, Anita Louise, Stanley Dale; m. George D. Rosel, Sept. 22, 1990 (dec. June 1995). Student, Ctrl. Coll., McPherson, Kans., 1961; BFA cum laude, Ft. Hays State U., 1994. Cert. machine embroidery instr. Dress designer Ms. Cosmo Ltd., Wichita, Kans., 1975-76; designer artistic embroidery garments, 1977-80; owner Carol Ann's Gallery, Liberal, Kans.; part-time art tchr. C.C.s, Baker Art Ctr., Seward County C.C., U.S. D 480, Liberal. One-woman show Ft. Hays Libr., 1993. Mem. Baker Art Ctr., Liberal, 1989—, Hays (Kans.) Arts Coun., 1993; tchr. Sunday sch.; counselor girls ch. camp; solo pianist ch. weddings and comty. functions. Recipient All Am. Scholar Collegiate award, 1994, Grand Champion award State Fair, 1989, 90, 95, Purple Champion award, 1990, others; named Woman of World, 1995-96. Mem. Mid. Am. Arts and Crafts Assn., Pinnacle Honor Soc., Art Club. Republican. Home and Office: 406 Harvard Ave Liberal KS 67901-3024

ROSEN, GERALD ELLIS, federal judge; b. Chandler, Ariz., Oct. 26, 1951; s. Stanley Rosen and Marjorie (Sherman) Cahn; m. Laurie DeMond. BA, Kalamazoo Coll., 1973; JD, George Washington U., 1979. Researchist Swedish Inst., Stockholm, 1973; legis. asst. U.S. Senator Robert P. Griffin, Washington, 1974-79; law clk. Seyfarth, Shaw, Fairweather & Gerardson, Wash., 1979; from assoc. to sr. ptnr. Miller, Canfield, Paddock and Stone, Detroit, 1979-90; judge U.S. Dist Ct. (ea. dist.) Mich., Detroit, 1990—; mem. Jud. Evaluation Com. (co-chmn. 1983-88), Detroit; adj. prof. law Wayne State U., 1992, 93, U. Detroit Law Sch., 1994—; mem. U.S. Jud. Conf. Com. on Criminal Law; lectr. CLE confs., others. Contbr. articles to profl. jours. Rep. candidate for U.S. Congress, Mich., 1982; chmn. 17th Congl. Dist. REp. Com., 1983-85; mem. Mich. Criminal Justice Commn., 1985-87; mem. Jewish Cmty. Ctr. Fellow Kalamazoo Coll. (sr. 1972). Jewish. Office: US Courthouse Rm 802 231 W Lafayette Blvd Detroit MI 48226-2799

ROSENBAUM, JOEL AARON, electrical engineer, consultant; b. Akron, Ohio, Aug. 9, 1942; s. Aaron W. and Nita E. (Johnson) R.; m. LaDonna Ann Kachurchak, July 24, 1971; children: Matthew Aaron, Michael Aaric. BSEE, Akron U., 1966. Cert. profl engr., Ohio, Ill. Elec. engr. Gen. Tire & Rubber Co., Akron, 1966; project engr. Hale & Kullgren, Inc., Akron, 1966-74; project mgr. Dalton-Dalton-Newport, Inc., Cleve., 1974-81; mgr. projects group Controlled Power (CPC), Canton, Ohio, 1981-87; chief engr. PAMCO divsn., Canton, 1987-92; contract mgr. Controlled Power (CPC), Canton, 1988-93, dir. quality assurance, 1993-95, mgr. contracts dept., 1995—. Author conf. report. Rubber & Plastics Industries, 1977. Sr. mem. IEEE (mem. rubber and plastics com. 1977—, chmn. 1991-93, land transp. com. 1984—). Home: 149 Schneiderman Dr Akron OH 44319-4038 Office: Controlled Power (CPC) 1501 Raff Rd Canton OH 44710

ROSENBERG, DALE NORMAN, psychology educator; b. St. Ansgar, Iowa, Dec. 12, 1928; s. Eddie Herman and Ella (Kirchgatter) R.; BS, Mankato State Coll., 1956; M.Ed., U. S.D., 1959; postgrad. Ball State Tchrs. Coll., 1962, U. Nebr., 1961, Colo. State Coll., 1963-67; D.Arts, U. Central Ariz., 1978; m. Delrose Ann Hermanson, Sept. 10, 1950; children—Jean Marie, James Norman, Julie Ann, Lisa Jo. Tchr. public schs., Holstein, Iowa, 1956-60; prin., guidance dir., Crystal Lake, Iowa, 1960-62; prin. Grafton (Iowa) Jr. High Sch., 1962-66; psychol. tester Dept. Rehab., State of Iowa, 1960-66; prof. psychology North Iowa Area Community Coll., Mason City, 1966—; vis. lectr. Buena Vista Coll., Storm Lake, Iowa, 1984; invited speaker Inst. Advanced Philosophic Research, 1984-85. Served with USAF, 1949-53. Mem. NEA, Iowa Edn. Assn., Kappa Delta Pi, Phi Delta Kappa. Lutheran. Author multi-media curriculum for teaching disadvantaged introductory welding; author textbook-workbook, 1985. Recipient Golden Apple award Iowa TV Channel 3, 1994. Home: RR 3 Box 295 12373 Thrush Ave Mason City IA 50401-9828 Office: N Iowa Area Cmty Coll Psychology Dept Mason City IA 50401

ROSENBERG, JACK MICHAEL, emergency physician; b. Cin., July 24, 1958; s. Philip Harry and Brigitte Ruth (Matern) R. BA, Johns Hopkins U., 1980; MD, Ohio State U., 1984. Diplomate Am. Bd. Emergency Medicine, Am. Bd. Anesthesiology. Intern Truman Med. Ctr., Univ. Mo., Kansas City, 1984, resident in emergency medicine, 1985-87; instr. in surgery Truman Med. Ctr., Kansas City, Mo., 1984-85, instr. emergency medicine, 1985-88; resuscitation fellow Henry Ford Hosp., Detroit, 1988-89; sr. staff fellow NIH, Bethesda, Md., 1989-91; staff physician Suburban Hosp., Bethesda, 1989-91; house officer U. Mich., Ann Arbor, 1991-94, asst. prof. dept. anesthesiology, 1994—. Contbr. articles to Annals Emergency Medicine, Jour. Biochemistry, Neurobiology, Jour. AMA. Mem. AMA, Am. Coll. Emergency Physicians, Soc. Acad. Emergency Medicine, Anesthesia and Analgesia. Office: Dept Anesthesia Univ Mich PO Box 0048 Ann Arbor MI 48109

ROSENBERG, JAMES DONALD, public relations executive; b. Milw., Mar. 23, 1956; s. Donald Alfred and Lois Marie (Koepke) R.; m. Karla Jane Johnsrud, Nov. 12, 1975; children: Jack, Katherine. BS, U. of the State N.Y., 1981. Editor Grissom (Ind.) CONTACT, 1975-78; news reporter Sta. WUPY, Ishpeming, Mich., 1979-80; pub. affairs 410th Bombardment Wing, K.I. Sawyer AFB, Mich., 1978-81; dir. pub. rels. Wis. Fuel & Light Co., Wausau, 1981—; mem. Wis. Utilities Assn. Energy Edn. Com., Madison, 1983—; chmn. WUA Edn. Com., 1989; mem. WUA legis. com., 1981—. Contbr. articles to profl. jours. Media coord. State Rep. John Robinson campaign, Wausau, 1984, 88; county coord. U.S. Senate campaign, Marathon County, 1988; mem. comm. com. United Way Marathon County, Wausau, 1982-87; bd. dirs. Zion Luth. Sch., Wausau, 1987-94; sec. Commn. on Ethics, City of Wausau, 1989. Mem. Outdoor Writers Assn. Am. Lutheran. Home: 1806 Plato St Wausau WI 54403-6750 Office: Wis Fuel & Light Co 211 Forest St PO Box 1627 Wausau WI 54402

ROSENBERG, JOHN ALAN (JACK ROSENBERG), business owner; b. Milw., Apr. 6, 1920; s. Louis and Mary (Lichtenstein) R.; m. Sue Miller, 1953 (div. 1979); 1 child, John; m. Lorraine Greenberg, 1981 (div. 1982); m. Lucille Barash Glicklich, Dec. 10, 1984. BA, U. Wis., 1941. Pres., owner Lavo Co., Milw., 1948-55, Jax Hi-Fi, Milw., 1958-62, Cen. Parking, Milw., 1960-63, Fox Co., Milw., 1969-75, Milw. Terminal Warehouse, Milw., 1969-70; CEO, co-owner Telechek/Wis., Milw., 1975-95. V.p. Childrens Outing, Milw., 1985—, Milw. Chamber Theatre, 1989—, Cmty. Advs., Milw., 1990—, Next Act Theatre, 1992—, Generations in Jazz, 1992—; bd. dirs., v.p. Wis. ACLU, 1982-92; bd. dirs., treas. Transcenter, 1993—; vol. SCORE, Milw., 1985-88, Victim Offender Reconcilation, 1990-92; sponsor, dir. The Chosen, 1991—. Democrat. Home: 3431 N Lake Dr Milwaukee WI 53211-2919 Office: 5401 N 76th St Milwaukee WI 53218

ROSENBERG, RICHARD ALLAN, research chemist; b. St. Louis, Sept. 13, 1948; s. William and Ruth (Mayer) R.; 1 child, Benjamin. BS, Northwestern U., 1971; PhD, U. Calif., Berkeley, 1979. Rsch. chemist Naval Weapons Ctr., China Lake, Calif., 1979-85; rsch. scientist U. Wis.-Synchrotron Radiation Ctr., Madison, 1985-91; rsch. scientist Advanced Photon Source Argonne (Ill.) Nat. Lab., 1991—; cons. Jet Propulsion Lab, Pasadena, Calif., 1989-91; proposal study panel Nat. Synchrotron Light Source, Upton, N.Y., 1990-91. Contbr. chpts. to books and numerous articles to profl. jours. Grantee Rsch. Corp., 1986, Dept. of Energy, 1988. Mem. Am. Phys. Soc., Am. Vacuum Soc. Office: Argonne Nat Lab Advanced Photon Source 9700 South Cass Ave Argonne IL 60439-4803

ROSENBERGER, CAROLYN A., art educator; b. Beaver Dam, Wis., Nov. 27, 1945; d. Gust Albert and Ethel May (Linck) Pomering; m. Randy Byron Rosenberger, Aug. 3, 1968; 1 child, Shiloh Rae. BS, U. Wis., 1967, postgrad., 1969-94. founder, advisor Ann. H.S. Art Show, Iola, Wis., 1967-96, H.S. Art Club, 1972-96; art tchr., supr. Summer Sch. Art Program, Amherst, Wis., 1969-71; art tchr. adult night sch. Fox Valley Tech., Iola, 1970-80; supr. to student who won Milw. Jour. Art Calendar Contest, 1971, 76, 82, 83, 85, Waupacha Fine Arts Festival, Waupaca, Wis., 1969-96, Statewide H.S. Art Day, Oshkosh, Wis., 1979, 93, 94, Bi-State X-mas Card Design Contest, Waupaca, Wis., 1985, 90, 91, 91, 93; accepted exhibitor Ctrl. Wis. Art Tchrs. Exhibit, Stevens Point, 1984; judge Wis. Regional Art Assn. Exhibit, Wausau, 1992; tchr. Wis. Valley Art Assn., Wausau, 1993, 94, 95, 96; founder, chmn. Art on Track Profl. Art/Craft Fair, Iola, 1991, 92, 93, 94, 95, 96. Exhbns. include WEA Art Edn. Exhibit, Madison, Wis., 1990 (2 Purchase awards), 92 (Purchase award), 93, 94 (Purchase award), Shawand Arts & Crafts Fair, 1990 (2d Place prize), Wis. Rapids Arts & Crafts Fair, 1990 (1st Place award), New London Mid-Winter Art Exhibit, 1991 (prize), Winnebagoland Art & Crafts Fair in Oshkosh, 1991 (prize), 10 State Art Fair, 1992 (Excellence award), Milw. War Meml. Mus., 1992 (Merit award), Art Works Gallery, Green Bay, 1993, Wausau Ctr. for Visual Arts, 1993, 94, Neville Mus., Green Bay, 1993, 94, Bonifas Art Ctr., Escanaba, Mich., Nat. Exhibit Mequon, Wis., 1993, Waupaca 31st Fine Arts Festival Exhibit, 1994 (prize and purchase award 1994, Marshfield's New Visions Gallery, 1994, Nicolet Coll. No. Waters Exhibit, Rhinelander, 1994, Wausau 8-State Mid-Winter Exhibit, Green Bay, 1995, Waupaca Pub. Library Exhbn. Room, 1996, Alexander House Gallery & Mus. in Port Edwards, 1996. Leader, camp councilor United Meth. Youth, Iola, 1967-68; founding mem. Iola Jaycettes, 1976, local dir.; organizer Art in the Park Iola Centennial, 1992. Named Jaycette of Yr. Iola Jaycettes, 1979, Tchr. of Yr. Iola-Scandinavia Tchrs. Assn., 1979; recipient Best of Show Trophy winner Scandinavian Fine Arts Show, 1977, 78, 79, 81, 82, 83. Mem. Wis. Art Edn. Assn., Nat. Art Edn. Assn., Wis. Women in the Arts, Midwest Watercolor Soc., Wis. Painters and Sculptors Inc., Ctr. for the Arts in Wausau. Methodist. Home: Box 203 Iola WI 54945 Office: Iola Scandinavia Sch 540 S Jackson Iola WI 54945

ROSENBLATT, PAUL CONRAD, family educator; b. Chgo., Sept. 25, 1938; s. Harry and Rose (Albaum) R.; m. Judith E. Spitzner, Jan. 29, 1958 (div. 1983); children: Seth, Ira; m. Sara E. Wright, June 9, 1984; 1 child, Emily. Student, U. Ill., Chgo., 1955-57; AB, U. Chgo., 1958; PhD, Northwestern U., 1962. From. asst. prof. to assoc. prof. U. Mo., Columbia, 1962-67; from. assoc. prof. to prof. U. Minn., St. Paul, 1969—; vis. prof. Northwestern U., Evanston, Ill., 1978; vis. assoc. prof., lectr. U. Calif., Riverside, 1966-69. Author: The Family in Business, 1985, Farming Is in Our Blood, 1990, Metaphors of Family Systems Theory, 1994, Multiracial Couples, 1995; editl. bd. Rural Sociology, 1993-95, Family Bus. Rev., 1991—, Jour. Personal and Interpersonal Loss, 1995—. Mem. APA, Soc. Cross-Cultural Rsch. (past pres.), Nat. Coun. Family Rels., Am. Anthropological Assn., Soc. Applied Anthroplogy, Rural Sociol. Soc. Office: U Minn Dept Family Social Sci 290 McNeal Hall Saint Paul MN 55108

ROSENBLUTH, MARION HELEN, educator, consultant, psychotherapist; b. Chgo., Apr. 4, 1928; d. Edwin William and Louise (Sulzberger) Eisendrath; m. Paul Richard Rosenbluth, June 16, 1950 (dec. Nov. 1972); children: Daniel, Jane Baldwin, Thomas, James, Catherine Rothschild. BA, Harvard U., 1949; MSW, Cath. U. of Am., 1951; PhD, U. Ill., 1986. Lic. clin. social worker, Ill. Clin. therapist Chgo. Dept. of Health, 1973-80; pvt. practice Chgo., 1980—; prof. Loyola U., Chgo., 1986—; cons. Inst. for Clin. Social Work, Chgo., 1988—; cons. student health Loyola U., 1978-80. Bd. dirs. Chgo. Area Project, 1978—, Rec. for the Blind, Chgo., 1980—, Inst. Psychiatry Northwestern U. Mem. NASW, Coun. on Social Work Edn., Bd. Examiners Clin. Social Work (diplomate), Ill. Soc. Clin. Social Work, Arts Club of Chgo., Cliff Dwellers, Friday Club. Office: 676 N Saint Clair St Chicago IL 60611

ROSENFELD, JOEL, ophthalmologist, lawyer; b. Jan. 27, 1957; s. Jacques Maurice and Mazal (Attia) R.; m. Amy Beth Garon. BS with high honors, U. Mich., 1976, MD, 1980; JD cum laude, U. Detroit, 1993. Diplomate Nat. Bd. Med. Examiners, Am. Bd. Ophthalmology; bar: Mich. 1994. Intern Baylor Coll. Medicine, Houston, 1980-81; resident in ophthalmology Kresge Eye Inst./Wayne State U., Detroit, 1981-84; fellow in ultrasound U. Iowa, Iowa City, 1984; chief of ophthalmology Wheelock Hosp., Goodrich, Mich., 1984—, Huron Meml. Hosp., Bad Axe, Mich., 1988—; St. Joseph Mercy Hosp., Pontiac, Mich., 1989—; co-founder, pres., gen. counsel Mktg. Systems, Inc., 1994—. Author rsch. reports. Supporting mem. Boys and Girls Club Am., Pontiac, Mich., 1984—, Pontiac Rescue Mission, 1988—. Recipient Man of Yr. award Boys and Girls Clubs Am., 1988; named Hon. Citizen, Father Flanagan Boys Home, Boys Town, Nebr., 1991, Ptnr. of Conscience, Amnesty Internat., N.Y.C., 1991. Fellow AMA, Am. Acad. Ophthalmology, Am. Coll. Legal Medicine; mem. ABA, FBA, Am. Soc. Law, Medicine and Ethics, Mich. State Med. Soc., Nat. Health Lawyers Assn. Jewish. Home: 4612 W Maple Rd Bloomfield Hills MI 48301-1415

ROSENFELD, JOEL CHARLES, librarian; b. Bklyn., June 16, 1939. BA, U. Mich., 1961, AM in L.S., 1964. Br. libr. Flint Pub. (Mich.) Libr., 1962-66; adult svcs. cons. Lincoln Trail Libr., Champaign, Ill., 1967-68; dir. Urbana (Ill.) Free Libr., 1968-74; exec. dir. Met. Libr. Svc. Agy., St. Paul, 1974-79; exec. dir. Rockford (Ill.) Pub. Libr. 1980—; pres. Rockford Area Literary Coun., 1986-88, 95-96. Mem. ALA (chmn. constl. and bylaws com. 1988-89), Ill. Libr. Assn., Pub. Libr. Assn. (dir.-at-large 1980-81, pres. met. library sect. 1979-80). Office: Rockford Pub Library 215 N Wyman St Rockford IL 61101-1023

ROSENFELD, MARTIN JEROME, executive recruiter, educator; b. Flint, Mich., Oct. 3, 1944; s. Israel Edward and Lillian Edith (Natchez) R.; m. Marcy Tucker Colman; 1 child, Joshua; stepchildren: Jessica Colman, Zachary Colman. BA Mich. State U., 1968; MHA, 1978, MBA with high honors, Ind. No. U., 1979. Adminstr., Care Corp., Grand Rapids, Mich., 1969-70, Chandler Convalescent Ctr., Detroit, 1970-71, Grand Community Hosp., Detroit, 1971-73; exec. v.p., chief exec. officer Msgr. Clement Kern Hosp. Spl. Surgery, Warren, Mich., 1973-84; pres. M.J. Rosenfeld Assocs., 1984-85; COO Dickinson, Wright, Moon, Van Dusen & Freeman, 1985-88; chmn. Rosenfeld Assocs., 1989—; pres. Sanford Rose Assocs., Detroit, 1991—; acting COO New Ctr. Hosp., Detroit, 1995—; instr. Marygrove Coll., 1975-80; assoc. prof. Mercy Coll., Detroit, 1978-80; mem. faculty Inst. on Continuing Legal Edn., Ann Arbor, Mich., Inst. Law Firm Mgmt., Ann Arbor; mem. faculty Inst. on Law Firm Mgmt., Ann Arbor; instr. Legal Tech '87, Chgo. V.p. Detroit chpt. Jewish Nat. Fund, 1978—; pres. Cranbrook Village Homeowners Assn., 1977; chmn. Community Hosps. of Southeastern Mich., 1981-84; mem. tech. work group Comprehensive Health Planning Coun. of Southeastern Mich., 1981-84; mem. fin. mgmt. com., mem. hosp. affairs bd. Greater Detroit Area Hosp. Coun., 1981-84; bd. dirs., com. chmn. Detroit Symphony Orch., 1984-90; bd. dirs., mem. fund raising com. Detroit Met. Orch., 1984-87 . Mem. ABA, Assn. Legal Adminstrs., Am. Assn. Health Care Cons., Royal Soc. Health, Am. Podiatry Assn. (com. hosps. 1981-84). Warren C. of C. (com. chmn. 1975), Nat. Assn. Legal Search Cons., Nat. Assn. Pers. Svcs., Mich. Assn. Pers. Svcs., Sanford Rose Assocs Dirs. Assn. (pres. 1993-95, treas. 1995—). Author papers in field. Mem. editorial bd. The Human-Size Hosp.; mem. panel of experts The Health Care News. Office: Sanford Rose Assocs 25900 Greenfield Rd Ste 236 Oak Park MI 48237-1267

ROSENHOFFER, CHRIS, lawyer; b. Cin., Apr. 19, 1913; s. Joseph and Barbara (Stitzel) R.; m. Alberta Arlene Jarvis, Dec. 28, 1935 (div. Apr. 1992); children: Chris Jr., Dennis P., Gary A., John J., Nancy A., Todd D. BS Commerce, Salmon P. Chase Coll. Commerce, Cin., 1948; JD, Salmon P. Chase Coll. Law, Cin., 1951. Bar: Ohio, 1951, U.S. Dist. Ct. (so. dist.) Ohio 1952. Acct., log buyer Al J. Boehm Walnut Co., Kenova, W.Va., 1938-44; acct. The Green Embry Co., Cin., 1948-51; judge Clermont County Ct., Batavia, Ohio, 1958-62, 67-86; pvt. practice law Batavia, 1951—; spl. counsel Atty. Gen. of Ohio, Batavia, 1963-64. Treas. Clermont County Rep. Club, Batavia, 1957-58; team mem. Citizens Amb. Program, Seattle, 1988, 93; mem. sch. bd. West Clermont Local Sch. Dist., Amelia, Ohio, 1958-74. With U.S. Army, 1944-46. Mem. Ohio State Bar Assn., Ohio Acad. Trial Lawyers, Clermont County Bar Assn. (pres. 1962), Cin. Bar Assn., Am. Legion. Methodist. Office: 97 Main St Batavia OH 45103

ROSENMANN, DANIEL, physicist, educator; b. Lima, Peru, Sept. 6, 1959; came to U.S., 1991; s. Lothar and Eva (Roiter) R.; m. Patricia Edith Alvarado, Jan. 21, 1989. BS in Physics, U. Nac. Mayor de San Marcos, Lima, Peru, 1986; postgrad., No. Ill. U., 1991-93. Instr. U. Nacional Mayor de San Marcos, Lima, 1982-91; tchr. Coll. Leon Pinelo, Lima, 1986-91; teaching asst. No. Ill. U., DeKalb, 1991-93, grad. rsch. asst., 1993; lab. grad. participantship Argonne Nat. Lab., 1993—; rsch. lab. mgr. physics dept. No. Ill. U., DeKalb, 1994—. Author: Lab. guide book, 1988, 89. Scholar, fellow Argonne Nat. Lab. 1993—. Mem. AAAS, Am. Phys. Soc., N.Y. Acad. Scis., Nat. Geographic Soc., Sigma Xi, Sigma Pi Sigma. Home: 630 Annie Glidden Rd Apt 405 De Kalb IL 60115-2136

ROSENTHAL, EDWARD LEONARD, secondary school educator; b. Chgo., June 15, 1948; s. Irving H. and Nina (Kritchevsky) R.; m. Hilary Rosenberg, June 29, 1969; children: Rachel, Rebecca. BS in Sci. and Letters, U. Ill., 1969; MEd in Earth Sci., Northern Ill. U., 1972. Tchr. St. Joseph Sch., Dyer, Ind., 1969-70; tchr., golf coach Joliet (Ill.) Cath. High Sch., 1970-77; tchr., girls golf coach Naperville (Ill.) N. High Sch., 1977—. Chmn. United Multi Family Homeowners, Bolingbrook, Ill., 1974-75; v.p. Ill. Jr. Miss Program, Bolingbrook, 1985-87; trustee Village of Bolingbrook, 1975-81, mayor, 1981-85; bd. dirs. West Suburban Temple Har Zion, 1988-92. Named one of Outstanding Young men Am., 1975, 82, Ill. Girls' Golf Coach of Yr., 1988-89; elected to Ill. Golf Coaches Hall of Fame, 1995; recipient Disting. Svc. award, 1974. Mem. NEA, Ill. Edn. Assn. (bd. dirs. 1992—, exec. com. 1994-96, chmn. legis. com. 1987-90), Ill. Earth Sci. Assn., Nat. Sci. Tchrs. Assn., Ill. Girls' Golf Coaches Assn. (pres. 1985-88), Naperville Unit Edn. Assn. (1st v.p. 1990-95), Cmty. Assn. Inst. Ill. (bd. dirs. 1980-83). Jewish. Home: 508 Clover Ln Bolingbrook IL 60440-1416 Office: Naperville N High Sch 899 N Mill St Naperville IL 60563-2909

ROSENTHAL, JOHN W., art slides producer; b. Munich, Germany, Mar. 25, 1928; s. Julius and Anny (Springer) R.; m. Patricia M. Murray, 1954; children: David, Judith, Sarah, John E. BA, U. Chgo., 1953. Profl. photographer Koopman-Neumer, Chgo., 1955-65; med. photographer St. Lukes Hosp., Chgo., 1950-55; pres. Rosenthal Art Slides, Inc., Chgo., 1965-95; cons. photo Art Inst. Chgo., 1970-75, U. Ctrl. Fla., Orlando, 1989-91. Prin. works include slide sets of Master Paintings in the Art Inst. of Chgo., Chgo. Hist. Soc., World's Columbian Exposition, Mus. of Contemporary Art, Corcoran Gallery of Art, Washington, Nat. Mus. of Am. Art, Washington, Hirshhorn Mus., Washington, Pierpont Morgan Libr., N.Y.C., Simply Stunning in Cin. Art Mus., Textile Sets in Art Inst., Jewelry in Walters Art Gallery, Balt., Am. Glass in Toledo Mus. of Art and miscellaneous others. Author: The '90's Catalog, 1992; prin. works include slide sets of Master Paintings in the Art Inst. Chgo., Chgo. Hist. Soc., World's Columbian Expn., Mus. Contemporary Art, Corcoran Gallery Art, Washington, Nat. Mus. Am. Art, Washington, Hirshhorn Mus., Washington,

Pierpont Morgan Libr., N.Y.C., Simply Stunning in Cin. Art Mus., Textile Sets in Art Inst., Jewelry in Walters Art Gallery, Balt., Am. Glass in Toledo Mus. Art, others. Office: Rosenthal Art Slides Inc 5456 S Ridgewood Ct Chicago IL 60615-5315

ROSENTHAL, LESLIE, brokerage house executive. Prin. Rosenthal Collins Group, Chgo., 1970—; chmn. ING Clearing Derivatives, Chgo., 1990—. Office: ING Clearing Derivatives 209 S La Salle St Ste 3 Chicago IL 60604*

ROSENTHAL, MARILYNN MAE, medical sociology educator; b. Detroit, May 10, 1930; d. Jacob J. and Helen (Link) Waratt; m. Avram Rosenthal, May 21, 1954 (div. 1978); children: Daniel (dec.), Joshua, Helen. BA in Sociology, Wayne State U., 1952; MA in Am. Lit., U. Mich., 1965, PhD in Am. Culture, 1976. Lectr., teaching fellow sociology dept. U. Mich., Ann Arbor, 1973-74, 74-75; instr. dept. community medicine Sch. of Medicine Wayne State U., 1975-76; asst. prof. behavioral scis. dept. U. Mich., Dearborn, 1976-82, assoc. prof. behavioral scis. dept., 1982-88, prof. behavioral scis. dept., 1988—; vis. scholar Wolfson Coll. Ctr. for Socio-Legal Studies, Oxford (Eng.) U., 1990, 91, 92, 93, SPRI and Swedish Med. Assn., Stockholm, 1990; vis. lectr. dept. health policy and mgmt. Harvard U. Sch. Pub. Health, 1984; dir. program in health policy studies U. Mich., Dearborn, 1980—; cons. Karolinska Hosp. Ctr. for Diabetes Edn. and Tng., Stockholm, 1984-88; assoc. dir. program in soc. and medicine U. Mich. Med. Sch., dir. U. Mich. Forum on Health Policy, 1995—; presenter in field. Mem. editorial bd. Jour. Med. Practice Mgmt., 1984; author: Health Care in the People's Republic of China; Moving Toward Modernization, 1987, Dealing With Medical Malpractice-The British and Swedish Experience, 1987, (with Irene Butter, Mark Field) The Political Dynamics of Physician Manpower Policy, 1990; co-editor: (with Marcel Frenkel) Health Care Systems and Their Patients: An International View, 1992, The Incompetent Doctor, 1995; contbr. chpts. to books; contbr. articles to profl. jours. Bd. govs. U. Mich. League, 1991-93; chair com. U. Mich., 1991-93; mem. AIDS Task Force, 1988, chair, 1993—; co-chair task force on a smoke-free environment U. Mich., Dearborn, 1991; outside reviewer sociology program divsn. social and econ. sci. NSF, 1988. King Edward Hosp. Trust grantee, 1992-93, Brit. Coun. Travel grantee, 1992, Office of V.P. for Rsch. Small Projects grantee U. Mich., 1991, Fulbright Western European Region Rsch. grantee, 1989-90, U. Mich. Rackham grantee, 1982-83, 89-90, U. Mich.-Dearborn Campus grantee, 1980-83, 90; Swedish Med. Rsch. Coun. Vis. Scientist fellow, 1984-87, Danforth Grad. fellow for women, 1970-75. Mem. APHA, Am. Sociol. Assn., Assn. for Health Svcs. Rsch., Soc. for the Advancement of Scandinavian Studies, Women's Rsch. Club U. Mich. (pres. 1988-89), Sigma Xi. Jewish. Home: 1712 Shadford Rd Ann Arbor MI 48104-4544 Office: U Mich Evergreen Rd Dearborn MI 48128 also: U Mich Med Ctr 115 Zina Pitcher Dearborn MI 48128

ROSENTHAL, SUSAN LESLIE, psychologist; b. Washington, Sept. 27, 1956; d. Alan Sayre and Helen (Miller) R. BA, Wellesley Coll., 1978; PhD, U. N.C., 1986. Postdoctoral fellow Yale Child Study Ctr., New Haven, 1986-88; asst. prof. clin. pediatrics U. Cin., 1988-93, dir. psychology div. adolescent medicine, 1988—, assoc. prof. clin. pediatrics, 1993—; adj. faculty dept. psychology Miami U., Oxford, Ohio, 1992—. Contbr. articles to profl. jours. Grantee NIH, 1994—, Merck & Co., Inc., 1995, Wyeth-Ayerst Labs., 1995-96. Mem. APA (program chair divsn. 37 1992, sec. 1996—), Cin. Soc. Clin. Child Psychologists (treas. 1992-94, pres. 1994-96), Ohio Psychol. Assn., Soc. Behavioral Pediatrics, Soc. Rsch. on Adolescence, Cin. Acad. Profl. Psychology. Office: Children's Hosp Med Ctr Div Adolescent Medicine 3333 Burnet Ave Cincinnati OH 45229-3026

ROSENWALD, JOHN, humanities educator; b. Oak Park, Ill., June 25, 1943; s. Robert Henry and Laura (Frost) R.; m. Ann Arbor, Aug. 7, 1976; 1 child, Heidi. BA, U. Ill., 1964, MA, 1965; Fulbright diploma, U. Tübingen, Germany, 1966; PhD, Duke U., 1969. Asst. prof. Assumption Coll., Worcester, Mass., 1969-75; asst. prof. English Beloit (Wis.) Coll., 1976-80, assoc. prof. English, 1980-85, prof. English, 1985—; fgn. expert Fudan U., Shanghai, China, 1987, 90; mem. staff Robert Bly's Ann. Conf. on the Great Mother and New Father, 1975-83. Mem. editorial bd. Beloit Poetry Jour., 1976—; editor/translator: (anthology) Smoking People, 1989; author: Patrick Henry at Scotchtown, 1976; contbr. poems to various mags. Fulbright scholar, Fudan U., 1996—. Mem. MLA. Home: Granite Rose Farm PO Box 389 Andover ME 04216-0389 Office: Beloit Coll Box 106 700 College St Beloit WI 53511-5596

ROSENWEIN, BARBARA H., history educator; b. Chgo., Mar. 1, 1945; d. Norman and Rosaline (Katz) Herstein; m. Thomas D. Rosenwein; children: Jessica, Frank. BA, U. Chgo., 1966, MA, 1968, PhD, 1974. Prof. Loyola U., Chgo., 1988—; bd. editors French Hist. Studies, 1993-96; prof. invité Ecole Des Hautes Etudes en Sciences Sociales, Paris, 1992; co-chair medieval studies com. Loyola U., 1994—. Author: Rhinoceros Bound, 1982, To Be the Neighbor of St. Peter, 1989; co-author: Challenge of the West, 1995. John Simon Guggenheim fellow, 1992; fellow for study and rsch. NEH, 1986-87. Mem. Medieval Acad. Am. (councillor 1989-92). Office: Loyola U 6525 Sheridan Rd Chicago IL 60626

ROSENZWEIG, NORMAN, psychiatry educator; b. N.Y.C., Feb. 28, 1924; s. Jacob Arthur and Edna (Braman) R.; m. Carol Treleaven, Sept. 20, 1945; 1 child, Elizabeth Ann. MB, Chgo. Med. Sch., 1947, MD, 1948; MS, U. Mich., 1954. Diplomate Am. Bd. Psychiatry and Neurology. Asst. prof. psychiatry U. Mich., Ann Arbor, 1957-61, asst. prof., 1963-67, assoc. prof., 1967-73; prof. Wayne State U., Detroit, 1973—; chmn. dept. psychiat. Sch. Med. Wayne State U., Detroit, 1987-90, Sinai Hosp., Detroit, 1961-90; spl. cons., profl. advisor Oakland County Community Mental Health Services Bd., 1964-65; mem. protem med. adv. panel Herman Kiefer Hosp., Detroit, 1970, psychiat. task force N.W. Quadrangle Hosps., Detroit, 1971-78, planning com. mental health adv. council Dept. Mental Health State of Mich., Lansing, 1984-90, tech. adv.rsch. com., 1978-82; psychiat. bed need task force Office Health and Med. Affairs State of Mich., 1980-84; bd. dirs. Alliance for Mental Health, Farmington Hills, Mich., 1986-94; speaker in field. Author: Community Mental Health Programs in England: An American View, 1975; co-editor: Psychopharmacology and Psychotherapy-Synthesis or Antithesis?, 1978, Sex Education for the Health Professional: A Curriculum Guide, 1978; contbr. articles to profl. jours. and chpts. to books. Mem. profl. adv. bd. The Orchards, Livonia, Mich., 1963. Served as capt. USAF, 1955-57. Recipient Appreciation and Merit cert. Mich. Soc. Psychiatry and Neurology, 1970-71, Career Svc. award Assn. Mental Health in Mich., 1994. Fellow Am. Coll. Mental Health Adminstrn., fellow emeritus Am. Coll. Psychiatrists (hon. membership com., com. on regional ednl. programs, liaison officer to The Royal Australian and New Zealand Coll. Psychiatrists 1984-88), Am. Psychiat. Assn. (life fellow, coun. on internat. affairs 1970-79, chmn. 1973-76, assembly liaison to coun. on internat. affairs 1979-80, 82-84, reference com. 1973-76, nominating com. 1978-79, internat. affairs survey team 1973-74, assoc. representing Am. Psychiat. Assn. to Inter-Am. Coun. Psychiat. Assns. 1973-75, treas. APA lifers 1991-94, v.p. 1994-95, pres. 1995—, com. on sr. psychiatrists 1993—, others, Rush Gold Medal award 1974, cert. Commendation, 1973-76, 78-80, Warren Williams award 1986); mem. AAUP, AMA (Physician's Recognition award 1971, 74, 77, 80-81, 84, 87, 90, 92), Am. Assn. Dirs. Psychiat. Residency Tng. (nominating com. 1972-74, task force on core curriculum 1972-74), Am. Assn. Gen. Hosp. Psychiatry, Puerto Rico Med. Assn. (hon., presdl. award 1981), Am. Hosp. Assn. (governing coun. psychiat. svcs. sect. 1977-79, ad hoc com. on uniform mental health definitions, chmn. task force on psychiat. coverage under Nat. Health Ins. 1977-79, others), Brit. Soc. Clin. Psychiatrists (task force on gen. hosp. psychiatry 1969-74), Can. Psychiat. Assn., Mich. Assn. Professions, Mich. Hosp. Assn. (psychiat. and mental health svcs. com. 1979-81), Mich. Psychiat. Soc. (com. on ins. 1965-69, chmn. com. on community mental health svcs. 1967-68, chmn. com. on nominations of fellows 1972-73, mem. com. on budget 1973-74, task force on pornography 1973-74, chmn. commn. on health professions and groups 1974-75, pres. elect 1974-75, pres. 1975-76, chmn. com. on liaison with hosp. assns. 1979-81, chmn. subcom. on liaison with Am. Hosp. Assn. 1979-81, numerous others, Past Pres. plaque, 1978, cert. Recognition, 1980, Disting. Service award 1986), Mich. State Med. Soc. (vice chmn. sect. psychiatry 1972-73, chmn. sect. psychiatry 1974-75, mem. com. to improve membership 1977-78, alt. del for Mich. Psychiat. Soc. to Ho. of Dels. 1978-79, del. from Wayne County Med. Soc. to Mich. Med. Soc. Ho. of Dels. 1982-88), N.Y. Acad. Scis., Pan Am. Med. Assn., Wayne County Med. Soc. (com. on hosp. and prof. rels., 1983-84, com. on child health advocacy 1983-87, med. edn. com. 1983-87, mental health com. 1983-87), Royal Australian and New Zealand Coll. Psychiatrists (hon.), Indian Psychiat. Soc. (hon. corr.), World Psychiat. Assn., Sect. GeHosp. Psychiat. Home: 1234 Cedarholm Ln Bloomfield Hills MI 48302-0902 Office: Ste 602 26211 Ctrl Park Blvd Southfield MI 48076-4107

ROSENZWEIG, PEGGY A., state legislator; b. Detroit, Nov. 5, 1936; married; 5 children. BS, U. Wis., Milw., 1978; postgrad., Wayne State U. Wis. state assemblyman Dist. 98, 1982-92, Dist. 14, 1993; Wis. state senator Dist. 5, 1993—; former ranking minority mem. Health Com. Former dir. comty. rels. Milw. Regional Med. Ctr.; former pres. Med. Coll. Wis. Mem. LWV. Address: 6236 Upper Pkwy N Wauwatosa WI 53213 Office: Wis State Assembly State Capitol Madison WI 53702*

ROSHEL, JOHN ALBERT, JR., orthodontist; b. Terre Haute, Ind., Apr. 7, 1941; s. John Albert and Mary M. (Griglione) R.; B.S., Ind. State U., 1963; D.D.S., Ind. U., 1966; M.S., U. Mich., 1968; m. Kathy Roshel; children—John Albert III, James Livingston, Angela Kay. Individual practice dentistry, specializing in orthodontics Terre Haute, 1968—. Mem. ADA, Am. Assn. Orthodontists, Terre Haute C. of C., Lambda Chi Alpha, Delta Sigma Delta, Omicron Kappa Upsilon. Clubs: Terre Haute Country, Lions, Elks, K.C. Roman Catholic. Home: 15 E Wedgeway Dr Terre Haute IN 47802-4983 Office: 4241 S 7th St Terre Haute IN 47802-4367

ROSINSKI, ROBERT J., consultant company executive; b. Detroit, May 1, 1959. Grad. in Metal Forming, Local # 80, Warren, Mich., 1983. V.p. Quality Cons. Co. Inc., Mt. Clemens, Mich., 1985—; owner RJ Cons., Mt. Clemens, Mich., 1985—. Cub master, com. chair Boy Scouts Am., Mt. Clemens, 1990—. Recipient Cert. of Recognition, ARC-City of Mt. Clemons, 1991. Lutheran. Home: 73 Smith St Mount Clemens MI 48043-7901 Office: Quality Cons Co Inc PO Box 46398 Mount Clemens MI 48046-6398

ROSKAM, PETER JAMES, state legislator, lawyer; b. Hinsdale, Ill., Sept. 13, 1961; s. Verlyn Ronald and Martha (Jacobsen) R.; m. Elizabeth Andrea Gracey, June 18, 1988; children: Gracey, James (dec.), Frances, Stephen. BA, U. Ill., 1983; JD, Ill. Inst. Tech., 1989. Bar: Ill. 1989. Tchr. All Saints Sch., St. Thomas, V.I., 1984-85; legis. asst. to Congressman Tom Delay U.S. Ho. of Reps., Washington, 1985-86, legal asst. to Congressman Henry Hyde, 1986-87; exec. dir. Ednl. Assistance Ltd., Glen Ellyn, Ill., 1987-93; ptnr. Salvi & Roskam, Wheaton, Ill., 1994—; mem. Ill. Gen. Assembly, Springfield, 1993—. Republican. Mem. Evangelical Covenant Ch. Office: Salvi & Roskam 1755 S Naperville Rd Wheaton IL 60187-8132

ROSNER, BERNARD, assistant attorney general; b. Detroit, Jan. 9, 1927; s. David and Bella (Matyas) R.; m. Collette Vivia Salon, Feb. 1, 1953; children: Cindy Karen, Kim Melanie. JD, Wayne State U., 1952. Bar: Mich. Ptnr. Rosner & Rosner, Detroit, 1955-64; asst. prosecutor Oakland County Prosecutor, Pontiac, Mich., 1965-67; asst. atty. gen. Atty. Gen. Mich., Detroit, 1967—; in charge Royal Oak (Mich.) office Oakland County Prosecutor, 1966; sect. head social svc. div. Atty. Gen.'s Office, Detroit, 1976-88, asst.-in-charge children and youth svcs. div., 1989—. Mem. Wayne County Children's Task Force, Detroit, 1962; mem. docket com. Wayne County Juvenile Ct., Detroit, 1990—, user's com., 1990—. Served to sgt. U.S. Infantry, 1945-46. Office: Atty Gens Office 1025 E Forest Detroit MI 48207

ROSNER, PATRICE LYNN, editor; b. Newark, Ohio, July 5, 1948; d. Wayne Clifford and Betty Louise (Born) Ramga; m. Charles Joseph Rosner, Mar. 29, 1980; 1 child, Kara Lynn; stepchildren: Deborah Wilson, Paul, Michael. BA, Bluffton Coll., 1970; MDiv, Christian Theol. Sem., 1975; postgrad., St. Louis U., 1984-88. Ordained to ministry, Christian Ch., 1975. Tchr. Spinning Hills Jr. High Sch., Dayton, Ohio, 1970-71; assoc. minister Glen Echo Christian Ch., Des Moines, 1975-76; co-pastor Villa Ridge (Mo.) Christian Ch., 1978-80; tchr. Adult Edn., St. Louis, 1978-80; interim minister Overland (Mo.) Christian Ch., 1990, Brighton (Mo.) Christian Ch., 1992-93; editor Wonder Words, St. Louis, 1993—; editor Christian Bd. Publ., St. Louis, 1977-95, v.p., dir. gen. editl. divsn., 1995; cons. S & S Crafts, Colchester, Conn., 1994, Wonder Words, 1993—. Author: Consider the Children, 1990. Dir. Pattonville Bd. Edn., Maryland Heights, Mo., 1993, sec., bd. trustees, 1994; treas. Pattonville Heights Mid. Sch. PTA, 1992-93. Mem. Mo. Sch. Bd. Assn., St. Louis United Ch. Educators, St. Louis Network Women in Edn. Adminstrn. & Leadership, Assn. Profs. and Researchers in Religious Edn., Assn. Christian Ch. Educators, Religious Edn. Assn. Office: Christian Bd Publ 1316 Convention Plz Dr Saint Louis MO 63103

ROSNER, ROBIN LISA ZISKIND, mental health technologist; b. Detroit, Nov. 12, 1956; d. Samuel and Lorraine (Ziskind) R. AAS, AA with honors, Cuyahoga Community Coll., 1982; B Gen. Studies, Kent State U., 1985. Lic. social worker. Pub. info. specialist Alzheimer's Assn., Cleve., 1989-90; homemaker svcs. coord. Tri-City Consortium on Aging, South Euclid, Ohio, 1991—; faculty mem., chairperson presentations Am. Psychiat. Assn. Ann. Meeting and Inst. Hosp. and Community Psychiatry, 1988—. Contbr. articles to local newspaper. Mem. Citizens Mental Health Assembly (trustee 1986-90), Cleve. Mental Illness and Chem. Dependency Task Force (sec. 1991—). Home: 1874 Aldersgate Dr Cleveland OH 44124-3804 Office: Tri City Consortium Aging 1370 Victory Dr South Euclid OH 44121-3629

ROSS, CARSON, state legislator; b. Warren, Ark., Dec. 15, 1946; m. Eloise E. Ross; children: Shelely, Carla, Diane. BS, BA, Rockhurst Coll., 1977. Mem. Mo. State Ho. of Reps. Dist. 55, 1990—, former minority whip, former mem. various coms.; with Corp. Diversity, Hallmark Cards. Recipient Black Achievement in Industry award SCLC, 1985, Spirit of Enterprise award Chamber, 1991. Home: 3305 SW Park Ln Blue Springs MO 64015-7146*

ROSS, CHARLES STANLEY, English educator; b. East Orange, N.J., Oct. 20, 1949; s. Ira Stanley and La Una (Coggins) R.; m. Clare Chadwick, June 1, 1978; children: Slaney, Sam. AB, Harvard Coll., 1971; PhD, U. Chgo., 1976; JD, Ind. U. - Indpsl., 1994. Prof. English and comparative lit. Purdue U., West Lafayette, Ind., 1977—. Author/translator: Boiardo's Orlando Innamorato, 1989; author: The Custom of the Castle, 1996. Fulbright scholar, Italy, 1974-75. Mem. MLA, Renaissance Soc. Am., Shakespeare Assn. Am. Home: 6406 Division Rd West Lafayette IN 47906 Office: Dept English Purdue Univ West Lafayette IN 47907

ROSS, CHESTER WHEELER, retired clergyman; b. Evansville, Ind., Nov. 3, 1922; s. Mylo Wheeler and Irma (Berning) R.; AB cum laude, Kans. Wesleyan U., 1952; MDiv, Garrett Theol. Sem., 1954; D Ministry, St. Paul Sch. Theology, 1979; postgrad. in Computers Kans. Vocat.-Tech, 1989.; m. Ruth Eulaine Briney, Aug. 30, 1949; children: James W., Deborah R., Judith R., Martha S., John W. Ordained to ministry United Meth. Ch., 1953; enlisted pvt. USAAF, 1942, advanced through grades to lt. col., 1968; chaplain, Africa, Europe, Alaska, Greenland, Taiwan; installation chaplain, Columbus AFB, Miss., 1972-75; ret., 1975; pastor Unity Parish, Iuka, Kans., 1975-80, Ness City (Kans.) United Meth. Ch., 1980-88. active ARC, Boy Scouts Am.; vol. parolee counselor; mem. USD 303 Sch. Bd. Paul Harris fellow Rotary Internat.; Decorated Air medal (2), Meritorious Svc. medal (2); recipient Silver Beaver award, Boy Scouts Am., 1975. Mem. PRIDE, Am. Police Assn., Rail to Trails, Ministers Assn., Mil. Chaplains Assn., Stephen Ministry, Rural Chaplins Assn., 301st Vets Assn., Acad. Parish Clergy, Ret. Officers Assn., Air Force Assn., Nat. Hist. Soc., Am. Assn. Christian Counselors, Cmty. Vol. Svcs., Air Force Gunners Assn., Appalachian Trail Conf., Menninger Found., Kans. Sheriffs Assn. Assn. Ret. Persons, Order Ky. Col., Am. Legion, VFW. Address: 1102 Arcade St Goodland KS 67735-3426

ROSS, DEBRA BENITA, marketing executive; b. Carbondale, Ill., May 1, 1956; d. Bernard Harris and Marian (Frager) R. BS, U. Ill., 1978; MS, U. Wis., 1979. Dir. mktg. Ambion Devel., Inc., Northbrook, Ill., 1983-89; dir. mktg. Fitness Horizons, Inc., Northbrook, 1989-91, v.p. mktg., 1991—; owner Benita Ross Designs, Northbrook, 1992—. Mem. Chgo. CitiWomen. Home: 1853 Mission Hills Ln Northbrook IL 60062-5760

ROSS, DONALD HUGH, fraternal organization executive; b. Delta, Ohio, Aug. 19, 1949; s. Hugh Archibald and Margaret Baker (Harlton) R.; m. Mary Lynn Feuerborn, Dec. 21, 1974; children: Jon, Michael. BS, Miami U., Oxford, Ohio, 1971. Auditor Moose Internat., Mooseheart, Ill., 1971-76, dep. supreme sec., 1976-78, asst. comptroller, 1978-83; supreme sec. Supreme Lodge, Mooseheart, Ill., 1983—; sec. Mooseheart Bd. Govs., Moosehaven Bd. Govs., 1983—. Mem. editorial bd. Moose Action publ.; contbr. articles to newspapers and profl. jours. Republican. Club: Interact (Delta) (pres. 1966-67). Lodge: Moose (past gov. 1976, Pilgrim Degree of Merit 1983). Home: 1119 Woodland Ave Batavia IL 60510-3049 Office: Supreme Lodge Moose Internat Mooseheart IL 60539

ROSS, DONALD ROE, federal judge; b. Orleans, Nebr., June 8, 1922; s. Roe M. and Leila H. (Reed) R.; m. Janice S. Cook, Aug. 29, 1943; children: Susan Jane, Sharon Kay, Rebecca Lynn, Joan Christine, Donald Dean. JD, U. Nebr., 1948, LLD (hon.), 1990. Bar: Nebr. bar 1948. Practice law Lexington, Nebr., 1948-53; mayor City of Lexington, 1953; assoc. Swarr, May, Royce, Smith, Andersen & Ross, 1956-70; U.S. atty. Dist. Nebr., 1953-56; gen. counsel Rep. party, Nebr., 1956-58; mem. Rep. Exec. Com. for Nebr., 1952-53; nat. com. mem. Rep. Nat. Com., 1958-70, vice chmn., 1965-70; sr. judge U.S. Ct. Appeals 8th cir., 1971—.

ROSS, DONALD T., designer; b. South Bend, Ind., Sept. 30, 1955. A in Tech. Drafting, Ferris State U., 1975. Designer Capitol Techs., South Bend, Ind., 1984-87; product designer Bosch Automation Products, Buchanan, Mich., 1987-94; designer Capitol Techs., South Bend, 1994—. Mem. Fernwood Bot. Gardens, Potawatomi Zool. Soc., Moose Lodge. Office: Capitol Techs 3615 Voorde Dr South Bend IN 46628-1644

ROSS, EDWARD, cardiologist; b. Fairfield, Ala., Oct. 10, 1937; s. Horace and Carrie Lee (Griggs) R.; BS, Clark Coll., 1959; MD, Ind. U., 1963; m. Catherine I. Webster, Jan. 19, 1974; children: Edward, Ronald, Cheryl, Anthony. Intern, Marion County Gen. Hosp., Indpls., 1963; resident in internal medicine Ind. U., 1964-66, 68, cardiology rsch. fellowship, 1968-70, clin. asst. prof. medicine, 1970; cardiologist Capitol Med. Assn., Indpls., 1970-74; pvt. practice medicine, specializing in cardiology, Indpls., 1974—; staff cardiologist Winona Meml. Hosp., Indpls.; staff Meth. Hosp., Indpls., chmn. cardiovascular sect., 1989—; dir. cardiovascular ctr. Meth. Hosp., 1990-92; bd. dirs. Meth. Hosp. Heart-Lung Ctr., 1990—, med. dir. cardiovascular svcs., 1991—. Mem. Cen. Ind. Health Planning Coun., 1972-73; bd. dir. Ind. chpt. Am. Heart Assn., 1973-74, multiphasic screening East Side Clinic, Flanner House of Indpls., 1968-71; med. dir. Nat. Ctr. for Health Service Rsch. and Devel., HEW, 1970; consumer rep. radiologic device panel health, FDA, 1988-92; dir. hyptertensive screening State of Ind., 1974; J.B. Johnson Cardiovascular lectr. Nat. Med. Assn., 1991. Assoc. editor Angiology, Jour. Vascular Disease. Capt., MC, USAF, 1966-68. Woodrow Wilson fellow, 1959; Nat. Found. Health scholar, 1955, Gorgas Found. scholar, 1955. Diplomate Am. Bd. Internal Medicine. Fellow Royal Soc. Promotion of Health (Eng.), Am. Coll. Angiology (v.p. fgn. affairs, sec. 1993—), Internat. Coll. of Angiology, Am. Coll. Cardiology, Assn. Black Cardiologists (mem. bd. dirs. 1990-94); mem. AMA, Am. Soc. Contemporary Medicine and Surgery, Nat. Med. Assn. (council sci. assembly 1985-89), Ind. Med. Soc., Marion County Med. Soc., Am. Soc. Internal Medicine, Am. Heart Assn., Ind. Soc. Internal Medicine (pres. 1987-89), Ind. State Med. Assn. (chmn. internal medicine sect. 1987-89), Aesculapean Med. Soc., Hoosier State Med. Assn. (pres. 1980-85, 90—), NAACP, Urban League, Ind. Med. Soc., Alpha Omega Alpha, Alpha Kappa Mu, Beta Kappa Chi, Omega Psi Phi. Baptist. Sr. editor Jour. Vascular Medicine, 1983—. Office: 3737 N Meridian St Ste 400 Indianapolis IN 46208-4348

ROSS, FRANK HOWARD, III, management consultant; b. Charlotte, N.C., Aug. 28, 1946; s. Frank Howard Jr. and Alma (Richardson) R.; BS in Engring., N.C. State U., 1968; m. Beverly Hazel Ross, June 30, 1973; children: Martha McCausland, Frank Howard IV. Cons., Fails & Assocs., Inc., Raleigh, N.C., 1968-73; ptnr. Ross-Payne & Assocs., Inc., Barrington, Ill., 1973—; pres., chmn. bd. dirs., Emerald Capital Investments, Inc., Barrington, 1993—; adviser, spkr. on constrn. and fin.; bd. dirs. Sherman Plumbing. Author: More $ Through $ Management, 1975, MIS and You, 1978, Planning and Budgeting, 1979, Profit by Design, 1981, Pricing for Profit, 1983, Wealthbuilding, 1984, Equipment Cost Analysis, 1988, Survival in a Tight Economy, 1988, Associated Landscape Contractors of America Operating Cost Survey, 1989, 91, Cash Flow, 1989, Dealing with the Competition of the 90's, 1990, Designing Your Accounting System, 1991, Bidding in a Tight Market, 1992, Industry's Wage and Benefit Study, 1992, Financing Your Business, 1993, Pricing, 1994, How Low Can You Go?, 1995. Mem. Presbyn. Ch. Barrington. Mem. Inst. Mgmt. Cons., Barrington Hills Country Club, Haig Point Country Club, Sigma Alpha Epsilon. Homeand Office: Ross Payne Assocs Inc 536 Eton Dr Barrington IL 60010-2017

ROSS, JOHN ALLAN, university director; b. Wakeeney, Kans., Dec. 14, 1955; s. John and Lorraine Nellie (Bell) R. Diploma, DeVry Inst. Tech., Chgo., 1979; BA, Ft. Hays State U., Hays, Kans., 1990, MS, 1994. Owner Home Electronics Svc., Wakeeney, Kans., 1976-95; mgr. microcomputer svcs. Ft. Hays State U., Hays, 1989-94, asst. to dean edn., 1994-95, dir. card tech. ctr., 1995—; chmn. com. on microcomputers Kans. Bd. of Regents, Topeka, 1990-91, card application tech. task force Ft. Hays State U., 1994-95; mem. steering com. Ft. Hays State U. Coll. of Edn., 1994, diversity awareness com., 1994-95; speaker in the field; policy fellow Docking Inst. Pub. Affairs, 1996. Co-author: Principles of Electronic Devices and Circuits, 1994; contr. articles in computing and tech. fields. Bd. dir. CASA of the High Plains, 1995—; mem. advisory com. Ellis County (Kans.) GIS, 1993, tech. com. U.S.D. 489, 1994-95. Named All Am. Scholar U.S. Achievement Acad., 1994. Mem. Nature Conservancy (Kans. chpt.), Soc. Tech. Comm., Phi Alpha Theta, Sigma Tau Delta, Phi Kappa Phi. Office: Fort Hays State Univ 600 Park St Hays KS 67601

ROSS, M. JOANNA, physical therapist; b. Louisville, Dec. 30, 1942; d. John Hollis and Mary Elizabeth (Sloane) R. BS in Phys. Therapy, Ind. U., 1964; MS in Anatomy, U. Mich., 1971. Lic. phys. therapist, Mich. Staff phys. therapist St. Alexis Hosp., Cleve., 1964-65; staff/sr. staff phys. therapist Highland View Hosp., Cleve., 1965-68; sr. staff and acting chief outpatient divsn. U. Hosp. of Cleve., 1968-71; asst. chief phys. therapist to sr. staff phys. therapist Bronson Meth. Hosp., Kalamazoo, 1971-95; adv. com. phys. therapy Kellogg C.C., Battle Creek, Mich., 1973—; ctr. clin. coord. for various sch. programs. Mem. ch. coun. First Congl. Ch., Battle Creek, 1991-95. Recipient Outstanding Svc. award Mich. Phys. Therapy Assn., 1983. Mem. Am. Phys. Therapy Assn. (del. nat. conv.). Home: 375 Garrison Rd Battle Creek MI 49017

ROSS, MICHAEL NEIL, publishing executive; b. Chgo., May 2, 1952; s. Edward Louis and Muriel (Dlugach) R.; m. Naomi Manaka, Aug. 24, 1983 (dec. 1988); 1 child, Monica Nina; m. Kathleen Schultz, June 14, 1992. BA, U. Minn., 1974; MA, Brandeis U., 1977. Editor Time-Life Books, Tokyo, 1979-83; editorial dir. NTC Pub. Group, Lincolnwood, Ill., 1983-92; v.p., edit. dir. World Book, Inc., Chgo., 1992—; bd. dirs. Internat. Edn. Svcs., Tokyo, 1983—; cons. Ricsher Enterprises, Washington, 1987—. Editor: iViva el Español!, 1987, World At Its Best, 1986, Everything Japanese, 1988, Early World of English, 1993, Wonderful World of English, 1994, Say It In English, 1995. Mem. Am. Coun. Teaching. Fgn. Langs., Chgo. Coun. Fgn. Rels., Chgo. Book Clinic. Home: 610 Kincaid St Highland Park IL 60035-5038 Office: World Book Inc 525 W Monroe St Chicago IL 60661-3629

ROSS, RICHARD FRANCIS, veterinarian, microbiologist, educator; b. Washington, Iowa, Apr. 30, 1935; s. Milton Edward and Olive Marie (Berggren) R.; m. Karen Mae Paulsen, Sept. 1, 1957; children: Scott, Susan. D.V.M., Iowa State U., 1959, M.S., 1961, Ph.D., 1965. Rsch. assoc. Iowa State U., Ames, 1959-61, asst. prof., 1962-65, assoc. prof., 1966-72, prof., 1972—, assoc. dir., assoc. dean, 1990—, interim dean, 1992-93, dean, 1993—; oper. mgr. Vet. Lab. Inc., Remsen, Iowa, 1961-62; postdoctoral fellow Rocky Mountain Lab., NIAID, Hamilton, Mont., 1965-66; sr. U.S. scientist Alexander von Humboldt Found., Bonn, Fed. Republic Germany, 1975-76; chmn. Internat. Research Program on Comparative Mycoplasmology, 1982-86; pres. Iowa State U. Research Found., Ames, 1984-86; Howard Dunne meml. lectr. Am. Assn. Swine Practitioners, 1984. Contbr. numerous articles to profl. publs., 1963—. Named Disting. Prof., Iowa State

U., 1982, Hon. Master Pork Producer, Iowa Pork Producers Assn., 1985; recipient faculty citation Iowa State U. Alumni Assn., 1984, Beecham award for rsch. excellence, 1985, Howard Dunne Meml. award Am. Assn. Swine Practitioners, 1988, Am. Feed Mfg. award for rsch., 1995, Sec. of Agr. award for personal and profl. accomplishment, 1996. Mem. Am. Coll. Vet. Microbiologists (diplomate, vice chmn. 1974-75, sec.-treas. 1977-83), Am. Soc. Microbiology (chmn. div. 1985-86), Internat. Orgn. Mycoplasmology (chair 1990-92), AVMA, AAAS, Osborn Research Club, Conf. Rsch. Workers in Animal Diseases (coun. mem., pres. 1992). Republican. Lutheran. Home: 2003 Northwestern Ave Ames IA 50010-4522 Office: Iowa State U Coll Vet Medicine Ames IA 50011

ROSS, ROBERT EVAN, bank executive; b. Alliance, Ohio, Sept. 22, 1947; s. James Jacob Ross and Eva Mae (Forsha) Bodo; m. Susan Margaret Burd, June 20, 1970; children: Margaret Mae, James William. BBA, Kent State U., 1970; MBA, U. Chgo., 1977. Advisor to fraternities, dean of men's office Kent (Ohio) State U., 1970-71; trainee, supr. of trainees Northern Trust Co., Chgo., 1971-73, jr. analyst, 1973-74, trust rep., 1974-77, trust officer, 1977-81, v.p., div. head for personal fin. planning, 1981-85; portfolio mgr., investment rep. Morgan Stanley, Chgo., 1985-89; pres. Northern Trust Bank in Winnetka, Ill., 1989-92; exec. v.p. Northern Trust Bank/Lake Forest, Ill., 1992—; vice chmn., 1995—; bd. dirs. No. Trust Bank, Lake Forest, O'Hare, Ill., DuPage, Ill. Bd. dirs. The Camerata Singers of Lake Forest, Lake Forest Symphony, 1992—; suburban chair United Way North Region, 1993-94, 94-95. Office: No Trust Bank Lake Forest Deerpath And Bank Ln Lake Forest IL 60045

ROSS, SALLY PRICE, artist, mural painter; b. Cleve., Oct. 25, 1949; d. Philip E. and Mimi (Einhorn) Price; m. Howard D. Ross, Mar. 3, 1979; children: Sasha, Emily. BFA, Kent State U., 1971; MA, U. Iowa, 1974, MFA, 1975; student, Art Students League, N.Y.C., 1976-78. art cons. Art Options, Cleve., 1990-96; 1st and only woman artist to paint murals in the U.S. Capitol/Ho. of Reps. corridors, 1978-79, Comm. to paint two Murals for Rainbow Babies Children's Hosp., (Univ. Hosp.), Cleve. Art exhbns. include Cain Park Art Gallery, Cleve., 1967, Jewish Cmty. Ctr. Cleve., 1967, 86, Canton (Ohio) Art Inst., 1969, Studio Theatre, Iowa City, 1973; designed and executed murals Montefiore Nursing Home, Cleve., 2 murals Rainbow Babies and Children's Hosp. New Bldg., Cleve., 1996. Edwin Abbey scholar, 1975-77, Fresco scholar Skowhegan Sch. Painting and Sculpture, 1977. Home: 25 Millcreek Ln Chagrin Falls OH 44022-1265

ROSSER, ANNETTA HAMILTON, composer; b. Jasper, Fla., Aug. 28, 1913; d. Carlos Calvin and Jermai Reuben (Gilbert) Hamilton; m. John Barkley Rosser, Sept. 7, 1935 (dec. Sept. 1989); children: Edwenna Merryday, John Barkley Jr. BM, Fla. State U., 1932. Cert. tchr., Fla. Tchr. music Kirby-Smith Jr. High Sch., Jacksonville, Fla., 1932-35; 1st violinist Santa Monica (Calif.) Symphony, 1949-50; concertmaster Ithaca (N.Y.) Chamber Orch., 1948-56; concertmaster Cornell Univ. Orch., Ithaca, 1948-56, soloist, 1957; 1st violinist Princeton (N.J.) Symphony, 1959-61; concertmaster Madison (Wis.) Symphony Orch., 1963-66, 1st violinist, 1967-82. Composer of over 100 vocal and instrumental compositions including Meditations on Cross, song cycle for 2 voices, flute and piano, 1976, An Offering of Song, book of 48 songs, 1977, Songs of a Nomad Flute, song cycle for soprano, flute and piano, 1978, Six Songs of the T'ang Dynasty for soprano and violin, 1983, Nocturne for violin and piano, 1989, Trio for flute, violin and piano, 1991, Scherzo for flute ensemble, 1991. Bd. dirs. Madison Opera Guild, 1972-86, Madison Civic Music Assn., 1983-85; past pres. Madison Symphony Orch. League, Ithaca Federated Music Club, Ithaca Composers Club; trustee Madison Art Ctr., 1979-83, Madison Civics Club, 1976-79, Madison Woman of Distinction, 1980. Recipient Sr. Svc. award Rotary Club, 1994. Mem. AAUW, Univ. League, Univ. League Bird Study Group, Madison Club, Madison Federated Music Club, PEO, Phi Kappa Phi, Pi Kappa Lambda, Sigma Alpha Iota. Republican. Presbyterian. Home: 4209 Manitou Way Madison WI 53711-3703

ROSSETTI, ROSEMARIE, teacher educator, writer, book publisher; b. Columbus, Ohio, Aug. 7, 1953; d. Fiorovante Dante and Rose (Mascari) R. BS, The Ohio State U., 1975, MS, 1979, PhD, 1982. Cert. interior horticulturist. Horticulture instr. Delaware (Ohio) Joint Vocat. Sch., 1975-78; interior horticulturist Stanford Interior Gardens, Columbus, 1978-86; teaching asst. The Ohio State U., Columbus, 1978-82; instr. Ohio State U., Columbus, 1986-87, vocat. edn. cons., 1987-90, asst. prof. tchr. edn., 1990—; pres. Rosewell Pub., Inc., Columbus, 1991—, Rossetti Enterprises, 1994—; chair adv. com. Ohio Jr. Hort. Assn.; trainer, spkr., cons. in field. Co-author: The Healthy Indoor Plant, 1992; researcher, author ednl. reports. Grantee Kellogg Found., 1990, Nat. FFA, 1990, Ohio State Dept. Edn., 1987, Springfield Vocat. Sch., 1989. Mem. Am. Assn. for Agrl. Edn. (com. chair 1988-90), Am. Vocat. Assn. (task force 1992), Am. Vocat. Edn. Rsch. Assn., Nat. FFA Orgn. (mem. task force 1991-92), Nat. Vocat. Agr. Tchrs. Assn., Ohio FFA Alumni Coun. (chair, officer 1988-92, com. chair 1976-92).

ROSSI, ENNIO C., internist, educator; b. Madison, Wis., Apr. 3, 1931; s. Joseph and Esther (D'Amelio) R.; m. Anna Maria Bianchi, June 22, 1957; children: Roberta, Marco. BA, U. Wis., 1951, MD, 1954. Diplomate Am. Bd. Internal Medicine. Intern Ohio State U. Hosps., 1954-55; resident medicine U. Wis. Hosps., 1958-61, fellow, 1961-63; instr. medicine Marquette U., Milw., 1963-64, asst. prof. medicine, 1964-66; assoc. prof. medicine Northwestern U., Chgo., 1966-72, prof. medicine, 1972—, chief hematology, 1967-84, chief transfusion medicine, 1984—; v.p. med. affairs Life Source Blood Ctr., Glenview, Ill., 1988-93; vis. scientist Mario Negri Inst., Milan, 1977. Co-editor: Haemostasis and the Kidney, 1989; sr. editor: Principles of Transfusion Medicine, 1991, 2d edit., 1996. Capt. U.S. Army, 1956-58. Fulbright scholar, U.S. Dept. State, U. Rome, 1955; Nat. Heart, Lung Blood Inst. Transfusion Medicine Acad. awardee, 1983; WHO travelling fellow, 1985. Fellow ACP; mem. Am. Soc. Hematology, Am. Soc. Pharmacology and Exptl. Therapeutics, Am. Assn. Blood Banks (chmn. acad. transfusion medicine com. 1988-93), Internat. Soc. Blood Transfusion. Office: Northwestern U 303 E Chicago Ave Chicago IL 60611-3008

ROSSI, HELEN GARLAND WOOLFENDEN, administrative secretary; b. Pontiac, Mich., May 26, 1950; d. George Arthur and Roberta Fulton (Latture) Woolfenden; m. Michael Charles Rossi, June 25, 1988. BA, Wayne State U., 1992. Legal sec. Liberty Mut. Ins. Co., Birmingham, Mich., 1978-83; legal sec. Gofrank & Kelman, Southfield, Mich., 1983-91, adminstrv. sec., 1991—. Adult literacy tutor Oakland Literacy Coun., Pontiac, 1993—, English as a second lang. tutor, 1993—. Mem. Golden Key, Phi Beta Kappa. Home: 16276 Beechwood Beverly Hills MI 48025 Office: Gofrank and Kelman 1050 Travelers Tower 26555 Evergreen Southfield MI 48076

ROSSIO, RICHARD DOMINIC, automobile company executive; b. Flint, Mich., May 11, 1933; s. Charles Joseph and Levia Desolina (Peroni) R.; m. Mary Patricia Miller, Aug. 27, 1960; children: Mark, Ronald, Richard, Martin. BME, U. Detroit, 1956; M Automotive Engrng., Chrysler Inst., 1958; MBA, U. Detroit, 1961. Registered profl. engr., Mich. Prodn. engr. spl. products Chrysler Corp., Highland Park, Mich., 1958-61, supr. elec. circuits, 1961-65, mgr. elec. sys., 1965-68, asst. chief engr. elec. mechanisms, 1968-71, asst. chief engr. advance engring., 1971-73, asst. chief engr. body elec., 1973-74, chief engr. body elec., 1974-87, dir. elec., 1987-89, gen. mgr. ops., 1989-92, gen. mgr. sci. labs. and proving grounds, 1992-95; bd. dirs. Engring. Sci. and Devel. Found. Mem. engring. alumni adv. coun. U. Detroit, 1987; mem. motor vehicle safety rsch. adv. coun. NHTSA, Washington, 1989. Named Alumnus of Yr., U. Detroit Engring. Coll., 1981. Mem. Soc. Automotive Engrs. (mem. tech. rev. bd. 1991-94, chmn. test methods 1965-68), Automotive Mfg. Assn. (chmn. h'lite rsch. 1968-71), Engring. Soc. Detroit (bd. dirs. 1991), Mich. Profl. Engrs. Bd., Great Oaks Country Club, Rochester Hills Tennis Club. Roman Catholic. Home: 852 Peach Tree Ln Rochester MI 48306-3359

ROSSON, DENNIS MCKINLEY, manufacturing company executive; b. Cushing, Okla., Nov. 26, 1938; s. Vivian McKinley and Ethyl Juanita (Harris) R.; m. Sharon Martin, June 5, 1960 (div. July 1965); children: Velisa Dawn, Lance Elliot; m. Linda Kay Gant, June 23, 1972; 1 child, Kari Cheree. AS in Diesel Engring., Okla. State U., 1960, BS, 1969. Diesel mechanic instr. Tulsavo Tech., Tulsa, 1969-70, Ctrl. Area Vo-Tech., Drumright, Okla., 1970-73, Del Mar Coll., Corpus Christi, Tex., 1973-75; mfg. rep. Outdoor Recreational Dist., Springfield, Mo., 1975-79; tech. sales engr. Cato Oil and Grease Co., Oklahoma City, Okla., 1979-81; tech. svc. mgr. S.W. Petro-Chem., Olathe, Kans., 1981-84, Dryden Oil Co., Balt., 1984-89; OEM rep. BP Oil Co., Clevel., Ohio, 1989-92; tech. dir. BG Products Inc., Wichita, Kans., 1992—. With U.S. NG, 1950-57. Fellow Nat. Lubricating Grease Inst.; mem. Soc. Automotive Engrs. Home: 1903 White Oak Wichita KS 67207 Office: BG Products Inc 701 S Wichita Wichita KS 67213

ROST, DAVID EDWARD, state official; b. St. Louis, June 14, 1955; s. Medard Wilbert and Dorothy Ann (Mehmert) R.; m. Pamela Joyce Kempker, July 3, 1982; 1 child, Sean Brendan. BS in Polit. Sci., Ctrl. Mo. State U., Warrensburg, 1977; MPA, U. Mo., 1991. Program specialist Mo. Coun. on Criminal Justice, Jefferson City, 1977-80; program specialist Office of the Dir., Mo. Dept. Pub. Safety, Jefferson City, 1980-81, program analyst, 1981-85, justice programs adminstr., 1985-95; dep. dir. Mo. Dept. Pub. Safety, Jefferson City, 1995—; tech. assistance provider Nat. Crime Prevention Coun., Washington, 1992—, rep. Region VII, 1991—, mem. steering com., 1991—; bd. dirs. Jefferson City Area Crime Stoppers, 1991-94. Mem. Nat. Affairs Policy Roundtable, 1989-92; mem. bd. regents St. Mary's Health Ctr., Jefferson City, 1989—; co-treas. Jaycee/Cole County Fair, Jefferson City, 1987-89. Mem. Internat. Soc. Crime Prevention Practitioners (pres. 1985-86, Pres.'s award of merit 1987), Mo. Crime Prevention Assn. (pres. 1985-86), Mo. Police Chiefs Assn., KC (chancellor), Jefferson City Jaycees (pres. 1988-89, Jaycee of Yr. 1987), Jr. Chamber Internat. (senator 1990), Mo. Jaycees (Outstanding Local Chpt. Pres. 1989), U.S. Jaycees (Outstanding Local Chpt. Pres. 1989). Roman Catholic. Office: Mo Dept Pub Safety 301 W High St Jefferson City MO 65101-1580

ROST, MARCIA VERLENE, secondary educator; b. Polk County, Nebr., June 24, 1927; d. Oliver Ellsworth and Alvena Bernice (Flodman) Adelson; m. John Waldo Rost, July 23, 1950; children: Genon Verlene Rost Murray, Monica Rae Rost Meusburger, Clendon Waldo. AA, Luther Acad. and Jr. Coll., Wahoo, Nebr., 1948; BA, Kearney (Nebr.) State U., 1956, MS, 1965; postgrad., U. Nebr. Cert. tchr., Nebr. Tchr. Riverside Sch. Dist. 28, Polk County, Nebr., 1944-45, Mickey Sch. Dist., Polk County, Nebr., 1945-46, Axtell (Nebr.) Elem. Sch., 1948-51, Loomis (Nebr.) Elem. Sch., 1953-56; tchr. English and history Wilcox (Nebr.) H.S., 1956-60; tchr. sr. and advanced placement English Holdrege (Nebr.) H.S., 1968-92; mem. exec. com. Nebr. State Edn. Assn., Tchr. Edn. and Sch. Accreditation, 1982-89. Author, editor: The Ancestry of Carl Ulrik Flodman and a Genealogical Record of His Descendants, 1989. Mem. bd. Cmty. Concert Assn.; active ARC; den mother, Bluebird leader. Grantee Nebr. Humanities Project, U. Nebr., Lincoln, 1989. Mem.AAUW, PEO (guard, chaplain chpt. H), Nebr. Coun. Tchrs. English (mem. exec. com. 1988-89), Nebr. Coun. Tchr. Edn. (mem. exec. com. 1982-89), Kearney County Edn. Assn. (pres. 1955-56). Republican. Lutheran.

ROSTBERT, JIM, state legislator; b. May 28, 1956; m. Kathy Rostbert; 2 children. AA, Cambridge C.C.; postgrad., Met. State U. Minn. state rep. Dist. 18A, 1994—; former vet. svc. officer. Address: 26450 Terrace Rd NE Isanti MN 55040

ROTCHFORD, PATRICIA KATHLEEN, lawyer; b. Chgo., Nov. 17, 1945; d. Charles E. Sr. and Mary (Rodde) R.; 1 child, John. BA with honors, Rosary Coll., River Forest, Ill., 1966; JD, No. Ill. U., 1979. Bar: Ill. 1979. Tchr. pub. schs. Schiller Park, Ill., 1966-76; sole practice Elmhurst, Ill., 1977-79; assoc. Shand, Morahan, Evanston, Ill., 1979-83; corp. counsel CNA Fin., Chgo., 1983-86; gen. counsel, v.p. and corp. sec. MMI Cos., Bannockburn, Ill., 1986-87; gen. counsel, v.p., corp. sec. Inland Group, Northbrook, Ill., 1987-90; pvt. practice fin. and ins. legal counsel Northbrook, 1990—; bd. dirs. Notre Dame Corp., Chgo.; mem. nat. bd. dirs. NAFWIC; U.S. rep. ins. claims Lloyds of London. Author: (pamphlet) Handle Your Own Claims, 1983, (book) Women's Resource Guide, 1988, Women's Insurance and Financial Resource Guide, 1988. Counselor for battered women. Mem. Mich. Bar, Womens Bar Assn. Ill. (active coms. and activities), Corp. Councils Am., Womens Exec. Network, Nat. Assn. Women in Careers. Office: PO Box 4422 Northbrook IL 60065-4422

ROTH, CAROLYN LOUISE, art educator; b. Buffalo, June 17, 1944; d. Charles Mack and Elizabeth Mary (Hassel) R.; m. Charles Turner Barber, Aug. 4, 1991. Student, Art Student's League N.Y., 1965, Instituto Allende, San Miguel de Allende, Mex., 1966; BFA, Herron Sch. Art, 1967; MFA, Fla. State U., 1969. Asst. prof. art U. Tenn., Chattanooga, 1969-72; lectr. art So. Ill. U., Carbondale, 1973-75; asst. prof. art U. Evansville, Ind., 1975-80; lectr. art U. So. Ind., Evansville, 1984—; exhbn. coord., gallery dir. Krannert Gallery, U. Evansville, 1977-79; exhbn. coord., conf. advisor Ind. Women in Arts Conf., Ind. Arts Commn., Evansville, 1978. One woman shows include Wabash Valley Coll., Mt. Carmel, Ill., 1994, So. Ind. Ctr. for Arts, Seymour, Ind., 1996; exhibited in group shows Liberty Gallery, Louisville, 1992, Artlink Contemporary Art Gallery, Ft. Wayne, Ind., 1994, S.E. Mo. Coun. on Arts, Cape Girardeau, 1994, Lexington (Ky.) Art League, 1996, Mills Pond Horse Gallery, St. James, N.Y., 1996, SOHO Gallery, Pensacola, Fla., 1996; works appeared in Contemporary Batik and Tie-Dye, 1973, Kalliope: A Journal of Women's Art, vol. XIV, no. 1, 1992, Jour. Am. Vet. Med. Assn., vol. 203, no. 3, 1993. Mem. Nat. Mus. Women in Arts, Met. Mus. Art, J. B. Speed Mus., Evansville Mus. Arts and Sci., New Harmony Gallery of Contemporary Art. Democrat. Mem. Unity Ch. Home: 10801 S Woodside Dr Evansville IN 47712-8422 Office: U So Ind 8600 University Blvd Evansville IN 47712-3534

ROTH, JOHN E., mechanical engineer; b. Cin., Sept. 14, 1933. BSME, U. Cin., 1962. Cert. in tool and die mfg., Ohio. Tool and die maker Batesville (Ind.) Casket, 1965-72, Nat. Casket, Erwin, Tenn., 1972-75; pres. Action Tool & Die, Miamitown, Ohio, 1976—. Patentee in field. Served with USN, 1952-56. Mem. Nat. Machine Tool Assn. (pres. 1985), Eagles. Republican. Office: Action Tool & Die Engring 5835 Hamilton PO Box 301 Miamitown OH 45041

ROTH, NANCY LOUISE, former nurse, veterinarian; b. Cin., June 24, 1955; d. Jack Leopold Jr. and Elsie Harriet (Shemin) R. BS in Agr., U. Mo., 1977, DVM, 1989; BSN, Avila Coll., 1980. Critical care RN. Staff nurse St. Louis Univ. Hosp., 1980-81, Barnes Hosp., St. Louis, 1981-85, U. Mo. Hosp. and Clinic, Columbia, 1985-89; assoc. veterinarian Ill. Equine Field Svc., North Aurora, 1989-95; proprietor Cedar Ln. Equine Clinic, New Haven, Mo., 1995—. Contbr. articles to profl. jours. Vol. instr. U.S. Pony Club, Wayne, Ill., 1991-95, 4-H Club, Wheaton, Ill., 1991-95; bd. dirs. Ill. Dressage and Combined Tng. Assn. Mem. AVMA, Am. Assn. Equine Practitioners (trails and events com.), Sigma Theta Tau, Phi Zeta. Home: 3134 Hwy E New Haven MO 63068 Office: Cedar Ln Equine Clinic PO Box 108 New Haven MO 63068-0108

ROTH, TOBY, congressman; b. Strasburg, N.D., Oct. 10, 1938; s. Kasper and Julia (Roehrich) R.; m. Barbara Fischer, Nov. 28, 1964; children: Toby Jr., Vicky, Barbie. B.A., Marquette U., 1961. Mem. 96th-104th Congresses from 8th Wis. dist. 96th-103rd Congresses from 8th Wis. dist., Washington, D.C., 1979—; mem. banking, fin., urban affairs com., subcoms. fin. instns. and consumer credit, internat. rels. com., chmn. econ. policy, trade coms., Africa. Served to 1st lt. USAR, 1962-69. Named Wis. Legislator of Yr. Wis. Towns Assn., 1978. Republican. Clubs: VFW (hon.), Optimists (hon.), Kiwanis (hon.). *

ROTH, VANESSA L., religious organization administrator; b. Cuba, N.Y., Dec. 19, 1961; d. Elmer W. and Wanda C. (Hill) R. BA in Psychology, Taylor U., Upland, Ind., 1984; MSW, U. Ill., Chgo., 1990. Coord. family svcs. Head Start/Bensenville (Ill.) Home Soc., 1984-87; cmty. rels. rep. Northeastern Ill. Area Agy. on Aging, West Chgo., Ill., 1987-90; coord. cmty. devel. Outreach Cmty. Ministries, Wheaton, Ill., 1990-93, program dir., 1993—; instr. Coll. of DuPage, Glen Ellyn, Ill., 1990-94, Aurora (Ill.) U., 1992—. Bd. dirs. LWV, 1994-95. Mem. NASW. Office: Outreach Cmty Ministries 122 W Liberty Wheaton IL 60187

ROTH, WILLARD EDWARD, clergyman; b. Washington, Iowa, Mar. 10, 1933; s. Elmer Graber and Minnie Fannie (Wenger) R.; m. Alice Marie metzler, Aug. 25, 1956; children: Carla Joy, Kevin Roy. AA, Hesston Coll., 1953; BA, U. Iowa, 1955; MDiv, Assoc. Mennonite Seminary, Elkhart, 1971. Ordained clergyman Mennonite Ch., 1963. Organizing pastor Mennonite Ch., Des Moines, 1956-58; comms. dir. Mennonite Cen. Com., Akron, Pa., 1959-60; youth publs. editor Mennonite Pub. House, Scottsdale, Pa., 1961-68; comms. cons. Ghana Christian Coun., Accra, Ghana, 1969-73; comms. dir. Mennonite Bd. Missions, Elkhart, 1974-89; internat. editor Mennonite World Conf., Elkhart, 1990—; pastor Southside Mennonite Ch., Elkhart, 1990—; Chmn. Mennonite Ch. Ministerial Com., Bluffton, Ohio, 1992—. Co-author: (book) Becoming God's People Today, 1966; author: (book) No More the Round Mud Hut, 1971; editor: (mags.) Companion, 1961-68, Courier, 1990—. Mem. Hermitage Bd. Dirs., Three Rivers, Mich., 1986-95, Bridgebuilders Adv. Bd., Plymouth, Ind., 1993—; vice-chmn. Ch. Community Svcs., Elkhart, 1992-95. Mem. Soc. Profl. Journalists (life), Am. Soc. Missiology (pub. 1975-85), Acad. Parish Clergy, World Assn. of Christian Comm., Elkhart Minister's Assn. (pres. 1986-87). Democrat. Home: 2313 Morehouse Elkhart IN 46517-2440

ROTHE, CARL FREDERICK, physiologist, biomedical engineer; b. Lima, Ohio, Feb. 6, 1929; s. Calvin H. and Katharine C. (Boegel) R.; m. Mary Louise Hawk, Aug. 16, 1952; children: Sarah Katharine Rothe Whitfield, Thomas Herbert. BS, Ohio State U., 1951, MS, 1952, PhD, 1955. Sr. asst. scientist USPHS, Savannah, Ga., 1955-58; instr. Ind. U. Sch. Medicine, Indpls., 1958-59, asst. prof., 1960-63, assoc. prof., 1963-70, prof. physiology and biophysics, 1970—; mem. cardiovascular study sect. NIH, 1971-75. Mem. gen. bd. Nat. Coun. Chs., 1963-68; moderator Ind.-Ky. Conf. United Ch. Christ, copr. bd. United Ch. Bd. Homeland Ministries. Achievements include measurement role and control of vascular capacitance; reflex control of cardiovascular system; author Handbook of Physiology, various reviews in physiology. Mem. Biomed. Engring. Soc. (bd. dirs. 1982-85), Am. Physiol. Soc. (circulation sect. fellow), Am. Heart Assn. (circulation coun. fellow). Mem. United Ch. of Christ. Home: 4649 Boulevard Pl Indianapolis IN 46208-3549 Office: Ind U Med Ctr Dept Physiology and Biophysics 635 Barnhill Dr Indianapolis IN 46202-5120

ROTHE, ERHARD WILLIAM, engineering educator; b. Breslau, Germany, Apr. 15, 1931; s. Erich Hans and Hildegard (Ille) R.; m. Daria A. Rothe, Aug. 29, 1959; children: Lisa Catherine Booth, Margaret Louise. BS in Chemistry, U. Mich., 1952, PhD in Chemistry, 1959. Staff scientist Gen. Dynamics/Convair, San Diego, 1959-69; Gershenson Disting. prof. Wayne State U., Detroit, 1986-88, prof. engring., 1969—; cons. Phys. Dynamics Corp., San Diego, 1975-88; summer rsch. fellow Max Planck Inst., Göttingen, Fed. Republic Germany, 1980—. Humboldt-Planck fellow Humboldt Found., Bonn, Fed. Republic Germany, 1990. Fellow Am. Phys. Soc. (elected); mem. ACS, AAAS, Sigma Xi. Office: Wayne State U Chem Engring Dept Detroit MI 48202

ROTHENBERG, ELLIOT CALVIN, lawyer, writer; b. Mpls., Nov. 12, 1939; s. Sam S. and Claire Sylvia (Feller) R.; m. Sally Smayling; children: Sarah, Rebecca, Sam. BA summa cum laude, U. Minn., 1961; JD, Harvard U. (Fulbright fellow), 1964. Bar: Minn. 1966, U.S. Dist. Ct. Minn. 1966, D.C. 1968, U.S. Supreme Ct. 1972, N.Y. 1974, U.S. Ct. Appeals (2d cir.) 1974, U.S. Ct. Appeals (8th cir.) 1975. Assoc. project dir. Brookings Inst., Washington, 1966-67; fgn. svc. officer, legal advisor U.S. Dept. State, Washington, 1968-73; Am. Embassy, Saigon; U.S. Mission to the UN; nat. law dir. Anti-Defamation League, N.Y.C., 1973-74; legal dir. Minn. Pub. Interest Rsch. Group, Mpls., 1974-77; pvt. practice law, Mpls., 1977—; adj. prof. William Mitchell Coll. Law, St. Paul, 1983—; faculty mem. several nat. communications law and First Amendment seminars. State bd. dirs. YMCA Youth in Govt. Program, 1981-84; v.p. Twin Cities chpt. Am. Jewish Com., 1980-84; mem. Minn. House of Reps., 1978-82, asst. floor leader (whip), 1981-82; pres., dir. North Star Legal Found., 1983—; Legal affairs editor Pub. Rsch. Syndicated, 1986—; briefs and oral arguments published in full Landmark Briefs and Arguments of the Supreme Court of the U.S., Vol. 200, 1992; Mem. citizens adv. com. Voyageurs Nat. Park, 1979-81. Fulbright fellow, 1964-65; recipient Legis. Evaluation Assembly Legis. Excellence award, 1980, Vietnam Civilian Service medal U.S Dept. State, 1970, North Star award, U. Minn., 1961. Mem. Am. Bar Assn., Harvard Law Sch. Assn., Minn. Bar Assn., Am. Legion, Mensa, Phi Beta Kappa. Jewish. Contbr. articles to profl. and scholarly jours. and books, newspapers, popular magazines; author: (with Zelman Cowen) Sir John Latham and Other Papers, 1965. Avocations: long distance running, classical music, baseball. Home and Office: 3901 W 25th St Saint Louis Park MN 55416-3803

ROTHERHAM-WHIPP, CHERYL KAY, mental heal administrator; b. Pueblo, Colo., Apr. 17, 1951; d. Joseph Kent and Mary Patricia (Beatty) Rotherham; m. (div. June 1985); children: Jennifer Whipp, Tara Whipp, Katie Whipp. BS in Human Growth and Devel., U. Wis., Green Bay, 1975; MS in Counseling, U. Wis., Milw., 1983. Lic. social worker, Wis. Instr. N.E. Tech. Coll., Green Bay, 1976-86; social worker St. Marys Hosp. Med. Ctr., Green Bay, 1986-94, EAP coord., counselor, 1987-94; counselor Family Life & Growth Clinic, Green Bay, 1986-94; counselor, owner Bay Psychiat. Svcs., Green Bay, 1994—; cons. in field. Co-author: Pregnancy: A Time for Caring, 1988. Mem. ACA, Nat. Assn. Forensic Counseling. Roman Catholic. Office: Bay Psychiat Svcs 301 E St Joseph Green Bay WI 54301

ROTHERING, LARRY P., mechanical engineer; b. Racine, Wis., Nov. 15, 1956. BSME, U. Wis., Platteville, 1979. Project engr. Walker Mfg., Racine, 1979-82, Enerpac Applied Power, Butler, Wis., 1983—. Office: Enerpac Applied Power 1300 W Silver Springs Dr Butler WI 53007

ROTHERT, CATHY COTTON, physical therapist; b. Kansas City, Oct. 20, 1955; d. John L. Cotton and Beverly Ann Mullin; m. Eugene A. Rothert Jr. BA in Biology cum laude, Avica Coll., 1976. Cert. phys. therapist. Staff phys. therapist Charity Hosp., New Orleans, 1977-78, Skokie (Ill.) Valley Hosp., 1979-80; mgr. quality assurance RSI, Oak Park, Ill., 1980-86; dir. rehab. svcs. In Home Health Care, Morton Grove, Ill., 1986-90; dir. profl. devel. CPT, Wooddale, Ill., 1990—; chair quality assurance Cmty. Home Health Practice, Alexandria, Va., 1992-95. Roman Catholic. Home: 356 Russet Ln Highland Park IL 60035 Office: CPT 199 S Addison Wood Dale IL 60191

ROTHLISBERGER, RODNEY JOHN, music educator; b. Bottineau, N.D., May 13, 1940; s. Forrest John and Ellen Rothlisberger; m. Gay Elaine Mohr, Dec. 20, 1975 (div.). BA, St. Olaf Coll., 1962; MA, Eastman Sch. Music, 1967; DMusA, U. Colo., 1978. Organist, choirmaster U.S. Mil. Acad., West Point, N.Y., 1965-67; instr., prof. Bowdoin Coll., Brunswick, Maine, 1967-70; instr. Melbourne (Australia) H.S., 1973-75; prof. Berea (Ky.) Coll., 1976-77; instr. Concordia Coll., Moorhead, Minn., 1979-81, Moorhead Pub. Schs., 1989-95; prof. Moorhead State U., 1995—. Bd. dirs. Red River Boy Choir, Moorhead, 1984—, Arts Coun., Moorhead, 1985-89, Luth. Brotherhood, Moorhead, 1988—. With U.S. Army, 1985-87. Recipient Achievement award Lake Agassiz Arts Coun., 1987. Mem. Am. Choral Dirs. Assn., Music Educators Nat. Conf., Coll. Music Soc., Am. Guild Organists (dean Red River Valley chpt. 1985-87, Minn. state chair 1995—). Presbyterian. Home: 1021 S River Dr Moorhead MN 56560 Office: Moorhead State U 1104 7th Ave S Moorhead MN 56563

ROTHMAN, JERRY JAY, health facility administrator; b. St. Louis, Nov. 13, 1939; s. Charles and Lillian Rothman; m. Fran Smith (div. Oct. 1990); m. Christina Lucia, Oct. 15, 1992. BA, Washington U., St. Louis, 1962; MSW, U. Mo., 1967; PhD, Northwestern U., Evanston, Ill., 1972. Lic. clin. social worker, Ill.; cert hypnotherapist. Exec. dir. So. Human Svcs., Chgo., 1974-91; pres. Ctr. for Grief Recovery, Chgo., 1991—; vis. assoc. prof. Boise (Idaho) State U., 1992. Author (audio tape series) Guided Imagery, 1994; reviewer books. Bd. dirs. Ill. State Adv. Coun. on Edn. Handicapped Children, Springfield, Ill., 1980-84, White Crane Wellness Ctr., Chgo., 1993-95, Goodwill Industries, Chgo., 1984-90; pres. Transpersonal Psychology Network, Chgo., 1992-94. Mem. Bereavement Svc. Providers Network. Office: Ctr for Grief Recovery 1263 W Loyola Chicago IL 60626

ROTHMEIER, STEVEN GEORGE, merchant banker, investment manager; b. Mankato, Minn., Oct. 4, 1946; s. Edwin George and Alice Joan (Johnson) R. BA, U. Notre Dame, 1968; MBA, U. Chgo., 1972. Corp. fin. analyst Northwest Airlines, Inc., St. Paul, 1973, mgr. econ. analysis, 1973-78, dir. econ. planning, 1978, v.p. fin., treas., 1978-82, exec. v.p., treas., dir., 1982-83, exec. v.p. fin. and adminstrn., treas., dir., 1983, pres., chief operating officer, 1984, pres., chief exec. officer, 1985-86, chmn., chief exec. officer, 1986-89, also bd. dirs.; pres. IAI Capital Group, Mpls., 1989-93;

chmn., CEO Great No. Capital, St. Paul, 1993—; bd. dirs. Honeywell Inc., Precision Castparts, E.W. Blanch Holdings Inc., Dept. 56 Inc. Chmn. St. Agnes Found., Channel 53 Cath. TV Minn. Decorated Bronze Star. Republican. Roman Catholic. Clubs: Mpls.; Minn. Office: Great Northern Capital 332 Minnesota St Ste W 1295 Saint Paul MN 55101-1305

ROTHSCHILD, BERYL ELAINE, mayor; m. Edmund W. Rothschild; children: Margaret, Dan. BS in Journalism, Ohio U., 1951. Councilman City of University Heights, Ohio, 1968-78, mayor, 1979—; sec. Regional Coun. of Govts. Former mem. legis. policy com. Ohio Mcpl. League; past mem. exec. bd. N.E. Ohio Areawide Coord. Agy.; former trustee Citizens League Greater Cleve. and Citizens League Rsch. Inst., YWCA (Metro) Cleve., Meridia Suburban Hosp., 1987-90, chmn., Meridia Health System, 1987-90; bd. dirs. Cuyahoga County Nursing Home; mem. community adv. bd. Coop. Human Tissue Network, Case Western Res. U.; mem. adv. bd. Adult Basic and Literacy Edn.; charter mem., v.p. Ind. Living Experience Achievement Program; mem. adv. com. John Carroll U. Edn. Dept., 1988-90; past mem. com. on svcs. to the disabled Jewish Cmty. Fedn. of Cleve., special needs adv. com. Jewish Cmty. Ctr., advanced program employer adv. coun. Jewish Vocat. Svcs.; active mem. Learning Disabilities Assn. of Greater Cleve., Friends of the Cleveland Heights-Univ. Heights Libr. System, Hadassah, Pioneer Women, Coun. of Jewish Women, Heights Y, Univ. Heights Club 100, Fairmount Temple, Women's Com. of The Cleve. Orchestra, Cleve. Mus. Art. Recipient Career Woman of Achievement award Cleve. YWCA, 1986, Woman of Achievement Recognition award Greater Cleve. chpt. Hadassah, Recognition cert. Cleveland Heights-University Heights Bd. Edn., 1980-81, City of Peace award State of Israel Bonds, 1984, Kenneth R. Oldman Meml. award (with husband) Cleve. Assn. for Children and Adults with Learning Disabilities, 1988; named one of Outstanding Women of Yr. Greater Cleve. State of Israel Bonds, 1988. Mem. Nat. League of Cities and U.S. Conf. of Mayors, Cuyahoga County Mayors and Mgrs. Assn. (exec. bd., waste mgmt. com., legis. com., cable TV com.), Women in Comms., Inc., Alpha Sigma Nu (hon.). Office: City of University Heights 2300 Warrensville Center Rd University Heights OH 44118-3825

ROTHSCHILD, CHERYL LYNN, marketing executive; b. N.Y.C., Jan. 28, 1967; d. Wallace Goodman and Pearl I. (Rosenberg) Taylor; m. Stephen A. Rothschild, Aug. 21, 1988; children: Andrew M., Zachary R. BS in Comm. Studies, Northwestern U., 1988. Mgmt. trainee Nat. City Bank, Toledo, 1988-91, with mktg., 1988-89, br. svc. rep., 1989, corp. svcs. support supr., 1989-90, purchasing mgr., 1990, comml. credit analyst, 1990-91, corp. cash mgmt. officer, mgr., 1991-93; dir. mktg. and membership Jewish Community Ctr. of Greater Toledo, 1993—; fin. advisor Jr. Achievement, Toledo, 1989-90; resident artist Toledo Opera, 1990-93, mem., 1988—. Chmn., co-chair Jamie Farr LPGA Silent Auction, Toledo, 1989-91, chmn. events Jamie Farr LPGA Golf Classic, Toledo, 1991-96, chmn. spectator svcs. Jamie Farr, 1994-95; mem. Women's ORT, Toledo, 1990—; mem. steering com. United Jewish Fedn., Toledo, 1991-93; mem. Northwestern Adv. Coun., Northwestern Alumni Group. Mem. Northwestern Alumni Group, Sigma Alpha Iota. Office: Jewish Community Ctr 6465 Sylvania Ave Sylvania OH 43560-3916

ROTMAN, CARLOS ALBERTO, obstetrician, gynecologist; b. Buenos Aires, Argentina, July 20, 1947; came to U.S., 1972; s. David and Rosa (Kolomietz) R.; m. Carlotta Hayes, July 31, 1980; 1 child, Robin Mercedes. MD, U. Buenos Aires, 1970. Diplomate Am. Bd. Ob/gyn. Intern Cook County Hosp., Chgo., 1971-72, resident in ob/gyn., 1973-76; asst. prof. ob/gyn. Rush Med. Coll., Chgo., 1982—; assoc. dir. gynecology, dir. sect. ambulatory care Rush-Presbyn.-St. Luke's Med. Ctr., Chgo., 1986-88, attending physician ob/gyn., 1986—; attending physician ob/gyn. Grant Hosp., Chgo., 1988—; assoc. dir., v.p. Inst. Study and Treatment of Endometriosis, Chgo., 1988—; pres. Oak Brook Inst. Endoscopy; guest speaker Rio de Janeiro, 1987, Curitiba, Brazil, 1987, Sao Paulo, Brazil, 1988, 89, 92, 93, Natal, Brazil, 1989, Mexico City, 1990, Buenos Aires, 1991, 1992, Chgo., 1991, Athens, Geece, 1992, 1993, 1994, Guatemala, 1992, Fresno, Calif., 1993, Bahia Blanca, 1993, Lahore, Pakistan, 1994. Author: (with others) Conn's Current Therapy, 1991, The Journal of Clinical Practice and Sexuality, 1991, 2nd edit., 1993, Immunology of Endometriosis, 1991, Operative Laparoscopy, 1994; patentee suturing and knot tying forceps for laparoscopy. Recipient Best Prodn. award Movie Festival, San Diego, Calif., 1993; Golden Laproscope award, 1st place, 1994. Fellow Am. Coll. Ob/gyn.; mem. AMA, Am. Fertility Soc., Am. Assn. Gynecologic Laparoscopists (2nd Place award 1993, Golden Laparoscope award 1994), Ill. Med. Soc., Fallopius Soc., Ibero Am. Soc. Gynecology Endoscopy (v.p.), Argentinean Endoscopy Soc., Argentinean Fertility Soc. Office: 3647 W 26th St Chicago IL 60623

ROTSTEIN, GUSTAVO ARIEL, electrical engineer; b. Bahia Blanca, Argentina, Nov. 5, 1962; came to U.S., 1993; s. Enrique and Clara Rita (Pritzker) R.; m. Marisol Ebe Veilla, Oct. 16, 1987; children: Teodoro Ian, Violeta. BS in elec. engring., Universidad Nacional Del Sud, Buenos Aires, Argentina, 1993. Electromechanical supr. Pagrun S.A., Guatrache, 1989-93; freelance elec. designer Bahia Blanca, 1987-93; control sys. design, elec. engr. Despatch Industries, Mpls., 1994—. With Argentine Army, Falklands, 1982. Mem. IEEE, Soc. for Advancement of Materials and Process Engring., Soc. Mfg. Engring. Home: 16796 Jonquil Trail Lakeville MN 55044 Office: Despatch Industries Inc 8860 207th St W Lakeville MN 55044

ROTTMANN, LEON HARRY, psychologist, educator; b. Table Rock, Nebr., Feb. 14, 1927; s. John Henry and Minnie Anna (Huntemann) R.; m. Clara Thoren, 1959 (div. 1967). BS, U. Nebr., 1955, MA, 1957, PhD, 1960. Lic. psychologist, Nebr.; cert. tchr., Nebr., Iowa. Asst. dir. guidance Albuquerque Pub. Schs., 1959-60; asst. prof. U. Minn., Mpls., 1960-67; lectr. U. Nebr., Omaha, 1968-75; ext. specialist in human devel., prof. U. Nebr., Lincoln, 1975-94, prof. emeritus, 1994—; del. Wellness Coun. of Midlands, Omaha, 1980-94. Editor Wellness Perspectives, 1984-89, consulting editor, 1989-92. Mem. APA, Am. Assn. Suicidology (exec. dir. 1982—), Celiac Sprue Assn. U.S.A. (editor Lifeline newsletter 1982—). Republican. Lutheran. Home: 745 N 58th St Omaha NE 68132-2003

ROULEAU, REYNALD, bishop; b. St.-Jean-de-Dieu, Que., Can., Nov. 30, 1935. Ordained priest, 1963, bishop, 1987. Bishop Churchill-Hudson Bay, 1987—. Office: Diocese of Churchill-Baie D'Hudson, C P 10, Churchill, MB Canada R0B 0E0

ROUND, ALICE FAYE BRUCE, school psychologist; b. Ironton, Ohio, July 19, 1934; d. Wade Hamilton and Martha Matilda (Toops) Bruce; children: Leonard Bruce, Christopher Frederick. BA, Asbury Coll., 1956; MS in Sch. Psychology, Miami U., Oxford, Ohio, 1975. Cert. tchr., sch. psychologist, supr., Ohio; cert. tchr., Calif. Tchr. Madison County (Ohio) Schs., 1956-58, Columbus (Ohio) Pub. Schs., 1958, San Diego Pub. Schs., 1958-60, Poway (Calif.) Unified Sch. Dist., 1960-64; substitute tchr. Princeton City Schs., Cin., 1969-75; sch. psychologist, intern Greenhills/Forest Park City Schs., Cin., 1975-76; sch. psychologist Fulton County Schs., Wauseon, Ohio, 1976-77, Sandusky (Ohio) pub. and Cath. schs., 1977-96; tchr. art cmty. group and pvt. lessons, Sandusky, 1962, Springdale, Ohio, 1962-69; mem. Youth Svcs. Bd., Sandusky, 1978-88; bd. dirs., cons. Sandusky Sch. Practical Nursing, 1983-91; presenter suicide prevention seminars for mental health orgns.; speaker at ch., civic and youth orgns., local radio and TV programs; cons. on teen pregnancy to various schs., health depts. Mem. Huron (Ohio) Boosters Club, 1978-92, Vols. in Action, Sandusky, 1987—. Mem. NAACP, NEA, Nat. Sch. Psychologist Assn., Ohio Sch. Psychologist Assn., Maumee Valley Sch. Psychologist Assn., Ohio Edn. Assn., Sandusky Edn. Assn., Phi Delta Kappa (historian 1984-88, Most Innovative Preservation of History award 1988). Home: 821 Seneca Ave Huron OH 44839-1842 Office: Sandusky Bd Edn 407 Decatur St Sandusky OH 44870-2442

ROUNDS, M. MICHAEL, state legislator; m. Jean Rounds; 4 children. Student, S.D. State U. Mem. S.D. State Senate; mem. legis. procedure, retirement laws & state affairs coms., ins. and real estate exec. Home: 806 Cherry Dr Pierre SD 57501-2316*

ROUNSLEY, ROBERT RICHARD, chemical engineer, educator; b. Detroit, Jan. 11, 1931; s. John Roland and Verna E. (Clark) R.; m. Beatrice Anne Fulton, Mar. 7, 1953; children: Richard, Suzanne, Pamela, Deborah, David. BSChemE, Mich. Tech., Houghton, 1952, MSChemE, 1954; PhD in Chem. Engr., Iowa State U., 1957. Registered profl. engr., Ohio. Assoc. Argonne Nat. Lab., Lemont, Ill., 1953-54; instr. Iowa State U., Ames, 1954-57; rsch. fellow Mead Corp., Chillicothe, Ohio, 1957—; instr. Ohio U., Chillicothe, 1963-68. Patentee in field; contbr. articles to profl. jours. Mem. AICE (sr., pres. ctrl. Ohio sect. 1977-78), TAPPI (editorial bd. 1988-89, chmn. simulation com. 1991-93), Am. Chem. Soc., Soc. for Computer Simulation (sr.), nst. Paper Sci. and Tech. (project adv. com. 1986-89), Lions (chmn. 1975-76, 92-93. Methodist. Home: 4 Edgewood Ct Chillicothe OH 45601-2246 Office: 4 Edgewood Ct Chillicothe OH 45601

ROUPP, ALBERT ALLEN, architect; b. Wichita, Kans., Sept. 12, 1930; s. Walter Roy and Bertha Pearl (Schantz) R.; m. Susan Carol Nagy, Sept. 3, 1966; children: Aimee, Christopher. Student, Staatliche Hochschule für Bildende Kunste, Hamburg, Germany; AA, Hesston Coll., 1950; BS in Architecture, Ill. Inst. Tech., 1964, Masters in Architecture, Bus. Registered architect, Ill. Project architect C. F. Murphy, Chgo., 1964-74; plan commr. Evanston (Ill.) Plan Commn., 1970-74; prof. Ill. Inst. Tech., Chgo., 1966-74; tech. procedures administr. Capital Devel. Corp., Chgo., 1974-78; sr. v.p. Coder Taylor Assn., Kenilworth, Ill., 1978-82, prin., pres., 1982-85; owner, pres. Albert A. Roupp Assocs., Inc., Northfield, Ill., 1985—. Mem. AIA, Ill. AIA, Chgo. AIA. Office: 550 W Frontage Rd Ste 2700 Northfield IL 60093-1238

ROUSH, EDWARD, mechanical engineer; b. Willimgtoh, Ohio, June 19, 1946. BS in Mech. Engring., U. Cin., 1985. Mech. engr. Milacron, Cin., 1965—. Sgt. U.S. Army, 1967-69. Office: Milacron 4701 Marburg Ave Cincinnati OH 45209

ROUSH, PHILLIP HENRY, state official; b. Hillsboro, Ohio, June 3, 1931; s. Deforest Robinson and Sarah Jane (Barker) R.; m. Sue Ellen Jackson, Aug. 14, 1954 (div. 1964); 1 child, Melody Rozann; m. Sandra Sue Wallace, Aug. 29, 1969; children: Anne Michelle, Matthew Phillip. AB, Milligan Coll., 1954; MS, St. Francis Coll., 1969. V.p. Angola (Ind.) Brick & Tile Co., 1956-64; dir. admissions Internat. Bus. Coll., Ft. Wayne, Ind., 1965-69; v.p. Hickey Sch., Clayton, Mo., 1969-77; commr. Ind. Commn. on Proprietary Edn., Indpls., 1977—. With U.S. Army, 1954-56; ETO. Home: 13425 Lantern Rd Fishers IN 46038-3522 Office: Ind Commn on Prop Edn 302 W Washington St # 201 Indianapolis IN 46204-2738

ROUSSEAU, MARK OWEN, sociologist; b. Ft. Wayne, Ind., Apr. 5, 1940; s. Richard Jackson and Wilma (Combs) R.; BA, Ind. U., 1962, MA, 1966; PhD, U. N.C., Chapel Hill, 1971; cert. III Dégré, Alliance Francaise, Paris, 1972; m. Marion Frances Pruss, Aug. 18, 1973; 1 son, Mark Owen. Asst. instr. U. N.C., 1966-68; mem. faculty U. Nebr., Omaha, 1968—, asst. prof. sociology, 1971-82, assoc. prof., 1982-89, prof., 1990—, dept. chair, 1993—, sabbatical rsch. leave, 1985, 1992; Nat. Endowment Humanities fellow, summer 1979; funded rsch., Paris, 1982, Montreal, Can., 1988, 90. Co-author: Regionalism and Regional Devolution in Comparative Perspective, 1987; contbr. articles to profl. jours. Mem. Am. Sociol. Assn., AAUP, Midwest Sociol. Soc., Am. Assn. Tchrs. French, Conf. Group on French Politics and Soc., Am. Coun. for Quebec Studies, Assn. for Can. Studies in U.S., Ind. U. Alumni Assn. Home: 5001 Izard St Omaha NE 68132-1425 Office: U Nebr Dept Sociology Omaha NE 68182

ROUW, CARLA SUE ROBERTS, medical nurse; b. Chariton, Iowa, June 5, 1968; d. Glen Marlin and Phyllis Darlene (Allison) Roberts. ADN, Indian Hills C.C., 1988. RN, Iowa. Float med.-surg. LPN; lic. practical nurse med.-surg. float Ottumwa (Iowa) Regional Health Ctr., 1987-88; adolescent and children's charge nurse Laughlin Pavilion, Kirksville, Mo., 1988-89; charge nurse, dir. med. records Monroe Care Ctr., Albia, 1989-91; gen. surgery/urology nurse, office nurse Dr. Edeliro A. Escobar, Fort Madison, Iowa, 1991-96; nursing svc. supr. Homestead Living & Learning Ctr.-Serving Iowans with Autism, Runnells, Iowa, 1996—.

ROUZE, JEFFREY ALAN, real estate executive; b. Rockford, Ill., Feb. 5, 1952; s. Robert Lloyd and Ellen Erma (Korpi) R. BBA in Real Estate Fin., U. Wis., 1974, MS in Bus. and Real Estate, 1977. Lic. real estate broker, Wis.; notary pub., Wis. Exec. mgmt. trainee Grootemaat Corp., Milw., 1977-79; real estate cons. CUNA Mut. Ins. Soc., Madison, Wis., 1979-84, real property and mortgage mgr., 1984-93, sr. asset mgr., 1994—. Treas. Strollers Theatre, Ltd., Madison, 1985-89. Mem. Nat. Assn. Corp. Real Estate Execs. (master corp. real estate), Inst. Real Estate Mgmt. (cert. property mgr.), Mortgage Bankers Assn. Am., Urban Land Inst. Methodist. Home: 18 Mondale Ct Madison WI 53705-1121 Office: CUNA Mut Ins Soc 5910 Mineral Point Rd Madison WI 53705-4456

ROVELSTAD, ANDREW, mechanical engineer; b. Elgin, Ill., Jan. 12, 1945. B. U. Ill., 1967, MME, 1968, M in Applied Mechanics, 1989. Registered profl. engr., Ill. Project engr. Inger Soll, Rockford, Ill., 1977-79; mech. engring. mgr. DeVlieg-Sundstrand, Belvidere, Ill., 1979-91; engring. mgr. Gardner Disk Grinders, South Beloit, Ill., 1991—. Mem. ASME, Soc. Mfg. Engrs. Lutheran. Office: Gardner Disk Grinders 481 Gardner St South Beloit IL 61080-1326

ROVIN, ADRIENNE LEE, school social worker; b. Cleve., Dec. 16, 1947; d. Morris William and Violet (Neer) Sirkin; m. Ronald Rovin, June 13, 1971; 1 child, Eric Michael. BA, Kent State U., Kent, 1966-70; MS, Case Western Res., Cleve., 1970-72. Social worker Jewish Family Svc., Cleve., 1972-73; sch. social worker Sch. Dist. 54, Schaumburg, Ill., 1976—. Field instr. Jane Addams Sch. of S.W., Chgo, George Williams Coll., Downers Grove, Ill. Mem. NASW, Ill. Assn. Sch. Social Workers, Delta Kappa Gamma (literacy chmn., social chmn.). Office: Sch Dist # 54 524 E Schaumburg Rd Schaumburg IL 60194

ROVNER, ILANA KARA DIAMOND, federal judge; b. Aug. 21, 1938; came to U.S., 1939; d. Stanley and Ronny (Medalje) Diamond; m. Richard Nyles Rovner, Mar. 9, 1963; 1 child, Maxwell Rabson. AB, Bryn Mawr Coll., 1960; postgrad., U. London King's Coll., 1961, Georgetown U., 1961-63; JD, Ill. Inst. Tech., 1966; LittD (hon.), Rosary Coll., 1989, Mundelein Coll., 1989; DHL (hon.), Spertus Coll. of Judaica, 1992. Bar: Ill. 1972, U.S. Dist. Ct. (no. dist.) Ill. 1972, U.S. Ct. Appeals (7th cir.) 1977, U.S. Supreme Ct. 1981, Fed. Trial Bar (no. dist.) Ill. 1982. Jud. clk. U.S. Dist. Ct. (no. dist.) Ill., Chgo., 1972-73; asst. U.S. atty. U.S. Atty.'s Office, Chgo., 1973-77; dep. chief of pub. protection, 1975-76, chief pub. protection, 1976-77; dep. gov., legal counsel Gov. James R. Thompson, Chgo., 1977-84; dist. judge U.S. Dist. Ct. (no. dist.) Ill., Chgo., 1984-92; cir. judge U.S. Ct. Appeals (7th cir.), Chgo., 1992—. Trustee Bryn Mawr Coll., Pa., 1983-89; mem. bd. overseers Ill. Inst. Tech./Kent Coll. Law, 1983—; trustee Ill. Inst. Tech., 1989—; mem. adv. coun. Rush Ctr. for Sports Medicine, Chgo., 1991-96; civil justice reform act adv. com. for the 7th cir., Chgo., 1991-95; bd. vis. No. Ill. U. Coll. Law, 1992-94; vis. com. Northwestern U. Sch. Law, 1993—, U. Chgo. Law Sch., 1993-96, 7th cir. race and gender fairness com., 1993—, U.S. Ct. Appeals (7th cir.) fairness com., 1996—, 7th cir. gender study task force, 1995—. Recipient Spl. Commendation award U.S. Dept. Justice, 1975, Spl. Achievement award 1976, Ann. Nat. Law and Social Justice Leadership award League to Improve the Cmty., 1975, Ann. Guardian Police award, 1977, Profl. Achievement award Ill. Inst. Tech., 1986, Louis Dembitz Brandeis medal for Disting. Legal Svc. Brandeis U., 1993, 1st Woman award, Valparaiso U. Sch. Law, 1993, ORT Women's Am. Cmty. Svc. award, 1987-88, svc. award Spertus Coll. of Judaica, 1987, Ann. award Chgo. Found. for Women, 1990; named Today's Chgo. Woman of Yr., 1985, Woman of Achievement Chgo. Women's Club, 1986, more. Mem. ABA, Fed. Bar Assn. (jud. selection com. Chgo. chpt. 1977-80, treas. Chgo. chpt. 1978-79, sec. Chgo. chpt. 1979-80, 2d v.p. Chgo. chpt. 1980-81, 1st v.p. Chgo. chpt. 1981-82, pres. Chgo. chpt. 1982-83, 2d v.p. 7th cir. 1983-84, v.p. 7th cir. 1984-85), Fed. Judges Assn., Nat. Assn. Women Judges, Ill. Bar Assn., Women's Bar Assn. Ill. (ann. award 1989, 1st Myra Bradwell Woman of Achievement award 1994), Chgo. Bar Assn. (commendation def. of prisoners com. 1987), Chgo. Coun. Lawyers, Decalogue Soc. (citation of honor 1991), Kappa Beta Pi, Phi Alpha Delta (hon.). Republican. Jewish. Office: 219 S Dearborn St Ste 2774 Chicago IL 60604-1803

ROWARK, MAUREEN, fine arts photographer; b. Edinburgh, Midlothian, Scotland, Feb. 28, 1933; came to U.S., 1960, naturalized, 1970; d. Alexander Pennycook and Margaret (Gorman) Prezdpelski; m. Robert Rowark, May 3, 1952 (div. July 1965). 1 child, Mark Steven. Student, Warmington Bus. Coll., Royal Leamington Spa, Eng., 1950-51, Royal Leamington Spa Art Sch.; diploma, Speedwriting Inst., N.Y.C., 1961; AS in Edn., St. Clair County Community Coll., Port Huron, Mich., 1977, AA, 1978. Supr. proof reading Nevin D. Hirst Advt., Ltd., Leeds, Eng., 1952-55; publicity asst. Alvis Aero Engines, Ltd., Coventry, Eng., 1955-57; adminstrv. asst. Port Huron Motor Inn, 1964-66; adminstrv. asst. pub. rels. dept. Geophysics and Computer Svcs., Inc., New Orleans, 1966-68; sales mgr. Holiday Inn, Port Huron, 1968-70; adminstrv. asst. Howard Corp., Port Huron, 1971-73; sales and systems coord. Am. Wood Products, Ann Arbor, Mich., 1973-74; systems coord. Daniels & Zermack Architects, Ann Arbor, 1974; systems coord., cataloger fine arts dept. St. Clair County Community Coll., Port Huron, 1976-79; freelance fine arts photographer Port Huron, 1978—; photographer Patterns mag. front cover, 1978, Erie Sq. Gazette, 1979, Bluewater Area Tourism Bur. brochure, 1989, Port Huron, Can. Legion, Wyo., Ont. Br., 1987, 88—, Grace Episcopal Ch. Mariner's Day, Port Huron, 1987, 92, 93, 94, 95, 96, Homes mag., 1989. One-woman shows at Grace Episcopal Ch., 1995, Port Huron Mus., 1995; Mich. Waterways Coun. Girl Scouts Exhibit, 1996; exhibited in internat. shows at Ann. Ea. Mich. Internat. Exhbn., 1982, 83, 84 (awards of excellence 1982, 83, Best Photography award 1995), St. Clair County C.C., 1983, 86 (award of excellence), Sarnia (Ont.) Gallery, 1983-92, 94 (honorable mention), Bluewater Bridge Exhibit, 1988, Kaskilaaksontie Exhibit, Finland, 1991 (Par Excellence award), Swann Gallery, 1996, others; contbr. short stories to mags. Cons., buyer interior decor Grace Episcopal Ch., 1994; active Port Huron Mus., 1985—. Recipient Hon. Mention award Sarnia Art Gallery, 1981; named Best Photographer, Sarnia Art Gallery, 1988; winner 2d and 3d Pl. awards Times Herald Newspaper, 1988. Mem. St. Clair County C.C. Alumni Assn., Phi Theta Kappa, Lambda Mu. Democrat. Episcopalian. Home and Office: 2005 Riverside Dr #15 Port Huron MI 48060-2677

ROWE, DONALD EUGENE, fundraising consultant; b. South Bend, Ind., Nov. 10, 1938; s. Devon Dolphia and Bessie Caroline (Brown) R.; m. Barbara Ann Bussey, Aug. 20, 1960; children: Michele Rene Kolsis, Sherri Rowe-Lopez. BS, Manchester Coll., 1961. Asst. youth dir. South Bend YMCA, 1961-62; program dir. Mishawaka (Ind.) Family YMCA, 1962-64; youth dir. YMCA of Metro. South Bend-Mishawaka, 1964-66; youth dir. Racine (Wis.) YMCA, 1966-71, assoc. exec. dir., 1971-74, exec. dir., 1974-82; sr. counsel Am. City Bur., Hoffman Estates, Ill., 1982-86; pres., CEO Michiana YMCA, South Bend, 1986-89; sr. counsel Am. City Bur., Hoffman Estates, Ill., 1989—; cons., campaign dir. Salvation Army, Hartford, Conn., 1994—, Dioces of Greensburg, Pa., 1992-94, Kenmore (N.Y.) Mercy Hosp., 1991-92; cons., dir. and assoc. dir. Archdiocese of Boston, 1989-91; cons., assoc. coun. Worcester YMCA, 1982. Mem. exec. coun. United Way, South Bend, 1986-89; chmn. Year Round Schs. Task Force, Racine, 1973-74. Named one of Outstanding Young Men Am., 1966; recipient Outstanding Svc. award Big Bros. Orgn., Racine, Wis., 1980, Disting. Svc. award Wis. Cluster YMCAs, Oshkosh, 1982; day of cmty. recognition named in his honor, 1982; Paul Harris fellow, 1992. Mem. South Bend Rotary, Rcine Rotary (pres. 1979-80), Racine Rotary Found. (bd. dirs. 1979-82). Republican. Evangel. Free Ch. Home: 100 Cold Spring Rd 105A Rocky Hill CT 06067 Office: Am City Bur 1721 Moon Lake Blvd Hoffman Estates IL 60194

ROWE, DONALD FRANCIS, priest, secondary educator, administrator; b. Chgo., Feb. 18, 1941; s. Donald Francis and Ann Bernice (Hyland) R. LittB, Xavier U., 1963; MA, Columbia U., 1967; MDiv, Loyola U., 1977. Joined Soc. of Jesus, 1959, ordained priest Roman Catholic Ch., 1972. Mem. faculty Loyola U., Chgo., 1967-81; dir., founder The Martin D'Arcy Gallery of Art Loyola U., Chgo., 1969-92; pres. St. Ignatius Coll. Prep., Chgo., 1981—. Author: Enamels: The XII-XVI Centuries, 1970, The Art of Jewelry, 1975, The First Ten Years, 1979. Recipient Disting. Svc. award AIA, Chgo., 1991. Mem. Coun. for Advancement and Support of Edn., Jesuit Secondary Edn. Assn. Home: 6525 N Sheridan Rd Chicago IL 60626-5311 Office: St Ignatius Coll Prep 1976 W Roosevelt Rd Chicago IL 60608-1230

ROWE, MAE IRENE, investment company executive; b. Gardner, Mass., Dec. 6, 1927; d. Clifford Wesley and Mertie (Moore) Mann; m. Willard Chase Rowe, June 18, 1951 (div. 1979); children: Gail B. Rowe Simons, Bruce C. BA with high honor, Am. Internat. Coll., 1949. Cert. real property adminstr. Social worker City of Montague, Turners Falls, Mass., 1949-51; mgr. Park Investment Co., Cleve., 1979-94; ret. 1994. Pres., v.p., bd. dirs. Park Ridge Counseling Svc., Ill., 1972-76; clk. Village of Kildeer, Ill., 1977; bd. dirs. Maine Township Mental Health Svc., Park Ridge, 1975-76; trustee Heathermore Condominium Assn., 1987, 93, pres. 1988, 93-94, sec.-treas., 1989. Mem. Cleve. Bldg. Owners Mgrs. Assn. (mem. edn. com. 1983—), Bldg. Owners Mgrs. Assn. Internat., Soc. Real Property Adminstrs. (cert.), LWV (v.p., mem. city adv. com. 1973-76), Am. Mensa Soc. Republican. Unitarian. Club: Cleve. Racquet. Lodge: Kiwanis (bd. dirs., pres., trustee, v.p. Kiwanis Found. Cleve.). Avocation: tennis. Home: 34108 Chagrin Blvd Apt 5103 Chagrin Falls OH 44022-1042

ROWLAND, HOWARD RAY, mass communications educator; b. Eddy County, N.Mex., Sept. 9, 1929; s. Lewis Marion and Ursula Lorene (Hunt) R.; m. Meredith June Lee, Apr. 19, 1951; children: Runay Ilene Smith, Rhonda Lee Fisher. B in Journalism, U. Mo., 1950; MS in Journalism, So. Ill. U., 1959; PhD, Mich. State U., 1969. Feature writer Springfield (Mo.) Newspapers, Inc., 1954; newspaper editor Monett (Mo.) Times, 1954-55; editorial writer So. Ill. U., Carbondale, 1955-59; pub. rels. dir. St. Cloud (Minn.) State U., 1959-86, asst. dean, 1986-87, 88-90; dir. Ctr. for British Studies, Alnwick, Eng., 1987-88, 90-91; adj. prof. Mass Comms., St. Cloud State U., 1986—; cons. Conf. of Campus Ombudsmen, Berkeley, 1971; recorder Seminar on Fund Raising, Washington, 1985; bibliographer Higher Edn. Bibliography Yearbook, 1987. Author: American Students in Alnwick Castle, 1990, St. Cloud State University--125 Years, 1994; editor: Effective Community Relations, 1980; sect. editor: Handbook of Institutional Advancement, 1986; author book revs. Chair All-Am. City Com., St. Cloud, 1973-74. With U.S. Army, 1951-53. NDEA doctoral fellowship Mich. State U., 1967-69; recipient Appreciation award Mayor of St. Cloud, 1974, Disting Svc. award Coun. for Advancement and Support of Edn., 1985. Mem. Soc. of Profl. Journalists (Minn. chpt. pres. 1963-64, dep. dir. 1965-67), Coun. for Advancement and Support of Edn. (dist. 5 chair 1977-79, Leadership award 1979), Rotary Internat., Phi Delta Kappa (Mich. State U. chpt. pres. 1968-69, St. Cloud State Univ. chpt. pres. 1978-79). Presbyterian. Home: 29467 Kraemer Lake Rd Saint Joseph MN 56374-9646

ROWLAND, JAMES LEONARD, family practice physician, surgeon, homeopathic physician; b. Fort Smith, Ark., Aug. 20, 1917; s. James Lenard and Sally Ann (Biggs) R.; m. Eva Louise Squires, June 7, 1942 (div. May 1969); m. Christy Ann Bennett, Febr. 20, 1974; children: James Gregory, Suzanne, Lynda. BS, Central Methodist Coll., Fayette, Mo., 1940; MPH, Loyola U., Chgo., 1943; D in Osteopathic Medicine, U. Health Scis., Kansas City, Mo., 1956; D in Acupuncture, Ryodoraku, Tokyo, Japan, 1975; MD (hon.), Ryodraku Inst., Tokyo, 1976. Cert. in Family Practice. Chief sanitarian Oak Park (Ill.) Health Dept., 1943-46; acting health dir. Cen. Fla. Health Dist., Ocala, Fla., 1949-50; dir. food & drugs Mo. State Health Dept., Jefferson City, 1950-52; prof. pub. health U. Health Scis., Kansas City, Mo., 1952-58; physician family practice Kansas City, 1957—; Pres. Ryodovaku Rsch. Inst. N.Am., 1966—. Capt. USPHS, 1943-49. Fellow Am. Osteopathic Coll. Family Practice (nat. pres. 1964-65; mem. AOA, Am. Coll. Clin. Hypnosis, Internat. Assn. for Advancement Hypnosis (internat. pres. 1967-68). Office: Rowland Med Clinic 8133 Wornall Rd Kansas City MO 64114

ROWLAND, ROBERT CHARLES, clinical psychotherapist, writer, researcher; b. Columbus, Ohio, Jan. 18, 1946; s. Charles Albert and Lorene Bernadine (Friedlinghaus) R.; m. Saundra Marie Gardner, Dec. 21, 1968 (div. Mar. 1987); children: Carrie Ann, Marcus Jules Harrad, Heather Renée. BS in Physiol. Psychology, Ohio State U., 1971, MSW, 1981. Cert. marital and family therapist; cert. in drug and alcohol treatment; cert. sex therapist; cert. hypnotist. Respiratory therapist Mt. Carmel Med. Ctr., Columbus, Ohio, 1965-68; adj. prof. Columbus Ctr. Sci. and Industry, Columbus, Ohio, 1968-71; researcher in tetrahydrocannabinol/learning experiments Ohio State U. Rsch. Ctr., 1970-71; secondary tchr. Columbus (Ohio) Pub. Schs., 1971-73; case cons. Bur. Disability Determination, Columbus, 1973-80; clin. social worker Clarke County Out-Patient Mental

Health Ctr., Springfield, Ohio, 1979-80, Upham Hall, Ohio State U. Hosps., 1980-81; clin. psychotherapist Psychol. Systems, Inc., Columbus, 1981-84; psychotherapist, cons. Columbus, 1974-87, 94—, Delray Beach, Fla., 1987-93; dir. social svc. and cmty. rels. Apple Creek (Ohio) Devel. Ctr., 1981-82; pres., rsch. dir. Neurosocial Scis. Inst., Delray Beach, 1987-93, Columbus, 1994. Author: Brain Wars-The End of the Drug Game, 1991; contbr. articles to profl. jours. Adv. Neighbor to Neighbor, Delray Beach, 1991-93. Recipient scholarship grant, Ohio State U. Coll. of Social Work, 1980-81. Mem. AAAS, NASW (chmn. Ohio Pace chpt., lobbyist 1980-81, Excellence award 1981, mem. Fla. chpt.), Fla. Freelance Writer's Assn., Union of Concerned Scientists, Palm Beach County Scis. Jour. Club, Alpha Delta Mu. Home: 6378 Busch Blvd Apt 386 Columbus OH 43229

ROWLES, ARLENE BEVERLY, geriatric social program administrator; b. Johnstown, Ohio, July 12, 1935; d. John Wesley and Ruth Margaret (Johnston) Thomas; m. Edward William Rowles, July 21, 1957; children: Kenneth Alan, Keith Thomas, Diane Elizabeth. BS in Home Econs., Ohio State U., 1957. Lic. dietitian. Tchr. home econs. Southwestern City Schs., Grove City, Ohio, 1958-59; dir. Meals on Wheels of Fairfield County, Inc., Lancaster, Ohio, 1975—; mem. state, area ext. adv. com. Ohio State Univ. Ext., 1980—, v.p., pres. state adv. com., 1993-96; mem., past officer Fairfield County Adv. Com., 1971—; adv. com. Vis. Nurses Fairfield County, Lancaster, 1983—, pres., 1993-96; mem., past officer Fairfield County Com. on Aging, Lancaster, 1975—; mem. Millersport United Meth. Ch. Fellow Nat. Assn. Meal Providers (presenter 1980), Nat. Assn. Nutrition and Svc. Providers, Ohio Assn. Nutrition and Svc. Providers. Republican. Office: Meals on Wheels Fairfield Cty Inc 253 Boving Rd SW Lancaster OH 43130-4240

ROWLES, JOANNE RUTH, adult nurse practitioner; b. Lancaster, Ohio, Aug. 25, 1954; d. Cyril S. and Ruth L. (Ransom) R. Diploma, Riverside Meth. Sch. Nursing, 1975; BSN, Ohio U., 1978; MSN, U. Nebr. Med. Ctr., 1996. Staff nurse Lancaster (Ohio)-Fairfield County Hosp., 1975-77; house supr., asst. head nurse Boone Hosp. Ctr., Columbia, Mo., 1979-93; clin. instr. Cen. Meth. Coll., Fayette, Mo., 1991-93. Mem. Oncology Nursing Soc., Sigma Theta Tau. Home: RR3 15550 N Fernwood Dr Hallsville MO 65255-9334

ROY, PAUL EMILE, JR., county official; b. Sumter, S.C., Dec. 18, 1942; s. Paul Emile and Harriette Orvilla (Sorenson) R.; m. Patricia Jane Stariha, July 2, 1977; 1 child, Jennifer Jo. AA, Grand Rapids Jr. Coll., 1963; student, Universidad de las Americas, Mexico City, 1963-64, Instituto Mexicano-Norteamericano de Relaciones Culturales, Mexico City, 1964-65; BA, Aquinas Coll., Grand Rapids, 1967; MA, U. Americas Escuela de Graduados, Mexico City, 1968; postgrad., U. Mich., 1977-79; MBA, Calif. Coast U., 1994. Asst. prin., instr. Spanish Muskegon (Mich.) Cath. Cen. High Sch., 1971-75; govt. offcl. County of Muskegon, 1975—, dir. employment and tng. Muskegon/Oceana Consortium, 1975-87, dir. employment and tng., 1988-95, dir. employment and tng. and facilities mgmt., 1995—; mem. Mich. Com. for Devel. of Romance Lang. Performance Objectives; adult edn. adv. com. Muskegon Pub. Schs.; appointee Mich. Youth Employment Coun.; v.p. regional adv. coun. U.S. Dept. Labor, 1981; mem. City of Muskegon Local Devel. Funding Authority, 1988—, Downtown Devel. Authority, 1988—, City of Whitehall (Mich.) Local Devel. Funding Authority, 1988—, Muskegon Econ. Growth Alliance Edn. Com.; cons. U.S. Dept. Labor, Washington, Mich. Dept. Labor, Lansing, Gov.'s Office Manpower, Ind., U. Mich., Ann Arbor, various pvt. cos., non-profit orgns. Campaign chmn. Muskegon County United Way, 1986-88, Pacesetter award, 1987. Mem. Am. Assn. Tchrs. Spanish and Portuguese, Mich. Assn. Tchrs. English as Second Lang., Mich. Assn. Employment and Tng. Dirs. (pres. 1980-81), Mich. Employment and Tng. Inst. (founding bd. dirs. 1980-81), Nat. Assn. Counties (employment steering com.), Nat. Assn. County Employment and Tng. Adminstrs. (nat. bd. dirs. 1979-80, nat. chmn. organizational resources com. 1981). Office: Muskegon Cty Dept Employment & Tng 20 W Muskegon Ave Muskegon MI 49440-1317

ROY, RANJIT KUMAR, mechanical engineer; b. Barisal, E. Bengal, India, Jan. 1, 1947; came to U.S., 1968; s. Rajani and Kumundini (Baral) R.; m. Krishna Majumder, Apr. 25, 1970; children: Purba, Paula. Student, Khulna U., East Bengal, India, 1963; BSME, Regional Enging. Coll., Durgapur, India, 1968; MSME, U. Mo., Rolla, 1970, PhD, 1972. Registered profl. engr., Mich. Sr. engr. Burroughs Corp., Detroit, 1972-76; sr. project engr. GM, Warren, Mich., 1976-79; staff engr. Chevrolet Motors GM, Warren, Mcih., 1979-82, mgr. reliability CPC engring., 1982-87; cons., trainer Nutek Inc., Birmingham, Mich., 1987—; adj. prof. Oakland U., Rochester, Mich., 1976-87. Author: A Primer On The Taguchi Method, 1990; author computer software Qualitek-4, 1991. Pres. Bichitra Inc., Troy, 1980-82. Mem. Am. Soc. Quality Control (sr.), Am. Soc. Quality Control (v.p. profl. devel. 1987-88), Soc. Automotive Engrs. Democrat. Hindu. Home: 3829 Quarton Rd Bloomfield Hills MI 48302-4059 Office: Nutek Inc Bingham Ctr 30600 Telegraph Rd Ste 2230 Franklin MI 48025-4532

ROY, ROBERT RUSSELL, toxicologist; b. Mpls., Sept. 14, 1957; s. Rudolph Russell and Arlene Charlotte (Miller) R.; m. Barbara Jane Richie, Oct. 10, 1987; children: Andrew, Katherine. BA cum laude, Augsburg Coll., 1980; MS, U. Minn., 1986, PhD, 1989. Bd. cert. in toxicology. Rsch. asst. U. Minn., Mpls., 1986-88; toxicologist, project mgr. Pace Labs., Inc., Mpls., 1989-90; toxicologist Minn. Dept. Health, Mpls., 1990-93, Minn. Regional Poison Ctr., St. Paul, 1990—; lectr. U. Minn., Mpls., 1986-90, Midwest Ctr. Occupl. Health and Safety, St. Paul, 1990—, instr., 1989; clin. asst. prof. U. Minn., 1993—; mem. grad. faculty in toxicology U. Minn.; adj. asst. prof. emergency medicine Oreg. Health Sci. U., Portland. Tutor Mpls. Pub. Schs., 1982; vol. U. Minn. Hosps., Mpls., 1983; mem. Waite Pk. Community Coun., Mpls., 1977-80, Mt. Carmel Luth. Ch. Coun., Mpls., 1983-85. Mem. Am. Coll. Toxicology, Soc. Toxicology, Am. Indsl. Hygiene Assn., Minn. Acad. Sci., Sigma Xi, Delta Omega. Home: 6201 Near Mountain Blvd Chanhassen MN 55317-9117 Office: Minn Regional Poison Ctr St Paul-Ramsey Med Ctr 640 Jackson St Saint Paul MN 55101-2502

ROYAL, WILLIAM HENRY, real estate developer, architect; b. Jackson, Tenn., Dec. 16, 1924; s. Joe Henry and Millie Earline (Anderson) R.; m. Odell Peebles, June 16, 1943; children: William H. Jr., Frederick E., Diana, Carolyn M., Wanda H. Diploma, Chicago Tech. Coll., 1959; student, MIT, 1969, '73, U. Neb., 1971-76, U. Minn., 1974-76. Reg. architect, Ill., Mo. Architect, engr. U.S. Army Engr. Dist., Detroit, 1957-61; gen. architect U.S. Army Engr. Dist., St. Paul, Minn., 1959-62; supr. architect U.S. Army Engr. Dist., Chgo., 1962-70; gen. architect U.S. Army Engr. Dist., Omaha, Neb., 1970-73; architect, job captain Ellerbe & Co., St Paul, 1962; cons. FREBO, U.S. Postal Svc., St. Paul, 1973-77; constr. mgr. H.Q. U.S. Postal Svc., Washington, 1977-80; pres. William H. Royal & Assoc., Inc., Lake St. Louis, Mo., 1987—, Chgo., 1995—; pres. St. Louis Airport Devel. Corp., 1988-89; v.p. Steelgrade Corp., Clayton, Mo., 1991-93; sec.-treas. Am. Community Telecomms. System, Inc., Ferguson, Mo., 1992—; pres. Royal King Constrn. Co., St. John, Mo., 1995—. Author: (tng. manual) Architect Engineer Contracts, 1970; editor: Master Planning, Kinloch Redevelopment, 1987. Steward, United Meth. Ch., Omaha, 1970-73; urban cons. United Meth. Ministries, Omaha, 1970-73, Youth Coord., United Meth. Ch., Omaha, 1971-73; mem. Douglas County Parole Bd., Omaha, 1971-72. Recipient Commendation U.S. Postal Svc., Washington, 1976, Svc. award, 1980, letter of Appreciation, 1982; nominee Rockefeller Pub. Svc. award, U.S. Postal Svc., St. Paul, 1976. Home: 1 Berry Ct Lake Saint Louis MO 63367-1921 Office: William H Royal & Assocs 1 Berry Ct Lake Saint Louis MO 63367-1921

ROYHAB, RONALD, journalist, newspaper editor; b. Lorain, Ohio, Oct. 6, 1942; s. Halim Farah and Elizabeth Della (Naiser) R.; m. Roberta Lee Libb, Apr. 20, 1969; children: David Libb, Aaron Nicholas. Student, Lorain County (Ohio) Coll., Kent State U.; postgrad., Am. U., Washington. Reporter Lorain Jour., 1966-69; chief bur. Scripps Howard Ohio Bur., Columbus, 1975-78; reporter spl. assignment Scripps Howard Cin. Post, 1971-72; investigative reporter Scripps Howard Cleve. Press, 1972-75; chief bur. Scripps Howard Ohio Bur., Columbus, 1975-78; asst. mng. editor Scripps Howard News Svc., Washington, 1978-81; mng. editor Scripps Howard El Paso (Tex.) Herald Post, 1981-83; asst. mng. editor Scripps Howard Pitts. Press, 1983-92; assoc. editor Pitts. Post Gazette, 1992-93; mng. editor Toledo Blade, 1993—; bd. dirs. Toledo Blade Co. Bd. dirs. Am. Lebanese Congress. With USAR, 1964-70. Recipient 7 awards for Excellence Cleve. Newspaper Guild, 1972-75; Spl. Sect. awards Pa. Newspaper Pubs. Assn., 1985, 86, 88; fellow Am. Polit. Sci. Assn., 1970-71. Mem. AP Mng. Editors Assn., AP Soc. Ohio. Eastern Orthodox. Home: 27262 Fort Meigs Rd Perrysburg OH 43551-1230 Office: Toledo Blade 541 N Superior St Toledo OH 43660-1000

ROYSE, LYNNE ELLEN, marketing professional; b. Wood River, Ill., July 4, 1951; d. Edward Franklin and Marcella Eileen R. BA, St. Mary of the Woods Coll., 1973. Asst. buyer Ayr-Way Stores, Indpls., 1973-74; personal banker Bank of St. Louis, 1974-76; sales adminstr. Barber-Colman Co., St. Louis, 1976-84; acct. exec. Ask Mr. Foster Travel Svc., St. Louis, 1984-85; donor recruiter ARC, St. Louis, 1986—; co-founder Profl. Saleswoman St. Louis, 1984. Vol. World Affairs Coun. Internat. Visitor's Program, St. Louis, 1994—; bd. dirs. Alliance, St. Louis, 1988. Recipient Outstanding Woman of Achievement award Alliance, St. Louis, 1984. Mem. Squires and Ladies Charitable Found. Office: ARC Mo/Ill Region 4050 Lindell Blvd Saint Louis MO 63108-3202

ROYSE, SUE MARION, special education educator; b. Ironton, Ohio, Oct. 28, 1944; d. Paul Hurt and Clyda (Forson) Marion; m. David T. Royse, May 20, 1972. BS in Edn., Concord Coll., Athens, W.Va., 1971; MS in Edn., Ind. U., 1977. Tchr. Greater Clark County Schs., Jeffersonville, Ind., 1977-88, Phoenix (Ariz.) Union Dist. 210, 1989-91, Warren Achievement Ctr., 1991-93, State of Ill. Dept., Corrections Hill Correction Ctr., 1993-94; Ind. Sch. Dist. # 196, Rosemount, Minn., 1994—. Recipient Olin Davis award State of Ind., 1982. Mem. Coun. for Exceptional Children, Correction Edn. Assn., Beta Sigma Phi. Home: 8090 170th St W Lakeville MN 55044-9367

ROYSTER, DARRYL, computer programmer and analyst; b. Chgo., July 22, 1954; s. David and Doris (McGee) R.; m. Toni Diane Wilson, Aug. 19, 1978; children: Danté Marques, Damon Matthew. BS in Psychology, MacMurray Coll., Jacksonville, Ill., 1976. Counselor River Edge Hosp., Forrest Park, Ill., 1975-76; adolescent counselor Northwestern Meml. Hosp., Chgo., 1976-78; social worker Cath. Charities, Chgo., 1978-79; counselor Ray Graham Assn., Addison, Ill., 1978-80; input/output clk. Automatic Data Processing, Oak Brook, Ill., 1980-83; computer programmer/analyst IRS, Chgo., 1983—, DMR Inc.; motivational speaker. Basketball ofcl. Ill. High Sch. Assn., Bloomington, 1972—, NCAA, Fedn. Internat. Basketball Assn., 1977—; pres. Royster Basketball Sch. Mem. Big Ten Assn., Psi Chi. Home: 105 Burlington Ave Western Springs IL 60558-1631 Office: IRS 350 E 22nd St Lombard IL 60148-4924

ROZANSKI, BARBARA ANN, administrative librarian; b. Chgo., Oct. 17, 1942; d. Carl Joseph and Alice Ann (Dwyer) Kopp; m. James Paul Rozanski, July 11, 1964 (dec. Sept. 1980); 1 child, Kenneth. BS, Marquette U., 1964; MBA, MLS, Rosary Coll., 1983. From head tech. svcs. to adminstrv. libr. Prospect Heights (Ill.) Pub. Libr. Dist., 1978—; from pres.-elect to pres. Coop. Computer Svcs., Arlington Heights, Ill., 1991-94; chmn. Suburban Librs. United for Regional Planning, 1988-89. Editor: (serial) World Opera Schedule, 1992—. Mem. ALA, Ill. Libr. Assn., Pub. Libr. Assn., Wagner Soc. Am., Prospect Heights-Wheeling C. of C., Beta Gamma Sigma. Office: Prospect Heights Libr Dist 12 N Elm St Prospect Heights IL 60070-1499

ROZELL, JOSEPH GERARD, accountant; b. Kansas City, Kans., Mar. 20, 1959; s. Joseph Frank and Frances Elizabeth (Gojmeric) R. BSBA, Rockhurst Coll., 1981; MBA, U. Mo., Kansas City, 1992. Staff acct. Donnelly, Meiners & Jordan, Kansas City, Mo., 1981-82, Francis A. Wright & Co., Kansas City, Mo., 1982-88, Libby Corp., Kansas City, 1988-90, Sprint Corp., Overland Park, Kans., 1990—. Mem. Greater Kansas City Young Reps., pres. 1988-89; treas. Jackson County Rep. Com., 1989—. Mem. AICPAs, Mo. Soc. CPAs (legis. com., liaison com.), Greater Kans. Jaycees (treas. 1988-89). Republican. Roman Catholic. Home: 12112 Madison Ct Kansas City MO 64145-1023

ROZGA, MARGARET, English language educator; b. Milw., July 6, 1945; d. Charles Aloysius and Jeannette Martha (Paradowski) R.; m. James E. Groppi, Apr. 22, 1976 (dec. Nov. 1985); children: Anna G. Groppi, Christine A. Groppi, Matthew V. Groppi. BA, Alverno Coll., 1967; MA, U. Wis., Milw., 1971, PhD, 1977. Lectr. ednl. opportunity program U. Wis., Milw., 1976-78; lectr. George Washington U., Washington, 1978-79; asst. prof. U. Wis. Ctr.-Waukesha County, Waukesha, 1984-90, assoc. prof., 1990—; cons. Nat. Ctr. for Urban Ethnic Affairs, Washington, 1973. Author: poems, short stories, essays. Coord. Father Groppi Action for Justice Com., Milw., 1987-88. Recipient Fair Housing award Milw. Met. Fair Housing Coun., 1987; summer rsch. grantee U. Wis. Ctrs., 1986, profl. devel. grantee U. Wis. Ctrs., 1990. Mem. MLA, Ozaukee Writers Group, Wis. Fellowship of Poets, Nat. Coun. Tchrs. English, Midwest MLA. Roman Catholic. Office: U Wis Ctr Waukesha 1500 N University Dr Waukesha WI 53188-2720

ROZRAN, JACK LOUIS, courier service executive; b. Chgo., Mar. 4, 1939; s. Philip Reuben and Rose (Rosenberg) R.; m. Dawn Faulkner, May 25, 1986; children: Justin Grant, Claire Ashley, Ryan Bjur. BA, Northwestern U., 1960; JD, Harvard U., 1963. Bar: Ill. 1963. Law clk. to judge U.S. Dist. Ct. Ill., 1963-64; v.p. Cannonball, Inc., Chgo., 1964-66, pres., 1966-92, chmn., 1992—. Trustee Hull House Assn., 1972-90, v.p. 1987; sec. Erikson Inst., 1982, trustee, 1971-92; mem. vis. com. Northwestern U., Evanston, Ill. Mem. Messenger Svc. Assn. Ill. (pres. 1987-89, v.p. 1990-92, bd. dirs. 1987—), Chgo. Assn. Commerce & Industry (chmn. motor transp. div.), Air Courier Conf. Am. (treas. 1980-82, pres. 1982-84, bd. dirs. 1976—), ABA, Expedited Package Ind. Contractors Coun. (co-chair 1992-95), Chgo. Bar Assn., Chgo Assn. Commerce Downtown Traffic Study, Economic Club, Beta Alpha Psi. Home: 579 W Hawthorne Pl Chicago IL 60657-2922 Office: Cannonball Inc 875 W Huron St Chicago IL 60622-5960

ROZWICK, DONALD JOSEPH, recycling company executive; b. Greenfield, Wis., May 6, 1970; s. Donald August Rozwick and Kathleen Lynn (Huth) Shumway. BSEE, Mil. Sch. Engring., 1994. Cathecist St. Mathias Parish, West Allis, Wis., 1987-93. Mem. Internat. Inst. Elec. Engrs. Home: 6169 S 38th St Greenfield WI 53221

RUBENSTEIN, ERIC DAVIS, real estate executive; b. Chgo., Oct. 21, 1952; s. Leonard S. and Ruth B. R.; m. Gail D. Harwood, Aug. 12, 1973 (div. 1978); m. Chaya Michelle Cohen, Dec. 22, 1985; children: Rebecca, Renee. BA, Drake U., Des Moines, 1971; student percussion, A. Conservatory of Music, Chgo., 1963-67. Media rels. dir. Ill. Inst. Tech., Chgo., 1972-78; owner Alpine Communications, Chgo., 1975—; pres. Alpine Realty and Management Co., Chgo., 1977—, Single Rm. Operators Assn., Chgo., 1985—; also bd. dirs.; pres. Carter Realty & Devel. Co., 1984—; bd. dirs. Single Rm. Housing Assistance Corp.; lectr. in field. Pub. Real Crime Book Digest, Chgo., 1993—; contbr. articles to profl. jours. Bd. dirs., pres. Job Resources for Disabled, Chgo., 1982-84, 90-92, treas., 1987-90; mem. Chgo. Mayor's Task Force on Homelessness, 1987-90, Task Force on SRO's, 1993-94; mem. forcible entry and retainer com. Cook County Cir. Ct., 1987-91, mem. housing and eviction ct. merger com., 1989-91; mem. Chgo. Single Room Occupancy Adv. Com., 1985-86, Evanston (Ill.) Bldg. Code Appeals Bd., 1982-92; mem. Nat. Alliance To End Homelessness, Skokie (Ill.) Bd. Health, 1992-94, Cook County State's Atty. Criminal Housing Task Force, 1994—. Recipient Disting. Svc. award Job Resources for Disabled, 1989, Cert. of Merit, Iowa Daily Press Assn., 1971, others. Mem. Chgo. Property Owners Assn., Ill. Coalition for the Homeless, Single Rm. Operators Assn., Edgewater Community Coun., Ill. Inst. Tech. Parents Assn. (exec. sec. 1972-78), Drake U. Journalism Alumni Coun. of Chgo., Zeta Beta Tau. Jewish. Office: Alpine Realty & Mgmt Co 4917 N Kenmore Ave Chicago IL 60640-3709

RUBENSTEIN, IRWIN, molecular biologist, educator; b. Kansas City, Mo., Sept. 6, 1931; s. Marion and Fannie (Bachus) R.; m. Ina Rosen, Feb. 19, 1956; children: Ione, Ira, Ilana. BS in Physics, Calif. Inst. Tech., 1953; PhD in Biophysics, UCLA, 1960. Asst. prof. dept. molecular biophysics Yale U., New Haven, 1963-68, assoc. prof., 1968-70; prof. dept. genetics and cell biology U. Minn., St. Paul, 1970-88, prof. dept. plant biology, 1988-95; mem. World Book Ency. Biol. Sci. Com., Chgo., 1970—; biomed sci. study sect. NIH, Washington, 1982-85. Co-author: Emergent Technology for the Genetic Improvement of Crops, 1980; contbr. articles to profl. jours. With U.S. Army, 1954-55. Grantee NIH, 1978-93, USDA, 1980-82, Dept. of Energy, 1985-88, NSF, 1976-80. Mem. Rotary, Gamma Sigma Delta (Merit award 1987). Democrat. Jewish. Office: Univ Minn Dept Plant Biology 220 Bio Science Saint Paul MN 55108

RUBIN, ALLAN MAIER, physician, surgeon; b. Bavaria, Germany, Aug. 4, 1947; s. Benjamin Rubin and Ida Spiegle; children: Alanna T., Marissa D., Sarina D.; m. Jean Tellander, Mar. 5, 1989. BS, McGill U., Montreal, Que., Can., 1968, MS, 1970; PhD, MD, U. Toronto, Ont., Can., 1979. Diplomate Am. Bd. Otolaryngology. Demonstrator neuroanatomy U. Toronto, 1971-73, resident, 1979-84; investigator Toronto Gen. Hosp., 1976-78; fellow otolaryngology Toronto East Gen. Hosp., 1985; asst. prof. dept. otolaryngology Creighton U., Omaha, 1986-87; assoc. prof. dept. surgery Med. Coll. Ohio, Toledo, 1987-88, chmn., prof. dept. otolaryngology, 1988—; mem. resident edn. com. Blue Cross N.W. Ohio, Toledo, 1992-93, HMO/Toledo Health Plan, 1989-93; pres. Acad. Senate Med. Coll. Ohio, Toledo, 1991-92; chmn. search for urology chair Med. Coll. Ohio, 1991-92, presdl. search com., 1991-93. Mem. internat. editl. adv. bd. Jour. Otolaryngology, 1991—, editl. rev. bd. Am. Jour. Otolaryngology, 1989-94. Rsch. grantee Biomed. Rsch. Support Grant, 1984, NIH, 1986, 87. Fellow ACS, Royal Soc. Medicine, Am. Neurotology Soc., Am. Acad. Otolaryngology-Head and Neck Surgery (subcom. on equilibrium 1988—, subcom. on med. aspects of noise, editl. rev. bd. 1993—); mem. Soc. Univ. Otolaryngologists (resident edn. com., membership com.), Barany Soc., Triological Soc., Sigma Xi, Alpha Omega Alpha (v.p. Delta of Ohio chpt. 1996—, chmn. search com. for orthopaedic surgery chmn.). Office: Med Coll Ohio 3000 Arlington Ave Toledo OH 43614-2595

RUBIN, DAVID C., biology educator, association administrator; b. Bklyn., Feb. 9, 1943; s. Harold and Julia (Kleiner) R.; m. Rebecca Lynne Allen, Jan. 26, 1968; children: Robert Edward, Beth Allyn. BS, Cornell U., 1963; MA, Ind. State U., 1965, PhD, 1969. Park ranger trainee Lassen Volcanic Nat. Pk., Calif., 1961, Olympic Nat. Pk., Wash., 1962; instr. life scis. Ind. State U., Terre Haute, 1966-67; project writer interrelated math.-sci., Ft. Lauderdale, Fla., 1969-70; from asst. prof. to assoc. prof. biology Ctrl. State U, Wilberforce, Ohio, 1970-84, prof., 1984-95; membership dir., exec. dir. U. Cin. AAUP, 1996—; mem. exec. com. Ohio Biol. Survey, Columbus, 1991-95. Author: Systematics: An Introduction to Classification, 1973; contbr. articles to profl. jours. Westinghouse grantee, 1989-93. Mem. AAUP (bd. dirs. Ohio conf. 1978—, pres. Ohio conf. 1992-93, pres. Ctrl. State U. chpt. 1975-77, 84-86, Tacey award 1994), Soc. for Study Amphibians and Reptiles, Ind. Acad. Sci., Herpetologists League, Nature Conservancy. Home: 120 Sheridan Ave Xenia OH 45385 Office: Univ Cin Biology Dept AAUP ML 176 Cincinnati OH 45221

RUBIN, E(RWIN) LEONARD, lawyer; b. Chgo., Jan. 11, 1933; s. Samuel and Frances Birdie (Rabin) R.; m. Stephanie Siegel, Mar. 4, 1961 (div. Dec. 1981); children: Matthew, Suzanne; m. Audrey Gay Holzer, May 8, 1983; children: Margot, Bette. Student, U. Ill., Urbana, 1948-51; AB, U. Miami, 1956, JD, 1959. s. N.Y. 1960, Ill. 1962, U.S. Dist. Ct. (no. dist.) Ill. 1962, U.S. Ct. Appeals (7th cir.) 1990. Assoc. Hays, St. John A&H, N.Y.C., 1960-62, Devoe, Shadur, Mikva & P., Chgo., 1962-65; gen. counsel Playboy Enterprises, Inc., Chgo., 1965-78; ptnr. E. Leonard Rubin Law Offices, Chgo., 1978-81, Epton, Mullin & Druth Ltd., Chgo., 1981-86, Brinks, Hofer, Gilson & Lione, Chgo., 1986—; adj. prof. U. Ill., John Marshall Law Sch. Pres. Lawyers for Creative Arts, Chgo., 1983-85; chmn. bd. dirs. Mus. Holography; bd. dirs. Wisdom Bridge Theatre, Chgo., 1983-85. Cpl. U.S. Army, 1953-5, ETO. Mem. ABA, Ill. Bar Assn., Chgo. Bar Assn. (bd. mgrs. 1983-85, chmn. various coms., dir. Christmas Spirits Satire Show 1965—), Union Internat. Des Avocats (v.p. intellectual property comm.), Copyright Soc. Am. (trustee, pres. midwest chpt.). Jewish. Home: 270 Sunset Dr Northfield IL 60093-1047 Office: Brinks Hofer Gilson & Lione 455 N Cityfront Plaza Dr Chicago IL 60611-5503

RUBIN, JOANNE LESLIE, psychologist; b. N.Y.C., Aug. 12, 1950; d. Seymour Solomon and Phyllis Dorothy (Fleischer) R.; m. Steven R. Bergmann, Aug. 15, 1975; children: Rachel Rubin Bergmann, David Rubin Bergmann. BA in Psychology, George Washington U., 1972; MS in Psychol. Svcs., U. Pa., 1974, PhD in Counseling Psychology, 1980. Lic. psychologist, Mo.; cert. program family therapist. Pvt. practice St. Louis, 1977-80; staff counselor St. Louis U. Counseling Ctr., 1979-81; clin. psychologist St. Louis County Child Mental Health Svcs., 1981-84; pvt. practice Webster Groves, Mo., 1984—; lectr., supr. in family therapy Menninger Found., 1986-87. Mem. coun. on child abuse and neglect St. Louis Mental Health Assn., 1981-86, rsch. chmn., 1984. Mem. APA, Transpersonal Psychology Assn., Inst. Noetic Scis. (coord. St. Louis local Noetic Scis. study group 1991—), Internat. Soc. for Study of Subtle Energies and Energy Medicine. Office: 8772 Big Bend Blvd Saint Louis MO 63119

RUBIN, MARK RICHARD, foreign languages administrator, educator; b. N.Y.C., Mar. 14, 1944; s. Barnet and Rose (Lazar) R. AB, Rutgers U., 1966; AM, Princeton (N.J.) U., 1968, PhD, 1978. Instr. in French Kent (Ohio) State U., 1972-79, asst. prof. French, 1979-88, assoc. prof. French, 1988—; assoc. dir. Lemnitzer Ctr. for NATO and EC Studies, Kent State U., dir. for internat. and comparative programs. Co-editor: Europe's Neutral and Nonaligned States: Between NATO and the Warsaw Pact, 1989, Dien Bien Phu & Crisis of Franco-American Relations, 1990, NATO After Forty Years, 1990; author, translator chpts. in books. Capt. U.S. Army, 1970-72. Rutgers U. scholar, 1965-66; Soc. des Prof. Francais grantee, 1969. Mem. Am. Soc. for 18th Century Studies, Am. Assn. Tchrs. of French, Soc. Retif de la Bretonne, Societe francaise d'etude du XVIIIeme siecle, Societe des professeurs francais et francophones en Amerique, Ohio Arms Control Seminar. Office: Kent State U Ctr Internat Programs Kent OH 44242-0001

RUBINSTEIN, DAVID A., legal administator; b. Fresno, Calif., July 8, 1946; s. Ned H. Rubinstein and Edwina A. Atherton; children: Ned, Deborah. BS, U. Wis., Superior, 1968; MPA, U. S.C., 1973. City supt. City of Zeeland (Mich.), 1973-77; city mgr. City of Englewood (Ohio), 1977-79, City of Walker (Mich.), 1981-89; dep. county adminstr. Montgomery County, Ohio, 1979-81; firm adminstr. Miller, Johnson, Snell & Cummiskey, 1989-92; exec. dir. Sommers, Schwartz, Silver & Swartz, 1992—; adj. prof. Grant Valley State U., 1989-92; lectr. Sinclair C.C., Dayton, Ohio, 1978-79, Aquinas Coll., Grand Rapids, Mich., 1982. Bd. dirs. Temple Emanuel, Grand Rapids, 1983-93, 3d v.p., 1985-87, 1st v.p. 1987-89, pres. 1989-91; bd. dirs. Michigan City Mgmt. Assn., 1988-89; vice-chmn. Policy and Rsch. Com. GGREAT, Grand Rapids; mem. Labor Rels. Adv. Com., Mich. Mcpl. League, 1981-89; chairperson Walker/Standard Downtown Devel. Authority, 1986-89; bd. dirs. Grand Rapids Child Guidance Clinic, 1983-91, treas. 1987-89, v.p. 1989-91. Served to capt. USAF, 1968-73, col. USAFR. Recipient Civic Svc. award City of Zeeland, 1976, Englewood City Coun., 1979, City of Waller, 1989. Mem. Internat. City Mgmt. Assn. (data and info. services adv. council 1984-85), Montgomery City Mayors and Mgrs. Assn. (sec.-treas. 1979), West Mich. City Mgrs. Assn. (pres. 1985), Am. Soc. Pub. Adminstrs., Assn. Legal Adminstrs. (pres. West Mich. chpt. 1992-93, pres.-elect Detroit chpt., edn. officer Region III). Avocations: astronomy, running, reading, scuba diving. Office: 2000 Town Ctr Ste 900 Southfield MI 48075-1142

RUBLE, BERNARD ROY, educator, minister, labor relations consultant; b. Greensburg, Ind., Apr. 4, 1923; s. Jesse Emery and Marietta (Ward) R.; B.S., Ind. U., Bloomington, 1949; postgrad. transactional analysis Midwest Inst. Human Understanding, 1972-75; m. Mary Helen Rullman, Dec. 22, 1946; children: Barry Reece, Blane Rodney. Asst. mgr. Morris 5 and 10 Stores, Greensburg, 1941; store keeper Public Service Co. Ind., Greensburg, 1941-43; asst. mgr. personnel Kroger Co., Cin., 1949-51, mgr., personnel, Madison, Wis., 1951-56, Ft. Wayne, Ind., 1956-58, Cleve., 1958-73, mgr. labor relations Erie Mktg. Area, Solon, Ohio, 1973-84; faculty Kroger Edn. Center, Cin., 1978—; trustee Meat Cutters Health and Welfare Fund, 1971-79, Retail Clks. Union Health and Welfare Fund, Akron, 1970-88, No. Ohio Hospice Council, 1981-84. Active United Appeal Greater Cleve., Community Chest Greater Cleve., Met. Health Planning Corp.; v.p. trustee Urban League Greater Cleve., 1968-75; adv. com. Family Health Care, Washington, 1977-78; trustee Community Health Found., Greater Cleve. Interchurch Coun., 1993—; bd. dirs., exec. com. Greater Cleve. Coun. Chs., 1994—; team rep. B.R. Ruble Racing, Burton, Ohio. Served with USAAF, 1943-45. Mem. Internat. Transactional Ana

RUBLE, RONALD MERLIN, humanities and theater communications educator; b. Mansfield, Ohio, July 4, 1940; s. Eldred Roy and Dessie Cedelia (Shaw) Briner; m. Nancy Kay Dillon, Aug. 29, 1970 (div. Apr. 1976); children: Eric Douglas, Kristofer Philip. BA, Otterbein Coll., 1962; MA, Bowling Green State U., 1966, PhD, 1975. Site coord. Arts Unltd. Firelands Coll. of Bowling Green U., Huron, Ohio, 1989-92, instr. speech and theater, 1970-75, program dir. speech and theater, 1970—, asst. prof. speech and theater, 1976-79, chmn. dept. humanities, 1976-80, assoc. prof. humanities and theater, 1979—, tchg. artist Arts Unltd., 1987-89; bus. mgr., play dir. Huron Playhouse Bowling Green U., 1966-78; artistic dir. Caryl Crane Children's Theatre, Huron, 1990—; co-chmn. Arts in the Parks Festival, North Ctrl. Ohio Arts Coun., Sandusky, 1976-78, v.p. bd. dirs., 1977-78; theater cons. Caryl Crane Children's Theatre, Sandusky, 1984-90. Dir. play The Gingerbread lady, 1978 (1st place N.W. region Ohio Cmty. Theatre Assn. 1978); contbr. poems, short story to profl. publs. Unit commr. Erie dist. of Firelands coun. Boy Scouts Am., Huron, 1984-87, mem. troop rev. bd., 1985—, merit badge counselor Firelands dist. Heart of Ohio coun., Vermilion, Ohio, 1984—; elder 1st Presbyn. Ch., Huron, 1988-90, 95—. Recipient Outstanding Educator in Arts award Ohio Ho. of Reps., 1975, Outstanding Young Man of Am. award Nat. Jaycees, 1977, Outstanding Cmty. Svc. award Huron C. of C., 1983, 84, 85. Mem. Am. Theatre in Higher Edn., Am. Alliance Theatre Edn., Am. Assn. Univ. Prof., Drama League, Ohio Theatre Alliance, Am. Film Inst., Children's Theatre Assn. Home: 729 Taylor Ave Huron OH 44839-2522 Office: Bowling Green State U Firelands Coll 901 Rye Beach Rd Huron OH 44839-9791

RUCH, RICHARD HURLEY, manufacturing company executive; b. Plymouth, Ind., Apr. 15, 1930; s. Dallas Claude and Mabel (Hurley) R.; m. Patricia Lou Overbeek, June 27, 1931; children: Richard, Michael, Christine, Douglas. BA, Mich. State U., 1952. Stores acctg. supr. Kroger Inc., Grand Rapids, Mich., 1954-55; chief acct. Herman Miller Inc., Zeeland, Mich., 1955-58, controller, 1958-63, dir. mfg., 1963-67, v.p. mfg., 1967-77, v.p. adminstrn., 1978, v.p. corp. resources, 1979-85, chief fin. officer, sr. v.p., 1985-87, chief exec. officer, 1988-92, pres, chief exec. officer, 1990-92, also vice chair bd. dirs., 1992-95; chmn. of bd., 1995—. Active Hope Coll., Twentieth Century Club, Holland, Mich.; formerly active Holland C. of C., Zeeland Planning Com. Mem. Scanlon Plan Assocs. (bd. dirs., past pres.). Office: Herman Miller Inc 855 E Main Ave Zeeland MI 49464-1366

RUCKER, DENNIS MORTON ARTHUR, telecommunications executive; b. Bloomington, Ind., Sept. 23, 1949; s. Arthur Morton and A. Ileen (Tiemeyer) R.; m. Barbara Rose Daniels, Mar. 1, 1986. BSEE, BS in Speech and English, Purdue U., 1972, MSEE, 1983. Staff assoc. engr. C&P Telephone Co. of Md., Balt., 1973-74; asst. plant engr. Ind. Telephone Corp., Seymour, 1974-76; transmissions and radio planning engr. United Telephone Co. of Ohio, Mansfield, 1976-78, network mgr., 1978-79, gen. mgr. rates and tariffs, 1979-82; dir. cellular engr. Western Union Corp., Upper Saddle River, N.J., 1982-84; dir. planning Ameritech Mobile Communications Inc., Schaumburg, Ill., 1984-90; sr. dir. sci. and tech. Ameritech Mobile Communications Inc., Hoffman Estates, Ill., 1990-93; dir. engring. and personal comms. U.S. Cellular Corp, Chgo., 1993—. Author: Balancing Wireless Systems, 1995; contbr. articles to profl. jours. Recipient awards for rsch. in optical comms. U.S. Army, USAF, and Nat. Aero. & Space Adminstrn. Mem. IEEE, Cellular Telecom. Industry Assn. (Industry Svc. award 1990, chmn. advanced radio techs. subcom. 1986-89, tech. com. 1985-93), Telecom. Industry Assn. (sec. tech. rev. com. 45.5 1992-93), Rutgers U. Wireless Info Network Lab (bd. industry advisors), Internat. Engring. Consortium (overseers coun. 1993—). Roman Catholic. Office: US Cellular Corp 8410 W Bryn Mawr Ave Ste 700 Chicago IL 60631-3402

RUCKER, RICHARD SIM, information systems executive; b. Dayton, Ohio, Sept. 4, 1947; s. Wilbert Hunter and Estelle Janet Rucker. BBA, Wright State U., Dayton, 1976; MBA, Cen. Mich. U., 1987; PhD in Mgmt. Info. Systems, Kennedy-Western U., 1990. Asst. program mgr. Synergy, Inc., Dayton, 1968-78; mgr. data processing Ledex, Inc., Vandalia, Ohio, 1978-83; cons. analyst NCR Corp., Dayton, 1983-85; mgr. info. systems SelectTech Corp., Dayton, 1985; dir. computing and tech. svcs. Dayton Bd. Edn., 1985-91, asst. supt. bus. and tech. svcs., 1991-92; pres. Richard S. Rucker & Assocs., Dayton, 1982—; v.p. Midwest region Metters Industries, Inc., 1992—. Bd. dirs. Dakota Youth Ctr., Dayton, 1983, Dayton Urban League, 1986—; mem. exec. council Congl. Adv. Council to U.S. Congressman Tony Hall, 1986. Named one of Outstanding Young Men Am., 1984, Man of Achievement, 1988. Mem. Kappa Alpha Psi. Democrat. Home: 2914 Forest Grove Ave Dayton OH 45406-4039

RUCKERT, RITA E., elementary education educator; b. Monett, Mo., Feb. 15, 1947; d. Wesley Swearengin and Eva Anna Harriet (Spradling) R. BS in Edn., U. Mo., 1969. Cert. tchr., Mo. Jr. high sch. tchr. Milw. (Wis.) Pub. Schs., 1969-70; high sch. tchr. Houston (Mo.) Schs., 1970-79, elem. tchr., 1979-95; volleyball ofcl. Mo. State High Sch. Activities Assn., Columbia, 1980-93, volleyball rules interpreter, 1983-93. Election judge Tex. County Clk.'s Office, Houston, 1987-95; mem. Houston (Mo.) Pk. Bd., 1988-92, pres., 1991-92. Recipient Fitness Ctr. grant Wells Fargo Bank, Calif., 1990; named Volleyball Outstanding Ofcl., Nat. Fedn. Interscholastic Ofcls. Assn., 1991. Mem. NEA (v.p. 1994-95, pres.-elect 1995-96, pres. 1996-97), AAHPERD, Mo. Assn. Health, Phys. Edn., Recreation and Dance (Dist. Elem. Phys. Educator of Yr. 1990, quality phys. edn. com. 1991-93), Optimist Internat., Delta Kappa Gamma. Republican. Home: 505 Hawthorn St Houston MO 65483-1721 Office: Houston Elem Sch 423 W Pine St Houston MO 65483-1147

RUD, ANTHONY GORDON, JR., university administrator; b. Pittsfield, Mass., Jan. 10, 1953; s. Anthony Gordon and Marianne (Ellis) R.; m. Rita Marian Long, Aug. 6, 1983; 1 child, Rachel Anne Elizabeth. AB, Dartmouth Coll., 1976; MA, Northwestern U., 1979, PhD, 1982. Asst. dir. admissions Dartmouth Coll., Hanover, N.H., 1982-86; fellow, sr. fellow N.C. Ctr. for Advancement of Teaching, Cullowhee, 1986-94; assoc. dean Purdue U., West Lafayette, Ind., 1994—; cons. U. South Fla., Tampa, 1995—, Boston U., 1990-93. Editor, author: A Place for Teacher Renewal, 1992, The Educational Conversation, 1995. Office: Purdue U 1440 LAEB West Lafayette IN 47907-1440

RUDA, NEIL MICHAEL, data processing executive, minister; b. Chgo., July 25, 1957; s. Anthony John and Bette (Crockett) R.; m. Deanna Lyndell Mather, Nov. 25, 1988. Student, U. So. Fla., 1975-78, Berean Coll., 1982-87. Ordained minister, Assemblies of God Ch., 1988. Sales trainer Ill. Bell Telephone, Arlington Heights, 1977-80; sales rep. David C. Cook Pub., Elgin, Ill., 1980-82; dir. edn. We. Mich. Teen Challenge, Muskegon, 1982-84; dir. computer ops. STAR Communications, Durant, Fla., 1984-89; mgr. info. svcs. Life Pubs. Internat. div. Fgn. Missions Assemblies of God, Springfield, Mo., 1989—; cons. Custom Processing, Washington, 1986-87, Custom Programming, Falls Church, 1986-87, Univ. Acad., Miami, 1985-87. Mem. Palm Beach County Ministers Fellowship. Republican. Home: 3216 W Whiteside St Springfield MO 65807-2144 Office: Gen Coun Assemblies of God Divsn Fgn Missions 1445 N Boonville Ave Springfield MO 65802-1894

RUDE, BRIAN DAVID, state legislator; b. Viroqua, Wis., Aug. 25, 1955; s. Raymond and Conelee (Johnson) R.; m. Karen Thulin; children: Erik, Nels. BA magna cum laude, Luther Coll., 1977; MA, U. Wis., Madison, 1994. Mem. Wis. Assembly, Madison, 1982-84; mem. Wis. Senate, Madison, 1984—, asst. minority leader, 1989-93; pres. Wis. State Sen., 1993—; with corp. communications The Trane Co., La Crosse, Wis., 1981-85. Bd. advisers Nat. Trust Historic Preservation, 1990—. Mem. Lions, Sons of Norway, Norwegian-Am. Hist. Assn. (trustee). Republican. Lutheran. Home: 307 Babcock St PO Box 367 Coon Valley WI 54623-0367 Office: Wis State Senate State Capitol Rm 239-S PO Box 7882 Madison WI 53703

RUDESILL, MATILDA, retired farm wife; b. Mannington Twp., N.J., Jan. 3, 1925; d. Leland Irwin and Hermione (Barker) Warner; m. Harley Eldon Rudesill, Mar. 29, 1947; children: Norma, Francine Meyer, Lanette Harsdorf, Joanne Dowdy. BS, Glassboro State Tchrs. Coll., 1945. Unit leader Camp Madeleine Mulford Montclaire Girl Scouts, Branchville, N.J., 1944-46; tchr. Concord Sch., Mannington Twp., N.J., 1945, Pennsville (N.J.) Sch., 1945-47; farm wife Maple Grove Farm, Pierce County, Wis., 1947-90; ret., 1990. Author: Hot Dogs in the Cave, 1992, Letters from Rolling Acres, 1995. Reporter Pierce-St. Croix Guernsey Breeders, Pierce County, 1970-80; com. mem. Pierce County Hwy. Safety Commn., 1973-83; womans chair, del. Wis. Farm Bur., Pierce County, 1986-91; vol. Wis. Breeding Bird Atlas, Pierce County, 1995. Republican. United Methodist. Home: W 4925 890th Ave Baldwin WI 54002

RUDISILL, JOHN RICHARD, clinical psychologist, educator; b. Tulia, Tex., Jan. 2, 1947; s. Ray Burnley and Ruth Arlene (Blackburn) R.; m. Marla Elifritz, Aug. 30, 1969; children—John Stephen, Matthew James, Alisha Dawn. BA in Psychology, Denison U., 1969; PhD, Ind. U., 1974. Lic. psychologist, Ohio. Chief psychologist, program dir. Dayton (Ohio) Mental Health Ctr., 1977-79; dir. med. student edn. dept. psychiatry Wright State U. Sch. Medicine, Dayton, 1979-93, coord. behavioral sci. of family practice, 1979-93; dir. divsn. applied psychology dept. of family medicine; pvt. psychology, Dayton, 1977—; cons. Dayton VA Ctr., 1983—, Wright AFB Med. Ctr., Dayton, 1982—, IAMS Co., Ohio; mem. Montgomery County Mental Health Bd., vice-chair, 1984. Served to capt. USAF, 1973-77. Denison U. Founders' scholar, 1965-69; NIMH fellow, 1971, grantee, 1972-73; named Tchr. of Yr., Wright State U. Sch. Medicine, 1981-82; recipient Wright State's Chmn. award psychiatry, 1982. Mem. Am. Psychol. Assn., Am. Bd. Adminstrv. Psychology, Nat. Registry Health Svc. Providers, Ohio Psychol. Assn., Dayton Area Psychol. Assn., Mental Health Assn. Methodist. Clubs: Ind. Alumni, Denison Alumni, D-Man. Contbr. articles in field to profl. jours. Home: 786 Autumn Leaf Dr Dayton OR 45430-1488

RUDNICK, ELLEN AVA, health care executive; b. New Haven; d. Harold and C. Vivian (Soybel) R.; children from previous marriage: Sarah, Noah; m. Paul W. Earle. BA, Vassar Coll., 1972; MBA, U. Chgo., 1973. Sr. fin. analyst Quaker Oats, Chgo., 1973-75; various positions Baxter Internat., Deerfield, Ill., 1975-80, dir. planning, 1980-83, corp. v.p., 1985-1990; pres. Baxter Mgmt. Svcs., Deerfield, 1983-1990, HCIA, Balt., 1990-92, CEO Advs., Northbrook, Ill., 1992—; prin., chmn. Pacific Biometrics, Irvine, Calif., 1993—; bd. dirs. NCCI. Chief crusader Met. Chgo. United Way, 1982-85; pres. coun. Nat. Coll. Edn., Evanston, Ill., 1983—; cir. of friends Chgo. YMCA, 1985-89; bd. dirs. Highland Park Hosp., 1990—, NCCI. Mem. Chgo. Network, Econs. Club Chgo. (officer, bd. dirs.). Office: CEO Advs 255 Revere Dr Ste 111 Northbrook IL 60062-1595

RUDOLPH, STEPHEN P., insurance company executive; b. LaCrosse, Wis., Feb. 28, 1949; s. Alois Joseph and Mary Louise (Brown) R.; m. Mary Ann Schwoegler, May 5, 1973; children: Scott, Amanda, James. BS, U. Wis., LaCrosse, 1971; MA, George Washington U., 1978. Planning analyst Western Wis. HEalth Planning Orgn., LaCrosse, 1972-74; coord. Wis. Regional Med. Ptogram, Madison, 1974-77; asst. exec. dir. Cath. Health Assn. Wis., Madison, 1978-79; asst. adminstr. Hosp. Coop. Am., King Khalid Mulitry City, Saudi Arabia, 1975-80, Beloit (Wis.) Meml. Hosp., 1981-84; sr. dir. plan devel. Wis. Physicians Svc., Madison, 1984-93; CEO Cmty. Fin. & Ins. Corp., Madison, 1994—. Author: The History of the Wisconsin Regional Medical Program, 1976; contbr. articles to profl. jours. Bd. dirs. Boy Scouts Am. Four Lakes Coun., Madison, 1990—. Recipient Legion of Merit award Boy Scouts Am. Fellow Am. Coll. Healthcare Execs.; mem. Am. Hosp. Assn., U. Wis. Alumni Assn. (bd. dirs. 1991—). Roman Catholic. Home: 6214 Pioneer Rd Madison WI 53711 Office: Cmty Fin & Ins Corp PO Box 8430 Madison WI 53708

RUDOLPH, SUSANNE HOEBER, political and social science educator; b. Mannheim, Fed. Republic of Germany, Germany, Apr. 3, 1930; (parents Am. citizens); d. Johannes and Elfriede (Fischer) H.; m. Lloyd I. Rudolph, July 19, 1952; children: Jenny W., Amelia C., Matthew C. J. AB, Sarah Lawrence Coll., 1951; MA, Radcliffe Coll., 1953; PhD in Polit. Sci., Harvard U., 1955. Instr., lectr. govt. Harvard U., Cambridge, Mass., 1957-64; assoc. prof. polit. and social scis. U. Chgo., 1964-72, prof., 1972—, master social scis. collegiate div., 1973-75, chair dept. polit. sci., 1976-79, 89, dir. South Asia Ctr., 1980—; bd. dir. Rockefeller Residency Inst., 1990-94; lectr. Phi Beta Kappa, 1977-79, 86-90; mem. Bd. Fgn. Scholarships, 1979-82; chmn. com. on problems and policy, Social Sci. Rsch. Coun., 1987-89. Author: (with Lloyd I. Rudolph) The Modernity of Tradition: Political Development in India, 1967, Education and Politics in India, 1972, The Regional Imperative: Foreign Policy in South Asia, 1980, Gandhi, 1983, Essays on Rajputana, 1984, In Pursuit of Lakshmi, 1987. Bd. dirs. Sarah Lawrence Coll., 1984-90, Kodaikanal-Woodstock Found., 1988—. Ford Found. fgn. area tng. fellow, India, 1956-57, Fulbright sr. fellow, India, 1962-63, 87-88, Am. Inst. Indian Studies faculty fellow, India, 1966-67, 83-84, 91-92, Guggenheim fellow, 1970-71; grantee NSF, 1973-75, NEH, 1977-79, 95. Mem. Am. Polit. Sci. Assn. (v.p. 1973-74), Assn. Asian Studies (bd. dirs. 1973-75, v.p. 1985-86, pres. 1986-87), Asia Soc. (bd. dirs. 1991—). Office: U Chgo Dept Polit Sci 5828 S University Ave Chicago IL 60637-1515

RUDY, KATHLEEN VERMEULEN, small business owner; b. Grand Rapids, Mich., Dec. 29, 1931; d. John Weston and Geneva (Swiet) Vermeulen; m. Fredrick Albers Yonkman, June 9, 1953 (div. Sept. 1980); children: Sara Yonkman Davis, Margriet Yonkman Finnegan, Nina Vermeulen Hovnanian; m. Raymond Bruce Rudy Jr., Nov. 14, 1981. BA, Hope Coll., Holland, Mich., 1953. Owner Kateis Antiques, Danby, Vt., 1974—. Editor mag. Jr. League of Boston, 1960's, Scarsdale Jr. League, 1960's. Bd. dirs. Jr. League of Boston, 1960s, Greenwich Cmty. for Human Svcs., 1970s-80s, Neighbor to Neighbor, Greenwich, 1980—; trustee Hope Coll., Holland, 1986—; chmn. Mary Fund com. Ladies Golf Tournament, 1985; mem. Women's Nat. Rep. Club, 1995—; mem. Sch. of Politics Fgn. Affairs. Mem. Greenwich Jr. League, Greenwich Country Club (house com. 1990—), Dorset Field Club, Kappa Alpha Theta (past com. mem.). Republican. Congregationalist. Home: 37 Lismore Ln Greenwich CT 06831-3741 Office: Kateis Antiques Danby Antique Ctr Danby VT 05730

RUEDEN, HENRY ANTHONY, accountant; b. Green Bay, Wis., Dec. 25, 1949; s. Bernard M. and Audrey Virgin R. BS, U. Wis., Green Bay, 1971; MBA, U. Wis., Oshkosh, 1973; postgrad., Internat. Grad. Sch., St. Louis, 1984—. CPA, Ill., Wis.; cert. mgmt. acct.; cert. internal auditor; cert. info. systems auditor; cert. cost analyst. Auditor U.S. Customs Svc., Chgo., 1974-86; systems acct. U.S. R.R. Retirement Bd., Chgo., 1986—. With USAR, 1972—, Desert Storm, 1991, Operation Joint Endeavor, Bosnia, 1996. Mem. CPAs For The Pub. Interest, Nat. Wildlife Fedn., Inst. Cost Analysis, Nat. Audubon Soc., Wis. Farm Bur., Wis. State Hist. Soc., Wis. Farm Bur. Fedn., Future Farmers Am., Am. Inst. CPAs, Wis. Inst. CPAs, Nat. Assn. Accts., Assn. Govt. Accts. Roman Catholic. Home: 2661 S Pine Tree Rd De Pere WI 54115-9028

RUEDENBERG, KLAUS, theoretical chemist, educator; b. Bielefeld, Germany, Aug. 25, 1920; came to U.S., 1948, naturalized, 1955; s. Otto and Meta (Wertheimer) R.; m. Veronika Kutter, Apr. 8, 1948; children: Lucia Meta, Ursula Hedwig, Annette Veronika, Emanuel Klaus. Student, Montana Coll., Zugerberg, Switzerland, 1938-39; licence es Scis., U. Fribourg, Switzerland, 1944; postgrad., U. Chgo., 1948-50; PhD, U. Zurich, Switzerland, 1950; PhD (hon.), U. Basel, Switzerland, 1975, U. Bielefeld, Germany, 1991, U. Siegen, Germany, 1994. Research assoc. physics U. Chgo., 1950-55; asst. prof. chemistry, physics Iowa State U., Ames, 1955-60; assoc. prof. Iowa State U., 1960-62, prof., 1964-78, disting. prof. in sci. and humanities, 1978-91, disting. prof. emeritus, 1991—, sr. chemist Ames Lab., U.S. Dept. Energy, 1964-91, assoc., 1991—; prof. chemistry Johns Hopkins, Balt., 1962-64; vis. prof. U. Naples, Italy, 1961, Fed. Inst. Tech., Zurich, 1966-67, Wash State U. at Pullman, 1970, U. Calif. at Santa Cruz, 1973, U. Bonn (Germany), 1974, Monash U. and CSIRO, Clayton, Victoria, Australia, 1982, U. Kaiserlautern, Germany, 1987; lectr. univs., rsch. instns. and sci. symposia, 1953—. Author articles in field; assoc. editor: Jour. Chem. Physics, 1964-67, Internat. Jour. Quantum Chemistry; Chem. Physics Letters, 1967-81, Lecture Notes in Chemistry, 1976—, Advances in Quantum Chemistry, 1987—; editor-in-chief Theoretica Chimica Acta, 1985—. Cofounder Octagon Center for the Arts, Ames, 1966, treas., 1966-71, also bd. dirs. Guggenheim fellow, 1966-67; Fulbright sr. scholar, 1982. Fellow AAAS, Am. Phys. Soc., Am. Inst. Chemists, Internat. Acad. for Quantum Molecular Scis.; mem. AAUP, Am. Chem. Soc. (Midwest award 1982), Sigma Xi, Phi Lambda Upsilon. Home: 2834 Ross Rd Ames IA 50014-4030 Office: Dept Chemistry Iowa State Univ Ames IA 50011

RUEGER, DANIEL SCOTT, horticulture educator; b. Flint, Mich., May 16, 1957; s. William John and Barbara Jane (Ledford) R.; m. Michel Sharon Holzbach, July 22, 1989; children: Danielle Sharon, Christina Anne, Michael Scott. BS in Agr., Ohio State U., 1980, MS in Agr. Edn., 1980. Cert. profl. vocational, horticulture teacher, Ohio. Mgr. Idle R's Farms, Plain City, Ohio, 1973-77; research services worker O.M. Scott & Sons. Co., Marysville, Ohio, 1977; tng. counselor Cen. Ohio Rural Consortium, Delaware, 1978; supt. parks grounds City of Delaware, 1979; tchr. horticulture Ashland (Ohio) City Schs., 1980—. Co-author: Success Handbook, 1980. Sustaining mem. Rep. Nat. Com., 1980-92; lay leader Emmanuel Meth. Ch., 1988-94; chmn. adminstrv. bd., 1990-91. Named Citizen of Yr. Citizens Commn. for the Right to Keep and Bear Arms, 1986, 87, 88, Disting. Patriot Concil for Inter-Am. Security. Mem. NEA, Nat. Vocat. Agrl. Tchrs. Assn., Ohio Edn. Assn. (state coun. ednl. polit. action com. 1988-91), North Cen. Ohio Edn. Assn. (exec. com. 1986—), Ohio Vocat. Agrl. Tchrs. Assn. (hort. state chmn. 1988-92, Outstanding Agrl. Edn. Program 1992), Am. Vocat. Assn., Ohio Vocat. Assn., Ashland City Tchrs. Assn. (pres. 1988-89), Ohio State U. Alumni Assn., Air Force Assn., Future Farmers Am. Alumni Assn., Orgn. for Secondary Students Enrolled in Agrl. Edn., Ohio Forestry Assn., Gamma Sigma Delta, Phi Delta Kappa. Office: Ashland High Sch 1440 King Rd Ashland OH 44805-3635

RUEGSEGGER, DONALD RAY, JR., radiological physicist, educator; b. Detroit, May 29, 1942; s. Donald Ray and Margaret Arlene (Elliot) R.; B.S., Wheaton Coll., 1964; M.S., Ariz. State U., 1966, Ph.D. (NDEA fellow), 1969. Diplomate Am. Bd. Radiology; m. Judith Ann Merrill, Aug. 20, 1965; children—Steven, Susan, Mark, Ann. Radiol. physicist Miami Valley Hosp., Dayton, Ohio, 1969—, chief med. physics sect., 1983—; physics cons. X-ray dept. VA Hosp., Dayton, 1970—; adj. asst. prof. physics Wright State U., Fairborn, Ohio, 1973—, clin. asst. prof. radiology, 1976-81, clin. assoc. prof. radiology, 1981—, group leader in med. physics, dept. radiol. scis. Med. Sch., 1978—. Mem. Am. Assn. Physicists in Medicine (pres. Ohio River Valley chpt. 1982-83, co-chmn. local summer sch. arrangements com. 1986), Am. Coll. Radiology, Am. Coll. Med. Physics (founding chancellor), Am. Phys. Soc., AAAS, Ohio Radiol. Soc., Health Physics Soc. Baptist. Home: 1613 E Mars Hill West Carrollton OH 45449 Office: Radiation Therapy Miami Valley Hosp 1 Wyoming St Dayton OH 45409-2722

RUEHLE, DIANNE MARIE, retired elementary education educator; b. Detroit, Aug. 14, 1943; d. Richard Francis and Luella Mary (Kopp) R. BS, Ea. Mich. U., 1966, MA, 1971, adminstrv. cert., 1990, renewed adminstrv. cert., 1995. Cert. tchr., adminstr., Mich. Tchr. Cherry Hill Sch. Dist., Inkster, Mich., 1966-85; tchr. elem. sch. Wayne-Westland (Mich.) Community Schs., 1985-95; dist. com. Pub. Act 25 for State of Mich., Westland, 1990-93, chair bldg., 1991-95. Improvement Instrn. grantee Wayne Westland Found., 1992-94. Mem. ASCD, NEA, Mich. Edn. Assn. Home: 26117 La Salle Ct Roseville MI 48066-3285

RUEHLMANN, VIRGINIA JUERGENS, foundation administrator, writer; b. Cin., Dec. 31, 1924; d. Arthur Henry and Florence Johanna (Doogan) Juergens; m. Eugene Peter Ruehlmann, Aug. 30, 1947; children: Virginia Wiltse, E. Peter, Margaret Straus, Andrea Cornett, Gregory, James, Mark, Rick. BS in Edn., U. Cin., 1946, M in Adminstrn., 1948. Swimming instr. Williams YMCA, Cin., 1942-43; recreation leader City of Cin., 1942-43; camp dir. U. Cin. Girls Summer Camp, 1943-45; instr. U. Cin., 1946-47, Wellesley Coll., Wellesley, Mass., 1947-48; homemaker Cin., 1948-84; adminstr., researcher, editor, writer Helen Steiner Rice Found., Cin., 1984—; contr. Revell Pub., Baker Book House, Grand Rapids, Mich., 1984—; cons. Gibson Greeting, Cin., 1989—. Editor, compiler devotional and inspirational books, author of prayers, researcher. Chair Spl. Olympics Greater Cin., Ohio, Ind., Ky., 1974; pres. Cin. chpt. Freedom Found. Valley Forge, 1974-76; pres. Cath. Social Svc. S.W. Ohio, 1984-86; trustee Glenmary Missions, 1989-91; mem. Western Hamilton County Econ. Coun., Nat. Fedn. Rep. Women, Rep. Women's Club Hamilton County; mem. nat. adv. bd. United Theol. Sem.; bd. dirs. Anthenaeum of Ohio. Named Woman of Yr. Cin. Enquirer, 1977, Lady Equestrian Order of Holy Sepulchre of Jerusalem, 1989; named to Ohio Women's Hall of Fame, 1991. Mem. Coun. on Founds., Cin. Woman's Club, Queen City Club, Argus Club, Donors Forum Ohio, Mortar Bd., Chi Omega, Kappa Delta Pi. Republican. Roman Catholic. Home: 1150 Gleneagles Ct Cincinnati OH 45233-4865 Office: Helen Steiner Rice Found Atrium 2 221 E 4th St # 2100 Cincinnati OH 45202

RUF, H(AROLD) WILLIAM, JR., lawyer, corporation executive; b. Madison, Wis., July 1, 1934; s. Harold W. and Margaret (Dottridge) R.; m. Suzanne Williams, Aug. 25, 1962 (div. Jan. 1978); m. Jocelyn C. Ruf, Nov. 21, 1981; children: David W., Margaret E., Katharine S. BS, U. Wis., 1960, JD, 1962. Bar: Wis. 1962, Ohio 1963. Field atty. N.L.R.B., Cleve., 1962-65; counsel Oglebay Norton Co., Cleve., 1965-74, dir. indsl. rels., 1974-78, v.p., 1978-94; v.p. adminstrn. and legal affairs Oblebay Norton Co., Cleve., 1994—. Trustee Shaker Lakes Nature Ctr., Cleve., 1986; pres. bd. trustees Moreland Ct. Condo. Assn. Clubs: Cleve. Skating, Cleve. Union. Home: 13515 Shaker Blvd Cleveland OH 44120-1506 Office: Oglebay Norton Co 1100 Superior Ave E Cleveland OH 44114-2518

RUFF, DUREEN ANNE, small business owner, operater; b. Grand Forks, N.D., Feb. 27, 1931; d. Conrad and Margaret (Johnson) A.; m. R. William Ruff, June 23, 1956; children: Susan Lynne, Kristine Louise, Steven W., Anne Marie. BS, U. N.D., 1953. Cert. tchr., N.D., Minn., Calif. Tchr. Roosevelt Elem. Sch., Grand Forks, 1953-56, San Miguel Elem. Sch., Sunny Vale, Calif., 1956-57, Regent Jr. High Sch., Robbinsdale, Minn., 1957-59, Carl Sandburg Jr. High Sch., Golden Valley, Minn., 1959-60; designer, mfr. d. Anne Ruff Miniatures, Plymouth, Minn., 1970—. Mem. Abbott Hosp. Aux., Mpls., 1968-78, Abbott Northwestern Aux., 1978—; elder Westminister Presbyn. Ch., 1981-87. Mem. Nat. Assn. Miniature Enthusists (Acad. Honor 1986—), Miniatures Industry Assn. Am., Cottage Industry Miniatures Trade Assn., Miniature Guild of Minn, Internat. Guild of Miniature Artisans (artisan status 1989—). Republican. Home and Office: 1100 Vagabond Ln N Minneapolis MN 55447-2560

RUFF, L. CANDY, state legislator; m. Gregory W. Ruff. Rep. dist. 40 State of Kans., 1993—. Democrat. Home: 321 Arch St Leavenworth KS 66048-3421 Office: Kans Ho of Reps State Capitol Topeka KS 66612*

RUFF, MELISSA BREDEMAN, county official; b. Castro Valley, Calif., Mar. 20, 1966; d. B. L. and Carolyn (Myers) Bredeman; m. Jesse David Ruff, Apr. 3, 1993. BA in Polit. Sci., Ill. State U., 1988. Econ. devel. dir. City of Chillicothe, Ill., 1990-95; exec. dir. Livingston County Coun. Econ. Devel., Pontiac, Ill., 1995—; bd. dirs. Ill. Revolving Loan Fund Assn. Mem. Optimist Club (bd. dirs. 1990-93), Rotary. Republican. Methodist. Office: Livingston Cty Courthouse 112 W Madison Pontiac IL 61764

RUFF, ROBERT LOUIS, neurologist, physiology researcher; b. Bklyn., Dec. 16, 1950; s. John Joseph and Rhoda (Alpert) R.; m. Louise Seymour Acheson, Apr. 26, 1980. BS summa cum laude, Cooper Union, 1971; MD summa cum laude, U. Wash., 1976, PhD in Physiology, 1976. Diplomate Am. Bd. Neurology and Psychiatry. Asst. neurologist N.Y. Hosp., Cornell Med. Sch., N.Y.C., 1977-80; asst. prof. physiology and medicine U. Wash., Seattle, 1980-84; assoc. prof. neurology Case Western Res. Med. Sch., Cleve., 1984-92, prof. neurology and neuroscis., 1993—, vice chair neurology dept., 1995—; chief dept. neurology Cleve. VA Med. Ctr., 1984—; adv. Child Devel. and Mental Retardation Ctr., Seattle, 1980-84, Burien Devel. Disability Ctr., Wash., 1982-84; mem. med. adv. bd. Muscular Dystrophy Assn., Seattle, 1984, NE Ohio chpt. Multiple Sclerosis Soc., 1986—; mem. adv. bd. for Neurology Dept. Vets. Affairs, 1989—; chmn. med. adv. bd. N.E. Ohio chpt. Myasthenia Gravis Found., 1987—, bd. trustees, 1993—, nat. med. adv. bd., 1988—, grant and fellowship com., 1990—. Assoc. editor: Neurology, 1994—; ad hoc reviewer various profl. and sci. jours.; contbr. articles to profl. jours. and chpts. to books. Nat. bd. dirs. Myasthenia Gravis Found., 1994—. Recipient Tchr. Investigator award NIH; NSF fellow, 1971; NIH grantee, Muscular Dystrophy Assn. grantee, Dept. Vets. Affair grantee; N.Y. State Regents med. scholar, 1971. Fellow Am. Heart Assn. (stroke coun.), Am. Acad. Neurology (scientific issues com., legis. action com.); mem. AMA, Am. Physics Soc., Neurosci. Soc., Biophys. Soc., Am. Neurol. Assn., N.Y. Acad. Sci., Am. Geriatrics Soc., Sigma Pi Sigma (v.p. 1970-71), Alpha Omega Alpha (v.p. 1975-76). Home: 2572 Stratford Rd Cleveland OH 44118-4063 Office: VA Med Ctr 10701 East Blvd Ste 127W Cleveland OH 44106-1702

RUFFING, JOHN JACOB, JR., family practice physician; b. Crawford, Nebr., Jan. 15, 1934; s. John Jacob and Jennie Rodella (Wilton) R.; m. Patricia Ruth Beehler, June 14, 1959; children: Michael, Carol, and Gregory. BA, Union Coll., 1956; MD, Loma Linda U., 1960. Diplomate Nat. Bd. Med. Examiners, Am. Bd. Family Practice. Intern Hinsdale (Ill.) Sanitarium and Hosp., 1960-61; pvt. practice Hemingford (Nebr.) Clinic, 1961—; Active staff Box Butte Gen. Hosp., Alliance; assoc. staff Regional West Med. Ctr., Scottsbluff, Nebr.; med. dir. Highland Park Care Ctr., Alliance, Good Samaritan Nursing Home, Alliance, Hemingford Cmty. Care Ctr. Mayor Village of Hemingford, Nebr., 1975-76; bd. dirs. Box Butte Gen. Hosp., Alliance, Nebr., 1986—. Fellow Am. Acad. Family Practice. Republican. Mem. Seventh Day Adventist Ch. Home: 916 Kearney St Hemingford NE 69348 Office: Hemingford Clinic 812 Laramie Ave Hemingford NE 69348

RUFFINI, RICHARD JOHN, family systems psychiatry and behavioral medicine clinician, educator; b. Detroit, June 9, 1954. BA in Philosophy, So. Ill. U., 1977, BA in Sociology, 1977, MS in Human Devel., 1981; postgrad., So. Calif. U., 1994—. Pastoral counselor, dir. counseling Christian Campus Ministry So. Ill. U., Carbondale, 1975-82; cons., program dir. Niles (Ill.) Family Clinic, 1985-87, The Counseling Ctr., Crystal Lake, Ill., 1986-89; cons., head trainer Gottleib Corp. Health, Melrose Park, Ill., 1988-89; cons. Gottleib Meml. Hosp., Melrose Park, 1985-90; dir. Agraphobic & Panic Attack Group Support, Chgo., 1989-92, Agoraphobics Learning and Living, Chgo., 1989-92; cons., dir. Mind, Body Health: Cortis Cardiology Clinic, River Forest, Ill., 1990-92; cons. Midwest Mental Health, Chgo., 1990-91; founder, pres. FIRCORTHE: Bus. Buyers, Ltd., 1995—; dir., founder Fircorthe Mental Health: Family-Systems-Teaching, Chgo., 1985-94, Fircorthe Ednl. Seminars, 1985—; sr. clinician, clin. edn. supr. human sexuality program, dept. psychiatry Loyola U. Med. Ctr., Maywood, Ill., 1986-93; presenter in field. Contbg. editor The Christian Catalyst, 1979-82. Mem. Nat. Task Force on Dr.-Patient Comm. Fellow Am. Orthopsychiat. Assn.; mem. ABA, Am. Assn. for Marriage and Family Therapy (cert. educator and clinician), Christian Legal Soc., Christian Assn. for Psychol. Studies, Am. Sci. Affiliation, Am. Assn. Sex Educators, Counselors and Therapists, Nat. Assn. Adult Children of Dysfunctional Families, The Ctr. for Adolescent Obesity, Fetzer Inst. for Advancement of Health: Mind and Body Medicine, Western Mich. Study Group (dir. 1993—). Office: Kent Co Internat Airport Office Complex 5500 44th St # 888611 Grand Rapids MI 49588-8611

RUFFOLO, PAUL GREGORY, police officer, educator; b. Chgo., Feb. 4, 1952; s. Dante William and Anne Marie (Paese) R.; m. Janet Louise Anderson, July 8, 1978; 1 child, Annemarie. BA, U. Ill., Chgo., 1973; grad. Traffic Inst., Northwestern U., 1986, postgrad., 1993; MA in Edn. and Human Resources Devel., U. Ill., 1994, doctoral studies, 1995—. Cert. tchr. and law enforcement officer, Ill. Singer, musician night club, Las Vegas, Nev., 1974; tchr. Chgo. Pub. Schs., 1976; officer Naperville (Ill.) Police Dept., 1978-86, sgt., 1986-94; comdr. Woodridge Police Dept., 1994-95; internat. lectr., police cons., 1995—; police instr. Chgo. City-Wide Colls., 1990—, Chgo. Police Acad., 1990—; lectr. Office Internat. Criminal Justice, Chgo., 1990—; talk show host Sta. WHBC-TV, Willowbrook, Ill., 1990—, Sta. WMRO, Aurora, Ill., 1990; team mem. Profl. Occult Response Team, Wheaton, Ill., 1990—; guest lectr., cons. South African Police Dept. Govt. South Africa, 1994; dir. Internat. Affairs; tng. specialist on gangs and counter-terrorism Ill. State Crime Commn. Columnist Chicagoland newspaper, 1990; contbr. articles to profl. publs. Mem. choir St. Michael's Ch., Orland Park, Ill., 1978—; prodr., dir. Summerfest Rock and Roll Show, Orland Park, 1984. Named Most Contbg. Speaker, Internat. Police Inst., Cologne, Germany, 1991; recipient Presdl. Comsn. award 1992. Mem. Internat. Assn. Chiefs Police, Internat. Police Assn., Ill. Police Assn., DuPage County Police Assn., Fraternal Order Police, Am. Fedn. Musicians, Am. Bartending Sch. Republican. Home: 7233 Oneill Rd Downers Grove IL 60516-3771

RUGGERE, DENNIS JOSEPH, computer company executive; b. Boston, Feb. 26, 1943; s. Dennis Charles and Alma Katherine (Lawrence) R.; m. Linda Mathieson, Feb. 15, 1979 (div. 1984); children: Cynthia Leigh, Dennis Jr.; m. Alma Katherine Lawrence, Nov. 7, 1987; children: Joanne Frances, Crotty. Grad. high sch., Brookline, Mass. DBA cons. GE, Cleve., Gulfstream, Savavanah, Ga., Transport Accident Commn., Melbourne, Australia, Computer Assoc., Singapore; tech. mgr. BDM, Puerto Rico; database adminstrn. cons. Jared Group, Beachwood, Ohio, 1995—. Home: 11470 Chippewa Rd Cleveland OH 44144

RUGGERO, MARIO ALFREDO, physiologist, educator; b. Resistencia, Argentina, Nov. 7, 1943; came to U.S., 1961; s. Juan M. and Carolina F. (Volpe) R.; m. Elsa L. Statzner, Apr. 2, 1973. BA, Cath. U. Am., 1965; PhD, U. Chgo., 1972. Rsch. assoc. U. Wis., Madison, 1975; asst. prof. otolaryngology U. Minn., Mpls., 1975-87, assoc. prof., 1987-92, prof., 1992-93; Hugh Knowles prof. hearing sci. dept. comm. scis. and disorders Northwestern U., Evanston, Ill., 1993—; mem. communication disorders rev. com. Nat. Inst. on Deafness and Other Communication Disorders, NIH, Bethesda, Md., 1990-94. Assoc. editor Jour. of Neurosci., 1989-95; co-editor: The Mechanics and Biophysics of Hearing; contbr. articles to profl. jours. including Nature Jour. Neurophysiology, Jour Acoustical Soc. Am. Grantee NIH, 1975—, NSF, 1983-87. Mem. Soc. for Neurosci., Acoustical Soc. Am., Assn. for Rsch. in Otolaryngology. Home: 1209 Central St # A Evanston IL 60201-1611 Office: Northwestern U Dept Comm Scis and Disorders 2299 N Campus Dr Evanston IL 60208-3550

RUGO, STEVEN ALFRED, architect; b. Washington, June 1, 1953; s. Alfred Joseph and Lena (Aubrey) R.; m. Mary Lourie Blackett, Nov. 11, 1967 (div. Jan. 1985); m. Laura Secord de Frise, June 25, 1988; children: Peter William, Aubrey Secord. Student, Ripon Coll., 1971-73, Harvard U., 1973; BArch, Syracuse U., 1976. Assoc. firms Booth/Hansen, Booth Nagle & Hartray, Booth & Nagle, Chgo., 1976-81; pvt. practice architecture Rugo/Raff Ltd., Chgo., 1982—. Assoc. Rush Presbyn., St. Lukes Med. Ctr., Chgo, Art Inst. Chgo. Mem. AIA, Met. Planning Coun., Chgo. Archtl. Club, Southeast Ravenswood Assn. (pres.), Racquet Club. Episcopalian. Office: 20 W Hubbard St Chicago IL 60610-4623

RUHL, HELENA MAE, business educator; b. Ottumwa, Iowa, Dec. 17, 1940; d. Herbert Glen and Alice Laveta (Reese) Watson; m. Kenneth Earl Ruhl, Sept. 8, 1963; children: Becky Jo Ruhl Zoll, Tony Arden, Peggy Lynn Ruhl Peterson. BS, Culver-Stockton Coll., 1962; MS, Ark. State U., 1985, Specialist, 1989, EdD, 1995. Adminstrv. asst. S.E. Ozark Mental Health Ctr., Poplar Bluff, Mo., 1979-84; area supr. Green Thumb of Mo., Buffalo, Mo., 1986-87; instr., div. chmn. bus. Three Rivers Community Coll., Poplar Bluff, 1987—. Bd. dirs. Mfrs. Assistance Group-Sheltered Workshop, Poplar Bluff, 1989-92; dir. Mo. Assn. Acctg. Educators, 1994—. Mem. Nat. Vocat. Assn., Mo. Vocat. Assn., Nat. Bus. Educators Assn., Mo. Bus. Educators Assn., Mo. Assn. Acctg. Edn., Delta Pi Epsilon, Beta Gamma Sigma, Phi Beta Lambda, Kappa Delta Pi. Office: Three Rivers Community Coll 2080 Three Rivers Blvd Poplar Bluff MO 63901

RUHLIN, PEGGY MILLER, investment adviser, financial planner; b. Dayton, Ohio, May 20, 1949; d. Charles Raymond and Shirlee E. (Menke) Miller; m. John B. Ruhlin Jr., June 19, 1982; 1 child, Megan Falla. BA magna cum laude, Otterbein Coll., 1979. CPA, Ohio; Cert. fin. planner. Acct. Borden, Inc., Columbus, Ohio, 1971-72; mgr. Intraspace Planning Group, Inc., Columbus, Ohio, 1972-74; v.p. Mgmt. Media, Inc., Columbus, Ohio, 1974-80, pres., 1980-87; prin. Budros & Ruhlin, Inc., Columbus, Ohio, 1987—; adj. prof. Capital U., Columbus, 1992—; mem. nat. adv. bd./coun. Schwab Instl., 1994-95. Columnist Bus. First of Greater Columbus, 1986; commentator Sta. WCBE-FM, 1989-91, 95—; contbr. articles to profl. jours. Mem. AICPA, Assn. for Investment Mgmt. and Rsch., Internat. Assn. Fin. Planning (chpt. pres. 1989-91, nat. bd. dirs. 1992—, pres. elect 1995-96, pres. 1996—), Nat. Assn. Prsonal Fin. Advisers (Fin. Planner of Yr. award 1988), Inst. Cert. Fin. Planners, Internat. Women's Forum. Office: Budros & Ruhlin Inc 1650 Lake Shore Dr Ste 150 Columbus OH 43204-4895

RUHNKE, WILLIAM PAUL, management executive; b. Eldora, Iowa, Oct. 25, 1941; s. Herbert Frederick and Louise Wilamena (Ziesman) R.; m. Laura Lea Cable, Feb. 7, 1960; children: Charm Naomi, Christopher Thomas. Student, U.S. Naval Acad., 1963. CPCU. Warehouse supr. Northrup King and Co., Eldoro, 1960-63; adjuster Cen. Claim Svc., Des Moines, 1963-64; claim adjuster Home Ins. Co., Des Moines, 1964-65; claim adjuster Home Ins. Co., St. Louis, 1965-66, claim supr., 1966-70, claim mgr., 1970-80; acct. mgr. Countrywide Svc., St. Louis, 1980-90, sr. acct. mgr., 1990—. Co-author: Earthquakes, 1987 (CPCU award 1987). With USN, 1959-60. Mem. CPCU (rsch. com. 1987). Lutheran. Home: 205 Albert Dr Florissant MO 63031-6317 Office: Countrywide Svc PO Box 120 Saint Louis MO 63166-0120

RUKAVINA, TOM, state legislator; b. Aug. 1950; m. Lenore Rukavina; 2 children. BA, U. Minn. Mem. Minn. Ho. of Reps. St. Paul; mem. govt. ops. com., econ. devel. com., taxes com., environ. and natural resources com., vice chair labor mgmt. rels. com.; legal asst. Democrat. Home: 6930 Highway 169 Virginia MN 55792-8040*

RULAU, RUSSELL, numismatic consultant; b. Chgo., Sept. 21, 1926; s. Alphonse and Ruth (Thorsen) R.; student U. Wis., 1946-48; m. Hazel Darlene Grizzell, Feb. 1, 1968; children by previous marriage: Lance Eric, Carla Rae, Russell A.W., Marsha June, Scott Quentin, Roberta Ann, Kyle Christopher, Yvonne Marie; 1 step-dau., Sharon Maria Kenowski. With U.S. Army, 1944-1950, master sgt. USAF, 1950-62; resigned active duty, 1962; asst. editor Coin World newspaper, Sidney, Ohio, 1962-74, editor World Coins mag., 1964-74, Numis. Scrapbook mag., 1968-74; editorial coordinator How to Order Fgn. Coins guidebook, 1966-74; editor in chief World Coin News newspaper, 1974-84, Bank Note Reporter, 1983-84; fgn. editor Numis. News newspaper, 1974-77; cons. editor Standard Catalog of World Paper Money, 1975-83; contbg. editor Standard Catalog of World Coins, 1974-81; pres. House of Rulau, 1984—, Alpha Enterprises Inc., 1989—; v.p. Keogh-Rulau Galleries, Dallas, 1984-85, Pobjoy Mint Ltd., Iola, Wis., 1985-96; U.S. agent Christie's Pty. Ltd, 1992-95. Recipient Clemy Literary award 1993, Smedley Lifetime Achievement award, 1994, Numiasmatic Ambassador award, 1995. Mem. U.S. Assay Commn., 1973. Sec., Numismatic Terms Standardization Com., 1966-74; vice-chmn. Waupaca County Republican party, 1977-79, 1988-89, chmn., 1979-82; chmn. county chairmen, 3d vice chmn. Wis. Rep. Party, 1981-83; del. Rep. Nat. Conv., 1980; exec. com. 6th Wis. Dist. Rep. Com., 1984-87 . Fellow Royal Numis. Soc., Am. Numis. Soc. (assoc.); mem. Token and Medal Soc. (editor 1962-63), Am. Numis. Assn. (Merit medal 1995), Canadian, S. African numis. assns., Mont. Hist. Soc., Am. Vecturist Assn., Numis. Lit. Guild (dir. 1974-78, editor 1984-86), VFW (post commdr. 1985-89, 96—), Am. Legion. Lutheran. Author: (with George Fuld) Spiel Marken, 1962-65, American Game Counters, 1972: World Mint Marks, 1966; Modern World Mint Marks, 1970; (with J. U. Rixen and Frovin Sieg) Seddelkatalog Slesvig Plebiscit Zone I og II, 1970; Numismatics of Old Alabama, 1971-73; Hard Times Tokens, 1980; Early American Tokens, 1981; U.S. Merchant Tokens 1845-1860, 1982; U.S. Trade Tokens 1866-1889, 1983, Tokens of the Gay Nineties, 1987, Discovering America: The Coin Collecting Connection, 1989, Latin American Tokens, 1992; (with George Fuld) Medallic Portraits of Washington, 1985, Standard Catalog of U.S. Tokens 1700-1900, 1994; contbr. numis. articles to profl. jours. Home: N7747 County J Iola WI 54945 Office: Pobjoy Mint USA Ltd PO Box 153 Iola WI 54945-0153

RULE-HOFFMAN, RICHARD CARL, art therapist, educator, counselor; b. Youngstown, Ohio, June 19, 1947; s. Carl Frank and Bernice Rita (Kubala) Hoffman; m. Gail Lillian Rule, Aug. 9, 1980. BA, Cleve. State U., 1973; MA, Goddard Coll., 1978; M of Herbology, Emerson Coll., 1989. Registered art therapist; bd. cert. art therapist; lic. profl. counselor. Art therapist Beech Brook, Pepper Pike, Ohio, 1970—; instr. art therapy Art Psychotherapy Inst. of Cleve., Cleveland Heights, Ohio, 1974-77; adj. prof. art therapy Ursuline Coll., Pepper Pike, 1978—, asst. dir. MA program in art therapy, 1986—; art therapy field faculty supr. Goddard Coll. and Norwich U., Plainfield and Montpelier, Vt., 1978—; cons. Fedn. Community Planning, Cleve., 1976-77, Case Western Reserve U., Cleve., 1976-77. Editor, creator (newsletter) The Palette, 1975-79. Mem. Am. Art Therapy Assn., Buckeye Art Therapy Assn. Ohio (publs. chmn. 1975-80), Jungian Edn. Ctr. Home: 3700 Walnut Hills Rd Orange Village OH 44122-4435 Office: Beech Brook 3737 Lander Rd Pepper Pike OH 44124-5712 also: Ursuline Coll 2550 Lander Rd Pepper Pike OH 44124-4318

RUMA, JAN LYNNE, college alumni administrator; b. Springfield, Mo., Jan. 22, 1964; d. Byron Henry and Ardith Emma (Knapheide) Nolte; m. Peter N. Ruma, Jr., June 10, 1989. BS, Bowling Green State U., 1986, MEd, 1992. Exec. trainee May Dept. Stores Co., Akron, Ohio, 1986-87; dir. devel. Multiple Sclerosis Soc., Toledo, 1987-88; asst. dir. alumni affairs Bowling Green (Ohio) State U., 1988-90, assoc. dir. alumni affairs, 1990-95; dir. devel. Mercy Coll. N.W. Ohio, Toledo, 1994—; faculty presenter Advancement and Support of Edn. conf., Providence, 1992; on-air presenter Sta. WBGU-TV (PBS), Bowling Green, 1992. Mem. Falcon Club, Phi Mu (house corp. bd. dirs., sec., v.p. 1987-90, 92-96). Home: 5162 Saddlecreek Rd Toledo OH 43623

RUMBLES, JOHN BRYCE, library director; b. Fontana, Calif., Apr. 2, 1959; s. John Barry and Beverly Kay (Wisdom) R.; m. Holly Beth Monroe, Oct. 1, 1983 (div. 1987); m. Lori Christine Gullickson, Feb. 16, 1992. BA, U. N.Mex., 1987; MEd, U. Ill., 1995. Cert. elem. edn., Ill. Libr. tech. Ctrl. N.Mex. Correctional Facility, Los Lunas, N.Mex., 1984-86; libr. clk. Zimmerman Libr., U. N.Mex., Albuquerque, 1987-88; libr. info. specialist CSEL, U. N.Mex., Albuquerque, 1988-91; head bindery unit Regenstein Libr., U. Chgo., 1991-93; libr. dir. Prairie Creek Pub. Libr. Dist., Dwight, Ill., 1995—. Mem. Rotary Internat. Home: 18371 West St Lansing IL 60438 Office: Prairie Creek Pub Libr Dist 501 Carriage House Ln Dwight IL 60420

RUMMELL, HELEN MARY, critical care and pediatrics nurse; b. Detroit, Dec. 5, 1942; d. William John and Helen (Robbins) Mohn; m. Larry L. Rummell, Aug. 1, 1964; children: Robin Renee, Richard William, Christopher Lee, Kathryn Elizabeth. BSN, U. Mich., 1964; MSN, UCLA, 1984. Cert. Brazelton newborn assessment examiner; cert. clin. nurse specialist; cert. PNP; cert. instr. pediat. advanced life support. Nurse specialist, neonatal intensive care Northridge (Calif.) Med. Ctr.; instr. pediat. Ohio State U., Columbus, 1985-87; neonatal nurse practitioner Riverside Meth. Hosp., Columbus, 1987-88; clin. nurse specialist, cardiac care coord. cardiology-cardio vascular surgery Children's Hosp., Columbus, 1988—. Contbr. articles to profl. jours. Mem. Am. Heart Assn., Soc. Pediat. Cardiovasc. Nurses, Sigma Theta Tau (chpt. pres.). Home: 793 Pinecliff Pl Worthington OH 43085-1906

RUNBECK, LINDA C., state legislator; b. June 11, 1946; m. Richard Runbeck; 1 child. BA, Bethel Coll. Former mem. Minn. Ho. of Reps. St. Paul; mem. various coms., U.S. senator from Minn., 1993—; mem. govt. ops. and reform com., mem. jobs, energy and cmty. devel com., others; advt. exec. Mem. League Women's Voters. Home: 48 E Golden Lake Rd Circle Pines MN 55014-1725 Office: Minn State Senate State Capitol Building Saint Paul MN 55155-1606*

RUNCIE, JOHN FRYER, manufacturing company executive; b. East Orange, N.J., Jan. 2, 1942; s. W. Erskine and Carol Glover (Stone) R.; children: Pamela, Devonne, Brenda, Craig. BA, Lehigh U., 1964; MA, U. Conn., 1966; PhD, Rutgers U., 1971. Assoc. prof. U. Mich., Flint, 1969-78; dir. social rsch. Devel. Analysis Assocs., Cambridge, Mass., 1978-80; sr. researcher Pub. Systems Evaluation, Cambridge, 1980-82; sr. orgn. devel. cons. Anheuser-Busch, St. Louis, 1982-85; v.p. human resources Doehler-Jarvis, Toledo, 1985-87; mgr. orgn. devel. and tng. Batesville (Ind.) Casket Co., 1987-90; human resources mgr. Keebler Co., Grand Rapids, Mich., 1990-94, Eagle Snacks, Inc., St. Louis, 1994-96; human resources dir. James N. Gray Constrn. Co., Lexington, Ky., 1996—. Contbr. articles to profl. publs. Mem. ASTD, Assn. Quality and Participation, Am. Soc. Pers. Adminstrn., Alpha Kappa Delta. Home: 4701 Sunny Point Lexington KY 40515 Office: 2500 Lexington Fin Ctr Lexington KY 40507

RUNGE, KAY KRETSCHMAR, library director; b. Davenport, Iowa, Dec. 9, 1946; d. Alfred Edwin and Ina (Paul) Kretschmar; m. Peter S. Runge Sr., Aug. 17, 1968; children: Peter Jr., Katherine. BS in History Edn., Iowa State U., 1969; MLS, U. Iowa, 1970. Pub. service librarian Anoka County Library, Blaine, Minn., 1971-72; cataloger Augustana Coll., Rock Island, Ill., 1972-74; dir. Scott County Library System, Eldridge, Iowa, 1974-85, Davenport (Iowa) Pub. Libr., 1985—; bd. dirs. Brenton Bank. Bd. dirs. River Ctr. for Performing Arts, Davenport, 1983—, Am. Inst. Commerce, 1989—, Quad-Cities Conv. and Visitors Bur., 1991—, Quad-Cities Grad. Study Ctr., 1992—, Downtown Davenport Devel. Corp., 1992—, Hall of Honor Bd. Davenport Ctrl. H.S., 1992-95, Brenton Bank, 1996—; mem. steering com. Quad-Cities Visions for the Future, 1987-91; bd. govs. Iowa State U. Found., 1991—. Recipient Svc. Key award Iowa State U. Alumni Assn., 1979. Mem. ALA (chmn. library adminstrs. and mgrs. div., fundraising section 1988), Iowa Library Assn. (pres. 1983), Pub. Library Assn. (bd. dirs. 1990-96), Iowa Edn. Media Assn. (Intellectual Freedom award 1984), Alpha Delta Pi (alumni state pres. 1978). Lutheran. Office: Davenport Pub Libr 321 N Main St Davenport IA 52801-1409

RUNGE, LAWRENCE DEAN, automotive company executive; b. Jan. 22, 1953; Divorced; 1 daughter. Tech. positions AM Internat., A. B. Dick, Collins Radio Co. (N.Am. Rockwell), Des Plaines, Ill.; engr. shuttle mission simulator Singer-Link Flight Simulation, Johnson Space Ctr., Houston, 1982-85; project leader bus. sys. devel. GE Spacecraft Ops., Houston, 1985-87; project mgr. exec. info. sys. GE Aerospace, King of Prussia, Pa., 1987-89; project mgr. software applications devel. GE Capital Corp. Info. Sys., Stamford, Conn., 1989-90; dir. advanced sys. and tech. GE Capital Fleet Svcs., Eden Prairie, Minn., 1990-92; v.p., chief info. officer Wheels, Inc., Des Plaines, Ill., 1993—; speaker Chgo. Computer Soc., 1994, Soc. Info. Mgrs. Conf., Chgo, 1994, Nat. Assn. Fleet Adminstrs. Conf., Orlando, Fla., 1995, Chgo. NT Users Group, 1995, etc. Author computer games; contbr. articles to profl. jours. Office: Wheels Inc 666 Garland Pl Des Plaines IL 60016

RUNKLE, JAMES READE, ecology educator, researcher; b. Grove City, Pa., July 3, 1951; s. Irvin Lester and Beverly Aliene (Bell) R.; m. Janet Lynn Kreps, June 9, 1973; children: Benjamin, Matthew, William, Jennifer. BA, Ohio Wesleyan U., 1973; PhD, Cornell U., 1979. Asst. prof. U. Ill., Chgo., 1978-79; asst. prof. Wright State U., Dayton, Ohio, 1979-85, assoc. prof., 1985-93, prof. ecology, botany, design of biol. experiments, 1993—; vis. researcher Forest Rsch. Ins., Christchurch, New Zealand, 1988-89. Contbr. articles to profl. jours. Mem. AAAS, Internat. Assn. for Vegetation Sci., Ecol. Soc. Am., British Ecol. Soc., Ohio Acad. Sci., Nat. Audubon Soc., Sierra Club, Optimists, Phi Beta Kappa, Pi Mu Epsilon. Presbyterian. Office: Wright State Univ Dept Biol Scis Dayton OH 45435

RUNKLE, ROBERT SCOTT, environmental company executive; b. Washington, Mar. 9, 1936; s. Lloyd Manor and Louise (Armstrong) R.; m. Betsy Grater, Mar. 26, 1960 (div. July 1983); children: Beth R. Mackey, Brynn A.; stepchildren: Lori Anne Thompson, Jay M. Thompson; m. Joan Lewis, Aug. 6, 1983 (dec. Nov. 1987); m. Mary Beth Jorgensen, July 12, 1992; stepchildren: Elizabeth Jorgensen Feild, David Jorgensen Feild. BS in Bldg. Constrn., Ga. Inst. Tech ., 1960. Draftsman Ted Englehardt AIA, Silver Spring, Md., 1960-62; engr. Research Facilties Planning BD. div. Research Service NIH, Bethesda, Md., 1962-64; vice chmn. biohazards sect. Nat. Cancer Inst., NIH, Bethesda, 1964-67; research contracts mgr. Becton Dickinson & Co., Rutherford, N.J., 1967-69; adminstrn. mgr. Becton Dickinson Research Ctr., Raleigh, N.C., 1969-73; dir. adminstrn. Huntington (Eng.) Research Ctr., 1974-75; dir. rsch. liaison Becton Dickinson Co, Rutherford, N.J., 1976-78; v.p. ops. BBL microbiology systems div., Becton Dickinson Co., Balt., 1978-85; pres., chief exec. officer, chmn. bd. Pharmplastics Closures Inc., Balt., 1985-88; v.p. EA Engring., Sci. and Tech., Inc., Balt., 1989-91; v.p. bus. devel., sr. office leader EA Labs, EA Engring., Sci. and Tech., Inc., Chgo., 1992-94; v.p. ops. Carnow, Conibear & Assocs., Ltd., Chgo., 1994—; cons. Am. Inst. Biological Scis., Bethesda, 1963-67, ind., Balt., 1982—. Author: Microbial Contamination Control Facilities, 1969, Biomedical Applications Laminar Airflow, 1973; contbr. articles to profl. jours. Mem. Assn. for Corp. Growth, Am. Chem. Soc., Bldg. Futures Coun., Ga. Tech. Nat. Alumni Assn., Raleigh (N.C.) C. of C. Democrat. Episcopalian. Home: 1228 Hinman Ave Evanston IL 60202-1313 Office: Carnow Conibear & Assocs 333 W Wacker Dr Ste 1400 Chicago IL 60606

RUNNING, RICHARD V., state legislator, college official; b. New Rockford, N.D., Jan. 22, 1946; s. Vernnon E. and Lucille M. (Allmaras) R.; m. Joan A. Meighan, May 18, 1968; children: Elizabeth, Stefanie, Kirsten, Chad. BS, U. Wis., La Crosse, 1973. Quality control technologists Wilson Foods Corp., Cedar Rapids, 1974-78; mem. staff Congressman Mike Blouin U.S. Ho. of Reps., Cedar Rapids, 1978; bus. and industry trainer in quality control Kirkwood C.C., Cedar Rapids, 1988—; mem. Iowa Ho. of Reps., Des Moines, 1981—. With USN, 1967-69, Vietnam. Mem. Am. Soc. for Quality Control, Nat. Coun. State Legislators (past chmn. labor com.), VFW, Am. Legion, Vietnam Vets., Eagles. Democrat. Roman Catholic. Home: 16 Roxbury Dr NW Cedar Rapids IA 52405-4417*

RUNQUIST, ALFONSE WILLIAM, chemist; b. Hibbing, Minn., Apr. 4, 1945; s. Henrik Alfonse and Eleanore Irene (Anderson) R.; m. Jennifer Agnes Jackson, July 13, 1974. BS, Hamline U., 1967; PhD, Northwestern U., 1974. Instr. Northwestern U., Evanston, Ill., 1973-74; postdoctoral researcher Johns Hopkins U., Balt., 1974-76; chemist-devel. dept. Aldrich Chem. Co., Milw., 1976-79, mgr. tech. svcs., 1979-90; mgr. chem. products Aldrich Chem. Co., 1990—. Contbr. articles to profl. jours. Served with U.S. Army, 1969-71. Recipient Scholastic award Am. Inst. Chemists, 1967; NIH fellow, Northwestern U., 1969, 71-73. Mem. Am. Chem. Soc., Florentine Opera Club, Milw. Curling Club, Water Tower Hist. Trust. Office: Aldrich Chem Co 1001 W St Paul Ave Milwaukee WI 53233-2641

RUOFF, CYNTHIA OSOWIEC, foreign language educator; b. Chgo., Mar. 1, 1943; d. Stephen R. and Estelle (Wozniak) O.; m. Gary Edward Ruoff, June 5, 1965; children: Gary S., Laura A. AB, Loyola U., 1965; MA, Western Mich. U., 1973; PhD in French Lang. and Lit., Mich. State U., 1992. Tchr. Kalamazoo (Mic.) Pub. Schs., 1965-68; instr. Western Mich. U., Kalamazoo, 1980—; nat. and internat. spkr. in field. Contbr. articles to profl. jours. Mem. MLA, N.Am. Soc. Seventeenth-Century French Lit., Am. Assn. Tchrs. of French, Mich. Fgn. Lang. Assn., Internat. Soc. Phenomenology and Lit., L'Alliance Française, Soc. Interdisciplinary French Seventeenth-Century Studies, Phi Sigma Iota, Pi Delta Phi. Office: Dept Fgn Langs & Lit Western Mich Univ Kalamazoo MI 49008

RUPORT, SCOTT HENDRICKS, lawyer; b. Paterson, N.J., Nov. 22, 1949; s. Fred Hendricks and Juyne (Kennedy) R.; m. Linda Darlene Smith, Sept. 12, 1970; children—Brittany Lyle, Courtney Kennedy. B.S. in Bus. Adminstrn., Bowling Green State U., 1971; J.D., U. Akron, 1974. Bar: Ohio 1974, Pa. 1984, U.S. Dist. Ct. for no. dist. Ohio 1974, U.S. Ct. Appeals for 6th circuit, 1975, U.S. Supreme Ct. 1978. Assoc. firm Schwab, Sager, Grosenbaugh, Rothal, Fort, Skidmore & Nukes Co., L.P.A., Akron, Ohio, 1974-76, Skidmore & George Co., L.P.A., Akron, 1976-79, Skidmore, Ruport & Haskings, Akron, 1979-83; ptnr. Roderick, Myers & Linton, Akron, 1983-85; Ruport Co. L.P.A.,Akron, 1985—; instr. real estate law U. Akron, 1976-77, adj. asst. prof. constrn. tech. Coll. Engring., 1983—. Served as capt., Fin. Corps, USAR, 1971-79. Mem. ABA, Akron Bar Assn., Ohio Bar Assn., Ohio Acad. Trial Lawyers (chmn. civil and bus. litigation sect. 1989), Assn. Trial Lawyers Am., Beta Gamma Sigma, Sigma Chi. Republican. Presbyterian. Office: Ruport Co LPA 1 Cascade Plz Fl 10 Akron OH 44308-1111

RUPPEL, WILLIAM J., state legislator; m. Miriam ruppel. BS, Butler U.; MS, Manchester Coll. Tchr., coach Tippecanoe Valley Sch. Corp.; mem. from 22d dist. Ind. State Ho. of Reps., 1992—; mem. aged and acing com., fin. instns. com., local govt., county and twp. coms., human affairs com., vice chmn. pub. safety com. Mem. North Manchester (Ind.) Vol. Fire Dept.; mem. North Manchester Police Res.; mem. Butler U. Alumni Bd. Mem. Ind. Vol. Fireman Assn., Farm Bur., Rotary. Home: 909 State Rd 13 W North Manchester IN 46962-9150*

RUPRECHT, AXEL, oral and maxillofacial radiologist; b. Fleestedt, Hanover, Germany, Oct. 13, 1944; arrived in Can., 1951, came to U.S., 1987; s. Guenther Gustav Victor and Margarete (Zollbrecht) R.; m. Barbara Joan Busby, Sept. 5, 1969; 1 child, Jason Alexander. DDS, U. Toronto, Can., 1968, M.Sc.D, 1972. Diplomate Am. Bd. Oral and Maxillofacial Radiology. Asst. prof. U. Western Ont., London, Can., 1972-75; assoc. prof. U. of Sask., Saskatoon, Can., 1975-79, prof., 1979-82, asst. dean of dentistry, 1980-81, dept. head diagnosis and oral radiology, 1977-82; prof. King Saud U., Riyadh, Saudi Arabia, 1981-86, dept. head biomed. dental sci., 1983-85; sect. head radiology ZMK-U. of Marburg, Fed. Republic Germany, 1986-87; prof. and dir. Oral and Maxillofacial Radiology, prof. radiology U. Iowa, Iowa

City, 1987—; bd. dirs. Am. Bd. of Oral and Maxillofacial Radiology, 1987-92, sec.-treas., 1988-91, pres., 1992; examiner oral radiology Royal Coll. Dentists Can. Authors: (with others) Fundamentals of Oral Radiology, 1976, Practical Radiation Physics, 1976, Basic Principles of Oral Radiography, 1981. Mem. ADA, Iowa Dental Assn., Am. Assn. of Dental Schs., Iowa Radiol. Soc., Internat. Assn. of Dento Maxillofacial Radiology, Can. Acad. Oral Radiology, Am. Acad. Oral and Maxillofacial Radiology (immediate past pres.), Am. Coll. Radiology, Am. Soc. Head and Neck Radiology. Office: U Iowa Coll of Dentistry Iowa City IA 52242

RUSH, BOBBY L., congressman; b. Ga., Nov. 23, 1946; m. Carolyn Rush; 5 children. BA in Polit. Sci., Roosevelt U., 1974; MA in Polit. Sci., U. Ill., 1992. Fin. planner Sanmar Fin. Planning Corp.; assoc. dean Daniel Hale Williams U.; ins. agent Prudential Ins. Co.; city alderman Chgo., 1984-93; democratic committeeman Chgo. 2nd ward, 1984, 88, Central Ill., 1990; dep. chmn. Ill. Democratic Party, 1990; mem. 103d Congress from 1st Ill. Dist., 1993—; chmn. Environ. Protection, Energy and Pub. Utilities com., Budget and Govt. Operations com., Capitol Devel. com., Hist. Landmark Preservation Com.; mem. Commerce com. Former mem. Student Non-Violent Coordinating com.; founder Ill. Black Panther Party; past coord. Free Breakfast for Children, Free Med. Clinic. With US Army, 1963-68. Recipient Ill. Enterprise Zone award Dept. Commerce and Community, Operation PUSH Outstanding Young Man award, Henry Booth House Outstanding Community Svc. award, Outstanding Bus. and Profl. Achievement award South End Jaycees, Chgo. Black United Communities Disting. Polit. Leadership award. Office: US Ho of Reps 131 Cannon Ho Office Bldg Washington DC 20515-1301*

RUSH, RICHARD R., academic administrator. Pres. Mankato (Minn.) U. Office: Mankato State U South Rd And Ellis Ave Mankato MN 56001

RUSHFORD, ELOISE JOHNSON, land manager; b. Elmwood, Ill.; d. Albert Earl and Edna Merle (Dixon) Johnson; (div. June 1967); children: Gregory Gene, Barbara Merle Rushford Grimes. BA, Bradley U., 1936. Cert. tchr., Ill. Tchr. English Manual High Sch. Dist. 150, Peoria, 1955-56; ptnr. Johnson Devel. Co., 1956-76; v.p. Johnson's Men's Store, 1972-74; land mgr. Peoria, 1974—. Bd. dirs. Crippled Children's Found., Peoria, organized vols., 1975-76; bd. dirs. Women's Civic Fedn.; pres. Women's Assn. 1st Federated Ch., Mothers' Club; mem. Women's adv. bd. Internat. Christian U., Tokyo; mem. chpt. AH PEO; spearheaded tchg. of French in 4th grade, Peoria, 1959; chmn. Symphony Guild student concerts, organized Peoria Symphony student concerts that included all grade sch. student concerts that included all grade sch. Mem. AAUW (pres. 1958-60, chmn. bd. dirs. Peoria br., award 1977), Univ. Women's Investment Club (founder, past pres.), Lasertoma (pres. Peoria chpt. 1961-63), Pi Beta Phi (pres. Peoria ALUM chpt. 1960-61), Lambda Phi. Republican. Congregationalist. Home: 220 W Merle Ln Peoria IL 61604-1617

RUSHING, JAMES TAYLOR, journalist; b. Lafayette, Ind., Oct. 19, 1971; s. Travis Taylor and Sylvia (Williams) R. BA in Comm., Purdue U., 1994. Reporter, journalist Lakeland Newspaper, Grayslake, Ill., 1989-90; reporter, editor Purdue Exponent, Lafayette, Ind., 1990-93; reporter Kenosha (Wis.) News, 1994—. Contbr. articles to profl. jours. Pulliam Journalism scholarship Pulliam Newspapers, 1993. Mem. Sigma Delta (chpt. pres. 1992-94). Democrat. Home: 431 44th St #3 Kenosha WI 53140 Office: Kenosha News 715 58th St Kenosha WI 53141

RUSHING, MICHELE RENEE, academic budget analyst, administrator; b. Cape Girardeau, Mo., Sept. 1, 1965; d. Kenneth G. and JoAnn (Enderle) Compas; m. Theron W. Rushing, Aug. 3, 1986. AS in Bus. Adminstrn. and Acctg., John A. Logan Coll., Carterville, Ill., 1985; BS in Acctg., So. Ill. U., 1992, BS in Fin., 1992, MBA, 1996. Sec. John A. Logan Coll., Carterville, 1983-85; intelligence analyst So. Ill. U. Security Police Dept., Carbondale, 1985-92; budget analyst Budget Office So. Ill. U., Carbondale, 1992-94, asst. exec. dir. budgeting and info. resources, 1994—. Mem. Beta Alpha Psi (C.O.B.A. rep. 1991), Beta Gamma Sigma, Golden Key Nat. Honor Soc. Home: RR 2 Box 322 # R Carbondale IL 62901-9544

RUSHING, PHILIP DALE, retired social worker; b. Carbondale, Ill., Mar. 15, 1932; S. Paul and Beulah Myrl (Benton) R.; m. Linda North, July 5, 1958 (div. July 1964); 1 child, Lisa Ann Rushing Burrow; m. Rosalie Anne Sturm, Aug. 20, 1966. BA, So. Ill. U., 1958; MSW, Washington U., St. Louis, 1960. Bd. cert. diplomate, ACSW; lic. social worker, Ill. Child welfare worker Ill. Dept. Pub. Welfare, Salem, E. St. Louis, 1958-60; child welfare supr. Ill. Dept. Pub. Welfare, E. St. Louis, 1960-63; field rep. Nat. Assn. for Retarded Children, Dallas, Denver, 1963-65; dir. social svcs. A.L. Bowen Children's Ctr., Harrisburg, Ill., 1965-68; asst. zone dir. for mentally retarded Ill. Dept. of Mental Health, Harrisburg, 1968-74; regional coord. for devel. disabilities Ill. Dept. of Mental Health & Dev. Disabilities, Marion, 1974-83; social work adminstr. Choate Mental Health & Devel. Ctr., Anna, Ill., 1983-95; ret., 1995; adj. asst. prof. So. Ill. U. Rehab. Inst., Carbondale, Ill., 1968-78. Bd. cert. diplomate ACSW; lic. clin. social worker. Bd. deacons First Presbyn. Ch., Harrisburg, 1974-77, bd. trustees, 1978-80, bd. elders, 1980-83, 96—. With USN, 1951-55, Korea. Fellow Am. Assn. on Mental Retardation (life, chmn. social work divsn. Ill. chpt. 1973-74); mem. NASW (chmn. East St. Louis br. 1962). Home: 6542 Highway 13 W Harrisburg IL 62946-4142

RUSHMORE, LOUIS EVERETTE, evangelist; b. Bremerton, Wash., Jan. 3, 1954; s. Clifford and Nina Mae (Porterfield) R.; m. Bonnie Sue Reed, July 14, 1973; children: Rebecca Lee, Raymond Louis, Robert Daniel. Grad. cert., Memphis Sch. Preaching, 1977. Evangelist Chs. of Christ, Mich., Tenn., Ark., Miss., Va., Pa., Ill., Ohio, S.C., 1973—; instr. W.Va. Sch. Preaching, Moundsville, 1995—. Author: The Cost of Discipleship, 1985, The Spirit Summarized, 1994, The Church Divine, 1994, Bible Geography, 1994; editor: Survey of the First 15 Years Memphis Schools of Preaching Lectures, 1982; assoc. editor Defender Ill. Right to Life, Zion, 1981-82, Gospel Gazette, Salineville, Ohio, 1986—. Home: 4325 Southeast Dr Steubenville OH 43952-3353

RUSK, KARLA MARIE, critical care nurse, research coordinator; b. Zanesville, Ohio, Sept. 7, 1956; d. Willard E. Jr. and Charlotte M. (Basford) King; m. Jason T. Rusk, Aug. 30, 1980; 1 child, Whitney Malone. AS Nursing, Ohio U., 1977, BSN, 1985; MS, Ohio State U., 1987. Cert. crticial care nurse. Grant Med. Ctr., Columbus, Ohio, 1977-80; Team leader ICU-recovery rm. Providence Hosp., Cin., 1980-81; staff nurse Bethesda Hosp., Zanesville, 1977-80; staff nurse open heart ICU Grant Med. Ctr., Cin., 1982-83; edn. coord., critical care Grant Med. Ctr., Columbus, 1984-88; critical care educator Lancaster, Ohio, 1985-90; staff nurse III CCU Riverside Meth. Hosp., Columbus, Ohio, 1988-92, staff nurse invasive recovery unit, 1992—; clin. rsch. coord., mgr., adminstrv. dir. Mid-West Cardiology Rsch. Found., 1990—; adminstrv. clin. dir. Midohio Cardiology Cons., Inc., Columbus, 1993—. Contbr. articles to profl. jours.; rsch. on perception of stressful life events and the onset of myocardial infarction. Mem. AACCN, ANA, Nat. League Nursing, Phi Kappa Phi, Sigma Theta Tau, Lambda Omega (pres.). Home: 1003 Sheridan Dr Lancaster OH 43130-1926

RUSNAK, MARTHA HENDRICK, reading education educator; b. Boston, Jan. 15, 1938; d. Ives and Marie (McClung) Hendrick; m. Robert J. Rusnak Sr., Nov. 14, 1964; children: Robert J. Jr., Jennifer Marie. AB, Mills Coll., 1959; MSEd, No. Ill. U., 1978, EdD, 1983. Primary tchr. Hawaiian Gardens, Calif., 1961-63; intermediate tchr. Mill Valley, Calif., 1963-65; jr. high tchr. Santa Barbara, Calif., 1965-68; intermediate tchr. Bensenville, Ill., 1974-77; instr. reading No. Ill. U., DeKalb, 1978-80; prof. Lewis U., Romeoville, Ill., 1980—, dir. graduate reading, 1983—; cons. in field. Contbr. articles to profl. jours. Mem. Internat. Reading Assn., Nat. Coun. Tchrs. English, No. Ill. Reading Coun. (exec. bd. 1988—), Ill. Reading Coun. (editorial bd. 1989—). Office: Lewis U Rte 53 Romeoville IL 60446

RUSOFF, MAURICE BORIS, retired physician; b. Columbus, Ohio, May 30, 1908; s. Boris Simon and Anna (Feldman) R.; m. Jo Ann Fondaw, Feb. 2, 1972; 1 child, Martin Hans. BA, Ohio State U., 1929, MD, 1933. Diplomate in Internal Medicine. Physician in pvt. practice Columbus, 1934-94. Charter mem. Republical Presdl. Task Force, 1982. Capt. U.S. Army, 1942-45. Fellow Am. Coll. Cardiology; mem. Am. Soc. Internal Medicine, Masons.

RUSS, CARY, lawyer, federal agency administrator; b. Chgo., Jan. 21, 1948; s. Maurice and Belle (Norinsky) R.; m. Lisbeth Merry Nathan, June 20, 1971; children: Rebecca Ann, Brian Andrew. BSBA, U. Denver, 1969; JD, Ill. Inst. Tech., Chgo., 1972. Bar: Ill. 1973, Mich. 1974, U.S. Dist. Ct. (no. dist.) Ill. 1973, U.S. Tax Ct. 1978. Atty. U.S. Treas. IRS, Chgo., 1972-75; supervisory atty. U.S. Treasury IRS, Chgo., 1975-81; supervisory internal revenue mgr. U.S. Treasury IRS, Skokie, Ill., 1981-82; fin. products industry specialist U.S. Treasury IRS, Morton Grove, Ill., 1985—; ptnr. Gottleib & Schwartz, Chgo., 1982-85; chief tech. field support, fin. products, asst. commr. internat. U.S. Treasury IRS, Morton Grove, Ill., 1994—. Recipient Citation Revenue Can., Ottawa, 1989; named Govt. Atty. of Yr. Fed. Bar Assn., 1988. Mem. Ill. State Bar Assn. Home: 2967 Parkside Dr Highland Park IL 60035-1036 Office: US Treasury 8125 River Dr Morton Grove IL 60053-2638

RUSS, EDMOND VINCENT, JR., marketing professional; b. Washington, Feb. 14, 1944; s. Edmond V. and Thayer Kennedy (Thompson) R.; divorced; children: Jamie L., Edmond V. III; m. Tena Marie Loveland, Dec. 26, 1982; children: Christina T. Russ, Cory S. BA, Kent (Ohio) State U., 1966; MBA, U. Pitts., 1967. Dir. mktg. Borg-Warner Ednl. Systems, Niles, Ill., 1969-74; v.p. mktg. Rusty Jones Inc., Chgo., 1974-83; gen. mgr. Signed, Sealed and Delivered, Melrose Park, Ill., 1983-86; v.p. mktg. Merchant Network Inc., Chgo., 1986-90; dir. mktg. Am. Appraisal Assocs., Milw., 1990-93, Coopers & Lybrand, 1993—. Mem. Am. Mktg. Assn., Direct Mktg. Assn., Chgo. Assn. Direct Marketers, Vintage Sports Car Drivers Assn., Porsche Club Am. Home: 470 Jackson Glencoe IL 60022

RUSSELL, ARMIDA MENDEZ, management consultant; b. El Paso, Tex., Oct. 9, 1950. BA, U. Tex., El Paso, 1980; MA in Hosp. Adminstrn., S.W. U., 1986. Dir. admissions E.R. Thomason Hosp., El Paso, 1979-82; mgr. tng. and devel. Pillsbury Co., Mpls., 1984-86; pres. Mendez Russell Tng. & Devel. Inc., Mpls., 1986—; mem. Nat. Bd. Multi-Cultural Tng. and Devel., Va., Washington, 1988-90. Co-author: (assessment tools) Discovering Diversity Profile, 1994, Integrating Diversity Profile, 1995, Diversity Management Profile, 1995. Mem. Am. Soc. Tng. and Devel. Republican. Roman Catholic. Home and Office: 4200 Trillium Ln E Minneapolis MN 55364

RUSSELL, DAVID WILLIAMS, lawyer; b. Lockport, N.Y., Apr. 5, 1945; s. David Lawson and Jean Graves (Williams) R.; AB, Dartmouth Coll., 1967, MBA, 1969; JD cum laude, Northwestern U., 1976; m. Frances Yung Chung Chen, May 23, 1970; children: Bayard Chen, Ming Rennick. Bar: Ill. 1976, Ind. 1983. English tchr. Talledega (Ala.) Coll., summer 1967; math. tchr. Lyndon Inst., Lyndonville, Vt., 1967-68; instr. econs. Royalton Coll., South Royalton, Vt., part-time 1968-69; asst. to pres. for planning Tougaloo (Miss.) Coll., 1969-71, bus. mgr., 1971-73; mgr. will and trust rev. project Continental Ill. Nat. Bank & Trust Co. Chgo., summer 1974; law clk. Montgomery, McCracken, Walker & Rhoads, Phila., summer 1975; with Winston & Strawn, Chgo., 1976-83; ptnr. Klineman, Rose, Wolf & Wallack, Indpls., 1983-87, Johnson, Smith, Pence, Densborn, Wright & Heath, 1987—; cons. Alfred P. Sloan Found., 1972-73; dir. Forum for Internat. Profl. Svcs., 1985—, sec., 1985-88, pres. 1988-89; U.S. Dept. Justice del. to U.S. China Joint Session on Trade, Investment & Econ. Law, Beijing, 1987; lectr. internat. Law, Gov's Ind. Trade Mission to Japan, 1986, bus. law Ind. Continuing Legal Edn. Forum, 1986-94, chmn., 1987, 89, 91; adj. prof. internat. bus. law Ind. U., 1993—; bd. dirs. Ind. ASEAN Coun., Inc., 1988—; nat. selection com. Woodrow Wilson Found. Adminstrv. Fellowship Program, 1973-76; vol. Lawyers for Creative Arts, Chgo., 1977-83; dir. World Trade Club of Ind., 1987-93, v.p., 1987-91, pres., 1991-92; dir. Ind. Swiss Found., 1991—; dir. Ind. Soviet Trade Consortium, 1991—, sec., 1991-92; v.p., bd. dirs. Ind. Sister Cities, 1988—; dir. Internat. Ctr. Indpls., 1988-92, v.p. 1988-89; Ind. dist. enrollment dir. Dartmouth Coll., 1990—; bd. dirs. Indpls. Sister Cities, 1992—, Carmel Sister Cities, 1993—, v.p. 1995—; v.p. gen. coun. Lawrence Durrell Soc., 1993—; mem. bd. advisors Ctr. for Internat. Bus. Edn. and Rsch. Krannert Grad. Sch. Mgmt. Purdue U., 1995—. Woodrow Wilson Found. Adminstrv. fellow, 1969-72. Mem. ABA, ACLU, Ill. Bar Assn., Ind. Bar Assn. (vice chmn. internat. law section, 1988-90, chmn. 1990-92), Indpls. Bar Assn., Dartmouth Lawyers Assn., Indpls. Assn. Chinese Ams., Chinese Music Soc., Dartmouth Club of Ind. (sec. 1986-87, pres. 1987-88), Zeta Psi. Presbyterian. Home: 10926 Lakeview Dr Carmel IN 46033-3937 Office: Johnson Smith Pence Densborn Wright & Heath 1800 NBD Tower One Indiana Sq Indianapolis IN 46204

RUSSELL, EUGENE ROBERT, SR., engineering educator, administrator; b. Cromwell, Conn., Aug. 24, 1932; s. Arland William and Annie Margaret (LeBlanc) R.; m. Mary Lou Conner, June 29, 1957; children: Theresa, Janice, Eugene Jr., Anna, Ruth, Julie, Susan, Paul, Carol, Cecilia. BSCE, U. Mo., Rolla, 1958; MS in Civil Engring., Iowa State U., 1965; PhD, Purdue U., West Lafayette, Ind., 1974. Registered profl. engr., Iowa, Ind. Asst. bridge engr. State of Calif. Pub. Works, Sacramento, 1958-62; asst. area constrn. engr. Iowa Hwy. Commn., Grinnell, 1962-63; rsch. asst. soils Iowa State U., Ames, 1963-65; asst. prof. Ind. Inst. Tech., Ft. Wayne, 1965-69; rsch. assoc. Purdue U., West Lafayette, 1969-74; assoc. prof. Kans. State U., Manhattan, 1974-80, prof. civil engring., 1980—, dir. Ctr. for Transp. Rsch. and Tng., 1980—. Contbr. more than 60 articles to profl. jours. With USN, 1951-53. Mem. ASCE (br. pres.), Inst. Transp. Engrs., Am. R.R. Engring. Assn., Transp. Rsch. Bd. (univ. rep.), Transp. Rsch. Forum, Am. Soc. Engring. Edn., Sigma Xi. Home: 3424 Dickens Ave Manhattan KS 66503-2413 Office: Kansas State Univ Dept Civil Engring Seaton Hall Manhattan KS 66506-2905

RUSSELL, GEORGE ALBERT, university president; b. Bertrand, Mo., July 12, 1921; s. George Albert and Martha (Cramer) R.; m. Ruth Ann Ashby, Nov. 11, 1944; children: George Albert, Frank Ashby, Ruth Ann, Cramer Anderson. B.S. in Elec. Engring, Mass. Inst. Tech., 1947; M.S., U. Ill., 1952, Ph.D. in Physics, 1955. Assoc. prof. So. Ill. U., 1960-62; faculty U. Ill., Urbana, 1962-72, prof. physics, 1963-72, assoc. dir. Materials Research Lab., 1963-68, assoc. head physics dept., 1968-70, assoc. dean Grad. Coll., 1970-72, vice chancellor research, dean Grad. Coll., 1972-77; chancellor U. Mo.-Kansas City, 1977-91; pres. U Mo. system admin., Columbia, Mo., 1991—; cons. Office Naval Research, 1961-76; dir. Microthermal Applications Inc.; dir. Kansas City Power and Light Co.; mem. adv. bd. dirs. Boatman's First Nat. Bank Kansas City; mem. acad. adv. panel Com. on Exchanges. Vice chmn. Illini Union Bd., 1970; pres. Levis Faculty Center, 1972; chmn. bd. trustees AUA, 1977; mem. Mo. Sci. and Tech. Corp.; trustee Midwest Research Inst.; bd. dirs. Edgar Snow Meml. Fund, Inc. Served with USN, World War II. Mem. Am. Assn. Physics Tchrs., Am. Phys. Soc. Clubs: Champaign Country (pres. 1972), Mission Hills Country, Rockhill Tennis. Home: 1900 S Providence Rd Columbia MO 65203-3544 Office: U of Mo 321 University Hall Columbia MO 65211

RUSSELL, HARRIET SHAW, social worker; b. Detroit, Apr. 12, 1952; d. Louis Thomas and Lureleen (Hughes) Shaw; m. Donald Edward Russell, June 25, 1980; children: Lachante Tyree, Krystal Lanae. BS, Mich. State U., 1974; AB, Detroit Bus. Inst., 1976; BA in Pub. Adminstrn., Mercy Coll. Detroit, 1988; MSW, Wayne State U., 1992. Factory employee Gen. Motors Corp., Lansing, Mich., 1973; student supr. tour guides State of Mich., Lansing, 1974; mgr. Ky. Fried Chicken, Detroit, 1974-75; unemployment claims examiner State of Mich. Dept. Labor, Detroit, 1975-77, asst. payment worker, 1977-84, social svcs. specialist, 1984-90; ind. contractor Detroit Compact pres. Victory Enterprises, 1991; sch. social worker Detroit Bd. of Edn., 1992—; moderator Michigan Opportunity Skills and Tng. Program, 1985-86. Vol. Mich. Cancer Soc., East Lansing, 1970-72, Big Sisters/Big Bros., Lansing, 1972-73; elected rep. Mich. Coun. Social Svcs. Workers; speaker Triumphant Bapt. Ch., Detroit, 1976-80; chief union steward Mich. Employees Assn., Lincoln Park, 1982-83; leader Girl Scouts U.S.; area capt. Life Worker Project Program. Recipient Outstanding Work Performance Merit award Mich. Dept. Social Services, 1979, Unsung Hero award Neighborhood Found., 1995; grad. profl. scholar, 1990-91, Dean's scholar, 1991-92; elected to Wayne State Sch. Social Work Bd., 1992—. Mem. NAFE, Am. Soc. Profl. and Exec. Women, Assn. Internat. Platform Speakers, Mich. Coun. Social Svcs. Workers, Nat. Fedn. Bus. and Profl. Women's Clubs, Inc. U.S.A. (elected del. to China), Nat. Assn. Black Social Workers, Wayne State U. Social Work Alumni Assn. (bd. dirs. 1992—), Delta Sigma Theta. Democrat. Baptist. Office: PO Box 361 Lincoln Park MI 48146-0361

RUSSELL, HENRY MICHAEL WOODROW, university educator; b. Harrisburg, Pa., Aug. 26, 1952; s. Max Matthew and E. Fern (Hart) R.; m. Crystal Marie Costin, Aug. 12, 1989; children: Thomas Paul, Maria Veronica, Gabriel Peter, Jude Anthony. BA, Princeton U., 1976; MA, U. S.C., 1981; PhD, La. State U., 1992. Asst. prof. and honors dir. Anderson (S.C.) Coll., 1992-94; asst. prof. Wingate (N.C.) U., 1994-96, Franciscan U. of Steubenville, Ohio, 1996—; vis. asst. prof. Wake Forest U., Winston-Salem, N.C., 1989-92. Contbr. articles to profl. jours.; assoc. editor The Formalist, 1990—. Recipient Kirby award S. Ctrl. Rev., 1990; summer grantee NEH, 1993. Fellow Fellowship Cath. Scholars; mem. Southea. Conf. Christianity and Lit. (Daub-Maher Meml. award 1995). Republican. Office: Franciscan U of Steubenville Steubenville OH 43952

RUSSELL, JOHN THOMAS, state legislator; b. Lebanon, Mo., Sept. 22, 1931; s. Aubrey F. and Velma F. (Johnson) R.; m. Margaret Ann Carr, 1951; children: John Douglas, Georgia Jeanette, Sarah Melissa. Student, Drury Coll. Mem. Mo. State Ho. of Reps., Laclede County, 1963-66, Mo. State Ho. of Reps. Dist. 125, 1967-72, Mo. State Ho. of Reps. Dist. 150, 1973-76, Mo. State Senate Dist. 33, 1977—; dir., officer Laclede Metal Product Co. and Detroit Tool & Engring. Co., Lebanon, 1957—, Gen. Alumni Supply Co., Kansas City, 1959—; with Mo. Transp. Co., Lebanon, 1960; ptnr. Faith Leasing Co., Lebanon, 1969—. del. Rep. Nat. Conv., 1972. Mem. Kiwanis, Am. Legion, Mason (32 degree), Scottish Rite, Lebanon C. of C. Office: PO Box 93 Lebanon MO 65536-0093 also: State Senate State Capitol Building Jefferson City MO 65101-1556*

RUSSELL, JULIE RAPP, broadcast executive; b. Peoria, Ill., Aug. 9, 1966; d. Frederick Weston and Mardell (Haughey) Rapp; m. Peter Reed Russell, Oct. 6, 1990. BS, Bradley U., 1988. Weather reporter WEEK-TV, Peoria, 1985-88; acct. exec. We Can Image Advt., Peoria, 1988-89, WMBD/WMXP, Peoria, 1989—. Bd. dirs., 2d v.p. pub. rels. Peoria YWCA; bd. dirs. Jr. League of Peoria. Mem. Women's Advt. Club Chgo., Peoria Advt. and Selling Club (bd. dirs. 1990—, pres. 1995-96), Am. Advt. Fedn. Home: 235 E Oak Park Dr Peoria IL 61614-7411 Office: WMBD/WMXP 3131 N University St Peoria IL 61604-1316

RUSSELL, LILLIAN, medical, surgical nurse; b. N.Y.C., Feb. 21, 1942; d. Joserelle Russell; 1 child, Evan Gregory. AAS, N.Y.C. Community Coll., 1973; BS, St. Xavier Coll., Chgo., 1986; MS, Spertus Coll. of Judaica, Chgo., 1989. Staff/charge nurse Beth Israel Med. Ctr., N.Y.C., 1973-76; charge nurse Roosevelt Hosp., N.Y.C., 1977-78; staff/charge nurse U. Ill. Hosp., Chgo., 1979—; asst. adminstrv. coord. Bethany Hosp., Chgo., 1990-91; adminstv. nurse I Mile Square Health Ctr. & U. Ill. Hosp., Chgo., 1991-95; asst. dir. nursing Mile Square Health Ctr., Chgo., 1995—; mem. instnl. rev. com. Bethany Hosp., 1987—; adj. asst. prof. Trinity Christian Coll., Palos Heights, Ill., 1996—. Mem. Great Cities Com., Chgo., 1994—. Mem. ANA, NAFE, AAUW, Ill. Nurses Assn., Res. Officers Assn. Home: 1342 N Oakley Blvd Chicago IL 60622-3048

RUSSELL, MARY ELIZABETH, admissions director; b. St. Louis, Nov. 29, 1964; d. Charles Albert and Betty Jean (Compton) Mueller; m. Douglas Franklin Russell, June 22, 1985. BM summa cum laude, Webster U., 1986, MA, 1990; PhD, St. Louis U., 1995. Program asst. Webster U., St. Louis, 1986-90, dir. grad. admissions, 1990—. Mem. Nat. Assn. Grad. Admission Profls. Home: 1105 Wilmington Saint Louis MO 63111 Office: Webster U 470 E Lockwood Saint Louis MO 63119

RUSSELL, MICHAEL ERWIN, industrial hygienist; b. Milwaukee, Dec. 13, 1955; s. Erwin D. Russell and Ann (McMullen) O'Rourke; m. Susan D. Ehlers, June 21, 1982. BS, Univ. Wis., 1979; MS, Univ. Minn., 1982. Cert. industrial hygienist. Sr. industrial hygienist PACE, Inc., Mpls., 1984-92, indsl. hygiene lab. dir., 1989-92; indoor air quality program mgr. SEC Donohue, Inc., Mpls., 1992-93, sr. indsl. hygienist, 1992-93; sr. indsl. hygienist, mgr. indoor air quality program RUST Environment & Infrastructure, Mpls., 1993—. Mem. Am. Indsl. Hygiene Assn. (mem. indoor environ. quality tech. com. 1993—, sec. local sect. 1992-93), Am. Acad. Indsl. Hygiene, Minn. Safety Coun., Human Factors and Ergonomics Soc., Am. Conf. of Govtl. Indsl. Hygienists, Phi Beta Kappa. Office: RUST Environ & Infrastruct Ste 175 3033 Campus Dr Minneapolis MN 55441-2651

RUSSELL, STEPHEN JAMES, health care products executive; b. Covington, Ky., Nov. 22, 1949. BS in Engring., U. Cin., 1972. Sect. supr. mfg. engring. Ford Motor Co., Batavia, Sharonville, Ohio, 1973-93; pres. Russell Engring., Milford, Ohio, 1993-95; treas., sec. Greene Respiratory Svcs., Milford, 1994—. Treas. Milford Theatre Guild, 1994-95. Republican. Roman Catholic. Office: Greene Respiratory Svcs 817 US 50 Milford OH 45150-9513

RUSSELL, VALERIE EILEEN, social service executive; b. Winchester, Mass., Apr. 28, 1941; d. John Randolph Russell and Carrie Belle (Finley) Jones. BA in Sociology, Suffolk U., 1967; postgrad., Columbia U.; D in Theology (hon.), LaFayette Coll., 1985. Program dir. Blue Hill Christian Ctr., Roxbury, Mass., 1965-67; racial justicestaff mem. Nat. Bd. YWCA, N.Y.C., 1967-72; cons. Riverside Ch., N.Y.C., 1972-73, nat. conf. organizer, 1980-81; asst. to pres. United Ch. of Christ, N.Y.C., 1973-79; pres., exec. dir. City Mission Soc., Boston, 1981-90; adj. prof. Union Theol. Sch., N.Y.C., 1976, Harvard U. Div. Sch., Cambridge, Mass., 1983—; bd. dirs. Ctr. Ministry of the Laity, Newton, Mass. Author: Laity in the Church, 1987; inventor simulation game on pluralism, 1973; regular panelist weekly TV program A Show of Faith, Boston; lectr. in field. Bd. dirs. United Way Mass. Bay, Boston, 1984-88, Women and Poverty Network, Boston, 1984—; co-founder Christians for Justice Action, United Ch. of Christ, 1980—. Named Outstanding Young Women in N.Y., 1969; Recipient Outstanding Alumni award Suffolk U., 1981, Outstanding Social Work award The Girl Friends, Boston, 1985, Outstanding Human Services award Delta Sigma Phi, Boston, 1986. Uniter Ch. of Christ. Office: Office for Ch in Soc United Ch of Christ 700 Prospect Ave E Cleveland OH 44115-1131

RUSSELL, WILLIAM RAY, clergyman; b. Windsor, Ont., Can., Sept. 10, 1939; came to U.S., 1989; s. William and Marion Rae (Kenyon) R.; m. Elizabeth Ann Trotter, Nov. 17, 1962; children: Sarah Elizabeth, William Kirk, Rebecca Ann. BA in Philosophy, U. Toronto, 1961; MDiv, Princeton Sem., 1964; DMin, Ecumenical Theol. Sem., Detroit, 1994. Ordained to ministry Presbyn. Ch., 1964. Asst. pastor Fifth Ave Presbyn. Ch., N.Y.C., 1964-68; sr. pastor Wyo. Presbyn. Ch., Millburn, N.J., 1968-73, Ch. of St. Andrew and St. Paul, Montreal, Que., Can., 1973-83; gen. sec. Can. Bible Soc., Toronto, Ont., 1983-88; sr. pastor First Presbyn. Ch., Deerfield, Ill., 1989—. Home: 728 Price Ln Deerfield IL 60015-4177 Office: First Presbyterian Ch 824 Waukegan Rd Deerfield IL 60015-3206

RUSSELL-RADER, KATHLEEN, secondary school educator; b. Dayton, Ohio, Jan. 23, 1954; d. Reid Jerome and Margie (Miller) Russell; m. Donald Mark Rader, July 9, 1977. BS, Bowling Green (Ohio) State U., 1975; MS, U. Dayton, 1987. Cert. tchr., Ohio. English tchr. Fairborn (Ohio) City Schs., 1976—, Sinclair C. C., Dayton, 1991—; dir., choreographer Fairborn High Sch. Flyerette Dance Corps, 1976-81; adv. Nat. Jr. Honor Soc., Fairborn, 1985—, student leadership, 1990—, mem. acad. coun., 1988—; adv./dir. Drama Club, Fairborn, 1991—; coach Power of the Pen Writing Team, Fairborn, 1987—. Recipient Golden Apple Tchr. Achiever award Ashland Oil Corp., 1996; named Tchr. of Yr. Fairborn City Schs., 1989-90, Tchr. Honor Roll, Ohio Interscholastic Writing League, Cleve., 1990; Vera Schneider Teaching grantee Fairborn City Schs., 1988-92. Mem. Nat. Coun. Tchrs. English (judge Promising Young Writers Program 1991-93), Western Ohio Coun. Tchrs. English, Ohio Coun. Tchrs. English, Ohio Coun. English and Lang. Arts (judge writing contest 1989-93), Dayton Area Coun. Internat. Reading Assn. (pres. 1991-92), Ohio Coun. Internat. Reading Assn., Internat. Reading Assn., Nat. Assn. Student Activity Advisers, Phi Delta Kappa. Republican. Roman Catholic. Home: 7667 Turtle Creek Dr Dayton OH 45414-1755 Office: Fairborn City Schs 200 Lincoln Dr Fairborn OH 45324-5349

RUSSI, GARY D., academic administrator. Pres. Oakland U., Rochester, Miss. Office: Oakland U Rochester MI 48309*

RUSSO, GILBERTO, engineering educator; b. Rome, Aug. 23, 1954; s. Guido and Maria (Mazzoni) R. Laurea, Poly. Inst. Turin, Italy, 1975; ScD, MIT, 1980; MD, U. Chgo. Pritaker Sch. of Medicine. Pres. Studio Russo, Inc. Engring. Cons., Turin, 1970; asst. prof. Poly. Inst. Turin, 1975-80; lectr. MIT, Cambridge, Mass., 1985-91; dr. dept. plastic and reconstructive surgery U. Chgo., 1992-95; mem. dept. surgery U. Calif., San Francisco, 1995—; mem. designer selection bd. State of Mass., Boston, 1989. Contbr. articles to profl. publs., chpts. to books. Pres. Dante Alisheri Soc., Cambridge, 1986-88; treas. MIT/Poly. Alumni Assn., Turin, 1970. Fulbright fellow, 1978. Fellow Nat. Coun. Engring. Examiners; mem. Mass. Soc. Profl. Engrs. (v.p. 1991—), Tau Beta Pi (chpt. advisor 1985, Eminent Engr. 1985). Office: U Chgo Dept Plastic-Reconstrv Surg Chicago IL 60637 also: U Calif Dept Surgery Rm S-343 Box 0470 513 Parnassus Ave San Francisco CA 94143

RUSSO, MICHAEL JOHN, manufacturing engineer, manufacturing company executive; b. Cin., Apr. 3, 1960; s. George Edward and Ann Marie (Cianciolo) R.; m. Catherine Lynn Brocker. BS in Indsl. and Systems Engring., Ohio State U., 1983; MS in Indsl. Engring., U. Cin., 1995. Indsl. engr. Liebert Corp., Columbus, Ohio, 1983-85, Tracewell Enclosures, Inc., Columbus, 1985-88; ops. mgr. mfg. Cin. Electronics Corp., 1988—. Home: 8132 Sacred Heart Ln Cincinnati OH 45255-3155 Office: Cin Electronics Corp 7500 Innovation Way Mason OH 45040-9695

RUSSOMONDO-MOREHEAD, ANNETTE MARIE, disabled children's facility administrator, child advocate; b. San Diego; d. Michael Peter and Katherine Helen (Keegan) Russomondo; m. Peter James Morehead; children: Bradley Michael Caloca, Katherine Dana. Student, Southwestern Coll., Grossmont Coll. Dir. Rayito Day Care Ctr., San Diego, 1981-85; instrnl. asst. for children with disabilities San Diego City Schools, 1985-88; owner, operator Scripps Ranch Childcare Ctr. for Disabled Children, San Diego, 1990—; child advocate; speaker San Diego Bd. Edn., 1986, News Eight Local TV News, 1989, Miramar Coll., 1991, Scottish Rite Charities, 1992, Exceptional Parents Found., 1993. vol. Schweitzer Ctr. for Disabled Children, San Diego, 1985, Stein Edn. Ctr. fof Autistic Children, San Diego, 1987-88. Mem. Autism Soc. Am. (bd. dirs.), Mensa. Democrat. Home and Office: 7230 Blaisdell Ave S Minneapolis MN 55423

RUST, EDWARD BARRY, JR., insurance company executive, lawyer; b. Chgo., Aug. 3, 1950; s. Edward Barry Sr. and Harriett B. (Fuller) R.; m. Sally Buckler, Feb. 28, 1976; 1 child, Edward Barry III. Student, Lawrence U., 1968-69; BS, Ill. Wesleyan U., 1972; JD, MBA, So. Meth. U., 1975. Bar: Tex. 1975, Ill. 1976. Mgmt. trainee State Farm Ins. Cos., Dallas, 1975-76; atty. State Farm Ins. Cos., Bloomington, 1976, sr. atty., 1976-78, asst. v.p., 1978-81, v.p., 1981-83, exec. v.p., 1983-85, chmn., 1987—; pres., CEO State Farm Life Ins. Cos., Bloomington, 1985—; now also pres., CEO, chmn. State Farm Mutual Auto Ins. Co.; pres. and bd. dirs. State Farm Investment Mgmt. Corp., State Farm Internat. Services, Inc., State Farm Cos. Found.; chmn. State Farm Mut. Automobile Ins. Co., 1987; bd. dirs. exec. and investment coms. State Farm Annuity and Life Ins. Co., State Farm Mut. Automobile Ins. Co., State Farm Life Ins. Co., State Farm Fire and Casualty, State Farm Gen. Trustee Ill. Wesleyan U., 1985—; mem. adv. coun. Grad. Sch. Bus. Stanford U.; mem. bus. adv. coun. Coll. Commerce and Bus. Adminstrn. U. Ill. Mem. ABA, Am. Enterprise Inst., Bus. Roundtable, Tex. State Bar Assn., Ill. Bar Assn., Am. Inst. Property and Liability Underwriters (trustee 1986—), Ins. Inst. Am. (trustee 1986—). Office: State Farm Ins Cos 1 State Farm Plz Bloomington IL 61701-4300*

RUST, ROBERT C., electonics engineer; b. Northwood, N.D., May 9, 1944; s. Clifton Enar and Ruby Alice (Welin) R.; m. Sheila Sabina Fleming, Apr. 27, 1974 (div. Mar. 1988); children: David Charles, Sarah Elizabeth. BSEE, U. N.D., 1966, postgrad., 1966-68. Elec. engr. Control Data Corp., Bloomington, Minn., 1968-78, Luchy Engring. Corp., Bloomington, 1978-79; sr. devel. engr. Cardiac Pacemakers Inc., St. Paul, 1979-87, IBM Corp., Rochester, Minn., 1988—. Co-inventor fault tolerant sys. of bubble memories, atrial rate sensitive cardiac pacer cir. Mem. IEEE. Home: 2810 25th St NW Rochester MN 55901

RUSTERHOLZ, PAUL OLIVER, conductor; b. St. Paul, Nov. 20, 1947; s. Theophil and Florence (Billing) R.; m. Barbara Lomas, July 20, 1974; 1 child, Timothy. BA, Macalester Coll., St. Paul, 1969; MA, U. Minn., Mpls., 1975; DMA, U. So. Calif., L.A., 1980. Asst. prof. music Coll. St. Teresa, Winona, Minn., 1978-89; vis. assoc. prof. music U. Wis., LaCrosse, 1989—; conductor LaCrosse Chamber Chorale, 1990—, The Choral Union, LaCrosse, 1989—; founder, condr. Winona (Minn.) Oratorio Chorus, 1980-91. Mem. Nat. Assn. Tchrs. Singing (state treas. Wis. chpt. 1992-96). Home: 138 S 17th Pl La Crosse WI 54601

RUTECKI, GREGORY WILLIAM, physician, educator; b. Chgo., Nov. 27, 1948; s. William John and Alice J. (Jankowski) R.; m. Janis Louise Howenstine, July 15, 1976; children: Jared, John. BS, DePaul U., 1970; MD cum laude, U. Ill., 1974. Diplomate Am. Bd. Internal Medicine, Am. Bd. Nephrology. Resident Ohio State U., Columbus, 1974-78; rsch. assoc. U. Minn., Mpls., 1978-80; asst. prof. medicine Northeastern Ohio U. Coll. Medicine, Rootstown, Ohio, 1982-86; assoc. prof. medicine Northeastern Ohio U. Coll. Medicine, Rootstown, 1986—; assoc. program dir. Internal Medicine Residency Affiliated Hosps., Canton, Ohio, 1992—. Contbr. articles to profl. jours., chpts. to books. Bd. trustees Ky. Christian Coll., 1992—; bd. dirs. Juvenile Diabetes Found., 1992—; elder Jackson Christian Ch., 1988—. Mem. Am. Soc. Nephrology, Christian Med. Soc., Am. Acad. Med. Ethics, Alpha Omega Alpha.

RUTENBERG-ROSENBERG, SHARON LESLIE, journalist; b. Chgo., May 23, 1951; d. Arthur and Bernice (Berman) Rutenberg; m. Michael J. Rosenberg, Feb. 3, 1980; children: David Kaifel and Jonathan Reuben (twins), Emily Mara. Student, Harvard U., 1972; B.A., Northwestern U., 1973, M.S.J., 1975; cert. student pilot. Reporter-photographer Lerner Home Newspapers, Chgo., 1973-74; corr. Medill News Service, Washington, 1975; reporter-newsperson, sci. writer UPI, Chgo., 1975-84. Interviewer: exclusives White House chief of staff, nation's only mother and son on death row; others. Vol. Chgo.-Read Mental Health Ctr. Recipient Peter Lisagor award for exemplary journalism in features category, 1980, 81; Golden Key Nat. Adv. Bd. of Children's Oncology Service Inc., 1981; Media awards for wire service feature stories, 1983, 84, wire service news stories, 1983, 84, all from Chgo. Hosp. Pub. Relations Soc. Mem. Profl. Assn. Diving Instrs., Nat. Assn. Underwater Instrs., Hon. Order Ky. Cols., Hadassah, Sigma Delta Chi, Sigma Delta Tau. Home: 745 Marion Ave Highland Park IL 60035-5123

RUTHERFORD, DAN, state legislator. Degree, Ill. State U., 1978. Legis. asst. for State Rep. Tom Ewing, Ill., 1978-80; exec. dir. Ill. Reagan/Bush Com., 1980; asst. dir. Gov.'s Office of Pers., Ill., 1981; mem. adv. com. on internat. trade U.S. Govt. and Adv. Com. on Sports Medicine; mem. Livingston County Coun. for Econ. Devel., Ill.; Ill. State rep. Named One of the People to Watch in 1986 Chgo. Tribune. Mem. Livingston County Farm Bur., Ill. Corn Growers Assn., Pontiac C. of C., Pheasants Forever, Japan-Am. Soc. Republican. Home: 927 E Water St Pontiac IL 61764-2148*

RUTHMAN, THOMAS ROBERT, manufacturing company executive; b. Cin., May 24, 1933; s. Alois H. and Catherine (Gies) R.; grad. LaSaile U., 1970; m. Audrey J. Schumaker, Mar. 17, 1979; children: Thomas G., Julia C., Theresa K. With Ruthman Pump and Engring. Inc. (formerly Ruthman Machinery Co.), Cin., 1953—, gen. mgr., 1964-70, v.p., 1970-74, pres., 1974—, pres., owner, 1981—; pres. Gusher Pumps, Inc., Fulflo Spltys. Co., Gusher Pumps of New Castle, Cin., Grant County, Dry Ridge, Calif.; pres., owner Vulcan Tool Corp., Dayton, Ohio; owner BSM Pump Corp, North Kingston, R.I. With U.S. Army, 1953-55. Mem. Cin. Council World Affairs, Navy League U.S. Club: Rotary. Home: 6858 Dimmick Rd West Chester OH 45069-3945 Office: 1212 Streng St Cincinnati OH 45223-2643

RUTHSATZ, RANDALL A., accountant; b. Sandusky, Ohio, Apr. 1, 1964; s. Kenneth Harold and Sylvia Ruth (Poeschl) R. BA, Heidelberg Coll., 1986; MBA, Case Western Res. U., 1988. CPA, Ohio. Tax cons. Deloitte & Touche, Cleve., 1988-93; sr. tax cons. Howard, Wershbale & Co., Beachwood, Ohio, 1994-95; pvt. practice Sandusky, Ohio, 1995—. Mem. AICPA, Ohio Soc. CPAs. Republican. Episcopalian. Home: 1005 Mills St Sandusky OH 44870-2821

RUTKOWSKI, JAMES ANTHONY, state legislator; b. Milw., Apr. 6, 1942. BS in Bus., Marquette U., 1964, JD, 1966. Former instr. Marquette U., Milw.; asst. instr. U. Wis., Milw.; state legis. State of Wis., Madison, 1970. With USAR, 1966-72. Recipient Clean 16 award, 1982, 88, 90, 94, Wis. Man of Achievement award, 1976. Mem. KC, Greendale Jaycee Roosters. Home: 4550 S 117th St Greenfield WI 53228-2451 Office: State Capitol 216 North PO Box 8953 Madison WI 53708

RUTLAND, MYRTLE PAULINE, mental health nurse; b. Lynchburg, Va., July 22, 1948; d. Samuel Joseph and Carrie Arlean (Phillips) Robinson; 1 child, Jason Rutland. Diploma, Bronson Sch. Nursing, 1975. Clin. instr. Kalamazoo Valley Community Coll., 1976-77; occupational nurse GM, Kalamazoo, 1977-81; RN program coord. Kalamazoo Regional Psychiat. Hosp., 1981-91; nurse Vis. Nurses Assn. Southwestern Mich., Kalamazoo, 1992-94, Advantage Home Health Care, Kalamazoo, 1994—. Mem. Mich. Black Nurses Assn.

RUTLEDGE, CHARLES OZWIN, pharmacology educator; b. Topeka, Oct. 1, 1937; s. Charles Ozwin and Alta (Seaman) R.; m. Jane Ellen Crow, Aug. 13, 1961; children: David Ozwin, Susan Harriett, Elizabeth Jane, Karen Ann. BS in Pharmacy, U. Kans., 1959, MS in Pharmacology, 1961; PhD in Pharmacology, Harvard U., 1966. NATO postdoctoral fellow Gothenburg U., Sweden, 1966-67; asst. prof. U. Colo. Med. Ctr., Denver, 1967-74, assoc. prof., 1974-75; prof., chmn. dept. pharmacology U. Kans., Lawrence, 1975-87; dean, prof. pharmacology Purdue U., West Lafayette, Ind., 1987—. Contbr. articles on neuropharmacology to profl. jours. Grantee: NIH, 1970, Kans. Heart Assn., 1978. Mem. Am. Soc. Pharmacology and Exptl. Therapeutics (councillor 1982-84, sec.-treas. 1990-93, pres. 1996—), Am. Assn. Coll. Pharmacy (chmn. biol. scis. sect. 1983-84, chmn. council of faculties 1986-87, chmn. coun. deans, 1993-94, commn. implement change pharm. edn. 1989-92, pres. 1996—), Soc. for Neurosci., Am. Pharm. Assn. AAAS. Avocations: gardening; skiing. Home: 40 Brynteg E West Lafayette IN 47906-5643 Office: Purdue U Office of Dean Sch Pharmacy 1330 R Heine Pharm Bldg West Lafayette IN 47907-1330

RUTLEDGE, JANET MARIE, county clerk and recorder; b. Monmouth, Ill., May 8, 1947; d. Harold W. and Frances L. (Taylor) Ross; m. David A. Ruttledge, Dec. 10, 1966; children: Karen, Christine. Grad. high sch., Kirkwood, Ill., 1965. Bookkeeper/teller Nat. Bank, Monmouth, Ill., 1965-69; teller Cmty. Nat. Bank, 1977-78; bookkeeper County of Warren, Monmouth, 1978-86, elected county clk., 1986—; mem. County Clerks/Recorders (legis. com. 1990—, election legis. com. 1991—, historian 1994—, budget com. 1994—); apptd. Nat. Voter Registration Act Task Force, 1993—. Mem. Warren County Rep. Women (historian 1993—), Warren County Cancer Com. (bd. dirs. 1993—), Am. Legion (treas. 1993—). Republican. Office: Warren County Clk/Recorder 100 W Broadway Monmouth IL 61462

RUTLEDGE, JOEL R., state legislator, small business owner; b. Paoli, Ind., July 19, 1965; s. Donavon R. and Carol Marie (Brunner) R.; m. Tracy Jo Giglio, Apr. 26, 1986; 1 child, Joseph Devon. Grad. high sch., Wichita, Kans. Owner, mgr. Award Specialists, Wichita, 1987—; mem. Kans. Ho. of Reps., Topeka, 1993—. Democrat. Address: 2645 S Washington St Wichita KS 67216-1142

RUTSTEIN, ALEXANDER, engineering consultant; b. Kharkov, USSR, Oct. 18, 1929; Came to U.S., 1974; s. Lev Rutstein and Tatiana Shechter; m. Sedmara Zakarian, Aug. 28, 1958; 1 child, Alla. MSME, Kharkov Poly. Inst., 1952. Chief turbine dept. Energochermet, Leningrad, USSR, 1965-73; pres. Compressor Controls Corp., Des Moines, 1974-77; staff cons. Energy Mgmt. Engring., Lorain, Ohio, 1977-81; pres. Energy Mgmt. Controls, Elyria, Ohio, 1981-83; owner Alex Rutstein & Assocs., Oberlin, Ohio, 1983—. Patentee in field; contbr. articles to profl. jours. Mem. ASME, Instrument Soc. Am., Am. Soc. Heating Refrigeration and Air Conditioning Engrs., Nat. Soc. Profl. Engrs.

RUTTER, ELIZABETH JANE, consulting firm executive; b. Lansing, Mich., June 27, 1955; d. Robert Emmett and Anna Lou (Edwards) Martin; m. David Bruce Rutter, June 25, 1988; children: Robert Corey Myers, Jacob Martin Myers, Laura June Rutter. Student, Harrisburg Area C.C., Pa., 1975-76, U. Mo., 1990-91, Stephens Coll., 1995—. Exec. sec. Timeter Instrument, Inc., Lancaster, Pa., 1983-85; editorial asst. U. Extension, Columbia, Mo., 1985-88; grants/contracts specialist U. Mo. Office of Sponsored Programs, Columbia, Mo., 1988-91; pres. Grants Link, Inc., Columbia, Mo., 1991—; mem. Econ. Devel. Com. Ashland (Mo.) C. of C., 1991-93; mem Columbia (Mo.) C. of C., 1991—; chair Fin. Com. Sacred Heart Cath. Ch., Columbia, Mo., 1996; officer Exec. Bd. Advent Enterprises, Inc., Columbia, Mo.. 1992-95. Editor: Corporate Funders Operating in Missouri, 1992, 3d edit., 1996, The Funding Connection Newsletter, 1994, Right on The Money Newsletter, 1994, Corporate Funders Operating in Texas, 1996, Corporate Funders Operating in Illinois, 1996. Named Small Svc. Bus. of Yr. Columbia C. of C., 1994. Mem. Nat. Soc. Fund Raising Execs. (chair ctrl. Mo. chpt. 1996). Roman Catholic. Office: Grants Link Inc 5650A S Sinclair Rd Columbia MO 65203

RUTZ, STEPHEN L., design draftsman; b. Junction City, Kans., Sept. 15, 1959. Grad., high sch., 1977. Design draftsman Tramco, Wichita, Kans., 1979—.

RUTZKY, RONALD, school district superintendent; b. Chgo., July 29, 1945; s. Jules Paul and Pearl (Rubin) R.; m. Alene Joyce Schneider, Dec. 22, 1968; children: Miriam Deena, Solomon Louis. BA, U. Ill., Chgo., 1967; MA, Roosevelt U., 1973; EdD, No. Ill.U., 1993. Cert. tchr., Ill. Tchr. math. Sch. Dist. 143.5, Posen, Ill., 1968-79; prin. Turner Elem. Sch. Dist. 143.5, Robbins, Ill., 1979-87, 90-92; prin. Gordon Jr. High Sch. Sch. Dist. 143.5, Posen, Ill., 1987-90, dist. chmn. State of Ill. Young Authors Program, 1982-94; prin. Garfield Sch., Sch. Dist. 143.5, Blue Island, Ill., 1992-94; chmn. prins. round table Posen-Robbins Dist. 143.5, 1993-94; supt. Braceville (Ill.) Elem. Sch. Dist. 75, 1994—; dist. co-chmn. Multi-Cultural Edn. Com., 1990-94; sec., treas. Vermillion Valley Conf., 1994—; mem. exec. bd. Grundy County Spl. Edn. Coop. Prin. Bd. Jewish Edn., 1980-83; tchr. Congregation Etz Chaim, Flossmoor, Ill., 1974-81; tchr. Congregation Am Echad, Park Forest, Ill., 1982-87, 90—, prin., 1983-86. Mem. ASCD, Am. Assn. Sch. Adminstrs., Ill. Assn. Sch. Adminstrs., Nat. Assn. Secondary Sch. Prins., Nat. Staff Devel. Coun., B'nai B'rith, Kappa Delta Pi, Phi Delta Kappa. Jewish. Home: 18046 Cherrywood Ln Homewood IL 60430-1503 Office: Braceville Sch Dist 75 PO Box 178 209 Mitchell St Braceville IL 60407-0178

RUWE, WILLIAM, insurance executive; b. Cin., July 13, 1937; s. Roy J. and Marian E. (Von Wyck) R.; m. Marcia Cogsdon, June 10, 1961; children: Laura M., Paul F., Miriam L. BSBA, Xavier U., Cin., 1961, MBA, 1979. Cert. ins. counselor; assoc. in risk mgmt. Sales mgr. Ins. Co. N.Am., Cin., 1962-72; terr. mgr. Lumberman's Mut. Ins. Co., Mansfield, Ohio, 1972-74; br. mgr. Loveland (Ohio) Ins. Agy., 1974-79; v.p. ops., COO Dentrex Inc., Harrodsburg, Ky., 1979-81; v.p. comml. lines Emory P. Zimmer Agy. Inc., Cin., 1981—. Bd. dirs., officer North Avondale Neighborhood Assn., Cin., 1979—; bd. dirs. Neighborhood Support Program, City of Cin., 1982-84. Mem. Risk Edn. Soc. (pres. elect 1991—), Greater Cin. Ins. Agt. Assn. (bd. dirs. 1981—), Soc. Cert. Ins. Counselors. Office: Emory P Zimmer Agy 500 Loveland-Madiera Rd Loveland OH 45140

RUWWE, WILLIAM OTTO, retired automotive engineer; b. Cuba, Mo., July 25, 1930; s. Otto Albert and Maude May (Hines) R.; m. Helen Leona Haynes, Jan. 1, 1958; children: Teresa Lynn, Nancy Jean. BS, Cen. Mo. State U., 1959. Engring. clk. Wagner Brake div. Cooper Industries, St. Louis, 1959-64, engr., 1964-67, quality control chemist, 1967-68, mfg. mgr., 1968-82, plant mgr., 1982-93; ret., 1993. Inventor electroless nickle plating process for cast iron, 1964, dissolution of crystal formation in brake fluid, 1971. With U.S. Army, 1951-53. Mem. Soc. Automotive Engrs. (cert., product bus. com.1985-90), St. Louis Geneal. Soc. Home: 540 Innsbrook Estates Wright City MO 63390-5325

RUYLE, KIM ERNEST, training and software development executive; b. Yakima, Wash., Dec. 17, 1953; s. Covey E. and Constance J. (Easter) R.; m. Mary B. Christenson, June 24, 1972; children: Benjamin, Emily, Nathanael, Christopher, Daniel, Rebecca, Jonathan, Thaddeus, Margaret, Madeline. BS, Winona State U., 1983; MS, Oregon State U., 1986; MEd, East Tex. State U., 1988; PhD, Oregon State U., 1990; postgrad., U. Wis. Mechanic Inland Machinery, Yakima, Wash., 1975-79, LaCrosse (Wis.) Concrete, 1979-80; welder Winona (Minn.) Attrition Mill, 1980-83; instr. Winona (Minn.) State U., 1983-84, Oregon State U., Corvallis, 1984-87; mgr. human resource devel. ICI/ Fiberite Composite Materials, Greenville, Tex., 1987-88; asst. prof. U. Wis., Platteville, 1988-90; pres. Plus Delta Performance, Inc., Galesville, Wis., 1990—; mem. editorial adv. bd. Tech & Skills Tng. Mag., Alexandria, Va., 1990—. With U.S. Army, 1972-75. Mem. ASTD (exec. com. for tech. and skills tng.), Nat. Soc. for Performance and Instrn., Soc. Mfg. Engrs., Soc. Maintenance and Reliability Profls. Home: 17152 Fairview St Galesville WI 54630 Office: Plus Delta Performance Inc 1500 Green Bay St La Crosse WI 54601

RUZBASAN, ANTHONY, distribution executive; b. East Chicago, Ind., Mar. 31, 1947; s. Anthony John and Mildred Marie (Jurek) R.; m. Susan Linda Glick, Oct. 6, 1990; children: Amy Lynn, Zachary Blair. BA in Speech and Theater, Ind. U., 1972, BA in Radio and TV, 1972. Radio newscaster Sta. WLTH, Gary, Ind., 1967-68; store mgr. Kustom Music Ctrs., Chgo., 1969-71; dist. mgr. WMI Corp., Chgo., 1972; pres. A.R. Musical Enterprises Inc., Indpls., 1973—; pres. Kay Guitar Co., Indpls., 1982—. Contbr. articles to mus. mags. Participant Footlite Musicals, Indpls., 1986-88; pres., dir. Marian Theatre Guild, Whiting, Ind., 1962-68. Mem. Mus. Distbr. Assn., Guitar and Accesories Mus. Mktg. Assn., Nat. Assn. Importers & Exporters, Am. Mus. Conf., Nat. Assn. Mus. Mchts. Avocations: acting, directing, gardening, travel. Office: A R Musical Enterprises Inc 9031 Technology Dr Fishers IN 46038-2886

RYAN, DANIEL LEO, bishop; b. Mankato, Minn., Sept. 28, 1930; s. Leonard Bennett and Irene Ruth (Larson) R. BA, Ill. Benedictine Coll., 1952; JCL, Pontificia Università Lateranense, Rome, 1960. Ordained priest Roman Cath. Ch., 1956, consecrated bishop, 1981. Parish priest Roman Cath. Diocese, Joliet, Ill, 1956-82, chancellor, 1965-78, vicar gen., 1977-79, aux. bishop, 1981-84; bishop Roman Cath. Diocese, Springfield, Ill., 1984—. Office: Diocese of Springfield PO Box 3187 1615 W Washington Springfield IL 62708-3187

RYAN, DONALD PATRICK, contractor; b. Janesville, Wis., July 13, 1930; s. William H. and Myrtle (Westrick) R.; B.S. in Civil Engring., U. Wis., 1953, B.S. in Naval Sci., 1953; m. Diana Houser, July 17, 1954; children—Patrick, Susannah, Nancy, David, Josephine, Rebecca, Polly, Adam. Ptnr. Ryan Bros. Co., Janesville, Wis., 1949—; dir.. Ryan, Inc. Cen., Janesville; dir. M & I, Janesville, U. Wis. Cancer Ctr. Adv. Bd., Elvehjem Mus. Art Council, U. Wis. Found. Served with USNR, 1953-55. Registered profl. engr., Wis., Ill. Mem. Nat. Soc. Profl. Engrs., Wis. Meml. Union Bldg. Assn. (trustee), U. Wis. Alumni Assn., Chi Epsilon, Phi Delta Theta. Home: 703 St Lawrence Ave Janesville WI 53545-4039 Office: PO Box 1079 Janesville WI 53545

RYAN, EARL M., public affairs analyst; b. Detroit, Oct. 23, 1942; s. Thomas M. and Margaret L. (Halsey) R.; m. Jo Ellen Junod, July 3, 1965; children: Andrew M., Jeffrey A. BA in Polit. Sci., U. Mich., 1964; MA in Polit. Sci., Wayne State U., 1968. Dir. rsch. Detroit Urban League, 1965-67; resch. assoc. Citizens Rsch. Coun. Mich., Lansing, 1967-70; budget analyst Dept. Social Svcs., Lansing, 1970-71; dir. rsch. Health Impact Project, Lansing, 1971, Office of Program Effectiveness Rev., Lansing, 1971-74, Legis. Program Effectiveness Rev., Lansing, 1974-77, Citizens Rch. Coun. Mich., Detroit, 1977-84; pres. Pub. Affairs Rsch. Coun. La., Baton Rouge, 1984-87, Ind. Fiscal Policy Inst., Indpls., 1987-94; exec. dir. Citizens Rsch. Coun. of Mich., 1994—; polit. analyst Sta. WWL-TV, New Orleans, 1986; mem. blue ribbon panel Indpls. Bus. Jour., 1992-94. Recipient disting. achievement award grad. program pub. adminstrn. Wayne State U., Detroit, 1991. Mem. Govtl. Rsch. Assn. (pres. 1985-86, Disting. rsch. award 1977), Govtl. Fin. Officers Assn. Home: 40292 Woodside Dr N Northville MI 48167-3431 Office: Citizens Rsch Coun Mich 625 Shelby St Ste 1B Detroit MI 48226-3206

RYAN, EDWARD JOSEPH, accountant; b. Danville, Ill., Aug. 3, 1956; s. Edward Joseph and Margaret Deneen (Gillen) R. BS in Acctg., U. Ill., 1990. Facilities mgr. U. Ill. Coll. Medicine, Urbana, 1978-89; exec. dir. Ea. Ill. Food Bank, Urbana, 1989-92; acct. in pvt. practice Champaign, Ill., 1992—. Active Champaign City Coun., Champaign. Mem. Nat. Soc. Pub. Accts., Ind. Accts. Assn. of Ill. Office: Ryan Acctg and Cons 41 E University Ave 2D-2 Champaign IL 61820

RYAN, GEORGE H., state government official, pharmacist; b. Maquoketa, Iowa, Feb. 24, 1934; s. Thomas J. and Jeanette (Bowman) R.; m. Lura Lynn Lowe, June 10, 1956; children: Nancy, Lynda, Julie, Joanne, Jeanette, George. BS in Pharmacy, Ferris State Coll., Big Rapids, Mich. Mem. Ill. Ho. of Reps., 1973-82, minority leader, 1977-80, speaker, 1981-82; lt. gov. State of Ill., 1983-91, sec. of state, 1991—. Mem. Kankakee County Bd., 1966-72, chmn., 1971-72; chmn. Ill. Literacy Coun., 1991—. With U.S. Army, Korea. Recipient Humphrey award Am. Pharm. Assn., 1980, Top award Ill. chpt. DARE, 1989, Govt. Leadership award Nat. Commn. Against Drunk Driving and MADD Govt. Leader Against Drunk Driving award, 1994-95, City Club of Chgo. Man of Yr. award, 1995. Mem. Am. Pharm. Assn., Ill. Pharm. Assn., One Hundred Club, Masons (33d degree). Republican. Methodist. Lodges: Elks, Moose, Shriners.

RYAN, JACK, physician, hospital corporation executive; b. Benton Harbor, Mich., Aug. 26, 1925; s. Leonard Joseph and Beulah (Southworth) R.; m. Lois Patricia Patterson; children: Michele, Kevin, Timothy, Sarah, Daniel. AB, Western Mich. U., 1948; postgrad., U. Mich. Law Sch., 1949-50, Emory U., 1950-51; MD, Wayne State U., 1955. Intern St. Luke's Hosp., Saginaw, Mich., 1955-56; pres. Meml. Med. Ctr., Warren, Mich., 1956-77; v.p. med. affairs Detroit-Macomb Hosps. Corp., 1976-77, pres. and chief exec. officer, 1977—; assoc. prof. medicine Wayne State U., Detroit, 1974—. Recipient Disting. Alumnus award Wayne State U. Med. Sch., 1974, Wayne State U., 1979, Western Mich. U., 1989, Disting. Key award Mich. Hosp. Assn., 1986. Fellow Am. Coll. Family Physicians, Am. Coll. Physician Execs., Detroit Acad. Medicine; mem. Internat. Health Econs. and Mgmt. Inst. (charter), Econ. Club Detroit, Detroit Athletic Club, Renaissance Club, Red Run Club. Home: 175 Hendrie Blvd Royal Oak MI 48067-2412 Office: Detroit-Macomb Hosp Corp 12000 E 12 Mile Rd Warren MI 48093-3570

RYAN, JAMES E., attorney general; married; 6 children. BA in Polit. Sci., Ill. Benedictine Coll., 1968; JD, Ill. Inst. Tech., 1971. Bar: Ill. 1971. Asst. state's atty. criminal divsn. DuPage County State's Atty.'s Office, 1971-74, 1st. asst. state's atty., 1974-76; founder Ryan & Darrah; state's atty. DuPage County State's Atty.'s Office, 1984-94; atty. gen. State of Ill., 1994—. Recipient numerous awards from various orgns. including Nat. Assn. Counties, Alliance Against Intoxicated Motorists. Republican. Office: Office of Atty General 500 S Second St Springfield IL 62706*

RYAN, JAMES ROGERS, state legislator; b. Detroit, May 16, 1963; s. James Leo and Mary (Rogers) R.; m. Terri Ann Anthony, 1991; 1 child, Sean Patrick. BS, Ea. Mich. U.; Cert. in Tchg., U. Detroit. Tchr., coach Detroit Cath. Ctrl. H.S., 1988-94; rep. Dist. 16 Mich. Ho. of Reps., 1995—. Trustee Charter Twp. Redford, 1988-92. Mem. Redford/Dearborn Hts. C. of C., Teamsters Internat., KC. Office: Mich House of Reps State Capitol Lansing MI 48913

RYAN, JOHN MICHAEL, landscape architect; b. Chgo., Sept. 27, 1946; s. Terrance Joseph and Norma (Morris) R.; m. Victoria Jean Wheetley, June 26, 1986; children: Micheline Giannasi-Mennecke, Tony Giannasi, Nick Giannasi, Andrew Morris Jennings, Melissa Contance Victoria, Cameron

Michael Montgomery. B in Landscape Architecture, U. Ill., 1969. Registered landscape architect, Ill., Mich., Ariz.; cert. CLARB. Assoc. landscape architect Carl Garnder & Assocs., Inc., Chgo., 1969-71; sr. landscape architect Collaborative Rsch. & Planning, Chgo., 1971-73; v.p. Michael L. Ives & Assocs., Inc., Downers Grove, Ill., 1973-84; pres. Ives/Ryan Group, Inc., Naperville, 1984—. Prin. works include renovation of Old Orchard Shopping Ctr., Skokie, Ill., Lake Katherine Nature Preserve, Palos Heights, Ill., Crystal Tree Residential Golf Course Cmty., Orland Park, Ill., Corporetum Office Campus, Lisle, Ill. Crew chief search and rescue USCG Aux., 1980—. Recipient Nat. Landscape award Am. Assn. Nurserymen, 1988, 92, Key award in landscape arch. Home Bldrs. Assn. Greater Chgo., 1981, 84, 90. Mem. Am. Assn. Landscape Archs. (Merit award 1991, 94, 96), Ill. Landscape Contractors Assn. (Gold award 1991, 96, Silver award 1986, 90, 93, Merit award 1988, 91), Chgo. Hort. Soc., Perennial Plant Assn. (Nat. Honor award 1993), Morton Arboretum.

RYAN, KENNETH ROBERT, JR., accountant, stockbroker; b. Salem, W.Va., Aug. 8, 1947; s. Kenneth Robert Sr. and Helen Lee (Middleton) R.; m. Judy Ann Grandon, May 16, 1970. AAS, W.Va. U., 1970; BS in Acctg., Marietta Coll., 1974; postgrad., W.Va. U., 1976-80. CPA, W.Va., N.C. Staff acct. Arthur Andersen & Co., Chattanooga, Tenn., 1974-75; sr. acct. Kaiser Aluminum, Ravenswood, W.Va., 1975-76; owner Ryan & Co., CPA's, Ravenswood, 1976-85; tax mgr. Doak, Cuppett & Poling, Clarksburg, W.Va., 1985-89; stockbroker Parker/Hunter Inc., 1989—. Contbr. articles to profl. jours. Bd. dirs. Jackson County Devel. Coun., W.Va., 1981-83; investment bd. Nat. Found. for the Prevention of Child Abuse. With USN, 1965-68, Vietnam. Mem. AICPA (tax divsn.), VFW, W.Va. Soc. CPAs, Am. Philatelic Soc., Exch. Club (pres. Ohio-W. Va. dist. 1993-94), Nat. Exch. Club (investment bd., planned giving bd.). Republican. Methodist.

RYAN, LEO VINCENT, business educator; b. Waukon, Iowa, Apr. 6, 1927; s. John Joseph and Mary Irene (O'Brien) R. BS, Marquette U., 1949; MBA, DePaul U., 1954; PhD, St. Louis U., 1958; postgrad., Catholic U. Am., 1951-52, Bradley U., 1952-54, Northwestern U., 1950; LLD, Seton Hall U., 1988. Joined Order Clerics of St. Viator, Roman Cath. Ch., 1950. Mem. faculty Marquette U., Milw., 1957-65; dir. continuing edn. summer sessions, coord. evening divs. Marquette U., 1959-65, prof. indsl. mgmt., 1964; prof. and chmn. dept. mgmt. Loyola U., Chgo., 1965-66; adj. prof. mgmt. Loyola U., 1967-69; dep. dir. Peace Corps, Lagos, Nigeria, 1966-67; dir. Western Nigeria Peace Corps, Ibadan, 1967-68; asst. superior gen. and treas. gen. Clerics of St. Viator, Rome, 1968-69; dir. edn. Am. province Clerics of St. Viator, Arlington Heights, Ill., 1969-74; pres. St. Viator High Sch., 1972-74; dean, prof. mgmt. Coll. Bus. Adminstrn. U. Notre Dame, Ind., 1975-80; dean Coll. Commerce DePaul U., 1980-88, prof. mgmt. Coll. Commerce, 1980—, Wicklander prof. profl. ethics, 1993-94; dir. Peace Corps tng. programs Marquette U., 1962-65; adj. prof. human devel. St. Mary's Coll., Winona, Minn., 1972-74; mem. sch. bd. Archdiocese Chgo., 1972-75, vice chmn., 1973-75, mem. nat. edn. com. U.S. Cath. Conf., 1971-75, mem. exec. com., 1973-75; mem. nat. adv. bd. Benedictine Sisters of Nauvoo, 1973-83; mem. nat. adv. coun. SBA, 1982-85, vice chmn. minority bus., 1982-85, exec. com. Chgo. chpt., 1982-84; vis. prof. U. Ife, Ibadan, 1967-68; mem. adv. bd. 1st Bank-Milw., 1991-93, chmn. trust audit com., 1980-85, chmn. audit and examination com., 1985-90, mem. bus. adv. coun., 1991-93; bd. dirs. Vilter Mfg. Co., external dir. Vilter ESOP, Filbert Corp., Vilter Internat. (now Vilter Export Corp.), Henricksen & Co., Inc.; mem. fin. commn. Clerics of St. Viator, 1978—, mem. provincial chpt., 1985—; cons. Pontifical Commn. on Justice and Peace, 1968-70; vis. prof. Helsinki Sch. Econs., Mikkeli, Finland, 1990, 91, 94, 96, Poznan (Poland) Sch. Mgmt., 1991, 92, 93; coord. Polish Am. summer program in econs. Acad. Econs., Poznan, 1991; Fulbright prof. Adam Mickiewicz U., Poland, 1993, 94, 95; co-chair bus. and profl. com. Archdiocese of Chgo. Sesquetennial Com. Out Reach Divsn. Ctrl. Planning Group, 1993-94. Mem. editl. bd. Internat. Jour. Value Based Mgmt., European Bus. Jour., Bus. Ethics Quar. Mem. Pres.'s Com. on Employment Handicapped, 1959-65, Wis. Gov.'s Com. on Employment Handicapped, 1959-65, Wis. Gov.'s Com. on UN, 1961-64, Burnham Park Planning Commn., 1982-88; bd. dirs. Ctr. Pastoral Liturgy U. Notre Dame, 1976-79, Lake Forest Grad. Sch. Mgmt., 1989-91; trustee St. Mary of Woods Coll., 1978-81; regent Seton Hall U., 1981-87, mem. acad. affairs com., 1981-87, chmn., 1983-87; trustee Cath. Theol. Union, U. Chgo., 1992-95; dir. Ctr. for Enterprise Devel., 1992-95; fellow St. Edmonds Coll. Cambridge U., 1992; mem. Cath. Commn. Intellectual and Cultural Affairs, 1992—, Cath. Campaign for Am., 1994—; bd. dirs. Internat. Bus. Ethics Inst., Am. Grad. Sch. Internat. Mgmt., 1995—, Assn. Profl. Ethics, 1995—; mem. adv. coun. Mgmt. Edn. in Poland, U. Md., College Park, 1995—. Recipient Freedom award Berlin Commn., 1961, chieftancy title Asoju Atoaja of Oshogbo Oba Adenle I, Yorubaland, Nigeria, 1967, B'nai B'rith Interfaith award, Milw., 1963, Disting. Alumnus award Marquette U., 1974, DePaul U., 1976, Tchr. of Yr. award Beta Alpha Psi, 1980, Centennial Alumni Achievement award Marquette U., 1981, Boland Meml. Disting. Alumni award, St. Louis, 1989, Disting. Alumni and Bicentennial awards Jesuit Bus. Schs., 1989, Pres.' award St. Viator H.S., 1992, Medal of Merit Adam Mickiewicz U., 1995, Excellence in Teaching award DePaul U., 1995; Brother Leo V. Ryan award created in his honor Cath. Bus. Edn. Assn., 1962; Ryan Scholars in Mgmt. established in his honor DePaul U., 1989, Outstanding Svc. award, 1991-93; Ryan Scholarship established in his honor St. Vinton High Sch., 1992; named Man of C. of C., Milw., 1959, Marquette U. Bus. Adminstrn. Alumni Man of Yr., 1974, Tchr. of Yr. U. Notre Dame, 1980; Milw. Bd. Realtors traveling fellow, 1964, Nat. Assn. Purchasing Agts. faculty fellow, 1958, German Am. Acad. Exch. Coun. fellow, summer 1983, Presdl. fellow Am. Grad. Sch. Internat. Mgmt., 1989, vis. scholar, 1995, Malone fellow in Islamic studies, 1990, fellow Kosciuszko Found. Adam Mickiewicz U., 1990; scholar-in-residence Mgmt. Sch. Imperial Coll. Sci. and Tech. U. London, 1988; vis. scholar U. Calif., Berkeley, spring 1989; USIA Acad. Specialists grantee (3), Poland, 1991, 92, 93; fellow St. Edmund's Coll. Cambridge U., 1992; named vis. rsch. fellow Von Hugel Inst., 1992-93; scholar-in-residence Am. Grad. Sch. Internat. Mgmt., 1995; guest scholar Kellogg Inst. Internat. Studies U. Notre Dame, 1997. Mem. Cath. Bus. Edn. Assn. (nat. pres. 1960-62, nat. exec. bd. 1960-64), Assn. Sch. Bus. Ofcls. (nat. com. chmn. 1965-67), Am. Assembly Collegiate Schs. Bus. (com. internat. affairs 1977-84, chmn. 1981-84, bd. dirs. 1981-87, program chmn. 1979-80, exec. com., chmn. projects/svc. mgmt. com. 1984-86), Am. Fgn. Svc. Assn., Am. Assn. Profl. Ethics (bd. dirs. 1996—), Allamakee County Hist. Soc. (charter life), Acad. Internat. Bus., Acad. Mgmt. (social issues div., chmn. membership com. 1990-91), Ancient Order of Hibernians, Nat. Returned Peace Corps Assn., Atomic Vets. Assn., August Derleth Soc., Chgo. Area Return Peace Corps Vols., Econ. Club Chgo., Chgo. Coun. Fgn. Rels., Coun. Fgn. Rels. (Chgo. com.), European Found. Mgmt. Edn., European Bus. Ethics Network, Soc. Bus. Ethics (mem. exec. com. 1991—, pres. 1993-94, adv. bd. 1995—), Assn. Social Econs. (life), Assn. Christian Economists, Inst. Global Ethics, Inst. Internat. Ethics (adv. bd.), Dubuque County Hist. Soc., Iowa Hist. Soc., Iowa Postal History Soc., Fulbright Assn. (life), Internat. Assn. for Bus. and Soc. (founder), Internat. Soc. for Bus., Econs. and Ethics (charter), Internat. Trade and Fin. Assn. (founder, bd. dirs. 1989-92, 96—, v.p. membership 1991-92), Internat. Assn. Environ. Ethics, Internat. Learned Soc. Praxiology, Polish Inst. Arts and Scis. in Am., Milw. Press Club (hon.), USS Mt. McKinley Reunion Assn. (hon. chaplain AGC-7 1989-96, Disting. Svc. award 1991), Alpha Sigma Nu, Alpha Kappa Psi (bd. dirs. found. 1985-91, vice chmn. 1987-91, chmn. scholarship com. 1987-91, chmn. devel. com. 1987, mem. exec. com. 1990-91, Bronze Disting. Svc. award 1949, Silver Disting. Svc. award 1958), Beta Alpha Psi, Beta Gamma Sigma (co-chair 75th Anniversary com. Ill., faculty advisor DePaul chpt. 1986-92), Delta Mu Delta, Pi Gamma Mu, Tau Kappa Epsilon.

RYAN, MARK ANTHONY, architect; b. Council Bluffs, Iowa, Sept. 6, 1964; s. Paul Elmer and Darreline Kay (Wyland) R.; m. Shelli Ann Hagerbaumer, Sept. 26, 1992. BA in Architecture with distinction, Iowa State U., 1987. Registered profl. architect, Wis. Project architect U.S. Army Corps. of Engrs., Omaha, 1987-90, architect, security engr., 1990-91, environ. project mgr., 1991—; owner Ryan Designs, Omaha, 1987—, The Ryan Co., Omaha, 1994—; bd. advisors Fitness Plus, Council Bluffs, Iowa, 1990-92; expert witness for pvt. attys., Iowa and Nebr., 1991—. Chmn. City Devel. Commn., Council Bluffs, 1992; bd. trustees San. and Improvement Dist. No. 142, Douglas County, Nebr., 1995-96. State of Iowa scholar, 1982. Mem. AIA (sec. S.W. Iowa sect. 1991, treas. 1992, v.p. 1993, pres. 1994-96), Soc. Am. Mil. Engrs., Nat. Trust for Hist. Preservation, Golden Key, Phi Kappa Phi, Tau Sigma Delta. Home: 9030 Raven Oaks Dr Omaha NE 68152-1759 Office: US Army Corps of Engrs 215 N 17th St Omaha NE 68102-4910

RYAN, MARY NELL H., training consultant; b. Milw., Oct. 17, 1956; d. Robert Healey and Elizabeth Anne (Schulte) R.; 1 child, Katharine Scarlett. BA, Marquette U., 1979; MS, U. Wis., Milw., 1991. Tchr. St. Francis Borgia Sch., Cedarburg, Wis., 1979-81; dir. pub. rels. Aerobics West Club, N.Y.C., 1981; unit head, team leader Northwestern Mut. Life Ins. Co., Milw., 1982-84, asst. supr., 1984-86, tng. coord., 1986-87, mgr. tng., 1987-92; tng. cons. for ins. industry Workplace Learning, Inc., Milw., 1992—; cons. Aetna Life and Casualty Co., Hartford, Conn., 1988, Robertson-Ryan & Co., Milw., 1989, Blue Cross/Blue Shield United of Wis., Northwestern Mut. Life Ins. Co., CMI Group, Inc., Homes for Ind. Living, Inc., Aurora Health Care, Literacy Svcs. Wis., Executrain, Inc., Milw. First in Quality, Wis. Quality Network, United Wis. Svcs., Inc., Ameritech, Milw. Art Mus., Blood Ctr. Southeastern Wis., Meretz, Inc., Radiology Assocs. Wis., Deluxe Data, Inc., Portable Solution, Inc., Hewlett-Packard Users Group of Wis., Miller Brewing Co.; guest lectr. U. Wis., Milw., 1989, Milw. Area Tech. Coll., 1990, Marquette U., 1990; speaker confs., developer/trainer workshops. Mem. exec. com. Lakefront Festival Arts, Milw., 1985—, vol. com. chair, silent auction chair; exec. fundraiser United Performing Arts Fund, Milw., 1986; com. chmn. Jr. League Milw., 1983-87; fundraiser YMCA Ptnr. Youth, Milw. 1987-88; tutorHead Start Read with Me program, 1993—. Recipient gold medal Life Communicators Assn., 1987. Mem. ASTD (bd. dirs. Wis. chpt., membership com. 1989-90, chmn. Train Am.'s Workforce and comty. svcs. 1992-94), Milw. Mgmt. Support Orgn. (bd. dirs. 1988), Wis. Ins. Club (spkr.), InRoads (bd. dirs. Wis. chpt.), Phi Kappa Phi. Office: Workplace Learning Inc 1426 W Westport Cir Mequon WI 53092-5753

RYAN, MICHAEL, investment management consultant; b. Evansville, Ind., Oct. 5, 1951; s. Mike and Mabel (Mason) R.; m. Pamela Marie Bogdalik, Aug. 19, 1973; children: Dylan Michael, Devin Michael. BA, Ind. U., 1974, MA, 1978. Cert. fin. planner; cert. investment mgmt. analyst. Filmmaker Image Makers, Bloomington, Ind., 1978-79; travel cons. Am. Express Co., Chgo., 1979; pvt. investor Wilmette, Ill., 1979-82; pres. Ryan Fin. Advisors, Ltd., Wilmette, 1983-92, Paragon Asset Mgmt., Wilmette, 1983—; bd. dirs. Fin. Svcs. Mut. Ins. Co., chmn., 1994—; mem. adj. faculty Coll. of Fin. Planning, Denver, 1984-90. Named One of Am's. Best Fin. Planners Money Mag., 1987. Mem. Investment Mgmt. Cons. Assn., Inst. Cert. Fin. Planners (v.p. greater Chgo. chpt. 1985-86, pres. 1986-87, chmn. 1987-88, nat. bd. dirs. 1989, 90, Svc. award 1988, 90, Ann. Retreat dean 1991, bd. dirs. 1996-97), Internat. Assn. Fin. Planners (bd. dirs. Greater O'Hare chpt. 1984-86, North Shore chpt. 1987-88, Svc. award 1986), Am. Assn. Ind. Investors (life), Mich. Shore Club. Office: Paragon Asset Mgmt 1000 Skokie Blvd Ste 570 Wilmette IL 60091-1154

RYAN, MICHAEL J., marketing professional; b. Jackson, Mich., May 20, 1946; m. Lynda Hovey, July 12, 1968; children: Bethany Lyn Ryan Thompson, Craig M., Kevin A. BBA, U. Mich., 1973. Data control analyst Consuemrs Power Co., Jackson, 1973-79, gas supply coord., 1979-80, coal contract adminstr., 1980-81, supr. gas aquisition, 1981-90; dir. gas mktg. Ward Lake Energy, Gaylord, Mich., 1990—. Mem. various bds., coms. and past officers Evangelical Free Ch., Gaylord, 1990—. With USAF, 1966-70. Mem. C. of C., Mich. Oil & Gas Assn., Petroleum Accts. Soc. Mich., Exch. Club. Evangelican. Home: 2520 Krys Rd Gaylord MI 49735 Office: Ward Lake Energy PO Box 1663 685 E M32 Gaylord MI 49735

RYAN, MIKE, health association administrator; b. Maysville, Ky., June 20, 1961; s. Robert Michael and Rose Marie (Maley) R. BA in Journalism, Ohio State U., 1983, MPA in Pub. Policy and Mgmt., 1990. Pub. rels. dir. Ohio affiliate Nat. Soc. to Prevent Blindness, Columbus, 1983-88; communications specialist Cen. Benefits Mut. Ins. Co., Columbus, 1988-91; exec. dir. Nat. Vol. Health Agys. of Ohio, Columbus, 1991—, nominating chair, 1988, pub. rels. chmn., 1984-85; vice chmn. Nat. Vol. Health Agys. Coun. of States, Washington, 1987. Mem. steering com. Ohio Devel. Disabilities Alliance for Svc. Eligibility, 1992-93. Mem. Internat. Assn. Bus. Communicators (dist. dir. 1992-93, treas. dist. 7, 1990-92, pres. Columbus chpt. 1991-92, v.p. 1990-91, rels. dir. 1987-88, comms. dir. 1986-87, accreditation bd. 1996-98), Am. Assn. Soc. Execs. Home: 495 W 4th Ave Columbus OH 43201-3176 Office: Nat Vol Health Agys PO Box 1263 Columbus OH 43216-1263

RYAN, RICHARD KIRK, mechanical engineer; b. Des Moines, Nov. 16, 1953. Student, Grandview Coll., Des Moines, 1973-74; BS in Mech. Design, ARcall Vocat. Sch., Ankeny, Iowa, 1975. Chief design drafter Amana Refrigeration Inc., Amana, Iowa, 1976—. Republican. Roman Catholic. Office: Amana Refrigeration Inc Hwy 220 Amana IA 52204

RYAN, ROBERT COLLINS, lawyer; b. Evanston, Ill., Sept. 15, 1953; s. Donald Thomas and Patricia J. (Collins) R.; m. Joanne Kay Holata, Nov. 5, 1983. BA in Econs., BSIE with high honors, U. Ill., 1976; JD, Northwestern U., 1979. Bar: Ill. 1979, U.S. Dist. Ct. (no. dist.) Ill. 1980, U.S. Ct. Appeals (Fed. cir.) 1982, U.S. Supreme Ct. 1984. Assoc., Allegretti, Newitt, Witcoff & McAndrews, Ltd., Chgo., 1979-83, ptnr. 1983-88; founding ptnr. McAndrews, Held & Malloy, Ltd., Chgo., 1988—; lectr. engring. law Northwestern U. Tech. Inst., Evanston, Ill., 1981-85, adj. prof. engring. law, 1985-90; lectr. patent law & appellate practice John Marshall Law Sch., 1991-93, adj. prof. patent law & appellate advocacy, 1993—. Exec. editor Northwestern Jour. Internat. Law & Bus., 1978-79. Contbr. articles to profl. jours. James scholar U. Ill., 1976. Mem. ABA, Fed. Cir. Bar Assn., Intellectual Property Law Assn. Chgo., Licensing Execs. Soc., Tau Beta Pi, Phi Eta Sigma, Alpha Pi Mu, Phi Kappa Phi. Home: 61 Hawkins Cir Wheaton IL 60187-8464 Office: McAndrews Held & Malloy Ltd Citicorp Ctr 34th Fl 500 W Madison St Chicago IL 60661-2511

RYAN, RONALD LEE, highway patrolman; b. Poplar Bluff, Mo., July 28, 1948; s. Arthur A. Ryan and Betty L. (Bollinger) Padgett; m. Brenda Pauline Ryan, Nov. 17, 1968; children: Ronald L. II, Christopher Scott, Trisha. BS, S.E. Mo. State U., 1980; M in Criminal Justice Adminstrn., Ctrl. Mo. State U., 1990. Patrolman Mo. State Hwy Patrol, Jefferson City, 1971—; firearms instr. Mo. State Hwy. Patrol, 1986-96; adj. instr. Mid. South Inst., Walls, Miss., 1992-94, MOCIC, Springfield, Mo., 1985-93; trainer, instr. Multiple Police Agys., 1985-96; creator Field Tng. Officer Program, 1986; co-creator drug interdiction Criminal Patrol Tactics, 1986-93; instr. USN Seals, Walls, 1992-94. Pres. Jefferson City High Sch. Booster Club, 1990-91; mem. PTO, Jefferson City, 1991-92. Sgt. USMC, 1967-70. Mem. Mo. State Troopers Assn. Republican. Baptist. Home: 309 Troy Jefferson City MO 65109 Office: Mo State Highway Patrol 1510 E Elm St Jefferson City MO 65101-4118

RYAN, STEPHEN COLLISTER, funeral director; b. Salina, Kans., Jan. 10, 1942; s. Kenneth Richard and Janys (Collister) R.; m. Lynne Katheryn Slease, June 18, 1966; children: Scott Richard, Carrie Anne. BS in Bus. Adminstrn., U. Kans., 1964; Cert. in Mortuary Sci., Kans. U. Med. Ctr., 1965. Cert. funeral svc. practitioner; lic. funeral dir. and embalmer. Sec.-treas. Ryan Mortuary, Inc., Salina, 1969-80, pres., COO, 1980—. Contbr. articles to profl. jours. Mem., chmn. City Planning Commn., Salina, 1981-85; mem. Salina City Commn., 1985-93, mayor, 1987-88, 91-92; chmn. Govt. Bldg. Authority, Salina, 1990-91, 92-93. Capt. USAF, 1965-69. Mem. Nat. Selected Morticians (bd. dirs. 1993—, pres. 1995—), Nat. Funeral Dirs. Assn. (Spl. Recognition award 1991), Kans. Funeral Dirs. Assn. (bd. dirs. 1984-92, pres. 1990-91), Morticians of the S.W. (Kans. Funeral Dir. of Yr. 1991), Salina Area C. of C. (bd. dirs. 1982-85, 94—, vice chair 1984-85, sec. treas. 1994-95, chmn. 1996—) Lions, Masons (Knight Cmmdrs. Ct. of Honor, 32 KCCH), Shriners, Phi Gamma Delta. Republican. Lutheran. Home: 2313 Melrose Ln Salina KS 67401-3546 Office: Ryan Mortuary Inc 137 N 8th St Salina KS 67401-2686

RYBA, JOHN J., state legislator; b. Aug. 10, 1929; m. Gertrude Ryba, 1954; children: Sue, Sandy, Steve. Former city councilman Green Bay; former mem. Green Bay Planning Commn. Met. Sewerage Commn. and Transit Authority; Wis. state assemblyman Dist. 90, 1992—. Co-author: Informent Bill, Legalizing Pepper Protection Spray; author: Responsible Beverage Survey. Recipient Spl. Olympics Achievement award, 1991-92. Mem. VFW (life), Elks (life mem. lodge 259, Elk of Yr. 1988-91), Am. Legion (life mem.). Address: 714 Wilson Ave Green Bay WI 54303*

RYCHECKY, HELEN ROSE, private school system administrator; b. Ohiowa, Nebr., May 28, 1922; d. Cyril Methodias and Helen (Votipka) Bernasek; m. Leo Rychecky, Oct. 6, 1945 (dec. 1988); 1 child, Jack A. BS, U. Nebr., 1960. Elem. tchr. rural schs. Fillmore County, Nebr., 1939-42; elem. tchr. Alliance (Nebr.) Pub. Schs., 1944-46, Ohiowa Pub. Schs., 1947; kindergarten tchr. Sunflower Rural Schs., Mitchell, Nebr., 1951-53; elem. tchr. Scottsbluff (Nebr.) Pub. Schs., 1953-72, jr. high counselor, 1972-73; co-mgr. Family Farms in Morrill, Kimball and Fillmore Counties, Nebr., 1973-88, mgr., 1988—; assoc. prof. U. Nebr. summer session, 1962. Mem. AAUW, Presbyn. Women Assn., Pi Lambda Theta. Republican. Home: 641 N Mineral Ave Apt 1416 Littleton CO 80120

RYDELL, CATHERINE M., state legislator; b. Grand Forks, N.D., May 8, 1950; d. Hilary Harold and Catherine F. (Ireland) Wilson; m. Charles D. Rydell, 1971; children: Kimberly, Jennifer, Michael. BS, U. N.D., 1971. Mem. N.D. Ho. of Reps., 1985—, mem. supreme ct. judicial planning, govt., vet. affairs com., past rep. caucus leader; coord. cmty. svc. Bismarck Jr. Coll.; bus. mgr. surg. svc. St. Alexius Med. Ctr. Bd. dirs. Mission Valley Family, YMCA, N.D. Early Childhood Tng. Ctr., Ronald McDonald Found., CHAND; mem. state adv. bd. Casey Family Program, Juvenile Justice; mem. lay adv. bd. St. Alexius; mem. regional adv. bd. Luth. Social Svcs.; mem. N.D. State Centennial Com., N.D. State Mus. Art. Recipient Outstanding Svc. award Tobacco Free N.D., Legislator of Yr. award Children's Caucus, Guardian of Bus. award Nat. Fedn. Ind. Bus. Mem. Philanthropic and Edn. Orgn. Sisterhood, N.D. Med. Assn. (v.p.), Gamma Phi Beta. Home: 535 Assiniboin Dr Bismarck ND 58501-0212 Office: ND House of Reps Office Of House Mems Bismarck ND 58505*

RYDER, TOM, state legislator; b. Medora, Ill., May 17, 1949; m. Peggy Ryder; 2 children. BA, No. Ill. U.; JD, Washington and Lee U. Ill. state rep. Dist. 97, 1983—; mem. appropriations II, human svcs. Ill. Ho. Reps., state govt. adminstrn. transp. and motor vehicles coms., chmn. house rep. policy com., mem. health care, labor and commerce com., pub. safety, infrastructure appropriations coms., joint com. adminstrn. rules, minority dep. leader; minority dept. leader, atty. Mem. Ill. Nat. Guard. Mem. Lions, Elks, Moose, Am. Legion. Republican. Home: 309 N Liberty St Jerseyville IL 62052-1516*

RYDHOLM, RALPH WILLIAMS, advertising agency executive; b. Chgo., June 1, 1937; s. Thor Gabriel and Vivian Constance (Williams) R.; m. Jo Anne Beechler, Oct. 5, 1963; children: Kristin, Erik, Julia. B.A., Northwestern U., 1958, postgrad. in bus. adminstrn, 1958-59; postgrad. Advanced Mgmt. Program, Harvard U., 1982. Acct. trainee, copywriter Young & Rubicam Advt., Chgo., 1960-63; copywriter Post-Keyes-Gardner Advt., Chgo., 1963, E. H. Weiss Advt., Chgo., 1963-65; copy group head BBDO Advt., Chgo., 1965-66; with J. Walter Thompson Advt., Chgo., 1966-86; creative dir., v.p. J. Walter Thompson Advt., 1969-76, exec. creative dir., 1976-86, sr. v.p., 1972-80, exec. v.p., dir., 1980-86; exec. v.p., chief creative officer, dir. Ted Bates Worldwide, N.Y.C., 1986-87; mng. ptnr., chmn. mgmt. com., chief creative officer, chmn., CEO Tatham EURO RSCG Advt., Chgo., 1987—; bd. dirs., ops. com., chmn. creative com., vice chmn., 1996, 4A's, guest spkr. Ad Age Workshop, 1969, 77, 86, Adweek Seminar, 1993; keynote spkr. Stephen B. Kelly Awards, 1993. Mem. assoc. bd. Newberry Libr. Assn. With USAFR, 1959-65. Recipient Clio awards, Internat. Broadcast award, Lion awards, Cannes Film Festival, Addy awards; named one of Top 100 Creative Ad People Ad Daily, 1972, Advt. Exec. of Yr. Adweek, 1991, Best Man in Advt. McCalls and Adweek, 1992, Creative Leader Wall St. Jour., 1994. Mem. ASCAP, Chgo. Advt. Fedn., Saddle and Cycle Club, Econ. Club Chgo. (bd. dirs.), Northwestern Club Chgo., Harvard Club Chgo., Exec.'s Club Chgo., Tavern Club, Carlton Club, Chikaming Country Club (Mich.), Dunes Club (Mich.), Phi Delta Theta. Office: Tatham EURO RSCG 980 N Michigan Ave Chicago IL 60611-4501

RYNTZ, ROSE ANN, chemist; b. Detroit, July 23, 1957; d. Raymond Leonard and Rose Marie (Schabel) R. BS, Wayne State U., 1979; PhD, U. Detroit, 1983. Rsch. chemist Dow Chem. Co., Midland, Mich., 1983-85; sr. rsch. chemist Ford Motor Co., Mt. Clemens, Mich., 1985-86; group leader DuPont, Mt. Clemens, 1986-88; coatings specialist Dow Corning Corp., Midland, 1988-89; lab. dir. Akzo Coatings, Inc., Troy, Mich., 1989; tech. dir. Akzo Coatings, Inc., Troy, 1990-92; tech. specialist Ford Motor Co., Dearborn, Mich., 1992—; adj. prof. U. Detroit, 1985—; cons. Maro Communications, Fla., 1990—. Patentee in field; contbr. articles to profl. jours. Tchr. Polymer Edn., Detroit, 1981. Mem. Am. Chem. Soc. (chem. chmn, 1988-90), Fed. Soc. Coating Tech. (tech. chmn. 1985-95, profl. devel. com. chmn. 1990—, editl. rev. bd. 1989—, tech. adv. bd. 1992-95), Soc. Automotive Engrs. Office: Ford Motor Co 401 Southfield Rd Dearborn MI 48120-9999

RYON, MORTIMER, lawyer; b. Scranton, Pa., July 15, 1929; s. John Lesley and Katherine (Hummel) R.; m. Kathleen Ferenbach, Aug. 22, 1953 (div.); children: Kathleen P., Carolyn L., Helen Jennifer, Mortimer Jr.; m. Sandra Lipson, July 3, 1971. AB, Lafayette Coll., 1951; JD, Cornell U., 1957. Sr. atty. Akzona Inc., Asheville, N.C., 1975-80, assoc. gen. counsel, 1980-83; counsel Internat. Salt Co., Clarks Summit, Pa., 1985—; sec., assoc. gen. counsel Akzo Am. Inc., N.Y.C., 1983—; sec. Akzo Am. Found., N.Y.C., 1983—; chmn. Akzo Am. Polit. Action Com., N.Y.C., 1984—. Pres. Asheville Symphony, 1978-80; vice chmn. Asheville Country Day Sch., 1980-82. Served with U.S. Army, 1952-54, Korea. Mem. ABA, Pa. Bar Assn., N.C. Bar Assn. Home: Paxson Rd PO Box 378 Solebury PA 18963-0378 Office: Akzo Am Inc 7 Livingstone Ave Dobbs Ferry NY 10522-3401

RYPIEN, MARK ROBERT, professional football player; b. Calgary, Alta., Can., Oct. 2, 1962. Student, Wash. State U. With Washington Redskins, 1987-94, Cleve. Browns, 1994—. Named to Pro Bowl team, 1989, 91; recipient Most Valuable Player award Superbowl, 1992. Office: Cleve Browns 80 1st Ave Berea OH 44017-1238*

RYU, KYOO-HAI LEE, physiologist; b. Seoul, Republic of Korea, Sept. 5, 1948; came to U.S., 1972; d. Hee Soon and Jung Ock Lee; m. David Tai-Hyung Ryu, May 13, 1978; children: Eugenia, Christina, John. BS, Yonsei U., Seoul, 1971; PhD, U. Minn., 1981. Postdoctoral fellow U. Minn., Mpls., 1980-81, staff scientist, 1981-82; sr. rsch. assoc. Wright State U., Dayton, Ohio, 1985-91; adminstr. Ohio Ctr. of Cosmetic Surgery, Bellefontaine, Ohio, 1991—. Mem. Am. Physiol. Soc., Biophys. Soc., Soc. Gen. Physiologists. Home: 15 Bexley Ave Springfield OH 45503-1103

SAAL, HOWARD MAX, clinical geneticist, pediatrician, educator; b. N.Y.C., Aug. 20, 1951; s. Josef and Ester (Morgenstern) S.; m. Cara Tina Schweitzer, May 3, 1987; 1 child, Rebecca. BS, U. Mass., Amherst, 1973, MS, 1975; MD, Wayne State U., 1979. Intern pediatrics U. Conn. Med. Ctr., 1979-80; resident pediatrics U. Conn. Health Ctr., 1980-82; fellow med. genetics U. Wash. Sch. Medicine, 1982-84; dir. cytogenetics U. Conn. Health Ctr., Farmington, 1984-87; vice chmn. med. genetics Children's Nat. Med. Ctr., Washington, 1987-93; head clin. genetics Children's Nat. Med. Ctr., Cin., 1993—; asst. prof. pediats. George Washington U., Washington, 1987-93, assoc. prof. pediats., 1993; assoc. prof. clin. pediats. U. Cin. Sch. Medicine, 1993—. Contbr. articles to profl. jours. Mem. med. adv. com. Nat. Neurofibromatosis Found., N.Y.C., 1987—; mem. health profl. adv. com. March of Dimes, Arlington, Va., 1991-93; bd. dirs. Capital Area March of Dines, 1993. Tng. grantee NIH, 1979-82. Fellow Am. Acad. Pediats., Am. Coll. Med. Genetics; mem. Am. Soc. Human Genetics, Soc. Craniofacial Genetics (sec.-treas. 1990—). Home: 3715 Monets Ln Cincinnati OH 45241-3847 Office: Childrens Hosp Med Ctr 3333 Burnet Ave Cincinnati OH 45229-3026

SAAM, ROBERT HARRY, human resources consultant; b. Toledo, Ohio, Mar. 7, 1947; s. Robert J. and Dorothy H. (Kinney) S.; B.A., U. Toledo, 1970; MS Edn1. Psychology U. Wis., 1993; m. Pamela Soder, Oct. 30, 1982; children—Robert C., Cara B., Stacia J. Investigative supr. Ohio Civil Rights Commn., Cleve., 1973-76; counciliator U.S. EEO Commn., Cin., 1976-79; mgr. labor relations Internat. Minerals & Chems., Mundelein, Ill., 1979-85; dir. Human Resource Svcs., Rexnord, Inc., Brookfield, Wis., 1985-87; v.p./owner Thompson Consulting Ltd., Brookfield, 1987—. Advisor to Cleveland Hts.-Univ. Hts. Bd. of Edn. Com. on Minority Employment, 1975-76. Mem. Indsl. Relations Research Assn., Am. Compensation Assn., Human Resources Mgmt. Assn. Democrat. Contbr. articles to profl. jours. Home:

646 N 77th St Milwaukee WI 53213-3512 Office: 17700 W Capitol Dr Brookfield WI 53045-2006

SAARI, JOHN WILLIAM, JR., lawyer; b. Jersey City, Oct. 12, 1937; s. John William Sr. and Ina Marie (Bain) S.; m. Susan Jo Olson, Aug. 27, 1967 (div. June 1971); m. Marjorie Ann Palm, Nov. 16, 1973. Student, Duke U., 1955-58, U. N.C., 1962-63; JD with honors, Ill. Inst. Tech., Chgo., 1972. Bar: Ill. 1972, U.S. Dist. Ct. (no. dist.) Ill. 1972, Wis. 1980, U.S. Dist. Ct. (ea. and we. dists.) Wis. 1980, U.S. Ct. Appeals (7th cir.) 1972. Assoc. Yates, Goff, Gustafson & Been, Chgo., 1972-76, Hubbard, Hubbard, O'Brien & Hall, Chgo., 1976-78; atty. Ill. Bell Telephone Co., Chgo., 1978-79; assoc. Cirilli Law Office, Rhinelander, Wis., 1979-83; pvt. practice Rhinelander, 1983-90; ptnr. Rodd, Mouw, Saari & Krueger, Rhinelander, 1990—. Bd. dirs. Northwoods United Way, 1980-88, pres., 1983-84. With U.S. Army, 1958-61, ETO. Mem. ABA, Ill. Bar Assn., Wis. Bar Assn., Oneida-Vilas-Forest Bar Assn. (pres. 1996—), Lions (pres. Sugarcamp 1983-84). Home: 7279 Arbutus Dr Eagle River WI 54521-9249 Office: Rodd Mouw Saari & Krueger 8A W Davenport St Rhinelander WI 54501-0757

SAARI, KATHRYN CELESTE, public health nurse; b. Chgo., Sept. 3, 1948; d. H. Thaine and Margaret F. (Sauntry) Lyman; m. Charles T. Saari, Feb. 2, 1974; children: Matthew, Julia. BS in Nursing, Coll. St. Teresa, Winona, Minn., 1970. RN, Minn.; cert. pub. health nurse. Asst. head nurse St. Mary's Hosp., Rochester, Minn., 1970-73; instr. Coll. St. Teresa, Winona, 1973-74, St. Cloud (Minn.) Hosp. Sch. Nursing, 1974-76; staff nurse St. Cloud Hosp., 1976-78; instr. Minn. Area Vocat. Tech. Inst. System, St. Cloud, Alexandria, 1974-80; charge nurse Long Prairie (Minn.) Meml. Hosp., 1980-86; pub. health nurse Polk County Nursing Svc., Crookston, Minn., 1986-94, Cen. for American Indian Resources, 1994—; mem. Minn. Perinatal Guidelines Task Force, Mpls., 1988-90; dir. Improved Pregnancy Outcome Program, Crookston, Minn., 1986-94; sexuality educator, workshop presenter, 1986—; mem. adv. bd. dirs. Early Childhood Family Edn.; mem. Polk County Child Protection Team, Family Resource Group; coord. Ptnrs. in Parenting; mem. Polk County HIV Task Force; co-founded Polk County Alliance for Youth and Families, 1991-94. Chmn. Cathedral Sch. Bd., Crookston, 1987-90; mem. Diocesan Sch. Bd., Crookston, 1988-90, Jr. High Action Bd., Crookston, 1988-90, 91-94, Sr. High Action Bd., 1990-94; co-chmn. Nurses Fun Night Scholarship, Crookston, 1989-90; cert. nurse ARC; mem. Diocesan Respect Life Commn., 1987-90, Diocesan Sexuality Task Force; mem. adv. com. March Dimes Health Profl., 1992-94. Named Nurse of Yr., Polk County Nursing Svc., 1993. Mem. Minn. Perinatal Orgn., Parents Active in Cath. Edn., Minn. Pub. Health Assn. Roman Catholic. Home: 1702 Fern Ave Duluth MN 55811-2107 Office: Ctr for Am Indian Resources 211 W 4th St Duluth MN 55806-2719

SAARIO, TERRY NATALIE TINSON, foundation executive; b. McKeesport, Pa., Nov. 16, 1941; d. John Thomas and Margaret Louise (Kanyusik) Tinson; m. Leland Theodore Lynch, Jan. 22, 1983. BA, U. Calif., Riverside, 1963, MA, 1966; PhD, Claremont (Calif.) Coll., 1970. Lectr. Claremont Coll., 1969-70; mem. rsch. team S.W. Regional Lab., Inglewood, Calif., 1969-70; asst. in fed. affairs A.E.R.A., Washington, 1970-71; mem. rsch. staff Rand Corp., Santa Monica, Calif., 1971-72; sr. program officer Ford Found., N.Y.C., 1971-80; dep. asst. sec. Edn. Dept. Carter Adminstrn., Washington, 1980-81; dir. corp. cont. Standard Oil Co., Cleve., 1981-83; v.p. Pillsbury Co., Mpls., 1983-84; pres. N.W. Area Found., St. Paul, 1984-96; bd. dirs. Cowles Media Co., Mpls., Minn. Mut. Life Ins. Co., St. Paul, Employee Benefit Life (now named 1st Data Card). Contbr. articles to profl. jours. Mem. Gov.'s Commn. on Univs., Mpls., 1988; chair, bd. dirs. St. Paul Chamber Orch., Minn. Women's Campaign Fund. Recipient One of 5 Best Found. Mgrs. award Bus. Week Mag., 1990; European Cmty. Brussels fellow, 1982, U.S.-Japan Leadership fellow Japan Soc., 1990. Mem. Minn. Women's Econ. Roundtable (pres. 1988), Tomas Rivera Ctr. (trustee emeritus). Democrat. Episcopalian.

SABAU, CARMEN SYBILE, chemist; b. Cluj, Romania, Apr. 24, 1933; naturalized U.S. citizen; d. George and Antoinette Marie (Chiriac) Grigorescu; m. Mircea Nicolae Sabau, July 11, 1956; 1 child, Isabelle Carmen. MS in Inorganic and Analytical Chemistry, U. C.I. Parhon, Bucharest, Romania, 1955; PhD in Radiochemistry, U. Fridericiana, Karlsruhe, Fed. Republic of Germany, 1972. Chemist, Argonne (Ill.) Nat. Lab., 1976—. Internat. Atomic Energy Agy. fellow, 1967-68, Humboldt fellow, 1970-72. Mem. Am. Chem. Soc., Am. Nuclear Soc., Am. Romanian Acad. Arts and Sci., Assn. for Women in Sci., N.Y. Acad. Sci., Internat. Soc. Intercomm. of New Ideas, Alexander von Humboldt Assn. Am., Sigma Xi. Author: Ion-exchange Theory and Applications in Analytical Chemistry, 1967; contbr. articles to profl. jours. Home: 689 Raintree Way Bolingbrook IL 60440-1057 Office: Argonne Nat Lab 9700 S Cass Ave Bldg 205 Argonne IL 60439-4803

SABBY, LELAND, state legislator; m. Ina M. Peterson, Aug. 27, 1950; 4 children. BA, Luther Coll., 1943; postgrad., U. Notre Dame, 1943, Harvard U., 1943; MA, U. No. Colo., 1953; postgrad., U. Ill., U. N.D., Stanford U., Denver U. Tchr., 1947-48; rep. Dist. 24 N.D. Ho. of Reps., 1948-50, mem. judiciary and govt. and vet. affairs coms., 1950-85. Recipient Presdl. Award for Excellence in Teaching Math. N.D. Coun. of Tchrs. of Math. Mem. Kiwanis. Home: 1133 Sixth Ave NE Valley City ND 58072

SABEE, JANET M., mechanical engineer; b. Appleton, Wis., Feb. 11, 1968. BSME, Marquette U., 1990, MSME, 1990. Project engr. Twin Disc Inc., Racine, Wis., 1990—. Patentee synchronized clutch, resilient drive ring. Mem. Soc. Automotive Engrs. (vice chmn. tech. com. 1994—). Roman Catholic. Office: Twin Disc Inc 1328 Racine St Racine WI 53403-1758

SABERS, RICHARD WAYNE, state supreme court justice; b. Salem, S.D., Feb. 12, 1938; s. Emil William and Elrena Veronica (Godfrey) S.; m. Colleen D. Kelley, Aug. 28, 1965; children: Steven Richard, Susan Michelle, Michael Kelley. BA in English, St. John's U., Collegeville, Minn., 1960; JD, U. S.D., 1966. Bar: S.D. 1966, U.S. Dist. Ct. S.D. 1966, U.S. Ct. Appeals (8th cir.) 1983. From assoc. to ptnr. Moore, Rasmussen, Sabers & Kading, Sioux Falls, S.D., 1966-86; justice Supreme Ct. S.D., Pierre and Sioux Falls, 1986—. Mem. editorial bd. U. S.D. Law Rev., 1965-66. State rep. March of Dimes, Bismarck, N.D., 1963; bd. dirs. St. Joseph Cathedral, Sioux Falls, 1971-86; trustee, bd. dirs. O'Gorman Found., Sioux Falls, 1978-86; active sch. bd. O'Gorman High Sch., Sioux Falls, 1985-86. Lt. U.S. Army, 1960-63. Named Outstanding Young Religious Leader, Jaycees, Sioux Falls, 1971. Mem. ABA, S.D. Bar Assn., Inst. Jud. Adminstrn., St. John's Alumni Assn. (pres. Sioux Falls chpt. 1975-91). Republican. Roman Catholic. Home: 1409 E Cedar Ln Sioux Falls SD 57103-4514 Office: SD Supreme Ct 500 E Capitol Ave Pierre SD 57501-5070

SABHARWAL, CHAMAN LAL, computer science educator; b. Ludhiana, Panjab, India, Aug. 15, 1937; came to U.S., 1963; s. Milkhi Ram and Tara Vanti (Kaura) S.; m. Chander Lekha Khosla, July 12, 1968; children: Anup K., Aman D. MS, U. Ill., 1966, PhD, 1967. Asst. prof. St. Louis U., 1967-71, assoc. prof., 1971-83; sr. systems analyst McDonnell Douglas Co., St. Louis, 1980-81, specialist, 1981-82, lead engr., 1984-85, sr. specialist, 1985-86; prof. computer sci. U. Mo.-Rolla, St. Louis, 1986—; cons. McDonnell Douglas Co., St. Louis, 1986-90. Home: 5892 Chrisbrook Dr Saint Louis MO 63128-4413 Office: U Mo-Rolla 8001 Natural Bridge Rd Saint Louis MO 63121-4401

SABLE, LOUIS ANTHONY, trade association executive; b. Wamego, Kans., June 16, 1934; s. Henry Francis and Alice Viola (Welstch) S.; m. Mary Therese Wieland; children: Jeffery Joseph, Angela Marie. BS in Tech. Journalism, Kans. State U., 1957. Cert. assn. exec. Reporter, photographer Pratt (Kans.) Daily News, 1957-58; advt. mgr. Richmond (Mo.) News, 1958-59, Liberty (Mo.) Tribune, 1959-60; asst. exec. pres. Real Estate Bd. of Kansas City, Mo., 1960-66; exec. v.p. Greater Springfield (Mo.) Bd. Realtors, 1966—. Mem. disaster team ARC, Springfield; group chmn. United Way, Springfield, 1991; bd. dirs. Heart Assn., Springfield, Greene County Extension, U. Mo., Springfield. With U.S. Army, 1957-63. Mem. Nat. Assn. Realtors (bd. dirs.), Mo. Assn. Realtors (bd. dirs.), C. of C., Home Builders Assn., Apt. and Housing Assn., K.C. (grand knight), Elks. Roman Catholic. Home: 2370 S Bonnie Lee Ln Rogersville MO 65742 Office: Greater Springfield Bd Realtors 1310 E Primrose Box 11045 Springfield MO 65808

SABO, MARTIN OLAV, congressman; b. Crosby, N.D., Feb. 28, 1938; s. Bjorn O. and Klara (Haga) S.; m. Sylvia Ann Lee, June 30, 1963; children: Karin, Julie. BA cum laude, Augsburg Coll., Mpls., 1959; postgrad., U. Minn., 1961-62. Mem. Minn. Ho. of Reps. from 57B Dist., 1960-78, minority leader Dem.-Farmer-Labor party, 1969-72, speaker, 1973-78; mem. 96th to 104th U.S. Congresses from 5th Minn. Dist., 1979—; chmn. Dem. Study Group 96th to 101st Congresses; dep. majority whip 96th to 103rd Congresses, mem. appropriations com.; mem. permanent select com. on intelligence 102d Congress; chmn. Ho. Budget Com. 103d Congress; former mem. Nat. Adv. Commn. on Intergovtl. Rels.; past pres. Nat. Legis. Conf.; bd. regents Augsburg Coll. Mgr., player Dem. Congl. Baseball Team, 1987—. Recipient Disting. Alumni citation Augsburg Coll., Arms Control Leadership award Employees Union, Local 113, SEIU, AFL-CIO; named One of 200 Rising Young Leaders in Am. Time mag., 1974; Man of Yr. Mpls. Jr. C. of C., 1973-74, One of Ten Outstanding Young Men of Yr. Minn. Jr. C. of C., 1974; inducted Scandinavian Am. Hall of Fame, 1994. Mem. Nat. Conf. State Legis. Leaders (past pres.). Office: 2336 Rayburn Bldg Office B Washington DC 20515-0005

SACCO, MARY KATHLEEN, nurse; b. Washington, Jan. 5, 1952; d. John Joseph and Maureen Josphine (Halpin) Bahr; m. Robert Paul Sacco, Dec. 28, 1973; 1 child, Anthony William. BSN, Coll. Mt. St. Joseph, Cin., 1973; MSN, U. Cin., 1981. RN, Ohio. Psychiatric staff nurse Jewish Hosp. Cin., 1973-74, mem. faculty Sch. Nursing, 1974-79, 85-86; supr. Univ. Hosp., Cin., 1979-83; mgr. nursing resources Children's Hosp Med. Ctr., Cin., 1983-85; asst. prof. No. Ky. U., Highland Heights, 1986-87; dir. nursing Hamilton County Health Dept., Cin., 1987—; chair Greater Cin. Immunization Coalition, 1994—. Vol. ARC, Cin., 1983—; past pres. Summit Elem. Sch. PTA; vol. Boy Scouts Am. Recipient Dist. Meritorious Svc. award Boy Scouts Am. Mem. Ohio Pub. Health Nursing Dirs. Liaison Forum, Greater Cin. Sch. Nurses Assn. Republican. Roman Catholic. Home: 1445 Hilltree Dr Cincinnati OH 45255-3226 Office: Hamilton County Health Dept 11499 Chester Rd Ste 1500 Cincinnati OH 45246-4012

SACCONE, VIVIAN RICH, retired elementary educator, author, illustrator; b. Akron, Ohio, Apr. 4, 1929; d. Newton Nelson and Mary L. (Nuosce) Rich; m. John Anthony Saccone, Jr., Aug. 22, 1953; children: Vivette, Rich, Vanessa Saccone Spring. BS, Kent State U., 1953; MA, U. Akron, 1978. Cert. elem. tchr., Ohio. Tchr. Akron Pub. Schs., 1953-87; author, illustrator V-Press Graphic Arts Studio, Akron, 1987—. Author, illustrator: ABC's of What is Black, 1994, ABC's of What is Kwanzaa, 1995, ABC's of Kwanzaa Activities, 1995, Bible Baffler Activities, 1993. Educator Nat. Edn. Assn. Retired, 1987. Mem. Delta Kappa Gamma (1st Pl. Fibers 1987, Hon. Mention Fibers 1987). Home and Office: 3044 Lake James Terr Akron OH 44312

SACHNOFF, LOWELL, lawyer; b. Chgo., Oct. 1, 1930; s. Joseph and Clara (Reiner) S.; m. Elaine Ades, Jan. 6, 1953 (div. June 10, 1967); children: Scott, Marc, Katherine; m. Fay Clayton, Jan. 10, 1987. BA magna cum laude, Harvard Coll., 1952, LLB, 1957. Assoc. Ross, McGowan & O'Keefe, Chgo., 1957-61; gen. counsel Ill. Dept. Mental Health, Springfield, 1961-63; ptnr. Sachnoff & Weaver, Chgo., 1963—. Contbr. articles to profl. jours. Chmn. Chgo. Lawyers Com. for Civil Rights, 1983; mem. Lawyers Coms. for Nuclear Arms Control, 1982-95; bd. dirs. Northwestern Psychiat. Inst., 1989-94, Coalition for New Priorities, 1992-95. Recipient Learned Hand award Am. Jewish Congress, Chgo., 1987. Mem. ABA (corp. law com. 1985-87), Chgo. Bar Assn. (chmn. securities law com. 1981-83), mem. Standard Club (Chgo.). Home: 1044 Lake Shore Blvd Evanston IL 60202 Office: Sachnoff & Weaver 305 Wacker Dr Chicago IL 60606

SACHS, MARJORIE BELL, vocational and educational counselor; b. Cleve., Aug. 16, 1926; d. Julius Mark and Molly Evelyn (Hascal) Bell; m. Sidney H. Sachs, Feb. 25, 1950 (dec.); children: Wendi Sachs Forman, Peter Bell. BA, Western Res. U., 1948; MEd, Cleve. State U., 1975. Lic. profl. counselor, Ohio. Rsch. assoc. Urban Reports Corp., Cleve., 1973-75; counselor Preterm Clinic, Cleve., 1974-76, Jewish Vocat. Svc., Cleve., 1975-76, Resource, Cleve., 1975-76; vocat./ednl. counselor At-Home rehab. project The Cancer Ctr., Inc., Cleve., 1976-79; project dir. At-Home rehab. program U. Hosps. Cancer Ctr., Cleve., 1979-80; dir. of devel. Jewish Community Ctr., 1980—; undergrad. admission adv. Case We. Res. U., Cleve., 1973-90. Life trustee Mt. Sinai Med. CTr. Aux.; trustee Cleve. Opera, 1983-94, The Temple, 1984-87, Cleve. Ctr. Contemporary Art, 1995—; mem. vis. com. Sch. Dentistry Case We. Res. U., Cleve., 1977, chmn., 1983-86, em. bd. overseers, 1984-90. Mem. Cleve. State U. Alumni Assn. (trustee 1992-95), Cleve. Soc. Contemporary Art (trustee, sec. 1992-95). Home: 20676 Fairmount Blvd Apt 302 Cleveland OH 44118-4856

SACHS, SAMUEL, II, museum director; b. N.Y.C., Nov. 30, 1935; s. James Henry and Margery (Fay) S.; m. Susan McAllen (div.); children: Katherine, Eleanor; m. Jerre S. Hollander (div.); 1 child, Alexander; m. Elizabeth M. Gordon; 1 child, Hadley Elizabeth. BA cum laude, Harvard U., 1957; MA, NYU Inst. Fine Arts, 1962. Asst. in charge prints and drawings Mpls. Inst. Arts, 1958-60; asst. dir. U. Mich. Mus. of Art, Ann Arbor, 1963-64; chief curator Mpls. Inst. Arts, 1964-73, dir., 1973-85; dir. Detroit Inst. Arts, 1985—. Bd. dirs. Ctr. for Creative Studies, Detroit, Univ. Liggett Sch., Grosse Pointe. Decorated knight 1st class Order North Star (Sweden); Order of Dannebrog (Denmark). Mem. Am. Assn. Museums, Coll. Art Assn., Assn. Art Mus. Dirs. Clubs: Detroit, Century Assn, Harvard, Grosse Pointe. Home: 19344 Cumberland Way Detroit MI 48203-1456 Office: Detroit Inst Arts 5200 Woodward Ave Detroit MI 48202-4008

SACHTLER, WOLFGANG MAX HUGO, chemistry educator; b. Delitzsch, Germany, Nov. 8, 1924; came to U.S., 1983; s. Gottfried Hugo and Johanna Elisabeth (Bollmann) S.; m. Anne-Lore Luise Adrian, Dec. 9, 1953; children: Johann Wolfgang Adriaan, Heike Kathleen Julia, Yvonne Rhea Valeska. Diplomchemiker, Tech. U., Braunschweig, Ger., 1949; Dr.rer.nat. (Ph.D), 1952. Research chemist Kon-Shell Lab., Amsterdam, Netherlands, 1952-71, dept. head, 1972-83; extraordinary prof. chemistry U. Leiden, Netherlands, 1963-83; V.N. Ipatieff prof. Northwestern U., Evanston, Ill., 1983-96; chmn. Gordon Research Conf. Catalysis, N.H., 1985; Rideal lectr. Faraday div. Royal Soc. Chemistry, 1981; F. Gault lectr., 1991. Mem. editl. bd. Jour. Catalysis, 1976-88, Applied Catalysis, 1983-87, Catalysis Letters, 1987—, Advances in Catalysis, 1987—; contbr. numerous articles to sci. jours. Recipient Deutsche Gesellschaft Mineraloel und Kohle Kolleg, 1991. Fellow AAAS; mem. Royal Netherlands Acad. Scis., Internat. Congress Catalysis (pres. coun. 1992-96), Royal Dutch Chem. Soc. (hon. mem. catalysis divsn.), Am. Chem. Soc. (E.V. Murphee award 1987, Petroleum Chemistry award 1992), Catalysis Soc. N.Am. (Robert L. Burwell award 1985, E. Houdry award 1993). Home: 2141 Ridge Ave Apt 2D Evanston IL 60201-2788 Office: Northwestern U Sheridan Rd Evanston IL 60208-0002

SACK, JAMES MCDONALD, JR., radio and television producer, marketing executive; b. London, Ky., Oct. 11, 1948; s. James McDonald and Ruth Elmore (Bryant) S.; m. Cheryl S. Gremaux, July 13, 1969 (div. June 1974); 1 child, Graehm McDonald. BA in History, Ind. U., 1975, MS in Telecommunications, 1976. Coordinator Latin Am. Ednl. Ctr., Ft. Wayne, Ind., 1979-81, Mayor's Office, Ft. Wayne, 1981-83; producer WMEE-WQHK Radio, Ft. Wayne, 1983-85; owner, operator Festival Mgmt. and Devel., Ft. Wayne, 1984—; ptnr. Lily Co., Fort Wayne, 1991—; v.p. communications, mktg. United Way of Allen County, Ft. Wayne, Ind., 1989—; owner The Sack Co., 1992; owner The Lily Co.; pub. affairs prodr. WBYR, Ft. Wayne; dir. Cable Access, Inc. Producer radio documentary, 1985 (First Place award Ind. Broadcasters Assn., 1985), producer WFWA-PBS Eye on the Arts, 1987-89. Founder, pres. Germanfest of Ft. Wayne, 1981-92; pres. cable TV program adv. coun. City of Ft. Wayne, mktg. dir., 1996; founder Ft. Wayne-Gera (Germany) Sister City Affilation; commr. Ind. Hoosier Celebration, 1988; dir. Ind. Highland Games, 1992, cons., 1993—. Named Ky. Col., 1991. Mem. German Heritage Soc. (founder, bd. dirs. 1986—), Ind. German Heritage Soc. (founder, bd. dirs. 1986-92, Gov.'s Commendation award 1983), N.Am. Sängerbund (sec. 1985-86), Männerchor Club (Ft. Wayne), Ft. Wayne Sport Club (sec. 1985-86, trustee 1987-89). Lutheran. Home and Office: 2502 S Harrison St Fort Wayne IN 46807-1318

SACKSTEDER, THOMAS M., sales executive; b. Dayton, Ohio, July 27, 1950; s. Harry Pius and Mary Kay (Liebhardt) S.; m. Teresa Ann Nevius, Oct. 12, 1968 (div. Sept. 1980); children: Lori Ann, Kristi Marie, Julie Kay; m. Helen L. Dansker, Mar. 7, 1992. Student, Sinclair Community Coll., 1968-72, Wright State U., 1972-73, Grand Valley State Coll., 1978-79; Lourdes Coll., 1994—. Installer Western Electric, Dayton, 1968-69; sales rep. Smith Corona Mcht., Dayton, 1969-70; office mgr. Indsl. Machinery, Dayton, 1970 71; advisor Bell Pub. Rels., Dayton, 1972-73; sales mgr. Washington Nat. Ins., Dayton, 1974-81, Am. Fidelity Assurance Co., 1981-95; gen. ptnr. Innovative Benefits Resource Ltd., 1995—; sales cons. Ind. State Tchrs. Assn. Ins. Trust, Indpls., 1986—. Bd. dirs. Mental Health Assn., Dayton, 1971-75, Good Samaritan Mental Health Ctr., 1972-75, State Ohio Young Dem., 1971-73. Mem. Ohio Assn. Sch. Bus. Ofcls. (legis. com. 1993-95), Buckeye Assn. Sch. Adminstrs., Jaycees, Kiwanis. Roman Catholic. Office: Innovative Benefits Resource Ltd 6218 Wexford Ct Maumee OH 43537-1366

SADD, JOHN ROSWELL, plastic surgeon; b. Chgo., Apr. 18, 1933; s. Sumner Harry and Louise Elizabeth (Beardsley) S.; m. Valerie Crim Lavery; children: Elizabeth, Katherine, Virginia, Dorothy. BS, Purdue U., 1955; MD, U. Rochester, 1959. Diplomate Am. Bd. Plastic Surgery. Resident in plastic surgery U. Wis., 1959-67; attending suregon Toledo Hosp., 1967—, chmn. surgery, 1972-86, trustee; asst. clin. prof. Med. Coll. Ohio, Toledo, 1972—; bd. dirs. P.I. E. Mus. Ins. Co., Cleve., pres. med. staff, 1989—; trustee Toledo Hosp., Promedica Health Care Systems, Vanguard Health Ins. Co. Contbr. articles to med. jours. Served to lt. USN, 1961-63. Fellow Am. Coll. Surgeons; mem. Am. Soc. Plastic and Reconstructive Surgeons, Ohio Valley Plastic Surgery Soc. Republican. Episcopalian. Lodge: Rotary. Office: 2121 Hughes Dr Toledo OH 43606-3845

SADEK, SALAH ELDINE, consulting pathologist; b. Cairo, Egypt, June 9, 1920; s. Ahmad A. and Zienab (Zahran) S.; D.V.M., U. Cairo, 1945; M.R.C.V.S., U. Edinburgh, 1948; M.S., Mich. State U., 1950; Ph.D., U. Ill., 1956; m. Helen Ann Phoenix, Apr. 12, 1952; children—Craig, Ramsay, Mark. Asst. prof. U. Cairo, 1945-48; asst. U. Ill., Urbana, 1953-55; pathologist Dow Chem. Co., Midland, Mich., 1956-67; head of pathology Hoffmann La Roche, Nutley, N.J., 1967-85, also asst. dir.; clin. prof. pathology N.J. Coll. Medicine and Dentistry, Newark; cons. in exptl. pathology and toxicology. Pres., Midland County Humane Soc., 1965-67. Diplomate Am. Bd. Indsl. Hygiene. Mem. Am. Vet. Med. Assn., N.Y. Acad. Sci., British Vet. Assn., Royal Coll. Veterinary Surgeons, Mich. Soc. Pathologists, N.Y. Pathol. Soc., Soc. Toxicology, Soc. Toxicologic Pathologists, Internat. Acad. Pathology, AAAS, Am. Acad. Indsl. Hygiene. Club: Midland Country. Home and Office: 3910 Valley Dr Midland MI 48640-6608

SADER, NEIL STEVEN, lawyer; b. Torrington, Conn., Oct. 10, 1958; s. Harold M. and Carol Hope (Shimkin) S.; m. Elizabeth Napshin, Jan. 3, 1988; children: Samantha Isabel, Daniel Scott. AB, Columbia U., 1980; JD, U. Kans., 1984. Bar: Mo. 1984, U.S. Ct. Appeals (10th cir.) 1988, U.S. Supreme Ct. 1993, Kans. 1994, U.S. Dist. Ct. (ea. dist.) Mich. 1995. Asst. White House Domestic Policy Staff, Washington, 1980-81; mem. Brown, Nachman & Sader, P.C., Kansas City, Mo., 1986—. Planning commr. Johnson County, Kans., 1986-90; mem. Overland Park City Coun., 1990—, pres., 1995-96; bd. dirs. Mid-Am. Regional Coun., 1993—; precinct committeeman Johnson County Dem. Party, 1983—, mem. exec. com., 1984-90, vice chmn., 1988-90; mem. Dem. com. State of Kans., 1988-90; bd. dirs. Jewish Family and Children's Svcs. Kansas City, 1986-90. Mem. Am. Bankruptcy Inst., Mo. Bar Assn., Kans. Bar Assn., Columbia U. Club Kansas City (bd. dirs.). Jewish. Home: 11736 W 102d St Overland Park KS 66214-2686 Office: Brown Nachman & Sader PC Crown Center Sq 2405 Grand Blvd Ste 300 Kansas City MO 64108-2527

SADLER, JAMES BERTRAM, psychologist, clergyman; b. Albuquerque, Mar. 29, 1911; s. James Monroe and Mary Agnes (English) S.; m. Vera Ellen Ahrendt, Apr. 10, 1938. AB, U. N.Mex., 1938; BD, Crozer Theol. Sem., 1941, ThM, 1948; MA, U. Pa., 1941, EdD, 1959. Lic. psychologist, S.D.; ordained to ministry Baptist Ch., 1941. Pastor First Bapt. Ch., Mt. Union, Pa., 1941-42; chaplain USAF, 1943-48; pastor Hatboro (Pa.) Bapt. Ch., 1948-61; chmn. dept. psychology Sioux Falls (S.D.) Coll., 1961-75; pvt. practice psychology, Sioux Falls, 1975—; cons. in psychology and religion. Contbr. articles to profl. jours. Mem. ministers coun. Am. Bapt. Conv. Mem. APA, ACA, Soc. for Sci. Study Religion, Masons, Rotary (pres. 1960). Home: 4312 Glenview Rd Sioux Falls SD 57103-4935

SAEED, MOHAMMED, Islamic historian, eqyptologist, educator; b. El Paso, Tex., Aug. 15, 1948; s. Willard Wood and Grace Margaret (Weddle) W.; m. Jeanne Burger, Apr. 2, 1970 (div. 1979); children: Grace Ann, Anabelle Jane; m. Katleen M. D'Annette, Dec. 12, 1992. Student, Fullerton Coll., 1973-76; AA, Wichita State U., 1983, BS, 1983; MA, Emporia State U., 1989; student, Am. U., Cairo, Egypt. Rschr. Lawrence (Kans.) Islamic Student Assn., 1989-92, Islamic Studies Student Assn., Lawrence, 1992—. Author: The Jayhawk Nazi, 1983, Perceptions: Vietnam Veterans, 1989, Allah, The Glorious Quran and the Muslim Family, 1995; contbr. articles to profl. jours. Mem. DAV, World Wildlife Fund, Nat. Parks and Conservation Assn., Blinded Veterans Assn., Nat. Wildlife Fedn., Nat. Audubon Soc., Hist. Preservation Soc., Emporia State Alumni Assn., Greenpeace, Amnesty Internat., Disabled Am. Blind Vets., Archeol. Inst. Am., Egypt Exploration Soc. Moslem. Home: PO Box 372 Lawrence KS 66044-0372

SAENZ, GILBERT, computer programmer and analyst, poet; b. Detroit, Oct. 17, 1941; s. Valentine and Lena (Mireles) S. BA in English Lit., Wayne State U., 1968, postgrad., 1979-81. U.S. diplomatic courier Dept. State, Washington, 1969-70; computer programmer/analyst Detroit IRS Computing Ctr., 1974—; mem. Fed. Exec. Bd./Hispanic Employment Program Com., Detroit, 1988—, also past chair. Author: (poetry) Where Love Is, 1988, Colorful Impressions, 1993, Moments in Time, 1995. Mem. IMAGE, Detroit, 1995; v.p., bd. dirs. Manic Depressive and Depressive Assn. Met. Detroit, 1983—. Mem. U.S. Diplomatic Courier Assn. Democrat. Roman Catholic. Home: 6237 Appoline St Dearborn MI 48126

SAFFELL, JOHN EDGAR, retired history educator; b. North Georgetown, Ohio, July 22, 1916; s. Byron Edgar and Athalia Isabel (Anderson) S.; m. Helen Weaver, Oct. 8, 1955. AB, Mount Union Coll., 1937; AM, Western Res. U., Cleve., 1938, PhD, 1965; HD of humane letters, Mount Union Coll., 1996. Elem. sch. prin. Bd. Edn., Stark County, Ohio, 1939-41; tchr. Harvey Sr. H.S., Painesville, Ohio, 1941-43; rsch. analyst U.S. Army, Tokyo, 1945-47; faculty mem. history Mt. Union Coll., Alliance, Ohio, 1948-82; ret., 1982—; owner cattle farm, Homeworth, Ohio, 1955-89. Author: Sesquicentennial History of Mount Union College, 1996, Title: Wake the Echoes. With U.S. Army, 1943-45. Mem. Free and Accepted Masons. Republican. Presbyterian. Home: 841 W Milton Alliance OH 44601

SAFFELS, DALE EMERSON, federal judge; b. Moline, Kans., Aug. 13, 1921; s. Edwin Clayton and Lillian May (Cook) S.; m. Margaret Elaine Nieman, Apr. 2, 1976; children by previous marriage: Suzanne Saffels Gravitt, Deborah Saffels Godowns, James B.; stepchildren: Lynda Cowger Harris, Christopher Cowger. AB, Emporia State U., 1947; JD cum laude, LLB cum laude, Washburn U., 1949. Bar: Kans. 1949. Pvt. practice law Garden City, Kans., 1949-71, Topeka, 1971-75, Wichita, Kans., 1975-79; U.S. dist. judge Dist. of Kans., Topeka, 1979—; county atty. Finney County, Kans., 1951-55; chmn. bd. Fed. Home Loan Bank Topeka, 1978-79; mem. Jud. Conf. Com. on Fin. Disclosure, 1993—. Mem. bd. govs. Sch. Law Washburn U., 1973-85; pres. Kans. Dem. Club, 1957; Dem. nominee Gov. of Kans., 1962; mem. Kans. Ho. of Reps., 1955-63, minority leader, 1961-63; mem. Kans. Corp. Commn., 1967-75, chmn., 1968-75; mem. Kans. Legis. Coun., 1957-63; Kans. rep. Interstate Oil Compact Commn., 1967-75, 1st vice chmn., 1971-72; pres. Midwest Assn. Regulatory Commn., 1972-73, Midwest Assn. R.R. and Utilities Commrs., 1972-73; trustee Emporia State U. Endowment Assn.; bd. dirs. Nat. Assn. Regulatory Utility Commrs., 1972-75. Maj. Signal Corps U.S. Army, 1942-46. Fellow Am. Bar Found., Kans. Bar Found.; mem. ABA, Kans. Bar Assn., Wichita Bar assn., Am. Judicature Soc., Delta Theta Phi. Lutheran. Home: 2832 SW Plass Ave Topeka KS 66611-1630 Office: US Dist Ct 420 Federal Bldg 444 SE Quincy St Topeka KS 66683

SAGAN, JOHN, former automobile company executive; b. Youngstown, Ohio, Mar. 9, 1921; s. John and Mary (Jubinsky) S.; m. Margaret Pickett, July 24, 1948; children: John, Linda, Scott. B.A. in Econs, Ohio Wesleyan U., 1948; M.A., U. Ill., 1949, Ph.D., 1951; Fellow, Ohio Wesleyan U., 1946-

48; scholar, fellow research, U. Ill., 1948-51. Various positions Ford Motor Co., Dearborn, Mich., 1951-66; v.p., treas. Ford Motor Co., 1966-86; pres. John Sagan Assocs., Dearborn, 1986—; bd. dirs. Telident Corp., Chartwell Corp., SBCM Derivatives Products, Ltd. Trustee Ohio Wesleyan U., 1964—, Com. Econ. Devel. U.S.A., Oakwood Hosp., Dearborn, Mich., YMCA Found., Detroit Fund for Henry Ford Hosp. Served with USNR, 1943-46. Mem. Am. Econ. Assn., Phi Beta Kappa, Phi Kappa Phi, Delta Sigma Rho. Home and Office: 22149 Long Blvd Dearborn MI 48124-1104

SAGAN, SANDRA JOYCE, artist, educator; b. Cleve., Nov. 28, 1945; d. Rudolph James and Genevieve Jane Frances Kouba; m. Robert James Sagan, Aug.31, 1968; 1 child, Stacey Elizabeth. BS in Edn., Kent State U., 1967; MA, St. Louis U., 1970; MA in Ednl. Adminstrn., Lindenwood Coll., St. Charles, Mo., 1994. Cert. tchr., Mo. Art tchr. Parma (Ohio) Pub. Schs., 1967-68; dir. Project Headstart Mo. Ozark Econ. Corp., Richland, 1970-71; housing planner Albany (Ga.)-Dougherty County Planning Dept., 1973-75; chief advanced planning sect. St. Clair County, Ill., 1976-78; chair secondary art dept. Valley Park (Mo.) Sch.Dist., 1986—, coord. grants, 1994; dir. The Tchrs. Acad., St. Louis, 1992-94; adj. faculty Lindenwood Coll., 1995; mem. design team Metro 2000/Am. 2000, St. Louis, 1992-93; mem. planning com. Mo. Student-At-Risk Conf., Jefferson City, 1993-95; presenter in field. Desigenr costumes for St. Louis Gateway Ballet Co., USSR trip, 1988; designer dance costumes for Beutell Dancers, 1987, 95. Recipient Innovators award Citicorp, 1993-94; NEH fellow, 1993. Home: 803 Stone Canyon Dr Manchester MO 63021 Office: Valley Park Sch Dist 356 Meramec Station Rd Valley Park MO 63088

SAGAR, PERCY K., mechanical engineer; b. India, Nov. 4, 1953; came to U.S., 1977; BS in Mech. Engring., U. Mysore, India, 1977. Engr. Stearns Block Equipment, Olathe, Kans., 1982-87; project engr. ABB Raymond, Abilene, Kans., 1987-94; specialist applications R.M. Taylor Inc., Kansas City, Mo., 1994—. Patentee in field.

SAGARIN, JAMES LEON, rabbi, author, editor; b. Oceanside, N.Y., Dec. 31, 1951; s. Lawrence and Ethel (Wallace) S.; m. Lori Beth Baumblatt, Aug. 31, 1986. BA, SUNY, Albany, 1974; MA in Hebrew Letters, Hebrew U. Coll. Jewish Inst. Religion, 1978. Ordained rabbi, 1979, Reform Jewish educator, 1992. Hillel dir., congl. rabbi So. Ill. U., Carbondale, 1979-80; dir. Young Judaea Jewish Community Ctrs. Assn., St. Louis, 1980-82; sr. adult coord., chaplain, dir. contg. edn. Cen. Agy. for Jewish Edn., St. Louis, 1982-88; prof. Hebrew langs. and lit. Washington U., St. Louis, 1985-88; assoc. rabbi Temple Beth-El, Chgo., 1988-91; rabbi Temple Menorah, Chgo., 1991—. Author: Hebrew Noun Patterns, 1987; co-author: Oseh Shalom, 1990; youth editor Sagarin Rev., 1991-95, contbr., 1992-94; asst. editor Pastoral Outreach Newsletter, 1992, 93; contbr. to Chgo. Jewish Star, 1991-93, Chgo. Jewish News, 1995. Mem. Cen. Conf. Am. Rabbis, Nat. Assn. Profs. Hebrew, Nat. Assn. Temple Educators, B'nai Brith. Home: 200 Valley Vw Wilmette IL 60091 Office: Temple Menorah 2800 W Sherwin Ave Chicago IL 60645-1238

SAGE, PAMELA KAY, small business owner; b. Lansing, Mich., Nov. 18, 1949. Mgr. John Anthony Florist, Lansing, 1975-81, co-owner, 1981-84; co-owner Sage Systems Inc., Grand Rapids, Mich., 1989—. Republican. Office: Sage Systems Inc 4695 44th St SE Ste 150 Grand Rapids MI 49512-4061

SAGER, DONALD JACK, publisher, former librarian; b. Milw., Mar. 3, 1938; s. Alfred Herman and Sophia (Sagan) S.; m. Sarah Ann Long, May 23, 1987; children: Geoffrey, Andrew. BS, U. Wis., Milw., 1963; MSLS, U. Wis., 1964. Sr. documentalist AC Electronics divsn. GM, Milw., 1958-63; teaching asst. U. Wis., Madison, 1963-64; dir. Kingston (N.Y.) Pub. Libr., 1964-66, Elyria (Ohio) Pub. Libr., 1966-71, Mobile Pub. Libr., 1971-75, Pub. Libr. Columbus and Franklin County, Ohio, 1975-78; commr. Chgo. Pub. Libr., 1978-81; dir. Elmhurst Pub. Libr., Ill., 1982-83, Milw. Pub. Libr., 1983-91; pub. Highsmith Press, Ft. Atkinson, Wis., 1991—; sec. Online Computer Libr. Ctr., 1977-78, disting. vis. scholar, 1982; chmn. mus. com. PLA Pub. Libr., 1989-91, history com., 1993-95, chmn. investment com., 1985-89, chmn. PLA nat. conf. com., 1986-88; bd. dirs. Coun. Wis. Librs., 1982-91, Urban Librs. Coun., 1985-93, sec., 1991-93; adj. faculty U. Wis., Milw., 1984-91; cons. in field. Author: Reference: A Programmed Instruction, 1970, Binders, Books and Budgets, 1971, Participatory Management, 1981, The American Public Library, 1982, Public Library Administrators Planning Guide to Automation, 1983, Managing the Public Library, 1984, 2d rev. edit., 1989, Small Libraries, 1992, 2d rev. edit., 1996; co-editor: Urban Library Management Trends, 1989; contbg. editor: Public Libraries, 1990—; contbr. articles to profls. publs. Bd. dirs. Goethe House, 1985-91; pres. Milw. Civic Alliance, 1990-91; chmn. Milw. United Way Campaign, 1984; pres. Milw. Westown Assn., 1987-90. With inf. AUS, 1956-58. Mem. ALA (coun. mem. 1995—), Pub. Libr. Assn. (bd. dirs., v.p., pres.-elect, pres. 1982-83), Ill. Libr. Assn., Chgo. Book Clinic, Wis. Libr. Assn., Wis. Libr. Assn. Found. (chmn. 1986-88), Libr. Adminstrn. Assn. Wis. (chmn. 1987-88), Exch. Club Milw. (pres. 1988-89). Home: 590 Wilmot Rd Deerfield IL 60015-4206 Office: Highsmith Press 5527W Highway 106 Fort Atkinson WI 53538

SAHA, BADAL CHANDRA, biochemist; b. Jamurki, Tangail, Bangladesh, July 1, 1949; came to U.S., 1984, naturalized; s. Kalachand and Milan (Deshmukhya) S.; m. Sarabi Roychowdhury, June 7, 1976; children: Susmita, Saroj. BS (with honors), Dhaka U., Bangladesh, 1969, MS, 1970; MS, Kyushu U., Fukuoka, Japan, 1981, PhD, 1984. Biochemist Dhaka (Bangladesh) Med. Coll. Hosp., 1972-73; rsch. scholar Dhaka U., 1973-74; lectr. Bangladesh Agrl. U., Mymensingh, 1974-75, asst. prof., 1975-79; rsch. assoc. U. Md., College Park, 1984-85, Mich. State U., East Lansing, 1985-86; rsch. scientist Mich. Biotech. Inst., Lansing, 1986-92; vis. scientist, rsch. chemist USDA Agrl. Rsch. Svc., Peoria, Ill., 1992—; asst. adj. prof. Mich. State U., East Lansing, 1988-92. Author: Clostridia, 1989, Biocatalysis, 1990, (with others) Mixed Cultures in Biotechnology, 1991; contbr. more than 50 articles to profl. jours. including Trends in Biotech., Biochem. Jour., Applied Environ. Microbiology, others. Recipient UNESCO fellowship Japanese Nat. Commn. for UNESCO, 1977-78, Rsch. scholarship Japanese Govt., 1979-84, Grad. scholarship Dhaka U., 1969-70, Dhaka Bd. scholarships, 1962-69. Mem. AAAS, Am. Chem. Soc., Am. Soc. for Microbiology, Soc. for Indsl. Microbiology. Hindu. Home: 6516 N University St Apt 303 Peoria IL 61614-2763 Office: USDA-ARS Nat Ctr. for Agrl Utilization Rsch 1815 N University St Peoria IL 61604-3902

SAHA, SANTOSH C., history educator. BA in History with honors, Calcutta (India) U., 1955, LLB, 1959, MA in History, 1960; Assoc. of Preceptors, Coll. of Preceptors, London, 1972; BA in History with honors, U. London, 1976; postgrad., U. Toledo, 1985-87; PhD, Kent State U., 1993. Asst. prof. history Bagula Degree Coll., West Bengal, India, 1960-62, Itachuna Coll., Burdwan U. India, 1962-65; head of dept., instr. history Miaza 27 Comprehensive Inst., Jimma, Ethiopia, 1965-68, Monze (Zambia) Secondary Sch., 1968-80; prin., instr. Adult Edn. Ctr., Monze, 1974-80; instr. history St. Paul's Cath. Sem., Gbarnga, Liberia, 1982-83; head of dept., asst. prof. history Cuttington U., Liberia, 1981-85; tchr. survey courses in European and U.S. history U. Toledo, 1985-88, instr. comty. and tech. coll., 1986-87; teaching fellow in history Kent (Ohio) State U., 1989-93; instr. African history Mt. Union Coll., Alliance, Ohio, 1994—; prin., coord. Adult Edn. Ctr., Monze, 1970-79; dep. headmaster Monze Secondary Sch., 1978-79; regional chief examiner Zambian Sch. Sys. Exam., South Region, 1970-79; mem. faculty rsch. forum Cuttington U., 1983-85, student debates chmn., 1981-85, editor-in-chief, bd. historians The History of Cuttington University, 1983-85, acting head dept. history, 1984-85, editor Cutting Rsch. Jour., 1981-85; conf. presenter Gt. Lakes History Conf., Alendale, Mich., 1993, Ohio Valley History Cnf., Murray, Ky., 1986, 87, 88, 89, U.S. Ednl. and Agrl. Found., Monrovia, Liberia, 1983, 84. Author: Indo-U.S. Relations, 1947-1989: A Guide to Information Sources, 1990, A History of Agriculture in West Africa: A Guide to Information Sources, 1990, A History of Agriculture in Liberia, 1822-1970: Transference of American Values, 1990, History of the Tonga Chiefs and Their People in the Monze District of Zambia, 1994; contbr. articles to profl. jours. including Can. Jour. African Studies, Jour. of Negro History, Internat. Jour. African Hist. Studies, Jour. of Pakistan Hist. Soc., Leaders of the World, Women in World History, Indian Jour. of Social Work; contbr. book revs. and conf. papers in field. Mem. African Studies Assn. (conf. presenter 1993), Am. Hist. Assn., Third World Studies Assn., Assn. for Bibliography of History, Indian Polit. Sci. Assn. (Univ. Madras, India), World History Assn.

SAHLER, CHRISTY LEE, real estate manager; b. Bangor, Maine, Dec. 16, 1962; d. James Howard and Diane Alma (Sandstrom) Sahler; divorced; 1 child, Tahler Diane. BS in Computer Sci., U.S. Naval Acad., 1985. Mdse. mgr. Lenscrafters, Cin., 1990-91, sr. acct., 1991-93; gen. mgr. LaSalle Ptnrs. Asset Mgmt., Chgo., 1994—. Lt. USN, 1985-90. Republican. Lutheran. Office: LaSalle Ptnrs Asset Mgmt 184 Shuman Blvd Ste 110 Naperville IL 60563

SAHU, SUNIL KUMAR, political science educator; b. Muzaffarpur, Bihar, India, May 25, 1948; came to U.S., 1975; s. Kapildeo Prasad and Vidya Sahu; m. Indu Vohra, Dec. 17, 1977; children: Munjot, Punita. BA with honors, Bihar U., Muzaffarpur, 1965, MA, 1968; MA, U. Chgo., 1979, PhD, 1990. Asst. prof. Shyamlal Coll., U. Delhi (India), 1972-78; lectr. polit. sci. Chgo. State U., 1980-82; instr. polit. sci. Columbia Coll., Chgo., 1982-85, St. Xavier Coll., Chgo., 1987-88; asst. prof. DePauw U., Greencastle, Ind., 1988-95, assoc. prof., 1995—. Author: Small States' External Behavior, 1994; contbr. articles to profl. jours. Mem. NAACP, Greencastle, 1990—; resource person Great-Decisions, Internat. Ctr., DePauw U., 1989—. Fellow Asian Rsch. Svc. Hong Kong; mem. Am. Polit. Sci. Assn., Assn. Asian Studies, Indian Coun. World Affairs. Home: 427 Anderson St Greencastle IN 46135-1726 Office: DePauw U 103 Asbury Hall Greencastle IN 46135

SAIA, RICHARD JON, physical therapist; b. Belleville, Ill., Aug. 1, 1959; s. Vincent James and Rita Jean (Lindow) S.; m. Marge LaVerne West, June 25, 1982; children: Jonathon Michael, Stephen Alan. AS in Pre-Medicine, Bellevile Area Coll., 1980; BS in Phys. Therapy, Maryville Coll., 1983. Lic. phys. therapist, Ill. Staff phys. therapist St. John's Regional Health Ctr., Springfield, Mo., 1983-84, St. Elizabeth's Med. Ctr., Granite City, Ill., 1984; supervisory phys. therapist Meml. Hosp., Belleville, 1984-86; dir. phys. therapy Edward Utlaut Meml. Hosp., Greenville, Ill., 1986-91; clinic dir. Tuckey and Assocs. Phys. Therapy, St. Louis, 1991-92; dir. phys. therapy Sparta (Ill.) Cmty. Hosp., 1992—. Leader Cub Scouts Am., Troy, Ill., 1990-95; merit badge counselor Boy Scouts Am., Troy, 1991—; baseball coach, bd. dirs. TBSA, Troy, 1991-94; vol. fire fighter Troy Fire Dept., 1991—; soccer coach Troy Soccer Club, 1994—. Mem. Am. Phys. Therapy Assn., Madison County Fireman's Assn. Republican. Roman Catholic. Home: 5 David Dr Saint Jacob IL 62281 Office: Sparta Cmty Hosp 818 E Broadway Sparta IL 62286

SAID, CLIFFORD EVERETT, seminar company executive, speaker; b. Dedham, Iowa, Dec. 6, 1937; s. Clifford William and Marjorie Lucille (Homrighouse) S.; m. Mildred Ann Hoyt, Apr. 13, 1958; children: Cynthia L. Said Mason, Tammara J. Said Schuett. Grad. high sch., Scranton, Iowa. Salesman Matt Furniture Co., Ft. Dodge, Iowa, 1960-66, Koos Bros. Carpet, Rahway, N.J., 1966-68; sales mgr. Matt Furniture Co., Ft. Dodge, 1968-70; gen. mgr. Matt Furniture Co., Sioux City, Iowa, 1970-73; chief exec. officr Wayne Jones Furniture, LeMars, Iowa, 1973-75; chief exec. officer, owner Cliff & Millies Furniture, Jefferson, Iowa, 1975-79; account exec. Herrigan Distbrs., Des Moines, 1979-85; pres. Cliff Said Seminars, Jefferson, Iowa, 1985—; chmn. Retail Bur., Jefferson, 1976-78; continuing edn. provider Iowa Bd. Nursing, Des Moines, 1989-93. Actor, mem. reading com. Community Theatre, Jefferson, 1975-79; co-chmn. Greene County Compensation Bd., 1987—; chmn. membership com. Iowa Elks Assn., 1993—; bd. dirs. Creative Arts Coun. Recipient Disting. Svc. award Iowa Sheriffs Assn., 1987. Mem. Iowa Hawkeye Floor Covering Assn. (pres. 1981-85, editor newsletter 1981-85), Jefferson C. of C. (assoc.), Elks (Elk of Yr. 1991, chmn. mem. com.). Presbyterian. Office: PO Box 388 Jefferson IA 50129-0388

SAIN, MICHAEL KENT, electrical engineering educator; b. St. Louis, Mar. 22, 1937; s. Charles George and Marie Estelle (Ritch) S.; m. Frances Elizabeth Bettin, Aug. 24, 1963; children: Patrick, Mary, John, Barbara, Elizabeth. BSEE, St. Louis U., 1959, MSEE, 1962; PhD, U. Ill., 1965. Engr. Sandia Corp., Albuquerque, 1958-61, Vickers Electric Corp., St. Louis, 1962; instr. U. Ill., Urbana, 1962-63; asst. prof. U. Notre Dame (Ind.), 1965-68, assoc. prof., 1968-72, prof., 1972-82, Frank M. Freimann prof. elec. engring., 1982—; vis. scientist U. Toronto, Ont., Can., 1972-73; disting. vis. prof. Ohio State U., Columbus, 1987; cons. Allied-Bendix Aerospace, South Bend, Ind., 1976—, Deere & Co., Moline, Ill., 1981, 82, Garrett Corp., Phoenix, 1984, GM, Warren, Mich., 1984-94; plenary spkr. IEEE Conf. on Decision and Control, 1990. Author: Introduction to Algebraic System Theory, 1981; editor: Alternatives for Linear Multivariable Control, 1978; hon. editor: Ency. of Systems and Control, 1987; editor jour. IEEE Trans. on Automatic Control, 1979-83; contbr. 275 articles to profl. jours., books and refereed proc. Grantee Army Rsch. Office, NSF, Ames Rsch. Ctr., Lewis Rsch. Ctr. NASA, Office Naval Rsch., Air Force Office Sci. Rsch., Law Enforcement Assistance Adminstrn., Clark-Hurth Components. Fellow IEEE (prize papers com. 1992-96, chair 1994-96, awards bd. 1994-96); mem. Control Sys. Soc. IEEE (bd. govs. 1978-84, Disting. Mem. award 1983, Centennial medal 1984, Axelby prize chair 1991-96, awards com. chair 1993-96), Circuits and Sys. Soc. IEEE (co-chair internat. symposium on circuits and sys. 1990, newsletter editor 1990-96, v.p. adminstrn. 1992-93, v.p. tech. activities 1994-95), Soc. Indsl. and Applied Math. Republican. Roman Catholic. Office: U Notre Dame Dept Elec Engring 275 Fitzpatrick Heights Notre Dame IN 46556-5637

ST. CLAIR, DONALD DAVID, lawyer; b. Hammond, Ind., Dec. 30, 1932; s. Victor Peter and Wanda (Rubinska) Small; m. Sergine Anne Oliver, June 6, 1970 (dec. June 1974); m. Beverly Joyce Tipton, Dec. 28, 1987. BS, Ind. U., 1955, MS, 1963, EdD, 1967; JD, U. Toledo, 1992. Bar: Ohio 1992, U.S. Dist. Ct. (no. dist.) Ohio 1993, U.S. Supreme Ct., 1996. Assoc. prof. Coll. Edn. Western Ky. U., Bowling Green, 1967-68; assoc. prof. U. Toledo, 1968-77, prof., 1977-92; atty., ptnr. Garand, Bollinger, & St. Clair, Oregon, Ohio, 1992—; bd. dirs. Toledo Mental Health Ctr., 1977-79; mem. Ohio Coun. Mental Health Ctrs., Columbus, 1978-79; dir. honors programs U. Toledo. Author: (poetry) Daymarks and Beacons, 1983; contbr. numerous articles to profl. jours. Organizer Students Toledo Organized for Peace, 1970-71; mem. Lucas County Dem. Party, 1990—. With U.S. Army, 1955-57. Mem. ABA, AAU (nat. bd. dirs. 1973-74), Ohio Bar Assn., Toledo Bar Assn., Ohio Acad. Trial Lawyers, Toledo Power Squadron (commdg. officer 1981), Bay View Yacht Club, Masons (32 degree), Shriners, Ancient Order Friars, Phi Alpha Delta Law Soc. Home: 3353 Christie Blvd Toledo OH 43606-2862 Office: Garand Bollinger & St Clair Charlesgate Commons Forum 860 Ansonia Ste 113 Oregon OH 43616

ST. CYR, JOHN ALBERT, II, cardiovascular and thoracic surgeon; b. Mpls., Nov. 26, 1949; s. John Albert and Myrtle Lavira (Jensen) St. C.; m. Mary Helen Malinoski, Oct. 29, 1977. BA summa cum laude, U. Minn., 1973, BS, 1975, MS, 1977, MD, 1980, PhD, 1988. Teaching asst. dept. biochemistry U. Minn., Mpls., 1973, rsch. asst. dept. surgery, 1977-78, intern surgery dept. surgery, 1980-81, resident surgery, 1981-88, cardiovascular rsch. fellow dept. surgery, 1983-86, with dept. surgery, 1991-92; rsch. assoc. fellow Cardiovasular Pathology, United Hosp., St. Paul, 1987-88; cardiovascular surg. resident U. Colo., Dept. Cardiovascular Surgery, Denver, 1988-91; med. advisor Organetics, Ltd., Mpls., 1992, med. dir., 1992; med. advisor Aor Tech., Inc., St. Paul, 1992; bd. dirs. Minn. Acad. Sci.; pres. Virotech, Inc., 1993-94; ind. rsch., 1992—; dir. R&D Medcorp Internat., 1996—. Contbr. more than 60 articles to profl. jours. Recipient NIH Rsch./Fellowship award, 1983-86, Grant in Aid Rsch. award Minn. Heart Assn., 1983-85, Med. Student Rsch. award Minn. Med. Found., 1980, Acad. Excellence award Merck Found., 1980. Mem. AAAS, ACS, AMA, Assn. Acad. Surgeons, Soc. Thoracic Surgeons, Am. Physiol. Soc., Am. Fedn. and Clin. Rsch., N.Y. Acad. Scis., Phi Kappa Phi. Republican.

ST. JOHN, CHARLES VIRGIL, retired pharmaceutical company executive; b. Bryan, Ohio, Dec. 18, 1922; s. Clyde W. and Elsie (Kintner) St. J.; m. Ruth Ilene Wilson, Oct. 27, 1946; children: Janet Sue St. John Amy, Debra Ann St. John Mishler. AB, Manchester Coll., 1943; MS, Purdue U., 1946. Asst. gen. mgr., dir. ops. Eli Lilly and Co., Clinton, Ind., 1971-75; gen. mgr. Eli Lilly and Co., Lafayette, Ind., 1975-77, v.p. prodn. ops. divsn., 1977-89; bd. dirs. Bank One of Lafayette, Lafayette Life Ins. Co., Lafayette Cmty. Found., Bioanalytical Sys., Inc., West Lafayette, Ind. Past pres. bd. dirs. United Way Greater Lafayette and Tippecanoe County; bd. trustees Lafayette Symphony Found.; past chmn. lay adv. coun. St. Elizabeth Hosp.; mem. pres.'s coun. Purdue U.; trustee Manchester (Ind.) Coll.; bd. dirs. Lafayette Cmty. Found. Recipient Elizabethan award, St. Elizabeth Hosp., Lafayette, 1985. Mem. Am. Chem. Soc., Purdue Rsch. Found., Greater Lafayette C. of C. (past bd. dirs.), Lafayette Country Club, Rotary (selected as Cmty. Hero Olympic Torch Bearer 1996). Republican. Methodist. Home: 321 Overlook Dr West Lafayette IN 47906-1249

ST. LOUIS, PAULA MARIE, journalist; b. Laconia, N.H., July 19, 1968; d. Robert Roger and Marcia Ann (Whedon) St. L. BA, U. N.H., 1993. Reporter The Citizen, Laconia, 1991-93; intern, reporter Copley News Svc., Springfield, Ill., 1994—. James Armstrong scholar Ill. Legis. Corr. Assn., 1993. Mem. Soc. Profl. Journalists, 1990. Office: Copley News Svc Press Rm Capitol Bldg Springfield IL 62704

SAK, MICHAEL GERARD, county government official; b. Grand Rapids, Mich., Oct. 20, 1959; s. Casimir W. and Salomae Rose (Kurlenda) S. AA, Grand Rapids Jr. Coll., 1979; BFA, Utah State U., 1982; MEd, Grand Valley State U., 1995—. Tchr. St. Francis Xavier, Grand Rapids, 1982-84, Blessed Sacrament Sch., Grand Rapids, 1984-92; afterschool program dir. Grand Rapids Pub. Schs., 1984—; Alexander Elem. Sch., 1992—; commr. County of Kent, Grand Rapids, 1986—; recreation supr. Grand Rapids Parks and Recreation Dept., 1987—; speaker in field, 1987—. Bd. dirs. Cath. Social Svcs., Grand Rapids, 1989-92, Alternative Methods for Internat. Stability, 1986—; mem. exec. bd. Grand Rapids Area Transit Authroity, 1987-91, West Mich. Tree Corps, Grand Rapids, 1986—; mem. adv. coun. West Side Health Clinic, 1993—; mem. screening com. Senator Donald W. Riegle, Jr., Mil. Acad.; mem. West Mich. Regional Fitness Coun., 1996—. Recipient Outstanding Educator award, Grand Rapids, 1996, Excellence in Edn. award Grand Rapids Found. Mem. Nat. Assn. County Ofcls., Mich. Assn. County Ofcls., Mich. Assn. for Local Pub. Health, Kenty County Dem. Exec. Com, 3d Dist. Dem. Com., Am. Coun. Polit. Leaders, Polish Heritage Soc. (pres. 1992). Home: 236 Valley Ave NW Grand Rapids MI 49504-5480 Office: County of Kent 300 Monroe Ave NW Grand Rapids MI 49503-2206

SAKER, JAMES ROBERT, music educator; b. Sharon, Pa., Apr. 13, 1945; s. James W. and Florence A. (Wray) S.; m. Cheryl Ann Mayer, Dec. 26, 1966; children: James R. Jr., Robert David. MusB, Bowling Green State U., 1967; MusM, Youngstown State U., 1975; PhD, U. Iowa, 1982. Dir. instrumental music Hillsdale Schs., Jeromesville, Ohio, 1967-70; chmn. music dept., dir. high sch. bands Champion Schs., Warren, Ohio, 1970-76; grad. teaching asst., mem. band staff U. Iowa, Iowa City, 1976-78; dir. bands U. Nebr., Omaha, 1978—, prof., chair dept. music, 1992—; regional dir. Music Bowl, Inc., Chgo., 1986-92; music dir. Nebr. Ambs. of Music, Omaha, 1986—; mem. Nebr. Consortium on Discipline Based Music Edn., Lincoln, 1988-92; pres. Windthyme, Inc., Omaha, 1984—; music dir. Plam Springs (Calif.) Internat. Children's Festival, 1989, Bluffs Run Iowa Charity Jazz Festival, 1991. Bd. dirs. Omaha Area Youth Orch., 1981-84; mem. parade com. River City Roundup, Inc., Omaha, 1983—; founding pre. Tiburon Home Owners Assn., 1996. Mem. Ohio Music Educators Assn. (pres.-elect local dist. 1974-76), Nat. Band Assb. (exec. bd. 1983-86, 90—, Citation of Excellence 1986), Nebr. Music. Educators Assn. (pres. 1987-89, Disting. Svc. award 1989), Nebr. Bandmasters Assn. (pres. 1983-84, Donald A. Lenta Outstanding Bandmaster award 1993), Coll. Band Dirs. Nat. Assn. (state chmn. 1981—), Coll. Music Soc., Omaha Jazz Soc. (v.p. 1981-86), Rotary (chmn. Rotaract 1988-90), Golden Key Honor Soc. (hon.), Omicron Delta Kappa (hon.). Episcopalian. Home: 17509 Riviera Dr Omaha NE 68136-1951 Office: Univ Nebr Dept of Music Omaha NE 68182-0139

SALAMON, MYRON BEN, physicist, educator; b. Pitts., June 4, 1939; s. Victor William and Helen (Sanders) S.; m. Sonya Maxine Blank, June 12, 1960; children—David, Aaron. B.S., Carnegie-Mellon U., 1961; Ph.D., U. Calif., Berkeley, 1966. Asst. prof. physics U. Ill., Urbana, 1966-72, assoc. prof., 1972-74, prof., 1974—, program dir. materials research lab., 1984-91; vis. scientist U. Tokyo, 1966, 71, Tech. U. Munich, Fed. Republic Germany, 1974-75; cons. NSF; Disting. Vis. Prof. Tsukuba (Japan) U., 1995-96. Editor: Physics of Superionic Conductors, 1979; co-editor: Modulated Structures, 1979; divisional assoc. editor: Phys. Rev. Letters, 1992-96; contbr. sci. papers to profl. jours. Recipient Alexander von Humboldt Sr. U.S. Scientist award, 1974-75; NSF coop. fellow, 1964-66; postdoctoral fellow, 1966; A.P. Sloan fellow, 1972-73; Berndt Matthias scholar Los Alamos Nat. Lab., 1995—; visiting scientist CNRS and Inst. Laue-Langevin Grenoble, France, 1981-82. Fellow Am. Phys. Soc. Office: U Ill Dept Physics 1110 W Green St Urbana IL 61801-3003

SALAMON, SONYA, anthropology educator; b. Pitts., Nov. 1, 1939; d. Marcus Blank and Ethel (Snider) Strasser; m. Myron Salamon, June 12, 1960; children: David, Aaron. BFA, Carnegie Inst. Tech., 1961; MA, U. Calif., Berkeley, 1965; PhD, U. Ill., 1974. Asst. prof. U. Ill., Urbana, 1974-80, assoc. prof., 1980-87, prof., 1987—; vis. scientist Econ. Rsch. Svc. USDA, Washington, 1988-89, 95-96; mem. Kellogg Nat. Rural Studies Com., 1987-96. Author: Prairie Patrimony, 1992; mem. editl. bd. Family Rels., 1988-94; contbr. over 50 articles to profl. jours., chpts. to books. Postdoctoral fellow German Acad. Exchange Program, Munich, 1975; recipient policy fellowship Rural Sociol. Soc., Washington, 1988-89. Fellow Am. Anthrop. Assn., Soc. for Applied Anthropology. Home: 715 W Pennsylvania Ave Urbana IL 61801-4820 Office: U Ill 1105 W Nevada St Urbana IL 61801-3814

SALAMUN, PETER J(OSEPH), botanist, consultant; b. La Cross, Wis., June 12, 1919; s. Peter and Melana (Hardi) S.; m. Lorraine Ann Saurman, June 6, 1946; children: Mary Salamun Conrad, Elizabeth, Charles, William, Edward, David, Lawrence, Katherine Salamun Garrity. BS, Wis. State Tchrs. Coll., Milw., 1941; MS, U. Wis., 1947, PhD, 1950. Instr. to assoc prof. Wis. State Coll., Milw., 1948-56; assoc. prof. to prof. U. Wis., Milw., 1956-60, prof., dir. of herbarium, 1960-84, prof. emeritus, 1984—; postdoctoral rsch. fellow, Artic-Alpine Inst., Boulder, Colo., 1965; bd. trustees The Nature Conservancy, Wis., 1962-84; researcher Sea Grant Coll. Program, 1978-83. Author: Lake Shore Vegetation Studies, 1978, Vegetational Changes, 1990; contbr. rsch. articles to Transactions of the Wis. Acad. Scis., Arts and Letters. Tech. sgt. USAF, 1941-45. Recipient Disting. Teaching award AMOCO, Milw., 1976. Mem. Am. Soc. Plant Taxonomists, Am. Inst. Biol. Scis., Am. Meteorol. Soc., Ecol. Soc. Am., Sigma Xi (pres. Marquette chpt. 1971-72, pres. U. Wis.-Milw. chpt. 1982-83). Roman Catholic. Home: 5013 N Elkhart Ave Milwaukee WI 53217-5606 Office: U Wis PO Box 413 Milwaukee WI 53201-0413

SALATA, WAYNE FRANK, engineering executive; b. Chgo., Mar. 27, 1958; s. George and Dorothy S.; m. Susan Victor, Apr. 21, 1990. BS, Ill. Inst. Tech., 1981. Technician Dyna Scan Corp., Chgo., 1976-82; mgr. engring. Zenith Electronics, Glenview, Ill., 1982-94; dir. engring. Oryx Power Products, Glenview, 1994—. Patentee in field. Vol. local church. Office: Oryx Power Products 1000 Milwaukee Ave Glenview IL 60025-2423

SALCEDO, RODOLFO NACINO, environmental scientist; b. Los Baños, Laguna, Philippines, Dec. 18, 1940; s. Felix Nacino and Julita Agustin (Nacino) S.; m. Conchita D'Bayan Yniguez, Feb. 22, 1964; children: Rudolph John Patrick, Cheryl Rosana. BS in Agrl. Edn. magna cum laude, Visayas Agrl. Coll., Baybay, Leyte, Philippines, 1960; MS, U. of the Philippines, College, Philippines, 1962; PhD, Mich. State U., 1968. Cert. hazardous materials exec., hazardous materials mgr.; registered environ. profl. Rsch. instr. U. of the Philippines, College, Laguna, The Philippines, 1963-65; rsch. asst. Mich. State U., East Lansing, 1966-68; asst. prof. U. Ill., Urbana, 1968-74; environ. scientist City of Milw., 1974—; curriculum cons. U.S. Office of Edn., East Lansing, Mich., 1968; coord. comm. sensitivity U. Ill., Urbana, 1970-72; coord. air quality studies City of Milw., 1975-79; cons. environ. assessments En-Tech, Inc., Milw., 1992-94. Sr. author: Fugitive Dust Sources and Their Control, 1981, Environmental Impacts Hazardous Waste Facilities, 1989; co-author: (book) Communications in Agriculture, 1974; contbr. more than 25 articles to profl. jours. Mem. Milw. River Remedial Action Plan, 1990—, Lake Mich. Pub. Participation Group, Chgo., 1992-93, Toxics Minimization Task Force, Milw. Met. Sewerage Dist., 1993-94. Recipient Environ. Achievement award Friends of Havenwoods, Miw., 1988, citation County Bd. Suprs., Milw., 1992, Editorial Excellence award Pollution Engring., Chgo., 1993, Cert. of Appreciation Wis. Assessors' Assn., 1994; rsch. fellow U. Philippines, 1960-62; grantee USDA, U.S. EPA, 1968-

72. Mem. Fedn. Environ. Technologists, Acad. Hazardous Materials Mgmt., Wis. Environ. Health Assn. Roman Catholic. Home: 7644 W Palmetto Ct Milwaukee WI 53218 Office: City of Milwaukee Health Dept Rm 105 Municipal Bldg Milwaukee WI 53202

SALE, SARA LEE, history educator; b. Neosho, Mo., Feb. 27, 1954; d. Onal Carter and Margaret Lee (Hyde) Sale. BA, Mo. So. State Coll., 1977; MA, Cen. Mo. State U., 1979; PhD, Okla. State U., 1991. Cert. tchr., Mo. Acad. adv. Longview Community Coll., Lee's Summit, Mo., 1978-81; adjunct history lectr. Longview Community Coll., Lee's Summit, 1979-85, Rockhurst Coll., Kansas City, Mo., 1980-85; social sci. instr. Neosho (Mo.) High Sch., 1985-86; history instr. Okla. State U., Stillwater, Okla., 1986-88; assoc. prof. history Mo. So. State Coll., Joplin, Mo., 1989--. Author: Harry S. Truman, the National Security Council and the Cold War, 1996; co-author: Neosho: City of Springs, 1984, Show Me Missouri Women, 1989; contbr. articles to profl. jours. Recipient rsch. grant Harry S. Truman Libr. Inst., Independence, Mo., 1988-89. Fellow Harry S. Truma Libr. Inst.; mem. Orgn. Am. Historians, State Hist. Soc. Mo., Soc. Historians for Am. Fgn. Rels., Phi Alpha Theta, Beta Sigma Phi, Phi Gamma Mu, Phi Kappa Phi. Democrat. Methodist. Office: Mo So State Coll Social Sci Dept 3750 Newman Rd Joplin MO 64801-1595

SALEE, JOSEPH CLAUDE, electrical engineering educator; b. Evansville, Ind., Nov. 4, 1960; s. Donald R. Salee and Sandee R. (Evans) Roberts; m. Barbara C. Geibel, May 27, 1989; children: Kathryn A., Paul E. BS in Elec. Engring. Tech., U. So. Ind., 1991. Assembler Potter and Brumfield, Evansville, 1986-88; drafter Ind. Tube Corp., Evansville, 1989-91; instr. U. So. Ind., Evansville, 1991—. Contbr. article to book Proceedings of the ARRL National Education Workshop, 1992. Sgt. U.S. Army, 1982-86. Mem. IEEE, Am. Soc. for Engring. Edn.

SALEM, RICHARD ALLEN, mediator; b. N.Y.C., Aug. 15, 1930; s. Louis H. and Catherine (Levy) S.; m. Greta Waldinger, June 26, 1955; children: Susanne, Peter, Erica. BA in Sociology, Antioch Coll., 1953; MS in Journalism, Columbia U., 1957. Reporter Washington Post, 1957-59; editor, publ. Washington SBIC Newsletter, 1960-62; spl. asst. to dep. dir. for investment Small Bus. Adminstrn., Washington, 1963-64, assoc. dir. Office of Equal Opportunity, 1964-67, regional dir., 1967-68; Midwest dir. Cmty. Rels. Svc. U.S. Dept. Justice, Chgo., 1968-82; pres. Conflict Mgmt. Initiatives, Evanston, Ill., 1982—; adj. prof. Loyola U., Chgo., 1986-90; mediator Wounded Knee Takeover, 1972, Skokie-Nazi Conflict, 1980. Co-author: Students Guide to Mediation and Law, 1987, Ctr. for Pub. Resources award, 1987; contbr. articles to profl. jours. With U.S. Army, 1953-55. Recipient Outstanding Performance award U.S. Sr. Exec. Svc., 1980. Mem. Soc. Profls. in Dispute Resolution (2d v.p. 1988, bd. dirs. 1982-89, Follett Mgmt. Tng. in South Africa award 1993), Acad. Family Mediation. Home and Office: 1225 Oak Ave Evanston IL 60202

SALEM, STEPHEN JOHN, employment agency administrator; b. Sioux City, Iowa, Mar. 12, 1956; s. Rudolph Charles and Mary Frances (Bendixen) S.; m. Denise Mardelle Harris, July 27, 1985; children: Caitlin Rose, Jillian Marie. BS in Bus. Adminstrn./Mgmt., U. S.D., 1983. Corr. Sioux City Jour., 1970-75; dir. sports info. Morningside Coll., Sioux City, 1975-77; dir. women's sports info. U. S.D., Vermillion, 1978-83; sports editor N.W. Ia. Rev., Sheldon, 1983-84, Denison (Iowa) Newspapers, 1984-85; claims supr. Federated Mut. Ins. Co., Des Moines, 1985-87; mgr. Rudy Salem Employment Agy., Sioux City, 1987-91, owner, 1991—; cons./assoc. Inter-Cities Temporary Svcs., Appleton, Pasadena, Tex., 1989—. Pres. Iowa Assn. Pers. Svcs., 1995—; chair Nat. Fedn. Ind. Bus. Guardian Adv. Coun., 1995—, del. White House Conf. on Small Bus., 1994-95. Mem. Sioux City C. of C. (small bus. com. 1989—, named Small Bus. of Yr. 1995), Nat. Newspaper Assn. (Best Sports Page award 1985), Iowa Newspaper Assn. (Best Sports Page award 1984). Roman Catholic. Office: Rudy Salem Employment Agy 403 Home Fed Bldg 300 Pioneer Bank Bldg Sioux City IA 51101-1049

SALERNO, AMY, state legislator; m. Joe Armeni. BA, Youngstown State U., 1979; JD, Ohio State U., 1982. Bar: Ohio. Lawyer, small bus. owner Columbus, Ohio; mem. Ohio Ho. of Reps., Columbus. Past chmn. Italian Village Commn; former mem. bd. dirs. St. Mark's Comty. HealthCtr.; former mem. Victorian Village Commn., Downtown Housing Task Force, Columbus. Recipient Appreciation cert. Italian Village Commn, Victorian Village Commn., Columbus City Coun., Outstanding Orgn. award Short North Bus. Assn.

SALISBURY, ALICIA LAING, state senator; b. N.Y.C., Sept. 20, 1939; d. Herbert Farnsworth and Augusta Belle (Marshall) Laing; m. John Eagan Salisbury, June 23, 1962; children: John Eagan Jr., Margaret Salisbury La Rue. Student Sweet Briar Coll., 1957-60; BA, Kans. U., 1961. Mem. Kans. Senate, 1985—, v.p., chmn. commerce com., telecomm. strategic planning com.; vice chmn. ways and means com., mem. legis. post audit com., mem. joint com. on econ. devel.(mem. orgn. and calendar rules comm.). Elected mem. State Bd. Edn., Topeka, 1981-85, Kans.,; past pres. Jr. League of Topeka; trustee Leadership Kans., 1982-89; bd. dirs. Topeka Community Found., 1983—, Topeka Pub. Sch. Found., 1985-89, Capitol Area Pla. Authority, 1989—, Mid-Am. Mfg. Tech. Ctr., mem. workers' compensation fund oversight com., mem. Kids Count steering com., mem. Stormont-Vail Hosp. Aux.; mem. adv. commn. Juvenile Offenders Program, Kans., 1985—; mem. adv. bd. Topeka State Hosp., Kans. Action for Children, 1982—, Kans. Ins. Edn. Found., 1984—, Youth Center at Topeka, 1987-95; steering com. One Stop Career Ctr., Interstate Cooperation Com. Coun. State Govts.; mem. Nat. Fedn. Rep. Women; past bd. mem. United Way Greater Topeka, ARC, Family Service and Guidance, Topeka, Shawnee County Mental Health Assn., Florence Crittenton Services, Topeka, Topeka City Commn. Govtl. Adv. Com. Mem. Nat. Conf. State Legislators (exec. com.), Nat. Rep. Legislators' Assn. (Nat. Rep. Legislator of Yr. 1993, Bus. Guardian award 1990, Outstanding Individual Legis. Achievement award 1989), Nat. Fedn. Ind. Bus., Shawnee County Rep. Women, Kappa Kappa Gamma. Episcopalian. Avocations: tennis; downhill skiing; water sports; horseback riding; gardening. Office: Kans State Senate State Capital Topeka KS 66612

SALITERMAN, RICHARD ARLEN, lawyer, educator; b. Mpls., Aug. 3, 1946; s. Leonard Slitz and Dorothy (Sloan) S.; m. Laura Shrager, June 15, 1975; 1 child, Robert Warren. BA summa cum laude, U. Minn., 1968; JD, Columbia U., 1971; LLM, NYU, 1974. Bar: Minn. 1972, D.C. 1974. Mem. legal staff U.S. Senate Subcom. on Antitrust and Monopoly, 1971-72; acting dir., dep. dir. Compliance and Enforcement div. Fed. Energy Office, N.Y.C., 1974; mil. atty. Presdl. Clemency Bd., White House, Washington, 1975; sr. ptnr. Saliterman & Siefferman, Mpls., 1975—; adj. prof. law Hamline U., 1976-81. Chmn. Hennepin County Bar Jour., 1985-87; trustee, sec. Hopkins Edn. Found. Author: Advising Minnesota Business Corporations, 4 vols., 1995. Bd. dirs. Mpls. Urban League, 1987-94; pres. Am. Jewish Com., Mpls. St. Paul chpt., 1988-90; v.p., trustee W. Harry Davis Found, 1989—; treas., bd. dirs. Pavek Mus. Broadcasting, 1992—. With USN, 1972-75. Mem. ABA, Minn. State Bar Assn., Hennepin County Bar Assn. (governing council 1987-89), Oakridge Country Club (Hopkins, Minn.), Mpls. Club, Wayzata Yacht Club.

SALLEE, DON, state legislator; m. Jean Sallee. Rep. dist. 49 State of Kans., 1983-88, senator dist. 1, 1989—. Republican. Home: RR 2 Box 79 Troy KS 66087-9624*

SALLEE, FRANK, securities and investment executive; b. Manhattan, Mont., Mar. 29, 1930; s. Frank and Mildred (Easton) S.; m. Nancy Ann Foster, Jan. 27, 1952; children: Debra Ann Cook, Linda Gail Robbins, Frank F., David R. BS in Agr., U. Mo., 1951. Dist. mgr. Investors Diversified Svcs., St. Joseph, Mo., 1956-62; pres., chmn. Camden County Bank, Camdenton, Mo., 1962-88; fin. cons. Merrill Lynch Pierce Fenner & Smith, Camdenton, 1989-91; gen. securities prin. Sentra Securities Corp., Camdenton, 1991—; pres. Frank Sallee and Assocs., Inc., Camdenton, 1993—; pres., chmn. loan rev. com. Cen. Ozarks Devel., Inc., Camdenton, 1993—. Adv. dir. Great Rivers Coun. Boy Scouts Am., Columbia, 1975—; dir. Nat. Bd. U. Mo. Alumni Assn., Columbia, 1994—; trustee Mo. 4-H Found., Columbia, 1988-97. 1st lt. U.S. Army, 1951-55, ETO. Mem. Mo. Bankers Assn. (assoc., bd. dirs. 1976-78), Lake of the Ozarks Assn. (disting. bd. mem., disting. svc. dir. 1963-93, bd. dirs., pres. chmn. 1975-77), Kansas City Club, Country Club of Mo. Disciples of Christ. Home: RR 1 Box 26 Camdenton MO 65020-9702 Office: Frank Sallee & Assocs Inc PO Box 1469 Camdenton MO 65020-1469

SALLEE, LYNN KANT, library director; b. Waupun, Wis., Jan. 20, 1945; d. Edward Kenneth and Ellen Mary (Blasing) Kant; m. Lorry Francis Sallee, June 14, 1964; children: Kelly Jean Sallee Jahn, Sean Christian. BS, U. Wis., Oshkosh, 1971, MA, 1992. Cert. libr. K-12, Wis. Freelance writer, 1965—; libr. dir. Brandon (Wis.) Pub. Libr., 1989-91; elem. libr. Sch. Dist. Omro, Wis., 1991-93; libr. dir. Neuschafer Cmty. Libr., Fremont, Wis., 1993—. Author: To God, From Mom, 1975, Coffee Time Prayers, 1977, The Collector's Guide to Antique Costume Jewelry; editor X-tra Spl. News, 1986—; contbr. articles to profl. jours. Dir. Klinefelter's Syndrome Assn., Inc., 1986—. Home: N5879 30th Rd Pine River WI 54965 Office: Neuschafer Cmty Libr 317 Wolf River Dr Fremont WI 54940

SALLEE, MARY LOU, state legislator. Mem. Mo. State Ho. of Reps. Dist. 144. Home: PO Box 128 914 NW 9th St Ava MO 65608 Office: Mo Ho of Reps State Capitol Building Jefferson City MO 65101-1556*

SALLEN, MARVIN SEYMOUR, investment company executive; b. Detroit, Oct. 15, 1930; s. Jack Samuel and Sara S.; m. Nancy Susan Berke; 1 child, Jack Samuel II. AB in Econs., U. Mich., 1952. V.p. Sonnenblick-Goldman Corp., Detroit, 1967-83; sr. v.p. Comerica Bank, Detroit, 1983-87; pres. Comerica Mortgage Corp., Detroit, 1983-87; mng. ptnr. Brick Ltd., Birmingham, Mich., 1988-90; mng. dir. Redcliffe Corp., Birmingham, 1990—. Office: Redcliffe Corp PO Box 817 Birmingham MI 48012-0817

SALMON, STUART CLIVE, manufacturing engineer; b. London, 1952. BTech in Prodn. Engring. and Engring. Mgmt. with honors, Loughborough U., 1975; PhD, Bristol U., 1979. Apprentice Rolls-Royce Ltd., Derby, Eng., 1969-79; with Gen. Electric Aircraft Engine Group, Cin., 1979-83; engr. Gen. Electric Aircraft Engine Group, Evendale, Ohio, 1980-83; prin. Advanced Mfg. Sci. and Tech., Cin., 1983—; presenter seminars. Author: Abrasive Machining Handbook, 1983, Modern Grinding Process Technology, 1992; contbr. articles to profl. jours., to McGraw-Hill Ency., 1982-83; patentee in field. Recipient Jim Bottorf award Abrasive Engring. Soc., 1986, Sir Walter Puckey prize, Inst. Prodn. Engrs., U.K., 1975; Rolls-Royce/Brit. Sci. Rsch. Coun. grantee, 1976. Fellow Soc. Mfg. Engrs. Office: Advanced Mfg Sci and Tech PO Box 40469 Cincinnati OH 45240-0469

SALOMON, FRANK LOEWEN, anthropology educator; b. N.Y.C., Apr. 13, 1946; s. George and Mathilde (Loewen) S.; children: Malka, Abraham. BA, Columbia U., 1968; MA, Cornell U., 1974, PhD, 1978. Vis. asst. prof. U. Ill., Urbana, 1978-82; asst. prof. U. Wis., Madison, 1982-84, assoc. prof., 1984-91, prof. anthropology, 1991—. Author: Native Lords of Quito, 1986, Spanish version, 1981, The Huarochiri Manuscript, 1991; mem. edit. bd. Ethnohistory, 1992-94; contbg. editor Handbook of Latin American Studies, 1980-88. Fellow Am. Anthrop. Assn., Soc. for Ethnohistory. Jewish. Office: Univ Wisconsin Dept Anthro 5240 Social Scis Madison WI 53706

SALT, ALFRED LEWIS, priest; b. Hackensack, N.J., Apr. 30, 1927; s. Alfred John and Lily (Tittle) S.; m. Elizabeth May Loveland, June 18, 1949; children: Richard John, Michael Rob, Christopher William, Katharine Anne. BA with honors, Bishop's U., Lennoxville, Can., 1949, MA in History, 1951, BD, 1960; grad. advanced mgmt. program, Harvard U., 1970; D Ministry, Grad. Theol. Found., 1988. Ordained to ministry Episcopal Ch. as deacon, 1951, as priest, 1952. Incumbent St. Philip's, Sawyerville, Que., Can., 1951-52, St. John the Evangelist, Portneuf, Que., 1952-54; rector Christ Ch., Stanstead, Que., 1954-62, St. Michael's Ch., Sillery, Que., 1962-72, All Sts.' Ch., Millington, N.J., 1972-93; bishop's chaplain Diocese of Que., 1962, hon. canon, 1970; pres. Morris Convocation. Morris County, N.J., 1974-78, retreat condr., 1979—; with Victorious Ministry Through Christ, Orlando, Fla., 1981-92, dir., 1986-92, v.p., 1989-92; dir. VMTC Can., 1995—; hon. asst. Grace Ch., Port Huron, Mich., 1993—. Author: Compass Book on Healing, 1996; contbr. articles to religious jour. Mem. Superior Coun. Edn., Que., 1964-70; commr. Que. Protestant Sch. Bd., 1970-72; trustee Heath Village, Hackettstown, N.J., 1974-76; mem. Passaic Twp. Welfare Bd., Millington, 1977-78, 82. With U.S. Army Air Corps Res., 1944-45; with USN, 1945-46. Mem. Blue Water Convocation, Order St. Luke (chaplain). Home: 4429 Gratiot Ave Fort Gratiot MI 48059-3926 also: 190 Chemin du Lac, North Hatley, Canada JO8 2CO

SALTER, CHRISTOPHER LORD, geography educator. BA, Oberlin Coll., 1961; MA, U. Calif. Berkeley, 1968, PhD, 1970. Prof. geography U. Mo., Columbia. Recipient George J. Miller award Nat. Coun. for Geog. Edn., 1992, Disting. Geography Educator award Nat. Geog. Soc., 1990. Office: Univ Mo Dept Geography Dept Geography 3 Stewart Hall Columbia MO 65211

SALTER, EDWIN CARROLL, physician; b. Oklahoma City, Jan. 19, 1927; s. Leslie Ernest and Maud (Carroll) S.; m. Ellen Gertrude Malone, June 30, 1962; children—Mary Susanna, David Patrick. B.A., DePauw U., 1947; M.D., Northwestern U., 1951. Intern Cook County Hosp., Chgo., 1951-53; resident in pediatrics Children's Meml. Hosp., Chgo., 1956-58, Cook County Hosp., Chgo., 1956-58; practice medicine specializing in pediatrics Lake Forest, Ill., 1958—; attending physician Lake Forest Hosp., 1958—, pres. med. staff, 1981-82; attending physician Children's Meml. Hosp., Chgo.; clin. faculty mem. dept. pediatrics Northwestern U. Med. Sch. Served to capt. M.C., U.S. Army, 1954-56. Mem. AMA, Ill. State Med. Soc., Lake County Med. Soc. (pres. 1984), Phi Beta Kappa. Republican. Methodist. Home: 19 N Maywood Rd Lake Forest IL 60045-3233 Office: 900 N Westmoreland Rd Ste 110 Lake Forest IL 60045-1688

SALTSMAN, DONALD L., state legislator; b. Peoria, Ill., Dec. 15, 1933; m. Eva Saltsman, 1956; 4 children. Student, Ill. Ctrl. Coll., U. Ill. Ill. state rep. Dist. 92, 1981—; vice chmn. pers. com., mem. appropriations I Ill. Ho. Reps., cities and villages, vet affairs, chmn. econ. devel., mem. labor coms., elections com., chmn. exec. mem. gen. appropriations, munic and conservation, space need com., horse racing com. Formerly firefighter. *

SALTZMAN, ARTHUR MICHAEL, English language educator; b. Chgo., Aug. 10, 1953; s. Robert and Marion (Coover) S.; m. Marla Jane Marantz, July 26, 1980; 1 child, Elizabeth. AB, U. Ill., 1975, AM, 1976, PhD, 1979. Teaching asst. English U. Ill., Urbana, 1975-80; asst. prof. English Mo. So. State Coll., Joplin, 1981-86, assoc. prof., 1986-92, prof., 1992—, acting dept. head, summers 1991,92; manuscript evaluator Style, 1988, Syracuse U. Press, 1990, Bucknell U. Press, 1991, U. S.C. Press, 1994, U. Pa. Press, 1995; co-sponsor MSSC Live Poets Soc., 1995—. Author: The Fiction of William Gass: The Consolation of Language, 1986, Understanding Raymond Carver, 1988, Designs of Darkness in Contemporary American Fiction, 1990, The Novel in the Balance, 1993; editor, advisor Winged Lion, 1981-91; guest editor Rev. Contemporary Fiction, 1989, 92; contbr. articles to profl. jours. Recipient Outstanding Tchr. award Mo. So. Found., 1992; summer grantee NEH, 1983. Mem. MLA, Mo. Philological Assn. Jewish. Home: 2301 W 29th St Joplin MO 64804-1423 Office: Mo So State Coll Dept English Newman and Duquesne Rds Joplin MO 64801

SALTZMAN, BARRY, actor; b. Chgo., Nov. 1, 1961; s. Bernard William and Cynthia Iris (Gordon) S. BA in Theatre and Drama, Ind. U., 1983. Appeared in theatrical prodns. Rosencrantz and Guilderstern Are Dead, Stage Left Theatre, Chgo., 1984, Chaos Doesn't Run the Whole Show, City Lit Theatre, Chgo., 1986, On the Verge, Body Politic Theatre, Chgo., 1986, The Skin of Our Teeth, Baliwick Repertory, 1987, The Magic Barrel and Other Stories, Nat. Jewish Theatre, Skokie, Ill., 1988, The Little Prince, Children's Classical Theatre Co., Chgo., 1990, Broadway Bound, Briar Street Theatre, Chgo., 1991, Owners, Buffalo Theatre Ensemble, Glen Ellyn, Ill., 1992, The Miser, The Liar, Green Stockings, Festival Theatre, Wis., 1992, Julius Caesar, Next Theatre, Evanston, Ill., 1992, The Real Lie Brady Bunch (nat. tour), 1993, Beachwood Palace Jubilee, L.A., 1994-95, Theft, Hudson Theatre, L.A., 1994, The Smell of Ennui, Theater/Theatre, L.A., 1995, The Big Time Jubilee, Acme Theatre, L.A., 1995-96, numerous others; on camera performances include Bradymania, ABC, 1993. Author, fundraiser The Hunger Project, 1986-88; fundraiser Youth at Risk, 1988, AIDS Walk Chgo., 1990; group discussion leader, fundraiser Stop AIDS Chgo., 1987-90; various adminstrv. and enrollment roles Werner Erhard and Assocs., Chgo., 1986-90; mem. Human Rights Campaign Fund, 1990—. Recipient Medallion for Acting Excellence, Amoco Cos./Am. Coll. Theatre Festival, Kennedy Ctr., Washington, 1982. Home: PO Box 432 Wheeling IL 60090-0432

SALVESEN, B(ONNIE) FORBES, artist; b. Elgin, Ill., Nov. 6, 1944; d. Donald Behan and Helen Elaine (Krajacik) Forbes; m. Bruce Michael Salvesen, Sept. 3, 1966. Studied with Elvira Spivey, Barrington, Ill., 1972-74; studied with Peter Schoelch, Cary, Ill., 1975-82; student, Am. Acad. Art, 1976, Sch. Art Inst. Chgo., 1980-82, Kulick-Startk Byzantine Jewelry Sch., 1983. Asst. to purchasing agt. Harnischfeger, Crystal Lake, Ill., 1962-64; rec. sec. Electric Mfrs. Credit Bur., Cary, Ill., 1964-66; student and practicing artist, 1968—. Illustrator: (book) There were Reasons, 1983. Recipient Award of Excellence, Ill.-Arlington Heights Fine Arts Festival, 1995, Best of Show award 20th Ann. Cambridge Art Fair, 1995, 19th Ann. Fine Arts Festival, Downers Grove, Ill., 1995. Democratic. Roman Catholic. Home and Office: 1312 Whippoorwill Dr Crystal Lake IL 60014-2614

SALVI, AL, state legislator. Student, U. Notre Dame, U. Ill. Committeeman Lake County Rep. Com. Ill., 1987-92; Ill. state rep. Dist. 52; ptnr. Albert J. Salvi and Assocs. Rep cand. for U.S. Senate, I.L., 1996. Home: 24558 W Lake Fairfield Ln Mundelein IL 60060-9501*

SALYERS, PERRY A., electronic design engineer; b. West Union, Ohio, Aug. 3, 1963. BSEE, U. Cin., 1990. Elec. engr. Dosimeter, Cin., 1984-85, R-K Electronics, Cin., 1986—; dir. R-K Electronics, Cin., 1995. Office: R-K Electronics 11560 Gold Coast Dr Cincinnati OH 45249

SALZER, MARGARET MAE, librarian; b. Pollock, S.D., May 7, 1934; d. Benhard and Bertha (Weber) Kruger; m. Irvin H. Salzer, May 29, 1953; children: Nanette, Cheryl, Mark, Benton, Deedra, Wendy. Tchrs. cert. (hon.), No. State Coll., 1952. Tchr. Pollock, S.D., 1952-53; acctg. clk. Dept. Audits and Accounts, Pierre, S.D., 1953-54; sec. Fin. and Loan Office, Greenville, S.C., 1954-56; owner, operator, bookkeeper, worker Farm, Pollock, 1956-68; bookkeeper, office mgr. Timber Lake (S.D.) Livestock Auction, 1968-78; cashier, clk., bookkeeper Salzer Auction Svc., Timber Lake, 1965-95; bookkeeper, sec. T.C. & G. Water Assn. Inc., Glencross, S.D., 1975-95; libr. dir. Dewey County Libr., Timber Lake, 1992—. Republican. Home: PO Box 323 Timber Lake SD 57656

SAMAREL, ALLEN MARK, physician, biochemistry and cell biology educator; b. N.Y.C., June 4, 1951; s. Victor and Dulcy (Saltiel) S.; m. Joan Werber, June 19, 1979; children: Michael, Darla. BS, Queens Coll., 1972; MD, Harvard U., 1976. Resident Mt. Sinai Hosp., N.Y.C., 1976-79; fellow Northwestern U. Med. Sch., Chgo., 1979-82; asst. prof. Northwestern U., Chgo., 1982-85, assoc. prof., 1985-88; prof. Loyola U., Chgo., 1988—; chmn. clin. scis. study sect. NIH, Washington, 1991-94. Recipient Rsch. Ctr. Devel. award NHLBI/NIH, 1985-90. Mem. Am. Heart Assn. (basic sci. coun.), Am. Soc. for Cell Biology, Internat. Soc. for Heart Rsch. Office: Loyola U Med Ctr 2160 S 1st Ave Maywood IL 60153-3304

SAMMAK, PAUL JOSEPH, cell biologist, pharmacologist; b. Dover, Del., Feb. 8, 1956; s. Emil G. and Juliette C. S.; m. Jeannene J. Krone; children: Rebecca Lee, Alexander Julian. MS in Physics, U. Wis., 1981, PhD in Biophysics, 1988. Rsch. asst. Lab. Molecular Biology, U. Wis., Madison, 1981-88, rsch. assoc., 1988; lectr. physiology U. Calif., Berkeley, 1989, rsch. physiologist, 1988-89; rsch. pharmacologist U. Calif., San Diego, 1989-90; fellow in cell physiology U. Calif., Berkeley, 1990-92; asst. prof. dept. pharmacology U. Minn., Mpls., 1992—. Contbr. articles to profl. jours. including Nature, Jour. Cell Biology, Jour. Biol. Chemistry, Cell Motility and the Cytoskeleton. Admissions advisor Hampshire Coll., Amherst, Mass., 1980—. Recipient awards Interam. Conf. Theoretical Physics, 1978, Am. Soc. Cell Biology, 1987, Sigma Xi dissertation excellence, 1988, Nat. Rsch. Svc. award NIH, 1990-92; Edward Livingston Trudeau scholar Am. Lung Assn. Mem. AAAS, Am. Soc. Cell Biology, Am. Soc. Pharm. Exptl. Therapeutics, Sigma Xi. Office: U Minn Dept Pharmacology 435 Delaware St SE Minneapolis MN 55455-0347

SAMPLE, DAN, alcohol and drug prevention professional; b. Topeka, Apr. 14, 1956; s. Glen and Donna Lea (Kinter) S.; m. Sandra Kay Young, Aug. 12, 1978; children: Amber Christine, Alisa Ann. BA, S.W. Bapt. U., 1979, postgrad., 1993. Ordained pastor, Bapt. Ch., 1980; cert. tchr., 1995. Pastor Friendship Bapt. Ch., Mountain Grove, Mo., 1980-85, Cross Timbers (Mo.) Bapt. Ch., 1985-89, High Point Bapt. Ch., Stoutland, Mo., 1991—; prevention specialist Drug Alcohol Tobacco Edn., Bridgeton, Mo., 1985-87; v.p. Christian Civic Found., Bridgeton, 1987-91, Drug, Alcohol, Tobacco Edn., Bridgeton, 1987-91; pres. Free Life Edn., Stoutland, 1991—; technology coord. Stoutland Camden R-2 Sch. Dist., 1994—. Co-author: Free Life Models, Grades K-6, 1993. Home: RR 1 Box 59 Stoutland MO 65567-9713 Office: Free Life Edn RR 1 Stoutland MO 65567-9801

SAMPLES, IRIS LYNETTE, elementary school educator; b. Ravenna, Ohio, July 28, 1948; d. Enzo Joseph and Iris Lynette (Wiley) Lanari; m. Charles Victor Samples, Aug. 24, 1968. BS in Edn., Kent State U., 1973; postgrad. in Reading Instruction, U. Akron, 1977-79; student, Gesell Inst. Human Devel., 1989. Cert. tchr., Ohio. Tchr. first grade Highland Local Schs., Medina County, Ohio, 1968-72; tchr. first grade Barberton (Ohio) City Schs., 1973-77, reading tchr., 1977—; mem. faculty adv. com. Woodford Sch., 1982-89, Right to Read activities coord., 1983—, Buckeye Book activities coord., 1990—, young authors coord., 1991—, tchr. kindergarten pilot program chpt. one students, 1987-88; sch. levy com. Barberton City Schs., 1982, 93, mem. reading curriculum com., 1987-88, mem. Right to Read dist. com., 1987—, reading textbook selection com., 1987-89. Tchr. Bible Sch., Sunday Sch. 1st Luth. Ch., 1978-82, coord. Christmas program, 1979-80; active Woodford PTA, past program chair; vol. various health founds., 1975—. Recipient Woodford Tchr. of Yr., Woodford PTA, 1994; nominated Am. Tchr. award Internat. Reading Assn., Akron chpt.; Jennings scholar, 1984. Mem. Kappa Delta Pi. Lutheran. Home: 670 E Paige Ave Barberton OH 44203-3439 Office: Woodford Elem Sch 315 E State St Barberton OH 44203-2964

SAMPSON, EARLDINE ROBISON, education educator; b. Russell, Iowa, June 18, 1923; d. Lawrence Earl and Mildred Mona (Judy) Robison; m. Wesley Claude Sampson, Nov. 25, 1953; children: Ann Elizabeth, Lisa Ellen. Diploma, Iowa State Tchrs. Coll., 1943, BA, 1950; MS in Edn., Drake U., 1954; postgrad., No. Ill. U., Iowa State U., 1965-66, 74. Cert. tchr., guidance counselor, Iowa. Tchr. elem. sch. various pub. sch. sys., 1943-48; cons. speech and hearing Iowa Dept. Pub. Instrn., Des Moines, 1950-52; speech therapist Des Moines Pub. Schs., 1952-54, 55; lectr. spl. edn. No. Ill. U., DeKalb, 1964-65; tchr. of homebound Cedar Falls (Iowa) Pub. Schs., 1967-68; asst. prof. edn. U. No. Iowa, Cedar Falls, 1968; asst. prof., counselor Wartburg Coll., Waverly, Iowa, 1968-70; instr. elem. edn., then head of advising elem. edn. Iowa State U., Ames, 1972-82; field supr. elem. edn. U. Toledo, 1988, 89; ind. cons. Sylvania, Ohio, 1989—; cons. Des Moines Speech and Hearing Ctr., 1958-59, bd. dirs., 1962, 63; cons. Sartori Hosp., Cedar Falls, 1967-69; bd. dirs. Story County Mental Health Ctr., Ames, 1972-74. NDEA fellow, 1965. Mem. AAUW, Univ. Women's Club, Zeta Phi Eta. Methodist. Home: 4047 Newcastle Dr Sylvania OH 43560-3450

SAMPSON, WESLEY CLAUDE, auditor; b. Terril, Iowa, Nov. 25, 1953; s. Truman Lester and Pauline Marie (Prichard) S.; m. Earldine Robison, Nov. 25, 1953; children: Ann Elizabeth, Lisa Ellen. B in Comml. Sci., Drake U., 1950; MBA, U. Minn., 1964; PhD, U. Mo., 1985. CPA, Iowa, Ohio; cert. data processor; cert. tchr., Iowa. Mgr. A.G. Kiesling, CPA, Des Moines, 1953-56; asst. gen. mgr. Grand River Mutual Telephone Co., Princeton, Mo., 1956-57; mgmt. cons. Des Moines, 1957-59; instr. Rockford (Ill.) Sch. Bus., 1959-60; head tax and data processing dept. Farmers Grain Dealers Assn., Des Moines, 1960-62; dir. fin. svcs. dept. Batten and Assocs., Inc., Des Moines and Mpls., 1962-64; instr. accountancy No. Ill. U., DeKalb, 1964-66; asst. prof. acctg. and data processing U. No. Iowa, Cedar Falls, 1966-70; v.p., trust officer Nevada (Iowa) Nat. Bank, 1970-71; instr. acctg. and data processing Des Moines Area C.C., Ankeny, 1972-75; chief internal auditor Iowa State U., Ames, 1975-76; asst. prof. accountancy U. Mo., Kansas City, Kans., 1979-83; vis. assoc. prof. U. Wis., La Crosse, 1985-87; assoc. prof.

acctg. U. Toledo, 1987-94; owner Matrix Auditor, Sylvania, Ohio, 1994—; owner Ctrl. Iowa Computer Svc. Co., Ames, 1970—; speaker in field. Author and designer software for telephone and grain industry; reviewer: Auditing, 1988, Financial Statement Analysis, 1990, EDP Auditing, 1992; contbr. articles to profl. jours.; patentee in field. Auditor United Campus Christian Fellowship, No. Ill. U., DeKalb, 1965, U. Toledo Found., 1991, U. Toledo Campus Fellowship, 1992, Epworth United Meth. Ch., Toledo, 1990-91, mem. fin. com., 1990-91; treas. Congrl. Ch., Cedar Falls, Iowa, 1968-70; mem. faculty senate U. Toledo, 1994. Price Waterhouse Found. scholar, 1977, Peat, Marwick, Mitchell Found. scholar, 1978. Mem. Iowa Soc. CPAs, Ohio Soc CPAs, Inst. Internal Auditors (pres.-elect 1995-96. chpt. pres. 1996—), New Enterprise Forum, Info. Sys. Audit and Control Assn. Methodist. Home: 4047 Newcastle Dr Sylvania OH 43560-3450

SAMPSON, WILLIAM ROTH, lawyer; b. Teaneck, N.J., Dec. 11, 1946; s. James and Amelia (Roth) S.; 1 child, Lara; m. Drucilla Jean Mort, Apr. 23, 1988. BA with honors in History, U. Kans., 1968, JD, 1971. Bar: Kans. 1971, U.S. Dist. Ct. Kans. 1971, U.S. Ct. Appeals (10th cir.) 1982, U.S. Ct. Claims 1985, U.S. Ct. Appeals (8th cir.) 1992. Assoc. Turner & Balloun, Gt. Bend, Kans., 1971; ptnr. Foulston & Siefkin, Wichita, Kans., 1975-86; shareholder Shook, Hardy & Bacon, Overland Park, Kans., 1987—; presenter legal edn. seminars and confs.; adj. prof. advanced litig. U. Kans., 1994; mem. faculty trial tactics inst. Emory U. Sch. Law, 1994, 95, 96; lectr. area law schs. Mem. Kans. Law Rev., 1969-71, editor, 1970-71; contbr. articles to legal jours. Chmn. stewardship com. Univ. Friends Ch., Wichita, 1984-86; bd. dirs. Friends U. Retirement Corp., Wichita, 1985-87; chmn. capital fund drives Trinity Luth. Ch., Lawrence, Kans., 1990-93, mem. ch. coun., 1990-92; bd. dirs. The Lied Ctr. of Kans., Lawrence. Lt. USNR, 1971-75. Fellow Kans. Bar Assn. (chmn. Kans. coll. advocacy 1986, long-range planning, CLE com. 1987-88); mem. ABA, Douglas County Bar Assn., Johnson County Bar Assn. (bench-bar com. 1989-96, Boss of Yr. award 1990), Wichita Bar Assn. (bd. dirs. 1985-86), Am. Bd. Trial Advs. (pres. Kans. chpt. 1990-91, nat. bd. mem. 1990-91), Internat. Assn. Def. Coun. (faculty mem. trial acad. 1994), Def. Rsch. Inst. (Kans. chmn. 1990-96, Exceptional Performance Citation 1990, Outstanding State Rep. 1991, 92, 94), Kans. Assn. Def. Counsel (pres. 1989-90, legis. coun. 1991, 93, William H. Kahrs Disting. Achievement award 1994), Kans. U. Law Soc. (bd. govs. 1993—), Am. Inn Ct. (Judge Hugh Means chpt., Master of Bench), Alvamar Country Club, Order of Coif, Delta Sigma Rho, Phi Alpha Theta, Omicron Delta Kappa. Republican. Lutheran. Office: Shook Hardy & Bacon 9401 Indian Creek Pky Overland Park KS 66210-2005

SAMS, DALLAS C., state legislator; b. Aug. 30, 1952; m. Elaine Sams; 4 children. Student, Brainerd (Minn.) Cmty. Coll.; BS, U. Minn., 1974. U.S. senator from Minn. St. Paul, 1991—; vice-chmn. health care com., mem. agrl. and rural devel. com., mem. govt. ops. and reform com., mem. health care com., family svc. fin. divsn. com., tax com., tax laws com.; farmer; farm bus. mgmt. instr. Home: RR 1 Box 258 Staples MN 56479-9801*

SAMSON, CARLA ELAINE, family practice physician; b. St. Louis, Sept. 14, 1951; d. Carl Earl and Constance Mae (Delbartes) Ruffing; m. Donald Michael Samson, Aug. 17, 1973; children: Joseph Carl, Zachary James, Emily Mae. BS in Biology, U. Houston, 1973; MD, Baylor Coll. Medicine, Houston, 1978. Diplomate Am. Bd. Family Practice. Resident in family practice Med. Ctr., Columbus, Ga., 1981; mem. staff Catherine Kasper Ctr., East St. Louis, Ill., 1982, 85-86, Belleville (Ill.) Family Med. Assocs., 1982-85, So. Ill. U. Family Practice Ctr., Belleville, 1985—; asst. prof. dept. family medicine So. Ill. U. Sch. Medicine, 1985—. Chmn. edn. com. breastfeeding task force Ill. Dept. Pub. Health, mem. Ryan White Adv. Com., 1992-94. Named Woman of Achievement, YWCA, 1992; honoree Cath. Social Svcs., 1994. Mem. AMA, Am. Acad. Family Physicians, Ill. Acad. Family Physicians (Physician of the Yr. 1991), Ill. State Med. Soc., St. Clair County Med. Soc., Soc. Tchrs. Family Medicine, Physicians for Social Responsibility, Docs Ought to Care, Am. Soc. for Colposcopy and Cervical Pathology, LaLeche League Internat. Med. Assn., ACLU, Nat. Wildlife Fedn. Lutheran. Office: SIU Belleville Family Practice Ctr 180 S Third St Belleville IL 62220-1987

SAMSON, JOSEPH MICHAEL, architect, educator; b. Cleve., July 28, 1954; s. George Joseph and Anna Rose (Jerdonek) S.; m. Cynthia Jean Videto, May 14, 1988; 1 child, Johanna Mary. BArch, Kent (Ohio) State U., 1977, MArch, 1988. Registered architect, Ohio, Mich. Drafter HWH Assocs., Cleve., 1977-78; designer R.L. Hunker Assocs., Peninsula, Ohio, 1978-81; drafter Univ. Hosps., Cleve., 1981-82, project coord., 1982-86; teaching fellow Kent State U., 1986-87; architect A. Luketic & Assocs., Kent, 1987-88, Cleve. Metro-Gen. Hosp., 1988; assoc. prof. archtl. tech. Ferris State U., Big Rapids, Mich., 1988—; pvt. practice Rockford, Mich., 1984—; book reviewer West Pub., Amherst, Mass., 1992-94. Mem. bd. zoning appeals City of Kent, 1987; design advisor City of Coopersville, 1993. Mem. Internat. Facilities Mgmt. Assn., Facilities Mgmt. Educators' Coun. (sec.-treas. 1994—), Tau Sigma Delta. Office: Ferris State U 312 Swan Bldg Big Rapids MI 49307

SAMUEL, ROBERT THOMPSON, optometrist; b. Kansas City, Mo., June 27, 1944; s. Manlius Thompson and Helen Evelyn (Syverson) S. B.A., William Jewel Coll., 1966; postgrad. U. Mo.-Kansas City, 1967, M.S. U. Mo., 1968; D. Optometry, U. Tenn.-Memphis, 1971. Cert. optometrist, Mo. Buyer Recco, Inc., Kansas City, Mo., 1963-67; histology lab. instr. William Jewell Coll., Liberty, Mo., 1965-66; pvt. practice optometry Gladstone, Mo., 1972—; panel Dr. Ford Motor Co., Claycomo, Mo., 1985—, Union Pacific R.R., Kansas City, 1985—, TWA Airlines, 1990, Union Carbide, 1990. Publicity coord. Rep. Party, Kansas City, Mo., 1975-76; chmn. Save Your Vision Week, Kansas City, 1977; mem. Theatre League of Kansas City, 1976—, Kansas City Mus., 1986—, Friends of Art, 1985, Friends of Mo. Town 1855, 1980—. Recipient Outstanding Young Men of Am. award Jaycees, 1978, Good Citizens award DAR, 1962. Mem. Am. Optometric Assn., Mo. Optometric Assn., Optometric Soc. Greater Kansas City, Heart of Am. Contact Lens Congress, Am. Acad. Sports Vision, Vol. Optometric Svcs. for Humanity, Smithsonian Assocs, Kappa Alpha Order (treas. 1966). Republican. Lutheran. Lodge: Lions (exec. bd. dirs. Lions Eye Clinic 1974-84, bd. dirs. Lions Eye Clinic 1982—, Outstanding Svc. award 1973, 74, editor Lions Optometric Ctr. Quar., 1974-84). Avocations: photography, music, piano, swimming, travel. Home: 6325 N Monroe Ave Kansas City MO 64119-1923 Office: 2700 NE Kendallwood Pky Ste 109 Kansas City MO 64119-2071

SAMUEL, ROGER D., newspaper publishing executive. Pub. The Flint (Mich.) Jour. Office: The Flint Jour 200 E 1st St Flint MI 48505-1911*

SAMUELSON, DON S., engineering manager; b. Storm Lake, Iowa, Sept. 20, 1959. BS, Iowa State U., 1987. Cert. tutor Iowa State U. Engring. mgr. Bobalee Hydraulics, Laurens, Iowa, 1990—. Vol. tutor Cmty Sch., Laurens, Iowa. Mem. Pi Tau Sigma. Mem. Ch. of Christ. Office: Bobalee Hydraulics 137 NE Street Laurens IA 50554-1515

SAMUELSON, DONALD B., state legislator; b. Brainerd, Minn., Aug. 23, 1932; s. Walter H. and Ellen (Gallagher) S.; m. Nancy O'Brien, 1952; children: Stephen, Laura, Paula, Christine. Chmn. 6th Dist. Com. on Polit. Edn. State of Minn., 1960-66; former mem. Minn. Ho. of Reps. St. Paul; U.S. senator from Minn., 1982—; chmn. Health & Human Svc. Fin. Div. Com., mem. Commerce and Consumer Protection, mem. Family Svc. Com., mem. Fin. and Health Care Com.; former foreman Bor-Son Construct Co.; union bus. mgr. Chmn. 6th Dist. Com. on Polit. Edn., Minn., 1960-66; mem. State Ctrl. Com. Dem-Farmer-Labor Party, 1964-66, former chmn. Crow Wing County. Mem. Housing and Redevel. Authority, Minn. AFL-CIO, Bricklayers Union, Elks, Eagles, Moose. Democrat. Office: 1018 Portland Ave Brainerd MN 56401-4133 also: State Senate State Capital Building Saint Paul MN 55155-1606*

SAMUELSON, ELLEN BANMAN, state legislator; b. Mathiston, Miss., Dec. 11, 1930; d. Alvin Kornelius and Florence Ellen (True) Banman; m. Armin Otto Samuelson, June 22, 1952; children: Alida Jayne, Ronald Ramin, Eric Carl, Mark Alan. BS, Kans. State U., 1952, MS, 1974. Tchr. elem. sch. Newton (Kans.) Pub. Schs., 1952-53, tchr. home econs., 1957-58; tchr. home econs. Hesston (Kans.) Unified Sch. Dist. 460, 1965-79; prof. home econs. Bethel/Hesston Coll., North Newton, Hesston, Kans., 1979-82, Bethel Coll., North Newton, 1982-87; cons., 1987-88; legislator ho. of reps. State of Kans., Topeka, 1989—; chmn. Joint Com. Children and Families, 1992-94. Precinct committeewoman Rep. Ctrl. Com., Harvey County, Kans., 1956-68, 88—; mem., sec. Harvey County Extension Coun., 1960-64; mem. Family Life Adv. Coun. for Community Mental Health, Kans., 1967-71, Ct. Appointed Spl. Advocate Adv. Bd., Harvey County, 1991—; mem. Hertzler Rsch. Found. Bd., 1993—. Mem. Am. Home Econs. Assn. (speaker ann. meeting student sect. 1989), Am. Vocat. Home Econs. Assn., Kans. Home Econs. Assn. (past sec., past pres., bd. dirs.), Kans. Vocat. Home Econs. Assn. (past pres. bd. dirs.), Kans. State U. Alumni Assn., Kans. State U. Coll. Human Ecology Alumni (bd. dirs. 1991-94), Harvey County Rural Life, Soroptomists, Delta Kappa Gamma (pres. 1984-86), Kappa Omicron Phi. Methodist. Office: House Reps State House Topeka KS 66612

SAMUELSON, LEONARD W., JR., construction executive; b. Mpls., Minn., Feb. 14, 1925. BCE, U. Minn., 1950. Registered prof. engr., Minn. Pres. L.W. Samuelson Constrn., Mpls. Pres. Ch. Redeemer, Fridley, Minn., 1966-69; mem. City Coun., Fridley, Minn., 1966-69. 1st Lt. USAF, 1943-45, 1950-52. Recipient Silver Beaver award, Outstanding Vol. award Boy Scouts Am., 1972. Republican. Lutheran. Office: L W Samuelson Constrn 7800 E River Rd Minneapolis MN 55432-2413

SANCAKTAR, EROL, engineering educator; b. Ankara, Turkey, July 13, 1952; came to U.S., 1974; s. Mehmet Ali and Ulker Mualla (Elveren) S.; m. Teresa Sue Sancaktar, Feb. 16, 1979; children: Orhan Ali, Errol Alan. BS in Mech. Engring., Robert Coll., Istanbul, Turkey, 1974; MS in Mech. Engring., Va. Poly. Inst. and State U., 1975, PhD, 1979. Teaching asst. Robert Coll., Istanbul, 1972-74; instr. Va. Poly. Inst. and State U., Blacksburg, Va., 1977-78; visiting scholar Kendall Co., Boston, 1985-86; assoc. prof. Clarkson U., Potsdam, N.Y., 1984-95; prof. U. Akron (Ohio), 1996—; cons. to the UN Devel. Programme, 1987, ALCOA, 1990-91, U.S. Army Benet Labs., 1991. Mem. editl. adv. bd. Jour. Adhesion Sci. Tech., 1993—; assoc. tech. editor Transactions of the ASME, Jour. of Mech. Design, 1995—; contbr. articles to profl. jours.; patentee in field. Recipient various rsch. grants awarded by NSF, NASA, U.S. Army, N.Y., Grumman Corp., Kendall Co., GE, IBM. Mem. ASME (assoc. tech. editor transactions of ASME Jour. of Mech. Design 1995—, editor Reliability, Stress Analysis and Failure Prevention Aspects of Composite and Active Materials, elected mem. RSAFP tech. steering com.). Home: 14 Spring St Potsdam NY 13676-2116 Office: Dept Polymer Engring U Akron Akron OH 44325-0301

SANCHEZ, GUADALUPE, dermatologist; b. Rio Verde, Mex., June 7, 1952; came to U.S., 1956; d. Jacinto and Mercedes (Iniguez) Sanchez; m. Joseph J. Billadello, June 24, 1979; 1 child, Laura. BA, Berry Coll., Mt. Berry, Ga., 1974; MD, Harvard U., 1978. Diplomate Am. Bd. Internal Medicine. Resident in internal medicine Duke U. Med. Ctr., Durham, N.C., 1978-81; fellow in dermatology Washington U., St. Louis, 1981-82, resident in dermatology, 1982-84, chief resident, 1984-85; pvt. practice dermatology Family Dermatology Ctr., St. Peters, Mo., 1985—; chief of medicine Barnes St. Peters Hosp., 1987; mem. clin. staff Washington U. Student Helath, 1995—. Contbr. articles to Jour. Investigative Dermatology. Mem. St. Louis regional interview panel Pres.'s Commn. on White House Fellowships, 1995. Mem. Am. Acad. Dermatology, St. Louis Dermatol. Soc. (polit. task force 1994-95), Harvard Club St. Louis (admissions com. 1994-95). Office: Family Dermatology Ctr 70 Jungermann Cir Ste 204 Saint Peters MO 63376

SAND, GREGORY WILLIAM, history educator, researcher; b. Newark, N.J., Oct. 22, 1935; s. John Ferdinand and Marie Catherine (Gallagher) S.; m. Mary Jane Arnold, Aug. 11, 1962; children: Christopher, Rachel, Thomas. BA, Seton Hall U., 1959; MA in History, Creighton U., 1963; PhD in Am.-Modern European History, St. Louis U., 1973. Instr. history Duchesne Coll., Omaha, 1965-66, Mt. Marty Coll., Yankton, S.D., 1966-67, So. Ill. U., 1969-70; grad. fellow in history St. Louis U., 1968-69; adj. prof. internat. rels. Webster U., St. Louis, 1986-90; adj. prof. history East Ctrl. Coll., Union, Mo., 1993, Concordia U. Wis. St. Louis Ctr., St. Louis, 1994—; vis. lectr. history U. Mo., Kansas City, 1982; ednl. sales rep. Concordia Pub. House, St. Louis, 1994—. Author: Soviet Aims in Central America, 1989, Truman in Retirement, 1993; editor, reviewer for hist. accuracy part II: Nobility and Analogous Traditional Elites, 1993. Fund-raising assoc. St. Louis Zoo, 1986, Repertory Theatre of St. Louis, 1987—; devel., exec. dir., Big River Assn., St. Louis, 1985-86. Asia fellow Hamline U., 1966, ; travel grantee Fritz Thyssen Found., 1981; gen. edn. grantee Marguerite Eyer Wilbur Found., 1986, rsch. grantee Truman Libr. Inst., 1989-90. Mem. Nat. Assn. Scholars, Phi Alpha Theta. Roman Catholic. Home: 28 Jeanette Dr Granite City IL 62040 Office: Concordia Pub House 3558 S Jefferson Ave Saint Louis MO 63118

SAND, HARVEY, state legislator; m. Eleanor; 5 children. Mem. N.D. Senate, 1993—, vice chmn. govt. affairs com., mem. bus., labor coms. Mem. Masonic Orders, Am. Legion. Home: HC 2 Box 28 Langdon ND 58249-9501*

SAND, PHYLLIS SUE NEWNAM (PHYLLIS SUE NEWNAM), retired special education educator; b. Epworth, N.D., Feb. 12, 1931; d. Zelnoe Jackson and Susie Ella (Lindley) Newnam; m. Shirley Sylvester Sand, Aug. 24, 1952; children: Thomas Richard, James Waldow, Catherine Roberta, Constance Renae. AA, Minot State Tchrs. Coll., 1952; BS in Edn., U. N.D., 1970, MEd, 1971. Cert. profl. educator, N.D., tchr., Minn. Tchr. various rural schs. Ward/Cavalier Counties, N.D., 1950-53; cons., tchr. Griggs, Steele, & Trail Spl. Edn. Unit, N.D., 1976-78; diagnostician, tchr. learning disabled Larimore (N.D.) Elem., 1978-92. Mem. NEA (life), N.D. Edn. Assn. (life), Coun. for Exceptional Children, N.D. Ret. Tchrs. Assn., Greater Grand Forks Sr. Citizens Assn., DAV Aux., North Star Quilters Guild (charter), Minnkota Geneal. Soc., Delta Kappa Gamma (pres. 1990-92, program chmn.). United Methodist. Home: 418 Conklin Ave Grand Forks ND 58203-1669

SANDA, KRIS(TA LINNEA), state commissioner; b. Detroit Lakes, Minn., Dec. 26, 1937; d. K.I. and Luella E. (Meyer) Gandrud; m. Donald J. Sanda, Dec. 28, 1957 (div. 1990); children: John, Karin Luebke, Steven, Timothy, Paul, David; m. Richard O. Johnson, June 15, 1991; children: Lisa Johnson Wahlberg, Scott Johnson. Student, St. Cloud State U., 1955-57; cert., Humphrey Inst. of Pub. Affairs, U. Minn., 1983. Substitute tchr. Staples (Minn.) Pub. Schs., 1957-67; with customer svc. dept. Benson Optical Co., Staples, 1968-79; reporter, columnist Staples World, 1962-68; officer Rep. Party of Minn. State, 1968-79; nat. conv. del., 1972, 76; consumer advocate State of Minn., St. Paul, 1979-83; commr. dept. pub. svc. State of Minn., 1991—; with sales dept. Rural Ventures Inc. (Control Data Corp.), Mpls., 1983-87; pres. Rural Tech. Partnership, St. Paul, 1987-91; bd. dirs. St. Paul Combined Charities State of Minn. Employees. Contbr. editorials and columns to local newspapers; polit. analyst Pub. TV Almanac, KTCA-TV, St. Paul. Bd. dirs. St. Paul Downtown Coun., 1991-93, Rasmussen Bus. Colls. Minn., St. Paul Area United Way, Boy Scouts Am. Indianhead Coun., St. Paul Conv. Bur.; officer Gloria Dei Luth. Ch., St. Paul; bd. dirs. Minnehaha Park Restoration; nat. conv. del. Reps., 1972, 76; Todd County chair woman 7th congl. dist., state vice chair, 1964-79; mem. Minn. Hist. Soc. Mem. Nuc. Waste Strategy Coalition (exec. com.), Nat. Assn. Regulated Utility Commrs., Nuc. Regulatory Commn. (Minn. state liason), State of Minn. Environ. Quality Bd., Rotary (treas. 1987-88, Youth Leadership award St. Paul chpt. 1990), St. Paul C. of C. (bd. dirs. 1987-91), Sons of Norway. Republican. Office: Minn Dept Pub Svc 200 Metro Sq Saint Paul MN 55101

SANDAGE, ELIZABETH ANTHEA, retired market research executive; b. Larned, Kans., Oct. 13, 1930; d. Curtis Carl and Beulah Pauline (Knupp) Smith; student Okla. State U., 1963-65; BS, U. Colo., 1967; MA, 1970; PhD in Communications U. Ill., 1983; m. Charles Harold Sandage, July 18, 1971; children by previous marriage: Diana Louise Danner Wilson, David Alan Danner. Pub. rels. rep., editor Martin News, Martin Marietta Corp., Denver, 1960-63, 65-67; retail advt. salesperson Denver Post, 1967-70; instr. advt. U. Ill., 1970-71, vis. lectr. advt., 1977-84; v.p., corp. sec., dir. Farm Rsch. Inst., Urbana, 1984-95, ret. 1995. Bd. dirs. U. Ill. Libr. Friends, 1991-95. Exec. dir. Sandage Charitable Trust, 1986—. Mem. U. Ill. Alumni Assn. (pres.'s coun.), Champaign Social Sci. Club., The Book Club, , Moneymakers Investment Club, Kappa Tau Alpha. Editor: Occasional Papers in Advertising, 1971; The Sandage Family Cookbook, 1976, 2d edit., 1986; The Inkling, Carle Hosp. Aux. Newsletter, 1975-76. Home: 106 Meadow Dr Urbana IL 61801-5822

SANDAHL, DAVID GORDON, correctional administrator, consultant, educator; b. Ligonier, Ind., Oct. 9, 1942; s. Hjalmar Gordon and Lillian (Patrick) S.; m. Marcille Marie Pasdertz, Aug. 5, 1967. AA, Joliet Jr. Coll., 1965; BA, Lewis U., 1968; MS in Edn., No. Ill. U., 1972. Cert. ednl. adminstr., Ill.; tchr., Ill.; specialist in continuing edn., U.S. Office of Edn. Tchr. Joliet (Ill.) Pub. Sch. Dist. 86, 1967-70; correctional counselor Ill. Dept. Corrections, Joliet, 1970-71, diagnostic team supr., 1971-72, clin. svcs. supr., 1972-73, asst. warden, 1973-78, 88; acting chief investigator Ill. Dept. Corrections, Springfield, 1978-79, ops. cons., 1979-83, mgr. ops. and program audits, 1983-88; warden Shawnee Correctional Ctr. Ill. Dept. Corrections, Vienna, 1989-93; adminstr. stds. and accreditation Ill. Dept. Corrections, Springfield, 1993—; cons. Coop. Ednl. Rsch. Labs., Northfield, Ill., 1968-70; adj. faculty Joliet Jr. Coll, 1970-76, Lewis U., Lockport, Ill., 1970-76, Coll. of St. Francis, Joliet, 1970-76; bus. adv. bd. Joliet Drama Guild, 1972-78. Conbg. author: (3 vols.) Program of Instruction, 1970; author (stds.) Administrative Directives, 1979-81, Americans With Disabilities Act Revisions, 1995. Bd. dirs. Citizens for Ill. Constnl. Conv., Will County, 1968; vol. Am. Cancer Soc., Johnson County, Ill., 1989-92; mem. exec. coun. Egyptian coun. Boy Scouts Am., 1990-93. Recipient Key Man award Joliet East Jaycees, 1972, Award of Merit award Joliet East Jaycees, 1975. Mem. Am. Correctional Assn. (cert. auditor, cons.), Am. Fedn. Tchrs. (pres. Local 604 1969, v.p. 1968), Ill. Correctional Assn. (exec. bd. 1981-82, del. assembly 1993, membership com. 1995), Ill. Police Assn., Will County Police Chiefs Assn., Correctional Accreditation Mgrs. Assn.

SANDBERG, JOHN ALDEN, quality control professional; b. Altoona, Pa., Jan. 30, 1947. BS, Hiram Coll., 1981. Mfg. exec. Delphi Packard Elec. Systems, Warren, Ohio, 1968-84, pers. adminstr., 1984-88, divisional auditor, 1988-92, supplier, quality mgr., 1992—. Vol. ARC. With U.S. Army, 1964-68. Office: Delphi Packard Elec Systems 408 Dana St NE # 93L Warren OH 44483-3852

SANDBERG, RICHARD A., manufacturing engineer; b. Providence, July 30, 1946; s. Arthur Eugene and Irene Mary (Roy) S.; m. Gayle Burnett, Aug. 22, 1976; children: Debbie, Renee, Wayne, Brenda. A in Elec. Engring., Rogers Williams Coll., 1967; BS in Mktg., Ind. U., 1973; BS in Mfg. Engr., Brigham Young U., 1976. Mech. engr. Westinghouse Hanford, Richland, Wash., 1977-81; sr. mech. engr. ISC Sys., Spokane, 1981-90; mgr. engring. group, group leader mech. engr. Bendix-King Radio Allied Signal, Lawrence, Kans., 1990—. Patentee in field. Mem., first counselor, Bishopric, Morman Ch., Lawrence, 1990—; dist. tng. chmn., scoutmaster Boy Scouts Am., Lawrence, 1990—; counselor Jr. Achievement, Lawrence, 1992—. With U.S. Army, 1969-71. Decorated Commendation medal U.S. Army, Ft. Harrison, Ind., 1971. Republican. Office: Bendix-King Radio 2901 Lakeview Rd Ste 100 Lawrence KS 66049-8952

SANDBORG, VERIE, environmentalist; b. St. Joseph, Mich.; d. Otto and Gretchen (Dase) Weimann; m. Alan Sandborg (div. 1978); children: Pamela Joy, David Alan. BS in Chemistry, Valparaiso (Ind.) U., 1959; MA in Liberal Studies, Loyola U., Chgo., 1987. Cert. naturalist Morton Arboretum, Lisle, Ill. Tech. libr. CPC Internat., Argo, Ill., 1959-62; copy editor Med. Digest, Northfield, Ill., 1978; mng. editor Preston Publs., Niles, Ill., 1978-79; legal assoc. Baxter Internat., Deerfield, Ill., 1979-81, mgr. environ. affairs, 1981—; rep. World Environment Ctr. Author: Starseeds, 1989; co-editor: Baxter Environmental Manual, 1993; contbr. articles in profl. jours. in field of environ. mgmt. Mem. Nat. Assn. Environ. Mgmt. (2d v.p.). Office: Baxter Internat Baxter Pkwy Deerfield IL 60015-4625

SANDERMAN, MAURICE, construction company executive; b. 1940. Acct. Shepard, Schwartz & Harris, Chgo., 1961-68; with Kaufmann Broad Homes, Oak Brook, Ill., 1968-74, B.A. Storms Cons., Chgo., 1974-76; pres. Northbrook (Ill.) Devel. Corp., 1976-86; chmn. bd. dirs., CEO, pres. Sundance Homes Inc., Schaumburg, Ill., 1981—. Office: Sundance Homes Inc 1375 E Woodfield Rd Schaumburg IL 60173*

SANDERS, BARRY, football player; b. Wichita, July 16, 1968; s. William and Shirley Sanders. Student, Okla. State U., 1986-89. With Detroit Lions, 1989—. Recipient Heisman Trophy award, 1988; named Sporting News Coll. Football Player of Yr., 1988, NFL Rookie of Yr., 1990; named to Sporting News Coll. All-Am. team, 1987, 88, All-Pro team, 1989-91, 93, Pro Bowl, 1989-95. Office: Detroit Lions 1200 Featherstone Rd Pontiac MI 48342-1938*

SANDERS, GARY GLENN, electronics engineer, consultant; b. Gettysburg, Pa., Dec. 21, 1944; s. James Glenn Sanders and Martha Maybelle (Fleming) Ehlert; m. Elizabeth Marie Rega, Sept. 9, 1977 (div. Sept. 1981). Cert. med. technologist, Chgo. Inst. Tech., 1970; AA, Mayfair Coll., 1972; BS in Electronic Engring., Cooks Inst., Jackson, Miss., 1982. Registered Internat. Med. Techs. Cons. engr. Electronics Design Services, Chgo., 1977-79; applications engr. Nationwide Electronics Systems, Streamwood, Ill., 1979-80; mng. engr. Electronics Design Ctr. Case Western Res. U., Cleve., 1980-82; sr. project mgr. Scott Fetzer Co., Cleve., 1982-89; v.p. engring. Penberthy, Inc., 1990—; comml. pilot; electronic transduction cons. Teltech Inc., Mpls., 1989—; mem. adv. bd. Electronics Search Group, Indpls., 1991—. Contbr. articles on electronics in medicine and biology to profl. confs. and pubs.; patentee in biomed. electronics and indsl. instrumentation, inventor, 1985—. Served with U.S. Army, 1962-68, Vietnam. Decorated DFC, Bronze Star, Air medal, Purple Heart. Fellow Internat. Coll. Med. Technologists; mem. IEEE, AAAS, NRA, DAV, VFW, Instrument Soc. Am. (sr. mem.), Internat. Soc. Hybrid Microelectronics, N.Y. Acad. Scis., Ohio Acad. Sci., Nat. Fire Protection Assn., Am. Legion, Am. Soc. Materials Internat., Boy Scouts Am. Alumni, Nat. Eagle Scout Assn. Republican. Home: 3104 Prophetstown Rd Rock Falls IL 61071-2556 Office: Penberthy Inc 320 Locust St Prophetstown IL 61277-1147

SANDERS, GERALD HOLLIE, communications educator; b. Mt. Vernon, Tex., Dec. 10, 1924; s. Elmer Hugh and Velma Mae (Hollowell) S.; m. Mary Dean Crew, July 18, 1947; children: Michael Dwaine, Rose Ann, Susan Kathleen, Randall Wayne. BA, Southeastern Okla. U., 1947; MA, Tex. Tech U., 1969; PhD, U. Minn., 1974. Program dir. Sta. WEWO, Laurenburg, N.C., 1947-49; sports dir. Sta. KFYO, Lubbock, Tex., 1949-50; gen. mgr. Sta. KLVT, Levelland, Tex., 1950-51, 53-54; sports dir. Sta. KCUL, Ft. Worth, 1954-55; asst. mgr. Sta. KDAV, Lubbock, 1955-57; mgr. Sta. KCBD, Lubbock, 1957-58; owner Sta. KSEL, Lubbock, 1958-67, Sta. KBUY, Amarillo, Tex., Sta. KERB, Kermit, Tex., Sta. KBEK, Elk City, Okla., Sta. KZZN, Littlefield, Tex.; lectr. communications The Coll. of Wooster, Ohio, 1967-68, asst. prof., 1968-75, assoc. prof., 1975-81, chmn. dept. communication, 1974-81; chmn. dept. communication Miami U., Oxford, Ohio, 1981-92, prof. emeritus comm., 1992—; disting. lectr. Jinan U., Zhong Shan U., Fudan U., Nanjing U., Beijing U., China, 1989; cons. in field, Oxford, 1982—; polit. and trial cons., 1996—. Author: Introduction to Contemporary Academic Debate, 1983; also articles. Active Political Campaigns. Served to col. USMC, 1943-46, PTO, 1951-53, Korea. Recipient Disting. Svc. award Delta Sigma Rho-Tau Kappa Alpha, 1991, Am. Forensic Assn., 1991. Mem. Am. Forensic Assn. (pres. 1978-82), Speech Communication Assn., Speech Communication Assn. of Ohio (pres. 1976-77), Disting. Svc. award 1978), Am. Inst. Parliamentarians, Soc. Trial Cons. Presbyterian. Home: 200 Country Club Dr Oxford OH 45056-9002 Office: Advocacy Unltd PO Box 457 Oxford OH 45056

SANDERS, JACQUELYN SEEVAK, psychologist, educator; b. Boston, Apr. 26, 1931; d. Edward Ezral and Dora (Zoken) Seevak; 1 son, Seth. BA, Radcliffe Coll., 1952; MA, U. Chgo., 1964; PhD, UCLA, 1972. Counselor, asst. prin. Orthogenic Sch., Chgo., 1952-65; research assoc. UCLA, 1965-68; cons. Osawatomie State Hosp. (Kans.), 1965-68; asst. prof. Ctr. for Early Edn., L.A., 1969-72; assoc. dir. Sonia Shankman Orthogenic Sch., U. Chgo., 1972-73, dir., 1973-93, dir. emeritus, 1993—; curriculum cons. day care ctrs. L.A. Dept. Social Welfare, 1970-72; instr. Calif. State Coll., L.A., 1972; lectr. dept. edn. U. Chgo., 1972-80, sr. lectr., 1980-93, clin. assoc. prof. dept. psychiatry, 1990-93, emeritus, 1993—; instr. edn. program Inst. Psychoanalysis, Chgo., 1979-82; reading cons. Foreman High Sch., Chgo. Author: Greenhouse for the Mind, 1989; editor: (with Barry L. Childress) Psychoanalytic Approaches to the Very Troubled Child: Therapeutic Practice

Innovations in Residential & Educational Settings, 1989, Severly Disturbed Children and the Parental Alliance, 1992, (with Jerome M. Goldsmith) Milieu Therapy: Significant Issues and Innovative Applications, 1993; contbr. articles to profl. jours. Mem. vis. com. univ. sch. rels. U. Chgo. UCLA Univ. fellow, 1966-68; Radcliffe Coll. Scholar, 1948-52; recipient Alumna award Girls' Latin Sch., Boston. Mem. Assn. Children's Residential Ctrs. (past pres.). Clubs: Quadrangle, Radcliffe of Chgo. (sec/treas. 1986-87, pres. 1987-89); Harvard of Chgo. (bd. dirs. 1986—). Home: 5842 S Stony Island Ave Apt 2G Chicago IL 60637-2023

SANDERS, JAMES EDWARD, family practice physician; b. Mpls., July 31, 1951; s. Grover Edward and Betty Jane (Butts) S. BA, U. Kans., 1974, JD, 1977; MD, U. Kans., Kansas City, 1986. Diplomate Am. Bd. Family Practice, Am. Bd. Legal Medicine. Reginald Heber Smith Cmty. Lawyer fellow, 1977-79; atty. Kans. Legal Svcs., Kansas City, 1979-82; clin. asst. prof. medicine U. Kans. Med. Sch., Kansas City, 1989-91; assoc. chief of staff, dir. ambulatory care and emergency Eisenhower VA Med. Ctr., Leavenworth, Kans., 1991—; adj. clin. asst. prof. medicine U. Kans., 1991—, adj. clin. instr. Wichita State U., Coll. of Health Professions, 1994—. Fellow Am. Coll. Legal Medicine, Am. Acad. Family Practice; mem. Order of the Coif Legal Honor Soc., Phi Beta Kappa, Alpha Omega Alpha. Home: 4405 Cambridge Kansas City KS 66103-3505 Office: Eisenhower Med Ctr 41015 S 4th Leavenworth KS 66048

SANDERS, JAMES RICHARD, education educator, consultant, researcher; b. Williamsport, Pa., Nov. 11, 1944; s. William Leon and Evelyn Louise (Hinkle) S.; m. Susan Angela Meyers, June 15, 1968; children: Jamie Kathryn, Jennifer Elaine. AB, Bucknell U., 1966, MS in Edn. with honors, 1968; PhD, U. Colo., 1970. Asst. prof. edn. Ind. U., Bloomington, Ind., 1970-73; sr. rsch. assoc. N.W. Regional Edn. Lab., Portland, Oreg., 1973-75; from assoc. prof. to prof. edn. Western Mich. U., Kalamazoo, 1975—; vis. scholar Utah State U., Logan, 1984, U. B.C., Vancouver, Can., 1984, St. Patricks Coll., Dublin, 1983; program dir. W.K. Kellogg Found., Battle Creek, Mich., 1991-92; chmn. Joint Com. on Standards for Ednl. Evaluation, Kalamazoo, 1987—. Author: Evaluating School Programs, 1992, A Model for School Evaluation, 1995; co-author: Educational Evaluation, 1973, 87, Competency Assessment, 1979. Com. mem. Ind. Sector, Washington, 1992—, NSF, Washington, 1991-93. Bucknell U. fellow, 1967-68; U. Colo. fellow, 1968-70. Mem. Am. Ednl. Rsch. Assn., Nat. Soc. for Study of Edn., Am. Evaluation Assn. (bd. dirs.), Nat. Coun. on Measurement in Edn., Phi Delta Kappa. Lutheran. Home: 57 1st St Plainwell MI 49080-9127

SANDERS, MARTHA J. MORGAN, nurse; b. Hutchinson, Kans., Oct. 13, 1935; d. Hubert E. and Anna E. (Briggs) Morgan; children: Max D. Harris, Melissa D. Harris Stockwell. BSN, Kans. State U., Manhattan, 1958, MS, 1984, PhD, 1993; cert. in nursing, U. Kans., Kansas City, 1957; MSN, Clarkson Coll., 1995. RN; cert. childbirth edn. specialist level III. Dir. edn. Pratt (Kans.) Reg. Med. Ctr., 1972-88; instr. Kans. State U., 1989; asst. prof. nursing, baccalaureate outreach coord. Ft. Hays State U., Hays, Kans., 1990-96; coord. health occupation specialty programs Pratt C.C., 1973-89. Contbr. articles to profl. jours. Mem. Am. Assn. Adult and Continuing Edn., Coun. for Adult and Experiential Learning, Nat. Assn. Childbirth Edn. Specialists, Kans. State Nurses' Assn., Kans. Assn. Nursing Continuing Edn. Providers, Phi Delta Kappa, Sigma Theta Tau, PEO.

SANDERSON, DAVID ALAN, training and development administrator; b. Kenton, Ohio, Apr. 17, 1951; s. George H. and Betty Lou (Kelley) S.; m. Carla Lynn Schwyn, Aug. 7, 1976; children: Rachel Ann, Jessica Lynn. BS, Bowling Green State U., 1973, MEd, 1975, postgrad. Tng. coord. Cummins Engine Co., Fostoria, Ohio, 1976-78; tng. mgr. Cummins Engine Co., Fostoria, 1978-82, Doehler-Jarvis Co., Toledo, 1982-87; tng. and devel. mgr. Gen. Mills, Inc., Toledo, 1987—; ptnr., co-founder Applied Technetronics, Cygnet, Ohio, 1987—; owner Sanderson Stables, Cygnet, 1982—; adv. bd. Owens C. C., 1982—, adj. prof., instr. statis. process control, 1991—; mem. edn. adv. com. Ohio Edison Indsl. Ctr.; mem. trades subcom. State of Ohio Apprenticeship Coun. Author: Basic. S.P.C., 1986, Basic Video, 1981, The Apprenticeship System: How It Works, 1996. Councilman Village of Cygnet, 1989; mem. Cygnet Centennial com., 1989; mem. U.S. Equestrian Team. Mem. ASTD, Assn. for Quality and Participation, U.S. Apprenticeship Assn., Internat. Voc. and Tech. Assn., Assn. Jr. Colls. and Vocat. Schs. Assn. Performance and Instrn. Democrat. Methodist. Home: PO Box 146 46 Washington St Cygnet OH 43413 Office: Gen Mills Inc 1250 W Laskey Rd Toledo OH 43612-2909

SANDHU, SARWAN SINGH, chemical engineering educator, researcher; b. Jalandhar, Panjab, India, Feb. 3, 1940; came to U.S., 1973; s. Gurbachan Singh and Kartar Kaur (Chatha) S.; m. Swaran Kaur Mathu, July 15, 1955; children: Balwinder, Harjinder, Jagjit, Sukhdev. BS, Panjab U., 1961, BS in Chem. Engring., 1966; MSChemE, U. New Brunswick, Can., 1970; PhD, Imperial Coll., London, 1973. Sci. tchr. Khalsa Higher Secondary Sch., Nangal Ambia, India, 1961-62; lectr. dept. chem. engring. Panjab U., Chandigarh, India, 1966-67; engr. No. Rsch. and Engring. Corp., Cambridge, Mass., 1974-75; combustion scientist, chem. engr. Energy Lab. MIT, Cambridge, 1977-80; asst. prof. dept. chem. engring. U. Dayton, 1980-85, assoc. prof., 1985-90, prof., 1990—, dir. grad. chem. engring., 1986-90. Contbr. articles to profl. jours. Recipient USAF-SCEEE fellowship, 1981, sr. investigator rsch. grants USAF, Wright Patterson AFB, 1982, 1988, 1991—. Mem. AICHE (profl. devel. recognition cert. 1985), The Combustion Inst., Math. Assn. Am. Office: U Dayton 300 College Park Ave Dayton OH 45469-0001

SANDLOW, LESLIE JORDAN, physician, educator; b. Chgo., Jan. 7, 1934; s. Harry H. and Rose (Ehrlich) S.; m. Joanne J. Fleischer, June 16, 1957; children; Jay, Bruce, Lisa. BS, U. Ill., 1956; MD, Chgo. Med. Sch., 1960. Intern Michael Reese Hosp. and Med. Ctr., Chgo., 1961, med. resident, rsch. fellow gastrointestinal rsch., 1961-64, physician-in-charge clin. gastroenterology lab., 1963-74, asst. attending physician, 1964-67, assoc. attending physician, 1967-72, vice chmn. divsn. gastroenterology, dir. ambulatory medicine, 1968, dir. ambulatory care, 1969-76, attending physician, 1972—, assoc. med. dir., 1972-73; clin. asst. Chgo. Med. Sch., 1963-68, clin. instr., 1966; asst. prof. dept. medicine Pritzker Sch. Medicine, U. Chgo., 1973-76, assoc. prof., 1976-85, prof., 1985-90; prof. clin. medicine and med. edn. U. Ill. Coll. Medicine, Chgo., 1990-91, prof. medicine and med. edn., 1992—, sr. assoc. dean for grad. and continuing med. edn., 1993—, head dept. med. edn., 1993—, sr. assoc. dean for med. edn., 1994—; dep. v.p. profl. affairs Michael Reese Hosp. and Med. Ctr., 1973-78, dir. Office Ednl. Affairs, 1976-81, assoc. v.p. acad. affairs, 1978-82, dir. quality assurance program, 1981-91, v.p. planning, 1982-83, v.p. profl. affairs and planning, 1983-88, dir. divsn. internal medicine, 1986-93, v.p. profl. and acad. affairs, 1988-91, med. dirs. acad. and med. affairs, 1992-94; med. dir. Michael Reese Health Plan, Inc., 1972-74, interim exec. dir., 1976-77; cons. gastroenterologist Ill. Ctrl. Hosp., 1978-80; vis. prof. Pontifica U. Catolica Rio Grande do Sul, Brazil, 1978, U. Fed. Espirito Santo, Brazil, 1978, Nordic Fedn. for Med. Understanding, Akureyri, Iceland, 1978, Seoul Nat. U. Sch. Medicine, 1981, Coll. Physicians and Surgsons, Kharachi, Pakistan, 1994, U. Tex., Ft. Worth, 1977, U. Ariz., Tucson, 1977, Loyola U. Med. Sch., Maywood, Ill., 1979; cons. in field; coord. Health Scis. Librs. in Ill.; mem. Midwest Med. Libr. Network; mem. subcom. on delivery of ambulatory med. care Inst. Medicine Chgo.; mem. cmty. resources task force Interinstnl. Cardiovascular Ctr.; chmn. steering group Ill. Regional Med. Program; past co-chmn. curriculum com. U. Chgo. Reviewer Rsch. in Med. Edn./Assn. Am. Med. Colls., 1985—, Acad. Medicine/Assn. Am. Med. Colls., 1989; contbr. numerous articles to profl. publs. Mem. Skokie (Ill.) Bd. Health, 1973-85, chmn., 1976-85; bd. dirs. Group Health Assn. Am., 1976-78, Portes Ctr., 1980—; bd. dirs. Good Health Program Skokie Valley Hosp., 1978-80; bd. dirs., exec. com. Rsch. and Edn. Found. of Michael Reese Hosp. Med. Staff, 1992—. Recipient numerous grants, including NIH, 1988, Michael Reese Hosp. Found., 1994-95, Chgo. Cmty. Trust, 1994-95. Fellow Am. Coll. Gastroenterology; mem. N.Y. Acad. Scis., Inst. Medicine, Assn. Am. Med. Colls., Am. Coll. Physician Execs. (co-chair resource mgmt. com. of quality assurance forum), Soc. Dirs. Med. Coll. Continuing Med. Edn., Soc. Dir. Rsch. in Med. Edn. Home: 2314 Lincoln Park West Chicago IL 60614 Office: U Ill Coll Medicine Med Edn M/C 784 1819 W Polk St Chicago IL 60612

SANDRY, KARLA KAY FOREMAN, industrial engineering educator; b. Davenport, Iowa, Apr. 2, 1961; d. Donald Glen and Greta Geniveve (VanderMaten) Foreman; m. William James Sandry, Oct. 12, 1985; children: Zachary Quinn, Skyler David. BS in Indsl. Engring., Iowa State U., 1983; MBA, U. Iowa, 1992. Quality control supr., indsl. engr. Baxter Travenol Labs, Hays, Kans., 1983-84; indsl. engr. HQ Amccom, Rock Island, Ill., 1984-86; mgmt. engr. St. Lukes Hosp., Davenport, 1986-90; adj. instr. engring. St. Ambrose U., Davenport, 1990—; chair space allocations St. Luke's Hosp., Davenport, 1987-90; pres. employee rels. coun. HQ Amccom, Rock Island, 1986, chair savings bonds, 1985; speaker in field. Vol., past counselor Fellowship Christian Athletes Ctrl. H.S., Davenport, 1984-87, vol., adult chpt., 1988—; counselor Explorer Scout Troop, Davenport, 1984-85; leader, counselor ch. youth group, 1985-89; v.p. Crisis Pregnancy Ctr., 1996—, co-chmn. walkathon, 1996, pres. ch. choir, 1992, 95-96, orch. ch., 1994—, fin. com. 1995, dream team, 1996—, security com. 1996—. Mem. Inst. Indsl. Engrs. (sr. mem.), Healthcare Info. & Mgmt. Systems Soc. (recognition & comms. com. 1988), Soc. for Health Systems (founding mem.), Found. for Christian Living, Iowa State U. Alumni Assn., U. Iowa Alumni Assn.; Positive Thinkers Club. Office: St Ambrose U 518 W Locust St Davenport IA 52803-2829

SANDS, DEANNA, editor. Mng. editor Omaha World Herald. Office: Omaha World-Herald World-Herald Sq Omaha NE 68102*

SANDS, GENE CAMERON, public relations executive, educator; b. Healdton, Okla., July 1, 1944; s. Harry J. and Melba (Cameron) S.; m. Constance E. Jackson, Jan. 2, 1982; children: David, Ryan, Claire. BA, U. Okla., 1966, MA, 1967; EdD, Cath. U., 1982. Commd. 2nd lt. USAF, 1967, advanced through grades to lt. col., 1983; chief media and comty. rels. hdqs. tactical air command USAF, Langley AFB, Va., 1980-83; dep. dir. office of asst. sec. of def. Dept. Def., Washington, 1983-87; ret. USAF, 1987; coord. comty. rels. Fairfax (Va.) County Pub. Schs., 1988-92; dir. pub. rels. and mktg. The Fairfax Network, 1992-93; exec. dir. pub. affairs Coll. of St. Benedict-St. John's U., St. Joseph, Minn., 1994—. Contbr. articles to profl. jours. Mem. Pub. Rels. Soc. Am. (accredited), Soc. Profl. Journalists (chpt. pres. 1964), Air Force Assn., U.S. Distance Learning Assn., Coun. for Advancement and Support of Edn., North Va. Press Club (pres. 1992). Office: Coll of St Benedict 37 College Ave S Saint Joseph MN 56374-2001

SANDS, M. DALE, engineering industry executive; b. Highland Park, Mich., Feb. 13, 1951; s. Maynard Duffy and Claire Tess (Martin) Sands; m. Debra H. Sands, Aug. 25, 1973; children: Hilaria E., Trenton D., Kendrick D. BS in Chemistry and Biology, Ctrl. Mich. U., 1973; MS in Environ. Scis., U. Mich., 1974; MBA, Calif State U., 1984. Chemist, lab. dir. Raytheon Ocean Environ. Scis., Portsmouth, R.I., 1974-77; scis. dir. Interstate Elect-Scis., Anaheim, Calif., 1977-81; v.p., gen. mgr. McKesson Environ. Scis., Pleasanton, Calif., 1981-88; v.p., ops. mgr. CH2M Hill, Montgomery, Ala., 1988-89; west regional v.p. ABB Environ. Svcs., Camarillo, Calif., 1989-90; pres. ABB Environ. Svcs., Portland, Maine, 1990-93; v.p., gen. mgr. Wheelabrator Clean Air, Schaumburg, Ill., 1993-95; v.p. regional mgr. Rust Environment & Infrastructure, Schaumburg, Ill., 1995—. Contbr. over 35 articles to profl. jours. Nat. bd. dirs. Episcopal Marriage Encounter, 1990-92, chair nat. bd., 1992-94. Recipient several acad. scholarships, 1969-74. Mem. Air and Waste Mgmt. Soc. Republican. Home: 23010 Thornhill Ct Barrington IL 60010 Office: Rust Environment & Infrastructure 3121 Butterfield Rd Oak Brook IL 60521

SANDSTROM, DALE VERNON, state supreme court judge; b. Grand Forks, N.D., Mar. 9, 1950; s. Ellis Vernon and Hilde Geneva (Williams) S.; m. Gail Hagerty, Mar. 27, 1993; children: Carrie, Anne; 1 stepchild, Jack. BA, N.D. State U., 1972; JD, U. N.D., 1975. Bar: N.D. 1975, U.S. Dist. Ct. N.D. 1975, U.S. Ct. Appeals (8th cir.) 1976. Asst. atty. gen., chief consumer fraud and antitrust div. State of N.D., Bismarck, 1975-81, securities commr., 1981-83, pub. svc. commr., 1983-92, pres. commn., 1987-91, justice Supreme Ct., 1992—; chair N.D. Commn. on Cameras in the Courtroom, 1993—, Joint Procedure Com., 1996—; mem. exec. com. N.D. Jud. Conf., 1995—; mem. Gov.'s Com. on Security and Privacy, Bismarck, 1975-76, Gov.'s Com. on Refugees, Bismarck, 1976; chmn. Gov's Com. on Comml. Air Transp., Bismarck, 1983-84. Mem. platform com. N.D. Reps., 1972, 76, exec. com., 1972-73, 85-88, dist. chmn., 1981-82; former chmn. bd. deacons Luth. Ch.; mem. ch. coun., chair legal and constl. rev. com. Evang. Luth Ch. Am., 1993—. Mem. ABA, N.D. Bar Assn., Big Muddy Bar Assn., Nat. Assn. Regulatory Utility Commrs. (electricity com.), N.A. Assn. Securities Adminstrs., Order of De Molay (grand master 1994-95, mem. Internat. Supreme coun., Legion of Honor award), Nat. Eagle Scouts Assn., Shriners, Elks, Eagles, Masons (chmn. grand youth com. 1979-87, Youth Leadership award 1986). Office: State ND Supreme Court Bismarck ND 58505

SANDVIG, SALLY, state legislator; m. Henry David Sandvig; 3 children. Student, N.D. State U. Sales rep. Avon; rep. Dist. 21 N.D. Ho. of Reps., mem. human svc. and govt. and vet. affairs coms. Precinct chmn., dist. sec. Dist. 21, Cass, N.D.; 4-H leader; client coun. mem. LAND; mem. Dem. Women. Soroptimist Internat. Tng. Awards scholar, 1988. Mem. Avon Pres.'s Club. Home: 914 26th St NW Fargo ND 58102

SANETO, RUSSELL PATRICK, pediatrician, neurobiologist; b. Burbank, Calif., Oct. 10, 1950; s. Arthur and Mitzi (Seddon) S.; m. Kathleen D. Saneto. BS with honors, San Diego State U., 1972, MS, 1975; PhD, U. Tex. Med. Br., 1981; DO U. Osteo. Medicine and Surgery, 1994. Teaching asst. San Diego State U. 1969-75; substitute tchr. Salt Lake City Sch. Dist., 1975; teaching and rsch. asst. U. Tex. Med. Br., 1976-77, NIH predoctoral fellow, 1977-81, postdoctoral fellow, 1981; Jeanne B. Kempner postdoctoral fellow UCLA, 1981-82, NIH postdoctoral fellow, 1982-87; asst. prof. Oreg. Regional Primate Rsch. Ctr. div. Neurosci., Beaverton, 1987-89; asst. prof. dept. cell biology and anatomy Oreg. Health Scis. U., Portland, 1988-90, U. Osteo. Medicine & Surgery, 1991-94, Cleve. Clinic, 1994—; lectr. rsch. methods Grad. Sch., 1982; vis. scholar in ethics So. Baptist Theol. Sem., Louisville, 1981. Contbr. articles to profl. jours. Recipient Merit award Nat. March of Dimes, 1978; named one of Outstanding Young Men in Am., 1979, 81, one of Men of Significance, 1985. Mem. AAAS, Am. Acad. Pediats., Bread for World, Save the Whales, Sierra Club, Am. Soc. Human Genetics, Winter Confs. Brain Rsch., Neuroscis. Study Program, N.Y. Acad. Scis., Am. Soc. Neurochem., Soc. Neurosci., Am. Soc. Neurochemistry, Soc. Neurosci., World Runners Club, Sigma Sigma Phi. Democrat. Mem. Evangelical Free Ch.

SANFILIPPO, JON WALTER, lawyer; b. Milw., Nov. 10, 1950; s. Joseph Salvator and Jeanne Catherine (Lisinski) S.; m. Pamela Joy Jaeger, July 8, 1972; children: Kerri, Jessica, Jennifer. AS, U. Wis., West Bend, 1972; BS, U. Wis., Milw., 1974, MS, 1978; JD, Marquette U., 1988. Bar: Wis. 1988, U.S. Dist. Ct. (ea. dist.) Wis. 1988, U.S. Dist. Ct. (we. dist.) Wis. 1989, U.S. Ct. Appeals (7th cir.) 1988, U.S. Supreme Ct. 1994; cert. elem. tchr., ednl. adminstr., Wis. Collection agt. West Bend Co., 1970-72; educator, athletic dir., coach St. Francis Cabrini, West Bend, 1974-77; clk. of cir. ct. Washington County, West Bend, 1976-89; judo tchr. City of West Bend, 1967—; ptnr. Schowalter, Edwards & Sanfilippo, S.C., West Bend, 1989-94; sch. prin.K-8 Campbellsport (Wis.) Sch. Dist., 1994-95; chief dep. clk. Cir. Ct. Milw. County, Milw., 1995—. Author: Judo for the Physical Educator, 1981, Proper Falling for Education Classes, 1981. Mem. sch. bd. West Bend Sch. Dist., 1979-80; dist. chmn. Wis. Clk. of Cts. Assn., 1976-79, mem. exec. com., 1976-82, mem. legis. com., 1982-84. Recipient cert. study internat. and Chinese law East Chinese Inst. Politics & Law, Willamette U. Law Sch., Shanghai, People's Republic China, 1988, Black Belt 6th Degree U.S. Judo Assn., 1995, Black Belt 3d Degree Universal Tae Kwon Do Assn., 1988. Mem. ABA, Wis. Bar Assn. (bench/bar com. 1986-88), Milw. Bar Assn. (cts. com. 1995—), Washington County Bar Assn., U. Wis.-Washington County Found. Inc. (bd. dirs. 1993-94), Assn. Wis. Sch. Adminstrs., Rotary (bd. dirs. West Bend Sunrise Club 1990-91, Paul Harris fellow). Roman Catholic. Office: Milw County Ct House Rm 104 901 N 9th St Milwaukee WI 53233

SANFORD, RUTH EILEEN, data processing company administrator; b. Two Harbors, Minn., Mar. 15, 1925; d. John Arvid and Helene (Lind) Bostrom; m. Keith N. Sanford, Sept. 21 1950 (div. Sept. 1960); m. Michael R. Notaro, Mar. 10, 1984. Degree in bus., Cable's Secretarial Coll., 1944; student, Northwestern U., 1966. Exec. sec. 1st Am. Nat. Bank, Duluth, Minn., 1944-48; pvt. sec. Adam Thomson, Duluth, Minn., 1948-52; exec. sec. and administrv. asst. Res. Mining Co., Silver Bay, Minn., 1952-62, United Calif. Bank, San Francisco, 1963-64; office mgr. Poly-Tech, Mpls., 1964-66; corp. sec. and administrv. asst. to pres. Statis. Tabulating Corp., Chgo., 1966-90. Mem. NAES. Roman Catholic. Club: Butterfield Country (Hinsdale, Ill.). Lodge: Women of Moose. Home: 1400 Bonnie Brae River Forest IL 60305-1202

SANFORD, WILBUR LEE, elementary education educator; b. Lexington, Ky., Aug. 2, 1935; s. Lloyd Daniel and Catherine (Kirtley) S.; m. Dorothy Moore; children: James, Venessa. BA, Ky. State Coll., 1958; MA in Adminstrn., Xavier U., 1969, cert. elem. counselor, 1973. Cert. elem. counselor, Ohio; cert. elem. tchr. and prin., Ohio. Elem. tchr. North Coll. Hill (Ohio) Sch., 1960-65, Cin. Pub. Schs., 1965-73, St. Joseph Elem. Sch., Cin., 1993—; adminstrv. intern Cin. Pub. Schs., 1983-85, asst. prin., 1975-80, elem. prin., 1980-92; cons. PTA, Cin., 1989-92, GED program, Cin., 1990-91; prin./instrnl. leader Windsor Sch. Meritorious Achievement, Cin., 1985-86; dir. After Sch. Evening Tutorial, Cin., 1988-92. Leader 4-H Club, Cin., 1991-92, Boy Scouts Am., Cin., 1985-89; mem. Walnut Hills Victory Community Coun., Cin., 1985-89, Avondale Community Coun., Cin., 1990-92; mem. Sinai Temple. Recipient Notable Recognition award Youth Crime Intervention, Cin., 1991, Community Svc. award So. Bapt. Ch., Cin., 1991, Outstanding Svc. award Cincinnatians Active to Support Edn., 1989. Mem. Ohio Assn. Elem. Sch. Adminstrs. (Exemplary Svc. award 1987), Cin. Assn. Adminstrs. and Suprs., Cin. Assn. Elem. Prins. Democrat. Methodist. Home: 6748 Stoll Ln Cincinnati OH 45236-4039 Office: St Joseph Elem Sch 745 Ezzard Charles Dr Cincinnati OH 45203-1410

SANGMEISTER, GEORGE EDWARD, congressman, lawyer; b. Joliet, Ill., Feb. 16, 1931; s. George Conrad and Rose Engaborg (Johnson) S.; m. Doris Marie Hinspeter, Dec. 1, 1951; children: George Kurt, Kimberley Ann. BA, Elmhurst Coll., 1957; LLB, John Marshall Law Sch., 1960, JD, 1970. Bar: Ill. 1960. Ptnr. McKeown, Fitzgerald, Zollner, Buck, Sangmeister & Hutchison, 1969-89; justice of peace, 1961-63; states atty. Will County, 1964-68; mem. Ill. Ho. of Reps., 1972-76, Ill. Senate, 1977-87, 101st-103rd Congresses from 4th (now 11th) Dist. Ill., 1989-95; ret., 1995. Chmn. Frankfort Twp. unit Am. Cancer Soc., Will County Emergency Housing Devel. Corp.; past trustee Will County Family Svc. Agy.; past bd. dirs. Joliet Jr. Coll. Found., Joliet Will County Ctr. for Econ. Devel., Silver Cross Found., Silver Cross Hosp. With inf. AUS, 1951-53. Mem. ABA, Ill. Bar Assn., Assn. Trial Lawyers Am., Am. Legion, Frankfort (past pres.), Mokena C. of C., Old Timers Baseball Assn., Lions. Home: 20735 Wolf Rd Mokena IL 60448-8927

SANITI, DANIEL JOSEPH, electronics engineer; b. White Bear Lake, Minn., Nov. 14, 1967; s. Richard Daniel and Beverly Joan (Sullivan) S. BSEE, U. Minn. Duluth, 1991. Design engr. Dimensions Unltd., St. Paul, 1992-96; sr. product design engr. Autocon Industries Inc., St. Paul, 1996—. Recipient Outstanding Leadership and Service award IEEE, 1991. Mem. White Bear Racquet & Swim Club. Roman Catholic. Home: 2304 Randy Pl White Bear Lake MN 55110 Office: Autocon Industries Inc 995 University Ave Saint Paul MN 55104

SANKOVITZ, JAMES LEO, development director, lobbyist; b. St. Paul, July 3, 1934; s. John L. and Mabel A. (Hanrahan) S.; m. Margaret E. Mathews, Aug. 3, 1957; children: Richard, Therese, Patrick, Margaret, Katherine. BS in Journalism, Marquette U., 1956; MA in Speech, U. Denver, 1963. Dir. pub. rels. Coll. of St. Mary of the Wasatch, Salt Lake City, 1956-57; dir. pub. info. Colo. Sch. of Mines, Golden, 1957-63; assoc. dir. devel. Marquette U., Milw., 1963-66, dir. alumni fund, 1966-67, dir. alumni rels., 1967-69, asst. v.p. univ. rels., 1969-70, v.p. univ. rels., 1970-78, v.p. govtl. rels., 1978-86, v.p. govtl. and community affairs, 1986—. Contbr. articles to profl. jours. Founding dir. Univ. Nat. Bank, Milw., 1971-74; bd. dirs. St. Coletta Sch., Jefferson, Wis., 1970-76, 86-93, chair, 1974-76. Mem. Nat. Assn. for Ind. Colls. and Univs. (bd. dirs. Washington 1986-90), Disting. Svc. award 1986), Assn. Jesuit Colls. and Univs. (fed. affairs cons. Washington 1974-90), Assn. Cath. Colls. and Univs. (fed. affairs cons. Washington 1974-85, Blue Key, Alpha Sigma Nu. Roman Catholic. Home: 4057 N Prospect Ave Milwaukee WI 53211-2121 Office: Marquette U 1324 W Wisconsin Ave Milwaukee WI 53233-2241

SANNERUD, PAUL DAVID, theater design educator; b. Mpls., Apr. 21, 1958; s. A. M. and Margaret E. (Moe) S.; m. Peggy A. Nelson, Aug. 11, 1984; children: Bryn, Mina, Alberta. BA, Augsburg Coll., 1980; MFA, U. Minn., 1983. Resident designer Mid-Am. Festival, Inc., Shakopee, Minn., 1983-84, Hickory (N.C.) Community Theatre, 1984-85; asst. prof. Luther Coll., Decorah, Iowa, 1987-89; asst. prof. theater design U. No. Iowa, Cedar Falls, 1985-87, 89-93; asst. prof. Cornell Coll., Mt. Vernon, Iowa, 1993—; adjudicator Am. Coll. Theatre Festival, 1989—; chair artist series U. No. Iowa, 1990-93; guest lectr. Arts Internat., Yorkshire, Eng., 1990; cons. in field; scenic designer operas. Mem. U.S. Inst. Theatre Tech. Lutheran. Home: 612 2nd Ave N Mount Vernon IA 52314-1311 Office: Cornell Coll Dept Theatre Mount Vernon IA 53214

SANTANGELO, MARIO VINCENT, dental association executive, educator; b. Youngstown, Ohio, Oct. 5, 1931; s. Anthony and Maria (Zarlenga) S.; student U. Pitts., 1949-51; D.D.S., Loyola U. (Chgo.), 1955, M.S., 1960. Instr. Loyola U., Chgo., 1957-60, asst. prof., 1960-66, chmn. dpt. radiology, 1962-70, dir. dental aux. utilization program, 1963-70, assoc. prof., 1966-70, chmn. dept. oral diagnosis, 1967-70, asst. dean, 1969-70; practice dentistry, Chgo., 1960-70; cons. Cert. Bd. Am. Dental Assts. Assn., 1967-76, VA Research Hosp., 1969-75, Chgo. Civil Service Commn., 1967-75; counselor Chgo. Dental Assts. Assn., 1966-69; mem. dental student tng. adv. com. Div. Dental Health USPHS, Dept. Health, Edn. and Welfare, 1969-71; cons. dental edn. rev. com. NIH, 1971-72; cons. USPHS, HEW, Region IV, Atlanta, 1973-76, Region V, Chgo., 1973-77; mem. Commn. on Dental Edn. and Practice, Fedn. Dentaire Internationale, 1984-92. Bd. visitors Sch. Dental Medicine, Washington U., St. Louis, 1974-76. Served to capt. USAF, 1955-57. Recipient Dr. Harry Strusser Meml. award NYU Coll. Dentistry, 1985. Fellow Am. Coll. Dentists; mem. AMA (mem. edn. work group 1982-86), Assembly Specialized Accrediting Bodies (council on postsecondary accreditation 1981-92, award of Merit 1992), Am. Assn. Dental Schs., Odontographic Soc. Chgo., Am. (asst. sec. council dental edn. 1971-81, acting sec. 1981-82, sec. 1982-90, dir., 1990-92, asst. sec. commn. on dental accreditation 1975-81, acting sec. 1981-82, sec. 1982-90, dir., 1990-92, acting sec. commn. on continuing dental edn. 1981-82, sec. 1982-85), Ill., Chgo. dental assns., Am. Acad. Oral Pathology, Am. Acad. Dental Radiology, Canadian Dental Assn. (commission on dental accreditation award of merit 1992), Am. Acad. Oral Medicine, Am. Assn. Dental Examiners (hon. 1993), Omicron Kappa Upsilon (pres. 1967-68), Blue Key, Xi Psi Phi. Contbr. articles to profl. jours. Home: 1440 N Lake Shore Dr Chicago IL 60610

SANTAPOALO, JULIE ANN, media production professional; b. Racine, Wis., Feb. 6, 1958; d. Frank Vincent and Joann Ruth (Becker) S. BA in Journalism, Marquette U., 1981. Prodn. coord. Sorgel-Lee, Inc., Milw., 1981-82, prodn. mgr., 1982-83; v.p. ops. Brien Lee & Co., Milw., 1983-84; exec. v.p., creative dir. Emmer-Santapoalo Prodns., Milw., 1984-90; creative dir., mktg. dir. MGI Comms., Inc., Milw., 1990-94; v.p. Visions MultiMedia, Inc., Northbrook, Ill., Milw., 1994—; instr., drill designer summer music program Kenosha (Wis.) Unified Sch. System, 1976-87. Recipient Leadership award DAR, 1973, Community Appreciation award Kenosha Unified Sch. System, 1979. Office: Visions MultiMedia Inc 205 W Highland Ave Milwaukee WI 53203

SANTEN, ANN HORTENSTINE, broadcasting executive; b. New Orleans, May 23, 1938; d. Jacob L. and Martha Taylor (Grace) Hortenstine; m. Harry H. Santen, Oct. 4, 1958; children: Edward, Sally, Matthew. Student Smith Coll., 1956-58; BFA, U. Cin., 1979. Assoc. producer Sta.-WGUC, Cin., 1974-77, chief music producer, 1977-79, music dir., 1977-89, internat. coordinator, 1981-89, exec. dir., gen. mgr., 1989—; cons. Radio Nederland, The Netherlands, 1978-94, Deutsche Welle, Fed. Republic Germany, 1980-95; v.p., dir. Am. Music. Ctr.; producer radio series Festival! (Oebie award 1982). Adviser Cin. Composers Guild League, 1979-94; head media panel Ohio Arts Coun., Columbus, 1987-88; trustee Cin. Opera, 1980-84; panelist Ohio Arts Coun., 1985-88; mem. radio projects adv. panel NEA, 1987, 88, 93. Named Producer of Yr., Ohio Ednl. Broadcasters, 1983; recipient Deems

Taylor Broadcast award ASCAP, 1989. Mem. Am. Assn. Advancement Edn., Coll. Conservatory Music Alumni Assn. (trustee 1981-85), Taft Mus. (bd. overseers 1991—). Avocations: skiing, climbing. Office: Sta WGUC-FM 1223 Central Pky Cincinnati OH 45214-2812

SANTER, RICHARD ARTHUR, geography educator; b. Detroit, Sept. 26, 1937; s. Arthur James and Hazel Luella (Houghten) S.; m. Ruth Margaret Boyce, Aug. 29, 1959; children: Carolyn M., Catherine R. BS, Ea. Mich. U., 1959, MS, 1965; PhD, Mich. State U., 1970. Cert. secondary tchr., Mich. Tchr. geography Wyandotte (Mich.) Pub. Schs., 1963-66; prof. geography Ferris State U., Big Rapids, Mich., 1969—; cons. Graphic Learning Corp., Tallahassee, 1983, Humanities Coun. West Cen. Mich., Big Rapids, 1987—; coord. govs. conf. Upper Great Lakes Commn., Bid Rapids, 1980. Author: Michigan: Heart of Great Lakes, 1977, Geography of Michigan and the Great Lakes Basin, 1993, (atlas) Green Township Atlas, 1974; contbg. author: Michigan Visions of Our Past, 1989; co-editor, team leader: The Autobiography of Woodbridge N. Ferris, 1995. Mem., mapper Green Twp. Plan Commn., Paris, Mi., 1973-74; co-chmn. Mecosta County Bicentennial Commn., Big Rapids, 1974-75; mem. Mecosta County Zoning Commn., Big Rapids, 1978-81; bd. dirs., elder United Ch., Big Rapids, 1970-81; mem. Mich. conf. United Ch. of Christ, Commn. of Ch. and Pastoral Ministries, 1988-91; chmn. 1993 commn. Ferris State U., 1990-93; mem. bd. of trust Hist. Soc. Mich., 1993—. 1st Lt. U.S. Army, 1959-62. Recipient Recognition award Population Action Coun., 1983, Certs. of Appreciation, Mich. Sesquicentennial Commn., 1987, The Population Inst., 1987, Nat. Geography Bee, 1989-96. Mem. Assn. Am. Geographers, Nat. Coun. for Geog. Edn. (Mich. coord. 1970-74), Mich. Acad. Sci., Arts and Letters (sect. chmn. 1974-75, 94-95, instn. rep. 1988-89), Phi Delta Kappa (chmn. 1990-91). Presbyterian. Office: Ferris State Univ Dept Social Scis Geography 901 S State St Big Rapids MI 49307-2251

SANTIAGO, MIGUEL A., state legislator; b. P.R., May 24, 1953; 2 children. BA, Northwestern Ill. U.; MA, Gov.'s State U. Ill. state rep. Dist. 3, 1989—; mem. exec. fin. inst., vice chmn. human svcs. appropriations Ill. Ho. Reps., mem. reapportionment, regist and regulation, transp. and motor vehicles coms.; tchr. Democrat. Home: 4502 W Fullerton Ave Chicago IL 60639-1934*

SANTO, RONALD JOSEPH, lawyer; b. Detroit, Jan. 11, 1940; s. Joseph P. and Mary L. (Benzi) Angelosanto; m. Donna L. Macidoni, May 15, 1965; children: Michael, Donielle, Jason. AB, U. Detroit, 1962; JD, U. Mich., 1965. Bar: Mich., U.S. Ct. Appeals (6th cir.). Ptnr. Dykema, Gossett, Spencer, Goodnow & Trigg, Detroit, 1965—; chmn. bd. Bon Secours Hosp., Grosse Pointe, Mich., 19846. Contbr. articles to profl. jours. Office: Dykema Gossett PLLC 400 Renaissance Ctr Detroit MI 48243-1507

SAPORTA, JACK, psychologist, educator; b. N.Y.C., Oct. 21, 1927; s. David and Victoria (Fils) S.; m. Judith Hammond, May 28, 1967 (div. 1979); children: David, Victoria. AB cum laude, Adelphi U., 1951; PhD, U. Chgo., 1962. Diplomate Am. Bd. Profl. Psychology; lic. clin. psychologist. Pvt. practice, 1962—; supt. Tinley Park (Ill.) Mental Health Ctr., 1975-78; chief manpower tng. and devel. Ill. Dept. Mental Health, Chgo., 1978-82; dean, prof. Forest Inst. Profl. Psychology, Des Plaines, Ill., 1982-85; coord. studies Fielding Inst., Santa Barbara, Calif., 1984—; prof. Ill. Sch. Profl. Psychology, Chgo., 1985—; mem. adj. faculty psychology Lake Forest Grad. Sch. Mgmt., 1987—; mem. Ill. State Clin. Psychology Lic. and Disciplinary Com., Springfield, 1984-93; profl. staff Forest Hosp., Des Plaines, 1977-96; mem. staff Luth. Gen. Hosp., Park Ridge, Ill., 1986—. Served with U.S. Army, 1946-47, Germany. Named Educator of Yr., Forest Inst., 1982, Outstanding Faculty Mem. Lake Forest Grad. Sch. Mgmt. Fellow Acad. Clin. Psychology, NTL-Inst. (faculty); mem. APA (accreditation site vis. team), Ill. Psychol. Assn., Chgo. Psychol. Assn. Home: 3201 California Ave Rolling Meadows IL 60008-2226

SAPPINGTON, LYNDA LOUISA BURTON, sculptor, freelance writer, photographer; b. Alexandria, Va., Jan. 31, 1950; d. Raymond David and Helen Geraldine (Lamphiear) Burton; m. John Oliver Sappington, July 17, 1971; children: Jennifer Louisa, David John. MusB, Furman U., 1971. Clk. typist, receptionist Naval Ship R&D Ctr., Carderock, Md., 1971-73; riding instr. Potomac Equitation, Centreville, Va., 1969, 73; clk. typist Wright-Patterson AFB, Dayton, Ohio, 1973-74; substitute tchr. New Lebanon (Ohio) Dixie Schs., 1982-91; freelance writer West Alexandria, Ohio, 1986—; stained glass artist Rocking Horse Studio, Lewisburg, Ohio, 1990-91; photographer, sculptor, stained glass artist, newspaper correspondent The Country Artists, Lewisburg, 1991—; sole propr. Whimsy Hill Studio, 1996—; represented by Wagner Gallery, Del Mar, Calif., BJ Clark Art Studio, Lebanon, Ohio, Ruttledge Gallery, Dayton, Ohio; bd. dirs. Gem Entertainment Media Svcs. Commn. Author: (novel) Across the Valley, 1991 (Fan-Q award 1991). Investigative reporter Save Our Schs. Com., New Lebanon, 1986. Recipient Best of Show and Res. Best of Show awards in photography Preble County Fair, 1992, 1st and 2d place awards for adult sculpture fine art div. Gt. Darke County Fair, 1993, 3 1st place awards in photography Equine Affair, Dayton, 1994, 1st place award in adult sculpture fine arts div. Gt. Darke County Fair, 1995. Me. Soc. Preservation of Variety Arts, Am. Quarter Horse Assn., Spotlight STARMAN (newsletter writer/editor 1986—, Fan Q Best Editor award 1991, Newsletter award 1992, 93, 94, 95), County Artists Coop. Baptist. Home and Office: 15401 Eaton Pike West Alexandria OH 45381-9610

SARANITA, TOM VITO, electrical engineer; b. St. Louis, July 24, 1943. AA, Harris Stowe Jr. Coll., St. Louis, 1963; BSEE, Rolla U. of Mo., 1966; M of Engring., St. Louis U., 1971. Applications engr. Century Electric, St. Louis, 1966-80; sr. applications engr. Emerson Motor Co., St. Louis, 1980—. Mem. St. Anthony of Padua, St. Louis. Mem. Emerson Engrs. Club, KC (Grand Knights 1971, dist. dep. 1981). Roman Catholic. Home: 3524 Kingsland Ct Saint Louis MO 63111-1041 Office: Emerson Motor Co 8050 W Florrissant Ave Saint Louis MO 63136

SARANOW, MITCHELL HARRIS, investment banker, business executive; b. Chgo., Oct. 14, 1945; B.S.B.A. with high distinction, Northwestern U., 1967; J.D. cum laude, Harvard U., 1971; M.B.A. with distinction (George F. Baker scholar), Harvard U. Bus. Sch., 1971; m. Linda Lee Billig, Sept. 8, 1973; children: Jennifer Wynne, Julie Ann, William L., David M. Bar: Ill. 1971, Mo. 1976, D.C. 1984; Assoc. firm Mayer, Brown & Platt, Chgo., 1971-73; investment banker Becker and Warburg, Paribas, Bicker Group, Inc., Chgo., 1973-75; v.p. fin. and law Sunmark Cos., St. Louis, 1975-79; v.p. fin., chief fin. officer CFS Continental, Inc., Chgo., 1979-83; pres., The Saranow Co., Chgo., 1983—; chmn. Fluid Mgmt. L.P., Wheeling, Ill. 1987; cons., dir. MidAtlantic Cable TV, Inc., Washington, 1983—. C.P.A., Ill. Mem. Am. Bar Assn., Beta Gamma Sigma, Phi Epsilon Pi. Clubs: Econs., Standard; Harvard Bus. Sch. Century. Office: Saranow Co 1023 Wheeling Rd Wheeling IL 60090-5768

SARAVOLATZ, LOUIS DONALD, epidemiologist, physician educator; b. Detroit, Feb. 15, 1950; s. Samuel and Saya Betty (Chonich) S.; m. Yvette Susanne Braymer, Oct. 6, 1990; children: Samuel Francis, Louis Donald II, Stephanie Nicole. BS, U. Mich., 1972, MD, 1974. Fellow Am. Coll. Epidemiology. Internship Henry Ford Hosp., 1974-75, residency, 1975-77, infectious disease fellowship, 1977-79; intern Henry Ford Hosp., Detroit, 1974-75, 1975-77, fellow, 1977-79; dir. hosp. epidemiology Henry Ford Hosp., 1979-82, divsn. head infectious diseases, 1982—, dir. infectious diseases rsch. lab., 1982—; prof. medicine Case-Western Res. U., 1993—; clin. prof. medicine U. Mich. Med. Sch., Ann Arbor, 1986—; mem. AIDS clin. drug devel. com. NIH, 1990-95. Contbr. over 100 articles to profl. publs. Active Blue Ribbon Com. on AIDS State of Mich., Detroit, 1990; chmn. physician com. on AIDS Greater Detroit Health Coun., 1989. Fellow ACP, Infectious Diseases Soc. Am. Office: Henry Ford Hosp 2799 W Grand Blvd Detroit MI 48202-2608

SARCHET, BERNARD REGINALD, retired chemical engineering educator; b. Byesville, Ohio, June 13, 1917; s. Elmer C. and Nellie Myrtle (Huff) S.; m. Lena Virginia Fisher, Dec. 13, 1941; children: Renee Erickson, Dawne, Melanie Koewing. BS in Chem. Engring., Ohio State U., 1939; MS in Chem. Engring., U. Del., 1941. From engr. to dir. comml. devel. Koppers Co., Inc., Pitts., 1941-67; prof. and founding chmn. dept. engring. mgmt. U. Mo., Rolla, 1967-88; mgmt. cons. Sarchet Assocs., Rolla, 1975—. Co-author: Supervisory Management (Essentials), 2nd edit. 1976, Management for Engineers, 1981; contbr. articles to profl. jours. Mem. Planning Commn. Beaver, Pa., 1955-58; dir. Billy Graham Film Crusades, Rolla, 1969-75; area dir. Here's Life America, Rolla, 1977. Recipient Profl. Achievement award U. Del., 1952, Freedom Found. awards, 1974-75, Fellow Mem. awd., Am. Soc. for Engineering Educ., 1992. Fellow Am. Soc. Engring. Mgmt. (founding pres., bd. dirs. 1979—), Am. Soc. Engring. Edn. (chmn. 1976). Home: PO Box 68 Rolla MO 65402-0068

SARGENT, LIZ ELAINE (ELIZABETH SARGENT), safety consulting executive; b. Meadville, Pa., Apr. 17, 1942; d. Melvin Ellsworth and Roberta Jean (Beach) Taylor; m. Lawrence Sargent, Sept. 6, 1969; 1 child, Kathy-Dawn. Attended, Allegheny Coll., 1964; AA cum laude, Cuyahoga C.C., Cleve., 1987, Assoc. in Transp. cum laude, 1989; BA, Ithaca Coll., 1993. Car distbr. Norfolk and Western R.R., Cleve., 1963-69; account mgr. Ill. Cen. R.R., Cleve., 1970-73; traffic coord. Carlon Pipe, Mantua, Ohio, 1973-75; chief dispatcher X.L. Trucking, Coshocton, Ohio, 1975-77; corp. log auditor Anchor Motor Freight, Beachwood, Ohio, 1977-78; cons. Saf-T, Parma, Ohio, 1978-84; v.p. safety Saf-T, Shaker Heights, Ohio, 1987-91; dir. safety Sherwin Williams, Cleve., 1984-87; pres. Safety Advisors for Transp., Inc., Beachwood, Ohio, 1991—; founder Love Keepers, 1996; speaker Coshocton (Ohio) Traffic Club, 1984, Am. Indsl. Hygiene, Cleve., 1985. Author: Hall Chemical-Safety Procedures, 1983-84, Progressive Insurance, 1987, RL Lipton Co. manual, 1995; contbr. articles to profl. jours. Chairperson intergenerational com. Ch. in Aurora, Ohio, 1984-86, Valley View Village Ch. libr. chairperson, mem. choir; bd. dirs. Shaker Heights Teen Recreational Com., 1984-87. Delta Nu Alpha scholar, 1977. Mem. Ohio Trucking Assn. (nat. safety coun.), Cleve. Bd. Realtors, Motor Fleet Safety Suprs. (nat. com.), Fleet Maintenance Coun., Phi Theta Kappa. Republican. Office: Saf-T 14716 Rockside Rd Maple Heights OH 44137-4016

SARGENT, NOEL BOYD, electrical engineer; b. Cleve., Dec. 5, 1943; s. William Boyd and Jennie Parkin (Wheeler) S.; m. Joan Marie Hodan, Aug. 21, 1965; children: Andrew, Jeffrey. BS in Engring., Cleve. State U., 1970. Broadcast engr. Stas. WVIZ-TV, WERE am-fm, WKSU, Cleve., 1960-65; electronics technician NASA-Lewis Rsch. Ctr., Cleve., 1965-70, engr. aero-acoustics, 1970-76, rsch. engr., 1976-83, sr. engr. launch vehicles, 1983-87, tech. asst., 1988—. Mem. IEEE, Soc. Automotive Engrs. (vice chmn. Com. AE-4, 1992—, sec. Com. AE-4R, 1988-92). Office: NASA-Lewis Rsch Ctr 21000 Brookpark Rd Cleveland OH 44135-3127

SARGENT, WILLIAM WINSTON, anesthesiologist; b. Oshkosh, Wis., Feb. 28, 1933; s. Sprague Spencer and Lila Jane (Gjermundson) S. BS in Medicine, U. Ill., Chicago, 1955, Md, 1957; MS in Anesthesiology, U. Minn., 1967. Diplomate Am. Bd. Anesthesiology. Staff anesthesiologist St. Anthony Hosp., Rockford, Ill., 1960-61, Swedish Am. Hosp., Rockford, 1960-61; instr. anesthesiology U. Minn., Mpls., 1967-74, asst. prof. anesthesiology, 1974-80; staff anesthesiologist St. Luke's Hosp., Duluth, Minn., 1980-95. Contbr. articles to profl. jours. Capt. USAF, 1961-64, France. Fellow Am. Coll. Anesthesiologists; mem. AMA, Am. Soc. Anesthesiologists, Minn. Soc. Anesthesiologists, Minn. State Med. Assn., St. Louis County Med. Soc. Presbyterian. Office: 915 E 1st St Duluth MN 55805

SARICKS, CHRISTOPHER LEE, transportation analyst; b. Columbus, Ohio, Apr. 19, 1948; s. Ambrose and Reese (Pyott) S.; m. Joyce E. Goering, Aug. 21, 1971; children: Brendan James, Margaret Katherine. BA summa cum laude, U. Kans., 1970; MPhil, London (Eng.) Sch. Econs., 1973. Dir. environ. planning Chgo. Area Transp. Study, 1975-77, regional planning consistency coord., 1977-78; group leader, planning and assessment Pacific Environ. Svcs., Elmhurst, Ill., 1978-79; assoc. transp. systems planner Argonne (Ill.) Nat. Lab., 1979-84, environ. scientist, 1984—; Rsch. project rev. and overssight panel Transp. Rsch. Bd., Washington, 1994—, air quality com., 1988—. Contbr. articles to profl. jours. Little league coach Downers Grove, Ill., 1991-92; v.p. Artists Showcase West, Downers Grove, 1988-90, 94—. Recipient Argonne Pacesetter award Argonne Nat. Lab., 1987, Winner Nat. Pub. Radio, 1987. Mem. Air Waste Mgmt. Assn. (land use and transp. com. chair 1988-91, mobile sources com. 1991—), Delta Upsilon (Outstanding Alumni Kans. chpt. 1994). Home: 1116 61st St Downers Grove IL 60516 Office: Argonne Nat Lab ES-362/2B 9700 S Cass Ave Argonne IL 60439

SARNA, JOHN J., state legislator; b. Mar. 1935; m. Ann Sarna; 2 children. Mem. Minn. Ho. of Repd., Mpls., 1972—, chmn. commerce com.; mem. appropriations com., labor mgmt. rels. com., internat. trade com., others; labor officer. Democrat. Office: 563 State Office Bldg Saint Paul MN 55155-1201*

SARRI, ROSEMARY CONZEMIUS ALCUIN, sociology and social work educator; b. St. Paul, Sept. 13, 1926; d. George Henry and Marguerite Jane (Driscoll) Conzemius; m. Romilos H. Sarri, Sept. 6, 1961; children: Catherine, Kristen. BA, U. Minn., 1947, MSW, 1955; PhD, U. Mich., 1962; LLD, Western Md., 1981. Group worker St. Paul Girl (Minn.) Scouts, 1947-49; county dir. 4-H U. Minn., Faribault, 1950-54; state 4-H dir. U. Conn., Storrs, 1955-58; rsch. assoc. U. Mich., Ann Arbor, 1958-60, lectr., 1960-62, asst. prof., 1962-64, assoc. prof., 1964-67, prof., 1968—, faculty assoc. ISR, 1979—; adj. prof. Washington U., St. Louis, 1986—; Belle Spafford Prof. Social Work and Women's Studies U. Utah, Salt Lake City, 1992-93; cons. Pres. Commn. on Crime, Washington, 1966-67, Australian Dept. Social Security, Canberra, 1977-78; vis. prof. Nat. U., Singapore, 1985, Washington U., St. Louis, 1985-94; mem. social welfare commn. Ministry on Higher Edn., Russia, 1992-93; cons. on social work edn. Peking (People's Republic of China) U., 1994. Author: Individual Change and Small Groups, 1974, The Entrapped Woman, 1988, Brought to Justice?, 1976, Statistical Profile of Women, 1987. Treas. Coun. on Social Work Edn., N.Y., 1980-83; nat. com. Edn. Commn. of States, Denver, 1975-76. Recipient Sr. Faculty award Silberman Found., 1990; named Mich. Social Worker of Yr., 1995; Fulbright sr. scholar Coun. Internat. Edn. Soc., 1977-78. Fellow Nat. Assn. Social Workers, Am. Sociol. Assn.; mem. Coun. on Social Work Edn. (officer), Nat. Coun. on Crime and Delinquency, others. Democrat. Roman Catholic. Home: 2730 Daleview Dr Ann Arbor MI 48105-9603 Office: U Mich Inst for Social Rsch 3014 Isr Ann Arbor MI 48106

SARRO, THOMAS LEE, software engineer, consultant; b. Chgo., Mar. 23, 1957; s. Carl Dominick and Joan Ruth (Morse) S. BS in Engring. Sci., Ill. Inst. Tech., Chgo., 1979; MS in Computer Sci., U. Ill., Chgo., 1988. Registered profl. engr., Calif. Mem. tech. staff TRW, Inc., Redondo Beach, Calif., 1979-82; rschr. Siemens Gammasonics, Inc., Des Plaines, Ill., 1982-83; programmer SPSS, Inc., Chgo., 1983-85, Interand Corp., Chgo., 1986-88; sr. cons. William M. Mercer, Inc., Chgo., 1988-92, Odesta Systems Corp., Northbrook, Ill., 1993-94; pres. Sarro Assocs., Inc., Chgo., 1994—; tech. program coord. Ford Motor Co., Dearborn, Mich., 1990-92; facilitator Marion Merrell Dow, Kansas City, Mo., 1993; application designer Brit. Petroleum, Anchorage, 1994-95; implementation cons. Ency. Brit., Chgo., 1995. Coord./mgr., designer/implementator software systems. Prin. guitarist Elk Grove Big Band, Elk Grove Village, Ill., 1991—; sailing instr. Am. Youth Hostels, Chgo., 1990—. Mem. IEEE, Assn. for Computing Machinery. Office: Sarro Assocs Inc 6311 Holbrook St Chicago IL 60646

SARVER, JERRY P., protective services official; b. Grand Rapids, Mich., Oct. 19, 1951; s. Russell Aron and Alberta Tesse (Gandy) S.; m. Linda Louise Sarver, Oct. 25, 1969; children: Cris Ann, Chad Lee. AA in Law Enforcement magna cum laude, Kellogg C.C., Battle Creek, Mich., 1991; BA in Mgmt. Orgn. Devel. cum laude, Spring Arbor (Mich.) Coll., 1995. Patrolman Hastings (Mich.) Police Dept., 1980-86, sgt., 1986-87, dep. chief, 1988-89, chief of police, 1989—. Mem. tech. com. Barry County E-911, 1989—, vice chmn. adminstrv. bd., 1994—; mem. Cmty. Corrections Bd., 1990—. Recipient Letter of Commendation, Hastings City Coun., 1983. Mem. Hastings Rotary (sgt.-at-arms 1994-95, pres.-elect). Office: Hastings Police Dept 102 S Broadway Hastings MI 49058

SARYAN, LEON ARAM, biochemical toxicologist; b. Wilmington, Del., July 18, 1948; s. Sarkis S. and Armine Saryan; m. Shirley A. Kalajian, Nov. 21, 1981; children: Ani L., Armen L. BA in Natural Scis., Johns Hopkins U., 1970, PhD in Biol. Chemistry, 1975. Lab. technician Allied Kid Co., Wilmington, Del., 1964-68; engr. DuPont Co., Deepwater, N.J., 1968-69; NSF fellow Roswell Park Meml. Inst., Buffalo, 1970; NIH postdoctoral fellow chemistry U. Wis., Milw., 1975-81; tech. dir. indsl. toxicology lab. West Allis (Wis.) Meml. Hosp., 1982—; clin. asst. prof. pathology Med. Coll. Wis., Milw., 1991—; adj. asst. prof. chemistry U. Wis., Milw., 1981-82. Recipient Ralston Purina Bright Idea award Ralston Purina Co., 1979. Mem. Am. Chem. Soc., Am. Indsl. Hygiene Assn., Armenian Engrs. and Scientists of Am. (environ. task force 1989—, coord. blood lead coop. testing project 1991—). Armenian Apostolic. Home: 5777 W Upham Ave Greenfield WI 53220-4917 Office: West Allis Meml Hosp Indsl Toxicology Lab Milwaukee WI 53227

SASS, MARY MARTHA, freelance writer, artist; b. Chgo.; d. George James and Arbutus Laraine (Schwartz) Harles; m. Roger Edward Sass, June 29, 1968. BS in Edn., U. Ill., 1965; MA in Guidance and Counseling, Northeastern Ill. U., 1977. Cert. secondary educator, guidance counselor, Ill. Tchr. English Kelvyn Park High Sch., Chgo., 1965-83; freelance writer, Skokie, Ill., 1983—; lectr. North Suburban Libr. Systems, Chgo., 1992. Contbr. numerous short stories, essays, articles, audio scripts to mags., newspapers, anthologies; exhibited in one-woman shows and group exhbns. at Oakton C.C., 1993, All Chgo. Juried Art Show, Skokie Pub. Libr., 1993, 94, 95, 96, Woman's Club Evanston Ann. Art Exhibit, 1994, 95, Skokie Hist. Soc., 1994, 95, 96 (painting award, hon. mention award 1994). Recipient Radio Script hon. mention award Take One Nat. Radio Theatre Competition, 1994; Nat. Pub. Radio scholar, 1984. Mem. Mystery Writers Am., Mystery Writers Am. Spkr.'s Bur., Chgo. Artist's Coalition.

SASS, WALTER J., marketing professional; b. Chgo., Oct. 16, 1943; s. Walter and Mary Sass; m. Judith M. Sass, Oct. 18, 1969; children: April, Aimee. BS, DePaul U., 1965, MBA, 1969; postgrad., Northwestern U., 1995. Market rsch. analyst Gamble-Aldens, Inc., Chgo., 1966-69; mdse. devel. mgr. Belscott, Inc., Chgo., 1969; product mgr. Helene Curtis Industries, Chgo., 1969-72; mktg. planner Continental Bank & Trust, Chgo., 1972-73; new product mgr. Alberto Culver, Inc., Melrose Park, Ill., 1973-76; sr. product mgr. Scholl div. Schering-Plough, Inc., Chgo., 1976-79; sr. product mgr. consumer products div. Abbott Labs, Inc., North Chgo., Ill., 1979-84; v.p. mktg. and sales adminstrn. Internat. Games/Mattel, Joliet, Ill., 1984-95; pres. Walter J. Sass & Assoc., Inc., 1995—; instr. mktg. Joliet Coll., 1973—, mem. mktg. mgmt. adv. com., 1986—; instr. mktg. Coll. of St. Francis, 1989—. Mem. Bolingbrook (Ill.) Econ. Devel. Commn., 1972-76, vice chmn., 1974, chmn., 1975-76. Roman Catholic. Home: 630 N Ashbury Ave Bolingbrook IL 60440-1163 Office: 800 Corporate Ctr 800 W 5th Ave Ste 201G Naperville IL 60563

SATHER, EVERETT NORMAN, accountant; b. Story City, Iowa, July 20, 1935; s. George John and Laura Josephine (Bakka) S.; m. Patricia Ann Johnson, Apr. 24, 1955; children: Kimberly L., Kristine J., Kendall D. Student, Am. Inst. Bus., Des Moines, 1953-55. CPA, Iowa, Nebr., Ill. Office mgr. Story Polk Farm Svc., Nevada, Iowa, 1955-57; office mgr., bookeeper Capital City Electric Co., Des Moines, 1958-59; staff acct. Willard C. Randol, CPA, Des Moines, 1959-60, Ryun, Givens and Co., Des Moines, 1960-63; acct. Everett N. Sather, CPA, Des Moines, 1963-66; acct., ptnr. Denman and Co., Des Moines, 1966—; pres., chmn. Ankeny (Iowa) Nat. Bank, 1972-82; pres. Triple K Ltd., Ankeny, 1983—, Boone (Iowa) Speedways, Inc., 1976—. Active Polk County Bd. Rev., Des Moines, 1970—; chmn. bd. Greater Des Moines Aviation Expo, 1989-95; treas. Des Moines Grand Prix, 1988-94; bd. dirs. Care Initiatives, 1995—. Mem. AICPA, Ill. Soc. CPAs, Iowa Soc. CPAs, Rotary (bd. dirs. 1990-93, pres. 1994-95), Zagszig Shrine, Scottish Rite, MAsons. Lutheran. Office: Denman and Co 1601 22nd St Ste 400 West Des Moines IA 50266-1408

SATTERTHWAITE, TOD, mayor; b. Sept. 25, 1954; s. Cameron and Helen (Foster) S.; m. Lisa Pettit, Nov. 29, 1986. Student, U. Ill., 1971-74. Self-employed Urbana, Ill., 1974-92; mayor City of Urbana; bd. dirs. C-U Econ. Partnership, Urbana, Project 2000, Champaign/Urbana; bd. dirs., chair Project 18, Champaign/Urbana, 1993—; mem. legis. com. Ill. Mcpl. League, 1993—. Vol. U.S. Peace Corps, Grenada, W.I., 1990-92; mem. cen. com. Champaign County Dems., 1994—. Office: City of Urbana 400 S Vine St Urbana IL 61801

SATTLER, NANCY JOAN, curriculum chair; b. Toledo, July 14, 1950; d. Thomas Joseph and Margaret Mary (Linenkugel) Ainsworth; m. Rudolph Henry Sattler, June 17, 1972; children: Cortlund, Clinton, Corinne. BS, U. Toledo, 1972, MEd, 1988. Office worker/bookkeeper Gilbert Mail Svc., 1967-71; computer typesetter Quality Composition, Toledo, 1971-89; instr. Terra Tech. Coll. (now Terra C.C.), Fremont, Ohio, 1988-89; dept. head Terra Tech. Coll., Fremont, Ohio, 1989-95, curriculum chair bus., social scis., math. and arts, 1995—; adj. instr. Terra Tech. Coll., Fremont, 1982-88, U. Toledo, 1988, Lucas County Bd. Edn. Gifted Program, Toledo, 1988-92; computer coord. St. Joseph Elem. Sch., Fremont, 1987-94, coord. quiz bowl, 1993; extern in quality control Atlas Crankshaft, Fostoria, Ohio, 1990; instr. devel. math. A.O. Smith, Bellevue, Ohio, 1991, 93, 94; adult edn. computer instr. St. Joseph Ctrl. Cath. Sch., Fremont, 1990-92, sec. sch. bd., 1989-94, pres., 1991-94; instr. devel. math. and sci. Whirlpool Corp., Findlay, Ohio, 1992; presenter Am. Math. Assn. Two-Yr. Colls., 1991-95, Nat. Coun. Tchrs. Math. Conf., 1993, 95; co-presenter Continuous Improvements Through Faculty Externship, League for Innovation, 1992; co-chmn. Ohio Gt. Tchrs. Seminar, 1993-96; chmn. Kids Coll., Fremont, 1993-95; facilitator Mo. Gt. Tchrs. Seminar, 1993, Ohio Gt. Tchrs. Retreat, 1994, 95, 96, N.Y. Gt. Tchrs. Seminar, 1994, Inventing Our Future, 1995—; co-chmn., presenter Ohiomatyc Winter Inst., 1994, 95, 96; TOM trainer Terra C.C., 1994-96. Author: The Implication of Math Placement Testing in the Two Year College, 1988, Applied Math for Industrial Technology, 1989; co-author: Math and Science Made Easy, 1992, The Metric System, Preparing for the Future, 1992, Workplace Literacy, 1994, The Basics of Using the TI-85 Graphing Calculator, 1995. Sec. St. Joseph Ctrl. Cath. Sch. Bd., 1989-94, pres., 1991-94; Sunday sch. dir. St. Joseph Ch., Fremont, 1977-87; pres. Plant 'N Bloom Garden Club, Fremont, 1977-79; clk. Sandusky County Fair, 1977—; rep. for deanery Early Childhood Devel., 1982-84; parliamentarian Welcome Wagon, 1980; Eucharistic min., 1991—; chair communications Inventing Our Future, 1996. Mem. Ohio Math. Assn. Two-Yr. Colls. (pres. 1992-95, NSF grant com. 1992), Am. Math. Assn. Two-Yr. Colls. (assessment com. 1990—, chmn. 1993—, program com. 1993), Nat. Coun. Tchrs. Math., Ohio Coun. Tchrs. Math., Ohio Assn. Garden Clubs, Alumni and Friends (bd. mem. 1995-96, bd. viss. 1995—), Ohio Math. and Sci. Coalition (co-chmn. collaboration com. 1996—). Democrat. Roman Catholic. Home: 712 Hayes Ave Fremont OH 43420-2914 Office: Terra C C 2830 Napoleon Rd Fremont OH 43420-9670

SATULA, KEITH O., electrical engineer; b. Milw., Apr. 29, 1955. BS in Biochemistry, Marquette U., 1977; BS in Medicine, U. Nebr., Omaha, 1981; BSEE, U. Wis., Milw., 1984. Lic. pilot, Wis. Rsch. technician Med. Coll. Wis., Milw., 1977-79; physician asst. Med. Assocs., Menomonee Falls, Wis., 1982-83; devel. engr. Eaton Corp., Milw., 1984—. Patentee for color sensor, adapter sensor, controller package design. Mem. IEEE. Office: Eaton Corp 4201 N 27th St Milwaukee WI 53216-1807

SAUDER, NEIL EUGENE, critical care nurse; b. Wauseon, Ohio, Aug. 27, 1956; s. Roy E. and Selma F. (Gautsche) S. AD in Liberal Arts, Hesston Coll., 1976, ADN, 1980. Cert. BLS, ACLS, TNCCP, CEN, ENPC. Staff nurse CCU/ICU Halstead (Kans.) Hosp., 1980-85, relief supr., 1983-85, cardiovascular cath. lab., 1985-88, cath. lab. coord., 1988-90; staff nurse ECS Joseph Med. Ctr., Wichita, Kans., 1990-91; charge nurse ECS St. Joseph Med. Ctr., Wichita, Kans., 1991—. Grantee Wesley Found., 1991, Mother Mary Ann Found., 1991, 92, St. Joseph Found., 1993-95. Mem. Emergency Nurses Assn., Emergency Nurses Assn. Ctrl. Kans. (pres. 1994), Kans. Emergency Nurses Assn. (pres.-elect 1995). Home: 3411 E Funston Wichita KS 67218 Office: Saint Joseph Med Ctr 3600 E Harry St Wichita KS 67218-3713

SAUER, HAROLD JOHN, physician, educator; b. Detroit, Dec. 1, 1953; s. Peter and Hildegard (Muehlmann) S.; m. Kathleen Ann Iorio, Sept. 4, 1982; children: Angela Karin Ferrante, Peter Rolf Jan Muehlmann, Josef Andrew John Iorio. BS, U. Mich., 1975; MD, Wayne State U., 1979. Diplomate Am. Bd. Ob-Gyn. Resident in ob-gyn William Beaumont Hosp., Royal Oak, Mich., 1979-83; fellow in reproductive endocrinology and infertility William Beaumont Hosp., Royal Oak, 1983-85; asst. prof. dept. ob-gyn and reproductive biology Mich. State U., East Lansing, 1985-91, assoc. prof. ob.-gyn, 1991—; chmn. group practice clinicians coun., 1995—; mem. staff St. Lawrence Hosp., Lansing, Mich., 1985—; Sparrow Hosp., Lansing, 1985—; cons. Mich. Dept. Social Svcs., Lansing, 1985—; mem. Mich. Bd. Medicine, 1992—, chairperson, 1994—; rschr. in field. Fellow Am. Coll. Ob.-Gyn. (sec. Mich. sect. 1990—); mem. AMA, Ingham County Med. Soc., Lansing Ob-Gyn. Soc., Am. Soc. Reproductive Medicine, Am. Assn. Gynecol. Laparoscopists, Wayne State U. Med. Alumni Assn., Mich. Soc. Reproductive Endocrinology (sec.-treas. 1991-93). Roman Catholic. Home: 2601 Creekstone Trl Okemos MI 48864-2455 Office: Mich State U Dept Ob-Gyn Reproductive Biology B-316 Clinic Ctr East Lansing MI 48824-1315

SAUER, JANE GOTTLIEB, artist, educator; b. St. Louis, Sept. 16, 1937; d. Leo and Sally (Walpert) Gottlieb; m. Martin Rosen, June 6, 1959 (div. 1967); children: Julie, Leo, Rachel; m. Donald Carl Sauer, Oct. 31, 1972; children: Jeffrey, Diane. BFA, Washington U., St. Louis, 1960; pvt. study with Leslie Laskey, 1976-78. Artist in residence New City Sch., St. Louis, 1976-78; artist in schs. Mo. Arts Council, St. Louis, 1979; studio artist St. Louis, 1979—; tchr. Craft Alliance Art Ctr., St. Louis, 1979-82; cons. Harris Stowe Tchrs. Coll., St. Louis, 1980-84; lectr. and workshop leader various orgns. throughout country, 1979—. Represented in collections Wash. U., Joseph & Emily Rauh Pulitzer, St. Louis, Nordenfjeldske Kunstindustrimuseum, Tronndheim, Norway, Vera Mott U. Mo., Columbia, Prudential Ins. Co. Am., Dallas, Erie (Pa.) Art Mus., Mus. of Nanjing, Republic of China, Mus. of Suwa, Japan, Wadsworth Atheneum Mus., Hartford, Conn., Jack Lenor Larsen, N.Y.C., others; one and two person exhibits Craft Alliance Gallery, St. Louis, 1981, The Hand and the Spirit Gallery, Scottsdale, Ariz., 1982, 85, Am. Craft Mus., N.Y.C., 1986, Miller Brown Gallery, San Francisco, 1987, Del. Ctr. for Contemporary Art, Johnson Mus. Art, Ithaca, N.Y., Chgo. Cultural Arts Ctr., Grand Rapids (Mich.) Art Mus., Ella Sharp Mus., Jackson, Mich., B.Z. Wagman Gallery, St. Louis, St. Louis Art Mus., 1988, Bellas Artes Gallery, Santa Fe, 1989, The Works Gallery, Phila., 1989, Folk & Craft Art Mus., San Francisco, 1989; numerous selected exhibitions, 1979—; contbr. articles to profl. publs. Mem. Sch. of Fine Arts Nat. Coun., Washington U., St. Louis. Recipient Critic's Choice award Christmas exhibit Craft Alliance Gallery, 1979-80, Vera Mott Purchase award, 1981, various others; Nat. Endowment for Visual Arts grantee, 1984, 90, Mo. Arts Council grantee, 1986. Mem. Am. Craft Coun. (trustee), Area Coordinating Coun. (sec. 1984-86, past bd. dirs.), St. Louis Weavers Guild. Home: 4492 Laclede Ave Saint Louis MO 63108-2204 Office: 510 N Compton Ave Saint Louis MO 63103-1224

SAUER, MICHAEL RICHARD, editor; b. West Bend, Wis., Jan. 27, 1966; s. Roy Edward and Kathleen Marcella (Schmitt) S. BA, Marquette U., Milw., 1988. Typesetter, prodn. asst. Cath. Herald Newspaper, Milw., 1985-89; youth minister St. Hubert Cath. Ch., Hubertus, Wis., 1985-88; typesetter, prodn. artist The Brady Co., Menomonee Falls, Wis., 1989-92; asst. editor Corp. Report Wis., Menomonee Falls, 1992-93, mng. editor, 1993-96, editor, 1996—. Mem. The Hartford Players, Lake Country Players, Phi Beta Kappa. Roman Catholic. Office: Corp Report Wis PO Box 878 N80w12878 Fond Du Lac Ave Menomonee Falls WI 53052-0878

SAUER, PETER WILLIAM, electrical engineering educator; b. Winona, Minn., Sept. 20, 1946; s. Alfred von Rohr and Eleanor Francis (Sawyer) S.; m. Sylvia Louise Stenzel, Aug. 23, 1969; children: Katherine Dora, Daniel Alfred. BSEE, U. Mo., 1969; MSEE, Purdue U., 1974, PhD, 1977. Registered profl. engr., Va., Ill. Design engr. Langley AFB, Hampton, Va., 1969-73; asst. prof. U. Ill., Champaign-Urbana, 1977-82, assoc. prof., 1982-85, prof. elec. engring., 1985—; elec. engr. Chanute AFB, Rantoul, Ill., 1983-89, res. dir. engring. ops., 1989-93; chief engring. programs, East HQ AMC, Scott AFB, Ill., 1993—. Contbr. articles to IEEE Transactions on Power Apparatus, IEEE Transactions on Power Systems, IEEE Transactions on Cirs. & Systems. Pres. Trinity Luth. Ch., Urbana, 1990-93, treas., 1994—. Maj. USAF, 1989-96, lt. col., 1996. Decorated USAF Commendation medal (2), Meritorious Svc. medal; rsch. grantee NSF, 1978—; named Outstanding Young Coll. Educator, Champaign-Urbana Jaycees, 1982; NSF Engring. Dir. Corp. Team Effort award, 1993. Fellow IEEE (chpt. chmn. Ctrl. Ill. sect. 1982-83, chmn. power engring. 1988—). Lutheran. Office: U Ill 1406 W Green St Urbana IL 61801-2918

SAUL, BARBARA ANN, English studies educator; b. Vincennes, Ind., Feb. 20, 1940; d. Charles Dudley and Essie Faye (York) Green; children: Beth Suzanne, Becca Lynn, Brian William. BA with honors, So. Ill. U., Carbondale, 1961; MS, So. Ill. U., Edwardsville, 1988. Cert. secondary English tchr., spl. reading K-12 tchr., Mo.; cert. lang. arts specialist, K-12, English 6-12, Ill. English tchr. James Island High Sch., Charleston, S.C., 1961-63, Waterloo (Ill.) High Sch., 1963-65; instr. rhetoric and composition Belleville Area Coll., 1966-67; homebound tchr. Belleville Twp. High Sch., 1966-73; Title I reading tchr. Freeburg (Ill.) Community High Sch., 1973-80; grad. asst. So. Ill. U., Edwardsville, 1986-87; reading specialist Hazelwood Schs., St. Louis, 1987-92; tchr. English East Richland H.S., Olney, Ill., 1995-96; instr. Lion's Quest, 1988-91; team mem. Write-On project Highland (Ill.) Cmty. Schs., 1980-83; clinician Edwardsville Adult Literacy Prescription Project, 1986-88; presenter Mo/IRA State Conv., 1991; coordinating tchr. Intergenerational Oral History Gateway Writing Project, 1991-92; securities rep. Equitable Assurance Co. Bd. dirs. presch. 1st Presbyn. Ch., Belleville, 1969-73; mem. coun., conf. del. Evang. United Ch. of Christ, Highland, 1979-85, mem. choir, 1985-87; mem. Jr. High Reading Curriculum Revision Com. Mem. Sigma Kappa, Phi Kappa Phi, Kappa Delta Pi, Beta Sigma Phi. Home and Office: 1209 N Morgan St Olney IL 62450-1941

SAUL, BRADLEY SCOTT, communications, advertising and entertainment executive; b. Chgo., June 29, 1960; s. Richard Cushman and Yolanda (Merdinger) S. BS, Northwestern U., 1981, MA, 1982; postgrad., Loyola U., 1983-84. With info. services dept. Sta. CBS/WBBM Radio, Chgo., 1978-80; gen. mgr. Sta. WEEF Radio, Highland Park, Ill., 1979-81, Sta. WONX, Evanston, Ill., 1981-83; faculty advisor Sta. WNUR Radio, Evanston, 1981-96; pres., ptnr., co-founder Pub. Interest Affiliates, Chgo., N.Y., 1981-96; pres. Chgo. Antique Radio Corp., 1986—; pres., owner Media Adventures, Chgo., 1996—; prof. Columbia Coll., Chgo., 1985-87; bd. dirs. Lake View Mental Health Ctr., Chgo. Contbr. articles to prof. jours. Bd. dirs. Mus. Broadcast Comm., Chgo., 1988-95. Named Outstanding Investigative Journalist, Warner Books, 1977. Mem. Nat. Assn. Broadcasters, Ill. Assn. Broadcasters. Jewish. Club: East Bank (Chgo.). Office: Media Adventures 680 N Lake Shore Dr Ste 1230 Chicago IL 60611-4402 also: 1 Bridge Plz Ste 610 Fort Lee NJ 07024

SAUNDERS, GEORGE LAWTON, JR., lawyer; b. Mulga, Ala., Nov. 8, 1931; s. George Lawton and Ethel Estell (York) S.; children: Kenneth, Ralph, Victoria; m. Terry M. Rose. B.A., U. Ala., 1956; J.D., U. Chgo., 1959. Bar: Ill. 1960. Law clk. to chief judge U.S. Ct. Appeals (5th cir.), Montgomery, Ala., 1959-60; law clk to Justice Hugo L. Black U.S. Supreme Ct., Washington, 1960-62; assoc. Sidley & Austin, Chgo., 1962-67, ptnr., 1967-90; founding ptnr. Saunders & Monroe, Chgo., 1990—. With USAF, 1951-54. Fellow Am. Coll. Trial Lawyers; mem. ABA, Ill. State Bar Assn., Chgo. Bar Assn., Order of Coif, Chgo. Club, Tavern Club, Point-O'Woods Club, Quadrangle Club, Law Club, Legal Club, Phi Beta Kappa. Democrat. Baptist. Home: 179 E Lake Shore Dr Chicago IL 60611-1351 Office: Saunders & Monroe 205 N Michigan Ave Chicago IL 60601-5925

SAUNDERS, JOHN KENNETH, research scientist; b. Melbourne, Australia, Apr. 28, 1944; s. James and Edith May (Andrews) S.; m. Jennifer Iris Anderson, Feb. 19, 1967; children; chantal, Monique, Blair. BS with 1st class honors, U. Melbourne, 1966; PhD in Organic Chemistry, McMaster U., Hamilton, Ont., 1970. Exptl. officer S.S.I.R.O., Australia, 1964-67; prof. chemistry U. Ottawa, Ont., Can., 1970-71; assoc. prof. chemistry U. Sherbrooke, 1971-84; assoc. rsch. officer NRC, Ottawa, 1985-86, sr. rsch. officer, 1986-92; group leader NRC, Winnipeg, MB, Can., 1990-92; group leader, sr. rsch. officer NRC, Winnipeg, MB, 1992—. Contbr. articles to profl. jours. Mem. Med. Rsch. Coun. Can. Office: NRC, 435 Ellice Ave, Winnipeg, MB Canada R3B 1Y6

SAUNDERS, JOHN L., state official. Dir. Agr. Dept., Jefferson City, Mo. Office: Agr Dept PO Box 630 Jefferson City MO 65102*

SAUNDERS, LONNA JEANNE, lawyer, newscaster, talk show host; b. Cleve.; d. Jack Glenn and Lillian Frances (Newman) Slaby. Student, Dartmouth Coll.; AB in Polit. Sci. with hons., Vassar Coll.; JD, Northwestern U., 1981; cert. advanced study in Mass Media, Stanford U., 1992. Bar: Ill. 1981. News dir., morning news anchor Sta. WKBK-AM, Keene, N.H., 1974-75; reporter Sta. KDKA-AM, Pitts., 1975; pub. affairs dir., news anchor Sta. WJW-AM, Cleve., 1975-77; morning news anchor Sta. WBBG-AM, Cleve., 1978; talk host, news anchor Sta. WIND-AM, Chgo., 1978-82; atty. Arvey, Hodes, Costello & Burman, Chgo., 1981-82; host, news anchor WCIU-TV, Chgo., 1982-85; staff atty. Better Govt. Assn., Chgo., 1983-84; news anchor, reporter Sta. WBMX-FM, Chgo., 1984-86; pvt. practice, Chgo., 1985—; news anchor Sta. WKQX-FM, Chgo., 1987; instr. Columbia Coll., Chgo., 1987-90; guest talk host Sta. WMCA, N.Y.C., 1983, Sta. WMAQ, Chgo., 1988, Sta. WLS, Chgo., 1989, Sta. WWWE, Cleve., 1989, Sta. KVI, Seattle, 1994; host, prodr. The Lively Arts, Cablevision Chgo., 1986; talk show host The Lonna Saunders Show, Sta. KIRO, Seattle, 1995—; atty. Lawyers for Creative Arts, Chgo., 1985-91. Columnist Chgo. Life mag., 1986—; editl. bd. Jour. Criminal Law and Criminology, 1979-81; contbr. articles to profl. jours.; creator pub. affairs program WBBM-AM, Chgo., 1985; guest talk host WMAQ-Am, Chgo., 1988, WLS-AM, Chgo., 1989, WWWE-AM, Cleve., 1989, Sta. KVI, Seattle, 1994; talk host The Lonna Saunders Show, KIRO-AM, Seattle, 1995—. Recipient Akron Press Club award for best pub. affairs presentation, 1978; grantee Scripps Howard Found., 1978-81; AFTRA George Heller Meml. scholar, 1980-81. Fellow Am. Bar Found.; mem. ABA (mem. exec. coms. Lawyers and the Arts, Law and Media 1986-92, chmn. exec. com. Law and Media 1990-91, 91-92, Young Lawyers divsn. liaison to Forum Com. on Communications Law 1991-93, Commn. for Partnership Programs 1993-94, regional divsn. chair Forum on Communications Law 1995-96), NATAS, Women's Bar Assn. Ill., Dartmouth Lawyers Assn., Investigative Reporters and Editors, Sigma Delta Chi. Roman Catholic. Office: 39 S La Salle St Ste 825 Chicago IL 60603-1603

SAUNDERS, LUCILLE MAE, elementary education educator, librarian; b. Sioux City, Iowa, Sept. 30, 1930; d. Merwin B. and Frances (Sapienza) S. BA, Clarke Coll., 1952; MA, Ft. Wright Coll., 1970; postgrad., U. Nebr., 1980. Dir., tchr. Sisters of Charity of the Blessed Virgin Mary, Dubuque, Iowa, 1952-70, Children's Discovery Ctr., Omaha, 1970-81, Open Elem. Sch., Omaha, 1981-82; head tchr. Friedel Jewish Acad., Omaha, 1982-93; libr. media specialist Minne Lusa Sch. Omaha Pub. Schs., 1993—. Mem. libr. com. Omaha Together One Cmty. Mem. Nebr. Assn. for Edn. of Young Children (officer, sec. 1970—), Nebr. Libr. Assn. (Golden Sower com.), Metro. Reading Coun. Home: 7011 S 142nd St Omaha NE 68138-6244 Office: Minne Lusa Sch Libr Media Ctr 30th and Ida Omaha NE 68112

SAUNDERS, NELSON W., state legislator; b. Detroit, July 10, 1949; s. Nelson W. and Louise (Swann) S.; m. Juanita Mazique, 1978; children: Windy, Alexis, Nathan. Student, Lawrence Inst. Tech., 1968-69, Wayne State U., 1971-74. Prodn. mgr. Linwood Industries, 1970-71; congl. asst. John Conyers, Jr., 1974-77, adminstrv. asst., 1977-82; rep. Mich. Dist. 7, 1983-94, Mich. Dist. 10, 1995—; exec. bd. first congl. dist. Dem. com. orgn., Mich., 1975—, Mich. State Ctrl. Com., 1979-83; precinct del. Detroit, 1979—; chmn. housing & urban affaris com. Mich. Ho. Reps., econ. devel. com., energy com., ins. & labor com. Bd. dirs. Urban Alliance, 1979-83; adult counselor Boniface Corp., 1971-72; adult counselor Detroit Drug Abuse Treatment Program, 1972-73, dir. counseling svc., 1973-74; chmn. old mus. com. Afro Am. Mus., 1982—; co-dir. Black Film Festival, 1975—); mem. Trade Union Leadership Coun. Mem. Alpha Phi Alpha, Continental Africa C. of C., 7 Mile Club. Home: 17545 Santa Barbara Dr Detroit MI 48221-2528 Address: PO Box 30014 Lansing MI 48909-7514*

SAUNDERS, THOMAS LEE, molecular biologist; b. Starkville, Miss., Oct. 23, 1955; s. John Van Dyke and Julia (Vissotto) S.; m. Susan Jane Allen, June 14, 1982; children: Grace, Marielle, Michael. BS, Miss. State U., 1976; PhD, U. Tex., 1984. Postdoctoral assoc. U. Minn., Mpls., 1984-87; rsch. assoc. Howard Hughes Med. Inst., Ann Arbor, Mich., 1987-89; mgr. transgenic animal model core facility U. Mich., Ann Arbor, 1989—. Contbr. numerous articles to sci. jours. Office: U Mich Biomed Rsch Core Facilities 1150 W Medical Ctr Dr Ann Arbor MI 48109-0674

SAVAGE, AUDREY C., psychotherapist; b. Mpls., July 12, 1931; d. Earl Dewey and Leona (Beske) Cotton; m. Frank Roland Savage, Oct. 15, 1954 (div. Feb. 1980) children: Antonia Ellen, Theresa Gail. BS, U. Minn., 1953; MA, DePaul U., 1964; PhD, Northwestern U., 1972. Cert. clin. therapist. Speech pathologist Pub. Schs., Ohio, Mich., and Tenn., 1955-65; dir. speech dept. Mercy Hosp., Chgo., 1965-69; instr., dir. clin. tng. DePaul U., Chgo., 1967-68; instr. Indpls. U. Med. Sch., 1972-74; pvt. practice Indpls., 1975—; dir. tng. Indpls. Gestalt Inst., 1977-83, Sch. of Gestalt and Experiential Teaching, San Francisco, 1990—. Author: The Fourth Woman, 1988 (Honorable Mention 1987), Twice Raped, 1990 (1st prize 1991), The Making of a Man, 1991. Mem. NOW, Am. Assn. Marriage and Family Therapists. Democrat. Home and Office: 6350 Guilford Indianapolis IN 46220

SAVAGE, PATRICK JOSEPH, secondary education educator; b. Bklyn., Mar. 5, 1944; s. Patrick John and Margaret Mary (Kearney) S.; m. Nancy Ann Sullivan, June 1, 1946; children: Patrick Gerald, Julie Kathleen, Daniel Joseph. BS in Bus. Edn., DePaul U., 1966, MS in Bus. Edn., 1971; postgrad., Northwestern U., 1971, 72, 73, Azusa Pacific Coll., 1972-73, DePaul U., 1974-76. Tchr., head coach DePaul Acad., Chgo., 1965-68, St. George High Sch., Evanston, Ill., 1968-69; head running coach Oakton Community Coll., Des Plaines, Ill., 1971—; tchr., head coach Niles West High Sch., Skokie, Ill., 1969—; head coach, dir. Niles West/Oakton Runners Club, Skokie, Ill., 1980—. Contbr. numerous articles to sports mags. Recipient Coach of Yr. Gold award Scholastic Mag., 1988, Track Alumni of Yr. award DePaul U., 1983-84; named 6 time NJCAA Region IV Coach of Yr., named to Hall of Fame Ill. Coaches, 1989, named to DePaul U. Hall of Fame, 1993. Mem. Nat. Jr. Coll. Athletic Assn. (cross country and track coaches assn.), Nat. Bus. Edn. Assn., North Cen. Bus. Edn. Assn., Ill. H.S. Cross Country and Track Coaches Assn. (pres. 1979-81), Ill. Jr. Coll. Cross Country and Track Coaches (pres. 1980-85), Chgo. Area Runners Assn. (pres. 1992-95), USA/Track and Field. Roman Catholic. Home: 6145-A Lincoln Ave Morton Grove IL 60053-2964 Office: Niles West H S 5701 Oakton St Skokie IL 60077-2630

SAVAGEAU, MICHAEL ANTONIO, microbiology and immunology educator; b. Fargo, N.D., Dec. 3, 1940; s. Antonio Daniel and Jennie Ethelwin (Kaushagen) S.; m. Ann Elisa Birky, July 22, 1967; children—Mark Edward, Patrick Daniel, Elisa Marie. B.S., U. Minn., 1962; M.S., U. Iowa, 1963; Ph.D., Stanford U., 1967, postgrad., 1968-70; postgrad., UCLA, 1967-68. Research fellow UCLA, Los Angeles, 1967-68; lectr. Stanford U., Calif., 1968-69; from asst. to full prof. U. Mich., Ann Arbor, 1970—; sr. research fellow Max Planck Inst., Göttingen, Fed. Republic of Germany, 1976-77; fellow Australian Nat. U., Canberra, 1983-84; prof. microbiology and immunology U. Mich., Ann Arbor, 1978—, chmn. dept., 1982-85, 92—, prof. chem. engring., dir. cellular biotech. labs., 1988-91; dir. NIH trng. program in Cellular Biotechnology, 1991-92; cons. Upjohn Co., Kalamazoo, 1979-81, NIH, Bethesda, Md., 1981-82, 94-95, Synergen, Boulder, Colo., 1985-87; Found. for Microbiology lectr., 1993-95; vis. prof. dept. biochemistry U. Ariz., Tucson, 1994. Author: Biochemical Systems Analysis, 1976; mem. editl. bd. Math. Scis., 1976-95, editor, 1995—; mem. editl. bd. Jour. Theoretical Biology, 1989-96, mem. adv. bd., 1996—; mem. editl. bd. Nonlinear World, 1992—, Nonlinear Digest, 1992—; co-editor Math. Ecology, 1986—; contbr. articles to profl. jours. Australian Nat. U. fellow, 1983-84; Guggenheim Found., fellow N.Y.C., 1976-77; Fulbright Found., sr. research fellow, Washington, Fed. Republic of Germany, 1976-77; sr. fellow Mich. Soc. Fellows, 1990-94; grantee NIH, NSF, 1964—. Mem. AAAS, Am. Chem. Soc., Am. Soc. Microbiology, IEEE (sr.), Soc. Indsl. and Applied Math., Biophys. Soc., Soc. Gen. Physiologists, Soc. Math. Biology (bd. dirs. 1987-90). Office: U Mich Dept Microbiology and Immunology 5641 Med Sci II Ann Arbor MI 48109-0620

SAVARDA, RAYMOND RICHARD, engineering consultant; b. Parma, Ohio, June 29, 1959; s. Robert and Henrietta S.; m. Melanie, Ovt. 14, 1989; children: Alexander, MAtthew. B, Ohio Inst. Tech., 1981. Mgr. display systems H.P.M. Corp., Mt. Gilend, Ohio, 1984-87; engring. mgr. Display Automation Group, Dublin, Ohio, 1987-91; engring. group mgr. Applied Inovation, Dublin, Ohio, 1991—. Patnetee in field. Mem. IEEE, Assn. Computing Machinery. Office: Applied Innovation 5800 Innovation Dr Dublin OH 43017-3271

SAVARINO, RONALD R., die designer; b. Milw., Wis., Dec. 14, 1945. Detail jr. draftsman Nordberg Mfg., Milw., 1964-67; layout draftsman Super Die Set, Oak Creek, Wis., 1967-70; sr. die designer Lakeside Mfg., Inc., Milw., 1970—. Umpire H.S. fast pitch softball. Sgt. U.S. Army, 1966-72. Mem. Soc. Mfg. Engr. Democrat. Office: Lakeside Designer 1977 S Allis St Milwaukee WI 53207-1248

SAVIANO, ANGELO, state legislator; b. May 20, 1958; m. Julia Thalji, 1987; 1 child, Bianca. BA, DePaul U., 1980. Supr. Leyden Twp., Franklin Park, Ill., 1989-93; Ill. state rep. Dist. 77, 1993—. Home: 2433 N 77th Ct Elmwood Park IL 60635-2564*

SAVIC, STANLEY DIMITRIUS, physicist; b. Belgrade, Yugoslavia, Dec. 30, 1938; came to the U.S., 1958; s. Dimitrius and Zorka (Vuckovic) S. BS, Roosevelt U., 1962; MS, U. Ill., 1969. Staff scientist Argonne Cancer Rsch. Hosp., Chgo., 1962-63; with radiology staff U. Chgo., 1963-64; v.p. Zenith Electronics Corp., Glenview, Ill., 1964—; chief U.S. del. Internat. Electrotech. Commn., Geneva, 1986-90; lectr. in field, 1984-91; mem. com. FDA, Washington, 1978-81; mem. faculty N.Y. Acad. Fire Scis., Albany, 1991. Author: X-Ray Conference Proceedings, 1968, co-author, 1968; contbr. chpt.: Standards Management, 1990. Apptd. by sec. Dept. Health & Human Svcs. to Tech. Electronic Products Radiation Safety Standards Com., Washington, 1978-81, 93; sec. Holy Resurrection Cathedral, Chgo., 1978-79; divsn. chmn. Crusade of Mercy, United Way, 1988. Mem. IEEE (sr.), N.Y. Acad. Scis., Nat. Fire Protection Assn., ASTM, Electronic Industries Assn. (chmn. safety com. 1983-87, mem. engring. policy coun. 1992—, Disting. Svc. award 1987). Republican. Serbian-Orthodox. Office: Zenith Electronics Corp 1000 Milwaukee Ave Glenview IL 60025-2423

SAVITT, STEVEN LEE, computer scientist; b. Mpls., May 25, 1949; s. Leonard Robert and Claire (Hurwitz) S.; m. Gloria Lynn Kumagai; children: Mariko, Leilani, Joshua. BSEE, U. Minn., 1971, PhD in Computer Sci., 1992. Founder, CEO Compmark I Corp., Mpls., 1972-83; rsch. sect. head Honeywell, Inc., Mpls., 1983-89; rsch. staff scientist Alliant Techsystems, Inc., Mpls., 1989—; co-chair database com. Automatic Target Recognizer Working Group, 1985-87. Mem. IEEE, Japanese-Am. Citizens League. Home: 332 Westwood Dr N Golden Valley MN 55422-5263

SAVOY, SUZANNE MARIE, critical care nurse; b. N.Y.C., Oct. 18, 1946; d. William Joseph and Mary Patricia (Moclair) S. BS, Columbia U., 1970; M in Nursing, UCLA, 1978. RN, CCRN, cert. CCRN, CS. Staff nurse MICU, transplant Jackson Meml. Hosp., Miami, 1970-72; staff nurse MICU Boston U. Hosp. (Mass.), 1972-74; staff nurse MICU VA Hosp., Long Beach, Calif., 1974-75; staff nurse MIRU Cedars-Sinai Med. Ctr., L.A., 1975-77; critical care clin. nursing specialist Anaheim (Calif.) Meml. Hosp., 1978-81; practitioner, instr. Rush-Presbyn.-St. Luke's Med. Ctr. Coll. Nursing, Chgo., 1982-88; rsch. assoc. dept. neurosurgery, Rush U., 1984-88; clin. rsch. assoc. Medtronic, Inc. Drug Adminstrn. Systems, Mpls., 1988-91; staff nurse critical care Harper Hosp., Detroit, 1992-93; clin. nurse specialist, surg./trauma critical care, Detroit Recieving Hosp., 1993-95; critical care clin. nurse specialist Saginaw (Mich.) Gen. Hosp., 1996—; clin. instr. Wayne State U. Coll. of Nursing, Detroit, 1991-96, adj. faculty, 1996—; program coord. Critical Care ACNP-CC MSN, Wayne State U., 1993-96; critical care CNS Saginaw Gen. Hosp., 1996—; neurosci. clinician acute stroke unit Harper Hosp., Detroit, 1989; edn. cons. Critical Care Svcs., Inc., Orange, Calif., 1979-81. Co-author articles for profl. jours. Mem. Am. Assn. Neurosci. Nurses (treas. Ill. chpt. 1983-85, pres. 1986-87, SE Mich. chpt. 1992—, bd. dirs., treas., program chair), Am. Assn. Critical Care Nurses (bd. dirs. Long Beach chpt. 1981-82), Am. Assn. Sci. Nursing (mem. rsch. com. 1993-95), Lambda Gamma Phi (bd. dirs. 1994—), Sigma Theta Tau. Roman Catholic. Office: Wayne State Univ Coll of Nursing 5557 Cass Ave Detroit MI 48202-3615 also: Saginaw Gen Hosp 1447 N Harrison Saginaw MI 48602

SAWATSKI, SHEILA MARIE, cardio-thoracic nurse; b. Lawnton, Okla., May 8, 1960; d. Thomas P. and Sharon M. (Hart) McKernin; m. Christopher James Sawatski; children: Jason, Eric, Adam. ADN, Thornton Community Coll., 1989, Assoc. Psychology, 1989. RN, Ill.; cert. critical care nurse, BLS, ACLS, nurse paramedic open heart team, trauma, moril intensive care nurse, rapid flight nurse. Staff nurse Christ Hosp., Oak Lawn, Ill., 1988-89, Ingalls Hosp., Harvey, Ill., 1989-92, South Suburban Hosp., Hazel Crest, Ill., 1992—; instr. cardiac care classes Ingalls Meml. Hosp., Harvey, 1991-92, preceptor, 1991. Mem. AACCN, ANA. Roman Catholic. Home: 4939 145th St Midlothian IL 60445-2455

SAWTELLE, EDWARD STEPHEN, human resources executive; b. Erie, Pa., Aug. 29, 1930; s. William Charles and Marie Pia (Kohler) S.; m. Dolores Ann Eicher, Apr. 11, 1953; children: Catherine, Stephen, Thomas, Robert, Edward. BA, Gannon U., 1952; postgrad., Pa. State U., 1953. Dir. pers. City of Erie, 1962-66; asst. to dir. univ.-wide pers. adminstrn. U. Ill., Champaign, 1966-77; dir. pers. Ind. State U., Terre Haute, 1977-82, Ea. Ill. U., Charleston, 1982-85; pres. Sawtelle Assocs., Terre Haute, 1985—; cons. Anne Arundel County, Annapolis, Md., 1966, Ohio Water Svc. Co., Boardman, 1985-92, Dept. Forestry State Ind., Indpls., 1991; co-developer wage/salary plan Wage and Salary Program City of Erie, 1963. Author: The Supervisor's Guide to Corrective Counseling, 1986, Understanding the Basics of Supervision, 1987. Mem. Coll. and Univ. Pers. Assn., State Univs. Annuitants Assn., Gannon Univ. Alumni Assn., Four Winds Harbor Club. Republican. Roman Catholic. Home and Office: Sawtelle Assocs 837 E Cambridge Dr Terre Haute IN 47802-9344

SAWYER, FRANK S., state legislator; m. Karen Sawyer. BA, Ohio State Univ. Pres. Mansfield City Coun., 1978-82; City Charter com., 1980, 82; state rep. Ohio Dist. 64, 1983-92, Dist. 79, 1993—; chmn. Pub. Utilities Com.; mem. Health & Retirement, Elections & Twps. & Reference Coms. Named Outstanding Young Am. U.S. C. of C., 1980. Mem. Mansfield-Richland & Shelby C. of C., Mansfield Sertoma, Mifflin Lions, Fraternal Order Police Assocs., Nat. Rifle Assn., Cent. Ohio Bus. Devel. Coun. *

SAWYER, JIM CHARLES, journalist; b. Springfield, Mo., Sept. 30, 1939; s. Hugh James Sawyer and Ruth Irene Dodson Houghton; m. Judith West Patrick, July 1, 1960 (div. 1987); children: Page, Jon, Summer; m. Margaret Epperson Sawyer, Feb. 5, 1996. AA, Indian Hills Coll., Centerville, Iowa, 1959; BA, Drury Coll., Springfield, Mo., 1962, MEd, 1965. Tchr. secondary edn. Mo. schs.; with Mo. Dept. Edn., Jefferson City, 1968; youth specialist U. Mo., Springfield, 1969-80, assoc. dir. extension programs, 1980, regional info. specialist, 1980—; ptnr. Mottram-Brown & Sawyer, Commd. Writers; internat. journalist; instr. newswriting workshops. Editor S.W. region U. Mo. Ext. News Svc.; contbr. articles to nat. and internat. publs.; co-founder, co-producer Salute To America bicentennial program, 1976. Bd. dirs. Greene County (Mo.) Farm Bur.; mem. adv. bd. U. Mo. Agrl. Rsch. Ctr.; advisory work with U. Mo. and Ireland coop. ednl. programs. Fellow Royal Soc. Arts, U.K.; mem. Soc. Profl. Journalists (bd. dirs. S.W. Mo. chpt.), Mo. Press Assn., Investigative Reporters and Editors, Ozark Press Assn., Royal Colonial Light Horse Brigade. Home: 711 S Main St Willard MO 65781 Office: U Mo Ext 833 N Boonville Ave Springfield MO 65802-3831

SAWYER, MICHAEL THOMAS, state legislator, accountant; b. Wichita, Kans., Apr. 15, 1958; s. John T. and Virginia (Martinez) S. BBA cum laude, Wichita State U., 1984. Pres. Property Tax Mgmt. Co., 1984—; mng. gen. agt. Am. Life Ins. Co., 1986-92; mem. from dist. 95 Kans. State Ho. of Reps., Wichita, 1986—, House minority leader, 1992—; cons. Vertex Cost Sys., 1987—. Chief dep. county clk. Sedgwick County, Kans., 1978-84, county clk., 1984-85; mem. Kans. State Dem. Com., 1978—; pres. Wichita State Young Dems., 1979-84, Sedgwick County Young Dems., 1984-88, Kans. State Young Dems., 1985-86; del. Dem. Nat. Conv., 1980; treas. Sedgewick County Dem. Ctrl. Com., 1982-84; treas. Wichita Cmty. Housing Resources, 1986—; mem. Wichita Planned Parenthood. David scholar U. Nebr., 1976, recognition scholar Wichita State U., 1976; recipient Letter of Appreciation, City of Wichita, 1980, Cert. of Award, Wichita Assn. Colored Women's Club, 1980, Cert. of Appreciation, Dem. Nat. Com., 1982. Mem.

NOW, Citizen Participation Orgn. (chmn. 1979-84), Progressive Dem. Quorum, Shocker Athletic Scholar Orgn., Westside Dem. Club. Address: 1041 S Elizabeth St Wichita KS 67213

SAWYER, RAYMOND TERRY, lawyer; b. Cleve., Oct. 1, 1943; s. R. Terry and Fanny Katherine (Young) S.; m. Katherine Margaret Schneider, Aug. 5, 1972; children: Margaret Young, John Terry. BA, Yale U., 1965; LLB, Harvard U., 1968. Bar: Ohio 1969, U.S. Dist. Ct. (no. dist.) Ohio 1970. Assoc. Thompson, Hine and Flory, Cleve., 1968-76, ptnr., 1976-83, 86—; exec. dir. Ohio Housing Fin. Agy., Columbus, 1983-84; counsel to gov. State of Ohio, Columbus, 1984, chief of staff, 1985-86; chmn. Gov.'s commn. on housing, 1989-90; bd. dirs. Premix, Inc., North Kingsville, Ohio. Vol. VISTA, East Palo Alto, Calif., 1968-69; mem. Tech. Leadership Coun., Leadership Cleve., 1986-87, Cleve. Found. Study Commn. on Med. Rsch. Edn., 1991-92; mem. Ohio Bd. Regents, Columbus, 1987-96, chmn., 1992-93; trustee Cleve. Ballet, 1987—, Cleve. Orch., 1993—, Western Res. Hist. Soc.; bd. dirs. Premix, Inc., North Kingsville, Ohio; chmn. George W. Codrington Charitible Found. Named Man of Yr. Womanspace, 1982. Mem. ABA, Ohio State Bar Assn. (chair corp. law com. 1993-95), Clevel. Bar Assn., Yale U. Alumni Assn. (pres. Cleve. chpt. 1980-81). Democrat. Presbyterian. Office: Thompson Hine Flory PLL 3900 Society Ctr Cleveland OH 44114-1216

SAWYER, THOMAS C., congressman; b. Akron, Ohio, Aug. 15, 1945; m. Joyce Handler, 1968; 1 child, Amanda. BA, U. Akron, 1968, MA, 1970. Pub. sch. tchr. Ohio; adminstr. state sch. for delinquent boys; legis. agt. Ohio Pub. Utilities Commn.; mem. Ohio House Reps., Columbus, 1977-83; mayor City of Akron, 1984-86; mem. 100th-104th Congresses from 14th Ohio dist., Washington, D.C., 1987—; mem. ec and ed opp com., subcom. employer-employee rels., mem. subcom. oversight and investigations com. stds. conduct, mem. transp. and infrastructure com., subcom. surf. transp.; mem. Transp. and Infrastructure com., subcom. surface transp. Democrat. Office: US Ho of Reps 1414 Longworth Bldg Washington DC 20515-3514

SAWYER-KOCH, BARBARA JO, government executive; b. Menominee, Mich., Dec. 7, 1948; d. Richard Alvah and Muriel Louise (Lundin) Sawyer; m. Donald Koch, June 19, 1993. BA in Polit. Sci. with honors, Alma Coll., 1971; MPA, Mich. State U., 1990. Field rep. Mich. Dem. Party, Lansing, 1972-75; county treas. Menominee County, Mich., 1976-83; dir. local fin. programs Mich. Dept. Treasury, Lansing, 1983-91; fin. analyst Office Community Corrections, Lansing, 1992-93; adminstrv. mgr. sales, use and withholding Mich. Dept. Treasury, Lansing, 1994, adminstr. collection divsn., 1994-96, dir. office of strategic planning, 1996—; mem. bd. trustees Mich. State U., 1978-94. Bd. dirs. United Way, Mich., 1978-92, Blood Ctr. ARC, Lansing chpt., 1992-94; vestry, sr. warden St. Paul's Episcopal Ch., 1988-91; mem. ministry of higher edn. Diocese of Mich., 1991-94; trustee Mich. Affiliated Health Sys., Inc., 1991—. Recipient Women's Ctr. award No. Mich. U., 1978, Cmty. Leadership award Lansing YWCA, 1988, 90, 92, 94. Mem. Soc. for Internat. Devel. (bd. dirs. Mich. State U. chpt. 1991-94), Zonta Club of East Lansing Area. Democrat. Home: 417 Wildwood Dr East Lansing MI 48823-3161

SAX, MARY RANDOLPH, speech pathologist; b. Pontiac, Mich., July 13, 1925; d. Bernard Angus and Ada Lucile (Thurman) TePoorten; m. William Martin Sax, Feb. 7, 1948. BA magna cum laude, Mich. State U., 1947; MA, U. Mich., 1949; cert. clin. competence in speech and language pathology. Supr. speech correction dept. Waterford Twp. Schs., Pontiac, 1949-69; lectr. Marygrove Coll., Detroit, 1971-72; pvt. practice in speech and lang. pathology, Wayne and Oakland Counties, Mich., 1973—; co-investigator Support Personnel Profl. Practice of Speech-Lang. Pathology; counselor to divsn. stroke liaisons Am. Heart Assn. Mich.; liaison, staff Scientific Coun. Stroke AHA Mich. and Dallas, 1996—; adj. speech pathologist Southfield, Mich.; lectr. on stroke Mich. Speakers Bur., Am. Heart Assn., 1990—; pub. speaking coach, 1989—; adj. faculty SS. Cyril and Methodius Sem., Orchard Lake, Mich., 1989-90, St. Mary's Preparatory Sch., Orchard Lake, Mich., 1990—; founder, mem. Stroke Project Task Force for Detroit, 1993—; com. mem. Charrette, study Architecture and Design for physical restructuring Franklin, Mich., 1993. Mem. sci. coun. stroke Am. Heart Assn. Grantee Inst. Articulation and Learning, 1969, others, project choices and funding Meadow Lake Cmty. Coun., Birmingham, Mich., 1989—; christian svc. commn. St. Owen, Birmingham co-chmn. blood drive Red Cross, Franklin, Mich., 1991—. Mem. Am. Speech-Lang.-Hearing Assn. (clin. competence cert.), Mich. Speech-Lang.-Hearing Assn. (com. cmty. and hosp. svcs., pvt. practitioner liaison 1991—), Am. Heart Assn. of Mich. (mem. stroke awareness seminar, planning and operation ednl., liaison sci. coun. stroke 1996—, counselor divsn. stroke liaisons), Stroke Com. of Am., Internat. Assn. Logopedics and Phoniatrics (Switzerland), Franklin Found. (mem. natural resources adv. coun. 1991—, bd. dirs. 1994—), Founders Soc. of Detroit Inst. Arts, Mich. Humane Soc., Theta Alpha Phi, Phi Kappa Phi, Kappa Delta Pi, Gamma Phi Beta Internat. Contbr. articles to profl. jours. including Language and Language Behavior Abstracts, Language Speech & Hearing Services, Speech Language Hearing Jour. Achievements include research in language and speech acquisition in children in reference to the development of and prediction of biological speech change; research interests developmental phonatory voice disorders in adult acquisition of language and speech relative to central and autonomic nervous systems. Home and Office: 31320 Woodside Dr Franklin MI 48025-2027

SAXENA, RAJIV, software engineer; b. Burhan Pur, India, June 12, 1966. BA in Mech. Engring., MACT, Bohpal, India, 1988; M in Mech. Engring., U. Md., 1991. Mech. engr. SDRC, Milford, Ohio, 1991—. Office: SDRC Product Devel 2000 Eastman Dr Milford OH 45150-2712

SAXENA, SATISH CHANDRA, chemical engineering educator; b. Lucknow, India, June 24, 1934; came to U.S., 1966; s. Raja Ram and Vidya Wati (Saxena) Sinha; m. Asha Saxena, Feb. 16, 1964; children: Alka, Alok, Anup, Anil. MS, Lucknow U., 1953; PhD, Calcutta (India) U., 1956. Rsch. assoc. U. Md., College Park, 1956-58, Columbia U., N.Y.C., 1958-59, Yale U., New Haven, 1959; rsch. officer Bhabha Atomic Rsch. Ctr., Bombay, 1959-61; reader Rajasthan U., Jaipur, India, 1961-66; assoc. prof. Purdue U., West Lafayette, Ind., 1966-68; prof. chem. engring. U. Ill., Chgo., 1968—; cons. to various cos., labs. and univs., 1969—; vis. prof. Banaras Hindu U., Varanasi, India, 1986-87, King Fahd U. Petroleum & Minerals, Dhahran, Saudi Arabia, 1993-94; guest scientist Nat. Chem. Lab., Pune, India, 1987; sr. resident rsch. assoc. NASA Ames Rsch. Ctr., 1969, 70. Co-author: Thermal Conductivity of Nonmetallic Liquids and Gases, 1970, Viscosity, 1975, Thermal Accommodation and Adsorption Coefficients of Gases, 1989; editor Internat. Jour. Thermophysics, 1980-85; co-editor: Proc. Internat. Thermal Conductivity Conf., 1979, 83; contbr. over 510 articles top tech. jours., over 30 chpts. to books. Pres. Hindu Soc., Chgo., 1974-76; founder Chitra Gupta Pariwar, Skokie, Ill., 1978; founder Skokie-India Assn., 1981. NSF fellow Argonne Nat. Lab., 1974; faculty travel scholar Oak Ridge Assoc. Univs., 1979-80; rsch. grantee NSF, 1970-85, Dept. Energy, 1975-78, 86-90, Ctr. for Rsch. on Sulfur Coal, 1986-91, Office Solid Waste Rsch., 1990-92. Mem. Am. Inst. Chem. Engrs. Home: 8321 Kilbourn Ave Skokie IL 60076-2636 Office: U Ill 810 S Clinton St Chicago IL 60607-7000

SAXTON, WILLIAM MARVIN, lawyer; b. Joplin, Mo., Feb. 14, 1927; s. Clyde Marvin and Lea Ann (Farnan) S.; m. Helen Grace Klinefelter, June 1, 1974; children: Sherry Lynn, Patricia Ann Painter, William Daniel, Michael Lawrence. A.B., U. Mich., 1949, J.D., 1952. Bar: Mich. Mem. firm Love, Snyder & Lewis, Detroit, 1952-53; mem. firm Butzel, Long, Detroit, 1953—, dir., chmn., CEO, 1989-96; lectr. Inst. Continuing Legal Edn.; sec., bd. dirs. Fritz Broadcasting, Inc., 1983—; mem. mediation tribunal hearing panel for 3d Jud. Dist. Mich., 1989—, 6th Jud. Dist., 1994—. Trustee Detroit Music Hall Ctr. Soc. for the Performing Arts, 1984—; trustee Hist. Soc. U.S. Dist. Ct. (ea. dist.) Mich., 1992-95, pres., 1993-95. Recipient Distinguished award Mich. Road Builders Assn., 1987. Master of Bench Emeritus Am. Inn of Court; fellow Am. Coll. Trial Lawyers, Am. Bar Found., Mich. Bar Found.; mem. ABA, Detroit Bar Assn. (dir. 1974-79), Mich. Bar (mem. atty. discipline panel), Detroit Indsl. Rels. Rsch. Assn. (treas. 1980—, v.p. 1982, pres. 1984-85), Mich. Young Lawyers (pres. 1954-55), Am. Law Inst., Fed. Bar Assn., Indsl. Rels. Rsch. Assn. Am. Arbitration Assn., U.S. 6th Cir. Ct. Appeals (life, mem. jud. conf., mem. bicentennial com.), Am. Inn Ct., Cooley Club, Renaissance Club, Detroit Golf Club (dir. 1983-89), Detroit Athletic Club. Office: Butzel Long 150 W Jefferson Ave Ste 900 Detroit MI 48226-4415

SAYLES, RONALD LYLE, computer executive; b. Waukesha, Wis., Oct. 12, 1936; s. Burton Lyall and Sophia (Lapaz) S.; m. Fumiko Soeda, Jan. 15, 1957. BS in Secondary Edn., U. Wis.-Milw., 1978. Computer operator Mortgage Assocs., Milw., 1966-71, Kohl's Food Stores, Wauwatosa, Wis., 1971-83; supr. computer ops. Kohl's Dept. Stores, Menomonee Falls, Wis., 1983-86, prodn. coord., 1986-87, scheduling coord., 1987—. Contbr. articles on old time radio programs. Vol. Jim Moody for Congress 1984, 86, 88, 90, 92, Moody for U.S. Senate, 1991, Shirley Krug for State Assembly, 1984, 86, 88, 90, Tom Barrett for State Senator, 1990, Tom Barrett for Congress, 1991, 92, 94-96, Bill Clinton for President, 1992. Served with USN, 1954-57. Mem. Milw. Zool. Soc., Smithsonian Instn., Wis. Hist. Soc., Milw. Area Radio Enthusiasts (treas.), Metro Washinton Old Time Radio Club, Revival of Creative Radio, Soc. to Preserve and Ecourage Radio Drama, Variety, and Comedy, U. Wis.-Milw. Alumni Assn. (life). Democrat. Mem. LDS Ch. Home: 4278 N 53rd St Milwaukee WI 53216-1343 Office: N 56 W 17000 Ridgewood Dr Menomonee Falls WI 53051

SAYLES, WILLIAM W., insurance company executive; b. Madison, Wis., Jan. 3, 1950. BBA, U. Wis., 1972, MS in Fin., 1973. CFA. Stock analyst Nat. Bank of Detroit, 1973-75, Newton Co., Milw., 1976-77; v.p. CUNA Mutual Ins. Group, Madison, Wis., 1977—. Vice chmn. Downtown Madison, Inc., 1994-95; mem. Conv. Ctr. Task Force, Madison, 1991. Mem. Milw. Investment Analyst Soc. Republican. Home: 5017 Flad Ave Madison WI 53711-3619 Office: CUNA Mutual Ins Group PO Box 391 Madison WI 53701-0391

SAYRE, JEFFREY DON, lawyer; b. Milan, Mo., Mar. 20, 1966; s. William Harrison Jr. and Joyce Elaine (Clawson) S.; m. Kimberly Sinclair, Sept. 24, 1994. BS in Agrl. Econs., U. Mo., Columbia, 1988; JD, U. Mo., Kansas City, 1991. Rsch. asst. U. Mo./USDA, 1986-88; legal rsch. asst. to prof. Kelly U. Mo. Kansas City Sch. of Law, 1990-91; law clk. Stockard, Andereck, Hauck, Sharp & Evans, Trenton, Mo., 1989-93; assoc. atty. Andereck, Evans, Milne, Peace and Baumhoer, Trenton, 1993-94, Gifford & Richardson, P.C., Green City, Mo., 1994—. 2d. lt. U.S. Army Res., 1988. Mem. NRA, 9th Jud. Bar Assn., Future Farmers of Am. Alumni (life), Mo. Sheriff's Assn., Omicron Delta Kappa, Delta Theta Phi, Gamma Sigma Delta. Republican. Southern Baptist. Office: Gifford & Richardson PC Farmers Bank Bldg PO Box 218 Green City MO 64683

SAYRE, RICHARD THOMAS, biochemist, plant molecular biologist; b. Iowa City, May 24, 1951; s. Lombard and Marilyn Joy (Jenks) S.; m. Kathleen Mary Slattery, June 8, 1974; children: Matthew Paul, Robert Lombard. BA in Biology, Humboldt State U., 1974; PhD in Botany, U. Iowa, 1978. Postdoctoral fellow Fla. State U., Talahassee, 1978-79, U. Ky., Lexington, 1979-82; postdoctoral fellow Harvard U., Cambridge, Mass., 1982-85, vis. scholar, 1985-86; asst. prof. biochemistry and plant biology Ohio State U., Columbus, 1985-91, assoc. prof. biochemistry and plant biology, 1991—. Mem. AAAS, Internat. Soc. Plant Molecular Biologists, Am. Soc. Plant Physiologists, Photosynthesis Rsch. (editorial bd. mem.). Democrat. Roman Catholic. Office: Ohio State U 2021 Coffey Rd Rm 202 Columbus OH 43210-1043

SCALES, RICHARD LEWIS, sales representative; b. Indpls., Nov. 16, 1928; s. Ortho Lorton and Nina L. (Julian) S.; m. E. Jean Rankin, Dec. 21, 1951; children: Richard, Allan, Anne. BSME, Purdue U., 1952. Rsch. and devel. engr. Bell Labs./Western Electric, Chgo., also Whippany, N.J., 1955-58; sales engr. Bodine Electric Co., Chgo., 1958-61; dist. sales mgr. Wabash (Ind.) Magnetics, 1961-66; founder, chmn. bd. (emeritus) Richard Scales Assocs., Wabash, 1966—, RSA Inc., Wabash, 1985—. Contbr. articles to mag. Elder, Presbyn. Ch. Lt. USNR, 1952-55, Korea. Mem. Rotary (past pres. Wabash club, Paul Harris fellow 1987). Republican. Home: 550 Sommers Ave Wabash IN 46992-2021 Office: Richard Scales Assocs Inc 84 W Market St Wabash IN 46992-3127

SCALETTA, HELEN MARGUERITE, volunteer; b. Sioux City, Iowa, Apr. 13, 1927; d. Ralph J. and Ruth Cora (Coyle) Beedle; m. Phillip Jasper Scaletta, May 21, 1946; children: Phillip Ralph, Cheryl Diane Kesler. AA in Bus., Edwards Coll. Bus., Sioux City, 1946. Acct. Towners Dept. Store, Iowa City, 1947-48; legal sec. Phillip Scaletta, Sioux City, 1950-74; service chmn. Easter Seal Soc., Lafayette, Ind., 1970-88; recording sec. Home Hosp. Aux., Lafayette, 1989; danced in Civic Theatre Follies, 1962. Orch. mem. June's All-Girl Ensemble, 1943-50. Pres. Newcomers club YWCA, Lafayette, 1967-68, mem. chmn., bd. dirs., 1979; leader Girl Scouts Am., Ft. Wayne, Ind., 1960-63; chmn. Mental Health Inc., Ft. Wayne, 1960-61, Cancer Crusade, West Lafayette, 1973-74; precinct worker Rep. Cen. Com., West Lafayette, 1974-76; Nat. Missions sec. 1st Presbyn. Ch., 1957. Recipient Citation Easter Seal Soc., 1981. Mem. Purdue U. Women's Club (pres. 1973-74), Lafayette Country Club (golf chmn. 1971, 90, bowling pres. 1992-93, golf co-chair Battleground 9-hole group 1996), Purdue Women's Bowling League (treas. 1978-79), Cosmopolitan Club, Sigma Kappa (corp. bd., sec., treas. 1971—), Kappa Kappa Sigma (pres. 1972), Sigma Kappa Lafayette Alumnae (pres. 1970, 1988-93). Home: One Via Verde Lafayette IN 47906

SCALISH, FRANK ANTHONY, labor union administrator; b. Cleve., Nov. 5, 1940; s. John T. and Tillie M. (Rockman) S.; m. Carla Rita Cinti, 1960; children: John M., Frank A., Tina Marie. Grad. high sch., Cleve. Bus. agt. Local Union #1 Textile Processors Svc. Trades, Health Care Profl. and Tech. Employees Internat., Cleve., 1962—; sec., treas. Local Union #1, Cleve., 1978—; v.p. Internat. Union, Chgo., 1969-84, gen. pres., 1984—. Bd dirs. Cleve. Opera Theater, 1981-84. Recipient Israel Solidarity award Israeli Bonds, 1983. Roman Catholic. Office: Texile Processors Service Trades Health Care Prof Tech Employees 303 E Wacker Dr Ste 1109 Chicago IL 60601-5212

SCALLEN, THOMAS KAINE, broadcasting executive; b. Mpls., Aug. 14, 1925; s. Raymond A. and Lenore (Kaine) S.; m. Bille Jo Brice; children by previous marriage: Thomas, Sheila, Patrick, Eileen, Timothy and Maureen (twins). BA, St. Thomas Coll., 1949; JD, U. Denver, 1950. Bar: Minn. Asst. atty. gen. State of Minn., Mpls., 1950-55; sole practice Mpls., 1955-57; pres. Med. Investment Corp., Mpls., 1957—, Internat. Broadcasting Corp., Mpls., 1977—; owner Harlem Globetrotters; pres., exec. producer Ice Capades; chmn. bd. dirs. Century Park Pictures Corp., Los Angeles, chmn. bd. dirs. Blaine-Thompson Co., Inc., N.Y.C; chmn. Apache Plastics, Inc., Stockton, Calif. Served with AUS. Mem. World Pres. Orgn., Minn. Club, Calhoun Beach Club, L.A. Athletic Club. Clubs: University (St. Paul, Mpls.), Rochester (Minn.) Golf and Country, Edina (Minn.) Country, Athletic (Mpls.). Home: Heron Cove Windham NH 03087 Office: Internat Broadcasting Corp 80 S 8th St # 4701 Minneapolis MN 55402-2100

SCANK, JANET MARIE, librarian; b. Rahway, N.J., Feb. 16, 1950; d. Robert Stewart and Florence Theresa (Markell) S. BS in Edn., Ind. U., 1972, MLS, 1990. Analyst N.Am. Van Line, Ft. Wayne, Ind., 1977-79; bus. mgr. Royal Volkswagen, Bloomington, Ind., 1979-88; dir. Peabody Pub. Libr., Columbia City, Ind., 1990—; adv. bd. INCOLSA, Ind., 1995; exec. com., pres. Wabash Valley/Tri-Area Libr. Svc. Authority, Ind., 1992-95. Bd. dirs. Vol. Adv. Coun., Columbia City, 1994-95; mem. allocations/solicitations com. United Way, Whitley County, Ind. Mem. ALA, Ind. Libr. Fedn., Pub. Libr. Assn. Home: 2220 Point West Dr # 2C Fort Wayne IN 46808 Office: Peabody Pub Libr 203 N Main St Columbia City IN 46725

SCANNELL, THOMAS JOHN, cold metal forming company executive; b. Detroit, Sept. 11, 1954; s. Robert Michael and Mary Frances (Chadwick) S. AS, Henry Ford Community Coll., Dearborn, Mich., 1982; BME, U. Detroit, 1988. Gen. laborer Fed. Screw Works, Romulus, Mich., 1973-82, supr. tool store, 1982-84, tool design engr. III, 1984-86, tool design engr. II, 1986-88, tool design engr. I, 1988-90, mgr. tool engring., 1990—; owner Great Lakes News Distributors, 1986—. Hockey coach Detroit Police Athletic League. Mem. Soc. Mfg. Engrs. Office: Fed Screw Works 34846 Goddard Rd Romulus MI 48174-3406

SCARFF, HOPE DYALL, photographer; b. Mt. Pleasant, Iowa, Oct. 25, 1952; d. Charles and Marjorie (Hope) Dyall; m. David L. Scarff, Oct. 20, 1972; children: Misty Michelle, Shasta Shannon. Student, Southeastern Community Coll., Burlington, Iowa, 1973. Receptionist Dyall Photography, Mt. Pleasant, 1974-78, photographer, 1978—, mgr., 1978-80, owner, 1980—; spkr. in field. Exhibited in group shows Epcot Ctr., Disneyworld, nat. convs. for Profl. Photographers Am., 1987—; portrait pub. in Eastman Kodak book The Portrait. Mem. Profl. Photographers Am., Am. Soc. Photographers, Profl. Photographers Iowa (One of Top 10 Photographers awards 1984, 90, Profl. Photographer of Yr. award 1988, 89, highest scoring portrait from Iowa for 1989 conv., M. Photography degree 1990, Iowa Masters Silver Cup 1992, Iowa Master Photographer of Yr. for highest scoring portrait 1996), S.E. Iowa Assn. Photographers (pres. 1984), Mt. Pleasant C. of C., Mt. Pleasant Athletic Boosters Club. Republican. Methodist. Home: RR 3 Mount Pleasant IA 52641-9803 Office: Dyall Photography 123 N Main St Mount Pleasant IA 52641-2027

SCARRITT, RICHARD WINN, lawyer; b. Enid, Okla., Dec. 13, 1938; s. Nathan Spencer and Rilla Fayette (Winn) S.; m. Gloria June Gaba, Nov. 7, 1966 (div. Nov. 1971); m. Deborah Louise Guillemot, Sept. 3, 1986; 1 child, Nathan Spencer IV. BA, Okla. U., 1960; JD, Harvard U., 1963. Bar: Mo. 1963, U.S. Dist. Ct. (we. dist.) Mo. 1964, U.S. Supreme Ct. 1971. Assoc. Spencer, Fane, Britt & Browne, Kansas City, Mo., 1963-68, ptnr., chmn. real estate sect., 1969—; guest lectr. real estate law U. Mo. Extension Ctr., Independence, 1966-68; mem. panel of arbitrators Am. Arbitration Assn.; chmn. standard forms com., mem. govt. affairs, zoning law and legis. coms. Met. Real Estate Bd. Greater Kansas City; panelist Plaza West Assn., Kansas City, 1971-78. Co-author: Missouri Real Estate Forms and Practice, 1988, supplements, 1989-95. Mem. Clay County Econ. Devel. Coun. Fellow Am. Coll. Real Estate Lawyers (attys.' opinions com.); mem. ABA (real property, probate and trust law sect., subcom. significant real property decisions, environ. law com. subcom. energy law and real property, corp., banking and bus. law sect.), Mo. Bar Assn. (property law com., adv. coun., energy law com.), Kansas City Met. Bar Assn. (real estate law com., chmn. com. coun.), Lawyers Assn. Kansas City, Mo. C. of C., Downtown Inc. Kansas City, SAR, Mensa, Phi Delta Theta. Republican. Episcopalian. Home: 825 W 53rd Ter Kansas City MO 64112-2327 Office: Spencer Fane Britt & Browne 1400 Commerce Bank Bldg 1000 Walnut St Kansas City MO 64106-2140

SCHACHT, HENRY BREWER, manufacturing executive; b. Erie, Pa., Oct. 16, 1934; s. Henry Blass and Virginia (Brewer) S.; m. Nancy Godfrey, Aug. 27, 1960; children: James, Laura, Jane, Mary. BS, Yale U., 1956; MBA, Harvard U., 1962; DSc (hon.), DePauw U., 1982; MA (hon.), Yale U., 1988. Sales trainee Am. Brake Shoe Co., N.Y.C., 1956-57; investment mgr. Irwin Mgmt. Co., Columbus, Ind., 1962-64; v.p. fin. Cummins Engine Co., Inc., Columbus, 1964-66; v.p., cen. area mgr. internat. Cummins Engine Co., Inc., London, 1966-67; group v.p. internat. and subsidiaries Cummins Engine Co., Inc., 1967-69; pres. Cummins Engine Co., Inc., Columbus, 1969-77, CEO, 1977-94, chmn., 1977-95; chmn., CEO, Lucent Techs., Murray Hill, N.J., 1995—; bd. dirs. AT&T, Chase Manhattan Corp., Chase Manhattan Bank N.A., Alcoa. Trustee emeritus The Culver Ednl. Found.; active Bus. Coun., Coun. Fgn. Rels.; mem. The Assocs., Harvard Bus. Sch., The Bus. Enterprise Trust; hon. trustee Brookings Instn., Com. Econ. Devel., Yale Corp.; chmn. trustees Ford Found.; sr. mem. Conf. Bd. With USNR, 1957-60. Mem. Tau Beta Pi. Republican. Office: Lucent Techs 600 Mountain Ave New Providence NJ 07974

SCHAEFER, HELENE G(ERALDINE), social services professional; b. Chgo., Apr. 4, 1948; d. Jerry and Helen (Hruska) Souta; m. Kenneth Schaefer (div.) June 4, 1972; children: Rebecca, Benjamin. BA, Valparaiso U., 1970; MA, Govs. State U., 1984. Registered social worker, Ill. Social worker Ill. Dept. of Children & Family Svcs., Chgo., 1970-76, Bodimetric Health Svcs., Hillside, Ill., 1984-86; counselor svc. dir. Crisis Ctr. For So. Suburbia, Worth, Ill., 1979-82; child protection investigator Ill. Dept. Children and Family Svcs., Chgo., 1987-93, supr., 1993—. Bd. dirs. Rainbow House Shelter for Battered Women; leader Girl Scouts of So. Cook County, Palos Heights, 1982-87; active No. Ill. Hockey League. Mem. AAUW, Parent Faculty Assn., Chgo. Met. Battered, Women's Movement, Ill. Juvenile Officers Assn. Office: Ill Dept Children & Family Svcs 6201 S Emerald Chicago IL 60621

SCHAEFER, JIMMIE WAYNE, JR., agricultural company executive; b. Anna, Ill., Dec. 26, 1951; s. Jimmie Wayne and Wilma Jean (Kinder) S.; m. Melanie Kugel, Apr. 19, 1981; 1 child Jyoti. BS in Agronomy, So. Ill. U., 1974; MSCI, MERU, Switzerland, 1979. Br. mgr. World Plan Exec. Coun., Nashville, 1975-79; pres. Schaefer & Assoc., Inc., Fairfield, Iowa, 1979-82, J.W. Schaefer Mortgage Co., Fairfield, 1981-1982; chmn., chief exec. officer Soil Techs. Corp., Fairfield, 1982—; chmn. bd. Radiance Dairy Coop., Fairfield, 1980—; bd. dirs. FAE Credit Union, Fairfield, 1982-84; cons. BioField Rsch. Inc., Ottawa, Ont., Can., 1985—; lectr. microalgal applications in agr. to ednl. and rsch. instns. in numerous developing countries; mem. adv. bd. Inst. for Agr. and Environ. Studies, Maharishi Internat. U., Fairfield. Author: (with others) Turf Integrated Pest Management Systems, 1988; patentee in field. Mem. Am. Soc. Agronomy, Am. Soc. Agrl. Cons. Home: RR 4 Box 134 Fairfield IA 52556-9204 Office: Soil Techs Corp RR# 4 Fairfield IA 52556-9804

SCHAEFER, MARY ANN, health facility administrator, consultant; b. Chgo., May 18, 1942; d. Joseph and Mary A. (Kozyra) Strosnik; m. Robert Earl Schaefer, May 18, 1963; children: Debra Ann, Robert Joseph. Diploma in nursing, St. Francis Hosp. Sch. Nursing, Evanston, Ill., 1962; BA, Nat. Coll. Edn., Evanston, 1980; MBA in Health Svc. Mgmt., Webster U., 1990; MJ in Health Law, Loyola U., Chgo., 1993. Med. and surg. nurse Resurrection Med. Ctr., Chgo., 1962-79, charge nurse labor and delivery, 1978-79; coord. maternal child care Humana, Hoffman Estates, Ill., 1979-81; nurse mgr. labor and delivery Resurrection Med. Ctr., Chgo., 1981-91; mgr. Family Birthplace Resurrection Med. Ctr., Chgo., 1991—; cons., prin. M/B Assocs.-Consultants Perinatal Healthcare and Edn., Barrington, 1994—; seminar leader on childbirth edn., legal issues in nursing. Contbr. to Motor Facilitation Handbook; editorial bd. Essentials publ., Resurrection Med. Ctr. Mem. NAFE, NAACOG (cert. in inpatient obstetric nursing), Ill. Pub. Health Assn., Nat. Perinatal Assn., Perinatal Assn. Ill. (mem. exec. bd.), Am. Orgn. Nurse Execs. Home: 23370 N Juniper Ln Barrington IL 60010-2936

SCHAEFER, PATRICIA, librarian; b. Ft. Wayne, Ind., Apr. 23, 1930; d. Edward John and Hildegarde Hartman (Hormel) S. MusB, Northwestern U., 1951; MusM, U. Ill., 1958; MLS, U. Mich., 1963. With U.S. Rubber Co., Ft. Wayne, 1951-52; sec. to promotion mgr. Sta. WOWO, Ft. Wayne, Ind., 1952, sec. to program mgr., 1953-55; coord. publicity and promotion Home Telephone Co., Ft. Wayne, 1955-56; sec. Fine Arts Found., Ft. Wayne, 1956-57; libr. asst. Columbus (Ohio) Pub. Libr., 1958-59; audio-visual librarian Muncie (Ind.) Pub. Libr., 1959-86, asst. libr. dir., 1981-86; libr. dir., 1986-95; chmn. Ind. Libr. Film Cir., 1962-63; treas. Ind. Libr. Film Svc. 1969-70, 83-85; mem. trustee adv. coun. Milton S. Eisenhower Libr., Johns Hopkins U.; mem. presdl. counsellors Johns Hopkins U., 1994—; bd. dirs. Franklin Electric Co., Inc.; cons. in field. Weekly columnist Libr. Lines, Muncie Evening Press, 1981-83; program annotator Muncie Symphony Orch. and Masterworks Chorale; contbr. articles to profl. jours. Bd. dirs. Muncie Symphony Assn., 1964-74, 85-91; bd. dirs. Cen. City Bus. Assn., 1986-92, Ind. Inst. Tech., Ptnrs. for the Enhancement of Cmty. Coop.; adv. coun. Coll. Fine Arts, Ball State U.; mem. bd. dirs. Sta. WIPB-TV; mem. adv. com., bookshop dir. Midwest Writers Workshop, 1976-77; sec. Del. County Coun. for the Arts, 1978-79, pres., 1979-81, bd. dirs., 1985-86; mem. pres.'s coun. Berea Coll.; bd. dirs. Muncie YWCA, 1977-82, 85-89, 95—, treas., 1981-82, 88-89; gen. chmn. Ind. Renaissance Fair, 1978-79; pres. Muncie Matinee Musicale, 1965-67; past pres. Ind. Film and Video Coun.; mem. adv. bd. Community Found. Muncie and Delaware County; bd. dirs. Wapehani coun. Girl Scouts U.S., 1989-96. Named Woman Achievement Pub. Svcs., 1986; recipient Sagamore of the Wabash award Gov. State of Ind., Outstanding Libr. award Ind. Library Fedn., 1995. Mem. ALA, Ind. Libr. Assn. (pres. 1987-88), Nat. League Am. Pen Women (pres. Muncie br. 1974-78), Altrusa (pres. 1986-87), Riley-Jones Club, Delta Zeta, Mu Phi Epsilon. Republican. Roman Catholic. Home: 5400 W Deer Run Ct Muncie IN 47304-5775

SCHAEFER, PATRICIA ANN, retired librarian; b. Lebanon, Ohio, Jan. 22, 1933; d. Riley Ray and Louise Collette (Fraher) Freeze; BS, Miami U., Oxford, Ohio, 1954; m. William H. Schaefer, Aug. 11, 1956; children: Susan P., Nancy A., William H. III (dec.). Med. technologist Mercy Hosp., Hamilton, Ohio, 1954-58, Middletown (Ohio) Hosp., 1958-62; libr. Middletown City Schs., 1979—, intermediate libr. McKinley Sch., 1982-93, retired 1993. Active YMCA, pres., 1977-79; bd. dirs. Middletown Symphony, 1974-78, Arts in Middletown, 1983—, Middletown Symphony Women, 1992—; hon. bd. dirs. Am. Cancer Soc., 1961—; chmn. legis. City Charter Rev. Com., 1970, charter revision com. 1989; residential chmn. United Way, 1976, residential-retiree chmn., 1990; chmn. Sch. Tax Levy, 1978; mem. Middletown City Commn., 1983-88; mem. exec. com. Ohio-Ky.-Ind. Regional Coun., 1986-88; mem. Bicentennial Com. of Middletown; mem. Citizen's Adv. Com. for Miami U.; pres. Middletown Needy Youth Bd.; mem. adv. bd. Manchester Tech. Ctr., Drug Task Force Bd., Middletown Schs; bd. dirs. Citizens Adv. Bd. Manchester Technical, 1991—, Middletown Fine Arts, 1993—, Dental Emergency Fund Area Children, 1994—, DEFAC Bd., 1994—; mem. Leadership Middletown Exec. Bd., Adminstrv. Bd. Meth. Ch. Recipient Stuart Ives Service to Youth award, 1980. Mem. LWV (pres. 1962-63), PEO (pres. 1995—), Am. Soc. Clin. Pathologists, Registry Med. Technologists, Am. Bus. Women's Assn. (pres. 1961-62), Middletown C. of C., Browns Run Country Club, Sigma Sigma Sigma. Methodist. Home: 1909 Antrim Ct Middletown OH 45042-2901

SCHAEFER, ROBERT JOHN, state agency administrator; b. Waukesha, Wis., Dec. 25, 1943; s. Wendellin M. Schaefer and Dora Ann (Netesheim) Schaefer-Gahun; div.; children: Derek James, Dennis Michael, Melissa Lynn. BBA, U. Wis., Eau Claire, 1971. CPA, Wis. Legis. auditor Legis. Audit Bur., Madison, Wis., 1971-73; audit supr. Wis. Coun. on Criminal Justice, Madison, 1973-78; audit mgr. Health Care Financing, State of Wis., Madison, 1978-83; audit dir. Employee Trust Funds, State of Wis., Madison, 1983—. With U.S. Army, 1965-67, Vietnam. Mem. AICPA, Inst. Internal Auditors (Madison chpt. bd. govs. 1992—), Assn. Pub. Pension Fund Auditors (bd. dirs. 1991—, pres. 1993-95). Roman Catholic. Office: Dept Employee Trust Funds 201 E Washington Ave Madison WI 53703-2867

SCHAEFER, SANDRA ELLEN, secondary education educator; b. Troy, Ohio, Oct. 19, 1945; d. Charles Donald and Maribelle (Morrin) Brown; m. James J. Wagner, Aug. 12, 1967 (div. 1975); m. Kenneth Lee Schaefer, Feb. 27, 1976; 1 child, Kenneth Charles. BS in Edn., Miami U., Oxford, Ohio, 1967, MEd in Ednl. Adminstrn., 1974, postgrad., 1974; postgrad., Wright State U., 1976-82. Cert. tchr., Ohio. Tchr. College Corner (Ohio) Schs., 1967-68, West Milton (Ohio) Pub. Schs., 1968-69, Smith Jr. High Sch., Vandalia, Ohio, 1969-73; math. coord. intermediate unit McGuffey Lab. Sch., Oxford, Ohio, 1973-74; math. coord. Vandalia-Butler City Schs., 1976-77; tchr. math., algebra Smith Jr. High Sch., Vandalia, Ohio, 1974-86; tchr. algebra and precalculus Butler High Sch., Vandalia, 1986—; participant profl. confs.; presenter workshops. Contbr. to profl. publs. Mem. fundraising com. Miami Montessori Sch., Troy, 1989-94; curriculum coordinating coun. Vandalia-Butler City Schs., 1985—; coach Mathcounts, 1983-87, Butler H.S. Acad. Challenge Team, 1990—; treas. GMVC Acad. Challenge League, 1992—. Mem. NEA, Am. Montessori Soc., Ohio Edn. Assn., Western Ohio Edn. Assn., Vandalia-Butler Edn. Assn., Assn. Supervision and Curriculum Devel., Sch. Sci. and Math. Assn., Nat. Coun. Tchrs. Math., Ohio Coun. Tchrs. Math. (Outstanding Math. Classroom Tchr. award 1986), Wright State U. Area Coun. Tchrs. Math. Home: 2610 Greenlawn Dr Troy OH 45373-4363 Office: Butler High Sch 600 S Dixie Dr Vandalia OH 45377-2550

SCHAEFFER, BRENDA MAE, psychologist, author; b. Duluth, Minn.; d. Ralph J. Bernice M. (Johnson) Furtman; children: Heidi, Gordon III. BA in Sociology, Psychology and English cum laude, U. Minn., 1962; MA in Human Devel., St. Mary's Coll., Winona, Minn., 1976. Lic. psychologist, Minn.; cert. addictions specialist. Mem. faculty Coll. St. Scholastica, Duluth, 1976—; trainer, therapist, communications cons. Transactional Analysis Inst., Mpls., 1984-88; owner, clin. dir. Brenda M. Schaeffer and Assocs., Inc., Healthy Relationships, Inc.; vis. prof. U. Minn., Duluth, 1976—; guest lectr. dep. counseling U. Wis., Superior, 1980-81; nat. and internat. lectr. Author: Is It Love or Is It Addiction, 1987, Loving Me, Loving You, 1991, Signs of Healthy Love, Signs of Addictive Love, Power Plays, Addictive Love, Help Yourself Out; mem. editorial bd. Transactional Analysis Jour.; editor Healthy Relationships newsletter. Planner Lake Superior Task Force, Duluth, 1980-83; bd. dirs., sec. Nat. Coun. Sexual Addictions/Compulsions, 1992—, sec. 1994-95; v.p. H. Milton Erickson Inst. Minn., 1992-93. Mem. Internat. Transactional Analysis Assn. (1975), Transactional Anaylsis Inst. Minn. (founder, pres. 1984-86), U.S. Assn. Transactional Analysis, Northeast Minn. Transactional Analysis Seminar (founder and chairperson 1977-83). Office: 27306 County Road A Spooner WI 54801-9019

SCHAFER, EDWARD T., governor; b. Bismarck, N.D., Aug. 8, 1946; s. Harold and Marian Schafer; m. Nancy Jones; children: Edward Thomas Jr., Ellie Sue, Eric Jones, Kari Jones. BSBA, U. N.D., 1969; MBA, Denver U., 1970. Quality control inspector Gold Seal, 1971-73, v.p., 1974, chmn. mgmt. com., 1975-78; owner/dir. H&S Distbn., 1976—; pres. Gold Seal, 1978-85, Dakota Classics, 1986—, TRIESCO Properties, 1986—, Fish 'N Dakota, 1990-94; gov. State of N.D., 1992—. Chmn. N.D. Micro Bus. Mktg. Alliance; pres. N.D. Heritage Group; adv. coun. Distributive Edn. Clubs of Am.; lectr. Hugh O'Brien Leadership Found.; counselor Junior Achievement; dir. Bismarck Recreation Coun.; trustee Missouri Valley Family YMCA; plankowner USS Theodore Roosevelt; ann. support com. Medcenter One Found.; mem. Bismarck State Coll. Found. Mem. NRA, Theodore Roosevelt Assn. (Theodore Roosevelt Medora Found., United Sportsman of N.D., U. N.D. Pres. Club, U. Mary Pres. Club, Bismarck-Mandan Rotary. Republican. Office: Office of Gov 600 E Boulevard Ave Bismarck ND 58505-0001*

SCHAFER, MICHAEL SHAWN, small business owner; b. Alliance, Ohio, Jan. 24, 1954; s. Robert Walter and Bonnie Mae (Kelly) S.; m. Susan Laurel Boehm, June 19, 1976; children: Jennifer Grace, Holly Michelle, Heather Katherine. BS in Edn., Kent State U., 1976. Owner, operator Signs 'N' Such of Alliance, 1978—. Author: 150 Years of Serving God, 1989; semiweekly hist. reflections column The Alliance Rev. newspaper, 1993—. Active Stark County (Ohio) Dem. Ctrl. Com., 1988-94; bd. dirs. Mt. Union Cemetery Lot Owners Assn., Alliance, 1989—, sec., 1993—; bd. dirs. Morgan Elem. Sch. PTO, Alliance, 1986-93, treas., 1992; mem. adminstrv. coun. Christ United Meth. Ch., Alliance, 1988—, chmn. history and records commn., 1990—, ch. historian, 1994—. Named one of Outstanding Young Men Am., 1985. Mem. Alliance Area Dem. Club (sec. 1984-86, v.p. 1987, pres. 1989, 92, Man of Yr., 1989). Office: Signs 'N' Such of Alliance PO Box 3013 Alliance OH 44601-7013

SCHAFER, WILLIAM HARRY, electric power industry administrator; b. South Portsmouth, Ky., Aug. 22, 1936; s. William Harry and Mary Minnie (Papillon) S. AS, Franklin U., 1980; BA, Capital U., 1987; MS, Greenwich U., 1992. Cert. fraud examiner; cert. protection profl.; cert. profl. mgr. With Columbus (Ohio) region Am. Electric Power (formerly Columbus So. Power), 1969—, risk mgmt. coord., 1989—; cons. in loss prevention field. First aid instr. Franklin County ARC, Columbus, 1965-93; mem. Simon Kenton coun. Boy Scouts Am., Columbus. Named Ky. Col., Gov. Ky., 1974, Ky. Adm., 1994, Hon. (Ohio) Lt. Gov., 1974; recupent Columbus Mayor's award for Voluntary Svc., 1982, Outstanding Comty. Svc. award Ohio Senate, 1982, Humanitarian Achievement award Columbus Dispatch newspaper, 1983, Silver Beaver award Boy Scouts Am., 1979, 45 Yr. Vets award, 1992; James E. West fellow Boy Scouts Am., 1995. Mem. Am. Soc. Indsl. Security, Nat. Assn. Cert. Fraud Examiners, Acad. Security Educators and Trainers, Inst. Cert. Profl. Mgrs., Valley Forge Hist. Soc. (life), Ky. Hist. Soc. (life), U.S. Capitol Hist Soc. (supporting founding mem.), Nat. Safety Coun. (camping com. 1974-86), Nat. Fire Protection Assn. (edn. com. 1989-93), Children's Club-Children's Hosp. (charter), Masons, Shriners. Methodist. Home: 60 Broadmeadows Blvd Apt 327 Columbus OH 43214-1152 Office: Am Electric Power Columbus Region 215 N Front St Columbus OH 43215-2255

SCHAFFER, HARWOOD DAVID, minister; b. Dayton, Ohio, Oct. 15, 1944; s. Phillip David and H. Ruth (Scheid) S.; BS in Math., Ohio State U., 1965; MDiv, Hartford Sem. Found., 1969; m. Polly Anna Francis, May 6, 1983; children: Rosita, Virginia, Chandra, Karen, Amy, Laura. Ordained to ministry United Ch. of Christ, 1969; chaplain, tchr. Austin Sch., Hartford, Conn., 1967-71; asst. pastor S. Congl. Ch., Middletown, Conn., 1967-71; pastor Trinity United Ch. of Christ, Hudson, Kans., 1971-79, Emma Lowery United Ch. of Christ, Luzerne, Mich., 1979-82, First Congl. United Ch. of Christ and Scambler Union United Ch. of Christ, Pelican Rapids, Minn., 1982-86, United Ch. of Mapleton, Minn., 1986-88, First Congl. United Ch. of Christ, Sherburn and St. John's United Ch. of Christ, Ceylon, Minn., 1988—; area counselor 17/76 Achievement Fund of United Ch. of Christ, 1974-75; co-owner, Polly's Printery, 1984—;co-pub. West Martin Weekly News, 1990—, United Ch. Christ Rural Jour., 1989-90; mem. Western Assn. council Kans.-Okla. Conf., United Ch. of Christ, 1, 1971-74, 76-79, sec.-treas., 1971-74, chmn. ch. and ministry com., 1976-79; mem. various bds. Mich. Conf., United Ch. of Christ, 1979-82; mem. ch. devel. com. Minn. Conf. United Ch. of Christ, 1984-89; conf. and assn. ch. and minister coms, 1989—; v.p., bd. dirs. Dale A. Gardner Aerospace Mus. & Learning Ctr., 1989—. Am. camp mgr. Joint Archaeol. Expdn. to Tel Aphek/Antipatris, Israel, 1978, 80. Bd. govs. Austin Sch., Hartford, 1970-71; mem. Stafford County Democratic Central Com., 1976-79, Dem. Farm Labor precinct chairperson House dist. 10B, 1984-86; Oscoda County Dem. Com., 1980-82; mem. Stafford Council Overall Econ. Devel. Planning Com., 1976-79, chmn., 1977-79; mem. Oscoda County Housing Commn., 1979-82, Pelican Rapids Library Com., 1986. Mem. Sherburn Area C. of C., Trimont Area C. of C., Ind. Order Odd Fellows. Home: PO Box 250 Sherburn MN 56171-0250 Office: PO Box 395 Sherburn MN 56171-0395

SCHAFFLER, MITCHELL BARRY, research scientist, anatomist, educator; b. Bronx, N.Y., Apr. 10, 1957; s. Walter and Shirley (Balter) S. BS, SUNY, Stony Brook, 1978; PhD, W.Va. U., 1985. Rsch. fellow in radiobiology U. Utah, Salt Lake City, 1985-87; asst. prof. U. Calif., San Diego, 1987-90; assoc. prof. and sect. head anatomy Bone and Joint Ctr. Henry Ford Health Scis. Ctr., Detroit, 1990—, Case Western Res. U., 1990—; adj. prof. Anatomy U. Mich., Ann Arbor, 1990—. Mem. editl. bd. Bone, Jour. Orthop. Rsch.; contbr. articles to profl. jours. Grantee Whitaker Found., 1988, NIH. Mem. Am. Assn. Anatomists, Am. Assn. Phys. Anthropology, Am. Soc. Bone Mineral Rsch., Orthop. Rsch. Soc., Sigma Xi, Phi Kappa Phi. Office: Case Western U Henry Ford Hlth Scis Bone & Joint Ctr 2799 W Grand Blvd Detroit MI 48202-2608

SCHAFFNER, JOHN ALBERT, retail merchandising executive, designer; b. Basil, Ohio, Dec. 24, 1937; s. Samuel Stanley and Pauline E. (Stalter) S.; m. Luray Schirtzinger, July 6, 1962; children: Shawn Michael, Jorn Michael. BS, Columbus Coll. Art and Design, 1960. Designer Dave Ellis Ind. Design Inc., Columbus, Ohio, 1960-62, Schwartz Showell Inc., Columbus, 1962-64; dir. of design F.R. Lazarus (Fed. Dept. Stores), Columbus, 1964-69; dir. store planning Hecht's (div. May Dept. Stores), Washington, 1969-81, v.p. dir. store planning, 1985-87; v.p. design and planning May Design & Constn. Inc. (div. May Dept. Stores), St. Louis, 1981-85, v.p. store planning, merchandising, 1987—. Group exhbns. include: Mo. State Coll., 1989, Evansville Art Mus., 1989, 90. Recipient Gardner award Va. Beach Artist Assn., 1973, Golden Dragon Sadler award. Mem. Inst. Store Planners (ways and means com. 1981-87), St. Louis Artist Coalition, No. Va. Art League, St. Louis Artists Guild (bd. govs. 1991-93, Boeschenstein Meml. award 1988, Annual Centennial Sculpture award, 1991), Art and Edn. Coun. Home: 14727 Chermoore Dr Chesterfield MO 63017-7901 Office: May Design and Constrn 611 Olive St Saint Louis MO 63101-1721

SCHAFFNER, JOHN T., state government administrator; b. Milw., Feb. 19, 1944; s. A.J. and Mary E. (Tracy) S.; m. Marjorie Ann Elliott, Oct. 15, 1966; children: Jennifer, Susan, Cathleen, Tracy. BA, St. Ambrose U., 1966. Lic. tchr. Iowa. Sr. H.S. tchr. Postville (Iowa) Schs., 1966-70; pub. adminstr. State of Iowa, Des Moines, 1970—; instr. Des Moines Area C.C., 1978—. Chair Polk County Rep. Party, 1991-93. Roman Catholic. Home: 1404 6th Ave SE Altoona IA 50009 Office: State of Iowa Lucas State Bldg Des Moines IA 50319

SCHAFRATH, RICHARD P., state legislator; b. Canton, Ohio, Mar. 21, 1937; s. Norman Leo and Mary Kathryn (Starr) S.; m. Jamie Schafrath; children: Jeffrey, Renee Schafrath Dean, Ty, Heidi, Bruin, Garrett, Isaac. Student, Ohio State Univ., 1955-58. State senator Ohio 19th Dist., 1985; owner, pres. Loudonville Canoe Libery, Inc., 1996—; chmn. state & local gov. com. & Vets. Affaris; mem. aging com., Energy & Natural Resources, Environ. Com., vice chmn. Edn., Retirement & Aging Com. Named All Pro Nat. Football League, 1963-65, Wooster Count Sports Hall of Fame, Watchdog of Treas. award, 1992; recipient Legis. award AmVets, 1992, Ohio Coalition of Edn. Handicapped Children Legis. award, 1993, Ohio Coalition for More Effective Sch. Dist. award, 1993, Robert E. Hughes Meml. award Ohio Assn. Elec. Officials, 1993. Mem. Am. Legion, Farm Bureau, Nat. Football League Players Assn., Am. Fedn. TV & Radio, Nat. Football League Alumni Assn., Loudonville C. of C., Alpha Kappa Sigma, Kappa Sigma. Office: State Senate State Capitol Columbus OH 43215*

SCHALLER, DORIS GLADYS, writer; b. Petoskey, Mich., Mar. 7, 1915; d. Harve and Edna (Covey) Frederickson; m. William Albert Schaller, Oct. 18, 1938; children: Kirk Karen, Brent. Student, Cleary Coll., 1936-37, North Cen. Mich. Coll., 1960-61, 66-69. Sec. Mr. Beebe, Dean Freshman Coll., Petoskey, Mich., 1934-35, Dr. Dean C. Burns, Burns Clinic, Petoskey, 1937-38; with Probate and Juvenile Ct. Register, Petoskey, 1956-60; sec. bd. No. Mich. Rev., Inc., Mich., 1960-93. Cub scout leader, Petoskey; treas. Camp Daggett Bd.; pres. Bus. and Profl. Women's Club, Petoskey, 1974-75; state bd. Don't Waste Mich., Riga and Lansing, 1989—, bd. dirs. No. bd., 1988—; civic gardening chair Petoskey Area Garden Club, sec., 1986; program chair Keenagers, First Christian Ch.; choir mem. First Christian Ch. Home: Unit #55 2310 M 119 Lakeside Condo Petoskey MI 49770 Office: Petoskey News Rev 319 State St Petoskey MI 49770-2746

SCHAMBURG, TRACY MARIE, professional counselor; b. Amarillo, Tex., Nov. 20, 1964; d. William Edward and Dorothy Dean (Lehman) C.; m. Theodore Gene Schamburg, Jr., July 4, 1992. B of Gen. Studies, West Tex. A&M, 1989, MEd, 1991. Nat. cert. counselor. Dir. social skills Tex. Panhandle Mental Health Authority, Amarillo, 1990-91; profl. counselor Human Support Svcs., Waterloo, Ill., 1992—. lectr., commentator St. Paul's Cath. Ch., St. Louis, 1994—; campaign vol. Gary Gill for Congress, St. Louis, 1994. Republican. Roman Catholic.

SCHANAFELT, TED KEITH, sales engineering executive; b. Salem, Ill., Aug. 14, 1936. Student, U. Ill., 1954-56; BS in Indsl. Engring., So. Ill. U., 1959. Field engr. Rochester and Goodall Cons. Engrs., Salem, Ill., 1960-62; office engr. City of St. Louis, Mo. Housing Authority, 1962-64; constrn. mgr. Clark, Dietz, Painter Cons. Engrs., Urbana, Ill., 1964-66; field engr. Am. Cyanamid Co., Wayne, N.J., 1966, PS Svcs. Inc. (formerly Growmark, Inc.), Bloomington, Ill., 1966-69; mgr. Growmark, Inc., Bloomington, 1969-85; mfg. and product engr. Loren Tyler Corp., Decatur, Ill., 1986; engr. Con-Fab, Inc., Albertsville, Ala., 1986-87; exec. recruiter Dunhill Pers., Huntsville, Ala., 1987-88; product engr. Layco Mfg. Co., Clark Center, Ill., 1988-89, P&H Mfg. Co., Shelbyville, Ill., 1989-90, CEI, Inc., Cedar Rapids, Iowa, 1990-92; sales engr. Vert-Tex Mktg., Inc., Marshall, Ill., 1992-96, Doyle Equipment Mfg. Co., Quincy, Ill., 1996—. Past freelance writer Bloomington/Normal daily newspaper; contbr. articles and stories to profl. jours.; patentee in field. With USNG, 1959-60. Recipient award for work with George Khoory Girls and Boys Baseball League, Clinton, Ill., 1982. Mem. Bloomington/Normal Bass Club (life), Ducks Unltd. Home: 624 S 15th St Quincy IL 62301

SCHANDELMEIER, CATHLEEN ANN, playwright, poet; b. Chgo., Aug. 28, 1959; d. Dale Theodore and JoAnn Marie (Curren) S.; 1 child Vincent James Peterson-Schandelmeier. BA in Theater, Northeastern Ill. U., 1989. Tchr. Chgo. Children's Mus., 1996—, Chgo. Hist. Soc. Kidstory, 1996—; poetry host Poetry on the Beach, Chgo., 1990—, artistic dir. Vince Charming Prodns., Chgo, 1991—; TV show Host, Venue, Chgo., 1992-93; artist in edn. Ill. Arts Coun. Playwright: Sandy and the Circus, 1993, (grant IAC), Santa Girl, 1993 (Peace Mus. 1994), Mmm..Tatoo Screams of Love, 1994 (Adade Wheeler 1995), The Christmas Pageant-St Matthias, 1995; poet: (Anthologies of Poetry) Stray Bullets, 1991, Step Into the Light, 1992; (book of poetry) Scream and I'll Believe You, 1993; also poetry in magazines and articles in Letter eX (Poetry News Mag.). Recipient cert. of leadership in racial justice YWCA, DuPage County, Ill., 1994, spl. assistance grant Ill. Arts Coun., Chgo., 1994; nominated for Adade Wheeler award Coll. of DuPage in Glen Ellyn, 1995; named Outstanding Local Leader in Peace, The Peace Mus., Chgo., 1994. Mem. Internat. Soc. to Prevent Child Abuse and Neglect, Guild Complex Literary Soc., Puppeteers of Am. Democrat. Home: 2108 W Ainslie Apt 1E Chicago IL 60625

SCHANFARBER, RICHARD CARL, real estate broker; b. Cleve., June 11, 1937; s. Edwin David and Helen (Newman) S.; m. Barbara A. Berger, Dec. 21, 1958 (div. Sept. 1981); children: Edwin Jeffrey, Lori Jo, Tammy Joy. Grad., NYU, 1959. Cert. profl. standards instr.; cert. energy instr.; cert. tchr. Ohio; lic. FCC broadcasters; lic. gun dealer. Pres. Erieview Realty Inc., Gates Mills, 1961—, Miller Warehouse, Gates Mills, 1968—, ERI Travel Co., Gates Mills, 1974—, ERI Sales Co., Gates Mills, 1979—; ptnr. Landwood Assocs. Ltd., Gates Mills, 1986—; pres. Eastgate Travel Svcs., Gates Mills, Ohio, 1987—. Pres. Shaker Hts. (Ohio) Alumni Assn., 1986—, Cleve. Area Bd. Realtors, 1981, Cleve. Warehouseman Assn., 1977-79; chmn. City of Cleve. Landmarks Commn., 1984—. Mem. NRA (life), Nat. Assn. Realtors, Ohio Assn. Realtors, Ohio Hist. Soc., Cleve. Growth Assn., Cleve. Area Bd. Realtors, Cleve. Zool. Soc., Cleve. Mus. Art, Mayfield Twp. Hist. Soc., Western Res. Hist. Soc. Republican. Jewish. Home: 6719 Sandalwood Dr Gates Mills OH 44040-9619

SCHANFIELD, FANNIE SCHWARTZ, community volunteer; b. Mpls., Dec. 25, 1916; d. Simon Zouberman and Mary (Schmilovitz) Schwartz; m. Melvin M. Stock, Oct. 27, 1943 (dec. Apr. 1944); 1 child, Moses Samuel Schanfield; m. Abraham Schanfield, Aug. 28, 1947; children: David Colman, Miriam Schanfield Kieffer. Student, U. Minn., 1962-75. Author: My Thoughts, 1996. Bd. dirs. Jewish Cmty. Ctr., Mpls., 1975-96, chairperson older adult needs, 1982-88; past pres. Bnai Emet Women's League, Mpls., 1988-90; rschr., advocate Hunger Hennepin County, Mpls., 1969-75; sec. Joint Religious Legis. Coalition; v.p., bd. dirs. Cmty. Housing Svc., Mpls., 1971-85. Recipient Citation of Honor, Hennepin County Commn., 1989, Lifetime Achievement award Jewish Comty. Ctr. Greater Mpls., 1995. Mem. NOW, Lupus Found. Minn., Internat. Soc. Poets, Hadassah (prs. 1967-69, Citation 1969). Jewish. Home: 3630 Phillips Pky Minneapolis MN 55426-3792

SCHANSTRA, CARLA ROSS, technical writer; b. Berwyn, Ill., Sept. 4, 1954; d. Caroles Schanstra and Heather Millar (Thomson) Alonso. BA, Western Ill. U., 1976; postgrad., U. Ill. Circle, Chgo., 1980-81. Assoc. editor Hitchock Pub., Wheaton, Ill., 1976-80; assoc. product mgr. Advanced Systems, Inc., Elk Grove Village, Ill., 1980-81; tech. writer Profl. Computer Resources, Oak Brook, Ill., 1982; sr. tech. writer AT&T Bell Labs., Naperville, Ill., 1982—; freelance writer, 1980-85. Author: (stage plays) A Little Bit of Both, The Reversible Play, Survivors, Snakes and Apple Pie, It Should Be Obvious, Pastiche, The Model Home; contbr. articles to profl. jours. Violist DuPage Symphony, Glen Ellyn, Ill., 1984-87, 90-93, Elgin (Ill.) Symphonette, 1985-87. Mem. So. Tech. Comm. Assn. (award of excellence 1985), Dramatists Guild, Feminist Writers Western Suburbs (founder), Feminist Writers Guild Chgo. (adv. panel), Internat. Soc. Dramatists, Ill. Theatre Assn., Writers Workshop (co-founder). Office: AT&T Bell Labs IH 2A-173 2000 N Naperville Rd Naperville IL 60563-1443

SCHARCHBURG, RICHARD P., history educator, automotive history writer; b. Ann Arbor, Mich., Feb. 5, 1932; m. Nancy D. Scharchburg, Apr. 18, 1960l children: Richard D., Jean Elizabeth. BA, Eastern Mich. U., 1957, MA, 1963; postgrad., Mich. State U., 1966-70. Tchr., chmn. dept. Birmingham (Mich.) Pub. Schs., 1957-62; asst. prof. social studies State Coll. Iowa, Cedar Falls, 1963-64; asst. prof. indsl. history Gen. Motors Inst., Flint, Mich., 1964-82; Thompson prof. indsl. history Gen. Motors Engring. and Mgmt. Inst., Flint, 1982—, dir. Alumni Found. Collection of Indsl. History, 1982—; trustee Nat. Automotive Hist. Collection, Detroit; cons. automotive history, Fint, 1990—. Author: W.C. Durant: The Boss, 1972, Under No Man's Shadow: Kettering, 1975, Carriages Without Horses: Durya, 1993, GMA: The First 75 Years, 1994. Cpt. U.S. Army, 1952-54. Recipient McKean Cup, Antique Automobile Club Am., 1993. Mem. Mich. Archival Assn., Soc. Automotive History (Cugnot award 1993), Soc. Automotive Engrs. (hist. com.), Hist. Soc. Mich. Republican. Episcopalian. Home: 12147 Pine Row Ln Grand Blanc MI 48439 Office: GMI Engring and Mgmt Inst 1700 W 3d Ave Flint MI 48504

SCHARENBERG, SANDRA LEE, nurse; b. Miami, Fla., Mar. 6, 1960; d. James Myron and Mary (Kohler) Titus; m. Jay Robert Scharenberg, Sept. 8, 1990. AD, Lima (Ohio) Tech. Coll., 1981. RN, Ohio. Staff nurse med.-surg. and telemetry Wilson Meml. Hosp., Sidney, Ohio, 1981-87, staff nurse CCU/ICU, 1987—. Mem. AACN. Republican. Home: 17389 Sharp Rd Sidney OH 45365-8571 Office: Wilson Meml Hosp 915 Michigan St Sidney OH 45365-3501

SCHARP-RADOVIC, CAROL ANN, choreographer, classical ballet educator, artistic director; b. Ypsilanti, Mich., Aug. 9, 1940; d. John Lewis and Mary Vivien (Alther) Keeney; m. Jack Laurel Scharp, July 28, 1958 (div. July 1970); children: Kathryn E., Mark A.; m. Srecko Radovic, Nov. 15, 1989. Studied with Pereslavic, Danilova; student, Harkness Ballet, N.Y.C., Joffrey Ballet, N.Y.C., Eglevsky Ballet, N.Y.C., Briansky Ballet, Darvesh Ballet, N.Y.C.; studied with Jurgen Schneider, Am. Ballet Theatre, 1983-93; studied with Janina Cunova, Luba Gulyeava, Australian Ballet Co., 1983-93; studied with Ninel Kurgapkina, Ludmila Synelnikova, Genhrich Mayorov, Kirov Ballet, 1987-89; studied with Ludmila Sakharova, Perm Ballet, 1993; studied with Ludmila Synelnikova, Bolshoi Ballet Sch., Moscow, 1989; studied with Inna Zubkhovskaya, Alex. Stiopin, Lydia Goncharova, Valentina Chistova, Mararita Zagurskaya, Valentina Rumyantsema, Vaganova Ballet Acad., St. Petersburg, Russia, 1993. Ballet mistress Adrian (Mich.) Coll., 1982-84; founder, artistic dir. Ann Arbor (Mich.) Ballet Theatre, 1980—; studied with Janina Cunova; studied with Luba Gulyeava Kirov Ballet, 1984; former regional field judge Nat. Ballet Achievement Fund; dir. seminars Marygrove Coll., Detroit. Choreographer Cinderella, 1980, Nightingale, 1980, Nutcracker, 1984, Carnival of the Animals, 1981, Carmen, 1983, Midsummer Nights Dream, 1982, Vivaldi's Spring, 1990, Opulence, 1984, La Boutique Fantasque, 1995, Handel's Alcina, 1985, Gymnopedie, 1985, others. Ruth Mott grantee for choreography, 1982. Mem. Mich. Dance Assn. Home: 6476 Huron River Dr Dexter MI 48130 Office: CAS Ballet Theatre Sch Ann Arbor Ballet Theatre 548 Church St Ann Arbor MI 48104-2514

SCHATTEN, GERALD PHILLIP, cell biologist, reproductive biologist, educator; b. N.Y.C., Nov. 1, 1949; s. Frank and Sylvia Schatten; m. Heather Aronson, July 4, 1994; 1 child, Daniel. BS, U. Calif., Berkeley, 1971, PhD, 1975. Instr. U. Calif., Berkeley, 1975; postdoctoral fellow Rockefeller Found., 1976-77; from asst. prof. to prof. Fla. State U., Tallahassee, 1979-86; prof. molecular biology, zoology and obstetrics gynecology U. Wis., Madison, 1986—, dir. integrated microscopy resource for biomed. rsch., 1986-92, dir. gamete and embryo biol. tng. program, 1989—; dir. gamete and embryo biol. tng. program U. Wis., Madison, 1989—; exec. bd. UNESCO Internat. Cell Rsch. Orgn., 1995—. Recipient Rsch. Career Devel. award NIH, 1981-86. Office: Univ Wis 1117 W Johnson St Madison WI 53706-1705

SCHATZ, JONATHAN HARRY, journalist; b. Charlottesville, Va., Aug. 17, 1967; s. Paul Namen and Virginia Margaret (Bogert) S. BA, U. Wis., 1991. Reporter Monroe (Wis.) Evening Times, 1991-92, Beloit (Wis.) Daily News, 1992-94, So. Illinoisan, Carbondale, 1994, The Herald-News, Joliet, Ill., 1994—. Mem. Soc. Profl. Journalists, Investigative Reporters and Editors. Home: 155 N Raynor Ave Apt 8 Joliet IL 60435 Office: The Herald-News 300 Caterpillar Dr Joliet IL 60436

SCHATZ, PAUL FREDERICK, laboratory director; b. Cin., Aug. 24, 1944; s. Frederick Vincent and Nell (Sarles) S.; m. Eleanor Mae Smith, Aug. 19, 1967; children: Alexander, Christopher. BA, Colgate U., 1966; PhD in Chemistry, U. Wis., 1971. Lab. dir. U. Wis., Madison, 1971—. Author various computer programs. Mem. Am. Chem. Soc. Office: Univ Wis Dept Chemistry 1101 University Ave Madison WI 53706-1322

SCHAUBERGER, AMANDA LOUISE, freelance writer; b. Swea City, Iowa, Feb. 11, 1925; d. William and Catherine (Mathies) S. Student, Hamilton Sch. Commerce, Mason City, Iowa, 1943-44. Assembly worker Gen. Dry Batteries, Dubuque, Iowa, 1945-46; sales David Lionel Press, Chgo., 1946-49; sewing machine operator Workshop for the Blind, Sioux City, Iowa, 1950-53, 57-58; phone solicitor Aetna Roof Svc., San Francisco, 1962-63, Blind and Handicapped Products, San Francisco, 1963-64, Blind Made Products, San Francisco, 1964, Vols. of Am., San Francisco, 1965, DAV Store, Mpls., 1972-92. Contbr. articles to The Ringsted Dispatch, Packs of Fun; columnist The Arlington Citizen, 1961-67, Dubuque Leader, 1984—. Vol. disc jockey KFAI-FM, Mpls., 1978-87. Home: 555 5th Ave Apt 1011 Des Moines IA 50309-2300

SCHAUBLE, JOHN EUGENE, physical education educator; b. Paterson, N.J., Aug. 14, 1949; s. Charles Eugene and Rosemary (White) S.; children: Sarah, Angela. BA, Bemidji State U., 1973, BS, 1974; MA, U. Ala., 1984. Cert. tchr. health, phys. edn., K-12; cert. swimming coach/level 4. Northeast area dir. Phys. Fitness Inst. of Am., Albany, N.Y., 1974-75; head swim coach Lake Forest (Ill.) Swim Club, 1975-78; asst. swim coach/grad. asst. U. Ala., Tuscaloosa, 1978-79; head swim coach Palm Springs (Calif.) Swim Team, 1979-80; asst. swim coach Ft. Lauderdale (Fla.) Swim Team, 1980-82; aquatic dir., head swim coach Briarwood of Richmond Aquatic Club, Richmond, Va., 1982-83; head swimming coach, intramural coord. William Rainey Harper Coll., Palatine, Ill., 1983-85; boys/girls asst. swim coach Sch. Dist. 211, Palatine, 1985-90; nat. coach Palatine Swim Team, 1983-92; aquatic coord., head coach swim team, asst. coach track Adlai E. Stevenson High Sch., Lincolnshire, Ill., 1990-93; head sr. coach Adlai E. Stevenson High Sch., 1993—; head coach Patriot Aquatic Club, 1992-94; fund raising com. U.S. Swimming, Inc., Colorado Springs, Colo., 1990—; coaches rep. Ill. Swimming, Inc., Aurora, 1990-94, bd. dirs., tech. planning com., others. Nominated Coach of Yr., Nat. Jr. Coll. Athletic Assn., Ft. Pierce, Fla., 1984; named Sectional Coach of Yr. Ill. High Sch. Assn. Mem. Ill. Swimming Assn. (nominated Coach of Yr. coll. div., 1984), Nat. Interscholastic Swimming Coaches Assn., Am. Swimming Coaches Assn., Am. Coll. Sports Medicine, Nat. Strength and Conditioning Assn., AAPHERD, NEA. Republican. Roman Catholic. Home: 504 Spruce Dr Apt 1A Palatine IL 60074-2315 Office: Stevenson High Sch 1 Stevenson Dr Lincolnshire IL 60069

SCHAUENBERG, SUSAN KAY, educational counselor, educator; b. Taylor Ridge, Ill., Oct. 23, 1945; d. Albert George and Elizabeth (Stedman) Grill; m. Robert Dale Schauenberg Jr.; 1 child, Trevor Alan. BA, Marycrest Coll., 1967; MA, U. Iowa, 1968. From assoc. prof. to prof. Black Hawk Coll., Moline, Ill., 1971—; bus. cons., Rock Island, 1984—; v.p. faculty senate Black Hawk Coll., 1980-82. Planning com. United Way Orgn., Quad-Cities, Ill., 1981-84, agy. rels. com., 1981-82, allocations com., 1980-82; den mother Rock Island chpt. Boy Scouts Am., 1978-79; sponsor Christmas fundraiser for 100 children, yearly. Named one of Most Admired Women of the Quad-Cities, 1975; won L.I.V.E. Volunteerism honor for peer counselor-aide program, 1991. Mem. Assn. of Psychol. Type, Friends of Jung, Am. Fedn. Tchrs., Ill. Guidance and Personnel Assn. (Black Hawk chpt.), U. Iowa Alumni Assn., Phi Gamma Delta (mem. Parents Assn.). Home: 8428 104th Ave W Taylor Ridge IL 61284-9210 Office: Black Hawk Coll 6600 34th Ave Moline IL 61265-5870

SCHAUER, THOMAS ALFRED, insurance company executive; b. Canton, Ohio, Dec. 24, 1927; s. Alfred T. and Marie A. (Luthi) S.; BSc, Ohio State U., 1950; m. Joanne Alice Fay, Oct. 30, 1954; children: Alan, David, Susan, William. Ins. agt., Canton, 1951—; with Ind. Ins. Svc. Corp., 1964—, with Ind. Benefit Svc. Corp., 1984—; dir. Bank One, Akron, N.A., Ohio, 1991—. Chmn., Joint Hosp. Blood Com., 1974; bd. dirs. McKinley Life Ins. Co., 1991-95; bd. dirs. Better Bus. Bur., Canton, 1970-81, chmn., 1979-80; bd. dirs. area YMCA, 1974-92, v.p., 1975-82, pres., 1982-84; trustee Canton Cemetery Assn., 1988-91, Stark County Blue Coats, 1987—; bd. dirs. Hosp. Bur. Cen. Stark City, 1972-78; vice chmn. bd. Aultman Hosp., 1981-84, chmn., 1984-87; chmn. Aultman Health Svcs. Assn., 1990-93; pres. Aultman Hosp. Found., 1987-90 ; chmn. bd. JMS Found., 1968—; bd. dirs. United Way, 1974-84, pres., 1976-78; mem. distbn. com. Stark County Found., 1977-87, chmn. distbn. com.; 1984-87; dir. Dime Bank, Canton, 1965-72, Ctrl. Trust Co. of NE Ohio, N.A., 1972-91; adv. bd. Malone Coll., 1979-92; trustee Kent State U., 1980-88, trustee emeritus, 1988—, N.E. Ohio Univs. Coll. Medicine, 1983-88; past trustee Canton Urban League, Boys Village (Smithville, Ohio), Canton Art Inst., Buckeye Council Boy Scouts Am. Served with USNR, 1946-48. Recipient Gold Key award United Way of Cen. Stark County, 1981, Award of Merit Canton C. of C., 1984, Red Triangle award Canton Area YMCA, 1985. Mem. Chartered Ins. Inst. London, Nat. Assn. Mfg., Am. Soc. CPCUs, Am. Soc. CLUs, Assn. Advanced Life Underwriters, Am. Risk and Ins. Assn., Am. Soc. Pension Actuaries, Stark County Accident and Health Underwriters (past pres.), Canton Club, Brookside Country Club, Atwood Yacht Club. Home: 1756 Dunbarton Ave NW Canton OH 44708-1807 Office: Carnegie Libr Bldg 236 3rd St SW Canton OH 44702-1622

SCHAUNAMAN, CRAIG D., state legislator; m. Carolyn Schaunaman. Student, No. State Coll. Mem. S.D. Ho. of Reps., mem. legis. procedure and state affairs coms.; farmer Aberdeen, S.D. Home: 1403 S 7th St Aberdeen SD 57401-6827*

SCHECTER, JERRY SHERWIN, psychologist; b. Chgo., Mar. 13, 1946; s. Rubin and Dorothy (Siegal) S.; m. Sheryl L. Feldman, Aug. 10, 1969; children: Noel, Bradley. BA, U. Ill., Chgo., 1968; MA, Roosevelt U., 1971; PhD, Loyola U., 1981. Lic. psychologist, Ill. Tchr. Chgo. Pub. Schs., 1968-74, psychologist, 1974—; pvt. practice, Skokie, Ill., 1981—; cons. Ctr. for Talent Deve., Northwestern U., Evanston, 1990—. Contbr. articles to profl. jours. Mem. APA, Ill. Assn. Gifted Children, Chgo. Area Sch. Psychology (pres. 1984-85). Jewish. Home: 7712 Maple Morton Grove IL 60053 Office: 9150 N Crawford Ste 105 Skokie IL 60076

SCHEER, ROBERT P., mechanical engineer; b. St. Louis, Mar. 24, 1938. Student, Washington U., 1960's. Draftsman Magretek Century Electronic, St. Louis, 1957—. Coach St. Louis (Mo.) Youth Soccer, 1992—. Sgt. USNG, 1960-66. Roman Catholic. Office: Magretek Century Electric 1881 Pine St Saint Louis MO 63103-2264

SCHEETZ, GEORGE HENRY, library director; b. Columbus, Ohio, July 27, 1952; s. Donald Jean and Betty Jane (Killeen) S.; m. Kathy Charlotte Durley, Apr. 28, 1979, (div.); children: Trevor Killeen, Avery Kathleen. AB, U. Ill., 1974, MS, 1976. Reference libr. Bradley U., Peoria, Ill., 1977-78; bus. libr. Peoria Pub. Libr., 1978-79, br. mgr., 1979-82; asst. dir. Ames (Iowa) Pub. Libr., 1982-85; dir. Sioux City (Iowa) Pub. Libr., 1985-92, Champaign (Ill.) Pub. Libr., 1992—; registered agt. Sioux City Pub. Libr. Found., 1990-92; ex officio bd. dirs. Champaign Pub. Libr. Found., 1993—. Author: Place Names of Story County, 1985, Trevor, 1986, Name's Names, 1988; editor: Riverworld War, 1980; contbr. articles to profl. jours. Rep. Jr. League Community Adv. Coun., Sioux City, 1985-89; bd. dirs. Sioux City Concert Course, 1991-92; bd. dirs. Va. Theatre Group, 1995—, sec. 1995—, pres., 1996—. Named one of Outstanding Young Men of Am., Jaycees, 1979. Mem. ALA, Ill. Libr. Assn. (mem. pub. policy com. 1994—), Am. Name Soc., Ill. State Libr. Adv. Com. (subcom. pub. libr. svc. 1992—), Sci. Fiction Rsch. Assn., Rotary, Sigma Tau Delta, Omicron Delta Kappa. Roman Catholic. Home: #163 310 S Prospect Ave Champaign IL 61820-4715 Office: Champaign Pub Libr 505 S Randolph St Champaign IL 61820-5137

SCHEEVEL, KENRIE JAMES, state legislator; b. July 7, 1956; m. Karen Dornink. BA, Northwestern Coll., 1978; BSME, S.D. State U., 1981. Minn. state sen. Dist. 31, 1994—. Address: Rte 2 Box 227 Preston MN 55965

SCHEFFLER, LEWIS FRANCIS, pastor, educator, research scientist; b. Springfield, Ohio, Oct. 13, 1928; s. Lewis Francis and Emily Louise (Kloker) S.; m. Willa Pauline Cole, Aug. 9, 1949 (div. 1978); children: Lewis F. Fischer, Richard Thomas, Gary Arlen, Tonni Kay; m. Mary Lee Smith, Apr. 18, 1978; stepchildren: Kimberly McCollum, Jeffrey McIlroy, Kerry Buell. BA in Liberal Arts, Cin. Bible Seminary, 1950; AA in Bus., Jefferson Coll., 1989; MAT, Webster U., 1989. Quality assurance Tectum Corp., Newark, 1954-57; rsch. group leader Owens-Corning Fiberglas, Granville, Ohio, 1957-64; tech. asst. to v.p. R&D and Engring., 1960-63; rsch. administr. Modiglas Fibers Corp., Bremen, Ohio, 1965-68; dir. R & D Flex-O-Lite Corp., St. Louis, 1968-71; pastor Christian Ch., St. Louis, 1972-75; police commns. Brentwood (Mo.) Police Dept., 1975-87; pastor Christian Ch., Potosi, Mo., 1988-89, Slater (Mo.) Christian Ch., 1989-93, Laddonia Christian Ch., 1994—; asst. prof. English lang. and lit. Mo. Valley Coll., Marshall, 1989-93; adj. prof. theology Mo. Sch. Religion, 1993—; organizing co-chmn. aerospace composite materials com. ASTM, 1961; mem. exec. bd. Northwest Area Christian Ch., 1989-93; mem. Coun. of Areas of Mid-Am. Region Christian Ch., 1990-93; cons. in field. Contbr. articles to profl. jours. Patentee in field. Money raiser United Appeal, chaplaincy Blessing Hosp., Quincy, Ill., 1974; vol. Ill. Divsn. Children and Family Svcs., 1972-75; sec. exec. com. N.W. Area Christian Ch. (Disciples of Christ). Mem. Medieval Acad. Am., Mo. Philol. Assn. Home: RR 1 Box 32A Laddonia MO 63352-9710

SCHEIDERER, PHYLLIS JACKSON, nursing administrator; b. Columbus, Ohio, Jan. 4, 1935; d. Ped Wilbur and Clara Maxine (Shopshear) Jackson; m. Reinhard C. Scheiderer, Nov. 27, 1955; children: John P., George C. Diploma in nursing tech., Marion (Ohio) Tech. Coll., 1984; student, Capitol U. RN, Ohio; cert. correctional health profl. Nursing supr. Ohio Reformatory for Women, Marysville; adminstr. health care, dir. nursing Franklin Pre-Release Ctr., Columbus; mem. nurses edn. com. Ohio Dept. Rehab. and Corrections; cert. AIDS counselor Franklin Pre-Release Ctr. Vol. Health Check, Delaware, Ohio, Columbus, 1988, 89, 90, Teddy Bear Day, Columbus Zoo; mem. Women's Health Network, Columbus. Recipient Dorothy Cornealous award Mid Ohio Dist. Nurses Assn., 1995. Mem. ANA (continuing edn. ind. rev. panelist), Ohio Nurses Assn. (legis. liaison), Mid.-Ohio Nurses Assn. (membership and media rels. com.), Am. Correctional Assn., Am. Correctional Health Svcs. Assn., Aids Svc. Connection, Take it to the Streets Found.

SCHEIDLER, JAMES EDWARD, physicians services company executive; b. Chippewa Falls, Wis., Mar. 11, 1946; s. Clifford James and Mary Margaret (Roch) S.; m. Ellen Marie Swiontek, Aug. 23, 1970; children: Matthew, Nathan, Mary. BA in Econs. and History, U. Wis., Eau Claire, 1968, MA in Tchg. in History, 1975. Tchr., coach Campbellsport (Wis.) Sch. Dist., 1968-69, Reedsburg (Wis.) Sch. Dist., 1969-72; salesman IBM, Madison, Wis., 1973-78; salesman, mktg. mgr. WAF Inst. Raltech, Madison, 1978-85; nat. accounts and sales mgr. Spacesaver Corp., Ft. Atkinson, Wis., 1985-92; mgr. plan devel. and govt. rels. Wis. Physican Svcs., Madison, 1992—. Chmn. Madison Night at County Stadium, 1980-84; mem. steering com. Wis. Basketball Coaches All Star Game, Madison, 1983—; founder, chmn. Badger Classic, high sch. basketball tournament, Madison, 1986—; mem. Queen of Peace Sch. Bd., Madison, 1987-89; pres. Edgewood H.S. Athletic Assn., Madison, 1991—; pres. U. Wis. Basketball Boosters, 1977, 88. Named to Hall of Fame, Wis. Basketball Coaches, 1993. Mem. U. Wis.-Eau Claire Alumni Assn. (bd. dirs. 1989—, pres. 1996-97), Mendota Gridiron Club. Roman Catholic. Home: 21 Frederick Cir Madison WI 53711

SCHELL, ALLAN CARTER, retired electrical engineer; b. New Bedford, Mass., Apr. 14, 1934; s. Charles Carter and Elizabeth (Moore) S.; m. Shirley T. Sardineer; children: Alice Rosalind, Cynthia Anne. B.S., MIT, 1956, M.S.E.E., 1956, Sc.D., 1961; student, Tech. U. Delft, Netherlands, 1956-57. Research physicist Air Force Cambridge Research Labs., Bedford, Mass., 1956-76; Guenter Loeser Meml. lectr. Air Force Cambridge Research Labs., 1965; dir. electromagnetics directorate Rome Air Devel. Ctr., Bedford, 1976-87; chief scientist Hdqrs. USAF Systems Command, 1987-92; chief scientist, dep. dir. sci. and tech. Hdqrs. USAF Materiel Command, 1992-94; dir. Electro; vis. assoc. prof. MIT, 1974; chair dept. of elec. engring. adv. coun. U. Pa., 1992-94. Contbr. articles to profl. jours.; patentee in field (9). Served as lt. USAF, 1958-60. Recipient Fulbright award, 1956-57, Meritorious Exec. award U.S. Govt., 1989; NSF fellow, 1955-56, 60-61. Fellow IEEE (bd. dirs. 1981-82, editor IEEE Press 1976-79, Procs. of IEEE 1990-92), Antennas and Propagation Soc. of IEEE (pres. 1978, editor tran. 1969-71, John T. Bolljahn award 1966), Internat. Sic. Radio Union (U.S. nat. com.), Air Force Assn., Sigma Xi, Tau Beta Pi.

SCHELLEN, NANDO, opera director; b. The Hague, The Netherlands, Oct. 11, 1934; came to U.S., 1993; m. Deborah Raymond, June 19, 1991; 4 children. Mng. dir. Netherlands Opera, 1969-79, assoc. gen. dir., 1979-87; gen. artistic dir. Sweelinck Conservatory of Music, Amsterdam, 1990-93; gen. dir. Indpls. Opera, 1993-96; freelance stage dir., 1982—. Home: 209 E 45th St Indianapolis IN 46205

SCHELLER, JIM, mechanical engineer; b. Belleville, Ill., Feb. 18, 1967. BS in Mech. Engring., U. Ill., 1989. Mech. engr. Emerson Elec. Co., St. Louis, 1989-91, U.S. Elec. Motors, St. Louis, 1991—. Mem. Emerson Engring. Club. Roman Catholic. Office: US Elec Motors PO Box 3946 Saint Louis MO 63136-0546

SCHELLIN, PATRICIA MARIE BIDDLE, educator; b. Columbus, Wis., Apr. 1, 1955; d. Charles Westly Sr. and Dorothy (Madigan) Biddle; m. Edwin O. Schellin, June 21, 1980; children: Jennifer, Jeremy, Jonathan. BS, U. Wis., LaCrosse, 1978. Cert. tchr., Wis. Tchr., coach Freedom (Wis.) Schs., 1978-80, Fall River (Wis.) Schs., 1983-84; tchr. St. Jerome's Sch., Columbus, 1984-86, 90—, Dickason Mid. Sch., Columbus, 1987; substitute tchr. Columbus Schs., 1980—; swimming instr. Columbus Recreation Dept., 1979—; coach girls basketball, Columbus High Sch., 1983—, varsity girls soccer, 1993—; instr. CPR ARC, Columbus, 1986—, water safety chair, 1984—. Coach soccer, baseball Columbus Recreation Dept., 1988—; recreation dir. City of Columbus, 1993—. Mem. AAHPERD. Lutheran. Home: 549 Hibbard St Columbus WI 53925-1241 Office: Saint Jeromes Sch 156 W James St Columbus WI 53925-1569

SCHELLPEPER, STAN, state legislator; b. Hoskins, Nebr., Jan. 27, 1934; m. Faye Wiedeman, 1957; children: Jeffrey, Thomas, Nancy (Mrs. Morfeld). Grad., Stanton H.S. Farmer, livestock breeder Nebr.; mem. from dist. 18 Nebr. State Senate, Lincoln, 1986—, mem. agr. and revenue coms., chmn. gov. affairs com. Past state pres. Nebr. Rural Elec. Assn.; past sec. Sch. Dist. 13, Nebr.; sec., mgr. Stanton County Fair Bd.; mem. Nebr. State Fair Bd. Named Area Farmer of Yr., Norfolk Kiwanis, 1985. Mem. Stanton County Livestock Feeders Assn. (past pres.). also: Nebr State Legislature State Capitol Lincoln NE 68509*

SCHEMMEL, RACHEL ANNE, food science and human nutrition educator, researcher; b. Farley, Iowa, Nov. 23, 1929; d. Frederic August and Emma Margaret (Melchert) Schemmel. BA, Clarke Coll., 1951; MS, U. Iowa, 1952; PhD, Mich. State U., 1967. Dietitian, Children's Hosp. Soc., L.A., 1952-54; instr. Mich. State U., East Lansing, 1955-63, from asst. prof. to prof. food sci., human nutrition, 1967—. Author: Nutrition Physiology and Obesity, 1980. Contbr. articles on obesity, clin. nutrition to profl. jours. Recipient Disting. Alumni award Mt. Mercy Coll., 1971, Borden award for rsch. in applied nutrition, 1986, Disting. Faculty award Mich. State U., 1991. Mem. Am. Inst. Nutrition, Inst. Food Technologists, Am. Diet Assn. (pres. Mich. 1975-76, Lansing 1960), Brit. Nutrition Soc., Soc. for Nutrition Edn., Sigma Xi (sr. rsch. award 1986, pres. Mich. State U. chpt. 1983-84), Phi Kappa Phi (pres. 1994-95). Roman Catholic. Home: 1341 Red Leaf Ln East Lansing MI 48823-1339 Office: Mich State U Dept Food Sci Nutrit East Lansing MI 48824

SCHENCK-HAMLIN, WILLIAM JOSEPH, rhetoric and communications educator; b. Norman, Okla., Feb. 28, 1947; s. Hubert J. and Maxine (Peterson) Hamlin; m. Donna Christine Schenck, Dec. 13, 1952. BS, Kans. State U., 1969, MA, 1971; PhD, U. Oreg., 1976. Teaching fellow U. Oreg., Eugene, 1973-76; asst. prof. rhetoric and comm. Kans. State U., Manhattan, 1976-81, assoc. prof., dir. rhetoric and comm. program, 1981-92. Author: Building Speeches: A Decision-Making Approach, 1992; contbg. author: Automated Decision Procedures, 1992. Recipient William L. Stamey Teaching award Kans. State U., 1992. MMem. Speech Comm. Assn., Internat. Comm. Assn., Cen. States Speech Comm. Assn., Amnesty Internat. Home: 1922 Leavenworth St Manhattan KS 66502-3817 Office: Kans State U Nichols Hall Manhattan KS 66506

SCHENZ, ANNE FILER, product research and development supervisor, educator; b. Sharon, Pa., Sept. 16, 1945; d. Robert Adam John and Marjorie Ruth (Hengstler) Filer; m. Timothy William Schenz, June 15, 1968. BS in Chemistry, Westminster Coll., 1967; PhD in Chemistry, Kent State U., 1974. Tchr. chemistry Springfield (Ohio) Twp. Schs., 1967-68; vis. prof. chemistry King's Coll., Briarcliff Manor, N.Y., 1975-76; prin. devel. chemist Lever Bros., Edgewater, N.J., 1976-78; project specialist Gen. Foods Corp., Tarrytown, N.Y., 1978-81; group leader Gen. Foods Corp., Tarrytown, 1981-87; sr. group leader Ross products divsn. Abbott Labs., Columbus, Ohio, 1987—; adj. asst. prof. Ohio State U., Columbus, 1989—. Patent Amino Acids as Dry Beverage Mix Ingredients, 1984, Fruit Flavored Beverages, 1984, Flavor and Mouthful Character of Beverages, 1986. Mem. Am. Chem. Soc., Assn. Chemoreception Sci., Inst. Food Technologists. Moravian. Office: Ross Labs Dept 105644/RP4-1 625 Cleveland Ave Columbus OH 43215-1754

SCHENZ, TIMOTHY WILLIAM, chemist; b. Washington, Jan. 2, 1946; s. William Pard and Oletta Faye (Thompson) S.; m. Anne Kathleen Filer, June 15, 1968. BS in Chemistry, Westminster Coll., 1968; PhD in Chemistry, Kent State U., 1973. Sr. chemist Gen. Foods Corp., Tarrytown, N.Y., 1974-77, project specialist, 1977-79, rsch. specialist, 1979-85, sr. scientist, 1985-87; sr. rsch. scientist Ross Labs., Columbus, Ohio, 1987-90, assoc. rsch. fellow Volwiler Soc., 1990-95; rsch. fellow Volwiter Soc., 1995—; adj. asst. prof. food sci. and nutrition Ohio State U., Columbus, 1989—. Author jour. and book articles; patentee in field. Mem. Am. Chem. Soc., Inst. Food Technologists, Sigma Xi. Office: Ross Labs 625 Cleveland Ave Columbus OH 43215-1754

SCHERDIN, MARY JANE LISKOVEC, librarian, information professional, researcher; b. LaCrosse, Wis., Sept. 29, 1940; d. Ambrose John and Martha Marie (Borgmeier) Liskovec; m. Arthur William Scherdin, Apr. 15, 1961 (div. 1976); children: James William, Laurette Therese (dec.), Amy Lynn. BS in Elem. Edn., U. Wis., LaCrosse, 1961; MS in Libr. Sci., U. Wis., Madison, 1972; MEd Profl. Devel. in Audiovisual Media, U. Wisc., Whitewater, 1980; PhD in Edn. Adminstrn., U. Wisc., Madison, 1989. Children's libr. LaCrosse Pub. Libr., 1961; sch. libr. LaCrosse Pub. Schs., 1961-64; media dir. Whitewater Pub. Schs., 1971-75; supr. arts media ctr. U. Wisc., Whitewater, 1975-79, head learning mater ctr., 1979-86, instr., 1976-78; asst. dean U. Wis., Milw., 1986-88; collection access coord. U. Wisc., Madison, 1988-92; libr. dir. Edgewood Coll., Madison, 1992—; researcher The Highsmith Co., Ft. Atkinson, Wis., 1983, ALA, Chgo., 1991-96, Cons. Psychologists Press, Palo Alto, Calif., 1991-96; cons. Myers-Briggs Type Indicator, 1992—; vis. prof. U. Wis., Madison, 1992. Co-author: K-12 Library Curriculum, 1974; author of bio-bibliographies of Wis. authors, 1981-83; designer; instructional computer programs 1983, 87, 89; author, editor: Discovering Librarians: Profiles of a Profession, 1994; contbr. articles to profl. jours. Pres. Jefferson (Wis.) Jaycettes, 1968-69; state and internal exec. v.p. Wis. Jaycettes, 1969-71; edn. chair Nat. Found. March of Dimes, Jefferson, 1970-74; vol. Nat. Found. Sudden Infant Death, Wis., 1975-83. Mem. AAUW (v.p. Ft. Atkinson 1974-75), Assn. Coll. and Rsch. Librs. (task force chair 1991-93), Libr. Adminstrv. and Mgmt. Assn. (pubs. and bibliography com.), Wis. Health Sci. Libr. Assn. (long range planning com. 1990-92, bd. mem. 1992-93), Wis. Libr. Assn. (chair lit. awards com. 1983, bd. dirs. 1987-88, chair edn. sect. 1993), Wis. Assn. Acad. Librs. (chair conf. planning 1985, 96, chair publs. 1993, chair 1988), U. Wis. Sch. Libr. and Info. Studies Alumni Assn. (sec. 1993-95); del. Coun. Wis. Librs., 1994—. Home: 6111 Winnequah Rd Madison WI 53716-3459 Office: Edgewood Coll 859 Woodrow St Madison WI 53711-1958

SCHERECK, WILLIAM JOHN, retired historian, consultant; b. Chgo., Dec. 22, 1913; s. Frank and Adele (Schubert) S.; m. Flora Blanche George, May 19, 1943; children: Linda, William John, Ralph, George. Student Wofford Coll., 1950-51; BS in Sociology, U. Wis., 1952, postgrad., 1952-53. With Crawford County (Wis.) Welfare Dept., 1938-42; with State Hist. Soc. Wis., Madison, 1953-79, rsch. asst., 1954-55, field services supr., 1956-59, head Office Local History, 1960-79, Wis. Coun. Local History, from 1961, ret.; now researcher ancient histories and religions. Active Girls Scouts U.S.A., Spartanburg, S.C., 1947-48, Boy Scouts Am., Madison, 1956-58. 2d lt. U.S. Army, 1942-45. Decorated Bronze Star; recipient 1st place award S.C. State Coll. Press Assn., 1951, Crusade for Freedom awards, 1951, 1st place award for Sounds of Heritage, Am. Exhbn. Ednl. Radio and TV, 1955. Author, distbr. Simplified System of Cataloging local Hist. Soc. and Mus. Mem. Am. Legion, Ret. Officers Assn., Am. Fedn. State, County and Mcpl. Employees, Am. Fedn. of Police, Wis. Alumni Assn., Am. Assn. Ret. Persons. Methodist. Author numerous publs. State Hist. Soc. Am.; award winning poet; contbr. articles to mags. and newspapers. Home: 11013 W Harmony Dr Lodi WI 53555

SCHERER, ANITA (ANITA STOCK), advertising executive; b. Cleve., Sept. 20, 1938; d. William John Stock and Gertrud Clara (Kaufmann) Bacher; m. Richard Phillip Scherer, Nov. 25, 1961; children: William Richard, Christopher Howard. Student U. Cin., 1956-57. AB Jones Bus. Coll., 1958. Account sec. Northlich, Stolley Inc., Cin., 1978-79, account asst., 1979-80, asst. account mgr., 1980-81, account mgr., 1981-84, mktg. svc. assoc., 1984-89, mgr., 1989—; lectr. local schs., univs., Cin. 1980—. Coeditor: monthly newsletter Badge, 1967-72; designer assorted notepads, 1986. Lector, Our Lady of Victory Roman Cath. Ch., Cin., 1972—; corr. sec. Delhi Police Assn. Inc., Ohio, 1967-72; pres. Delhi Hills Community Coun., Ohio, 1974-75; adv. bd. mem. Coll. Mount St. Joseph, Ohio, 1974-80; v.p. adminstr. Stagecrafters, Cin., 1983-85, publicity chmn., 1984-89; mktg. bd. mem. Contemp. Arts Ctr., 1985—, chmn. Advt./Graphic Arts div. Fine Arts Fund Campaign, 1988; trustee Arts and Humanities Resource Ctr. for Elderly, 1990—, bd. chmn., 1991-93. Winner nat. competition Am. Assn. Advt. Agys., 1980; recipient Outstanding Performance award Assn. Community Theatres, Cin., 1983, Excellence in Acting award Ohio Community Theatres Assn., 1984. Mem. Cin. Direct Mktg. Assn., Am. Mktg. Assn., Acad. Health Services Mktg. (adv. bd. dirs. 1989-91), Am. Coll. Healthcare Mktg., Cin. C. of C. (lectr. 1984-86). Avocations: travel, reading, medieval/renaissance history, community theater, archaeology. Home: 5511 Palomino Dr Cincinnati OH 45238-4143 Office: Northlich Stolley LaWarre Inc 200 W 4th St Cincinnati OH 45202-2602

SCHERER, CHRISTIAN MACARTHUR, marketing consultant; b. Olney, Ill.; s. Arthur Ludwig and Edna Oliva Scherer; m. Jane Ann Buford, Nov. 28, 1970. BS, U. Ill., 1964; MExtEd, —, 1975. Extension advisor U. Ill. Coop. Extension, Freeport, 1967-71; assoc. prof., comms. specialist U. Ill. Coop. Extension, Urbana, 1972-88; info. dir. Ill. Dept. Agr., Springfield, 1971-72; support svcs. head Ill. Water Survey, Champaign, 1988-89; CEO Scherer Comms. Co., Urbana, 1989—. 1st lt. U.S. Army, 1965-67, Vietnam. Mem. Rotary (exec. sec. 1993—, Paul Harris fellow), Symphony Bd., Master Communicators (award excellence 1992), Advt. Club Champaign-Urbana (award excellence 1993). Lutheran.

SCHERER, GEORGE ROBERT, retired secondary education educator; b. Marion, Ill., Sept. 2, 1923; s. Herman Albert and Alice Madora (Bulliner) S.; m. Margaret Mary Brzozowski, Dec. 31, 1945; children: Marion, Anne Madora. BS in Piano, Juilliard Sch., N.Y.C., 1948; MMus in Piano, Roosevelt U., 1952. Cert. elem. and secondary tchr., Ill. Tchr. Chgo. Bd. Edn., 1954-85; profl. chorister Chgo. Symphony Orch. Chorus, 1965-70; instr. Fenger Jr. Coll., Chgo., 1971-73. Composer music for chorus and piano; author: Scherer A Genealogy, 1996. Mem. Am. Guild of Music Artists, Juilliard Sch. Music Alumni Assn., Roosevelt U. Alumni Assn. Avocation: profl. genealogist. Home: 17841 Anthony Country Club Hills IL 60478

SCHERER, VICTOR RICHARD, physicist, computer specialist, musician; b. Poland, Feb. 7, 1940; came to U.S., 1941, naturalized, 1951; s. Emanuel and Florence B. Scherer; m. Gail R. Dobrofsky, Aug. 11, 1963; children: Helena Cecille, Markus David. BS magna cum laude, CCNY, 1960; MA, Columbia U., 1962; PhD, U. Wis., 1974. Health physics asst. Columbia U., N.Y.C., 1961-63; research asst. dept. physics U. Wis., Madison, 1967-74, project assoc., project mgr. Inst. for Environ. Studies, World Climate-Food Rsch. Group, 1974-78, specialist computer systems U. Wis. Acad. Computing Ctr., 1978—, coord. divsn. info. tech. help desk, U. Wis., Madison. Concert pianist; tchr., promoter contemporary composers. AEC fellow, 1960-61. Mem. AAAS, Am. Phys. Soc., Am. Meteorol. Soc., Am. Soc. Agronomy,

Assn. Computing Machinery, Nat. Computer Graphics Assn., Sigma Xi, Phi Beta Kappa. Researcher in particle physics, agroclimatology, soil-yield relationships and computer graphics; cons. on computer sys., electronic mail, geographic analysis and supercomputing applications. Office: U Wis-Madison Divsn Info Tech 1210 W Dayton St Madison WI 53706-1685

SCHEUERMAN, DAVID ELMER, sales executive; b. Elmhurst, Ill., Nov. 13, 1967; s. Elmer Lee and Judith Ann (Strathmann) S. BSEE, Purdue U., 1990. Regional sales mgr. Littelfuse Inc., Des Plaines, Ill., 1991—. Mem. IEEE, Internat. Assn. Elec. Inspectors. Lutheran. Home: 2002 Stillwater Rd Arlington Heights IL 60004 Office: Littelfuse Inc 800 E Northwest Hwy Des Plaines IL 60016-3049

SCHEVE, ADDIE R., author; b. Madison, Nebr., Mar. 30, 1919; d. Walter Herman and Lena (Emrich) Freidenburg; m. Alvin I. Scheve, Mar. 2, 1941; children: Kathy, Gary, Jean (dec.). Grad. high sch., Battle Creek, Nebr. Author: That Extra Touch, 1979, He Says It With Flowers, 1981, Listen to the Talking Trees, 1991; contbr. articles to mags. Vol. sec. St. John's Luth. Ch., Battle Creek; pres. Battle Creek Betterment,. Named Nebr. Mother of the Yr., 1980. Lutheran. Home: 315 Valley View Dr Norfolk NE 68701

SCHEVE, MAY E., state legislator; b. St. Louis, June 27, 1964; d. Robert Anthony and May Ellen (Braun) S. BA, St. Louis U., 1987; postgrad., Webster U. Rep. Mo. State Ho. Reps. Dist. 98, 1991—. Committeewoman Gravois Twp. Dem. Club. Mem. Women Legislators (v.p.), Third Congl. Women's Club (sec.), Women's Dem. Forum, Alpha Gamma Delta, Kappa Beta Phi. Office: Mo Ho of Reps State Capitol Building Jefferson City MO 65101-1556*

SCHICHTEL, BARBARA NAN, college library administrator; b. Grand Rapids, Mich., Feb. 16, 1958; d. Robert Reynold and Esther Ann (Shears) S. BA summa cum laude, Western Mich. U., 1979, MS in Librarianship, 1982. Cert. profl. pub. libr., AMT, CMT, CNT. Tchr., libr. Grand Rapids (Mich.) Cath. Schs., 1978-80; circulation supr. Aquinas Coll., Grand Rapids, 1980-82, serials libr., 1982-89, sys., serials libr., 1989-91, asst. dir., 1991-95; access libr. Grand Valley State U., Allendale, Mich., 1995—; freelance cons., Grand Rapids, 1987—; region rep. USJCC Outstanding Metro Conf., 1996. Editor Lakenet Calendar of Events, 1986-93, Grand Rapids Bus. Jour. Index, 1987-95. Founder, chmn. Wayland (Mich.) Area Jaycees; participant Western Mich. Learning Initiative Learning Ecosystem Project, Grand Rapids, 1994. Mem. Mich. Database Users Group, Mich. Archival Assn., Mich. Libr. Assn., Grand Rapids Jaycees Found. (sec. 1994-96, trustee 1996—), Grand Rapids Jaycees (bd. dirs. 1990-92, exec. bd. mem. 1992-94), U.S. Jr. C. of C. (metro conf. dir. 1995-96, Outstanding Metro State Rep 1994), Mich. Jaycees (Outstanding Writing 1992, Armbruster 1992, metro conf. dir. 1994-95, grandnet steering com. 1994-95). Republican. Roman Catholic. Home: 2652 Ridgecroft Dr SE Grand Rapids MI 49546 Office: Grand Valley Ste U Zumberge Libr 113 1 Campus Dr Allendale MI 49401

SCHICK, PAUL WALTER, project engineer; b. S.I., Aug. 13, 1951; s. Walter and Sophia (Pablos) S. BS in Physics, Cooper Union Coll., 1972; MS in Physics, U. Wis., 1976. Engr., technician Madison (Wis.) Computer, 1977-83, prin., software engr., 1983-85; computer writer Enteleki, Inc., 1986-87; project engr. Locus, Inc., 1987—. Mem. Internat. Loran Assn., Sigma Pi Sigma. Home: 507 W Wilson St Apt 307 Madison WI 53703-3635

SCHIEFFER, JAMES MICHAEL, electrical engineer; b. Sioux City, Iowa, Feb. 27, 1955; s. James Michael and Lucile Louise (Hayslip) S.; m. Jacqui A. Ellis, Dec. 26, 1995. BSEE, S.D. Sch. Mines and Tech., 1982. Rschr. S.D. Sch. Mines and Tech., Rapid City, 1981-82; lead elec. engr. Boeing Mil. Airplane Co., Wichita, 1982-85, Smiths Industries, Grand Rapids, Mich., 1985—. Mem. IEEE, Order of Engrs., Order of Arrow. Roman Catholic.

SCHIER, STEVEN EDWARD, political science educator, political consultant; b. Mt. Pleasant, Iowa, Oct. 1, 1952; s. James Edward and Marjorie Ilean (Tomb) S.; m. Mary Lahr, Aug. 10, 1986; children: Anne Maria, Teresa Amaranta. BA summa cum laude, Simpson Coll., Indianola, Iowa, 1974; MA, U. Wis., 1975, PhD, 1978. Asst. prof. polit. sci. Wittenberg U., Springfield, Ohio, 1978-81; asst. prof. polit. sci. Carleton Coll., Northfield, Minn., 1981-87, assoc. prof., 1987-95, prof., 1995—, chmn. dept. polit. sci., 1996—; polit. analyst WCCO TV, Mpls., 1992—, Minn. Pub. Radio, 1993—, WCAL Radio, 1995—; cons. Mondale Forum Mpls., 1991-92. Author: The Rules and the Game, 1980, A Decade of Deficits, 1992; co-author: Congress: Games and Strategies, 1995, Payment Due: A Nation in Debt, A Generation in Trouble, 1996; co-editor: Political Economy in Western Democracies, 1985; author numerous newspaper columns. Profl. Devel. grantee Carleton Coll., 1986, 94, 95. Mem. Am. Polit. Sci. Assn. (pubs. com. 1993—), Concord Coalition, Friends of Montpelier. Roman Catholic. Home: 1200 Washington St Northfield MN 55057-2823 Office: Carleton Coll One N College St Northfield MN 55057

SCHILLING, DON RUSSELL, electric utility executive; b. Greenburg, Ind., June 11, 1951; s. Cloyd H. and Ruth V. (Knarr) S.; m. Teri L. Edwards, July 14, 1973; children: Jaclyn, Christopher. BS in Elec. Engring., Purdue U., 1973; MS in Bus. Adminstrn., Ind. U., Fort Wayne, 1977. Registered profl. engr., Ind. Elec. engr. Ind. and Mich. Electric Co., Fort Wayne, 1973-79; asst. gen. mgr. Decatur County REMC, Greensburg, Ind., 1979-86, pres., gen. mgr., 1986—; v.p. Ind. Rural TV, Inc., 1989-91; pres. Ind. Rural TV, Inc., 1988-89. Mem. IEEE, Greensburg Area C. of C. (pres. 1994), Lions, Masons. Baptist. Office: Decatur County REMC PO Box 46 Greensburg IN 47240-0046

SCHILLING, KATHERINE LEE TRACY, retired principal; b. Mitchell, S.D., May 31, 1925; d. Ernest Benjamin and Mary Alice (Courier) Tracy; BA, Dakota Wesleyan U., 1947; MA, U. S.D., 1957; postgrad. U. Wyo., U. Nebr., Kearney State Coll.; m. Clarence R. Schilling, Oct. 14, 1951; 1 child, Keigh Leigh. Tchr. elem. and secondary schs., also colls., S.D. and Nebr. Mem. staff S.D. Girls' State, 1950-51; mem. S.D. Gov.'s Com. on Library, Nebr. Gov.'s Com. on Right to Read; prin. Mitchell (S.D.) Christian Sch., 1987-94; ret., 1994. Recipient Outstanding Tchr. award S.D. High Sch. Speech Tchrs., 1966. Mem. NEA, Nebr., Thurston County (pres.) edn. assns., Winnebago Tchrs. Assn., Delta Kappa Gamma. Clubs: Internat. Toastmistress (internat. dir. 1963-65, Mitchell Toastmistress of Year 1959), Order Eastern Star. Contbr. articles to profl. jours., also poetry. Home: 39 S Harmon Dr Box 578 Mitchell SD 57301

SCHILLING, MIKE, state legislator. Rep. Mo. State Ho. Reps. Dist. 136. Home: 1027 S New Ave Springfield MO 65807-1346*

SCHILPLIN, YVONNE WINTER, educational administrator; b. Mahnomen, Minn., May 26, 1946; d. Milo Joseph and Lucille Margaret (Schoenborn) Winter; m. Frederick Colegrove Schilplin III, Dec. 30, 1975; children: Frederick IV, Chad. Student, St. Cloud State U., 1964. Retail fashion buyer Fandel's Dept. Store, St. Cloud, Minn., 1968-75; mem. graduation standards exec. com. Minn. Dept. Edn., Mpls., 1988—; mem. Annandale (Minn.) Sch. Bd. Dist. 876, 1988-94, chmn., 1991-94; co-owner, cons. Am. Rsch. Grant Writing & Tng., Inc., 1993—. Edn. chmn. Minn. PTA, Mpls., 1989-91; mem. legis. com. St. Cloud Reading Rm., 1991-92, v.p., 1996—; liaison for sch. bd. Annandale PTA, 1989-94; co-chmn. Living Wax Mus., Minn. Pioneer Park, 1991-92; mem. facilities planning com. Sch. Dist. 876, mid. sch. steering com. Recipient Minn. Sch. Bd. Mem. of Yr., 1994. Mem. Stearns County Hist. Soc., Minn. Sci. Mus., St. Cloud Country Club. Home: RR 3 Annandale MN 55302-9803

SCHIMBERG, BARBARA HODES, organizational development consultant; b. Chgo., Nov. 30, 1941; d. David and Tybe Zisook; children from previous marriage: Brian, Valery; m. A. Bruce Schimberg, Dec. 29, 1984. BS, Northwestern U., 1962. Ptnr. Just Causes, cons. not-for-profit orgns., Chgo., 1978-86; cons. in philanthropy, community involvement, and organizational devel., 1987—; Chgo. cons. Population Resource Ctr., 1978-82. Woman's bd. dirs. Mus. Contemporary Art; bd. dirs., vice chmn. Med. Rsch. Inst. Coun., Michael Reese Med. Ctr.; bd. dirs., chmn. Midwest Women's Ctr.; trustee Francis W. Parker Sch.; bd. dirs. Women's Issues Network, 1991—, pres., 1993-94; mem. honorary bd. Med. Rsch. Inst. Coun., Children's Meml. Hosp. Mem. ACLU (adv. com.). Office: 132 E Delaware Pl Apt 5002 Chicago IL 60611-1442

SCHIMEK, DIANNA RUTH REBMAN, state legislator; b. Holdrege, Nebr., Mar. 21, 1940; d. Ralph William and Elizabeth Julia (Wilmot) Rebman; m. Herbert Henry Schimek, 1963; children: Samuel Wolfgang, Saul William. AA, Colo. Women's Coll., 1960; student, U. Nebr., Lincoln, 1960-61; BA magna cum laude, U. Nebr., Kearney, 1963. Former tchr. and realtor; mem. Nebr. Legislature, Lincoln, 1989—, chmn. govt., mil. and vets. affairs com., 1993-94, vice chair urban affairs com., 1995—. Chmn. Nebr. Dem. Com., 1984-88, mem. exec. com., 1987-88; past pres., sec. bd. dirs. Downtown Sr. Ctr. Found.; mem. exec. bd. Midwest Conf. of State Govts., co-chair health and human svcs. com. Mem. Nat. Conf. State Legislators Women's Network (bd. dirs.), P.E.O., Soroptomists. Democrat. Unitarian. Home: 2321 Camelot Ct Lincoln NE 68512-1457 Office: Dist # 27 State Capital Lincoln NE 68509

SCHIMKE, DENNIS J., state legislator; m. Olive Schimke; 3 children. BS, U. N.D., MS. Bison rancher, tchr. physics; rep. Dist. 28 N.D. Ho. of reps., 1990-92, rep. dist. 26, 1995—, mem. edn. and agr. com. Home: PO Box 525 Edgeley ND 58433

SCHINDLER, JUDI(TH KAY), public relations executive, marketing consultant; b. Chgo., Nov. 23, 1941; d. Gilbert G. and Rosalie (Karlin) Cone; m. Jack Joel Schindler, Nov. 1, 1964; 1 child, Adam Jason. BS in Journalism, U. Ill., 1964. Assoc. editor Irving Cloud Publs., Lincolnwood, Ill., 1963-64; asst. dir. publicity Israel Bond Campaign, Chgo., 1965-69; v.p. pub. relations Realty Co. of Am., Chgo., 1969-70; dir. pub. relations Pvt. Telecommunications, Chgo., 1970-78; pres. Schindler Communications, Chgo., 1978—; del. White House Conf. on Small Bus., Washington, 1980, 86; mem. adv. bd. Entrepreneurship Inst., Chgo., 1988-92. Bd. dirs. Family Matters Comty. Ctr.; mem. Chgo. bd. Roosevelt U.; leader luncheon coun. YWCA, Chgo., 1987, 89-90, 92; appointee small bus. com. Ill. Devel. Bd., 1988-89. Named Nat. Women in Bus. Adv. SBA, 1986, Chgo. Woman Bus. Owner of Yr., Continential Bank and Nat. Assn. Women Bus. Owners, 1989, Ill. Finalist Entrepreneur of Yr. award, 1991, 92. Mem. Nat. Assn. Women Bus. Owners (pres. Chgo. chpt. 1980-81, nat. v.p. membership 1988-89), Small Bus. United of Ill., Ill. Coun. Growing Cos. (vice chair 1993-94), Publicity Club Chgo., Alpha Epsilon Phi. Office: Schindler Comm 500 N Clark St Chicago IL 60610-4202

SCHIRO-GEIST, CHRISANN, rehabilitation counselor; b. Chgo., Dec. 31, 1946; d. Joseph Frank and Ethel (Fortunato) Schiro; m. John J. Conway Sr., Oct. 26, 1985; children: Jennifer, Daniel; stepchildren: Patricia, Nicole, John Jr., Denise, Christine. BS, Loyola U., Chgo., 1967, MEd, 1970; PhD, Northwestern U., 1974. Registered psychologist, Ill.; cert. sex edn. cons. Tchr. sci. Northbrook (Ill.) Jr. High Sch., 1967-70; dir. career counseling and placement Mundelein Coll., Chgo., 1972-74; counselor human devel. Regional Service Agy., Skokie, Ill., 1975-87; assoc. prof. psychology, rehab. counselor Ill. Inst. Tech., Chgo., 1975-87; full prof. rehab. U. Ill., Champagne-Urbana, 1987—. Co-author: Placement Handbook for Counseling Disabled Persons, 1982; author, editor: Vocational Counseling with Special Populations, 1990. Rsch. grantee Northwestern U., 1974; Region V Short-Term Tng. grantee Rehab. Svcs. Adminstrn., 1978-79, Long-Term Tng. grantee, 1983—; Mary E. Switzer fellow NIDRR, 1989-90, VA, 1991-92, World Rehab. Fund fellow, 1993. Mem. APA, ACA, Nat. Rehab. Assn., Nat. Coun. Rehab. Edn. (named Educator of Yr. 1987), Ill. Rehab. Counseling Assn. (pres. 1979-80), Coun. on Rehab. Edn. (pres. 1982-85, editor jour. 1986-92), Ill. Rehab. Assn. (pres.-elect), Kappa Beta Gamma Alumni Assn. (nat. officer). Office: U Ill Divsn Rehab Edn 1207 S Oak St Champaign IL 61820-6901

SCHLANSER, THERESA DIANNE, speech-language pathologist; b. Bardstown, Ky., July 31, 1963; d. James Robert and Mary Frances (Hardin) Greenwell; m. Michael Gerard Schlanser, Mar. 14, 1987; children: Kristen Marie, David Michael, Lauren Nicole. BS, Ea. Ky. U., 1985, MA, 1986. Speech-lang. pathologist Comm. Disorders Inst., Columbus, Ohio, 1987-88, Columbus Speech and Hearing Ctr., Columbus, 1988-89, South-Western City Schs., Grove City, Ohio, 1989—. Mem. NEA, Am. Speech and Hearing Assn., Ohio Speech and Hearing Assn. Roman Catholic. Home: 6239 Brookmeade Cir Grove City OH 43123-9085

SCHLATHER, MARY AGNES, librarian; b. Berea, Ohio, Jan. 12, 1961; d. Bernard Paul and H. Virginia (Bilskey) S. BA, Walsh Coll., 1983; MLS, Kent State U., 1986. Cert. elem. tchr., Ohio, Ill.; cert. media, Ohio, Ill. Tchr. St. Mary's Elem. Sch., Lorain, Ohio, 1983-84, Avon, Ohio, 1984-85; student ref. asst. Kent (Ohio) State U., 1985-86; youth svcs. libr. Granite City (Ill.) Pub. Libr. Dist., 1987-90, St. Charles (Ill.) Pub. Libr. Dist., 1990-91; youth svcs. libr., asst. dir. East Alton (Ill.) Pub. Libr. Dist., 1991-93; west br. libr. supr. Belleville (Ill.) Pub. Libr., 1993—, interim dir., 1995—; project dir. Door to Learning family literacy grant, 1992-93; mem. adv. com. Ill. Family Edn. Tng. Inst. Project, 1995—; citizen amb. to Peoples Republic of China, 1993. Mem. So. Ill. U. at Edwardsville Cmty. Choral Soc., 1988-90, 92—; mem. Southwestern Adv. for Youth Svcs. (SWAYS), 1991—; mem. Gateret Adv. Coun., 1995—. Mem. ALA, Assn. for Libr. Svcs. to Children, Pub. Libr. Assn., Young Adult Libr. Svcs. Assn., Libr. Adminstrn. and Mgmt. Assn., Ill. Libr. Assn. (youth svcs. forum, chmn. 1995-96, mem. I-read com. 1990-92, conf. com. 1993-94), Metro Area Pub. Librs. Roman Catholic.

SCHLEGEL, FRED EUGENE, lawyer; b. Indpls., July 24, 1941; s. Fred George and Dorothy (Bruce) S.; m. Jane Wessels, Aug. 14, 1965; children: Julia, Charles, Alexandra. BA, Northwestern U., 1963; JD with distinction, U. Mich., 1966. Bar: Ind. 1966. Assoc. lawyer Baker & Daniels, Indpls., 1966-72, ptnr., 1972—; vice chmn. Meridian St. Preservation Commn., Indpls., 1975-90; bd. dirs. Indpls. Water Co., IWC Resources Corp. Contbr. articles to profl. jours. Chmn. Indpls. Pub. Schs. Edn. Found., 1988-90; pres. Festival Music Soc., 1974-75, 79, 86-87; bd. dirs. Indpls. Symphony Orch., 1991—, Arts Coun. Indpls. Mem. ABA, Ind. Bar Assn., Fed. Energy Bar Assn., Northwestern U. Alumni Club Indpls. (pres. 1992-94). Republican. Presbyterian. Office: Baker and Daniels 300 N Meridian St Ste 2700 Indianapolis IN 46204-1755

SCHLEICHER, SUSAN L., critical care nurse; b. Dodgeville, Wis., Dec. 15, 1959; d. Norbert F. and Rose B. (Winters) Kreul. ADN, Madison Area Tech. Coll., 1981; grad. EMT, MATC, Madison, Wis., 1983. Cert. critical care nurse, emergency nurse, TNCC, basic life support-I, advanced cardiac life support-I, emergency med. technician-D. Staff nurse St. Mary Hosp., Madison; emergency med. technician Oregon (Wis.) EMS Dist.; staff nurse U. Wis. Hosp. and Clinic, Madison; staff ICU nurse St. Elizabeth Hosp., Appleton, Wis.; ICU nurse Norrell Helath Care, Milw.; paramedic Gold Cross Ambulance, Appleton, Wis.; BLS and ACLS instr. Fox Valley Tech. Inst., Appleton; camp nurse Easter Seal of Wis., Madison; evening supr. Clintonville (Wis.) Community Hosp.; hosp. supr. St. Mary Hosp., Green Bay, Wis.; staff nurse Stat Temporary, Appleton, 1995—; eye nucleator Wis. Eye Bank. Mem. AACN (nat., local sec.), Emergency Nurses Assn., Am. Heart Assn. Home: W 9828 Elm Rd Bear Creek WI 54922

SCHLENK, FRITZ, retired biochemistry educator; b. Munich, Nov. 26, 1909; came to U.S., 1940; s. Wilhelm and Mathilde (von Hacke) S.; m. Tilde Eberle, 1940; children: Margaret Karin, Edward Frederick. PhD, U. Berlin, 1934. Rsch. assoc. U. Stockholm, 1934-40; asst. prof. U. Tex. Med. Sch., Galveston, 1940-43; prof. of biochemistry U. Tex. Med. Sch., Houston, 1943-47; prof. of bacteriology Iowa State U., Ames, 1947-54; rsch. assoc. prof. U. Chgo., 1954-74; prin. biochemist Argonne (Ill.) Nat. Lab., 1954-74; vis. prof. U. Ill., Chgo., 1975-90; retired, 1990. Contbr. over 170 rsch. articles, chpts. to profl. publs. Mem. Am. Soc. Biol. Chemistry, Soc. Am. Microbiology (Pasteur medal 1968), Am. Acad. Microbiology (charter mem.), Sci. and Medicine Acad. (fgn. mem., Naples, Italy). Home: 3460 Saratoga Ave Apt 4 Downers Grove IL 60515-1199

SCHLENKER, ROBERT ALISON, environment, safety and health administrator; b. Rochester, N.Y., Oct. 25, 1940; s. Martin and Ruth (Isler) S.; m. Sara Elizabeth Law, June 8, 1968; children: Martin, Laura. BS in Physics, MIT, 1962, PhD in Nuclear Physics, 1968. Rsch. assoc. MIT Radioactivity Ctr., Cambridge, 1968-69; asst. physicist radiol. and environ. rsch. divsn. Argonne (Ill.) Nat. Lab., 1970-75, biophysicist, 1975-84, biophysicist, group leader biol. and med. rsch. divsn., 1984-89, sect. head, 1985-87, biophysicist environ., safety and health divsn., 1989-91, assoc. divsn. dir., 1991—, chmn. dir.'s ad hoc com. on human health rsch., 1994-96; pres. Madison Rsch. Group, Willowbrook, Ill., 1993—; instr. tech., engring., math. Coll. DuPage, Glen Ellyn, Ill., 1975-78; mem. sci. com. 57 Nat. Coun. on Radiation Protection and Measurements, Bethesda, Md., 1978-94; co-chmn. organizing com. Internat. Conf. on Radiobiology of Radium and the Actinides in Man, Lake Geneva, Wis., 1980-81; com. mem. BEIR IV, NAS Nat. Rsch. Coun., Washington, 1985-88; mem. internal radiation dose group U.S. Dept. Energy, Washington, 1985-90; cons. Sci. Com. 83, Identification of Rsch. Needs for Radiation, Nat. Coun. on Radiation Protection and Measurements, Bethesda, 1989-91; cons. Picillo, Harvey, Bromberg and Caruso, Passaic, N.J., 1990-92, Ctrs. for Disease Control, Atlanta, 1991-92, Schmeltzer, Aptaker and Shepard, Washington, 1995—. Contbr. over 100 sci. and tech. publs. in the fields of nuclear physics, biophysics and others to profl. jours. Mem. Am. Geophys. Union, AAAS, Am. Assn. Physicists in Medicine, Health Physics Soc., Radiation Rsch. Soc., Soc. for Risk Analysis. Office: Argonne Nat Lab 9700 Cass Ave Lemont IL 60439-4803 Office: Madison Rsch Group 6412 Madison St Willowbrook IL 60521

SCHLESINGER, CAROLE LYNN, elementary education educator; b. Detroit, May 13, 1961; d. Robert Schlesinger and Regenia Compere. Student, Kalamazoo Coll., 1981-84; BA, U. Mich., 1986; teaching cert., Eastern Mich. U., 1992. Cert. elem. tchr., Mich. Bank teller U. Mich. Credit Union, Ann Arbor, 1987; rsch. asst. dept. postgrad. medicine U. Mich., Ann Arbor, 1987; fin. planner IDS Fin. Svcs., Ann Arbor, 1988-89; telemarketer U. Mich. Telefund, Ann Arbor, 1989-90; enumerator U.S. Bur. Census, Ann Arbor, 1990; reading and math. tutor Reading and Learning Skills Ctr., Ann Arbor, 1991-92; interpreter Living Sci. Found., Wixom, Mich., 1992-94; intern planning and mgmt. info. div. Peace Corps., Washington, 1985; intern Com. for Econ. Devel., Washington, 1985. Elder 1st Presbyn. Ch., Ann Arbor, 1992-94; canvasser, vol. Pub. Interest Rsch. group in Mich., Ann Arbor, 1986-87; trainee Groundwater Edn., Esatern Mich. U., Ypsilanti, 1991, mem. dean's adv. com., 1992; mem., group leader Ann Arbor Dems., 1984-87. Mem. ASCD, Mich. Reading Assn., Washtenaw Reading Coun., Mich. Coun. Tchrs. Math., Nat. Coun. Tchrs. Math., Mich. Sci. Tchrs. Assn., Kappa Delta Pi.

SCHLESINGER, KEITH ROBERT, historian, educator; b. Detroit, Aug. 26, 1957; s. Robert Schlesinger and Regena Compere; m. Martha Ellen Kline, June 29, 1985; children: Andrew Cook, Sarah Cook. BA, Oberlin U., 1979; MA in History, Northwestern U., Evanston, Ill., 1981, PhD in History, 1985. Editor, proof reader Am. Libr. Assn., Chgo., 1981-82; asst. editor Mass. Hist. Soc., Boston, 1984-86; instr. U. Dayton, Ohio, 1987-94; asst. prof. Wilberforce (Ohio) U., 1991—, rschr., evaluator, technologist, curriculum developer; cons. Lexis-Nexis, Dayton. Author: The Power That Governs, 1990; mng. editor: Strategy and Tactics, Los Angeles, 1992-94; contbr. articles to profl. jours. Organizing mem. Miami Valley Unity Project, Dayton, 1993-94; vol. Hale Ch., Dayton, 1994-95. Recipient Charles Thomson award Orgn. Am. Historians, 1981; Comfort Starr scholar, 1979. Mem. Phi Beta Kappa. Mem. Baha'i Ch. Office: Wilberforce U North Bickett Rd Wilberforce OH 45384

SCHLESSER, JERLEEN ETHEL, information systems executive; b. Great Lakes, Ill., Apr. 6, 1953; d. James Edward and Jerleen Shirley (Zahrte) S. BS in Bus. Mgmt., Bradley U., Peoria, Ill., 1977, BS in Computer Sci., 1977; MBA, Ill. Inst. Tech., Chgo., 1988. Asst. membership coord. WTVP-TV, Peoria, 1976-77; application analyst Caterpillar, Peoria, 1978-84; tech. cons. Baxter, Deerfield, Ill., 1984-86; instr. Webster U., St. Louis, 1990—; v.p. Harris Bank, Chgo., 1986—. Mem. NAFE, Data Processing Mgmt. Assn. Office: Harris Bank 700 E Lake Cook Rd Buffalo Grove IL 60089

SCHLESSINGER, NATHAN, psychoanalyst; b. Ciechanow, Poland, Oct. 31, 1924; came to U.S., 1938; s. Morris and Eleanor (Ciechanower) S.; m. Alice Wiley Schlessinger, Sept. 7, 1947; children: Henry Joseph, Daniel Isaac, Judith Hannah, Michael Raphael, Gideon Kai. MD, U. Cin., 1949. Diplomate Am. Bd. Neurology and Psychiatry; cert. psychoanalyst. Pvt. practice Chgo., 1962—; faculty, tng. analyst supr. Inst. for Psychoanalysis, Chgo., 1965—, dir. of clinic, 1980-94; sr. attending psychiatrist Michael Reese Hsop., Chgo., 1970—; clin. prof. psychiatry U. Ill. Coll. of Medicine, Chgo., 1970—. Author: A Developmental View of the Psychoanalytic Process, 1983; contbr. articles to profl. jours. With U.S. Army, 1943-46, USN, 1954-56. Fellow Am. Psychiat. Assn.; mem. AMA, Am. Psychoanalytical Assn. (councilor 1970-74), Chgo. Psychoanalaytic Soc. (pres. 1976-78). Jewish. Home: 1441 E 56th St Chicago IL 60637 Office: 35 E Wacker Dr Chicago IL 60601

SCHLEUTER, LOIS JEAN, music educator; b. Chariton, Iowa, Feb. 27, 1943; d. Otto Leon and Esther Mina (Rogers) Hutchison; m. Stanley Leroy Schleuter, Aug. 14, 1965; children: Monika Jean Schleuter Spangler, Scott Leroy. BM, U. Iowa, 1965; MFA, SUNY, Buffalo, 1976; PhD, Kent State U., 1988. From jr. high gen. music and choral tchr. to 1st grade tchr. Sch. Dist. 89, Maywood and Melrose Park, Ill., 1965-68; gen. music tchr. Iowa City Cmty. Schs., 1968-70; substitute tchr. Verona (Wis.) Pub. Schs., 1973-74; from tchg. asst. to instr. music edn. SUNY, Buffalo, 1974-77; from instr. to asst. prof. music Kent (Ohio) State U., 1978-89; instr. childrens choir, introduction to music edn. Ind. U., 1990-92; asst. prof. music dept. U. Toledo, 1992—; instr. Woodridge Local Schs., Northampton, Ohio, 1978-79; adj. instr. Jordan Coll. Fine Arts, Butler U., Indpls., 1989-90, adj. assoc. prof. Ind. U. Sch. Edn., Bloomington, 1990-92. Co-author: (with S. Schleuter) Teaching and Learning Music Performance: What, Where, and How, 1988; A Nichol's Worth, Piano Accompaniments, vol., I and II, 1976; contbr. articles to profl. jours. Mem. Am. Orff-Schulwerk Assn., Early Childhood Music Assn., Music Educators Nat. Conf., Ohio Music Educators Assn., Coun. Rsch. in Music Edn. (com. mem.), Phi Delta Kappa. Home: 3165 Middlesex D Toledo OH 43606 Office: Univ Toledo 2801 W Bancroft Toledo OH 43606

SCHLICHTING, CATHERINE FLETCHER NICHOLSON, librarian, educator; b. Huntsville, Ala., Nov. 18, 1923; d. William Parsons and Ethel Louise (Breitling) Nicholson; BS, U. Ala., 1944; MLS, U. Chgo., 1950; m. Harry Fredrick Schlichting, July 1, 1950 (dec. Aug. 1964); children: James Dean, Richard Dale, Barbara Lynn. Asst. librarian U. Ala. Edn. Library, Tuscaloosa, summers 1944-45; librarian Sylacauga (Ala.) High Sch., 1944-45, Hinsdale (Ill.) High Sch., 1945-49; asst. librarian Centre for Children's Books, U. Chgo., 1950-52; instr. reference dept. library Ohio Wesleyan U., Delaware, 1965-69, asst. prof., 1969-79, assoc. prof., 1979-85, prof., 1985—, curator Ohio Wesleyan Hist. Collection, 1986—, student personnel librarian, 1966-72, adviser Mortar Bd., 1969-72, mem. exec. com., 1973-79, 85-86, sec. com., 1973-74, 76-77. Mem. adminstrv. bd. Methodist Ch., 1963-81, chmn. adminstrv. bd., 1985—, mem. Council on Ministries, 1975-81, chmn., 1975-77. Recipient Algernon Sidney Sullivan award U. Ala., 1944. Ohio Wesleyan U.-Mellon Found. grantee, 1972-73, 84-85; GLCA Teaching fellow, 1976-77. Mem. ALA, Ohio Library Assn., Midwest Acad. Librarian Conf., Acad. Librarians Assn. Ohio (dir. 1984-86), AAUP (chpt. sec. 1967-68, chpt. exec. com. 1973-78), United Meth. Women (v.p. Mt. Vernon dist. 1989-92, pres. 1994—), Kappa Delta Pi, Alpha Lambda Delta. Democrat. Clubs: Ohio Wesleyan U. Womans (exec. bd. 1969-72, 77-79, 81-84, pres. 1969-70, sec. 1977-78), History (pres. 1971-72, v.p. 1978-79), Fortnightly (pres. 1975-76, 87-88), Am. Field Service (pres. Delaware chpt. 1975-76) (Delaware). Author: Introduction to Bibliographic Research: Basic Sources, 4th edit., 1983; Checklist of Biographical Reference Sources, 1977; Audio-Visual Aids in Bibliographic Instruction, 1976; Introduction to Bibliographic Research: Slide Catalog and Script, 1980; info. cons. (documentary) Noble Achievements: The History of Ohio Wesleyan 1942-92, 1992, 150 Years of Excellence: A Pictoral View of Ohio Wesleyan University, 1992. Home: 414 N Liberty St Delaware OH 43015-1232 Office: Ohio Wesleyan U La Beeghly Library Delaware OH 43015

SCHLICK, THOMAS LEROY, marketing executive; b. Red Wing, Minn., Mar. 18, 1950; s. Gerard Arthur and Carol Betty (Lundell) S.; m. Kathryn Ann Petitt, May 27, 1971; children: Brian Thomas, Anna Kathryn, Heather Leah, Kevin Christopher. BS in Engring. and Mktg., U. Minn., 1972, MBA, 1977. Design engr. Gen. Electric Co., Erie, Pa., 1972; product service specialist Gen. Electric Co., Bridgeport, Conn., 1973; industry mktg. specialist Gen. Electric Co., Fort Wayne, Ind., 1974; mktg. engr. Rosemount, Inc., Mpls., 1974-77, mgr. bus. planning, 1977-81, dir. planning and new bus. devel., 1981-88, dir. svc. and support divsn., 1988-94; v.p., gen. mgr. svc. and support divsn. Fiber-Rosemount Group, Emerson Electric Co., Mpls., 1994—; bd. dirs. Azonix Corp., Burlington, Mass. Author: Product Development Guidelines, 1980. Recipient Outstanding Tech. Mktg. award Gen. Electric Co., 1973, 74. Mem. Instrument Soc. Am. (sr.), Am. Mgmt. Assn., Strategic Leadership Forum, Am. Field Svc. Mgmt. Assn. Lutheran. Home: 15213 Edgewater Cir NE Prior Lake MN 55372-1100 Office: Rosemount Inc 12001 Technology Dr Eden Prairie MN 55344-3620

SCHLIECKERT, MARY JEAN, software development professional; b. Belleville, Ill., Nov. 20, 1947; d. Oliver Theodore and Anna Eleanora (Keller) S.; m. Gary John Schlieckert, June 28, 1969; children: Rebecca Anne, Christopher John. BS in Teaching of Math. with distinction, U. Ill., 1969; MS in Computer Sci. with distinction, Rivier Coll., Nashua, N.H., 1986. Computer specialist VA Med. Ctr., Mpls., 1988-89; software test engr. Archetype Sys., Inc., Mpls., 1989-92; sr. software engr. Diametrics Med., Inc., St. Paul, 1992—. Contbr. articles to profl. jours. Mem. IEEE. Office: Diametrics Med Inc 2658 Patton Rd Saint Paul MN 55113

SCHLIPF, FREDERICK ALLEN, library administrator; b. Fargo, N.D., Sept. 14, 1941; s. Stewart and Ruth (Sulerud) S.; m. Diane Hillard, Aug. 7, 1965; 1 child, Karl Frederick Hillard. AB, Carleton Coll., Northfield, Minn., 1963; AM, U. Chgo., 1966, PhD, 1973. Instr. Grad. Libr. Sch. U. Chgo., 1966-70; asst. prof. Grad. Sch. Libr. and Info. Sci. U. Ill., Urbana, 1970-74, adj. prof., 1974—; exec. dir. Urbana Free Libr., 1974—; mem. adv. com. Ill. State Libr., 1977-81. 89-92, also vice chair; mem. Champaign County Network Planning Com., 1993—; libr. archtl. cons., 1987—; spkr. in field. Co-author, editor 7 books; contbr. articles to profl. jours., chpts. to books. Bd. dirs. Urbana Promotion Corp., 1987-93; bd. dirs., pres. Champaign County Hist. Mus., Champaign, Ill., 1979-87; founder Urbana Mcpl. Documents Ctr. Mem. ALA, Ill. Libr. Assn., Exchange Club Urbana. Home: PO Box 816 Urbana IL 61801-0816 Office: Urbana Free Libr 201 S Race St Urbana IL 61801-3283

SCHLOSS, NATHAN, economist; b. Balt., Jan. 14, 1927; s. Howard L. and Louise (Levi) S.; BS in Bus., Johns Hopkins U., 1950; m. Rosa Montalvo, Mar. 1, 1958; children: Nina L., Carolyn D. Buyer, Pacific Coast gen. merchandise office Sears Roebuck & Co., Los Angeles, 1955-60, staff asst. econ. research dept., Chgo., 1960-63; sr. market analyst corp. rsch. dept. Montgomery Ward & Co., Chgo., 1963-65; rsch. mgr. real estate dept. Walgreen Co., Chgo., 1970-72; v.p. rsch. and planning Maron Properties Ltd., Montreal, Que., Can., 1972-74; corp. economist, fin. analyst Real Estate Rsch. Corp., Chgo., 1974-88, sr. v.p., 1986-88, treas., chief fin. analyst, 1982-88; economist Office of Ill. Atty. Gen., Chgo., 1988—; cons. economist, since 1965—; mem. com. on price indexes and productivity fgn. labor Bus. Research Adv. Council of Bur. Labor Stats., Dept. Labor, 1979-88, also chairperson (1985-86), com. on employment and unemployment. Recipient Commendable Svc. award Dept. Labor, 1987. Mem. Plan Commn., Village of Wilmette, Ill., 1975-77, mem. tech. adv. com. on employment and tng. data Ill. Employment and Tng. Coun., 1979-82; mem. tech. adv. com. Ill. Job Tng. Coordinating Council, 1983-87. Mem. Am. Mktg. Assn., Nat. Assn. Bus. Economists, Lambda Alpha. Contbr. articles on fin. and market analysis of real estate to profl. jours. Home: 115 Hollywood Ct Wilmette IL 60091-3122 Office: 100 W Randolph St Chicago IL 60601-3218

SCHLOSSBERG, HOWARD BARRY, editor, freelance writer; b. Bklyn., Nov. 10, 1950; s. Murray Bernard and Henrietta (Kamen) S.; m. Eva Rose Levin, Aug. 4, 1974 (div. May 1984); 1 child, Erin Rachel; m. Jocelyn Marguerite Stroupe, Nov. 2, 1990. BA in History, SUNY, Albany, 1972; MA in Journalism, No. Ill. U., 1974. Coord. print traffic Incentive Svcs., Inc., Chgo., 1975-77; staff sports writer Countryside Newspapers, Barrington, Ill., 1977-84; sr. editor Cahners Pub., Des Plaines, Ill., 1984-87; news editor Lerner-Life Newspapers, Chgo., 1987-88; dir. pub. Technomic, Inc., Chgo., 1988-89; editor spl. projects publs. group Am. Mktg. Assn., Chgo., 1989-94; sports reporter Pioneer Press, Inc., Barrington, 1984-94; sports writer Paddock Pubs. "Daily Herald", Arlington Heights, Ill., 1994—; adj. prof. journalism William Rainey Harper Coll., Palatine, Ill., 1994, Columbia Coll., Chgo., 1995—, DePaul U., Chgo., 1996; contbg. editor Bill Pub., N.Y.C., 1988-89, Jour. Promotion Mgmt., Binghamton, N.Y., 1991; mem. editl. adv. bd. Sports Mktg. Quar., Morgantown, W.Va., 1991—; syndicated sports columnist The Sports Network, Phila., 1993—. Author: Sports Marketing, 1994. Bd. dirs., editor newsletter Homeowners Assn., Cary, Ill., 1981-83; bd. dirs., v.p., editor newsletter Homeowners Assn., Schaumburg, Ill., 1992; mem. sport adminstrn. adv. bd. Robert Morris Coll., 1992. Recipient award for best sports photography Ill. Press Assn., 1978, Nat. Assn. Softball Writers and Broadcasters, 1979, award for best sports writing and features No. Ill. Newspaper Assn., 1979, 81, 83. Mem. Am. Mktg. Assn. (sports mktg. planning com. 1991, 92), SUNY Alumni Assn., Hanover Park Racquet Club. Home: 2358 County Farm Ln Schaumburg IL 60194-4807

SCHLUETER, ROBERT ANTHONY, electrical engineer, educator; b. Buffalo, N.Y., May 11, 1942; s. Albert Joseph and Dorothy Eleanor (Then) S.; m. Karen Mildred Quedens, Jul. 9, 1967; children: Ellen, Paul, John. BSEE, Rensselaer Poly. Inst., 1964, MSEE, 1967; PhD, Polytech. Inst. Bklyn., 1972. Registered profl. engr., Mich. Engr. Grumman Aircraft Engr. Corp., Bethpage, N.Y., 1964-66; assoc. engr. Sperry Gyroscope Co., Great Neck, N.Y., 1967; analyst Mobil Oil Corp., N.Y., 1969; asst. prof. Mich. State U., East Lansing, 1971-76, assoc. prof., 1976-81, prof., 1981—. Assoc. editor: Electric Machines and Power Systems; contbr. over 50 articles to profl. jours. Mem. IEEE (sr.), Eta Kappa Nu, Sigma Xi. Lutheran. Home: 1936 Heatherton Dr Holt MI 48842 Office: Mich State U Dept Engring East Lansing MI 48824

SCHLUP, LEONARD C., librarian, researcher, writer, historian; b. Barberton, Ohio, Feb. 22, 1943; s. Clarence Leonard and Addie May (Roberts) S. BA magna cum laude, U. Akron, 1965; MA, Kent State U., 1967; PhD, U. Ill., 1973; MLS, Ind. U., 1983. Instr. Tarleton State U., Stephenville, Tex., 1980-81; chmn. UMS Prep Sch., Mobile, 1981-82; librarian Marshall U., Huntington, W. Va., 1984-85, Akron-Summit County (Ohio) Pub. Lib., 1985—. Contbr. 200 articles to profl. jours., chpts. to directories. Mem. Am. Polit. Sci. Assn., Am. Hist. Assn., Orgn. Am. Historians, Ctr. Study of the Presidency, Soc. Historians of the Gilded Age, Ohio Acad. History, Genealogical Soc., YMCA, Animal Shelter. Democrat. Methodist. Office: Akron Pub Lib 55 S Main St Akron OH 44326

SCHLUTTER, LOIS COCHRANE, psychologist; b. Indpls., Oct. 18, 1953; d. Roy and Mavis (Wolfe) Cochrane; m. Dennis James Schlutter, Oct. 30, 1976; 1 child, Nathan Paul. BS, U. S.D., 1974, MA, 1975, PhD, 1978. Lic. psychologist, Minn. Psychologist, asst. Neurol. Inst. and Pain Ctr., Sioux City, Iowa, 1975-77; staff Mpls. Psychotherapy Inst., St. Louis Park, Minn., 1978-80; with strategic planning Vail Place, Mpls. and Hopkins (Minn.), 1988-90; owner Schlutter & Assocs., St. Louis Park, Minn., 1994—; bd. dirs. Vail Pl.; allied health staff, disability cons. Meth. Hosp., St. Louis Park, 1978—, mem. hospice adv. com., 1984—, mem. child abuse consortium, 1985-89; staff psychologist Sister Kenny Inst., Mpls., 1980-81; cons. Dept. Vocat. Rehab., St. Paul, 1984-93; supr. pastoral care AAPC, St. Louis Park, 1984—; lectr. St. Mary's Hosp. and Coll., Mpls., 1984-90; psychologist, dir. Family Dynamics, St. Louis Park, 1980-94; owner Employee Assistance Programs; presenter in field. Co-author: (play) The Extrapolator, 1968; contbr. articles to profl. jours. Mem. task force Vinland Nat. Ctr.; chmn. adult edn., Hopkins United Meth. Ch., 1988-91. Recipient rsch. grant Lederle Pharms., 1979. Mem. APA, Am. Coll. Forensic Examiners, Mental Health Assn. Minn., Minn. Psychol. Assn., Am. Assn. Pastoral Counselors (profl. affiliate), Brookside Condominium Assn., Blvd. Condominium Assn., Internat. Platform Assn., Rotary, Twin West C. of C., Phi Beta Kappa, Kappa Alpha Theta, Alpha Lambda Delta, Psi Chi. Office: Schlutter & Assocs 6200 Excelsior Blvd Ste 202 Saint Louis Park MN 55416-2730

SCHMAHL, STEPHANIE HELENE, school social worker; b. Watertown, N.Y., Dec. 14, 1941; d. John Schmahl and Helene (Mosely) Kay. AB in Elem. Edn., Ripon Coll., 1964; MSW, U. Wis., Milw., 1969, MA in Urban Affairs, 1973; cert. in marriage and family studies, Chgo. Family Inst., 1983. Diplomate Am. Bd. Examiners in Clin. Social Work; cert. marriage and family therapist, cert. ind. clin. social worker, Wis. Clinician Philstan Psychiat. Clinic, Milw., 1977-86; psychotherapist Psychiat. Consultation Assocs., Milw., 1986—; sch. social worker Milw. Pub. Schs., 1989—; case work supr. Milwaukee County Dept. Social Svcs., Milw., 1974-77; psychotherapist Charter Counseling Svcs., 1990—; field instr. Sch. Social Welfare, U. Wis., Milw.; presenter workshops; pvt. practice psychotherapy. Mem. Nat. Assn. Social Workers (past state and local chpt. officer), Am. Assn. Mental Health Counselors, Acad. Cert. Social Workers. Democrat. Unitarian-Universalist. Office: Milw Pub Schs Victory 2222 W Henry Ave Milwaukee WI 53221-4920

SCHMALE, ALLEN LEE, financial services company executive; b. Addieville, Ill., Feb. 12, 1933; s. Arnold August and Leona Karoline (Becker) S.; m. Lorraine Marie Loyet, July 19, 1952; children: Judith Ann, Arnold August II, Michelle Lee, René Cerise, Allen Kent. CLU, ChFC. Salesman Western & So. Life Ins. Co., St. Louis, 1955-56, Monarch Life Ins. Co., St. Louis, 1956-58, Mass. Indemnity & Life Ins., St. Louis, 1958-65; pres. Schmale Fin. Svcs., Inc., Okawville, Ill., 1965-88, chmn., 1988—, also bd. dirs. Trustee Village of Okawville, 1976-80, mem. bus. devel. com.; vice chmn. Washington County (Ill.) Rep. Com.; coord. Edgar for Gov., Ill., 1990, 94; pres. St. Peters Ch., 1975-77; br. officer Walnut St. Securities Inc. Recipient Contbns. to Growth award Belleville (Ill.) Area Coll., 1977. Mem. Am. Soc. CLU and ChFC, East Side Life Underwriters (pres. 1971-72), Million Dollar Roundtable, Ill. Life Underwriters (bd. dirs. 1975-78), Nat. Assn. Life Underwriters (del. 1971), Estate Planning Coun. St. Louis, Okawville Comty. Club (pres. 1974-76). Republican. Home: 5304 County Highway 6 Okawville IL 62271-2530 Office: Schmale Fin Svcs Inc 611 S Front St Okawville IL 62271-2121

SCHMELTZER, JOHN CHARLES, financial writer; b. Davenport, Iowa, Sept. 30, 1945; s. J. Howard and Virginia Marie (Smith) S. BA, Wartburg Coll., Waverly, Iowa, 1967; MA, No. Ill. U., 1974. Reporter Davenport Times-Democrat, 1967, Lynchburg (Va.) News, 1968-69; dir. pub. rels. Doane Coll., Crete, Nebr., 1967-68; news editor Belvidere (Ill.) Daily Rep., 1971-72; reporter Chgo. Tribune Co./The Trib, Hinsdale, Ill., 1973-76; area editor Suburban Trib, Hinsdale, 1976-82; reporter, asst. bur. chief Chgo. Tribune, 1982-88, bur. chief, 1988-91, fin. writer, 1991—; instr. McHenry County Coll., Crystal Lake, Ill., 1970-74, Coll. of DuPage, Glen Ellyn, Ill., 1982-86. Recipient 1st place award for spot news Iowa AP, 1967, 1st place award for feature writing No. Ill. Newspaper Assn., 1972, for editl. writing, 1981, 1st place award for pub. svc. Ill. AP, 1984, Peter Lisagor award Bus. Journalism, 1993, 94. Mem. Nat. Assn. Hispanic Journalists, Wartburg Coll. Alumni Assn., Soc. Profl. Journalists, Chgo. Headline Club. Lutheran. Home: 400 N McClurg Ct Apt 1314 Chicago IL 60611-4338 Office: Chgo Tribune 435 N Michigan Ave Chicago IL 60611-4001

SCHMEROLD, WILFRIED LOTHAR, dermatologist; b. Munich, Germany, Dec. 30, 1919; came to U.S., 1956; s. Wilhelm and Frieda (Hinterwinkler) S.; m. Perlette J. Joers, 1962 (div. Apr. 1974); children: Klaus, John, Will, James, Susan, Paul, Carl, Mike, Tom, Marianne. Abiturient, Altes Realgymnasium, 1938; MD, U. Munich, 1945. Bd. cert. dermatologist, dermatopathologist. Intern U Munich Med. Faculty, 1945-46; asst. UN Hosp., Munich, 1946-50, Max Plank Inst., Munich, 1951-52, U. Erlangen, Germany, 1952-53, U. Munich, 1953-56; intern Fairview Park Hosp., Cleve., 1956-57; asst. U. Ill., Chgo., 1957-60, instr., 1960-75, clin. asst. prof., 1975—; dermatologist pvt. practice, Carol Stream, Ill., 1959—, dermatopathologist, 1978—. Contbr. articles to profl. jours. Charter mem. founders club Ctrl. DuPage Hosp., Winfield, Ill., 1963. Fellow AMA, Am. Acad. Dermatology (life), German Dermatological Soc. (life), Am. Soc. Dermatopathology, Ill. Dermatological Soc., Ill. State Med. Soc., Chgo. Dermatological Soc. Roman Catholic. Office: Mona Kea Med Park 507 Thornhill Dr # B Carol Stream IL 60188-2703

SCHMERSE, TRACI JO, financial services company executive; b. Rockford, Ill., Jan. 24, 1959; d. Paul Eugene and Barbara Jean (Nelson) Hutmacher; m. Micke Schmerse, May 10, 1986 (div. Jan. 1988). AS, Rock Valley Coll., Rockford, Ill., 1982; BS in Biology, Rockford Coll., 1985. Mktg. asst. Pioneer Fin. Svcs., Rockford, 1989-90, mktg. analyst, 1990-91, exec. adminstrv. asst., 1991—, asst. corp. sec., 1994—. Office: Pioneer Fin Svcs Inc 304 N Main St Rockford IL 61101

SCHMETZER, ALAN DAVID, psychiatrist; b. Louisville, Sept. 3, 1946; s. Clarence Fredrick and Catherine Louise (Wootan) S.; m. Janet Lynn Royce, Aug. 25, 1968; children: Angela Beth, Jennifer Lorraine. BA, Ind. U., 1968, MD, 1972. Diplomate Am. Bd. Psychiatry and Neurology with added qualifications in addictions psychiatry. Intern, Ind. U. Hosps., Indpls., 1972-73, resident, 1972-75; dir. clinics PCI, Inc., Anderson, Beech Grove and Kokomo, Ind., 1975-79; psychiat. cons. Community Addiction Svcs. Agy., Indpls., 1975-80; instr. psychiatry in primary care Family Practice Residency Programs, St. Francis Hosp., St. Vincent's Hosp. and Ind. U. Hosps., Indpls., 1975-91; med. dir. Child Guidance Clinic of Marion County, Indpls., 1980-81; chmn. psychiatry dept. St. Francis Hosp., Beech Grove, 1980-82; med. dir. Crisis Intervention Unit, Midtown Mental Health Ctr., 1980-90; dir. Midtown Mental Health Ctr., 1990-96, med. dir. 1996—; coord. emergency psychiat. svcs. Ind. U. Med. Ctr., Indpls., 1980-90; asst. prof. psychiatry, 1975-94, assoc. prof. psychiatry, 1994—, coord. psychiat. edn. of med. students, 1989-95, asst. chmn. dept. psychiatry, 1993-96, dir. psychiatric edn., 1995—; chief psychiatry Wishard Meml. Hosp., 1990—; primary psychiat. cons. Ind. Dept. of Mental Health, 1988-89. Maj. Ind. N.G., 1972-79. Decorated Army Commendation medal; recipient Residents award for outstanding teaching 1985, 90, Roeske Excellence in Teaching award 1992. Fellow Am. Psychiat. Assn., Am. Ortho-psychiat. Assn.; mem. AMA (Physicians Recognition award 1978—), Ind. Med. Assn., Indpls. Med. Soc., Am. Psychiat. Assn., Ind. Psychiat. Soc. (pres. 1989-90), Am. Orthopsychiat. Assn., Am. Acad. Clin. Psychiatry, Alpha Phi Omega, Phi Beta Pi, Psi Chi, Alpha Epsilon Delta. Presbyterian. Clubs: Athenaeum Turnverein, Columbia. Contbr. articles to profl. jours. Office: Midtown CMHC 1001 W 10th St Indianapolis IN 46202-2859

SCHMID, LYNETTE SUE, child and adolescent psychiatrist; b. Tecumseh, Nebr., May 28, 1958; d. Mel Vern John and Janice Wilda (Bohling) S.; m. Vijendra Sundar, June 13, 1987; children: Jesse Christopher Mikaéle, Eric Lynn Kalani, Christina Elizabeth Ululani. BS, U. Nebr., 1979; MD, U. Nebr., Omaha, 1984; postgrad., U. Mo., 1984-89. Diplomate Am. Bd. Med. Examiners, Am. Bd. Psychiatry and Neurology. Child and adolescent psychiatrist Fulton (Mo.) State Hosp., 1990-91, Mid-Mo. Mental Health Ctr., Columbia, Mo., 1991—; clin. asst. prof. psychiatry U. Mo., Columbia, 1990—. Contbr. articles to profl. jours. Mem. Am. Psychiat. Assn., Am. Acad. Child and Adolescent Psychiatry, Ctrl. Mo. Psychiat. Assn. (sec.-treas. 1992-93, pres.- elect 1993-94, pres. 1994-95), U. Nebr. Alumni Assn., Phi Beta Kappa, Alpha Omega Alpha. Republican. Baptist.

SCHMID, THOMAS HENDERSON, clergyman; b. Houston, Aug. 6, 1943; s. Albert Darwin and Nancy Bell (Hunter) S.; m. Elizabeth Anne Wheatcroft, Sept. 6, 1966; children: Albert, Gretchen, Rachel, Bennett. BA, Austin Coll., 1965; MDiv, Austin Presbyn. Theol. Sem., 1971; D Ministry, McCormick Theol. Sem., 1979. Ordained to ministry, Presbyn. Ch., 1971. Assoc. pastor Grace Presbyn. Ch., Lafayette, La., 1971-73; pastor Eastminster Presbyn. Ch., New Orleans, 1973-77; pastor, sr. minister San Pedro Presbyn. Ch., San Antonio, 1977-88, 1st Presbyn. Ch., Lincoln, Nebr., 1988-96; Mechanicsburg (Pa.) Presbyn. Ch., 1996—; trustee Austin (Tex.) Presbyn. Theol. Sem., 1974-83, 84-93. Author: Dawn in the Afternoon, 1995. With USCGR, 1966-68. Mem. Acad. Homiletics. Democrat. Home: 4217 Nantucket Dr Mechanicsburg PA 17055 Office: First Presbyn Ch 300 E Simpson St Mechanicsburg PA 17055

SCHMIDT, ALVIN J., educator; b. Waldersee, Manitoba, Can., Sept. 28, 1932; came to U.S., 1963; s. John and Lydia (Dreger) S.; married, Aug. 15, 1964; children: Timothy John, Mark Alvin. BA, Valparaiso U., 1962; Bof Div., Concordia Sem., 1964; MA, U. Nebr., 1967, PhD, 1970. Assoc. prof. sociology Concordia Coll., Seward, Nebr., 1963-73, Lenoir-Rhyne Coll., Hickory, N.C., 1973-75; prof. sociology and social ethics Concordia Sem., Ft. Wayne, Ind., 1975-89; prof. sociology Ill. Coll., Jacksonville, 1989—. Author: Oligarchy in Fraternal Organizations, 1973, Fraternal Organizations, 1980, Veiled and Silenced: How Culture Shaped Sexist Theology, 1989, The Menace of Multiculturalism: Trojan Horse in America, 1996. Mem. Rotary (bd. dirs. 1995—). Republican. Lutheran. Home: 7 Audubon Dr Jacksonville IL 62650

SCHMIDT, ARLO E., state legislator; m. Marion Schmidt; 6 children. Grad., Am. Sch. Auctioneering. Auctioneer; rep. Dist. 12 N.D. Ho. of Reps., mem. indsl. bus. and labor and govt. and vet. affairs coms. Named to N.D. Auctioneers Hall of Fame. Mem. N.D. Auctioneers Assn. (past pres.), Legionnaires. Home: PO Box E Maddock ND 58348

SCHMIDT, ARTHUR IRWIN, steel fabricating company executive; b. Chgo., Sept. 9, 1927; s. Louis and Mary (Fliegel) S.; m. Mae Rosman, July 25, 1950; children: Jerrold, Cynthia, Elizabeth, Richard. Student, Colo. A. and M. Coll., 1946-47; BS in Aero. Enging., U. Ill., 1950. Sec. Rosman Iron Works, Inc., Franklin Park, Ill., 1950-86; pres. Rosman-Schmidt Steel Corp., 1986—. Served with USNR, 1944-46, 51-52. Mem. U. Ill. Alumni Assn. Lodge: B'nai B'rith (trustee, past pres. Lincolnwood chpt.). Home and Office: 1901 Somerset Ln Northbrook IL 60062-6067

SCHMIDT, CARL ANTHONY, locomotive engineer; b. Cleve., Sept. 20, 1948; s. Carl Edward and Adele Lillian (Centa) S.; m. Barbara Lee Uselis, Apr. 24, 1971; children: Stacey Anne, Kevin Anthony. Grad. h.s., Mayfield Heights, Ohio. Cert. locomotive engr. Locomotive engr. Consolidated Rail Corp. (formerly Penn. Ctrl.), Cleve., 1968—; sec., treas. United Transp. Union Local 1498, Cleve., 1989-93. Mem. Order of DeMolay (past master coun. Coeur de Lion chpt., Chevalier award 1967), Masons (Collinwood Lodge #582), Order of Ea. Stars (Western Res. chpt. #71, 1995). Democrat. Presbyterian.

SCHMIDT, CLARENCE ANTON, financial consultant; b. Chgo., Nov. 28, 1935; s. Clarence Lawrence and Anna Elizabeth (Leske) S.; m. Anne Louise Wolfer, Feb. 28, 1959; children: J. Paul, Carolyn Anne Schmidt Noll. BS in Indsl. Mgmt., Carnegie-Mellon U., 1957, MS in Indsl. Adminstrn., 1958. ChFC; CLU. Cost engr. Eastman Kodak Co., Rochester, N.Y., 1958-65; supr. cost engring. Eastman Kodak Co., Rochester, 1965-67; corp. mgr. fin. plans Litton Industries, Beverly Hills, Calif., 1967-69; v.p. fin. machine tool group Litton Industries, Hartford, Conn., 1969-72; v.p. fin., CFO, Hillenbrand Industries, Batesville, Ind., 1972-76, Consol. Aluminum Corp., St. Louis, 1976-79; spl. agt. Northwestern Mut. Life, St. Louis, 1979-85; fin. counselor Cigna Fin. Advisors, St. Louis, 1985-93; fin. cons. Clarence A. Schmidt, ChFC, St. Louis, 1994—. Bd. dirs. Luth. Ministries Assn., St. Louis, 1983-91, pres., 1988-90. Mem. Am. Soc. CLU's and ChFC's (instr. wealth accumulation 1994), Internat. Assn. for Fin. Planning, Nat. Assn. Life Underwriters, Estate Planning Coun. St. Louis. Republican. Office: 139 Ladue Oaks Dr Saint Louis MO 63141-8129

SCHMIDT, DANNY R., engineering designer; b. Canton, Ohio, Aug. 31, 1949. Designer Dundee (Mich.) Cement, 1972-86; engr. Sponseller Engring., Maumee, Ohio, 1986-91; designer Glasstech, Perrysburg, Ohio, 1991—. Vol. ARC; vol., mem. Jaycees.

SCHMIDT, DAVID JOSEPH, special education educator, consultant; b. Columbus, Ind., Nov. 22, 1950; s. Richard Everett and Norma (Waggoner) S. BS, Ball State U., 1973, MA, 1975. Tchr. Lakeland Sch. Corp., Lagrange, Ind., 1975—. Mem. edn. adv. com. U.S. Congress 4th Dist., Ft. Wayne, Ind., 1989-94; mem. edn. com. Ind. State, Indpls., 1989—; pres. Assn. for Retarded Citizens, Lagrange, 1982-94, v.p., sec., Indpls., 1986-90; vice-chair Ind. Adv. Coun. on Edn. of Handicapped Children and Youth, 1985—; chmn., bd. dirs. ARC Opportunities, Inc., 1994—. Recipient Outstanding Alumnus award Ball State U., 1988, Alumni Achievement award Delta Chi Fraternity, 1990, Dekko Internat. Found. award for excellence, 1992. Mem. Ind. State Tchrs. Assn. (spl. edn. com. 1984—, chmn. 1986-89, legal def. panel 1981-89, chmn. 1984-89, dir. 1989-95, bd. mgmt. pers. com. 1989-95, governance com. 1995—), Lakeland Edn. Assn. (pres. 1981-83). Republican. Presbyterian. Home: Dallas Lake 30 W 625 S Wolcottville IN 46795-9527 Office: Lakeland High Sch 805 E 75 N Lagrange IN 46761-9360

SCHMIDT, DEBRA JEAN, college official; b. Huron, S.D.. BA in Psychology magna cum laude, Hanover Coll., 1980; MS in Personnel Svcs. and Counseling, Miami U., Oxford, Ohio, 1983. Partial hospitalization therapist Jefferson Mental Health and Guidance Ctr., Ind., 1980-81; head resident Miami U., Oxford, 1981-83; asst. dean students Centre Coll., Danville, Ky., 1983-86; dir. student support svcs. U. Minn., Waseca, 1986-91; asst. dean students Carleton Coll., Northfield, Minn., 1991-94, ind. cons., trainer and career counselor, 1994—. Bd. dirs. Ctrl. for PRevention of Child Abuse, 1987-90; bd. dirs. Family Focus Chem. Dependency Svcs., 1992-94. Ednl. devel. grantee, U. Minn., 1987, 88, 90. Mem. Minn. Coll. Personnel Assn., Mortar Bd., Psi Chi, Gamma Sigma Pi, Exch. Club. Office: Carleton Coll Dept Career Counseling Northfield MN 55057

SCHMIDT, DIANE CAROL, librarian; b. Ortonville, Minn., Dec. 8, 1956; d. F. Leigh and Elizabeth Nellie (Pierce) S. BA in Biology and Psychology, Hamline U., 1978; MS in Biology, Purdue U., 1982; MA in Libr. and Info. Studies, U. Wis., 1987. Ref. libr. and bibliographer sci. and tech. U. Miss., Oxford, 1987-90; asst. biology libr. U. Ill., Urbana, 1990—. Co-author: Using The Biological Literature: A Practical Guide, 2d edit., 1995, Guide to Information Sources in The Botanical Sciences, 2d edit., 1995. Mem. Spl. Libr. Assn. Office: U Ill 101 Burrill Hall 407 S Goodwin Urbana IL 61801

SCHMIDT, EDWARD G., astronomer; b. Cut Bank, Mont., Dec. 13, 1942; s. Donald J. and Kathryn (Frevert) S.; m. Sandy L.Ramsey, July 9, 1988. BSc, U. Chgo., 1965; PhD, Australian Nat. U., 1970. Rsch. assoc. U. Ariz., Tucson, 1970-72; sr. rsch. fellow Royal Greenwich Obs., Herstmonceux, Sussex, Sussex, Eng., 1972-74; from asst. prof. to prof. astronomy U. Nebr., Lincoln, 1974—; program dir. NSF, Washington, 1992-94; assoc. dean Coll. Arts and Scis. U. Nebr., Lincoln, 1996—; mem. users com. Cerro Tololo InterAm. Obs., La Serena, Chile, 1978-80; mem. rev. com. NASA, Greenbelt, Md., 1983-84, 93-94. Editor: The Use of Pulsating Stars in Astronomy, 1989; contbr. articles to profl. jours. USN fellow, 1991, 92; grantee NSF, 1978-91, NASA, 1978-90.

SCHMIDT, GUNTER, dentist; b. Nuremberg, Germany, Aug. 22, 1913; s. Willy and Irma (Treumann) S.; m. Corinne Mitchell, May 26, 1944; children: Carol, Linda. Student, U. Munich, 1932-33, U. Wurzburg, 1933; DDS, Washington U., St. Louis, 1937. Gen. practice dentistry, St. Louis, 1937-59, Clayton, Mo., 1959-86; dentist Shriner's Hosp. for Crippled Children, 1938-43; staff dentist Jewish Hosp., 1938-78, sr. dentist, 1978—. Past editor Newsletter of Am. Acad. of Oral Medicine, Greater St. Louis Dental Soc. Bull.; contbr. articles to profl. jours. Past chmn. United Fund Dental Div., Arts and Edn. Fund Dental Div.; mem. adv. com. on dental techs. St. Louis C.C.; trustee Temple Emanuel, 1993-96. Maj. AUS, 1943-46. Recipient Diamond Pin award Am. Acad. Oral Medicine, 1976, Gold medal Greater St. Louis Dental Soc., 1985, Herschfus Meml. award Am. Acad. Oral Medicine, 1986; Am. Acad. Oral Medicine fellow, 1964, Am. Coll. Dentists fellow, 1980. Mem. AARP (pres. chpt. 4048 1992-94, cmty. coord. dist. 8 1994-96). Mem. ADA, Am. Acad. Oral Medicine (sec., trustee, pres. 1962-63), Am. Soc. Geriatric Dentistry (past pres.), Pierre Fauchard Acad., Acad. Gen. Dentistry, Fedn. Dentaire Internat., St. Louis Dental Soc. (chmn. 1989-93, mem. coun. on legis. 1988-91, parliamentarian 1989-96), Mo. Dental Assn. (chmn. coun. on legis. 1970-84, mem. coun. on Constn. 1988-92, Disting. Svc. award 1985), Temple Emanuel Men's Club (founder, bd. trustees 1993—), Temple Israel Men's Club (past pres.). Home: 15 Princeton Ave Saint Louis MO 63130-3158 Office: 7777 Bonhomme Ave Ste 1400 Saint Louis MO 63105-1911

SCHMIDT, KARL JOSEPH, historian, educator; b. Pt. Pleasant, N.J., Nov. 3, 1963; s. Joseph Herbert and Jacquelyn Louise (Bower) S.; m. Nadine Lea Purvis, Dec. 11, 1993. BA in Geography cum laude, U. South Fla., 1985; MA in Internat. Affairs, Fla. State U., 1987, PhD in History, 1994. Asst. prof. history Mo. So. State Coll., Joplin, 1994—; adj. instr. Tallahassee (Fla.) C.C., 1989-93. Author: An Atlas and Survey of South Asian History, 1995. Dissertation fellow Fla. State U., 1993-94. Mem. Am. Hist. Assn., World History Assn, Soc. South Asian Studies, Indo-British Hist. Soc., Phi Alpha Theta, Phi Kappa Phi, Gamma Theta Upsilon. Home: 322 N Pearl

Ave Joplin MO 64801 Office: Mo So State Coll Dept Social Sci 3950 E Newman Rd Joplin MO 64801

SCHMIDT, KATHLEEN MARIE, lawyer; b. Des Moines, June 17, 1953; d. Raymond Driscoll and Hazel Isabelle (Rogers) Poage; m. Dean Everett Johnson, Dec. 21, 1974 (div. Nov. 1983); children: Aaron Dean, Gina Marie; m. Ronald Robert Schmidt, Feb. 7, 1987. BS in Home Econs., U. Nebr., 1974; JD, Creighton U., 1987. Bar: Nebr. 1987, U.S. Dist. Ct. Nebr. 1987, U.S. Ct. Appeals (8th cir.) 1989, U.S. Supreme Ct. 1991. Apprentice printer, journeyman Rochester (Minn.) Post Bull., 1978-82; dir. customer info. Cornhusker Pub. Power Dist., Columbus, Nebr., 1982-83; artist Pamida, Omaha, 1983; offset artist Cornhusker Motor Club, Omaha, 1983-84; assoc. Lindahl O. Johnson Law Office, Omaha, 1987-88; pvt. practice Omaha, 1988-90; ptnr. Emery, Penke, Blazek & Schmidt, Omaha, 1990-91; pvt. practice, Omaha, 1992—; atty. in condemnation procs. Douglas County Bd. Appraisers, Omaha, 1988—. Mem. Millard Sch. Bd., Omaha, 1989-96, treas. 1991, 92; mem. strategic planning com. Millard Sch. Dist., 1990; mem. Omaha Mayor's Master Plan Com., 1991-94. Named hon. mem. Anderson Mid. Sch., Omaha, 1991. Mem. Nebr. Bar Assn., Omaha Bar Assn. (spkrs. bur. 1992—), Nat. Sch. Bd. Assn. (del. federal rels. network 1991-96, cert. recognition 1991), Nebr. Sch. Bd. Assn. (presenter 1991, 92, award of achievement 1991, 94). Republican. Lutheran. Home: 15936 Cuming St Omaha NE 68118-2241 Office: 399 N 117th St Ste 305 Omaha NE 68154-2507

SCHMIDT, LYNN MARIE LAMMER, business owner; b. Menomonie, Wis., Mar. 14, 1951; d. John Francis and Willa Barbara (Rayburn) Lammer; m. E. Peter Matrejek (div. May 1986); m. Gregory J.L. Schmidt, Jan. 1, 1987; children: Tara, Richard, Tiffany. BA, U. Wyo., 1973; JD, William Mitchell Coll. Law, 1984. Law clk. 10th Jud. Dist. Ct. Minn., Stillwater, Minn., 1984-87; dir. mail mgr. West Pub. Co., St. Paul, 1987-88, mktg. coord., 1988-90; pres., CEO ENCO, Stillwater, 1988-93; CEO EnviroHealth Cons., Inc., Stillwater, 1993-95; homeopathic cons., 1996—; bd. dirs. L-Mark Shopping Ctr.; cons. H.E.A.L., Atlanta, 1990-92. Mem. Sch. Bd. Ind. Sch. Dist. 834, Stillwater, 1990-93, sec., 1990-91, treas., 1991-92, trustee, bd. dirs., 1990—; officer Minn. Women's Polit. Caucus, St. Paul, 1990-93, cons., 1989—. Mem. AAUW, Stillwater C. of C., Rotary, Alpha Chi Omega. Home: 10571 Penfield Avenue Cir N Stillwater MN 55082-9218

SCHMIDT, PATRICIA ANN, geriatrics nurse; b. Garden City, Kans., Mar. 2, 1952; d. Forest Wayne Uthe and Grace Edith Lydia (Nusser) Uthe-Greenwood;m. Douglas E. Schmidt, June 11, 1977 (div.); 1 child, Tiffany Dawn. ADN, Garden City Community Coll., Kans., 1977; student, Hays State Coll. Cert. nurses' aide instr. Kans., 1992. Med. asst. Wiley Clinic, Garden City, 1971-76; nurse's aide and nurse tech. St. Catherine's Hosp., Garden City, 1976-77, staff nurse surgery, 1977-83, staff nurse nursery, normal newborn, 1983-84; office nurse Plaza Med. Ctr., Garden City, 1984-88; contract nurse Wichita County Hosp., Leota, Kans., 1988-89; DON High Plains Retirement Village, Lakin, Kans., 1989-92; quality assurance coord. Garden Valley Retirement Village, Garden City, Kans., 1992-94; home health coord. Garden Valley Home Health Agy., Garden City, 1994—. Mem. Kans. Assn. for Homes of the Aging. Republican. Mem. Assembly of God. Home: 1006 Long Blvd Garden City KS 67846-7309

SCHMIDT, PATRICIA JEAN, medical lab technician; b. Cleve., June 15, 1941. Cert. applied lab. tech., Cuyahoga C.C., Cleve., 1967. Lic. student driver instr. Lab. sect. supr. Meridia Euclid (Ohio) Hosp., 1968-74; gen. lab. technician, 1974-94; student driving instr. Cleve., 1994—; tutor deaf students in coll. math.; designer including vet.'s memls. Author: A Manual of Disciplines for Interpreters of the Deaf; composer, vocal and stage presentation coach; sculptor and designer. Active voter registration Rep. Party. Recipient Acad. award Math. Assn. Am., Washington, 1959. Mem. Nat. Assn. of the Deaf, Nat. Head Injury Found., Sweet Adeline Internat. Home: PO Box 43123 Cleveland OH 44143-0123

SCHMIDT, RICHARD HEINRICH, taxidermist, educator; b. Goessel, Kans., Jan. 25, 1909; s. Peter U. and Anna (Unruh) S.; m. Tina Bergen, Apr. 3, 1931 (dec. Mar. 1979); children: Richard, Frances, Donald, Elizabeth, Kathryn, Glenda (dec.); m. Ruth Banman, May 27, 1990. Instr. taxidermy Emporia (Kans.) State U., 1956-76; collector, preparer mus. specimens for Richard H. Schmidt Natural History Mus. Emporia State U.; founder Morris Yoder Meml. Mus. Heston (Kans.) Coll., 1948-56. Author: How to Mount Birds and Prepare Bird Study Skins, 1969, Collecting and Mounting Butterflies, 1970, How to Mount Fish, 1971, How to Prepare Mammal Study Skins and Tan Furs, 1986. Recipient Conservation Edn. award Kans. Wildlife Fedn., Nat. Wildlife Fedn., Sears Roebuck Found., 1968, Colman Jones award, 1982. Mem. (charter) Kans. Ornithol. Soc., Kans. Assn. Taxidermists. Mennonite. Home: 716 N Ash Newton KS 67114

SCHMIDT, RUSSEL ALAN, II, sales executive; b. Stuttgart-Bad Canstatt, Germany, Nov. 18, 1953; Came to U.S., 1954.; s. Russell Allen and Phyllis (Coty) S.; m. Christie Ellen Duncan, Oct. 18 1975; children: Rachel Lea, Russell Alan III. BS, U. Minn., 1984. Lic. federal communications commn. gen. radiotelephone operator; cert. Motorola Effective Presentations, Successful Negotiator. Pres. Electronic Engring. Inds. Co., St. Paul, Minn., 1971-77, Dis-Com Inc., St. Paul, Minn., 1978-81; sales engr. Motorola Inc., Mpls., 1984-85, dist. sales engr., 1985-86, dist. sales mgr.(IBM), 1987-89; sr. account sales mgr. (IBM) Motorola Inc., 1989-93, sr. acct. sales mgr., 1993-95, power PC market devel. mgr., 1995—; bd. dirs. Dis-Com Inc. 1978-81; chief TV engr. Renewal Internat. Inc., St. Paul, Minn., 1984-87. Mem. Nat. Small Bus.Assn.; St. Paul Chamber Commerce, North Suburban Chamber Commerce, Mpls. Chamber Commerce, North Oaks Golf Club. Republican, Lutheran. Office: Motorola Semiconductor Products 5620 Smetana Dr Minnetonka MN 55343

SCHMIDT, VICTORIA, educator, author, consultant; b. St. Louis, July 19, 1908; d. Gottfried and Anna Christina (Juenger) S. AB, Harris Tchrs. Coll., St. Louis, 1929; MA, Columbia U., 1930; EdD, U. Colo., 1952. Tchr. pub. schs., St. Louis, 1929-48; prof. Harris Tchrs. Coll., 1949-78; prof. emeritus Harris-Stowe Coll., St. Louis, 1978—. Author: Victoria's Story--Reincarnation--God's Love Returned, 1992, (poetry) Matrix of Our Lives, 1995, (poetry) Life--Death, 1995, (poems) The Mind, 1996, Time, 1996. Primary candidate for U.S. Congress from St. Louis, 1974, 76, 78, primary candidate for Mo. State Rep., 1980. Mem. Libr. of Congress Assocs., Internat. Soc. Poets, Explorers Club, Am. Mus. Natural History, Ret. Sch. Employees of St. Louis (parliamentarian 1990—). Democrat. Home: 3667 Liermann Ave Saint Louis MO 63116-4511

SCHMIDT, WAYNE WALTER, legal association executive; b. St. Louis, Feb. 8, 1941; s. Warren W. and Geneva N. (Walker) S.; children: Andrew M., Nancy K. Diploma in English and Comparative Law, City of London Coll., 1963; BA, U. N.Mex., 1964; JD, Oklahoma City U., 1966; LLM, Northwestern U., 1974. Bar: N.Mex. 1966, Ill. 1968, D.C. 1970, N.Y. 1982. Dir. police legal advisor program Northwestern U., 1968-70; counsel Internat. Assn. Chiefs of Police, 1970-73; exec. dir. Am. for Effective Law Enforcement, Inc., Chgo., 1973—; pres. Pub. Safety Pers. Rsch. Inst., 1974—, Govt. Employment Rsch. Inst., Inc., 1986-89, Lauterbrunnen Properties, 1990-93; dir. Comprehensive Ensurers Market Syndicate, Inc., 1984-91, 93-94, Capital Exch. Mgmt., Inc., 1988-91; cons. Uniform Code of Criminal Procedure. Co-author: Legal Aspects of Criminal Evidence, 1978, Introduction to Criminal Evidence, 1982; editor Fire and Police Personnel Reporter, 1975—, Pub. Employment Health Law and Benefits, 1986-89. Served with U.S. Army, 1966-67. Mem. ABA (liaison to criminal justice council 1973—). Office: 5519 N Cumberland Ave Ste 1008 Chicago IL 60656-1480

SCHMIDTLEIN, MARY VIRGINIA, lawyer; b. Columbia, Mo., Aug. 20, 1958; d. Eugene Francis and Mary Virginia (Holland) S.; m. James Everett Rhodes, Oct. 20, 1990; children: Matthew Francis, Andrew James, John Joseph. BA, U. Notre Dame, 1980; JD, U. Mo., 1983. Bar: Mo. 1983, U.S. Dist. Ct. (ea. and we. dists.) Mo. 1983, Ill. 1984. Assoc. Evans & Dixon, St. Louis, 1983-88; of counsel, 1996—; counsel The May Dept. Stores Co., St. Louis, 1988-96; part-time prof. St. Louis C.C. at Meramec, 1988, 90, 91, 92; speaker in field. Vol. Spl. Olympics, St. Louis, 1987-89; bd. dirs. Mo. Spl. Olympics, Inc., 1994—; mem. Immacolata Choir, St. Louis, 1988-89, cantor, 1995—. Mem. Bar Assn. Met. St. Louis (chmn. trial practice young lawyers sect. 1986), Lawyers Assn. St. Louis (exec. com. 1986-89, sec. 1990-91, v.p. 1992-93, pres.-elect 1993-94, pres. 1994-95), St. Thomas More Soc. (sec. 1994-95), Mo. Bd. Law Examiners. Roman Catholic. Office: Evans & Dixon 200 N Broadway #1200 Saint Louis MO 63102

SCHMIT, DAVID MICHAEL, retired secondary educator, artist, designer; b. Pearl Lake, Minn., May 17, 1925; s. August Louis and Exilda Delia (Picard) S.; m. Mary Anna Kranz; children: Stephen, Peter, John. A in Liberal Arts, U.Minn., 1950, BS, 1951, MEd, 1961. Cert. tchr., Minn. Photo lab. technician Christianson Studio, St. Cloud, Minn., 1942-43; phys. therapy asst. Elizabeth Kenny Inst., Mpls., 1946-47; sales clk. J.C. Penney Co., Mpls., 1947-48; tchr., elem. art supr. Cherryvale (Kans.) Pub. Schs., 1951-53; tchr. art and English Mpls. Pub. Schs., 1953-54; tchr. art, drama and social studies Edina (Minn.) Pub. Schs., 1954-89, chair dept. art, 1965-70, dir. dramatics, 1957-87; founding mem., designer Edina Hist. Soc., 1969; bd. dirs., actor, technician Edina Cmty. Theater, 1961-66. Designer logo and charter Edina Hist. Soc., 1969; stage set designer. Bd. dirs. South Metro Airport Action Coun., Mpls., 1989-93; dir. Mpls. chpt. Earth Save Found., 1994-95. With U.S. Army, 1945-46. Recipient Century Club award Ind. Reps. of Minn., 1991. Mem. Art Educators of Minn., Am. Legion, Minn. Packard Club (dir. 1973), Minn. Geneal. Soc., KC, Ind. Reps. of Minn. Roman Catholic. Home: 5025 Morgan Ave S Minneapolis MN 55419

SCHMITT, JERRY, state legislator; b. Oak, Nebr., Aug. 28, 1938; m. Lavonne R. Holmes; children: Dennis, Bruce. Constrn. worker; mem. Nebr. State Patrol; mem. from dist. 41 Nebr. State Senate, Lincoln, 1992—, mem. govt., mil. and vet. affairs com., transp. com. Mem. Ordinance City Bark Bd. Mem. NRA, Nebr. Hist. Soc., VFW, State Troopers Assn. Nebr. Office: Nebr State Senate State Capitol Rm 1117 Lincoln NE 68509*

SCHMITT, MARY ELIZABETH, postal supervisor; b. Detroit, Sept. 16, 1948; d. Jerome Ferdinand and Margaret Ellen (Beauregard) S. BS, Ea. Mich. U., 1979. Waitress, hostess Mr. Steak, Westland, Mich., 1969-70; mgr. housewares K-Mart, Ypsilanti, Mich., 1971, asst. mgr., jewelry, 1972; postal clk. U.S. Postal Svc., Ann Arbor, Mich., 1972-88, postal supr., 1988—. Crisis intervention counselor Ozone House, Ann Arbor, 1978; convenor Gray Panthers of Huron Valley, Ann Arbor, 1979-80; active Greenpeace. Mem. LWV, Nat. Assn. Postal Suprs., Ann Arbor Postal Fed. Credit Union (v.p. 1987—), Sierra Club, Ancestry Club. Roman Catholic. Home: PO Box 1833 Ann Arbor MI 48106-1833 Office: US Postal Svc 2075 W Stadium Blvd Ann Arbor MI 48103-7011

SCHMITT, WOLFGANG RUDOLF, consumer products executive; b. Koblenz, Germany, Mar. 12, 1944; s. Josef H. and M.H. (Baldus) S.; m. Toni A. Yoder, June 30, 1974; children: Christopher, Corey, Clayton. BA, Otterbein Coll., 1966; AMP, Harvard U. Bus. Sch., 1986. With Rubbermaid Inc., Wooster, Ohio, 1966—, pres., gen. mgr. housewares products div., 1984-91, exec. v.p., bd. dirs., 1987-91, pres., chief operating officer, 1991—; chmn., CEO, 1993—; bd. dirs. Parker Hannifin Corp., Kimberly-Clark Corp. Bd. dirs. Otterbein Coll., 1992—. Office: Rubbermaid Inc 1147 Akron Rd Wooster OH 44691-6000

SCHMITZ, SHIRLEY GERTRUDE, marketing and sales executive; b. Brackenridge, Pa., Dec. 19, 1927; d. Wienand Gerard and Florence Marie (Grimm) S. BA, Ariz. State U., 1949. Tchr., guidance counselor Mesa High Sch., Ariz., 1949-51; area mgr. Field Enterprises Ednl. Corp., Phoenix, 1951-52, dist. mgr., 1952, regional mgr., 1953-55, br. mgr., Montreal, Que., Can., 1955-61, nat. supr., Chgo., 1961-63, asst. sales mgr., 1963-65, nat. sales mgr., 1965-70; v.p., gen. sales mgr. F.E. Compton Co. div. Ency. Brit., Chgo., 1970-71, exec. v.p., dir. sales, 1971-73; pres. CHB Port-A-Book Store, Inc., 1973-76; gen. mgr. Bobbs-Merrill Co., Inc., Indpls., 1976-82; v.p. sales U.S. Telephone Communications of Midwest, Inc., Chgo., 1982-83; exec. v.p. sales and market devel. Entertainment Publs., Corp., Birmingham, Mich., 1983-89, sr. v.p. mktg. and sales, Troy, Mich., 1989-92; prin. S.G. Schmitz and Assocs., Chgo., 1992—; bd. dirs. Ariz. Tech. Incubator; bd. advisors Ctr. Advancement of Small Bus., Ariz. State U. Sch. Bus; bd. dirs. Spectral, Inc., Colourtech, Inc. Recipient Twin award Nat. Bd. YWCA, 1987. Recipient Honors award Beta Gamma Sigma, 1995, Disting. Achievement award Sch. Bus. Ariz. State U., 1995; Angel award Nat. Assn. Women Bus. Owners, 1996. Mem. USGA (assoc.), Internat. Platform Assn., Am. Mgmt. Assn., Nat. Bus. Incubation Assn., Nat. Geographic Soc., Nat. Space Soc., World Future Soc., Ariz. State U. Alumni Assn. Republican. Roman Catholic. Home: 93 Miller Rd Lake Zurich IL 60047-1395

SCHMOCKER, KENNETH ERNEST, financial planner, underwriter; b. Mauston, Wis., July 9, 1953; s. Ernest A. and Audrey J. (Clary) S.; children: Ryan K., Jerod M. BS, U. Wis., La Crosse, 1975. CLU; cert. Nat. Health Underwriter; ChFC. Night mgr. Ernies Shell, Mauston, 1971-76; pres. Schmocker Fin. Svcs., Inc., La Crosse, 1976—. Pres. St. Patrick's Home and Sch., Am. Heart Assn. Mem. Nat. Assn. Life Underwriters (past pres.), Western Wis. Life Underwriters (past pres.), LaCrosse Estate Planning Coun. Office: Schmocker Financial Svcs PO Box 401 La Crosse WI 54602-0401

SCHMUCKER, RUBY ELVY LADRACH, nurse, educator; b. Sugarcreek, Ohio, Nov. 17, 1923; d. Walter F. and Carrie M. (Mizer) Ladrach; R.N., Aultman Hosp., Canton, Ohio, 1945; B.S. in Nursing, U. Akron, 1970, M.S. in Edn., 1973; children: Gary, David, Barbara, Steven. Cert. psychiat. nurse. Gen. duty nurse, head nurse Aultman Hosp., 1945-47, part-time, 1950-62, instr. nursing, 1962-64, 69-74, part-time psychiat. nurse, 1991—; instr. nursing Coll. Nursing, U. Akron (Ohio), 1974-76; instr. div. nursing edn. Children's Hosp., Akron, 1976-78; psychiat. nurse and supr. Massillon (Ohio) State Hosp., 1978-80, cons. to nursing dept., 1980-81, dir. nursing edn., 1981-84; supr. Molly Stark Hosp., 1984-88; charge nurse, individual and group therapist Cuyahoga Falls Gen. Hosp., 1984-90, part-time psychiat. nurse; cons. Stark-Tuscarawas Counties Student Nurses Assn., 1973-74. Health chmn. Avondale Sch. PTA, Canton, 1956, mem. coms., 1954-70; vol. instr. home nursing courses ARC, 1959-62, instr. CPR, 1979-83. Cert. psychiat. nurse. Mem. Aultman Hosp. Sch. Nursing Alumni Assn., Am. Nurses' Assn., Nat. League Nursing, Am. Personnel and Guidance Assn., Am. Coll. Personnel Assn., U. Akron Alumni Assn., Alpha Sigma Lambda, Pi Lambda Theta. Mem. Ch. of Christ. Office: 4214 Bellwood Dr NW Canton OH 44708-1656

SCHMUTZ, CHARLES REID, university foundation executive; b. Youngstown, Ohio, Jan. 26, 1942; s. Charles Edward and Alice Mae (Bliss) S.; m. Judith Rhodes Seiple, June 19, 1965; children: Charles Reid Jr., Andrew Edward, Jill Caroline. AB in Econs., Brown U., 1964. Lab. technician The Standard Slag Co., Youngstown, 1964-65; direct salesman The Standard Slag Co., Cleve., 1965-69; mktg. and prodn. scheduler The Standard Slag Co., Youngstown, 1969-73, mktg. and indsl. engr., 1973-85, gen. mgr., v.p. ops., 1985-89; pres. Youngstown State U. Found., 1989—; bd. dirs. StanCorp., Youngstown. Bd. dirs. Youngstown Playhouse, Jr. Achievement Mahoning Valley. Named to Hall of Fame, Ohio Aggregates Assn., 1990. Mem. Rotary. Methodist.

SCHNECK, TODD M., manufacturing engineer; b. Louisville, Ky., May 22, 1964. A, Purdue U., 1987, postgrad. Project mgr. Engineered Conveyors Inc., Kokomo, Ind., 1986—. Office: Engineered Conveyors Inc 1055 Home Ave Kokomo IN 46902-1624

SCHNEIDER, ALEXANDER WILLIAM, reliability engineer; b. Kalamazoo, Nov. 25, 1945; s. Alexander William and Jennylouise Standish (Lockwood-White) S.; m. Lauretta Ann Gerretse, Sept. 18, 1971; children: Alexander W. III, James A. BSEE, Northwestern U., Evanston, Ill., 1967, MS, 1968; MBA, U. Chgo., 1972. Registered profl. engr., Ill. Engr. Commonwealth Edison Co., Chgo., 1968-75, statis. analyst, 1975-80, sr. engr., 1980-92; reliability engr. Mid-Am. Interconnected Network, Lombard, Ill., 1992—. Contbr. articles to profl. jours. Elder session Addison (Ill.) Presbyn. Ch., 1985-87, 93—. Recipient 1st Use award Elec. Power Rsch. Inst., 1985, Dist. award of merit Boy Scouts Am., 1992. Mem. IEEE (sr., Working Group Recognition award 1991, 95, applications of probability methods subcom. 1985—). Presbyterian. Office: Mid-Am Interconn Network Main Coordination Ctr 939 Parkview Blvd Lombard IL 60148

SCHNEIDER, ALLAN FRANK, geology educator and researcher; b. Chgo., Feb. 7, 1926; s. Emory Francis and Esther Marie (Westgard) S.; m. Betty-Louise Dorn, Aug. 26, 1950; children: David Emory, Doris Jane Schneider Rossmann, James Allan. BS, Beloit (Wis.) Coll., 1948; MS, Pa. State U., 1951; PhD, U. Minn., 1957. Grad. asst. Pa. State U., State College, 1948-50, instr. geology, 1950-51; geologist U.S. Geol. Survey, Lexington, Ky., 1949-50; instr. geology U. Minn., Mpls., 1951-54; geologist Minn. Geol. Survey, Mpls., 1951-54; from instr. to asst. prof. Wash. State U., Pullman, 1954-59; geologist Ind. Geol. Survey, Bloomington, 1959-70; assoc. prof. geology U. Wis.-Parkside, Kenosha, 1970-80, prof., 1980-93, prof. emeritus, 1993—; map and illustrations editor Ind. Geol. Survey, 1961-66; lectr. Ind. U., Bloomington, 1969; geol. cons. Town of Paris, Kenosha County, Wis., 1981-83; dist. geologist Lake Michigan Dist., Wis. Dept. Natural Resources, Green Bay, 1986—. Author: Pleistocene Geology of the Randall Region, Central Minnesota, 1961; editor, author: (guidebook) Geologic Tales along Hoosier Trails, 1967, Late Quaternary History of the Lake Michigan Basin, 1990, Pleistocene Geomorphology and Stratigraphy of the Door Peninsula, Wisconsin, 1993; contbr. articles to profl. jours. Vol. geologist The Ridges Sanctuary, Baileys Harbor, Wis., 1979—, bd. dirs., 1995—; mem. adv. com. Racine County (Wis.) Coastal Mgmt. Program, 1976-86. Grantee Geol. Soc. Am., 1956, 58, Wis. Alumni Rsch. Found., 1971, 72, NOAA, 1976, U. Wis.-Parkside. Fellow Geol. Soc. Am., Ind. Acad. Sci.; mem. Am. Quaternary Assn., Wis. Acad. Scis., Arts and Letters, Nat. Assn. Geosci. Tchrs., Sigma Xi. Republican. Lutheran. Office: U Wis-Parkside Dept Geology Box 2000 Wood Rd Kenosha WI 53141-2000

SCHNEIDER, BRYAN A., lawyer; b. Aurora, Ill., May 17, 1967; s. G. Allan and Barbara J. (Koehler) S. BS, Tri-State U., 1989; JD, U. Wis., 1992. Bar: Ill., Wis.; CPA, Ill. Law clk. to judge Chgo., 1992-93; assoc. Sidley & Austin, Chgo., 1993—; atty. office of speaker Ill. Ho. of Reps., Springfield, 1995. Mem. Federalist Co. Chgo. Lawyers (pres. 1995). Republican. Lutheran. Office: Sidley & Austin 1 1st National Plz Chicago IL 60603

SCHNEIDER, JAMES JOSEPH, military theory educator, consultant; b. Oshkosh, Wis., June 18, 1947; s. Joseph Edward and Virginia Gertrude Schneider; m. Peggy L. Spees, July 28, 1973 (dec. May 1976); m. Claretta Virginia Burton, Nov. 11, 1984; children: Kevin, Jason, Jenifer, Julie. BA, U. Wis., Oshkosh, 1973, MA, 1974; PhD, U. Kans., 1992. Planning evaluator Winnegago County, Oshkosh, 1978-80; ops. rsch. analyst Tng. and Doctrine Command Analysis Ctr., Ft. Leavenworth, Kans., 1980-84; prof. mil. theory Sch. Advanced Mil. Studies U.S. Army Command and Gen. Staff Coll., Ft. Leavenworth, 1984—; adj. assoc. prof. history Russian and East European Studies Ctr., U. Kans., 1994—. Author: (monograph) Exponential Decay of Armies in Battle, 1985, The Structure of Strategic Revolution, 1994; also numerous articles. With U.S. Army, 1965-68, Vietnam. Recipient medal for civilian achievement Dept. Army, 1989, Bronze Order of St. George, U.S. Cav. Assn., 1990. Mem. Am. Hist. Assn., Mil. Ops. Rsch. Soc. Office: U S Army Command/Gen Staff Coll Sch Advanced Mil Studies Fort Leavenworth KS 66027

SCHNEIDER, JEANNE ANNE, nursing educator; b. Columbus, Ohio, Dec. 23, 1950; d. Paul Leroy and Dorothy Alice (Humphrey) Miller; m. Norman Edward Schneider II, Mar. 30, 1974; children: Jason Edward, Seth Jared, Rachel Anne. LPN, Columbus Sch. Nursing, 1970; Assoc. degree, Columbus State Coll., 1973; student, Franklin U., 1983-85; BSN, Capital U., 1989. RN, Ohio. LPN Grant Hosp., Columbus, Ohio, 1970-73; RN Grant Hosp., Columbus, 1973-74, 76-79, Heinzerling Inst., Columbus, 1979-81, Riverside Hosp., Columbus, 1987-90; instr. maternity nursing Columbus (Ohio) Sch. Practical Nursing, 1990-92; nurse critical care unit Doctos Hosp. West, Columbus, 1992—; vol. RN, Guam, 1976. Mem. AACN. Republican. Baptist. Home: 638 Darlene Pl Galloway OH 43119-9464

SCHNEIDER, JOHN DURBIN, state legislator; b. St. Louis, Mar. 1, 1937; s. F. John and Kathleen (Durbin) S.; m. Mary Jo Steppan; children: Anne Marie, John Steppan, Robert Durbin. BS, JD, St. Louis U., 1960. Atty. Transit Casualty Co., 1960-65, chief trial atty., 1965-70; rep. Mo. State Ho. Reps. Dist. 26, 1969-70; senator Mo. State Senate Dist. 14, 1970—. Mem. St. Louis Bar Assn., Phi Delta Phi. Address: 3520 Tremont Dr Florissant MO 63033-3057 also: State Senate State Capitol Building Jefferson City MO 65101-1556*

SCHNEIDER, JOHN DAVID, theatre director, playwright, actor, jazz singer; b. Fond du Lac, Wis., June 7, 1948; s. David Elmer and Bernice Catherine (Pable) S. BA, St. Norbert Coll., 1970. Mem. Theatre X, Milw., 1971—; also artistic dir., 1978—, profl. playwright, 1973—; vocalist, leader John Schneider Orch., Milw., 1988—. Author: (plays) Scenarios For the Living/For the Dead, 1983; author numerous plays. Recipient New Works award Wis. Arts Bd., 1990; NEA fellow, 1988, Milwaukee County fellow, 1991, Program Devel. grantee Theatre Comms. Group-Pew Charitable Trust, 1992. Office: Theatre X 158 N Broadway St Milwaukee WI 53202

SCHNEIDER, JUDITH LYNN, mathematics educator; b. Lima, Ohio, June 15, 1944; d. Walter Harmon Branscome and Mary Lucille Mills Elsea; m. Barry Michael Schneider, June 10, 1967 (div. 1972); 1 child, Leah Elizabeth. BS, Bowling Green State U., 1966. Tchr. Euclid (Ohio) Pub. Schs., 1966-67; tchr. math. Chagrin Falls (Ohio) Schs., 1967—; mem. evaluation team State Dept. Edn., Columbus, 1990-92. Trustee Cleve. Bur. Jewish Edn., 1983-85; mem. edn. com. Cleve. Bicentennial Commn.; mem. adv. com. John Carroll U., 1989—; interface participant Martha Holden Jennings Found., Cleve., 1990-91; precinct committeeperson Dem. Ctrl. Com., Cleveland Heights, Ohio, 1991-94; mem. Ohio State Dem. Exec. Com. Mem. NEA, Pub. Sector Labor Rels. Assn., Nat. Coun. Tchrs. Math., Ohio Coun. Tchrs. Math., Greater Cleve. Coun. Tchrs. Math., Coalition for Sch. Funding Reform (steering com. 1990—), Ohio Edn. Assn. (exec. com. 1987-93), North Eastern Ohio Edn. Assn. (exec. com. 1979-85, 87-95, pres.-elect 1992-93, pres. 1993-94, past pres. 1994-95), Chagrin Falls Edn. Assn. (pres. 1974-78). Office: Chagrin Falls Schs 77 E Washington St Chagrin Falls OH 44022-3001

SCHNEIDER, MARK P., design engineer; b. Milw., Dec. 19, 1949. A. Internal Combustion, Milw. Sch. Engring., 1971. Engring. clk. Am. Motors, Kenosha, Wis., 1972-74; engring. designer J.I. Case, Racine, Wis., 1974-87; OEM sales engr. Karl Schmidt, Wayne, Pa., 1987-88; design engr. Cooper Energy Svcs., Springfield, Ohio, 1989—. Mem. Soc. Automotive Engrs., Exptl. Aircraft Assn., Porch Club. Office: Cooper Engring 1401 Sheridan Ave Springfield OH 45505-2255

SCHNEIDER, MARK STEVEN, telecommunications company executive; b. Devils Lake, N.D., Nov. 11, 1951; s. Adam Louis and Lucille Mary (Grasser) S.; m. Kristing Louise Olson, Apr. 15, 1972; children: Jennifer Kristen, Brittany Marie. BS in econs., Colo. State U., 1975, MBA, 1976. Grad. tchg. asst. Coll. Bus. Colo. State U., 1975-76, grad. rsch. technician Expt. Sta., 1976; analyst futures planning Frontier Airlines, 1977-78, asst. mgr., 1978-79, mgr. pricing and capacity control, 1979-80, dir., 1980-83, dir. product planning, 1984; independent bus. cons., 1985-87; dir. pricing and revenue mgmt. Braniff, Inc., 1987-88; v.p. planning revenue, mktg., devel., 1988; v.p. mktg. GTE Airfone, 1988—. Bd. dirs. United Charities Family Svcs. Dupage, 1994—, Knolls Huntington Home Owners Assn, 1992—; ski instr. for blind and handicapped Winter Park Recreation.

SCHNEIDER, MARLIN DALE, state legislator; b. La Crosse, Wis., Nov. 16, 1942; s. Donald M. and Elva M. (Peterson) S.; m. Georgia Jean Johansen, 1973; children: Jeanine Marie, Molly Anne. BS, U. Wis., La Crosse, 1965; MST, U. Wis., Stevens Point, 1976; MS, U. Wis., 1979; cert. Police Acad., Madison Area Tech. Coll., 1982. Wis. state assemblyman Dist. 72, 1970—, Dist. 59, 1971-72; asst. majority leader, 1970—, asst. minority leader; tchr. Lomira H.S., Wis., 1965-66, Lincoln H.S., Wisconsin Rapids, 1966-71. Mem. Nat. Conf. State Legis. NSF grantee in sociology La. State U., 1970; named one of Outstanding Young Men of Am., 1973, Wis. Men of Achievement, 1976. Mem. Moose (local 819), Sigma Tau Gamma. Address: 3820 Southbrook Wisconsin Rapids WI 54494*

SCHNEIDER, MELVIN FREDERICK, retired secondary music educator; b. Lark, Wis., Mar. 7, 1904; s. Charles Phillip and Amelia (Thiele) S.; m.

Naomi Jessie Manshardt, Sept. 14, 1940. BMus, U. Wis., 1930, MA, 1948, postgrad., to 1955. Tchr. orch., chorus and math. high sch., South Beloit, Ill., 1930-32; tchr. orch., band and social studies high sch., Oregan, Wis., 1932-35, Wisconsin Dells, Wis., 1935-37, Prairie du Sac, Wis., 1937-40; rschr. in music edn. U. Wis., Madison, 1940-45, U. No. Iowa, Cedar Falls, 1945-60; ind. rschr. in music edn. Cedar Falls, 1960—; voice and string instr., instrument repair instr. Mem. String Tchrs. Assn. (a founder), Music Educators Nat. Conf. (award for 50 yrs. of svc.), Cedar Falls C. of C., Phi Delta Kappa. Republican. Congregationalist. Home: 1615 Merner Ave Cedar Falls IA 50613

SCHNEIDER, ROBERT STEVEN, electrical engineer, educator; b. Chippewa Falls, Wis., Nov. 8, 1960; s. Robert Edward and Ruth Marcella (Hurth) S.; m. Denise Sue Mortensen, Aug. 12, 1983; children: Adam Christopher, Lucas Robert. BS in physics, math. magna cum laude, U. Wis., Eau Claire, 1982; MS in elec. engring., U. Wis., 1986. Physics tchr. Redwood Falls (Minn.) H.S., 1982-83; test engr. J.I. Case Co., Racine, Wis., 1983-84; sr. devel. engr. UNICO, Inc., Franksville, Wis., 1986-90; sr. project engr. Omnion Power Engring. Corp., Mukwonago, Wis., 1990-92, sr. devel. engr., 1994-95; cons. power electronics East Troy, Wis., 1992-94; sr. design engr. Soft Switching Techs. Corp., Middleton, Wis., 1995—; cons. Teltech-Tech. Knowledge Svc., Mpls., 1993—; seminar instr. U. Wis., Madison, 1992—; chmn. seminar U. Wis. Milw., 1994-96. Big bro. Big Bros.-Big Sisters Am., Racine, 1988-90; coach Odyssey of the Mind East Troy Mid. Sch., 1992; presch. Sunday Sch. tchr. Mt. Olive Luth. Ch., Mukwonago, 1994-96. Mem. IEEE. Home: 1628 Mayflower Dr Middleton WI 53562 Office: Soft Switching Techs 2224 Evergreen Rd Middleton WI 53562

SCHNEIDER, THOMAS AQUINAS, surgeon, educator; b. St. Charles, Mo., Dec. 22, 1934; s. Vincent Augustine and Anna Maria (Marheineke) S.; m. Joyce Elaine Diehr, June 7, 1958; children: Lisa, Thomas, Dawn, Tracy. BS, Loras Coll., 1954; MD, St. Louis U., 1958. Diplomate Am. Bd. Surgery. Resident surgery St. Louis City Hosp., 1958-63; pvt. practice St. Charles, 1963—; clin. instr., St. Louis U., 1966-91, asst. clin. prof. 1991—; med. dir. vascular lab. St. Joseph Health Ctr., St. Charles, 1991—, dir. trauma svc. 1981-91. Fellow ACS; mem. Mo. Com. on Trauma, St. Louis Surg. Soc. (councilor 1988-91, v.p. 1996—), St. Louis Vascular Soc. (pres. 1993-95), Hodgen Club (pres. 1988), Alpha Omega Alpha. Roman Catholic. Office: 2850 W Clay St Saint Charles MO 63301-2536

SCHNEIDER, THOMAS PATRICK, financial planner; b. St. Louis, July 14, 1948; s. Maurice Jacob and Josephine C. (Flynn) S.; m. Rachel Marie Samel, June 27, 1969; children: Jacob, Zachary, Marc, Claire, Julie, Paul. BS in Civil Engring., U. Mo., Rolla, 1975. Cert. fin. planner. City engr. Florissant, Mo., 1975-78; mfg. rep. Sprayial Sys., St. Louis, 1978-81; fin. planner First Fin. Group, Clayton, Mo., 1982-86, Wamhoff Fin. Planning Co., Florissant, 1987—. Coun. rep. City of Florissant, Mo., 1979—. Petty officer 2nd class USN, 1967-72, Viet Nam; lt. (j.g.) USNR, 1976-79. Mem. Internat. Assn. Fin. Planners, NALU, Inst. CFP, Florissant C. of C., Rotary Internat. (sgt.-at-arms 1992), VFW, Optimist Internat. Roman Catholic. Office: Wamhoff Fin Planning Co 3224 N Us Highway 67 Florissant MO 63033-1646

SCHNEIDER, WESLEY CLAIR, marketing communications company executive; b. Chgo., May 2, 1953; s. Clair A. and Ruth (Jenks) S.; m. Jeanie A. Tomaino, Nov. 23, 1990. BA magna cum laude, Ill. Wesleyan U., 1975. Sales rep. confectionery div. Am. Home Products, Chgo., 1975-77; midwest regional sales mgr. confectionery & snacks div. Beatrice Foods, Denver, 1977-78, mktg. analyst, 1978-80; product mgr. Tootsie Roll Industries, Chgo., 1980-85, mgr. internat. mktg., 1985-88; v.p., gen. mgr. Marden-Kane, inc., Chgo., 1988-91; pres., owner Creative Mktg. Comms., Inc., Chgo., 1991—; bd. dirs. Wesleyan Co., Inc., Chgo.; speaker Inst. for Internat. Rsch. and Promotion Mktg. Assn. Am., N.Y.C., 1991. Patentee in field. Cubmaster Boy Scouts Am., Chgo., 1991. Recipient Best Design award retail food category Nat. Flexible Packaging Assn., 1979, Indian statue Point of Purchase Advt. Inst., 1986, 87. Mem. Am. Def. Preparedness Assn., Exec. Club Chgo. (comms. com.) Internat. Platform Assn., Masons, Shriners, Sigma Chi. Republican. Episcopalian. Office: Creative Mktg Comms Inc 25 E Washington St Ste 1500 Chicago IL 60602-1804

SCHNEIDER-CRIEZIS, SUSAN MARIE, architect; b. St. Louis, Aug. 1, 1953; d. William Alfred and Rosemary Elizabeth (Fischer) Schneider; m. Demetrios Anthony Criezis, Nov. 24, 1978; children: Anthony, John and Andrew. BArch, U. Notre Dame, 1976; MArch, MIT, 1978. Registered architect, Wis. Project designer Eichstaedt Architects, Roselle, Ill., 1978-80, Solomon, Cordwell, Buenz & Assocs., Chgo., 1980-82; project architect Gelick, Foran Assocs., Chgo., 1982-83; asst. prof. Sch. Architecture U. Ill., Chgo., 1980-86; exec. v.p. Criezis Architects, Inc., Evanston, Ill., 1986—. Graham Found. grantee MIT, 1977, MIT scholar, 1976-78; Prestressed Concrete Inst. rsch. grantee, 1981. Mem. AIA, Chgo. Archtl. Club, Chgo. Women in Architecture, Am. Solar Energy Soc., NAFE, Jr. League Evanston, Evanston C. of C. Roman Catholic. Office: 1007 Church St Ste 101 Evanston IL 60201-5910

SCHNEIDERS, LOLITA, state legislator; b. Chgo., Mar. 3, 1931; d. Albert and Eve (Lis) Krell; m. Don A. Schneiders, 1954; children: Nancy, Donna, Lita Sue. Student, Mundelein Coll., 1948-50; BE, Wis. State U., Stevens Point, 1952. Cert. tchr. Wis., Minn., Mich. Wis. state assemblywoman Dist. 24, 1981—. Mem. AAUW, Bus. and Profl. Women, Met. Builders Aux., Omega Mu Chi. Home: W136 N8019 Eagle Ct Menomonee Falls WI 53051-2010 Office: Wis State Assembly State Capitol Madison WI 53702*

SCHNEIR, STEVEN RICHARD, psychiatrist; b. Akron, Ohio, Aug. 28, 1955; s. Edward Sol and Eileen (Welsh) S.; m. Dawn Elaine Pearlstein, May 28, 1978; children: Jordan, Katrina, Lauren. BA, Miami U., Oxford, Ohio, 1977; MD, Ohio State U., 1982. Diplomate Am. Bd. Psychiatry and Neurology. Intern Ohio State U. Hosp., Columbus, 1982-83, resident, 1983-86; cons. Athens (Ohio) Mental Health Ctr., 1984-86; pvt. practice Columbus, 1986—; clin. asst. prof. psychiatry Ohio State U., Columbus, 1986—; cons. psychiatrist Heritage House, Columbus, 1987-92; vice chmn. Mt. Carmel Med. Ctr., Columbus, 1987-92, chmn., 1992—. Mem. AMA, Am. Psychiat. Assn., Ohio Psychiat. Assn., Psychiat. Soc. Cen. Ohio, Ohio Med. Assn., Franklin County Med. Soc. Office: Cen Ohio Psychiat Assocs 6484 E Main St Reynoldsburg OH 43068-2349

SCHNIER, DAVID CHRISTIAN, marketing executive, author; b. Marion, Ohio, Aug. 26, 1942; s. Frederick George William and Dorothy LaVerne (Keller) S. AA, Sinclair Community Coll., Dayton, Ohio, 1976; BS in Edn., U. Dayton, 1979. Adminstr. various depts. VA Ctr., Dayton, 1964-66; tutorial dir. Sinclair Community Coll., 1975-81; pres. Go Blue Enterprises, Dayton, 1987—, Bobby Driscoll Fan Club, Dayton, 1988—; minister of music Ch. of the Holy Angels, Dayton, 1980—. Author: The Sea Eagle, 1951; soloist, Hope Luth. Ch., Dayton, 1995—; contbr. articles to profl. jours. Active Am. Gay/Lesbian Atheists, Inc., Freedom From Religion Found., Inc., Fundamentalists Anonymous; soloist St. Paul Evang. Ch., 1996—, St. Luke's United Ch. of Christ, Dayton, 1996—. Mem. ASPCA, People for Ethical Treatment of Animals, N.Am. Man/Boy Love Assn., Circus Hist. Soc., The Cousteau Soc., Greenpeace, Scrabble Players Club No. 215 (dir. Dayton chpt. 1983-85), Nat. Geographic Soc., Columbus Assn. Performing Arts, Fellowship Christian Magicians, Dayton Mus. Natural History (life). Roman Catholic. Home and Office: 601 Bowen St Dayton OH 45410-2422

SCHNOBRICH, ROGER WILLIAM, lawyer; b. New Ulm, Minn., Dec. 21, 1929; s. Arthur George and Amanda (Reinhart) S.; m. Angeline Ann Schmitz, Jan. 21, 1961; children: Julie A. Johnson, Jennifer L. Holmers, Kathryn M. Kubinski, Karen L. Holetz. BBA, U. Minn., 1952, JD, 1954. Bar: Minn. 1954. Assoc. Fredrikson and Byron, Mpls., 1956-58; pvt. practice Mpls., 1958-60; ptnr. Popham Haik, Schnobrich & Kaufman, Mpls., 1960—; bd. dirs. numerous corps., Mpls. With U.S. Army, 1954-56. Mem. ABA, Minn. Bar Assn., Hennepin County Bar Assn., Order of Coif, Law Rev. Roman Catholic. Home: 530 Waycliff Dr N Wayzata MN 55391-1385 Office: Popham Haik Schnobrich & Kaufman 3300 Piper Jaffray Tower 222 S 9th St Minneapolis MN 55402-3389

SCHNOES, MARK ALLAN, middle school educator, baseball coach; b. Cherokee, Iowa, Jan. 19, 1956; s. John Alfred and Kathryn (Traver) S.; m. Pamela Jean Larson, Nov. 17, 1954; children: Michael Traver, Sara Ann, Amy Beth. BA, Northwestern Coll., Orange City, Iowa, 1979. Cert. tchr., Iowa. Tchr. South O'Brien High Sch., Paullina, Iowa, 1979-94; mid. sch. tchr. O'Brien Mid. Sch., Primghar, Iowa, 1994—. Steward Zion Luth. Ch., 1992-93; bd. dirs. Paullina Golf Course, 1992-96. Recipient Coaching Merit award Northwestern Coll. Alumni Club, 1986. Mem. Iowa Baseball Coaches Assn., Paullina Edn. Assn. (negotiations com. 1988-89, 91-92). Republican. Home: PO Box 77 107 S Willow Paullina IA 51012-0077 Office: South O'Brien Mid Sch PO Box P Primghar IA 51245

SCHNOOR, JERALD LEE, environmental engineering educator; b. Davenport, Iowa, Aug. 26, 1950; s. Vincent Leo and Emma Clara (Gross) S.; m. Jana Lynn Johnson, Feb. 26, 1972; children—Benjamin Carl, Britta Anne. B.S., Iowa State U., 1972; M.S., U. Tex., 1974, Ph.D., 1975. Registered profl. engr. Iowa. Process engr Procter & Gamble Co., Cin., 1972-73; chem. engr. EPA, Dallas, summer 1974; NSF postdoctoral fellow Manhattan Coll., N.Y.C., 1976; asst. to assoc. prof. U. Iowa, Iowa City, 1977-83, prof. environ. engring., 1983—, chmn. civil and environ. engring. dept., 1985-90; cons. EPA, Washington, 1982—, Homestake Mining Co., Lead, S.D., 1983—, Monsanto/St. Louis, 1982-83, Battelle Northwest Labs., Richland, Washington, 1982-83, Calif. Air Rsch. Bd., Sacramento, 1986—; exch. scientist NAS/NRC, Czechoslovakia, 1991. Author: Environmental Modeling, 1996; editor: Modeling Total Acid Precipitation, 1985, Environmental Science and Technology, 1992—; assoc. editor Environ. Sci. and Tech., 1990; contbr. articles to profl. jours. U. Iowa scholar, 1981-84; fellow NSF, 1976, ASCE, 1975; EPA grantee, 1978-90; recipient Merit award Environ. div. Am. Chem. Soc., 1981, Walter L. Huber Rsch. prize ASCE, 1985, Profl. Progress in Engring. award Iowa State U., 1989. Mem. NRC Panel Lake Acidification, Water Pollution Control Fedn. (exec. com. 1984-89—, editor rsch. jour. 1989-91), Iowa Groundwater Assn. (pres. 1985), Am. Acad. Environ. Engrs. (diplomate). Democrat. Lutheran. Home: 18 Heather Dr Iowa City IA 52245-3227 Office: U Iowa Dept Civil And Engring Iowa City IA 52242

SCHNUCK, CRAIG D., grocery stores company executive; b. 1948. MBA, Cornell U., 1971. With Schnuck Markets, Inc., Hazelwood, Mo., 1971—, v.p., 1975-76, exec. v.p., sec., 1976-83, pres., chief exec. officer, 1983—, also bd. dirs. Office: Schnuck Markets Inc 11420 Lackland Rd Saint Louis MO 63146-6928

SCHNUCK, SCOTT C., grocery store executive; b. 1950. Pres., COO Schnuck Markets, Inc., St. Louis. Office: Schnuck Markets Inc 11420 Lackland Rd Saint Louis MO 63146-3559*

SCHNUCK, TERRY EDWARD, lawyer; b. St. Louis, Oct. 10, 1952; s. Donald Otto and Doris Irene (Letson) S.; m. Sally Barrows Braxton, May 24, 1980; children: Hadley Braxton, Terry Edward Jr. BA in Econs., Tulane U., 1975; MBA, Washington U., St. Louis, 1980; JD, St. Louis U., 1980. Bar: Mo. 1980. Assoc. Greensfelder, Hemker, Wiese, Gale & Chappelow, St. Louis, 1980-84; with Schnuck Markets Inc., Bridgeton, Mo., 1980—, chief legal counsel, sec.; bd. dirs. Arts and Edn. Coun. of Greater St. Louis, 1991—. Bd. dirs. Urban League of Met. St. Louis, 1987—. Mem. ABA, Mo. Bar Assn., Bar Assn. of Met. St. Louis, Better Bus. Bur. (bd. dirs. 1990—), Mo. Retailers Assn. (exec. bd. 1984—), Beta Theta Pi. Republican. Presbyterian. Club: Bellerive Country (St. Louis). Office: Schnuck Markets Inc 11420 Lackland Rd Saint Louis MO 63146-6928*

SCHOBER, WILLIAM RUDOLPH (BUD), retired physical therapist; b. Clear Lake, Iowa, Nov. 18, 1933; s. William Christian and Catherine Ellen (Reents) S.; m. Betty Lee Ballew, June 15, 1955 (div. May 1981); children: Julie Ann, Patty Lee; m. Carol Claudette Auringer, June 1, 1982. AA, Mason City (Iowa.) Jr. Coll., 1958; BA in Biology, Wartburg Coll., Waverly, Iowa, 1959; Cert. in Phys. Therapy, Herman Sch. Phys. Therapy, Houston, 1960. Lic. phys. therapist, Iowa; cert. respiratory therapy technician Nat. Bd. Respiratory Therapy. Phys. therapist Younker Meml. Rehab. Ctr., Des Moines, 1960-61, Cedar Valley Hosp., Charles City, Iowa, 1961-62; adminstr. Americana Nursing Ctr., Mason City, Iowa, 1962-64; ops. dir. Americana Nursing Ctr., Monticello, Ill., 1962-64; ptnr., co-owner Rehab Cons., Mason City, 1964-68, Schober Grant & Assocs., Charles City, Iowa, 1968-96; pres. Spl. Med. Svcs. Corp., Charles City, 1968-96; co-dir. phys. therapy dept., respiratory therapy dept. Floyd County Meml. Hosp., Charles City, 1968-96; co-dir. cardio-pulmonary dept. St. Joseph Cmty. Hosp., New Hampton, Iowa, 1968-96, Floyd County Meml. Hosp.; past pres., bd. dirs. Iowa Phys. Therapy Examining Bd., Des Moines, 1968-71; co-owner C&W Investments, Charles City and Clear Lake, Iowa. Contbr. articles to profl. jours. Pres. Charles City YMCA, 1971, 72, 91, 93, bd. dirs., 1971—, Family YMCA Found., 1993—. With USN, 1952-56. Angus McNider scholar, 1958. Mem. Am. Phys. Therapy Assn. (Iowa chpt. dist. chmn., bd. dirs.), Nat. Bd. Respiratory Therapy, Beta Beta Beta. Republican. Methodist. Home: 206 Park Dr Charles City IA 50616 Office: Special Med Svcs Corp 800 11th St Charles City IA 50616

SCHOBINGER, RANDY ARTHUR, state legislator. Student, Minot State U., 1991-96. Warehouseman Minot; senator State of N.D., Bismarck; Movers, Inc.; vice chmn. transp. com. State Senate of N.D., mem. edn. com.; endorsed candidate of the N.D. Repub. Party for State Treasurer, 1996. Office: ND State Capitol 600 East Blvd Bismarck ND 58505

SCHOECK, RICHARD J(OSEPH), English and humanities scholar; b. N.Y.C., Oct. 10, 1920; s. Gustav J. and Frances M. (Kuntz) S.; m. Reta R. Haberer, 1945 (div. 1976); children: Eric R., Christine C., Jennifer A.; m. Megan S. Lloyd, Feb. 19, 1977. M.A., Princeton U., 1949, Ph.D., 1949. Instr. English Cornell U., 1949-55; asst. prof., then assoc. prof. U. Notre Dame, 1955-61; prof. English U. Toronto, 1961-71; head dept. English St. Michael's Coll., 1965-70; prof. vernacular lit. Pontifical Inst. Mediaeval Studies, Toronto, 1964-71; dir. rsch. activities Folger Shakespeare Libr., also dir. Folger Inst. Renaissance and 18th Century Studies, 1970-74; adj. prof. English Cath. U. Am., 1972; prof. English, medieval and renaissance studies U. Md., 1974-75; prof. English and humanities U. Colo., Boulder, 1975-89, prof. emeritus, 1987—; chmn. dept. integrated studies U. Colo., 1976-79; chmn. comparative lit., 1983-84; prof. Anglistik Universität Trier, 1987-90, head dept., 1988-89; adj. prof. English U. Kans., Lawrence, 1990—; Vincent J. Flynn prof. Letters Coll. St. Thomas, 1969; vis. prof. Princeton U., 1964, U. Dallas, 1985; vis. fellow Inst. Advanced Studies in Humanities, Edinburgh, 1984-85; vis. scholar Corpus Christi Coll., Oxford, 1994; fellow Assn. Advancement Edn., 1952-53, Yale U., 1959-60, Can. Coun. 1967-68, Ctr. for the Book, Brit. Libr., 1995-96; cons. NEH: bd. dirs. Natural Law Inst. U. Notre Dame; advisor Italian Acad. for Advanced Studies in Am., 1993. Author: The Achievement of Thomas More, 1976, Intertexuality and Renaissance Texts, 1984, Erasmus Grandescens, 1988 (poems) The Eye of a Traveller, 1992, The Knights Book, 1993; contbr. numerous articles, papers, revs. to jours. and mags.; editor: Delehaye's Legends of the Saints, 1961, Editing 16th Century Texts, 1966 (Roger Ascham), The Scholemaster, 1966, Shakespeare Quar., 1972-74, Acta Conventus Neo-Latini Bononiensis, 1985; gen. editor: The Confutation of Tyndale, 3 vols., 1973; co-editor: Voices of Literature, 2 vols., 1964, 66, Chaucer Criticism, 2 vols, 1960, 61, Style, Rhetoric and Rhythym: Essays by M.W. Croll, 1966, Acta Conventus Neo-Latini Torontonensis, 1991; former gen. editor: Patterns of Literary Criticism; spl. editor Canada vol. Rev. Nat. Literatures, 1977, Sir Thomas Browne and the Republic of Letters, 1982, A Special Number of English Language Notes, 1982; gen. editor (series) Renaissance Masters, 1992—; mem. editl. bds. profl. jours. Served with U.S. Army, 1940-46. Guggenheim Found. fellow, 1968-69, Fulbright fellow, 1983; recipient Centennial medal U. Colo., 1976; grantee: Can. Coun., UNESCO, Am. Coun. Learned Socs., U. Toronto, U. Colo. Fellow Royal Soc. Can., Royal Hist. Soc.; mem. Internat. Assn. Neo-Latin Studies (pres. 1976-79), MLA, Renaissance Soc. Am., PEN (N.Y.), Can. Humanities Assn., Internat. Assn. U. Profs. English, Assn. Can. Studies in U.S. Home: 232 Dakota St Lawrence KS 66046-4710

SCHOEDINGER, DAVID STANTON, funeral director; b. Columbus, Ohio, Nov. 27, 1942; s. John Frederick and Juliet Ellen (Stanton) S.; m. Jeanne Winfield Northrup, Dec. 18, 1965; children: Michael, Kellie, Kevin. BA, U. Colo., 1964; postgrad., Cin. Coll. Mortuary Sci., 1965. Cert. funeral service practitioner; lic. funeral dir. and embalmer. Chmn. bd. Schoedinger Funeral Svc., Columbus, Ohio, 1965—; pres. Nat. Selected Morticians, 1992-93, Nat. Security Reassurance Co.; sec., bd. dirs. Consumer Info. Bur. Funeral Svc., Evanston, Ill., 1976-80; mem. Young Pres. Orgn., 1983-93, treas., 1989-93. Contbr. articles to textbooks and mags. Bd. trustees Cin. Coll. Mortuary Sci., 1977-86; bd. dirs. Allied Meml. Council Ohio, 1985-87; pres. Hospice Adv. Council, Columbus Bd. Health, 1983; pres., bd. trustees The Community health and Nursing Service, 1971-72; bd. trustees Children's Hosp., 1972-84, exec. com., 1975-77; bd. trustees Columbus Zool. Park Assn., 1967-86, exec. com., 1970-74; co-chmn. Burbank Sch. Parent Adv. Council, 1977-78; bd. trustees, exec. com. Hospice Columbus, 1978-81. Recipient Disting. Alumni award Cin.; named one of Ten Outstanding Young Citizens of Columbus, Ohio, 1976. Mem. Nat. Selected Morticians (regional chmn. Ohio, W.Va. 1977-78, bd. dirs., pres. 1992-93), Ohio Funeral Dirs. Assn. (pres. 1986-87, bd. dirs. 1980-88), Nat. Funeral Dirs. Assn., Cen. Ohio Funeral Dirs. Assn., Ohio Hist. Soc., Nat. Wildlife Fedn., Am. First Day Cover Soc., Royal Order Scotland, Upper Arlington Civic Assn., Ohio State U. Alumni Assn., Columbus Acad. Alumni Assn. (bd. trustees 1972-76), Jaycees (past v.p. 1969-70), Kappa Sigma, Phi Sigma Eta, Mu Sigma Alpha, U. Colo. Alumni Assn., Young Pres. Orgn. (treas. 1987-88), Capital Club, Scioto Country Club, City Club, Upper Arlington Booster Club, Club of Ohio State U. (pres.), Masons (hon.), Shriners. Republican. Presbyterian. Home: 2470 Stonehaven Ct S Columbus OH 43220-2854 Office: Schoedinger Funeral Svc 229 E State St Columbus OH 43215-4330

SCHOEFFEL, STEVEN SCOT, policy analyst; b. Alton, Ill., Jan. 29, 1971; s. Richard D. and Cynthia L. (Perica) S. MusB, So. Ill. U., 1994. Campaign coord. Citizens for Prehn, Alton, 1994; doorkeeper of the house Ill. Ho. of Reps., Springfield, Ill., 1995; policy analyst Office of the Spkr., Springfield, 1995—; panelist So. Ill. Rep. Tng. Seminar, Collinsville, Ill. Vice chmn. So. Ill. U.-Edwardsville Coll. Reps., 1992-94; dep. registrar Madison County (Ill.) Rep. Party, 1994, Alton Rep. precinct committeeman, 1994-95; chmn. Letters to the Editor, Citizens for Towse for Mayor, Alton, 1993; mem. Rep. Nat. Com. Mem. NRA. Presbyterian. Office: House Rep Policy 402 N Stratton Bldg Springfield IL 62706

SCHOELD, CONSTANCE JERRINE, financial planner; b. Wichita, Kans., July 20, 1935; d. Joe Delos and Volna May (Liston) Lumbert; m. Edmund Allan Schoeld, Oct. 4, 1953 (div. Dec. 1974); children: Nancy Ann., Elsa Charlene, Jennie Marie, Brian Shelton, Richard Zweibruck. Student, St. Olaf Coll., 1953-54, Lindenwood Coll., 1960-62, U. Mich., 1967-68, Harper Jr. Coll., 1970. Cert. fin. planner. Mgr. Walden Books, Schaumburg, Ill., 1972-74; owner Books, Etc., Mt. Prospect, Ill., 1974-77; sales rep. Fawcett Books/CBS, N.Y.C., 1977-78, Lawyers Cooperative Pub., Rochester, N.Y., 1978-83; owner Associated Lawyers Svc., Palatine, Ill., 1982-86; broker, v.p. investments A.G. Edwards & Sons, Aurora and Roselle, Ill., 1983—. Sec. Northwest Mental Health/Retardation Ctr., Arlington Hts., Ill., 1971, Mental Health Ctr., Elk Grove/Schaumburg Twp., Ill., 1970-72, vice chmn., bd. dirs.; v.p. PTA, St. Charles, Mo., 1964; pres. St. Charles coun. Girls Scouts U.S., 1965-66; mem. com. Dist. 54 Bd. Edn., Schaumburg, 1969-72; bd. dirs. Mental Health Ctr. St. Charles, 1963-66, Mental Health Ctr. Schaumburg Twp., chmn., 1969-72; bd. dirs. Planetary Studies Found., 1992—, Am. Cancer Soc., 1993—. Named one of Outstanding Young Women Am., 1964. Mem. Internat. Bd. Cert. Fin. Planners, Internat. Soc. Retirement Planners, LWV (bd. dirs. St. Charles 1964-66, Hoffman Estates-Schaumburg 1969-71), DAR (Outstanding Mem. award 1964), Greater O'Hare Assn. (bd. dirs. 1990-93, ambassador, co-chmn. 1989), Nat. Assn. Women in Careers, NAFE, N.W. Bus. and Profl. Women (rec. sec. 1988-89, asst. treas. 1989-90), Hoffman Estates C. of C. (chmn. women's coun. 1990-94), Rotary, Epsilon Sigma Alpha. Republican. Episcopalian. Office: AG Edwards & Sons 1350 Lake St Roselle IL 60172-3370

SCHOELL, RICHARD MARTIN, university administrator; b. Burlington, Iowa, Feb. 28, 1953; s. Richard Milton and Juanita Delores (Simms) S.; m. Rebecca Jean Rath, Jan. 28, 1978; children: Elizabeth Ann, William Walker. BA, U. Iowa, 1975, MA, 1976. State govt. rels. mgr. Household Internat., Prospect Heights, Ill., 1977-79; rsch. assoc. Ill. Commn. Intergovtl. Cooperation, Springfield, 1979-82; dir. Washington office Ill. State Legis., 1983-87; dir. fed. rels. U. Ill., Urbana-Champaign, 1987—; mem. exec. com. Nat. Conf. State Legislators, Denver, 1986-87; bd. dirs. Internat. Arid Lands Consortium, Tucson. Bd. dirs., sec. Windsor Park Home Owners Assn., Champaign, 1988-89. Recipient Disting. Pub. Svc. award U.S. Army Corps Engrs., 1991. Mem. Nat. Assn. State Univ. and Land Grant Colls. (bd. dirs. 1994-95, co-chair coun. govt. affairs 1994-95). Episcopalian. Home: 802 Park Lane Dr Champaign IL 61820 Office: U Ill 441 Henry Adminstrn Blvd 506 S Wright St Urbana IL 61801

SCHOEN, CARL PATRICK, mathematics educator; b. Rawlins, Wyo., Nov. 18, 1947; s. Frank Carl and Annalee (Bauer) S. BS in Physics, USAF Acad., 1970; MS in Math., U. Wyo., 1979, PhD in Math., 1985. Commd. 2d lt. USAF, 1970, advanced through grades to capt., 1973; assigned to Vietnam, 1973; ret., 1977; instr. math. U. Wis., Eau Claire, 1982-85, asst. prof., 1985-89, assoc. prof., 1989—. Contbr. articles to profl. jours. Mem. Math. Assn. Am., Epsilon Tau Sigma (faculty advisor 1988—). Libertarian. Home: 2113 Providence Ct Eau Claire WI 54703-4104 Office: U Wis Dept Math Eau Claire WI 54701

SCHOEN, CHARLES JUDD, service executive; b. Owatonna, Minn., Sept. 6, 1943; s. John Nicholas and Dorothy Georgine (Jacobson) S.; m. Birgitta Marianne Haggren, Dec. 15, 1972; 1 child, Vanja Karina. BA, U. Minn., 1965. Stockbroker Harris, Upham and Co., Mpls., 1967-70; with Litton Industries, Sydney, Australia, 1970-71; gen. mgr. Westinghouse Electric, Mpls., 1971-77; pres. Westco Security, Mpls., 1977—, Automatic Alarm Corp., 1986—; bd. chmn. SpyderNet, Minn., 1993. With USN, 1966-67. Mem. Ctrl. Sta. Alarm Assn. (chmn. polit. action com.), Assn. Former Intelligence Officers. Office: Westco Security 401 Lake St E Wayzata MN 55391-1610

SCHOENBECK, LEE, state legislator. Senator S.D. State Dist. 1; govt. ops. and audit com. S.D. State Senate, jud. com., local govt. com.; pvt. practice law. Address: PO Box 181 Webster SD 57274

SCHOENBECK, PAUL JOHN, transportation executive; b. Hinsdale, Ill., June 3, 1959; s. Delbert Louis and Joyce Marie (Kolzow) S. Pres., owner Uni-Carrier Inc., Willowbrook, Ill., 1977—; commr. Tri-State Fire Prot. Dist., 1996—. Asst. fin. sec. Good Shepherd Ch., Downers Grove, Ill., 1984-87; pres., bd. trustees Clarendon Hgts. Fire Dept. Mem. Am. Mktg. Assn. (cons. 1985—), Fleet Owners (Community Svc. awards 1985, 86, 88, 89), Inc. Forum, Willowbrook C. of C., Ill. C. of C. Lutheran. Home: 218 Brookside Ln # C Clarendon Hills IL 60514-2907 Office: Uni Carrier Inc 7886 S Quincy St Hinsdale IL 60521-5534

SCHOENBERG, JEFFREY M., state legislator; b. Chgo., July 28, 1959. BA, Columbia U., 1983, Rugers U. Ill. state rep. Dist. 58, 1991—; mem. aging com. appropriations, edn. fin. Ill. Ho. Reps., environ. and energy, health care, human svcs. com.; dir. Roosevelt Ctr. for Am. Policy Studies. Democrat. Home: 3114 Hartzell St Evanston IL 60201-1126*

SCHOENBERG, MARLENE COHEN, speech pathologist; b. Bronx, N.Y., May 7, 1950; d. Louis and Rose Peskin (Levine) Cohen; m. Michael Schoenberg, Jan. 23, 1972; children: Jordan, Naomi. BA in Speech Lang. Pathology, CCNY, 1972; EdM in Comm. Disorders, Boston U., 1973. Registered speech pathologist, Minn. Speech clinician Peabody (Mass.) Pub. Schs., 1973-75; pathologist speech/lang. St. Paul Rehab. Ctr., 1975-86; pres., cons. ETHCOM, St. Paul, 1987—; mgr., dir., founder Yiddishe Foldsmenshn Klezmer Bank, St. Paul, 1984-94; instr. pronunciation Minn. C.C. Sys., St. Paul, 1992—. Author: Pronunciation for Career Growth, 1988, 95, Pronunciation for Academic Success, 1990; prodr., narrator (video) Understanding Accented Speakers, 1986, Yiddish Songs for a New Generation. Vol. Ctr. for Victims of Torture, Mpls., 1990-93. Grantee Minn. State Arts Bd., 1986. Mem. ASTD, NAFE, Am. Speech Hearing Assn. (cert.), Minn. World Trade Ctr., Twin Cities Speech Hearing Assn. (pres. 1984). Democrat. Jewish. Office: ETHCOM 411 Warwick Saint Paul MN 55105

SCHOENBURG, BERNARD ALAN, reporter, columnist; b. Chgo., June 26, 1954; s. William B. and Edith (Youngmann) S.; m. Kim Susan Yaffe, Dec. 14, 1985; children: Samuel Ernest, Elyse Lauren. BJ, U. Ill., 1976. Reporter, polit. columnist Bloomington (Ill.) Pantagraph, 1976-86; reporter, supr. AP, Chgo., 1986-90; reporter State Jour.-Register, Springfield, Ill., 1990—; also polit. columnist, 1992—. Jewish. Office: State Jour-Register PO Box 219 Springfield IL 62705-0219

SCHOENE, KATHLEEN SNYDER, lawyer; b. Glen Ridge, N.J., July 24, 1953; d. John Kent and Margaret Ann (Bronder) Snyder. BA, Grinnell Coll., 1974; MS, So. Conn. State Coll., 1976; JD, Washington U., St. Louis, 1982. Bar: Mo. 1982, U.S. Dist. Ct. (we. and ea. dists.) Mo. 1982, Ill. 1983. Head libr. Mo. Hist. Soc., St. Louis, 1976-79; assoc. Peper, Martin, Jensen, Maichel & Hetlage, St. Louis, 1982-88, ptnr., 1989—; bd. dirs. Legal Svcs. of Eastern Mo. Author: (with others) Missouri Corporation Law and Practice, 1985; contbr. articles to profl. jours. Trustee Grinnell (Iowa) Coll., ex officio voting mem., 1991-93; bd. dirs. Jr. League St. Louis, 1995-96, Leadership Ctr. Greater St. Louis, 1995—. Mem. ABA, Nat. Health Lawyers Assn., Nat. Assn. Bond Lawyers, The Mo. Bar, Ill. State Bar Assn., Bar Assn. Met. St. Louis (treas. 1991-92, sec. 1992-93, v.p. 1993-94, pres.-elect 1994-95, pres. 1995-96, chairperson small bus. com. 1987-88, mem. exec. com. 1988-96, chairperson bus. law sect. 1988-89, mem. exec. com. young lawyers sect. 1988-90), St. Louis Bar Found. (bd. dirs. 1994—, v.p. 1995-96, pres. 1996—). Home: 7824 Cornell Ave Saint Louis MO 63130-3701 Office: Peper Martin Jensen Maichel & Hetlage 720 Olive St Fl 24 Saint Louis MO 63101-2338

SCHOENE, MARY PATRICIA, artist; b. St. Louis, Apr. 9, 1919; d. Joseph Valerian and Lillian Mary (Kearney) S. BS in English, Washington U., St. Louis, MA in English; art student, Corcoran Art Sch., Washington, D.C., St. Louis Sch. Fine Arts, St. Louis U. Art Sch. Ordained min. Ind. Spiritualist Assn., 1987. Dir. pub. rels. Gen. Contract Corp., St. Louis, 1959-61; tchr. English Pontbonne Coll., St. Louis, 1961-62; sec., asst. Ctrl. West End Bank, St. Louis, 1965-74; sec. Mo. State Employment, St. Louis, 1975-84; freelance artist St. Louis, 1984—. Prin. works include portrait of Edgar Mitchell, Vincent Price; author: (poem) Move Among Stars, 1975, and others. With USN, 1943-45. Mem. Theosophical Soc. (St. Louis lodge pres. 1992-94, lectr.), Amnesty Internat. (freedom writer).

SCHOENEBERG, JOYCE EILEEN, secondary school biology educator; b. St. Louis, Jan. 13, 1944; d. John F. and Sophie A. (Nachowiak) Zielinski; m. Carl M. Schoeneberg, Dec. 18, 1971; children: C. Jason, Jennifer. BA in Zoology, Washington U., St. Louis, 1965; MEd in Biology, So. Ill. U., 1972. Cert. secondary biology tchr., Mo. Life sci. tchr. Normandy (Mo.) Sch. Dist., 1965-69; biology tchr. Hazelwood (Mo.) Sch. Dist., 1969-73, Parkway Sch. Dist., St. Louis County, Mo., 1983—; sci. chair Parkway Sch. Dist., St. Louis County, Mo., 1992—. Mem. Sci. Tchrs. Mo., Nat. Assn. Biology Tchrs., Phi Mu (pres. 1964-65). Methodist. Office: Parkway N High Sch 12860 Fee Fee Rd Saint Louis MO 63146-4431

SCHOENECKER, MARTIN J., design engineer; b. Milw., Oct. 23, 1959. BSME, Marguette U., 1983. Design engr. Allise-Chalmers, Appleton, Wis., 1983-90, Waukesha (Wis.) Engring., 1990—. Mem. Soc. Automotive Engrs.

SCHOENFELDER, JOHN ROBERT, pharmaceutical executive; b. Cedar Rapids, Iowa, July 2, 1950; s. Robert Carl and Mary Margaret (Mahan) S.; m. Carol Ann Barnes, June 21, 1975; children: Brian, Jason, Laura. BA, Cornell Coll., 1972; MS, U. N.C., 1974, PhD, 1981. Sr. statistician Burroughs Wellcome Co., Research Triangle Park, N.C., 1980-88; assoc. dir., biostats. Glaxo Inc., Research Triangle Park, 1988-90, Pharmaria, Inc., Dublin, Ohio, 1990-93; dir. biometrics Pharmaria, Inc., Dublin, 1993—. Co-author: Presentation of Clinical Data, 1989, Data Collection Forms in Clinical Trials, 1991. Mem. Am. Statis. Assn. (pres. N.C. chpt. 1989-90), Inst. Math. Stats., Biometric Soc., Drug Info. Assn., Ctrl. Ohio SAS Users Group. Home: 6378 Newgrange Dr Dublin OH 43016 Office: Pharmacia Inc 7001 Post Rd Dublin OH 43017

SCHOENHARD, WILLIAM CHARLES, JR., health care executive; b. Kansas City, Mo., Sept. 26, 1949; s. William Charles S. and Joyce Evans (Thornsberry) Bell; m. Kathleen Ann Klosterman, June 3, 1972; children: Sarah Elizabeth, Thomas William. BS in Pub. Adminstrn., U. Mo., 1971; M of Health Adminstrn. with honors, Washington U., St. Louis, 1975. V.p., dir. gen. svcs. Deaconess Hosp., St. Louis, 1975-78; assoc. exec. dir. St. Mary's Health Ctr., St. Louis, 1978-81; exec. dir. Arcadia Valley Hosp., Pilot Knob, Mo., 1981-82, St. Joseph Health Ctr., St. Charles, Mo., 1982-86; exec. v.p., COO SSM Health Care Sys., St. Louis, 1986—; bd. dirs. Mark Twain Bank, 1986—. Contbr. articles to profl. jours. Pres. Shaw Neighborhood Improvement Assn., St. Louis, 1979-80; mem. adv. bd. St. Louis chpt. Lifeseekers, 1985-94; mem. bd. mgrs. Kirkwood-Webster (Mo.) YMCA, 1990—, sec., 1996—; mem. bd. mgrs. Nat. Affairs Round Table Sen. Christopher Bond, St. Louis, 1990; mem. nat. adv. coun. Healthcare Forum, 1992—; mem. healthcare adv. bd. Sanford Brown Colls., 1992-94; mem. leadership excellence com. Cath. Health Assn. U.S., 1993—; mem. steering com. Greater St. Louis Healthcare Alliance, 1994-95; bd. dirs. St. Andrews Mgmt. Svcs., Inc., 1994-95. With USN, 1971-72, Vietnam. Fellow Am. Coll. Health Care Execs.; mem. Mid-Am. Transplant Assn. (bd. dirs. 1995—), Am. Legion, Navy League U.S., Univ. Club St. Louis, Phi Eta Sigma, Pi Omicron Sigma, Delta Upsilon, Delta Sigma Pi. Roman Catholic. Home: 420 Fairwood Ln Saint Louis MO 63122-4429 Office: SSM Health Care System 477 N Lindbergh Blvd Saint Louis MO 63141-7813

SCHOENROCK, TRACY ALLEN, airline pilot, securities trader; b. Oshkosh, Wis., Jan. 11, 1960; s. Elder Roy and Shirley Mae (Rutz) S.; m. Kathleen Mary Neumann, Oct. 8, 1983; children: Amanda Beth, Veronica Grace, Shannon Traci. BS in Geography summa cum laude, U. Wis., Oshkosh, 1982. Charter pilot Basler Airlines, Oshkosh, 1977-82; pilot Simmons Airlines, Marquette, Mich., 1982-84, Northwest Airlines, St. Paul, 1984—; owner flt. sch. and charter operation. Lutheran. Home and Office: 1345 Maricopa Dr Oshkosh WI 54904-8150

SCHOETTLE, FREDERICK JOHN, insurance company executive; b. Indpls., July 6, 1939; s. Harold Francis and Jeanette F (Sims) S.; m. Sonja Fay O'Brien, Nov. 30, 1957; children: William H. Christopher P., Lora M, Karen A. John F. Grad. high sch., Indpls., 1957. Mgr. mortgage loan United Home Life Ins. Co., Greenwood, Ind., 1957-75; with sales dept. Townsend Bus. Forms, Indpls., 1975-79; v.p. George M. Bindner Assocs., Indpls., 1979-84; sec. United Home Life Ins. Co., Greenwood, 1984—, sr. v.p., 1987—; bd. dirs. United Home Life Ins. Co., Greenwood. Bd. dirs. Cath. Social Svcs., Wishing Wells, Inc. Mem. Nat. Assn. Life Underwriters, KC. Roman Catholic. Home: 6020 Shelby St Indianapolis IN 46227-4780 Office: United Home Life Ins Co 1499 Windhorst Way Ste 200 Greenwood IN 46143-8800

SCHOFIELD, EILEEN KATHRYN, editor; b. Worcester, Mass., Apr. 6, 1939; d. Thomas James and Margaret Mary (Steele) Carroll; m. Edmund Acton Schofield, May 28, 1966 (div. Oct. 1971); m. Theodore Mitchell Barkley, Feb. 7, 1981. AB, Clark U., 1960; MS, Columbia U., 1966. Rsch. asst. Harvard U., Cambridge, Mass., 1960-64; rsch. assoc., dept. zoology Ohio State U., Columbus, 1966-71; herbarium supr. N.Y. Botanical Garden, Bronx, 1971-81; assoc. editor, agrl. experiment sta. Kans. State U., Manhattan, 1981—. Author and illustrator: Plants of the Galapagos Islands, 1984, Roadside Wildflowers of the Southern Great Plains, 1991; illustrator: Field Guide to the Common Weeds of Kansas, 1983; assoc. editor: Brittonia, 1979-81, Flora of the Great Plains, 1981-85; contbg. editor: Curriculum Innovations, Inc., 1979-82; contbr. articles to profl. jours. Mem. Manhattan Arts Coun., Kans., 1982—. Grantee Nat. Museum Act, 1970; assistantship in taxonomy, N.Y. Botanical Garden, Bronx. 1964-66; scholarship Clark U., Worcester, 1956-60. Mem. Am. Soc. Plant Taxonomists, Bot. Soc. Am., Coun. Biology Editors, Assn. Women in Sci. (sec. Manhattan chpt. 1992-94), AAUW (sec. Manhattan chpt. 1989-90), Kans. Wildflower Soc., Audubon Soc., Torrey Bot. Club (treas. 1978-79). Office: Dept Communications Kans State U Manhattan KS 66506-3402

SCHOLER, SUE WYANT, state legislator; b. Topeka, Oct. 20, 1936; d. Zint Elwin and Virginia Louise (Achenbach) Wyant; m. Charles Frey Scholer, Jan. 27, 1957; children: Elizabeth Scholer Truelove, Charles W., Virginia M. Scholer McCal. Student, Kans. State U., 1954-56. Draftsman The Farm Clinic, West Lafayette, Ind., 1978-79; assessor Wabash Twp., West Lafayette, 1979-84; commr. Tippecanoe County, Lafayette, Ind., 1984-90; state rep. Dist. 26 Ind. Statehouse, Indpls., 1990—; asst. minority whip, 1992-94, majority whip, 1994—; mem. Tippecanoe County Area Plan Commn., 1984-90. Bd. dirs. Crisis Ctr., Lafayette, 1984-89, Tippecanoe Arts Fedn., 1990—, United Way, Lafayette, 1990-93; mem. Lafayette Conv. and Visitors Bur., 1988-90. Recipient Salute to Women Govt. and Politics award, 1986, United Sr. Action award, Outstanding Legislator award, 1993, Small Bus. Champion award, 1995, Ind. Libr. Fedn. Legislator award, 1995. Mem. Ind. Assn. County Commrs. (treas. 1990), Assn. Ind. Counties (legis. com. 1988-90), Greater Lafayette C. of C. (ex-officio bd. 1984-90), Sagamore Bus. and Profl. Women, LWV, P.E.O., Purdue Women's Club (past treas.), Kappa Kappa Kappa (past pres. Epsilon chpt.), Delta Delta Delta (past pres. alumnae, house corp. treas.). Republican. Presbyterian. Home: 807 Essex St West Lafayette IN 47906-1534 Office: Indiana Statehouse Rm 3A-4 Indianapolis IN 46204

SCHOLIN, RAY ALBERT, printing company executive; b. Waterloo, Iowa, Apr. 20, 1924; s. Carl Albert and Ruth Beatta (Worley) S.; m. Virginia Lena Youngman, Sept. 9, 1952; children: Suzanne, Marianne, James, Christopher. Student, U. Mo., 1942, 46-48. Pres. Scholin Bros. Printing Co., Inc., St. Louis, 1948—; pres. C. Albert Scholin & Sons Music Publs., St. Louis, 1955-58, Sho-Pac Packaging Co., St. Louis, 1960-70, Whitehead & Sholin Advt., St. Louis, 1960-80, Jubilee Packaging Co., St. Louis, 1991—; chmn. bd. Vi-Jon Printing and Packaging, Fenton, Mo., 1991—; bd. dirs. Vi-Jon Labs., St. Louis. Pres. Webster Groves C. of C., St. Louis County, 1972; ruling elder Trinity Presbyn. Ch., 1956—; bd. dirs. Camp Wyman for At Risk Children, 1988—; bd. dirs. Eden Theol. Sem., Webster Groves, 1993. With USAF, 1943-45. Named Bus. Person of Yr., St. Louis County League C. of C., 1990. Mem. Master Printers St. Louis (bd. dirs., pres. 1975-85), Printing Industry St. Louis (pres. 1979), Daniel Webster Soc. of Webster U. (bd. dirs. 1990—), Kiwanis (pres. Hampton-Tower Grove chpt. 1952, Ambassador award 1991). Home: 3002 Frisco Hill Rd Imperial MO 63052-2045 Office: Scholin Bros Printing Co Inc 45 E Lockwood Ave Saint Louis MO 63119-3019

SCHOLL, JESSE MYRON, retired agronomy educator; b. Richland Center, Wis., Feb. 5, 1913; s. Harry Talbot and Mildred (Mason) S.; m. Irma Estelle Scholl, Aug. 23, 1939; children: Stanley, Philip, Dennis, Norman. BS, U. Wis., 1943, MS, 1944, PhD, 1947. Tchr. elem. sch., 1932-39; rsch. agronomist Auburn (Ala.) U., 1947-49; assoc. prof. Iowa State U., Ames, 1949-60; prof. U. Wis., Madison, 1960-78, prof. emeritus, 1978—; cons. U.S. AID, Argentina, 1959, 61, 63; exch. prof., cons. Rio Grande do Sul, Brazil, 1966, 70-73; cons. Mainland China, 1979, 81. Fellow Am. Soc. Agronomy. Republican. Presbyterian. Home: 1400 W Seminary St Richland Center WI 53581-2036 Office: Scholl and Sons Orchards RR 4 Richland Center WI 53581-9804

SCHOLL, MARILYN DARBY, publishing company executive; b. Algona, Iowa, Dec. 13, 1942; d. Don Darby and Isabel (Greenberg) Alt; m. David Edward Scholl, Feb. 5, 1966; children: Katherine Darby, Mark David. AB, Grinnell Coll., 1964. Cert. finance. Assoc. A.G. Becker & Co. Inc., Chgo., 1964-67; assoc. dir. admission Grinnell (Iowa) Coll., 1971-82; pres. Scholl Comm. Inc., Deerfield, Ill., 1982—. Editor Jour. Coll. Admissions, 1984-89, Harmony jour. Symphony Orch. Inst. mem. adv. coun. Northea. Ill. U., Chgo., 1985-93; mem. Deerfield plan commn., 1990-92; bd. dirs. LWV, Deerfield, 1975-88, 91-96, mem. state voter svc. com., 1996—; bd. dirs., v.p. Moraine coun. Girl Scouts U.S., 1976-81; trustee Deerfield Park Found., 1994—. Mem. Internat. TV Assn., Nat. Assn. Coll. Admission Counselors, Ill. Assn. Coll. Admissions Counsellors (bd. dirs. 1976-81), Northea. Ill. Norwegian Elkhound Assn. (bd. dirs. 1991-94). Democrat. Roman Catholic. Office: Scholl Communications Inc PO Box 560 Deerfield IL 60015-0560

SCHOLLER, THOMAS PETER, lawyer; b. Big Rapids, Mich., Aug. 15, 1937; s. Clarence Leo and Ruth Winona (Williams) S.; m. Marcia Kay Harman, June 25, 1960; children: Susan, Mark, Katrina, Laura, Emily. BS in Acctg., Ferris State U., 1959, LLD (hon.), 1984; JD, U. Mich., 1962. CPA, Mich. Staff acct. Arthur Andersen & Co., Detroit, 1962-63, sr. acct., 1963-66, tax mgr., 1966-72, tax ptnr., 1972-91; dir. tax div. Arthur Andersen & Co., Grand Rapids, Mich., 1982-85, 88-91; of counsel Smith, Haughey, Rice & Roegge, Grand Rapids, 1992—. Contbr. articles to profl. jours. Chmn. bd. control Ferris State U., Big Rapids, 1978-83; mem. taxation adv. com. Walsh Coll., 1972-92; trustee Grand Rapids Art Mus., 1989-95. Mem. AICPA, Assn. Corp. Growth (pres. Detroit chpt. 1984-87), Grand Rapids Bar Assn., Mich. Assn. CPAs, Mich. Oil and Gas Assn., State Bar Mich., Healthcare Fin. Mgmt. Assn., Western Mich. Estate Planning Coun., Peninsular Club, Serra Club (pres. Grand Rapids Club 1992-94, gov. Dist. 15 1995—), U. Mich. Club, Egypt Valley Country Club. Republican. Roman Catholic. Office: Smith Haughey Rice & Roegge 200 Calder Pla Bldg Grand Rapids MI 49503-2251

SCHOLTEN, MENNO NICO, mortgage banker; b. Assen, Drenthe, Netherlands, June 18, 1943; came to U.S., 1949; s. Nico Menno and Hennie (Nienhuis) S.; m. Susan Sumnar, Aug. 11, 1973; 1 child, Paul Menno. BArch., U. Calif., Berkeley, 1967; MBA, DePaul U., 1980. Registered architect. Architect various, including Skidmore, Owings & Merrill, others, Chgo., 1968-78, Knight Architects, Engrs. and Planners, Chgo., 1978-81, 1989-92; asst. v.p. constrn. lending adminstr. First Nat. Bank of Chgo., 1981-85; v.p. real estate group First Tex. Savs., Dallas, 1985-87; mgr. constrn. lending Household Internat. (Household Bank), Prospect Heights, Ill., 1992—. Patentee chair design, 1979. Recipient award of merit Chgo. Assn. of Commerce and Industry and Internat. Trade Club of Chgo., 1979. Mem. AIA (Chgo. chpt.), Homebuilders Assn. of Greater Chgo., Am. Guild Organists (bd. dirs., treas. 1991-94), Calif. Scholarship Fedn. (life mem.), Delta Mu Delta.. Home: 3521 Central St Evanston IL 60201

SCHOMMER, DENNIS HAROLD, physical education educator; b. Marshall, Minn., Jan. 19, 1962; s. Harold Lander and Nora Marie (Dolan) S.; m. Susan Carol O'Conner, Aug. 10, 1991. BS, S.W. State U., 1987; MS, St. Cloud State U., 1992. Asst. women's basketball coach S.W. State U., Marshall, Minn., 1987-89; phys. edn. tchr. St. Mary's Grade Sch., Sleepy Eye, Minn., 1989-90; asst. men's basketball coach St. Johns Univ., Collegeville, Minn., 1990-92, 94-95; phys. edn. tchr. Echo Park Elem. Sch., Burnsville, Minn., 1994-95; assoc. head men's basketball coach North Ctrl. Bible Coll., Mpls., 1995; collegiate instr. North Hennepin Cmty. Coll., Brooklyn Park, Minn., 1995; phys. edn. tchr. St. John Vianney Grade Sch., South St. Paul, Minn., 1995—; adj. prof., asst. basketball coach S.W. State U., 1991-94; phys. edn. cons. Schommer Enterprises, Coon Rapids, 1992—; presenter in field. Com. Respect Life Group, Coon Rapids, Minn., 1995; founder SSU Pro-Life Student Group, 1993-94. Mem. NEA, Minn. Edn. Assn., Nat. Assn. of Basketball Coaches, K.C. Republican. Roman Catholic. Home: 9950 University Ave NW #104 Coon Rapids MN 55448

SCHOMMER, JON CLIFFORD, pharmaceutical administration educator; b. Fond du Lac, Wis., June 8, 1962; s. Elwyn G. and Janet E. (Gunderson) S.; m. Lisa R. Bath, Aug. 20, 1988. BS in Pharmacy, U. Wis., 1985, MS in Pharmacy, 1989, PhD in Pharmacy, 1992. Pharmacist Kremer Pharmacy, Fond du Lac, 1985-87; cons. Konsult Data Systems, Oshkosh, Wis., 1986-88; fellow U. Wis., Madison, 1987-88, 89-92, teaching asst., 1988-89; asst. prof. Ohio State U., Columbus, 1993—, The Ohio State U., Columbus, 1993—; adv. com. Pharmacy Examining Bd., Madison, 1990—. Ad hoc mem. Wis. Pharmacy Internship Bd., Madison, 1986; coord. Inter Varsity Christian Fellowship Married Couples Group, Madison, 1990—. Recipient Eli Lilly Co. Achievement award, Madison, 1985; named fellow Wis. Alumni Rsch. Found., 1987-88, Am. Found. Pharm. Edn., 1989—, Robert W. Hammel fellow, 1992, Springboard to Teaching fellow Am. Found. Pharm. Edn., 1993-94. Fellow Am. Coll. Apothecaries (assoc.); mem. Am. Pharm. Assn., Am. Assn. Colls. Pharmacy, Am. Assn. Pharm. Scientists, Am. Soc. Con. Pharmacists, Christian Pharmacists Felowship Internat., Rho Chi (v.p. Wis. chpt. 1989-90). Home: 3220 Needham Dr Dublin OH 43017-1767 Office: Ohio State U Coll Pharmacy 500 W 12th Ave Columbus OH 43210-1214

SCHONDELMEYER, BRENT LEE, communications consultant; b. Independence, Mo., Dec. 16, 1953; s. William Lee and Wilma Lee (Siegrist) S.; m. Lee Ann Williams, Aug. 24, 1989. BA, Grinnell Coll., 1976; MSc, London Sch. Econs., 1981. Reporter Missouri Valley (Iowa) Times News, 1977-78, Keokuk (Iowa) Daily Gate City, 1978-79, Burlington (Iowa) Hawk Eye, 1979-80, Kansas City (Mo.) Star, 1982-84, Kansas City Bus. Jour., 1987-91; editor Kansas City Health Care Times, 1992-93, Budapest Bus. Jour., Hungary, 1994; comms. dir. Local Investment Commn., Kansas City, 1995—; adj. faculty Webster U., Kansas City, 1989-90; health care cons. Author: Independence, 1985, Building a First Class Bank, 1986; contbr. article sto profl. publs. Bd. dirs. Christian Ch., Indpls., 1972-80; organizer Pub. Safety First, Independence, 1994; sec. Midtown/Truman Rd. Adv. Com., Independence, 1995; deacon First Christian Ch., 1995, exec. com., 1995. Recipient investigative journalism awards Kansas City Press Club, 19989, 90, Internat. Assn. Bus. Publs., 1989. Mem. Jackson County Hist. Soc. (v.p. 1990-92), Investigative Reporters and Editors, Midwest Bioethics Ctr. Home: 501 N Union Independence MO 64050

SCHOOFS, GERALD JOSEPH, pilot; b. Kewaskum, Wis., May 11, 1954; s. Francis Christ and Bernice Mary (Kowanda) S.; m. Nancy Lynn Thompson, June 7, 1975; children: Matthew, Katherine. AS in Aeronautics, Gateway Tech. Inst., 1974. Lic. airline transport pilot, instrument flight instr., ground instr. Asst. chief flight instr. West Bend flying Service, 1974-78; dir. ops. Brennan Air Flight, Clintonville, Wis., 1978-80; capt. pilot Miss. Valley Airlines, Moline, Ill., 1985-95, Air Wis., Appleton, 1985—; pilot United Air Lines, 1995—; chief pilot Advanced Tech. Aircraft Design, Hartford, Wis., 1984—. Scoutmaster troop 643 Boy Scouts Am., 1993-95, asst. scoutmaster, 1995—. Mem. Airline Pilots Assn. (sec.-treas. coun. 21 1990, chmn. coun. 46 1990-92, sec.-treas. master exec. coun. 1990-93), Exptl. Aircraft Assn. Roman Catholic. Home and Office: E2170 Crystal River Ln Waupaca WI 54981-8374

SCHOOLMAN, ARNOLD, neurological surgeon; b. Worcester, Mass., Oct. 31, 1927; s. Samuel and Sarah (Koffman) Schulman; m. Gloria June Feder, Nov. 10, 1963; children: Hugh Sinclair, (Jill) Annette. Student, U. Mass., 1945-46; BA, Emory U., 1950; PhD, Yale U., 1954, MD, 1957. Diplomate Am. Bd Neurol. Surgery, Nat. Bd. Med. Examiners. Intern U. Calif. Hosp., San Francisco, 1957-58; resident in neurol. surgery Columbia-Presbyn. Med. Ctr., Neurol. Inst. N.Y., N.Y.C., 1958-62; instr. neurol. surgery U. Kans. Sch. Medicine, Kansas City, 1962, asst. prof. surgery, 1964; assoc. prof. U. Mo. Sch. Medicine, Kansas City, 1976; chief sect. neurosurgery Research Med. Ctr., Kansas City, 1982; dir. Midwest Neurol. Inst., 1982-83. Patentee in field. Served with USN, 1946-48. Fellow ACS (mem. Mo. chpt.); mem. AMA, Mo. State Med. Assn., Kansas City Med. Soc., Kansas City Neurosurg. Soc. (pres. 1984-85), Kansas City Neurol. Soc., Rocky Mountain Neurosurg. Soc., Am. Assn. Neurol. Surgeons, AAAS, Mo. Neurol. Soc., Internat. Coll. Surgeons, Congress Neurol. Surgeons, Brit. Royal Soc. Medicine, Phi Beta Kappa, Sigma Xi. Home: 8705 Catalina St Shawnee Mission KS 66207-2351 Office: 1000 E 50th St Ste 310 Kansas City MO 64110-2215

SCHOONHOVEN, RAY JAMES, retired lawyer; b. Elgin, Ill., May 24, 1921; s. Ray Covey and Rosina Madeline (Schram) (White) S.; m. Marie Theresa Dunn, Dec. 11, 1943; children: Marie Kathleen, Ray James, Jr., Pamela Suzanne, John Philip, Rose Lynne. B.S.C., U. Notre Dame, 1943; J.D., Northwestern U., 1948. Bar: Ill. 1949, U.S. Supreme Ct. 1954, D.C. 1973, U.S. Ct. Mil. Appeals 1954. Assoc. Seyfarth, Shaw Fairweather & Geraldson, Chgo., 1949-57, ptnr., 1957-92; ret.; chief rulings and ops. br. Wage Stabilization Bd. Region VII, Chgo., 1951-52. Book rev. editor: Ill. Law Rev., 1948. Served to lt.comdr. USNR, 1942-62. Mem. ABA, Ill. State Bar Assn., Chgo. Bar Assn., D.C. Bar Assn., Chgo. Athletic Assn., Univ. Club. Chgo., Order of Coif. Republican. Roman Catholic. Home: 6636 N Ponchartrain Blvd Chicago IL 60646-1428 Office: Seyfarth Shaw Fairweather & Geraldson 55 E Monroe St Ste 4200 Chicago IL 60603-5803

SCHORGL, THOMAS BARRY, arts administrator; b. St. Louis, Mar. 1, 1950; s. Francis William and Janet Sarah (Peterson) S.; m. Elizabeth Ann Eades, Aug. 6, 1977; children: Matthew, Ann, Joseph. BFA, U. Iowa, 1973, MA in Drawing, 1974; MFA in Printmaking, Miami U., Oxford, Ohio, 1976; apprenticeship, Atelier, Garrigue, France, 1976; postgrad., U. Notre Dame, 1979. Comml. artist R.H. Donnelly, Chgo., 1977; curator Art Ctr. Inc., South Bend, Ind., 1977-78, dir. acting, 1978, exec. dir., 1978-81; account exec. James P. Carroll & Assocs., South Bend, 1981-83; exec. dir Ind. Arts. Commn., Indpls., 1983-94; pres., CEO Culture Works, Dayton, Ohio, 1994—; cons. in field. Chmn. Arts Midwest, 1989-91, treas., 1987, 88; panelist Nat. Endowment for Arts, 1985-90, chmn. grants panel Art is Basic to Edn., 1986-89. Mem. Great Lakes Arts Alliance (sec., treas. 1983-85, merger com.), Affiliated State Arts Agys. Upper Midwest (chmn. program com. 1985—), Arts Midwest (chmn. 1989-91), Nat. Assembly of State Arts Agys. (bd. dirs. 1991—). Office: Culture Works 126 N Main St Ste 100 Dayton OH 45402-1766

SCHOTT, MARGE, professional baseball team executive; b. 1928; d. Edward and Charlotte Unnewehr; m. Charles J. Schott, 1952 (dec. 1968). Owner Schottco, Cin.; ltd. ptnr. Cin. Reds, 1981-84, gen. ptnr., 1984-85, owner, pres., 1985—, chief exec. officer. Office: Cin Reds 100 Riverfront Stadium Cincinnati OH 45202*

SCHOTTELKOTTE, ALBERT JOSEPH, broadcasting executive; b. Cheviot, Ohio, Mar. 19, 1927; s. Albert William and Venetta (Mentrup) S.; m. Elaine Green, Jan 2, 1988; children: Paul J., Carol A., Matthew J., Joseph G., Louis A., Mary J., Ellen E. Noble, William E., Michael H., Linda Brewer, Martha Schottelkotte, Amy Wholeber. Student pub. and parochial schs. With Cin. Enquirer, 1943-61, successively copy boy, city-wide reporter, columnist, 1953-61; news broadcaster Sta. WSAI, Cin., 1953-59; news broadcaster Sta. WCPO-TV, 1959-94, dir. news-spl. events, 1961-83, sta. dir., 1983-88; gen. mgr. news div. Scripps-Howard Broadcasting Co., 1969-81, v.p. for news, 1971-81, sr. v.p., 1981-93; pres., chief exec. officer, trustee Scripps Howard Found., 1986—. Served with AUS, 1950-52. Recipient Nat. CD award for reporting on subject, 1958, Disting. Broadcaster award Alpha Epsilon Ro, 1990, Carr Van Anda award E.W. Scripps Sch. Journalism Ohio U., 1996—; charter inductee Cin. Journalism Hall of Fame Soc. Profl. Journalists, 1990; inducted into Cin. Broadcasting Hall of Fame, 1992. Mem. Bankers Club, Maketewah Country Club (Cin.), Sea Pines Country Club (Hilton Head, S.C.), Hidden Valley Country Club (Lawrenceburg, Ind.), Hidden Valley Golf Club. Roman Catholic. Home: 1032 St Moritz Ct Lawrenceburg IN 47025 Office: Scripps Howard 312 Walnut St Cincinnati OH 45202-4024

SCHOTTENSTEIN, IRVING E., construction company executive; b. 1920. Apt. bldg. developer, 1966-73; pres., CEO M/I Schottenstein Homes Inc., Columbus, Ohio, 1973—; chmn. bd. dirs. M/I Real Estate Co., Inc., Columbus, Ohio; ptnr. Brothers Realty Co., Columbus, Ohio. Office: M/I Schottenstein Homes Inc 41 S High St Ste 2410 Columbus OH 43215-6101*

SCHOU, CHARLENE MAE, federal goverment official, consultant; b. Fremont, Nebr., Aug. 10, 1954; d. Charles William and Dorothy Marian (Van Scoyoc) Greenfield; children: Elizabeth Ann, Daniel B., Jonathan R. B degree, U. Nebr., 1988; M in Human Rels., U. Okla., 1991. Staff adminstrn. specialist DOD, USAR, Omaha, 1985-88; equal opportunity specialist Dept. Labor/OFCCP, Omaha, 1988-91; compliance specialist officer Dept. Labor/OFCCP, St. Louis, 1991—; trainer, facilitator Def. Equal Opportunity Mgmt. Inst., Patrick AFB, Fla., 1990-91,. black studies dept. U. Nebr., Omaha, 1990-91, Group Dynamics and Strategy Trainers, Orlando, Fla., 1988-92. Contbr. articles to profl. publs. Pres. PTA, Fremont, 1990-91; mem. NAACP, Omaha and St. Louis, 1990-92, Urban League, Omaha and St. Louis, 1990-92. Master sgt. USAR, 1976-96. Mem. Mensa (new mem. officer 1988). Democrat. Presbyterian. Home: 13270 Shady Green Dr Saint Louis MO 63128-3842

SCHOVILLE, KEITH N., Hebrew and Semitic studies educator; b. Soldiers Grove, Wis., Mar. 3, 1928; s. Harley Leonard and Viva Ruth (Banta) S.; m. Merrlyn June Mitchell; children: Kenneth, Mary Lee, Harley, John, Robert. BA, Milligan Coll., Johnson City, Tenn., 1956; MA, U. Wis., 1966, PhD, 1969. Isntr. U. Wis., Madison, 1968-70, asst. prof., 1970-74, assoc.prof., 1974-81, prof., 1981—, dir. faculty advising svc., 1987—, chair

Hebrew and Semitic studies, 1977-82; panel mem. NEH, Washington, 1985-94; project dir. Sign, Symbol, Script Exhibit, 1982-86. Author: Biblican Archaeology in Focus, 1978, Exodus and Leviticus Commentary, 1988, Sign, Symbol, Script Catalog, 1984; editor jour. Hebrew Studies, 1982. Served with U.S. Army, 1946-47, Philippines. Grantee NEH, 1982, Wis. Humanities Com., 1987, Wis. Soc. for Jewish Learning, 1977—. Mem. Am. Oriental Soc. (pres. Midwest sect.), Am. Schs. of Oriental Rsch., Archaeol. Inst. Am., Nat. Assn. Profs. of Hebrew (pres.), Inst. for Bibl. Rsch., Soc. Bibl. Lit. Christian. Home: 5689 Sun Valley Pkwy Oregon WI 53575 Office: U Wis Dept Hebrew and Semitic Studies 1344 Van Hise Hall 1220 Linden Dr Madison WI 53706

SCHOWENGERDT, DONALD EUGENE, management consultant; b. Independence, Mo., Dec. 23, 1935. BS in Acctg., Rockhurst Coll., 1970. CPA, Kans., Mo. Ptnr. Arthur Young and Co., Kansas City, Mo., 1969-88; exec. dir. Stinston Mag & Fizzell, Kansas City, 1988-91; mgmt. cons. Grant Thornton, Kansas City, 1991-93; v.p. Impact Group, Shawnee Mission, Kans., 1993—. Mem. AICPA. Presbyterian. Office: Impact Group 5100 W 95th St Ste 200 Shawnee Mission KS 66207-3305

SCHRADER, DAVID F., congressman; b. Oct. 23, 1952; s. Hubert F. and Violet L. (Marshall) S.; m. Roberta J. Sterling, July 15, 1974; children: Todd, JoAnna, Heather, Melissa. Grad. high sch., Monroe, Iowa, 1970. Owner, operator automotive fabrication bus. Monroe, 1970-93, owner, operator amusement and vending bus., 1980-88; mem. Iowa Ho. of Reps., Des Moines, 1987-90, asst. majority leader, 1991-92, asst. minority leader, 1993—. Named Legis. Conservationist of 1993, Iowa Wildlife Fedn. Mem. Internat. Motor Contest Assn., NASCAR, Kiwanis. Democrat. Methodist. Office: Iowa Ho Of Reps Des Moines IA 50319*

SCHRADER, HELEN MAYE, retired municipal worker; b. Akron, Ohio, June 8, 1920; d. Simon P. and Helen Cecelia (Fennessy) Eberz; widowed; children: Alfred E., Kathleen Therese Schrader Wein. Notary pub. Insp., clk. Fed. Govt. agys., 1940; stenographer Chem. Warfare divsn. USAF, Akron, 1954; clk., stenographer VA; elected clk./treas. of twp. Springfield (Ohio) Twp., 1956-92. Sec. Springfield Dem. Club, Akron, 1957—; sec., treas. Springfield Twp. Civic Club, 1980—. Mem. Summit County Assn. of Trustees and Clks. (sec. 1959-78, 83-92, Svc. plaque 1979, 92). Roman Catholic. Home: 693 Neal Rd Akron OH 44312-3709

SCHRADER, THOMAS F., utilities executive; b. Indpls., 1950. Grad., Princeton U., 1972, 78. Pres., chief exec. officer Wis. Gas Co., Milw. Office: Wis Gas Co 626 E Wisconsin Ave Milwaukee WI 53202-4603

SCHRAM, BRIAN T., drafting supervisor; b. Davenport, Iowa, Apr. 7, 1965. B, Northwest Mo. State U., 1988. Draftsman Ryke Mfg., Grimes, Iowa, 1988-90, elec. designer, 1990-93, drafting supr., 1993—.

SCHRAM, GERALDINE MOORE, security consultant; b. Kinde, Mich., Jan. 1, 1935; d. Charles Harold and Stella Mary (Horetski) Moore; children: Robert Charles, Kelly Jo. Cert. Bus., Cleary Coll., Ypsilanti, 1954; BAA in Bus., Delta Coll., University Center, Mich., 1983; BS in Mgmt./Mktg., Northwood Inst., Midland, Mich., 1988. Registered med. sec. Hubbard Meml. Hosp., U. Mich., Ann Arbor, 1955-58; account mgr. Bloom Assocs., Detroit, 1960-62; pub. rels. staff Dow Chem. Co., Midland, Mich., 1970-80; govt. security adminstr. Dow Corning Corp., Midland, 1980-95; cons./lectr. Janus Assocs., Midland, 1977—; lectr. in field; facilitator World Assn. Document Examiners, Chgo., 1989—. Author: Personalities at Risk, 1993; contbr. articles to profl. jours. Mem. Am. Def. Preparedness Assn., World Assn. Document Examiners, Internat. Graphoanalysis Soc. (instr. 1976—), C. of C., Am. Soc. Indsl. Security. Republican. Roman Catholic. Home and Office: 302 Hollybrook Dr Midland MI 48642-3350

SCHRAM, JOSEPH H., retired sales executive; b. N.Y.C., Feb. 17, 1927. BBA, Iona Coll., 1950. V.p. sales John V. McCarthy & Assocs., Southfield, Mich., 1955—. With USN, 1945-46. Roman Catholic. Home: 34612 Grove St Livonia MI 48154-2443

SCHRAMM, BEATRICE G., retired teacher; b. Clinton, Ohio, June 6, 1914; d. Tully and Mary Griffin; m. Marvin C. Schramm, Sept. 13, 1939 (dec. Oct. 1963); children: Ellen McGlothin, Roselyn Drew, Janice Hultman. BE, Ill. State U., Normal, 1933; MS, Purdue U., Lafayette, 1968; postgrad, Ball State U., Muncie, 1966. Cert. tchr., Ill., Ind. Tchr. rural schs., Ill., Ind., 1934-76. Author: Sounds and Symbols in American English, 1994. Home: 1705 S 12th St Lafayette IN 47905

SCHRAMM, DAVID NORMAN, astrophysicist, educator; b. St. Louis, Oct. 25, 1945; s. Marvin M. and Betty Virginia (Math) S.; m. Judith J. Gibson, 1986; children from previous marriage: Cary, Brett. SB in Physics, MIT, 1967; PhD in Physics, Calif. Inst. Tech., 1971. Rsch. fellow in physics Calif. Inst. Tech., Pasadena, 1971-72; asst. prof. astronomy and physics U. Tex., Austin, 1972-74; assoc. prof. astronomy, astrophysics and physics U. Chgo., 1974-77, prof., 1977—, Louis Block prof. phys. scis., 1982—, prof. conceptual founds. of sci., 1983—, acting chmn. dept. astronomy and astrophysics, 1977, chmn., 1978-84, v.p. for rsch., 1995, Louis Block disting. svc. prof. in phys. scis., 1996—; resident cosmologist Fermilab, 1982-84; cons., lectr. Adler Planetarium, Lawrence Livermore Lab., Los Alamos Nat. Lab.; organizer sci. confs.; frequent lectr. in field; chmn. bd. trustees Aspen Ctr. for Physics; bd. on physics and astronomy, exec. com. NRC, 1990—, chair, 1993—, mem. com. aviation weather systems aeronautics and space engrng. bd., 1994—; bd. dirs. Astron. Rsch. Consortium, 1990—; pres. Big Bang Aviation, Inc.; bd. overseers Fermi Nat. Accelerator Lab., 1990—. Co-author: The Advanced Stages of Stellar Evolution, 1977, From Quarks to the Cosmos: Tools of Discovery, 1989, The Shadows of Creation: Dark Matter and the Structure of the Universe, 1991; co-editor: Supernovae, 1977, Fundamental Problems of Stellar Evolution, 1980, Essays in Nucleosynthesis, 1981, Gauge Theory and the Early Universe, 1988, Dark Matter in the Universe, 1990; editor profl. jours.; columnist Outside mag.; contbr. over 350 articles to profl. jours. Recipient Gravity Rsch. Found. prize, 1980, Humboldt award Fed. Republic Germany, 1987-88, Einstein medal Evotos U., Budapest, Hungary, 1989, Grad. Teaching award U. Chgo., 1994. Fellow Am. Acad. Arts and Scis., Am. Phys. Soc. (Lilienfeld prize 1993), Meteor. Soc.; mem. Nat. Acad. Sci., Am. Astron. Soc. (Helen B. Warner prize 1978, exec. com. planetary sci. divsn. 1977-79, sec.-treas. high energy astrophysics divsn. 1979-81), Am. Assn. Physics Tchrs. (Richtmeyer prize 1984), Astron. Soc. Pacific (Robert J. Trumpler award 1974), Internat. Astron. Union (commns. on cosmology, stellar evolution, high energy astrophysics), Aircraft Owners and Pilots Assn., British-N Am. Com., Hungarian Acad. Scis. (hon.), Alpine Club, Sigma Xi. Home: 155 N Harbor Dr Apt 5203 Chicago IL 60601-7326 Office: U Chgo AAC 140 5640 S Ellis Ave Chicago IL 60637-1433 also: 150 Pitkin Mesa Dr Aspen CO 81611-1075

SCHRAND, RICHARD HENRY, broadcaster; b. Cin., Nov. 1, 1957; s. Edward August and Jane Marie (Scheib) S.; m. Deborah Fortner, 1979 (div. 1985); 1 chld, Cynthia Lanette; m. Sharon Lynn Lassandro, Dec. 24, 1986; 1 child, Courtney Lynne. Student, Ohio State U., 1975-76, No. Ky. U., 1976-77. Producer WKRC-TV, Cin., 1975-79; reporter, anchor WCSC-TV, Charleston, S.C., 1979-83; actor Phila. Experiment, L.A., 1984; asst. promotion dir. WLWT-TV, Cin., 1983-86; spl. projects coord. KXAS-TV, Dallas/Ft. Worth, 1986-87; mgr. media svcs. NBC TV Network, Burbank, Calif., 1987-89; pres. Cyn-Court Enterprises, Burbank, 1989-91; mktg. dir. WPTA-TV, Ft. Wayne, Ind., 1991-92; v.p., gen. mgr. Branson (Mo.) Broadcasting Corp., 1992-95; dir. spl. projects/nat. media, graphics and advt. creator, 1995—; v.p., gen. mgr. Jim Owens & Assocs., Nashville, 1992—. Bd. dirs. Project Graduation, Dallas/Ft. Worth, 1986-87; mem. Muscular Dystrophy Assn., Charleston, 1980-83; publicist Housing Now, L.A., 1988. Recipient Local Emmy awrd NATAS, 1975, award Broadcast Promotion and Mktg. Execs., Seattle, 1992.

SCHRAUT, SHERRY JO, marketing executive; b. Thief River Falls, Minn., May 21, 1965; d. Frank Adam and Lucille Alta (Brosseau) Passa; m. Brad Evan Schraut, Apr. 30, 1994. AA, Northland C.C., 1985; BS, Mayville State U., 1988. Mktg. mgr. Rovak, Inc., Lake Elmo, Minn., 1988—. Home: 8645 Lake Jane Tr Lake Elmo MN 55042 Office: Rovak Inc 3549 Lake Elmo Ave Lake Elmo MN 55042

SCHRECK, ROBERT, commodities trader; b. 1944. With Pillsbury Co., Mpls., 1968-93, v.p.; exec. v.p. Commodity Specialists Co., Mpls., 1993—. Office: Commodity Specialists Co 301 4th Ave S Minneapolis MN 55415*

SCHREIBER, BARBARA LOUISE, civic worker; b. Canton, Ohio, Apr. 10, 1915; d. Ralph Mitchell and Lela May (Hower) Fawcett; m. Robert Edward Schreiber, June 17, 1938 (dec. Oct. 1974); children: Ralph F., Barbara Binkley, Susan Spring, Linda Parkos. BA, Conn. Coll., New London, 1937; student, Kent State U., 1937-38. Cert. tchr., Ohio. Mem. Bd. Edn., Canton City Schs., 1964—, pres., 1967, 70, 75, 78, 80, 86, 89, 91; trustee Ohio Sch. Bds. Assn., Westerville, 1967—, mem. policies and legislation, 1975—, mem., past pres. N.E. region exec. com., 1966—; cons. to bd. dirs. Nat. PTA, Chgo., 1982-83; bd. dirs. Nat. Sch. Bds. Assn., Alexandria, Va., 1978-84; mem. Large City Schs. Commn., Ohio, 1967—, pres., 1974, 90; mem. bd. advisors, treas. Philomatheon Soc. of the Blind, Canton, 1957—; chmn. pers. Gt. Trail coun. Girl Scouts U.S., Ohio, 1982—, pres., 1976-82; life mem. Ohio PTA; bd. dirs. Malone Coll., 1986-92, sec. bd.; mem. women's adv. coun. Malone Coll., 1966—, pres., 1967; chmn. lay adv. com. dept. edn. Walsh Coll., 1983-93; sec. adv. com. Walsh U., 1980-90; mem. women's com. Walsh U., 1968—. Recipient Appreciation award Greater Canton C. of C., 1981, Recognition award Phi Delta Kappa, 1978, Ohio Oaktree award Ohio PTA; named in her honor Barbara F. Schreiber Elem. Sch. Mem. Jr. League of Canton (pres. 1954-56, Woman of Yr. 1968), Coll. Club of Canton (pres. 1961-63), Rotary (Paul Harris fellow), Delta Kappa Gamma (hon.), Kappa Delta Pi. Republican. Presbyterian (elder, Sunday sch. tchr.). Home: 408 23rd St NW Canton OH 44709-3818

SCHREIBER, LOLA F., state legislator; m. Marion Schreiber; 2 children. Student, S.D. State U. Mem. S. D. Ho. Reps., vice-chmn. edn. com., mem. state affairs com.; chmn. edn. com., mem. judiciary com., mem. tax com., chmn. legislators exec. bd., 1995, 96, chmn. edn. com. Nat. Conf. State Legislators; commr. Edn. Commn. States; mem. policy and priorities com.; mem. adv. bd. Policymakers Inst., Danforth Found.; mem. Fin. Project. Home: 30045 173d St Gettysburg SD 57442-9735*

SCHREIER, BRADLEY, finance company executive; b. Aug. 19, 1951; m. Marge Schreier; children: Ryan, Kyle. BS in Social Studies/Econs., Mankato State U. Letterpress supr. Carlson Craft, 1973-74, custom svc. supr., 1974-76, office mgr., 1976-79; v.p. sales and mktg. Taylor Corp., Mankato, Minn., 1980-85, pres., 1985—. bd. dirs. Mankato Area United Way, 1975-81, v.p., 1979, 80, pres. bd. dirs., 1981; bd. dirs. YMCA, 1983-92, chmn. fin. com., co-chair spl. gifts divsn. 1 million dollar bldg. expansion capital campaign; bd. dirs. Immanuel-St. Joseph's Hosp., 1984-94, treas., 1988, vice chmn., treas, 1989, chmn. med. office bldg. task force, 1990, vice chmn., 1990, chmn. bd. dirs., 1991, 92, mem. exec. com., 1993-94; bd. dirs. Mankato Area Cath. Sch. Found., 1988—; pres. parish coun., mem. coun. Holy Rosary Ch., 1988—, chmn. fin. com., mem. com., 1989—; mem. pers. com. Loyola Cath. High Sch., 1989-90, mem. sch. bd., 1989-90; chmn. Mankato Area Cath. Sch. Bd., 1990—; coach Mankato Area Youth Baseball Assn., 1986—, bd. dirs., 1991—; pres. Mankato Royals Baseball, 1989, 90, bd. dirs., 1989-93; Fitzgerald 7th and 8th grade basketball coach, 1988, mem. Loyola Booster Club; bd. dirs. Mankato Basketball Assn., 1989—, traveling team coach, 1989—; basketball team coach Holy Rosary. Recipient Book of Golden Deeds award for Outstanding Cmty. Svc., Mankata Exch. Club, 1994. Mem. KC. Office: Taylor Corp 1725 Roe Crest Dr Mankato MN 56003-1807

SCHRENK, LORENZ PHILIP, human resources executive; b. Utica, N.Y., Feb. 8, 1932; s. Matthew Henry and Katheryn Charlotte (Hess) S.; m. Ann Reed Sweeney, Apr. 28, 1956; children: Janet, Stephen, Lisa. AB, George Washington U., 1954; MA, Ohio State U., 1962, PhD, 1964. Assoc. scientist System Devel. Corp., Santa Monica, Calif., 1956-57, Ramo-Woolridge, Inc., Denver, 1959-60; rsch. scientist Honeywell, Inc., Mpls., 1964-70, mgr. life scis., 1970-78, mgr. tng. systems office, 1978-80, mgr. human resources planning, 1980-83, mgr. health care, 1983-86, dir. human resources planning and talent, 1987-88, dir. exec. devel., 1987-93; dir., treas. Infrared Solutions, Inc., Mpls., 1994—. Author: Northern Pacific: Supersteam Era, 1985, Northern Pacific: Diesel Era, 1988; inventor: automatic tng., 1980; contbr. articles to profl. jours. Lt. j.g. USNR, 1954-56, USS Bennington. Mem. Human Factors Soc., Lexington Group.

SCHRIMSHER, KANDACE PEARSON, sociology educator, researcher; b. Wis., Mar. 23, 1963; d. Douglas Charles and Sharon Lee (Smith) Pearson; m. Neil A. Schrimsher, Feb. 16, 1991. BGS, U. Iowa, 1986; postgrad., U. Wis., Madison, 1986-87; MA in Sociology, U. Wis., Milw., 1990; PhD, Loyola U., Chgo., 1996. Teaching asst. dept. sociology U. Wis., Milw., 1987-89; rsch. asst. dept. sociology Loyola U., 1989-91, tchg. fellow Grad. Sch., 1991-92; instr. sociology Coll. of DuPage, Glen Ellyn, summer 1990; instr. Elgin (Ill.) Coll., fall 1990; instr. sociology John Carroll U., Cleveland, Ohio, 1991-94, Oakland U., Rochester, Mich., 1995—; dir. project on study of career patterns Sch. Law, Case Western Res. U., 1991—. Chairperson survey coordination com., mem. steering com. task force on gender fairness Ohio State Bar and Supreme Ct., 1991-93, cons., 1993. Mem. Am. Sociol. Assn. (sex and gender sect., occupations and orgn. sect., undergrad. tchg. sect.), Sociologists for Women in Soc., Midwest Sociol. Soc., North Ctrl. Sociol. Soc. Democrat. Home: 2146 Willow Leaf Ct W Rochester Hills MI 48309-9999

SCHROCK, JOHN RICHARD, biology educator; b. Goshen, Ind., Oct. 23, 1946; s. Cletus Paul and Vera Idelle (Green) S.; m. Lois Sue West, Feb. 2, 1968; children: John Richard II, Donna Sue. BS in Biology, Ind. State U., 1971, MS in Sci. Edn., 1973; PhD in Entomology, U. Kans., 1983. Tchr. Campbell County Schs., Alexandria, Ky., 1968-73; instr. Lab. Sch. Ind. State U., Terre Haute, 1973-75; tchr. Hong Kong Internat. Sch., 1975-78; from asst. to assoc. prof. Emporia (Kans.) State U., 1986—. Co-author: Controlled Wildlife: State Wildlife Regulations, 1985; co-editor: A Guide to Museum Pest Control, 1988; editor: Kansas School Naturalist, 1990—; contbr. over 20 articles to profl. jours. Fellow Ind. Acad. Sci.; mem. Kans. Assn. Biology Tchrs. (editor). Office: Emporia State U Biol Div PO Box 4050 Emporia KS 66801

SCHROCK, J(OSEPH) BYRON, real estate broker; b. Bloomington, Ill., July 24, 1945; s. Joseph B. and Esther A. (Rassi) S.; m. Mary Jean Rinkenberger, Sept. 4, 1966; children: Todd M., Troy D., Trent D., Lanae M., Larissa R. BS, Univ. Ill., 1967. With Cen. Ill. Land Inc., Congerville, 1967—, elected pres., 1981—; pres. Schrock Realty Inc., Morton, Ill., 1982—; bd. dirs. Tri-County Investment Exchs., Peoria, 1978—. Scoutleader Boy Scouts of Am., Congerville, 1973-83, com. chair., bible class tchr. Apostolic Christian Ch., Congerville, 1970-86. Named Best Managed project Dist. #3, USDA Farmers Home Adminstrn., Galesburg, 1992; recipient Pres.'s award Peoria Area Assn. Realtors, 1992-93. Mem. Cert. Comml. Investment, Nat. Assn. Realtors, Ill. Assn. Realtors, Peoria Assn. Realtors (bd. dirs. 1987—, sec. 1994-95, treas. 1995-96, pres.-elect 1996-97). Republican. Home: 29509 Allentown Rd Mackinaw IL 61755-9404 Office: Schrock Realty Inc 117 N Main St Morton IL 61550-2051

SCHRODER, BARRY CHARLES, lawyer; b. New Buffalo, Mich., Apr. 26, 1955; s. Charles William and Veronica Helen (Bigda) S.; m. Nancy Lee Vincent, Sept. 6, 1980; 1 child: Erika. BA with high honors, Mich. State U., 1977; JD, Wayne State U., 1980. Bar: Mich. 1980, U.S. Dist. Ct. (we. dist.) Mich. 1980, U.S. Ct. Appeals (6th cir.) 1983. Assoc., Rhoades, McKee & Boer, Grand Rapids, Mich., 1980-86; mem. Mich. Worker's Compensation Appeal Bd., Grand Rapids, 1986-87; magistrate, Mich. Worker's Compensation Bd. Magistrates, Grand Rapids, 1987-93; prin. shareholder and CEO Schroder Law Offices, P.C., 1993—. Pres., trustee New Sch. for Creative Learning, Grand Rapids, 1993-95, co-founder, v.p., bd. trustees, The New Sch. Charter Acad., 1995-96. Mem. Mich. Bar Assn. (com. on medicolegal problems 1991-92), mem. Am. Trial Lawyer Assoc. Democrat. Roman Catholic. Office: 6731 28th St SE Grand Rapids MI 49546

SCHRODER, PAUL D., mechanical engineer; b. Tyndall, S.D., June 2, 1956. BSME, S.D. Sch. of Mines and Tech., 1978. Project engr. Pella (Iowa) Corp., 1978-92, Pella (Iowa) Electronics Co. Inc., 1992—. Patentee in field. Republican. Office: Pella Electronics Co Inc PO Box 556 Pella IA 50219

SCHROEDER, CHARLES EDGAR, banker, investment management executive; b. Chgo., Nov. 17, 1935; s. William Edward and Lelia Lorraine (Anderson) S.; m. Martha Elizabeth Runnette, Dec. 30, 1958; children: Charles Edgar, Timothy Creighton, Elizabeth Linton. BA in Econs., Dartmouth Coll., 1957; MBA, Amos Tuck Sch., 1958. Treas. Miami Corp., Chgo., 1969-78, pres., 1978—; chmn., bd. dirs Blvd. Bank of Chgo., 1981-91; chmn. Blvd. Bancorp., Inc., 1991-94; bd. dirs. Nat.-Standard Co., Niles, Mich. Trustee Northwestern Meml. Hosp., 1985-93, Northwestern U., 1989—. Lt. (j.g.) USN, 1958-60. Mem. Fin. Analysts Soc. of Chgo., Chgo. Club, Glen View Club, Michigan Shores Club, Comml. Club. Office: Miami Corp 410 N Michigan Ave Chicago IL 60611-4211

SCHROEDER, DAVID HAROLD, health care facility executive; b. Chgo., Oct. 22, 1940; s. Harry T. and Clara D. (Dexter) S.; m. Clara Doorn, Dec. 27, 1964; children: Gregory D., Elizabeth M. BBA, Kans. State Coll., 1965; MBA, Wichita State U., 1968; postgrad., U. Ill., 1968-69. CPA, Ill. Supt. cost acctg. Boeing Co., Wichita, Kans., 1965-68; sr. v.p., treas. Riverside Med. Ctr., Kankakee, Ill., 1971—; treas. Riverside Health System, 1982—, Kankakee Valley Health Inc., 1985—, Health Info. Systems Coop., 1991—; v.p., treas. Oakside Corp., Kankakee, 1982—; bd. dirs. Harmony Home Health Svc., Inc., Naperville, Ill.; mem. faculty various profl. orgns.; adj. prof. econs. divsn. health adminstrn. Gov.'s State U., University Park, Ill., 1990-95; trustee Riverside Found. Trust, 1989—, RMC Found., 1989—, Sr. Living Ctr., 1989—. Contbg. author: Cost Containment in Hospitals, 1980; contbr. articles to profl. jours. Trustee Riverside Found. Trust, 1989—, RMC Found., 1989—, Sr. Living Ctr., 1989—; pres. Riverside Employees Credit Union, 1976-79; founder Kankakee Trinity Acad., 1980, Riverview Hist. Dist., Kankakee, 1982; pres. Kankakee County Mental Health Ctr., 1982-84, United Way Kankakee County, 1984-85; chmn. Ill. Provider Trust, Naperville, 1983-85; mem. adv. bd. Students in Free Enterprise, Olivet Nazarene U., Kankakee, 1989—; pres. adv. coun. divsn. health adminstrn., preceptor Gov.'s State U., 1987—; trustee, treas. Am. Luth. Ch.; wish granter Make a Wish Found., 1994—; dir. Kankakee County Hist. Soc., 1995. Capt. U.S. Army, 1969-71. Fellow Am. Coll. Healthcare Execs., Halthcare Fin. Mgmt. Assn. (pres. 1975-76, cert. mgr. patient accounts 1981), Fin. Analysts Fedn.; mem. AICPA, Ill. Hosp. Assn. (chmn. coun. health fin. 1982-85), Inst. Chartered Fin. Analysts, Nat. Assn. Accts., Fin. Exec. Inst., Ill. CPA Soc., Healthcare Fin. Mgmt. Assn. (William G. Follmer award 1977, Robert H. Reeves award 1981, Muncie Gold award 1987, Founders medal of honor 1990), Investment Analysts Soc. Chgo., Inc., Kankakee County Hist. Soc. (dir. 1995—), Classic Car Club Am., Packard Club, Kiwanis (pres.), Masons, Alpha Kappa Psi, Sigma Chi. Home: 901 S Chicago Ave Kankakee IL 60901-5236 Office: Riverside Med Ctr 350 N Wall St Kankakee IL 60901-2901

SCHROEDER, DONALD LEE, farm manager; b. McPherson, Kans., Mar. 20, 1951; s. Milo Henry and Leatrice (Peters) S.; m. Janice Lee Goertzen, Dec. 28, 1971; children: Deborah Lynn, David Henry. Student, Tabor Coll., 1969-70, Hutchinson (Kans.) C.C., 1970. Owner, mgr. Heartland Farms, Inc., Inman, Kans., 1973—; bd. dirs. Multi-Comty. Diversified Svcs. Bd. dirs., pres. Unified Sch. Dist. 448, Inman, 1991—, Pleasant View Home of Inman, 1992—; precinct committeeman, McPherson County (Kans.) Rep., 1984-88, 91—; mem. Leadership McPherson C. of C., 1995. Mem. Kans. Corn Growers (bd. dirs.), McPherson County Small Bus. Devel. Assn. (bd. dirs. 1996—). Mennonite. Home: 131 14th Ave Inman KS 67546

SCHROEDER, GREGG LEROY, critical care nurse; b. Newton, Kans., Feb. 26, 1958; s. Delmar LeRoy and Barbara Jean (Unruh) S.; m. Cynthia Jo Scheller, Oct. 28, 1978; 1 child, Jason Peter. ADN, Hesston (Kans.) Coll., 1986; BSN, Bethel Coll., Newton, Kans., 1992; MSN, Wichita State U., 1994. RN, Kans.; cert. ARNP-CNS; cert. ACLS, BLS, critical care nursing, respiratory therapy technician. Staff nurse Halstead (Kans.) Hosp., 1986-87, staff critical care nurse, 1987-89, charge nurse coronary ICU, coord. quality assurance, 1989—, edn. resource person coronary ICU, 1988—, instr. BLS, 1985—, instr. ACLS, 1991-92; clin. nursing instr. Bethel Coll., 1992-94, asst. prof. nursing, 1994—, clin. nurse specialist for ICU, 1995—. Mennonite. Home: 105 S Summit Goessel KS 67053 Office: Bethel College 300 E 27th St North Newton KS 67117-9989

SCHROEDER, HANS, retired electrical engineering educator; b. Cologne, Germany, May 14, 1929; came to U.S., 1949; s. Cloyde Paul and Margaret Alice (Guthmann) S.; m. Janet C. Steil, Sept. 25, 1954. BS, Milw. Sch. Engring., 1955; MS, U. Wis., 1970. Registered profl. engr. Wis., Ohio. Sect. head NCR Corp., Dayton, Ohio, 1955-65; project engr. Astronautices Corp. Am., Milw., 1965-69; prof. Milw. Sch. Engring., 1970-95, prof. emeritus, 1995. Patentee in field. Mem. IEEE (sr. mem., life), Am. Soc. Engring. Edn., Am. Radio Relay League, League Am. Bicyclists.

SCHROEDER, HENRY WILLIAM, publisher; b. Cleve., Wis., Sept. 7, 1928; s. Henry and Esther Julia (Kammann) S. ; m. Dorothy Hildebrand, Aug. 18, 1956 (div.); children: Susan Schroeder Smith, Katherine Jean Duhamel; m. Elizabeth Churbuck, Aug. 15, 1977 (dec.); children: Joy, Bill, Stephen; m. Mary Vae Legler, Feb. 15, 1992; 1 child, Derek Legler. BS, U. Wis., 1957, MS, 1959. Info. dir. Wis. Farm Bur., Madison, 1960-63; asst. dir. pub. rels. Credit Union Internat., Madison, 1963-65; editor, co-pub. Verona Press (Wis.), Oreg. Observer (Wis.), 1966—, also v.p. Southwest Suburban Publs., Inc., 1966-80; co-pub. Fitchburg Star, 1974—, also pres. Southwest Suburban Publs. and Schroeder Publs., Inc., 1980—; pub. Blade-Atlas, Blanchardville, Wis., 1977-83; pres., pub. Leader Publ. Corp., Evansville, Wis., 1981-88; pub. Cmty. Herald Newspapers Corp., 1988—, Monona Herald and McFarland Life newspapers, Clinton (Wis.) Topper, 1994—; pub. Country Courier, Hinckley, Ill. Mem. Gov.'s UN Commn., 1974. Served with USNR, 1949-53. Mem. Wis. Newspaper Assn. (pres. 1983-84), Wis. Newspaper Assn. (bd. dir. 1973-86, 94—), WNA Found. (pres. 1990-91), Madison Press Club, Madison Advt. Fedn., Nat. Newspaper Assn. (govt. affairs conf., chmn. services com., state chmn., Better Newspaper Contest), Suburban Newspapers Am., Verona C. of C. (pres. 1970, 91), Madison Club, East Madison Optimists (bd. dirs. 1993—, pres. 1995-96), Masons (master 1970, bd. dirs. jour. 1990-93, pres. jour., bd. dirs. 1993—), Shriners, Royal Order Jesters. Republican. Office: Verona Press 120 W Verona Ave Verona WI 53593-1315

SCHROEDER, JOANNE FRANCES, librarian; b. Frankfort, Mich., Dec. 17, 1940; d. Raymond Clemens and Frances Judith (Jirik) Johnson; m. Sydney Allen Schroeder, Jan. 31, 1962; children: Daniel Charles, Nicholas Allen. BA in Edn. and LS, U. Cen. Fla., 1974. Cert. libr., psychology, Fla., Tex. Audio-visual specialist Brevard County Schs.s, Titusville, Fla., 1968-72, libr., 1974-75; libr. Friendswood (Tex.) Pub. Libr., 1976-81; sch. libr. Pasadena (Tex.) Sch. Dist., 1981—; cons. reading program Fisher Elem. Sch., Pasadena, 1988-91; regional dir. Puppeteers Am., Friendswood, 1985-88, workshop dir., Tahlequah, Okla., 1990-91. Editor Puppet News. Bd. dirs. Friendswood Heritage Mus., 1978, Children's Mus., Houston, 1987. Recipient Tapper award Dallas Puppet Guild, 1986. Mem. Tex. Libr. Assn., Greater Houston Puppetry Guild (pres. 1983-85, Outstanding Contbn. award 1990). Republican. Home: 2 Whittier Dr Friendswood TX 77546-4021 Office: Fisher Elem Sch 2220 Grunewald Dr Pasadena TX 77502-5604

SCHROEDER, JOHN H., university chancellor; b. Twin Falls, Idaho, Sept. 13, 1943; s. Herman John and Azalia (Kimes) S.; m. Sandra Barrow; children: John K., Andrew Barrow. BA, Lewis and Clark Coll., Portland, Oreg., 1965; MA, U. Va., 1967, PhD, 1971. Instr. history U. Wis., Milw., 1970-71, asst. prof., 1971-76, assoc. prof., 1976-86, prof., 1986—, Am. Coun. on Edn. fellow, 1982-83, assoc. dean, 1976-82, asst. to vice chancellor, 1982-85, acting vice chancellor, 1985-87, vice chancellor, 1987-90, chancellor, 1990—; Louis M. Sears Meml. lectr. Purdue U., 1978; bd. dirs. Columbia Health Sys., Inc. Author: Mr. Polk's War: American Opposition and Dissent, 1973, The Commercial and Diplomatic Role of the American Navy 1829-1861, 1985. Bd. dirs. Greater Milw. Com., Milw. Boys and Girls Club, Milw. Pub. Policy Forum, Greater Milw. Edn. Trust, Wis. Jr. Achievement, Commn. on Urban Agenda; mem. Milw. Conf. on Employment, Edn. and Race, Milw. Quality Edn. Commn. Recipient Edward and Rosa Uhrig award U. Wis.-Milw., 1974, Disting. Teaching award AMOCO/U. Wis.-Milw., 1975. Mem. Orgn. Am. Historians, Soc. for History of Early Republic, Soc. for History Am. Fgn. Rels., Nat. Assn. State Univs. and Land Grant Colls. (bd. dirs.), Rotary. Office: U Wis 2310 E Hartford Ave Milwaukee WI 53211-3165

SCHROEDER, JOHN LORREN, computer programmer; b. Neenah, Wis., Nov. 29, 1954; s. Lorren Arlin and Gwyneth Katherine (Thomas) S.; m. Margaret Ann Ruoff, Aug. 7, 1983; 1 child, Zina Katherine. BS in Computer Sci., U. Wis., 1979. Rsch. assoc. U. Wis., Madison, 1975-82; computer programmer DNA STAR, Inc., Madison, 1982—, also bd. dirs. Inventor algorithm for solving restriction maps. Grantee NIH, 1988. Office: DNA STAR Inc 1228 S Park St Madison WI 53715

SCHROEDER, JON HENRY, public affairs professional; b. Fergus Falls, Minn., Jan. 19, 1950; s. Henry W. and Delores E. (Johnson) S.; m. Dana M. Schenker, Dec. 27, 1975; children: Erin, Carl, Helen. BA, Macalester Coll., 1972. Comm. dir. Minn. Constitutional Study Com., St. Paul, 1972; rsch. assoc. Citizens League, Mpls., 1972-77; pub. Grant County Herald, Elbow Lake, Minn., 1977-84; comm. dir. Sen. Dave Durenberger, Mpls., 1984-88, sr. edn. advisor, 1989-94, Minn. dir., 1993-94; v.p. for pub. affairs and comm. Citizen's Scholarship Found. of Am., Mpls., 1994—; v.p., dir. Jefferson Ctr., Mpls., 1989—. Co-chair S.W. H.S. Baccalaureate Parent Com., Mpls., 1995-96; dir., Nat. Youth Leadership Coun., 1995—. Mem. Citizens League. Home: 4011 York Ave S Minneapolis MN 55410 Office: Citizens Scholarship Found of Am 7600 Parklawn Ste 248 Minneapolis MN 55435-5128

SCHROEDER, JOYCE KATHERINE, research analyst; b. Moline, Ill., Apr. 1, 1951; d. Reinhold J. and Miriam-May Schroeder. BS in Math., U. Ill., 1973, MA in Ops. Rsch., 1978. Underwriter/programmer Springfield, Ill., 1973-76; ops. rsch. analyst Ill. Dept. Transp., Springfield, 1976-78, data analyst, 1978-80, team leader, fatal accident reporting sys., 1980-83, mgr. safety project evaluation, 1983-92, mgr. accident studies and investigation, 1992—; sys. engring. del. to China China Assn. for Sci. and Tech., 1986; mem. staff Driving While Intoxicated Adv. Coun. and Task Force, State of Ill., 1983-86, 89-92, Gov. Task Force on Occupant Protection, 1988-90; active Ill. Traffic Safety Info. Sys. Coun., 1993—. Vol. Animal Protective League, Springfield; leaderbd. co-chairperson LPGA Rail Classic, Springfield, 1983-87; amb. of goodwill Lions of Ill. Found., 1993, trustee, 1995—. Lions Clubs Internat. Melvin Jones fellow, 1993, Lions of Ill. Found. fellow, 1995. Mem. Lions of Ill. Found. (amb. of goodwill 1993, trustee 1995—), Springfield Lincoln Land Lions Club (charter pres. 1988-90, treas. 1993-95, news editor 1995—), Lions Club (dist. gov. Ill. 1992-93, state membership coord. 1994—, Melvin Jones fellow 1993), Past. Dist. Gov. Assn. (sec.-treas. 1993—, Phi Kappa Phi, Kappa Delta Pi. Office: Ill Dept Transp 3215 Executive Park Dr Springfield IL 62703-4509

SCHROEDER, KORY DEAN, electrical engineer; b. Beatrice, Nebr., Aug. 16, 1969; s. Dale and Dorothy S. BS in Elec. Engring., U. Nebr., Lincoln, 1994. Application engr. Am. Shizuki Co., Ogallala, Nebr., 1994—. Mem. IEEE (rep. exec. bd. 1989-95). Lutheran.

SCHROEDER, MICHAEL JAY, history educator; b. Mpls., Mar. 13, 1958; s. Harold F. Schroeder Jr. and Betty (Delehanty) Schroeder-Tedmon; m. Denise Knuth, Oct. 8, 1988; children: Sarah Elizabeth, Timothy Delehanty. BA in History, BA in Econs., U. Minn., 1987; PhD in History, U. Mich., 1993. Asst. prof. history U. Mich., Flint, 1993—, dir. Mex.-Am. and Latino/Latina studies program, 1995—. Mellon fellow in humanities Woodrow Wilson Nat. Fellowship Found. 1987-93. Mem. Am. Hist. Assn., Resource Ctr. of the Ams., Latin Am. Studies Assn., Congress on Latin Am. History. Office: U Mich-Flint Dept History 322 CROB Flint MI 48502

SCHROEDER, NICHOLAS JOHN, engineer; b. Bklyn., Oct. 29, 1955; s. Nikolaus and Hildegarde (Edelmann) S.; m. Gerri L. Roadarmel, Mar. 4, 1985; children: Kate Marie, Emma Jeanne. BS in Environ. Sci., L.I. U., 1977. Lab. chemist Aerotech Labs., N.Y.C., 1980-89; measurement and quality control technician Buckeye Pipe Line Co., Huntington, Ind., 1987-89; regional engr. Buckeye Pipe Line Co., Lima, Ohio, 1989-94, ops. supr., 1994—; regional environ. coord. T.E. Products Pupiline Co. LP, Seymour, Ind., 1994—. Contbr. articles to Oil and Gas Jour.; contbg. editor Liquefied Petroleum Gas and Automotive Gasoline chpts. to ASTM Significance and Use Manual. Mem. ASTM (chmn. subcom. on liquefied petroleum gasses 1989-94, sec. subcom. fluid, rubber interaction 1989-91). Office: TE Products Pipeline Co LP PO Box 426 Seymour IN 47274

SCHROEDER, RAYMOND ERNEST, educational administrator; b. South Bend, Ind., Dec. 8, 1949; s. Marvin Klopsch and Jean (Hirsch) S.; m. Gail Arnsdorf, Mar. 5, 1977; children: Geneva Marie, Mary Lynn. BA in Speech, Augustana Coll., Rock Island, Ill., 1970; MS in Radio-TV, U. Ill., 1972. Reporter Sta. WOWO, Ft. Wayne, Ind., 1969; gen. mgr. Sta. WVIK, Rock Island, 1970; news reporter Sta. WILL-AM-FM, Urbana, Ill., 1971-74; instr. radio-TV U. Ill., Urbana, 1975-77; asst. prof. communication Sangamon State U., Springfield, Ill., 1977-83, assoc. prof. comm., 1983-95, dir. TV Office, 1984—, faculty assoc. to v.p. for acad. affairs, 1984—; prof. comm. U. Ill., Springfield, 1995—; interim exec. dir. Inst. for Pub. Affairs, 1992-93; part-time photographer Sta. WAND-TV, Decatur, Ill., 1975-77; coordinator community access Dimension Cable, Springfield, 1984—. Editor, cons. TV documentary Breadbasket or Dustbowl, 1983; tech. cons. TV documentary Illinois Prairies: Sense of Place, 1986; co-dir. TV documentary Mr. Lincoln of Illinois, 1986 (Spl. Achievement award 1987); creative cons. TV documentary The Lincolns of Springfield, Illinois, 1990 (Spl. Achievement award 1991). V.p. Holy Spirit Frat., 1986-87. Grantee Ill. State Bd. Edn., 1994; recipient Finalist award Nat. Fedn. Local Cable Programmers, 1987, 88, 93. Mem. Internat. TV Assn., Broadcast Edn. Assn., Sangamon State U. Faculty Union (pres. 1993). Roman Catholic. Office: Sangamon State U TV Office Springfield IL 62794-9243

SCHROEDER, ROBERT LOUIS, engineering executive; b. Cleve., Mar. 24, 1927; s. Harry Ernest and Ruth Loretta (Nienhuser) S.; m. Elaine Lois Thunhorst, June 14, 1974 (dec. 1988); children: Gary R., Mark L., Gail L., Susan E.; m. Pauline Schaum, Jan. 28, 1989. BS in Engring. Adminstrn., Case Inst. Tech., 1950. Mgr. Ostendorf-Morris Co., Cleve., 1950-51; dir. sales and engring. Pesco Products-Bong Warner, Bedford, Ohio, 1951-72; v.p. sales and engring. Lake Shore Electric Co., Bedford, Ohio, 1972-74; product mgr. TRW-Power Accessories div., Cleve., 1974-86; v.p. Argo-Tech. Corp., Cleve., 1986-90, exec. v.p., 1990—; pres. R.L. Schroeder & Assocs., 1990-93; pres. Upsilon Internat. Corp., L.A., 1991-94. V.p., bd. dirs. Cleve. Air Show, 1988—; bd. dris. Jr. Achievement, Cleve., 1984—. Mem. Case Alumni (trustee 1976—, past pres.). Republican. Lutheran. Home: 770 Emerald Harbor Dr Longboat Key FL 34228-1610

SCHROEDER, SHARI, software analyst; b. Kans., Nov. 29, 1957; d. Edgar and Patricia Schroeder; m. Donald L. Brown, Sept. 20, 1980. B in med. tech., Wichita State U., 1980; MSEE, Kans. State U., 1992. Cert. med. technologist Am. Soc. Clin. Pathologists. Med. technologist Wamego (Kans.) City Hosp., 1980-82, Kans. State U., Manhattan, 1983-88; software analyst Cerner Corp., Kansas City, Mo., 1992—. Office: Cerner Corp 2800 Rockcreek Kansas City MO 64117

SCHROEDER, WILLIAM ARTHUR, law educator; b. Chgo., Mar. 19, 1943; s. Arthur C. Schroeder; m. Connie Koshiol; children: Elizabeth, Matthew, David, Sara. BA, U. Ill., Champaign, 1966, JD, 1969; LLM, Harvard U., 1977. Bar: Mass. 1972, Mo. 1990, U.S. Supreme Ct. 1978. Instr. law Boston Coll., 1970-71; practicing atty. various firms, Mass., 1972-80; assoc. prof. law U. Ala., Tuscaloosa, 1980-84; prof. law So. Ill. U., Carbondale, 1984—; visiting prof. law U. Mo.-Columbia, 1983; Washington U. 1991. Co-author: Alabama Evidence, 1987; author: Missouri Evidence, 1991; contbr. articles to profl. jours. Mem. ABA, Harvard Club of St. Louis, Lions. Home: 370 N Mill St Nashville IL 62263-1743 Office: So Ill U Lesar Law Bldg Carbondale IL 62901

SCHROEK, ED, state legislator; b. Holdrege, Nebr., Aug. 20, 1943; m. Judith M. Grove, 1965; children: Ted, Tom. BA, Nebr. Wesleyan U., 1965. Farmer Phelps County, Nebr.; senator Nebraska Senate, Lincoln, 1994—. Mem. Phelps County Sch. Bd. Dist. R-4. Mem. Holdrege Area C. of C., Natural Resources Commn., Nebr. Corn Growers Assn., Nebr. Corn Developers (utilization and mkt. coms. bds.), Ctrl. Irrigators Assn., Nebr. Cattlemens Assn.

SCHROER, EDMUND ARMIN, utility company executive; b. Hammond, Ind., Feb. 14, 1928; s. Edmund Henry and Florence Evelyn (Schmidt) S.; m. Lisa V. Strope; children: James, Fredrik, Amy, Lisa, Timothy, Suzanne. BA, Valparaiso U., 1949; JD, Northwestern U., 1952. Bar: Ind. 1952. Pvt. practice law Hammond, 1952—; assoc. Crumpacker & Friedrich, 1952; ptnr. Crumpacker & Schroer, 1954-56; assoc., then ptnr. Lawyer, Friedrich, Petrie & Tweedle, 1957-62; ptnr. Lawyer, Schroer & Eichhorn, 1963-66; sr. ptnr. Schroer, Eichhorn & Morrow, Hammond, 1967-77; pres., chief exec. officer No. Ind. Pub. Svc. Co., Inc., Hammond, 1977-93; chmn. No. Ind. Pub. Svc. Co., Hammond, 1978-93, chmn., chief exec. officer, 1989-93, also bd. dirs.; chmn., pres., chief exec. officer NIPSCO Industries, Inc., 1987-93; cons. NIPSCO Industries Inc., Hammond, 1993-96; also bd. dirs.; asst. dist. atty., No. Ind., 1954-56; trustee Ill. Ins. Exch., 1993-95. Trustee Sch. Bd., Munster, Ind., 1969-71, pres., 1971; fin. chmn. Rep. Party, Hammond, 1958-62; del. Ind. Rep. Conv., 1958, 60, 64, 66, 68. Mem. Fed. Bar Assn., Am. Gas Assn. (chmn. 1986), Rotary (pres. Hammond club 1968). Lutheran. Home and Office: No Ind Pub Svc Co 5265 Hohman Ave Hammond IN 46320-1722

SCHROER, LAURIE ANN, investment broker; b. Columbus, Ind., Jan. 1, 1973. AS in Acctg., Ind. Bus. Coll., 1992. Investment broker J.J.B. Hilliard W.L. Lyons Inc., Columbus, 1991-96, Linsco/Pvt. Ledger, Columbus, 1996—. Lutheran. Office: Home Fed Savs Bank 501 Washington St Columbus IN 47201

SCHROER, MARY, state legislator; b. St. Marys, Ohio, Feb. 11, 1947; m. J. Michael Schroer; children: Jennifer, Amy, Rebecca. Student, Washtenaw C.C., Ea. Mich. U. Legis. asst. to State Sen. Lana Pollack Inst. Study of Mental Retardation and Related Disabilities, 1983-92; state rep. 52d dist. State of Mich., 1992—. Mem. Washtenaw County (Mich.) Dem. Party, Washtenaw County Area Auto Plant Coaltion, Ann Arbor, Pittsfield Twp. Econ. Deve. Corp. Bd.; past pres. Carpenter Sch. PTO, Ann Arbor; former bd. dirs. Ann Arbor (Mich.) Cmty. Ctr. Roman Catholic. Office: 907 Olds Plz Bldg Lansing MI 48913

SCHROM, ELIZABETH ANN, educator; b. Princeton, Minn., June 7, 1941; d. Raymond Alois and Grace Eleanor (Hayes) S. Student, U. Minn., 1960; BA, St. Scholastica Coll., Duluth, Minn., 1963; postgrad., Princeton U., 1965; MEd, Temple U., 1972; MLS, Drexel U., 1974; postgrad., NYU, 1981, Russian Temple U., 1983. Tchr. Strandquist (Minn.) H.S., 1963-64, Hutchinson (Minn.) H.S., 1964-65, Peace Corps, Ankara, Turkey, 1965-67, Phila. Sch. Dist., 1968-80; children's libr. Laurel (Del.) Pub. Libr., 1983. Mem. Jewish Com. on Middle East, Washington, 1988-90, 93, Nat. Coun. Returned Peace Corps. Vols., Washington, 1989-96, Nat. Taxpayers Union, Washington, 1988-92; mem. bd. policy Liberty Lobby, Washington, 1989-96; mem. Emergency Com. to Stop Immigration, Marietta, Ga., 1989-91. Populist. Roman Catholic. Home: RR 2 Box 206 Ortonville MN 56278-9784

SCHROTH, JOHN HENRY, associate lawyer; b. Hinsdale, Ill., Jan. 24, 1968; s. Stanley Edward and Janis Kay (Hardin) S. BA, Marquette U., 1990; JD, U. Minn., 1994. Bar: Wis. 1994, Minn. 1995. Law clk. Parke, O'Flaherty, Heim, Koby, O'Keefe, La Crosse, Wis., 1993-94; assoc. Parke, O'Flaherty Ltd., La Crosse, Wis., 1994—. Mental health job coach, Jesuit Vol. Corps, Juneau, Alaska, 1990-91. Mem. La Crosse Optimist's Club, Phi Beta Kappa, Alpha Sigma Nu. Republican. Roman Catholic. Home: 814 W Parkway Blvd Appleton WI 54914 Office: Parke O'Flaherty Ltd 201 Main St 10th Fl La Crosse WI 54601

SCHROTT, JANET ANN, human resources specialist, administrator, consultant; b. Cleve., Dec. 11, 1941; d. Louis Vincent and Amelia Jane (Lauko) Cupolo; BA, Flora Stone Mather Coll. of Case Western Res. U., 1963, MS in Social Adminstrn., 1974; MBA, Baldwin-Wallace Coll., Berea, Ohio, 1986; m. Norman Schrott, July 25, 1964. Lic. ind. social worker. Rsch. asst. Aging Baseline Study, HEW Grant, Miami, Fla., 1964-65; caseworker Div. Social Svcs., Cuyahoga County Welfare Dept., Cleve., 1965-72, protective svcs. supr., 1974-78; dir. social svcs. Luth. Housing Corp., Cleve., 1973-74; dir. travelers aid svcs. and quality assurance Ctr. for Human Svcs., Cleve., 1978-86; tng. analyst Cleve. Electric Illuminating Co., Perry, Ohio, 1985-86, supr. support svcs., tng., 1986-96; mgr. quality assurance Lorain County Children Svcs., 1996—; adj. faculty Lakeland (Ohio) C. C. Kirkland, 1995—; mgr. quality assurance Lorrain County Children's Svcs., 1996—. Bd. dirs. adv. council Adult Rehab. Svcs., Salvation Army, 1978-85. Cuyahoga County Welfare Dept. grantee, 1972-74. Mem. Assn. MBA Execs., Acad. Cert. Social Workers, Nat. Assn. Social Workers, Am. Evaluation Assn., Nat. Geographic Soc., Travelers Aid Assn. Am. (bd. dirs., Steering com. 1982-85), Theta Phi Omega. Home: 25925 Lake Rd Cleveland OH 44140-2563 Office: 226 Middle Ave Elyria OH 44035

SCHROTT, NORMAN, clinical social worker; b. N.Y.C., Jan. 26, 1938; s. Walter Quido Otto and Anna (Klein) S.; B.A. in Sociology, Cleve. State U., 1972; M.S. in Social Planning and Adminstrn. (grantee State of Ohio 1974-76), Case Western Res. U., 1976; m. Janet Ann Cupolo, July 25, 1964. Lic. Ind. Social Worker, Ohio. Adminstrv. specialist div. social services Cuyahoga County Welfare Dept., Cleve., 1972-74, foster care specialist, 1976-79, child abuse supr., 1979-80, protective services supr., 1980—. Served with U.S. Army, 1962-65. Mem. Acad. Cert. Social Workers, Nat. Assn. Social Workers, Nat. Conf. Social Welfare, Am. Pub. Welfare Assn., Am. Acad. Polit. and Social Scis., Nat. Audubon Soc., Am. Orchid Soc. Club: Kiwanis. Home: 25925 Lake Rd Cleveland OH 44140-2563 Office: 3955 Euclid Ave Cleveland OH 44115

SCHROY, JERRY MICHAEL, chemical engineer; b. Dayton, Ohio, Nov. 6, 1939; s. Lloyd Felton and Georgia (Kostoff) S.; m. Barbara Ann Meyrose, Jan. 11, 1969; children: Catherine Marie, David Michael, Mark Alan. B-ChemE, U. Cin., 1963; postgrad., Bklyn. Poly. Inst., 1970-71, Washington U., St. Louis, 1974-75. Registered profl. engr., N.Y., Ill., Ohio, Iowa, Mo. Process engr. Inorganic Chems. divsn. Monsanto Chem. Co., St. Louis, 1963-67, supr. plant tech. svcs. group, 1967-69; process engring. specialist Monsanto Biodize Systems Inc. and Monsanto Enviro-Chem System Inc., L.I. and Chgo. Monsanto Co., St. Louis, 1969-72, mgr. process engring. Monsanto Enviro-Chem System Inc., Chgo., 1972; prin. engring. specialist Monsanto EnviroChem Systems, Inc., St. Louis, 1972-75; prin. engring. specialist Monsanto Co., St. Louis, 1976-81, fellow, 1981-89, sr. fellow, 1989—. Mem. AAAS, AICE (dir. L.I. chpt. 1969-71, dir. safety and health divsn. 1987-89, dir. environ. divsn. 1987-89, 2d vice chair 1990, vice chair 1991, chair 1992, vice chair continuing edn. com. 1993-94, chair continuing edn. com. 1995-96), Water Environment Fedn. (Water Environment Found. Rsch. coun. 1989-96), Am. Chem. Soc., Soc. Risk Analysts, Nat. Assn. Environ. Profls., Chem. Mfrs. Assn., Internat. Soc. Exposure Analysts (pres. 1992-93), Sigma Xi, Alpha Chi Sigma. Home: 5 Springlake Ct Ballwin MO 63011-3549

SCHUBEL, DIAN, construction company manager; b. Detroit; d. Edgar Auger; m. Jeffrey Allen Schubel, June 28, 1969; children: Adam, Regan. BA, Stephens Coll., 1969; teaching cert., Mich. State U., 1971. Retail mgr. Montgomery Ward, Southfield, Mich., 1969-70; tchr. Royal Oak (Mich.) Pub. Sch., 1970-76; builder Dian Schubel, Inc., Marshall, Mich., 1989—. Mem. devel. coun. Oaklawn Hosp., Marshall; mem. Marshall Hist. Soc. Mem. Nat. Assn. Homebuilders, Mich. Assn. Homebuilders (del. 1994—), Battle Creek Homebuilders Assn. (sec., v.p. 1989—), Jr. League of Battle Creek. Office: Dian Schubel Inc 740 Allison Dr Marshall MI 49068-9610

SCHUBERT, ESTHER VIRGINIA, psychiatrist, physician; b. Glendale, Calif., Mar. 29, 1945; d. William Everett and Katherine (McCoy) S.; m. David A. Chambers, Jan. 15, 1971; children: Daniel, John, Tony, Jeff. AB, Asbury Coll., 1966; MD, Ind. U., 1970; FACEP, Am. Coll. Emergency Physicians, Dallas, 1981; FAAFP, Am. Acad. Family Practice, Kansas City, Mo., 1990; postgrad., Ind. U., 1992-95. Diplomate Am. Bd. Emergency Medicine, Am. Bd. Family Practice, Am. Bd. Psychiatry and Neurology. Family practice Indpls., 1972-73; pvt. practice emergency medicine Ind., Republic of China, 1973-92; pvt. practice psychiatry, cons. for missions Anderson, Ind., Republic of China, 1989—; resident in psychiatry, 1992-95; clin. asst. prof. psychiatry Ind. U., 1995—; cons. physician Ctr. for Mental Health, Anderson, 1989-92. Mem. Youth Task Force, New Castle, Ind., 1977, Rape Crisis Coun., New Castle, 1975, Child Abuse Panel, New Castle, 1977; bd. dirs. Christian & Missionary Alliance Ch., New Castle, 1988-92. Named one of Outstanding Young Women of Am., 1975, Mother of Yr., Jaycees, Middletown, Ind., 1977. Fellow Am. Psychiat. Assn., Am. Acad. Family Practice, Am. Coll. Emergency Physicians (bd. dirs. Ind. chpt. 1976-82), Christian Med. and Dental Soc. Home and Office: 2239 N Cadiz Pike New Castle IN 47362-9743

SCHUBERT, WILLIAM HENRY, curriculum studies educator; b. Garrett, Ind., July 6, 1944; s. Walter William and Mary Madeline (Grube) S.; children by previous marriage: Ellen Elaine, Karen Margaret; m. Ann Lynn Lopez, Dec. 3, 1977; children: Heidi Ann, Henry William. BS, Manchester Coll., 1966; MS, Ind. U., 1967; PhD, U. Ill., 1975. Tchr., Fairmount, El Sierra and Herrick Schs., Downers Grove, Ill., 1967-75; clin. instr. U. Wis., Madison, 1969-73; teaching asst., univ. fellow U. Ill., Urbana, 1973-75; asst. prof. U. Ill., Chgo., 1975-80, assoc. prof., 1981-85, prof., 1985—, coord. secondary edn., 1979-82; coord. instrl. leadership, 1979-85, dir. grad. studies Coll. Edn., 1983-85, coord. grad. curriculum studies, 1985—, coord. edn. studies, 1990-94, chair area curriculum and instruction, 1990-94; vis. assoc. prof. U. Victoria (B.C., Can.), 1981; disting. vis. prof. U. S.C., 1986. Mem. Profs. of Curriculum (factotum 1984-85), Soc. for Study of Curriculum History (founding mem., sec.-treas. 1981-82, pres. 1982-83), Am. Ednl. Rsch. Assn. (chmn. creation and utilization of curriculum knowledge 1980-82, program chmn. curriculum studies div. 1982-83, sec. Div. B 1989-91), Am. Assn. Colls. for Tchr. Edn., John Dewey Soc. (bd. dirs. 1986-95, chair awards com., 1988-90, co-chair lectures commn., 1989-91, pres. elect, 1990-91, pres. 1992-93), ASCD (steering com. of curriculum com. 1980-83, pubs. com. 1987-90, internat. polling panel 1990—), Am. Ednl. Studies Assn., World Coun. for Curriculum and Instrn., Soc. for Profs. of Edn., Nat. Soc. for Study of Edn., Inst. Dem. in Edn., Masons, Scottish Rite, Phi Delta Kappa, Phi Kappa Phi (pres. U. Ill.-Chgo. chpt. 1981-82). Author: (with Ann Lopez) Curriculum Books: The First Eighty Years, 1980; author: Curriculum: Perspective, Paradigm, and Possibility, 1986; (with Edmund C. Short and George Willis) Toward Excellence in Curriculum Inquiry, 1985; editor: (with Ann Lopez) Conceptions of Curriculum Knowledge: Focus on Students and Teachers, 1982, (with George Willis) Reflections from The Heart of Ednl. Inquiry: Understanding Curriculum and Teaching Through the Arts, 1991, (with William Ayers) Teacher Lore: Learning From Our Own Experience, 1992, (with George Willis, R. Bullough, C. Kridel, J. Holton) The American Curriculum: A Documentary History, 1993; assoc. editor: Ednl. Theory; former mem. editl. bd. Ednl. Studies; cons. editor Phenomenology Pedagogy; adv. bd. Teaching Edn., Pi Lamda Theta Pubs., 1995—; mem. editl. bd. Ednl. Theory; cons. editor Jour. Curriculum and Supervision; editorial bd. Curriculum and Teaching; reviewing editor Jour. Gang Behaviour; editor: book series Student Lore, SUNY Press, 1990—; cons. editor Jour. Curriculum Discourse and Dialogue; contbr. over 150 articles to profl. pubs. Home: 727 S Ashland Ave Chicago IL 60607-3165 Office: U Ill Coll Edn M/C 147 1040 W Harrison St Chicago IL 60607-7129

SCHUCHART, JOHN ALBERT, JR., utility company executive; b. Omaha, Nov. 13, 1929; s. John A. and Mildred Vera (Kessler) S.; m. Ruth Joyce Schock, Dec. 2, 1950; children: Deborah J. Kelley, Susan K. Felton. BS in Bus, U. Nebr., 1950; grad., Stanford U. Exec. Program, 1968. With No. Natural Gas Co., Omaha, 1950-71, asst. sec., 1958-60, mgr. acctg., 1960-66, adminstrv. mgr., 1966-71; v.p., treas. Intermountain Gas Co., Boise, Idaho, 1972-75, chief fin. officer, 1973-75; fin. v.p. and treas., chief fin. officer Mont.-Dakota Utilities Co. (now MDU Resources Group, Inc.), Bismarck, N.D., 1976-77, pres., chief oper. officer, 1978-80, pres., 1980-92, CEO, 1980-94, chmn. bd., 1983—, also dir. Contbr. articles to profl. jours. Trustee Bismarck YMCA, N.D. chpt. Nature Conservancy; mem. bd. regents U. Mary, Bismarck; bus. adv. bd. Coll. Bus., Mont. State U., Billings. With AUS, 1951-53. Recipient Am. Gas Assn. Order of Acctg. Merit award, 1968, 78, Scroll and Merit award Adminstrv. Mgmt. Soc., 1972, U. Nebr. at Omaha citation of Alumnus Achievement, 1987, Coll. of Bus. Disting. Achievement award, 1989, CEO of Yr. award Fin. World Mag., 1993, Commn. and Leadership award Dist. 20 Toastmasters Internat., 1994. Mem. Apple Creek Country Club, Mpls. Athletic Club, Elks, Delta Sigma Pi. Republican. Methodist. Home: 1014 Cottage Dr Bismarck ND 58501-2458 Office: MDU Resources Group Inc 400 N 4th St Bismarck ND 58501-4022

SCHUCHERT, BART O., product engineering manager; b. Iowa City, Iowa, Feb. 12, 1938. B, U. Iowa, 1960. Project engr. Iowa State Hwy. Commn., Columbus Junction, 1960-65; mfg. engr. Amana (Iowa) Refrigeration, 1965-70, sr. equipment engr., 1970-80, mgr. prodn. engring., 1980—. Patentee in field. With Iowa Nat. Guard, 1953-65. Mem. Soc. Plastics Engrs. Home: 3911 Schuchert Dr SE Iowa City IA 52246-5888

SCHUCK, WILLIAM, state legislator; b. Findlay, Ohio, Dec. 12, 1951; s. Robert and Margaretta (Beynon) S. BA, Harvard Univ., 1974; MBA, JD, Cornell Univ., 1982. Mem. Columbus Devel. Com., Ohio, 1985-86; State Rep. Ohio Dist. 29, 1987—; lawyer Porter, Wright, Morris & Arthur, 1984—. Named Outstanding Citizen of Columbus, Jaycees, 1986. Mem. Columbus Athletic Club, Aladdin Shrine, Delta Epsilon. *

SCHUCKMAN, BARBARA ANNE, psychology instructor; b. Livonia, Mich., Sept. 13, 1967; d. Richard William Pierce and Susan Grace (Farquhar) MacDavitt; m. Mark Joseph Schuckman, Dec. 11, 1993. BA, Central Mich. U., Mt. Pleasant, 1985-90, MA, 1990-93. Instr. psychology Saginaw Valley State U., Univ. Ctr., Mich., 1992-95, Delta Coll., Univ. Ctr., 1993-95, Lorain County Cmty. Coll., Elryia, Ohio, 1995—. Home: 10617 Station Rd Columbia Station OH 44028

SCHUERING, MARK ALLEN, judge, educator; b. Quincy, Ill., Sept. 7, 1953; s. Robert A. and Norma C. (Terwelp) S.; m. Kate Orlet, May 14, 1977; children: Emily K., Julie A., Maggie E., Laura M., Lucy E. BA in Polit. Sci., Quincy Coll., 1975; JD cum laude, St. Louis U., 1978. Bar: Ill. 1978, U.S. Dist. Ct. (cen. dist.) Ill. 1982, Mo. 1982. Assoc. Goehl, Adams & Schuering, Quincy, 1978-82; pub. defender Adams County, Quincy, 1980-84; ptnr. Goehl & Schuering, Quincy, 1983-86; assoc. cir. judge 8th Jud. Cir. State of Ill., Quincy, 1986-90; cir. judge State of Ill., Quincy, 1990—; instr. Quincy (Ill.) U., Quincy, Ill., 1989—. Trustee St. Francis Solanus Ch., Quincy, 1987-90. Mem. ABA, Ill. Judges Assn., Am. Judicature Soc., Ill. State Bar Assn., Adams County Bar Assn., Mart Heinen Club. Office: Adams County Courthouse Quincy IL 62301

SCHUERMAN, NORBERT JOEL, school superintendent; b. DeWitt, Nebr., Dec. 26, 1934; s. Edwin J. and Martha (Finkbeiner) S.; m. Charlette Ann Detling, Aug. 6, 1960; children: Robert, Brenda, Todd. B of Music Edn., U. Nebr., 1957, MEd, 1959, EdS in Ednl. Mgmt. and Supervision, 1964, EdD, 1967. Cert. profl. tchr. (life), Nebr. Tchr. Clatonia-Bennet (Nebr.) Pub. Sch., 1954-58; tchr., prin. Mullen (Nebr.) Pub. Sch., 1958-61; prin. Ainsworth (Nebr.) Pub. Sch., 1961-63; sr. high sch. vice prin. Lincoln (Nebr.) Pub. Sch., 1963-66, 67-69; sr. high sch. prin. Arapahoe County Sch. Dist. 6, Littleton, Colo., 1969-74; from asst. supt. to assoc. supt. to supt. Omaha Pub. Schs., 1974—; trustee, mem. exec. com. Nebr. Coun. Econ. Edn., 1985—; bd. dirs. Nat. Study Sch. Evaluation, 1986-90, Charles Drew Health Ctr., 1985-95, Fontenelle Forest, 1987-92, 95—; bd. trustees Western Heritage Mus., 1994—; mem. exec. com. Coun. Gt. City Schs., 1988—; mem. Nat. Urban Edn. Task Force, 1990—; mem. Nat. Adv. Bd. for Active Citizenship Today, 1992—; mem. bd. advisors Close Up Found., 1992—; mem. adminstrs. adv. com. U. Nebr.-Lincoln Tchrs. Coll. Mem. adv. com. Mid-Am. coun. Boy Scouts Am., 1984—; coun. regents Big Bros./Big Sisters of Midlands, Omaha, 1986—; bd. dirs. United Way of Midlands, 1985—; adv. bd. Omaha Children's Mus., 1988—. Named Nebr. Supt. of Yr., 1991; recipient Disting. Svc. award Nebr. Coun. Sch. Adminstrs., 1988, awards of honor Nat. Sch. Pub. Rels. Assn., 1991, Nebr. PTA Outstanding PTA Advocate award; named to Exec. Educator mag.'s Top 100 Sch. Execs., 1993. Mem. Am. Assn. Sch. Adminstrs. (urban schs. com. 1992—), Nebr. Coun. Sch. Adminstrs., Omaha Sch. Adminstrs. Assn., North Ctrl. Assn. (bd. dirs. 1983-89, chmn. 1987-88), Large City Schs. Supts. (pres. 1992-93), NCCJ (bd. dirs. 1990—), Nebr. Schoolmasters Club, Urban League of Nebr., Nat. Congress Parents and Tchrs. (hon. life), Nebr. Congress Parents and Tchrs. (hon. life), Phi Delta Kappa, Omicron Delta Kappa. Home: 4007 N 94th St Omaha NE 68134-3927 Office: Omaha Sch Dist 3215 Cuming St Omaha NE 68131-2000

SCHUETTE, BILL, state senator; b. Midland, Mich., Oct. 13, 1953. Student, U. Aberdeen, 1974-75; B.S. in Fgn. Svc., Georgetown U.,

1976; J.D., U. San Francisco, 1979. Bar: U.S. Supreme Ct. 1985. Atty. Midland, Mich., 1981—; Mich. field coordinator George Bush for Pres., 1979; Mich. polit. dir. Reagan/Bush for Pres., 1980; mem. 99th-101st Congresses from 10th Mich. dist., Washington, 1985-91, Mich. Senate, 1994—. Office: PO Box 30036 Lansing MI 48909-7536

SCHUH, JOSEPH FRANCIS, weed scientist; b. Green Bay, Wis., Aug. 11, 1963; s. Frank C. and Janet H. S. BS, U. Wis., Platteville, 1985; MS, U. Wis., Madison, 1988, PhD, 1990. Grad. rsch. asst. U. Wis., Madison, 1985-90; postdoctoral scientist Am. Cyanamid Co., Lincoln, Nebr., 1990-91; field rsch. agriculturist Am. Cyanamid Co., Sioux Falls, S.D., 1991—. Contbr. articles to Weed Sci. Jour., Weed Tech. Jour., other profl. publs. Mem. Am. Soc. Agronomy, Weed Sci. Soc. Am., North Cen. Weed Sci. Soc., North Cen. Entomological Soc. Am.

SCHUL, BILL DEAN, psychological administrator, author; b. Winfield, Kans., Mar. 16, 1928; s. Fred M. and Martha Mildred (Miles) S.; B.A., Southwestern Coll., 1952; M.A., U. Denver, 1954; Ph.D., Am. Internat. U., 1977; m. Virginia Louise Duboise, Aug. 3, 1952; children—Robert Dean, Deva Elizabeth. Reporter and columnist Augusta (Kans.) Daily Gazette, 1954-58, Wichita (Kans.) Eagle-Beacon, 1958-61; Kans. youth dir. under auspices of Kans. Atty. Gen., 1961-65; Kans. state dir. Seventh Step Found., Topeka, 1965-66; mem. staff Dept. Preventive Psychiatry, Menninger Found., Topeka, Kans., 1966-71; dir. cons. Ctr. Improvement Human Functioning, Wichita, 1975—; psychologist Ctr. for Human Devel., Wichita, Kans. Mng. editor: The Register, Oxford, Kans., 1988—; author: (with Edward Greenwood) Mental Health in Kansas Schools, 1965; Let Me Do This Thing, 1969; (with Bill Larson) Hear Me, Barabbas, 1969; How to Be An Effective Group Leader, 1975; The Secret Power of Pyramids, 1975; (with Ed Pettit) The Psychic Power of Pyramids, 1976, Pyramids: The Second Reality, 1979; The Psychic Power of Animals, 1977; Psychic Frontiers of Medicine, 1977, Animal Immortality, 1990, Life Song, 1995. Bd. dirs. Recreation Commn., Topeka, United Funds, Topeka, Adamic Inst., Trees for Life; v.p. Pegasus Way; pres. Intraface Corp., 1989—; mem. adv. bd. Clayton U. Served with USN, 1945-46. Recipient John H. McGinnis Meml. award for Nonfiction, 1972, Am. Freedom Found. award, 1966, Spl. Appreciation award Kans. State Penitentiary, 1967. Mem. Acad. of Parapsychology and Medicine, Kans. Council for Children and Youth (pres. 1965-66), Assn. for Strenghtening the Higher Realities and Aspirations of Man (pres. 1970-71), Smithsonian Inst., Lions (pres. 1957). Address: RR 3 Winfield KS 67156-9803

SCHULER, ROBERT LEO, appraiser, consultant; b. Cin., June 15, 1943; s. Del D. and Virginia D. (Heyl) S.; m. Shelagh J. Moritz, Aug. 11, 1962; children: Robert C., Sherry L. V.p. Comprehensive Appraisal Service, Inc., Cin., 1977—; bd. dirs. Hamilton County Regional Planning Commn., Cin., 1987-88; mem. exec. com., past pres. OKI Regional Coun. Govts., Cin., 1981-92. Councilman City of Deer Park, Ohio, 1979-86; trustee Sycamore Twp., 1988-92; Ohio state rep. 36th dist. Mem. Am. Assn. Cert. Appraiser (sr.), Cin. Bd. Realtors, Ohio Assn. Realtors, Jaycees (v.p.). Republican. Roman Catholic. Home: 3648 Jeffrey Ct Cincinnati OH 45236-1544 Office: PO Box 36442 Cincinnati OH 45236-0442

SCHULFER, ROCHE EDWARD, theater executive director; b. Chgo., Sept. 26, 1951; s. Thomas Florian and Tess (Ronk) S.; m. Arlene Lencioni, June 2, 1973 (div. 1979); m. Linda Kimbrough, Aug. 2, 1986. BA in Econs., U. Notre Dame. Box office asst. Goodman Theatre, Chgo., 1973-74, asst. to mng. dir., 1974-77, gen. mgr., 1977-80, mng. dir., producer, producing dir., exec. dir., 1980—. Mem. exec. com. League of Resident Theatres, Chgo., 1981, 83; pres. League of Chgo. Theatres, 1983-85, pres. Chgo. Theatre Found., 1985-87 ; bd. dirs. Chgo. Theatre Group, Lifeline Theatre, Theatre Comm. Group, Lawyers for Creative Arts. Mem. Am. Arts Alliance (chair), Ill. Art Alliance (pres.), Ill. Arts Coun. Office: Goodman Theatre 200 S Columbus Dr Chicago IL 60603-6402*

SCHULMAN, ALAN MICHAEL, small business owner; b. Chgo., Feb. 5, 1946; s. Aaron and Anne (Bendersky) S.; m. Barbara Picard, May 27, 1984; 1 child, Jeffrey. BBA, Roosevelt U., 1968. Salesman Dictaphone Corp., Chgo., 1968-69; sales engr. Boston Gear, Chgo., 1969-70; mgr. Imperial Packaging, Chgo., 1970-71; owner A.M.S. Distbg., Skokie, Ill., 1971-77; owner, pres. Greater Distbn. Svcs., Glenview, Ill., 1977-90, The Battery Bank div. Jalco, Inc., Glenview, 1982-92, Glentronics Inc., Glenview, 1989—; host tv gardening program. Author (newspaper column) Gardening Information, 1980; host numerous TV fishing programs; contbr. articles on battery to nat. mags.; patentee in field; subject of mag., newspaper articles. Named to Freshwater Fishing Hall of Fame for world record catch. Mem. Entrepreneurs Network. Club: Men's Garden of North Shore (Highland Park) (pres. 1984-85). Office: Glentronics Inc 2053 Johns Dr Glenview IL 60025-1654

SCHULMAN, TAMMY BETH, communications executive; b. Queens, N.Y., Sept. 1, 1960; d. David Abraham and Diane Lois (Herman) Schulman; m. Kurt James Anderson, Sept. 14, 1986 (div. 1990); m. Kenneth Steven Peterson, 1990; stepchildren: Tanya, Kathleen, Amanda. Degree in comml. art, Hennepin County Vocat.-Tech., Eden Prairie, Minn., 1978; postgrad., Coll. St. Catherine, St. Paul, 1985-88, Augsburg Coll., 1991—. Corr. sec. Ross Investment Co., Edina, Minn., 1980; quality control rep. Hubbard Milling Co., Minnetonka, Minn., 1980-81; ins. insp. Underwriters Svc. Co., Hopkins, Minn., 1982-83; dir. publs., communications mgr. Lifetouch Nat. Sch. Studios, Mpls., 1984—. Author, editor: Versatile Beans, 1978, Exposure mag., 1986-92, Life Lines mag., 1995—. Tutor Glenwood-Lyndale Community Ctr., Mpls., 1982; women's advocate Sojourner Shelter, Minnetonka, 1984—; active Sta. KFAI-Radio, Mpls., Simon Weisenthal Ctr., Mpls., 1985-86. Mem. Women in Communications Inc., Upper Miss. Blues Soc. Democrat. Jewish. Office: Lifetouch Nat Sch Studios 7800 Picture Dr Minneapolis MN 55439-3149

SCHULSINGER, MICHAEL ALAN, data processing executive; b. Springfield, Ohio, Dec. 2, 1952; s. Gerald Morton and Dolores Mae (McLendon) S. AS, SUNY, Albany, 1977, BS, 1985; BA, Wittenberg U., 1984. Technician Dimension Electronics, Dayton, Ohio, 1977-78; electronics technician Yellow Springs (Ohio) Instrument Co., 1978-79, 80-81; lab. technician Scripps Inst. Oceanography U. Calif., San Diego, La Jolla, 1979; electronics technician Nu-Tech Industries, Inc., Trotwood, Ohio, 1981-82; project dir. Clark County Hist. Soc., Springfield, 1983; editor Scott Pub. Co., Sidney, Ohio, 1985; facilities supr. Inst. Communications and Media Arts Antioch Coll., Yellow Springs, 1986-87; designer Analytical Rsch., Yellow Springs, 1988-89, Huntington Instruments Inc., Yellow Springs, 1989—. Editor Australasian Informer, 1977-78, Scott Stamp Monthly, 1985. Treas. Citizen's Arcade Alliance, Springfield, 1986-87; planning officer Clark County Civil Def., 1970-71; vol. disaster relief ARC, 1993-96. Recipient Staff award Clark County Civil Def., 1972; named Vol. of Yr., Clark County chpt. ARC, 1996; grantee Ohio Humanities Coun., 1983. Mem. IEEE Computer Soc., Assn. for Computing Machinery, Ind. Radion Assn., Inc. (pres. 1993, sec. 1993-96), N.Y. Acad. Scis. Democrat. Jewish. Home: 1002 Woodlawn Ave Springfield OH 45504-2140 Office: Huntington Instruments Inc PO Box 718 Yellow Springs OH 45387-0718

SCHULTE, GARY RODGER, consumer products company executive; b. Detroit, Feb. 25, 1949; s. Rodger Louis and Helen May (Byrd) S.; m. Felicia Delores Gillish, Sept. 5, 1970; children: Kimberly Kathleen, Keith Daniel. BS in Architecture, Lawrence Technol. U., Southfield, Mich., 1972. Registered architect, Mich. Project engr. Ford Motor Co., Dearborn, Mich., 1972-74; project engr. Dow Chem. Co., Midland, Mich., 1974-79, engring. mgr., 1979-84; project mgr. Dow Consumer Products, Bay City, Mich., 1984-86, supt., 1986-88; ops. dir. Dow Brands, Mpls., 1988-93; ops. mgr. Dow Brands, Urbana, Ohio, 1993—. Bd. dirs. Mid-Mich. Health Care Systems, Midland, 1978-88; vice chmn. bd. Stratford Pines Nursing Home, Midland, 1984-87; chmn. bd. Gladwin (Mich.) Nursing Home, 1987-88; vice chmn. bldg. com. Midland Hosp. Ctr., 1982-88; elder Midland Reformed Ch., 1986-88, deacon, 1980-83; bd. dirs. Leadership Bay County, 1985-88; loaned exec. United Way, 1979-80. Evangelical Christian. Home: 5852 Rushwood Dr Dublin OH 43017 Office: Dow Brands 801 State Rte 55 Urbana OH 43078

SCHULTE, WILLIAM PAUL, religious fund raiser; b. St. Paul, Apr. 1, 1947. BA in Theology, Quincy U., 1970. Vice rector Our Lady of Angels Sem., Quincy, Ill., 1971-75; dir. student activities Quincy U., 1975-78, asst. dir. admissions, 1978-81, dir. alumni, 1981-83, dir. devel., 1982-83; dir. devel. The Franciscans, St. Louis, 1983—; trustee Cath. Theol. Union, Chgo., 1988-94; dir., bd. dirs. Doorways, St. Louis; cons. religious orgns., 1983—. Pub. Novena Book, 1994, note cards, 1990. Named Ky. Col., State of Ky. Mem. Alliance of Nonprofit Mailers, Conservation Internat., Nat. Cath. Devel., Rainforest Alliance, Direct Mktg. Assn., Nat. Soc. Fund Raising Execs. Republican. Roman Catholic. Home and Office: The Franciscans 3140 Meramec St Saint Louis MO 63118

SCHULTZ, ARNOLD J., JR., linguistic programmer and designer; b. N.Y.C., Jan. 24, 1932; s. Arnold J. and Ragnhild (Fogelberg) S.; m. Darlene Burbeck. BA, U. Minn., 1958, MA, 1968. Pres. Syntactic Analyzer, Inc., Minnetonka, Minn., 1972-92. Creator/inventor Syntactica, a linguistic program for indexing and abstracting of English lang. text data. With U.S. Army, 1956-58, West Germany. Recipient Best New Software of 1995 award Byte Mag., 1995. Address: 333 8th St SE Apt 104 Minneapolis MN 55414-1254

SCHULTZ, BARBARA MARIE, insurance company executive; b. Chgo., Sept. 9, 1943; d. Edwin and Bernice (Barstis) Legner; m. Ronald J. Schultz Sr., May 1, 1965; 1 child, Ronald J. Grad. high sch., Chgo. Account rep. Met. Ins. Co., Aurora, Ill., 1981—; qualifier Met. Life Leaders Conf., 1990. Fellow Nat. Assn. Life Underwriters (edn. chmn. 1988-91, nat. quality award Robert L. Rose award 1990), Life Underwriters Tng. Coun. (chmn. 1986-88, citation 1987), South Cook County Assn. Life Underwriters (edn. chmn. 1988-91). Roman Catholic. Office: Met Ins Co 15255 94th Ave Orland Park IL 60462-3800

SCHULTZ, BRYAN CHRISTOPHER, dermatologist, educator; b. Evergreen Park, Ill., June 29, 1949; s. Warren H. and Norinne A. (McNamara) S.; m. Cathleen T. Fitzgerald, May 14, 1977; children: Carrie T., Megan C., Erin L. B.S., Loyola U., Chgo., 1971; M.D., Loyola Stritch Sch. Medicine, 1974. Diplomate Am. Bd. Dermatology. Intern St. Joseph's Hosp., Chgo., 1975; resident Northwestern U., Chgo., 1976-79; assoc. clin. prof. Loyola U., Maywood, Ill., 1979—; practice medicine specializing in dermatology, Oak Park, Ill., 1979—; cons. dermatologist West Suburban Hosp., Oak Park Hosp., Gottlieb Hosp., Westlake Hosp., MacNeal Hosp., 1979—. Author: Office Practice of Skin Surgery, 1985. Patentee surgical instrument. Contbr. articles to sci. publs. Supr., founder pub. awareness program for skin cancer Loyola U. Stritch Sch. Medicine, 1983—; operator Ultraviolet-Ozone meter, Ill., 1983—. Mem. Am. Acad. Dermatology, Am. Soc. Dermatologic Surgery, Internat. Soc. Dermatologic Surgery, Soc. Investigative Dermatology, Chgo. Dermatologic Soc., AMA (del. intern and resident sect. 1975), Ill. Dermatologic Soc. (exec. com. 1981, chmn. membership com. 1983-84), Soc. Cosmetic Chemists, Royal Soc. Medicine, Alpha Sigma Nu. Office: Affil in Dis & Skin Surg SC 159 Westgate Oak Park IL 60301

SCHULTZ, CHARLES EDWARD, state official; b. Canton, Ohio, Aug. 23, 1951; s. Charles Frederick and Lillian Rose (Hudkins) S.; m. Cynthia Ann Wildroudt, Mar. 29, 1980; children: Charles Andrew, Colleen Elizabeth. BS in Labor Econs., U. Akron, 1974. Agt. Prudential Ins., Canton, 1974-76; retail sales mgr. We. Auto Supply Co., Cleve, 1976-79; cons. John A. Day & Assocs., Akron, 1979-81; adminstr. Summit County Engr., Akron, 1981-91; chief Office of Employee Svcs., Ohio Dept. Natural Resources, Columbus, 1991—; pres. Akron Fraternal Homeholding, 1979-83, treas., 1977-79; treas. Hy Comp Enterprises, Cuyahoga Falls, Ohio, 1987-89. Participant Leadership Akron Prog., 1984-85;l candidate Ohio State Rep., 39th dist., 1980, 43rd dist. 1982. Mem. Phi Kappa Tau. Republican. Roman Catholic. Home: 6876 Bowerman St E Worthington OH 43085-2490 Office: Ohio Dept Natural Resources Fountain Sq Columbus OH 43224

SCHULTZ, DALE WALTER, state legislator; b. Madison, Wis., June 12, 1953; s. Walter Albert and Lillian (Fortman) S.; m. Rachel Weiss, June 20, 1981; children: Katherine Ann, Amanda. BBA, U. Wis., 1975. Farm mgr. Hillpoint, Wis., 1975—; adminstrv. and legis. asst. Wis. State Senate, Madison, 1976-79; planning analyst State of Wis., Madison, 1979-82, rep., 1982-91; senator Wis. State Senate, Madison, 1991—; chair ins. com. Wis. State Seante, Madison, 1995—; mem. joint com. fin., com. ins., Mississippi River pky. commn., Minn.-Wis. boundary commn. Wis. State Senate. Mem. citizens adv. bd. Sauk County (Wis.) Health Care Ctr.; mem. Sauk County Farm Bur. Recipient Disting. Svc. award FFA, 1994; named Legislator of Yr., Wis. Tech. Coll. Assn., 1994-95, Guardian of Small Bus., Nat. Fedn. Ind. Bus., 1994, Legislator of Yr., Vietnam Vets. Assn., 1994. Republican. Club: Rod & Gun (Hillpoint, Wis.). Lodges: Lions, Masons. Home: 515 N Central Ave Richland Center WI 53581-1702 Office: PO Box 7882 Madison WI 53707-7882

SCHULTZ, DANIEL JOSEPH, manufacturing executive, writer; b. St. Louis, Dec. 10, 1945; s. Abraham Y. and Isabelle (Balk) S.; m. Karen Lynn Hanson, Aug. 3, 1980; children: Brian, David, Rebecca, Jacob. BA, Pershing Coll., 1968; MA, Webster U., 1974, MBA, 1975; PhD, Greenwich U., Hilo, Hawaii, 1992. Exec. Std. Register Co., St. Louis, 1972-75, Schultz Co., St. Louis, 1975—; cons. in field, 1975—. Author: The Crisis Within, 1993. Leader Boy Scouts Am., St. Louis, 1980—. Capt., pilot USAF, 1968-72, Vietnam. Decorated DFC. Fellow Internat. Soc. for Philos. Inquiry (dir. pub. rels. 1994—); mem. Am. Fighting Arts Assn. (Shodan 1st degree Black Belt, 1986, Nidan 2nd Degree Black Belt, 1990). Republican. Home: 60 Muirfield Ct Town and Country MO 63141 Office: Schultz Co 14090 Riverport Dr Maryland Heights MO 63043

SCHULTZ, GERALD A. (JERRY SCHULTZ), graphic designer; b. St. Paul, Jan. 29, 1934; s. Adolph E. and Ida Louise (Grunewald) S.; m. Mary Lu Seiler, Oct. 17, 1953; children: Pamela Jean, Gayle Marie, Kari Lynn (Dec.), Stephanie Lu, Bryon Anthony. A, Art Instrns., Mpls., 1947-51; BA, St. Paul Sch. Associated Arts, 1953. Cert. graphic designer, design illustrator, Minn. Designer, illustrator Brown & Bigelow, St. Paul, 1951-59; art dir. 3M Co., St. Paul, 1959-65; v.p., creative dir. Louis F. Dow Co., St. Paul, 1965-68; exec. v.p., creative dir. Elliot & Assocs., St. Paul, 1968-70; creative art dir. Swansen, Sinkey, Ellis, Lincoln, Nebr., 1970-71; v.p., sr. art dir. Darcey, Mac Manos, Masius Internat., 1971-75; sr. art dir. Peterson-Morris Internat., St. Paul, 1975-78; v.p. creative svcs. Stevenson & Assocs., Mpls., 1978-81; sr. v.p., creative dir. Adhouse, Inc. Internat., St. Paul, 1981-85; chief exec. officer, pres. One Plus Two, Inc., St. Paul, 1985—; part-time design instr. St. Paul Sch. Associated Arts, St. Paul 1951-53, Mpls. Art Sch., 1964-65. Comml. artist Art Direction Mag., Mag. & Graphics Internat; creator brochures, greeting cards, print advt., corp. logo designs. Coach Roseville (Minn.) Youth Hockey Assn., 1974-87, 90—, bd. dirs.; coach North Star Youth Baseball Assn., Roseville, 1976-83. With U.S. Army, 1954-56. Recipient Design awards; named Community Youth Leader of Yr. KSTP Broadcasting, St. Paul, 1985. Mem. Art Dirs. Twin Cities, N.Y. Art Dirs. Club, Chgo. Art Dirs. Club. Roman Catholic.

SCHULTZ, GREGORY, company executive; b. Chgo., July 15, 1962. BA in Journalism, Roosevelt U., 1987. V.p. Sherwood Group Inc., Northbrook, Ill., 1984—. Contbr. over 100 articles to profl. jours. Office: Sherwood Group Inc 60 Revere Dr Ste 500 Northbrook IL 60062-1577

SCHULTZ, KAREN ROSE, clinical social worker, author, publisher, speaker; b. Huntington, N.Y., June 16, 1958; d. Eugene Alfred and Laura Rose (Palazzolo) Squeri; m. Richard S. Schultz, Apr. 8, 1989. BA with honors, SUNY, Binghamton, 1980; MA, U. Chgo., 1982. Lic. clin. social worker, Ill. Unit dir., adminstr. Camp Algonquin, Ill., 1981; clin. social worker United Charities Chgo., 1982-86; social worker Hartgrove Hosp., Chgo., 1986-87; pvt. practice, Oak Brook, Ill., 1987—; trainer, speaker various groups, schs. and orgns., DuPage County, Ill., 1988-89; group leader Optifast Program, Oak Park and Aurora, Ill., 1989-90; instr. social work Morraine Valley C.C., Palos Hills, Ill., 1989-90; instr. eating disorders Coll. of Dupage, Glen Ellyn, Ill., 1990-92, mem. eating disorder com., 1989—, tchr. intuition and counseling, 1995—. Editor, contbg. author The River Within newsletter, 1989—. Com. mem. DuPage Consortium, 1987-89. Mem. NASW (registerd, diplomate), acad. Cert. Social Workers, Nat. Speakers Assn., Profl. Speakers Ill., Toastmasters Interant., Women Entrepreneurs DuPage. Office: 900 Jorie Blvd Ste 234 Oak Brook IL 60521-2230

SCHULTZ, LOUIS EDWIN, management consultant; b. Foster, Nebr., Aug. 8, 1931; s. Louis Albert and Lula Pusey (Cox) S.; m. Mary Kathleen Peck, Mar. 3, 1962; children: Kurt Michael, Kristen Leigh. BSEE, U. Nebr., 1959; MBA, Pepperdine U., 1974. Mktg. mgr. Bell & Howell, Pasadena, Calif., 1962-70; dir. mktg. Cogar Corp., Utica, N.Y., 1970-71; product mgr. Pertec Corp., L.A., 1971-73; gen. mgr. Control Data Corp., Mpls., 1973-84; founder, CEO Process Mgmt. Inst. Inc., Mpls., Minn., 1984—; adv. bd. Inst. for Productivity Through Quality, U. Tenn., Knoxville, 1982-84. Author: Managing in the Worldwide Competitive Society, 1984, Quality Management Philosophies, 1985, Profiles in Quality, 1994; co-author: Quality Handbook for Small Business, 1994, Deming, The Way We Knew Him, 1995. Mem. Gov.'s Commn. on Productivity, St. Paul, 1986; chmn. Wirth Park Tree Restoration Com., Mpls., 1983; mem. Productivity Planning Com., St. Paul, 1985—. Staff sgt. USMC, 1952-54; advisor to Deming Forum, 1985—; judge Minn. Quality award, 1992. Recipient Profl. Partnership award U. Minn., 1987. Mem. Am. Soc. Performance Improvement (bd. dirs. 1984-89, outstanding svc. award), Minn. Coun. for Quality (bd. dirs. 1987—), Human Sys. Mgmt. (edtl. bd.), Asia-Pacific Orgn. Quality Control, Toastmasters Internat. Republican. Methodist. Office: Process Mgmt Inst 7801 E Bush Lake Rd Ste 360 Minneapolis MN 55439-3113

SCHULTZ, LOUIS WILLIAM, judge; b. Deep River, Iowa, Mar. 24, 1927; s. M. Louis and Esther Louise (Behrens) S.; m. D. Jean Stephen, Nov. 6, 1949; children: Marcia, Mark, Paul. Student, Central Coll., Pella, Iowa, 1944-45, 46-47; LL.B., Drake U., Des Moines, 1949. Bar: Iowa. Claims supr. Iowa Farm Mut. Ins. Co., Des Moines, 1949-55; partner firm Harned, Schultz & McMeen, Marengo, Iowa, 1955-71; judge Iowa Dist. Ct. (6th dist.), 1971-80; justice Iowa Supreme Ct., 1980-93; county atty. Iowa County, 1960-68; ret., 1993. Served with USNR, 1945-46. Mem. Am. Bar Assn., Iowa Bar Assn. (bd. govs.), Iowa Judges Assn. (pres.). Office: U Iowa Coll Law # 1488 Iowa City IA 52242

SCHULTZ, RICHARD DALE, national athletic organizations executive; b. Grinnell, Iowa, Sept. 5, 1929; s. August Henry and Marjorie Ruth (Turner) S.; m. Jacquilyn Lu Duistermars, June 26, 1949; children: Robert Dale, William Joel, Kim Marie. BS, Cen. Coll., Pella, Iowa, 1950; EdD Honoris Causa, Cen. Coll., 1987; LLD (hon.), Wartburg Coll., 1988, Alma Coll., 1989, Luther Coll., 1991; Phd, U.S. Sports Acad., 1993. Head basketball coach, athletic dir. Humboldt (Iowa) High Sch., 1950-60; freshman basketball coach U. Iowa, Iowa City, 1960-62; head baseball coach, assoc. basketball coach U. Iowa, 1962-70, head basketball coach, 1970-74, asst. v.p., 1974-76; dir. athletics and phys. edn. Cornell U., Ithaca, N.Y., 1976-81; dir. athletics U. Va., Charlottesville, 1981-87; exec. dir. NCAA, Mission, Kans., 1987-94; pres. Global Sports Enterprises, 1994-95; exec. dir. U.S. Olympic Com., Colorado Springs, Colo., 1995—; mem. honors ct. Nat. Football Found. and Hall of Fame, Nat. Basketball Hall of Fame, 1992; chmn. bd. NCAA Found., 1989; organizer Iowa Steel Mill, Inc. Author: A Course of Study for the Coaching of Baseball, 1964, The Theory and Techniques of Coaching Basketball, 1970; Contbr. articles to mags. Bd. dirs. Fellowship of Christian Athletes, 1986, chmn., 1990; chmn. Multiple Sclerosis, 1974-75; mem. Knight Found. Commn. on Intercollegiate Athletics, 1990—; mem. adv. com. on svc. acad. athletic programs Def. Dept. Recipient Disting. Alumni award Ctrl. Coll., Pella, 1970, Lifetime Svc. award U. Iowa, 1994, Corbett award NCADA, 1994; mem. Basketball Hall of Fame Honor Ct., 1992; inducted into Iowa Baseball Hall of Fame, 1993. Mem. Nat. Assn. Coll. Basketball Coaches, Ea. Coll. Athletic Assn. (mem. exec. com. 1980-81), Am. Basketball Coaches Assn. (Award of Honor 1994), Am. Football Coaches Assn. (lifetime membership award 1995). Home: 3670 Twisted Oak Cir Colorado Springs CO 80904-2138 Office: US Olympic Com One Olympic Plz Colorado Springs CO 80909

SCHULTZ, ROBERT J., retired automobile company executive; b. 1930. BSME, Mich. State U., 1953, MBA, 1969. With GM Corp., 1955-92, chief engr., 1977-81, gen. mgr. Delco Elecs. div., 1981-84; group dir. engr. Chevrolet, Pontiac, Can. Group, 1984-85; group v.p. GM of Canada Group GM Corp., 1985-90; vice chmn. GM Corp., Detroit, 1990-92; ret., 1993; also chmn., pres., chief exec. officer GM Hughes Electronics Corp.; bd. dirs. OEA, Inc., Nat. Digitronics Corp. Bd. trustees Calif. Inst. Tech. With USAAF, 1953-55. Mem. NAE.

SCHULTZ, ROBERT VERNON, entrepreneur; b. Sterling, Ill., July 2, 1936; s. Wilbur Henry and Eleanor Grace (Love) S.; m. Shelly I. Shaw, Feb. 12, 1970; children: Robert G., Trina R., Cherie A. BBA, Lincoln Mgmt. Sch. of Chgo., 1971; BA in Acctg., Rockford Sch. of Bus., 1975; BS in Christian Edn., Moody Bible Inst., 1980. Asst. to v.p. DeKalb Ogle Tel. Co., Rochelle, Ill., 1969-74; mktg. mgr. Chambers Owen Inc., Rockford, Ill., 1960-69; owner, pres. Schultz Mgmt. and Mktg., St. Charles, Ill., 1970—; pres., owner Investment Internat. Inc., North Aurora, 1988—, Diamond Publs. Inc., North Aurora, 1987—; owner Schultz Internat. Inc., Princeton, Ill.; bus. cons. Network Bus. Opportunity Entrepreneurs Chgo. 1970—; owner Schultz Internat. Inc., Princeton. Editor-in-chief, owner, pres., chmn. bd. Ill. Car Mart, 1988. With U.S. Army, 1957-59. Recipient Quick Silver award Ambs. Internat., 1990. Mem. Internat. Platform Assn., Internat. Speakers Platform Assn., Jaycees (pres. 1968). Republican. Home: PO Box 185 Princeton IL 61356-0185 Office: Schultz Internat Inc PO Box 185 Princeton IL 61356-0185

SCHULTZ, ROGER C., career officer; b. LeMars, Iowa, Oct. 13, 1945; s. Harry Willis and Sylvia Dorothy (Aronson) S.; m. Barbara J. Kaiser, Feb. 14, 1969. BS, Upper Iowa U., 1988; MPA, Shippensburg U., 1992. Commd. USNG, advanced through grades to brig. gen., 1996; rifle platoon leader Co. A 2d Bn., 133d Inf., Ft. Carson, Colo., 1968-69; scout leader Hdqs. and Hdqs. Co. 2d Bn., 22d Inf., Vietnam, 1969; logistics, personnel, intelligence officer HHC 2d Bn., 133d Inf., Sioux City, Iowa, 1970-75; rifle co. comdr. Co. B 2d Bn., 133d Inf., Sheldon, Iowa, 1975-76; ops. and tng. officer HHC 2d Bn., 133d Inf., Sioux City, Iowa, 1976-78; brigade ops. and tng. officer 34th Brigade, 47th Inf., Boone, Iowa, 1978-81, exec. officer, 1981-82; bn. comdr. 1st Bn., 168th Inf., Council Bluffs, Iowa, 1982-84; dir. op. and tng. Iowa Army Nat. Guard, Johnston, Iowa, 1984-88, chief of staff, 1988-95, dep. adjutant gen., 1995—. Lobbyist Dept. Pub. Def., Des Moines, 1996. Decorated Silver Star, 1969, Bronze Star, 1969, Purple Heart (2 awards), 1969, Legion of Merit, 1995. Presbyterian. Home: 7728 NW Beaver Dr Johnston IA 50131 Office: Iowa Nat Guard, Camp Dodge 7700 NW Beaver Dr Johnston IA 50131

SCHULTZ, THEODORE WILLIAM, retired economist, educator; b. Arlington, S.D., Apr. 30, 1902; s. Henry Edward and Anna Elizabeth (Weiss) S.; m. Esther Florence Werth; children: Elaine, Margaret, T. Paul. Grad., Sch. Agr., Brookings, S.D., 1924; B.S., S.D. State Coll., 1927, D.Sc. (hon.), 1959; M.S., U. Wis., 1928, Ph.D., 1930; LL.D. (hon.), Grinnell Coll., 1949, Mich. State U., in 1962, U. Ill., 1968, U. Wis., 1968, Cath. U. Chile, 1979, U. Dijon, France, 1981; LL.D., N.C. State U., 1984. Mem. faculty Iowa State Coll., Ames, 1930-43; prof., head dept. econs. and sociology Iowa State Coll., 1934-43; prof. econs. U. Chgo., 1943-72, chmn. dept. econs., 1946-61, Charles L. Hutchinson Disting. Service prof., 1952-72, prof. emeritus, 1972—; econ. adviser, occasional cons. Com. Econ. Devel., U.S. Dept. Agr., Dept. State, Fed. Res. Bd., various congl. coms., U.S. Dept. Commerce, FAO, U.S. Dept. Def., Germany, 1948, Fgn. Econ. Adminstrn., U.K. and Germany, 1945, IBRD, Resources for the Future, Twentieth Century Fund, Nat. Farm Inst., others.; dir. Nat. Bur. Econ. Research, 1949-67; research dir. Studies of Tech. Assistance in Latin Am.; bd. mem. Nat. Planning Assn.; chmn. Am. Famine Mission to India, 1946; studies of agrl. developments, central Europe and Russia, 1929, Scandinavian countries and Scotland, 1936, Brazil, Uruguay and Argentina, 1941, Western Europe, 1955. Author: Redirecting Farm Policy, 1943, Food for the World, 1945, Agriculture in an Unstable Economy, 1945, Production and Welfare in Agriculture, 1950, The Economic Organization of Agriculture, 1953, Economic Test in Latin America, 1956, Transforming Traditional Agriculture, 1964, The Economic Value of Education, 1963, Economic Crises in World Agriculture, 1965, Economic Growth and Agriculture, 1968, Investment in Human Capital: The Role of Education And of Research, 1971, Human Resources, 1972, Economics of the Family: Marriage, Children, and Human Capital, 1974, Distortions of Agricultural Incentives, 1978, Investing in People: The

Economics of Population Quality, 1981, Restoring Economic Equilibrium: Human Capital in the Modernizing Economy, 1990, The Economics of Being Poor, 1993, Origins of Increasing Returns, 1993; co-author: Measures for Economic Development of Under-Developed Countries, 1951; editor: Jour. Farm Econs., 1939-42; contbr. articles to profl. jours. Research fellow Center Advanced Study in Behavioral Sci., 1956-57; recipient Nobel prize in Econs., 1979. Fellow Am. Acad. Arts and Scis., Am. Farm Econs. Assn., Nat. Acad. Scis.; mem. Am. Agrl. Econ. Assn., Am. Econ. Assn. (pres. 1960, Walker medal 1972), Am. Philos. Soc., Royal Econ. Soc., Nat. Acad. Edn., others. Home: 5620 S Kimbark Ave Chicago IL 60637-1606 Office: U Chgo Dept Econs 1126 E 59th St Chicago IL 60637-1580*

SCHULTZ, WARREN ROBERT, manufacturing administrator; b. Chgo., June 29, 1949; s. Warren Gimbel and Helen Catherine (Mattes) S.; m. Mary Elise Nunnally, Mar. 31, 1973; children: Warren Thomas, Gregory James. BS in Aerospace Engring., U.S. Naval Acad., 1971. Commd. ensign USN, 1971, advanced through grades to lt., 1975, resigned, 1976; process engr. Corning Glass Works, Harrodsburg, Ky., 1976-78, quality control supr., 1978; project engr., elec. supr. Manville Corp., Etowah, Tenn., 1978-82; plant engr. Manville Corp., Waterville, Ohio, 1982-86, prodn. supt., 1986-89, furnace expansion project spl. assignment coordinator, 1989-92, prodn. supt. fiberglass dept., 1992-93; prodn. supt. material and sliver depts., 1993; plant mgr. Manville Corp., Waterville, Ohio, 1993—; Waterville Planning Commn., 1995—; mem. Waterville Planning Commn., 1995—. Religious tng. instr. St. Joseph's Ch., Maumee, Ohio, 1984-85, mem. parish coun., 1989-91; little league coach Anthony Wayne Area Baseball Assn., Waterville, 1983-86. Republican. Roman Catholic. Home: 201 Harvest Ln Waterville OH 43566 Office: Schuller Corp PO Box 517 Toledo OH 43697-0517

SCHULZ, KRAIG FRANKLYN, Peace Corps volunteer; b. Mpls., May 15, 1969; s. Franklyn A. and Ann Carol (Frolund) S. BS, U. Minn., 1992. With Peace Corps, Mali, 1992—. Mem. Phi Beta Kappa.

SCHULZ, MICHAEL JOHN, fire and explosion analyst, consultant; b. Milw., Oct. 7, 1958; s. John F. and JoAnn E. (Carlson) S.; m. Donna M. Guzman; children: Kari L., Brian M. BS in Fire and Safety Engring. Tech., U. Cin., 1996; grad., U.S. Fire Adminstrn. Acad. Cert. fire and explosion investigator; cert. fire protection specialist; cert. fire investigation instr.; cert. fire svc. instr. II. Fire investigator Cedarburg (Wis.) Police Dept., 1979-90; capt., fire investigator Cedarburg (Wis.) Fire Dept., 1981-90; sr. staff expert John A. Kennedy & Assoc., Hoffman Estates, Ill., 1990—; cons. U.S. Fire Adminstrn.; instr. fire tech. and police sci. depts. Milw. (Wis.) Area Tech. Coll.; instr. fire sci. tech. dept. William Rainey Harper C.C.; lectr. in field. Author: Manual for the Determination of Electrical Fire Causes, 1988, Guide for Fire and Explosion Investigations, 1992. Recipient Common Coun. Commendation, City of Cedarburg, Wis., 1986; named Firefighter of Yr., Ozaukee County Assn. Fire Depts., 1985. Mem. ASTM, Nat. Assn. Fire Investigators (bd. dirs. 1987—, nat. cert. bd. 1987—, chmn. edn. com., editor The Nat. Fire Investigator, Man of Yr. 1991), Nat. Fire Protection Assn. (tech. com. on fire investigations 1985—, fire svc. sect., sect. rep. tech. com. on fire investigations 1985-92, sec. rep. nat. conf. on fire investigation instrn., mem. bd. dirs. fire sci. and tech. educators sect.), Fire Marshal's Assn. N.Am. (assoc.), Nat. Inst. Bldg. Scis. (reviewing mem. fire rsch. sub-com.), Bldg. Ofcls. and Code Adminstrs. Internat., So. Bldg. Code Congress Internat., Internat. Bldg. Code Ofcls., Internat. Assn. Arson Investigators (John Charles Wilson scholarship award 1982), Ill. Chpt. Internat. Assn. Arson Investigators, Internat. Soc. Fire Svc. Instrs., Nat. Conf. Fire Investigation Instrn. (bd. dirs.), Wis. Soc. Fire Svc. Instrs., Ky. Cols. Republican. Lutheran. Office: John A Kennedy & Assocs 2155 Stonington Ave Ste 118 Hoffman Estates IL 60195

SCHULZ, STANLEY DEAN, library director; b. Norfolk, Nebr., June 1, 1969; s. Alfred W. and Lucille B. (Boehmlehner) S.; m. Grace I. Loschen, June 1, 1969; children: Christina, John, Joseph, Catherine. BA, U. Nebr., 1969, MA, 1971; MLS, Emporia State U., 1972. Circulation libr. Keene Meml. Libr., Fremont, Nebr., 1972-75, asst. dir., 1975-83; dir. Kilgore Meml. Libr., York, Nebr., 1983—; mem. adv. com. for pub. librs. Online Computer Libr. Ctr., Inc., Dublin, 1985-89. Sec. 1st Evang. Luth. Ch., york, 1995. Mem. ALA, Nebr. Libr. Assn. (chairperson pub. libr. sect. 1981, mem. various coms.), Sertoma (life, 2nd v.p. York Sunrise chpt. 1995). Office: Kilgore Meml Libr 6th & Nebraska York NE 68467

SCHULZE, MARK HOWARD, secondary school educator; b. Omaha, Sept. 10, 1950; s. Gerald Edward and Mary Elizabeth (Sorensen) S. BS, Nebr. Wesleyan U., 1972; postgrad., U. Nebr., Omaha. Tchr. Omaha Tech. High Sch., 1973-84, Omaha North High Sch., 1984—. Bd. dirs. United Ministries N.E. Omaha, 1989—, Camp Fontanelle, 1983—. Mem. NEA, Nebr. Ednl. Assn., Nat. Coun. Social Studies, Circus Fans Am., UN Assn. U.S.A., Nebr. Hist. Soc., Omaha Ednl. Assn. (bd. dirs. polit. action com., chmn.), United Ministries N.E. Omaha (bd. dirs., chmn.), Douglas County Hist. Soc., Camp Fontanelle (bd. dirs.), Kappa Delta Pi. Avocations: performing as a clown, sports announcing and score keeping. Home: 2721 Bauman Ave Omaha NE 68112-3315 Office: Omaha North High Sch 4410 N 36th St Omaha NE 68111-2207

SCHUMACHER, ERVIN, retired social services administrator; b. Eureka, S.D., Apr. 16, 1926; s. Christ and Christina (Klooz) S.; m. Gertrude H. Klipfel, Nov. 2, 1946; children: Candace Schumacher Hilmoe, Randall Ervin. BS in Edn., Bus. and Social Sci., U. N.D., 1961. Lic. cert. social worker, S.D. Farmer, Eureka, 1945-57; counselor McIntosh (S.D.) High Sch., 1961-63; social worker S.D. Dept. Social Svcs., Mobridge, 1963-64; coord. med. svcs. S.D. Dept. Social Svcs., Pierre, 1964-67, dir. medicaid, 1967-90; mem. S.D. Nursing Home Licensing Bd., Pierre, 1971-90. Recipient svc. award S.D. Med. Assn., 1990, S.D. Found. for Med. Care, 1990, S.D. Health Care Assn., 1990. Mem. State Medicaid Dirs. Assn. (Disting. Svc. award 1990), Rotary. Republican. Lutheran. Home: 20375 Cendok Rd Pierre SD 57501

SCHUMACHER, LESLIE, state legislator, artist; b. Oct. 4, 1955; m. Byron Schumacher; 2 children. Freelance artist, Princeton, Minn.; mem. Minn. Ho. of Reps., St. Paul, 1994—. Mem. Dem.-Farmer-Labor Party.

SCHUMACHER, MARVIN W., manufacturing exective; b. Denver, Iowa, Mar. 10, 1936. BS, U. Iowa, 1962. Pres. Schumacher Elevator Co., Inc., Denver, Iowa, 1962—; bd. dirs. Fredirica State Bank. Pres. Winnebago Coun. Boy Scouts Am., Denver, Iowa; vol. elderly adv. bd., Denver. Sgt. U.S. Army, 1955-56, Korea. Recipient Silver Beaver award Boy Scouts Am. Mem. Rotary Club Interntat., Lions Club, Elks Club. Republican. Office: Schumacher Elevator Co 240 E Main St Denver IA 50622-9504

SCHUMAKER, DENNIS J., nuclear engineer; b. Port Clinton, Ohio, Oct. 5, 1949. BS in Mech. Engring., Ohio State U., 1972, M in Nuclear Engring., 1972; MBA, U. Mich., 1977. Exec. v.p. Schumaker & Co. Inc., Ann Arbor, Mich., 1985—. Office: Schumaker & Co Inc 1000 Victors Way Ann Arbor MI 48108-2743

SCHUMAN, LEROY, mechanical engineer; b. Watertown, Wis., Jan. 29, 1934. BSME, Marquette U., 1956. Quality control engr. Ladish Co., Kudahy, Wis., 1956-60; design engr. mgr. Telsmith, Milw., 1960-74; project engr. Bacyrus-Erie, South Milwaukee, 1974-78; engring. mgr. Lippmann-Milw., 1977-85; product design engr. Logemann Bros. Co., Milw., 1989—; cons. E.L. Jay divsn. Cedar Rapids, Eugene, Oreg., 1985. Holder 7 patents in field. Lutheran. Office: Logemann Bros Co 3150 W Burleigh St Milwaukee WI 53210-1903

SCHUMANN, ALICE MELCHER, medical technologist, educator, sheep farmer; b. Cleve., Sept. 1, 1931; d. John Henry and Marian Louise (Clark) M.; m. Stuart McKee Struever, Aug. 21, 1956 (div. June 1983); children: Nathan Chester, Hanna Russell; m. John Otto Schumann, July 3, 1985. BS, Colby Coll., New London, N.H., 1953. Cert. tchr.; cert. med. technologist. Rschr. Lakeside Hosp., Cleve., 1953-54, Bambridge (Ohio) Schs., 1954-55, Shalersville (Ohio) Schs., 1955-56, Richtnior Sch., Overland, Mo., 1956-57; sci. tchr. Tonica (Ill.) High Sch., 1956-58, Morton Grove (Ill.) High Sch., 1958-60, Univ. Chgo. Lab Sch., 1960-65; co-founder Ctr. for Am. Archeology, dir. flotation rsch. U. Chgo. Campus, Kampsville, Ill., 1957-71, head of supplies distbn., dir. food svcs. dept.; head mailing dept. Found. for Ill. Archeology, Evanston and Kampsville, Ill., 1971-83; sheep farmer, wool processor Gravel Hill Farm, Kampsville, 1983—. Vol. Mt. Sinai Hosp., Cleve., 1948-49; tchr. Title I Dist. 40, Kampsville, 1970-71. Recipient Beverly Booth award Colby Coll., 1953, 1st prize for hand spun yarn DeKalb County Fair, Sandwich, Ill., 1987, 88. Mem. Precious Fibers Found., Natural Colored Wool Growers Assn., Farm Bur. of Calhoun County. Home and Office: Gravel Hill Farm RR 1 Box 121A Kampsville IL 62053-9720

SCHUMANN, MARK WOLFGANG, computer programmer, consultant; b. Hartford, Conn., Sept. 3, 1965; s. Roy Wesley and Ruth Elaine (Hills) S.; m. Judith Ellen Mravetz, July 2, 1988; children: Adele, Benjamin. BA in Math., Grinnell Coll., 1988. Sec. Jewish Community Fedn., Cleve., 1985-87; fin. analyst Victoria Fin. Corp., Cleve., 1988-89; programmer Victoria Fin. Corp., Mayfield Heights, Ohio, 1989-90; programmer, analyst, network/Unix mgr. STR, Inc., Bath Twp., Ohio, 1990-96; pres. Software Under Flap, Cleve., 1991—; spkr. CA-Technicon, New Orleans, 1994—. Editor Alternatives Jour., 1988; contbr. articles to various publs. Mem. Crossroads Devel. Corp., Cleve., 1986—, Grassroots Polit. Action Com., Cleve., 1986-91; chmn. bd. deacons Archwood United Ch. of Christ, Cleve., 1990-94. Mem. Clipper Developers Assn. Greater Cleve., Victoria Alumni Assn. (sgt.-at-arms 1990-92). Home: 3111 Mapledale Ave Cleveland OH 44109-2447

SCHUNCK, JAMES RICHARD, business executive; b. Cleve., Jan. 5, 1944; s. Charles Eugene and Mary Loretta (Laughrin) S. m. Nina Margarita Mason, June 7, 1966 (div. June 1978); children: Hannah Jean, Rebecca Anne. BA, Cleve. State U., 1971. City rm. clk. Cleve. Plain Dealer, 1966-67; underwriting dept. clk. Untied Transp. Union, Cleve., 1967-68; pers. dir. Romac Containers, Cleve., 1968-71; HMO devel. Met. Gen. Hosp., Cleve., 1971-73; project mgr. Dept. of Pub. Health, Cleve., 1973; exec. dir. Vis. Nurse Assn., Kansas City, Mo., 1974-79; pvt. mgmt. cons. Overland Parks, Kans., 1979-81; CEO, owner Phoenix-Hudson Corp., Overland Parks, Kans., 1981—. With USAF, 1962-66. Mem. U.S. Trotting Assn., Ohio Harness Horsemans Assn., Kansas City Regional Home Health Assn. (bd. dirs. 1977), Nat. Assn. Home Health, Nat. Assn. Rehab. Agys. Office: Phoenix-Hudson Corp 6900 College Blvd Overland Park KS 66211

SCHUNCK, RICHARD A., research engineer; b. Milw., Wis., Oct. 12, 1943. BSME, U. Wis., 1966, MSME, 1967. Rsch. engr. Falk Corp., Milw., 1967. Contb. article to profl. jour. Achievements include patent for gearbox cooling device. Office: Falk Corp dept 621 P O Box 492 Milwaukee WI 53201-0492

SCHUPP, KEITH LOWELL, general contractor; b. Litchfield, Minn., Aug. 31, 1953; s. Lowell Henry and Alice Mae (Draxten) S.; m. Judith M. Peters; children: Jami, Jennifer. Degree in Bldg., Constrn., Drafting and Estimating, St. Cloud (Minn.) Vo-Tech. Inst., 1973. Sec., treas. Winkelman Bldg. Corp., St. Cloud, 1973—. Mem. Sys. Bldg. Assn. (pres. 1991-92), Nat. Sys. Builders (pres. 1993), Lions, Sertoma, KC, Ducks Unltd. Office: Winkelman Bldg Corp 1025 Rook Rd NE Sauk Rapids MN 56379-9684

SCHUPP, RONALD IRVING, clergyman, civil rights leader; b. Syracuse, N.Y., Dec. 10, 1951; s. George August and Shirley Louise (Mitchell) S. Ordained ministry, Old Country Ch., 1972; ordained Bapt. ministry, 1976; cert., Moody Bible Inst., 1986, 1988; advanced cert., Evang. Tng. Assn., 1992. Missionary, asst. pastor The Old Country Ch. Inc., Chgo., 1972-76; missionary Solid Rock Bapt. Ch., Chgo., 1976-89, Marble Rock Missionary Bapt. Ch., Chgo., 1990—; asst. dir. Uptown Community Orgn., Chgo., 1974-76; dir. Chgo. Action Ctr., 1978-80; bd. dirs. West Englewood United Orgn./Clara's House Shelter, 1991-95 (Recipient Appreciation award, 1992), assoc. chaplain, 1991-95; bd. dirs. America's Soup Kitchen on Wheels, Inc., 1996—, organizer, 1996—, nat. chaplain 1996—; mem. steering com. 1st Congl. Dist. Ministerial Assn., Chgo., 1993-95, chair housing com., 1993-95. Contbr. articles and poems to numerous periodicals. Mem. Nat. Coalition for the Homeless, 1991—, Nat. Union of the Homeless, 1992—, Chgo. Coalition for the Homeless, 1988—, vol. organizer, 1988-94, mem. empowerment adv. com., 1991-94; mem. Homeless on the Move for Equality, 1990-92, bd. dirs. 1991-92; mem. Chgo. Peace Coun., 1984-87, Voice of Homeless, San Jose, Calif., 1993—, Kansas City Union of Homeless, 1993—; active Pledge of Resistance, Chgo., 1985—; rep. Chgo. Welfare Rights Orgn., 1986-88; activist Chgo. Clergy and Laity Concerned, 1981-87; founding mem. People's Campaign for Jobs, Housing and Food, Chgo., 1992—, chaplain, 1992—; founding mem., missionary People's Ministry Without Walls, Chgo., 1993—; rep. Lakota Nat. Organizing Com., 1993—, League of Indigenous Sovereign Nations of Western Hemisphere, 1993—; supporting mem. Autonomous Chgo. chpt. Am. Indian Movement of Ill., 1994—, Chgo. Native Am. Urban Indian Retreat, 1994—; rep. Kasigluk Elders Conf., Alaska, 1994—; pres., co-founder Citizens Taking Action, Chgo., 1995—, chair, steering com., 1995—, mem. action com., 1995—; mem., nat. organizer and outreach coord. Nat. People's Campaign, 1995—; organizer Chgo. Pure Food Campaign, 1995—, Chgo. People's Conv. Coalition, 1996. Recipient letter of commendation Chgo. Fire Dept., 1983, proclamations Mayor Richard M. Daley, Chgo., 1991, 92, 93, 94, Mayor Joan Barr, Evanston, Ill., 1993, Mayor Lorraine H. Morton, Evanston, 1994, letters of support for anti-apartheid and related work Operation Push 1985-95, Yogesh K. Gandhi 1987, 1994, Nat. Black United Front, 1989, Cesar Chavez, 1990, NAACP, 1991, Indian Treaty Rights Com., Chgo, 1993, Am. Indian Ctr., Chgo., 1993, Am. Indian Movement, Chgo., 1994, various U.S. senators and congresspersons 1990-93, Coretta Scott King, 1992, Nelson Mandela, Archbishop Desmond Tutu, Janusz Ziolkowski, 1993, The Dalai Lama, 1994, 95; commendation resolution Chgo. City Coun., 1993, South African elections vigil support resolution Chgo. City Coun., 1994; tribute in congl. record Congressman Bobby L. Rush, 1993, Sen. Carol Moseley Braun, 1994; initiated Wa-kin-ya-wicha-ho Thunder Voice by trad. Lakota Elders, 1993; initiated Kiyuyakki Aurora by Inuit Elder Etok, 1994; porfolio on file Smithsonian Instn., 1996, Nat. Civil Rights Mus., 1996, UN Libr., 1996. Mem. Operation Push, Inc., 1985— (citation 1990), NAACP, ACLU, Chgo. Free South Africa (steering com. 1984-94), UN Assn. of USA, World Jewish Congress (diplomat), Transafrica. Democrat. Home and Office: 6412 N Hoyne Ave Apt 3A Chicago IL 60645-5638

SCHURING, J. KIRK, insurance company executive; b. Canton, Ohio, Sept. 17, 1952; s. James A. and D. Margaret (Felton) S.; m. Darlene K. Newkirk, Mar. 2, 1976; children: J. Derrick, Kristin. Student, Kent State U., 1970-74. Sec., treas. The Schuring Agy., Inc., Canton, 1978-80, pres., 1980—; ins. cons. Stark Devel. Bd., Canton, 1985—. Bd. dirs., v.p. Canton Urban League, 1983—, v.p. Stark/Wayne Am. Lung Assn., 1984—; bd. dirs. Canton Players Guild, 1986—; mem. adv. bd. Walsh Coll., 1988; mem. exec. bd. Stark County Rep. Orgn., Canton, 1981—; chmn. Stark County Reagan-Bush Com., Canton, 1984. Mem. Ind. Ins. Agts. Canton (bd. dirs. 1982-85), Jaycees Internat. (Sen. 1984), U.S. Jaycees (Charles Kulp, Jr. award 1983, Gordon B. Thomas award 1983), Ohio Jaycees (James Lammermier award 1982), Canton Jaycees (pres. 1982-83, recipient Disting. Service award 1987). Republican. Mem. Ch. Christ. Clubs: Canton (pres. 1988, bd. dirs. 1986—); Brookside Country. Home: 1817 Devonshire Rd NW Canton OH 44708-1907

SCHUTTA, JAMES T., quality assurance executive; b. Milw., Jan. 11, 1944; s. Roman Anthony and Anna (Klaus) S.; m. Mary Jane Davis; children: Jamie Lynn, Michael James. BSEE, Milw. Sch. Engring., 1978, MSEM, 1988. Mgr. quality assurance Johnson Controls, Milw., 1965-88; dir. quality assurance Premark Internat., Troy, Ohio, 1988-95; cosn. S&S Assocs., Inc., Kettering, Ohio, 1988—; pres. S&S Consulting Assocs., Inc., Kure Beach, N.C.; mem. adv. bd. Milw. Sch. Engring., 1980-88, U. Dayton, Ohio, 1990-94; mem. exam. bd. Malcolm Baldrige Award, Washington, 1992-95; auditor Registrar Accreditation Bd., 1995—; assessor Internat. Quality Audit, 1994—. Mem. IEEE, Am. Soc. for Quality Control. Home: 102 Leeward Ct Kure Beach NC 28449 Office: S&S Consulting Assocs Inc 102 Leeward Ct PO Box 105 Kure Beach NC 28449

SCHUTTER, DAVID JOHN, banker; b. Erie, Pa., Apr. 21, 1945; s. Donald John and Ruth Margaret (Hilbert) S. m. Ellen Carol Hoffman, June 18, 1967; children: David, Erica. BS with honors and distinction, Pa. State U., 1967; postgrad., Mich. State U., 1967-68, Ohio State U., 1973-75; cert., Stonier Grad. Sch. Banking, 1981. Asst. v.p. Huntington Nat. Bank, Columbus, Ohio, 1973-80; v.p. Ameritrust Co., Cleve., 1980-81, v.p., mgr. asset based lending dept., 1981-86, sr. v.p. secured lending div., 1986-89, dep. sr. loan adminstr., 1989-90, sr. cred. pol. off., 1990-92; sr. v.p., regional credit exec. Soc. Nat. Bank, Cleve., 1992-94; exec. v.p., chief credit officer, 1994—; pres. AT Comml. Corp., 1986—; panelist Robert Morris Assocs., Cleve., 1981, 93, mem., 1986—, Cleve. Bar Assn., 1986. Served to capt. U.S. Army, 1968-72. Mem. Nat. Comml. Fin. Assn. (bd. dirs. 1986—), Beta Gamma Sigma, Omicron Delta Epsilon. Office: Soc Nat Bank 127 Public Sq Cleveland OH 44114-1216

SCHUTZ, ROBERT J., municipal government official; b. Dayton, Ohio, Feb. 4, 1947; s. Robert Lawrence and Dorothy May (Turnbull) S.; m. Valeria D'Ann Yehoda, May 14, 1974; 1 child, Krischelle Alyse. BSCE, Ohio No. U., 1972; EMC, U. So. Calif., 1975; advanced engr. officer, U.S. Army Engr. Sch., 1977. Registered profl. engr., Ohio, Fla.; registered profl. surveyor, Ohio; registered sanitarian, Ohio; cert. chief blg. ofcl., Ohio, electrical safety inspector, Ohio, plumbing inspector, Ohio. Lab. tech. Martin Marietta Corp., Woodville, Ohio, 1966-67; journeyman, operator Graffice & Son, Woodville, 1966-67; engring. tech. Lester H. Poggemeyer, P.E., P.S., Bowling Green, Ohio, 1967-70; engr. planner Office of Comprehensive Health Planning, Columbus, Ohio, 1972-75; chief engr. Ohio Dept. Health, Columbus, 1975-81; project mgr. Poggemeyer Design Group, Columbus, 1989-90; dir. pub. svcs. Village of Powell, Ohio, 1990—; chief bldg. ofcl. Powell/ Liberty Twp. Bldg. Dept., 1989—. Major U.S. Army, 1981-89; with Army Nat. Guard, 1969-91. Mem. Ohio Bldg. Ofcls. Assn. (pres. 1996—), Ctrl. Ohio Code Ofcls. Assn. (pres. 1995—), Ohio Consultative Coun. Nat. Insts. Bldg. Scis. (sec.-treas. 1994—), Am. Pub. Works Assn. (pres. 1995—). Home: 3100 Scioto Trace Columbus OH 43221 Office: Village of Powell 260 Village Park Dr Powell OH 43065

SCHUYLER, DANIEL MERRICK, lawyer, educator; b. Oconomowoc, Wis., July 26, 1912; s. Daniel J. and Fannie Sybil (Moorhouse) S.; m. Claribel Seaman, June 15, 1935; children: Daniel M., Sheila Gordon. AB summa cum laude, Dartmouth Coll., 1934; JD, Northwestern U., 1937. Bar: Ill. 1937, U.S. Supreme Ct. 1942, Wis. 1943. Tchr. constl. history Chgo. Latin Sch., 1935-37; assoc. Schuyler & Hennessy (attys.), 1937-42, ptnr., 1946-48; ptnr. Schuyler, Richert & Stough, 1948-58, Schuyler, Stough & Morris, Chgo., 1958-76, Schuyler, Ballard & Cowen, 1976-83, Schuyler, Roche & Zwirner, P.C., 1983—; treas., sec. and controller B-W Superchargers, Inc. div. Borg-Warner Corp., Milw., 1942-46; lectr. trusts, real property, future interests Northwestern U. Sch. Law, 1946-50, asso. prof. law, 1950-52, prof., 1952-80, prof. emeritus, 1980—. Author: (with Homer F. Carey) Illinois Law of Future Interests, 1941; supplements, 1947, 54; (with William M. McGovern, Jr.) Illinois Trust and Will Manual, 1970; supplements, 1972, 74, 76, 77, 79, 80, 81, 82, 83, 84; contbr. to profl. jours. Rep. nominee for judge Cook County Cir. Ct., 1958; bd. dirs., life mem. United Cerebral Palsy Greater Chgo., Lawrence Hall Youth Svcs. Fellow Am. Bar Found.; mem. ABA (past mem. ho. of dels., past chmn. sect. real property, probate and trust law), Chgo. Estate Planning Coun. (past pres., Dist. Svc. award 1977), Am. Coll. Trust and Estate Counsel (past pres.), Chgo. Bar Assn. (past chmn. coms. on trust law and post-admission edn., past bd. mgrs.), Ill. Bar Assn. (past chmn. real estate and legal edn. sects., past bd. govs.), Wis. Bar Assn., Legal Club, Law Club, Univ. Club, Order of Coif, Phi Beta Kappa, Phi Kappa Psi. Home: 909 W Foster Ave Apt 403 Chicago IL 60640-2510 Office: Schuyler Roche & Zwirner PC Ste 3800 130 E Randolph St Chicago IL 60601-6342

SCHWAB, DAVID, state legislator; b. 1944; m. Phyllis Schwab, 1966; three children. Owner Schwab's Pines; farmer and businessman; rep. Mo. State Ho. Reps. Dist. 157. Former chmn. Farmers for Emerson Com.; former mem. Farmers for Ashcroft Com., Farmers to Elect Sen. Bon State Com.; mem. Mo. State Agr. Stabilization Conservation Com., Gov. Ashcroft's Adv. Coun. on Agr.; former committeeman Ward 6, Byrd; former pres. congregation St. Paul Luth. Ch., Jackson, Mo., Sunday sch. tchr., chmn. bd. elders, chmn. men's club; former mem. St. Paul Sch. Bd. Edn. Mem. Nat. Fedn. Ind. Businessmen, Am. Tree Farm Sys., Mo. State Christmas Tree Growers Assn., Cape County Far Bur. (past pres.), Jackson C. of C., NRA. *

SCHWAB, JAMES CHARLES, urban planner; b. Oceanside, N.Y., Dec. 20, 1949; s. Charles Francis and Hazel Dorothy (Waters) S.; m. Jean Catlett, June 8, 1985; 1 child, Jessica. BA in Polit. Sci., Cleve. State U., 1973; MA in Urban & Regional Planning, U. Iowa, 1985, MA in Journalism, 1985. Purchasing agt. Kaufman Container Co., Cleve., 1973-75; rsch. assoc. No. Ohio Project on Nat. Priorities, Cleve., 1975-76; sales rep. Met. Life Ins. Co., Willoughby Hills, Ohio, 1976-78; exec. dir. Iowa Pub. Interest Rsch. Group, Iowa City, 1979-81; rsch. asst. Legis. Extended Assistance Group, Iowa City, 1982-85; asst. editor Am. Planning Assn., Chgo., 1985-90, sr. rsch. assoc., 1990—. Author: Raising Less Corn and More Hell, 1988, Industrial Performance Standards for a New Century, 1993, Deeper Shades of Green, 1994; editor Zoning News, 1990—, Environment and Devel., 1992—; contbr. articles to profl. publs. Chmn. Environ. Concerns Working Group, Met. Chgo. synod Evang. Luth. Ch. Am., 1989—; chmn. Task Force on Care of Creation, Region 5, Dubuque, Iowa, 1992-93; chmn. ch. coun. Augustana Luth. Ch., Chgo., 1990-93. Mem. Soc. Midland Authors (bd. dirs., newsletter editor 1990-95, membership sec. 1995—, chmn. biography awards, v.p. 1996—), Soc. Environ. Journalists, Soc. Profl. Journalists, Investigative Reporters and Editors, Am. Planning Assn., Am. Inst. Cert. Planners. Lutheran. Home: 1755 N Campbell Ave Chicago IL 60647-5205 Office: Am Planning Assn 122 S Michigan Ave Ste 1600 Chicago IL 60603

SCHWAB, MAUREEN DOLAN, nursing educator; b. Cin., May 11, 1955; d. J. Vincent and Adele Marie (Behler) Dolan; m. Steven Thomas Schwab, Dec. 28, 1991. BSN, Ea. Ky. U., 1977; MEd, Xavier U., Cin., 1986; MS, Wright State U., Dayton, Ohio, 1992. RN, Ohio. Staff nurse St. George Hosp., Cin., 1978-79; staff nurse med. ICU-CCU, Christ Hosp., Cin., 1979-81, asst. head nurse, 1981-82, asst. head nurse med. ICU stepdown, 1982-84, instr. orientation, 1984-88, mem. adj. faculty, 1987-88, instr. Sch. Nursing, 1988—. Marion C. Atkins scholar Christ Hosp., 1988-92. Mem. AACN, Sigma Theta Tau, Phi Kappa Phi. Office: Christ Hosp Sch Nursing 2139 Auburn Ave Cincinnati OH 45219-2906

SCHWAB, PAUL JOSIAH, psychiatrist, educator; b. Waxahachie, Tex., Jan. 14, 1932; s. Paul Josiah and Anna Marie (Baeuerle) S.; m. Martha Anne Beed, June 8, 1953; children: Paul Josiah III, John Conrad, Mark Whitney. BA, N. Cen. Coll., 1953; MD, Baylor U., 1957. Diplomate Am. Bd. Psychiatry and Neurology. Intern Phila. Gen. Hosp., 1957-58; clin. assoc. Nat. Cancer Inst., Bethesda, Md., 1958-60; resident in internal medicine U. Chgo., 1960-62, resident psychiatry, 1962-65, chief resident and instr. psychiatry, 1965; pvt. practice Naperville, Ill., 1965—; lectr. psychiatry U. Chgo., 1968-74, assoc. prof., 1974-79; clin. assoc., 1979-86, clin. assoc. prof., 1986—; dir. residency tng. U. Chgo., 1976-79, dir. in-patient unit and day treatment program, 1975-79. Contbr. articles to profl. jours. Bd. trustees North Ctrl. Coll., chair liaison com., 1983—, vice-chmn. acad. and student affairs com., 1983-92, vice chair admissions, fin. aid and student devel., 1992-95. Fellow Am. Psychiat. Assn. (Nancy C.A. Roeske award 1991); mem. AMA, Am. Soc. Clin. Psychopharmacology, Acad. Clin. Psychiatrists, Alpha Omega Alpha. Republican. Methodist. Office: 1200 Tall Oaks Ct Naperville IL 60540-9494

SCHWABE, JOHN BENNETT, II, lawyer; b. Columbia, Mo., June 14, 1946; s. Leonard Wesley and Hazel Fern (Crouch) S. A.B., U. Mo.-Columbia, 1967, J.D., 1970. Bar: Mo. 1970, U.S. Dist. Ct. (we. dist.) Mo. 1970, U.S. Ct. Mil. Appeals 1971, U.S. Supreme Ct. 1973. Owner, prin. John B. Schwabe, II & Assocs., Columbia, 1974—, St. Louis, 1984—. Trustee, lay leader, mem. adminstrv. bd. Wilkes Blvd. United Meth. Ch., 1974-79, chmn. pastor-parish relations com., 1984-85 ; mem. Friends of Music, Columbia, 1979—; bd. dirs., 1979-81; bd. dirs. Mo. Symphony Soc., 1984-85 . Served to capt. JAGC, USAF, 1970-74. Mem. ABA, Boone County Bar Assn. (sec. 1977-79), Bar Assn. Met. St. Louis, Assn. Trial Lawyers Am., Mo. Assn. Trial Attys., Personal Injury Lawyers Assn., Lawyers Assn. St. Louis, Columbia C. of C., Am. Legion, Phi Delta Phi. Republican. Club: Wilkes Men's (pres. 1977-79) (Columbia). Office: John B Schwabe II & Assocs Locust Bldg 1015 Locust St Ste 900 Saint Louis MO 63101-1323

SCHWAN, JOHN J., sales executive; b. Elmhurst, Ill., Nov. 10, 1949; s. John James and Josephine (Nuzzo) S.; m. Susan Elizabeth Schwan, Aug. 11, 1982; children: John James, Robert, Josianna, Catherine. BS in Mktg., Morehead State U., 1971; MBA, No. Ill. U., 1973. V.p. mktg. AM Bruning, Chgo., 1977-80; v.p., gen. mgr. Bausch & Lomb, Austin, Tex., 1980-83, Lockheed-Calcomp, Anaheim, Calif., 1983-85; pres. Tech. Group, Chgo., 1985-87; dir. mktg. and devel. Computer Assocs., Lisle, Ill., 1987-90; v.p. sales EMC, Washington, 1990-93, Dynatech Video Group, Salt Lake City, 1993—; mktg. com. chair ARMM, Washington, 1977-80. Contbr. articles and papers to profl. publs. Bd. dirs. U. Ill. Parents Assn., Champaign, 1995. Recipient Emmy award NATAS, 1992. Home: PO Box 195 Gilberts IL 60136 Office: Dynatech Video Group 11W356 Williamsburg Gilberts IL 60136

SCHWANK, JOHANNES WALTER, chemical engineering educator; b. Zams, Tyrol, Austria, July 6, 1950; came to U.S., 1978; s. Friedrich Karl and Johanna (Ruepp) S.; m. Lynne Violet Duguay; children: Alexander Johann, Leonard Friedrich, Hanna Violet. Diploma in chemistry, U. Innsbruck, Austria, 1975, PhD, 1978. Mem. faculty U. Mich., Ann Arbor, 1978—, assoc. prof. chem. engring., 1984-90, acting dir. Ctr. for Catalysis and Surface Sci., 1985-90, prof., interim chmn. dept. chem. engring., 1990-91, assoc. dir. Electron Microbeam Analysis Lab., 1990-91; chmn. dept. chem. engring., 1991-95; prof. chem. engring. U. Mich., Ann Arbor, 1995—; vis. prof. U. Innsbruck, 1987-88, Tech. U. Vienna, 1988; cons. in field. Patentee bimetallic cluster catalysts, hydrodesulfurization catalysts and microelectronic gas sensors; contbr. over 70 articles to sci. jours. Fulbright-Hays scholar, 1978. Mem. AAAS, Am. Chem. Soc., Am. Inst. Chem. Engrs., Mich. Catalysis Soc. (sec.-treas. 1982-83, v.p. 1983-84, pres. 1984-85), Am. Soc. Engring. Edn. Home: 2335 Placid Way Ann Arbor MI 48105-1295 Office: U Mich Dept Chem Engring 2300 Hayward St Ann Arbor MI 48109-2136

SCHWARTZ, BARRY M., iron and metal company executive; b. Detroit, Dec. 21, 1947. BABA, Wayne State U., 1972; MBA in Fin., Rice U., 1976. Fin. analyst C.I.W., Houston, 1972-76; CEO Schwartz Iron and Metal Co., Detroit, 1977—. Office: 20300 Mount Elliott St Detroit MI 48234-2743

SCHWARTZ, CHARLES PHINEAS, JR., replacement auto parts company executive, lawyer; b. Chgo., Apr. 23, 1927; s. Charles Phineas and Lavinia Duffy (Schulman) S.; m. Joan Straus, Aug. 12, 1954 (div. 1971); children: Alex, Ned, Debra, Emily; m. Susan Lamm Hirsch, Dec. 18, 1976. A.B., U. Chgo., 1945; LL.B., Harvard U., 1950. Bar: Ill. 1950, N.Y. 1951, U.S. Supreme Ct. 1955. Assoc. Szold & Brandwen, N.Y.C., 1950-52; rsch. associ., teaching fellow Harvard U. Law Sch., Cambridge, Mass., 1952-56; pvt. practice Chgo., 1956-61; ptnr. Straus, Blosser & McDowell, Chgo., 1961-67; fin. and bus. cons. Chgo., 1967-75, 93—; pres., chief exec. officer Champion Parts Inc., Oak Brook, Ill., 1975-86, chmn. bd., chief exec. officer, 1986-92; chmn. emeritus Champion Parts Inc., Oak Brook, 1992—; dir. Supercrete Ltd., Winnipeg, Man., Can., 1964-80, Athey Products Corp., Raleigh, N.C., 1967-86. Trustee, officer Hull House Assn., Chgo., 1958-70; dir., officer Chgo. Fedn. Settlements, 1972-79; dir., officer, pres. Friends of the Parks, Chgo., 1982—; dir., officer, pres. Hyde Park Coop. Soc., 1962-68; pres. U. Cho. Lab. Schs. Parents Assn., 1970-72, 75-77; trustee KAM Isaiah Israel Congregation, 1975-85; bd. dirs. Chgo. Hearing Soc., 1996—. Served with USNR, 1945-46. Recipient Boulton Meml. award for disting. bus. statesmanship and dedicated service rendered to the entire auto parts rebuilding industry Automotive Parts Rebuilders Assn., 1987. Mem. ABA, Motor Equipment and Mfrs. Assn. (dir. 1977-81), Automotive Pres. Coun., Heavy Duty Bus. Forum, Automotive Sales Coun., Soc. Automotive Engrs., Automotive Parts Rebuilders Assn. (dir., officer, chmn. 1988—), Chgo. Coun. Lawyers, Heavy Vehicle Maintenance Group (officer 1994—), Chgo. Hearing Soc. (dir. 1996—), Quadrangle Club (Chgo.), Harvard Club (N.Y.C.). Jewish. Clubs: Quadrangle (Chgo.); Harvard (N.Y.C.). Office: 230 E Ohio St Ste 120 Chicago IL 60611-3201

SCHWARTZ, ELIEZER LAZAR, psychologist, educator; b. Arad, Romania, Dec. 14, 1947; came to U.S., 1974; s. George and Elka (Rothchild) S.; m. Susan Ellen Lorge; children: Dafna, Michal, Amitai. BA in Psychology, Hebrew U., Jerusalem, Israel, 1973; MS in Psychology, Ill. Inst. Tech., 1975, PhD in Psychology, 1977. Cert. clin. psychologist, Ill. Psychologist, chief svc. Chgo.-Read Mental Health Ctr., 1979-80; core faculty Ill. Sch. Profl. Psychology, Chgo., 1981—; clin. psychologist Ray Graham Assn. for Handicapped, Elmhurst, Ill., 1981-89; dir. clin. svcs. Michael Solomon Psychology Ctr., Chgo., 1989-91; instr. Northwestern U., Evanston, Ill., summers 1988—; dir. neuropsychology Brownstone Ctr., Chgo., 1991-92; cons. Jewish Vocat. Svcs., Chgo., 1983-84, 91-92, North Suburban Spl. Edn. Orgn., Arlington Heights, Ill., 1985-91, Grant Hosp., Chgo., 1991-95; dir. clin. tng. Ill. Sch. Profl. Psychology. Author: (with others) Severe Developmental Disabilities, 1987, The Mental Status Exam, 1989; contbr. articles to profl. jours. Mem. APA, ASCD, Ill. Psych. Assn., Coun. for Exceptional Children. Jewish. Office: 20 S Clark St Chicago IL 60603

SCHWARTZ, GARRY ALBERT, advertising executive; b. Toledo, Ohio, Jan. 4, 1949; s. Albert Theodore Otto and Ethel Anna (Weiler) S. BA in Speech, Adrian Coll., 1971; MA in Communication, Bowling Green State U., 1972; postgrad., Ind. U., 1974. Creative dir. S & L Advt. & P.R., Toledo, 1976-78; instr. U.S. Savings League Inst., Toledo, 1977; conf. leader Aeroquip Corp., Jackson, Mich., 1978-79; sales promotion supr. Aeroquip Corp., Jackson, 1979-87, advt. display mgr., 1987-88, sr. writer, producer, video, pub. rels., 1988-89, advt. prodn. supr., 1989-91; sr. copywriter Donald L. Arends, Inc., Oak Brook, Ill., 1992-96, Alexander Mktg. Svcs., Inc., Grand Rapids, Mich., 1996—. Mem. Lambda Iota Tau, Iota Beta Sigma, Pi Kappa Delta. Home: 2745 Birchcrest Dr SE Grand Rapids MI 49510 Office: Alexander Mktg Svcs Inc 277 Crahen Ave Grand Rapids MI 49516

SCHWARTZ, HOWARD WYN, health facility administrator; b. Mpls., June 12, 1951; s. Jerry Schwartz and Geraldine (Berg) Brooks; m. Jeannie Marie Holtzmann, Aug. 2, 1975; children: Abigail Jorene, Rachel Elizabeth. BA cum laude, U. Minn., 1973, MBA, 1982. Acct. Med. Sch., Univ. Minn., 1973-77; bus. mgr. Neurology Dept., Univ. Minn., 1977-79; administra. Found. Edn. Dept., Univ. Minn., 1979-82; sr. adminstrv. dir., instr. Radiology Dept. Univ. Minn., 1982—; pres. Bus. Mgmt. Svcs., Golden Valley, Minn., 1979—; lectr., author Topics in Radiology Adminstrn., 1984—. Editor-in-chief: RADWORKS Workload Measurement Manual, 1985-87; editor: Radiology Management, 1985-87, Purchasing the Radiology Information System, 1991, Current Concepts in Radiology Management, 1991; contbr. articles to profl. jours. Mem. Cystic Fibrosis Found., Minn., 1980—; chmn. Human Rights Commn., Robbinsdale, 1982-84; sec. Coord. Coun. Minority Concerns, 1984-85; chmn. imaging tech. adv. com. Univ. Hosp. Consortium, 1989-92; dir. Univ. Hosp. Consortium Svcs. Corp., 1990-92, Nat. Summit on Manpower, 1989-92; treas. Tech. Learning Campus Site Coun., Dist. 281, 1990-91, chmn. Bond Referendum campaign, 1995; pres. Armstrong H.S. Parent Assn., Dist. 281, 1991-92. Fellow Am. Healthcare Radiology Adminstrn. (regional pres. 1986-87, nat. pres. 1988-89, sec. edn. found. 1990-91, bd. dirs. edn. found. 1993-95, Outstanding Author award 1990, 93, 96, Midwest Region Disting. Mem. award 1991, Gold award 1991); mem. Radiologists Bus. Mgrs. Assn., Delta Kappa Epsilon. Home: 7400 Winnetka Heights Dr Golden Valley MN 55427-3549 Office: U Minn Hosp 420 Delaware St SE Minneapolis MN 55455-0374

SCHWARTZ, JOEL BARRY, psychologist, educational researcher; b. N.Y.C., Nov. 20, 1950; s. Howard Spencer and Annette Gertrude (Williams) S.; m Gwynne Ellen Ellis, June 27, 1987; children: Natalie, Douglas. BA, Alfred U., 1971, MA, 1976; MBA, Ind. U., 1987; PhD, Ball State U., 1987. Lic. sch. psychologist, Ind., N.Y. Tchr. N.Y.C. Bd. Edn., 1971-74; staff psychologist Porter County Spl. Edn. Coop., Valparaiso, Ind., 1976-78; supr. cope program Gary Community Sch. Corp., Ind., 1978-79, supr. evaluation and rsch., 1980-89, dir. evaluation and rsch., 1989—; ednl. cons. Chesterton, Ind., 1990—. Mem. Gary Reading Coun., Gary, 1990. Mem. Am. Assn. Sch. Adminstrs., Assn. for Supervision/Curriculum Devel., Gary Sch. Adminstrs'. Assn. (exec. bd. 1987-89), Phi Delta Kappa, Beta Gamma Sigma. Office: Gary Community Sch Corp 620 E 10th Pl Gary IN 46402-2731

SCHWARTZ, KARON STITT, nursing educator; b. Muskegon, Mich., Nov. 10, 1943; d. Samuel James and Jewel LaVern (Zeckzer) Stitt; m. James Allen Schwartz, Nov. 23, 1972; children: James Allen Jr., Theodore Joel. AD in Religion, Ky. Mountain Bible Coll., Vancleve, 1964; BSN, BA in Social Svcs., Goshen Coll., 1971; MSN, Andrews U., 1990; doctoral student, Wayne State U., 1992—. RN, Mich., Ind. Staff nurse Three Rivers (Mich.) Hosp., 1977-87; nurse educator Three Rivera Area Hosp., 1987-89, Three Rivers Manor, 1989-90; instr. nursing Glen Oaks C.C., Centreville, Mich., 1990—; cons. HCR,Toldeo, 1989-90; guest lectr. Emergency Nurses Assn. Symposium, San Francisco, 1991; co-presenter "Gender and Caring Constructs Through History", Internat. Assn. for Human Caring, Inc., 1995. Contbr. articles to profl. jours. Guest lectr. on personal loss syndrome, 1989—; vol. St. Joe County (Mich.) Hospice, 1991—, cmty. liason, Reach to Recovery, 1994—; Sunday sch. tchr. Ch. of Nazarene, Three Rivers, 1991-95. Recipient Rumble award Wayne State U., 1992; grantee Kalamazoo Rsch., 1991. Mem. ANA, Mich. Nurses Assn., Nat. League Nursing, Mich. League Nursing, Transcultural Nursing Soc., Future Farmers Am. Alumni, Sigma Theta Tau (presenter "Evaluation of Bhola's Change Theory"), Phi Kappa Phi. Home: 60128 Klinger Lake Rd Centreville MI 49032 Office: Glen Oaks CC 62449 Shimmel Rd Centreville MI 49032

SCHWARTZ, LINDA EVELYN, insurance executive; b. Chgo., Mar. 9, 1951; d. Robert John Hogan and Evelyn Anna (Redel) Heidke; m. Steven Mark Schwartz, July 22, 1972. BA in English with honors, U. Ill., 1972. Lic. all-lines producer, Ill. Editorial proofreader Commerce Clearing House, Chgo., 1972-73; direct response copywriter Combined Ins. Co. of Am., Chgo., 1973-77, Nat. Ben Franklin Life Ins. Co., Chgo., 1977-78; mktg. communications supr. Am. Res. Corp., Chgo., 1978-79; sr. v.p. mktg. Sedgwick James Group Svc., Inc., Chgo., 1979-95; v.p. property/casualty-north Alexander & Alexander, Chgo., 1995; sr. v.p. affinity group mktg. Near North Ins. Brokerage, Inc., 1995—. Vol. Blind Svc. Assn. Recipient award for Excellence in Mass Mktg., Profl. Inss. Mass Mktg. Assn., 1980, 86, 87, 88, 91, 92, 93, 94. Fellow Life Office Mgmt. Assn.; mem. Chgo. Assn. Direct Mktg. (judge creative awards competition 1982, awards com. 1983), Metropolitan Club. Office: Near North Ins Brokerage 875 N Michigan Ave Chicago IL 60611

SCHWARTZ, MICHAEL, university president, sociology educator; b. Chgo., July 29, 1937; s. Norman and Lillian (Ruthenberg) S.; m. Ettabelle Slutsky, Aug. 23, 1959; children: Monica, Kenneth, Rachel. BS in Psychology, U. Ill., 1958, MA in Indsl. Relations, 1959, PhD in Sociology, 1962; LLD (hon.), Youngstown State U., 1990. Asst. prof. sociology and psychology Wayne State U., Detroit, 1962-64; asst. prof. sociology Ind. U., Bloomington, 1964, assoc. prof. sociology, 1966-70; prof., chmn. dept. sociology Fla. Atlantic U., Boca Raton, 1970-72, dean Coll. Social Sci., 1972-76; v.p. grad. studies and research Kent (Ohio) State U., 1976-78, interim pres., 1977, acting v.p. acad. affairs, 1977-78, v.p. acad. and student affairs, 1978-80, provost, v.p. acad. and student affairs, 1980-82, pres., 1982-91; pres. emeritus and trustee's prof. Kent State U., 1991—; acting dir. Inst. for Social Rsch., Ind. U., 1966-67; tng. cons. Operation Head Start in Ind., 1964-70; cons. Office of Manpower, Automation and Tng., U.S. Dept. Labor, 1964-65. Cons. editor, Sociometry, 1966-70, assoc. editor, 1970; reader Am. Sociol. Rev. papers; author: (with Elton F. Jackson) Study Guide to the Study of Sociology, 1968; contbr. articles to profl. jours., chpts. to books. Chmn. Mid-Am. Conf. Coun. Pres.; rep. Nat. Coll. Athletic Assn. Pres.'s Commn.; corps evaluators North Ctrl. Assn. Colls. and Schs.; mem. bd. visitors Air U., USAF; mem. Akron (Ohio) Regional Devel. Bd., N.E. Ednl. TV of Ohio, Inc., N.E. Ohio Univs. Coll. Medicine; trustee Akron Symphony Orch. Assn.; mem. State of Ohio Post-Secondary Rev. Entity, 1995; mem. Assn. of Governing Bds. Commn. on Strengthening the Presidency. Recipient Disting. Tchr. award Fla. Atlantic U., 1970-71, Meritorious Svc. award Am. Assn. State Colls. and Univs., 1990; Michael Schwartz Ctr., Kent State U., named in his honor, 1991. Mem. Ohio Tchr. Edn. and Cert. Adv. Commn., Akron Press Club, Cleve. Press Club, Pine Lake Trout Club. Office: Kent State U 405 White Hall Kent OH 44242

SCHWARTZ, RICHARD ABRAM, psychiatrist; b. Boston, Jan. 19, 1935; s. Earl Samuel and Ruth (Leventhal) S.; m. Ilze Knezinskis, June 15, 1960; children: Anna, Katrina, Mara. BA, Harvard U., 1957; MD, Tufts U., 1961. Diplomate Am. Bd. Psychiatry and Neurology. Intern Boston City Hosp., 1961-62; resident Mass. Mental Health Ctr., Boston, 1962-65; asst. chief psychiatry USPHS, S.I., N.Y., 1965-67; clin. dir. Fairhill Mental Health Ctr., Cleve., 1967-70; staff psychiatrist Cleve. Clinic Found., 1970-78, Euclid Clinic Found., Cleve., 1978-85; dir. dept. psychiatry Univ. Mednet, Euclid Clinic Found., 1985—, trustee, 1990-93; chief geropsychiatry Laurelwood Hosp., Willoughby, Ohio, 1988—. Contbr. articles to med. jours., chpt. to book. Fellow Am. Psychiat. Assn.; mem. Cleve. Psychiat. Soc. (past. pres.), Ohio Psychiat. Assn., Acad. Medicine Cleve., Alpha Omega Alpha. Office: Univ Mednet 18599 Lake Shore Blvd Cleveland OH 44119-1039

SCHWARTZ, ROBERT CHARLES, communications and business consultant; b. Bridgeport, Conn., Apr. 27, 1936; s. Robert Daniel and Kathryn Arlene (Melville) S.; m. Barbara Diane Manhart, May 28, 1958 (dec. July 1985); children: Michael, Charles; m. Mavis Joy Shurson, July 26, 1986. BSEE, Purdue U., 1962. Engr. Gen. Electric, Lynchburg, Va., 1962-65, product planner, 1965-75, product mgr., 1975-82; mgr. product line mgmt. E.F. Johnson Co., Waseca, Minn., 1983-88; dir. advanced comms. E.F. Johnson Co., Eden Prairie, Minn., 1988-92; dir. market devel. E.F. Johnson Co., Burnsville, Minn., 1992-95; comms. cons. in pvt. practice Bloomington, Minn., 1995—; chmn. APCO 25 Interface Com., 1994—. Patentee battery saving sys. Served with U.S. Army, 1954-57. Mem. IEEE, Assn. Pub. Safety Comm. Officers, Radio Club. Am., Amateur Radio Relay League. Republican. Methodist. Home: 10517 Zinran Ave S Bloomington MN 55438

SCHWARTZ, SHIRLEY E., chemist; b. Detroit, Aug. 26, 1935; d. Emil Victor and Jessie Grace (Galbraith) Eckwall; m. Ronald Elmer Schwartz, Aug. 25, 1957; children: Steven Dennis, Bradley Allen, George Byron. BS, U. Mich., 1957, Detroit Inst. Tech., 1978; MS, Wayne State U., 1962, PhD, 1970. Asst. prof. Detroit Inst. Tech., 1973-78, head divsn. math. sci., 1976-78; mem. rsch. staff BASF Wyandotte (Mich.) Corp., 1978-81, head sect. functional fluids, 1981; sr. staff rsch. scientist GM, Warren, Mich., 1981—. Contbr. articles to profl. jours.; patentee in field. Recipient Gold award Engring. Soc. Detroit, 1989. Fellow Soc. Tribologists and Lubrication Engrs. (treas. Detroit sect. 1981, vice chmn. 1982, chmn. 1982-83, chmn. wear tech. com. 1987-88, bd. dirs. 1985-91, assoc. editor 1989-90, contbg. editor 1989—, Wilbur Deutsch award 1987, P.M. Ku award 1994); mem. Am. Chem. Soc., Soc. In Vitro Biology, Soc. Automotive Engrs. (Excellence in Oral Presentation award 1986, 91, 94, Arch T. Colwell Merit award 1991, Lloyd L. Withrow Disting. Spkr. award 1995), Mensa, Classic Guitar Soc. Mich., U.S. Power Squadrons, Detroit Navigators, Sigma Xi. Lutheran. Office: GM NAO Rsch & Devel Ctr 30500 Mound Rd Warren MI 48092-2031

SCHWARTZ, SUSAN LYNN HILL, principal; b. Portland, Ind., Aug. 15, 1951; d. Leland Alfred and Marjorie (Halberstadt) Hill; m. William Samuel Schwartz, July 6, 1974; children: Angelica Martinique, Allysia Dominica. BA, DePauw U., 1973; MA, Ball State U., 1976; postgrad., Tri-Coll. U., Fargo, N.D., 1986, Ind. U., 1993—. Cert. tchr. and aminstr., Ind., N.D. 2d and 3d grade tchr. Jay Sch. Corp., Portland, 1973-76; 1st to 3d grade tchr. Minot (N.D.) Pub. Schs., 1976-80; prin. elem. sch. Ward County Schs., Minot, 1980-82, LaPorte (Ind.) Schs., 1988-89; prin. 3d to 4th grade and spl. edn. Western Wayne Schs., Cambridge City, Ind., 1989—; mem. State Sch. Evaluation Team, Bismarck, N.D., 1980-81. Bd. dirs. Am. Cancer Soc., Muncie, Ind., 1985-88, Richmond, Ind., 1992—, Suzuki Music Assn., Muncie, 1986-87; mem./leader Work Area on Edn.-Meth., Muncie, 1985-87; philanthropic chair Delaware County Welcome Wagon, Muncie, 1982-88; treas./fin. sec. Christian Women's Club, Muncie, 1983-86; pres. N.D. State U. Sch. Adminstrs. Assn., Fargo, 1980-81; mem. Wayne County Step Ahead Edn. Com., 1991—. Named Outstanding Young Educator, Jaycees, 1980, Outstanding Young Career Woman, Bus. and Profl. Women, 1981. Mem. Phi Delta Kappa, Pi Lambda Theta, Delta Kappa Gamma, Psi Iota Xi. Methodist. Home: 12522 W Us Highway 40 Trlr 30 Cambridge City IN 47327-9481 Office: Milton Elem Sch PO Box 308 Milton IN 47357-0308

SCHWARZ, JOHN J.H., state senator, surgeon; b. Chgo., Nov. 15, 1937; s. Frank William and Helen Veronica (Brennan) S.; m. Anne Louise Ennia, Jan. 16, 1971 (dec. Feb. 1990); 1 child, Brennan Louise. BA, U. Mich., 1959; MD, Wayne State U., 1964. Physician, surgeon Battle Creek, Mich., 1974—; mayor City of Battle Creek, 1985-87; senator State of Mich., 1987—, pres. pro tempore, 1994—. Trustee Olivet Coll., 1991—, Wayland Acad., 1992—. Lt. comdr. USN, 1965-67. Mem. AMA, Am. Coll. Surgeons, Am. Soc. for Head & Neck Surgery. Republican. Roman Catholic. Office: State Senate State Capital Lansing MI 48909

SCHWARZE, ROBERT FRANCIS, osteopath, dermatologist; b. St. Louis, Aug. 13, 1949; s. William Casper and Mary Constance (Glaser) S.; m. Donna Lea Jakubiak, Nov. 3, 1990; children: William, Michael. BS, Maryville Coll., 1971; DO, U. Health Sciences, Kansas City, 1980; Cert. in Dermatology, 1990. Intern Normandy Osteo. Hosp., St. Louis, 1980-81; resident in surgery Deaconess West Hosp., St. Louis County, 1982-83, resident in dermatology, 1986-89; emergency physician St. Louis Regional, Dexter Meml., Met. and other hosps., 1981-89; dir. emergency dept. Lincoln County Meml. Hosp., 1985-87; preceptor in dermatology Met. Hosp., St. Louis, 1986-89; dermatologist St. Louis, 1989—; trainer dermatology residency program, lectr. in dermatology Deaconess West Hosp., St. Louis. Contbr. articles to profl. jours. Vol. Variety Club, St. Louis, 1989—; lectr. Jr. League, St. Louis, 1989; bd. dirs. Maryville Coll., St. Louis, 1971-74; fundraiser Incarnate Word Hosp., 1973-74, Chaminade Coll. Prep. Mem. Am. Osteo. Assn., Am. Coll. Osteo. Dermatology (trustee), St. Louis Met. Med. Soc., Am. Acad. Dermatology, Mo. Med. Soc., Mo. Osteo. Soc., St. Louis Osteo. Assn. Roman Catholic. Home: 17 Godwin Ln Saint Louis MO 63124-1591 Office: North County Dermatology 1120 Graham Rd Florissant MO 63031-8013 also: 11245 St Charles Rock Rd Saint Louis MO 63141

SCHWARZKOPF, GLORIA A., education educator, psychotherapist; b. Chgo., Apr. 20, 1926; m. Alfred E. Grossenbacher. BE, Chgo. State U., 1949, MEd in Libr. Sci., 1956. Cert. nat. recovery specialist, reality therapist; libr. sci. endorsement; cert. hypnotherapist; nat. forensic counselor. Tchr. Chgo. Bd. Edn., 1949-91, inservice trainer in substance abuse, 1990, 91; co-therapist ATC outpatient unit Ingalls Meml. Hosp., Chgo., 1981-86; recovery specialist Interaction Inst., Evergreen Park, Ill., 1993-95; instr. Govs. State U., University Park, Ill., 1987, 91, South Suburban Coll., South Holland, Ill., 1991, Prairie State Coll., Chicago Heights, Ill., 1993, 96. columnist Peoples Choice Weekly, 1991-93. Citizens Amb. Program del. to Russia and Czechoslovakia, 1996. Recipient Sci. Tchr. of Yr. award, 1976, Svc. Recognition award, 1985, IMSA Recognition award, 1988; grantee Chgo. Pub. Sch., 1981. Mem. NEA, Nat. Assn. Forensic Counselors, Sci. Tchrs. Assn., Ill. Alcoholism Counselors Alliance, Nat. Alcoholism Coun., Am. Assn. Hypnotherapists, Am. Assn. Behavioral Therapists, Soc. of Am. for Recovery (nat. cert. recovery specialist). Home: 2216 W 91st St Chicago IL 60620-6238

SCHWARZLOSE, RICHARD ALLEN, journalism educator; b. Chgo., Mar. 18, 1937; s. Paul Fowler and Muriel Beth (Kingsley) S.; m. Sally Jean Frye, July 27, 1963; children: Daniel Frye, Rebecca Frye. BS in Journalism, U. Ill., 1959, MA in Polit. Sci., 1960, PhD in Communications, 1965. Reporter, telegraph editor News-Gazette, Champaign, Ill., 1955-62; asst. prof. journalism Purdue U., West Lafayette, Ind., 1965-68; from asst. prof. to prof. journalism Northwestern U., Evanston, Ill., 1968—, assoc. dean Sch. Journalism, 1989-93. Author: Newspapers: A Reference Guide, 1987, Nation's Newsbrokers, 2 vols., 1989-90; author monograph; contbr. numerous articles to profl. jours. Peterson rsch. grantee Am. Antiquarian Soc., Worcester, Mass., 1984. Mem. Assn. for Edn. in Journalism and Mass Communications, Soc. Profl. Journalists. Unitarian. Home: 2712 Payne St Evanston IL 60201-2028 Office: Northwestern U Medill Sch Journalism Evanston IL 60208

SCHWARZROCK, SHIRLEY PRATT, author, lecturer, educator; b. Mpls., Feb. 27, 1914; d. Theodore Ray and Myrtle Pearl (Westphal) Pratt; m. Loren H. Schwarzrock, Oct. 19, 1945 (dec. 1966); children: Kay Linda, Ted Kenneth, Lorraine V. BS, U. Minn., 1935, MA, 1942, PhD, 1974. Sec. to chmn. speech dept., U. Minn., Mpls., 1935, instr. in speech, 1946, team tchr. in creative arts workshops for tchrs., 1955-56, guest lectr. Dental Sch., 1967-72, asst. prof. (part-time) of practice adminstrn. Sch. Dentistry, 1972-80; tchr. speech, drama and English, Preston (Minn.) H.S., 1935-37; tchr. speech, drama and English, Owatonna (Minn.) H.S., 1937-39, also dir. dramatics, 1937-39; tchr. creative dramatics and English, tchr.-counselor Webster Groves (Mo.) Jr. H.S., 1939-40; dir. dramatics and tchr.-counselor Webster Groves Sr. H.S., 1940-43; exec. sec. bus. and profl. dept. YWCA, Mpls., 1943-45; tchr. speech and drama Covent of the Visitation, St. Paul, 1958; editor pro-tem Am. Acad. Dental Practice Adminstrn., 1966-68; guest tchr. Coll. St. Catherine, St. Paul, 1969; vol. mgr. Gift Shop, Eitel Hosp., Mpls., 1981-83, Edina Cmty. Resource Pool, 1992-95; cmty. citizen mem. planning, evaluating, reporting com. Edina Pub. Sch. System, 1993-96; tutor for reading, writing, and speaking, 1993-96; cons. for dental med. programs Normandale C.C., Bloomington, Minn., 1968; cons. on pub. rels. to dentists, 1954-96; guest lectr. to various dental groups, 1966-95; lectr. Internat. Congress on Arts and Communication, 1980, Am. Inst. Banking, 1981; condr. tutorials in speaking and profl. office mgmt., 1985-96; owner Shirley Schwarzrock's Exec. Support Svc., 1989—; cons. to mktg. communications mgr. Ergodyne Corp., St. Paul, 1991-92; freelance editor med. support bus., 1992. Author books (series): Coping with Personal Identity, Coping with Human Relationships, Coping with Facts and Fantasies, Coping with Teenage Problems, 1984; individual book titles include: Do I Know the "Me" Others See?, My Life-What Shall I Do With It?, Living with Loneliness, Learning to Make Better Decisions, Grades, What's So Important About Them, Anyway?, Facts and Fantasies About Alcohol, Facts and Fantasies About Drugs, Facts and Fantasies About Smoking, Food as a Crutch, Facts and Fantasies About the Roles of Men and Women, You Always Communicate Something, Appreciating People-Their Likenesses and Differences, Fitting In, To Like and Be Liked, Can You Talk With Someone Else? Coping with Emotional Pain, Some Common Crutches, Parents Can Be a Problem, Coping with Cliques, Crises Youth Face Today, Effective Dental Assisting, (with L.H. Schwarzrock) 1954, 59, 67, (with J.R. Jensen) 1973, 78, 82, (with J.R. Jensen, Kay Schwarzrock, Lorraine Schwarzrock) 1990, Workbook for Effective Dental Assisting, 1960, 68, 73, (with Lorraine Schwarzrock), 1978, 82, 90, Manual for Effective Dental Assisting, 1968, 73, 78, 82, 90; (with Donovan F. Ward), Effective Medical Assisting, 1969, 76; Workbook for Effective Medical Assisting, 1969, 76, Manual for Effective Medical Assisting, 1969, 76; (with C.G. Wrenn) The Coping With Series of Books for High School Students, 1970, 73; The Coping With Manual, 1973, Contemporary Concerns, of Youth, 1980. Pres. University Elem. Sch. PTA, 1955-56. Fellow Internat. Biog. Assn.; mem. Minn. Acad. Dental Practice Adminstrn. (hon.), Minn. Historical Soc., 1992—, Minn. Geneaolgical Soc., 1992—, Zeta Phi Eta (pres. 1948-49), Eta Sigma Upsilon. Home: 7448 W Shore Dr Edina MN 55435-4022

SCHWEICKERT, RICHARD JUSTUS, psychologist, educator; b. Madison, Wis., July 19, 1946; s. Carl E. and Marie E. (Dilzer) S.; m. Carolyn M. Jagacinski, Dec. 27, 1980; children: Patrick, Kenneth. BS in Math., U. Santa Clara, 1968; MA in Math., Ind. U., 1972; PhD in Psychology, U. Mich., 1979. Statistician Bellevue Psychiatric Hosp., N.Y.C., 1969-71; asst. prof. Purdue U., West Lafayette, Ind., 1978-83; assoc. prof. Purdue U., West Lafayette, 1984-91, prof., 1992—; mem. adv. panel on human cognition & perception NSF, 1993-96. Author: (with others) Handbook of Human Factors, 1987; assoc. editor Psychol. Bull. and Rev., 1993—; mem. editl. bd. Jour. Exptl. Psychology; Learning, Memory & Cognition, 1985-89, 91-94, Jour. Math. Psychology, 1986-94; contbr. articles to profl. jours. Grantee NSF, 1981-84, 92—, NIMH, 1983-86, 87-89. Fellow AAAS, Am. Psychol. Soc.; mem. Soc. for Math. Psychology (pres. 1990-91, bd. dirs.), Psychonomic Soc., Informs. Office: Purdue U Dept Psychol Scis West Lafayette IN 47907

SCHWEIKLE, PAUL DOUGLAS, genealogist; b. Celina, Ohio, Mar. 17, 1954; s. Floyd Arnold and Geraldine Mary Alice (Leach) S. BBA with honors, U. Miami, 1975, postgrad. in hist. linguistics, 1975; studies with Dr. Gerhard Wein, Germany, 1984. Owner Crown & Sceptre Numismatics, Van Wert, Ohio, 1976-85; profl. genealogist, hist. researcher Van Wert, 1985—; chmn. Van Wert County chpt. Ohio Geneal. Soc. First Families of Ohio, 1981-82. Author: A Line of Descent from Lt. Edward Ricketts, Revolutionary War Officer, of Maryland, Pennsylvania, and Ohio 1758 to date, 1982, Captain Ezra Ricketts, Civil War Hero, 1982, Tracing Your Ancestors, 1991;

contbr. articles to profl. jours. Mem. The Monarchist League (London, life fellow), First Families of Ohio (writer's award 1981), Univ. Miami Alumni Assn., Phi Kappa Phi, Beta Gamma Sigma, Beta Alpha Psi. Republican. Quaker. Home: 142 East Maple Ave Van Wert OH 45891

SCHWENDAU, MARK STEVEN, computer graphics educator; b. Evanston, Ill., Apr. 12, 1954; s. Edward Herbert and Vada E. Schwendau; m. Karen M. Duffy, Oct. 11, 1954 (div.); children: Kendra Ann, Trevor Brandon. BS in Indsl. Edn., No. Ill. U., 1976, MS in Indsl. Mgmt., 1990. CAD/drafting instr. Ind. Valley Area Vocat. Ctr., Sandwich, Ill., 1977-90, Kishwaukee Coll., Malta, Ill., 1990—; indsl. edn. dir. Kishwaukee Edn. Consortium, DeKalb, Ill., 1992—. Author: Autocad Fundamentals, 1992, From Campus to Career: A Hire Education, 1994; co-author: Drafting Fundamentals and Industrial Applications, 1989, Drafting Fundamentals, 1986. Alderman City of Plano, Ill., 1979-89. Recipient 1990 Outstanding Young Alumnus No. Ill. U. Mem. Am. Vocat. Assn., Ill. Vocat. Assn., Vocat. Indsl. Clubs of Am., Ill. Drafting Educator's Assn., Ill. Indsl. Tech. Edn. Assn. (community coll. membership com. 1991—). Office: Kishwaukee Coll 21193 Malta Rd Malta IL 60150-9600

SCHWEPKER, CHARLES HENRY, JR., marketing educator; b. St. Charles, Mo., Jan. 21, 1963; s. Charles Henry Sr. and Mary Regina (Halter) S.; m. Laura Ann Pirrone, Dec. 1992. BSBA, S.E. Mo. State U., 1984, MBA, 1988; PhD, U. Memphis, 1992. Asst. mgr. WalMart, Lubbock, Tex., 1985; asst. prof. mktg. Cen. Mo. State U., Warrensburg, 1992—; student coord. Small Bus. Inst., Cape Girardeau, 1986-87; exec. asst. Mktg. and Small Bus. Conf., Cape Girardeau, 1986, 87; ad hoc reviewer Jour. of Personal Selling and Sales Mgmt., 1991, 92. Mem. editl. rev. bd. Jour. Personal Selling and Sales Mgmt., 1993—, Jour. Mktg. Theory & Practice, 1993—, So. Bus. Rev.; contbr. articles to profl. jours. Chpt. advisor for Student Am. Mktg. Assn. at Ctrl. Mo. State U., 1992—. Mem. Am. Mktg. Assn., Acad. Mktg. Sci., So. Mktg. Assn. (procs. reviewer 1991), Atlantic Mktg. Assn. (procs. reviewer 1991, nat. conf. in sales mgmt. procs. reviewer 1993, 94, 95). Roman Catholic. Office: Ctrl Mo State U Coll Bus & Econs Dept Mktg and Legal Studies Warrensburg MO 64093

SCHWERDTNER, FREDERICK HOWARD, retired police commander, lawyer; b. Chgo., Oct. 13, 1949; s. Fred and Lydia (Tatz) S.; m. Julie Anne Carramusa, Oct. 21, 1990; 1 child, Sarah Elizabeth. BS, Loyola U., Chgo., 1973, JD, 1989; MBA with distinction, DePaul U., 1983. Bar: Ill. 1989, U.S. Dist. Ct. (no. dist.) Ill. 1989. Officer Oak Park (Ill.) Police Dept., 1973-93, commdr., 1989-93. Contbr. articles to profl. jours. Tutor inner city high sch. students, Chgo., 1988. With USMC, 1965-69, Vietnam. Mem. ABA, Fraternal Order Police, Marine Corps League (DuPage County chpt.), Ill. State Bar Assn., Chgo. Bar Assn., DuPage County Bar Assn., Viet-Now (Cook County chpt.), Beta Gamma Sigma. Republican. Lutheran. Office: 28-32 W Lake St Oak Park IL 60302-2606

SCHWIER, PRISCILLA LAMB GUYTON, television broadcasting company executive; b. Toledo, Ohio, May 8, 1939; d. Edward Oliver and Prudence (Hutchinson) L.; m. Robert T. Guyton, June 21, 1963 (dec. Sept. 1976); children—Melissa, Margaret, Robert; m. Frederick W. Schwier, May 11, 1984. B.A., Smith Coll., 1961; M.A., U. Toledo, 1972. Pres. Gt. Lakes Communications, Inc., 1982—; vice chmn. Seilon, Inc., Toledo, 1981-83, also dir. Contbr. articles to profl. jours. Trustee Wilberforce U., Ohio, 1983—, Planned Parenthood, Toledo, 1979-83, Maumee Valley Country Day Sch., Toledo; bd. dirs. N.W. Ohio Hospice, 1991—. Episcopal Ch., Maumee, Ohio, 1983—; bd. trustees Toledo Hosp., Maumee Country Day Sch., 1986-92; pres. Edward Lamb Found., 1987—. Democrat. Episcopalian. Home: 345 E Front St Perrysburg OH 43551-2131 Office: 129 W Wayne St Ste 100 Maumee OH 43537-2150

SCHWING, RICHARD CHARLES, chemical engineer; b. Buffalo, N.Y., Dec. 8, 1934; s. Charles Vincent and Ruth Mary (Geschwender) S.; m. Joan Cathryn Baker, June 16, 1956 (div. Nov. 1969); children: Mark, Cathryn; m. Patricia Ann Stevenson, Dec. 17, 1971; children: Michelle, Michael. BS in Chem. Engring., U. Mich., 1957, MS in Chem. Engring., 1959, PhD in Chem. Engring., 1963. Sr. rsch. engr., fuels and lubricants dept. R & D Ctr. GM, Warren, Mich., 1963-71; sr. rsch. engr. societal analysis dept. (ops. scis. dept.) GM Rsch. Labs., Warren, Mich., 1971-87, prin. rsch. engr. operating scis. dept., 1987—. Editor: Societal Risk Assessment: How Safe is Safe Enough, 1980, Human Behavior and Traffic Safety, 1985. 1st lt. U.S. Army, 1962-63. Fellow Soc. for Risk Analysis (pres. 1988-89); mem. AAAS, Internat. Assn. for Impact Assessment (pres. 1984-85), Am. Chem. Soc., World Future Soc., Sigma Xi. Unitarian-Universalist. Office: GM R & D Ctr MC480-106-359 Tech Forecast & Soc Trends Warren MI 48092-2031

SCHWINGENDORF, KEITH EUGENE, mathematician, educator, researcher; b. Chgo., May 9, 1948; s. Paul Dawson and Laverne Marie (Reber) S.; m. Susan Kay Wilcox, aug. 22, 1970 (div. Apr. 1981); children: Karen Marie, Jeffrey Paul; m. Lisa Gaye Mannering, May 7, 1989; children: Jessica Lynn, Ryan Keith. BS in Math., Purdue U., 1970, MS, 1971, PhD in Math., 1978. Counselor, instr. math. Purdue U., West Lafayette, Ind., 1978-91; assoc. prof. Purdue U., Westville, Ind., 1991-96, prof., 1996—. Author: Precalculus, Concepts and Computers, 1996, (Math. Assn. Am. notes series) Calculus, Concepts and Computers-Innovations in Learning, 1990, Constructing Calculus Concepts in a Computer Laboratory, 1991, Horizontal and Vertical Growth of the Student's Conception of Function, 1992, A Practical Guide to Cooperative Learning in Collegiate Mathematics, 1995; contbr. articles to profl. jours. Grantee NSF, 1988-89, 90-94, 92-95, 94-96. Mem. Am. Math. Soc., Math. Assn. Am., Nat. Coun. Tchrs. Math., Ind. Coun. Math. Home: 1101 Sunset Ct West Lafayette IN 47906-2454 Office: Mathematics Tech 277 Purdue U North Central 1401 S US Highway 421 Westville IN 46391-9528

SCHWINN, DAVID RONALD, management consultant; b. Dayton, Ohio, Sept. 10, 1944; s. Arthur Leonard and Mary Anna (Reger) S.; m. Marilyn Esther Durst, Oct. 6, 1966 (div. June 1986); children: Steven, Jeffrey, Timothy; m. Carole Joyce Bly, Aug. 16, 1986; stepchildren: Kristi, Randy, Lisa. BME, Gen. Motors Inst., 1967; MBA, Wright State U., 1971. Registered profl. engr., Ohio. Supr., engr. Gen. Motors Corp., Dayton, 1966-72; exec. Ford Motor Co., Dearborn, Mich., 1972-86; prin. cons., Transformation of Am. Industry Community Colls. Nat. Tng. Project, Jackson Community Coll., Jackson, Mich., 1984—; instr. Schoolcraft & Henry Ford Colls., Detroit, 1982-84; cons. Tel Tech Resource Network, Mpls., 1987—. Co-author: (video and print tng. system) Transformation of American Industry, 1984, Total Quality Transformation Training System, 1991; author, producer various video tapes, 1979-90; contbr. articles to profl. jours. Mem. Am. Civil Liberties Union, Washington, Common Cause, Washington, current. Recipient Quality Leadership award Am. Soc. Tng. & Devel., 1989, Fulbright scholarship Coun. for Internat. Exchange of Scholars, Washington, 1989-90. Mem. Am. Soc. for Quality Control (Craig award 1982), Nat. Soc. Profl. Engrs. (Am. Quality and Productivity Inst. liaison 1988—), World Ctr. for Community Excellence (bd. advisors), Assn. for Quality and Participation. Office: Jackson Community Coll 2111 Emmons Rd Jackson MI 49201-8335

SCISCOE, JASON WILLIAM, clergy member; b. St. Louis, Aug. 22, 1970; s. William Leo and Nancy Ellen (Jordan) S. Youth worker United Pentecostal Ch. Internat., Atlanta, 1988; youth pastor United Pentecostal Ch. Internat., New Orleans, 1989, Witchita, Kans., 1989; minister United Pentecostal Ch. Internat., Hazelwood, Mo., 1989—. Republican. Home: 1381 Marchfield Way Columbus OH 43204 Office: United Pentecostal Ch Inter 8855 Dann Rd Hazelwood MO 63042

SCOBBA, JUDY, credit collections executive; b. Marshalltown, Iowa, July 31, 1944; d. Edward Elmer and Lois Wilma (Strohschoen) Grimes; m. Alfred Verne Scobba, May 23, 1963 (div. May 1973); children: Montgomery Scott, Lance Alfred. Student, U. Wis., 1981, Iowa Western Coll., 1985, 88. Cert. collection agy. exec. Office mgr. Gamble-Skogmo Inc., Algona, Iowa, 1962-69; auditor Look Mag., Des Moines, 1969; from cashier to adminstrv. asst. Avco Fin., Des Moines, 1969-75; mgr. Avco Fin., Indianola, Iowa, 1975, Atlantic, Iowa, 1975-78; loan mgr. Walnut Grove Credit Union, Atlantic, 1978-84; gen. office mgr. Collection Specialist Inc., Omaha, 1984-86; account exec. Nat. Account Systems, Omaha, 1986-90, dep. legal systems mgr., 1990-95, v.p., 1995—; paralegal Law Office Joseph Louis Vacca, 1995—; cashier Target, Inc., Des Moines, 1973; inventory clk. RGIS, Atlantic, 1981-82; asst. mgr., cashier Casey's Gen. Store, 1982-84; night office mgr. No Frills Supermarket, 1984—. Sec., v.p., pres. Bus. Profl. Women, Atlantic, 1975-80; bd. dirs. Am. Bus. Women, Omaha, 1989-91; bd. dirs., sec. CWI Credit Profls., Omaha, 1986-90. Mem. Am. Guild Patient Account Mgrs. (mem. awards 1984—), Internat. Credit Assn. of Midlands (treas., bd. dirs.), Am. Bus. Women's Assn. (Omaha chpt., corr. sec., bd. dirs.), CWI: Credit Profls. Omaha. Office: Joseph L Vacca Atty at Law 2819 S 125 Ave Ste 256 Omaha NE 68144

SCOBIE, CRAIG K., computer company executive; b. Toledo, June 3, 1942; s. James Hall and Minnie Emma (Olsen) S.; m. Betty Gayle Gorley, Jan. 6, 1966 (div. Nov. 1978); children: Timothy Craig, Jill Anne; m. Therese Anne Martin, June 3, 1983. BS in Math., Wittenberg U., 1964. Computer programmer, analyst civilian USAF, WP AFB, Ohio, 1964-66; sys. mgr. RCA, Chgo., 1966-71; dir. Comshare Inc., Chgo., 1971-85; v.p. sales Artificial Intelligence Corp., Boston, 1985-87; dir. Infonet, Chgo., 1987-94; dir. sales SCO, Chgo., 1994—. Home: 1318 Brighton Dr Wheaton IL 60187 Office: SCO 8725 W Higgins Ste 595 Chicago IL 60631

SCOBY, DONALD R., environmental biologist; b. Sabetha, Kans., Mar. 18, 1931; s. Otis C. and Stella R. (McClanahan) S.; m. Glenna J. Norrie, 1 child, Meloyde J. Scoby Hansen. BS, Kans. State U., 1957; MS, Nebr. State Tchrs. Coll., 1960; postgrad., U. Tex., 1960-61; PhD, N.D. State U., 1968. Cert. sec. tchr., Kans., Colo.; lic. in real estate. Farmer Sabetha, 1954-60; biol. farmer Lake Park, Minn., 1968-88; tchr. sci. Sabetha High Sch., 1957-60; instr. biology/ chmn. dept. sci. Colorado Springs (Colo.) Sch. Dist., 1961-66; prof. biology N.D. State U., Fargo, 1966-89, prof. emeritus biology and edn., 1989—; prof. biology Moorhead (Minn.) State U., 1988-95. Editor: Environmental Ethics, 1971; contbr. articles to profl. jours. With USAF, 1951-54. Named Conservationist of the Yr. N.D. Wildlife Fedn., 1971; recipient Friends of Sci. Edn. award N.D. Sci. Tchrs., 1984, Odney Award for Teaching Excellence, N.D. State U., 1986, Partner in Edn. award Fargo Pub. Schs., 1988. Methodist. Home: 3302 2nd St N # 22 Fargo ND 58102

SCOGIN, ROBERT ERWIN, actor; b. Moulton, Ala., Nov. 15, 1937; s. Allison Parker and Bessie Elise (Bowden) S. BA in English, Florence (Ala.) State U., 1960. Actor Am. Shakespeare Theatre, Stratford, Conn., 1968-69, Mo. Repertory Theater, Kansas City, 1970-74, Gt. Lakes Shakespeare Festival, Cleve., 1976, Ind. Repertory Theater, Indpls., 1973-77, Goodman Theater, Chgo., 1978-93, Shakespeare Repertory, Chgo., 1986-96, Guthrie Theater, Mpls., 1980-81, Wisdom Bridge Theater, Chgo., 1992; tchr. Shakespeare Repertory, Chgo., 1988-96, Roosevelt U., 1995-96. 1st lt. U.S. Army, 1961-63. Home: 919 W Argyle St Chicago IL 60640-3805 Office: Shakespeare Repertory 820 N Orleans St Chicago IL 60610-3051

SCOLARO, JOSEPH ALAN, journalist; b. Racine, Wis., July 20, 1970; s. Martin and Arlene (Kunhart) S. BS in Journalism with honors, U. Wis., 1992. City Hall reporter Beloit (Wis.) Daily News, 1993-94; govt. reporter Jour.-Times, Racine, Wis., 1994—. Mem. Soc. Profl. Journalists. Home: 3311 Debra Ln Apt 3 Racine WI 53403 Office: Jour-Times 212 4th St Racine WI 53403

SCOLES, CLYDE SHELDON, library director; b. Columbus, Ohio, Apr. 14, 1949; s. Edward L. and Edna M. (Ruddock) S.; m. Diane Francis, July 14, 1976; children: David, Kevin, Karen, Stephen. BS, Ohio State U., 1971; MLS, U. Mich., 1972. Librarian Columbus Pub. Library, 1972-74; library dir. Zanesville (Ohio) Pub. Library, 1974-78; asst. dir. Toledo-Lucas County Pub. Library, 1978-85, dir., 1985—; adj. lectr., libr. bldg. cons. U. Mich.; v.p. bd. dirs. Read for Literacy. Mem. ALA, Ohio Libr. Assn., Ohio Libr. Coun., Toledo C. of C., Com. of 100, Maumee Hist. Soc. Club: Torch (Toledo). Lodge: Rotary.

SCOLLARD, DIANE LOUISE, retired elementary school educator; b. Seattle, Mar. 12, 1945; d. James Martin and Viola Gladys (Williams) S. BA in Edn., Wash. State U., 1967; 5th yr. cert. in edn., U. Wash., 1970; cert. edn., Oakland U., 1977. Tchr. Battle Ground (Wash.) Sch. Dist., 1967-70, Lapeer (Mich.) Cmty. Schs., 1970-95; ret. Mem. AAUW, NEA, NAFE, Nat. Assn. Career Women, Am. Bus. Women's Assn., Mich. Edn. Assn., Lapeer Edn. Assn. (bldg. rep. 1985, 89), Beta Sigma Phi. Democrat. Episcopalian.

SCOTT, AMY ANNETTE HOLLOWAY, nursing educator; b. St. Albans, W.Va., Apr. 10, 1916; d. Oliver and Mary (Lee) Holloway; m. William M. Jefferson, June 22, 1932, (div. Oct. 1933); 1 child, William M. Jefferson, m. Vann Hyland Scott, Mar. 15, 1952, (dec. Dec. 1972). BS in Nursing Edn., Cath. U., Washington, 1948; cert. in psychiat. nursing, U. Paris, Paris, 1959. Indsl. nurse Curtiss Wright Air Plane Co., Lambert Field, St. Louis, 1941-44; faculty St. Thomas U., Manila, Philippines Island, 1948-50; pub. health nurse St. Louis Health Dept., 1951-56; capt. USAF Nursing Corps, Paris, 1956-60; resigned as maj. USAF (Nurse Corps), 1960, 1960; faculty St. Louis State Hosp., 1960-67; dept. head St. Vincents Hosp., St. Louis, 1967-68; faculty RN, creator psychiat. program sch. of Nursing Jewish Hosp., 1968-72; adminstrv. nurse St. Louis State Hosp., 1972-84; initiated first psychiatric program sch. nursing, Jewish Hosp. Author: (short story) Two Letters, 1962, (novel) Storms, 1987, Life's Journey, 1993. Past bd. dirs. county bd. Mo. U., 1984-88; hon. citizen Colonial Williamsburg, Va.; mem. Rep. Presdl. Task Force; mem. Women in the Arts '94. Recipient Key to Colonial Williamsburg, Va., Medal of Merit, Rep. Presdl. Task Force, 1992; named to Rep. Presdl. Task Force Honor Roll, 1993, Nat. Women's Hall of Fame, 1995, Women's Hall of Fame, 1996. Mem. AAUW, NAFE, Internat. Fedn. Univ. Women, Internat. Soc. Quality Assurance in Health Care, N.Y. Acad. Scis., Am. Biog. Inst. (life, governing bd.), Women in the Arts, Cambridge Centre Engring., Internat. Platform Assn. Roman Catholic.

SCOTT, CRAIG, superintendent; b. Marshalltown, Iowa, July 4, 1945; s. Vernon S. and Vivian F. (Atkinson) S.; m. Mary K. Taylor, June 3, 1967; children: Angela, Christopher, Dawn. BA, Simpson Coll., 1968; MA, U. No. Iowa, 1974; PhD, Drake U., 1988. Tchr., coach Allison-Bristow Sch. Dist., Allison, Iowa, 1970-71, Auleuy (Iowa) Sch. Dist., 1971-79; prin. Underwood (Iowa) Sch. Dist., 1979-81, supt., 1981-83; supt. Red Oak (Iowa) Sch. Dist., 1983-86, Ballard Sch. Dist., Huxley, Iowa, 1986-93, Oregon (Ill.) Unit Sch. Dist., 1993-94, Fort Madison (Iowa) Sch. Dist., 1994—; chair First in Nation in Edn., Des Moines, 1991-92, AEA Supts. Adv., Johnston, Iowa, 1990-91; advisor grad. program U. No. Iowa, Cedar Falls, 1989-95. Apptd. Legis. Adv. Panel, Des Moines, 1986-87; bd. dirs. YMCA, 1995, Meth. Ch., Huxley, 1993. Sgt. U.S. Army, 1968-70. Mem. C. of C. (v.p. 1995), Rotary (vocat. chmn. 1986), Masons, Ambassadors Club. Republican. Home: 3315 203d St Fort Madison IA 52627 Office: Fort Madison Cmty Schs 1930 Ave M Fort Madison IA 52627

SCOTT, DELBERT LEE, state legislator. Rep. Mo. State Ho. Reps. Dist. 119. Home: PO Box 147 700 E 7th St Lowry City MO 64763*

SCOTT, DOUGLAS PATRICK, lawyer, state representative; b. Rockford, Ill., Jan. 17, 1960; s. Robert Wallace and Janice Elaine (Baldwin) S.; m. Tammy Raye Johnson Scott, July 20, 1985. BA, U. Tulsa, 1982; JD, Marquette U., Milw., 1985. Asst. city atty. City of Rockford, Ill., 1985-87; city atty., 1987-95; state rep. State of Ill., Rockford, 1995—; mem., pres.-elect. bd. Ill. Recycling Assn., Mokena, Ill., 1994-95. Bd. mem. Discovery Ctr. Mus., Rockford, Ill., 1993-94; bd. mem., pres. Ken-Rock Cmty. Ctr., Rockford, Ill., 1991-95; mem. Cmty. Edn. Task Force, Rockford, Ill., 1993-94. Mem. Ill. State Bar Assn., Wis. Bar Assn. Democrat. Home: 130 N Prospect St Rockford IL 61107 Office: 200 S Wyman St Ste 304 Rockford IL 61101

SCOTT, JACK CHARLES, dermatologist, educator; b. Altus, Okla., Jan. 27, 1945; s. John Louis and Mary I. (Grone) S.; m. Nancy J. Gray, Aug. 23, 1969; children: John E. Jay, Kirstin T. BA, St. Mary's U. Minn., Winona, 1966; MD, UCLA, 1966-70. Diplomate Am. Bd. Dermatology. Intern L.A. County Harbor Gen. Hosp., Torrance, Calif., 1970-71; flight surgeon Sch. Aerospace Med., Brooks AFB, San Antonio, 1971; resident in dermatology U. Minn., Mpls., 1973-76; physician Skin Diseases, PA., Mpls., 1976-80; pvt. practice Mpls., 1980-85; ptnr., physician Associated Skin Care Specialists, Fridley, Minn., 1985—; cons., contbg. dermatologist Star Tribune Newspaper, Mpls., 1983—. Author: (monograph) Dermatology I & II, Am. Acad. Family Practice Home Study Program, 1995; contbr. articles to profl. jours. mem. Twin Cities adv. counc. St. Mary's U. of Minn., Mnpls., 1990—. Capt., flight surgeon USAF, 1971-73. Fellow Am. Acad. Dermatology (Bronze award, 1985, 86), Minn. Dermatol. Soc. (v.p. 1991), Minn. Med. Assn. Roman Catholic. Office: Associated Skin Care Spec 7205 Univ Ave NE Fridley MN 55432

SCOTT, JAMES WHITE, newspaper editor; b. Lebanon, Kans., Feb. 22, 1926; s. James Malcolm and Bernice (White) S.; m. Sammy Peete, June 9, 1950; children: James Peete, Thomas Whiteford, Edward English. B.J., U. Kans., 1950. Reporter Kansas City (Mo.) Times, 1950-54; editorial writer Kansas City (Mo.) Star, 1954-93, nat. affairs writer, arts and entertainment assoc. editor, 1968-77, v.p., 1987-93; editor editorial pages Star and Times, 1977-93, sr. editor, 1993-96. Served with AUS, 1944-46, ETO. Mem. Delta Upsilon. Episcopalian. Home: 3204 W 83rd Ter Leawood KS 66206-1304 Office: Kansas City Star 1729 Grand Blvd Kansas City MO 64108-1413

SCOTT, JOHN CARL, educator; b. Norfolk, Va., Feb. 17, 1958; s. Ivan Carl and Melvia Mary (Atta) S. BA in History, U. Toledo, 1981, MEd in Counseling, 1984, PhD in Higher Edn. Adminstrn., 1991. Grad. asst. U. Toledo, 1984-89; cons. ShopAmerica, Toledo, 1989-92; adj. prof. Greenwich U., Hilo, Hawaii, 1991-93; instr. Northwest State C.C., Archbold, Ohio, 1994-95. Author: (book) The Influence of the Medieval University on the Latin Church & Secular Government Politics, 1992, (scholarly paper) Medieval Universities and Cities Interwoven, 1993, The Medieval University: 'Ivory Tower' or Professional Training Ground?, 1994. Mem. Assn. for the Study of Higher Edn., Am. Assn. for Higher Edn., Phi Alpha Theta. Episcopalian.

SCOTT, JOHN E., state legislator. Rep. Mo. State Ho. Reps., 1971-76; senator Mo. State Senate Dist. 3, 1977—. Office: 6038 Guilford Pl Saint Louis MO 63109-3316*

SCOTT, LINDA ANN, assistant principal, elementary education educator; b. St. Louis, Jan. 21, 1955; d. Jay R. and Bernadette (Hogan) S. BS, Youngstown State U., Ohio, 1979; MS, Gov.'s State U., Park Forest, Ill., 1991. Tchr. Bishop Blanchette, Joliet, Ill., 1981-85, St. Joseph's, Joliet, Ill., 1985-86, Hufford Jr. H.S., Joliet, Ill., 1986-92; asst. prin. Washington Jr. H.S., Joliet, 1992—; ednl. coord. Warren-Sharpe Community Ctr., Joliet, 1990—. Mem. life PTA, 1990—. No. Ill. U. grantee, 1990, Argonne Nat. Lab. grantee, 1990, U. Ill. grantee, 1991. Mem. Ill. Coun. Tchrs. of Math. Home: 7324 Heritage Ct Frankfort IL 60423-9587 Office: Washington Jr HS 402 Richards St Joliet IL 60433-2218

SCOTT, MARTHA G., state legislator; b. Ware Shoals, S.C., Nov. 10, 1935; d. Harold and Pearl (Wardlaw) Smith; children: Marion Jr., Deborah Ann Gilmore. Student, Highland Park Jr. Coll., 1952-54; DHH, Tenn. Sch. Religion, 1990; DHL, Urban Bible Inst., Detroit, 1994. With Mich. Bell Telephone Co., 1960-86; rep. Mich. Ho. of Reps. Mem. Mich. State Dem. Ctrl. Com., 1974-82; commr. Wayne County Bd. Commrs., 1977-80, chairwoman Human Resources Com., 1978-80; vice chairwoman Wayne County Civil Svc. Commn., 1980-82; pres. Highland Park City Coun., 1984-87; mayor City of Highland Park, 1988; Dem. precinct del. 1st Congl. Dist.; bd. dirs. Nat. Coun. Alcoholism and Other Dependencies, 1979, Detroit Osteopathic Hosp., 1990; vice chairwoman Mich. Women in Mcpl. Govt.; founding mem. Nat. Polit. Congress Black Women; adv. bd. Met. Region Bus. Alliance; vol. Residential Care Alternatives. Recipient Plaque Highland Park Sch. Bd., 1977, Nat. Polit. Congress of Black Women award, 1981, Resolution, Wayne County Bd. Commrs., 1981, Wayne County Auditors, 1981, Dollars and Sense Mag. award, 1989, Spl. Achievement award Amvets, Golden Heritage award for excellence in svc., 1988, Cmty. Svc. award Knoxville Coll. Alumni, 1988. Mem. Gamma Phi Delta. Office: Michigan House of Reps State Capitol Lansing MI 48909

SCOTT, MILDRED HOPE, nurse; b. Miami, Fla., July 5, 1926; d. Enos R. and Ruth (Sommers) Eby; m. Thomas Wayne Scott, Dec. 19, 1958; children: Linda Joy Scott Day, Daniel Dean. ThB in Bible Theology, Internat. Bible Inst. and Sem., Plymouth, Fla., 1982. Lic. practical nurse, Fla. Lic. practical nurse various hosps. and nursing homes, Fla. and Mo., 1969-86; sch. nurse Orange County Sch. Bd., Orlando, Fla., 1974-78; pvt. duty nurse Upjohn Healthcare Services, Kansas City, Mo., 1985-89; allergy nurse Agarwal Allergy Clinic, Raytown, Mo., 1987-89, 92—; sec. to Dr. Lottie McWherter Mission, Kans., 1989-92; staff writer Majestic Records-Countrywine Pub., Linden, Tex., 1987—. Served as cpl. USMC, 1957-59. Mem. ASCAP, Assn. Internat. Gospel Assemblies Ind. (ordained minister). Democrat. Home: PO Box 183 43 Aspen St Belton MO 64012-2091

SCOTT, RAYMOND GERALD, management executive; b. Presho, S.D., Dec. 1, 1916; s. Ray Bruce and Elsa M. (Sehnert) S.; m. Gladys May Frederick, Dec. 1, 1939; children: Pamela Rae Scott Swierzb, David Bruce. Student, Nettleton Comml. Coll., Sioux Falls, S.D., 1934-36. Adminstrv. asst. John Deere Plow Co., Sioux Falls, 1940-41, USAF, various locations, 1942-57, The Strategic Air Command, Offutt AFB, Nebr., 1958-72, Henry Doorly Zoo, Omaha, 1973-74; exec. dir. Midlands Community Hosp. Found., Papillion, Nebr., 1974-85, U.S. Badminton Assn., Papillion, Nebr., 1986-89; pres., owner R&G Enterprises, Papillion, Nebr., 1990—. Bd. dirs. Civil Svc. Commn., Papillion, 1979-81, Econ. Devel. Coun., Papillion, 1984—; mem. Papillion City Coun., 1982-84; chmn. local orgn. Boy Scouts Am., Omaha, 1960—; mayor Orchard Park, N.Mex. Recipient Silver Beaver award Boy Scouts Am., Omaha, 1970, Meritorious Svc. award Internat. Badminton Fedn., Glouchestershire, Eng., 1989, Nat. Ken Davidson trophy for Sportsmanship; decorated Legion of Merit, USAF. Mem. Am. Legion (adjutant, fin. officer Harry Bossard Post 32, Papillon, 1960-85), C. of C. (bd. dirs., sec./treas., Outstanding Svc. award 1976, Disting. Svc. award 1984). Republican. Lutheran. Office: R&G Enterprises 501 W 6th St Papillion NE 68046-2220

SCOTT, REBECCA ANDREWS, biology educator; b. Sunny Hill, La., June 4, 1939; d. Hayward and Dorothy (Nicholson) Andrews; m. Earl P. Scott, June 8, 1957; children: Stephanie Scott Dilworth, Cheryl L. BS, So. U., 1962; MS, Eastern Mich. U., 1969. Biology tchr., Detroit, 1966-68; sci. tchr. Ann Arbor (Mich.) Pub. Schs., 1968-69; biology tchr. North High Sch., Mpls., 1972—, coord. math., sci. tech. magnet, 1986—, advisor Jets Sci. Club. Mem. LVW (pres. 1981-83, 87-89, treas. 1989-94), Nat. Sci. Tchrs. Assn., Minn. Sci. Tchrs. Assn., Minn. Acad. Sci., Nat. Assn. Biology Tchrs., Iota Phi Lambda (pres. 1995—). Democrat. Presbyterian. Home: 3112 Wendhurst Ave Minneapolis MN 55418-1726 Office: 1500 James Ave N Minneapolis MN 55411-3161

SCOTT, RICHARD LYNN, data processing executive; b. Ora, Ind., Mar. 1, 1941; s. Harold Hophius and Maxine Louise (Strevey) S.; m. Karen Louise Kamp, Aug. 9, 1963; 1 child, Jonathon William. Student, Purdue U., 1959-61. Design engr. Kaydon, Muskegon, Mich., 1961-63; mgr. data processing Bastian Blessing, Grand Haven, Mich., 1963-79; dir. data programming Oliver Machine Co., Grand Rapids, Mich., 1979-82; mgr. CAD/CAM-CIM Steelcase, Inc., Grand Rapids, 1983—. Cons. United Way Kent County, Grand Rapids, 1986. Mem. Data Processing Mgmt. Assn. (pres. 1984-85), Am. Prodn. and Inventory Control Soc. (regional dir. 1984-85), Soc. Mfg. Engrs. (sr.), Computer and Automated Systems Assn. (sr.). Home: 18063 Lake Hills Dr Spring Lake MI 49456-9412 Office: CO-3N-14 901 44th St SE Grand Rapids MI 49508-7575

SCOTT, RONALD HUBERT, geriatrics physician, surgeon; b. Rocky Ford, Colo., Jan. 3, 1912; s. Robert Hetherington and Bessie Estelle (Searls) S.; m. Hazel Louise Wiler, Aug. 15, 1937 (dec. Oct. 1993); 1 child Ronalyn Louise Scott Des Pres. AB, Western State Coll., 1935; DO, Kirksville Coll. Osteo. Medicine, 1945; postgrad. Kans. U-Med. Ctr., 1970-82. Practice osteo. medicine specializing in geriatrics, Sullivan, Mo., 1947—; Sullivan Cmty. Hosp. Dir. Presbyn. Chancel Choir, Sullivan Cmty. Chorus, 1956-85; bd. dirs. Dist. CII Sch., Sullivan, Mo., 1957-72, pres. bd., 1960-70. Fellow Internat. Coll. Gen. Practitioners; mem. Am. Acad. Osteopathy, Nat. Assn. Watch and Clock Collectors Assn., Am. Osteo. Assn., (life), Mo. Osteo. Assn. (life; trustee 1957-72), Am. Coll. Gen. Practitioners, Am. Acad. Osteopathy, Am. Coll. Advancement of Medicine, Great Lakes Assn. of Clin. Medicine,

Psi Sigma Alpha. Republican. Presbyterian. Lodges: Rotary (pres. 1959-60, dist. gov. 1965-66), Odd Fellows. Home: 131 Meredith Ln Sullivan MO 63080-1654

SCOTT, STEPHEN BRINSLEY, theater producer; b. Pitts., Aug. 27, 1950; s. Robert Crawford and Lucille (Hendrickson) S. BS in Edn., U. Kans., 1972; MA, U. Denver, 1973. Artistic dir. Creede (Colo.) Repertory Theatre, 1976-78; chair dept. theatre Baker U., Baldwin, Kans., 1978-80; dir. edn. and cmty. svcs. Goodman Theatre, Chgo., 1980-84, dir. arts in edn., 1986-88, artistic assoc., 1988-94, assoc. producer, 1994—; dir. ednl. programs Chgo. Internat. Theatre Festival, 1985-86; spl. instr. Loyola U. Chgo., 1987-95; instr. Columbia Coll., Chgo., 1981-85, 92-94, Latin Sch. Chgo., 1984-86; mem. arts in edn. panel Nat. Endowment for Arts, Washington, 1990-91. Mem. adv. panels Ill. Arts Coun., Chgo., 1984-87; mem. com. League Chgo. Theatres, 1990—; cmty. rep. local sch. coun. Franklin Sch., Chgo., 1990-94. pres. Chgo. Coalition for Arts in Edn., 1983-85. Mem. Ill. Theatre Assn. (exec. com. 1987-90), Soc. Stage Dirs. and Choreographers, Ill. Alliance for Arts in Edn., Ill. Arts Alliance, Phi Beta Kappa. Democrat. Home: 124 W Polk # 207 Chicago IL 60605 Office: Goodman Theatre 200 S Columbus Dr Chicago IL 60603

SCOTT, SUSANNAH C., transportation engineering consultant; b. Ames, Iowa, Apr. 18, 1966; d. Thomas and Lelia (Gentry) S. BA in Economics, Northwestern U., 1988; MS in History, Spertus Coll., Chgo., 1991. Rsch. analyst Refco, Chgo., 1987-91; mgr., venture devel. Shields Enterprises, Inc., Rosemont, Ill., 1991—; U.S. del. ISO Tech. Com. 211. Fellow VERTIS; mem. IEEE Computer Soc., SAE (vice chmn. navigation com.), Internat. Cartographic Assn. (exec. sec. standards commn.), Assn. Computing Machinery.

SCOTT, THEODORE R., lawyer; b. Mount Vernon, Ill., Dec. 7, 1924; s. Theodore R. and Beulah (Flannigan) S.; m. Virginia Scott, June 1, 1947; children: Anne Laurence, Sarah Buckland, Daniel, Barbara Gomon. AB, U. Ill., 1947, JD, 1949. Bar: Ill. 1950. Law clk. to judge U.S. Ct. Appeals, 1949-51; pvt. practice Chgo., 1950—; assoc. Spaulding Glass, 1951-53, Loftus, Lucas & Hammand, 1953-58, Ooms, McDougall, Williams & Hersh, 1958-60; ptnr. McDougall, Hersh & Scott, Chgo., 1960-87; of counsel Jones, Day, Reavis & Pogue, 1987—. 2nd lt. USAAF, 1943-45. Decorated Air medal. Fellow Am. Coll. Trial Lawyers; mem. ABA, Ill. Bar Assn., Chgo. Bar Assn., 7th Cir. Bar Assn. (past pres.), Legal Club Chgo., Law Club Chgo., Patent Law Assn. Chgo. (past pres.), Union League Club, Exmoor Country Club (Highland Park, Ill.), Phi Beta Kappa. Home: 1569 Woodvale Ave Deerfield IL 60015-2350 Office: Jones Day Reavis & Pogue 77 W Wacker Dr Chicago IL 60601-1692

SCOTT, WILLIAM PAUL, lawyer; b. Staples, Minn., Nov. 8, 1928; A.L.A., U. Minn., 1949; B.S.L., St. Paul Coll. Law, 1952, J.D., 1954; m. Elsie Elaine Anderson, Feb. 7, 1968; 1 son, Jason Lee; children: William P., Mark D., Bryan D., Scott; stepchildren: Thomas J. (dec.), Terri L. Weeding-Berg. Bar: Minn. 1954. Atty. right of way div. Minn. Hwy. Dept., 1945-52, civil engr. traffic and safety div., 1953-55; practice law Arlington, Minn., 1955-61, Gaylord, Minn., 1963-67; sr. partner firm Scott Law Offices and predecessors, Pipestone, Minn., 1967—; probate, juvenile judge Sibley County, Minn., 1956-61; Minn. pub. examiner, 1961-63; county atty. Sibley County, 1963-68, city atty., Pipestone, 1978—. Formerly nat. committeeman Young Rep. League; Sibley County Rep. chmn., 1961. Served with USMCR, 1946-50; from 2d lt. to lt. col. USAF Res., 1950-77; ret. Recipient George Washington Honor medal Freedoms Found., 1970, 72. Mem. Minn. Bar Assn., TROA, Mensa, V.F.W., DAV, Am. Legion, Res. Officers Assn. Home: PO Box 704 Pipestone MN 56164-0704 Office: Park Plz Offices Pipestone MN 56164

SCOTT-CONNER, CAROL ELIZABETH HOFFMAN, surgeon, educator; b. Towanda, Pa., June 24, 1946; d. Charles Wesley and Mary Elizabeth (Lord) Hoffman; m. Christopher Scott, Jan. 29, 1967 (dec. May 1971); m. Harry Faulkner Conner, Aug. 24, 1974. BS, MIT, 1969; MD, NYU, 1976; PhD, U. Ky., 1988. Cert. Nat. Bd. Med. Examiners, 1977, Am. Bd. Surgery, 1982, 90; cert. surg. critical care Am. Bd. Surgery, 1990. Asst. prof. surgery Marshall U., Huntington, W.Va., 1981-85, assoc. prof. surgery, 1985-86; assoc. prof. surgery U. Miss., Jackson, 1986-91, prof. surgery, 1991-95; prof., head surgery U. Iowa, Iowa City, 1995—; W.Va. State Councillor, Am. Coll. Surgery, 1985-86; USMLE testing com., 1994—, mem. Halsted Soc., 1995—. Mem. editl. bd. Clin. Anatomy mag., 1987—; contbr. over 90 articles to profl. jours. Bd. dirs. Am. Cancer Soc., 1988-90. Fellow ACS (young surgeon rep. 1984), Am. Coll. Gastroenterology; mem. Am. Surg. Assn., Soc. for Surgery Alimentary Tract, Soc. Univ. Surgeons, So. Surg. Assn., Internat. Soc. Surgery. Office: U Iowa Coll Medicine Dept Surgery 1516 JCP 200 Hawkins Dr Iowa City IA 52242-1086

SCOVILLE, GEORGE RICHARD, adhesive company product manager; b. Ashtabula, Ohio, May 18, 1954; s. George Rueben and Lois Jean (Prince) S.; m. Cindy Leah Thayer, Aug. 2, 1975; children: Kimberly Michelle, Karolyn Marie, Richard Michael. Cert. indsl. engr., Lakeland Coll., 1979. Quality mgr. Geneva (Ohio) Rubber Co., 1974-81, dir. quality, 1982-84; quality mgr. Mich. Rubber Co., Cadillac, 1981-82; tech. sales rep. Whittaker Corp., West Alexandria, Ohio, 1984-90; product mgr. Morton Internat., West Alexandria, 1990-93; nat. accounts mgr. Moton Internat., West Alexandria, 1993—. Mem. Am. Chem. Soc., Boston Rubber Group, N.E. Ohio Rubber Group, Ft. Wayne Rubber & Plastics Group, Detroit Rubber Group. Republican. Methodist. Home: 248 Porter Dr Englewood OH 45322-2452 Office: Morton Internat 10 Electric St West Alexandria OH 45381-1212

SCOVILLE, JAMES GRIFFIN, economics educator; b. Amarillo, Tex., Mar. 19, 1940; s. Orlin James and Carol Howe (Griffin) S.; m. Judith Ann Nelson, June 11, 1962; 1 child, Nathan James. B.A., Oberlin Coll., 1961; M.A., Harvard U., 1963, Ph.D., 1965. Economist ILO, Geneva, 1965-66; instr. econs. Harvard U., Cambridge, Mass., 1964-65; asst. prof. Harvard U., 1966-69; assoc. prof. econs. and labor and indsl. relations U. Ill.-Urbana, 1969-75, prof., 1975-80; prof. indsl. rels. Indsl. Rels. Ctr., U. Minn., Mpls., 1979—, dir., 1979-82, dir. grad. studies, 1990—; cons. ILO, World Bank, U.S. Dept. Labor, Orgn. for Econ. Cooperation and Devel., AID; labor-mgmt. arbitrator. Author: The Job Content of the US Economy, 1940-70, 1969, Perspectives on Poverty and Income Distribution, 1971, Manpower and Occupational Analysis: Concepts and Measurements, 1972, (with A. Sturmthal) The International Labor Movement in Transition, 1973, Status Influences in 3rd World Labor Markets, 1991. Mem. Am. Econ. Assn., Indsl. Rels. Rsch. Assn., Internat. Indsl. Rels. Assn. Home: 4849 Girard Ave S Minneapolis MN 55409-2214 Office: U Minn Ind Rels Ctr 271 19th Ave S Minneapolis MN 55455-0430

SCRABECK, JON GILMEN, dental eductor; b. Rochester, Minn., Dec. 6, 1938; s. Clarence and Nancy Alma (Brown) S.; m. DeAnn Louise Jacks, June 16, 1962; children: Joan Louise, Erik Jon. Student, Contra Costa Coll., San Pablo, Calif., 1964-66, U. Calif., Berkeley, 1966-67; DDS, UCLA, 1971; MA in Edn., U. Colo., 1985. Pvt. practice, Santa Rosa, Calif., 1971-78; sr. instr. U. Colo. Sch. Dentistry, Denver, 1978-79, asst. prof., 1980-86, dir. patient care, 1979-80, acting dir. clin. affairs, 1980-81; acting assoc. dean U. Colo. Sch. Dentistry, Denver, 1983-84; acting div. chmn. U. Colo. Sch. Dentistry, Denver, 1984-85; dept. chmn. Marquette U. Sch. Dentistry, Milw., 1986-90, assoc. prof., 1986—, assoc. prof. tenure, 1989, curricular head, 1990—; cons. Dental Student mag.,1983-86, Colo. Bd. Dentistry, Denver, 1985-86, Dentist mag., 1986-90, VA, Milw., 1987-90. Editor Jour. Colo. Dental Assn., 1980-86; contbr. articles and abstracts to dental jours. mem. vol. staff Morey Dental Clinic, Denver, 1982-85, Health Fair, Denver, 1983-85; ofcl. judge S.E. Wis. Sci. Fair, Milw., 1988—. Fellow Internat. Coll. Dentists, Acad. Dental Materials, Am. Coll. Dentists, Pierre Fauchard Acad.; mem. ADA (coun. on journalism 1984-86, coun. on dental rsch. 1986-88, manuscript reviewer 1988—), Acad. Operative Dentistry, Wis. Dental Assn. (assoc. editor Jour. 1987—), Omicron Kappa Upsilon, Alpha Gamma Sigma. Roman Catholic. Home: W349s10140 Bittersweet Ct Eagle WI 53119-1851 Office: Marquette U Sch Dentistry 604 N 16th St Milwaukee WI 53233-2117

SCRANTON, LYNDA KAY, secondary education educator; b. Quincy, Ill., Aug. 6, 1947; d. Charles Leslie and Dorothy Blanche (Schnellbecher) S. BS in Phys. Edn., U. Ill., 1970; MA in Guidance, Roosevelt U., 1981. Cert. tchr., Ill. Phys. edn. tchr., coach Barrington (Ill.) High Sch., 1970-94, guidance counselor, 1994—; orchesis sponsor Barrington (Ill.) High Sch., 1971-78, girls tennis coach, 1973-88; mem. adv. bd. Ill. High Sch. Assn. Tennis, Bloomington. Mem. NEA, Ill. Edn. Assn., Am. Assn. Health, Phys. Edn., Recreation and Dance, Ill. Assn. Health, Phys. Edn., Recreation and Dance. Home: 670 South Rd Palatine IL 60074-1070 Office: Barrington High Sch 616 W Main St Barrington IL 60010-3015

SCRIBBINS, JIM, writer; b. Milw., Sept. 1, 1928; s. Ralph and Katherine (Graf) S.; m. Barbara Claire Driscoll, Feb. 25, 1956. H.S. grad., Milw. Various positions from operating to pub. rels. Milwaukee RR, 1948-85. Author: (books) The Hiawatha Story, 1970 (Merit award State Hist Soc. Wis. 1971), The 400 Story, 1982 (Commendation from Am. Assn. for State and Local History 1983), Milwaukee Road Remembered, 1990 (Merit award State Hist. Soc. Wis., Commendation Am. Assn. State and Local History, Outstanding Achievement Wis. Libr. Assn. 1991); contbr. articles to mags.: Trains, Bluegrass Unlimited, Passenger Train Jour., 1983—; lectr. in elem. schs., Milw. and Chgo., U. Wis., Milw., 1991—. Vol. Milw. Rd. Archives Pub. Libr., 1983—. Mem. Milw. Rd. Hist. Assn. (life), Chgo. and North Western Hist. Soc. (editl. staff 1992—). Methodist. Home: 101 Cedar Ridge Dr West Bend WI 53095

SCRIPTER, FRANK C., manufacturing company executive; b. Dansville, Mich., June 21, 1918; s. Edgar and Maggie Alice (Havens) S.; student Warren's Sch. of Cam Design, 1946. Lic. firmarms mfg.; m. Dora Maebelle Smalley, Nov. 2, 1940 (dec. Sept. 1945); 1 child, Karen Scripter Allen; m. Elvira Elaine Taylor, Aug. 6, 1951; children: James Michael, Mark Lee, Anita Elaine, Warren Arthur, Charles Edward. Apprentice, Lundberg Screw Products Co., 1940-41; set-up man Reo Motors, Inc., 1942-43; night supt. Manning Bros. Metal Products Co., 1943; with McClaren Screw Products Co., 1946-47; ptnr. Dansville Screw Products Co., 1946-54, pres., dir. Scripco Mfg. Co., Laingsburg, Mich., 1954-88, ret. 1988; mfg. of ASP Pistol, 1980-81. Chmn., Citizens Com. Laingsburg, 1956-58; mem. Laingsburg Community Schs. Bd. Edn., 1971-75, sec., 1973-74, pres., 1974-75. With USNR, 1944-45. Mem. Nat. Rifle Assn. (life), Mich. Antique Arms Collectors (life), The Am. Leopard Horse Assn. (founder 1967), N.Am. Hunting Club (life), Am. Legion (life mem.). Republican. Methodist. Patentee in field. Home: 9701 Round Lake Rd Laingsburg MI 48848-9404

SCUPIN, RAYMOND URBAN, anthropology educator; b. Detroit, Dec. 26, 1944; s. Urban Joseph and Donna Sue (Jackson) S.; m. Susan Marilyn Libner, Oct. 1, 1971; children: Jonathan, Derek. BA, UCLA, 1972; MA, U. Calif., Santa Barbara, 1974, PhD, 1978. Lectr. U. Calif., Santa Barbara, 1975-76, Ramkhamhaeng U., Bangkok, Thailand, 1976-77; instr. No. Ky. U., Highland Heights, 1980-81; prof. anthropology Lindenwood Coll., St. Charles, Mo., 1981—; cons. Procter and Gamble, Cin., 1980-81. Author: (textbooks) Anthropology, 2d edit., 1995, Cultural Anthropology, 2d edit., 1995; editor: (anthology) Islam in Southeast Asia, 1988. Trustee St. Charles City-County Libr., 1990-95. With U.S. Army, 1966-68. Fulbright fellow, 1986. Fellow Am. Anthropology Assn.; mem. Asian Studies Assn., Coun. Thai Studies. Office: Lindenwood Coll Sociology/Anthropology Dept Saint Charles MO 63301

SEABOLT, CLARENCE, management executive; b. Bergoo, W.Va., Oct. 5, 1929. Cert. traffic mgr., Nebr. Mgr. traffic and purchasing Seiberling Rubber Co., Barberton, Ohio, 1954-67; rechr. Ea. Ctrl. Motor Carrier Assn., Akron, Ohio, 1967-72; distbn. mgr. Hedgestrom Corp., Ashland, Ohio, 1972-92; v.p. Logistics Mgmt. Inc., Ashland, Ohio, 1992—. Served to cpl. U.S. Army, 1951-53. Mem. Distbn. and Transp. Assn. (pres. 1980-81, 86-87), Ctrl. Ohio Traffic Club (pres. 1987-88, Hall of Fame 1989). Republican. Office: Logistics Mgmt Inc PO Box 585 Ashland OH 44805-0585

SEABROOKS, NETTIE HARRIS, government executive; b. Mt. Clemens, Mich., Feb. 22, 1934; d. Ivan Joseph and Katherine Marshall (Davis) Harris; m. Aug. 23, 1958 (div. 1986); children: Victoria D., Franklyn E. BS in Chemistry, Marygrove Coll., Detroit, 1955, PhD (hon.), 1995; AM in Library Sci., U. Mich., 1957. Librarian Detroit Pub. Library, 1956-58; instr. Tenn. State U., Nashville, 1958-62; libr. GM, Detroit, 1962-72, mgr. pub. rels. staff libr., 1972-84, dir. pub. affairs info. svcs., 1985; dir. govt. and civic affairs Chevrolet/Pontiac/Can. group GM, Warren, Mich., 1985-92, dir. govt. rels. N.Am. ops. passenger car platforms, 1992-93; dep. mayor City of Detroit, 1994—. Trustee Marygrove Coll., Detroit, 1986-95; bd. dirs. Barat Human Svcs., 1991—, Detroit Inst. Arts Friends of African and African-Am. Art, Detroit Med. Ctr., Karmanos Cancer Inst., Music Hall. Mem. Links. Office: City of Detroit 1126 City County Bldg Detroit MI 48226

SEAGLE, DENNIS ALAN, chemicals executive, chemical engineer; b. Lafayette, Ind., Mar. 4, 1956; s. Stan Robert and Joyce Alene (Smith) S.; m. Carol Sue Vargo, May 25, 1978; children: Christopher Timothy, Jennifer Elizabeth. BS in Chemical Engring., Purdue U., 1978; MBA, U. Chgo., 1985. Sr. engr. Brown & Root, Inc., Naperville, Ill., 1978-85; mgr. engring. The NutraSweet Co., Deerfield, Ill., 1985-94; dir. supply chain Monsanto Co., Mt. Prospect, Ill., 1994—. Mem. AIChE.

SEAGREN, ALICE, state legislator; b. 1947; m. Fred Seagren; 2 children. BS, SE Mo. State U. Mem. Minn. Ho. of Reps., 1993—. Active Bloomington (Minn.) Sch. Bd., 1989-92. Mem. Bloomington C. of C. (bd. dirs. 1990-92), Phi Gamma Nu, Alpha Chi Omega. Republican. Home: 9730 Palmer Cir Bloomington MN 55437-2017 Office: Minn Ho of Reps State Capital Building Saint Paul MN 55155-1606

SEALINE, RON L., chief engineer; b. Ames, Iowa. BS, Iowa State U., 1964; MA, Iowa U., 1984. Chief engr. J.I. Case, 1965—. Inventor: holds patent on operator control. Mem. SAE (mem. com.). Lutheran. Office: J I Case 1930 Des Moines Ave Burlington IA 52601-4441

SEALTS, MERTON MILLER, JR., English language educator; b. Lima, Ohio, Dec. 8, 1915; s. Merton Miller and Daisy (Hathaway) S.; m. Ruth Mackenzie, Nov. 17, 1942 (dec. 1995). BA, Coll. of Wooster, 1937, DLitt (hon.), 1974; PhD, Yale U., 1942. Instr. in English U. Mo., Columbia, 1941-42, Wellesley Coll., 1946-48; asst. prof. English Lawrence Coll., Appleton, Wis., 1948-51; assoc. prof. English, 1951-58; prof. English Lawrence Coll./U., Appleton, Wis., 1958-65; prof. English U. Wis., Madison, 1965-75, Henry A. Pochmann prof. English, 1975-82, Henry A. Pochmann prof. English emeritus, 1982—. Author: Melville as Lecturer, 1957, Melville's Reading, 1966, The Early Lives of Melville: Nineteenth-Century Biographical Sketches and Their Authors, 1974, Pursuing Melville: Chapters and Essays, 1982, Melville's Reading: Revised and Enlarged Edition, 1988, Emerson on the Scholar, 1992, Beyond the Classroom: Essays on American Authors, 1996; editor: The Journals and Miscellaneous Notebooks of Ralph Waldo Emerson, vol. V (1835-1838), 1965, vol. X (1847-1848), 1973; co-editor: Billy Budd, Sailor (by Herman Melville), 1962, Emerson's Nature: Origin, Growth, Meaning, 1969, 79. Pvt.-maj. USAAC, 1942-46. Fellow Ford Found., 1953-54, J. S. Guggenheim Found., 1962-63, NEH, 1975; Am. Coun. Learned Socs. grantee, 1970; recipient Tchg. award E. and R. Uhrig Found., 1965, Disting. Alumni award Coll. of Wooster, 1994. Mem. MLA (Jau B. Hubbell medal Am. Lit. sect. 1992), Am. Lit. Assn., Melville Soc. (pres. 1953), Ralph Ealdo Emerson Soc. (Disting. Achievement award 1995), Thoreau Soc. Home and Office: Apt 1106/08 6209 Mineral Point Rd Madison WI 53705-4556

SEAMAN, JEROME FRANCIS, actuary; b. Oak Park, Ill., Nov. 4, 1942; s. William Francis and Bernice Florence (Haughey) S.; m. Jacquelyn Ann Robinson, Aug. 22, 1970; children: Carolyn, John. BA, U. Notre Dame, 1964; MA, Northwestern U., 1991. Asst. actuary Combined Ins. Co. of Am., Chgo., 1966-73; v.p., actuary United Equitable Life Ins. Co., Skokie, Ill., 1975-77; mgr. Peat Marwick Mitchell & Co., Chgo., 1973-75, 77-78; nat. dir. actuarial svcs. Arthur Young & Co., Chgo., 1978-83; pres., cons. actuary Jerome F. Seaman & Assocs., Northfield, Ill., 1983—; dir. Polysystems, Inc., Chgo., 1987-91. Contbr. articles to profl. jours. Recipient Commendation for Svc. Pres. Ronald Reagan, 1982. Fellow Soc. of Actuaries, Conf. of Cons. Actuaries; mem. Am. Acad. Actuaries (task force on risk based capital health orgns. 1993-95). Democrat. Unitarian Universalist. Home: 1550 Asbury Ave Winnetka IL 60093 Office: Jerome F Seaman & Assocs 550 Frontage Rd Northfield IL 60093

SEAMAN, WILLIAM CASPER, retired news photographer; b. Grand Island, Nebr., Jan. 19, 1925; s. William H. and Minnie (Cords) S.; m. Ruth Witwer, Feb. 14, 1945; 1 son, Lawrence William. Grad. high sch. Photographer Leschinsky Studio, Grand Island; news photographer Mpls. Star & Tribune, 1945-82; ret., 1982. Recipient Pulitzer prize, 1959; also awards Nat. Headliners Club; also awards Nat. Press Photographers Assn.; also awards Inland Daily Press Assn.; also awards Kent State U.; also awards Mo. U.; also awards Local Page One; State A.P. contest; Silver Anniversary award Honeywell Photog. Products, 1975. Mem. Nat. Press Photographers Assn., Sigma Delta Chi. Home: 8206 Virginia Cir S Minneapolis MN 55426-2458

SEAMONS, QUINTON FRANK, lawyer; b. Idaho Falls, Idaho, Mar. 5, 1945; s. Eldon Monroe and Lois (Merrill) S.; m. Michele Geyer Seamons. BA cum laude with honors, Brigham Young U., 1968; JD, U. Utah, 1971. Bar: Utah 1971, D.C. 1976, Ill. 1977, U.S. Supreme Ct. 1975, U.S. Ct. Appeals (7th cir.) 1979, U.S. Dist. Ct. (no. dist.) Ill. 1978. Legis. asst. to Senator Wallace F. Bennett of Utah U.S. Senate, Washington, 1969-71; law clk. Utah Atty. Gen., Salt Lake City, 1970-71; staff atty. divsn. mkt. regulation, legal counsel SEC, Washington, 1971-76; ptnr. Wilson & McIlvaine, Chgo., 1976—; arbitrator NASD Proceedings; adj. prof. Chgo. Kent Coll. Law, 1996—. Asst. editor: The Summation: A Journal of Utah Law; Contbr. articles to profl. jours. Trustee Riverwoods Homeowners Assn., Ill., 1992, Ill. Cancer Coun., 1980-84; bd. dirs. Vol. Legal Svcs., Chgo., 1993; coach Northfield Park Dist., 1978-84. Hinckley scholar, U. Utah, 1969; recipient Outstanding Young Men of Am. award, 1970, Am. Jurisprudence award Bancroft-Whitney Co. and U. Utah, 1971. Mem. ATLA, ABA (bus. law sect., litigation sect.), Chgo. Bar Assn. (securities law com., corps. com., class actions com.), Blue Key, Phi Kappa Phi, Phi Alpha Delta, Phi Sigma Alpha. Office: Wilson & McIlvaine 500 W Madison St Ste 3700 Chicago IL 60661-2511

SEARLES, LYNN MARIE, nurse; b. Cherryvale, Kans., Oct. 29, 1949; d. Darrell Eugene and Beva Caroline (Waller) Stringer; m. Martin Dale Searles, Aug. 23, 1970; children: Jeremy Dale, Michelle Le Anne. Assoc. in Fine Arts, Labette Cmty. Jr. Coll., Parsons, Kans., 1969, ADN, 1970. RN, Kans., Calif. Evening med.-surg. charge nurse Coffeyville (Kans.) Meml. Hosp., 1970-72, med.-surg. head nurse, 1972-73, relief evening house supr. and emergency rm. nurse, 1974, head nurse recovery rm., 1974-81; head nurse recovery rm., ambulatory care unit Coffeyville Meml. Med. Ctr., 1981-83, head nurse recovery rm., ambulatory care unit and surgery, 1983-84; dir. family planning, rural home health aide and multi phasic screening clinics, AIDS edn. and counseling Jefferson County Health Dept., Oskaloosa, Kansas, 1984-87; nurse III, health facility surveyor Lawrence dist. Kans. Dept. Health and Environ., Lawrence, Kans., 1988—. Nazarene Healthcare fellow. Mem. Nazarene Healthcare Fellowship, Kans. Pub. Health Assn., Am. Soc. Post Anesthesia Nurses (charter mem.). Republican. Nazarene Ch. Office: Kans Dept Health and Environment 808 W 24th St Lawrence KS 66046-4417

SEARS, DONNA MAE, technical writer and illustrator; b. St. Paul, Oct. 23, 1951; d. Raymond and Shirley Marie (Dupre) Waldoch; m. Mark D. Sears, Sept. 4, 1993. BA in Art and Edn., Cardinal Stritch Coll., Milw., 1969-73; postgrad., Rock Valley Coll., Rockford, Ill., 1985, 87, 89-90, So. Ill. U., 1983; cert. of tng., Computervision Tech. Ctr., Itasca, Ill., 1986, 88. Electronic assembler Warner Electric Co., Marengo, Ill., 1973-75, machine hand, 1976-78, quality assurance lead insp., 1978-80, draftswoman, 1980-86, CAD-sr. draftswoman, 1986-87; tchr. art Stephen Mack Sch. Dist., Rockford, 1975, Harrison Sch. Dist., Wonder Lake, Ill., 1975-76; CAD specialist Greenlee Textron Inc., Rockford, 1988-89, resigned, 1989; asst. buyer Ingersoll Milling, Rockford, 1989-90; asst. office mgr. and sign maker Shake-A-Leg Signs, Rockford, 1990-92; tech. writer and illustrator Mathews Co., Crystal Lake, Ill., 1992; tech. writer and CAD support Clinton Electronics, Loves Park, Ill., 1993—. Author: (with others) Treasured Poems of America, 1990, Poetic Voices of America, spring 1992, Anthology of American Poetry, fall 1991 (awards of Poetic Excellence 1992), Distinguished Poets of America, spring 1993, The Sound of Poetry, spring 1993. Vol. Boone County Conservation Dist.; mem. choir St. James Ch., Belvidere, Ill., 1985-93; assoc. mem. Spl. Olympics; mem. Macktown Restoration Found. Recipient Leadership award YWCA, Rockford, 1988. Mem. Internat. Soc. Poets, Exptl. Aircraft Assn., Nat. Right to Life Assn., Macktown Restoration Found. Roman Catholic.

SEARS, JIM, state legislator. Rep. dist. 1 State of Mo. Office: 314 S Adams St Memphis MO 63555

SEARS, JOHN D., state legislator; b. Dec. 7, 1944; m. Kristen Sears; 2 children. Student, Creighton U., 1963-64, U. S.D., 1964-68. Mem. S.D. State Ho. of Reps., 1985-92, 93—; asst. majority whip, 1987—, sys. salesman and designer; mem. govt. oper. and audit, retirement laws and state affairs coms. Home: 3023 Sunny Hill Cir Rapid City SD 57702-9202*

SEATON, SCOTT B., construction company executive; b. Missouri Valley, Iowa, Jan. 25, 1961. AS in Engring., U. Nebr., 1986. Pres. Diver Con Constrn., Omaha, 1980—. Republican. Office: 10547 Bondesson Cir Omaha NE 68122-9703

SEATOR, LYNETTE HUBBARD, freelance writer; b. Chgo., Mar. 23, 1929; d. Alvin Glen and Thelma May (Mulnix) Hubbard; m. Gordon Douglas Seator, June 8, 1949 (dec. 1988); children: Pamela, Penelope, Patricia, Glen. BS, Western Ill. U., 1963; MA, U. Ill., 1965, PhD, 1972. Teaching asst. U. Ill., Champaign-Urbana, 1963-66; instr. Western Ill. U., Macomb, 1966-67; prof. Spanish, Ill. Coll., Jacksonville, 1967-89, Dunbaugh disting. prof., 1976, Pixley prof. humanities, 1988, prof. emeritus, 1989—; columnist Jacksonville Jour.-Courier, 1991—; symposium dir. New Understandings of Experience of Women, Moscow, 1991, Jacksonville, 1992; dir. poetry workshop Jacksonville (Ill.) Correctional Facility. Author: (poetry) After the Light, 1992; also articles to profl. jours. and newspaper. Pub. rels. dir. Habitat for Humanity, Jacksonville, 1992—; translator Amnesty Internat., Jacksonville, 1992; bd. dirs. Ill. Writers, Inc., Planned Parenthood Springfield Area, Friends of the Libr., Jacksonville, West Ctrl. Ill. Coun. on Fgn. Affairs. Recipient Sears-Roebuck faculty award Ill. Coll., 1988. Mem. MLA, Poets and Writers, Ill. Writers (bd. dirs. 1983-87, 92—), Midwest L.Am. Studies Assn., Feministas Unidas, Midwest Concerns, Phi Kappa Phi. Democrat. Home: 1609 Mound Ave Jacksonville IL 62650-2257 Office: Ill Coll Jacksonville IL 62650

SEAVER, ALBERT EDWARD, engineer; b. Boston, Apr. 19, 1941; s. Albert Edward and Antonina Seaver; m. Antoinette Ruth Wolkowich, June 14, 1970; children: Craig Alan, Brian Paul. BSEE, N.Mex. State U., 1967; MSEE, Northeastern U., 1969; PhDEE, Rensselaer Poly. Inst., 1973. Engr. DuPont, Wilmington, Del., 1967-69; sr. engr. 3M, St. Paul, 1973-77, devel. specialist, 1977-80, rsch. specialist, 1980-83, sr. rsch. specialist, 1983-90, 1990—; affiliate prof. Dept. of Chem. Engring., U. Washington, 1983-92. Contbr. articles to profl. publs.; patentee in field. Coach Woodbury Athletic Assn., 1980-87, mgr. hockey, 1989-91; cubmaster Boy Scouts Am., Woodbury, 1983-86. With USAF, 1959-63. Mem. IEEE, IEEE Industry Application Soc. (mem. stds. com. 1991—, electrostatic processes com. 1990—), Electrostatics Soc. of Am. (exec. coun. 1993—, pres. 1995—), Am. Assn. Aerosol Rsch., Eta Kappa Nu, Sigma Xi. Home: 7861 Somerset Ct Woodbury MN 55125 Office: 3M 3M Center 518-1-01 Saint Paul MN 55144

SEAVER, FRANK ALEXANDER, III, retired medical center administrator; b. Detroit, Aug. 13, 1940; s. Frank A. Jr. and Emily Eugenia (Stafford) S.; m. Ellison Murton, Aug. 1967 (div. Jan. 1979); children: Frank A. IV, Dean, Claire; m. Robin Millan, May 17, 1980. BA cum laude, Mich. State U., 1965, MA, 1967. Pers. adminstr. Ford Motor Co., Mt. Clemens, Mich., 1965-67; pers. mgr. Allied Supermarkets, Detroit, 1967-76; dir. human resources Harper-Grace Hosps., Detroit, 1976-85; v.p. human resources Detroit Med. Ctr., 1985-92. Contbr. articles to profl. jours. Mem. vocat. edn. adv. bd. Detroit Pub. Schs., 1976-92. Sgt. USMC, 1958-61. Mem. Am. Soc. Human Resource Adminstrs. (pers. rsch. com. 1980-86), Mich. Hosp. Assn. (ins. com. 1984-88), Hosp. Pers. Assn. SE Mich. (President's citation 1983, Profl. Achievement award 1984).

SEAVY, MARY ETHEL INGLE, art educator; b. Alpena, S.D., Mar. 23, 1910; d. James Albert and Mollie (Ceny) Ingle; m. Donald Lee Seavy, Mar. 19, 1940; 1 child, Judith Ann. BS, No. State Tchrs. Coll., Aberdeen, S.D., 1934; MA in Art, U. Iowa, 1937, postgrad., 1949-53; postgrad., Columbia U., 1940. Cert. permanent profl. tchr., Iowa. Art coord. pub. schs., Decorah, Iowa, 1937-38, Waterloo, Iowa, 1938-40, Whiting, Ind., 1940-41; instr. art Luther Coll., Decorah, 1942-43, U. Iowa, Iowa City, 1945-47; tchr. Solon (Iowa) Elem. Sch., 1949-53; art coord. Mil. Sch., Aschaffenburg, Fed. Republic Germany, 1962-64; tchr. Iowa City Pub. Schs., 1965-75; artist, tchr. Stauffenburg Studio, Marengo, Iowa, 1987-90. One-woman show Hawkeye State Bank, Coralville, Iowa, 1987; exhibited in group shows State Fair, Des Moines, 1989, Cmty. Theatre, 1990, Heart Ctr. for Arts, Cedar Falls, 1992, Fern Hill Gallery, 1992, Dubuque (Iowa) Art Show, 1993, Iowa City Art Ctr., 1994, Hawkeye State Bank, 1994, art show, Iowa City, 1994, Cedar Rapids Art Show, 1994. Recipient award for short story State Federated Women's Club, 1987, 90, award for essay, 1987, 90, 1st place award for short story, 1996; 1st place print award, 2d place oil award State Regional Art Show, Dubuque, 1994, 2d place award, Cedar Rapids, 1994; Mil. Edn. Achievement award, 1994; 1st and 2d oil and watercolor awards Iowa Artists State Regional Ar t Show, 1995; 2d place watercolor award Federated Woman's Art Club Show, Des Moines, 1995, 96; named to Internat. Profl. and Bus. Women's Hall of Fame, 1994. Mem. AAUW, DAR (past regent Iowa City), Iowa Watercolor Soc., Iowa City Women's Club, Order Ea. Star, Order White Shrine of Jerusalem (past worth high priestess), Order of Amaranth, Delta Kappa Gamma, Zeta Tau Alpha (v.p. Alpha Omicron chpt. 1970-71). Christian Scientist. Home and Studio: 534 Clark St Iowa City IA 52240-5616

SEBELA, VICKI D., association executive, freelance writer; b. Des Plaines, Ill., Mar. 7, 1964; d. James Edward and Mary Nell (Davis) S.; m. Julius Michael Colangelo, Oct. 8, 1988. AA, AS, Harper Coll., 1984; BS, Roosevelt U., 1986; student, Inst. Orgnl. Mgmt., Boulder, Colo., 1991-93. Adminstrv. asst. McDonald's Corp., Rolling Meadows, Ill., 1979-83; info. specialist William Rainey Harper Coll., Palatine, Ill., 1983-84; teller Arlington Fed. Savs. and Loan, Arlington Heights, Ill., 1984-85; asst. to the pres. Ill. Women's Agenda, Chgo., 1984-85; student outreach coord. William Rainey Harper Coll., Palatine, 1985-86; adminstrv. asst. women's affairs Office of the Gov., Chgo., 1986-88; exec. adminstr. Social Enging. Assocs., Inc., Chgo., 1988-89; exec. dir. Greater Wheaton (Ill.) C. of C., 1989-94; internat. conf. dir. Environ. Planning Group, Barrington, Ill., 1994-95; pres. SEBCO Enterprises, Wheaton, Ill., 1995—; freelance writer, 1996—; founder Wheaton Womens Bus. Coun., Greater Wheaton Cycle Classic; freelance writer, Wheaton, Ill., 1996—. Columnist Daily Herald, 1992—; corr. Wheaton Leader, Warrenville Post, Winfield Estate, 1996—; contbr. articles to Ency. Brit. Cert. paraprofl. Talk Line/Kids Line Crisis Hot Line, Elk Grove Village, Ill., 1983; plan commr. City of Wheaton, 1994—, vice chair plan commn., 1995, chair, 1996—; mem. Wheaton History Ctr., chair Silver and Gold Ball Auction, 1995, publicity coord. Heritage Tour, 1996. Harper Coll. scholar, 1982, Roosevelt U. scholar, 1984. Mem. APA, Chgo. Women in Govt. Rels. (membership chair, bd. dirs. 1988-89), Women's Opportunity Internat., Greater Wheaton C. of C. (hon. life, chair clubs and orgn. autumnfest 1995), South Wheaton Bus. Assn., Phi Theta Kappa. Republican.

SEBELIUS, KATHLEEN GILLIGAN, insurance commissioner; b. Cin., May 15, 1948; d. John J. and Mary K. (Dixon) Gilligan; m. Keith Gary Sebelius, 1974; children: Edward Keith, John McCall. BA, Trinity Coll., 1970; MA, U. Kans., 1977. Dir. planning Ctr. for Cmty. Justice, Washington, 1971-74; spl. asst. Kans. Dept. Corrections, Topeka, 1975-78; mem. Kans. Ho. of Reps., 1987-95. Founder Women's Polit. Caucus; mem. Friends of Cedar Crest, Florence Crittendon Svcs.; precinct committeewoman, 1980-86; mayor-elect, Potwin, 1985-87; exec. com. NAIC, Kans. Health Care Commn. Mem. Common Cause (state bd., nat. gov. bd. 1975-81), Kans. Trial Lawyers Assn. (dir. 1978-86). Democrat. Roman Catholic. Home: 224 SW Greenwood Ave Topeka KS 66606-1228

SEBELL, TELLERVO MARIA, musician; b. Ashtabula, Ohio, Nov. 6, 1915; d. Walter Evald and Aino Irene (Glantz) Lakari; m. William Lauri Raske, Aug. 1, 1936 (dec. 1940); 1 child, Elaine; m. Raymond George Sebell, Dec. 15, 1951 (dec. 1969). Student, Cleve. Inst. Music, 1957-58. Sec., clerk-custodian Ashtabula Area City Schs., 1947-73; violinist, mem. chamber and local orchs., Ashtabula, 1940—, Am. Community Symphony Orch., 1968, Finlandia Trio, Ashtabula, 1968-82; violinist, charter mem. Ashtabula Chamber Orch., 1980-92. Sec. Ashtabula chpt. Finlandia Found., 1958-59, corr. newsletter, 1958-89. Mem. Harbor Coalition (Ashtabula), Finnish-Am. Heritage Assn. Republican. Lutheran. Home: 1833 W 5th St Ashtabula OH 44004-2837

SECHRIST, CHALMERS FRANKLIN, JR., electrical engineering educator; b. Glen Rock, Pa., Aug. 23, 1930; s. Chalmers F. and Lottie V. (Smith) S.; m. Lillian Beatrice Myers, June 29, 1957; children: Jonathan A., Jennifer N. BEE, Johns Hopkins U., 1952; MS, Pa. State U., 1954, PhDEE, 1959. Sr. engr. Bendix Corp., summers 1952, 53, 54; instr. elec. engring. Pa. State U., 1954-55; staff engr. HRB-Singer, Inc., State College, Pa., 1959-65; asst. prof. elec. engring. U. Ill., Urbana, 1965-67, assoc. prof., 1967-71, prof., 1971-96, assoc. head instructional programs dept. elec. and computer engring., 1984-86, asst. dean engring., 1986-96; program dir. divsn. undergrad. edn. NSF, Washington, 1992-96; acting sci. sec. Sci. Com. on Solar-Terrestrial Physics, 1981; chmn. publs. com. Middle Atmosphere Program, 1980-86, editor handbook, 1981-86. Editor: Proc. Aeronomy Confs, 1965, 69, 72; contbr. articles to profl. jours. NSF grantee. Mem. Edn. Soc. of IEEE (v.p. 1989-90, pres. 1991-92, mem. IEEE edn. activities bd. 1990, 92, 93, mem. tech. activities bd. 1991-92), Am. Geophys. Union, Am. Meteorol. Soc., Am. Soc. for Enging. Edn. Home: 12767 Yacht Club Cir Fort Myers FL 33919

SECHRIST, ROBERT EARL, industrial engineer; b. Carthage, Ill.. BS, U. Ill., 1987. Submarine officer U.S.N., Charleston, S.C., 1988-93; indsl. engr. Michelin Tire Corp., Greenville, S.C., 1993; mgr. Comml. Pest Control, Millersburg, Ohio, 1993-95. Lt. USN, 1983-88. Mem. Nat. Pest Control Assn., Ohio Pest Control Assn., Rotary (bd. dirs. 1993—). Home: PO Box 238 Holmesville OH 44633

SECREST, PATRICIA K., state legislator. Rep. Mo. State Ho. Reps. Dist. 93. Home: 723 Country Heights Ct Ballwin MO 63021-5623 Office: Mo Ho of Reps State Capitol Building Jefferson City MO 65101-1556*

SEDGWICK, ALICE JANE, librarian; b. Oconto, Wis., Feb. 29, 1936; d. Wilbur Norman Viestenz and Ruby Frances Schmolinske; m. Steven King Sedgwick, Dec. 23, 1967. BS in Edn., U. Wis., Stevens Point, 1961; MLS, U. Wis., Milw., 1971. Classroom tchr. Neenah (Wis.) Pub. Schs., 1961-67, Mequon-Thiensville Schs., 1971; libr. youth svcs. Manitowoc (Wis.) Pub. Libr., 1971-78; libr. dir. Weyenberg Pub. Libr., Mequon, 1978—; alumni adv. bd. U. Wis., Milw., 1980-84; bd. dirs. Libr. Coun. of Met. Milw. Mem. U.S. and Wis. Internat. 4-H Youth Exch., 1963—, exch. del., 1963. Mem. ALA (mem. best books com. 1974-78), Rotary (bd. dirs. 1994—). Lutheran. Office: Weyenberg Lib Mequon-Thiensville 11345 N Cedarburg Rd Mequon WI 53092

SEDLAK, RICHARD, naturopath, physical therapist; b. Berwyn, Ill., July 7, 1944; s. Richard and Alice H. (Tejcek) S. D in Naprapathy, Nat. Coll. Naprapathy, Chgo., 1966; D in Chiropractic Medicine, Palmer Coll. Chiropractic Medicine, 1970; BS in Phys. Therapy, Wheatfield Coll., 1975, MS in Phys. Therapy, 1978, PhD, 1979; D in Nutrimedicine, John F. Kennedy Ctr. Acad., 1989; PhD in Psychology and Clin. Nutrition, Notre Dame De Lafayette U., 1989; postgrad., Mazinic Ctr., Berwyn, Ill., 1993-94. Diplomate Nat. Bd. Chiropractic and Phys. Therapy, Am. Bd. Phys. Therapy Examiners; cert. naprapath, myotherapist. Phys. therapist West Suburban Hosp., Oak Park, Ill., 1964-66; pvt. practice naprapath, phys. therapist Berwyn, Ill., 1970—; cons. phys. therapist Pershing Convalescent Home, Stickney, Ill., 1985-87; assoc. dean Nat. Coll. Naprapathy, 1966-69, prof. endocrinology and diagnosis, 1968-71, prof. naprapathy, 1973; founder United Health Assn., 1976; counselor holistic health Bernadine U., 1989. Spl. police officer City of Cicero, 1968-90. Recipient Cert. of Merit, Am. Massage Therapy Assn., 1969, Cert. of Achievement Palmer Coll. of Chiropractic Medicine, 1970, Cert. Achievement AMA, 1980. Fellow Soc. for Nutrition and Preventive Medicine, Ill. Naprapathic Assn., Am. Back Soc.; mem. Acad. Holistic Practitioners, Am. Assn. Nutritional Cons., Interant. Assn. Counselors and Therapists. Democrat. Presbyterian. Home: 5537 W 24th Pl Cicero IL 60650-2733 Office: 3223 Harlem Ave Berwyn IL 60402-2807

SEDLAK, S(HIRLEY) A(GNES), freelance writer; b. Chgo., Sept. 6; d. Frederick Jesse and Agnes (Baum) Machacek; m. Harold Otto Sedlak; 1 child, Linda Carol. Student, Morton Jr. Coll., Cicero, Ill. Editor children's books Benefic Press subs. Harcourt Brace Jovanovich, Westchester, Ill., 1973-75; publicity and pub. rels. The Nat. League of Am. Pen women, Inc., Chgo. br., 1987-89. Home: 2226 S 9th Ave North Riverside IL 60546

SEDLER, ROBERT ALLEN, law educator; b. Pitts., Sept. 11, 1935; s. Jerome and Esther (Rosenberg) S.; m. Rozanne Friedlander, Jan. 24, 1960; children: Eric, Beth. BA, U. Pitts., 1956, JD, 1959. Bar: D.C. 1959, Ky. 1968, Mich. 1979; U.S. Supreme Ct. 1969. Asst. prof., assoc. prof. law St. Louis U., 1961-65; assoc. prof. law, asst. dean Addis Ababa U., Ethiopia, 1963-66; assoc. prof. to prof. law U. Ky., Lexington, 1966-77; prof. law Wayne State U., Detroit, 1977—. Author: American Constitutional Law, 1994, Across State Lines, 1989: Applying the Conflict of Law to Your Practice, 1989 (with R. Cramton) The Sum and Substance of Conflict of Laws, 1987, Ethiopian Civil Procedure, 1968; contbr. articles to profl. jours. Gen. counsel ACLU Ky., 1971-76. Gershenson Disting. Faculty fellow, Wayne State Univ., 1985-87. Mem. ABA, AAUP, Phi Beta Kappa, Order of the Coif. Democrat. Jewish. Home: 18851 Capitol Dr Southfield MI 48075-2680 Office: Wayne State U 468 E Ferry Mall Detroit MI 48202-3814

SEDLOCK, MICHAEL EUGENE, information systems executive; b. Scranton, Pa., Aug. 7, 1942; s. Michael J. and Claire J. (Gorny) S.; children: Michelle A., Michael J. II. BS, U. Scranton, 1963; MS, Marywood Coll., 1975. Data processing cons. Industry Data Systems, Inc., Cin., 1969-70; adv. systems analyst Bro-Dart, Inc., Williamsport, Pa., 1970-74; dir. MIS Snacks Group, Borden, Inc., Atlanta, 1974-82; v.p. Metro-Mark Integrated Systems, Inc., Albertson, N.Y., 1982-90, Sterling Software Inc., Cleve., 1990-93; pres. Next Edition Inc., Moreland Hills, Ohio, 1993—. Capt. U.S. Army, 1963-69. Home and Office: 4245 Som Center Rd Moreland Hills OH 44022-2313

SEE, ALAN JEFFERY, marketing executive; b. Pekin, Ill., Jan. 4, 1959; s. Harold Joseph and Flora Loetta (Lawrence) S.; children: Austin, Taylor, Victoria. BBA, Abilene Christian U., 1981, MBA summa cum laude, 1986. Mktg. dir. Standard Perforators, Inc., Abilene, Tex., 1982-86; dir. mktg. channels NCR (formerly AT&T Global Info. Solutions), Dayton, Ohio, 1987—; cons. mktg. Chlorofluorocarbons Reclamation and Recycling, Inc., Abilene, 1989—; cons. Corp. Cons., Abilene, 1989—. Mem. Sunrise Optimist Club (bd. dirs. 1990-91), Alpha Chi. Republican. Mem. Ch. of Christ. Home: 2461 Rosina Dr Miamisburg OH 45342 Office: NCR 1334 S Patterson Blvd USG-2 Dayton OH 45479

SEE, WILLIAM MITCHEL (W. MIKE SEE), cardiovascular and thoracic surgeon; b. Columbia, Mo., Jan. 10, 1952; s. William Bernard and Maribeth (Sapp) S. BA in Zoology, U. Mo., 1974, MD, 1980. Diplomate Am. Bd. Surgery, Am. Bd. Thoracic Surgery. Resident in gen. surgery Mayo Grad. Sch. Medicine, Rochester, Minn., 1980-85; chief resident in gen. surgery Mayo Clinic, Rochester, 1984-85; chief resident in cardiothoracic surgery Med. Coll. of Wis., Milw., 1985-87; chief resident and instr. cardiothoracic surgery U. Colo., Denver, 1987-89; with Mo. Cardiovascular and Thoracic Surgeons, Columbia, 1989—. Mem. AMA (mem. governing coun. resident physician's sect. 1984-87, vice-chmn. 1985-87), ACS, Am. Coll. of Chest Physicians. Home: 3100 Woodbine Dr Columbia MO 65203-0932 Office: Mo Cardiovascular and Thoracic Surgeons 1701 E Broadway Columbia MO 65201-8018

SEEBER, WILLIAM THADEN, retired university development director; b. Atchison, Kans., Sept. 1, 1924; s. William August and Charlotte Katherine (Thaden) S. BS, U.S. Mil. Acad., West Point, 1946; MBA, U. Ala., Tuscaloosa, 1956. Ch. exec. Luth. Ch., St. Louis, 1970-74; univ. devel. dir. Valparaiso (Ind.) U., 1974-92; deacon Immanuel Luth. Ch., Valparaiso, 1993—. Col. U.S. Army, 1946-69, Korea, Vietnam. Luth.

SEEBERT, KATHLEEN ANNE, international sales and marketing director; b. Chgo.; d. Harold Earl and Marie Anne (Lowery) S. BS, U. Dayton, 1971, MA, U. Notre Dame, 1976; MM, Northwestern U., 1983. Registered commodity rep. Publs. editor ContiCommodity Services, Inc., Chgo., 1977-79, supr. mktg., 1979-82; dir. mktg. MidAm. Commodity Exchange, 1982-85; internat. trade cons. to Govt. of Ont., Can., 1985-90; dir. mktg. and program devel. Internat. Orientation Resources. 1990-94; v.p. Am. Internat. Group, 1995—. guest lectr. U. Dayton, U. Notre Dame, Northwestern U., Kellogg Alumni Chgo., French-Am. C. of C., Internat. Employee Relocation Coun., Soc. Intercultural Educators, Trainers and Researchers, Am. Soc. Tng. and Devel., Ill. CPA Soc., SBA, KPMG Peat Marwick, Price Waterhouse, Arthur Andersen, Coopers & Lybrand, Nat. Fgn. Trade Coun., William M. Mercer, Inc., Minn. Employee Relocation Coun., MRA, CRC, Chgo. Relocation Coun., Ky. Relocation Coun., Mpls. Employee Relocation Coun., Chgo.-Midwest Credit Mgmt. Assn. Mem. Futures Industry Assn. Am. (treas.), Greater Cin. C. of C., Notre Dame Club Chgo., Kellogg Mgmt. Club Chgo. Republican. Roman Catholic. Office: 500 W Madison St Ste 1000 Chicago IL 60611

SEEDER, RICHARD OWEN, infosystems specialist; b. Chgo., May 4, 1947; s. Edward Otto and Betty Jane (Reamer) S. BA, Trinity U., 1969; M in Mgmt., Northwestern U., 1979; MS, DePaul U., 1993. Programmer, analyst R.R. Donnelley & Sons Co., Chgo., 1972-76, project mgr., 1977-80; mgr. systems devel. Joint Commn. Accreditation of Healthcare Orgns., Chgo., 1980-84, dir. mgmt. info. systems, 1985-89; dir. info. svcs., 1989-92; v.p. AApex Info. Systems., Skokie, Ill., 1992—; cons. Internat. Printworks, Newton, Mass., 1981-82. Served to 1st lt. U.S. Army, 1969-71, Korea. Mem. Assn. MBA Execs., Healthcare Info. and Mgmt. Systems Soc., Am. Mgmt. Assn., Mensa. Club: Northwestern U. Mgmt. Home: 2224 Maple Ave Northbrook IL 60062-5208 Office: AApex Info Systems 9230 Lotus Ave Skokie IL 60077-1150

SEEHAUSEN, RICHARD FERDINAND, architect; b. Indpls., Mar. 17, 1925; s. Paul Ferdinand and Melusina Dorothea (Nordmeyer) S.; student DePauw U., 1943-44, Wabash Coll., 1944, State U. Iowa, 1944; B.Arch., U. Ill., 1949; m. Phyllis Jean Gates, Dec. 22, 1948; children: Lyn, Dirk. Ptnr., Johnson, Kile, Seehausen & Assocs., Inc., architects, engrs., Rockford, Ill., 1949-82, pres., 1974-82; pres. Richard F. Seehausen-Architect, Inc., 1983—. Mem. com. jail planning and constrn. standards Bur. Detention Facilities, Ill. Dept. Corrections, 1970-73; analyst Fed. Fall-Out Shelter, 1962—. Bd. dirs. Rockford Boys Club, Lincola Pk. Boys Club, past mem; trustee Emmanuel Luth. Ch., Rockford, Ill., 1989—. Served with USNR, 1943-45, USAF, 1949-55. Mem. AIA (dir. No. Ill. chpt. 1966-68, 75—, pres. chpt. 1978—), Ill. Coun. of Am. Inst. Architects, Univ. Ill. Alumni Assn., Lambda Chi Alpha. Lutheran. Mason (Shriner), Kiwanian. Club: Forest Hills Country (gov. 1970-72), Prin. works include No. Ill. U. Center, also Health Svc. Bldg., DeKalb, Winnebago County Courthouse, Rockford, St. Mark Luth. Ch., Rockford, Christ Meth. Ch., Rockford, 1st Presbyn. Ch., Rochelle, Ill., McHenry County Ct. House, Woodstock, Ill., Stephenson County Courthouse, Freeport, Ill., Ogle County Pub. Safety Bldg., Oregon, DeKalb High Sch., Page Park Spl. Edn. Sch., Rockford, Oak Crest Retirement Ctr., Sycamore/DeKalb, Ill., Social Security bldgs. in Racine, Sheboygan, Oshkosh and Janesville, Wis., Freeport YWCA Bldgs., renovation of Carroll County Ct. House, DeKalb Area Retirement Center; renovation Old Winnebago County Courthouse. Rockford, Rockford Mut. Ins. Home Office Bldg., Court Street Meth. Ch., Rockford, Willows Personal Care Ctr., Rockford, others. Office: Richard F Seehausen Arch Inc 36 Briar Ln Rockford IL 61103-1601

SEELBACH, WILLIAM ROBERT, management executive; b. Lakewood, Ohio, Apr. 26, 1948; s. William Fowler and Carolyn (Paisley) S.; m. Nancy Chockley, June 28, 1969; children: Scott, Ryan. BS, Yale U., 1970; MBA, Stanford U., 1972. Assoc. Intasa, Menlo Park, Calif., 1972-74; sr. assoc. Griffenhagen-Kroeger, San Francisco, Calif., 1974-75; assoc. to ptnr. McKinsey & Co., Cleve., 1975-86; pres. Parkwood Corp., 1986-88; chmn. Inverness Ptnrs. and Inverness Castings Group, Cleve., 1988—; bd. dirs. Lumitex, Inc., Cleve. Trustee Work in N.E. Ohio Coun., Cleve., 1984—, Enterprise Devel. Inc., Cleve., 1985—, Playhouse Sq. Found., Cleve., 1986—, Univ. Sch., Cleve. Office: Inverness Ptnrs 25700 Science Park Dr Beachwood OH 44122-7312 Also: Inverness Castings Group Inc 65059 M 43 Bangor MI 49013-9674

SEELEY, MARK, agronomist; b. Gary, Ind., May 3, 1942; s. Clayton Barron and Margaret Louise (Cook) S.; BS, Purdue U., 1967; MA in Edn., Austin Peay State U., 1971. Staff asst. Purdue U., 1962; sci. tchr. Lake Central Sch. Corp., St. John, Ind., 1967-68; sci. tchr., Gary Ind., 1972-73; mgr. agronomic crops R.L. Schultz Farms, Hobart, Ind., 1973-94, dir. Lupin introduction and devel., 1980-94; bd. dirs. On Line Electric Inc., mem. exec. steering com. corp. svcs. Mem. Lake Area United Way Vol. Service, Lake County Health Fair, 1974; sci. and engring. judge 26th and 27th Calumet Regional Sci. Fairs. Mem. AAAS, NSPE, Am. Inst. Biol. Scis., Am. Soc. Hort. Sci. (Food Qulality and Nutrition Working Group), Am. Soc. Agrl. Engrs. (pres.'s club 1980-94), Ind. Soc. Profl. Engrs. (mem. scholarship com. Calumet chpt. 1982-83, co-chmn. 1984-85), Am. Soc. Agronomy, Am. Soc. Plant Physiologists, Council Agrl. Sci. and Tech. (mem. Century Club 1983), Crop Sci. Soc. Am., Fedn. Am. Scientists, Internat. Soc. Hort. Sci., Soil Sci. Soc. Am., Lake Michigan Flyers Assn., U.S. Hang Gliding Assn. Address: 6126 Sykes Rd Route 1 Hobart IN 46342

SEELY, BRUCE EDSALL, historian, educator; b. Chgo., Jan. 10, 1953; s. Horace Edsall and Carolyn Louise (Miller) S.; m. Sara Lynn Crowell, June 1975 (div. 1984); m. Nancy Lynne Smith, Sept. 21, 1985; children: Michael Stephen, Karen Lynne. BA, St. Lawrence U., 1975; MA, U. Del., 1977, PhD, 1982. Historian Historic Am. Engring. Record U.S. Dept. Interior, Wilmington, Del., 1976, Washington, 1977; project supr. and historian Historic Am. Engring. Record U.S. Dept. Interior, Blue Mountain Lake, N.Y., 1978; asst. prof. history Tex. A&M U., College Station, 1981-86; historian Mich. Tech. U., Houghton, 1986-88, assoc. prof., 1988—; project assoc. for policy analysis Interstate Hwy. Rsch. Project Pub. Works Hist. Soc., 1987-88. Author: Building the American Highway System: Engineers as Policy Makers, 1987; contbr.: World Book Encyclopedia, Dictionary of American Industrial Language, 1988, The Iron and Steel Industry in the Nineteenth Century: The Encyclopedia of American Business History and Biography, 1989, Harry S. Truman Encyclopedia, 1989; editor: The Iron and Steel Industry in the Twentieth Century: The Encyclopedia of American Business History and Biology, 1994; contbr. chpts. to books and articles to profl. jours. Trustee Grace United Meth. Ch., Houghton, 1992—. Grantee NSF, 1980, 90, 91; rsch. fellow Dibnor Inst. for the History of Sci. and Tech., 1996. Mem. AAAS, Soc. for History of Tech. (sec. 1990-95, Abbott Payson Usher prize 1987), Pub. Works Hist. Soc. (trustee 1992—, Abel Wolman award 1988), Bus. History Conf. (dir. 1992-95), Soc. for Indsl. Archaeology (Norton prize 1984), Orgn. Am. Historians, Lexington Group for Transp. History, Omicron Delta Kappa (Copper Scroll award 1990). Democrat. Home: 212 Hubbell St Houghton MI 49931-1210 Office: Mich Tech U Dept Social Sci 1400 Townsend Dr Houghton MI 49931-1200

SEGAL, JOYCE TRAGER, communications director; b. Phila., July 30, 1943; d. Irving and Elizabeth (Lerner) Trager; m. Feb. 26, 1965 (div. Apr. 5, 1976); children: Ethan Isaac, Michael Zachary. BA in English and Psychology cum laude, Temple U., 1965; B of Hebrew Lit., Gratz Hebrew Coll., 1965; MA, Western Mich. U., 1974. Cert. secondary educator, Pa., N.Y. Tchr. English Long Beach (N.Y.) High Sch., 1965-68; instr. Detroit Coll. of Bus., Kalamazoo, Mich., 1975-78; freelance writer, cons. self-employed The Upjohn Co., Kalamazoo, 1977-79; instr. coll. bus. Western Mich. U., Kalamazoo, 1979-83; instr. Davenport Coll., Kalamazoo, 1983-84, dir. pub. info., instr., 1984-87, dir. communications, 1987—; workshop leader Western Mich. U., Kalamazoo, 1982-89, Van Buren County Mental Health, Paw Paw, Mich., 1988, Kalamazoo Pub. Schs., 1986, Legal Secs. Assn., 1986. Host, producer cable access TV show Student Life in Kalamazoo, 1986; editor: Computers, Society and Learning, 1984, Business Reporting: A Management Tool, 1983; contbr. articles to profl. jours. Vol. Am. Lung Assn., Kalamazoo, 1988; bd. dirs. Kalamazoo Women's Festival, 1986; participant YMCA Corp. Olympics, 1990, 91; mem. Kalamazoo & Battle Creek C. of C., 1986—. Recipient "Best" award for TV Ad, 1986, Silver Addy award, 1985, Scholarship, 1961. Mem. Kalamazoo Consortium for Higher Edn., Kalamazoo Network, Intercom, Women in Communications, Am. Bus. Communications Assn. Office: Davenport Coll 4123 W Main St Kalamazoo MI 49006-2748

SEGALE, JOHN P., computer system administrator; b. N.Y.C., Mar. 22, 1966; s. Victor E. and Sarah L. (Gourley) S. BS in Computer Sci., U. Kans., 1990. Team mgr. Cerner Corp., North Kansas City, Mo., 1990—. Precint com. person Dem. Party, Shawnee, Kans., 1993—. Mem. World Federalist Assn. (v.p. 1993-95), Amnesty Internat., U.S. Rowing Assn., Kansas City Rowing Club (v.p., pres. 1993-94), Sierra Club. Home: 11425 W 50th Terr Shawnee KS 66203

SEGAR, FLOYD, engineering manager; b. Marine City, Mich., Sept. 2, 1942. B, U. Ariz., 1966; M, Trinity Evang. Sch., 1974. Supr. engring. Volvo GM Heavy Truck, Orville, Ohio, 1986-93; mgr. engring. Transp. Mfg. Corp., Roswell, N.Mex., 1993-94, Universal Coach Parts, Des Plaines, Ill., 1994—. Maj. U.S. Army, 1966-70. Mem. Lions. Office: Universal Coach Parts Inc 105 E Oakton St Des Plaines IL 60018-1946

SEGEDY, JAMES A., urban planning educator; b. Detroit, Jan. 24, 1951; s. James and Esther Clara (Jahn) S.; m. Janis Bernice Dail, June 29, 1974; 1 child, David James. BS, Mich. State U., 1973; BS in Architecture with honors, Lawrence Inst. Tech., 1983; M in Urban Planning, U. Mich., 1983, PhD, 1988. Cert. Am. Inst. Cert. Planners. Microbiologist Children's Hosp. Mich., Detroit, 1973-75, Beaumont Hosp., Royal Oak, Mich., 1975-80; arch. Beaumont Hosp., Royal Oak, 1980-82; grad. asst. U. Mich., Ann Arbor, 1982-86; assoc. prof. Ball State U., Muncie, Ind., 1986—; sr. ptnr. The Cmty. Partnership, Muncie, 1990—; adj. assoc. prof. U. Mich., Ann Arbor, 1992—; pres. Ind. Cmty. Devel. Soc., Indpls., 1993-94. Contbr. chpts. to books. Active Muncie/Delaware County Planning Commn., Ind., 1994—. Named Hon. citizen LaGrange (Ind.) County Commrs., 1990. Mem. Am. Planning Assn. (chpt. pres., chair small town and rural planning divsn. 1994—, Outstanding Planning award Small Town Divsn. 1994), Urban Land Inst., Ind. Planning Assn. (pres. 1994—, Outstanding Planning award 1994). Home: 1418 W North Muncie IN 47303 Office: Ball State Univ Dept Urban Planning Muncie IN 47306

SEGREST, KATRINA ANN WORDLAW, academic administrator; b. Chgo., Nov. 2, 1959; d. Obie Cleveland and Maudine (McCurine) Wordlaw; m. James Ellis Segrest, Sept. 12, 1981; children: Jakara Marie, James Alexander. AA, Wright Coll. Asst. tchr. Marillac House, Chgo., 1975-77; caregiver St. Vincent DePaul Ctr. Child Care, 1989-90; asst. dir. Rainbow House Daycare, Indpls., 1990-91; tchr. Head Start, Indpls., 1991-95; site dir. after sch. program YMCA, Indpls., 1995—. Mem. Friends of Libr., Indpls., 1995. Mem. Nat. Assn. Edn. Young Children, Child Devel. Assn. Home: 618 W 30th Indianapolis IN 46208-5032

SEGULJA, DANNY D., manufacturing engineer; b. Bakar, Croatia, June 10, 1935; came to U.S., 1957; B, U. Mich., 1969. Lead engr. Willobrader Corp., Mishawaka, Wis., 1960—; sr. project engr. United McGill Corp., Columbus, Ohio, 1972—; mem. adv. bd. Nat. Mgmt. Assn., 1970—. Vol. Cancer Rsch. Ctr., Columbus, Ohio, local chs. Lt. Croatia Coastal Art., 1956. Mem. NSPE, Soc. Naval Architects and Marien Engrs. Democrat. Roman Catholic. Office: United McGill Corp 1779 Refugee Rd Columbus OH 43207-2119

SEHEULT, MALCOLM MCDONALD RICHARDSON, lawyer; b. Port of Spain, Trinidad, July 18, 1949; s. Errol Andre and Laura (Laltoo) S.; m. Robin Lynn Montanye; children: Kristie, Julie, Laura, Aimée. BA in Sociology magna cum laude, U. Toronto, 1971, BEd, 1972, MA, 1973; LLB, U. Toronto, Ottawa, 1976; DJuris, Kensington U., 1988. Bar: Ontario, Can. 1978, N.Y. 1987; cert. tchr., Toronto, Can. Pvt. practice Toronto, 1978-85; assoc. Outerbridge, Barristers & Solicitors, Mississauga, Ont., Can., 1985-86, Don Brown, Mississauga, 1986—; lectr. numerous profl. and cmty. groups and orgns. Producer, editor Where Is Tomorrow?, 1969; editor Ottawa Law

Rev.; also articles. Mem. Justice for Children, Vanier Inst. of Family, Ont. Sch. Tchrs. Fedn.; bd. dirs. North York Branson Hosp. Mem. ABA, N.Y. State Bar Assn., Can. Bar Assn., Assn. Trial Lawyers Am., Law Soc. Upper Can., Medico-Legal Soc., Lawyers Club, Can. Civil Liberties Union, Royal Soc. Arts (fellow 1979), Mensa Internat., Can. Sociology and Anthropology Assn., Nat. Directory Sociology of Edn. and Ednl. Sociology, Am. Philatelic Soc., Phi Kappa Phi. Home: 25623 State St Loma Linda CA 92354-2443 Address: 2638 Victoria Park Ave, Willowdale, ON Canada M2J 4A6

SEIBERT, EARL HENRY, JR., financial planner, lecturer; b. Evansville, Ind., July 10, 1952; s. Earl Henry Sr. and Elaine Doris (Connor) S.; m. Christine Natalie Haynie, Aug. 17, 1972 (div. 1982); children: Heather Lea, Megan Natalie; m. Dawn Lori Duenke, Jan. 2, 1986. BS in Bus., Ind. U., 1974. Sales rep. Hormel & Co., Cleve., 1974-76; key account exec. Hormel & Co., Chgo., 1976-79; product mktg. mgr. Hormel & Co., Austin, Minn., 1979-82; dist. sales mgr. Hormel & Co., St. Louis, 1982-84, Mich., 1984-86; dir. sales, mktg. Habbersett Sausage, Media, Pa., 1986-88; pres. The Seibert Group, St. Louis, 1988—; v.p. mktg. M.F.G. Mgmt., Manchester, 1989-91; v.p. Delta First Fin., Inc., 1991-92; pres. Strategic Asset Mgmt., Inc., 1993—. Group leader Jr. Achievement, Austin, 1982. Named Mr. Jr. Achievement, Evansville, Ind., 1970. Mem. Internat. Assn. Fin. Planners, Wilmington/Chester County Delta Group (bd. dirs. 1988-89), Share the Wealth (bd. dirs. 1989-92), Charles J. Givens Orgn., Phila. Food Trades Orgn., Internat. Assn. Registered Fin. Cons. Mem. Ch. of Christ. Home: 13615 Peacock Farm Rd Saint Louis MO 63131-1231

SEIDEL, ROBERT WAYNE, science historian, educator, institute administrator; b. Kansas City, Mo., June 9, 1945; s. Wayne Herman and Harriet Anita (Day) S.; m. Alison Publicover, Aug. 26, 1972 (div. 1989); 1 child, Mary Ruth; m. Christine Ruth Stack, July 1, 1992. BA, Westmar Coll., 1967; MA, U. Calif., Berkeley, 1968, PhD, 1978. Exhibit designer Lawrence Hall Sci., Berkeley, 1970-72; specialist Poland 4-city tour USIA, Warsaw, 1971-72; grad. rsch. and teaching asst. U. Calif., 1972-78; asst. prof. Tex. Tech U., Lubbock, 1978-83, dir. rsch., 1979-83; rsch. historian U. Calif., Berkeley, 1980-82, Laser History Project, Albany, Calif., 1983-85; adminstr. Bradbury Sci. Mus., Los Alamos, N.Mex., 1985-90, project leader, 1990-92; sr. staff mem. Ctr. Nat. Security Studies, Los Alamos, N.Mex., 1992-94; dir. Charles Babbage Inst., U. Minn., Mpls., 1994—; ERA Land Grant prof. History of Tech. U. Minn., Mpls., 1994—. Author: Lawrence and His Laboratory: A History of the Lawrence Berkeley Laboratory, 1989, Los Alamos and the Making of the Atomic Bomb, 1995. Mem. Lubbock Heritage Soc., 1983, N.Mex. Sci. Ctr. Commn., 1989—; mem. adv. com. County Cultural Ctr., Los Alamos, 1986-89. Woodrow Wilson fellow, 1967, U. Calif. Regent's fellow, 1968, German Marshall Fund fellow, Grenoble, France, 1975. Mem. History Sci. Soc., Soc. for History Tech., Am. Hist. Assn., Soc. for Philosophy Tech., N.Mex. Acad. Scis. Democrat. Home: 5625 Woodlawn Blvd Minneapolis MN 55417-2667 Office: Charles Babbage Inst 103 Walter Libr, U Minn Minneapolis MN 55455

SEIDEL, WOLFGANG, design engineer; b. Manitoba, Can., Aug. 23, 1962. BA in Engring., Bradley U., 1982. Design engr. Catapiller, Peoria, Ill., 1985-94, J I Case, Burlington, Iowa, 1994—. Mem. KC.

SEIDMAN, DAVID N(ATHANIEL), materials science and engineering educator; b. N.Y.C., July 5, 1938; s. Charles and Jeanette (Cohen) S.; m. Shoshanah Cohen-Sabban, Oct. 21, 1973; children: Elie, Ariel, Eytan. BS, NYU, 1960, MS, 1962; PhD, U. Ill., Urbana, 1965. Postdoc. assoc. Cornell U., Ithaca, N.Y., 1964-66, asst. prof. materials sci. and engring., 1966-70, assoc. prof. materials sci. and engring., 1970-76, prof. materials sci. and engring., 1976-85; prof. materials sci. and engring. Northwestern U., Evanston, Ill., 1985-96, Walter P. Murphy prof. materials sci. and engring., 1996—; vis. prof. Technion, Haifa, 1969, Tel-Aviv U., Ramat-Aviv, 1972; Lady Davis vis. prof. Hebrew U., Jerusalem, 1978, 80-81, prof. materials sci., 1983-85; vis. scientist C.E. de Grenoble, 1981, C.N.E.T.-Meylan, 1981, C.E. de Scalay, 1989, U. Goettingen, 1989, 92; sci. cons. Argonne (Ill.) Nat. labs., 1985-94. Spl. issues editor, editl. bd. Interface Sci., 1993—; contbr. numerous articles on internal interfaces, atomic-scale imperfections in metals and semicondrs., radiation effects, field-ion, atom-probe and electron microscopy, 1964—. Recipient Max Planck Rsch. prize Max-Planck-Gesellschaft and the A. von Humboldt-Stiftung, 1993; Guggenheim fellow, 1972-73, 80-81, Humboldt fellow, 1989, 92; named chair for phys. metallurgy Gordon Conf., 1982. Fellow Am. Phys. Soc.; mem. AAAS, Metall. Soc. (Hardy Gold medal 1967), Materials Rsch. Soc., Microscopy Soc. Am., A. von Humboldt Soc. Am. Democrat. Jewish. Home: 9056 Tamaroa Ter Skokie IL 60076-1928 Office: Northwestern U Engring Dept MLSF Bldg Evanston IL 60208-3108

SEIDNER, ALLEN PAUL, food products executive, computer consultant; b. Chgo., May 22, 1962; s. Frederic Jay and Eloise Ann (Albert) S. Student, U. Iowa, 1980-85. Editl. asst. Sta. WBBM-CBS, Inc., Chgo., 1983; editl. page editor The Daily Iowan, Iowa City, 1983-85; campaign coord. Simon for Pres., Des Moines, 1987; radio producer Sta. WBEZ/Chicagoland Pub. Radio, 1987-89; news archivist Mus. of Broadcast Comms., Chgo., 1989; campaign mgr. Baum for State Rep., Evanston, Ill., 1989-90; restaurant mgr. Blind Faith Cafe, Evanston, Ill., 1988-93; computer cons. Seidner Comms., Evanston, Ill., 1992—; deli and human resources mgr. Oak Street Market, Evanston, Ill., 1993—. Mem. Dem. Party of Evanston, 1988—. Recipient scholarship U. Iowa, 1985, Am. Express Customer Svc. award, 1987. Home: 1612 Wesley Ave Evanston IL 60201 Office: Oak St Market 1615 Oak Ave Evanston IL 60201

SEIFARTH, MARK EVAN, state agency administrator; b. Youngstown, Ohio, July 5, 1957; s. John Paul and Evelyn Marie (Magni) S.; m. Lucy Carroll Gettman, Oct. 17, 1987. BA in Polit. Sci., Kent State U., 1986, postgrad., 1979-83. Dir. residence halls Kent (Ohio) State U., 1979-83; legis. intern Ohio Legis. Svc. Commn., Columbus, 1983-84; program coord. Gov.'s Office of Advocacy, Columbus, 1984; exec. asst., legis. aide Ohio State Senator Oliver Ocasek, Columbus, 1985-86; asst. dir. Ohio Employee Assistance Program, Columbus, 1987-88; govt. affairs coord. Ohio Rehab. Svcs. Commn., Columbus, 1989—. Pres. bd. trustees MOBILE Ind. Living Ctr., Columbus, 1986-87, bd. trustees, 1985-89; legis. com. Mid-Ohio Multiple Sclerosis Soc., Columbus, 1989—. Named one of Outstanding Young Men Am., 1979, 81, 83, 85, 86. Mem. Univ. Club Columbus, Ohio LWV, Ohio Rehab. Assn. (bd. dirs. 1992-95, exec. bd. 1992, 93, Meritorious Svc. award 1993). Methodist. Home: 4499 Danforth Rd Columbus OH 43224 Office: Ohio Rehab Svcs Commn 400 E Campus View Blvd Columbus OH 43235-4604

SEIFERT, ACHIM G., commercial real estate lender; b. Germany, Apr. 9, 1955; came to U.S., 1957; s. Erich and Christa (Stöhr) S.; m. Kathleen McCarron, July 19, 1980; children: Emily Ann, Molly Kate, Matthew Erich. B Landscape Architecture, Ball State U., 1978; MBA, Emory U., 1982. Cert. comml. investment mgr. Land planner Heery and Heery Architects, Atlanta, 1980-82; regional mgr. Cairn Co., Atlanta, 1982-84; acquisitions mgr. Equitec Co., Atlanta, 1984-85; asset mgr. Mass. Mut. Life Ins. Co., Atlanta, 1985-87, acquisition dir., 1987-90; regional dir., sr. v.p. Mass. Mut. Life Ins. Co., Chgo., 1990—. Mem. Ill. Mortgage Bank Assn., Nat. Assn. Indsl. & Office Parks, Internat. Coun. of Shopping Ctrs. Office: Mass Mut Life Ins Co 100 S Wacker Dr Ste 2000 Chicago IL 60606-4005

SEIFERT, CAROLINE HAMILTON, community health nurse, school nurse; b. Warren, Ohio, May 28, 1937; d. Oliver L. and Martha (Moran) Hamilton; m. Dale E. Seifert, Sept. 5, 1959; children: Brian Dale, Joan Kimberly. Diploma, Youngstown (Ohio) Hosp. Assn., 1959; BSN, U. Cin., 1964, MEd, 1979. Cert. sch. nurse, health educator, spl. edn. educator. Caseworker Children's Svcs. div. Dept. Health and Human Svcs., Batavia, Ohio, 1966-68; dir. Happy Days Nursery Sch. Bethel (Ohio) United Meth. Ch., 1970-73; social worker Clermont County Bd. Mental Retardation/Devel. Disabilities, Batavia, 1973—; sch. nurse, health educator Thomas A. Wildey Sch., Owensville, Ohio, 1973—; instr. Sch. Health Svcs. U. Cin., 1976, preceptor nursing students, 1992—. Mem. Hamilton/Clermont Sch. Nurses Orgn. (v.p.), S.W. Ohio Sch. Nurses Assn. (program chmn.), Profl. Assn. for Retardation (v.p. nursing div., Nurse of Yr.). Home: 2631 Oldforge Ln Cincinnati OH 45244-2831 Office: Thomas A Wildey Sch PO Box 8 Owensville OH 45160-0008

SEIFERT, KARL E., geology educator; b. Orangeville, Ohio, Mar. 16, 1934; s. Allan L. and Elma I. (Cassidy) S.; m. Norma L. Scroggy, Dec. 18, 1954 (div. 1981); children: Keith Alan, Lynnette Kay, Kendall Curtis; m. Carole Ann Aselman, June 19, 1981. BS, Bowling Green State U., 1956; MS, U. Wis., Madison, 1959, PhD, 1963. Asst. prof. geology Iowa State U., Ames, 1965-68, assoc. prof., 1968-72, prof. geology, 1972—, chair dept. geology, 1988-91; Shipboard scientist Deep Sea Drilling Project, Pacific Ocean, 1978, Ocean Drilling project, Atlantic Ocean, 1993; vis. sci. fellow Geol. Mus., Oslo, 1979; speaker in field. Contbr. to profl. publs. Capt. USAF, 1961-65. Disting. visitor Washington U., St. Louis, 1980-81. Fellow Geol. Soc. Am.; mem. Geochem. Soc., Am. Geophys. Union. Office: Iowa State Univ Dept Geol Scis Ames IA 50011

SEIFERT, TIMOTHY MICHAEL, infosystems specialist; b. Marengo, Iowa, Jan. 17, 1951; s. Henry George and Margy Elaine (Gerard) S. BS, U. Iowa, 1973. Sr. clerical asst. Sears, Roebuck & Co., Chgo., 1973-74, asst. div. head, 1973-76, div. head, 1976-77; operator word processing Arnstein & Lehr, Chgo., 1978-80, supr. word processing dept., 1980-85, mgr. systems and procedures, 1985-89, mgr. tech. svcs., 1989-91, mem. adminstrv. com., 1988—, dir. of ops., 1991—. Mem. Assn. Legal Adminstrs., C/T 3000 User's Group, Internat. HP User's Group, Netware Users Internat. Democrat. Methodist. Home: 2150 N Lincoln Park W Apt 1312 Chicago IL 60614-4647 Office: Arnstein & Lehr 120 S Riverside Plz Ste 1200 Chicago IL 60606-3910

SEILER, CHARLOTTE WOODY, retired English language educator; b. Thorntown, Ind., Jan. 20, 1915; d. Clark and Lois Merle (Long) Woody; m. Wallace Urban Seiler, Oct. 10, 1942; children: Patricia Anne Seiler Bootzin, Janet Alice Seiler Sawyer. AA, Ind. State U., 1933; AB, U. Mich., 1941; MA, Cen. Mich. U., 1968. Tchr. elem. schs., Whitestown, Ind., 1933-34, Thorntown, Ind., 1934-37, Kokomo, Ind., 1937-40, Ann Arbor, Mich., 1941-44, Willow Run, Mich., 1944-46; instr. English div. Delta Coll., University Center, Mich., 1964-69, asst. prof., 1969-77, ret., 1977; organizer, dir. Delta Coll. Puppeteers, 1972-77. Mem. Friends of Grace A. Dow Meml. Library, 1974—, treas. 1974-75, 77-79, corr. sec., 1975-77; mem. Midland Art Assn.; adv. bd. Salvation Army, 1980-91, sec., 1984-87; leader Sr. Ctr. Humanities program Midland Sr. Ctr., 1977—. Mem. AAUW (fellowship honoree 1979), Mich. Libr. Assn., Midland Symphony League, Tuesday Rev. Club (pres. 1979-80), Seed and Sod Garden Club (v.p. 1986-87, pres. 1987-88), Pi Lambda Theta, Chi Omega. Presbyterian. Home: 5002 Sturgeon Creek Pky Midland MI 48640-2284 also: 652 Blackburn Blvd Harbor Cove North Port FL 34287

SEILER, WALLACE URBAN, chemical engineer; b. Evansville, Ind., Aug. 31, 1914; s. Samuel Alfred and Anna Beatrice (Grossman) S.; student U. Evansville, 1932-34; BS, Purdue U., 1937; postgrad. U. Mich., 1945-46; m. Charlotte Woody, Oct. 10, 1942; children: Patricia Anne, Janet Alice. With Dow Chem. Co., 1937-80, engr., Midland, Mich., 1937-39, cons. rsch. engr., Ann Arbor, Mich., 1939-49, tech. svc. engr., Midland, 1950-55, mgr. solvents field svc., 1955-64, contract R & D specialist, 1964-80. Mem. AAAS, Am. Chem. Soc., Am. Inst. Chemists, Sigma Xi, Tau Beta Pi, Phi Lambda Upsilon. Home: 5002 Sturgeon Creek Pky Midland MI 48640-2284 Home (winter): 652 Blackburn Blvd North Port FL 34287

SEILHAMER, RAY A., bishop. Bishop United Brethren in Christ. Office: United Brethren in Christ 302 Lake St Huntington IN 46750-1264

SEITZ, FLORIAN CHARLES, retired banker; b. Mattoon, Wis., May 31, 1926; s. Andrew Charles and Veronica Ann (Koch) S.; m. Phyllis Anne Smith, Feb. 3, 1949; children: Blake Howard, Todd Charles. Student, Am. Mgmt. Assn., Chgo., 1972, U. Chgo., 1972, U. Va., 1979. Cert. consumer credit exec. Field supr. Beneficial Fin. Corp., Morristown, N.J., 1952-68; owner, pres. Credit-Wise, Inc., Racine, Wis., 1968-69; v.p. 1st Wis. Nat. Bank, Milw., 1969-89; ret., 1989; cons. bank card program The Gulf Bank, Kuwait City, Kuwait, 1978; bd. dirs. Milw. Lenders Exch., 1965-68. Editor Skip Tracing Procedures jour., 1986. Bd. dirs. Kenosha (Wis.) Civic Com., 1961-62; com. mem. Kenosha County CD, 1963. Sgt. USA-Airborne Paratroopers, 1944-46, ETO. Recipient spl. recognition Boy Scouts Am., Kenosha, 1965, Christian Youth Coun., Kenosha, 1972, citation United Fund Greater Milw., 1974. Mem. Internat. Credit Assn., Wis. Assn. Credit Grantors (pres. 1985-87, bd. dirs.), Milw. Credit Assn. (hon. life, pres. 1981-83), Lions (life Kenosha, newsletter editor, charter pres. 1967, treas., charter pres. Found. 1969). Home: 2532 32nd Ave Kenosha WI 53144-1424

SEITZ, JAMES EUGENE, retired academic administrator, freelance writer; b. Columbia, Pa., July 27, 1927; s. Joseph Stoner and Minnie (Frey) S.; m. Florence Arlene Dutcher, Apr. 6, 1950; children: Diane Louise, Ellen Kay, Linda Marie, Karl Steven. BS, Millersville State Coll., 1950; MEd, Pa. State U., 1952; PhD, So. Ill. U., 1971. Tchr. pub. schs., Pa., 1950-56; lectr. Temple U., Phila., 1956-62; asst. prof. engr. tech. Kans. State U., Pitts., 1962-65; dean Mineral Area Coll., Flat River, Mo., 1965-69, Coll. of Lake County, Gravslake, Ill., 1969-73; founding pres. Edison State Community Coll., Piqua, Ohio, 1973-85; freelance writer Sidney, Ohio, 1985—; founding sec./treas. Ohio Tech. and C.C. Assn., Columbus, 1976; speaker at nat. confs. of educators, 1960-85. Author: Woodcarving: A Designer's Notebook, 1989, Country Creations, 1991, Selling What You Make, 1992, Effective Board Participation, 1993; contbr. articles to profl. jours. Founding pres. Exch. Club Grayslake, 1970; pres. Epicurian Soc., Sidney, Ohio, 1978-79; mediator Mcpl. Ct., Sidney, 1992—; sr. citizen's steering com. Arbor Day Found. Recipient Leadership and Svc. award Pa. State U. Alumni Soc., 1990. Mem. AARP (founding chpt. pres. 1990-91), VFW, Am. Vocat. Assn., Am. Legion, Iota Lambda Sigma. Home: 55 Brown Rd Sidney OH 45365-2557

SEITZ, MELVIN CHRISTIAN, JR., distributing company executive; b. Indpls., Aug. 9, 1939; s. Melvin Christian and Francis Sue (Lee) S.; m. Bette Louise Pierson, May 5, 1941; children: David, Mark, Keith, Cindy. Student Butler U., 1957-60. Salesman, Service Supply Co., Inc., Indpls., 1963-71, sec.-treas., 1971-74, v.p., 1974-81, exec. v.p., 1981-83, pres., 1983-94, COO, 1995, dir. corporate rels. Pres. Seitz-Owings Found.; active Met. Devel. Commn. Indpls., 1994—. Served with U.S. Army. Mem. Nat. Fastener Distributor Assn. (bd. dirs.), Cole Roster (bd. dirs.), Sigma Nu. Republican. Mem. Disciples of Christ. Lodges: Masons, Shriners, Scottish Rite. Home: 4716 Northeastern Ave Indianapolis IN 46239-1665 Office: Svc Supply Co Inc Ind 603 E Washington St Indianapolis IN 46204-2620

SEKHON, JASMEET M., psychologist; b. Pathankote, Punjab, India, Dec. 10, 1937; came to U.S., 1968; d. Jagat Singh Manku and Shakuntala (Nagi) Duggal; m. Kuldip Singh Sekhon, May 7, 1964; children: Sanjiv, Ajay. BA, Govt. Coll. for Women, Chandigarh, India, 1959; MA, Punjab U., Chandigarh, 1961; PsyD, Forest Sch. Profl. Psychology, Wheeling, Ill., 1984. Cert. clin. psychologist. Lect. in psychology Govt. Coll. for Women, Patiala, India, 1961-65; psychodiagnostician, intern Psychiat. Hosp., Hamilton, Ont., Can., 1966-68; psychologist Trumbull County Mental Health Ctr., Warren, Ohio, 1977-78; psychologist Elgin (Ill.) Mental Health Ctr., 1979-88, psychologist, adminstr., 1988—, chief psychologist, 1990—; cons. psychologist Trumbull County Juvenile Ct., Warren, 1977-78. Mem. APA, Ill. Psychol. Assn., Soc. Psychologists in Addictive Behavior. Office: Elgin Mental Health Ctr 750 S State St Elgin IL 60123-7612

SELBO, RAY GORDON, training director; b. Jamestown, N.D., Mar. 23, 1940; s. Arthur Gordon Selbo and Helen Evelyn (Peterson) Johnson; m. Joy Marget Bostrom, May 29, 1964; children: Jon Gordon, James Everett. Student, U. Minn., 1958-59. Various positions Am. Hardware Mut. Ins. Co., Mpls., 1959-70, dir. tng., 1970-77; dir. tng., regional v.p. Collateral Control Corp., St. Paul, Chgo., 1977-79; sales cons. Universal Tng. Systems, Wilmette, Ill., 1980-81; dir. tng. Schwan's Sales Enterprises Inc., Marshall, Minn., 1981-95, mgr. human resource devel., 1995—; cons. in field, 1973—; bd. dirs., treas. Rural Mktg. Inc., 1994—. Rep. precinct chmn., Bloomington, Minn., 1974-77; pres. Marshall United Fund, 1985-87; master of ceremonies United Fun Telethon, 1984—; fund raising host Pioneer Pub. TV, 1989—, bd. dirs., 1994—, v.p., 1995—. Named Minn. Sales and Mktg. Trainer of Yr., 1986. Mem. ASTD (pres. Mpls./St. Paul 1974-75, Nat. Torch award 1974), Marshall C. of C. (chmn. leadership devel. 1991-92). Republican. Lutheran. Home: RR 1 Box 21 Lynd MN 56157-9710 Office: Schwan's Sales Enterprises Inc 115 W College Dr Marshall MN 56258-1747

SELBY, BARBARA KENAGA, bank executive; b. San Francisco, July 14, 1942; d. George W. and Margaret (Spencer) Kenaga; m. Robert I. Selby, June 19, 1965; 1 child, Michael S. BBA, Ill. Wesleyan U., 1964. Corp. activities analyst Harris Bank, Chgo., 1969-77; asst. to gen. mgr. Harriscorp Fin., Inc., Chgo., 1978-80; with Bank Ill., Champaign, 1984-86; pers. officer BankIll., Champaign, 1986-87, asst. v.p. human resources, 1988-95, v.p. human resources, 1995—. Mem. Champaign-Urbana Pers. Assn. (treas. 1987-88), Women's Bus. Coun. (treas. 1991, bylaws chairperson 1996). Home: 909 W Union St Champaign IL 61821-3323 Office: BankIll 100 W University Champaign IL 61820

SELBY, ROBERT IRWIN, architect, educator; b. Evanston, Ill., Jan. 26, 1943; s. William Martin and Alice (Irwin) S.; m. Barbara Jean Kenaga, June 19, 1965; 1 child, Michael Scott. BArch, U. Ill., 1967, MArch, 1985. Registered architect, Ill., Wis., Ind., Colo., Fla., Pa., Idaho, N.C., Mich., Mo., Ohio. V.p. The Hawkweed Group Ltd., Chgo., Soldiers Grove and Osseo, Wis., 1971-84; prin. Robert I. Selby, Architect, Champaign, Ill., 1984—; asst. prof. architecture U. Ill., Champaign, 1984-88, assoc. prof., 1988—, chmn. design divsn., 1988-93, coord. China program, 1988-91; cons. housing rsch. and devel. program U. Ill., Urbana, 1985—; bd. editors U. Ill. Sch. Architecture jour., 1986-89, 96—; chair exec. com. East St. Louis action rsch. project, 1995—. Author: (with others) The Hawkweed Passive Solar House Book, 1980; editor: (monograph) Urban Synergy: Process, Projects and Projections, 1993; contbr. articles to profl. jours.; exhbn. of work (with E.N. Bacon) New Visions for Phila., 1993. Served with USAFR, 1966-72. Mem. AIA (corp. sec. Champaign-Urbana sect. 1985, pres. 1987, v.p., pres.-elect Ctrl. Ill. chpt. 1989, pres. 1990, bd. dirs. 1995—), Environ. Design Rsch. Assn. (chmn. 21st ann. internat. conf., co-editor conf. procs. 1988-90), Gargoyle Honor Soc., Alpha Rho Chi, Delta Upsilon (bd. dirs. U. Ill. 1991). Home: 909 W Union St Champaign IL 61821-3323 Office: U Ill 611 Taft Dr Champaign IL 61820

SELBY, RONALD JAY, electrical engineer; b. Huntington, Ind., Nov. 9, 1952; s. Jerrod and Avonelle (Scott) S.; m. Janet Ann Hollis, Sept. 25, 1982; 1 child, Laura Elizabeth. BSEE, Purdue U. of Indpls., 1985; MSEE, Rochester Inst. Tech., 1991. Engr.-in-tng., Ind. Apprentice/journeyman electrician Internat. Brotherhood Elec. Workers, Indpls., 1976-84; devel. engr. mfg. R&D orgn. Eastman Kodak, Rochester, N.Y., 1985-92; project engr. Prologix Sys. Integration, Indpls., 1992-96; sr. engr. Ind. Automation, Noblesville, 1996—. Mem. IEEE, Instrument Soc. Am., Ctrl. Ind. Bycycling Assn., Purdue U. at Indpls. Engring. Sch. Alumni Assn. (bd. dirs. 1995). Home: 10901 Marquette Rd Zionsville IN 46077 Office: Indiana Automation 8001 E 196th St Noblesville IN 46060

SELIG, ALLAN H. (BUD SELIG), professional baseball team executive; b. Milw., July 30, 1934; s. Ben and Marie Selig; m. Suzanne Lappin Steinman, Jan. 18, 1977; children: Sari, Wendy. Grad., U. Wis., Madison, 1956; LHD (hon.), Lakeland Coll., 1989. With Selig Ford (became Selig Chevrolet 1982), West Allis, Wis., 1959-90, pres., owner, 1966-90; with Selig Exec. Leasing Co., West Allis, 1959—, pres., owner, 1977—; part owner Milw. Braves (became Atlanta Braves 1965), 1963-65; co-founder Teams, Inc., 1964; co-owner, pres., chief exec. officer Milw. Brewers Baseball Club, Inc., 1970—; interim commr. Maj. League Baseball, 1991—; bd. dirs. Green Bay Packers Profl. Football Team. Co-founder Child Abuse Prevention Fund, 1988. With U.S. Army, 1956-58. Recipient Major League Exec. of Yr. award UPI, 1978, Internat. B'nai B'rith Sportsman of Yr. award 1981, Sportsman of Yr. award U.S. Olympic Com., 1988, August A. Busch, Jr. award for long and meritorious svc. to baseball, 1989, Ellis Island Congl. medal of honor, 1993, Anti-Defamation League's "A World of Difference Award" 1994. Office: Milw Brewers Milw County Stadium PO Box 3099 Milwaukee WI 53201-3099

SELIGMAN, COLETTE ARLENE, library director; b. Davenport, Iowa, Feb. 28, 1959; d. Carl Gene and Margrett L. (Barker) Green; m. Michael Wayne Seligman; children: Josh, Abbey. Diploma, AIC Bus. Sch., Davenport; libr. cert., Muscatin C.C. Sales clk. Spencer Gifts, Davenport, 1975-77; cashier McDonald's, Davenport, 1980-82; bookkeeper OK Welding, Davenport, 1982-83; accounts payable clk. Hormel Corp., Davenport, 1983-85; bookkeeper Silver Creek Mobile Pk., Davenport, 1986-87, Live Stock Svcs., Tipton, Iowa, 1990-91; libr. Bennett (Iowa) Pub. Libr., 1992—. Sec. Bennett Cmty. Club, 1988; mem. Pilots, Bennet's School, 1992. Office: Bennett Pub Libr 203 Main St Bennett IA 52721

SELL, NANCY JEAN, chemistry, physics and engineering educator; b. Milw., Jan. 18, 1945; d. Homer Paul and Jeanette Rose (Karrels) S. B.A., Lawrence U., 1967; M.S., Northwestern U., 1968, Ph.D., 1971; M.S. Inst. Paper Chemistry, Appleton, Wis., 1987. Registered profl. engr., Wis. Teaching asst. Northwestern U., Evanston, Ill., 1967-71; asst. prof. U. Wis.-Green Bay, 1971-77, assoc. prof., 1977-82, prof. Natural & Applied Scis., 1982—; pres. N.J. Sell & Assocs., Green Bay, 1984—. Author: Industrial Pollution Control: Issues and Techniques, 1981, 2d edit., 1992; (with others) Energy: A Conceptual Approach, 1985. Contbr. articles to profl. jours. Patentee in field. Recipient Excellence in Scholarship award U. Wis., Green Bay, 1982; named Alumnus Honoris, Clintonville Sr. High Sch., Wis., 1982. Mem. Am. Chem. Soc. (local chmn. 1982), TAPPI (chair process simulation com. 1993-95), ASTM (com. chmn. 1981-87), Sigma Xi (local chmn. 1979-80). Avocation: dog training. Home: 3244 Peterson Rd Green Bay WI 54311-7238 Office: U Wis Green Bay ES 317 Green Bay WI 54311

SELLARS, JAMES ALLEN, landmark director; b. Mitchell, S.D., Apr. 2, 1958; s. Arleigh V. and Berniece (Brown) S.; m. Tamara R. Peterson, Apr. 10, 1976 (div. 1987); children: Christopher, Stephanie. Student, U. S.D., 1977. Cashier World's Only Corn Palace, Mitchell, 1975-76, asst. mgr., 1977-79, tourism dir., 1980—. Chmn. Mitchell Hist. Preservation Commn., Mitchell Conv. and Visitors Bur.; bd. dirs., exec. com., chmn. Dakota Heritage and Lakes Assn., Sioux Falls, S.D.; bd. dirs., exec. com. Gt. Lakes S.D. Assn., Pierre; S.D. Tourism Edn. Coun.; bd. dirs., exec. com., past chmn. Black Hills Badlands and Lakes Assn., Rapid City, S.D. Mem. Am. Bus. Assn. (mem. orientation com.), S.D. Restaurant Assn. (bd. dirs., past pres., past chmn.), Am. Fedn. Musicians (bd. dirs. Mitchell chpt.). Home: 617 E Hanson St Mitchell SD 57301-3552 Office: World's Only Corn Palace 604 N Main St Mitchell SD 57301-2620

SELLERS, GREGORY JUDE, physicist; b. Far Rockaway, N.Y., June 20, 1947; s. Douglas L. and Rita R. (Dieringer) S.; m. Lucia S. Kim, Nov. 26, 1983; 1 child, Kristin Kim. AB in Physics, Cornell U., 1968; MS, U. Ill., 1970, PhD, 1975. Sr. scientist B-K Dynamics, Inc., Rockville, Md., 1974-76; with Allied-Signal Corp., Morristown, N.J., 1976-88, applications physicist, 1977-88; pres. Fotron, Inc. Naperville, Ill., 1995—; product supr. amphenol fiber optic product, 1985-88; mgr. Cinch Connectors, 1988-91; pres. Forss, Inc., Naperville, 1991—, Fotron, Naperville, 1995—; bd. dirs. Thermo-Tek, Inc., Forss, Fotron. Mem. AAAS, IEEE, Am. Phys. Soc. Home and Office: Fotron Inc 7S 515 Oak Trails Dr Naperville IL 60540

SELLMYER, DAVID JULIAN, physicist, educator; b. Joliet, Ill., Sept. 28, 1938; s. Marcus Leo and Della Louise (Plumhoff) S.; m. Catherine Joyce Zakas, July 16, 1962; children: Rebecca Ann, Julia Maryn, Mark Anthony. BS, U. Ill., 1960; PhD, Mich. State U., 1965. Asst. prof. MIT, Cambridge, 1965-72, assoc. prof., 1972; assoc. prof. U. Nebr., Lincoln, 1972-75, prof., 1975—, chmn. dept. physics, 1978-84, George Holmes disting. prof., 1987, dir. Ctr. Materials Rsch., 1988—; cons. Dale Electronics, Norfolk, Nebr., 1980—. Contbr. articles, book revs. to refereed jours. Recipient tech. award NASA, 1972; disting. vis. prof. S.D. Sch. Mines and Tech., Rapid City, 1981. Fellow Am. Phys. Soc. Office: U Nebr Ctr Materials Rsch 112 Brace Lab Lincoln NE 68588-0113

SELLON, JENNIFER PARKER, marketing professional; b. Muskegon, Mich., Jan. 21, 1967. BA, DePauw U., 1989; MBA, U. Notre Dame, 1991. V.p. Thomas F. Parker & Assocs., Grand Haven, Mich., 1992-95, Bowman Inc., Grand Haven, 1995—; cons. various firms, Mich., 1988—. Mktg. vol. Kids Hope USA, Muskegon, Mich., 1994, Am. Cancer Soc., Western Mich., 1991; Sunday sch. tchr. Christ Cmty. Ch., Spring Lake, Mich., 1994—. Mem. Am. Mktg. Assn., Counterpart Grand Haven. Mem. Reformed Ch. Am. Office: Thomas F Parker & Assocs 1810 Industrial Dr Grand Haven MI 49417-9429

SELMENSBERGER, JAMES, design engineer; b. Buffalo, N.Y., Sept. 20, 1968. BSEE, U. Dayton, 1991. Staff elec. engr. N.Y. Power Authority, N.Y.C., 1989-90, Dayton (Ohio) Power & Light, 1990-95; application/design engr. Square D, Middletown, Ohio, 1995—. Roman Catholic. Office: Square D 1500 S University Blvd Middletown OH 45044-5968

SELZLE, KURT ANDER, sales executive; b. Aberdeen, S.D., June 28, 1964; s. Norman Robert and Nina Lee (Brandenburger) S. BSME, S.D. Sch. Mines and Tech., 1986. Sales rep. Trane Co., Tyler, Tex., 1986-87; mgr. engineered sales Matheny Heating & Cooling, St. Louis, 1987-91; sr. sales engr. Jarrell Contracting Co., Inc., St. Louis, 1991—. Pres. Coll. Reps., Rapid City, S.D., 1986; Bible group leader St. Louis Ch. of Christ, 1989—, v.p. singles ministry, 1989—; legis. lobbyist SHED, Rapid City, Pierre, S.D., 1983-86. Named one of Outstanding Young Men Am., 1989. Home: 12309 Rule Hill Ct Maryland Heights MO 63043-4523 Office: Jarrell Contracting Svc Co 4208 N Rider Trl Earth City MO 63045-1105

SEMANIK, ANTHONY JAMES, university program administrator; b. Cleve., Mar. 2, 1942; s. Anthony Joseph and Angela Theresa (Peters) S.; m. Elaine Maria Christian, Apr. 20, 1968. BS in Edn., Kent State U., 1965, MEd, 1969. TV coord. Kent (Ohio) State U., 1967-71; TV producer/dir. High/Scope Ednl. Rsch. Found., Ypsilanti, Mich., 1971-72; dir. learning resource ctr. Mercy Coll. of Detroit, 1972-78; ind. media designer/cons. Detroit, 1972—; pub. affairs specialist Detroit bn. recruiting command U.S. Army, 1980-84; pub. affairs specialist tank-automotive command U.S. Army, Warren, Mich., 1984-85; dir. learning resource ctr. U. Detroit Mercy, 1985—; chair Detroit Ednl. Cable Consortium, 1992—. Producer, designer, dir., editor instructional-educational multimedia and video programs-series for univ. and cable TV, 1985—; editor: (video programs) Elders in the New Japan, 1987, China and its Elders, 1989. Chmn. Detroit Ednl. Cable Consortium, 1992—. With U.S. Army, 1965-67. Mem. Consortium of Coll. and Univ. Media Ctrs., Assn. for Ednl. Comms. and Tech., Mich. Assn. Media in Edn., Phi Delta Kappa. Home: 7176 Green Farm Rd West Bloomfield MI 48322-2824 Office: U Detroit Mercy PO Box 19900 Detroit MI 48219-0900

SEMION, A. KAY, editor; b. New Castle, Ind., July 27, 1944; d. Lowell Ernest and T. Byrneta (Byrne) Hooker; m. William Alexander Semion, June 21, 1969; children: Justin Alexander, Sonja Katherine. BA, Purdue U., 1966; AA, Delta Coll., 1974; MA, Wayne State U., 1981. Reporter The Flint (Mich.) Jour., 1966-70, The Daily Eagle, Wayne, Mich., 1970-71, The Bay City (Mich.) Times, 1971-72; copy editor The Ann Arbor (Mich.) News, 1979-83, editl. page editor, 1983—. Newsletter chmn. Lamaze Wayne County, Canton, Mich., 1977-80; leader La Leche League, Canton, 1978-81. Recipient Orthy awards Ch. 19 PBS, Bay City, 1973, 74. Mem. Soc. Profl. Journalists, Nat. Conf. Editl. Writers (chair mgmt. com., 1993-95, co-chair, mem. svcs. com. 1995—). Home: 41629 Larimore Ln Canton MI 48187-3921 Office: The Ann Arbor News PO Box 1147 Ann Arbor MI 48106-1147

SEMION, WILLIAM ALEXANDER, magazine editor; b. Northville, Mich., Sept. 13, 1947; s. Alexander Alexis and Lillian May (Hulle) S.; m. Anyta Kay Semion, June 21, 1969; children: Justin, Sonya. BA in Journalism, Wayne State U., 1969. Reporter Saginaw (Mich.) News, 1969, 71-75; contbg. editor AAA Mich. Living Mag., Dearborn, 1975-82; assoc. editor Mich. Living Mag., Dearborn, 1982-85, sr. assoc. editor, 1985—. Author: Michigan Family Adventure Guide, 1996; contbr. articles on travel and outdoors to mags. With U.S. Army, 1970-71. Recipient award State Bar of Mich., 1975, 82. Mem. Soc. Profl. Journalists (Detroit chpt. sec. 1982-87, pres. 1987-89, bd. dirs. 1989—), Mich. Outdoor Writers Assn. (sec., v.p. 1996—, award 1994, 95), Outdoor Wriers Am., Automotive Press Assn. Office: Mich Living Mag 1 Auto Club Dr Dearborn MI 48126

SEMPLE, HARRY D., business executive; b. Chgo., Apr. 5, 1932. BBA, Ohio U., 1954. V.p. Nat. Drug Stores, Inc., Marietta, Ohio, 1957-67, Performance Incentives Corp., Detroit, 1970-78; sr. v.p. Flaghren & Swink Advt., Marion, Ohio, 1978-88; pres. The Incentive Works, Inc., Cin., 1988—. Inventor Hide-A-Spike. Dir. Marca Industries, Marion, 1978-88; fin. com. dir. United Meth. of Cin., 1994—. Capt. USAF, 1954-57. Mem. Cin. C. of C. Office: 9640 Rexford Dr Cincinnati OH 45241-3364

SEN, ASHISH KUMAR, urban planner, educator; b. Delhi, India, June 8, 1942; came to U.S., 1967, naturalized, 1985; s. Ashoka Kumar and Arati Sen; m. Colleen Taylor. BS with honors, Calcutta U., 1962; MA, U. Toronto, Ont., Can., 1964, PhD, 1971. Research assoc., lectr. dept. geography Transp. Center, Northwestern U., 1967-69; mem. faculty Center Urban Studies, U. Ill., Chgo., 1969—; prof. Center Urban Studies, U. Ill., 1978—, dir. Sch. Urban Planning, 1991; dean Center Urban Studies, U. Ill. (Sch. Urban Scis.), 1977-78, acting dir., 1992; pres. Ashish Sen. and Assocs., Chgo., 1977—. Author: Regression Analysis: Theory, Methods and Applications, 1990, Gravity MOdels of Spatial Interaction Behavior, 1995; also articles. Mem. Chgo. Bd. Edn., 1990-95; chmn. budget com. 1992-94; bd. trustees Asian Inst., 1993—. Fellow Royal Statis. Soc.; mem. Am. Statis. Assn., Inst. Math. Stats., Am. Soc. Planning Ofcls., Regional Sci. Assn., Transp. Rsch. Forum, Transp. Rsch. Bd., Cliffdwellers. Hindu. Home: 2557 W Farwell Ave Chicago IL 60645-4617

SENDAK, THEODORE LORRAINE, lawyer; b. Chgo., Mar. 16, 1918; s. Jack and Annette (Frankel) S.; m. Tennessee Elizabeth Read, Sept. 13, 1942; children: Theodore T., Timothy R., Cynthia L. AB cum laude, Harvard U., 1940; LLB, JD, Valparaiso U., 1958. Bar: Ind. 1959. Chief editl. writer Hammond (Ind.) Times, 1940-41; pub. rels. dir. Ind. Dept. Vets. Affairs, Indpls., 1946-48; pres. Gary (Ind.) Electric Co., 1948-59; pvt. practice law Crown Point, Ind., 1959-69; atty. gen. Ind., 1969-81; of counsel Sendak, Sendak, Neff & Rominger, Crown Point, 1981—; bd. mem. Ams. for Effective Law Enforcement, Chgo.; adv. bd. mem. The Salvation Army, Indpls., 1970—. Author: Olive But Not Drab, 1943, Pilgrimage Through the Briar Patch, 1990; columnist The Propaganda Analyst, 1981. Supr. U.S. Census, First Congl. Dist., Ind., 1960; chmn. Lake County (Ind.) Rep. Party, 1962-70. Col. USAR, 1941-72. Mem. ABA, Ind. Bar Assn., Indpls. Press Club, Masons (Scottish Rite, 33 Degree), Roosevelt Lodge F&AM (life mem.), Am. Legion (life mem. post 369), Elks (life mem.). Republican. Methodist. Office: Sendak Sendak Neff & Rominger 219 S Main St Crown Point IN 46307

SENEFF, SMILEY HOWARD, business owner; b. Odon, Ind., June 28, 1925; s. Smiley and Ada Fern (Howard) S.; m. Barbara Jean Daum, July 17, 1950 (div. 1966); children: Nancy Kay Secrest, Cheryl Evans; m. Mary Ann Beeler, Mar. 12, 1966; children: Jill Midtbo, Judy Hiland, Jacalyn Harness, Jennifer Sillery, Donald. Student, Duke U., 1945; BS, Ind. U., 1950. Mem. acctg. staff Armour and Co., Indpls., 1950-52, Chevrolet Comml. Body Co., Indpls., 1952-54; owner, mgr. Seneff Hardware and Appliance, Plainfield, Ind., 1955-66, Catalina Motel, Indpls., 1966-73, Smiley's Pancake and Steak, Indpls., 1972—, Smiley's Car Wash, Indpls., 1972—. Mem. County Zoning Bd., 1959-63; Rep. precinct committeeman, del. to state Rep. conv., 1959-63. Mem. Elks, Rotary (pres.), Masons, Scottish Rite, Shriners. Home: 6002 Mt. Auburn Dr Indianapolis IN 46224 Office: Seneff Inns Inc 1307 S High School Rd Indianapolis IN 46241-3128

SENGPIEHL, PAUL MARVIN, lawyer, former state official; b. Stuart, Nebr., Oct. 10, 1937; s. Arthur Paul and Anne Marie (Andersen) S.; B.A., Wheaton (Ill.) Coll., 1959; M.A. in Pub. Adminstrn., Mich. State U., 1961; J.D., Ill. Inst. Tech.-Chgo. Kent Coll. Law, 1970; m. June S. Cline, June 29, 1963; children—Jeffrey D., Chrystal M. Bar: Ill. 1971, U.S. Supreme Ct. 1982. Adminstrv. asst. Chgo. Dept. Urban Renewal, 1962-65; supr. Ill. Municipal Retirement Fund, Chgo., 1966-71; mgmt. officer Ill. Dept. Local Govt. Affairs, Springfield, 1971-72, legal counsel, Chgo., 1972-73; spl. asst. atty. gen. Ill. Dept. Labor, Chgo., 1973-76; asst. atty. gen. Ct. of Claims div. Atty. Gen. of Ill., 1976-83; hearing referee Bd. Rev., Ill. Dept. Labor, 1983-84; local govt. law columnist Chgo. Daily Law Bull., 1975-84; instr. polit. sci. Judson Coll., Elgin, Ill., 1963. Republican candidate for Cook County Recorder of Deeds, 1984; dep. committeeman Oak Park Twp Rep. Orgn.; elected alt. del., served as del. Rep. Nat. Conv., 1992; People's Choice candidate pres. Oak Park Village, 1993; committeeman Oak Park Twp., 1994—. Mem. Ill. Bar Assn. (local govt. law sect. council 1973-79, vice chmn. 1976-77, co-editor local govt. newsletter 1976-77, chmn. 1977-78, editor newsletter 1977-78, state tax sect. council 1979-82, 84-85), Chgo. Bar Assn. (local govt. com., chmn. legis. subcom. 1978-79, sec. 1979-80, vice chmn. 1980-81, chmn. 1981-82, state and mcpl. tax com.),Internat. Platform Assn., John Ericsson Rep. League Ill. (state sec. 1983-85, 95—, sec. Cook County 1982—), Oak Park-River Forest C. of C. (sm. bus. coun., 1991—). Baptist (vice chmn. deacons 1973-76, 79-80, moderator 1983-86, supt. sunday sch. 1986-93). Home: 727 N Ridgeland Ave Oak Park IL 60302-1735

SENGSTACKE, FREDERICK D., newspaper publishing executive. Now pub. Chgo. Defender. Office: Sengstacke Enterprises 2400 S Michigan Ave Chicago IL 60616-2329

SENGSTACKE, JOHN HERMAN HENRY, publishing company executive; b. Savannah, Ga., Nov. 25, 1912; s. Herman Alexander and Rosa Mae (Davis) S.; 1 son, Robert Abbott. B.S., Hampton (Va.) Inst., 1933; post-grad., Ohio State U., 1933. With Robert S. Abbott Pub. Co. (publishers Chgo. Defender), 1934—, v.p., gen. mgr., 1934-40, pres., gen. mgr., 1940—; chmn. bd. Mich. Chronicle, Detroit; pres. Tri-State Defender, Defender Pubs., Amalgamated Pubs., Inc.; pub. Daily Defender; pres. Sengstacke Enterprises, Inc., Sengstacke Pubs., Pitts. Courier Newspaper Chain; dir. Ill. Fed. Savs. & Loan Assn., Golden State Mut. Life Ins. Co. Mem. exec. bd. Nat. Alliance Businessmen; bd. govs. USO; mem. Ill. Sesquicentennial Commn., Pres.'s Com. on Equal Opportunity in Armed Services; mem. pub. affairs adv. com. Air Force Acad.; trustee Bethune-Cookman Coll., Daytona Beach, Fla., Hampton Inst.; bd. dirs. Washington Park YMCA, Joint Negro Appeal; chmn. bd. Provident Hosp. Recipient Two Friends award Nat. Urban League, 1950; Hampton Alumni award, 1954; 1st Mass. Media award Am. Jewish Com. Mem. Negro Newspaper Pubs. Assn. (founder), Nat. Newspaper Pubs. Assn. (founder, pres.), Am. Newspaper Pubs. Assn., Am. Soc. Newspaper Editors (dir.). Congregationalist. Clubs: Royal Order of Snakes, Masons, Elks, Econs, Chgo. Press. Office: Sengstacke Enterprises Inc 2400 S Michigan Ave Chicago IL 60616-2329

SENIOR, RICHARD JOHN LANE, textile rental services executive; b. Datchet, Eng., July 6, 1940; came to U.S., 1972, naturalized, 1977; s. Harold Denis Senior and Jane Lane Dorothy (Chadwick) Senior Rigg; BA, Oxford U., 1962; M.I.A., Yale U., 1964; m. Diana Morgan, Dec. 19, 1966; children: Alden, Alicia, Amanda. Mgmt. cons. McKinsey & Co., Inc., London and Chgo., 1967-74; pres., CEO Morgan Svcs., Inc., Chgo., 1974—; bd. dirs. Geo. J. Ball, Inc., 1990-95, Northwestern Mem. Corp., 1992—, Ball Hort. Co., 1996—; mem. regional adv. bd. Kemper Ins. Cos., 1994-96. Pres. bd. trustees Latin Sch., Chgo., 1979-83; bd. dirs. Chgo. Crime Commn., 1994—. Mem. Textile Rental Svcs. Assn. Am. (pres. 1983-85, dir., mem. exec. com. 1978-86), Racquet Club (bd. govs. 1983-91), Chicago Club, Glen View Club, Casino (bd. govs., 1991-96, treas. 1993-94), Econ. Club. Home: 1420 N Lake Shore Dr Chicago IL 60610-1628 Office: Morgan Svcs Inc 323 N Michigan Ave Chicago IL 60601-3798

SENN, RICHARD ALLAN, environmental safety professional; b. LaCrosse, Wis., Dec. 20, 1946; s. Hugo and Evelyn Ruth (Winters) S.; m. Denise Marie Corriveau, May 6, 1989; 1 stepchild, Danelle Marie Wiersma. BS in Chemistry and Bus., U. Wis., 1970, BS in Environ. Scis., 1975, MBA in Mgmt., 1980. Cert. hazardous materials mgr. Analytical chemist Warf Inst., Madison, Wis., 1970-75; scientist Warf Inst., Madison, 1975-77; scientist II Raltech Scientific Svcs., Madison, 1977-78, herbicide sect. leader, 1978-82; environ. chemist III U. Wis., Madison, 1982-84; pres. 4 Lakes Volleyball Assn., Madison, 1981-83; owner Sports Mgmt. Svcs., Madison, 1981-83; lab/safety mgr. Madison, 1984-86; environ. health safety mgr. Agracet U.S., Inc., Middleton, Wis., 1986—; pres. 4 Lakes Recreation Inc., Verona, Wis., 1984—. Author: (with others) Waste Minimization in Research and Academic Institutions, 1995. Vol. WHA-Pub. TV, Madison, 1991—. Mem. Fedn. Environ. Techs. (Madison chpt. program chmn. 1986—, pres., founder 1990-92), Nat. Safety Coun., Acad. Cert. Hazardous Materials Mgrs. (bd. dirs. Greater Wis. chpt. 1993—), Am. Biol. Safety Assn., Madison Area Safety Coun. (bd. dirs. 1994—), U.S. Wis. Madison Volleyball Booster Club (bd. dirs. 1987-95). Home: 6066 Whalen Rd Verona WI 53593 Office: Agracentus Inc 8520 University Green Middleton WI 53562

SENNER, ROBERT WILLIAM, secondary education educator; b. Freeman, S.D., Mar. 19, 1912; s. William Jacob and Elizabeth Pandora (Graber) S.; m. Rachel Bertha Epp, Aug. 15, 1943; children: John William, Rachel Ann, Roberta Ann, Stanley Epp. BA, Bethel Coll., 1942; MusM, Wichita STate U., 1953. Tchr. music Fowler (Kans.) High Sch., 1942-43, Buhler (Kans.) High Sch., 1943-74; adjudicator Okla. Secondary Sch. Activities, 1960-85. Contbr. articles to profl. jours.; conductor concerts including Handel's Messiah, DuBois' Seven Last Words, Haydn's Creation, 1957-75. Pres. Mennonite Song Festival Soc., Newton, Kans., 1947-50; vol. Mennonite Disaster svcs., Kans. and Colo. Named to Music Tchrs. Hall of Fame, Kans. Music Edn. Assn., 1978. Mem. Music Educators Nat. Conf., S.D. Music Edn. Assn., Am. Choral Dirs. Assn. (Harry Robert Wilson award 1981), Nature Conservancy S.D., Hawk Mountain Sanctuary Assn. Democrat. Home and Office: 220 E 7th St Freeman SD 57029-2303

SENNET, CHARLES JOSEPH, lawyer; b. Buffalo, Aug. 7, 1952; s. Saunders M. and Muriel S. (Rotenberg) S. AB magna cum laude, Cornell U., 1974; JD with high honors, George Washington U., 1979. Bar: Ill. 1979, U.S. Dist. Ct. (no. dist.) Ill. 1979, U.S. Ct. Appeals (7th cir.) 1982, U.S. Ct. Appeals (D.C. cir.) 1993. Assoc. Reuben & Proctor, Chgo., 1979-83; assoc. counsel Tribune Co., Chgo., 1984-91, sr. counsel, 1991—; adj. faculty Medill Sch. Journalism, Northwestern U., 1991—; co-chair Television Music Lic. Com., 1995—. Contbr. articles to profl. jours. Mem. ABA (spkr. 1984-88, 91-96), NATAS, Ill. Bar Assn. (chmn. media law com. 1989-91, mem. gov. bd. Forum on Comms. Law, 1995—), Chgo. Bar Assn., Fed. Comms. Bar Assn. Office: Tribune Co 435 N Michigan Ave Chicago IL 60611-4001

SENSENBRENNER, FRANK JAMES, JR., congressman, lawyer; b. Chgo., June 14, 1943; s. Frank James and Margaret Anita (Luedke) S.; m. Cheryl Lynn Warren, Mar. 26, 1977; children: Frank James III, Robert Alan. AB in Polit. Sci., Stanford U., 1965; JD, U. Wis., 1968. Bar: Wis. 1968, U.S. Supreme Ct. 1972. Mem. firm McKay and Martin, Cedarburg, Wis., 1970-75; mem. Wis. Assembly, 1969-75; mem. Wis. State Senate, 1975-79, asst. minority leader, 1977-79; mem. 96th-104th Congresses from 9th Wis. dist., Washington, 1979—; mem. House Jud. Com., House Sci. Com., chmn. subcom. on space and aeronautics. Mem. Am. Philatelic Soc. Republican. Episcopalian. Club: Capitol Hill. Office: US Ho of Reps 2332 Rayburn House Bldg Washington DC 20515-4909

SENTER, KAROLYN ELIZABETH, protection services officer; b. St. Louis, Feb. 28, 1959; d. Harold Ewing and Ola Mae (Watkins) S.; m. Mark Stephen Travis, Sep. 14, 1985 (div. July 1987). BA in Adminstrn. of Justice, U. Mo., Kansas City, 1982; MEd in Counseling with honors, U. Mo., St. Louis, 1994. Investigator State of Mo., St. Louis, 1984-85; patient educator Planned Parenthood of Greater Dallas, 1985-86; counselor First Offender Program Dallas Police Dept., 1986-89; agent Mo. Divn. of Child Support Enforcement, St. Louis, 1989-90; dep. juvenile officer Family Ct. 22d Judd. Circuit of Mo., St. Louis, 1991-94, asst. mgr. probation dept. Family Ct., 1994—; cmty. spkr. juvenile divn. Family ct. spkr's. bur., St. Louis, 1992—. Co-host A Different Point of View, weekly cmty. edn. radio program on WGNU Radio, St. Louis, 1996—. Active Mo. Juvenile Justice Assn., 1995—. Mem. ACA, Am. Coll. Couns. Assn., Delta Sigma Theta. Office: Family Ct Juvenile Divn 920 N Vandeventer Saint Louis MO 63108

SEPPALA, KATHERINE SEAMAN (MRS. LESLIE W. SEPPALA), retail company executive, clubwoman; b. Detroit, Aug. 22, 1919; d. Willard D. and Elizabeth (Miller) Seaman; B.A., Wayne State U., 1941; m. Leslie W. Seppala, Aug. 15, 1941; children: Sandra Kay, William Leslie. Mgr. women's bldg. and student activities adviser Wayne State U., 1941-43; pres. Harper Sports Shops, Inc., 1947-85, chmn. bd., treas., sec., v.p. 1985—; ptnr. Seppala Bldg. Co., 1971—. Mich. service chmn. women grads. Wayne State U., 1962—, 1st v.p., fund bd., Girl and Cub Scouts; mem. Citizen's adv. com. on sch. needs Detroit Bd. Edn., 1957—, mem. high sch. study com., 1966—; chmn., mem. loan fund bd. Denby High Sch. Parents Scholarship; bd. dirs., v.p. Wayne State U. Fund; precinct del. Rep. Party, 14th dist., 1956—, del. convs.; mem. com. Myasthenia Gravis Support Assn. Recipient Ann. Women's Service award Wayne State U., 1963. Recipient Disting. Alumni award Wayne State U., 1971. Mem. Intercollegiate Assn. Women Students (regional rep. 1941-45), Women Wayne State U. Alumni (past pres.), Wayne State U. Alumni Assn. (dir., past v.p.), AAUW (dir. past officer), Council Women as Public Policy Makers (editor High lights) Denby Community Ednl. Orgn. (sec.), Met. Detroit Program Planning Inst. (pres.), Internat. Platform Assn., Detroit Met. Book and Author Soc. (treas.), Mortar Bd. (past pres.), Karyatides (past pres.), Anthony Wayne Soc., Alpha Chi Alpha, Alpha Kappa Delta, Delta Gamma Chi, Kappa Delta (chmn. chpt. alumnae adv. bd.). Baptist. Clubs: Zonta (v.p., dir.); Les Cheneaux. Home: 22771 Worthington Ct Saint Clair Shores MI 48081-2603 Office: Harper Sport Shop Inc 23208 Greater Mack Ave Saint Clair Shores MI 48080-3422

SEPRODI, JUDITH CATHERINE, accounting administrator; b. Terre Haute, Ind., June 16, 1955; d. Ferris Lee and Mary Ann (Tully) Roberson; m. Donald Matthew Seprodi, Aug. 1, 1972 (div. Oct. 1994); children: Antoinette, Autumn, Jacob, Brooklyn. AA, Ivy Tech., 1990; grad., Dale Carnegie Course. Lic. property/casualty ins. agt.; notary public. Sec. Equifax, Oklahoma City, 1975-76; ins. clk. Northside Family Medicine, Del City, Okla., 1976; office mgr. Dick Clark Ins., Terre Haute, 1981, Simrell's, Terre Haute, 1981-85; ADC acctg. clk./typist V Vigo County Welfare, Terre Haute, 1985-86, head ADC acctg., clk./typist IV, 1986-87; purchasing agt. Bruce Fox, Inc., New Albany, Ind., 1987-88; acctg. mgr. Terre Haute Coke and Carbon, 1988-96, acting sec. bd. dirs., 1989; ptnr., owner Thistlehare; office mgr. Terre Haute (Ind.) Truck Ctr., 1996—; ptnr., owner Thistlehare; bookkeeper Seprodi Constrn., Terre Haute, 1989—; grad. asst. Dale Carnegie Inst.; owner Take-A-Letter. Author employee manuals. Coach, Terre Haute Youth Soccer Assn., 1979-82, bd. dirs., 1979-82; player North Tex. Women's Soccer Assn., Plano, 1977-78. Recipient Dale Carnegie higehst award for achievment. Mem. NAFE, AIPB, Am. Notary Assn., Profl. Bookkeepers Assn., Vigo County Taxpayers Assn. Democrat. Roman Catholic.

SERAFYN, ALEXANDER JAROSLAV, automotive executive, retired; b. Stare Selo, Ukraine, Mar. 27, 1930; came to U.S., 1949; s. Leon and Ahaphia (Peretiatko) S.; m. Zenia Maria Sylvestruk, July 5, 1958; children: Lesia, Lidia, Myron, Roman. BA, Wayne State U., 1954, MBA, 1960; PhD, Kensington U., 1983. Mgr. fin. analysis Ford (France) S.A., Paris, 1964-66; budget analysis mgr. Ford Motor/Indsl. and Chem. Div., Southfield, Mich., 1967; asst. ops. controller Ford Motor/Paint and Vinyl Ops., Mt. Clemens, Mich., 1968, ops. controller, 1969-71; controller Ford South Africa, Port Elizabeth, 1972-73; asst. div. controller Ford Motor/Metal Stamping Div., Dearborn, Mich., 1974-80, Ford Motor/Body and Assembly Ops., Dearborn, 1981-82; bus. plans and adminstrv. mgr. Ford Motor/Mfg. Ops., Dearborn, 1983-84; program mgr. Mazda Ford Motor/Body and Assembly Ops., Dearborn, 1985-90; bd. dirs. Selfreliance Fed. Credit Union, Warren, Mich. Contbr. articles to profl. jours. Adviser Ukrainian Nat. Assn., 1994—, pres. Detroit dist., 1989—, exec. v.p., 1987-89; treas. Shevchenko Sci. Soc., Detroit, 1989—. Named Ukrainian of Yr., Ukrainian Grads. of Detroit and Windsor, 1980, Disting. Alumnus, Wayne State U. Sch. Bus., 1995. Mem. Acad. Engring. Scis. of Ukraine, Ukrainian Engrs. Soc. Am. (sr. mem., bd. dirs. 1991—), Ukrainian Engring. Soc. (pres. Detroit br. 1978-79), Ukrainian Nat. Assn. (Fraternalist of Yr. award 1991), others. Republican. Ukrainian Catholic. Home: 2565 Timberwyck Trail Dr Troy MI 48098-4103

SERATTI, LORRAINE M., state legislator; b. Oct. 30, 1949. V.p. Wis. Fedn. Taxpayers Orgn.; pres. Florence County Taxpayers Alliance; Wis. state assemblywoman dist. 36, 1992—; small bus. owner. Mem. Florence Hist. Soc. Mem. NRA. Address: HC-2 Box 588 Florence WI 54121*

SERDAN, MARK I., design engineer; b. West Bend, Wis., Nov. 2, 1967. Draftsman Ward Tool & Die, West Bend, 1988-90; design engr. Capitol Stampings, Milw., 1990—. Recipient Ulbrich Stainless Steel award Precision Metal Forming Assn., 1993. Mem. Auto Cad Users Group. Republican. Roman Catholic. Office: Capitol Stampings PO Box 12365 Milwaukee WI 53212-0365

SERMERSHEIM, J. SCOTT, manufacturing engineer; b. Huntingburg, Ind., Apr. 15, 1954. BS, Purdue U., 1976, MS, 1979. With United Techs., Converse, Ind., 1979-81; mfg. engr. Hurco Mfg., Indpls., 1981-83; mfg. product engr. AES Interconnects, Plaainfield, Ind., 1983—. Mem. Wire Harness Mfrs. Assn. (bd. dirs. 1993—), Soc. Automotive Engrs., Soc. Mfg. Engrs. (sr.). Home: 14706 Laredo Ct Carmel IN 46032-5154 Office: AES Interconnects PO Box 248 12675 W Hwy 36 Plainfield IN 46168

SERNETT, RICHARD PATRICK, lawyer; b. Mason City, Iowa, Sept. 8, 1938; s. Edward Frank and Loretta M. (Cavanaugh) S.; m. Janet Ellen Ward, Apr. 20, 1963; children: Susan Ellen, Thomas Ward, Stephen Edward, Katherine Anne. BBA, U. Iowa, 1960, JD, 1963. Bar: Iowa 1963, Ill. 1965, U.S. Dist. Ct. (no. dist.) Ill. 1965, U.S. Supreme Ct. 1971. House counsel, asst. sec. Scott, Foresman & Co., Glenview, Ill., 1963-70; sec., legal officer Scott, Foresman & Co., Glenview, 1970-80; v.p., law sec. SFN Cos., Inc., Glenview, 1980-83, sr. v.p., sec., gen. counsel, 1983-85, exec. v.p., gen. counsel, 1985-87; pvt. practice Northbrook, Ill., 1988-90; v.p., sec., gen. counsel Macmillan/McGraw-Hill Sch. Pub. Co., 1990-92; v.p. Bert Early Assoc., Chgo., 1992-93; ptnr. Sernett & Blake, Northfield, Ill., 1993-95; ret., 1995; mem. U.S. Dept. State Adv. Panel on Internat. Copyright, 1972-75. Chmn. bd. dirs. Iowa State U., Broadcasting Co., 1987-94. Mem. ABA (chmn. copyright div. 1972-73, com. on copyright legis. 1967-68, 69-70, com. on copyright office affairs 1966-67, 79-81, com. on program for revision copyright law 1971-72), Am. Intellectual Property Law Assn., Am. Soc. Corp. Secs., Ill. Bar Assn. (chmn. copyright com. 1971-72), Chgo. Bar Assn., Patent Law Assn. Chgo. (bbd. mgrs. 1979-82, chmn. copyright law com. 1972-73, 77-78), Copyright Soc. U.S.A. (trustee 1972-75, 77-80), North Shore Country Club (Glenview, Ill.), Eagle Ridge Country Club (Galena, Ill.), Wyndemere Country Club (Naples, Fla.), Met. Club Chgo. Home: 2579 Fairford Ln Northbrook IL 60062-8101

SEROCKY, WILLIAM HOWARD, retired sales professional; b. Waukegan, Ill., Nov. 3, 1936; s. William John and Rose Marie (Grahek) S.; m. Cherylin Kresten, Apr. 11, 1970. AS in Mid Mgmt., Coll. of Lake County, 1979; BA in Applied Scis., Nat. Coll. of Edn., 1982. Supr. planning, scheduling and customer svc. Manville Corp., Waukegan, 1954-87; sales assoc. Atwood Pitcher & Assocs., Zion, Ill., 1988-92, James H. Pitcher & Assocs., Zion, 1992-96; ret., 1996. Mem. Young Reps. Club, Waukegan, 1962. Mem. Moose. Lutheran.

SERPE-SCHROEDER, PATRICIA L., elementary education educator; b. La Porte, Ind., Feb. 1, 1949; d. Fred J. and Priscilla (Nowak) Serpe; children: Matthew Aaron, Scott Allan. BA, Purdue U., 1971, MS in Edn., 1976. Cert. tchr., administr., Ind. Tchr., grades 1-2 Westville (Ind.) Sch.; tchr., grade 2 Lincoln Sch., Highland, Ind.; tchr. grades 1, 2, 4 Iddings Sch., Merrillville, Ind., 1985-92; prin. Hudson Lake Elem. Sch., New Carlisle, Ind., 1992-94; title I coord. New Prairie Sch. Corp., New Carlisle, 1994—; mem. drug-free, sci. textbook, elem. computer coms. New Prairie United Sch. Corp.; presenter in field. Recipient Ind. State grant. Mem. NEA, ASCD, Ind. Tchrs. Assn., Merrillville Tchrs. Assn. (sec., membership chmn., mem. computer and tech. coms. for sch. corp., bldg. adv. com.), Nat. Assn. Sch. Prins., Ind. Assn. Sch. Prins., Ind. Prins. Leadership Acad., Kappa Delta Pi, Delta Kappa Gamma, Pi Delta Phi. Home: PO Box 1076 New Carlisle IN 46552-1076 Office: Olive Twp Elem Sch 300 W Ben St New Carlisle IN 46552-9505

SERRAGLIO, MARIO, architect; b. Bassano, Veneto, Italy, Apr. 13, 1965; came to U.S., 1972; s. Luciano G. and Maria P. (Bellon) S. BS in Architecture, Ohio State U., 1988. Real estate agent Four Star Realty, Columbus, Ohio, 1984—; treas. Columbus Masonry, Inc., 1985-86; v.p. Serraglio Masonry, Inc., Columbus, 1986—; pres. Serraglio Builders, Inc., Columbus, 1987—; residential designer Gary A. Bruck, SGR, Inc., Columbus, 1988-89, Sullivan Gray Ptnrs., Columbus, 1989-92; project mgr. John Regan Architects, Columbus, 1992-93. Mem. AIA, Columbus Bd. Realtors. Office: Mario Serraglio Inc 515 Green Meadow Dr S Westerville OH 43081

SERRATTO-BENVENUTO, MARIA, pediatric cardiologist; b. Genova, Italy; came to U.S. 1962; d. Tito and Gemma (Macaluso) Serratto; m. Riccardo Benvenuto. BA, Liceo A. Doria, Genoa, Italy, 1949; MD magna cum laude, U. Genoa. Cert. Am. Bd. Pediatrics, Am. Bd. Pediatric Cardiology. Rsch. assoc. U. Ill. Hosp., Chgo., 1963-67; asst. prof. of Pediatrics U. Ill., Chgo., 1967-73, assoc. prof. of Pediatrics, 1974-80, prof. of Pediatrics, 1981—; faculty mem. Rush Med. Sch., Chgo., 1980—; assoc. attending physician Cook County Children's Hosp., Chgo., 1967-73, sr. attending physician, 1974-93, vis. attending physician, 1993—; assoc. attending physician Rush Presbyn. St. Luke's Hosp., Chgo., 1982-94, sr. scientist, 1994—; attending physician U. Ill. Hosp., 1995—; coord. Nat. Ctr. Advanced Med. Edn., Chgo., 1975—; cons. Cardiothoracic Ctr., Monte Carlo, Monaco, 1988—, Grant Hosp., Ill., 1968—, Masonic Hosp., 1978—; attending physician Michael Reese Hosp., 1995—; former cons. Chgo. Bd. Edn. Co-author: (books) Congenital Heart Disease Under 3 Months of Age, 1981, Pathophysiology of Intraventricular Conduction Disturbances, 1982, Tricuspid Atresia, 1982, Drug Therapy in the Neonate and Small Infant, 1985, Neonatal Therapeutics, 1991. Past chmn. subcom. on registry delinquency, rheumatic fever com. Chgo. Heart Assn., past cons. Internat. Symposium on Primary Prevention in Childhood of Atherosclerotic and Hypertensive Diseases, former mem. heart disease in young, steering com. congenital heart disease registry. Recipient Cert. of Award Meritorious Svc., Am. Heart Assn., Chgo., 1965, 86. Fellow Am. Coll. Cardiology, Am. Acad. Pediatrics, Am. Coll. Chest Physicians; mem. AMA, Am. Pediatric Soc., Am. Fedn. for Clin. Rsch., Sigma Xi. Roman Catholic. Office: Cook County Hosp 700 S Wood St Chicago IL 60612-3834

SERSTOCK, DORIS SHAY, retired microbiologist, educator, civic worker; b. Mitchell, S.D., June 13, 1926; d. Elmer Howard and Hattie (Christopher) Shay; BA, Augustana Coll., 1947; postgrad. U. Minn., 1966-67, Duke U., summer 1969, Communicable Disease Center, Atlanta, 1972; m. Ellsworth I. Serstock, Aug. 30, 1952; children: Barbara Anne, Robert Ellsworth, Mark Douglas. Bacteriologist, Civil Service, S.D., Colo., Mo., 1947-52; research bacteriologist U. Minn., 1952-53; clin. bacteriologist Dr. Lufkin's Lab., 1954-55; chief technologist St. Paul Blood Bank of ARC, 1959-65; microbiologist in charge mycology lab. VA Hosp., Mpls., 1968-93; instr. Coll. Med. Scis., U. Minn., 1970-79, asst. prof. Coll. Lab. Medicine and Pathology, 1979-93. Mem. Richfield Planning Commn., 1965-71, sec., 1968-71. Contbr. articles to profl. jours. Extended ministries commn. Wood Lake Luth. Ch., Richfield, Minn., 1993-94; rep. religious coun. Mall Am., Bloomington, Minn., 1993-94, chief nursery caregiver Christ the King Lutheran Ch., Bloomington, Minn. 1994—. Fellow Augusta Coll.; named to Exec. and Profl. Hall of Fame; recipient Alumni Achievement award Augustana Coll., 1977; Superior Performance award VA Hosp., 1978, 82, Cert. of Recognition, 1988; Golden Spore awards Mycology Observer, 1985, 87. Mem. Minn. Planning Assn. Republican. Clubs: Richfield Women's Garden (pres. 1959), Wild Flower Garden (chmn. 1961). Home: 7201 Portland Ave Minneapolis MN 55423-3218

SERVER, GREGORY DALE, state legislator, guidance counselor; b. Mpls., Jan. 27, 1939; 3 children. BA, U. Evansville, Ind., 1962; MS, Ind. State U., 1968, Ind. State U., 1970; EdS, Ind. State U., 1981. Guidance counselor Cen. High Sch., Evansville, 1976; mem. Ind. State Senate, 1973—; bd. dirs. Sta. WNIN-TV. Mem. New Harmony (Ind.) Commn. Served with USN. Mem. Edn. Commn. of States, Evansville Tchrs. Assn., VFW, Phi Delta Kappa. Republican. Methodist. Home: 5601 Spring Lake Dr Evansville IN 47710-4241

SERVIES, CAROL, academic program director; b. East Chicago, Ind., July 19, 1944; m. Richard Servies, Aug. 7, 1965; children: Scott Christopher, Tammy Elizabeth. AA in Gen. Sci., Ctrl. Ariz. Coll., 1971; BA in Clin. Psychology, Purdue U., 1982, MS in Edn., 1987. Advisor, coord. tutoring Purdue U. Calumet, Hammond, Ind., 1983-88, dir., 1988—. Picture lady Hammond Art in Action, 1990-92; vol. U.S. Peace Corps, Ghana, West Africa, 1992-94. Mem. Nat. Tutoring Assn. (chair constitution and bilaws com. 1993-), Nat. Assn. Devel. Edn., Ind. Assn. Devel. Edn. (Outstanding Svc. award 1991-92, Spin Chairperson Assessment 1993-), Midwest Profl. Assn. Coll. Testing Pers. Office: Purdue U Calumet Skills Assess & Devel Ctr Hammond IN 46323

SERVINSKI, SARAH JANE (JEROUE), language arts educator; b. Detroit, Sept. 13, 1944; d. Edward Lawrence and Frances Elizabeth (Henne) Jeroue; m. Leonard Charles Servinski, July 31, 1965; children: Charles, Mary, Michael, Katherine, Andrew. BA, Mich. State U., 1965, MA, 1978; EdS, Cen. Mich. U., 1990. Cert. tchr., adminstr., Mich. Tchr. elem. and secondary schs. Mich., 1965-80; assoc. prof. lang. arts Northwood U., Midland, Mich., 1980-90; field placement coord. Saginaw Valley State Univ./Coll. of Edn., University Center, Mich., 1991-95; owner Maple Hill Farm, Midland, Mich., 1990—; communications cons.; co-founder Maple Hill Nursery and Flowers, Midland, 1977, Maple Hill Equip. Sales and Svc., Midland, 1987; founder Maple Hill Children's Shop, Midland, 1983; adj. prof. lang. arts Delta Coll., University Center, Mich., 1990—. mem. Dow Corning Citizens Community Adv. Panel, Midland, Mich, 1991-92. Republican. Roman Catholic. Home: 2674 N Eastman Rd Midland MI 48640-8833

SERWY, ROBERT ANTHONY, accountant; b. Chgo., Mar. 26, 1950; s. Anthony J. and Bernice (Zubek) S.; m. Margaret A. Smejkal, Aug. 12, 1972; children: Karen, Steven. BS in Engring., U. Ill., 1972; M Mgmt., Northwestern U., 1974. Mgr. cons. Arthur Andersen & Co., Chgo., 1974-83; dir. fin. planning Teepak, Inc., Oak Brook, Ill., 1983-85; sr. mgr. cons. Peat Marwick & Mitchell, Chgo., 1985-86; dir. cons. Warady & Davis, Lincolnwood, Ill., 1986—. F.C. Austin scholar, 1972. Mem. AICPA, Ill. CPA Soc. Roman Catholic. Home: 721 Valley Rd Lake Forest IL 60045-2981 Office: Warady & Davis 108 Wilmot Rd Ste 500 Deerfield IL 60015

SESSLER, DONNA JEAN HOTZ, secondary education educator; b. Iowa City, May 3, 1954; d. Raymond Louis and Marie Frances (Klouda) Hotz; m. Allen Henry Sessler, Aug. 8, 1992. BA in Psychology, U. Iowa, 1975; MA in Spl. Edn., U. No. Iowa, 1981. Multicategorial resource tchr. grades 6-12 Beaman-Conrad-Liscomb Community Schs., Conrad, Iowa, 1978-84; multi-categorial resource tchr. grades 6-8 Iowa Falls (Iowa) Community Sch., 1984—. Mem. NEA, Iowa Falls Edn. Assn. (negotiations team 1988-90), Iowa Edn. Assn., Coun. for Exceptional Children, Delta Kappa Gamma (treas. 1994-96, sec. 1996—). Roman Catholic. Office: Riverbend Mid Sch 1124 Union St Iowa Falls IA 50126-1435

SESTINA, JOHN E., financial planner; b. Cleve., Mar. 17, 1942; s. John J. and Regina Sestina; BS, U. Dayton, 1965; MS in Fin. Svc., Am. Coll, 1982; m. Mary Barbara Jezek, Dec. 20, 1970; 1 child, Alison. Cert. fin. planner, chartered fin. cons. With John E. Sestina and Co., Columbus, Ohio, 1967—. Author: Complete Guide to Professional Incorporation, 1970, Managing To Be Wealthy, 1988, Fee-Only Financial Planning, How To Make It Work For You, 1991; (video tape series) Managing To Be Wealthy (4 series), 1987; contbr. articles to profl. jours.; contbr. weekly fin. planning segment AM Columbus, WOSU-AM, 1979—. Mem. Soc. Ind. Fin. Advisers (past pres., Fin. Planner of Yr. award 1982), Internat. Assn. Fin. Planners, Nat. Assn. Personal Fin. Advisors (founder, pres.), Inst. Cert. Fin. Planners, Fin. Planning Clubs Internat. (founder). Office: 7677 Tamarisk Ct Dublin OH 43017-9295

SESTRIC, ANTHONY JAMES, lawyer; b. St. Louis, June 27, 1940; s. Anton and Marie (Gasparovic) S.; student, Georgetown U., 1958-62; JD, Mo. U., 1965; m. Carol F. Bowman, Nov. 24, 1966; children: Laura Antonette, Holly Nicole, Michael Anthony. Bar: Mo. 1965, U.S. Ct. Appeals (8th cir.) 1965, U.S. Dist. Ct. Mo., 1966, U.S. Tax Ct. 1969, U.S. Supreme Ct. 1970, U.S. Ct. Appeals (7th cir.) 1984, U.S. Dist. Ct. (no. dist.) Tex. 1985, U.S. Claims Ct. 1986. U.S. Dist. Ct. Ill., 1994, Minn. 1996. Law clk. U.S. Dist. Ct., St. Louis, 1965-66; ptnr. firm Sestric, McGhee & Miller, St. Louis, 1966-77; spl. asst. to Mo. atty. gen., St. Louis, 1968; ptnr. Fordyce and Mayne, 1977-78, Sestric & Garvey, St. Louis, 1978-96, Sestric Law Firm, 1996—; hearing officer St. Louis Met. Police Dept.; active Fed. Jud. Selection Commn., 1993; bd. dirs. Marquett Learning Ctr.; gen. chmn. 22nd jud. cir. bar com., 1995. Contbr. articles to profl. jours. Mem. exec. com. Nat. Caucus of Met. Bar Leaders, 1987-90; mem. Fed. Judicial Commn., 1993, mem. St. Louis Air Pollution Bd. Appeals and Varience Rev., 1966-73, chmn., 1968-73; mem. St. Louis Airport Commn., 1975-76; dist. vice chmn. Boy Scouts Am., 1970-76; bd. dirs. Full Achievement, Inc., 1970-77; bd. dirs. Legal Aid Soc. of St. Louis, 1976-77, Law Library Assn. St. Louis, 1976-78; v.p. bd. St. Elizabeth Acad., 1985-86; bd. dirs. Thomas Dunn Memls., 1995—, Marquette Learning Ctr., 1995—; mem. U.S. Judicial Selections Commn., 1993—. Mem. ABA (state chmn. judiciary com. 1973-75, cir. chmn. com. condemnation, zoning and property use 1975-77, standing com. bar activities 1982-88), Nat. Conf. Bar Pres.'s (exec. coun. 1987-90), Mo. Bar (vice chmn. young lawyers sect. 1973-76, bd. govs. 1974-77), Bar Assn. Met. St. Louis (chmn. young lawyers sect. 1974-75, exec. com. 1974-83, 94-95, pres. 1981-82, bd. govs. 1995—). Home: 3967 Holly Hills Blvd Saint Louis MO 63116-3135 Office: Sestric & Garvey 22 Morgan St Saint Louis MO 63102-2558

SETZER, KIRK, religious leader. Pres. Amana (Iowa) Ch. Soc. Office: Amana Church Society Amana IA 52203

SETZLER, EDWARD ALLAN, lawyer; b. Kansas City, Mo., Nov. 3, 1933; s. Edward A. and Margaret (Parshall) S.; m. Helga E. Friedemann, May 20, 1972; children: Christina, Ingrid, Kirstin. BA, U. Kans., 1955; JD, U. Wis., 1962. Bar: Mo. 1962, U.S. Tax Ct. 1962. Assoc. Spencer, Fane, Britt & Browne, Kansas City, 1962-67, ptnr., 1968—, mng. ptnr., 1974-77, 78-82, chmn. trust and estate sect., 1974—; lectr. U. Mo. and Kansas City Sch. Law Continuing Edn. programs, 1983-95; mem. Jackson County Probate Manual com., 1988—; Mo. State rep. Joint Editl. Bd./Uniform Probate Code, 1989—. Co-author: Missouri Estate Administration, 1984, supplements, 1985-93; co-author, co-editor, reviewer Missouri Estate Planning, 1986, supplements, 1987-93; contbg. editor: A Will Is Not The Way -- The Living Trust Alternative, 1988; contbg. editor: Understanding Living Trusts, 1990, expanded edit., 1994; bd. editors Wis. Law Rev., 1961-62. Amb., bd. govs., bd. dirs., chmn. found. com. Am. Royal, 1982—; mem. planning giving com., bus. coun. Nelson Atkins Mus. Art, 1984—; mem. deferred giving com. Children's Mercy Hosp., 1991—; mem. Kansas City Estate Planning Symposium Com., 1984-92, chmn., 1991. Fellow Am. Coll. Trust and Estate Counsel (state chmn. 1992—); mem. ABA, Mo. Bar Assn. (lectr., vice chmn. probate and estate planning com. 1994—), Lawyers Assn. Kansas City, Kansas City Met. Bar Assn. (lectr., chmn. probate and trust 1979, 92, vice chmn. 1983-85, 91, legis. rev. com. 1991—), Estate Planning Soc. Kansas City (co-founder 1965, pres. 1983-84, dir. 1984-85, mem. social com. 1968—), Order of Coif, Sigma Chi, Phi Delta Phi. Office: Spencer Fane Britt & Browne 1000 Walnut St Ste 1400 Kansas City MO 64106-2140

SEVELAND, JOHN WALLACE, college administrator; b. Phila., Dec. 25, 1943; s. Forrest John and Helen Virginia (Muir) S.; m. Linda Jeanne Behncke, Feb. 21, 1970 (dec. Mar. 1995); children: Sean Keith, Chad Forrest. BA, George Williams Coll., 1968, MS, 1972. Admissions counselor to assoc. dir. admissions George Williams Coll., Downers Grove, Ill., 1971-76; dir. admissions Dakota Wesleyan U., Mitchell, S.D., 1976-79, dean of admissions, asst. prof. psychology, 1979-81; dir. admissions Aurora (Ill.) Coll., 1981-85, v.p. enrollment and admissions, 1985-88; v.p. enrollment and student affairs Alma (Mich.) Coll., 1988—; cons. colls. Iowa, Colo., N.C., Nebr., S.C. and Ohio, 1986—. Bd. dirs. Ill. hdqs. Mich. Act Coun., 1993-95, United Way Gratiot County, Alma, 1990—, Alma Symphony Orch., 1989-92, pres., 1991; big brother Big Brother/Big Sisters, Alma, 1993-95. Corp. USMC, 1969-70. Mem. Gratiot County Optimist Club (bd. dirs. 1992-95, v.p. 1992-94). Presbyterian. Home: 928 W Center Alma MI 48801 Office: Alma Coll Alma MI 48801

SEVERNS, PENNY L., state legislator; b. Decatur, Ill., Jan. 21, 1952. BS in Polit. Sci. and Internat. Relations, So. Ill. U., 1974. Spl. asst. to adminstr. AID, Washington, 1977-79; city councilwoman Decatur, from 1983; mem. 51st dist. Ill. State Senate, 1987—, chief budget negotiator for Senate Dems., 1993—, minority spokesperson appropriations com., 1994—. Office: Ill State Senate State Capitol Springfield IL 62706

SEVERSON, GLEN ARTHUR, circuit court judge; b. Sioux Falls, S.D., Mar. 9, 1949; s. Arthur and Muriel (O'Hara) S.; m. Mary K. Schweitzer, May 24, 1975; children: Thomas, Kathryn. BS, U. S.D., 1972, JD, 1975. Bar: S.D. 1975, U.S. Dist. Ct. S.D., 1976, U.S. Ct. Appeals (8th cir.) 1989, Minn. 1990. Dep. states atty. Beadle County, Huron, S.D., 1975-76; ptnr. Benson, Wehde, Martin & Severson, Huron, 1976-82, Fingerson, Severson & Nelson, Huron, 1982-93; cir. ct. judge Sioux Falls, 1993—; city atty. City of Huron, 1977-92; pres. S.D. Mcpl. Attys. Assn., Pierre, 1985. Bd. dirs. S.D. Bd. Water and Natural Resources, Pierre, 1986-92, Huron Area C. of C., 1983-86. Name one of Oustanding Young Men of Am., 1977. Mem. ABA, S.D. Bar Assn., Minn. Bar Assn. Roman Catholic. Office: 415 N Dakota Ave Sioux Falls SD 57102-0136

SEVERSON, WAYNE LARSON, retired physician; b. Slater, Iowa, Mar. 7, 1921; s. George James and Minnie Christina (Larson) S.; m. Dorothy Weeks, Dec. 1943 (div. 1974); children: Allan, Richard, Brenda, Kelli; m. Eyleen Bond, Aug. 1975 (dec. 1987); m. Maxine Sturdivant, Feb. 14, 1990. BS, Iowa State U., 1943; MD, U. Iowa, 1946. Intern Broadlawns Gen. Hosp., Des Moines, 1946-47; resident St. Joseph's Hosp., Flint, Mich., 1948; pvt. practice, Slater, Iowa, 1948-68; med. dir. Iowa Blue Cross Blue Shield, Des Moines, 1968-83; med. cons. Iowa Found. Med. Care, Des Moines, 1983-86; mem. med. adv. bd. Nat. Blue Cross-Blue Shield, Chgo., 1976-81, pres. bd., 1980-81. Capt. M.C., USAF, 1955-56. Mem. AMA, Am. Acad. Family Practice, Iowa Acad. Family Practice, Iowa Med. Assn., Polk County Med. Assn. Home: 1652 Rio Valley Dr Des Moines IA 50325-6541

SEWARD, JEFFREY JAMES, lawyer, protective services official, educator, administrator; b. Rochester, Pa., Aug. 21, 1953; s. Kelson Charles and Virginia Emma (McConnell) S. BA, Ohio No. U., 1975, JD, 1986; MS, U. Nebr., 1979. Bar: Iowa 1990. Security cons. North Hills Passavant Hosp., Pitts., 1975-77; state trooper Nebr. State Patrol, Omaha, 1977-84; pvt. practice law Omaha and Council Bluffs, 1986—; cons. Overland Corp., 1988-89, Fire Photo Corp., Omaha, 1980-91; instr. law enforcement State Nebr., 1979; instr. environ. law and hazardous materials Nebr. State Patrol, 1979-92, technician hazardous material, 1979-84, investigator accidents, 1978-84; adj. faculty U. Nebr., Omaha, Lincoln, Southwestern Community Coll., Iowa, Lakeland Coll., West Allis, Wis.; corp. counsel Farmers Telephone Co., 1990-93, S&M Oil Co., 1990—, Environ. Protection Instrn. Cons. Corp., 1991—, GSI-Environ. Cons. Corp., 1991—, Environ. Assessment Group, 1990—, Firstier Bank, 1990-92, Bank One Trust Co., 1992-95, Merrill Lynch Trust Co., 1995—. Law Enforcement Assistance Adminstrn. scholar, 1978-79; recipient Life Saving award Am. Heart Assn., 1982, Am. Jurisprudence award Bancroft-Whitney Co., 1986, 87. Mem ABA, Nat. Assn. Chiefs of Police, State Troopers Assn. Nebr., Peace Officers Assn. Nebr., Am. Trial Lawyers Assn., Iowa State Bar Assn., Omaha Bar Assn., Delta Theta Phi. Republican. Lutheran. Home and Office: 5683 Moorgate Dr Columbus OH 43235-2507

SEWARD, JOHN EDWARD, JR., insurance company executive; b. Kirksville, Mo., June 12, 1943; s. John Edward and Ruth Carol (Connell) S.; children: Mitch, Justina. BS in Fin., St. Joseph's Coll., 1968. CLU, CPCU, cert. profl. ins. agent; Mgr. acctg. svcs. Guarantee Res. Life Ins. Co., Hammond, Ind., 1965-69; asst. contr. Gambles Ins. Group, Mpls., 1969-71, N.Am. Cos., Chgo., 1971-73; v.p., treas. Home & Auto. Ins. Co., Chgo., 1973-75, bd. dirs., 1974-83, pres., chief exec. officer, 1975-83; pres., chief exec. officer, dir. Universal Fire & Casualty Ins. Co., 1983-88, acting chmn. bd., pres., chief exec. officer, 1988, chmn. bd., pres., chief exec. officer, 1989-92; co-founder, pres., CEO J&J Underwriting Svcs. Inc., 1992-93, chmn., CEO, 1994; v.p. Concord Gen., 1993—; pres. Classictire & Marine Ins. Co., 1994. Bd. dirs., v.p., treas., v.p. fin. Calumet Coun. Boy Scouts Am., 1981-85; mem. Shriners Hosp.-Teddy Bear Club, 1980; mem. exec. com. Chgo. Baseball Cancer Charities, 1981—; co-chmn. Ron Kittle's Ind. Sports Charities, 1989. Named to Wall of Fame, T.F. South High Sch., 1993. Fellow Life Mgmt. Inst.; mem. Ind. C. of C., Munster C. of C., Am. Biog. Inst. (dep. gov.). Home: 1124 Lisa Ln Schererville IN 46375-1183 Office: 5261 Fountain Dr Crown Point IN 46307-1089

SEWARD, STEVEN LE MAR, optometrist; b. Ft. Wayne, Ind., Oct. 26, 1946; s. George Winn and Eva (Olive) S.; children: Heidi Elaine, James Lemar; 1 child, Robert Nathaniel. AB in Math., Knox Coll., 1968; OD cum laude, Ohio State U., 1972, MS in Physiol. Optics, 1972. Cert. Ocular Disease and Treatment. Pvt. practice optometry North Manchester, Ind., 1972—; counselor Am. Dr. of Optometry, 1989—. Chmn. Task Force on Housing North Manchester Town Forum, 1989-90; bd. dirs. Wabash County United Fund, pres., 1978; mem. North Manchester Community Found., 1982-93, pres., 1985-89; mgr. Kiwanis Little League Baseball Team, 1981-83, Seward Eye Care Little League Baseball Team, 1992-93. Fellow Am. Coll. Optometric Physicians, Am. Acad. Optometry; mem. Am. Optometric Assn. (Recognition award 1980-93), Gesell Inst. Child Devel., Vol. Optometric Svcs. for Humanity, Wabash Valley Optometric Soc. (pres. 1977-78), Ind. Optometry Assn. (v.p. 1981-82, pres. 1983-84, chmn. and del. various coms., citation 1978), Coll. Optometrists Vision Devel. (assoc.), Beta Sigma Kappa. Republican. Home: 1303 Westchester Dr North Manchester IN 46962-2209 Office: Seward Eye Care Inc 1201 State Rd 114 E North Manchester IN 46962-9393

SEWELL, PHYLLIS SHAPIRO, retail chain executive; b. Cin., Dec. 26, 1930; d. Louis and Mollye (Mark) Shapiro; m. Martin Sewell, Apr. 5, 1959; 1 child, Charles Steven. B.S. in Econs. with honors, Wellesley Coll., 1952. With Federated Dept. Stores, Inc., Cin., 1952-88, research dir. store ops., 1961-65, sr. research dir., 1965-70, operating v.p., research, 1970-75, corp. v.p., 1975-79, sr. v.p., research and planning, 1979-88; bd. dirs. Lee Enterprises, Inc., Davenport, Iowa, Pitney Bowes, Inc., SYSCO Corp. Bd. dirs. Nat. Cystic Fibrosis Found., Cin., 1963—; chmn. divsn. United Appeals, Cin., 1982; mem. bus. adv. coun. Sch. Bus. Adminstrn., Miami U., Oxford, Ohio, 1982-84; trustee Cin. Cmty. Chest, 1984-94, Jewish Fedn., 1990-92, Jewish Hosp., 1990—; mem. bus. leadership coun. Wellesley Coll., 1990—, Fordham U. Grad. Sch. Bus., 1988-89. Recipient Alumnae Achievement award Wellesley Coll., 1979, Disting. Cin. Bus. and Profl. Woman award, 1981, Directors' Choice award Nat. Women's Econ. Alliance, 1995; named one of 100 Top Corp. Women Bus. Week mag., 1976, Career Woman of Achievement YWCA, 1983, to Ohio Women's Hall of Fame, 1982.

SEWELL, WILLIAM HAMILTON, JR., historian; b. Stillwater, Okla., May 15, 1940; s. William Hamilton and Elizabeth Lucille (Shogren) S.; m. Ellen Martha Wheeler, June 16, 1962; children: Jessica Ellen, Adrienne Felicity. BA, U. Wis., 1962; MA, U. Calif., 1963, PhD, 1971. Instr. of history U. Chgo., 1968-71, asst. prof. of history, 1971-75; mem. Sch. Social Sci. Inst. Advanced Study, Princeton, N.J., 1975-80; assoc. prof. of history U. Ariz., Tucson, 1980-83, prof. of history, 1983-85; dir. d'etudes associe Ecole de Hautes Etudes en Scis. Sociales, Paris, 1984, 88; prof. of history and sociology U. Mich., Ann Arbor, 1985-90; prof. polit. sci. and history U. Chgo., 1990—; mem. bd. of editors Jour. Modern History, 1984-86, French Hist. Studies, 1985-88; mem., bd. dirs. Social Sci. Rsch. Coun., N.Y.C., 1986-92; dir. Program in Comparative Study of Social Transformations, U. Mich., Ann Arbor, 1987-90, Ctr. for Rsch. Social Orgn., U. Mich., Ann Arbor, 1988-90. Author: Work and Revolution in France, 1980, Structure and Mobility, 1985, A Rhetoric of Bourgeois Revolution, 1994. Recipient Herbert Baxter Adams prize Am. Hist. Assn., 1981, William Koren Jr. prize Soc. for French Hist. Studies, 1982; grantee Nat. Sci. Found., 1972-75. Mem. Am. Hist. Assn., Soc. for French Hist. Studies, Am. Sociol. Assn., Social Sci. History Assn., Coun. for European Studies, Am. Polit. Sci. Assn. Office: U Chgo Dept Polit Sci 5828 S University Ave Chicago IL 60637-1515

SEYMOUR, RICHARD DEMING, technology educator; b. Shelby, Ohio, Oct. 3, 1955; s. G. Deming and Elizabeth (Peterson) S.; m. Vicki Stebleton. BS in Edn., Ohio State U., 1978; MA, Ball State U., 1982; EdD, W.Va. U., 1990. Tchr. Crestview Sr. High Sch., Ashland, Ohio, 1978-81; from instr. to assoc. prof. Ball State U., Muncie, Ind., 1982—; vis. instr. W.Va. U., Morgantown, 1985, Oreg. State U., 1990-91. Co-author: Exploring Communications, 1987, rev. edit., 1996; co-editor: Manufacturing in Technology Education, 1993. Advisor 4-H Clubs, Richland County, Ohio, 1978-81; dir. in-svc. workshops Ind. Dept. Edn., Indpls., 1988-93. Mem. Internat. Tech. Edn. Assn. (bd. dirs. 1992-94), Soc. Mfg. Engrs., Coun. on Tech. Tchr. Edn., Ind. Math., Sci., Tech. Alliance (bd. dirs. 1994—), Tech. Educators Ind. (pres. 1995—), Am. Soc. Engring. Edn., Tech. Edn. Collegiate Assn. (internat. advisor 1990-92), Epsilon Pi Tau, Phi Delta Kappa. Methodist. Office: Ball State U Dept Industry/Tech Muncie IN 47306

SGRO, GREGORY PETER, lawyer; b. Springfield, Ill., Dec. 24, 1961; s. Sam P. and Jeanette C. (Kieffer) S.; m. Leslie A. Cutler, Feb. 15, 1987; children: Benjamin M., Sarah M., Nicholas G. Northwestern U., 1983, Washington U., St. Louis, 1986. Bar: Ill. 1986, U.S. Dist. Ct. (cen. dist.) Ill. 1986, U.S. Supreme Ct. 1995. Pvt. practice, pvt. practice, Springfield, 1986-89; mng. ptnr. Sgro & LaMarca, Springfield, 1990—. Bd. dirs. Springfield Parks Found., 1991-96, Sangamon State U. Found., 1990, chmn., 1992-95. Mem. ABA, Assn. Trial Lawyers Am., Ill. Bar Assn., Sangamon County Bar Assn. (pres. young lawyers divsn. 1991), Sangamon County Bar Assn. (sec.-treas. 1991-93, dir. 1995-96). Office: Sgro & LaMarca 1119 S 6th St Springfield IL 62703-2405

SHAAR, H. ERIK, academic administrator. V.p. acad. affairs Shippensburg U. of Pa., until 1986; pres. Lake Superior State U., Sault Sainte Marie, Mich., 1986-92, Minot (N.D.) State U., 1992—. Office: Minot State U Office of Pres Minot ND 58707

SHABEL, DENNIS JOSEPH, printing executive; b. Chgo., Dec. 18, 1944; s. Clemens Paul and Florence Ann (Jendro) S.; m. Karen May Lind, Mar. 6, 1976; children: Jeffrey Clemens, Daniel Earl. Diploma, Gordon Tech., Chgo., 1958-62; student, Wright Jr. Coll., Chgo., 1963-64. Organizer Wallace Press, Chgo., 1962-64; printer W.F. Hall, Chgo., 1964-74; sales mgr. Consumer Co-op, Chgo., 1974-75; print mgr. Pettibone Corp., Chgo., 1974-77; bus. founder Communicate, Inc. (C.I. Printing), Westchester, Ill., 1977—; print mgr. U.S. Army, Hawaii, 1965-67; cons., troubleshooter printing equipment various small bus., 1988. Contbr. articles in field, 1972-75. Sunday sch. tchr. Grace Luth. Ch., LaGrange, Ill., 1986-87; speaker, career day presenter local schs., Westchester and Westmont, Ill.; mem. Zoning Bd. of Appeals, Village of Westmont, 1992—. Mem. Am. Youth Soccer Assn. (coach 1986-87), Better Bus. Bur. Chgo., Chgo. Zool. Soc., Nat. Geographic Soc., Westchester C. of C. (bd. dirs., v.p., parade chmn. 1978-82). Office: CI Printing 10407 W Cermak Rd Westchester IL 60154-5211

SHACKELFORD, MARTIN ROBERT, social worker; b. Boonville, Mo., May 22, 1947; s. Hugh and Carol Lois (Schoene) S. BA in History, U. Mich., 1969. Driver Yellow Cab, Saginaw, Mich., 1969-70; sales clk. Waldenbooks, Saginaw, Mich., 1972; eligibility worker Saginaw County Dept. Social Svcs., 1972-73, employment worker, 1973-77, delinquency svcs. worker, 1977—; charter mem. social work adv. com. Saginaw Valley State U., 1981—. Contbr. articles on JFK assassination to profl. jours. Bd. dirs. Valley Film Soc., Saginaw, 1978—, ACLU, Cen. Mich. Br., 1978—; vice chmn. Lone Tree Coun. Home: 216 N Webster St # 2 Saginaw MI 48602-4243

SHACKLETON, MARY JANE, small business owner; b. Colorado Springs, Colo., Oct. 20, 1934; d. James Emrie and Thelma Isabella (Vittetoe) Mc Carty; m. William H. Shackleton, Apr. 25, 1953; children: Denise, Dennis, Danette, Donna, Donald. Grad. high sch., Montebello, Calif. Owner Chi Town/Radio Shack, Oscoda, Mich., 1978—, East Tawas, Mich., 1983—. Bd. dirs. Oscoda Downtown Devel. Authority. Mem. Toastmasters (competent, sec. Lake Huron chpt. 1988-89, sec.-treas. 1991-92), Oscoda C. of C. (bd. dirs. 1985-90), Oscoda Mchts. Assn. (sec.-treas.), Quota Club Iosco (bd. dirs. 1990-91). Republican. Roman Catholic. Home: 3852 N Huron Rd Oscoda MI 48750-9480

SHADID, GEORGE P., state legislator; b. Clinton, Iowa, May 15, 1929; m. Lorraine; two children. Sheriff Peoria County, Ill., 1976-93; mem. Ill. State Senate Dist. 46, 1993—, mem. judiciary, higher edn. and exec. appts. coms.

SHADLE, DONNA A. FRANCIS, principal; b. Canton, Ohio, Oct. 29, 1944; d. Gerald W. and Virginia M. (Kerker) Francis; m. Joseph E. Shadle, Apr. 24, 1965; children: Joseph, Paul, Ann, Mary. Student, Walsh Coll., 1964; BS in Edn., Kent State U., 1980, MS in Edn., 1989. Cert. early childhood, kindergarten, elementary edn., Ohio. Tchr. grade 4 St. Joseph's Elem., Canton, Ohio, 1964-65; dir., adminstr. Community Pre-sch., Canton, 1969-79; substitute tchr., K-8 Diocese of Youngstown, Canton, 1965-80; tchr. kindergarten St. Paul's Elem., North Canton, Ohio, 1980-95; prin. Sacred Heart of Mary Elem. Sch., Harrisburg, Ohio, 1995—; reading pubs. cons.; tchr. rep. Home & Sch. Assn., North Canton, 1985; tech. com., 1992—; dir. drama Ctrl. Cath. H.S., Canton, 1987—; workshop presenter various ednl. conventions, 1989—; adv. bd. ADD Partnership of Ohio, North Canton, 1992—; invited to participate in various dept. projects Ohio State Dept. Edn.; cons. Sadlier Pub. editor, pub. (newsletter) KinderKindlings, 1989—, pub. cons., 1994. Troop Leader Girl Scouts Am.,

North Canton, 1977-93; dir. Mime Easter drama, North Canton, 1983-89; vol. United Way, March of Dimes, Heart Fund Canton, Canton, 1965—. Recipient spl. recognition award for Ohio Tchr. of Yr. Ashland Oil, 1989. Mem. ASCD, Assn. Childhood Edn. Internat., Nat. Assn. Edn. Young Children, Nat. Cath. Ednl. Assn., Ohio Assn. Edn. Young Children, Canton Area Assn. Edn. Young Children. Home: 5544 Frazer Ave NW North Canton OH 44720-4040 Office: Sacred Heart of Mary 8276 Nickel Plate Ave NE Louisville OH 44641

SHAFER, RANDALL WILLIAM, home health nurse; b. Springfield, Mo., Feb. 1, 1953; s. Ralph James and Lola Mae (Nall) S.; m. Susan Mary Bianco, June 21, 1980; children: Jonathan Randall, Harrison James. BS in Edn., U. Mo., 1975; MS in Counseling, Troy State U., 1978; Diploma in Nursing, St. Lukes Sch. Nursing, Kansas City, Mo., 1984. Psychiat. team leader Rsch. Med. Ctr., Kansas City, 1984-85; oncology staff nurse Trinity Luth. Hosp., Kansas City, 1985-88; home health nurse Kimberly Quality Care, Leavenworth, Kans., 1988-91, Clinicare, Kansas City, Kans., 1992-94; adminstr. McCurry's Cmty. Health Svcs., Kansas City, 1995—. With USN, 1976-78. Office: McCurrys Cmty Health Svcs 1021 N 7th St Kansas City KS 66101

SHAFFER, PAUL E., retired banker; b. Rockford, Ohio, Aug. 3, 1926; s. Randall J. and Zelah V. (Alspaugh) S.; m. Dorothy L. Schumm, June 26, 1951; children: Paula Kay, Patti Lee. Grad., U. Wis. Sch. Banking, 1954; cert., Am. Inst. Banking; DHL (hon.), Purdue U., 1985. With Rockford Nat. Bank, 1945-48; asst. nat. bank examiner Treasury Dept., 1948-52; with Ft. Wayne (Ind.) Nat. Bank, 1952-65, from exec. v.p. to vice-chmn., 1965-93, chmn. emeritus, 1993-95, ret., 1995; ret., 1996; bd. dirs. Old First Nat. Bank, Bluffton, Ind. Pres. Downtown Fort Wayne Assn., 1965, Credit Bur., Fort Wayne, 1962, Jr. Achievement, 1967-69; treas. Fort Wayne Better Bus. Bur., 1968, Ind.-Purdue Devel. Fund; mem. regional adv. com. Comptroller Currency, 1968-70; commr. Ft. Wayne Conv. and Tourism Authority.; past bd. dirs. Fort Wayne Conv. Bur., Fort Wayne Philharmonic Orch., Parkview Meml. Hosp.; bd. dirs. Caylor-Nickel Hosp., Ft. Wayne campus Ind. U., Ind.-Purdue Found., Taxpayers Research Assn.; past bd. dirs. United Community Services, chmn. drive, 1970-71; past bd. dirs. Fort Wayne YMCA, v.p., 1964-67; bd. adviser Ind. U.-Purdue U., Ft. Wayne; mem. fin. adv. bd. Luth. Social Services; bd. govs. Assn. Colls. Ind.; chmn. vol. com. U.S. Savs. Bonds, Allen County, Ind., numerous other civic activities. Served with USAAF, 1945. Mem. Am. Inst. Banking (past pres. Ft. Wayne chpt.), Am. Bankers Assn. (governing coun. 1978-79), Ind. Bankers Assn. (past pres., bd. dirs.), Ft. Wayne C. of C. (past v.p., bd. dirs.), Ind. C. of C. (state dir.), Execs. Club (past pres.), Ft. Wayne Country Club, Summit Club, Quest Club, Ft. Wayne Press Club, Mad Anthonys Club, Sycamore Hills Country Club, Masons, Shriners. Home: 11132 Carnoustie Ln Fort Wayne IN 46804-9014

SHAFFER, STEVE J., control engineer manager; b. Toledo, Nov. 26, 1961. AD, U. Toledo, 1985. Design engr. tech. Kaufman Co., Toledo, 1981-87; controls engr. mgr. Automatic Handling Inc., Erie, 1987—. Office: Automatic Handling Corp 360 La Voy Rd Erie MI 48133-9638

SHAH, JAMES M., actuarial consultant; b. Amadhara, India, Feb. 4, 1943; came to U.S., 1980; s. Manekchand Keshrichand and Kamuben Manekchand Shah S.; m. Urmila Jashwantlal Shah, May 16, 1966; children: Meeta, Keena, Jatin. BS, Gujarat U., India, 1965; MS, Gujarat U., 1969; MA, Georgetown U., 1983; MS, U. Nebr., 1986. Sr. rsch. asst. Nat. Inst. Rural Devel., Hyderabad, India, 1972-74; rsch. officer Population Ctr. World Bank Population Project, Bangalore, India, 1974-77; actuarial analyst Shelby (Ohio) Ins. Co., 1987-90; actuary ins. dept. State of N.D., Bismarck, 1990-91; pres. A S D Consulting Svcs., Mansfield, Ohio, 1991—. Contbr. articles to profl. jours. UN fellow Ministry of Fgn. Affairs, 1978; recipient Outstanding Young Person award Garden City Jaycees, 1977, 7th Summer Seminar award U. Hawaii, 1976. Mem. Internat. Union for Sci. Study of Population, Soc. Actuaries (cert. 1994), Am. Acad. Actuaries (cert. 1994). Home: 3381 Clearview Ave Columbus OH 43221-1623 Office: A S D Consulting Svcs 91 S Ireland Blvd Mansfield OH 44906-2220

SHAH, SURENDRA POONAMCHAND, engineering educator, researcher; b. Bombay, Aug. 30, 1936; s. Poonamchand C. and Maniben (Modi) S.; m. Dorothie Crispell, June 9, 1962; children: Daniel S., Byron C. BE, B.V.M. Coll. Engring., India, 1959; MS, Lehigh U., 1960; PhD, Cornell U., 1965. Asst. prof. U. Ill., Chgo., 1966-69, assoc. prof., 1969-73, prof., 1973-81; prof. civil engring Northwestern U., Evanston, Ill., 1981—, dir. Ctr. for Concrete and Geomaterials, 1987—; dir. NSF Sci. and Tech. Ctr. for Advanced Cement-Based Materials Northwestern U., 1989—, Walter P. Murphy prof. of engring., 1992—; cons. govt. agys. and industry, U.S.A., UN, France, Switzerland, People's Republic China, Denmark, The Netherlands; vis. prof. MIT, 1969, Delft U., The Netherlands, 1976, Denmark Tech. U., 1984, LCPC, Paris, 1986, U. Sidney, Australia, 1987; NATO vis. sci. Turkey, 1992. Co-author: Fiber Reinforced Cement Composites, 1992, High Performance Concrete and Applications, 1994, Fracture Mechanics of Concrete, 1995; contbr. more than 400 articles to profl. jours.; editor 12 books; mem. editorial bds. 4 internat. jours.; editor-in-chief Jour. Advanced Based Materials. Recipient Thompson award ASTM, Phila., 1983, Disting. U.S. Vis. Scientist awrd Alexander von Humboldt Found., 1989, Swedish Concrete award, Stockholm, 1993, Engring. News Record award of Newsmaker, 1995. Fellow Am. Concrete Inst. (chmn. tech. com., Anderson award 1989), Internat. Union Testing and Rsch. Labs. Materials and Structures (chmn. tech. com. 1989—, Gold medal 1980); mem. ASCE (past chmn. tech. com., mem. exec. com.). Home: 921 Isabella St Evanston IL 60201-1773 Office: Northwestern U Tech Inst Rm A130 2145 Sheridan Rd Evanston IL 60208-0834

SHALALA, DONNA EDNA, federal official, political scientist, educator, university chancellor; b. Cleve., Feb. 14, 1941; d. James Abraham and Edna (Smith) S. AB, Western Coll., 1962; MSSC, Syracuse U., 1968, PhD, 1970; 16 hon degrees, 1981-91. Vol. Peace Corps, Iran, 1962-64; asst. to dir. met. studies program Syracuse U., 1965-69; instr. asst. to dean Syracuse U. (Maxwell Grad. Sch.), 1969-70; asst. prof. polit. sci. CUNY, 1970-72; assoc. prof. politics and edn. Tchrs. Coll. Columbia U., 1972-79; asst. sec. for policy devel. and research HUD, Washington, 1977-80; prof. polit. sci., pres. Hunter Coll., CUNY, 1980-88; prof. polit. sci., chancellor U. Wis., Madison, 1988-93; sec. Dept. HHS, Washington, 1993—. Author: Neighborhood Governance, 1971, The City and the Constitution, 1972, The Property Tax and the Voters, 1973, The Decentralization Approach, 1974. Bd. govs. Am. Stock Exch., 1981-87; trustee TIAA, 1985-89, Com. Econ. Devel., 1981-93; bd. dirs. Inst. Internat. Econs., 1981-93, Children's Def. Fund, 1980-93, Am. Ditchley Found., 1981-93, Spencer Found., 1988-93, M&I Bank of Madison, 1991-93, NCAA Found., 1991; mem. Trilateral Commn., 1988-93, Knight Commn. on Intercollegiate Sports, 1990-93; trustee Brookings Inst., 1989-93. Ohio Newspaper Women's scholar, 1958, Western Coll. Trustee scholar, 1958-62; Carnegie fellow, 1966-68; Nat. Acad. Edn. Spencer fellow, 1972-73; Guggenheim fellow, 1975-76; recipient Disting. Svc. medal Columbia U. Tchrs. Coll., 1989. Mem. ASPA, Am. Polit. Sci. Assn., Nat. Acad. Arts & Scis., Nat. Acad. Pub. Adminstrn., Coun. Fgn. Rels., Nat. Acad. Edn., Nat. Acad. Arts and Scis. Office: Dept Health and Human Svcs Office of Sec 200 Independence Ave SW Rm 615F Washington DC 20201-0004

SHALLENBURGER, TIM, state legislator; m. Linda N. Shallenburger. Rep. dist. 1 State of Kans. Republican. Home: 2027 Fairview Ave Baxter Springs KS 66713-2264*

SHANAFIELD, HAROLD ARTHUR, educator; b. South Bend, Ind., Nov. 26, 1912; s. Harry Bacon and Anna (Paulsen) S.; m. Margaret Ann Goodman, Nov. 23, 1939; 1 child, Harold A. BA, U. Notre Dame; MSJ, MA, Northwestern U.; MEd, Chgo. State U. Copy editor Chgo. Herald Am., 1945-46; night picture editor Chgo. Sun-Times, 1946-47; mng. editor Elec. Dealer, Chgo., 1947-52; editor, mgr. Florists' Transworld Delivery News, Detroit, 1952-61; asst. mng. editor AMA Jour., Chgo., 1961-62; asst. dean Northwestern U., Chgo.-Evanston campus, evening divs., 1962-73; with Chgo. Bd. Edn., 1973—. Editor-in-chief news bull. Retired Tchrs. Assn. Chgo., 1984—; Vice chmn., bd. visitors Freedoms Found. at Valley Forge. Served to capt. USCG, 1945—. Bd. dirs. Ret. Tchrs. Assn. Chgo., Northwestern U. and Alumni Coun., Am. Bus. Writing Assn., Assn. Evening Univs., Quill and Scroll (lifetime faculty mem.), Nat. Sojourners (pres. Chgo. chpt. 1971), Ind. Soc. Chgo. (resident v.p. 1975—), U.S. Coast Guard League (nat. comdr. 1954-55, 59-60, Res. Officers Assn., Am. Legion, Mol. Order of World Wars, Masons (33 degree, editor Scottish Rite mag. 1973—, meritorious svc. award 1986, St. John's conclave, red cross of Constantine, 1989, knight of the York rite cross of honor, 1991, Sovereign Grand Insp. Gen. 33rd degree, 1992— hon. mem. Scottish Rite Supreme Coun. 1992—), Shriners (pres. 1970, editor Medinah Temple mag. 1987-91), KT (comdr. 1981), Societas Rosicruciana Civitatibus Foederatis, Chgo. Press Club, Chgo. Headline Club, Star Craft Club of Ill. (sec. 1972-77, pres. 1977-78), SAR (Ft. Dearborn chpt.), Delta Mu Delta, Phi Chi Theta, Delta Sigma Pi, Sigma Delta Chi, Iota Sigma Epsilon. Home: 2515 Marcy Ave Evanston IL 60201-1111

SHANAHAN, ROBERT E., plastic surgeon; b. Charleuoix, Mich., Feb. 21, 1931; s. Edward Kim and Phila Averill (Armstrong) S.; m. Mary Lou Moss, June 26, 1954; children: Patrick Q., Mary Kim, Edward L., Robert H., Kathleen A. BS, U. Mich., 1954, MD, 1958. Diplomate Am. Bd. Plastic Surgery, Am. Bd. Surgery. Staff surgeon Burns Clinic, Petoskey, Mich., 1963-74; resident plastic surgery Med. Coll. Wis., Milw., 1974-76; staff plastic surgeon Burns Clinic, 1976-81; clin. assoc. prof. surgery Med. Coll. Ohio, Toledo, 1982—; pvt. practice plastic surgery, Toledo, 1982—. Edtl. adv. bd. Internat. Dictionary Medicine & Biology, 1981-82. Mem. AMA, ACS, Am. Soc. Plastic & Reconstructive Surgery, Am. Fedn. Musicians. Home: 5945 Barkwood Ln Sylvania OH 43560-2213

SHANAHAN, THOMAS M., judge; b. Omaha, May 5, 1934; m. Jane Estelle Lodge, Aug. 4, 1956; children: Catherine Shanahan Trofholz, Thomas M. II, Mary Elizabeth, Timothy F. A.B. magna cum laude, U. Notre Dame, 1956; J.D., Georgetown U., 1959. Bar: Nebr., Wyo. Mem. McGinley, Lane, Mueller, Shanahan, O'Donnell & Merritt, Ogallala, Nebr.; assoc. justice Nebr. Supreme Ct., Lincoln, 1983-93; judge U.S. Dist. Ct. Nebr., Omaha, 1993—. Office: US Dist Ct PO Box 457 Omaha NE 68101-0457

SHANE, SANDRA KULI, postal service administrator; b. Akron, Ohio, Dec. 12, 1939; d. Amiel M. and Margaret E. (Brady) Kuli; m. Fred Shane, May 30, 1962 (div. 1972); 1 child, Mark Richard; m. Byrl William Campbell, Apr. 26, 1981 (dec. 1984). BA, U. Akron, 1987, postgrad., 1988-90. Scheduler motor vehicle bur. Akron Police Dept., 1959-62; flight and ops. control staff Escort Air, Inc., Akron and Cleve., 1972-78; asst. traffic mgr. Keen Transport, Inc., Hudson, Ohio, 1978-83; mem. ops. and mktg. staff Shawnee Airways and Essco, Akron, 1983-86; in distbn. U.S. Postal Svc., Akron, 1986—; rec. sec. Affirmative Action Coun., Akron, 1988-90. Asst. art tchr. Akron Art Mus., 1979; counselor Support, Inc., Akron, 1983-84; com. chmn. Explorer post Boy Scouts Am., Akron, 1984-85. Mem. Bus. and Profl. Women's Assn. (pres.), Delta Nu Alpha. Democrat. Roman Catholic. Home: 455 E Bath Rd Cuyahoga Falls OH 44223-2511

SHANKEL, DELBERT MERRILL, microbiology and biology educator; b. Plainview, Nebr., Aug. 4, 1927; s. Cecil Wilfred and Gladys Dalton (Dodd) S.; m. Carol Jo Mulford, Sept. 10, 1962; children: Merrill, Jill, Kelley. BA, Walla Walla Coll., 1950; PhD, U. Tex., 1959. Tchr. Walla Walla Coll. Acad., College Place, Wash., 1950-51; instr. San Antonio Coll., 1954-55; asst. prof., assoc. prof. microbiology and biology U. Kans., Lawrence, 1959-68, prof., 1968—, asst. dean, assoc. dean arts and sci., 1966-72, acting dean, 1973, exec. vice chancellor, 1974-80, 86, 90-92, acting chancellor, 1980-81, chancellor, 1994-95, prof. and cancellor emeritus, 1996; cons., evaluator, commr. North Cen. Assn. Colls. and Schs., Chgo., 1969-96. Editor: (conf. procs.) Antimutagenesis and Anticarcinogenesis: Mechanisms, Vols. 1-3, 1986, 89, 93; assoc. editor Mutation Rsch. Active numerous civic orgns. With U.S. Army, 1952-54. Named Outstanding Educator award Mortar Bd., U. Kans., 1982, 85, 90, Disting. Alumnus of Yr., Walla Walla Coll., 1989; recipient numerous grants for sci. rsch. Fellow Am. Acad. Microbiology; mem. Am. Soc. for Microbiology (past chmn. edn. com., mem., chmn. numerous coms.), Environ. Mutagen Soc. (chmn. pub. policy com. 1991-93, mem., chmn. numerous coms.), Genetics Soc. Am., Soc. Gen. Microbiology (Gt. Britain), Radiation Rsch. Soc., Sigma Xi (pres. U. Kans. chpt. 1967). Republican. Unitarian. Office: U Kans 7035 Haworth Hall Lawrence KS 66045

SHANNON, JAMES NEIL, educator; b. St. Louis, Feb. 5, 1954; s. Lawrence James and Clair Gay (Cox) S.; m. Denise Dawn Braim, Apr. 24, 1974 (div. Mar. 1993); children: Kristen Marie, Ryan Michael, Kelleen Ann; m. Michele Gould, May 24, 1993. Degree in Nuclear Engring., NTC Bainbridge, Md., 1974. Enlisted USN, 1978; naval nuclear power instr. USN, Ballston Spa, N.Y., 1978-84; EDEA USS submarines USN, San Diego, 1984-93; tng. mgr. APTUS Environ. Svcs., Coffeyville, Kans., 1993—; adv. bd. hazardoux material Coffeyville (Kans.) C.C., 1993—, adv. bd. adult edn., 1993—. Mem. Lions Club, Coffeyville Cmty. Theatre (best new actor 1994). Home: 516 N 5th Independence KS 67301 Office: APTUS Environ Svcs Inc PO Box 1328 Coffeyville KS 67337

SHANNON, WILLIAM NORMAN, III, marketing and international business educator, food service executive; b. Chgo., Nov. 20, 1937; s. William Norman Jr. and Lee (Lewis) S.; m. Bernice Urbanowicz, July 14, 1962; children: Kathleen Kelly, Colleen Patricia, Kerrie Ann. BS in Indsl. Mgmt., Carnegie Inst. Tech., 1959; MBA in Mktg. Mgmt., U. Toledo, 1963. Sales engr. Westinghouse Electric Co., Detroit, 1959-64; regional mgr. Toledo Scale, Chgo., 1964-70; v.p. J. Lloyd Johnson Assoc., Northbrook, Ill., 1970-72; mgr. spl. projects Hobart Mfg., Troy, Ohio, 1972-74; corp. v.p. mktg. Berkel, Inc., La Porte, Ind., 1974-79; gen. mgr. Berkel Products, Ltd., Toronto, Can., 1975-78; chmn. Avant Industries, Inc., Wheeling, Ill., 1979-81; chmn., pres. Hacienda Mexican Restaurants, South Bend, Ind., 1978—; chmn. Ziker Shannon Corp., South Bend, 1982-88, Hacienda Franchising Group, Inc., South Bend, Ind., 1987—; assoc. prof. mktg. and internat. bus. St. Mary's Coll., Notre Dame, Ind., 1982—; chmn. Hacienda Franchise Group, Inc., 1987—, Hacienda Mex. Restaurants Mgmt., Inc., 1994—; mem. London program faculty, 1986, 89, 92, 94, coord. internat. bus. curriculum, 1989—, mktg. curriculum, 1983, 88, 95—; advisor Coun. Internat. Bus. Devel., Notre Dame, 1991—; mng. dir. Alden & Torch Lake Railway, 1995—. Co-author: Laboratory Computers, 1971; columnist small bus. Bus. Digest mag., 1988—; bd. editors Jour. Bus. and Indsl. Mktg., 1986—; mem. bd. editorial advisors South Bend Tribune Business Weekly, 1990—; contbr. articles to profl. jours. V.p. mktg. Jr. Achievement, South Bend, Ind., 1987-90; pres. Small Bus. Devel. Coun., South Bend., 1987-90; bd. dirs. Ind. Small Bus. Coun., Indpls., 1986—, Mental Health Assn., South Bend, 1987-90, Michiana World Trade Orgn., Internat. Bus. Edn., 1989-91; Entrepreneurs Alliance Ind., 1988-92, Nat. Small Bus. United, Washington, 1989-92, Women's Bus. Initiative, 1986-90, dir. ednl. confs., 1986-90; chmn. bd. trustees, Holy Cross Coll., Notre Dame, Ind., 1987—, chmn. edn. com., 1993—; chmn. St. Joseph County Higher Edn. Coun., 1988-91, Nat. Coun. Small Bus., Washington, 1988—; Midwest region adv. coun. U.S. SBA, 1988-91; at-large mem. U.S. Govt. Adv. Coun. on Small Bus., Washington, 1988-90, 1994—, chmn. Bus. and Econ. Devel. Com., 1988-90, 1994—; vice chmn. Internat. Trade Com., 1994—; mem. nat. adv. coun. Women's Network for Entrepreneur Tng., 1991—; mem., vice chmn. State of Ind. Enterprise Zone Bd., 1991—; elected del. White House Conf. Small Bus., Washington, 1986; bd. dirs. Ind. Small Bus. Devel. Ctrs. Adv. Bd. Named Small Bus. Person of the Yr., City of South Bend, 1987, Small Bus. Advocate of the Yr., State of Ind., 1987, Ind. Entrepreneur Advocate of the Yr., 1988. Mem. Am. Mktg. Assn. (chmn. Mich./Ind. chpt., pres. 1985-86), U.S. Assn. Small Bus. and Entrepreneurship (nat. v.p. for entrepreneurship edn. 1991-92, nat. v.p. entrepreneurship devel. 1992—), Ind. Inst. New Bus. Ventures (mktg. faculty 1987-91), Michiana Investment Network (vice chmn. 1988-91), SBA (adminstrn. adv. coun. 1988—, contbg. editor Our Town Michiana mag. 1988-91), U.S. C. of C., Nat. Coun. Small Bus. (Washington), South Bend C. of C. (bd. dirs. 1987—, vice chmn. membership 1993—), Assn. for Bus. Communications (co-chmn. Internat. Conf. 1986), Univ. Club Notre Dame (vice chmn.), Shamrock Club Notre Dame (exec. dir., trustee 1993—), Rotary. Roman Catholic. Home: 2920 S Twyckenham Dr South Bend IN 46614-2116 Office: Saint Mary's Coll Dept Bus Adminstrn Eco Notre Dame IN 46556

SHAPERO, JAMES ALLEN, psychiatrist; b. Cleve., Oct. 31, 1943. BA, Washington and Jefferson Coll., 1965; MD, Ohio State U., 1969. Diplomate Am. Bd. Psychiatry and Neurology. Intern Cleve. Met. Gen. Hosp., 1969-70; resident dept. psychiatry U. Mich. Hosp., Ann Arbor, 1970-73; chief resident in psychiatry U. Mich., Ann Arbor, 1972-73; asst. prof. U. Mo., Columbia, 1975-77; pvt. practice Columbia, 1978-93; cons. Ellis Fischel State Cancer Hosp., 1981-91; staff physician Boone Hosp. Ctr., 1978—, Columbia Regional Hosp., 1978—. Maj. U.S. Army, 1973-75. Mem. AMA, Am. Psychiat. Assn.

SHAPIRO, HERBERT, history educator; b. Jamaica, N.Y., June 14, 1929; s. Max and Sophie (Mirkin) S.; m. Judith Lee Stock, Feb. 3, 1957; children: Mark Steven, Nina Ellen. BA, Queens Coll., 1952; MA, Columbia U., 1958; PhD, U. Rochester, 1964. Instr., asst. prof. Morehouse Coll., Atlanta, 1962-66; asst. prof. U. Cin., 1966-71, assoc. prof., 1971-88, prof., 1988—; faculty rep. U. Cin. Bd. of Trustees, 1985-87; fellow W.E.B. DuBois Inst., Harvard U., 1990-91. Author: White Violence and Black Response, 1988; editor: Muckraking and American Society, 1968, The World of Lincoln Steffens, 1962; co-editor: Black Americans and American Communism, 1991, Autobiography of Rose Pastor Stokes, 1992; co-editor: Northern Labor and Antislavery: A Documentary History, 1994, Culture Gender, Race and U.S. Labor History, 1993; contbr. numerous articles to profl. jours. Home: 3990 Beechwood Ave Cincinnati OH 45229-1408 Office: U Cincinnati Cincinnati OH 45221

SHAPIRO, RICHARD CHARLES, sales and marketing executive; b. Bklyn., May 28, 1936; s. Isidore and Sylvia (Rappaport) S.; m. Marilyn Joyce Bialy, Feb. 17, 1957 (div. 1974); children: Joseph, Scott; m. Francine L. Shaw, Sept. 19, 1975. BS in Edn., Golden State U., 1978, MBA, 1981; PhD in Bus. Adminstrn., Honolulu U., 1987. Lic. real estate broker, Ill. Affiliate Effective Motivation Assocs./Success Motivation inst., Bethpage, N.Y., 1965-68; v.p. sales Field Enterprises, Chgo., 1962-78; pres., CEO Snack-In, Inc., Detroit, 1978-82; sr. ptnr. Directions Growth and Strategy Cons., Chgo., 1982-95; CEO America's Home Detailing Corp., 1995—; v.p. domestic & internat. mktg. & sales Ency., oper. officer Ency. Brit.-Compton's Learning Co., 1991-93, specialist network mktg. & relationship mktg., pres., bd. dirs.; CEO Am.'s Home Detailing Corp., 1995, 1995—; pres., COO Am.'s Deep Clean Divsn., Deerfield, Ill., 1995—; instr. planning Life Underwriter Tng. Coun., L.I., 1965-66; assoc. editor Media Technics Pub. Assn., Lake Forest, 1988; bd. dirs. Master Deep Clean Co., Nat. Video Libr.; spkr. on mktg., sales and leadership. Author various self-improvement cassettes; contbr. articles to profl. jours. Active Explorers, high schs., youth clubs, 1965-74; founder, pres. Abundance and Goodwill Soc., 1968—. Served with USAF, 1957-60. Recipient Leadership award Am. Sales Masters, 1968; named Sales/Mktg. Execs. Leadership Recruiter/Trainer of Decade award. Mem. Salesmen With a Purpose, Chgo. Computer Soc., Effective Motivation Assocs.

SHAPIRO, ROBERT DONALD, management consultant; b. Milw., Sept. 11, 1942; s. Leonard Samuel and Adeline Ruth (Arnovitz) S.; m. Karen Jean Hubert, Apr. 14, 1979; children: Lee Evan, Stacy Ellen, Jenifer Erin, Tracy Elizabeth, Jeffrey Eric. BS with honors, U. Wis., 1964. CLU. Cons. actuary Milliman & Robertson, Inc., Milw., 1965-80; dir. Life Ins. Cons., TPF&C, Milw., 1980-85; mng. dir. Merrill Lynch Capital Markets, Milw., 1986-87; pres. The Shapiro Network, Inc., 1987—; bd. dirs. John Deere Ins. Group, First Colony Corp., Pacific Ins. Conf. Contbr. articles to profl. lit. Fellow Am. Soc. Actuaries (bd. dirs.); mem. Am. Acad. Actuaries (conf. actuaries in pub. practice, Pacific ins. conf.), Internat. Actuarial Assn. Home: 4923 N Oakland Ave Milwaukee WI 53217-6052 Office: 312 E Wisconsin Ave Ste 700 Milwaukee WI 53202-4305

SHAR, BRIAN DOMINIC, product engineer; b. Salem, Ohio, Mar. 21, 1971. BS in Engring. Physics, John Carroll U., 1993; Assoc. Pharmacy Tech, U.S. Army Am Acad. Health Sci., 1993. Product engr. Alphabet Inc., Warren, Ohio, 1994—. Tchr. catechist St. Patrick Cath. Ch., Leetonia, Ohio, 1995. Specialist USAR, 1991-95. Mem. Soc. Automotive Engring. Roman Catholic. Office: Alphabet Inc 8700 E Market St Warren OH 44484-2340

SHARBONEAU, LORNA ROSINA, artist, educator, author, poet, illustrator; b. Spokane, Wash., Apr. 5, 1935; d. Stephen Charles Martin and Midgie Montana (Hartzel) Barton; m. Thomas Edward Sharboneau, Jan. 22, 1970; children: Curtis, Carmen, Chet, Cra, Joseph. AA in Arts, Delta Coll., 1986; studies with Steve Lesnick, Las Vegas, Nev.; studies with Bette Myers/Zimmerman, Phoenix and Bonners Ferry, Idaho. Prin. Sharboneau's Art Gallery, Spokane, 1977-80; tchr. art Michell's Art Gallery, Spokane, 1978-79; art therapist Vellencino Sch. Dist., Calif., 1981-83; ind. artist Lind, Wash., 1948—; dir., producer, stage designer Ch. of Jesus Christ of LDS, San Jose, Sonora, Modesto, Calif., 1978 (1st. place road show San Jose); dir. Sharboneau's Art Show, Spokane, 1979, Hands On-Yr. of the Child; platform spkr., poet, fundraiser, libr., 1984-87; asst., apprentice to Prof. Rowland Cheney, Delta Coll., Stockton, Calif., 1985, 86, 87; demonstrated drip oil technique, Bonners Ferry, Idaho, Spokane, Wash., Stockton, Calif., Delta Coll. Author, illustrator: Through the Eyes of the Turtle Tree, The One-Armed Christmas Tree, The Price of Freedom, William Will, Bill Can, Song of the Turtle Tree, Chet's Ottle-Bottle: The Unbreakable Bottle, One Drop of Water and a Grain of Sand; poet; prolific artist completed over 4000 paintings and drawings, displayed works in galleries through western states; featured in Magnolia News, Seattle, Delta Coll. Impact, Stockton, Calif., Stockton Record, Union Democrat, Sonora, Calif., Lincoln Center Chronicle, Stockton, Calif., Spokesman Rev., Spokane, Wash., Modesto (Calif) Bee, Angels Camp, Calif., Union Democrat, Sonora, Calif., New-Letter, Ch. of Jesus Christ of L.D.S 1st ward, Sonora; artist mixed media, oil, drip oil works, sculptures, pastel, watercolor; illustrations pen and ink, acrylic; sculptor bronze, lost wax method, ceramic art, soap stone, egg-tempra, original techniques, collage, variation on a theme. Dir., programmer, fundraiser Shelter Their Sorrows, Sonora, Calif., 1989-92, vol. Community Action Agency and Homeless Shelter. Recipient Golden Rule award J.C. penny, 1991, Recognition award Pres. George Bush, cert. Spl. Congl. Recognition Congressman Richard H. Lehman, 3rd Pl. Best Show East Valley ARtists/Pala Show, 1973, 74, 75, 3d Pl. Artist of Yr., 1974, Valley Fair, Santa Clara, Calif., 1974, 1st and 2d Pl. Spokane County Fair, 1978, 3 honorable mentions, 4 premiums, 1979, 3 1st Pl., 3 2d Pl., 2 3rd Pl., honorable mention Calaveras County Fair/Angels Camp, Calif., 1983, 1st and 3rd Pl. Unitarian Art Festival, Stockton, Calif., 1984, 2d Pl., 1985, 3d Pl., 1986, 1st Pl. Lodi Art Ann., 1985, 3rd Pl., 1986, 1st Pl. 1987, 1st Pl., 1988, honorable mention SJCAC Junque Art Show, Stockton, 1985, 1st Pl Ctrl. Calif. Art League, Modesto, 1986, 88, 2d Pl. 1995; 3d Pl. Camilla Art Show, San Jose, Calif., 1974, and numerous others; 1st, 2d, and 3d Pl., Spokane County Fair, 1978; 4 honorable mentions, Sonora, Calif., 1993, 2nd Pl. Ctrl. Calif. Art Show, 1996. Mem. Ctrl. Sierra Arts Coun., Mother Lode Artists Assn., Sacramento Fine Arts Ctr., Inc., Internat. Platform Assn. (Judges Choice conv. arts competition 1993), The Planetary Soc., The Nat. Mus. of Women of Arts. Mem. Ch. of Jesus Christ of LDS. Office: Internat Platform Assn PO Box 250 Winnetka IL 60093-0250

SHARKEY, KATHLEEN, accountant; b. Phila., Jan. 25, 1951; d. Joseph Philip and Florence Veronica (Noykoff) Sharkey; m. Joel David Delpha, Sept. 24, 1977; children: Daniel Joseph, Madeleine Day. BA, John Carroll U., 1973. Tchr. St. Michael's Sch., St. Louis, 1976-79; acct. Citicorp Acceptance, St. Louis, 1986-89; fin. dir., adminstr. Women's Self Help Ctr., St. Louis, 1989—. Bd. dirs. Mo. Religious Coalition for Reproductive Choice, St. Louis, 1992—; co-chair St. Louis Caths. for a Free Choice, 1992—; treas. Shaw Neighborhood Improvement Assn., 1994—, Mo. Coalition Against Domestic Violence, 1995—. Democrat. Roman Catholic. Home: 4047 Magnolia Pl Saint Louis MO 63110-3914 Office: Women's Self Help Ctr Inc 2838 Olive St Saint Louis MO 63103-1428

SHARKEY, LEONARD ARTHUR, automobile company executive; b. Detroit, May 21, 1946; s. Percy and Lillian (Peros) S.; m. Irene Johnson, Aug. 9, 1969 (div. Nov. 1991); children: Michelle, Wesley Tucker (step-son). Cert. pvt. pilot. Tool and diemaker Ford Motor Co., Dearborn, Mich., 1965-85; indsl. hazardous substance educator Ford Motor Co., Dearborn, Mich., 1985-86, indsl. health, safety and energy control educator, 1987-88, tool and diemaker leader, 1989—; non-fiction author Individual Initiative, Brighton, Mich., 1989—. Author: Journey Into Fear, 1995, Hidden Shadows - An Opening to the Windows of the Mind, 1996. Mem. Nat. Geog. Soc., Livingston Players, Nat. Rifle Assn., Boat U.S., Drummond Island Sportsman's Club, Mich. United Conservation Clubs.

SHARMA, HARI CHAND, geneticist, researcher; b. Himachal, India, Mar. 22, 1949; came to U.S., 1976; s. Ram and Manso (Devi) S.; m. Madhu Veena, Feb. 5, 1976; children: Seema, Kiran, Nikki, Jay. BS, Punjab Agrl. U., Palampur, India, 1970; MS, Indian Agr. Rsch. Inst., New Delhi, 1976; PhD, U. Calif., Riverside, 1980. County agt. Himachal Dept. of Agr., Chamba, India, 1970-73; rsch. asst. U. Calif., 1976-80; postdoctoral fellow Kans. State U., Manhattan, 1980-83; sr. rsch. biologist Monsanto Co., St. Louis, 1983-86; rsch. agronomist Purdue U., West Lafayette, Ind., 1986—; adj. asst. prof. U. Mo., St. Louis, spring 1986; tchr. genetics Purdue U., 1987—; speaker in field. Contbr. articles to profl. jours. Demonstrator, vol. 4-H Club, West Lafayette, 1988, 89; vol. Program for Retarded Citizens, Lafayette, 1989. Recipient gold medal, scholarship, honors and rsch. grant awards including internat. coop. rsch. grant with Morocco. Fellow Indian Soc. Genetics and Plant Breeding; mem. Am. Soc. Agronomy, Crop Sci. Soc. Am. Home: 525 N 7th St Lafayette IN 47901-1087 Office: Purdue U Dept of Agronomy Dept Agronomy West Lafayette IN 47907

SHARP, CHARLES EUGENE, minister; b. Roswell, N.Mex., Jan. 7, 1937; s. Oran Clay and Harriet Darlyne (Chaney) S.; m. Peggie Anne Brewer, Aug. 30, 1957; children: Cynthia Louise, Lori Kay, Jason Charles. BMus, Henderson State U., 1959; MEd, East Tex. State U., 1962, PhD, 1969. Cert. chaplain. Band dir. Gurdon (Ark.) H.S., 1957-59; jr. high band & orch. dir. Agnew Jr. High, Mesquite, Tex., 1959-62; chmn. music dept. Decatur (Tex.) Bapt. Coll., 1962-63; H.S. band dir. Anadarko (Ark.) H.S., 1963-64; assoc. prof. music East Tex. Bapt. Coll., Marshall, Tex., 1964-74; pastor Bellwood Bapt. Ch., North Syracuse, N.Y., 1974-76; chmn. music edn. Mobile (Ala.) Coll., 1976-78; dir. ch. tng. & music No. Plains Bapt. Conv., Rapid City, S.D., 1978-82; exec. dir. Colo. Bapt. Gen. Conv., Denver, 1982-92; dir. missions Western Kans. Bapt. Assn., Garden City, 1993—; adj. prof. Southwestern Bapt. Sem., Ft. Worth, 1992; vis. prof. Bapt. Theol. Sch., Johannesburg, South Africa, 1985, Zimbabwe, 1987, Russia, 1995, Romania, 1996. Conductor Marshall Civic Symphony, 1965-67, Onondaga Civic Symphony, North Syracuse, 1975-76; mem. Housing Adv. Bd., North Syracuse, 1975-76. Chaplain CAP, 1994—. Mem. Nat. Band Assn., Orgn. Dirs. Missions, Mil. Chaplains Assn., Phi Delta Kappa, Kappa Delta Pi. Office: Western Kans Bapt Assn 1008 N Main Garden City KS 67846

SHARP, GLENN (SKIP SHARP), vocational education administrator; b. Stroud, Okla., Nov. 19, 1938; s. Charles W. and Adeline M. (Jenisch) S.; m. Sherry Caroline Waddle, Aug. 29, 1959; children: Stephanie, Patricia, Nancy, Christopher. BS, Emporia State U., 1960, MS, 1966. Bus. educator Windthorst High Sch., Spearville, Kans., 1960-64; Bus. educator Northwest Kans. Area Vocat. Tech. Sch., Goodland, 1964-66, asst. dir., 1966—. Commr. Goodland City Commn., 1986-87; mem. state Scholar Com., Topeka, 1984-85; county chmn. Am. Cancer Soc., Sherman County, Kans., 1981-82; bloodmobile chmn. ARC, Sherman County, 1978-80; cubmaster Boy Scouts Am., Goodland, 1976— (Silver Beaver award 1992, Award of Merit 1989, James E. West Fellowship 1995); bd. dirs. N.W.K. Regional Med. Ctr., 1993—. Recipient Outstanding Svc. award Kans. Jaycees, 1972, silver Beaver award Boy Scouts Am., 1992, Award of Merit, 1989, named Employee of Yr. Goodland C. of C., 1988; James E. West fellowship, 1995. Mem. Nat. Assn. Fin. Aid (bd. dirs. 1988-91), Am. Vocat. Assn. (life, Nat. Leadership award 1995), Am. Vocat. Assn. (life), Rocky Mountain Assn. Fin. Aid (pres., bd. dirs. 1985-91, Disting. Svc. awards 1985, 87, Hall of Fame 1992), Kans. Vocat. Assn. (life), Kans. Assn. Fin. Adminstrs. (pres., bd. dirs. 1983-93, Outstanding Svc. award 1986, Hall of Fame 1996, Meritorious Achievement award 1995), Kiwanis (pres. 1968-69, 92-93, Outstanding Kiwanian 1968, 94, 95), Phi Delta Kappa (pres. 1983-84, Outstanding Educator 1985-86, Svc. Key 1991). Democrat. Christian. Home: 702 Walnut St Goodland KS 67735-2048

SHARP, PAUL DAVID, institute administrator; b. Youngstown, Ohio, Nov. 3, 1940; s. Robert Henderson and Kathryn (Tadsen)S.; m. Carole G. Graff, Sept. 16, 1967; children: David Allen, Kathryn Elizabeth. BA cum laude, Kenyon Coll., Gambier, Ohio, 1962; MPA, Auburn U., 1974. Commd. 2d lt. USAF, 1962, advanced through grades to col., 1983, intelligence officer, 1962-80; comdr. Detachment 1, 7450th Intelligence Squadron USAF, Neubruecke, Germany, 1980-83; comdr. 480th Reconnaissance Tech. Group USAF, Langley AFB, Va., 1983-85, dir. intelligence systems HQ Tactical Air Command, 1985-86, dep. chief intelligence Tactical Air Command, 1986-88; mgr. operational intelligence group Battelle Meml. Inst., Columbus, Ohio, 1988-89, mgr. fgn. tech. assessment group, 1989-91, mgr. intelligence projects/programs, 1991-92, v.p. bus. devel. fgn. sci. and tech., 1992-95; dir. fgn. sci. and tech. programs Battelle Meml. Inst., Columbus, Ohio, 1995—; mem. student career coun. Kenyon Coll., Columbus, 1992-95. Trustee Brandywine Assn., Yorktown, Va., 1987, Chase Assn., Powell, Ohio, 1991. Decorated Legion of Merit, Meritorious Svc. medals. Mem. Nat. Mil. Intelligence Assn., Armed Forces Communications and Electronics Assn., Air Force Assn., Sigma Pi (pres. Lambda chpt. 1961-62). Republican. Episcopalian. Office: Battelle Meml Inst 505 King Ave Columbus OH 43201-2696

SHARP, WILLIAM CHARLES, systems engineer; b. Cambridge, N.Y., Dec. 2, 1953; s. William Leland and Phyllis Evelyn (Burns) S.; children: William Welsey Leland, Natasha Nicole Nativa. BS in System Engring., Rensselaer Poly. Inst., 1976. Engr. Applicon, Burlington, Mass., 1976-78, Xylogics, Burlington, 1978, McDon, Long Beach, Calif., 1978-81, Hughes Aircraft Co., Fullerton, Calif., 1981-82; engring. mgr. Able Computer, Irvine, Calif., 1982-84; engr. Sierra Cybernetics, Brea, Calif., 1984-86; pres. Glacier Blue, Rancho Santa Margarita, Calif., 1986-93, Fairview Hts., Ill., 1994—; cons. Midcom Corp., Anaheim Hills, Calif., 1986-91, Jet Propulsion Lab., Pasadena, Calif., 1986-91, Tech. Advancements Inc., Playa del Rey, Calif., 1994—, Digital Equipment Corp., St. Louis, 1994—, Scott AFB, Ill., 1994—. Mem. Armed Forces Comm. and Electronics Assn., Digital Equipment Corp. User's Soc., Order of DeMolay (adult advisor, chevalier). Libertarian. Home and Office: 320 Frey Ln Fairview Heights IL 62208-2823

SHARROCK, ANITA KAY, computer specialist; b. Logan, Ohio, Dec. 3, 1955; d. Lloyd Earl and Gayle Irene (Daubenmier) Wrentmore; m. Jerry Dale Sharrock, June 4, 1994. BS, Ohio U., Lancaster and Athens, 1978; MS, Ohio U., Athens, 1979. Cert. secondary tchr., Ohio. Tchr. gen. and basic math. Circleville (Ohio) City Schs., 1979-80; vis. lectr. in math. scis. Denison U., Granville, Ohio, 1980; lectr., instr. Ctrl. Ohio Tech. Coll., Newark, 1981-83; lectr. dept. math. Ohio State U., Newark, 1980-83; instr. dept. gen. studies Ctrl. Ohio Tech. Coll., Newark, 1983-86; substitute tchr. Newark (Ohio) City Schs., 1986-87, various sch. dists., Ohio, 1987; computer specialist Info. Processing Ctr., Columbus, Ohio, 1987-90, Info. Porcessing Ctr., Columbus, 1990-92, DLA Sys. Design Ctr., Columbus, 1992—. Mem. steering com. Women's Changing World, 1987-95, active United Way, others. Mem. AAUW (pres. 1990-92), Licking County Bus. and Profl. Women's Club (treas. 1990-92, 96-97), Nat. Coun. Tchrs. Math. (life), Ohio Coun. Tchrs. Math. (life) Assn. Tchr. Educators (life), Assn. for Computing Machinery, Nat. Ret. Tchrs. Assn., IEEE Computer Soc., Kappa Delta Pi, Phi Kappa Phi. Home: 103 Ramona Ave Newark OH 43055 Office: DLA Sys Design Ctr RDCAO 3990 E Broad St PO Box 1605 Columbus OH 43216

SHARROW, LEONARD, musician, educator; b. N.Y.C., Aug. 4, 1915; s. Saul and Sonia (Berson) S.; m. Emily M. Kass, Oct. 22, 1942; 1 son, Neil Jason. Grad., Juilliard Sch. Music, 1935. Prin. bassoonist Nat. Symphony Orch., Washington, 1935-37; bassoonist NBC Symphony, N.Y.C., 1937-41; prin. bassoonist NBC Symphony, 1947-51, Detroit Symphony, 1946-47, Chgo. Symphony Orch., 1951-64, Pitts. Symphony Orch., 1977-87; mem. faculty Juilliard Sch. Music, 1949-51; mem. faculty, performer Gunnison Music Camp, Western State Coll., Colo., 1962-63; pvt. teaching, 1946—; tchr. bassoon Ind. U. Sch. Music, Bloomington, Ind., part-time 1963-64; prof. music (bassoon) Ind. U. Sch. Music, 1964-77; assoc. prof. Indiana U. of Pa., 1979-80; part-time faculty Pa. State U., 1979-80, 80-81; adj. prof. Sch. of Music, Carnegie Mellon U., 1981-86; mem. bassoon faculty New Eng. Conservatory Music, Boston, 1986-89; faculty, performer New Coll. Summer Music Festival, 1976, 77, 79-86, Aspen Music Festival, 1967—, Waterloo Music Festival, 1979, 80, 83, 86, Banff Ctr. for Arts, Can., 1982, Johannesen Internat. Sch. Arts Summer Festival, Victoria, B.C., Can., 1984; solo bassoonist World Philharm. Orch., Stockholm, 1985; Alan R. Rose fellow, guest artist, lectr., performer Victorian Coll. Arts, Melbourne, Canberra, Sydney, Australia, 1989; mem. faculty, performer Nagano Aspen Music Festival, Japan, 1990-94; mem. faculty Marrowstone Music Festival, Port Townsend, Wash., 1995—. Mem. Am. Woodwind Quintet, 1964-77; Editor: major works for bassoon; performances chamber music groups, Washington, N.Y.C., Chgo. others; participant, Pablo Casals Festival, Prades, France, 1953, soloist, NBC Symphony, Chgo. Symphony Orch., Pitts. Symphony, Aspen Festival Orch.; TV concerts, Chgo. and Pitts. symphonies; solo recs.: Mozart Bassoon Concerto in B flat Major, with Arturo Toscanini and NBC Symphony, Vivaldi Concerti for Bassoon with Max Goberman and N.Y. Symphonietta, Leonard Sharrow Plays Bassoon Solos, with piano, Concerto da Camera for Bassoon and Orch. (Dan Welcher), Concerto for bassoon and orch. (Ray Luke); assisting artist: A Baroque Trumpet recital with Gerard Schwarz. Served with AUS, 1941-45. Recipient award Toscanini Collection Assn., 1985. Mem. AAUP, Pi Kappa Lambda. Office: 3153 Coppertree Dr Bloomington IN 47401-9699

SHATZ, MARILYN JOYCE, psychologist; b. N.Y.C., Mar. 4, 1939; d. Morris and Freida Reva (Levinthal) Karpman; m. Stephen Sidney Shatz, Dec. 21, 1958 (div. July 1977); children: Geoffrey Ian, Adria Beth; m. Richard Feingold, Jan. 1, 1995. BA, U. Pa., 1971, MA, 1973, PhD, 1975. Asst. prof. Grad. Ctr. NYU, 1975-77; asst. prof. to prof. U. Mich., Ann Arbor, 1977—, dir. linguistics program, 1995—; assoc. editor Lang. Jour. Linguistic Soc. Am., Washington, 1991-93; vis. scholar Inst. Human Devel., Berkeley, Calif., 1991-92. Author: A Toddler's Life: Becoming a Person, 1994; contbr. articles to profl. jours. Fellow Guggenheim, Harvard U., 1980, Nat. Inst. Edn., U. Wis., 1981; Fulbright scholar Cambridge U., 1985; named First Alternate James McKean Cattell, 1991. Home: 2730 Maitland Dr Ann Arbor MI 48105-1565 Office: 525 E University Ave Ann Arbor MI 48109-1109

SHAW, BRUCE LLOYD, restaurant manager; b. Oklahoma City, July 25, 1960; s. William E. and Sharon R. (Fales) S.; m. Tina M. Thompson, Nov. 24, 1978 (div.); children: Joshua Bruce, Jeremiah Daniel, Shara Marie, Caleb James, Rachel Renae. Diploma, Broken Bow High Sch., 1978. Sales trainer, mgr. Cen. Nebr. Fire Equipment, Broken Bow, 1979-83; restaurant owner Broken Bow, 1981-83; ins. agt. Guideline Ins. and Fin. Svcs., Broken Bow, 1983-91; gen. mgr. Super 8 Lodge, Restaurant & Lodge/So. Hills Inestment Co., Hot Springs, S.D., 1991-95, Hardee's of Hot Springs, S.D., 1996—. Bd. dirs. Hot Springs Area 2000, 1992; pres. So. Hills Pool League, 1994-95; bd. dirs. Black Hills Badlands & Lakes Assn., 1994-95, Oyate Trail Assn., 1995; co-chmn. Econ. Devel. Com., 1995; bd. dirs. Visitor Industry Alliance, 1994-95, Mueller Civic Ctr., 1995. Mem. Hot Springs C. of C. (v.p. 1992, tourism chmn. 92, pres. 1993). Republican. Office: LLL Investment Co 901 Jensen Hwy Hot Springs SD 57747

SHAW, CHARLES RUSANDA, government investigator; b. Detroit, Aug. 17, 1914; s. Leonard George and Harriet (Kratzer) S.; m. Sally Madeline Jock, May 3, 1947; children: Patrick R., Sandra L. Keding (dec.), Janice L., Lisa Keding; stepchildren: Lillian Genna, Ruth Czenkus. Cert., Wicker Sch. of Fine Arts, 1936, Mich. Acad. Advt. Art, 1937; student, Intelligence Corps Sch., 1947. Freelance artist Detroit, 1936-39; spl. agt. U.S. Army Counter Intelligence Corps, Washington, 1947-48, Office Spl. Investigations, USAF, Washington, 1948-66; pvt. investigator Charles Shaw Assocs., Mt. Clemens, Mich., 1966-84; contract investigator USAF & U.S. Customs Svc., Washington, 1984-94; entrepreneur-inventor neoteric products, patents pending, 1994—. Master sgt. U.S. Army, 1939-45, PTO, ETO. Mem. Assn. Former OSI Spl. Agts. (chartered). Democrat. Roman Catholic. Home and Office: 59295 Bates Rd New Haven MI 48048-1728

SHAW, DANNY WAYNE, secondary education educator; b. Detroit, Jan. 18, 1947; s. George L. and Nina Margarete (Smith) S.; m. 2d Nancy Rivard Shaw, Feb. 29, 1980; 1 dau., Christina Marie. B.S., Wayne State U., 1973, M.Mus., 1975, Ed.S., 1979, Ph.D., 1982. Tchr. Dearborn Pub. Schs. (Mich.), 1973-74, Lincoln Park (Mich.), Schs. 1974—; pres. System Support Services, Lincoln Park, Trenton, Mich., 1982—; research asst. Wayne State U., 1980-81, now adj. faculty; adj. faculty Marygrove Coll., Detroit, 1984. Mem. music adv. panel Mich. Council Arts, 1976-84. Served with USMC, 1965-68; Vietnam. Decorated Vietnam Service medal, Nat. Def. Service medal, Presdl. Unit citation, Campaign medal Republic of Vietnam; recipient cert. for outstanding acad. achievement Mich. Ho. Reps., 1975. Mem. NEA, Wayne State U. Alumni Assn., Phi Delta Kappa. Lodge: Masons. Home: 1999 Church Pl Trenton MI 48183-2148

SHAW, DOROTHY RUTH, library director, social worker; b. Fargo, N.D., Aug. 12, 1926; d. Arthur and Mae Estelle (Holbert) Harms; m. Edgar Allen Shaw, Dec. 22, 1950; children: Alan, Laurie, Gordon. BA, Hamline U., St. Paul, 1947. Child welfare and social worker Becker County, Detroit Lakes, Minn., 1947-50; social worker Hennepin County, Mpls., 1951; social worker in child welfare Stevens County, Morris, Minn., 1952-55; libr. City of Hancock, Minn., 1975—; city forester City of Hancock, 1985—. Pres. Hancock Sr. Citizens, 1994—; sec. Hancock Dining Coun., 1994—; election judge City of Hancock, 1975—; sec. Stevens County Red Cross, Morris, 1986-95. Mem. Minn. Libr. Assn. Republican. Congregationalist. Office: Hancock Cmty Libr 652 6th St Hancock MN 56244

SHAW, JANNÉTTE SUE, mental health nurse; b. Battle Creek, Mich., Apr. 26, 1956; d. James Henry Jr. and Laura Melrose (Everett) Shaw; children: Mathew Buchanan. LPN with honors, Kellogg Community Coll., 1978, ADN, 1983; BSN, Nazareth Coll., 1990. RN, Mich.; cert. psychiat./mental health nurse; cert. 1st level healing touch practitioner. LPN surg.-post operative Lelia Hosp., Battle Creek, 1980-83; charge nurse substance abuse unit Borgess Hosp., Kalamazoo, 1983-84; staff nurse, charge nurse, supr. psychiat. unit VA Med. Ctr., Battle Creek, 1984-91; commd. capt.nurse corps Air Nat. Guard, 1991—; mem. ethics com. VA Med. Ctr., 1987-90; v.p. Nazareth Student Nurses Assn.; clin. instr. ADN, Kellogg Cmty. Coll. Author: (text) Sleep Enhancement, 1990, Standardized Care Plan for Post Traumatic Stress Disorder, 1989. Health chairperson Battle Creek Road Runner, 1987-91; vol., peer, leader Critical Incident Stress Debriefing team S.W. Mich., Kalamazoo, 1989—. Named Outstanding Young Am. Woman, Outstanding Young Women Am., 1991. Mem. Air N.G. Nurses Assn., Battle Creek Balloon Club (sec. 1992—); Holistic Nurses Assn. Democrat. Home and Office: 513 S Main St Bellevue MI 49021-1418

SHAW, JOSEPH THOMAS, Slavic languages educator; b. Ashland City, Tenn., May 13, 1919; s. George Washington and Ruby Mae (Pace) S.; m. Betty Lee Ray, Oct. 30, 1942; children: David Matthew, Joseph Thomas, James William. AB, U. Tenn., 1940, AM, 1941; AM, Harvard, 1947, PhD, 1950. Asst. prof. Slavic langs. Ind. U., 1949-55, assoc. prof., 1955-61; prof. Slavic langs. U. Wis., 1961-89, prof. emeritus, 1989—, chmn. dept. Slavic langs., 1962-68, 77-86, chmn. div. humanities, 1964-65, 72-73, assoc. dean Grad. Sch., 1965-68. Author: The Letters of Alexander Pushkin, 1963, Pushkin's Rhymes: A Dictionary, 1974, Baratynskii: A Dictionary of the Rhymes and a Concordance to the Poetry, 1975, Batiushkov: A Dictionary of the Rhymes and a Concordance to the Poetry, 1975, Pushkin: A Concordance to the Poetry, 1985, American Association Teachers Slavic and East European Languages: The First Fifty Years 1941-91, 1991, Pushkin's Poetry of the Unexpected: The Nonrhymed Lines in the Rhymed Poetry and the Rhymed Lines in the Nonrhymed Poetry, 1994, Pushkin, Poet and Man of Letters, and His Prose (Collected works, vol. 1), 1995; editor: The Slavic and East European Jour., 1957-70; contbr. articles to profl. jours. Served to capt. USNR, 1942-46, 51-53. Mem. Am. Assn. Tchrs. Slavic and East European Langs. (mem. exec. council 1953-70, 73-80, pres. 1973-74). Home: 4505 Mineral Point Rd Madison WI 53705-5071

SHAW, LARRY A., health facility administrator. BA, Capital U., 1982; MA, Ctrl. Mich. U., 1987. Mgr. receiving and shipping St. Anthony Med. Ctr., Columbus, Ohio, 1982-84, supr. ctrl. sterile supply, 1984-86, supr. bus. office, 1986-88, dir. patient acctg., 1988-90; v.p. Patient Acctg. Mgmt. Systems, Inc., Columbus, 1990—. Contbr. articles to profl. jours. Mem. Am. Guild Patient Account Mgrs., Ctrl. Ohio Patient Account Mgrs. Republican. Lutheran. Office: Patient Account Mgmt System PO Box 9766 Columbus OH 43209-0766

SHAW, PATRICIA MARIE, home care nurse; b. McLeansboro, Ill., Oct. 4, 1950; d. Henry Paul and Rita Marie (Rapp) Kiefer; m. Charles H. White, Aug. 26, 1970 (div. Sept. 1979); children: Christopher, Gregory; m. Larry N. Shaw, Nov. 27, 1981; children: Mark, Angie, Sarah. Student, Rend Lake Coll., 1969-71; ADN, Frontier Community Coll., Fairfield, Ill., 1980; student, McKendree Coll., 1993-95. From CNA to lic. practical nurse to RN Good Samaritan Hosp., Mt. Vernon, Ill., 1972-80; RN Hamilton Meml. Hosp., McLeansboro, Ill., 1980-81, Crossroads Hosp., Mt. Vernon, 1981-84, Jeffersonian Nursing Home, Mt. Vernon, 1985-88, Olson Kimberly Quality Care, Marion, Belleville, Ill., 1988-94, Staff Builders, Edwardsville, Ill., 1989—, Ptnrs. Home Health, Marion, Ill., 1989—; nurse Home House Calls, Fairview Heights, Ill., 1993-95, Olsten Kimberly Quality Care, Marion, 1995—. Former head birthday com., charge Sunday sch. class activity, choir mem. First Freewill Bapt. Ch. Mem. Ladies Aux. (former sec.-treas.). Baptist. Home: PO Box 185 Ina IL 62846-0185 also: Staff Builders 8 Cottonwood Rd Ste 1 Glen Carbon IL 62034

SHAW, RANDY LEE, human services administrator; b. Revenna, Ohio, Oct. 18, 1945; s. Robert and Dorothy Mae (Turner) S.; m. Terri Marie Richardson, July 4, 1988; 1 child, Garrett Samuel. BTh, Ridgedale Sem., 1975, ThM, 1977. Cert. social worker. Exec. dir. Boy's Recovery Home, Detroit, 1979; clin. dir. Boniface, Detroit, 1979-83; unit dir. Problem Daily Living, Detroit, 1983-84; clin. dir. Calvin Wells, Detroit, 1984-86; exec. dir. Children Youth Equal Rights Adv. House, Pontiac, Mich., 1986-87, Touch of Hope, Hartford, Mich., 1988-89; program supr. New Ctr. Community Mental Health, Detroit, 1989-91; exec. dir. Nat. Inst. Hypertension Studies, Detroit, 1979-88. Local rep., magician for Make-A-Wish Found.; exec. dir. Magicians Against Gangs, Ignorance, and Crime Intervention Program, M.A.G.I.C., 1991—. Mem. Soc. Am. Magicians (local pres. 1993-94), Magic Circle, Internat. Brotherhood of Magicians (local pres. 1993-94), Supreme Magic Club of U.K. Home and Office: 249 Lolly Pop St Westland MI 48186-6849

SHAW, RICHARD DAVID, marketing and management educator; b. Pitts., Kans., Aug. 25, 1938; s. Richard Malburn and Jessie Ruth (Murray) S.; m. Adolphine Catherine Brungardt, Aug. 21, 1965; children: Richard David Jr., John Michael, Shannon Kathleen. BSBA, Rockhurst Coll., 1960; MS in Commerce, St. Louis U., 1964. Claims adjuster Kemper Ins. Group, Kansas City, Mo., 1961; tchr. acctg. Corpus Christi High Sch., Jennings, Mo., 1961-63; assoc. prof. econs. Fontbonne Coll., St. Louis, 1963-70; chmn. social behavioral sci. dept. Fontbonne Coll., 1968-70; mem. faculty, chmn. bus. div. Longview Community Coll., Lee's Summit, Mo., 1970-81, coord. mktg., 1979-81; assoc. prof. mktg. Rockhurst Coll., Kansas City, 1981—, chmn. mgmt. and mktg., 1983-85; workshop leader Rockhurst Coll., 1975—, faculty moderator Jr. Execs. Assn., The Rock yearbook, Students in Free Enterprise, Rockettes; pvt. cons., 1981—, chmn. freshman seminar com., 1994; instr. principles of mktg. on The Learning Channel on Cable TV for the PACE Program, 1994; chmn. sch. mgmt. curriculum com., 1993—. Author: Personal Finance, 1983, Principles of Marketing Study Guide, 1993, Contemporary Marketing Study Guide, 1994, Consumer Behavior Study Guide, Instructor's Manual for Michael Solomon's Consumer Behavior; cooperating author: Philip Kotler's Marketing Management. Mem. alumni bd. assessment task force Rockhurst Coll., 1971-73, 78-80, chmn. 30 yr. reunion com., 1990, 35 yr. reunion com., 1995, chmn. curriculum com., curriculum task force; chmn. Eastwood Hills Coun., Kansas City, 1974-76, bd. dirs., 1988-91, co-chmn. of Solid Rocks Faculty-Staff Fund Raising Campaign, 1994; lead couple Marriage Preparation Classes, Kansas City St. Joseph Dioceses; co-chmn. Kansas City Vols. Against Hunger, 1975-80; campaign mgr. Larry Ferns for City Coun., Kansas City, 1975; bd. govs. Citizens Assn., 1976—. With USAR, 1960-64. Recipient Gov.'s Excellence in Teaching award, Mo., 1993; Hallmark fellow Rockhurst Coll.; faculty devel. grantee Sch. Mgmt., Rockhurst Coll., 1984, 93, 95. Mem. Am. Mktg. Assn., Soc. for Advancement of Mgmt., Mid-Am. Mktg. Assn., Alpha Sigma Nu. Roman Catholic. Home: 11014 Washington St Kansas City MO 64114-5177 Office: Rockhurst Coll 1100 Rockhurst Rd Kansas City MO 64110-2508

SHAW, ROBERT EUGENE, minister, administrator; b. Havre, Mt., Apr. 8, 1933; s. Harold Alvin and Lillian Martha (Kruse) S.; m. Marilyn Grace Smit, June 14, 1957; children—Rebecca Jean, Ann Elizabeth, Mark David, Peter Robert. B.A., Sioux Falls Coll., 1955; M.Div., Am. Baptist. Sem. of West, 1958; D.D. (hon.), Ottawa U., 1976, Judson Coll., 1984. Ordained to ministry Am. Bapt. Chs. U.S.A., 1958; pastor First Bapt. Ch., Webster City, Ia., 1958-63, Community Bapt. Ch., Topeka, Kans., 1963-68; sr. pastor Prairie Bapt. Ch., Prairie Village, Kans., 1968-78; pres. Ottawa U., Kans., 1978-83; exec. minister Am. Bapt. Chs. Mich., East Lansing, 1983—; mem. gen. bd. Am. Bapt. Chs. U.S.A., Valley Forge, Pa., 1972-80, nat. v.p., 1978-80; nat. v.p. Am. Bapt. Minister Council, Valley Forge, 1969-72, nat. pres., 1972-75; nat. chair Am. Bapt. Evang. Team, 1988—; mem. Internat. Commn. on Edn. and Evangelism, Bapt. World Alliance, 1990—; mem. nat. exec. com. Am. Bapt. Adminstrs. Colls. and Univs., 1980-82; bd. dirs. Kans. Ind. Colls. Assn., 1980-82. Trustee No. Bapt. Theol. Sem., Lombard, Ill., 1983—, Kalamazoo Coll., Mich., 1983—, Judson Coll, Elgin, Ill., 1983—; dir. Webster City C. of C., 1961-62, Ottawa C. of C., 1980-82. Office: Am Baptist Chs of Mich 4578 S Hagadorn Rd East Lansing MI 48823-5355

SHAW, WILLIAM, state legislator; b. Fulton, Ark., July 31, 1937; s. McKinley and Gertrude (Henderson) S.; m. Shirley Shaw, 1957; children: Gina, Victor, Shawn, 3 stepchildren. Grad. high sch. Adminstrv. asst. to Alderman Wilson Frost 34th Ward; precinct capt. 24th ward and inspector City of Chgo.; pres. 9th ward Regional Dem. Orgn.; Ill. state rep. Dist. 34, 1983—; mem. appropriations I com. labor and commerce com. Ill. Ho. Reps., exec. and vet. affairs com., registration com., vice chmn. fin. insts. com., chmn. ins. com.; mem. Ill. State Senate Dist. 15, 1993—; asst. dir. Supportive Svcs., Chgo. Mem. Masons, C. of C. Home: 12126 S Perry Ave Chicago IL 60628-6627•

SHAWSTAD, RAYMOND VERNON, business owner, retired computer specialist; b. Brainerd, Minn., Mar. 17, 1931; stepson Klaas Ostendorf, s. Ruth Catherine Hammond. Student, San Bernardino Valley Coll., 1959-60, 65, West Coast U., 1960-62, UCLA Extension, 1966-81, Liberal Inst. Natural Sci. and Tech., 1973-83, Free Enterprise Inst., 1973-83, Kingsway Christian Coll., 1994—. Salesman Marshalltown, Iowa, 1952-53; asst. retail mgr. Gamble-Skogmo, Inc., Waverly, Iowa, 1953-54; retail mgr. Gamble-Skogmo, Inc., Iowa Falls, Iowa, 1954-57; sr. programmer County of San Bernardino (Calif.), 1958-64; info. systems cons. Sunkist Growers, Inc., Van Nuys, Calif., 1965-75, sr. systems programmer, 1975-92; univ. extension instr. UCLA, 1980-81; propr. artificial intelligence rschr. Lang. Products Co., 1980—; propr., fin. educator Pennyseed Mgmt. Co., 1987—; reader in geriatrics, propr., instr. econs. Liberal Pentagon, 1991-93, Liberal Propr., 1993-94; propr. Med. Investments, 1993—; distbn. specialist, propr. Networking Group Co., 1992—. Author numerous software programs; editor VM Notebook of GUIDE Internat. Corp., 1982-92. Vol. bedside music therapist VA Hosp., 1984—; musician Project Caring, 1984-87; mentor The Caring Connection; vol. Meals-on-Wheels; rep. U.S. Senatorial Bus. Adv. Bd., Calif., 1988-92; mem. data processing adv. bd. City of Marshalltown, Iowa, 1993—; vol. League of Mercy of Salvation Army; patron DAV. With Iowa N.G., 1948-57; 1st lt. USAR, 1957-63. Mem. Am. Def. Preparedness Assn., Res. Officers Assn., Am. Legion, U.S. Naval Inst., Assn. U.S. Army, Toastmasters, Kiwanis. Home and Office: 303 Sunset Ln Marshalltown IA 50158-5146

SHAWVER, STANLEY WALTER, county planner; b. Fountainbleau, France, Apr. 28, 1954; came to U.S., 1955; s. James Lloyd Jr. and Margaret Ruth (Ivie) S.; m. Earlene Nina Newcomb, Feb. 14, 1974 (div. Sept. 1983); m. Anna Louise Brown, Oct. 2, 1983. BA in Polit. Sci., U. Mo., 1980. Community planner Mid-Mo. Coun. Govt., Jefferson City, 1980-82; county planner Boone County Pub. Works, Columbia, Mo., 1982-85; dir. planning and bldg. inspection Boone County Commn., Columbia, 1985—. Sgt. U.S. Army, 1973-76. Mem. Am. Planning Assn., Mo. Assn. of Code Adminstrs. Office: Boone County Planning Bldg 801 E Walnut Rm 210 Columbia MO 65201-7730

SHAY, DAVID E., lawyer; b. Scranton, Pa., Nov. 9, 1962; s. Howard E. Jr. and Arlene (Pace) S.; m. Kimberly R. Grow, June 22, 1985; children: Daniel E., Andrew W., Matthew D. BS in Journalism, Kans. U., 1984, JD, 1988. Bar: Mo. 1988, U.S. Dist. Ct. (we. dist.) Mo. 1988, U.S. Ct. Appeals (5th and 8th cirs.) 1991. Reporter KDXE, Sulphur Springs, Tex., 1984, KTTR/KZNN, Inc., Rolla, Mo., 1984-85; shareholder Shughart, Thomson & Kilroy, P.C., Kansas City, Mo., 1988—. Contbr. articles to profl. publs., chpt. to Mo. Bar Deskbook, 1991. Chmn. gen. bd. Hillcrest Christian Ch., Overland Park, Kans., 1992. Mem. ABA, Mo. Bar Assn. (chair environ. and energy law com. 1995—), Lawyers Assn. Kansas City/Young Lawyers (bd. dirs. 1991—, officer 1993—, pres. 1996—), Kansas City Met. Bar Assn., Order of Coif, Phi Kappa Phi. Republican. Mem. Christian Ch. (Disciples of Christ). Office: Shughart Thomson & Kilroy 120 W 12th St Ste 1500 Kansas City MO 64105-1917

SHEA, DANIEL FRANCIS, mathematician, educator; b. Springfield, Mass., Aug. 2, 1937; m. Gail Frances Benkert, Aug. 27, 1966; children: Darrell Daniel, Leslie Frances. BA, Am. Internat. Coll., 1959; PhD, Syracuse U., 1965. Asst. prof. U. Wis., Madison, 1965-69; assoc. prof. U. Wis., 1969-72, prof., 1972—; vis. assoc. prof. Purdue U., Lafayette, Ind., 1970-71; vis. prof. Calif. Inst. Tech., Pasadena, 1974-75, U. Hawaii, Honolulu, 1979, U. Wurzburg, Germany, 1991. Editor: Complex Variables, Anniversary Issue, 1989; assoc. editor Analysis, 1981—; contbr. articles to Mich. Math. Jour., Jour. of Analysis, Annales Fourier Inst., Am. Jour. Math. Rsch. grantee NSF, 1966-85, Swedish NFR, 1982, Deutsche Forschungs, 1991. Mem. Am. Math. Soc. Office: U Wis Dept Math Madison WI 53706

SHEA, REX TUNGSHENG, research engineer, educator; b. Taipei, Taiwan, Mar. 29, 1952; came to U.S., 1980; s. Chin-Yuan and Chi Chin (Young) Shea; m. Ellin T. Chu, Dec. 26, 1981; 1 child, Brian J. BS, Nat. Cheng-Kung U., Tainan, Taiwan, 1974, MS, 1976; PhD, Northwestern U., 1986. Design engr. Nat. Chung Shan Inst. Sci. and Tech., Lun Tan, Taiwan, 1976-80; staff engr. GM R&D Ctr., Warren, Mich., 1985—. Contbr. articles to profl. jours. Bd. dirs. Am. Chinese Assn., 1994-96; chmn. Nat. Cheng Kung U. Alumni Assn., Royal Oak, Mich., 1994-95; prin. Ann Arbor (Mich.) Chinese Sch., 1994-95. Recipient Outstanding Svc. award Nat. Cheng Kung U. Alumni Assn., 1994, 95. Mem. ASME, Soc. Automotive Engrs. (Arch T. Colwell award 1987). Office: GM R&D Ctr 30500 Mound Warren MI 48090-9055

SHEAR, S. SUE, state legislator; b. Mar. 17, 1918; m. Harry Shear; three children. Student, Wash. U. Del. Dem. Nat. Conv., 1976; rep. Mo. State Ho. Reps. Dist. 83. Mem. Am. Jewish Com. Home: 200 S Brentwood Blvd Saint Louis MO 63105-1601 Office: Mo Ho of Reps State Capitol Building Jefferson City MO 65101-1556*

SHECTERLE, LINDA MARIE, biologist; b. Milw., Jan. 24, 1956; d. Norman Daniel and Jane Ann (Reynolds) S.; m. Steven Earl Shelton, July 20, 1984 (div. Aug. 1990); 1 child, Alexander. BS, U. Stevens Point, 1974. Account coord. Miller Brokerage, St. Louis, 1974-77; clinic advisor and rschr. U. Wis., Madison, 1978-80, program coord., 1980-86; dir. R & D Enthermics Inc., Madison, 1986-93; exec. v.p. Virotech, Mpls., 1993-94; pres. Jacqmar, Mpls., 1993—; mem. adv. bd. Virotech, Mpls., 1993-94; cons. Bioenergy, Mpls., 1994-95, Med Corps, Annapolis, Md., 1995—. Author: (with others) Advances in Comparatvie Leuk Research, 1983; reviewer jour.; contbr. articles to profl. jours. Vol. tchr. Math. Club, Mpls., 1995—. Recipient Wis. Clin. Cancer Ctr. Merit award, 1984. Mem. Am. Soc. Clin. Hyperthermic Oncology, N.Am. Hyperthermia, Minn. Acad. Scis., Regulatory Affairs Profl. Soc. Home and Office: Jacqmar Inc 940 Fernbrook Ln N Minneapolis MN 55447

SHEEHAN, DENNIS WILLIAM, SR., lawyer; b. Springfield, Mass., Jan. 2, 1934; s. Timothy A. and H. Marjorie (Kelsey) S.; m. Elizabeth M. Hellyer, July 27, 1957; children: Dennis William Jr., Catherine Elizabeth, John Edward. BS, U. Md., 1957; JD, Georgetown U., 1960, LLM, 1962. Bar: D.C., Md. 1960, Mo. 1976, Ohio 1977. Legal asst. to chmn. NLRB, Washington, 1960-61; trial atty. U.S. SEC, Washington, 1962-63; corp. atty. Martin Marietta, Balt., N.Y.C., 1963-64; v.p., gen. counsel, sec. Bunker Ramo Corp., Oak Brook, Ill., 1964-73; exec. v.p., gen. counsel, dir. Diversified Industries, Inc., St. Louis, 1973-75; v.p., gen. counsel, dir. N-ReN Corp., Cin., 1975-77; v.p., gen. counsel, sec., dir. AXIA Inc., Oak Brook, Ill., 1977-84, chmn., pres., chief exec. officer, 1984—; bd. dirs. Andamios Atlas, Mexico City, Compagnie Fischbein (S.A.), Brussels, Greenfield Industries, Augusta, Ga., CST, Inc., Wheeling, Ill., Bradington-Young, Inc., Hickory, N.C.; chmn. Allied Healthcare Sys., St. Louis. Bd. dirs. St. Margaret's Sch. Found., MAPI, Washington; chmn. U.S. C. of C., Nat. Coun. on Crime and Delinquency. Mem. ABA, Chgo. Club, St. Louis Club, Econ. Club Chgo., Met. Club Washington, Downtown Club Richmond, Met. Club Chgo., Univ. Club Balt., Phi Delta Pi, Sigma Alpha Phi, Delta Sigma Phi. Republican. Home: 450 Lexington Dr Lake Forest IL 60045-1563 Office: Axia Corp 2001 Spring Rd Ste 300 Hinsdale IL 60521-1879

SHEEHAN, MICHAEL GILBERT, utilities executive; b. Peoria, Ill., Oct. 26, 1952; s. Jerry James and Mary Ellen (Murrin) S.; m. Debra Lynn England, Apr. 12, 1975; children: Mark Michael, Lisa Michele. AS, Ill. Cen. Coll., 1972; BS, Bradley U., 1974. Cert. purchasing mgr., Nat. Assn. Purchasing Mgmt., adult literacy tutor Laubach Literacy Action. Sta. clk. Cen. Ill. Light Co., Canton, 1975, office and stores supr., 1975-79; purchasing agt. Cen. Ill. Light Co., Peoria, 1979-81, bldg. mgr., 1981-85, sr. investment recovery adminstr., 1985-90; sr. fuel supply adminstr. Cen. Ill. Light Co., Peoria, 1990-92; supr. D.C. Fuel Mgmt., Peoria, Ill., 1992—. Advisor Jr. Achievement, Peoria, 1980, cons. project bus., 1987, 88; student tutor adult literacy program YWCA, Pekin, Ill., 1988-90; mem. Friends Pekin Pub. Libr., 1989—, Lakeview Mus., Peoria, 1989—. Mem. Bldg. Owners and Mgrs. Assn., Invesment Recovery Assn. Republican. Roman Catholic. Office: Cen Ill Light Co 300 Liberty St Peoria IL 61602-1400

SHEEHAN, ROBERT MERRILL, JR., executive director; b. Columbus, Ohio, June 8, 1957; s. Robert M. and M. Ellen (Thompson) S.; m. Donna A. Charles, July 18, 1992; stepchildren: Janelle, Amber, Kendra. BA, Westminster Coll., 1979; MA, Ohio State U., 1989, PhD, 1994. Exec. dir. Alpha Sigma Phi Fraternity and Ednl. Found., Delaware, Ohio, 1981-90, LeaderShape, Inc., Champaign, Ill., 1992—. Fellow NIF Found., 1990. Mem. Nat. Soc. Fund Raising Execs. (cert., chpt. pres. 1989, 96), Rotary Internat. Office: LeaderShape Inc Ste 101 1801 Fox Dr Champaign IL 61820

SHEEHAN, STEPHEN D., airport commissioner; b. Oct. 29, 1942. BS, USAF Acad., 1965; M in Aviation Mgmt. with honors, Embry Riddle Aero. U.; postgrad., Air War Coll., 1982-83. Commd. officer USAF, 1965, advanced through grades to col., ret., 1992, chief test pilot, instr., flight examiner, 1965-75; chief Air Base Plans Divsn., Incirilik, Turkey, 1975-76; pilot, action officer, exec. officer, dept. chief staff Hdqrs. USAF Tactile Air Command, 1977-80; pilot, chief air ops. tng., comdr. air support ops. squadron, 1980-82; asst. inspector gen. Unified Command Hdqrs., 1983-86; group comdr. USAF, 1986-89, base comdr., 1989-91; faculty mem., dir. Tactical Air Ops., U.S. Army War Coll., 1991-92; dep. commr. ops. Safety and Security Cleve. Hopkins Internat. Airport, 1992-94; commr. Cleve. Hopkins Internat. Airport, 1994—. Decorated Legion of Merit, 3 Disting. Flying Crosses, 13 Air medals. Office: 5300 Riverside Dr Cleveland OH 44135

SHEEHY, PATRICK DAVID, organizational and fundraising consultant; b. Phila., Apr. 2, 1951; s. Patrick Joseph and Kathryn (Walsh) S.; m. Wendy Margaret O'Leary, June 18, 1977; children: Mariah, Dylan. AAS, Grahm Jr. Coll., Boston, 1971; BJ, U. Mont., 1978. Govt. reporter The Montana Standard, Butte, 1978-79; city editor, mng. editor Havre (Mont.) Daily News, 1979-83; mgr. pub. rels. No. Mont. Hosp., Havre, 1983-85; dir. cmty. rels. St. Joseph Regional Med. Ctr., Lewiston, Idaho, 1985-89; asst. dir. devel. The Menninger Found., Topeka, Kans., 1989-90; dir. devel. Hillcrest Family Svcs., Dubuque, Iowa, 1990-95; cons. Dubuque, 1995—. Dir. Iowa United Meth. Found., Des Moines, 1992-95, Big Brothers/Big Sisters No. Mont., v.p., 1979-80; past chair Task Force to Overcome Racism in Topeka (Kans.), 1989, Topeka Dist. Religion and Race Com. United Meth. Ch., Topeka Dist. Convocation on Racism United Meth. Ch.; bd. dirs. Brown Found., Topeka, 1990; founder Dubuque Edn. Coalition, 1993, Dubuque Area Peace Coalition, Mont. 1st Amendment Fund, Buffalo Berry Food Coop.; mem. Dubuque Cmty. Sch. Dist. Bd. Edn., 1995. Mem. Soc. Profl. Journalists (pres. Mont. chpt. 1983), Mont. Soc. Hosp. Cmty. Rels. and Devel. (pres. 1982). Democrat. United Methodist. Home and Office: 1018 W 5th St Dubuque IA 52001

SHEELER, JOHN BRIGGS, retired chemical engineering educator; b. Anita, Iowa, Oct. 25, 1921; s. Ivan Howard and Mildred Lucile (Briggs) S.; m. Charlsee A. Pitt (div. 1960); m. Mary Irene Squire, July 18, 1970; children: John R., Daniel, Anne, Robert, William, Diane, James, John E. BS, Iowa State U., 1950, PhD, 1956. Rsch. asst. Iowa Engring. Experiment Sta., Ames, 1950-56; asst. prof. Iowa State U., Ames, 1956-59, assoc. prof., 1959-88, prof. emeritus, 1988—; cons. Iowa Dept. Transp., Ames, 1950-88. Contbr. scientific articles to profl. jours. Coach, vol. NROTC (Rifle and Pistol Team) Iowa State U., 1947-88. Sgt. USMC, 1941-47. Fellow Iowa Acad. Sci. (emeritus); mem. AAAS, AIChE, Masons, Moose, Kiwanis, Sigma Xi (emeritus). Presbyterian. Home: 505 Bel Air Dr Marshalltown IA 50158-2314

SHEEN, DAN ROGER, research engineer; b. Columbia, Mo., June 30, 1959; s. Edwin Martin and Shirley Mae (Yagel) S.; m. Kimberly Hazen Sheen, Jan. 24; 1 child, Emily Marie. BS in Elec. Engring., Washington State U., Pullman, 1981; MS in Elec. Engring., U. Ill., Urbana, 1983; PhD in Elec. Engring., 1987. Rsch. asst. U. Ill., Urbana, 1981-87; Environmental Rsch. Inst. Mich., Ann Arbor, 1987—. Contbr. articles to profl. jours. Recipient NASA Tech. Brief award, 1991, E. Allen Phillips scholarship Washington State U., 1980, Departmental Fellowship U. Ill., 1985. Mem. IEEE, Am. Geophys. Union. Home: 1434 Roxbury Rd Ann Arbor MI 48104 Office: ERIM 1975 Green Rd Ann Arbor MI 48105

SHEERER, JUDY B., state legislator; m. Ben Sheerer; 1 child, Morgan. BA summa cum laude, Cleveland State Univ. State rep. Ohio Dist. 18, 1983-92; state senator Ohio Dist. 25, 1993; mgmt. cons. Exec. Com. Cuyahoga County Dem. Party Women's Polititcal caucus; past pres. Moreland PTA. Recipient Award for Excellence Ohio Assn. Deaf, 1984, Achievement award Cuyahoga County Women's Political Caucus, 1990, Josephine Irwin award Womenspace, 1992. Mem. Friends of Shaker. Home: 17115 Lomond Blvd Shaker Heights OH 44120 Office: Ohio House of Reps Office of House Mems Columbus OH 43215*

SHEETS, STANLEY STUART, retired construction company executive; b. Beaver City, Nebr., Apr. 18, 1927; s. Emmett Ira and Bernice (Leach) S.; m. Ruth Elaine Bomberger, Jan. 26, 1951; children: Michael Jon, James Stuart. Student, MIT, 1947-49, U. Nebr., 1949-51. Ptnr. Valley Lumber Co., Superior, Nebr., 1951-71; from pres. to sec. bd. dirs. Valley Bldg. Ctr., Inc., Superior, 1971—; v.p. Valley Construction, Inc., Superior, 1963-76. Author: A History of Superior, Nebraska, 1995. Mem. City Coun., Superior, 1954-55; bd. dirs. Indsl. Devel. Corp., Econ. Devel. Coun., Superior, 1968-70, 90—, Judicial Nominating Com., Lincoln, Nebr., 1981-84. Served to cpl. USAF 1945-47, Germany. Mem. Nebr. Lumber Mchts. Assn. (bd. dirs. 1966-76, pres. 1973-74), Mid-Am. Lumbermen's Assn. (bd. dirs. 1974-78), Nat. Lumber & Bldg. Material Dealers Assn. (bd. dirs. 1973-74, lobbyist 1973-74), Am. Legion, VFW, Eagles, Superior Ambassadors, Nebr. Dems., Elds. Home: 10 Random Rd RR 1 Box 89 Superior NE 68978

SHEETZ, ERNEST AUSTIN, academic administrator, educator; b. McKeesport, Pa., June 23, 1929; s. Ernest Austin and Grace Manley S.; m. Betty Ann Hixenbaugh, Nov. 24, 1956; children: Craig Thomas, Kenneth Lee, Brian Douglas. BS, Mt. Union Coll., 1951. Alumni sec. Mt. Union Coll., Alliance, Ohio, 1955-62, asst. to pres., 1962-68, dir. devel., 1968-82, v.p. devel., 1982-91, sr. v.p., 1991-95; ret., 1994. Campaign coord. Ohio Found. Ind. Coll., Columbus, 1979; bd. dirs. Alliance City Hosp., 1982—, ARC, Alliance, 1975-80; chmn. bd. Alliance Area United Way, 1981; mem. exec. com. Buckeye coun. Boy Scouts Am., 1984—; pres. elect Nat. Soc. Profl. Fund Raisers North Cen. Ohio chpt., 1988—. Named Citizen of Yr. Alliance Area United Way, 1981; recipient Alumni Svc. award Mount Union Coll., 1991. Mem. Nat. Soc. Fund Raiser Execs., Council for Advancement and Support Edn. (cons. 1977-79, dist. bd. dirs. 1983-84, fund raising com., summer faculty). Republican. Methodist. Club: Alliance Country (bd. dirs. 1982). Lodges: Filibusters (pres. 1979-80), Alliance Ruritans (Service to Youth award 1983). Home: 2500 Crestview Ave Alliance OH 44601-4600 Office: Mt Union Coll 1972 Clark Ave Alliance OH 44601-3929

SHEFFIELD, JAMES FRANKLIN, JR., political science educator; b. Cleveland, Miss., June 11, 1946; s. James Franklin and Annie Lea (Coleman) S.; m. Patsy Dale Posey (div.); children: Mark, Susan. BA, Miss. State U., 1969; MS, Fla. State U., 1970, PhD, 1973. Asst. prof. U. Tenn., Knoxville, 1973-74, Wichita (Kans.) State U., 1974-81; vis. assoc. prof. U. New Orleans, 1981-83; assoc. prof. Wichita State U., 1981—, chairperson dept. politcal scis., 1994—; assoc. faculty Ctr. for Urban Studies, Wichita State U., 1974-80; ptnr., rsch. dir. Sheffield, Carpenter & Assocs., Wichita, 1991-94. Contbr. articles to profl. jours. Participant Wichita Assembly, 1992; precinct committeeman Dem. Party, Kans., 1986—. 1st lt. USAR, 1974. Woodrow Wilson fellow Woodrow Wilson Found., 1969-70. Mem. Am. Polit. Sci. Assn. (co-editor newsletter of Urban Politics Sect.), Midwest Polit. Sci. Assn., So. Polit. Sci. Assn., Southwestern Polit. Sci. Assn. (v.p. 1994-95, nominating com. 1991-92, exec. coun. 1983-85), Western Polit. Sci. Assn. Democrat. Baptist. Office: Wichita State U Dept Polit Sci Wichita KS 67260

SHEFFIELD, JOHN WILLIAM, mechanical engineering educator; b. Ft. Worth, May 3, 1950; s. James G. and Sarah E. (Laney) S.; m. Mary White, May 21, 1977; children: Jennifer Marie, Katherine Elaine, Christopher William robert. B of Engring. Sci., U. Tex., 1971; M of Engring. Mechanics, N.C. State U., 1973, PhD in Engring. Sci. and Mechanics, 1975. Sr. analytical engr. Pratt & Whitney Aircraft, United Tech. Corp., East Hartford, Conn., 1975-76; sr. exptl. engr. Pratt & Whitney Aircraft, United Tech. Corp., West Palm Beach, Fla., 1976-78; rsch. asst. prof. of mech. engring. U. Miami, Coral Gables, Fla., 1978-80; asst. prof. U. Mo., Rolla, 1980-84, assoc. prof., 1984-89, prof. of mech. and aerospace engring., 1989—; asst. dir. Indsl. Assessment Ctr., 1994—; asst. editor Internat. Assn. for Hydrogen Energy, 1978-82; assoc. editor Internat. Assn. Hydrogen Energy, 1983—. Contbr. numerous articles to profl. jours. Mem. ASHRAE (Dist. Svc. award 1991, mem. various coms.), ASME, AIAA, Am. Soc. Engring. Edn., Sigma Xi, Phi Kappa Phi, Tau Beta Pi, Pi Tau Sigma. Home: 11870 Forest Lake Dr Rolla MO 65401-9372 Office: Univ Mo Rolla Dept Mech & Aerospace Engrg 207 Mech Engring Bldg A Rolla MO 65409-0050

SHEFFIELD, LESLIE FLOYD, retired agricultural educator; b. Orafino, Nebr., Apr. 13, 1925; s. Floyd L. and Edith A. (Presler) S.; BS with high distinction in Agronomy, U. Nebr., 1950, MS, 1964; postgrad. U. Minn., summer 1965; PhD, U. Nebr., 1971; m. Doris Fay Fenimore, Aug. 20, 1947; children: Larry Wayne, Linda Faye (Mrs. Bernard Eric Hempelman), Susan Elaine (Mrs. Randy Thorman). County extension agt. Lexington and Schuyler, Nebr., 1951-52; exec. sec. Nebr. Grain Improvement Assn., 1952-56; chief Nebr. Wheat Commn., Lincoln, 1956-59; exec. sec. Great Plains Wheat, Inc., market devel., Garden City, Kans., 1959-61; asst. to dean Coll. Agr., U. Nebr. at Lincoln, 1961-66, supt. North Platte Expt. Sta., 1966-71, asst. dir. Nebr. Coop. Extension Service, Nebr. Agrl. Expt. Sta., Lincoln, 1971-75, asst. to vice chancellor Inst. Agr. and Natural Resources, 1975-84, also extension farm mgmt. specialist and assoc. prof. agrl. econs., 1975-94; ret. U. Nebr., Lincoln, 1994. v.p. U. Nebr. Found., 1982-86; sec.-treas. Circle 4S-L Acres, Wallace, Nebr., 1973-87; cons. econs. of irrigation in N.D., Minn., S.D. and Brazil, 1975, 88, Sudan, Kuwait and Iran, 1976, People's Republic of China, 1977, 81, Can., 1977, 78, 79, 80, Mex., 1978, 79, Argentina, 1978, Hong Kong, 1981, Japan, 1981, Republic of South Africa, 1985, Argentina, Brazil and Paraguay, 1992, Australia, 1994, New Zealand, 1994. Author: Economic Impact of Irrigated Agriculture, 1985; co-author: Flat Water-A History of Nebraska and Its Water, 1993; author chpt. to book; editor: Procs. of Nebr. Water Resources and Irrigation Devel. for 1970's, 1972; contbg. editor Irrigation Age Mag., St. Paul, 1974-86; contbr. articles to various publs. With U.S. Army, 1944-46; ETO. Recipient Hon. State Farmer award Future Farmers Am., 1955, Hon. Chpt. Farmer award, North Platte chpt., 1973; fellowship grad. award Chgo. Bd. Trade, 1964, Agrl. Achievement award Ak-Sar-Ben, 1969, Citizen award U.S. Dept. Interior Bur. Reclamation, 1984; Pub. Svc. award for contbns. to Nebr. agr. Nebr. Agribus. Club, 1984, Ditch Rider award Four States Irrigation Coun., 1988, Disting. Svc. award Am. Soc. Farm Mgrs. & Rural Appraisers Nebr. chpt., 1993, Alumnus of Yr. award U. Nebr.-Lincoln Coll. Agr. & Natural Resources Alumni Assn., 1993, Headgate award Four States Irrigation Coun., 1995, Pioneer Irrigation award Nebr. Water Conf. Coun. and U. Nebr. Lincoln, 1995 ; NASA Rsch. grantee, 1972-77; inducted Nebr. Hall of Agrl. Achievement, 1988; named Irrigation Man of Yr. Irrigation Assn., 1988; honoree Disting. Svc. Nebr. Hall Agrl. Achievement, 1996. Mem. Am. Agrl. Econs. Assn., Am., Nat., Nebr. Water Resources Assns. (Pres.'s award 1979, award for Commitment to Irrigated Agriculture 1993), Nebr. Irrigation Assn., Nebr. Assn. Resource Dists., Am. Soc. Farm Mgrs. Rural Appraisers, Orgn. Profl. Employees of U.S. Dept. Agr., Lincoln C. of C. (chmn. agrl. com. 1974-77), Rotary (dir. 1965-66), Gamma Sigma Delta, Alpha Zeta (v.p. Nebr. agrl. rels. coun., 1993-94). Home: 3800 Loveland Dr Lincoln NE 68506-3842

SHEFT, MARK DAVID, market analyst, consultant, product manager; b. Racine, Wis., Dec. 10, 1953; s. Max Morris and Ruth (Milman) S.; m. Susan Barbara Fisher, Sept. 16, 1984; children: Alexander Franklin. BSEE, Purdue U., 1976; MBA in Mktg., Loyola U., Chgo., 1982. Proposal engr. ITT Telecommunications, Des Plaines, Ill., 1977-78, software engr., 1978-80; software engr. Motorola, Inc., Schaumburg, Ill., 1980-83; product planner AT&T Teletype, Skokie, Ill., 1983-86; bus. analyst Ill. Inst. Tech. Research Inst., Chgo., 1986-87; market rsch. mgr. Videojet Systems Internat., Wood Dale, Ill., 1987-92; mktg. cons., prin. Advanced Bus. Concepts, Inc., Hawthorn Woods, Ill., 1992-94; product mktg. mgr. Printek, Inc., Wheaton, Ill., 1992-93; product mgr. Follett Software Co., McHenry, Ill., 1993—. Mem. U.S. Chess Fedn., Am. Radio Relay League. Office: 1391 Corporate Dr Mc Henry IL 60050-7040

SHEHAN, WAYNE CHARLES, lawyer; b. Miami, Fla., Nov. 25, 1944; s. Joseph L. Shehan and Louise A. Salloum; m. Sherrin M. Graham, May 21, 1981; children: Christopher, Kevin. BS, U. Detroit, 1966, JD, 1969. Bar: Mich. 1969. Prin. Wayne C. Shehan, P.C., St. Clair Shores, Mich., 1969—; prof. U. Detroit, 1969-70; mediator Macomb County Cir. Ct., Mt. Clemens, Mich., 1988—; lectr. People's Law Sch., St. Clair Shores, 1987—. Precinct del. Macomb County Rep. Party, St. Clair Shores, 1974-80. Mem. State Bar Assn. Mich. (family law sect., estate planning sect., gen. practice sect.), Macomb County Bar Assn. (speakers bur.), Macomb County Trial Lawyers Assn. Office: 22420 Greater Mack Ave Saint Clair Shores MI 48080-2012

SHEHORN, HENRY WAYNE, real estate developer; b. Lawton, Okla., Jan. 22, 1935; s. Henry E. and Una Irene Shehorn; m. Gina Barclay, June 9, 1972; 1 child, Hollister Ann. BA in Bus., U. Nebr., 1969; MPA, U. Okla., 1973. Enlisted U.S. Army, 1960, advanced through grades to lt. col., 1984; pres. G & W Properties Corp., Leavenworth, Kans., 1978—; owner Fire Restoration Co., Leavenworth, 1981—; bd. dirs. Leavenworth Nat. Bank. Bd. dirs. Neighborhood House, Leavenworth; pres. Unified Sch. Dist. Bd., Leavenworth, 1989—. Mem. Assn. U.S. Army (pres. 1987-88), Leavenworth Rotary Club # 210, Leavenworth-Lansing Area C. of C. (pres. 1995, bd. dirs.). Republican. Home: 215 Elm St Leavenworth KS 66048 Office: G & W Properties Inc 779 Metropolitan Leavenworth KS 66048

SHEIKH, SUNEEL ISMAIL, aerospace engineer, researcher; b. Bristol, Gloucester, Eng., Jan. 21, 1966; came to U.S., 1975, U.S. Citizen 1987; s. Hyder Ismail and Joan Mary (Duncan) S. BS in Aerospace Engring, Maths., U. Minn., 1988; MS in Aeronautics and Astronautics, Stanford U., 1990. Lic. pvt. pilot, U.S. Student intern Honeywell, Inc., Mpls., 1989-90; assoc. engr. Martin Marietta Corp., Denver, 1990-91; prin. rsch. scientist Honeywell, Inc., Mpls., 1991—; cons., engr. Honeywell, Inc., Mpls., 1991. Recipient Honorable Mention award NSF, 1988. Mem. AIAA, Inst. Navigation, Planetary Soc., Nat. Space Soc. Home: 1012 Thomas Ave S Minneapolis MN 55405-2113 Office: Honeywell Inc 3660 Technology Dr Minneapolis MN 55418-1006

SHEKLETON, MAUREEN E., respiratory nurse, educator; b. Cleve., Oct. 26, 1947; d. Raymond S. and Marjorie Anne (Hogue) Gurnick; m. Gerald T. Shekleton, Dec. 27, 1968; 1 child, Thomas. BSN, Coll. Mt. St. Joseph, 1969; MSN, Case Western Res. U., 1973; DNSc, Rush U., 1982. RN, Ill. Dir. nursing grad. program Coll. Nursing Rush U., Chgo., 1984-85; asst. chair dept. oper. rm., surg. nursing Rush Presbyn. St. Luke's Med. Ctr., Chgo., 1983-85, practitioner, tchr., 1981-83, 85-86; asst. prof. nursing U. Ill., Chgo., 1989-92; adj. clin. faculty Rush U. & U. Ill., Chgo., 1992—; satellite site coord. DuPage Cmty. Clinic, Wheaton, Ill., 1992—. Author: (with M. Groer) Basic Pathophysiology: A Holistic Approach, 1989; (with K. Litwack) Critical Care Nursing of the Surgical Patient, 1991. Named Med. Surg. Nurse of Yr. ANA, 1989, Disting. Alumna Rush U., 1992, Nat. Academies of Practice Disting. Practitioner in Nursing, 1995; recipient Golden Apple award for excellence in teaching, 1991, Jesse Scott award ANA, 1994; postdoctoral fellow Nat. Rsch. Svc., 1987-88, fellow Am. Acad. Nursing, 1995. Mem. Ill. Nurses Assn. (pres. 1989-91), Respiratory Nursing Soc. (pres. 1992-94), Sigma Theta Tau (ANF Internat. scholar 1987). Home: 805 Edgewood Dr Glen Ellyn IL 60137-4214

SHELBY, CHARLES FRANCIS, priest, fundraising executive; b. L.A., Feb. 18, 1941; s. Peter Paul and Ruth (Russell) S. Student, St. John's Sem. Coll., Camarillo, Calif., 1959-62; BA, St. Mary's Sem., Perryville, Mo., 1964; MDiv, De Andreis Sem., Lemont, Ill., 1984; MS, DePaul U., 1972. Ordained priest Roman Cath. Ch., 1968. Adminstr., mem. faculty St. Vincent's Sem., Montebello, Calif., 1971-73; mem. faculty St. Mary's Sem., Perryville, 1973-79; assoc. dir. Assn. of Miraculous Medal, Perryville, 1980-82, dir., 1983—; bd. dirs. Nat. Cath. Devel. Conf., Hempstead, N.Y., v.p., 1992—. Mem. fin. com. Congregation of the Mission, St. Louis, 1980—; trustee Lazarist Trust, St. Louis, 1990—; treas. Ministerial Alliance, Perryville, 1975—. Mem. AAAS, Am. Mgmt. Assn., Advt. Mail Mktg. Assn., Perryville C. of C. Office: Assn of Miraculous Medal 1811 W Saint Joseph St Perryville MO 63775-1598

SHELDON, MARK PETER, philosophy educator; b. Camp Blanding, Fla., Dec. 17, 1944; s. Marvin Paul and Georgianna (Steinman) S.; children: Ivan, Noah. AB, Shimer Coll., Mt. Carroll, Ill., 1967; postgrad. (Sachar fellow), Oxford (Eng.) U., 1972-73; PhD, Brandeis U., 1975. Sr. policy analyst AMA, Chgo., 1987-88; assoc. prof. ethics Rush-Presbyn.-St. Luke's Med. Ctr., Chgo., 1989—; prof. philosophy, adj. prof. medicine Sch. Medicine Ind. U. N.W., Gary, Ind., 1991—; adj. lectr. Northwestern U., Evanston, Ill., 1985—; adj. prof. philosophy Loyola U. Chgo., 1989—. Guest editor Theoretical Medicine; contbr. articles to profl. jours., chpts. to books. 2d lt. U.S. Army, 1968-70. NDEA Title IV fellow, 1971-73, Sachar internat. fellow Brandeis U., 1972-73; grantee Ind. Com. for Humanities, 1975, 87, Coun. Philos. Studies, 1975, NEH, 1977, Lilly Endowment grantee Eli Lilly Co., 1990-93. Mem. N.Am. Soc. Social Philosophy (bd. mem. ctrl. div. 1989-90), Am. Philos. Assn., Soc. Health and Human Values (planning com. 1985-92). Jewish. Home: 2910 Simpson St Evanston IL 60201-2000 Office: Ind U NW 3600 Broadway Gary IN 46408-1603

SHELDON, NORMAN E., state legislator; b. DeSoto, Mo., May 31, 1936; m. Bernna Bourbon; 1 child, Lisa. Rep. Mo. State Ho. Reps. Dist. 107, 1988-93; rep. Mo. State Ho. Reps. Dist. 104, 1993—, mem. consumer protection, motor vehicle, labor coms., mem. fed.-state rels. and vet. coms. Mem. AMVETS, Elks Lodge. Home: 5201 State H Rd De Soto MO 63020*

SHELEY, WAYNE MCDOWELL, academic administrator; b. Ellenville, N.Y., Apr. 23, 1943; s. George L. and Adele (McDowell) S.; m. Nancy L. Stroud, Mar. 3, 1970; children: Jennie K., Justin W., Joanthan S. BS, Hartwick Coll., 1963; MusB, Yale U., 1964, MusM, 1965; MusD, Eastman Sch. Music, 1968. From asst. prof. to prof. music Murray (Ky.) State U., 1967-72; prof., chmn. music Appalachian State U., Boone, N.C., 1972-74; prof., head dept. music U. Ala., Tuscaloosa, 1974-81; dean coll. creative arts W.Va. U., Morgantown, 1981-84; dean coll. arts Calif. State U., Long Beach, 1984-91; provost, v.p. acad. affairs Washburn U., Topeka, 1991—; cons. in field. Editor: An Annotated Bibliography on LEadership, 1989, 2d edit., 1991. Mem. adv. com. Tuurnaround Topeka Team, 1993—; exec. com. Long Beach Symphony, 1986-91; exec. bd. Coalition Urban & Met. Univs., Washington, 1993—. Fulbright scholar, Italy. Mem. Am. Assn. Applied Editors (exec. bd. 1989—), Rotary (fellow chair 1995—), Phi Kappa Phi (v.p. 1993-95), Kappa Kappa Psi. Methodist. Office: Washburn U Morgan Hall College Ave Topeka KS 66621

SHELFFO, JULIE ANN, accountant; b. Chgo., Feb. 11, 1955; d. Loren E. and Patricia A. (Thompson) S.; m. John Z. Margold, May 23, 1988; 1 child, Matthew. BA, Seton Hall U., S. Orange, N.J., 1990. CPA, N.J., Ill. Accts.

records mgr. Leasing First Fidelity Bank, Newark, N.J., 1986-90; acct. Falk & Fisher, Millburn, N.J., 1990-92; acctg. mgr. Friendship Village, Schaumburg, Ill., 1993—. Literacy vol. Sr. Outreach, E. Orange, N.J., 1992. Mem. Ill. CPA Soc. Home: 704 S Patton Buffalo Grove IL 60089 Office: Friendship Village 350 W Schaumburg Rd Schaumburg IL 60194

SHELTON, O. L., state legislator; b. Greenwood, Miss., Feb. 6, 1946; s. Obie and Idell (McClung) S.; m. Linda Kay, July 21, 1980; children: Eric, Jaimal, Schron, Kiana. AB, Lincoln U., 1970. Youth specialist Mo. Ext. Svc., St. Louis, 1972-82. Committeeman 4th ward Dem. party, St. Louis, 1988—; vice-chmn. Dem. Party; advisor Ville Area Neighborhood Housing Assn.; active Black Leadership Roundtable, Mary Rydar Homes, Williams Community Sch. Mem. Early Childcare Devel. Corp. Home: 1803A Cora Ave Saint Louis MO 63113-2221

SHELTON, SAMUEL TERRANCE, court administrator; b. Boynton Beach, Fla., Sept. 5, 1948; s. Clarence Wilton, Sr. and Lou Anna (Ward) S.; 1 child, Jair Dasilva Shelton. BA, Emory U., 1970; MPA, Am. U., 1971; EdD, U. Tenn., 1978. Dist. ct. adminstr. Sixth Judicial Dist., Stevens Point, Wis., 1980—; organizing com. 2d Midwest Conf. on Ct. Mgmt., Milw., 1987-89; bd. dirs. Nat. Assn. Ct. Mgmt., 1990-92, mem. com. on preparing record on appeal Am. Bar. Assn., Chgo., 1992-94. Editor conf. report 2d Midwest Conf. on Ct. Mgmt., 1989; contbr. articles to profl. jours. Bd. dirs. CAP Svcs. Inc., Stevens Point, 1986-89; pres., bd. dirs. Beaver Dam Cmty. Theatre, Wis., 1981-84, area cmty. theatre, Stevens Point, 1989-92; mem. area sch. bd., Stevens Point., 1994-95. Recipient Outstanding Leadership award, Nat. Assn. for Ct. Mgmt., 1990. Mem. Am. Soc. Pub. Adminstrn., Am. Judicature Soc., Phi Kappa Phi, Omicron Delta Kappa, Phi Delta Kappa, Pi Sigma Alpha. Episcopalian.

SHEN, JEROME TSENG YUNG, pediatrician; b. Shanghai, China, Aug. 5, 1918; came to U.S., 1947; s. John G.K. and Agnes (Yao) S.; m. Theresa D.S. Yao, Oct. 10, 1938; children: Jerome L., Elizabeth Burke, Frances Schuman, Li Poppen, Thomas. BS, St. John's U., Shanghai, 1942, MD, 1945; MS in Pediatrics, St. Louis U., 1949. Lic. physician, Mo.; diplomate Am. Bd. Pediatrics 1951. Instr. dept. pediatrics St. Louis U. Sch. Medicine, 1949-52, sr. instr., 1952-60, asst. clin. prof., 1960-70, assoc. clin. prof., 1970-76, clin. prof., 1976-93, clin. prof. emeritus, 1994—; grad. fellow adolescent medicine Harvard Grad. Sch., Boston, 1958-59; vis. prof. Nat. Coll. Juvenile Ct. Judges, Reno, Nev., 1973, adj. prof. jud. adminstrn., 1981-82; cons. adolescent medicine St. Louis State Hosp. and Mo. Inst. Psychiatry, St. Louis, 1973-80; head dept. pediatrics St. Louis City Hosp., 1959-63; chief dept. pediatrics and outpatient dept. Scott Field Air Force Hosp., Belleville, Ill., 1956-58; chief dept. pediatrics St. Lous Labor Health Inst., 1967-90; sr. cons. adolescent clinic Cardinal Glennon Children's Hosp., St. Louis, 1977-90; hon. staff Cardinal Glennon Children's Hosp., St. Mary's Health Ctr., St. John's Mercy Health Ctr.; emeritus staff Jewish Hosp. St. Louis, 1993—; chmn., Expert Advisors Medicine and Pub. Health Rep. China (Taiwan), 1978; bd. dirs., mem. exec. com. Children's Lobby, Washington, 1972; mem. planning com. Mo. State Conf. on Crime, Delinquency and System of Justice; mem. adv. com. Mo. Divsn. Family Svcs., 1973-80; pres. Bi-State Interagy. Coun. on Smoking and Health, 1971-74; Mo. del. to White House Conf. on Children and Youth, 1970; mem. Gov. Com. for Children and Youth, chmn. subcom. on health, 1972-81; chmn. Midwest Regional Conf. Smoking and Health, 1972. Author, editor: Clinical Practice of Adolescent Medicine, 1980, Spanish edit., 1983; editorial bd. Postgrad. Medicine, 1977-88; contbr. articles to profl. jours. Coord. Mother Teresa's Gift of Mary Ctr., St. Louis; founder, bd. dirs. past pres. Pro Life Citizens Polit. Action Com., St. Louis, 1986—; chmn. Mo. Task Force on Unwed Adolescent Sexual Activity and Pregnancy, Jefferson City, 1987; hon. mem. Nat. Coun. Juvenile and Family Ct. Judges, Reno, 1982—; bd. dirs. Birthright Counseling, 1965—; Westminster Day Ctr. for the Poor, St. Louis, 1969-72, St. Louis Archdiocesan Pro Life Com., 1974—, co-chmn. 1981-82; Lady's Inn, St. Lousi, 1981—, co-chmn, 1974-75; bd. dirs.; Mo. and Nat. Drs. for Life, 1980—; mem. Bd. of Health, City of University, 1974-80; bd. dirs. Our Lady's Inn, St. Louis, 1981—; chmn. Midwest Regional Conf. on Smoking and Health, 1972. Maj. USAF, 1956-58. Recipient Cardinal Carberry Pro Life award Archdiocese of St. Louis, 1978, Citation for Outstanding Achievement Senate State of Mo., Jefferson City, 1988, Svc. award St. Louis U. Fellow Am. Acad. Pediat. (now emeritus; liaison rep. to various couns., mem. Nat. Com. on Youth 1970-76, com. on adolescence 1977-80, chmn. Mo. com. on youth 1969-70, co-chmn. youth and sch. com. 1971); charter mem. Soc. Adolescent Medicine (treas. 1973-75, chmn. pvt. practice com. 1976-75, historian 1982-90). Republican. Roman Catholic. Home: 7132 Kingsbury Blvd University City MO 63130-4306

SHENEFIEL, CHRIS ALLEN, software engineering administrator, educator; s. Aubrey and Marilou (Geyer) S.; m. Rebecca Elena Davis, May 28, 1983. BS in Psychology, U. Ill., 1981, MS in Engring. Psychology, 1982. Human factors mgr. AT&T Comm., Piscataway, N.J., 1983-87; sr. technologist in user interfaces Southwestern Bell Tech., St. Louis, 1987-94; software engring. mgr. Motorola Cellular Infrastructure, Arlington Heights, Ill., 1994—. Mem. Assn. Computer Machinery, Human Factors Assn. Office: Motorola Cellular 1475 Shure Dr Arlington Heights IL 60004

SHENK, RICHARD LAWRENCE, real estate developer, photographer, artist; b. Columbus, Ohio, Jan. 26, 1940. BBA, Tulane U., 1961, U. of Va., 1961-62, Ohio State U., 1962-65. Plant mgr. S.A. Shenk Co., Columbia and U.S., 1962-65; v.p. Konter Corp., Cin., 1965-70; owner Richard L. Shenk Devel., Cin., 1970—; bd. dirs. Consol. Stores Corp., Columbus; co-founder Images Photographic Gallery, Cin., 1980; pres. Cmty. Improvement Corp., Springdale, Ohio, 1989-93; past. pres., bd. dirs., chmn. fin. com. Talbert House, Inc., Cin. Author: Different Way of Seeing, 1989. Mem. program com. Judaic studies program U. Cin.; mem. bd. overseers Cin. Campus Hebrew Union Coll.; bd. dirs., chmn. fin. com. Jewish Home of Cin., past campaign chmn., pres. Jewish Fedn. of Cin.; bd. dirs. Adath Israel Synagogue, Israil Ednl. Fund, Simon Wiesenthal Ctr., L.A. Mem. United Jewish Appeal (nat. vice chmn.), Rotary (past pres. Springdale chpt.). Home: 2349 Grandin Rd Cincinnati OH 45208

SHEPARD, IVAN ALBERT, securities and insurance broker; b. Springfield, Mass., Sept. 28, 1925; s. Albert Joseph and Mary (Harrigan) S.; m. Miriam Murray, May 20, 1950; children: Kirk, Robin, Mark. BS in Edn., Ohio State U., 1949. Registered rep. Divisional mgr. Confedn. Life, Columbus, Ohio, 1953-62; regional v.p. Western Res. Life, Cleve., 1962-69; v.p. Computer Life-Pan Western, Columbus, 1969-74; ins. broker Shepard and Assocs., Rocky River, Ohio, 1974—; bd. dirs., v.p., sec. Computer Life Ohio, 1969-72. With U.S. Navy, 1943-45. Home: 29318 Lake Rd Cleveland OH 44140-1321 Office: Shepard and Assocs 20525 Center Ridge Rd Cleveland OH 44116-3424

SHEPARD, RANDALL TERRY, judge; b. Lafayette, Ind., Dec. 24, 1946; s. Richard Schilling and Dorothy Ione (Donlen) S.; m. Amy Wynne MacDonell, May 7, 1988; one child, Martha MacDonell. AB cum laude, Princeton U., 1969; JD, Yale U., 1972; LLM, U. Va., 1995; LLD (hon.), U. So. Ind., 1995. Bar: Ind. 1972, U.S. Dist. Ct. (so. dist.) Ind. 1972. Spl. asst. to under sec. U.S. Dept. Transp., Washington, 1972-74; exec. asst. to mayor City of Evansville, Ind., 1974-79; judge Vanderburgh Superior Ct., Evansville, 1980-85; assoc. justice Ind. Supreme Ct., Indpls., 1985-87, chief justice, 1987—; instr. U. Evansville, 1975-78, Indiana U., 1995. Author: Preservation Rules and Regulations, 1980; contbr. articles to profl. publs. Bd. advisors Nat. Trust for Hist. Preservation, 1980-87, chmn. bd. advisors, 1983-85, trustee, 1987—; dir. Hist. Landmarks Found. Ind., 1983—, chmn., 1989-92, hon. chmn., 1992—; chmn. State Student Assistance Commn. on Ind., 1981-85; chmn. Ind. Commn. on Bicentennial of U.S. Constn., 1986-91; vice chmn. Vanderburgh County Rep. Ctrl. Com., 1977-80. Recipient Friend of Media award Cardinal States chpt. Sigma Delta Chi, 1979, Disting. Svc. award Evansville Jaycees, 1982, Herbert Harley award Am. Judicature Soc., 1992. Mem. ABA (coun. mem. sect. on legal edn. 1991—, vice chair appellate judges conf. 1992—), Ind. Bar Assn., Ind. Judges Assn., Princeton Club (N.Y.), Capitol Hill Club (Washington), Columbia Club (Indpls.). Republican. Methodist. Home: 4057 N Meridian St Indianapolis IN 46208-4012 Office: Ind Supreme Ct 304 State House Indianapolis IN 46204-2213

SHEPARDSON, DANIEL PHILIP, science education educator; b. DeKalb, Ill., May 26, 1957; s. Philip Raymond and Mary Ellen (Garrison) S. BS in Wildlife Sci., Utah State U., 1980, MEd in Secondary Edn., 1984; PhD in Sci. Edn., U. Iowa, 1990. Cert. tchr., Utah. Sci. tchr. Grand County Mid. Sch., Moab, Utah, 1981-83; dir. curriculum Nat. Energy Found., Salt Lake City, 1984-87; assoc. prof. sci. edn. Purdue U., West Lafayette, Ind., 1990—; adj. instr. Utah State U., Logan, 1984-85; instr. Project Learning Tree, West Lafayette, Ind., 1990—, Project Wild, West Lafayette, 1990—; cons. Project STEPS problem solving, Iowa City, 1987—; presenter in field. Contbr. articles to profl. jours. Mem. NSTA (sci. tchr. edn. com. 1991-93), ASCD, Nat. Assn. for Rsch. in Sci. Tchg. (assoc. editor Jour. 1993—), Am. Ednl. Rsch. Assn., Assn. for Edn. Tchrs. in Sci. (reviewer 1991, editl. bd. 1992-96, bd. dirs.-at-large north ctrl. region 1992-95), Sch. Sci. and Math. Assn. (reviewer 1990—), Assn. for Advancement Computers in Edn. (editor Jour. Computers in Math. and Sci. Tchg. 1992—), Nat. Wildlife Fedn. Home: 32 Scarborough Ct Lafayette IN 47905-7623 Office: Dept Curriculum and Instrn 1442 Laeb West Lafayette IN 47907-1442

SHEPHERD, BYRD, systems analyst; b. Gulston, Ky., Feb. 22, 1931; s. Albert and Elva (Fee) S.; m. Mary Lou Jackson, Nov. 28, 1963; children: Cassandra Dee, Scott Byrd. B of Gen. Studies, Chaminade Coll., 1970; MBA, So. Ill. U., 1975; M of Data Processing, Washington U. St. Louis, 1979. System analyst Southwestern Bell Telephone Co., St. Louis, 1980-91, retired, 1991. Capt. USAF, 1957-80, Vietnam. Mem. Counterparts Assn., Vietnam Vets. Am. (chpt. treas.), Air Force Photo Mapping Assn., Mil. Order World Ward, SAR, Soc. War of 1812, Descendents of Washington Army Valley Forge, Am. Legion. Baptist. Home: 417 Todd Ln Belleville IL 62221

SHEPHERD, ELSBETH WEICHSEL, manufacturing consultant; b. Youngstown, Ohio, Dec. 5, 1952; d. Richard Henry and Lesley Frances (Lynn) Weichsel; BS in Math., Carnegie-Mellon U., 1974; MBA, U. Cin., 1979; m. Gordon Ray Shepherd, Aug. 28, 1976. Asst. indsl. engr. Armco, Inc., Middletown, Ohio, 1974-76, asso. indsl. engr., 1976-78, indsl. engr., 1978-82, sr. ops. engr., 1982-86, supr. process planning, 1986-88; project mgr. Integrated Mfg., 1988-91, supt. primary ops. scheduling, 1991-92; sr. assoc. Coopers & Lybrand, Cin., 1992-93, mng. assoc., 1993-94; sr. cons. CSC Consulting, 1995—. Mem. news mag. staff Jr. League Cin., 1980-81; vol. Miami Purchase Assn. Am. Iron and Steel Inst. fellow, 1978-81. Mem. Soc. Women Engrs. (pres. sect. 1981-82, provisional regional dir. 1983-84), Assn. Computing Machinery, Am. Inst. Indsl. Engrs. (v.p. services, pres. 1985-86), Tech. Socs. Council of Cin. (pres. 1986-87, 1st v.p. 1985-86, 2d v.p. 1984-85, treas. 1983-84), Engrs. and Scientists of Cin. (sec. 1986-87, pres. elect 1987-88, pres. 1988-89, treas. 1990-95). Home: 7382-4 Ridgepoint Dr Cincinnati OH 45230-4398 Office: 27th Flr 255 E 5th St Cincinnati OH 45202-4122

SHEPHERD, LEWIS EDWARD, portfolio manager; b. Kansas City, Mo., Nov. 21, 1946; s. Leo D. and Ruth M. (Ragan) S.; m. Janet E. Schindler, June 20, 1968; 1 child, Christine. AB, William Jewell Coll., 1968. Underwriter Aetna Casualty & Surety, Hartford, Conn., 1968-74, Shand, Morahan & Co., Evanston, Ill., 1974-80; portfolio mgr., pvt. investor Shepherd Investments, Deerfield, Ill., 1980—. Mem. Presdl. Roundtable, Washington, 1993—, House Majority Trust, Washington, 1995, 2d Amendment Task Force, Washington, 1994. Recipient Senatorial Medal of Freedom U.S. Senate GOP Mems., 1994, Ronald Reagan Eternal Flame of Freedom, 1995. Republican. Presbyterian. Home and Office: 221 Pine St Deerfield IL 60015

SHEPHERD, MARY ANNE, elementary education educator; b. Washington, Jan. 26, 1950; d. Edwin Joseph and Louise Therese (McKay) Zabel; m. Robert A. Shepherd, June 25, 1988. BS, U. Md., 1972; MEd, George Mason U., 1976; postgrad., U. Akron, 1991-93. Tchr. elem. schs. Montgomery County Public Schs., Rockville, Md., 1972-74, Fauquier County Pub. Schs., Warrenton, Va., 1974-76, Wooster (Ohio) Pub. Schs., 1976—. Advisor 4-H Club, Apple Creek, Ohio, 1982-87; vestrywoman St. James Episcopal Ch., Wooster, 1984-86, 88-91, St. Paul's Episcopal Ch., Akron, Ohio, 1996—. Mem. Wooster Edn. Assn. (treas. 1984-91). Republican. Home: 4872 Medina Rd Akron OH 44321-1122 Office: Wooster City Schs 144 N Market St Wooster OH 44691-4810

SHEPLER, JOHN EDWARD, engineering executive; b. Freeport, Ill., June 23, 1950; s. Edward Charles and Joyce Margaret (Wagner) S.; m. Barbara Jeanne Heinrich, Sept. 11, 1976. BSEE, Milw. Sch. Engring., 1972. Lic. FCC gen. class radiotelephone operator. Disc jockey, chief engr. Sta. WACI, Freeport, 1972-73, owner, ops. mgr., 1974-75; asst. chief engr. Sta. WROK, Rockford, Ill., 1973-74, chief engr., 1975-79; project engr. Martin Automatic, Rockford, 1979-80; engring. mgr. Pacific Scientific, Rockford, 1984-86; design engr. Sundstrand Corp., Rockford, 1980-84, engring. mgr., 1986—; tech. instr. Rock Valley Coll., Rockford, 1981-84; tech. cons. various broadcasters, 1979-94; columnist Electronic Servicing and Tech. Mag., 1990-94. Author: Sensational Sound Handbook, 1981; columnist Radio World mag., 1982-94; tech. illustrator, cartoonist, 1989-94; also articles; patentee in field. Named Outstanding Alumnus Milw. Sch. Engring., 1987. Club: Broadcast (v.p. 1971-72). Home: 5653 Weymouth Dr Rockford IL 61114-5544 Office: Sundstrand Corp 4747 Harrison Ave Rockford IL 61108-7929

SHEPLEY, CAROL FERRING, writer, art critic, magazine editor; b. St. Louis, Dec. 21, 1949; d. John Henry III and Georgene Emma (Otto) Ferring; m. William H. Starbuck, Jr., Sept. 8, 1973 (div.); 1 child, Caroline; m. John H. Shepley, Mar. 21, 1986; 1 child, Lucy. BA, Wellesley Coll., 1972. Staff lectr. Phila. Mus. Art, 1972-73; staff writer, art critic Caracas (Venezuela) Daily Jour., 1973-76; freelance writer, 1977--; editor corp. newspaper Monsanto Co., St. Louis, 1983, Southwestern Bell, St. Louis, 1984; editor alumnae mag. Mary Inst., St. Louis, 1986-89; art writer St. Louis Sun, 1989-90, St. Louis Mag., 1990-92; home design writer 1991-92; St. Louis corr. Money mag., 1991—; art critic New Art Examiner, 1989-94, St. Louis Post-Dispatch, 1991—; part-time prof. art history Maryville U., 1993—. Author: Miami for Kids, 1981, The Gentle Spirit and the Understanding Heart, 1984. Pub. rels. vol. Jr. League, Miami, Fla., 1982, March of Dimes, St. Louis, 1985, Good Shepherd Sch., St. Louis, 1988, St. Louis Libr., 1989, Goodwill, 1989, Kidney Found., 1991, 92; bd. dirs. women's cancer support SHARE, 1989-91. Mem. Alumnae Assn. Mary Inst. (officer 1987-88, 89-96, v.p. 1991-94, pres. 1994-96), Wellesley Club (v.p. 1986-88, officer 1989-91). Republican. Presbyterian.

SHEPP, CONNIE ANN, information systems specialist; b. Sedalia, Mo., May 28, 1965; d. Hiram Wilbert and Joan Elizabeth (Nolting) S. BS in Computer Info. Sys., Columbia (Mo.) Coll., 1992. Asst. dir. data processing Columbia (Mo.) Regional Hosp., 1987-88; computer operator Boone Hosp. Ctr., Columbia, 1988-91, programmer, 1991-93, info. sys. support ctr. mgr., 1993—; bus. mgr. Village Glass Works, Columbia, 1993.

SHEPPARD, JOAN LOCKER, activist; b. Oak Park, Ill., Jan. 26, 1932; d. Calvin Arthur and Anna Irene (Dost) S.; m. Charles Leland Sheppard, Dec. 23, 1953; children: Charles Arthur, Sarah Locker Sheppard Graham, Amy Jo, Rachel Morgan Sheppard Hyland. Student, U. Ill., 1953. Co-founder, charter mem. Alton Area Aid Assn., 1959, pres., 1962-63, 91, bd. dirs., 1990-91; mem. costume com. Alton Children's Theater, 1961; mem. gen. planning com. Alton City Sesquicentennial Celebration, 1986; bd. dirs. Alton Comty. Svc. League, 1981-82, 85-88, v.p., 1985, 86, adv. bd., 1990-91; bd. dirs. Gilson Brown Mother's Club, 1971-73, pres., 1971-72; bd. dirs. North Jr. H.S. PTA, 1969-71, West Jr. H.S., 1976-80, nominating com. parents group, 1976-77; facilitator Alton Lake Heritage Pkwy. Commn., 1992-93, strategic planning, 1992-93; mem. props com. Alton Little Theater, 1980, patrons chair, 1990, constitution revision com., 1995; bd. dirs. Alton Mus. History and Art, 1973-74, nominating com., 1975, ways and means com., 1977; bd. dirs. Am. Field Svc., 1976-77; celebrity waitress Am. Heart Assn., 1991; bd. dirs. ARC, 1979-85, sec., bd. dirs., 1982-85; bd. dirs. Better Homes for Alton, 1977-80; bd. dirs. Creative Express-Children's Drama Workshop, 1985; v.p. Gt. Rivers Preservation, Inc., 1993-95, newsletter com., 1995; chair vols. tax referendum Hayner Pub. Libr., 1988; bd. dirs. Lewis & Clark C.C. Found., 1985-95; comty. bd. St. Anthony's Health Ctr., 1991-95; bd. dirs. Urban League, Madison County, 1990-95; bd. dirs. YMCA, 1970-77, 81-82; bd. dirs. YWCA, 1959, 60, 64, 66, 68, numerous others. Home: 3514 Rosenberg Ln Godfrey IL 62035

SHERBY, KATHLEEN REILLY, lawyer; b. St. Louis, Apr. 5, 1947; d. John Victor and Florian Sylvia (Frederick) Reilly; m. James Wilson Sherby, May 17, 1975; children: Michael R.R., William J.R., David J.R. AB magna cum laude, St. Louis U., 1969, JD magna cum laude, 1976. Bar: Mo. 1976. Assoc. Bryan Cave, St. Louis, 1976-85; ptnr. Bryan Cave LLP, St. Louis, 1985—. Contbr. articles to profl. jours. Bd. dirs Jr. League, St. Louis, 1989-90, St. Louis Forum, 1992—, pres., 1995—); vice chmn. Bequest and Gift Coun. of St. Louis U., 1995—. Fellow Am. Coll. Trust and Estate Coun., Estate Planning Coun. of St. Louis (pres. 1986-87), Bar Assn. Met. St. Louis (chmn. probate sect. 1986-87), Mo. Bar Assn. (probate coun. 1985-87, 89—, chmn. probate law revision subcom. 1988—). Episcopalian. Home: 47 Crestwood Dr Saint Louis MO 63105-3032 Office: Bryan Cave LLP 1 Metropolitan Sq Ste 3600 Saint Louis MO 63102-2733

SHERBY, LOUISE SHARON, librarian; b. Bridgeton, N.J., Feb. 2, 1947; d. David and Edith (Fisher) S. BA, Hofstra U., 1969; MA in Libr. Sci., U. Denver, 1970; DLS, Columbia U., 1988. Adult svcs. libr. Chgo. Pub. Libr., 1970-73; reference libr. R.I. Coll. Libr., Providence, 1973-77, head reference libr., 1977-82; reference libr. Columbia U. Librs., N.Y.C., 1982-87, dep. head for adminstrn., 1987-88; asst. dir. for pub. svcs. U. Mo.-Kansas City Librs., 1988—; adj. prof. U. R.I. Grad. Libr. Sch., Kingston, 1981-82, U. Mo. Sch. Libr. and Info. Sci., 1989—. Co-editor (books) P.G. Wodehouse: A Comprehensive Bibliography, 1990, Who's Who of Nobel Prizes, 1901-95, 1996; contbr. chpt. to Basic Bus. Libr., 1983, 89, 95. Mem. Am. Libr. Assn., Assn. of Col. & Rsch. Librs. (bd. dirs. univ. libr. sci. 1994—, exec. bd. reference and adult svcs. divsn., 1991-92), Phi Kappa Phi. Office: Univ Mo Kansas City Librs 5100 Rockhill Rd Kansas City MO 64110

SHERIDAN, MARK WILLIAM, mechanical engineer, strategic planner; b. Bryn Mawr, Pa., July 9, 1959; s. Phillip Frederick and Shirley (Fraser) S. BSME, Lafayette Coll., 1981; MBA, Cornell U., 1987, M. Engring. (Mech.), 1988. Registered profl. engr., Ohio. Project engr. Internat. Paper Co., Mobile, Ala., 1981-83, sr. process engr., 1983-85; assoc. Booz-Allen & Hamilton, Cleve., 1988-90; coord. long range planning appliance motor divsn. Emerson Electric Co., St. Louis, 1990-93, resident engr. Paragould Plant, 1993—; summer intern Saturn Corp., Troy, Mich., 1986, 87. Bd. dirs. ABC Condominium Assn., St. Louis, 1992—; chmn. JGSM Student Faculty Com./Quality of Life Com., Ithaca, N.Y., 1985-87; pres. Mobile Soap Box Derby, 1983-85; v.p. ways and means, bd. dirs. Mobile Jaycees, 1984-85. Lester B. Knight scholar Cornell U., 1986-88, J. Stanford Smith scholar Cornell U., 1985-87; named Outstanding Young Man of Am., 1984, 85, 87. Mem. ASME, Inst. Indsl. Engrs., The Planning Forum, Gateway Area Macintosh Users Group, Soc. Indsl. Archaeology, World Future Soc., St. Louis Jaycees (bd. dirs. 1992-94), Am. Mensa. Republican. Presbyterian. Home: 7302 Tory Ln Paragould AR 72450 Office: Emerson Elec Pekin and Scott Sts Paragould AR 72450

SHERIDAN, SINCLAIR, healthcare administrator; b. Clinton, Ind., July 22, 1949; d. Harvey Roger and Martha (Gressmire) Sutliff; divorced; children: Bethann, Rebecca Ann. Diploma in nursing, St. Anthony Hosp. Sch. Nursing, Terre Haute, Ind., 1970; BSN, Ind. State U., 1978; MBA, Ctrl. Mich. U., 1982. RN, Ind. Operating rm. nurse Union Hosp., Terre Haute, 1975-80; mgr. program Rehab. Inst. of Pacific, Hawaii, 1983-87; exec. dir. New Medico Healthcare Sys., Fla.; regional dir. New Medico Healthcare Sys., Midwest, 1990-92; dir. oprs. Visitors Hosp., Buchanan, Mich., 1992-93; clin. dir. Rehab. Inst. Tri-State Hosp., Buchanan, Mich., 1993-94; pres., CEO Electronic Payment Svcs., Chgo., 1994-95; dir. medgridge ops. Manor Helathcare Inc., Arlington Heights, Ill., 1995-96; dir. subacate programs ops. support HCR, Toledo, Ohio, 1996—; profl. advisor Nat. Head Injury Assn., 1987—. Contbr. articles to profl. jours. Capt. U.S. Army, 1980-83. Decorated Meritorious Svc. award, 1983. Mem. Nat. Assn. Consumer Shows (assoc.), Am. Coll. Healthcare Execs., Greater Chgo. C. of C. Home: 505 N Lake Shore Dr # 2217 Chicago IL 60611 Office: HCR One SeaGate Toledo OH 43604-2616

SHERIFF, KENNETH WAYNE, social services administrator; b. Carthage, Mo., Dec. 27, 1942; s. Albert Edward and Veda Marie (Holcomb) S.; m. Shirley Ann Wingler, Oct. 3, 1964; children: Wendy Ann, Bradley Wayne. BA, Greenville Coll., 1965; MSW, U. Mo., 1970; M in Pub. Adminstrn., Sangamon State U., 1983. Lic. clin. social worker, Ill. Social worker Ill. Dept. Pub. Aid, Centralia, 1965-70, social svcs. cons., 1970-71; asst. regional dir. Ill. Dept. Pub. Aid, Springfield, 1971-72, sect. supr., 1972-79, program mgr., 1979-82, asst. bur. chief, 1982—; bd. dirs. Woodstock (Ill.) Christian Care Inc., 1981-94; exec. dir. Christian Counseling and Ednl. Ministries, Springfield, 1985-87; exec. dir. Keep In Touch Svcs., Inc., Springfield, 1983—. Bd. edn. Community Unit Dist. 8, Pleasant Plains, Ill., 1981-87; com. chmn. Citizens Com. for Better Schs., Pleasant Plains, 1979-80; bd. dirs. ministerial edn. and guidance Free Meth. Cen. Ill. Conf., Greenville, 1980—; alumni bd. mem. Greenville Coll., 1975-78. Mem. Nat. Assn. Social Workers. Free Methodist. Home: 1201 Larchmont Dr Springfield IL 62704-2109

SHERLOCK, JOHN MICHAEL, bishop; b. Regina, Sask., Can., Jan. 20, 1926; s. Joseph and Catherine S. Student, St. Augustine's Sem., Toronto, Ont., Can., 1950; student canon law, Catholic U. Am., 1950-52; LLD (hon.), U. Windsor, 1986; DD (hon.), Huron Coll., London, Ont., 1986. Ordained priest Roman Catholic Ch., 1950, bishop, 1974; asst. pastor St. Eugene's, Hamilton, Ont., 1952-59, St. Augustine's, Dundas, Ont., 1959-63, Cathedral Christ the King, Hamilton, also, Guelph and Maryhill, Ont., 1950-52; pastor St. Charles Ch., Hamilton, 1963-74; aux. bishop London, Ont., 1974-78; bishop, 1978—; chaplain Univ. Newman Club, McMaster U., Hamilton, 1963-66; pres. Canadian Conf. Cath. Bishops, 1983-85, liaison with U. Chaplains Can. and Pres. Cath. Coll. and Univs.; chmn. social affairs com. commn. Ont. Conf. Cath. Bishops, edn. commn., family life com.; adv. judge for the Regional Marriage Truban, 1954-72. Mem. Wentworth County Roman Cath. Separate Sch. Bd., 1964-74, chmn., 1972-73; chmn. Nat. Cath. Broadcasting Found., 1995—. Fellow honoris cause U.St. Michael's Coll., Toronto, 1994. Address: Chancery Office, 1070 Waterloo St, London, ON Canada N6A 3Y2

SHERMAN, ELAINE C., gourmet foods company executive, educator; b. Chgo., Aug. 1, 1938; d. Arthur E. and Sylvia (Miller) Friedman; m. Arthur J. Spiegel, Jan. 1989; children: Steven J., David P., Jaime A. Student, Northwestern U., 1956-58; diploma in cake decorating, Wilton Sch. Profl. Cake Decorating, 1973; diploma, Dumas Pere, L'école de la Cuisine Française. Tchr. cooking and adult edn. Maine, Oakton, Niles Adult and Continuing Edn. Program, Park Ridge, Ill., 1972-82; corp. officer The Complete Cook, Glenview, Ill., 1976-82, Madame Chocolate, Glenview, 1983-87; food columnist Chgo. Sun Times, 1985-87; dir. mktg. Sue Ling Gin, Chgo., 1987-88; co-owner Critical Eye, Chgo., 1988—; v.p., dir. merchandising, gen. mgr. Foodstuffs, Inc., Evanston, Ill., 1990-91, food cons. mgmt. and mktg., 1991—. Author: Madame Chocolate's Book of Divine Indulgences, 1984 (nominated Tastemaker award 1984). Bd. dirs. Chgo. Fund on Aging and Disability, 1989—; co-chmn. Meals on Wheels, 1989-90, 91. Mem. Les Dames D'Escoffier (founding pres.), Women's Foodservice Network (pres.), Confrerie de la Chaine Des Rotisseurs (vice conselliere gastronomique), Am. Inst. Wine and Food (bd. dirs.). Home and Office: 1728 Wildberry Dr # D Glenview IL 60025-1748

SHERMAN, FRANK WILLIAM, engineer; b. Ft. Dodge, Iowa, Nov. 15, 1946; s. Frank LaSalle and True Rosemary (Miller) S.; m. Joan Frances Van Bruaene, Aug. 21, 1971; children: Emma Daun, Joshua Frank. BS, Iowa State U., 1970; MS, So. Ill. U., 1991. Registered profl. engr., Ill. Air pollution engr. Ill. Environ. Protection Agy., Springfield, 1970-84; mgr. Ill. Vehicle Emission Test Program, Springfield, 1984-89; self-employed internat. environ. engring. practice Springfield, Ill., 1990-92; bd. dirs., pres. Sherman Engring., Inc., 1992—; chmn. Air Quality Adv. Com. Chgo. Area Transp. Study, 1976-84; bd. dirs., pres. Decatur Bicycle Shoppe Ltd. Contbr. articles to profl. jours. Pres. Pasfield Neighborhood Assn., Springfield, 1979; active 1st Congl. Ch., Springfield, 1985-88, host sponsor Youth for Understanding Fgn. Lang., 1987-88; vol. capt. Am. Heart Assn. Mem. Am. Assn. Motor Vehicle Adminstrs. (chmn. vehicle emissions subcom. 1988-90), Nat. Soc. Profl. Engrs., Ill. Soc. Profl. engrs., Air and Waste Mgmt. Assn.

SHERMAN, JAMES LEROY, engineering manager; b. Des Moines, Oct. 15, 1946; s. Eldon E. and Marian J. S.; m. Joan M., Sept. 2, 1989; children: Lori Heiser, Scott J., Jeffrey A.; Engring. mgr. Little Giant Crane & Shovel, Des Moines, 1967-74, 79—; engr. Eagle Iron Works, Des Moines, 1974-79;

mem. adv. bd. T.R.P. Project, Iowa CIty, Iowa, 1993. Republican. Methodist.

SHERMAN, JOHN KINGSLEY, retired industrial sales executive; b. Jackson, Mich., Nov. 8, 1914; s. Hugh Kingsley and Hetty Myra (Brittingham) S.; m. Dorothea von der Halben; 1 child, William Hugh. BS in Mech. Engring., U. Cin., 1938. Registered profl. engr., Ohio. Draftsman William Powell Co., Cin., 1933-37, Cin. Gas and Electric Co., 1937-41; sales engr. White Indsl. Sales and Equipment Co., Cin., 1943-64; pres., chmn. bd. dirs. Sherman & Schroder Equipment Co., Cin., 1964-84; ret., 1984. With USN, 1941-43. Mem. Ret. Engrs. and Scientists of Cin. (pres. 1993-94), Engrs. and Scientists of Cin. (bd. dirs.), Masons. Republican. Presbyterian. Home: 543 Terrace Ave Cincinnati OH 45220

SHERMAN, JOSEPH OWEN, pediatric surgeon; b. Chgo., Aug. 15, 1936; s. Joseph Owen and Mary Elizabeth (Kelly) S.; m. June Marie Martin, Mar. 16, 1963; children: Brian William, Lee Ann. Student, U. Ill., 1955-58; BS, Northwestern U., 1959, MD, 1962. Diplomate Am. Bd. Surgery, Am. Bd. Pediatric Surgery; lic. physician, Ill. Rotating intern Passavant Meml. Hosp., Chgo., 1963-64; resident in gen. surgery VA Rsch. Hosp., Chgo., 1964-65, 67-68; Am. Cancer Soc. clin. fellow Northwestern U. Med. Sch., Chgo., 1965-66; resident in pediatric surgery Children's Meml. Hosp., Chgo., 1966, 68-69; resident in thoracic surgery Mcpl. Tb San., Chgo., 1967; from instr. to assoc. prof. surgery Northwestern U. Med. Sch., 1967-86, prof. clin. surgery, 1986—; emeritus staff dept. surgery Children's Meml. Hosp., 1995—, Evanston (Ill.) Hosp., 1995—. Contbr. articles to profl. jours. Served with Ill. Army N.G., 1953-69, Ill. Air N.G., 1966-67. Fellow ACS, Inst. Medicine Chgo.; mem. AMA, Am. Pediat. Surg. Assn., Assn. for Acad. Surgery, Chgo. Med. Soc., Chgo. Surg. Soc., Ill. Pediat. Surg. Assn., Ill. State Med. Soc.

SHERMAN, KENNETH ELIOT, medicine educator, researcher; b. Long Branch, N.J., Dec. 21, 1955; s. Emanuel and Gertrude Sherman; m. Susan Nacht, Nov. 30, 1980; children: Marc, Amy. BS, Rutgers U., 1976, PhD, 1980; MD, George Washington U., 1985. Diplomate Am. Bd. Internal Medicine, Am. Bd. Gastroenterology. Commd. capt. U.S. Army, 1985, advanced through grades to lt. col., 1995; intern, then resident in medicine Tripler Army Med. Ctr., Honolulu, 1985-88; fellow in gastroentrology Fitzsimmons Army Med. Ctr., Aurora, Colo., 1989-91; gastroenterologist Fitzsimons Army Med. Ctr., Aurora, Colo., 1991-94, chief dept. clin. investigation, 1992-94; resigned, 1994; assoc. prof. medicine U. Cin. Med. Ctr., 1994—. Author, editor: Viral Insecticides for Biological Control, 1985; reviewer Hepatology, 1993—, Am. Jour. Gastroentrology, 1994—; contbr. articles to med. jours., chpt. to book; inventor composition and method. Asst. cubmaster Boy Scouts Am., Aurora, 1993-94. Recipient heroism award Kiwanis, 1982, rsch. award William Beaumont Soc., 1991; Busch predoctoral fellow Waksman Inst. Microbiology, 1976. Fellow ACP; mem. Am. Assn. for Study Liver Disease, Am. Soc. for Microbiology, Am. Gastroent. Assn. Office: U Cin Med Ctr Liver Unit Div Digestive Diseases Cincinnati OH 45267-0595

SHERMAN, MARK A., insurance company executive; b. Buffalo, Nov. 16, 1924; m. Kathleen Ann Laughlin, Feb. 17, 1951; children: Ann, John. AB, Oberlin Coll., 1948; MBA, U. Mich., 1949. CPCU, CLU. Office mgr., dir. tng. and pers. Citizens Ins. Co. Am., Howell, Mich., 1949-59; program developer Allstate Ins. Group, Skokie, Ill., 1959-60; sec./treas. Farmland Ins. Group, Des Moines, Iowa, 1960-67; dir. orgn. planning, regional dir. mktg. Country Cos., Bloomington, Ill., 1967-80; v.p. mktg. Union Ins. Group, Bloomington, 1980-90, ret., 1990—; adj. prof. Ill. State U. Editor quar. in-house publ.; contbr. articles to profl. jours. Bd. dirs. United Way McLean County, Bloomington, 1972-81, v.p. planning, 1973; v.p. Bloomington-Normal Symphony Soc., 1985-86, pres., 1986-88, bd. dirs. 1982-92; elder Presbyn. Ch. Sgt. U.S. Army, 1943-46, ETO. Mem. Soc. Ins. Trainers and Educators (life, pres. 1975-76), Soc. CPCU's, Nat. Assn. Profl. Ins. Agts., Sr. Profls. Ill. State U., Coll. Alumni Club (pres. 1972), Rotary (v.p. 1959, 90, pres. 1991, bd. dirs. 1984-93). Home: 1013 Barton Dr Normal IL 61761-4212

SHERMAN, MONA DIANE, school system administrator; b. N.Y.C., Aug. 28, 1941; d. Hyman and Lillian (Baker) Ginsberg; m. Richard H. Sherman, May 9, 1964; children: Holly Baker, Andrew Hunter. BS, Hunter Coll., CUNY, 1962; MS, CUNY, 1965. Cert. elem. tchr., K-12 reading endorsement specialist, ESL tchr., elem. adminstrn. and supervision, instrnl. supervision, spl. edn. learning disabilities and neurologically impaired edn., Ind. Elem. tchr. N.Y.C. Pub. Schs., 1962-77; team leader Tchr. Corps Potsdam (N.Y.) State Coll., SUNY, 1977-79; dir. Tchr. Ctr., Sch. City of Hammond, Ind., 1979-87; lab. coord. PALS, Gary (Ind.) Sch. Corp., 1987-93, mentor, 1988—, facilitator of staff devel., 1993—; instr. Tex. Instrument Computer Co., Lubbock, 1983-84, Performance Learning Sys., Emerson, N.J., 1984—; cons. in classroom discipline and computer instrn. Gary Staff Devel. Ctr., 1987—; mentor Urban Tchr. Edn. program Ind. U. N.W., Gary, 1991—; chair sch. improvement team, tchr. of yr. com., 1993-94; mem., grantswriter Gary Tech. Com., Gary Distance Learning Com. Mem. Lake Area United Way Lit. Coalition NW Ind., 1990, Gary Reading Textbook Adoption Com.; sec. Martin Luther King Jr. Acad. PTSA, mem. sch. improvement team. Recipient Recognition NW Ind. Forum, 1988, Tchr. of Yr. award Merrillville (Ind.) Lions Club, 1988, Outstanding Tchr. of Yr. award Inland Ryerson, East Chicago, Ind., 1989. Mem. Ind. Reading Assn., Gary Reading Assn., Phi Delta Kappa, Delta Kappa Gamma. Home: 1112 Fran Lin Pky Munster IN 46321-3607

SHERMAN, RICHARD H., education educator; b. Yonkers, N.Y., Jan. 5, 1941; m. Mona D. Sherman, May 9, 1964; children: Holly Baker, Andrew Hunter. BA, Hunter Coll., 1962; MA, Iowa U., 1965; MS, Queens Coll., 1970; EdD, Yeshiva U., 1977. Cert. tchr., Ind., Ill., N.Y. Asst. prof. edn. SUNY, Potsdam; instr. Herbert H. Lehman Coll., CUNY; asst. prof. edn. Purdue U., Hammond, Ind.; assoc. dean Ind. Vocat. Tech. Coll., Gary; chmn., assoc. prof. Calumet Coll. St. Joseph, Whiting, Ind.; edn. dir. Mus. Broadcast Communications, Chgo.; dir. Zarem/Golde ORT TECH Inst., Chgo.; workshop leader; presenter and speaker in field; exec. dir. Allied Ednl. Svcs. Author, playwright, poet, critic. Bd. dirs. Jewish Fedn. N.W. Ind.; chmn. events "Walk for Israel", Lake Area United Way, v.p. mobilization and resources devel, needs and assessment priorities com., chmn. section campaign; active Lake County chpt. ARC, N.W. Ind. Film Commn. Recipient N.W. Ind. Forum Svc. Recognition award, Jewish Fedn. N.W. Ind. Young Leadership award, Harlem Arts Svc. award. Mem. Internat. Reading Assn., Am. Assn. Theatre Critics, Dramatists Guild, Ind. Reading Coun., Ind. Reading Profs. (treas.), Hammond Reading Coun. (pres.), Ind. State Coun., N.W. Ind. Arts Assn. (subcom.), Rotary Club, Sigma Tau Delta, Phi Delta Kappa.

SHERMAN, THOMAS FRANCIS, education educator; b. Salamanca, N.Y., Dec. 20, 1946; s. Harry and Ione (Schultz) S.; m. Janice Ann Wade, Aug. 17; children: Piper Lee, Wade Thomas. AA, Paul Smith's Coll., 1967; BA, SUNY, Buffalo, 1970; MEd, Colo. State U., 1975; EdD, U. Colo., 1980. Tchr. Buffalo Pub. Schs., 1970; tchr. Poudre R.I. Pub. Schs., Ft. Collins, Colo., 1971, tchr., reading specialist, 1973-80; sr. resident supr. Lookout Mountain Schs. for Boys, Golden, Colo., 1972; faculty, dir. reading ctr. Ea. N.Mex. U., Portales, 1981-84; faculty Bemidji (Minn.) State U., 1985-90, Winona State U., Rochester, Minn., 1990-92; interim asst. v.p. acad. affairs S.W. State U., Marshall, Minn., 1992-93; interim asst. vice chancellor acad. affairs Minn. State Univ. System, St. Paul, 1993; mem. system quality facilitator team Minn. State U.; chair Winona State Outcomes/Indicators; coord. WSU/Minn. High Success Consortium Grad. Program. Contbr. articles on reading edn. to profl. jours. Bd. mem. Dodge/Fillmore/Olmstead Counties Corrections Bd., 1990-93; elder Presbyn. Ch. Mem. Internat. Reading Assn. (v.p. Minn. Coun., cert. of merit, sub chair evaluation team Nat. Coun. Accreditation Tchr. Edn., mem. nat. media award com.), Rochester Kiwanis (bd. dirs. 1992-95), Alpha Upsilon Alpha Internat. (steering com.). Democrat. Home: 1735 Walden Ln SW Rochester MN 55902-0901 Office: Winona State U Highway 14 E Rochester MN 55904

SHERMIS, ROBIN BARRY, radiologist; b. Fontana, Calif., Sept. 28, 1956; s. Stewart Shermis and Barbara Gail (Thompson) Townend; m. Denise Renae Thorson, May 27, 1988; children: Paige, Nicholas. BS, U. Calif., Davis, 1979; MPH, UCLA, 1982; MD, Case Western Res., 1986. Diplomate Am. Bd. Radiology, Am. Bd. Diagnostic Radiology. Resident in radiology U. Mich. Hosp., Ann Arbor, 1986-90; fellowship in cross-sectional radiology Henry Ford Hosp., Detroit, 1990-91; pvt. practice radiology Toledo Radiol. Assocs., Inc., 1991—; sect. head mammography Toledo Hosp., 1992—. Mem. AMA, Am. Coll. Radiology, Radiol. Soc. of N.Am., Am. Roentgen Ray Soc., Soc. of Breast Imaging, Acad. of Medicine Toledo. Office: TRA Inc 4841 Monroe Toledo OH 43623

SHERREN, ANNE TERRY, chemistry educator; b. Atlanta, July 1, 1936; d. Edward Allison and Annie Ayres (Lewis) Terry; m. William Samuel Sherren, Aug. 13, 1966. BA, Agnes Scott Coll., 1957; PhD, U. Fla.-Gainesville, 1961. Grad. teaching asst. U. Fla., Gainesville, 1957-61; instr. Tex. Woman's U., Denton, 1961-63, asst. prof., 1963-66; rsch. participant Argonne Nat. Lab., 1973-80, 93, 94; assoc. prof. chemistry N. Cen. Coll., Naperville, Ill., 1966-76, prof., 1976—. Ruling elder Knox Presbyn. Ch., 1971—, clk. of session, 1976-94. Mem. AAAS, AAUP, Am. Chem. Soc., Am. Inst. Chemists, Ill. Acad. Sci., Sigma Xi, Delta Kappa Gamma, Iota Sigma Pi (nat. pres. 1978-81, nat. dir. 1972-78, nat. historian 1989—). Presbyterian. Contbr. articles in field to profl. jours. Office: North Ctrl Coll Dept Chemistry Naperville IL 60566

SHERRILL, H. VIRGIL, securities company executive; b. Long Beach, Calif., 1920. Grad., Yale U., 1942, JD, 1948. Sr. dir. Prudential Securities Inc., N.Y.C. Office: Prudential Securites 199 Water St Fl 34 New York NY 10292

SHERRILL, THOMAS BOYKIN, III, newspaper publishing executive; b. Tampa, Fla., Nov. 19, 1930; s. Thomas Boykin Jr. and Mary Emma (Addison) S.; m. Sandra Louise Evans, Dec. 27, 1969; children: Thomas Glenn, Stephen Addison. Circulation dir. Tampa (Fla.) Tribune, 1962-67, Sarasota (Fla.) Herald-Tribune, 1967-75; v.p. circulation The Dispatch Printing Co., Columbus, Ohio, 1975-78, v.p. mktg., 1978—, bd. dirs., 1977—; v.p., bd. dirs. Ohio Mag., Inc., Columbus, 1979—. Chmn. bd. dirs. Salvation Army; trustee, past chmn. bd. dirs. Better Bus. Bur. Ctrl. Ohio, Inc.; bd. dirs. Ctrl. Ohio Ctr. Econ. Edn.; v.p., trustee Columbus Dispatch Charities; exec. bd. mem. Simon Kenton coun. Boy Scouts Am.; past pres. Wesley Glen United Meth. Retirement Ctr.; pres.'s adv. bd. mem. Meth. Theol. Sch.. With USN, 1951-56. Recipient Disting. Svc. award Editor and Pub. Mag., 1978; named hon. pres. Troy State U., 1979, hon. Ky. Col., 1980, hon. lt. col. aide-to-camp to Gov. State of Ala., 1984. Mem. Internat. Circulation Mgrs. Assn. (pres. 1975, Pres's. award 1989), Internat. Newspaper Mktg. Assn., Ohio Newspaper Assn. (bd. dirs., pres. 1986-88, Pres.'s award 1990), So. Circulation Mgrs. Assn. (pres. 1967-68, C.W. Bevinger Meml. award 1972), Audit Bur. Circulations (bd. dirs. 1980-90), Am. Advt. Fedn., Navy League, Ohio Newspapers Found., Ohio Circulation Mgrs. Assn (Pres.' award 1989), Columbus Area C. of C., SAR, Internat. Platform Assn., Columbus Met. Club, Athletic Club of Columbus, Muirfield Village Country Club, Kiwanis (pres. 1982). Republican. Home: 5215 Hampton Ln Columbus OH 43220-2270 Office: Columbus Dispatch 34 S 3rd St Columbus OH 43215-4201

SHERRY, PAUL HENRY, minister, religious organization administrator; b. Tamaqua, Pa., Dec. 25, 1933; s. Paul Edward and Mary Elizabeth (Stein) S.; m. Mary Louise Thornburg, June 4, 1957; children: Mary Elizabeth, Paul David. BA, Franklin and Marshall Coll., 1955; ThM, Union Theol. Sem., N.Y.C., 1958, PhD, 1969; hon. doctorate, Ursinus Coll., 1981, Elmhurst Coll., 1990, Defiance Coll., 1991, Lakeland Coll., Sheboygan, Wis., 1991, Reformed Theological Acad., Debrecen, Hungary, 1994, United Theol. Sem. Twin Cities, 1995. Ordained to ministry United Ch. of Christ, 1958. Pastor St. Matthew United Ch. of Christ, Kenhorst, Pa., 1958-61, Community United Ch. of Christ, Hasbrouck Heights, N.J., 1961-65; mem. staff United Ch. Bd. Homeland Ministry, N.Y.C., 1965-82; exec. dir. Community Renewal Soc., Chgo., 1983-89; pres. United Ch. of Christ, Cleve., 1989—; mem. gen. bd. Nat. Coun. Chs., N.Y.C., 1989—; mem. cen. com. World Coun. Chs., Geneva, 1991—, del. 7th Assembly, Canberra, Australia, 1991; bd. dirs. Ind. Sector, Washington, 1991—. Editor: The Riverside Preachers; editor Jour. Current Social Issues, 1968-80; contbr. numerous articles to religious jours.; host weekly radio programs local sta., 1974-78, 84-85, 93—. Mem. Soc. Christian Ethics. Democrat. Home: 13400 Shaker Blvd Cleveland OH 44120-1599 Office: United Ch of Christ 700 Prospect Ave E Cleveland OH 44115-1131

SHERRY, RICHARD JAMES, English language educator; b. Richland, Wash., May 14, 1949; s. Charles Ernest and Margery Grace (Sabiston) S.; m. Candice Elaine Shearer, Jan. 23, 1971; children: Peter Douglas, Emily Grace. BA, Wash. State U., 1971; MA, U. Ill., 1973, PhD, 1978. Instr. English Asbury Coll., Wilmore, Ky., 1977-78, asst. prof., 1978-83, assoc. prof., 1983-87, prof., 1987-94; dean of Faculty Growth and Assessment Bethel Coll., St. Paul, 1994—; trustee The Christian Scholars Rev., Chgo., 1987-94. Editor: Tragedy of the Lady Jane Gray, 1980; assoc. editor The Classical Bull., 1982-86; editor Ky. Philol. Assn. Bull., 1984-86; contbr. articles to profl. jours. NEH grantee, U. Minn., 1980, U. Conn., 1983, UCLA, 1985. Mem. Nat. Coun. Tchrs. English, Assn. Depts. English, Am. Soc. 18th Century Studies, Midwest Soc. 18th Century Studies. Republican. Mem. Christian and Missionary Alliance. Office: Bethel College 3900 Bethel Dr Saint Paul MN 55112-6902

SHERWIN, BYRON LEE, religion educator, college official; b. N.Y.C., Feb. 18, 1946; s. Sidney and Jean Sylvia (Rabinowitz) S.; m. Judith Rita Schwartz, Dec. 24, 1972; 1 child, Jason Samuel. BS, Columbia U., N.Y.C., 1966; B of Hebrew Lit., Jewish Theol. Sem. of Am., 1966, M of Hebrew Lit., 1968; MA, NYU, 1969; PhD, U. Chgo., 1978. Ordained rabbi, 1970. Prof. Jewish philosophy and mysticism Spertus Coll. Judaica, Chgo., 1970—, v.p. acad. affairs, 1984—. Author: Judaism, 1978, Encountering the Holocaust, 1979, Abraham Joshua Heschel, 1979, Garden of the Generations, 1981, Jerzy Kosinski: Literary Alarm Clock, 1981, Mystical Theology and Social Dissent, 1982, The Golem Legend, 1985, Contents and Contexts, 1987, Thank God, 1989, In Partnership with God: Contemporary Jewish Law and Ethics, 1990, No Religion Is an Island, 1991, Toward a Jewish Theology, 1991, How To Be a Jew: Ethical Teachings of Judaism, 1992, The Theological Heritage of Polish Jews, 1995, Sparks Amongst the Ashes: The Spiritual Legacy of Polish Jewry, 1996, also articles. Recipient Man of Reconciliation award Polish Coun. Christians and Jews, 1992, Presdl. medal, Officer of Order of Merit, Republic of Poland, 1995. Mem. Midwest Jewish Studies Assn. (founding pres.), Am. Philos. Assn., Assn. for Jewish Studies, Rabbinical Assembly, Am. Acad. Religion, Religious Ednl. Assn. Republican. Office: Spertus Coll Judaica 618 S Michigan Ave Chicago IL 60605-1901

SHERWOOD, LILLIAN ANNA, librarian, retired; b. South Bend, Ind., Dec. 22, 1928; d. Julius Andrew and Mary (Kerekes) Takacs; m. Neil Walter Sherwood, May 31, 1953; children: Susan Kay Huff, Nancy Ellen Coney, James Walter. AB in Home Econs., Ind. U., 1951, postgrad., 1978-83. Cert. libr. IV, Ind., 1984. Lab. tech. Lobund Inst., Notre Dame (Ind.) U., 1951-53; substitute tchr. Plymouth (Ind.) Community Schs., 1969-73; bookkeeper, processing clk. Plymouth (Ind.) Pub. Libr., 1973-76, audio-visual coord., 1976-79, reference and genealogical libr., 1980-93; retired, 1994; project dir. Ind. Heritage rsch. grant, Ind. Humanities Coun. and Ind. Hist. Soc., 1992-93; orgn. and verification com. Geneal. Socs., Pioneer Soc., Marshall County, Ind., Plymouth, 1988—. Mem. bd. dirs. Child Day Care Ctr. of Plymouth, 1971-75, pres., 1974. Mem. AAUW (v.p. 1966-68, pres. 1971-73, 85-87, 91-93), Marshall County Geneal. Soc. (v.p. 1986-87), Omicron Nu. Methodist. Home: 808 Thayer St Plymouth IN 46563-2859

SHERWOOD, PETER MILES ANSON, chemistry educator; b. London, July 12, 1945; came to U.S., 1985; s. Denis William and Merlyn E. (Green) S.; m. Gillian Thomson Taylor, Dec. 18, 1982. BSc, St. Andrews (Scotland) U., 1967; MA, PhD, Cambridge (Eng.) U., 1970; ScD, Cambridge (Eng.) U., England, 1995. Fellow Downing Coll., Cambridge U., 1970-72; lectr. dept. chemistry U. Newcastle upon Tyne, Eng., 1972-84, sr. lectr., 1984-85; program officer chemistry div. NSF, Washington, 1990-91; assoc. prof. chemistry Kans. State U., Manhattan, 1985-90, prof., 1991—; cons. W.R. Grace Co., 1986, E.I. Du Pont de Nemours & Co., 1988-90. Author: Vibrational Spectroscopy of Solids, 1972; editor: Critical Reviews in Surface Chemistry; also numerous articles. Fellow Salter's Co., London, 1970-72. Fellow Royal Soc. Chemistry, Inst. of Physics, Camridge Philos. Soc.; mem. Am. Chem. Soc., Soc. Applied Spectroscopy, Materials Rsch. Soc., Electrochem. Soc., Sigma Xi. Episcopalian. Home: 5811 Tuttle Cove Rd Manhattan KS 66503-8432 Office: Willard Hall Kans State U Dept Chemistry Manhattan KS 66506

SHETLER, CHRISTOPHER DAVID, chiropractor; b. Oneida, N.Y., Apr. 8, 1960; s. Harold Henry and Theila Marie (Bowman) S. AAS, Ricks Coll., 1984; D of Chiropractic, Tex. Chiropractic Coll., 1987. Lic. chiropractic physician, Ill. Physician Head-to-Toe Chiropractic, Hillsboro, Ill., 1988-89, Shetler Health Ctr., Irving, Ill., 1991-93, Shetler Clinic, Johnston City, Ill., 1993-94; physician, ctr. dir. Shetler Chiropractic Ctr., Effingham, Ill., 1994—. Capt. CAP. With U.S. Army, 1989-91. Mem. Motion Palpation Inst., Zone Fitness Ctr., C&S Self Defense Assn., Rotary Internat. Home: RR2 Box 147 Neoga IL 62447 Office: Shetler Chiropractic Ctr 811 W Fayette Effingham IL 62401

SHETTY, MULKI RADHAKRISHNA, oncologist, consultant; b. Hiriadka, Karnataka, India, July 10, 1940; came to U.S., 1974; s. Mulki Sunderram and Kusumavati Shetty. MBBS, Stanley Med. Coll., Madras, 1964; DTM, U. Liverpool, Eng., 1968; LMCC, Med. Coun., Can., 1975. House surgeon and physician Bombay Hosp., 1965-66; sr. house officer Manor Pk. Hosp., Bristol, Eng., 1966-67, Torbay Hosp., 1967-68, St. Lukes Hosp., Huddersfield, 1969-70; sr. resident Gen. Hosp. Meml. U., New Foundland, 1971-72; intern Ottawa Gen. Hosp., 1972-73; fellow in chemotherapy Ont. Cancer Found., Ottawa, Can., 1973-74; fellow in clin. oncology U. Fla., Gainesville, 1974-75; attending oncologist N.W. Community Hosp., Arlington Heights, Ill., 1975—; cons. N.W. Community Hosp., 1975—. Author: Lung Cancer, 1980, Recent Advances in Chemotherapy, 1985; contbr. numerous articles to profl. jours.; coined new ord calcifectomy; writer lyrics for Love Can Make a Grown Up Cry. Recipient Cert. for Outstanding Svc., Am Cancer Soc., 1982. Fellow Royal Soc. Medicine; mem. Internat. Assn. for Study of Lung Cancer, Chgo. Med. Soc. Hindu. Office: NW Community Hosp 800 W Central Rd Arlington Heights IL 60005-2349

SHEW, ROSE JEAN, nurse; b. Clinton, Ind., June 21, 1952; d. Paul James and Norma Jean (Bonomo) Duchene; m. Robert Morgan Roberts, Aug. 26, 1972 (div. May 1979); children: Joy Lynn, Robert John; m. Howard Edward Shew II, May 4, 1987 (div. Mar. 1994); 1 child, Sara Rose. Student, Ind. Vocat. Tech. Coll., Terre Haute, 1982-83. Float nurse Union Hosp., Terre Haute, 1983-88, ob.-gyn. nurse, 1988—; intensive coronary care Vermillion Country Hosp., Clinton, 1984-88; sec. Shew Excavating, Universal, Ind., 1987-93; ob nurse Union Hosp., 1990—. Chmn. Boy Scouts Am., 1985; troop leader Girl Scouts U.S.A., 1991-92. Mem. Daus. of Nile, Kappa Delta Phi. Roman Catholic. Home: 1440 S 4th St Clinton IN 47842-2232

SHIBLEY, RALPH EDWIN, JR., special education educator; b. Columbus, Ohio, Dec. 31, 1944; s. Ralph Edwin and Dorothy Ann (Evans) S.; m. P. Kathleen Phillips, July 23, 1966; children: Christine Marie, Margot Marie. BSc in Edn., Ohio State U., 1971, MA, 1981, PhD, 1984. Cert. spl. edn. supr., Ohio. Spl. edn. tchr. Columbus City Schs., 1974-80; dir. rsch. and devel. Six Pence Sch., Columbus, 1980-81; grad. rsch. assoc. Ohio State U., Columbus, 1980-84, program dir. Nisonger Ctr., 1984-87; prof. U. Rio Grande (Ohio), 1987—; adj. prof. Bowling Green State U., 1994—; cons. Gallipolis (Ohio) Devel. Ctr., 1989-90; project site coord. U. Cin., Gallipolis, 1990-91. Author articles and textbook revs. Named Tchr. of Yr. Cen. Ohio Soc. for Autistic Children, 1977; recipient cert. of appreciation Coalition of Handicapped Students, 1988. Mem. ASCD, Coun. for Exceptional Children (pres.-elect, editor Ohio fedn. tchr. edn. divsn.), Ohio Fedn. Coun. for Exceptional Children (pres.-elect, chmn. human rights task force), Am. Assn. Mental Retardation, Assn. for Children with Learning Disabilities, Interuniv. Coun. for Tchr. Edn., Epsilon Pi Tau. Democrat. Roman Catholic. Home: 3590 Milton Ave Columbus OH 43214-4045 Office: U Rio Grande Coll Edn Rio Grande OH 45674

SHIDE, DON, state legislator; m. Marijo; 4 children. Degree, U. N.D. Mem. N.D. Ho. of Reps., 1983—, vice chmn. agr. com., mem. indsl., bus., labor com.; farmer. Mem. Twp. Bd.; trustee St. Stephens Cath. Ch. Agriculturist award N.D. State U. Mem. Lions, Elks, Farm Bur. Home: RR 1 Box 92-c Larimore ND 58251-9769*

SHIELDS, CHARLES W., state legislator; b. Kansas City, Mo., July 25, 1959; m. Brenda Shields; 1 child, Brandt. BA, U. Mo., BS, MA. Real estate agt. Century 21 Cornerstone; rep. Mo. State Ho. Reps. Dist. 9, 1991-93; rep. Mo. State Ho. Reps. Dist. 28, 1993—, mem. commerce, edn., govt. orgn. coms., mem. joint com. on econ. devel. Mem. Lions Club (v.p.). Home: RR 4 Box 59 Saint Joseph MO 64507-9610*

SHIELDS, JAMES RICHARD, alcohol and drug counselor, consultant; b. Milw., Mar. 1, 1935; s. Edmund and Louise S.; m. Marlene Brietkreutz, Nov. 20, 1957. Grad. high sch., Hartford, Wis. Cert. alcohol and drug counselor, Wis.; nat. cert. addiction counselor, alcohol and drug counselor; cert. employee asst. profl.; cert. addictions specialist. Cons. Wis. Energy Corp., Milw., 1979—. With U.S. Army, 1959-66. Mem. Occupational Programing Cons. Assn., Employee Assistance Soc. N.Am., Employee Assistance Program Assn. (cert.). Home: 7230 Maple Ln Hartford WI 53027-9703 Office: Wis Energy Corp A-149 333 W Everett St Milwaukee WI 53203

SHIELDS, PATRICK THOMAS, JR., property manager; b. San Antonio, Sept. 5, 1935; s. Patrick Thomas and Mary Belle (Carson) S.; m. Mary Lou Sechrist, Mar. 28, 1964; children: Llewellyn Sechrist, Patrick Terrence. BBA in Real Estate, U. Tex., 1959. Loan officer Oak Cliff Savs., Dallas, 1962-65; appraiser assessor's office City of Richmond, Va., 1965-68; tax mgr. Sears, Roebuck & Co., Chgo., 1968-93; property tax adminstr. O'Keefe, Ashenden, Lyons & Ward, Chgo., 1993—. Plan commr. Village of Buffalo Grove, Ill., 1973-85, chmn., 1978-85, trustee, 1985-89. Mem. Inst. Property Taxation (cert., membership com. 1985, CMI com. 1986), Appraisal Inst., Internat. Assn. Assessors Officers (chmn. subscribing mem. com. 1985-87, membership svc. com., 1984, adj. assoc. mem. bd. dirs. 1989-91, Harry Galkin award 1984, Presdl. citation 1985). Presbyterian. Home: 1016 Whitehall Dr Buffalo Grove IL 60089-1934 Office: O'Keefe Ashenden et al 30 N LaSalle St Chicago IL 60602

SHIELDS, VALERIE LYNNE, public relations professional; b. Chgo., Jan. 26, 1967; d. Phillip Michael and Judith Ann (Schmitz) S. BA in Journalism, Ind. U., 1988. Sr. account exec. Golin/Harris Comms., Chgo., 1988-91; pres. Shields Comms., Chgo., 1991—. Freelance reporter The Chgo. Sun-Times, 1989-90. Chair pub. rels. Around the Coyote Arts Festival, Chgo., 1992-94; v.p. Ulrich Children's Home Aux. Bd., Chgo., 1991-92; Stagenotes editor Jr. League of Chgo., 1991; bd. dirs. Around the Coyote, 1992-94; contbg. arts editor: Roy Leonard's Going Out Guide, 1993-94. Office: Shields Comms 225 W Huron St Ste 511 Chicago IL 60610-3653

SHIER, GLORIA BULAN, mathematics educator; b. The Philippines, Apr. 20, 1935; came to U.S., 1966.; d. Melecio Cauilan and Florentina (Cumagun) Bulan; m. Wayne Thomas Shier, May 31, 1969; children: John Thomas, Marie Teresita, Anna Christina. BS, U. Santo Tomas, Manila, Philippines, 1956; MA, U. Ill., 1968; PhD, U. Minn., 1986. Tchr. Cagayan (Philippines) Valley Coll., 1956-58, St. Paul Coll., Manila, 1959-62, Manila Div. City Schs., 1958-64; asst. prof. U. of East, Manila, 1961-66; rsch. asst. U. Ill., Urbana, 1968-69; instr. Miramar Community Coll., San Diego, 1974-75, Mesa Community Coll., San Diego, 1975-80, Lakewood Community Coll., St. Paul, 1984, U. Minn., Mpls., 1986-87, North Hennepin Community Coll., Brooklyn Park, Minn., 1987—; cons. PWS Kent Pub. Co., Boston, 1989—. Chairperson Filipino Am. Edn. Assn., San Diego, 1978-79. Fulbright scholar U.S. State Dept., U. Ill., 1966-70; fellow Nat. Sci. Found., Oberlin Coll., 1967; recipient Excellence in Teaching award UN Ednl. Scientific Cultural Organ., U. Philippines, 1960-62, Cert. Commendation award The Gov. of Minn., 1990, Outstanding Filipino in the Midwest Edn. Cat. award 1992, Cavite Assn. Mem. Am. Math. Soc., Math. Assn. Am., Phi Kappa Phi, Sigma Xi Rsch. Honor Soc., Nat. Coun. Tchrs. Math., Am. Math. Assn. for Two Yr. Colleges, Internat. Group for Psychology of Math. Edn., Minn. Coun. of Tchrs. Math., Minn. Math. Assn. of Two Yr. Colleges, Filminnesotan Assn (bd.dirs. 1991—), Am. Statistical Assn. Roman Catholic. Home: 210 Wexford Heights Dr New Brighton MN 55112

SHIFFERD, KENT DRUMMOND, history educator; b. Chgo., Dec. 29, 1940; s. Stanley John and Frances (Drummond) S.; m. Patricia Jane Allen, Dec. 29, 1962; children: Sania, Sarah. BA, No. Ill. U., 1963, MA, 1965, PhD, 1974. Prof., dir. peace studies Northland Coll., Ashland, Wis., 1968—; exec. dir. Wis. Inst., Stevens Point, 1993-95; bd. dirs. Midwest Peace Inst., Chgo., 1987-88; v.p. Wis. Acad., Madison, 1977. Co-author: Dilemmas of War and Peace, 1993; contbr. articles to profl. jours. and chpts. to books. Mem. Phi Alpha Theta, Kappa Delta Pi. Buddhist. Home: Rt 1 Box 196 Ashland WI 54806 Office: Northland Coll Off of Dir Peace Studies Ashland WI 54806

SHILANDER, JIM R., mechanical engineer; b. Maryville, Tenn., Mar. 25, 1950. BS, U. Mich., 1976; postgrad., Ea. Mich. U. Draftsman LaSalle Machine Tool, Troy, Mich., 1978-85; engr. Parker-Majestic Inc., Troy, 1985—. Vol. Ann Arbor Jr. Football. Mem. ASME. Home: 3230 N Prospect St Ypsilanti MI 48198-9480

SHIMANDLE, FRANCIS EDWARD, advertising agency executive, writer, illustrator; b. Chgo., Nov. 20, 1942; s. Leonard Thomas and Margaret Frances (Voda) S.; m. Sally Ann Callanan, Sept. 5, 1963 (dec. July 1975); children: Shannon Mary, Del Francis, Tara Janine; m. Constance D. Baker, June 26, 1976 (div. Feb. 1984); 1 child, Christopher Jaime; m. Mary P. McCarthy, Feb. 27, 1988; 1 child, Thomas Justin. Student Chgo. Acad. Fine Arts, 1960-61. Prin. v.p., The Art Guys, Inc., Evansville, Ind., 1967-69; art dir. Albert Jay Rosenthal & Co., Chgo., 1969-70; exec. art dir. Rothenberg, Feldman & Moore, Chgo., 1970-73; creative dir. Scussell/Miller, Chgo., 1973-76, PGM, Inc., Chgo., 1976-83, v.p. creative svcs., 1989-95; prin. Our Co., Inc., Chgo., 1983-88, Shimandle Mktg., Des Plaines, Ill., 1995—. Author, illustrator: Dreamoirs, 1996; co-author, illustrator: Chocolate Mooselaneous, 1984. Songwriter popular songs. Recipient awards in field. Roman Catholic. Club: Naturals Social and Athletic (sec. 1981-83) (Chgo.).

SHIMANDLE, SHARON ANNE, critical care nurse; b. Cleve., Mar. 12, 1959; d. Harry William and Dorothy May (McGivney) Dowdell; m. James Edward Shimandle Jr., Dec. 22, 1979; children: Jason Michael, Jillian Lyn. ADN, Cuyahoga C.C., Parma, Ohio, 1980; MSN, Case Western Reserve U., 1990. RN, Ohio; cert. ACLS, BLS instr. Staff nurse SICU St. Vincent Charity Hosp., Cleve., 1980; staff nurse ICU Kaiser Hosp., Parma, 1981-82, staff nurse oper. rm., 1982-85; staff nurse post anesthesia care unit/ambulatory surgery unit Deaconess Hosp., Cleve., 1985-86, asst. dir. post anesthesia care unit/ambulatory surgery unit, 1986-87, critical care educator, 1987-90; critical care instr. Mt. Sinai Med. Ctr., Cleve., 1990-92; critical care educator Lorain (Ohio) Cmty. Hosp., 1992-94, Lorain Cmty./St. Josephs Regional Health Ctr., 1994—. Mem. AACN, Nursing Staff Devel. Orgn. Home: 290 B2 Yorktown Pl Vermilion OH 44089 Office: Lorain Cmmty St Joe Reg Health Ctr 3700 Kolbe Rd Lorain OH 44053-1611

SHIMKUS, JOHN MONDY, county treasurer; b. Collinsville, Ill., Feb. 21, 1958; s. Gene Louis and Kathleen (Mondy) S.; m. Karen Kay Muth; children: David, Joshua. BS, U.S. Mil. Acad., 1980. Advanced through grades to capt. U.S. Army, 1980-86; stationed at U.S. Army Base, Columbus, Ga., 1980-81, 85; served at U.S. Army Base, Bamberg, Germany, 1981-84; stationed at U.S. Army Base, Monterey, Calif, 1985-86; tchr. Metro East Luth. H.S., Edwardsville, Ill., 1986-90; treas. Madison County, Edwardsville, 1990—; liaison officer U.S. Mil. Acad., 1987—; treas. So. Ill. Law Enforcement Commn., 1990—. Bd. dirs. Sr. Citizen Companion Program, Belleville, Ill., 1991; trustee Collinsville Twp., Ill., 1989-93; Rep. precinct committeeman, Collinsville, 1988—. Maj. USAR. Rep Cand. for U.S. House 20th dist I.L., 1996. Mem. Nat. Assn. County Treas. and Fin. Officers (bd. dirs.), Ill. County Treas. Assn., Am. Legion Post 365. Lutheran. Home: 504 Sumner Blvd Collinsville IL 62234 Office: Madison County Treasurer Suite 125 157 N Main St Edwardsville IL 62025*

SHIMODA, THOMAS EDWARD, dentist, lawyer; b. Gt. Lakes Naval Base, Ill., Apr. 2, 1952; s. Noboru and Chieko (Furusawa) S.; m. Barbara F. De Kerf, July 14, 1984; children: Thomas Edward II, Clark Nicholas. BS in Biology with honor, Loyola U., Chgo., 1973; BS in Dentistry, U. Ill., Chgo., 1977, DDS, 1978; JD, DePaul U., 1987. Am. Coaching Effectiveness Program cert. coach. Pvt. practice, Chgo., 1978—; clin. asst. prof. oral medicine and diagnostic scis. U. Ill. Coll. of Dentistry, Chgo.; law clk. Fed. Pub. Defender, L.A., 1986; guest spkr. DePaul U. Health Law Inst., Chgo., 1988. Sr. editor, contbg. editor Hosp. Law Jour., 1986-87; contbr. articles to profl. jours. Vol. Health Fair, Chgo. Mem. ADA, ABA, Ill. Dental Soc., Chgo. Dental Soc., Ill. State Bar Assn., Chgo. Bar Assn., U.S. Judo Assn. (life, 3d degree black belt), U. Ill.-Chgo. Alumni Assn. (life), DePaul U. Alumni Assn., Loyola U. Alumni Assn., Japan Am. Soc., Beta Beta Beta. Office: Ste 1420 55 E Washington Chicago IL 60602-2109

SHIN, WILLIAM DONG MOON, brokerage house executive; b. Seoul, Korea, Apr. 12, 1944; came to the U.S., 1970; s. Kyung Soon and Il Soon (Kim) S.; m. Jeanie C. Youn, Jan. 30, 1971; children: Laura, Melissa. BSBA, Youngstown State U., 1977, MBA, 1986. Cert. money mgr. Payroll auditor Gen. Motors, Lordstown, Ohio, 1978-82; steel cost analyst Gen. Motors, Mansfield, Ohio, 1982-87; fin. cons. Merrill Lynch, Cleve., 1987-89, fin. mgr., 1989-90, asst. v.p., 1990-91, v.p., 1991-94; first v.p. Merrill Lynch, Pepper Pike, Ohio, 1994—. Pvt. Korean Army, 1966-69. Presbyterian. Home: 32081 Meadow Lark Way Pepper Pike OH 44124-5507 Office: Merrill Lynch 30100 Chagrin Blvd Pepper Pike OH 44124-5705

SHINE, NEAL JAMES, journalism educator, former newspaper editor, publisher; b. Grosse Pointe Farms, Mich., Sept. 14, 1930; s. Patrick Joseph and Mary Ellen (Conlon) S.; m. Phyllis Theresa Knowles, Jan. 24, 1953; children: Judith Ann, James Conlon, Susan Brigid, Thomas Patrick, Margaret Mary, Daniel Edward. BS in Journalism, U. Detroit, 1952; PhD (hon.), Cleary Coll., 1989, Siena Heights Coll., 1995, U. Mich., 1995, U. Detroit Mercy, 1996, Ctrl. Mich. U., 1996. Mem. staff Detroit Free Press, 1950-95, asst. city editor, 1963-65, city editor, 1965-71, mng. editor, 1971-82, sr. mng. editor, 1982-89, pub., 1990-95; prof. journalism Oakland U., Rochester, Mich., 1995—. Host, moderator Detroit Week in Rev., Sta. WTVS-TV, 1981-89, host Neal Shine's Detroit, 1989-91. Trustee, vice chmn. bd. trustees Youth for Understanding, 1973-75, chmn., 1975-78; mem. bd. for student publs. U. Mich.; bd. dirs. Children's Hosp., Econ. Club Detroit, Detroit Renaissance, New Detroit, Inc., Detroit Symphony Orch., Detroit Inst. Arts, Detroit Hist. Soc., United Way of Southeastern Mich., Met. Detroit Conv. and Visitors Bur., Operation ABLE, Detroit Press Club Found. With U.S. Army, 1953-55. Inducted Mich. Journalism Hall of Fame, 1990. Mem. Am. Soc. Newspaper Editors, Am. Newspapers Pubs. Assn., Mich. Press Assn. (bd. dirs. 1990-95), AP Mng. Editors, Sons of Whiskey Rebellion (comdr.-in-chief 1979—), Inc. Soc. Irish-Am. Lawyers, Detroit Press Club (charter, bd. govs. 1966-89, sec. 1957-68, v.p. 1969-71, pres. 1971-73). Home: 11009 Harbor Place Dr Saint Clair Shores MI 48080-1527 Also: Rathclaire, Gen Delivery, Pointe aux Roches, ON Canada N0R 1N0

SHINGLEDECKER, LEON G., podiatrist; b. Brookville, Pa., Feb. 9, 1949; s. Daniel G. and Flora B. (Brooks) S.; children: Dustin, Carly. BA in Biology, Clarion U., 1972; postgrad., Ill. State U., 1973-75; DPM, Pa. Coll. Podiatric Medicine, 1980. Diplomate Am. Bd. Podiatric Surgery. Resident Moss Rehab. Hosp., Phila., 1980-81; pvt. practice Allegheny Podiatry, Clarion, Pa., 1981-84; asst. prof. podiatric medicine and surgery U. Osteopathic Medicine, Des Moines, 1984-88; pvt. practice Ctrl. Iowa Foot and Ankle Assocs., Des Moines, 1988—; adj. clin. prof. Pa. Coll. Podiatric Medicine, Phila., 1981-84. Contbr. articles to profl. jours. Fellow Am. Coll. Foot and Ankle Surgeons; mem. Am. Podiatric Med. Assn., Iowa Podiatric Med. Soc. Republican. Presbyterian. Office: CtrlIowa Foot & Ankle Assoc 4900 Franklin Des Moines IA 50310

SHIPLEY, ANNA FRANCES, human environmental sciences educator; b. Maryville, Mo., July 17, 1939; d. Robert Willie and Helen Catherine (Batt) S. B Sci. Edn., N.W. Mo. State U., 1961; MS, Iowa State U., 1967; PhD, U. Mo., 1975. Cert. family and consumer sci. 7-12th grade home econs. tchr. Coon Rapids (Iowa) schs., 1961-66; rsch. asst. Iowa State U., Ames, 1966-67; H.S. home econs. tchr. Grundy Center (Iowa) schs., 1967-68; tchr. educator human environ. scis. N.W. Mo. State U., Maryville, 1968—, chair dept. human environ. scis., 1978—, grad. dean, 1988—, dean faculty and instrn., acting v.p. acad. affairs, 1994-95, interim dean Coll. Arts and Scis., 1995; del. U.S.-China Joint Conf. on Women's Issues, Beijing, 1995. Parliamentarian, exec. bd. Nat. Coun. Home Econs. Adminstrs., 1986-91; pres. AAUW, Maryville, 1989-90; trustee 1st Christian Ch., Maryville, 1989-92, elder, 1992—. Grantee Develop Model STAR Events Mo., 1984-85. Mem. Am. Assn. Family Consumer Scis. (mem. ethics com. 1993-95), Mo. Assn. Family Consumer Scis. (pres. 1989-90), Coun. Adminstrs. Family Consumer Scis., Kappa Omicron Nu (v.p. program 1982-84, dir. nat. rsch. project 1984). Mem. Christian Ch. (Disciples of Christ).

SHIPMAN, DAVID NORVAL, healthcare consultant; b. Henderson, Tex., Aug. 1, 1939; s. Norval Stewart Shipman and Dixie Juinita (VanNastrum) Retherford; m. Helen Morgan Suggs, July 1, 1960; children: Jeffrey David, Kimberly Kaye. Student, So. Ill. U., 1958-59, Okla. Bapt. U., 1959-61. Cert. Fin. Planner, CLU. Agt. Mutual Benefit Life Ins. Co., Oklahoma City, 1960-68; ptnr. Med. Cons. Inc., Oklahoma City, 1968-70; supr. Mutual Benefit Life Ins. Co., Oklahoma City, 1970-72; gen. agt. Mutual Benefit Life Ins. Co., Wichita, Kans., 1972-79; v.p. Mutual Benefit Life Ins. Co., Kansas City, Mo., 1979-83; pres. Fin. Group Inc., Kansas City, 1983-84; cons. Physicians Fin. Analysis Corp. (now Integrated Strategies), Kansas City, 1984—; charter mem. practice support initiative Am. Acad. Family Practice; mem. doctor's adv. network AMA. Contbr. articles to profl. jours. Bd. dirs. Young Dems., Oklahoma City, 1959-62, River Festival, Wichita, 1973-79, founding dir. Wichita Wagonmasters, 1975-79, Fellowship Christian Athletes, Wichita, 1976-79, Historic Wichita Cowtown, 1977-79. Mem. Am. Soc. CLU's, Internat. Assn. Fin. Planning, Inst. Cert. Fin. Planners, Nat. Assn. Securities Dealers (registered rep. 1969—), Nat. Assn. Life Underwriters, Gen. Agts. and Mgrs. Assn. (pres., bd. dirs. 1973-80), Profl. Assn. Health Care Office Mgrs., Jaycees (bd. dirs., pres. 1961-65), C. of C., Leawood Country Club. Republican. Baptist. Home: 8914 Cedar Dr Shawnee Mission KS 66207-2216 Office: 10100 Santa Fe Dr Ste 101 Overland Park KS 66212-4628

SHIPSHOCK, MICHAEL DONALD, engineer; b. Milw., July 6, 1973; s. Donald and Susan Shipshock. BSEE, Milw. Sch. of Engring. Engr. asst. Wilinski Assocs., Wauwatosa, Wis., 1993-94; assoc. engring. intern Controls Group - Johnson Controls, Milw., 1994-95; software engr. Motorola CSG, Libertyville, Ill., 1995—. Mem. IEEE, Eta Kappa Nu. Home: N93 W25180 Crestwood Dr Sussex WI 53089 Office: Motorola CSG Rm AN-273 600 N US45 Libertyville IL 60048

SHISLER, SISTER MARY PAUL, elementary school administrator, educator; b. Chgo., Dec. 6, 1948; d. Charles Robert and Henrietta Amelia (Precourt) S. BS, Coll. St. Francis, 1975; MS, Purdue U., 1982. Cert. tchr. K-9, adminstr. K-12. File/corr. clerk Met. Life Ins. Co., Des Plaines, Ill., 1966; elem. tchr. St. Joseph Sch., Dyer, Garrett, Ind., 1969-81; prin., jr. high math. tchr. St. Mary Sch., Park Forest, Ill., 1981-84; prin., jr. high math tchr. Peru (Ill.) Cath. Sch., 1984-92; prin. St. Mary Sch., Mundelein, Ill., 1992—; Assoc. Ill. Adminstr. Acad., 1989—. Recipient Outstanding Educator award LaSalle County, 1992. Mem. ASCD, Nat. Cath. Edn. Assn., Nat. Assn. Elem. Sch. Prins., U.S. Cath. Conf., The Smithsonian Assocs. Roman Catholic. Office: St Mary Sch 22277 W Erhart Rd Mundelein IL 60060-9551

SHIVELY, DANIEL JEROME, retired transportation executive; b. Akron, Ohio, Sept. 2, 1924; s. Richard Miles and Josephine (Pellicer) S.; m. Pamela Marion Kurfess, July 31, 1954; children: Jennifer, Laurie, Thomas. Grad., U.S. Mcht. Marine Acad., King's Point, N.Y., 1945. Chief officer (tanker) Trinidad Corp., N.Y.C., 1946-51; co-owner, mgr. Shively Bros. Jersey Farm, Quaker City, Ohio, 1952-54; staff asst. Gulf Oil Corp., Phila., 1955-57; distbn. coord. Standard Oil Co., Cleve., 1957-73; budget coord. BP Oil Co., Wilmington, Del., 1973-79; mgr. mktg. budget and planning Standard Oil Co., Cleve., 1979-85; owner, mgr. Shively & Assocs., Cleve., 1985-88. Served to lt. (j.g.) USNR, 1945-61. Mem. Transp. Practitioners Assn. (exec. com. 1984-90, pres. local chpt. 1984-85), Kings's Point Club (treas. N.E. Ohio chpt. 1989-94), KC (chancellor 1986, dep. grant knitght 1987-91). Republican. Roman Catholic. Home: 21347 Erie Rd Rocky River OH 44116-2133

SHIVELY, ELAINE MARIE, university official; b. Youngstown, Ohio, Apr. 6, 1946; d. Willis John and Beatrice (Riebe) Welch) S. AB in Math., Youngstown State U., 1968, MS in Math., 1970; postgrad., Kent (Ohio) State U., 1970-73; devel. edn. specialist, Appalachian State U., 1988. Cert. 7-12 math. tchr., Ohio. Sr. programmer Universal-Rundle Corp., New Castle, Pa., 1977-78, Sharon (Pa.) Steel Corp., 1978-80, Gen. Am. Transp., Masury, Ohio, 1981-82; programmer, analyst Youngstown Hosp. Assn., 1980-81, Dynacom Systems, Hubbard, Ohio, 1983; instr. math. Kent State U., 1984—, coord. devel. edn., 1990—; project coord. tech. intervention and support program Kent State U., Warren, Ohio, 1990—, dir. Trumbull Campus Skill Ctr., 1990—, coord. orientation and curriculum Trumbull Campus, 1991—. Mem. AAUW (sec. 1989-91, chmn. women's issues mentoring program 1991-92), Coll. Media Advisors, Nat. Assn. for Devel. Edn., Math. Assn. Am., Ohio Assn. for Devel. Edn., Ohio Acad. Sci., Phi Kappa Phi. Home: 61 Placid Dr Youngstown OH 44515-1638 Office: Kent State U Trumbull Campus 4314 Mahoning Ave NW Warren OH 44483-1998

SHOAF, BRUCE ALLEN, instrument engineer; b. Meadville, Pa., Apr. 8, 1950; s. Nevin Gray Shoaf and Nellie Adrienne (Rickard) S.; m. Jane Irene Miniaci, Nov. 6, 1971; children: Christine, Brenda, Michael, Benjamin; 1 stepson: Brian. Student, Erie (Pa.) Inst. Tech., 1968-70. Machine tool operator Teledyne Penn Union Electric, Edinboro, Pa., 1972; welder GE, Erie, 1972-73; sr. instrument technician Elkem Metals Co., Ashtabula, Ohio, 1973-94; engring. technician Cleve. Electric Illuminating Co., Ashtabula, Ohio, 1994; instrument engr. Elkem Metals Co., Marietta, Ohio, 1994—. Recipient cert. of merit Western Pa. Physics Tchrs. Assn. Mem. Instrument Soc. Am. (sr.), Indsl. Computing Soc. (founding), IEEE Computer Soc., Elkem Metals Co. Quality Club, Nuc. & Plasma Scis. Soc., Aerospace & Electronic SYstems Soc. Republican. Office: Elkem Metals Co Rt 7 South Riverview Marietta OH 45750

SHOAFF, THOMAS MITCHELL, lawyer; b. Ft. Wayne, Ind., Aug. 21, 1941; s. John D. and Agnes H. (Hanna) S.; m. Eunice Swedberg, Feb. 7, 1970; children: Andrew, Nathaniel, Matthew-John. BA, Williams Coll., 1964; JD, Vanderbilt U., 1967. Bar: Ind. 1968. Assoc. Isham, Lincoln & Beale, Chgo., 1967-68; ptnr. Baker & Daniels, Ft. Wayne, Ind., 1968—; bd. dirs. Ft. Wayne Nat. Bank, Ft. Wayne Nat. Corp., Weaver Popcorn Co., Inc., Ft. Wayne, Dreibelbiss Title Co., Inc., Ft. Wayne, Am. Steel Investment Corp., Ft. Wayne. Bd. dirs. McMillen Found., Ft. Wayne, Wilson Found., Ft. Wayne. Mem. ABA, Allen County Bar Assn., Ind. State Bar Assn. Presbyterian. Office: Baker & Daniels Ste 800 111 E Wayne St Fort Wayne IN 46802

SHOAFSTALL, EARL FRED, entrepreneur, consultant; b. Des Moines, Jan. 26, 1936; s. Ralph Paul and Josephine E. (Carnes) S.; m. Sharon I. Vannoy, Mar. 21, 1962 (div. 1980); children: Michael E., Angela R.; m. Carlene Christenson, Dec. 11, 1980; 1 child, Trace Herman. BA, MBA, Drake U., 1962. Enlisted USAF, Des Moines, 1954; advanced through grades to sgt. USAF, 1961, resigned, 1962; underwriter Hawkeye Security Ins., Des Moines, 1962-65; mgr., owner B & B Transfer and Storage Inc., West Des Moines, Iowa, 1965—; cons., owner B & B Mini Storage Inc., West Des Moines, 1975—. Inventor pressure gage, control valve for air and liquid. Republican. Club: Des Moines Golf and Country. Lodges: Masons (32 degree), Shriners. Home: 802 Irvindale SW Ankeny IA 50021-4500 Office: B&B Transfer and Storage Inc 536 S 19th St West Des Moines IA 50265-5547

SHOCK, DAVID HARRY, police officer; b. South Band, Ind.; s. Charles Albert and Emily (Wunsch) S.; m. Kathleen M. Kohen, Aug. 6, 1970 (div. Dec. 1976); 1 child, Emily; m. Wanda Paul, Dec. 1982. AS, Ind. U., 1975, BA in Sociology, 1981. Police officer South Bend (Ind.) Police Dept., 1970—. Sgt. U.S. Army, 1967-70. Mem. Rotary, Optimists. Home: 701 W Sample St South Bend IN 46601

SHOCKLEY, EARL MCCOY (COY SHOCKLEY), jazz musician, educator; b. East Orange, N.J., Dec. 30, 1930; s. Hurley Anderson and Lucy Jane (Cooper) S.; m. Elizabeth Allen, Nov. 10, 1987. Student, Hertz Sch. Music, Newark, 1948, U. Md., 1948-51. Composer: Miss Liz, 1986, Alabama Liz, 1987, N.J. Blues, 1990, Home Boy Blues, 1991; appeared at Bourbon Club, New Orleans, Hotel Fountainebleu, Miami, Le Bistro, Atlantic City, Club 500, Atlantic City, El San Juan Hotel, San Juan, P.R., The Dunes, Las Vegas, Caesar's Palace, Las Vegas, Meridian Hotel Chain, Paris and Nice, Satch's Boston, also in Catskill Mountains, numerous others; appeared at Newport Jazz Festival, MIT, Harvard U., Carnegie Hall; appeared on radio and TV; host TV series World of Coy Shockley, 1991—; recorded (with Jimmy McGriff) Billy & Lillie. With USMP MP, 1956-62. Recipient Lifetime Achievement award Al Stiles Talent Factory, Ft. Wayne, 1950. Mem. Musicians Union.

SHOEMAKER, DIANE MARIE, goldsmith, designer; b. Columbus, Ohio, Oct. 25, 1959; d. Wendell Eugene and Georgia June (Porschet) S. BA and BFA with distinction, Ea. Ky. U., 1983; MFA, Ohio U., 1986. Art dir. Action Group, Inc., Columbus, Ohio, 1986-87; stone setter The Trading Corp., Columbus, 1987-89; goldsmith, designer Michael W. Hayes Designer-Goldsmith, Woodmere, Ohio, 1991—; adj. faculty Ashland U., Ohio, 1989-94, Lorain County C.C., Ohio, 1990, 94, Ohio U., Lancaster, 1987-89; treas./exhbn. coord. E10 Gallery, Cleve., 1992—; curator Contrapposto Gallery, Cleve., 1995; instr. Esteem, Inc., Cleve., 1990-92. Exhibitor Millworks Gallery, Akron, Ohio, 1995, Bath, Ohio, 1995, Colonial Arcade, Cleve., 1994; solo exhibitor, E10 Gallery, 1995. Vol. Cleve. Pub. Theatre, 1995. Named Outstanding Alumnus, Sch. of Art, Ohio U., for yr. 1986, 1995; recipient Hon. Mention, Greater Lafayette (Ind.) Mus. of Art, 1990, Best of Show, Three Rivers Fine Arts Festival, Pitts., 1989, Westinghouse Purchase award, Pitts, 1989. Mem. Coll. Art Assn., Cleve. Mus. of Art. Home: 3620 Archwood Ave Cleveland OH 44109

SHOEMAKER, JAMES MICHAEL, aerospace engineer, researcher; b. Scott County, Va., Sept. 20, 1960; s. James Howard and Betty Ann (Grimm) S.; m. Suzanne Massey, Feb. 18, 1983; children: Christopher Michael, Timothy Howard. BS, Va. Poly. Inst. and State U., 1982, MS, 1984; MBA, Rollins Coll., 1990. Engr. Naval Surface Weapons Ctr., Dahlgren, Va., 1984-85; sr. engr. Martin Marietta Corp., Orlando, Fla., 1985-91; rsch. engr., turbomachinary analysis CFD ADF Inc.- NASA Lewis Rsch. Ctr., Brook Park, Ohio, 1991-93; sect. head secondary payloads sect., space experiments dept. ADF, Brook Park, Ohio, 1994—; mgmt. cons. Rollins Cons. Group, 1986-91; cons. Applied Tech. Assocs., Orlando, 1986-88; adj. prof. fin. and computer sci. U. Akron-Wayne Coll., 1993—. Patentee in microgravity two-phase fluid separation. Mem. student scholarship com. Orange County (Fla.) Sch. Bd., 1988-90; active Medina Vol. Tutor Program. Mem. AIAA (sr.), N.E. Ohio VPISU Alumni (exec. com.), Sigma Gamma Tau, Beta Gamma Sigma. Republican. Office: ADF Inc 2001 Aerospace Pky Cleveland OH 44142-1002

SHOEMAKER, MICHAEL C., state legislator; b. Nipgen, Ohio, July 2, 1945; m. Vicki Shoemaker; children: Michale Todd, Angela Lynn. BS, Capital Univ., 1967; MEd, Xavier Univ., 1973. Tchr. Paint Valley H.S., 1967-70, Waverly H.S., 1970-72, Smith Jr. H.S., 1972-73, Unioto H.S., 1973-77; carpenter, 1977; state rep. Ohio Dist. 88, 1983-92, Ohio Dist. 91, 1993; vice chmn. Health & Retirement Com., mem. Edn. Pub. Utilities & Fin. & Appropriations com., mem. Coll. & Univ. com. Named Athletic of Yr. Capital Univ.; recipient Svc. to Edn. award Ohio Univ. 1989, Friend of Edn. award, COTA, 1989. Mem. Bainbridge Hist. Soc., Paint Valley Athletic Boosters, Ross County Farm Bureau, Twp. Trustee & Clerks Assn., Scioto Valley Habitat for Humanity. Home: 10989 Cropp St Bourneville OH 45617*

SHOEMAKER, REBECCA SHEPHERD, history educator; b. Franklin, N.C., May 10, 1947; d. Charles Crawford and Mildred Maggie (Shuler) Shepherd; m. Carl Dahmer Cunningham, Dec. 20, 1972 (div. Mar. 1980); m. Raymond Leroy Shoemaker, Feb. 14, 1981. BA, Berea Coll., 1969; MA, Ind. U., 1970, PhD, 1976. Instr. U. N.C., Wilmington, 1973-74; asst. prof. Ill. State U., Normal, 1974-77; rsch. historian Ind. Gen. Assembly, Indpls., 1977-79; asst. prof. Ind. State U., Terre Haute, 1979-82, assoc. prof., 1972-92, prof., 1992—. Editor: (book) Biographical Directory of the Indiana General Assembly, Vol. I, 1814-1900, 1980. Chair, editorial bd. Vigo County Hist. Soc., Terre Haute, 1980-88. Recipient Summer Rsch. fellowship Ind. Humanities Coun., 1986, Clio Rsch. grant Ind. Hist. Soc., 1992. Mem. Ind. Hist. Soc., Orgn. Am. Historians, Ind. Assn. Historians. Disciples of Christ. Home: 7521 Heartland Rd Indianapolis IN 46278-1776 Office: Ind State U Dept of History Terre Haute IN 47809

SHOEMAKER, ROBERT SHERN, architect; b. Omaha, Sept. 9, 1953; s. Donald Shern and Peggy (Farnam) S. Student, Bethany Coll., 1971-72; pvt. pilot cert., Penn Valley Coll., 1975; BArch, Kans State U., 1977. Cert. architect Nat. Cert. Archtl. Registration Bd.; registered architect, Kans., Mo., Tex. Assoc. planner W.G. Roeseler, Kansas City, Mo., 1973-76; asst. project mgr. McCloskey Devel., Phila., 1976-77; project architect Fullerton Carey & Oman Architects, Kansas City, 1977-79; project mgr. HNTB Architect/Engineer/Planner, Kansas City, 1979-86; prin. Robert S. Shoemaker & Assocs., Kansas City, 1986—. Mem. City Coun. of Fairway, Kans., 1979-80. Mem. AIA (pres. Kans. State U. 1975-76, jurer Homes for Better Living 1976), Mo. Council Architects, Am. Arbitration Assn., Constrn. Specifications Inst., Kans. Soc. Architects (assoc.), Phi Kappa Tau. Home: 450 W 68th St Kansas City MO 64113-1919 Office: P O Box 22477 2200 Commerce Tower Kansas City MO 64113

SHOENER, JERRY J., state legislator. Mem. S.D. State Senate, mem. taxation and transp. coms.; newspaper exec. Home: 4012 Clover St Rapid City SD 57702-0252*

SHOFFER, JEFFREY DAVID, financial planner; b. Toledo, Ohio, Sept. 4, 1951; s. Norman and Marilyn (Fingerhut) S.; m. Kathleen R. Morrison, Sept. 20, 1975; children: Sarah E., Steven A., John E. BS, U. Toledo, 1975, MBA, 1976. Cert. fin. planner. Agt., registered rep. Mfrs. Life/Manequity, toledo, 1976-81; asst. br. mgr. Mfrs. Life/Manequity, New Orleans, 1981-83; dept. head, agt. Savage & Assocs. Inc., Toledo, 1983-86; fin. planner, v.p. Bolanis Fin. Planning Group, Toledo, 1989-94; fin. planner, pres. Strategic Resources Planning, Toledo, 1986-89, 94—. Contbr. articles to profl. jours. Charter mem., mem. program com. Toledo Planned Giving Coun., 1994—; mem. fin. bd. Oblates of St. Francis, Toledo, 1991—; bd. dirs. St. Pius X Sch., Toledo, 1990—, Internat. Inst., Toledo, 1994—; fund raiser Republican Party, Toledo, 1989-90. Mem. Internat. Assn. for Fin. Planning (vice chair chpt. adv. coun. 1990—). Jewish. Office: Strategic Resources Planning Inc 3341 W Bancroft St Toledo OH 43606

SHOGREN, JASON FREDRICK, economics educator; b. Cloquet, Minn., Sept. 29, 1958; s. Travis L. and Lou Ann (Provost) S.; m. Deborah Riley, June 16, 1984; children: Maija Liisa, Riley Travis. BA, U. Minn., Duluth, 1980; PhD, U. Wyo., 1986. Asst. prof. Appalachian State U., Boone, N.C., 1986-90; assoc. prof. economics Iowa State U., Ames, 1990—; head resource environ. policy Ctr. for Agrl. and Rural Devel. Iowa State U., Ames, 1990-92; vis. prof. Yale U., 1993; Stroock Disting. Prof. natural resource conservation and mgmt. dept. econs. and fin. U. Wyo., 1995—. Author/editor 4 books on environ. econs.; contbr. articles to profl. jours. Mem. Assn. Environ. Resource Econs. (editor newsletter 1992—). Office: Dept Econs U Wyoming Laramie WY 82071

SHOLAR, MARGERIE ELEANOR, elementary education educator; b. Wauwatosa, Wis., June 27, 1951; s. John W. and Eleanor I. (Rogers) Schaller; m. Michael L. Sholar Sr., Dec. 4, 1976; children: Michael L., Matthew J. BA, U. Wis., Eau Claire, 1973. Cert. tchr., Wis. Tchr. 6th grade Wautoma (Wis.) Area Schs., 1974—; bd. dirs. Living Environ. Facility, Wautoma, 1974-80. Troop leader Boy Scouts Am., Wautoma, 1987-92; active Habitat for Humanity, Wautoma, 1995. Mem. NEA, Wautoma Edn. Assn. (v.p. and pres. 1989-90). Lutheran. Home: 8406 Majestic Pines Circle Wautoma WI 54982 Office: Wautoma Area Schs PO Box 870 Wautoma WI 54982

SHOLITON, MARILYN COHEN, psychiatrist; b. Cin., Mar. 8, 1935. BS in Zoology, U. Cin., 1957, MD, 1961. Intern Christ Hosp., Cin., 1962; resident Rollman's Psychiat. Inst., 1973-75; fellow in indsl. psychiatry U. Cin., 1975-76; pvt. practice Cin., 1988—; med. dir. NORCE Behavioral Health Sys., 1988—; attending staff Jewish Hosp. Cin., 1988—; courtesy staff

Good Samaritan Hosp., Cin., 1991—, Christ Hosp., 1994—; lectr. U. cin., 1988—, assoc. prof. clin. psychiatry, 1982-88, student advisor, 1984-86; attending staff Holmes Hosp., 1976-88; mem. criteria com. Medco Peer Rev., Inc., Cin., 1980-83; mem. rehab. svcs. com. Comty. Chest and Coun. of Cin. Area, 1977-80; mem. med. adv. bd. Cin. Multiple Sclerosis Soc., 1977-80. Contbr. articles to profl. jours. and chpts. to books. Active occupational health com. Acad. Medicine, Cin., 1985—; bd. dirs. Orthodox Jewish Home for Aged, Cin., 1984—. Mem. Acad. Medicine Cin., Am. Psychiat. Assn., Ohio Psychiat. Assn., Ohio State Med. Assn.

SHONDELL, DONALD STUART, physical education educator; b. Fort Wayne, Ind., Jan. 1, 1929; s. Howard David and Elizabeth (Jones) S.; m. Betty Lou Hudson, Dec. 30, 1951; children: Steven, Kim, David, John. BS, Ball State U., 1952, MS, 1955; PED, Ind. U., 1970. Tchr. Brook (Ind.) High Sch., 1956-58; instr. Ball State U., Muncie, Ind., 1958--; pres. U.S. Volleyball Assn., Colorado Springs, Colo., 1979-80, v.p. 1972-80; ch mn. NCAA Volleyball Com., Overland, Kans. Author: Volleyball, 1970. Recipient Leader in Volleyball award, 1971, William Morgan Pres.'s award U.S. Volleyball Assn., 1981, Tachikara 600 Victory Club award, 1989, H.T. Friermood award U.S. Volleyball Assn., Outstanding Faculty Tchr. award Ball State U, 1980; named to Ball State Athletic Hall of Fame, 1984, Del. County Athletic Hall of Fame, 1987, Disting. Alumni award Ball State U., 1994; named outstanding alumnus Ball State Tchrs. Coll. Alumni Assn., 1980. Methodist. Home: 1315 N Winthrop Rd Muncie IN 47304-2960 Office: Ball State U Muncie IN 47306

SHOOK, ANN JONES, lawyer; b. Canton, Ohio, Apr. 18, 1925; d. William M. and Lura (Pontius) Jones; m. Gene E. Shook Sr., Nov. 30, 1956; children: Scott, William, Gene Edwin Jr. AB, Wittenberg U., 1947; LLB, William McKinley Law Sch., 1955. Bar: Ohio 1956, U.S. Dist. Ct. (no. dist.) Ohio 1961, U.S. Ct. Appeals (6th cir.) 1981. Cost acct. Hoover Co., North Canton, Ohio, 1947-51; asst. sec. Stark County Prosecutor's Office, Canton, Ohio, 1951-53; ins. adjuster Traveler's Ins. Co., Canton, 1953-56; ptnr. Shook & Shook Law Firm, Toledo, 1958-62, North Olmsted, Ohio, 1962—. Mem. at large coun. Olmsted Community Ch., Olmsted Falls, Ohio, 1987-90; chmn. ways and means com. North Olmsted PTA, 1968; area chmn. United Way Appeal, North Olmsted, 1963; v.p. LWV, Toledo, 1960-62. Mem. Cleve. Bar Assn.

SHOOK, JAMES CREIGHTON, real estate executive; b. Lafayette, Ind., May 19, 1931; s. Charles Wheeler and Jane Creighton (Peffer) S.; m. Mary Weil, Apr. 12, 1958 (dec. Jan. 1987); children: James C. Jr., Kathryn S. Bates, Stephen H., Sara Jane; m. Janice Warren, Feb. 13, 1988. BS in Bus., Ind. U., 1952. Ptnr. The Shook Agy., Lafayette, 1954-86; pres. The Shook Agy., Inc., Lafayette, 1986—; bd. dirs. NBD Inc., N.A., Indpls., Ind. Gas Co. Inc., Indpls., Ind. Energy Inc., Indpls., Crossman Cmtys., Inc., Indpls., Lafayette Life Ins. Co. Pres. Greater Lafayette United Way, 1965-66, Lafayette Home Hosp., Inc., 1973-74; chmn. North Ctrl. Health Svcs., 1989-91. 1st lt. USAF, 1952-54. Mem. Ind. C. of C. (bd. dirs. 1975—), Lafayette Country Club (pres. 1969-70), Crystal Downs Country Club (Frankfort, Mich.). Republican. Office: Shook Agy Inc 427 Main St Lafayette IN 47901-1369

SHOOK, JERRY L., company executive; b. Jefferson, Iowa, Dec. 23, 1949. Engraver Gardner Industries, Independence, Mo., 1974-88; owner Gardner Industries, Independence, 1988—. With U.S. Army, 1970-72. Mem. Nat. Tooling and Maching Assn. Office: Gardner Industries 9508 E Truman Rd Independence MO 64052-1862

SHOOP, L. JANE, nurse; b. Findlay, Ohio, Nov. 15, 1933; d. Victor Davis and Dora (Dukes) Johnson; m. June 12, 1955 (div. 1970); children: Julie Dawn, Jodi Anne. RN, Lima Meml. Sch. Nursing, Lima, Ohio, 1954. Office nurse L.H. Goodman, M.D., Findlay, Ohio, 1954-55; staff nurse Ohio State U. Hosp., Columbus, 1955-57; head nurse surgery clinic Ohio State U. Hosp., 1957-59; office nurse C.R. Coleman, M.D., Columbus, 1959-65; office mgr., nurse Othopedic & Trauma Surgeons, Inc., Columbus, 1965-96, ret., 1996; staff nurse First Community Village, Columbus, 1996. Mem. Orthopedic Nurses Assn. Republican. Home: 2368 Cambridge Blvd Columbus OH 43221-4001 Office: Orthopedic & Trauma Surgeons Inc 3600 Olentangy River Rd Columbus OH 43214-3437

SHORE, CARON DEAN, commercial real estate executive; b. Tillamook, Oreg., Oct. 24, 1949; d. Wayne Dickerson and Louise Margaret (Burge) Dean; 1 child, Jacqueline Lisa. BS, U. Oreg., 1971; MA, Washington U., 1973. Rsch. analyst Ind. Colls. and Univs. of Mo., St. Louis, 1972-74; purchasing agt. Paragon Group, Inc., St. Louis, 1974-75, property mgr., 1975-77, mgr. of residential adminstrn., 1977-81, mgr. of corp. adminstrn., 1982-84; asst. v.p. corp. adminstrn. and human resources Paragon Group, Inc., 1984-91; v.p. adminstrn. and human resources Paragon Group Inc., St. Louis, 1991-94, Paragon Group Property Svcs., Inc., St. Louis, 1994—; v.p. Paragon Group Property Svcs., Inc., Dallas, 1995—; v.p. Tex. PGI, Inc., St. Louis, 1994—, Dallas, 1995—; mem. nat. adv. bd. Paragon Comml. Contbr. articles to profl. jours. Course dir. Paragon Run for Juvenile Diabetes, St. Louis, 1985, Paragon Run for Spl. Olympics, St. Louis, 1986, Paragon Run to benefit U.S. Olympics, St. Louis, 1987-88, Old Newsboys; Day for United Way, 1987-94; vol. Berean House, 1991-93, U.S. Olympic Festival, 1994. Mem. Paragon Comml. Nat. Adv. Bd., Comml. Real Estate Women (bd. dirs. 1993-95), Soc. for Human Resource Mgmt., Assn. Legal Adminstrs., Order Ea. Star. Republican. Home: 5750 E University Blvd Apt 524 Dallas TX 75206-4283 Office: Paragon Group Property Svcs Inc 7557 Rambler Rd Ste 1300 Dallas TX 75231-2306

SHORE, EUGENE L., state legislator; b. Mar. 24, 1936; m. Janet Shore. BS, State U. Kans. Rep. dist. 124 State of Kans., 1985—. Mem. NRA, Kans. Farm Bur., Kans. Livestock Assn., Kans. Wheat Growers, Kans. Irrigators, Lambda Sigma Tau. Republican. Home: RR 2 Johnson KS 67855*

SHORES, ROBERT PHELPS, pharmacist, business owner; b. Burlington, Iowa, Apr. 27, 1942; s. Sumner Phelps and Lenore (Smith) S.; m. Patricia Ann Bellew, June 5, 1965; children: Christine, Susan, Robyn. BS in Pharmacy, Drake U., 1965. Registered pharmacist. Staff pharmacist Shores Pharmacy, Inc., New London, Iowa, 1965-72, chief pharmacist, 1972-78, pres. and CEO, 1978—; cons., Danville (Iowa) Care Ctr., 1973—, New London Care Ctr., 1975—; pres. New London Health Care, Inc., 1975-82. Mem. New London Fire and Rescue, 1969—, treas., 1980-84, pres. 1984-88; trustee New London Mcpl. Utility Bd., 1993-95. Named Friend of Edn., New London Edn. Assn., 1987, Hon. Grand Marshal, New London Day Com., 1990. Fellow Am. Soc. of Cons. Pharmacists; mem. Am. Pharm. Assn., Nat. Assn. Retail Pharmacists, Iowa Pharmacists Assn. (Ho. of Delegates 1965-95, bd. trustees 1985-87, chmn. Long Term Care Acad. 1988-92), Sigma Alpha Epsilon. Roman Catholic. Home: 201 S Chestnut St New London IA 52645-1606 Office: Shores Pharmacy Inc 134 W Main St New London IA 52645-1334

SHORROCK, WILLIAM IRWIN, history educator, academic administrator; b. Milw., June 16, 1941; s. William Joseph and Helen Louise (Irwin) S.; m. Marjorie Jean Britnall, Aug. 29, 1964; children: David William, Kimberly Lynn. BA, Denison U., 1963; MA, U. Wis., 1965, PhD, 1968. Asst. prof. history U. Wis.-Marathon County, Wausau, 1967-69; asst. prof. history Cleve. (Ohio) State U., 1969-73, assoc. prof. history, 1973-82, prof. history, 1982—, chair dept. history, 1980-87, vice provost for acad. affairs, 1989—; bd. dirs. Denison U. Rsch. Found., Granville, Ohio, 1988—. Author: French Imperialism in the Middle East, 1990-14, 1977, From Ally to Enemy, 1988 (French Colonial History Book prize 1989); editor: Ohio Coun. Social Studies Rev., 1982-94. Named Fulbright Rsch. fellow US Information Agy., Washington, 1985. Mem. Phi Beta Kappa. Office: Cleveland State Univ Cleveland OH 44115

SHORT, ANN MARIE HEROLD, library director; b. Richmond, Ind., June 15, 1957; d. Clarence Ferdinand and Dorothy Joyce (Holaday) H.; m. Michael Estill Short, May 7, 1977; 1 child, Wenona Jeannette. BFA, Ind. U., Indianapolis, 1979; MLS, Ind. U., Bloomington, 1986. Cert. libr. I, Ind. Libr. dir. Rauh Meml. Libr. Indpls. Children's Mus., 1980; children's libr. Shelbyville-Shelby County (Ind.) Pub. Libr., 1981-84, reference libr., 1987-88, libr. dir., 1988—; — Rushville (Ind.) Pub. Libr., 1984-87; mem. exec. com. Ind. Visual and Audio Network, Indianapolis, 1995—. Mem. Ind. Libr. Fedn., DAR, ACLU, Ind. Civil Liberties Union, People for Ethical Treatment of Animals. Roman Catholic. Office: Shelbyville-Shelby County Pub Libr 57 W Broadway Shelbyville IN 46176

SHORT, JOEL BRADLEY, lawyer, consultant, software publisher; b. Birmingham, Ala., Dec. 27, 1941; s. Forrest Edwin and Laura Elizabeth (Bradley) S.; m. Georgianna Pohl, June 5, 1965 (div. Apr. 1973); m. Nancy Ann Harty, Dec. 17, 1977; children: Christopher Bradley, Matthew Douglas. BA, U. Colo., 1963, LLB, 1966, JD, 1968. Bar: Kans. 1966, U.S. Dist. Ct. Kans. 1966, U.S. Ct. Appeals (10th cir.) 1975, U.S. Supreme Ct. 1976. Ptnr. Short & Short, Attys., Fort Scott, Kans., 1966-77, Nugent & Short, Overland Park, Kans., 1977-83; pvt. practice J. Bradley Short & Assoc., Overland Park, Kans., 1983-91; ptnr. Short & Borth, Overland Park, Kans., 1991—; owner Bradley Software; mem. tech. adv. com. Kans. Jud. Coun., Topeka, 1991-95. 1st lt. U.S. Army, 1967-73. Fellow Am. Acad. Matrimonial Lawyers; mem. Johnson County Bar Assn. (ethics and family law coms. 1983—). Office: Short and Borth Attys 32/1111 Corporate Woods 9225 Indian Creek Pky Overland Park KS 66210-2009

SHOTWELL, MALCOLM GREEN, minister; b. Brookneal, Va., Aug. 14, 1932; s. John Henry and Ada Mildred (Puckett) S.; m. LaVerne Brown, June 19, 1954; children: Donna (dec.), Paula. BA in Sociology, U. Richmond, 1954; MDiv, Colgate Rochester Div. Sch., 1957; D Ministry, Ea. Bapt. Theol. Sem., 1990; DD (hon.), Judson Coll., 1990. Ordained to ministry Am. Bapt. Ch. in U.S.A., 1957. Student asst. Greece Bapt. Ch., Rochester, N.Y., 1954-57; pastor 1st Bapt. Ch., Cuba, N.Y., 1957-62; sr. pastor 1st Bapt. Ch., Galesburg, Ill., 1962-71, Olean, N.Y., 1971-81; area minister Am. Bapt. Chs. of Pa. and Del., 1981-90; regional exec. minister Am. Bapt. Chs. of Great Rivers Region, Ill. and Mo., 1990—; mem. Midwest Commn. on Ministry, Am. Bapt. Chs. U.S.A., 1990—, mem. task force for So. Bapt.Am. Bapt. Chs. Relationships, 1990—. Author: Creative Programs for the Church Year, 1986, Renewing the Baptist Principle of Associations, 1990. Trustee No. Bapt. Theol. Sem., Lombard, Ill., 1993—, Judson Coll., Elgin, Ill., 1990—, mem. gen. bd. ABC, 1990—, mem. gen. exec. coun., 1990—, regional exec. ministers coun., 1990—; bd. dirs. Cen. Bapt. Theol. Sem., Kansas City, Kans., 1990—; sec. bd. dirs. Shurtleff Fund, Springfield, Ill., 1990—. Walter Pope Binns fellow William Jewell Coll., 1995. Mem. Ministers Coun. Ill. and Mo. Office: Am Bapt Chs of Great Rivers 225 E Cook St Springfield IL 62704-2509

SHOU, SHARON LOUISE WIKOFF, rehabilitation counselor; b. Mpls., Oct. 23, 1946; d. Wallace S. and Phyllis (Ireland) Wikoff; m. James Kouping Shou, Dec. 27, 1969 (dec. June 4, 1989); children: Michelle, Darren. Student, U. Colo., 1971-72, Chinese U. Hong Kong, 1966-67; BA, Macalester Coll., 1968; MA, U. Denver, 1975. Cert. rehab. counselor, case manager, employment counselor; lic. clin. profl. counselor. Employment counselor Colo. Dept. of Employment, Denver, 1971-74; acad. advisor U. Ky., Lexington, 1978-81; employment advisor DeVry Inst. Tech., Lombard, Ill., 1985-86; trainee asst. specialist County of DuPage, Wheaton, Ill., 1987; sr. rehab. case mgr. CRA Managed Care (Comprehensive Rehab. Assoc.), Boston, 1987—; vocat. rehab. expert witness. Mem. AAUW (internat. rels. com. 1983), Naperville (Ill.) Chinese Assn. (adminstrv. com. 1984), Nat. Assn. Rehab. Profls. in the Pvt. Sector. Office: CRA 9801 W Higgins Rd Ste 500 Rosemont IL 60018-4726

SHOUP, CHARLES SAMUEL, JR., chemicals and materials executive; b. Nashville, Dec. 10, 1935; s. Charles Samuel and Leola Ruth (Turner) S.; m. Frances Carolyn DiCarlo, June 7, 1958; children: Mark Steven, Elizabeth Ann Shoup Kehoe, Margaret Carol Shoup Meyer. AB, Princeton U., 1957; MS, U. Tenn., 1961, PhD, 1962. Rsch. chemist Oak Ridge (Tenn.) Natl. Lab., 1962-67; mgr. special projects Union Carbide Corp., N.Y.C., 1967-68; mgr. planning and controls Bell and Howell Co., Lincolnwood, Ill., 1968; v.p. Bell and Howell Sch. Inc., Chgo., 1968-69; mgr. tech. planning Cabot Corp., Boston and Cambridge, Mass., 1969-70, dir. corp. rsch., Mass., 1970-73, gen. mgr. E-A-R div., 1973-87, v.p., Indpls., 1984-87; pres. Alphaflex Ind. Inc., Indpls, 1987-88, bd. dirs., 1988, Cemkote Corp., Indpls., 1988-91; chmn. bd. dirs. Blasterz Corp., Carmel, Ind., 1992—; bd. dirs. Exec. Svc. Corps, Indpls., 1993—, mem. exec. com., 1994—; mem. bd. visitors Coll. Arts and Scis., U. Tenn., Knoxville, 1994—. Contbr. articles to profl. jours.; patentee in field. Treas. Oak Ridge Community Arts Ctr., 1965-67; pres. Sherborn Edn. Found., 1974-76; chmn. Met. Div. United Way, 1982; bd. trustees, Ind. Safety Equipment Assn. 1978-81. Fellow Am. Inst. Chemists; mem. AAAS, Am. Chem. Soc., Noise Control Products and Materials Assn. (trustee 1977-87, pres. 1982-84), Sigma Xi. Presbyterian. Home: 13019 Andover Dr Carmel IN 46033-2419

SHRAUNER, BARBARA WAYNE ABRAHAM, electrical engineering educator; b. Morristown, N.J., June 21, 1934; d. Leonard Gladstone and Ruth Elizabeth (Thrasher) Abraham; m. James Ely Shrauner, 1965; children: Elizabeth Ann, Jay Arthur. BA cum laude, U. Colo., 1956; AM, Harvard U., 1957, PhD, 1962. Postdoctoral researcher U. Libre de Bruxelles, Brussels, 1962-64; postdoctoral researcher NASA-Ames Rsch. Ctr., Moffett Field, Calif., 1964-65; asst. prof. Washington U., St. Louis, 1966-69, assoc. prof., 1969-77, prof., 1977—; sabbatical Los Alamos (N.Mex.) Sci. Lab., 1975-76, Lawrence Berkeley Lab., Berkeley, Calif., 1985-86; cons. Los Alamos Nat. Lab., 1979, 84, NASA, Washington, 1980, Naval Surface Weapons Lab., Silver Spring, Md., 1984. Contbr. articles on transport in semiconductors, hidden symmetries of differential equations, plasma physics to profl. jours. Mem. IEEE (exec. com. of standing tech. com. on plasma sci. applications), AAUP (local sec.-treas. 1980-82), Am. Phys. Soc. (divsn. plasma physics, exec. com. 1980-82, 96—), Am. Geophys. Union, Univ. Fusion Assn., Phi Beta Kappa, Sigma Xi, Eta Kappa Nu, Sigma Pi Sigma. Home: 7452 Stratford Ave Saint Louis MO 63130-4044 Office: Washington U Dept Elec Engring 1 Brookings Dr Saint Louis MO 63130-4862

SHRESTHA, BIJAYA, nuclear scientist; b. Kathmandu, Nepal, July 8, 1955; came to U.S., 1985; s. Kalidas and Kamala M. (Joshi) S.; m. Puja, May 7, 1975; children: Anjana, Anjaya, Srijana, Samjhana. MS in Plasma Physics, Tribhuvan U., Kathmandu, Nepal, 1978; MS in Nuclear Physics, La. State U., 1988; PhD, U. Mo., Rolla, 1995. Asst. lectr. Tribhuvan U., Kathmandu, Nepal, 1979-82, lectr., 1982-85; teaching asst. La. State U., Baton Rouge, 1985-88; rsch. teaching asst. U. Mo., Rolla, 1988-95, postdoctoral fellow, 1995—. Author: Campus Physics, 1982. Treas. Univ. Tchrs. Assn., Kathmandu, 1982. Recipient Fulbright scholarship, 1985. Mem. Am. Phys. Soc., Am. Nuclear Soc., Nepal Phys. Soc., Am. Math. Soc., Sigma Pi Sigma, Alpha Nu Sigma (pres. U. Mo. at Rolla chpt.), Tau Beta Pi. Home: 1602 N Cedar Rolla MO 65401 Office: U Missouri Dept Nuclear Engring Rolla MO 65401

SHREVE, ALLISON ANNE, former air traffic control specialist; b. Sturgeon Bay, Wis., Aug. 29, 1961; d. Kendil McLaren and Barbara Gail (Kellner) S. Student, U. Wis., Oshkosh, 1979-82, 95—, Madison Area Tch. Coll., 1993. Cert. control tower operator. Air traffic asst. FAA, Green Bay, Wis., 1985-87, air traffic control specialist, 1987-96. Active Earth Share Fund, Humane Assn., ASPCA; animal care vol. Wildlife Sanctuary, Green Bay, Wis. Mem. Wis. Wildlife Rehabilitator's Assn. Home: 411 S Francis St Brillion WI 54110-1338

SHREVE, GENE RUSSELL, law educator; b. San Diego, Aug. 6, 1943; s. Ronald D. and Hazel (Shepherd) S.; m. Marguerite Russell, May 26, 1973. AB with honors, U. Okla., 1965; LLB Harvard U., 1968, LLM, 1975. Bar: Mass. 1969, Vt. 1981. Appellate atty. and state extradition hearing examiner Office of Mass. Atty. Gen., 1968-69; law clk. U.S. Dist. Ct., Dallas, 1969-70; staff and supervising atty. Boston Legal Assistance Project, 1970-73; assoc. prof. Vt. Law Sch., Royalton, 1975-81; vis. assoc. prof. George Washington U., Washington, 1981-83; assoc. prof. law N.Y. Law Sch., N.Y.C., 1983-84, prof., 1984-87; vis. prof. law Ind. U., Bloomington, 1986, prof., 1987-94, Ira C. Batman faculty fellow, 1988-89, Charles L. Whistler faculty fellow, 1992-93, also dir. grad. studies; Richard S. Melvin Prof. of law, 1994—; cons. Conn. Bar Examiners, Hartford, 1978—. Co-author: Understanding Civil Procedure, 2nd edit., 1994; bd. editors Am. Jour. Comparitive Law, 1994—; contbr. numerous articles to legal jours. Mem. Am. Law Inst., Am. Soc. for Pol. & Legal Phil. Bd. Edn., Am. Jour. Corp. Law. Democrat. Episcopalian. Office: Ind U Sch Law Bloomington IN 47405

SHREVE, MICHAEL GERALD, computer consultant; b. La Porte, Ind., July 11, 1948; s. Russell Eugene and Elizabeth Ledeema (Masterson) S.; m. Virginia Louise Oliver, Apr. 13, 1950; children: Janine Marie Shreve Larkin, Michael Gerald II. BA in Psychology, Forensic Studies, Ind. U., 1974, MPA, 1988. Cert. law enforcement officer, Ind.; peace officer, Colo. Marshal Wanatah (Ind.) Police, 1974; police officer Purdue U., Ft. Wayne, Ind., 1975-76; dep. sheriff Gilpin County, Central City, Colo., 1977-79; dir. security Mark Resort, Vail, Colo., 1980; police officer Notre Dame (Ind.) Police, 1981-94; owner PC Fix, La Porte, Ind., 1989—. Sgt. USAF, 1968-72, Vietnam. Recipient Silver Safety Belt, Hoosiers for Safety Belts, 1988, 89. Mem. VFW, NRA, Law Enforcement Alliance, Mensa (coord. N.W. Ind. 1989—). Republican. Home: 2962 E 850 N La Porte IN 46350-8994

SHRIVER, DUWARD FELIX, chemistry educator, researcher, consultant; b. Glendale, Calif., Nov. 20, 1934; s. Duward Laurence and Josephine (Williamson) S.; m. Shirley Ann Clark; children: Justin Scott, Daniel Nathan. BS, U. Calif., Berkeley, 1958; PhD, U. Mich., 1961. From instr. to assoc. prof. chemistry Northwestern U., Evanston, Ill., 1961-70, prof., 1970-87, Morrison prof. of chemistry, 1987—, chmn. dept. chem., 1992-95; mem. Inorganic Syntheses Inc., 1974—, pres., 1982-85; vis. staff mem. Los Alamos (N.Mex.) Nat. Lab., 1976-85, cons., 1985-92; vis. prof. U. Tokyo, 1977, U. Wyo., 1978, U. Western Ont., Can., 1979. Author: The Manipulation of Air-Sensitive Compounds, 1969, edit., 1987; co-author: Inorganic Chemistry, 1990, 2d edit., 1994; editor-in-chief Inorganic Syntheses, vol. 19, 1979; co-editor: The Chemistry of Metal Cluster Complexes, 1990, Inorganic Synthesis, 1979—, Advances in Inorganic Chemistry, 1986—, Jour. Coordination Chemistry, Inorganic Chimca Acta, 1988—, Chemistry of Materials, 1988-90, 92—, Jour. Cluster Sci., 1990—, Organometallics, 1993-95; contbr. articles to profl. jours. Alfred P. Sloan fellow, 1967-69; Japan Soc. Promotion of Sci. fellow, 1977; Guggenheim Found. fellow, 1983-84. Fellow AAAS; mem. Am. Chem. Soc. (Disting. Svc. in Inorganic Chemistry award 1987), Royal Soc. Chemistry London (Ludwig Mond lectr. 1989), Electrochem. Soc., Materials Rsch. Soc. (medal 1990). Home: 1100 Colfax St Evanston IL 60201-2611 Office: Northwestern U Dept Chemistry Evanston IL 60208-3113

SHRIVER, JOSEPH DUANE, state legislator; b. Arkansas City, Kans., Oct. 13, 1959; s. John Francis and Carolyn Joan (Thornhill) S.; m. Mindi Sue Peterson, 1982; 1 child, Jayme Dawn. AA, Cauley County C.C., 1981. Mem. from dist. 79 Kans. State Ho. of Reps., 1994—, mem. tax and judiciary coms.; mem. Kans. Joint Commn. on Adminstv. Rules and Regulations and Spl. Com. on Motor Fuel Tax, U.s. Dept. Revenue. Recipient Outstanding Svc. award Kans. Dem. Party, 1990. Mem. Arkansas City C. of C. (legis. chmn. 1990-91), Firefighter Relief Assn. (pres. 1991-94), Firefighters Local 2101. Address: PO Box 1324 Arkansas City KS 67005

SHUCK, D(EE) R(OSS), industrial exhibit designer; b. Logansport, Ind., Oct. 19, 1941; s. Donald Ray and Dorothy (Ross) S.; m. Martha Scott, Feb. 14, 1975. Diploma, Ind. U., 1963; postgrad., Art Ctr. Coll. Design, 1967-68. Pres. Dimensional Designs, Inc., Indpls., 1971-75; designer/model builder Giltspur Exhibits, Chgo., 1979-81; designer, model builder Exhibitgroup Chgo., 1981-86; pres. D.R. Shuck and Assocs., Indianapolis, Ind., 1986—; mgr. display products group Delta Faucet Co., Indianapolis, 1988—; cons. Exhibitgroup, Chgo., 1986-89; artist-in-residence N.E. Mo. State U., Kirksville, 1987. Advisor J. Everett Light Career Ctr., Indpls., 1974-79, Ind. Evaluation Team on Higher Edn., 1979, Ind. Vocat. Tech. Coll., South Bend, 1979-81; bd. dirs. Elburn/Countryside (Ill.) Cmty. Ctr., 1985-90. With U.S. Army, 1963-66. Mem. Internat. Exhibitors Assn., Exhibit Designers and Prodrs. Assn. (bd. dirs. 1996—), Soc. Illustrators (Nat. Exhbn. Cert. of Merit 1972, 75), Art. Dirs. Club Ind. (pres. 1976), Oak Park/Forest River Art League (bd. dirs. 1981-82), Herron Sch. Art Alumni Assn. (pres. 1975). Republican. Methodist. Office: 300 S County Line Rd Indianapolis IN 46229-2974

SHUEY, JOHN HENRY, diversified products company executive; b. Monroe, Mich., Mar. 14, 1946; s. John Henry and Bertha (Thomas) S.; children: Katherine, John Henry, John Joseph Satory. B.S. in Indsl. Engring., U. Mich., 1968, M.B.A., 1970. With Tex. Instruments Co., Dallas, 1970-74; asst. treas. The Trane Co., La Crosse, Wis., 1974-78, treas., 1978-81, v.p., treas., 1981-83, v.p. fin., chief fin. officer, 1983-86; also v.p., group exec. Am. Standard; sr. v.p. and chief fin. officer AM Internat. Inc., Chgo., 1986-91; exec. v.p. Amcast Indsl. Corp., Dayton, Ohio, 1991-93, pres., COO, 1993-95, pres., CEO, 1995—, also bd. dirs.; dir., chmn. audit com. State Bank of La Crosse, 1981-87. Bd. dirs. Pub. Expenditure Survey of Wis., La Crosse, 1980-83; bd. dirs., pres. Luth. Hosp. Found., 1983-87. Mem. Fin. Execs. Inst., Machinery and Allied Products Inst. Congregationalist. Office: Amcast Indsl Corp PO Box 98 Dayton OH 45401-0098 Also: Elkhart Products Corp 1255 Oak St Elkhart IN 46514-2277

SHUGARS, DALE L., state legislator; b. May 6, 1953; m. Debra; 1 child, Meaghan. BSBA, Western Mich. U. CPA. Rep. Mich. State Dist. 47, 1991-92; rep. Mich. State Dist. 61, 1993-94, sen., 1994—; chmn. health policy & sr. citizens com. Mich. State Senate, vice chmn. econ. delvel. com., vice chmn. internat. rels. com., vice chmn. regulatory affairs com., mem. fin. com. Vol. Big Brothers and Big Sisters of Kalamazoo. Mem. Lions Club, Rotary, Kalamazoo C. of C. Home: 5315 Angling Rd Portage MI 49008-3450 Address: 709 Olds Plz Lansing MI 78909*

SHULKIN, NEIL HOWARD, dentist; b. Chgo., Oct. 30, 1940; s. Joseph Morton and Beatrice Beverly (Schneidman) S.; m. Rhoda Frances Mamett Dec. 22, 1962; children: Glenn, Arnold, Susan, Elizabeth. DDS, U. Ill., Chgo., 1964. Pvt. practice Assocs. for Gen. Dentistry Ltd. DBA Dental Store, Elk Grove Village, Ill., 1964-90, Deerfield, 1972-84, Skokie, Ill., 1973-75; pvt. practice The Dental Store Ltd., Schaumburg, Ill., 1990—. Recipient TAD Gold awards for Dental Advt. and Pub. Rels., 1982, 85. Office: The Dental Store 1061 S Roselle Rd Schaumburg IL 60193

SHULTZ, KENNETH LOWELL, athletic director; b. St. Louis, Aug. 15, 1948; s. Lowell Vern and Nellie Pauline (Rusk) S.; m. Kathleen Mary McElderry, Sept. 10, 1967; children: Amy Kathleen, Brandy Lynn, Michael Kenneth. BS with high honors, U. Ill., 1970, MS, 1971. Cert. tchr., adminstr., athletic adminstr., Ill. Instr. Western Ill. U., Macomb, 1972-73; tchr., coach Morris (Ill.) High Sch., 1973-79; assoc. athletic dir. Homewood-Flossmoor (Ill.) High Sch., 1979-81; athletic dir. North Olmsted (Ohio) City Schs., 1981-83, Homewood-Flossmoor (Ill.) High Sch., 1983—; speaker 5 clinics athletic drug testing program Homewood-Flossmoor High Sch., 1990-91. Contbr. articles to athletic jours. Mem. AAHPERD, Nat. Strength and Conditioning Assn., Nat. Interscholastic Athletic Dirs. Assn., Ill. Athletic Dirs. Assn. (Athletic Dir. of Yr. 1992), Ill. Assn. Health, Phys. Edn., Recreation and Dance, Nat. Coun. Secondary Sch. Athletic Dirs. (named midwest regional athletic dir. of the year 1993). Home: 9078 Charrington Dr Frankfort IL 60423-9449

SHULTZ, LINDA JOYCE, library director; b. South Bend, Ind., Aug. 25, 1931; d. Justin Russell and Gladys Ernstine (Miller) Nash; m. Dale Jay Shultz, Apr. 20, 1952; children: Donald Jay, Sally Janine, William Justin, Alan Joel, Kent Jon. AA, Stephens Coll., 1951; BS in Edn., Ind. U., Ft. Wayne, 1971, Cert. I in Libr. Edn., 1975. Sec. John R. Worthman, Inc., Ft. Wayne, 1951-54; farm wife, mother Noble County, Ind., 1954-68; libr. Noble County Pub. Libr., Albion, Ind., 1968—; mem. exec. bd. Tri-Alsa Libr. Svc. Authority, Ft. Wayne, 1988-90. Editor: Albion Memories, 1977. Mem. Albion Local Devel. Corp., 1989-92; sec. Cen. Noble Jr. Achievement, 1988-92. Named Albion Citizen of the Yr. Albion Rotary Club, 1977. Mem. DAR, Ind. Libr. Assn., Ind. Hist. Soc., Albion C. of C., Order Ea. Star, Rotary (pres. Albion club 1993-94), Toastmasters (pres. U.S. Six Shooters chpt. 1988-89), Gene Stratton Porter Meml. Soc., Ind. Soc. Mayflower Descendants. Republican. Methodist. Office: Noble County Pub Libr 813 E Main St Albion IN 46701-1038

SHULTZ, RETHA MILLS, retired missionary; b. Anderson, Ind., Apr. 22, 1914; d. Raymond White and Mary Beulah (Yoder) Mills; m. Clair Wilson Shultz, Dec. 25, 1935; children: Carol Ann Shultz Lehner, David Clair. BA, Anderson U., 1937. Missionary, bookkeeper Ch. of God Mission, Trinidad, W.I., 1945-58, Jamaica, W.I., 1958-62, Kenya, East Africa, 1962-70, 85-86; co-founder, tchr. music, bookkeeping W.I. Bible Inst., Trinidad, 1950-58;

mem. missionary bd. Ch. of God, Anderson, Ind., 1980-90; missionary speaker, various churches in U.S., W.I., East Africa. Republican.

SHUMPERT, EVERETT DRAYDEN, minister; b. Chgo., Mar. 15, 1951; s. Autrie Samuel and Margaret (Hobson) S.; m. Maudestine Hobbs; children: Drayden Douglas, Kimberly Evette, Evonne Nicole. Student, So. Utah State U., U. Chgo.; PhD in Criminal Justice Mgmt., LaSalle U. Deputy sheriff Cook County Jail, Chgo., 1973; campus policeman U. Chgo., 1973-75; patrolman, investigator Chgo. Police Dept., 1973-92; chief security Harold Washington Party, Chgo., 1989-91; dir. security, CEO West Bur. Security Agy., Chgo., 1995; CEO Literary Enterprises, Chgo., 1985—; — Shakden Safety Systems, Orlando, Fla., 1984—; assoc. pastor St. Mark A.M.E. Ch., Milw., 1995—. Author: War of the Sons of Light, 1995, For Whom It Is Prepared; author of poems; inventor in field. Founder Free African Soc. Today, Milw., 1995; bodyguard Mayor Harold Washington, Chgo., 1983, Pres. Anwar Sadat, U. Chgo., 1974, Ambassidor Dr. Guannau, UN, Chgo., 1979; aldermanic candidate Regular Dem. Orgn., 6th Ward, Chgo., 1989. Mem. Ministrial Alliance Chgo., Black Panther Party for Self Defense 1968. Home: 8735 N 73d St #306 Milwaukee WI 53223 Office: Literary Enterprises 1324 W 111 Pl Chicago IL 60643

SHUTER, ADRIENNE JOAN, real estate broker; b. N.Y.C., May 20, 1937; d. Samuel Ralph and Gerturde Florence (Krinsky) Bertenthal; m. Eli Ronald Shuter, june 16, 1958; children: Anne Pride, Lynn Dale Buchholz, Beth. BA, Cornell U., 1958; MA, Case Western Reserve U., 1966; postgrad., Washington U., St. Louis, 1967-70; grad., Realtors Inst., 1988. Real estate sales lic., Mo.; real estate broker lic., Mo. Substitute tchr. Ithaca High Sch., Ithaca, N.Y., 1957-58; elem. sch. tchr. Park Sch., E. St. Louis, Ill., 1958-60; religious edn. dir. First Unitarian Ch., St. Louis, 1970-74; columnist West End Word, 1974—; broker-salesperson Feinberg Real Estate Co., Inc., St. Louis, 1975—; v.p. St. Louis Bd. Edn.; bd. dirs. Coun. of Great City Schs.; mem. St. Louis Heritage and Urban Design Commn., 1993—, St. Louis Planned Indsl. Expansion Authority, 1991-94. Mem. adv. bd. Housing Solutions, St. Louis, 1989; bd. dirs., exec. com. Interfaith Partnership Met. S. Louis, 1989-94; trustee Thompson Ctr., St. Louis, 1992-96; mem. secondary sch. com. Cornell Univ. Club, St. Louis, 1970—; chair facilities com. First Unitarian Ch., St. Louis, 1993—; grad. Coro Women in Leadership; bd. dirs. Adequate Housing for Missourians, 1992—. Mem. St. Louis Met. Real Estate Bd., Mo. Real Estate Bd., Nat. Real Estate Bd., Mo. Million Dollar Club (life), Media Club, St. Louis Ambs. Office: Feinberg Real Estate Co 360 N Skinner Blvd Saint Louis MO 63130-4831

SIARNY, WILLIAM DONALD, librarian, archivist; b. Chgo., Apr. 11, 1945; s. William D. and Ann E. (Walczyk) S.; m. Cynthia A. Skarbek, Oct. 6, 1973; children: Gerard B., David B., Matthew A., Monica R., Elizabeth M. BA, DePaul U., 1971; MA in Libr. Sci., Rosary Coll., River Forest, Ill., 1974. Asst. libr. Nat. Dairy Coun., Rosemont, Ill., 1974-79; libr. dir. Nat. Livestock & Meat Bd. (now Nat. Cattlemen's Beef Assn.), Chgo., 1979—; libr., archivist Am. Meat Sci. Assn., Chgo., 1980—; archivist Am. Meat Sci. Assn., Chgo., 1980—; coord. Ill. Health Librs. Consortium, Chgo., 1975—; chmn. map workshop com. Ill. Documents Librs., Chgo., 1973. Editor: Am. Meat Sci. Assn. Proc. (microfilm edit.), 1983. Chmn. troop com. Boy Scouts Am., River Forest, Ill., 1990-93, pack com. chmn., Oak Park, Ill., 1986-89; religious edn. tchr. Ascension Parish, Oak Park, Ill., 1978-94. With USAR, 1965-74. Mem. ALA, Med. Libr. Assn. (bylaws com. 1977-79), Spl. Librs. Assn., Acad. of Health Info. Profls., Spl. Librs. Assn., Soc. Am. Archivists, Am. Soc. Info. Sci., Assn. Records Mgmt. Adminstrn. Roman Catholic. Home: 715 S Grove Oak Park IL 60304 Office: Nat Livestock and Meat Bd 444 N Michigan Ave Chicago IL 60611

SIBBET, LORRAINE ALBERTA, academic administrator; b. Pitts., Aug. 6, 1939; d. Howard Alexander Sibbet and Helen Theresa (Muzyk) Dunbar. BA in English, Allegheny Coll., 1961; MEd in Counseling, U. Pitts., 1967, PhD in Higher Edn. Adminstrn., 1976. Asst. dean women U. Pitts., Pa., 1964-65; dir. women's housing U. Pitts., 1965-68, assoc. dir. univ. housing, 1968-69; asst. dean students Westminster Coll., New Wilmington, Pa., 1969-71; assoc. dean students Westminster Coll., New Wilmington, 1971-79; dean students D'Youville Coll., Buffalo, N.Y., 1979-87; v.p. for student affairs D'Youville Coll., Buffalo, 1987-88; v.p. for student devel. Notre Dame Coll., South Euclid, Ohio, 1989-94; dean of student Tex. State Tech. Coll., Sweetwater, 1996—; exec. bd. mem. Nat. Lambda Sigma Soc., Atlanta, 1962-74, Pa. Assn. Women Deans, Adminstrs. and Counselors, Pitts., 1964-70; treas. Substance Abuse Consortium, Buffalo, 1987-88. Editor: (newsletter) Cwen Tid, 1962-72. Recipient chpt. citation Mortar Bd., Westminster Coll., 1978; named Outstanding Dean Student, Christopher Columbus Soc., Buffalo, 1986. Mem. Nat. Assn. Student Pers. Adminstrs., Ohio Coll. Pers. Assn., Assn. for Student Judicial Affairs. Republican. Presbyterian. Home: 406 E New Mexico St Sweetwater TX 79556

SIBENER, STEVEN JAY, chemistry educator; b. Bklyn., Apr. 3, 1954; s. Daniel Irving and Gerie S.; m. Linda Young, May 29, 1990. BA in Physics, BS in Chemistry, U. Rochester, 1975; MS, U. Calif., Berkeley, 1977, PhD, 1979. Postdoctoral fellow Bell Labs., Murray Hill, N.J., 1979-80; asst. prof. U. Chgo., 1980-85, assoc. prof., 1985-89, prof. chemistry, 1989—; vis. fellow Joint Inst. for Lab. Astrophysics, Boulder, Colo., 1992-93; cons. Dow Chem. Co., Midland, Mich., 1982-85, Teltech Resource Network, Chgo., 1985—, Inst. Def. Analyses, Alexandria, Va., 1985—. Contbr. over 70 sci. articles to profl. publs. Alfred P. Sloan Found. fellow, 1983-87; recipient Camille Henry Dreyfus Young Faculty in Chemistry award, Dreyfus Found., 1980, IBM Faculty Devel. award, 1984-86. Mem. AAAS, Am. Chem. Soc., Am. Phys. Soc. (chmn. chem. physics divsn. 1996), royal Soc. Chemistry (Marlow medal 1988), Sigma Xi, Phi Beta Kappa. Office: Univ Chgo The James Franck Inst 5640 S Ellis Ave Chicago IL 60637-1433

SICARD, GUILLERMO RAFAEL, dermatologist; b. LaVega, Dominican Republic, Oct. 25, 1937; came to U.S., 1963; s. Fausto A. and Margarita (Moya) S.; m. Emilia Cordova, Jan. 11, 1963; children: Fausto Antonio, Julia Margarita. BS, Norman Sch., La Vega, Dominican Republic, 1954; MD, U. St. Domingo, Dominican Republic, 1960. Diplomate Am. Bd. Dermatology, Am. Bd. Dermatopathology. Chief of health Health Dept., La Vega, 1960-63; intern Franklin Sq. Hosp., Balt., 1963-64; resident Cleve. Metro Gen. Hosp., 1966-69; ptnr. Gardner, Sicard DMD, Inc., Canton, Ohio, 1969-82; practice medicine specializing in dermatology Canton, 1982—; cons. Aultman Hosp., Canton, 1969—, Timken Mercy Hosp., Canton, 1969—, Massillow Community Hosp., 1982—; asst. prof. Northeastern Ohio U. Coll. Medicine, Rootswoen, 1984—, sect. chief dermatology, 1985—. Investigator medication evaluation, 1984-85. Mem. Stark County Historical Soc., 1972—; sustaining mem. Republican Nat. Com., 1986—. Served to capt. U.S. Army, 1964-66. Fellow Am. Acad. Dermatology; mem. Canton Acad. Medicine (pres. 1981-82, Tennis Champion 1991), Stark County Med. Soc. (sec. 1979-80, pres. 1980-81), Smithsonian Inst., Ohio Dermatol. Assn., Cleve. Dermatol. Soc., Dermatology Found., Leaders Soc. Roman Catholic. Club: Hall of Fame Fitness (Canton). Home: 10695 Kent Ave NE Hartville OH 44632-8756 Office: 4825 Munson St NW Canton OH 44718-3614

SICHERMAN, MARVIN ALLEN, lawyer; b. Cleve., Dec. 27, 1934; s. Harry and Malvina (Friedman) S.; m. Sue Kovacs, Aug. 18, 1957; children: Heidi Joyce, Steven Eric. B.A., Case Western Res. U., 1957, LL.B., 1960, J.D., 1968. Bar: Ohio 1960. Mng. prin. Dettelbach, Sicherman & Baumgart, Cleve., 1971—. Editorial bd.: Case-Western Res. Law Rev, 1958-60; Contbr. articles to legal jours. Mem. Beachwood (Ohio) Civic League, 1972—; mem. Beachwood Bd. Edn., 1978-86, pres., 1981, 85, v.p., 1984; trustee Beachwood Arts Council, 1977-84. Mem. ABA, Ohio Bar Assn. (lectr. truth in lending 1969, lectr. bankruptcy 1972, 81, 84; Meritorious Service awards 1971, 77, 78, 79, 83, 84, 85, 86, 87), Cleve. Bar Assn. (lectr. practice and procedure clinic 1960-80, 82-87, chmn. bankruptcy ct. com. 1971-73), Jewish Chautauqua Soc., Tau Epsilon Rho, Zeta Beta Tau. Jewish (trustee Temple brotherhood 1968-76, sec. 1971-73). Home: 24500 Albert Ln Cleveland OH 44122-2302 Office: Dettelbach Sicherman & Baumgart 1100 Ohio Savings Plz Cleveland OH 44114

SICILIANO, ELIZABETH MARIE, secondary education educator; b. Mansfield, Ohio, Apr. 22, 1934; d. Samuel Sevario and Lucy (Sferro) S. BS in Edn., Ohio State U., 1957; MA in Edn., Ea. Mich. U., 1971; MFA, Bowling Green U., 1975. Cert. tchr., Mich. Instr. adult edn. The Toledo (Ohio) Mus. Art, 1972-81; tchr. art Monroe (Mich.) Pub. Schs., 1975—; workshop facilitator; presenter in field; art tchr. computer graphics. Artist, working in oils, pastels and fabricating jewelry. Judge Monroe Bicentennial, Monroe Arts and Crafts League, other shows. Mem. NEA, Mich. Edn. Assn., Nat. Art Edn. Assn., Mich. Art Edn. Assn., Stratford Festival for the Arts, Toledo Craft Club, Toledo Fedn. Art Socs., Toledo Mus. Art. Home: 7179 Edinburgh Dr Lambertville MI 48144-9539 Office: Monroe High Sch 901 Herr Rd Monroe MI 48161-9702

SICKINGER, TIMOTHY, advertising executive. BA in Journalism, U. Iowa, 1960. Salesman Am. Hosp. Supply Corp., 1960-64; asst. account exec. Benton & Bowles, 1965-66; account exec. Ogilvy & Mather, N.Y.C., 1966, Chgo., 1967; account exec. Ogilvy & Mather, N.Y.C., 1968-69, account supr., 1970-71, v.p., account supr., 1972-75, v.p., mgmt. supr., 1975-76; v.p., regional mgmt. supr. Europe, Mid. East., Africa Ogilvy & Mather, London, 1976-79, sr. v.p., 1979-81, bd. dirs., 1981—, dir. agy. tng. program, 1981-83; gen. mgr. Ogilvy & Mather, N.Y.C., 1983-87, sr. v.p., dir. client svcs., 1987—, gen. mgr., 1988, mem. operating bd., 1989, exec. v.p., 1990. Recipient Ad Man of Yr. award Omaha chpt. Am. Fedn. Advt., 1991, Outstanding Svc. Advt. Profession award U. Nebr., 1994. Office: Bozell Worldwide Inc 800 Blackstone Ctr 302 S 36th St Omaha NE 68131-3800*

SIDAWAY, BRUCE A., mechanical engineer; b. Cleve., Sept. 1, 1946. BSME, Cleve. State U., 1979. Registered profl. engr., Ohio. Sys. engr. Meier Transmission, Cleve., 1983-92; mech. engr. Mill & Motion Inc., Cleve., 1992—, also bd. dirs. With U.S. Army, 1968-71, Vietnam. Mem. Assn. Iron and Steel Engrs., Cleve. Engring. Soc. Office: Mill & Motion Inc 5415 E Schaaf Rd Cleveland OH 44131-1333

SIDON, CLAUDIA MARIE, psychiatry, mental health nursing educator; b. Bellaire, Ohio, Feb. 6, 1946; d. Paul and Nell (Bernas) DePaulis; m. Michael Sidon; children: Michael II, Babe. Diploma, Wheeling (W.Va.) Hosp. Sch., 1966; BS in Nursing summa cum laude, Ohio U., Athens, 1979; MS in Nursing, W.Va. U., Morgantown, 1982. Cert. social worker. Various staff positions Bellaire City Hosp., 1966-67, 72-77; adj. nursing faculty W.Va. No. Community Coll., Wheeling, 1977-82; nurse clinician, psychotherapist Valley Psychol. and Psychiat. Svcs., Moundsville, W.Va., 1984; psychotherapist, nurse clinician, case mgr. No. Panhandle Behavioral Health Ctr., Wheeling, 1984-88; assoc. prof. ADN program Belmont Tech. Coll., St. Clairsville, Ohio, 1988—; presenter in field. Mem. Tri-State Psychiat. Nursing Assn. (pres., v.p., program chmn.), Nat. League for Nursing (presenter), Phi Kappa Phi, Sigma Theta Tau. Home: 52295 Sidon Rd Dillonvale OH 43917-9538 Office: Belmont Tech Coll 120 Fox Shannon Pl Saint Clairsville OH 43950-8751

SIEBEN, TODD, state legislator; b. Geneso, Ill., July 11, 1945; m. Kay Sieben; children: Rachel, Brandon, Meredith. BS, Western Ill. U., 1967. Commnr. Geneso Park Dist., 1977-87; mem. Henry County Planning Commn., 1978-80, 85-86; Ill. state rep. Dist. 73, 1987-92; vice chmn. fin. inst. com., mem. pub. utilities com. Ill. Ho. Reps., state govt. adminstrn. com., energy, environ. com., natural resources com., aging com., children com., small bus. com.; mem. Ill. State Senate Dist. 37, 1993—; co-owner, v.p. Sieben Hybrids, Inc. Mem. Am. Legion, Geneso Rotary, VFW, Farm Bur., Masons. Home: 129 S College Ave Geneseo IL 61254-1317*

SIEBERT, THEODORE BRIAN, sculptor; b. Portland, Oreg., May 7, 1958; s. Harlan Anton and Barbara Lou (Richardson) S.; m. Colette Teresa Graham, Nov. 5, 1989 (div. Jan. 1991); 1 child, Cody James; m. Laura Lee Czaja, Dec. 31, 1993. AA, North Idaho Coll., 1978; BA, U. Wash., 1985. Author: The Art of Sandcastling, 1991; illustrator Diving the San Juan Islands, 1990. Holder World Record Longest Sand Sculpture Guiness Bood of Records, 1989, 90, World Record Tallest Sand Castle, 1990, 91, 93. Republican. Roman Catholic. Home and Office: 3321 Riverdale Mc Henry IL 60050

SIEDLECKI, NANCY THERESE, lawyer, funeral director; b. Chgo., May 30, 1954; d. LeRoy John and Dorothy Josephine (Wilczynski) Schielka; m. Jonathan Francis Siedlecki, June 18, 1977; children: Samantha Ann, Abigail Marie. Student Triton Jr. Coll., 1971-73; grad. funeral dir., Worsham Coll., 1974; student Loyola U., Chgo., 1974-76., U. Ill.-Chgo., 1976-77; JD with honors, Chgo.-Kent Coll. Law, 1980. Bar: Ill. 1980. Paralegal in real estate Rosenberg, Savner & Unikel, Chgo., 1974-77; pvt. practice law, Burr Ridge, Ill., 1980—; cons. probate and various small bus. corps., Chgo., 1980—. Mem. ABA, Ill. State Bar Assn., Chgo. Bar Assn. Roman Catholic. Office: 5300 Main St Downers Grove IL 60515

SIEFERS, ROBERT GEORGE, banker; b. Pitts., Aug. 28, 1945; s. George Francis and Idella Alice (Eiler) S.; m. Janice Lynn Kirkpatrick, Mar. 25, 1970; children—Robert Scott, Jillian Stewart. B.A., Mt. Union Coll., 1967; M.B.A., Kent State U., 1971; J.D., Cleveland Marshall Law Sch., 1976. Security analyst Nat. City Bank, Cleve., 1971-76, v.p., investment rsch. dir., 1976-80, v.p. adminstrn. and rsch., 1980-82; sr. v.p. corp. planning Nat. City Corp., Cleve., 1982-85; sr. v.p. corp. banking Nat. City Bank, Cleve., 1985-86; pres., chief exec. officer Ohio Citizens Bank (affiliate Nat. City Corp.), Toledo, 1986-90; exec. v.p., chief fin. officer Nat. City Corp., Cleve., 1990—; bd. dirs. HCR Corp. Bd. trustees Mt. Union Coll. Republican. Presbyterian Club: Chagrin Valley Country. Home: 10 Pebblebrook Ln Chagrin Falls OH 44022-2380 Office: Nat City Corp Nat City Ctr Cleveland OH 44022

SIEGEL, BARRY ALAN, nuclear radiologist; b. Nashville, Dec. 30, 1944; s. Walter Gross Siegel and Lillian B. (Tumbarello) Ivener; m. Pamela M. Mandel, Aug. 18, 1968 (div. Mar. 1981); children: Peter A., William A.; m. Marilyn J. Siegel, Jan. 29, 1983. AB, Washington U., St. Louis, 1966, MD, 1969. Diplomate Am. Bd. Nuclear Medicine, Am. Bd. Radiology. Intern Barnes Hosp., St. Louis, 1969-70; resident in radiology and nuclear medicine fellow Mallinckrodt Inst. Radiology, Washington U., 1970-73, dir. div. nuclear medicine, 1973—, asst. prof., 1973-76, assoc. prof., 1976-79, prof. radiology, 1979—, assoc. prof. medicine, 1980-83, prof. medicine, 1983—; dir. Am. Bd. Nuc. Medicine, L.A., 1985-90, sec., 1990; chmn. adv. com. on med. uses of isotopes NRC, Washington, 1990-96; chmn. radiopharm. drugs adv. com. U.S. FDA, Rockville, Md., 1982-85, radiol. devices panel, 1992-95; mem. U.S. Pharmacopeia Adv. Panel on Radiopharms., 1975—, Armed Forces Radiobiol. Rsch. Inst., Bethesda. Author, editor 26 books; contbr. articles to profl. jours., chpts. to books. Maj. USAF, 1974-76. Recipient Commr.'s Spl. citation U.S. FDA, 1988, Honor citation U.S. Pharmacopeial Conv., 1995. Fellow ACP, Am. Coll. Radiology (vice chmn. commn. on nuclear medicine 1981—, editor in chief self evaluation program 1988—), Am. Coll. Nuclear Physicians; mem. AMA, Am. Roentgen Ray Soc., Assn. Univ. Radiologists, Radiol. Soc. N.Am., Soc. Nuclear Medicine (trustee 1981-85, 87-91). Office: Washington U Mallinckrodt Inst Radiology 510 S Kingshighway Blvd Saint Louis MO 63110-1016

SIEGEL, HARVEY ROBERT, engineering and product development executive; b. Chgo., Jan. 9, 1928; s. Emanuel and Jean (Ochstein) S.; m. Babette Wax, Apr. 18, 1948; children: Alan, Vicki Siegel Goltz. BSME, Wash. U., 1952, M in Engring. Adminstrn., 1966. Registered profl. engr., Mo. COOP engr. trainee McDonnel/Wash. U., St. Louis, 1950-52; design engr. McDonnell Aircraft Helicopter Div., St. Louis, 1952-54, Kennard Corp./Air Conditioning, St. Louis, 1954-56; chief product engr. Kennard Div. Am. Air Filter, St. Louis, 1956-61; mgr. quality/reliability Am. Air Filter Def. Products, St. Louis, 1961-71, Am. Air Filter, Herman Nelson Group, Moline, Ill., 1971-73; gen. mgr. Ft. Wayne (Ind.) Truck Parts, 1973-83; v.p. engring. Coachmen RV Div., Coachmen Ind., Middlebury, Ind., 1983-85; asst. v.p. engring. Coachmen, Inc., Corp. Engring., Middlebury, Ind., 1985-90; v.p. engring. product devel. Clarion div. Coachmen Industries, Elkhart, Ind., 1990-94; v.p. corp. engr. Coachmen Industries, 1994—; cons. quality assurance, numerous cos., St. Louis, 1972-73; instr. Wash. U., St. Louis, 1960-71, Ivy Tech., 1992—; corp. officer Coachmen Industries, Elkhart, Ind., 1985—. Inventor press brake safety device; patentee Clarion Motor Vehicle. Bd. dirs. Temple Edn. Com., Ft. Wayne, 1980-83, 96—, Ft. Wayne Jewish Found., 1979-81; instr. Temple Sunday Sch., Ft. Wayne, 1975-83; adv. coun. tech. asst. program Purdue U. , 1994—. Mem. Am. Soc. Quality Control, Soc. Automotive Engrs., Ft. Wayne C. of C. (economic devel. com. 1979-80). Jewish. Home: 3651 Kirkwood Ct Elkhart IN 46514-4706 Office: Coachmen Industies PO Box 30 Middlebury IN 46540-0030

SIEGEL, HOWARD JEROME, lawyer; b. Chgo., July 29, 1942; s. Leonard and Idele (Lehrner) S.; m. Diane L. Gerber; children: Sari D., Allison J., James G. BS, U. Ill., 1963; JD, Northwestern U., 1966. Bar: Ill. 1966, U.S. dist. Ct. (no. dist.) Ill. 1967. Assoc., Ancel, Stonesifer & Glink, Chgo., 1966-70; ptnr. Goldstine & Siegel, Summit, Ill., 1970-75; sole practice, Chgo., 1975-77; pres. Wexler, Siegel & Shaw, Ltd., Chgo., 1978-82; ptnr. Keck, Mahin & Cate, Chgo., 1982-95, Neal Gerber & Eisenberg, Chgo., 1995—; dir. various corps. Mem. ABA, Chgo. Bar Assn., Ill. Bar Assn., Internat. Council Shopping Ctrs., Urban Land Inst., Chgo. Real.Estate Bd. Clubs: Standard (Chgo.); Ravisloe Country (Homewood, Ill.). Office: Neal Gerber & Eisenberg 2 N LaSalle St Ste 2100 Chicago IL 60602

SIEGEL, JEANNE BERYL, furniture appraiser; b. Chgo., Feb. 28, 1932; d. Walter J. and Florence B. (Goldenberg) Cohen; m. Jack M. Siegel, Sept. 9, 1952; children: Julie Siegel Halpern, Philip. Student, U. Wis., 1949-50, Art Inst. Chgo., 1950-51. Ind. appraiser Wilmette, Ill., 1980-95; lectr. Oakton Coll., Des Plaines, Ill., 1992-95. Author-illustrator: How to Speak Furniture with an Antique American Accent, 1991, How to Speak Furniture with an Antique English Accent, 1992, How to Speak Furniture with an Antique French Accent, 1994, Selling Your Valuables, 1996. Sec. Midwest Shakespeare Globe Ctr., U.S., 1990-96; bd. dirs. Milw. Art Mus. Print Forum, 1992-96, Auschwitz Drawings. Mem. Midwest Antique Club, Mich. Shores Club, Art Inst. Chgo. (life). Home: 2406 Meadow Dr Wilmette IL 60091

SIEGLER, LAWRENCE NOAH, financial consultant; b. Cleve., Nov. 4, 1930; s. Edward N. Siegler and Rose C. Chait; m. Myrna K. Kursh, Aug. 16, 1961; children: Ellery, Edward. BS, Ohio State U., 1953; MA, Kent State U., 1971. V.p. Merrill Lynch, Cleve., 1978—. Trustee, pres. Cleveland Heights Pub. Libr., 1977-83, Cleve. Chamber Music Soc., 1989—. With U.S. Army, 1955-57. Mem. City Club of Cleve. (adv. com. 1979-83), Rowfant Club (pres. 1992-93). Home: 3012 Fairmount Blvd Cleveland Heights OH 44118-4129 Office: One Cleveland Center 1375 E 9th St Cleveland OH 44114

SIEKMANN, DONALD CHARLES, accountant; b. St. Louis, July 2, 1938; s. Elmer Charles and Mabel Louise (Blue) S.; m. Linda Lee Knowles, Sept. 10, 1966; 1 child, Brian Charles. BS, Washington U., St. Louis, 1960. CPA, Ohio, Ga. Regional mng. ptnr. Arthur Andersen & Co., Cin., 1960—. Columnist Cin. Enquirer, 1983-86, Gannett News Services, 1983-86; editor "Tax Clinic" column Tax Advisor mag., 1974-75. Mem. bd. Cin. Zool. Soc., 1985-88; officer, bd. dirs. Cin. Found. for Pub. TV, 1984-88, Cin. Symphony Orch., 1973-85, Cin. Ballet Co., 1973-88, Cin. Theatrical Assn., Jewish Hosp., 1993—, Cin. Assn. for Performing Arts, 1992—, Cin. United Way, 1992—, Cin. Pk. Bd. Found., 1995—. Mem. AICPA, Ohio Soc. CPAs, Cin. Country Club (trustee 1983-88), Optimists Club (pres. Queen City chpt. 1986). Lutheran. Club: Cin. Country (trustee 1983-88). Home: 5495 Waring Dr Cincinnati OH 45243-3933 Office: Arthur Andersen & Co 425 Walnut St Ste 1500 Cincinnati OH 45202-3916

SIELA, DEBRA LYNNE, pulmonary nurse specialist; b. Bluffton, Ind., July 9, 1952; d. Leo Frederick Siela Jr. and Naomi Mae (Yake) Siela Shilling. BSN, Ind. U., Indpls., 1974; MN, UCLA, 1980; cert. in respiratory therapy, East L.A. Coll., 1983. Cert. CCRN, BLS instr., ACLS instr., CS, CRTT, RRT. Staff nurse intensive care unit Luth. Hosp., Ft. Wayne, Ind., 1974-77; critical care nurse Critical Care Svcs., L.A., 1977-79, Staff Builders, Sherman Oaks, Calif., 1977-79; nurse Meml. Hosp. of Glendale (Calif.), 1979-82; staff nurse Hollywood (Calif.) Community Hosp., 1983-85; nurse Ask-A-Nurse, L.A., 1986-90; pulmonary nurse specialist, nurse educator Glendale Adventist Med. Ctr., 1980-90; asst. prof. nursing Ball State U. Sch. Nursing, Muncie, Ind., 1990—; call RN Caylor-Nickel Med. Ctr., Bluffton, Ind., 1991—. Literacy tutor Literacy Coun. Mem. AACN, Am. Assn. Respiratory Care, Respiratory Nursing Soc., Sigma Theta Tau. Home: 3935 E Elm Grove Rd Bluffton IN 46714-9312 Office: Ball State U 2000 W University Ave Muncie IN 47306-1022

SIENKEWICZ, THOMAS JEROME, classics educator; b. Hoboken, N.J., Apr. 29, 1950; s. Edmund R. and Maria F. (Liguori) S.; m. Anne Waterman, June 10, 1972; children: Marie Kathleen, Julia Alice, Richard Oscar. BA in Classics, Coll. Holy Cross, Worcester, Mass., 1971; MA in Classics, Johns Hopkins U., 1973, PhD in Classics, 1975. Asst. prof. classics Howard U., Washington, 1975-81, assoc. prof. classics, 1981-84; vis. assoc. prof. classics Monmouth (Ill.) Coll., 1984-85, Minnie Billings Capron prof. classics, 1985—; vis. dir. Assoc. Colls. Midwest Programs in Florence, Italy, 1992-93. Author: Classical Epic, 1991, World Mythology, 1996; co-author: Classical Gods and Heroes, 1983, Oral Cultures Past and Present, 1990. Mem. Am. Philological Assn., Am. Inst. Archeology, Ill. Classical Conf. (pres.), Ill. Coun. Teaching Fgn. Langs., Classical Assn. Middle West and South (state and regional v.p.), Phi Beta Kappa. Roman Catholic. Home: 1103 E 2d Ave Monmouth IL 61462 Office: Monmouth Coll 700 E Broadway Monmouth IL 61462

SIERACKI, ALOYSIUS ALFRED, religious organization administrator; b. Chgo., Nov. 5, 1929; s. Peter Paul and Mary Ann (Kroll) S. BS in Chem. Engring., Ill. Inst. Tech., 1951; cert. in theology, Whitefriars Hall, Washington, 1960; MS in Math., U. Notre Dame, 1962. Ordained priest Roman Cath. Ch., 1959. Secondary sch. tchr. Mt. Carmel High Sch., Chgo., 1960-67; instr. chemistry and math. Mt. Carmel Coll., Niagara Falls, Ont., Can., 1967-68; instr. math. Marquette U., Milw., 1968-75; assoc. pastor St. Agnes Parish, Phoenix, 1975-81; provincial dir. lay Carmelites in U.S. and Can. Aylesford Carmelite Ctr., Darien, Ill., 1981—; chmn. Lay Carmelite Commn., 1987—. Author: Songs for God, 1990; editor: Carmel's Call, 10th edit., 1991; editor Aylesford Carmelite Newsletter, 1984—; contbr. articles to profl. jours. With U.S. Army, 1951-53. Democrat. Office: Aylesford Carmelite Ctr 8501 Bailey Rd Darien IL 60561-8418

SIERRA, EDWARD, physician; b. Defiance, Ohio, June 5, 1956; s. Alfredo Palma and Oralia (Munoz) S.; m. Jacqueline Frances Clouse, Oct. 5, 1991. BA, Defiance Coll., 1978; MA, Ball State U., 1980; MD, Med. Coll. of Ohio, 1986. Diplomate Am. Bd. Family Practice. Physician Leipsic, Ohio; staff physician Lima Meml. Hosp. Mem. AMA, Ohio Student Med. Assn., Ohio Acad. Family Practice, Nat. Lang. Honor Soc. (pres. 1977-78). Home: 321 Hedgewyck Dr Findlay OH 45840-7466

SIGAL, MICHAEL STEPHEN, lawyer; b. Chgo., July 9, 1942; s. Carl I. and Evelyn (Wallack) S.; m. Kass M. Flaherty, May 16, 1971; 1 child, Sarah Caroline. BS, U. Wis.-Madison, 1964; JD, U. Chgo., 1967. Bar: Ill. 1967, U.S. Dist. Ct. (no. dist.) Ill. 1967. Assoc. firm Sidley & Austin and predecessor firm, Chgo., 1967-73, ptnr., 1973—. Mem. U. Chgo. Law Rev., 1965. Bd. dirs. EMRE Diagnostic Services, Inc., affiliate Michael Reese Hosp., Chgo., 1982-91, The Mary Meyer Sch., Chgo., 1986-87. Mem. ABA, Chgo. Bar Assn., Phi Beta Kappa, Phi Kappa Phi, Phi Eta Sigma. Jewish. Clubs: Law, Monroe (Chgo.); Mill Creek Hunt (bd. dirs. 1992—, Wadsworth, Ill.). Home: 2180 Wilmot Rd Deerfield IL 60015-1556 Office: Sidley & Austin 1 First Nat Plz Chicago IL 60603

SIGMON, JOYCE ELIZABETH, professional society administrator; b. Stanley, N.C., Oct. 4, 1935; d. Rome Alfred and Pearl Elizabeth (Beal) S. BS, U. N.C., 1971; MA, Loyola U., 1980. Cert. dental asst., assn. exec. Dental asst. Dr. Paul A. Stroup, Jr., Charlotte, N.C., 1953-63; instr. Wayne Tech. Inst., Goldsboro, N.C., 1963-65, Ctrl. Piedmont Community Coll., Charlotte, 1965-69; dir. Dental Assisting Edn. ADA, Chgo., 1971-85, asst. sec. Coun. Prosthetics Svcs., 1985-87, mgr. Office Quality Assurance, 1987-80, exec. dir. Aux., 1990-92; dir. adminstrv. activities Am. Acad. of Implant Dentistry, Chgo., 1993—; exec. sec. Am. Bd. of Oral Implantology/Implant Dentistry, 1993—. Deacon 4th Presbyn. Ch., 1973-75, elder 1975-77, 88-91, trustee, 1991-94; moderator Presbyn. Women in 4th Ch., 1987-91. Mem. Am. Soc. Assn. Execs., Chgo. Soc. Assn. Execs. (chair CAE com. 1991-92), Am. Dental Assts. Assn., N.C. Dental Assn. (pres. 1968-69), Charlotte Dental Assts. Soc. Presbyterian. Home: 260 E Chestnut St Chicago IL 60611-2423 Office: Am Acad Implant Dentistry 211 E Chicago Ave Chicago IL 60611-2616

SIGNORILE, EUGENE ROBERT, business executive, product designer; b. Chgo., Jan. 3, 1937; s. William Victor and Elizabeth (Evans) S.; m. Choi Keun Jom, Sept. 29, 1959 (div. May 1983); children: Susan, Deborah, Lisa, David. BSEE, Kans. State U., Manhattan, 1963. Owner Signorile Co.,

Chgo., 1969-76; pres. Mechelle Toy Corp., Chgo., 1976-81; pres. Mechelle Corp., Chgo., 1986—, new product cons., 1989—; inventor elec. pet toys, differential relay, others. Sgt. U.S. Army, 1956-63, Korea. Recipient award Sci. Am., 1968. Home and Office: 2838 N Sayre Ave Chicago IL 60634-3655

SIGWART, CHARLES DALLAS, computer scientist, educator; b. Durand, Mich., July 27, 1941; s. Dallas Charles and Dorothy Lucille (Bonneville) S.; m. Gretchen L. Van Meer, Oct. 18, 1976; 1 child, Julia Dorothy. SB, MIT, 1967; PhD, Northwestern U., 1976; MS, W.Va. U., 1984. Staff engr. Draper Lab., Cambridge, Mass., 1967; grad. teaching asst. Northwestern U., Evanston, Ill., 1968-75; postdoctoral fellow U. Cin. Med. Ctr., 1976-79; rsch. assoc. W.Va. U. Med. Ctr., Morgantown, 1980-81; grad. teaching asst. W.Va. U., Morgantown, 1982; asst. prof. Cen. Mich. U., Mt. Pleasant, 1983-88; assoc. prof. computer sci. No. Ill. U., DeKalb, 1988-94; pvt. practice computer cons. De Kalb, 1994—; activist rights for the disabled, adaptive computer aids for the blind; cons. in field. Author: Software Engineering, 1990; contbr. articles to tech. publs. Newsletter editor Sierra Club, Ohio, 1976-79, Coalition of Citizens with Disabilities in Ill., DeKalb, 1989—, pres. DeKalb County chpt., 1995—; coach Odyssey of the Mind, Mt. Pleasant, 1985-87; coord. phys. handicaps Learning About Disabilities, DeKalb, 1990—. Nat. Inst. Environ. Health Scis. fellow, 1976-79; grantee Benjamin-Cummings Pub. Co., 1986. Mem. IEEE Computer Soc., Assn. Computing Machinery, Sigma Xi. Home and Office: 110 E Sunset Pl De Kalb IL 60115-4424

SIH, CHARLES JOHN, pharmaceutical chemistry educator; b. Shanghai, China, Sept. 11, 1933; s. Paul Kwang-Tsien and Teresa (Dong) S.; m. Catherine Elizabeth Hsu, July 11, 1959; children—Shirley, Gilbert, Ronald. A.B. in Biology, Caroll Coll., 1953; M.S. in Bacteriology, Mont. State Coll., 1955; Ph.D. in Bacteriology, U. Wis., 1958. Sr. research microbial biochemist Squibb Inst. for Med. Research, New Brunswick, N.J., 1958-60; mem. faculty U. Wis.-Madison, 1960—, Frederick B. Power prof. pharm. chemistry, 1978, Hilldare prof., 1987—. Recipient 1st Ernest Volwiler award, 1977; Roussel prize, 1980, Am. Pharm. Assoc. award 1987. Mem. Am. Chem. Soc., Soc. Am. Biol. Chemists, Acad. Pharm. Scis., Soc. Am. Microbiologists. Home: 6322 Landfall Dr Madison WI 53705-4309

SIITARI, DAVID WILLIAM, materials scientist, consultant; b. Milw., Apr. 11, 1952; s. Ahti John and Ruth Jean (Goell) S.; m. Elizabeth Sandberg, July 24, 1982; children: Kathryn, Stephanie, William, Alison, Erica, Andrew. B-SChemE, U. Minn., 1974; PhD, U. Ill., 1979. Rsch. engr. Nat. Steel Corp., Weirton, W.Va., 1979-83, sr. rsch. engr., 1983-84; sr. rsch. engr. 3M Co., St. Paul, 1984-87, engring. specialist, 1987-88; rsch. scientist Rolscreen Co., Pella, Iowa, 1988-92; cons. Phenix Composites, Mankato, Minn., 1993-94; prof. Mankato State U., 1994—; exch. rschr. Nat. Steel Co. and Nippon Kokan K.K., Japan, 1981-82; mem. del. vacuum sci. to USSR, People to People Internat., 1990. Contbr. articles to profl. jours. Mem. Electrochem. Soc. (Young Author's award 1982), Materials Rsch. Soc., Soc. Photo-Optical Instrumentation Engrs. Home and Office: 417 Hummingbird Ln Madison WI 53714

SIKKEMA, KENNETH R., state legislator; b. Cadillac, Mich., Feb. 10, 1951; s. Peter John and Kathryn Mae (Laarman) S.; m. Carla Chase, Oct. 12, 1985; 1 child, Zachary Chase. BA in History cum laude, Harvard U., 1974; MBA with distinction, U. Mich., 1984. Legis. asst. Mich. Ho. of Reps., Lansing, 1974-75; adminstrv. asst. Mich. State Senate, Lansing, 1975-79; mktg. mgr. Herman Miller, Inc., Zeeland, Mich., 1984-86; exec. dir. West Mich. Environ. Action, Grand Rapids, 1979-82; state rep. State of Mich., Lansing, 1987—. Republican. Mem. Reformed Ch. in Am. Home: 3885 Omaha SW Grandville MI 49418 Office: Ho of Reps 505 Olds Plz Lansing MI 48913

SIKORA, LARRY ARTHUR, mechanical engineer; b. Milw., July 11, 1954. Assoc. in Internal Combustion Engring., Milw. Sch. Engring., 1975, BSME, 1977. Sr. project engr. Jacobsen Mfg., Racine, wis., 1977-80, George J. Meyer Co., Cudahy, Wis., 1980-83; contract engr. J.I. Case, Racine, 1983-85; sr. design engr. Interlake Packaging Corp., Racine, 1985—. Co-patentee for magnetic rotator, jogger/stitcher/stacker. Lutheran. Office: Interlake Packaging Corp 718 S Marquette St Racine WI 53403-1108

SIKORA, SUZANNE MARIE, dentist; b. Kenosha, Wis., Dec. 4, 1952; d. Leo F. and Ida A. (Dupuis) S. BS, U. Wis., Parkside, 1975; DDS, Marquette U., 1981. Assoc. Paul G. Hagemann, DDS, Racine, Wis., 1981-84; pvt. practice dentistry Racine, 1984—; cons. Westview Health Care Ctr., Racine, 1981-89, Lincoln Luth. Home, Racine, 1981—, Becker-Shoop Ctr., Racine, 1981—, Lincoln Village Convalescent Ctr., Racine, 1986—, Racine Community Care Ctr., 1989—. Mem. ad hoc study com. County Health Dept., Racine, 1982-83. Mem. ADA, Wis. Dental Assn. (coun. on access prevention and wellness com. 1984-86, impaired provider program intervenor 1990—, del. 1993—). Office: 1900 Lathrop Ave Racine WI 53405-3707

SILETS, HARVEY MARVIN, lawyer; b. Chgo., Aug. 25, 1931; s. Joseph Lazarus and Sylvia (Dubner) S.; m. Elaine L. Gordon, June 25, 1961; children: Hayden Leigh, Jonathan Lazarus (dec.), Alexandra Rose. BS cum laude, DePaul U., 1952; JD (Frederick Leicke scholar), U. Mich., 1955. Bar: Ill. 1955, U.S. Dist. Ct. (no. dist.) Ill. 1955, N.Y. 1956, U.S. Tax Ct. 1957, U.S. Ct. Mil. Appeals 1957, U.S. Ct. Appeals (7th cir.) 1958, U.S. Supreme Ct. 1959, U.S. Ct. Appeals (6th cir.) 1965, U.S. Ct. Appeals (2d cir.) 1971, U.S. Ct. Appeals (5th cir.) 1972, U.S. Ct. Appeals (11th cir.). Assoc. Paul, Weiss, Rifkind, Wharton & Garrison, N.Y.C., 1955-56; asst. atty. U.S. Dist. Ct. (no. dist.) Ill., 1958-60; chief tax atty. U.S. atty. No. Dist. Ill., Chgo., 1960-62; ptnr. Harris, Burman & Silets, Chgo., 1962-79, Silets & Martin, Ltd., Chgo., 1979-92; asst. advance tng. program IRS, U. Mich., 1952-53; law lectr. advance fed. taxation John Marshall Law Sch., 1962-66; adj. prof. taxation Chgo.-Kent Coll. Law, 1985—; gen. counsel Nat. Treasury Employees Union, 1968-92; mem. adv. com. tax litigation U.S. Dept. Justice, 1979-82; mem. Tax Reform Com., State of Ill., 1982-83; mem. Speedy Trial Act Planning Group U.S. Dist. Ct. (no. dist.) Ill., 1976-79; mem. civil justice reform act adv. com. U.S. Dist. Ct. (no. dist.) Ill., 1991-94; lectr. in field. Contbr. articles to profl. jours. Trustee Latin Sch., Chgo., 1970-76; active Chgo. Crime Commn., 1975-93, Govv.'s Commn. Reform Tax Laws, Ill., 1982-83. With AUS, 1956-58. Fellow Am. Coll. Trial Lawyers (chmn. com. on fed. rules of criminal procedure 1982-91, fed. rules of evidence com. 1988-93, mem. judiciary com., Upstate Ill. com. chmn. 1990-91), Am. Coll. Tax Counsel, Internat. Acad. Trial Lawyers; mem. ABA (active various coms.), Bar Assn. 7th Fed. Cir. (chmn. com. criminal law and procedure 1972-82, bd. govs. 1983-86, sec. 1986-88, v.p. 1989-90, pres. 1990-91), Fed. Bar Assn. (bd. dirs. 1971—, pres. 1977-78, v.p. 1976-77, sec. 1975-76, treas. 1974-75, active various coms.), Chgo. Bar Assn. (tax com. 1958-66, com. devel. law 1966-72, 78—, com. fed. taxation 1968—, com. evaluation candidates 1978-80, exec. com. tax sect. 1994—), Am. Bd. Criminal Def. Lawyers, Chgo. Soc. Trial Lawyers, Decalogue Soc. Lawyers, Bar Assn. N.Y. City, Nat. Assn. Criminal Def. Lawyers, Standard Club, Cliff Dwellers Club, Chgo. Club, Phi Alpha delta, Pi Gamma Mu. Office: Katten Muchin & Zavis 525 W Monroe St Ste 1600 Chicago IL 60661-3629

SILINS, ASTRIDA ILGA, retired anesthesiologist; b. Talsi, Latvia, July 9, 1928; came to U.S. 1951; d. Wilhelm and Zigrida (Skrebers) Grikmanis; m. V. Raymond Silins, Mar. 26, 1926; 1 child, Karen Ingrid. Cand.med., Baltic U., Hamburg, W. Ger., 1949; MD, U. Kiel, W. Ger., 1955. Diplomate Am. Bd. Anesthesiology. Resident in anesthesiology Presbyn.-St. Luke's Hosp., Chgo., 1960-61; asst. attending anesthesiologist Presbyn.-St. Luke's Hosp., 1962-67; assoc. attending anesthesiologist Highland Park (Ill.) Hosp., 1967-75, Presbyn. St. Luke's Hosp., 1975-95; ret., 1995; asst. prof. Anesthesiology Rush Med. Coll., Chgo., 1975-95; sr. attending anesthesiologist Rush Presbyn.-St. Luke's Hosp. Mem. Am. Cardiovascular Anesthesiologists Soc. Republican. Lutheran. Home: 277 Hibbard Rd Winnetka IL 60093-3507 Office: Univ Anesthesiologists 1753 W Congress Pky Chicago IL 60612-3809

SILKWOOD-SHERER, DEBORAH JO, dean; b. Ypsalanti, Mich., Apr. 6, 1956; d. Joseph Dennis Sr. and Ida Yvonne (Skaggs) Silkwood; m. Robert Calvin Sherer Jr., Oct. 1, 1983; children: Kaitlyn Ruth, Jessica Mae. Student, We. Ky. U., 1974-76; B in Health Sci., U. Ky., 1978; MS, DePaul U., 1991. Lic. phys. therapist, Mich. Phys. therapist Mount Sinai Hosp., Chgo., 1978-80; clin. coord. edn. Schwab Rehab. Svcs., Chgo., 1980-82; clin. coord. edn., inpatient supr. phys. therapy Ingham Med. Ctr., Lansing, Mich., 1982-87; dir. rehab. svcs. Ingham Med. Ctr., Lansing, 1987-92; dean Allied Health Baker Coll., Flint, Mich., 1992—; cons. Forest Hills Pain Clinic, Chgo., 1979-80; profl. adv. com. mem. Vis. Nurse Svcs., Lansing, 1988-93; phys. therapist Pacemaker Wheelchair Basketball Team, Chgo., 1980-81. Contbr. articles to profl. jours. Bd. trustees Mich. chpt. Multiple Sclerosis Soc., Southfield, 1986-95, sec., 1990-94, chair chpt. svcs., 1989-93. Mem. Am. Phys. Therapy Assn., Soc. Health Care Adminstrs., Mich. Phys. Therapy Assn. (coms.), Order Ky. Cols., Omicron Delta Kappa. Office: Baker Coll of Flint 1050 W Bristol Rd Flint MI 48507

SILL, LARRY ROBERT, physics educator; b. Fairmont, Minn., Sept. 10, 1937; s. Robert Ellis and Marie Victoria (Keeler) S.; m. Judith Ann Larson, Aug. 29, 1959; children: Jennifer, Stephen. BA, Carleton Coll., 1959; PhD, Iowa State U., 1964. Prof. physics No. Ill. U., DeKalb, 1964-95, assoc. dean Coll. Liberal Arts and Scis., 1969-80, dir. Tech. Commercialization Ctr., 1985-95, prof. emeritus physics, 1995—; scientist-in-residence Argonne (Ill.) Nat. Lab., 1983-84. Contbr. articles to profl. jours. Mem. Am. Assn. Physics Tchrs., Am. Inst. Phys., Assn. of Univ. Tech. Mgrs., Tech. Transfer Soc., Licensing Execs. Soc., Sigma Xi, Sigma Pi Sigma, Lions (local pres. 1981-82). Presbyterian. Lodge: Lions (local pres. 1981-82). Office: No Ill U Dept Physics De Kalb IL 60115

SILLS, WILLIAM HENRY, III, investment banker; b. Chgo., Jan. 2, 1936; s. William Henry II and Mary Dorothy (Trude) S.; children: William Henry IV, David Andrew Henry. AB, Dartmouth Coll., 1958; MA, Northwestern U., 1961. Stockbroker Bache & Co., Chgo., 1961-64; co-founder and investment banker Chgo. Corp., 1964-84, First of Mich. Corp., Chgo., 1984-86, Sills & Co., Inc., Zenda, Wis., 1986-90, exec. v.p. Beijing Hong Fei Econ. and Technol. Firm, Beijing, 1990—, vice chmn, 1991—. Nat. vice commodore of Sea Exploring Boy Scouts Am., 1992—, mem. 1965—; with Chgo., Harvard and Geneva Lake R.R. Co., 1962—; cons. in field. Author papers in field; vice-chmn. bd. dirs. Honduras-Am. Securities, Ltd.; dir. Honduran-Am. Real Estate Programs; chmn. bd. dirs., pres. Cen. Am. Fund, Ltd., INVI, S.A., Honduras, San Pedro Sula, Cortes, 1990—. Chmn. Geneva Lake (Wis.) Area Joint Transp. Commn., 1965-86, 90-92, sec. 1992—, Wisconsin River Rail Transit Commn., 1975—, Ferro Carreal Nacional de Honduras Acquiring Corp., 1992—; pres. PRC, U.S., Cen. Am. Transp. Co., 1988—. With USMCR, 1955-61. Mem. NRA (benefactor), Am. Soc. Traffic and Transp., Am. Sail Tng. Assn., U.S. Coun. Cmty. Sailing Orgns., Am. Short Line R.R. Assn., Coun. Am. Master Mariners, U.S. Sailing Assn. (sr. judge), Wis. Rifle and Pistol Assn. (charter), Inland Lake Yachting Assn.(sr. judge), Lake Geneva Yacht Club (past commodore), Chgo. Lions Rugby Football Club (founder), Chgo. Area Rugby Football Union-Referees Soc., Lake Geneva Country Club, Skeeter Ice Boat Club. Republican. Episcopal. Avocations: sailing, ice boating, chess, hunting, rugby. Mailing: PO Box 40 Zenda WI 53195-0040

SILVA, PAUL DOUGLAS, reproductive endocrinologist; b. Durban, Natal, Republic South Africa, Oct. 29, 1956; came to U.S., 1968; s. George Douglas and Georgette Marie (Schedivetz) S.; m. Diane Elisabeth Deterville, June 28, 1980; children: Julie Renee, Jennifer Marie, Dawn Elisabeth. BA in Biology, UCLA, 1976; MD, U. Calif., Davis, 1981. Diplomate Am. Bd. Ob-Gyn, Am. Bd. Reproductive Endocrinology. Resident in ob-gyn U. Calif., Irvine, 1981-85; fellow in reproductive endocrinology U. So. Calif., L.A., 1985-87; reproductive endocrinologist Gundersen/Luth. Med. Ctr., La Crosse, Wis., 1987—; med. researcher Gundersen Med. Found., La Crosse, 1987—; cons. St. Francis Med. Ctr., La Crosse, 1988—. Coontbr. articles to Jour. Am. Acad. Dermatology, Am. Jour. Ob-Gyn, Jour. Clin. Endocrinology and Metabolism, Acta Endocrinology, also others. Lectr. to community orgns. Recipient Geog. Acad. award U. Calif., Irvine, 1984, rsch. award Soc. for Gynecologic Investigation, 1987, svc. award Pacific Coast Fertility Soc., 1987; Gundersen Med. Found. grantee, 1989-93. Fellow Am. Coll. Ob-Gyn., Am. Fertility Soc.; mem. Am. Assn. Gynecologic Laparoscopists, Soc. Reproductive Endocrinologists. Roman Catholic. Office: Gundersen Clinic 1836 South Ave La Crosse WI 54601-5429

SILVEOUS, C(HARLES) DANIEL, mortgage company executive, financial consultant; b. Columbus, Ohio, July 6, 1944; s. Charles Daniel and Lura Jane (Anderson) S.; m. Carolee Kelly Herning, Feb. 14, 1966; children: Brant D., Brooke N. Student, Ohio Wesleyan U., 1962-67. Br. mgr. Capital Fin. Svc., Columbus, 1967-76; asst. v.p. Assocs. Fin. Svcs., Columbus, 1976-85; sr. v.p., chief lending officer Freedom Fed. Savs. & Loan, Columbus, 1985-88; CEO, Merc. Mortgage Co., Columbus, 1988—; pres. Merc. Fin. Group, Inc., Columbus, 1989—; fin. advisor C. Daniel Silveous Fin., Delaware, Ohio, 1989—; cons. Oxford Bldg. & Remodeling, Delaware, 1990—. Mem. Soc. Mortgage Cons., Ohio Assn. Mortgage Brokers (bd. dirs., v.p., exec. com. 1991-93, pres.-elect 1993), Am. Conservative Union. Republican. Home: 690 Bunty Station Rd Delaware OH 43015 Office: Merc Morgage Co 8101 N High St Ste 380 Columbus OH 43235

SILVER, BELLA WOLFSON, daycare center executive, educator; b. N.Y.C., Mar. 10, 1937; d. David Michael and Edith (Bienenstock) Wolfson; m. Kenneth A. Silver, Oct. 19, 1958; children: James, Daniel. BS, Adelphi U., 1958; postgrad. Bank St. Coll., 1958-59, Nova U. Cert. tchr., N.Y., Ill., Wis. Kindergarten tchr., N.Y.C., 1958, Madison (Wis.) Pub. Schs., 1959-61, White Fish Bay (Wis.) Public Schs., 1961-65; nursery sch. tchr., Deerfield, Ill., 1975-77; substitute tchr. Deerfield Pub. Schs., 1975-77; founder., dir., pres. Deerfield Day Care Ctr., 1978-94; founder Bella W. Silver and Assocs., 1990-94, child care cons. for the nineties; pres., founder B & K E.C.E Enterprises 1993—; corp. cons. Day Care/Child Care Svcs., 1983—; pub. speaker on child care to North Shore High Schs., 1984; speaker, presenter Hawaiian Assn. for Edn. Young Children, 1992, 93, Chgo. Assn. for Edn. Young Children, 1993—, Mid West Assn. for Edn. Young Children, 1994; chmn. publicity, fundraiser, promoter 1st Ann. Craft Show, Deerfield Day Care Ctr., 1978-94. Author series of books on child care, 1993—. Mem. Deerfield Caucus; active Cub Scouts, Deerfield, Outstanding Service award 1973-77; mem. exec. bd. Jewish United Fund; sec. Parents-Tchrs. Orgn. Recipient award Bahais of Deerfield, 1981; mem. "Com. of 200" Child Care Info. Exchange Mag., 1985—. Mem. NAFE, AAUW, ASCD, Assn. Childhood Edn. Internat., Nat. Assn. Edn. Young Children, Chgo. Assn. Edn. Young Children (early childhood conf. presenter 1993-96), Assn. Child Care Con. Internat., Nat. Assn. Child Care Profl., Wis. Early Childhood Assn., Dirs. Network of Childcare Info. Exch., Deerfield C. of C., Phi Sigma Sigma (Pyramid award 1965). Jewish. Home: 459 Williamsburg Ln Rob Roy Country Club Village Prospect Heights IL 60070

SILVER, GEORGE, metal trading and processing company executive; b. Warren, Ohio, Dec. 17, 1918; s. Jacob and Sophie (Bradlyn) S.; m. Irene Miller, Aug. 5, 1945. Student U. Ala., 1938; BA, Ohio U., 1940, postgrad. law sch. Ohio State U., 1940-41; grad. Adj. Gen. Sch., 1944. Pres., Riverside Indsl. Materials, Bettendorf, Iowa, 1947-70, Metalpel subs. Continental Telephone Co., Bettendorf, 1970-71, Riverside Industries Inc., Bettendorf, 1971—; pres. Scott Resources Inc., Davenport, Iowa; v.p. Durbin Midwest, Davenport, 1987-90; mktg. dir. NAMCO Internat., Miami; cons. Waste Mgmt.-non Ferrous Mktg., 1990—, Snyer Steel Casting, Iowa, Riverside Products, Ill., 1992-93; founder Iowa Steel Mills (name changed to North Star Steel), Cargill and Wilton; mktg. dir. NAMCO Environ. Svcs. Corp., Miami, Fla.; bd. dirs. NAMCO Trading Co., Miami; cons. metal trading Cricket Club, Miami, Fla. Contbr. articles to profl. jours. Mem. Nat. UN Day Com., 1975-83. Served to capt. AC, USAF, 1941-46, 50-51, Korea. Named to Hon. Order Ky. Cols., 1991. Mem. Nat. Assn. Recycling Industries (co-chmn. nat. planning com., bd. dirs.), Copper Club, Paper Stock Inst. Am. (mem. exec. com.), Bur. Internat. de la Recuperation (chmn. adv. com.), Inter Global Trading Group (chmn. bd. dirs.), Mining Club N.Y.C., Outing Club, Hatchet Men's Chowder and Protective Assn., Copper Club, Jockey Club Miami, Williams Island Club, Rock Island Arsenal Officer's Club, Chemist Club (N.Y.C.), Crow Valley Country Club, Elks, Phi Sigma Delta. Republican. Jewish. Office: Cricket Club 1800 NE 114th St Apt 608 Miami FL 33181-3417

SILVER, NEIL MARVIN, manufacturing executive; b. Bklyn., June 2, 1928; s. Jack and Rose (Eisenberg) S.; m. Leah Rebecca Coffman Silver, Sept. 4, 1949; children: Pamela Sue, Carole Beth. Student. U. Mich., 1945-46, 48-49; BS, Ind. U., 1951. Asst. mgr. Wolvering Parking Co., Lansing, Mich., 1951-54; treas. Capitol Parking Co., Indpls., 1955-60; controller, asst. to pres. Eberhart Steel Products, Inc., Mishawaka Tool & Die, Inc., Ind., 1961-63; PRES. Allied Quality Products, Inc., Mishawaka, Ind., 1964-67; treas. Allied Screw Products, Inc., Mishawaka, Ind., 1968-88, chmn., sec., 1989—. Bd. dirs. Ind. State Anti-Defamation League, 1955-57; bd. dirs., treas., pres., chmn. Fin. Commn., Family and Children's Ctr., Inc., Mishawaka, Ind., 1957-77; bd. dirs., treas. Family Svc. Assn. St. Joseph County, Ind., 1955-57. With U.S. Army, 1946-48. Mem. AIAA, Soc. Mfg. Engrs., SAE Internat., Internat. Computing Soc., ASM Internat., B'nai B'rith. Office: Allied Screw Products Inc PO Box 543 815 E Lowell Ave Mishawaka IN 46546-0543

SILVER, RALPH DAVID, distilling company director; b. Chgo., Apr. 19, 1924; s. Morris J. and Amelia (Abrams) S.; m. Lois Reich, Feb. 4, 1951; children: Jay, Cappy. B.S., U. Chgo., 1943; postgrad., Northwestern U., 1946-48; J.D., DePaul U., 1952. Bar: Ill. bar 1952. Staff accountant David Himmelblau & Co. (C.P.A.'s), 1946-48; internal revenue agt. U.S. Dept. Treasury, 1948-51; practice in Chgo., 1952-55; atty. Lawrence J. West, 1952-55; fin. cons., bd. dirs. Barton Inc., Chgo., 1955-92; bd. dirs. Stone Fin. Corp., Stone Fin. II Corp., 1992-95; arbitrator N.Y. State Exch., Cir. Ct. of Cook County, Ill., Nat. Assn. Securities Dealers. Bd. dirs., pres. Ralph and Lois Silver Found. Lt. (j.g.) USNR, 1943-46. Mem. ABA, Chgo. Bar Assn., AICPA. Club: Green Acres Country. Home: 1124 Old Elm Ln Glencoe IL 60022-1235

SILVERBERG, ALAN BERNARD, endocrinology educator; b. St. Louis, Nov. 17, 1946; s. Hymen Dorf and Dorothy (Nathanson) S.; m. Devorah Sonenschein, 1969; children: Amy Mara, Rachel Dena. AB in Biology, Washington U., St. Louis, 1968; MD, U. Kans., 1972. Diplomate Nat. Bd. Med. Examiners, Am. Bd. Internal Medicine, Am. Bd. Endocrinology and Metabolism. Intern dept. medicine U. Minn. Sch. Med., Mpls., 1972-73; fellow in internal medicine U. Minn. Sch. Med., 1973-75; fellow in endocrinology and metabolism dept. medicine, divsn. metabolism Washington U. Sch. Med., St. Louis, 1975-76; staff assoc., Lab. Environ. Toxicology Nat. Inst. Environ. Health Svcs., Research Triangle Park, N.C., 1976-78, endocrinologist Lab. Environ. Toxicology, 1978-79; asst. prof. dept. internal medicine, divsn. endocrinology St. Louis U. Sch. Med., 1979-85, assoc. prof., 1985—; cons., mem. med. adv. com., physician reviewer Med. Rev. Svc. Mid-Am., Jefferson City, Mo., 1989—; physician advisor Mo. Patient Care Rev. Found., 1989—; physican cons. div. med. svc. Mo. Dept. Social Svcs., 1990—; mem. ambulatory care quality assurance com. St. Louis U. Med. Ctr., 1990—; mem. clin. evaluative sci. coun. Univ. Hosp. Consortium, 1991—; v.p. med. staff St. Louis U. Hosp., 1995-96, pres., 1996—. Contbr. articles to prof. jours. Lt. comdr. USPHS, 1976-79. Recipient Physician's Recognition award AMA, 1977, 81, 84, 88, 91, 93. Fellow ACP, Am. Col. Endocrinology, Am. Assn. Clin. Endocrinologists; mem. Endocrine Soc., Am. Diabetes Assn., Am. Fertility Soc., Ctrl. Clin. Rsch. Club, (chmn. St. Louis U. chpt. 1986, 87), St. Louis U. Internists Club (sec.-treas. 1985, v.p. 1986, pres. 1987, 88), Sigma Xi, Alpha Chi Sigma. Jewish. Office: Divsn Endocrinology St Louis U 1402 S Grand Blvd Saint Louis MO 63104

SILVERMAN, ELLEN, speech and language pathologist; b. Milw., Oct. 12, 1942; d. Roy and Bettie (Schlaeger) Loebel; m. Feb. 5, 1967 (div.); 1 child, Catherine Bette. BS, U. Wis., Milw., 1964; MA, U. Iowa, 1967, PhD, 1970. Rsch. assoc. U. Ill., Urbana, 1969-71; asst. prof. speech pathology Marquette U., Milw., 1973-79; assoc. prof. speech pathology Marquette U., 1979-85; pvt. practice speech and lang. pathology, Milw., 1985—; owner, pres. The Speech Source, Inc. Contbr. articles to profl. jours., chpts. to books. Marquette U. grantee, 1982. Fellow Am. Speech, Hearing, Lang. Assn.; mem. Wis. Speech, Hearing, Lang. Assn., Sigma Xi.

SILVERMAN, HARRY MARK, physical therapist; b. Chgo., July 26, 1954; s. Edward Karl and Shirley (Shapiro) S.; m. Nancy Shalowitz, June 6, 1993. BA in Bus. and Fin., U. Ill., 1976; BS in Phys. Therapy, Northwestern U., 1987. Lic. phys. therapist, Ill. Phys. therapist Condell Med. Ctr., Libertyville, Ill., 1987-90, Edgewater Rehab. Assoc., Northbrook, Ill., 1987-95, U.S. Med. Placements, Chgo., 1992-94; prin. Regency Rehab. Svc., Inc., Niles, Ill., 1994—. Mem. AMA, NRA, Am. Phys. Therapy Assn. Home: 1030 N State St Chicago IL 60610 Office: Regency Rehab Svc 6625 N Milwaukee Ave Niles IL 60714

SILVEY, RONALD L., project engineer; b. Versailles, Mo., July 7, 1958. BS in Environ. Chem. Tech., S.W. Mo. U., 1980. Project engr. Eagle-Picher Industries Inc., Joplin, Mo., 1980—. Contbr. articles to profl. jours. Mem. Second Assembly of God, Joplin, 1980—; mem., state level officer Royal Rangers, Second Assembly of God, So. Mo. Dist., 1980-94. Republican. Office: Eagle-Picher Industries Inc 1215 W B St Joplin MO 64801-2869

SIMES, STEPHEN MARK, pharmaceutical products executive; b. N.Y.C., Nov. 23, 1951; s. Herbert H. and Mimi (Maurer) S.; m. Anita H. Herzog, Aug. 23, 1975. BS in Chemistry, Bklyn. Coll., 1973; MBA in Mktg., NYU, 1980. Sales rep. G.D. Searle and Co., N.Y.C., 1974-78; supr. sales tng. G.D. Searle and Co., Chgo., 1978-79; dist. sales mgr. G.D. Searle and Co., N.Y.C., 1979-81; product mgr. G.D. Searle and Co., Chgo., 1981-82, sr. product mgr., 1982-83, dir. pub. affairs and communications, 1983-84; v.p. Gynex Inc., Chgo., 1984-88; dir. Gynex Pharms. Inc., Deerfield, 1985-93; pres., dir. Gynex Labs., Chgo., 1985-88; pres., CEO Contracap Inc., Ill., 1988-89; pres., CEO Gynex Pharms., Inc., Chgo., 1989-93, chmn., 1992-93; sr. v.p., dir. Bio-Technology Gen. Corp., 1993-94; pres., CEO, dir. Unimed Pharms., Inc., 1994—. Mem. Chgo. Coun. Fgn. Rels., Licensing Exec. Soc. Home: 1173 Rd Long Grove IL 60047-9524 Office: Unimed Pharms Inc 2150 E Lake Cook Rd Buffalo Grove IL 60089-1862

SIMMONS, BARBARA JAYNE, physical therapist assistant; b. Jackson, Mich., Feb. 29, 1960; d. Robert J. and Kaylene A. Myers; m. Jerry L. Simmons, May 6, 1983; children: Lisa M., Heather L., Anthony J. AAS, Kellogg C.C., 1980; BA, Spring Arbor (Mich.) Coll., 1994. Phys. therapist asst. Ottawa Area Ctr., Zeeland, Mich., 1980-81, Mary Free Bed/St. Mary's Hosp. Sys., Grand Rapids, Mich., 1981-83, Battle Creek (Mich.) Pub. Sch., 1983-95; part time faculty Kellogg C.C., Battle Creek, 1984—; phys. therapist asst. Rehab. Assocs., Battle Creek, 1987-93, Vis. Nurse Svcs., Battle Creek, 1995—. Editor (newsletter) Western Lines, 1992-94. Chairperson Indian Trails Camp Fund of Calhoun County, Battle Creek, 1985-95. Mem. Am. Phys. Therapy Assn. (on-site evaluator Commn. on Accreditation for Phys. Therapy Edn. 1991—, Mich. del. 1982, 85, 86, 89, 92, edn. sect.), Mich. Phys. Therapy Assn. (affiliate v.p., liaison 1992-94, Outstanding Phys. Therapist Asst. Western Mich. award 1991, Outstanding Phys. Therapist Asst. Mich. award 1994), We. Dist. and Mich. Phys. Therapy Assn., Mobility Internat. USA, Health Promotion and Wellness Coun. Mich., Kenny Found., Physically Impaired Assn. Mich. Home: 244 Feld Ave Battle Creek MI 49017-1342

SIMMONS, CHUCK, state official. Sec. Dept. Corrections, Topeka, Kans. Office: Corrections Dept 900 SW Jackson St #400 Topeka KS 66612-1284*

SIMMONS, DEBORAH ANNE, education educator; b. Oroville, Calif., Oct. 9, 1950; d. Daniel Fredrick and Jeanne (Marlow) Simmons; m. Ronald Eugene Widmar, May 17, 1980. BA in Anthropology, U. Calif., Berkeley, 1972; MS, Humboldt State U., Arcata, Calif., 1977, PhD in Natural Resources, 1983. Cert. secondary tchr., Calif. TESOL instr. U.S. Peace Corps, South Korea, 1973-75; postdoctoral scholar U. Mich., Ann Arbor, 1983-84; asst. prof. Montclair State Coll., Upper Montclair, N.J., 1984-87; asst. prof. dept. curriculum and instrn. No. Ill. U., DeKalb, 1987-92, assoc. prof., 1992—; cons. Mendocino County Schs., Ukiah, Calif., 1977-78, Acad. for Ednl. Devel., Washington, 1994-95, Lincoln Park Zoo, Chgo., 1990-92, Chgo. Acad. Scis., 1992—. Author monograph; contbr. numerous articles to Jour. Environ. Edn., Environment and Behavior, Children's Environments, Women in Natural Resources, others. Recipient Rsch. award Progressive Architecture, 1987, 88; U.S. Forest Svc. grantee, 1991—. Mem. N.Am. Assn. for Environ. Edn. (treas. 1991-95, pres. 1996). Office: No Ill U Dept Curriculum & Instrn De Kalb IL 60115

SIMMONS, ETHEL LORETTA, journalist; b. Detroit, Mar. 15, 1933; d. John and Elizabeth (Kotulis) Smilick. BA in Journalism, Wayne State U., 1954. Assoc. editor Guest, Skyliner, On Stage, Detroit, 1954-56; publicity dir. WJBK-TV, Channel 2, Detroit, 1956-57; staff writer Pictorial Living, Detroit Times, 1957-60; arts editor, news editor The Eccentric Newspapers,

Birmingham, Mich., 1962-72, mng. editor, 1972-75; food & entertainment editor Observer & Eccentric Newspapers, Livonia, Mich., 1975-90; suburban life editor The Eccentric Newspapers, 1991—. Mem. Soc. Profl. Journalists (past treas., past bd. dirs.). Office: The Eccentric Newspapers 805 E Maple Birmingham MI 48009

SIMMONS, JOSEPH THOMAS, accountant, educator; b. Forest Lake, Minn., Jan. 23, 1936; s. Roland Thomas and Erma (Rabe) S.; m. Winola Ann Zwald, Aug. 18, 1962 (div.); children: Thomas E, Kevin M. BS in Bus. and Econs., Morningside Coll., 1964; MBA, U. S.D., 1965; PhD in Bus., U. Nebr., 1974. CPA, S.D. Prof. acctg. and fin. U. S.D., Vermillion, 1966-69, 75—, dir. Sch. Bus., 1975—; prof. U. Nebr., Lincoln, 1969-71, U. Man., Winnipeg, Can., 1971-75; prin. Simmons and Assocs. Mgmt. Cons., Rapid City, S.D., 1981—; pvt. practice acctg. Rapid City, 1982—; pres. Simmons Profl. Fin. Planning, Vermillion, 1983—; bd. dirs. Powerhouse Computers, Sioux Falls, N.D., v.p. fin., 1992-93; bd. dirs. MDU Resources Inc., Bismarck, N.D., RE/spec, Rapid City, Gro-Tech, Rapid City, Dairlean Inc., Sioux Falls; vis. prof. U. Warsaw, Poland, 1994. Served with U.S. Army, 1958-60. Mem. AICPA, Am. Acctg. Assn., Fin. Mgmt. Assn., S.D. Soc. CPA's. Republican. Methodist. Home and Office: Ponderosa Acres Lot 2 Burbank SD 57010-9731

SIMMONS, LAWRENCE WILLIAM, health care company executive; b. Omaha, May 7, 1947; s. Albin Pachola and Leella Clarice (Franklin) S.; m. Leanna Carol McGee, Nov. 3, 1968; children: Scott, Anthony. Assoc. Gen. Studies, U. Nebr., 1977, B Gen. Studies, 1978. Pharm. sales rep. 3M Pharms., Omaha, 1972-83; dist. sales mgr. 3M Pharms., Chgo., 1983-89; regional sales mgr. midwest region 3M Pharms., St. Paul, 1989-92; group bus. mgr. pharm. and personal care 3M Pharms., Mexico City, 1992-95; group bus. dir. 3M Mexico/Div. V Health Care, 1995—; cluster mem. Xavier U., New Orleans, 1987—; minority outreach rep. 3M, St. Paul, 1987—. With U.S. Army, 1968-71, Vietnam. Mem. Kappa Alpha Psi (polemarch 1981-83, best chpt. award 1983). Office: 7525 Currell Blvd Woodbury MN 55125

SIMMONS, PATRICIA ANN, employment services manager; b. Sioux City, Iowa, Dec. 18, 1946; d. Milford Orland Rogers and Betty Jane Harrison; m. Michael Steven Trexel, Sept. 5, 1965 (div. June 1978) children: Kimberly Ann, Matthew Allen, Nathan Andrew, Michael Steven; m. Bruce Howard Simmons, Aug. 23, 1979. BS in Edn., Morningside Coll., 1969, MS in Edn., 1973. Tchr. St. Boniface Sch., Sioux City, 1968-69; substitute tchr. Lawton-Bronson, Lawton, Iowa, 1969-75; interviewer Dept. Employment Svcs., Sioux City, 1975-78, counselor, 1978-81; counselor Dept. Employment Svcs., Iowa City, 1982-85; office mgr. Dept. Employment Svcs., Atlantic, Iowa, 1985—. Foster parent Luth. Social Svcs., 1986—; mem. city coun. City of Atlantic, 1991—; mem. Gov.'s Commn. Persons with Disabilities, State of Iowa, 1992-95. Mem. AAUW (membership chair State of Iowa 1993-94), Internat. Assn. Pers. in Employment Security (disability chair 1988, state pres. 1990), Toastmasters (pres. 1987-88, area gov. 1988-89, dist. gov. 1989-90), Atlantic C. of C. (bd. dirs. 1986-90). Lutheran. Home: 802 W 10th St Atlantic IA 50022-2045 Office: 508 Poplar Atlantic IA 50022

SIMMONS, RALPH OLIVER, physics educator; b. Kensington, Kans., Feb. 19, 1928; s. Fred Charles and Cornelia (Douglass) S.; m. Janet Lee Lull, Aug. 31, 1952; children: Katherine Ann, Bradley Alan, Jill Christine, Joy Diane. B.A., U. Kans., 1950; B.A. (Rhodes scholar), Oxford U., 1953; Ph.D., U. Ill., 1957. Research assoc. U. Ill., Urbana, 1957-59, faculty physics, 1959—, assoc. prof., 1961-65, prof. physics, 1965—, head physics dept., 1970-86; vis. scientist Ctr. for Study Nuclear Energy, Mol, Belgium, 1965; mem. governing bd. Internat. Symposia on Thermal Expansion, 1970-88; cons. Argonne Nat. Lab., 1978-86, Los Alamos Nat. Lab., 1983-84; chmn. Office of Phys. Scis., NRC, 1978-81; mem. Assembly of Math. and Phys. Scis., 1978-81, Geophysics Rsch. Bd., 1978-81; trustee Argonne Univs. Assn., 1979-83. Mem. internat. adv. bd.: Jour. Physics C (Solid State Physics), 1971-76; mem. editorial bd.: Physical Review B, 1978-81. Recipient Sr. U.S. Scientist Rsch. award Alexander von Humboldt Found., 1992; sr. postdoctoral fellow NSF, 1965. Fellow Am. Phys. Soc. (vice chmn., chmn. divsn. solid state physics 1975-77, coun. 1988), AAAS (chmn. sect. B Physics 1985-86); mem. Am. Crystallographic Assn., Am. Assn. Physics Tchrs., Phi Beta Kappa, Sigma Xi, Pi Mu Epsilon. Home: 1005 Foothill Dr Champaign IL 61821-5622

SIMMS, AMELIA MOSS, publishing executive; b. Detroit, Nov. 12, 1954; d. Leonard W. and Beebe (Gottesman) Moss; m. Steven W. Simms, June 19, 1977; 1 child, Jennifer Rachel. BA, Kalamazoo Coll., 1976; cert. in teaching, Western Mich. U., 1977; postgrad., U. Mich., Flint, 1984-86. Tchr. Davison (Mich.) Community Schs., 1978-81, Mott Adult High Sch., Flint, 1982-83; owner Mallery Press, Flint, Mich., 1986—; lectr., workshop leader various quilt guilds, U.S. and overseas, 1982—. Author: How to Improve Your Quilting Stitch, 1987, Invisible Applique, 1988, Every Trick in the Book, 1990, Classic Quilts: Patchwork Design from Ancient Rome, 1991, Creating Scrapbook Quilts, 1993, How NOT to Make a Prize-Winning Quilt, 1994; creator Worst Quilt In The World Contest, yearly 1995—. Mem. Am. Quilters Soc., Internat. Quilt Assn., Nat. Quilting Assn., Quilters Network. Home and Office: Mallery Press 4206 Sheraton Dr Flint MI 48532-3557

SIMON, DAVID LEO, physician; b. Middletown, Ohio, July 21, 1923; s. Frank and Mary (Chapman) S.; m. Mary Stern, 1946 (div. 1966); m. Jane Currell, 1966; children: Frank Simon II, Barbara Simon Woodward. BS, Harvard Coll., 1943; MD, U. Cin., 1948. Intern Jewish Hosp., Cin., 1948-49, resident, 1949-51; fellow Cin. Gen. Hosp., 1951-55; active staff Univ. Hosp., Cin.; courtesy staff Jewish Hosp., Cin., Mercy Anderson Hosp., Cin., Brown County Hosp., Georgetown, Ohio; instr. medicine U. Cin. Contbr. articles to profl. jours. Mem. exec. com. Rep. Party, Hamilton County, 1965-69; mem. Ourteach Com. to Elect Ronald Reagan. With U.S. Army, 1942-44, maj. USAF, 1953. Mem. AMA, Ohio State Med. Assn., Acad. of Medicine, Soc. Internal Medicine, N.Y. Acad. Scis., Coldstream Country Club, Harvard Club, Harvard Club of Cin., Masons (32 deg.), Shriners, Sigma Xi. Jewish. Home: 7336 Sanderson Pl Cincinnati OH 45243 Office: 2427 Auburn Ave Cincinnati OH 45219

SIMON, MELVIN, real estate developer, professional basketball executive; b. Oct. 21, 1926; s. Max and Mae Simon; m. Bren Burns, Sept. 14, 1972; children: Deborah, Cynthia, Tamme, David, Max. Bs in Acctg., CCNY, 1949, M in Bus., Real Estate, 1983; PhD (hon.), Butler U., 1986, Ind. U., 1991. Leasing sgt. Albert Frankel Co., Indpls., 1955-60; pres. Melvin Simon & Assocs., Indpls., 1960-73, chmn. bd., 1973—; co-owner Ind. Pacers, Indpls., 1983—; mem. adv. bd. Wharton's Real Estate, Phila., 1986—. Mem. adv. bd. dean's council Ind. U., Bloomington; bd. dirs. United Cerebral Palsy, Indpls., Muscular Dystrophy Assn., Indpls., Jewish Welfare Found., Indpls.; trustee Urban Land Inst., Internat. Council Shopping Ctrs. Recipient Horatio Alger award Boy's Club Indpls., 1986; named Man of Yr., Jewish Welfare Found., 1980. Democrat. Jewish.

SIMON, MICHAEL PAUL, general contractor, realtor; b. Madison, Wis., Sept. 23, 1941; s. Michael Francis and Ferne Doris (DeBower) S.; m. Sharon Lee Hackbart, Aug. 31, 1963; children: René M., Michael V. BS in Bldg. Constrn., Bradley U., 1964. Designer, estimator Michael F. Simon Builders, Inc., Waunakee, Wis., 1964-67, v.p., 1967-73, pres., 1973—. Commentator St. John's Cath. Ch., Waunakee, 1975-93. Named Bus. Man of Yr., Waunakee C. of C., 1980, One of Top Dane County Execs., Madison Mag. Poll, 1994. Mem. Nat. Assn. Home Builders (bd. dirs. 1985—), Wis. Builders Assn. (bd. dirs. 1980-85, membership chair 1981), Madison Area Builders Assn. (pres. 1980, chair arbitration com. 1992-94, Builder of Yr. 1980), Waunakee Rotary. Roman Catholic.

SIMON, NEIL JEROME, consulting company executive; b. Detroit. BS in Spl. Edn., Ea. Mich. U., Ypsilanti, 1970, MA in Ednl. Psychology, 1974. Co-dir., clinician pvt. clin. practice Ypsilanti, 1971-74; CEO Cons. & Learning Ctr., Inc., Ypsilanti, 1974-84; pres. Bus. Devel. Group, Inc., Ann Arbor, Mich., 1984—; instr. Washtenaw C.C., Ann Arbor, 1975—; facilitator workshops; work with designing orgnl. performance, large sys. change and orgn. process; mem. instrnl. staff U. Mich., Ann Arbor, 1987—, Am. Mgmt. Assn.. Author: Navigating in a Sea of Change, 1996; contbr. articles to profl. jours. Mem. ASTD, Orgnl. Devel. Network, Soc. Competitive Intelligence Profls. (lectr., presenter 1993—), Southeastern Mich. Health Exec. Forum, U.S. Judo Fedn. (bd. govs. Konan region 1990—), Judo Assocs. Mich. (bd. trustees, chmn. ways and means 1989—). Home: 17340 W 12 Mile Rd Ste 102 Southfield MI 48076 Office: Bus Devel Group Inc 122 S Main Ste 360 Ann Arbor MI 48104

SIMON, PAUL, senator, educator, author; b. Eugene, Oreg., Nov. 29, 1928; s. Martin Paul and Ruth (Troemel) S.; m. Jeanne Hurley, Apr. 21, 1960; children: Sheila, Martin. Student, U. Oreg., 1945-46, Dana Coll., Blair, Nebr., 1946-48; 39 hon. doctorates. Pub. Troy (Ill.) Tribune and 14 other So. Ill. weeklies., 1948-66; mem. Ill. Ho. of Reps., 1955-63, Ill. Senate, 1963-69; lt. gov. Ill., 1969-73; fellow John F. Kennedy Sch. Govt., Harvard U., 1972-73; founded pub. affairs reporting program Sangamon State U., Springfield, Ill., 1972-73; mem. 94th-98th Congresses from 22d and 24th Dists. 94th-98th Congresses from 24th and 22d Dists. Ill., Ill., 1975-85; U.S. Senator from Ill., 1985-96; U.S. presdl. candidate, 1987-88. Author: Lovejoy: Martyr to Freedom, 1964, Lincoln's Preparation for Greatness, 1965, A Hungry World, 1966, You Want to Change the World, So Change It, 1971, The Tongue-Tied American, 1980, The Once and Future Democrats, 1982, The Glass House, Politics and Morality in The Nation's Capitol, 1984, Beginnings, 1986, Let's Put America Back to Work, 1986, Winners and Losers, 1989; (with Jeanne Hurley Simon) Protestant-Catholic Marriages Can Succeed, 1967; (with Arthur Simon) The Politics of World Hunger, 1973, Advice and Consent, 1992, Freedom's Champion: Elijah Lovejoy, 1994. With CIC, AUS, 1951-53. Recipient Am. Polit. Sci. Assn. award, 1957; named Best Legislator by Ind. Voters of Ill., 7 times. Mem. Luth. Human Rels. Assn., Am. Legion, VFW, NAACP, Urban League. Democrat. Lutheran. Office: US Senate 462 Dirksen Senate Bldg Washington DC 20510

SIMON, PAUL JEROME, holding company executive, accountant; b. Detroit, May 23, 1954; s. George Anthony and Shirley Ann (Priester) S.; m. Cynthia Ann Scott, June 25, 1976; children: Michael, Paul Jr., Kristen, Alyssa, Patrick. BS magna cum laude, Georgetown U., 1975; MBA, U. Pa., 1977. CPA, Mich. Staff acct. Alexander Grant & Co., Detroit, 1976; sr. cons. Touche Ross & Co., Detroit, 1977-80; treas. U.S. Equipment Co., Detroit, 1980-83; pres. U.S. Group, Inc., Detroit, 1983—; bd. dirs. U.S. Real Estate Co., Detroit, Star Engring. and Machine, Bluffton, Ind. Bd. dirs. St. Jude Children's Rsch. Hosp., Memphis, 1986—, Am. Lebanese-Syrian Assoc. Charities, Memphis, 1986, 2d v.p., 1988-89, 1st v.p., 1990-91, chmn. bd. dirs., 1992—; treas. pack 39, Cub Scouts Am., Grosse Pointe, Mich., 1988-89. Mem. AICPA, Mich. Assn. CPA's, Young Pres. Orgn., Econ. Club Detroit, Lochmoor Club. Republican. Roman Catholic. Home: 63 Michaux Ct Grosse Pointe MI 48236-1461 Office: US Group Inc 20580 Hoover St Detroit MI 48205-1064

SIMON, ROBERT H., JR., journalist; b. Elyria, Ohio, Mar. 18, 1962; s. Robert Henry and Patricia Ann (Carter) S. BA, Ohio State U., 1984. Aide Ohio Senate, Columbus, 1985-87; sr. rsch. asst. George Bush for Pres., Washington, 1987-88; researcher, speechwriter The White House, Washington, 1989-92; speechwriter NASA, Washington, 1992-93; asst. to the mayor Columbus, 1993-95; editl. writer Columbus Dispatch, 1995—. Press sec. Watts for State Senate, Columbus, 1984; sr. adv. Dana Preisse for Coun., Columbus, 1995; dir. ops. Republican Senate Campaign Commn., Columbus, 1986. Recipient NASA exceptional svc. medal, 1993. Mem. Bush-Quayle Alumni Assn., Athletic Club Columbus, Phi Beta Kappa. Home: 2132 Firestone St Columbus OH 43228

SIMON, ROBERT MICHAEL, manufacturing company executive; b. Chgo., Aug. 24, 1947; s. Frank Michael and Emily Eleanor (Malinauskas) S.; m. Wendelin Theresa Lang, May 17, 1969; 1 child, Heather Lee. BS in Chemistry, John Carroll U., 1969; MBA, Roosevelt U., 1972. Account exec. Richardson Corp., Madison, Conn., 1973-76; sr. mktg. specialist Mobay div. Bayer A.G., Pitts., 1976-79; v.p. Transmet div. Battelle, Columbus, Ohio, 1979-85; pres., sr. cons. Indsl. Mktg. Mgmt. Systems, Dublin, Ohio, 1985-87; pres. USTEK Inc., Columbus, 1987—. Editor, author Designing with Flake Filled Plastic, 1986. Mem. Soc. Plastic Engrs. (bd. dirs.), Soc. Plastics Industry (chmn. N.Y.C. 1974), Bus. Tech. Ctr. (bd. dirs. 1986—), Technology Alliance Cen. Ohio. Republican.

SIMON, SEYMOUR, lawyer, former state supreme court justice; b. Chgo., Aug. 10, 1915; s. Ben and Gertrude (Rusky) S.; m. Roslyn Schultz Biel, May 26, 1954; children: John B., Nancy Simon Cooper, Anthony Biel. B.S., Northwestern U., 1935, J.D., 1938; LL.D. (hon.), John Marshall Law Sch., 1982, North Park Coll., 1986, Northwestern U., 1987. Bar: Ill. 1938. Spl. atty. Dept. Justice, 1938-42; practice law Chgo., 1946-74; judge Ill. Appellate Ct., Chgo., 1974-80; presiding justice Ill. Appellate Ct. (1st Dist., 3d Div.), 1977, 79; justice Ill. Supreme Ct., 1980-88; ptnr. Rudnick & Wolfe, Chgo., 1988—; former chmn. Ill. Low-Level Radioactive Waste Disposal Facility Siting Commn.; former dir. Nat. Gen. Corp., Bantam Books, Grosset & Dunlap, Inc., Gt. Am. Ins. Corp. Mem. Cook County Bd. Commrs., 1961-66, pres., 1962-66; pres. Cook County Forest Preserve Dist., 1962-66; mem. Pub. Bldg. Commn., City Chgo., 1962-67; Alderman 40th ward, Chgo., 1955-61, 67-74; Democratic ward committeeman, 1960-74; bd. dirs. Schwab Rehab. Hosp., 1961-71, Swedish Covenant Hosp., 1969-75. Served with USNR, 1942-45. Decorated Legion of Merit; recipient 9th Ann. Pub. Svc. award Tau Epsilon Rho, 1963, Hubert L. Will award Am. Vets. Com., 1983, award of merit Decalogue Soc. Lawyers, 1986, Judge Learned Hand award Am. Jewish Com., 1994, Frances Feinberg Meml. Crown award Associated Talmud Torahs of Chgo., 1995; named to Sr. Citizen's Hall of Fame, City of Chgo., 1989, Hall of Fame Jewish Comty. Ctrs. Chgo., 1989. Mem. ABA, Ill. Bar Assn., Chgo. Bar Assn., Chgo. Hist. Soc., Decalogue Soc. Lawyers (Merit award 1986), Izaak Walton League, Chgo. Hort. Soc., Comml. Club Chgo., Standard Club, Variety Club, Order of Coif; Phi Beta Kappa, Phi Beta Kappa Assocs. Home: 1555 N Astor St Chicago IL 60610-1673 Office: Rudnick & Wolfe Ste 1800 203 N La Salle St Chicago IL 60601-1210

SIMONEAU, DANIEL ROBERT, accountant, watercolorist, educator; b. Lewiston, Maine, Aug. 3, 1962; s. Robert Eugene and Rolande Muriel (Plante) S. BFA, U. So. Maine, 1984. Reconciling specialist Fleet/Norstar Bank of Maine, Lewiston, 1981-84, acct., 1984-88; acct. Sterling Engineered Products, Auburn, Maine, 1988-89; fin. analyst Pioneer Plastics Corp., Auburn, Maine, 1989-91; acct. Aeroquip Corp., New Haven, Ind., 1992; adminstrv. sys. coord. Aeroquip Corp., Maumee, Ohio, 1992-93, acct., 1993-94; acct. Trinova Corp., Maumee, Ohio, 1994-96; chmn. employee activities com. ann. outing Trinova Corp., Toledo, 1995; fin. edn. specialist PeopleSoft, Inc., Westchester, Ill., 1996—; dir. Spectrum Gallery, 1995-96; pres. Pioneer Mgmt. Assn., 1991. Contbr. article to mag. Chmn. award winners show Spectrum Friends of Fine Art, Toledo, 1995. Recipient Recognition award Spectrum Friends of Fine Art, 1994, Com. award Spectrum Gallery, 1994, 3d pl. award Toledo Fedn. Art Socs., 1992, 3d Judge's award Lewiston Art Festival Com., 1988, 90, 91, Purchase award Portland Art Festival Com., 1981, 91. Mem. Northwestern Ohio Watercolor Soc., Coll. Art Assn. Home: 6033 N Sheridan Rd Unit 31G Chicago IL 60660 Office: PeopleSoft Inc 2 Westbrook Corporate Ctr Ste 400 Westchester IL 60154

SIMONEAU, WAYNE ANTHONY, state legislator; b. Ashland, Wis., Jan. 17, 1935; s. Rex Robert and Helen Leigten S.; m. Jane Jarzyna, 1958; children: lisa, Laura, Anthony, Paul, Matthew, Leslie. Grad., Dunwoody Inst., Mpls., 1957. Chmn. Dist. 46 Dem./Farmer-Labor Com., Minn., 1972-75; Minn. State rep. Dist. 52A, 1975—; cons. Workers Compensation Claims Adminstr.; fastener salesperson; chmn. govt. ops. com., health and human svc. com.; mem. environ. and natural resources com., local govt. and met. affairs com., rules and legis. adminstrn. com., ways and means, capital investments coms. Rec. sec. local teamsters Union; adv. bd. Pine City Area Vocat.-Tech. Inst.; mem. Hennepin County Vocat.-Tech. Inst.; bd. dirs. Fridley Bldg. Stds. and Design Control. *

SIMONELLI, MICHAEL TARQUIN, chemical engineer; b. Chgo., July 27, 1946; s. Michael Eugene and Caroline S.; m. Nancy Jo Garnaas (div.); 1 child, Kimberly; m. Tania Kalikin, Nov. 15, 1986; children: Nicole, John. BS in Chem. Engring., U. Ill., Chgo., 1968; BA, Elmhurst Coll., 1969. R & D mgr. plastic divsn. product devel. Masonite Corp., St. Charles, Ill., 1968-71; dist. sales mgr. DeGaynor and Co., Hillside, Ill., 1971-75; chem. salesman Dearborn Chem. Co., Arlington Hgts., Ill., 1975-77; waste water divsn. mgr. H-O-H Chemicals, Inc., Palatine, Ill., 1977-80; pres. N. Am. Waste Systems, Inc., Rolling Meadows, Ill., 1980-84; product reliability mgr. Modular Controls, Inc., Carol Stream, Ill., 1984-89; sr. vendor quality engr., R&D project engr. Blaw-Knox Constrn. Equipment Corp., Mattoon, Ill., 1989-94, sr. vendor quality engr., 1994—. Author: (book) Hydraulics Manual, 1991; inventor: waste mgmt. system, 1981, burner controls (patent pending), hydraulic controls (patent pending), cardinogenic fume extraction unit (patent in U.S. and Europe). Recipient flying honors, USCG Aux., Glenview Naval Air Sta., 1978, valor award, USCG Aux., Glenview Naval Air Sta., 1980. Mem. Am. Std. for Testing Methods, Nat. Asphalt Paving Assn., Aircraft Owners & Pilots Assn., Exptl. Aircraft Assn., Delta Tau Alpha (pres. 1965-67). Home: 320 N 35th St Mattoon IL 61938-2147

SIMONI, MARY HOPE, university official; b. Great Blanc, Mich., Aug. 2, 1954; d. Lewis Eugene and Ann Elizabeth (Allwein) S.; m. Kevin Thomas Dowd; children: Shannon Elise, Sarah Kathryn. MusB, Mich. State U., 1977, MusM, 1981, PhD, 1983. Tchr. Saginaw (Mich.) Cath. Schs., 1977-79; asst. dir. Mich. State U., East Lansing, 1979-81; instr. Lansing (Mich.) C.C., 1981-85; assoc. prof. Berklee Coll. Music, Boston, 1985-86; supr. pub. computing U. Mich., Ann Arbor, 1986-94, dir. Ctr. for Performing Arts and Tech., 1994—, mem. adj. faculty, 1991-93; cons. Ctr. for Performing Arts, Ann Arbor, 1990-91; lectr. in field. Composer orchestral, band, synthesizers and computer-generated scores. Mich. Coun. for the Arts grantee, 1986. Mem. Internat. Computer Music Assn. (regional chair 1989-90, bd. dirs., publs. coord.), Assn. for the Mgmt. Info. Tech. in Higher Edn., Educom, Pi Kappa Lambda. Office: Univ Mich 3213 Moore Ann Arbor MI 48109-2085

SIMONS, DIANA LEE, counselor clerk specialist; b. Shenadoah, Iowa, Mar. 12, 1951; d. Lloyd and Georgia (Cozad) Braymen; m. Ronald Simons, Aug. 1975 (div. Aug. 1985); children: Gia, Michael, Matthew, Crystal, Carrie, Benjamin. Cert. bookkeeper, Metro C.C., Omaha, 1989, Cert. retailer, 1992, AAS in Merchandising Mgmt., 1992, AAS in Bus. Mgmt., 1992. Tutor Metro C. C., Omaha, 1989-95, counsel clk. specialist, 1993-95. Home: 3420 Ave B Council Bluffs IA 51501 Office: Metro Cmty Coll 29th & Ed "Babe" Gomez Ave Omaha NE

SIMONS, HELEN, school psychologist, psychotherapist; b. Chgo., Feb. 13, 1930; d. Leo and Sarah (Shrayer) Pomper; m. Broudy Simons, May 20, 1956 (May 1972); children: Larry, Sheri. BA in Biol., Lake Forest Coll., 1951; MA in Clin. Psychology, Roosevelt U., 1972; D of Psychology, Ill. Sch. Profl. Psychology, 1980. Intern Cook County Hosp., Chgo., 1979-80; pvt. practice psychotherapist Chgo., 1980—; sch. psychologist Chgo. Bd. Edn., 1974-79, 80—. Contbr. articles on psychotherapy of A.D.D. and P.T.S.D. children to profl. jours. Mem. APA, Internat. Coun. Psychologists, Nat. Sch. Psychologists Assn., Midwestern Psychol. Assn., Mental Health Assn. Ill., Ill. Psychol. Assn., Ill. Sch. Psychologists Assn., Chgo. Psychol. Assn., Internat. Coun. of Psychologists, Chgo. Sch. Psychol. Assn. Home: 6145 N Sheridan Rd Apt 29D Chicago IL 60660-2883 Office: Brennemann Sch 4251 N Clarendon Ave Chicago IL 60613-1523

SIMONS, R. KAYE, healthcare administrator; b. Marquette, Mich.; d. William and Dorothy (Maynard) S.; 1 child, Eric Thomas. BSN, Mich. State U., 1961; M in Health Care Adminstrn., Johns Hopkins U., Balt., 1981. Health sys. cons. Pub. Sector Cons., Lansing, Mich.; exec. dir. E. Cen. Mich. Health Sys. Agy., Saginaw, Mich.; dir. Dept. Health Sys. Planning, Rockville, Md.; ind. health cons. Bridgeport, Mich.; regional dir. for expanded svcs. ABC Home Health. Mem. Am. Assn. Critical Care Nurses, Am. Assn. Nurse Execs.

SIMONSEN, ROBERT ALAN, marketing executive; b. Cherokee, Iowa, Apr. 8, 1956; s. Earl Dean and Betty (Gabrielson) S.; m. Shawn Marie Beck, June 11, 1983; children: Adam David, Patrick Robert, Brian Matthew. BS in Bus. with honors, Iowa State U., 1978, BA in Econs. with honors, 1978; MBA in Mktg. with honors, U. Colo., 1982. Cost acct. Simonsen Mfg. Co., Quimby, Iowa, 1978-81, mktg. mgr., 1983-87; mgr. corp. mkt. Simonsen Mill, Simonsen Mfg., Simonsen Propane, Quimby, 1987-94; pres. Simbec, Inc., Cherokee, Iowa, 1994—; mktg. mgr. R.J. Thomas Mfg. Co., Inc., Cherokee, Iowa, 1995—. Fin. chmn. Cherokee County Rep. Party, 1992—; chmn. Quimby Centennial Com., 1983-87; precinct chmn. Cherokee County Reps., Quimby Twp., 1980, 88, Cherokee Twp., 1990—; trustee Quimby United Meth. Ch., 1983-89; bd. dirs. Cherokee Area Econ. Devel. Corp., 1993—. Recipient First Pl. award for Radio Advt. Cen. Iowans in Radio and TV, 1988, Iowa chpt. of Nat. Agr. Mktg. Assn., 1990, Addy Citation of Excellence award Advt. Profls. of Des Moines, Inc., 1989, First Pl. for Radio Series and Best Show award, Nat. Agr. Mktg. Assn., 1990, Merit award for Print Advt. Iowa chpt., 1992. Mem. Cherokee C. of C. (bd. dirs. 1995—), Iowa State U. Alumni Assn., Beta Gamma Sigma. Home: 1567 520th St Cherokee IA 51012-7228 Office: Simbec Inc 1401 N 2nd St Cherokee IA 51012-2201

SIMONSON, LLOYD GRANT, microbiologist; b. San Jose, Calif., Dec. 1, 1943; s. Rolfe Lau and Dorothy Fay (Scully) S.; m. Katherine Lenora Peck, Aug. 24, 1968. PhD, Ill. State U., 1974; MBA with honors, Roosevelt U., 1984. Prin. investigator Naval Dental Rsch. Inst., Great Lakes, Ill., 1968-88, chief scientist, 1988—; adj. prof. Dental Sch., Northwestern U., Chgo., 1990—; cons. Chgo. Med. Sch., North Chicago, 1977-80; reviewer grant applications Med. Rsch. Coun. of Can. Contbr. articles to profl. jours. Mem. Internat. Assn. Dental Rsch. (pres. microbiology-immunology group 1988-89), Am. Assn. Dental Rsch. (pres. Chgo. chpt. 1988-89, Young Investigator 1979), Am. Soc. Microbiology, Sigma Xi. Office: Naval Dental Rsch Inst Bldg 1-H Great Lakes IL 60088-5259

SIMOVIC, LASZLO, architect; b. O Becej, Yugoslavia, May 11, 1957; s. Mihaly and Eva (Daku) S.;. BArch, Ill. Inst. Tech., 1982; postgrad., Mass. Inst. Tech., 1984. Architect Marton Sass & Assoc., Chgo., 1974-82, Imre & Anthony Halasz Inc., Boston, 1984-85; architect Skidmore, Owings & Merrill, N.Y.C., 1985-86, Chgo., 1986-87; architect Loebl, Schlossman & Hackl, Chgo., 1987-89; pvt. practice Chgo., 1989—. Home: 1932A W Greenleaf Ave Chicago IL 60626-2306

SIMPKINS, JOHN ROBERT, machine designer; b. Youngstown, Ohio, Feb. 16, 1956. Grad., Ohio Peace Officers Basic Tng. Program, 1978; A in Archtl. and Mech. Design, Youngstown State U., 1979. Lic. fireworks display operator Ohio. Sr. draftsman Aetna Std., Ellwood City, Pa., 1981-85, GenDynamics, Grotton, Conn., 1984; draftsman Perrine Engring., Poland, Ohio, 1985-87; sales engr. United Engring., Youngstown, Ohio, 1987-91; machine designer Glowe-Smith Ind., Warren, Ohio, 1991—; res. dep. sherrif, Mahoning County, Ohio, 1978-85. Social chmn. Divorces Aren't Really the End, Boardman, Ohio, 1987-89. Mem. Pyro Technique Guild Internat. Republican. Methodist. Home: 200 E Philadelphia Youngstown OH 44507

SIMPSON, ART, agricultural products supplier; b. 1950. Grad., U. Ark., 1973, Purdue U., 1978. Rschr. U. Ark., Fayetteville, 1978-83; with Marked Tree (Ark.) Coop. Inc., 1983—, now mgr. Office: Marked Tree Coop Inc 110 W 2d St Marked Tree AR 72365*

SIMPSON, HOWARD MATTHEW, textbook publisher; b. Peoria, Ill., Apr. 29, 1918; s. Laurens Luther and Pearl Claudia (Howard) S.; m. Kathryn Lucia Jacquin, Nov. 25, 1948; children: John Niehaus, James Patrick (dec.), Cory Jane, Michael Howard, David Matthew, Dana Kathleen. Student U. Ill., 1937-41. Shipping clk. Manual Arts Press, Peoria, 1933-37, advt., 1945-49, salesman, 1946-53, dir., 1949-83; advt. mgr. Chas. A. Bennett Co., Inc. (formerly Manual Arts Press), 1949-53, sales mgr., 1953-64, treas., 1962-72, v.p., 1970-75, pres., 1975-83, dir., 1949-83, cons., 1983-85; organizer, dir., sec., pres. CABCO, Inc., Peoria, 1964-76. Mem. exec. bd. W.D. Boyce coun. Boy Scouts Am., Peoria, 1966-89, rep. nat. coun., 1985-89, mem. adv. coun., 1989—; mem. capital projects com., United Way Peoria, 1978-80, spl. fund raising com., 1978-80; mem. YMCA Leader Luncheon Com.; mem. chmns. coun. Crow Canyon Archeol. Ctr., Cortez, Colo., 1987—. Served to capt., cav. armor U.S. Army, 1941-46; Africa, Italy. Decorated Purple Heart, 6 battle stars; recipient Silver Beaver award Boy Scouts Am., Peoria, 1969, also Order of Arrow. Mem. Am. Legion, The Ship, Kiwanis (dir. local club 1965-68), Willow Knolls Country Club, Pi Beta Alpha, Sigma Alpha Epsilon.

SIMPSON, JACK BENJAMIN, medical technologist, business executive; b. Tompkinsville, Ky., Oct. 30, 1937; s. Benjamin Harrison and Verda Mae (Woods) S.; student Western Ky. U., 1954-57; grad. Norton Infirmary Sch. Med. Tech., 1958; m. Winona Clara Walden, Mar. 21, 1957; children: Janet Lazann, Richard Benjamin, Randall Walden, Angela Elizabeth. Asst. chief med. technologist Jackson County Hosp., Seymour, Ind., 1958-61; chief med. technologist, bus. mgr. Mershon Med. Labs., Indpls., 1962-66; founder, dir., officer Am. Monitor Corp., Indpls., 1966-77; founder, pres., dir. Global Data, Inc., Ft. Lauderdale, Fla., 1986—; mng. partner Astroland Enterprises, Indpls., 1968—, 106th St. Assocs., Indpls., 1969-72, Keystones Ltd., Indpls., 1970-82 Delray Rd. Assoc., Ltd., Indpls., 1970-71, Allisonville Assocs. Ltd., Indpls., 1970-82, Grandview Assocs. Ltd., 1977—, Rucker Assocs., Ltd., Indpls., 1974—; mng. ptnr. Raintree Assocs., Ltd., Indpls., 1978—, Westgate Assocs., Ltd., Indpls., 1978—; pres., dir. Topps Constrn. Co., Inc., Bradenton, Fla., 1973-91, Acrouest Corp., Asheville, N.C., 1980—; dir. Indpls. Broadcasting, Inc.; founder, bd. dirs. Bank of Bradenton, 1986-92. Mem. Am. Soc. Med. Technologists (cert.), Indpls. Soc. Med. Technologists, Ind. Soc. Med. Technologists, Am. Soc. Clin. Pathologists, Royal Soc. Health (London), Internat. Platform Assn., Am. Mus. Natural History. Republican. Baptist. Clubs: Columbia of Indpls.; Harbor Beach Surf, Fishing of Am., Marina Bay (Fort Lauderdale, Fla.). Lodge: Elks.

SIMPSON, VINSON RALEIGH, manufacturing company executive; b. Chgo., Aug. 9, 1928; s. Vinson Raleigh and Elsie (Passeger) S.; m. Elizabeth Caroline Matte, Sept. 9, 1950; children: Kathleen Simpson Jackson, Nancy Simpson Ignacio, James Morgan. S.B. in Chem. Engring, Mass. Inst. Tech., 1950; M.B.A., Ind. U., 1955. With Trane Co., LaCrosse, Wis., 1950-75, mgr. mktg. services, 1957-64, mgr. dealer devel., 1964-66; mng. dir. Trane Ltd., Edinburgh, Scotland, 1966; v.p. internat. Trane Co., LaCrosse, Wis., 1967, exec. v.p., 1968-70; exec. v.p., gen. mgr. comml. air conditioning div., 1970-73, pres., 1973-75; pres. Simpson and Co., La Crosse, 1975-76; pres., chief operating officer Marathon Electric Mfg. Corp., Wausau, Wis., 1976-80; chmn., pres., chief exec. officer Marion Body Works, Inc., Wis., 1980-93, chmn., 1993—; bd. dirs. Clintonville Area Found. Regional chmn. edn. coun. MIT; trustee Northland Coll.; bd. dirs., v.p. Fox Valley Tech. Coll. Found.; past pres., bd. dirs. Wausau Area Jr. Achievement; mem. Marion Minutemen, Adv. Team, U. Wis. Served with USAF, 1951-53. Decorated Korean War Commendation ribbon. Mem. Fire Apparatus Mfrs., Nat. Truck Equipment Assn., Am. Legion, Kappa Kappa Sigma, Alpha Tau Omega, Beta Gamma Sigma (mem. dirs. table). Congregationalist. Lodges: Masons, Shriners, Jesters, Rotary (past. pres. Marion club, Paul Harris fellow). Home: 171 Fairway Dr Clintonville WI 54929-1071 Office: Marion Body Works Inc 211 W Ramsdell PO Box 500 Marion WI 54950-0500

SIMS, BETTY, state legislator. Senator dist. 24 State of Mo., St. Louis, 1994—. Active United Way, Girl Scout Coun., Jr. League Girls, Inc., 1972—. Office: State Capitol Rm 425 Jefferson City MO 65101

SIMS, TERRE LYNN, insurance company executive; b. Madison, Wis., Dec. 26, 1951; d. Roy Charles and Ruth Marie (McCloskey) Pierstorff; m. Gary Peter Laufenberg, Feb. 15, 1969 (div.); children: Amie, Monte, Tawna; m. Perry Allen Sims, May 3, 1994. Sales agt. Bankers Life and Casualty, Madison, 1977-80, asst. mgr., 1981-84; br. mgr. Bankers Life and Casualty, Peoria, 1984-91; co-owner Complete Ins. Svcs., Inc., Madison, Wis., 1991—; owner, operator Ohio Tavern, Madison, 1993—. Office: Complete Ins Svcs Inc 6400 Gisholt Dr Madison WI 53713-4800

SIMS, VICTOR DWAYNE, lawyer; b. Middletown, Ohio, Aug. 1, 1959; s. Gerald Clifton and Ethel Ree (Bruce) S. Student, Am. U., 1980; BA, Heidelberg Coll., 1981; JD, Howard U., 1987. Bar: Ohio, 1989; U.S. Dist. Ct. (so. dist.) Ohio, 1990. Congl. intern U.S. Congress, Washington, 1980; fundraiser Telecommunications Rsch. and Action Ctr., Washington, 1984; assoc. Leslie I. Gaines & Assoc., Cin., 1989-91; ptnr. Sims and Assocs., Cin., 1991—; mng. atty. Leslie I. Gaines & Assoc., 1990—; ptnr. Sims and Asmah Law Firm. Author poetry. Mem. Nat. Bar Assn., ABA, Ohio Bar Assn., Cin. Bar Assn. Home: 7501 Granby Way West Chester OH 45069-2368 also: Grand Baldwin Bldg 655 Eden Park Dr Ste 100 Cincinnati OH 45202-6008

SIMS, WENDY L., music educator; b. Cleve., Jan. 4, 1956; d. Philip S. and Barbara A. (Less) S. B in Music, Music Edn., Kent (Ohio) State U., 1978, M in Music, Music Edn., 1981; PhD in Music Edn., Fla. State U., Tallahassee, 1985. Elem. music specialist Norton (Ohio) City Schs., 1978-79, Nordonia Hills City Schs., Northfield, Ohio, 1979-81; univ. fellow Fla. State U., Tallahassee, 1982-85; assoc. prof. music edn. U. Mo., Columbia, 1985—; manuscript reviewer Prentice Hall, Inc., N.Y.C., 1987—, Oxford Univ. Press, N.Y.C, 1995—; curriculum cons. Clayton (Mo.) Public Schs., 1995—; asst. cons. Kansas City (Mo.) Pub. Schs., 1996. Author, editor: (book) Music in Pre-Kindergarten, 1993, Strategies For Teaching Pre-Kindergarten Music, 1995; editor: (rsch. jour.) Missouri Journal of Research in Music Edn., 1990-92; contbr. articles to profl. jours. Treas. bd. dirs. Hillel Found. of Columbia, Mo., 1993—. Recipient Gov's. award for Teaching Excellence Gov. State of Mo., 1993, Disting. Alumnus award Kent State U. Sch. Music, 1995. Mem. Music Educator's Nat. Conf. (music edn. rsch. coun. 1976—), Mo. Music Edn. Assn. (rsch. chair 1985—), Internat. Soc. for Music Edn. (commn. chair 1982—), Phi Delta Kappa, Pi Kappa Lambda, Delta Omicron Profl. Music Fraternity (edn. chair 1975—). Office: U Mo 138 Fine Arts Ctr Columbia MO 65211

SINACORE, JANIE MARIOL, surgical nurse; b. Canton, Ohio, May 12, 1956; d. Paul Frederick Mariol and Helen Jean (Weisent) Race; children: Lauren Michelle, Julie Nicole. Diploma, Idabelle Firestone Sch Nursing, Akron, Ohio, 1978; BS, St. Joseph's Coll., North Windham, Maine, 1989; MSA, Cen. Mich. U., Columbus, Ohio, 1994. RN, Ohio; CNOR; cert. BLS instr. Surg. technician Akron City Hosp., 1975-78, staff nurse oper. rm., 1978-79, head nurse oper. rm., 1979-81; sales rep. Richards Mfg., Cleve., 1981-82; staff nurse oper. rm. Akron Gen. Med. Ctr., 1982-83, Staff Devel. Inst., 1983-90, acting head nurse orthopedics, 1984-85; dir. surg. svcs. and interim dir. pediatric ICU Children's Hosp. Med. Ctr., Akron, 1990—; mem. Telethon adv. com. Children's Hosp., Akron, 1991-92; presenter in field. Mem. Assn. Oper. Rm. Nurses (newsletter chmn. 1989-90), Am. Orgn. Nurse Execs., Ohio Orgn. Nurse Execs., Am. Coll. Health Care Execs. Home: 4016 Highpoint Dr Uniontown OH 44685-7950 Office: Children's Hosp Med Ctr One Perkins Sq Akron OH 44302-1813

SINCOFF, MICHAEL Z., human resources and marketing professional; b. Washington, D.C., June 28, 1943; s. Murray P. and Anna F. (Jaffe) S. m. Kathleen M. Dunham, Oct. 9, 1983. BA, U. Md., 1964, MA, 1966; PhD, Purdue U., 1969. Instr. U. Tenn., Knoxville, 1968; asst. prof. Ohio U., Athens, 1969-74, dir. Ctr. for Comm. Studies, 1969-76, assoc. prof., 1974-76; vis. prof. U. Minn., St. Paul, 1974; dir. personnel devel. Celanese Corp., N.Y., 1976-79; dir. employee comm. Hoechst-Celanese formerly The Mead Corp., Dayton, Ohio, 1979-81; dir. edn., tng. The Mead Corp., Dayton, Ohio, 1981-83; assoc. dean Sch. of Bus. Adminstrn. Georgetown U., Washington, 1983-84; v.p. human resources ADVO-System, Inc. now ADVO, Inc., Hartford, 1984-87; v.p. human resources, corp. officer DIMAC Direct Inc., St. Louis, 1987-88; sr. v.p. human resources and adminstrn., sr. corp. officer DIMAC Corp. (parent of DIMAC Direct Inc.), St. Louis, 1988—; also sec., asst. treas. DIMAC Corp. (parent of DIMAC Direct, Inc.), St. Louis, 1988—. Author, editor human resources sect. Am. Mgmt. Assn. Mgmt. Handbook, 3d edit., 1994; author approximately 50 books and articles; mem. edtl. adv. bd. Jour. Applied Comm. Rsch., 1991—. Life mem. Internat. Comm. Assn. (bus. mgr.-exec. sec. 1969-73, fin. com. 1982-85); mem. Am. Mgmt. Assn. (human resources coun. 1990—), Direct Mktg. Assn., Printing Industries of Am. (employer resources group 1989—).

SINES, RAYMOND E., state legislator; m. Suanne Sines; children: Stephanie, Amanda, Victoria. Student, Lakeland Coll., Aldenson-Broadus Coll. State rep. Ohio Dist. 61, Ohio Dist. 69, 1993; owner SInes & Sons, Inc. Mem. Am Legion, United Way, C. of C., Farm Bureau, Ahtletic Assocs., Humane Soc. (bd. mem.). Home: 4287 Harper St Perry OH 44081*

SINGER, MARCUS GEORGE, philosopher, educator; b. N.Y.C., Jan. 4, 1926; s. David Emanuel and Esther (Kobre) S.; m. Blanche Ladenson, Aug. 10, 1947; children: Karen Beth, Debra Ann. A.B., U. Ill., 1948; Ph.D. (Susan Linn Sage fellow), Cornell U., 1952. Asst. in philosophy Cornell U., Ithaca, N.Y., 1948-49; instr. philosophy Cornell U., 1951-52; instr. philosophy U. Wis.-Madison, 1952-55, asst. prof., 1955-59, assoc. prof., 1959-63, prof. philosophy, 1963-92, prof. emeritus, 1992—, chmn. dept. philosophy, 1963-68; chmn. philosophy dept. U. Wis. Center System, 1964-66; dir. pub. lectr. series Royal Inst. Philosophy, London, 1984-85; vis. fellow Birkbeck Coll., U. London, 1962-63; research assoc. U. Calif.-Berkeley, 1969; vis. Cowling prof. philosophy Carleton Coll., Northfield, Minn., 1972; vis. prof. humanities U. Fla., Gainesville, 1975; vis. fellow U. Warwick, 1977, 84-85; vis. Francis M. Bernardin disting. prof. humanities U. Mo., Kansas City, 1979; hon. research fellow Birkbeck Coll., U. London, 1984-85; acad. visitor London Sch. Econs., U. London, 1984-85. Author: Generalization in Ethics, 2d edit., 1971, Verallgemeinerung in der Ethik, 1975; editor: Morals and Values, 1977, American Philosophy, 1986, Reason, Reality, and Speculative Philosophy, 1996; contbr. Essays in Moral Philosophy, 1958, Ency. of Philosophy, 1967, Law and Philosophy, 1970, Skepticism and Moral Principles, 1973, Morals and Values, 1977, Acad. Am. Ency., 1982, 84, 89, World Book Ency., 1984, 86, Gewirth's Ethical Rationalism, 1984, Morality and Universality, 1985, American Philosophy, 1986, New Directions in Ethics, 1986, The Handbook of Western Philosophy, 1988, Applying Philosophy, 1988, Moral Philosophy: Historical and Contemporary Essays, 1989, Key Themes in Philosophy, 1990, Essays on Henry Sidgwick, 1992, Ency. of Ethics, 1992, A History of Western Ethics, 1992, Ethics, 1993, Cambridge Dictionary of Philosophy, 1995, Biographical Dictionary of Twentieth Century Philosophers, 1996; co-editor: Introductory Readings in Philosophy, 2d edit., 1974, Reason and the Common Good, 1963, Belief, Knowledge and Truth, 1970, Legislative Intent and other Essays on Law, Politics and Morality, 1993. Served with USAAF, 1944-45. Am. Philos. Assn. Western Div. fellow, 1956-57; Summer Research grant Social Sci. Research Council, 1958; Guggenheim fellow, 1962-63; Inst. for Research in Humanities fellow U. Wis., 1984. Mem. Am. Philos. Assn. (v.p. Western divsn. 1984-85, pres. Ctrl. divsn. 1985-86, bd. officers 1991-94), Royal Inst. Philosophy, AAUP, Aristotelian Soc., Mind Assn., Wis. Acad. Scis., Arts and Letters, Sidgwick Soc. (exec. dir.), Phi Beta Kappa, Phi Kappa Phi. Home: 5021 Regent St Madison WI 53705-4745

SINGER, NORMAN MARVIN, international education consultant; b. Boston, Mar. 21, 1940; s. Meyer and Libby (Seltzer) S.; m. Barbara Horwitz, Aug. 20, 1957; children: Debra, Todd. BA, U. Miami, 1962, MEd, 1968; EdD, U. Tenn., 1972. Tchr. English Dade County Pub. Schs., Miami, 1961-64, studio tchr. humanities, 1963-67; grad. fellow U. Tenn., Knoxville, 1968-72; sr. R & D specialist Ohio State U., Columbus, 1972-86; sr. assoc. Powell (Ohio) Internat., 1989—; ind. cons. Columbus, 1972—; cons. Turkish Ministry Edn., N.Y. Inst. Work, Trade and Tech., Ankara, Turkey, 1990-91; statewide curriculum specialist Ohio Bd. Regents, Columbus, 1992—. Author: Explore Your Future: Careers in the Natural Gas Industry, 1988; contbr. 53 articles and monographs to profl. pubs. Exec. dir. Columbus Pub. Schs. Fund of the Columbus Found., 1987-88. Recipient fellowship U.S. Office Edn., 1968, Doctoral fellowship in Curriculum Instrn., Nat. Def. Edn. Act, 1968, Disting. Svc. award, 1984. Mem. Worthington Community Theatre, Internat. Vocat. Edn. Tech. Assn., Kappa Delta Pi. Home: 2323 Haviland Rd Upper Arlington OH 43220-4625 Office: 30 E Broad St 36th Fl Columbus OH 43266

SINGER, NORMAN SOL, food products executive, inventor; b. Phila., Dec. 10, 1937; s. Herman and Thelma (Scheinberg) S.; m. Anne Goldstein, Aug. 23, 1959; children: Amy Debra, Judith Ellen. BS, Rutgers U., 1961. Sr. lab. technician Bur. Biological Rsch., New Brunswick, N.J., 1960-61; food scientist Thomas J. Lipton, Inc., Englewood Cliffs, N.J., 1961-68; rsch. dir. McCain Foods, Florenceville, Can., 1968-70; sr. scientist John Labatt Ltd., London, Ontario, Can., 1970-84; fellow/dir. exploration The NutraSweet Co., Deerfield, Ill., 1984-94; pres. Ideas Workshop Cons., Inc., Highland Park, Ill., 1994—; co-founder, CEO Sous Chef Culinary Supply, Inc., Highland Park, Ill., 1994—. Patentee in field. Recipient Outstanding Am. Inventor award Intellectual Property Owners Found., Washington, 1989. Mem. Inst. Food Technology, Product Devel. and Mgmt. Assn., Chgo. Horticultural Soc., Sigma Xi. Home: 40 Ridge Rd Highland Park IL 60035-4337 Office: Sous Chef Culinary Supply Highland Park IL 60035

SINGER, SANDRA MANES, university administrator; b. Washington, Jan. 24, 1942; d. Joseph Gabriel and Rebekah Mary (Miller) Manes; m. Malcolm Singer; children: Cathryn, Scott; m. Allan Robert Kuse, July 5, 1978. BA, U. Colo., 1969, MA, 1972, PhD, 1975. Instr. dept. psychology U. Colo., Boulder, 1975-77, mem. rsch. faculty Inst. for Behavioral Genetics, 1978-80; postdoctoral fellow in psychiat. genetics U. Iowa, Iowa City, 1977-78; prof. psychology U. So. Ind., Evansville, 1980-92, chair dept. psychology, 1985-86, dir. grad. studies, 1986-92, asst. v.p. acad. affairs, 1987-92; vice chancellor for acad. affairs Purdue U., Hammond, Ind., 1992—; mem. adv. bd. Ind. Resource Ctr. for Autism, Bloomington, 1987-93; cons. to youth leadership programs Nat. Crime Prevention Coun., Washington, 1987-93. Author: Heredity of Behavior Disorders in Adults and Children, 1986; reviewer Teaching of Psychology, 1986—; contbr. articles to profl. jours. Bd. dirs., mem. exec. com. Greater Evansville Cmty. Found., 1991-93; bd. dirs. St. Anthony's Med. Ctr., Crown Point, Ind., 1995—, Calumet coun. Girl Scouts U.S., 1993—, Ind. Humanities Coun., 1993—, Lake Area United Way, Lake County, 1994—. NIMH postdoctoral fellow, 1977-78. Mem. Am. Psychol. Soc., Behavior Genetics Assn., Ind. Assn. for Instnl. Rsch. (sec. 1987-89), Southwestern Ind. Psychol. Assn. (pres. 1986-87), Leadership Evansville (v.p. 1987-88), Kiwanis, Sigma Xi. Office: Purdue Univ-Calumet 308 Lawshe Hall Hammond IN 46323

SINGERMAN, DONA FATIBENO, reading specialist; b. Cleve., July 6, 1939; d. Pasquale and Mary (Del Priore) Fatibeno; children: Camille Swartz, David E. BA, Lake Erie Coll., 1967; MEd, Cleve. State U., 1977; cert. in supervision, John Carroll U., 1985; student, Cambridge (Eng.) U., 1990-91. Cert. tchr. and supr., Ohio. Tchr. Painesville-Mentor Schs., Ohio; tchr. Mentor (Ohio) Schs., tchr. chpt. I reading, 1986—; mem. Gephart Symposium, U. Colo., summer 1992; chmn. Internat. Literacy, OCIRA, 1995. Vol. Lake County Hist. Soc.; sec. Friends of Mentor Pub. Libr., 1990-91. Joseph Nemeth scholar (OCIRA), 1995. Mem. AAUW (legis. chair Mentor br. 1990-91, treas. 1991-93), Coun. Exceptional Children, Internat. Reading Assn. (v.p. Lake-Geauga unit 1990-91, 91-92, pres. 1992-93), Phi Delta Kappa (program v.p. N.E. Ohio unit 1990-91, pres. 1991-92, Gerald Read Internat. scholar 1992).

SINGH, MANMOHAN, orthopedic surgeon, educator; b. Patiala, Punjab, India, Oct. 5, 1940; came to U.S., 1969; s. Ajmer and Kartar (Kaur) S.; m. Manjit Anand, Jan. 1, 1974; children: Kirpal, Gurmeet. MB, BS, Govt. Med. Coll., Patiala, 1964; MSurgery, Panjab U., Chandigarh, India, 1968. Diplomate Am. Bd. Orthopaedic Surgery. Rsch. fellow Inst. Internat. Edn., Chgo., 1969-74; resident in orthopedic surgery Michael Reese Hosp. and Med. Ctr., Chgo., 1974-78, mem. attending staff, dir. orthopedic rsch., 1979-94; fellow in orthopedic oncology Mayo Clinic and Mayo Found., Rochester, Minn., 1979-80; assoc. prof. U. Ill., Chgo., 1996—; pvt. practice, Chgo.; mem. vis. faculty Mayo Grad. Sch., Rochester, 1969. Developer x-ray method (Singh Index) and bone density method (Radius Index) for diagnosis of osteoporosis. Fulbright travel grantee, 1968. Fellow Am. Acad. Orthop. Surgeons, Am. Orthop. Foot and Ankle Soc.; mem. Orthop. Rsch. Soc., Am. Soc. for Bone and Mineral Rsch., Internat. Bone and Mineral Soc. Democrat. Sikh. Office: 443 E 31st St Chicago IL 60616-4051

SINGHAM, MANO, physicist; b. Colombo, Sri Lanka, July 22, 1950; s. Leonard P. and Gneneswari (Somasunderam) S.; m. Shermila Brito, Dec. 22, 1977; children: Devaushi, Ashali. BSc, U. Colombo, 1973; MS, U. Pitts., 1976, PhD, 1980. Lectr. U. Colombo, 1980-83; vis. scientist U. Pitts., 1983; vis. asst. prof. Drexel U., Phila., 1984; postdoctoral staff mem. Los Alamos (N.Mex.) Nat. Lab., 1984-86; sr. rsch. assoc. U. Rochester, N.Y., 1986-88; rschr. in physics Case Western Res. U., Cleve., 1989—; scientist-educator Project Discovery, 1992—. Contbr. articles to Annals of Physics, Jour. Chem. Phys. and Phys. Rev. Letters, Phi Beta Kappa. Mem. Am. Phys. Soc. (com. on internat. sci. affairs 1986-89, internat. freedom of scientists com. 1990-92), Am. Assn. Physics Tchrs. Home: 3681 Townley Rd Shaker Heights OH 44122-5119 Office: Case Western Res U Dept Physics Cleveland OH 44106

SINGHVI, SURENDRA SINGH, finance and strategy consultant; b. Jodhpur, Rajasthan, India, Jan. 16, 1942; came to U.S., 1962, naturalized 1986; s. Rang Raj and Ugam Kanwar (Surana) S.; m. Sushila Bhandari, July 7, 1965; children: Seema, Sandeep. B in Commerce, Rajasthan U., 1961; MBA, Atlanta U., 1963; PhD, Columbia U., 1967. CPA, Cert. Mgmt. Acct. Asst. prof. fin. Miami U., Oxford, Ohio, 1967-69, assoc. prof., 1969-70; adj. prof. fin., 1970-95; fin. mgr. ARMCO Inc., Middletown, Ohio, 1970-79, asst. treas., 1979-83, gen. fin. mgr., 1983-86; v.p. and treas. Edison Bros. Stores, Inc., St. Louis, 1986-90; pres. Singhvi & Assocs., Inc., Dayton, Ohio, 1990—; bd. dirs. Columbia Indsl. Sales Corp., Hauer Music Co., Oasis Property Inc. Author: Planning for Capital Investment, 1980; co-editor: Frontiers of Financial Management, 4th edit., 1984, Global Finance 2000-A Handbook of Strategy and Organization (The Conference Board), 1996; contbr. over 90 articles to profl. jours. Recipient Chancellor's Gold medal Rajasthan U. Mem. Planning Forum, Inst. Mgmt. Accts. (Bayer Silver medal 1978), Fin. Execs. Inst., Rotary (dir. internat. program Middletown chpt. 1973-86, Dayton chpt. 1995—), India Club (pres. Dayton chpt. 1980). Home: 439 Ridge Line Ct Dayton OH 45458 Office: Singhvi and Assocs Inc 515 Windsor Park Dayton OH 45459

SINGLETON, DONNA MARIE, travel agency executive; b. Dowagiac, Mich., Sept. 14, 1960; d. Lester Allen and Betty Lorella (Fryman) Stover; m. Mark Steven Singleton, Sept. 1, 1979; children: Christina Marie, Christopher Michael. BA, Assoc. Travel Sch., Miami, 1979. Cert. travel cons. Travel cons. Signal Travel & Tours, Inc., Niles, Mich., 1979-80; mgr. Signal Travel & Tours, Inc., Niles, 1980-94, Dowagiac, Mich., 1985—; key coord. Am. Airlines, Signal Travel, Niles, 1988—; coord. Cert. Travel Cons., Niles, 1989—; sabre master local leval Am. Airlines, 1983-86. Vol. United Way, Dowagiac, 1988; sec. bd. Christian edn. Federated Ch., 1988-90, moderator, 1995-96; bd. dirs. Dowagiac Rocket Football, 1995-96. Mem. Dowagiac C. of C. (bd. dirs. 1987-90). Bus. and Profl. Women (chmn. young careerists 1988-91). Office: Signal Travel & Tours Inc 146 S Front St Dowagiac MI 49047-1737

SINGLETON, MARVIN AYERS, otolaryngologist, senator; b. Baytown, Tex., Oct. 7, 1939; s. Henry Marvin and Mary Ruth (Mitchell) S.; B.A., U. of the South, 1962; M.D., U. Tenn., 1966. Intern, City of Memphis Hosps., 1966-67; resident in surgery Highland Alameda City Hosp., Oakland, Calif., 1967-68, resident in otolaryngology U. Tenn. Hosp., Memphis, 1968-71; Am. Acad. Otolaryngology and Ophthalmology fellow in otolaryngic pathology Armed Forces Inst. Pathology, Washington, 1971; fellow in otologic surgery U. Colo. at Gallup (N.Mex.) Indian Med. Center, 1972; practice medicine specializing in otolaryngology and allergies, Joplin, Mo., 1972—; founder, operator Home and Farm Investments, Joplin, 1975—, staff mem. Freeman Hosp., St. John's Hosp., Joplin, Oakhill Hosp.; cons. in otolaryngology Parsons (Kans.) State Hosp. and Tng. Center, Mo. Crippled Children's Service, Santa Fe R.R.; pres. Ozark Mfg. Co., Inc., Joplin. Mem. Internat. Arabian Racing Bd., 1983-88; mem. Mo. State Senate, 1990—, chmn. Senate Rep. Caucus; del. Rep. Nat. Conv., 1988, 92. Served with USNG, 1966-72. Diplomate Am. Bd. Otolaryngology. Fellow A.C.S., Am. Acad. Otolaryngologic Allergy (past pres.), Am. Assn. Clin. Immunology and Allergy; mem. AMA (Mo. del.), Mo. State, So., Jasper County med. assns., Council of Otolaryngology, Mo. State Allergy Assn., Ear, Nose and Throat Soc. Mo. (past pres.), Joplin C. of C., Masons (32 degree), Sigma Alpha Epsilon, Phi Theta Kappa, Phi Chi. Methodist. Club: Elks. Contbr. articles to profl. jours. Home: 4476 Five Mile Rd Seneca MO 64856 Office: 114 W 32nd St Joplin MO 64804-3651

SINHA, RANENDRA NATH, ecologist, stress management consultant; b. Calcutta, India, Jan. 25, 1930; came to U.S. 1952; s. Sachindra Nath and Indu Bala (Majumder) S.; m. Helen Luella Sinha, June 23, 1963; children: Mala Marie, Jay Christopher. BSc with honors, Calcutta U., 1950; PhD, U. Kans., 1956. Instr. biology St. Xavier Coll., Calcutta, 1951-52; rsch assoc. zoology McGill U., Montreal, 1956-57; hon. lectr. entomology Kyoto (Japan) U., 1966-67; rsch. officer Rsch. Sta., Can. Dept. Agr., Winnipeg, Man., 1956-67, sr. rsch. scientist, 1967-76; prin. rsch. scientist Rsch. Sta., Can. Dept. Agr., Winnipeg, 1976-93; pres. Ranen Sinha Stress Mgmt. Cons., Winnipeg, 1993—; hon. prof., faculty grad. studies U. Man., Winnipeg, 1961—. Author: Yoga: Two Concepts and Four Choices, 1975; co-author: Insect Pests of Flour Mills, Grain Elevators and Feed Mills, and Their Control, 1985; mem. editl. bd. Jour. Stored Products Rsch., 1976-94, Scis. des Alimentes, Paris, 1975—; contbr. over 220 articles to profl. jours. Recipient Gold Medal award, Entomol. Soc. Can., 1985. Mem. Entomol. Soc. Am., Ecol. Soc. Am., Soc. Population Ecology, Sigma Xi (Sr. Scientist award 1991). Hinduism. Home and Office: 582 Queenston St, Winnipeg, MB Canada R3N 0X3

SINICROPI, STEPHEN ANTHONY, radio station executive; b. Olean, N.Y., June 9, 1957; s. Anthony Vincent and Margaret Frances (Michienzi) S.; m. Laura Marie Schwaigert, Jan. 8, 1983. BBA in Indsl. Relations, U. Iowa, 1983. Account exec. Sta. KKRQ-FM, Iowa City, Iowa, 1982-83, sales mgr. Cedar Rapids, 1983-84, gen. sales mgr., 1984-86; gen. mgr. Stas. KKRQ-FM and KXIC-AM, Iowa City, 1987; v.p., gen. mgr. Sta. WLUM-AM-FM, Milw., 1987—. Republican. Roman Catholic. Home: 1601 E Blackthorne Pl Milwaukee WI 53211-1139 Office: Sta KKRQ-KXIC Interstate 80 N Iowa City IA 52240 Office: Sta WLUM-FM 2500 N Mayfair Rd Milwaukee WI 53226-1409*

SINKS, JOHN R., JR., state legislator; b. Ft. Wayne, Ind., Dec. 3, 1929; m. Mary Louise Sinks; 1 child, John Robert III. Student, Wabash Coll.; BS, Ind. U.; MS, Ball State U. Guidance counselor Elmhurst H.S., Ft. Wayne; mem. Ind. State Ho. of Reps., 1964-76; mem. Ind. State Senate, 1976—, chmn. edn. com. mem. legis. appts. and elections com., mem. fin. com., rules and legis. procedures com. Mem. NEA, Ind. State Tchrs. Assn., Masons, Shriners. Office: 4965 W Woodland Dr Bloomington IN 47404-8935 also: 6414 E Canal Pointe Ln Fort Wayne IN 46804-4700 also: State Senate State Capitol Indianapolis IN 46204*

SINN, JAMES MICHEAL, manufacturing executive; b. Wichita, Kans., Oct. 1, 1950; s. James Howard Sinn and Mary Anne (Harris) Hahner; m. Alice Marie Moss, Feb. 28, 1970; 1 child, Kelly Marie. AA in Psychology, Columbia Coll., 1976, BA in Psychology, Bus. Adminstrn., 1979. Project engr. Instrument and Flight Rsch., Wichita, 1973-75; mech. designer, draftsman Kice Metal Products, Wichita, 1976-79; mfg. engr. Cessna Aircraft, Wichita, 1979-80; mgr. hardware, ops. Boeing Mil. Aircraft, Wichita, 1980-82, engr., 1982-91; indsl. engr. Learjet, Inc., Wichita, 1984—, mgr. procurement, 1991—. Contbr. articles to profl. jours. Acct. exec. United Way, 1989—, allocation commn. With USMC, 1967-69, Vietnam. Mem. Soc. Mfg. Engrs., Soc. Automotive Engrs. Internat., Acad. of Model Aeros. (contest dir. 1978—), Nat. Assn. Purchasing Mgmt. Home: 9831 Harvest Ln Wichita KS 67212-4220 Office: Learjet Corp PO Box 7707 Wichita KS 67277-7707

SINNER, GEORGE ALBERT, former state governor, farmer, corporate executive; b. Fargo, N.D., May 29, 1928; s. Albert and Katherine (Wild) S.; m. Elizabeth Jane Baute, Aug. 10, 1951; children: Robert, George, Elizabeth, Martha, Paula, Mary Jo, Jim, Jerry, Joe, Eric. BA in Philosophy, St. Johns U., St. Cloud, Minn., 1950. Farmer Sinner Bros. and Bresnahan, Casselton, N.D., 1952-93; mem. N.D. Senate, 1962-66; mem. N.D. Ho. of Reps., 1982-84, chmn. fin. and tax com., 1983; gov. State of N.D., Bismarck, 1985-93; v.p. pub. & govt. affairs Am. Crystal Sugar Co., Moorhead, Minn., 1990—; U.S. del. Inter-Am. Food and Agr. Conf., 1966; founder, chmn. N.D. Crops Coun., Fargo, 1978-83; chmn. No. Crops Inst. Coun., Fargo, 1980-83; mem. Interstate Oil Compact Commn., 1986-88; chmn. Am. Energy Assurance Coun., 1987-89; presdl. appointee to Adv. Commn. on Govtl. Rels., 1989-92. Candidate for U.S. Congress, 1964; chmn., bd. dirs. S.E. Region Mental Health and Retardation Clinic, Fargo, 1964-66; mem. N.D. Bd. Higher Edn., Bismarck, 1966-75, chmn., 1970, Broadcasting Coun., 1968-73; co-founder bd. dirs. Tri-Coll. Univ. Bd., Fargo, N.D., and Moorhead, Minn., 1970-84; del. N.D. Constl. Conv., Bismarck, 1972; mem. Casselton Planning and Zoning Commn., 1982-85. With N.D. N.G., 1950-51. Recipient Rotary Diversified Farming award, 1960, Outstanding Farming award N.D. State U., 1964, L.B. Hartz Profl. Achievement award Moorhead (Minn.) State U., 1980, EPA Nat. Wetlands award, 1992, Nat. Ducks Unltd. Wetlands Conservation award, 1992; named Nat. Water Statesman of Yr., 1992, Doctor of Law, St. John's U., 1992, Doctor of Humanities, N.D. State U., 1993. Mem. Nat. Gov.'s Assn. (chmn. com. agr. 1987-89, chmn. com. energy and environment, lead gov. out-of-state sales tax collection), Western Govs. Assn.

(chmn. 1989-90, lead gov., mem. water pollution com. 1985-93, chmn. 1989-90), N.D. Cattle Feeders' Assn. (farm prodn.), Red River Valley Sugarbeet Growers Assn. (pres. bd. dirs. 1975-79), Greater N.D. Assn. (bd. dirs. 1981), N.D. Farm Bur. (farm prodn.), N.D. Wheat Producers (farm prodn.), N.D. Crop Improvement Assn. (farm prodn.), N.D. Stockmen's Assn. (farm prodn.), Am. Soybean Assn. (farm prodn.), N.D. Barley Coun. (farm prodn.), N.D. Farmers Union (farm prodn.), Am. Legion. Office: 101 3rd St N Moorhead MN 56560-1952

SIPE, ROGER WAYNE, accountant, consultant; b. Ft. Wayne, Ind., Dec. 5, 1950; s. Robert Wayne and Esther Lenore (Allen) S.; m. Gwen Sue Mays, June 2, 1973; children: Andrew, Allison, Aaron. BS, Manchester (Ind.) Coll., 1973. CPA, Ind. Staff acct. Koeneman, Krouse, Dinius, Erb, Conrad & Kauffman, Ft. Wayne, Ind., 1973-80; audit mgr. Baden, Conrad, Gage & Schroeder, Ft. Wayne, 1980-87; prin. Roger W. Sipe, CPA, Ft. Wayne, Ind., 1987-91; mng. ptnr. Sipe CPA Firm, Ft. Wayne, 1992—; instr. Advanced Tng. Seminars, Inc.; cons. small bus. seminars for entrapreneurs; cons. and seminar instr. in field. Contbr. articles to profl. jours. and newspapers. Bd. dirs. Christian Bus. Men's Com., Ft. Wayne, 1982-84, mem. Time Corner, 1984-90; bd. dirs. Park Ctr., Inc., chmn. svcs. com., 1986-87, mem. exec. com., 1986-92, treas., 1987-92; mem. adv. com. Daybreak Children's Home, 1985-93; bd. dirs. Daybreak Childrens Found., Inc., 1994—, Portage Creek coun. Boy Scouts Am., 1984-86, asst. scoutmaster, cubmaster, 1994—. Mem. AICPA (pvt. co. practice sect.), Ind. Soc. CPAs (com. chmn. 1980-84, mgmt. adv. svcs. com. 1984-87, bd. dirs. 1985-89, pres. 1987-88), Ft. Wayne Estate Planning Coun., Masons, Shriners. Republican. Home: 14431 Winters Rd Roanoke IN 46783-9644 Office: 4646 W Jefferson Blvd Ste 140 Fort Wayne IN 46804-6832

SIPES, THEODORE LEE, educator; b. Galion, Ohio, Apr. 24, 1944; s. Clarence Lloyd and Miriam Juanita (Ness) S.; m. Josephine Marie Bunde, Feb. 11, 1967; 1 child, Lisa Lynn. BS in Edn., Bowling Green (Ohio) State U., 1967, MEd, 1970; EdD, Wayne State U., 1975. Indsl. arts tchr. Otsego local schs., Tontogany, Ohio, 1965-66, 1968-69; spl. edn. tchr. Otsego local schs., Tontogany, 1969-70; indsl. arts tchr. Springfield local schs., Holland, Ohio, 1967-68, N. Dearborn Heights (Mich.) Schs., 1970-74; instr. Fla. Internat. U., Miami, 1974-75; asst. prof. Bowling Green State U., 1975-79; Options IV job tng. coord. Findlay (Ohio) City Schs., 1979—. Editor, narrator audio-visual prodn. Onan Engine Tng. Program, 1979-80. Pres. Wood Lane Industries Sheltered Workshop, Bowling Green, 1979-80, 86-87, trustee, 1975-92, Wood County ARC, 1992—, bd. dirs., 1985-89; mem. bd. Wood County bd. Mental Retardation and Developmental Disabilities, 1993—. Mem. Am. Vocat. Assn. (life), Ohio Vocat. Assn. (life, trade and indsl. divsn., treas. 1995—, Pacesetter award 1992, 94, 95, 96), Gideons Internat., Phi Lambda Theta, Iota Lambda Sigma. Republican. Methodist. Home: 818 W Wooster St Bowling Green OH 43402-2601 Office: Millstream South 1100 Broad Ave Findlay OH 45840-2651

SIPLEY, NANCY E. YOUNG, career development trainer, writer, consultant; b. Austin, Minn., May 29, 1929; d. Frederick Lloyd and Pruda Armington (Moulton) Y.; 1 child, John F. Student, The King's Coll., 1946-47, Bryant Coll., 1947-48; BA, Bethel Coll., 1990. Exec. sec. Indsl. Trust Co., Providence, 1948-50, Geo. A. Hormel & Co., Austin, 1954-72; adminstrv. asst. N.W. Dist. Christian and Missionary Alliance, St. Paul, 1972-82; self-employed counselor St. Paul, 1982-84; adminstrv. asst. The St. Paul Cos., 1984-87; adminstrv. asst. vol. Campus Crusade, Limassol, Cyprus, 1987-88; Cyprus Am. Archeol. Rsch. Inst. Cyprus Am. Archeological Rsch. Inst., Nicosia, 1987-88; info. specialist US West 9-1-1, Mpls., 1989-91; sr. trainer HIRED, Mpls., 1991—; testing adminstr. for physically and mentally disadvantaged Mower County Social Svcs., Austin, 1946; counselor for low-income Salvation Army, Austin, 1955-72; fin. mgmt. cons. Minn. Extension Hennepin County, 1991—; cons., speaker, tchr. Prison Fellowship, Mpls., 1991—; mem. com. Mpls. Jobs and Tng. Demand Occupations; cons. in field. Author: (curricula) Children's Youth Groups, 1960-87, Job Retention, Interviewing, Resume Writing, Time Management, Money Management, 1991, Career Exploration, 1992, Youth Employability, 1995. Residential chair United Way; active Salvation Army, 1955-87. Mem. AAUW, Cyprus Am. Archeol. Rsch. Inst., Minn. Hist. Soc., Minn. Assn. Counseling and Devel., Minn. Landscape Arboretum Found., Greater St. Paul Assn. Evangs. (bd. mem., exec. com. 1991-92), Death Valley Natural Hist. Assn. Baptist. Home: 6273 W Broadway Ave Brooklyn Park MN 55428-2821

SIPPEL, WILLIAM LEROY, lawyer; b. Fond du Lac, Wis., Aug. 14, 1948; s. Alfonse Aloysious and Virginia Laura (Weber) S.; m. Barbara Jean Brost, Aug. 23, 1970; children: Katharine Jean, David William. BA, U. Wis., JD. Bar: Wis. 1974, U.S. Dist. Ct. (we. dist.) Wis. 1974, Minn. 1981, U.S. Dist. Ct. Minn. 1981, U.S. Ct. Appeals (10th cir.) 1984, U.S. Ct. Appeals (8th cir.) 1985. Research assoc. dept. agrl. econs. U. Wis., Madison, 1974-75; counsel monopolies and comml. law subcom. Ho. Judiciary Com., Washington, 1975-80; spl. asst. to asst. gen. antitrust div. U.S. Dept. of Justice, Washington, 1980-81; from assoc. to ptnr. Doherty, Rumble & Butler, Mpls. and St. Paul, Minn., 1981—. Co-author: The Antitrust Health Care Handbook, 1988. Mem. program com. Minn. World Trade Assn., Mpls., St. Paul, 1985-86, bd. dirs., 1986, Minn. With USAR, 1971-77. Mem. ABA (vice chmn. ins. industry com. 1990-91), Minn. Bar Assn. (co-chmn. antitrust sect. 1986-88, internat. law sect. coun. 1986-89, treas. 1989-90, sec. 1990-91, vice chmn. 1995-96, chmn. 1996-97), Minn. Med. Alley Assn. (co-chmn. internat. bus. com. 1990-95, Hennepin County Office Internat. Trade (bd. dirs. 1988-93), Phi Beta Kappa. Roman Catholic. Home: 1448 Pinewood Dr Saint Paul MN 55125-2063 Office: Doherty Rumble & Butler PA 2800 Minnesota World Trade Ctr Saint Paul MN 55101

SIPPO, ARTHUR CARMINE, occupational medicine physician; b. Jan. 30, 1953; s. Carmine Constantine and Mildred Angela (Musto) S.; m. Katherine Velma Sager, Jan. 87, 1987; children: Sean, Tiffany, Courtney. BS in Chemistry magna cum laude, St. Peter's Coll., Jersey City, 1974; MD, Vanderbilt U., 1978; MPH, Johns Hopkins U., 1983. Diplomate Am. Bd. Preventive Medicine. Commd. 2d lt. U.S. Army, 1978, advanced through grades to lt. col., 1992; intern in ob-gyn. Walter Reed Army Med. Ctr., 1978-79; 1st brigade surgeon 101st Airborne Div., Ft. Campbell, Ky., 1979-81; resident in aerospace medicine USAF Sch. Aerospace Medicine, Brooks AFB, Tex., 1981-83; dir. biodynamics rsch. div. U.S. Army Aeromed. Rsch. Lab., Ft. Rucker, Ala., 1983-86; exch. officer RAF Inst. Aviation Medicine, Farnborough, Hants., Eng., 1986-90; ret., 1990; occupational medicine physicians Occupational Care Cons., Holland, Ohio, 1990-92; comdr. 145th M.A.S.H., Camp Perry, Ohio, 1992-94; dep. comdr. for clin. svcs. 112th Med. Brigade Ohio Army Nat. Guard, Columbus, 1994-95; asst. state surgeon Ohio Army N.G., Columbus, 1995—; med. dir. Libbey Glass, Inc., Toledo, 1990—, Clyde (Ohio) divsn. Whirlpool Corp., 1990—; mem. aerospace cons. adv. panel U.S. Army Surgeon Gen.'s Office. Author: Arthropometic Considerations of the U.S. Army, 1988. Mem. Ohio N.G., 1990—. Master Am. Coll. Occup. and Environ. Medicine; fellow Am. Coll. Preventive Medicine, Aerospace Med. Assn.; mem. Soc. U.S. Army Flight Surgeons, Am. Coll. Emergency Physicians, Fellowship Cath. Scholars. Roman Catholic. Office: Occupational Care Cons 6855 Spring Valley Dr Ste 160 Holland OH 43528-9374

SIROTKO, THEODORE FRANCIS, priest, retired military officer; b. Muskegon, Mich., Oct. 5, 1936; s. Theodore Felix and Dorothy Mary (Bray) S.; m. Phyllis Anne Bourziel, May 5, 1962; children: Mary Anne, Kathleen, Stephen, Michael. BS, Ferris State U., 1958, MDiv, Nashotah House Theol. Sem., 1965; D in Ministry, San Francisco Theol. Sem., 1982; MSA, U. Notre Dame, 1982. Ordained to ministry Episcopal Ch., 1965. Vicar St. Matthew Ch., Sparta, Mich., 1965-68; rector St. Mark Parish, Howe, Ind., 1968-70; sr. chaplain Howe Mil. Sch., 1968-70; served with U.S. Army, 1959-61, advanced through grades to lt. col., 1985, chaplain, 1970-93, chief parish/profl. devel., Europe, 1982-85, chief pastoral ministry and counselling Chaplain Ctr. and Sch., Ft. Monmouth, N.J., 1985-88, asst. dir. dept. mil. ministry, 1988-89, dir., 1989; chief Resource Mgmt. Br., Ft. Knox, Ky., 1989-91; chief adminstrn./ops br., dep. post chaplain, Ft. Knox, 1991-93, ret., 1993; rector St. Peter's-by-the-lake, Montague, Mich., 1993—. Bd. dirs. LaGrange County Mental Health Assn., Ind., 1969-70, Sch. Opportunity, LaGrange, 1969-70; chaplain Montague Fire Dept., 1995—. Decorated Bronze Star with 1 bronze oak leaf cluster, Air medal with 3 bronze oak leaf clusters, Meritorious Svc. medal with 3 bronze oak leaf clusters, Army Commendation medal with 1 oak leaf cluster, parachutist badge. Mem. Mil. Chaplains Assn., Evang. and Cath. Mission, Order St. Benedict. Mem. DAV (life), U.S. Army Chaplain Mus. Assn. (bd. dirs. 1986-88), Am. Soc. Mil Comptrollers. Home: 8381 Old Channel Trl Montague MI 49437-1536

SISBARRO, THOMAS A., business executive; b. Newark, N.J., Oct. 11, 1946. BSME, Newark Coll. Engring., 1969. Corp. mfg. engr. White Consolidated Industry, Mansfield, Ohio, 1984-87; plant engr. GE Aircraft Engines, Cin., 1987-91; pres. Environ. Closure Systems, Inc., Reynoldsburg, Ohio, 1991—; cons. Flexible Technologies, Inc., Reynoldsburg, 1987-91. Patent degreaser door system; contbr. articles to profl. jours.

SISCO, ROGER D., minister, marriage and family therapist; b. Siloam Springs, Ark., Nov. 22, 1950; s. Rex Emmanuel and Elizabeth Marie (Mitchell) S.; m. Karen S. Dees, Dec. 31, 1992; 1 stepdau., Bridget. BA, Mo. So. Coll., 1972; MS, Pitts. State U., 1976; DD (Hon.), World Christianship Ministries, 1990. Lic. Marriage and Family Therapist. Freelance artist Webb City, Mo.; lay minister Carterville (Mo.) First Baptist Ch.; sch. psychologist Reno County Edn. Coop., Hutchinson, Kans.; detention counselor Children's Ct. Ctr., Pitts., Kans.; psychology tchr. Bartlesville Wesleyan Coll., 1982; marriage and family therapist Washington County Youth and Family Svcs., Bartlesville, Okla., 1982-85; adminstrv. asst. Family Care Ministries, Bapt. Boys Ranch Town, Edmond, Okla., 1985-92; marriage & family therapist pvt. practice, Carterville, Mo.; lay minister Carterville (Mo.) First Baptist Ch.; animal therapy cons. Bapt. Boys Ranch Town, Edmond, Okla., 1987-92, recreation dir., 1987-88, chess program supr., 1989-92, music therapy dir., 1991-92; dir. social svcs. Sterling Home Health Care, Inc., 1993—; breeder quarter horses Sisco Quarter Horses, Webb City, Mo., 1993—; with Sisco Home Health Care, Inc., 1995. Mem. So. Bapt. Ch., deacon, Chrisitan counselor. Mem. Am. Checker Fedn., U.S. Chess Fedn. (named chess master), Nat. Coll. Martial Arts (named Black Belt, 7th degree), Okla. Songwriters Assn.

SISKA, RICHARD STANLY, marketing professional; b. Chgo., June 6, 1948; s. Stanly J. and Anna Marie (Czelka) S.; m. Christine Alexandria Plodzin, Sept. 7, 1969; children: Cara, Kylene. BSBA, Christian Bros. Coll., 1969. Tech. sales rep. Advance Process Supply, Chgo., 1971-73; nat. sales mgr. premium/incentives R.A. Briggs Co., Lake Zurich, Ill., 1974-77, nat. sales mgr. retail div., 1977-80, dir. sales, mktg., 1980-82, v.p., 1983-87; v.p. sales and nat. accounts Wilton Enterprises, Woodridge, Ill., 1987-93; sr. v.p. nat. sales Ben Franklin Retail Stores Inc., 1994—. Contbr. articles to profl. jours. Campiagn dir. Rep. Com. to Elect Jim Kay for Lake Zurich Mayor, 1982. Served to sgt. U.S. Army, 1970-71. Mem. Nat. Premium Sales Execs., Chgo. Textile Assn., Bed and Bath Linen Assn., Lake Zurich Indsl. Coun., Chgo. Housewares Assn., Christian Bros. U. Alumni Assn. (sec. 1980-81), Delta Sigma Pi. Home: 36 Pheasant Run Lake Zurich IL 60047-9785 Office: Ben Franklin Retail Stores 500 E North Ave Carol Stream IL 60188

SISSON, MARY WINIFRED, retired elementary education educator; b. Decatur, Ill., Oct. 8, 1919; d. Leland Eugene and Amy Gertrude (Chaplin) Jayne; m. Lewis Milton Sisson, June 30, 1962 (dec.). BS, Bradley U., 1948. Elem. tchr. Milford (Ill.) Sch., 1941-43, Pekin (Ill.) Douglas Sch., 1943-58, Lake Weston Sch., Orlando, Fla., 1958-60, various, San Jose, Calif., 1960-61, White Sch., Peoria, Ill., 1960-65, Blaine-Sumner Sch., Peoria, 1965-67; adult tutor Common Place, Peoria, 1985-89, 92-94; leader summer playgrounds, Pekin, Ill., 1954-58. Active Cedars of Lebanon Residents' Assn. Recipient scholarships Ill. State U., Normal. Mem. DAR, Naomi Cir., Peoria Area Retired Tchrs. Assn., Ill. Retired Tchrs. Assn. Republican. Presbyterian. Home: 1047 N Emily Pl Apt 316 Peoria IL 61604-4684

SIT, EUGENE C., investment executive; b. Canton, China, Aug. 8, 1938; s. Hom Yuen and Sue (Eng) S.; B.S.C., DePaul U., 1960, postgrad. Grad. Sch. Bus., 1962-65; m. Gail V. Chin, Sept. 14, 1958; children: Ronald, Debra, Roger, Raymond, Robert, Richard. CPA, Ill.; CFA. Fin. analyst Commonwealth Edison, Chgo., 1960-66, fin. asst. to chmn. finance com., 1966-68; asso. portfolio mgr. Investors Stock Fund, Investors Diversified Services, Mpls., 1968-69; portfolio mgr. IDS New Dimensions Fund, Mpls., 1969, v.p., portfolio mgr., 1970-72; v.p., sr. portfolio mgr. IDS New Dimensions, IDS Growth Fund, Mpls., 1972-76; pres. IDS Adv., 1976-77, pres., CEO, 1977-81; CEO IDS Trust Co., 1979-81; chmn., CEO IDS Adv./Gartmore Internat. Ltd., 1979-81; chmn., CEO, chief investment officer Sit Investment Assocs., Inc., Mpls., 1981—; chmn. Sit/Kim Internat. Investment Assocs., Inc.; chmn., pres., dir. Sit Mut. Fund Group; trustee Carleton Coll., Minn. Orchestral Assn.; active Minn. Hist. Soc., Mlps. Inst. Fine Arts. Mem. Inst. Chartered Fin. Analysts (trustee, past chmn. Rsch. Found.), Twin Cities Soc. Security Analysts, Univ. Club (N.Y.), Chgo. Club, Mpls. Club, Edina Country Club, World Trade Club (San Francisco), Indian Ridge Country Club (Palm Desert). Home: 6216 Braeburn Cir Minneapolis MN 55439-2548 Office: 4600 Norwest Ctr 90 S 7th St Minneapolis MN 55402-3903

SITA, MICHAEL JOHN, pharmacist, educator; b. St. Louis, Apr. 28, 1953; s. Julianne Gail Sita; m. Nora Ann Dillon, June 1, 1974; children: Michael John, Paul Thomas, Julianne Joyce. BS, St. Louis Coll. Pharmacy, 1976; MBA, So. Ill. U., 1983. Registered pharmacist, Mo., Ill. Staff pharmacist Luth. Med. Ctr., St. Louis, 1976-78, asst. chief pharmacist, 1978-81, adminstrv. coord. pharmacy svcs., 1981-85; dir. pharmacy svcs. Jefferson Meml. Hosp., 1985—; instr. St. Louis Coll. Health Careers, 1983-86; adj. instr. pharmacy practice St. Louis Coll. Pharmacy, 1980—; relief pharmacist Dolgins Apothecary, St. Louis, 1976-86, Best Pharmacy, 1986-88, Carraige Drugs, 1989-93, Medicine Shoppe, Festus, Mo., 1990—. Author/editor Pharmacy Capsule quar., 1977-85. Mem. St. Louis Soc. Hosp. Pharmacists (treas. 1985-87, pres. 1988-89, sec. 1990-92, Pharmacist of Yr. 1994-95), Mo. Soc. Hosp. Pharmacists, Am. Soc. Hosp. Pharmacists, Am. Pharm. Assn., Hosp. Assn. Met. St. Louis (chmn. pharmacy tech. adv. com. 1985-86). Avocations: carpentry, rehabbing. Home: 1345 Mccausland Ave Saint Louis MO 63117-1945 Office: PO Box 350 Crystal City MO 63019-0350

SITARZ, DARRELL EDWIN, company executive; b. Oak Park, Ill., Apr. 7, 1946; s. Edwin Carl and Violet (Carlson) S. AA, Coll. of DuPage, 1980; BA, Nat.-Louis U., 1986. Lic. real estate agt., Ill. Machinist GEM Products, Glen Ellyn, Ill., 1965-66; asst. credit mgr. W. T. Grant & Co., Glen Ellyn, Ill., 1967-69; tax acct. Kroehler Mfg. Co., Naperville, Ill., 1969-70; gen. mgr. GEM Products, Inc., Carol Stream, Ill., 1970-89; exec. dir. Kart Mktg. Assn., Wheaton, Ill., 1990-92; pres. Kart Expo Internat. Corp., 1992—; co-pub., co-owner Kart Mktg. Internat. Author: Official Karting Directory and Guide, 1991, 92, 93, 94; contbr. articles to profl. jours. Mem. Wheaton Community Assn., 1972-77. Named Coach of Yr., W.I.A. Baseball, 1988, Champion 1st Pl., Chgo. White Sox Fantasy Camp, 1986. Mem. World Karting Assn., Internat. Karting Fedn., River Valley Kart Assn. Republican. Lutheran. Office: Kart Mktg Group Inc PO Box 101 Wheaton IL 60189-0101

SITZ, MARK, state legislator; m. Linda; 2 children. Mem. N.D. Ho. of Reps., mem. fin., taxation, agr. coms.; farmer. Supr. Twp. Bd.; dir. McHenry County Farmers Union. Mem. Anamoose Wildlife Club. Home: PO Box 40A Drake ND 58736-0040*

SITZMAN, JERRY CLAYTON, consulting electrical engineer; b. Sheboygan, Wis., July 16, 1936; s. John and Elizabeth Sitzman. BS, U. Wis., 1963, MS, 1969. Project asst. Elec. Stds. and Instrumentation Lab., Madison, Wis., 1965-67; project engr. Space Sci. & Engring. Ctr., U. Wis., Madison, 1967-78, chief engr., 1978-95; pres. Primetics, engring. cons., Madison, 1995—; cons. JCS Cons. Co., Madison, 1976-88. Patentee in field. Mem. IEEE, U. Wis. Flying Club Inc. (pres. 1971-73), Eta Kappa Nu, Tau Beta Pi, Phi Kappa Phi. Office: Primetics 506 Clifden Dr Madison WI 53711-1531

SIVE, REBECCA ANNE, public affairs company executive; b. N.Y.C., Jan. 29, 1950; d. David and Mary (Robinson) S.; m. Clark Steven Tomashefsky, June 18, 1972. BA, Carleton Coll., 1972; MA in Am. History, U. Ill., Chgo., 1975. Asst. to chmn. of pres.' task force on vocations Carleton Coll., Northfield, Minn., 1972; asst. to acquisitions librarian Am. Hosp. Assn., Chgo., 1973; rsch. asst. Jane Addams Hull House, Chgo., 1974; instr. Loop Coll., Chgo., 1975, Columbia Coll., Chgo., 1975-76; cons. Am. Jewish Com., Chgo., 1975, Ctr. for Urban Affairs, Northwestern U., Evanston, Ill., 1977, Ill. Consultation on Ethnicity in Edn., 1976, MLA, 1977; dir. Ill. Women's History Project, 1975-76; founder, exec. dir. Midwest Women's Ctr., Chgo., 1977-81; exec. dir. Playboy Found., 1981-84; v.p. pub. affairs/pub. rels. Playboy Video Corp., 1985; v.p. pub. affairs Playboy Enterprises, Inc., Chgo., 1985-86; pres. The Sive Group, Inc., Chgo., 1986—; guest speaker various ednl. orgns., 1972—; instr. Roosevelt U., Chgo., 1977-78; dir. spl. projects Inst. on Pluralism and Group Identity, Am. Jewish Com., Chgo., 1975-77; cons. Nat. Women's Polit. Caucus, 1978-80; bd. dirs. NOVA Health Systems, Woodlawn Community Devel. Corp.; trainer Midwest Acad.; mem. adv. bd. urban studies program Associated Colls. Midwest; proposal reviewer NEH. Contbr. articles to profl. jours. Commr. Chgo. Park Dist., 1986-88; mem. steering com. Ill. Commn. on Human Rels., 1976; mem. structure com. Nat. Women's Agenda Coalition, 1976-77; del.-at-large Nat. Women's conf., 1977; mem. Ill. Gov.'s Com. on Displaced Homemakers, 1979-81, Ill. Human Rights Com., 1980-87, Ill. coordinating com., Internat Womens Yr.; coord. Ill. Bicentennial Photog. Exhbn., 1977; mem. Ill. Employment and Tng. Coun.; mem. employment com. Ill. Com. on Status of Women; bd. dirs. Nat. Abortion Rights Action League and NARAL Found., Ill. div. ACLU, Midwest Women's Ctr. Recipient award for outstanding community leadership YWCA Met. Chgo., 1979, award for outstanding community leadership Chgo. Jaycees, 1988. Home: 3529 N Marshfield Ave Chicago IL 60657-1224 Office: The Sive Group 359 W Chicago Ave Ste 201 Chicago IL 60610-3025

SIWICKI, BILL, journalist; b. Berkeley, Ill., Nov. 27, 1966; s. Donald Joseph and Rachel Marilyn (Ary) S.; m. Dori Carolyn Adams, May 22, 1993. BA in Polit. Sci., Loyola U., Chgo., 1988. Chief bus. writer Press Publs., Elmhurst, Ill., 1989; mng. editor Jobber Exec. Mag., Des Plaines, Ill., 1989-90; mng. editor internat. divsn. Hunter Pub., Des Plaines, 1990-92; assoc. editor Healthcare Fin. Mgmt. Mag., Westchester, Ill., 1992-94; sr. editor Health Data Mgmt. Mag., Chgo., 1994—. Active Chgo. Coun. Fgn. Rels., 1995—. Roman Catholic. Office: Health Data Mgmt Mag 300 S Wacker Dr 18th Fl Chicago IL 60606

SIX, FRED N., state supreme court justice; b. Independence, Mo., Apr. 20, 1929. AB, U. Kans., 1951, JD with honors, 1956; LLM in Judicial Process, U. Va., 1990. Bar: Kans. 1956. Asst. atty. gen. State of Kans., 1957-58; pvt. practice Lawrence, Kans., 1958-87; judge Kans. Ct. Appeals, 1987-88; justice Kans. Supreme Ct., Topeka, 1988—; editor-in-chief U. Kans. Law Review, 1955-56; lectr. on law Washburn U. Sch. Law, 1957-58, U. Kans., 1975-76. Maj. USMC, 1951-53; USMCR, 1957-62. Recipient Disting. Alumnus award U. Kans. Sch. Law, 1994. Fellow Am. Bar Found. (chmn. Kans. chpt. 1983-87); mem. ABA (jud. adminstrn. divsn.), Internat. Law Assn. (Am. br.), Am. Judicature Soc., Kans. Bar Assn., Kans. Bar Found., Kans. Law Soc. (pres. 1970-72), Kans. Inn of Ct. (pres. 1993-94), Order of Coif, Phi Delta Phi. Office: Kans Supreme Ct 301 SW 10th Ave Topeka KS 66612-1507

SJOGREN, DONALD ERNEST, farmer; b. Holdrege, Nebr., Jan. 3, 1932; s. Ernest V. and Ellen M. (Peterson) S. AA, Luther Jr. Coll., Wahoo, Nebr., 1951; BS in Agr., U. Nebr., Lincoln, 1953. Owner, farmer Funk, Nebr., 1954—; bd. dirs Nebr. Corn Devel. Utilization and Mktg. bd., Phelps Co. Livestock Feeders, 1975-78. Mem. Ch. Coun., 1962-65, 69-72, 75-78, 89-92, ch. coun., 1996—; active Rep. Nat. Com., Washington, 1978—; pres. Phelps County Farm Bur., 1989-91. Mem. Holdrege C. of C., Nebr. Corn Growers Assn. (bd. dirs. 1974-90, Golden Ear award 1988), Nat. Corn Growers Assn. (v.p. rsch. 1982-85, bd. dirs. 1978-88), Lions, South. Cen. Nebr. Corn Growers Assn. (pres. 1988, Jerry Johnson Meml. Achievement award 1990), Phelps County Farm Bur. (bd. dirs. 1985—, pres. 1989-92). Republican. Lutheran. Home: PO Box 165 Funk NE 68940-0165

SKAGGS, BILL, state legislator; b. Sylacanga, Ala., Jan. 24, 1942. Student, Ctrl. Mo. State U. Rep. Mo. State Ho. Reps. Dist. 34, 1983-93, Mo. State Ho. Reps. Dist. 31, 1993—. Home: 3613 N Park Ave Kansas City MO 64116-2831*

SKAGGS, JIMMY M., economics educator; b. Gorman, Tex., June 13, 1940; s. Clarence E. and Bessie (Lee) S.; m. Janette Johnson, Mar. 30, 1961 (div. Jan. 1976); children: Janeen Skaggs Longfellow, Jessica Skaggs Waltmon, Joy Skaggs Schreiber. AAS, Odessa Coll., 1960; BS cum laude, Ross State Coll., 1962; MA, Tex. Tech. U., 1965, PhD, 1970. Tchr. history Lubbock (Tex.) Pub. Schs., 1962-65; instr. dept. history Tex. Tech. U., Lubbock, 1965-70, dep. archivist S.W. collection, 1968-70; asst. prof. econs. Wichita (Kans.) State U., 1970-73, assoc. prof., 1973-77, assoc. prof. Am. studies, 1975-77, chmn. dept., 1975-81, prof., 1977-89, prof. econs., 1977—; hist. cons. Phillips Petroleum Co., Barltesville, Okla., 1978-81; dir. Historic Wichita-Cowtown, Inc., 1980-82. Co-editor: (with Glenn W. Miller) Metropolitan Wichita; past, present, future, 1978; (with Fane Downs and Winifred Vigness) Chronicles of the Yaqui Expedition, 1972; editor: The Ranch and Range in Oklahoma, 1978; author: (with Melvin H. Witrogen and Dennis C. Duell) An Act of Faith, 1984; (with David B. Gracy II and Roy Sylvan Dunn) Irrigation in the Southwest: A Center for Historical Research in the Southwest Collection, 1968, A Cattle-log of the Southwest Collection: a Repository for Ranch Research, 1968; (with Seymour V. Connor) Broadcloth and Britches: The Santa Fe Trade, 1977; Prime cut: Livestock Raising and Meatpacking in the Unied States, 1607-1983, 1986, An Interpretive History of the American Economy, 1975, The Great Guano Rush: Entrepreneurs and American Overseas Expansion, 1994, Clipperton: A History of the Island the World Forgot, 1989, The Cattle-Trailing Industry: Between Supply and Demand, 1866-1890, 1973, paperback edit., 1991; contbr. articles to profl. jours., chpts. to books; assoc. editor Mil. History of Tex. and Southwest, 1967-76, book rev. editor, 1970-74; editor Bus. and Econ. Report, 1984-91; mem. editl. bd. Regents Press of Kans., 1978-83, Great Plains Jour., 1972-89, Jour. of West, 1988-89; manuscript referee Agrl. History. Mem. Red. River Valley Hist. Assn. (dir., assoc. editor 1974-81). Office: Wichita State U Dept Econs Box 78 WSU Sta Wichita KS 67208

SKALA, GARY DENNIS, electric and gas utilities executive management consultant; b. Bay Shore, N.Y, Oct. 15, 1946; s. Harry A. and Emily Skala. BS in Mgmt. Engring., Rensselaer Polytech. Inst., 1969; MA in Psychology, Hofstra U., 1972; postgrad., Chgo. Theol. Sem., 1996. Engr. L.I. Lighting Co., Hicksville, N.Y., 1969-71; labor rels. coord. L.I. Lighting Co., 1971-73; mgmt. cons. Gilbert/Commonwealth, N.Y.C., 1973-74; sr. mgmt. cons. Booz, Allen & Hamilton, San Francisco, 1974-78; mgr. utility cons. A.T. Kearney, Chgo., 1978-81; mng. cons. Cresap, div. Towers Perrin, Chgo., 1981-85; pres. Gary D. Skala & Assocs. Mgmt. Cons., Chgo., 1985—; lectr. on utility bus. issues Edison Electric Inst., Utility Exec. Mgmt. Com., Internat. Maintenance Conf., Assn. Rural Electric Coops., Inst. Indsl. Engrs.; subcontracting cons. Arthur D. Little Inc., Liberty Cons. Group, Ernst & Young, Cresap, A.T. Kearney, Towers Perrin, Michael Paris Assocs. Ltd., Planmetrics. Contbr. articles to profl. jours. Trustee, strategic planning com. Samaritan Inst. for Religious Studies; mem. bd. Ordained Ministry of Great Lakes Dist. of Universal Fellowship Met. Cmty. Chs.; vice moderator bd. dirs. Good Shepherd Parish Met. Cmty. Ch. of Chgo; vol. The Night Ministry of Chgo. Mem. Inst. Indsl. Engrs. (sr. mem. utility div. 1978—, charter), Am. Inst. Indsl. Engrs. (chmn. Midwest chpt. utility div. 1980-81).

SKARPHOL, ROBERT J., state legislator; m. Diana; 3 children. Mem. N.D. Ho. of Reps., 1993—, mem. indsl., bus., labor, transp. coms.; farmer; ind. oil contract pumper. Vice chmn. Tioga Area Econ. Devel. Corp. Mem. Kiwanis, Farm Bur. Home: PO Box 725 Tioga ND 58852-0725*

SKAU, MICHAEL W., English educator; b. Chgo., Jan. 6, 1944; s. Walter Francis and Martha Catherine (Marich) S. BA, U. Ill., 1965, MA, 1967, PhD, 1973. Rsch. asst. U. Ill., Urbana and Champaign, 1965-66, teaching asst., 1966-73; asst. prof. English U. Nebr., Omaha, 1973-78, assoc. prof. English, 1978-85, prof. English, 1985—. Author: Constantly Risking Absurdity: The Writings of Lawrence Ferlinghetti, 1989; Me and God Poems, 1990; author poems; contbr. articles to profl. jours. Mem. MLA, AAUP. Home: 4913 Chicago St Omaha NE 68132-2914 Office: U Nebr 60th & Dodge Sts Omaha NE 68182

SKAVERY, STANLEY, school system administrator. BS, Ctrl. Mich. U., 1967; MA, Ea. Mich. U., 1975; EdD, U. Mich., 1986; postgrad., U. Ctrl. Fla., 1993, 94. Tchr. grades 3 and 5 Utica Community Schs.-Walter Flickinger Elem., 1967-71; tchr. grades 3 and 6 Utica Community Schs.-Edward

DeKeyser Elem., 1971-73; dir. community edn. Holly Area Schs., 1973-75; dir. community edn. Avondale Sch. Dist., 1975—, acting early childhood prin., 1981-85; coord. for Title IX, Title VI and sect. 504 programs Avondale Sch. Dist.; mem. Oakland C.C. Child Care Task Force; mem. conf. planning com. Mich. Assn. Community and Adult Edn., 1990. Newsletter editor: Avondale Sch. Dist., 1980-86; contbr. articles to profl. jours. Vol. alumni recruiter U. Mich., 1993—; charter mem. Avondale Fine Arts Coun., Shelby Twp. Youth Football League, Avondale Youth Soccer League, Rochester Younger Persons Com.; chmn., bd. dirs. Rochester Avon-Recreation Authority. Mem. ASCD, Nat. Community Edn. Assn., Mich. Assn. of Community and Adult Educators (presenter), Oakland County Community and Adult Educators (past pres.), Mich. Sch. Pub. Rels. Assn. (Commendable Publ. award 1984, 85, 86, 89, Disting. Publ. award 1989, 92), Mich. Pks. and Recreation Assn., Ctrl. Mich. U. Nat. Alumni Assn. (bd. dirs.). Home: 53295 Freda Dr Macomb MI 48042-2829

SKELLY, JOSEPH PATRICK, radio personality; b. Amityville, N.Y., Mar. 21, 1956; s. Joseph Edward and Claire May (Muller) S. AA, Suffolk County C.C., Selden, N.Y., 1976; BS, SUNY, Oneonta, 1978; student, May Sch. Broadcasting, Billings, Mont., 1986. Cons. geologist Continental Labs., Inc., Billings, 1979-85; radio personality Sta. KBIT, Billings, 1985-86, Sta. KORN, Mitchell, S.D., 1986—; program dir., 1996—. Vol. Davison County 4-H, Mitchell, 1986—; trustee S.D. 4-H Found., Mitchell, 1987-91; treas. Mitchell Area Crimestoppers, Inc., 1990—. Named Friend of 4-H, Davison County 4-H leaders, 1987, Hanson County 4-H Leaders, Alexandria, S.D., 1988. Mem. Mitchell C. of C. (Amb.'s Club 1992—), Toastmasters Internat. (gov. area VI 1992-93, gov. divsn. B 1993-94, Area Gov. of Yr. 1993, Divsn. Gov. of Yr. 1994, Table-Topics champion dist. 41 1995), Mitchell Toastmasters (local pres. 1995—, Toastmaster of Yr. 1991), Balloon Fedn. of Am. Republican. Roman Catholic. Home: PO Box 877 Mitchell SD 57301-0877 Office: Korn Palace Broadcasting 319 N Main St Mitchell SD 57301-2611

SKELTON, ISAAC NEWTON, IV (IKE SKELTON), congressman; b. Lexington, Mo., Dec. 20, 1931; s. Isaac Newton and Carolyn (Boone) S.; m. Susan B. Anding, July 22, 1961; children: Ike, Jim, Page. AB, U. Mo., 1953, LLB, 1956. Bar: Mo. 1956. Pvt. practice Lexington; pros. atty. Lafayette County, Mo., 1957-60; spl. asst. atty. gen. State of Mo., 1961-63; mem. Mo. Senate from 28th dist., 1971-76; mem. 95th-104th Congresses from 4th Mo. Dist., 1977—, ranking minority mem. nat. security subcom. on mil. procurement. Active Boy Scouts Am. Mem. Phi Beta Kappa, Sigma Chi. Democrat. Mem. Christian Ch. Clubs: Masons, Shriners, Elks. Home: 1814 Franklin St Lexington MO 64067-1708 Office: US Ho of Reps 2227 Rayburn House Bldg Washington DC 20515*

SKELTON, ROBERT EUGENE, aeronautics and astronautics educator; b. Elberton, Ga., Mar. 21, 1938; s. Sara (Dickerson) Clardy; children: Leigh, David; m. Judith King, June 26, 1971; children: Jeff, Buzz. BSEE, Clemson U., 1963; MSEE, U. Ala., 1970; PhD, UCLA, 1976. From asst. to assoc. prof. Sch. Aeronautics & Astronautics Purdue U., West Lafayette, Ind., 1975-82, prof. Sch. Aeronautics & Astronautics, 1982—, dir. Space Systems Control Lab., Inst. Interdisciplinary Engring. Studies, 1991—; appointee Aeronautics and Space Engring. Bd., 1983-88; mem. ad hoc com. NASA-Univs. Rels. in Aero/Space Engring., Nat. Rsch. Coun., 1984-85; mem. univ. senate Purdue U., 1983-86, mem. ednl. com., 1983-86; vice chmn. applications tech. com. Internat. Fedn. of Automatic Control; Russell Severance Springer prof. U. Calif., Berkeley, 1991. Recipient Sr. U.S. Scientist award Alexander von Humboldt Found., 1991; W.F. Poole Alumni scholar Clemson U., 1962-63, Clemson Engring. Found. scholar, 1961-62; fellow Japan Soc. for Promotion of Sci., 1986. Fellow AIAA, IEEE, Phi Kappa Phi, Phi Eta Sigma, Sigma Gamma Tau, Sigma Xi, Tau Beta Pi (chmn. Clemson chpt. 1962-63). Office: Purdue Univ Space Sys Control Lab 334 Grissom Hall West Lafayette IN 47907-1282

SKILBECK, CAROL LYNN MARIE, elementary educator and small business owner; b. Seymour, Ind., May 1, 1953; d. Harry Charles and Barbara Josephine (Knue) S.; div.; 1 child, Michael Charles. Postgrad., U. Cin., 1977, No. Ky. U., 1985-86, Northern Ky. U. Cert. tchr., Ohio. Sec. Procter & Gamble, Cin., 1971-76; classified typist The Cin. Enquirer, Cin., 1976; tchr. St. Aloysius Sch., Cin., 1977-79, St. William Sch., Cin., 1979-82; legal sec. County Dept. Human Svcs., Cin., 1982-86; tchr. St. Jude Sch., Cin., 1986-91; educator, owner CLS Tutoring Svcs., Cin., 1991—; photographer Interstate Studio and Am. Sch. Pictures, 1994—; tchr. St. Martin Gifted Program, Cin., 1992-93, Oak Hills Schs. Community Edn., Cin., 1990—, Super Saturday Gifted Program, Cin., 1990—; adult leader antidrug program Just Say No, Cin., 1989-92. Author: Study Skills Workshop, 1993; writer, dir. Christmas play, 1993. Vol. interior designer for homeless shelter St. Joseph's Carpenter Shop, Cin., 1990; mem. LaSalle PTA, 1993—; vol. Habitat for Humanity. Mem. Nat. Tchrs. Assn. Democrat. Roman Catholic. Home and Office: 3801 Dina Ter Cincinnati OH 45211-6527

SKILES, JAMES JEAN, electrical and computer engineering educator; b. St Louis, Oct. 16, 1928; s. Coy Emerson and Vernetta Beatrice (Maples) S.; m. Deloris Audrey McKenney, Sept. 4, 1948; children: Steven, Randall, Jeffrey. BSEE, Washington U., St. Louis, 1948; MS, U. Mo.-Rolla, 1951; PhD, U. Wis., 1954. Registered profl. engr., Wis. Engr. Union Electric Co., St. Louis, 1948-49; instr. U. Mo.-Rolla, 1949-51; prof. elec. engring. U. Wis., Madison, 1954-89, prof. emeritus, 1989—, chmn. Dept. Elec. Engring., 1967-72, dir. Univ. Industry Rsch. program, 1972-75, dir. Energy Rsch. Ctr., 1975-95; cons. in field. Contbr. articles to profl. jours. Mem. Monona Grove Dist. Schs. Bd., Wis., 1961-69; mem. adv. com. Wis. Energy Office, Madison, 1979-80, Wis. Pub. Service Commn., 1980-81. Recipient Wis. Electric Utilities Professorship in Energy Engring. U. Wis., 1975-89; recipient Benjamin Smith Reynolds Teaching award, 1980, Kiekhofer Teaching award, 1955, Acad of Elec. Engring. award U. Mo.-Rolla, 1982. Mem. IEEE (sr.), Am. Soc. Engring. Edn. Home: 8099 Coray Ln Verona WI 53593-9073 Office: Univ of Wisconsin Dept Elec & Computer Engring 1415 Engineering Dr Madison WI 53706-1691

SKILLICORN, JUDY PETTIBONE, gifted and talented education coordinator; b. Cleve., June 16, 1943; d. C. Arthur and Dorothy Laura (Parratt) Pettibone; m. Robert Charles Skillicorn, Aug. 21, 1965; children: Jodie Lynn, Brian Jeffrey, Jennifer Laura. BS in Edn., Ohio State U., 1965; MEd, Cleve. State U., 1988. 6th grade tchr. Windermer Sch., Upper Arlington, Ohio, 1965-68; pvt. tutor, 1968-71; adminstr. Westshore Montessori Sch., Elyria, Lorain & Amherst, Ohio, 1981; ch. educator First Congl. Ch., Elyria, 1982-84, St. Peters United Ch. of Christ, Amherst, Ohio, 1984; tchr. gifted Clearview Local Schs., Lorain, 1985-90; coord. gifted Lorain County Bd. Edn., Elyria, 1990—, planning dir. county-wide sch. creative & performing arts; founder Arts Advocacy of Lorain County, 1994, pres. 1996; founder Arts Connected Tchg. pilot program in 4 sch. dists., 1995-96. Author: Young Authors Handbook, 1991, 92, 93, 94, 95, 96. Chairperson tickets Elyria 150th Bicentennial Celebration; pageant dir. Ch. Medieval Feast, Elyria, 1988-91; chmn. diaconate First Congl. Ch., Elyria, 1990-93; mem. com. Lorain County Beautiful, Seventh Generation, 1995—. Recipient Partnership in Edn. for Young Authors Program grades K-6 Nat. Assn. Coll. Stores, Oberlin, 1993-96, for Writers conf. Program grades 7-9, 1993-96; Jennings scholar tchr. Martha Holden Jennings Found., 1990-91. Mem. Writing Tchrs. Network (publ. com. 1991-93), North Ctrl. Consortium for Gifted (treas., v.p. 1991-93), Lorain County Elem. Sch. Adminstrs. (sec.-treas. 1993, v.p. 1993-94, pres. 1994-95), Consortium Ohio Coords. for Gifted, Ohio Assn. Gifted Children, Chautauqua Lit. Soc., Internat. Network for Visual and Performing Arts Schs., Phi Delta Kappa. Office: Lorain County Office Edn 1885 Lake Ave Elyria OH 44035-2551

SKILLING, RAYMOND INWOOD, lawyer; b. Enniskillen, U.K., July 14, 1939; s. Dane and Elizabeth (Burleigh) S.; m. Alice Mae Welsh, Aug. 14, 1982; 1 child by previous marriage, Keith A. F. LLB, Queen's U., Belfast, U.K., 1961; JD, U. Chgo., 1962. Solicitor English Supreme Ct. 1966. Bar: Ill 1974. Assoc. Clifford-Turner (now Clifford Chance), London, 1963-69, ptnr., 1969-76; exec. v.p., chief counsel Aon Corp. (and predecessor cos.), Chgo., 1976—; bd. dirs. Aon Corp. (and predecessor cos.). Commonwealth fellow, U. Chgo., 1961-62, Bigelow teaching fellow U. Chgo. Law Sch., 1962-63; Fulbright scholar U.S. Ednl. Commn., London, 1961-63; recipient McKane medal Queen's U., Belfast, 1961. Mem. ABA, Ill. Bar Assn., Chgo. Bar Assn., The Casino Chgo., Chgo. Club, Econ. Club Chgo., Racquet Club Chgo., The Carlton Club London. Office: Aon Corp 123 N Wacker Dr Chicago IL 60606-1700

SKINDRUD, RICK, state legislator; b. Sept. 15, 1944. Bd. dirs. Dane County, Wis.; planning commn. Town of Primrose, Wis.; assemblyman Wis. State Dist. 79, 1993—; farmer. Past pres. Mt. Vernon Park Assn. Address: 1261 LaFollette Rd Mount Horeb WI 53572

SKINLO, MICHELLE ELAINE, data entry clerk; b. Springfield, Ohio, June 19, 1950; d. Richard Lamar and Ruth Pauline (Miller) Kiger; m. Donald Thomas Skinlo, Dec. 31, 1993; children: Meredith Ann Spitz, Hilary Paige Spitz. AS, Lakeland Jr. Coll., 1988; postgrad., Ea. Ill. U., 1988—. Data entry clk. City of Mattoon (Ill.) Water Dept., 1974—. Pres., bd. dirs. Cmty. Unit 2 Bd. Edn., Mattoon, 1990—; chmn. Parade Orgn., Mattoon, 1970—; sec., bd. dirs. Am. Cancer Soc., Mattoon, 1992—; mem. March of Dimes; bd. dirs. Dist. 10 PTA; Sunday sch. tchr.; youth group dir.; basketball coach; dir. Girls Ch. League Basketball; ponytail coach; vol. ICTC Spl. Olympics, Jump Rope for Heart; pres. Mattoon Band Parents; sec. Mattoon Rep. Women. Recipient Book of Golden Deeds award Mattoon Exch. Club, 1993, Life Mem. award Mattoon Jr. High PTA, 1978; named Master Sch. Bd. Mem., Ill. Assn. Sch. Bd., 1994. Mem. Am. Bus. Women's Assn., Am. Heart Assn., Am. Legion Aux. Republican. Home: 2501 Dakota Mattoon IL 61938 Office: City of Mattoon Water Dept 1201 Marshall Mattoon IL 61938

SKINNER, CALVIN L., JR., state legislator; b. Easton, Md., June 11, 1942; s. Calvin L. Sr. and Eleanor (Stevens) S.; m. Robin Meredith Geist, 1977 (div.); m. Michele M. Giangrasso, 1990; 1 child, Alexandra. BA, Oberlin Coll., 1964; MPA, U. Mich., 1971. Treas. McHenry County, 1966-70; Ill. state rep. Dist. 33, 1973-81, Dist. 64, 1993—; candidate State Comptr. Ill., 1982; committeeman Algonquin Rep. Precinct, Ill., 1986—; mem. Ill. AIDS Adv. Coun., 1988-92. Mem. Crystal Lake-Cary LWV. Mem. McHenry County Defenders. Republican. Home: 275 Meridian St Crystal Lake IL 60014-5411*

SKINNER, SAMUEL KNOX, utilities executive, lawyer; b. Chgo., June 10, 1938; s. Vernon Orlo and Imelda Jane (Curran) S.; m. Mary Jacobs, 1989; children: Thomas, Steven, Jane. B.S., U. Ill., 1960; J.D., DePaul U., 1966. Bar: Ill. 1966. Asst. U.S. atty. No. Dist. Ill., Chgo., 1968-74, 1st asst. U.S. atty., 1974-75, U.S. atty., 1975-77; ptnr. Sidley & Austin, Chgo., 1977-89; chmn. Regional Transp. Authority, Chgo., 1984; U.S. sec. of transp., 1989-91; chief of staff White House, Washington, 1991-92; gen. chmn. Republican Nat. Com., Washington, 1992-93; pres. Commonwealth Edison Co., Chgo. Chmn. Ill. Capitol Devel. Bd., 1977-84. Served as 1st lt. U.S. Army, 1960-61. Mem. ABA, Ill. Bar Assn., Chgo. Bar Assn., Chgo. Club, Shoreacres Club. Republican. Presbyterian. Office: Commonwealth Edison Co 1 1st Nat Plz Chicago IL 60603

SKINNER, WILLIS DEAN, consulting engineering company executive; b. Council Grove, Kans., Feb. 9, 1932; s. Leonard Leroy and Bertha Marie (Young) S.; m. Constance Irena Wilcox, Apr. 9, 1955; children: Kimberly, Karen, Kurt. BSCE, Kans. State U., 1955. Diplomate Am. Acad. Environ. Engrs.; registered profl. engr., Mo. Civil engr. Black & Veatch, Kansas City, Mo., 1955-72; resident dir. Black & Veatch Internat., Bogota, Colombia, 1973-75; project mgr. Black & Veatch Internat., Kansas City, 1976-77, v.p., 1978-80; ptnr. Black & Veatch, Boston, 1981-83, Cairo, 1984-85, Kansas City, 1986—; exec. v.p. Black & Veatch Internat., Kansas City, 1993—. Mem. Dist. 110 Sch. Bd., Overland Park, Kans., 1964-68. 1st lt. U.S. army, 1957-58. Mem. NSPE, Am. Water Works Assn., Water Environ. Fedn. Office: Black & Veatch 8400 Ward Pky Kansas City MO 64114-2031

SKIRVIN, ROBERT MICHAEL, college professor; b. Burlington, Wash., Oct. 27, 1947; s. Orval Cecil and Sylvia Edella (Reynolds) S.; m. Mary Margaret Van Horn, May 4, 1973; children: Timothy, Daniel. BS, So. Ill. U., Carbondale, 1969, MS, 1971; Phd, Purdue U., West Lafayette, 1975. Asst. prof. Purdue U., West Lafayette, 1975-76, U. Ill., Urbana, Ill., 1976-81; assoc. prof. U. Ill., Urbana, 1981-88, prof., 1988—. Co-inventor Illini Hardy Blackberry. Office: Univ Ill 1201 Gregory Dr Urbana IL 61801

SKJERVOLD, GERALDINE REID See REID, GERALDINE WOLD

SKOGLUND, WESLEY JOHN, state legislator; b. Mpls., June 9, 1945; s. John and Edith Peterson S.; m. Linda; children: Anne, Jenny. BA, U. Minn., 1967. Park commr. Hennepin County, Minn., 1974-75; Minn. State rep. Dist. 62B, 1975—; personnel-employee rels. Control Data Corp., 1967-75; businessman; chmn. ins. com. and fin. inst. com., Nat. Conf. of Ins. Legislators, Nat. Conf. of State Legislators; mem. capitol area archtl. and planning bd.; legis. audit com. and judiciary coms; mem. edn. and ways and means coms. Active YMCA, Bicentennial Commn., Hennepin County Study Group, Adoptive Families of Am. Recipient Anti-Smoking Group awards, Hennepin County award, Airport Noise Control award, United Way awards. Office: 409 State Office Bldg Saint Paul MN 55155-1201*

SKOGMAN, DALE R., bishop. Bishop No. Great Lakes Synod, Marquette, Mich. Address: Evangelical Lutheran Church 1029 N 3rd St Marquette MI 49855-3509

SKOLNICK, ANDREW ABRAHAM, science and medical journalist, photographer; b. N.Y.C., Oct. 21, 1947; s. Solomon and Blanche (Blidner) S. Cert. profl. photography, Paier Art Sch., Hamden, Conn., 1974; BA in Liberal Arts, Charter Oaks State Coll., Farmington, Conn., 1978; MS in Journalism, Columbia U., 1981. Photographer biology dept. Yale U., New Haven, 1975-76; sci. writer March of Dimes Birth Defects Found., White Plains, N.Y., 1981-85; life scis. editor-news bur. U. Ill., Urbana-Champaign, 1985-87; assoc. sci. news editor AMA, Chgo., 1987-89; assoc. news editor Jour. of AMA, Chgo., 1989—; vis. instr. Trumbull Coll. Yale U., New Haven, Conn., 1976-77; vis. lectr. dept. internat. journalism Shanghai (China) Internat. Studies U., 1996. Contbg. author Collier's Ency., Merit Students' Ency., Macmillan, Inc., N.Y.C.; contbr. articles, op-eds and photographs to mags., newspapers and books. Recipient (with others) 1st Ann. Cmty. Health award for journalistic excellence Nat. Assn. Cmty. Health Ctrs., 1992, Responsibility in Journalism award Com. for Sci. Investigation of Claims of Paranormal, Buffalo, 1992, Morris Fishbein award in med. comm. Am. Med. Writers Assn., 1994, Harry Chapin Media award World Hunger Yr., 1996; Nate Haseltine Meml. fellow in sci. writing Coun. for Advancment of Sci. Writing, 1980-81. Mem. Nat. Assn. Sci. Writers. Home: 328 Des Plaines Ave Forest Park IL 60130-1405 Office: Jour of AMA 515 N State St Chicago IL 60610-4320

SKOLNIK, DAVID ERWIN, financial analyst; b. Cleve., Oct. 31, 1949; s. Marvin and Ruth (Kovit) S.; m. Linda Susan Pollack, Mar. 31, 1973; children: Carla Denise, Robyn Laurel. BS in Acctg., Ohio State U., 1971. CPA, Ohio. Chief acct. Gray Drug Fair, Cleve., 1976-82, mgr. acctg. systems, 1982-84; fin. systems analyst Soc. Corp., Cleve., 1984, fin. systems officer, 1984-86, fin. systems rsch. officer, 1986-90, sr. fin. systems officer, 1990-91, strategic rsch. officer, 1991-92; mgmt. acctg. officer Keycorp, Cleve., 1992-96; asst. v.p., 1996—. Scoutmaster Boy Scouts Am., Cleve., 1971-77. Mem. AICPAs, Ohio Soc. CPAs, Am. Inst. Banking, Am. Mgmt. Assn., Tau Epsilon Phi. Jewish. Home: 4130 Stonehaven Rd Cleveland OH 44121-3163 Office: Keycorp 127 Public Sq Cleveland OH 44114-1216

SKORICH, ARLENE RITA MAE, labor union bookkeeper; b. Mpls., July 4, 1936; d. William Vladimir and Irene Lenore (Johnson) S.; m. Wes Poeschl (div. 1974); children: Ann Mary, Michael Joseph. B of Elected Studies, U. Minn., 1975. Cert. real estate broker, Minn. Sec., book-keeper Harris-Matteson Ins. Agy., St. Paul, 1956; sec. Zurich Am. Ins. Co., St. Paul; owner Arlene's of Roseville, 1959-66; office clk. Louiselle Agy., Mpls., 1974-75, Viking Electric, St. Paul, 1975-76; real estate agt. Ed Bossard Realty Co. Vol. Dem. Farm Labor Party Com., 1963; charter pres. Suburban Ramsey Bus. and Profl. Womens Club; fin. chairwoman Roseville LWV, 1964-66; vice chair Roseville Growth Com., 1962-63. Mem. AFL-CIO, NOW (charter), Minn. DFL Feminist Caucus (charter), Internat. Women's Rights Action Watch, Minn. Internat. Ctr., Mpls. Downtown Residents Assn., Neighborhood Salon Assn., Planned Parenthood, Dem. Farm Labor Union, Office Profl. Employees Internat. Union, Nat. Abortion Rights Action League, U. Minn. Alumni Assn., Quota Club Mpls. Lutheran. Home: 19 S 1st St Towers 2206B Minneapolis MN 55401 Office: Teamsters Local 1145 2636 Portland Ave Minneapolis MN 55407-1019

SKORUPA, CHRIS, mechanical engineer; b. Hamand, Ind., Jan. 14, 1949. BA in Mech. Engring., Wabash U., 1969; postgrad., Purdue U., 1971. Draftsman No. Ind. Pub. Svc., Hammond, 1967-73; designer Abex Co., Chicago Heights, Ill., 1973-75; chief draftsman Carter Control, Lansing, Ill., 1975-81; draftsman Ortman, Hammond, 1981—; engr. Sheffer, Cin., 1981—. Mem. Internat. Brotherhood Magicians.

SKOWRONSKI, VINCENT PAUL, concert violinist, recording artist, executive producer, producer classical recordings; b. Kenosha, Wis., Jan. 22, 1944. MusB, Northwestern U., 1966, MusM, 1968. V.p. Eberley-Skowronski, Inc., Evanston, Ill., 1973-92; internat. dir. mktg. and pub. rels. Vincent Skowronski: Producer of Classical Recordings, Evanston, 1993—; internat. broker rare instruments Strings & Things, Evanston, 1973-92; owner Vincent Skowronski: Fine Violins, Evanston, 1993—; internat. dir. mktg. and pub. rels. EB-SKO Prodns., Evanston, 1978-92; dir. media comm. E-S Mgmt., Evanston, 1985-92; instr. violin Northwestern U., 1969-71; asst. prof. violin U. Wyo., 1971-72; pvt. violin tchr., chamber music coach, lectr., master classes. Solo violinist debut Chgo. Youth Orch., 1959; soloist Chgo. Civic Orch., 1968, guest solo artist Am. Artist Gala, Nat. Puerto Rican TV, 1960; solo guest artist Young Am. Musicians Sta. WKAR-TV Mich. State U., 1966, N.Am. premiere R. Nanes' Rhapsody Pathetique for violin and orch., Chgo. Cultural Ctr., 1994, Beijing, 1994, DePaul U. Ctr., Chgo., 1994, Skowronski in Recital: 20 Years Remembered, Northwestern U., Evanston, Ill., 1994, IV Internat. Tchaikovsky Competition Commemorative Recital-Moscow Remembered: 1970-95, Evanston, Ill., 1995; featured solo artist Artist Showcase, Sta. WGN-TV Chgo., 1966-71; featured soloist Honors Concert-Northwestern U., 1966, guest solo artist A.M. Am., Sta. ABC-TV, 1977—; numerous concerts and recitals in Europe, Cen.Am., Mex. and U.S.; solo guest artist radio appearances include Continental Bank Concerts, Sta. WFMT-FM Chgo., 1983, 85-86, 88, 90, United Airlines Presents, Live!, Sta. WFMT-FM Chgo., Schumann, 1986, Szymanowski, 1987, Bloch, 1988, Saint-Saens, 1989, Grieg, 1991, Excursions in Music: The Artistry of Vincent P. Skowronski, Sta. KQED-FM San Francisco, 1979, Skowronski: Musical Giant, Interlake Profiles, Sta. WFMT-FM Chgo., 1980, Skowronski at 50: A Birthday Celebration Sta. WNIB-FM, Chgo., 1994; guest solo artist, producer, annotator Separate but Equal, 1976, All Brahms, 1977; solo artist, exec. producer, annotator Gentleman Gypsy, 1978, Strauss and Szymanowski, 1979, Franck and Szymanowski, 1982, Skowronski Alone, 1995; producer, annotator Opera Lady I, 1978, Eberley Sings Strauss, 1980, American Girl, 1983, Opera Lady II, 1984; guest performances numerous TV stas. Bd. dirs. Chgo. Youth Orch., 1973-77, v.p., 1974-77; artistic cons. Classical and Protege Symphony Orchs., Chgo., 1994—; adjudicator ice skating shows and competitions Wilmette (Ill.) Park Dist., 1985-89; guest panelist classical performance-career forum Sch. of Music, Northwestern U., Evanston, 1992, 94; guest cons. career symposium Edwin G. Foreman High Sch., Chgo., 1989; mem. mayor's founding com. Evanston Arts Coun., 1974-75. Recipient Roy Harris award Inter-Am. U., San German, P.R., 1960, award Am. Fedn. Musicians, 1961, award Soc. Am. Musicians, 1961, McCormick Found. award Chgo. Tribune, 1965, Wade Fetzer award for excellence in performance Northwestern U., 1966, award Crescendo Musical Club, 1967; selected as one of 7 violinists chosen to represent U.S. in IV Internat. Tachaikovsky Competition, Moscow, 1970. Mem. Sigma Nu, Internat. Platform Assn.

SKRAMSTAD, HAROLD KENNETH, JR., museum administrator, consultant; b. Washington, June 3, 1941; s. Harold K. and Sarah (Shroat) S.; m. Susan Chappelear, Dec. 28, 1963; children: Robert, Elizabeth. AB, George Washington U., 1963, PhD, 1971. Asst. dir. Am. studies program Smithsonian Instn., Washington, 1969-71, spl. asst. to dir. Nat. Mus. Am. History, 1971, chief spl. projects Nat. Mus. Am. History, chief exhibit programs Nat. Mus. Am. History, 1971-74; dir. Chgo. Hist. Soc., 1974-80; pres. Henry Ford Mus. and Greenfield Village, Dearborn, Mich., 1981—; mem. Nat. Coun. on Humanities, 1994; mem. mus. mgmt. adv. com. J. Paul Getty Trust, L.A., 1984-90. Chmn. bd. Met. Detroit Conv. and Visitors Bur., 1993, chmn., mem. exec. com., 1985—; trustee Coll. Art and Design, Detroit, 1981—; mem. Mich. Travel Commn., 1989—. Recipient Charles Frankel prize Nat. Endowment for the Humanities, 1992. Mem. Am. Assn. Mus. (v.p. 1984-88, accreditation commn. 1982, ethics commn. 1992-93), Smithsonian Instn. Nat. Air and Space Mus. (pub. programming adv. com. 1990—), Nat. Coun. on the Humanitites, 1994, Greater Detroit and Windsor Japan-Am. Soc. (bd. dirs. 1989—), Detroit Club, Cosmos Club (Washington). Home: Stone Mill 20900 Oakwood Blvd Dearborn MI 48124 Office: Henry Ford Mus Greenfield Village Dearborn MI 48124

SKROMME, ARNOLD BURTON, educational writer, engineering consultant; b. Zearing, Iowa, Apr. 1, 1917; s. Austin and Belle (Holmedal) S.; m. Lois Lucille Fausch, Sept. 14, 1940; children: Roger, Keith, Deborah, Erik. Agrl. Engr., Iowa State U., 1941. Engr. Firestone Tire & Rubber Co., Akron, Ohio, 1941-45, Auto Splty. Mfg., St. Joseph, Mich., 1945-46; rsch. engr. Pineapple Rsch. Inst., Honolulu, 1946-50; asst. chief engr. John Deere, Ottumwa, Iowa, 1950-55; chief engr. John Deer Spreader Works, East Moline, Ill., 1955-70; mgr. value engring. John Deere Harvester Works, East Moline, 1970-84; writer and cons. East Moline, 1984—; cons. to corps., 1984—. Author The 7-Ability Plan, 1989; holder 44 patents. Chmn. Citizens Adv. Com., Moline, 1964-66. Mem. Am. Soc. Agrl. Engrs. (v.p. 1965-68). Lutheran. Home: 2605 31st St Moline IL 61265

SKULINA, THOMAS RAYMOND, lawyer; b. Cleve., Sept. 14, 1933; s. John J. and Mary B. (Vesely) S. AB, John Carroll U., 1955; JD, Case Western Res. U., 1959, LLM, 1962. Bar: Ohio 1959, U.S. Supreme Ct. 1964, ICC 1965. Ptnr. Skulina & Stringer, Cleve., 1967-72, Riemer Oberdank & Skulina, Cleve., 1978-81, Skulina, Fillo, Walters & Negrelli, 1981-86, Skulina & McKeon, Cleve., 1986-90, Skulina & Hill, Cleve., 1990—; atty. Penn Cen. Transp. Co., Cleve., 1960-65, asst. gen. atty., 1965-78, trial counsel, 1965-76; with Consol. Rail Corp., 1976-78; tchr. comml. law Practicing Law Inst., N.Y.C., 1970; practicing arbitrator Am. Arbitration Assn., Fed. Mediation and Conciliation Svc., 1990—; arbitrator Mcpl. Securities Rulemaking Bd., 1994—, N.Y. Stock Exch., 1995—, NASD, 1996—. Contbr. articles to legal jours. Income tax and fed. fund coord. City of Warrensville Heights, Ohio, 1970-77; spl. counsel City of North Olmstead, Ohio, 1971-75, spl. counsel to Ohio Atty. Gen., 1983-93, Cleve. Charter Rev. Commn., 1988; pres. Civil Svc. Commn., Cleve., 1977-86, referee, 1986—; fact-finder State Employees Rels. Bd., Ohio, 1986—. With U.S. Army, 1959. Mem. ABA (R.R. and motor carrier com. 1988—, jr. chmn. 1989—), Soc. Profls. in Dispute Resolution, Cleve. Bar Assn. (grievance com. 1987-93, chmn. 1989-90, trustee 1993—), Ohio Bar Assn. (bd. govs. litigation sect. 1986—, negligence law com. 1989—, ethics and profl. responsibility com. 1990—), Fed. Bar Assn., Ohio Trial Lawyers Assn., Am. Arbitration Assn. (labor panel 1988—), Nat. Assn. R.R. Trial Counsel, Internat. Assn. Law and Sci., Pub. Sector Labor Rels. Assn., Indsl. Rels. Rsch. Assn. Democrat. Roman Catholic. Home: 3162 W 165th St Cleveland OH 44111-1016 Office: Skulina & Hill 24803 Detroit Rd Cleveland OH 44145-2512

SKUTT, RICHARD MICHAEL, lawyer; b. Pontiac, Mich., Sept. 25, 1947; s. Milton E. and Esther R. (Kayner) S.; m. Joe Ellen Bissel; 1 child, Sabra Morman. BS, Ea. Mich. U., 1969; JD cum laude, Wayne (Mich.) State U., 1972. Bar: Mich. 1972. Dir. Food Task Force, N.Y.C., 1974-76; atty. Food Rsch. and Action Ctr., Washington, 1976-78; dir. Mich. Legal Svcs., Detroit, 1978-82; sole practice Detroit, 1982-85; ptnr. Glotta, Rawlings & Skutt, Detroit, 1985—. Pres. LaSalle Townhouses Coop., Detroit, 1982-84. Mem. ABA, NAACP (life) NOW, Nat. Lawyers Guild, Nat. Legal Aid and Defenders Assn., Mich. Bar Assn. (past chmn. com. pro bono involvement, past chmn. standing com. civil liberties, John W. Cummiskey award), Mich. Trial Lawyers Assn. (pres.), Fed. Fly Fishers, Anglers of the Ausable, Ruffed Grouse Soc., Trout Unltd. Democrat. Home: 1507 Chateaufort Pl Detroit MI 48207-2717 Office: Glotta Rawlings & Skutt Ste 808 220 Bagley Ave Detroit MI 48226-1409

SKUTT, THOMAS JAMES, insurance company executive; b. Omaha, Nov. 1, 1930; s. Vestor Joseph and Angela (Anderson) S.; m. Jeanne Cecille Plunkett, Sept. 3, 1955; children: Mary Elizabeth Sutton, Kimberly Ann

Davis, Thomas V.J. BA, Yale U., 1952; LLB, Creighton U., 1957; post-grad., Harvard U., 1979. Ptnr. Spire, Morrow & Skutt, Omaha, 1961-69; with Mut. of Omaha, 1969—, exec. v.p., sec., 1980-81, vice chmn. bd. dirs., 1981-84, 1st vice chmn. bd. dirs., chief exec. officer, 1984-86; chmn. bd. dirs., chief exec. officer Mutual of Omaha Ins. Co., 1986-96; chmn. bd. dirs., chief exec. officer United of Omaha subs. Mut. of Omaha, 1986-96; chmn. bd. dirs. United Mutual of Omaha Life Ins. Co., 1996—; chmn. bd., dir. United of Omaha Life Ins. Co., 1996—; bd. dirs. United of Omaha, Mut. Omaha Ins. Co., Companion Life Ins. Co., United World Life Ins. Co. Past pres., selected Citizen of Yr., Mid-Am. Coun. Boy Scouts Am., 1987, 89, 93.mem. exec. bd. 1980—; mem. consultation com. SAC, Omaha, 1984; bd. dirs. Omaha Zool. Soc., 1978—, pres., 1987-88, past. bd. dirs.; gen. chmn. campaign United Way of Midlands, 1979-80, bd. dirs., 1981—; bd. dirs. Creighton U., Omaha, 1983—. Recipient Humanitarian award Nat. Conf. Christians and Jews, 1992. Mem. Greater Omaha C. of C. (bd. dirs. 1979—, chmn. 1983, past chmn.), Mpls. Club, Yale Club N.Y.C., Knights of Ak-Sar-Ben (bd. govs. 1985, King XCVI 1992). Republican. Roman Catholic. Home: 400 N 62nd St Omaha NE 68132-1955 Office: Mut Omaha Ins Co 10250 Regency Cir Ste 175 Omaha NE 68114

SLABY, FRANK, financial executive; b. South Bend, Ind., Aug. 3, 1936; s. Frank A. and Alice E. (Michalec) S.; m. Carolyn Kay Carr, Jan. 20, 1960 (div. Sept. 1977); children: Cami Lynn, Keriann; m. Kristi Lynn Courtright, May 18, 1978, 1 child, Joy Marie. BS, Ind. U., 1961, MBA, 1963; ABD, U. Cin., 1970. CLU, Chartered Fin. Cons. Prof. bus. adminstrn. Ill. Inst Tech., Chgo., 1970-72; spl. asst. to pres. St. Mary's Coll., Notre Dame, Ind., 1972-74; dean, grad. studies coll bus. adminstrn. Ind. U. Northwest, Gary, 1974-78; prof. bus. adminstrn. Valparaiso (Ind.) U., 1978-81; prof. bus. adminstrn. and exec. dir. inst. entrepreneurial edn. St. Joseph's Coll., Rensselaer, Ind., 1981-95, coord. div. of commerce, 1985-91, chair bus. adminstrn. dept., 1991-95; pres., CEO Mark-Killian Fin. Group, Rensselaer, Ind., 1978—; owner H&R Block, Kentland, Ind., 1995—; mem. adv. subcom. continuing edn. to commr. ins. State of Ind. Contbr. articles to profl. jours. Del. Rep. State Conv., Indpls., 1972-86; mem. Jasper County Rep. Ctrl. Com., 1982-90; mem. adv. coun. Union Twp. Jasper County, 1982—, chmn., 1986—; life mem. Rep. Presdl. Task Force; chair bd. dirs. Lincoln Econ. Area Devel. Area, 1992-94; mem. adv. com. SBDC, N.W., Ind. With USAF, 1954-58, USN, 1968-70, USNR, 1963-68, 70-95, ret. 1995. Named Ky. Col. by Gov. State of Ky., 1968, Ky. Admiral, 1969; Sagamore of the Wabash by Gov. State Ind., 1981. Mem. Midwest Bus. Adminstrn. Assn., Midwest Bus. Econ. Assn. (adv. com., pres., program chmn., exec. com.), Ind. U. Alumni Assn. (life), Masons, Alpha Kappa Psi, Beta Gamma (life, chpt. pres., bronze medal), Kappa Delta Rho (life, alumni pres.). Home: Stonehendge Glen 5669 W County Rd 200 N Rensselaer IN 47978-7432

SLABY, LILLIAN FRANCES, home finance counselor, real estate professional; b. Cleve., June 9, 1931; d. Bismarck Otto and Marie Theresa (Emo) Newman; m. Jack Glenn Slaby, Sept. 22, 1951; children: Lonna, Jan, Jeffrey, James, Jack. Student, Dyke Coll., 1949-50. Lic. realtor, Ohio. Home fin. counselor, real estate assoc. HGM Hilltop, Rocky River, Ohio, 1978-88, Realty One, Westlake, Ohio, 1988-91; with Riveredge Realty, Rocky River, Ohio, 1993—. Mem. Internat. Graphoanalysis Soc. (cert.), World Assn. of Document Examiners. Roman Catholic. Home: 5106 NW 16th Pl Gainesville FL 32605-3302 Office: Riveredge Realty Detroit Rd Rocky River OH 44116

SLACK, FRED PAUL, global industrial sales executive; b. Detroit, Aug. 2, 1953; s. Fred Paul and Patricia Helen (Belton) S.; m. Linda Diane Micek, July 12, 1975; children: Lauren M., Ian F. BA in internat. rels., Northwestern U., 1975; MBA in indsl. econs., U. Ill., 1981. Dir. internat. sales Dumond Co., Downers Grove, Ill., 1976-81; v.p. project sales dept. Dept St, Downers Grove, Ill., 1983-85; fgn. svc. officer Dept. State, Washington, 1981-83; v.p. sales & mktg. Rockware Internat., Oklahoma City, Okla., 1985-89; dep. dir.-internat. Fairbanks Scales, Kansas City, Mo., 1989-92; v.p. internat. sales Rice Lake (Wis.) Weighing Systems, 1992-93, v.p. sales, 1994—. Mem. polit. action com. Rice Lake Sch. Bd., 1995. Mem. MENSA, Internat. Soc. Weighing and Measurement. Republican. Roman Catholic. Office: Rice Lake Weighing Systems 230 W Coleman Rice Lake WI 54868

SLACK, JERALD DAVID, adjutant general of Wisconsin, civil engineer; b. Peoria, Ill., Feb. 14, 1936; s. Clarence E. and Lois M. (Pearson) S.; m. Sherill Ann Cordts, Mar. 26, 1959; children: Ann, Sara Slack Lenz, John Cordts. BS in Civil Engring., Bradley U., 1959. Profl. engr., Wis. Commd. 2d lt. USAF, 1961, advanced through grades to maj. gen., 1990, vice wing comdr. 128th Tactical Fighter Wing, 1983-85, dir. ops. Wis. Air Nat. Guard, 1985-87, chief of staff Wis. Air Nat. Guard, 1987-89; adj. gen. Wis. Dept. Mil. Affairs, Madison, 1989—; chief engr. Wis. Dept. Natural Resources, Madison, 1973-86; adminstr. Div. Facilities Mgmt., Madison, 1986-89. Decorated Legion of Merit, Meritorious Svc. medal. Mem. Nat. Guard Assn. U.S., Adj. Gen. Assn., Wis. Nat. Guard Assn. Unitarian. Office: Mil Affairs Dept PO Box 8111 2400 Wright St Madison WI 53708-8111

SLADE, ROY, artist, college president, museum director; b. Cardiff, U.K., July 14, 1933; came to U.S., 1967, naturalized, 1975; s. David Trevor and Millicent (Stone) S. N.D.D., Cardiff Coll. Art, 1954; A.T.D., U. Wales, 1954; D of Arts, Art Inst. So. Calif., 1994. Tchr. art and crafts Heolgam High Sch., Wales, 1956-60; lectr. art Clarendon Coll., Nottingham, Eng., 1960-64; sr. lectr. fine art Leeds Coll. Art, Eng., 1964-67; prof. painting Corcoran Sch. Art, Washington, 1967-68, assoc. dean, 1969-70, dean, 1970-77; dir. Corcoran Gallery of Art, Washington, 1972-77; pres., dir. Cranbrook Acad. Art, Bloomfield Hills, Mich., 1977-94; sr. lectr. Leeds Coll. Art, Eng. 1968-69; vis. Boston Mus. Fine Arts, 1970. Exhibited one-man shows Howard Roberts Gallery, Cardiff, Wales, 1958, New Art Ctr., London, 1960, U. Birmingham, 1964, 69, Herbert Art Gallery and Mus., Coventry, 1964, Va. State Art League, 1967, Mus. of Arts and Crafts, Columbus, Ga., 1968, Jefferson Place Gallery, Washington, 1968, 70, 72, 73, Park Sq. Gallery, Leeds, 1969, St. Mary's Coll., Md., 1971, Guelph U., Ont., Can., 1971, Hood Coll., 1974, Pyramid Gallery, Washington, 1976, Robert Kidd Gallery, 1981, 92, Herman Miller, Inc., Mich., 1985; group shows in U.K., Washington, Can.; represented in permanent collections Arts Council Gt. Brit., Contemporary Art Soc., Nuffield Found., Ministry of Works, Eng., Brit. Embassy, Washington, Brit. Overseas Airways Corp., U. Birmingham, Wakefield City Art Gallery, Clarendon Coll., Cadbury Bros., Ltd., Eng., Lord Ogmore, Local Edn. Authorities. Mem. D.C. Commn. on Arts.; bd. dirs. Artists for Environment Found., Nat. Assn. Schs. Art; chmn. Nat. Council Art Adminstrs., 1981. Served with Brit. Army, 1954-56. Decorated knight 1st class Order of White Rose (Finland), Royal Order of Polar Star (Sweden); recipient award Welsh Soc., Phila., 1974, Gov.'s Arts Orgn. award, 1988; Fulbright scholar, 1967-68. Mem. Nat. Soc. Lit. and Arts, AIA (hon. Detroit chpt.), Assn. Art Mus. Dirs. (hon.). Home: PO Box 48 Harsens Island MI 48028-0048

SLADEK, MARTHA J., lawyer; b. Columbus, Ohio, Sept. 24, 1946; d. Keith Lloyd and Phyllis Elaine (Clayton) McClatchie; m. Don Sladek, Nov. 6, 1970. BS in Edn., Kent State U., 1968; MA in Journalism, Ohio State U., 1969; JD, Loyola U. Sch. Law, Chgo., 1994. News and talk show producer, 1969-75; dir. pub. relations Ill. State Office Tourism, Chgo., 1975-79; pub. relations supr. AT&T, Chgo., 1979-86; dir. univ. relations Northeastern Ill. U., Chgo., 1986-93; cons. Kraft Co., Glenview, Northbrook, Ill., 1986, AT&T, Chgo., 1986, Ill. Nature Conservancy, OpenLands Project, Downers Grove, Park Dist., 1989-91 (pro bono). Author: Two Weeks With the Psychic Surgeons, 1976. Active various polit. campaigns DuPage and Cook Counties, Ill.; bd. dirs. Ill. Coll. Rels. Coun., 1986-93, DuPage Environ. Awareness Ctr., 1988—, chairperson, 1995—. Mem. DuPage Bar Assn. (1st v.p.), DuPage Assn. Women Lawyers, Ill. State Bar Assn. Presbyterian.

SLADEN, BERNARD JACOB, psychologist; b. Chgo., Mar. 30, 1952; s. Mayer and Anne S. BA, U. Ill., 1974; PhD, Washington U., St. Louis, 1979. Intern U. Minn., Mpls., 1976-77; psychologist Mental Health Ctr., Inc., Ft. Wayne, Ind., 1978-80, Hines (Ill.) VA Hosp., 1980—; pvt. practice psychology Chgo., 1982—; asst. prof. Northwestern U. Med. Sch., Chgo., 1983-92; cons. Assocs. in Adolescent Psychiatry Mental Health Resources, Forest Park, Ill., 1985—, Assoc. in Clin. Psychology, Westchester, Ill., 1985-87. VA traineeship, 1974-76; NIMH fellow, 1977-78. Mem. APA, Am. Orthopsychiat. Assn. Home: 421 W Melrose St Apt 12 D Chicago IL 60657-3806 Office: 421 W Melrose St Apt 12 B Chicago IL 60657-3809

SLAGTER, KEITH EUGENE, manufacturing company executive; b. Pella, Iowa, Apr. 1, 1966; s. Marion and Cordillia June Slagter. Technician Pella Motor Co., 1984; painter, welder, fabricator Ring-O-Matic, 1985-87; designer Vermeer Mfg. Co., Pella, 1987—. Patentee (4) in field. Mem. Tin Car Club. Republican. Christian Ref. Ch. Office: Vermeer Mfg Co PO Box 200 Pella IA 50219-0200

SLATER, WILLIAM ADCOCK, social services organization executive; b. Kiangsu, People's Republic China, July 26, 1933; (parents U.S. citizens); s. Paul Raymond and Daisy Roberta (Butcher) S.; m. Karen C. Crutchfield, Sept. 4, 1956; children: Kathleen Ann, Bryan Paul. BA in Sociology and History, Wichita State U., 1958; MSW, Denver U., 1960. Juvenile probation officer Hennepin County Dept. Ct. Svcs., Mpls., 1960-63, program dir., 1963-65, dir. social svcs., 1965-67; clin. dir. St. Cloud (Minn.) Children's Home, 1967-70; exec. dir. Gillis Ctr., Women's Christian Assn., Kansas City, Mo., 1970-88, mng. exec. dir., 1988-95; team leader Coun. on Accreditation Svcs. for Families and Children, Washington, 1975—; presenter various child welfare confs., Okla., Kans., Mo., 1980-88; mem. Mo. Residential Treatment Task Force, Mo. Licensing Standards Task Foprce; mem. levels of care com. Kans. Dept. Social Svcs.; mem. EEO panels Fed. Exec. Bd., 1978, 79; mem. mental health tour People to People, People's Republic China, 1990. Contbr. articles to profl. jours. Mem. Speaker's Bur., United Way Kansas City, 1970—, chmn. agy. rels. com., agys. div., mem. homeless com.; mem. adv. bd. Bingham Jr. High Sch., Kansas City, 1984-86. With U.S. Army, 1953-55. Mem. Nat. Assn. Social Workers, Acad. Cert. Social Workers, Mo. Assn. Social Welfare, Mo. Child Care Assn. (bd. dirs. 1972-74, 84-88), Kans. Assn. Lic. Pvt. Child Care Agys., Children's Residential Treatment Assn. Kansas City (chmn.), Child Welfare League Am. (steering com. midwest region, nat. adv. coun. to exec. dir. 1976-80), Waldo Bus. Assn. (v.p.), Alpha Kappa Delta. Mem. Christian Ch. (Disciples of Christ). Home: 9328 Woodson Dr Shawnee Mission KS 66207-2437 Office: Women's Chrstian Assn 8150 Wornall Rd Kansas City MO 64114-5806

SLATKIN, LEONARD EDWARD, conductor, music director, pianist; b. L.A., Sept. 1, 1944; s. Felix Slatkin and Eleanor Aller; m. Linda Hohenfeld, Mar. 29, 1986. Began violin study, 1947; piano study with, Victor Aller and Selma Cramer, 1955; composition study with, Castelnuovo-Tedesco, 1958; viola study with, Sol Schoenbach, 1959; conducting study with, Felix Slatkin, Amerigo Marino and Ingolf Dahl; student, Ind. U., 1962, L.A. City Coll., 1963, Juilliard Sch.; student (Irving Berlin fellow in musical direction), beginning 1964; student of, Jean Morel and Walter Susskind. Founder, music dir., condr. St. Louis Symphony Youth Orch., 1969—, mus. advisor, 1979-80; mus. dir., condr. St. Louis Symphony Orch., 1979-96; mus. dir. Nat. Symphony Orch., Washington, 1996—; current mgmt. ICM Artist, Ltd., Harold Holt, Ltd., Konzertdirektion/Schmidt. Conducting debut as asst. condr., Youth Symphony of N.Y., Carnegie Hall, 1966; asst. condr., Juilliard Opera Theater and Dance Dept., 1967, St. Louis Symphony Orch., 1968-71, assoc. condr., 1971-74; guest conductor Concertgebouw, Royal Danish Orch., Tivoli, English Chamber Orch., BBC Manchester, London Philarmonic, London Synphony Orch., Philarmonia Orch., Nat. Orch. Paris, Stockholm, Oslo, Goetborg, Scottish Nat. Orch., NHK Tokyo, Israel, Berlin, Vienna State Opera, Lyric Opera Chgo., Stuttgart Opera and throughout the world; debut with Chgo. Symphony Orch., 1974, N.Y. Philharmonic, 1974, Phila. Orch., 1974, European debut with Royal Philharmonic Orch., 1974, debut with USSR orchs., 1976-77, Tokyo debut, 1986, Met. Opera debut, 1991; prin. guest condr. Minn. Orch., beginning 1974; summer artistic dir., 1979-89, music dir., New Orleans Philharmonic Symphony Orch., 1977-78, artistic dir. Great Woods, 1990; artistic adminstr. Blossom, 1991; composer: The Raven, Dialogue for Two Cellos and Orchestra, (string quartets) Extensions 1, 2, 3, 4; numerous recordings for RCA, Angel EMI, Vox. Telarc, Philips, Warner Bros. and others. Recipient 2 Grammy awards for Prokofiev Symphony No. 5 with St. Louis Symphony Orch. Nat. Acad. Rec. Arts and Scis., 1985, Declaration of Honor in Silver Austrian Govt., 1986, 5 Honorary Doctorates. Mem. Nat. Acad. Rec. Arts and Scis. (Chgo. chpt. bd. govs.). Office: St Louis Symphony Orch Powell Symphony Hall 718 N Grand Blvd Saint Louis MO 63103-1011 also: National Symphony Orchestra John F Kennedy Ctr Washington DC 20566

SLAUGHTER, JAMES LUTHER, III, graphic designer; b. Jenkins, Ky., Aug. 22, 1944; s. James Luther and Loretta (Winchester) S.; m. Susan Lee Brundige, Sept. 16, 1972. BS in Graphic Design, U. Cin., 1967. Graphic designer Shaw Studio Advt., Cin., 1967-69, E.F. MacDonald Co., Dayton, Ohio, 1969-70; ptnr., designer Slaughter & Slaughter, Inc., Cin., 1970—; cons. NIOSH, Cin., 1979; adj. faculty mem. No. Ky. U., Highland Heights, 1978-80. Contbr. articles to profl. jours. Mem. Concours Com. Arthritis Found., Cin., 1980-86; trustee Unity Ctr., Cin., 1986-89, 90-93; bd. dirs. Appalachian Cmty. Devel. Assn., Cin., 1985-86, A Day in Eden, Cin., 1986-88, Eastwood Cmty. Urban Redevel. Corp., 1991-93. Recipient Silver and Bronze medals The Advt. Club, Cin., 1980, Design Excellence award Internat. Typographic Composition Assn., 1980. Mem. Bus. and Profl. Advt. Assn. (workshop chmn. 1986), The Art Dirs. Club (Merit award 1970-85), Am. Inst. Graphic Arts, Nat. Model RR Assn.

SLEGMAN, BETTY HARVEY, publicist; b. N.Y.C., Aug. 19, 1922; d. Gerald Joseph and Dorothy (Bienenstok) Horvitz; m. Robert Morris Slegman, Sept. 9, 1946; children: John Robert, Dorothy Slegman Brewer, Ann Slegman Isenberg. BA, U. Mich., 1944. Writer UPI, N.Y.C., 1944-46; ptnr. Slegman, Laner Pub. Rels., Shawnee Mission, Kans., 1980—; free lance writer, Shawnee Mission, 1948—, writer, broadcaster sta. KCMO, radio, Shawnee Mission, 1984-85. Pres. Shawnee Mission Area PTA, 1964-65; v.p. Girl Scouts U.S., Kansas City, Mo., 1952-60; v.p. Am Field Svc., Kansas City, 1965-67; mem. Nelson Atkins Mus. Art, Soc. Fellows. Recipient citation Girl Scouts Am., 1960. Mem. Oakwood Country Club.

SLEMMONS, ROBERT SHELDON, architect; b. Mitchell, Nebr., Mar. 12, 1922; s. M. Garvin and K. Fern (Borland) S.; AB, U. Nebr., 1947, BArch, 1948; m. Dorothy Virginia Herrick, Dec. 16, 1945; children: David (dec.), Claire, Jennifer, Robert, Timothy. Draftsman, Davis & Wilson, archs., Lincoln, Nebr., 1947-48; chief designer, project arch. Office of Kans. State Arch., Topeka, 1948-54; asso. John A. Brown, arch., Topeka, 1954-56; partner Brown & Slemmons, arch., Topeka, 1956-69; v.p. Brown-Slemmons-Kreuger, archs., Topeka, 1969-73; owner Robert S. Slemmons, A.I.A. & Assos., archs., Topeka, 1973—. Cons. Kans. State Office Bldg. Commn., 1956-57; lectr. in design U. Kans., 1961; bd. dirs. Kaw Valley State Bank & Trust Co., Topeka, 1978-92. Bd. dirs. Topeka Civic Symphony Soc., 1950-60, Midstates Retirement Cmtys., Inc., 1986-92, Topeka Festival Singers; cons. Ministries for Aging, Inc., Topeka, 1984—; mem. Topeka Bd. Bldg. and Fire Appeals, Kans. Com. for Employer Support of the Guard and Res., With USNR, 1942-48. Mem. AIA (Topeka pres. 1955-56, Kans. dir. 1957-58, mem. com. on housing, com. for hist. resources), Internat. Conf. Bldg. Ofcls., Topeka Art Guild (pres. 1950), Am. Corrections Assn., Kans. Coun. Chs. (dir. 1961-62), Shawnee County Hist. Soc. Topeka, Greater Topeka C. of C. (mil. affairs task force), Downtown Topeka, Inc. (v.p. 1992—), Topeka, Shawnee County Libr. (dir. friends of the libr.), St. Andrews Soc. (pres.), SAR (v.p state soc., pres. chpt.), U. Nebr. Alumni Assn. (life), Band Alumni Assn., Kiwanis (pres. 1966-67), Topeka Knife and Fork Club. Presbyterian (elder, deacon, chmn. trustees). Prin. archtl. works include: Kans. State Office Bldg., 1954, Topeka Presbyn. Manor, 1960-74, Meadowlark Hills Retirement Cmty., 1979, Shawnee County Adult Detention Facility, 1985. Office: Slemmons Assocs Archs 534 S Kansas Ave Topeka KS 66603-3406

SLETNER, BARBARA MARIE, credit professional; b. Eau Claire, Wis., Nov. 30, 1939; d. Edwin Conval and Ida Elizabeth (Peterson) Sletner; m. Robert A. Skifstad, Dec. 7, 1957 (div. 1977); children: Steven, Sindi, Scott, Staci and Shari (twins). Grad. high sch., Eau Claire. Sales mgr. Genie Sales-Tupperware, Eau Claire, 1966-68; underwriting clk. John F. Nauss & Assocs./Mut. of Omaha, Eau Claire, 1968-70; office mgr. Skoglund Advt., Eau Claire, 1970-72, Janeway Real Estate, Eau Claire, 1977-78; credit mgr. Farm House Foods, Eau Claire, 1978-84; exec. sec. Chippewa County Coun. AODA, CHippewa Falls, Wis., 1984-85; credit mgr. Aslesen's, Mpls., 1985-86, Northwest Racquet, Swim and Health Clubs, Inc., Mpls., 1986-95; sr. credit rep. ChemRex Inc., 1995—; presenter workshops on single parenting; drafter grassroots programs for schs. and single parents Internat. Conv. Parents Without Ptnrs., Chgo., 1984. Bd. dirs., sec., v.p., leader Camp Fire Girls, Eau Claire, 1972-79, dir. C.F. Day Camp, 1977. Recipient Seaton Nat. award Camp Fire Girls, Eau Claire, 1977, Community Svc. award I-94 WEAQ Radio, Eau Claire, 1983. Mem. Nat. Assn. Credit Mgrs. (chair Mpls. chpt. 1985-86), Nat. Assn. Credit Mgrs. (vice-chair Mpls. chpt. 1985), Parents Without Ptnrs. (chpt. pres. 1977-89, v.p. Northland Regional Coun. 1983-85, Single Parent of Yr. 1983). Lutheran. Home: 1837 Deer Hills Trl Eagan MN 55122-2252

SLEVIN, TARA MARGARUITE, volunteer coordinator; b. N.Y.C., Apr. 16, 1971; d. James Anthony and Teresa Ann (Walsh) S. BA, U. Nebr. Vol. coord. Jennie Edmundson Hosp., Council Bluffs, Iowa, 1989-94, asst. dir. vol. svc., 1994—; advisor for teen coun., Jennie Edmundson Hosp., Council Bluffs, Iowa, 1989—; active Omaha 2000, Vol. Outreach Task Force, Omaha, 1995—. Mem. Am. Soc. Dirs. Vol. Svcs., Iowa Dirs. of Vol. Svcs. (treas., mem. 1994—), Nebr. Soc. for Vol. Svcs., Midplains Dirs. (teen coord. chair 1994—), Omaha Panhellenic (card file chmn. 1995-96), Zeta Tau Alpha Alumni Assn. (v.p. 1995-96, pres. 1996—). Republican. Roman Catholic. Home: 3209 Renner Dr Council Bluffs IA 51501

SLICHTER, D.J., electrical engineer; b. Erie, Pa., Sept. 6, 1940. BSEE, Pa. State U., 1966. Grad. apprentice GE, Erie, 1960-66; supervising engr. Eaton Corp., Milw., 1966—. Mem. IEEE. Office: Eaton Corp 4265 N 30th St Milwaukee WI 53216-1821

SLINEY, JAMES GILMORE, JR., laser electro-optic engineer, educator; b. Evanston, Ill., Jan. 16, 1940; s. James Gilmore and Lauretta Margaret (Bremner) S.; m. Nancy Ann Calabretta, Oct. 16, 1976 (div. Dec. 1990, annulled Jan. 1996); children: Katherine Calabretta, Rachel Calabretta. AB in Philosophy, Springhill Coll., 1964; BS in Physics, U. So. Calif., 1968, MS in Physics, 1970, MSEE, 1975, PhD in Elec. Engring., 1978; STM, Jesuit Sch. Theology, 1974. Cert. community coll. credential, Calif. Tchr. math. Bellarmine Coll. Prep. Sch., San Jose, Calif., 1965-67; rsch. asst. U. So. Calif., L.A., 1973-77; work study fellow Aerospace Corp., L.A., 1975-77; specialist on tech. staff Aerojet Electro Systems Co., Azusa, Calif., 1977-82; rsch. engr. Allied Techs., Allied Corp., Westlake Village, Calif., 1982-84; sr. optical engr. Rocketdyne div. Rockwell Internat., Canoga Park, Calif., 1984-91; instr. laser and electro-optics Moorpark (Calif.) Coll., 1985-91; assoc. prin. engr. Collins Commercial Avionics, Cedar Rapids, Iowa, 1991—. Patentee flexible, resilient anti-contamination baffle. Mem. IEEE, Optical Soc. Am., Laser Inst. Am., Sigma Xi. Home: 460 Beverly St Robins IA 52328-9735 Office: Collins Commercial Avionics 400 Collins Rd NE Cedar Rapids IA 52498-0001

SLOAN, JEANETTE PASIN, artist; b. Chgo., Mar. 18, 1946; d. Antonio and Anna (Baggio) Pasin; children: Eugene Blakely, Anna Jeanette. BFA, Marymount Coll., Tarrytown, N.Y., 1967; MFA, U. Chgo., 1969. Exhibited in one-woman shows G.W. Einstein Gallery, N.Y.C., 1977-85, Landfall Press Gallery, Chgo., N.Y.C., 1978, 87, Frumkin & Struve Gallery, Chgo., 1981, Roger Ransay Gallery, Chgo., 1987, 89, 92, Adams-Middleton Gallery, Dallas, 1987, Tatischeff Gallery, Santa Monica, Calif., 1989, Steven Scott Gallery, Balt., 1989, Butters Gallery, Portland, Oreg., 1989, 91, 94, 96, Tatischeff Gallery, N.Y.C., 1995, Ouarter Editions, N.Y.C., 1995, Elliot Smith Gallery, St. Louis, 1994, Peltz Gallery, Milw., 1994-95; represented in permanent collections Art Mus. Chgo., Cleve. Mus. Art, Ill. State Mus., Indpls. Mus. Art, Canton (Ohio) Art Inst., Ball State Bus., Mpls., Inst. Art, Fogg Mus. Harvard U., Yale U. Art Gallery, Snite Mus. U. Notre Dame, Met. Mus. Art, N.Y.C., Herbert F. Johnson Mus. Cornell U., Ithaca, N.Y.; exhibited in group shows. Studio: 535 Keystone Ave River Forest IL 60305-1611

SLOAN, TOM, state legislator; m. Gail Sloan. Rep. dist. 45 State of Kans., Lawrence; comm. cons. in field. Republican. Office: So Farmers Assn 824 N Palm St North Little Rock AR 72114-5134*

SLOANE, PHYLLIS LESTER, artist; b. Worcester, Mass., Sept. 27, 1921; d. Nathan and Goldie (Pollock) Lester; m. David J. Sloane, Nov. 25, 1943 (div. July 1986); children: Ginna, Nathaniel, Lisa. BFA, Carnegie Mellon U., 1943. Freelance product designer N.Y.C., 1944-45; co-owner PDA Design Co., Cleve., 1946-48, Sloane O'Sickey Gallery, Cleve., 1970-72; gallery dir. New Orgn. for Visual Arts, Cleve., 1972-74; freelance artist Cleve., 1974—. One woman shows include Gallery 200, Cleve. Play House Gallery, 1972, 74, 76, 81, 83, 85, Columbus, Ohio, 1974, 78, Mansfield (Ohio) Art Ctr., 1977, 96, Wooster (Ohio) Coll. Art Mus., 1978, Massillon (Ohio) Mus., 1979, Janus Gallery, Santa Fe, 1981, Women's City Club, 1982, 88, Florence O'Donnell Wasmer Gallery, Ursiline Coll., 1987, Frank Croft Fine Art, Santa Fe, 1987, 88, 96, William Engle Gallery, Indpls., 1987, 88, Bonfoey Gallery, Cleve., 1990, 92, 94, 96; group shows include Mansfield (Ohio) Art Ctr., 1984, 93, Pratt Graphics Ctr., N.Y., 1986, Calif. Coll. Arts & Crafts, 1987, Oreg. Sch. Arts & Crafts, Portland, 1987, Hudson River Mus., Yonkers, N.Y., 1987, Cleve. Ctr. Contemporary Art, 1987, Sigma Gallery, N.Y., 1990; included in permanent collections including Cleve. Mus. Art, Hunterdon Art Ctr., Clinton, N.J., Phila. Art Mus., Massillon (Ohio) Mus., Rutgers (N.J.) U. Archives, Cleve. Pub. Libr., N.Mex. Mus. Fine Arts, Santa Fe, U. N.Mex. Art Mus. Recipient Purchase award Hunterdon Nat. Print Exhbn., 1977, Print Club of Phila., 1977, Graphics award Cleve. Mus. Art, 1978, Cleve. award Okla. Nat. Exhbn., 1981, City of Cleve. Visual Arts award, 1982, Purchase award Boston Printmakers, 1984, 1st Prize, Miami Internat. Print Biennial, 1984, Nationwide Ins. award Ohio Watercolor Soc., 1984, Purchase award Anderson Winter Show, 1985, N.C. Print and Drawing Ann., 1985. Mem. Boston Printmakers, Cleve. Soc. for Contemporary Art, Print Club Cleve. (trustee 1991—). Home: 13800 Shaker Blvd Apt 1204 Cleveland OH 44120-1576

SLOCUM, ROSEMARIE R., physician management search consultant; b. Port Arthur, Tex., Dec. 19, 1948; d. Edly and Ella (McNeely) Raccard; m. James Rubenstein; 1 child, Blair Ashton. BS, La. State U., Baton Rouge, 1971. Cert. tchr., La. Edn. specialist La. Dept. Occupational Standards, Baton Rouge, 1971-74; account exec. Uarco, Inc., Baton Rouge, 1974-77; owner, broker Rosemarie Slocum Real Estate, Baton Rouge, 1977-91; physician recruiter MSI, New Orleans, 1985-86; assoc. dir. physician recruitment Physician Search, Inc., Fairfax, Va., 1986-88; spl. cons. Caswell/Winters Physician Search Cons., Milw., 1988-89; v.p. U.S. Med. Search, Inc. subs. of Caswell/Winters, Milw., 1988-89; dir. physician recruitment/mktg. East Range Clinics, Ltd., Virginia, Minn., 1989-91; pres. Rosemarie Slocum, Inc., Virginia, Minn., 1991—. Office: RSI 817 S 5th Ave Virginia MN 55792-2804

SLODERBECK, PHILLIP EUGENE, entomologist; b. Marion, Ind., Aug. 31, 1952; s. Burnham Doyle and Levina Elizabeth (Lightle) S.; m. Paula Adelle Bertin, July 12, 1975; children: Caroline Elizabeth, Christina Marie. BS in Biology Edn., Purdue U., 1974, MS in Entomology, 1977; PhD in Entomology, U. Ky., 1981. Survey entomologist U. Ky., Lexington, 1977-81; extension specialist Kans. State U., Garden City, 1981—. Contbr. articles, reports, bulls. to profl. publs. Pres. Jaycees, Garden City, 1984-85; treas. Garden City Ambucs, 1992-93. Recipient Horizon award Alpha Rho chpt. Epsilon Sigma Phi, 1984. Mem. Entomol. Soc. Am., Bd. Cert. Entomologists (pres. Mid-Am. chpt. 1992-93). Home: 1606 E Johnson St Garden City KS 67846-4746 Office: Kansas State U 1501 E Fulton Ter Garden City KS 67846-6165

SLOGGY, JOHN EDWARD, engineering executive; b. Mpls., Aug. 2, 1952; s. William Edwin and Dorthea Ann (Darling) S.; m. Vivian Arlene Gilles, Aug. 9, 1975; children: Cheryl Ann, JoAnna Ellen, Laura Ann, William Harrison, Sarah Ellen, Andrew Harrison. Assoc. in Mech. Design, Superior Inst. of Tech., 1974; BS in Indsl. Tech. summa cum laude, U. Wis., Stout, 1976; MBA, U. Wis., 1982. Mech. design engr. Gilman Engring., Janesville, Wis., 1977-79, sr. mech. design engr., 1979-80; sys. project mgr. Giddings & Lewis, Janesville, 1982-84; sr. project engr. Black & Decker, Fayetteville, N.C., 1984-85, mfg. engring. supr., 1985-86, mfg. engring. mgr., 1986-89, adv. mfg. engring. mgr., 1989-90, productivity engring. mgr., 1990-92; modernization engring. mgr., 1992-93; engring. mgr. Gen. Corp., Marion, Ind., 1993—. V.p. country club North Cmty. Assn., Fayetteville, 1985—, Cmty. Watch Assn., Fayetteville, 1985—; advisor PTA, Fayetteville, 1986—. Mem. Soc. Mfg. Engrs., Am. Soc. Quality Control, Soc. Plastics Engrs., Am. Soc. Value Engrs., Am. Soc. Materials, Inst. Indsl. Engrs., N.Am. Diecasting Assn.

SLONIM, ARNOLD ROBERT, biochemist, physiologist; b. Springfield, Mass., Feb. 15, 1926; s. Sam and Esther (Kantor) S.; married, 1951; 3 children; m. 1984. BS, Tufts Coll., 1947; AM, Boston U., 1948; PhD, Johns Hopkins U., 1953. Rsch. asst. nutrition Sterling-Winthrop Rsch. Inst., Rensselaer, N.Y., 1948-49; rsch. asst. pharmacology George Washington U. Med. Sch., Washington, 1949-50; rsch. asst., jr. instr. biology Johns Hopkins U., Balt., 1950-53; rsch. assoc. chemotherapy Children's Cancer Rsch. Found. Harvard U., Boston, 1953-54; head chem. lab. Lynn (Mass.) Hosp., 1955-56; various positions including chief applied ecology, supervisory rsch. biologist, physiologist & biochemist, phys. sci. adminstr., biotech. mgr. Aerospace Med. Rsch. Lab., Wright-Patterson AFB, Ohio, 1956-86; cons., pres. ARSLO Assocs., Columbus, Ohio, 1987—; lectr. Mass. Sch. Physiotherapy, Boston, 1955-56, Antioch U., 1984-85; mem. internat. bioastronautics com. Internat. Astronautical Fedn., 1966—; mem. environ. carcinogens program Internat. Agy. for Rsch. on Cancer/WHO, Paris, 1981—. Mem. com. on biol. handbooks Fedn. Am. Socs. for Exptl. Biology, 1966-71; mem. editorial bd. Aerospace Medicine, 1967-71; contbr. articles to profl. jours. Served with USN, 1944-46. Mem. Aerospace Med. Assn., Am. Soc. Biochemistry and Molecular Biology, Am. Physiol. Soc., N.Y. Acad. Sci., Internat. Acad. Aviation and Space Medicine, Sigma Xi, Masons, Scottish Rite, Shriners. Office: 630 Cranfield Pl Columbus OH 43213-3407

SLOTKOWSKI, KENNETH GEORGE, electronics engineer; b. Detroit, Feb. 22, 1942; s. Albin Lambert and Laddie M. (Nyklewicz) S.; m. Elaine F. Donaldson, Apr. 1, 1966 (dec. Apr. 1979); children: Kenneth George, Kurt James; m. Marcia Ellen Nowicki, May 29, 1993. BSEE, Lawrence Tech. U., Southfield, Mich., 1963; MBA, Wayne State U., 1966. Project engr. Bendix Aerospace, Ann Arbor, Mich., 1967-68; chief engr. Auto-Flo Co., Redford, Mich., 1968-70; product mgr. Masco Corp., Taylor, Mich., 1970-71; product design engr. Body Engring. Ford Motor Co., Dearborn, Mich., 1971-94, tech. specialsit EESE/AVT, 1994—. Patentee automatic headlamp dimmers, decoding circuit, others. Mem. IEEE (sr.), Audio Engr. Soc., Ford Yacht Club.

SLOWINSKI, THOMAS FRANK, priest; b. Detroit, Nov. 23, 1955; s. John Walter and Pauline (Januszczak) S. BA in History, Sacred Heart Sem. Coll., 1977; MDiv, St. John Provincial Sem., 1981. Ordained priest, Roman Cath. Ch., 1981. Deacon intern St. Agatha Ch., Redford, Mich., 1981-82; assoc. pastor St. Sylvester Ch., Warren, Mich., 1982-85, St. Edith Ch., Livonia, Mich., 1985-88, St. Anastasia Ch., Troy, Mich., 1988-90; pastor St. Agatha Ch., Redford, Mich., 1990—; seminary prof. Sacred Heart Sem., Detroit, 1985, 90, St. John Provincial Sem., Plymouth, Mich., 1984-85; advocate and defender of the bond Met. Tribunal, Detroit, 1981-86. Pres., bd. dirs. Living Concepts, Inc., Livonia, 1988—. Lt. USNR, 1988—. Mem. Mil. Chaplains Assn., Priests Conf. for Polish Affairs, Founders Soc. Detroit Inst. of Arts, Redford C. of C., Assn. Death Educators and Counselors. Home and Office: 19750 Beech Daly Rd Redford MI 48240-1348

SLUTSKY, JEFF L., marketing executive. AB, Ind. U., 1977. Exec. v.p. H.P.N. Advt., Ft. Wayne, Ind., 1977-80; pres. Streetfighter Mktg. Inc., Columbus, Ohio, 1980—; bd. dirs. Ohio Speakers Forum, Columbus. Contbg. author: Street Fighting, 1983, Streetsmart Teleselling, 1990, How To Get Clients, 1992, Streetfighter Marketing, 1994. Contbr. WOSU Pub. TV, Columbus, 1993. Mem. Nat. Speakers Assn. (cert.). Office: Retail Mktg Inst 467 Waterbury Ct Columbus OH 43230-5313

SMALL, BRUCE W., sales and marketing executive; b. Waltham, Mass., Oct. 3, 1950; s. W. Harold Jr. and Ruth M. (Lovejoy) S.; m. Ursula E. Briggs, Sept. 7, 1974. BA in English, BA in Psychology, Gettysburg Coll., 1972. Cert. hotel sales exec. Sales mgr. Boston (Mass.) Statler Hilton, 1972-75; dir. of sales Logan Airport Hilton, Boston, 1975-77, Dallas (Tex.) Hilton, 1977-80, Fontainebleau Hilton, Miami Beach, Fla., 1980-81; dir. of mktg. Fontainebleau Hilton, Miami Beach, 1981-84; dir. sales and mktg. Hyatt Regency Grand Cypress, Orlando, Fla., 1984-88; corp. dir. sales and mktg. pre-openings and acquistions Hyatt Hotels Corp., Chgo., 1988-92, divisional dir. sales and mktg., 1992-96; dir. sales and mktg. nat. sales force Hyatt Hotels and Resorts, Chgo., 1996—. Mem. Profl. Conv. Mgmt. Assn. (assoc.), Am. Soc. Assn. Execs. (assoc.), Relig. Conv. Mgmt. Assn. (assoc.), Mtg. Planners Internat. (assoc.). Office: Hyatt Hotels & Resorts Nat Sales Force 200 W Madison Chicago IL 60606

SMALL, DEBRA JEAN, public service professional; b. Bloomington, Ill., June 27, 1960; d. Jerry Gene and H. Corrine (Thomas) S. Student, Lincoln Coll., Bloomington, 1983. Cert. Life Office Mgmt. Assn. File clk. Ill. Farm Bur., Bloomington, 1978-82, order clk., 1982-87, acquistions clk., 1987-91, pub. svc. asst., 1991—. Libr. Colfax (Ill.) Chrisition Ch., 1992—. Home: 201 W Main Colfax IL 61728 Office: IAA & Affiliated Libr PO Box 2901 Bloomington IL 61702

SMALL, MARVIN BURTON, retired industrial chemicals company executive; b. Chgo., Apr. 9, 1926; s. Harry William and Janet (Udell) S.; m. Marion Isabel Greenwald, Aug. 21, 1949 (div. Aug. 1981); m. Doris Emil Malecek, Nov. 21, 1982; children: Richard, Ronald, Davida, Pamela, William, Deborah. BS in Chemistry, Ill. Inst. Tech., Chgo., 1950. With Velsicol Chems. Corp., Chgo., 1950-52, City Svc. Oil Co., Chgo., 1952-54, Stauffer Chems., Chgo., 1954-56, Big Ben Chems. & Solvents (Ashland Oil), Chgo., 1956-72, Gt. Lakes Solvents, Chgo., 1970-72, EMCO, North Chicago, (Il., 1972-78; owner B&D Indsl. Chems., Vernon Hills, Ill., 1978—. Pres. Brotherhood, Nroth Shore Congregation Israel; pres. Parents Club, No. Ill.; pres. Jewish Chapel Coun., Gt. Lakes Naval Tng. Ctr.; area chmn. New Trier Rep. Party. Served with USN, 1944-46. Mem. Chgo. Drug and Chem. Soc., Soc. Cosmetic Chemists, Chgo. Hide and Leather Assn., Am. Indsl. Hygiene Assn., Chgo. Perfumery, Soap and Extract Assn. (pres.), Chgo. Printing Ink Prodn. Club (pres.). Republican. Jewish. Home: 205 Crabtree Ln Vernon Hills IL 60061-2106

SMALL, RICHARD DONALD, travel company executive; b. West Orange, N.J., May 24, 1929; s. Joseph George and Elizabeth (McGarry) S.; A.B. cum laude, U. Notre Dame, 1951; m. Arlene P. Small; children: Colleen P., Richard Donald, Joseph W., Mark G., Brian P. With Union-Camp Corp., N.Y.C., Chgo., 1952-62; pres. Alumni Holidays, Inc., 1962—, AHI Internat. Corp., 1962—, All Horizons, Inc., 1982—; chmn. AHI, Inc., 1982-89; bd. dirs. French Cruise Lines, Des Plaines, Ill., Russian Cruise Lines. Recipient Munich Ptnr. award, 1989. Mem. Univ. Club (Chgo.), Alumni Campus Abroad (bd. dirs. 1994). Home: 190 N Sheridan Rd Lake Forest IL 60045-2429 also: 2202 Wailea Elua Wailea Maui HI 96753 Office: 1st National Bank Bldg 701 Lee St Des Plaines IL 60016-4539

SMALL, ROGER STEVEN, middle school educator; b. Hawthorne, Calif., Mar. 19, 1947; s. Roger Joseph and Mary Alice (Lilly) S.; m. Lois Jean Davis, June 9, 1966 (div. June 1975); m. Janet K. Raber, July 4, 1975; children: Steven Joseph, Jennifer Lynn, Erik Jason. BA, Mich. State U., 1969, MA, 1975. Cert. tchr., Mich. Tchr. Hoover Jr. H.S., Montgomery County, Md., 1969-70; tchr. Gardner Mid. Sch., Lansing, Mich., 1971—, chair dept. social studies, 1985—; chair curriculum dept. Lansing Schs., 1992-95; coord. Gardner Earth Expo, Lansing, 1990-91. Editor, author: Playoffs for Officials, 1984-1995, creator course guide Creative World History, 1990, creator course guide World Literature/World History block, 1991, Gardner Enrichment Plan Social Studies, 1996. Active Advent House, Lansing, 1994-95; coord. Sch. Improvement, Gardner-Lansing, 1990-92; Gardner coord. Japanese Exch., Lansing, 1988—. Mem. NEA, Mich. Edn. Assn., Lansing Edn. Assn., Capital Area Ofcls. Assn. (sec. 1990—, Ofcl. of Yr. 1994, 95), Mich. H.S. Athletic Assn. Presbyterian. Home: 338 Chanticleer Trail Lansing MI 48917

SMALL, WILLIAM L., electrical engineer; b. Warren, Ohio, Mar. 27, 1961. BEE, Youngstown State U., 1984. Project engr. Delphi Packard Electric, Warren, Ohio, 1984—; adv. rep. from Packard, Corp. Pelay Com., GMC Packard, Warren, 1985-86. Office: Delphi Packard Electric PO Box 431 Warren OH 44486

SMALLEY, WILLIAM EDWARD, bishop; b. New Brunswick, N.J., Apr. 8, 1940; s. August Harold and Emma May (Gleason) S.; m. Carole A. Kuhns, Sept. 12, 1964; children: Michelle Lynn, Jennifer Ann. BA in Sociology, Lehigh U., 1962; MDiv, Episcopal Theol. Sch., 1965; MeD, Temple U., 1970; D of Ministry, Wesley Theol. Sem., 1987. Ordained to ministry Episcopal Ch., 1965, bishop, 1989. Vicar St. Peter's Episcopal Ch., Plymouth, Pa., 1965-67, St. Martin-in-the-Fields Ch., Nuangola, Pa., 1965-67; rector All Saints' Episcopal Ch., Lehighton, Pa., 1967-75; fed. program adminstr. Lehighton Area Schs., 1970-72; rector Episcopal Ministry of Unity, Palmerton, Pa., 1975-80; bishop Episcopal Diocese Kans., Topeka, 1989—. Pres. Gaithersburg (Md.) Pastoral Counseling Inc., 1986-89; bd. dirs. Washington Pastoral Counseling, 1988-89; chmn. Turner House Inc., Kansas City, Kans., 1989—, Episcopal Social Svcs., Wichita, Kans., 1989—; bd. dirs. Christ Ch. Hosp., Topeka, 1989—, St. Francis Acad., Atchison, Kans., 1989—; v.p. Province VII, The Episcopal Ch., 1993-95, pres. Province VII, 1995—; pres. Province VII Hosp of Bishops; mem. Ch. Devel. Bd.; chair Presiding Bishop's Coun. Advice; mem. joint nominating com. for Presiding Bishop. Mem. Omicron Delta Kappa. Democrat.

SMALLWOOD, GLENN WALTER, JR., utility marketing management executive; b. Jeffersonville, Ind., Oct. 12, 1956; s. Glenn Walter and Darlene Ruth (Zeller) S. BSBA, S.E. Mo. State U., 1978; MA in Bus., Webster U., 1992, MBA, 1993. Cert. counselor. Customer svc. advisor Union Electric Co., Mexico, Mo., 1979-95, Cape Girardeau, Mo., 1995—; instr. Mexico Vo-Tech Sch., 1981; panelist on home design Mo. Extension Svc., 1984; co. advisor Mo. Bus. Week. Coord. local United Way, 1984; mem., chair Gt. Rivers coun. Boy Scouts Am.; panelist Mo. Freedom Forum, 1990; charter mem. class Mo. Leadership; chmn. Leadership Mexico Program; coordinating advisor Jr. Achievement, Mexico H.S.; committeeman, chmn. Republican Party of Audrain County; bd. dirs. Mo. Rep. Grassroots Caucus. Named among Ten Outstanding Young Missourians, Mo. Jaycees, 1993; recipient Disting. Svc. award Mexico, Mo. Jaycees, 1993. Mem. Am. Mktg. Assn. (profl.), Nat. Eagle Scout Assn., Cooper Dome Soc., Boy Scouts Am. Alumni Family, Mexico Area C. of C. (bd. dirs.), Semo U. Aumni Assn., Inst. Cert. Profl. Mgrs. (cert. mgr.), Adminstrv. Mgmt. Soc., Optimists (youth appreciation award 1974), Kiwanis (cert. appreciation 1984), Mexico Noon (bd. dirs. 1990, treas. 1990-91, v.p. 1991-92, pres. 1993-94), Audrain County Pachyderm Club (bd. dirs., 2d v.p. 1990-92, pres. 1993), Sons of Confederate Vets., Honorable Order Ky. Cols. Republican. Office: Union Electric Co PO Box 40 Cape Girardeau MO 63701-0040

SMARR, JANET LEVARIE, comparative literature educator; b. Chgo., May 20, 1949; d. Siegmund and Norma (Cohn) Levarie; m. Larry Lee Smarr, June 3, 1973; children: Joseph, Benjamin. BA, Brown U., 1970; PhD, Princeton U., 1975. Instr. Princeton (Ill.) U., 1975-76, U. Mass., Boston, 1976-77; Mellon faculty fellow Harvard U., Cambridge, Mass., 1977-78; asst. prof. Yale U., New Haven, 1978-80; asst. prof. comparative lit. U. Ill., Urbana, 1980-86, assoc. prof., 1986-92, prof., 1992—, acting dir. comparative lit. program, 1992-93; dir., 1994—; mem. exec. com. Ctr. for Renaissance Studies, Newberry Libr., Chgo., 1989—. Author: Bocaccio and Fiammetta, 1986; author, translator: Boccaccio's Eclogues, 1987; translator: Italian Renaissance Tales 1983 (award Am. Assn. Italian Studies 1984); editor: Historical Criticism and the Challenge of Theory, 1993. Fellow AAUW, Princeton U., 1974-75, Ctr. for Advanced Study, U. Ill., 1986. Mem. MLA, Am. Assn. Italian Studies, Am. Boccaccio Assn., Am. Renaissance Soc., Phi Beta Kappa. Office: U Ill 2070 Fgn Langs Bldg 707 S Mathews Ave Urbana IL 61801-3625

SMART, DENISE TORVIK, marketing educator; b. Sisseton, S.D., Oct. 5, 1951; d. Ober Lawrence and Maxine Catherine (Dady) T.; m. Dennis Lee Smart, Aug. 16, 1975; children: Peter, Christopher. BS, S.D. State U., 1973; MBA, U. S.D., 1976; PhD, Tex. A&M U., 1984. Asst. buyer Joslin's Dept. Store, Denver, 1973-74; career edn. specialist N.W. Area Schs., Lemmon, S.D., 1974-75; grad. rsch. asst. bus. rsch. bur. U. S.D., Vermillion, 1975-76; instr. Sioux Falls (S.D.) Coll., 1977; lectr. Tex. A&M U., College Station, 1978-84, vis. asst. prof., 1986-92; assoc. prof. U. Nebr., Omaha, 1992—, chair mktg. dept., 1995—; seminar presenter Army/Air Force Exch. System, College Station, 1989-90, Dallas Apparel Mart, 1988. Pres. Meml. Student Ctr. Opera and Performing Arts Soc., College Station, 1990-91; v.p. Brazos Valley Arts Coun., College Station, 1986-90; regional chair Tex. State Arts Coun., Austin, 1988-90; bd. mem. Reading is Fundamental, College Station, 1985-88. Recipient Student-Community Rels. award Meml. Student Ctr. Opera and Performing Arts Soc., 1986; Consortium fellow Tex. A&M U. Mktg. Dept., 1980. Mem. Am. Mktg. Assn. (best conf. paper edn. track 1988, Educator of Yr. award Greater Omaha chpt. 1994), So. Mktg. Assn. (sec. 1993-94, pres.-elect 1994—, pres. 1995—), Acad. Mktg. Sci., Am. Acad. Advt. Assn. for Creativity, Beta Gamma Sigma, Mu Kappa Tau. Roman Catholic. Home: 3305 Armbrust Dr Omaha NE 68124-2728 Office: U Nebr at Omaha Dept Mktg Omaha NE 68182

SMART, KATHRYN ALENE, rehabilitation nurse; b. Chgo., Dec. 30, 1959; d. David W. and Grace E. (Walther) S. BSN, North Park Coll., Chgo., 1982; MS, Rush U., Chgo., 1991. CRRN. Staff nurse Rehab. Inst. of Chgo., 1982-87; staff nurse Bowman Health Ctr. for Elderly Rush Presbyn.-St. Luke's Med. Ctr., Chgo., 1987-91, rehab. clin. nurse specialist Bowman Health Ctr. for Elderly, 1991—; lectr. in field. Mem. Assn. Rehab. Nurses. Office: Bowman Health Ctr Elderly 710 S Paulina St Chicago IL 60612-3808

SMARTE, CHARLOTTE ELIZABETH, educator, journalist; b. Winter Haven, Fla., June 23, 1959; d. Freddie Lee Alexander and Ruthie Lee (Wilson) Smarte; m. Samba A. Faal, Mar. 1983 (div. Aug. 1989). BA, Fla. State U., Tallahassee, 1981; M in Journalism, Northwestern U., 1983; psotgrad., Roosevelt U., 1993—. Cert. tchr., spl. edn. evaluator, Ill. Copy editor Chgo. Daily Defender, 1989; tchr. Upward Bound project Roosevelt U., Chgo., 1989-91; lectr. Chgo. State U., 1991-92; mng. editor Catalyst Mag., Chgo., 1989-92; interim edn. dir. Chgo. Urban League, 1992-95; dir. edn. The Better Boys Found., Chgo., 1995-95; dir. vocat. and ednl. tng. Midwest Women's Ctr., Chgo., 1995—; commr. desegregation Chgo. Pub. Schs., 1994-95; chair edn. com. LWV, Chgo., 1993-94; mem. Ill. Coun. on Coll. Attendance, 1994—. Author articles. Journalism scholar Northwestern U., 1982-83; Ill. Bd. Higher Edn. doctoral fellow, 1993—. Mem. DuSable Mus. African Am. History. Home: 2851 S King Dr Apt 1610 Chicago IL 60616

SMAYLING, LYDA MOZELLA, speech pathologist; b. Britton, Okla., Apr. 19, 1923; d. Miles and Evelyn (King) Maxwell; m. George F. Smayling, Sept. 12, 1944 (dec. 1985); children: Sally, Michael, Miles. BA magna cum laude, U. Wichita, Wichita, Kans., 1944; MA summa cum laude, U. Wichita, 1947. Dir., cons., assoc. U. Kans. Med. Ctr., Kans. City, 1947-56; cons. Westchester County Cerebral Palsy Assn., Bedford Village, N.Y., 1947-54; asst. dir. Inst. Logopedics, Wichita, 1957-68; instr. Wichita (Kans.) State U., 1957-68; cons. Wichita, 1957-68; pvt. practice Mpls., 1968—. Contbr. articles to profl. jours. V.p. PTA, Wichita, 1957-64, tchr. Unitarian Ch., Wichita, 1959-64;. Mem. Am. Speech-Lang. Hearing Assn., Kans. Speech-Lang. Hearing Assn. (v.p., bd. dirs., treas.). Unitarian Universalist. Home and Office: 3145 Dean Ct # 903 Minneapolis MN 55416-4390

SMEDINGHOFF, THOMAS J., lawyer; b. Chgo., July 15, 1951; s. John A. and Dorothy M.; m. Mary Beth Smedinghoff. BA in Math., Knox Coll., 1973; JD, U. Mich., 1978. Bar: Ill. 1978, U.S. Dist. Ct. (no. dist.) Ill. 1978. Assoc. McBride, Baker & Coles and predecessor McBride & Baker, Chgo., 1978-84, ptnr., 1985—. adj. prof. computer law John Marshall Law Sch., Chgo.; chair Ill. Commn. on Electronic Commerce and Crime, 1996—. Office: McBride Baker & Coles 500 W Madison St Ste 40 Chicago IL 60661-2511

SMELCER, GLEN ERNEST, mechanical engineer; b. Beaver Dam, Wis., May 3, 1931; s. Archibald J. Smelcer and Edna Emma (Schreiber); divorced; children: Steven A., Michele B., Suzanne C. BSME, U. Wis., 1955; postgrad., State U. Iowa, 1962; MSME, U. Ill., State U. of Iowa. Reg. profl. engr., Ill., Iowa, Wis. Rsch. asst. Atomic Energy Commn., Madison, Wis., 1955; illustrator Wis. Alumni Rsch. Found., Madison, 1956; draftsman Brandes Co., Madison, 1956; design engr. Internat. Harvester Co., East Moline, Ill., 1956-59; design analyst Internat. Harvester Co., Hinsdale, Ill., 1959-70; sr. reliability engr. John Deere Dubuque (Iowa) Works, 1970-86, sr. engr., 1986-89; chief design analyst Mechanical Design Analysis Consultants, Beaver Dam, Wis., 1989—. Inventor, patentee in field. Ecumenical organizer Social Concerns Commn., Dubuque, 1986. Mem. Soc. Automotive Engrs. (transaction rev. com.), NSPE, Ill. Soc. Profl. Engrs. Republican. Methodist. Office: Mechanical Design Analysis Consultants 254 Walnut St Beaver Dam WI 53916-1810

SMELTZER, PENELOPE SUE, marketing professional; b. Jackson, Mich., Mar. 16, 1947; d. Elwyn V. and Bertha (Koch) Stoneburner; m. John James Smeltzer Jr., Apr. 16, 1966; 1 child, Laura Ann Hayes. BA in English, Ctrl. Mich. U., 1970. Proposal coord. Gilbert/Commonwealth Assocs., Inc., Jackson, Mich., 1973-79, comms. specialist, 1979-80, mgr. mktg. svcs., 1980-88; asst. product mgr. Camp Internat., Jackson, Mich., 1988-89; tech. editor, mktg. specialist Commonwealth Cultural Resources Group, Jackson, Mich., 1989-90; adminstrv.-mktg. mgr. Cummins & Barnard, Inc., Ann Arbor, Mich., 1990—. Bd. dirs. Jr. Achievement, Jackson, 1984-88. Mem. Soc. for Mktg. Profl. Svcs., Soc. for Coll. and Univ. Planning. Mem. United Ch. of Christ. Home: 352 Oakwood Jackson MI 49203 Office: Cummins & Barnard Inc 2058 S State St Ann Arbor MI 48104

SMERCINA, CHARLES JOSEPH, mayor, accountant; b. Cleve., Sept. 18, 1932; s. Edward Steven and Barbara Rose (Vincik) S.; m. Dorothy Rita Pazdernik, May 9, 1953; children: Cynthia Bomeli Smercina, David. ABA in Acctg., Fenn Coll.; ABA in Mgmt., BBA in Acctg., Cleve. State U.; postgrad., Kent State U., Case Western Res. U., Youngstown (Ohio) State U. CPA, Ohio. Chmn. CSC, Solon, 1956-66; councilman City of Solon, Ohio, 1966-68, vice mayor, 1966-67, income tax adminstr., 1968-73, mayor, 1974-75, 78-87; cons. taxation, mcpl. fin. various Ohio communities, 1970—; lectr. polit.. sci., corp. fin. Case Western Res. U. Mem. Am. Soc. Pub. Adminstrs., Mayors Assn. Ohio, Cuyahoga County Mayors and City Mgrs. Assn., Mcpl. Fin. Officers Am., Nat. League of Cities, Nat. Soc. Pub. Accts., Ohio Assn. Pub. Safety Dirs., Ohio Assn. Tax Adminstrs. (past pres.), Ohio Mcpl. League, Water Pollution Control Fedn., Solon C. of C., VFW, Council on Human Relations, Ohio Nature Conservancy, Nat. Arbor Day Found. Democrat. Roman Catholic. Lodges: Rotary, KC. Home: 5075 Brainard Rd Cleveland OH 44139-1101

SMEREK, WILLIAM JOHN, communications executive, electrical engineer; b. Youngstown, Ohio, June 2, 1958; s. John Joseph and Blanche Margaret (Terihay) S.; m. Mariellen Patricia Andrich, July 2, 1983; children: Andrea, Courtney. BEE, Youngstown State U., 1984; MEE, Clemson U., 1991. Occupational engr. AT&T Network Systems, Columbus, Ohio, 1984-90; engring. mgr. AT&T Network Systems, Whippany, N.J., 1990-93; tech. mgr. AT&T Network Systems, Columbus, 1993—. Mem. IEEE. Home: 829 Hensel Woods Rd Gahanna OH 43230 Office: AT&T Network Systems 6200 E Broad St Columbus OH 43213

SMERLING, DAVID WARREN, manufacturing executive; b. Chgo., July 3, 1933; s. Manuel and Marie (Steinberg) S.; m. Rae Livingston, Aug. 1, 1933; children: Linda Schapiro, Michael, Janet LeVee. AB in Econs., U. Mich., 1955; JD, Northwestern U., Chgo., 1958. Bar: Ill., 1958. V.p. Ogden Foods, Div. Ogden Corp., Chgo., 1958-67; pres. City Bonded Messengers Svc., Chgo., 1967-85; chmn. L.C. Industries, Inc., Chgo., 1988—. Pres. Jewish Fedn. Metro Chgo., 1979-80, Jewish Family and Community Svc., 1970-72. Mem. Standard Club of Chgo. (pres. 1990-92). Home: 799 Moseley Rd Highland Park IL 60035-4633 Office: LC Industries Inc 401 W Western Ave Chicago IL 60612

SMILEY, DAVID BRUCE, administrative director; b. Pitts., Aug. 6, 1942; s. Alan Gary and Sarah Marie (Frank) S.; m. Eleanor Gayle Houk, Feb. 10, 1966 (dec.); children: Linda Marie, Jonathan David; m. Peggy N. Dannar, June 24, 1995. BS in Edn., Ind. State Coll., 1964; MBA, St. Louis U., 1975. Commd. 2d lt. U.S. Army, 1964, advanced through grades to lt. col., 1981, ret., 1984; dir. adminstrn. Sherman, Wickens, Lysaught & Speck, P.C., Kansas City, Mo., 1984-86, Armstrong, Teasdale, Schlafly & Davis, Kansas City, Mo., 1986—. Decorated Bronze Star medal. Mem. Assn. Legal Adminstrs. (pres. Kansas City chpt. 1990). Republican. Methodist. Office: Armstrong Teasdale Schlafly & Davis 2345 Grand Blvd Ste 2000 Kansas City MO 64108

SMILEY, JANE GRAVES, author, educator; b. L.A., Sept. 26, 1949; d. James La Verne and Frances Nuelle (Graves) S.; m. John Whiston, Sept. 4, 1970 (div.); m. William Silag, May 1, 1978 (div.); children: Phoebe Silag, Lucy Silag; m. Stephen Mark Mortensen, July 25, 1987; 1 child, Axel James Mortensen. BA, Vassar Coll., 1971; MFA, U. Iowa, 1976, MA, 1978, PhD, 1978. Asst. prof. Iowa State U., Ames, 1981-84, assoc. prof., 1984-89, prof., 1989-90, Disting. prof., 1992—; vis. asst. prof. U. Iowa, Iowa City, 1981, 87. Author: (fiction) Barn Blind, 1980, At Paradise Gate, 1981 (Friends of American Writers prize 1981), Duplicate Keys, 1984, The Age of Grief, 1987 (Nat. Book Critics Cirle award nomination 1987), The Greenlanders, 1988, Ordinary Love and Goodwill, 1989, A Thousand Acres, 1991 (Pulitzer Prize for fiction 1992, Nat. Book Critics Cirle award 1992, Midland Authors award 1992, Amb. award 1992, Heartland prize 1992), Moo: A Novel, 1995; (non-fiction) Catskill Crafts: Artisans of the Catskill Mountains, 1987. Grantee Fulbright U.S. Govt., Iceland, 1976-77, NEA, 1978, 87; recipient O. Henry award, 1982, 85, 88. Mem. Author's Guild, Screenwriters Guild. Office: Iowa State U Dept English 201 Ross Ames IA 50011-1401

SMILEY, PETER C., manufacturing executive; b. Ashtabula, Ohio, Sept. 13, 1944. Journeyman tool and diemaker, Ohio. Plant mgr. Phoenix Machine & Foundry Co., Ashtabula, 1964—; treas. Signet Bldg. Co., Ashtabula, 1992—. Mem. Grotto (treas. 1980—), Masons. Republican. Office: Phoenix Machine & Foundry 620 W 48th St Ashtabula OH 44004-6911

SMILEY, WYNN RAY, director of communications; b. Danville, Ill., May 18, 1961; s. Arthur Glen and Lois Jean (Lawrence) S. BS in Agriculture Comms., U. Ill., 1983. Asst. prodr. Sta. WCIA-TV, Champaign, Ill., 1982-83, news prodr., 1983-87, gen. assignments reporter, 1987-91, host, anchor news show, 1988—; founder, owner, pres. Advisory Inc., Champaign, 1989—; dir. communications Alpha Tau Omega Nat. Hqrs., Champaign, 1991—; facilitator Leadershape Inc., Champaign, 1990—. Editor: The Positive Experience, 1992, 96. Chmn. bd. Am. Cancer Soc., Champaign, 1991-93; bd. dirs., sec. Meadowbrook Cmty. Ch., 1994—. Mem. Assembly of God. Office: Advisory Inc 303 Burwash Ave Savoy IL 61874

SMITH, ALAN BRONSON, JR., military officer, farm executive; b. Milw., Aug. 7, 1917; s. Alan Bronson and Claire Christie (Lund) S.; m. Harriett Ellen Rittenour, July 10, 1943; children: Alan Bronson III, Christie, Kyle, Kerry. BA, Ohio Wesleyan U., 1940; grad., Air Command and Staff Coll., Maxwell AFB, Ala., 1951, Naval War Coll., Newport, R.I., 1963; MBA, George Washington U., 1959. Commd. 2d lt. USAF, 1940, advanced through grades to col., 1962; ret., 1969; assoc. dir. Grant Hosp., Columbus, Ohio, 1969-74; owner, producer Meadowbrook Farms, Circleville, Ohio, 1974-91; researcher in low cholestrol, low-fat beef and pork. Decorated DFC, Air medal with 3 oakleaf clusters, Legion of Merit; recipient Pub. Rels. award Am. Hosp. Assn., 1970, 73. Mem. Air Force Assn. (life), Navy League U.S. (life; bd. dirs. Columbus coun. 1969-76), Ret. Officers Assn. (life), Rotary (com. chmn. Columbus 1982-95), Sigma Alpha Epsilon. Republican. Methodist. Home and Office: 5755 Flintlock Ln Columbus OH 43213-2626

SMITH, ALMA WHEELER, state legislator; b. Aug. 6, 1941. BA, U. Mich. Legis. coord. Senator Lane Pollack; senator Dist. 18 Mich. State Senate, 1995—, mem. appropriations com. Mem. South Lyon (Mich.) Bd. Edn.

SMITH, ARTHUR B(EVERLY), JR., lawyer; b. Abilene, Tex., Sept. 11, 1944; s. Arthur B. and Florence B. (Baker) S.; children: Arthur C., Sarah R. BS, Cornell U., 1966; JD, U. Chgo., 1969. Bar: Ill. 1969, N.Y. 1976. Assoc. Vedder, Price, Kaufman & Kammholz, Chgo., 1969-74; asst. prof. labor law N.Y. State Sch. Indsl. and Labor Rls., Cornell U., 1975-77; ptnr. Vedder, Price, Kaufman & Kammholz, Chgo., 1977-86; founding mem. Murphy, Smith & Polk, Chgo., 1986—; guest. lectr. Northwestern U. Grad. Sch. Mgmt., 1979, Sch. Law, spring 1980; mem. hearing bd. Ill. Atty. Registration and Disciplinary Commn. Recipient award for highest degree of dedication and excellence in teaching N.Y. State Sch. Indsl. and Labor Relations, Cornell U., 1977. Mem. ABA (co-chmn. com. on devel. law under Nat. Labor Relations Act, Sect. Labor Rels. Law 1976-77), N.Y. State

Bar Assn., Phi Eta Sigma, Phi Kappa Phi. Presbyterian. Clubs: Chgo. Athletic Assn., Monroe (Chgo.). Author: Employment Discrimination Law Cases and Materials, 4th edit., 1994; Construction Labor Relations, 1984, supplement, 1993; co-editor-in-chief: 1976 Annual Supplement to Morris, The Developing Labor Law, 1977; asst. editor: The Developing Labor Law, 3d edit., 1992; contbr. articles to profl. jours. Office: Murphy Smith & Polk 2 First National Plz Fl 25 Chicago IL 60603

SMITH, ARTHUR E., counseling educator, vocational psychologist; b. St. Louis, Feb. 28, 1926; s. Lee L. and Dorothea M. (Debrecht) S.; m. Jane C. Dooley; children: Greg, Laura, Terry, Chris. BS, St. Louis U., 1949, MEd, 1951, PhD, 1962. Diplomate Am. Bd. Vocational Experts; lic. psychologist. Tchr., counselor St. Louis Pub. Schs., 1949-60; Evening Coll. dir. and assoc. prof., St. Louis U., 1960-66; grad. dean St. Mary's Coll., Notre Dame, Ind., 1966-68; chmn. behavioral studies U. Mo., St. Louis, 1968—; pres. Clayton Bus. Sch., St. Louis, 1983—; dir. Affiliates in Psychology and Counseling, St. Louis, 1970-78. Contbr. articles to profl. jours. Served with USNR, 1944-46, PTO. Recipient Recognition award Am. Soc. Tng. Dirs. and Am. Pers. and Guidance Assn. Mem. AACD (pres. St. Louis 1965), Nat. Vocat. Guidance Assn., Assn. Counselor Educators and Supvs., Am. Coll. Vocat. Experts, Nat. Rehab. Assn. (pres. St. Louis 1979-80, Recognition award 1980). Office: U Mo 8001 Natural Bridge Rd Saint Louis MO 63121-4401

SMITH, BARBARA ANN, gifted education coordinator; b. Oak Park, Ill., Mar. 20, 1950; d. William J. and Mary T. (Barlow) S. BS in Edn., No. Ill. U., 1971, MS in Edn., 1974, cert. advanced study in edn., 1977, EdS, 1988, EdD, 1994; EdD, No. Ill. U., 1994. Cert. tchr., adminstr. gifted edn., verification, Ill.; lic. counselor, Ill. Coord. gifted edn. Dist. 45 Elem. Schs., Villa Park, Ill., 1986—, counselor to group on leadership devel., tchr. Author numerous articles on gifted edn., self-esteem enhancers, sch.-bus. partnerships. Mem. AACD, ASCD, NEA (chpt. sec., treas.), ACA, Ill. West Suburban Reading Coun., AAUW (coord. families facing change group), Delta Kappa Gamma (chpt. pres.), Phi Delta Kappa. Office: Sch Dist 45 255 W Vermont St Villa Park IL 60181-1943

SMITH, BARBARA MARTIN, art educator; b. St. Louis, Feb. 3, 1945; d. Charles Landon and Mary Louise (Nolker) Martin; m. Timothy Van Gorder Smith, Nov. 27, 1976; children: Brian Eliot, Marjorie Van Gorder. BA, Lawrence U., 1967; MFA, So. Ill. U., 1975. Cert. tchr., Mo. Art instr. Horton Watkins High Sch., Ladue, Mo., 1968-76; leader Experiment in Internat. Living, Brattleboro, Vt., 1974; art tchr. Michigan City (Ind.) Ctr. for the Arts, 1979-80, Cleve. Mus. of Art, 1981-83; art instr. Villa Duchesne, St. Louis, 1986—; edn. dir. Dunes Art Found., Michigan City, 1979; co-chmn. Internat. Wives Group, Cleve. Coun. on World Affairs, 1982-84; bd. dirs. Webster Groves (Mo.) Sch. Found., 1992. Exhibited in shows at Art Inst. of Chgo., 1979, So. Ill. U. Alumnae Exhibit, 1982, Focus Fiber, Cleve. Mus. of Art, 1982, Nova, Wearable Art, Kuban Gallery, Cleve., 1983, Drawings & Prints, St. Louis Artist's Guild, 1986. Recipient Grad. Fellowship Ann. Grad. award So. Ill. U., 1975; named Artist in Residence/ Artist in Schs. Ind. Arts Commn./NEA, 1978-79; named to Honors Seminar for Advancement of Art Edn., R.I. Sch. of Design, 1988, Mem. Art Edn. Delegation to Japan, 1992. Mem. Nat. Art Edn. Assn., Internat. Soc. for Edn. through Art, St. Louis Art Mus., St. Louis Artist Guild. Home: 135 Jefferson Rd Webster Grv MO 63119-2934 Office: Villa Duchesne Oak Hill Sch 801 S Spoede Rd Des Peres MO 63131-2606

SMITH, BENNETT HOLLY, biological anthropologist; b. Detroit, Mar. 12, 1952; d. Frederick Janney and Colleen Francis (Forney) S.; m. Philip Derstine Gingerich, June 12, 1982; children: Daniel Gingerich, Matthew Gingerich. BA, U. Tex., 1975; MA, U. Mich., 1976, PhD, 1983. Asst. rsch. scientist U. Mich., Ann Arbor, 1983-88, assoc. rsch. scientist, 1989—; vis. asst. prof. Ariz. State U., Tempe, 1984-85. Assoc. editor Am. Jour. Phys. Anthropology, 1987-92, Jour. Human Evolution, 1990-93, Evolutionary Anthropology, 1995-96; contbr. articles to Nature, Am. Jour. Phys. Anthropology, Evolution. NSF grantee, 1979, 84, 87, 91, 94. Mem. Am. Anthrop. Assn., Am. Assn. Phys. Anthropologists, AAAS, Human Biology Coun., Dental Anthropology Assn. (sec.-treas. 1988-90). Office: Univ Mich Mus Anthropology Ann Arbor MI 48109

SMITH, BONNIE BEATRICE, corporate communications executive; b. Dayton, Ohio, July 22, 1948; d. Joseph Edward and Phyllis Jean (Shook) S. BS in Journalism, Ohio U., 1970. Accredited bus. communicator. Reporter Piqua (Ohio) Daily Call, 1970-71; asst. dir. pub. rels. Bethesda Hosps., Cin., 1971-76; dir. communication St. Joseph's Hosp., Ft. Wayne, Ind., 1976-81; publs. editor E. Ohio Gas Co., Cleve., 1981-88, coord. customer communications, 1988-90; mgr. employee communication Picker Internat., Inc., Highland Heights, Ohio, 1990—; speaker, seminar leader various hosps., bus. and profl. orgns., 1975—. Outreach vol. Cleve. Children's Mus., 1986-88, co-chmn. outreach program, mem. speaker's bur., 1988-89, mem. pub. rels. task force, 1989-92. Recipient numerous awards Ohio Hosp. Assn., Ohio Press Women, Acad. Hosp. Pub. Rels., Cin. Editors Assn., also others. Mem. Internat. Assn. Bus. Communicators (dir. mem. svcs. internal communications coun. 1985-88, chmn. directory mktg. coun. 1988-90, dir. examiners accreditation bd. 1986-88), numerous awards 1975—). Home: 1700 E 13th St Apt 22S Cleveland OH 44114-3238 Office: Picker Internat Inc 595 Miner Rd Cleveland OH 44143-2131

SMITH, BRUCE VAUGHAN, electrical engineer; b. Kingsville, Tex., July 28, 1953; s. Robert Vaughan and June Estelle (Link) S.; m. Astrid Marie Ryerson, June 18, 1976; 1 child, Leslie Michelle. BSEE, Iowa State U., 1975, MSEE, 1980, PhD, 1991. Prof. engr., Iowa. Engring. mgr. Rockwell-Collins Avionics, Cedar Rapids, Iowa, 1975—; adj. prof. Iowa State U., Ames, 1991—; program evaluator Accreditation Bd. Sci. & Tech., Balt., 1995—. Bd. dirs. North Linn Sch. Dist., Troy Mills, Iowa, 1993-95. Mem. IEEE, Nat. Coun. Sys. Engring., Sigma Xi. Office: Rockwell 400 Collins Rd NE Cedar Rapids IA 52498

SMITH, CARL EDWIN, electronics company executive; b. Eldon, Iowa, Nov. 18, 1906; s. Seldon L. and Myra (Hutton) S.; BS in Elec. Engring., Iowa State U., Ames, 1930; MS in Elec. Engring., Ohio State U., 1932, EE, 1936; m. Hannah B. McGuire, Sept. 3, 1932; children: Larc A., Darwin W., Barbadeen Jo, Margene Sue, Ada Kay, Ramona Lee. Draftsman, Iowa Electric Co., Fairfield, summer 1929; student engr. RCA Victor Co., Camden, N.J., 1930-31; engr. Radio Air Service Corp., Cleve., 1932; radio operator WGAR, Cleve., 1933; engr. United Broadcasting Corp., Cleve., 1933-36, asst. chief engr., 1936-41, chief engr., 1941-45, v.p., 1946-53; owner, mgr. Carl E. Smith Consulting Radio Engrs., Cleve., 1935-80; pres. Smith Electronics, Cleve., 1956-88; pres. Carl Smith Electronics, Inc., Cleve., 1988-91; owner Carl E. Smith Electronics, 1991—; founder Cleve. Inst. Electronics Inc., 1934, chmn. ednl. com., 1970—. Served with Office of Chief Signal Officer, U.S. Army, World War II. Recipient Dist. Alumnus award Ohio State U., 1974, Disting. Achievement award, Iowa State U., 1980, Disting. Service award Nat. Religious, 1984, Engring. Achievement award Nat. Assn. Broadcasters, 1985; named to Broadcasters Hall of Fame, 1992, Nat. Religious Broadcasters Hall of Fame, 1994. Registered profl. engr., Ohio, D.C. Fellow IEEE (life), Radio Club Am. (Jack Poppele Broadcast award 1995); mem. Cleve. Engring. Soc., Brecksville C. of C. Republican. Presbyterian. Ch. Am. Author 53 tech. papers and books including: Directional Antenna Patterns, Theory and Design of Directional Antennas, Applied Mathematics, Communications Circuit Fundamentals; Contbr. articles to tech. jours. Patentee electromech. calculators; elliptical polarization electromagnetic energy radiation systems; slotted cylindrical antenna; three-slot cylindrical antenna; spiral slot antenna; short low loss antenna system. Home: 8704 Snowville Rd Cleveland OH 44141-3468 Office: 8200 Snowville Rd Cleveland OH 44141

SMITH, CAROLE DIANNE, legal editor, writer; b. Seattle, June 12, 1945; d. Glaude Francis and Elaine Claire (Finkenstein) S.; m. Stephen Bruce Presser, June 18, 1968 (div. June 1987); children: David Carter, Elisabeth Catherine. AB cum laude, Harvard U., Radcliffe Coll., 1968; JD, Georgetown U., 1974. Bar: Pa. 1974. Law clk. to Hon. Judith Jamison Phila., 1974-75; assoc. Gratz, Tate, Spiegel, Ervin & Ruthrouff, Phila., 1975-76; freelance editor, writer Evanston, Ill., 1983-87; editor Ill. Inst. Tech., Chgo., 1987-88; mng. editor LawLetters, Inc., Chgo., 1988-89; editor ABA, Chgo., 1989-95; product devel. dir. Gt. Lakes Divsn. Lawyers Coop. Pub., Deerfield, Ill., 1995—. Author Jour. of Legal Medicine, 1975, Selling and the Law: Advertising and Promotion, 1987; (under pseudonym Sarah Toast) 61 children's books, 1994-96; editor The Brief, 1990-95, Criminal Justice, 1989-90, 92-95 (Gen. Excellence award Soc. Nat. Assn. Pubs. 1990, Feature Article award-bronze Soc. Nat. Assn. Pubs. 1994), Franchise Law Jour., 1995; mem. editl. bd. The Brief, ABA Tort and Ins. Practice Sect., 1995—. Dir. Radcliffe Club of Chgo., 1990-93; mem. parents council Latin Sch. Chgo., 1995-96. Mem. ABA, Chgo.-Lincoln Inn of Ct. Office: Lawyers Coop Pub 155 Pfingsten Rd Deerfield IL 60015

SMITH, CLYDE CURRY, historian, educator; b. Hamilton, Ohio, Dec. 16, 1929; s. Charles Clyde and Mabel Ethel Ola (Curry) S.; m. Ellen Marie Gormsen, June 13, 1953; children: Harald Clyde, Karen Margaret Evans. BA in Physics cum laude and MS, Miami U., Oxford, Ohio, 1951; BDiv, U. Chgo., 1954, MA, 1961, PhD, 1968. Ordained to ministry Christian Ch. (Disciples of Christ), 1954. Exec. asst. to dean Disciples Div. House, Chgo., 1956-57; lectr. in O.T., Univ. Coll. U. Chgo., 1957; asst. prof. St. John's Coll. U. Manitoba, Winnipeg, Can., 1958-63; instr. Brandeis U., Waltham, Mass., 1963-65; prof. ancient history and religions U. Wis., River Falls, 1965-90, prof. emeritus, 1990—; vis. prof. religious studies Culver-Stockton Coll., Canton, Mo., 1990, U. Newcastle-upon-Tyne, Eng., 1992-94; vis. lectr. div., Edge Hill Coll. of Edn., Ormskirk, Eng., 1970-71; postdoctoral fellow Johns Hopkins U., Balt., 1977; NEH fellow-in-residence U. Calif., Santa Barbara, 1978-79; vis. rsch. fellow, lectr. religious studies U. Aberdeen, Scotland, 1980, 85-86. Contbr. articles to profl. publs. Mem. Pierce County Hist. Assn., River Falls, 1965—, Wis. Dems., 1965—, Dem. Nat. Com., 1983—; charter mem. Sci. Mus. of Minn., St. Paul, 1973—; founding mem. River Falls Cmty. Arts Base, 1996—. Recipient Gov.'s Spl. award State of Wis., 1990, several grants. Mem. Assn. Ancient Historians, Can. Soc. Ch. History (founder, treas. 1960-63), N.Am. Patristic Soc., Can. Soc. for Mesopotamian Studies, Soc. for Promotion Roman Studies of London, Hellenic Soc. London, Brit. Sch. Archaeology in Iraq, Brit. Inst. Archaeology in Ankara, Oriental Inst. U. Chgo., Phi Beta Kappa. Democrat. Home: 939 W Maple St River Falls WI 54022-2055

SMITH, CRAIG MALCOLM, architect, consultant; b. Bloomington, Ind., Nov. 4, 1952; s. Ned Myron and Virginia (Reuter) S.; m. Carolyn Guth, Sept. 3, 1983; children: Natalie Fern, Julia. BArch, U. Ill., 1974, MArch, 1976. Registered architect, Ill., Mich., Fla. Design instr. U. Ill., Urbana, 1974-76; intern Piano & Rogers, Paris, 1974; designer Bertrand Golberg, Chgo., 1976-77; architect Schipporeit Inc., Chgo., 1977-83; prin. Smith-Smith, Chgo., 1983; dir. architecture Bevins Cons. Inc., Chgo., 1983-88, Griskelis and Smith, Ltd., Chgo., 1988—; mem. aux. bd. Chgo. Archtl. Found., 1993—; mem. Newhouse Commn., 1995—. Planner City of Hammond and Ind. Arts Coun., 1977; mem. Friends of Downtown, Chgo., 1981-85. Mem. AIA (grantee 1977, chmn. office practice commn. 1985-86, chmn. exhibit Chgo. chpt. housing trends, 1986), Nat. Coun. Archtl. Accreditation Bds. (cert.), Chgo. Archtl. Found. Aux. Bd. (v.p. 1994-95, Newhouse com. 1995—), Phi Kappa Phi. Democrat. Office: Griskelis and Smith 400 N Michigan Ave Chicago IL 60611-4104

SMITH, CRAIG RICHEY, machinery executive; b. Cleve., May 30, 1925; s. Wilbur Thomas and Helen (Stearns) S.; m. Mary Wood Glover, Dec. 17, 1945; children: Timothy VanGorder, Craig Richey, Patricia Sodon, Marcia Colby. B.S. in M.E, Case Inst. Tech., 1945; postgrad., Harvard Bus. Sch., 1974. Mem. Warner & Swasey Co. (merger Bendix Corp. 1980, Allied Corp. 1983), 1946-84; gen. mgr. Wiedemann div. Warner & Swasey Co., King of Prussia, Pa.; v.p. Turning Machine Div. Warner & Swasey Co., Cleve., 1969-73, group v.p. machine tools, 1973-77, pres., chief operating officer, 1977-79, chmn., chief exec., 1979-80, pres. indsl. group, 1980-82, chmn. indsl. group, 1982-84; chmn. Prodn. Pub. Co., 1985-86; chmn., chief exec. officer Ransburg Corp., 1988-89, bd. dirs., 1979-89; chmn., chief exec. officer Ameritrust Corp., 1992, bd. dirs., 1990-92; bd. dirs. Lincoln Elec. Co., Soc. Corp., Cleve. Machine Controls Co. Campaign leader United Way Svcs., 1977-83; trustee Judson Park, 1977-84, Greater Cleve. Growth Assn., 1979-84, Case Western Res. U., 1979-95; trustee Vocat. Guidance & Rehab. Svcs., 1972-79, 1st v.p. 1976-79. Served with USN, 1943-46, 52-53. Mem. Soc. Mfg. Engrs. (hon.), MAchien Tool Builders Assn., (dir. 1971-74, 79-84, chmn. 1980-81), Machinery and Allied Products Inst. (mem. exec. coun. 1979-84). Clubs: Union, Chagrin Valley Hunt, Cleve. skating. Home: 13754 County Line Rd Chagrin Falls OH 44022-4008

SMITH, CURTIS ALFONSO, JR., university administrator; b. Hot Springs, Ark., Jan. 28, 1934; s. Curtis Alfonso and Claudine (Collins) S.; m. Willa Mae Steger, May 16, 1956 (div. Sept. 1962); 1 child, Pamela Yvette; m. Barbara Joan Brunious, Dec. 20, 1962; children: Curtis Alfonso, Tasya Ayesha. Assoc. deg., Kans. Tech., Topeka, 1955; BE, Chgo. Tchr. Coll., 1963; MA, Roosevelt U., Chgo., 1968; EdD, Nova U., Ft. Lauderdale, 1985. Commercial Rated Pilot. Water safety instr. ARC, Chgo., 1951-67; tchr. Chgo. Pub. Schs., Chgo., 1964-70; staff asst. Chgo. Pub. Schs., 1970-74, dir. govt. fund, 1974-76, adminstr., 1976-81, asst. to deputy, 1981-85, adminstr., 1985-91; instr. Roosevelt U., Chgo., 1977-92; cluster coord. Nova U., Ft. Lauderdale, 1990—; dir. Chgo. sch. adminstrn. programs Concordia U., River Forest, Ill., 1992—. Author: Slang Soul & Soup, 1968, Help for the Bereaved, 1973, Loved Ones Remembered, 1987. Treas. Evang. Child & Family Agy., Chgo., 1977-82. Named Outstanding Tchr. Chgo City Bank & Trust, 1967. Mem. NAACP, Aircraft Owners and Pilots Assn., The Rosicrucian Order, Urban League, Am. Assn. Sch. Educators, Ednl. Devel. Assn. (pres. 1982-94), Phi Delta Kappa (v.p. NIU chpt., Svc. award 1986, Outstanding Educator 1988). Democrat. Home: 16645 Paxton Ave South Holland IL 60473-2634 Office: Concordia U 7400 Augusta St River Forest IL 60305-1402

SMITH, DANIEL LYNN, lawyer; b. Ottawa, Kans., June 22, 1952; s. Daniel H. and Mary K. (Lynn) S.; m. Alana A. Windhorst, Aug. 15, 1981; children: Tricia, Lauran, Alexa. BA, U. Kans., 1973; JD, Duke U., 1976. Bar: Kans. 1976, U.S. Dist. Ct. Kans. 1976, U.S. Ct. Appeals (10th cir.) 1977, U.S. Tax Ct. 1977. Assoc. Bronston Law Offices, Overland Park, Kans., 1976-78; ptnr. Oliver, Smith & Oliver, Overland Park, 1978-80, Bronston and Smith, Overland Park, 1981-92, Ankerholz & Smith, Overland Park, Kans., 1992—; pvt. practice Westwood, Kans., 1980-81. Mem. Kans. Bar Assn., Kans. Trial Lawyers Assn. (bd. govs. 1981—), Civil War Roundtable Kansas City, Phi Beta Kappa. Home: 10075 Goodman Dr Shawnee Mission KS 66212-3432 Office: Ankerholz & Smith 6900 College Blvd Overland Park KS 66211-1547

SMITH, DANIEL WALKER, financial services company executive; b. Des Moines, Oct. 15, 1931; s. Daniel Fuller and Gladys Rosalind (Walker) S.; m. Lois Grace Gooder, Nov. 25, 1954; children: David, Gregory, Bradley, Marsha. BCS, Drake U., 1953, JD, 1955. FLMI, CLU, ChFC, CFP, bar: Iowa, 1955. Trainee The Principal Fin. Group, Des Moines, 1957-64, legal asst., 1964-65, legal assoc., 1965-69, asst. dir. sales/svcs., 1969-70, dir. sales/ svcs., 1970-74, asst. v.p., 1974-87, 2nd v.p., 1987-90; v.p. Prin. Fin. Advisors, Inc., Des Moines, 1987-93; advanced mkts. counsel Principal Fin. Group, Des Moines, 1990-93, advanced mktg. cons., 1993—. Contbr. articles to profl. jours. Vol. Planned Parenthood of Mid-Iowa, Des Moines. 1st lt. USAF, 1955-57. Mem. Am. Soc. CLUs and ChFCs, Iowa Bar Assn., Polk County Bar Assn., Des Moines Estate and Fin. Planners, Internat. Assn. Fin. Planning,. Office: The Principal Fin Group Ste 100 555 Walnut St Des Moines IA 50309-4199

SMITH, DARRYL D., business executive; b. Friend, N.C., May 16, 1939. CLU, CFP. Pres. Dairy Smith Co., Inc., Atlantic, Iowa, 1982—; chmn. Rolling Hills Nat. Bank, Atlantic, 1985—. Mem. Atlantic Golf and Country Club, Rotary Club, C. of C. Office: PO Box 478 Atlantic IA 50022-0478

SMITH, DAVID BERN, electronic design engineer; b. Huntington, W.Va., Nov. 29, 1953. BS, Marshall U., 1977; AS, Columbus State U., 1981. Electronic design engr. HDR Power Sys., Hilliard, Ohio, 1983—. Home: 3424 Parkbrook Dr Grove City OH 43123-1885 Office: HDR Power Sys 4242 Reynolds Dr Hilliard OH 43026-1260

SMITH, DAVID E., secondary education educator, English; b. Middlesboro, Ky., Aug. 10, 1944; s. Kenneth Claude and Joanna (Rosenbaum) S.; m. Sharon Louise Morency, June 22, 1977 (div. Dec. 1981); m. Sandra Joy, Feb. 12, 1982; children: Todd Taylor, Jennifer Taylor. BS in Edn., Wayne State U., 1966, MA, 1979. Cert. secondary educator, Mich.; cert. journalism educator. Tchr. Lamphere Pub. Schs., Madison Hgts., Mich., 1966—; newsletter adviser Lamphere Schs., Madison Hgts., 1966—, mentor tchr., 1991-94, high sch. English dept. chair, 1969-78; dir. Directional Strategies, Pleasant Ridge, Mich., 1990—. Author: (book) The Future Teacher Manual, 1985; editor: (sch. newsletter) ExPress, 1986—, (dist. newsletter) Lamphere Dateline, 1995; contbr. articles to profl. jours. Del. for City of Pleasant Ridge Intergovernmental Cable Comm. Authority, Huntington Woods, Mich., 1982—; mem. City Planning Commn., Pleasant Ridge, 1984-87; dep. mayor City of Pleasant Ridge, 1988, 90, 92, 95 city commr., 1987—. Recipient Best editorial award Union Tchrs. Press Assn., 1978, PM Salutes award WJBK-TV, 1984; named Host/Commentator of Yr., TCI Cablevision of Oakland County, 1993, 94, 95, disting. advisor Dow Jones Newspaper Fund, 1994. Mem. Mich. Interscholastic Press Assn., Journalism Edn. Assn., World Future Soc. (Detroit area coord. 1979—), Pleasant Ridge Found. (trustee 1978-87). Home: 38 Oxford Blvd Pleasant Ridge MI 48069 Office: Lamphere H S 610 West 13 Mile Rd Madison Heights MI 48071

SMITH, DAVID JOHN, JR., plastic surgeon; b. Indpls., Feb. 20, 1947; s. David John and Carolyn (Culp) S.; m. Nancy Loonsten, June 7, 1975; children: Matthew, Peter, Hadley. BA, Wesleyan U., 1969; MD, Ind. U., 1973. Diplomate Am. Bd. Plastic Surgery. Resident Emory U.-Grady Hosp., Atlanta, 1973-78; resident Ind. U. Med. Ctr., Indpls., 1978-80; Christine Kleinert fellow in hand surgery, 1979; asst. prof. surgery Ind. U. Sch. Medicine, 1980-84; assoc. prof. of surgery Wayne State U. Sch. Medicine, 1984-87; assoc. prof. plastic surgery, surgery sect. head U. Mich. Med. Ctr., Ann Arbor, 1987-92, prof. surgery sect. head, 1992—; mem. Residency Rev. Com. for Plastic Surgery, 1992, vice chmn., 1994, chmn. 1996—. Mem. editl. bd. Jour. of Surg. Rsch., 1989-95, Annals of Plastic Surgery, 1992—, assoc. editor, 1994, Yearbook of Hand Surgery, 1989—; guest reviewer Surgery, 1988—, Plastic and Reconstructive Surgery, 1988—; contbr. articles to profl. jours. Recipient numerous grants. Fellow ACS (many coms.), Soc. Univ. Surgeons, Am. Assn. Plastic Surgeons, Am. Surg. Assn., Am. Bd. Plastic Surgeons, Assn. for Acad. Surgery, Western Surg. Assn., Ctrl. Surg. Assn., Am. Soc. for Surgery of the Hand, Am. Soc. Plastic and Reconstructive Surgeons, Plastic Surgery Ednl. Found. (bd. dirs. 1988—, treas. 1994, v.p., pres.-elec., other coms.), Plastic Surgery Rsch. Coun., Am. Burn Assn., Am. Burn Life Support Nat. Faculty, Am. Assn. for Hand Surgeons (pres. 1994). Home: 769 Heatherway St Ann Arbor MI 48104-2731 Office: U Mich Med Ctr 2130 Taubman Health Ctr 1500 E Medical Center Dr Ann Arbor MI 48109-0340

SMITH, DEAN GORDON, economist, educator; b. Flint, Mich., Feb. 23, 1959; s. David Wade and Janet Pearl (Hendrickson) S. AB, U. Mich., 1981; PhD, Tex. A&M U., 1985. Economist RRC, Inc., Bryan, Tex., 1984-85, Parke-Davis, Ann Arbor, 1995-96; from rsch. investigator to asst. prof. U. Mich., Ann Arbor, 1985-94, assoc. prof., 1994—; faculty fellow Lincoln Nat. Life Ins. Co., Ft. Wayne, Ind., 1990. Contbr. articles to profl. jours. Economist, Mich. Med. Liability Rsch. Program, Lansing, 1990, Gov.'s Healthcare Cost Mgmt. Team, Lansing, 1989; bd. dirs. Care Am. Mich., Inc. Grantee Mercy Consortium for Rsch., 1990, Robert Wood Johnson Found., 1992-95. Mem. APHA, Am. Coll. Healthcare Execs., Am. Econ. Assn., Am. Fin. Assn., Assn. Univ. Programs in Health Adminstrn. (chair fin. faculty com. 1992-93). Office: Dept HSMP U Mich Dept HSMP 109 Observatory Ann Arbor MI 48109-2029

SMITH, DELANCEY ALLAN, retired business executive; b. Leavenworth, Wash., Jan. 8, 1916; s. Christopher Allan Smith and Lois Leigh (DeLancey) Carpenter; m. Emily Louise Fountain, May 27, 1939; children: Stephanie Ann, DeLancey Allan Jr., Kevin Leigh. Student, Rockhurst Coll., 1936-38. Br. mgr. Kansas City (Mo.) Power & Light Co., 1933-45; asst. sales mgr. Donnelly Garment Co., Kansas City, 1946-50; v.p., gen. mgr. Superior Distbg. Co., Kansas City, 1950-57; pres. D.A. Smith Co., Kansas City, 1957-73, Am-Foam Products Co., Kansas City, 1973-84; ret., 1984; bd. dirs. Am.-Foam div. Cramer Products Co., Kansas City, Metal Doors & Frame Co., Kansas City. Mem. adv. bd. dirs. Empire State Bank, Kansas City, 1974-80, Mark Twain Banks, 1980-83, 88-91. Cpl. U.S. Army, 1945-46. Mem. Nat. Home Furnishing Reps. Assn. (bd. dirs. 1960-61, pres. 1962-63), Plaza Mchts. Assn. (pres. 1946), Kiwanis (pres. 1944), Rotary. Republican. Mem. Disciples of Christ Ch. Home: 6529 Mission Rd Shawnee Mission KS 66208-1748

SMITH, DELOS V., JR., actor, producer, director; b. Hutchinson, Kans., June 2, 1906; s. Delos V. and Beatrice Caroline (Von Blume) S. Student, NYU, 1926-27; BA, Kans. U., 1928; postgrad., Harvard U., 1929, Sorbonne U., Paris, 1930, Coll. De France, Paris, 1931. Producer, dir. Osborne & Souvaine Radio Prodns., N.Y.C., 1931-41. Appeared in (Broadway plays) Three Sisters, Front Page, Our Town, Fun Couple; London Aldwych Theatre on the Strand: Blues for Mr. Charlie, Three Sisters, (movies) One Flew Over the Cuckoo's Nest, Bound for Glory, 1976, Silver Streak, 1976, The Pack, 1977, (TV shows) Kojak, 1977, WKRP in Cincinnati, 1978, Studs Lonergan, 1978, Brave New World, 1978, (radio shows) The GM Symphony Hour, Metropolitan Opera of The Air, The Road Ahead, The Chevrolet Hour, Voice of America. Dir., trustee Kans. Pub. TV, Wichita, 1981—; civic adviser Mayor's Com., Hutchinson, 1987-88; founder, treas. Delos V. Smith Sr. Ctr., 1987. mem. Actors Studio Inc. (life), Lambs Club, Order DeMolay, Masons, Phi Beta Kappa. Republican. Presbyterian. Home: 700 Monterey Pl Hutchinson KS 67502 Office: Delos V Smith Sr Ctr Inc 101 W 1st Ave Hutchinson KS 67501-5235

SMITH, DOLORES MAXINE PLUNK, dancer, educator; b. Webster City, Iowa, Dec. 22, 1926; d. Herschel Swanson and Kathryn (Wilke) Hassig; m. Del O. Furrey, Aug, 26, 1945 (div. Feb. 1960); children: Bob H. Furrey, Jon B. Furrey, Kathryn E. Furrey; m. Dewey Pechota, 1962 (div. 1963); m. Leon Plunk, 1965 (div. 1966); m. Harold Burdick, 1974 (div. 1977); m. Floyd E. Smith, July 13, 1985. BS in Edn., Black Hills Tchrs. Coll., 1962; MA, Tex. Woman's U., 1964, PhD, 1974. Owner, operator pvt. dance studios, S.D., 1953-62; tchr. rural schs. Rosebud Reservation, S.D., 1945-49; tchr. Mellette County Pub. Schs., White River, S.D., 1958-60, St. Francis Indian Day Sch., 1960-61, Converse County (Wyo.) High Sch., 1961-62; grad. asst. Tex. Woman's U., Denton, 1962-64, 71; asst. prof. dance Sam Houston U., Huntsville, Tex., 1964-65; prof. Ctrl. Mo. State U., Warrensburg, 1965—; judge dance contest Kansas City Dance Theatre Co., 1987, 88, World Dance Assn., 1988, Mo. State Fair, 1989; judge Miss Am. Co-ed Pageants, 1991-93; dir. Dance Partisans Assn., Ctrl. Mo. State U., 1982—, cmty. children's gymnastics program, 1982—, tchr. cmty. dance program, 1988—, dir. show dance team, 1991—; dance coord. Internat. Coun. Health, Phys. Edn., Recreation, Sport and Dance, 1991—; presenter Japanese Asia Dance Events, Malaysia, 1994, Dance Edn. Conf., Mich. State U., 1994. Contbr. articles to profl. jours. Bd. dirs. Kansas City Dance Theatre Co.; dir. Commn. on Dance, 1991-96, co-dir., 1994-96. Coun. for Health, Phys. Edn., Recreation, Sport and Dance scholar, 1995. Mem. Dance Masters Am. (sec. 1985-87, chmn. Mr. and Miss Dance Contest 1985, scholarships com. 1988-90), AAHPERD (honors award cen. dist. chpt., cen. dist. presentor 1991-92, dance chair, coll. chair, dance performance chair 1989-90, v.p. dance edn. 1991-93), Mo. Assn. Health, Phys. Edn., Recreation and Dance (pres. 1972, svc. award), Nat. Dance Assn. (v.p. dance edn. 1991-93, chmn. Heritage luncheon 1968, 78, 87, Heritage award com. 1988-89, mem. ad hoc spl. svcs. com. 1989—, pub. Spotlight 1989-90), Mid-Am. Dance Network (on-site coord. choreographers/dancers workshop 1992, bd. dirs., sec. 1992-94), Mo. Art Coun. Basic Arts Edn. (basic arts edn. task force higher edn.), Dance and Child Internat. (display chair, presider 1991), Asian Pacific Conf. Arts Edn. (presenter 1989), Assn. Supervision and Curriculum Devel., Internat. Congress Health, Phys. Edn. and Recreation Presenters (congress dels. representing dance, presenter 1991, 93), Internat. Phys. Edn. and Sports for Girls and Women, Phys. Edn. and Recreation, Mo. Alliance for Arts Edn. Home: 130 SW 400th Rd Warrensburg MO 64093-8109 Office: Ctrl Mo State U Dept Physical Education Warrensburg MO 64093

SMITH, DON C., state legislator; m. Hildred A. Smith. Rep. dist. 116 State of Kans. Democrat. Home: 2206 Roanoke Rd Dodge City KS 67801-2734*

SMITH, DONALD ARTHUR, electrical engineer, educator; b. Hudson, Wis., Dec. 23, 1935; s. Charles Phillip and Marguerite Evelyn (Harsh) S.; m. Joan Mary Kaehn, Apr. 26, 1958 (div. 1983); children: Michael, Daniel,

Teresa, Susan, Anne, Jessica; m. JoEllen Margaret Leintz, July 16, 1988; stepchildren: Charles Kranz, Nicholas Kranz, Melissa Kranz. BEE, U. Minn., 1957, MEE, 1960, PhD, 1968. Instr. U. Minn., Mpls., 1959-64; electonics engr. U.S. Army Electronics Command, Ft. Monmouth, N.J., 1964-68; rsch. staff mem. corp. R&D Gen. Electric, Schenectady, N.Y., 1968-74; assoc. prof. N.D. State U., Fargo, 1974-81, chmn. elec. engring. dept., 1990, 95; prof., 1981—; assoc. dean N.D. State U., Fargo, 1991-94; cons. Stieger Tractor, Branick Industries, Fargo, 1983-89. Contbr. numerous articles to profl. jours.; patentee in field. Active electronics adv. com. Fargo Pub. Schs., 1982-94. NSF summer fellow, 1975, USAF summer fellow, 1976. Mem. IEEE (sr., paper reviewer 1985-90), N.D. Acad. Sci., KC (grand knight 1978-79, dist. dep. 1988-92, 4th degree honor guard 1983—), Tau Beta Pi, Eta Kappa Nu, Sigma Xi. Roman Catholic. Home: 1123 5th Ave S Fargo ND 58103-1725 Office: ND State U Elec Engring Dept Fargo ND 58105

SMITH, DONALD C., business executive; b. Detroit, Oct. 30, 1939. BSBA, Ea. Mich. U., 1963. Treas. Great Scott Supermarkets, Detroit, 1973-76; sr. v.p. of fin. and ops. Coca Cola, Detroit, 1976-95; pres. Donald C. Smith & Assoc., Southfield, Mich., 1985—; adj. faculty Wayne State U., Detroit, 1986—, Walsh Coll., Detroit, 1988-93. Author: (booklet) The Business Checkup, 1994. Treas. Farmington Rockets Jr. Football League, 1985-90. Office: Ste 625 24901 NW Hwy Southfield MI 48075

SMITH, DONALD ROY, public relations professional; b. Hudson, Colo., Aug. 1, 1926; s. Roy Cannon and Blanche Ethel (Rouse) Strauss; m. Helen George Caldes, Mar. 19, 1955; children: Ronald, Richard, Melissa. BA, U. Denver, 1950. Dir. publicity Denver Bears baseball team, 1951-55; athletic info. dir. U. Denver, 1955-62; asst. commr. Western Athletic Conf., Denver, 1962-64; dir. pub. rels. Denver Broncos football team, 1964-66, New Orleans Saints football team, 1967-68; v.p. pub. rels. Pro Football Hall of Fame, Canton, Ohio, 1968—; ofcl. scorer, Super Bowl, NFL, 1968—, mgr. promotional activities, 1970—. Co-author: Their Deeds and Dogged Faith, 1984; author: Pro Football Hall of Fame All-Time Greats, 1988, Official Encyclopedia of Football, 1989; inventor forward passing rating system for NFL, 1973; host Baseball TV Show, 1952-55. With USN, 1944-46. Mem. Football Writers Assn. Am., NFL Alumni Assn., Cleve. Touchdown Club, Hall of Fame Luncheon Club, Phi Beta Kappa, Omicron Delta Kappa. Republican. Home: 601 Furbee Ave SW Canton OH 44720-2801 Office: Pro Football Hall of Fame 2121 George Halas Dr NW Canton OH 44708-2630

SMITH, DWYANE, university administrator; b. St. Louis, Feb. 16, 1961; s. Magnolia Smith. BS in Psychology, N.E. Mo. State U., 1983, MA in Edn. Adminstrn., 1991. Intern IRS, St. Louis, 1983; minority counselor N.E. Mo. State U., Kirksville, 1983-88, dir. minority svcs., 1988-91, asst. dir. admissions, 1991—. Mem. Alpha Phi Alpha (chair statewide conv. 1990, Mo. Man of Yr. 1985), Alpha Phi Omega. Home: 1601 S Franklin St Kirksville MO 63501-4401

SMITH, E. BERRY, television and radio executive; b. Daytona Beach, Fla., Feb. 21, 1926; s. Samuel Rogers and Rosemary (Berry) S.; m. Mary Terese Hoffman, Apr. 3, 1948 (dec.); children: Kevin B., Martin J. BS, Butler U., 1949. Account exec. Sta. WIRE Radio, Indpls., 1949-54; dir. advt. and pub. relations Franklin Fin. Co., Hartford City, Ind., 1954-56; account exec. CBS Radio Network, Detroit, 1956-57; v.p. Sta. WFIE-TV, Evansville, 1957-61, Sta. WFRV-TV, Green Bay, Wis., 1961-62; exec. v.p. Sta. WLKY-TV, Louisville, 1962-64; pres. Sta. WTVW-TV, Evansville, 1964-80, Sta. WSBT, South Bend, Ind., 1981-89; sr. v.p. Schurz Comm. Inc., South Bend, 1989—; dir. adv. bd. CBS-TV Affiliates Assn., 1984-87, sec., treas., 1988-90, chmn., 1990-91. Dir. Goodwill Industries, South Bend, 1984-85, Jr. Achievement Michiana, South Bend, 1984-91. Served to 1st lt. U.S. Army, 1944-46, PTO. Recipient Silver medal Am. Advt. Fedn., Evansville, Ind., 1973; named to Ind. Broadcasters Assn. Hall of Fame, 1989; appointed Sagamore of the Wabash, 1993. Mem. South Bend C. of C. (bd. dirs. 1988-92), Ind. Soc. Chgo., Morris Park Country Club, Nat. Press Club, Summit Club, Notre Dame U. Club. Roman Catholic. Home: 5182 Finch Dr South Bend IN 46614-5491 Office: Schurz Comm Inc 225 W Colfax Ave South Bend IN 46626-1000

SMITH, ELIZABETH BARKER, psychiatrist; b. Knoxville, Tenn., Mar. 17, 1930; d. Robert Monroe and Myrtle (Dekle) Bell; m. James Benton Barker (div.); children: Jennifer, Susan; m. Othello Dale Smith, Feb. 26, 1971 (dec. May 1994). BA, Johnson Bible Coll., Knoxville, 1950, U. Tenn., 1952; MD, U. Tenn., Memphis, 1955. Intern John Gaston Hosp., Memphis, 1956; resident U. Tenn. Hosp., Memphis, 1957-60; pvt. practice Tripoli, Libya, 1960-63, Memphis, 1964-65; psychiatrist Johnson County Mental Health Ctr., Prairie Village, Kans., 1966; pvt. practice Prairie Village, 1967—; chair program for women Sch. Medicine U. Mo., Kansas City, 1986—; chair Advocacy and Intervention for Med. Students Coun., Kansas City, 1990—. Chair bd. trustees Baker U., Baldwin City, Kans., 1991-93. Mem. AMA, Am. Psychiat. Assn., Am. Med. Women's Assn. (br. 9 pres. 1991-92), Kans. Med. Assn., Johnson County Med. Assn. Republican. Methodist. Address: 3709 Somerset Prairie Village KS 66208 Office: Gestalt Found Kans 7301 Mission Rd Ste 248 Prairie Village KS 66208-3005

SMITH, EVAN SHREEVE, university official; b. Lawrence, Kans., Oct. 9, 1951; s. Carlyle S. and Judith (Pogany) S.; m. Marlene Mannella, Oct. 16, 1982; 1 child, Nathan Mannella. BA in Anthropology and Linguistics, U. Kans., 1973, MA in Linguistics, 1975; MA in Linguistics, Ind. U., 1978, PhD in Linguistics, 1982. Asst. instr. linguistics dept. U. Kans., Lawrence, 1974-75; assoc. instr. linguistics dept. Ind. U., Bloomington, 1976-79, proofreader/editor or mng. editor, 1978-84, vis. asst. prof., 1983-84, editor ind. study program, 1984-87, devel. coord., 1987-89; univ. and non-credit curriculum specialist U. Mo., Columbia, 1989—. Editor: (course study) Consumer Education, 1985; co-editor: Lingua Franca, Son of Lingua Franca, 1978, 79, Proc. 1992 Mid-Am. Linguistics Conf. and Conf. Siouan/Caddoan Langs., 1993; contbr. articles to profl. newsletters and jours. Mem. Nat. Univ. Continuing Edn. Assn., Phi Beta Kappa.

SMITH, FRANK EARL, retired association executive; b. Fremont Center, N.Y., Feb. 4, 1931; s. Earl A. and Hazel (Knack) S.; m. Caroline R. Gillin, Aug. 14, 1954; children—Stephen F., David S., Daniel E. B.S., Syracuse U., 1952. With Mellor Advt. Agy., Elmira, N.Y., 1954-55; asst. mgr. Assn. of Commerce, Elmira, N.Y., 1955-56, C. of C., Binghamton, N.Y.; mgr. Better Bus. Bur., Broome County, N.Y., 1956-60; exec. v.p. C. of C., Chemung County, Elmira, 1960-65, Schenectady County (N.Y.) C. of C., 1965-69, Greater Cin. C. of C., 1969-78; pres. Greater Detroit C. of C., 1978-95. Served to 1st lt. USAF, 1952-54. Named Young Man of Yr. Jr. C. of C. Elmira, 1964. Mem. C. of C. Execs. Mich., Am. C. of C. Execs. (past chmn.), N.Y. State C. of C. Execs. (past pres.), Ohio C. of C. Execs. (past pres.), C. of C. of U.S. (past bd. dirs., past chmn. nat. bd. regents), Inst. for Orgn. Mgmt., Lochmoor Golf Club. Presbyterian. Home: 59 Greenbriar St Grosse Pointe Shores MI 48236-1507

SMITH, FRANK EDMUND, English educator; b. Conneaut, Ohio, Apr. 20, 1943; s. Frank Ernest and Gertrude Helen (Stickney) S.; m. April Rose Kendziora, June 18, 1966; children: Paul Andrew, Thomas More. BA, Gannon U., 1965; PhD, Loyola U., Chgo., 1973. Prof. English W.M.R. Harper Coll., Palatine, Ill., 1968—; pub. White Eagle Coffee Store Press, Fox River Grove, Ill., 1992—. Mem. MLA, Nat. Coun. Tchrs. English. Office: WM R Harper Coll 1200 W Algonquin Palatine IL 60067

SMITH, GEORGE CURTIS, judge; b. Columbus, Ohio, Aug. 8, 1935; s. George B. and Dorothy R. S.; m. Barbara Jean Wood, July 10, 1963; children: Curtis, Geoffrey, Elizabeth Ann. BA, Ohio State U., 1957, JD, 1959. Bar: Ohio 1959, U.S. Dist. Ct. (so. dist.) Ohio 1987. Asst. city atty. City of Columbus, 1959-62; exec. asst. to Mayor of Columbus, 1962-63; asst. atty. gen. State of Ohio, 1964; chief counsel to pros. atty. Franklin County, Ohio, 1965-70, pros. atty., 1971-80; judge Franklin County Mcpl. Ct., Columbus, 1980-85; judge Franklin County Common Pleas Ct., 1985-87; mem. Ohio Supreme Ct. Coun. on Victims Rights, 1988-94; judge in residence Law Sch. U. Cin., 1993; faculty Ohio Jud. Coll., Litigation Practice Inst.; chmn. 1994, Fed. Bench-Bar Conf., 1995; lectr. ABA Anti-Trust Sec., 1995; alumni spkr. law graduation Ohio State U., 1995; pres. Young Rep. Club, 1963, Perry Group, 1996; exec. com. Franklin County Rep. Party, 1971-80; Elder Presbyn. Ch. Recipient Superior Jud. Service award Supreme Ct. Ohio; Resolution of Honor, Columbus Bldg. and Constrn. Trades Coun. Mem. Ohio Pros. Attys. Assn. (pres., Ohio Prosecutor of Yr, Award of Honor, Leadership award), Columbus Bar Assn., Assn. Trial Lawyers Am., Columbus Bar Found., Fed. Bar Assn., Ohio Mcpl. Judges Assn. (v.p. 1983), Columbus Athletic Club (pres., dir.), Lawyers Club of Columbus (pres. 1975), Masons (33d degree), Aladdin Shrine. Presbyterian. Office: 85 Marconi Blvd Columbus OH 43215-2823

SMITH, GERARD VINTON, chemistry educator; b. Delano, Calif., Oct. 14, 1931; s. Marion Lew and Marjorie Elsie (Ryland) S.; m. Jolynn Clayton Fenn, June 22, 1956; children: Kenneth Paul, Craig Stephen, Elise Patricia. BA in Chemistry, Coll. of Pacific, 1953, MS in Chemistry, 1956; PhD in Chemistry, U. Ark., 1959. Rsch. assoc. Northwestern U., Evanston, Ill., 1959-60, instr. chemistry, 1960-61; asst. prof. chemistry Ill. Inst. Tech., Chgo., 1961-66; assoc. prof. chemistry So. Ill. U., Carbondale, 1966-73, prof. chemistry, 1973—, dir. molecular sci. program, 1978-96; tech. cons. to ins. adjusters and attys. and industry in So. Ill.; chemistry tutor local high sch.; rsch. collaborator Jozsef Attila U., Szeged, Hungary, 1980—; instr. organic catalysis Pohang (Korea) U. Sci. and Tech., 1994, vis. prof., 1996. Author: Catalysis in Organic Syntheses, 1977; contbr. over 115 articles and book revs. to sci. jours. Elder Ch. of Christ. Recipient Outstanding Rschr. award So. Ill. U. Coll. Sci., 1990, Kaplan rsch. award Sigma Xi, 1992, Paul N. Rylander award Organic Reactions Catalysis Soc. div. N.Am. Catalysis Soc., 1995; grantee Free U. Iran, 1978-81, Monsanto Co., 1962-63, ACS-PRF, 1963-66, USPHS-NIH, 1963-66, W.R. Grace Co., 1966-72, Ill. State Geol. Survey, Dept. Energy, 1981-84, 86-87, Ill. Coal Rsch. Bd., 1982—, ORR, 1967-69, Materials Tech. Ctr., So. Ill. U., 1983—, Uniroyal Chem. Co., 1989-92, CRSC, 1987—, numerous others. Home: 106 N Lark Ln Carbondale IL 62901-2017 Office: So Ill U Mailcode 4409 Carbondale IL 62901

SMITH, GLENN SANBORN, plant breeder, university administrator; b. Antler, N.D., Dec. 21, 1907; s. Ralph Waldo and Effie Frances (Christian) S.; m. Doris Elaine Abel, July 25, 1930; children: Nancy Ann, Ronald Glenn, Robert Paul. BS, N.D. State U., 1929, DSc, 1990; MS, Kans. State U., 1931; PhD, U. Minn., 1947. Agronomist USDA, Fargo, 1929-47; prof. agronomy N.D. State U., Fargo, 1947-78, assoc. dir., assoc. dean, 1947-51, dean grad. sch., 1954-73, prof. emeritus agronomy, 1978—; cons. plant breeding U.S. AID, Uruguay, 1977-78; curriculum cons. agr. Facultad of Agriculture, Uruguay, 1979, People to People, China, 1983. Publisher Smith Family Rhymes, 1995; contbr. articles to profl. jours. Fellow Am. Soc. Agronomy, Crop Sci. Soc. Am.; mem. N.D. Acad. Sci. (pres. 1952), Sigma Xi. Methodist. Home: 3140 10th St N Fargo ND 58102-1336 Office: ND State U Univ Sta Fargo ND 58102

SMITH, HARRY BUCHANAN, JR., graphic designer, painter, photographer, writer; b. Springfield, Ill., Aug. 30, 1924; s. Harry Buchanan and Cordelia Warren (Birchall) S.; divorced; 1 child, Mark Savolainen. B of Design, U. Mich., 1947; MS in Design, Ill. Inst. Tech., 1948. Designer Chgo. Plan Commn., 1948-49, Warren Wetheral & Assocs., Chgo., 1949-50; dir. design Dekovic-Smith Design Orgn., Chgo., 1951-58; prin. H.B. Smith & Assocs., Chgo., 1959-87. Author: Contemporary Fables, 1988; works include graphic design (with Mortimer Adler) Encyclopaedia Britannica, 15th edit., 1975, 176 exhibitions, 1951-87; redesigned YMCA internat. symbol, numerous corporate identity programs, publs. Served to lt. (j.g.) USNR, 1943-47, PTO. Mem. Am. Inst. Graphic Arts, Am. Ctr. for Design (steering com.). Home and Office: 2417 N Burling St Chicago IL 60614-2615

SMITH, HENRY CHARLES, III, symphony orchestra conductor; b. Phila., Jan. 31, 1931; s. Henry Charles Jr. and Gertrude Ruth (Downs) S.; m. Mary Jane Dressner, Sept. 3, 1955; children—Katherine Anne, Pamela Jane, Henry Charles IV. BA, U. Pa., 1952; artist diploma, Curtis Inst. Music, Phila., 1955. Solo trombonist Phila. Orch., 1955-67; condr. Rochester (Minn.) Symphony Orch., 1967-68; assoc. prof. music Ind. U., Bloomington, 1968-71; resident condr., ednl. dir. Minn. Orch., Mpls., 1971-88; prof. music U. Tex., Austin, 1988-89, Frank C. Erwin Centennial Prof. of Opera, 1988-89; music dir. S.D. Symphony, Sioux Falls, 1989—; prof. Ariz. State U., Tempe, 1989-93, prof. emeritus, 1993—; vis. prof. U. Tex., Austin, 1987-88; founding mem. Phila. Brass Ensemble, 1956—. Composer 5 books of solos for trombone including Solos for the Trombone Player, 1963, Hear Us As We Pray, 1963, First Solos for The Trombone Player, 1972, Easy Duets for Winds, 1972; editor 14 books 20th century symphonies lit. Served to 1st lt. AUS, 1952-54. Recipient 3 Grammy nominations, 1967, 76, 1 Grammy award for best chamber music rec. with Phila. Brass Ensemble, 1969. Mem. Internat. Trombone Assn. (dir.), Am. Symphony Orch. League, Music Educators Nat. Conf., Am. Guild Organists, Am. Fedn. Musicians, Tubist Universal Brotherhood Assn., Acacia Fraternity. Republican. Congregationalist. Home: 8032 Pennsylvania Rd Bloomington MN 55438

SMITH, IAN CORMACK PALMER, biophysicist; b. Winnipeg, Man., Can., Sept. 23, 1939; s. Cormack and Grace Mary S.; m. Eva Gunilla Landvik, Mar. 27, 1965; children: Brittmarie, Cormack, Duncan, Roderick. BS, U. Man., 1961, MS, 1962; PhD, Cambridge U., England, 1965; Filosophie Doktor (hon.), U. Stockholm, 1986; DSc (hon.), U. Winnipeg, 1990; Diploma Tech. (hon.), Red River Coll., 1996. Fellow Stanford U., 1965-66; mem. rsch. staff Bell Tel. Labs., Murray Hill, N.J., 1966-67; rsch. officer divsn. biol. scis. NRC, Ottawa, 1967-87, dir. gen., 1987-91; dir.-gen. Inst. Biodiagnostics, Winnipeg, 1992—; adj. prof. chemistry and biochemistry Carleton U., 1973-90, U. Ottawa, 1976-92; adj. prof. chemistry, physics and anatomy U. Man., 1992—; adj. prof. biophysics U. Ill., Chgo., 1974-80; allied scientist Ottawa Civic Hosp., 1985—, Ottawa Gen. Hosp., 1989—, Ont. Cancer Found., 1989-91, St. Boniface Hosp., 1992—, Health Scis. Ctr., 1993—, Econ. Tech. Innovation Coun., Man., 1994—, exec. com., 1995—, Man. Health Rsch. Coun., 1995—. Contbr. chps. to books, articles in field to profl. jours. Recipient Barringer award Can. Spectroscopy Soc., 1979, Herzberg award, 1986, Organon Teknika award Can. Soc. Clin. Chemists, 1987, Sr. Scientist award Sigma Xi, 1995. Fellow Chem. Inst. Can. (Merck award 1978, Labatt award 1984), Royal Soc. Can. (Flavelle medal 1996), Soc. Magnetic Resonance Medicine (exec. com. 1989-94); mem. Internat. Coun. Sci. Unions (gen. com. 1993—), Am. Chem. Soc., Biophys. Soc., Can. Biochem. Soc. (Ayerst award 1978), Biophys. Soc. Can. (pres. 1992-94), Internat. Union Pure and Applied Biophysicis (coun. 1993—), U. Man. Alumni Assn. (bd. dirs. 1993—). Office: Inst Biodiagnostics, Winnipeg, MB Canada R3B 1Y6

SMITH, JAMES E., music educator, jazz guitarist; b. San Diego, Aug. 2, 1952; s. Jaems E. and Dorothy A. (Worden) S.; m. Gloria Curtis; children: Shelley, Bryan, Aaron, Rachel. BA, U. N.Mex., 1974; MM, Wis. Conservatory of Music, Milw., 1980. Assoc. prof. music Ctrl. State U., Wilberforce, Ohio, 1980—; adj. asst. prof. music Coll. Conservatory of Music, U. Cin., 1984—; pub. Jazz from The Conservatory Press, Bellbrook, Ohio, 1985—. Author: Jazz Guitar: Theory and Technique, 1981, Chord Thesaurus for Jazz Guitar, 1986, Guitarist's Guide to Technique, 1989; musician (CD) Cin. Seven, 1987. NEH grantee, 1984. Office: Central State U Dept Music Wilberforce OH 45384

SMITH, JANE SCHNEBERGER, retired city clerk; b. Chgo., Aug. 9, 1928; d. Frank R. and Marion (Durante) Schneberger; m. Z. Erol Smith, Jr., Oct. 28, 1950 (div. 1974); children: Suzan McCue Kuester, Tracy Smith Cawley, Cameron Farley, Z. Erol III, Kimberly Van Den Elzen, Scott. BA in Chemistry, U. Colo., 1950; MA in Communication, Mich. State U., 1978, PhD in ednl. adminstrn. Mich. State U., 1987. Chemist, Kellogg Switchboard, Chgo., 1950-51; tchr. Crab Orchard Sch., Palos Heights, Ill., 1969-70; v.p. South Cook County Girl Scouts, Harvey, Ill., 1967-69, (Thanks badge 1972), staff advisor, 1970-72; program and tng. dir. Mich. Capitol coun. Girl Scouts U.S., Lansing, 1972-75; dir. svc. learning ctr. Mich. State U., East Lansing, 1975-81; city clk. City of Ashland, Wis., 1981-89; interim city adminstr., 1989-90, ret. 1990; cons. vol. adminstrn., Mich., Wis., 1975—. Co-editor Looking Backward Moving Forward; Contbr. articles to profl. jours. V.p. Mich. Capitol Girl Scout Council, Lansing, 1976-78 (cert. appreciation 1975); bd. dirs. Lansing RSVP, 1976-81, Ashland Mus., 1985-87, Ptnrs. in Recovery, 1985-87; v.p. Friends of the Libr., 1992—; sec. New Horizons, 1985-90, New Day Shelter, 1990—, v.p., 1993-95, pres., 1995—; pres. LWV of Ashland Bayfield County, 1992-93; sec. No. Wis. History Ctr., 1992-94; commr. Ashland Water & Wastewater Utility, 1993—; mem. Ashland Beautification Com., 1993—, Big Top Chautauque, 1996, vice chair Allaince for Sustainability, 1994—; v.p. GFWC/Ashland Monday Club, 1994—. Mem. Internat. Assn. Mcpl. Clks., Wis. Mcpl. Clks. Assn. (dist. dir. 1984-86). Roman Catholic. Club: Am. Bus. Women's Assn. (scholarship chmn. 1985) (Ashland). Lodge: Zonta (pres. 1979-81). Avocations: stained glass, gardening, stamp collecting, genealogy. Home: 700 MacArthur Ave Ashland WI 54806-2903

SMITH, JEFFREY HOWARD, accountant; b. Des Moines, Dec. 3, 1956; s. Richard Howard and Helen Louise (Shepley) S.; m. Carol Sue Lippens, Sept. 7, 1985; children: Crystal, Stephanie, Travis. AA in Liberal Arts, Des Moines Area Community Coll., 1977; BA in Acctg., U. No. Iowa, 1979. CPA, Iowa. Sr. staff acct. Dee, Gosling and Co., Maquoketa, Iowa, 1980-84; pvt. practice tax acctg. Jeffrey H. Smith, Tax Practice, Maquoketa, Iowa, 1984-85; acct., treas. West Des Moines (Iowa) Water Works, 1985—. Mem. Am. Inst. CPA's, Iowa Soc. CPA's, Maquoketa Jaycees. Democrat. Roman Catholic. Home: 1035 22nd St West Des Moines IA 50265-2220 Office: West Des Moines Water Works PO Box 65610 West Des Moines IA 50265-0610

SMITH, JOAN H., women's health nurse, educator; b. Akron, Ohio; d. Joseph A. and Troynette M. (Lower) McDonald; m. William G. Smith; children: Sue Ann, Priscilla, Timothy. Diploma, Akron City Hosp., 1948; BSN in Edn., U. Akron, 1972, MA in Family Devel., 1980. Cert. in inpatient obstetric nursing. Mem. faculty Akron Gen. Med. Ctr. Sch. Nursing, 1964; former dir. obstet. spl. procedures Speakers Bur., Women's Health Ctrs. Akron Gen. Med. Ctr., 1988;, 1990; cons., speaker women's health care. Mem. Assn. Women's Health, Obstet. and Neonatal Nursing (charter, past sec.-treas., past vice chmn. Ohio sect., chmn. program various confs.). Home: 873 Kirkwall Dr Copley OH 44321-1751

SMITH, JOHN FRANCIS, JR., automobile company executive; b. Worcester, Mass., Apr. 6, 1938; s. John Francis and Eleanor C. (Sullivan) S.; children: Brian, Kevin; m. Lydia G. Sigrist, Aug. 27, 1988; 1 stepchild, Nicola. B.B.A., U. Mass., 1960; M.B.A., Boston U., 1965. Fisher Body div. mgr. Gen. Motors Corp., Framingham, Mass., 1961-73; asst. treas Gen. Motors Corp., N.Y.C., 1973-80; comptroller Gen. Motors Corp., Detroit, 1980-81, dir. worldwide product planning, 1981-84; pres., gen. mgr. Gen. Motors Can., Oshawa, Ont., Can., 1984-85; exec. v.p. Gen. Motors Europe, Glattbrugg, Switzerland, 1986-87, pres., 1987-88; exec. v.p. internat. ops. Gen. Motors Corp., Detroit, 1988-90; vice chmn. internat. ops. Gen. Motors Corp., 1990, bd. dirs., mem. fin. com., 1990—, pres., COO, 1992—; CEO, pres., 1992-95; chmn. bd. Gen. Motors Corp., Detroit, 1996—; pres.'s coun. Global Strategy Bd.; bd. dirs. EDS, Hughes Electronics Corp., Gen. Motors Acceptance Corp.; mem. Bus. Roundtable Policy Com.; mem. U.S. Japan Bus. Coun., Am. Soc. Corp. Execs.; mem. Bd. of Detroit Renaissance; bus. coun. Meml. Sloan-Kettering Cancer Ctr.; bd. dirs. Procter & Gamble Co. Mem. chancellor's exec. com. U. Mass., dir.; trustee United Way S.E. Mich., New Am. Revolution, Boston U. Mem. Am. Soc. Corp. Execs., Am. Auto Mfrs. Assn. (bd. dirs.), Econ. Club Detroit (bd. dirs.), Beta Gamma Sigma (pres.), Dirs. Table. Roman Catholic. Office: GM 3044 W Grand Blvd Detroit MI 48202-3091*

SMITH, JOHN WALLACE, surgeon, educator; b. Hutchinson, Kans., Feb. 18, 1931; s. W. Donald and Claramary (Smith) S.; m. Margaret Lee, Dec. 26, 1959; children: John Wallace Jr., Frances, George MacDonell. AB, Harvard U., 1952; MD, U. Nebr., 1956. Diplomate Am. Bd. Surgery, Am. Bd. Gen. Vascular Surgery. Intern San Francisco Hosp., 1956-57; resident Stanford U. Hosps., San Francisco, 1957-60, U. Calif. Hosps., San Francisco, 1960-62; pvt. practice in gen. surgery Omaha, 1964-70; practice specializing in vascular surgery, pres. Vascular Surgery, P.C., Omaha, 1970-96; clin. assoc. prof. surgery Coll. Medicine U. Nebr., Omaha, 1966—; pres. med. staff Meth. Hosp., Omaha, 1986-87. Contbr. articles to profl. jours. Bd. dirs. Omaha Symphony Assn. Served to capt. Med. Corps U.S. Army, 1962-64. Fellow ACS (gov. 1987-92); mem. Midwestern Vascular Surg. Soc. (chmn. membership com. 1982), Internat. Soc. Cardiovascular Surgery, Western Surg. Assn. (chmn. membership com. 1995), Alpha Omega Alpha (pres. 1982-83). Office: 8111 Dodge St Omaha NE 68114

SMITH, JOHN WILLIAM, political scientist; b. Jamestown, N.D., Oct. 31, 1938; s. John William and Lena R. (Jordheim) S.; AA, U. N.D., 1958; BA, Northwestern U., 1960; MA, U. Mich., 1963; m. Therese Al Hout, Nov. 22, 1980; children: Lena Jordan, Galen Dakota. Instr., U. Detroit, 1962-63, No. Mich. U., 1965-67; asst. prof. Indiana (Pa.) U., 1967-69; adj. prof. U. Detroit, 1970-82; vis. lectr. U. Mich., Dearborn, 1975—; instr. polit. sci. Henry Ford C.C., Dearborn, 1969—. Mem. Am. Polit. Sci. Assn., So. Polit. Sci. Assn., Western Polit. Sci. Assn., Assn. for Asian Studies, Mich. Soc. Planning Ofcls., Mich. Conf. Polit. Sci. (pres. 1986-87). Contbr. chpts. to Riot in the Cities, 1970, City-Surburban Relations, 1979; co-author: (with John S. Klemanski) The Urban Politics Dictionary, 1990. Contbr. articles to profl. jours. Home: 21652 N Riverview Ct Beverly Hills MI 48025-4864 Office: Henry Ford Community Coll Dept Polit Sci Dearborn MI 48128

SMITH, JOHN WILLIAM HUGH, civil engineer; b. Port Arthur, Ont., Can., Oct. 16, 1937; s. George Edward and Nina Edith Smith; m. Anne Patten; children: Scott, Steven, Richard. AA with honors, Lakehead U., Thunder Bay, Ont., 1959; BSCE with honors, Mich. Tech. U., 1962. Proposal engr. surface combustion div. Midland-Ross Corp., Toledo, 1962-65; sr. project engr. surface combustion div. Midland-Ross Corp., Toronto, Ont., 1965-70; div. mgr. Holcroft & Co. (Can.) Ltd., London, Ont., 1970-76; mgr. engring. Holcroft, Livonia, Mich., 1976-81, tech. dir., mgr., sales and mktg., v.p., tech. dir., 1981-93; pres. Sterling Systems, Royal Oak, Mich., 1993—. Contbr. chpts. to books; patentee in field. Mem. Assn. Profl. Engrs. of Province Ont., Am. Soc. Metals Internat. Office: 5060 Delemere Ave Royal Oak MI 48073-1005

SMITH, JOSEPH W., elementary education educator; b. Kansas City, Mo., Apr. 14, 1937; s. Oren Zelus and Nellie Catherine (Floyd) S. BS in Elem. Edn., Ctrl. Mo. State U., 1964; MA in Coll. & Univ. Adminstrn., Mich. State U., East Lansing, 1990. Tchr. elem. sch. Raytown (Mo.) Sch. Dist. # 2, 1964-66, Villa Park (Ill.) Sch. Dist. # 45, 1966-88; grad. dir. Mich. State U., East Lansing, 1988-90; area dir., residence life Calif. State U., Sacramento, 1990-92; tchr., asst. spl. edn. Independence (Mo.) Pub. Schs., 1992—; tchr. Willowbrook H.S., Villa Park, 1975-85; area dir. residence life multicutlural choir Calit. State U., Sacramento, 1991. Editor newsletter Up to Date Inof. and Humor, 1980. Mem. NEA, AACD, Am. Coll. Student Pers. Assn. Home: 16901 Larkspur Ln # 4 Independence MO 64055

SMITH, JUDY ANN, insurance broker; b. Cape Girardeau, Mo., Oct. 16, 1948; d. James William and Gladys Marie Lawrence; m. Gary L. Smith, June 8, 1968 (div. 1983); children: Scott David, Ricky Alan, Robert Daryl. Student, S.E. Mo. State U., 1969-70. Ins. broker Shelter Ins. Co., Columbia, Mo., 1979—; owner ABC Mini-Storage Complex, Dexter, Mo. Home: 11455 S Lakeview Dr Dexter MO 63841 Office: Shelter Ins/Judy Smith Agy 915 Smith Ave Dexter MO 63841

SMITH, J.W., mechanical engineer; b. Columbus, Ohio, Jan. 28, 1936. BSBA, Ohio State U., 1960; BSME, U. Detroit, 1966. Cert. fluid power engr. Fluid Power Soc. Engring. mgr., mktg. mgr. Jeffrey divsn. Indressco Inc., Columbus, Ohio, 1975—; gen. mgr. Rotary Power, Columbus, 1983-86; chmn. control stds. com. Am. Mining Congress, Washington, 1989—, chmn. diesel com., 1981-82. Contbr. articles to profl. pubs. Mem. Rep. Nat. Glee Club, Columbus, 1984—. 2d lt. U.S. Army, 1952-54, Korea. Mem. NSPE, Am. Soc. Safety Engrs., Soc. Automotive Engrs., Soc. Mining Engrs. Methodist. Office: Indressco Inc Jeffrey Divsn 274 E 1st Ave Columbus OH 43201-3673

SMITH, KENARD EUGENE, marketing professional; b. L.A., July 28, 1946; s. Charles Howard and Dorothea (Tanquist) S.; m. Joanne Halvorsen, Aug. 8, 1969; children: Tracy, Lisa, Evan. BA, Bethel Coll., 1968; MA, U. Minn., 1971, PhD, 1974. From instr. to asst. prof. Va. Polytech Inst. and State U., Blacksburg, 1973-79; from sr. analyst to mgr. area rsch. and planning Dayton Hudson Corp., Mpls., 1979-88; dir. May Dept. Stores Co., St. Louis, 1988-93, v.p. area rsch., 1993—; adj. assoc. prof. Bethel Coll., St. Paul, 1981-83; guest lectr. in field. Contbr. articles to profl. jours. Capt. USAFR, 1972-82. Mem. Internat. Coun. Shopping Ctrs. (rsch. adv. task force 1991—), The Profl. Geographer (editl. bd. 1991—). Office: May Dept Stores Co 611 Olive St Saint Louis MO 63101-1721

SMITH, KIRK BERTON, judge; b. Cogswell, N.D., Feb. 5, 1930; s. Harry William and Adeline Marie (McCauley) S.; m. Mary Joan Bushaw July 2, 1960; children: Ellen, Thomas, James. PhB, U. N.D., 1956, JD, 1957. Bar: N.D. 1957. Law clk. to presiding justice U.S. Ct. Appeals (8th cir.), Fargo, N.D. and St. Louis, 1957-58; ptnr. Bangert & Smith, Enderlin, N.D., 1958-59, Arnason & Smith, Grand Forks, N.D., 1959-63; judge Grand Forks County Ct., 1963-77; judge N.D. Dist. Ct., Grand Forks, 1977—, presiding judge, 1987-90; mem. N.D. Spl. Procedures Commn., Bismarck, 1967—; chmn. N.D. Sentencing Commn., Bismarck, 1975-77, N.D. Jud. Immunity Commn., Bismarck, 1985—; chair-elect N.D. Jud. Conf., 1995—; internat. speaker U.S. legal system USIA, Kathmandu, Nepal, 1993. With USN, 1951-54, Korea. Mem. ABA, Am. Judicature Soc. (bd. dirs. N.D. chpt. 1982-86), Kiwanis (pres. Grand Forks 1975). Roman Catholic. Office: Dist Ct Courthouse 125 S 4th St PO Box 6347 Grand Forks ND 58206-6347

SMITH, LAUREN ASHLEY, lawyer, journalist, clergyman, physicist; b. Clinton, Iowa, Nov. 30, 1924; s. William Thomas Roy and Ethel (Cook) S.; m. Barbara Ann Mills, Aug. 22, 1947; children: Christopher A., Laura Nan Smith Pringle, William Thomas Roy II. BS, U. Minn., 1946, JD, 1949; postgrad., U. Chgo., 1943-49; MDiv, McCormick Theol. Sem., 1950; postgrad., U. Iowa, 1992. Bar: Colo. 1957, Iowa 1959, Ill. 1963, Minn. 1983, U.S. Supreme Ct. 1967; ordained to ministry Presbyn. Ch., 1950. Pastor Presbyn. Ch., Fredonia, Kans., 1950-52, Lamar, Colo., 1952-57; pastor Congl. Ch., Clinton, 1975-80; editor The Comml., Pine Bluff, Ark., 1957-58; pvt. practice Clinton, 1959—; internat. conferee Stanley Found., Warrenton, Va., 1963-72; legal observer USSR, 1978; co-sponsor All India Renewable Energy Conf., Bangalore, 1981; law sch. conferee U. Minn., China, 1983; sr. assoc. Molecular Nanotech. Foresight Inst., Palo Alto, Calif. Author: (jurisprudence treatise) Forma Dat Esse Rel, 1975, (monograph) First Strike Option, 1983; co-author: India On to New Horizons, 1989; columnist Crow Call, 1968—; co-editor Press and News of India, 1978-82; pub. Crow Call; pseudonym Christopher Crow, 1981—; editor Asian Econ. Community Jour.; contbr. articles to religious publs. Minister-at-large Presbyn. Ch. U.S.A., Iowa, 1987—, mem. nat. New Spiritual Formation Network; bd. dirs. Iowa divsn. UN Assn. U.S.A., Iowa City, 1970-85; sr. assoc. Molecular Nanotechnology Foresight Inst., Palo Alto, Calif.; Franciscans United Nations Non Govt. Orgn. Mem. Iowa Bar Assn., Ill. Bar Assn., St. Andrews Soc., Clinton County Bar Assn. (pres. 1968, Best in Iowa citation), Clinton Ministerial Assn., Samaritan Health Systems Chaplain Corps., Quaker Internat. Yokefellow, Nat. Network for New Spiritual Formation Presbyn. Ch. USA, Molecular Nanotechnology Foresight Inst. (sr. assoc.), Franciscans Internat.

SMITH, LEILA HENTZEN, artist; b. Milw., May 20, 1932; d. Erwin Albert and Marian Leila (Austin) Hentzen; m. Richard Howard Smith, Sept. 12, 1959; 1 child, Jennie. BFA, Miami U., 1955; cert., Famous Artists Schs., 1959. Quilting tchr. Milw. Pub. Schs., 1975-79. One-woman shows include Boerner Bot. Gardens, Whitnall Park, Wis., 1995; 2-woman show West Bend (Wis.) Gallery Fine Arts, 1963, Mapledale Sch. Gallery, Bayside Wis., 1981; exhibited in group shows, Including Milw. Art Ctr., 1961, Mustum Mus. Art, Racine, Wis., 1966, 77, Artist's World Gallery, Cedarburg, Wis., 1975, Ozaukee Art Ctr., Cedarburg, 1982-86, 93, John Michael Kohler Arts Ctr., Sheboygan, Wis., 1984, 87, 89-96, Cedarburg Cultural Ctr., 1988-96, West Bend Gallery Fine Arts, 1993, 96, Rahr-West Art Mus., Manitowoc, Wis., 1994, Gallery 110 North, Plymouth, Wis., 1996; represented in permanent collections Milw. County Art Commn., Wheaton Franciscans. Women's aux. vol. Salvation Army, Milw. Recipient Honorable Mention for painting Bayshore Merchants Assn, 1969, Delta Gamma Art Fair, 1981, Best of Show for painting John Michael Kohler Arts Ctr., 1988. Mem. AAUW, Cedarburg Artists Guild, Wis. Watercolor Soc., Seven Arts Soc. Milw. (pres. 1967-68, painters group chmn. 1962-63), Wis. Watercolor Soc., DAR (Milw. chpt. Holiday Folk Fair chmn. 1965-76, libr. historian 1974-77, corr. sec. 1977-80, dir. 1983-86, rec. sec. 1992-95, regent 1995—, Outstanding Jr. Mem. 1966), Wis. Soc. Daus. of Founders and Patriots of Am. (pres. 1964-66, 2d v.p. 1966-68, 70-73, corr. sec. 1976-79), Wis. Ct. Assts., Nat. Soc. Women Descendants Ancient and Hon. Artillery Co. Boston, Wis. Soc. Mayflower Descendents, Delta Zeta. Congregationalist. Home and Studio: 9966 N Corey Ln Mequon WI 53092-6207

SMITH, MARGARET, state legislator; b. Chgo.; m. Fred J. Smith; 2 sons, (dec.). Student, Tenn. State U. Mem. Ill. Ho. of Reps., 1981-83; mem. Ill. Senate, dist. 12, 1983—. Trustee Chgo. Bapt. Inst. Democrat. Office: State Senate State Capital Springfield IL 62706 Address: 4949 N Melvina Ave Chicago IL 60630-2907

SMITH, MARK ANTHONY, biochemist, educator; b. Leicester, Eng., Aug. 15, 1965; came to U.S., 1992; s. John and Rita Joyce (Haywood) S. BSc with honors, Durham (U.K.) U., 1986; PhD, Nottingham (U.K.) U., 1990. Postdoctoral biochemist Sandoz Forschungsinstitut, Vienna, Austria, 1990-91, Karl Landsteiner rsch. fellow, 1991-92; rsch. assoc. Case Western Res. U., Cleve., 1992-94, instr. in biochemistry, 1994-95; asst. prof., 1995—. Editor Biomed. Jour., 1994-95; guest editor Molecular Chemistry Neuropathology; contbr. articles to profl. jours.; rsch. findings presented on WQHS-TV 61 sta. Dalland fellow Am. Philos. Soc., 1995. Mem. AAAS, N.Y. Acad. Scis., Internat. Soc. Neurochemistry. Home: 2666 N Moreland Blvd Ste 14 Shaker Heights OH 44120 Office: Case Western Res U Inst Pathology 2085 Adelbert Rd Cleveland OH 44106

SMITH, MARK MAURICE, marketing professional; b. N.Y.C., Feb. 26, 1944; s. Maurice Fredrick and Catherine (Hanley) S.; m. Catherine Boaz White, Dec. 13, 1963 (div. June 1973); children: Renee Theresa, Tammy Marie; m. Christine Ellen Raubinger, May 30, 1975. BBA, Western Mich. U., 1971; MBA, U. Mich., 1974. Supt. Perini Corp., Boston, 1966-71; assoc. instr. Western Mich. U., Kalamazoo, 1971-74; dist. sales mgr. Poorman-Douglas Corp., Portland, Oreg., 1974-75; pres. Mktg. Mgmt., Inc., Kansas City, Mo., 1975-86; gen. mgr. Rollins Protective Svc., Overland Park, Kans., 1986-89; pres. Internat. Mktg., Ltd., Kansas City, 1989—; pres., gen. mgr. Weathershield Corp., 1993—. Mem. Jaycees, Kansas City Internat. Club (adv. 1990—). Office: Weathershield Corp Executive Hls Kansas City MO 64153 Office: Internat Mktg Ltd Executive Hls Kansas City MO 64153

SMITH, MARK STEVEN, lawyer; b. Cinn., Dec. 11, 1950; s. Roy and Burnetta (Rosenbaum) S.; m. Holly Sider, Oct. 10, 1981; children: Aaron, Jenna. BA, Ohio State U., 1972; JD, IIT, 1976. Bar: Ill. 1976, Ohio 1976, U.S. Ct. Appeals (7th cir.). Atty., ptnr. Engelman & Smith, Evanston and Skokie, Ill., 1976—. Mem. Am. Trial Lawyers Assn., Ill. State Bar Assn. (com. mem. alternate dispute resolution com. 1991-92), Chgo. Bar Assn. Democrat. Jewish. Home: 704 Michigan Ave Evanston IL 60202-2512 Office: Engelman & Smith 4711 Golf Rd Ste 907 Skokie IL 60076-1247

SMITH, MARK STEVEN, sales manager; b. Flint, Mich., Aug. 29, 1955; s. Pleasant Edward Jr. and Carole Jean (Ragan) S.; m. Pina Smith, Aug. 1, 1975; children: Zachary Wayne, Matthew Brice. BS in Indsl. Engring. summa cum laude, So. Ill. U., 1992; MS in Mfg. Sys. Engring., Oakland U., 1994. Project engr. mining divsn. Brit. Petroleum, Benton, Ill., 1977-90; applications engring. mgr. Automation Software, Inc., Farmington Hills, Mich., 1992-94; sales mgr. Detroit Testing Lab., Warren, Mich., 1994—; cons. CAD-CAM for various cos. Author: (tech. manual) Robotic Programming Using CAD Data, 1993. With U.S. Army, 1973-76, Vietnam. Mem. Soc. Mech. Engrs., Soc. Automatic Engrs. Home: 2345 Harness Dr West Bloomfield MI 48324 Office: Detroit Testing Lab Inc 7111 E Eleven Mile Rd Warren MI 48090

SMITH, MARY LOU BRAUN, psychiatric-mental health nurse; b. Burlington, Iowa, Oct. 3, 1935; m. Jack E. Smith, Feb. 12, 1966; children: Susan, Michael. Diploma, Mercy Hosp. Sch. Nursing, Davenport, Iowa, 1956; BSN, St. Ambrose Coll., Davenport, 1959; MA in Nursing, U. Iowa, 1971. RN, Iowa; cert. psychiat.-mental health nurse. Asst. prof. nursing U. Iowa, Iowa City, 1972-79; instr. psychiat. nursing Indian Hills Community Coll., Ottumwa, Iowa, 1983-84; clin. supr. psychiatry Burlington Med. Ctr., 1985; surveyor health facilities State of Iowa, Des Moines, 1985—. Contbr. articles to nursing jours. Named Iowa Surveyor of Yr., Iowa Dept. Inspections and Appeals, 1990. Mem. Am. Psychiat. Nurses Assn., Sigma Theta Tau. Home: 2616 Hickory Ave Mount Pleasant IA 52641

SMITH, MARYA JEAN, writer; b. Youngstown, Ohio, Nov. 12, 1945; d. Cameron Reynolds and Jean Rose (Sause) Argetsinger; m. Arthur Beverly Smith Jr., Dec. 30, 1968 (div. 1996); children: Arthur Cameron, Sarah Reynolds. BA, Cornell U., 1967. Editorial asst. Seventeen Mag., N.Y.C., 1967-68; promotion writer U. Chgo. Press, 1968-70; asst. account exec. Drucilla Handy Co., Chgo., 1970-72; feature writer various mags. Chgo., 1972-74; freelance writer Cornell U., Ithaca, N.Y., 1975-76, lectr., 1976-77; playwright Playwrights' Ctr. Prodn., Chgo., 1978; humor columnist various jours. Chgo., 1979-81, freelance writer, 1982—. Author: Across the Creek, 1989, Winter-Broken, 1990, Danish edit., 1991; contbr. poetry Primavera, Ariel VI and VIII, 1974, 87, 89; contbr. articles to mags. and papers, 1984—. Vol. reading tutor Literacy Vols. Western Cook County, Oak Park, Ill., 1988-89, Oak Park Pub. Libr. Reading Program, 1990-94. Recipient 1st Pl. for News Writing Associated Ch. Press, 1986, Poetry award Poets and Patrons, 1986, Triton Coll. Salute to Arts, 1987, 89. Mem. Nat. Writers Union, Soc. Children's Book Writers, Author's Guild, Chgo. Women in Pub., Children's Reading Round Table. Roman Catholic.

SMITH, MERILYN ROBERTA, art educator; b. Tolley, N.D., July 24, 1933; d. Robert Coleman and Mathilda Marie (Staael) S. BA, Concordia Coll., Minn., 1953; MA, State U. of Iowa, Iowa City, 1956, MFA, 1966. Tchr. Badger (Minn.) High Sch., 1954; instr. in art Valley City (N.D.) State Tchrs. Coll., 1957, 58; instr. in art U. Wis., Oshkosh, 1967, asst. prof. art, 1969, assoc. prof., 1977-91, prof., 1991-93, prof. emeritus, 1993—; represented by Miriam Perlman Gallery, Chgo.; counselor Luth. Student Ctr., U. Iowa, 1959-65, rsch. asst. in printmaking, 1960-65; owner, dir. James House Gallery, Oshkosh, 1972-77; dir. Allen Priebe Gallery, U. Wis., Oshkosh, 1975. Exhibited in group shows at N.W. Printmakers Internat., Seattle and Portland, Oreg., 1964, Ultimate Concerns 6th Nat. Exhbn., Athens, Ohio, 1965, 55th Nat. Exhbn., Springfield, Mass., 1974, 11th An. So. Tier Arts and Crafts, Corning, N.Y., 1974, Soc. of the Four Arts, Palm Beach, Fla., 1974, Appalachian Nat. Drawing Competition, Boone, N.C., 1975, Rutgers Nat. Drawing Exhbn., Camden, N.J., 1975, 8th and 9th Biennial Nat. Art Exhibit, Valley City, N.D., 1973, 75, Clary-Miner Gallery, Buffalo, 1988, Nat. Art Show, Redding, Calif., 1989, Internat. Printmaker, Buffalo, 1990, Westmoreland Nat. Juried Competition, Youngwood, Pa., 1990, Ariel Gallery, Soho, N.Y., 1990, Grand Prix de Paris Internat., Chapelle De La Sorbonne, Paris, 1990, Nat. Juried Exhbn., Rockford, Ill., 1991, Nat. Invitational Exhbn., Buffalo, 1991, East Coast Artists Nat. Invitational Art Exhbn., Havre de Grace, Md., 1991, Ariel Gallery, Soho, N.Y., 1991, N.Y. Art Expo, 1991, Milw. Art for AIDS Auction, 1991, 92, 94. Mem. Winnebago Hist. Soc., Oshkosh, 1987—. Lutheran. Home: 226 High Ave Oshkosh WI 54901-4734 Office: U Wis Dept Art Oshkosh WI 54901

SMITH, MICHAEL DALE, insurance agency executive; b. Rensselaer, Ind., Sept. 17, 1953; s. Hamlin Henry and Phyllis Joan (Hall) S.; m. Gretchen Zuege, Sept. 1, 1973; children—Mandy, Joshua. Grad. Internat. Coll., 1973. Mem. mgmt. program Household Fin. Corp., 1973-74; owner Credit Bur. Rensselaer, 1974-79; pres. Smith Realty, Rensselaer, 1974—; v.p., owner Consol. Ins. Agy., Rensselaer, 1975—. Mem. Ind. Gen. Assembly, 1993—. Precinct committeeman Reps., Rensselaer, del. state conv., 1978, 82. Mem. Ind. Ins. Agts. Assn. (bd. dirs.), Soc. Cert. Ins. Counselors (cert.), Profl. Ins. Agts. Assn., Rensselaer C. of C. (past v.p.). Lodges: Rotary (dir. 1982—), Masons, Shriners (Rensselaer). Home: P O Box 1 Rensselaer IN 47978 Office: 116 W Washington St Rensselaer IN 47978-2820

SMITH, MICHAEL KENT, state legislator; b. Canton, Ill., May 23, 1966; m. Donna Shaw. BA, Bradley U., 1988. Legis. asst. to Rep. Thomas J. Homer Ill. State Ho. of Reps., Springfield, 1986-92, mem. from dist. 91, 1994—, mem. agr., mem. consumer protection, mem. elem. and secondary sch. com., mem. judiciary criminal law com. Trustee Graham Hosp.; field coord. Dukakis/Bentsen Presdl. Campaign, 1988; precinct committeeman Dem. Com., 1984—; chmn. Fulton County Dem. Ctrl. Com., 1990—; trustee Canton Twp., 1991-94; citizen's advocate Ill. Atty. Gen., Peoria, 1992-95. Mem. Canton Area C. of C. (past pres.), Am. Heart Assn., Dem. County Chmn.'s Assn. (v.p. 1992—). Address: 2 N Main St Canton IL 61520

SMITH, MICHAEL LAWRENCE, computer company executive, consultant; b. Sheboygan, Wis., Aug. 29, 1958; s. Lawrence Eugene Patrick and Velma Mary (Baltus) S. BS in Computer Sci., U. Wis., 1980; MS in Computer Sci., U. So. Calif., 1988. Lab. asst. McArdle Lab. for Cancer Rsch., Madison, Wis., 1978-80; systems programmer/analyst Controls and Data Systems, Belvidere, Ill., 1980-82; sr. systems software engr. Ex-Cell-O Mfg. Systems Co., Rockford, Ill., 1982-85; artificial intelligence cons. McDonnell-Douglas Artificial Intelligence Ctr., Cypress, Calif., 1985-88; sr. artificial intelligence engr. Eaton Corp., Milw., 1988-92; sr. knowledge engr. Inference Corp., L.A., 1992-93, sr. cons., 1993-94; sr. cons. Compuware Corp., 1994—. Author: (chpt.) Cooperating Artificial Neural and Knowledge-Based Systems in a Truck Fleet Brake-Balance Application, 1991; contbr. articles to profl. jours. Founder, chmn. Computer Profls. for Social Responsibility, Milw., 1989-90. Mem. AAAS, Am. Assn. for Artificial Intelligence, N.Am. Fuzzy Info. Processing Soc., Internat. Neural Network Soc. Home: Apt 1212 111 Marquette Ave S Minneapolis MN 55401 Office: Compuware Corp Northstar Ctr E Ste 585 608 Second Ave S Minneapolis MN 55402

SMITH, MICHAEL MORGAN, management consultant; b. Mpls., Apr. 13, 1948; s. Theodore Sprague and Constance Vivian (Morgan) S.; m. Charlotte Jean Mitchell, May 17, 1970; 1 child, Edward Allan. BA, Macalester Coll., 1970; MHA, Duke U., 1972. Acct. N.C. Blue Cross and Blue Shield, Chapel Hill, 1972-73; ptnr. Peat, Marwick, Mitchell & Co., Chgo., 1973-85; v.p. higher edn. David M. Griffith & Assocs. Ltd., Northbrook, Ill., 1985—; pres. Chgo.-Orleans Housing Corp., 1987—; mem. adv. bd. Ill. Designated Accounts Purchase Program/Ill. Student Fin. Assistance Commn., Deerfield, 1980—. Office: David M Griffith & Assocs 630 Dundee Rd Northbrook IL 60062-2747

SMITH, MICHAEL WILLIAM, biomedical engineer, consultant; b. Hancock, Mich., Mar. 14, 1957; s. Jackson B. and Vivian Elizabeth (Pier) S. AAS in Biomed. Engring., Western Wis. Tech. Coll., 1977; B of Biomed. Engring. Tech., Milw. Sch. Engring., 1983. Registered profl. engr., Wis. Quality engr. GE Med. Sys., Waukesha, Wis., 1984-85, supr., 1985-87, project leader, 1987-91; dir. engring. Miller Med. Sys., Indpls., 1991-93; med. sys. engr. Comdisco Med. Exch., Wood Dale, Ill., 1993—. Pres. Madison Home Owners Assn., Waukesha, 1989-91. Mem. IEEE, NSPE. Office: Comdisco Med Exch 1421 N Wood Dale Rd Wood Dale IL 60191-1078

SMITH, MICHELLE M., marketing executive; b. Kewanee, Ill., Dec. 27, 1956; d. Robert Edward and Alvina L. (Bevard) Miller; m. William H. Smith, July 8, 1978; children: Lance, Jaclyn. AA, Black Hawk Coll., 1991. Pub. rels. dir. Henry County Youth Svcs. Bur., Kewanee, 1991-93; advt./graphics tech. Star Courier, Kewanee, 1993-94; mktg./ops. mgr. Henry County Youth Svcs. Bur., 1994—; pub. info. chair Kewanee Bd. Pub. Works, 1993-94, corr. sec., 1994-95; pub. rels com. Kewanee ABCD Program, 1992—; mem. Kewanee Drug & Alcohol Task Force, 1994—; coord. corp. image seminar Kewanee, 1993. Mem. Bradley U. Women's Choir, Peoria, Ill., 1992; leader Girl Scouts U.S., Galva, Ill., 1985-90. Mem. LVW, Kewanee Bus. & Profl. Women (corr. sec.). Office: Henry County Youth Svcs Bd 600 N Lexington Ave Kewanee IL 61443

SMITH, MURRAY THOMAS, transportation company executive; b. Hudson, S.D., 1939; s. Rex D. and Frances M. Smith; m. Diane R. Cramer, Dec. 4, 1959 (div. June 1994); children: Lisa B., Thomas M., Amy R.; m. Donna Thomas Kjonaas, Jan. 1995. V.p. Overland Express Inc., Indpls., 1978-82; v.p. ops. R.T.C. Transp. Inc., Forest Pk., Ga., 1982-83; with Midwest Coast Transport L.P., Sioux Falls, S.D., 1983—, sr. v.p., 1983-84; pres. Midwest Coast Transport L.P., Sioux Falls, S.D., 1984-89, prin., pres., chief exec. officer, 1989—, also bd. dirs.; bd. dirs. Interstate Carrier Conf., Nat. Perishable Logistics Assn. Bd. dirs. Sioux Valley Hosp., 1991—, United Way, Sioux Falls, 1991—. Office: Midwest Coast Transport LP 1600 E Benson Rd Sioux Falls SD 57104-0871

SMITH, NANCY HOHENDORF, sales and marketing executive; b. Detroit, Jan. 30, 1943; d. Donald Gerald and Lucille Marie (Kopp) Hohendorf; m. Richard Harold Smith, Aug. 21, 1978 (div. Jan. 1984). BA, U. Detroit, 1965; MA, Wayne State U., 1969. Customer rep. Xerox Corp., Detroit, 1965-67; mktg. rep. Univ. Microfilms subs. Xerox Corp., Ann Arbor, Mich., 1967-73, mktg. coord., 1973-74, mgr. dir. mktg., 1975-76; mgr. mktg. Xerox Corp., Can., 1976-77; major account mktg. exec. Xerox Corp., Hartford, Conn., 1978-79, New Haven, Conn., 1979-80; account exec. State of N.Y. Xerox Corp., N.Y.C., 1981; N.Y. region mgr. customer support Xerox Corp., Greenwich, Conn., 1982, N.Y. region sales ops. mgr., 1982; State of Ohio account exec. Xerox Corp., Columbus, 1983; new bus. sales mgr. Xerox Corp., Dayton, Ohio, 1983, major accounts sales mgr., 1984; info. systems sales and support mgr., quality specialist Xerox Corp., Detroit, 1985-87, new product launch mgr., ops. quality mgr., 1988, dist. mktg. mgr., 1989-91, major accounts sales mgr., 1992—. Named to Outstanding Young Women of Am., 1968, Outstanding Bus. Woman, Dayton C. of C., 1984, Women's Inner Circle of Achievement, 1990. Mem. NAFE, Am. Mgmt. Assn., Women's Econ. Club Detroit, Detroit Inst. Arts Founders' Soc., Detroit Hist. Soc., Greater Detroit C. of C. Republican. Roman Catholic. Home: 23308 Reynard Dr Southfield MI 48034-6924 Office: Xerox Corp 300 Galleria Officentre Southfield MI 48034-4700

SMITH, NEIL, professional football player; b. New Orleans, Apr. 10, 1966. Student, U. Nebr. Defensive end Kansas City Chiefs, 1988—. Played in Pro Bowl, 1991-93; named defensive lineman The Sporting News All-America team, 1987. Office: Kansas City Chiefs 1 Arrowhead Dr Kansas City MO 64129-1651*

SMITH, OZZIE (OSBORNE EARL SMITH), professional baseball player; b. Mobile, Ala., Dec. 26, 1954; m. Denise Jackson, Nov. 1, 1980; children: Osborne Earl Jr., Dustin Cameron. Grad., Calif. State Poly. U., San Luis Obispo. Shortstop San Diego Padres Baseball Club, Nat. League, 1977-82, St. Louis Cardinals Baseball Club, Nat. League, 1982—. Player Nat. League All-Star Team, 1981-92, 94, All-Star Team Sporting News, 1982, 84-87, World Series Championship Team, 1982; recipient Most Valuable Player award Nat. League Championship Series, 1985, Gold Glove award, 1980-92, Silver Slugger award, 1987. Office: St Louis Cardinals Busch Meml Stadium 250 Stadium Plz Saint Louis MO 63102-1722*

SMITH, PATRICIA J., educational consultant; b. Chgo., Aug. 19, 1946; d. Joseph Peter and Jean Gloria (Sturmer) S. BA in English, Siena Heights Coll., 1970; MA in Spl. Edn., Eastern Mich. U., 1972. Cert. elem., spl. edn. tchr., Mich. Tchr. St. Theresa Sch., Detroit, 1970-71, Wayne County Child Devel. Ctr., Northville, Mich., 1971-73, Detroit Pub. Schs., 1981-82; tchr., advisor Met. State Hosp., Waltham, Mass., 1973-78; ednl. supr. Children's Friend and Svcs., Warwick, R.I., 1978-81; recruiter Mgmt. Support Svcs., Southfield, Mich., 1982-86; cognitive therapist Rehab. Resources, Inc., Southfield, 1985-86; ednl. coord. Fedn. Girls' Homes, Detroit, 1986-87, Davenport Shelter, Spectrum Youth Svcs., Highland Park, Mich., 1987-92; ednl. cons. Beverly Hills, Mich., 1988—; tchr. Detroit House of Corrections, Plymouth, Mich., 1971-73. Mem. Mich. Assn. Tchrs. of Emotionally Disturbed Children, Networks of Educators and Therapists Working in Orgns. for Rehab., Corrections and Spl. Edn. (sec. 1989—).

SMITH, PATRICIA NEWELL, training and development manager; b. Alton, Ill., Mar. 17, 1943; d. George Washington and Anna Lee (Phillips) Newell; m. Richard C. Smith, Sept. 1, 1962; 1 child, Steven. BS in Edn., U. Mo., 1971. Tchr. social studies Pkwy. Schs., St. Louis, 1971-73; freelance cons. comm., 1974-79; tchr. writing Normandy (Mo.) Schs., 1981-86; edn. cons. Newsweek Mag., N.Y.C., 1983-87; freelance writer, 1984—; bus. communicator, trainer Edward D. Jones & Co., St. Louis, 1987-91; tng. coord. Save-A-Lot Ltd., St. Louis, 1991—, mgr. staffing and devel., 1993—. Writer ednl. column St. Louis Parent Mag.; ednl. writer Newsweek Mag.; contbr. articles to profl. jours. Trustee, town clk. Village of Glen Echo Park, Mo., 1977-81. Mem. ASTD, Assn. Bus. Communicators (presenter internat. conv. 1990). Roman Catholic. Home: 939 Pavillion Dr Creve Coeur MO 63141-6032 Office: Save A Lot Ltd 8474 Delport Dr Saint Louis MO 63114-5904

SMITH, PATRICK S., art history educator; b. Evanston, Ill., Aug. 17, 1949; s. Stanley J. and Dolores (Bannon) S. BA, Notre Dame U., 1972; MA, U. N.C., 1975; PhD, Northwestern U., 1982. Asst. prof. U. North Tex., Denton, 1981-88; vis. lectr. U. Ariz., Tucson, 1989; vis. asst. prof. Fla. State U., Tallahassee, 1991; from asst. to assoc. prof. Wichita State U., Kans., 1991—. Author: Andy Warhol's Art and Films, 1986, Warhol: Conversations About the Artist, 1988. Mem. Kans. Contemporary Art Assn. (pres. 1994—), Phi Beta Kappa. Office: Wichita State U Sch Art & Design Wichita KS 67260-0067

SMITH, PAUL MARTIN, physical therapist, athletic trainer; b. Huntington, N.Y., Feb. 21, 1964; s. Joseph Anthony and Mary Jean (Antenucci) S. BS in Biochemistry, Case Western Res. U., 1986; MS in Phys. Therapy, U. Miami, Coral Gables, Fla., 1989. Cert. phys. therapist Am. Phys. Therapy Assn., athletic trainer Nat. Athletic Trainer Assn. Athletic trainer U. Miami, Coral Gables, 1987-89; athletic trainer Ohio Phys. Therapy and Sports Medicine, Cleve., 1983-87, phys. therapist, 1990—. Organizer Wheelchair Challenge U. Miami, 1987-89, Jr. Orange Bowl Ability Games, Fla., 1988-89. Roman Catholic. Office: Ohio Phys Therapy/Sports Medicine Ste 1 6990 Lindsay Dr Mentor OH 44060-4981

SMITH, PAUL W., information systems professional; b. Columbus, Ohio, Aug. 30, 1946. BA, Ohio State U., 1972. Account rep. Dunn & Bradstreet, Cleve., 1972-78; dist. sales mgr. MDB Systems, Orange, Calif., 1980-85; major account rep. IBM, Akron, Ohio, 1985-88; v.p. Midrange Computer Solutions Inc., Cleve., 1988—. With USAF, 1965-69, Vietnam. Mem. Data Processing Mgrs. Assn., Soc. Mfg. Engrs.

SMITH, PETER WILSON, symphony orchestra administrator; b. Utica, N.Y., Mar. 15, 1938; s. Stanley W. and Frances (Brown) S.; m. Kay Gardner, 1960 (div. 1972); children: Juliana, Jennifer; m. Lynn Perrott, 1976. B.Mus., U. Mich., 1965. Asst. mgr. Indpls. Symphony, 1966-67; asst. mgr. St. Louis Symphony, 1967-68; exec. dir. Norfolk Symphony, Va., 1968-72; ops. mgr. Buffalo Philharmonic, 1972-74; ops. adminstr. Carnegie Hall Corp., N.Y.C., 1974-76; mng. dir. Ft. Wayne (Ind.) Philharmonic, 1976-85; exec. dir. Grand Rapids (Mich.) Symphony, 1985-95, pres., 1995—. Served to airman 1st class USAF, 1961-64. Mem. Met. Orch. Mgrs. Assn. (pres. 1979-81), Regional Orch. Mgrs. Assn. (v.p. 1987-89), Am. Symphony Orch. League (bd. dirs. 1989-91), Mgrs. Am. Orch. (vice-chmn. 1989-91). Office: Grand Rapids Symphony 169 Louis Campau Promenade Ste 1 Grand Rapids MI 49503

SMITH, PHILIP G., state legislator; b. Louisiana, Mo., Oct. 4, 1946; m. Andrea K. Smith; children: Andrew Gentry, James Lyndon. BS, N.E. Mo. State U., 1968; JD, U. Mo., 1972. Atty.; rep. Mo. State Ho. Reps. Dist. 11. Mem. Rotary Club, Elks, Masons, Mo. Alumni Assn., Mo. State U. Alumnus Assn. Home: PO Box 486 Louisiana MO 63353-0486*

SMITH, PHILIP LUTHER, molecular geneticist; b. Milan, Ind., Dec. 23, 1956; s. Donald Walter and Evelyn Emma (Vornheder) S.; m. Mary Ann Radike, Feb. 9, 1985; children: Martha Jesse, Philip Benjamin. BS, Purdue U., 1980. Rsch. asst. U. Cin. Coll. of Medicine, Cin., 1981-84; sr. phys. biochemist Med. Coll. of Ohio, Toledo, 1985-89; sr. rsch. molecular geneticist Marion Merrell Dow Rsch. Inst./Hoechst Marion Roussel Inc., Cin., 1990-95; patent info. scientist Hoechst Marion Roussel, Cin., 1996—. Contbr. articles to profl. jours. Mem. AAAS, Am. Radio Amateur Satellite Corp., Am. Chem. Soc., The Prot. Soc., Am. Radio Relay League, Purdue U. Alumni Assn. (life). Roman Catholic.

SMITH, PHYLLIS ELIZABETH, community volunteer; b. Cedar Rapids, Iowa, Aug. 3, 1928; d. Elza Raymond and Wilma Grace (Walrath) Potter; m. Willard Gregg Smith, June 11, 1949; children: Willard Mark, Kevin, Sara Blair, Andrew, David. BA, U. Kans. City, 1950. Personnel asst. The Jones Store Co., Kansas City, Mo., 1950-51; purchasing clk. Hallmark Cards, Kansas City, Mo., 1950-52; ptnr., owner, cons. Doncaster Clothing, Overland Park, Kans., 1990—. Bd. dirs. Am. Cancer Soc., 1987-93, 79—; trustee

St. Paul Sch. Theology, Kansas City, 1983—; adv. bd. breast cancer ctr. U. Kans. Med. Ctr., 1993—. Mem. Kappa Delta. Democrat. Methodist. Home: 5118 W 120th Terr Overland Park KS 66209-3550

SMITH, RALPH EDWARD, psychology assistant; b. Bellfountaine, Ohio, May 19, 1953; s. Ralph Raymond and Virginia (Picklesimer) S.; m. Melody Lee Welbaum Smith, Sept. 3, 1988. B of Gen. Studies, Ohio U., 1980; MS in Edn., U. Dayton, 1987. Houseparent Roweton Boys Ranch, Chillicothe, Ohio, 1974-86, social worker, 1981-82; employment counselor Ross County Community Action, Chillicothe, 1980-81, 83; social worker Roweton Residential Ctr., Chillicothe, 1986-87; psychology asst. Ross Correctional Inst., Chillicothe, 1988-89, Chillicothe Correctional Inst., State of Ohio, 1989—; pres. H.Y.S. Fed. Credit Union, Chillicothe, 1981-86. Vol. Ross County Community Action, Inc., Chillicothe, 1983-87, commodity distbn. vol. Office: Chillicothe Correctional Inst PO Box 5500 Chillicothe OH 45601-0990

SMITH, RICHARD CONRAD, JR., telecommunications company executive; b. Gadsden, Ala., Feb. 10, 1942; s. Richard Conrad and Anne Ruth (McFarlin) S.; m. Mary Elizabeth Dale, Mar. 18, 1967; children: Corinne Craig, Andrea Dale, Jason McFarlin. B Engring., Vanderbilt U., 1964; MS, MPhil, Yale U., 1966, PhD, 1970. Salesman Ins. Sys. Am., Atlanta, 1970-73, adminstr., 1973-76, sr. v.p., 1976-80; pres., CEO, ISACOMM, Inc., Atlanta, 1980-83; pres. U.S. Telecom-Corp. Network Svcs., Atlanta, 1983-86; pres. nat. accounts div. U.S. Sprint, Atlanta, 1986-89; pres. nat. markets div. U.S. Sprint, Kansas City, Kans., 1989-91; sr. v.p. quality devel. and pub. rels. Spring Corp., Kansas City, Mo., 1991—. Bd. advisors Ctr. for Entreprenurial Leadership, Kansas City, Mo., 1992; bd. dirs. Pvt. Industry Coun., Kansas City, Mo., 1992, Kansas City Crime Commn., 1992, St. Lukes Hosp., 1995; trustee U. Kansas City, 1993; mem. commn. on ministry Episcopal Diocese We. Mo., 1993. Mem. Kansas City (Mo.) C. of C. (bd. dirs.), Carriage Club, Mission Hills Country Club, Sigma Xi, Tau Beta Pi. Episcopalian. Office: Sprint Corp PO Box 11315 Kansas City MO 64112

SMITH, RICHARD HARDING, analytical biochemist; b. Phila., Apr. 27, 1950; s. Richard Harding and Doris Reese (Putsche) S. BS in Chemistry, Millersville U., 1978; PhD in Biology, Wesleyan U., 1983. Lab. asst. Millersville (Pa.) U., 1975-78; postdoctoral fellow dept. pathology U. Mich., Ann Arbor, 1983-86, rsch. assoc. dept. internal medicine, cons., 1986-88; sr. rsch. scientist BioQuant, Inc., Ann Arbor, 1986-95; sr. scientist Selective Technologies, Inc., Ann Arbor, 1995—; cons. Defined Healthcare Rsch., Inc., Summit, N.J., 1990—; mem. inst. rev. bd. Lancaster (Pa.) Osteo. Hosp., 1977-78. Contbr. articles to profl. jours. Foster parent Plan Internat., Warwick, R.I., 1988—; tchr. Sun. sch. 1st Unitarian Universalist Ch., Ann Arbor, 1990—. NSF fellow, 1978; Sigma Xi grantee, 1980. Mem. AAAS, Am. Clin. Chemists, Am. Chem. Soc., Pa. Acad. Sci., Rotary. Office: Selective Technologies Inc 50 Enterprise Dr Ann Arbor MI 48103

SMITH, RICK A., mechanical engineer, consultant; b. Shelby, Ohio, Sept. 10, 1948; s. Reginald A. and Ella Mae (Bolin) S.; m. Rhea Dawn Wilcox, Dec. 15, 1973. BSME, Purdue U., 1976; M of Engring., Ohio State U., 1988. Registered profl. engr., Ohio. Project engr. Armour-Dial, Inc., Montgomery, Ill., 1976-77, Purdue U., West Lafayette, Ind., 1977-79; plant energy engr. ALCOA, Lafayette, Ind., 1979-81; facility project mgr. Cummins Engine Co., Columbus, Ind., 1981-83; project mgr., sr. engr. Ohio State U., Columbus, 1983-88; pres., cons. mech. engr. Applied Thermal Engring., Ostrander, Ohio, 1988—. Mem. Mayor's Dist. Heating Task Force, Columbus, Ohio, 1984-86. 1st lt. USMC, 1968-72, Vietnam. Mem. ASME, Am. Cons. Engrs. Coun., Am. Inst. Plant Engrs., Pi Tau Sigma. Republican. Office: Applied Thermal Engring Inc PO Box 212 Ostrander OH 43061-0212

SMITH, ROBERT BURNS, newspaper magazine executive; b. Columbus, Ohio, Feb. 24, 1929; s. Edwin Clyde and Blanche (Burns) S.; m. Marjorie Ann Otten. BS, Ohio State U., 1949. Reporter, then asst. news editor Ohio State Jour., Columbus, 1948-59; with Columbus Dispatch, 1959—, mng. editor, 1968-80; editor-in-chief Living Single mag., 1980-86, Ohio mag., 1980-89; editor Columbus Dispatch, 1989-95, editor-in-chief, 1995—, 1996—; v.p. Dispatch Features, Columbus, 1968—, Dispatch Charities, Columbus, 1990—; bd. dirs. Dispatch Printing Co.; v.p. Ohio Mag. Inc., 1990-95, pres., 1995—; pres. Dispatch Consumer News Svcs., Inc., 1996—. Sec.-treas. James Faulkner Meml. Fund, Columbus, 1967—; trustee Ohio Hist. Soc., 1986—, pres., 1988-95; trustee Dawes Arboretum, 1988-96, Hayes Presdl. Ctr., 1995—; active Ohio Privacy Bd., 1977-81. Mem. Blue Pencil Ohio (v.p. 1969, pres. 1970), AP Ohio (v.p. 1974, pres. 1975), Mag. Pub. Assn., Am. Soc. Mag. Editors, Am. Soc. Newspaper Editors, Regional Pubs. Assn. (bd. dirs. 1986-89), York Temple Country Club, Masons, Rotary, Sigma Delta Chi, Delta Tau Delta. Presbyterian. Home: 1456 Sandalwood Pl Columbus OH 43229-4445 Office: The Columbus Dispatch 34 S 3rd St Columbus OH 43215-4201

SMITH, ROBERT FRANCIS, psychologist, consultant, account representative; b. Independence, Mo., May 4, 1943; s. Ernest L. and Grace Evelyn (Buck) S.; m. Susan Marie Quanty, Sept. 3, 1976; children: Justin Quanty, Natalie Christine. BA, U. Mo., Kans. City, 1973, MA, 1976; PhD, U. Kans., 1984. Assoc. field svc. engr. Diamond Power Speciality Corp., Lancaster, Ohio, 1968-71; rsch. assoc. Kans. U. Med. Ctr. Otolaryn. Dept., Kansas City, Kans., 1973-78; rsch. psychologist VA Behavioral Radiology Labs., Kans. City, Mo., 1978-95; chmn. subcom. working group on biorhythms for C95-1-IV, Am. Nat. Stds. Inst., Washington, 1983-91; cons. Midwest Rsch. Inst., Kansas City, Mo., 1982—, West Assocs. Energy Task Force, Rosemead, Calif., 1984-86; guest speaker NAS Workshop, Washington, 1985. Contbr. articles to profl. jours. Served in USN, 1962-68. Mem. Bioelectromagnetics Soc., Psi Chi. Home: 9351 E 60th Ter Raytown MO 64133-3803 Office: Ste 820 4240 Blue Ridge Blvd Kansas City MO 64133

SMITH, ROBERT FRANKLIN, mechanical designer; b. Toledo, Ohio, Dec. 16, 1934. Engr. Libby Glass divsn. Owens Ill., Toledo, 1972-82; designer Bartlett & Collins divsn. Ind. Glass, Dunkirk, Ind., 1982-87, Glasstech, Inc., Perrysburg, Ohio, 1987—. Patentee for solar cell stand, glass manufacturing process. Staff sgt. USAF, 1957-61. Mem. Riverview Yacht Club (sgt.-at-arms 1994-95). Democrat. Lutheran. Home: 5412 Edgewater Dr Toledo OH 43611-2642

SMITH, ROBERT FREEMAN, history educator; b. Little Rock, May 13, 1930; s. Robert Freeman and Emma Martha Gottlieb (Buerkle) S.; m. Alberta Vester, Feb. 1, 1950 (dec. 1985); children: Robin Ann, Robert Freeman III; m. Charlotte Ann Coleman, Sept. 9, 1985. BA, U. Ark., 1951, MA, 1952; PhD, U. Wis., Madison, 1958. Instr. U. Ark., Fayetteville, 1953; asst. prof. Tex. Luth. Coll., Seguin, 1958-62; assoc. prof. U. R.I., Kingston, 1962-66, U. Conn., Storrs, 1966-69; prof. history U. Toledo, 1969-86, disting. univ. prof., 1986—; vis. prof. U. Wis., Madison, 1966-67. Author: The United States and Cuba: Business and Diplomacy 1917-1960, 1961 (Tex. Writers' Roundup award 1961), What Happened in Cuba: A Documentary History of U.S.-Cuban Relations, 1963, The United States and Revolutionary Nationalism in Mexico, 1916-1932, 1973 (Ohio Acad. History award 1973), The Era of Caribbean Intervention, 1890-1930, 1981, The Era of Good Neighbors, Cold Warriors, and Hairshirts, 1930-82, 1983, The Caribbean World and the United States: Mixing Rum & Coca-Cola, 1994; contbr. to numerous publs. Lt. col. 43rd Mil. Police Bn., Ohio Mil. Res. 1st lt. U.S. Army, 1953-55. Knapp fellow in history U. Wis., 1957; Tom L. Evans rsch. fellow Harry S. Truman Libr., Independence, Mo., 1976-77, Mexican Ministry Fgn. Rels. fellow, 1991-92. Mem. Soc. Historians of Am. Fgn. Rels., Soc. Mil. History, U.S. Naval Inst., Ohio Acad. History, So. Hist. Assn., Orgn. Am. Historians, Assn. U.S. Army, State Guard Assn. of U.S., Am. Legion, Masons, Scottish Rite, Shriners, Phi Beta Kappa, Phi Alpha Theta. Episcopalian. Home: 4110 Dunkirk Rd Toledo OH 43606-2217 Office: U Toledo Dept History Toledo OH 43606

SMITH, RONALD LOUIS, stockbroker; b. Ravenna, Ohio, Oct. 25, 1949; s. Elmer Louis and Mary Elizabeth (Barnes) S.; children: Ian Louis, Austen Weaver. BA in History, Allegheny Coll., Meadville, Pa., 1972; student, Oxford (Eng.) U., 1971; MA in Pub. Adminstrn., Ohio State U., 1974. Adminstr. Ohio EPA, Columbus, 1974-75; v.p. Merrill Lynch, Columbus, 1975-85, E.F. Hutton, Columbus, 1985-88; v.p. investments Dean Witter Reynolds, Columbus, 1988-92; 1st v.p. investments Prudential Securities, Columbus, 1992—; pres. bd. dirs. Willoway Villas Condominium Assn., Columbus, Arbor Village Condominium Assn., Columbus. Mem. Upper Arlington (Ohio) Civic Assn., 1980—; mem. So. Poverty Law Ctr., Montgomery, Ala., 1975—, First Community Ch. Recipient Humanity award So. Poverty Law Ctr., Montgomery, 1990. Mem. Ohio State U. Alumni Assn., Ohio State U. Golf Club, Columbus Touchdown Club (bd. trustees 1994-96). Home: 2626 Wexford Rd Columbus OH 43221-3216

SMITH, RONALD NOEL, facilities manager; b. Beech Grove, Ind., Oct. 10, 1946; s. Clayton Marion and Fannie Lee (Ashley) S.; m. Susan Jean Lauterborn, Dec. 15, 1972; children: Jennifer Lynn, Jessica Lee. A in Archtl. Engring. Tech., Sams Tech. Inst., 1966; cert., Ind. U., 1978, BS, 1980. Draftsman Elliot-Williams Co., Indpls., 1967-68; chief designer Acme Corp., Indpls., 1973-77; supr. contract maintenance, improvements and alterations Indpls. Pub. Schs., 1977-82; dir. physical plant to dir. facilities planning and constrn. Sinclair Community Coll., Dayton, 1982-90; dir. phys. plant Kearney (Nebr.) State Coll., 1990-91; dir. facilities U. Nebr., Kearney, 1991—. Leader Royal Rangers, Beech Grove, 1972-74; coll. rep. Miami Valley River Corridor Com., Dayton, 1982. Served to staff sgt. USAF, 1968-72. Mem. Assn. Higher Edn. Facility Officers, Am. Inst. Plant Engrs. (editorial bd. 1984), Profl. Ground Mgmt. Soc., Internat. Facility Mgmt. Assn., Ctrl. Assn. Plant Adminstrs. Coll. and Univs., Nebr. Phys. Plant Assn. (pres. 1993), TIAA-CREF, Ctrl. Assn. Phys. Plant Adminstrs. Republican. Mem. Assembly of God Ch. Office: U Nebr Office of Facilities Dir Kearney NE 68849

SMITH, SIDNEY TALBERT, biomedical engineer; b. Decatur, Ill., Oct. 30, 1954; s. Sidney Paulsen and Patricia Louise (Talbert) S.; m. Katherine Louise Wolf, June 24, 1989. BS, Millikin U., 1976; postgrad., Washington U., St. Louis, 1976-78; MBA with honors, Lake Forest (Ill.) Sch. Mgmt., 1985. Rsch. asst. Baxter Travenol, Morton Grove, Ill., 1980-82; devel. engr. Fenwal divsn. Travenol Labs., Round Lake, Ill., 1982-83, sr. devel. engr., 1983-84; prin. engr. Fenwal divsn. Baxter Healthcare, Round Lake, 1984-88; project mgr. biotech. systems Baxter Healthcare, Round Lake, 1988-89; dir. devel. Applied Immune Scis., Menlo Park, Calif., 1990-91; prin. Smith Engring., Lake Forest, Ill., 1989-96; mgr. container devel. advanced engr. Baxter Healthcare Corp., Deerfield, Ill., 1996—; cons. Safety Diagnostics, Evanston, Ill., 1989-91, Clintec Nutrition, Deerfield, Ill., 1991—, Baxter Healthcare Corp., Deerfield, Ill., 1993—, Teltech Resource Network Corp., Mpls., 1995—. Patentee in field. Mem. Lake Forest/Lake Bluff Running Club (bd. mem. 1995), Vintage Sports Car Drivers Assn., Porsche Club Am. Presbyterian. Home: 1326 W Everett Rd Lake Forest IL 60045-2610

SMITH, STAN, state offical. Commr. Dept. Transp., Indpls. Office: IGCN 755 100 N Senate Ave Indianapolis IN 46204*

SMITH, STEVE C., lawyer, state legislator; b. Hutchinson, Minn., Nov. 29, 1949; s. Charles H. and Laura G. Smith; married; 1 child, Ryan. BA, U. Minn., 1972; JD, Oklahoma City U., 1975. City coun. mem. City of Mound, Minn., 1984-86, mayor, 1986-90; state rep. Minn. Ho. of Reps., St. Paul, 1990—. Served with U.S. Army, 1971-75. Republican. Home: 2710 Clare Ln Mound MN 55364-1812 Office: 353 State Office Bldg Saint Paul MN 55155-1201

SMITH, STEVEN ANTONIO, engineer; b. Dayton, Ohio, Sept. 26, 1958; s. George E. and Cecilia Ester (Arnedo) S. Student, Greenejoint Vocat. Sch., Xenia, Ohio, 1974-76. Draftsman Scott Equip. Co., Dayton, 1975-76; elec./mech. draftsman SRL Med. Inc., Beavercreek, Ohio, 1976-78, Staco Energy Products Co., Dayton, 1978-88; project engr. STACO, Dayton, 1988—; R&D staff Hobart, Dayton, 1979-80. Sec. Cub Scout Pack 40 Boy Scouts Am., Waynesville, Ohio, 1995—. Mem. Miami Valley Astron. Soc. (pres. 1984, 87). Office: STACO Energy Products Co 301 Gaddis Blvd Dayton OH 45403-1314

SMITH, STUART ALLAN, groundwater scientist, consultant, educator; b. Ashland, Ohio, Feb. 25, 1955; s. Walter and Margaret Eleanor (Sparr) S.; m. Julianne DiRocco, June 21, 1980; children: Jessica, Sarah. BA, Wittenberg U., 1977; MS, Ohio State U., 1984. Cert. groundwater specialist. Tchr. secondary sci. Mechanicsburg (Ohio) Village Sch., 1978-79; rsch. assoc. Nat. Water Well Assn., Worthington, Ohio, 1979-83; adj. assoc. prof. Wright State U., Dayton, 1981-85; tech. writer and editor Battelle Meml. Inst., Columbus, 1985-86; cons. scientist S.A. Smith Cons. Svcs., Ada, 1986—; instr. biology Ohio No. U., Ada, 1991—. Author: Hydraulic Fracturing, 1989, Monitoring and Remediation Wells Problem Prevention, 1995; editor: Water Publ. Digest, 1994—; co-author, editor: Australian Drilling Manual, 1992, Drilling, 1996; co-author: Evaluation and Restoration of Water Supply Wells, 1993; contbr. over 100 articles to profl. jours. Mem. Ada Town and Gown Com., 1992-93. Mem. ASTM, Nat. Ground Water Assn., Am. Soc. for Microbiology, Soc. for Tech. Comm. (sr.), Am. Water Works Assn., Ohio Acad. Sci., Ohio Rural Water Assn., Kiwanis (pres. Ada 1992). Lutheran. Office: PO Box 88 Ada OH 45810-0088

SMITH, SYDNEY DAVID, data processing executive; b. San Antonio, Tex., Nov. 25, 1947; s. Sydney Philip and Doris Annette (King) S.; m. Helen Louise Smith; 1 child, Anne. BBA, Baylor U., 1969; MBA, Northwestern U., 1973. CPA, Ill. Sr. cons. Arthur Andersen & Co., Chgo., 1973-76; sr. systems engr. Bd. Edn., Chgo., 1976-77; applications mgr. Estech, Inc., Chgo., 1977-84; info. ctr. mgr. GATX Corp., Chgo., 1984-85; N.Am. support mgr. Trinzic Corp., Chgo., 1986-95; region support mgr. HPR Inc. (Health Payment Rev.), Chgo., 1995—. Served with U.S. Army, 1969-71. Mem. AICPA, Ill. CPA Soc. Office: HPR Inc Ste 301 650 Warrenville Rd Lisle IL 60532

SMITH, TERRY DAVIS, quality engineer; b. Springfield, Mo., Feb. 16, 1944. BS in Mgmt., S.W. Mo. State U., 1993. Quality engr., SPC coord. Litton Advanced Circuitry Divsn., Springfield, 1964—. Republican. Office: Litton Advanced Circuitry Divsn 4811 W Kearney St Springfield MO 65803-9579

SMITH, TERRY G., insurance sales professional; b. Fairfield, Ill., Aug. 14, 1954; s. Lester G. and Lois L. (Porter) S.; m. Connie S. Eikenhorst, May 24, 1981; children: James T., Adam W., Melissa J. Student, Frontier Community Coll., Fairfield. Adminstr. asst. Pillsbury Co., Mpls., 1981-83; field rep. Woodmen of the World, Fairfield, 1983-86, area mgr., 1986—. Supr., mgr. youth lodges, Woodmen of the World, Fairfield, 1987—, adult lodges, Mt. Carmel, Ill., 1987—. Recipient 1 Million Club award Nat. Assn. Fraternal Ins. Counselors, 1986, Top Area Mgr. in Ill. awards, 1991, 92, 93. Fellow Fraternal Ins. Counselors; mem. Am. Legion, Multi-Millionaire Club (pres.'s cabinet 1986), Ill. Fraternal Ins. Counselors Orgn. (pres. 1992-93). Home: RR 5 Box 44 Fairfield IL 62837-9805 Office: Woodmen of World PO Box 44 609 W Main Fairfield IL 62837

SMITH, TERRY LYNN, information scientist; b. La Porte, Ind., Dec. 8, 1944; s. Paul F. and Ferne R. (Eplett) S.; m. Mary Jo Hartley, Jan. 31, 1970; children: Todd Alan, Timothy Eric. BS, Butler U., 1968. Programmer LTV Steel Co., East Chicago, Ind., 1971-74; systems analyst Allis Chalmers Co., Harvey, Ill., 1974-76; mgr. finished inventory La Salle Steel Co., Hammond, Ind., 1976-80; internal cons. Wheelabrater-Frye Co., Harvey, 1980-82; dir. mgmt. info. systems Trailmobile, Inc., Chgo., 1982-83; prin., cons. Arthur Young & Co., Chgo., 1983-86; sr. mgr. Peat Marwick, Chgo., 1986-88; prin. Arthur Young & Co., Chgo., 1988—, CSC Cons., 1988-90, Mfg. Mgmt. Assocs., Oakbrook, Ill., 1992-96; sr. prin. Tech. Solutions Co., 1996—; mem. client strategy com., Arthur Young & Co., Chgo., 1986, peer rev. team, Orange County, Calif., 1986. Mem. Com. for Strategic Ednl. Planning Lake Cen. Ind. Sch., 1987, 88. Served as sgt. U.S. Army, 1968-71. Mem. Am. Prodn. and Inventory Control Soc. (edn. com. 1981, cert.), Data Processing Mgmt. Assn., Spl. Interest Group for Cert. Data Processors, Assn. Inst. Cert. Group Computer Profls. (cert.). Republican. Methodist. Club: East Bank (Chgo.). Home: 8752 Lantern Dr Saint John IN 46373-9316

SMITH, TONI COLETTE, government official, social worker; b. Columbus, Ohio, Oct. 31, 1952. BA, Ohio State U., Columbus, 1974, postgrad., 1975-76; postgrad., Ohio State U., Columbus, 1978-90; MS in Edn., U. Dayton, 1993. Lic. social worker, Ohio. Cons. Ohio Dept. Human Svc., Columbus, 1974-75; mgr. Fisher Body Div., Columbus, 1977-78; with Franklin County Human Svc., Columbus, 1975—, supr., 1979-86, adminstr., 1986-91, asst. dep. dir., 1991-95, dep. dir., 1996—; pub. speaker human svcs. program Franklin County Human Svc., 1988—; instr., human svc. devel. Columbus State C.C., 1990—; grad. United Way Project Diversity Leadership Program. Mem. adv. bd. Columbus City Comprehensive Plan, 1989—, Syntaxis Group Home, Columbus, 1989—; Informed Neighbors Com., 1989—, Berwick Civic Assn., Columbus (v.p. 1990-92, pres. 1992—); trustee Mental Health Assn., Columbus. Mem. AAUW (corr. sec. Columbus Chpt. 1988—), NAFE, LWV, Columbus Women's Network, Berwick Civic Assn. (pres. 1992-94). Democrat. Roman Catholic. Home: 2665 Mitzi Dr Columbus OH 43209-3263 Office: Franklin County Dept Human Svc 80 E Fulton St Columbus OH 43215-5127

SMITH, TROY D., engineering manager; b. Vicksburg, Mich., Sept. 1, 1965. AS, Kalamazoo C.C., 1984. Tool designer Beacon Tool, Vicksburg, Mich., 1984-86; corp. CAD mgr. FabriKal Corp., Kalamazoo, 1986-89; engring. mgr. Bond Tool & Engring., Kalamazoo, 1989—. Chmn. adv. com. Kalamazoo C.C.; asst. scoutmaster Boy Scouts of Am. Mem. Soc. Plastic Engrs., Soc. Mfg. Engrs. Office: Bond Tool & Engring 6190 N Riverview Dr Kalamazoo MI 49004-1574

SMITH, VERNON G., education educator, state representative; b. Gary, Ind.. BS, Ind. U., 1966, MS, 1969, EdD, 1978; postgrad., Ind.U.-Purdue U., 1986-90. Tchr. Gary Pub. Schs. Systems, 1966-71, resource tchr., 1971-72; asst. prin. Ivanhoe Sch., Gary, 1972-78; prin. Nobel Sch., Gary, 1978-85, Williams Sch., Gary, 1985-92; part-time counselor edn. div. Ind. U. N.W., Gary, 1967-69, adj. lectr., 1987-92, asst. prof., 1992—; mem. Ind. Ho. of Reps., Indpls., 1990—; columnist Gary Crusader, 1969-71; speaker Devel. Tng. Inst., 1986—. Author: (with D. McClam) Building Bridges Instead of Walls—History of I.U. Dons, Inc., 1979; also articles. Mem. Gary City Coun., 1972-90; precinct committeeman Gary Dem. Com., 1972-92; founder, chmn. Gary City-wide Festival Com.; bd. dirs. N.W. Ind. Urban League; founder, pres. I.U. Dons, Inc.; past pres. Gary Cmty. Mental Health Bd.; v.p. Gary Common Coun., 1982, 85-87, pres., 1976, 83-84, 88; past mem. bd. dirs. Little League World series; founder, past sponsor Youth Ensuring Solidarity, Young Citizens' League; chmn. Ind. Commn. on Status of Black Males, 1992—; mem. Gov.'s Commn. for Drug-Free Ind., 1990—. Recipient citation in edn. Gary NAACP, 1970, Good Govt. award Gary Jaycees, 1977, Outstanding Svc. award Gary Young Dems., 1979, Businessman of Yr. award Gary Downtown Mchts., 1979, Bd. Dirs. Svcs. award Gary Cmty. Health Ctr., 1982, G.O.I.C. Dr. Leon H. Sullivan award, 1982, Gary Jaycees Youth award, 1983, Info Newspaper Outstanding Citizen of N.W. Ind. and Info. Newspaper's Outstanding Educator award, 1984, Post Tribune Blaine Marz Tap award, 1984, Gary Cmty. Sch. Corp. Speech Dept. Recognition award, 1984, Gary Cmty. Mental Health Ctr.'s 10th Yr. Svc. award, 1985, Roosevelt H.S. Exemplary Svc. award, 1985, Gary Crusader 25th Anniversary award, 1986, Purdue U. Ednl. Opportunity Programs Black History Svc. award, 1986, Educator Par Excellence awa4rd Williams Sch., 1987, Black Woman Hall of Fame Found. Success award, 1987, Black Women Hall of Fame Bethune-Tubman-Truth award, 1987, Our Lady of Perpetual Help Ch. Hon. Mem. award, 1987, Gary Educator of Christ Adminstr. Leadership award, 1988, NBC-LEO Appreciation award, 1988, Omega Psi Phi Citizen of Yr., 1989, Omicron Rho chpt. Appreciation award, 1991, Gary Cmty. Schs. Presenters award, 1991, Mr. G.'s Svc. award, 1991, Appreciation award Ind. Assn. Chiefs Police, 1992, Meth. Hosp., 1992, Bros. Keeper, 1992, Svc. award Ind. Assn. Elem. and Mid. Sch. Prins., 1992, I.U. N.W. Alumni Assn. Divsn. of Edn. Disting. Educator award, 1992, N.W. Ind. Black Expo's Sen. Carolyn Mosby Above and Beyond award, 1995. Mem. NAACP (life), Ind. Assn. Sch. Prins., No. Ind. Assn. Black School Educators (founder), Ind. U. N.W. Alumni Assn. (life, Disting. Educator award 1992), Phi Delta Kappa, Omega Psi Phi (life, Omega Man of Yr. award 1974, Citizen of Yr. award 10th dist. 1989, appreciation award Omicrono Rho chpt. 1991). Baptist. Home: PO Box M622 Gary IN 46401-0622 Office: Ind U NW 3400 Broadway Hawthorn #339 Gary IN 46408

SMITH, VIRGIL CLARK, state legislator; b. Detroit, July 4, 1947; s. Virgil Columbus and Eliza (Boyer) S.; m. Evelyn Owens (div.); children: Virgil Kai, Adam Smith; m. Elizabeth Ann Little. BA in polit. sci., Mich. State U., 1969; JD, Wayne State U., 1972. Legal advisor various community groups, Detroit, 1972-73; supervising atty. Wayne County Legal Svcs., Detroit, 1973-74; sr. asst.corp. counsel law dept. City of Detroit, 1974-75; mem. Mich. State Ho. Reps., 1976-88, Mich. State Senate, 1988—; mem. Appropriations Comm. Mem. Nat. Caucus Black State Legislators, Nat. Caucus of State Legistlators, Mich. Legis. Black Caucus (2d chair 1991-92). Democrat. Office: State Senate PO Box 30036 Lansing MI 48909-7536 Address: 19316 Norwood St Detroit MI 48234-1820

SMITH, VIRGINIA BROWN, classical musician; b. Nashville, July 24, 1954; d. Jordan Stokes and Annie Frances (Sory) Brown; m. Mark Brampton Smith, Feb. 28, 1976 (div. 1986); 1 child, Evelyn Anne. MusB, Eastman Sch. Music, 1976; MusM, U. Mich., 1979. Dir. music Good Shepherd United Meth. Ch., Dearborn, Mich., 1977-81, Westminster Presby. Ch., Ann Arbor, Mich., 1981-84; instr. voice Schoolcraft Coll., Livonia, Mich., 1986-89; pvt. practice voice instr. Ann Arbor, 1976—; adj. instr. Albion (Mich.) Coll., 1991—; solo recitals, performances Ann Arbor, Detroit, Mpls., Nashville, Washington, 1977—. Soprano soloist Christ Ch. Cranbrook, Bloomfield Hills, Mich., 1984—, U. Mich. Early Music Ensemble, 1977-89, Ann Arbor Cantata Singers, 1981-89, Ars Musica Choir, Ann Arbor, 1984-85, 94—, Vocal Arts Ensemble, 1995—. Mem. Nat. Assn. Tchrs. Singing (bd. dirs. Mich. chpt.), Music Tchrs. Nat. Assn. (nat. profl. cert. 1989), Acad. for Study and Performance Early Mus. (bd. dirs. and sec. 1994), Early Mus. Am., Mich. Music Tchrs. Assn. (bd. dirs., cert. 1988, state voice chairperson 1989-95), Ann Arbor Piano Tchrs. Guild (treas. 1983-85), Livonia Area Piano Tchrs. Forum (pres. 1991-93), Detroit Musicians League, Pi Kappa Lambda, Sigma Alpha Iota. Democrat. Episcopalian. Home: 3730 Burns Ct Ann Arbor MI 48105

SMITH, WALTER DELOS, accountant, professional speaker; b. Rensselaer, Ind., June 7, 1936; s. Walter Myron and Evelyn Geraldine (Murphy) S.; m. Yvonne Marie Dietz, Sept. 24, 1960; children: Michele, Michael, Kevin, Bryan, Denise, Derek. BS in Acctg., Walton Sch. Commerce, Chgo., 1960. CPA, Wis., Ill. Acct. Frazer & Torbet CPAs, Chgo., 1960-66; asst. contr. Rath-Packing Co., Waterloo, Iowa 1966-68; contr., treas. DeLeuw, Cather & Co., Chgo., 1968-72; corp. contr. Mohawk Data Scis., Utica, N.Y., 1972-75; mgmt. cons. Walter D. Smith & Assocs., New Hartford, N.Y., 1975-76; v.p., gen. mgr. Flambeau-Plastics, Baraboo, Wis., 1976-83; prin. Walter D. Smith, CPA, Baraboo, 1983—; ad hoc faculty Univ. Wis. Mgmt. Inst., 1988—; dir. Trachte Bldg. Systems, Sun Prairie, Wis., Baraboo Mutual Fire Ins. Co., Baraboo, Wis.; bd. dirs. New Hartford Sch. Dist., 1974-76, Baraboo Sch. Dist., 1980-83. Served with AUS, 1955-56, Korea. Mem. Nat. Soc. Pub. Accts., Nat. Conf. CPA Practitioners, Nat. Speakers Assn., Wis. Profl. Speakers Assn., Inst. Mgmt. Accts., Alliance Practicing CPA's, Baraboo Toastmasters, Am. Legion, VFW, Kiwanis, Elks. Republican. Roman Catholic. Home: 809 Iroquois Cir Baraboo WI 53913-1248 Office: Walter D Smith CPA 102 4th Ave Baraboo WI 53913-2175

SMITH, WARING GRANT, graphic arts designer, advertising executive; b. Cleve., Dec. 2, 1916; s. Earl Grant and Marguerite Gladys (Herrick) S.; m. Thelma Edith Mansbridge, Aug. 11, 1945 (dec. Apr. 1979); children: Mark Leland, Quentin Grant, Grant Waring; m. Lillian Griffin St. John, May 16. 1981 (div. June 1985); 1 stepchild, Anne. Student, Cleve. Sch. Art, 1934; BFA, Miami U., Oxford, Ohio, 1938; postgrad., John Huntington Poly. Inst., 1939-40, Fenn Coll., 1942. Cert. scuba diver. Br. adv. mgr. Kroger Grocery and Baking Co., Cleve., 1939-41; asst. adv. mgr. Iron Fireman, Cleve., 1949-50; account exec. Batten, Barton, Durstine and Osborne, Cleve., 1950-56; account supr. Ketchum, MacLeod and Grove, Pitts., 1956-70; owner, mgr. Skipper's Cottage Resort, Marblehead, Ohio, 1971-77; owner Waring Advt. Agy. and Studio, Akron, Ohio, 1971—; cons. Boy Scouts of Am., Pitts, 1963-70; instr. U.S. Power Squadron, 1974-81; dir communications Peace Grows Inc., Akron, 1985—; mgr. pub. rels. Alternatives to Violence, 1985—. Founder, dir. Youth-Adult Coun., 1948-52; treas. East Harbor Improvement Assn., 1972-75; mem. City Charter Commn., Eastlake, Ohio; scout master, explorer post advisor, Boy Scouts Am., 1957-70. Lt. USCG, 1941-45. Recipient award Am. Bus. Press, 1966, Scouter's Key Boy Scout Am., 1962, mention Freedom Found., 1964, various adv. and graphic arts awards, 1952—; named Hon. Order Ky. Cols. Mem. C&D Investment

Club (pres. 1958-59), Assn. Indsl. Advertisers (bd. dirs. 1967-70), Sierra Club (dir. Portage Trail Group). Democrat. Home: 2027 Ayers Ave Akron OH 44313-7205

SMITH, WAYNE ARTHUR, export company executive; b. Detroit, Jan. 28, 1945; s. Edson Alvin Smith and Helen Margaret (Hofer) McKnight. PhB, Wayne State U., 1966, JD, 1969. Bar: Mich. 1969, U.S. Dist. Ct. (ea. dist.) Mich. 1969, U.S. Ct. Appeals (6th cir.) 1970. V.p. R.G. Corace, P.C., Detroit, 1970-76; pvt. practice, Detroit, 1976-80; pres. Tech. Pers. Svcs. of Mich., Ltd., Royal Oak, Mich., 1980-81; v.p. McRae Energy Resources, Inc., Harper Woods, Mich., 1981-82; pres. Diversified Energy Corp. and subs., Troy, Mich., 1982—. Mem. ABA, State Bar of Mich., World Trade Club, Can. Legion, Elks (P.E.R. 1990-91, Elk of Yr. Royal Oak chpt. 1992-93). Republican. Office: Diversified Energy Corp 105 Futura Office Ctr 671 E Big Beaver Rd Troy MI 48083-1421

SMITH, WAYNE RICHARD, lawyer; b. Petoskey, Mich., Apr. 30, 1934; s. Wayne Anson and Frances Lynetta (Cooper) S.; m. Carrie J. Swanson, June 18, 1959; children: Stephen, Douglas (dec.), Rebecca. AB, U. Mich., 1956, JD, 1959. Bar: Mich. 1959. Asst. atty. gen. State of Mich., 1960-62; pros. atty. Emmet County (Mich.), 1963-68; dist. judge 90th Jud. Dist. Mich., 1969-72; sr. ptnr. Smith & Powers, Petoskey; city atty. City of Petoskey, 1976—; lectr. real estate law U. Mich. Trustee North Central Mich. Coll., 1981—, chmn., 1992—; mem. No. Mich. Cmty. Mental Health Bd., 1972-92, chmn. 1979-81. Mem. ABA, Am. Judicature Soc., Emmet-Charlevoix Bar Assn. (pres. 1967). Presbyterian. Home: 201 Sunset Petoskey MI 49770-0111 Address: PO Box 636 2 Pennsylvania Plz Petoskey MI 49770-0636

SMITH, WENDY L., foundation executive; b. Chgo., Sept. 12, 1950; d. John Arthur and Dolores Mae (Webb) Rothenberger; m. Alan Richard Smith; children: Angela Fuhs, Erica Smith. Ed., Oakton C.C., Des Plaines, Ill., 1986, Mundelein Coll., 1990. Purchasing clk. AIT Industries, Skokie, Ill., 1975-76; purchasing agt. MCC Powers, Skokie, 1976-78; office mgr. Spartan Engring., Skokie, 1978-80, Brunswick Corp., Skokie, 1980—; successively sr. sec., coord. indsl. rels., dir. Brunswick Found., Lake Forest, Ill., 1982-89; pres. Brunswick Found., Lake Forest, 1989—; asst. sec. Brunswick Pub. Charitable Found., Lake Forest, 1989—; mem. adv. com. Found. for Ind. Higher Edn., Stamford, Conn., 1989—, Coun. Better Bus. Burs., Arlington, Va., 1988-90; bd. dirs. Associated Colls. of Ill., 1991—; bd. dirs., mem. trustees com., mem. compensation and benefits com. Donors Forum of Chgo., 1988-93. Bd. dirs. INROADS/Chgo., Inc., 1994—; mem. steering com. Dist. 57 Edn. Found., Mt. Prospect, Ill., 1996—. Recipient Pvt. Sector Initiative Commendation, U.S. Pres., 1987-89. Mem. Donors Forum Chgo. (treas. 1988-91, bd. dirs., mem. exec. com., chairperson audit and fin. com., mem. trustees com. 1992—), Coun. on Founds., Ind. Sector Suburban Contbns. Network (chairperson 1987-89), Women in Philanthropy Corp. Founds. (mem. cmty. rels. com. 1985-87), Chgo. Women in Philanthropy. Office: Brunswick Found 1 N Field Ct Lake Forest IL 60045-4810

SMITH, WESLEY HAROLD, physics educator; b. San Francisco, June 14, 1954; s. Harold Allison and Anita (Koryn) S.; m. Stephanie Joy Smith, Jan. 1, 1983; 1 child, Jennifer Arlene. AB, Harvard U., 1975, AM, 1976; PhD, U. Calif., Berkeley, 1981. Rsch. assoc. Lawrence Berekely Lab., 1976-81; rsch. assoc. Columbia U., N.Y.C., 1981-82, asst. prof., 1982-87, assoc. prof., 1987-88; assoc. prof. U. Wis., Madison, 1988-92, prof. physics, 1993—; trigger project mgr. mgmt. bd. Compact Moon Solenoid Expt. CERN, Switzerland; high energy adv. panelist Dept. Energy. Contbr. articles to profl. jours. Named NSF Presdl. Young Investigator, 1986, Outstanding Jr. Investigator Dept. Energy, 1987; recipient Investigator award Exxon Edn. Found., 1984. Mem. Am. Phys. Soc., Div. of Particles and Fields. Home: 2525 Marshall Pky Madison WI 53713-1030 Office: U Wis Physics Dept 1150 University Ave Madison WI 53706-1302

SMITHBURG, DONALD ROWAN, hospital executive; b. Pomona, Calif., Oct. 18, 1960; s. Donald Winston and Mary Harper (McAnlis) S.; m. Susan Jane Swafford, July 7, 1984; children: Devon Marie, Chase Ewing, Hunter Rowan. BA in Anthropology, Colo. Coll., 1983; MA in Pub. Adminstrn., U. N.Mex., 1985. Asst. to chief adminstr. City of Albuquerque, 1983-85; dir. adminstrv. affairs sch. medicine U. Mo., Kansas City, 1985-87; city adminstr. City of Mission Hills, Kans., 1987-88; assoc. exec. dir. Truman Med. Ctr. Inc., Kansas City, Mo., 1988—; exec. dir. Truman Med. Ctr. Charitable Found., 1988—; chief adminstrv. officer U. Mo. Sch. Medicine, Kansas City, 1988—; vice chmn. adv. bd. Health Care for Homeless, Albuquerque, 1984-85; mem. adv. bd. Western Mo. Mental Health Ctr.; v.p Wee Friends Hosp. Hill Corp. Mem. Lenexa (Kans.) Safety Coun., 1986-87, Greater Kansas City Coun. on Philanthropy; chmn. Centurions Leadership Program Kansas City, 1991-92. Fellow Newberry Libr., 1983, Mgmt. fellow Nat. Assoc. Pub. Hosps., 1992, Sr. Policy fellow Nat. Assn. Pub. Hosps./NYU, 1995. Mem. Internat. Rels. Coun., Am. Soc. Pub. Adminstrn. (elected coun. N.Mex. chpt.), Assn. Am. Med. Colls., Assn. Healthcare Philanthropy, Phi Alpha Alpha, Phi Kappa Phi, Phi Delta Theta. Democrat. Episcopalian.

SMITHBURG, WILLIAM DEAN, food manufacturing company executive; b. Chgo., July 9, 1938; s. Pearl L. and Margaret L. (Savage) S.; children: Susan, Thomas. BS, DePaul U., 1960; MBA, Northwestern U., 1962. With Leo Burnett Co., Chgo., 1961-63, McCann-Erickson, Inc., Chgo., 1963-66; various positions Quaker Oats Co., Chgo., 1966-71, gen. mgr. cereals and mixes divsn., 1971-75, pres. food divsn., 1975-76, exec. v.p. U.S. grocery products, 1976-79, pres., 1979-83, chief exec. officer, 1979—, chmn., 1983—, also bd. dirs. Served with USAR, 1959-60. Roman Catholic. Office: Quaker Oats Co 321 N Clark St Chicago IL 60610-4714

SMITHKEY, JOHN, III, public health nurse, consultant; b. Akron, Ohio, Nov. 14, 1953; s. John C. and Catherine V. (Ennis) S.; m. Kathleen Ann Cuenot, Apr. 9, 1994. BS in Edn., U. Akron, 1977, BS in Nursing, 1988; Med. Lab. Specialist, U.S. Acad. Health Scis., Ft. Sam Houston, Tex., 1983. RN, Ohio; cert. ARC nurse, advanced cardiac life support; cert. instr., trainerCPR, HIV/AIDS, sch. nurse. Med. asst. instr. So. Ohio Coll., Mogadore, 1984-86; EMT Plain Twp. Fire Dept., 1985-88; commd. 2d lt. USAF, 1988, advanced through grades to lst lt., 1990; staff nurse USAF, Goldsboro, N.C., 1988-91; pub. health nurse Summit County Health Dept., 1991-96, Physicians Indsl. and Instnl. Svcs., 1996—, Carriere Care Svcs., 1996—. Author: Prevention is the Cure for Hearing Loss Caused by Noise in the Lab, 1991, The Use of Narcotics in Controlling Patient Pain, 1993; contbr. articles to profl. jours. Home: 4242 20th St NW Canton OH 44708-2847

SMITTLE, NELSON DEAN, electronics executive; b. Peebles, Ohio, Sept. 19, 1934; s. Nelson John and Alma Katherine (Green) S.; m. Claire Wiggins, May 5, 1973. BS, BFA, U. Cin., 1962, MA, 1971. Commd. 2d lt. U.S. Army, 1962; staff officer U.S. Army Photo Agy. Pentagon, Washington, 1966; detachment comdr. tactical comms. Republic South Vietnam, 1967-68; comdr. 907th communications squadron Rickenbacker AFB, Ohio, 1972; dir. ops. fixed communications Air Combat Command Langley AFB, Va., 1982; dir. info. systems AWACS Saudi Arabia, 1984-85; dep. chief of staff standard systems Air Material Command Wright-Patterson AFB, Ohio, 1985; comdr. engring. installation divsn. Tinker AFB, Okla., 1988; commn. transferred to USAF, 1970, commd. col., 1988; ret. USAF, Cin., 1991; pres. Falcon Techs., Cin., 1991—; tchr. Princeton City Sch. Dist., Cin., 1992-94; cons. Air War Coll., Air Univ., Maxwell AFB, Ala., 1987—, Defense Systems Mgmt. Coll., Ft. Belvior, Va., 1988—. Author: (books) Army Visual Presentation, 1966 (medal 1966), Famous Movements in Aviation History, 1997. Mem. Batavia (Ohio) City Coun., 1972; pres. Ohio Buckeye Wing Assn., Columbus, 1973; mem. Air Force Policy Coun., Washington, 1978; congl. campaign mgr., 1993; bd. dirs. Cin. Art Club, 1995—. Decorated Commendation medal; recipient Meritorious Svc. medal Dept. Def., 1986, 91. Mem. DAV, Air Force Assn., Res. Officers Assn., Am. Soc. Aviation Artists. Home and Office: Falcon Techs 159 Francisridge Dr Cincinnati OH 45238-6051

SMOKE, RICHARD EDWIN, lawyer, investment adviser; b. Detroit, Sept. 16, 1945; s. Bruno Donald and Else Marie (Reinvaldt) S.; m. Evelyn Panagsagan Navarro, Jan. 24, 1986. BA, Kalamazoo (Mich.) Coll., 1967; JD, Wayne State U., 1970. Bar: Mich. 1970, Calif. 1975, U.S. Supreme Ct. 1980. Assoc. Hill Lewis, Detroit, 1970-75; gen. counsel Grosse Ile (Mich.) Bridge Co., 1975-78, pres., 1980-83, v.p., 1989—; gen. counsel Campbell-Ewald Co., Warren, Mich., 1978-80; pvt. practice law, investment adviser Grand Rapids, Mich., 1985—; dir. Kent County Cmty. Mental Health, 1996—; adj. faculty Davenport Coll., 1993—; trustee Grand Rapids Charter Twp., 1991—. Bd. dirs. World Affairs Coun. Western Mich., Grand Rapids, 1988-93, pres., 1991-92; mem. exec. com. Kent County Rep. Party, Grand Rapids, 1989-92; trustee Kalamazoo Coll., 1970-79. London-Sloan fellow, 1983. Mem. State Bar Mich., State Bar Calif., Investment Analysts Chgo., Peninsular Club. Office: 500 Peoples Bldg Grand Rapids MI 49503

SMOLEN, CHERYL HOSAKA, special education educator; b. Fairview, Ohio, Dec. 17, 1959; d. James Yukio and Midori (Osaki) Hosaka; m. Alan Smolen; 1 child, Tyler. BA, Ohio U., 1983; M in Curriculum and Instrn., Cleve. State U., 1992. Tchr. devel. handicapped Scioto Valley Sch. Dist., Piketon, Ohio, 1983-85; tchr. learning disabled Darlington County Sch. Dist., Darlington, S.C., 1985-88; small group instrn. tchr. Upper Arlington (Ohio) Sch. Dist., 1988-89; tchr. handicapped presch. Euclid (Ohio) Sch. Dist., 1989-91, Cuyahoga County Bd. Edn., North Olmsted, Ohio, 1991—; tutor learning disabled Avon Lake City Schs., Ohio, 1991-92; coord. Spl. Olympics, Darlington County, 1987-88; counselor Snoopy Camp, Hartsville, S.C., 1987; tchr. Spl. Horizon, North Olmsted, Ohio, summer, 1992; tutor Project LEARN, Cleve., 1990-92; mem. spl. edn. curriculum devel. com., handicapped presch. curriculum devel. com., coord. spl. edn. newsletter; ESL tutor, 1992—. Active North Olmsted Preschool PTA. Mem. Coun. for Exceptional Children, North Olmsted Presch. PTA. Home: 5630 Revere Dr North Olmsted OH 44070-4472

SMOOT, JOSEPH GRADY, university administrator; b. Winter Haven, Fla., May 7, 1932; s. Robert Malcolm and Vera (Eaton) S.; m. Florence Rozell, May 30, 1955 (dec.); m. Irma Jean Kopitzke, June 4, 1959; 1 child, Andrew Christopher. BA, So. Coll., 1955; MA, U. Ky., 1958, PhD, 1964. Tchr., Ky. Secondary Schs., 1955-57; from instr. to assoc. prof. history Columbia Union Coll., Takoma Park, Md., 1960-68, acad. dean, 1965-68; prof. history Andrews U., Berrien Springs, Mich., 1968-84, dean Sch. Grad. Studies, 1968-69, v.p. acad. adminstrn., 1969-76, pres., 1976-84; v.p. for devel. Pittsburg State U., Kans., 1984—; exec. dir. Pitts. State U. Found., 1985—; bd. dirs. 1st State Bank and Trust Co., Pitts., 1994—; founder Pitts. State U. Radio Sta.-KRPS-FM, 1988; commr. North Cen. Assn., 1987-91, cons., evaluator, 1978—; cons. internat. edn; trustee Loma Linda U., 1976-84, U. Ea. Africa, Baraton, Kenya, 1979-84, Hindsdale Hosp., Ill., 1973-84; chmn., bd. trustees Andrews Broadcasting Corp., 1976-84; bd. dirs. Internat. U. Thailand Found., 1987-95, trustee, 1994-95. Contbr. articles to profl. jours; editor: Spottiswoode Soc. Record, 1990—. Active Pitts. Area Festival Assn., 1984-86, bd. dirs. Pitts. United Way, 1987-92, Pitts. C. of C. Found., 1990-93; bd. advisors Pitts. Salvation Army, 1987-92, vice-chmn., 1990-91, chmn., 1991-92; bd. trustees Mt. Carmel Med. Ctr. Found., 1991-95; bd. dirs. S.E. Kans. Symphony Orch., 1995—, bd. trustees, 1996—. Recipient Disting. Pres. award Mich. Coll. Found., 1984. Mem. Inst. Early Am. History and Culture (assoc.), Am. Hist. Assn., So. Hist. Assn., Orgn. Am. Historians, Soc. for Historians of Early Am. Rep., Soc. History of Authorship, Reading & Pub., Phi Alpha Theta. Club: Crestwood Country. Lodge: Rotary (dist. chmn. scholarship com. 1986-88, Paul Harris Fellow) Home: 1809 Heritage Rd Pittsburg KS 66762-3556 Office: Office of V.P. for Development Pittsburg State U Pittsburg KS 66762

SMUTNY, JOAN FRANKLIN, academic director, educator; b. Chgo.; d. Eugene and Mabel (Lind) Franklin; m. Herbert Paul Smutny; 1 child, Cheryl Anne. BS, Northwestern U., MA. Tchr., New Trier High Sch., Winnetka, Ill.; mem. faculty, founder, dir. Nat. High Sch. Inst., Northwestern U. Sch. Edn., Chgo.; mem. faculty, founder dir. high sch. workshop in critical thinking and edn., chmn. dept. communications Nat. Coll. Edn., Evanston, Ill., exec. dir. high sch. workshops, 1970-75, founder, dir. Woman Power Through Edn. Seminar, 1969-74, dir. Right to Read seminar in critical reading, 1973-74, seminar gifted high sch. students, 1973, dir. of Gifted Programs for 6, 7 and 8th graders pub. schs., Evanston, 1978-79, 1st-8th graders, Glenview (both Ill.) 1979—; dir. gifted programs Nat.-Louis U., Evanston, 1980-82, dir. Center for Gifted, 1982—; dir. Bright and Talented and Project 1986—, North Shore Country Day Sch., Winnetka, 1982—; dir. Job Creation Project, 1980-82; dir. New Dimensions for Women, 1973, dir. Thinking for Action in Career Edn. project, 1974-77 , dir. Individualized Career Edn. Program, 1976-79, dir. TACE, dir. Humanities Program for Verbally Precocious Youth, 1978-79; co-dir., instr. seminars in critical thinking Ill. Family Svc., 1972-75 . Writer ednl. filmstrips in Lang. arts and Lit. Soc. for Visual Edn., 1970-74 ; mem. speakers bur. Counc. Fgn. Rels., 1968-69 ; mem. adv. com. edn. professions devel. act U.S. Office Edn., 1969—; mem. state team for gifted, Ill. Office Edn., Office of Gifted, Springfield, Ill., 1977; writer, cons. Radiant Ednl. Corp., 1969-71 ; cons. ALA, 1969-71 , cons., workshop leader and speaker in area of gifted edn., 1971—; coord. of career edn. Nat. Coll. Edn., 1976-78, dir. Project 1987—, dir. Summer Wonders, 1986—, Creative Children's Acad., bd. dirs., Worlds of Wisdom and Wonder, 1978—; dir. Future Tchrs. Am. Seminar in Coll. and Career, 1970-72; cons. for research and devel. Ill. Dept. Vocat. Edn., 1973—; cons. in career edn. U.S. Office Edn., 1976—; evaluation cons. DAVTE, IOE, Springfield, Ill., 1977, mem. Leadership Tng. Inst. for Gifted, U.S. Office Edn., 1973-74; dir. workshops for high sch. students; cons., speaker in field; dir. Gifted Young Writer's and Young Writer's confs., 1978, 79; dir. Project '92 The White House Conf. on Children and Youth; mem. adv. bd. Educating Able Learners, 1991—; chmn. bd. dirs. Barbereux Sch., Evanston, 1992—; asst. editor, mem. editl. bd. Understanding Our Gifted, 1994—. Mem. AAUP, Nat. Assn. for Gifted Child (nat. membership chmn. 1991—, co-chmn. schs. and programs, co-editor newsletter early childhood divsn.), Nat. Soc. Arts and Letters (nat. bd., 1st and 3d v.p. Evanston chpt., dir. 1983-92, pres. Evanston chpt. 1990-92), Mortar Bd., Outstanding Educators of Am. 1974, Pi Lambda Theta, Phi Delta Kappa (v.p. Evanston chpt., rsch. chmn. 1990-92). Author: (with others) Job Creation: Creative Materials, Activities and Strategies for the classroom, 1982, A Thoughtful Overview of Gifted Education, 1990, Your Gifted Child - How to Recognize and Develop the Special Talents in Your Child from Birth to Age Seven, 1989, paperback, 1991, Education of the Gifted: The Young Gifted Child: An Anthology, 1990, Potential and Promise: The Young Gifted Child, 1996; contbg. editor Roepper Review, 1994—; asst. editor Understanding a Gift, 1995—; editor, contbr. Maturity in Teaching; writer ednl. filmstrips The Brother's Grimm, How the West Was Won, Mutiny on the Bounty, Dr. Zhivago, Space Odessey 2001, Christmas Around the World; editor Jour. for Gifted, Ill., 1984—, Ill. Coun. Gifted Jour., 1985-93; contbg. editor Roeper Review, 1994—; editor IAGC Jour. for Gifted, 1994—; contbg. editor numerous books in field; contbr. articles to profl. jours. including Chgo. Parent Mag. Reviewer of Programs for Gifted and Talented, U.S. Office of Edn., 1976-78. Home: 633 Forest Ave Wilmette IL 60091-1713

SMYTH, WILLIAM, machine designer; b. Stanton, Ky., June 29, 1932. BS, Ea. Ky. State U., 1958. Machine designer Voith Sulzer Paper Tech., Middletown, Ohio, 1959—; indsl. arts tchr. Jr. H.S., Lexington, Ky., 1958-59. Cpl. U.S. Army, Korea. Mem. VFW, Eagles. Democrat. Presbyterian. Office: Voith Sulzer PO Box 509 Middletown OH 45042

SMYTHE, THOMAS, advertising executive; b. 1941. Attended, U. Evansville. V.p. account supr. Keller-Crescent Co. Inc., Evansville, Ind., 1974, pres., COO, 1980, pres., CEO, dir., 1984—. Office: Keller-Crescent Co PO Box 3 1100 E Louisiana St Evansville IN 47711*

SMYTHE ZĂJC, M. CATHERINE, research librarian, administrator; b. Washington, Jan. 5, 1956; d. William Sterling Jr. and Anna Rosamund (Johnson) S. BA in History, Westminster Coll., 1976; MLS, Syracuse U., 1982. Rsch. libr. White House Libr., Washington, 1982-86; dep. dir., rsch. libr. Time, Inc. Sports Libr., N.Y.C., 1986-89; dir. libr. svcs. Nat. Sports Daily, N.Y.C., 1989-90; rsch. assoc. Jury Verdict Rsch., Solon, Ohio, 1990-91; cons., owner Sports Source, Inc., Painesville, Ohio, 1990-92; dir. of prospect rsch. Baldwin-Wallace Coll., Berea, Ohio, 1992—; cons. Bowman Gray Sch. Medicine/Bapt. Hosp. Med. Ctr., Winston-Salem, N.C., 1990-93. Author: Geothesaurus, 1982. Mem. Assn. of Profl. Rschrs. for Advancement, Coun. for Advancement and Support of Edn., Ohio Prospect Rschrs. Network, Ind. Coll. Advancement Assocs., Soc. for Am. Baseball Rsch., Ch. St. Ministries (fund raising adv. bd.), Cleve. Sight Ctr., Radio Reading Svc. Presbyterian. Home: 2672 W 14th St #2 Cleveland OH 44113

SNAVELY, WILLIAM BRANT, management educator and consultant; b. Balt., June 18, 1951; s. Charles Albert and Helen (Morris) S.; m. Bretta Kay Smith, Aug. 16, 1974; children: Michael David, Sarah Anne. BS, Ill. State U., 1973; MA, W.Va. U., 1974; PhD, U. Nebr., 1977. Vis. asst. prof. Miami U., Oxford, Ohio, 1977-80; asst. prof. mgmt. Miami U., Oxford, 1980-82, assoc. prof. mgmt., 1982—; pvt. practice mgmt. cons., 1976—; dir. Labor Mgmt. Ctr., Oxford, 1987-89; pres. Talawanda Band Boosters, 1995—; v.p. Oxford Kiwanis, 1995-97. Author: Interpersonal Communication Experiences, 1980; contbr. articles to various jours. Mem. Oxford Planning Commn., 1987-88, 90-91, Oxford City Coun., 1987-95; vice mayor City of Oxford, 1989-91, mayro, 1991-93; bd. dirs. Oxford Sr. Citizens, Inc., 1988-90, Woodside Cemetery, Oxford, 1988-90, Cmty. Improvement Corp., 1990-91, 93—, Oxford Area Cmty. Theatre, 1990-92; mem. Firefighters Dependents Bd., 1989-93; mem. exec. com. Butler County Land Use Coordinating Com., 1993-95, chair, 1995; mem. Ohio-Ky.-Ind. regional Coun. Govts., 1993-95, Retirement Cmty. Adv. Com., 1992—; mem. Butler County Regional Transit Auth., 1996—. Mem. Acad. Mgmt. (div. program chmn. 1988-89, div. chmn 1989-91, local chair. 1995-96), Internat. Comm. Assn., Cen. States Comm. Assn. (div. chmn. 1979-80), Beta Gamma Sigma, Alpha Tau Omega. Presbyterian. Office: Miami U Dept Mgmt Oxford OH 45056

SNEARY, MAX EUGENE, retired physician; b. Zanesfield, Ohio, Oct. 13, 1930; s. Kenneth Douglas and Grace Agnes (Yeiser) S.; m. Joy Ann Preston, Apr. 4, 1950; children: Candice Barbulesco, Jennifer Laur. Student, Wabash Coll., 1949-52; MD, Ind. U., 1956. Pvt. practice Avilla, Ind., 1957-95; retired, 1995; coroner Noble County (Ind.) Coroner's Office, 1960-64, 72-76; pres. bd. dirs. McCray Meml. Hosp., Kendallville, Ind., 1961-64; mem. Noble County Bd. of Health, 1962-65, 76-80, health officer, 1965-67. Bd. dirs. Kendalville Bank & Trust Co., 1980-88, chmn., 1987-88. Named Citizen of the Yr., Town of Avilla, 1988, Indian Family Physician of the Yr., 1990. Fellow Am. Acad. Family Physicians; mem. AMA, Am. Bd. Family Physicians (charter), Ind. Med. Assn., Noble County Med. Soc., Alpha Omega Alpha. Home: 205 Baum St #140 Avilla IN 46710

SNEED, MARIE ELEANOR WILKEY, retired secondary education educator; b. Dahlgren, Ill., June 12, 1915; d. Charles N. and Hazel (Miller) Wilkey; student U. Ill., 1933-35; B.S., Northwestern U., 1937; postgrad. Wayne State U., 1954-60, U. Mich., 1967; m. John Sneed, Jr., Sept. 18, 1937; children: Suzanne (Mrs. Geoffrey B. Newton), John Corwin. Tchr. English, drama, creative writing Berkley (Mich.) Sch. Dist., 1952-76. Mem. Mich. Statewide Tchr. Edn. Preparation, 1968-72, regional sec. 1969-70; mem. Pleasant Ridge Arts Council, 1982—; mem. Pleasant Ridge Parks and Recreation Commn., 1982-88, sr. citizen cons., 1989—. Mem. NEA, Mich., Berkley (pres. 1961-62, 82-87) edn. assns., Oakland Tchr. Edn. Council (exec. bd. 1973-76), Student Tchr. Planning Com. Berkley (chmn. 1971-72), Farm Bureau Ill., Founder's Soc., Phi Alpha Chi, Pi Lambda Theta, Alpha Delta Kappa, Alpha Omicron Pi. Club: Pleasant Ridge Woman's (pres. 1980-83), Royal Oak Republican Woman's, Nomad's. Home: 21 Norwich Rd Pleasant Ridge MI 48069-1027 also: Heritage Farm Dahlgren IL 62828

SNEERINGER, STEPHEN GEDDES, lawyer; b. Lancaster, Ohio, Mar. 27, 1949; s. Stanley Carlylle and Mary Eleanor (Fry) S.; m. Kristine Karen Serfling, Oct. 6, 1974; children: Mary Rhonda, Robyn Kathleen. BA magna cum laude, Denison U., 1971; JD, Washington U., 1974. Bar: Mo. 1974. V.p. A.G. Edwards & Sons Inc., St. Louis, 1974—; arbitrator N.Y. Stock Exchange, Nat. Assn. Securities Dealers, Nat. Futures Assn., Am. Arbitration Assn. Editor: Urban Law Ann., 1973-74. Am. Jurisprudence scholar, 1974. Mem. ABA, Mo. Bar Assn. (securities Industries Assn. (arbitration subcom.), Futures Industries Assn., Nat. Assn. Securities Dealers (past mem. arbitration com.).. Office: AG Edwards & Sons Inc 1 N Jefferson Ave Saint Louis MO 63103-2205

SNEIDERMAN, MARILYN SINGER, secondary and elementary school educator; b. Erie, Pa., Jan. 13, 1943; d. Albert E. and Nettie (Levick) Singer; m. Donald G. Sneiderman, Aug. 15, 1965; children: Steven, Russell. BA in Edn., Mercyhurst Coll., 1965. Cert. tchr., Ohio. Substitute tchr. Beachwood (Ohio) Sch. System, 1980-87; tutor Hilltop Sch., Beachwood, 1987-91, instnl. tutor, ESL tchr., 1991—. Mem. ASCD, Greater Cleve. Coun. Tchrs. Math., Phi Delta Kappa. Home: 26200 Fairmount Blvd Beachwood OH 44122-2220

SNELL, BRUCE M., JR., state supreme court justice; b. Ida Grove, Iowa, Aug. 18, 1929; s. Bruce M. and Donna (Potter) S.; m. Anne Snell, Feb. 4, 1956; children: Rebecca, Brad. AB, Grinnell Coll., 1951; JD, U. Iowa, 1956. Bar: Iowa 1956, N.Y. 1958. Law clk. to presiding judge U.S. Dist. Ct. (no. dist.) Iowa, 1956-57; asst. atty. gen., 1961-65; judge Iowa Ct. Appeals, 1976-87; justice Iowa Supreme Ct., 1987—. Comments editor Iowa Law Rev. Mem. ABA, Iowa State Bar Assn., Am. Judicature Soc., Order of Coif. Methodist. Home: PO Box 192 Ida Grove IA 51445-0192 Office: Iowa Supreme Ct St Capitol Bldg Des Moines IA 50319

SNELLING, NORMA JUNE, retired music educator, English educator; b. Brooten, Minn., June 1, 1928; d. Harold Melvin and Mabel Olga (Markuson) Hellickson; m. Douglas Howard Snelling, June 27, 1953; children: Julie Marie, Mary Merced, Steven Douglas. BA, Concordia Coll., Moorhead, Minn., 1949. Cert. tchr., Minn. Tchr. Wolverton (Minn.) Sch. Dist., 1949-51, Kimball (Minn.) Sch. Dist., 1951-52, Benson (Minn.) Sch. Dist., 1952-53, Belgrade (Minn.) Sch. Dist., 1953-57, Hutchinson (Minn.) Sch. Dist., 1964-66, Litchfield (Minn.) Sch. Dist., 1966-92; mem. staff edn. liaison 2d Congl. Dist. Minn., Litchfield, 1992—. Assoc. chairperson county level, del. Dem. Farmer Labor Party, Minn., 1992—, chair 1994; del. to Dem. Nat. Conv., 1984; co-chairperson Concert Series, Litchfield, 1962, Cancer Dr., Litchfield, 1960; dir. Choralaires, Eden Valley, Minn., 1976—; dir. music Zion Luth. Ch., Litchfield, 1962-85, poet ch. pubs., dedications, etc., also Big Grove Luth. Ch.; speech coach Litchfield Jr. H.S., 1972-77; mem. VFW Aux., Am. Legion Aux. 94m. NEA (life, congl. contact person 1985-90), Minn. Edn. Assn. (govtl. rels. uniserve chairperson, Leadership award medal 1986), Ret. Educators Minn. (legis. chairperson 1993—), Internat. Platform, Sons of Norway (musician, pres. Vannland Lodge 1993-94, Bronze medal 1993-94), Gen. Fedn. Women's Study Clubs, Halling Laget, Delta Kappa Gamma. Home: 621 W Crescent Ln Litchfield MN 55355-1830

SNODGRASS, KLYNE RYLAND, seminary educator; b. Kingsport, Tenn., Dec. 28, 1944; s. Charles Sidney and Wanda Virginia (Lauderback) S.; m. Phyllis Parks, Aug. 28, 1966; children: Nathan, Valerie. BA, Columbia Bible Coll., 1966; MDiv magna cum laude, Trinity Evang. Div. Sch., 1969; PhD, St. Andrews U., 1973. Instr. N.T. Georgetown (Ky.) Coll., 1973-74; asst. prof. bibl. lit. North Park Sem., Chgo., 1974-78, assoc. prof., 1978-84, prof., 1984-89, Paul Brandel prof. N.T. studies, 1989—, dean of faculty, 1988-93. Author: The Parable of the Wicked Tenants, 1983, Between Two Truths, 1990; contbr. articles to profl. jours. Assn. Theol. Schs. grantee, 1981, PEW Evang. Scholars Program grantee, 1995. Fellow Inst. Bibl. Rsch. (exec. sec. 1989-93, pres. 1993-95); mem. Chgo. Soc. Bibl. Rsch. (pres. 1990-91), Soc. Bibl. Lit., Assn. Bapt. Profs. of Religion, Studiorum Novi Testamenti Societas. Office: North Park Theol Sem 3225 W Foster Ave Chicago IL 60625-4810

SNOUFFER, CHET ALAN, coach, manufacturing executive; b. Columbus, Ohio, Sept. 22, 1956; s. Richard Kendall and Patti Janice S.; m. Maria del Carmen Foster, Oct. 19, 1985; children: Cody Alan, Lydia Rae. BS, Wheaton Coll., 1979. Cert. phys. edn. tchr., Ohio; cert. safety U.S. Gymnastics Fedn. Tchr. phys. edn. Delaware (Ohio) Joint Vocat. Schs., 1979-80; coach men's gymnastics Hayes High Sch., Delaware, 1979-86; coach women's gymnastics Hayes High Sch., 1987—; supr. gymnastics Delaware Parks and recreation dept., 1979-93; owner, boomerang mfr., editor newsletter Leading Edge Boomerangs, Delaware, 1979—; co-owner C & C Sch. Gymnastics, 1993—. Bd. dirs. Ohio H.S. Gymnastics, Columbus. Mem. U.S. Boomerang Assn. (v.p. 1983-85, 88-94, pres. 1994—), World Boomerang Assn. (v.p. 1991—), Free Throwers Boomerang Soc. (founder), U.S. Boomerang Team (U.S. Nat. champion 1983, 87-95, U.S. Open champion 1992-96, Internat. Team champion 1981, 87, 88, 91, 94, World champion overall 1985, 89, 94, World champion fastcatch & triclecatch 1996). Office: US Boomerang Assn PO Box 182 Delaware OH 43015-0182

SNOW, JOEL ALAN, research director; b. Brockton, Mass., Apr. 1, 1937; s. George H. and Mary W. (Sproul) S.; m. Laetitia Harrer, June 29, 1957 (div. 1983); children: Jonathan, Nicholas; m. Barbara Kashian, Feb. 7, 1992; stepchildren: James, Alexander. BS in Physics, U. N.C., 1958; MA in Physics, Washington U., St. Louis, 1963, PhD in Physics, 1967. Program dir. for theoretical physics NSF, Washington, 1968-70, head office of interdisciplinary rsch., 1970-71, dep. asst. dir. for sci. and tech., rsch. applications, 1971-74, dir. office of planning and resources, 1974-76, dir. div. of policy rsch. and analysis, 1976; sr. policy analyst, office of sci. and tech. policy Exec. Office of the Pres., Washington, 1976-77; assoc. dir. for rsch. policy U.S. Dept. Energy, Washington, 1977-81, dir. sci. and tech. affairs, 1981-88; assoc. v.p. for rsch. and Argonne, U. Chgo., 1988-92; dir. Inst. for Phys. Rsch. and Tech. Iowa State U., Ames, 1993—, prof. elec. and computer engring., 1993—; rsch. assoc. dept. physics U. Ill., Urbana, 1967-68; instr. physics and electronics U.S. Navy Nulcear Power Shc., New London, Conn., 1958-61; sci. organizer Pres.'s Conf. on Superconductivity, 1987, NSF program rsch. applied to nat. needs, 1971, NSF program interdisciplinary rsch. relevant to problems of society, 1969. Contbr. over 130 articles to mags. and profl. jours. Lt. (j.g.) USN, 1958-61. Recipient Meritorious Svc. award NSF, 1972, Meritorious award William A. Jump Found., 1973, Arthur S. Fleming award Downtown Jaycees, 1974; NSF postdoctoral fellow Ctr. for Advanced Study U. Ill., 1967-68; NSF fellow, 1963-65. Fellow AAAS, Am. Phys. Soc.; mem. Am. Chem. Soc., Am. Nuc. Soc., World Future Soc., Sigma Xi, Phi Beta Kappa. Office: IPRT/Iowa State U 112 Office Lab Bldg Ames IA 50011

SNOW, JOSEPH THOMAS, language educator; b. Atlantic City, N.Y., Sept. 21, 1941; s. Lockyer and Ruth Irene (Patton) S. BA, Montclair State Coll., 1963; MA, U. Iowa, 1965; PhD, U. Wis., 1972. Asst. prof. U. Minn., Mpls., 1970-72; from asst. prof. to prof. U. Ga., Athens, 1973-91; prof. Mich. State U., East Lansing, 1991—; test maker, chief reader Coll. Bd., Ednl. Testing Svcs., N.Y.C., 1977-91; fellow Fulbright/Spain Joint Commn., Washington and Madrid, 1984. Editor jour. Celestinesca, 1977—; author, editor 5 books in field; contbr. articles to profl. publs. Reader Rec. for the Blind, Athens and East Lansing, Mich., 1978—. NEH grantee, 1979. Mem. MLA, Mediaeval Acad. Am., Conf. Editors Learned Jours., Internat. Assn. Hispanists, Southeastern Medieval Assn. (councilor 1989-92), Internat. Courtly Lit. Soc. (hon. pres.), Hispanic Soc. Am. (corr.). Home: 1850 Abbott Rd #D8 Lansing MI 48823-1465 Office: Mich State U 161 Old Horticulture East Lansing MI 48824-1112

SNOWBARGER, VINCENT KEITH, lawyer, state representative; b. Kankakee, Ill., Sept. 16, 1949; s. Willis Edward and Wahnona Ruth (Horger) S.; m. Carolyn Ruth McMahon, Mar. 25, 1972; children: Jeffrey Edward, Matthew David. BA in History, So. Nazarene U., 1971; MA in Polit. Sci., U. Ill., 1974; JD, U. Kans., 1977. Bar: Kans. 1977, U.S. Dist. Ct. Kans. 1977, Mo. 1987. Instr. Mid-Am. Nazarene Coll., Olathe, Kans., 1973-76; ptnr. Haskin, Hinkle, Slater & Snowbarger, Olathe, 1977-84, Dietrich, Davis, Dicus et al, Olathe, 1984-88, Armstrong, Teasdale, Schafly & Davis, Overland Park, Kans., 1989-92; Holbrook, Heaven & Fay, P.C., Merriam, Kans., 1992-94; ptnr. Snowbarger & Veatch LLP, Olathe, Kans., 1994—. Mem. Kans. Legislature, Topeka, 1985—; majority leader Ho. of Reps., 1993—; mem. Olathe Planning Commn., 1982-84, Leadership Olalthe; bd. dirs. Johnson County Cert. Devel. Corp.; divsn. chmn. United Way, Olathe, 1985-88, chmn. citizen rev. com., 1991—. Mem. Kans. Bar Assn., Kans. Assn. Hosp. Attys., Johnson County Bar Assn., Olathe Area C. of C. (bd. dirs. 1984). Republican. Nazarene. Home: 1451 E Orleans Dr Olathe KS 66062-5728 Office: PO Box 10121 110 S Cherry Ste 103 Olathe KS 66051-1421

SNUFFER, DANIEL HADEN, process engineer; b. Alexandria, La., Apr. 19, 1962; s. Ira Haden Jr. and Dixie June (Atwood) S.; m. Joyce Evelyn Dolinger, Feb. 5, 1983; children: Desiree, Daniel Jr. BS in Materials Engring., Va. Poly. and State U., 1985. Cert. electroplater finisher, quality engr., reliability engr., quality auditor, mfg. engr. Materials and process engr. Inland Motor, Radford, Va., 1985-93; project engr. Marathon Electric, Wausau, Wis., 1993—. Cubmaster pack 439 Boy Scouts Am., Weston, Wis., 1994-95. Mem. Am. Soc. for Quality Control, Am. Electroplaters Soc., Soc. for Advancement of Materials and Process Engrs., SME, Am. Welding Soc. Republican. Home: 6204 Shawna St Schofield WI 54476 Office: Marathon Electric 100 E Randolph St Wausau WI 54401

SNYDER, CAROLYN ANN, university dean, librarian; b. Elgin, Nebr., Nov. 5, 1942; d. Ralph and Florence Wagner; m. Barry Snyder, Apr. 24, 1969. Student, Nebr. Wesleyan U., 1960-61; BS cum laude, Kearney State Coll., 1964; MS in Librarianship, U. Denver, 1965. Asst. libr. sci. and tech. U. Nebr., Lincoln, 1965-67, asst. pub. svc. libr., 1967-68, 70-73; pers. libr. Ind. U. Librs., Bloomington, 1973-76, acting dean of univ. librs., 1980, 88-89, assoc. dean for pub. svcs., 1977-88, 89-91, interim devel. officer, 1989-91; adminstrv. army libr. Spl. Svcs. Agy., Europe, 1968-70; dean libr. affairs So. Ill. U., Carbondale, 1991—; team leader Midwest Univs. Consortium for Internat. Activities-World Bank IX project to develop libr. system and implement automation U. Indonesia, Jakarta, 1984-86; libr. devel. cons. Inst. Tech. MARA/Midwest Univs. Consortium for Internat. Activities Program in Malaysia, 1985. Contbr. chpt. to book and articles to profl. jours. Mem. Humane Assn. Jackson County, 1991—, Carbondale Pub. Libr. Friends, 1991—. Recipient Cooperative Rsch. grant Coun. on Libr. Resources, Washington, 1984. Mem. ALA (councilor 1985-89, Bogle Internat. Travel award 1988, H.W. Wilson Libr. Staff devel. grantee 1981), Libr. Adminstrn./Mgmt. Assn. (pres. 1981-82), Com. on Instnl. Coop./Resource Sharing (chair 1987-91), Coalition for Networked Info. (So. Ill. U. at Carbondale rep. 1991—), Coun. Dirs. State Univ. Librs. in Ill. (chair 1992-93), Ill. Asn. Coll. and Rsch. Librs. (chair Ill. Bd. Higher Edn. liaison com. 1993-94), Ill. Network (bd. dirs.), Ind. Libr. Assn. (chair coll./univ. divsn. 1982-83), U.S. Grant Assn. (bd. dirs. 1992—), Ill. Libr. Computer Sys. Orgn. (policy coun. 1992-95), Nat. Assn. State Univs. and Land-Grant Colls. (commn. on info. tech. and its distance learning bd. 1994—), NetIllinois (bd. dirs. 1994—), OCLC Users Coun. (elected rep. 1995—). Office: So Ill U Morris Libr Carbondale IL 62901-6632

SNYDER, DONALD MARK, research chemist; b. Johnstown, Pa., July 31, 1952; s. Donald Clyde and Mabel Carol (Hunt) S.; m. Cheryl Ann Coryer, May 27, 1977; 1 child, Jennifer. BS, U. Pitts., 1974; PhD, Purdue U., 1980. Project leader R & D Va. Chems. Inc., Portsmouth, 1980-85; rsch. scientist Basic Rsch. Group Armstrong World Industries, Inc., Lancaster, Pa., 1985-93; asst. prof. dept. chemistry Eastern Mich. U., 1993—. Contbr. articles to Jour. Macromolecular Sci.-Chemistry, Jour. Chem. Edn. Mem. Am. Chem. Soc. (organic div., treas. S.E. Pa. sect. 1987-90, contbr. articles to jour.), Phi Lambda Upsilon (alumni sec. Purdue U. chpt. 1979-80). Office: Eastern Mich U Dept Chem Mark Jefferson Sci Bldg Ypsilanti MI 48197

SNYDER, GARY LAINE, electronics company project leader; b. Portsmouth, Va., Mar. 19, 1954; s. William Travis and Leona (Tyler) S.; m. Wendy Beth Webb, Nov. 29, 1980; children: Lindsay Paige, Mary Elizabeth. Cert. computer sci., Electronic Computer Inst, Virginia Beach, Va., 1977; BS in BA summa cum laude, Ind. Wesleyan U., Marion, 1993. Prodn. follower GE, Portsmouth, 1972-74, warehouseman, stockkeeper, 1974-78, computer operator, 1978-81, computer operator leader, 1981-85, programmer, 1985-86; programmer analyst Thomson Consumer Electronics, Indpls., 1986-87, systems analyst I, 1987-89, systems analyst, 1989-91, systems designer, 1991-93; project leader, 1993—; focus site coord. Thomson Consumer Electronics, Indpls., 1986—. Electoral John Anderson Campaign, Va., 1980. Republican. Episcopalian. Home: 7691 Creekside Dr Fishers IN 46038-1354

SNYDER, HARRY COOPER, retired state senator; b. July 10, 1928. Student, Wilmington Coll., Ohio U. Mem. Ohio State Senate, Columbus, 1979-96; ret., 1996; chmn. edn. and retirement com. Ohio State Senate, Columbus. Former mem. exec. com. Ohio Sch. Bds. Assn.; commr. Ohio High Speed Rail Devel. Authority; mem. Edn. Commn. of the States; chmn. Ohio Retirement Study Commn.; chmn. Legis. Office on Edn. Oversight; ad hoc mem. State Bd. Edn., Ohio Bd. Regents; mem. Jobs for Ohio Grads.; founder Clinton County Family Y; mem. Clinton County Bd. Edn. Recipient Outstanding Legis. Svc. award Citizens United for Responsible Edn., Ohio Ret. Tchrs. Assn., Ohio Coalition for Edn. of Handicapped Children, Ohio Assn. Civil Trial Attys., Guardian of Small Bus. award Nat. Fedn. Ind. Bus., Outstanding Contbr. to Edn. in Ohio award Ohio Confedn. Tchr. Edn. Orgn., Disting. Govtl. Svc. award Ohio Coun. Pvt. Colls. and Schs., Legis. of Yr. Ohio Sch. and Transit Assn. Mem. Am. Legis. Exch. Coun. (edn. com., Outstanding State Legis.-Jefferson award), Nat. Conf. State Legislatures (state/fed. assembly, edn. and job tng. com., assembly of legislature, edn. com.), Rotary Club (pres.), Great Oaks Task Force. Republican. Methodist. Home: 6508 Spring Hill Dr Hillsboro OH 45133-9209

SNYDER, LEWIS EMIL, astrophysicist; b. Ft. Wayne, Ind., Nov. 26, 1939; s. Herman Lewis and Bernice (McKee) S.; m. Doris Jean Selma Lautner, June 16, 1962; children: Herman Emil, Catherine Jean. BS, Ind. State U., 1961; MA, So. Ill. U., 1964; PhD, Mich. State U., 1967. Research assoc. Nat. Radio Astronomy Obs., Charlottesville, Va., 1967-69; prof. astronomy dept. U. Va., Charlottesville, 1969-73, 74-75; vis. fellow Joint Inst. for Lab. Astrophysics, U. Colo., Boulder, 1973-74; prof. astronomy dept. U. Ill., Urbana, 1975—. Co-editor: Molecules in the Galactic Environment, 1973; contbr. articles to sci. jours. NASA-Am. Soc. Engring. Edn. summer fellow, 1972, 73; Alexander von Humboldt Found. sr. U.S. scientist award, 1983-84. Mem. AAAS, Astron. Soc. Pacific, Am. Phys. Soc., Am. Astron. Soc., Internat. Astron. Union, Union Radio Scientifique Internationale. Lutheran. Office: U Ill 1002 W Green St Urbana IL 61801-3074

SNYDER, NANCY MARGARET, translator, language services company executive; b. Detroit, Sept. 24, 1950; d. Estle M. and Noreen V. (Woodruff) S.; m. P. W. Denton, July 15, 1972 (div. Feb. 1980); 1 child, Virginia. BA in German, Mich. State U., 1972; cert. in programming and ops., Control Data Inst., 1984. Office mgr. Detroit Translation Bur., Southfield, Mich., 1980-82; bilingual sec. Volkswagen Am., Troy, Mich., 1984-85, translator, 1985-88; owner, operator Tech. Lang. Svcs., Birmingham, Mich., 1988—; guest speaker Kent State U. Inst. Applied Linguistics, 1992, Ferndale (Mich.) High Sch., 1992. Contbr. articles to profl. jours. Stadium usher Olympic Games, Munich, 1972; mem., worker Cass Corridor Food Coop., Detroit, 1986-90. Mem. S.E. Mich. Translators and Interpreters Network (newsletter editor 1993), Am. Translators Assn. (accredited German to English translator), Chgo. Area Translators Assn., Am. Mensa Ltd., Amherst Block Club. Office: Tech Lang Svcs 600 S Adams Rd Ste 210 Birmingham MI 48009-6863

SNYDER, ROBERT LEE, anesthesiologist; b. Midland, Mich., Aug. 26, 1952; s. Robert M. and Kathleen M. (Bogan) S.; m. Shelley Ann Marquiss, June 29, 1974; children: Kenneth Robert, Kacie Lee Ann. BS in Zoology, Mich. State U., 1974, D of Osteopathy, 1979. Diplomate Am. Osteopathic Bd. Anesthesiology. Intern Saginaw (Mich.) Osteo. Hosp., 1979-80, cons., 1982—; resident in anesthesia Flint (Mich.) Osteo. Hosp., 1980-82; staff anesthesiologist McPherson Community Health Ctr., Howell, Mich., 1982-88, chief of anesthesia services, 1986-88, chmn. dept. anesthesia, 1986-87; chmn. dept. anesthesia McPherson Cmty. Health Ctr., 1988-89; staff anesthesiologist Mid-Mich. Regional Med. Ctr., Midland, Mich., 1988—; cons. privileges anesthesia Mid-Mich. Regional Med. Ctr., Clare, Mich., 1991—; med. dir. Mid-Mich. Regional Med. Ctr., Midland, Mich., 1994—; examiner Am. Osteo. Bd. Anesthesiologists, 1989—; cons. Herrick Meml. Hosp., Tecumseh, Mich., 1982; assoc. clin. prof. Mich. State U. East Lansing, 1982—; lectr. Mich. Osteo. Med. Ctr., Detroit, 1986; program chmn. Am. Osteo. Coll. Anesthesiologist Ann. Conv. and Sci. Seminar, 1990. Legis. asst. to Thomas Holcomb State Rep., 1974-75; physician liaison United Way, Livingston County, Mich., 1986. Recipient Richard P. Alper Meml. award for Community Service, Mich. State U., 1979. Fellow Am. Osteo. Coll. Anesthesiologists (bd. govs.); mem. Am. Osteo. Assn., Mich. Assn. Osteo. Physicians and Surgeons (del. 1985-89, numerous coms.), Livingston County Osteo. Assn. (sec.-treas. 1984-86), Mich. Soc. Osteo. Anesthesiologists (pres. 1988-90, chmn. bd. trustees 1990-92), Mich. Soc. Anesthesiologists, Am. Soc. Anesthesiologists, Mich. State Med. Soc. (del. 1992—), Midland County Med. Soc. (sec.-treas. 1993, v.p. 1994, pres. 1995—), Mich. State U. Alumni Assn., Jaycees, Sigma Sigma Phi (founding chpt. pres. 1977). Methodist. Home and Office: 2367 N Deer Valley Dr Midland MI 48642-8800

SNYDER, TERESA ANN, medical surgical nurse; b. Evansville, Ind., Mar. 4, 1946; d. Stephen Michael and Fredricka Otilia (Memmer) Kurtz; m. James Howard Snyder, June 12, 1976; children: Katrina Michelle, Jacqueline Sue. Diploma, Lakewood (Ohio) Sch. Practical Nursing, 1965; BSN, U. Akron, 1989. Emergency room nurse Parma (Ohio) Community Hosp., Cleve. Clinic Found., Akron (Ohio) City Hosp.; acting mem. Summa Nursing Senate, Summa Health Care, Akron City Hosp. Active fire and rescue Chatham Vol. Fire Dept. Mem. Sigma Theta Tau. Home: 10145 Shaw Rd Spencer OH 44275-9739

SNYDER, VIRGINIA LEA, anatomist, educator; b. Coldwater, Ohio, July 30, 1957; d. William Runkle and Madelyn Anne (Nonte) S. BS, Defiance Coll., 1979; PhD, Med. Coll. Ohio, 1988. Med. technologist, assoc. prof. U. Wis., Platteville, 1988—. Mem. AAAS, NACTA, Human Anatomy Physiology Soc., Sigma Xi. Office: Univ Wis Rm 249 Gardner Biology Platteville WI 53818

SNYDER, WILLARD BREIDENTHAL, lawyer; b. Kansas City, Kans., Dec. 18, 1940; s. N.E. and Ruth (Breidenthal) S.; m. Lieselotte Dieringer, Nov. 10, 1970 (dec. Nov. 1975); 1 child, Rolf; m. T.J. Sewall, May 17, 1996. BA, U. Kans., 1962, JD, 1965; postgrad., Hague Acad. Internat. Law, The Netherlands, 1965-66, U. Dijon, France, 1966; grad., Command and Gen. Staff Coll., Ft. Leavenworth, Kans., 1977. Bar: Kans. 1965, Mo. 1986, U.S. Tax Ct. 1977, U.S. Ct. Mil. Appeals 1981, U.S. Dist. Ct. Kans. 1965, U.S. Supreme Ct. 1977. Atty. Kansas City, 1970-80, 85—; trust officer, corp. trust officer Security Nat. Bank., Kansas City, 1980-83, corp. sec., 1983-85; pres. Real Estate Corp. Inc., Leawood, Kans., 1984—; dir., mem. trust and investment com. Blue Ridge Bank; German Consul (H) for Kans., Western Mo., 1972—. Mem. Platte Woods (Mo.) City Coun., 1983-84; mem. exec. bd. dirs. regional coun. Boy Scouts Am.; bd. govs. Liberty Meml. Assn.; bd. dirs., v.p. MacJannett Found., Talloires, France; pres. Breidenthal-Snyder Found.; bd. dirs., mem. exec. com. CORO Found.; trustee Hoover Pres. Libr. Decorated Bundesverdienst Kreuz, 1982, BVK 1KL (Germany), 1992, Bundeswehr Kreuz (silver), 1987, Ge. Abn., Legion of Merit, Meritorious Svc. medal, Army commendation medal; named to Hon. Order Ky. Cols., 1988; recipient Golden Honour badge German Vet. Orgn., Bavaria, 1988, Mil. Order of WW award, OCS Hall of Fame. Mem. Mo. Bar Assn., Kansas City Bar Assn., Kansas City Hosp. Attys., Kansas City Bd. Trade, Mil. Order of World Wars (chpt. comdr. 1983-84, regional comdr. 1987-91, Patrick Henry award), Nat. Eagle Scout Assn. Office: 8014 State Line Rd Ste 203 Leawood KS 66208-3712

SOBCZAK, DARLENE MARIE, police officer; b. Chgo., Nov. 17, 1956; d. Richard and Marilyn (Fuesting) Dvorak; children: Christopher B., Gina K. A of Criminal Justice, Morton Coll., 1991; B in Criminal Justice, U. Ill., Chgo., 1993. Police officer Town of Cicero, Ill., 1984—; field tng. officer Cicero Police Dept., 1989—, detective, 1992-95, sgt., 1995—; bd. dirs. Cicero Police Pension Bd. Active PTA, Cicero, 1984—. Fellow Ill. Police Assn., Fraternal Order Police; mem. Cicero Police Benevolent Assn. (pres. 1985—), Cicero Police Pension Bd. (bd. dirs. 1992—).

SOBCZAK, JUDY MARIE, clinical psychologist; b. Detroit, Dec. 28, 1949; d. Thaddeus Joseph and Bernice Agnes (Sowinski) Gorski; m. John Nicholas Sobczak, Aug. 17, 1974. BE cum laude, U. Toledo, 1971; postgrad., Ea. Mich. U., 1980-82; PhD, U. Toledo, 1987. Lic. psychologist. Tchr. Ottawa (Ohio)-Glandorf Schs., 1971-73; prin., tchr. St. Mary Sch., Assumption, Ohio, 1973-77; tchr. Our Lady of Perpetual Help Sch., Toledo, 1978-79; staff psychologist Outer Dr. Hosp., Lincoln Park, Mich., 1987-90; psychologist Adult/Youth Devel. Svcs., Farmington, Mich., 1991-95, Daivs Counseling Ctr., Farmington Hills, Mich., 1996—; with Northwestern Cmty. Svcs., Livonia, Mich., 1996—, Orchard Hills Psychiat. Ctr., Plymouth, Mich., 1996—; adj. asst. prof. Madonna U., Livonia, Mich., 1987-94. Eucharistic minister St. Anthony Cath. Ch., Belleville, Mich., 1991—, parish coun. 1993-96; Cath. Svc. Appeal co-chmn., 1993—; sec. bd. dirs. Children Are Precious Respite Care Ctr., 1995. Fellow Mich. Women Psychologists (charter; newsletter editor 1987-92, treas 1989-93, Plaque of Appreciation 1992-96, sec. 1993—); mem. Mich. Psychol. Assn., Phi Kappa Phi. Home: 41498 Mckinley St Belleville MI 48111-3439 Office: Davis Counseling Ctr 37923 W Twelve Mile Rd Farmington Hills MI 48331

SOBIE, ROBERT FRANSIS, educator; b. Oak Park, Ill., June 17, 1955; s. Richard and Margaret (Houda) S.; m. Martha Lee Olson, Mar. 20, 1982; children: Carl Lee, Roger Fransis. AAS, Waubonsee Coll., 1975; BS in Edn., No. Ill. U., 1979; MS in Edn., Chgo. State U., 1991. Instr. Waubonsee C.C., Sugar Grove, Ill., 1977-79; pres. Sobie Cons. Svc., Glen Ellyn, Ill., 1990—; prof. Coll. of DuPage, Glen Ellyn, 1979—. Bd. dirs. Am. Lung Assn., Glen Ellyn, 1979—. Recipient Vol. of Yr. Am. Lung Assn., 1987. Mem. Nat. Inst. for Automotive Svc. Excellence (master technician), Soc. Automotive Engrs. (assoc.), Ill. Coll. Automotive Instrs. Assn. (bd. dirs. 1982-93, pres. 1982, 89). Office: Coll of DuPage 22d and Lambert Rd Glen Ellyn IL 60137

SOBOLEWSKI, JANE ANN, business educator; b. Ironwood, Mich., May 24, 1958; d. Edward A. and Betty A. (Olson) Blomquist. AA, Gogebic Community Coll., 1978; BS, Ferris State Coll., 1980; MA, Northern Mich. U., 1987. Instr., bus. Ironwood (Mich.) High Sch., 1980-84, Gogebic Community Coll., Ironwood, 1983—; sec. Mich. Assn. Higher Edn., Ironwood, 1985-93. Tchr., Sunday Sch., Salem Luth. Ch., Ironwood, 1990-91. Mem. Nat. Bus. Educators Assn., Mich. Bus. Educators Assn. (regional fall conf. co-chmn. 1989-90), Delta Pi Epsilon. Home: 139 E Michigan Ave Ironwood MI 49938-1225 Office: Gogebic Community Coll 4946E Jackson Rd Ironwood MI 49938-1300

SOBOTTKA, FRED HERMAN, systems analyst; b. Eau Galle, Wis., Jan. 25, 1956; s. Fred Cleve and Darlene May (Bauer) S.; m. Sandra Francis Meyer, May 5, 1985; 1 child, Kristin Lee. BS, U. Wis., Stout, 1978; MBA, Coll. St. Thomas, St. Paul, 1984. Programmer/analyst Sperry, Eagan, Minn., 1978-83; sr. programmer/analyst Unisys, Eagan, Minn., 1983-87, prin. systems analyst, 1987-94; sr. programmer, analyst West Publishing, Eagan, 1994—. Chmn. UCP fundraiser One Block Run, 1993; chmn. Hudson Pepperfest, 1993; mgmt. devel. v.p. Hudson Jaycees, 1993-94, treas., 1995-96. Mem. Hudson Jaycees. Roman Catholic.

SOCIER, MICHAEL JAMES, television executive; b. Bay City, Mich., Nov. 12, 1957; s. James R. Socier and Sandra Stanos; m. Connie Marie Filipiak, July 5, 1985; children: Nyssa Marie, Laken Nicole. A., Delta Coll., 1978. Mem. staff Sta. WUCM-TV, Univ. Ctr., Mich., 1975-78, Sta. WNEM-TV, Saginaw, Mich., 1978; prodn. mgr. Inner-City Media, Inc., Chgo., 1979-83, Sta. WBKB-TV, Alpena, Mich., 1983-85; sta. mgr. Sta. WAQP-TV, Saginaw, 1985—. Mem. Nat. Edn. and Employment Devel. Found. Mem. Soc. Motion Picture and TV Engrs., Alpha Epsilon Rho (pres. local chpt. 1977). Office: Sta WAQP TV PO Box 2215 Saginaw MI 48605-2215

SOCOL, MICHAEL LEE, obstetrician, gynecologist, educator; b. Chgo., Oct. 3, 1949; s. Joseph and Bernice (Bofman) S.; m. Donna Kaner, Dec. 17, 1972. BS, U. Ill., 1970; MD, U. Ill., Chgo., 1974. Diplomate Am. Bd. Ob-Gyn., Am. Bd. Maternal-Fetal Medicine. Resident obstetrics and gynecology U. Ill. Hosp., Chgo., 1974-77; clin. rsch. fellow dept. obstetrics and gynecology L.A. County-U. So. Calif. Med. Ctr., 1977-79; assoc. attending physician Northwestern Meml. Hosp., Chgo., 1980-86, attending physician dept. ob-gyn., 1986—; co-dir. Northwestern Perinatal Ctr., Chgo., 1987—; head maternal-fetal medicine, chief obstetrics Northwestern U. Med. Sch., Chgo., 1987—, dir. maternal-fetal medicine fellowship program, 1987—, asst. prof. obstetrics and gynecology, 1979-84, assoc. prof., 1984-92, prof., 1992—; mem. appointment and promotions and departmental com. on clin. privileges Northwestern Meml. Hosp., Chgo., 1987—, vice-chmn. dept. ob-gyn., 1992—; mem. residencey edn. com., 1987—; mem. appointments, promotions and tenure com., 1991—. Author: (with others) Clinical Obstetrics and Gynecology, 1982, 1984, Diagnostic Ultrasound Applied to Obstetrics and Gynecology, 1987, Principles and Practice of Medical Therapy in Pregnancy, 1992; peer reviewer Am. Jour. Obstetrics and Gynecology, 1980—, Obstetrics and Gynecology, 1984—; contbr. numerous articles to profl. jours. Fellow Am. Coll. Ob-Gyn., Soc., Perinatal Obstetricians, Ctrl. Assn. Ob-Gyn., Chgo. Gynecol. Soc., Soc. for Gynecol. Investigation, Am. Gynecol. and Obstetrical Soc.; mem. AMA, Assn. Profs. of Gynecology and Obstetrics, Ill. State Med. Assn., Chgo. Med. Soc. Office: 333 E Superior St # 410 Chicago IL 60611-3015

SOCOLOFSKY, MARTHA ANN, physician; b. Kansas City, Kans., Oct. 18, 1958; d. Jackie Andrew and Dianna Louise (Lynch) Teeter; m. Paul R. Simony, July 22, 1980 (div. 1982); m. Edward Terrill Socolofsky, June 28, 1986; children: Jason A., Justin A. BS in Agrl., Kans. State U., 1980, BA in Biology, 1988; MD, U. Kans. Med. Ctr., 1988. Intern U. Kans. Med. Ctr., Kansas City, 1989-90, resident, 1992-94; physician Kaiser Permanente, Overland Park, Kans., 1993—; staff physician Douglass Cmty. Health Ctr., Kansas City, 1995; med. dir. Topeka Correctional Facility, 1995-96; acting state med. dir. Prison Health Svcs., Kans., 1996—. Council of lore, sr. clergy, grove organizer Ar nDraiocht Fein, 1984—. Mem. Am. Acad. Family Physicians, Am. Holistic Med. Soc., Paleo Pathology Soc., Wilderness Med. Soc.

SOCOLOW, ELIZABETH ANNE, poet, educator, artist, writer; b. N.Y.C., June 15, 1940; d. Ralph Maurice and Frances Irene (Goldberg) Sussman; m. Robert H. Socolow, June 10, 1962 (div. Apr. 1982); children: David Jacob, Seth Louis. BA, Vassar Coll., Poughkeepsie, N.Y., 1962; MA, Harvard U., Cambridge, Mass., 1963, PhD, 1967. Lectr. in English and composition U. Mich., Dearborn, 1993—; lectr. in English Lawrence Technological U., Southfield, Mich., 1994—; poetry editor newsletter Soc. for Lit. and Science, Athens, Ga., 1989—. Author: (book) Laughing at Gravity: Conversations With Isaac Newton, 1988. Home: 29550 Franklin Rd Apt 228 Southfield MI 48034

SODER-ALDERFER, KAY CHRISTIE, counseling administrator; b. Evanston, Ill., Oct. 25, 1949; d. Earl Eugene and Alice Kathryn (Lien) Soder; m. David Luther Alderfer, May 15, 1976. BSE, No. Ill. U., 1972; postgrad., Luth. Sch. Theology, Phila., 1973; MA, Gov.'s State U., University Park, Ill., 1978; PhD, Walden U., 1985. Consecrated deaconess Luth. Ch., 1974. News reporter Suburban Life Newspaper, La Grange Park, Ill., 1972; counselor various orgns. Ill. & Pa., 1973—; parish worker Luth. Ch., De Kalb, Ill., 1973-74; pub. rels. asst. Luth. Ch. Women, Phila., 1974-76; editor Luth. Ch., Chgo., 1979—; spiritual dir. Gentle Pathways, Downers Grove, Ill., 1988—, counseling psychologist, 1990—, also bd. dirs.; cons. Evang. Luth. Ch. in Am., Chgo., 1988—, Lehigh Valley Hosp. Assn., Allentown, Pa., 1986. Author: Gentle Journeys, 1993, With Those Who Grieve, 1995, Help! There's a Monster in My Head, 1996; editor Entree, 1988-93, Multicultural Jour., 1992—; graphic designs exhbn. Franklin Mus., Phila., 1981. Spokeswoman Progressive Epilepsy Network, Phila., 1980-85; chair spiritual life com. Luth. Deaconess Cmty., Gladwyne, Pa., 1990-92; founder Teens with Epilepsy and Motivation, 1995; vol. March of Dimes, Ill., 1991-93; amb. of goodwill Good Bears of the World, 1993-94; spiritual dir. Evang. Luth. Ch. in Am. Recipient Silver award Delaware Valley Neographics Soc., 1981; 50th anniversary scholar Luth. Deaconess Community, 1983. Mem. AAUW, APA (div. women and psychology, div. psychology and the arts, div. psychology and religion). Office: Gentle Pathways 1207 55th St Downers Grove IL 60515-4810

SOERGEL, KONRAD HERMANN, physician; b. Coburg, Germany, July 27, 1929; came to U.S., 1954, naturalized, 1962; s. Konrad Daniel and Erna Henrietta (Schilling) S.; m. Rosina Klara Rudin, June 24, 1955; children: Elizabeth Ann, Karen Theresa, Marilyn Virginia, Kenneth Thomas. M.D., U. Erlangen, Germany, 1954, Dr. med., 1958. Intern Bergen Pines County Hosp., Paramus, N.J., 1954-55; resident in pathology West Pa. Hosp., Pitts., 1955-56; resident in medicine Mass. Meml. Hosp., Boston, 1957-58; fellow in gastroenterology Boston U. Med. Sch., 1958-60, instr., 1960-61; mem. faculty Med. Coll. Wis., Milw., 1961—, prof. medicine, 1969—, prof. physiology, 1993—; chief sect. gastroenterology Med. Coll. Wis., 1961-93, dir. fellowship program, dept. medicine, 1993—; chmn. gastroenterology and clin. nutrition study sect. NIH, 1979-80. Contbr. articles to profl. jours., chpts. to books. Recipient Research Career Devel. award USPHS, 1963-72; Alexander von Humboldt Found. sr. fellow, 1973-74. Mem. Am. Gastroenterol. Assn., Am. Soc. Clin. Investigation, Am. Assn. Physicians, German Soc. for Digestive and Metabolic Disorders (hon.), Ger. Soc. Internal Medicine (hon.). Home: 14245 Hillside Rd Elm Grove WI 53122-1677 Office: Med Coll Wis 9200 W Wisconsin Ave Milwaukee WI 53226-3522

SOETER, JOHN RANDOLPH, cardiothoracic surgeon; b. Teaneck, N.J., May 12, 1935; s. John Jacob and Esther (Fitzrandolph) S.; m. Marianne Hageman (div. Mar. 1985); children: John Matthew, Mary E., Caroline

Benjamin. BA, Hope Coll., Holland, Mich., 1957; MD, Union U., Albany, N.Y., 1962. Rsch. fellow U. Hawaii, Honolulu, 1972-73, asst. prof. surgery Sch. Medicine, 1973-75; attending surgeon Bellin & St. Vincent Hosps., Green Bay, Wis., 1975—; chmn. dept. cardiac medicine and surgery Bellin Hosp., Green Bay, 1991—. Lt. comdr. USNR, 1963-65. Fellow ACS; mem. AMA, Soc. Thoracic Surgeons, Wis. Surg. Soc., Am. Heart Assn. Home: 2501 Ducharme Ln Green Bay WI 54301-1913

SOKOL, DENNIS ALLEN, hospital administrator; b. Chgo., May 3, 1945; s. Stanley John and Mildred Veronica (Krenslake) S.; m. Gwen Noble, Dec. 19, 1971 (div.); children: Anne, Ellen; m. Jolene K. Buehrer, Jan. 28, 1989. BS in Bus., No. Ill. U., 1968; MBA, U. Nebr., Omaha, 1974; M of Hosp. Adminstrn., U. Minn., 1976. Radio personality various stas., Ill., Iowa and Nebr., 1968-72; pub. relations officer Children's Meml. Hosp., Omaha, 1972-73, Meth. Hosp., Omaha, 1973-74; v.p. adminstrn. Golden Valley (Minn.) Health Ctr., 1976-82; pres. Sacred Heart Health Svcs., Yankton, S.D., 1982—; regional pres. Presentation Health Sys., 1996; instr. health care mgmt. Mt. Marty Coll., 1986-87, U. Minn., 1986-88. Pres. Valley Health Svcs., Inc., 1984—, Health Mgmt. Svcs., 1987—. Fellow Am. Coll. Health Care Execs. (regent 1991-95); mem. S.D. Hosp. Assn. (trustee 1990—), Missouri Valley Health Network (v.p. 1986—), Yankton Area C. of C. (pres. 1989-90), Rotary. Republican. Roman Catholic. Office: Sacred Heart Hosp 501 Summit St Yankton SD 57078-3855

SOKOL, ROBERT JAMES, obstetrician/gynecologist, educator; b. Rochester, N.Y., Nov. 18, 1941; s. Eli and Mildred (Levine) S.; m. Roberta Sue Kahn, July 26, 1964; children: Melissa Anne, Eric Russell, Andrew Ian. BA with highest distinction in Philosophy, U. Rochester, 1963, MD with honors, 1966. Diplomate Am. Bd. Ob-Gyn (assoc. examiner 1984-86), Sub-Bd. Maternal-Fetal Medicine. Intern Barnes Hosp., Washington U., St. Louis, 1966-67, resident in ob-gyn., 1967-70, asst. in ob-gyn., 1966-70, rsch. asst., 1967-68, instr. clin. ob-gyn., 1970; Buswell fellow in maternal fetal medicine Strong Meml. Hosp.-U. Rochester, 1972-73; fellow in maternal-fetal medicine Cleve. Met. Gen. Hosp.-Case Western Res. U., Cleve., 1974-75, assoc. obstetrician and gynecologist, 1973-83, asst. prof. ob-gyn., 1973-77; asst. program dir. Perinatal Clin. Rsch. Ctr., 1973-78, co-program dir., 1978-82, program dir., 1982-83, acting dir. obstetrics, 1974-75, co-dir., 1977-83, assoc. prof., 1977-81, prof., 1981-83, assoc. dir. dept. ob-gyn., 1981-83; prof. ob-gyn. Wayne State U., Detroit, 1983—, chmn. dept. ob-gyn., 1983-89, mem. grad. faculty dept. physiology, 1984—, interim dean Med. Sch., 1988-89, dean, 1989—, pres. Fund for Med. Rsch. and Edn., 1988—; chief ob-gyn. Hutzel Hosp. Detroit, 1983-89; dir. C.S. Mott Ctr. for Human Growth and Devel., 1983-89; interim chmn. med. bd. Detroit Med. Ctr., 1988-89, chmn. med. bd., 1989—, sr. v.p. med. affairs, 1992—, trustee, 1990—; past pres. med. staff Cuyahoga County Hosps.; mem. profl. adv. bd. Educated Childbirth Inc., 1976-80; sr. Ob cons. Symposia Medicus; cons. Nat. Inst. Child Health and Human Devel., Nat. Inst. Alcohol Abuse and Alcoholism, Ctr. for Disease Control, NIH, Health Resources and Services Adminstrn., Nat. Clearinghouse for Alcohol Info., Am. Psychol. Assn.; mem. alcohol psychosocial research rev. com. Nat. Inst. Alcohol Abuse and Alcoholism, 1982-86; mem. ob/gyn adv. panel U.S. Pharmacopeial Conv., 1985-90. Mem. internat. editorial bd. Israel Jour. Obstetrics and Gynecology; reviewer med. jours.; mem. editorial bd. Jour. Perinatal Medicine; editor-in-chief Interactions: Programs in Clinical Decision-Making, 1987-90; researcher computer applications in perinatal medicine, alcohol-related birth defects, perinatal risk and neurobehavioral devel.; contbr. articles to profl. jours. Mem. Pres.'s leadership council U. Rochester, 1976-80; mem. exec. com. bd. trustees Oakland Health Edn. Program, 1987—; mem. voluntary alumni admissions com. U. Rochester, 1986—. Served to maj. M.C. USAF, 1970-72. Mem. AMA, NAS (Inst. of Medicine), ACOG (chmn. steering com. drug and alcohol abuse contract 1986-87), Am. Med. Informatics Assn., Soc. Gynecologic Investigation, Perinatal Rsch. Soc., Assn. Profs. Gyn.-Ob, Royal Soc. Medicine, Mich. Med. Soc., Wayne County Med. Soc., Detroit Acad. Medicine, Cen. Assn. Obstetricians-Gynecologists, Rsch. Soc. Alcoholism, Soc. Perinatal Obstetricians (v.p., pres.-elect 1987-88, pres. 1988-89, achievement award 1995), Liaison Com. for Ob-Gyn., Am. Gynecol. and Obstetrical Soc., Neurobehavioral Teratology Soc., APHA, Am. Med. Soc. on Alcoholism and Other Drug Dependencies, Soc. for Neurosci. (Mich. chpt.), Internat. Soc. Computers in Obstetrics, Neonatology, Gynecology (v.p. 1987-89, pres. 1989-92, immediate past pres. 1992—), World Assn. Perinatal Medicine, Soc. Physicians Reproductive Choice and Health, Am. Assn. Med. Colls. (coun. of deans), Detroit Physiol. Soc. (hon.), Polish Gynecologists World Club, Phi Beta Kappa, Sigma Xi, Alpha Omega Alpha. Republican. Jewish. Home: 5200 Rector Ct Bloomfield Hills MI 48302-2654 Office: Wayne State U Sch Medicine 540 E Canfield St Detroit MI 48201-1928

SOLATKA, MATT FRANCIS, laboratory executive; b. Blue Island, Ill., Sept. 23, 1963. BA in Environ. Biology, St. Mary's Coll., 1985. Lic. asbestos profl., Ill. Observer U.S. Dept. Commerce, Seattle, 1985-88; v.p. RCM Labs., Brookfield, Ill., 1988—. Contbr. articles to profl. jours. Mem. Environ. Info. Assn., Chicagoland Indoor Air Quality Assn. (founding mem.). Democrat. Roman Catholic. Home: 5529 E Lake Dr E Lisle IL 60532 Office: RCM Labs 9431 Ogden Ave Ste 2E Brookfield IL 60513-1819

SOLBERG, KEN, state legislator; b. Minot, N.D., Jan. 10, 1940; m. Chris; children: Tom, Brad, Stacy. Mem. N.D. Senate, 1991—, mem. judiciary, agr., transp., joint constn. rev. coms., mem. appropriations com.; owner, mgr. Rugby Livestock Sales, 1965—. Mem. Rugby City Coun., 1966-72; bd. dirs. Regional Selective Svc., 1980, Good Samaritan Hosp., 1981-87, pres., 1985-86, chmn. health found., 1988; alt. del. Nat. Rep. Conv., 1988. Recipient DSA award N.D. Jaycees, 1965. Mem. Eagles Club, Am. Legion, Stockmens Assn. (bd. dirs. 1985), Cattlemen's Assn., Rugby C. of C. Home: 207 Sunset Ln Rugby ND 58368-2510*

SOLBERG, LOREN ALBIN, state legislator, secondary education educator; b. Blackduck, Minn., Nov. 3, 1941; s. Albin Andy and Mabel Ethel (Bergen) S.; m. Joan Maxine Olsen, Aug. 9, 1969; children: Sean, John, Previn, Kjirstin. BS, Bemidji (Minn.) State U., 1965, MS, 1974; MPA, Harvard U., 1990. Tchr. math. Ind. Sch. Dist. 316, Coleraine, Minn., 1965—; mem. Minn. Ho. of Reps., St. Paul, 1983—; instr. math. Itasca C.C., Grand Rapids, Minn., 1981-83; instr. computer sci. Harvard U., Cambridge, Mass., 1988. Mayor City of Bovey, Minn., 1970-82. Democrat. Lutheran. Home: PO Box 61 Bovey MN 55709-0061 Office: Minn Ho of Reps State Office Bldg Saint Paul MN 55155-1201

SOLBRIG, INGEBORG HILDEGARD, German literature educator, author; b. Weissenfels, Germany, July 31, 1923; came to U.S., 1961, naturalized, 1966; d. Reinhold J. and Hildegard M.A. (Ferchland) S. Grad. in chemistry, U. Halle, Germany, 1948; BA summa cum laude, San Francisco State U., 1964; postgrad., U. Calif., Berkeley, 1964-65; MA, Stanford U., 1966, PhD in Humanities and German, 1969. Asst. prof. U. R.I., 1969-70, U. Tenn., Chattanooga, 1970-72, U. Ky., Lexington, 1972-75; assoc. prof. German U. Iowa, 1975-81, prof., 1981-93, prof. emerita, 1993—. Author: Hammer-Purgtall und Goethe, 1973; main editor Rilke Heute, Beziehungen und Wirkungen, 1975; translator, editor: (bilingual edit.) Reinhard Goering: Seeschlacht/Seabattle, 1977, Orient-Rezeption, 1995; contbr. numerous articles, revs. and transls. to profl. jours., chpts. to books. Mem. Iowa Gov.'s Com. on 300th Anniversary German-Am. Rels. 1683-1983, 1983. Recipient Hammer-Purgstall Gold medal Austria, 1974; named Ky. col., 1975; fellow Austrian Ministry Edn., 1968-69, Stanford U., 1965-66, 68-69; Old Gold fellow Iowa, 1977; Am. Coun. Learned Socs. grantee; German Acad. Exch. Svc. grantee, 1980; sr. faculty rsch. fellow in the humanities, 1983; NEH grantee, 1985; May Brodbeck fellow in the humanities, 1989; numerous summer faculty rsch. grants. Mem. MLA (life), Internat. Verein fur Germanishce Sprach und Lit. Wiss., Goethe Gesellschaft, Deutsche Schiller Gesellschaft, Am. Soc. for 18th Century Studies, Can. Soc. for 18th Century Studies, Goethe Soc. N.Am., Inc. (founding mem.), Internat. Herder Soc. Prin. Rsch. Interest: contact of eastern and western cultures. Home: 1126 Pine St Iowa City IA 52240

SOLIWON, LOTHAR ERNST, marketing professional; b. Herne, Germany, Nov. 21, 1948; came to U.S., 1949; s. Jan Stanislaw and Gerda (Radtke) S.; m. Audrey Bernadette Butkunas, Dec. 7, 1974; children: Diana Karin, Erik Ernst. BA, U. Ill., 1970, M of Social Scis., 1974; MBA, Sangamon State U., 1985. Asst. editor Std. Ednl. Corp., Chgo., 1972-73; project mgr. Ill. Dept. Transp., Chgo., 1974-77; aviation planner Ill. Dept. Transp., Springfield, 1978-81, mktg. mgr., 1982—; cons. Biok Ltd., Vilnius, Lithuania, 1992—. Contbr. articles to profl. publs. Mem. U. Ill. Alumni Assn. Roman Catholic. Home: 2150 S Illini Rd Springfield IL 62704-4366 Office: U Ill Dept Transp 2300 S Dirksen Pky Springfield IL 62764

SOLOMON, BARRY DAVID, geography and environmental policy educator; b. L.A., Dec. 26, 1955; s. Philip and Marcella Solomon. Student, UCLA, 1973-74; BA in Social Ecology, U. Calif., Irvine, 1977; MPA in Environ. Policy, Ind. U., 1979, PhD in Regional Analysis & Planning, 1983. Rsch. asst. waste mgmt. project Nat. Gov.'s Assn., Washington, 1978; assoc. instr., rsch. asst. dept. geography Sch. Pub. & Environment Affairs, Ind. U., Bloomington, 1979-82; vis. asst. prof. geography and energy econs., rsch. assoc. Regional Rsch. Inst., W.Va. U., Morgantown, 1982-84; industry economist Office of Electric Power Regulation Fed. Energy Regulatory Commn., Washington, 1984-86; economist Office Energy Markets & End Use Energy Info. Adminstrn., U.S. Dept. Energy, Washington, 1986-89; internat. energy economist climate change divsn. U.S. EPA, Washington, 1989-91, sr. economist acid rain divsn. Office Atmospheric Programs, 1991-95; assoc. prof. geography and environ. policy Mich. Tech. U., Houghton, 1995—; proposal reviewer NSF; mem. com. Am. Planning Assn.; lectr. colloquium series Pi Alpha Alpha, Ind. U., 1978-80. Co-author: The International Politics of Nuclear Waste, 1991; co-editor: Geographical Dimensions of Energy, 1985; mem. editorial adv. bd. Computers, Environment and Urban Systems, 1989—, consulting editor Energy Svcs Jour.; manuscript reviewer for numerous profl. jours. including Annals of Assn. Am. Geographers, Jour. Environ. Econs. and Mgmt., Worldwatch Papers; contbr. chpts. to books, articles to profl. jours. Commr. Coop. Recycling Ctr., U. Calif.-Irvine, 1976-77, Environ. Quality and Conservation Commn., Bloomington, Ind., 1980-82, chmn., 1982; mem. citizen's adv. com. Bloomington Sludge Mgmt. Plan, Utilities Svc. Bd., Bloomington, 1980; mem. tech. adv. com. Bloomington Area Transp. Study, Planning Dept., City of Bloomington, 1982; mem. planning com. Greenbelt Conf. on New Towns, 50th Anniversary Com., City of Greenbelt, 1985-87; mem., sec. City Parks and Recreation Adv. Bd., Greenbelt, 1987-89. Recipient Best Article award Nat. Coun. Geographic Edn., 1987-88; SPEA fellow Ind. U., 1980-81; grantee Ind. U. and W.Va. U., 1978-84; travel grantee Am. Ctr. for Internat. Leadership, 1991. Mem. AAAS, Assn. Am. Geographers (chmn. energy and environ. splty. group 1988-90, grantee 1978-84), Nat. Assn. Environ. Profls., Assn. Energy Svc. Profls. Democrat. Jewish. Office: Mich Tech U Dept Social Scis Houghton MI 49931-1295

SOLOMON, GLEN DAVID, physician, researcher; b. Jersey City, Mar. 24, 1955; s. Ernest and Shirley (Schlosky)S. BA, Northwestern U., 1976; MD, Rush Med. Coll., 1980. Diplomate Am. Bd. Internal Medicine, Nat. Bd. Med. Examiners. Intern and resident in internal medicine USAF Med. Ctr., Wright-Patterson AFB, Ohio, Wright State U. Affiliated Hosps., Dayton, Ohio, 1980-83; physician Diamond Headache Clinic, Chgo., 1986-88; internist Headache Sect. Cleve. Clinic Found., 1988—; internist, dir. headache sect., 1994—; adj. asst. prof. Chgo. Med. Sch., 1987-88; prof. medicine Pa. State U., 1989—; assoc. prof. medicine Ohio State U., 1992—; attending staff Louis A. Weiss Hosp., Chgo., 1986-88; lectr. sci. and lay orgns. in fields of headaches, pain mgmt., internal medicine, pharmacology; med. educator in internal medicine and headache medicine. Contbr. chpts. to books and articles to profl. jours. Maj. USAF, 1980-86. Named one of Outstanding Young Men of Am., 1986; recipient tchg. award Am. Acad. Family Physicians, 1984, 85, 86. Fellow ACP, Am. Assn. for Study of Headache (bd. dirs. 1990-95); mem. Internat. Headache Soc., Am. Soc. Clin. Pharmacology and Therapeutics (chmn. headache sect.), Nat. Headache Found. (bd. dirs. 1995—), Alpha Omega Alpha, Psi Upsilon. Office: Cleve Clinic Found 9500 Euclid Ave Cleveland OH 44195-0001

SOLOMON, JOHN DAVIS, aviation executive; b. Kingfisher, Okla., Oct. 22, 1936; s. Edward Dempsey and Mary Blanche (Smith) S.; m. Mildred Oraline Brammer, July 16, 1968 (div. Mar. 1984); children: Jennifer Leigh, Jason Lewis; m. Sheila Mary McLeod, Nov. 23, 1985. BA, Okla. State U., 1958. Asst. mgr. airport City of Oklahoma City Dept. Aviation, 1963-66, City of Tulsa Airport Authority, 1966-70; dir. aviation City of Oklahoma City., 1970-77, Clark County Dept. Aviation, Las Vegas, Nev., 1977-86; dir. environ. planning Landrum & Brown, Aviation Planners, Cin., 1986-88; dep. dir. aviation City of Houston Airport System, 1988-90; dir. aviation City of Kansas City, Mo., 1990—. Editor Airport Mgmt. Jour., 1975; contbr. articles to aviation jours. Mem. Am. Assn. Airport Execs. (bd. dirs., ex-officio, accredited 1965, pres. 1979, Pres.'s award 1975, Disting. Svc. award 1991), Airports Coun. Internat. (bd. dirs. 1985-86), Kappa Sigma. Office: Dept Aviation Kansas City Internat. Airport PO Box 20047 Kansas City MO 64195-0047

SOLOMON, MARILYN KAY, educator, consultant; b. Marshall, Mo., Oct. 16, 1947; d. John W. and Della M. (Dille) S. BS, Ctrl. Mo. State U., 1969; MS, Ind. U., 1974. Cert. in early childhood and nursery sch. edn., Mo., Ind. Tchr. Indpls. Pub. Schs., 1969-74; dir. Singer Learning Ctrs., Indpls., 1974-78; v.p. ECLC Learning Ctrs., Inc.; Early Learning Ctrs., Inc., Indpls., 1995—; pres., CEO, owner Solomon Antique Restoration, Inc., Indpls., 1996—; owner, pres., CEO, Early Learning Ctrs., Inc., Indpls., 1995—, Solomon Antique Restoration, Inc., Indpls., 1996—; mem. OJT tng. task force Dept. Labor, Washington; mem. nat. task force for parenting edn. HEW, Washington; cons. to numerous corps. on corp. child care. Co-author curricula. Founding bd. dirs. Mid City Pioneer, Indpls., 1977, Enterprise Zone Small Bus. Incubator, Indpls., 1995—, Family Support Ctr., Indpls., 1983, pres. bd. dirs., 1985-87. Recipient Outstanding Leadership award Ind. Conf. on Social Concerns, 1975, 76, 77, Children's Mus. Edn. award, 1974; named to Outstanding Young Women of Am., 1984. Mem. Indpls. Mus. Art, Ind. Lic. Child Care Assn. (v.p. 1992, pres. 1974, 75), State of Ind. Quality and Tng. Coun. (chair 1992), Step Ahead-Marion County (rep. for child care 1992—), Ind. Alliance for Better Child Care (bd. dirs. 1992), Order Eastern Star, Indpls. Zool. Soc. (charter). Office: Early Learning Ctrs Inc 1315 S Sherman Dr Indianapolis IN 46203-2210

SOLON, SAM GEORGE, state legislator; b. Duluth, Minn., June 25, 1931; s. Nick and Demitra (Stasinopooulos) S.; m. Carole Wedan, 1958 (div.); m. Paula Korhonen, 1974; children: Jon, Nicholas, Chris, Dina, Vicki. BS, U. Minn., 1958. Minn. State rep. Dist. 7, 1971-72, Minn. State sen., 1973—; ret. tchr. Duluth Bd. Edn.; chmn. com. and consumer protection com.; mem. edn., higher edn. divsn., family svc., health care and family svc. fin. divsn. and rules and adminstrn. coms. Mem. VFA, Eagles, Am. Hellenic Edn. Progressive Assn., Am. Legion, Moose, Duluth Hall of Fame Com. Office: 616 W 3rd St Duluth MN 55806-2404 also: State Senate State Capital Building Saint Paul MN 55155-1606*

SOLTI, SIR GEORG, conductor; b. Budapest, Hungary, Oct. 21, 1912; naturalized Brit. citizen, 1972; s. Mor Stern and Theres (Rosenbaum) S.; m. Hedi Oechsli, Oct. 29, 1946; m. Anne Valerie Pitts, Nov. 11, 1967; 2 daus. Ed., Budapest Music High Sch.; MusD (hon.), Leeds U., 1971, Oxford U., 1972, DePaul U., Yale U., 1974, Harvard U., 1979, Furman U., 1983, Sussex U., 1983, London U., 1986, Rochester U., 1987, Bologna (Italy) U., 1988, Roosevelt U., Chgo., 1990. Music dir. Chgo. Symphony Orch., 1969-91, music dir. laureate, 1991—; MusD (hon.) U. Durham, 1995. Mus. asst. Budapest Opera House, 1930-39, pianist, Switzerland, 1939-45; gen. music dir. Munich (Germany) State Opera, 1946-52, Frankfurt (Germany) City Opera, 1952-60; mus. dir. Royal Opera House Covent Garden, London, 1961-71, Orchestre de Paris, 1972-75; prin. condr. and artistic dir. London Philharm., 1979-83; condr. emeritus London Philharm., 1983-90, music dir. laureate Royal Opera House Covent Garden, London, 1992—; pianist Concours Internat., Geneva, 1942; guest condr. various orchs. including N.Y. Philharm., Vienna Philharm., Berlin Philharm., London Symphony, Bayerischer Rundfunk, Norddeutscher Rundfunk, Salzburg, Edinburgh, Glyndebourne, Ravinia and Bayreuth Festivals, Vienna State, Met. Opera; condr. concert tours with Chgo. Symphony to Europe, 1971, 74, 78, 81, 85, 89, 90, Chgo. Symphony to Japan, 1977, 86, 90, Chgo. Symphony to Australia, 1988; artistic dir. Salzburg Easter Festival and Whitsun Concerts, 1992-93; prin. guest condr. Paris Opera Bicentennial Tour, 1976, rec. artist for London Records. Recipient 31 Grammys, Lifetime Achievement Grammy award, 1996, Gold medal Royal Philharm. Soc., Gt. Britain, 1992, honored by John F. Kennedy Ctr. for Performing Arts, Washington, for lifetime achievement in music. Hon. fellow Royal Coll. Music (London). Office: care Chgo Symphony Orch 220 S Michigan Ave Chicago IL 60604-2508

SOLTYS, ANDRZEJ, industrial engineer; b. Krakow, Poland, Nov. 9, 1949; came to U.S., 1985; B, AGH U., 1975, M, 1976. Machinist Harold Hays Co., Harold Heights, Ill., 1985-87; indsl. engr. Grot Tool & Mfg., Morton Grove, Ill., 1987—. Home: 235 Renee Ter Wheeling IL 60090-4624

SOLYMOSSY, EMERIC, management consultant, engineer; b. Wolfratshausen, Germany, Dec. 1, 1948; came to U.S., 1952; s. Martin Akos V. and Maria Rosalia (Mailath) S.; m. Sharon Dale Fults, Aug. 3, 1974; children: Christine Maria, Martin Emeric. Cert. in Energy Mgmt., NYU, Chgo., 1979; BS in Engring., Century U., 1991; MBA, Colo. State U., Denver, 1994; postgrad., Case Western Res. U., 1994—. Registered master electrician, Wyo. Chief estimator Carlton Electric, Denver, 1974-76; coord. Amco Electric, Denver, 1976-77; chief estimator Modern Electric Inc., Casper, Wyo., 1977-83; pres., CEO A & E Electric/A & E Petroleum, Casper, Wyo., 1983-90, Custom Electronics, Casper, Wyo., 1986-92; prin. Emeric Solymossy, Cons., Grand Junction, Colo., 1989—; cons. Moores-Eikenhorst, Denver, 1989-92; turnaround cons. Redlands Video and Tan, Grand Junction, Colo., 1991, cons. in electronic sys. Denver Internat. Airport, 1992-94. Author: Organization Values—Individual Values, 1966: Hungarian Enterprises—Marketing in Transition, 1966, Project Management, 1988, Ethics in Entrepreneurship: The Present State of the Art, 1995, Entrepreneurial Ethics: The Impact of Accountability and Independence, 1996. Dir. Panorama Improvement Dist., Mesa County, Colo., 1990-92; bd. dirs. Casper, Natrona County Licensing Bd., 1985-89; co-chmn. Tourism Com. Wyo. Centennial, 1985-86; scoutmaster Boy Scouts of Am., Grand Junction, 1989-92. Named Outstanding Young Man of Am., 1978; recipient Paul Harris fellowship Rotary, 1988. Mem. Associated Bulders and Contractors (pres. 1987-88), Acad. Mgmt., Acad. Internat. Bus., Internat. Coun. for Small Bus., Strongville Rotary. Office: Emeric Solymossy Cons 18336 Cook Ave Strongsville OH 44136-5221

SOMBART, PAUL C., state legislator; b. Boonville, Mo., Dec. 24, 1920; s. Bernice Sombart; children: Lisa, Kevin. Dairy farmer; former cir. clk. and recorder Cooper County, Mo.; rep. Mo. State Ho. Reps. Dist. 117, 1991—, mem. agr., children, youth and families coms., mem. correctional inst. and fees and salaries Coms. Mem. Boonville and Calif. C. of C., Cooper County Farm Bur. *

SOMER, THOMAS JOSEPH (TJ SOMER), police officer, lawyer; b. Chicago Heights, Oct. 13, 1953; m. Cynthia Flamini; 2 children. BA, Nat. Louis U., 1987; JD, John Marshall Law Sch., 1991. Republican candidate for U.S. House, 2d dist., Ill., 1996. Roman Catholic. Address: Com to Elect Thomas Joseph Somer PO Box 36 Olympia Fields IL 60461*

SOMERS, JOSEPH MOORE, retired librarian; b. Portland, Maine, July 21, 1933; s. William Joseph and Nora Mae (Moore) S.; m. Sheila Millicent Chapman, Feb. 11, 1960; children: James, Pierce, David, Sharon. AAS, Coll. of Lake County, Grayslake, Ill., 1985; BA, Barat Coll., 1987; MEd, DePaul U., 1992. Libr. Barat Coll., Lake Forest, Ill., 1987-93, ret., 1993. Assoc. Smithsonian Instn.; mem. DAV, Archaeol. Inst. Am., Nat. Trust Hist. Press, Wilson Ctr. Assocs., Fleet Res. Assn., Ill. Sheriffs Assn., Law Enforcement Officers Meml. Fund. Mem. Am. Legion. Roman Catholic.

SOMERVILLE, DEBORAH MARIE-MARGARET, state agency administrator; b. Lakewood, Ohio, Mar. 23, 1957; d. Joseph George Herzberger and Sophie Marie (Herzeberger) Albrecht; m. Robert L. Scheuneman, Jan. 15, 1982 (div. Apr. 1983); m. Lane E. Somerville, Apr. 17, 1986; children: Maggie, Molly. BS, Ohio State U., 1984; MA, Antioch U., Yellow Springs, Ohio, 1992. Devel. specialist Ohio Housing Fin. Agency, Columbus, 1984-89, acting dir. Office of Policy, 1990, sr. housing planner, 1991-95, mgr. low income housing tax credit program, 1995—; mem. Columbus Bldg. Code Review Task Force, 1989; chair Columbus Coord. Coun. for the Homeless, 1989-91; cons. local devel. corps., Columbus, 1991-94. Neighborhood commr. North Linden, Columbus, 1990-91; mem. devel. bd. Children's Hosp., 1996—. Office: Ohio Dept of Devel 77 S High St 26 Floor Columbus OH 43215

SOMERVILLE, WILLIAM H., academic administrator; b. Blanshard Twp., Ontario, Canada, Apr. 25, 1921; s. John and Mary (Taylor) S.; m. Jean Fawcett, June 16, 1945; children: John, Karen. St. Mary's Collegiate Inst., St. Mary's, Ontario, Canada, 1939. Proprietor of drug store U. Windsor, St. Mary's, Ontario, Can., 1946-55; exec. Drug Trading Co., London, Ontario, Can., 1956-62; mgr. St. Marys Br. Brit. Mortgage & Trust Co., 1962, mgr. Stratford Br., 1963-67, asst.gen. mgr., 1968-72, v.p., 1973-75, v.p. mortgages, 1976, exec. v.p., 1977; pres., CEO Victoria and Grey Trustco Ltd., 1978-82; chmn., CEO The Premier Trust Co., 1983; pres., CEO Nat. Trustco Inc. and Nat. Trust Co., 1984; pres. Victoria and Grey Mortgage Co., The Premier Trust Co., 1985-88; chmn. Pension Commn. of Ontario, Toronto, Ontario, Can., 1989—. past pres., bd. govs. Stratford Shakespearean Festival; dir. St. Joseph's Health Ctr.; chancellor emeritus U. of Windsor; councillor St. Mary;s, 1962-64, mayor, 1965-66; liberal candidate for Perth Riding, Fed. Election, 1968; alderman City of Stratford, 1970-73. Mem. Internat. Accts. Soc., Ontario Club. Office: Ontario Pension Bd, 1 Adelaide St E Ste 1100, Toronto, ON Canada M5C 2X6

SOMES, JOAN MARIE, emergency nurse; b. St. Paul, Aug. 17, 1952; d. Richard and Jane (Blaiser) Friesen; m. Michael Somes, Nov. 15, 1975. BA in Nursing, Coll. of St. Catherine, St. Paul, 1974; paramedic cert., Inver Hills C.C., Inver Grove Heights, Minn., 1976; MSN, U. Minn., 1989. RN, Minn.; nat. registered EMT-paramedic; cert. ACLS instr., PALS instr.; cert. TNCC instr. Paramedic A.L.F. Ambulance, Apple Valley, Minn., 1987—; charge nurse emergency dept. Divine Redeemer Hosp., South St. Paul, Minn., 1974-94; staff nurse emergency dept. St. Joseph's Hosp., St. Paul, 1994—; instr. numerous local cmty. colls., hosps. and ambulance svcs.; item writer CEN exam., 1994-96. Author nursing home study courses; contbr. articles to profl. jour. Grantee Glaxo Pharm. Co., 1989, Health East Found. 1991, 94, recipient Mary Piner award Minn. Emergency Nurses Assn. State Coun. 1994. Mem. Emergency Nurses Assn. (CEN, dir./state coun. liaison Greater Twin Cities chpt., mem. Minn. state coun., chair state trauma com. 1994-95).

SOMMER, SCOTT WILLIAM, control systems integrator manager; b. Peoria, Ill., Mar. 26, 1959; s. William Alvin and Claudia (Almand) S.; m. Julia Ann Kyburz, May 19, 1984; children: Meghann Claire, Logan Scott. BSChemE, U. Ill., 1981; M in Engring. Chem. Engring., McNeese State U., 1983; postgrad., U. Phoenix, 1994—. Registered profl. engr., Ohio, Ill. Process engr. Conoco Chems. Co., Westlake, La., 1981-84; sys. engr. Celanese, Bishop, Tex., 1984-85; sr. automation engr. Fluor-Daniel, Cin., 1985-88; project mgr. Asea-Brown-Boveri, Columbus, Ohio, 1988-90; v.p. The Delta Group, Cin., 1990-93, 95—; dir. ops. PID, Inc., Cin., 1993-95, bus. process improvement leader, sr. tech. cons., 1995. Mem. NSPE, AICE, Instrument Soc. Am., Tau Beta Pi. Republican. Evangelical. Home: 6058 Hillsdale Ln West Chester OH 45069 Office: The Delta Group Ste 200 9933 Alliance Rd Cincinnati OH 45242

SOMMERS, BAMBI VAIL, radio executive; b. Salem, Ohio, Aug. 20, 1955; d. James Paul and Cora Alice (Brown) Gorby; m. John N. Vail, Dec. 15, 1972 (div. Dec. 1981); m. Larry L. Sommers, Feb. 29, 1996. Sales rep., producer, promotion dir. WQXK K-105, Salem, Ohio, 1981—. Office: K-105 WQXK 465 E State St Salem OH 44460-2848

SOMMERS, DANA EUGENE, insurance agency executive; b. Marion, Ind., Oct. 15, 1953; s. Darlton L. and Martha F. (Bontrager) S.; m. Judy L. Grotenhuis, Aug. 21, 1976; children: Erin L., Danae N. BA in Social Work, Taylor U., 1976; MA in Student Personnel Adminstrn., Ball State U., 1977. Resident dir., coordinator Calvin Coll., Grand Rapids, Mich., 1977-79; ins. agt. The Grotenhuis Group, Grand Rapids, 1979-80; ops. mgr., agt. F.W. Grotenhuis Underwriters, Grand Rapids, 1980-81; v.p. adminstrn., treas. F.W Grotenhuis Underwriters, Inc., Grand Rapids, 1981-82, exec. v.p., treas., 1982-83, pres., treas., 1983—; mem. Mich. agts. adv. com. Firemans Fund Ins. Co., Detroit, 1986-88, chmn., 1986; mem. Jonathan Trumball coun. Hartford Ins. Co., Grand Rapids, 1986-88; agts. adv. coun. Aetna Ins. Co., Grand Rapids, 1986. Vice chmn. bd. dirs. Grand Rapids Area Youth for Christ, 1986; chmn. Grand Rapids campaign Mich. Colls. Found., Southfield, 1985-87, 93; bd. dirs., exec. com. Marantha Bible Conf., 1995—, chmn. pers. com., 1987, selection com., 1988, bus. com., 1990-91; devel. coun. St. Mary's Hosp., Grand Rapids, 1987—, co-chair corp. campaign, 1991, 93; exec. bd., chmn. Leader Grand Rapids, 1990—, chmn. program com., 1987-88, selection com. 1988-89, immediate past chair 1991-92; active Greater Grand Rapids Chamber Found. Bd., 1987-88, 90—, v.p., 1989, pres., 1992-93. Mem. Grand Rapids C. of C. (bd. dirs. 1990—, vice chmn. adminstrn., treas. 1993-94, sr. vice chmn. 1995, chair 1996), Cascade Hills Country Club, Grant Rapids Downtown Rotary (bd. dirs. 1991-94, program chair 1995-96), Econ. Club of Grand Rapids (bd. dirs. 1992-96, vice chair 1996—), Greater Pub. Edn. Fund (bd. dirs. 1995-98, sec. 96). Republican. Office: The Grotenhuis Group 660 Cascade West Pky SE Grand Rapids MI 49546-2147

SOMMERS, DAVID LYNN, architect; b. Salem, Ohio, June 17, 1949; s. Carl Ervin and Jean (Mohr) S. BArch, Kent State U., 1974. Registered architect, Ohio. Designer, draftsman Rice & Stewart, Architects, Painesville, Ohio, 1974-76; assoc. architect Prentiss Brown Assoc., Kent, Ohio, 1977-81; project architect Edward W. Prusak, Assoc., Ravenna, Ohio, 1982-83; pvt. practice Kent, 1983—. Mem. archtl. adv. com. Kent Planning Commn., 1985—; mem. Franklin Twp. Bd. Zoning Appeals; bd. bldg. appeals, City of Kent Bldg. Dept.; bd. dirs. Townhall II Drug and Crisis Intervention Ctr., Kent, 1986. Named one of Outstanding Young Men of Am., 1979-81. Mem. AIA (pres. Akron chpt. 1991—), Archs. Soc. Ohio, Jaycees (pres. Kent chpt. 1981-82, Jaycee of Yr. 1980, Keyman of Yr. 1981), Rotary (bd. dirs. 1994—). Office: 136 N Water St # 208 Kent OH 44240-2450

SONDEREGGER, THEO BROWN, psychology educator; b. Birmingham, Ala., May 31, 1925; d. Ernest T. and Vera M. (Sillox) Brown; children: Richard Paul, Diane Carol, Douglas Robert. BS, Fla. State U., 1946; MA in Chemistry, U. Nebr., 1948, MA in Exptl. Psychology, 1960; PhD in Clin. Psychology, U. Nebr., 1965. Lic. psychologist, Calif; clin. lic., cert. Nebr. Asst. prof. U. Nebr. Med. Ctr., Omaha, 1965-71, Nebr. Wesleyan U., Lincoln, 1965-68; asst. prof. U. Nebr., Lincoln, 1968-71, assoc. prof., 1971-76, prof., 1976-94; ret., 1994, prof. emeritus, 1995—; vol. assoc. prof. U. Nebr. Med. Ctr., 1972-77, courtesy prof. med. psychology, 1977-95. Editor: Nebr. Symposium on Motivation, 1974, 84, 91, Problems of Perinatal Drug Dependence: Research and Clinical Implications, 1986, Neurobehavioral Toxicology and Teratology vol. 8, 1988-89, Problems of Perinatal Drug Dependence, 1979, 82, 84, Feminist Therapy Interchange, 1988-89, 91, Perinatal Substance Abuse: Research and Clinical Implications, 1992, Agendas for Aging, 1994—. Mem. grant rev. coms. Nat. Inst. Drug Abuse, 1983-84, 85, 91-94. Tribute to Women award Lincoln YMCA, 1985, named Outstanding Rsch. Scientist Nebr. Chpt. Sigma Xi, 1991, Outstanding Contbn. to Status of Women, N N-L Chancellors Commn. on Status of Women, 1994, Pound Howard Disting. Career Achievement award, 1996. Fellow AAAS, Am. Psychol. Assn., Am. Psychol. Soc.; mem. Midwestern Psychol. Assn., Internat. Soc. Devel. Psychobiology, Internat. Soc. Psychoneuroendocrinolty, Nebr. Psychol. Assn. (pres. 1972), Soc. Neurosci., Advanced Feminist Therapy Inst., Region V Adv. Coun. on Drugs, Fetal Alcohol Adv. Coun., Phi Beta Kappa (sec. Nebr. chpt. 1974), Sigma Xi (pres. 1986). Club: Altrusa YWCA.

SONDEY, MARGARET ELLEN, historian, educator; b. Meriden, Conn., Aug. 20, 1955; d. Walter Theophilus and Eleanor May (Schumacher) S.; m. Gregory Roland Coleman, June 16, 1979 (div. Sept. 1984); m. William Lon Hines, June 20, 1987; children: Evangeline Marie Hines, Jacob Lee Hines. AB, Lake Erie Coll., 1977; MA, Ohio U., 1979; postgrad., Ohio State U., 1985—. With personnel, cost acctg., advt. and sales promotion depts Lincoln Electric Co., Cleve., 1979-84; residence dir. Lake Erie Coll., Painesville, Ohio, 1984-85; sales cons. Workbench/Arhaus, Columbus, Ohio, 1985-86; hist. cons. Edison Welding Inst., Columbus, 1988-90; staff writer Tri-County Chronicle, 1990-91. Canvasser Madison (Ohio) Sch. Levy Com., 1988; active Lake County La Leche League. Mem. Orgn. Am. Historians, Bus. History Conf. (rsch. fellow 1988-89), Soc. for History of Tech. United Methodist. Home and Office: 5967 Silver Ct Mentor OH 44060-2317

SONG, RENMING, mathematics educator, researcher; b. Linzhang, Hebei, China, Apr. 6, 1963; came to U.S., 1988.; s. Yufu and Xiourong (Meng) S.; m. Junge Guo Song, July, 15, 1986. BS, Hebei U., Boading, Hebei, China, 1983, MS, 1986; PhD, U. Fla., 1993. Lectr. Hebei U., 1986-94; asst. prof. math. U. Mich., Ann Arbor, 1994—. contbg. author to profl. jours. Mem. Am. Math. Soc. Office: Univ Mich Dept Math Ann Arbor MI 48109

SONGER, HUGO CHARLES, judge; b. Duff, Ind., Apr. 11, 1931; s. Hugo Elijah and Clarissa (Bretz) S.; m. Lillian Mae Chinn, Oct. 13, 1979; children: Julie, James. BS, Ind. U., 1958, LLB, 1960. Bar: Ind. 1960, U.S. Dist. Ct. (so. and no. dists.) Ind., 1960. Assoc. Iglehart, Hewin & Songer, Evansville, Ind., 1960-81; ptnr. Nordhoffs & Songer, Jasper, Ind., 1981-84; cir. judge Dubois Cir. Ct., Jasper, 1985—. Author: Duff - A Continuum, 1983, History of Huntingburg, 1987. Active in past various civic orgns. With U.S. Army, 1951-54. Recipient James Bethel Gresham award, Evansville Bar Assn., 1969. Mem. Ind. Bar Assn., Dubois County Bar Assn. Democrat. Office: Courthouse Jasper IN 47546

SONGSIRIDEJ, VANEE, physician; b. Bangkok, Thailand, Feb. 21, 1949; Came to US 1977; d. Songsakdi and Mayuree (Wasantachat) S. MD, Siriraj Med. Sch Mahidol U., Bangkok, 1974. Residency in internal medicine St. Joseph Hosp. Affil. with Northwestern U., Chgo., Ill., 1977-80; fellow in allergy and clinical immunology U. Wis., Madison, 1980-82; allergist internist Gundersen Clinic, La Crosse, Wis., 1982—, chief sect. allergy, 1994—; med. dir. Stress Reduction and Relaxation Clinic, 1993—, chief sect. allergy, 1994—; clin. asst. prof. U. Wis., Madison, 1995—. Fellow Am. Coll. Chest Physicians; mem. AMA, ACP, Am. Lung Assn. Wis. (bd. dirs. 1989-94), Am. Coll. Physician Execs., Am. Acad. Allergy and Clin. Immunology, Wis. Med. Soc., Wis. Allergy Soc., La Crosse County Med. Soc. Office: Gundersen Clinic 1836 South Ave La Crosse WI 54601-5429

SONKA, STEVEN T., agricultural economics educator, consultant; b. Cedar Rapids, Iowa, July 4, 1948; s. Jerome and Marcella (Pickert) S.; m. Karilyn Mae Stephen, June 5, 1970; children: Tracy, Melissa, Julie, Teresa. BS in Agrl. Bus., Iowa State U., 1970, PhD in Econs., 1974. Resident assoc./staff economist Iowa State U., 1971-75; asst. prof. U. Ill., Urbana, 1975-79, assoc. prof., 1979-83, prof. agr. econ., 1983—; ptnr. Agrl. Edn. and Cons., Champaign, Ill., 1983—; vis. faculty in residence Arthur Andersen & Co., summer 1982, Monstanto Co., summer 1993; resident assoc. Ctr. for Advanced Study, Champaign, fall 1986; vis. prof. Inst. Agrl. Bus., Santa Clara, Calif., 1986-87; cons. Orgn. Econ. Coop. and Devel., Paris, 1989, office tech. assessment U.S. Congress, Washington, 1989-90. Author: (books) American Farm Size, 1975, Hail Suppression, 1977, Computers in Farming, 1983. Task force mem. U.S. Senate, Washington, 1982-83. Recipient Van Nostrand Reinhold/A V I Press Teacher awd., Nat. Assn. of Colleges and Teachers of Agriculture, 1992. Mem. Am. Agrl. Econ. Assn. (chair 1987-90). Office: U Ill 1301 W Gregory Dr Urbana IL 61801-3608

SONNENSCHEIN, HUGO FREUND, academic administrator, economics educator; b. N.Y.C., Nov. 14, 1940; s. Leo William and Lillian Silver S.; m. Elizabeth Gunn, Aug. 26, 1962; children: Leah, Amy, Rachel. AB, U. Rochester, 1961; MS, Purdue U., 1963, PhD, 1964; PhD (hon.), Tel Aviv U., 1993; D (honoris causa), U. Autonoma Barcelona, Spain, 1994; hon. degree, Purdue U., 1996. Mem. faculty dept. econs. U. Minn., 1964-70, prof., 1968-70; prof. econs. U. Mass., Amherst, 1970-73, Northwestern U., 1973-76; prof. econs. Princeton U., 1976-87, Class of 1926 prof., 1987-88; dean and Thomas S. Gates prof. Sch. Arts and Scis. Sch. Arts & Scis., U. Pa., Phila., 1988-91; provost Princeton (N.J.) U., 1991-93; pres., prof. dept. econs. and Coll., U. Chgo., 1993—; vis. prof. U. Andes, Colombia, 1965, Tel-Aviv U., 1972, Hebrew U., 1973, U. Paris, 1978, U. Aix-en-Provence, France, 1978, Stanford U., 1984-85. Editor: Econometrica, 1977-84; asso. editor: Jour. Econ. Theory, 1972-75; bd. editors: Jour. Math. Econs, 1974—, SIAM Jour, 1976-80; Contbr. articles to profl. jours. Trustee U. Rochester, 1992, U. Chgo., 1993—. Social Sci. Research Council fellow, 1967-68; NSF fellow, 1970—; Ford Found. fellow, 1970-71; Guggenheim Found. fellow, 1976-77. Fellow Am. Acad. Arts and Scis., Econometric Soc. (pres. 1988-89); mem. NAS.

SONNHALTER, CAROLYN THERESE, physical therapist, consultant; b. Bedford, Ohio, Apr. 26, 1942; d. Gabriel Edward Jr. and Josephine Irene (Kubera) Farkas; m. Donald Joseph Lippert, June 11, 1966 (div. June 1981); 1 child, Kevin Michael; m. Robert Louis Sonnhalter, Aug. 31, 1985. BS, Ohio State U., 1964. Lic. phys. therapist, Ohio. Staff and sr. phys. therapist Akron (Ohio) City Gen. Hosp., 1964-69; asst. dir. phys. therapy Akron Gen. Med. Ctr., 1975-82; dir. phys. therapy Litchfield Rehab. Ctr., Akron, 1983-87; phys. therapist HMO Health Ohio, Akron, 1987—, Phoenix-Hudson Corp., Middleburg Heights, Ohio, 1993—; devel. phys. therapy first outpatient Chronic Pain Mgmt. Program, Ohio, 1983. Mem. Am. Phys. Therapy Assn., Alpha Gamma Delta. Home: 3631 Oak Rd Stow OH 44224 Office: HMO Health Ohio 676 S Broadway Akron OH 44311

SOPER, DONALD ARTHUR, geologist; b. L.A., Oct. 26, 1947; s. Arthur Hobart and Eleanor (Williams) S. BS, U. Fla., 1972, MS, 1974. Sr. geologist Aluminum Co. Am., Phoenix, 1974-79, Fluor Mining & Metals, Inc., Tucson, 1979-81; sr. mining geologist Bechtel Civil & Minerals, Inc., San Francisco, 1981-85; mining geologist China-Am. Internat. Engring., Inc., Shenzhen, China, 1985; chief mining geologist Antaibao Island Creek of China Coal, Ltd., Pingshuo, China, 1985-91; sr. geologist Arch Mineral Corp., Turtle Creek, W.Va., 1992-93, mgr. exploration and geology W.Va., 1993-94; mgr. computer mapping Arch Mineral, St. Louis, Ill., 1994—; freelance cons., Boise, Idaho, 1991-92. Sgt. U.S. Army, 1965-68, Vietnam. Mem. Am. Assn. Petroleum Geologists, Soc. Mining, Metallurgy and Exploration, Soc. Sedimentary Geology. Office: City Place One Ste 300 Saint Louis MO 63141

SORBO, ALLEN JON, actuary, consultant; b. Blue Earth, Minn., Aug. 7, 1953; m. Karen Lee Anderson, June 5, 1982; children: Matthew Allen, Sunny Lynn. BA, Gustavus Adolphus Coll., 1975; MS, U. Wis., 1976. Cons. Stennes and Assocs., Mpls., 1976-78; cons. Towers Perrin Forster and Crosby, Mpls., 1978-86, prin., 1986-87; prin.-in-charge health care actuarial svcs. Ernst and Whinney, Chgo., 1987-89; prin. Tillinghast, Towers, Perrin, Mpls., 1989-94; prin. and mgr. Towers Perrin Integrated Health Systems Cons., Mpls., 1995—. Mem. Am. Acad. Actuaries, Soc. Actuaries. Republican. Office: Towers Perrin Integ Health 8300 Norman Center Dr Minneapolis MN 55437-1027

SORELL-JENSEN, INEZ MARIE, photography studio executive; b. Troy, N.Y., June 18, 1947; d. Henry Paul Sorell and Peggy Jeanne (Tompkins) Lill; m. Robert George Jensen; children: William, Erik, Therese, Daniel, Kurt. AAS, Oakton C.C., Niles, Ill., 1978; BA, Nat. Coll. Edn., Evanston, Ill., 1987; BA (hon.), Nat. Lewis U., Evanston, Ill., 1990. Lic. phys. therapist asst., Ill., Tenn. Phys. therapist asst. Bethany Meth. Corp., Chgo., 1978-89, Excellcare, Inc., Northbrook, Ill., 1989—; mgr./agt. Bob Jensen Photography, Chgo., 1992—. Mem. Salvation Army Med. Fellowship, 1991—; founder, pres. Talk T.U.F.F., Incorp., Chgo., 1995—. Mem. Am. Phys. Therapy Assn., United Phys. Therapy Assn. (asst. treas. 1979-80), Chgo. ARea Camera Clubs Assn., Wright Coll. Cambera Club. Home: 2527 N Ridgeway Ave Chicago IL 60647 Office: PO Box 578760 Chicago IL 60657

SORENSEN, JIMMY LOUIS, management consultant; b. Chgo., June 11, 1927; s. Soren Johannes and Jensine Elizabeth (Jensen) S.; m. Esther Nancy Sorensen, Nov. 27, 1954; children: Nancy, Mark, Karen, Ruth. BA cum laude, Dana Coll., 1951. CPA, Ill. Asst. dir. data processing Continental Assurance Co., Chgo., 1951-57; spl. rep. UARCO, Chgo., 1957-59; asst. treas. Signode Steel, Glenview, Ill., 1959-60; ptnr. Arthur Young & Co., Chgo., 1960-84; dir. mgmt. info. services Cotter & Co., Chgo., 1984-90. Bd. dirs. Luth. Gen. Health Care System, Park Ridge, Ill., 1980-95; chmn. bd. trustees Danish Old People's Home, Chgo., 1976—; chmn. bd. dirs. Pioneer Ministries, Inc. Decorated Order Ridder of Dannebrog, Queen Margrethe II of Denmark, 1991. Mem. AICPA, Ill. Soc. CPAs, Midwest Danish Am. C. of C. (treas.), Medinah Country Club. Home and Office: 329 Carter Ave Wood Dale IL 60191-1934

SORENSEN, KELD, biochemist; b. Copenhagen, June 5, 1953; came to U.S. 1987; s. Alf and Karin (Bendtsen) S.; m. Susan Linda Hom, June 3, 1980; 1 child, Kasper. PhD, U. Copenhagen, 1980. Research assoc. U. Bern, Switzerland, 1980-82; postdoctoral researcher Tex. A&M U., Temple, 1982-83; asst. prof. U. Bern, 1983-87; dir. biochemistry and immunology NTD Labs., Carle Place, N.Y., 1987-89; lab. dir. Equichem. Rsch. Inst., Carle Place, N.Y., 1989-91; sr. rsch. scientist Pierce Chem. Co., Rockford, Ill., 1991—; asst. prof. Coll. Medicine, U. Ill., 1993—. Editorial bd. Clinica Chemica Acta, Glasgow, 1987-89; referee several sci. jours.; contbr. articles to profl. jours.; patentee in field. Mem. Am. Assn. Clin. Chemistry. Unitarian Universalist. Home: 11637 Chatt Dr Roscoe IL 61073-9207 Office: Pierce Chem Co PO Box 117 Rockford IL 61105-0117

SORENSEN, MARK WAYNE, archivist, historical researcher; b. Chgo., Jan. 20, 1947; s. Aener Victor and Elizabeth (Huska) S.; m. Kathy Lee Owen, July 4, 1969; children: Jennifer, Erika. BS in Edn., Ea. Ill. U., 1969; MA in History, U. Ill., Springfield, 1978. Tchr. Decatur (Ill.) Pub. Schs. and Richland C.C., 1969-86; supr. records mgmt. Ill. State Archives, Springfield, 1982-86, asst. dir., 1987—; bd. dirs. Ill. Hist. Soc. Author: Illinois Local Records Management Handbook, 1984; editor: Capitol Centennial Papers, 1989; creator 5 exhibits Ill. History Topics, 1986—; contbr. articles to profl. jours. Trustee Decatur Libr. Bd., 1986-93; mem. Decatur Hist. and Archtl. Sites Commn., 1993—; bd. dirs. Decatur Fine Arts Film Series, 1983-95; Rep. candidate for county clk., Macon County, Ill., 1990. Recipient Disting. Leadership award Decatur Leadership Inst., 1987, Outstanding Individual award Decatur Area Arts Coun., 1989. Mem. Acad. Cert. Archivists (cert.), Soc. Am. Archivists, Ill. Humanities Coun., Phi Delta Kappa. Home: 289 S Westlawn Ave Decatur IL 62522-2540 Office: Ill State Archives Springfield IL 62756

SORENSEN, NELS PETER, JR., dentist; b. Greenville, Mich., Apr. 4, 1938; s. Nels Peter and Kathryn Adelia (Baylis) S.; m. Carol Ann Mount, July 30, 1960; children: Christopher N., Eric P., Lisle E. BS, U. Mich., 1960, DDS, 1964. Lic. dentist, Mich. Gen. practice dentistry Greenville, Mich. Treas., Greenville Band Boosters, 1978-91; trustee, sec.-treas. Greenville Bd. Edn., 1982—. Mem. ADA, Mich. Dental Assn. (del. alt. hos. of dels. 1980-81), U. Mich. Dental Sch. Alumni Assn. (bd. govs. 1985-91), West Mich. Dental Soc. (rep. 1977-81). Home: 1217 Frank Dr Greenville MI 48838

SORGEN, RICHARD JESSE, architect; b. Toledo, Ohio, Aug. 4, 1945; s. William C. and Frances Louise (Lederhaus) S.; m. Ellen Kathleen Mumma, Aug. 19, 1972; children—Brian Richard, Neal Andrew. B.S. in Arch., U. Mich., 1972, M.Arch. with high distinction, 1973, postgrad. U. Toledo, 1974, 80. Registered architect, Ohio and 38 additional states. Designer, Schauder & Martin, Architects, Toledo, Ohio, 1972; project mgr. SSOE, Inc., Toledo, 1972-76; v.p. Harris Builders, Inc., Toledo, 1976-77; ptnr. Troy Partnership, Toledo, 1977-83; dir. archtl. svcs, Johnson Architects, Monroe, Mich., 1983-88; prin. Sorgen Architect, Sylvania, Ohio, 1988-89; instr. archtl. tech. Monroe County Community Coll., 1987-89; chief architect, dir. bus. devel., prin. GPD Assocs., Akron, Ohio, 1989-93; bus. developer AVCA Corp., Sylvania, Ohio, 1993—. Served with USN, 1965-69. Recipient Scholastic award AIA Found., 1972. Mem. AIA (nat. design com.), Soc. Mktg. Profl. Svcs., Architects Soc. Ohio (trustee 1980), Nat. Council Archtl. Registration Bds. Republican. Methodist. Maj. works include: Toledo Engring. Co. Hdqrs., YMCA, Oregon, Ohio, Ohio Citizens Bank, Owens Tech. Coll., Jefferson High Sch., Monroe, Davis-Besse Nuclear Power Sta. Access Facility, U. Toledo-Bowman Oddy Labs. addition, City of Sylvania Adminstrn. Bldg.

SORTEBERG, KENNETH WARREN, executive accountant; b. Mpls., July 26, 1945; s. Kenneth L. and Ellen L. (Moynihan) S.; m. Karon L. Burmeister, Dec. 2, 1972; children: Samuel T., Garrett W. BA in Acctg., St. Cloud (Minn.) State U., 1967, MBA, 1968. CPA, Minn. Sr. auditor Arthur Andersen & Co., Mpls., 1969-72; asst. v.p. Eberhardt Co., Edina, Minn., 1972-75; pvt. practice acctg. Edina, 1975-80; pres. Diamond S. Livestock Equipment, Watertown, Minn., 1981-84; ter. mgr. Snell Systems, San Antonio, 1985-87; pres., dir. Equity Lending, Inc., Mpls., 1990—; real estate cons., Watertown, 1985—; dir. Mountain Parks Fin. Svcs., Inc. Mem. Minn. Assn. Realtors, Minn. Consumer Fin. Conf., Minn. Ducks Unltd. (com. chmn. 1972-80). Roman Catholic. Home: 7430 Sherrys Arm Rd Grand Rapids MN 55744-8547 Office: 7350 France Ave Ste 100 Minneapolis MN 55435-2004

SORTLAND, ALLAN BERDETTE, pastor; b. Litchville, N.D., Jan. 26, 1928; s. John and Hulda Louise (Teigland) S.; m. Eunice Elizabeth Nystuen, Feb. 8, 1952; children: Paul, John, Mary, David. BA, Concordia Coll., 1950; BTh, Augsburg Theology Sem., Mpls., 1953; DMin, Luth. Sch. Theology, Chgo., 1977. rdained Luth. Ch., 1953. Pastor Powers Lake (N.D.) Luth. Parish, 1953-57, Sharon Luth. Ch., Grand Forks, N.D., 1957-65; assoc. pastor 1st Luth. Ch., Albert Lea, Minn., 1965-72; sr. pastor Am. Luth. Ch., Lincoln, 1972-78; pastor, min. for pastoral care Calvary Luth. Ch. of Golden Valley, Mpls., 1978-94. Staff sgt. U.S. Army, 1946-49. Home: 2045 Zealand Ave N Golden Valley MN 55427

SORTLAND, PAUL ALLAN, lawyer; b. Powers Lake, N.D., July 30, 1953; s. Allan Berdette and Eunice Elizabeth (Nystuen) S.; m. Carolyn Faye Anderson, June 23, 1979; children: Joseph Paul, Martha Marie, Nicholas John, Benjamin David. BA, St. Olaf Coll., 1975; JD, U. Minn., 1978. Bar: Minn. 1978, N.D. 1981, U.S. Dist. Ct. Minn. 1979, U.S. Dist. Ct. N.D. 1980, U.S. Ct. Appeals (8th cir.) 1987, U.S. Supreme Ct. 1991. Assoc. Alderson & Ondov, Austin, Minn., 1978-80, Qualley, Larson & Jones, Fargo, N.D., 1980-83; ptnr. Holand, Lochow & Sortland, Fargo, 1983-85; pres. Sortland Law Office, Fargo, 1985-88; ptnr. Messerli & Kramer, Mpls., 1988-92; Sortland Law Office, Mpls., 1993—; adj. prof. bus. law Moorhead State U., 1987. Mem. N.D. Bar Assn., Minn. Bar Assn. (cert. civil trial specialist), Assn. Trial Lawyers Am., Horseshoe Bay Yacht Club, Kiwanis, Gamma Eta Gamma. Lutheran. Home: 120 Quebec Ave S Minneapolis MN 55426-1509 Office: 701 4th Ave S Ste 500 Minneapolis MN 55415-1810

SOSKA, GEARY VICTOR, robotics consultant; b. Sewickley, Pa., June 30, 1948; s. Victor Andrew and Evelyn Olga (Dugan) S.; m. Carolyn Ann Huppenthal, Sept. 20, 1969; children: Christopher Michael, Aaron Patrick. BS in Indsl. Engring., Southwestern U., Tucson, 1984; BS in Tech. Edn., U. Akron, 1990, MS in Tech. Edn., 1993. Field svc. engr. Unimation Inc., Farmington, Mich., 1972-73; automation specialist Ford Motor Co., Kansas City, Mo., 1973-79; mfg. R & D engr. John Deere, Waterloo, Iowa, 1979-81; dir. mktg. and sales Cybotech Corp., Indpls., 1981-86; cons. Goodyear Tire & Rubber Co., Akron, Ohio, 1986—; pvt. cons., 1982—; pub. speaker, 1982—; instr. Stark Tech. Coll., Canton, Ohio, 1989—; cons. on automated mfg., robotics and mfg. engring. curriculum, 1983. Author: Implementing Industrial Robots, 1987; contbr. articles to profl. jours; patentee robot arm. Advisor Indpls. Pub. Schs., 1983-86, Walker Career Ctr., Indpls., 1983-86, Childrens' Mus., Indpls., 1984-86, U. Akron, 1991—, Akron Pub. Schs., 1993—; asst. coach Community Soccer League, North Canton, 1990. Sgt. USAF, 1968-72. Recipient Internat. Golden Robot award, 1991. Mem. Am. Mgmt. Assn., Soc. Mfg. Engrs. (cert.), Robotics Internat. of Soc. Mfg. Engrs. (bd. dirs. 1989—), Robotics Industries Assn., Soc. Competitive Intelligence Profls., Masons, Shriners, Golden Key. Republican. Roman Catholic. Home: 7388 Ashburton Cir NW North Canton OH 44720-5914 Office: Goodyear Tire & Rubber Co 1144 E Market St Dept 453C Akron OH 44316-0002

SOSNIECKI, GARY STUART, newspaper editor, publisher; b. Chgo., Jan. 3, 1951; s. Walter F. and Lillian M. (Hornburg) S.; m. Helen Louise Stephens, May 15, 1973. BJ, U. Mo., 1973. Reporter Columbia Missourian, 1972; bur. chief Jackson (Tenn.) Sun, 1973-74; reporter So. Illinoisan, Carbondale, 1974-77, assoc. sports editor, 1977-78, sports editor, 1978-80; co-pub., owner Humansville (Mo.) Star-Leader, 1980-86; editor, gen. mgr. Hillsboro (Kans.) Star-Jour., 1986-88; co-pub., owner Webster County Citizen and Advertiser, Seymour, Mo., 1988—. Bd. dirs. Seymour Merchants Assn., 1989-90; chmn. Seymour Cmty. Libr. Com., 1993-94. Recipient numerous journalism awards Ill. AP Editors, So. Ill. Edit. Assn., Ill.Press Assn., Nat. Newspaper Found., Internat. Soc. Weekly Newspaper Editors, Kansas City Press Club, Kans. Newspaper Advt. Assn., Kans. Press Assn., Others, 1976—. Mem. Internat. Soc. Weekly Newspaper Editors, Mo. Press Assn. (chmn. better newspaper contest com. 1991-93, numerous awards), Ozark Press Assn. (bd. dirs. 1990-92, sec.-treas. 1992-93, v.p. 1993-94, pres. 1994-95, past pres. 1995-96), Nat. Newspaper Assn. (numerous awards), Humansville C. of C. (v.p. 1981), Hillsboro C. of C. (bd. dirs. 1987-88), Seymour C. of C. Office: Webster County Citizen 221 S Commercial St Seymour MO 65746-0190

SOSNIECKI, HELEN LOUISE STEPHENS, newspaper editor, publisher; b. Clinton, Mo., June 19, 1951; d. Charles Edward and Frances Louise (Barker) Stephens; m. Gary Stuart Sosniecki, May 15, 1973. BJ, U. Mo., 1973. Reporter, copyeditor Columbia (Mo.) Missourian, 1972-73; copyeditor Jackson (Tenn.) Sun, 1973, asst. chief copy desk, 1974; reporter, Family Living editor Marion (Ill.) Daily Rep., 1973-74, wire editor, 1974-79, mng. editor, 1979-80; co-pub., owner Humansville (Mo.) Star-Leader, 1980-86; copyeditor, state wire editor Wichita (Kans.) Eagle-Beacon, 1986-87; dir. promotion Salem Hosp. Inc., Hillsboro, Kans., 1987-88; co-pub., owner Webster County Citizen & Advertiser, Seymour, Mo., 1988—. Mem. editl. adv. bd. Mo. Comty. Mag., 1990-92. Vol. Tiger Tracker, U. of Mo., Columbia, 1995—; mem. comms. com. U. Mo. Alumni Assn., Columbia, 1992—. Recipient numerous awards So. Ill. Editl. Assn., Nat. Newspaper Found., Kansas City Press club, 1979—. Mem. Nat. Newspaper Assn. (awards), Internat. Soc. Weekly Newspaper Editors, Mo. Press Assn. (awards), Ozark Press Assn. (bd. dirs.), Seymour Merchants' Assn. (publicity co-chair Apple Festival 1989-90, 92—), Seymour Area C. of C. (pres. 1990, v.p. 1994, bd. dirs. 1991-93, 95—). Office: Webster County Citizen 221 S Commercial PO Box 190 Seymour MO 65746

SOTH, LAUREN KEPHART, journalist, economist; b. Sibley, Iowa, Oct. 2, 1910; s. Michael Ray and Virginia Mabel (Kephart) S.; m. Marcella Shaw Van, June 15, 1934; children: John Michael, Sara Kathryn, Melinda. BS in Journalism, Iowa State U., 1932, MS in Econs., 1938; LHD (hon.), Grinnell Coll., 1990. From instr. to assoc. prof. journalism and econs. Iowa State U., Ames, 1933-46; from editorial writer to editorial page editor Des Moines Register and Des Moines Tribune, 1947-75; columnist Des Moines Register/Extra Newspaper Features syndicate, 1976-94; chmn. agr. com., bd. dirs. Nat. Planning Assn., Washington, 1953-76; bd. dirs. Resources for the Future, Washington, 1956-76; mem. Am. Soc. Newspaper Editors, 1954-75. Author: Farm Trouble, 1957, An Embarrassment of Plenty, 1965, The Farm Policy Game--Play by Play, 1989. Maj. U.S. Army, 1942-46, PTO. Decorated Bronze star medal; recipient Pulitzer prize for editorial writing, 1956. Mem. Nat. Conf. Editorial Writers (pres. 1961), Am. Agrl. Econs. Assn. Episcopalian. Home: 907 Ashworth Rd West Des Moines IA 50265-3673

SOTHERN, ROBERT B., chronobiologist; b. Mpls., Oct. 30, 1946; s. Bruce S. and Margaret I. (Satt) S. BA in Psychology, U. Minn., 1969; PhD in Medicine, U. Bergen (Norway), 1992. From lab. asst. to jr. scientist chronobiology lab. U. Minn., Mpls., 1965-76, assoc. scientist chronobiology lab., 1977-85, scientist, assoc. dir. med. chronobiology lab., 1986-88, scientist, dir. rhythmometry lab., 1989—; cons. Hines (Ill.) VA Hosp., 1988—, Ill. Inst. Tech. Rsch. Inst., Chgo., 1989—, dept. pathology U. Bergen, Norway, 1992—, arctic chronobiology sect. Finnmark Coll., Norway, 1995—, bioengring. and chronobiology lab. U. Vigo, Spain, 1995—. Contbr. numerous articles and abstracts to profl. jours. Active Big Bros., St. Paul, 1983-86. Recipient Chronobiology award Hoechst Found., Italy, 1979; Sci. Fair Tchr. Commendation Internat. Sci. and Engring. Fair, 1977, 78, 81. Mem. Internat. Soc. for Chronobiology, 1971—, Sigma Xi, 1973—. Democrat. Home: 1903 Selby Ave Saint Paul MN 55104-5945 Office: U Minn Rhythmometry Lab UMHC Box 609 420 Delaware St SE Minneapolis MN 55455-0374

SOTO, RAMONA, training specialist; b. East Chicago, Ind., Apr. 14, 1963; d. Robert Rudy and Antonia (Perez) S. Student, Purdue U., 1982-86, U. Ill., Chgo., 1990, DePaul U., 1992-95. Salesperson The Gap, Inc., Ind., 1979-84; asst. mgr. The Gap, Inc., Ind. and Ill., 1984-88; tng. mgr. The Gap, Inc., Ill., 1988-90; tng. specialist Montgomery Ward & Co., Ill., 1990-93; temp. worker The Richard Michael Group, Chgo., 1993, Resort Travel Corp, Oakbrook Terrace, Ill., 1993; ind. tng. cons. Chgo., 1994—; tutor tng. mgr. The Cabrini Green Tutoring Program, Chgo., 1991-94, jr. asst. coord., 1995—, tutor Preparing An Attitude for Learning, Leadership and Success,

1991-94, jr. asst. advisor, 1995—. Mem. ASTD. Home: 3550 N Lake Shore Dr Chicago IL 60657-1916

SOTTILE, BENJAMIN JOSEPH, greeting card company executive; b. Bklyn., 1937; s. John and Nicoletta Sottile; m. Ileana Nardone; children: John, Robert. BSEE, U.S. Naval Acad., 1961. With Colgate Palmolive, 1965-68, Vick Chem. co., 1968-69, Warner Lambert, 1969-80, Warner Communications, Inc., 1980-83; sr. v.p. Revlon, Inc., 1983-86; pres., chief operating officer Gibson Greetings, Inc., Cin., 1986, pres. chief exec. officer, 1987, chief exec. officer, pres., chmn. bd., 1989—; also bd. dirs.; bd. dirs. Decker Communications, San Francisco. Bd. govs. USO, Washington, 1989—. Lt. USN, 1961-65. Mem. Nat. Assn. Chain Drug Stores (adv. bd.). Office: Gibson Greetings Inc 2100 Section Rd Cincinnati OH 45237-3510

SOUDER, MARK EDWARD, congressman; b. Ft. Wayne, Ind., July 18, 1950; s. Edward Getz and Irma (Fahling) S.; B.S., Ind. U., Ft. Wayne, 1972; M.B.A., U. Notre Dame, 1974; m. Diane Kay Zimmer, July 28; children—Brooke Diane, Nathan Elias. Mgmt. trainee Crossroads Furniture Co., Houston, 1974; mktg. mgr. Gabberts Furniture & Studio, Mpls., 1974-76; mktg. mgr., exec. v.p. Souder's Furniture & Studio, Grabill, Ind., 1976-80, pres., 1981-84; econ. devel. liaison for U.S. Rep. Dan Coats, 1983—; U.S. congressman, Ind. 4th Dist., 1995— . Publicity chmn. Grabill County Fair, 1977—; advisor Dan Coats for Congress Com., 1980-81; mem. Ind. Area Devel. Council; mem. bus. alumni adv. com. Ind. U.-Ft. Wayne. Mem. Midwest Home Furnishings Assn. (dir. 1976-84, past treas., exec. v.p.), Ft. Wayne, Grabill chambers commerce, Allen County Hist. Soc., Alumni Assn. Ind. U. at Ft. Wayne (dir., past pres.), Alumni Assn. U. Notre Dame. Republican. Mem. Apostolic Christian Ch. Home: 13733 Ridgeview Ct Grabill IN 46741 Office: US House Reps 508 Cannon House Office Bldg Washington DC 20515-1404

SOUERS, MARJORIE ELAINE, education educator; b. Lake James, Ind., Aug. 19, 1936; d. Kenneth E. and Eloise (Johnson) Gillespie; m. Dewey L. Souers, Aug. 17, 1957; children: Steven M. and Linda D. BS magna cum laude, Butler U., 1958; MA summa cum laude, Ball State U., 1965; PhD summa cum laude, Case Western Res. U., 1976. Elem. tchr. Indpls., 1958; elem. tchr. Dugway Proving Grounds, Utah, 1958-59, kindergarten tchr., 1959, asst. prin., elem. tchr., 1959-60; elem. tchr. North Manchester, Ind., 1960-61; assoc. faculty mem. Ind. U.-Purdue U., Ft. Wayne, 1966-73, lectr. edn., 1973-76, asst. prof., 1976-82, assoc. prof., 1982-90, prof., 1990—, coord. student teaching and field experiences, 1982-85; dean, 1985-94; lectr., presenter in field; cons. Author: (monographs) Training Teachers and Administrators to Be Decision Makers, 1980, (with others) Pre-Student Teaching Laboratory Experiences, 1979; contbr. articles to profl. jours. Mem. cert. and lic. commn. Ind. Dept. Edn., 1989-91; del. Ind. Congress Edn., 1986, Gov.'s Conf. Children and Youth, 1981; mem. citizens adv. group Ft. Wayne Community Schs., 1990, Women's Orgn. Nat. Assn. Retail Druggists, 1963—; cons., reader U.S. Dept. Edn., 1988-89; trustee Carpetland USA Scholarship Trust, 1987-92. Grantee Midwest Univs. Consortium Internat. Activities, 1978, Libr. Resource Devel. Fund, 1986-87, 89-90, Jour.-Gazette Found., 1991-94; Gerald Howard Read Internat. Seminar scholar, 1988; named Hon. Ky. Col. Commonwealth of Ky., 1987, Pioneer in Collaboration honoree Pres. Forum Tchg. Profession, 1990. Mem. ASCD (nat. polling panel 1987-89), AAUW (Am. fellowships reader cons. Ednl. found. 1986-94), Assn. Tchr. Educators (instnl. rep. 1983—), Nat. Assn. Women Deans, Adminstrs. and Counselors (jour. bd. 1988-89), Am. Assn. Colls. Tchr. Edn. (chief instnl. rep. 1985-94), Ind. Assn. Colls. Tchr. Edn. (exec. com. 1989-91, v.p. 1990-91), Ind. Assn. Tchr. Educators, Ind. Assn. Elem. Sch. Prins., Kappa Delta Pi, Pi Lambda Theta (pres. 1985-87, Disting. Pi Lambda Thetan award 1995), Phi Delta Kappa. Home: 1115 Pelham Dr Fort Wayne IN 46825-4115 Office: Ind U Office of Edn 2101 E Coliseum Blvd Fort Wayne IN 46805-1499

SOUKUP, AL, state legislator; m. Evie; 6 children. Studetn, Dakota Bus. Coll., N.D. State U. Mem. N.D. Ho. of Reps., 1989—, vice chmn. polit. subdivsn. com., mem. indsl., bus. and labor coms.; past mem. security adv. group N.D. Atty. Gen. Past bd. dirs. Shanley H.S.; past scout leader; past pres. Turtle Lake (Minn.) Improvement Assn., Shanley Grow, past bd. dirs., Cent. Crime Conf., past bd. dirs.; dir. Roger Maris Celebrity Golf. Recipient Shanley Hall of Fame award 1983. Mem. KC, Am. Legion, Elks, Telephone Pioneers. Home: PO Box 446 Fargo ND 58107-0446*

SOULE, GEORGE ALAN, literature educator; b. Fargo, N.D., Mar. 3, 1930; s. George Alan and Ruth Georgia (Knudsen) S.; m. Carolyn Richards, Nov. 24, 1961; 1 child, Katherine. BA, Carleton Coll., 1947; postgrad., Corpus Christi Coll., Cambridge (Eng.) U., 1952-53; MA, Yale U., 1956, PhD, 1960. Instr. English lit. Oberlin (Ohio) Coll., 1958-60; asst. prof. U. Wis., Madison, 1960-62; from asst. prof. to prof. Carleton Coll., Northfield, Minn., 1962-95, prof. emeritus, 1995—, dir. Centennial, 1965-67; chair English dept. Carleton Coll., Northfield, 1980-83; dir. summer writing program Carleton Coll., Northfield, Minn., 1980-86; cons. Ednl. Testing Svc., Princeton, N.J., 1967-84, 94—. Editor (book) Theatre of the Mind, 1974; contbr. articles, revs. to profl. jours. With U.S. Army, 1954-55. Internat. fellow Rotary, 1952-53, Sterling pre-doctoral fellow Yale U., 1957-58. Mem. Johnson Soc. of Lichfield, Boswell Soc. of Auchinleck, Friends of Dove Cottage, The Charles Lamb Soc., Rotary. Episcopalian. Home: 313 Nevada St Northfield MN 55057-2346 Office: Carleton Coll 1 N College St Northfield MN 55057-4001

SOURBRINE, RICHARD DON, II, architect; b. Akron, Ohio, Aug. 26, 1965; s. Richard Don and Clara Violet (Garritano) S. BS, Kent State U., 1987, BArch, 1988. Lic. architect, Ohio, Calif.; cert. architect Nat. Coun. Archtl. Registration Bds. Intern-architect James Reinbolt Architect, Inc., Akron, Ohio, 1986-88, Reinbolt, Evans & Mann Inc, Akron, 1988-94; architect David Pelligra and Architects, Inc., Cuyahoga Falls, Ohio, 1994-95, Ziska Architects and Assocs., Cleve., 1995—; bd. trustees LeBlond Housing Corp., 1996—. Mem. Historic Warehouse Dist. Devel. Corp., Cleve. Ctr. for Contemporary Art. Scholar Kent (Ohio) State U., 1983. Mem. AIA, Nat. Trust for Hist. Preservation, Alfa Romeo Owners Club. Republican. Roman Catholic. Home: 1235 W 6th St # 2A Cleveland OH 44113-1301 Office: Ziska Architects & Assocs 5325 Naiman Pkwy Ste A Cleveland OH 44139

SOUTHARDS, WILLIAM THOMAS, mechanical engineer; b. Lawndale, N.C., July 14, 1952; s. John Jackson and Floye Mildrid (Martin) S.; m. Mary Jane Stapel, Oct. 22, 1983. BE with high honors, U. N.C., Charlotte, 1974; ME, U. Fla., 1976. Rsch. engr. Babcock & Wilcox, Alliance, Ohio, 1976-81, rsch. and devel. ops. planner, 1981-87, sr. rsch. quality engr., 1987-90, group supr. quality assurance sect., 1990-92; sr. rsch. engr. C & AES, 1993—. Mem. ASHRAE, ASME (chmn. Ohio coun.), Am. Soc. Quality Control, Phi Kappa Phi. Home: 1122 Vincent Rd NW North Canton OH 44720-4357 Office: Babcock & Wilcox 1562 Beeson St NE Alliance OH 44601-2165

SOUTHWICK, CHRISTOPHER LYN, anesthesiologist; b. Salina, Kans., Jan. 12, 1956; s. Forest Arthur II and Carolyn Kay (Kauth) S.; m. Laura Lee Stuck, Nov. 17, 1984; children: Andrew William, Kylie Marie, Caitlin Lee. BS in Chem. Sci., Kans. State U., 1978; MD, U. Kans., 1984. Certified Am. Bd. Anesthesiology. Intern Western Res. Care System, Youngstown, Ohio, 1984-85, resident, 1985-87; anesthesiologist Columbia (Mo.) Regional Hosp., 1987-88, Boone Hosp. Ctr., Columbia, 1988—. Mem. AMA, Am. Soc. Anesthesiologists, Mo. Med. Soc. (sec./treas. 1996—), Theta Xi, Alpha Delta Epsilon (pres. 1976-78). Republican. Home: 1001 Lake Point Ln Columbia MO 65203-2900 Office: Columbia Anesthesia Assoc Inc 1506 E Broadway Ste 302 Columbia MO 65201-8078

SOWA, JULIE HOLMES, journalist; b. High Point, N.C., Apr. 17, 1953; d. Clayton Carr and Betty Page (Holderby) Holmes; m. Donald Higgie; children: John Clayton, William Arthur. BS in Journalism, Ohio U., 1975. Copy editor, columnist, reporter Sun Newspapers, Cleve., 1985—; career advisor Polaris Vocat. Sch., Middleburg Heights, Ohio. Recipient Excellence in Journalism award Press Club Cleve., 1993. Mem. Soc. Profl. Journalists. Office: Sun Newspapers 29336 Buckthorn Pl Westlake OH 44145

SOWASH, BECKY MARIA, physical therapist; b. Mansfield, Ohio, Mar. 9, 1967; d. Robert Lee and Diana Amelia (Hubner) S. BS cum laude, U. Toledo, 1990; cert. musculoskeletal evaluation/rehab., U. Fla., 1993. Lic. phys. therapist, Ohio, Ind. Phys. therapist Betty Jane Rehab. Ctr., Tiffin, Ohio, 1990-91; phys. therapist Kokomo (Ind.) Rehab. Ctr., 1991-96, clin. coord. phys. therapist Workable of Ctrl. Ind., 1992-96; phys. therapist Huntington (Ind.) Meml. Hosp., 1996—. Mem. Am. Phys. Therapy Assn. Home: 1417 W Jefferson St Kokomo IN 46901 Office: Huntington Meml Hosp 1215 Etna Ave Huntington IN 46750

SOWD, DAVID HOWARD, writer; b. Canton, Ohio, Jan. 15, 1946; s. William Howard and Ruth Geiger (Smith) S.; m. Judith Ann Kovacs, Sept. 16, 1967 (div. May 1980); children: Aaron, Hannah. BA in Philosophy, Ohio State U., 1967; MA in English, Kent State U., 1970; PhD in English, Bowling Geen State U., 1973. Clk. U.S. Postal Svc., Canton, Ohio, 1974-81; instr. Kent State U. and U. Akron, Ohio, 1981-84; libr., br. head Stark County Dist. Libr., Canton, 1984-87; reporter The Plain Dealer, Cleve., 1987-91; mem. mktg. com. Ohio Ballet, Akron, 1989-90; cons. Booksellers, Cleve., 1991-93. Free-lance writer Cleve. Plain Dealer, Cleve. Mag., Radio World, Libr. Jour., 1984—, Akron Beacon Jour., Scene Entertainment Weekly, Sun Newspapers, Akron and Cleve., 1991—; reviewer books. Sigma Delta Chi scholar, 1963-67. Mem. Cleve. Music Group (bd. dirs. 1989), Stark County Arab-Am. Assn. (sec. 1987), Canton Fedn. Musicians, Soc. Profl. Journalists, Jazz Journalists Assn., Press Club Cleve. Home and Office: 1309 Fulton Rd NW Apt 5 Canton OH 44703

SOWDER, FRED ALLEN, foundation administrator, alphabet specialist; b. Cin., July 17, 1940; s. William Franklin and Lucille (Estes) S.; m. Sandra Ann Siegman, July 15, 1961 (div. Sept. 1963); 1 child, William. Student, Cin. Sch. Ct. Reporting, 1975; diploma Self-Health Insts., Sch. of Med. Masso-Therapy, 1985; diploma, Cin. Sch. Hypnosis, 1989. Founder World Union Universal Alphabet, Cin., 1981—, Internat. Assn. Sch. Massage, Cin., 1988—. Inventor of hundreds of published and unpublished alphabets and writing systems, including light wave, color and musical tone systems and tactile systems for the blind; author: Sowder Shorthand, 1980, Universal Alphabet: What and Why, 1981, Your Intimacy Quotient: The Symptoms, Causes & Consequences of Intimacy Deprivation, 1996; contbr. numerous articles to mags. State dir. Soc. Separationists, Cin., 1967-70; bd. dirs. ACLU of Ohio, ACLU Found., 1984-89, sec., Cin. chpt., 1984-89. Mem. AAAS, Amnesty Internat., Ohio Com. to Abolish Capital Punishment, Assn. for Humanistic Psychology, Internat. Soc. for Gen. Semantics, Am. Sunbathing Assn., The Naturist Soc., Am. Massage Therapy Assn., Urban Appalachian Coun. Democrat. Home: PO Box 252 Cincinnati OH 45201-0252 Office: World Union Universal Alphabet PO Box 252 Cincinnati OH 45201-0252

SPADY, DALE ROLAND, sociology educator; b. Oakland, Calif., May 29, 1941; s. Roland Raymond and Beulah (Anderson) S.; m. Pamela Jean Lazowski, Aug. 6, 1988; 1 child, Victoria Anne. BA, San Jose State U., 1965, MA, 1967; PhD, U. Oreg., 1972. Rsch. assoc. Econ. Opportunity Commn., San Jose, Calif., 1965-67; instr. U. Oreg., Eugene, 1969-71; assoc. prof. sociology No. Mich. U., Marquette, 1972—, dir. Inst. Finnish-Am. Studies, 1976-78. Author: Social Problems, 1980; contbr. articles to profl. jours. With U.S. Army, 1959-62, Germany. Mem. Am. Sociological Assn. Democrat. Home: 228 W Nicolet Blvd Marquette MI 49855 Office: No Mich U Dept Sociology Marquette MI 49855

SPAETH, MARY SHEPARD, marketing communications executive; b. Evanston, Ill., Apr. 25, 1957; d. Kenneth Sihler and Helen (Reis) Shepard; m. Alan Colin Spaeth, May 27, 1978; children: Erika Leigh, Daniel Barrett. BA in English, So. Meth. U., 1978, MA, 1982. Cert. secondary edn. tchr., Tex., Ill. Pub. info. officer Hockaday Sch. for Girls, Dallas, 1978-79; French tchr. Episcopal Sch. Dallas, 1979-80; teaching fellow So. Meth. U., Dallas, 1980-82, English instr., 1982-83; English lectr. Loyola U., Chgo., 1984-92; adj. prof. Nat. Louis U., Evanston, 1989—; pres. Communication Resource Group, Evanston, 1989—; dir. pub. rels. Northwestern U./Evanston Rsch. Park, 1994—; mem. English dept. writing com. Loyola U., Chgo., 1987-89; pres. Savoy-aires Light Opera Co., 1990-92, 93-94. Author: The Fiery Collaboration of Gilbert and Sullivan, 1991; author numerous articles and poems; editor: Hockaday, 1978-79; assoc. editor: Brides Today, 1993-94. Active Chgo. Coun. on Fgn. Rels., 1993—; chair Lincoln Sch. PTA Lang. Bd., 1990—. 1st lt. CAP. Loyola U. fellow, 1990-91; named one of Outstanding Young Women of Am., 1991. Mem. MLA, DAR, Internat. Assn. Bus. Communicators, Nat. Coun. Tchrs. English, Westminster Club, Technology Execs. Roundtable (bd. dirs.), Young Execs. Club Chgo. (v.p. comms. 1992-94, exec. v.p. 1994-95, dir. 1995-96, v.p. pub. rels. 1996—), Sigma Tau Delta, Pi Delta Pi. Home: 1214 Lake Shore Blvd Evanston IL 60202-1415

SPAETH, NICHOLAS JOHN, lawyer, former state attorney general; b. Mahnomen, Minn., Jan. 27, 1950. A.B., Stanford U., 1972, J.D., 1977; B.A., Oxford U., Eng., 1974. Bar: Minn. 1979, U.S. Dist. Ct. (Minn.) 1979, U.S. Ct. Appeals (8th cir.) 1979, N.D. 1980, U.S. Dist. Ct. (N.D.) 1980, U.S. Supreme Ct. 1984. Law clk. U.S. Ct. Appeals (8th cir.), Fargo, N.D., 1977-78; law clk. to Justice Byron White U.S. Supreme Ct., Washington, 1978-79; pvt. practice, 1979-84; atty. gen. State of N.D., Bismarck, 1984-93; ptnr. Dorsey & Whitney, Fargo, 1993—; adj. prof. law U. Minn., 1980-83. Rhodes scholar, 1972-74. Democrat. Roman Catholic. Office: Dorsey & Whitney PO Box 1344 Fargo ND 58107-1344

SPAFFORD, EUGENE HOWARD, computer science educator, consultant, author; b. Rochester, N.Y., Mar. 26, 1956; s. Howard Franklin and Elizabeth Ann (Gallagher) S.; m. Kathleen Ann Heaphy, Nov. 2, 1985. BS in Math.-Computer Sci. summa cum laude, SUNY, Brockport, 1979; MS in Info. and Computer Sci., Ga. Inst. Tech., 1981, PhD in Info. and Computer Sci., 1986. Rsch. scientist II Software Engring. Rsch. Ctr., Ga. Inst. Tech., Atlanta, 1986-87; asst. prof. computer sci. Purdue U., West Lafayette, Ind., 1987-93, assoc. prof. computer sci., 1993—; founder, dir. COAST Lab., 1993—; mem. adv. bd. Jour. Info. Systems Security, 1991—; presenter, keynote speaker confs. in field; mem. evaluation team N.Y. State Sci. and Tech. Found., Columbia U., 1990; mem. evaluation team computer sci. dept. SUNY, 1991. Co-author: Computer Viruses, 1989, Practical Unix and Internet Security, 2d edit., 1996; mem. editl. bd. Computing Systems, 1987-95, Jour. Computer and Software Engring., 1990—, Virus Bull., 1991—, Computers and Security, 1995—; assoc. editor: Computing Systems, 1992-94; contbr. chpts. to books and articles to profl. jours. Instr. ARC, Atlanta, 1984-87, Lafayette, Ind., 1987-89. Named one of Top 10 Outstanding Tchrs. Purdue U. Sch. Sci. Student Coun., 1990, 92; Pres.' fellow Ga. Inst. Tech., 1979; grad. fellow NSF, 1980-83; recipient Meritorious Svc. award IEEE, 1992, Award of Merit Soc. Tech. Communications, 1991. Mem. IEEE (sr., Golden Care award 1996), Assn. for Computing Machinery (chmn. self-assessment com. 1991-96, Internat. Sci. and Engring. Fair awards com. 1992-94), USENIX Assn., Rsch. Ctr. on Computers and Soc. (assoc., nat. adv. bd. 1989—), Computer Security Inst., Computer Soc. of IEEE, Sigma Xi, Upsilon Pi Epsilon. Office: Purdue U Dept Computer Scis West Lafayette IN 47907

SPAHR, SIDNEY LOUIS, agricultural research and education; b. Bristol, Va., Sept. 5, 1935; s. Ralph Hunt and Margie Leona (Pettijohn) S.; m. Mary Ann Harsh, June 8, 1961 (div. June 1974); children: Douglas Eric, Diane Lynn; m. Gladys Ruth Spencer, June 14, 1975. BS, Va. Polytech. Inst., 1958; MS, Pa. State Univ., 1960, PhD, 1964. Instr. dept. of dairy sci. Pa. (University Pk.) State Univ., 1961-64; asst. prof. dept. of dairy sci. Univ. Ill., Urbana, 1964-70; staff officer Nat. Acad. Sci., Washington, D.C., 1970-72; assoc. prof. dept. of dairy sci. Univ. Ill., 1970-81, prof. dept. of dairy sci., 1982-85, prof. dept. of animal scis., 1985—. Author: The Dairy Cow Today, 1988, 2d edit., 1996; editor: Degradation of Synthetic Organic Molecules in the Biosphere, 1972, Productive Agriculture and Quality Environment, 1972. Recipient Paul A. Funk award, Univ. Ill., 1987, MSD AgVet Dairy Mgmt. award, Am. Dairy Sci. Assn., 1987. Mem. Am. Dairy Sci. Assn., Am. Soc. Animal Sci., U.S. Animal Health Assn., Livestock Conservation Inst., Am. Assn. Advancement Sci. Office: U Ill Dept Animal Sci 1207 W Gregory Dr Urbana IL 61801-3838

SPAINHOUR, (DALLAS) KYLE, international division controller; b. Winston-Salem, N.C., Oct. 8, 1960; s. Dallas Marvin and Rachel Lee (Jones) S. BS in Acctg., U. N.C., 1982; MBA in Internat. Fin., U. Chgo., 1990. CPA, N.C. Auditor U.S. Dept. Defense, Washington, 1983-85; cons. Peat, Marwick, Mitchell & Co., Washington, 1985-86; fin. analyst Motorola, Inc., Schaumburg, Ill., 1986-89; mgr. cost and investment policy Motorola Inc., Arlington Heights, Ill., 1990-91, ops. contr. Cellular Joint Ops., 1992-95, divsn. contr. for Europe, Middle East and Africa, 1995—; bd. dirs. Pakistan Mobile Comms. Ltd., St. Petersburg Telecom., Omnitel; chmn. bd. Jordan Mobile Telephone Svcs.; mem. Chgo. adv. coun. to the bd. dirs. Motorola, Inc., 1991-93. Author, editor: PMM & Co. Government Contracts Hotline newsletter, 1985-86. Vol. U.S. Spl. Olympics, Washington, 1986, Chgo., 1987; advisor Jr. Achievement, Chgo., 1990, 91. Mem. AICPA. Democrat. Methodist.

SPALT, STELLA MICKEY, medical nurse, nursing educator; b. Houston, Nov. 24, 1943; d. Morris Elwood and Lena (Borzilleri) Mickey; m. Donald Fredrick Spalt, June 13, 1963; children: Gretchen, Derrick, Heidi. ADN, Marymount Coll., 1978; BA in Humanities, St. Louis U., 1981, BSN summa cum laude, 1987; MS in Adminstrn., Lindenwood Coll., 1985. Staff RN, surg. ICU St. Louis U. Hosp., 1978-79; head nurse, ICU Bethesda Gen. Hosp., 1979-80; staff RN, neonatal ICU U.S. Naval Regional Med. Ctr., Okinawa, Japan, 1981-83; head med. nurse Bethesda Gen. Hosp., St. Louis, 1983-84; staff RN, neonatal ICU St. John's Mercy Med. Ctr., St. Louis, 1984-85, coord. mgmt. devel. instr., level II, 1985-89; mgr., mgmt. devel. ARC St. Louis Bi-State Chpt., 1989-91; dir. employee devel./dir. patient care svcs. Deaconess Health System, St. Louis, 1992-93, dir. patient care svcs., 1993—; pres. Tng. 2000, St. Louis, 1994—. Mem. ASTD (membership com. 1989, pres.-elect 1992, pres. 1993—), Am. Soc. Health Care Edn. Tng. Am. Hosp. Assn., Soc. Human Resources Mgmt., Greater St. Louis Soc. Health Educators Trainers (treas. 1985—), Delta Lambda Chpt. Sigma Theta Tau. Republican. Episcopalian. Home: 229 E Argonne Dr Saint Louis MO 63122-4309 Office: Tng 2000 229 E Argonne Dr Saint Louis MO 63122-4309

SPANGLER, DOUGLAS FRANK, state legislator; m. Mary Clare Spangler. Small bus. owner; mem. from dist. 36 Kans. State Ho. of Reps., Topeka. Address: 3026 N 54th St Kansas City KS 66104

SPANGLER, STEPHEN ALAN, state legislator; m. Sherri Spangler; children: Amy, Erik. Student, Joliet Jr. Coll., 1973; BS, No. Ill. U., 1976, postgrad. Mem. Ill. State Ho. of Reps. Dist. 75, 1995—. Trustee Nettle Creek Twp.; bd. mem., mem. local emergency planning com., regional planning com. Grundy County. Mem. Am. Soc. Safety Engr., Lower Fox Valley Mutual Aid Assn. (v.p.).

SPANN, WILMA NADENE, educational administrator; b. Austin, Tex., Apr. 24, 1938; d. Frank Jamison and Nadene (Burns) Jamison Plummer; m. James W. Spann II, Aug. 2, 1958; children: James III, Timothy, Terrance, Kemberly, Kelby, Elverta, Peter, Margo. BA, Marquette U., 1974; MS, U. Wis., 1985. Sec. Spandagle Coop., Milw., 1969-89; tchr. adult basic edn. Milw. area Tech. Coll., Milw., 1975-80; tchr. Milw. Pub. Sch. System, 1975-90, adminstrv. intern, 1990-91; asst. prin. Clara Barton Elem. Sch., Milw., 1992-93; asst. prin. in charge Greenfield Montessori Sch., Milw., 1993-94, 1993-94, prin., 1993—; prin. Greenfield Montessori Sch., 1993—; del. Inter Group Coun. Contbr. articles to profl. jours. Dir. Vacation Bible Sch., Tabernacle Cmty. Bapt. Ch., Milw., 1977-80, bd. dirs. Christian edn., 1981-90; v.p. women's aux. Wis. Gen. Bapt. State Conv., 1985-95, pres. women's aux., 1995—; instr. Wis. Congress Christian Edn., 1982—; asst. dean Wis. Gen. Bapt. State Congress Christian Edn., 1985; mem. sr. retreat com. Nat. Bapt. Youth Camp; fin. sec. Interdenominational Min.'s Wives Wis. Recipient cert. of Recognition, women's auxiliary Wis. Gen. Bapt. State Conv., 1986, Bd. Edn. Tabernacle Bapt. Ch., 1990. Mem. NAACP, Internat. Assn. Childhood Edn. (sec. 1990-92), Met. Milw. Alliance Black Sch. Educators, Nat. Bapt. Conv. (life, del. intergroup coun., Myra Taylor shcolar com.), Marquette U. Alumni Assn., Assn. Childhood Edn. Internat. (sec. 1990-92), Interdenominational Alliance Minister's Wives & Widows of Wis. (fin. sec.), Assn. Women in Adminstrn., N.Am. Baptist Women's Union, Ch. Women United (life, del. to intergroup), Phi Delta Kappa, Eta Phi Beta. Democrat. Home: 1906 W Cherry St Milwaukee WI 53205-2046 Office: Greenfield Montessori Sch 1711 S 35th St Milwaukee WI 53215-2004

SPARKS, BILLY SCHLEY, lawyer; b. Marshall, Mo., Oct. 1, 1923; s. John and Clarinda (Schley) S.; A.B., Harvard, 1945, LL.B., 1949; student Mass. Inst. Tech., 1943-44; m. Dorothy O. Stone, May 14, 1946; children: Stephen Stone, Susan Lee Sparks Raben, John David. Admitted to Mo. bar, 1949; partner Langworthy, Matz & Linde, Kansas City, Mo., 1949-62, firm Linde, Thomson, Fairchild Langworthy, Kohn & Van Dyke, 1962-91, ret., 1991. Mem. Mission (Kans.) Planning Council, 1954-63; mem. Kans. Civil Service Commn., 1975-90. Mem. dist. 110 Sch. Bd., 1964-69, pres., 1967-69; mem. Dist. 512 Sch. Bd., 1969-73, pres., 1971-72; del. Dem. Nat. Conv., 1964; candidate for representative 10th Dist., Kans., 1956, 3d district, 1962; treas. Johnson County (Kans.) Dem. Central com., 1958-64. Served to lt. USAAF, 1944-46. Mem. Kansas City C. of C. (legis. com. 1956-82), Am., Kansas City bar assns., Mo. Bar, Law Assn. Kansas City, Harvard Law Sch. Assn. Mo. (past dir.), Nat. Assn. Sch. Bds. (mem. legislative com. 1968-73), St. Andrews Soc. Mem. Christian Ch. (trustee). Clubs: Harvard (v.p. 1953-54), The Kansas City (Kansas City, Mo.); Milburn Golf and Country, American Legion. Home and Office: 8517 W 90th Ter Shawnee Mission KS 66212-3053

SPARKS, (LLOYD) MELVIN, appraiser; b. Putnam County, Mo., Sept. 12, 1921; s. Whitlow Vane and Anna Jane (Hart) S.; m. Naomi Nadine Wiles, Jan. 3, 1942; children: Beverly, Richard, Jill. Grad. high sch., Unionville, Mo. Lic. real estate appraiser, Mo. Farm operator Unionville, 1942-77; pres. Northeast Mo. Telephone Co., Green City, Mo., 1961-77; asst. cashier Farmers Bank, Unionville, 1967-77; appraiser Sparks Appraisal, Inc., Unionville, 1983—. Mem. sch. bd. Putnam County Rt. I, Unionville, 1967-72. Mem. Nat. Assn. Ind. Fee Appraisers, Rotary (pres. Unionville 1982-83). Republican. Mem. Ch. of Christ. Home: RR 2 Box 38 Unionville MO 63565-9712

SPARKS, (THEO) MERRILL, entertainer, translator, poet; b. Mount Etna, Iowa, Oct. 5, 1922; s. David G. and Ollie M. (Hickman) S.; student U. Besançon (France), 1945; BA, U. So. Calif., 1948; postgrad. U. Iowa, 1948-51, Columbia U., 1951-52. Entertainer as singer, pianist, L.A., Midwest, Fla., N.Y., N.J. areas, 1953—. With AUS, 1942-46, ETO, MTO. Co-recipient P.E.N. transl. award, 1968, Cross of Merit with Vernon Duke for cantata Anima Eroica, Order of St. Brigida, Rome, 1966. Bd. mem. Adams County Compensation Bd. Mem. ASCAP, ACLU, Am. Fedn. Musicians, Authors Guild, The Songwriters Guild, Vista, The Nat. Icarian Heritage Soc, Adams Co. Hist. Soc., Icarian Players, Alliance Francaise Modern Poetry Assn., Iowa Friends of the Library, Iowa Geneal. Soc., Cert. Local Govt., (moderator Great Books program), Rotary (Paul Harris fellow). Composer songs including Sleepy Village, 1942, Christmas Came Early This Year, 1946, A Heart of Gold, 1956, Anima Eroica, 1966, An Italian Voyage, 1976, O Come and Join the Angels, 1982, Ballad of Ollie and Bart, 1983, Elegy, 1987, Ave Maria, 1988, I Must Remember The Cross, 1991. poems pub. in mags. including Western Rev., Choice, Coastlines, South & West, N.Y. Rev. Books; poems included in: Arts of Russia, Primer of Experimental Poetry, The Portable 20th Century Russian Reader, 20th Century Russian Poetry, play (musical) Icaria, 1986; co-editor, co-translator (with Vladimir Markov) Modern Russian Poetry, 1967. Democrat. Avocations: opera, gardening, reading, swimming, sunning, Home: 1266 Water St Mount Etna IA 50841-8345

SPARKS, RICHARD EDWARD, aquatic ecologist; b. Kingston, Pa., Apr. 19, 1942; s. Raymond Earl and Marjory Bernice (Coffey) S.; m. Ruth Marie Cole, Dec. 30, 1966; children: Amelia Mary, Carolyn Denise. BA, Amherst Coll., 1964; MS, U. Kans., 1968; PhD, Va. Poly Inst., 1971. Instr. Meth. Tchr. Tng. Coll., Uzuakoli, Nigeria, 1964-66; rsch. assoc. Va. Poly. Inst. and State U., Blacksburg, 1971-72; asst. aquatic biologist Ill. Natural History Survey, Champaign, 1972-77, assoc. aquatic biologist, 1977-80, aquatic biologist, 1980—. Contbr. articles to profl. jours.; author and co-author 11 spl. publs. and refereed symposia. Mem. Ill. Chpt. Am. Fisheries Soc. (pres. 1980, north cen. div. exec. com. 1980), Sigma Xi. Home: RR 1 Ipava IL 61441-9801 Office: Ill Natural History Survey River Rsch Lab Box 590 Havana IL 62644

SPARROW, LARRY CLINTON, marketing executive; b. Louisville, Aug. 30, 1947; s. Ezra Clinton and Audrey Catherine (Lee) S.; m. Carol Anne McClung, Sept. 13, 1980; 1 child, Kelsey Leigh. BA in Sociology/

Psychology, Western Ky. U., 1969. Sales rep. Diamond Sci., Des Moines, 1985-87, biol. product mgr., 1987-88, nat. sales tng., mktg. mgr., 1988-89, nat. sales mgr., 1989-90; mgr. sales tng. Diamond Sci./Haver/Cuter a Bayer Co., Shawnee Mission, Kans., 1990-92, mgr. sales/mktg. tng., 1992—. Co-recipient 21 Gold Addy awards, 19 Silver Addy awards, 9 Bronze Addy awards. Mem. Am. Mgmt. Assn. Republican. Mem. Disciples of Christ. Home: 6210 W 158th Pl Overland Park KS 66223-3488 Office: Bayer Agr Divsn/Animal Health PO Box 390 Shawnee Mission KS 66201-0390

SPARTZ, ALICE ANNE LENORE, retired retail executive; b. N.Y.C., May 14, 1925; d. John Francis and Alice Philomena (Murray) Rattenbury; m. George Eugene Spartz, Oct. 29, 1949; children: Mary Elizabeth, James, Barbara, Anne, Thomas, William, Michael, John, Matthew, Clare, Robert, Richard. Student, Wright Coll., 1945-47, No. Ill. U., 1950; AA, Triton Coll., 1987. Svc. rep. Ill. Bell Tel., Chgo., 1945-46; stewardess United Airlines, Denver, 1947-49; mgr. Family Life League Resale Shop, Oak Park, Ill., 1987-95; retired, 1995. Mem. Cicero (Ill.) Cmty. Coun., 1967-69; mem. Park Dist. Oak Park Com., 1973-74; active Ill. Right to Life Com., Chgo., 1971—, Com. Pro-Life Caths., Chgo., 1992—; former bd. dirs. Ill. Pro-Life Coalition, Family Life League; vol. canteen workers ARC, Chgo., 1942-45. Mem. St. Edmunds Womens Club. Democrat. Roman Catholic. Office: 226 N Ridgeland Oak Park IL 60302

SPAULDING, DANIEL ALEXANDER, small business owner; b. San Juan, P.R., June 28, 1963; s. Marcel George and Frances Wilma (Small) S. BA, Beloit (Wis.) Coll., 1986. Account mgr. Internat. Bus. Cons., Wilmette, Ill., 1986-88; pres. Creditel, Inc., Oak Park, Ill., 1988—. Bd. dirs. Episcopal Charities, 1987-91, Anti-Cruelty Soc., 1988—; trustee Beloit Coll., 1994—. Mem. Ill. Mortgage Bankers Assn., N.W. Assn. Realtors (bd. dirs. 1989—), Assn. Profl. Mortgage Women (bd. dirs. 1990—), Ill. Assn. Mortgage Brokers, Soc. Loan Underwriters, Nat. Corvette Restorers Soc., Rotary. Office: Creditel 6429 North Ave Oak Park IL 60302-1028

SPEAK, THOMAS JOHN, software engineer; b. St. Paul, May 29, 1958; s. John Stephen and Gladys Mae (Specker) S.; m. Janice Marie Holzrichter, Oct. 8, 1988; children: Jennifer Marie, Kathleen Ann. BEE, U. Minn., 1980, MS, 1982. Software engr. Siemens, Mpls., 1983—. Mem. IEEE. Home: 4575 Arrowood Ln Plymouth MN 55442

SPEAR, ALLAN HENRY, state senator, historian, educator; b. Michigan City, Ind., June 24, 1937; s. Irving S. and Esther (Lieber) S. BA, Oberlin Coll., 1958; MA, Yale U., 1960, PhD, 1965. Lectr. history U. Minn., Mpls., 1964-65, asst. prof., 1965-67, assoc. prof., 1967—; mem. Minn. State Senate, St. Paul, 1973—, chmn. jud. com., 1983-93; chmn. crime prevention com., 1993—; pres. Minn. State Senate, 1993—; vis. prof. Carleton Coll., Northfield, Minn., 1970, Stanford U., Palo Alto, Calif., 1970. Author: Black Chicago, 1967. Mem. Internat. Network Gay and Lesbian Elected Offcls., Com. on Suggested State Legislation of Coun. of State Govts.; bd. dirs. Family and Children's Svc. of Mpls. Mem. Dem. Farm Labor Party. Home: 2429 Colfax Ave S Minneapolis MN 55405-2942 Office: Minn State Senate 27 State St Saint Paul MN 55107-1408

SPEARMAN, DAVID LEROY, elementary education educator, administrator; b. Chgo., June 4, 1959; s. Lee Roy and Florida Lee (Gordon) S.; m. Tina R. Smith, Aug. 20, 1994; 1 child, David Gordon. Student, Loyola U., Chgo., 1977-78, Moody Bible Inst., 1978-81; BA in Comm., Columbia Coll., Chgo., 1986; postgrad., DePaul U., 1987-89, Chgo. City Wide Colls., 1988—, Chgo. State U., 1992-93; MA in Ednl. Adminstrn., Governor's State U., 1994. Cert 03 tchr., lang. arts endorsement K-8, adminstrv. 020 endorsement, speech endorsement, Ill. Prodr., announcer, talk show host Sta. WYCA, Hammond, Ind., 1983-88; music dir., announcer Sta. WCFJ, Chicago Heights, Ill., 1988-89; tchr. Evangelical Christian Sch., Chgo., 1987-89; truant officer Chgo. Bd. of Edn., 1990-92; tchr. Truth Elem. Sch., Chgo., 1992—; 4th grade facilitator Truth Elem. Sch., Chgo., 1994-95, 3rd grade facilitator 1995-96, chair dept. sci., 1993—, chair social com., 1994-95, dir. summer sch., 1994, coord. social ctr., 1994; freelance camera operator Sta. WCFC-TV, Chgo., 1989—, Cen. City Prodns., Chgo., 1992—, Chgo. Cable Acess Prodns., 1992—; CEO Dana Prodns. Inc. Author: (booklet) Teacher's Opinions of the Security and Safety Climate in Chicago Public Schools at Cabrini Green, 1993; contbr. articles to profl. jours., mags. and newspapers. Youth counselor Cook County Juvenile Detention Ctr., 1979-80; scoutmaster Boy Scouts Am., Chgo., 1992-94, asst. scoutmaster Chgo. Housing Authority scouting program, 1992-94; bd. dirs. ISO Aeronautics Chgo. Bd. Edn., 1994—. Recipient Tchr. Incentive award Oppenheimer Found., 1993-94, 95-96, Rochelle Lee Found. award, 1996-97; named one of Outstanding Young Men of Am., 1989; chgo. Found. for Edn. grantee, 1993-94, 94-95, 95-96; tchr. honoree Chgo. State of City Address Dinner by Mayor Richard Daley, 1995; honored by visitation by U.S. Sec. of Edn. Richard Riley and Chgo. Pub. Schs. CEO Paul Vallas, 1995. Mem. Chgo. Tchrs. Union, Moody Bible Inst. Alumni, Columbia Coll. Alumni Govs. State U. Alumni, Internat. Platform Assn. Pentecostal. Office: Sojourner Truth Elem Sch 1443 N Ogden Ave Chicago IL 60610-1007

SPEARS, LAURA ELIZABETH, special education educator; b. Osawatomie, Kans., Jan. 21, 1953; d. Jonathan Henry and Hazel Irene Spears. BSE, Emporia State U., 1979; postgrad., Kans. State U., 1983, Wichita State U., U. Kans., 1989. Tchr. spl. edn., dept. chmn. Unified Sch. Dist. 261, Haysville, Kans., 1975—; cons. dir. Kans. State H.S. Activities Assn., Topeka, 1990—. Bd. dirs. Am. Cancer Soc., Wichita, 1991-92; dir. competition Kans. Spl. Olympics. Mem. Haysville Edn. Assn. (negotiation team 1975—), Transition Coun. Mentally Retarded. Office: USD # 261 2100 W 55th St S Wichita KS 67217-4165

SPEARS, RICHARD R., bank executive; b. 1939. Pres., CEO First Am. Bank Mich. NA, Kalamazoo. Office: First Am Bank Mich NA 108 E Michigan Ave Kalamazoo MI 49007*

SPEAS, CHARLES STUART, personnel director; b. Phila., Jan. 1, 1944; s. Austin LeRoy and Peggy Elaine (Drake) S.; m. Julie Ellen Royce, Apr. 10, 1965; children: Eric S. Speas, Robert Austin Speas. Student, Tri-State Coll., U. Notre Dame, Purdue U. Lic. agt. in life, accident and health ins., Ind. Sr. scheduling coord. Excel Industries, Elkhart, Ind., 1966-73; corp. dir. pers. EFP Corp., Elkhart, 1973—; cons. various Elkhart, Goshen area bus., 1980—. Contbr. articles profl. jours. Participant Soviet/Am. Conf. on Trade and Econ. Cooperation, Kremlin, 1991. With USAF, 1962-66. Mem. Ind. Pers. Assn., Goshen Indsl. Club (recipient cert. of appreciation 1990), Soc. for Human Resources Mgmt., Elkhart C. of C. (task force on healthcare availability/cost). Republican. Home: 23683 River Dr Goshen IN 46526-9000 Office: EFP Corp 223 Middleton Run Rd Elkhart IN 46516-5429

SPECK, HILDA, retired social services administrator; b. Stalybridge, Cheshire, Eng., Mar. 2, 1916; came to U.S., 1923; d. John Robert and Rose Ethel (Tymns) Smith; m. Willmot Hilton Speck, Sept. 4, 1937 (dec. Jan 1968); foster children: Barbara Ann Beranek Renfrow, Winifred June Beranek Aguilar. Student, Community Coll., Flint, Mich. Lic. social worker, Mich. Founder of Social Svc. Dept. and dir. social svcs. The Salvation Army, Flint, 1945-86; mem. establishing com. 4C Child Care Agy.; life mem. Salvation Army Adv. Bd., Flint, Mich. Acting founding Safe House for domestic violence victims, Flint, 1976-80; mem. convalescent home com. Ch. Women United; adminstr. clothing distbn.; dir. disaster rehab. program Salvation Army; mem. original planning com. Planned Parenthood Orgn.; mem. aux. McLaren Regional Med. Ctr., Salvation Army, Flint, League of Mercy, Ch. Salvation Army, Centennial Planning Com., Flint; mem. Genesee County CD; mem. organizing com. Big Sisters Agy., Flint, Shelter for Homeless Women. Recipient Hands of Mercy award The Salvation Army, 1967, Centennial Youth award The Salvation Army, 1965, 20 Yr. Svc. award Big. Bros. of Genesee County, award for exceptional svc. The Salvation Army, 1993, Mich. Cmty. Svc. award Ky. Col's. Way, 1996; named Women of Week local radio sta., 1957, Mich. winner Sr. Citizens KFC Colonel's award program for comty. svc., 1996. Mem. Coun. Social Agys., Genesee County Commn. on Aging (v.p. 1971—), GLS Counties Health Planning Coun. Bd., Genesee County Emergency Task Force, Zonta. Salvation Army. Home: 1041 Leisure Dr Flint MI 48507-4058

SPEDALE, VINCENT JOHN, manufacturing executive; b. Chgo., Dec. 2, 1929; s. Joseph and Mildred (Satarino) S.; m. Joan Deeny, Apr. 11, 1953; children: Kathleen, Joseph, Barbara, Judith, Robert, Anthony. BSME, Ill. Inst. Tech., 1952; MS in Indsl. Engring., Wayne State U., 1959; postgrad. in mgmt., MIT, 1977. With Chrysler Corp., 1952-70; v.p. mfg. solar gas turbine div. Internat. Harvester Co., San Diego, 1971-73; v.p. mfg. truck div. Internat. Harvester Co., Chgo., 1973-78, v.p., gen. mgr. engine div., 1978-81; pres. machine tool div. ACME Precision Products, Inc., Detroit, 1982-87; v.p. ops. ICM Industries, Inc., Chgo., 1987-91; CEO, K-Whit Inc, air conditioning equipment mfrs., Fishers, Ind., 1993-94; pres. Hwy. Recycling Sys. Corp., Wasau, Wis., Vinco Mgmt. Cons., Wheaton, Ill.; bd. dirs. Spartan Diesel Co., Harbor Beach, Mich.; CEO Forum Group, Inc., Indpls., 1991-92, Union City (Ind.) Body Co., 1992-93; mfg. cons. Kamaz Truck and Diesel Engine Mfr., Naberezhniye-Chelny, Tartarstan, Russia, 1995—. Mem. Soc. Automotive Engrs. Roman Catholic. Home: 1260 Shady Ln Wheaton IL 60187-3722

SPEER, HUGH W., education educator; b. Olathe, Kans., May 28, 1906; s. Henry W. and Amelia (Shonehair) S.; m. Catherine Edwards (dec. May 1995); children: Marcia Speer Snook, Mary Lynn Shea. AB, Am. U., 1928; MA, George Washington U., 1933; PhD, U. Chgo., 1950. From tchr. to prin. Fredonia (Kans.) H.S., 1928-36; prin. Hays (Kans.) Jr.-Sr. H.S., 1936-42; Am. field dir. ARC, Italy, 1943-45; from dir. veterans advisement to prof. U. Mo., Kansas City, 1945-76; trustee, chmn. Johnson County C.C., Overland Park, Kans., 1967—; trustee Faith Village, Overland Park, 1979-84; columnist Olathe Daily News, 1988-95. Author: Case of the Century, 1968, Funny Things on the Way to the Supreme Court, 1988. Fulbright grantee, 1951, 61, 64. Democrat. Avocations: woodworking, farming. Home: 6304 Sherwood Ln Shawnee Mission KS 66203 Office: Johnson County C C 12345 College Blvd Overland Park KS 66210

SPEER, MAX MICHAEL, special education educator; b. Granite City, Ill., Nov. 10, 1949; s. Max J. and Betty L. (Butler) S.; m. Anita Christine Patton, June 12, 1971; children: Michael, Max. BS in Edn., So. Ill. U., Edwardsville, 1973. Cert. tchr. elem. social and emotional disorders. cert. tchr. learning disabled and educable mentally handicapped, Ill. Tchr. jr. high spl. edn. Granite City Sch. Dist., 1973—. With U.S. Army, 1969-70. Mem. Coun. for Exceptional Children. Episcopalian.

SPEER, NANCY GIROUARD, educational administrator; b. Mankato, Minn., Sept. 14, 1941; d. Jared and Katherine (Schmitt) How; m. Robert L. Girouard, Aug. 29, 1964 (dec. Mar. 1983); children: Robert James Girouard, Mark Jared Girouard; m. David J. Speer, Dec. 21, 1985. BA, Wellesley Coll., 1963; MA in Tchg., Wesleyan U., 1965; cert. mgmt., Smith Coll., 1985. Tchr. secondary sch. Bunnell H.S., Stratford, Conn., 1964-65; tchr., class advisor Lincoln Sch., Providence, 1965-69; substitute tchr. Mankato, 1972-74; pub. info. dir. City of Mankato, 1974-78; univ. editor, dir. pub. affairs forum Mankato State U., 1978-79; comms. mgr. Humphrey Inst., U. Minn., Mpls., 1980-83, dir. external rels., 1983-87, dir. devel. and external rels., 1987—; dir. devel. Breck Sch., Mpls.; mem. steering com. Minn. Meeting, Mpls., 1990—; chair bd. Minn. Newspaper Found., St. Paul, 1985-91. Contbr. articles to mags. and periodicals; photographer for publs. and newspapers. Bd. dirs., vice-chair Cabrini House, Mpls., 1993—; bd. dirs., sec. Minn. Ctr. for Book Arts, Mpls., 1990—; bd. dirs. Minn. Landmark Ctr., St. Paul, 1994—; dir. Minn. Women's Campaign Fund, Mpls., 1994—; mem. Leadership Mpls., Mpls. C. of C., 1982. Bush Leader fellow, 1985-87. Home: 23235 St Croix Trail N Scandia MN 55073 Office: Breck Sch 123 Ottawa Ave N Minneapolis MN 55422

SPEICHER, CARL EUGENE, pathologist; b. Carbondale, Pa., Mar. 21, 1933; s. William Joseph and Elizabeth Marcella Speicher; m. Mary Louise Walsh; children: Carl Jr., Gregory, Erik. BS in Biology, Kings Coll., 1954; MD, U. Pa., 1958. Diplomate Am. Bd. Pathology. Rotating med. intern U. Pa. Hosp., Phila., 1958-59, resident in pathology, 1959-63; commd. 2d lt. USAF, 1963, advanced through grades to col., 1977; chief lab svcs. 7520th USAF Hosp., N.Y.C., 1963-66, USAF Wright-Patterson, Dayton, Ohio, 1966-70; fellow clin. pathology Upstate Med. Ctr., Syracuse, N.Y., 1970-71; chair pathology Wilford Hall USAF Med. Ctr., Lackland AFB, Tex., 1971-77; fellow in clin. pathology SUNY, Syracuse, 1970-71; dir. clin. labs. Ohio State U. Hosps., Columbus, 1977—; prof. pathology Ohio State U., Columbus, 1977—; dir. clin. labs. VA Outpatient Clinic, Columbus, 1989-94; co-dir. clin. labs. James Cancer Hosp., Columbus, 1990—; vice chair pathology Ohio State U., 1992—. Co-author: Choosing Effective Laboratory Tests, 1983; author: The Right Test, 1990, 2d edit., 1993; mem. editl. bd. Am. Jour. Clin. Pathology, 1983-91, Archives of Pathology and Lab. Medicine, 1984-95. Fellow Am. Coll. Pathologists, Royal Soc. Medicine (Eng.); mem. AMA, Am. Soc. Clin. Pathologists, Ohio State Med. Assn., Ohio Soc. Pathologists, Ctrl. Ohio Soc. Pathologists, Acad. Medicine Columbus and Franklin County, Alpha Omega Alpha. Office: Ohio State U Hosps 410 W 10th Ave Columbus OH 43210-1240

SPEICHER, GARY DEAN, financial planner; b. Marshalltown, Iowa, Oct. 13, 1947; s. Rodney William and Pearl Arlene (Gunderson) S.; m. Susan R. Lorensen, Aug. 25, 1968; children: Christopher, Amy, Matt, Sarah. BS in Agr. Journalism, Iowa State U., 1969. With sales Northwestern Mut. Life, Cedar Rapids, Iowa, 1972-75; mgr. New Eng. Life, Cedar Rapids, 1975-79; field v.p. All Am. Life, Chgo., 1979-82; owner, mgr. Fin. Planning Svcs., Cedar Rapids, Iowa, 1982—. With Iowa Army N.G., 1970-78. Mem. Am. Soc. CLU and ChFC, Nat. Assn. LifeUnderwriters; Internat. Assn. Fin. Planners. Republican. Methodist. Home: 3222 Lindsay Ln SE Cedar Rapids IA 52403-1956

SPEIER, JOHN LEO, JR., retired chemist; b. Chgo., Sept. 29, 1918; s. John L. and Mary Jane (Dickman) S.; m. A. Louise Kimmel, Oct. 21, 1944; children—Susan, Genevieve, Dorothy, Margaret, John L. III, Thomas J. B.Sc., St. Benedict's Coll., 1941; M.Sc., U. Fla., 1943; Ph.D., U. Pitts., 1947. Naval Stores research fellow U. Fla., 1941-43; research fellow Mellon Inst., Pitts., 1943; sr. fellow Mellon Inst., 1947-56; mgr. organic research Dow Corning Corp., Midland, Mich., 1956-69; scientist in corp. research Dow Corning Corp., 1969-75, sr. scientist in corp. research, 1975-93; retired, 1994. Contbr. numerous articles to profl. jours., 1950—; holder 100 patents prodn. organosilicon compounds and allied products. Named Indsl. Research and Devel. Scientist of Yr. Indsl. Research/Devel. mag., 1978. Mem. AAAS, Am. Chem. Soc. (Frederick Stanley Kipping award 1990), Sigma Xi. Office: Dow Corning Corp Dept Research Midland MI 48640

SPEISER, JAMES WARREN, electrical engineer, computer systems consultant; b. N.Y.C., Sept. 2, 1949; s. Warren Henry and Eileen Catherine (Lupo) S.; m. Phoebe Louise Winholt, Nov. 25, 1977; children: Selene Elizabeth, Samantha Emily, Jonathan David. BEE, U. Mo., Rolla, 1977, MEE, 1979. Owner Speiser's Dental Lab., 1974—; engr. McDonnell Douglas Astronautics Co., St. Louis, 1979-81; sr. engr. McDonnell Douglas Missile Systems Co., St. Louis, 1981-83; lead engr. McDonnell-Douglas Astronautics Co., St. Louis, 1983-86, unit chief, 1986-89; cons., developer microcomputer database mgmt. applications systems, 1986—; St. Louis sect. chief McDonnell Douglas Tng. Systems, 1990-92; cons. Computer Applications Cons., St. Louis, 1993—. With USCG, 1970-74. Mem. IEEE, AIAA, Assn. for Computing Machinery, Am. Legion, Eta Kappa Nu. Republican. Methodist. Home: 721 Stone Canyon Dr Ballwin MO 63021-7163 Office: Computer Applications Cons 2129 Barrett Station Rd Saint Louis MO 63131-1606

SPELLMAN, GEORGE GENESER, SR., internist; b. Woodward, Iowa, Sept. 11, 1920; s. Martin Edward and Corinne (Geneser) S.; m. Mary Carolyn Dwight, Aug. 26, 1942; children: Carolyn Anne Spellman Rambow, George G. Jr., Mary Alice, Elizabeth Spellman-Chrisinger, John Martin Pile-Spellman, Loretta Suzanne Spellman Hoffman. B.S., St. Ambrose Coll., 1940; M.D., State U. Iowa, 1943. Diplomate Am. Bd. Internal Medicine. Intern Providence Hosp., Detroit, 1944; resident in internal medicine State U. Iowa, Iowa City, 1944-46; practice medicine specializing in internal medicine Mitchell, S.D., 1948-50, Sioux City, Iowa, 1950-91; instr. Coll. Medicine U. Iowa, 1975-77, clin. assoc. Coll. Medicine, 1977-95, ret., 1995; mem. Iowa Bd. Med. Examiners, 1989-95; instr. schs. nursing St. Vincent Hosp. and Luth. Hosp.; bd. dirs. St. Joseph Mercy Hosp. (merged with St. Vincent's Hosp. into Marian Health Ctr. 1977), 1977-80, 87-90, mem. staff, 1950-91, chief of staff, 1963; bd. dirs. St. Vincent's Hosp., 1965-77, also bd. dirs.; clin. assoc. prof. medicine State U. Iowa; bd. dirs. Mid-Step Svcs. Mentally Handicapped, Hospice of Siouxland, Marian Health Ctr., 1974-80, 89-91, also co-founder, 1st pres., chmn. dependency unit, founder renal dialysis unit, 1964, St. Joseph Mercy-St. Vincent's Hosps., 1977-89. Contbr. articles to med. jours. Ordained deacon Cath. Ch., 1988; vol. cons. Siouxland Community Health Ctr., 1993—. Capt. M.C., U.S. Army, 1946-48. Decorated Knight of St. Gregory (Vatican); named Internist of Yr., Iowa Soc. Internal Medicine, 1987; recipient Laureate award Iowa Chpt. ACP, 1991, Humanitarian award Siouxland Community, 1991. Fellow ACP; mem. AMA, Am. Acad. Scis., Iowa State Med. Soc., Woodbury Med. Soc., Am. Soc. Internal Medicine, Iowa Soc. Internal Medicine, Am. Thoracic Soc., Iowa Thoracic Soc., Am. Heart Assn., Iowa Heart Assn., Am. Geriatric Soc., Alpha Omega Alpha. Home: 3849 Jones St Sioux City IA 51104-1447

SPELLMAN, ROBERT LUTHER, journalism educator; b. Grandfield, Okla., Apr. 8, 1937; s. Robert L. and Flossie (Crane) S.; m. Susan O'Rilla Edwards, Dec. 27, 1958; children: Virginia Black, Robin, Elizabeth Spellman, Catherine Roberts. BA, Baldwin-Wallace Coll., 1959; MS, Mich. State U., 1966; JD, Cleve. State U., 1977. Bar: Ohio 1979. Reporter Lima (Ohio) Citizen, 1959-62, Democrat and Chronicle, Rochester, N.Y., 1962-68; pure waters dir. County of Monroe, Rochester, N.Y., 1968-70; dep. city mgr. City of Rochester, 1970-72; v.p., gen. mgr. Bldg. Systems Park Ctr., Cleve., 1972-78; dir. real estate devel. Nationwide Devel. Co., Columbus, Ohio, 1978-82; pvt. practice law Columbus, Ohio, 1981-85; assoc. prof. journalism So. Ill. U., Carbondale, 1985—. With USAR, 1954-62. Mem. Soc. Profl. Journalists. Home: 301 W Broad St Jonesboro IL 62952 Office: So Ill Univ Sch of Journalism Carbondale IL 62901

SPELLMIRE, SANDRA MARIE, systems analyst, programmer; b. San Francisco, Feb. 20, 1950; d. Robert Joseph and Catherine Louise (Sockett) S. BS, Calif. State U., L.A., 1977. Project controls analyst Ralph M. Parsons Co., Pasadena, Calif., 1978-81, C.F. Braun & Co., Alhambra, Calif., 1981-84; configuration mgr. software systems Burroughs Corp., Santa Ana, Calif., 1984-85; sr. scientific analyst, programmer Electronic Data Systems, L.A., 1985, Denver, 1985-87, Mpls., 1987-89; software cons. Shared Resource Mgmt., St. Louis Park, Minn., 1989-91, Shoreview, Minn., 1991-92, TWF & Assocs., Edina, Minn., 1992-93; sr. programmer analyst Harmon Glass, Golden Valley, Minn., 1993-94, Keane Inc., Bloomington, Minn., 1994—.

SPELSON, NICHOLAS JAMES, engineering executive, retired; b. Oak Park, Ill., Sept. 10, 1923; s. James and Constance (Rellos) S. BS in Mech. Engring., Ill. Inst. Tech., Chgo., 1947. Mech. engr. pvt. industry Chgo., 1947-60; mech. engr. USAF, 1960-65, Def. Logistics Agy., Dept. of Def., Chgo., 1965-82; br. chief ops. Def. Logistics Agy.-Def. Contract Adminstrn. Svcs. Region, Chgo., 1982-90; br. chief quality assurance engring. Def. Logistics Agy.-Def. Contracts Dist., Chgo., 1990-94. With U.S. Army, 1943-45. Mem. Am. Legion, Hellenic Profl. Soc. Ill. Greek Orthodox.

SPENCE, JOSEPH PATRICK, advertising executive; b. Wilmington, Ohio, Oct. 26, 1964; s. Phillip and Esther Ann (Brannon) S.; m. Lynnette Sue Eury, Nov. 7, 1987; 1 child, Nicholas. Student, So. State U., 1988. Farm hand Family Garm, Martinsville, Ohio, 1973-81; mgr. used parts Martinsville Auto Parts, 1979-84; ramp loader, sorter Airborne Express, Wilmington, Ohio, 1982-95; CEO, owner Hot Looks Products, Fayetteville, 1993—. Office: Hot Looks Products 5415 Murray Corner Rd Fayetteville OH 45118

SPENCE, MICHELE JEANNE, editor, writer; b. Smithville, N.C., July 14, 1940; d. Grant Fletcher Mollring and Margaret Mary (Kuhl) Baker; m. Stan Stephen Spence, Apr. 14, 1960; children: Scott David, Robert Lewis. BA summa cum laude, U. Md., 1970. Sr. editor Cliffs Notes, Inc., Lincoln, Nebr., 1979—. Author: Shadow Play, 1981, Rebekka Moon, 1983. Miller Analogies Test Preparation Guide, 1992. Democrat. Home: 5147 S 37th St Lincoln NE 68516-4527 Office: Cliffs Notes Inc 4851 S 16th St Lincoln NE 68512-1211

SPENCE, WAYNE JAY, naval aviation officer; b. Willow Springs, Mo., Dec. 14, 1924; s. Lyman Cecil and Charlotte May (Pottle) S.; m. Sibyl Jean Lovan, Dec. 23, 1945; children: Ronald Jay, Deborah Jean Spence Mast, Mary Judith. BS in Edn., Southwestern Mo. U., 1948. Commd. ensign USN, 1945, advanced through grades to lt. comdr., 1972, retired, 1995. Author book of poems. Srs. tchr. Trinity Bapt. Ch., Willow Springs, 1994-95; lay minister So. Bapt. Ch., 1980-95. Mem. Ozarks Genealogical Soc., S.W. Ozarks Genealogical Soc. Democrat. Home: PO Box 37 Willow Springs MO 65793

SPENCER, BETTY K., marketing professional; b. Portsmouth, Ohio, May 8, 1929. BA, Ohio State U., 1951, MBA, 1953. V.p. Dwight Spencer & Assocs., Columbus, Ohio, 1958—. Mem. Am. Mktg. Assn., Chi Omega. Office: Dwight Spencer & Assocs 1240 Grandview Ave Columbus OH 43212-3428

SPENCER, CLYDE DAVID, civil engineer, land surveyor; b. Hazard, Ky., Sept. 16, 1963; s. Clyde and Mattie C. (Gabbard) S. BS in Engring., U. Alaska, 1986. Lic. profl. engr. Civil engr. Rogina & Assoc., Joliet, Ill. With USAF. Home: 230 Moore Ct Apt 1C Grayslake IL 60030-2744

SPENCER, DALE A., medical products executive; b. 1945. BS in Engring., U. Maine, 1968; MBA, So. Ill. U., 1973. With Kuken Steel Co., Cin., 1973-75; sales and mktg. mgr. Baxter Travenol Labs., Mpls., 1975-80; with Scimed Life Systems Inc., Osseo, Minn., 1980—, pres., CEO, 1982, now chmn. and CEO, 1994; also, pres. (subsidiary) Scimed, Inc., Osseo, Minn. With USAF, 1968-73. Office: Scimed Life Systems Inc 1 Scimed Pl Osseo MN 55311-1565

SPENCER, DONALD SPURGEON, historian, academic administrator; b. Anderson, Ind., Jan. 29, 1945; s. Thomas E. and Josephine (Litz) S.; m. Pamela Sue Roberts, June 19, 1965; 1 child, Jennifer Wynne. BA, Ill. Coll., 1967; PhD, U. Va., 1973. Asst. prof. history Westminster Coll., Fulton, Mo., 1973-76, Ohio U., Athens, 1976-77; from asst., assoc. to full prof., assoc. dean, asst. provost U. Mont., Missoula, 1977-90; provost SUNY, Geneseo, 1990-93; pres. Western Ill. U., Macomb, 1994—. Author: Louis Kossuth and Young America, 1978, The Carter Implosion: Jimmy Carter and the Amateur Style of Diplomacy,1989; contbr. articles to jours. in field. With U.S. Army, 1968-71, Korea. Woodrow Wilson Found. fellow, 1968; Danforth Found. univ. teaching fellow, 1971. Mem. Phi Beta Kappa. Congregationalist. Home: 2001 Wigwam Hollow Rd Macomb IL 61455-9336 Office: W Ill Univ Office of the President Sherman Hall Macomb IL 61455

SPENCER, JOHN ROBERT, social service administrator; b. Kansas City, Mo., July 8, 1949; s. Howard Laurence and Elizabeth Wilma (Lehmuth) S.; m. Janice Lynn Bingaman, Dec. 26, 1968 (div. Sept. 1981); children: Christopher John, Matthew Gerald, Heather Elizabeth; m. Candice Rae Hogden, Oct. 8, 1988. BA, U. No. Colo., 1971; MDiv, Nashotah (Wis.) House, 1974. Vicar St. Michael & All Angels Ch., Denver, 1974-75; rector St. Andrews Ch., La Junta, Colo., 1975-78; detective La Junta Police (Colo.) Police Dept., 1978-83; investigator Denver County Coroner, 1983-84; F & I mgr. Sanchez Car/Truck Ctr., La Junta, 1984-86; detective La Junta Police Dept., 1986-89; program supr. Homme Home for Boys, Wittenberg, Wis., 1990-94; sect. chiff Wis. Divsn. Youth Svcs., Wausau, Wis., 1994—. Author: Icequake!, 1995. Pres. bd. Picketwire Players, La Junta, 1982-88; sec. Lake Jacqueline Protection Dist., Sharon, Wis., 1991-95; bd. dirs. Ctrl. Wis. Area Cmty. Theatre, Stevens Point, Wis., 1994-96. Mem. Colo. Criminal Intelligence Assn. (bd. dirs. 1987-89). Lutheran. Home: 7208 S Jacqueline Lake Custer WI 54423

SPENCER, MARK EDWARD, management consultant; b. Ann Arbor, Mich., Nov. 24, 1954; s. Robert and Patricia (McIlharge) S.; 1 child, Gabrielle. BA, Eastern Mich. U., 1977. Sr. mgr. Great Lake Shipping Co., Ann Arbor, 1973-83; cons. A.T. Hudson, Paramus, N.J., 1983; food and beverage mgr. Ann Arbor Inn, 1984; treas. S.S.& H. Mgmt., Ann Arbor, 1984-86; pres. C.T. Mgmt., Ann Arbor, 1986-88; dir. ops. Epicuren Mgmt., Kalamazoo, 1988-89, A.T. Hudson, Paramus, N.J., 1989—. Mem. Nat. Restaurant Assn., Mich. Restaurant Assn. (bd. dirs. Detroit chpt. 1982-85), Washtenaw Restaurant Assn. (pres. 1982), Traverse City Restaurant Assn.

(pres. 1981). Roman Catholic. Home: 1215 W Washington Ann Arbor MI 48103-4245

SPENCER, MILTON HARRY, economics and finance educator; b. N.Y.C., Mar. 25, 1926; m. Roslyn Pernick; children: Darcy, Robin, Cathy. BS, NYU, 1949, MA, 1950; PhD, Cornell U., 1954. Instr. econs., fin. Queens Coll., N.Y.C., 1949-52; research asst. Cornell U., Ithaca, N.Y., 1952-54; economist Armour & Co., Chgo., 1954-55; assoc. prof. Wayne State U., Detroit, 1955-62, prof., 1962-91, prof. emeritus, 1991—; vis. prof. U. Hawaii, Honolulu, 1965-66; lectr., U.S., Australia, Europe, Asia, Africa, South Am.; cons. U.S. Dept. State, Washington, 1959—, govts. of Chile, Israel, Eng., France, Italy, Australia, Hong Kong, Japan, Rep. of China and various domestic and fgn. corps. Author: Basic Economics, 1951, Economic Thought, 1954, Business and Economic Forecasting, 1958, Managerial Economics, 3 edits., 1959-68, Contemporary Economics, 8 edits., 1971-93; various monographs: contbr. numerous articles to profl. jours. Served as cpl. U.S. Army, 1943-45. Recipient Disting. Service awards from U.S. Dept. State, Govts. of Chile, Israel, France, Spain, England, Italy, Belgium. Mem. Am. Econ. Assn., Am. Fin. Assn., Nat. Assn. Bus. Economists.

SPENCER, REX LEROY, secondary education educator; b. Kendallville, Ind., Jan. 29, 1944; s. Richard Donald and Mildred Francis (Fourman) S.; m. Diana Carole Land, Nov. 21, 1981; children: Katie Jo, Emily Paige. BS, The Defiance Coll., 1966; MA, Ball State U., 1970. Cert. tchr., Ohio. Tchr. Ansonia (Ohio) High Sch., 1966-80, Ansonia (Ohio) Middle Sch., 1982-86, Ansonia (Ohio) High Sch., 1986—; instr. Edison State C.C., Piqua, Ohio, 1983-88, Defiance (Ohio) Coll., summer 1989-92. Named Outstanding Am. History Tchr., Darke County DAR, 1992. Mem. NEA, Ohio Edn. Assn., Ansonia Edn. Assn. (pres. 1976-77, treas. 1991—), Nat. Coun. for the Social Studies, Ohio Coun. for the Social Studies, Defiance Coll. Alumni Assn. (bd. mem. 1976-79, v.p. 1979-80, pres. 1980-82). Methodist. Office: Ansonia High Sch 200 W Canal St Ansonia OH 45303-0279

SPENCER, WILLIAM EDWIN, telephone company executive, engineer; b. Kansas City, Mo., Mar. 22, 1926; s. Erwin Blanc and Edith Marie (Peterson) S.; student U. Kansas City, 1942; A.S., Kansas City Jr. Coll., 1945; BEE, U. Mo., 1948; postgrad. Iowa State U., 1969; m. Ferne Arlene Nieder, Nov. 14, 1952; children: Elizabeth Ann, Gary William, James Richard, Catherine Sue. Registered profl. engr., Kans. With Southwestern Bell Telephone Co., Kansas City, Mo., 1948-50, Topeka, 1952-61, sr. engr., 1966-69, equipment maintenance engr., 1969-76, engring. ops. mgr., 1976-79, dist. mgr., 1979—; mem. tech. staff Bell Telephone Labs., N.Y.C., 1961-62, Holmdel, N.J., 1962-66; pres., owner W.E. Spencer Co.; mem. U.S. Senatorial Club, 1985—. Mem. Rep. Presdl. Task Force, 1984—; supervising judge Shawnee County Election Commn.; trustee, bd. dirs. Brookwood Covenant Ch. With AUS, 1950-52. Recipient Best Kans. idea award Southwestern Bell Telephone Co., 1972, cert. of appreciation Kans. Miss Teen Pageant, 1984, Rep. Presdl. Legion of Merit, 1992—. Mem. IEEE, Kans. Engring. Soc., Nat. Soc. Profl. Engrs., Topeka Engrs. Club (pres.), Telephone Pioneers Assn. (pres., life Sunflower Chpt.), Nat. Geog. Soc., Kans. Hist. Soc., Am. Assn. Ret. Persons, U. Mo.-Columbia Alumni Assn., Nat. Travel Club. Republican. Patentee in field. Home: 3201 SW Macvicar Ct Topeka KS 66611-1800 Office: 220 SE 6th Ave Topeka KS 66603-3507

SPERO, KEITH ERWIN, lawyer; b. Cleve., Aug. 21, 1933; s. Milton D. and Yetta (Silverstein) S.; m. Carol Kohn, July 4, 1957 (div. 1974); children: Alana, Scott, Susan; m. 2d, Karen Weaver, Dec. 28, 1975. BA, Western Res. U. 1954, LLB, 1956. Bar: Ohio 1956. Assoc. Sindell, Sindell & Bourne, Cleve., 1956-57, Sindell, Sindell, Bourne, Markus, Cleve., 1960-64; ptnr. Sindell, Sindell, Bourne, Markus, Stern & Spero, Cleve., 1964-74, Spero & Rosenfield, Cleve., 1974-76, Spero, Rosenfeld & Bourne, L.P.A., Cleve., 1977-79, Spero & Rosenfield Co. L.P.A., 1979—; tchr. bus. law U. Md. overseas div., Eng., 1958-59; lectr. Case-Western Res. U., 1965-69; instr. Cleve. Marshall Law Sch. of Cleve. State U., 1968-75; nat. panel arbitrators Am. Arbitration Assn. Trustee Western Res. Hist. Soc., 1984—, exec. com., 1992—, v.p., chmn. libr. display and collections com., 1992-95, chmn. history mus. com., 1995—. 1st lt. JAGC, USAF, 1957-60; capt. Res., 1960-70. Fellow Am. Acad. Matrimonial Lawyers; mem. ABA, Ohio Bar Assn., Cleve. Bar Assn., Cuyahoga County Bar Assn., Ohio Acad. Trial Lawyers (pres. 1970-71), Assn. Trial Lawyers Am. (state committeeman 1971-75, bd. govs. 1975-79, sec. family law litigation sect. 1975-76, vice-chmn. 1976-77, chmn. 1977-79), Am. Bd. Trial Advs., Order of Coif, Cleve. Racquet Club, The Club at Soc. Ctr., Hawthorne Valley Country Club, Dugway Creek Yacht Club (commodore 1984-88), Masons, Phi Beta Kappa, Zeta Beta Tau, Tau Epsilon Rho. Jewish (trustee, v.p. congregation 1972-78). Author: The Spero Divorce Folio, 1966, Hospital Liability for Acts of Professional Negligence, 1979. Home: 2 Bratenahl Pl Cleveland OH 44108-1183 Office: Spero & Rosenfield 440 Leader Bldg E 6th and Superior Cleveland OH 44114-1214

SPERO, LESLIE WAYNE, linen service and distribution company executive; b. Youngstown, Ohio, July 3, 1926; s. Harry and Sadie (Weiskopf) S.; m. Elaine Grossfield, Jan. 25, 1953; children: Rand Kevin, Laurie Diane. BA summa cum laude, UCLA, 1948; postgrad., Harvard U. Purchasing agt. United Svc. Co., Youngstown, 1948-53, v.p., dir., 1953-68, chmn., pres., 1968—; v.p., dir. United Paper Svc. Co., Youngstown, 1953-68, chmn., pres., 1968—; pres. TRSA, Hallendale, Fla., 1982-83; bd. dirs. Dollar Savs. and Trust, Youngstown., Performance Plus Advisors Inc., Palm Beach, Fla., Performance Plus Asset Mgmt. Corp. Past pres. Child Guidance Ctr., Jewish Federation Youngstown, Community Relations Council, Am. Jewish Com., Youngstown; past bd. dirs. Child and Adult Mental Health Ctr., March of Dimes Nat. Found., Youngstown, Friends Am. Art Butler Art Gallery, Jewish Community Ctr.; past chmn. Community Chest, March of Dimes Nat. Found., Com. Heritage Manor; past trustee Rodef Sholem Temple, Bellfaire Home for Exceptional Children, Cleve.; past commdr. U.S. Power Squadron, Youngstown; past mem. Am. Jewish Com., Young Leadership Cabinet Nat. United Jewish Appeal; bd. dirs. Heritage Manor Home for Aged; bd. dirs. Frenehman's Creek Property Owners Assn. Served to lt. (j.g.) USN., 1944-47. Mem. MENSA, Youngstown C. of C., Gold Key, Phi Beta Kappa, Phi Eta Sigma. Clubs: Youngstown, Squaw Creek Country, Frenchmens Creek Country. Lodges: Rotary, Elks. Home: Frenchman's Creek Palm Beach Gardens FL 33410 Office: 555 N Meridian Rd Youngstown OH 44509-1232

SPETH, GERALD LENNUS, education and business consultant; b. Logan, Utah, July 14, 1934; s. Fredrick William and Elizabeth LaVern (Nuttall) S.; m. Dora Goff, Aug. 11, 1955; children: Camille, Michael Gerald, Mark Alan, Janell, Doreen. BS, Utah State U., 1956; MBA, Ind. U., 1969; EdD, Ball State U., 1988. Auditor Ernst & Ernst, Salt Lake City, 1956, 58-59; officer 1st and 2d lt. U.S. Army, 1956-58, officer capt. to col., 1959-82; controller Columbia Club, Indpls., 1982-83; sr. v.p. Allied Fidelity Corp., Indpls., 1983-85; adj. faculty Ind. Cen. U., Indpls., 1982-85; prof., dir. grad. bus. progs. U. Indpls., 1985—; cons. in mgmt. and strategic planning. Counselor in stake presidency, bishop, welfare dir., mission pres., high councilor LDS Ch., 1965—. Recipient Legion of Merit, 1971-80, Bronze Star medal, 1966. Mem. Am. Soc. Mil. Comptrollers, U.S. Govt. Accts. Assn., Beta Gamma Sigma, Sigma Iota Epsilon, Alpha Kappa Psi, Kappa Delta Psi, Delta Mu Delta. Home: 8337 Goldfinch Cir Indianapolis IN 46256-1629 Office: U Indpls 1400 E Hanna Ave Indianapolis IN 46227-3630

SPHIRE, RAYMOND DANIEL, anesthesiologist; b. Detroit, Feb. 12, 1927; s. Samuel Raymond and Nora Mae (Allen) S.; m. Joan Lois Baker, Sept. 5, 1953; children—Suzanne M., Raymond Daniel, Catherine J. BS, U. Detroit, 1948; MD, Loyola U., Chgo., 1952. Diplomate Am. Bd. Anesthesiology. Intern Grace Hosp., Detroit, 1952-53; resident Harvard Anesthesia Lab.-Mass. Gen. Hosp., 1953-55; attending anesthesiologist Grace Hosp., Detroit, 1955-72, dir. dept. inhalation therapy, 1968-70; sr. attending anesthesiologist, dir. dept., dir. dept. respiratory therapy Detroit-Macomb Hosps. Assn., 1970—, trustee, 1978—, chief of staff, 1980—; clin. asst. prof. Wayne State U. Sch. Medicine, 1967—; clin. prof. respiratory therapy Macomb Community Coll., Mount Clemens, Mich., 1971—; examiner Am. Registry Respiratory Therapists, 1972—; insp. Joint Rev. Com. Respiratory Therapy Edn., 1972—. Co-author: Operative Neurosurgery, 1970, First Aid Guide for the Small Business or Industry, 1978. With AUS, 1944-45; 1st lt. M.C., USAF, 1952. Fellow Am. Coll. Anesthesiologists, Am. Coll. Chest Physicians; mem. AMA, Am. Soc. Anesthesiologists, Wayne County Soc. Anesthesiologists (pres. 1967-69), Am. Assn. Respiratory Therapists, Soc. Critical Care Medicine, Detroit Athletic Club, Country Club of Detroit, Cumberland Club (Portland, Maine), Severance Lodge. Roman Catholic. Home: 19874 Westchester Dr Clinton Township MI 48038 Office: 119 Kercheval Ave Grosse Pointe MI 48236-3618

SPICE, DENNIS DEAN, financial marketing consultant; b. Rochester, Ind., Feb. 7, 1950; s. Donnelly Dean and Lorene (Rhodes) S.; m. Linda Kay Buehler, Oct. 1, 1971; children: Kristie Lorene, Danielle Deanne. AA, SUNY, Albany, 1974; BA, Eastern Ill. U., 1978; MBA, U. Ill., Urbana, 1985. Employee benefits mgr. Eastern Ill. U., Charleston, 1977-80; disbursements officer State Univs. Retirement System, Champaign, Ill., 1980-81, asst. dir. adminstrn., 1981-85, assoc. exec. dir., 1985-90, exec. dir., 1991-95; pres., CEO Instnl. Advisors, Ltd., Champaign, 1995—; mem. dean's adv. bd. Ea. Ill. U. Lumpkin Coll. Bus. and Applied Scis.; bd. dirs. Ea. Ill. Univ. Found. Staff sgt. USMC, 1968-77; Vietnam. Mem. Econ. Club Chgo., Champaign C. of C., Execs. Club of Chgo., Rotary. Republican. Home: 5008 W Bluebill Rd Champaign IL 61821-9512 Office: Instnl Advisors Ltd 1909 Fox Dr Champaign IL 61820-1909

SPICER, JOHN AUSTIN, physicist; b. Rock Springs, W.Va., Sept. 25, 1930; s. Ernest Marvin and Ruth (Stevens) S.; m. Erika Gruendig, 1959; children: Cynthia, Michael, Marilynn. BS, U. Wyoming, 1956, MS, 1957; PhD, U. Freiburg, Germany, 1962. Mathematician Geotech. Corp., Laramie, Wyo., 1956-57; physicist Goodyear Aerospace Corp., Litchfield, Ariz., 1962-63; head engr. Aeroject Gen. Corp., Azusa, Calif., 1963-64; mathematical analyst North Am. Aviation Info. Systems Div., Downey, Calif., 1973-76; program mgr. Chrysler Space Systems Div., New Orleans, La., 1966-68; sr. research mathematician U. Dayton Research Inst., Ohio, 1968-70; ops. research analyst U. McCall Printing Corp. Systems Dept., Dayton, 1970-71; mathematician Systems Dyamics Br. AF Flight Dynamics La., 1971-72; physicist Radar and Microwave Tech. Br. Af Avionics lab., 1972-74, Analysis and Evaluation Br. AF Avionics Lab., 1974-89; physicist tech group, target recognition br. AF Avionics Lab., Dayton, Ohio, 1989—. Contbr. articles on neural networks, wavelets and fractal methodology to profl. jours. Home: 4666 North St Rt 235 Conover OH 45317-9601 Office: WL/AARA Bldg 23 2010 5th St Dayton OH 45433-7001

SPIDELL, DANIEL M., JR., business executive; b. Grand Rapids, Mich., Feb. 9, 1924; s. Daniel M. and Nell C. (Vandenberg) S.; children: Lori, Lance (dec.). Gen. mgr. Byrne Electric, Rockford, Mich., 1982-86; pres. Code Cons., Inc., Grand Rapids, 1986—; mem. adv. bd. Underwriters Labs., Northbrook, Ill., 1989—; other testing labs.; liaison Montec-elcon, Germany, 1990—. Patentee cutting process for stencils for cemetery markers. Mem. 1st ward Zoning Bd., Grand Rapids. Buck sgt. U.S. Army, 1943-46. Mem. The Edelweis (founding 1980). Lutheran. Office: Code Cons 1345 Monroe Ave NW Grand Rapids MI 49505-4670

SPIEGELBERG, HARRY LESTER, retired paper products company executive; b. New London, Wis., Apr. 24, 1936; s. Harry Henry and Gladys Louise (Kalt) S.; m. Bonnie Faye Ludden, Jan. 23, 1960; children: Susan Faye Spiegelberg Schuldes, Sharon Louise Spiegelberg Kozlowski, Stephen Harry, Scott Charles. BSChemE, U. Wis., 1959; MS, Inst. Paper Chemistry, Appleton, Wis., 1963, PhD, 1966; MBA, U. Chgo., 1980. Teaching asst. U. Wis. Coll. Engring., Madison, 1957-59; engr. Kimberly-Clark Corp., Neenah, Wis., 1959-61, rsch. scientist, 1965-68, mgr. new concepts, 1968-73, dir. R & D, 1973-84, v.p. consumer tissue rsch., 1985-92; v.p. tech. and patent strategy Kimberly-Clark Corp., 1992-93, v.p. tech. transfer, 1993-96, ret., 1996; mem., past chmn. vis. com. dept. chem. engring. U. Wis., 1985—, mem., past chmn. indsl. liaison coun. Coll. Engring., 1987-93; founder, vice chmn. Paper Industry Hall of Fame; pres. Ctr. Project Inc. Contbr. chpt. to book; patentee in nonwovens and tissue fields. Pres. Ctr. Project, Inc. Capt. C.E. USAR, 1959-67. Recipient Disting. Svc. citation U. Wis., 1986. Congregationalist. Home: 3624 S Barker Ln Appleton WI 54915-7038

SPIEGEL-HOPKINS, PHYLLIS MARIE, psychotherapist; b. Chgo., Oct. 28, 1947; d. Joseph Frank and Marie Ann (Hejhal) Spiegel; m. Daniel Mark Hopkins, Jan. 14, 1984. BSE, Chgo. State U., 1968, MA in History, 1972; MA in Clin. Psychology, Ill. Sch. Profl. Psychology, Chgo., 1988; D in Clin. Hypnotherapy, Am. Inst. Hypnotherapy, Santa Ana, Calif., 1991. Cert. tchr., Ill; cert. clin. hypnotherapist. Tchr. Holy Cross Grammar Sch., Chgo., 1968-69, Chgo. Bd. Edn., 1969-81, Mt. Asissi Acad., Lemont, Ill., 1981-82; police officer Chgo. Police Dept., 1982—; psychotherapist pvt. practice Chgo., 1988—; mem. Am. Bd. Hypnotherapy. Mem. ACA, Nat. Guild Hypnotists, S.W. Hypnosis Soc., Assn. for Study Dreams, Internat. Med. and Dental Hypnotherapy Assn., C.G. Jung Inst. Chgo., Assn. Past-Life Therapy and Rsch. (life), Internat. Assn. Counselors and Therapists (life), Am. Psychotherapy and Med. Hypnosis Assn., Fraternal Order Police. Office: PO Box 185 Bedford Park IL 60499-0185

SPIEK, JOHN ROBERT, JR., accountant; b. Evergreen Park, Ill., Sept. 23, 1947; s. John Robert and Wilma Ann (Korienek) S.; m. Joanne L. Markowski, Apr. 29, 1972; children: Jennifer Lynn, Christopher Jon, Rebecca Ann. Student, U. Ill., Chgo., 1965-66, Chgo. Jr. Coll., 1966-68; BS in Acctg., No. Ill. U., 1970; MBA in Acctg., DePaul U., 1974. Asst. mgr. plant acctg. Sherwin-Williams Co., Chgo., 1970, mgr. plant acctg., 1970-74; plant contr. Sherwin-Williams Co., Dayton, Ohio, 1974-77; fin. analyst Sherwin-Williams Co., Cleve., 1977, mgr. gen. acctg., 1977-78, dir. acctg. and planning, 1978-87; acctg. mgr. Sola Ophthalmics, Phoenix, 1987-88; contr. Sola/Barnes-Hind, Phoenix, 1988-89; pvt. practice, Peoria, Ariz., 1989-91; dir. finance Curtis Industries, Inc., Eastlake, Ohio, 1991-93; v.p. mktg. Acctg. Practice Builders, Inc., Medina, Ohio, 1993-95; sec./treas. North Coast Bus Svcs., Inc., Concord, Ohio, 1995—; cons. Cactus Collection Specialists, Glendale, Ariz., 1988-90. Treas. St. Ambrose Youth Ministry, Brunswick, Ohio, 1983-87; pres. Eagle Lakes Homeowners Assn., Brunswick, 1986-87; mem. fin. coun. St. Gabriel's Ch., 1995—. Recipient Jaycee of Month award Northmont Jaycees, 1975, Keyman award, 1977. Mem. Inst. Mgmt. Accts. Roman Catholic. Office: North Coast Bus Svcs Inc 9895 Weathersfield Rd Concord OH 44060-6827

SPIELMAN, CHRIS, professional football player; b. Canton, Ohio, Oct. 11, 1965. Student, Ohio State U. With Detroit Lions, 1988—. Recipient Lombardi award, 1987; named to Sporting News Coll. All-Am. team, 1986, 87, Pro Bowl team, 1989-91. Office: Detroit Lions 1200 Featherstone Rd Pontiac MI 48342-1938*

SPIER, ROBERT FOREST GAYTON, anthropologist, educator; b. Seattle, June 12, 1922; s. Leslie and Erna (Gunther) S.; m. Veva Drake, Mar. 15, 1951; children—Martha, Stephen. B.A., U. Calif. at Berkeley, 1947; M.A., Harvard, 1949, Ph.D., 1954. Instr. U. Minn., Mpls., 1951-52; mem. faculty U. Mo., Columbia, 1949-51, 52—; prof. U. Mo., 1966—, prof. emeritus, 1987—; acting dir. U. Mo. (Coll. Gen. Studies), 1980-81; vis. asso. prof. U. Oreg., Eugene, 1962-63; tchr. summers Portland (Oreg.) State Coll., 1957, U. Wis., Madison, 1958, U. Calif. at Berkeley, 1965, 66, 73, Ind. U., Bloomington, 1967. Author: From Hand of Man, 1970, Surveying and Mapping, 1970. Pres. Friends of Pub. Library, Columbia, 1969, Columbia Swim Parents Assn., 1970; mem. Bd. Elec. Examiners Columbia, 1971-77; trustee Norwegian-Am. Mus., Decorah, Iowa, 1985—. Served with AUS, 1942-46. NATO fellow, 1960-61. Fellow Am. Anthrop. Assn. Club: Columbia Track. Home: 708 Morningside Dr Columbia MO 65201-5987

SPIERING, NANCY JEAN, accounting executive; b. Park Ridge, Ill., Apr. 15, 1958; d. Richard Arthur and Helen Mary (Henry) S. BS, De Paul U., 1982; postgrad., U. Minn., North Ctrl. Coll., 1989-90. CPA, Ill. Staff acct. Ruzicka & Assocs., Inc., Chgo., 1980-84; supr. acctg. Cargill, Inc., Carpentersville, Ill., 1984-87, regional asst. acctg. mgr., 1988-89; sr. internat. tax acct. Cargill, Inc., Minnetonka, Minn., 1989-90; acctg. mgr. Barnant Co. divsn. Cole Parmer, Barrington, Ill, 1990—; mgr. Twin Pines Janitorial Service, Elgin, Ill., 1980-89; pvt. practice tax service, Elgin, 1984-89. Official Michael Bakalis campaign, Chgo., 1980; vol. Disabled Am. Vets., Cin., 1987. Mem. Am. Soc. CPA's, Ill. Soc. CPA's, Chgo. Soc. Women CPA's. Roman Catholic. Club: Dundee Dart (Ill). Home: 7521 Gilmore Ave Las Vegas NV 89129 Office: Bonanza Materials Inc PO Box 92170 Henderson NV 89009-2170

SPIESS, ELIOT BRUCE, biologist, educator; b. Boston, Oct. 13, 1921; s. George Nicholas and Rena (Bunce) S.; m. Luretta Davis; children: Arthur Eliot, Bruce Davis. AB, Harvard Coll., 1943; AM, Harvard U., 1947, PhD, 1949. Instr. biology Harvard U., Cambridge, Mass., 1947-52; asst. prof. U. Pitts., 1952-56, assoc. prof., 1956-65, prof., 1965-66; prof. U. Ill., Chgo., 1966-89, prof. emeritus, 1989—. Editor: Papers on Animal Polulation Genetics, 1962; author: (book) Genes in Populations, 1977, 2d edit., 1989; contbr. articles to profl. jours. 1st lt. U.S. Army Air Force, 1943-45. Grantee NSF, 1972-83, U.S. Atomic Energy Commn., 1966-72. Fellow AAAS; mem. Soc. for the Study of Evolution (assoc. editor 1956-58, 67-69, editor of Evolution 1975-78), Am. Soc. Naturalists (pres. 1981).

SPINA, ANTHONY FERDINAND, lawyer; b. Chgo., Aug. 15, 1937; s. John Dominic and Nancy Maria (Ponzio) S.; m. Anita Phyllis, Jan. 28, 1961; children—Nancy M. Spina Okal, John D., Catherine M. Spina Samatas, Maria J. Spina Samatas, Felicia M. B.S. in Social Sci., Loyola U., Chgo., 1959; J.D., DePaul U., 1962. Bar: Ill. 1962. Assoc. Epton, Scott, McCarthy, & Bohling, Chgo., 1962-64; sole practice, Elmwood Park, Ill., 1964-71; pres. Anthony & Spina, P.C., 1971-84, Spina, McGuire & Okal, P.C., 1985—; atty. Leyden Twp., Ill., 1969-89, Village of Rosemont, Ill., 1971; counsel for Pres. and dir. Cook County Twp. Ofcls. of Ill., 1975—; counsel for exec. dir. Ill. State Assn. Twp. Ofcls., 1975-96; counsel Elmwood Park Village Bd., 1967-89, Norwood Park St. Lighting Dist., 1988—, various Cook County Twps. (including DuPage, 1980-82, Maine, 1981—, Norwood Park, 1982—, Wayne, 1982-84), all Cook County Hwy. Commrs. Traffic Fine Litigation, Hanover Twp. Mental Health Bd., 1991—, Glen Edens Assn., 1994—; mem. Elmwood Park Bldg. Code Planning Commn. Bd. Appeals. Recipient Lacodaire medal, Dean's Key Loyola U.; Loyola U. Housing awards, 1965, 71, 76; award of appreciation Cook County Twp. Ofcls., av rating Martindale-Hubbel. Mem. Ill. Bar Assn., ABA, Chgo. Bar Assn., West Suburban Bar Assn. of Cook County (past chmn. unauthorized practice of law sect.), Am. Judicature Soc., Justinian Soc. Lawyers, Ill. State Twp. Attys. Assn. (past v.p., pres. 1982-86, dir. 1986—), Nat. Inst. Town and Twp. Attys. (past v.p., pres. 1993-95, Ill. del.), Montclare/Leyden C. of C., Edgebrook C. of C. (past bd. dirs.), Nat. Assn. Italian Am. Lawyers, World Bocce Assn. (dir.), Blue Key, Delta Theta Phi, Tau Kappa Epsilon, Pi Gamma Mu. Roman Catholic. St. Rocco Soc. of Simbario (auditor-trustee Chgo.), KC (scribe, trustee, past grand knight, bldg. corp. dir. 1967—, Calabresi in Am. Orgn. (bd. dirs. 1990—). Author Rosemont Village Ordinances, 1971; Elmwood Park Bldg Code, 1975, Leyden Twp. Codified Ordinances, 1987. Office: 7610 W North Ave Elmwood Park IL 60707

SPINNER, LEE LOUIS, accountant; b. Hillsboro, Ill., Nov. 9, 1948; s. John Louis and Clara Mae (Brown) S. BS in Acctg., U. Ill., 1971, MAS in Acctg., 1972; MS in Taxation, DePaul U., 1983. CPA, Ill. Sr. tax acct. Ernst & Young, Chgo., 1972-78; dir. tax returns and audits Sunbeam Corp., Chgo., 1978-82; dir. tax compliance Sara Lee Corp., Chgo., 1982-83; mgr. tax compliance AM Internat., Inc., Chgo., 1983-85; mgr. taxes Household Mfg., Inc., Prospect Heights, Ill., 1985-89; mgr. internat. taxes Pittway Corp., Chgo., Ill., 1990—; instr. tax tng. program Ernst & Young, 1975-78. Tax advisor Sta. WIND, Call Your Acct., Chgo., 1977-78; sec. Grant Park Accts. Softball League, Chgo., 1976-77. Mem. AICPA, Ill. C.P.A. Soc. Democrat. Roman Catholic. Club: Top Social Athletic (Chgo.). Lodges: Moose, K.C. Home: 923 Stonehedge Ln Palatine IL 60067-7114

SPIRES, ROBERTA LYNN, court clerk; b. Gary, Ind., Sept. 4, 1952; d. Merle Russell and Kathryn Dias (Felts) Harris; m. Richard John Badovinich, Aug. 16, 1975 (div. 1989); m. Patrick Robert Spires, Mar. 14, 1992; 1 child, Zachary Robert. Grad. high sch., Griffith, Ind. Dep. clk. U.S. Bankruptcy Ct., Gary, 1970-80; chief dep. clk. U.S. Bankruptcy Ct., 1980—. Mem. Fed. Ct. Clks. Assn., Fed. Bar Assn. (lectr., cert. 1984). Democrat. Roman Catholic. Home: 719 N Rueth Dr Griffith IN 46319-3817 Office: US Bankruptcy Ct 610 Connecticut St Gary IN 46402-2550

SPITSBERGEN, DOROTHY MAY, children's healthcare specialist; b. Eaton Rapids, Mich., May 13, 1932; d. Herbert Madison and Eva (Bunker) Van Aken; m. Merlin D. Spitsbergen, Dec. 27, 1952; children: Karen Richardson, Jan, Raymond (dec.), John, Claire Cooper. Student, Mich. State U., 1950-53; BS in Sociology, Oakland U., 1973, MA in Teaching Early Childhood Edn., 1980. Cert. child life specialist. Child life specialist Crittenton Hosp., Rochester, Mich., 1980-94; hosp. play cons. Hong Kogn Hosps., 1994-95; instr. Oakland U., 1996—; lectr. Oakland U., 1981—, Wayne State U., Macomb C.C., 1982—, Mott C.C., Flint, Mich., 1992; creator Pediatric Edn. Program, 1981—, Child Body Safety Program, 1985—; state presentor in field. Co-author: Infants and Toddlers in the Hospital, 1993. Bev Erikson Meml. grantee, 1987. Mem. Assn. for Care Children's Health (sec. state chpt. 1984-86, nat. presenter 1984, 87, state presentor 1983, 86), Child Life Coun., Rochester Tuesday Musicale Club (past pres., v.p., sec.), Delta Psi Kappa. Democrat. Home: 3959 Ella Mae St Oakland MI 48363-2854 Office: 3959 Ellamae Oakland MI 48363

SPITZ, TIMOTHY JOE, banker; b. Mattoon, Ill., Feb. 15, 1962; s. Daniel Steven and Essie Annabel (Thornton) S.; m. Renee Ann Lindsay, Sept. 8, 1984; children: Lindsay Renee, Andrew Thornton. AS, Lake Land Coll., Mattoon, Ill., 1982; BS in Fin., Ea. Ill. U., 1984. Loan officer Heartland Fed. Savs. and Loan, Mattoon, 1984-87, asst. v.p., 1987-89; asst. sec. Okaw Bldg. and Loan, s.b., Mattoon, 1989-91, v.p., 1991—. Bd. dirs. Consol. Unified Sch. Dist. #2 Sch. Bd., Mattoon, 1991-93, Am. Cancer Soc., Mattoon, 1986-92. Mem. Mattoon C. of C. (mem. housing devel. com. 1992-93), Kiwanis (Disting. Svc. award 1985-86). Home: 408 Wabash Ave Mattoon IL 61938 Office: Okaw Bldg and Loan sb 720 Broadway Mattoon IL 61938

SPLAWN, P. JANE, English language educator; b. Campobello, S.C., Aug. 12, 1956; d. Boyzillie and Ossie L. (Burgess) S. BA, Queens Coll., 1980; MA, Marquette U., 1982; PhD, U. Wis., 1988. Rsch. asst. Marquette U., Milw., 1980-82; tchg. asst. U. Wis., Madison, 1982-87; asst. examiner Ednl. Testing Svc., Princeton, N.J., 1988-89; asst. prof. Purdue U., West Lafayette, Ind., 1989—; intern U.S. C. of C., Washington, 1980; initiator, judge Helen Bass Williams Award, Purdue U., 1989—; initiator Leonora Woodman Women's Lit. Award, Purdue U., 1995; judge Gwendolyn Brooks Lit. Awards, Purdue U., 1993—. Editor: (newsletters) Reaching Out to Deaf and Hard of Hearing Citizens, 1986, Equity, 1984-86; author: (critical edit.) Black Women Writers: Carrie L.M. Figgs and Carrie Williams Clifford, Vol. 3, 1996, (chpt.) Black Women Film & Video Artists, 1996; mem. adv. bd. Collegiate Press, 1992—, Modern Fiction Studies, 1992—. Vol. direct svcs. Women's Transit Authority, Madison, 1986, bd. dirs., 1986-87; vol. Centro Hispano, Madison, 1987; mem. Wis. Coalition for Minorities with Disabilities, Madison, 1986-88, African Am. studies com., Purdue U., 1989-92, women's studies com., 1990—; mem. Poverty & Race Rsch. Coun., Washington, 1992—; faculty advisor Students in Liberal Arts Minorities, Purdue U., 1991-93; mem. 1,604 African American Women in Defense of Ourselves, 1991. Spartan Mills scholar, 1973, Milliken scholar, 1973, tuition scholar Dartmouth Sch. of Criticism, 1988; internat. travel grantee Purdue Rsch. Found., 1992, 93; faculty exchange U. Hamburg/Purdue U., 1993; Ford Found. fellow Ctr. for Study of Black Lit. and Culture, U. Pa., 1992. Mem. MLA, Coll. Lit. Assn., African Lit. Assn. (women's caucus 1995—), Women in Theatre Project, Black Theatre Network, Women & Minorities Adv. Com. (chair 1990—), Sigma Upsilon. Home: 201 Trace Two West Lafayette IN 47906 Office: Purdue U Dept English West Lafayette IN 47907

SPLETE, HOWARD HENRY, JR., counselor educator; b. Watertown, N.Y., Nov. 7, 1931; s. Howard Henry and Minnie Bertha (Peterjohn) S.; m. Marlene Barbara Rebits Mar. 4, 1961; children: Andrew, Charles, Nancy. BA, St. Lawrence U., 1953; MS, Syracuse U., 1956; PhD, Mich. State U., 1968. Counselor pub. schs., N.Y., Mich., Fed. Republic Germany, 1958-70; counselor educator Wayne State U., Detroit, 1970-78, Oakland U., Rochester, Mich., 1978—. Served with U.S. Army, 1953-55. Mem. Nat. Career Devel. Assn. (pres. 1993), Am. Counseling Assn. (cert.), Mich. Personnel and Guidance Assn. (Disting. Service award 1979), Internat. Assn. Ednl. and Vocat. Guidance. Author: The Consulting Process 1975; Career Development, 1975; Counseling: An Introduction, 1984. Office: Oakland U 522 O'Dowd Hall Rochester MI 48309

SPLINTER, JOHN PAUL, clergy member, minister; b. Redwing, Minn., Aug. 18, 1945; s. Gerrald Edward and Eileen Eloise (McCreary) S.; m. Marcia Lee Carlson, Aug. 10, 1968; children: Gretchen Nicole, Kirsten

Erica, Megan Alison. BA, Bethel Coll., 1968; MCE, Bethel Sem., 1970; MA, Lindenwood Coll., 1988. Ordained to ministry Presbyn. Ch., 1972. Area dir. Evang. Ch. Alliance, Winnipeg, Manitoba, Can., 1970-75, Young Life Campaign, St. Louis, 1975-80; broker Lawton-Byrne-Bruner, St. Louis, 1980-84; clergy Ctrl. Presbyn. Ch., St. Louis, 1984—; dir. "Second Chpt." divorce recovery, St. Louis, 1985-91; bd. dirs. Nat. Assn. Single Adult Leaders, Grand Rapids, Mich., 1989-90, New Identity, St. Louis, 1986-90. Author: Second Chapter, 1987, Complete Divorce Recovery Handbook, 1992, The Healing Path, 1993; contbg. author: Singles Ministry Handbook, 1988, Single Adult Ministry, 1989;. Mem. Second Chpt. (bd. dirs., founder 1985-92), Nat. Assn. Single Adult Leaders. Presbyterian. Office: Ctrl Presbyn Ch 7700 Davis Dr Clayton MO 63105-2616

SPODEN, JAMES EDWARD, otolaryngologist; b. Guttenberg, Iowa, Jan. 16, 1949; s. John Michael and Elinor Theresa (Adams) S.; m. Janet Lynn Thompson, Apr. 22, 1978; children: Elizabeth, Erika, Natalie. BA, U. Iowa, 1971, MD, 1974. Diplomate Am. Bd. Otolaryngology. Intern Butterworth Hosp., Grand Rapids, Mich., 1974-75; resident in otolaryngology U. Iowa, Iowa City, 1976-79, assoc. fellow, 1979-80; emergency physician Galesburg (Ill.) Cottage Hosp., 1975-76; otolaryngologist Finley Hosp., Dubuque, Iowa, 1980-84, Mercy Hosp., Dubuque, 1980-84, Mercy and St. Luke's Hosp., Cedar Rapids, Iowa, 1984—; cons. otolaryngologist Delaware County Hosp., Manchester, Iowa, 1982—, Anamosa Cmty. Hosp., Anamosa, Iowa, 1984—. Contbr. articles to profl. jours. Bd. dirs. Amana Colonies Golf Course, Amana, Iowa, 1995—, Linn County Iowa Club, Cedar Rapids, 1995—. Served with USAF, 1967-69. Fellow ACS, Am. Acad. Facial Plastic Surgery; mem. Pinehurst Country Club, Amana Colonies Golf Club (bd. dirs. 1990—), Cedar Rapids Country Club. Roman Catholic. Home: 2260 Country Club Pkwy SE Cedar Rapids IA 52403-1639

SPOHR, FREDERICK STEPHEN, sales professional; b. Cin., July 23, 1949; s. Frederick Andrew and Alice Marie (Rengers) S.; m. Joyce Wyse, Feb. 16, 1991; 1 child, Andrea. BSBA, Miami U., Oxford, Ohio, 1971, MBA in Mgmt., 1977. Account mgr. Pease Co., Hamilton, Ohio, 1972-77; mgr. ops. Farera Enterprises, Cin., 1977-78; sales mgr. Continental Can Co., Chgo., 1978-88; regional mgr. Graco/LTI, Franklin Park, Ill., 1988-89; sales mgr. Safelite Glass Co., Chgo., 1990; dir. sales Packaging Resources, Lake Forest, Ill., 1991-93; mid-west regional mgr. Advanced Monobloc, Inc., Hermitage, Pa., 1993—. Mem. Soc. for Advancement of Mgmt. (bd. dirs. Cin. chpt. 1976-82, internat. bd. dirs. 1989-93), Inst. Packaging Profls., Miami U. Alumni Assn. (bd. dirs. Chgo. chpt. 1988—, nat. bd. dirs. 1995—). Roman Catholic. Home and Office: 1721 E Suffield Dr Arlington Heights IL 60004-2253

SPORE, KEITH KENT, newspaper executive; b. Milw., May 29, 1942; s. G. Keith and Evelyn A. (Morgan) S.; divorced; children: Bradley, Julie; m. Kathy Stokebrand. BS in Journalism, U. Wis., Milw., 1967. City editor Milw. Jour. Sentinel, 1977-81, asst. mng. editor/news, 1981-89, mng. editor, 1989-91, editor, 1991-95, editl. page editor, 1995, pres., 1995—. Author: (novels) The Hell Masters, 1977, Death of a Scavenger, 1980. With U.S. Army, 1961-64. Recipient Freedom of Info. award Soc. Profl. Journalists, 1995; named Mass Comms. Alumnus of Yr., U. Wis.-Milw., 1994. Mem. Milw. Press Club. Office: Milw Jour Sentinel 333 W State St PO Box 661 Milwaukee WI 53203-1500

SPOTTSVILLE, SHARON ANN, counselor; b. St. Louis; d. Robert F. and Elberta M. (Thompson) Hunter; children: Raymon L., Rodney L. BA, Cleve. State U., 1980, MEd, 1984. Lic. clin. counselor, Ohio. Counselor asst. pvt. practice psychiatry Cleve., 1980-84; counselor, social worker Harambee Svcs. to Black Families, Cleve., 1984-89; coord. parenting devel. rsch. projects Child Guidance Ctr., Cleve., 1989-94; case mgr. supr. Murtis H. Taylor-Multi Svcs. Ctr., Cleve., 1994—; presenter workshops; cons. and trainer in field. Co-author: Parenting Plus. Mem. ACA, Assn. Multi-Cultural Counseling and Devel., Ohio Mental Health Counselors Assn. Home: 19014 Winslow Rd Shaker Heights OH 44122 Office: Murtis H Taylor Multi Svcs Ctr 13422 Kinsman Rd Cleveland OH 44120-4410

SPRADLEY, DAVID LEE, music producer; b. Seoul, Democratic Republic of Korea, May 18, 1954; came to U.S., 1958; s. Russell Lee and Nancy Ann (Monesmith) S.; m. Judy Myland, Nov. 17, 1983; 1 child, Bruce. Student, Oakland U., Rochester, Mich., 1972-75. Composer Atomic Dog, 1981 (Number 1 Billboard charts); producer Let's Go All the Way, 1985 (Top Ten Billboard); producer, composer Fly Girls, 1986 (Number 1 Billboard charts); performer: (albums) George Clinton, Parliament-Funkadelic, Michael Henderson, Bootsy Collins, Chapter 8, Our Daughters Wedding, Sly Fox, Tom Browne, Boogie Boys, numerous others. Office: Spraad Prodns PO Box 37419 Oak Park MI 48237-0419

SPRAGUE, DONALD EUGENE, educational administrator; b. Boston, Sept. 16, 1955; s. Ronald James and Evelyn Marie (O'Connell) S. BA in Classics, Williams Coll., 1977; M Pastoral Studies, Loyola U., Chgo., 1981. Cert. 6-12 tchr., Ill. Tchr. classics Loyola Acad., Wilmette, Ill., 1977—, dir. testing, 1978—, dir. honors program, 1984—, dir. student activities, 1995-96, assoc. headmaster for student life, 1996—. Recipient Educator of Yr. award Loyola Acad., 1983, Language Leadership award Ill. Fgn. Lang. Leadership Coun., 1991. Mem. Ill. Classical Conf. (sec. 1981-84, treas. 1984—, Latin Tchr. of Yr. award 1990), Chgo. Classical Club (pres. 1995—), Williams Coll. Alumni Assn. Chgo. (admission chmn. 1980-86, exec. bd. 1980-86). Roman Catholic. Office: Loyola Acad 1100 Laramie Ave Wilmette IL 60091-1021

SPRANDEL, DENNIS STEUART, management consulting company executive; b. Little Falls, Minn., June 1, 1941; s. George Washington and Lucille Margaret (Steuart) S.; AB, Albion Coll., 1963; MEd, U. Ariz., 1965; PhD, Mich. State U., 1973. Grad. teaching asst. U. Ariz., Tucson, 1964-65; dir. athletics, Owen Grad. Center Mich. State U., East Lansing, 1965-68; prof., dir. student teaching Mt. St. Mary's Coll., 1968-70; exec. dir. Mich. AAU, 1974-81, mem. numerous nat. coms., 1974-81; mem. U.S. Olympic Com., 1974-77; pres., chmn. bd. Am. Sports Mgmt., Ann Arbor, 1976—, Am. SportsVision, 1981—, Am. Sports Rsch., 1977—, Sprandel Group, 1984—; pres. Nat. Sports & Entertainment, Inc., 1984—, Sprandel Assocs., 1984—, registered rep., 1988—; bd. dirs. Nat. Golden Gloves, 1980—, bd. trustees, 1986, Port Huron TV Project, 1985—; pres. Detroit Golden Gloves Charities; pres. adminstrv. bd. Detroit Golden Gloves, 1985—; Bd. dirs. Mich. Sports Hall of Fame, 1976—; Cons. in field. Recipient Detroit Striders award, 1978; Emerald award, 1979; World TaeKwonDo award, 1979; Detroit Spl. Olympics award, 1978; Cmty. Svc. award Mich. State U., 1985. Mem. Am. Soc. Assn. Execs., Nat. Assn. Phys. Edn. in Higher Edn., AAHPER, Nat. Recreation and Parks Assn., Nat. Assn. Life Underwriters, Internat. Boxing Fedn., N.Am. Boxing Fedn., U.S. Boxing Assn., World Boxing Assn., World Boxing Coun., Nat. Assn. for Girls and Women in Sport, Psi Chi. Contbr. articles to profl. jours. Home: 4439 Hunt Club Dr Apt 1B Ypsilanti MI 48197-9121 Office: Sprandel & Assocs PO Box 6047 Ann Arbor MI 48106

SPRANG, MILTON LEROY, obstetrician, gynecologist, educator; b. Chgo., Jan. 15, 1944; s. Eugene and Carmella (Bruno) S.; m. Sandra Lee Karabelas, July 16, 1966; children: David, Christina, Michael. Student, St. Mary's Coll., 1962-65; MD, Loyola U., 1969. Diplomate Am. Bd. Ob-gyn; Nat. Bd. Med. Examiners; CME accreditation. Intern St. Francis Hosp., Evanston, Ill., 1969-70, resident, 1972-75, sr. attending physician, 1985—; assoc. attending phsycian Evanston Hosp., 1975-79, attending physician, 1980-84, sr. attending physician, 1985—, v.p. med. staff, 1990-91, pres.-elect, 1991-92, pres., 1992-93; also bd. dirs., 1991-94; sec. exec. com. Evanston Hosp., 1993-94; chmn. ob-gyn Cook County Grad. Sch. Medicine,, Chgo., 1983-91; instr. Northwestern U. Med. Sch., Chgo., 1975-78, asst. prof., 1984-85, assoc. prof., 1995—; pres. Northwestern Healthcare Network Physician Leadership, 1994; lectr. acad. and civic groups OB-Gyn. Nat. Ctr. Advanced Med. Edn., 1991—; bd. dirs. Ill. Found. Med. Rev.; bd. trustees Ill. State Ins. Svcs., 1992-96; bd. govs. Ill. State Med. Inter-Inst. Exch., 1987-92. Editor: Profl. Staff News, 1992-93; chmn. editorial bd. Jour. Chgo. Medicine, 1986-91; contbr. articles to profl. jours. Bd. dirs. Am. Cancer Sooc., chmn. profl. edn. com. North Shoore unit, 1982-85; bd. dirs. Chgo. Community Info. Network, 1994-95; mem. Nat. Rep. Congrl. Com., 1981—, Ill. Med. Polit. Action Com. With USN, 1970-72. Fellow ACS, Am. Coll.Ob-Gyn. (chmn. Ill. sect. 1975-76), Am. Soc. Colposcopy and Cervical Pathology; mem. AMA (Physician Recognition award 1977, 80, 83), Ill. Med. Soc. (del. to AMA 1987, 91—, ho. dels., govt. affairs com. 1988-96, chmn. reference com. 1989, chmn. bd. trustees 1996—, chmn. fin. com. 1992-94, sec.-treas. 1994-96), Chgo. Med. Soc. (v.p. 1984-85, adv. com. advt. stds. 1978-84, counselor, physician's rev. com. 1980-85, chmn. 1985, , sec. 1989—, exec. coun. north suburban br. 1981-82, 86, chmn. 1985, trustee ins. bd. 1982—, nominating com. 1985-96, trustee 1986-92, treas. 1986-89, sec. 1989-90, pres.-elect 1990-91, pres. 1991-92, chmn. fin. com. 1986-89, pres. 1991-93, chmn. ethical rels. com. 1994-96, chmn. bd. trustees 1990-91), Chgo. Found. Med. Care (nominating com. 1980-84, med. care evaluation and edn. com. 1980-83, practice guidelines com. 1984), Physician Benefit Trust (chmn. fin. com. 1993-96). Roman Catholic. Home: 4442 Concord Ln Skokie IL 60076-2606 Office: AGSO 1000 Central St Evanston IL 60201-1777

SPRANKEL, WILLIAM ALBERT, project engineer; b. Bellevue, Ohio, July 18, 1931; s. William A. and Winifred C. (Smith) S.; m. Charlene M. Eitel, June 30, 1969; children: Charles, Melanie, Steven, Tara. BS in Indsl. Sci., Letournea U. Coll., 1954. Project engr. Kobelco Steel, Kobelco Stewart Bolling Inc., Hudson, Ohio, 1969—. 2d lt. USAF, 1955-58. Home: 1245 Summit Ave Lakewood OH 44107-2442 Office: Kobelco Stewart Bolling Inc 1600 Terex Rd Hudson OH 44236-4070

SPRINGER, HARRY AARON, surgeon; b. El Paso, Tex., Nov. 23, 1937; s. Moses David and Louise S.; m. Nancy K. Springer, Sept. 1, 1958 (div. 1977); children: Rhonda Springer Levin, Michael R., Steven. m. Mavis Leona Springer, May 4, 1980; children: Margo Louise, David Lee. DDS, Northwestern U., 1960; MD, U. Tex., 1964. Diplomate Am. Bd. Plastic Surgery. Intern Cook County Hosp., Chgo., 1964-65, resident in gen. surgery, 1964-69; resident in plastic surgery Northwestern U., 1968-71; practice medicine specializing in plastic surgery, Evanston, Ill. Contbr. articles to med. jours. Served with USAR, 1965-71, 1981-84. Fellow ACS; mem. Am. Soc. Plastic and Reconstructive Surgeons, AMA, Ill. State Med. Soc. (trustee 1983-90, 2d v.p. 1985-86, 1st v.p. 1986-87, pres. 1988-89), Chgo. Med. Soc. (pres. 1983-84). Office: 1000 Skokie Blvd Wilmette IL 60091

SPRINGER, THOMAS J., state legislator; b. Apr. 25, 1968. BA, U. Wis. Wis. state assemblyman dist. 86, 1991—; mem. Agr. Rural Affairs and Natural Resources Coms. Address: 1701 16th St Mosinee WI 54455*

SPRINGSTED, ERIC OSMON, minister, philosophy and religion educator; b. St. Paul, May 27, 1951; s. Osmon Rutherford and Elaine B. (Kirchhoff) S.; m. Brenda Margaret Lockhart, June 11, 1976; children: Simone Anne, Mary Leidy, Elspeth Elaine. BA, St. John's Coll., Santa Fe, N.Mex., 1973; MDiv, Princeton Theol. Sem., 1976, PhD, 1980. Ordained to ministry Presbyn. Ch., 1981. Supply pastor Calvary United Presbyn. Ch., Jersey City, 1976-77; interim pastor The Congregational Ch., Jacksonville, Ill., 1983-84, 88-89; chaplain, prof. philosophy and religion Ill. Coll., Jacksonville, 1981—; mem. com. on higher edn. Synod of Lincoln Trails, Indpls., 1982-88; del. Assn., Presbyn. Colls. and Univs., 1983-87; mem. com. on preparation for ministry Presbytery of Great Rivers, 1992-95; gen. editor SUNY Series, Simone Weil Studies, SUNY Press. Author: Christus Mediator, 1983, Simone Weil and the Suffering of Love, 1986, Who Will Make Us Wise? How the Churches Are Failing Higher Education, 1988, Primary Readings in Philosophy for Understanding Theology, 1992, Spirit, Nature & Community, 1994, The Beauty That Saves, 1996; contbr. articles to profl. jours. Pres. Friends of the Libr., Jacksonville, 1990-91; steering com. Clergy and Laymen Concerned About Vietnam, Santa Fe, 1971-73; sec. Youth Attention Ctr. Bd., Jacksonville, 1992—. Mem. Am. Weil Soc. (pres. 1981—), Ctr. Theol. Inquiry, Am. Acad. Religion, Am. Philos. Assn., Presbyn. Coll. Chaplains Assn. Democrat. Office: Ill Coll 1101 W College Ave Jacksonville IL 62650-2212

SPROLES, KENNETH RAY, insurance agent; b. Dayton, Ohio, Oct. 22, 1949; s. Charles K. Sproles and Opal Jean (Adams) Greer; m. Karen Sue Beck; children: Krista Rae, Kelli Sue. AS, Sinclair Coll., 1969; BS, Wright State U., 1975; postgrad., Tulane U., 1976. Psychotherapist Good Sam Mental Health Ctr., Dayton, Ohio, 1969-75; asst. coroner investigator Coroner's Office, New Orleans, 1980; instr. Tulane U., New Orleans, 1980; dir. New Orleans Suicide Prevention, 1977-80; therapist/educator Starr Commonwealth Schs., Van Wert, Ohio, 1978-82; fin. planner Prudential Securities, Springfield, Ohio, 1982—; cons. Dayton (Ohio) Police Dept., 1974-75, U.S. Coast Guard, 1978; lectr. Sinclair Coll., Dayton, 1970-75, Wright State U., 1972-75, Wright State U., Dayton, 1972-75. Mem. Nat. Assn. Life Underwriters (ethics com. 1983-94, chmn. 1994-95), Nat. Assn. Securities Dealers. Home: 2132 Hoppes Ave Springfield OH 45503 Office: Prudential 674 N Limestown St Springfield OH 45503

SPROTBERRY, STEVEN J., product designer; b. St. Clair, Mich., Nov. 4, 1964. Product designer BTM Corp., Marysville, Mich., 1984—; tchr. course in computer-aided drafting at local coll. Baptist. Office: BTM Corp 300 Davis Rd Marysville MI 48040-1955

SPRUNGER, DONALD J., construction executive; b. Monroe, Ind., Apr. 16, 1915. Constrn. supr. Ind. Constrn., Fort Wayne, 1943-83; v.p., treas. Swiss Properties, Inc., Berne, Ind., 1986—. With U.S. Army, 1944-46. Mem. Lions. Mennonite. Home: 838 W 500 S Berne IN 46711-9704

SPRUNGL, KATHERINE LOUISE, nurse; b. Sandusky, Ohio, May 29, 1961; d. Karl William and Patricia Carol (Addy) Steuk; m. Jeffery Alan Sprungl; children: Diana Kristine, Alixandra Marie. AA, Cuyahoga Community Coll., 1982; BS, Bowling Green State U., 1986. RN, Ohio; cert. inpatient obstetric nurse. Med. technician Fairview Gen. Hosp., Cleve., 1983-84; staff nurse labor, delivery Fairview Gen. Hosp., 1984-86; office staff nurse Dr. T. J. Wasserbauer, M.D., Inc., Cleve., 1984-85; counselor, instr. Far West Ctr. Project Find, Westlake, Ohio, 1986—; instr. Am. Heart Assn., Cleve., 1983—, Well Aware, Westlake, Ohio, 1986-88; staff nurse-labor, delivery SW Gen. Hosp., Middleburg Heights, Ohio, 1987, St. Joseph Hosp., Lorain, Ohio, 1988, Cleve. Metrohealth System, 1988-95; nurse Profl. Nursing Svc., Cuyahoga Falls, Ohio, 1995—; cons. Well Aware, 1985, Far West Ctr., 1986. Author: Living with Arthritis, 1986, Teen Contact, 1991. Project founder, dir. Teen Contact, 1991. Mem. Assn. Women's Health, Obstetrics and Neonata Nurses. Home: 1545 King Rd Hinckley OH 44233-9773

SPURGEON, KATHERINE J., library director, consultant; b. Williamsport, Ind., Sept. 29, 1948; d. Elbert Glenn and Jane Elizabeth (Wilber) Odle; m. David Wells Spurgeon, Feb. 13, 1977. BS, Ball State U., 1970; MLS, U. Ky., 1971. Cert. I Ind. State Libr. Libr. dir. Greenwood (Ind.) Pub. Libr., 1971-79; bookstore mgr. Chapman Booksellers, Carmel, Ind., 1980-82; libr. cons. Hamilton County Librs., Ind., 1982; libr. dir. Westfield (Ind.) Publ Libr., 1982—; libr. cons. pvt. practice, Westfield, 1995—; bd. dirs. Ctrl. Ind. ALSA, Indpls., 1973-95, Ind. Visual Network, 1986—, Ind. Coop. LSA, 1991—. Pres. Bus. and Profl. Women, Greenwood, Ind., 1975-79. Recipient Outstanding Contbn. award Westfield Sesquicentenniel, 1984; named Young Profl of Yr., Bus. and Profl. Women, Greenwood, Ind., 1976. Mem. ALA, Ind. Visual Network (pres. 1996), Main St. Productons Westfield (sec. 1993—), Westfield C. of C. (bd. dirs. 1993—, pres. 1995-96), Ind. Libr. Fedn. (Dist. IV officer 1995—). Home: PO Box 646 Carmel IN 46032 Office: Westfield Pub Libr 333 W Hoover St Westfield IN 46074

SPURGEON, NANNETTE SUANN (SUSIE SPURGEON), special education educator; b. Crawfordsville, Ind., Nov. 15, 1962; d. Dwight Cordell and Nancy Mae (Meagher) Spurgeon. BS, Stephen F. Austin State U., 1985; MS, Purdue U., 1990. Cert. elem. edn. tchr., deaf edn. tchr., learning disabilities educator. Tchr. 1st grade Aldine Ind. Sch. Dist., Houston, 1985-86; tchr. pre-Kindergarten Cypress-Fairbanks Ind. Sch. Dist., Houston, 1986-88, Disabilities Svcs., Inc., Crawfordsville, Ind., 1989; elem. hearing impaired tchr. Pleasant Hill Elem. Sch. North Montgomery Community Sch. Corp., Crawfordsville, Ind., 1990-91; tchr. learning disabilites, chpt. 1, hearing impaired, reading recovery Hoover Elem. Sch. Crawfordsville Community Sch. Corp., Crawfordsville, 1991—; tchr. aide Crawfordsville Community Sch. Dist., 1988-89; interpreter Christ the Good Shepard Cath. Ch., Houston, 1986-87; coach 7th grade volleyball Northridge Mid. Sch., 1990, Tuttle Mid. Sch., Crawfordsville, 1991—. Named to Alpha Chi, Kappa Delta Pi. Mem. Coun. for Exceptional Children, Kappa Sigma Phi. Home: 307 Jennison St Crawfordsville IN 47933-2748

SPURGEON, WESLEY C., material handling administrator; b. Clarksville, Ill., Apr. 30, 1937. AD, Louisville Tech. Inst., 1968. Designer Conveyorization, Inc., Louisville, 1988-93; material handling engr. Precision Automation Co., Jeffersonville, Ind., 1993—. Clk., S.E. Ind. Bapt. Assn., 1980—; deacon local ch., 1975—. Baptist. Home: 633 N Fairbanks Ave Clarksville IN 47129-2423

SPURRIER, JAMES JOSEPH, theater educator; b. Mexico, Mo., Oct. 1, 1946; s. Jack Joseph and Ruth Marilyn (Mundy) S.; m. Jean Madelon Alkire, June 5, 1976; children: Jenna, Jamie. BA, U. Mich., 1968; MA, UCLA, 1970; PhD, So. Ill. U., 1979. Tchr., dept. chmn. Alemany High Sch., Mission Hills, Calif., 1968-74; prof. speech, dir. theater Vincennes (Ind.) U., 1977—. Composer various music selections, 1974-79. Choir dir. First Christian Ch., Vincennes, 1977—; bd. dirs. Arts Coun. Southwestern Ind., 1991—. Recipient Dir. Best Musical award Northridge (Calif.) Arts Coun., 1971; named Outstanding Young Man of Am., 1979, 82. Mem. Nat. Assn. Schs. of Theatre (ethics com. 1987-93, chmn. ethics com. 1990-93, nominations com. 1993-94), Assn. for Theater in Higher Edn. (com. chmn. 1986-88), Ind. Theater Assn., Phi Kappa Phi, Kiwanis. Roman Catholic. Home: 114 Seminole Dr Vincennes IN 47591-1922 Office: Vincennes U Shircliff # 15 Vincennes IN 47591

SQUIRES, GORDON WAYNE, federal agency executive; b. Detroit, Jan. 21, 1939; s. Elmer Wayne and Geraldine Elizabeth (Carpenter) S.; m. suann Kay Guenther, Jan. 11, 1947; 1 child, Jennifer Margene. BS, Western Mich. U., 1972, MS, 1974. Lic. airline transport pilot, comml. pilot, airframe and power plant mechanica. Advanced through grades to maj. USMC, 1962-77; auto/race car mechanic Taylor, Mich., 1967-70; instr. Western Mich. U., Kalamazoo, 1972-76; engr./supr. Parker-Hannefin Corp., Otsego, Richland, Mich., 1976-79; plant engr./project engr. Kal-Equip Co., Otsego, 1979-82; plant engr. Union Pump Co., Battle Creek, Mich., 1982-84; asst. engring. mgr./project engr. Valley Plastics Corp., Kalamazoo, 1984-86; project engr. Am. Fibrit, Battle Creek, 1986-88; procedures specialist/pilot BTLFIFO/FAA, Battle Creek, 1988-95, procedures specialist, 1995—. V.p., ops. officer Plainwell (Mich.) Music Soc., 1995, pres., ops. officer, 1995—. Duke Harrah scholar, 1971. Mem. vFW (adj.). Roman Catholic. Home: 2990 E Baseline Rd Plainwell MI 49080 Office: BTLFIFO/DOT/FAA 2800 W Territorial Battle Creek MI 49017

SRESTY, GUGGILAM CHALAMAIAH, environmental engineer; b. Perala, India, Nov. 11, 1954; came to U.S., 1976; s. Ramasubbarao and Suseela (Utakuri) Guggilam; m. Annapurnadevi Guggilam Madipalli, Nov. 7, 1979; children: Padma, Hema. B in Tech., Banaras Hindu U., Varanasi, India, 1975; MS, Columbia U., 1978. Assoc. engr. Ill. Inst. Tech. Rsch. Inst., Chgo., 1979-80, rsch. engr., 1980-85, sr. engr., 1985-91, mgr. environ. technologies sect., 1991-92, mgr. energy and environ. scis. dept., 1992—; mem., sr. tech. com. Nat. Inst. for Petroleum and Energy Rsch., Bartlesville, Okla., 1984-86. Author: Size Reduction, 1985; co-author: Particle Size Analysis, 1980. Pres. India Club of Columbia U., N.Y.C., 1978; student coord. Andhra Samithi, Varanasi, India, 1974. Recipient Best Presentation award Am. Inst. Mining, Metallurgy and Petroleum Engrs., 1978, Gold medal Banaras Hindu U., 1975, Hadfield medal, 1975. Mem. AICE, Am. Inst. of Mining, Metallurgy and Petroleum Engring. Hindu. Home: 8241 Mason Ave Burbank IL 60459-1955 Office: Ill Inst Tech Rsch 10 W 35th St Chicago IL 60616-3703

SRINIVASA, VENKATARAMANIAH, engineer; b. Mysore, India, Aug. 30, 1941; came to U.S., 1968; s. Venkataramaniah and Gowramma S.; m. Janakimala Muthiah, June 1972; children: Supreeth, Suman. BSc, Mysore U., 1962, MSc, 1964; MS, Rutgers U., 1972, PhD, 1975. Rsch. fellow CFTRI, Mysore, 1964-67; tech. officer Indian Inst. Packaging, Bombay, 1967; rsch. intern, rsch. and tching. asst. Rutgers U., New Brunswick, N.J., 1972-75, rsch. intern, tching. asst., rsch. fellow Bur. Engring. Rsch., 1970-75; sr. packaging engr. Abbott Labs., Abbott Park, Ill., 1975-78, sr. project engr., 1978-83, mgr., 1983—. Mem. Inst. Packaging Profls., Soc. Plastics Engrs., Am. Chem. Soc., Sigma Xi. Home: 2729 Sallmon Ave Waukegan IL 60087-3514

SRISKANDARAJAH, JEGANATHAN, mathematics educator; b. Colombo, Sri Lanka, Oct. 30, 1949; came to U.S., 1982; s. Coomarasamy and Rajeswarie (Kanagaratnam) J.; m. Gowrigambikai Katheravel, May 19, 1979; children: Mayuran, Aingaran. BS, U. Sri Lanka, Colombo, 1974; diploma, U. Sri Lanka, Nugegoda, 1977; MS, U. Sri Lanka, Colombo, 1978, U. Del., 1985. Instr. U. Sri Lanka, Colombo, 1974-78; lectr. U. Zambia, Kitwe, 1979-80; system analyst ops. rsch. N.C.C.M. Ltd., Kitwe, Chingola, 1980-82; teaching asst. U. Del., Newark, 1983-85; assoc. chair math., assoc. prof. math. U. Wis., Richland Center, 1985—; state coord. Am. High Sch. Math. Exam., Am. Jr. High Sch. Math. Exam.; mem. exec. adv. com. for region V, Am. Math. Competitions. Author: Optimality Pays an Introduction to Linear Programming, 1992, American High School Mathematics Examination in Wisconsin, Summary of Results and Awards, 1993, 94, 95, Lab-Manual: Derive, 1995; cons Ednl. Testing Svcs.--AP Calculus, 1996. Mem. Math. Assn. Am., Am. Math. Assn. Two-Yr. Colls. (referee 1991—), Sch. Sci. and Math. Assn., Wis. Math. Coun., Wis. Math. Assn. Two-Yr. Colls. (Mo. Jour. Math. Scis.), Kappa Mu Epsilon. Home: 1 Eastbourne Cir Madison WI 53717-1094 Office: U Wis Hwy 14 W Richland Center WI 53581

STAAB, MICHAEL JOSEPH, lawyer; b. Hays, Kans., Oct. 12, 1955; s. Robert Joseph and Beatrice Agnes (Schenk) S.; m. Kathy Lee Brock, Jan. 11, 1986; children: Colton Brock, Matthew Michael. BA magna cum laude, Ft. Hays State U., 1978; JD, Drake U., 1981; LLM in Health Law, DePaul U., 1993. Bar: Idaho 1981, U.S. Dist. Ct. Idaho 1981, Utah 1986, U.S. Dist. Ct. Utah 1986, Ill. 1990, U.S. Dist. Ct. (no. dist.) Ill. 1990. Assoc. Quane, Smith, Howard and Hull, Boise, Idaho, 1981-83, Meuleman & Miller, Boise, Idaho, 1983; pvt. practice Boise, Idaho, 1983-85; ptnr. Biele, Haslam & Hatch, Salt Lake City, 1985-89, Parsons, Behle & Latimer, Salt Lake City, 1989-90; assoc. Steinberg, Polacek & Goodman, Chgo., 1990-93, Ruff, Weldenaar and Reidy, Ltd., Chgo., 1994—; legal advisor Ill. Pediatric Brain Injury Resource Ctr., Algonquin, Ill., 1991—. Contbr. articles to legal publs. Bd. dirs. Winnetka Village Caucus, 1992-94, Big Bros./Big Sisters, Salt Lake City, 1985-89, Utah Head Injury Assn., Salt Lake City, 1988-90, Pediat. Brain Injury Assn., Salt Lake City, 1988-90. Mem. ABA, Ill. Bar Assn., Chgo. Bar Assn., Nat. Health Lawyers Assn., Nat. Order of Barristers, Order of Omega, K.C., Phi Kappa Phi, Phi Alpha Theta, Phi Eta Sigma. Roman Catholic. Home: 173 De Windt Rd Winnetka IL 60093 Office: Ste 4400 One N LaSalle St Chicago IL 60602

STAAKE, BOB TED, cartoonist, writer; b. Santa Monica, Calif., Sept. 26, 1957; s. Alfred Thedor Staake and Bridgette M. Baigert Faulkner; m. Paulette Fehlig, 1990; children; Ryan, Kevin. Student, U. So. Calif., L.A., 1978-80. Cartoons, illustrations and writings in Washington Post, Chgo. Tribune, L.A. Times, Parents Mag., Time, SF Weekly, St. Louis Post-Dispatch, Asahi-Shimbum; author: The Complete Book of Caricature, 1991, The Complete Book of Humorous Art, 1996; illustrator: Headlines by Jay Leno, 1990, True and Tacky II, 1991. Student Press Law Ctr. intern Robert F. Kennedy Meml., Washington, 1978. Mem. Nat. Cartoonists Soc., Nat. Stereoscopic Assn. Democrat. Office: Bob Staake Cartoons 726 S Ballas Rd Saint Louis MO 63122

STABEJ, RUDOLPH JOHN, computer consultant; b. Milw., Dec. 14, 1952; s. Rudolf and Katharina (Schaab) S. BS in Acctg., U. Ill., Chgo., 1975; MBA in Fin., De Paul U., 1981, MS in Computer Sci., 1986. Gen. acct. Field Mus. Nat. History, Chgo., 1975-77, Victor Bus. Products, Chgo., 1977-80, Northrop Def. Systems, Rolling Meadows, Ill., 1981-82; programmer Fed. Reserve Bank, Chgo., 1983-84; programmer/analyst Arthur Andersen & Co., Chgo., 1984-85; cons./programmer Sycomm Systems Corp., Chgo., 1985-86; pvt. practice computer cons. Chgo., 1986—. Mem. Ind. Computer Cons. Assn., Data Processing Mgmt. Assn. Home: 1004 Bayshore Dr Schaumburg IL 60194-1304

STABLER, NANCY RAE, infosystems specialist; b. Elgin, Ill., June 15, 1946; d. Raymond Herman and Eleanora Marie (Gaedke) Redmer, m. Jay Stabler, Mar, 28, 1970; 1 child: Andrea Marie. AAS with honors, Elgin Community Coll., 1982, AA with Honors, 1985. Programmer, analyst Houghton-Mifflin, Geneva, Ill., 1966-77; project leader Kane County, Geneva, 1978-83; systems designer Burgess Norton, Geneva, 1983-87; human resources telecommunication specialist Recon/Optical, Barrington, Ill., 1987-91; MIS project leader, sales and mktg. Advance Transformer, Rosemont, Ill., 1991—; tutor Elgin (Ill.) Community Coll., 1983—. Home: 2305 Blue Jay Trail Elgin IL 60123 Office: Advance Transformer 10275 W Higgins Rd Rosemont IL 60018-5625

STACK, PAUL FRANCIS, lawyer; b. Chgo., July 21, 1946; s. Frank Louis and Dorothy Louise Stack; m. Nea Waterman, July 8, 1972; children: Nea Elizabeth, Sera Waterman. BS, U. Ariz., 1968; JD, Georgetown U., 1971. Bar: Ill. 1971, U.S. Ct. Claims 1975, U.S. Tax Ct. 1974, U.S. Ct. Internat. Trade 1977, U.S. Supreme Ct. 1975. Law clk., U.S. Dist. Ct., Chgo., 1971-72; Asst. U.S. Atty. No. Dist. Ill., Chgo., 1972-75; mng. dir. Stack & Filpi, Chgo., 1976—. Bd. dirs. Riverside (Ill.) Pub. Libr., 1977-83, Suburban Libr. Sys., Burr Ridge, Ill., 1979-82; mem. Mayor's ad hoc adv. com. on Ctrl. Libr., Chgo., Ill., 1987-88; mem. bd. edn. Twp. H.S. Dist. 208, Riverside, Ill., 1989—. Mem. Chgo. Zoological Soc. (governing mem.), Brookfield, Ill., 1982—, Chgo. Bar Assn., Union League Club of Chgo. (bd. dirs. 1986-89). Presbyterian. Home: 238 N Delaplaine Rd Riverside IL 60546-2035 Office: 140 S Dearborn St Ste 411 Chicago IL 60603-5892

STACKHOUSE, DAVID WILLIAM, JR., retired furniture systems installation contractor; b. Cumberland, Ind., Aug. 29, 1926; s. David William and Dorothy Frances (Snider) S.; B.S., Lawrence Coll., Appleton, Wis., 1950; m. Shirley Pat Smith, Dec. 23, 1950; 1 son, Stefan Brent. Indsl. designer Globe Am. Co., Kokomo, Ind., 1951-53; product designer, chief engr. Midwest Foundry & Workwall divsn. L.A. Darling Co., Bronson, Mich., 1954-66; contract mgr. Brass Office Products, Indpls., 1966-73; mfrs. rep., Nashville, Ind., 1973-78; mktg. exec. Brass Office Products, Inc., Indpls., 1978-80; office furniture systems installation contractor, 1980-92; founder This Great House, The Story of This Home, 1995, Half-High Hill Prodns., Inc., 1996. Served with USNR, 1944-46; Beta Theta Pi. Anglican. Clubs: Lions, Masons, Shriners. Patentee interior structural systems. Home: 4617 N Helmsburg Rd Nashville IN 47448-8227

STADELMANN, EDUARD JOSEPH, plant physiologist, educator; b. Graz, Austria, Sept. 24, 1920; s. Eduard Joseph and Josefa (Eigner) S.; m. Ok Young Lee, Mar. 22, 1975. BS, Bundesrealgymnasium, Graz, Austria, 1939; PhD, U. Innsbruck, Austria, 1953; Pvt. Docent, U. Freiburg, Switzerland, 1957; PhD (hon.), Agrl. U. Vienna, 1989. Sr. asst. U. Freiburg, 1962-63; rsch. assoc. U. Minn., Mpls., 1963, asst. prof., 1964-66, assoc. prof., 1966-72, prof. hort. sci., 1972-91, prof. emeritus, 1991—. Muellhaupt Scholar in Biology, Ohio State U., 1958-59; Humboldt Found. awardee, 1974-75; Fulbright award, Coun. Internat. Exchange, 1979-80, 87-88. Mem. Am. Inst. Biology, Am. Soc. Plant Physiologists, German Bot. Soc., Swiss Bot. Soc., Sigma Xi. Roman Catholic. Office: Univ Minn Dept Hort Sci 1970 Folwell Ave Saint Paul MN 55108-6007

STADLMAN, REBECCA MURPHY, federal agency administrator; b. Lemars, Iowa, June 2, 1952; d. John J. and Verna M. (Wulf) Murphy; m. Evan G. Stadlman, June 28, 1975; children: Sean, Megan, Marisa. BA, Iowa State U., 1974. Cert. sr. profl. in human resources. Svc. rep. Social Security Adminstrn., Ft. Dodge, Iowa, 1975-76, claims rep., 1976-78; field rep. Social Security Adminstrn., Ames, Iowa, 1979-83; ops. supr. Social Security Adminstrn., Des Moines, Iowa, 1984-91; chief pers. IRS, Des Moines, 1991-94, asst. to dir., 1994—; fund raising chmn. Fed. Exec. Coun., Des Moines, 1984—, mem. policy coun., 1990, v.p., 1991-96, pres., 1996—; diversity cons. Author: Development Clerk Training Course, 1990. Active Leadership Iowa, 1990—; div. chmn. United Way, Des Moines, 1988, 91, bd. of dirs., 1991—. Named Ctrl. Iowa Fed. Employee of Yr., 1993. Mem. Am. Soc. Quality Control, Soc. for Human Resource Mgmt.

STADTFELD, RICHARD LOUIS, church administrator; b. Riverside, Ill., July 13, 1934; s. William Louis and Elizabeth Jane (Diedrich) S.; m. Marcella Rita Steward, July 14, 1953; 1 child, Dorothy Angela. JCD, Athanaeum Pontificium Internat, 1957. Prof., dean Coll. Gaztelueta, Las Arenas, Vizcaya, Spain, 1957-62; mgr. cmty. rels. Chgo. Housing Authority, 1962-64; dir., city planner Dept. Urban Renewal City of Chgo., 1964-75; city planner Dept. Cmty. Devel. City of Claremont, Calif., 1975-76; coord. housing devel. Housing Authority City of Santa Barbara, Calif., 1977-81; purchasing agt., mgr. devel. Marvin Co. Diversified, Inc., Camarillo, Calif., 1982-88; coord. Housing Authority City of Berkeley, Calif., 1982-85; asst. housing mgr. San Francisco Housing Authority, 1986-87; acting housing mgr. San Diego Housing Commn., 1987-94; dir. Office of Planned Giving Diocese of Crookston, Minn., 1994—. Inventor Modular Building System, 1957. Recipient Cert. of Appreciation U.S. Drug Enforcement Adminstrn., 1994, Southwestern Coll., 1991. Mem. Nat. Soc. Fund Raising Execs. (N.D. chpt.), Nat. Cath. Stewardship Coun., Cath. Orgn. Devel. Execs. for Schs., MinnDak Assn. Planned Giving Execs. (pres., founder 1994—). Home: 1823 Washington St N 52 Grand Forks ND 58203-1452 Office: Diocese of Crookston Office Planned Giving PO Box 610 Crookston MN 56716

STAEBELL, RONALD THOMAS, life insurance agent; b. Vallejo, Calif., July 8, 1945; s. Fred Michael and Delores Mary (Hanisch) S.; m. Janice Kay Nordling, Apr. 1, 1980 (div.); children: Chad, Dan, Audra; m. Virginia Rae Blosmo, Nov. 7, 1981. BBA, No. State Coll., Aberdeen, S.D., 1969. CLU. Group ins. rep. Aetna Life & Casulty, St. Paul, 1969-72; agt. Dornberger Ins. Agy., Sioux Falls, S.D., 1972-74; br. mgr. N.Am. Life & Casualty, Sioux Falls, 1974-80; brokerage supr. MONY, Sioux Falls, 1980-81; agt. Williams Ins. Agy., Inc., Sioux Falls, 1981—. Bd. dirs. Sioux Falls Area Found., 1982-93, O'Gorman H.S. Found., Sioux Falls, 1982-90, Sioux Falls Girls Club, 1979-85, S.D. Guardianship Program, Pierre, 1988—. Mem. Am. Soc. CLU's and Chartered Fins. Cons. (pres. local chpt. 1986-88, cert.), Nat. Assn. Life Underwriters (pres. local chpt. 1978-79), S.D. Assn. Life Underwriters (pres. 1983-84), Sioux Falls Estate Planning Coun. (pres. 1985-86). Republican. Roman Catholic. Office: Williams Ins Agy Inc 300 S Phillips Ave Sioux Falls SD 57102

STAFFORD, ARTHUR CHARLES, medical association administrator; b. Cleve., May 10, 1947; s. Charles Arthur and Florence Mildred (Hovey) S.; m. Patricia Anne Cz, Dec. 20, 1991. BS, Kent State U., 1977; MBA, Lake Erie Coll., 1984. Med. tech. VA, Cleve., 1977-81, supr. med. tech., 1981—; instr. Lake Erie Coll., Painesville, Ohio, 1980-82, Cuyahoga C.C., Cleve., 1988-91; pres. Kent State U. Veterans Assn., 1974, mem. Kent State U Budget Review Com., 1975. Contbr. articles to profl. jour. Mem. Am. Legion, 1974, VFW, 1973. With USN, 1968-72. Mem. Am. Soc. Clin. Pathologists, Clin. Lab. Mgmt. Assn. (treas. Cleve. chpt. 1990—), Founders Club, Rock and Roll Hall of Fame. Republican. Home: 2193 Chimney Ridge Dr Madison OH 44057-2588 Office: VA Med Ctr 10701 East Blvd Cleveland OH 44106-1702

STAFFORD, JAMES DUARD, advertising executive; b. Des Moines, Nov. 24, 1947; s. Harry Duard Stafford and Beverly Rogene (Blake) Everett; m. Nancy Louise Heger, Nov. 25, 1969 (div. Mar. 1982); children: Cory James, Sara Louise; m. Lila Beard Porter, Aug. 12, 1982; children: Ashley Porter, Tyler Porter. BA, Drake U., 1972. Acct. mgr. Young & Rubicam, Cedar Rapids, Iowa, 1972-75; v.p. ATS&H Inc., Moline, Ill., 1975-79, Cooper Jenner Stafford & Assocs., Waterloo, Iowa, 1979-83; dir. mktg. support ISC Sys. Corp., Spokane, 1983-87; mktg. comms. dir. Applied Comms., Omaha, 1987-89; sr. v.p. Thomas C. Porter & Assocs., Des Moines, 1989—. Bd. dirs. Waterloo/Cedar Falls Symphony, 1981-83, Powell III Assn., Des Moines, 1991-93, Bernie Lorenz Recovery, Des Moines, 1992-95. Mem. Am. Mktg. Assn., Advt. Profls. Des Moines, Am. Advt. Fedn. (Addy awards 1972—), Des Moines Golf & Country Club, Sunnyside Country Club, Glen Oaks Country Club. Republican. Office: Thomas C Porter & Assoc 4900 University Ave #101 West Des Moines IA 50266

STAFFORD, JOYCE RUTH, artist; b. Springfield, Mo., Apr. 13, 1932; d. August Karl and Ada Lou (Brundrett) Luebke; m. John Warner Stafford, June 28, 1958; 1 child, Charles August. BA, Denver U., 1954, MA, 1957. Tchr. Denver Pub. Schs., 1955-57, San Leandro (Calif.) Unified Schs., 1958-59; toy designer Effanbee Doll Co., N.Y.C., 1982-83; pvt. practice Wheaton, Ill., 1967—. Artistic work represented in Teddy Bear Artists, 1984, Effanbee Collectors Encyclopedia, 1983, Modern Collectors Doll, 1975; contbr. articles to profl. jours. Mem. Nat. Inst. Am. Doll Artists (west coast v.p. 1974-76, grantee), Internat. Doll Acad. (bd. dirs. 1987-93), United Fedn. Doll Club (chmn. modern doll exhibit 1991-92), Original Doll Artists Coun. Am. (sec. 1995-96). Republican. Episcopalian. Home: 26w126 Mohican Dr Wheaton IL 60187-7917 Office: 3270 Whitbeck Blvd Eugene OR 97405-1938

STAGE, RICHARD LEE, consultant, retired utilities executive; b. Byesville, Ohio, Nov. 5, 1936; s. Clifford Earl Stage and Evelyn Virginia (Nunley) Rolston; m. Joan Eleanor Bednarz, Feb. 1, 1958; 1 child, Julie Marie. B in Mgmt., Malone Coll., 1987. Fleet office supr. Ohio Power Co., Canton, 1954-77; supr. automotive acctg. and leasing Am. Electric Power, Canton, 1977-83; dir. fleet mgmt. Am. Electric Power, Columbus, 1983-95; fleet mgmt. cons., Canton, 1995—. Mem. Soc. Automotive Engrs. (chmn. utilities com. 1988-89, exec. com.), Edison Electric Inst. (fleet mgmt. com. 1983-95), Masons. Republican. Home and Office: 1329 Davis St SW Canton OH 44706-4503

STAGGERS, KERMIT LEMOYNE, II, history and political science educator; b. Washington, Pa., Nov. 2, 1947; s. Kermit LeMoyne and Christine Ruby (Scherich) S.; m. June Ann Wenda, Aug. 22, 1970; children: Ayn Kristen, Kyle Lee. BS, U. Idaho, 1969, MA, 1975; PhD, Claremont Grad. Sch., 1986. Instr. history Troy (Ala.) State U., 1975-76, U. Idaho, Moscow, 1977, Northwestern Coll., Orange City, Iowa, 1979-80, Coll. Lake County, Grayslake, Ill., 1981-82; lectr. history Chapman Coll., Orange, Calif., 1979, U. Md.-Europe, Heidelberg, Germany, 1988-89; vis. instr. history Trinity Coll., Deerfield, Ill., 1980; ad. instr. history Coll. St. Francis, Joliet, Ill., 1982; assoc. prof. history and polit. sci. U. Sioux Falls (S.D.), 1982—; state senator, 1995—; expert analyst on polit. and social issues for local radio and TV. Contbr. to profl. publs. Capt. USAF, 1970-76. Malone Faculty fellow, 1993. Mem. Orgn. Am. Historians, Conf. on Faith and History, Federalist Soc., Am. Legis. Exch. Coun., Kiwanis, Phi Alpha Theta, Phi Kappa Phi. Republican. Disciples of Christ. Home: 1135 S Walts Ave Sioux Falls SD 57105-0543 Office: U Sioux Falls Dept History/Polit Sci 1101 W 22nd St Sioux Falls SD 57105-1699

STAHL, DEBORAH ANN, clinical psychologist; b. Harrisburg, Pa., Dec. 9, 1950; d. Robert Edward and Ruth (Rolin) S; m. Joseph Erlanger, June 4, 1944. BA with distinction/honors in psychology, Mary Washington Coll., U. Va., 1972; PhD, Washington U., St. Louis, 1981. Lic. psychologist, Mo.; cert. forensic examiner, Mo. Child psychology intern Wash. U. Child Guidance, St. Louis, 1975-76; psychologist Potential Psychol. Cons., St. Louis, 1978-80; instr. psychology Washington U., St. Louis, 1980, supr. in clin. psychology, 1986-90; psychologist St. Louis State Hosp., 1980-87, supervising psychologist, 1987—; pvt. practice Sunset Hills Psychol. Svcs., St. Louis, 1991—; clin. psychologist St. Anthony's Med. Ctr., Inst. for Marriage and the Family, St. Louis, 1990-91. Vol. facilitator Pet Loss Support Group. Washington Univ. fellow, 1973-77. Mem. APA, Mo. Psychol. Assn., Am. Contract Bridge League (life master 1979). Office: Sunset Hills Psychol Svcs 3555 Sunset Office Dr Ste 203 Sunset Hills MO 63127-1021

STAINBROOK, JAMES RALPH, JR., educator; b. Indpls., Dec. 8, 1936; s. James Ralph, Sr., and Alta Marie (Doty) S.; m. Barbara Sue Miller, Dec. 17, 1988; children—Susan Ann, Steven James. A.B., Butler U., Indpls., 1959; M.A., U. Wis., Madison, 1964; Ed.D., Ind. U., Bloomington, 1970. Cert. Latin tchr., secondary sch. adminstr., counselor guidance and social studies, Ind. Tchr. Indpls. public schs., 1963-68; teaching asst. Ind. U., 1968-70; prof. edn. Ball State U., Muncie, Ind., 1970—. Served as officer USAF, 1959-62. Mem. Assn. Teacher Educators, Assn. for Supervision and Curriculum Devel., Phi Delta Kappa, Kappa Delta Pi, Phi Kappa Phi. Republican. Methodist. Clubs: Scottish Rite, Shriners. Masons. Contbr. numerous articles to profl. jours. Home: 8225 Lockwood Ln Indianapolis IN 46217-4242 Office: Teachers Coll 822 Ball State U Muncie IN 47306

STAINES, MICHAEL LAURENCE, oil and gas production executive; b. Guildford, Eng., May 30, 1949; came to U.S., 1958; s. John Richard and Myrra (Smith) S.; m. Laura Catherine Terdoslavich, May 11, 1974; children: Leslie Myrra, Claire Alexandra, Julia Wallis, Cameron Sutton. BS, Cornell U., 1971; MBA, Drexel U., 1976. Asst. comptr. grants U. Pa., phila., 1976-78; sr. analyst Sun Co., Radnor, Pa., 1978-80, Penn Cen. Energy Group, Radnor, 1980-83; v.p., sec. Bryn Mawr Energy Co., Bala Cynwyd, Pa., 1983-88; sr. v.p., dir., sec. Resource Am., Inc., Phila. and Akron, Ohio, 1988—. Chmn. stewardship com. St. Mary's Episc. Ch., Radnor, 1990. Winner Silver medal in coxless pair rowing, 1976 Olympic Games, Montreal; named Oarsman of Yr. Schuylkill Navy, Phila., 1976; U.S. Nat. Rowing Champion, 1971, 72, 73. Mem. Soc. Corp. Secs., Ohio Oil and Gas Assn., Oil and Gas Assn. N.Y., Havre de Grace (Md.), Yacht Club, Bachelors Barge Club (Phila.), Vesper Boat Club (capt. 1973). Office: Resource Am Inc 2876 S Arlington Rd Akron OH 44312-4716

STAKER, GEORGE V., vocational rehabilitation coordinator; b. Portsmouth, Ohio, Dec. 19, 1950; s. George Victor and Anita Lorraine (Smith) S.; m. Carolyn Kaye, Dec. 19, 1971; 1 child, V. Lorraine. BS Edn., Ohio U., 1973, MEd, 1990. Cert. rehab. counselor, lic. profl. clin. counselor. Tchr. Notre Dame High Sch., Portsmouth, 1972-75; ins. sales rep. Nat. Life & Accident, Portsmouth, 1975-78, sales mgr., 1978-86; tchr. Southeastern Bus. Coll., New Boston, Ohio, 1986-87, job placement dir., 1987-90, br. dir., 1990; case mgr. Shawnee Mental Health, Portsmouth, 1990-91, vocat. rehab. coord., 1991-92, outpatient therapist, 1992-95, asst. dir. of case mgmt. svcs., 1995—; mem. clin. records com. Shawnee Mental Health, Portsmouth, 1991—. Praise Acad. scholar in spl. edn. Ohio U., 1990. Mem. Nat. Rehab. Assn., Counselor's Profl. & Acad. Honor Soc. Lutheran.

STALEY, MARSHA LYNN, elementary school educator; b. California, Mo., July 19, 1950; d. David D. and Jenny L. (Howard) Hutchison; divorced; children: Timothy Jay Turley, Damon Andrew Turley; m. Richard Lynn Staley, June 30, 1989. AA, State Fair C.C., Sedalia, Mo., 1982; BS in Edn., Drury Coll., 1984; MS in Elem. Adminstrn., S.W. Mo. State U., 1993; doctoral student, U. Mo., 1994—. Cert. tchr. grades 1-8, Mo. Tchr. grade 5 Newburg (Mo.) Elem. Sch., 1986-88; tchr. grades 1, 4, 5 and 6 Sherwood Elem. Sch., Springfield, Mo., 1988-93, Westport Elem. Sch., Springfield, 1993—. Mem. Pi Delta Kappa, Pi Lambda Theta (v.p. Alpha chpt. 1995—). Office: U Mo 209C Townsend Columbia MO 65211

STALEY, R(OBERT) ERIC, academic administrator; b. Phila., Aug. 4, 1947; s. Walter Frederick and Mildred Clara (Rahas) S.; m. Melinda Louise Keach, Dec. 10, 1977; children: Amanda, Gretchen, Tucker. BA with honors, U. Mo., 1969; postgrad., Oxford (Eng.) U., 1969; MA, U. Mo., 1970, PhD, 1993; Cert. in Mgmt., Harvard U., 1990. Teaching fellow U. Mo., Columbia, 1970-73, dir. program advancement, 1973-82; exec. dir. Assoc. Writing Programs, Norfolk, Va., 1982-86; exec. dir. devel. and coll. relations Mary Baldwin Coll., Staunton, Va., 1986-91; v.p., dean of advancement N.E. Mo. State U., Kirksville, 1991-93; v.p. mktg. & enrollment mgmt. William Woods U., Fulton, Mo., 1994—; exec. dir. Mo. Peace Studies Inst., Columbia, 1970-71; assoc. prof. English Old Dominion U., Norfolk, 1982-86; cons. to various arts orgns., 1977—; bd. dirs. ShenanArts Inc., Staunton, 1987-89. Author numerous fiction and nonfiction works; editor The Mo. Rev., 1975-80, Singing Winds Publs., 1970-75. Mem. Staunton City Mgr.'s Com. on Econ. Devel., 1987; mem. Staunton City Coun., 1990-91; pres. bd. Mo. Rev. Trust Fund, 1994—. Nat. Endowment for Arts fellow, 1970, 72. Mem. Coun. for Advancement and Support of Edn., Staunton C. of C. (bd. dirs. 1987-91, Outstanding Community Leader 1988), Kiwanis (pres. Staunton chpt. 1989-90, v.p. 1988-89). Democrat. Episcopalian. Office: William Woods U Office of Enrollment Mgmt Fulton MO 65251

STALKER, JACQUELINE D'AOUST, academic administrator, educator; b. Penetang, Ont., Can., Oct. 16, 1933; d. Phillip and Rose (Eaton) D'Aoust; m. Robert Stalker; children: Patricia, Lynn, Roberta. Teaching cert., U. Ottawa, 1952; tchr. music, Royal Toronto Conservatory Music, 1952; teaching cert., Lakeshore Tchrs. Coll., 1958; BEd with honors, U. Manitoba, 1977, MEd, 1979; EdD, Nova U., 1985. Cert. tchr. Ont., Man., Can. Adminstr., tchr., prin. various schs., Ont. and Que., 1952-65; area commr. Girl Guides of Can., throughout Europe, 1965-69; administr., tchr. Algonquin Community Coll., Ottawa, Ont., 1970-74; tchr., program devel. Frontenac County Bd. Edn., Kingston, Ont., 1974-75; lectr., faculty advisor dept. curriculum, edn. U. Man., Can., 1977-79; lectr. U. Winnipeg, Man., Can., 1977-79; cons. colls. div. Man. Dept. Edn., 1980-81, sr. cons. programming br., 1981-84, sr. cons. post secondary, adult and continuing edn. div., 1985-88, dir. post secondary career devel. br. and adult and continuing edn. br., 1989; asst. prof. higher edn., coord. grad. program in higher edn. U. Man., 1989-92, assoc. prof., coord. grad. program in higher edn., 1992-95; cons. lectures, seminars, workshops throughout Can. Contbr. articles to profl. jours.; mng. editor Can. Jour. of Higher Edn., 1989-93. Mem. U. Man. Senate, 1976-81, 86-89, bd. govs., 1979-82; Can. rep. Internat. Youth Conf., Garmisch, Fed. Republic of Germany, 1968; vol. Can. Cancer Soc.; mem. Assn. RN Accreditation Coun., 1980-85; chair Child Care Accreditation Com., Man., 1983-90; chair Task Force Post-Secondary Accessibility, Man., 1983; vol. United Way Planning and Allocations; provincial dir., mem. nat. bd. Can. Congress for Learning Opportunities for Women. Recipient award for enhancing the Outreach activities of the univ. U. Man., 1994. Mem. Can. Soc. Study Higher Edn., Man. Tchrs. Soc., U. Man. Alumni Assn., Women's Legal Edn. and Action Fund, Am. Assn. Study Higher Edn. Home: 261 Baltimore Rd, Winnipeg, MB Canada R3L 1H7

STALL, ALAN DAVID, packaging company executive; b. Moose Jaw, Sask., Can., June 14, 1951; came to U.S., 1982; s. Joel and Evelyn (Schwartz) S.; m. Carol I. Johnston; children: Jeffrey, Jennifer, Michael, Timothy. BSME, U. Sask., 1973; MBA, Lewis U., 1986. Registered profl. engr., Ont. Devel. engr. DuPont Can., North Bay, Ont., 1973-76; project engr. Union Carbide Corp. Can., Lindsay, Ont., 1976-79, engring. mgr., 1979-82; mgr. shirring rsch. Union Carbide Corp., Chgo., 1982-85; dir. engring. tech. Viskase Corp., Chgo., 1985-90, v.p. engring., 1990-95; gen. mgr. Kuko Corp., Gross-Gerau, Germany, 1995-96; pres. Films Casings Tech. Inc., Woodridge, Ill., 1996—. Patentee breathable plastic, shirring apparatus, sausage stuffing machine. Rotary bus. exchange fellow, London, 1982. Mem. Engring. Inst. Can., Can. Soc. Mech. Engrs., Soc. Plastics Engrs., Assn. Profl. Engrs., Ont., Assn. Energy Engrs., Am. Mensa, Can. Club Chgo. Home: 23W540 James Way Naperville IL 60540-9552 Office: Films Casings Tech Inc Po Box 5415 Woodridge IL 60517

STALLARD, WAYNE MINOR, lawyer; b. Onaga, Kans., Aug. 23, 1927; s. Minor Regan and Lydia Faye (Randall) S.; B.S., Kans. State Tchrs. Coll., Emporia, 1949; J.D., Washburn U., 1952; m. Wanda Sue Bacon, Aug. 22, 1948; children: Deborah Sue, Carol Jean, Bruce Wayne (dec.). Bar: Kans. 1952. Pvt. practice, Onaga, 1952—; atty. Community Hosp. Dist. No. 1, Pottawatomie, Jackson and Nemaha Counties, Kans., 1955—; Pottawatomie County atty., 1955-59; city atty. Onaga, 1953-79; atty Unified School Dist. 322, Pottawatomie County, Kans., 1966-83; bd. dirs. North Central Kans. Guidance Ctr., Manhattan, 1974-78; lawyer 2d dist. jud. nominating commn., 1980—; atty. Rural Water Dist. No. 3, Pottawatomie County, Kans., 1974—, Rural Water Dist. No. 4, Pottawatomie County, 1995—; chmn. Pottawatomie County Econ. Devel. Com., 1986-92, atty., 1992—. Fund dir. chmn. Pottawatomie County chpt. Nat. Found. for Infantile Paralysis, 1953-54. Served from pvt. to sgt., 8th Army, AUS, 1946 to 47. Mem. ABA, Pottawatomie County, Kans. bar assns., Onaga C. of C., , Am. Judicature Soc., City Attys. Assn. Kan. (dir. 1963-66), Masons, Shriners, Order Ea. Star, Gamma Mu, Kappa Delta Pi, Delta Theta Phi, Sigma Tau Gamma. Mem. United Ch. of Christ. Home: 720 High St Onaga KS 66521 Office: 307 Leonard St Onaga KS 66521-9734

STALLINGS, HENRY, state legislator; b. Dec. 30, 1950. BA, Western Mich. U.; JD, Detroit Coll. Law. Bus. owner; fellow Congl. Black Caucus; senator Dist. 3 Mich. State Senate, 1995—, mem. econ. devel., internat. trade, regulator affairs coms., mem. human resources, fin., labor and vets. affairs coms., asst. Dem. whip.

STALLWORTH, ALMA GRACE, state legislator. Grad., Highland Park Community Coll., 1956; student, Wayne State U., 1956. Mem. Mich. Ho. of Reps., Lansing, 1970-74, 81—; dep. dir. Hist. Dept. City of Detroit, 1975-78, job developer, 1978-79; mem. exec. com. Nat. Conf. State Legislatures, 1986-89. Commr. Wayne County Charter, Detroit, 1978-79, Martin Luther King Commn., Detroit, 1987; chairperson bd. dirs. task force on infant mortality Mich. Legislature, 1987; pres. Nat. Black Child Devel. Inst., Detroit; vol. United Negro Coll. Fund, 1987—; founder, adminstr. Black Caucus Found. of Mich., 1987—. Recipient cert. of appreciation Mich. Dept. Edn., 1986, Advs. award Mich. Health Mothers, Health Babies Coalition, 1987; named Woman Leader in Pub. Health, Mi ch. Assn. Local Pub. Health, 1987, Woman of Yr., Minority Women's Network, 1988. Mem. NAACP, Nat. Conf. State Legislators (exec. commr. 1986), Nat. Black Caucus State Legislators, (sec. women's caucus), Mich. Legis. Black Causus (chair 1987), Alpha Kappa Alpha. Democrat. Clubs: Cameo, Top Ladies of Distinction. Home: 19793 Sorrento Detroit MI 48235 Office: Mich Ho of Reps State Capitol Lansing MI 48909

STALOCH, JAMES EDWARD, JR., vocational educator; b. Worthington, Minn., Aug. 14, 1946; s. James Edward and Cecil Ilo (Rist) S.; m. Susan Kay Schroeder, June 8, 1968; children: Paul, Jennifer, Michael. BS, Moorhead (Minn.) State U., 1971; MEd, U. Minn., 1986. Asst. constrn. engr. Ford Motor Co., Dearborn, Mich., 1968-69; tchr. St. Paul Pub. Schs., 1971-72; mgr. Litho Shop, Mpls., 1972-74; trade and indsl. supr. Dakota County Vocat. Sch., Rosemount, Minn., 1974-93; customized tng. & devel. coord., 1993—. Sr. mem. Civil Air Patrol, cert. flight instr.; pres. Northview Elem. PTA, Eagan, Minn.; pres. Rosemount Youth Hoc Assn.; v.p., bd. dirs. Metro Ringette Coun. Served with U.S. Army, 1966-68, Vietnam. Mem. ASCD, Am. Legion, VFW, Dakota County Vocat. Inst. Alumni Assn. (bd. dirs.), Nat. Assn. Flight Instrs., Am. Vocat. Assn., Minn. Vocat. Assn., Phi Kappa Phi. Roman Catholic. Office: 1300 145th St E Rosemount MN 55068-2932

STAMBAUGH, PEGGY GENE, mental health nurse; b. Omaha, Nebr., Aug. 27, 1952; d. Harold Edward Nicklen and Mary Elizabeth (Davis) Wiese; m. Rick Lynn; children: Darren, Michelle, Stacey, Anthony Cook, Kevin Kersch. B.S. in Nursing and English, Mount Marty Coll., Yankton, S.D., 1980. R.N., Nebr; cert. mental health nursing. Psychiat. technician Douglas County Hosp., Omaha, 1970-75; tutor Aid the Vietnamese, Yankton, S.D., 1978-80; psychiat. charge nurse St. Joseph Hosp., Omaha, 1980-82; med. charge nurse Luth. Community Hosp., Norfolk, Nebr., 1982-85; psychiat. nurse Norfolk Regional Ctr., 1985-91. Editor mag. Mid Stream, 1976-80. Sec., Young Republicans, Yankton, 1979. Named Outstanding Young Woman Am., 1980. Mem. Am. Nurses Assn., Nat. Nurses Assn., Norfolk Bus. and Profl. Women. Democrat. Roman Catholic. Avocations: writing nursing articles; crocheting; reading. Home: 55826 853rd Rd Hoskins NE 68740-9726

STAMBERGER, EDWIN HENRY, farmer, civic leader; b. Mendota, Ill., Feb. 16, 1916; s. Edwin Nicolaus and Emilie Anna Marie (Yost) S.; m. Mabel Edith Gordon, Oct. 6, 1937; 1 child, Larry Allan. Farmer seed corn, livestock, machinery devel. Mendota, 1939—; bd. dirs. Mendota Coop. & Supply Co., 1949-67, pres., 1958-67. Mem. coun. Mendota Luth. Ch., 1958-64, chmn., 1964, treas. N.W. conf., 1966-68, trustee Bible camp; mem. Mendota Watershed and Flood Ctrl. Com., 1966-73, 77-79, started flood control City of Mendota, Ill., rev. and comment com. subregion and region Ill. Ctr. Comprehensive Health Planning Agy., 1974-76; asst. in devel. Mendota Hosp., Mendota Lake; chmn. bldg. com. Mendota Luth. Home, 1972-73; bd. dirs. LaSalle County Mental Health Bd., 1969-74, U. Ill. County Extension, 1963-67, chmn., 1966-67; bd. dirs. Soil and Water Dist., 1968-73, vice chmn., 1971-73. Recipient Future Farmers Am. award. Mem. Am. Soc. Agrl. Engrs., Ill. Coun. Watersheds, Smithsonian Inst., Mental Health Assn., People-to-People Internat., Internat. Platform Assn., Mendota C. of C. (Honor award 1974), Mendota Sportsman's Club, Loyal Order of Moose, Odd Fellows, Lions (bd. dirs. Mendota chpt. 1965-67, Honor award 1981). Home and Office: Sabine Farm 4429 E 250th Rd Mendota IL 61342-9426

STAMOS, JOHN JAMES, judge; b. Chgo., Jan. 30, 1924; s. James S. and Katherine (Manolopoulos) S.; m. Helen Voutiritsas, Sept. 3, 1955 (dec. 1981); children—James, Theo, Colleen, Jana; m. Mary Sotter, March 21, 1986. LL.B., DePaul U., 1948. Bar: Ill. 1949. Since practiced in Chgo.;

asst. corp. counsel City Chgo., 1951-54; asst. states atty. Cook County, 1954-61; chief criminal div. States Attys. Office, 1961-64, 1st asst. states atty., 1964-66, states atty., 1966-68; judge Appellate Ct. of State of Ill., 1968-88; Judge Ill. Supreme Ct., Springfield, 1988-90; ret., 1990; of counsel Stamos and Trucco, Chgo., 1991—. Served with AUS, 1943-45.

STAMOS, PETER, telecommunications executive; b. Jamaica, N.Y., May 7, 1958; s. George Peter and Georgia (Rahaniotes) S.; m. Elizabeth Alison Murphy, May 1, 1993. BS, St. John's U., Jamaica, N.Y., 1980. Sales rep. Phoenix Mutual Life Ins., N.Y.C., 1980-84; regional mgr. Cuffs Notes, Inc., Lincoln, Nebr., 1984-86; v.p. sales DAta Clean Corp., Bensenville, Ill., 1986-94; dir. SkyTel Corp., Chgo., 1995—; ins. broker, N.Y.C., 1981-84; telecom. cons. VTE, Chgo., 1994—. Vol. youth counselor 61st Precinct Youth Program, Bklyn., 1983-86, Chgo. Dist., 1993—. Mem. Data Processing Mgrs. Assn., Am. Mktg. Assn., Bus. Resumption Planners Assn. (bd. dirs. 1989-92), Am Mktg. Assn. Office: SkyTel Corp 1600 Golf Rd Ste 1100 Rolling Meadows IL 60008

STAMPER, JAMES M., retired English language educator; b. Roxana, Ky., Sept. 26, 1917; s. Marion and Amanda (Combs) S.; m. Diane C. Mahoney, Aug. 12, 1967. BS in Edn., Union Coll., 1941; MA in English, U. Ky., 1946. Subs. tchr. Ermine Elem. Sch., Dry Fork Elem. Sch., 1936-37; elem. tchr. various schs., 1937-41; h.s. Eng. tchr. Whitesburg H.S., Ky., 1941-46; instr. English U. Ky., Lexington, 1946-49, U. Md., College Park, 1949-52; instr. bus. English DePaul U., Chgo., 1952-62; English tchr., cons. in high sch. English Bd. Edn., Chgo., 1962-72; ret. Chgo. Area Schs., 1972; subst. tchr. Chgo. Area schs., 1972-82; vis. instr. in English Jacksonville (Fla.) U. Co-author: A Handbook on Oral Reading Diagnosis, Resource Materials for Essential English in the Secondary Schools, A Syllabus in Basic English; contbr. articles to profl. jours. Scholar Knights of Columbus, Union Coll., U. Ky. Mem. AARP. Home: 1448 N Picadilly Cir Mount Prospect IL 60056-1028

STAMPLE, JAMES M., plant engineer; b. St. Charles, Ill., Dec. 16, 1960. Student, Coll. DuPage. Maintenance supr., technician solder wave ops. Tellabs, Lisle, Ill., 1984-86; plant engr. Morey Corp., Downers Grove, Ill., 1986—. With USN, 1979-86. Mem. Am. Inst. Plant Engrs. Office: Morey Corp 2659 Wisconsin Ave Downers Grove IL 60515-4244

STAMSTA, DUANE ROBERT, commissioner; b. Chgo., Apr. 15, 1931; s. Marius and Stella (Rollofson) S.; m. Jean F. Nagel, Aug. 16, 1956; children: Marc Jon, David Tom. BS, U. Wis., Milw., 1958. Asst. v.p. Time Ins. Co., Milw., 1959-89; commr. planning commn. Town of Merton, Wis., 1989—; supr. dist. 3 Waukesha County Bd., 1990—, exec. com., 1991-93, chmn. health and human svcs. com., 1991-93, mem. fin. com., 1993—. Chmn. North Lake (Wis.) Sch. Bd., 1978-88. With U.S. Army, 1950-52. Home: W299N 9313 Center Oak Rd Hartland WI 53029

STANBERY, ROBERT CHARLES, veterinarian; b. Conneaut, Ohio, Apr. 5, 1947; s. Robert James and Ruth Virginia Stanbery; student Miami U., Oxford, Ohio, 1965-67; D.V.M., Ohio State U., 1971; m. Constance Ann Coutts, July 24, 1971; children: Scott Andrew, Mark Donald. Veterinarian, Lexington (Mass.) Animal Hosp., 1971-74, Avon Lake Animal Clinic Inc. (Ohio) 1974-76; pres., treas. Bay Village Animal Clinic Inc., Ohio, 1976—. Mem. AVMA, Ohio Vet. Med. Assn., Animal Hosp. Assn. Cleve. Acad. Vet. Medicine, Lorain County Vet. Assn. Internat. Platform Assn., Bay Village C. of C. (bd. dirs., pres.), U.S. Jaycees (Outstanding Young Man of Am. 1976). Fundamentalist Christian. Home: 309 Timberlane Dr Avon Lake OH 44012-1541 Office: 627 Clague Pky Bay Village OH 44140-3004

STANCATI, JOHN F., municipal official; b. Swickley, Pa., Jan. 18, 1935; s. Anthony J. and Anna A. (DeMarco) S.; m. Joan G. Stancati, July 12, 1957; children: Cathryn, Susan, Nancy. Student, Ind. U., Bloomington, Ind. U., South Bend, Western Mich. U. Dir. South Bend (Ind.) Water Wks. Vice pres. St. Joseph River Basin Commn., South Bend, 1993—; state treas. Dem. Party, Indpls., 1983-85. Mem. South Bend C. of C. (pres. 1973-75), Am. Water Wks. Assn., Sumit Club (pres. 1975-76). Office: South Bend Water Wks 224 N Main St South Bend IN 46601-1217

STANCZYK, BENJAMIN CONRAD, judge; b. Detroit, Apr. 4, 1915; s. Bruno and Josephine (Tarczynski) S.; m. Stephanie W. Wojsowski, June 4, 1946; children: Benjamin Conrad Jr., Kathy Jo Thibault. AB, Wayne State U., 1936; JD, U. Mich., 1939. Bar: Mich. 1939, U.S. Dist. Ct. (ea. and we. dists.) Mich. 1939, U.S. Ct. Appeals (6th and 10th cir.) 1943. Pvt. practice Detroit, 1939-49, asst. pros. atty., 1949-57; judge Common Pleas Ct., Detroit, 1957-75; vis. judge State of Mich., Detroit, 1975—; chair Income Tax Study Commn., Detroit, 1960-62; adv. bd. Madonna Coll., 1961-65; chair Tri-County Dental Health Coun., Detroit, 1962-68, pres., 1962-65. Pub. Poles in Michigan. Pres. Polish Nat. Alliance 167, Detroit, 1949-57, Ctrl. Citizens Commn., Polish Coordinating Coun., Detroit, 1951-58, Cass Tech H.S. Assn., 1964-65; spokesmen Detroit's Polish Cmty. in Pol. and Cult. Matters, 1950-75, mem. Adv. Com. on Sch. Needs, Detroit, 1956-58; trustee Hist. Soc. Mich., 1988—; adv. dem. Platform Comm. of Fgn. Affairs, 1952, 56; mem. exec. bd. Detroit's 250th Birthday Com., 1951; mem. Mich. Soccer and Football Commn., 1956-58; pres., mem. adv. bd. Vols. Am., 1977-80; organizer family music concerts Detroit Symphony Orch., 1954; active NAACP. With U.S. Army, 1942-46. Mem. ABA, NRA, NAACP, Grosse Point Camera Club (pres. 1993-94, 96—), Lions (pres. Detroit chpt. 1966-67, 96—), Pi Sigma Alpha, Delta Sigma Rho. Democrat. Roman Catholic. Office: 22811 Mack Ste 211 Saint Clair Shores MI 48080

STANDBERRY, HERMAN LEE, school system administrator, consultant; b. Oran, Mo., Feb. 22, 1945; s. Willie Standberry and Bettie Mae (Thompson) Standberry-Taylor; m. Barbara Irene Palmer, July 1, 1942; children: Donna, Debra, Nina, Miriam, Miranda, Gretchen, Charles, Mary, Dwayne, Helena, Regina, Lakesha. BS, So. Ill. U., 1968; MA, Newport U., 1981, LHD (hon.), 1990; EdD, Walden U., 1992; D Ministry, U. Bibl. Studies and Sem., 1996. Cert. supt., gen. adminstr., curriculum, tchr. Tchr. Community H.S. Dist. 428, Blue Island, Ill., 1968-70; exec. dir. Kane County Coun. for Econ. Opportunity, Batavia, Ill., 1970-75; dep. dir./program planner, Head-Start dir., casemgr., youth supr., educator State of Ill., Dept. Pub. Aid., Dept. Corrections, Chgo., Joliet and St. Charles, Ill., 1975-85; adminstrv. asst. to prin. Bloom High Sch. Dist. 206, Chicago Heights, Ill., 1992-93; asst. prin. Rogers High Sch., Michigan City, Ind., 1994-95; prin. Mich. City (Ind.) Area Alternative H.S., 1995—; chmn. bd. dirs. Greater Chgo. Coun. of Religious Orgns., 1985-89; mem. George Bush's Rep. Presdl. Task Force, Washington, 1989; nominated mem. U.S. Rep. Senatorial Inner Cir., Washington, 1989. Author (curriculum) Business Law I & II, 1968, Career Counseling and Survival, 1978. Bd. dirs. United Way, Elgin, Ill, 1972, City of Elgin-Fremont Youth Orgn., 1971-72; host agy. rep. Dept. Human Svcs., Chgo., 1985-90; sustaining mem. Ill. Rep. Party, Springfield, 1989; host agy. Percy Julian High Sch., Chgo., 1989-90, Ill. Dept. Pub. Aid, Chgo., 1987. Recipient grant Ill. Dept. Pub. Aid, 1984-87, hon. award Christian World Affairs Conf., 1985-86. Mem. Internat. Assn. Police and Community Rel. Officers, United Evangelistic Consulting Assn. (chmn. bd. dirs., pres. 1985—). Home: 803 E 193rd St Glenwood IL 60425-2011 Office: United Evangelistic Assn 1236-42 W 103d St Chicago IL 60643

STANDIFER, SABRINA, state legislator; m. Brad Barkley. Mem. Kans. Ho. of Reps., 1993—; self-employed computer cons. Democrat. Home: 317 W 41st St N Wichita KS 67204-3203 Office: Kans Ho of Reps State Capitol Topeka KS 66612

STANEVICH, KENNETH WILLIAM, staff engineer; b. Berwyn, Ill., June 12, 1958; s. William George and Susanna Regina (Logins) S.; m. Jill Elaine Dahlberg, June 2, 1990; 1 child, Kyle. AS, Morton Coll., 1981; student, U. Ill., Chgo., 1981-85. Designer, prodn. coord. Grayhill, Inc., LaGrange, Ill., 1983; product engr. Molex, Inc., Lisle, Ill., 1985-88; supr. product devel. engring. Augat Automotive Divsn., Mt. Clemens, Mich., 1988-92; mgr. mech. design Robertshaw Controls Co.-Simicon Divsn., Holland, Mich., 1992-94; staff engr. TRW-Transp. Electronics Divsn., Farmington Hills, Mich., 1994-95; mgr. new connector devel. Ideal Industries, Inc., Sycamore, Ill., 1996—. Patentee in field. Co-chmn. study-a-thon Muscular Dystrophy Assn., 1981. Mem. Soc. Plastics Engrs., Soc. Auto. Engrs. (student chpt. pres. 1984-85), Mensa.

STANFILL, BRIAN EUGENE, county official; b. Oxford, Ohio, June 26, 1958; s. Kenneth Dean and Barbara Jean (Tope) S.; m. Nancy Hall, June 25, 1983; children: Timothy Andrew, Katherine Ann, Amy Elizabeth. BS in Fin., Ohio State U., 1985; MBA, U. Dayton, 1987. Mgr. Wendy's Internat., Columbus, Ohio, 1979-83; mgr. retail lockbox BancOhio Nat. Bank, Columbus, 1983-86; county adminstr. County of Delaware, Ohio, 1987—; dir. emergency mgmt. Delaware County Emergency Mgmt., 1987—. Bd. dirs. Recreation Unltd., Ctrl. Ohio Symphony Orch., treas. Named Eagle Scout with Double Silver Palms Boy Scouts Am., 1973, God and Country award, 1975. Mem. Nat. Assn. County Adminstrs., Ohio Assn. County Adminstrs. (sec.-treas. 1989, v.p. 1990, pres. 1991), Delaware Area C. of C. (bd. dirs.), Rotary (team mem. group study exch. with Denmark 1992, pres. Del. club 1996—). Republican. Mem. Grace Brethren Ch. Office: County of Delaware 101 N Sandusky St Delaware OH 43015-1732

STANFORD, MELVIN JOSEPH, retired dean, educator; b. Logan, Utah, June 13, 1932; s. Joseph Sedley and Ida Pearl (Ivie) S.; m. Yvonne Watson, Feb. 8, 1951 (div. 1956); children: Connie Stanford Tendick, Cheryl Stanford Bohn; m. Linda Barney, Sept. 2, 1960; children: Joseph Barney Stanford, Theodore Barney Stanford, Emily Stanford, Charlotte Stanford Vaughan, Charles Barney Stanford, Sarah Stanford. B.S. (First Security Found. scholar), Utah State U., 1957; M.B.A. (Donald Kirk David fellow), Harvard U., 1963; Ph.D., U. Ill., 1968. CPA, Utah. Asst. audit supr. Utah Tax Commn., 1959-61, auditor, 1958-59; acct. Haskins & Sells, C.P.A.s, Boston, 1961-62; acctg. staff analyst Arabian Am. Oil Co., Dhahran, Saudi Arabia, 1963-66; teaching and rsch. asst. U. Ill., Urbana, 1966-68; mem. faculty Brigham Young U., Provo, Utah, 1968-82; dir. mgmt. devel. programs Brigham Young U., 1970-73, prof. bus. mgmt., 1974-82; dean Coll. Bus., Mankato (Minn.) State U., 1982-89, prof. mgmt., 1989-94, prof. emeritus, 1994—; mem. adv. bd. M.L. Bigelow & Co., Inc., Organ Builders; cons. Strategic Planning, Decision Case Mgmt., New Enterprise Mgmt.; vis. prof. mgmt. Boston U., Europe, 1975-76; vis. prof. agrl. mgmt. U. Minn., 1991-92. Author: New Enterprise Management, 1975, 82, Management Policy, 1979, 83; co-author: Cases in Business Policy and Strategy, 1990, Decision Cases for Agriculture, 1992, Business Plan Guidebook, 1995; also articles, mgmt. cases; founder Midwestern Jour. Bus. and Econs., 1985. Bishop, Mankato ward LDS Ch., 1987-91. With USAF, 1951-55, USAR, 1956-80. Named Amb. of City of Mankato, 1988. Fellow N.Am. Case Rsch. Assn. (v.p. for rsch. 1985-86, pres. 1987-88, Curtis E. Tate Jr. Outstanding Case Writer award 1992); mem. SAR (pres. Utah 1978-79, nat. trustee 1979-81, Meritorious Svc. medal 1981, Patriot medal 1991), Kiwanis, Sons of Utah Pioneers, Alpha Kappa Psi, Phi Kappa Phi. Home: 1754 Cobblestone Dr Provo UT 84604-1155

STANFORTH, STEVEN RICHARD, electronics executive, accountant, consultant; b. Wilmington, Ohio, June 22, 1959; s. John Richard and Patricia Elizabeth (Griffith) S. BSB, Wright State U., 1981. CPA, Ohio; CMA. Staff acct. Kentner & Sellers, CPA, Dayton, Ohio, 1980-81; audit sr. Ernst & Whinney, Dayton, 1981-85; mgr. Stout & Duncan, CPAs, Dayton, 1985-87; tax sr. mgr. Ernst & Young, Dayton, 1987-94; v.p. fin., CFO Tech. Devices N.A. Inc., Dayton, 1994—; bus. and tax cons. Steven R. Stanforth CPA, Dayton, 1986—. Com. mem. United Way, Dayton, 1992-94; fin. advisor Montgomery County Housing Bd., 1989. Mem. AICPA, Ohio Soc. CPA's (chair mem. com. 1987), Inst. Mgmt. Accts. (v.p. 1992-93, pres. 1993-94), Miami Valley Golf Club, Kettering Tennis Ctr. Home: 4500 Rean Meadow Dr Kettering OH 45440 Office: Tech Devices NA Inc 9181 N Dixie Dr Dayton OH 45414

STANLEY, ARTHUR JEHU, JR., federal judge; b. nr. Lincoln, Kans., Mar. 21, 1901; s. Arthur and Bessie (Anderson) S.; m. Ruth Willis, July 16, 1927; children: Mary Louise Stanley Andrews, Carolyn Stanley Lane, Constance Stanley Yunghans, Susan Stanley Hoffman. LL.B., Kansas City Sch. Law (U. Mo.), Kansas City, 1928. Bar: Kans. bar 1928. County atty. Wyandotte County, Kans., 1935-41; U.S. dist. judge Dist. of Kans., Leavenworth, 1958-71; chief judge Dist. of Kans., 1961-71, sr. U.S. dist. judge, 1971—; mem. Jud. Conf. U.S., 1967-70, chmn. com. on operation jury system, 1973-78, mem. bicentennial com., 1975-78. Mem. Kans. Senate, 1941. Served with 7th U.S. Cav. Can. Army, World War I; with USN, 1921-25; Yangtze Patrol Force 1923-25; 9th Air Force USAAF, 1941-45; disch. to Inf. Res. as lt. col. Fellow Am. Bar Found.; mem. ABA, Kans. Bar Assn., Wyandotte County Bar Assn. (past pres.), Leavenworth County Bar Assn., Am. Judicature Soc., Kans. Hist. Soc. (pres. 1974-75), Am. Legion. Anglican. Home: 501 N Esplanade St Leavenworth KS 66048-2027 Office: US Dist Ct 235 Fed Bldg Leavenworth KS 66048

STANLEY, CHRISTOPHER DENNIS, religious studies educator; b. Birmingham, Ala., Mar. 2, 1955; s. Donald and Mary Evelyn (Jones) S.; m. Laurel Virginia O'Brien, May 7, 1976; children: Jeremy Adam, David Joseph. BS in Commerce, U. Va., 1976; M of Christian Studies, Regent Coll., 1983; PhD of Religion, Duke U., 1990. From adminstrv. asst. to asst. v.p. AMVEST Corp., Charlottesville, Va., 1976-80; instr., adminstr. Ctr. for Christian Study, Charlottesville, 1982-85; resident dir. Emmaus with Child, Scottsville, Va., 1985-86; tchg. asst., rsch. asst. Duke U., Durham, N.C., 1986-90; lectr. religious studies U. N.C., Greensboro, 1990-91; vis. asst. prof. religious studies N.C. State U., Raleigh, 1991-92; asst. prof. religious studies Hastings (Nebr.) Coll., 1992-93, McKendree Coll., 1993—. Author: Paul and the Language of Scripture, 1990; contbr. articles to books and jours. Mem., bd. dirs. Washington Park (Ill.) Comty. Coalition, 1995. Travel grantee Midwest Faculty Seminar, U. Chgo., 1994. Mem. Internat. Orgn. for Septuagent and Cognate Studies, Soc. Bib. Lit., Phi Beta Kappa. Home: 2408 Richland Prairie Blvd Belleville IL 62221 Office: McKendree Coll 701 College Rd Lebanon IL 62254

STANLEY, MARGARET DURETA SEXTON, retired speech therapist; b. Wells County, Ind., Aug. 7, 1931; d. James Helmuth and Bertha Anna (Kizer) Roberts; m. Gale Sexton, Nov. 21, 1950; children: Cregg Alan, Donna Sue, Sheila Rene; m. Charles Stanley, Mar. 24, 1979. BS, Ball State U., 1952, MA, 1963. Speech and hearing clinician Hamilton (Ohio) City Schs., 1955-59, Kettering (Ohio) Pub. Schs., 1959-60; speech, lang. and hearing clinician Muncie (Inc.) Community Schs., 1960-93; asst. prof. speech pathology Ball State U., 1993—; dir. Psi Iota Xi Summer Clinic, Decatur, Ind., 1964, Ball State U., 1965-77, asst. prof., 1993—; supr. clinician Tri-County Hearing Impaired Assn., 1978-81. Compiler, editor curriculum for speech, lang. and hearing clinicians of Muncie Community Schs. Mem. NEA, Am. Speech and Hearing Assn., Ind. Edn. Assn., Ind. Coun. Suprs. Speech and Hearing (pres. 1982-84), Speech and Hearing Area Educators Ind. (founder, 1st pres. 1984-86, Disting. Svc. award 1991, Honors of Assoc. 1992), Delta Kapa Gamma (1st v.p. 1992-94, pres. 1994-96). Republican. Methodist. Home: 10871 W St Rd 32 Parker City IN 47368-9721 Office: Dept of Speech Pathology and Audiology Ball State U Muncie IN 47306

STANLEY, MICHAEL FRITZ, production engineer; b. Wichita Falls, Tex., July 2, 1952. Student, Purdue U., 1970; Assoc. Digital Electronics, Ind. Vocat. Tech. Coll., 1986. Electronic technician State of Ind. Toll Rds., Elkhart, 1985-89; prodn. engr. Shuttleworth Inc., Huntington, Ind., 1989—. Staff sgt. USAF, 1972-76. Mem. Kiwanis. Mem. Christian Ch. (Disciples of Christ). Office: Shuttleworth Inc 10 Commercial Rd Huntington IN 46750-8805

STANLEY, RICHARD HOLT, consulting engineer; b. Muscatine, Iowa, Oct. 20, 1932; s. Claude Maxwell and Elizabeth Mabel (Holthues) S.; m. Mary Jo Kennedy, Dec. 20, 1953; children: Lynne Elizabeth, Sarah Catherine, Joseph Holt. BSEE and BSME, Iowa State U., 1955; MS in Sanitary Engring., U. Iowa, 1963. Lic. profl. engr., Iowa, other states. With Stanley Cons. Inc., Muscatine, Iowa, 1955—, pres., 1971-87, chmn., 1984—; also bd. dirs. Stanley Cons. Inc.; bd. dirs. HON Industries, Inc., vice-chmn., 1979—; chmn. Nat. Constrn. Industry Coun., 1978, Com. Fed. Procurement Archtl.-Engring. Svcs., 1979; pres. Ea. Iowa C.C., Bettendorf, 1966-68; mem. indsl. adv. coun. Iowa State U. Coll. Engring., Ames, 1969—, chmn., 1979-81. Contbr. articles to profl. jours. BD. dirs. N.E.-Midwest Inst., 1989-95, treas., 1991-93, chmn., 1993-95; bd. dirs. Stanley Found., 1956—, pres., 1984—; bd. dirs. Muscatine Health Support Found., pres., 1984—; bd. dirs. Muscatine United Way, 1969-75, Iowa State U. Meml. Union, 1968-83, U. Dubuque, Iowa, 1977-93, Inst. Social and Econ. Devel., 1992-; bd. govs. Iowa State U. Achievement Found., 1982-96. Recipient Young Alumnus award Iowa State U. Alumni Assn., 1966, Disting. Svc. award Muscatine Jaycees, 1967, Profl. Achievement citation Coll. Engring., Iowa State U., 1977, Anson Marston medal Iowa State U., 1991; named Sr. Engr. of Yr., Joint Engring. Com. Quint Cities, 1973. Fellow ASCE, Am. Cons. Engrs. Coun. (pres. 1976-77), Iowa Acad. Sci.; mem. IEEE (sr.), ASME, Am. Soc. Engring. Edn., Nat. Soc. Profl. Engrs., Cons. Engrs. Coun. Iowa (pres. 1967), Iowa Engring. Soc. (pres. 1973-74, John Dunlap-Sherman Woodward award 1967, Disting. Svc. award 1980, Voice of Engr. award 1987, Herbert Hoover Centennial award 1989), Muscatine C. of C. (pres. 1972-73), C. of C. of U.S. (constrn. action coun. 1976-91), Tau Beta Pi, Phi Kappa Phi, Pi Tau Sigma, Eta Kappa Nu. Presbyterian (elder). Club: Rotary. Home: 601 W 3rd St Muscatine IA 52761-3119 Office: Stanley Cons Inc Stanley Bldg Muscatine IA 52761

STANNY, GARY, infosystems specialist, rocket scientist; b. Detroit, Aug. 2, 1953; s. Richard Telesfor and Gertrude Mildred (Eisenbach) S. AS, Washtenaw Community Coll., 1973; B in Computer Sci., Ea. Mich. U., 1975. Programmer Ann Arbor (Mich.) Terminals, 1976-78; sr. programmer, analyst Mfg. Data Systems Inc., Ann Arbor, 1978-83; sr. software specialist Digital Equipment Corp., Farmington Hills, Mich., 1983-85; sr. systems cons. Tierra del Fuego Ltd, Whitmore Lake, Mich., 1985-87, v.p. rsch. and devel., 1987—, also bd. dirs.; bd. dirs. RTS Enterprises, South Lyon, Mich.; dir. rsch. & devel., Lynn-Arthur Assocs., 1993—. Author: Ingres RMS Benchmarks, 1986, The S&P Premium Matrix, 1991; inventor in field; developer software TDF-lib, 1993. Counselor Drug Help, Ann Arbor, 1971-77, Rep. candidate senate, Ann Arbor, 1976; mem. Students Dem. Soc. State of Mich. Competitive Sci. grantee, 1971. Mem. Am. Assn. Artificial Intelligence Rsch. (computing machinery), Digital Equipment Computer Users Soc., Decus Artificial Intelligence Spl. Interest Group, Soc. Machine Intelligence, Mensa. Office: Tierra del Fuego Ltd 7725 Shady Beach St Whitmore Lake MI 48189-9514

STANTON, JANET LYN, social service administrator; b. Pana, Ill., Apr. 20, 1943; d. Reginald E. and Eva Vivian (Abernathy) Culberson; children: Steven Blaine, Matthew Wayne. AA, Stephens Coll., 1963; BA, U. Ill., Springfield, 1985; MA, Sangamon State U., 1990. Interior designer Springfield, Ill., 1965-72; florist Illiopolis, Ill., 1972-80; prevention specialist Rape Info., Springfield, Ill., 1982-84; project dir. ISEARCH Sangamon County, Springfield, Ill., 1984-85; trainer, adminstr. Ill. State Police, Springfield, 1985-90; adminstr. Ounce of Prevention Fund, Chgo., 1990—. Bd. dirs. Youth Svc. Bur., Springfield, 1985-91, Nat. Orgn. on Adolescent Pregnancy, Parenting and Prevention, 1995—; bd. dirs., chair Ill. Caucus Adolescent Health, Chgo., 1991—; mem. gov.'s task force on teen suicide State of Ill., Springfield, 1987-88; mem. libr. bd. Illipolis (Ill.) Libr., 1975-85. Mem. Ill. Caucus Adolescent Health, Am. Profl. Soc. on the Abuse of Children. Methodist. Office: Ounce of Prevention Fund 122 S Michigan Ste 2050 Chicago IL 60603

STANTON, JEANNE FRANCES, retired lawyer; b. Vicksburg, Miss., Jan. 22, 1920; d. John Francis and Hazel (Mitchell) S.; student George Washington U., 1938-39; BA, U. Cin., 1940; JD, Salmon P. Chase Coll. Law, 1954. Admitted to Ohio bar, 1954; chief clk. Selective Svc. Bd., Cin., 1940-43; instr. USAAF Tech. Schs., Biloxi, Miss., 1943-44; with Procter & Gamble, Cin., 1945-84, legal asst., 1952-54, head advt. svcs. sect. legal div., trade practices dept., 1954-73, mgr. advt. svcs., legal div., 1973-84, ret., 1984. Team capt. Community Chest Cin., 1953; mem. ann. meeting com. Archaeol. Inst. Am., 1983; trustee, asst. corr. sec., statutory agt. Friends of Bronze Age Archaeology in the Aegean area, 1987—. Mem. ABA (chmn. subcom. D of com. 307 copyright sect. 1987-88, 89, 90), Ohio Bar Assn. (chmn. uniform state laws com. 1968-70), Cin. Bar Assn. (sec. law day com. 1965-66, chmn. com. on preservation hist. documents 1968-71), Vicksburg and Warren County Hist. Soc, Cin. Hist. Soc., Intercontinental Biog. Assn., Lawyers Club Cin. (exec. com. 1979—, pres. 1983), Cin. Women Lawyers (treas. 1958-59, nominating com. 1976), Terrace Park Country Club. Personal philosophy: Most people are good and honest. If a person does the honorable thing, that is its own reward. Home: 2302 Easthill Ave Cincinnati OH 45208-2608

STANTON, ROGER D., lawyer; b. Waterville, Kans., Oct. 4, 1938; s. George W. and Helen V. (Peterson) S.; m. Judith L. Duncan, Jan. 27, 1962; children: Jeffrey B., Brady D., Todd A. AB, U. Kans., 1960, JD, 1963. Bar: Kans. 1963, U.S. Dist. Ct. Kans. 1963, U.S. Ct. Appeals (10th cir.) 1972, U.S. Supreme Ct. 1973. Assoc. Stanley, Schroeder, Weeks, Thomas & Lysaught, Kansas City, Kans., 1963-68; ptnr. Weeks, Thomas, Lysaught, Bingham & Johnston, Kansas City, 1968-72, Weeks, Thomas & Lysaught, 1969-80, also bd. dirs., chmn. exec. com., 1981-82, Stinson, Mag & Fizzell, 1983—; chmn. products practice group, also bd. dirs., 1993-95. Active Boy Scouts Am., 1973-79; pres. YMCA Youth Football Club, 1980-82; co-chmn. Civil Justice Reform Act com. Dist. of Kans., 1991-95. Fellow Am. Coll. Trial Lawyers (state chmn. 1984-86); mem. Internat. Assn. Def. Counsel, Am. Bd. Trial Adv., Def. Rsch. Inst. (state co-chmn. 1979-90, Exceptional Performance award 1979), Kans. Bar Assn. (Pres.'s award 1982), Johnson County Bar Found. (v.p., trustee), Kans. Assn. Def. Counsel (pres. 1977-78), Kans. Inn. Ct., U. Kans. Sch. Law Alumni Assn. (bd. dirs. 1972-75). Chmn. bd. editors Jour. Kans. Bar Assn., 1975-83; contbr. articles to legal jours. Office: Stinson Mag & Fizzell 7500 W 110th St Overland Park KS 66210-2328

STANTON, SANDRA SUNQUIST, school counselor, consultant, educator; b. Morris, Minn., Nov. 4, 1946; d. Herbert Charles and Marie C. (Johnson) Sunquist; m. Robert David Stanton, Apr. 15, 1967; children: Dawn, Jennifer, Heidi. BA, U. Wis., Eau Claire, 1968; MS, U. Wis., Stout, 1980. Cert. tchr., Wis.; cert. counselor, Wis.; cert. elem. adminstr., Wis.; cert. curriculum dir., Wis., Nat. Cert. Counselor, N.C.C., 1984—. Counselor, tchr. Bitburg Am. Dependent Sch., Bitburg AFB, West Germany, 1968-70; sch. counselor Osseo-Fairchild (Wis.) Sch. Dist., 1981-89, Eau Claire Area Pub. Schs., 1989—; project dir. Osseo-Fairchild Devel. Guidance Curriculum K-12, 1985-89; cons. Coop. Edn. Soc. Agy. 10, Chippewa Falls, Wis., 1986-89; final rev. team Wis. Devel. Guidance Model, Madison, 1987; mem. Eau Claire Edn. for Employment coun., 1989-93, Sch. to Work coun., 1993—; mem. Young-Am. Partnership com., 1995—; group leader Applied Acads., 1996—. Contbr. articles to profl. jours. Pres. bd. dirs. telephone counseling svc. T-A-P Line, Eau Claire, 1982-84; mem. Wis. Tchr.'s Forum. Wis. Dept. Pub. Inst. Project grantee, 1985-89, 87, alcohol and drug abuse project mini grantee, 1991. Mem. NEA, ACA, ASCD, Am. Sch. Counselor Assn., Assn. Spritual, Ethical and Religious Values in Counseling, Internat. Alliance for Invitational Edn., Wis. Sch. Counselors Assn. (elem. v.p. 1991-92, chair profl. recognition 1992—, spkr.). Home: E 4520 Woodfield Rd Eau Claire WI 54701 Office: Longfellow Elem Sch 512 Balcom St Eau Claire WI 54703-3201

STANTON, WILLIAM TAYLOR, manufacturing engineer; b. Detroit, Oct. 27, 1926; s. Luther Dill and Maggie Ethel (Smith) S.; m. Sue Carol Reed, Feb. 19, 1960 (div. Jan. 1983); children: Terry, Steven, William. Registered profl. engr., Calif. Contract engr. various locations, 1966—. Lodge: Eagles, Moose. Home: PO Box 1124 Connersville IN 47331-8124

STANTON-HICKS, MICHAEL D'ARCY, anesthesiologist, educator; b. Adelaide, Australia, June 3, 1931; came to U.S., 1972; s. Cedric Stanton-Hicks and Florence (Haggett) Perrin; m. Kristina Litsmark, Aug. 4, 1969 (div. Aug. 1984; children: Erik Michael, Leif Neal; m. Ursula Koch, Aug. 27, 1985. MB, BS, Adelaide U., 1962; Dr. of medicine, U. Dusseldorf, 1984. Bd. equivalent Am. Bd. Anesthesiology; diplomate Am. Bd. Pain Medicine. Intern Queen Elizabeth Hosp., Adelaide, 1961-62, tutor, staff anesthesiologist, 1970-72; resident Royal Postgrad. Med. Sch., London and Lasarettet Köping, 1966-68; asst. dir. anesthesiology intensive care Södersjükhuset, Stockholm, 1968-69; instr. anesthesiology U. Wash. Med. Sch., Seattle, 1969-70, asst. prof., 1972-75; prof., chmn. dept. U. Mass. Med. Sch., Worcester, 1975-83; prof. U. Colo. Health Scis. Ctr., Denver, 1983-86, vice chmn. dept., 1983-85, acting chmn., 1985-86; prof., dir. pain clinic and rsch. Johannes Gutenberg U., Mainz, Fed. Republic Germany, 1986-88, prof., 1986—; dir. pain mgmt. ctr. Cleve. Clinic Found., 1988—. Author, editor: Regional Anesthesia: Advances and Selected Topics, 1978; (with Boas) Chronic Low Back Pain, 1982; author: (with Raj and Nolte) Illustrated Manual of Regional Anesthesia, 1988 (Most Beautiful Book of Yr. award Frankfurt, Fed. Republic Germany Pubs. Book Conv. 1989), Pain and Sympathetic Nervous System, 1989; (with Janig and Boas) Reflex Sympathetic Dystrophy, 1989;

(with Janig) Reflex Sympathetic Dystrophy: A Reappraisal, 1996. Squadron leader res. Royal Australian Air Force, 1962-65. Australian Univs. Commn. mature age scholar, 1953-60. Fellow Royal Coll. Surgeons (faculty anesthetists), Royal Coll. Anesthetists, Am. Acad. Pain Medicine; mem. Internat. Assn. Study Pain (chmn. spl. interest group on sympathetically maintained pain 1990—), Am. Soc. Regional Anesthesia (bd. dirs. 1979-91, pres. 1989-90), Am. Soc. Anesthesiologists, Assn. Anesthetists Gt. Britain and Ireland, Ohio State Med. Assn., Cleve. Acad. Medicine, Am. Acad. Med. Infrared Imaging (bd. dirs. 1991—, pres. 1994-95), Am. Pain Soc., Am. Acad. Pain Medicine, Am. Neuromodulation Soc. (pres. 1994—), Army-Navy-Air Force Club. Republican. Anglican. Home: 198 Woodsong Way Chagrin Falls OH 44023-6703 Office: Cleve Clinic Found 9500 Euclid Ave Cleveland OH 44195-0001

STAPLES, DANNY LEW, state senator; b. Eminence, Mo., Apr. 1, 1935; s. Harvey R. and Edna O. (Smith) S.; m. Barbara Ann Salisbury, 1966; children: Jeannine Shaffer Spurgin, Janet Shaffer, Robin Staples, Joe Shaffer, Richard Staples. Student Southwest Mo. State U., 1952-54, Ark. State U., 1954. Mem. Mo. State Ho. of Reps., 1977-82, Mo. State Senate, Dist. 20, 1983—. Democrat. Methodist. Mem. Sigma Pi. Office: Rte 3 Box 18 Eminence MO 65466 also: State Senate State Capitol Building Jefferson City MO 65101-1556

STARACE, ANTHONY FRANCIS, theoretical atomic physicist; b. N.Y.C., July 24, 1945; s. Louis J. and Ione A. (Liva) S.; m. Katherine Anne Fritz, June 25, 1968; children: Alexander Fritz, Anne Katherine. AB cum laude, Columbia Coll., 1966; MS, U. Chgo., 1967, PhD, 1971. Rsch. assoc. Imperial Coll., London, 1971-72; asst. prof. Dept. Physics & Astronomy, U. Nebr., Lincoln, 1973-75, assoc. prof., 1975-81, prof., 1981—, chmn., 1984-95; mem. adv. bd. Inst. Theoretical Atomic and Molecular Physics Harvard-Smithsonian Ctr. Astrophysics, 1993-96, chmn., 1994-95; vis. fellow Harvard-Smithsonian Inst. Theoretical Atomic and Molecular Physics, Cambridge, Mass., 1995-96. Author: Theory of Atomic Photoionization, 1982; assoc. editor Revs. of Modern Physics, 1996—; mem. editl. bd. Phys. Rev. A, 1993—. Rsch. fellow Albert-Ludwigs U., Freiburg, Germany, 1979-80; fellow Alexander von Humboldt, 1979-80, Alfred P. Sloan Found., 1975-79; Joint Inst. for Lab. Astrophysics vis. fellow U. Colo., Boulder, 1992-93. Fellow Am. Phys. Soc. (chmn. div. atomic molecular and optical physics 1990-91). Office: U Nebr Dept Physics and Astronomy 116 Brace Lab Lincoln NE 68588-0111

STARK, JAY IRWIN, automotive company executive; b. Detroit, Mar. 11, 1944; s. Sidney S. and Bluma (Pupko) S.; m. Sandra R. Yanitz, Aug. 5, 1967; children: Eric, Michael. AB, Wayne State U., 1965; AM, U. Mich., 1967, PhD, 1969. Mgr. econ. and sales F/C GMC, Detroit, 1973-78, dir. overseas sales analysis, 1978-85, gen. dir. overseas mktg. product planning, 1985-87, exec. dir., NA vehicle ops. mktg. and product planning, 1988-92, exec. dir. worldwide market analysis, 1992-94; exec. dir. N.Am. market analysis, 1994—. Exec. com. Boy Scouts Am., Clinton Valley Coun., Pontiac, Mich., 1990. Mem. Am. Econs. Assn., Am. Statis. Assn. Home: 4221 Margate Ln Bloomfield Hills MI 48302-1627 Office: GM Corp Cadillac World Hdqrs 203-11 30009 Van Dyke Ave Warren MI 48090-9025

STARK, JOAN SCISM, education educator; b. Hudson, N.Y., Jan. 6, 1937; d. Ormonde F. and Myrtle Margaret (Kirkey) S.; m. William L. Stark, June 28, 1958 (dec.); children: Eugene William, Susan Elizabeth, Linda Anne, Ellen Scism; m. Malcolm A. Lowther, Jan. 31, 1981. B.S., Syracuse U., 1957; M.A. (Hoadly fellow), Columbia U., 1960; Ed.D., SUNY, Albany, 1971. Tchr. Ossining (N.Y.) High Sch., 1957-59; free-lance editor Holt, Rinehart & Winston, Harcourt, Brace & World, 1960-70; lectr. Ulster County Community Coll., Stone Ridge, N.Y., 1968-70; asst. dean Goucher Coll., Balt., 1970-73; asso. dean Goucher Coll., 1973-74; assoc. prof., chmn. dept. higher postsecondary edn. Syracuse (N.Y.) U., 1974-78; dean Sch. Edn. U. Mich., Ann Arbor, 1978-83, prof., 1983—; dir. Nat. Ctr. for Improving Postsecondary Teaching and Learning, 1991-96. Editor: Rev. of Higher Edn., 1991-96; contbr. articles to various publs. Leader Girl Scouts U.S.A., Cub Scouts Am.; coach girls Little League; dist. officer PTA, intermittently, 1968-80; mem. adv. com. Gerald R. Ford Library, U. Mich., 1980-83; trustee Kalamazoo Coll., 1979-85; mem. exec. com. Inst. Social Research, U. Mich., 1979-81; bd. dirs. Mich. Assn. Colls. Tchr. Edn., 1979-81. Mem. Am. Assn. for Higher Edn., Am. Ednl. Rsch. Assn., Assn. Study Higher Edn. (dir. 1977-79, v.p. 1983, pres. 1984, Rsch. Achievement award 1992), Assn. Innovation Higher Edn. (nat. chmn. 1974-75), Assn. Instl. Rsch. (disting. mem.), Assn. Colls. and Schs. Edn. State Univs. and Land Grant Colls. (dir. 1981-83), Acctg. Edn. Change Commn., Phi Beta Kappa, Phi Kappa Phi, Sigma Pi Sigma, Eta Pi Upsilon, Lambda Sigma Sigma, Phi Delta Kappa, Pi Lambda Theta. Office: Univ Mich 2002 Sch of Edn Ann Arbor MI 48109-1259

STARK, PATRICIA ANN, psychologist, educator; b. Ames, Iowa; d. Keith C. and Mary L. (Johnston) Moore. BS, So. Ill. U., Edwardsville, 1970, MS, 1972; PhD, St. Louis U., 1976. Counselor to alcoholics Bapt. Rescue Mission, East St. Louis, 1969; researcher alcoholics Gateway Rehab. Center, East St. Louis, 1972; psychologist intern Henry-Stark Counties Spl. Edn. Dist. and Galesburg State Research Hosp., Ill., 1972-73; instr. Lewis and Clark Community Coll., Godfrey, Ill., 1973-76, asst. prof., 1976-84, assoc. prof., 1984, coordinator child care services, 1974-84; mem. staff dept. psychiatry Meml. Hosp., St. Elizabeth's Hosp., 1979—; supr. various workshops in field, 1974—; dir. child and family services Collinsville Counseling Center, 1977-82; clin. dir., owner Empas-Complete Family Psychol. and Hypnosis Services, Collinsville, 1982—; cons. community agys., 1974—; mem. adv. bd. Madison County Council on Alcoholism and Drug Dependency, 1977-80. Mem. Am. Psychol. Assn., Ill. Psychol. Assn., Midwestern Psychol. Assn., Nat. Assn. Sch. Psychologists, Am. Soc. Clin. Hypnosis, Internat. Soc. Hypnosis. Office: 2802 Maryville Rd Maryville IL 62062

STARK, ROHN TAYLOR, professional football player; b. Mpls., May 4, 1959; m. Ann Stark; 1 child, Rohn Jr. BS in Finance, Fla. State U., 1982. With Indpls. Colts, 1982-84; punter Indpls. Colts (formerly Balt. Colts), 1984—. Punter on the Sporting News Coll. All-Am. Team, 1981, NFL All-Pro team, 1992; played in Pro Bowl 1985, 86, 90, 92. *

STARKE, SHIRLEY DIANA, composer, harpist; b. Valley City, N.D., July 3, 1950; d. Anthony Frank and Edith Louise (Collings) S. BA, Valley City State U., 1979. Author: Red Hugh: The Story of Hugh Roe O'Donnell, 1985, Voices of the Trees: Songs for the Harp, 1989, Celtica: Songs for the Harp, 1990, Song for the White Rider, 1992, The Black Bull of Norroway, 1993, How to Play the Folk Harp from Chord Symbols, 1995, Angel-Chief of Many Names, 1995. Mem. Mensa (editor Litir Scèala, The Prairie Dawg newsletter, coord. Irish spl. interest group Am.), Aodh Ruadh O'Domhnaill Guild (coord.), Nat. Hon. Soc., Phi Alpha Theta. Roman Catholic. Home: RR 2 Box 230 Valley City ND 58072-9802

STARKMAN, BETTY PROVIZER, genealogist, writer, educator; b. Detroit, July 18, 1929; d. Jack and Rose (Bodenstein) Provizer; m. Morris Starkman, Dec. 25, 1952; children: Susan Lynn Starkman Rott, Robert David Starkman. AB, Wayne State U., 1951; postgrad., U. Wis., 1949; MA, Wayne U., 1954. Cert. social worker. Social worker Wayne County Social Aid, Detroit, 1951-54, B'nai B'rith Youth Orgn., Detroit, 1951-54; genealogist, historian Birmingham, Mich., 1979—; tchr. Midrasha Coll., Southfield, Mich., 1986-88, Coll. Jewish Studies, Birmingham, 1986-88; lectr. Jewish Cmty. Ctr., West Bloomfield, Mich., 1986-89. Editor jour. Generations, 1986; contbr. articles to Jwish News, Generations, Search, others. Bd. dirs. Anti Defamation League,Detroit, 1980—, Jewish Cmty. Coun., Southfield, 1980—, Tribute Fund, Detroit, 1979-85; v.p. Maimonides, Detroit, 1966-67; bd. dirs. Am. Mogen David for Israel, Mich. br.; del. 1st conf. Jewish of Old China, Harvard U., 1992; mem. archives com. Jewish Welfare Fedn. Mich., 1993—. Recipient 8 Gold Keys for debate and oratory Wayne U., 1947-51; Humanitarian award State of Israel Bonds, 1980, Helping Hand award, Israel Red Cross, 1980, Humanitarian award, 1991. Mem. Jewish Genealogy Soc. Mich. (founder, pres. 1984-86, bd. dirs. 1995—), Jewish Genealogy Soc. Ill., Jewish Genealogy Soc. Inc., Jewish Hist. Soc. (Mich. bd. dirs. 1986-88), Jewish Genealogy Soc. L.A., Jewish Genealogy Soc. Phila., Jewish Genealogy Soc. Washington, Jewish Genealogy Soc. Toronto, Polish Genealogy Soc. Mich. Home and Office: 1260 Stuyvessant Rd Bloomfield Hills MI 48301-2141

STARN, BARBARA JEAN, nursing administrator; b. Elyria, Ohio, June 1, 1948; d. Andrew and Eugenia Tomoko; m. Richard W. Starn, Feb. 13, 1971; children: Heather, DeAnna, Jennifer. Student, M.B. Johnson Sch. Nursing, 1969, Baldwin Wallace Coll., 1970. RN, Ohio, Mo., Pa. Staff nurse Elyria Meml. Hosp.; supr. Medi Ctr. of Am., Springfield, Mo.; asst. dir. nursing Manor Care Nursing Ctr., Olmsted, Ohio; nurse coord. Parkside Health Mgmt. Corp., Middleburg Heights, Ohio; client svc. rep. Parkside Health Mgmt. Corp.; asst. dir. nursing The Oakridge Home, Westlake, Ohio; DON Oakridge Home, Edinboro (Pa.) Manor, 96—. Zaharas scholar. Home: 10783 Konneyaut Trail Ext Conneaut Lake PA 16316

STARNES, JAMES WRIGHT, lawyer; b. East St. Louis, Ill., Apr. 3, 1933; s. James Adron and Nell (Short) S.; m. Helen Woods Mitchell, Mar. 29, 1958 (div. 1978); children: James Wright, Mitchell A., William B. II; m. Kathleen Israel, Jan. 26, 1985. Student St. Louis U., 1951-53; LLB, Washington U., St. Louis, 1957. Bar: Mo. 1957, Ill. 1957, Fla. 1992. Assoc. Stinson, Mag & Fizzell, Kansas City, Mo., 1957-60, ptnr., 1960-90; ptnr. Mid-Continent Properties Co., 1959-90, Fairview Investment Co., Kansas City, 1971-76, Monticello Land Co., 1973—, of counsel Yates, Mauck, Bohrer, Elliff, Croessmann & Wieland, P.C., Springfield, Mo., 1995—; sec. Packaging Products Corp., Mission, Kans., 1972-89; chmn., treas. Galerie of Naples (Fla.), Inc., 1990-92. Bd. dirs. Mo. Assn. Mental Health, 1968-69, Kansas City Assn. Mental Health, 1966-78, pres., 1969-70; bd. dirs. Heed, 1965-73, 78-82, pres., 1966-67, fin. chmn. 1967-68; bd. dirs. Kansas City Halfway House Found., exec. com., 1966-69, pres., 1966; bd. dirs. Joan Davis Sch. for Spl. Edn., 1972-88, v.p., 1972-73, 79-80, pres., 1980-82; bd. dirs. Sherwood Ctr. for Exceptional Child, 1977-79, v.p., 1978-79. Served with AUS, 1957. Mem. ABA, Mo. Bar, Fla. Bar, Springfield Bar Assn., Kansas City Bar Assn., Washington U. Law Alumni Assn. (bd. govs. 1990-92). Presbyterian (deacon). Mem. adv. bd. Washington U. Law Quar., 1957-90. Home: 2657 E Wildwood Rd Springfield MO 65804-5271 Office: Yates Mauck Bohrer Elliff Croessmann & Wieland 3333 E Battlefield Rd Ste 1000 Springfield MO 65804-4048

STARR, DAVID EVAN, corporate executive; b. Muscatine, Iowa, May 4, 1962; s. Walter C. and Ruth E. (Hayes) S. Grad. high sch., Marion, Iowa. Telemktg. dir. East-West Theatrical Prodns., West Port, Conn., 1983-85, WRG Enterprises, Sarasota, Fla., 1985-86; CEO Wolf Entr., 1982-84, Nat. Labyrinth Cos., Cedar Rapids, Iowa, 1989—, Megaplex Industries, Marion, Iowa, 1992—. Author: Girls of the Deep, 1989. Charter mem. Repub. Presdl. Task Force, Washington, 1982—; sustaining mem. Repub. Nat. Com., Washington, 1984—. Mem. Assn. MBA Execs., U.S. Jaycees. Methodist. Office: Megaplex Industries PO Box 604 Marion IA 52302-0604

STARR, STEPHEN FREDERICK, academic administrator, historian; b. N.Y.C., Mar. 24, 1940; s. Stephen Z. and Ivy (Edmondson) S.; children: Anna, Elizabeth. B.A. in Ancient History, Yale U., 1962; M.A. in Slavonic Langs. and Lit., King's Coll., Cambridge U., 1964; Ph.D. in History, Princeton U., 1968. Assoc. prof. dept. history Princeton U., 1968-74; sec. Kennan Inst. for Advanced Russian Studies, Woodrow Wilson Internat. Center for Scholars, Washington, 1974-79; v.p. acad. affairs Tulane U., New Orleans, 1979-82; prof. history, adj. prof. architecture Tulane U., 1979-83; scholar-in-residence Historic New Orleans Collection, 1982-84; pres. Oberlin (Ohio) Coll., 1983-94, The Aspen Inst., Washington, 1994—; spl. cons. President's Commn. Fgn. Langs. and Internat. Studies, 1978-81; v.p. Nat. Council for Soviet and East European Rsch., 1978-80. Author: Decentralization and Self Government in Russia, 1830-1870, 1972, Konstant in Melnikov: Solo Architect in a Mass Society, 1978, 2nd edit., 1981, Il padiglione di Melnikov, 1979, Bamboula! The Life and Times of Louis Moreau Gottschalk, 1994, (with Hans von Herwarth) Against Two Evils, 1981, The Russian Avant-Garde, 1981, Red and Hot: The Fate of Jazz in the USSR, 1983, New Orleans Unmasqued, 1985, Southern Comfort, The Garden District of New Orleans, 1800-1900, 1990. Mem. Greater New Orleans Regional Found., 1983—, La. Repertory Jazz Ensemble, 1980—; bd. dirs. Rockefeller Bros. Fund, 1984-94. Mem. Am. Assn. Advancement Slavic Studies, Coun. Fgn. Rels., Internat. Rsch. and Exch. Bd. (trustee), Nat. Fgn. Lang. Ctr. (bd. advisers). Office: The Aspen Inst 1818 N St NW Ste 701 Washington DC 20036-2406

STARTT, JAMES DILL, history educator; b. Balt., July 26, 1932; s. William Andrew Jr. and Viola (Dill) S.; m. Catherine Louise Felten, Apr. 10, 1960; children: James Nelson, Jennifer Leigh. BA, U. Md., 1957, MA, 1961, PhD, 1965. Asst. prof. history Murray (Ky.) State U., 1964-66; assoc. prof. Valparaiso (Ind.) U., 1966-71, prof., 1971—. Author: Journalists for Empire, 1991, Journalism's Unofficial Ambassador: A Biography of Edward Price Bell, 1980; co-author: Historical Methods in Mass Communication, 1989; co-editor: The Significance of the Media in American History, 1994; contbr. articles to profl. jours. Active adminstrv. bd. First United Meth. Ch., Valparaiso, 1976-86. With U.S. Army, 1953-55. Endowment grantee Eli Lilly Co., 1983. Mem. Am. Hist. Assn., Am. Journalism Historians Assn. (bd. dirs. 1985-88, 90-93, v.p. 1995—). Home: 1806 Earthstone Dr Valparaiso IN 46383 Office: Valparaiso U History Dept Huegli Hall Valparaiso IN 46383

STARZYNSKI, CHRISTINE JOY, secondary educator; b. Chgo.; d. Stanley J. and Lottie (Wnek) Dudek; children: Karolyn, Katherine, Jeanne. BA, Northeastern U.; MA in Teaching, Webster U. Tchr. Des Plaines (Ill.) Dist. 62 Schs.; tchr. Spanish, Dist. 211 Schs., Hoffman Estates, Ill., dept. chmn.; with Spanish program Schaumburg (Ill.) Schaumburg Pub. Libr., 1984-92; bd. dirs. Kohl Internat. Teaching Awards, 1992-94. Recipient Kohl Exemplary Teaching award, 1986; inducted into Adminstr's. Acad. Mem. Am. Assn. Tchrs. Spanish and Portuguese (conv. presenter), Am. Coun. Tchrs. Fgn. Langs., Ill. Coun. Tchrs. Fgn. Langs. Home: 319 Mendon Ln Schaumburg IL 60193-1037 Office: Hoffman Estates High Sch 1100 W Higgins Rd Hoffman Estates IL 60195-3050

STASHOWER, DAVID L., advertising executive. Chmn., CEO Liggett-Stashower Inc., Cleve. Active Cleve. Play House, Cleve. Opera. Inducted into Cleve. Advt. Club Hall of Fame, 1986. Mem. Am. Assn. Advt. Agys. (nat. sec./treas., trustee pension & profit sharing plans), Advt. & Mktg. Internat. Network, Ohio Motorists Assn., Cleve. Advt. Club, Neighborhood Ctrs. Assn. Office: Liggett-Stashower Inc 1228 Euclid Ave Cleveland OH 44115-1831*

STASTNY, CHARLES JOSEPH, musician; b. Parkston, S.D., Aug. 2, 1964; s. Joseph James and Mary Ann Wilhemena (Kathol) S. BA, Mt. Marty Coll., 1987; M of Music, U. S.D., 1990. Cert. music tchr. S.D. Subs. tchr. Wagner (S.D.) Schs., Andes Ctrl., 1988-92; tchr. Dell Rapids Sch., 1992-94; grad. asst. U. S.D., Vermillion, 1988-90; tchr. Parkston (S.D.) High Sch., 1990-91; asst. dir. U. S.D. Music Camp, 1988-93; mgr. Yankton (S.D.) Area Summer Band, 1990—; radio DJ WNAX Radio-570 AM, Yankton, 1987—; adjudicator various music contests, 1990—; reviewer various recordings, Wagner, 1990—; profl. musician over 75 bands, 1974—. Contbr. articles to profl. jours. Mem. Internat. Polka Assn. (sgt.-at-arms), U.S. Polka Assn., Cleve. Polka Assn., Polka Club Iowa, #1 Okal. Polka Club, KC. Independent. Roman Catholic. Home and Office: PO Box 7075 Yankton SD 57078-7075

STAUBER, JOEL VINCENT, urban planner, architect; b. Portland, Oreg., Feb. 21, 1954; s. Leo Vincent and Marilyn Joyce (Foote) S.; m. Camille Judith Lee, June 24, 1984; 1 child, Jacob Louis. BArch, U. Oreg., 1977; MArch in Urban Design, Harvard U., 1984. Registered architect, Ill. Project mgr. Moreland/Unruh/Smith P.C., Eugene, Oreg., 1978-80; designer The Grad Partnership, Newark, 1980-82; project mgr. Notter, Finegold & Alexander, Boston, 1984-85; sr. planner, urban designer Lohan Assocs., Chgo., 1985-92; dir. planning O'Donnell, Wicklund, Pigozzi & Peterson, Deerfield and Chgo., 1992—. Bd. dirs. Friends of Downtown, 1993—; mem. Met. Planning Coun. Mem. AIA (bd. dirs. Chgo. chpt. 1992-94, chmn. planning and urban affairs com. 1991-92), Am. Inst. Cert. Planners, Am. Planning Assn., Urban Land Inst., Execs. Club Chgo. Office: O'Donnell Wicklund Pigozzi & Peterson 1 N Franklin St Ste 850 Chicago IL 60606

STAUBER, MARILYN JEAN, secondary and elementary school; b. Duluth, Minn., Feb. 5, 1938; d. Harold Milton and Dorothy Florence (Thompson) Froelich; children: Kenneth D. and James H. Atkinson; m. Lawrence B. Stauber Sr., Jan. 11, 1991. BS in K-6 Edn., U. Minn., Duluth, 1969, MEd in Math., 1977. Cert. elem. and secondary reading tchr., remedial reading specialist, devel. reading tchr., reading cons. Sec. div. vocat. rehab. State Minn., Duluth, 1956-59; sec. Travelers Ins. Co., Duluth, 1962-66; lead tchr. Title 1 reading and math. Proctor, Minn., 1969—. Mem. choir, comm. coord. Forbes Meth. Ch., Proctor. Mem. NEA, Internat. Reading Assn., Nat. Reading Assn., Minn. Arrowhead Reading Coun., Elem. Coun. (pres. 1983-84, 86-87), Proctor Fedn. Tchrs. (recert. com. 1980—, treas. 1981-86), Proctor Edn. Assn. Home: 6713 Grand Lake Rd Saginaw MN 55779-9782

STAUFF, JON WILLIAM, history educator; b. Toms River, N.J., Sept. 5, 1965; s. John Henry and Regina (Fox) S. AA, Ocean County Coll., 1984; AB, Coll. William and Mary, 1986; MA, SUNY, Buffalo, 1990, PhD, 1994. Grad. teaching asst. SUNY, Buffalo, 1986-89, 90, lectr. history Millard Fillmore Coll., 1991; rsch. asst. German Bundestag Christian Dem. Union, Bonn, Germany, 1991; instr. history Ocean C.C., Toms River, 1992-93; asst. prof. history St. Ambrose Univ., Davenport, Iowa, 1993—. Tchg., rsch. fellow SUNY, 1986-89, Milton Plesur Dissertation fellow SUNY, 1990-91; Dissertation grantee German Acad. Exch. Svc., 1989-90; participant Fulbright German Studies Summer Seminar, 1995. Mem. AAHPERD, Am. Hist. Assn., German Studies Assn., World History Assn., Phi Beta Kappa, Phi Alpha Theta (Lynn Turner prize 1986). Address: St Ambrose Univ History Dept 518 W Locust St Davenport IA 52803-2829

STAUFFACHER, ALBERT HERBERT, resource company executive. Dir. labor rels. Pontiac (Mich.) Motor div. GM, 1975-78; dir. personnel Terex div. GM, Hudson, Ohio, 1978-80; v.p. personnel I.B.H., Hudson, Ohio, 1980-82; pres. Employers Resource Coun., Cleve., 1983—. Tchr. Jr. Achievement, Twinsburg, Ohio, 1989-92; v.p. adminstrn., bd. trustees United Way, Akron, Ohio, 1978-85; bd. trustees Health Action Coun. 1st lt. U.S. Army, 1954-56. Mem. Nat. Assn. MFg. (bd. dirs. 1992—), Am. Mgmt. Assn., Employers Assn. Group (exec. com. 1990—, chmn. 1993-94). Republican. Unitarian. Office: Employers Resource Coun 5700 Lombardo Ctr Ste 200 Cleveland OH 44131-2545

STAUFFACHER, TRUDY SHARRON, hospice coordinator; b. Hettinger, N.D., Nov. 8, 1941; d. Vinton Merle and Madeline Othelia (Felt) Henderson; m. Lyndon E. Stauffacher Jr., Mar. 4, 1967 (div. 1983); children: DeAnn, Robert. BSN, S.D. State U., 1964; M Mgmt., U. Mary, Bismarck, N.D., 1992. RN, N.D., S.D., Minn., Mich., Fla., Alaska. Nursing instr. Saginaw (Mich.) Gen. Hosp., 1964-65, St. John's Sch. Nursing, Rapid City, S.D., 1965-67; pub. health nurse Pennington County Health Dept., Rapid City, 1967-68, Hernando County Health Dept., Brooksville, Fla., 1982-83; indsl. nurse Sears, Roebuck and Co., Mpls., 1968-71; staff nurse Pasco Humana Hosp., Dade City, Fla., 1984-86; CPR and emergency med. technician instr. Pasco-Hernando C.C., Brooksville, 1982-86; dir., assoc. Gulf Coast Home Health, Brooksville, 1983-86; staff nurse St. Alexius Home Health Care, Bismarck, N.D., 1987—; hospice coord. St. Alexius Home Health Care and Hospice, Bismarck, 1994—; pub. health cons. N.D. State Dept. Health, Bismarck, 1986-92, maternal/child health and primary care cons., 1992-93, dir. optimal pregnancy outcome program & adolescent health, 1993-94; cons. bd. of health 12 counties, N.D., 1986-94; home health cons. all N.D. home health agys., 1986-94. Pianist, organist, Sunday sch. tchr., mem. ch. coun. 1st Luth. Ch., Brooksville, 1982-86, Good Shepherd Luth. Ch., 1986—. Mem. ANA, N.D. Pub. Health Assn., N.D. Nurses Assn., Sigma Theta Tau, Beta Sigma Phi. Democrat. Home: 719 N 32nd St Bismarck ND 58501-3218 Office: Saint Alexius Home Health Care and Hospice 1120 E Main St Bismarck ND 58502

STAUFFER, KATHLEEN, editor, author; b. Pottstown, Pa., Feb. 7, 1963; d. Willard Henry and Margaret Mary (Henry) S. BA in Journalism, Point Park Coll., 1985. Intern The Pitts. Press, 1983, Reader's Digest, Pleasantville, N.Y., 1984, Prevention Mag., Emmaus, Pa., 1985; asst. editor Cath. Digest, St. Paul, 1986-89, assoc. editor, 1989-93, mng. editor, 1993—. Co-author: Womansport: The Women's Sports Bible, 1994, Facing Life's Challenges, 1996; cartoonist Minn. NOW Times, 1994—. Coord. Police-Cmty. Storefront, St. Paul, 1995—; phone vol. Minn. AIDS Project, Mpls., 1995—. Mem. NOW, Cath. Press Assn. (lidge 1995), Soc. Profl. Journalists. Office: Cath Digest PO Box 64090 Saint Paul MN 55164

STAUFFER, STANLEY HOWARD, newspaper and broadcasting executive; b. Peabody, Kans., Sept. 11, 1920; s. Oscar S. and Ethel L. (Stone) S.; m. Suzanne R. Wallace, Feb. 16, 1945 (div. 1961); children: Peter, Clay, Charles; m. Elizabeth D. Priest, July 14, 1962 (div. 1991); children: Elizabeth, Grant; m. Madeline A. Sargent, Nov. 27, 1992. AB, U. Kans., 1942. Assoc. editor Topeka State Jour., 1946-47; editor, pub. Santa Maria (Calif.) Times, 1948-52; rewrite and copy editor Denver Post, 1953-54; staff mem. AP (Denver bur.), 1954-55; exec. v.p. Stauffer Publs., Inc., 1955-69; gen. mgr. Topeka Capital-Jour., 1957-69; pres. Stauffer Comm., Inc., 1969-86, chmn., 1986-92; bd. dirs. Topeka/Shawnee County Devel. Corp.; chmn. bd. dirs. Stauffer Comm. Found. Past pres. Topeka YMCA; past chmn. adv. bd. St. Francis Hosp.; past chmn. Met. Topeka Airport Authority; trustee William Allen White Found., Menninger Found., Midwest Rsch. Inst., Washburn U. Endowment Assn. With USAAF, 1942-45. Named Chpt. Boss of Yr. Am. Bus. Women's Assn., 1976, Outstanding Kans. Pub. Kappa Tau Alpha, 1980, Legion of Honor De Molay, Topeka Phi of Yr., 1971. Mem. Kans. Press Assn. (past pres.), Inland Daily Press Assn. (past dir.), Air Force Assn. (past pres. Topeka), Kans. U. Alumni Assn. (past dir.), Kans. C. of C. and Industry (past chmn.), Def. Orientation Conf. Assn., Topeka Country Club, Top of the Tower Club, Garden of the Gods Club, La Quinta (Calif.) Country Club, Masons (32d deg.), Shriners, Phi Delta Theta (past chpt. pres.), Sigma Delta chi (past chpt. pres.). Episcopalian (past sr. warden). Office: Stauffer Comm Inc 6th & Jefferson St Topeka KS 66607

STAUNTON, JOHN JOSEPH JAMESON, electrical engineer; b. Binghamton, N.Y., July 4, 1911; s. Henry Capen and Florence Eliza (Jameson) S.; m. Eileen Mary Humiston, May 3, 1939; children: Susan, John Jr., Harold, Joanne, Douglas, Ralph. BSEE, U. Notre Dame, 1932, MS in Physics, 1934, EE, 1941; DEng, Midwest Coll. Engrs., 1969. Registered profl. engr., Ill. Jr. engr. Bantam Ball Bearing Co., South Bend, Ind., 1935-36; head physics dept. DePaul U., Chgo., 1936-38; dir. rsch. Coleman Instruments, Inc., Maywood, Ill., 1938-64; sr. staff scientist Perkin-Elmer Corp., Oakbrook, Ill., 1964-78; cons. Perkin-Elmer Corp., Oak Pk., Ill., 1978—; councilor, chmn. Optical Soc. Chgo., 1955-56, 56-60; dir. Physics Club of Chgo., 1954-57, 65-68, 78-81; patent rev. panel Applied Optics, 1967—. Contbr. articles to profl. jours. Recipient Annual Merit award Chgo. Tech. Soc. Coun., 1969. Fellow IEEE (life), Optical Soc. Chgo.; mem. Optical Soc. Am. (emeritus life), Sigma Xi (life). Roman Catholic. Home: 310 Wesley Ave Oak Park IL 60302-3510

STAVROPOULOS, ROSE MARY GRANT, community activist, volunteer; b. Decatur, Ill.; d. Walter Edwin and Ora Lenore (Kepler) Grant; m. Stan Stavropoulos; children: Becky Ann Stavropoulos Betian, Stephanie Diane. BS, Ea. Ill. U., 1954. Cert. elem. edn. Tchr. 2nd grade Garfield Sch., Decatur, 1954-55; bd. dirs. Wilmot Sch. Bd. PTA, Deerfield, 1971-73, Moraine Girl Scout Coun., Deerfield, 1968-75; also bd. dirs. Moraine Girl Scout Coun., Deerfield, Ill., 1984-89; chmn. Human Rels. Commn., Deerfield, 1975-84; mem. sr. citizen adv. com. Deerfield Park Dist., 1984-89; pres. Lake County (Ill.) LWV, 1979-81; chmn. Deerfield Village Caucus, 1980-82; pres. Caring For Others, Inc., Deerfield, 1986-88, Deerfield Area LWV, 1989; bd. mem. Deerfield Area United Way, 1976-93, pres., 1991-93; Mem. Deerfield Village Caucus Adv. Coun., 1980-81, 92—. Recipient Deerfield Human Rels. Humanitarian award, 1984, Lerner Life's Citizen of Month, 1987. Mem. Deerfield Area Hist. Soc., Highland Park Hosp. Aux, Delta Zeta. Home: 1629 Village Green Ct Deerfield IL 60015-2638

STAYTON, MICHAEL BRUCE, financial entrepreneur, corporate professional; b. Battle Creek, Mich., June 1, 1946; s. Chester Arthur Jr. and Betty Zane (Redwine) S.; m. Carol Sue Root, Dec. 23, 1978; children: Alison Bryn, Melissa Cristine, Michael Bruce Jr. BA in Biology, Wabash Coll., 1969; MS in Internat. Bus., George Washington U., 1973. Fin. planning mgr. Ford Motor Co., Dearborn, Mich., 1973-80; v.p. Biologicals Inc., Toronto, Ont.,

Can., 1980-82; pres. M.B. Stayton & Assocs. Inc., Indpls., 1982-92; exec. v.p. T.M. Englehart Corp., Indpls., 1986—; treas. Labthermics Techs. Inc., Champaign, Ill., 1986-92; v.p. Lab. Equipment Corp., Mooresville, Ind., 1988-91, also bd. dirs.; dir. Indpls. Dept. Pub. Works, 1993-95; exec. v.p. SM & P Utility Resources, Carmel, Ind., 1995—; bd. dirs. Thomas L. Green & Co., Indpls., T.M. Englehart Corp., Indpls. 1st lt. U.S. Army, 1969-72. Republican. Episcopalian. Home: 6180 Meridian West Dr Indianapolis IN 46208-1539

STEAD, JAMES JOSEPH, JR., securities company executive; b. Chgo., Sept. 13, 1930; s. James Joseph and Irene (Jennings) S.; m. Edith Pearson, Feb. 13, 1954; children: James, Diane, Robert, Caroline. BS, DePaul U., 1957, MBA, 1959. Asst. sec. C. F. Childs & Co., Chgo., 1957-62; exec. v.p., sec. Koenig, Keating & Stead, Inc., Chgo., 1962-66; 2d v.p., mgr. midwest mcpl. bond dept. Hayden, Stone Inc., Chgo., 1966-69; sr. v.p., nat. sales mgr. Ill. Co. Inc., 1969-70; mgr. instl. sales dept. Reynolds and Co., Chgo., 1970-72; partner Edwards & Hanly, 1972-74; v.p., instnl. sales mgr. Paine, Webber, Jackson & Curtis, 1974-76; v.p., regional instl. sales mgr. Reynolds Securities, Inc., 1976-78; sr. v.p., regional mgr. Oppenheimer & Co., Inc., 1978-88; sr. v.p., regional mgr. fixed income Tucker Anthony, 1988—; instr. Mcpl. Bond Sch., Chgo., 1967—. With AUS, 1951-53. Mem. Security Traders Assn. Chgo., Nat. Security Traders Assn., Am. Mgmt. Assn., Mcpl. Fin. Forum Washington. Clubs: Execs., Union League, Mcpl. Bond, Bond (Chgo.); Olympia Fields Country (Ill.); Wall Street (N.Y.C.). Home: 1005 Hickory Ridge Ct Frankfort IL 60423-2114 Office: 1 S Wacker Dr Chicago IL 60606-4614

STEADMAN, DAVID WILTON, museum official; b. Honolulu, Oct. 24, 1936; s. Alva Edgar and Martha (Cooke) S.; m. Kathleen Carroll Reilly, Aug. 1, 1964; children: Alexander Carroll, Kate Montague. B.A., Harvard U., 1960, M.A.T., 1961; M.A., U. Calif.-Berkeley, 1966; Ph.D., Princeton U., 1974. Lectr. Frick Collection, N.Y.C., 1970-71; asst. dir., acting dir., assoc. dir. Princeton U. Art Mus., 1971-73; dir. galleries Claremont Colls. (Calif.), 1974-80; art cons. Archtl. Digest, L.A., 1974-77; rsch. curator Norton Simon Mus., Pasadena, Calif., 1977-80; dir. Chrysler Mus., Norfolk, Va., 1980-89, Toledo Mus. Art, Ohio, 1989—. Author: Graphic Art of Francisco Goya, 1975, Works on Paper 1900-1960, 1977, Abraham van Diepenbeeck, 1982. Chester Dale fellow Nat. Gallery Art, Washington, 1969-70. Mem. Coll. Art Assn., Am. Assn. Mus. Dirs. Episcopalian. Office: Toledo Mus Art PO Box 1013 Toledo OH 43697-1013

STEADMAN, JACK W., professional football team executive; b. Warrenville, Ill., Sept. 14, 1928; s. Walter Angus and Vera Ruth (Burkholder) S.; m. Martha Cudworth Steinhoff, Nov. 24, 1949; children: Thomas Edward, Barbara Ann, Donald Wayne. B.B.A., So. Methodist U., 1950. Accountant Hunt Oil Co., Dallas, 1950-54; chief accountant W.H. Hunt, Dallas, 1954-58, Penrod Drilling Co., Dallas, 1958-60; gen. mgr. Dallas Texans Football Club, 1960-63; gen. mgr. Kansas City Chiefs Football Club, 1963-76, exec. v.p., 1966-76, pres., 1976-88; also chmn. bd., 1988—; chmn. benefit com. NFL; chmn. Hunt Midwest Enterprises, Inc., Kansas City; dir. Commerce Bank of Kansas City, Pvt. Industry Coun.; former chmn. Full Employment Coun. Former bd. dirs. Children's Mercy Hosp., bd. dirs. Civic Council, Starlight Theatre Assn., Kansas City, Am. Royal Assn.; pres. Heart of Am. United Way, 1981; adv. trustee Research Med. Ctr., Kansas City; trustee Midwest Research Inst.; mem. Village Presbyn. Ch.; past chmn. C. of C. of Greater Kansas City. Recipient Kans. Citian of Yr. award, 1988. Mem. Indian Hills Country Club, Kansas City Club (pres. 1988), 711 Inner, River, Carriage, Man-of-the-Month Fraternity. Home: 6436 Wenonga Ter Shawnee Mission KS 66208-1732 Office: Kansas City Chiefs 1000 Walnut St Ste 1528 Kansas City MO 64106-2123

STEAGALL, M. SUSAN, management services executive; b. Decatur, Ill., May 14, 1949; d. Robert Bendorf and Alice Virginia (Davern) Coble; m. Mark Dennis Steagall, Nov. 23, 1993. AB in English, U. Calif., Riverside, 1971; postgrad, Golden Gate U., San Francisco, 1983. Claims examiner State Compensation Ins. Fund, Los Angeles, 1971-75; asst. claims mgr. State Compensation Ins. Fund, Oakland, Calif., 1975-79; claims mgr. Transamerica Corp., San Francisco, 1979-83; v.p., claims Sedgwick James, Chicago, 1983-86, sr. v.p., 1986—; bd. dirs. Workers Compensation Rsch. Inst. Cambridge, Mass. Mem. MENSA, Nat. Trust for Historic Preservation, Nat. Coun. of Self-Insurers, Chgo. Architecture Found., Blanchard Assn. (cert. quality leadership trainer). Office: Sedgwick James Inc Claims Mgmt Svcs 230 W Monroe St Chicago IL 60606

STEAR, CINDY ANN, clinical psychologist; b. Ft. Eustice, Va., Nov. 10, 1963; d. Richard Wilburt and Darla Ann (Smith) L. BS with honors, U. Iowa, 1985; MS, Nova U., 1992; PsyD, Nova Southeastern Univ., 1995. Behavior specialist Assn. Retarded Citizens of Rock Island County, Ill., 1988-89, birth-to-three coord., 1989-90; founder, exec. dir. Quad Cities Child and Family Support Ctr. Inc., Davenport, Iowa, 1988-95; clinical psychologist Singer Mental Health Ctr., Lake Villa, Ill., 1995—; spkr.'s bur. Coun. on Children at Risk, Moline, Ill., 1988-90. Bd. dirs. Dirs. of Vols. in Agys., Davenport, 1989-90.

STEARNS, CAROL KEISER, architect; b. St. Louis, Nov. 19, 1957; d. Bernhard Edward and F. Evelyn (Koenig) Keiser; m. Steven Bryan Stearns, Apr. 5, 1986; children: Elizabeth Ann, Bryan William. BS in Architecture, U. Va., 1979; MArch, Wash. U., St. Louis, 1985. Registered architect, Mo. Project architect, job capt. Thomas G. Georgelas & Assoc., McLean, Va., 1979-83, Mitchell Wall & Assocs., St. Louis, 1987-88; pvt. practice St. Peters, Mo., 1988-90; cons. mem. Trinity Luth. Ch. Bldg. Com., Bridgeton, Mo., 1988-90. Author: Lutheran Home School Planner, 1995. Counselor young people's group Immanuel Luth. Ch., Alexandria, Va., 1979-83, H.S. tchr. Sunday sch., 1981-83; mem. Trinity Young Adults, Bridgeton, 1983-94; program coord., nominating com. mem. Trinity Luth. Women's Missionary League, Bridgeton, 1990-92, zone rep., 1992-94, dist. conv. del., 1994, Overland Zone devel. chmn., 1994-96, effective soc. planning zone trainer, 1994-96, leader neighborhood Bible study, St. Peter's, 1991-94; active mem. Trinity Luth. Ch. Ladies Cir., Orchard Farm, 1996—; youth advisor LC-MS Cir. 9 SE Dist., No. Va., 1980-83; del. 1996 Rep. Congl. Dist. Conv. 2nd Dist.; del. 1996 Mo. Rep. State Conv. Mem. Aux. of Gideons Internat. (St. Ann camp v.p. 1988-90, St. Ann camp pres. 1994-96, new mem. plan follow-up rep. Kirkwood Camp 1991-92). Republican. Lutheran.

STEARNS, CHARLES RICHARD, meteorologist, educator, farmer; b. McKeesport, Pa., May 21, 1925; s. Fenton Verle and Lois Annette (Sellers) S.; children: James, Laura. BS, U. Wis., 1950, MS, 1952, PhD, 1967. Farmer Princeton, Wis., 1952-55; physicist Winzen Rsch., Mpls., 1955-57; project asst. U. Wis., Madison, 1957-65, asst. prof. meteorology, 1965-70, assoc. prof., 1970-75, prof., 1975—. Author, editor: Antarctic Meteorology, 1993. Chair Plan Commn., Oregon, Wis., 1970-85. Served with inf. U.S. Army, 1943-46, PTO. Decorated Bronze Star. Mem. AAAS, Am. Meteorol. Soc., Am. Geophys. Union. Office: U Wis 1225 W Dayton St Madison WI 53706

STEARNS, ROBERT LELAND, curator; b. L.A., Aug. 28, 1947; s. Edward Van Buren and Harriett Ann (Hauck) S.; m. Sheri Roseanne Lucas, Oct. 2, 1982 (div. 1994); children: Marissa Hauck, Caroline Lucas. Student, U. Calif., San Diego, 1965-68, BFA, 1970; student, Calif. Poly. State U., San Luis Obispo, 1968. Asst. dir. Paula Cooper Gallery, N.Y.C., 1970-72; prodn. asst. Avalanche Mag., N.Y.C., 1972; dir. Kitchen Ctr. for Video/Music, N.Y.C., 1972-77, Contemporary Arts Ctr., Cin., 1977-82; dir. performing arts Walker Art Ctr., Mpls., 1982-88; dir. Wexner Ctr. for Arts, Columbus, Ohio, 1988-92; mem. Wexner Ctr. Found., Columbus, 1990-92; dir. Stearns & Assocs./Contemporary Exhbn. Svcs., Lancaster, Ohio, 1992—; adj. prof. dept. art, assoc. dean Coll. Art, Ohio State U., Columbus, 1988-92; cons. McKnight Found., St. Paul, 1978, Jerome Found., 1978-79; chmn. Artists TV Workshop, N.Y.C., 1976-77; bd. dirs., chmn. Minn. Dance Alliance, Mpls., 1983-88; bd. dirs. Haleakala, Inc., N.Y.C.; mem. various panels Nat. Endowment for Arts, Washington, 1977— ; mem. pub. arts policy Greater Columbus Arts Coun., 1988-90; adv. coun. Bklyn. Acad. Music, 1982-84, Houston Grand Opera, 1991-93. Author, editor: Robert Wilson: Theater of Images, 1980, Photography and Beyond in Japan, 1995; editor: Dimensions of Black, 1970; exec. editor: Breakthroughs, 1991; author and editor numerous catalogues. Decorated chevalier Order of Arts and Letters (France); Jerome Found. travel grantee, 1986, Japan Found. travel grantee, 1991.

STEAVENS, ALAN D., customer service administrator; b. Lansing, Mich., Jan. 21, 1937. Field svc. rep. Unisys, Battle Creek, Mich., 1966-74; mgr. document processing Burroughs, Deerborn, Mich., 1974-83; mgr. customer svc. satisfaction Unisys, Plymouth, Mich., 1983—. Treas. United Way, Plymouth, 1994—, bd. dirs., 1992—). Staff sgt. USAF, 1959-66. Office: Unisys 41100 Plymouth Rd Plymouth MI 48170-1856

STEC, JOHN ZYGMUNT, real estate executive; b. Stalowawola, Poland, Jan. 21, 1925; Came to U.S.A. 1947.; s. Valenty and Maria (Madej) S. m. Wanda G. Baca, Oct. 13, 1956; children: David, Maria, Monica. Student, Poland, 1941-44, Kent St. U., Oh., 1965-66, Kent St. U., Oh., 1966-67. Cert. Master of Corporate Real Estate. With The Singer Co., Cleve., 1952-54, dis. mgr., 1954-60, sales supr., 1960-67; dir. real estate The Singer Co., Detroit and Chgo., 1967-73; v.p. Fabri Center of Am., Beachwood, Ohio, 1973—; sr. v.p. real estate Fabri-Centers of Am., Inc., Beachwood, Ohio, 1987—; With U.S. Army 1950-52. With U.S. Army, 1950-52. Mem. Nat. Assoc. of Corporate Real Estate (speaker, organizer 1974-77, audit Com. 1977-79, bd. dirs. 1970-82, Outstanding Achievement award 1982). Chagrin Valley Club. Repulican. Roman Catholic. Home: 9630 Stafford Rd Chagrin Falls OH 44023-5302 Office: Fabri-Ctrs Am Inc 5555 Darrow Rd Hudson OH 44236-4011

STECICH, JOHN PATRICK, structural engineer; b. Chgo., Nov. 1, 1949; s. William Frank and Margaret Mary (Hanrahan) S.; m. Rita Louise Fahey, July 1, 1972; children: Eric John, Thomas John. BSCE, Ill. Inst. Tech., 1971, MSCE, 1972. Lic. profl. engr., Ill., Ind., Pa.; lic. structural engr., Ill. Design engr. Chgo. Bridge and Iron Co., Oak Brook, Ill., 1971-79; adjunct prof. Midwest Coll. Engring., 1976-77; sr. cons. Wiss, Janney, Elstner Associates, INc., Chgo., 1979—; speaker in field. Contbr. papers to prof. publs. Recipient Repair Project of Yr. award Internat. Concrete Repair Inst., 1993, McGraw Hill/CIS Boston Advanced Constrn. Tech. First Place award, 1994, Diehaus Preservation Project of Yr. award, 1994, Ill. Ind. Masonry Coun. 1993 Honorable Mention award, Amoco Bldg. Facade Recladding. Fellow ASCE (design of steel bldg. structures com.); mem. ASTM (dimension stone com.), Am. Inst. Steel Constrn., Am. Concrete Inst. (steel reinforcement com.), Am. Soc. for Metals, Chgo. Com. on High Rise Bldgs., Structural Engrs. Assn. Ill. (1st prize award 1988, Meritorious Publ. award 1991, award of merit for Amoco Bldg. facade 1993, award of merit for Bahai House of Worship restoration 1994). Home: 11306 S Central Park Ave Chicago IL 60655-3416 Office: Wiss Janney Elstner Assocs 29 N Wacker Dr Chicago IL 60606-3203

STEELE, BRENT E., state legislator; m. Sally Steele. BS, Ind. U., JD. Atty. Steele, Steele, McSoley & McSoley; mem. Ind. State Ho. of Reps. Dist. 65, mem. agr. and rural devel. com., mem. cts. and criminal code com., mem. judiciary com., vice-chmn. fin. inst. com. Vice precinct committeeman, Ind.; former pres. Bedford City Planning Bd.; mem. Rep. Ctr. Fin. Com. Mem. Lions Club.

STEELE, CARL LAVERN, academic administrator; b. Patoka, Ill., Aug. 22, 1934; s. Boyd Alfa and Effie Jane (Corson) S.; m. Lula Irene Saliba, June 11, 1961; children: Jeffrey Van, Gregory Michael, Douglas Alan. BEd, So. Ill. U., 1956, MEd, 1960; MLS, No. Ill. U., 1971. Tchr. Shawneetown (Ill.) Community High. Sch., 1956-57; GED instr. U.S. Army, Ft. Hood, Tex. and Ulm, Fed. Republic of Germany, 1957-59; tchr. Forrest-Strawn-Wing Unit Dist., Forrest, Ill., 1959-61, Richwoods Community High Sch., Peoria, Ill., 1961-66; asst. dir. instructional materials Sauk Valley Coll., Dixon, Ill., 1966-68; dir. Ednl. Resources Ctr., Rock Valley Coll., Rockford, Ill., 1968-93; ret., 1993; part-time traffic safety instr. Rock Valley Coll., 1992—. Asst. World Record sec. Nat. Fresh Water Fishing Hall of Fame, Hayward, Wisc., 1977-79. Served with U.S. Army, 1957-59. Mem. ALA, Assn. Ednl. Communications and Technology, Ill. Assn. Ednl. Communications and Technology (conv. chmn. 1976), No. Ill. Media Assn. (conv. chmn.), Learning Resource Commn. ICCCA (chmn. 1981). Democrat. Presbyterian. Home: 5758 Weymouth Dr Rockford IL 61114-5569

STEELE, CHARLES EDWARD, industrial designer; b. Cristobel, Panama, Oct. 5, 1943; s. Russell Dean and Dorothy Mae (Lipp) S.; m. Ramona Dolores Wizner, Sept. 20, 1975; children: Angela Natalie, Katrina Linda, Mary Christine. BS in Indsl. Design, U. Cin., 1968. Product designer AMF Wheel Goods Divsn., Olney, Ill., 1967-69; interior design GM Design Staff, Warren, Mich., 1973-76; staff designer Mel Boldt & Assocs., Mt. Prospect, Ill., 1976-79; sr. designer KMH Design, Ceresco, Mich., 1978-88; sr. project engr. Kerr Corp., Romulus, Mich., 1988—. Patentee in field. Active Common Cause. Staff sgt. USAF, 1969-73. Mem. Am. Materials Soc. Internat., Indsl. Designers Soc. Am. (Bronze medal 1987), Soc. Mfg. Engrs., Soc. Plastics Engrs., Planetary Soc. Office: Kerr Corp 28200 Wick Rd Romulus MI 48174

STEELE, DAVID FRANK, elementary education educator; b. Hiawatha, Kans., Sept. 10, 1952; s. Dale William and Jean Elizebeth (Thompson) S. AA, Highland C.C., 1972; BS, Kans. State U., 1974. Cert. elem. tchr., Kans. Elem. tchr. St. Marys (Kans.) Grade Sch., 1974—. Mem. PTO, St. Marys Elem. Sch., 1974—; bd. dirs. St. Marys Hist. Soc., 1985—, archivist/display coord., 1990—; treas., coord. Muscular Dystrophy Telethon Com., St. Marys, 1981-90; dir. Pottowatomie County (Kans.) Spelling Bee, 1980-92; Dem. precinct committeeman St. Marys, 1984-90; sec. Pottowatomie Dem. Com., 1992—, 2d. Congl. Dist., Topeka, 1984—; vol. Slattery for Congress, 1984, 86, 88-90, Docking for Gov., 1986, Rezac for State Rep., 1986-90; active N.E. Kans. United Tel. Customer Coun.; mem. choir Immaculate Conception Ch., 1978—; mem. Kans. Dem. Century/Star 34; contbg. mem. Dem. Nat. Com. Recipient Alice Klingery and William H. Wells State Aerospace award Kans. Dept. Transp., 1992, Vol. award Muscular Dystrophy Assn., 1989, Cmty. Svc. award Mod. Woodmen Am., 1994; named Kaw Valley Tchr. of Yr., Tchrs. Assn., 1982, Outstanding Young Educator, St. Marys Jaycees, 1977. Mem. Kans. Nat. Edn. Assn. (Lakeland/Konza Uniseve dist. coordinating coun.), Kaw Valley Edn. Assn. (pres. 1979-80), St. Marys C. of C. (treas. 1981-92, v.p. 1980-81, Cmty. Svc. award 1991, Outstanding Tchr. award 1995), Kans. State U. Alumni Assn., Phi Kappa Phi (Kans. State U. chpt.). Home: 104 N 5th St Saint Marys KS 66536-1505 Office: St Marys Grade Sch 312 Grand Ave Saint Marys KS 66536-1754

STEELE, DIANA MARIE, nurse; b. Branson, Mo., Sept. 24, 1960; d. Benton Leon and Dorothy Mae (Selsor) Craig; divorced; children: Brian, Adam. AS, Penn Valley Community Coll., Kansas City, Mo., 1983. Nurse ICU, gynecol. North Kansas City (Mo.) Meml. Hosp., 1983-84; nurse ICU, shock trauma Suburban Hosp., Bethesda, Md., 1984-85; nurse ICU Potomac Hosp., Woodbridge, Va., 1985-86; nurse ICU and critical care, clin. preceptor Holy Cross Hosp., Silver Spring, Md., 1986-87; nurse ICU Stat Nurse, Silver Spring, 1988—; pub. rels. profl. Regional Computer Svcs. Author publs. in field. Past sec. County Geneal. Soc.; guest speaker and insvc. coord. genealogists; vice-chmn. Colonial Cape Found.; bd. dirs. Women In Need. Mem. Am. Assn. Critical Care Nurses, Phi Beta Kappa (pres. nursing sch. class Kansas City chpt. 1981-83). Home: 3703 Stonebridge Dr Cape Girardeau MO 63703

STEELE, HILDA BERNEICE HODGSON, farm manager, retired home economics supervisor; b. Wilmington, Ohio, Mar. 24, 1911; d. George Sanders and Mary Jane (Rolston) Hodgson; m. John C. Steele, Jan. 10, 1963 (dec. Jan. 1973). BS, Wilmington Coll., 1935; MA, Ohio State U., 1941; postgrad., Ohio U., 1954, Miami U., Oxford, Ohio, 1959. Cert. elem. and high sch. gen. tchr. and vocat. supr., Ohio. Part-time tchr. Wilmington Pub. Schs., Midland Elem. Sch., 1931-32; tchr. Brookville (Ohio) Pub. Schs., 1932-37, Dayton (Ohio) Pub. Schs., Lincoln Jr. High Sch., 1937-40; tchr. practical arts, coord. home econs. Dayton Pub. Schs., 1940-45, supr. home econs., 1945-81; mgr. Steele's Farm, Xenia, Ohio, 1972—; mem. home econs. adv. com. Cen. State U., Wilburforce, Ohio, 1941-92, Miami Valley Hosp. Nursing Sch., Dayton, 1951-63; mem. adv. bd. Dayton Sch. Practical Nursing, 1951-92. Mem. adv. com. Montgomery County ARC, Dayton, 1940-80; mem. town and country career com. Miami Valley Br. YMCA, Dayton, 1948-59; mem. Ohio Electrification Com., Dayton, 1964-66; mem. corp. com. United Way, Dayton, 1970-96; bd. dirs. Ohio Future Homemakers of Am.-Home Econs. Related Occupations, Columbus, 1979-81; chmn. home econs. adv. com. Ohio Vets. Children Home, 1987-95. Recipient Outstanding Contbns. award Girls Scouts U.S., 1987, Appreciation award Dayton Practical Nursing Program, 1989; named Ohio Vocat. Educator of the Yr., 1981. Mem. NEA, Ohio Edn. Assn., Am. Home Econs. Assn. (Appreciation award 1990), Am. Vocat. Assn., Ohio Home Econs. Assn. (various coms., Friend of Family award 1994), Ohio Vocat. Assn. (life), Ohio Dist. C Home Econs. Assn., Ohio Ret. Tchrs. Assn. (life), Montgomery County Ret. Tchrs. Assn., Dayton Pub. Schs. Adminstrv. Assn., Met. Home Econs. Assn. (pres. 1949-50, 60-61), Greene County Landmark Assn., Electric Womens Roundtable Assn. (Dayton-Cin. chpt. 1951-72, mem.-at-large 1972—), U.S. C. of C., Phi Upsilon Omicron (hon.), Ea. Star, Zonta (pres. Dayton chpt. 1950-52). Mem. Ch. of Christ. Home: 1443 State Route 380 Xenia OH 45385-9789

STEELE, JACK ELLWOOD, surgeon, medical researcher; b. Lacon, Ill., Jan. 27, 1924; s. Maurice Edgar and Ruth Naomi (Feller) S.; m. Ruth Eleanor (Kelley), Oct. 1, 1955; children: Jill Mayer, Suzy Ruth Ellen Steele. MD, Northwestern U., 1950; MS in Sys. Engring., Wright State U., 1977. Intern Cin. Gen. Hosp., 1949-50; fellow in rsch., tchg. Northwestern U., Chgo., 1950-51; psychiat. ward officer USAF Hosp., Wright Patterson AFB, Ohio, 1951-53; rsch. officer with numerous titles Aerospace Med. Lab., Wright Patterson AFB, Ohio, 1953, rsch. neurologist, flight surgeon, asst. chief math and analysis sect., lab. bionicist, 1971; advanced through grades to col. USAF, 1971; psychiat. physician Dayton (Ohio) Mental Health Ctr., 1973-91; med. dir. BUDA Methadone Clinic, Dayton, 1988, Nova House drug treatment, Dayton, 1988-90; pres. Gen. Bionics Corp., Dayton, 1991—; contbr. articles to profl. pubs. Editor: Bionics Symposium, 1960. Mem. AMA, IEEE, Am. Soc. of Clin. Hypnosis, Swedish Soc. of Clin. Hypnosis, Am. Legion, Loyal Order of Moose. Winter Home: 436 Airport Dr S Summerland Key FL 33042-4421 Office: Gen Bionics Corp 2313 Bonnieview Ave Dayton OH 45431-1987

STEELE, KATHLEEN FRANCES, federal official; b. Kansas City, Mo., Oct. 28, 1960; m. Steve Danner, Jan. 18, 1996. Admissions counselor N.E. Mo. State U., Kirksville, 1980-83, assoc. dir. admissions, 1983-86, programming coord. dept. pub. svcs., 1986-87; Iowa, N.H. dir. Gephardt for Pres., St. Louis, 1987-88; mem. Mo. Ho. of Reps., Jefferson City, 1988-94; state dir. Clinton for Pres., 1991-92; regional dir. U.S. Dept. Health and Human Svcs., Kansas City, Mo., 1994—; chair Freshman Dem. Caucus, 1989, chair sci., tech. and critical issues com. Bd. dirs. Adair County chpt. ARC, 1987. Recipient Young Careerist award Kirksville Bus. and Profl. Women, 1988. Mem. Nat. Order Women Legislators, Women Legislators of Mo. (pres. 1989-92). Roman Catholic. Home: 6 Nantucket Ct Smithville MO 64089-9605 Office: US Dept Health and Human Svcs 601 E 12th St Ste 210 Kansas City MO 64106-2808

STEELE, SARAH JANE, elementary school educator; b. Scottsbluff, Nebr., May 28, 1947; d. Earl Roe and Mary Eleanor (Blakey) Cherry; m. Gary Gene Steele, May 19, 1968; children: Jason Linn, Sally Suzanne. BS, Chadron State Coll., 1970, MS, 1994. Tchr. k., 1, 2 grades Chadron (Nebr.) Elem. Sch., 1970-71; tchr. 6th grade Morrill (Nebr.) Elem. Sch., 1971—. Mem. NEA, Nebr. State Edn. Assn., Morrill Edn. Assn. (pres. 1983-84), Alpha Delta Kappa (pres. 1994-96), Phi Delta Kappa. Republican Congregationalist. Home: 100777 County Road D Morrill NE 69358-2105 Office: Morrill Pub Schs Box 486 Morrill NE 69358

STEELMAN, JOHN ROBERT, real estate broker, entrepreneur; b. Cleve., June 5, 1948; s. Walter B. and Thelma E. (Dietrick) S. BA in Psychology, BS in Bus. Econs., Ala.-Athens Coll., 1971; postgrad., Xavier U. Lic. real estate broker, Ohio, Ky.; candidate cert. property mgr. Mgmt. cons. Consol. Pers. Svcs. Corp., Cin., 1973-75; mfg. rep. Steelman and Co., Cin., 1975-78; exec., sales assoc. Hauge, Inc. Realtors, Cin., 1978-80; adminstrv. mgr. Queen City, Realtors, Cin., 1980-82; gen. mgr. The Frederick A. Schmidt Co., Realtors, The Hammond North, Cin., 1982-83, J.R. Steelman, Realtor, The Regency, Cin., 1984-86, J.R. Steelman, Realtor, Kroger Farm Estate, Cin., 1987-89; broker, realtor J.R. Steelman, Coldwell Banker Real Estate, and ReMax, Cin., 1989-96. Pres., chmn. bd. dirs. Mt. Airy Town Coun., Inc., Cin., 1989-96, trustee, chmn. transp. and safety com.; chmn. Pres.'s Coun., Cin., 1992; chmn. rev. com. Neighborhood Support Programs, Inc., 1991, chmn. mgmt. selection com., 1991; trustee Invest In Neighborhoods, 1994-96, bd. dirs., 1994-96; bd. dirs. A Day in Eden, 1995-96; mem. Rep. Nat. Com., 1988—. Mem. Nat. Assn. Realtors, Ohio Assn. Realtors (trustee 1994), Cin. Bd. Realtors (legis. com. 1976-96, vice chmn. 1992), Cin. C. of C. (local govt. com.). Presbyterian. Home: 5688 Colerain Ave Cincinnati OH 45239-6746

STEEN, DON, state legislator; b. Tuscumbia, Mo., Nov. 16, 1949; m. Alisa Steen; children: Amy, Darrick, Scott, Katie. BS, U. Mo. Farmer; mem. Mo. Ho. of Reps. from 115th dist., 1991—; mem. Agr., Bus., Fees & Salaries, Misc. Bills and Resolutions, State Instns. and Property & Tourism, Recreational and Cult Affairs Coms Mo. Ho. of Reps. Mem. Osage (Mo.) Sch. Bd., Miller County Hist. Soc. Republican. Home: RR 3 Eldon MO 65026-9803*

STEEN, LOWELL HARRISON, physician; b. Kenosha, Wis., Nov. 27, 1923; s. Joseph Arthur and Camilla Marie (Henriksen) S.; m. Cheryl Ann Rectanus, Nov. 20, 1969; children—Linda C., Laura A., Lowell Harrison Jr., Heather J., Kirsten M. B.S., Ind. U., 1945, M.D., 1948. Intern Mercy Hosp.-Loyola U. Clinics, Chgo., 1948-49; resident in internal medicine VA Hosp., Hines, Ill., 1950-53; pvt. practice, Highland, Ind., 1953—; pres., chief exec. officer Whiting Clinic, 1960-85; mem. sr. staff St. Catherine Hosp., East Chicago, Ind.; staff Community Hosp., Munster, Ind.; bd. commrs. Joint Commn. Accreditation of Hosps. Served with M.C., AUS, 1949-50, 55-56. Recipient Disting. Alumni Service award Ind. U., 1983. Fellow ACP; mem. AMA (trustee 1975, chmn. bd. trustees 1979-81), Ind. Med. Assn. (pres. 1970, chmn. bd. 1968-70), World Med. Assn. (dir. 1978-82, chmn. 1981-82, del. world assembly), Ind. Soc. Internal Medicine (pres. 1963), Am. Soc. Internal Medicine (Disting. Internist award 1981), Lake County Med. Soc., Ind. U. Sch. Medicine Alumni Assn. (pres. 1989-90, Disting. Alumnus award 1981). Presbyterian. Home: 8800 Parkway Dr Hammond IN 46322-1520 also: Gateway 11481 Waterford Village Dr Fort Myers FL 33913-7917 Office: 3641 Ridge Rd Hammond IN 46322-2064

STEFANIK, JANET RUTH, realtor; b. Harrisville, W.Va., Apr. 25, 1938; d. John Jackson Davis Jr. and Helen Virginia (Waller) D.; m. Robert John Stefanik, Oct. 13, 1956 (div. Apr. 1977); children: Robert Mark, Deborah Ruth, Perry Wayne, David Lee, Susan Irene. Grad., Midview High Sch., Grafton, Ohio; student, Lorain County Community Coll., Elyria, Ohio, 1982, 85, 90-91. Salesperson Demby Real Estate, Elyria, 1970-71, Schwed Real Estate, Elyria, 1971-93; mem. women's coun. Lorain County Bd. Realtors, 1971-74, past pres., 1974. Toll collector Ohio Turnpike Commn., 1975. Mem. Gibson Girls Variety Chorale Group, Nat. Arbor Day Found., AARP. Mem. Women of the Moose, United Electrical Radio & Machine Workers of Am. (treas.). Republican. Roman Catholic. Home: PO Box 1556 Elyria OH 44036-1556

STEFFANNI, BRETT A., business manager; b. Tiffin, Ohio, Apr. 25, 1955. BS, Bowling Green State U., 1979. Mgr. CMC Whirlpool Corp., Clyde, Ohio, 1976—. Vol. United Way; vol. coach girls basketball. Mem. ASQC, SME. Office: Whirlpool Corp 119 Birdseye St Clyde OH 43410-1301

STEFFEN, ALAN LESLIE, entomologist; b. Ansonia, Ohio, Feb. 27, 1927; s. Henry William and Maude Moiselle (DuBois) S.; m. Genevieve Carlyle, Dec. 27, 1950 (dec. Jan. 6, 1989); m. Doris Mae Rable, Jan. 20, 1990. AB, Miami U., 1948; MSc in Entomology, Ohio State U., 1949; diploma, Malaria Tng. Ctr., 1959; postgrad., WHO, Sri Lanka and The Philippines, 1967, 68. Registered profl. entomologist. Malaria specialist Agy. for Internat. Devel., Jakarta, Indonesia, 1959-65; chief malaria advisor Agy. for Internat. Devel., Kathmandu, Nepal, 1966-72, Addis Ababa, Ethiopia, 1972-76, Kathmandu, 1976-78, Islamabad, Pakistan, 1978-80; malaria specialist Ctr. Disease Control, Songkhla, Thailand, 1965-66; tropical disease cons. Ill., 1981—; cons. U.S. AID, Port Au Prince, Haiti, 1981, WHO, Geneva, 1981—, Tifa, Ltd., Millington, N.J., 1982, John Snow, Inc., Boston, 1984, Vector Biology and Control Project, Arlington, Va., 1986. Mem. Nature Conservancy, Washington, 1986-88. With U.S. Army, 1945-46, ETO. Recipient Meritorious Honor award U.S. Dept. State, 1972. Fellow Royal Soc. Tropical Medicine; mem. Entomol. Soc. Am., Am. Registry Profl. Entomologists, Nat. Assn.

Ret. Fed. Employees (life), Am. Fgn. Svc. Assn. Home and Office: 303 Hickory Bnd Belleville IL 62223-3474

STEFFENS, JOHN HOWARD, cytotechnologist; b. Glendale, Calif., Aug. 5, 1941; s. Amzel Emmet Steffens and Wanda Elgain (Haylock) Clark; m. Yvonne Marie Croxen, Sept. 9, 1966; children: Roberta Mae, Deena Marie, Adam Kemp. BS, Warner Pacific Coll., Portland, Oreg., 1970; cert. cytotech., U. Kans., 1973. Cert. cyto-technologist. Messenger, orderly Palo Alto (Calif.) Stanford Hosp., 1957-62; warehouse worker Loma Linda Foods, Riverside, Calif., 1962-64; apiary worker Albert Knoefler Honey Co., Riverside, 1962-65; cyto-technician United Med. Labs., Portland, 1966-70; mgr. Independence (Mo.) Fire & Safety Equipment Co., 1970-72; res. and substitute tchr. Independence Sch. System, 1970-72, 90-95; cyto-technologist, med. technologist U. Health Scis., Kansas City, Mo., 1973-85; cyto-technologist Kansas City VA Hosp., 1973—, Rsch. Med. Ctr., Kansas City, 1984-90, Johnson Med. and Reference Labs., Independence, 1990—; cons. Univ. Diagnostics, Independence, 1991—; quality control supr. United Med. Labs, Portland, 1968-70; lab. safety officer U. Health Scis., Kansas City, 1980-84. Mem. Burroughs Aubudon Soc., Kansas City, Cmty. Assn. for the Arts. Recipient Performance award Kansas City City VA Hosp., 1987, Svc. award, 1988, Outstanding Rating Cert., 1988, 94, 95. Mem. Heart of Am. Assn. Cytotechnologists, Am. Beekeeping Fedn., Mo. Beekeepers Assn., Midwestern Beekeepers Assn. (bd. dirs. 1987-89, pres. 1990, honey plants com., Beekeeper of Yr. award 1990), Nat. Audubon Soc., Pathfinder Club (bd. dirs. 1973-76, dep. dir. 1974-76). Republican. Seventh Day Adventist. Home: 913 Main Rd Independence MO 64056-2417 Office: Kansas City VA Hosp 4801 E Linwood Blvd Kansas City MO 64128-2226

STEFFES, DON CLARENCE, state senator; b. Olpe, Kans., Jan. 13, 1930; s. William A. and Marie M. (Dwyer) S.; m. Janie L. Steele, Oct. 10, 1953; children: Michael, Steve, David, Andrew, Nancy, Terrence, Jennifer. BS, Kans. State Tchrs. Coll., 1952, MS, 1958. Mgr. Abilene C. of C., Kans., 1955-57; mem. staff Topeka C. of C., 1957-60; mgr. McPherson C. of C., Kans., 1960-65; exec. v.p. Kans. Devel. Credit Corp., Topeka, 1965-68, McPherson Bank & Trust, 1968-73; pres., CEO BANK IV McPherson (formely McPherson Bank & Trust), 1973-91; mem. Kans. State Senate, Topeka, 1992—. Mem. Kans. Main St. Adv. Counsel, Topeka, 1978-82; pres., bd. dirs. Mingenback Found., McPherson, Kans., 1970—; vice chmn. Nat. Commn. Agrl. Fin., Washington, 1987-89; v.p. McPherson Indsl. Devel. Co., 1970-75. Named Man of Yr. McPherson Coll., 1989. Mem. Kans. Bankers Assn. (pres. 1985), KC. Roman Catholic. Home: 1008 Turkey Creek Dr Mc Pherson KS 67460-9763

STEGER, JOSEPH A., university president. Formerly sr. v.p. and provost U. Cin., pres., 1984—. Office: U Cin PO Box 210063 Cincinnati OH 45221-0063

STEGNER, LYNN NADENE, treasurer; b. Bethlehem, Pa., Aug. 20, 1955; d. Edmund Joseph and Evelyn Virginia (Shelbo) S.; m. Frederick Gerald Freitag, Sept. 10, 1977; children: Crescentia Adela Stegner-Freitag, Abigail Amadea Stegner-Freitag, Genevieve Angelica Stegner-Freitag. BBA, U. Wis., 1977; MBA, U. Chgo., 1979. Sr. cons. Arthur Andersen & Co., Cleve., 1979-82; mgr. of fin. Morton Internat. (Morton Thiokol), Chgo., 1982-89; asst. treas. Eclipse, Inc., Rockford, Ill., 1989-90; CFO Bd. of Jewish Edn. and Community Found. for Jewish Edn., 1991-96; cons. Diamond Headache Clinic, Chgo., 1989-93. Mem. U. Chgo. Alumni Bd., 1986-88. Recipient Cert. Merit YWCA, Cleve., 1981, Cert. Leadership, Chgo., 1984. Mem. Treasury Mgmt. Assn. (prog. chmn. 1987), Chgo. Assn. Soc. Execs.

STEIGER, SHERRY HANSEN, author, lecturer, counselor; b. Dearborn, Mich., Apr. 24, 1945; d. Greg Michie and Lorraine Ruth Johnson; adopted by Paul Lippold; m. Brad. Steiger; children: Erik (dec.), Melissa; stepchildren: Bryan, Kari, Steve, Julie Olson. Student, No. Ill. U.; postgrad., Lutheran Sch. Theology, U. Chgo., Ohio State U. Staff mem. Luth. Sch. Theology; counselor SUNY, Stony Brook; creator Celebrate Life multi-media program; stress mgmt. cons.; speaker in field; bd. dirs. various health ctrs.; model, actress. Author: Seasons of the Soul, Starborn, Hollywood and the Supernatural, The Philadelphia Experiment and Other UFO Conspiracies, The Teaching Power of Dreams, Mystical Legends of the Shamans, Indian Wisdom and Its Guiding Power, Montezuma's Serpent-Supernatural Tales of the Southwest, The Strange Powers of Pets, Undying Love, Super Scientists of Atlantis and Other Worlds, The Mystery of Animal Intelligence, Amazing Moms, Angels Over Their Shoulders, Demon Deaths, More Powers of Pets, The Rainbow Conspracy, More Strange Powers of Pets, Angels Around the World, Children of Light; editor: The Fellowship. Counselor, cmty. worker Smithtown, L.I. Address: 505 W M St Forest City IA 50436

STEIGERWALDT, DONNA WOLF, clothing manufacturing company executive; b. Chgo., Apr. 2, 1929; d. Harry Hay and Donna (Currey) Wolf; m. William Steigerwaldt, Dec. 31, 1969; children: Debra, Linda. BA, U. Colo., Colo. Springs, 1950, LHD (hon.), 1987. Ins. broker Conn. Mut. Life Ins. Co., Chgo., 1950-53; vice chmn. Jockey Internat., Inc., Kenosha, Wis., 1978-80, chmn., chief exec. officer, 1980—. Pres. Donna Wolf Steigerwaldt Found., Inc.; mem. Infant Welfare Soc., Evanston Hosp.-Glenbrook Hosp. Corp., N.W. Cmty. Hosp. Aux., Aid to Animals No. Ill., Inc.; vice chmn. Carthage Coll., 1982-92, chmn., 1992—; bd. dirs. Century Club Sarasota Meml. Hosp. Paul Harris fellow, Rotary, 1984. Mem. Am. Apparel Mfrs. Assn., Navy League U.S., Glenview Hist. Soc., Exec. Women Internat. (hon.), Rotary (Paul Harris fellow 1984). Republican. Episcopalian. Clubs: North Shore Country, Plaza, Valley Lo Sports; Meadows Country (Sarasota, Fla.). Office: Jockey Internat Inc 2300 60th St Kenosha WI 53140-3822

STEIGMAN, GARY, physics and astronomy educator; b. N.Y.C., Feb. 23, 1941. BS in Physics magna cum laude, CCNY, 1961; MS in Physics, NYU, 1963, PhD in Physics, 1968. Rsch. asst. Brookhaven Nat. Lab., 1961; teaching asst. physics dept. Cornell U., 1961-62; rsch. scientist Aerospace Corp., 1962; teaching asst. physics dept. NYU, 1963-64, rsch. asst. physics dept., 1966-67, instr. physics dept., 1967-68; vis. fellow Inst. Theoretical Astronomy, Cambridge, Eng., 1968-70; rsch. fellow physics Calif. Inst. Tech., 1970-72; asst. prof. astronomy Yale U., 1972-78; assoc. prof. physics Bartol Rsch. Found., 1978-80, prof. physics, 1980-86; prof. physics and astronomy Ohio State U., 1986—; vis. scientist Nat. Radio Astronomy Obs., 1975-76; vis. prof. Stanford U., 1979; dir. early universe program Inst. for Theoretical Physics, U. Calif., Santa Barbara, 1981; George Ellery Hale dist. vis. prof. Enrico Fermi Inst., U. Chicago, 1983; mem. adv. bd., bd. trustees Aspen Ctr. Physics, organizing com. Astrophysics Workshops, 1973-83, 86—. Assoc. editor Nuclear Physics B, 1984—. Recipient NSF fellowship, 1963, 64, 65, 65-66, N.Y. State Regents Coll. Teaching fellowship, 1961-62, 62-63, 64-65, 1st prize Gravity Rsch. Found. Essay Competition, 1980, first E.A. Yunker Lectr. in Physics award, Oreg. State U., 1985, Alexander von Humboldt-Stiftung Sr. U.S. Scientist award, 1986, Disting. Scholar award Ohio State U., 1992; named Del. Scientist of Yr., Sigma Xi, 1979. Fellow Am. Phys. Soc.; mem. Am. Astron. Soc., Internat. Astron. Union. Home: 43 Campus View Blvd Columbus OH 43235 Office: Ohio State Univ Dept Physics 174 W 18th Ave Columbus OH 43210-1106

STEIL, GLENN, state legislator; b. Aug. 29, 1940. AAS, Davenport Coll.; BSBA, Aquinas Coll. Bus. owner; senator Dist. 30 Mich. State Senate, 1995—, mem. appropriations and legis. coun. coms., vice chmn. govt. ops. com.

STEIL, MICHELLE DIANNE DUNAGAN, nurse; b. Des Moines, Apr. 11, 1962; d. Carl Duane and Sharon Ann (Richardson) Dunagan; m. Alan Ray Steil, Oct. 9, 1982; children: Ashleigh Rae, Alan "Blake". ADN, Des Moines Area Community Coll, 1983. RN, Iowa. Staff nurse med.-surg., psychiatric, emergency rm. Skiff Med. Ctr., Newton, Iowa, 1983-88; staff nurse Nelson Manor, Newton, Iowa, 1989; nurse floor supr. Willowbrook Residential Care Ctr., Cedar Rapids, Iowa, 1990-92; nurse clinician skilled nursing unit Mercy Med. Ctr, Cedar Rapids, 1992-94; charge RN skilled nursing Mercy Med. Ctr., Cedar Rapids, Iowa, 1994, charge RN SNF unit, 1994—. Independent. Methodist. Home: PO Box 8237 Cedar Rapids IA 52408-8237

STEIN, BOB, lawyer. Degree, U. Minn. Lawyer Minn. Timberwolves; former NFL player; former pres. Minn. Timberwolves; former pres. Target Ctr. Arena, Mpls., 1967-68. Home: Minn Timberwolves Wayzata Blvd Ste 700 Minneapolis MN 55416-1233

STEIN, ELEANOR BANKOFF, judge; b. N.Y.C., Jan. 24, 1923; d. Jacob and Sarah (Rashkin) Bankoff; m. Frank S. Stein, May 27, 1947; children: Robert B., Joan Jenkins, William M. Student, Barnard Coll., 1940-42; BS in Econs., Columbia U., 1944; LLB, NYU, 1949; grad. Ind. Jud. Coll., 1986. Bar: N.Y. 1950, Ind. 1976, U.S. Supreme Ct. 1980. Atty. Hillis & Button, Kokomo, Ind., 1975-76, Paul Hillis, Kokomo, 1976-78, Bayliff, Harrigan, Kokomo, 1978-80; judge Howard County Ct., Kokomo, 1981-89; ret., 1989; co-juvenile referee Howard County Juvenile Ct., 1976-78. Mem. Republican Women's Assn. Kokomo, 1980—; bd. dirs. Howard County Legal Aid Soc., 1976-80; dir. Howard County Ct. Alcohol and Drug Svcs. Program, 1982-89; bd. advisors St. Joseph Hosp., Kokomo, 1979—; bd. dirs. Kokomo Human Rels. Commn., 1967-70, Howard County Children's Ctr., 1993—. Mem. law rev. bd. NYU Law Rev., 1947-48. Mem. Am. Judicature Soc., Ind. Jud. Assn., Nat. Assn. Women Judges, ABA (apptd. Ind. del. jud. adminstrn. div. 1987), Ind. Bar Assn., Howard County Bar Assn. Jewish. Clubs: Kokomo Country, Altrusa. Home: 3204 Tally Ho Dr Kokomo IN 46902-3985

STEIN, ERIC, retired law educator; b. Holice, Czechoslovakia, July 8, 1913; came to U.S., 1940, naturalized, 1943; s. Zikmund and Hermina (Zalud) S.; m. Virginia Elizabeth Rhine, July 30, 1955. JUD, Charles U., Prague, Czechoslovakia, 1937; JD, U. Mich., 1942; Dr. honoris causa, Vrije U., Brussels, 1978, U. Libre, Brussels, 1979. Bar: Ill. 1946, D.C. 1953. Practiced law Prague, 1937; with State Dept., 1946-55; acting dep. dir. Office UN Polit. Affairs, 1955; mem. faculty U. Mich. Law Sch., Ann Arbor, 1956, prof. internat. law and orgn., 1958-76; Hessel E. Yntema prof. law U. Mich. Law Sch., 1976-83, emeritus prof., 1983—; co-dir. internat. legal studies, 1958-76, dir., 1976-81; vis. prof. Stanford Law Sch., 1956, 77, Law Faculties, Stockholm, Uppsala and Lund, Sweden, 1969, Inst. Advanced Legal Studies U. London, 1975, U. Ariz., 1991, 92; lectr. Hague Acad. Internat. Law, summer 1971; vis. lectr. European U. Inst., Florence, Italy, 1983, Beijing, Shanghai, Wuhan, 1986, U. Tokyo, Kyoto, 1986, Coll. of Europe, Bruges, Pontificia, Madrid, 1988; Jean Monnet prof. European U. Inst., Florence, Italy, 1991, Henry Morris lectr. Kent Coll. of Law, Chgo., 1992, Jeanne Kiewit Taylor disting. vis. lectr. U. Ariz., winter 1993; adviser U.S. delegation UN Gen. Assembly, 1947-55; mem. adv. panel, cons. Bur. European Affairs, State Dept., 1966-73; cons. U.S. rep. for trade negotiations, 1979; vice chmn. com. Atlantic studies Atlantic Inst., 1966-68; mem. adv. council Inst. European Studies, Free U., Brussels, Belgium, 1965-70; mem. U.S. Com. for Legal Edn. Exchange with China, 1983-91; lectr. Acad. of European Law, Florence, Italy 1990. Author: (with others) American Enterprise in the European Common Market-A Legal Profile, vols. I, II, 1960, (with H.K. Jacobson) Diplomats, Scientists and Politicians: The United States and the Nuclear Test Ban Negotiations, 1966, Harmonization of European Company Law: National Reform and Transnational Coordination, 1971, Impact of New Weapons Technology on International Law-Selected Aspects, 1971, Un Nuovo Diritto per l'Europa, 1991; editor: (with Peter Hay) Law and Institutions in the Atlantic Area Readings, Cases and Problems, 1967, (with Peter Hay and Michel Waelbroeck) European Community Law and Institutions in Perspective, 1976; co-author, co-editor: Courts and Free Markets-Perspectives From the United States and Europe, 1982; bd. editors: Am. Jour. Internat. Law, 1965—; mem. adv. bd. Common Market Law Rev., 1964—, Legal Issues of European Integration, 1974—, Rivista di Diritto Europeo, 1978—, Columbia Jour. East European Law, 1994—, Columbia Jour. European Law, 1994—; contbr. articles to profl. jours. Mem. Internat. Com. for Revision Czechoslovak Constn., 1990-92. With AUS, 1943-46. Decorated Bronze Star, Order Italian Crown, Italian Mil. Cross; Guggenheim fellow, 1962-63; Social Sci. Rsch. Coun. grantee; Rockefeller Found. scholar-in-residence, 1965, 73; Alexander von Humboldt Stiftung awardee, 1982; fellow Inst. Advanced Study, Berlin, 1984-85, IREX rsch. grant, 1995. Mem. ABA (co-chmn. European law com. 1982, mem. coun. sect. on internat. law and practice 1983-84), Internat. Law Assn., Coun. Fgn. Rels., Am. Soc. Internat. Law (exec. coun. 1954-57, bd. rev. and devel. 1965-67, 70-75, hon. v.p. 1982—), Brit. Inst. Internat. and Comparative Law, Internat. Acad. Comparative Law (assoc.). Home: 2649 Heatherway St Ann Arbor MI 48104-2850

STEIN, GARY ALECK, electrical engineer; b. Roseau, Minn., Mar. 16, 1961; s. Walter Allan and Avis Ione (Palm) S.; m. Judith Ann Hanzlik, May 25, 1985; children: Tracy Ann, Katie Jo. BSEE, N.D. State U., 1983. Assoc. engr. 3M Co., St. Paul, 1982; sr. engr. Sperry Corp., Eagan, Minn., 1983-87; prin. engr. Unisys Corp., Eagan, 1987-91; sr. engr. Tricord Systems, Inc., Plymouth, Minn., 1991—. Mem. IEEE. Office: Tricord Systems Inc 2800 Northwest Blvd Plymouth MN 55441

STEIN, LARRY ARDEN, electrical engineer; b. Roseau, Minn., May 29, 1964; s. Walter Allen and Avis Ione (Palm) S.; m. Joan Annette Goossen, Oct. 21, 1989. BSEE, N.D. State U., 1986. Engr. Control Data Corp., Arden Hills, Minn., 1986-89; sr. engr. Rosemount Inc., Burnsville, Minn., 1989-95; cons. Embedded Micro Designs Inc., St. Paul, 1995—; prin. engr. XIOtech Corp., Eden Prairie, Minn., 1995—. Mem. IEEE. Home: 1859 Nebraska Ave E Saint Paul MN 55119-4222 also: XIOtech Corp 6509 Flying Cloud Dr Eden Prairie MN 55344

STEIN, MYRON SANFORD, art educator, social worker; b. Detroit, Oct. 7, 1941; s. Nathan and Celia (Mendelson) S.; m. Nancy Louise Trewern, Jan. 31, 1971; children: David, Tobey. BA, Detroit Inst. Tech., 1964; BA and cert. art edn., Wayne State U., 1990, postgrad., 1983-86. Cert. social worker, Mich.; cert. secondary provisional tchr., Mich. Probation officer, social worker Wayne County Juvenile Ct., Detroit, 1968-86; substitute tchr. Livonia (Mich.) and Hazel Pk. (Mich.) Pub. Schs., 1990-94; art tchr., counselor St. Scholastics Sch., Detroit, 1994—; tchr. art Temple Beth El, Bloomfield, Mich., 1990—. Author: (books) A Guide to Step-Parent and Related Adoption, 1985, Professional Sports Word Search Puzzles, 1993, Word Search Puzzles Younger Kids Love, 1994, (children's play) The Lunch Bag Genie, 1995. Jewish. Home: 28219 Berkshire Dr Southfield MI 48076

STEIN, PAUL CLINTON, financial planner; b. Mpls., Feb. 27, 1960; s. Clinton W. and Pauline Stein; m. Jann Marie Matheis, Mar. 23, 1983; children: Michelle, Andrew. BS in Math. Edn., U. Minn., 1983. Registered investment advisor, series 7 rep.; lic. life, health and variable ins. rep., CFP. Orgnl. mgr. Southwestern Co., Nashville, 1980-85; sr. acct. rep. Gt. Am. Opportunities, Nashville, 1985-90; assoc. gen. agt. Luth. Brotherhood, Balt., 1990-92; assoc. adviser Swenson Anderson Fin. Group, Mpls., 1992—; spkr. on money and fin. to various schs., colls., banks and pvt. corps, and radio, Ill. and Minn., 1985—. Singer, songwriter, performer various ch. and comty. concerts, corp. banquets, 1980—. V.p. Ellicott Mills Homeowners Assn., Balt., 1990-92. Mem. Internat. Assn. Fin. Planning, Inst. CFPs, Nat. Assn. Life Underwriters. Republican. Office: Swenson Anderson Fin Planners 1221 Nicollet Ave Ste 400 Minneapolis MN 55403-2474

STEIN, PAUL DAVID, cardiologist; b. Cin., Apr. 13, 1934; s. Simon and Sadie (Friedman) S.; m. Janet Louise Tucker, Aug. 14, 1966; children: Simon, Douglas, Rebecca. BS, U. Cin., 1955, MD, 1959. Intern Jewish Hosp., Cin., 1959-60, med. resident, 1961-62; med. resident Gorgas Hosp., C.Z., 1960-61; fellow in cardiology U. Cin., 1962-63, Mt. Sinai Hosp., N.Y.C., 1963-64; rsch. fellow Harvard Med. Sch., Boston, 1964-66; asst. dir. cardiac catheterization lab. Baylor U. Med. Ctr., Dallas, 1966-67; asst. prof. medicine Creighton U., Omaha, 1967-69; assoc. prof. medicine U. Okla., Oklahoma City, 1969-73; prof. rsch. medicine U. Okla. Coll. Medicine, Oklahoma City, 1973-76; dir. cardiovascular rsch. Henry Ford Hosp., Detroit, 1976-94, med. dir. cardiovascular rehab., 1994—; adj. prof. physics Oakland U., Rochester, Mich., 1985—; prof. medicine (Henry Ford) Case Western Res. U., Cleve., 1994—. Author: A Physical and Physiological Basis for the Interpretation of Cardiac Ausculation: Evaluations Based Primarily on Second Sound and Ejection Murmurs, 1981; contbr. articles to profl. jours. Coun. on Clin. Cardiology fellow Am. Heart Assn., 1971, Coun. on Circulation fellow, 1972. Fellow ACP, Am. Coll. Cardiology, Am. Coll. Chest Physicians (pres. 1993), Internat. Acad. Chest Physicians and Surgeons (pres. 1993); mem. ASME, Am. Physiol. Soc., Ctrl. Soc. Clin. Rsch. Office: Henry Ford Hosp New Center Pavillion 2921 W Grand Blvd Detroit MI 48202-2691

STEIN, PAUL LLOYD, insurance company executive; b. Bklyn., Sept. 23, 1943; s. Nathan and Mollie (Zucker) S.; m. Margaret R. Malachek, Sept. 22, 1950; children: Nathan, Hilary. BS, So. Ill. U., 1966. CLU, 1973. Spl. agt. Northwestern Mut. Life Ins. Co., Ann Arbor, Mich., 1969-77, field dir., 1977-78, dir. coll. unit, 1978-80, dist. agt., 1980-85; gen. agt. Northwestern Mut. Life Ins. Co., Detroit and S.E., Mich., 1985—. Contbr. articles to profl. jours. Pres., bd. dirs. Project Grow, Ann Arbor, 1973-74. Mem. Million Dollar Round Table (life), Am. Soc. of CLU's, Greater Detroit Assn. of Life Underwriters, Gen. Agts. and Mgrs. Assn. Master Agency Builder, Ann Arbor Art Assn. (v.p., bd. dirs. 1984-85), Ann Arbor C. of C. (treas., bd. dirs. 1984-86). Jewish. Office: Northwestern Mut Life Ins Co 2701 Troy Center Dr Ste 300 Troy MI 48084-4741

STEIN, PAULA JEAN ANNE BARTON, hotel real estate consultant; b. Chgo., July 29, 1929; m. Marshall L. Stein; children: Guy G., George L. BA, Lake Forest (Ill.) U., 1951; postgrad., Roosevelt U., Chgo., 1955-77, UCLA, 1978-79. Lic. internat. hotel and mgmt. cons./broker, Ill. Adminstrv. asst. publicity Kefauver for Pres., Chgo., 1951; adminstrv. asst. Wells Orgns., Chgo., 1952; rschr., writer Employers Assn. Am., Chgo.; writer Woodworking Jobbers Assn., Chgo., 1953; cons. L.A., 1978-80; founder, pres., ptnr., cons. internat. hotel real estate Steinvest, Inc., Chgo., 1980—; cons., hotels Nat. Diversified Svcs., Inc., Chgo., 1990—, Chatmar, Inc., Bayview Hotels, Monterey, Calif. IBA fellow, 1990. Mem. World Future Soc. (profl.). Home and Office: Steinvest Inc 641 W Willow St House 202 Chicago IL 60614-5176

STEIN, THOMAS HENRY, social science educator; b. Elmhurst, Ill., May 17, 1949; s. Peter Leonard and Marion Edith (Zirbel) S.; m. Alberta Piazza, July 10, 1971; 1 child, Heather. BA in Polit. Sci., Loyola U., Chgo., 1971; postgrad., Loyola U., 1972-76; MS in Edn., Pacific Western U., 1988, PhD in Edn., 1989. Cert. tchr., Ill. Budget analyst U.S. Dept. Def., Gt. Lakes Naval Sta., Ill., 1971-72; tchr. social sci., coach bowling, softball Mother Guerin High Sch., River Grove, Ill., 1972—; tchr. Highland Park (Ill.) High Sch., 1981-84; instr. Franklin Park (Ill.) Park Dist., 1977—; tchr. Triton Coll., River Grove, 1990-91; evaluator Chgo. Met. History Fair, 1980-89; faculty adviser Scholastic, Inc., N.Y.C., 1990—; dir. Students Against Animal Cruelty, River Grove, 1991—; mod. Nat. Honor Soc., 1993—. With Ill. N.G., 1971-77. Recipient Outstanding Achievement award Am. Express/Assn. Am. Geographers, 1989. Fellow Acad. Polit. Sci.; mem. ASCD, Nat. Coun. Social Studies, Nat. Hist. Soc., Ctr. Study of the Presidency, Nat. Cath. Edn. Assn., Orgn. History Tchrs., Am. Polit. Sci. Assn. Democrat. Roman Catholic. Home: 3601 Emerson St Franklin Park IL 60131-1713 Office: Mother Guerin High Sch 8001 W Belmont Ave River Grove IL 60171-1012

STEIN, TIMOTHY ANDREW, copy editor; b. Milw., Oct. 14, 1970; s. Neil Richard and Barbara Joann (Rosenow) S.; m. Kimberly Jean Murphy, Aug. 22, 1992; 1 child, Adam Joseph. BA, U. Wis., Eau Claire, 1992. Copy editing intern N.Y. Newsday, N.Y.C., summer 1991; mgr. Rocky Rococo's, Eau Claire, Wis., 1991-93; proofreader Nat. Bus. Inst., Eau Claire, 1993; freelance newsletter editor, 1994—; copy editor Leader-Telegram, Eau Claire, 1993—. Recipient internship/scholarship Dow Jones Newspaper Fund, 1991, 2nd Place headline writing Wis. Newspaper Assn. Writing awards, 1996. Lutheran. Office: Leader-Telegram PO Box 570 Eau Claire WI 54702

STEINBERG, JOEL, physician, psychiatrist; b. Miami, Jan. 13, 1934; s. Leo Charles and Fannie (Goldstein) S.; m. Marta C. Steinberg, Sept. 16, 1955 (div. 1987); children: Karl, Debbie, Clif, Leslie. BS, U. Fla., 1954; MD, Emory U., 1958. Diplomate Am. Bd. Internal Medicine, Am. Bd. Psychiatry and Neurology. Resident in internal medicine U. Hosps., Atlanta, 1958-62; dir. med. clinics Grady Meml. Hosp., Atlanta, 1962-67; resident in psychiat Cleve., 1967-70; dir. mental health City of Cleve., 1970-72; pvt. practice Cleve., 1972-75; dir. med. psychiat St. Luke's Hosp., Cleve., 1976-85; pvt. practice Cleve., 1986—. Fellow Am. Coll Physicians, Am. Psychiat. Assn. Home and Office: 5370 SOM Center Rd Willoughby OH 44094

STEINBERG, LOIS SAXELBY, marketing executive; b. New Rochelle, N.Y., Sept. 13, 1926; d. John J. and Ruth (Taussig) Saxelby; m. Jack Steinberg, Nov. 27, 1947 (div. 1980); children: Eric, Mark. BA, Hunter Coll., N.Y.C., 1952; MA, Columbia U., N.Y.C., 1964; PhD, Fordham U., Bronx, 1978. Account exec. The Rowland Co., N.Y.C., 1956-64; rsch. asst. Columbia U., N.Y.C., 1965-67; rsch. assoc. CUNY, 1967-72; staff asst. Community Svc. Soc., N.Y.C., 1972-74; rsch. assoc. Inst. for Responsive Edn., Boston, 1976-77, Designs for Change, Chgo., 1977-78; sr. study dir. Nat. Opinion Rsch. Ctr., U. Chgo., 1979-81; rsch. spr. BBDO, N.Y.C., 1981-82, Marsteller, Inc., Chgo., 1982-83; v.p. Sorkin-Enenstein Rsch. Svc., Inc., Chgo., 1984—. Contbr. articles to profl. jours. Fordham U. fellow, 1974; Columbia U. fellow, 1964. Mem. Am. Sociol. Assn., Am. Mktg. Assn. Office: Sorkin-Enenstein Rsch Svc 500 N Dearborn St Chicago IL 60610-4901

STEINEGER, MARGARET LEISY, non-profit organization officer; b. Newton, Kans., Feb. 8, 1926; d. Ernest Erwin and Elva Agnes (Krehbiel) L.; m. John Francis Steineger, Dec. 2, 1949; children: John Steineger III, Cindy Blair, Melissa, Chris. B., So. Meth. U., 1947; M. in Social Work, U. Kans., 1949. County vice-chair United Way, Kansas City, Kans., 1960-61; bd., sec., treas. Wyandotte County Bar Aux., Kans., 1960-63; bd. Jr. League of Kansas City, 1962-66, County Coun. PTA, Wyandotte County, 1963-66, KCK Friends of the Arts, Kansas City, 1974-77; pres. Grinter Place Mus. Friends, Kans., 1977-78; bd. Kaw Valley Arts Coun., Kansas City, 1982-86; commr. Landmarks Commn., Kansas City, 1985-87; bd. Arts with the Handicapped, Wyandotte County, 1986—; bd. dirs. Kans. Arts Adv. Bd., Grinter Place Friends, Kans., Tri-County Tourism Coun., Kans. V.p. Kans. Legis. Wives, Topeka, 1975-76; bd. dirs. KCK Friends of the Libr., Kansas City, 1984—, Shepherd's Ctr., 1996—; founder Wyandotte County Libr., 1963-64, Creative Experiences, Kansas City, 1967; commr. Kans. Arts Commn., 1965-85; mem. Kaw Valley Arts and Humanities Bd., 1988-92; mem. adv. bd. Parents as Tchrs., 1992—; mem. KCK C.C. Endowment Bd., 1989—. Recipient Humanities award Kans. Com. for the Humanities, 1989; named Citizen of Yr. Kansas City, Kans., 1978. Democrat. Methodist. Home: 6400 Valleyview St Kansas City KS 66111-2013 Office: Security Bank Building Ste 600 Kansas City KS 66101

STEINER, JEFFERY ALLEN, project engineer, executive; b. Longview, Wash., June 22, 1954; s. Glyn Elmer and Betty Jean (Shuster) S.; m. Cynthia Gene Schoppey, June 5, 1976; children: Peter, David, Scott. BSME, U.S. Naval Acad., 1976; MSCE, Oreg. State U., 1982. Registered profl. engr., Calif., Minn. Commd. ensign USNR, 1976; gunnery officer U.S.S. Bradley, San Diego, 1976-79; maintenance officer Naval Base, Guantanamo Bay, Cuba, 1979-81; co. comdr. Amphibious Constrn., San Diego, 1982-85; engr. City of Chula Vista (Calif.), 1985-86; project mgr. Mayo Clinic, Rochester, Minn., 1986—; tech. advisor Minn. Pollution Control Agy., St. Paul, 1988-93. Bd. trustees Ronald McDonald House, Rochester, Minn., 1990—, pres. 1995-96; bd. govs. Grace Evang. Free Ch., Stewartville, Minn., 1990-94. Decorated Navy Achievement, Navy Battle Excellence. Mem. Minn. Soc. Profl. Engrs. (sec.-treas. 1992, v.p. 1993, pres. 1994), Toastmasters (Competent Toastmaster). Office: Mayo Clinic 200 1st St SW Rochester MN 55905-0001

STEINER, KAREN RUTH, physician's assistant; b. Milw., Nov. 25, 1953; d. Carl Gustav Martin and Lois Pauline Edna (Koch) S.; m. Christian Joseph Nichols, Sept. 15, 1990. AA in Sci., Glendale Community Coll., 1974; cert. of surg. tech., Maricopa County Tech. Coll., 1976; AA physician asst. pgrm., Essex Community Coll., Balt., 1980. Registered physician asst., Ariz.; lic. phys. asst., Mich.; cert. Nat. Commn. Cert. Physician's Assts. and Nat. Bd. Examiners. Operating room technician Maricopa County Gen. Hosp., Phoenix, 1976-77, Greater Balt. Med. Ctr., 1977-78; resident dept. surgery Franklin Square Hosp., Balt., 1980-811; physician's asst. urgent care unit Ariz. Health Plan, Phoenix, 1981-82; physician's asst. family practice unit CIGNA Healthplan, Tempe, Ariz., 1982-83; physician's asst. cardiac-thoracic surgery dept. Henry Ford Hosp., Detroit, 1983-87, Thoracic Surgeon's Assocs., Grand Rapids, Mich., 1987-88; physician's asst. surg. White Mountain Hosp., 1988-89; physicians asst. Grace Hosp., Detroit, 1989-91, St. John Hosp., 1991—, Women's Health Ctr., Clarkston, Mich., 1993, Livonia (Mich.) Family Physicians, 1994—. Choral Mem. Ariz. State U.,

Tempe, 1977, 82, Balt. Choral Arts Soc., 1978, White Mtn. Chorale, 1988. Fellow Am. Acad. Physician's Assts., Assn. Physician Assts. in Cardiovascular Surgery, Mich. Acad. Physician Assts. Democrat. Lutheran.

STEINER, PAUL ANDREW, retired insurance executive; b. Woodburn, Ind., Feb. 17, 1929; s. Eli Gerig and Emma Mae (Yaggy) S.; m. Ruth Edna Henry, Sept. 1, 1950; children: Mark, Nancy, Jonathan, David. AB, Taylor U., 1950. C.P.C.U. Owner feed and grain, lumber and constrn. firms, Bluffton, Ohio, 1951-64; home office rep. Brotherhood Mut. Ins. Co., Ft. Wayne, Ind., 1964-65, dir. claims, 1966-71, v.p., treas., 1968-71, pres., 1971-94, chmn. bd., 1974—. Past treas., Nat. Assn. Evangels., bd. trustees Am. Bible Soc.; past chmn. Summit Christian Coll.; trustee Taylor U. Named Layman of Yr., Nat. Assn. Evangelicals, 1977. Mem. Nat. Assn. Mut. Ins. Cos. (past chmn. bd.; Merit award 1973), DEVCO Mut. Assn. (past chmn.) Conf. Casualty Ins. Cos. (past pres.), Mut. Ins. Cos. Assn. Ind. (past pres.), Soc. C.P.C.U.s (past nat. ethics com. past pres. No. Ind. chpt.), Ft. Wayne Rotary (past pres.). Republican. Evang. Mennonite. Club: Christian Bus. Men's Com. (Ft. Wayne). Home: 1825 Florida Dr Fort Wayne IN 46805-5036 Office: Brotherhood Mut Ins Co 111 E Ludwig Rd Ste 100 Fort Wayne IN 46825-4240

STEINER, RUSSELL A., lawyer, judge; b. Lewisburg, Ohio, Nov. 27, 1935; s. Glenn Victor and Alice Mae (Bridenbaugh) S.; m. Lois Jean Spatz, June 22, 1963; children: Russell S., Marlise M., Vicki A., Leanna M., Lori, Julia K., Tim P. BSChemE, U. Dayton, 1965; JD, Capital U., 1972. Bar: Ohio, U.S. Dist. Ct. (so. and ea. dists.) Ohio, U.S. Supreme Ct. Prodn. engr. Western Electric, Columbus, Ohio, 1965-67, Ross Labs., Columbus, Ohio, 1967-72; atty. pvt. practice Columbus, Ohio, 1972-74, Newark, Ohio, 1974-83; judge Mcpl. Ct., Newark, Ohio, 1983-91, Domestic Rels., Newark, Ohio, 1991—; first group of attys. Columbus Mini-Arbitration Panel, 1975-83; group leader Nat. Jud. Coll., San Diego, 1994; faculty presenter Ohio Jud. Coll., Columbus, 1994. Contbr. articles to profl. jours. With U.S. Army, 1958-60. Mem. ABA, Ohio State Bar Assn., Am. Judges Assn., Assn. Family and Conciliation Cts., Ohio Domestic Rels. Judges Assn. (exec. com., v.p.). Office: Domestic Rels Ct Courthouse Newark OH 43055

STEINHAUS, CAROLYN PINKERTON, computer science educator; b. Madison, Wis., Jan. 29, 1950; d. John Edward and Mila Jean (Pinkerton) S. BS, Emory U., 1972; MS, U. Mich., 1974, postgrad., 1978. Programmer Emory U., Atlanta, 1969-72; grad. asst. U. Mich., Ann Arbor, 1973-83; instr. part-time Ga. State U., Atlanta, 1983-86, instr., 1986-89; rsch. asst. Ga. Tech. U., Atlanta, 1984-85; asst. prof. computer sci. Morningside Coll., Sioux City, Iowa, 1989—, mem. bd. Ctr. for Women, 1991—, pres. of Ctr., 1992-94. Trustee 1st Unitarian Ch., Sioux City, 1991-94, sec., 1991-93, pres., 1993-94, dir. religious edn., 1994-96. GE fellow, 1972, Bouroughs fellow, 1979. Mem. Assn. for Computing Machinery. Democrat. Office: Morningside Coll Dept Math Scis 1501 Morningside Ave Sioux City IA 51106-1717

STEINLEY, LORI ANDERSON, physical therapist; b. Milaca, Minn., July 17, 1965; d. Oscar John and Peggy Marie (Jennison) A.; m. Maurie Shawn, Sept. 3, 1994. BA in Biology and Phys. Therapy, Coll. of St. Scholastica, 1988; MS, St. Cloud State U., 1994. Registered phys. thereapist, exercise physiologist. Phys. therapist Meth. Hosp., St. Louis Park, Minn., 1988-90; cast mem. Up With People, 1990-91; phys. therapist Fairview Princeton (Minn.) Hosp., 1991-92, Ctrl. Minn. Group Health Plan, St. Cloud, 1992-94, Park Nicollet Med. Ctr., Minnetonka, Minn., 1994; teaching asst. coll. level Coll. of St. Catherine, Mpls., 1994; phys. therapist Brookings (S.D.) Ctr. for Phys. Therapy, 1995—; part-time tchr. phys. therapy assistance Lake Area Tech. Inst., 1995. Vol. work Up With People, 1990. Mem. Am. Phys. Therapy Assn. (temporomandibular joint study group 1994-95, clin. coord., guest lectr.). Baptist. Home: 1924 Orchard Dr Brookings SD 57006

STEINMAN, CHARLES HUNTER, electrical engineer; b. Pocahontas, Ark., May 18, 1958; s. Hunter Andrew and Serena Bea (Miller) S.; m. Jane Ellen Tabor, Sept. 15, 1984; children: Valerie Clason, Kenneth Clason, Christopher Steinman. Postgrad., North Ctrl. Tech. Coll., 1984, 1986—. Electronics salesman Servex Electronics, Mansfield, Ohio, 1977-83; instrumentation engr. City of Mansfield, 1984-85; with svc. dept., engr. Universal Enterprises, Mansfield, 1985-86, rsch. and devel. engr., 1986-87, mgr. electronic rsch. and devel., 1987-89, v.p. product devel., 1989—; cons. engr. Consumer Elec. Mfg., Ontario, Ohio, 1984-95; instr. North Ctrl. Tech. Coll., Mansfield, 1987-89; ptnr. Lex-Tronics, 1991—. Author (programs) Diskfile, Disksplit, Whodos, Turbo-Os; inventor 4/8 Point Temperature Monitor, Turbo-816 Adapter, Programmer's Pal, 1988. Mem. Nat. Arbor Day Found., 1987-89. Mem. Ctrl. Ohio 6502 Users Group (pres. 1984-85), Mid-Ohio Atari Users Gruop (pres. 1988—), Mid-Ohio Sysops Club. Home: 345 Westlawn Dr Mansfield OH 44906-2313 Office: Lex-Tronics 1780 W 4th St Mansfield OH 44906-1705

STEINMETZ, JON DAVID, mental health executive, psychologist; b. N.Y.C., June 4, 1940; s. Lewis I. and Rose (Josefsberg) S.; m. Jane Audrey Hilton, Dec. 24, 1964; children: Jonna Lynn, Jay Daniel. BA, NYU, 1962; MA, Bradley U., 1963. Lic. psychologist, Ill. Intern in psychology Galesburg (Ill.) State Rsch. Hosp., 1963-64; staff psychologist Manteno (Ill.) State Hosp., 1964-68, program dir., 1968-70, asst. dir., 1970-72; dep. dir. Manteno Mental Health Ctr., 1972-80, Tinley Park (Ill.) Mental Health Ctr., 1980-88; dir. Chgo. Read Mental Health Ctr., 1988-91; ret., 1991; clin. dir. Jane Addams Hull House Assn., 1992—. Trustee Village of Park Forest, Cook and Will Counties, Ill.; officer, bd. dirs. various civic orgns., Park Forest. Home: 200 Hickory St Park Forest IL 60466-1016

STEINMETZ, THOMAS SCOTT, electrical engineer; b. Cin., Nov. 26, 1965. BS, U. Cin., 1989. Registered engr.-in-tng., Ohio. Elec. engr. U.S. Turbine Corp., Mainville, Ohio, 1989-91; supr. elec. engring. Systecon Inc., West Chester, Ohio, 1991-96, Genesis Engring., Inc., Cin., 1996—. Vol. local ch. Mem. IEEE, ASHRAE. Republican. Home: 6334 Tara Brooke Ct Indian Spgs OH 45011-7156 Office: Genesis Engring Inc 6840 Ashfield Dr Cincinnati OH 45242

STEINMILLER, JOHN F., professional basketball team executive; b. Mt. Prospect, Ill.; m. Corinne Steinmiller; children: John Henry, Mary Kate. V.p. bus. ops. Milw. Bucks, 1977—. Bd. dirs. M.W. Athletes Against Childhood Cancer Fund, Milw. Big Bros.-Big Sisters, Metro Milw. YMCA; mem. Greater Milw. Com. Recipient Contardi Commitment award MACC Fund, 1991. Mem. Milw. Pen and Mike Club (pres.). Office: Milw Bucks 1001 N 4th St Milwaukee WI 53203-1314

STELLA, FRANK DANTE, food service and dining equipment executive; b. Jessup, Pa., Jan. 21, 1919; s. Facondino and Chiara (Pennoni) S.; m. Martha Theresa Yetzer (dec. Apr. 1994); children: Daniel (dec.), Mary Anne, William J., Philip J., Marsha, James C., Stephen P. Student, U. Detroit, 1937-41, Washington and Lee, 1944; D in Bus. and Industry (hon.), Gentium Pacem U., Rome, 1979; D in Sci. and Bus. Adminstn. (hon.), Cleary Coll., 1985. Pres., chmn., CEO F.D. Stella Products Co., Detroit, 1946—; founding ptnr. The Fairlane Club (sold to Club Corp. Am., 1979); chmn. bd., CEO Stella Internat., N.Y.C.; mem. Mich. Higher Edn. Facilities Commn., Area-Wide Water Quality Bd., Fed. Statis. Commn., White House Fellows Commn. and others; chmn. Detroit Income Tax Rev. Bd.; instr. orgn. and mgmt. sch. bus. U. Detroit; vice chmn., bd. dirs. Met. Realty Corp.; bd. dirs. Fed. Home Loan Bank Indpls., Computer Bus. Solutions Inc. Bd. dirs. March of Dimes Mich., 1976, mem. exec. com., 1984; corp. bd. dirs. Boys Club Met. Detroit., 1979; bd. dirs., exec. com. Orchestra Hall, 1974, vice chmn., 1979-82, chmn. 1982—; trustee U. Detroit, 1971-80, 82—, exec. com. 1971-77, chmn. devel. com. 1971-80, chmn. nominating com. 1971-78; chmn. Nat. Vol. Commn., Nat. Rep. Heritage Council, 1985—, chmn. 1991—; trustee Sacred Heart Rehab. Ctr., 1981—, St. Gabriel Media, Inc., 1980—; group chmn. food and drug div. United Found., 1978-79; mem. adv. bd. dirs. Bishop Borgess High Sch., 1984-88; bd. dirs. Ctr. for Ind. Living, Detroit Rehab. Inst., 1977-82, New Detroit Inc., Detroit Econ. Growth Corp., 1983, Detroit Econ. Growth Fund, 1983, Mich. Opera Exec. Com.; mem. St. John's Hosp. Guild, Friend of the Folger Libr., Washington, 1978-80; vice chmn. Detroit Symphony Orch. Hall Bd.; mem. divisional bd. trustees Mt. Carmel Mercy Hosp., 1979-90; founding chmn. 1979-82, mem. exec. com. 1979—; mem. exec. com. Nat. Rep. Com. 1985—; active Mich. Rep. Com.; apptd. Presdl. Commn. on Fed. Stats.; chmn. Nat. Vol. Svc. Comm.; presdl. commn. White House fellows; apptd. by Gov. Mich. Higher Edn. Facilities Commn.; mem. Area-wide Water Quality Bd., founding pres. Legatus Mich. chpt., internat. bd. dirs.; chmn. bd. Mercy Hosp. Detroit and Health Svcs., 1987-90; Nat. Italian Am. Found., Washington, 1992; former mem. Detroit Renaissance, Inc.; appointed by Gov. John Engler to chair Mich. Christopher Columbus Quincentenary Commn., 1991; appointed by President George Bushto Christopher Columbus Presdl. Quincentenaery Jubilee Commn., 1991; chmn. Nat. Rep. Heritage Groups Coun., 1991; bd. dirs. Oakland Children's Svcs., 1992, Metro Detroit Juvenile Diabetes, 1991, Complete Bus. Solutions, Inc., 1993; mem. bd. trustees Merrill Palmer Inst. Wayne State U., chmn. 1996. Recipient over 35 awards from local, nat. and internat. civic and profl. orgns. including Ellis Island medal of Honor, 1995. Mem. Alliance for Mich. (bd. dirs. 1984—), Detroit Ctrl. Bus. Dist. Assn., Nat. Comml. Refrigerator Sales Assn. (bd. dirs., pres. 1953-54, adv. bd. 1954—), Nat. Assn. Wholesaler-Distbrs. (del. 1982—), Wholesale Distbrs. Assn. (bd. dirs. 1973—, v.p. 1976, pres. 1977-79), Bus. Edn. Alliance (various offices), Mich. Restaurant Assn., Food Svc. Execs. Assn., Italian-Am. C. of C. Mich., Nat. Italian-Am. Found. (charter, bd. dirs., exec. com., pres. 1979—), Hispanos Organized to Promote Entrepreneurs (bd. dirs. 1976-81), Econ. Club Detroit (bd. dirs. 1982—), Air Force Assn. (charter), Am. Soc. Legion Merit, Greater Detroit C. of C. (chmn. 1980-81, bd. dirs.), Wayne County C.C. Found. (pres.), Young Pres.'s Orgn., Detroit Club, Detroit Athletic Club, Detroit Golf Club, The Fairlane Club, Capitol Hill Club, Skyline Club (Southfield). Home: 19180 Gainsborough Rd Detroit MI 48223-1344 Office: 7000 Fenkell St Detroit MI 48238-2052

STELMACK, GLORIA JOY, elementary education educator; b. Chgo., Oct. 1, 1933; d. Raymond Thomas and Bess (Henneberry) Ibison; m. Carl Francis McGarrity, Feb. 7, 1953; children: Maureen, Thomas, Stephen, John; m. Stephen Stanley Stelmack, Dec. 22, 1979. BA with honors, U. Ill., 1972; MA in Reading, Northeastern Ill. U., 1977. Cert. tchr., Ill. Tchr., reading specialist St. Pius Sch., Chgo., 1972-82, St. Jane de Chantal Sch., Chgo., 1982—; adv. com. St. Jane de Chantal Sch., Chgo., 1986—; v.p. Nat. Coun. of Tchrs. of English, Chgo., 1980-81. Nominated for Golden Apple award, 1990. Office: Saint Jane de Chantal Sch 5201 S Mcvicker Ave Chicago IL 60638-1424

STENBERG, DONALD B., state attorney general; b. David City, Nebr., Sept. 30, 1948; s. Eugene A. and Alice (Kasal) S.; m. Susan K. Hoegemeyer, June 9, 1971; children: Julie A., Donald B. Jr., Joseph L., Abby E. BA, U. Nebr., 1970; MBA, Harvard U., 1974, JD cum laude, 1974. Bar: Nebr. 1974, U.S. Dist. Ct. Nebr. 1974, U.S. Ct. Appeals (fed. cir.) 1984, U.S. Ct. Claims 1989, U.S. Ct. Appeals (8th cir.) 1989, U.S. Supreme Ct., 1991. Assoc. Barlow, Watson & Johnson, Lincoln, Nebr., 1974-75; ptnr. Stenberg and Stenberg, Lincoln, 1976-78; legal counsel Gov. of Nebr., Lincoln, 1979-82; sr. prin. Erickson & Sederstrom, Lincoln, 1983-85; pvt. practice law Lincoln, 1985-90; atty. gen. State of Nebr., Lincoln, 1991—. Mem. Phi Beta Kappa. Republican. Office: Office of Atty Gen 2115 State Capitol Lincoln NE 68509

STENDER, MARK V., electrical engineer; b. Toledo, Ohio, July 1, 1952. BSEE, U. Toledo, 1975. Design engr. Surface Combustion, Inc., Maumee, Ohio, 1976—. Deacon United Ch. of Christ, Sylvania, Ohio, 1990—. Mem. Instrument Soc. Am. Office: Surface Combustion Inc PO Box 428 Maumee OH 43537-0428

STENEHJEM, ALLAN, state legislator; m. Lisa; 1 child. Student, N.D. State U., N.D. State Coll. Sci. Mem. N.D. Ho. of Reps., 1989-90, 93—, past mem. human svc., vet. affairs coms.; vice chmn. govt., vet affairs coms., mem. judiciary com.; dir. student union N.D. State Coll. Sci.; mgr. retail bus. Mem. Elks, Toastmasters (pres.), Kiwanis, Wahpeton C. of C. (ambassador). *

STENEHJEM, BOB, state legislator; m. Kathy; 4 children. Degree, Bismarck State Coll. Mem. N.D. Senate, mem. human svc. com., chmn. transp. com. Mem. NRA, Elks, Ducks Unlimited, N.Am. Boone and Crockett Club. Home: 7475 41st St SE Bismarck ND 58504-3200*

STENEHJEM, WAYNE KEVIN, state senator, lawyer; b. Mohall, N.D., Feb. 5, 1953; s. Martin Edward and Marguerite Mae (McMaster) S.; m. Tama Lou Smith, June 16, 1978 (div. Apr. 1984); 1 child, Andrew; m. Beth D. Bakke, June 30, 1995. AA, Bismarck (N.D.) Jr. Coll., 1972; BA, U. N.D., 1974, JD, 1977. Bar: N.D. 1977. Ptnr. Kuchera & Stenehjem, Grand Forks, N.D., 1977—; spl. asst. atty. gen. State of N.D., 1983-87; mem. N.D. Ho. Reps., 1976-80, N.D. State Senate, 1980—; chmn. Senate Com. on Social Svcs., 1985-86, Senate Com. on Judiciary, Interim Legis. Judiciary Com., 1995—, Legis. Coun., 1995—; mem. Nat. Conf. Commrs. on Uniform State Laws, 1995—; mem. Gov.'s Com. on Juvenile Justice. Chmn. Dist. 42 Reps., Grand Forks, 1986-88; bd. dirs. N.D. Spl. Olympics, 1985-89, Christus Rex Luth. Ch., pres., 1985-86. Named Champion of People's Right to Know, Sigma Delta Chi, 1979, Outstanding Young Man of N.D., Grand Forks Jaycees, 1985, N.D. Friend of Psychology, N.D. Psychol. Assn., 1990; recipient Excellence in County Govt. award N.D. Assn. Counties, 1991, Legis. Svc. award State Bar Assn. N.D., 1995. Mem. N.D. State Bar Assn. (Legis. Svc. award), Grand Forks County Bar Assn., Mental Health Assn. (bd. dirs.). Home: 2204 12th Ave N Grand Forks ND 58203-2251 Office: Kuchera Stenehjem & Walberg PO Box 6352 212 S 4th St Grand Forks ND 58206-6352

STENGER, VERNON ARTHUR, analytical chemist, consultant; b. Mpls., June 11, 1908; s. Laurence Arthur and Effie Harriet (Dahlberg) S.; m. Ruth Luella Day, Aug. 2, 1933 (dec. Oct. 1994); children: Robert, Emilie, Alan, Gordon, David. BS, U. Denver, 1929, MS, 1930; PhD, U. Minn., 1933; DSc (hon.), U. Denver, 1971. Chemist Eastman Kodak Co., Rochester, N.Y., 1929-30, N.W. Rsch. Inst., U. Minn., Mpls., 1933-35; chemist Dow Chem. Co., Midland, Mich., 1935-40, tech. expert, 1940-53, asst. lab. dir., 1954-61, rsch. scientist, 1961-73, cons., 1973—; chmn. subcom. on magnesium alloy analysis ASTM, Phila., 1941-54. Author: (with I.M. Kolthoff) Volumetric Analysis, Vol. I, 1942, Vol. II, 1947, (with Kolthoff and R. Belcher) Volumetric Analysis, Vol. III, 1957; contbr. 10 encyclopedia articles, 6 chpts. to books and articles to profl. jours. Bd. mem. Midland (Mich.) Symphony Orch., hon. mem. 1990—. Recipient Anachem award Soc. Analytical Chemists, Detroit, 1970. Fellow Am. Inst. Chemists, N.Y. Acad. Sci.; mem. Am. Chem. Soc. (chmn. com. on analytical reagts. 1967-73, mem. adv. bd. Analytical Chemistry 1953-56, Midland sect. award 1979), Geochem. Soc., Sigma Xi. Baptist. Home: 1108 E Park Dr Midland MI 48640-4275

STENULSON, SONYA HELEN, advertising executive; b. Black River Falls, Wis.; d. Theodore Wilhelm and Amelia Gladys (Krametbauer) S.; m. William Edward Overmyer, July 16, 1981; stepchildren: Scott H., Susannah K. Student, U. Minn., 1959-62. Exec. asst. to pres. Knox Reeves Advt., Mpls., 1962-68; acct. executive Wheaties Sports Fed., Mpls., 1968-70; exec. dir. Concept Prodns., Mpls., 1970-80; pres. Chatham Corp., Mpls., 1980—; exec. dir., founding mem. Bob Richards Attainment Inst., Mpls., 1970-80; v.p. Bozell Jacobs Advt., Mpls., 1975-80; bus. agt. Olympic Champion Bob Richards, Mpls., 1970—. Co-chair Silver Medal Award Commn., Mpls., 1976. Mem. Rocky Mountain Ski Instrs. Assn., Cen. Ski Instrs. Assn., Jr. Ad Club (founding officer 1964-67), The Lotos Club of N.Y. Lutheran. Home: 1605 Yuma Ln N Plymouth MN 55447-2846

STENWICK, MICHAEL WILLIAM, internist, geriatric medicine consultant; b. Red Wing, Minn., Nov. 12, 1941; s. Vincent Ferdinand and Geraldine Frances (Veith) S.; m. Judith Ann Nelson, June 10, 1961; children: Scott Michael, Gregg William. BS cum laude, Hamline U., 1963; MD, U. Minn., 1969. Diplomate Am. Bd. Internal Medicine. Fellow dept. pharmacology U. Minn., Mpls., 1966-68; intern in internal medicine Northwestern Hosp., Mpls., 1969-70, resident in internal medicine, 1970-73; sr. internist internal medicine sect. Bloomington Lake Clinic, Mpls., 1973—; bd. dirs. Bloomington Lake Clinic, Mpls., pres. 1977, v.p. 1989—, fin. com., 1987—, chmn. properties, 1984—, chmn. trustees profit sharing; med. adviser Kimberly Quality Care, St. Paul, 1990-94; internal medicine cons. Fairview Multiple Sclerosis Ctr. and Rehab. Unit, Mpls., 1986—; informal adviser internal medicine sect. Minn. Relative Value Index, Mpls., 1971; mem. task force Riverside Med. Ctr., Mpls., 1988-91, chmn. critical care com., 1986-91, reviewer quality assurance subcom., 1989-90. Contbr. articles to profl. jours. Mem., co-organizer, 1st pres. Cyrus Barnum Soc., U. Minn. Med. Sch., Mpls.; bd. dirs. Signal Inn Beach and Racquetball Club, Sanibel Island, Fla., 1983-84, 89—, Signal Inn Condominium Assn., Sanibel Island, 1983-84, 89—; co-emcee Nursing Talent Show, Northwestern Hosp., Mpls., 1969; 1st med. dir. Beltrami Health Ctr., Mpls., 1970-72. Recipient scholarship Charles and Alora Allis Found., 1960-63, Walter Kenyon award, 1963, grant U. Minn., 1963. Fellow Am. Coll. Physicians; mem. AMA, Am. Soc. Internal Medicine, Minn. Med. Assn., Hennepin County Med. Assn., Mpls. Soc. Internal Medicine. Republican. Lutheran. Office: Bloomington Lake Clinic 3017 Bloomington Ave Minneapolis MN 55407-1715

STEP, EUGENE LEE, retired pharmaceutical company executive; b. Sioux City, Iowa, Feb. 19, 1929; s. Harry and Ann (Keiser) S.; m. Hannah Scheuermann, Dec. 27, 1953; children—Steven Harry, Michael David, Jonathan Allen. BA in Econs., U. Nebr., 1951; MS in Acctg. and Fin., U. Ill., 1952. With Eli Lilly Internat. Corp., London and Paris, 1964-69; dir. Elanco Internat. Eli Lilly Internat. Corp., Indpls., 1969-70, v.p. marketing, 1970-72, v.p. Europe, 1972; v.p. mktg. Eli Lilly and Co., Indpls., 1972-73, pres. pharm. div., 1973-86, exec. v.p., 1986—, also dir.; bd. dirs. Scios-Nova Cell-Genesys, Medco Rsch. Pathogenesis, Guidant Corp., GMIS Inc. 1st lt. U.S. Army, 1953-56. Mem. Pharm. Mfrs. Assn. (bd. dirs. 1980-92), Internat. Pharm. Mfrs. Assn. (pres. 1991-92). Home: 741 Round Hill Rd Indianapolis IN 46260-2917

STEPAN, FRANK QUINN, chemical company executive; b. Chgo., Oct. 24, 1937; s. Alfred Charles and Mary Louise (Quinn) S.; m. Jean Finn, Aug. 23, 1958; children: Jeanne, Frank Quinn, Todd, Jennifer, Lisa, Colleen, Alfred, Richard. A.B., U. Notre Dame, 1959; M.B.A., U. Chgo., 1963. Salesman Indsl. Chems. div. Stepan Chem. Co., Northfield, Ill., 1961-63, mgr. internat. dept., 1964-66, v.p. corporate planning, 1967-69, v.p., gen. mgr., 1970-73, pres., 1973-84; pres., chmn., chief exec. officer Stepan Co., Northfield, Ill., 1984—, also bd. dirs. Mem. liberal arts council Notre Dame U., South Bend, Ind., 1972—; bd. dirs. Big Shoulders, Chgo. Served to 1st lt. AUS, 1959-61. Mem. Chem. Mfrs. Assn. (bd. dirs.), Soap and Detergent Assn. (bd. dirs.), Ill. Bus. Roundtable, Econ. Club Chgo., Exmoor Country Club, Bob O'Link Golf Club, Everglades Club. Home: 200 Linden St Winnetka IL 60093-3862 Office: Stepan Co Edens & Winnetka Rds Northfield IL 60093

STEPANSKI, EDWARD JEROME, psychologist; b. Royal Oak, Mich., Aug. 3, 1957; s. Edward Jerome and Janice Sheila (Kline) S.; m. Nancy Wood, June 14, 1982; children: Christine, Kathryn. BA, U. Detroit, 1979; MA, Bowling Green State U., 1983, PhD, 1985. Lic. psychologist, Ill.; diplomate Am. Bd. Sleep Medicine. Dir. insomnia clinic Henry Ford Hosp., Detroit, 1985-93; clin. dir. Ctr. for Sleep and Ventilatory Disorders U. Ill. Hosp., Chgo., 1993—; assoc. prof. clin. psychology in medicine U. Ill. at Chgo. Coll. of Medicine, 1994—; Reviewer scientific articles for profl. jours.: Sleep, Chest, Human Psycho Pharmacology. Co-author: (book) A Step-By-Step Guide to SAS System for Univariate and Multivariate Statistics, 1994; contbr. articles to profl. jours. and book chpts. Recipient Trustee's Insignes scholarship U. Detroit, 1975-79. Fellow Am. Sleep Disorders Assn.; mem. Sleep Rsch. Soc., Am. Psychol. Assn., Mich. Sleep Disorders Assn. (sec./treas. 1990-93). Office: Univ Ill Hosp 1740 W Taylor (M/C 787) Chicago IL 60612

STEPHAN, DANIEL L., state legislator; b. Huntington, Ind., Nov. 26, 1947; s. Richard D. and Audrey (Neher) S.; m. Linda S. Gallaway, 1969; children: D.J., Stuart Kete. BS, Ball State U., 1969. Gen. mgr. Beaty Assocs., Inc., Syracuse, Ind., 1973-77; pres. D.L. Stephan & Assocs., 1977—; farmer; mem. from 50th dist. Ind. State Ho. of Reps., 1980—, mem. agr. and rural devel. com., pub. health com., mem. ins., corp. and small bus. com., pub. safety com.; bd. dirs. First Fed. Savs. Bank, Lime City Econ. Devel. Corp. Mem. Kosciusko County Reassessment Bd., 1976; bd. dirs. Otis R. Bowen Ctr. for Human Svc., 181-82, Ind. Rehab. Svc. Adv. Com., 1981-82. Recipient Leadership award Am. Security Coun. Home: 5573 W 700 N Huntington IN 46750-8822*

STEPHANI, NANCY JEAN, social worker, journalist; b. Garden City, Mich., Feb. 19, 1955; d. Ernest Helmut Schulz and Margaret Mary Fowler Thompson; m. Edward Jeffrey Stephani, Aug. 29, 1975; children: Edward J., Margaret J., James E. AA, Northwood Inst., Midland, Mich., 1975; student in theology, Boston Coll., 1991; BS summa cum laude, Lourdes Coll., Sylvania, Ohio, 1992; MSW, Ohio State U., 1995. Lic. social worker. Profl. facilitator Parents United, Findlay, Ohio, 1989-94; contbg. writer Cath. Chronicle, Toledo, 1988-95; mem. ministry formation faculty Cath. Diocese of Toledo, 1992-96, mem. accreditation com., ministry formation program, 1996-97; crisis intervention specialist John C. Hutson Ctr., 1994—; social work clinician Family Svc. Hancock County, Blanchard Valley Home Health Social Svc.; trustee, bd. dirs. Hope House for the Homeless, Findlay, 1990—, v.p. 1996-97; adult edn. coord. St. Michael Parish, Findlay, 1986-93, mem. strategic plan core com., 1989-91, v.p., pres. parish coun., 1985-89; program planning com. Family Life Conf., Cath. Diocese, 1994-95, mem. accreditation com. ministry formation dept.; profl. facilitator Hope Plus Program through Hancock County Common Pleas Ct., 1996—. Founder Food Coop., MPBA, Findlay, 1981; founding mem. Chopin Hall, Findlay, 1983; mem. Hancock County AIDS Task Force, 1994—; strategic planning com. mem., co-chair goal setting com. Findlay Pub. Schs., 1994. Nat. Inst. Food Svcs. grantee, 1974; Diocese of Toledo grantee, 1991; Ohio State U. Coll. Social Work grantee, 1994. Mem. NOW, NASW, Am. Assn. on Child Abuse, Transpsychol. Assn., Friends of Creation Spirituality, Cognitive/Behavioral Profl. Soc., Call to Action, Pax Christi. Home: 2615 Goldenrod Ln Findlay OH 45840-1025

STEPHEN, RICHARD JOSEPH, oral and maxillofacial surgeon; b. Joliet, Ill., Jan. 2, 1945; s. Joseph E. and Marcella M. (Pearson) S.; children: Anne, Susan, George. Student, Lewis U., Lockport, Ill., 1962-65; DDS, Loyola U., Chgo., 1969; Cert. in Oral and Maxillofacial Surgery, Loyola U., Maywood, Ill., 1972. Practice dentistry specializing in oral and maxillofacial surgery Mt. Vernon, Ill., 1972—; cons. Ill. Cancer Council, Chgo., 1979—; Centralia (Ill.) Correctional Facility, 1980—, Vandalia (Ill.) Correctional Facility, 1980—. Fellow Am. Coll. Stomatologic Surgeons, Am. Coll. Oral and Maxillofacial Surgeons, Am. Soc. Oral and Maxillofacial Surgeons, Am. Dental Soc. of Anesthesiology, Internat. Assn. Oral Surgery, Internat. Assn. Maxillofacial Surgery, Lions, Elks. Home: RR 5 Box 226 Mount Vernon IL 62864-9323 Office: 2413 Broadway St # 582 Mount Vernon IL 62864-2917

STEPHENS, GAY, public administrator; b. Aurora, Ill., Sept. 29, 1951; d. Benjamin Mark Jr. and Joyce Audrey (Sinclair) S. BA magna cum laude, George Williams Coll., 1973, MS summa cum laude, 1975. Clin. dir. Village of Downers Grove (Ill.) Dept. Health and Human Svcs., 1975-78; exec. dir. Villages of Bloomingdlae (Ill.) Police Program, 1978-81, Family Support Ctr., Aurora, 1981-83; devel. dir. Family Svc. & Mental Health Ctr. of Oak Park, Ill., 1983-88; mgmt. cons. United Way of Chgo., 1988-89; exec. Office of Inspector Gen. Ill. Dept. Mental Health and Devel. Disabilities, Chgo., 1989-96; exec. office inspector gen. Ill. Dept. Pub. Aid. Mem. Unitarian Ch. of Naperville, 1973—; vol. Girl Scouts U.S. of DuPage County, Naperville, 1973-77; bd. dirs. Horizons, 1991-92. Mem. Nat. Soc. Fundraising Execs., Women in Mgmt., Chgo. Area Runners Assn., Kappa Delta Phi. Democrat.

STEPHENS, JAMES LINTON, mechanical engineer; b. Stamford, Conn., Nov. 1, 1956; s. James Regis and Beatrice Helen (Johnson) S.; m. Laura Lynn Holmes, Sept. 6, 1980; children: Mark Linton, Jaimee Lee, Matthew James. BS in Mech. Engring., BS in Biomed. Engring., Northwestern U., 1980. Registered profl. engr., Wis. Mfg. engr. Parker Hannifin Corp., Des Plaines, Ill., 1980-81, St. Mary's, Ohio, 1981-84; mfg. engr. Ohmeda divsn. BOC Group, Madison, Wis., 1984-91, sr. mfg. engr. Ohmeda divsn., 1991-95; sr. engr. Case Corp., Racine, Wis., 1995—. Mem. steering com. for engring. profl. devel. program U. Wis., Madison, 1994. Ill. State scholar, 1975. Mem. Soc. Mfg. Engrs. (treas. Madison chpt. 1984-85, 2d vice chmn. 1985-86, 1st vice chmn. 1986-87, chmn. 1987-88, certification chmn. 1988—, fundraiser 1987—, seminar and workshop leader 1987—, Chmn. plaque 1988). Office: Case Corp 7000 Durand Ave Racine WI 53406

STEPHENS, PAUL ALFRED, dentist; b. Muskogee, Okla., Feb. 28, 1921; s. Lonny and Maudie Janie (Wynn) S.; m. Lola Helena Byrd, May 7, 1950; children: Marsha Stephens Wilson, Paul Alfred Jr., Derek M. BS cum laude, Howard U., 1942, DDS, 1945. Instr. dentistry Howard U., Washington, 1945-46; gen practice dentistry Gary, Ind., 1947—; chmn. bd. Assocs. Med. Ctr., Inc., Gary; Sec. Gary Ind. Sch. Bldg. Corp., 1967-85; pres. Bd. Health,

1973-81; Ind. State Bd. Dental Examiners, 1975-83. Mem. adv. bd. Ind. U.-Purdue U. Calumet Campus, 1973; bd. dirs. Urban League Northwest Ind.; pres. Gary Ednl. Devel. Found., 1990—. With AUS, 1942-44. Fellow Internat. Coll. Dentists, Acad. Dentistry Internat., Acad. Gen. Gen. Dentistry (pres. chpt. 1973, nat. chmn. dental care com. 1977, Midwestern v.p., nat. bd. dirs. 1984-89, v.p. 1990-91, pres. 1992-93), Am. Coll. Dentists; mem. ADA, Nat. Dental Assn., N.W. Ind. Dental Assn. (bd. dirs., pres. 1976-77, Disting. Svc. award 1993), Am. Soc. Anesthesia in Dentistry, Am. Acad. Radiology, Gary C. of C., Alpha Phi Alpha (pres. Gary Ednl. Found. 1988, pres. Gary Ednl. Devel. Found. 1990—), Acad. Gen. Dentistry (pres. 1992-93). Baptist. Home: 1901 Taft St Gary IN 46404-2759 Office: 2200 Grant St Gary IN 46404-3439

STEPHENS, RONALD EARL, state legislator; b. East St. Louis, Ill., Feb. 19, 1948; s. Earl Evered and Velma Juanita (Wills) S.; m. Karen Kay Angleton, 1975; children: Wendi, Chad, Kent, Tod, Molly. BS, St. Louis Coll. of Pharmacy. Pres., CEO Stephens Pharmacy, Inc., 1975, Freedom Pharmacy, Inc., 1982; pres. Caseyville Township Rep., Ill., 1980-82; trustee Caseyville Township Rep., 1981-82; Ill. state rep. Dist. 110, 1985-89, 93—. Rep. candidate Ill. House, 1982. Decorated Purple Heart, Bronze Star. Mem. Nat. Pharmacists Assn., Lions, Jaycees (state dir. 1982), Shriners, Kiwanis, Kappa Psi (Man of Yr. 1980). Office: 1004 S Lincoln Ste 10 O'Fallon IL 62269*

STEPHENS, SHERYL LYNNE, family practice physician; b. Huntington, W.Va., Dec. 11, 1949; d. William Clayton Stephens and Virginia Eleanor (Hatten) Stephens Terry; 1 child, William Earl Hicks III (dec.); m. Lannie Dale Rowe, Jan. 17, 1981; 1 child, Seton Christopher. BA, U. Ky., 1972; MA, Marshall U., 1982, MD, 1988. Tchr. Wayne County Bd. Edn., Ceredo, W.Va., 1973-83; real estate developer Huntington, 1981-88; resident in family practice Grant Med. Ctr., Columbus, Ohio, 1988-91; gen. practice physician Columbus (Ohio) Health Dept., 1991—; med. dir. Billie Brown Jones Family Health Ctr., 1992—; sch. physician Columbus Bd. Edn., 1994—; med. dir. St. Stephens Health Care Ctr., Columbus, 1995—; chairperson Coll. Health Dept. Com. on Pharmacy and Therapeutics, 1994—; rschr., 1976-81. Counselor, instr. Contact of Huntington, 1975-88; polit. activist pro choice movement and ratification of equal rights amemdment, 1976-81. Recipient Leadership award Marshall U., 1985. Mem. Am. Assn. Family Practitioners (pres. 1984-85, Leadership award 1985), Am. Med. Women's Assn. (sec. 1985-86), NOW (pres. 1976-78, 79-81, v.p. Huntington 1978-79, sec. 1981-82), Nat. Abortion Rights Action League. Democrat. Home: 9323 McCord Rd Orient OH 43146 Office: Columbus Health Dept 181 S Washington Ave Columbus OH 43215-5327 Office: St Stephens Health Care Ctr 1824 Cleveland Ave Columbus OH 43211

STEPHENS, STEVE ARNOLD, real estate broker; b. Irby, Cheshire, Eng., May 25, 1945; came to U.S., 1983; s. Harold Dennis George and Hilda Leonora (Howell) S.; m. Lynn Williams, Apr. 14, 1983. Student, Manchester U., Eng., 1967-69. Lic. pvt. detective, Ill. From cadet to detective Cheshire (Eng.) Police, 1961-69; acting detective sgt. Merseyside (Eng.) Police, 1969-75; acting sgt. Hampshire (Eng.) Police, 1975-77; retail store owner Horsham, West Sussex, Eng., 1977-79; pvt. detective Carratu Internat., London, 1979-83, D.A.C. Stephens, Aurora, Ill., 1983-86; broker Primus Coml., Oswego, Ill., 1986—. Bd. dirs. Aurora Crimestoppers, pres., 1995—. Recipient Republican Legion of Merit award. Mem. Nat. Assn. Realtors (CCIM), Comml. Investment Real Estate Inst. (cert., bd. dirs. Ill. CCIM chpt. 1992——, sec.-treas. 1994, v.p. 1995, pres. 1996), No. Ill. Comml. Assn. Realtors (dir. 1995—), Internat. Assn. Chiefs of Police, Ill. Assn. Realtors, Greater Aurora C. of C., Aurora Country Club. Home: 7 Saddlewood Ct Aurora IL 60506 Office: Primus Comml Real Estate 13 W Merchants Dr Oswego IL 60543-9456

STEPHENSON, DOROTHY MAXINE, volunteer; b. Hanna, Ind., July 16, 1925; d. William John and Inez Louisa (Werner) Hunsley; m. Orville Lee Stephenson, Mar. 10, 1945 (dec. Oct. 1985). Grad. high sch., Hanna. Postal clk. U.S. Post Office, Hanna, 1943-44; bookkeeper LaPorte Co Farm Bur. Coop Assn., Hanna, 1944-45; news correspondent Hanna, Ind., 1950—; organist Wanatah (Ind.) United Meth. Ch., 1959-60, Bethel Presbyn. Ch., Union Mills, Ind., 1960—. Compiler: Werner-Wentz Connections, 1982, Inez Scribblins/Dot's Jottings, 'N Nibblins, 1986, abstractions Hanna H.S. Alumni records, 1990, record books II, III and IV for Bethel Presbyn. Ch., 1992; compiler, pub. Poetry, Music of the Soul, 1995. Publicity person Am. Heart Assn. (Ind. affiliate), LaPorte, 1982-85, LaPorte County Geneal. Soc., 1984—. Recipient Golden Poet award World of Poetry, 1988, hon. mention, 1987-88, Editor's Choice award Nat. Libr. of Poetry, Best Poems of 90's and the 1990 Nat. Anthology award, Echoes of Yesterday, 1994; Voices of America by Sparrowgrass Poetry anthologies, 1989, 90, 91, 92, Amherst Soc. anthologies, 1990, 92, Iliad Press anthologies, 1992, 93, Quill Books, 1993, Outstanding Poets of Am. anthology, 1994, Distinguished Poets of America anthology, 1993. Mem. Merry Prairie (treas. 1964—), Order Ea. Star (worthy matron 1953, 85-90). Democrat. Presbyterian. Home and Office: 12805 S Hunsley Rd Hanna IN 46340-9736

STEPNITZ, SUSAN STEPHANIE, special education educator; b. Detroit, Mar. 1, 1948; d. N. Thomas and Dorothy (Richardson) Wagner; m. Kenneth H. Stepnitz Jr., July 25, 1970; children: Joshua, Zachary. BA in Polit. Sci., Olivet Coll., 1970; MA in Spl. Edn., Wayne State U., 1972. Tchr. Traverse Bay Area Intermed. Sch. Dist., Traverse City, Mich., 1973—; negotiator, ednl. profl. and support staff Traverse Bay Area Intermed. Sch. Dist., Travere City, Mich., 1982—; mem. spl. edn. adv. com. Mich. Bd. Edn., 1992—; mem. spl. delivery sys. edn. task force Mich. Dept. Edn., 1993-94, mem. spl. edn./gen. edn. com. Office of Spl. Edn. Dir. Handicapped Accessibility Awareness Special Kid's Day Nat. Cherry Festival, 1987—. Recipient Anne Sullivan award Mich. Edn. Assn., 1993, Friend of the Physically Impaired Assn. of Mich. award, 1994. Mem. AAUW (pres. Mich. chpt. 1987-89, Outstanding Person in Edn. award 1986, strategic planning com.), Mich. Edn. Assn. (spl. edn. tng. cadre 1990—). Home: 10729 Wood View Ter Traverse City MI 49686-9203

STERLING, DAVID A., environmental and occupational health science educator; b. Tuscaloosa, Ala., Jan. 12, 1955; s. Theodor D. and Nora M. S.; m. Linda S. Leason, Mar. 31, 1979; children: Callen S., Ryan A. BS in Biol. Scis., U. Oreg., 1978; MS in Environ. Health/Sci., U. Cin., 1982; PhD in Environ. Occupl. Health Sci., U. Tex. Sch. Pub. Health, Houston, 1986. Environ. and occupl. health/indsl. hygiene cons. TDS Ltd., Vancouver, B.C., Can., 1975-81; sr. rsch. asst., field studies dir. Tex. Indoor Air Quality U. Tex., Houston, 1982-83, grad. instr. Indsl. Hygiene Lab., 1981-84; rsch. chemist IIT Rsch. Inst., Chgo., 1984-87, coord. Chgo. divsn. environ. health and safety program, 1986-87; asst. prof., asst. dir. for programs Environ. Health Old Dominion U., Norfolk, Va., 1987-93; asst. prof. environ., occupl. health Saint Louis U., 1993—. Contbr. articles to profl. jours./publs. Grantee in field, including Old Dominion U. Rsch. Found., 1993-94. Mem. Am. Indsl. Hygiene Assn., Air and Waste Mgmt. Assn., Am. Occupl. Med. Assn., Am. Conf. Govtl. Indsl. Hygienists, ASTM, Am. Bd. Indsl. Hygienists, Am. Acad. Indsl. Hygiene, AAAS, Soc. Toxicology. Office: Saint Louis Univ Sch of Pub Health 3663 Lindell Blvd Saint Louis MO 63108

STERLING, DUANE RAY, university administrator; b. Tipton, Mo., Jan. 18, 1938; s. Raymond Alger and Opal Josephine (McBroom) S.; m. Patricia Jo Allison, Apr. 20, 1962; children: Allison Lee Sterling Ludlam, Shannon Kay, Tiffany Ann. Student, Ctrl. Coll., Fayette, Mo., 1955-56; BS in Edn., S.W. Mo. State U., Springfield, 1962; MS, La. State U., 1964, PhD, 1969. Tchr., coach Birch Tree (Mo.) High Sch., 1962, Appleton City (Mo.) High Sch., 1962-63; grad. asst. La. State U., Baton Rouge, 1963-64, rsch. asst., 1964-65; asst. prof. Ctrl. Mo. State U., Warrensburg, 1965-70, asst. v.p., 1970-72, asst. to pres., 1972-86, univ. dir., 1986—; mem. adv. com. Missourians for Higher Edn., 1990-96; mem. exec. com. Mo. Assn. for Affirmative Action, 1974-80. Campaign chmn. Johnson County United Way, Warrensburg, 1983, pres., 1984. With U.S. Army, 1957-60; exec. com. Mo. Boys State, 1972—; chmn. Warrensburg First Christian Ch., 1993. Mem. Soc. Coll. and Univ. Planning (program com. 1991-92), Warrensburg C. of C. (dir. 1979-81, 93-96), Rotary (dist. gov. 1987-88, pres. Show Me Planning Coun. 1992-93, Dist. Rotarian of Yr. 1985, regional rotary found. coord. 1995-97, group discussion leader 1995, 96), Phi Delta Kappa. Office: Ctrl Mo State U Administration 206 Warrensburg MO 64093

STERLING, HARRY JOSEPH, JR., environmental engineer; b. Ashland, Ky., May 15, 1950; s. Harry Joseph and Mary Catherine (Hulett) S.; m. Peggy Sue Cornette, June 20, 1981; children: Joseph Patrick Riley, Robert E. Riley, Lauren Ashley. BS in Civil Engring., U. Ky., 1972, MS in Civil Engring., 1974, PhD, 1976. Registered profl. engr. Environ. engr. GRW, Inc., Lexington, 1976-77; project mgr. Mason & Hanger-Silas Mason Co., Lexington, 1977-80; asst. prof. civil engring. U. Ky., Lexington, 1981-84; prin. environ. engr. Fluor Daniel, Greenville, S.C., 1985-88, mgr. environ. info. mgmt. group, 1988-92, sales mgr., 1987-90; sr. mgr. info. systems Fermco, Cin., 1992-95, sr. mgr. records, 1995—; researcher U. Ky., 1981-84. Author: MicroStation Database Book, 1992; contbr. articles to profl. jours. Cubmaster Boy Scouts Am., Lexington, 1982; com. mem. LaValle Sch., Fairfield, Ohio, 1992-95. Mem. Am. Soc. Civil Engrs., Nat. Soc. Profl. Engrs., Am. Records Mgmt. Assn., Nuclear Info. & Recrods Mgmt. Assn. Baptist. Home: 112 Pinnacle Peak Fairfield OH 45014 Office: Fermco PO Box 538704 Cincinnati OH 45253-8704

STERN, CARL WILLIAM, JR., management consultant; b. San Francisco, Mar. 31, 1946; s. Carl William and Marjorie Aline (Gunst) S.; m. Karen Jaffe, Sept. 7, 1966 (div. Mar. 1972); 1 child, David; m. Holly Drick Hayes, Mar. 21, 1985; 1 child, Matthew. BA, Harvard U., 1968; MBA, Stanford U., 1974. Cons. Boston Cons. Group, Inc., Menlo Park, Calif., 1974-77, mgr., 1977-78; mgr. Boston Cons. Group, Inc., London, 1978-80; v.p. Boston Cons. Group, Inc., Chgo., 1980-87, sr. v.p., 1987—. Lt. USNR, 1968-71. Office: Boston Consulting Group Inc 200 S Wacker Dr Chicago IL 60606-5802

STERN, DANIEL HENRY, ecologist; b. Richmond, Va., June 18, 1934; s. Henry Sycle and Adele (Lewit) S.; m. Michele Suchard, June 20, 1963 (div. 1982); 1 child, Alexander; m. Ann Binswanger, Aug. 2, 1983; children: Jeff, Brian, John Levinson. BS in Chemistry, U. Richmond (Va.), 1955, MS in Biology, 1959; PhD in Zoology, U. Ill., 1964. Asst. prof. Tenn. Tech. U., Cookeville, 1964-66, U. New Orleans, 1966-69; asst. prof. to prof. biology U. Mo., Kansas City, 1969-95, prof. emeritus, 1995—; co-dir. U. Mo.-Kansas City Asbestos Analysis Lab., 1982-92; cons. in field. Contbr. articles to profl. jours. Trustee Nature Conservancy, 1990—; mem. Kansas City Consensus, 1989—, Ct. Appointed Spl. Advocate, Jackson County, 1985—. Named Outstanding Tchr., Best of Kansas City, 1987, La. State U., New Orleans, 1968. Mem. Ecol. Soc. Am., N. Am. Benthological Soc., Am. Soc. Limnology and Oceanography. Office: Univ of Mo Divsn Molec Biology and Biochem Kansas City MO 64110-2499

STERN, EDWARD, performing company executive. Producing artistic dir. Cin. Playhouse in the Park. Office: Cincinnati Playhouse in the Park PO Box 6537 Cincinnati OH 45206-0537

STERN, GRACE MARY, former state legislator; b. Holyoke, Mass., July 10, 1925; d. Frank McLellan and Marguerite M. (Nason) Dain; m. Charles H. Suber, June 21, 1947 (div. 1959); children: Ann, Peter, Thomas, John; m. Herbert L. Stern, May 13, 1962; stepchildren: Gwen, Herbert III, Robert. Student, Wellesley Coll., 1942-45; LLD (hon.), Shimer Coll., 1984. Asst. supr. Deerfield Twp., Lake County, Ill., 1967-70; county clk. Lake County, Ill., 1970-82; mem. Ill. Ho. of Reps., Springfield, 1984-92, Ill. State Senate, 1993-95. Author: With a Stern Eye, 1967, Still Stern, 1969. Candidate lt. gov. State of Ill., 1982. Democrat. Presbyterian. Home: 291 Marshman Ave Highland Park IL 60035-4732 Office: 540 W Frontage Rd Ste 1000 Northfield IL 60093-1201

STERN, MICHAEL DAVID, dentist; b. Cleve., Feb. 26, 1946; s. Milton B. and Harriette (Hoffman) S.; m. Ellen Weiner, June 9, 1968; children: Gregory, Stephanie, Jeffrey. BS, Ohio State U., 1968, DDS, 1972; cert., L.I. U., N.Y.C., 1981. Cert. pain mgmt., Am. Acad. Pain Mgmt., instruction in temporomandibular joint disfunction syndrome, L.I. U. Staff dentist Office of Drs. Rhodes and Rinaldi, Cleve., 1972-73; assoc. dentist Office of William Rothkopf, DDS, Cleve., 1973-75; practice dentistry specializing in temporomandibular joint disorders Wickliffe, Ohio, 1975-93, Willoughby Hills, Ohio, 1993—; resident in cranio facial pain Coll. Dentistry U. Fla., Gainsville, 1989; media spokesperson Morning Exch., WEWS-TV, Cleve., 1981-85; cons. Richmond Hts. (Ohio) Hosp., 1983; adj. grad. lectr. Cleve. State U., 1983-84; preceptorship lectr. Case Western Res. U., Cleve., 1986-95; mem. staff Pain Ctr., Meridia South Pointe Hosp., 1991-96. Fellow Am. Endodontic Soc., Acad. Gen. Dentistry, Internat. Coll. Craniomandibular Orthopedics; mem. ADA, Ohio Dental Assn., N.E. Ohio Dental Soc. (pub. rels. chmn. 1979—). Jewish. Office: 34950 Chardon Rd Ste 209 Willoughby OH 44094-9162

STERN, ROY DALTON, manufacturing financial executive; b. Beulah, N.D., July 24, 1943; s. Earhart G. Stern and Eleanora (Trusskey) Moonen; m. Donna Lynne Blickenstaff, June 20, 1970; children: Heather Lynne, Courtney Mae. BSME, N.D. State U., Fargo, 1965; MSME, Colo. U., 1967; MBA, Ohio State U., Columbus, 1971. CPA, Ind.; cert. managerial acct., Ind.; lic. profl. engr, Ohio. Fin. mgr. Cummins Engine Co., Inc., Columbus, Ind., 1971-83; chief fin. officer Micro Sonics, Inc., Indpls., 1983-85; v.p. fin. & treas. Seradyn, Inc., Indpls., 1985-89; v.p. fin. Ind. RR Co., Indpls., 1989-90; trustee, employee 401K plan Indpls.; dir. fin. Cummins Mil. Systems Co., 1991-93; v.p. fin. and acctg. Reyco Industries, Springfield, Mo., 1994—; instr. Ind. U.-Purdue Extension, Columbus, 1975-80. Advisor Jr. Achievement, Columbus, 1981. Served to capt. USAF, 1967-71. Recipient Sylvia Farney award ASME, 1963, Marjorie Roy Rothermal award ASME, 1965. Mem. Ind. CPAs Soc., Fin. Exec. Inst., Inst. Mgmt. Accts. Republican. Presbyterian. Home: 4955 S Glenhave Ave Springfield MO 65804

STERN, STEPHEN LEWIS, psychiatry educator; b. N.Y.C., Apr. 13, 1946; s. William B. and Mary (Weinstein) S.; m. Marion B. Goertzel, Jan. 2, 1972; 1 child, David. BA cum laude, Columbia U., 1967; MD, NYU, 1971. Diplomate Am. Bd. Psychiatry and Neurology. Intern in medicine and psychiatry U. Pa. div. Phila. Gen. Hosp., 1971-72; resident in psychiatry Hosp. of U. Pa. and VA Med. Ctr., Phila., 1972-75; sr. resident for rsch. dept. psychiatry U. Pa., 1974-75, asst. prof., 1977-79, asst. prof. clin. psychiatry, 1979-80; assoc. prof. Ohio State U. Coll. Medicine, Columbus, 1980—; cons. physician Good Samaritan Hosp., Mt. Vernon, Ill., 1976-77; cons. psychiatrist Comprehensive Svcs., Inc., Mt. Vernon, 1976-77, Chester County Mental Health Svcs., West Chester, Pa., 1978; instr. clin. psychiatry Washington U. Sch. Medicine, St. Louis, 1976-77; dir. mood disorders clinic Ohio State U. Hosps., 1980—; staff psychiatrist lithium clinic VA Outpatient Clinic, Columbus, 1980—; presenter in field. Contbr. articles and astracts to med. jours. Mem. adv. bd. Mental Health Assn. Franklin County, 1990-93. Maj. M.C., USAF, 1975-77. N.Y. State Regents scholar, 1963-71; grantee NIMH, 1979, Bremer Found., 1980-81, Ohio Dept. Mental Health, 1982-85, Merrell Dow Pharms., 1982, Pfizer Pharms., 1985, 92—, McNeil Pharm., 1986-88. Fellow Am. Psychiat. Assn.; mem. Soc. Biol. Psychiatry, Ohio Psychiat. Assn. (mem. iiaison com. 1989-92), Neuropsychiat. Soc. Ctrl. Ohio (sec. 1982-84, pres. 1985-86), Am. Soc. Clin. Psychopharmacology, Am. Psychosomatic Soc., Phi Beta Kappa. Office: Univ Hosps Clinic 456 W 10th Ave # 2B Columbus OH 43210-1228

STERNBERG, DAVID EDWARD, psychiatrist; b. Norfolk, Va., Jan. 18, 1946; s. Theodore and Bella (Rosenblatt) S.; m. Frances Toby Glazer; children: Jonathan Theodore, Daniel Alexander. BA in Biopsychology, U. Chgo., 1967; MD, Tufts U., 1971. Fellow in psychiatry Yale U., New Haven, 1972-75; staff psychiatrist, dir. alcohol rehab. Nat. Naval Med. Ctr., Bethesda, Md., 1975-77; rsch. coord., staff psychiatrist Biol. Psychiatry br. NIMH, Bethesda, 1977-79; asst. prof., chief clin. rsch. unit Yale U., New Haven, 1979-83; med. dir. Falkirk Hosp., Central Valley, N.Y., 1983-88, Kansas Inst., Olathe, 1988-90; dir. Assocs. for Psychiatry and Psychotherapy, Overland Pk., Kans., 1990—; lectr. Karl. Menninger Sch. Psychiatry, Topeka, 1988-91, dept. psychiatry Yale U., New Haven, 1983-92; assoc. clin. prof., U. Kans., Kansas City, 1988—. Author: Evaluation and Treatment of Drug Abuse, 1990, (with others) Dual Diagnosis: Addiction and Psychiatric Disorders, 1988; contbr. 87 articles to profl. jours. Lt. comdr. USN, 1975-77, comdr. USPHS, 1977-79. Mem. Am. Psychiat. Assn., Soc. for Biol. Psychiatry, Soc. Neurosci., Acad. Clin. Psychiatrists, Am. Acad. Psychiatrist in Alcoholism and Addictions. Office: Assocs for Psychiatry 6900 College Blvd Ste 850 Shawnee Mission KS 66211-1536

STERNLIEB, LAWRENCE JAY, marketing professional; b. Akron, Ohio, Aug. 19, 1951; s. Max and Mollie (Atleson) S. BA in English, Kent State U., 1974, BA in Sociology, 1974, MA in Sociology, 1977. Lic. social worker, Ohio. Social program specialist State of Ohio, Cleve., 1976-79; sr. mktg. exec. Xerox Corp., Cleve., 1979-82; nat. acct. mgr. NCR Corp., Independence, Ohio, 1983-85; sr. acct. mgr. McDonnell Douglas Corp., Independence, Ohio, 1985-87; sr. mktg. rep. Prime Computer Inc., Independence, Ohio, 1987-90; acct. exec. GE Cons. Svcs., Independence, Ohio, 1990-94; sr. sales and mktg. exec. Decarlo, Paternite and Assoc., Independence, Ohio, 1994—; instr. Cuyahoga C.C., Cleve., 1980-81, 92. Author: Barry Storm, 1995. Mem. Cleve. Playhouse. Home: 8694 Broadview Apt 228H Broadview Heights OH 44147

STETTES, GREGORY G., mechanical engineer; b. St. Louis, Jan. 25, 1967. AA, East Ctrl. Coll., Union, Mo., 1987; BS in Mech. Engring., U. Mo., Rolla, 1989. Engr. McDonnell Douglas, St. Louis, 1990-93; sr. design engr. Crane Natl. Vendors, Bridgeton, Mo., 1993—. Lutheran. Office: Crane Nat Vendors 12955 Enterprise Way Bridgeton MO 63044-1206

STEVENS, C. GLENN, judge; b. Rockford, Ill., Oct. 29, 1941; s. Robert W. and Mary Louise (Shaughnessy) S.; m. Suzanne Ruth Corkery, July 4, 1967; children: Robert W., Angela M. BS, St. Louis U., 1964, JD, 1966. Bar: Ill. 1966, Mo. 1966, U.S. Dist. Ct. (so. dist.) Ill. 1966, U.S. Dist. Ct. (ea. dist.) Ill. 1968. Law clk. to judge U.S. Dist. Ct. (so. dist.) Ill., Springfield, Ill., 1966-67; instr. St. Louis U., 1967-68; assoc. Pope & Driemeyer, Belleville, Ill., 1967-74; ptnr. Pope & Driemeyer, Belleville, 1974-77; judge State of Ill., Belleville, 1977—. Bd. editors St. Louis U. Law Rev., 1965-66. Arbitrator Am. Arbitration Assn., St. Clair County, Ill, 1970-77. With U.S. Army, 1958-66. Mem. Mo. Bar Assn., Ill. Judges Assn., Am. Judges Assn., Ill. State Bar Assn., St. Clair County Bar Assn., East St. Louis Bar Assn., Phi Delta Phi (pres. Murphy Inn 1965-66). Democrat. Roman Catholic. Office: Saint Clair County Courthouse Public Sq Belleville IL 62220

STEVENS, CHESTER WAYNE, real estate executive; b. Milw., May 24, 1925; s. Daniel Augusta and Genevieve (Kingston) S.; m. Bernice Louise Limberg, Nov. 8, 1947; 1 child, Doreen Louise Scholtes. Student, Augustana Coll., 1944. Mgr. ops. Plankinton Bldg., Milw., 1962-72; v.p. 1st Wis. Devel. Corp., Milw., 1972-78; pres., chief exec. officer Stevens Carley Co., Milw., 1978-81, C.W. Stevens Co., Milw., 1981-85; v.p. Towne Realty Inc., Milw., 1985-91; cons. Milw. Redevel., 1981-82, Milw. Ins., 1983, Towne Realty Inc., 1991, 92. Pres. Milw. Westown Bd., 1990—. With USAAF, 1943-46. Mem. Bldg. Owners and Mgrs. Assn. (pres. 1972-73, dir. exec. com. 1976-82), Inst. Real Estate Mgmt. (pres. 1982, Mgr. of Yr. 1981). Democrat. Lutheran. Home: 4439 N Friedel Cambridge WI 53523

STEVENS, DAN, state legislator; b. Feb. 23, 1950; m. Barbara; four children. Student, U. Minn. Minn. State Sen. Dist. 17, 1993—; bus. mgr., farmer. *

STEVENS, DOUGLAS R., business owner; b. Gothenburg, Nebr., July 29, 1941. Mgr. Timpte Trailer Co., Denver, 1968-79; foreman Coloyo Coal Co., Craig, Colo., 1979-82; owner Etna Engine and Machine, Gothenburg, 1982—. Inventor automotive transmission part. With U.S. Army, 1969-73. Democrat. Baptist. Office: Etna Engine and Machine HC 79 Box 40 Gothenburg NE 69138-9103

STEVENS, JAMES HERVEY, JR., financial advisor; b. Balt., June 22, 1944; s. James H. and Hilda (Pearce) S.; m. Patricia Carol Donohue, Aug. 27, 1967 (div. Mar. 1983); children: James III, Carol; m. Lisa Gay Landrum, Apr. 29, 1984. BA, Duke U., 1966; MS in Fin. Scis., Am. Coll., Bryn Mawr, Pa., 1981. CLU; ChFC; CFP; registered health underwriter. Supr. New Eng. Life, Overland Park, Kans., 1969-75, agt., 1969—; v.p., treas. Creative Planning, Inc., Overland Park, 1980—; pres. Hokanson, Lehman & Stevens, Inc., Overland Park, 1982—, Wings Over Mid-Am., Inc., 1995—. Contbg. editor monthly tax topics Kansas City Bus. Jour.; contbr. articles to profl. jours. Bd. dirs. Mo. div. Am. Cancer Soc., Kans. and Mo., 1982-84, Apple Valley Homes Assn., Overland Park, 1990—, pres. 1992, Cen. United Meth. Ch., Kansas City, Mo., 1990-92., North Cross United Meth., 1991—. Recipient Outstanding Young Man award, 1977; named one of Top 200 Fin. Advisors, Money Mag., 1987, Boss of Yr., Kansas City LICOMA, 1983. Mem. Kansas City Life Underwriters (pres. 1980-82, Herbert A. Hedges award 1987), Kansas City CLU & ChFC Soc. (pres. 1981-83), Mo. Life Underwriters (pres. 1984-86), Am. Soc. CLU & ChFC (vice chmn., bd. dirs.). Republican. Home: 5200 W 98th Ter Shawnee Mission KS 66207-3221 Office: Creative Planning Inc 5340 College Blvd Shawnee Mission KS 66211-1621

STEVENS, JOAN D., design company executive; b. Chilton, Wis., Mar. 12, 1933. BA in Music Edn., Wis. State Coll., 1955. Owner, designer Options In Design, Milw., 1988—. Chmn. tree commn. City of Greenfield, Wis., 1992—; dir., founder City of Greenfield Beautification Org. Recipient Global Relief award Internat. Soc. Arborists, 1993, Lawrence Enerson award Nat. Arbor Found., 1995. Home and Office: Options In Design 4059 S 99th St Milwaukee WI 53228-2144

STEVENS, JOSEPH EDWARD, JR., federal judge; b. Kansas City, Mo., June 23, 1928; s. Joseph Edward and Mildred Christian (Smith) S.; m. Norma Jeanne Umlauf, Nov. 25, 1956; children: Jennifer Jeanne, Rebecca Jeanne. B.A., Yale U., 1949; J.D., U. Mich., 1952. Bar: Mo. 1952, U.S. Supreme Ct. 1973. Assoc. Lombardi, McLean, Slagle & Bernard, Kansas City, Mo., 1955-56; assoc. then ptnr. Lathrop, Koontz, Righter, Clagett & Norquist, Kansas City, Mo., 1956-81; judge U.S. Dist. Ct. (we. dist.) Mo., Kansas City, 1981—, chief judge, 1992-95; mem. adv. com. on Fed. Rules of Civil Procedure, Washington, 1987-92; bd. trustees Harry S. Truman Scholarship Found., 1995—. Bd. govs. Citizens Assn. Kansas City, 1959-70; bd. dirs., exec. com. Truman Med. Ctr., Kansas City; trustee Central United Methodist Ch., Kansas City, 1978—, Barstow Sch., Kansas City, 1978-87. Served with USNR, 1952-55. Recipient Lon O. Hocker Meml. Trial Lawyer award Mo. Bar Found., 1963, Spurgeon Smithson award, 1987, Charles E. Whittaker award Kansas City Lawyers Assn., 1996. Mem. ABA (ho. dels. 1982-88), Kansas City Met. Bar Assn., Lawyers Assn., Mo. Bar (pres. 1980-81, bd. govs. 1976-82, Pres.'s award 1995), Univ. Club, Carriage CLub, Vanguard Club, Mercury Club, Beta Theta Pi, Man-of-Month Fraternity. Office: US Dist Ct 811 Grand Blvd Ste 404 Kansas City MO 64106-1909

STEVENS, KATHLEEN M., nurse; b. Chgo.; m. Robert F. Stevens; children: Eric, Karl. AAS, Prairie State Coll., 1979. RN Ill. Staff nurse South Suburban Hosp., Olympia Fields Osteopathic Hosp.; emergency rm. nurse St. James Hosp.; staff nurse HPI, Pasadena, Calif.; supr. Intracorp, Lisle, Ill.; nurse specialist Ellis & Assocs., Chgo.; br. mgr., med. investigations Corvel Corp., Oak Brook, Ill.; Pres., CEO Shorman Stevens Assocs., Inc., Elk Grove, Ill. Mem. Internat. Assn. Quality Assurance, Midwest Assn. Billing Auditors (past pres.), Assn. Health Care Internal Auditings, Ill. C. of C. (workers' compensation taskforce), Ind. Workers' Compensation Inst., Ind. C. of Cl, Workers' Compensation Claims Assn., Nat. Assn. Blud Goose (mem. bd.).

STEVENS, LEOTA MAE, retired elementary education educator; b. Waverly, Kans., Mar. 27, 1921; d. Clinton Ralph and Velma Mae (Kukuk) Chapman; m. James Oliver Stevens, Nov. 7, 1944 (dec.); children: James Harold, Mary Ann Hooker Tibbit. BA, McPherson Coll., 1954; MS, Emporia U., 1964, postgrad., 1969-77; postgrad., Wichita U., 1977. Educator Pleasant Mound Sch., Waverly, 1940-41; prin. educator Halls Summit Sch., Waverly, 1941-42; educator Waverly Grade Sch., 1942-43, Ellinwood (Kans.) Jr. H.S., 1943-45, Hutchinson (Kans.) Grade Sch., 1945-48, Lincoln Sch., Darlow, Kans., 1948-49; educator prin. Mitchell-Yaggy Consol. Sch., Hutchinson, 1949-57; educator elem. Hutchinson Sch. Dist. 308, 1957-85, ret., 1985; v.p. Reno County Tchrs. Assn. Hutchinson, 1956-57, pres. Assn. Childhood Edn. Internat., 1978-79. Author of numerous poems; compiler The Alexander-Kukuk Descendants: 1754 to 1990. Mem. Worker ARC Blood Mobile, 1986—, Hutchinson Cmty. Concerts 1970—; ch. sch. tchr. Trinity United Meth. Ch., 1959-71. (attendance chair, 1994); historian Women's Civic Ctr., 1988-92, art com. chmn., 1992-96; den mother Cub Scouts, 1963-66, leader Girl Scouts Ellinwood, 1944-45. Mem. AAUW (news reporter 1984-87, legis. chmn. program com. 1991—, 2d v.p., 1994—),

Ret. Nation State and Local Edn. Assn., Reno County Tchrs. Assn. (v.p. 1956-57), Assn. Childhood Edn. Internat. (pres. 1978-79), Reno County Extension Homemaker Coun. (rep. 1987—), Rainbow Extension Club (pres. 1986-92), Hutchinson Area Ret. Tchrs. Assn. (historian 1996—), Am. Legion Aux., Friends of Preservation, Delta Kappa Gamma (sec., v.p. 1972-80, grant chmn. 1980-88, publicity com. 1990-93, legis. chmn. 1994—). Republican. Home: 805 W 23rd Ave Hutchinson KS 67502-3765

STEVENS, PAUL G., JR., brokerage house executive; b. 1944. With Saul Lerner Co., N.Y.C., 1968-71, Lombard Saint Inc., N.Y.C., 1971-72, Ragner Option Corp., N.Y.C., 1975-89; with Am. Stock Exch., N.Y.C., 1989—, pres., COO, treas. Office: Options Clearing Corp 440 S La Salle St Chicago IL 60605*

STEVENS, ROBERT EDWARD, engineering company executive; b. Kansas City, Mo., Oct. 30, 1957; s. Kenneth E. and Nina (France) S. BS in Chem. Engring., U. Mo.-Rolla, 1980, MS in Engring. Mgmt., 1985. Process design engr. The Pritchard Corp., Kansas City, Mo., 1981-83; process engr. Procter & Gamble, Cape Girardeau, Mo., 1986-87; tech. mgr. Procter & Gamble, 1987-90; project engring. mgr. Bechtel, 1990, mgr. engring., 1990-93, project mgr., 1993—. Contbr. to Physical Properties of Gases and Liquids, 1987. Chairperson bd. dirs. Wesley Found., St. Louis, 1993—; mem. corp. devel. coun. U. Mo.-Rolla, 1996—. Recipient Stan Adams Reliability award P & G Paper Div., 1990; Nat. Merit scholar, 1976. Mem. AIChE, Am. Soc. Engring. Mgmt., U. Mo. Rolla-Wesley Found. Alumni Assn. (pres. 1988—), Alpha Chi Sigma (Cert. Appreciation 1991). Methodist. Home: 2908 Wind Flower Dr Florissant MO 63031-1042 Office: Hwy 111 and Madison Wood River IL 62095

STEVENS, WILLIAM ALAN, computer consultant; b. Kew Gardens, N.Y., Feb. 2, 1946; s. Raloh Alfred and Mary Louise (McManamy) S.; m. Joyce Marie Pattison Stevens, Apr. 22, 1985 (div.); 1 child, Megan Marie Stevens; m. Sharon Rae Constable Stevens, Dec. 20, 1991. BS in Computer Tech., N.Y. Inst. Tech., 1969. Fin. analyst IBM Corp., Poukeepsie, N.Y., 1969-80; sys. analyst, 1980-83; sys. engr. Indpls., 1983-92; owner Stevens Consulting Svcs., Indpls., 1992—; mem., chmn. Facilities and Curriculum Com., Bus. Adv. Coun. Crossroads Rehab. Ctr., Indpls., 1990—. Author: Supporting and Troubleshooting OS/2, 1993, Inside OS/2 WARP, 1994. Mem. Broad Ripple Village Assn., Indpls., 1994—. Recipient Eagle Scout Boy Scouts Am., N.Y.C.,1960, Divsn. award Data Sys. Divsn. IBM, Poughkeepsie, N.Y., 1980. Mem. Indpls. OS/2 Users Group, Indpls. Computer Soc., U.S. Auto Club, Sports Car Club Am. Mem. LDS Ch.

STEVENSON, DAN CHARLES, state legislator; m. Dawn Stevenson. Student, Calumet Coll. Steelworker Inland Steel Co.; mem. Ind. State Ho. of Reps. Dist. 11, mem. labor and employment com., mem. local govt. and pub. safety com. Mem. Jaycees, Ind. Young Dems. (former pres.), Hessville Dem. Club.

STEVENSON, HAROLD WILLIAM, psychology educator; b. Dines, Wyo., Nov. 19, 1924; s. Merlin R. and Mildred M. (Stodick) S.; m. Nancy Guy, Aug. 23, 1950; children: Peggy, Janet, Andrew, Patricia. BA, U. Colo., 1947; MA, Stanford U., 1948, PhD, 1951; ScD (hon.), U. Minn., 1996. Asst. prof. psychology Pomona Coll., 1950-53; asst. to asso. prof. psychology U. Tex., Austin, 1953-59; prof. child devel. and psychology, dir. Inst. Child Devel., U. Minn., Mpls., 1959-71; prof. psychology, fellow Center for Human Growth and Devel., U. Mich., Ann Arbor, 1971—; dir. program in child devel. and social policy U. Mich., 1978-93; adj. prof. Tohoku Fukushi Coll., Japan, 1989—, Peking U., 1990—, Inst. Psychology Chinese Acad. Scis.; mem. tng. com. Nat. Inst. Child Health and Human Devel., 1964-67; mem. personality and cognition study sect. NIMH, 1975-79; chmn. adv. com. on child devel. Nat. Acad. Scis.-NRC, 1971-73; exec. com. div. behavioral scis. NRC, 1969-72; mem. del. early childhood People's Republic of China, 1973, mem. del. psychologists, 1980; mem. vis. com. Grad. Sch. Edn., Harvard U., 1979-86; fellow Center Advanced Studies in Behavioral Scis., 1967-68, 82-83, 89-90. Recipient J.M. Cattell Fellow award in applied psychology Am. Psychol. Soc., 1994, William James Fellow award, 1995, Quest award Am. Fedn. Tchrs., 1995. Fellow Am. Acad. Arts and Scis., Nat. Acad. Edn.; mem. APA (pres. divsn. devel. psychology 1964-65, G. Stanley Hall award 1988), Soc. Rsch. Child Devel. (mem. governing coun. 1961-67, pres. 1969-71, chmn. long-range planning com. 1971-74, mem. social policy com. 1977-85, mem. internat. affairs com. 1991-94, Disting. Rsch. award 1993), Internat. Soc. Study Behavioral Devel. (mem. exec. com. 1972-77, pres. 1987-91), Phi Beta Kappa, Sigma Xi. Home: 1030 Spruce Dr Ann Arbor MI 48104-2847

STEVENSON, JAMES LARAWAY, communications engineer, consulting; b. Detroit, Oct. 25, 1938; s. Joseph Morley and Kittie Harriet (Laraway) S.; m. Jeanie Lorraine Minkstein, Aug. 7, 1965; children: Amy Jean, Brian Morley. AAS, U.S. Armed Forces Inst., 1958; BSEE, MIT, 1960, MSEE, 1962. Cert. master radio and telecommunications engr. FCC. With USN Mercury Space Project, 1957-63; engr. Sta. WBCM-FM, Bay City, Mich., 1964-65; chief engr. Sta. WCRM, Clare, Mich., 1965-66, Sta. WSMA, Marine City, Mich., 1966; engr. Sta. WWJ-AM-FM-TV, Detroit, 1966-79; owner, mgr. Twin Oaks Comms. Engring. (name now Twin Oaks Comms. Engring. P.C.), North Branch, Mich., 1972—; charter pilot, flight & ground instr. G. B. DuPont Co., Almont Marlette Aviation Inc., 1977-82; cons. electronics engr. various cos., 1968—; expert legal witness, 1968—. Sr. div. judge Detroit Met. Sci. and Engring. Fair, 1975—; search & rescue pilot, mission comdr., capt. Mich. wing CAP, 1961-81; cubmaster Pack 457 Boy Scouts Am., North Branch, 1983-85. Recipient appreciation award CAP, 1980, North Branch Area Schs., 1985, Century award Boy Scouts Am., 1984. Mem. AIAA, IEEE (sr., chmn. N.E. Mich. sect. 1987-88, 95—, bd. dirs. 1984—), NSPE, Nat. Assn. Radio Telecomm. Engrs. (sr.), Mich. Soc. Profl. Engrs. (flint chpt.), Saginaw Valley Engring. Coun. (chmn. 1990-91, sec.-treas. 1992—), Engring. Soc. Detroit (profl.), Profl. Activities Coun. Engrs. (chmn. U.S. activities bd. 1985—), Nat. Pilots Assn. (sr. pilot citation, safe pilot award 1978), Aircraft Owners and Pilots Assn., North Branch C. of C. (charter), Am. Legion, Lions (pres. North Br. club 1990-91), Radio Club Am. Office: Twin Oaks Comms Engring PC 2465 Johnson Mill Rd PO Box 340 North Branch MI 48461-0340

STEVENSON, JOANNE S., older adults care provider, educator, researcher; b. Steubenville, Ohio, June 8, 1939; d. Joseph A. and Susan (Ploskunak) Sabol; m. Robert J. Stevenson, Aug. 6, 1966; children: James J., Michael J. BS, Ohio State U., 1963, MS, 1964, PhD, 1970. Prof., dir. Ctr. for Nursing Rsch. Coll. Nursing Ohio State U., Columbus, prof. dept. adult health and illness. Author books; editor Ann. Rev. of Nursing Rsch.; contbr. articles to profl. jours. Pres. bd. trustees Friendship Village Columbus. NIH predoctoral fellow; Fulbright scholar to Brazil; recipient Am. Jour. Nursing Book of Yr. award, 1977, 94, 95, 96, others. Fellow AAAS, Am. Acad. Nursing (chmn. knowledge devel. and utilization think tank); mem. AAUP, ANA (cabinet on rsch., coun. nurse researchers), Ohio Nurses Assn., Midwest Nursing Rsch. Soc. (pres. 1991-93), Am. Coll. Sports Medicine, Sigma Theta Tau (chmn. rsch. com.), Alpha Tau Delta, Phi Beta Delta. Home: 4954 Wintersong Ln Westerville OH 43081-4440

STEVENSON, ROBERT BENJAMIN, III, prosthodontist, writer; b. Topeka, Feb. 13, 1950; s. Robert Benjamin and Martha (McClelland) S.; m. Barbara Jean Sulick, June 6, 1975; children: Jody Ann, Robert Woodrow. BS, U. Miami, Coral Gables, Fla., 1972; DDS, Ohio State U., 1975, MS, MA, 1980, cert. in prosthodontics splty. tng., 1980. Practice dentistry specializing in prosthodontics Columbus, Ohio, 1981—; clin. asst. prof. Ohio State U., Columbus, 1981-87; chmn. oral cancer com. Columbus Dental Soc., 1981-85, Am. Cancer Soc., Columbus, 1985—; vol. dentist Provodencialis Ctr., Turks and Chicos Islands, Brit. West Indies, 1982-87. Editor: Columbus Dental Soc. Bull., 1981-87, 89-92; assoc. editor Ohio State U. Dental Alumni Quar., 1982—, Am. Med. Writer's Assn. Ohio Newsletter, 1983-86, Ohio State Journalism Alumni Assn. Newsletter, 1986-88; assoc. editor Jour. Prosthetic Dentistry, 1987-92; inventor intraoral measuring device. Vol. Am. Cancer Soc., Columbus, 1982—, Gahanna and Reynoldsburg, Ohio, 1983, 84; fundraiser Columbus council Boy Scouts of Am., 1984. Served to capt. USAF, 1975-78. Mem. ADA, Am. Coll. Prosthodontists, Ohio Dental Assn. (alt. del. 1982-89, del. 1990-92, new products editor newsletter 1988—), Carl Boucher Prosthodontic Conf. (editor 1987-92, sec. 1992-94, sec. 1994—), Proscrastinator's Club Am. Home: 1300 Southport Cir Columbus OH 43235-7642 Office: 3600 Olentangy River Rd Columbus OH 43214-3437

STEVENSON, THOMAS HERBERT, management consultant, writer; b. Covington, Ohio, Oct. 16, 1951; s. Robert louis and Dolly Eileen (Minnich) S. BA in Econs./Comm., Wright State U., 1977; cert. bank compliance officer, Bank Adminstrn. Inst., 1990. Cert. regulatory compliance mgr. Teaching asst., rsch. asst. Wright State U., Dayton, Ohio, 1975-77; teaching asst. Bowling Green (Ohio) State U., 1978; loan officer Western Ohio Nat. Bank & Trust Co., 1979-80, asst. v.p. adminstrs., 1981-82, v.p. mgmt. svcs. div., 1983-85; v.p., bank mgmt. cons. Young & Assocs., Inc., Kent, Ohio, 1985-86, exec. v.p., 1987—; legis. impact analyst Community Bankers Ohio, 1985—, Community Bankers Ga., 1988—; mem. exec. com. Owl Electronic Banking Network, 1981-85. Author: Compliance for Community Banks, 1987, Compliance Deskbook, 1988, Internal Audit for Community Banks, 1989, Truth in Lending for the Community Bank, 1989, Bank Protection for the Community Bank, 1989, Community Reinvestment Act for the Community Bank, 1989, Executive Management Guide to an Executive Board of Directors, 1990, The Board of Directors, 1990, The Home Mortgage Disclosure Guide, 1990, A Guide to Flood Insurance, 1990, Insider Lending, 1990, A Guide to the Equal Credit Opportunity Act, 1990, Investment Management, 1990, Contingency Planning, 1990, Insider Conduct, 1990, Currency Transaction Reporting Deskbook, 1990, Property Appraisal Deskbook, 1991, Bank Protection Deskbook, 1991, Regulatory Management Deskbook, 1991, Record Retention Deskbook, 1991, Environmental Deskbook for Financial Institutions, 1992, Deposit Compliance Deskbook, 1992, Fair Housing Deskbook, 1992, Insider Lending Deskbook, 1992, CRA Deskbook, 1992, Investment Mgmt. Deskbook, 1992, Internal Audi Deskbook, 1993; contbr. articles to profl. jours. Mem. adv. bd. Upper Valley Joint Vocat. Sch. for Fin. Instns., 1981-85. Cpl. USMC, 1972-73. Recipient George Washington medal of Honor Freedom's Found., 1974. Mem. Am. Inst. Banking (adv. bd. 1982-85), Community Bankers Assn. Ohio, Community Bankers Assn. Ga., Community Bankers Assn. Ill., Bank Adminstrn. Inst., Profl. Stds. Bd., Cert. Bank Compliance Officers, Eagles Club. Republican. Mem. Ch. of Brethren. Home: 3750 Chagrin River Rd Chagrin Falls OH 44022 Office: 121 E Main St Kent OH 44240-2524

STEVENSON, WARREN HOWARD, mechanical engineering educator; b. Rock Island, Ill., Nov. 18, 1938; s. Joseph Howard and Camilla Irene (Darnall) S.; m. Judith Ann Fleener, June 7, 1959; children: Kathleen, Kevin, Kent. BSME, Purdue U., 1960, MSME, 1963, PhD, 1965. Engr. Martin Co., Denver, 1960-61; rsch. asst., instr. Purdue U., West Lafayette, Ind., 1961-65, asst. prof., 1965-68, assoc. prof., 1968-74, prof., 1974—, asst. dean engring., 1992—; guest prof. U. Karlsruhe, Germany, 1973-74; vis. prof. Ibaraki U., Hitachi, Japan, 1993; mem. tech. conf. coms. various profl. groups. Editor: Laser Velocimetry and Particle Sizing, 1979; mem. editorial bd. Jour. Laser Applications, 1988—; contbr. articles to profl. jours.; patentee in field. U.S. sr. scientist Alexander von Humboldt Found., Fed. Republic Germany, 1973. Fellow Laser Inst. Am. (bd. dirs. 1984—, pres. 1989); mem. ASME, Optical Soc. Am. Office: Purdue U Sch Mech Engring Applied Optics Lab West Lafayette IN 47907

STEVIE, RICHARD GEORGE, economist; b. Covington, Ky., Sept. 15, 1951; s. Robert Joseph and Freda Rose (Luther) S.; m. Carol Ann Schwab, Aug. 10, 1973; children: Elizabeth, Laura. AB, Thomas More Coll., 1971; MA, U. Cin., 1973, PhD, 1977. Economist USEPA, Cin., 1976-78; economist Economic Rsch. div. N.C. Utility Commn., Raleigh, 1978-81, dir., 1981-82; economist Cin. Gas and Electric Co., 1982-84; lectr. Thomas More Coll., Crestview Hills, Ky., 1984-92, U. Cin., 1985—; sr. economist Cin. Gas and Electric Co., 1984-94; mgr. retail market analysis Cinergy Svcs. Corp., 1994-95; gen. mgr. retail mktg. Cinergy Svcs. Corp., Cin., 1995—. Mem. Hamilton County Census Areas Commn., Cin., 1985, Cin. Post Econs. Adv. Bd., 1987-88, Jr. Achievement Applied Econs., Cin., 1986-94; parish coun. mem. Our Lady Victory, Cin., 1988-91. Mem. Am. Econ. Assn., Internat. Assn. Energy Econs., ECAR Commn. on Load Forecasting (chmn. 1988-90), Nat. Assn. Bus. Econs., Ctr. for Electric Eud Use Data, Greater Cin. C. of C. (chmn. econ. adv. com. 1991—), Cin. Enquirer (bd. economists 1991—). Home: 5412 Casual Ct Cincinnati OH 45238-4229 Office: Cin Gas and Electric Co 139 E 4th St Cincinnati OH 45202-4003

STEWARD, JAMES BRIAN, lawyer, pharmacist; b. Cleve., Mar. 25, 1946; s. Louis Fred and Helen Elaine (Goodwin) S.; m. Betty Kay Krans, Dec. 14, 1968; children: Christina Lynn, Brian Michael. BS in Pharmacy, Ferris State Coll., 1969; JD, U. Mich., 1973. Bar: Mich. 1973, U.S. Dist. Ct. (we. dist.) Mich. 1979, U.S. Cir. Ct. (6th Cir.) 1980, U.S. Supreme Ct. 1986. Pharmacist Revco Pharmacies, Grand Rapids, Mich., 1969-70, Coll. Pharmacy, Ypsilanti, Mich., 1970-73; assoc. Bridges & Collins, Negaunee, Mich., 1973-80; ptnr. Steward, Peterson, Sheridan & Nancarrow, Ishpeming, Mich., 1980-94, Steward & Sheridan, Ishpeming, 1995—. Mem., chmn. Negaunee Commn. on Aging, 1974-86; mem., chmn., sec. Marquette County Commn. on Aging, 1976-82; trustee, v.p., pres. Negaunee Bd. Edn., 1984-88, 91-95; adv. bd. trustee Ishpeming Area Cmty. Fund, 1995—. Mem. Mich. Bar Assn., Marquette County Bar Assn. (sec.- treas., v.p., pres.), Am. Soc. for Pharmacy Law, Ishpeming Cross County Ski Club, Wawonowin Country Club, Phi Delta Chi, Rho Chi. Office: Steward & Sheridan 205 S Main St Ishpeming MI 49849-2018

STEWART, ALBERT ELISHA, safety engineer, industrial hygienist; b. Urbana, Mo., Dec. 20, 1927; s. Albert E. and Maurine (Lighter) S.; m. Elizabeth O. Tice, May 31, 1958 (div.); children: Sheryl E., Mical A. BA, U. Kans., 1949; MS, U. Mo., 1958, MBA, 1970; PhD, Western States U., 1984. Registered profl. engr., Calif., cert. safety engr., cert. indsl. hygienist. Sales engr. Kaiser Aluminum and Chem. Co., Toledo, 1949-56; tchr. Kansas City (Mo.) Pub. Schs., 1959-65; indsl. hygienist Bendix Corp., Kansas City, 1960-65; safety adminstr. Gulf R&D, Merriam, Kans., 1968-71; sr. indsl. hygienist USDOL-OSHA, Kansas City, 1971-77; pres. Stewart Indsl. Hygiene, Kansas City, 1977—; adj. prof. Cen. Mo. State U. Mem. Boy Scouts Am. With U.S. Army, 1950-53. Mem. Am. Indsl. Hygiene Assn., Am. Chem. Soc., Am. Acad. Indsl. Hygiene, Am. Soc. Safety Engrs., Am. Welding Soc., Nat. Mgmt. Assn., Nat. Sci. Tchrs. Assn., Adminstrv. Govt. Soc., Am. Legion Post 596, DAV, ARC, Alpha Chi Sigma. Episcopalian. Office: 8029 Brooklyn Ave Kansas City MO 64132-3516

STEWART, BARBARA ELLEN, media specialist; b. Wilmington, Del., Oct. 20, 1939; d. William Thompson Stewart and Barbara Frances (Kelsey) Madison. BA, Alma (Mich.) Coll., 1962; MLS, Cen. Mich. U., 1980. cert. sec. tchg., Mich. English tchr. Owosso (Mich.) Pub. Schs., 1962-80, media specialist, 1981—. Mem. Am. Business Women's Assn. (at-large, head scholarship com. 1975, 79, v.p. 1978).

STEWART, BARBARA LYNNE, geriatrics nursing educator; b. Youngstown, Ohio, May 10, 1953; d. Carl Arvid and Margaret (Ashton) Swanson; m. James G. Stewart, Mar. 17, 1973; children: Trevor J., Troy C. AAS, Youngstown State U., 1973, BS, 1982. Cert. gerontol. nurse, ANCC. Asst. dist. office supr. divsn. quality assurance Bureau of Healthcare Stds. and Quality; supr., dir. nursing svcs. Peaceful Acres Nursing Home, North Lima, Ohio; nurse repondent Health Sci. Ctr. U. Colo., Denver; charge nurse Westwood Rehab. Med. Ctr., Inc., Boardman, Ohio, Park Vista Health Care Ctr., Youngstown, Ohio; dir. nursing Rolling Acres Care Ctr., North Lima, Ohio; primary instr. Alliance (Ohio) Tng. Ctr., Inc.; asst. dist. office supr. divsn. of quality assurance Bureau Healthcare Stds. and Quality, Akron, Ohio. Former instr. CPR, ARC. Mem. Tri County Dir. Nurses Assn., Nat. Gerontol. Nursing Assn. (nomination com.), Youngstown State U. Alumni Assn.

STEWART, BERNARD FRANCIS, lawyer; b. Janesville, Wis., May 16, 1928; s. John Malcolm and Florence Claire (Ford) S.; m. Ruth Inga Kjornes, Aug. 19, 1950; children: Tamara Anne, Deborah Marie, Charles Arthur, Suzanne Elizabeth. BS, U. Wis., 1951, JD, 1954. Pvt. practice law Chgo., 1954-82; v.p., sec., gen. counsel ITT Auto., Inc., Auburn Hills, Mich., 1983-91; exec. v.p., sec., gen. counsel Exide Corp., Troy, Mich., 1992—. Contbr. articles to profl. jours. With USNC, 1946-48. Republican. Roman Catholic. Home: 500 Overbrook Rd Bloomfield Hills MI 48302-2142 Office: Exide Corp 1400 N Woodward Ave Bloomfield Hills MI 48304-2854

STEWART, BRUCE EDMUND, SR., retired mechanical designer, writer; b. Mpls., Nov. 9, 1930; s. Milford James and Ivah Delano (Gallant) S.; m. Mary Incornata Christofore Stewart, May 25, 1957; children: Bruce Edmund Stewart Jr., Robert Daniel Stewart. AA, U. Minn., Mpls., 1950. Mem. engring. dept. St. Paul Divsn. Whirlpool Corp., St. Paul, 1959-85; contractor Possis Tech. Svcs., Mpls., 1986-87; contract designer St. Croix Personnel, Inc., St. Paul, 1987-88; designer Distinction in Design, Mpls., 1988, St. Paul, 1988-91, Distinction in Design, Mpls., 1991; engr. Possis Tech. Svcs., Mpls., 1991, Source Tech., Mpls., 1992. Patentee in field. Sgt. Army Security Agy., 1950-53. Mem. Moose Lodge #963, Inventor's Network, Night Scribes. Home: 771 Belland Ave Saint Paul MN 55127

STEWART, DAVID DICKSON, psychologist; b. Sharon, Pa., Aug. 19, 1949; s. Thomas Dickson and Mary Ella (Rodecker) S.; m. Jodi Anne Martin, Dec. 13, 1970. BA, Mich. State U., 1971; MS, George Williams Coll., Downers Grove, Ill., 1974; PhD, U.S. Internat. U., San Diego, 1981. Lic. psychologist, Minn. Family therapist, team leader Youth in Crisis, Berwyn, Ill., 1974-75, counseling coordinator, 1975-77; program coordinator Harmonium, Inc., Poway, Calif., 1979-80; psychology intern Hennepin County Med. Ctr., Mpls., 1980-81; staff psychologist Dakota Mental Health Ctr., South St. Paul, Minn., 1981-86, dir. psychol. services, 1986, clin. dir., 1987-92; clin. dir. Linden Ctr. Psychol. Health, Eagan, Minn., 1992—. Mem. Am. Psychol. Assn., Minn. Psychol. Assn. Democrat. Office: Linden Ctr Psychological Health 3459 Washington Dr Saint Paul MN 55122-1347

STEWART, DAVID MACK, childbirth educator, seismologist, author; b. St. Louis, Sept. 20, 1937; s. Harold Mack and Lora Mae (Coil) S.; m. Lee Frances Pomeroy, Sept. 1, 1962; chidlren: Jonathan, LoraLee, Keith, Benjamin, Anthony. BS, U. Mo., Rolla, 1965, MS, 1969, PhD, 1971. Cert. childbirth educator, Mo. Asst. prof. U. N.C., Chapel Hi'l, 1971-78; exec. dir. Internat. Assn. Parents and Profls. for Safe Alternatives in Childbirth, Marble Hill, Mo., 1978-88; dir. Ctr. Earthquake Studies, 1989-91; assoc. prof. Southeast Mo. State U., 1988-93. Author: Five Standards for Safe Childbearing, Damages and Losses from Future New Madrid Earthquakes, 1991, 5th edit., 1996, The Earthquake That Never Went Away, 1993, 2d edit., 1996, The Earthquake America Forgot, 1995, Teh New Madrid Fault Finders Guide, 1995; author (booklets) God's Existance: Can Science Prove It?, Fathering and a Career: Keeping a Health Balance, Earthquake Guide for Home and Office; co-author: The Childbirth Activists handbook, Salfe Alternatives in Childbirth, 1976 (Book of Yr. award Am. Jour. Nursing), 21st Century Obstetrics Now!, 1977, Compulsory Hospitalization or Freedom?, 1979 (Book of Yr. award Am. Jour. Nursing); contbr. over 200 articles, pamphlets and booklets. Former local pastor United Meth. Ch., Scott City, Mo. Mem. Optimists (v.p. Marble Hill 1981-89). Republican. Home: Rt 1 Box 646 Marble Hill MO 63764

STEWART, FRANKLIN DAVID, social worker; b. Covington, Ky., May 23, 1945; s. Kaiser and Ethel (Ford) S. BA, St. Martin's Coll., Milw., 1982; Cert., U. Ill., Chgo., 1983, U. Chgo., 1993. Exec. dir., founder Social Svcs. and Cmty. Devel., Joliet, Ill., 1979-90; social worker Salvation Army, Joliet, 1991, Hamilton Behavior Health Care Ltd., Chgo., 1994—; dir., founder Work Release Cons., Chgo., 1993-95. Mem. Sch. Bd., Joliet, 1980—; vice chmn. Operation P.U.S.H., Joliet, 1980—; bd. dirs. Nat. P.U.S.H., Chgo., 1980—; mem. Nat. Black Elected Ofcls., 1980—. Mem. NAACP, Elks (chaplain 1989-90), Masons (32 degree, chaplain 1981-89), Shriners (sec. 1989-90). Baptist. Home: 622 Norton Joliet IL 60432

STEWART, JEFFREY K., quality improvement manager; b. Parsons, Kans., Mar. 1, 1958; s. Wilson K. and Betty J. (Robinson) S.; m. Cherryll E. Doughty, Sept. 5, 1992; children: Kesha, Brandon, Jason, Chaynler. BBA in Fin. and Econs., Wichita State U., 1988; MS of Bus. Mgmt., Friends U., Wichita, Kans., 1993; cert., George Washington U. Boeing cert. instr. continuous quality improvement. Bookeeper 1st Nat. Bank, Parsons, Kans., 1976-77; br. mgr. Univ. Bank, Wichita, 1978-79, Cen. Bank & Trust, Wichita, 1979-80; control mgr. Bank IV, Wichita, 1980-81; cost analyst Boeing Co., Wichita, 1981—, proposal adminstr., sr. cost analyst, quality improvement adminstr., quality improvement mgr.; developer, facilitator workshop between Kans. univs./colls. and Boeing Engring., 1994; cons. Kans. Dept. Social and Rehab. Svcs., Wichita area office, 1994; bus. advisor Jr. Achievement of Wichita Inc., 1992, 93, 94; cons./facilitator Unified Sch. Dist. 259, Wichita, 1993, Unified Sch. Dist. 358, Oxford, Kans., 1990; panelist ASTD, Oklahoma City, 1992. Mem. adv. coun., cons./facilitator Child Care Assn.-Head Start; bd. trustees, chmn. men's mentor program Tabernacle Bapt. Ch. Mem. Wichita Alumni chpt. Kappa Alpha Psi. Republican. Office: Diversified Assocs PO Box 20821 Wichita KS 67205

STEWART, PAUL ARTHUR, pharmaceutical company executive; b. Greensburg, Ind., Sept. 28, 1955; s. John Arthur and Alberta Jeannette (Densford) S.; m. Susan Rhodes, Dec. 20, 1975; children: John Rhodes, Daniel Robbins; BS, Purdue U., 1976; MBA, Harvard Bus. Sch., 1987. Grad. asst. Purdue U., West Lafayette, Ind, 1977; asst. treas. Stewart Seeds, Inc., Greensburg, Ind., 1977-82, sec., treas., 1982-84; cons. The Boston Cons. Group, Inc., Chgo., 1986; founder, owner PASCO Group, mgmt. and computer cons., aircraft leasing, 1979-87; mgr. bus. planning-agrichems. Eli Lilly & Co., Indpls., 1987-88, dist. sales mgr. agrichems., 1989-90, tech. acquisition mgr. med. devices and diagnostics divsn., 1990-92; dir. mktg. info. and bus. devel. IVAC Corp. subs. Eli Lilly & Co., 1992-94, advisor corp., fin. and investment banking, 1994-96, mgr. global bus. devel. (animal health), 1996—. Mem. Greensburg-Decatur County Bd. of Airport Commrs., 1980-85, pres., 1980, 81, 83; mem. Decatur County Data Processing Bd., 1982-85; deacon 2nd Presbyn. Ch. of Indpls., 1991-92, elder, 1996—. Mem. Alpha Gamma Rho. Republican. Presbyterian. Office: Eli Lilly & Co Lilly Corp Ctr Indianapolis IN 46285

STEWART, ROBERT ALVIN, auditor; b. Gainesville, Fla., Aug. 19, 1963; s. John Harris and Elizabeth Ann (Staudt) S. Grad., high sch., 1981. Floor staff Plitt Theatres, Inc., Ocala, Fla., 1979-81, asst. theatre mgr., 1982-83; theatre mgr. Plitt Theatres, Inc., Hollywood, Fla., Atlanta, 1983-87; dist. supr. Cineplex Odeon Corp., Dallas and Washington, 1987-90; theatre auditor Cineplex Odeon Corp., Chgo., 1990-95, sr. ops. auditor, 1995—.

STIBBE, AUSTIN JULE, accountant; b. St. Paul, Mar. 29, 1930; s. Austin Julius and Agnes Dorothea (Delaney) S.; m. Mary Elizabeth King, May 29, 1952; children: Anne Marie, Craig Jule, David King, Karen Lee. BBA in Acctg., U. Minn., 1952. CPA, Minn., Wis. Tax acct. Ernst & Ernst, Mpls., 1955-60; corp. tax mgr. EcoLab, Inc., St. Paul, 1960-65; audit mgr. Coopers & Lybrand, Mpls., 1965-74; v.p. Wilkerson, Guthmann & Johnson, Ltd., St. Paul, 1974-93, of counsel, 1993—. Exec. officer Twin Cities Squadron, U.S. Naval Sea Cadet Corps, Mpls., 1974-80; bd. dirs., treas., mem. Twin Cities coun. Navy League, 1970—, pres., 1979-81, treas., 1975-79, 81-91; mem. adv. coun. to dept. acctg. U. Minn., Mpls., 1983-86; bd. dirs., chmn. audit com. St. Paul Area Coun. Chs., 1985-87; mem. adv. bd. Headwaters Soc., 1987-88; mem. fin. reporting com. United Way St. Paul Area, 1981-93, mem. audit com., 1991-93. Lt. USN, 1952-55. Mem. Minn. Soc. CPAs (life), Belle Taine Lake Assn. (dir. 1995—), Hubbard County COLA Print Com. Presbyterian. Office: PO Box 41 Nevis MN 56467-0041

STIEFF, JOHN JOSEPH, legislative attorney, educator; b. Indpls., Feb. 28, 1952; s. James Frederick and Mary Therese (Bisch) S.; m. Dusty Lee-Ann Warner, Apr. 21, 1989. BA with Distinction, Ind. U., 1973, JD, 1977. Bar: Ind. 1977. Sr. atty. Office of Bill Drafting & Rsch., Legislative Svcs. Agy., Indpls., 1977-86; dep. dir. and asst. revisor of statutes Office of Code Revision, Legislative Svcs. Agy., Indpls., 1986-92, dir. and revisor of statutes, 1992—; adj. prof. law Ind. Univ., Bloomington, 1985-86; instr. continuing legal edn. Ind. Gen. Assembly, Indpls., 1987-91; faculty mem. Nat. Conf. State Legislatures, Denver, Colo.; assoc commr. Nat. Conf. Commrs. on Uniform State Laws, Chgo., 1993—. Editor in chief: (books) The Acts of Indiana, 1986—, The Indiana Code, 1993—; ast. editor, The Indiana Code, 1986-92. Poetry instr. Gage Inst. for Gifted Children, Indpls., 1982-86. Named Hoosier Scholar, Indiana Commn. for Higher Edn., 1970-73. Mem. Writer's Ctr. of Indpls. (founding mem.), Ind. U. Varsity Club. Home: 7707 Windy Hill Way Indianapolis IN 46239 Office: Legislative Svcs Agy Office Code Revision 302 State House Indianapolis IN 46204

STIFTER, GERARD EDWARD, accountant; b. Hutchinson, Minn., Oct. 14, 1941; s. Eugene John and Angela Christina (Fasching) S.; m. Rosemary

Ann Bispring, Aug. 19, 1961; children: John, Michael, Thomas, Barbara, Eugene. BS, St. Cloud (Minn.) State U., 1976. CPA, Minn. Staff auditor Anderson & Sieberlich, St. Paul, 1976-79, audit mgr., 1979-80; audit mgr. McGladrey & Puller n, St. Paul, 1980-84, ptnr., 1984—; trustee mentor Am. Hosp. Assn., Chgo.; trustee edn. com. mem. Minn. Hosp. Assn., Mpls.; bd. chair St. Mary's Residence, Winstead, Minn. Author: Audits of Health Care Providers, 1991; (material for tng. seminar) Government Auditing for In-Charges, 1992; co-author: (tech. booklet) An Executive Summary of Financial Accounting Standards 116 and 117, 1994. Bd. mem. St. Mary's Hosp. & Home, Winsted, 1978-85, bd. chair, 1985-90; bd. trustee Health Ctrl. Inst., Mpls., 1980-81, HealthCtrl., Inc., Mpls., 1985. Mem. AICPA, Govt. Fin. Officers Assn. (spl. com., reviewer 1989-95), Healthcare Fin. Mgmt. Assn. (chpt. bd. 1996), Minn. Soc. CPAs. Republican. Roman Catholic. Home: 362 S Shore Dr Winstead MN 55395 Office: McGladrey & Pullen LLP 800 Marquette Ave Ste 1300 Minneapolis MN 55402

STILES, DONALD ALAN, insurance company executive; b. Waukegan, Ill., June 19, 1951; s. James Fuller and Helen Alma (Ferry) S.; m. Leslie Ann Herzog, June 24, 1978; children: Peter Alan, Thomas Joseph. BA, Carleton Coll., 1973; MBA, U. Minn., 1979. With Nat. Theatre Co., N.Y.C., 1973-74; corp. acct. Ministers Life Ins. Co., Mpls., 1974-81; sr. tax cons. Touche Ross & Co., Mpls., 1981-83; mgr. tax planning Northwestern Nat. Life Ins. Co., Mpls., 1983-86, dir. tax svcs., 1986-87; asst. v.p. corp. tax svcs. ReliaStar Fin. Corp., Mpls., 1987—. Bd. dirs. Minn. Opera, 1989-92. Mem. Tax Execs. Inst. (bd. dirs. Minn. chpt. 1987-92, 94-96, sec. 1988-89, v.p. 1989-91, pres. 1991-92, internat. bd. dirs. 1994-96), Minn. Acctg. Aid Soc. (bd. dirs. 1987—, pres. 1989-90), Minn. Taxpayers Assn. (bd. dirs. 1993—). Office: ReliaStar Fin Corp 20 Washington Ave S Minneapolis MN 55401-1908

STILL, CHRISTOPHER GENE, industrial designer; b. Independence, Mo., Oct. 18, 1968. BS in Indsl. Tech. and Mgmt., N.W. Mo. State U., 1991. Product designer Heatron, Leavenworth, Kans., 1992—. Mem. Phi Sigma Kappa (alumni v.p. 1992—). Republican. Roman Catholic. Office: Heatron 3000 Wilson PO Box 45 Leavenworth KS 66048

STILLE, LEON E., state legislator; b. Olive, Mich., Nov. 21, 1939; m. Zinnie; four children. BS, Mich. State U. Market rep., mgr. IBM, 1966-92; mayor Ferrysburg, Mich.; rep. Mich. Dist. 89, 1993-94; Rep. asst. whip, 1993-94; sen. Mich. Dist. 32, 1995—; chair regularity subcom. 1993-94, transportation subcom., 1993-94; mem. higher edn. subcom., 1993-94, gen. govt. subcom., 1993-94. Mem. Rotary. Home: 17386 Hazel St Spring Lake MI 49456-1222*

STILWELL, MARTHA ANN, academic administrator; b. Ypsilanti, Mich., Sept. 5, 1951; d. Donald Hugh and Winifred (Bergstrom) Cramton; m. Roy Eric Johnson, Dec. 21, 1974 (div. June 1980); m. Donald Bain Stilwell III, Jan. 22, 1988. BA, Western Mich. U., 1974, MA, 1976. Cert. tchr., libr., Mich. Librarian Harper Creek High Sch., Battle Creek, Mich., 1974-81, Kalamazoo Valley Commun. Coll., Kalamazoo, 1982; coord. media Kalamazoo Coll., 1982-84; dir. learning resources Danville (Va.) Commun. Coll., 1984-87, Kellogg Commun. Coll., Battle Creek, 1987—; mem. exec. bd. Mich. Libr. Consortium, Lansing, 1990-93. Bd. dirs. Calhoun Child Abuse/Neglect Coun., Battle Creek, 1992-93; vol. United Way of Greater Battle Creek, 1990—, Cereal City Festival, Battle Creek, 1991—; mem. Commun. Leadership Acad., Battle Creek, 1991—. Mem. AAUW, ALA, Mich. Libr. Assn. (exec. bd. 1991—, pres. 1995—), Assn. for Ednl. Communications and Tech., Nat. Coun. for Learning Resources, Mich. Tutorial Assn., Jr. League of Battle Creek (bd. dirs. 1990-92). Methodist. Office: Kellogg CC 450 North Ave Battle Creek MI 49017-3306

STINSON, DALE BERNARD, lawyer; b. Emporia, Kans., Sept. 27, 1926; s. Dale Bernard and Anna May (Bowersox) S.; m. Melva Delores Mayes Stinson, Aug. 6, 1949; children: Jeffrey Stephen, Dale Bernard III, Melissa LoAnn, Bradford Charles. AB, Emporia State U., Kans.; LLB, JD, Washburn U. Bar: Kans., 1951, U.S. Dist. Ct. Kans., 1951, U.S. Ct. Appeals (10th cir.), 1966, U.S. Supreme Ct., 1981. Clk. Land Dept. Phillips Petroleum Co., Bartlesville, Okla., 1951-53; atty. assoc. Ratner, Mattox & Ratner, Wichita, 1953-58; atty. pvt. practice, 1958-62; atty. ptnr. Foster & Stinson, 1962-66; Stinson, Lasswell & Wilson, 1966—; chmn. Legal Econ. Commn., Lans. bar Assn., Wichita, 1959; judge Pro Tem Probate, Juvenile Ct., Wichita, 1960-64; speaker Seminar Wills, Trusts Probate, Wichita, Topeka, 1985; speaker, participant Wichita Bar Assn Seminars, 1995. Supporter, campaigner Sedgwick County Kans Rep. Party, Wichita, 1954-74; mem., officer Downtown Optimist Club, Wichita, 1955-90; mem., bd. dirs. Starkey Developmental Ctr., Wichita, 1974-80, Sedgwick County Assn. for Retarded Citizens, Wichita, 1989-94; trustee Bd. Trustees Endowment Assn. Emporia (Kans.) State U., 1985-90; elder Presbyn. Ch. Recipient Disting. Svc. award Jr. C. of C., Wichita, 1959; pres. Wichita Estate Planning Coun., 1966, The Wichita Club, 1984; Outstanding Svc.award Kans. Bar Assn., Wichita, 1974; Svc. award Sedgwick County Assn. for Retarded Citizens, Wichita, 1994; Howard C. Kline Svc. award Wichita Bar Assn., 1995; 33rd Degree Supreme Coun. Scottish Rite Masonry, Wichita, 1995. Mem. ABA, C. of C., Kans. Bar Assn., Albert Pike Lodge AF&AM, Wichita Bar Assn. (pres. 1974), Wichita Estate Planning Coun., Wichita Consistory-Scottish Rite; fellow Kans. Bar Found. Republican. Presbyterian. Home: 150 S Dellrose Wichita KS 67218

STINSON, KAREN, education educator; b. Caldwell, Kans., Sept. 4, 1950; d. Robert Warren and Frances Jane (Korbel) S.; children: Bradley, Kathryn, Michael. BA in English and Speech, U. No. Iowa, 1971, MA in Spl. Edn., 1980, EdD, 1988; adminstrv. endorsement, Wartburg Coll., 1979. Cert. flight instr.; lic. comml. pilot. Head speech dept. Aplington (Iowa) Schs., 1971-73; head English dept. East Buchanan Schs., Winthrop, Iowa, 1973-74; spl. edn. tchr. Area VII Edn. Agy., Cedar Falls, Iowa, 1974-82; dir. reading clinic U. No. Iowa, Cedar Falls, 1982-83; elem. spl. edn. tchr. Cedar Heights Sch., Cedar Falls, 1983-86; elem. tchr. Castle Hill Sch., Waterloo, 1990-91; dir. tchr. edn. Upper Iowa U., Fayette, 1991—; dental cons. Insights Out Assocs., Newark, 1991—, Schs. in NE Iowa, 1987—. Assoc. editor Reading Tchr. Jour., 1991-93. Mem. Iowa Reading Assn. (pres. 1991-92, rsch. award 1987), Learning Disabilities of Iowa (pres. 1991-92), Iowa Assn. Women Pilots-99s (pres. 1980-82), CAP (pilot, officer 1979-81), Alpha Upsilon Alpha. Lutheran. Office: Upper Iowa U PO Box 1857 Fayette IA 52142-1857

STINSON, MARY FLORENCE, nursing educator; b. Wheeling, W.Va., Feb. 11, 1931; d. Rolland Francis and Mary Angela (Voellinger) Kellogg; m. Charles Walter Stinson, Feb. 12, 1955; children: Kenneth Charles, Karen Marie, Kathryn Anne. BSN, Coll. Mt. St. Joseph, 1953, postgrad., 1983; MEd, Xavier U., Cin., 1967; postgrad. U. Cin., 1981. Staff nurse contagious disease ward Cin. Gen. Hosp., 1953-54, asst. head nurse med. and polio wards, 1955, acting head nurse, clin. instr., 1955-56; instr. St. Francis Hosp. Sch. Practical Nursing, Cin., 1956-57; instr. Good Samaritan Hosp. Sch. Nursing, Cin., 1957-65; instr. refresher courses for nurses Cin. Bd. Edn. and Ohio State Nurses Assn. Dist. 8, 1967-70; coord. sch. health office Coll. Mt. St. Joseph (Ohio), 1969-72, instr. dept. nursing, 1974-79, asst. prof., 1979-89; part-time staff nurse St. Francis/St. George Hosp., Cin., 1988-89; RN assessor Passport program Ohio Coun. on Aging, 1989-90, quality assurance coord., 1990-93; quality assurance supr. Passport and Elderly Svcs. Program, 1993-94; quality assurance mgr. Coun. Aging, Cin., 1995—. Charter mem. Adoptive Parents Assn. St. Joseph Infant and Maternity Home; active Women's Com. for Performing Arts Series, Coll. Mt. St. Joseph; mem. St. Antoninus Rosary Altar Rosary and Sch. Soc., St. Antoninus Athletic Club, com. chmn., 1969-70; bd. dirs. Coll. Mt. St. Joseph Alumnae Assn., 1982-84, sec., 1968-69, v.p., 1969-70, pres., 1970-71, chmn. revision of constn., 1976-77; homecoming chmn. Coll. Mt. St. Joseph, 1970, co-chmn., 1977; mem. Gamble Nippert YMCA. Mem. O.K.I. Gerontol. Nursing Assn. Democrat. Roman Catholic. Club: River Squares (v.p. 1967). Home: 5549 Cleander Dr Cincinnati OH 45238-4266 Office: Coun on Aging of Cin Holiday Office Pk 644 Linn St Cincinnati OH 45203-1720

STINSON, THOMAS FRANKLIN, economist, educator; b. Puyallup, Wash., July 17, 1942; s. John F. and Mildred F. (Thomas) S.; m. Susie Smith, Aug. 22, 1964. BA, Wash. State U., 1964; PhD, U. Minn., 1972. Economist econ. rsch. svc. USDA, Washington, 1965-69, St. Paul, 1970-85; full prof. econs. U. Minn., St. Paul, 1985—; with State of Minn. Economist, St. Paul, 1987—; cons. U.S. Senate Intergovtl. Rels. Subcom., Washington, 1986, Minn. Tax Study Commn., St. Paul, 1984; mem. econ. panel Pioneer Press, St. Paul, 1987—; mem. bd. economists Star-Tribune, Mpls., 1987—. Contbr. numerous articles to profl. jours. Mem. Am. Econ. Assn., Am. Agrl. Econs. Assn., Nat. Tax Assn., Minn. Econs. Assn. (pres. 1990).

STIRITZ, WILLIAM P., food company executive; b. Jasper, Ark., July 1, 1934; s. Paul and Dorothy (Bradley) S.; m. Susan Ekberg, Dec. 4, 1972; children—Bradley, Charlotte, Rebecca, Nicholas. B.S., Northwestern U., 1959; M.A., St. Louis U., 1968. Mem. mktg. mgmt. staff Pillsbury Co., Mpls., 1959-62; account mgmt. staff Gardner Advt. Co., St. Louis, 1963—; with Ralston Purina Co., St. Louis, 1963—; pres., chief exec. officer, chmn. Ralston Purina Co., 1981—; bd. dirs. Angelica Corp., Ball Corp., Boatmen's Bancshares, Inc., Gen. Am. Life Ins. Co., May Dept. Stores, S.C. Johnson & Son. With USN, 1954-57. Mem. Grocery Mfrs. Assn. (dir.). Office: Ralston Purina Co Checkerboard Sq Saint Louis MO 63164

STIRLER, KAREN SUE, special education educator, adult education educator; b. Waterloo, Iowa, June 25, 1951; d. Walter Henry and Nadine Augusta (Boege) S. BS in Vocat. Home Econs., U. No. Iowa, 1973, MA in Spl. Edn., 1982. Tchr. vocat. home econs. and sci. Randolph (Nebr.) Pub. Schs., 1976-77; tchr. spl. edn. Highland Community Sch., Riverside, Iowa, 1978-82, New Hampton (Iowa) Schs., 1982-86, Roosevelt Mid. Schs., Cedar Rapids, Iowa, 1986-92, Kennedy High Sch., Cedar Rapids, 1992—; tchr. adult basic edn. Kirkwood C.C., Cedar Rapids, 1987—. Mem. NEA, Am. Home Econs. Assn., Coun. for Exceptional Children, Iowa Edn. Assn., Cedar Rapids Home Econs. Assn., Cedar Rapids Tchr. Edn. Assn. Lutheran. Office: Kennedy High Sch 4545 Wenig Rd NE Cedar Rapids IA 52402-2212

STITES, SUSAN KAY, human resources consultant; b. Colorado Springs, Colo., Sept. 20, 1952; d. William Wallace and Betty Jane (Kosley) Stites; m. Gerald Frederick Simon, Aug. 14, 1988. BA, Wichita State U., 1974; MA, Northwestern U., 1979. Benefits authorizer Social Security Adminstrn., Chgo., 1974-77; trainer Chgo. Urban Skills Inst., 1977-79; human resources mgr. Montgomery Ward, Chgo., 1979-83; mgr. tng. Lands' End, Dodgeville, Wis., 1983-87; dir. human resources Cen. Life Assurance, Madison, Wis., 1988-90; owner Mgmt. Allegories, Madison, Wis., 1987—. Author: Delegating for Results, 1992, Business Communications, 1992, Managing with a Quality Focus, 1994, Training and Orientation for the Small Business, 1994, Powerful Performance Management, 1994, Safety Management Techniques, 1995, Teaching First Aid and CPR, 1995, Alive at 25, 1995, Strategic Thinking and Planning, 1995, Teaching Alice at 25, 1996, Fundamendals of Industrial Hygiene, 1996, Recruiting, Developing, and Retaining Volunteers, 1996. Vol. tutor Japanese Students in English, Evanston, Ill., 1977-80; read to blind Chgo. Coun. for the Blind, 1974-76. Named Outstanding Woman of the Yr. Wichita State U., 1974. Mem. ASTD (chpt. pres. 1988, v.p. membership 1986, region V awards chair 1992), Soc. Applied Learning Tech., Madison Area Quality Improvement Network, Assn. for Quality and Participation, Rotary (vol. fund raiser), Mendota Yacht Club (treas. 1990-94). Home: 3788 Highridge Rd Madison WI 53704-6206 Office: Mgmt Allegories 3788 Highridge Rd Madison WI 53704-6206

STITLEY, JAMES WALTER, JR., food manufacturing executive; b. York, Pa., May 23, 1944; s. James Walter and Geraldine Salome (Horn) S.; BS in Chemistry, Millersville U., 1970. Med. technician York Hosp., 1962-66; research biochemist Carter-Wallace, Inc., Cranbury, N.J., 1970-75; mgr. Ward Labs. div. Ward Foods, East Orange, N.J., 1975-77; mgr. tech. services Pepperidge Farm, Inc., Norwalk, Conn., 1977-86; dir. tech. devel. Am. Inst. Baking, Manhattan, Kans., 1986-88; dir. baking and cereal sci. research and biscuit product devel. internat., Campbell Soup Co., Camden, N.J., 1988-90; nat. dir. rsch. and tech. Domino's Pizza, Inc., 1990-91, div. v.p. consumer and product rsch., 1992—; pres., CEO TechnoVation Network, Inc., 1992—; cons. biochemistry and toxicology. Asst. scoutmaster Boy Scouts Am. Nominee Presidential Merit award Campbell Soup Co., 1982; mem. Am. Chem. Soc., Am. Mgmt. Assn., Am. Assn. Cereal Chemists, Am. Inst. Baking (ednl. adv. com. 1978—), Instrument Soc. Am. (assoc. dir.-food industry liaison), AAAS, Am. Astron. Research Group, York Astron. Soc. (v.p. 1960). Contbr. articles to profl. jours.; patentee in field. Home: 9061 Matthews Hwy Tecumseh MI 49286-8708 Office: TechnoVation Network Inc Box 384 24 Frank Lloyd Wright Dr Ann Arbor MI 48106

STITNIZKY, JOHN LOUIS, health facilities and hospital services professional; b. Chgo., Oct. 10, 1939; s. John and Laura Lucille (Elzroth) S.; m. Yasuko Terada, June 2, 1961; children: Janet Laura, Diane Lynn, Sherry Jean. BA in Bus., Chaminade U. of Honolulu, 1977, postgrad., 1980-81. Enlisted USN, 1956, advanced through grades to sr. chief, ret., 1977; ins. underwriter Conn. Mut., Honolulu, 1977-80; gen. mgr. Waikiki Grand Hotel, Honolulu, 1980-81; auditor, night mgr. Outrigger Hotel, Honolulu, 1981-86; asst. dir. environ. svcs. St. Mary Med. Ctr. United Health Services, Inc., Long Beach, Calif., 1987-88; dir. environ. svcs. Fairview Devel. Ctr., Costa Mesa, Calif., 1988-89, Marriott Facilities Mgmt., Camarillo State Hosp., 1989-91; mgr., dir. environ. svcs. L.A. Dodgers Stadium, 1991-92; mgr. Gene Autry Western Heritage Mus., 1993-94; ops. mgr. Marriott Mgmt. Svcs./St. Francis Hosp., Evanston, Ill., 1994—, Rush-Presbyn. Hosp., Chgo., 1996—. Big brother Big Bros. of Hawaii, Honolulu, 1975-76; del. Rep. Conv., Honolulu, 1980. Mem. Navy League U.S. (life, sec., v.p. 1978-79, Sailor of Yr. award 1977), Am. Legion (comdr., dist. vice comdr. Post 56 1979), Fleet Res. (bd. dirs. bd. 46 1978), VFW, NRA (Cert. saftey instructor), Nat. Exec. Housekeepers Assn. (reg. mem.), Elks. Lutheran. Office: Mariott Helath Care Svcs 3020 Woodcreek Dr Ste B Downers Grove IL 60515

STIVALE, CHARLES JOSEPH, French language and literature educator; b. Glen Ridge, N.J., Dec. 13, 1949; s. Joseph John and Olive Martha (Playfoot) S. BA, Knox Coll., 1971; MA, Sorbonne-Paris U., 1973, Maîtrise, 1974; PhD, U. Ill., 1981. Teaching asst. U. Ill., Urbana, 1977-78, 79-80, rsch. asst., 1978-80; resident dir. jr. yr. abroad program Knox Coll., Besancon, France, 1976-77; instr. French Western Mich. U., Kalamazoo, 1980-81; resident dir. CIEE Coop. Study Ctr., Rennes, France, 1981-82; asst. prof. Franklin & Marshall Coll., Lancaster, Pa., 1982-86, Tulane U., New Orleans, 1986-90; assoc. prof. Wayne State U., Detroit, 1990-96, prof., 1996—, dept. chair, 1996—. Author: La Trilogie de Jules Valles, 1988, La Temporalité romanesque chez Stendhal, 1989, The Art of Rapture: Narrative Desire and Duplicity in the Tales of Guy de Maupassant, 1994; guest editor: Substance 44/45, 1984, Substance 66, 1992, Works & Days 25/26, 1995-96; mem. editl. bd. Works & Days, 1995—; adv. bd. Alternative Ednl. Environs., 1995. Univ. fellow U. Ill., 1975-76, Rsch. fellow Tulane U., 1988, 89, Wayne State U., 1992, 93, 94, 95. Mem. MLA (field bibliographer MLA Internat. Bibliographer Internat. Bibliography 1990-95), Midwest Modern Lang. Assn., Soc. for Study of Narrative Lit. Office: Wayne State Univ Dept Romance Langs Detroit MI 48202

STIVER, JAMES FREDERICK, pharmacist, health physicist, administrator, scientist; b. Elkhart, Ind., Jan. 27, 1943; s. Melvin Hugh and Pauline Anna (Schrock) S.; m. Joan Louise Trindle, Aug. 14, 1965; children: Gregory James, Richard Frederick, Kristin Louise, Elizabeth Ann. BS in Pharmacy and Pharm. Scis., Purdue U., 1966, MS, 1968, PhD, 1970. Lic. pharmacist, Ind., N.D. Asst. prof. N.D. State U., Fargo, 1969-73, assoc. prof., 1973-76, radiol. safety officer, 1969-76; radiation safety officer KMS Fusion Inc., Ann Arbor, Mich., 1976-80; mgr., pharmacist Kroger Sav-On Pharmacy Co., Elkhart, Ind., 1980-81; pharmacist Elkhart Gen. Hosp., 1981; environ. regulatory affairs adminstr. Upjohn Co., Kalamazoo, Mich., 1981-88; patent liaison scientist, 1988-92; sr. patent liaison scientist, 1992-94; pharmacist, asst. mgr. Judd Drugs, Elkhart, 1994-95; pharmacist Meijer Pharmacy, Goshen, Ind., 1995—; cons., lectr. Mem. Trinity Luth. Ch., Goshen, Ind. Named to Honorable Order Ky. Cols. Fellow Am. Inst. Chemists; mem. AAAS, Am. Pharm. Assn., Ind. Pharmacists Assn., N.D. Pharm. Assn., Am. Chem. Soc., Health Physics Soc., Internat. Radiation Protection Assn., Am. Biol. Safety Assn., N.Y. Acad. Scis., Kappa Psi, Rho Chi, Phi Lambda Upsilon, Sigma Xi. Contbr. articles, abstracts to publs. Home: 505 Skyview Dr Middlebury IN 46540-9427 Office: Meijer Inc Goshen IN 46526

STOA, TERRY A., chemical engineer; b. Northwood, N.D., Aug. 28, 1952; s. Gordon Adolph and Donna Germayne (Johnson) S.; m. Heather Hastings Hutchison, June 8, 1974; children: Kristen Nicole, Ryan Allen. BS, U. N.D., 1974. Prof. engr. Ill. Process engr. DuPont, Kinston, N.C., 1974-75; from prodn. asst. to mgr. constn. engring. Archer-Daniesl-Midland, Decatur, Ill., 1975—. Del. Parent's Adv. Coun., Decatur, 1986. Mem. Ill. Soc. Prof. Engrs. (young profl. engr. of yr. 1982). Office: Archer-Daniels-Midland Co 4666 Faries Pkwy Decatur IL 62526

STOCK, ANITA See SCHERER, ANITA

STOCK, SIDNEY R., systems engineer; b. Logan, Utah, Dec. 3, 1961. BS in Sys. Engring., Utah State U., Logan, 1986. Sys. engr. Delco Systems, Santa Barbara, Calif., 1986-88, Delco Elec., Kokomo, Ind., 1989—. Scoutmaster Boys Scouts Am., Santa Barbara, 1986-89; missionary Ch. of Latter-day Saints, Chile, 1981-82. Republican. Mormon.

STOCKERT, TERRY J., electrical engineer; b. Bismark, N.D., Jan. 27, 1968. BS in Elec. Engring., U. N.D., Grand Forks, 1990; postgrad., U. Iowa, 1991—. Assoc. design engr. Rockwell Internat., Cedar Rapids, Iowa, 1991—. Office: Rockwell Internat Corp 400 Collins Rd NE Cedar Rapids IA 52402

STOCKGLAUSNER, WILLIAM GEORGE, accountant; b. St. Louis, Dec. 25, 1950; s. William George and Mary Virginia (Lopez) S.; m. Vickie Kay Mackler, Nov. 17, 1973; children: Tyson Marshall, Jacob Cameron. BS summa cum laude, Columbia (Mo.) Coll., 1985. CPA, Mo. Staff acct. Wright-Price Inc., Jefferson City, Mo., 1974-77; staff acct. Williams-Keepers CPAs, Columbia, 1977-81, supr. acctg. svc., 1981-85, auditor, 1985-86; acct. Don Landers & Co. CPAs, Columbia, 1986-89; ptnr. Columbia, 1990—. Coach Daniel Boone Little League, Columbia, 1986-90, 94-95, Diamond Coun., 1994-95, Columbia Soccer Club, 1988-90, divsn. coord., 1991-92; campaign vol. United Way, 1991-94; mem. fin. adv. com. City of Columbia, 1996—. Mem. AICPA, Mo. Soc. CPAs (tech. standards rev. com. 1989-90), Lions (sec. Columbia club 1983-85, bd. dirs. 1986-88). Republican. Roman Catholic. Office: Don L Landers & Co 33 E Broadway Ste 190 Columbia MO 65203-4207

STOCKLEY, DARLEEN J., lawyer; b. Champaign, Ill., July 14, 1943; d. John Ted and Florence Belle (Gadberry) Dixon; m. Dale Leon Stockley, June 12, 1965; children: James Dale, Robert DeLeon. Student, U. Ill.; BS in Edn., No. Ill. U., 1973, MS, 1980; JD, De Paul U., 1984; MSEE, No. Ill. U., 1993; MBA, U. Chgo., 1996. Bar: Ill. 1984, U.S. Dist. Ct. (no. dist.) Ill. 1984, U.S. Patent Ct., 1990. Research asst. U. Ill., Champaign, 1960-62, researcher, 1962-69; tchr. Ottawa (Ill.) Pub. Schs., 1973-84; ptnr. Pool & Stockley, Ottawa, 1984-89; patent atty. Motorola, Inc., Schaumburg, Ill., 1990—. Contbr. research articles to profl. jours. Coordinator Citizens for Stockley for (Ill. State) Senate, 1985-86. Mem. ABA, Ill. Bar Assn., LaSalle County Bar Assn. Club: Zonta (Ottawa). Office: Motorola Inc 1303 E Algonquin Rd Schaumburg IL 60196-4041

STOECKLE, MARY L., critical care nurse, nursing educator; b. Cin., Nov. 14, 1956; d. Melvin and Margaret Mary (Atkins) S. BSN, Coll. Mt. St. Joseph, Ohio, 1979; MSN, U. Cin., 1988, PhD, 1993. BLS instr., trainer. Staff nurse St. Francis Hosp., Cin., 1979-81; charge relief nurse Shriners Burns Inst., Cin., 1981-85; staff nurse Univ. Hosp., Cin., 1985; staff, charge nurse St. Elizabeth Med. Ctr., Edgewood, Ky., 1985-88; critical care instr. Mercy Hosp. Anderson, 1988-93; instr. Am. Healthcare Inst., Silver Springs, Md., 1989—; asst. prof. Wright State U., Dayton, Ohio, 1993—; bd. dirs. Kidney Found. of Greater Cin., 1988-94; bd. dirs. Miami Valley chpt. Nat. Kidney Found., 1994—; mem. Organ Donor Awareness Coun., 1988—; mem. ECC task force Am. Heart Assn., 1988-91. Author: (with others) Organ & Tissue Transplantation, 1991; contb'r. of articles to jours. Mem. Ohio Burn Team, 1981-86. Grantee Kidney Found. Greater Cin., 1992, Wright State U., 1994, Ortho-Biotech, 1996. Mem. AACN, Midwest Nursing Rsch. Soc., Assn. Nurses Endorsing Transplantation, Nat. Student Nurses Assn. (sustaining), Ohio Nurses Assn., Sigma Theta Tau (rsch. award Beta Iota chpt. 1989). Home: 5625 Eula Ave Cincinnati OH 45248-4201 Office: Wright State U Miami Valley Coll Nursing and Health Dayton OH 45435

STOEFFLER, DAVID BRUCE, newspaper editor; b. Boscobel, Wis., Mar. 8, 1959; s. Raymond Elwood and Arlene Mary (Laufenberg) S.; m. Rose Mary Hromadka, June 9, 1978; 1 child, Christine Elizabeth. BA in English, Viterbo Coll., LaCrosse, 1981. Reporter LaCrosse Tribune, LaCrosse, Wis., 1979-81, Wis. State Jour., Madison, Wis., 1981-88; asst. city editor Wis. State Jour., Madison, 1988-93, city editor, 1993-95; editor LaCrosse Tribune, LaCrosse, 1995—. Recipient Cmty. Svc. award Inland Daily Press Assn., 1990, 94. Mem. Soc. of Profl. Journalists (pres. Madison Pro chpt.; mem. chmn. Region 6). Catholic. Office: La Crosse Tribune 401 N 3rd St La Crosse WI 54601

STOERMER, EUGENE FILMORE, biologist, educator; b. Webb, Iowa, Mar. 7, 1934; s. Edward Filmore and Agnes Elizabeth (Ekstrand) S.; m. Barbara Purves Ryder, Aug. 13, 1960; children: Eric Filmore, Karla Jean, Peter Emil. BS, Iowa State U., 1959, PhD, 1963. Assoc. rsch. scientist, rsch. scientist U. Mich., Ann Arbor, 1965-79, assoc. prof., 1979-85, prof., 1985—; editl. advisor Jour. Paleolimonology. Contbr. over 190 articles to profl. jours. Fellow Acad. Natural Scis., Phila., 1980; recipient Darbaker prize, Bot. Soc. Am., 1993. Mem. Phycological Soc. Am. (pres. 1988-89), Internat. Assn. for Diatom Rsch. (pres. 1992-94). Home: 4392 Dexter Ave Ann Arbor MI 48103-1636 Office: U Mich Ctr for Great Lakes Ann Arbor MI 48109

STOFER, KATHRYN TAMARA, communication arts educator; b. Hyannis, Nebr., Jan. 17, 1948; d. Robert J. Bunner and Gail R. (Jennings) Reichert; m. John W. Wood, Mar. 25, 1994. BA in English and Journalism, Hastings (Nebr.) Coll., 1983; MA in English, U. Nebr., 1987, MA in Journalism, 1993. Tchr. N.W. High Sch., Grand Island, Nebr., 1983-88; prof. Hastings Coll., 1988—; presenter in field. Editor (newsletter) Acad. Freedom Coaliton of Nebr., 1989—; contbr. articles to profl. jours. Pres. Hastings Coll. Women's Club, 1990; bd. dirs. Hastings Cmty. Theatre, 1991—, YMCA, 1993-96. Mem. ACLU, Bus. and Profl. Women (chair 1990-91), Adams County Hist. Soc., Nebr. Collegiate Media Assn. (exec. dir.), Order of Eastern Star, Delta Kappa Gamma. Republican. Methodist. Home: 913 Richmond Hastings NE 68901-3327 Office: Hastings Coll 7th & Turner Hastings NE 68901

STOGSDILL, FRANK JO, design engineer; b. Susanville, Calif., May 31, 1948. BS in Design, S.W. Mo. State U., 1972. Engring. supr. Paul Mueller Co., Springfield, Mo., 1973-86; project engr. Precision Stainless, Springfield, 1986-88, Custom Metal Craft Inc., Springfield, 1988—. Leader Boy Scouts Am. Republican. Office: Custom Metal Craft Inc 2332 E Div Springfield MO 65803

STOHLER, MICHAEL JOE, dentist; b. Anderson, Ind., Mar. 26, 1956; s. Herbert Warren and Mary Jo (Philbert) S.; m. Mary Anne Poinsette, May 16, 1981; children: James Lawrence, Maria Christine, Benjamin Joseph. Student, Lake-Sumter C.C., Leesburg, Fla., 1974-76; BS, Ball State U., 1978; DDS, Ind. U., 1982. Gen. practice dentistry Anderson, 1982—. Mem. ADA, Ind. Dental Assn., East Ctrl. Dental Assn., Madison County Dental Assn., Acad. Gen. Dentistry, Acad. Dentistry for Handicapped, Ind. U. Alumni Assn. (assoc., life), Rotary (sgt.-at-arms Anderson Suburban chpt. 1986), Psi Omega. Home: 2829 W Ridge Ln Anderson IN 46013-9749 Office: 2012 E 53rd St Anderson IN 46013-3102

STOHLMAN, CONNIE SUZANNE, obstetrical gynecological nurse; b. Tucson, Sept. 27, 1960; d. Irvin Wendell and Betty Jo (Stewart) Holmes; m. Bruce R. Stohlman, Sept. 14, 1991. BSN, Bishop Clarkson Coll. Nursing, 1987; BA, U. Nebr., 1982; cert. med. asst., Omaha Coll. Health Careers, 1983. Primary nurse I U. Md. Med. System, Balt., 1987-90; staff nurse St. Joseph Hosp., Omaha, 1990—; mem. quality assurance task force U. Md. Med. System, 1987-90; mem. quality assurance com. St. Joseph Hosp., 1992—. Named to Outstanding Young Women of Am., 1986.

STOHRER, PHILIP CHARLES, media specialist; b. Kalamazoo, Sept. 8, 1950; s. Frederic Charles and Thelma Imojean (Triestram) S.; m. Annamae Keiser, June 20, 1981; children: Jonathan, David. Student, Kalamazoo Valley C.C., 1968-70; BS, Western Mich. U., 1972, MA, 1976. Cert. secondary tchr., Mich. Libr. Cen. Jr. High Sch., Portage, Mich., 1977-82; libr. Hartford (Mich.) High Sch., 1982-86, cable acess adminstr., 1984-86; media specialist West Middle Schs., Portage, 1986—; cons. Project TIME, Lansing, Mich., 1984-87. Author computer programs. Mem. Mich. Assn. of Computer Users in Learning, MIch. Assn. for Media in Edn. (regional pres. 1990-92). Mem. Reformed Ch. in Am. Home: 5314 Rugby St Portage MI 49024 Office: Portage Pub Schs 7145 Moors Bridge Rd Portage MI 49024-4025

STOHS, SIDNEY JOHN, dean; b. Ludell, Kans., May 24, 1939; s. John H. and Lydia E. S.; m. Susan J. Stehl; children: Sarah, Tim. BS in pharmacy, U. Nebr., Lincoln, 1962, MS in natural products, 1964; PhD in biochemistry, U. Wis., Madison, 1967. Asst. prof. U. Nebr. Coll. of Pharmacy, Lincoln, Nebr., 1967-72; assoc. prof. U. Nebr. Coll. of Pharmacy, Lincoln, 1972-74; prof. Coll. of Pharmacy - U. Nebr. Med. Ctr., Omaha, 1974-85; asst. dean, prof. Coll. of Pharmacy and Eppley Inst., U. Nebr. Med. Ctr., Omaha, 1985-87, prof., 1987-89; asst. dean, prof. Creighton U., Omaha, 1989-91, dean, prof., 1991—; mem. EPA Dioxin Sci. Adv. Bd., Washington, 1995—, USP Nat. Adv. Com., Washington, 1995—. Author: (with others) Oxidative Stress and Antioxidant Defenses, 1995,; contbr. articles to profl. jours. Honor Soc. for Internat. Scholars, Phi Beta Delta, 1992. Mem. Am. Pharm. Assn. (Rsch. award 1985), Am. Assn. Coll. of Pharmacy (Tchr. award 1987), Soc. of Toxicology, Assn. Sch. Allied Health Professions (ethics com. 1994—), Phi Lambda Sigma (Excellence in Leadership award 1994, 95, Outstanding Svc. to Nebr. Pharmacy award 1996), Rho Chi. Office: Creighton Univ 2500 California Pl Omaha NE 68178

STOIA, VIOREL G., life underwriter; b. Aberdeen, S.D., Feb. 13, 1924; s. John and Seana (Biliboca) S.; m. Donna Marie Maurseth Stoia, Sept. 10, 1949; children: Marsha Jo, Nancy Kay, Gregory Allen, Thomas John, James Vincent. BBA, U. Minn., 1949. CLU, ChFC, Am. Coll. Special agent Northwestern Mutual Life, Mil., Wis., 1950—, district agent, 1960-89; broker Aetna Life Ins. Co., Hartford, Conn., 1960—, Principal Mutual Life, Des Moines, Iowa, 1967—; with Northwestern Natl. Life, Mpls., Minn., 1971—; co-founder, chmn. bd. Student Loan Fin. Corp., 1978—; ptnr. Aberdeen Real Estate, Ltd.; co-founder, mng. ptnr. Tel Serv, 1983—. Co-founder, pres. Northeastern Mental Health Ctr., 1957-59, North Plains Hospice, 1980-84; sec. Edn. Asst. Corp., 1978—; bd. dirs. S.D. Crippled Children's Hosp.; trustee Aberdeen YMCA, 1969-73, St. Luke's Hosp., 1969—; co-founder, trustee Northern State U. Found., 1972—. Named Outstanding Civic Leader of Am., 1967; recipient, Jefferson award Nat. Inst. of Pub. Svc., Sioux Falls, 1980, George award Aberdeen C. of C., Aberdeen, 1979, 94. Mem. Aberdeen Devel. Corp. (pres. 1972-87), Aberdeen Jr. C. of C. (pres. 1956), S.D. Jr. C. of C., Aberdeen C. of C., S.D. Soc. CLU's (co-founder, pres. 1958-59), Nat. Assn. Life Underwriters, Aberdeen Dist. Life Underwriters (pres. 1953-54), S.D. Assn. Life Underwriters (pres. 1959-60), Million Dollar Round Table (life), Moccasin Creek Country Club (v.p. 1969-75). Republican. Roman Catholic. Home: 1022 N Main St Aberdeen SD 57401-2426 Office: Stoia Seiler & Assoc PO Box 98 304 1/2 S Main St Aberdeen SD 57401-4146

STOIKES, MARY ELOISE, pharmacy researcher; b. Madison, Wis., May 23, 1960; d. Gerald Leonard and Dorothy Jane (Dunn) S. BS in Pharmacy, Drake U., 1983; MS in Pharmacy Practice, N.D. State U., 1985; postgrad., U. Minn., 1994—. Resident VA Med. Ctr., Fargo, N.D., 1983-85; staff pharmacist Strong Meml. Hosp., Rochester, N.Y., 1985-86; staff pharmacist Park Ridge Hosp., Rochester, 1986-88, clin. coord., 1988-89; supr. clin. svcs. Sisters of Charity Hosp., Buffalo, 1989-91; dir. pharmacy St. Francis Med. Ctr., Buffalo, 1989-91; clin. pharmacist A.O. Fox Meml. Hosp., Oneonta, N.Y., 1991-92; pharmacy supr. St. Joseph's Hosp., St. Paul, 1992-94. Contbr. articles to profl. jours. E.R. Squibb & Sons scholar, 1985; recipient Albert P. Prescott/Glaxo Leadership award, 1993, Albert B. Prescott Leadership award; N.Y. State Rsch. and Edn. Found., 1990. Fellow Am. Soc. Health-Sys. Pharmacists; mem. AAUW, N.Y. State Coun. Hosp. Pharmacists (pres. 1990-92), Rochester Area Soc. Hosp. Pharmacists (pres. 1987-89), Minn. Soc. Hosp. Pharmacists, Am. Soc. Hosp. Pharmacists (com. 1991—), N.D. Soc. Hosp. Pharmacists, Minn-Dakota Soc. Hosp. Pharmacists (sec. 1984-85), Gamma Phi Beta, Lambda Kappa Sigma, Rho Chi. Home: 3107 4th St SE Apt 5 Minneapolis MN 55414-3333

STOKAN, LANA, state legislator. Rep. dist. 76 State of Mo. Office: 3555 Amblewood Dr Rm 305 A Florissant MO 63033

STOKEN, JACQUELINE MARIE, physician; b. Beaver Falls, Pa., Sept. 29, 1948; d. Jack Marc and Lillian Marie Stoken; m. John F. Edge, June 2, 1990; children: Randi Elizabeth; stepchildren: Lisa Adrienne, Alexander Joseph. Nursing diploma, Presbyn.-U. Hosp. Sch. Nursing, Pitts., 1970; BS in Biology with honors, Chatham Coll., Pitts., 1986; DO, U. Osteo. Med. & Health Scis., Des Moines, 1990. RN, Pa., Iowa; cert. ACLS, BCLS. Home care staff nurse South Hills Health System, Pitts., 1976-89; intern internal medicine Des Moines Gen. Hosp., 1990-91; resident physician dept. phys. medicine and rehab. U. Minn., Mpls., 1991-94; lectr. Internat. Rehab. Med. Assn., Des Moines, 1994—; physiatrist Iowa Orthopaedic Ctr., Des Moines, 1994—; guest lectr. dept. phys. therapy U. Minn., Mpls., 1991-94, dept. ocupational therapy, 1991-94, U. Osteo. Medicine and Health Sci., Des Moines, 1990, 95, 96, IOFP, 1996—; chief resident dept. phys. medicine and rehab. U. Minn., Mpls., 1992-93; mem. Iowa Gov.'s Task Force on Rural Health, 1989. Mem. AMA, Am. Acad. Phys. Medicine and Rehab., Am. Osteo. Assn. (sec. coun. student coun. pres. 1988-89), Iowa Osteo Med. Assn. (student del. ho. of dels. 1987-88, student coun. rep. 1987-88), Am. Med. Women's Assn., Am. Holistic Med. Assn., Am. Acad. Osteopathy, Cranial Acad., Sigma Sigma Phi.

STOKES, LOUIS, congressman; b. Cleveland, Ohio, Feb. 23, 1925; s. Charles and Louise (Stone) S.; m. Jeanette Frances, Aug. 21, 1960; children: Shelley, Louis C., Angela, Lorene. Student, Case Western Res. U., 1946-48; JD, Cleve. Marshall Law Sch., 1953; LLD (hon.), Wilberforce U., 1969, Shaw U., Livingstone Coll., Morehouse Coll., Meharry Coll. Medicine. Bar: Ohio 1953. Mem. 91st-104th Congresses from 21st (now 11th) Ohio dist., Washington, D.C., 1969—; ranking minority mem. appropriations subcom. on Vets. Affairs, HUD & Ind. Agys.; guest lectr., 1960—. Mem. adv. council African-Am. Inst. Internat.; mem. exec. com. Cuyahoga County Democratic Party, Ohio State Dem. Party; bd. dirs. Karamu House; trustee Martin Luther King, Jr. Center for Social Change, Forest City Hosp., Cleve. State U. Served with AUS, 1943-46. Recipient numerous awards for civic activities including Distinguished Service award Cleve. br. NAACP; Certificate of Appreciation U.S. Commn. on Civil Rights. Fellow Ohio State Bar Assn.; mem. Am., Cuyahoga County, Cleve. bar assns., Nat. Assn. Def. Lawyers Criminal Cases Fair Housing (dir.), Urban League, Citizens League, John Harlan Law Club, ACLU, Am. Legion, Kappa Alpha Psi. Clubs: Masons (Cleve.), Plus (Cleve.). Office: US Ho of Reps 2365 Rayburn House Bldg Washington DC 20515

STOKES, ROBERTA ANNE, clinical nurse specialist, manager; b. Phila.; d. Robert Thomas and Anne Louise (Kurtz) Park; children: Tracey Jane, Suzanne Lee. ADN, Lakeland Community Coll., Mentor, Ohio, 1972; BSN, Ursuline Coll. Ctr. for Nursing, 1983; MSN, Case Western Res. U., 1987. Cert. clin. specialist gerontology nursing ANCC; cert. hemodialysis nurse Bd. Nephrology Examiners; cert. nephrology nurse Nephrology Nursing Cert. Bd. With Cleve. Clinic Found., 1972—, clin. instr. acute hemodialysis, 1985-87, nurse educator transition care, 1987-93; clin. faculty Frances Payne Bolton Sch. Nursing Case Western Res. U., Cleve., 1990—; del. nephrology nursing del. Citizen Amb. Program, Berlin, Budapest, Hungary, Prague, Czech Republic, Moscow, 1991; mem. advanced practice coun. divsn. patient care ops. Cleve. Clinic Found., 1994—; presenter in field of nephrology nursing topics. Author: Competency-Based Orientation Manual for Hemodialysis Nursing, 1991; editor Cleve. Clinic Nurse jour. Cleve. Clinic Found., 1992-94, mem. editl. bd., 1994-95; contbr. articles to profl. jours., chpt. to books. Recipient Emma Barr Excellence in Clin. Practice award, 1990; Stewart fellow, 1991-92; Fenn scholar Greater Cleve. Citizens League for Nursing, 1970-71, 71-72, 82-83. Mem. ANA, Ohio Nurses Assn. (Vol. Recognition awards 1989, 91, 93, 95), Greater Cleve. Nurses Assn., Am. Nephrology Nurses Assn. (AMGEN Ednl. scholar 1990, 1st pl. writing award 1991, chpt. coord. elect North Ctrl. Region 1992-93, chpt. coord. 1993-94, continuing edn. approval bd. 1990-93, manuscript rev. panel jour. 1993-95, asst. editor 1995—, program com. clin. concerns 1995), Sigma Theta Tau (Alpha Mu chpt. 1987—, corr. sec. 1988-90, newsletter editor 1989-92, Iota Psi chpt. 1988-94, Media Print award 1990). Home: 246 Hawthorne Dr Chagrin Falls OH 44022-3326 Office: Cleve Clinic Found 9500 Euclid Ave Cleveland OH 44195-0001

STOLL, JOHN HENRY, psychologist, theologian; b. Oxford, Pa., Feb. 22, 1925; s. Ralph Henry and Lula Irene (Beckley) S.; m. Irma Dreipelcher, Oct. 22, 1977; children: Kenneth, Jane, Kevin, Carolyn. Student, Wheaton Coll., 1942-45; BA, Manchester Coll., 1949; MDiv, Grace Theol. Sem., 1949, ThM, 1960; PhD, U. Notre Dame, 1975. Theology tchr. Wheaton (Ill.) Coll., 1949-51; chmn. dept. religion Cedarville (Ohio) Coll., 1951-57, Grace Coll., Winona Lake, Ind., 1966-75; v.p. acad. affairs Calvary Bible Coll., Kansas City, Mo., 1961-66; exec. dir. counseling clinic A.S.K., Inc., Mpls., 1979—; pastor Grace Chapel, West Liberty, Ohio, 1957-61; dir. counseling Camp Forest Springs, Westboro, Wis., 1967-75. Author: Exposition of Habakkuk, 1970, Old Testament History, 1972, Biblical Principles for Christian Maturity, 1996. Mem. Am. Sci. Affiliation, Am. Assn. Pastoral Counselors, Christian Assn. for Psychol. Studies (nat. bd. dirs. 1981-87), Evangelical Theol. Soc. Baptist. Home: 1618 Amy Ln Minneapolis MN 55430-1135 Office: ASK Inc 1405 N Lexington Ave #320 Saint Paul MN 55126

STOLL, JOHN ROBERT, lawyer, educator; b. Phila., Nov. 29, 1950; s. Wilhelm Friedrich and Marilyn Jane (Kremser) S.; m. Christine Larson, June 24, 1972; children: Andrew Michael, Michael Robert, Meredith Kirstin, Alison Courtney. BA magna cum laude, Haverford Coll., 1972; JD, Columbia U., 1975. Bar: Ind. 1975, U.S. Dist. Ct. (no. and so. dists.) Ind. 1975, U.S. Ct. Appeals (7th cir.) 1978, U.S. Dist. Ct. (no. dist.) Ill. 1980, (so. dist.) N.Y. 1993, Ill. 1981, N.Y. 1989. Atty. Barnes & Thornburg, South Bend, Ind., 1975-80, Mayer, Brown & Platt, Chgo., 1980—; adj. prof. law Northwestern U., Chgo., 1985—, DePaul U., Chgo., 1987; lectr. in bus. St. Mary's Coll., Notre Dame, Ind., 1977-78. Contbr. articles to profl. jours. Mem. ABA, Ind. State Bar Assn., Am. Bankruptcy Inst., Phi Beta Kappa. Office: Mayer Brown & Platt 190 S La Salle St Chicago IL 60603-3410

STOLL, STEVE, state legislator; b. St. Louis, Apr. 3, 1947; m. Kathleen Woods; children: Emily, Laura, Amy, Andrew. Student, S.E. Mo. State U., 1965-67; BA, U. Mo., 1970, postgrad., 1979. Tchr.; mem. Mo. Ho. of Reps. from 103d dist.; mem. Appropriations, Natural and Econ. Resources, Edn., Labor, Profl. Registration, Licensing and Budget Coms. Mo. Ho. of Reps. Councilman Ward II, Crystal City, Mo., 1983, 85, 87, 89, 91, Mayor Pro Tem, 1987-92. Mem. KC, Am. Legion. Democrat. Home: 716 Richard Dr Festus MO 63028-1077*

STOLLER, PATRICIA SYPHER, structural engineer; b. Jackson Heights, N.Y., Dec. 16, 1947; d. Carleton Roy and Mildred Vivian (Ferron) Sypher; m. David A. Stoller Sr.; children: Stephanie Jean, Sheri Lynn. BSCE, Washington U., St. Louis, 1975; M in Mgmt., Northwestern U., 1989. R&D engr. Amcar div. ACF Industries, St. Charles, Mo., 1972-79; project engr. Truck Axle div. Rockwell Internat., Troy, Mich., 1979-81; sr. engr. ABB Impell, Norcross, Ga., 1981-83; supervising engr., client mgr., div. mgr. ABB Impell, Lincolnshire, Ill., 1983—; dir. bus. devel., v.p. VECTRA (formerly ABB Impell), Lincolnshire, 1991-94; pres., CEO ASC Svcs. Co., LLC, Chgo., 1994—; Author computer program Quickpipe, 1983; numerous patents in field. Mem. ASCE, NAFE, Soc. Women Engrs., Am. Nuclear Soc. (exec. bd. Chgo. sect. 1991-93). Office: ASC Svcs Co LLC 300 W Washington St Ste 200 Chicago IL 60606-1720

STOLOV, JERRY FRANKLIN, healthcare executive; b. Kansas City, Mo., Jan. 31, 1946; s. I. Paul and Marion R. (Rothberg) Stolov. BA, Washington U., 1968; MPA, Roosevelt U., 1972. Adminstrv. asst. U. Ill. Chgo. Circle & Med. Sch. Campuses, Chgo., 1970-75; exec. dir. Hosp. Hill Health Svcs. Corp., Kansas City, Mo., 1976—; also bd. dirs. Hosp. Hill Health Svcs. Corp., Kansas City, 1976—; bd. dirs. Kansas City Psychoanalytic Found., 1996—; adv. dir. Mchts. Bank Corp., Kansas City, 1985-92. Leadership tng. C. of C., Kansas City, 1977-78. Mem. Assn. Am. Med. Colls. (group on faculty practice), Med. Group Mgmt. Assn., Internat. City Mgrs. Assn., Am. Soc. Pub. Health Adminstrs., Acad. Polit. Sci. (contbg. mem.). Office: Hosp Hill Health Svcs Corp 800 Hospital Hill Ctr 2310 Holmes St Kansas City MO 64108-2634

STOLTE, LARRY GENE, marketing executive, former computer and publishing company executive; b. Cedar Rapids, Iowa, Sept. 17, 1945; s. Ed August and Emma Wilhelmena (Tank) S.; BBA with highest distinction (FS Svcs. scholar), U. Iowa, 1971; CPA, CMA, CME, CSE; m. Rebecca Jane Tappmeyer, June 13, 1970; children: Scott Edward, Ryan Gene. Tax and auditing acct. McGladrey Pullen & Co., Cedar Rapids, 1971-73; v.p., gen. mgr. TLS Co. (subs. CCH Computax Inc.), Cedar Rapids, 1973-92, also bd. dirs.; re-engring. cons. Commerce Clearing House., Inc., Riverwoods, Ill., 1992-94; regional dir. mktg. McGladrey & Pullen, Cedar Rapids, Iowa, 1994—. Sgt. USMC, 1964-67. CPA, Iowa, Ill., Mo., Minn., Mich., Wis.; cert. mgmt. acct. Mem. Nat. Assn. Computerized Tax Processors (pres.), Nat. Assn. Accts., AICPA, Am. Mgmt. Assn., Am. Mktg. Assn., Direct Mktg. Assn., Sales & Mktg. Execs., Inc. Republican. Methodist. Address: 3000-A Towne House Dr NE PO Box 2026 Cedar Rapids IA 52406-2026 Office: McGladrey & Pullen LLP Town Ctr Ste 300 221 3rd Ave SE Cedar Rapids IA 52401-1512

STOMBAUGH, JAY A., manufacturing engineer, consultant; b. Eustis, Nebr., Nov. 30, 1943. Mgr. tool and dye Orthman Mfg., Lexington, Nebr., 1965—, plant mgr., R & D cons., 1988—. With U.S. Army, 1967-73. Mem. Soc. Mfg. Engrs., AWS. Home: 43620 Road 757 Lexington NE 68850-3813 Office: Orthman Mfg PO Box B Lexington NE 68850-0030

STOMMA, PETER CHRISTOPHER, lawyer; b. Milw., May 29, 1966; s. Thaddeus and Hedwig Wanda (Struszczyk) S. BSEE, Marquette U., 1988; JD, Drake U., 1991. Bar: Wis. 1991, U.S. Dist. Ct. (ea. and we. dists.) Wis. 1991, U.S. Ct. Appeals (fed. cir.) 1991, U.S. Patent and Trademark Office 1991. Assoc. Andrus, Sceales, Starke and Sawall, Milw., 1991—. Vol. Discovery World, Milw., 1991-94, Lawyers' Hotline Wis., Madison, 1991—; mem. devel. com. Legal Aid Milw., 1991-93; recruiting rep. Drake U., Des Moines, Iowa, 1992-94. Mem. ABA, Am. Intellectual Property Law Assn., Wis. Intellectual Property Law Assn., St. Thomas More Lawyer's Soc., Marquette Minuteman Club, Marquette Tip Off Club. Office: Andrus Sceales Starke and Sawall 100 E Wisconsin Ave Ste 1100 Milwaukee WI 53202-4107

STONE, ALAN JAY, college administrator; b. Ft. Dodge, Iowa, Oct. 15, 1942; s. Hubert H. and Bernice A. (Tilton) S.; m. Jonieta J. Smith; 1 child, Kirsten K. Stone Morlock. BA, Morningside Coll., 1964; MA, U. Iowa, 1966; MTh, U. Chgo., 1968, DMin, 1970; PhD (hon.), Kyonggi U., Korea, 1985; LLD, Stillman Coll., 1991, Sogong U., Korea, 1992. Admissions counselor Morningside Coll., Sioux City, Iowa, 1964-66; dir. admissions, asso. prof. history George Williams Coll., Downers Grove, Ill., 1969-73; v.p. coll. relations Hood Coll., Frederick, Md., 1973-75; v.p. devel. and fin. affairs W.Va. Wesleyan Coll., Buckhannon, 1975-77; dir. devel. U. Maine, 1977-78; pres. Aurora (Ill.) U., 1978-88, Alma (Mich.) Coll., 1988—; bd. dirs. Bank of Alma. Chmn. bd. Mich. Intercollegiate Athletic Assn.; bd. dirs. Mich. Coll. Found., Assn. Ind. Colls. and Univs. of Mich., Mich. Campus Compact, Korean Social Policy Inst., Seoul; chmn. United Way Gratiot County, Strategic Planning Group Gratiot County, Assn. Presbyn. Coll. Pres. Mem. Am. Assn. Higher Edn., Am. Assn. Colls., Renaissance Club, Alma Country Club. Home: 313 Maple Ave Alma MI 48801-2234 Office: Alma Coll Off of Pres Alma MI 48801

STONE, BARBARA SUZANNE, educator, dean; b. Cambridge, Mass., Feb. 18, 1951; d. Walter and Maria (Schweinburg) Grossmann; m. Harold Samuel Stone, July 22, 1978 (div. Mar. 1988). BA cum laude, U. Mass., Boston, 1972; MA, Northwestern U., 1976, PhD, 1985. Lectr. Northwestern U., Evanston, Ill., 1980-81, U. Chgo., 1983-85; faculty Shimer Coll., Waukegan, Ill., 1985—; assoc. dean Shimer Coll., Waukegan, 1989-91, dean of the coll., 1991—. Author: Adalbert Stifter and the Idyll: A Study of Witiko, 1989. Grantee Germanic Soc. Am., 1978-79, Fulbright-Hays, 1978-79. Office: Shimer Coll PO Box A-500 Waukegan IL 60079-7997

STONE, JAMES HOWARD, management consultant; b. Chgo., Mar. 4, 1939; s. Jerome H. and Evelyn Gertrude (Teitelbaum) S.; m. Carole Marlen David, Apr. 21, 1972; children: Margaret Elisa, Emily Anne, Phoebe Jane. AB cum laude, Harvard U., 1960, MBA, 1962. Cert. mgmt. cons., CMC, 1977. Staff analyst Stone Container Corp., Chgo., 1962-64, gen. mgr., Kansas City Div., 1964-66, asst. treas., 1966-68, dir., 1969—, with exec. com., 1983—; founder, owner, CEO Stone Mgmt. Cons., 1969—; mem. strategic alliance Boston Cons. Group, 1990—, trustee, sec., exec. com. Roosevelt U., Chgo., 1983—, exec. com. edn. alliance, 1994—; co-chmn. commn. fgn. and domestic affairs Northwestern U., Evanston, Ill., 1981-85, bus. plan judge Kellog Grad. Sch. Mgmt., 1994—; mem. vis. com. libr. U. Chgo., 1980—, The Chgo. Com., 1986—, Mid-Am. Com., Chgo., 1993—; bd. overseers IIT Stuart Sch. Bus., 1994—; bd. dirs. Fullerton Metals Corp., 1986—, Berteau Corp. Mem. Chgo. Coun. Fgn. Rels., 1967, bd. dirs., 1974-78; bd. dirs., mem. exec. com. NCCJ, Chgo., 1985, presiding co-chmn., 1990—; trustee Hadley Sch. Blind, Winnetka, Ill., 1985, chmn. planning com., 1989—. Mem. Warehousing Edn. and Rsch. Coun., Inst. Mgmt. Cons. (pres. Chgo. chpt. 1981-83, regional dir. 1983-86), Coun. Logistics Mgmt. (dir. Roundtable-Chgo. 1990-94), Assn. of Corp. Growth, The Exec. Club Chgo., Econs. Club, Harvard Club Chgo., Harvard Bus. Sch. Assocs. Chgo. (dir. 1992), Traffic Club Chgo., Standard Club, Northmoor Country Club. Home: 83 Woodley Rd Winnetka IL 60093-3746 Office: Stone Mgmt Corp 208 S La Salle St Chicago IL 60604-1003

STONE, JOHN TIMOTHY, JR., writer; b. Denver, July 13, 1933; s. John Timothy and Marie Elizabeth (Briggs) S.; m. Judith Bosworth Stone, June 22, 1955; children: John Timothy III, George William. Student Amherst Coll., 1951-52, U. Mex., 1952; BA, U. Miami, 1955; postgrad., U. Miami 1955, U. Colo., 1959-60. Sales mgr. Atlas Tag, Chgo., 1955-57; br. mgr. Household Fin. Corp., Chgo., 1958-62; pres. Janeff Credit Corp., Madison, Wis., 1962-72; pres. Recreation Internat., Mpls., 1972-74; pres. Continental Royal Services, N.Y.C., 1973-74; dir. devel. The Heartlands Group/Tryon Mint, Toronto, Ont., Can., 1987-89; spl. cons. Creative Resources Internat., Madison, 1988-90, Pubs Adv. Group, 1990—; spl. cons. art and antiques Treasure Hunt Assocs., 1994—; bd. dirs. Madison Credit Bur., Wis. Lenders' Exchange. Author: Mark, 1973, Going for Broke, 1976, The Minnesota Connection, 1978, Debby Boone So Far, 1980, (with John Dallas McPherson) He Calls Himself "An Ordinary Man", 1981, Satiacum, The Chief Who's Winning Back the West, 1981, Runaways, 1983, (with Robert E. Gard) Where The Green Bird Flies, 1984, The Insiders Guide to Buying Art, 1993, Anyone's Treasure Hunt, 1995; syndicated columnist The Great American Treasure Hunt, 1983-87. Served with CIC, U.S. Army, 1957-59. Mem. Sigma Alpha Epsilon. Republican. Presbyterian. Clubs: Minarani, African First Shotters. Home: 1009 Starlight Dr Madison WI 53711-2724 Office: Pubs Adv Group 1009 Starlight Dr Madison WI 53711-2724

STONE, LISA JANE, data processing executive; b. N.Y.C., June 30, 1944; d. Charles Haskel and Edith (Karlitz) Wald; m. Stephen Paul Stone, Mar. 1, 1969; children: Jason Harris, Erica Lauren, Charles David. BA in Spanish, Beaver Coll., Glenside, Pa., 1965; MBA, Sangamon State U., 1979. Systems analyst Ill. Dept. Pub. Health, Springfield, 1976—. Bd. dirs., sec., v.p., pres. Jr. League, Springfield, 1984-88; bd. dirs. Springfield Pub. Sch. Found., 1981—, sec., v.p., pres., 1988-90; bd. dirs., sec. Habitat for Humanity-Sangamon County, Springfield, 1989-92, Springfield Bd. Jewish Edn., 1981-83; mem. Young Women's Leadership Cabinet, United Jewish Appeal, 1981-84; bd. dirs., v.p. Springfield Jewish Fedn., 1984-87, 88—, campaign chmn., 1989-90, pres., 1992-94, major gifts chair, 1994, nominating chair, 1994, exec. bd., 1995—; bd. dirs., v.p. Temple B'rith Sholom Sisterhood, pres., 1990, treas., 1992-96, fundraising chair, 1997, trustee, 1993, exec. com., 1990, choir, soloist, 1985—, Temple B'rith Sholom, 1990—; human svcs. com. United Way, 1988-92; class agt. Beaver Coll., 1980-85, 90-95; bd. dirs., sec. Springfield Children's Mus., 1994, pres., 1995—; mem. selection com. Mayor's Award for Arts, 1993-95; mem. grant review com. Springfield Area Arts Coun., 1990—; bd. dirs., mem. combined budgeting coun. Coun. of Jewish Fedns., 1994—. Named Vol. of Yr. Sch. Dist. 186, Springfield, 1985, YMCA, 1985, Cmty. Svc. award Ill. Dept. Pub. Health, 1987, Springfield Jewish Fedn., 1991, Temple B'rith Sholom, 1995. Mem. Orgn. for Rehab. and Tng., Hadassah, Go For Broke Investment Club (chair 1992-93), Rotary (Paul Harris fellow 1995). Home: 3013 Mill Bank Ln Springfield IL 62704-1020 Office: Ill Dept Pub Health 535 W Jefferson St Springfield IL 62702-5058

STONE, MICHELLE YVONNE, broadcast executive; b. Trenton, Mich., Dec. 13, 1966; d. Arlie Edd and Arlene Dolores (McAfee) S. BA, Spring Arbor Coll., 1989; MA, Mich. State U., 1996. Music dir. Radio Sta. KNIS, Carson City, Nev., 1989-91; program dir. Radio Sta. WUNI, Saginaw, Mich., 1991-92; news anchor Radio Sta. WMAX, Saginaw, 1992; program dir. Radio Sta. WSAE, Spring Arbor, Mich., 1993—; instr. communication Spring Arbor (Mich.) Coll., 1993—; speaker in field. Author, dir.: (play) I Saw Christmas, 1989. Recipient Mich. Assn. Broadcasters Merit award for excellence in news, 1993. Office: Spring Arbor College Wsae Radio Spring Arbor MI 49283

STONE, ROGER WARREN, container company executive; b. Chgo., Feb. 16, 1935; s. Marvin N. and Anita (Masover) S.; m. Susan Kesert, Dec. 24, 1955; children: Karen, Lauren, Jennifer. BS in Econs., U. Pa., 1957. With Stone Container Corp., Chgo., 1957—, dir., 1968-77, v.p., gen. mgr. container div., 1970-75, pres., chief operating officer, 1975-79, pres., chief exec. officer, 1979—, chmn. bd., chief exec. officer, 1983—; bd. dirs. Morton Internat., McDonald's Corp., Option Care, Inc. Past trustee Glenwood (Ill.) Sch. for Boys; trustee Chgo. Symphony Orch. Assn.; fellow Lake Forest (Ill.) Acad.; mem. bd. overseers Wharton Sch. Bus., U. Pa.; mem. adv. coun. Econ. Devel. Named Best or Top CEO in firm's industry Wall Street Transcript, 1981-86; recipient Top CEO award in Forest and Paper Specialty Products Industry, Fin. World Mag., 1984, Bronze award in Paper and Packaging Category, 1996. Mem. Am. Forest and Paper Assn. (chmn. bd. 1985-86, bd. dirs), Chief Execs. Orgn., Corrugated Industry Devel. Corp. (past pres.), Inst. Paper Sci. and Tech. (former trustee), The Chgo. Com., Mid-Am. Com., Chgo. Coun. Fgn. Rels., Standard Club, Tavern Club, Comml. Club, Econ. Club, Lake Shore Country Club. Republican. Office: Stone Container Corp 150 N Michigan Ave Chicago IL 60601

STONE, STEPHEN PAUL, dermatologist; b. N.Y.C., Aug. 22, 1941; s. C. Sidney and Sylvia (Alpher) S.; m. Lisa Jane Wald, Mar. 1, 1969; children: Jason Harris, Erica Lauren, Charles David. AB cum laude, Tufts U., 1963; MD, NYU, 1967. Diplomate Am. Bd. Dermatology, Nat. Bd. Med. Examiners. Intern Lincoln Hosp., Bronx, N.Y., 1967-68, resident in internal medicine, 1968-69; resident in dermatology Mayo Grad. Sch. Medicine, Rochester, Minn., 1971-74; pres. Dermatology Ctr. Ltd., Springfield, Ill., 1974—; clin. assoc. prof. medicine, former chief dermatology So. Ill. U. Sch. Medicine, Springfield. Editor-in-chief: Dialogs in Dermatology, 1993-97, assoc. editor, 1976-93; contbr. articles to profl. jours. Pres. Springfield Jewish Cmty. Rels. Coun., 1986-88, 90-91; mem. adv. coun. Nat. Jewish Cmty. Rels., vice chair, 1993—, mem. exec. com., 1990-93; bd. dirs. Coun. of Jewish Fedns., 1981-83, 85-95, chmn. small cities nat. com., 1987-88, nat. com. leadership devel., 1981-87, v.p., 1988-91; bd. dirs. Springfield Jewish Fedn., 1976—, v.p., 1977-79, pres., 1980-83; bd. dirs. Springfield Jewish Fedn. Found., 1983-93, pres., 1984-85; bd. dirs. Springfield Zool. Soc., 1983-86, United Way of Greater Sangamon County, 1985-91, Planned Parenthood, Springfield area, 1979-80; trustee, bd. dirs. Temple B'rith Sholom, 1984-90; trustee Lincoln Libr., 1991—, v.p., 1993-94, pres., 1995-96; mem. United Jewish Appeal, Nat. Young Leadership Cabinet, 1977-82, reginal chmn., 1980-81, midwest regional cabinet, 1980-94, midwest project renewal cabinet, 1986-88, region II small cmtys. chmn., 1991-93; sec. B'nai Israel Synagogue, Rochester, Minn., 1973-74; bd. dirs. West Ctrl. Ill. Health Sys. Agy., 1978-83, exec. bd., 1978-84, v.p., 1982-84; mem., treas. Springfield Parks Found., 1992-95. Mem. AMA, Chgo. Dermatological Soc. (plans and policy com. 1982-84), Ill. Dermatologic Soc. (sec.-treas. 1978-80, pres. 1981), Ill. State Med. Soc. (alternate del. 1984-85, coun. on govtl. affairs 1983-86), Internat. Soc. Tropical Dermatology, Noah Worcester Dermatological Soc. (trustee 1987-90, continuing med. edn. com. 1982-83), Sangamon County Med. Soc. (chmn. liason com. 1985), Soc. for Investigative Dermatology, N.Y. Bd. Med. examiners (cert.), Minn. Bd. Med. Examiners, Calif. Bd. Med. Examiners, Ill. Bd. Med. Examiners, Am. Acad. Dermatology (coun. on communicaitons 1980-84, chmn. 1987-89). Lodge: Emes, B'nai Brith (v.p. Springfield, 1975-76, pres. 1976-77). Home: 3013 Mill Bank Ln Springfield IL 62704-1020 Office: 630 N 1st St Springfield IL 62702-4934

STONE, TIMOTHY DONALD, JR., health care executive; b. St. Louis, Mar. 12, 1956; s. Timothy Donald Sr. and Mary Catherine (Stretch) S.; m. Georgia Elizabeth Michael, Sept. 18, 1981; children: Lauren Marie, Ryan Nicholas. BA in bus. mgmt., Webster U., 1985, MA in healthcare adminstrn., 1987. Supr. Jewish Hosp., St. Louis, 1977-86; mgr. Barnes Hosp., St. Louis, 1987-90, dir., 1990-94; v.p. Decatur (Ill.) Meml. Hosp., 1994—. Author: Galaxy of Verse, 1991. Mem. Holy Family Cath. Ch., 1995—. Acad. scholar Webster U., 1983. Mem. Am. Coll. Healthcare Execs. (assoc.), Am. Hosp. Assn., Mo. Hosp. Assn., Creve Coeur Am. Legion, Decatur C. of C., Webster U. Alumni Assn. Republican. Home: 1505 Ashland Ave Mount Zion IL 62549 Office: Decatur Meml Hosp 2300 N Edward St Decatur IL 62529

STONEHILL, LLOYD HERSCHEL, gas company executive, mechanical engineer; b. South Bend, Ind., May 20, 1927; s. Charles Myers and Louise Mary (Reed) S.; m. Jean Carole Herzer, Dec. 30, 1961; children: Mark, Bill, John, Rob. BS in Mech. Engring., Purdue U., 1949. Registered profl. engr., La. Chief engr. Rothschild Boiler & Tank Works, Shreveport, La., 1949-54; chmn. bd. Frankfort (Ind.) Bottle Gas, Inc., 1956—. Patentee in field. Founding prs. Clinton County Hosp. Authority, Frankfort, 1974; membership chmn. Clinton County Hosp. Found., Frankfort, 1982-83, 89. With U.S. Army, 1954-56. Recipient Heroism award Elks Lodge, Frankfort, 1959. Mem. VFW, Nat. Propane Gas Assn. (mktg. awards 1986, 87), Am. Legion, Purdue Alumni Assn. (Clinton County chpt. mem. pres.' coun.), Hudson Inst., Rotary (sec. 1963-65, Paul Harris fellow), Lambda Chi Alpha (sec. 1946-47). Republican. Mem. Christian Ch. Home: 1258 Forest Dr Frankfort IN 46041-3230 Office: Frankfort Bottle Gas Inc 1555 McKinley Ave Frankfort IN 46041-1805

STONER, LEONARD D., novelty company executive; b. Galion, Ohio, Feb. 19, 1950; s. Kenneth M. and Delores I. (Fix) S.; m. Katharine I. Wiese, Feb. 14, 1980; children: Elisha, Cameron, Aaron. AS in Electronics Engring. Tech., Bell Howell U., 1974-76; student, U. Nebr., 1976-80; BS of Bus. Adminstrn. in Tech. Svcs., Bellevue U., 1995. Maintenance stores Keeper Control Data Corp., Omaha, 1978-85; prodn. control mgr. Douglas and Lamason, Richmond, Mich., 1986-87; ops. mgr. Johnson Controls, Lapeer, Mich., 1987-89; project mgr. Dohrman Machine Prodn. Inc., Omaha, 1990-92; mgr. prodn. and inventory control Stuart Entertainment, Inc., Council Bluffs, Iowa, 1995—; assoc. cons. Internat. Purchasing Svc., Dearborn. With USAF, 1970-77. Mem. Am. Prodn. & Inventory Control Soc., Am. Radio Relay League. Home: 8605 Raven Oaks Dr Omaha NE 68152-1827 Office: Stuart Entertainment Inc 3211 Nebraska Ave Council Bluffs IA 51501

STONEROOK, ELEANOR RAE, librarian; b. Clarence, Iowa, Mar. 22, 1929; d. Orba Alvin and Erma Catherine S.; children: Franklin Port, Eleanor Rae. Grad. high sch., Clarence, 1946. Mem. Am. Legion Auxiliary #286 (past pres.). Republican. Methodist. Home: 318 6th Ave #6 Clarence IA 52216

STOPPER, HERBERT, electronics company executive, research educator; b. Hamburg, Germany, Apr. 14, 1931; s. Karl Johann and Helene Petra (Roth) S.; m. Elisabeth Gertrude Tesarczyk, Jan. 14, 1961; children: Andrea Ulrike, Sabina Monica Kesling. M in Elec. Engring., Tech. U., Karlsruhe, Germany, 1955, PhD, 1968. Dept. mgr. AEG-Telefunken, Konstanz, Germany, 1955-62, 65-69; sect. head Gen. Electric, Phoenix, 1962-65; dir. engring. Burroughs Co., Detroit, 1969-82; v.p. R&D Mosaic Sys., Inc., Troy, Mich., 1982-89, Pico Sys., Inc., Toledo, 1994—; chief sci. Environ. Rsch. Inst., Ann Arbor, Mich., 1989-94; adj. prof. U. Detroit, 1974-84, U. Toledo, 1995—. Contbr. articles to profl. jours.; patentee in field. Mem. IEEE (mem. panel confs. 1979-87). Roman Catholic. Home: 1324 Pinetree Trl Harbor Springs MI 49740 Office: 329 14th St Toledo OH 43624

STORCH, JOHN GARY, biomedical engineer; b. Milw., Jan. 10, 1965; s. Jerome Gilbert and Eleanor (Steliga) S.; m. Roseann Myszewski, Aug. 3, 1991. BS in Biomed. Engring., Milw. Sch. Engring., 1988. Counselor Camp Wil-O-Way, Wauwatosa, Wis., 1985-88; biomed. coord. No. Ill. Med. Ctr., McHenry Ill., 1988-90; clin. engr. Criticare Sys., Waukesha, Wis., 1990-93; biomed. engr. St. Mary's Hosp., Mequon, Wis., 1994-95, Milw., 1995; biomed. engr. West Allis (Wis.) Meml. Hosp., 1995—. Vol. Camp Wil-O-Way, Wauwatosa, 1980-84. Mem. Am. Soc. Healthcare Engring. (mem. comm. com., subcom. newsletters 1995), Am. Coll. Clin. Engrs., Assn. Advancement Med. Instrumentation (mem. equipment mgmt. std. com. 1995), Biomed. Assn. Southeastern Wis. (v.p. 1995—), Engring. in Medicine and Biology Soc. (sec.-treas., 1994-95, vice chair 1995—), Soc. Biomed. Equipment Technicians. Home: 2469 N 66th St Milwaukee WI 53213 Office: West Allis Meml Hosp 8901 W Lincoln Ave West Allis WI 53227

STORCK, JOHN W.P., librarian; b. Bklyn., Mar. 9, 1947; s. John Norman and Elizabeth Marian (Gabbert) S. BA, Haverford Coll., 1969; MLS, Kent State U., 1974. Instr. English and music Olney Friends Sch., Barnesville, Ohio, 1969-71; head libr. North Baltimore (Ohio) Pub. Libr., 1974-76; dir. Martins Ferry (Ohio) Pub. Libr., 1976—; bd. dirs. Ohio Libr. Coun., Columbus, 1995, Ohio Pub. Libr. Info. Network, Columbus, 1995—; treas. East Ohio Arts Coun./James Wright Poetry Festival, Martins Ferry, 1981—. Classical music reviewer Wheeling (W.Va.) Intelligencer, 1993—. Mem. Martins Ferry Rotary Club (pres. 1988-89, bd. dirs. 1994—, Paul Harris fellow 1990), Phi Beta Kappa. Democrat. Episcopalian. Home: PO Box 475 Martins Ferry OH 43935 Office: Martins Ferry Pub Libr PO Box 130 20 James Wright Pl Martins Ferry OH 43935

STORFJELL, JOHAN BJORNAR, archaeology educator; b. Ballangen, Norway, Mar. 9, 1944; came to U.S., 1962; s. Arthur Hagrup and Margit (Pedersen) S.; m. Judith Irene Lloyd, July 14, 1963; children: Troy Alan, Thor Leif Erik. BA, Walla Walla Coll., 1966; student, Portland State U., 1969; BD, Andrews U., 1969, PhD, 1983. French and German tchr. Auburn (Wash.) Acad., 1968-69; from instr. to asst. prof. biblical langs., archeology and ancient history Mid. East Coll., Beirut, 1970-73; contract tchr. Theol. Sem. Andrews U., Berrien Springs, Mich., 1977, 78, asst. curator Siegfried H. Horn Archaeol. Mus., 1980-84, editor Siegfried H. Horn Archaeol. Mus. newsletter, 1980-85; asst. prof. archaeology and history of antiquity Seventh-day Adventist Theol. Sem., Berrien Springs, Mich., 1981-85, libr., 1984-85, acting dir. Inst. Archaeology, 1986-89, assoc. prof., 1985-89, prof., 1989—, dir. religion, 1987-93; vol. Wymer Indian Site Excavation Andrews U., 1976; contbg. speaker various lectr. series and seminars on archaeology and religion, 1983-86; cons. Frankinsense and Myrrh exhibit Kresge Art Mus. Mich. State U., 1986; adminstrv. dir. Tell el-Umeiri Excavation, Jordan, 1987; vol. diver underwater archaeol. project South Haven Maritime Mus., 1987; ceramicist Mt. Carmel Project, Haifa, Israel, 1988-90; dir. Grove Park Archaeol. Project, Berrien Springs, 1988-91. Mem. Mich. Maritime Mus., Berrien County Hist. Assn. Rsch. grantee Nat. Endowment for the Humanities, 1978. Mem. Nat. Assn. Profs. of Hebrew, Soc. Biblical Lit., Biblical Archaeology Soc., Israel Exploration Soc., Am. Schs. Oriental Rsch., Adventist Soc. Religious Studies. Home: 4720-1 E Hillcrest Dr Berrien Springs MI 49103-9583 Office: Seventh Day Adventist Theol Sem Andrews U Berrien Springs MI 49104-1500

STORM, SANDY LAMM, secondary education educator; b. Shelbyville, Ill., Aug. 6, 1949; d. Raymond Ralph and Hazel Clara (Sands) Lamm; m. David Michael Storm, Aug. 24, 1968; children: Michael Lee, Marc David, Michelle Kimberly. BS in Edn., Eastern Ill. U., 1967-70, MSEd, 1990-91. Cert. tchr. and sch. guidance, Ill. Substitute tchr. Shelby County, Shelbyville, Ill., 1989-90; home econs. tchr. Shelbyville Sch., Shelbyville, 1990—; counselor, sports cons. Human Excellence, Shelbyville, 1991—. Mem. NEA, Internat. Assn. Neuro-Linguistical Programming, Ill. Edn. Assn. Democrat. Home and Office: P O Box 506 1102 N Long Shelbyville IL 62565

STOTLER, EDITH ANN, grain company executive; b. Champaign, Ill., Oct. 11, 1946; d. Kenneth Wagner and Mary (Odebrecht) S. Student, Mary Baldwin Coll., 1964-66; BA, U. Ill., 1968. Asst. v.p. Harris Trust and Savs. Bank, Chgo., 1969-83; mgr. Can. Imperial Bank of Commerce, Chgo., 1983, sr. mgr., 1983-85, asst. gen. mgr. group head, 1985-88, v.p., dir. utilities, 1988-90; ptnr. Stotler Grain Co., Champaign, Ill., 1990—; pres. Homer Grain Co., 1990—; bd. dirs., mem. exec. compensation com., nominating com. Southeastern Mich. Gas Enterprises, Inc. Mem. investment com. 4th Presbyn. Ch.; past pres. liberal arts and scis. constituent bd. U. Ill., mem. pres.' coun.; mem. Friends of Libr. Bd., U. Ill. Mem. U. Ill. Found., Champaign Country Club, Art Club. Home: 900 N Lake Shore Dr Apt 2106 Chicago IL 60611-1523

STOTT, DIANA ELLEN, social services advocate; b. Cedarville, Calif., Apr. 14, 1934; d. I.A. and Lois A. (Tyeryar) Barber; m. Norman K. Stott, June 29, 1956; children: Charlotte, Russell. BA, U. Calif., Berkeley, 1956; BS in Metaphysics, Am. Inst. Holistic Theology, Berkeley, 1996, Am. Inst. Holistic Theology, 1996; BA in Holistic Theology, Am. Inst. Holistic Theology, 1996. Cert. pre-sch., elem., adult edn. Tchr. Tsuda Sch., Tokyo, 1956, Colegio Americano, Durango, Mex., 1968, Mt. Diablo Schs., Concord, Calif., 1964-74; founder, owner Sunbonnet Sue Templates, Willits, Calif., 1970-89; owner, operator 3T Sheep Ranch, Willits, 1974-89; founder, dir. Animal Crackers PreSch., Willits, 1979-89; dir. of shelter svcs. CATRL, Kimberling City, Mo., 1992—; co-founder Harbor Lights Shelter Svcs., Stone County, Mo., 1994; com. Mo. Coalition Against Domestic Violence, 1992—, Nat. Coalition Against Domestic Violence; sch./cmty. organizer for drug and alcohol prevention, 1993—. Editor newsletter The Quilting Room, 1974-80. Patron Friends of the Libr., Kimberling City, Mo., 1989-94; legis. chmn. Bus. & Profl. Women, Tri-Lakes Area, 1993-94; publicity chmn. Welcome Wagon, Tri-Lakes Area, 1992. Recipient quilting awards Guild of Quilters, 1975-76, Premium Wool award Mendocino County Fair, 1986-88. Mem. AAUW (founder, chmn. Tri-Lakes 1993-94), Bus. and Profl. Women's Club (Woman of Yr. 1996), Kimberling Area C. of C. (rep. 1993-96), Phi Mu, Pi Lambda Theta. Mem. Unity Ch. Office: Christian Assocs of Table Rock Lake Country Club Shopping Ctr Kimberling City MO 65686

STOUGH, CHARLES DANIEL, lawyer; b. Mound Valley, Kans., Dec. 6, 1914; s. Charles Daniel and Narka Pauline (Ice) S.; m. Mary Juliet Shipman, Feb. 13, 1936 (dec. 1986); children: Vera Rubin, Sally Randall Stough Bartlett; m. Edith Gray, Nov. 19, 1988. AA, Kemper Mil. Sch., 1934; AB, U. Kans., 1936, LLB, 1938, JD, 1968. Bar: Kans. 1938, Ill. 1938. City atty. City of Lawrence, Kans., 1947-67, City of Eudora (Kans.), 1949-85; spl. counsel, Douglas County Kans., 1951-85; pvt. practice, Lawrence, 1939-82; with Stough & Heck, 1982-88, Stough & Catt, 1988—; prof. local govt. law U. Kans., 1969-70. Mem. U. Kans. Spencer Mus., 1986; mem. Kans. Ho. of Reps., 1947-55, majority leader, 1951-53, speaker of house, 1953-55. Trustee, U. Kans. Endowment Assn., Nat. Parks and Conservation Assn., Washington; bd. govs. Adams Alumni Ctr. U. Kansas, 1988; bd. dirs. Mus. Natural History, Anthropology Mus., Lawrence Arts Ctr., Kans. State Hist. Soc.; bd. govs. U. Kans Law Soc., 1990. Served to lt. j.g. USNR, 1943-46. Recipient Ellsworth award U. Kans., 1980, Svc. to Mankind award Lawrence Sertoma Club, 1991, Citizen of Yrs. award Lawrence C. of C., 1993; named one of Outstanding Kansans U. Kans., 1986; named to Gallary of Outstanding Kansans, 1986. Trustee Hertzler Rsch. Found., Halstead, Kans., 1983-90. Mem. ABA (charter, chmn. Local Govt. Law Sect. 1964-67, charter World Peace through Law sect.), Kans. Bar Assn. (chmn. world Peace Through Law Sect. 1970-89), Nat. Inst. Mcpl. Law Officers (trustee 1964-65), City Attys. Assn. (exec. com.), Kans. Wildscape Found. (bd. dirs.), Kiwanis (substantial citizen award, 1970), Masons (Lawrence), Rep. Vets. of Kans (state pres. 1959-60). Republican. Congregationalist.

STOUT, DONALD EVERETT, real estate developer, environmental preservationist; b. Dayton, Ohio, Mar. 16, 1926; s. Thorne Franklin and Lovella Marie (Sweeney) S.; m. Gloria B. McCormick, Apr. 10, 1948; children: Holly Sue, Scott Kenneth. BS, Miami U., 1950. Mgr. comml.-indsl. div. G.P. Huffman Realty, Dayton, 1954-58; leasing agt., mgr. Park Plaza, Dayton, 1959-71; pres. various real estate groups; developer 1st transp. ctr. for trucking in Ohio; pres. The Falls Estates, Wright Gate Tech. Ctr., Edglo Land Recycle, pres. Donald E. Stout, Inc. Contbr. articles to profl. jours. Served with U.S. Army 1944-45, USN 1945-46. Named Outstanding Real Estate Salesman in Dayton, Dayton Area Bd. Realtors, in Ohio, Ohio Bd. Realtors, 1961. Lic. real estate broker, Ohio, U.S. V.I.; cert. gen. appraiser, Ohio. Mem. Dayton Area Bd. Realtors (founder, 1st pres. salesman div., gen. appraiser), Nat. Assn. Real Estate Bds., Appraisal Inst., Sr. Residential Appraiser, Soc. Indsl. Office Realtors, Res. Officers Assn., Masons (32 degree), Shriners, Phi Delta Theta. Office: 1344 Woodman Dr Dayton OH 45432-3442

STOUT, EDWARD IRVIN, medical manufacturing company executive; b. Washington, Iowa, Mar. 2, 1939; s. George L. and M. Gladys (Gorsh) S.; m. Dixie Lee Farris (div.); children: Deborah Lee Stout Poole, Cathy Ann Stout Phillips, Angela Fay; m. Marjorie Soria. BS, Iowa Wesleyan Coll., 1960; MS in Chemistry, Bradley U., 1968; PhD in Organic Chemistry, U. Ariz., 1973. Analytical chemist Lever Bros. Rsch., Edgewater, N.J., 1961-62; rsch. chemist USDA, Peoria, Ill., 1962-78; dir. rsch. Spenco Med. Corp., Waco, Tex., 1978-81; pres. S.W. Techs. Inc., Kansas City, Mo., 1981-96, chmn. bd., 1996—; dir. rsch. Chemstar Product Co., Mpls., 1982-86, cons., 1979-81; cons. Stout Supply Co., Ainsworth, Iowa, 1985—; instr. Bradley U., Peoria, 1970-78. Contbr. articles to profl. jours.; patentee in field. Mem. Am. Chem. Soc., Inst. Food Technologists, Am. Assn. Cereal Chemists, Am. Burn Assn., Soc. Plastic Engrs., Mid-Am. Inventors Assn. (v.p. 1988). Home: 10590 Haskins St Shawnee Mission KS 66215-4306 Office: SW Techs Inc 2018 Baltimore Ave Kansas City MO 64108-1914

STOUT, FREDERICK HUBBELL, artist; b. St. Louis, Sept. 30, 1935; s. Frederick Hubbell Stout and Viola Marie (Wulfert) Schumann; m. Patsy Jean McClure, Aug. 10, 1960 (div. Aug. 1969); children: Catherine, Elisabeth; m. Shirley Jean Marie Collette Keefe, Sept. 24, 1983. BFA, Washington U., St. Louis, 1957. Art dir. Perceptual Devel. Labs., St. Louis, 1960-63; ptnr. RSR Assocs., Maplewood, Mo., 1963-85; proprietor Raceart, Manchester, Mo., 1985—. Artist: (historical paintings) Open Wheel Mag., Indpls. 500 Program. LTJG U.S. Navy, 1957-60. Mem. Nat. Automotive Artist Assn. (v.p. 1995). Mem. Libertarian Party. Home: 939 Chestnut Ridge Ballwin MO 63021

STOUT, MARK ORREN, marketing professional; b. Cin., Jan. 28, 1955. BFA, Ohio U., 1978. Dir. food and beverage Hilton Hotel Corp., Cin., 1973-88; v.p. Stout & Gallant Assocs., Cin., 1988—. Past com. chmn. Downtown Coun. City of Cin., 1993. Office: Stout & Gallant Assocs 617 Vine St Ste 1430 Cincinnati OH 45202-2416

STOUT, MAYE ALMA, educator; b. Reliance, S.D., Mar. 3, 1920; d. Jesse Wilbur and Susie Maude (Fletcher) Moulton; m. Dennis William Stout, Jan. 6, 1943; children: Perry Wilbur, David Jay. BA, Dakota Wesleyan U., Mitchell, S.D., 1969. Tchr. Rural Lyman County Sch., Iona/Oacoma, S.D., 1939-42, Vivian (S.D.) Pub. Sch., 1942, Rural Lyman County Sch., Reliance, S.D., 1944-45, Reliance Cons. Dist., 1945-46, 49-51, Ft. Pierre (S.D.) Ind. Sch. Dist., 1954-67, Kadoka (S.D.) Ind. Sch., 1967-82; ret. Asst. editor: Jackson/Washabaugh County History 2, 1989; contbr. articles to publications. Pres. Kadoka Community Betterment Assn., 1987. Mem. Am. Legion Aux. (dist. pres. 1985-89, chmn. com. Dept. Fgn. Rels. 1990-91, dept. chmn. constitution and by-laws com. 1992-93). Republican. Methodist. Address: 6 Poplar St W Po Box 231 Kadoka SD 57543

STOVALL, CARLA JO, state official, lawyer; b. Hardner, Kans., Mar. 18, 1957; d. Carl E. and Juanita Jo (Ford) S. BA, Pittsburg (Kans.) State U., 1979; JD, U. Kans., 1982. Bar: Kans. 1982, U.S. Dist. Ct. Kans. 1982. Pvt. practice, Pittsburg, 1982-85; atty. Crawford County, Pittsburg, 1984-88; gov. Kans. Parole Bd., Topeka, 1988-94; attorney general State of Kansas, Topeka, 1995—; lectr. law Pittsburg State U. 1982-84; pres. Gilston Internat. Mktg., Inc., 1988—. Bd. dirs., sec. Pittsburg Family YMCA, 1983-88. Mem. ABA, Kans. Bar Assn., Crawford County Bar Assn. (sec. 1984-85, v.p. 1985-86, pres. 1986-87), Kans. County and Dist. Attys. Assn., Nat. Coll. Dist. Attys., Pittsburg State U. Alumni Assn. (bd. dirs. 1983-88), Pittsburg Area C. of C. (bd. dirs. 1983-85, Leadership Pitts. 1984), Bus. and Profl. Women Assn. (Young Careerist 1984), Kans. Assn. Commerce and Industry (Leadership Kans. 1983), AAUW (bd. dirs. 1983-87). Republican. Methodist. Home: 3561 SW Mission Ave Topeka KS 66614-3637 Office: Atty Gen Office Kansas Judicial Ctr 2nd Fl Topeka KS 66612*

STOVALL, DORIS GRACE, performing arts association executive; b. Toccoa, Ga., May 26, 1934; d. Clyde and Grace (Adams) Edwards; m. Ernice Stovall, Jr., Oct. 16, 1954 (div. Feb. 14, 1961); children: James Michael, William Brett. Secretarial degree, Harrison-Draughon Sch. Commerce, 1953. Cert. facilities exec. Adminstrv. asst. Am. Cryogenics, Inc., Atlanta, 1965-70, Atlanta Symphony Orchestra, Atlanta, 1970-73; gen. mgr. Long Beach (Calif.) Symphony Orchestra, 1973-74; exec. dir. Long Beach Regional Arts Coun., 1974-76; event sales coord. Long Beach Conv. & Entertainment Ctr., 1976-78; asst. mgr. Music Ctr., L.A., 1978; auditorium mgr. Pasadena (Calif.) Civic Auditorium, 1978-91; distbr. Phonic Ear Hearing Assistance Systems, Atlanta, 1991-92; exec. dir. Embassy Theatre Found., Ft. Wayne, Ind., 1992—. Recipient Commendation, Long Beach City Coun., 1976, Pasadena City Bd. Dirs., 1991. Mem. Internat. Assn. Auditorium Mgrs. (dist. v.p. 1989-91, 1st v.p. 1996-97), Rotary (Paul Harris fellow). Republican. Episcopalian. Office: Embassy Theatre Found 125 W Jefferson Blvd Fort Wayne IN 46802-3010

STOVALL, RICHARD L., academic administrator; b. Springfield, Mo., Mar. 28, 1944; s. Wilbern Lee and Ernestine Patricia (Putman) S.; m. Susannah K. Young; children: Richard Christopher, Stacy Suzanne. BA, SW Mo. State U., 1966; MA, C.W. Post Coll. L.I. U., 1969; PhD, Ohio State U., 1975. Instr. SW Mo. State U., Springfield, 1969-72; asst. prof. U. S.C., Columbia, S.C., 1975-77; prof., asst. dept. head SW Mo. State U., Springfield, 1977—; cons. Cedar Hills High Sch., Dallas, 1986, Andrews Ins. Agy., 1984, Mo. Cosmetology Assn., 1983-84, Springfield Pers. Assn., 1982, Syntex Corp. 1981-82; pub. rels. Halcyon of Dallas, 1988-96, Hawthorne Group of Washington, 1995-96. Contbr. articles to profl. jours. Tabulation room coord. for MSHSAA Dist. Speech Festival; lectr. Springfield Pub. Schs., City Utilities Citizens Adv. Bd.; pres. Boy Scouts Am. With ES USNR-TAR, 1962-69. Mem. Am. Forensics Assn., Speech Communication Assn. Am., So. Speech Communication Assn., Speech Communication Assn. Ohio, Cen. States Speech Assn., Speech and Theatre Assn. Mo., Cherokee Homeowners Assn. (pres.). Episcopal. Home: 1131 E Meadowlark St Springfield MO 65810-2961 Office: SW Mo State U 901 S National Ave Springfield MO 65804-0027

STOVER, DONALD RAE, software engineering executive, retired; b. Ponca City, Okla., Oct. 6, 1934; s. Frederick Edward and Myrtle Inez (Grantham) S.; m. Velma June Kirkpatrick, June 10, 1961; 1 child, Roy James. BSEE with high distinction, U. Iowa, 1956; MA in Math., UCLA, 1959; PhD in EE, U. Iowa, 1968. Mem. tech. staff Hughes Aircraft Co., Culver City, Calif., 1956-59; logic designer Emerson Electric, St. Louis, 1959-62; project engr. Collins Radio Co., Cedar Rapids, Iowa, 1962-71; tech. staff mem. Rockwell Avionics Group, Cedar Rapids, 1971-79, software mgr., 1979-91; mem. Rockwell tech. panel on Artificial Intelligence, 1984-89, on Software, 1989-90; responsible for validated Ada Compiler devel., 1985-91. Contbr. articles to profl. jours. Tennis program coord. YMCA, Marion, Iowa, 1973, canvasser, Cedar Rapids, 1968. Mem. Pi Mu Epsilon, Eta Kappa Nu. Republican. Methodist. Home: 2270 26th St Marion IA 52302-1639

STOVER, P. E., standards engineer; b. Bradford, Ohio, May 30, 1933. A. in Engring., DeVry Tech., Chgo., 1951. Stds. engr. Hobart Bros. Co., Troy, Ohio, 1960—. Mem. Bradford Bd. of Edn., 1961-69. With U.S. Army, 1954-66. Republican. Methodist. Office: Hobart Bros Co Dept 702 600 W Main St Dept 702 Troy OH 45373-2975

STOWE, CAROL ANN, education educator; b. Evanston, Ill., Nov. 25, 1951; d. Irwin and Albina (Podstupka) Orzech; m. Timothy J. Stowe, July 10, 1971; children: Elspeth Liane, Alyssa Joy, Abaigeal Louise. BA, Nat. Coll. Edn., Evanston, 1983, MSEd, 1987; PhD, Northwestern U., 1994. Cert. elem. tchr., gen. adminstr., early childhood tchr., Ill. Tchr. Ctr. for Life, Palatine, Ill., 1978-83; dir. learning resource ctr. Creative Children's Acad., Arlington Heights, Ill., 1983-84; adminstr. Spectrum Ednl. Ct., Palatine, 1985-87; adj. faculty Ctr. for Gifted, Nat. Coll. Edn., Evanston, 1985-89; asst. dir. ctr. ednl. rsch. and svcs. Nat. Coll. Edn., 1988-90; grad. asst. Northwestern U., Evanston, 1989-91, rsch. asst., 1990-94, mgr. tchr. certification, 1991-92, instr., 1992-94; asst. prof. interdisciplinary studies curriculum & instrn. Nat. Coll. Edn. Nat.-Louis U., Wheeling, Ill., 1994-95; dir. Northwestern U. Consortium of Sch. Dists., Evanston, Ill., 1995-96; coord. early childhood edn. Columbia Coll., Chgo., 1996—; advisor Golden Apple Found. for Excellence in Teaching, Chgo., 1990-93; cons. Chgo. Found. for Edn., 1990—; adj. faculty Nat.-Louis U., Evanston, Ednl. Founds., 1993-96. Contbr. articles to profl. jours. Mem. AAUP, APA (affiliate), AAUW, ASCD, Am. Ednl. Rsch. Assn., Am. Ednl. Studies Assn., Assn. for Edn. Young Children, Assn. for Childhood Edn. Internat., Soc. for Rsch. in Child Devel., Assn. Tchr. Educators, Phi Delta Kappa. Home: 514 W Center Rd Palatine IL 60074-1020

STOWE, DAVID HENRY, JR., agricultural and industrial equipment company executive; b. Winston-Salem, N.C., May 11, 1936; s. David Henry and Mildred (Walker) S.; m. Lois Burrows, Nov. 28, 1959; children: Priscilla, David Henry. BA in Econs., Amherst Coll., 1958. V.p. First Nat. Bank Boston, 1961-68; mgr. Deere & Co., Moline, Ill., 1968-71; dir. Deere & Co., Moline, 1971-77, v.p., 1977-82, sr. v.p., 1982-87, exec. v.p., 1987-90, pres., COO, 1990-96; ret., 1996. Home: 4510 5th Ave Moline IL 61265-1904

STOWE, ROBERT ALLEN, catalytic and chemical technology consultant; b. Kalamazoo, July 26, 1924; s. Allen Byron Stowe and Doris Alfreda (Wood) Stowe Weber; m. Dorothea May Davis, Aug. 23, 1947 (div. 1973); children: Michael, Randall, Catherine, Robert; m. Marion June Smith, Oct. 20, 1973 (div. 1980). AB, Kalamazoo Coll., 1948; PhD, Brown U., 1953. Phys. chemist Dow Chem. Co., Midland, Mich., 1952-58; rsch. chemist Dow Chem. Co., Ludington, Mich., 1958-64, sr. rsch. chemist, 1964-69; sr. rsch. chemist Dow Chem. Co., Midland, 1969-72, assoc. scientist, 1972-88; ret., 1988; pres. Bobcat Techs. Ltd., Cross Village, Mich., 1988—; sr. consulting assoc. Omnitech Internat. Ltd., Midland, 1989—; bd. dirs., mem. oper. bd., chief scientist Van Tek Corp. (formerly VF Sales), 1990—; chief exec. scientist Environ. Assessments Ltd., Midland, 1990—. Contbr. articles to sci. jours.; numerous patents in U.S. and fgn. countries. Treas. Ludington Bd. Edn., 1960-63, pres., 1963-68. With USAAF, 1943-45; mem. Nat. Ski Patrol. Recipient Victor J. Azbe award Nat. Lime Assn., 1964. Fellow Am. Inst. Chemists (cert. profl. chemist); mem. Am. Chem. Soc. (program sec. divsn. indsl. and engring. chemistry 1972-82, chmn. 1982-83, councilor 1986—, sec. gen. Catalysis Secretariat 1990, 94, Joseph P. Stewart award 1984), N.Am. Catalysis Soc., N.Am. Thermal Analysis Soc., Mich. Catalysis Soc. (sec.-treas. 1987-88, pres. 1988-89). Home and Office: Box 173 5680 Chippewa Dr Cross Village MI 49723-0173

STOWELL, EWELL ADDISON, botany educator, forestry consultant; b. Ashland, Ill., Sept. 2, 1922; s. Leslie Rockwell and Margaret Virginia (Flatt) S.; m. Barbara Joanne Edwards, June 21, 1953. BEd, Ill. State Normal U., Normal, 1943; MS in Botany, U. Wis., 1947, PhD, 1955. Instr. botany U. Wis., Milw., 1947-49; teaching asst. U. Wis., Madison, 1949-53; from instr. to assoc. prof. biology Albion (Mich.) Coll., 1953-65, prof., 1965-88, prof. emeritus, 1988—, chmn. dept., 1972-76; vis. lectr. U. Wis., Madison, 1963; vis. prof. U. Mich., Ann Arbor, 1964. Co-author lab. manuals; contbr. articles to profl. jours. Cpl. U.S. Army, 1943-46, ETO. Stowell Arboretum at Albion Coll. named in his honor, 1988. Mem. Am. Inst. Biol. Sci., Mich. Acad. Sci., Arts and Letters (chmn. botany sect. 1970-71, 89-90), Mich. Bot. Club (v.p. 1981-85), Mycological Soc. Am., Nat. Audubon Soc., Sigma Xi (local pres. 1961, 73). Methodist. Home: 1541 E Michigan Ave Albion MI 49224-9200 Office: Albion Coll 611 E Porter St Albion MI 49224-1831

STOWERS, JAMES, III, data processing company executive; b. 1958. With Twentieth Century Svcs., Kansas City, Mo., 1979—, pres. Office: 20th Century Cos Inc 4500 Main St Ste 1500 Kansas City MO 64111-1800*

STOWERS, JAMES EVANS, JR., investment company executive; b. Kansas City, Mo., Jan. 10, 1924; s. James Evans Sr. and Laura (Smith) S.; m. Virginia Ann Glasscock, Feb. 4, 1954; children: Pamela, Kathleen, James Evans III, Linda. A.B., U. Mo., 1946, B.S. in Medicine, 1947. Pres. Twentieth Century Svcs., Kansas City, 1956—, Survivors Benefit Ins. Co., Kansas City, 1956-80, 20th Century Investors, Inc., Kansas City, 1957—, Investors Research Corp., Kansas City, 1958—, Twentieth Century Cos. Inc., Kansas City, 1984—; chmn. bd., CEO Twentieth Century Svcs., 20th Century Investors, Investors Rsch. Group, Twentieth Century Cos. Inc., Kansas City, 1993—. Author: Why Waste Your Money on Life Insurance, 1967, Principles of Financial Consulting, 1971, Yes, You Can....achieve financial independence, 1992. Co-founder, pres. Stowers Inst. for Med. Rsch., Kansas City, 1995—. Capt. USAAF, 1943-45; with USAFR, 1945-57. Mem.

Kansas City C. of C., Sigma Chi. Republican. Office: Twentieth Century Svcs 4500 Main St Kansas City MO 64111-1800

STRAIN, HERBERT ARTHUR, III, plastic surgeon; b. St. Louis, Dec. 26, 1954; s. Herbert Arthur Jr. and Roberta (Heller) S.; m. Constance Ann Dziuk, Oct. 10, 1981; children: Nicholas Andrew, Ryan Arthur, Kathleen Elizabeth. BA in Biology, U. Mo., Kansas City, 1977, MD, 1979. Diplomate Am. Bd. Plastic Surgery, Am. Bd. Med. Examiners. Intern, then resident in gen. surgery St. Luke's Hosp., Kansas City, 1979-82; fellow in plastic and reconstructive surgery U. Mo., Kansas City, 1982-84; practice medicine specializing in plastic surgery Kansas City, 1984—; assoc. clin. prof. plastic surgery U. Mo., 1984—; affiliated staff mem. St. Luke's Hosp., Rsch. Med. Ctr., Truman Med. Ctr. West, North Kansas City Meml. Hosp., Trinity Luth. Hosp., Menorah Med. Ctr., Bapt. Med. Ctr., Children's Mercy Hosp.; vis. prof. plastic surgery, Rijeka, Croatia, 1993, 95. Mem. AMA, Mo. Med. Assn., Met. Med. Soc. of Greater Kans., Am. Soc. Plastic and Reconstructive Surgeons, Kansas City Plastic Surg. Soc., Assn. Acad. Chmn. Plastic Surgery, Mo. Assn. Plastic and Reconstructive Surgeons, Am. Coll. Occupational and Environ. Medicine, Lipoplasty Soc. N.Am. Episcopalian. Home: 13033 Catalina St Leawood KS 66209-2394 Office: 4320 Wornall Rd Ste 420 Kansas City MO 64111-3210

STRAND, DEAN PAUL, disc jockey, audio engineer; b. Robbinsdale, Minn., Sept. 23, 1963; s. Gerald Everett and Sharron Elaine (Ubelhoer) S. Grad. high sch., Pine City, Minn., 1981. Lic. radio FCC. Disc jockey Skateland, Osseo, Minn., 1984-88, Glitz DJ Sound & Light Show, Mpls., 1984-89, Sta. KMOJ Radio, Mpls., 1986-88, Today's Music Prodns., Mpls., 1989—; audio engr., instr. Glitz DJ Sound & Light Show, Mpls., 1986-89, Today's Music Prodns., Mpls., 1989—. Actor-dir. (cable TV music video) Tyrant Rocks the Oldies, 1984; disc jockey, audio engr. Fester's Lab, 1985—, Fester's Ravemixes, 1994—. Democrat. Mem. New Age Ch. Home: 3327 Lee Ave N Golden Valley MN 55422-3144 Office: Today's Music Prodns 3327 Lee Ave N Golden Valley MN 55422-3144

STRAND, NEAL ARNOLD, county government official; b. Canton, S.D., Mar. 25, 1924; s. Henry N. and Alma Augusta E. Strand; m. Alice E. Wolden, Aug. 19, 1979. Student, S.D. State U. County auditor Lincoln County, Canton, 1960-62; state senator S.D. State Legislature, Pierre, 1963-69; treas. State of S.D., Pierre, 1969-73; exec. dir. S.D. Assn. County Commrs., Pierre, 1973-89; county commr. County of Pennington, Rapid City, S.D., 1991-94; mem. S.D. Ho. of Reps., 1994—; mem. coun. Bur. Land Mgmt., Miles City, Mont., 1986-92; clk. sch. bd., Canton, 1966. Sgt. U.S. Army, 1945-46, PTO. Republican. Home: 4822 Powderhorn Dr Rapid City SD 57702-4801 Office: Pennington County Courthouse E Saint Joe Rapid City SD 57702

STRANG, CHARLES DANIEL, marine engine manufacturing company executive; b. Bklyn., Apr. 12, 1921; s. Charles Daniel and Anna Lincoln (Endner) S. B.M.E., Poly. Inst. Bklyn., 1943. Mem. mech. engring. staff MIT, 1947-51; v.p. engring., exec. v.p. Kiekhaefer Corp. div. Brunswick Corp., Fond du Lac, Wis., 1951-64; v.p. marine engring. Outboard Marine Corp., Waukegan, Ill., 1966-68; exec. v.p. Outboard Marine Corp., 1968-74, pres., gen. mgr., 1974-80, pres., CEO, 1980-82, chmn., CEO, 1982-90, chmn., 1990-93; bd. dirs., chmn. mgmt. rev. com. Outboard Marine Corp., Waukegan, 1993—. Patentee engine design and marine propulsion equipment; contbr. research papers to sci. publs. Bd. dirs. Poly. Inst. N.Y. Served with USAAF, 1944-47. Mem. Am. Power Boat Assn. (past pres.), Soc. Automotive Engrs., Union Internat. Motorboating (continental v.p. N.Am.), Sigma Xi. Club: Waukegan Yacht. Home: 25679 W Florence Ave Antioch IL 60002-8734

STRANG, PHILIP ANDREW, recording company executive; b. Flushing, N.Y., Nov. 24, 1949; s. Lloyd Robert and Margaret Ann (Bonadurer) S.; m. Tamera Lee Little, Apr. 13, 1991; children: Joseph David, Teresa Margaret. BS, U. Ill., 1972. Pres. Edible Records, Urbana, Ill., 1979-90; founder, pres., co-mgr. Record Svc., Inc., Champaign, Ill., 1969—. Author: (poetry) Hole in the Clouds, 1973; lead singer Rocking Clones, Champaign-Urbana, 1978-82; actor, dir. Station Theatre, Urbana, 1981-91; singer-songwriter; producer compact disc Record Svc. 20th Birthday, 1990. Bd. dirs. Cmty. Devel. Commn., Urbana, 1980-86, Celebration Co., Urbana, 1992—; asst. coach Park Dist. T-Ball, Urbana, 1995. Recipient Cert. of Merit, Am. Songwriting Festival, 1976. Home: 1703 Eagle Ridge Rd Urbana IL 61802 Office: Record Svc 621 E Green Champaign IL 61820

STRANG, WILLIAM M., electrical engineer; b. Washington, May 19, 1944; s. William C. and Janet R. Strang; 1 child, Karyn L. BSEE, Purdue U., 1967; MSEE, U. Mo., 1972. Registered profl. engr. Sr. engr. Emerson Elec., St. Louis, 1968-69; engr. McDonnell Douglas, St. Louis, 1969-71; rsch. asst. U. Mo., Columbia, 1971-72; sales/application engr. GE Co., Atlanta, 1972-75; sr. design engr. GE Co., Burlington, Iowa, 1975-77; application engring. mgr. Beckwith Elec., Largo, Fla., 1977-78; regional sales/mktg. mgr. Baslen Elec., Highland, Ill., 1978-90; regional sales mgr. Dowty Control Tech., Edwardsville, Ill., 1990-92; owner Mktg. and Mgmt. Cons., Ltd., Glen Carbon, Ill., 1988—. Contbr. articles to profl. jours. Mem. IEEE, IEEE Power Engring. Soc. (working group chair 1988—), Masons, Shriner. Office: Mktg and Mgmt Cons Ltd PO Box 787 8 Athena Dr Glen Carbon IL 62034

STRAPP, NAOMI ANN, women's health nurse; b. Mt. Vernon, Ohio, Apr. 26, 1964; d. Harold Perry and Naomi Lysbeth (Houpt) D. AAS, Ctrl. Ohio Tech. Coll., 1984. Cert. neonatal resuscitation; cert. inpatient obstetric nursing Nat. Cert. Corp. Staff nurse med.-surg. Riverside Hosp., Columbus, Ohio, 1984-85; telemetry nurse intermediate care St. Ann's Hosp., Westerville, Ohio, 1986-88, staff nurse labor and delivery, 1988-96, staff nurse high risk antepartum, 1996—. Office: St Ann's Hosp 500 S Cleveland Ave Westerville OH 43081-8726

STRATTON, JULIUS AUGUSTUS, psychologist, consultant; b. Norfolk, Va., July 9, 1924; s. Julius Augustus and Annie (Thornton) S. BS, Hampton U., Va., 1947; MEd, Cornell U., 1957; postgrad., Harvard U., 1966-67, U. Chgo., 1965. Instr., chmn. dept. counseling Roosevelt High Sch., Gary, Ind., 1952-68; assoc. faculty Ind. U. N.W., Gary, 1971-74; research dir. Gary Sch. Corp., 1968-76; v.p. Cornell Urban Cons., Chgo., 1976—. Author: Nonintellectual Factors Associated with Academic Achievement, 1957; contbr. articles to profl. jours. Mem. Nat. Coun. Tchrs. of Math., Assn. for Measurement and Evaluation in Counseling & Devel., Alpha Phi Alpha, Phi Delta Kappa, Sigma Gamma Mu. Democrat. Episcopalian. Office: Cornell Urban Cons PO Box 16651 Chicago IL 60616-0651

STRATTON, RICHARD LEROY, optometrist, educator; b. Springfield, Ill., Oct. 19, 1925; s. Solon Clifford Stratton and Alice Leora (Beeler) Harrison; m. Jeanette Elaine Duda, Aug. 9, 1945; children: Pamela, Richard L. II, Janna, Kenneth W., James T. OD, Ill. Coll. Optometry, 1948. Optometrist Dr. Chas R. Lenz & Assocs., Springfield, 1949-61, Drs. Irvine & Stratton, Springfield, 1961-65; gen. practice optometry Springfield, 1965-89; gen. practice optometry, asst. prof. Sch. Medicine So. Ill. U., Springfield, 1989—; chmn. State Bd. Optometry, Ill., 1972-87. Past officer Sangamon/Menard Coun. on Alcohol and Drugs, Springfield; past pres., bd. mem. Triangle Ctr., Springfield; mem. bd. Blood Bank Springfield, Springfield Eye Bank. Staff sgt. U.S. Army Air Corps, 1943-45, ETO. Mem. Am. Optometric Assn.(contact lens sect.), Internat. Optometric and Optical League, Ill. Optometric Assn. (Optometrist of Yr. 1983), Midstate Optometric Soc., Internat. Assn. of Bds. of Examiners in Optometry. Methodist. Lodges: Lions (pres. 1965-66), Elks (exalted ruler 1966-67). Home: 100 Circle Dr Springfield IL 62703-4807 Office: So Ill U Sch Medicine PO Box 19230 Springfield IL 62794-9230

STRAUB, LARRY GENE, business executive; b. Great Bend, Kans., Aug. 25, 1959; s. Walter Joseph and Barbara Jane (Schartz) S.; m. Julie Ann Miller, May 25, 1985; children: Hillary Ann, Brantley Joseph. BA, Ft. Hays State U., 1988, MS, 1990, postgrad., 1992—; MBA, Friends U., 1995. V.p., CFO Straub Internat., Great Bend, Kans., 1983—; bus. mgr. Lords & Ladys Hair Care, Great Bend, Kans., 1984—; trustee Barton County C.C., Great Bend, 1995—. Pres., bd. dirs. Kiwanis Club, Great Bend; bd. dirs. Great Bend Jaycees. Mem. Western Retailers Assn., Great Bend C. of C. (amb., pres.), Masons (32nd degree, bd. dirs.), Pi Kappa Phi (v.p. recruitment). Republican. Roman Catholic. Home: 3220 Broadway Ave Great Bend KS 67530-3716

STRAUS, HELEN LORNA PUTTKAMMER, biologist, educator; b. Chgo., Feb. 15, 1933; d. Ernst Wilfred and Helen Louise (Monroe) Puttkammer; m. Francis Howe Straus II, June 11, 1955; children: Francis Howe III, Helen E., Christopher M., Michael W. AB magna cum laude, Radcliffe Coll., 1955; MS in Anatomy, U. Chgo., 1960, PhD in Anatomy, 1962. With U. Chgo., 1964—, asst. prof. anatomy, 1967-73, dean of students, 1971-82, assoc. prof., 1973-87, dean of admissions, 1975-80, prof. anatomy and biol. scis., 1987—; bd. govs. U. Chgo. Internat. House, 1987—. Trustee Radcliffe Coll., Cambridge, Mass., 1973-83. Recipient Quantrell Award for Excellence in teaching, U. Chgo., 1970, 87, Silver medal Case Outstanding Tchr. Program, 1987. Mem. AAAS, NCAA (acad. requirements com. 1986-92, chmn. 1990-92, rsch. com. 1996—), Nat. Sci. Tchrs. Assn., Am. Assn. Anatomists, Harvard U. Alumni Assn. (bd. dirs. 1980-83), Phi Beta Kappa (sec., treas. U. Chgo. chpt. 1984—). Home: 5642 S Kimbark Ave Chicago IL 60637-1606 Office: U Chgo 5845 S Ellis Ave Chicago IL 60637-1404

STRAUSS, ERIC JAMES, urban planning educator, lawyer, consultant; b. Chgo., Apr. 14, 1947; s. Harold Richard and Irene (Jacobson) S.; m. Emily Jane Fisher, July 3, 1971; children: Rebecca, Janet, Karen. BA, U. Wis., 1968, PhD, 1981; JD, Northwestern U., Chgo., 1971. Bar: Tex. 1971, Wis. 1972, Kans. 1987. Specialist U. Wis. Extension, Madison, 1971-78; prof. urban planning U. Kans., Lawrence, 1978—; vis. lectr. Queen's U., Belfast, No. Ireland, 1983, U. Wis.-Madison, 1993—, Ind. U., Bloomington, 1995; cons. City of Eudora, Kans., 1988—, City of Hillsboro, Kans., 1992—; site vis. Planning Accrediation Bd., 1986—. Contbr. articles to profl. jours. Recipient Energy Ordinance award City of Lawrence, 1981, Govtl. Tng. award State of Kans., 1984, Profiles of Innovations award Am. Pub. Power Assn., 1986, Pub. Svc. award City Attys. Assn. of Kans., 1992. Mem. Am. Inst. Cert. Planners, Am. Planning Assn. (v.p. Kans. chpt. 1983-85). Democrat. Jewish. Home: 971 E 1338 Rd Lawrence KS 66046-9630 Office: U Kans 415 Marvin Hall Lawrence KS 66045

STRAUSS, JAMES LESTER, investment sales executive, accountant; b. Indpls., Aug. 24, 1944; s. Lester H. and Rosalie (Grossman) S. BS, Ind. U., 1966; MBA, Columbia U., 1968. CPA, Ohio. Acct. Deloitte Haskins & Sells, Dayton, Ohio, 1975-79, Main Hurdman, Cin., 1979-83; mng. exec. Royal Alliance Assocs., Inc., Cin., 1983—; gen. securities prin. Nat. Assn. Securities Dealers; trustee Judah Touro Cemetary Assn.; speaker in field. With USAR, 1968-74. Mem. Am. Inst. CPA's, Ohio Soc. CPA's, Alliance Francaise, Mensa, Cin. Racquet Club. Republican. Home: 2324 Madison Rd Apt 904 Cincinnati OH 45208-2640 Office: Royal Alliance Assocs Inc 414 Walnut St Ste 502 Cincinnati OH 45202-3913

STRAUSS, JEFFREY LEWIS, healthcare executive; b. Balt., Aug. 16, 1963; s. Ronald Jay and Roberta Maude (Henriques) S.; m. Melissa Marie Nieding, Sept. 2, 1990. AA in Acctg., Purdue U., Westville, Ind., 1984, BA in Acctg., 1985. Staff acct. Bon Secour Hosp., Balt., 1986-88, Helix Health Systems/Franklin Sq. Hosp. Ctr., Balt., 1988-89; budget mgr., dir. provider svcs. Rush Prudential Health Plans, Chgo., 1989-93; dir. managed care fin. ops. West Suburban Hosp. Med. Ctr., Oak Park, Ill., 1993-94; dir. West Suburban Health Providers, Inc., Oak Park, 1995—. Mem. Antique Automobile Club Am. (life). Democrat. Jewish. Home: 497 Grosse Pointe Cir Vernon Hills IL 60061-3405 Office: West Suburban Health Providers Inc 1000 Lake St Oak Park IL 60301

STRAWBRIDGE, JESSE RONALD, management consultant; b. Mineral Wells, Tex., Aug. 2, 1950; s. Jesse Elvis and Theresa Erlyne (Logan) S.; m. Beverly Jean Beck, June 27, 1986; 1 child, Tara Michelle. BS, Okla. Christian Coll., 1972; Student, U. Okla., 1974-76, U. Tex., Dallas, 1978-79, Cen. State U., 1984--. Cert. Data Processor, Okla., Tex., Ohio. Chemist Okla. State Dept. Health, 1973-76; sr. programmer Enserch Corp., Dallas, 1976-78; mgr. electronic data processing Ensearch Corp., San Angelo, Tex., 1978-80; data processing specialist Informatics Gen. Corp., Houston, 1980-82; accts. mgr. Informatics Gen. Corp., Dallas, 1982-86; sr. staff mem. The BDM Corp., Ohio, 1986-87; project mgr. RAH Software Technol., Inc., Dayton, Ohio, 1987-89; sr. project mgr. Centech, Inc., Dayton, Ohio, 1989—; program dir. Greater SW Regional Mark IV User Group Dallas, 1983-84; cons., ptnr. Wonder Info. Technol., Dayton, 1988; owner The Concept Beyond, Dayton, 1989—. Author: Book, A C.I.C.S. Primer, 1986; contbr. articles to profl. jours. With U.S. Army 1971-72. Home: 1223 Ringwalt Dr Dayton OH 45432-1738 Office: Century Tech Inc 4060 Executive Dr Dayton OH 45430-1061

STRAWDER, JIMMY LEE, publisher, author; b. Canton, Ohio, July 16, 1954; s. Robert Lee and Roxie Ann (Moyer) S.; divorced. Author J.S. Pub., Carrollton, Ohio, 1988-92; artist Carrollton, 1980—. Author: (poetry) Constantly Changing, 1988. Recipient Photo awards. Democrat. Home: PO Box 434 Carrollton OH 44615-0434

STRAYER, BRETT ALLEN, mechanical engineer; b. Lime Springs, Iowa, Aug. 2, 1958. B, U. No. Iowa, 1980. Mgr. engring. Douglas Corp., Mpls., 1987-92; lead engr. Whirlpool Corp., Benton Harbor, Mich., 1992-94; mgr. mech. engring. E.F. Johnson Co., Waseca, Minn., 1994—. Vol. local ch. Mem. ASME, Soc. Plastics Engrs. Evangelican. Home: 16895 Westbury Ave SW Prior Lake MN 55372-2395 Office: E F Johnson Co M D 5020 Dept 598 299 Johnson Ave SW Waseca MN 56093-2539

STREETER, JOHN WILLIS, information systems manager; b. Topeka, Sept. 3, 1947; s. Jack and Edith Bernice (Vowels) S.; m. Nancy Ann Buck, June 15, 1968 (div. 1985); children: Sarah Beth, Timothy Paine; m. Linda Lea Wenrich Weisbender, Sept. 13, 1986; stepchildren: Michael Leon Weisbender II, Debra Ann Weisbender Johnson, Dawn Marie Weisbender. BS in Computer Sci., Kans. State U., 1973, MBA in Mgmt., 1974; postgrad., Harvard U., 1992. Computer programmer U.S.M.C., 1965-70, Kans. State U., Manhattan, 1970-74; cons., mgr., prin. Am. Mgmt. Systems, Inc., Arlington, Va., 1974-83; systems planning analyst Fed. Nat. Mortgage Assn., Washington, 1983-85; assoc. dir. computing and telecomm. Kans. State U., Manhattan, 1985-91, dir. info. systems, 1991—. Author: Streeter Genealogy, 1985. Staff sgt. USMC, 1965-70. Recipient Navy Achievement medal in data processing Sec. Navy, 1971. Mem. IEEE Computer Soc. (affiliate), Assn. for Computing Machinery, Am. Inst. Cert. Computer Profls., Cause Inc. (Kans. State U. voting mem. rep. 1987—, liaison com. 1987-89), Streeter Family Assn. (bd. dirs. 1988—, v.p. 1990-95), Am. Legion, S.R., KC. Republican. Roman Catholic. Home: 6765 Salzer Rd Wamego KS 66547-9636 Office: Kans State U Info Sys 2323 Anderson Ave Ste 215 Manhattan KS 66502-2947

STREETER, VICTOR JOHN, information systems educator; b. El Paso, Sept. 15, 1940; s. Victor Lyle and Evelyn Maria (Hoody) S.; m. Renate Hundertmark, Dec. 24, 1971 (div. 1976); 1 child, David V.; m. Kazuko Hokama, Oct. 23, 1982. BA, U. Mich., 1961, MA, 1962, PHD, 1969. Rsch. asst. U. Mich. Computing Ctr., Ann Arbor, 1963-67; assoc. prof. U. Mich., Dearborn, 1964—. Exch. scholar German Acad. Exch. Svc., 1962. Mem. IEEE Computer Soc., Assn. for Computational Linguistics, Assn. for Computing Machinery, Soc. for Info. Mgmt., Internat. Bus. Schs. Computing Assn., Assn. for Info. Sys., Upsilon Pi Epsilon. Home: 4980 S Ridgeside Cir Ann Arbor MI 48105 Office: U Mich 4901 Evergreen Rd Dearborn MI 48128-2406

STREETMAN, JOHN WILLIAM, III, museum official; b. Marion, N.C., Jan. 19, 1941; s. John William, Jr. and Emily Elaine (Carver) S.; children: Katherine Drake, Leah Farrior, Burgin Eaves. BA in English and Theatre History, Western Carolina U., 1963; cert. in Shakespeare studies, Lincoln Coll., Oxford (Eng.) U., 1963. Founding dir. Jewett Creative Arts Ctr., Berwick Acad., South Berwick, Maine, 1964-70; exec. dir. Polk Mus. Art, Lakeland, Fla., 1970-75; dir. Mus. Arts and Sci., Evansville, Ind., 1975—; chmn. mus. adv. panel Ind. Arts Commn., 1977-78. Mem. Am. Assn. Museums, Assn. Ind. Museums (bd. dirs.). Episcopalian. Office: Evansville Mus Arts & Scis 411 SE Riverside Dr Evansville IN 47713-1037

STREETO, JOSEPH MICHAEL, catering company official; b. New Haven, Dec. 12, 1942; s. Pasquale Joseph and Marie Veronica (Matazzaro) S. BS, Quinnipiac Coll., Mt. Caramel, Conn., 1964. Mng. dir. spl. events divsn. Culinary Enterprises, Inc., Chgo., 1986—. Co-chmn. telethon Muscular Dystrophy Assn., Chgo., 1989; mem. benefit com., vol. Horizon Hospice, Chgo., 1990, 96; co-chmn. gourmet dinner Blackstone benefit DePaul U.; chmn. comms. com., bd. dirs. Horizon Hospice, 1995—; active Cooks by the Books/The Chgo. Fund on Aging, 1994-95. Home: 253 E Delaware Pl Apt 10E Chicago IL 60611-1733

STREIBEL, BRYCE, state senator; b. Fessenden, N.D., Nov. 19, 1922; s. Reinhold M. and Frieda I. (Broschat) S.; m. June P. Buckley, Mar. 23, 1947; 1 child, Kent. Attended U. N.D., Grand Forks; BS, San Francisco State Coll., 1947. Engr. U.S. Govt., Napa, Calif., 1943-46; dir. Martin Funeral Home, Stockton, Calif., 1946-55; owner Streibel Twin Oaks Farm, Fessenden, N.D., 1955—; state sen. State of N.D., Bismarck, 1981—, pres. pro tempore, 1995, state rep., 1957-75. Author: Pathways Through LIfe, 1983. Chmn. N.D. Legis. Coun., Bismarck, 1969-75; councilman Town of Fessenden, 1976-84; former pres. 20-30 Internat. Group, Sacramento, trustee, 1952-54; dir. World Coun., Sacramento, 1951-53; bd. dirs. U. N.D. Fellows, Grand Forks, 1982-86; pres. Fessenden Airport Authority, 1980—; mem. N.D. Bd. Higher Edn., 1977-81; chmn. N.D. adv. commn. U.S. Commn. on Civil Rights, 1988-93. Recipient Sioux award U. N.D. Alumni Assn., 1976, Benefactor award U. N.D. Found., 1982, William Budge award, 1983, Outstanding Svc. award Jaycees, 1988; named Outstanding Alumnus Theta Chi, 1987. Mem. Masons (Master), Elks, Kiwanis, Shriners, Farm Bur. Republican. Baptist. Home and Office: 226 2nd St N Fessenden ND 58438-7204 Office: PO Box 467 Fessenden ND 58438-0467

STREKAL, DEBRA JOAN, producer, writer, director, actress; b. Cleve., Apr. 3, 1952; d. Carl and Lillian Ida (Levine) Wiener; m. John Strekal, Jan. 28, 1979; 1 child, Alexander. BFA in Theatre cum laude, Ohio U., 1973; MA in Humanities and Higher Edn., Fla. State U., 1975; M in Non-profit Orgns., Case Western Res. U., 1992. Lic. social worker. Admissions dir. ADONEX: External Coll. Degree Ctr., Cleve., 1980; dept. asst. sch. applied social scis. Case Western Res. U., Cleve., 1981-83; v.p. AHZ Computers, Lakewood, Ohio, 1983-84; copy editor health pubns. Harcourt Brace Jovanovich, Berea, Ohio, 1984-85; edt. libr. asst. Cleve. Clinic Found., 1988-90; dir. drama program Oasis, Cleve., 1984-86; communications cons., Cleve., 1985-87; drama tchr. Willoughby (Ohio) Sch. Fine Arts, 1987, drama tchr. Andrews Sch., Willoughby, 1987; speaker in field. Producer, dir., actress numerous theatrical and mus. prodns. specializing in prodn. of original work including Shadows, 1989, A Discarded Rose Petal, 1988, dir. A Lie of the Mind, 1987, All My Sons, 1987, A View From the Bridge, 1986 (Ohio Community Theatre Assn. regional awards for directing, acting, 1986), My Cup Runneth Over, 1985; presenter papers on the homeless. Pres. Euclid Little Theatre, 1986-88; founder Thespians for the Homeless; founder, exec. dir. ESTEEM: Establishing Svcs. to Enhance Esteem and Motivation, 1990; mem. Mayor's Task Force on Homeless Families, 1990, N.E. Ohio Coalition for the Homeless, Cleve., 1990, Substance Abuse Initiative, Cleve. Recipient Point of Light award Pres. George Bush, 1991. Mem. Nat. Coun. Jewish Women (homeless rsch. com.), Nonprofit Mgmt. Assn. Home: 22020 Maydale Ave Cleveland OH 44123-1931

STRENTZ, HERBERT J., educator, journalist; b. Chgo., Dec. 18, 1938; s. Raymond T. and Mildred E. (Savol) S.; m. Joan M. Pflueger, Dec. 17, 1966; children: Tamra, Laura. BA, Fresno (Calif.) State Coll., 1960; MA, Syracuse (N.Y.) U., 1964; PhD, Northwestern U., 1970. Reporter Fresno Bee, 1959-63, Associated Press, Albany, N.Y., 1964-65; asst. prof. sch. journalism U. Ky., Lexington, 1968-69; chmn. dept. journalism U. N.D., Grand Forks, 1969-75; dean sch. journalism Drake U., Des Moines, 1975-88; prof. sch. journalism Drake U., 1975—; dir. grad. studies Drake U., Des Moines, 1993—; exec. sec. Iowa Freedom Info. Coun., Des Moines, 1976—; v.p., dir. Quill and Scroll Found., Iowa City, 1987—. Author: News Reporters and News Sources, 1978, 2d edit., 1989; author, editor Iowa Open Meetings and Open Records Law Handbook, 1979, 1982, 1991, 1993, 94, 96. Chmn. Iowa Citizens Privacy Task Force, Des Moines, 1978-80, Supreme Ct. Adv. Com., Des Moines, 1984-85, Iowa Pub. TV Editorial Integrity Com., Des Moines, 1989—; bd. dirs. Nat. Freedom Info. Coalition, 1993—. With USANG, 1960-66. Named to Hall of Fame Iowa Broadcasters Assn., 1982; recipient Disting. Svc. award Iowa Newspaper Assn., 1989. Mem. Am. Civil Liberties Union, Assn. for Edn. in Journalism and Mass Communication, Soc. Profl. Journalists, Phi Kappa Phi. Democrat. Lutheran. Home: 9306 Greenbelt Dr Des Moines IA 50322-7448 Office: Sch Journalism and Mass Communication Drake U Des Moines IA 50311

STRESEN-REUTER, FREDERICK ARTHUR, II, metal fabricating company executive; b. Oak Park, Ill., July 31, 1942; s. Alfred Procter and Carol Frances (von Pohek) S.-R.; cert. in German, Salzburg (Austria) Summer Sch., 1963; BA, Lake Forest Coll., 1967. Mgr. advt. Stresen-Reuter Internat., Bensenville, Ill., 1965-70; mgr. animal products mktg. Internat. Minerals & Chem. Corp., Mundelein, Ill., 1971-79, dir. animal products mktg., 1979-87; dir. communications Pitman-Moore, Inc. subs. IMCERA, Inc., 1987-92; pres. I&A Metal Works, Inc., Racine, Wis., 1993—. Trustee governing mem. Libr. Internat. Rels., Chgo., 1978; founding pres. Woodstock (Ill.) Mozart Festival, 1988-90; bd. dirs. Woodstock Opera House, Ill. Arts Alliance Found., Ill. Arts Alliance, 1993-94. Decorated Cross of Honor for sci. and art (Austria), 1995. Mem. Rolls Royce Owner's Club. Episcopalian. Club: Sloane (London), The Chgo. Farmer's Club. Contbr. articles to profl. jours. Home: Tryon Grove Farm PO Box 218 Ringwood IL 60072-0218

STREVEY, GUY DONALD, insurance company executive; b. Norcatur, Kans., Mar. 8, 1932; s. Guy Ross Strevey and Maxine Elizabeth (Johnson) Gruse.; m. Irene Franklyn Corey Nov. 7, 1953; children: Richard A., Janet E. Bolte, Philip E., Melinda K. Halvorson. BS, Okla. A&M U., 1953. Cert. CFP, CLU, ChFC. Agt. Penn Mut. Life Ins. Co., Tulsa, 1955-62, regional mgr., 1958-62; gen. agt. Penn Mut. Life Ins. Co., Omaha, 1962-69, agt., 1969—; ptnr. Strevey and Assocs., Omaha, 1979—; agt. Various Cos., Omaha, 1979—; registered rep. Hornor, Townsend & Kent, Inc., Omaha, 1985—; Deacon Hillcrest Bapt. Ch., Omaha, 1960, Westside Bapt. Ch., Omaha, 1978, chmn. 1979-81. 1st lt. U.S. Army, 1953-55. Mem. NALU (Nat. Quality award 1970-94), Am. Soc. CLUs, Omaha Assn. Life Underwriters, Million Dollar Roundtable (life), Inst. CFPs (pres.-elect N.E. chpt. 1996—). Republican. Home: 3518 S 106th St Omaha NE 68124-3614 Office: Strevey & Assocs 11422 Miracle Hills Dr Ste 508 Omaha NE 68154-4420

STREZLEC, JOHN ALLEN, social worker; b. Astoria, Oreg., Aug. 26, 1945; s. Bernard Leo Strezlec and Donna Christine (Reynolds) Strezlec Ulrich; m. Sharon Lee Kassner, June 20, 1970; children: Michael J., Robert S., Megan C. BS, U. Wis., Stevens Point, 1968; MSW, U. Wash., 1971. Cert. social worker; bd. cert. diplomate social work. Social worker Luth. Social Svcs. Wis./Upper Mich., Stoughton, 1971-75; clin. instr. Dept. Family Medicine, U. Wis., Madison, 1987—; coord. pediatric adolescent svcs. U. Hos. and Clinics, Madison, 1976-80, dir. dept. social work, 1980-87; mgr. mental health Group Health Coop., Madison, 1987—; lectr. social wk. U. Wis., Madison, 1979-86; cons. Southwest Health Ctr., Platteville, Wis., 1981-87, Lancaster (Wis.) Living Ctr., 1986-87. Mem. NASW. Home: 1138 N Westfield Rd Madison WI 53717-1038 Office: Group Health Coop 8202 Excelsior Dr Madison WI 53744-4971

STRICK, CYNTHIA LEE, elementary education educator; b. Dennison, Ohio, Jan. 15, 1962; d. John Lee and Donna Elaine (Ross) Kilpatrick; m. Thomas Stephen Strick, Dec. 28, 1985; children: Curtis Russell, Victoria Lynn. BS in Edn., Akron U., 1984; M of Curriculum Instrn., Ashland U., 1995. Day care tchr./aide U. Akron, 1980-84; developmentally handicapped tchr. Lorain (Ohio) City Schs., 1984-90, 6th grade tchr., 1990—. Mem. Internat. Reading Assn. Roman Catholic. Home: 212 Moorewood Ave Avon Lake OH 44012-1418 Office: Longfellow Elem Sch 1800 Cleveland Blvd Lorain OH 44052

STRICKLER, IVAN K., dairy farmer; b. Carlyle, Kans., Oct. 23, 1921; s. Elmer E. and Edna Louise (James) S.; m. Madge Lee Marshall, Aug. 7, 1949; children—Steven Mark, Thomas Scott, Douglas Lee. B.S., Kans. State U., 1947. Owner, mgr. dairy farm Iola, Kans., 1947—; tchr. farm tng. to vets. World War II, 1947-54; judge 1st and 2d Nat. Holstein Show, Brazil,

1969-70, Internat. Holstein Show, Buenos Aires, 1972, Nat. Holstein Show, Ecuador, 1978, 10th Nat. Holstein Show, Brazil, 1980; judge Holstein Show, Australia, Mex. and Argentina, 1981, Lang Lang, 1984; judge Adelaide (Australia) Royal Show, 1987; pres Mid-America Dairymen, Inc., Springfield, MO, 1981—; appointed chmn. Nat. Dairy Bd., 1985-90; dairy leader 4-H Club, 1962-75; dir. Iola State Bank; rep. U.S. Internat. Dairy Symposium, 1994, Belo Horinzote, Brazil. Trustee Allen County Community Jr. Coll.; mem. agr. edn. and rsch. com. Kans. State U., U.S. Agrl. Trade and Devel. Mission, Algeria and Tunisia, 1989. With USN, 1942-46, PTO. Recipient Silver award Holstein Friesian Assn. Brazil, 1969, Top Dairy Farm Efficiency award Ford Found., 1971, Master Farmer award Kans. State U. and Kans. Assn. Commerce and Industry, 1972, Gold award Holstein Friesian Assn. Argentina, 1972, Richard Lynng award Nat. Dairy Bd., 1990, award of merit Gamma Sigma Delta, 1987; named Man of Yr. World Dairy Exposition, 1978; portrait in Dairy Hall of Fame Kans. State U., 1974; Guest of Hon. Nat. Dairy Shrine, 1985. Mem. Mid Am. Dairymen (sec. corporate bd. 1971-81, pres. 1981—), Holstein Friesian Assn. Am. (nat. dir. 1964-72), Dairy Shrine (nat. dir. 1971-81), United Dairy Industry Assn. (dir. 1971—), Nat. Holstein Assn. Am. (pres. 1979-80), Alpha Gamma Rho. Mem. Christian Ch. (elder, bd. dirs.). Club: Nat. Dairy Shrine (pres. 1978). Home: PO Box 365 Iola KS 66749-0365 Office: Mid America Dairymen Inc 3253 E Chestnut Expy Springfield MO 65802-2540

STRICKLIN, REBECCA ELLEN, chemistry educator; b. New Albany, Ind., Feb. 4, 1954; d. Ernest and Mary Ellen (Burnett) S. BS in Chemistry, Ohio U., 1974, MS in Inorganic Chemistry, 1976, EdD in Sci. Edn., 1993. Grad. asst. Ohio U., Athens, 1974-76; quality control lab. technician Procter and Gamble, Cin., 1978; chemistry tchr. Oak Hills High Sch., Cin., 1976—; chemistry instr. Cin. Tech. Coll., 1978-82; vis. instr. chemistry Miami U., Middletown, Ohio, 1989, Hamilton, 1989—; presenter in field; mem. Sci. Com. Greater Cin., 1980-86, chair tchrs. resources and safety com. 1980-82. Author News for the Classroom column Am. Chem. Soc. Newsletter. Mem. curriculum coun. Ohio U., 1975-76, mem. individual course subcom., 1975-76; advisor Future Tchrs. Am., 1976-79; v.p. local PTA, 1977-79. Tandy Tech. scholar, 1995; grantee Dreyfus Outreach, 1986; Woodrow Wilson Found. fellow, 1985; recipient Catalyst award Chem. Mfrs. Assn., 1995. Mem. NEA, ASCD, AAAS, Am. Chem. Soc. (high sch. planning com. Cin. sect., scholarships and grants com. 1987, ednl. svc. chair 1989—), Am. Inst. Chemists, Am. Nuclear Soc., Cin. Hist. Soc., Nat. Sci. Tchrs. Assn. (sci. edn. coun. Ohio), Ohio Acad. Sci. (v.p. sci. ednl. sect. 1989-90, chair coun. S.W. Ohio dist. 1989-92), Ohio Edn. Assn., Southwestern Ohio Edn. Assn., Oak Hills Edn. Assn., World Wildlife Fedn. Democrat. Office: Oak Hills High Sch 3200 Ebenezer Rd Cincinnati OH 45248-4038

STRIGGOW, KEITH GREGORY, education educator, provost; b. Chgo., Nov. 23, 1941; s. Chester Gustav and Charlotte Anna (Mollenhauer) S.; m. Carol Lou Sorensen, Dec. 17, 1966; 1 child, Kay Ellen. AB, Harvard U., 1965; MDiv, Garrett Sem., 1968; MA, Northwestern U., 1971, PhD, 1973. Chair behavioral scis. dept. Lakeland Coll., Sheboygan, Wis., 1973-80, tenured prof. sociology, 1979, chair social scis. divsn., 1980-81, dean of the coll., 1981-93, provost, 1993—. Adult edn. instr. First United Luth. Ch., Sheboygan, 1985-93; chair Mayor's Task Force on Downtown Renewal, Sheboygan, 1986, C. of C. Leadership Devel. Program, Sheboygan, 1990-92. Mem. Am. Assn. Higher Edn., Soc. for the Sci. Study of Religion. United Ch. of Christ. Home: 1701 N 25th St Sheboygan WI 53081 Office: Lakeland Coll PO Box 359 Sheboygan WI 53082

STRIGLIS, DIMOS, company executive; b. Athens, Greece, July 5, 1959; came to the U.S., 1980; MA in Mech. Engring., W.Va. Inst. Tech., 1987. Sr. R&D engr. DynaTherma, Balt., 1988-89, Bowles Fluidics Corp., Balt., 1989-91, The Campbell Group, Harrison, Ohio, 1991-95; Mid-East European ops. dir. The Campbell Group, Harrison, 1995—. Mem. ASME.

STRINGHAM, EVELYN L., financial services executive; b. Vinton, Iowa, Aug. 5, 1930; d. Victor Vern and Leora Evelyn (Moyer) Uthoff; m. Walter Gene Stringham, Feb. 25, 1967; children: Willard Garrett. Pediat. dept. Mercy Hosp., Mason City, Iowa, 1948-50; tech. Kans. U. Med. Ctr., Kansas City, 1957-62; from office mgr. to fin. mgr. Cardiovascular Cons., Inc., Kansas City, 1962—. Mem. Am. Inst. Profl. Bookkeepers. Democrat. Home: 320 4th Ave Bucyrus KS 66013 Office: Cardiovascular Cons Inc 4330 Wornall Rd Ste 2000 Kansas City MO 64111

STROBECK, CHARLES LEROY, real estate executive; b. Chgo., June 27, 1928; s. Roy Alfred and Alice Rebecca (Stenberg) S.; m. Janet Louise Halverson, June 2, 1951; children: Carol Louise, Nancy Faith, Beth Ann, Jane Alison, Jean Marie. BA, Wheaton (Ill.) Coll., 1949. Mgr. Sudler & Co., Chgo., 1949-50, ptnr., 1951-63; chmn. bd. Strobeck, Reiss & Co., Chgo., 1964-82; pres. Strobeck Real Estate, Chgo., 1983-94, chmn. bd. dirs., 1994—; bd. dirs. Am. Slide-Chart Corp., Carol Stream, 1971—. Bd. dirs. YMCA, Ill. Humane Soc., 1982—; pres. Chgo. Youth Ctrs., 1981-83, bd. dirs., 1985—; trustee Wheaton Sanitary Dist., 1976-91. Mem. Inst. Real Estate Mgmt. (pres. 1970-71), Am. Soc. Real Estate Counselors, Mental Health Assocs. Greater Chgo. (bd. dirs.), Am. Arbitration Assn., Chgo. Club, Chgo. Golf Club (bd. dirs. 1984-86), Union League Club (pres. 1975-76), Mid-Am. Club, Laurel Oak Country Club, Long Boat Key Club, Mill Creek Club, Lambda Alpha. Republican. Home: 1 S 751 Hawthorne Ln Wheaton IL 60187 Office: 104 S Michigan Ave Chicago IL 60603

STROBEL, RUDOLF GOTTFRIED KARL, biochemist; b. Kiessling Thuringia, Germany, Feb. 7, 1927; came to U.S. 1958, naturalized 1968; s. Karl M.F. and Frida L. (Weber) S.; m. Josefine M. Haunschild, Sept. 2, 1958; children: Wolfgang R., Christine B., Oliver K., Roland W. B. Sci., U. Regensburg, Bavaria, 1953; Dipl. Chem., U. Munich, Fed. Republic Germany, 1956, Ph.D., 1958. Biochemist, The Procter & Gamble Co., Cin., 1958-75, group leader, 1975-81, sect. head, 1981-93; ind. cons. in beverage tech., chemistry, physiology, 1993—. Patentee in fields of flour tech., emulsion tech., coffee aroma and flavor tech., tea and fruit juices. Mem. Am. Chem. Soc., Assn. Scientifique Internat. du Café, Internat. Apple Inst. Avocations: farming, gardening, pomology, machine design, classical music.

STROBL, RUDOLF, business strategist; b. Eisenerz, Austria, Nov. 9, 1954; came to U.S., 1979; s. Johann Loberauer and Liselotte (Strobl) Beck; m. Margaret G. Saville, May 31, 1986; 1 child, Beatrice Saville. BA, BS, Eisenerz Coll., 1973; PhD in Telecommunications, U. Salzburg, Austria, 1979. Dir. data communications rsch. tech. The Yankee Group, Boston, 1983-84; product mgr. Software Rsch. Corp., Natick, Mass., mgr. bus. planning, sales cons. software, 1984-86; sr. mgmt. cons. Arthur D. Little, Cambridge, Mass., 1986-87; mgr. strategy and bus. devel. GE Transp. Systems, Erie, Pa., 1987-90; dir. backhoe loader and forklift product lines J.I. Case Constrn. Equipment Group subs. Tenneco, Racine, Wis., 1990-92, dir. corp. devel., 1992; prin. strategy consulting Gemini Consulting mem. of Cap Gemini SoGeti (CGS), Chgo., 1992-93; mng. dir. The Windpoint Group, Strategy Cons. and Interim Corp. Mgmt., Racine, Wis., 1993—; bd. dirs. Daffodill Hill Inc. Mem. Strategic Leadership Forum. Home: 5225 Hunt Club Rd Racine WI 53402-2334 Office: The Windpoint Group Racine WI

STRODA, JURGEN H., owner small business; b. Hamburg, Germany, Sept. 27, 1946; came to U.S., 1950; AS, Muscatine (Iowa) C.C., 1970; BS, U. Wyo., 1972; postgrad., C.S.I., 1977. Sr. service engr. Banding Triangle, Davenport, Iowa, 1978-86; pres. Jurgen Stroda, Inc., Muscatine, Iowa, 1986—; owner Gun Shop, Muscatine, 1992—. Inventor: holds 7 patents in retreading equipment. Vol. Starter Kids Gun Control.

STRODER, BARBARA G., federal agency auditor, consultant; b. Gary, Ind., Jan. 19, 1941; d. Clayton and Susie Williams. BS, Roosevelt U., 1970; postgrad., Govs. State U., 1995—. Revenue agent IRS, Chgo., 1989—; cons. College Grants, Gary, 1989—; area v.p., exec. bd. dirs. Nat. Treas. Employees Union, Chgo., 1993-95. Mem. NAFE, Froebel H.S. Alumni Assn. (exec. bd. dirs. 1992-95). Home: PO Box 4072 Mission Viejo CA 92690

STROGER, TODD H., state legislator. BA, Xavier U.; postgrad., DePaul U. Adminstrv. asst. Chgo. Park Dist.; jury supr. Cook County Jury Commn.; statistician Office of Chief Judge Cook County Cir. Ct.; 2nd v.p. Young Dems. of Ill.; Ill. state rep. Dist. 31. HOme: 8534 S Blackstone Ave Chicago IL 60619-6527*

STROH, RAYMOND EUGENE, personnel executive; b. Bloomington, Ill., Aug. 13, 1942; s. Harry William and Felcie Cleo (Weaver) S.; m. Peggy Jane Whitacre, June 12, 1966; children: Rebecca Jane, David Ray. BA, So. Ill. U., 1966, U. Ill., 1977. Pers. technician Ill. Dept. Mental Health, Springfield, Ill., 1966-67; pers. officer Andrew McFarland Mental Health Ctr., Springfield, 1967-68, Manteno (Ill.) State Hosp., 1968-69; chief pers. officer Ill. Dept. Law Enforcement, Springfield, 1969-75, Ill. Dept. Revenue, Springfield, 1975-81, Ill. Dept. Mental Health, Springfield, 1981-82; pers. exec. Ill. Dept. Cen. Mgmt. Svcs., Springfield, 1982—; state govt. chmn. U.S. Savs. Bond Campaign, Springfield, 1978-82. Bd. dirs. Consumer Credit Counseling Svc., Springfield, 1988-94, sec., 1994; coun. exec. bd. Boy Scouts Am., Springfield, 1987—, v.p., 1987-94, 96—, dist. commr., 1979-86, unit commr., 1970-79; bd. dirs. Ill. State Employees Credit Union, 1984-85. Recipient Patriotic Svc. awards U.S. Treasury Dept., 1979-82, Silver Beaver award Boy Scouts Am., 1987, Dist. award of merit, 1981, Area Pres. awards, 1985, 86, Scouters Key award, 1976. Mem. NRA, U. Ill. Alumni Assn., So. Ill. U. Alumni Assn., Exptl. Aircraft Assn., Aircraft Owners and Pilots Assn., Ponce De Leon Inlet Lighthouse Assn., Nat. Geog. Soc., Cornell U. Lab. of Ornithology Project Feederwatch, Abraham Lincoln Gun Club, Appalachian Trail Conf., Union County (Tenn.) Hist. Soc., Bass Anglers Sportsman Soc., Lionel Railroader Club, Wabash R.R. Hist. Soc., Theta Delta Chi. Republican. Lutheran. Home: 2111 Warwick Dr Springfield IL 62704-4147 Office: Ill Dept Cen Mgmt Svcs 501 Stratton Ofc Bldg Springfield IL 62706

STROHMAIER, THOMAS EDWARD, designer, educator, photographer; b. Cin., Aug. 26, 1943; s. Charles Edward and Margaret Mary (Meyers) S.; m. Margaret Ann Haglage, June 7, 1980; children: Paige Maura, Edward Michael, Phoebe Greer, Michael Thomas. BFA, U. Cin., 1969, MFA, 1973. Lectr. in design U. Cin. City Outreach Program, 1975-76; instr. in design U. Dayton, Ohio, 1976-80, asst. prof. design, 1980-83; pres. Strohmaier Design, Cin., 1983—; cons. City Arts Corp., Cin., 1977-78, City Beautiful Program, Dayton, 1982; adj. prof. design U. Cin., 1983—, mem. lecture outreach program, 1995. Designer urban wall projects Ohio Arts Council, Columbus, 1974, Corbet award, Cin., 1977; patentee in field. U. Dayton grantee, 1980. Mem. Contemporary Arts Ctr., Design, Architecture, Art and Planning Alumni Com., Internat. Freelance Photographers Orgn., Associated Photographers Internat., U. Cin. Decade Club. Republican. Roman Catholic. Club: Decade. Home: 7311 Redondo Ct Cincinnati OH 45243-1247 Office: Strohmaier Design 4612 Kellogg Ave Cincinnati OH 45226

STROHMEIER, KARL WILHELM, pharmaceutical industry executive; b. Chgo., July 22, 1957; s. Wilhelm and Gertrude (Brandmaier) S.; m. Julie Marie McClure, Nov. 7, 1981; children: Sofie Josephine, Stephen Lawrence, Wilhelm Karl. MS in Pharmacy, U. Ill., Chgo., 1980; MBA, U. Chgo., 1985. Registered pharmacist, Ill. Pharmacist U. Chgo. Hosps. and Clinics, 1980-85; fin. analyst Marion Merrell Dow, Kansas City, Mo., 1985-86, sr. fin. analyst, 1986-87, sr. market rsch. analyst, 1987-89, strategic bus. analysis mgr., 1989-91, mgr. global comml. devel., 1991-92; dir. global comml. devel., 1992-94; dir. corp. bus. analysis Hoechst Marion Roussel, Kansas City, 1994-95; bus. mgr. Teva Marion Partnership, Kansas City, 1995—. Pres. Old Surrey Owners Assn., Hinsdale, Ill., 1984; mem. Capital Funds Dr. Ch. of Pilgrimage, Overland Park, Kans., 1991, mem. pastor parish rels. com., 1994—. Office: Hoechst Marion Roussel PO Box 9627 Kansas City MO 64134-0627

STROHMER, GERHARD OTTO, mathematics educator; b. Fulda, Hessen, Germany, Mar. 2, 1953; came to U.S., 1986; s. Willi and Rosemarie (Ackermann) S.; m. Margaret Schutter, May 7, 1988; children: Daniel, Andrew. Diplom-Mathematiker, U. Göttingen, 1976, doctor rer. nat., 1978. Asst. Inst. of Tech., Aachen, Germany, 1977-86; asst. prof. math. U. Iowa, Iowa City, 1986-88, assoc. prof., 1988—. Contbr. articles to profl. jours. Mem. Deutsche Mathematiker Vereinigung, Am. Math. Soc. Office: Univ of Iowa Dept Of Math Iowa City IA 52242

STROM, ELWOOD MALCOLM, soil and water conservationist, consultant; b. Dwight, Kans., Mar. 24, 1918; s. Elwood Earnest Magnus and Albena Aurora Johanna (Rundquist) S.; m. Edith Kelley, Dec. 17, 1942; children: Byron Malcolm, Katharine Elaine Strom-Renes. BS in Agr., Kans. State U., 1939. Cert. agronomist, Am. Registry Cert. Profls. Work unit conservationist USDA/Soil Conservation Svc., Kadoka, S.D., 1946-50, 52-54; area conservationist USDA/Soil Conservation Svc., Mobridge, S.D., 1955-60, Pierre, S.D., 1960-64; asst. state conservationist USDA/Soil Conservation Svc., N.H., 1964-69; team leader soil and water conservation project USAID, Nigeria, West Africa, 1970-71; asst. state conservationist USDA Soil Conservation Svc., N.H., 1972-73; cons. agronomist Agri Svc. Assocs., Manhattan, Kans., 1975-87. Mem. Rural Life Fellowship, Kans. East Conf. United Meth. ch., pres. 1993-95, mem. hunger commn., chmn. round-up com., 1984-89; bd. dirs. Heifer Project Internat., Kans., 1989—; dir. Morris County Kans., Hist. Soc., Council Grove, 1988—, Moris County Conv. and Visitors bur., Council Grove, 1994—; pres. Meml. Hosp. Assn., Kadoka, S.D., 1953-54; bd. dirs. Bapt. Hosp., Winner, S.D., 1964; scoutmaster Boy Scouts Am., Kadoka, 1947-50. With U.S. Army, 1941-45 ETO, Capt. U.S. Army, 1950-51. Recipient Goodyear Conservation award Goodyear Tire Co., Morris County Kans. Conservation Dist., 1980, Conservation award Kans. Bankers Assn., 1986; named Area Rep. of Yr. Photographic Soc. Am., 1994. Mem. Soil and Water Conservation soc. (sec. S.D. chpt. 1950, pres. 1953), S.D. sect. Soc. Range Mgmt. (chmn. 1960). Republican. Home and Office: 1545 D Ave Dwight KS 66849

STROM, LYLE ELMER, federal judge; b. Omaha, Nebr., Jan. 6, 1925; s. Elmer T. and Eda (Hanisch) S.; m. Regina Ann Kelly, July 31, 1950; children: Mary Bess, Susan Frances, Amy Claire, Cassie A., David Kelly, Margaret Mary, Bryan Thomas. Student, U. Nebr., 1946-47; AB, Creighton U., 1950, JD cum laude, 1953. Bar: Nebr. 1953. Assoc. Fitzgerald, Brown, Leahy, Strom, Schorr & Barmettler and predecessor firm, Omaha, 1953-60, ptnr., 1960-63, gen. trial ptnr., 1963-85; judge U.S. Dist. Ct. Nebr., Omaha, 1985-87, chief judge, 1987-95, sr. judge, 1995—; adj. prof. law Creighton U., 1959-95, prof., 1996—; mem. com. pattern jury instrns. and practice and proc. Nebr. Supreme Ct., 1965-91; spl. legal counsel Omaha Charter Rev. Commn., 1973. Mem. exec. com Covered Wagon Coun. Boy Scouts Am., 1953-57, bd. trustees and exec. com. Mid-Am. Coun., 1988—; chmn. bd. trustees Marian High Sch., 1969-71; mem. pres. coun. Creighton U., 1990—. Ensign USNR and with U.S. Maritime Svc., 1943-46. Fellow Am. Coll. Trial Lawyers, Internat. Acad. Trial Lawyers; mem. ABA, Nebr. Bar Assn. (ho. of dels. 1978-81, exec. coun. 1981-87, pres. 1989-90), Omaha Bar Assn. (pres. 1980-81), Am. Judicature Soc., Midwestern Assn. Amateur Athletic Union (pres. 1976-78), Alpha Sigma Nu (pres. alumni chpt. 1970-71). Republican. Roman Catholic. Lodge: Rotary (pres. 1993-94). Office: US Dist Ct PO Box 607 Omaha NE 68101-0607

STROME, STEPHEN, distribution company executive; b. Lynn, Mass., June 20, 1945; s. David and Rose (Cantor) S.; m. Phyllis Ruth Fields, Jan. 14, 1967; children: Michael, Rochelle. BA, Hillsdale (Mich.) Coll., 1967; MBA, Wayne State U., 1968. Trainee KMart Corp., Detroit, 1968-69; mgr. work measurement KMart Corp., Troy, Mich., 1970-73; mgr. tng., edn. Fruehauf Corp., Detroit, 1974-76, regional mgr. labor relations, 1976-78; dir. ops. Handleman Co., Clawson, Mich., 1978-80, account exec., 1980-82; v.p. computer software div. Handleman Co., Troy, 1983-85, pres. computer software/video div., 1986-87, exec. v.p., 1987-89, exec. v.p., chief oper. officer, 1990, pres., CEO, 1991—. Home: 4597 Kiftsgate Bnd Bloomfield Hills MI 48302-2331 Office: Handleman Co 500 Kirts Dr Troy MI 48084-5225

STRONG, DOROTHY SWEARENGEN, educational administrator; b. Memphis, Feb. 3, 1934; d. John Harrison and Willie Beatrice (Hawkins) Swearengen; m. Joseph Nathaniel Strong, Mar. 19, 1953; 1 child, Joronda Ramette Crawford. BS in Edn., Chgo. State U., 1958; MA in Math. Edn., 1964; EdD, Nova U., 1985. Elem. and secondary tchr. Chgo. Pub. Schs., 1958-65, dir. math., 1976-94; co-principal investigator Access 2000, 1991-93; cons. math, 1965-76; dir. Pre-Algebra Devel. Ctrs., 1967-84, NSF Urban Systemic Initiative, 1993-94, regional coord., 1994—; instr. Chgo. State U., 1969-71; mem. Commn. on Tchr. Edn., Task Force on Math. in Urban Centers, Ill. Basic Skills Adv. Coun., Nat. Inst. Edn. Conf. on Basic Skills; mem. coun. acad. affairs Coll. Bd., v.p., 1983-86; bd. dirs. Allendale Sch. for Boys, 1974—, mem. com. educating tchrs. math., 1974-77, in-svc. handbook com., chmn. exhibits, 1972, ann. meeting and math. in-svc. conf., 1978, speaker ann., regional meetings, 1977-84. Author: Modern Mathematics Structure and Use-Spirit Masters, 1977, Pre-Algebra Unit Packs: Ratios and Proportions, Fractions, Decimals, Percent, Measurements; author Chgo. Pub. Schs. curriculum materials; co-author: Bible Mathematics, Book I, 1995; contbg. author Algebra For Everyone; contbr. articles to profl. publs.; coord. devel. numerous curriculum guides. Bible class tchr. Assemblies of God Inc., 1979-89, Full Gospel Pentecostal Ch.; pres. midwest dist. United Pentecostal Coun. Recipient Edn. PaceSetter award President's Nat. Adv. Coun. on Supplementary Ctrs., 1973, Anderson medal Bus. Higher Edn. Forum, 1993. Mem. ASCD, Nat. Coun. Tchrs. Math. (bd. dirs. 1987-90), Nat. Coun. Suprs. Math. (sec. chpt. 1973-75, pres. chpt. 1977-79), Elem. Sch. Math. Advs. Chgo. Area, Met. Math. Club, Math. Club Chgo. and Vicinity, (ednl. equality projects, vice chmn. coun. for acad. affairs coll. bd., nominating com., program com. ICTM, pres. NCSM 1977-79, NIE conf. on basic skills and learning, speaker NASA educators conf.), Nat. Alliance Black Sch. Educators, Ill. Coun. Tchrs. Math., Benjamin Banneker Assn. (nat. pres. 1991-93), Delta Sigma Theta, Kappa Delta Pi, Kappa Mu Epsilon. Home: 2820 Paris Rd Olympia Fields IL 60461-1826 Office: 1819 W Pershing Rd # 4cw Chicago IL 60609-2317

STRONG, HERBERT E., JR., plumbing supply distributing company executive; b. Indpls., Oct. 2, 1925; s. Herbert E. and Margaret Katherine (Welch) S.; m. Shirley Kay Stephenson, Aug. 9, 1953 (div. Jan. 1988); children: Elizabeth Ann, John Stephenson; m. Ann Elizabeth Bowman, Oct. 22, 1988. BSME, Purdue U., 1946; postgrad., Ind. U., Indpls., 1947-49, Butler U., 1950. Salesman Economy Plumbing Supply Co., Indpls., 1946-48, ptnr., 1948-61, pres., 1961—. Pres. Riley Area Revitalization Program, Indpls., 1982-83. Lt. USN, 1943-46, 51-53, PTO. Mem. Am. Supply Assn. (pres. 1996, exec. com. 1990—), Ctrl. Wholesalers Assn. (nat. pres. 1988-89), Ind. Assn. Credit Mgmt. and Svc. (pres. 1988-90), Svc. Club Indpls. (pres. 1990-91), Contemporary Club Indpls. (pres. 1985-85, exec. com. 1990—). Republican. Presbyterian. Office: Economy Plumbing Supply Co Inc PO Box 217 Indianapolis IN 46206-0217

STRONG, JOHN DAVID, insurance company executive; b. Cortland, N.Y., Apr. 12, 1936; s. Harold A. and Helen H. S.; m. Carolyn Dimmick, Oct. 26, 1957; children: John David Jr., Suzanne. BS, Syracuse U., N.Y., 1957; postgrad, Columbia U., 1980. With Kemper Group, 1957-90, Kemper Corp., 1990-96, Empire div. sales mgr., 1972-74, exec. v.p. Fed. Kemper Ins. Co., Decatur, Ill., 1974-79, pres., bd. dirs., 1979-93, CEO, 1988-93, chmn. bd., 1989-93; vice chmn. Millikin Assocs., 1993-96, chmn., 1996—; exec. v.p., dir. Facilitators, Inc., 1995—; bd. dirs. First of Am. Bank, Decatur, 1994. Mem. adv. council Sch. Bus. Millikin U., 1975-79, 84—; bd. dirs. United Way of Decatur and Macon County, Ill., 1976-83, campaign chmn., 1978-79, pres. bd. dirs., 1979-81; pres. United Way of Ill., 1981-83; bd. dirs. DMH Commn. Svcs. Corp., 1985—, chmn., 1988-90; bd. dirs. Decatur-Macon County Econ. Devel. Found., 1983-88, DMH Health Systems, 1987-94, Richland C.C. Found., 1987-90, Symphony Ord. Guild of Decatur, 1992-96, DMH Found., 1988—; bd. dirs. Ill. Ednl. Devel. Found., 1983-90, pres., 1986-87; bd. dirs. Decatur Meml. Hosp., 1985-94, vice-chmn., 1988, chmn. 1990-92; bd. dir. Ctrl. Ill. Health Assocs., Inc., 1994, vice chmn. 1994-96; mem. steering com. Decatur Advantage, 1981-93, pres., 1988-93. Capt. USAR, 1958-69. Mem. Metro Decatur C. of C. (bd. dirs. 1977-80, 2d vice chmn. 1981-82, 1st vice chmn. 1982-83, chmn. 1983-84), Alpha Kappa Psi. Club: Decatur (bd. dirs. 1980-83, pres. 1983), Country of Decatur (bd. dirs. 1993—, pres. bd. 1995—). Office: Ste 366 First Am Ctr 250 N Water Decatur IL 62523

STRONG, STEVEN PHILIP, account executive, consultant, optician; b. Gary, Ind., Jan. 28, 1967; s. John Philip and Rose Marie (Mastrionni) S. AA, Fla. C.C., Jacksonville, 1990; student, Ind. U., Indpls., 1995—. Lic. ins. agt., Ind., Mo., Kans.; lic. optician. Retail mgr. Pearle Vision, Inc., Calumet City, Ind., 1990-94; sales agt. Trustgard Ins. Co., Indpls., 1994-96; account exec. Lincoln Tech. Inst., Indpls., 1996—. Precinct committeeman Highland (Ind.) GOP, 1993-94, Marion County GOP, Indpls., 1995—. With USN, 1985-90. Recipient Cert. of Merit, Duval County Sch. Corp., Jacksonville, 1990. Mem. Circle City Cigar Club, Ft. Wayne Cigar Connoiseurs, Police Athletic League, Italian Heritage Soc. Home: 4817 College Ave Indianapolis IN 46205

STRONSKI, ANNA MARIA NIEDŹWIEDZKA, language professional; b. Starachowice, Poland, Aug. 17, 1940; came to U.S., 1954; d. Antoni Niedzwiedzki and Wanda Gluszkiewicz; divorced; 1 child, Alexandra Joanna Paszkowski. BA, Wayne State U., 1963, MA, 1972. Cert. secondary edn. tchr., Mich. Tchr. French and Spanish Ford Mid. Sch., Highland Park, Mich., 1965-66; tchr. fgn. lang. dept. Highland Park Cmty. H.S., 1966—, head fgn. lang. dept., 1968-70, 73-78, lang. arts facilitator, 1991-94; owner, founder Horizons-Internat., Grosse Pointe Park, Mich., 1993—; dist.-wide lang. cons./coord. Highland Park Pub. Schs., 1994—; ind. contractor/cons. Langs. and Svcs. Agy., 1993—; assessor, field study, tchr. performance lang. arts Nat. Bd. Profl. Tchg. Stds., Mich., 1994; scorer writing proficiency assessments Mich. Dept. Edn., 1994-95, trainer of tchrs., 1995; mem. in-strnl./profl. devel. task force Mid. Cities Assn., Lansing, Mich., 1995—; mem. North Ctrl Accreditation Evaluations Teams, 1970—. Advisor: (high sch. yearbook) Polar Bear, 1985-86 (Big E award Josten's Printing Divsn. 1986); editor: (newsletter) Happenings, 1977-79, Mich. Writing Assessment News, 1994—. Bd. dirs. French Inst. Mich., Southfield, 1985—, Friends of Polish Art, Mich., 1995—. Recipient cert. appreciation for participation in Classrooms of Tomorrow program, Mich. Gov., 1990. Mem. Alliance Francaise: Detroit/Grosse Pointe, AAUW. Roman Catholic. Home: 790 Middlesex Blvd Grosse Pointe MI 48230-1742 Office: Horizons Internat 790 Middlesex Blvd Grosse Pointe Park MI 48230-1742

STROUD, BRADLEY LYN, ballet company executive; b. Three Rivers, Mich., Oct. 3, 1958; s. Harley Allen Stroud and Sandra Lou (Hill) Hansen; m. Claudia Marie Doll, Aug. 2, 1980; children: Carolyn, Matthew, Michael. BS, Ctrl. Mich. U., 1980. Regional adminstrv. mgr. Harris/Lanier, Boston, 1982-86; exec. dir. Met. Ballet Theatre, Detroit, 1992—; compt. Comcast Cablevision, Flint, Mich., 1986-87; asst. compt. M&B Distbg., Flint, 1987-91; compt. Midwest Wholesale Foods, Flint, 1991-92. Co-dir. Cath. Youth Group St. Ives Cath. Ch., Southfield, Mich., 1986-92. Mem. Detroit Club. Home: 16250 Locherbie Birmingham MI 48025 Office: Met Ballet Thetre 229 Gratiot Detroit MI 48226

STROUD, HERSCHEL LEON, dentist; b. Peabody, Kans., Sept. 21, 1930. Student, U. Kans., 1948-50; BS, U. Mo., Kansas City, 1952; OD cum laude, Ill. Inst. Tech., 1954; DDS magna cum laude, U. Mo., Kansas City, 1961. Diplomate Nat. Dental Bd. Officer, founder Topeka Dental Lab., Inc., 1971; ptnr. Gage Ctr. Dental Group, P.A., Topeka, 1979—; pres., bd. dirs. Delta Dental Ins. of Kans. Corp., 1974-92; mem. dental staff St. Francis Hosp. and Med. Ctr., Topeka, 1963—, C.F. Menninger Meml. Hosp., Topeka, 1964—; cons., lectr. in field. Contbr. articles to profl. publs. Vesteryman St. David's Episcopal Ch., 1966-68, dir. Rejoice folk mass, 1967-74, mem. choir; dir. music for blessing of animals Friends of Topeka Zoo, 1983—; mem. U. Kans. Alumni Marching Band. With USNR, 1950-54; capt. USAF, 1954-57, USAR, 1957-70. Fellow Am. Coll. Dentists, Internat. Coll. Dentists; mem. Soc. Preservation Oral Health (bd. dirs. 1965, exec. sec.-treas. 1966-70), Kans. State Dental Assn. (chmn. coun. on dental care plans 1972-76, state peer rev. com. 1974-76), Am. Dental Assn., Chgo. Dental Soc., Midwest Soc. Peridontology, Am. Prosthodontic Soc., Am. Equilibration Soc., Acad. Gen. Dentistry, Am. Pain Soc., Soc. for Preservation Barbership Quartet Singing Am. (chorus dir.), Shawnee Yacht Club, Masons, shriner, Tau Kappa Epsilon, Tau Kappa Nu, Xi Psi Phi. Home: 3640 SW Drury Ln Topeka KS 66604-2550 Office: Gage Ctr Dental Group PA 1271 SW Woodhull St Topeka KS 66604-1849

STROUD, JAMES CLYDE, early childhood educator; b. Paoli, Ind., Sept. 9, 1952; s. Clyde J. and Delores Jane (Dailey) S.; m. Judith Elaine Little, Aug. 23, 1986; children: Elizabeth Elaine, Rebecca Jane. Degree in elem. edn., Ind. State U., 1974, degree in early childhood/elem. edn., 1978, degree early childhood/child psychology, 1988. Tchr. Vigo County Schs., Terre Haute, Ind., 1974-78; tchr. Early Childhood Program, Indpls., 1978-82, asst. dir., 1982-85; doctoral fellow Ind. State U., Terre Haute, 1985-86; assoc. prof. Ball State U., Muncie, Ind., 1988—; adj. instr. Butler U., Indpls., 1984-88; cons. Head Start, various locations in Ind., 1985-95, Muncie Cmty. Schs., 1995—; adv. bd. mem. Ivy Tech. Prep. Sch., Muncie, 1989-94, Apple Tree

Child Care, Muncie, 1991-95. Author: (video script) Science and Nature, 1995; co-author: (video script) Outdoor Environments, 1993; contbr. articles to profl. jours. Mem. Nat. Fatherhood Initiative, Pa., 1994—, Nat. Ctr. Fathering, Kans., 1995—. Recipeint Excellence in Teaching award Student Edn. Assn., Muncie, 1989, 90, 91, 93, 94, Outstanding Tchr. award Tchrs. Coll. Alumni Assn., Ball State U., 1993; named Oustanding Faculty mem. Mortar Bd., Muncie, 1991. Mem. Nat. Assn. Early Childhood Tchr. Edn., Nat. Assn. Edn. of Young Children, Ind. Assn. Edn. Young Children (past v.p. and state membership chairperson), Midwest Assn. Edn. of Young Children, So. Early Childhood Assn. Roman Catholic. Office: Ball State Univ Teachers Coll 218C Muncie IN 47306

STROUP, KALA MAYS, state education official. BA in Speech and Drama, U. Kans., 1959, MS in Psychology, 1964, PhD in Speech Comm. and Human Rels., 1974. V.p. acad. affairs Emporia (Kans.) State U., 1978-83; pres. Murray State U., Ky., 1983-90, S.E. Mo. State U., Cape Girardeau, 1990-95; commr. of higher edn. State of Mo., Jefferson City, 1995—; pres. Mo. Coun. on Pub. Higher Edn.; mem. pres.'s commn. NCAA; cons. Edn. Commn. of States Task Force on State Policy and Ind. Higher Edn.; adv. bd. NSF Directorate for Sci. Edn. Evaluation; adv. com. Dept. Health, Edn. and Welfare, chair edn. com.; citizen's adv. coun. on state of Women U. S. Dept. Labor, 1974-76. Mem. nat. exec. bd. Boy Scouts Am., nat. exploring com., former chair profl. devel. com., mem. profl. devel. com., exploring com., Young Am. awards com., 1986-87, north ctrl. region strategic planning com., bd. trustees, nat. mus. chair; mem. Gov.'s Cabinet, Gov.'s Coun. on Workforce Quality, State of Mo.; bd. dirs. Midwestern Higher Edn. Commn.; chair ACE Leadership Commn.; mem. bd. visitors Air U.; v.p. Missourians for Higher Edn.; mem. bd. dirs. St. Francis Med. Ctr. Found., 1990-95, Cape Girardeau C. of C., 1990-95, U. Kans. Alumni Assn.; pres. Forum on Excellence, Carnegie Found.; adv. bd. World Trade Ctr., St. Louis; mem. Mo. Higher Edn. Loan Authority, 1995—, depts. econ. devel. & agrl. Mo. Global Partnership, 1995—, Mo. Tng. & Employment Coun., 1995—, Concordia U. Sys. Advancement Cabinet, State Higher Edn. Exec. Officers; bd. govs. Heartland Alliance Minority Participation, 1995—. ACE fellow; recipient Alumni Honor Citation award U. Kans. and U. Kans. Womans Hall of Fame. Mem. Am. Assn. State Colls. and Univs. (past bd. dirs., mem. Pres.'s Commn. on Tchr. Edn., Task Force on Labor Force Issues and Implications for the Curriculum), Mortar Board, Phi Beta Kappa, Omicron Delta Kappa, Phi Kappa Phi, Rotary (found. Ednl. awards com.). Office: Southeast Missouri State Univ 1 University Plz Cape Girardeau MO 63701

STROZIER, ROBERT MANNING, II, retired English literature educator; b. Rock Hill, S.C., Dec. 30, 1934; s. Ben Lovett and Katharine Madison (Kinard) S.; m. Geraldine Mary Russell, Apr. 5, 1966 (div. Aug. 16, 1981); children: Jessica Sarah, Adam Nathaniel. B of Mech. Engring., Ga. Inst. Tech., 1958; MA in English, U. Chgo., 1961; PhD in English, 1970. From instr. English dept. to assoc. prof. Wayne State U., Detroit, 1967-88, prof., 1988-96. Author: Epicurus and Hellenistic Philosophy, 1984, Saussure and Derrida, 1988; co-editor: The Ends of Theory, 1996. With USMC, 1958-59. Woodrow Wilson fellow U. Chgo., 1959-60, fellow Sch. Criticism and Theory, NEH, U. Calif., Irvine, 1976. Mem. MLA, Internat. Assn. Philosophy of Lit. Home: 730 Indianwood Lake Orion MI 48362 Office: Wayne State U English Dept 51 W Warren Detroit MI 48202

STRUBE, CHRISTOPHER WILLIAM, pastor; b. Clinton, Iowa, Nov. 4, 1963; s. LeRoy Henry Strube and Becky Jane (Hansen) Emerson; m. Ruth Effie Kaufman, Apr. 27, 1985; children: Elizabeth, Anna, Aimee, Jonathan. AA, World Harvest Bible Coll., South Bend, Ind., 1985; BA, World Harvest Bible Coll., 1986; MA, Ind. Christian U., 1991. Ordained minister. Founder, pastor Good Samaritan Ch. Inc., Centerville, Iowa, 1990—; founder, pres. Tower Ministries, Inc., Centerville, Iowa, 1986—; founder Good Samaritan Ctr., Centerville, 1993—. Mem. Internat. Conf. Faith Ministries (dist. dir. 1991—). Republican. Office: Good Samaritan Ch Inc RR#3 Box 122 Centerville IA 52544

STRUCKHOFF, DAVID RAYMOND, sociology educator; b. St. Louis, Aug. 16, 1942; s. Clarence Emil and Aurelia Cecilia (Atteln) S.; m. Georgia Ann Gustafson, Nov. 26, 1966; children: Andrew David, Rachael Margaret. BA, Quincy U., 1966; MS, Ill. Inst. Tech., 1975; PhD, So. Ill. U., 1977. Sociologist Ill. Dept. Corrections, Joliet, Ill., 1967-77; assoc. prof. Loyola U., Chgo., 1977—; dir. Justice Rsch. Inst., Joliet, 1984—; adj. prof. Coll. St. Francis, Joliet, 1975—, Union Inst., Cin., 1994—; vis. prof. Gov. State U., University Park, Ill., 1993—; expert witness, cons. in field. Author: Criminal Motivation, 1992, The American Sheriff, 1994; editor monographs. Active Sheriff's Adv. Bd., Will County, Ill., 1986-92, Joliet Police Bd., 1993—. Mem. Am. Correctional Assn., Ill. Correctional Assn. (pres. 1985), Ill. Acad. Criminology (pres.), Elks. Office: Justice Rsch Inst 306 N Raynor Ave Joliet IL 60435 also: Loyola U Dept Criminal Justice 820 N Michigan Ave Chicago IL 60611-2103

STRUIF, L. JAMES, lawyer; b. Alton, Ill., Sept. 18, 1931; s. Leo John and Clara Lillie (Bauer) S.; m. Shirley Ann Spatz, Mar. 24, 1965; children: Scott B., Jamie Lynn, Susan Marie, Jeffrey James. BS, Northwestern U., 1953; JD, U. Ill., Champaign, 1960. Bar: Ill. 1960, U.S. Dist. Ct. (so. Dist.) Ill. 1960. Gen. counsel So. Ill. U., 1960-64; pvt. practice Struif Law Offices, Alton, Ill., 1964—; lectr. So. Ill. U., Edwardsville, 1960-65. Author: Guide to Law for Laymen, 1987, Field Guide to 150 Prairie Plants of S.W. Ill., 1989. Scoutmaster Boy Scouts Am., Alton, 1966-69; active civil rights worker, Miss., 1964. With USN, submarines 1953-57, Pacific. Recipient Chmns. award Madison County Urban League, 1989, Blazing Star award The Nature Inst., 1990. Mem. Assn. Trial Lawyers Am., Ill. Trial Lawyers Assn., Ill. Bar Assn. Democrat. Mem. United Ch. of Christ.

STRUTZ, THOMAS EDWARD, association administrator; b. Oakland, Calif., Nov. 14, 1956. BS in Engring., U.S. Mil. Acad., 1978; MS, Fla. Internat. U., 1985. Commd. 2d lt. U.S. Army, 1978, advanced through grades to maj., 1990, ret., 1989; sr. v.p. McMahon Group Inc., St. Louis, 1990—. Office: McMahon Group Inc 12977 N Outer 40 Dr Saint Louis MO 63141

STRYKER, JAMES WILLIAM, automotive executive, former military officer; b. Grand Rapids, Mich., Apr. 20, 1940; s. John Alvin and Marian (Anderson) S.; m. Eleanor Marie Finger, Sept. 26, 1964; children: James William II, Marian Marie, Kathryn Alison Greenbauer. BS, U.S. Mil. Acad., 1963; MA, U. Mich., 1972; postgrad., U.S. Army Command and Gen. Staff Coll., 1978. Commd. 2d lt. U.S. Army, 1963; battery exec. officer 6th/20th field arty. U.S. Army, Ft. Carson, Colo., 1964-65; advisor U.S. Army, Vietnam, 1965-66; battery comdr. 4th/3d field arty. U.S. Army, Ft. Hood, Tex., 1967-68; advisor U.S. Army, Thailand, 1969-70; S-3 ops. officer 1st/7th F.A., Ft. Riley, Kans., 1972-73; assoc. prof. history U.S. Mil. Acad., West Point, N.Y., 1973-77; chief nuclear ops. Ctrl. Army Group NATO, Heidelberg, Germany, 1978-81; dir., project mgr. tank-automotive command U.S. Army, Warren, Mich., 1981-86; ret. U.S. Army, 1986; program mgr. military vehicles operation GMC Truck, Pontiac, Mich., 1987-95; cross brand portfolio mgr. Pontiac-GMC Divsn. GM Corp., Pontiac, Mich., 1996—. Author: (with others) Encyclopedia of Southern History, 1977; co-author: Early American Wars, 1978. Decorated Legion of Merit, Bronze Star medal, Def. Meritorious Svc. medal, Meritorious Svc. medal with oakleaf cluster, Army Commendation medal with oakleaf cluster, U.S. Army/Vietnamese Cross of Gallantry with palm and gold star. Mem. NRA (life), Am. Def. Preparedness Assn. (dir. Detroit chpt. 1991-92, 94—, 2d v.p. 1995, 1st v.p. 1995-96, pres. 1996—), Assn. U.S. Army (dir. Detroit chpt. 1990-95), Gordon Setter Club Am., Nodrog Setter Club Mich. Home: 168 First St Romeo MI 48065-5000 Office: Pontiac-GMC Divsn 31 E Judson St MC 3103-12 Pontiac MI 48342-2230 Office: Pontiac GMC Divsn Gen Motors Corp MC 3103-12 31 E Judson St Pontiac MI 48342-2230

STUART, GORDON EDGAR, dentist; b. St. Louis, Feb. 7, 1951; s. Gordon Edgar and Iris (Bass) S.; m. Marcia Jane Meier, Aug. 5, 1977; children: Gordon Geoffrey, Catherine Marie. BA cum laude, St. Louis U., 1973, grad. fellow in organic chemistry, 1973-74; DDS magna cum laude, U. Mo., Kansas City, 1978. Gen. practice dentistry St. Louis, 1978—; dentist II St. Louis Health/Hosp., 1978-83, Michael Sch. Handicapped Children, St. Louis, 1980-81; mem. staff Christian Hosp. N.E./N.W., St. Louis, 1990—. Mem. ADA, Acad. Gen. Dentistry, Am. Assn. Hosp. Dentists, Psi Omega. Republican. Lutheran. Office: 6182 Howdershell Rd Hazelwood MO 63042

STUART, SANDRA JOYCE, computer information scientist; b. Wheatland, Mo., Aug. 15, 1950; d. Asa Maxville and Inez Irene (Wilson) Friedley; m. John Kendall Stuart, Apr. 17, 1971; 1 child, Whitney Renee. Student, Cen. Mo. State U., 1968-69; AA (hon.), Johnson County Community Coll., 1980; BS in Bus. Adminstrn. cum laude, Avila Coll., 1992. Statis. asst. Fed. Crop Ins. Corp., Kansas City, Mo., 1978-83; mgr. Fed. Women's Program, Kansas City, 1979-80; mgmt. asst. Marine Corps Fin. Ctr., Kansas City, 1983-85, analyst computer systems, 1985-88; computer programmer analyst Corps. of Engrs., Kansas City, 1988-91; regional program mgr. FAA, Kansas City, 1991—. Author: The Samuel Walker History, 1983. Asst. supt. Sunday sch. Overland Park (Kans.) Christian Ch., 1979-80, supt., 1980-82. Mem. Wheatland High Sch. Alumni Assn. (pres. 1990-91).

STUART, WILLIAM CORWIN, federal judge; b. Knoxville, Iowa, Apr. 28, 1920; s. George Corwin and Edith (Abram) S.; m. Mary Elgin Cleaver, Oct. 20, 1946; children: William Corwin II, Robert Cullen, Melanie Rae, Valerie Jo. BA, State U. Iowa, 1941, JD, 1942. Bar: Iowa 1942. Pvt. practice Chariton, 1946-62, city atty., 1947-49; mem. Iowa Senate from, Lucas-Wayne Counties, 1951-61; justice Supreme Ct. Iowa, 1962-71; judge U.S. Dist. Ct., So. Dist. of Iowa, Des Moines, 1971-86, sr. judge, 1986—. With USNR, 1943-45. Recipient Outstanding Svc. award Iowa Acad. Trial lawyer, 1987, Iowa Trial Lawyers Assn., 1988, Spl. award Iowa State Bar Assn., 1987, Disting. Alumni, U. Iowa Coll. Law, 1987. Mem. ABA, Iowa Bar Assn., Am. Legion, All For Iowa, Order of Coif, Omicron Delta Kappa, Phi Kappa Psi, Phi Delta Phi. Presbyterian. Club: Mason (Shriner). Home: 216 S Grand St Chariton IA 50049-2139 Office: US Dist Ct 103 US Courthouse E 1st & Walnut Sts Des Moines IA 50309

STUBBS, JAN DIDRA, retired travel industry executive, travel writer; b. Waseca, Minn., June 19, 1937; d. Gordon Everett and Bertha Margaret (Bertsch) Didra; m. James Stewart Stubbs, Nov. 24, 1962; children: Jeffrey Stewart, Jacqueline Didra. BA in Speech/English, U. Minn., 1961; cert. travel counselor, Inst. Cert. Travel Agts., 1988. Sales agt. United Airlines, Mpls., 1961-64; interior decorator Lloyd and Assocs., St. Paul, 1964-66; v.p. Stubbs and Assocs., Textiles, St. Paul, 1966-83; account exec. Twin Cities Mag., Mpls., 1983-85; account exec. Internat. Travel Arrangers, St. Paul, 1985-86, asst. dir. sales, 1986-88; mgr. Dayton's Group Holidays, Mpls., 1988-96; writer for Mgmt. Assistance Project. V.p. Jr. Women's Assn. of Minn. Symphony Orch.; chairperson 60th anniversary Jr. League of St. Paul, sec., 1967—, sustaining mem.; deacon Ho. of Hope Presbyn. Ch., St. Paul, 1970; mem. Unied Way adv. bd. corporate giving Dayton Hudson Corp. Named Outstanding Alumni, Coll. Liberal Arts, U. Minn., 1995. Mem. AAUW, Inst. Cert. Travel Agts., Am. Soc. Travel Agts., Minn. Exec. Women in Tourism (publicity com. 1987-88, by-laws chmn. 1989-90, sec. 1988-89, 90, fedn. dir. 1990—, v.p., 1993, pres. 1993-94), Internat. Fedn. Women in Travel (alt. gov. Mid-Am. region, standing com. dir. historian, gov. mid-Ams. area I 1994, 95), Jr. Assistance League, St. Paul Pool and Yacht Club, Alpha Omicron Pi (pres. 1958-59, alumni pres. 1962), Whitefish Chain Yacht Club (sec.), U. Minn. Alumni Assn. Republican. Home: 1575 Boardwalk Ct Saint Paul MN 55118-2747 Office: Dayton's Group Holidays 320 Plymouth Bldg 12 S 6th St Minneapolis MN 55402-1508

STUCKEY, HELENJEAN LAUTERBACH, counselor educator; b. Bushnell, Ill., May 17, 1929; d. Edward George and Frances Helen (Simpson) Lauterbach; m. James Dale Stuckey, Sept. 30, 1951; children: Randy Lee, Charles Edward, Beth Ellen. BFA, Ill. Wesleyan U., 1951; MEd, U. Ill., 1969. Cert. art tchr., guidance, psychology instr.; lic. clin. profl. counselor, Ill. Display designer Saks Fifth Ave., Chgo., 1951; interior designer Piper City, Ill., 1953-63; art tchr. Forrest (Ill.)-Strawn-Wing Schs., 1967-68; tchr., counselor Piper City Schs., 1969-74; counselor, art tchr. Ford Cen. Schs., Piper City, 1974-85; psychiatric counselor Community Resource Counseling Ctr., Ford County, Ill., 1985-87; history tchr., counselor Iroquois West High Sch., Gilman, Ill., 1987-88; spl. needs coord. Livingston County Vocat., Pontiac, Ill., 1988-93; ret., 1993; clin. profl. counselor, pvt. practice Piper City, 1995—. Job skills coord. Livingston Area Edn. for Employment, 1994. Mem. AACD, Am. Vocat. Assn., Ill. Counseling Assn., Ill. Vocat. Assn., Ill. Mental Health Counselors Assn., Ill. Assn. Vocat. Spl. Needs Pers. (membership com.), Ill. Ret. Tchrs., Delta Kappa Gamma (v.p., sec., program chmn., pres.). Presbyterian.

STUDEBAKER, GLENN WAYNE, steel company executive; b. Jefferson City, Mo., Oct. 12, 1939; s. Glenn Noble and Dora Mabel (Scrivner) S.; m. Regina Louise O'Kane Buckmaster, Jan. 28, 1961 (div. 1977); children: Glenn Wayne, Ted William, John Christopher, Patrick O'Kane; m. Harriet Jean Hansen, Aug. 7, 1978; stepchildren: Scott Robert Jundt, Jill Michelle Jundt. BSCE, U. Mo., 1962. Bridge design engr. Mo. Hwy. Dept., Jefferson City, 1962-66; sales engr. Vulcraft div. Nucor corp., Norfolk, Nebr., 1966-67, engring. mgr., 1967-70, mgr. rsch., 1970-78; mgr. rsch. and devel. Nucor Corp., Norfolk, Nebr., 1978-82, gen. mgr. rsch. and devel., 1982—; chmn. rsch. com. Steel Joist Inst., Myrtle Beach, S.C., 1972—; rsch. overseer Iowa State U., Okla. U., U. Minn., Va. Poly., Washington U., U. Wis., 1970—. Adv. dir. Luth. Community Hosp., Norfolk, 1985—; trustee York (Nebr.) Coll., 1989—. Mem. NSPE, Am. Welding Soc., Am. Soc. Metals, Wire Assn. Internat., Soc. Mfg. Engrs., Norfolk Country Club (bd. dirs. 1987-89), Kiwanis, Chi Epsilon. Republican. Mem. Ch. of Christ.

STUDER, PATRICIA S., psychologist; b. Ft. Scott, Kans., Sept. 3, 1942; d. Herb E. Studer and Mary Edith (McElroy) Cook; children: Mary Paige, Catherine Ann. BS, Cen. Mo. State U., Warrensburg, 1964; MS, Pittsburg (Kans.) State U., 1975. Lic. psychologist, Mo.; cert. elem. tchr., Mo. Supervisory tchr. Cen. Mo. State U., 1966; tchr. Consolidated Sch. Dist. 1, Hickman Mills, Mo., 1964-68; clin. psychologist Nevada (Mo.) State Hosp., 1977-80, chief unit psychologist, 1980-83; dir. psychology dept., staff psychologist Raphael Ctr. Hosp., Nevada, 1982-83; dir., psychologist Nevada Counseling Ctr., 1983-91; adj. med. staff Nevada Regional Med. Ctr., 1983—; dir. Ctr. for Human Devel., Nevada, Mo., 1992—; guest lectr. Cottey Coll., Nevada, 1983-91; practicum supr. Pittsburg State U., 1980—; clin. supr. Cmty. Counseling Cons., Cinton, Mo., 1987-88; cons. psychologist Barton County Meml. Hosp., 1993—, Heartland Hosp., Nevada, 1995—; mem. Com. for Drug Free Schs., Nevada, 1988—, cons. psychologist, 1988-90; cons. psychotherapist Nevada Child Abuse Coun., 1981-82. Mem. The Nelson-Adkins Mus. Art; mem. Mo. Regional Adv. Coun. on Alcohol and Drug Abuse, 1985-94, v.p., 1988, 92; bd. dirs. Mental Health Adv. Bd., 1993—, Sch. Health Adv. Com., 1994—. Mem. APA (assoc.), Mo. Psychol. Assn., Soroptimist Internat. of Nevada (pres. 1992-93), Rotary Internat., Nevada Vernon County C. of C. Home: RR 2 Box 113C Nevada MO 64772-9670 Office: Ctr for Human Devel PO Box 472 Nevada MO 64772-0472

STUDNIARZ, ROBERT ANTHONY, manufacturing executive; b. Cleve., June 13, 1954; s. Ted Joseph and Marie Anita (Fioritto) S.; m. Rosa Maria Ciancibello, May 20, 1978; children: Marie Elizabeth, Theresa Catherine. BBA in Acctg., Cleve. State U., 1976; MBA, John Carroll U., 1987. CPA. Corp. acct. Parker-Hannifin Corp., Cleve., 1976-79; staff analyst TRW Automotive Worldwide, Solon, Ohio, 1979-81; sr. acctg. analyst TRW Valve Div., Cleve., 1981-83; fin. analyst TRW Indsl. & Energy, Pepper Pike, 1983-86; mgr.. budgets Union Carbide Corp., Parma, 1986-91; site controller UCAR Carbon Co., Parma, 1992—; pres. Carbide Toastmasters, Parma, 1989-90, treas., 1987-88. Advisor Parma City Schs. Ptnrs. in Edn., 1989—, INROADS, Cleve., 1990-93. Mem. AICPA, Ohio Soc. CPA's, St. Anselm Parish. Republican. Roman Catholic. Office: UCAR Carbon Co Inc 12900 Snow Rd Cleveland OH 44130-1012

STUDWELL, WILLIAM EMMETT, librarian, author; b. Stamford, Conn., Mar. 18, 1936; s. Alfred Theodore and Mary Alice (Baker) S.; m. Ann Marie Stroia, Aug. 28, 1965; 1 child, Laura Ann. BA, U. Conn., 1958, MA, 1959; MLS, Cath. U. Am., 1967. Tech. abstracter Libr. Congress, Washington, 1963-66; asst. editor decimal classification office, 1966-68; head libr. Kirtland C.C., Roscommon, Mich., 1968-70; head/prin. cataloger No. Ill. U., DeKalb, 1970—; mem. U.S. Adv. Com. to Chemistry Sects., Universal Decimal Classification, 1968-72; chmn. adv. group Libr. Rsch. Ctr., Urbana, Ill., 1982-84. Author: Chaikovskii, Delibes, Stravinskii, 1977, Christmas Carols, 1985, Adolphe Adam and Leo Delibes, 1987, Ballet Plot Index, 1987 (named One of Outstanding Academic Books by Choice mag. 1988-89), Cataloging Books, 1989, Library of Congress Subject Headings, 1990, Opera Plot Index, 1990, Christmas Card Songbook, 1991, Subject Access to Films and Videos, 1992, Popular Song Reader, 1994, Christmas Carol Reader, 1995, National and Religious Song Reader, 1996; asst. editor Western Assn. of Map Librs. Info. Bull., 1989-94; editor Music Reference Services Quarterly, 1991—; contbr. over 270 articles music history and libr. sci. to profl. jours.; over 250 radio, TV and print media appearances. Internat. leader to devel. standardization code for libr. congress subject headings. Named most productive author among librs. in U.S., Coll. and Rsch. Librs. Mag., 1983-87. Mem. Ill. Assn. Coll. and Rsch. Librs. (exec. bd. 1980-85, newsletter editor 1980-85, lifetime achievement award 1992), Ill. Libr. Assn., Librs. for Social Responsibility (editor newsletter 1986-87, bd. dirs. 1986-94). Home: 15354 Plank Rd Sycamore IL 60178-8743 Office: No Ill U U Librs De Kalb IL 60115-2868

STUEBNER, JAMES CLOYD, real estate developer, contractor; b. Phila., Dec. 15, 1931; s. Erwin A. and Frances (Quinn) S.; children: Kathleen, Stephen, James, Susan, Elizabeth; m. Susan Rae Peterson, June 16, 1990. BA, Dartmouth Coll., 1953. Sales engr. Rohm & Haas Co., Phila., 1956-69; pres. Structural Plastics Corp., Mpls., 1961-69; pres., gen. ptnr. Stuebner Properties, Mpls., 1969—; pres. Northland Inn and Exec. Conf. Ctr., 1988—. Mem. Minn. Conv. Ctr. Commn., St. Paul, 1988; commr. Minn. Econ. Devel. Commn., St. Paul, 1985; bd. dirs. Bach Soc. of Minn., Mpls., 1986—, Minn. Orchestral Assn., Mpls., 1988-91. Sgt. U.S. Army, 1953-55. Mem. Nat. Assn. Office and Indsl. Parks (bd. dirs. Minn. chpt. 1976-85, 81-90, pres. 1978-80, 92-93, nat. pres. 1983-84, v.p. 1981-81, Developer of Yr. award 1987, Minn. Bus. Person of Yr. award 1990, vice chmn. indsl. devel. forum 1996). Office: Five Star Rental and Development Co 7000 Northland Dr N Minneapolis MN 55428-1502

STUECK, WILLIAM NOBLE, small business owner; b. Elmhurst, Ill., May 20, 1939; s. Otto Theodore and Anna Elizabeth (Noble) S.; m. Martha Lee Hemphill Stueck, June 2, 1963; children: Matthew Noble, Erika Lee. BS, U. Kans., 1963. Owner, pres. Suburban Lawn & Garden, Inc., Overland Park, Kans., 1953—; chmn. bd. Mark Twain Bank South, Kansas City., Mo., 1984—. Bd. dirs. Ronald McDonald House, Kansas City; ambassador Am. Royal, Kansas City, 1983. Mem. Am. Assn. Nurserymen, Mission Valley Hunt Club (master 1986—), Leavenworth Hunt Club, Saddle & Sirloin Club. Home: 6701 W 167th St Stilwell KS 66085-9235 Office: Suburban Lawn & Garden Inc 13635 Wyandotte St Kansas City MO 64145

STUERKE, KENNETH W., electrical engineer; b. Lexington, Mo., July 19, 1951; s. Marvin William and Anna Marie (Schaefer) S.; m. Stacie Ann Long, Mar. 18, 1979; 1 child, Carl William. BS, Western Ky. U., 1983. Registered profl. engr., Kans. Design engr. Cessna Aircraft, Wichita, Kans., 1983-85, Raytheon (Beech) Aircraft, Wichita, 1985-94; sr. engr. Raytheon Aircraft, Wichita, 1994—. Mem. IEEE (v.p. 1995-96). Home: 1031 S Cypress Wichita KS 67207-3601 Office: Raytheon Aircraft PO Box 85 Wichita KS 67201

STUEVER, ANITA CAROL, trade association executive; b. Yale, Mich., Jan. 22, 1956; d. Alfred Charles and Doris Estella (Brennan) S. BS, Mich. State U., 1978, MA, 1982. Cert. tchr. secondary and vocat. edn., Mich.; cert. assn. exec. Tchr. vocat. agrl., Future Farmers Am. advisor Breckenridge (Mich.) High Sch., Lakeshore High Sch., Stevenville, 1978-81; FFA projects asst., exec. dir. Mich. FFA Found. Mich. Assn. FFA, Mich. State U., East Lansing, 1981-82; dir. comm. N.E. Dairy Herd Improvement Assn., Ithaca, N.Y., 1983-86; editor Cornell U., Ithaca, N.Y., 1986-91; exec. dir. Ind. Soybean Growers Assn., Lebanon, 1991—; bd. dirs., student mem. State Career Edn. Adv. Commn., Lansing, Mich., 1977-78; freelance editor various clients, Ithaca, 1986-91; editorial/media cons. Nat. FFA Orgn., Alexandria, Va., 1986-90; computer tng. cons. Bd. Coop. Ednl. Svcs., Ithaca, 1990-91; state sec. Mich. Assn. FFA, East Lansing, 1974-75. Author: Agriscience Laboratory Manual, 1991, (mag.) Teaching Fin. Responsibility through Supervised Occupational Experience, 1983; editor (alumni newspaper) Human Ecology News, 1990-91; contbr. over 250 articles to publs. 4-H leader, adv. com. Tompkins County Ext., Ithaca, 1984-86; Sunday sch. supt., youth group advisor, Bible sch. tchr. Stevensville, East Lansing, 1970-74, 80-85; sec. Mich. Future Farmers Am. Alumni Coun., 1981-82; pres. Press Club, 1990. Mem. Am. Soc. Assn. Execs., Ind. Soc. Assn. Execs., Alpha Zeta.

STUEWER, ROGER HARRY, physics historian; b. Shawano, Wis., Sept. 12, 1934; s. Martin and Esther (Westphal) S.; m. Helga Schmeidel, Apr. 8, 1960; children: Marcus Lee, Suzanne Audrey. BS, U. Wis., 1958, MS, 1964, PhD, 1968. Tchr. Germantown (Wis.) High Sch., 1958-59; instr. Heidelberg Coll., Tiffin, Ohio, 1960-62; asst. assoc. prof. U. Minn., Mpls., 1967-71, assoc. prof., 1972-74, prof., 1974—; assoc. prof. Boston U., 1971-72; hon. rsch. assoc. Harvard U., Cambridge, Mass., 1974-75; Volkswagen vis. prof. Deutsches Mus., Munich, 1981-82; vis. prof. Universities of Vienna and Graz, Austria, 1989. Author: The Compton Effect, 1975; editor: Historical and Philosophical Perspectives of Science, 1970, Nuclear Physics in Retrospect, 1979; co-editor: Springs of Scientific Creativity, 1983, The Michelson Era in American Science 1870-1930, 1988, The Invention of Physical Science, 1992; editor Am. Jour. Physics Resource Letters, 1978—; mem. editl. bd. Arch. Hist. Exact Sci., NTM: Schrift. Ges. Naturw. With U.S. Army, 1954-56. Recipient Disting. Svc. citation Am. Assn. Physics Tchrs., 1990; fellow AAAS, 1983, Am. Coun. Learned Socs., 1974, 83, Am. Phys. Soc., 1991. Mem. Am. Phys. Soc. (chmn. divsn. history of physics1986-88), Soc. for History of Sci. (Germany), Brit. Soc. History of Sci., History of Sci. Soc. (sec. 1972-78), Am. Inst. Physics (chmn. adv. com. history of physics 1980-93), Sigma Xi, Sigma Pi Sigma. Home: 124 Windsor Ct Saint Paul MN 55112-3372 Office: U Minn Sch Physics and Astronomy 116 Church St SE Minneapolis MN 55455-0149

STUHR, ELAINE, state legislator; b. Polk County, Nebr., June 19, 1936; m. Boyd E. Stuhr, 1956; children: Cynthia (Stuhr) Hendricks, Teresa (Stuhr) Robbins, Boyd E., Jr. Student, U. Nebr. Tchr. jr. and sr. vocat. h.s. Lincoln (Nebr.) Schs.; senator Nebr. State Senate, Lincoln, 1994—; farmer Bradshaw, Nebr.; former asst. instr. U. Nebr., Lincoln; participant farmer to farmer assignment to Russia with Winrock, Internat., 1993, to Lithuania with Vol., 1993; former pres. Agrl. Womens Leadership Network; former mem. bd. dirs. Feed Grains Coun., Nebr. Corn Bd.; currently mem. York News-Times edtl. bd., agrl. adv. com. for Congressman Doug Bereuter and Gov. Ben Nelson. Past pres., bd. dirs. Found. for Agrl. Edn. and Devel.; former mem. exec. com. and bd. dirs. Agrl. Coun. Am.; leader 4H Club; mem. adv. com. Nebr. Extension Svc.; bd. dirs. Nebr. Family Cmty. Leadership Program; chmn. Nebr. Agrl. Leadership Coun.

STUKEL, JAMES JOSEPH, academic administrator, mechanical engineering educator; b. Joliet, Ill., Mar. 30, 1937; s. Philip and Julia (Mattivi) S.; m. Mary Joan Helpling, Nov. 27, 1958; children: Catherine, James, David, Paul. B.S. in Mech. Engring, Purdue U., 1959; M.S., U. Ill., Champaign-Urbana, 1963, Ph.D., 1968. Research engr. W.Va. Pulp and Paper Co., Covington, Va., 1959-61; mem. faculty U. Ill., 1968—, prof. mech. engring., 1975—, dir. Office Coal Research and Utilization, 1974-76, dir. Office Energy Research, 1976-81, dir. pub. policy program Coll. Engring., 1981-84, assoc. dean Coll. Engring. and dir. Expt. Sta., 1984-85; dean Grad. Coll., vice chancellor for research U. Ill. at Chgo., 1985-86, exec. vice chancellor, vice chancellor academic affairs, 1986-91, interim chancellor, 1990-91, chancellor, 1991-95, pres., 1995—; v.p. Chgo. Tech. Park Corp., 1985-88, pres., 1990-91; exec. sec. midwest Consortium Air Pollution, 1972-73, chmn. bd. dirs., 1973-75; mem. adv. bd. regional studies program Argonne (Ill.) Nat. Lab., 1975-76; adv. com. Energy Resources Commn., 1976; chmn. panel on dispersed electric generating techs. Office Tech. Assessment, U.S. Congress, 1980-81; chmn. rev. adv. bd. tech. rev. dist. heating and combined heat and power systems Internat. Energy Agy, OECD, Paris, 1982-83; cons. in field. Contbr. articles to profl. jours. Pres. parish council Holy Cross Roman Cath. Ch., Urbana, 1967-68. Mem. ASCE (State-of-the-Art of Civil Engring. award 1975), ASME, AAAS, Sigma Xi, Phi Kappa Phi, Pi Tau Sigma. Home: 2650 N Lakeview Ave Apt 1610 Chicago IL 60614-1819 Office: PO Box 4348 2833 Univ Hall M/C 105 Chicago IL 60680-4348

STULL, DANIEL RICHARD, retired research thermochemist, educator, consultant; b. Columbus, Ohio, May 28, 1911; s. Lucius Walter and Irene Mabel (Haldeman) S.; m. Ruth Louise Keck, Sept. 26, 1936 (dec. 1982); children: Louise Irene Stull Hassman, Richard Walter; m. Mary Morton

Lowe, Apr. 28, 1984. BS in Chemistry, Math., Baldwin-Wallace Coll., 1933; PhD in Chemistry, Johns Hopkins U., 1937. Asst. prof. chemistry East Carolina U., Greenville, N.C., 1937-40; rsch. crew leader Dow Chem. Co., Midland, Mich., 1940-50, rsch. tech. expert, 1950-60, dir. thermal lab., 1960-69, rsch. scientist, 1969-76, cons., 1976-77; ret., 1976; rsch. adv. com. Mfg. Chemists Assn., Washington, 1958-65, NRC rev. bd. Nat. Bur. Stds., Washington, 1959-70; rsch. mem., commr. Internat. Union Pure and Applied Chemistry, 1963-72; printer Hobby Print Shop, Alembic Press, 1954-92; plenary spkr. 50th Calorimatry Conf., Washington, 1995. Author: Fundamentals of Fire and Explosion, 1976; author, editor books Joint Army Navy Airforce Rocket Propulsion Group, 1958-76; co-author: Chemical Thermodynamics of Organic Compounds, 1948-69; contbr. to more than 70 sci. rsch. publs. Fin. chmn. 1st United Meth. Ch., Midland, 1948-58; mem. Cosmos Club, Washington, 1967-72; mem. ch. choir various cmtys., 1928-96. Recipient Hugh Huffman Meml. award Calorimetry Conf., Ames, Iowa, 1965, Alumni Merit award Baldwin-Wallace Coll., Berea, Ohio, 1968, Book award Rsch. Soc. Am., 1969. Fellow Am. Inst. Chemists; mem. AAAS, Am. Chem. Soc. (local sect. award 1980), Sigma Xi, Phi Beta Kappa, Phi Lambda Upsilon. Home: 1113 W Park Dr Midland MI 48640-4277

STULLKEN, IDA MARIE, auditing clerk; b. Kansas City, Kans., Jan. 4, 1966; d. Lloyd Edward and Lorna Marie (Craig) S. AS, Garden City (Kans.) C.C., 1986; BS in Psychology, Emporia (Kans.) State U., 1989. Sales rep. Squire Men's Wear, Garden City, 1984-85, J.C. Penney Co., Garden City, 1985-86; display designer, men's wear sales rep. J.C. Penney Co., Emporia, 1989-91; houseware sales rep. J.C. Penney Co., Topeka, 1991-92; fragrance cons. The Jones Store, Topeka, 1989; waitress, cashier Marshall's of Emporia, Inc., 1989; youth care worker United Meth. Youthville, Emporia, 1989-90; fin. cons., collector Sallie Mae, Lawrence, Kans., 1991-93; lead auditing clk., collector Nat. Credit Svc. Corp., Overland Park, Kans., 1993—; model John Casablanca's of Kansas City, Mo., 1994—; movie extra Violent New Breed. Actress, mem. Garden City Community Theatre, 1984-86; treas. Emporia State U. Stingers Dance and Spirit Squad, 1987-88. Singing scholarship Garden City C.C., 1984-85, Drama and Dance scholarship, 1984-86. Fellow Internat. Thespian Soc.; mem. NAFE. Lutheran. Home: Apt 1225 12273 S Strang Line Rd Olathe KS 66062-5235

STUMP, DONALD WAYNE, forester, real estate broker; b. Hammond, Ind., Nov. 1, 1947; s. Donald Eugene and Yvona June (Michaels) S.; m. Susan Louise Sinclair, June 12, 1970; children: Michael Robert, Steven Thomas, Eric Wayne. BS in Forest Prodn., Purdue U., 1970. Dist. forester Ind. Dept. Natural Resources-Div. Forestry, Henryville, 1971—; mem., chmn. State Forester's Adv. Commn., Indpls., 1991-94; dist. chmn. State Tree Farm Commn., Scottsburg, Ind., 1986—. Creator: Indiana Big Tree Register, 1973; author: How We Use Trees, 1991; co-author: Forest Improvement Handbook, 1992; contbr. articles to profl. jours. Pres. Scottsburg Youth Baseball Assn., 1988-93; chmn. transp. ministry First Christian Ch., Scottsburg, 1988—; adv. Scottsburg Park Bd., 1993—; mem. Scottsburg Beautification Com., 1992—. Recipient Tree Farm Incentive award State Tree Farm Commn., 1976, Nat. Tree Farmer of Yr. nominee Nat. Tree Farm Orgn., 1984, Tom Wallace Farm Forestry Contest nominee Louisville Courier-Jour., 1976, 80, 84. Mem. Hist. Hoosier Hills Woodland Resource Commn. (charter mem., organizer), Ind. Forestry and Woodland Owners Assn., Scott County Bd. Realtors (sec. 1980), Soc. Am. Foresters. Home: 150 E Lovers Ln Scottsburg IN 47170 Office: Div Forestry PO Box 119 Henryville IN 47126

STUMP, EARL SPENCER, psychologist; b. Parkersburg, W.Va., Dec. 12, 1943; s. Amos Earl Stump and Harriet Gertrude (White) Stiff; m. Ann Chadwick, Sept. 30, 1967 (div. 1985); 1 child, Andrea Renee; m. Joan Irene Croft, Sept. 28, 1985. BA, Ohio State U., 1966; MS in Corrections, Xavier U., 1971. Lic. psychologist, Ohio, profl. clin. counselor. Psychiat. aide Harding Hosp., Worthington, Ohio, 1965-67; psychology trainee Athens (Ohio) State Hosp., 1966-67; psychologist Ohio Dept. Rehab. and Correction, Columbus, 1967—; supr. psychology Chillicothe (Ohio) Correctional Inst., 1977—; pvt. practice psychology Columbus Mental Health Clinic, Columbus, 1976-77; instr. psychology Hocking Tech. Coll., Chillicothe, 1973-78; instr. diagnostics Ohio U., Athens, 1983-84. Mem. Biofeedback Soc. Ohio, Antique Wireless Assn., Nat. Acad. Neuropsychology (affiliate). Home: 15 N May Ave Athens OH 45701-1817 Office: Chillicothe Correctional Inst Box 5500 Chillicothe OH 45601

STUMPF, LEROY A., state legislator; b. May 29, 1944; m. Carol; three children. BA, St. Paul Seminary; MPA, Syracuse U. Former Minn. State rep.; Minn. State Sen. Dist. 1, 1982—; farmer; chmn. higher edn. divsn.; co-chmn. edn. mem. edn. funding divsn.; mem. fin., govt. ops. and reform and rules and adminstrn. coms. Office: 428 Riverside Ave Thief River Falls MN 56701-3521 also: State Senate State Capital Building Saint Paul MN 55155-1606*

STUNZ, JOHN HENRY, JR., physician; b. Freeland, Pa., May 20, 1921; s. John Henry and Anna Amelia (Gross) S.; m. Geraldine Kutz, July 2, 1944; children: Beverly A. Stunz Boyd, Geri Stunz Konstantin. BA, U. Pa., 1943, MD, 1946. Diplomate Am. Bd. Occupational Medicine. Intern U.S. Naval Hosp., Saint Albans, N.Y., 1946-47; pvt. practice Freeland, 1949-50; plant physician Harrison Radiator div. Gen. Motors Corp., Lockport, N.Y., 1950-52, med. dir., 1952-78; med. dir. Cadillac Motor Car div. Gen. Motors Corp., Detroit, 1978-86; occupational medicine cons. Preferred Med. Assocs., Southfield, Mich., 1987—; pres. Niagara County (N.Y.) Bd. Health, 1966; acting commr. health Niagara County, 1972-73. Lt. (j.g.) M.C., USNR, 1946-49. Fellow Am. Coll. Occupl. and Environ. Medicine; mem. Mich. State Med. Soc., Oakland County Med. Soc. (environ. health com. 1988), Mich. Occupl. and Environ. Med. Assn. (bd. dirs. 1985-88), Detroit Occupl. Physicians Assn. Republican. Presbyterian. Home: 735 Ardmoor Dr Bloomfield Hills MI 48301-2417 Office: Preferred Med Assocs 29200 Southfield Rd Southfield MI 48076-1906

STURGEON, MARTY ROGER, career military officer; b. Marengo, Iowa, Apr. 17, 1961; s. Arlo Owen and Donna Jean (Adolf) S.; m. Beth Ann Gilmer, Sept. 30, 1994; children: Tara Lee, Carissa Lee. BS, Embry-Riddle Aeronautical U., 1994. Enlisted USAF, 1979; air traffic controller 1926 Comms. Squadron, Rogins AFB, Ga., 1979-81, 5th Combat Comms. Group, Rogins AFB, 1981-83; supply supervisor Supply Squadron, Dyess AFB, Tex., 1983-87; supply supt. 50th Supply Squadron, Hahn AFB, Germany, 1987-91; from non-commd. officer in charge to 1st sgt. 20th Intelligence Squadron, Offitt AFB, Nebr., 1991-94; resource advisor 20th Intelligence Squadron, 1995—; co-champion quality bd. 20th Intelligence Squadron, 1995; base fin. working group 55th Wing, Offitt AFB, 1994-95; group fin. mgmt. group 480th Intelligence Group, Offitt AFB, 1994-95. Troop co-leader Girl Scouts U.S., Hahn AFB, 1987-91. Recipient leadership award 55th Tactical Fighter Wing, 1990; named noncommissioned officer of yr. 55 Supply Squadron, 1990, 20th Intelligence Squadron, 1994. Mem. Assn. Old Crows, Noncommissioned Officers Assn., Toastmasters. Republican. Baptist. Home: 408 W 30th Ave Bellevue NE 68005 Office: 20th Intelligence Squadron 106 Peacekeeper Dr Ste 2N3 Offutt AFB NE 68113-4037

STURGES, GLORIA JUNE, learning disabilities educator; b. Ingallas, Kans., Nov. 10, 1937; d. Donald Nathan and Dorothy Ellen (Whaley) Kitch; m. W.G. Bray, Jan. 22, 1960 (div. Apr. 1978); children—Lori Lynn, William Don; m. Sidney James Sturges. B.S. in Edn., Southeastern State U., 1959; M.A. in Edn., Webster U., 1975; postgrad. U. Kans., 1978-84, cert. learning disabilities specialty, 1984. Cert. tchr. elem. edn., Colo., Mo., reading and learning disabilities specialist, Mo. Tchr., Jefferson County Schs., Denver, 1959-60, Briggsdale, Colo., 1960-63, Colo. Sch. for Deaf and Blind, Colorado Springs, 1963-66, Bertha Heid Sch., Thornton, Colo., 1966-70; reading specialist Center Sch. Dist., Kansas City, Mo., 1970-78, learning disabilities specialist, 1985—; bus. exec. Sturges Co., Independence, Mo., 1982—. Active ARC, 1984—, Nat. Polit. Action, Kansas City, Mo., 1970—. conference presenter Emporia State U. Recipient Excellence in Edn. award ARC, 1984-85; Outstanding Achievement award Colo. for Deaf and Blind, 1963. Mem. Nat. Assn. Females Execs., NEA, Kappa Delta Pi. Republican. Baptist. Avocations: gourmet cooking; tennis; swimming; antiques. Home: 16805 E Cogan Rd Independence MO 64055-2815 Office: Red Bridge Sch 418 E 106th Ter Kansas City MO 64131-4318

STURMON, PATRICIA MONTGOMERY, public relations executive; b. Springfield, Ill., Aug. 27, 1945; d. David Thomas and Mary Jane (McBride) Montgomery; m. Daniel Eugene Sturmon, Nov. 16, 1991. BA, U. Ky., 1967; EdM, U. Cin., 1970. Mgr. edn. rels. Ill. Bell, Homewood, 1971-72; mgr. comm. rels. Ill. Bell, Chicago Heights/Wheaton, 1972-75; editor Telenews Ill. Bell, Chgo., 1975-76; mgr. comm. rels. Ill. Bell, Joliet, 1976-78; mgr. media rels. Ill. Bell, Chgo., 1978-83, dir. media rels., 1983-90; sr. dir. external rels. Ameritech, Chgo., 1990-94; dir. corp. comm. ANTEC Corp., Rolling Meadows, Ill., 1994—. Bd. dirs. Girl Scouts of Chgo., pres. 1988-90, Vol. Network, chair, 1992-93; bd. dirs. United Cerebral Palsy, 1990-93, Abraham Lincoln Ctr., 1990-94, Ada S. McKinley Community Ctrs., 1990-94, Girl Scouts of DuPage, 1992—. Mem. PRSA, Chgo. Pub. Rels. Forum, Women in Communications, Phi Alpha Theta, Delta Delta Delta. Office: ANTEC 2850 Golf Rd Ste 600 Rolling Meadows IL 60008-4032

STURTEVANT, WILLIAM T., fundraising executive, consultant; b. Balt., Feb. 2, 1947; s. Charles N. and Mary Jane (Thomson) S.; m. Teresa L. Woollen Sturtevant, Apr. 8, 1988; children: Stephanie A., Robert E., Melissa N. BBA, Western Mich. U., Kalamazoo, 1969; MBA, Wayne State U., Detroit, 1971. Cert. Fin. Planner. Devel. officer WTVS, Detroit, 1969-71; legis. aide Mich. House of Reps., Detroit, 1971-73; pres. Portage Rubber Co., Kalamazoo, Mich., 1973-76; sr. devel. officer Western Mich. U., Kalamazoo, Mich., 1976-79; v.p. devel. Lake Erie Coll., Painesville, Ohio, 1979-80; dir. planned giving U. Ill. Found., Urbana, 1980—; bd. dirs. Warren and Clara Cole Found., Chgo., 1989—, Jagdish N. Sheth Found., Urbana, Ill., 1991—, The Lauritsen Family Found., Urbana, 1994—; cons. pvt. practice, Mahomet, Ill., 1990—; pres. Inst. for Charitable Giving, Chgo., 1990—. Mem. Union League Club, Chgo., 1990—. Named Planned Giving Prof. of Yr., Planned Giving Today, 1995. Mem. Nat. Soc. Fundraising Execs., Coun. for Advancement and Support of Edn. Home: 702 S Mahomet Rd Mahomet IL 61853 Office: U Ill Found Harker Hall MC-386 1305 W Green St Urbana IL 61801-2919

STURTZ, W. DALE, state legislator; m. Fay Sturtz. Grad., Nat. Sheriffs Inst., FBI Acad. Sheriff LaGrange County, Ind., 1980-90; investigator, legal adminstr. Yoder Law Offices, 1990—; mem. from 52d dist. Ind. State Ho. of Reps., 1992—, vice chmn. govt. affairs com.; mem. county and twp., local govt., cts./crinal code coms. Mem. Nat. Sheriffs Inst., Fraternal Order of Police, Meridian Sun Lodge, Exch. Club, Scottish Rite. Home: 2770 N 200 E Lagrange IN 46761-9154*

STYRSKY, DENNIS MARTAN, company executive; b. Oak Park, Ill., Feb. 28, 1944; s. Jerry B. and Slavka M. (Martan) S.; m. Jerrolyn M. Vavricka, July 19, 1969 (div. May 1983); children: Jennifer B., Christopher J.; m. Donna Lee Letrich, Dec. 29, 1984. BS, U. N.Mex., 1971. Cert. contracting officer U.S. Govt. Cert. Program. Clk. VA, Hines, Ill., 1972, chief mktg. drugs, 1978-94; trainee supply mgmt. VA, Chgo., 1972-74; specialist contract VA, Nashville, 1974-75, chief. inventory mgmt., 1975-76; asst. chief supply VA, Birmingham, Ala., 1976-78; pres. MDG Assocs., Willow Springs, Ill., 1995—; co-chmn. Dept. Def./VA/Pub. Health Svc. Procurement, Washington, 1979-94; mem. VA Task Force Pres.'s Pvt. Sector Study on Cost Containment (Grace Commn.) Washington, 1985; founder Milden Group. Served as specialist 5th class U.S. Army, 1966-69. Recipient Presdl. Quality and Mgmt. Improvement award Pres.' Coun. on Mgmt. Improvement, 1992. Mem. NAPM, Am. Mgmt. Assn., Am. Mktg. Assn., Acad. Healthcare Svcs. Roman Catholic. Clubs: South Wilmington (Essex, Ill.), Sportsman's. Home: 8310 Regency Ct Willow Springs IL 60480-1166

STYVE, ORLOFF WENDELL, JR., electrical engineer; b. Winnebago, Minn., Feb. 1, 1936; s. Orloff Wendell and Katharine (Drake) S.; m. Jane Carol Meister, Feb. 25, 1961 (div. 1981); children: Elizabeth Anne, David John, Robert Peter, Susan Katharine. BEE, U. Minn., 1959. Registered profl. engr., Wis. Dist. distbn. engr. Wis. Electric Power Co., Menomonee Falls, 1959-69; div. distbn. engr., then svc. ctr. engring. supr. Wis. Electric Power Co., West Bend, 1969-73; planning engr. Wis. Electric Power Co., Milw., 1973-76, sr. underground dist. engr., 1976-84, elec. engr. underground dist., 1984-94; cons. elect. distbn. engr. Slinger (Wis.) Utilities, 1995-96, utility mgr., 1996—; dir. WPPI, 1996—; mem. elec. bd., West Bend, 1972-94; dir. WPPI, 1996—. Mem. IEEE (voting mem. 1993, insulated conductors com. 1991—), Assn. of Edison Illuminating Cos. (cable engring. sect. 1991-94), Am. Nat. Stds. Inst. (distbn. transformer stds. com. 1985-88), Masons, Scottish Rite (com. stage properties & elec. effects com. 1986—, Wis. Player's award Valley of Wis. 1989, Svc. award 1991), Shriners (potentate's aide emeritus Tripoli Shrine 1986), Nat. Honor Soc. Office: Slinger Utilities PO Box 227 Slinger WI 53086-0227

SUAREZ, PATRICK JOSEPH, technology company executive; b. Canton, Ohio, Mar. 17, 1948; s. Benjamin and Mary Suzanne (DeBord) S.; m. Nola Jean Pencil, Apr. 29, 1972; children: Gregory Edmund, Justin Gabriel. BA in Polit. Sci., Wright State U., 1975; MS in Adminstrn., Cen. Mich. U., 1989. Contract specialist Aero. Systems div. Wright-Patterson AFB, Ohio, 1976-83; contract adminstr. Northrop Corp., Hawthorne, Calif., 1983-84; sr. contract adminstr. Gould Navcom Systems div., El Monte, Calif., 1984; sr. buyer EG&G Mound Applied Technologies, Miamisburg, Ohio, 1984-92, sr. tng. analyst, 1992-95; owner Suarez Assocs., Springfield, 1990—; adj. prof. Urbana (Ohio) U., 1990—; adj. instr. Wright State U., OHio, 1994—. Author: (software) The Beginner's Introduction to the Personal Computer, 1992, The Beginner's Guide to the Internet (Windows, DOS, Mac), 1993—; author: (books) The Beginner's Guide to the Internet, 1995, The Beginner's Guide to the Internet for Mac Users, 1995. Bd. founders Sta. WDPR-FM, Dayton, 1980; founder Radio Broadcasts of the Springfield Symphony Orch., 1973. With USAF, 1968-72. Home: 3703 Marbella St Springfield OH 45502-9443 Office: Knowledgelink Inc 3020 S Tech Blvd Miamisburg OH 45343

SUBER, TOMMIE LEE, union organizer, writer; b. Toledo, Ohio, Oct. 26, 1947; s. Leon Levon and Shirley Ann (Remmert) S.; m. Ileana V. Zoubareff, Oct. 26, 1969; 1 child, Victoria Allyson. Student, Wayne State U., Detroit, 1965-68; MA in Legal Studies, Antioch Coll., 1985. Libr. asst. City of Detroit, 1968-72; child support specialist, social svc. investigator Mich. Dept. Social Svcs., 1972-86; social prog. developer Ohio Dept. Human Svcs., 1988—; internat. staff rep. Am. Fedn. State, County and Mcpl. Employees, AFL-CIO, 1979-80; dep. dir. safety and regulatory bargaining unit Mich. State Employees Assn., AFSCME AFL-CIO, 1980-85; rep. United Auto Workers, AFL-CIO, 1985-87; del. Local 1199, Svc. Employees Internat. Union, AFL-CIO, Columbus, Ohio, 1988-90; full time adminstrv. organizer Local 1199, Svc. Employees Internat. Union, AFL-CIO, 1990; nat. field organizer Nat. Treasury Employees Union, Chgo., 1990-92; organizer United Elec., Radio and Machine Workers Am., 1994—. Recipient Legis. commendation Mich. State Senate, 1987, Mich. State Ho. of Reps., 1987. Home and Office: 6939 Eastview Dr Worthington OH 43085-2306

SUCH, MARY JANE, nurse, service executive; b. Chgo., Dec. 15, 1942; d. Dr. Leon Raymond Wasielewski and Jane Genevieve (Guzik) Wallace; children from previous marriage: Jennifer, Kenneth, Christopher. BSN, Loyola U., Chgo., 1965; MS HSA, Coll. St. Francis, 1996. Clinical Instr. Dept. of Mental Health, Chgo., 1964-69, asst. chief of svc., 1969-72; charge nurse Luth. Gen. Hosp. Alcohol Treatment Ctr., Park Ridge, Ill., 1973-77; program coord. Malayali Cultural Assn., Chgo., 1977-79; psychiat. nurse con. Blue Cross Ill., Chgo., 1979-85; corp. adminstr. Forest Health Systems, Des Plaines, Ill., 1985-91; chief exec. officer Managed Behavioral Care Inc., Oak Park, Ill., 1991-92; pres. Managed Health Systems, Inc., Park Ridge, Ill., 1993—; adminstrv. dir. Divsn. Child and Adolescent Psychiatry Children's Meml. Hosp., Chgo., 1995; exec. dir. Compsych, Chgo., 1995—. Officer Parent-Tchrs. Coun., Sch. Dist. 64, Park Ridge, Ill., 1972-84; mem. Girl/Boy Scouts, Park Ridge, 1972-79. Mem. NAFE, Am. Hosp. Assn., Am. Coll. Utilization Rev. Physicians (cons. 1979-85), Am. Mgmt. Assn., Am. Coll. Healthcare Execs., Chgo. Healthcare Execs. Forum.

SUCHECKI, LUCY ANNE, elementary education educator; b. East Cleveland, Ohio, May 3, 1945; d. Ben and Adelaide V. (Maneri) Urban; m. Robert K. Suchecki, Aug. 19, 1972. BS, Bowling Green State U., 1967; MA, Oakland U., 1981. Cert. elem. tchr., Mich. Elem. tchr. L'Anse Creuse Pub. Schs., Mt. Clemens, Mich., 1967—; grade cons. (book) Michigan, 1991. Active Immaculate Conception Ch., 1969—, Anchor Bay Women's Pool League, 1972—. Mem. NEA, MEA, MEA-NEA (local 1), L'Anse Creuse Ednl. Assn. (sec. 1968—), New Baltimore Hist. Soc. Roman Catholic. Home: 8504 Anchor Bay Dr Clay MI 48001-3507 Office: Marie C Graham Elem Sch 25555 Crocker Blvd Harrison Township MI 48045-3443

SUCHOMEL, JEFFREY RAYMOND, accountant, business consultant; b. Chgo., Dec. 17, 1956; s. Raymond T. and Mary R. (Vachout) S.; m. Connie Rae Lighty, July 4, 1987; 1 child, Matthew. BS in Accountancy, U. Ill., 1980, MBA, 1983. CPA, Ill. Grad. teaching asst. U. Ill., Urbana, 1982-83; staff acct. Peat Marwick, Chgo., 1983-85; sr. acct. Seidman and Seidman, Chgo., 1986-87; sr. bus. cons. Deloitte & Touche, Oak Brook, Ill., 1987-88, supr., 1988-90; mgr. Deloitte & Touche, Oakbrook Terrace, Ill., 1990-92; mgr. Deloitte & Touche, Detroit, 1992-95, dir. recruiting Mich. region, 1995—, mgr. internat. China practice unit, 1994—; regional dir. recruiting-Midwest, 1996—. Mem. adv. bd. U. Ill. Coll. Bus., 1993—; mem. bus. adv. bd. Ptnrs. Plus program U. Mich., 1994—; exec. in residence Oakland U., 1994-95. Mem. AICPA, Ill. CPA Soc. (membership chmn. Salt Creek chpt. 1990-91, constrn. com. 1991-92, internal auditors com. 1992-94), Mich. Assn. CPAs, U. Ill. MBA Alumni Assn. (bd. dirs. 1991-92), U. Ill. Alumni Assn., Nat. Eagle Scout Assn., Rotary (program com. Oak Brook 1987-89, treasury com. 1989-91, program com. 1991-92), Delta Kappa Epsilon (internat. alumni bd. 1993-94), Delta Pi (bd. dirs. 1986-87). Home: 715 Avondale Ln Aurora IL 60504

SUCHY, SUSANNE N., nursing educator; b. Windsor, Ont., Can., Sept. 20, 1945; d. Hartley Joseph and Helen Viola (Derrick) King; m. Richard Andrew Suchy, June 24, 1967; children: Helen Marie, Hartley Andrew, Michael Derrick. Diploma, St. Joseph Sch. Nursing, Flint, Mich., 1966; BSN, Wayne State U., 1969, MSN, 1971. RN, Mich. Afternoon supr., staff nurse oper. and recovery rm. St. John Hosp., Detroit, 1966-70; nursing instr. Henry Ford Community Coll., Dearborn, Mich., 1972—, on leave 1988-90; CNS/case mgr. surg. nursing Harper Hosp., Detroit, 1988-89; CNS case mgr. oncology, 1989—; mem. Detroit Demonstration Site Team for defining and differentiating ADN/BSN competencies, 1983-87. Contbr. articles to profl. jours. Past bd. dirs., pres. St. Pius Sch. Mem. ANA, AACH, N.Am. Nursing Diagnosis Assn. (by-law com. chmn. 1992—), Mich. Nursing Diagnosis Assn. (pres. 1987-90, elected by-law chmn. 1991-92, treas. 1993—), NLN, Detroit Dist. Nurses Assn. (past chmn. nominating com., legis. com., sec. 1994-96), Oncology Nursing Soc. (gov. rels. chmn. 1992—, presenter abstract conf. 1991, 95, poster presentations ann. conf. 1991-93, 95, 96), Daus. of Isabella (internat. dir. 1992—, past regent 1992—, state recording sec. 1995—), Wayne State U. Alumni Assn., Sigma Theta Tau (nominating com. 1991-93). Roman Catholic. Home: 12666 Irene St Southgate MI 48195-1765 Office: Henry Ford CC 5101 Evergreen Rd Dearborn MI 48128-2407

SUDBRINK, BECKY L., medical, surgical nurse; b. Pontiac, Ill., June 1, 1956; d. Alvin D. and Jo Ann (Totten) Kobernus; m. Steven R. Sudbrink, Mar. 12, 1978; children: Lauren D., Taylor S. AS in Nursing, Lincolnland C.C., Springfield, Ill., 1977. RN, Ill. RN 1 health care asst. Dr. S. David Ross Physician Group Clinic, Springfield, Ill., 1977-91; RN Dr. William Coughlin, Doctors' Hosp. Network, Springfield, 1991—. Chairman Ways and Means Com. Sesquecentennial Com., Virginia, Ill., 1986; co-chair Little Miss Virginia Pageant, 1992-93; bd. edn. Virginia Cmty. Unit Sch., 1989—, pres. 1990-92, 94—. Methodist. Home: RR 2 Box 58 Virginia IL 62691

SUDBRINK, JANE MARIE, sales and marketing executive; b. Sandusky, Ohio, Jan. 14, 1942; niece of Arthur and Lydia Sudbrink. BS, Bowling Green State U., 1964; postgrad. in cytogenetics Kinderspital-Zurich, Switzerland, 1965. Field rep. Random House and Alfred A. Knopf Inc., Mpls., 1969-72, Ann Arbor, Mich., 1973, regional mgr., Midwest and Can., 1974-79, Can. rep., mgr., 1980-81; psychology and ednl. psychology adminstrv. editor Charles E. Merrill Pub. Co. div. Bell & Howell Corp., Columbus, Ohio, 1982-84; sales and mktg. mgr. trade products Wilson Learning Corp., Eden Prairie, Minn., 1984-85; fin. cons. Merrill Lynch Pierce Fenner & Smith, Edina, 1986-88; sr. editor Gorsuch Scarisbrick Pubs., Scottsdale, Ariz., 1988-89; regional mgr. Worth Publs., Inc. - von Holtzbrinck Pub. Grp., N.Y.C., 1988—. Lutheran. Home and Office: 3801 Mission Hills Rd Northbrook IL 60062-5729

SUDHOLT, BRYAN F., electronic engineer; b. Belleview, Ill., Dec. 22, 1962. BSEE, So. Ill. U., Edwardsville, 1995. Sr. electronic engr. Basler Electric, Highland, Ill., 1983—. Office: Basler Electric Power Products Hwy 143 Highland IL 62249

SUDOW, THOMAS NISAN, marketing services company executive, broadcaster; b. Stevens Point, Wis., Nov. 7, 1952; s. Noah and Gertrude (Fein) S.; m. Michele Ross, Aug. 8, 1976; children: Erin, Noah, Nathaniel. Student, U. Wis., 1971, Jerusalem Inst., Israel, 1972; BA, Kent State U., 1976; MSW, Yeshiva U., N.Y.C., 1980. Tchr. Akron (Ohio) Hebrew High Sch., 1976-78; sr. assoc. Jewish Cmty. Fed. of Cleve., 1978-85; exec. dir. Am. Friends of Hebrew U., Beachwood, Ohio, 1986-88; v.p. Cleve. Coll. of Jewish Studies, Beachwood, 1988-93, Solid Sound Rec. Studio, Chgo., 1980—; pres. T.N.S. and Assocs., 1993—; exec. producer, host Sports Talk for Kids, Cleve., 1993—; instr. Kent (Ohio) State U., 1976-78. Exec. bd. dirs. Kent Sunday Sch., 1976-78; bd. dirs. Park Synagogue, Cleveland Heights, Ohio, 1986—, pres. Men's Club, 1989-91; bd. dirs. Cleve. Pops Orch.; regional program chair FJMC Conv., v.p. Gt. Lake region, 1992—, pres. cabinet, 1995—, chmn. Cleve. region, 1995—; founding dir. Congregation Cmty. Inst. Adult Jewish Studies, 1988-93; hon. dir. Bejing Ctr. for Jewish Studies, 1993—; mem. bd. trustees Beachwood C. of C., 1993—, v.p., 1995—. Recipient Young Leadership award, United Jewish Appeal, N.Y.C., 1976; named Man of the Yr. Park Synagogue, Cleveland Heights, 1986, Sherman Fellow Brandeis U., Waltham, Mass., 1986. Mem. NASW, Conf. Jewish Communal Svc. Workers (chmn. 1986-93), Assn. Jewish Communal Orgn. Profs. (regional chmn. 1981-85), Conf. Alternatives in Jewish Edn., Glass Inst. (chmn. 1986-87), Wahoo Club (pres.), Cleve. Indians Heavy Hitters, Nat. Soc. Fundraising Exec., Ohio Fundraising Exec. Coun., Beachwood C. of C. (v.p.). Office: TNS and Assocs 3665 Tolland Rd Cleveland OH 44122-5140

SUELFLOW, AUGUST ROBERT, historian, educator, archivist; b. Rockfield, Wis., Sept. 5, 1922; s. August Henry and Selma Hilda (Kressin) S.; m. Gladys I. Gierach, June 16, 1946; children: August Mark, Kathryn Lynn Du Bois. BA, Concordia Coll., Milw., 1942; BDiv, MDiv, Concordia Sem., St. Louis, 1946, fellow, 1947, STM, 1947; DivD, Concordia Sem., Springfield, Ill., 1967. Asst. curator Concordia Hist. Inst., St. Louis, 1946-48, dir., 1948-95, cons., 1995—; guest lectr. Concordia Sem., St. Louis, 1952-69, 74-75, adj. prof., 1975—; asst. pastor Luther Meml. Ch., Richmond Heights, Mo., 1948-56, Mt. Olive, St. Louis, 1958-75; archivist Western Dist. Luth. Ch.-Mo. Synod, 1948-66, archivist Mo. Dist., 1966-87, 88-95; instr. Washington U., St. Louis, 1967-82. Inst. Mem. Am. Assn. Museums, Nat. Trust for Hist. Preservation, Soc. Am. Archivists, Orgn. Am. Historians, Western History Assn., Luth. Hist. Conf. Lutheran. Author: A Preliminary Guide to Church Records Depositories, 1969, Religious Archives: An Introduction, 1980, Heart of Missouri, 1954; cons., contbr. Luth. Cyclopedia, 1975; contbr. Moving Frontiers, 1964, Ency. of the Luth. Ch., 1965, The Luths. in N.Am., 1975, C.F.W. Walther: The American Luther, 1987; mng. editor Concordia Hist. Inst. Quar., 1950-95, assoc. editor., 1950—; Archives & History: Minutes and Reports, 1952-89; editor: Directory of Religious Hist. Depositories in America, 1963, Microfilm Index and Bibliography, vol. I, 1966, vol. II, 1978, Luth. Hist. Conf. Essays and Reports, 1964-92; series editor: Selected Writings of C.F.W. Walther, 6 vols., 1981; vol. editor, translator: Walther's Convention Essays, vol. III, 1981; sec., mem. editorial com. Concordia Jour., 1976-81; mem. editorial/adv. com. Luth. Higher Edn. in N.Am., 1980; mem. editorial com., contbr. Moving Frontiers, 1964. Office: Concordia Hist Inst 801 De Mun Ave Saint Louis MO 63105-3168

SUESS, PATRICIA ANN, software systems consultant; b. St. Louis, Feb. 11, 1956; d. John Andrew and Betty Lee (Allen) Leonard; m. Robert Gerard Suess, Nov. 24, 1984; children: Laura Elizabeth, Amanda Michelle, Robert Gerard Jr. BS in Education and Math, U. Mo., 1976, MS in Nuclear Engring., 1981, MS in Indsl. Engring., 1984. Grad. cert. in Artificial Intelligence, Washington U., 1987. Tchr. Math. St. Thomas Aquinas High Sch., Florissant, Mo., 1976-79; instr. computer programming U. Mo., Columbia, 1979-84; sr. engr. McDonnell Aircraft Co., St. Louis, 1984-86, tech. specialist, 1986-88; mfg. systems specialist Digital Systems Cons., St. Louis,

1988-89; pres. Software Systems Specialists, Inc., 1989—; adj. faculty Maryville Univ., St. Louis, 1989—; McDonnell Aircraft Co. rep. McDonnell Douglas Corp. Artificial Intelligence External Relations Com., St. Louis, 1987—. Contbr. articles to profl. jours. Active Girl Scout Coun. of Greater St. Louis; bd. curator's telecomm. com. U. Mo., 1994—, chancellor's com. on sci. and tech., 1994—; exec. bd. St. Louis County Econ. Coun.'s Small Bus. Devel. Partnership, 1994—; chair Sacred Heart Edn. Commn., 1994-96. Mem. IEEE, Inst. Mng. Scis. (vice chair 1989), Women's Commerce Assn. (scholarship com. 1989-91), Am. Inst. Indsl. Engrs. (bd. dirs., v.p. chpt. devel. 1986-87, sec. 1987-88, v.p. community affairs, C.D. award of Excellence 1987), Soc. Mfg. Engrs. (cert. of Appreciation 1986-88), Am. Assn. Artificial Intelligence, Mensa, McDonnell Douglas Corp. Mgmt., Soroptimists Internat. of the Ams. (sec. 1990-91, dir. 1995-97), Assn. for Corp. Growth. Roman Catholic. Club: McDonnell Douglas Corp. Mgmt. Office: Software Systems Specialists Inc Ste 110 11970 Borman Dr Saint Louis MO 63146

SUGAR, JONATHAN AKIBA, child psychiatrist; b. Santa Monica, Calif., Sept. 29, 1953; s. Carl and Sylvia (Reiner) S.; m. Nan R. Barbas, June 3, 1984; children: Abby, Leigh. BA, U. Calif., Irvine, 1975; MHSA, U. Mich., 1978, MD, 1984. Diplomate in psychiatry and child and adolescent psychiatry Am. Bd. Psychiatry and Neurology. Pub. health analyst HEW, Washington, 1976; asst. planner Comprehensive Health Planning Coun. S.E. Mich., Detroit, 1977-78; transitional intern Henry Ford Hosp., Detroit, 1984-85; resident in psychiatry Mass. Gen. Hosp., Boston, 1985-87, resident in child psychiatry, 1987-89, clin. fellow in psychiatry, 1989-91; rsch. fellow in social medicine Harvard Med. Sch., 1989-91; dir. pediatric consultation-liaison psychiatry U. Mich. Med. Ctr., Ann Arbor, 1991-95; dir. resident-fellowship tng., child psychiatry svc. U. Mich. Med. Sch., Ann Arbor, 1992-94; clin. asst. prof. psychiatry U. Mich. Med. Sch., 1991—; dir. med. svcs. Mass. Soc. Prevention of Cruelty to Children Mental Health Clinic, Brockton, 1989-91; candidate Mich. Psychoanalytic Inst., 1993—. Burroughs-Wellcome fellow, 1985. Mem. Am. Acad. Child and Adolescent Psychiatry, Am. Orthopsychiat. Assn., Am. Psychiat. Assn., Am. Psychoanalytic Assn., Physicians for Social Repsonsibility. Office: 202 E Washington Ste 208 Ann Arbor MI 48104

SUGDEN, RICHARD LEE, pastor; b. Compton, Calif., Apr. 13, 1959; s. L. Fred Sugden and Nancy Jane (Motherwell) Coulter; m. Rebecca Lynn Travis, June 1981; children: Richard Lee II, Ryan Leon, Rachel Lynn, Lawrence Fred, Nicole Irene. BA, Pensacola (Fla.) Christian Coll., 1981. Ordained pastor, 1985. Assoc. pastor Chippewa Lake Bapt. Ch., Medina, Ohio, 1981-84; dir., evangelist Victory Acres Christian Camp, Warren, Ohio, 1985; asst. pastor Bible Bapt. Temple, Campbell, Ohio, 1985-93; missionary evangelist Sugden Evang. Ministries, Struthers, Ohio, 1993—; del. pastors' sch. 1st Bapt. Ch., Hammond, Ind., 1982—. Author: Philippians on Your Level, 1990, James on Your Level, 1991, I Timothy On Your Level, 1991. Founder, dir. Penn-Ohio Bapt. Youth Fellowship. Mem. Christian Law Assn., Buckeye Ind. Bapt. Fellowship. Republican. Home and Office: Sugden Evang Ministries 71 Harvey St Struthers OH 44471-1538

SUGINTAS, NORA MARIA, veterinarian, scientist, medical company executive; b. Evergreen Park, Ill., Mar. 12, 1956; d. George and Mary (Navickas) S. BS in Biol. Scis. with highest distinction, U. Ill., Chgo., 1978; DVM, U. Ill., 1982. Lic. veterinarian, Ill. Profl. hosp. specialist Abbott Labs., Detroit, 1983-87; anes./crit. care patient monitoring equipment acct. exec. Shiley, Inc., Detroit, 1987-91; anesthesia and critical care monitoring equipment sales exec. and cons. Ohmeda, Detroit, 1991-94; regional mgr. Criticare Systems, Detroit, 1994-95, nat. acct. dir., 1995—. Journalist The Lithuanian World-Wide Daily Newspaper, 1975; author: The Production S-Adenosylmethionine by Saccharomyces cerevisiae and Candida utilis. Troop leader Girl Scouts Lithuanian, Chgo., 1972-77, camp dir., 1977. Recipient Louis Pasteur award for Academic Excellence in the Biol. Scis. and Ind. Rsch. U. Ill., 1978. Mem. NAFE, Econ. Club Detroit, Phi Beta Kappa. Republican. Office: 6284 Aspen Ridge West Bloomfield MI 48322-4433

SUGRUE, MARY SHARON, epidemiology nurse; b. Detroit; d. James Joseph and Geraldine Grace Sugrue. ADN, Schoolcraft Coll., 1974; BSN, Ea. Mich. U., 1986; MS, Wayne State U., 1992. Staff nurse intensive care Botsford Hosp., Farmington Hills, Mich., 1974-80, infection control coord., 1981-84; infection control practitioner St. Joseph Mercy Hosp., Pontiac, Mich., 1984-86; coord. infection control and employee health Huron Valley Hosp., Milford, Mich., 1986-89, coord. infection control and nursing quality assurance, 1990-91, coord. epidemiology and regulatory compliance, 1991-92; nursing continuous improvement coord. Harper Hosp., Detroit, 1992—; premarital counselor AIDS and sexually transmitted diseases Huron Valley Hosp., Milford, 1988-92; cons. infection control and hazardous waste to physician offices, Novi, Mich., 1988—. Contbg. author: Management of Methicillin Resistant Staphylococcus, 1992. Named Disting. Alumna Ea. Mich. U., 1995. Mem. Quality Assurance Nursing Network, Mich. Nursing Assn. (HIV task force), Nat. Nursing Assn., Mich. Soc. for Infection Control Mktg. (program chmn. 1986-89), Assn. for Practitioners in Infection Control. Office: Harper Hosp 3990 John R St Detroit MI 48201-2018

SUITS, MIKE A., engineering executive; b. Utica, Mich., Nov. 20, 1962. CAD/CAM mgr. Hi Tech Mold & Engring. Inc., Rochester, Mich., 1982—. Office: Hi Tech Mold & Engring Inc 2775 Commerce Dr Rochester MI 48309-3815

SULICK, ROBERT JOHN, general contractor; b. Columbus, Ohio, Jan. 2, 1947; s. Edward Joseph and Elizabeth Jane (Winters) S.; m. Patricia J. Taylor, Dec. 2, 1965 (div. 1989); children: Roberta Michelle (dec.), Melissa Marie; m. Christine Heidy Morton, Oct. 29, 1994. AD in Architecture, Columbus Coll., 1966; photography student, Ohio U., Lancaster, 1987. Elec. engr. Metzger and Blackburn, Columbus, Ohio, 1965-67; archtl. draftsman Van Buren and Firestone, Columbus, 1967-69; asst. ops. mgr. Capp Homes, Columbus, 1969-76; plant mgr. Parsons Floors and Cabinet Co., Columbus, 1976-81; gen. contractor, photographer R.J. Co., Lancaster, Ohio, 1981—; part-time photography bus. Mayor Village of Brice, Ohio, 1974-79. Democrat. Roman Catholic. Home and Office: 547 Tarkiln Rd SE Lancaster OH 43130-9653

SULKIN, HOWARD ALLEN, college president; b. Detroit, Aug. 19, 1941; s. Lewis and Vivian P. (Mandel) S.; m. Constance Annette Adler, Aug. 4, 1963; children—Seth R., Randall K. PhB, Wayne State U., 1963; MBA, U. Chgo., 1965, PhD, 1969; LHD (hon.), De Paul U., 1990. Dir. program rsch., indsl. rels. ctr. U. Chgo., 1964-72; dean Sch. for New Learning, De Paul U., Chgo., 1972-77; v.p. De Paul U., Chgo., 1977-84; pres. Spertus Inst. Jewish Studies, Chgo., 1984—; St. Paul's vis. prof. Rikkyo U., Tokyo, 1970—; cons., evaluator North Central Assn., Chgo., 1975—. Contbr. articles to profl. jours. Sec.-treas. Grant Park Cultural and Ednl. Cmty., Chgo., 1984—; bd. dirs. Chgo. Sinai Congregation, 1972—, pres., 1980-83; bd. dirs. S.E. Chgo. Commn., 1980—, United Way, 1984—, Crusade of Mercy United Way, 1990—; bd. dirs., chmn. Parliament of World's Religions, 1989—. Mem. Adult Edn. Assn. U.S.A., Acad. Internat. Bus. Club: Cliff Dwellers (Chgo.). Office: Spertus Inst. of Jewish Studies 618 S Michigan Ave Chicago IL 60605-1901

SULLENBARGER, PEGGY ANN, nurse manager, rehabilitation consultant; b. St. Louis, Feb. 21, 1954; d. Arthur Ernst and Betty Alice (Smith) Koenig; divorced; children: Kristina Robyn, Sean David; m. Stuart Sullenbarger, De. 5, 1992. BSN, U. Tex., Arlington, 1977; postgrad., Wright State U., Dayton, Ohio, 1986—. RN, Ohio; cert. rehab. cons., case mgr., rehab. RN. Primary nurse Hospice of Dayton, 1982-86, Miami Valley Hosp., Dayton, 1986-89; grad. teaching asst. Wright State U., 1986; ind. rehab. nurse cons., 1987—; mgr. employee health svcs. Emery Worldwide., 1993—. Contbr. short stories and poems to various publs. Chmn. pub. info. Am. Cancer Soc., 1987-88, chmn. pub. issues, 1988—. Mem. NAFE, Assn. Rehab. Nurses, Ohio Nurses Assn. (alt. 1989), LWV. Office: One Emory Plz Vandaba OH 45377

SULLIVAN, AUSTIN PADRAIC, JR., diversified food company executive; b. Washington, June 26, 1940; s. Austin P. Sullivan and Janet Lay (Patterson); m. Judith Ann Raab, June 8, 1968; children: Austin P. III, Amanda, Alexander. AB cum laude, Princeton U., 1964. Spl. asst. to dep. dir. N.J. Office Econ. Opportunity, Trenton, 1965-66; prof. staff mem. Com. on Edn. and Labor, U.S. Ho. of Reps., Washington, 1967-71, legis. dir., 1971-76; dir. govt. relations Gen. Mills, Inc., Mpls., 1976-78,, 1977-78, v.p., corp. dir. govt. relations, 1978-79, v.p. pub. affairs, 1979-93, v.p. corp. comms. and pub. affairs, 1993-94, sr. v.p. corp. rels., 1994—; lectr. fed. labor market policies Harvard U., 1972-76, Boston U., 1972-76. Bd. dirs., exec. com. Guthrie Theatre, Mpls., 1978-84, Minn. Citizens for the Arts, 1980-83, Mpls. Cmty. Bus. Employment Alliance, 1982-84, Urban Coalition Mpls., 1978-80; chnn. Pub. Affairs Coun., 1993-94—; chmn. Mpls. Pvt. Industry Coun.,1983-87; mem. nat. Commn. on Employment and Tng., 1979-81; chmn. Gov.'s Coun. on Employment and Tng., 1976-82; 1, co-chmn. gov's Comn. on Dislocated Workers, 1988-89; mem. steering com. Minn. Meeting, 1982-94; bd. advisors Dem. Leadership Coun., 1986—; Minn. C. of C., bd. dirs. 1993—; prin. the Coun. for Excellence inGovt., 1988—; With USMC, 1957-59. Eleanor Roosevelt fellow in interracial relations, 1964-65. Mem. conf. bd., Coun. of Pub. Affairs Execs. (chmn. 1989-90) Grocery Mfrs. Assn. (chmn. state govt. task force 1989-90, govt. affairs coun. 1991—), Bus. Roundtable (pub. info. com. 1987—), Greater Mpls. C. of C. (bd. dirs. and exec. com,. 1980-86, 90-93). Home: 17830 County Rd 6 Minneapolis MN 55447-2905 Office: Gen Mills Inc One Gen Mills Blvd Minneapolis MN 55426

SULLIVAN, BERNARD JAMES, accountant; b. Chgo., June 25, 1927; s. Bernard Hugh and Therese Sarah (Condon) S.; m. Joan Lois Costello, June 9, 1951; children: Therese Lynn Scanlan, Bernard J., Geralyn M. Snyder. BSC, Loyola U., Chgo., 1950. CPA, Ill. Staff Bansley and Kiener, Chgo., 1950-66, ptnr., 1966-82, mng. ptnr., 1982—; bd. dirs. Associated Acctg. Firms, Internat.; exec. com. Moore Stephens and Co., U.S.A., 1984—, Arbitrator Nat. Assn. Security Dealers. Served with USN, 1945-46. Mem. Am. Inst. CPA's, Ill. Soc. CPA's, Govt. Fin. Officer Assn., Internat. Found. Employee Benefit Plans, Delta Sigma Pi. Clubs: Beverly Country (Chgo.), Metropolitan (Chgo.). Lodges: Elks, K.C. Home: 9636 S Kolmar Ave Oak Lawn IL 60453-3214 Office: Bansley & Kiener 125 S Wacker Dr Chicago IL 60606-4402

SULLIVAN, CAROLINE ELIZABETH, nursing educator; b. Milw., May 23, 1925; d. Chester and Agnes Walczak; m. Robert J. Sullivan, May, 13, 1950; children: Cynthia, Timothy, Michael. BS in Nursing, Marquette U., 1947; MS in Adminstr. Lead and Supervision, U. Wis., Milw., 1980. GI asst. St. Luke's Hosp., Racine, Wis., 1986-88, mem. faculty nursing, 1972-86; operating room supr. St. Joseph Hosp., Milw.; cons. Ostomy Club, Racine, 1980-86; advisor student nursing, Racine, 1975-86; organizer continuing edn. in nursing Marquette U., 1971; mem. study group SE Wis. Blood Pressure; adj. faculty Gateway Tech. Coll., 1989—, Nursing Edn. Inst. Lincoln Lutheran Racine, Inc., 1989—. Author textbook Nutrition for Nurses, 1983. Rep. Women's Civic Soc., Racine, 1983—; mem. Parish Council. Mem. ANA (dist. del. 1978, 89-91), Nurses Found. Racine, Inc. (sec.-treas. 1981—), Kenosha-Racine Nurses Assn. (legis. chair 1990—), Marquette U. Nurses Alumni Assn. (pres. 1972), WINPAC (vice chair, trustee). Roman Catholic. Home: 5522 Willowview Rd Racine WI 53402-1948

SULLIVAN, CHARLES BRONSON, microelectronic researcher, engineer; b. Lafayette, Ind., Feb. 28, 1960; s. James Jerry and Betty Jane (Bronson) S. BSEE, Purdue U., 1982; postgrad., Butler U., 1993—. Semiconductor engr. Naval Avionics Ctr., Indpls., 1983-88; spl. program engr. Naval Air Warfare Ctr., Indpls., 1989-93, lead technologist, 1993-94, project leader small bus. innovation rsch., 1994—; tech. cons. Def. Advanced Rsch. Projects Agy., Washington, 1988-91; mem. rev. com. Def. Advanced Rsch. Projects Agy. Millimeter/Microwave Integrated Circuits, 1989-91. Keeper Indpls. Zoo, 1994-95. Mem. IEEE, Soc. Mfg. Engrs., Ind. Entrepreneur Alliance, U.S. Naval Inst. Home: 1523 Norfolk Dr Zionsville IN 46077 Office: Naval Air Warfare Ctr 6000 E 21st St Indianapolis IN 46219

SULLIVAN, CONNIE CASTLEBERRY, artist, photographer; b. Cin., Jan. 8, 1934; d. John Porter and Constance (Alf) Castleberry; m. John J. Sullivan, June 6, 1959; children: Deirdre Kelly, Margaret Graham. BA, Manhattanville Coll., 1957. spl. lectr. Cin. Contemporary Art Ctr., 1984, Toledo Friends of Photography, 1991, U. Ky. Art Mus., 1993, Dennison U. Sch. Art, 1993, El Instituto de Estudios Norte Americanos, Barcelona, 1994. One-woman shows include Contemporary Art Ctr. Cleve., 1982, Cin. Contemporary Arts Ctr., 1983, Fogg Art Mus., Cambridge, Mass., 1983, 90, Camden Arts Ctr., London, 1987, Jean-Pierre Lambert Galerie, Paris, 1988, 96, David Winton Bell Gallery, Brown U., Providence, 1989, Toni Burckhead Gallery, Cin., 1989, Rochester Inst. Tech., 1991, Fotomus. im Münchner Stadtmus., Munich, 1992, U. Ky. Art Mus., Lexington, 1993, Internat. Photography Hall, Kirkpatrick Mus. complex, Oklahoma City, 1993, Institut d'Estudios Fotografics de Catalunya, Barcelona, Spain, 1994, Cheekwood Art Mus., Nashville, 1994, Museo Damy di Fotografia Contemporanea, Brescia, Italy, 1995, Photography Gallery U. Notre Dame, Ind., 1995, Louisville Visual Art Assoc., Watertower, Louisville, KY, 1995; exhibited in numerous group shows including Dayton (Ohio) Art Inst., 1987, J.B. Speed Art Mus., Louisville, 1988, Ohio U., Athens, 1989, Centre Nat. Photographie, Paris, 1989, Cleve. Ctr. for Contemporary Art, 1991, Tampa Mus. Art, 1991, 93, Images Gallery, 1991, Dayton Art Inst./Mus. Contemporary Art Wright State U., Dayton, 1992, Bowling Green State U. Sch Art, 1992, Carnegie Arts Ctr., Covington, Ky., 1993, Cin. Art Mus., 1993, POLK Mus. Art, Lakeland, Fla., 1993, Tampa (Fla.) Mus. Art, 1993, Adams Landing Fine Art Ctr., Cin., 1995, Cheekwood Mus. Art, Nashville, 1995, Photo Forum Gallery, 1995, Jean-Pierre Galerie, 1996, Soros Ctr. Contemporary Art, Kiev, Ukraine, 1996, Dom Khudozhnikiv, Kharkiv, Ukraine, 1996; represented in numerous permanent collections Tampa Mus. of Art, Münchner Stadt Mus., Munich, Germany, Museo Damy, Brescia, Italy, Ctr. Creative Photography, Tucson, Detroit Inst. Arts, Biblioteque National, Paris, Internat. Photography Hall of Fame and Mus., Kirkpatrick Ctr. Mus. Complex, Okla. City, Nelson Gallery-Atkins Mus., Kansas City, Ctr. for Photography, Bombay, Milw. Art Mus., Mus. Photography Arts, San Diego, Musee Nat. D'Art Modern, Centre Georges Pompidou, Paris, Denver Art Mus., Boston Mus. Fine Arts, Stanford U. Mus. Art, Palo Alto, Indpls. Art Mus., New Orleans Mus. Art, Fogg Mus., Cambridge, Mass., numerous others; also pvt. collections; author: Petroglyphs of the Heart, Photographs by Connie Sullivan, 1983; work represented in numerous publs. Trustee Images Ctr. for Fine Photography, Cin., 1986-94. Arts Midwest fellow NEA, 1989-90; recipient award Toledo Friends Photography Juried Show, 1986, Best of Show award, 1988, Images Gallery, 1986, Pres.'s Coun. for Arts award Manhattanville Coll., 1991, Treasure of the Month award Mus. Fine Arts St. Petersburg, Fla., 1995; Aid to Individual Artists grantee Summerfair, 1987; named Hyde Park Living Person of Yr., 1996. Mem. McDowell Soc. Home and Studio: 9 Garden Pl Cincinnati OH 45208-1056

SULLIVAN, DAVID P., electrical engineer; b. Cleve., Dec. 29, 1967. BSEE, Engring. and Mgmt. Inst., 1991. Elec. controls engr. Wandorn DeMag, Cleve., 1991—. Democrat. Roman Catholic. Office: Van Dorn DeMag 11791 Alameda Dr Cleveland OH 44136-3010

SULLIVAN, ERNEST LEE, human resources director; b. Columbus, Ohio, Dec. 17, 1952; s. Robert Lee and Emma Jane (Phillips) S. BA, Capital U., Columbus, 1980. Cert. profl. in human resources. Mgmt. trainee Bank One Corp., Columbus, 1971-73, personnel generalist, 1973-77, profl. recruiter, 1977-79, employment mgr., 1979-81, v.p. employment mgr., 1981-87; mgr. staffing, employee rels. and labor rels. Rockwell Internat., Columbus, 1988—; v.p. of exec. selection Banc One Corp.; personnel cons. Martin Luther King Ctr., Columbus, 1989—, bd. dirs.; advisor United Negro Coll. Fund, Columbus, 1983—; bus. adv. bd. Cen. State U., Wilberforce, Ohio, 1989—. Pres. bd. Jobs for Columbus Grads., 1995—; v.p. St. Stephen's Cmty. House Bd. Named to Hall of Fame Columbus Met. Housing, 1989-92; recipient Outstanding Bus. and Profl. award, 1993—, Pinnacle award, Eagle award, 1995. Mem. Soc. Human Resources and Mgmt., Employment Mgrs. Assn., Personnel Soc. Columbus. Office: Bank One Columbus 800 Brookedge Ln Columbus OH 43271

SULLIVAN, FAITH H., elementary education educator, writer; b. Pipestone, Minn., Oct. 1, 1933; d. Edgar William Scheid and Helen Florence (Howes) Page; m. Daniel Joseph Sullivan, Oct. 22, 1935; children: Maggie, Ben, Kate. BS, Mankato (Minn.) State U., 1956. English and history tchr. Cambridge, Minn., Evanston, Wyo., Minn., 1956—. Author: Repent, Lanny Merkel, 1981, Watchdog, 1982, Mrs. Demming an The Mythical Beast, 1985, The Cape Ann, 1988, The Empress of One, 1996. Mem. PEN, Womens Nat. Book Assn.

SULLIVAN, F(RANK) VICTOR, retired dean; b. Wichita, Kans., Mar. 5, 1931; s. Frank Townsend and Olive Mae (Kinseley) S.; m. Mary-Kate Larson, June 2, 1956; children: Mark Kenneth, Olive Louise. BS, Friends U., 1953; MA, U. No. Colo., 1957; EdD, U. Ill., 1964. Tchr. indsl. arts Minneha Pub. Schs., Wichita, 1953-56; instr. indsl. arts Friends U., Wichita, 1956-60; instr. U. Ill. H.S., 1960-63; rsch. assoc. Illini Blind Project, U. Ill., 1963-64; asst. prof. Sch. Tech. Pitts. State U., 1964-66, assoc. prof., 1966-68; prof. Sch. Tech., 1968-96; chair dept. tech. studies Pitts. State U., 1978-85, interim dean Sch. Tech. and Applied Sci., 1980-82, dean Sch. Tech. and Applied Sci., 1985-96; prof. and dean emeritus Pitts. (Kans.) State U., 1996—; bd. dirs. Am. Inst. Design and Drafting, Bartlesville, Okla., Kans. Tech. Enterprise Corp., Topeka. Mem. ESEA (dir./author secondary exploration of tech. project III 1971-74, dir. curriculum from contemporary industry summer 1967), Am. Soc. for Engring. Edn., Phi Delta Kappa (coord. Kans. area 3-B 1974-79, bd. dirs. dist. III 1979-85). Mem. ESEA (dir./author secondary exploration of tech. project III 1971-74, dir. curriculum from contemporary industry summer 1967), Am. Soc. for Engring. Edn. Home: 510 Thomas St Pittsburg KS 66762-6526 Office: Pittsburg State Univ Wilkerson Alumni Ctr Pittsburg KS 66762

SULLIVAN, GEORGE FINLEY, athletic trainer, physical therapist; b. Rockville, Nebr., May 6, 1927; s. Samuel Dempsey and Bessie N. (Nelson) S.; m. Emogene May Pearson, June 10, 1951; children: Gregory Francis, Gary Scott, Glen Lee. BSc in Edn., U. Nebr., 1951; Phys. Therapy Cert., U. Iowa, 1953; MA in Edn., U. Nebr., 1974. Lic. phys. therapist; cert. athletic trainer. Trainer, therapist U. Nebr., Lincoln, 1953-75, head trainer, therapist, 1975—, asst. athletic dir., 1978-95, assoc. prof. phys. edn., 1974-95; prof. emeritus athletic medicine U Nebr., Lincoln, 1995—; mem. Nebr. State Bd. Examiners in Phys. Therapy, 1966-70; mem. Nebr. State Bd. Health Phys. Therapy, 1974-80; mem. Nebr. State Bd. Health Athletic Tng., 1983-86. Author, producer: (film) Care of Athletic Injuries, 1966. Recipient Disting. Svc. award Am. Ortho Soc., 1988, Tim Kerin award for excellence Nat. Athletic Trainers, 1994, medal of honor Nebr. Baseball Assn., 1983, Huskers Track and Field award, 1993, others; named to Nebr. Hall of Fame, Rebounder Club, 1994, Citizens Savs. Found. Hall of Fame. Mem. Am. Phys. Therapy Assn., Nat. Athletic Trainers Assn. (named to Hall of Fame 1978), Am. Legion, Masons (32 deg.), Scottish Rite, Royal Order of Jesters. Republican. Office: U of Nebraska Athletic Dept Lincoln NE 68505

SULLIVAN, JAMES GERALD, business owner, postal letter carrier; b. Bad Axe, Mich., Sept. 13, 1935; s. John Thomas and Frances Eugena (O'Henley) S.; m. Florence Marie Tack, Sept. 12, 1959; children: Kevin Michael, Kathleen Marie. Student, U. Detroit, 1957-58, Highland Park Coll., 1959-60. Owner Jerry's Barber Shop, Kinde, Bad Axe, Mich., 1963-66, 79—; purchasing agt. Thumb Elec. Coop., Ubly, Mich., 1966-79, Walbro Corp., Cass City, Mich., 1979-80; sales rep. Thumb Blanket, Bad Axe, Mich., 1980-81, Sta. WLEW, Bad Axe, 1981-82; sr. regional mgr. Pri Am. Fin. Svcs., Bad Axe, 1985—; treas. Colfax Twp., Bad Axe, 1979-90; rural letter carrier PO, Bad Axe, 1982—; loss clk., Toplis & Harding Wagner & Gliddon, Detroit, 1959-61; inventory control clk., Carrick Products Co., Royal Oak, Mich., 1957-59. pres., Huron County (Mich.) Twp. Assn., 1988-90; leader Boy Scouts Am., Bad Axe,1975-77. Served in U.S. Army, 1954-56. Mem. Huron County Rural Letter Carriers Assn. (pres. 1990—), Armed Forces Vets. Club of the Nat. Rural Letter Carriers Assn. (Mich. divsn.), Am. Legion, 4-H Club (pres. 1948-50), Lions (pres. 1979-80), Cmty. Club (pres. 1976-77), KC (mem. coun. #1546), Ushers Club Sacred Heart Ch. Republican. Roman Catholic. Home: 122 W Richardson Rd Bad Axe MI 48413-9108

SULLIVAN, JAMES MICHAEL, association executive; b. Key West, Fla., Oct. 1, 1950; s. Woodrow and Elizabeth (Holder) S.; divorced; 1 child, Esther Marie. BA, Toccoa Falls Coll., 1974; MDiv, Columbia (S.C.) Sem., 1975; MA, U. Chgo., 1983, PhD, 1993; MLitt (hon.), Xavier Univ., Philippines, 1978. Missionary linguist Overseas Missionary Fellowship, Badak, Maguindanao, The Philippines, 1975-80; rsch. fellow Dansalan Coll., Marawi City, The Philippines, 1978—; coord. field mgmt. Nat. Opinion Rsch. Ctr. U. Chgo., 1984-88; sr. rsch. assoc. United Charities, Chgo., 1988-92; dir. rsch. Ounce of Prevention Fund, Chgo., 1992—; cons. Asian Devel. Bank, Manila, 1984—, United Charities, 1988—. Contbr. articles to profl. publs. With U.S. Army, 1968-70, Vietnam. Decorated Bronze Star, Purple Heart, Gallantry Cross, Presdl. Citation; U. Chgo. overseas rsch. grantee, 1984. Mem. Am. Ethnol. Assn., Am. Anthropol. Assn., Am. Evaluation Assn., Soc. for Applied Anthropology, Am. Statis. Assn., Am. Assn. Pub. Opinion Rsch., Amnesty Internat., Nat. Def. Resource Coun., Soc. for Rsch. in Child Devel., Sierra Club, Yale Club Chgo. Democrat. Episcopalian. Home: 6052 S Ingleside Ave Chicago IL 60637-2618 Office: Ounce of Prevention Fund 122 S Michigan Ste 2050 Chicago IL 60603

SULLIVAN, KATHRYN ANN, librarian, educator; b. Elmhurst, Ill., Jan. 22, 1954; d. Joseph Terrence and Rose Marie (Wright) S. Student, Triton Jr. Coll., 1972-73; BA, No. Ill. U., 1975, MLS, 1977; D of Sci. in Info. Sci., Nova U., 1991. Chief periodicals clk. No. Ill. U., Dekalb, 1976-77; periodicals librarian West Chgo. (Ill.) Pub. Library, 1977-78, Winona (Minn.) State U., 1978—. Contbr. articles to profl. jours. Grantee Winona State U., 1986, 88, 92, 94. Mem. ALA, Minn. Libr. Assn., Libr. and Info. Tech. Assn., N.Am. Serials Interest Group. Home: 670 Winona St Winona MN 55987-3353 Office: Winona State U Maxwell Libr Winona MN 55987

SULLIVAN, MICHAEL PATRICK, food service executive; b. Mpls., Dec. 5, 1934; s. Michael Francis and Susan Ellen (Doran) S.; m. Marilyn Emmer, June 27, 1964; children: Katherine, Michael, Maureen, Bridget, Daniel, Thomas. BS, Marquette U., 1956; JD, U. Minn., 1962. Bar: Minn. 1962, U.S. Dist. Ct. Minn. 1962, U.S. Supreme Ct. 1975, U.S. Ct. Appeals (8th cir.) 1978. Assoc., Gray, Plant, Mooty, Mooty & Bennett, Mpls., 1962-67, ptnr., 1968-87, mng. ptnr., 1976-87; pres., chief exec. officer Internat. Dairy Queen, Inc., 1987—; bd. dirs. The Valspar Corp., Allianz Life Ins. Co. N.Am., Opus U.S. Corp.; instr. U. Minn. Law Sch., 1962-67; lectr. continuing legal edn.; spl. counsel to atty. gen. Minn., 1971-79, 82-84. Contbr. articles to profl. jours. Bd. dirs. Legal Aid Soc. Mpls.; bd. trustees Fairview Hosps., St. Paul Sem; bd. govs. Children's Miracle Network; bd. dirs. Met. Mpls.YMCA; pres. Uniform Law Commn., 1987-89. Served with USN, 1956-59. Mem. ABA (ho. of dels., 1984-89), Minn. Bar Assn. (gov. 1974-86), Hennepin County Bar Assn. (pres. 1978-79), Am. Bar Found., Am. Law Inst., Order of Coif. Roman Catholic. Office: Internat Dairy Queen 7505 Metro Blvd Minneapolis MN 55439-3020

SULLIVAN, ROGER JOHN, radar engineer, researcher; b. Newport, R.I., Feb. 8, 1941; s. John Francis Jr. and Barbara (Williams) S.; m. Susan Dulaney Goodpaster, Aug. 27, 1966; children: Andrew, Barbara, Catherine. BS in Physics, MIT, 1962, PhD in Physics, 1969. Assoc. scientist Ill. Inst. Tech. Rsch. Inst., Chgo., 1969-73; scientist System Planning Corp., Arlington, Va., 1973-86; rsch. mgr. Environ. Rsch. Inst. of Mich., Ann Arbor, 1986-94; mem. rsch. staff Inst. Def. Analyses, Alexandria, Va., 1994—. Contbr. articles to profl. jours. Fulbright scholar Cambridge (Eng.) U., 1962-63. Mem. IEEE, Am. Astron. Soc.

SULLIVAN, SARAH LOUISE, management and technology consultant; b. Wilmington, Del., Sept. 24, 1954; d. Frederick William III and Ruth (Swavely) S. BS, Bowling Green U., 1975; MS, Ill. Inst. Tech., 1986, PhD, 1990. Programmer Computer Sci. Corp., Langley AFB, Va., 1975-77; sr. systems programmer JPLRCC, Perrysburg, Ohio, 1977-80; sr. systems engr. Kraft Inc., Glenview, Ill., 1980-83; project leader Siemens Gammasonics, Des Plaines, Ill., 1983-85; sect. mgr. Zenith Electronics, Glenview, Ill., 1985; mem. tech. staff AT&T Bell Labs., Naperville, Ill., 1986-87; cons., trainer Sarah L. Sullivan & Assocs., Morton Grove, Ill., 1987-90; instr. Ill. Inst. Tech., Chgo., 1988; asst. prof. dept. computer sci. North Cen. Coll., Naperville, 1988-89, Ind.-Purdue U., Ft. Wayne, 1990-94; prin. engr. Boeing Info. Svcs., Dayton, Ohio, 1995-96, Rockwell Collins, Cedar Rapids, Iowa, 1996—; presenter in field. Mem. IEEE, Assn. for Computing Machinery, Oasis Ctr. for Human Potential.

SULLIVAN, THOMAS PATRICK, academic administrator; b. Detroit, July 8, 1947; s. Walter James and Helen Rose (Polosky) S.; m. Barbara Jean

Fournier, Aug. 9, 1968; children: Colleen, Brendan. BA in English, U. Dayton, 1969; M. Edn. and Adminstrn., Kent State U., 1971; postgrad., U. Mich., 1988. Tchr. Resurection Elem. Sch., Dayton, Ohio, 1968-69; adminstr. residence hall Kent (Ohio) State U., 1969-71; program mgr. residence hall Ea. Mich. U., Ypsilanti, 1971-73, adminstrv. assoc., 1973-76, dir. housing, 1976-83; assoc. provost Wayne County Community Coll., Belleville, Mich., 1983-84; dir. budget and mgmt. devel. Wayne County Community Coll., Detroit, 1984-85, sr. v.p. acad. affairs, acting provost, 1985-86; acting exec. dean Wayne County Community Coll., Belleville, 1986-88; dir. budget and mgmt. devel. Wayne County Community Coll., Detroit, 1988-89; pres. Cleary Coll., Ypsilanti, 1989—; part-time instr. English and math. Schoolcraft Coll., Livonia, Mich., 1980-90. Home: 44954 Patrick Dr Canton MI 48187-2551 Office: Cleary Coll 2170 Washtenaw Rd Ypsilanti MI 48197-1744

SULLWOLD, CORLISS KAY, history educator; b. Kearney, Nebr., Feb. 9, 1946; d. Theodore Roslin and Floretta (Record) S.; 1 child, Christa Marie Britton. BA in Internat. Studies, Kearney State Coll., 1987, secondary teaching cert., 1989; MA in History, U. Nebr., Kearney, 1993; postgrad., U. Nebr., Lincoln, 1993—. Bank & loan officer Elm Creek (Nebr.) State Bank, 1968-72; statis. analyst Eaton Corp., Kearney, 1979-86; livestock producer Sullwold Farms, Inc., Elm Creek, 1985—; grad. teaching asst. history dept. Kearney (Nebr.) State Coll., 1990-91; tchr. history, student advisor U. Nebr., Kearney, 1995—; mem. grad. coun. U. Nebr., Kearney, 1989-90, mem. chancellor's planning coun., 1989—; coord. Great Plains Nietzche Conf., 1993. Mem. Nebr. State Hist. Soc., Buffalo County Hist. Soc. Gene Hamacker scholar Kearney State Coll., 1989. Mem. AAUW (pres. 1989-90), Orgn. Am. Historians, N.Am. South Devon Assn., Nebr. Draft Horse Assn., Oral History Assn., Phi Alpha Theta (chpt. v.p. 1989-91, pres. 1990-91, historian 1991-92, editor 1992-93), Alpha Mu Gamma. Democrat. Home: 910 W 22nd St Kearney NE 68847-5049 Office: Student Support Svcs U Nebr at Kearney Kearney NE 68849-2365

SULLY, IRA BENNETT, lawyer; b. Columbus, Ohio, June 3, 1947; s. Bernie and Helen Mildred (Koen) S.; m. Nancy Lee Pryor, Oct. 2, 1983. B.A. cum laude, Ohio State U., 1969, J.D. summa cum laude, 1974. Bar: Ohio 1974, U.S. Dist. Ct. (so. dist.) Ohio 1974. Assoc. Schottenstein, Garel, Swedlow & Zox, Columbus, 1974-78; atty. Borden Inc., Columbus, 1978-80; sole practice, Columbus, 1980—; instr. Real Estate Law Columbus Tech. Inst., 1983-88; title ins. agt. Sycamore Title Agy., Columbus, 1983—. Active Ohio Dem. Bldg. Com., 1995; commentator Sta. WOSU, Columbus, 1980. Treas. Leland for State Rep., Columbus, 1982, 84, Leland for City Atty., Columbus, 1985; asst. treas. Pamela Conrad for City Council, Columbus, 1979; bd. dirs. Research Franklin County Celeste for Gov., Columbus, 1978. Mem. Columbus Bar Assn., Ohio Bar Assn., ABA. Democrat. Jewish. Club: Agonis (Columbus). Avocations: running, coin collecting. Home: 200 Reinhard Ave Columbus OH 43206-2616 Office: 844 S Front St Columbus OH 43206-2543

SUMMER, NANCY L., electrical engineer; b. Indpls., Oct. 4, 1960; d. Leroy William Ratliff and Veda Mae (Fechner) Ehrlich; m. Scott L. Summer, Nov. 29, 1991. BSEE, Wichita State U., 1983. Registered profl. engr., Ill. Elec. engr. The Boeing Co., Wichita, 1983-91, Cochran & Wilken, Inc., Springfield, Ill., 1991—. Mem. IEEE, Eta Kappa Nu. Office: Cochran & Wilken Inc 3009 S 6th St Springfield IL 62703

SUMMERS, DON, state legislator. Rep. dist. 2 State of Mo. Office: Rte 4 Box 209 Unionville MO 63565

SUMMERS, PATSY JO, educator; b. Springfield, Mo., Sept. 26, 1942; d. Wesley Edward and Virginia Maledia (Chranford) Shean; m. Gail Eugene Summers, June 27, 1964; children: Gena Jo, Wesley Eugene. BA, Drury Coll., Springfield, 1964, postgrad. Cert. tchr., Mo. Tchr. pub. schs. Springfield, 1965—; Summer Queest educator Drury Coll., Springfield, 1987—; supervising tchr. Drury/SMSU Colls., Springfield, 1980—; v.p., bd. dirs. S&S Investments, Ozark, Mo., 1990—; presenter in field. Mem. adv. bd., officer P.A.L.S./Arts Coun., Ozarks area, 1990—; mem. bd. Christian edn. Coun. of Chs., Ozarks area, 1988-92; spokesperson, vol. Crosslines, 1991—. Recipient teaching awards. Republican. Mem. United Ch. of Christ. Home: 1340 S Delaware Springfield MO 65804

SUMMERS, WILLIAM B., brokerage house executive; b. 1950. With McDonald & Co. Investments Inc., Cleve., 1971—; pres., CEO McDonald & Co. Securities, Cleve., 1983—. Office: McDonald Securities 800 Superior Ave E Cleveland OH 44114-2601*

SUMMERSETT, KENNETH GEORGE, psychiatric social worker, educator; b. Marquette, Mich., Mar. 9, 1922; s. Frank Elger and Ruth H. (Fairbanks) S.; B.S., No. Mich. U., 1948, M.A. in Sociology, 1964; M.S.W., Wayne State U., 1951; student U. Puget Sound, 1942-43; m. Vivian M. Wampler, June 17, 1950 (dec. 1980); children—Nancy M., Kenneth R., Mark G.; m. Donna Mae Gerhett, May 25, 1985. With Mich. Dept. Mental Health, 1950—, Marquette (Mich.) Child Guidance Clinic, 1950-52; chief psychiat. social worker Battle Creek (Mich.) Child Guidance, 1952-54; dir. social services Newberry (Mich.) State Hosp., 1954-66, dir., cons. social services, 1966-73, adminstrv. dir. community psychiatry, 1973—, mental health exec., 1975-82, dir. community services div., 1975-82; extension prof. sociology dept. No. Mich. U., 1962-70; lectr. sociology Lake Superior State Coll., 1968—; pvt. practice marriage and family counseling, 1982—; v.p. Luce County Social Services, 1985—, vice-chmn., 1988; adv. com., bd. dirs. Mich. County Social Services, 1985—. Mem. Upper Peninsula Mental Health Planning Com., 1964-65, Mich. Task Force Com. Mentally Retarded, 1964-65, Upper Peninsula Mental Health Com. for Comprehensive Health Planning, 1972-75, Mich. Dept. Mental Health Legis. Planning Com. Release Planning, 1975—. Bd. dirs. Eastern Upper Penninsula Mental Health Clinic, v.p., 1970-72; bd. dirs. Luce County Extension Program, sec. bd., 1972-75; bd. dirs. Luce County Social Svcs., 1983—, Mich. Dept. Social Svcs., v.p. dist. X. Served with AUS, 1943-46. Certified marriage counselor. Mem. Nat. Assn. Social Workers (chmn. upper Peninsula chpt. 1957-59, 64-65, vice chmn. 1972-73), Acad. Cert. Social Workers, Mich. County Social Services Assn., Theta Omicron Rho. Clubs: Lions (pres. 1959-60), Elks (maj. projects chmn. 1968-70). Author various articles pub. in profl. jours. Home: PO Box 14 Newberry MI 49868-0014

SUMNER, DAVID EDWARD, journalist, educator; b. Bushnell, Fla., June 24, 1946; s. Joseph David Sumner and Ruth (Sumner) Hoffman; m. Elise Carr, Aug. 14, 1983. BA, Stetson U., DeLand, Fla., 1969; MDiv, S.E. Baptist Theol. Sem., Wake Forest, N.C., 1979; MST, U. of the South, Sewanee, Tenn., 1983; PhD, U. Tenn., 1989. Editor, pub. Christian Writers Newsletter, Knoxville, Tenn., 1988-89; dir. comms. Episcopal Diocese of So. Ohio, Cin., 1981-86; assoc. prof. journalism Ball State U., Muncie, Ind., 1990—; coord. Nixon Newspapers Nat. Journalism Writing Award, Muncie, 1993—. Author: Graduate Programs in Journalism and Mass Communications, 1996, The Episcopal Church's History 1945-1985, 1987; contbr. Encyclopedia Britannica Yearbook, over 250 articles to profl. jours. Mem. Assn. Edn. Journalism Mass Comms. (rsch. chair magazine divsn. 1993-94, chair mem. com. 1993-95). Episcopalian. Office: Ball State Univ Dept Journalism Muncie IN 47306

SUN, JING, electrical engineering educator; b. Hefei, Anhui, Peoples Republic of China, Apr. 7, 1961; came to U.S., 1984; d. Hansheng Sun and Xingzhen Xu; m. Bingchang Xu, July 4, 1986; 1 child, Alexander M. Xu. BS in Elec. Engring., U. Sci. and Tech. of China, Heifei, 1982, MS, 1984; PhD, U. So. Calif., 1989. Teaching asst. U. So. Calif., L.A., 1985-87, rsch. asst., 1988-89; asst. prof. elec. engring. Wayne State U., Detroit, 1989-93; cons., lectr. Ford Motor Co., Dearborn, Mich., 1991-93, engring. specialist, 1994—. Assoc. editor IEEE Transactions of Automatic Control, 1994—; contbr. articles to profl. jours. Mem. IEEE, Detroit Soc. Engrs. Office: Control Systems Dept PO Box 2053 MD1170 SRL Dearborn MI 48121

SUNAMI, JOHN SOICHI, designer; b. N.Y.C., June 10, 1949; s. Soichi and Suyeko (Matsushima) S.; m. Marialyce Norman, Apr. 21, 1973; children: Christopher Andrew, Jennifer Kiyoko. BA, CCNY, 1969. Cert. Gemological Inst. Am. Vol. Peace Corps, Jamaica, W.I., 1969-71; jeweler N.Y.C. and Columbus, Ohio, 1971-82; dir. mktg. Knight's Inn/Cardinal Industries, Columbus, 1982; founder, exec. designer Nimbus, Columbus, 1983—. Designer/sculptor pub. artwork IntroCenter, 1990; designer logo identities for various cos.; exhibited paintings and sculpture; author poems and essays. Bd. dirs. William H. Thomas Gallery, Columbus, 1992-93; v.p., bd. dirs. South Side Settlement House, Columbus, 1982-93; mem. cultural diversity outreach com. United Way of Franklin County, 1993—. Recipient 1st prize Macworld Gallery/Macworld Mag., 1985. Mem. Columbus C. of C., Columbus Art League. Home: 419 Fairwood Ave Columbus OH 43205-2202 Office: Nimbus 413 Fairwood Ave Columbus OH 43205-2202

SUND, JEFFREY OWEN, publishing company executive; b. Bklyn., June 19, 1940; children: Catherine, Meredith. BA, Dartmouth Coll., 1962. Sales rep. Prentice-Hall, Englewood Cliffs, N.J., 1967-73; sales rep. Houghton Mifflin, Boston, 1973-74, coll. div. editor, 1974-77, editor-in-chief, 1977-86, v.p., editorial dir., 1986-89; pres., chief exec. officer Richard D. Irwin, Burr Ridge, Ill., 1989—. Lt. USN, 1962-66. Office: Richard D Irwin 1333 Burr Ridge Pky Burr Ridge IL 60521-6489

SUNDE, MILTON LESTER, retired poultry science educator; b. Volga, S.D., Jan. 7, 1921; s. Andrew Carl and Clara Josephine (Mehl) S.; m. Genevieve O. Larson, Dec. 29, 1946; children: Roger, Scott, Robert. BS in Poultry Sci., S.D. State Coll., 1947; MS in Biochemistry, U. Wis., 1949, PhD in Nutrition, 1950. Instr. in poultry sci. U. Wis., Madison, 1949-51, asst. prof., 1951-55, assoc. prof., 1955-57, prof., 1957-64, 66-71, prof., chmn. dept. poultry sci., 1964-66, 71-85, prof. emeritus, 1987—; mem. nutrition adv. bd. Nat. Rsch. Coun., Washington, 1970-78; cons. Min. of Agriculture Govt. of Venezuela, 1964, FAO, India, 1977; poultry scientist Rockefeller Found., 1960. Patentee Vitamin D compounds; assoc. editor: Poultry Sci. Jour., 1964-72, 77-83; contbr. articles to profl. jours. and chpts. to books. Inducted into Am. Poultry Hall of FAme, 1992. Fellow Poultry Sci. Assn. (pres. 1967-68, v.p. 1965-67), World Poultry Sci. Assn. (coun. 1970—, chmn. nutrition program com. 1974, chmn. scientific papers 1981-84, v.p. U.S. br. 1979-84, pres. 1984-89, v.p. 1988—). Lutheran. Office: U Wis Poultry Sci Dept Madison WI 53706

SUNDEEN, ANN LOWRY, writer, community volunteer; b. Kansas City, Mo., Sept. 24, 1962; d. Jack William and Catherine Ann (Griffith) Lowry; m. John Earl Sundeen Jr., May 4, 1991. BA in French with honors, U. Kans., 1984, BS in Journalism, 1984. Sr. writer Kansas City Mag., 1983-87; asst. editor Vance Pub., Overland Park, Kans., 1984-85; coord. corp. pubs. United Telecom, Inc., Westwood, Kans., 1986-89; internal communications coord. Hallmark Cards Inc., Kansas City, 1989-93. Chmn. Encore Young Friends of Kansas City Symphony, 1986-89; fundraiser Children's Mercy Hosp., 1995-96, DeLaSalle Edn. Ctr., Cir. of Friends Bd., 1996—; mothers' group Curé of Ars Ch., 1995—. Mem. Internat. Assn. Bus. Communicators, Jr. League of Kansas City (v.p. 1993-94, bd. dirs. 1994-95), Pi Beta Pi Alumni Assn. (v.p. programs 1988-90). Republican. Roman Catholic.

SUNDERLAND, ROBERT, cement company executive; b. Omaha, Dec. 21, 1921; s. Paul and Avis Marie (Peters) S.; m. Terri Reed, Nov. 21, 1959; children—Sharon Marie, Lori Diane. B.S. in Bus. Adminstrn, Washington U., St. Louis, 1947; LL.D. (hon.), Bethany Coll., Lindsborg, Kans., 1980. With Ash Grove Cement Co., Overland Park, Kans., 1947—; sec., asst. treas. Ash Grove Cement Co., 1953-57, treas., 1957-61, v.p., treas., 1961-67, chmn. bd., 1967-91, hon. chmn., 1992—. Trustee Lester T. Sunderland Found., Kansas City. Served with USAAF, 1942-46, Philippines. Mem. Kansas City Club, Shadow Glen Golf Club, Sigma Chi. Republican. Presbyterian. Office: Ash Grove Cement Co 8900 Indian Creek Pky Ste 600 Shawnee Mission KS 66210-1513

SUNDGREN, ANN CHRISTINE, physical therapist; b. Manhattan, Kans., July 24, 1962; d. Eldon E. and Beverly (Specht) J. S. BA in Biology, Cornell Coll., 1984; BS in Phys. Therapy, Wichita State U., 1986. Registered phys. therapist. Staff phys. therapist Susan B. Allen Meml. Hosp., El Dorado, Kans., 1986-89; staff phys. therapist Mid-Kans. Therapy, 1989-92; staff PT, clinic mgr. Rehab Clinics, Inc., 1992-94; clinic mgr. Novacare Outpatient Rehab. Divsn., Wichita, 1994—; clin. instr. Wichita State U. Dept. Phys. Therapy, 1987—; ctr. coord. clin. edn. Novacare Outpatient Rehab. Divsn., 1992—. Mem. Am. Phys. Therapy Assn. (Sports Phys. Therapy sect.), Kans. Phys. Therapy Assn. (chair edn. com. 1992-95, treas. 1995—, Disting. Svc. award 1995). Office: Novacare Outpatient Rehab Divsn 728 N Emporia St Wichita KS 67214

SUNDLING, MARY JO, community volunteer; b. Milw., Sept. 19, 1950; d. Joseph Matthew and Joyce Lorrayne (Scott) Kachelmeyer; m. Ralph Walter Sundling, July 11, 1970; children: Robert John, Thomas Joseph. BS in Med. Tech. with honors, U. Wis., Milw., 1972. Med. technologist VA Hosp., Wood, Wis., 1972-73, Luther Hosp., Eau Claire, Wis., 1973-74, Kenosha (Wis.) Meml. Hosp., 1974-76; beauty cons., Stoughton, Wis., 1980—; proof cons. The Portrait Co., Stoughton, 1989-93; cons. polit. campaigns, Stoughton, 1988—; polit. and ednl. pub. speaker, Stoughton, Madison, Wis., 1989—. Vol. Stoughton Pub. Schs., 1982—, sch. bd. mem., 1987-93; vol. Stoughton Sr. Ctr., 1992-94; coord. Working for Kids Parent Group, Kengosa Elem. Sch., Stoughton, 1985-87; coord. Cmty. Vol. Reading Program, 1988-89. Recipient devel. award level I, Wis. Assn. Sch. Bds., 1990, level II, 1991, level III, 1992. Mem. Stoughton Bus. and Profl. Women (pres., Woman of Yr. award 1995). Home: 200 Rowe St Stoughton WI 53589-2352

SUNDSTROM, RICHARD CARL, police analyst, writer; b. Duluth, Minn., Mar. 16, 1953; s. George B. and Ellyn B. Sundstrom. BA, U. Minn., 1976; MA, No. Mich. U., 1984. Program coord. Arrowhead Econ. Opportunity, Virginia, Minn., 1976-86; ops. mgr. Tex. Relief Pharmacists, Dallas, 1986-88; fin. officer Garden City (Mich.) Police Dept., 1988-93; budget analyst City of Dallas, 1993—; pres. Richard Sundstrom and Assocs., Garden City, Mich.; cons. Garden City Pub. Sch. Dist., 1990—. Mem. Garden City Chemically Free Task Force. No. Mich. U. scholar, 1979; Office of Criminal Justice grantee, 1989, 90, 91. Republican. Home: 609 N Kristi Ln Cedar Hill TX 75104

SUNDY, GEORGE JOSEPH, JR., engineering executive; b. Nanticoke, Pa., Apr. 22, 1936; s. George Joseph Sr. and Stella Mary (Bodurka) S.; m. Stella Pauline Miechur, May 21, 1966; children: Sharon Ann, George Joseph III. BS, Pa. State U., 1958. Rsch. engr. Bethlehem (Pa.) Steel Corp., 1959-85; reliability engr. Flo-Con Systems, Inc. (name now Vesuvius USA), Champaign, Ill., 1985-90; reliability mgr., 1990—. Patentee in field. Mem. Am. Soc. Materials, Am. Ceramics Soc., Iron and Steel Soc. AIME, Keramos, Sigma Tau. Democrat. Roman Catholic. Home: 604 E South Mahomet Rd Mahomet IL 61853-3602 Office: Vesuvius USA 1404 Newton Dr Champaign IL 61821-1069

SUNSHINE, IRVING, toxicologist; b. N.Y.C., Mar. 17, 1916; s. Samuel Sunshine and Sara Kanter; m. Helen Rogoff, Dec. 24, 1939, (dec.); children: Jonathan Howard, Carl Alan; m. June Singer, Oct. 20, 1985. BS, NYU, 1937, MA, 1941, PhD, 1950. Diplomate Am. Bd. Forensic Toxicology (dir. 1979—), Am. Bd. Clin. Chemistry. Prof. toxicology emeritus Case Western Res. U., Cleve., 1951—; chief toxicologist emeritus Coroner's Office, Cleve., 1951—; toxicologist Univ. Hosps., Cleve., 1951-85; cons. toxicologist VA Hosp., Cleve., 1979-85; vis. prof. U. Ghent, Belgium, 1976; Fulbright prof. Vrije U., Brussels; cons. toxicologist PharmChem, Menlo Park, Calif., 1985—. Author: Handbook of Analytical Toxicology, 1969, Handbook of Spectrophotometric Data of Drugs, 1981, Handbook of Mass Spectra of Drugs, 1981, Methods for Analytical Toxicology Vol. 1, 1975, Vol. 2, 1982, Vol. 3, 1985. Fellow Am. Acad. Forensic Sci. (chmn. 1969-71, Gettler award 1980), Am. Assn. Clin. Chemistry (bd. dirs. 1981-84, Internat. fellowship 1984, Ames award 1973); mem. Am. Chem. Soc. (chmn. Cleve. sect. 1968), Calif. Assn. Toxicologists (bd. dirs. 1986-87), Internat. Assn. Forensic Toxicologists. Home: 28150 S Woodland Rd Pepper Pike OH 44124

SUNSHINE, RON LEON, executive search consultant; b. N.Y.C., Dec. 19, 1940; s. Meyer Sunshine and Mildred Rubin Reiskin; m. Barbara Ellen Blake, Aug. 16, 1967; children: Matthew Jay, Stacy Loren. Student, U. Okla., 1958-61. Mgr. Premier Talent Assocs., N.Y.C., 1964-70, Creative Mgmt. Assocs., N.Y.C., 1970-75; pres. The Sunshine Agy., St. Louis, 1975-79; cons. Profl. Career Devel., St. Louis, 1979-82; pres. Ron Sunshine Associs., St. Louis, 1982—. Vice pres. Creve Coeur Athletic Assn., 1978-84. Mem. nat. Assn. Pers. Cons. Office: Ron Sunshine Assocs 20 N Wacker Dr Ste 1731 Chicago IL 60606

SUOMI, PAUL NEIL, alumni association director; b. Ishpeming, Mich., July 15, 1937; s. Niilo John and Florine Blanche (LaCombe) S.; m. Martha Jean Banaglio, July 18, 1964; children: Michael Paul, Mark Joseph, Matthew John. Student, William & Mary Coll., Norfolk, Va., 1957-58; BA, No. Mich. U., 1962, MA in Ednl. Adminstrn., 1972. Asst. to v.p. adminstrv. affairs No. Mich. U., Marquette, 1969-72, asst. to asst. to pres. of univ. rels., 1972-76, news bur. chief, 1976-82, dir. comm., acting dir. alumni rels., 1982-84, dir. alumni rels., 1984—; panelist The Coun. for the Advancement & Support of Edn., 1973, 75, 79, 83, 88, 94; panelist, cons. Midwest Labor Press Assn., 1975. Editor: (book) Coaching Better Basketball, 1964; co-publ., contbg. writer: (quarterly newspaper) Horizons, 1984—. Trustee Am. Lung Assn., 1981-89, pres., 1986-88; trustee Upper Mich. Lion's Eye Bank, 1983-85; bd. dirs. K.I. Sawyer AFB Heritage Mus., 1994—. With USN, 1955-58. Recipient Exceptional Achievement award Coun. Advancement & Support Edn., 1976, 83. Mem. Air Force Assn. (bd. dirs. Northland chpt. 1992—), Econ. Club of Marquette County (bd. dirs. 1986—, pres. 1995-96). Roman Catholic. Home: 44 Elder Dr Marquette MI 49855 Office: No Mich U Alumni Assn Presque Isle Ave Marquette MI 49855

SUPER, WILLIAM ALAN, manufacturing executive; b. Evergreen Park, Ill., Dec. 9, 1953; s. Peter and Adeline Marie (Gulch) S.; m. Terrie Elaine Helms, Sept. 22, 1979; children: Emilee Erin, Nicholas William. BS in Indsl. Mgmt., Purdue U., 1975; MBA, No. Ill. U., 1976; MS in Indsl. Tech., U. Wis., Platteville, 1980; postgrad. in indsl. engring., U. Iowa, 1983—. Indsl engr., analyst John Deere Dubuque (Iowa) Works, 1977-79; sr. indsl. engr., analyst Deere Co. Corp., Moline, 1979-81, advanced indsl. engr., analyst, 1981-85; mgr. indsl. engring. Sheller Globe, Iowa City, 1985-88; v.p. mfg. Snappy Air Distbn. Products, Detroit Lakes, Minn., 1988—; instr. St. Ambrose Coll., Davenport, Iowa, 1983-84. Mem. Holy Rosary Sch. Bd., 1996—. Mem. Inst. Indsl. Engrs. (sec. 1978-79), Soc. Mfg. Engrs., No. Ill. U. Alumni Assn. (bd. dirs. 1981-86), Sertoma (sec.-treas. Davenport 1982-83), Masons, Rotary (sec. 1993-94, pres. 1995-96). Republican. Roman Catholic. Home: 1030 Summit Ave Detroit Lakes MN 56501-3320 Office: Snappy Air Distbn Products 1011 11th Ave SE Detroit Lakes MN 56501-3711

SUPROCK, DAVID M., mechanical engineer; b. Sewickley, Pa., June 21, 1947. BS, U. Cin., 1974; MS, Xavier U., Cin., 1978. Gen. mgr. XTEK, Cin., 1984-86, mgr. internat. bus., 1986-89; mgr. Cin. Milacron Inc., 1989—; lectr. on tech. subjects. Coach Little League; vol. fundraiser local ch. Capt. U.S. Army, 1967-70. Mem. ASME. Office: Cin Milacron Inc 4701 Marburg Ave Cincinnati OH 45209-1025

SURDIN, DENNIS R., laboratory technician; b. N.Y.C., Apr. 27, 1944. Student, U. Philippines, Manila, 1966-68. Engr. technician Rival Mfg., Kansas City, Mo., 1966-78; sr. engring. lab. technician Toastmaster Inc., Columbis, Mo., 1978—. Served with USAF, 1965-68, S.E. Asia. Office: Toastmaster Inc 1801 N Stadium Blvd Columbia MO 65202-1330

SURESH, NALINA, mathematics educator; b. Tamil Nadu, India, Sept. 5, 1958; d. A. and Bhavani Rajagopalan; m. T.S. Suresh, Sept. 1, 1982 (dec. Oct., 1984). BS in Edn., Lakshmi Coll. Edn., Gandhigram, India, 1981; MS in Math., Madurai (India) U., 1981; MA in Math., U. South Fla., 1988, PhD in Math. and Stats., 1992. Tchr. Freetown, Sierra Leone, 1982-84; teaching asst. U. South Fla., Tampa, 1984-90; assoc. prof. U. Wis., Eau Claire, 1990—; mem. Gold Coun. for Excellence, U. South Fla., Tampa, 1989-90; reviewer Quality and Productivity Track, Decision Scis. Inst. meeting, 1993, 94; presenter numerous confs., seminars. Statis. reviewer Am. Jour. Psychiatry; contbr. articles to profl. jours. Mem. IEEE, Am. Statis. Assn., Am. Soc. Quality Control, Am. Math. Soc., Assn. Women in Math., Univ. Women Assn. Eau Claire, Pi Mu Epsilon. Home: 2828 Claudette St # 31 Eau Claire WI 54701-6208 Office: U Wis Eau Claire Dept Math Eau Claire WI 54702

SURFACE, CHUCK L., state legislator; b. Webb City, Mo., Feb. 5, 1944; s. Hubert Basil and Hazel (Ulmer) S.; m. Sherry Louzader, 1978; children: Jason, Christi, Kimberly. BS, So. State Coll., 1969. Agt. Shelter Ins., 1970—; mem. Mo. Ho. of Reps. from 129th dist., 1985—. Mem. Joplin (Mo.) Zoning and Planning Commn., 1977-82, chmn., 1981-82; mem. Joplin City Coun., 1982-85. Mem. Am. Legion, Sertoma, Mo. So. State Coll. Alumni Assn. (past bd. dirs.), Jaycees (past pres. Joplin chpt.), Elks. Republican. Home: 2401 W 29th St Joplin MO 64804-1425*

SURGI, ELIZABETH BENSON, veterinarian; b. New Orleans, June 11, 1955; d. Andrew Ernest Jr. and Mary Elizabeth (Steinlage) Benson; m. Marion Rene Surgi, May 22, 1981; children: Reneé Elizabeth, Sara Elizabeth. BS in Med. TEch., U. New Orleans, 1977; DVM, La. State U., 1984. Assoc. veterinarian West Park Vet. Svcs., Houma, La., 1984, Animal Emergency Svc., Schaumburg, Ill., 1984-85; staff veterinarian Anti-Cruelty Soc., Chgo., 1985-86; assoc. veterinarian Terry Animal Hosp., Wilmette, Ill., 1986-89; owner, chief veterinarian Sauganash Animal Hosp., Chgo., 1989—. Mem. Am. Vet. Med. Assn., Am. Vet. Dental Soc., Ill. Acad. Vet. Medicine (pres. 1992), Assn. Avian Veterinarians, Ill. State Vet. Med. Assn., Chgo. Vet. Med. Assn. Republican. Episcopalian. Office: Sauganash Animal Hosp 4054 W Peterson Ave Chicago IL 60646-6019

SURGI, MARION RENE, chemist; b. New Orleans, Dec. 19, 1956; s. George Edward and Barbara Ruth (Pearce) S.; m. Elizabeth Benson, May 22, 1981; children: Reneé Elizabeth, Sara Elizabeth. BS, U. New Orleans, 1979; PhD, La. State U., 1981-84. Gen mgr. Superior Amusement Co., New Orleans, 1975-80; rsch. assoc. U. New Orleans, 1980-81; grad. asst. La. State U., Baton Rouge, 1981-84; sr. rsch. chemist Signal Cos., Des Plaines, Ill., 1984-86; rsch. specialist Allied Signal Corp, Des Plaines, 1986-90; rsch. mgr. in math. simulation sci. AlliedSignal Corp, Des Plaines, 1990-94; pres. Analytical and Environ. Svcs., Inc., Chgo., 1994—; bd. dirs. SAH, P.C., Chgo. Contbr. articles to profl. jours. Patentee in field. Recipient Merck award, 1981, others. Mem. Am. Chem. Soc., Phi Lambda Upsilon. Republican. Episcopalian. Office: 503 Oakdale Ave Glencoe IL 60022-2180

SUROVELL, EDWARD DAVID, real estate company executive; b. Washington, Mar. 20, 1940; s. Samuel and Florence Deborah (Starfield) S.; m. Barbara Ann Bartelmes, Apr. 26, 1958 (div. Jan. 1974); children: David Alexander, Claire Katherine. AB, Columbia U., 1962; postgrad., U. Mich., 1968-71. Lic. real estate broker, Mich. Copy editor Harcourt, Brace & World, Inc., N.Y.C., 1963-65; editor Princeton (N.J.) U. Press, 1965-67, Scott, Foresman Co., Glenview, Ill., 1967-68, U. Mich., Ann Arbor, 1970-73; real estate agt. Fletcher & Klein, Inc., Ann Arbor, 1973-75; sales mgr. Charles Reinhart Co., Ann Arbor, 1975-82; pres. Edward Surovell Co., Realtors, Ann Arbor, 1982—. Chmn. Ann Arbor City Planning Commn., 1988; active Downtown Devel. Authority, Ann Arbor, 1991-95, vice chair, 1994-95; trustee Ann Arbor Dist. Libr., 1996—. Mem. Nat. Assn. Realtors (bd. govs. RB coun. 1987-91), Mich. Bd. Profl. Cmty. Planners, Hist. Soc. Mich. (trustee 1992—), Ann Arbor Bd. Realtors (v.p. 1984, pres. 1985, Realtor of Yr. 1990), Univ. Mus. Soc. (bd. dirs. 1992—). Democrat. Jewish. Home: 2024 Vinewood Blvd Ann Arbor MI 48104-3614 Office: Edward Surovell Co/Realtors 1886 W Stadium Blvd Ann Arbor MI 48103-7007

SURSA, CHARLES DAVID, banker; b. Muncie, Ind., Nov. 5, 1925; s. Charles Vaught and Ethel Fay (Schukraft) S; m. Mary Jane Palmer, Feb. 2, 1947; children: Ann Elizabeth, Janet Lynne, Charles Vaught, Laura Jane. BSChemE, Purdue U., 1946; MBA, Harvard, 1948. Executive NBD Bank N.A. (formerly Summit Bank, Indsl. Trust & Savings), Muncie, Ind., 1946-51, pres., 1951-80; chmn. bd., pres. NBD Bank N.A. (formerly Summit Bank, Indsl. Trust & Savings), Muncie, 1980-88, chmn. bd., CEO, 1988-90, chmn. bd., 1990-94, chmn. emeritus, 1994—; bd. dirs. Old Rep. Life Ins. Co., Chgo., Home Owners Life Ins. Co., Chgo., Old Rep. Internat. Corp., Chgo., Ball Meml. Hosp., Inc., Old Rep. Ins. Co., Greensburg, Pa., Old Rep. Life Ins. Co. N.Y.C., Am. Bus. & Merc. Ins. Group, Chgo., Am. Bus. & Merc. Reassurance Co., Chgo., bd. dirs., pres. Com. Svcs. Coun. of Del. County, 1973-74. Treas. Muncie Symphony Assn., 1949-62, pres., 1962-72,

2d v.p., 1978-80, dir., 1991—; bd. dirs., pres. The Community Found. of Muncie and Del. County, Inc., 1985—. Recipient Outstanding Young Man award Ind. Jr. C. of C., 1956, Hon. Jaycees award, 1974. Mem. Ind. Banker's Assn., Ind. Pres.'s Orgn. (treas. 1980-86), Ind. Soc. of Chgo., Internat. Wine and Food Soc., Delaware County C. of C., Ind. State C. of C., Muncie C. of C. (pres. 1959-60), Rotary (pres. 1964-65), Delaware Country Club (pres., bd. dirs. 1964), Elks, Phi Gamma Delta. Republican. Presbyterian. Home: 3410 W University Ave Muncie IN 47304-3970 Office: NBD Bank NA 220 Walnut Plz Muncie IN 47305-2804

SURZ, RONALD JOSEPH, financial consultant; b. Chgo., Jan. 14, 1945; s. Erwin Norbert Surz and Harriet Nowicki; m. Eloise Krase, Dec. 8, 1966 (div. 1968); 1 child, Lisa; m. Barbara Jane Haik, May 18, 1985. BS in Math., U. Ill., Chgo., 1967, MS in Math., 1969; MBA in Finance, U. Chgo., 1974. Cons. engr. Northrop, Rolling Meadows, Ill., 1969-71; pesnion cons. A. G. Becker/SEI, Chgo., 1971-86; pension cons., co-owner Becker, Burke Assocs., Chgo., 1986-91; owner PPCA, Wheaton, Ill., 1992—; salesman Glenwood Trust, 1991—; mng. dir. Roxbury Capital Mgmt., Santa Monica, Calif., 1996—; mem. investment adv. com. State of Alaska Retirement Sys., 1992-95; mng. dir. Roxbury Capital Mgmt., 1996—; spkr. in field. Contbr. articles to profl. jours. and books. Office: Performance Presentation Cons Alliance 2152 Belleau Woods Dr Wheaton IL 60187-6023

SUSHKA, THEODORE WILSON, civil engineer, county engineer; b. Martins Ferry, Ohio, Aug. 28, 1942; s. Theodore L. and Elizabeth (Scotka) S.; m. Beverly R. McClelland Loery, 1964 (div. 1969); children: Louis, Roberta; m. Barbara L. Farnsworth, July, 1970; 1 child, Steve. BS in Civil Engring., Tri-State Coll., 1964. Registered profl. engr. and surveyor, Ohio. Engring. technician Wash. State Hwy. Dept., Yakima, Wash., 1965, Ohio Dept Hwys., Dist. 11, New Phila., Ohio, 1965-69; engr. in tng. Ohio Dept. Hwys., Columbus, 1967-69; right-of-way plans engr. Ohio Dept. Transp. Dist. 10, Marietta, 1991-92, dist. traffic engr., 1978-91; traffic field engr. Ohio Dept. Transp., Columbus; county engr. Washington County, Marietta, Ohio, 1993—. Pres. Muskingum Valley chpt. Ohio Soc. Profl. Engrs., 1978. Republican. Office: Washington County Engr 217 Putnam St Marietta OH 45750

SUSOR, DONALD J., testing and support administrator; b. Perrysburg, July 8, 1938. B, U. Toledo, 1975. Supr. engine test Champion Spark Plugs, Toledo, 1982-87, mgr. aviation, 1987-93, mgr. testing & support, 1993—; mem. adv. bd. U. Toledo, 1985—. With USAF, 1956-64. Mem. SAE (com. mem. 1988—). Republican. Roman Catholic. Office: Champion Spark Plugs 900 Upton Ave # 910 Toledo OH 43661-1000

SUSTER, RONALD, state legislator; b. Cleveland, Oct. 31, 1942; s. Joseph and Frances (Pryatel) S.; m. Patricia Hocevart, 1974; children: Jennifer, Joseph, Michael. BA, Western Res. Univ., 1964, JD, 1967. Lawyer, 1967; asst. law dir. City of Cleveland, 1967; asst. county prosecutor Cuyahoga, Ohio, 1968-71; law dir. City of Highland Heights, 1976-80; asst. atty. gen. Ohio, 1971-80; legal adv. Euclid Dem. Exec. Com., Ohio, 1975-76; state rep. Ohio Dist. 19, 1981-92, Ohio Dist. 14, 1993; mem. Labor-Mgmt. Rels. subcom., chmn. ethics com. 1983-84, chmn. Civil & Comml. Law com., 1985-87; chmn. Fin. Inst. Com., 1987; exec. com. mem. Cuyahoga County Dem., 1974-78. Mem. Am. Fedn. of State, County & Mcpl. Employees, Fraternal Order of Police Auxiliary, Northern Ohio Patrolmen Benevolent Assn., Internat. Assn. Firefighters, Am. Arbit Assn. Home: 18519 Underwood Ave Cleveland OH 44119*

SUTHERLAND, JEFFREY W., electrical engineer; b. East Liverpool, Ohio, June 12, 1953. BA in Telecom., Kent State U., 1981; postgrad., Akron U., 1983-84. Sr. engr. technician Westinghouse Broadcasting, Pitts., 1981-82; prin. engr. Telxon Corp., Akron, Ohio, 1983—; pvt. practice computer cons., Akron, 1989—. Patentee in field. Mem. Trinity Presbyn., East Liverpool. With USCG, 1974-78. Recipient Achievement award USCG, Hawaii, 1978, Rescue Accomdation Unit award USCG, Hawaii, 1978. Office: Texlon Corp PO Box 5582 Akron OH 44334-0582

SUTTER, ELIZABETH HENBY (MRS. RICHARD A. SUTTER), civic leader, management company executive; b. St. Louis, May 15, 1912; d. William Hastings and Alvina (Steinbreder) Henby; AB, Washington U., St. Louis, 1931; m. Richard A. Sutter, June 15, 1935; children: John Richard, Jane Elizabeth, Judith Ann Hinrichs. Sec.-treas. Sutter Mgmt. Co., St. Louis, , until 1985. Chmn. com. on mental health AMA Aux., 1960-62, v.p., 1962-63, 63-64, pres. 1965-66, editor Direct Line newsletter, 1967-74; assoc. editor MD's Wife, 1973-80; mem. adv. bd. Deaconess Hosp. Sch. of Nursing, St. Louis; trustee John Burroughs Sch., 1958-61, v.p. 1959, devel. commn., 1960-61; mem. Hist. Bldgs. Commn. St. Louis County, 1957-91, chmn., 1973-91; bd. dirs. Gamma Phi Beta House Corp. Washington U., St. Louis, 1989-93; chmn. Com. for Preservation Children's Teeth; mem. planning bd. Health, Hosp. Health, Welfare Coun. Met. St. Louis, 1955-64; pres. Aux. Cen. States Soc. Indsl. Medicine and Surgery, 1960-61; pres. St. Louis County Med. Soc. Aux., 1948-49, Mo. Med. Soc. Aux., 1952-53; sec. St. Louis County Health and Hosp. Bd., 1956-61, chmn., 1961; bd. dirs. Am. Lung Assn. Eastern Mo., exec. com., 1956-85, v.p., 1960-61; pres. Tb and Health Soc. of St. Louis, 1962-65; adv. coun.vol. svcs. Nat. Assn. Mental Health, 1962-64; bd. dirs. Am. Cancer Soc., St. Louis, exec. com., 1954-64; bd. dirs. Mental Health Assn. St. Louis, 1960-61; mem. Practical Nursing Edn. Coun., chmn. exec. com., 1959-60; mem. AMA Coun. on Mental Health Planning for Nat. Conf. on Mental Health, 1961; mem. adv. com. on women in svcs. Dept. Def., 1969-72, vice chmn., 1971; participant 24th ann. global strategy discussion U.S. Naval War Coll., 1972; bd. govs. Washington U. Alumni, 1970-71, 75—, vice chmn. 1979-80, chmn., 1980-81; trustee Washington U., 1979-81; pres. Washington U. Arts and Scis. Century Club, 1970-71; bd. dirs. St. Louis Conv. and Tourist Bur., 1975-83, sec., 1980-82; bd. dirs. Health Svcs. Agy., 1975-82; mem. East West Gateway Coordinating Coun. Task Force on Hist. Preservation, 1975-81, U. City Hist. Preservation Commn., 1977-85; bd. dirs. Whitney Beach III Assn., Longboat Key, Fla., 1984-87, 91-94; del. Mo. Rep. Conv., 1972, 76, 80, 84, 88, 92, del. Nat. Rep. Conv., 1984. Named 1 of 10 Women of Achievement in good citizen category St. Louis Globe-Democrat, 1961; Alumna of Yr., Gamma Phi Beta, St. Louis, 1966; recipient St. Louis County Med. Soc. award of merit, 1964; Disting. Alumni citation Washington U., 1968, Disting. Alumni Svc. citation, 1977; Life Style award Eastern Mo. chpt. Am. Lung Assn., 1982; Meritorious Svc. award Am. Park and Recreation Soc., 1985; Endowed Richard A. and Elizabeth H. Sutter chair in Occupational, Industrial and Environ. Med., Washington U., St. Louis, 1993. Mem. Mo. Hist. Soc., St. Louis Symphony Soc., AMA Aux. (hon. life), Mo. Med. Aux. (hon. life), Met. St. Louis Med. Aux. (hon. life), Gamma Phi Beta (bd. found. St. Louis chpt. 1989). Presbyterian.. Home: 7215 Greenway Ave Saint Louis MO 63130-4126

SUTTER, JANE ELIZABETH, artist, educator; b. St. Louis, Nov. 27, 1939; d. Richard Anthony and Elizabeth Henby Sutter. AB in Sociology and English, Vassar Coll., 1961; MA in Health Facilities Mgmt., Webster U., St. Louis, 1979. Healthcare analyst Chgo. and St. Louis, 1966-83; asst. dir. radio, TV and motion picture dept. AMA, Chgo., 1966-67; staff coord., rsch. assoc. environ. health study Inst. of Medicine of Chgo., 1967-69; environ. health dir., planning assoc. Comprehensive Health Planning, Inc., Chgo., 1969-73; planning assoc., spl. asst. to med. dir. Sutter Clinic, Inc., St. Louis, 1975-84; vol. tchr., naturalist Shaw Arboretum, ext. of Mo. Bot. Garden, 1984—; vol. activist, educator. Chmn. Opera Guild St. Louis Newsletter, Vol. 1, No. 1, 1980, Vol. 1, No. 2, 1980; co-founder, com. mem. 1st Internat. Alewife Festival of Chgo., Chgo. Yacht Club, summer 1968; appointee Gov.'s Com. for Pure Air and Water, Chgo., 1968; dir. enrivon. health planning Comprehensive Health Planning, Inc., Chgo., 1969-73. Mem. Nat. Coun. State Garden Clubs, Inc., Federated Garden Clubs of Mo., Inc., Clayton Garden Assn., Mo. Bot. Garden-Shaw Arboretum, St. Louis Artists' Guild (mem. artists' sect. 1992-95, portraitist), Inst. Religion in an Age of Sci., The Racquet Club. Home: 7376 Pershing Blvd Saint Louis MO 63130

SUTTINGER, MARY CATHERINE, media specialist; b. Chgo., Aug. 5, 1945; d. Edward Lawrence and Juanita (Lavalle) White; m. Leonard Wayne Suttinger, Nov. 5, 1966. BA in English, St. Joseph's Coll., 1967; MA in English, Purdue U., 1973, MS in Media Sci., 1981. Juvenile cataloger Hammond (Ind.) Pub. Libr., 1967-68; grad. teaching asst. Purdue U., 1968-73, grad. instr. in English, 1979-85; tchr. English Highland (Ind.) Pub. Schs., 1973-79; tchr. English Crown Point (Ind.) Community Sch. Corp., 1985-86, media specialist, 1986—. Mem. AAUW, Assn. Ind. Media Specialists, Phi Kappa Phi. Roman Catholic. Home: 9015 Hess Dr Highland IN 46322-2132 Office: Taft Jr High Sch Libr 1000 S Main St Crown Point IN 46307-4830

SUTTON, BETTY, state legislator; married. BA, Kent State Univ., 1985; JD, Univ. Akron, 1990. Coun.-at-larte Barberton City Coun., 1990-91; v.p. Summit County Coun., 1991-92; state rep. Ohio Dist. 47, 1993—; vice chmn. Judiciary & Criminal Justice Com., mem. Civil & Comml. Law, Ways & Means, Ins. Pub. Utilities & Elec. Twp. Com. Recipient Outstanding Performance in Const. Law Fed. Bar Assn., 1989, Am. Jurisprudence award, 1989. Mem. ABA, Akron Child Guidance Adv. Coun., Assn. Trial Lawyers Am., Ohio Acad. Trial Lawyers, Summit County Trial Lawyers, Fed. Dem. Women. Home: OH Ho of Reps 338 Baird Ave Barberton OH 44203*

SUTTON, JAMES HERCULES, educational association administrator; b. Boston, Jan. 8, 1943; s. Hercules James and Paras (Zingovas) S.; m. Nancy Mona Kohrt, June 8, 1982; children: Michael, Raphael, Robert, Thessaly, Athena, Thalia. Cert. des solfèges, South End Music Ctr., Boston, 1958; BA, Brown U., 1964; MFA, U. Iowa, 1968, PhD, 1988. Lic. C.C. teaching, regional supt. and evaluator, Iowa. Asst. to dir. Textual Ctr., U. Iowa, Iowa City, 1966-68; labor organizer Iowa Higher Edn. Assn., Des Moines, 1971-73, exec. dir., 1973-74; lobbyist Iowa State Edn. Assn., Des Moines, 1974-80, dir. profl. devel., 1980-83, state agy. liaison, 1983-87, sr. policy analyst, 1987-94; orgn. specialist profl. issues, 1994—; licensure cons. NEA, Washington, 1989. Author: Sonnets for Athena, 1991, Prometheus, 1995. Office: Iowa State Edn Assn 4025 Tonawanda Dr Des Moines IA 50312-2909

SUTTON, JOHN MARTIN, industrial food broker, consultant; b. Indpls., July 21, 1922; s. Martin Luther and Margaret Louise (O'Conner) S.; m. Charlotte Jane Lewis, Feb. 9, 1944; children: Nancy Ann, Margaret Jane, John Jr., Mary Janet, Barbara Gail, Linda Sue, Richard Lewis. BS in Chemistry, Purdue U., 1948; postgrad., Ind. U., 1962-63. Office sales Hydraulic Press Brick Co., Indpls., 1946-52; dist. mgr. Union Starch & Refining Co., St. Louis, 1952-68; regional mgr. Union Div. Miles Labs., Chgo., 1968-71; dir. bulk sales Corn Sweeteners Inc., Cedar Rapids, Iowa, 1971-72, Corn Refining Div. ADM, Cedar Rapids, 1972; v.p., gen. mgr. Edible Soy Products, Waterloo, Iowa, 1972-76; exec. v.p., sec., treas. Scholl-Sutton, Inc., St. Louis, 1976-91; pres., CEO Sutton & Heinz, Inc., St. Louis, 1991—; also bd. dirs.; bd. dirs. Scholl-Sutton, Inc.; chmn. bd., pres., CEO Sutton Food Ingredients Inc.; pres. and CEO Sutton & Heinz, Inc., also bd. dirs. V.p. Brentwood (Mo.) Optimist Club, 1962-67; mem. Elks Lodge, Waterloo, 1974-76. 1st sgt. U.S. Army, 1943-46. Mem. Am. Assn. Cereal Chemists, Inst. Food Techs. (exec. com. St. Louis sect. 1980—, nat. counselor Chgo. 1985-89), Mo. Food Processors Assn., Cherry Hills Country Club, Scottish Rite, Masons. Republican. Home: 702 Lofty Point Dr # D Ballwin MO 63021-7726 Office: Sutton & Heinz Inc 614 S Kirkwood Rd Saint Louis MO 63122

SUTTON, MARY ELLEN, organist, educator; b. Butler, Mo., Nov. 7, 1940; d. Algie Charles and F. Elinor (Padley) S. AA, Graceland Coll., Lamoni, Iowa, 1960; BMus, U. Mo., Kansas City, 1963, MMus, 1968; DMA, U. Kans., 1975. Elem. music specialist Independence Mo. Pub. Schs., 1964-67; from instr. to prof. music Mo. Valley Coll., Marshall, 1968-73; prof. organ Kans. State U., Manhattan, 1974—. Composer ch. music; recitals include Internat. Summer Organ Acad., The Netherlands, 1978, 82; contbr. articles to profl. jours. organist 1st Presbyn. Ch., Manhattan, Kans., 1975-77, 1st United Meth. Ch., Manhattan, 1977—. Mem. Am. Guild Organists (dist. convenor 1983-89, dean Topeka chpt., chair task force on young organist 1984-86), Music Tchrs. Nat. Assn., Kans. Music Tchrs. Assn. (exec. bd., state sec.). Office: Kans State U Music Dept McCain Auditorium Manhattan KS 66506

SUTTON, PEGGY ROSE, critical care nurse; b. Zanesville, Ohio, Dec. 8, 1955; d. Rudolph and Rosie Lee (Lancaster) Boykin Foos; m. Mark A. Sutton, Apr. 8, 1978; 1 child, Luke Markus. Diploma, Mansfield Gen. Hosp., 1977; BS Profl. Arts in Health Care Adminstrn., St. Joseph's Coll., Windham, Maine, 1989. CCRN. Staff nurse Galion (Ohio) Community Hosp., 1978; charge and staff nurse intensive care and critical care units Marion (Ohio) Gen. Hosp., 1978-79, asst. head nurse intensive care and critical care units, 1981-85, head nurse intensive care and critical care units, chmn. head nurse group, 1985-92; nurse mgr. intensive care, post anesthesia care, endoscopy, 1992—. Mem. AACN. Home: 4445 State Route 309 Galion OH 44833-9616

SUTTON, PETER ALFRED, archbishop; b. Chandler, Que., Can., Oct. 18, 1934. BA, U. Ottawa, 1960; MA in Religious Edn, Loyola U., Chgo., 1969. Ordained priest Roman Catholic Ch., 1960, bishop, 1974; oblate of Mary Immaculate; high sch. tchr. St. Patricks, Ottawa, Ont., 1961-63, London (Ont.) Cath. Cen. Sch., 1963-74; bishop of Labrador-Schefferville, Que., Can., 1974—; archbishop Missionary Diocese of Keewatin-Le Pas, Man., 1986, apptd. coadjutor archbishop, 1986—, archbishop, 1986—; mem. Can. Conf. Cath. Bishops, Western Cath. Conf. of No. Bishops, Man. Bishops; accompanying Bishop L'Arch Internat. (homes for mentally handicapped), 1983—. Contbr. religious articles to newspapers. Address: PO Box 270, 108 1st St W, The Pas, MB Canada R9A 1K4

SUTTON, SHARON EGRETTA, architect, educator, artist; b. Cin., Feb. 18, 1941; d. Booker and Egretta (Sutton) Johnson. Student, Manhattan Sch. Music, 1959-62; MusB, U. Hartford, Conn., 1963; postgrad., Parson's Sch. Design, N.Y.C., 1967-69; MArch, Columbia U., 1973; PhM, CUNY, 1981, MA, PhD in Psychology, 1982. Registered architect, N.Y., Mich. Pvt. practice architect N.Y.C. and Dexter, Mich., 1976—; vis. asst. prof. Columbia U., N.Y.C., 1981-82; asst. prof. U. Cin., 1982-84; assoc. prof. U. Mich., Ann Arbor, 1984-94, prof., 1994—; architect-in-residence NEA, N.Y.C., 1978-82; keynote spkr., lectr. colls. and profl. meetings. One-woman shows include Nat. Urban League, N.Y.C., 1980, Your Heritage House, Detroit, 1986, June Kelly Gallery, N.Y.C., 1987; exhibited in group shows at Studio Mus., N.Y.C., 1979, U. Mich. Mus. Art, Ann Arbor, 1988, Art-in-Gen. Gallery, Soho, N.Y.C., 1990; represented in permanent collections Mint Mus., Charlotte, N.C., Wadsworth Atheneum, Hartford, Conn., Balt. Mus. Art; Author: Learning Through The Built Environment, 1985, Weaving a Tapestry of Resistance, 1996; mem. editl. bd. Jour. Archtl. Edn., 1984-87; contbr. articles to profl. jours. Coord. The Urban Network-an urban design program for youth funded by NEA Design Cities Program Kellogg Found., U. Mich., 1988—. Recipient Postbaccalaureate award Danforth Found., 1977-81, Design Rsch. award NEA, 1983, Edn. award Am. Planning Assn., 1991, Regents award for disting. pub. svc. U. Mich., 1992, Mich. Humanities award, 1995, Disting. Prof. award Assn. Collegiate Schs. Architecture, 1996; grantee NEA, 1988-90; W.K. Kellogg Found. fellow, 1986-89. Fellow AIA; mem. APA, Am. Ednl. Rsch. Assn., Nat. Archtl. Accreditation Bd. (bd. dirs. 1995-98). Democrat. Home: 8071 Main St Dexter MI 48130-1027 Office: Coll Architecture/Urban Planning U Mich Ann Arbor MI 48109-2069

SUVA, SUZANNE, personnel relations executive, consultant, educator; b. Cleve., Feb. 15, 1947; d. James Patrick and Marie (Kohut) Monnolly; m. Robert J. Suva; children: Heather Marie, Sara Beth. BA in Psychology and Bus., Baldwin Wallace Coll., 1984; postgrad., Cleve. Marshall Law Sch., 1987-90. Cert. sr. profl. in human resources. Pers. asst. J.M. Smucker Co., Medina, Ohio, 1973-76; asst. mgr pers. Eaton Corp., Aurora, Ohio, 1976-85; mgr. personnel, supr. employee rels. Lubrizol Corp., Wickliffe, Ohio, 1985—; mem. adv. bd. Women Starting Over for Success, Cleve. State U., 1985-93. Dep. registrar Summit County Bd. Elections, Akron, 1984—; clinic leader freedom from smoking Am. Lung Assn., Cleve., 1984-94. Mem. Soc. Human Resource Mgrs., Am. Humane Soc., Alpha Lambda Sigma. Roman Catholic. Home: 801 Silverberry Ln Hudson OH 44236-4621 Office: Lubrizol Corp 29400 Lakeland Blvd Wickliffe OH 44092-2201

SUZUKI, TSUNEO, molecular immunologist; b. Nagoya, Aichi, Japan, Nov. 23, 1931; s. Morichika and Toshiko (Kita) S.; widowed; children: Riichiro, Aijiro, Yozo. BS, U. Tokyo, 1953, MD, 1957; PhD, U. Hokkaido, 1967. Asst. prof. U. Kans. Med. Ctr., Kansas City, 1970-79, assoc. prof., 1979-83, prof., 1983—, interim chair, 1994—; mem. NIH Study Sect., Washington, 1983-87. Contbr. articles to profl. jours. Postdoctoral fellows U. Wis., 1963-66, 69-70, U. Lausanne, Switzerland, 1966-67, U Toronto, 1969; recipient Fulbright Travel award, 1962, Sr. Investigator award, U. Kans. Med. Ctr., 1990. Mem. Am. Assn. Immunologists, Am. Soc. Biological Chemists (Travel award 1988). Home: 3620 W 73rd St Prairie Vlg KS 66208-2903 Office: U Kans Med Ctr Dept Microbiology 3901 Rainbow Blvd Kansas City KS 66160-0001

SVARD, TRYGVE N., electrical engineer; b. Gothenburg, Sweden; came to U.S., 1973; s. Owe V. and Berit S. (Heden) S. m. Janet M. Ziemer, July 18, 1969; children: Michael, Stefan. BEE, Gothensburg U., Sweden, 1966. Registered profl. engr. Engr. Volvo Car Div., Gothenburg, 1969-73; from project engr., sr. sect. engr. to program mgr. Honeywell Inc., Mpls., 1973-90; sr. program mgr., internat. programs Alliant Techsystems, Inc., Mpls., 1990—; pres. Nord Mark Inc., Mpls, 1986--. Sgt. Swedish Coast Arty., 1967-68. Mem. Am. Swedish Inst. Republican. Home: 12075 48th Ave N Minneapolis MN 55442-2129

SVEDJAN, KEN, state legislator; m. Lorrtta; 1 child. BS, Valley City State Coll., U. N.D.; MS, U. N.D. Mem. N.D. Ho. of Reps., 1991—, vice chmn. human svcs. com., mem. vet. affairs, polit. subdivsns., nat. resources coms. Pres. United Health Found.; chmn. bd. Third St. Clinic. Recipient Disting. Svc. award Am. Diabetes Assn. Mem. Rotary Internat. (bd. dirs.), Grand Forks C. of C., Elks. Home: 1300 Lincoln Dr Grand Forks ND 58201-5645*

SVEEN, GERALD O., state legislator; m. Ruth Ellen; 3 children. Student, U. N.D., Temple U. Dentist, mayor; mem. N.D. Ho. of Reps., 1993—, mem. edn., transp. coms. With USAF, Korea. Recipient Cmty. Svc. award. Mem. Am. Legion, Lions, Creek Cemetery Assn. (pres.). Home: 411 5th St E Bottineau ND 58318-1403*

SVENDSEN, DALE PHILLIP, psychiatrist, health care administrator, educator; b. Chgo., May 12, 1942; s. Fred Gunnar Svendsen and Margaret (Fletcher) Hansen; m. Gail Elise Michalsen, July 2, 1966; children: Margot, Kirsten, Peter. BA, No. Ill. U., 1964; MD, Ohio State U., 1967, MS in Psychiatry, 1971. Diplomate Am. Bd. Psychiatry and Neurology. Asst. prof. psychiatry Pa. State U., Hershey, 1973-75; sr. psychiatrist and chief Ohio State U. Mental Health Clinic, Columbus, 1975-91; med. dir. Ohio Dept. Mental Health, Columbus, 1991—; clin. asst. prof. psychiatry Ohio State U., Columbus, 1975—; staff psychiatrist Riverside Meth. Hosp., Columbus, 1975—, psychiat. teaching liaison to family practice, 1983—. Investigator and rschr. eating behaviors of coll. students, 1979-91. Maj. U.S. Army, 1971-73. Fellow Am. Psychiat. Assn. (rep. from Ohio to assembly 1993—); mem. Am. Assn. Cmty. Psychiatrists, Nat. Assn. State Mental Health Program Dirs. (med. dirs. divsn. 1993—), Am. Coll. Physician Execs., Ohio Psychiat. Assn. (pres. 1990-91), Ohio State Med. Assn., Psychiat. Soc. Ctrl. Ohio, Franklin County Med. Soc., Scandinavian Club of Columbus (pres. 1981-82), Alpha Omega Alpha. Home: 1487 Guilford Rd Columbus OH 43221-3884 Office: Ohio Dept Mental Health 30 E Broad St Columbus OH 43266-0414

SVIHLIK, SUSAN JESSUP, editor; b. Richmond, Ind., Apr. 26, 1947; d. Richard Albert and Alice (Eby) J.; m. Charles Edward Svihlik, Aug. 30, 1969 (div. May 1991); children: Charles Richard, Sarah Lorraine, Thomas Joseph. BS, Northwestern U., 1969. Copy editor, asst. Sunday editor Indpls. Star, 1969-86; Sunday editor, features editor Richmond (Ind.) Palladium-Item, 1986-91; mng. editor, exec. editor Tribune Chronicle, Warren, Ohio, 1991—. Bd. dirs. LEadership Mahoning Valley, Youngstown, Ohio, 1996—; mem. exec. bd. Chamber Orch., Warren, 1996—; mem. govt. affairs com. Warren C. of C., 1996—. Mem. Am. Soc. Newspaper Editors, Associated Press Soc. Ohio (bd. dirs. 1994—), Soc. Profl. Journalists. Episcopalian. Office: Tribune Chronicle 240 Franklin St SE Warren OH 44482

SVOBODA, DONNA LEE, neonatal nurse; b. St. Clair County, Ill., Aug. 28, 1951; d. James F. Sr. and Pat Lee (Souchek) Durer; m. John R. Svoboda, July 25, 1970; 1 child, Jennifer Lynn. BS in Edn., So. Ill. U., 1973; BSN, So. Ill. U., Edwardsville, 1987. Neonatal staff nurse, parenting skills coord. and educator Anderson Hosp., Maryville, Ill. Recipient Esther Ott Estes award in nursing, 1987, Outstanding Nurse Recognition award March of Dimes Birth Defects Found., 1995. Mem. Nat. Assn. Neonatal Nurses, Sigma Theta Tau (Granting Body Esther Ott Estes award Epsilon Eta chpt.), Phi Kappa Phi. Home: 106 Dunlap Cove Ct S Edwardsville IL 62025-2491

SVOBODA, JANICE JUNE, nurse; b. Dorchester, Wis., June 13, 1933; d. Alfred A. and Jessie (Boor) Hinke; m. Glenn R. Svoboda, July 20, 1957; children: Melora, Kevin, Craig. Diploma, Luther Hosp., 1954; cert., U. Wis., 1955; student, U. Wis., Madison; BS in Health Edn. cum laude, U. Wis., Milw., 1980; student, Alverno Coll., 1991-92. Pub. health nurse Ozaukee County, Wis., 1979, 86; asst. instr. nursing Milw. Area Tech. Coll., 1979-83; instr. seminar Cardinal Stritch Coll., Milw., 1985-87; nutritional counselor Nutri-Sys., Grafton, Wis., 1987-90; instr. seminar Milw. Area Tech. Coll., 1983, 90, health seminars Alverno Coll., Milw., 1991-95, designed and implemented alternative health and healing seminar,Alverno Coll., 1994—. Mem. Am. Holistic Nurses Assn., N.Am. Nutrition Preventive Medicine Assn., Ctr. for Sci. in the Pub. Interest.

SWADENER, JOHN REA, product development engineer; b. Mishawaka, Ind., July 12, 1969; s. James Leonard and Virginia Lenore (Rea) S.; m. Staci Lynn Lymangrover, Oct. 2, 1993. BS, Ind. U., South Bend, 1991; M of Computer Sci. and Engring., U. Notre Dame, 1994. Engr. Allied Signal-ALS, South Bend, 1990-94, product devel. team leader, 1994-95; product devel. engr. Allied Signal-Aircraft Landing Sys., South Bend, 1995—. Vol. Battell Cmty. Ctr., Mishawaka, Ind., 1993—. Mem. IEEE. Democrat. Roman Catholic. Office: Allied Signal/ Aircraft Landing Sys 3520 Westmoor St South Bend IN 46628

SWAIMAN, KENNETH FRED, pediatric neurologist, educator; b. St. Paul, Nov. 19, 1931; s. Lester J. and Shirley (Ryan) S.; m. Phyllis Kammerman Sher, Oct. 1985; children: Lisa, Jerrold, Barbara, Dana. B.A. magna cum laude, U. Minn., 1952, B.S., 1953, M.D., 1955; postgrad., 1956-58; postgrad. (fellow pediatric neurology), Nat. Inst. Neurologic Diseases and Blindness, 1960-63. Diplomate: Am. Bd. Psychiatry and Neurology, Am. Bd. Pediatrics. Intern Mpls. Gen. Hosp., 1955-56; resident pediatrics U. Minn., 1956-58, neurology, 1960-63; postgrad. fellow pediatric neurology Nat. Inst. Neurologic Diseases and Blindness, 1960-63; asst. prof. pediatrics, neurology U. Minn. Med. Sch., Mpls., 1963-66; asso. prof. Nat. Inst. Neurologic Diseases and Blindness, 1966-69; prof., dir. pediatric neurology U. Minn. Med. Sch., 1969—; interim head Dept. Neurology, U. Minn. Med. Sch., 1994-96; interim head dept. neurology U. Minn. Med. Sch., 1994—, mem. internship adv. council exec. faculty, 1966-70; interim head dept. neurology, 1994—; cons. pediatric neurology Hennepin County Gen. Hosp., Mpls., St. Paul-Ramsey Hosp., St. Paul Children's Hosp., Mpls. Children's Hosp.; vis. prof. Beijing U. Med. Sch., 1989. Author: (with Francis S. Wright) Neuromuscular Diseases in Infancy and Childhood, 1969, Pediatric Neuromuscular Diseases, 1979, (with Stephen Ashwal) Pediatric Neurology Case Studies, 1978, 2d edit., 1984, Pediatric Neurology: Practice and Principles, 1989; editor: (with John A. Anderson) Phenylketonuria and Allied Metabolic Diseases, 1966, (with Francis S. Wright) Practice Pediatric Neurology, 1975, 2d edit., 1982; mem. editorial bd.: Annals of Neurology, 1977-83, Neurology Update, 1977-82, Pediatric Update, 1977-85, Brain and Devel. (Jour. Japanese Soc. Child Neurology), 1980—, Neuropediatrics (Stuttgart), 1982-92; editor-in-chief: Pediatric Neurology, 1984—; contbr. articles to sci. jours. Chmn. Minn. Gov.'s Bd. for Handicapped, Exceptional and Gifted Children, 1972-76; mem. human devel. study sect. NIH, 1976-79, guest worker, 1978-81. Served to capt. M.C. U.S. Army, 1958-60. Fellow Am. Acad. Pediatrics, Am. Acad. Neurology (rep. to nat. council Nat. Soc. Med. Research); mem. Soc. Pediatric Research, Central Soc. Clin. Research, Central Soc. Neurol. Research, Internat. Soc. Neurochemistry, Am. Neurol. Assn., Minn. Neurol. Soc., AAAS, Midwest Pediatric Soc., Am. Soc. Neurochemistry, Child Neurology Soc. (1st pres. 1972-73, Hower award 1981, chmn. internat. affairs com., 1991—, mem. long range planning com. 1991—), Internat. Assn. Child Neurologists (exec. com. 1975-79), Profs. of Child Neurology (1st pres. 1978-80, mem. nominating com. 1986—), Japanese Child Neurology Soc. (Segawa award 1986, mem. nominating com. 1986—, chair internat. affairs com. 1991—, mem. long range planning com. 1991—), Soc. de Psiquiatria y Neurologia de la Infancia y Adolescencia, Phi Beta Kappa, Sigma Xi.

Home: 420 Delaware St SE Minneapolis MN 55455-0374 Office: U Minn Med Sch Dept Pediatric Neurology Minneapolis MN 55455

SWAISGOOD, BRUCE WILLIAM, mechanical engineer; b. Ashland, Ohio, Aug. 5, 1964; s. Donald William and Pauline Janet S. AAS, North Ctrl. Tech. Coll., Mansfield, Ohio, 1984; BSME, Franklin U., Columbus, Ohio, 1995. Product engr. Neer Mfg. Co., Inc., Mansfield, 1984—. Mem. Jeromesville (Ohio) Christian Ch., 1984—. Office: Neer Mfg Co Inc PO Box 3089 265 S Mill St Mansfield OH 44904-9572

SWAN, JAMES BYRON, agronomy educator, soil scientist; b. Normal, Ill., Dec. 9, 1933; s. Emmett B. and Kathryn (Barth) S.; m. Patricia E. Brintnall, Apr. 23, 1962. BS, U. Ill., 1955, MS, 1959; PhD, U. Wis., 1964. Asst. prof. soil sci. U. Minn., St. Paul, 1964-68, assoc. prof. soil sci., 1968-75, prof. soil sci., 1975-89; prof. agronomy and assoc. dir. Leopold Ctr. for Sustainable Agr., Iowa State U., Ames, 1989—; study team mem., co-author report and recommendations on organic farming Agrl. Rsch. Svc., USDA, 1980. Contbr. articles to Soil Sci. Soc. Am. Jour., Soil & Tillage Rsch., Agronomy Jour. With U.S. Army, 1955-57. Coop. States Rsch. Svc. grantee USDA, 1988, 90, 93. Mem. Am. Soc. Agronomy, Soil Sci. Soc. Am., Sigma Xi. Office: Iowa State U Dept Agronomy Ames IA 50011

SWAN, PETER MICHAEL, engineering executive; b. London, Dec. 6, 1934; s. Percy Joseph and Eileen Penrose (Damerall-Stevens) S.; m. Rosalba Wilma Arauco, Nov. 8, 1967; children: Heather Marina, Lois Vivian. BSME, Brighton Tech. Coll., 1960. Design engr. British Rail, Brighton, England, 1958-63; chief mech. engr. Bolivian Railroads, La Paz, 1963-65; maintenance mgr. Marcona Mining Co., San Juan, Peru, 1965-69; from plant mgr. to dir. ops. Internat. Mill Svc., Munster, Ind., 1969—. Mem. Inst. Mech. Engrs. (U.K.). Home: 1324 Tamarack Dr Munster IN 46321 Office: Internat Mill Svc PO Box M824 Gary IN 46401

SWANK, DAVID BRIAN, telecommunications industry executive; b. Akron, Ohio, June 15, 1957; s. Roland D. and Norma L. (Adams) S.; m. Clare M. Paquelet, Jan. 2, 1982; children: Katherine R., Andrew D. BSBA, Ohio State U., 1980; MBA, So. Meth. U., Dallas, 1989. CPA, Tex. Mgr. Peat, Marwick, Mitchell & Co., Dallas, 1980-85; CFO AVM Syss., Inc., Ft. Worth, 1985-86; audit mgr. Pepsico, Inc., Dallas, 1986-89; regional contr. Pepsico Foods Internat., Dallas, 1989-92; CFO Teledyne Fluid Syss., Brecksville, Ohio, 1994; CFO Telxon Corp., Akron, Ohio, 1994-95, exec. v.p. corp. devel., 1995—; chmn. Virtual Vision, Inc., Seattle, 1995—; bd. dirs. Metanetics Corp., Ft. Meyers, Fla. Mem. Beta Alpha Psi, Beta Gamma Sigma. Office: Telxon Corp 3330 W Market St Akron OH 44333

SWANN, MICHAEL M., geographer, educator; b. Kansas City, Mo., Feb. 10, 1950; s. Maurice M. and Jeanette M. (Ziegel) S.; m. Patricia Ann Lambert, Dec. 30, 1978. BA in History and Geography, U. Kans., 1972; MA in Geography, Syracuse U., 1975, Cert. Latin Am. Studies, 1975, PhD in Geography, 1980. Thomas Watson grad. fellow Syracuse U., 1972-75, Shell rsch. fellow, 1975-76, instr., 1977-78; vis. asst. prof. U. Okla., Norman, 1978-79; asst. prof. U. Nebr., Lincoln, 1979-85; dir. Regents Ctr. for Archtl. Studies, Kansas City, Mo., 1988-92; asst. prof. Kans. State U., Kansas City, 1989; dir. grad. program in archtl. mgmt. U. Kans., Kansas City, 1991—; asst. dean and assoc. prof. U. Kans., Lawrence, 1991—; dir. Kansas City Ctr. for Design Edn. & Rsch., 1992—; adj. assoc. prof. U. Mo.-Kansas City, 1992—. Author: Tierra Adentro, 1982, Migrants in the Mexican North, 1989, Design for the Displaced, 1991, Making Urban and Rural Landscapes on the Prarie-Plains, 1996; contbr. articles to profl. jours. Bd. dirs. Kansas City (Mo.) Planning Ctr., 1988-90, Carnegie Ctr. for the Arts, Leavenworth, Kans., 1990-91, Kansas City Archtl. Found., 1990—, Ctr. for Understanding the Built Environment, 1994—; mem. steering com. Wayside Waifs Animal Shelter, Kansas City, 1992—; mem. adv. bd. U. Kans. Regents Ctr. Recipient Presdl. Recognition award Am. Soc. Landscape Architects, 1991; George Holmes faculty fellow U. Nebr., 1983; Newberry Libr. vis. fellow, 1982. Mem. AIA (hon.), Am. Hist. Assn., Assn. Am. Geographers, Assn. Borderlands Scholars, Latin Am. Studies Assn., Historic Kansas City Found., U. Kans. Alumni Assn., Nat. Trust for Historic Preservation, Vernacular Arch. Forum. Home: 6444 Summit St Kansas City MO 64113-1558 Office: Univ of Kans Sch Arch & Urban Design Lawrence KS 66045

SWANSEN, ANITA C., educator; b. Almena, Wis., Aug. 14, 1940; d. Henry John and Theresa Marie (Naser) S. B of Elem. Edn., Mt. Senario Coll., Ladysmith, Wis., 1970; M in Religious Edn., Seattle U., 1978; Pastoral Ministry Cert., Trinity Coll., Washington, 1974. Cert. tchr., Wis., Minn., N.J. Tchr. elem. grades Cath. Schs., Wis., Minn., N.J., 1960-75; elem. prin. St. Joseph Annes, Carteret, N.J., 1970-71; dir. religious edn. St. Thomas Parish, St. Paul, 1975-92; pres. Sisters Servants of Mary, Ladysmith, 1992—; coun. rep. Sisters coun. Archdiocese of St. Paul, 1977-91; vol. night chaplain St. John's Hosp., St. Paul, 1981; mem. jusice and peace com. Servants of Mary, Ladysmith, 1974-87. Democrat. Roman Catholic. Office: Servants of Mary 1000 College Ave W Ladysmith WI 54858

SWANSON, DARLENE MARIE CARLSON, speech therapist, educator, speaker, writer; b. Boone, Iowa, Aug. 8, 1925; d. Arvid Wilhelm and Edith Marie (Peterson) Carlson; m. Reuben Theodore Swanson, Aug. 8, 1948; children: Conrad T., Joyce Marie Swanson Jobson. BA, Augustana Coll., 1947; postgrad., U. Chgo., 1949, Creighton U., 1972; student, Joslyn Art Mus., Omaha, 1975. Cert. tchr., Ill., Nebr. Speech therapist Rock Island and Rockford (Ill.) Pub. Sch. System, 1946-51, Omaha (Nebr.) Pub. Sch. System, 1963-64; ch. organist Calvary Luth. Ch., Moline, Ill., 1944-46; asst. organist Augustana Luth. Ch., Omaha, 1956-63; mortuary organist Swanson-Golden Mortuary, Omaha, 1956-63; freelance lectr., 1960—; freelance writer, 1960—; chalk artist lectr. and pub. speaker, retreat leader; observer Luth. World Fedn. Assembly, Budapest, Hungary, 1984. Sunday sch. tchr. Kountze Mem. Luth. Ch., Omaha, 1964-74; Sunday sch. supr. St. Andrew's Luth. Ch., West Hemstead, N.Y., 1951-54; sec. Omaha PTA, 1968-70; mem. adv. coun. Cen. High Sch., Omaha, 1971-74, Omaha Pub. Schs., 1971-74; bd. dirs., sec. Luth. Summer Music Program, 1990—; active Met. Opera Guild, 1986-90, Omaha Opera Guild, 1990—, Omaha Symphony Guild, 1990—; bd. dirs. Bethpage Mission Gt. Britain, sec., 1994—. Named Vol. of Yr. Omaha Head Start Program, 1965. Address: PO Box 37448 Omaha NE 68137-0448

SWANSON, DAVID HEATH, agricultural company executive; b. Aurora, Ill., Nov. 3, 1942; s. Neil H. and Helen J. (McKendry) S.; children: Benjamin Heath, Matthew Banford. B.A., Harvard U., 1964; M.A., U. Chgo., 1969. Account exec. 1st Nat. Bank Chgo., 1967-69; dep. mgr. Brown Bros. Harriman & Co., N.Y.C., 1969-72; asst. treas. Borden, Inc., N.Y.C., 1972-75; v.p., treas. Continental Grain Co., N.Y.C., 1975-77, v.p., CFO, 1977-79, gen. mgr. European div., 1979-81, exec. v.p. and gen. mgr. World Grain div., 1981-83, corp. sr. v.p., chief fin. and adminstrv. officer, 1983-86, group pres., 1985-86; pres., CEO Cen. Soya, Ft. Wayne, Ind., 1986-93; chmn. Premiere Agri Tech., Inc., Ft. Wayne, 1994—; chmn., CEO Explorer Nutrition Group, N.Y.C., 1995-96; pres., CEO, Countrymark Coop., Inc., Indpls., 1996—; mem. adv. bd. U.S. Export-Import Bank, 1985-86; mem. Gov.'s Agrl. Bd. Ind.; bd. dirs. Fiduciary Trust Internat., Conrail. Mem. Internat. Policy Coun. on Agr. and Trade; mem. adv. bd. Purdue U. Agr. Sch.; mem. Gov.'s Econ. Devel. Ind. Bd.; bd. govs. Exec. Coun. on Fgn. Diplomats and U.S. Agr. Libr.; gov. Found. for U.S. Constn. Mem. Coun. Fgn. Rels., Nat. Assn. Mfrs. (bd. dirs.), Ind. C. of C. (bd. dirs.), Am. Alpine Club (bd. dirs.), Links Club, Racquet and Tennis Club, Explorers Club (bd. dirs., sec., pres.). Republican. Congregationalist. Office: Countrymark Coop Inc 950 N Meridian St Indianapolis IN 46204-3909

SWANSON, DONALD FREDERICK, retired food company executive; b. Mpls., Aug. 6, 1927; s. Clayton A. and Irma (Baiocchi) S.; m. Virginia Clare Hannah, Dec. 17, 1948; children—Donald Frederick, Cynthia Hannah Lindgren, Janet Clare Webster. B.A., U. Minn., 1948. With Gen. Mills, Inc., 1949-85, div. v.p., dir. marketing flour, dessert and baking mixes, 1964-65, v.p., gen. mgr. grocery products div., 1965-68, v.p., corporate adminstrn. officer consumer foods group, fashion div., transp. and purchasing depts., advt. and marketing services, 1969, exec. v.p. craft, game and toy group, fashion group, direct marketing group, travel group, dir., 1968-76, sr. exec. v.p. consumer non-foods, 1976-85, chief financial officer, 1977-79, sr. exec. v.p. restaurants and consumer non-foods, 1980-81, vice chmn. restaurants and consumer non-foods, 1981-85; ret. chmn. bd. Soo Line Corp. Served with AUS, 1946-47. Mem. Lafayette Club, Mpls. Club, Wayzata Country Club, Royal Poinciana Golf Club, Phi Kappa Psi. Home: Apt 504 2171 Gulf Shore Blvd N Naples FL 34102 Office: 641 Lake St E Wayzata MN 55391-1760

SWANSON, JACK LEE, chemistry educator; b. Aurora, Nebr., Oct. 22, 1934; s. Kermit Seander and Blanch Mertyl (Hansen) S.; m. Myrna Rose Schaffert, June 3, 1956; children: Jacqueline Lee, Julie Lynn, Jane Louise. BA, Kearney (Nebr.) State Coll., 1956; MS, U. Nebr., 1959, PhD, 1967. Lab. asst. U. Nebr., Lincoln, 1956-58; prof. chemistry U. Nebr., Kearney, 1958-71; dean Chadron (Nebr.) State Coll., 1971-87, prof., 1987-95. Mem. Chadron Sch. Bd. Dist. 2, 1981—. Mem. NEA, Am. Chem. Soc., Nebr. Acad. Sci. (pres. 1990), Chadron C. of C. (pres. 1976), Gideons Internat. (pres. Chadron 1992), Kiwanis (pres. Chadron 1975, lt. gov. Rocky Mountain dist. 1990-91), Sigma Xi. Republican. Lutheran. Home: 801 Maple St Chadron NE 69337-2554

SWANSON, KATHRYN ANN, communications executive; b. Chgo., Dec. 5, 1961; d. Paul Sigfrid and Marilyn Laverne Swanson; children: Andrew Mankivsky, Matthew Mankivsky. BA in Polit. Sci., Wheaton Coll., 1983; MPA, No. Ill. U., 1989. Dir. DuPage Office House Minority Leader Lee Daniels, Addison, Ill., 1983-88; dep. chief staff House Minority Caucus, Chgo., 1988-91; proprietor KSM Consulting, Wheaton, Ill., 1992-95; pres. Strategic Comms. Inc., Wheaton, 1994—; asst. to pres. for govtl. rels. No. Ill. U., DeKalb, 1995—. Mem. Ill. City Mgmt. Assn., Sycamore C. of C. (bd. dirs.). Office: Strategic Comm Inc 1547 Huntleigh Dr Wheaton IL 60187

SWANSON, RAYMOND E., pathologist; b. Chgo., Dec. 8, 1927; s. Elmer B. and Doris M. (Leichtfeld) S.; m. Joanne Lankenau, Dec. 16, 1950; children: Raymond, Randall, Richard, Rebecca. BA, Valparaiso U., 1951; MS, Wayne State U., 1954; MD, U. Md., 1958. Diplomate Am. Bd. Pathology, Am. Bd. Anatomical and Clin. Pathology. Resident in pathology Wayne State U., Detroit, 1960-64; assoc. pathologist, instr. med. tech. Hackly Hosp., Muskegon, Mich., 1964-77; pathologist Med. Pathfinders Inc., Fennville, Mich., 1977-79; dir. labs. Goshen (Ind.) Hosp., 1980-89; cons. pathologist Mich. and Ind., 1989—; chief med. examiner Muskegon County, 1973-77; pres. Elkhart County (Ind.) Bd. Health, 1989. With USN, 1945-47; with USMC, 1951-52, Korea. With USN, 1945-47; with USMC, 1951-52, Korea. Fellow Coll. Am. Pathologists, Am. Soc. Clin. Pathologists; mem. Mich. Soc. Pathologist, Ind. Assn. Pathologists, Ind. Med. Soc. Methodist. Home: 207 Island View Dr Goshen IN 46526

SWANSON, ROBERT LEE, lawyer; b. Fond du Lac, Wis., July 15, 1942; s. Walfred S. and Edna F. (Kamp) S.; m. Mary Ruth Francis, Aug. 19, 1967; children: Leigh Alexandra, Mitchell Pearson. BS, U. Wis., 1964; JD, Valparaiso U., 1970; LLM, Boston U., 1979. Bar: Wis. 1970, U.S. Dist. Ct. (ea. dist.) Wis. 1970, U.S. Dist. Ct. (we. dist.) Wis. 1974, U.S. Dist. Ct. (cen.) Ill. 1988, U.S. Tax Ct. 1981. Atty. Kasdorf, Dahl, Lewis & Swietlik, Milw., 1970-73; atty., ptnr. Wartman, Wartman & Swanson, Ashland, Wis., 1973-80; city atty. City of Ashland, Wis., 1976-80; atty., ptnr. DeMark, Kolbe & Brodek, Racine, Wis., 1980-95; ptnr. Hartig, Bjelajac, Swanson & Koenen, Racine, 1995—; lectr. civil rights and discrimination laws, 1980—. Columnist (legal) Burlington Std. Press, 1991—, Wis. Restaurant Assn. Mag., 1986. Vice comdr. USCG Aux. Bayfield (Wis.) Flotilla, 1975-81; v.p., bd. dirs. Meml. Med. Ctr., Ashland, 1975-80; chmn. Ashland County Rep. Party, 1976-79; vol. atty. ACLU Wis., 1975—. 1st lt. U.S. Army, 1964-66. Named one of Outstanding Young Men of Am., Jaycees, 1978; recipient Disting. Achievement in Art and Sci. of Advocacy award Internat. Acad. Trial Lawyers, 1970. Mem. Racine County Bar Assn. (bd. dirs. 1986-89), Wis. Acad. Trial Lawyers, Def. Rsch. Inst., Am. Hockey Assn. U.S. (coach, referee 1983—), Am. Legion, The Federalist Soc. Home: 333 Hollow Creek Rd Racine WI 53402-2637 Office: Hartig Bjelajac Swanson and Koenen 601 Lake Ave Racine WI 53401-0038

SWANSON, ROBERT MARTIN, medical center administrator, ordained priest; b. Bell, Calif., Oct. 14, 1940; s. Harold M. and Elsie Lorraine (Allison) S.; AB, Long Beach (Calif.) State Coll., 1963; MA, U. Iowa, 1965; PhD, UCLA, 1970; m. Katharine Vivian Martin, Feb. 16, 1980. Dir., Office of Mental Health Rsch., U. Iowa, Iowa City, 1966-70; rsch. dir. Health Planning Coun., St. Paul, 1970-73; exec. dir. Kansas City (Mo.) Health Plan, 1973-75; asst. dir. St. Louis U. Hosps., 1975-80; asst. v.p. and chief planning officer St. Louis U. Med. Ctr., 1981-87, assoc. v.p., 1988—; pastor St. Basil the Great Orthodox Ch., 1987—; dir. Organizational Rsch. & Devel. Corp., Kansas City; dir., sec., chmn. awards com. Group Health Found. of Greater St. Louis; dir., sec., alliance for community health; dir. Family Care Ctr. Carondelet; clin. prof. St. Louis U. Grad. Sch. Pub. Health, 1980—; adj. prof. Webster Coll., St. Louis, 1975-82; spl. cons. to Kansas City (Mo.) Health Dept., 1974-75; tech. cons. Health Services Adminstrn., HEW, 1973-75; coord. St. Louis Community-Univ. Conf., 1977-80; mem. health affairs task force Mo. Cath. Conf., 1977. Named Adm. in Nebr. Navy, 1971; State of Iowa grantee, 1969. Mem. Nat. Assn. Hosp. Devel. (cert.), Am. Mgmt. Assn., Soc. for Advancement Mgmt., N.Am. Soc. Corp. Planners, Internat. Platform Assn., Advt. Club Greater St. Louis, Zeta Beta Tau. Republican. Eastern Orthodox. Contbr. articles on health services to profl. jours. Office: 3556 Caroline St Saint Louis MO 63104-1008

SWANSON, ROBERT MCLEAN, retired business educator; b. Union City, Pa., Aug. 11, 1920; s. Peter Leonard and Mary Edna (McLean) S.; m. Marie Manda, May 25, 1946; children: Catherine, Robert Jr., Mary Ann, Christina. BS in Edn., Ind. U. of Pa., 1942; MA, Columbia U., 1949, EdD, 1953. Bus. tchr. Darlington (Pa.) Joint Schs., 1946-48; prof. bus. Thiel Coll., Greenville, Pa., 1948-52; vis. prof. Teachers Coll. Columbia U., N.Y.C., 1953; prof. bus. Ball State U., Muncie, Ind., 1954-85, head dept. bus. edn., 1961-67, prof. emeritus, 1985—. Author: (with others) Century 21 Accounting, 1967, 72, 77, 82, 87, 92, 95. Charter bd. dirs. Muncie Hosp. Hospitality House, 1983-86. Maj. U.S. Army, 1942-46, ETO. Mem. Nat. Bus. Edn. Assn., Ind. Bus. Edn. Assn., Delta Pi Epsilon. Roman Catholic. Home: 1719 E Wexley Rd Bloomington IN 47401-4357

SWANSON, ROY ANDREW, music educator; b. Royal Oak, Mich., Dec. 11, 1964; s. James Richard and Joan Elizabeth Swanson. MusB, U. Dayton, 1988; MusM, U. Mich., 1990. Cert. tchr., Mich., Ohio. Musician, trumpet player Miami Valley Dinner Theatre, Springboro, Ohio, 1988-89; instr. music Wilberforce (Ohio) U., 1990-94, asst. prof. music, 1994—; dir. music Meml. Presbyn. Ch., Dayton, Ohio, 1992—; trumpet player Renaissance Brass, Vandalia, Ohio, 1993—, Tom Daugherty Orch., Dayton, 1994—; adj. prof. music U. Dayton, 1995. Composer choral anthems. Vol. food bank ARC, Dayton, 1991-92; mem. U. Dayton Band Alumni, 1988—. Mem. Coll. Music Soc. Home: 1827 Gondert Ave Dayton OH 45403

SWANSON, ROY ARTHUR, classicist, educator; b. St. Paul, Apr. 7, 1925; s. Roy Benjamin and Gertrude (Larson) S.; m. Vivian May Vitous, Mar. 30, 1946; children: Lynn Marie (Mrs. Gerald A. Snider), Robin Lillian, Robert Roy (dec.), Dyack Tyler, Dana Miriam (Mrs. Jon Butts). B.A., U. Minn., 1948, B.S., 1949, M.A., 1951; Ph.D., U. Ill., 1954. Prin. Maplewood Elementary Sch., St. Paul, 1949-51; instr. U. Ill., 1952-53, Ind. U., 1954-57; asst. prof. U. Minn., Mpls., 1957-61; assoc. prof. U. Minn., 1961-64, acting chmn. classics, 1963-64, prof. classics, chmn. comparative lit., 1964-65; prof. English Macalester Coll., St. Paul, 1965-67; coord. humanities program, 1966-67; prof. comparative lit. and classics U. Wis.-Milw., 1967—, prof. English, 1990—, chmn. classics dept., 1967-70, 86-89, chmn. comparative lit., 1970-73, 76-83, coord. Scandinavian studies program, 1982-96; cons. St. Paul Tchrs. Sr. High Sch. English, 1964. Author: Odi et Amo: The Complete Poetry of Catullus, 1959, Heart of Reason: Introductory Essays in Modern-World Humanities, 1963, Pindar's Odes, 1974, Greek and Latin Word Elements, 1981, The Love Songs of the Carmina Burana, 1987, Pär Lagerkvist: Five Early Works, 1989; editor Minn. Rev., 1963-67; Classical Jour., 1966-72; contbr. articles to profl. jours. With AUS, 1944-46. Decorated Bronze Star; recipient Disting. Teaching award U. Minn., 1962, Disting. Teaching award U. Wis.-Milw., 1974, 91. Mem. Am. Philol. Assn., Am. Comparative Lit. Assn., Modern Lang. Assn., Soc. for Advancement Scandinavian Study, Phi Beta Kappa (pres. chpt. 1975-76). Home: 11618 N Bobolink Ln Mequon WI 53092-2804 Office: U Wis Dept Classics & Comp Lit PO Box 413 Milwaukee WI 53201-0413

SWANSON, THOMAS RICHARD, manufacturing, supply chain and systems executive; b. St. Paul, June 4, 1954; s. John Richard and Lorraine Ann (Meline) S.; m. Carol Ann Kraemer, June 26, 1976; children: Brian, Christopher. BS in Mech. Engring., U. Minn., 1976. Engring. positions 3M Co., St. Paul, 1976-79, supr. positions, 1979-81, office supr., 1981-84, materials control mgr., 1984-92, mfg. systems mgr., 1992—; ptnr. T.R.S. Enterprises, Shoreview, Minn., 1981-84; pres. T.R.S. Enterprises, Forest Lake, Minn., 1984—, chief exec. officer, 1990-91; chief fin. officer MTR Holdings Ltd., St. Paul, 1990—; v.p., CFO Lake Country Marine, Inc., 1994—; speaker-cons. Council of Logistics Mgmt., Oak Brook, Ill., 1985, Minn. Soc. Packaging and Handling, Mpls., 1985, Material Handling Inst., Pitts., 1984—, Am. Prod. and Inventory Control Soc., Oaks Church, Va., 1987—; pres. MTR Holdings, Ltd., 1989—; corp. cons., 1992—. Contbr. articles to profl. jours. Mem. Coun. Logistics Mgmt., Minn. Snowmobilers Assn., Am. Power Boat Assn. (chair region 8), Twin City Power Boat Assn. (bd. dirs.), Deep South Racing Assn. Republican. Methodist. Home: 6725 N Lake Blvd Forest Lake MN 55025 Office: 3M Co 3M Ctr Bldg 290-3-01 Saint Paul MN 55144-1000

SWANSON, WILLIAM RUSSELL, marketing professional; b. Omaha, July 22, 1949; s. Verlyn Russel and Marilyn Joan (McCormick) S.; m. Peggy Lynn O'Connor, May 30, 1976; children: Erin Eileen, Sean Russell. BSBA, U. Nebr., Omaha, 1978; MBA, U. Nebr., Lincoln, 1991. Cert. Purchasing Manager, Nebr. Graphics mgr. Snow Corp., Omaha, 1971-73, asst. purchasing agent, 1973-75; asst. purchasing mgr. McMartin Industries, Omaha, 1976-80; buyer Valmont Industries Inc., Valley, Nebr., 1980-81; purchasing mgr. Valmont Industries Inc., Valley, 1981-88, sales mgr., 1988-89, quality assurance mgr., 1989-93; ter. mgr. Castle Metals (A.M. Castle & Co.), Kansas City, 1994-95; exec. in residence dept. mktg. Coll. Bus. U. Nebr., Omaha, 1995—; instr. S.E. C.C., Lincoln, 1984-87, Metro C.C., Omaha, 1988-91; instr. U. Nebr., 1993—, chairperson EMBA adv. com., 1993. Divsn. campaign chairperson United Way Midlands Valley, 1986; mem. bus. dept. adv. com. Metro C.C., 1988-91, mem. bd. govs., 1992-93; corp. sec. N.W. Omaha Renegades Youth Athletic Assn., 1993—. Mem. Am. Mktg. Assn. (mem. recognition com. Omaha chpt. 1995—), Am. Prodn. Inventory Control Soc., Nat. Assn. Purchasing Mgmt. (chmn. budget com. dist. III), Am. Soc. Quality Control, Nebr. Assn. Purchasing Mgmt. (pres. 1987-88), Jr. Achievement Project Bus. (cons. 1992-93). Republican. Roman Catholic.

SWANTON, VIRGINIA LEE, author, publisher, bookseller; b. Oak Park, Ill., Feb. 6, 1933; d. Milton Wesley and Eleanor Louise (Linnell) S. BA, Lake Forest (Ill.) Coll., 1954; MA in English Lit., Northwestern U., 1955; cert. in acctg., Coll. of Lake County, Ill., 1984. Editorial asst. Publs. Office, Northwestern U., Evanston, Ill., 1955-58; reporter Lake Forester, Lake Forest, 1959; editor Scott, Foresman & Co., Glenview, Ill., 1959-84; copy editor, travel coord. McDougal Littell/Houghton Mifflin, Evanston, 1985-94; sr. bookseller B. Dalton Bookseller, Lake Forest, Ill., 1985—; author, pub. Gold Star Publ. Svcs., Lake Forest, 1994—. Contbr. articles to profl. jours. Mem. bd. deacons First Presbyn. Ch. of Lake Forest; mem., sec. bd. dirs., newsletter editor Career Resource Ctr., Inc., Lake Forest. Mem. Internat. Reading Assn., Deerpath Art League, Chgo. Women in Pub. Presbyterian. Office: Gold Star Publ Svcs PO Box 125 Lake Forest IL 60045

SWARTZ, JACK, fraternal organization administrator; b. Dodge City, Kans., Nov. 24, 1932; s. John Ralph and Fern (Cave) S.; m. Nadine Ann Langlois, Aug. 4, 1956; children: Dana, Shawn, Tim, Jay. A.A., Dodge City Community Coll., 1953; student St. Mary of Plains Coll., 1953-55, 58; B.A. in Econs., Washburn U., 1974, B.B.A., 1973. Vice pres. D.C. Terminal Elevator Co., Dodge City, Kans., 1957-65; exec. v.p. Kans. Jaycees, Hutchinson, 1965-68, Kans. C. of C. and Industry, Topeka, 1968-82; pres. Nebr. C. of C. and Industry, Lincoln, 1982—. Past chmn., bd. regents U.S. C. of C. Inst. U. Colo. Served with U.S. Army, 1955-57. Named Outstanding Local Pres. in State, Kans. Jaycees, 1961, Outstanding Young Man of Yr., Dodge City Jaycees, 1961; Outstanding State Vice Pres., U.S. Jaycees, 1962, Outstanding Nat. Dir., 1963. Mem. Am. Soc. Assn. Execs. (cert.), Am. Chamber Commerce Execs. (bd. dirs., cert.), Nebr. Chamber Commerce Execs. (sec.-treas.), Nebr. Soc. Assn. Execs. (past pres.), Nebr. Fedn. Bus. Assns. (pres. 1986-88), Washburn U. Alum. (bd. dirs.). Republican. Roman Catholic. Lodge: Rotary. Home: 2744 Laurel St Lincoln NE 68502-5142 Office: Nebr C of C and Industry 1320 Lincoln Mall PO Box 95128 Lincoln NE 68509

SWARTZ, MICHAEL ALLEN, minister; b. Indpls., May 21, 1946; s. Vern Edward and Irma Lee (Stokes) S.; m. Nancy Louise McConnell, Sept. 18, 1982; children: Taylor Katherine, Rebecca Sommerville. AB, Calif. State U., 1969; MDiv, Pacific Sch. Religion, Berkeley, Calif., 1978; DMin, Austin (Tex.) Presbyn. Theol. Sem., 1995. Assoc. pastor California Heights United Meth. Ch., Long Beach, Calif., 1975-77, St. John United Meth. Ch., Davenport, Iowa, 1990-91; pastor Legrand/Chowchilla (Calif.) United Meth. Ch., 1978-81, Redwood City (Calif.) United Meth. Ch., 1981-87, Hillsdale United Meth. Ch., San Mateo, Calif., 1987-90, Ch. of Peace United Ch. of Christ, Rock Island, Ill., 1991—; mem. mission com., bd. dirs. Ill. Conf. United Ch. of Christ, Chgo., 1994—; mem. adj. faculty Scott C.C., Bettendorf, Iowa, 1995—. Editor Occasional Bull., Guatemala Relief Ministries, 1994—. Bd. dirs. Child Abuse Coun., Moline, Ill., 1990—. Mem. Kiwanis. Office: Ch of Peace United Ch of Christ 1114 12th St Rock Island IL 61201

SWARTZ, PAUL FREDERICK, clergyman; b. New Philadelphia, Ohio, Mar. 2, 1943; s. Luther Franklin and Dorothy Mae (Keppler) S.; m. Betty Lou Lacina, Apr. 24, 1965; children: Aaron Joel, Lynnea Renee. Student, Bowling Green State U., 1963-64; BA, Wittenberg U., 1965; BD, Trinity Luth. Sem., 1968, MDiv, 1976. Ordained to ministry Luth. Ch. in Am., 1968. Pastor Trinity Luth. Ch., Sebring, Ohio, 1968-72; mission developer Christ the Redeemer Luth. Ch., Brecksville, Ohio, 1972-73, pastor, 1973-75; asst. to bishop, mem. exec. bd. Ohio Synod, Luth. Ch. in Am., Columbus, Ohio, 1975-88; sr. pastor St. Matthew's Luth. Ch., Urbana, Ill., 1989—; cons. Profl. Leadership, Columbus, 1981-87; treas., bd. dirs. Midwest Career Devel. Svcs., Columbus and Chgo., 1981-87; del. Luth. Ch. in Am. Conf., Toronto, Ont., Can., 1984, mem. Cen. So. Ill. Synod, 1989—; dean E. Cen. Conf. Cen./So. Ill. Synod Coun., Evang. Luth. Ch. Am., 1990; news corr. The Luth., 1970-75. Contbr. articles to religious publs., chpt. to book. Vice pres. Community Action Ctr., Sebring, 1969-72; bd. dirs. Luth. Children's Aid and Family Svcs., Cleve., 1973-75, Luth. Social Svcs. N.E. Ohio, 1980-84, Luth. Metro Ministries, Cleve., 1980-85; mem. Goals for Greater Akron (Ohio), 1982; cons. Greater Cleve. East Strategy, 1984-87, Greater Akron Strategy, 1985-87. Bowling Green State U. President's scholar, 1962-64; Nat. Luth. Coun. European study grantee, 1963. Office: Saint Matthew Luth Ch 2200 Philo Rd Urbana IL 61802-6923

SWARTZ, WILLIAM JOHN, transportation resources company executive/retired; b. Hutchinson, Kans., Nov. 6, 1934; s. George Glen and Helen Mae (Prather) S.; m. Dorothy Jean Parshall, June 5, 1956; children: John Christopher, Jeffrey Michael. BSME, Duke U., 1956; JD, George Washington U., 1961; MS in Mgmt. (Alfred P. Sloan fellow), MIT, 1967. With AT & SF Ry., 1961-78, 79—, asst. v.p. exec. dept., 1973-77, v.p. adminstrn., 1977-78, exec. v.p., 1979-83; exec. v.p. Santa Fe Industries, Chgo., 1978-79, pres., 1983-90; vice chmn. Santa Fe So. Pacific, 1983-90; pres. AT & SF Ry., 1986-89. Past bd. dirs. Chgo. Mus. Sci. and Industry; mem. Dean's Coun. Duke U. Sch. Engring. With USMC, 1956-59. Mem. Assn. Am. R.R. (past bd. dirs.). Republican. Methodist. Home: 914 Paseo del Sur Santa Fe NM 87501

SWARTZEL, STAN J., electrical engineer; b. Hendersonville, N.C., Jan. 8, 1963. BSEE, Clemson (S.C.) U., 1984. Sr. engr. Cin. Milacron, 1984-87, PMI Hobart, Troy, Ohio, 1987—.

SWEARINGEN, HAROLD LYNDON, oil company executive; b. Independence, Kans., Sept. 17, 1937; s. Luther and Dorothy Grace (Swalley) S.; m. Charlene Faye Meyer, Oct. 17, 1959; children: Renee (Mrs. Michael Readinger), Lisa (Mrs. Dick Drumeller), Shari (Mrs. Dustin Garrett), Kurtis. AA, Independence Jr. Coll., 1957; BSEE, Kans. State U., 1960. Lic. gen. radio telephone operator, FCC. Microwave technician Sinclair Pipe Line Co., Indpendence, 1960-61, sr. telecomm. engr., 1961-67; adminstr. telecomm. ops. Sinclair Oil Corp., N.Y.C., 1967-69; sr. telecomm. system design engr. Trans Alaska Pipe Line Co., Houston, 1969-72; project mgr. telecomm. Atlantic Richfield Co., Tulsa, 1972-75; mgr. telecomm. ops. Arco

Pipe Line Co., Independence, 1975-89, mgr. telecomm., 1989-92; ret., 1992; bd. dirs. First Fed. Savs. & Loan, Indpendence. Sch. bd. mem. Unified Sch. Dist. # 446, Independence, 1991-93. Sgt. U.S. Army, 1955-63. Mem. IEEE. Republican. Lutheran. Home: RR 2 Box 240 Independence KS 67301-9412

SWEENEY, ASHER WILLIAM, state supreme court justice; b. Canfield, Ohio, Dec. 11, 1920; s. Walter William and Jessie Joan (Kidd) S.; m. Bertha M. Englert, May 21, 1945; children: Randall W., Ronald R., Garland A., Karen M. Student, Youngstown U., 1939-42; LL.B., Duke U., 1948. Bar: Ohio 1949. Practiced law Youngstown, Ohio, 1949-51; judge adv. gen. Dept. Def., Washington, 1951-65; chief Fed. Contracting Agy., Cin., 1965-68; corp. law, 1968-77; justice Ohio Supreme Ct., Columbus, 1977—. Democratic candidate for Sec. of State Ohio, 1958. Served with U.S. Army, 1942-46; col. Res. 1951-68. Decorated Legion of Merit, Bronze Star; named to Army Hall of Fame Ft. Benning, Ga., 1981. Mem. Ohio Bar Assn., Phi Delta Phi. Democrat. Home: 6690 Drake Rd Cincinnati OH 45243-2706 Office: Ohio Supreme Ct 30 E Broad St Fl 3D Columbus OH 43215-3414

SWEENEY, DENNIS JOSEPH, educator, author; b. Des Moines, Iowa, Oct. 5, 1941; s. James P. and Gladys K. (Gunderson) S.; m. Cheryl J. Strom, Nov. 26, 1964; children: Mark, Linda, Brad, Tim, Scott, Lisa. BS, Drake U., 1968; MBA, Ind. U., 1970, DBA, 1971. Asst. prof. U. Cin., 1971-74, assoc. prof., 1974-77, prof., 1977—, head dept. quantitative analysis, 1979-84, assoc. dean, 1985-88; vis. prof. Duke U., Durham, N.C.; cons. Procter & Gamble, Cin., 1977—, Champion Internat., Hamilton, Ohio, 1976—, Cin. Dept. Health, 1975; prin. investigator IBM grant U. Cin., 1985. Author: Statistics for Business and Economics, 6th edit., 1996, Production and Operations Management, 1993, Management Science, 7th edit., 1994, Quantitative Methods for Business, 6th edit., 1995. Pres., mem. parish coun. St. Andrew's Ch., Milford, Ohio, 1988-91; dir. Ctr. Productivity Improvement, 1993—. Grantee CG&E, 1991-92, Procter & Gamble, 1993, Federated Dept. Stores, 1994, Kroger Co., 1995. Mem. Omicron Delta Kappa. Roman Catholic. Home: 7357 Eastborne Rd Cincinnati OH 45255-3962 Office: U Cin Mail Loc 130 Cincinnati OH 45221

SWEENEY, JAMES LEE, retired government official; b. Rocky River, Ohio, Mar. 23, 1930; s. John H. and Mary J. (Walkinshaw) S.; m. Marion J. Ridley, Oct. 4, 1958; children: John A., James L. BBA, Case-Western Res. U., 1959. Cost acct. AFB, Dayton, Ohio, 1959-62; acct. Def. Electronics Supply Center, Dayton, 1962-64, budget analyst, 1964-67, budget officer, 1967-74, supervisory budget analyst, 1974-82, supervisory mgmt. analyst, 1982, supervisory program analyst, 1983—; pres. 3001 Hoover Inc.; mem. tax adv. com. Dayton-Montgomery County, 1967-70. Bd. dirs. Dayton Human Rels. Commn., 1970-74, Model Cities Housing Corp., 1972-74, M & M Broadcasting Co., Ohio Valley Broadcasting Co., 1979-81; vestryman, treas. St. Margaret's Episc. Ch., 1984-88. Served with U.S. Army, 1952-54. Recipient Pub. Svc. award Def. Electronics Supply Ctr., 1972, Meritorious Civilian Svc. award, 1981, Unity award in Media, Lincoln U., 1982-83, Disting. Career award Def. Electonics Supply Ctr., 1986, Martin Luther King Jr. award Gov. State of Ohio, 1995. Mem. Alpha Phi Alpha. Prodr., commentator Spl. Cmty. Report Sta. WHIO-TV, twice weekly 1970-76, daily, 1976—, prodr., commentator Spotlight; spl. cons. Sta. WHIO-TV. Home: 743 Argonne Dr Dayton OH 45408-1501

SWEENEY, JERRY KENT, history educator; b. Pratt, Kans., July 13, 1941; s. Charles E. and Maxine V. (Parcel) S.; m. Mira Clark, Mar. 13, 1964; children: Matthew, Whitney, Jennifer. BA, Ft. Hays Kans. State Coll., 1962; MA, Kans. State U., Manhattan, 1967; PhD, Kent State U., 1970. Asst. prof. S.D. State U., Brookings, 1970-75, assoc. prof., 1975-80, prof. history, 1980—, adminstrv. assoc., 1987. Co-author: Handbook of American Diplomacy, 1993, Handbook of American Military History, 1995; contbr. articles to profl. jours. Trustee Brookings Pub. Libr., 1974-79; mem. Historic Preservation Commn., Brookings, 1986-90. With U.S. Army, 1962-65. Rsich. grantee Eleanor Roosevelt Inst., 1975, Am. Coun. Learned Socs., 1976, 78, Harry S. Truman Found., 1978, S.D. State U. Rsch. Fund, 1978, 80, 90, 93, Danforth Found., 1980, S.D. Com. on Humanities, 1983, 85, 86, 87, 91; Danforth assoc. Danforth Found., 1977, 87. Mem. Conf. Group on Portugal, Soc. Historians of Am. Fgn. Rels., Soc. Mil. History, KC. Roman Catholic. Office: SD State U Dept History Brookings SD 57007

SWEENEY, NANCY L., psychiatric nurse; b. Sewickley, Pa., Mar. 16, 1947; d. Thomas P. and Josephine M. Tarquinio; m. John F. Sweeney, June 21, 1969; children: Kevin Patrick, Kimberly Marie. BSN, St. John Coll., 1969; MSN, Ohio State U., 1977, PhD in Preventive Medicine, 1995. RN, Ohio; cert. family nurse practitioner ANCC. Asst. head nurse inpatient psychiat. unit St. Rita's Med. Ctr., Lima, Ohio, 1969-71, staff developer, 1970, dir. behavioral svcs., 1991-95; nursing instr. Lima (Ohio) Tech. Coll., 1971-77; assoc. prof. Bluffton (Ohio) Coll., 1977-89, DON, 1989-91; assoc. prof. nursing Med. Coll. of Ohio, Toledo, 1990-91; clin. specialist Lindenview Behavioral Health Ctr., Ft. Wayne, Ind., 1995; adj. prof. Wright State U., Dayton, Ohio, 1995—; adv. bd. Lima Area Health Edn. Ctr., Mercy Home Health Care; regional coord. for heart at work program Am. Heart Assn.; chmn. Ohio Dept. Health Edn. & Practice Task Force; adj. assoc. prof. Capital U., Med. Coll. of Ohio, Wright State U., 1995. Mem. ANA, Assn. Community Health Nurse Educators, Assn. Mental Health Adminstrs., Nat. League for Nursing, Midwest Alliance in Nursing, Midwest Nursing Rsch. Soc., Ohio Nurses Assn., Nurse Practitioners Assembly, Sigma Theta Tau. Home: 2967 Canterbury Dr Lima OH 45805-2904

SWEENEY, PATRICK A., state legislator; b. Cleveland, Ohio, 1941; m. Emily Mirsky; 1 child, Margaret Anne. Student, Kennedy Sch. Govt.; MPA, Harvard Univ.; LLD, Cleveland State Univ. State rep. Ohio Dist. 9, 1966-92, Ohio Dist. 19, 1993—; majority whip Ohio House Rep., 1996—; vice chmn. Fin. & Appropriations com., mem. Health & Retirement Com., Ins. Com. & Fin. Inst. Com., Legis. Budget Com.; mem. Devel. & Fin. adv. bd., mem. Legis. Svc. Com. Pres. PASCO Cons., bd. trustees Rock & Roll Hall Fame, Ohio Arts Coun. Named Legis. of Yr. Acad. Nursing Homes, 1986, 90. Home: 16529 St Anthony Ln Cleveland OH 44111*

SWEENEY, ROBERT KEVIN, lawyer; b. St. Louis, Dec. 26, 1959; s. Robert Vincent Sweeney and Kathleen Patricia (Rush) Rhymer; m. Donna Marie Anvender, Nov. 23, 1979; children: Allison Marie, Molly Clare. BS, So. Ill. U., 1987; JD, St. Louis U., 1990. Bar: Mo. 1990, U.S. Dist. Ct. (ea. and we. dists.) Mo. 1990, U.S. Ct. Appeals (8th cir.) 1990. Assoc. Linde, Thomson, Kansas City, Mo., 1990-91, Craig & Craig, St. Louis, 1989-91, 91-93, Franz, Franz & Sweeney, St. Louis, 1993-95; ptnr. Spector & Sweeney, Kirkwood, Mo., 1995—. Mem. presdl. trust fund Dem., Washington, 1991—. Mem. ABA, AFL-CIO, Am. Judicature Soc., Lawyers Coord. Com., Mo. Bar Assn., St. Louis Met. Bar Assn., Kansas City Met. Bar Assn., Order of Woolsack, Alpha Sigma Nu, Phi Kappa Phi. Roman Catholic. Home: 1338 Libra Dr Arnold MO 63010-3009 Office: Spector & Sweeney 333 S Kirkwood Rd Kirkwood MO 63122

SWEET, ARTHUR, orthopedist; b. Chgo., Aug. 30, 1920; s. Mandel and Yetta (Spector) S.; m. Natalie Levy, Feb. 21, 1964; 1 child, Margaret Helaine. BS, U. Ill., 1941; MD, 1944. Diplomate Am. Bd. Orthopaedic Surgery. Instr. Northwestern U., 1947-52; mem. staff Decatur (Ill.) Meml. Hosp., 1954—, St. Mary's Hosp., Decatur, 1954—; cons. Wabash Hosp. Assn., Decatur, 1954—; instr. U. Ill., 1972—; pres. med. staff St. Mary's Hosp., Decatur, Ill. Capt. M.C., U.S. Army, 1946-48, 51-53, Korea. Mem. Acad. Orthopaedic Surgery, Decatur Club. Jewish. Home: 245 N Park Pl Decatur IL 62522-1951

SWEET, JERRY JAMES, clinical psychologist; b. East Stroudsburg, Pa., Dec. 1, 1951; s. Waldo Thomas and Betty Jane (Flory) S.; m. Nancy Ann Sullivan, July 9, 1971; children: Christopher, Jamie. BS with distinction, Pa. State U., 1973; MS, Western Wash. U., 1975; PhD, U. S.D., 1979. Lic. clin. psychologist, Ill.; diplomate Am. Bd. Profl. Psychology in Clin. Neuropsychology. Sr. psychologist pain ctr., neuropsychologist dept. psychiatry Ill. Masonic Med. Ctr., Chgo., 1979-86; dir. psychol. evaluation and testing svc. Evanston (Ill.) Hosp., 1986-89, co-dir. Ctr. Psychol. Evaluation and Learning, 1989-91, dir. neuropsychology svc., 1991—; clin. assoc. prof. psychiatry med. sch. Northwestern U., adj. assoc. prof., 1982—. assoc. dir. clin. tng., 1986—; neuropsychology cons. Cook County Hosp., Chgo., 1983-87, 93—; lectr. psychology Loyola U., Chgo., 1983, 85, 87, 91; neuropsychol. seminar instr. Ill. State Psychiat. Inst., Chgo., 1986. Co-editor Handbook of Clin. Psychology in Med. Settings, 1991; founding assoc. editor Jour. Clin. Psychology in Med. Settings, 1993—; contbr. articles to profl. jours. and chpts. to profl. texts. Fellow Nat. Acad. Neuropsychology; mem. APA, Internat. Neuropsychol. Soc., Assn. Postdoctoral Tng. Programs in Clin. Neuropsychology. Office: Evanston Hosp Dept Psychiatry 2650 Ridge Ave Evanston IL 60201-1718

SWEET, LOWELL ELWIN, lawyer; b. Flint, Mich., Aug. 10, 1931; s. Leslie E. and Donna Mabel (Latta) S.; m. Mary Ellen Ebben, Aug. 29, 1953; children: Lawrence Edward, Diane Marie, Sara Anne. BA in Psychology, Wayne State U., 1953, LLB, U. Wis., 1955. Bar: Wis. 1955, U.S. dist. ct. (ea. dist). Wis. 1955, U.S. dist. ct. (no. dist.) Ill. 1958. Ptnr., Morrissy, Morrissy, Sweet & Race and predecessors, Elkhorn, Wis., 1957-70; shareholder, pres. Sweet & Reddy, S.C., Elkhorn, 1970—; instr. gen. practice sect. U. Wis. Law Sch. 1978, 79, 86, 90; lectr. real estate law Wis. Bar, Gateway Tech. Carthage Coll. Inst., 1974—. Author Phased Condominiums for Matthew Bender, 1992; co-editor: Condominium Law Handbook, 1981, 93; mem. editorial bd. Workbook for Wis. Estate Planners, 1990. Mem. Walworth County Republican Com.; sect. Wis. Joint Survey Commn. on Debt Mgmt. Served with CIC, U.S. Army, 1955-57. Named Outstanding Young Man, Elkhorn Jaycees, 1966; recipient citation for service in drafting Wis. Condominium Law, Wis. Legislature, 1978. Mem. ABA, Wis. Bar Assn. (gov. 1972-75, 91-93), Walworth County Bar Assn., Am. Judicature Soc., Assn. Trial Lawyers Am., Am. Coll. Real Estate Lawyers, Kiwanis, Lions, Moose, KC. Home: 411 W Marshall St Elkhorn WI 53121-1624 Office: Sweet & Reddy SC 114 N Church St Elkhorn WI 53121-1202

SWEET, PHILIP W. K., JR., former banker; b. Mt. Vernon, N.Y., Dec. 31, 1927; s. Philip W.K. and Katherine (Buhl) S.; m. Nancy Frederick, July 23, 1950; children—Sandra H., Philip W.K. III, David A.F. AB, Harvard U., 1950; MBA, U. Chgo., 1957. Pres., dir. The No. Trust Co., Chgo., 1975-81; chmn., chief exec. officer No. Trust Corp., 1981-84. Alderman City of Lake Forest, Ill., 1972-74; adv. com. United Negro Coll. Fund; vis. com. U. Chgo. Grad. Sch. Bus.; trustee Chgo. Zool. Soc., past chmn. 1988-93; life trustee Rush-Presbyn.-St. Luke's Med. Ctr.; vestryman Episc. Ch., 1971-74, 86-89. Mem. Soc. Colonial Wars (gov. Ill. chpt. 1978-80), Chgo. Sunday Evening Club (trustee, treas.), Econ. Club, Comml. Club, Chgo. Club, Commonwealth Club (past pres.), Old Elm Club (Highwood, Ill.), Onwentsia Club (gov.), Shoreacres Club (past pres. Lake Bluff).

SWEET, SHIRLEY MARIE, psychology and social studies educator, consultant; b. Chippewa Falls, Wis., Jan. 20, 1934; d. John Emanual and Marie Edith (Flanigan) Brask; m. Donald Edgar Sweet, June 16, 1956; children: William John, Steven Alan. BS, U. Wis.-Stout, Menomonie, 1955, MS, 1963; postgrad., U. Wis.-Stout and U. Wis., Oshkosh, 1963-89. Cert. adult counseling and guidance; cert. social studies, psychology, natural scis., home econs. tchr., Wis. Instr. home econs. Thorp (Wis.) Pub. High Sch., 1955-56, Chippewa Falls Pub. High Sch., 1956-59; counselor acad. Blackhawk Tech. Coll., Janesville, Wis., 1959-75, instr. psychology, 1975-92; ednl. cons., Beloit, Wis., 1991—. Author: (student study packets) Psychology/Devel. Psychology/Telecourses/Human Sexuality/Sociology, 1975-92, (telecourse study guides) Psychology, Sociology, Human Relations, 1995. Recipient Nat. Teaching Excellence award U. Tex., Austin, 1989, Outstanding Tchr. of Yr. award Wis. State Bd. of Vocat., Tech. Edn., 1992. Mem. Am. Assn. Women in Cmty. Colls., Am. Vocat. Assn., Wis. Vocat. Assn. (v.p. 1961-63), Wis. Assn. Vocat. Adult Edn., Blackhawk Tech. Assn. (pres. 1975-76, Profl. Excellence award 1984, 92), Wis. Ret. Educators, Beloit Area Ret. Educators (pres. 1996), Altrusa Internat. of Beloit (pres. 1986, 95—), Phi Delta Kappa. Methodist. Home and Office: 1517 Highland Ave Beloit WI 53511-5945

SWEEZY, JOHN WILLIAM, political party official; b. Indpls., Nov. 14, 1932; s. William Charles and Zuma Frances (McNew) S.; BS in Mech. Engring., Purdue U., 1956; MBA, Ind. U., 1958; student Butler U., 1953-54, U. Ga., 1954-55, Ind. Cen. Coll., 1959; m. Carole Suzanne Harman, July 14, 1956; children: John William, Bradley E. Design, test engr. Allison div. GM, Indpls., 1953-57; power sales engr. Indpls. Power & Light Co., 1958-69; dir. pub. works City of Indpls., 1970-72; chmn. Marion County Rep. Cen. Com., 1972—; bd. dir. Lorco Engring., Indpls., Indpls. Industrial Products, Acme Screw & Mfg., Inc., Telnet, Inc., Landmarks Ltd.; ptnr. Arch. Products, Innovative Investment Co. Bd. dirs. Indpls. Humane Soc.; chmn. 11th Dist. Rep. Com., 1970, 73—; chmn. Nat. Assn. Urban Rep. County Chmn.; alt. del. Rep. Nat. Conv., 1968, del., 1972, 76, 80, 84, 88, 92, del., mem. credentials com., 1984, 88; mem. credentials com., 1980; mem. Rep. Nat. Com., 1984—, exec. com., 1984—; mem. Warren Schs. Citizens Screening Com., 1958-72; bd. dirs. Warren Devel. Com. With AUS, 1953-55. Mem. AMA, Mensa, Sigma Iota Epsilon. Home: 2089 S German Church Rd Indianapolis IN 46239-9620 Office: 12 N Delaware St Indianapolis IN 46204-3205

SWEGLE, DAVID B., engineering executive; b. Corydon, Iowa, Aug. 28, 1962. BS in Indsl. Tech., Iowa State U., 1987. Indsl. engr. Ritchie Mfg. Co., Conrad, Iowa, 1988; engring. mgr. Indsl. Electric Reel, Omaha, 1990-91; v.p. mfg. GMI Industries, Inc., Union, Iowa, 1992—. Sunday sch. tchr. Conrad Meth. Ch., 1995—. Republican. Office: GMI Industries Inc PO Box D Union IA 50258-0904

SWENSON, DALE, state legislator; m. Roberta Swenson. Mem. from dist. 97 Kans. State Ho. of Reps., Topeka. Address: 3145 S Fern Wichita KS 67217

SWENSON, DOUGLAS, state legislator; b. Aug. 1945; m. Sandie; two children. BS, Gustavus Adolphus Coll.; JD, William Mitchell Coll. Minn. State Rep. Dist. 51B, 1987—; atty.; mem. edn., health and human svc., judiciary, environ. and natural resources and local govt. and met. affairs coms. Home: 9429 Jewel Lane Ct N Forest Lake MN 55025-9169*

SWENSON, FAYE LORENE, executive management development firm; b. Springfield, Minn., Sept. 19, 1964; d. Charles Kenneth and Faith Lorene (Seymour) Pederson; m. Timothy Dennis Swenson, June 6, 1987. BA magna cum laude, Luther Coll., Decorah, Iowa, 1987. Psychometrist Personnel Decisions Internat., Mpls., 1987-88, assoc. cons., 1988-89, client rels. cons., 1989-94, sales trainer, 1991-94, acct. mgr., 1995—. Mem. Sales and Mktg. Execs., Phi Beta Kappa. Home: 5613 Sherwood Ave Edina MN 55424 Office: Pers Decisions Internat 45 S 7th St Minneapolis MN 55402

SWENSON, HOWARD, state legislator, farmer; b. Dec. 20, 1930; m. Jane Swenson; 5 children. Farmer, Nicollet, Minn.; mem. Minn. Ho. of Reps., St. Paul, 1994—. Independent-Republican.

SWENSON, RICHARD ALAN, physician educator; b. Elgin, Ill., Feb. 1, 1948; s. Warren Lloyd and Ruth Caroline (Ostrom) S.; m. Linda Carol Wilson, Aug. 16, 1970; children: Adam John, Matthew Erick. BS in Physics, Denison U., 1970; MD, U. Ill., 1974. Diplomate Am. Bd. Family Practice. Resident in family practice Cedar Rapids (Iowa) Med. Edn. Consortium, 1977; pvt. practice Red Cedar Clinic, Menomonie, Wis., 1977-82; asst. prof. clin. health scis. U. Wis. Med. Sch., Eau Claire, 1982-89, assoc. prof. clin. health scis., 1989—; bd. dirs. Red Cedar Clinic, 1980-82. Author: Margin, 1992. Med. rep. Child Abuse Coun., Menomonie, 1977-79; governing bd. Menomonie Alliance Ch., 1981-86, 90—; mem. Menomonie Christian Sch. Bd., 1986-92. Fed. Tng. grantee, 1984-87. Mem. Christian Med. and Dental Soc., Am. Acad. Family Practice, Soc. of Tchrs. of Family Medicine, Internat. Ctr. for Family Medicine, Phi Beta Kappa. Home: 2503 Aurora Cir Menomonie WI 54751-2398 Office: Eau Claire Family Med Clin 807 S Farwell St Eau Claire WI 54701-3832

SWENSON, RUTH WILDMAN, cell biologist, educator; b. Wilkes-Barre, Pa., July 16, 1924; d. Charles Harkness and Dorothy Eulalie (Carpenter) Bowman; m. William Cooper Wildman, Aug. 21, 1947 (div. 1979); m. Clayton Albert Swenson, Jan. 1, 1980. AB, Mt. Holyoke Coll., 1946; MS, U. Ill., 1947; PhD, Iowa State U., 1969. Asst. chemist Ill. Geol. Survey, Urbana, 1947-49; rsch. asst. biochem. dept. U. Wis., Madison, 1949-50; instr., adviser Iowa State U., Ames, 1966-69, asst. prof. botany, 1969-72, assoc. prof., 1972-77, prof., 1977-87, prof. emerita, 1987—, asst. dean Coll. Sci. and Humanities, 1975-84, assoc. dean Coll. of Sci. and Humanities, 1984-87, assoc. dean emerita Coll. Liberal Arts and Scis., 1987—, mem. liberal arts and scis. dean's adv. coun., 1994—; state coord. nat. identification program Am. Coun. Edn., 1983-84; vis. scientist Los Alamos (N.Mex.) Nat. Lab., 1984; mem. del. sci. deans China Assn. Sci. and Tech., People's Republic of China, 1986; co-dir. career workshop NSF, 1977. Bd. dirs. Women in Sci. and Engring. Archives, 1993—, ARC, Story County, Iowa, 1963-72, chair, 1971-72; bd. dirs. Ames Town & Gown Chamber Music Assn., 1980-86, 92-95, pres., 1983-84, sec. 1993—; bd. dirs. Ames Internat. Orch. Festival Assn., 1979-85, 87-90, treas. 1988-90; bd. dirs. Ctrl. Iowa Symphony, Ames, 1990-93, v.p., 1991-92; bd. dirs. Emergency Residence Project, Ames, 1988-92, pres., 1990-91. Named to Iowa Women's Hall of Fame, Iowa Commn. Status Women, 1989. Fellow Iowa Acad. Sci. (bd. dirs. 1985-88, pres. 1989-90); mem. AAUW, LWV (pres.-elect 1994-95, pres. 1995-96), Assn. for Women in Sci., Nat. Acad. Advising Assn. (bd. dirs. 1986-89), Argonne Univs. Assn. (trustee 1977-80), Iowa Natural Heritage Found., Audubon Soc., The Nature Conservancy (life), Phi Beta Kappa (Zeta of Iowa chpt. pres. 1985-86), Sigma Xi, Phi Kappa Phi (sec.-treas. 1988-91), Iota Sigma Pi (life). Democrat. Episcopalian. Home: 2102 Kildee St Ames IA 50014-7027

SWERDLOW, MARTIN ABRAHAM, physician, pathologist, educator; b. Chgo., July 7, 1923; s. Sol Hyman and Rose (Lasky) S.; m. Marion Levin, May 19, 1945; children—Steven Howard, Gary Bruce. Student, Herzl Jr. Coll., 1941-42; BS, U. Ill., 1945; MD, U. Ill., Chgo., 1947. Diplomate: Am. Bd. Pathology. Intern Michael Reese Hosp. and Med. Center, Chgo., 1947-48; resident Michael Reese Hosp. and Med. Center, 1948-50, 51-52, mem. staff, 1974—, chmn. dept. pathology, v.p. acad. affairs, 1974-90; pathologist Menorah Med. Ctr., Kansas City, Mo., 1954-57; asst. prof., pathologist U. Ill. Coll. Medicine, Chgo., 1957-59, assoc. prof., 1959-60, clin. assoc. prof., 1960-64, clin. prof., 1964-66, prof., pathologist, 1966-72, assoc. dean, prof. pathology, 1970-72; prof. pathology, chmn. U. Mo., Kansas City, 1972-74; prof. pathology U. Chgo., 1975-89, Geever prof., head pathology U. Ill., 1989-93, Geever prof., head pathology emeritus, 1993—; mem. com. standards Chgo. Health Systems Agy., 1976—. Served with M.C. U.S. Army, 1944-45, 50-54. Recipient Alumnus of Yr. award U. Ill. Coll. Medicine, 1973; Instructorship award U. Ill., 1960, 65, 68, 71, 72. Mem. Chgo. Pathology Soc. (pres. 1980—), Am. Soc. Clin. Pathologists, Coll. Am. Pathologists, Internat. Acad. Pathology, Am. Acad. Dermatology, Am. Soc. Dermatopathology, Inst. Medicine, AMA. Jewish. Office: U Ill Coll Medicine Dept Pathology 1819 W Polk St Chicago IL 60612-7331

SWETLAND, DAVID WIGHTMAN, investment company executive; b. Cleve., Apr. 13, 1916; s. Fredrick L. and Pauline (Wightman) S.; m. Mary Ann Sears, May 15, 1943 (dec. July 1969); children: David S., Ruth W., Polly M.; m. Jean Thomas, Sept. 23, 1971; stepchildren: Christine Anderson, Dane Anderson, Carol Anderson, Chace Anderson. AB, Williams Coll., 1938. Mgr. Swetland Co./Park Investment Co., Cleve., 1939-60; owner Park Investment Co., Cleve., 1960—. Trustee Cleve. Mus. Natural History, Holden Arboretum, Vocat. Guidance Svcs., Cleve. Soc. for the Blind, Emeritus Western Res. Acad.; hon. turstee Cleve. Garden Ctr., Ohio chpt. Nature Conservancy; trustee emeritus Univ. Circle, Inc. Capt. USAF, 1942-46. Mem. Cleve. Assn. Bldg. Owners and Mgrs. (trustee), The Pepper Pike Club, Rowfant Club (Cleve.), Biscayne Bay Yacht Club, Wiscasset Yacht Club, Union Club. Home: 3505 Main Lodge Dr Miami FL 33133-5918 Office: Pk Investment Co 140 Public Sq Cleveland OH 44114-2213

SWETLIK, WILLIAM PHILIP, orthodontist; b. Manitowoc, Wis., Jan. 31, 1950; s. Leonard Alvin and Lillian Julia (Knipp) S.; m. Cheryl Jean Klein, June 30, 1973 (div.); children: Alison Elizabeth, Lindsey Ann, Adam William Swetlik. Student, Luther Coll., Decorah, Iowa, 1968-70; DDS, Marquette U., 1974; MS in Dentistry, St. Louis U., 1977. Diplomate Am. Bd. Orthodontics. Resident in gen. dentistry USPHS, Norfolk, Va., 1974-75; practice dentistry specializing in orthodontics Green Bay, Wis., 1977—; instr. oral pathology NE Wis. Tech. Coll., Green Bay, 1979-86. Author: (with others) Orthodontic Headgear, 1977. Mem. Prevention Walking Club, Family Crisis Ctr. of Green Bay. Served as lt. USPHS, 1974-75. Fellow Coll. Diplomates Am. Bd. Orthodontics; mem. ADA, Am. Assn. Orthodontists, Wis. Dental Assn. (Continuing Edn. award 1986), Wis. Soc. Orthodontists, Orthodontic Edn. and Research Found., Brown Door Kewaunee Dental Soc. (program chmn. 1985-86, sec., treas. 1986-87, v.p. 1987-88, pres. 1988-89), St. Louis U. Orthodontic Alumni Assn. (pres. 1988-89), Acad. Gen. Dentistry, Violet Club of Am. Roman Catholic. Home: 2160 Green Leaf Rd DePere WI 54115-8621 Office: 2654 S Oneida St Green Bay WI 54304-5302

SWIDEN, LADELL RAY, travel company executive; b. Sioux Falls, S.D., June 17, 1938; s. Alick and Mildred Elizabeth (Larson) S.; m. Phyllis Lorriane Enga, Sept. 10, 1961; children: David, Daniel, Shari. BSEE, S.D. State U., 1961; MBA, U. S.D., 1982. Registered profl. engr., S.D., Minn. Instrument engr. Honeywell, Mpls., 1962-67; v.p. sales Swiden Appliance and Furniture, Sioux Falls, 1967-68; engring. mgr. Raven Industries, Inc., Sioux Falls, 1968-84; v.p. engring. Beta Raven Inc., St. Louis, 1984-85; pres. Delta Systems, Inc., St. Louis, 1985-86; acting dir. Engring. and Environ. Rsch. Ctr. S.D. State U., Brookings, 1986-94, dir. univ./industry tech. svc., 1986-94; v.p. Village Travel Inc., Brookings, 1994—; bd. dirs. Brookings Econ. Devel. Ctr. Patentee in field. Chmn. Indsl. Devel. Com., Brookings, 1989-90, vice-chair, 1988-89; chmn. bldg. com. Ascension Luth. Ch., 1988-90. Mem. NSPE, Nat. Assn. of Mgmt. and Tech. Assistance Ctrs. (bd. dirs.), Instrument Soc. Am., Aircraft Owners and Pilots Assn., Exptl. Aircraft Assn., Am. Bonanza Soc., S.D. Engring. Soc. (pres. N.E. chpt. 1991-92), Rotary, Elks. Home: 105 Heather Ln Brookings SD 57006-4123 Office: Village Travel Inc 1715 6th St Brookings SD 57006

SWIFT, DOLORES MONICA MARCINKEVICH, public relations executive; b. Hazleton, Pa., Apr. 3, 1936; d. Adam Martin and Anna Frances (Lizbinski) Marcinkevich; student McCann Coll., 1954-56; m. Morden Leib Swift, Dec. 18, 1966. Pub. rels. coord. Internat. Coun. Shopping Ctrs., N.Y.C., 1957-59, Wendell P. Colton Advt. Agy., N.Y.C., 1959-61, Sydney S. Baron Pub. Rels. Corp., N.Y.C., 1961-65, Robert S. Taplinger Pub. Rels., N.Y.C., 1965-66; prin. Dolores M. Swift, Pub. Rels., Chgo., 1966—. Bd. dirs. Welfare Pub. Rels. Forum, 1971-79, treas., 1975-77; mem. pub. rels. adv. com. Mid-Am. chpt. A.R.C., 1973—; mem. women's com. Mark Twain Meml., 1968-69; pub. rels. dir. N.J. Symphony, Bergen County, 1969-70, mem. pub. rels. and promotion com.; mem. Wadsworth Atheneum, 1968-69; bd. dirs. Youth Guidance, 1972-75, Camp Fire, Met. Chgo. Coun., Inc., 1990-91; mem. NCCJ Labor, Mgmt. and Pub. Interest Conf., 1977-78; mem. pub. rels. com. United Way/Crusade of Mercy, 1979-80, 83, chmn. health svcs. com., 1984, direct mail com. 1985-86. Mem. Pub. Rels. Soc. Am. (accredited, coll. of fellows, Disting. Svc. award 1988, chmn. subcom. Nat. Ctr. for Vol. Action 1971-72, pub. svcs. com. Chgo. chpt. 1971-72, dir. 1975-82, chmn. counselors sect. 1976-77, assembly del. 1976, 79-81, 84-89, sec. 1977-78, v.p. 1978-79, pres.-elect 1979-80, pres. 1980-81, Midwest dist. chmn. 1984, nat. bd. dirs. 1985-89, sec. 1987-89, host chpt. chmn. 1981 conf., chmn. Midwest Dist. Conf. 1983, chmn. ethics awareness com. 1990-92, chmn. sr. forum com. 1993-94, 95-96, chmn. past pres. coun. 1995-96, mem. sr. forum com. 1995—, ednl. affairs com. 1990—, chmn., past pres. coun. 1995—), Women's Club (publs. chmn. Englewood, N.J., 1970-71), Publicity Club (chmn. pub. info. com. 1975-76). Mem. editorial bd. Public Relations Jour., 1978.

SWIHART, FRED JACOB, lawyer; b. Park Rapids, Minn., Aug. 19, 1919; s. Fred and Elizabeth Pauline (Judnitsch) S.; m. Edna Lillian Jensen, Sept. 30, 1950; 1 child; Frederick Jay. BA, U. Nebr., 1949, JD, 1954; M in Russian Lang., Middlebury Coll., 1950; grad., U.S. Army Command and Staff Coll., 1965. Bar: Nebr. 1954, U.S. Dist. Ct. Nebr. 1954, U.S. Ct. Appeals (8th cir.) 1977, U.S. Supreme Ct. 1972. Claims atty. Chgo. & Eastern Ill. R.R., 1954-56; atty. Assn. Amer. R.R.s, Chgo., 1956-60; assoc. Wagener & Marx, Lincoln, Nebr., 1960-61; prosecutor City of Lincoln, 1961-68; sole practice Lincoln, 1968—. Editor Law for the Aviator, 1969-71. Served to lt. col. U.S. Army, 1943-46, ETO, Korea, ret. col., USAR, 1979. Fellow Nebr. State Bar Found.; mem. ABA, Nebr. Bar Assn., Fed. Bar Assn., Assn. Trial Lawyers Am., Am. Judicature Soc., Aircraft Owners and Pilots Assn. (legis. rep.), Nebr. Criminal Def. Attys. Assn., Nat. Assn. Criminal Def. Lawyers, Mercedes Benz Club Am., Nebr. Assn. Trial Attys., Nat. Assn. Uniformed Svcs., Res. Officers Assn., Nat. Assn. Legion of Honor, Internat. Footprint Assn., Am. Legion (adm. Nebr. Navy), Mason (knight comdr. of ct. of honor), Shriners, The Cabiri. Republican.

Presbyterian. Home: 1610 Susan Cir Lincoln NE 68506-1854 Office: 4435 O St Ste 130 Lincoln NE 68510-1864

SWINDELL, WARREN C., humanities educator; b. Kansas City, Mo., Aug. 22, 1934; s. John Truman and Estella Juanita (McKittrick) S.; m. Monica S. Streetman, June 25, 1967; children: Warna Celia, Lillian Ann. BS, Lincoln U., 1956; MusM, U. Mich., 1964; PhD, U. Iowa, 1970. Dir. band and choir, musical activities Ctrl. H.S., Hayti, Mo., 1956-57, 59-60; specialist instrumental music Flint (Mich.) Pub. Schs., 1961-67; chairperson music, prof. Ky. State U., Frankfort, 1970-80; chairperson Dept. Africana Studies Ind. State U., Terre Haute, 1980-96. Contbr. articles to profl. jours. With U.S. Army, 1957-59. Recipient Disting. Tchr. award Caleb Mills, 1996; fellow Lilly Endowment Inc., 1994; grantee Nat. Rsch. Coun., 1989. Mem. NAACP (v.p. Terre Haute br. 1995), Ind. Coalition of Blacks in Higher Edn. (v.p. 1995-96), Prince Hall Grand Lodge (chair Masonic edn., historian 1995). Home: 14 Douglas Dr Terre Haute IN 47803 Office: Indiana State Univ Terre Haute IN 47809

SWINGLEY, SHERYL ANN, journalism educator, consultant; b. Columbus, Ind., Dec. 30, 1951; d. Emil Monroe and Clara (McClellan) Stace; m. Phillip Allen Swingley, Aug. 14, 1977; 1 child, Derek Ryan. BS, Ball State U., 1974, MA, 1982. Asst. to dir. of pub. rels. Muncie (Ind.) Community Schs., 1970-74; tchr. Warren Cen. High Sch., Indpls., 1974-77; publs. editor St. John's Med. Ctr., Anderson, Ind., 1978-79; instr. Ball State U., Muncie, 1990—; asst. dir. pub. rels. Ball Meml. Hosp., Muncie, 1979-88; dir. mktg. div. Parkview Meml. Hosp., Muncie, 1988-90. Editor: Spirit mag., 1979, (newsletter)(Rounds, 1981-85; mem. editorial bd. Health Focus mag., 1984-88, Parkviews mag., 1988-90. Active journalism alumni bd. Ball State U., 1984-94; bd. dirs., fundraising chair Hillcroft Ctr. for Devel. Disabled, Muncie, 1987-89, 91-92, 94-95. Recipient MacEachern award Acad. Hosp. Pub. Rels., 1984. Mem. Nat. Fedn. Press Women (7 nat. comm. awards 1982-84), Women in Comm., Inc. (chpt. pres., v.p. programs, past chair nominations com. Gt. Lakes region), Starsoccer Club (bd. dirs., sec. 1991—), Ctrl. Ind. Youth Soccer League (bd. dirs., sec. 1995—), Mortar Board, Kappa Tau Alpha, Lambda Iota Tau, Delta Zeta (adv. bd. Muncie chpt. 1991-94). United Methodist. Home: 3908 N Vienna Woods Dr Muncie IN 47304-1779 Office: Ball State U Journalism Dept West Quad Muncie IN 47306

SWISHER, PHILLIP M., company executive; b. Detroit, Dec. 9, 1940. BS, Wayne State U., 1966. Registered profl. engr., Mich. Dir. venture devel. Vickers Inc., Rochester Hills, Mich., 1966—. Active St. Paul's United Meth. Ch.; coach Little League. Mem. IEEE.

SWITZER, JON REX, architect; b. Shelbyville, Ill., Aug. 22, 1937; s. John Woodrow and Ida Marie (Vadalabene) S.; m. Judith Ann Heinlein, July 7, 1962; 1 child, Jeffrey Eric. Student, U. Ill., 1955-58; BS, Millikin U., 1972; MA, Sangamon State U., 1981. Registered architect Ill., Mo., Ohio, Colo.; registered interior designer, Ill. Architect Warren & Van Praag, Inc., Decatur, Ill., 1970-72; prin. Decatur, 1972-81, Bloomington, Ill., 1981-83; architect Hilfinger, Asbury, Cufaude, Abels, Bloomington, 1983-84; ptnr. Riddle/Switzer, Ltd., Bloomington, 1984-86; with bldg., design and constrn. div. State Farm Ins. Cos., Bloomington, 1986-89; architect The Riddle Group, Bloomington, 1989-91; prin. J. Rex Switzer, Architect, Bloomington, 1991—. Elder Presbyn. Ch., 1996. With U.S. Army, 1958-61. Mem. AIA (pres. Bloomington chpt. 1983, Decatur chpt. 1976, v.p. Ill. chpt. 1986-87, sec. 1985, treas. 1984), Am. Archtl. Found., Chgo. Architecture Found., Nat. Trust Hist. Preservation, Frank Lloyd Found., Decatur C. of C. (merit citation 1974, merit award 1979), Masons (32d degree). Republican. Presbyterian (elder). Home: 9 Mary Ellen Way Bloomington IL 61701-2014 Office: 2412 E Washington St Ste 6A Bloomington IL 61704-4497

SWITZER, SAMUEL THOMAS, non-profit administrator; b. Cowgill, Mo., Feb. 5, 1951; s. William Thomas and Lova Nadine (Hayden) S.; m. Carolyn Beth Stephens, Aug. 7, 1971; children: Samuel Andrew, Jennifer Elaine. BSBA summa cum laude, William Jewell Coll., 1973; cert. mgmt. program, Rockhurst Coll., 1978. CPA, Mo. Asst. bank examiner Fed. Res. Bank St. Louis, 1973-74; cashier, asst. contr. Kansas City (Mo.) Life Ins. Co., 1974-77; contr., asst. treas. Belsaw Machinery Co., Kansas City, Mo., 1977-80; coord. spl. projects Kansas City Power and Light Co., 1980-81; dir., sec.-treas. Scudder Communications Assocs., Inc., Gladstone, Mo., 1982-87; treas. Midwestern Sem. Housing Corp., Kansas City, Mo., 1981-93; v.p. Midwestern Bapt. Theol. Sem., Kansas City, 1981-93; dir. Open Options, Inc., 1993—; chmn. So. Bapt. Sems. Bus. Officers Coun., 1986, 91; notary pub., State of Mo., 1982—. Bd. govs. William Jewell Coll. Alumni Assn., Liberty, Mo., 1973—; bd. dirs. Kearney (Mo.) Devel. Corp., 1977-80; ordained deacon 1st Bapt. Ch., Kearney, 1977, chair fin. com., pers. com., tchr. Sunday sch.; league treas., dir. of ofcls., coach Kearney Holt Youth Soccer Club, 1982-93; league coord., coach Kearney Holt Recreation Assn., 1985-91; chair religious life commn. William Jewell Coll., 1989-92; bd. dirs. Kearney R-1 Sch. Bd., 1991-94, liaison mem. strategic planning com., 1992; mem. Sr. Link Adv. Bd., 1994—; pres. William Jewell Coll. Soccer Booster Club, 1995—. Mem. Kansas City C. of C., Clay County Devel. Commn. (gold crown mem.), Phi Beta Kappa, Phi Mu Alpha. Republican. Home: 17009 NE 134th Ter Kearney MO 64060-8910 Office: Open Options Inc Ste 100 3217 Broadway Kansas City MO 64111

SWOBODA, LARY JOSEPH, state legislator; b. Luxemburg, Wis., May 28, 1939; s. Joseph Francis and Catherine Magdalene (Daul) S.; m. Janice Marie Hendricks, Nov. 16, 1968. BS in Speech and Edn., U. Wis., Milw., 1963, MS in Polit. Sci., 1965, EdS, 1988; postgrad., U. Wis., Madison, 1988—. Cert. ednl. specialist. Speech and English tchr. So. High Sch., Brussels, Wis., 1963-67; tchr. Luxemburg Schs., 1967-70; mem. Wis. State Legislature, Madison, 1970—; chair adminstrv. rules com. Wis. State Assembly, Madison, 1993—; exec. dir. Wis. Nat. and Cmty. Svc. Bd., Madison. Active Dem. County Unit. Mem. K.C., Luxemburg C. of C., Lions, Phi Eta Sigma, Kappa Delta Pi, Phi Kappa Phi, Phi Delta Kappa. Roman Catholic. Home: 1835 Broadway Dr Sun Prairie WI 53590-1758 Office: Wis Nat and Cmty Svc Bd 101 E Wilson St Madison WI 53703-3422

SYDNOR, SYNTHIA, kinesiology educator; b. Chester, Pa., Apr. 2, 1956; d. Alvin Griffith and Mary Elizabeth (Kounnas) S.; m. James Alan Slowikowski, Nov. 19, 1983; children: Jesse Francis, Journey Elizabeth. BS, U. Del., 1978; MS, U. Wash., 1982; PhD, Pa. State U., 1988. Tchr. phys. edn. and art Deer Park (Wash.) Middle Sch., 1978-80; dir. Laotian Refugee Project, Raymond, Wash., 1982-83; asst. prof. kinesiology U. Ill., Urbana-Champaign, 1988-94, assoc. prof. kinesiology, theory and interpretive criticism, 1994—. Mem. editorial bd. Play and Culture, 1991—; contbr. articles to profl. jours. Periklean Athens Summer Inst. fellow Nat. Endowment for Humanities, 1991; Pa. State U. fellow, 1984-85; Internat. Program in Humanities and Arts grantee, 1988-92. Mem. N.Am. Soc. for Sport History (editor ann. procs. 1988-93, book rev. editor Jour. Sport History), Assn. for Study of Play, Internat. Sociol. Assn., Internat. Assn. for Study of History of Sport and Phys. Edn., Philosophic Soc. Study of Sport. Office: U Ill Dept Kinesiology 225B Freer 906 S Goodwin Urbana IL 61801

SYFERT, SAMUEL RAY, retired librarian; b. Beecher City, Ill., July 20, 1928; s. Fred and LaVonne Mildred (High) S.; B.S. in Edn., Eastern Ill. U., 1957, M.S., 1961; M.S. in Edn., Calif. Christian U., 1979. Tchr. bus. Geneseo (Ill.) Community Unit schs., 1957-59; tchr. English, Bethany (Ill.) Community Unit schs., 1961-77, sch. librarian, 1977-95; ret., 1995; bd. dirs., treas. Marrowbone Twp. Library, Bethany, 1978-84, sec., 1984-85, pres., 1985—. Served with AUS, 1950-52. Named Tchr. of Yr., Moultrie County (Ill.), 1975. Mem. NEA, ALA, Ill. Edn. Assn., Ill. Library Assn., Bethany C. of C. (sec. 1977-81, pres. 1982), Am. Legion. Republican. Mem. Christian Ch. (Disciples of Christ) (bd. chairperson). Home: PO Box 402 Bethany IL 61914-0402 Office: PO Box 97 Bethany IL 61914-0097

SYKES, VERNON L., state legislator; b. Oct. 2, 1951; m. Barbara Sykes; children: Stancy, Emilia. BS, Ohio Univ., 1974; MS, Wright State Univ., 1980; MPA, Harvard Univ., 1986. Planner, rsch. & eval., asst. Fiscal Officer Summit Coun. Criminal Justice Com., Akron, Ohio, 1976-79; city councilman Akron, 1980-83; Ohio State Rep. Dist. 42, 1983-92, Dist. 44, 1993—; chmn. Interstate Coop Com.; real estate agt. Clarence K. Allen Realty, Akron, 1982; mem. Ohio Housing Fin. Agy., Econ. Devel. & Small Bus, Financial Inst., Econ. Affairs & Fed. Rels., Transp. & Urban Affairs Com., mem. jt. Com. on Agy. Rule Rev; tchr. Akron Bd. Edn., Ohio, 1974-75, sr. mgmt. specialist United Neighborhood Coun. Inc., Akron, 1975-76; instr. Univ. Akron & Southern Ohio Coll., 1980; pres. Harvard Group, 1987, mem. BancOne Cmty. adv. bd., 1996—. Named Legis. of Yr. Nat. Assn. Social Workers, 1986. Mem. Akron Pvt. Indsl. Coun., Akron Cmty. Action Agy., Western Econ. Assn. Internat. Cuyahoga Valley Assn. Home: 615 Diagonal Rd Akron OH 44320*

SYKORA, BARBARA ZWACH, state legislator; b. Tracy, Minn., Mar. 5, 1941; d. John M. and Agnes (Schueller) Zwach; m. Robert G. Sykora, 1965; children: Mona, John, Kara, Mary. BA, St. Catherine Coll., 1963. Tchr. Springfield (Mass.) Sch., 1963-64, Roseville (Minn.) Sch., 1964-66; mem. Minn. Ho. of Reps., St. Paul, 1994—. Vice chmn. 2d Congl. Dist. Rep. Com., Minn., 1978-82; chmn. 6th Congl. Dist. Rep. Com., 1982-86, 2d congl. dist. Senator Durenberger Campaign, 1980-82, Senator Pillsbury Campaign, Wayzata, Minn., 1980, Ind. Rep. State Com., Minn., 1987-93; dist. dir. Office Congressman Rod Grams, 1993-94. Mem. Kappa Gamma Phi.

SYLKE, LORETTA CLARA, artist; b. Parkston, S.D., Nov. 4, 1926; d. Jacob and Maria Magdelin (Frey) Sprecher; m. Arthur C. Sylke, Apr. 26, 1961; children: Michael Arthur, Patricia, Constance, Sharon, Catherine, Charles (dec.). Grad. H.S., Chgo. Represented by Becca Gallery Berlin, Wis. Works have appeared at N.Mex. Art League, Albuquerque, 1991, El Dorado Gallery, Colorado Springs, Mont. Miniature Show, Billings, The New Eng. Fine Art Inst., The N.E. Trade Ctr., Woburn, Mass., 1993, El Dorado Gallery, Colorado Springs, 1993, 20th Annual Am. Nat. Miniature Show, Laramie, Wyo., Art in the Park, Lenexa, Kans., Gov.'s office, Madison, Wis., Custer County Art Ctr., Miles City, Mont., 1995, Laramie (Wyo.) Miniature Show, 1995; juried exhibns., Beloit, Wis., Miniature Show: Custer County Art Ctr., Miles City, Mont., 1995, 96; represented in pvt. collections. Recipient Masco award Madison Art Supply, 1982. Mem. Nat. Mus. Women in the Arts, Soc. Exptl. Artists, Wis. Women in the Arts, Catherine Lorillarr Wolfe Art Club (N.Y.C.). Home: N4392 Wicks Lndg Princeton WI 54968-8508 Office: 1714 Studio Princeton WI 54968

SYLVESTER, NANCY KATHERINE, speech educator, management consultant; b. Evansville, Ind., July 17, 1947; d. Leonard Nicholas and Marjoire (Moore) Jochim; m. James Andrew Sylvester, Aug. 21, 1971; children: Marcy Dee, Holly Nicole. BS, Ind. State U., 1969; MA, U. Mich., 1970. Registered profl. parliamentarian; cert. prof. parliamentarian; team/meeting mgmt. specialist. Assoc. prof. speech Rock Valley Coll., Rockford, Ill., 1970—; co-owner Jimmy's Frozen Custard, 1996—; bd. dirs. First Fed. Savs. Bank, Belvidere, Ill. Author: Basics of Parliamentary Procedure, 1983, Handbook for Effective Meetings, 1993; contbr. articles to profl. jours. Bd. dirs. Jr. League Rockford, 1974-78, Rock River Homeowners Assn., 1990-91; pres. Children's Devel. Ctr. Aux. Bd., Rockford, 1984-85; parliamentarian Winnebago County Dem. Caucus, 1991; vice-chmn. Commn. on Am. Parliamentary Practice, 1989-90, chmn., 1990-91; nat. parliamentarian Girl Scouts U.S., 1996—, bd. dirs. Rock River coun., 1979-81. Recipient Jardene medal Ind. State U., 1969, RVC Faculty of Yr. award, 1994; Rockham scholar U. Mich., 1969-70. Mem. Am. Inst. Parliamentarians, Am. Soc. Women Accts. (parliamentarian 1980—), Am. Women Soc. CPAs (parliamentarian 1991—), Nat. Coun. State Bds. Nursing (parliamentarian 1992—), Ill. Assn. Parliamentarians, Nat. Assn. Ins. Women (parliamentarian 1983-91), Nat. Assn. Parliamentarians, Assn. Quality and Participation, Speech Commn. Assn., Coun. Better Bus. Burs. (parliamentarian 1993), Nat. League Nursing (parliamentarian), Rockford C. of C. (ex-officio bd. dirs.), Phi Rho Pi (region 4 v.p. 1972-73, nat. v.p. 1973-74), Am. Soc. Pain Mgmt. Nurses (nat. parliamentarian 1994—), Ind. Accts. Assn. Ill. (parliamentrian 1990—), Info. Sys. Audit and Control Assn. (parliamentarian 1994—). Roman Catholic. Home: 4826 River Bluff Ct Rockford IL 61111-5836

SYLVESTER, TERRY LEE, controller, business administrator, school system administrator; b. Cin., June 12, 1949; s. Wilbert Fairbanks and Jewell S.; m. Janet Lynn Brigger, Nov. 29, 1975; children: Carisa, Laura, Jason, Katherine. BS in Bus. Accounting, Miami U., Oxford, Ohio, 1972, student, 1993—; MBA in Fin., Xavier U., Cin., 1983; MEd Xavier U., 1991. Staff accountant Alexander Grant & Co., CPAs, Cin., 1972; treas., controller Imperial Cmty. Developers, Inc., Cin., subs. of Chelsea Moore Devel. Corp., 1972—; controller home bldg. div. Chelsea Moore Devel. Corp., 1978—; controller, CFO Armstrong Cos., apt. mgmt., 1978-79, Dorger Investments, Cin., 1979-81, Delta Mechanical Constructors, Inc., Fairfield, Ohio, 1981-83; bus. mgr. Oak Hills Local Schs., Cin., 1983-87; treas. Lockland City Schs., Cin., 1987-91, 91-93; dir. budget Cin. Pub. Schs., 1993-94; budget mgr. Seattle Pub. Schs., Seattle, 1994—; CFO Davenport Cmty. Schs., 1995—. Home: 31 Woodmont Court Fairfield OH 45014 Office: 1001 Harrison St Davenport IA 52803

SYMENS, MAXINE TANNER, restaurant owner; b. Primghar, Iowa, June 12, 1930; d. George Herman and Irene Marie (Dahnke) Brinkert; m. Jack Frederiksen Tanner, Dec. 28, 1950 (dec. Oct. 1976); m. Delbert Glenn Symens, Sept. 26, 1981. BS magna cum laude, Westmar Coll., 1970. Cert. tchr., Iowa. Elem. tchr. Rural Sch. O'Brien Co., Primghar, 1949-54, Gaza (Iowa) Com. Sch., 1954-60; secondary tchr. Primghar Com. Sch., 1960-81; fitness salon owner Slim 'N' Trim, George, Rock Rapids, Iowa, 1982-87; restaurant owner George Cafe, 1985-90, Pizza Ranch, 1988-96; with network mktg. divsn. Espial and STS, 1996—. Pres. Primghar Edn. Assn., 1970-71. Mem. George C. of C., George Kiwanis Club (sec. 1991-95), Delta Kappa Gamma. Lutheran. Home: 307 Dell St NE George IA 51237-1030

SYMENS, RONALD EDWIN, electrical engineer, consultant; b. Britton, S.D., Jan. 16, 1951; s. Edwin Donald and Dora Marie (Larson) S.; children: Amy Marie, Chad Ronald. BSEE, S.D. Sch. Mines and Tech., 1973. Jr. engr. Firestone Tire Co., Akron, Ohio, 1973-74; engr. Firestone Tire Co., Akron, 1974-76, sr. engr., 1977-78; systems engr. Hewlett Packard, Cleve., 1977-79; pres. Comml. Timesharing Inc., Akron, 1980—. Inventor defect marker. Deacon Manchester Trinity Chapel, Akron, 1984-88, chmn. deacon bd., 1987-88; mem. Akron Regional Bd. Republican. Office: Comml Timesharing Inc 2650 S Arlington St Akron OH 44319-2049

SYMULESKI, RICHARD ALOYSIUS, chemical engineer; b. N.Y.C., June 21, 1947; s. Samuel Michael and Josephine Rose (Koda) S.; m. Mary Susan Sommers, Aug. 24, 1974; 1 child, Margaret Joan. BSChemE, Cath. U. Am., 1970, MSChemE, 1973, PhD in ChemE, 1977. Rsch. engr. Nat. Bur. Standards, Washington, 1972-77; rsch. chem. engr. Amoco Chems. Co., Naperville, Ill., 1977-78; coordinator environ. affairs Amoco Chems. Co., Chgo., 1978-80, dir. environ. affairs, 1980-83; dir. environ. planning and permitting Amoco Corp., Chgo., 1983-86, dir. product safety, 1986-89, mgr. environ. affairs and safety, 1989-91, gen. mgr., environ. cons., product steward and toxicology, 1991-93, mgr. environ. projects (Mex.), 1992—; gen. mgr. environ. tech. devel., 1994—; editl. advisor Chem. Processing mag., 1987—; mem. joint U.S.-USSR com. on civil engring. constrn. NAS, 1977—; vice chmn. N.Am. Environ. Adv. Bd., 1995—. Contbr. articles to profl. jours. Mem. Air Pollution Control Assn., Am. Chem. Soc., Am. Inst. Chem. Engrs., Chem. Mfrs. Assn. (environ. mgmt. com. 1984-87, exec. com. product liability tort reform, chmn. product safety com. 1987-89, internat. affairs group 1989—), Internat. Petroleum Industry Environ. Conservation Assn. (chmn. environ. health group 1988—), Sierra Club, Sigma Xi. Roman Catholic. Office: Amoco Corp Mail Code H-7 150 W Warrenville Rd Naperville IL 60563

SYROPOULOS, MIKE, school system director; b. Kato Hora, Navpactos, Greece, Jan. 18, 1934; came to U.S., 1951; s. Polykarpos Dimitri and Constantoula P. (Konstantinopoulos) S.; m. Sandra Francis Flick, Jan. 3, 1942; children: Pericles, Connie, Tina. BS, Wayne State U., 1960, MEd, 1965, EdD, 1971. Cert. secondary tchr., Mich. Tchr. Detroit Pub. Schs., 1960-66, dept. head, 1966-67, acting supr., 1967-69, rsch. asst., 1969-74, program assoc., 1976—; asst. dir. Wayne (Mich.) County Intermediate Dist., 1974-76. Contbr. articles to reports. V.p. St. John Greek Orthodox Ch., Sterling Heights, Mich., 1987, pres., 1988. With U.S. Army, 1956-58. Mem. ASCD, Am. Edn. Rsch. Assn., Am. Hellenic Edn. Progressive Assn. (athletic dir. 1992, treas. 1994, sec. 1995), Mich. Assn. Supervision Curriculum (bd. dirs. 1994-95, 95-96), Mich. Edn. Rsch. Assn. Greek Orthodox. Home: 46602 Red River Dr Macomb MI 48044 Office: Detroit Pub Schs 5035 Woodward Ave Detroit MI 48202-4015

SYVERSON, DAVE, state legislator; b. June 29, 1957; m. Shirley Syverson. Student, Rock Valley Coll. Mem. Ill. State Senate, Dist. 34; ptnr. Market Ins. Group. Mem. Rockford Boys and Girls Club; bd. govs. Luth. Social Svc. Recipient Humanitarian award Office Internat. Conf., 1994, Activator award Famr Bur., Voice of Employer award; named Freshman Legislator of Yr. Hosp. Assn. Home: 6757 Flowerhill Rd Rockford IL 61114*

SZABO, JOSEPH CLARK, labor lobbyist; b. Evergreen Park, Ill., Dec. 26, 1957; s. Joseph Frank and Shirley Jean (Clark) S. AAS, South Suburban Coll., 1984; BA, Governors State U., 1990. Train condr. Metra/ICG, Chgo., 1976-96; state dir. Ill. legis. bd. United Transp. Union, 1996—; mem. labor/mgmt. com. Metra, Chgo., 1988—. Chmn. Riverdale (Ill.) Zoning Bd./Plan Commn., 1981-86; commr. Ivanhoe Park Bd., Riverdale, 1982-87; trustee Village of Riverdale, 1987—. Mem. United Transp. Union (sec.-treas. local 1290 1984-90, legis. rep. 1987-96, vice chmn. state legis. bd. 1992-96), Calumet Region Enterprise Zone (bd. dirs. 1989—), Calumet Region Indsl. Assn. (bd. dirs. 1990-92, 95—), Dolton Riverdale Jaycees (treas. 1979-80, v.p. 1980-81, pres. 1981-82, Jaycee of Yr. 1980, 81, Disting. Svc. award 1981, Outstanding Loca. Pres. 1982, Outstanding Jaycee 1990), Elks. Methodist. Home: 14211 S Tracy Ave Riverdale IL 60627-2341

SZALLER, JAMES FRANCIS, lawyer; b. Cleve., Jan. 22, 1945; s. Frank Paul and Ellen Grace (O'Malley) S.; m. Roberta Mae Curtin, Oct. 23, 1967 (div. Aug. 1975); m. Charlene Nancy Smith, Apr. 28, 1984. AA, Cuyahoga Community Coll., 1967; BA, Cleve. State U., 1970, JD cum laude, 1975. Bar: Ohio 1975, U.S. Dist. Ct. (no. dist.) Ohio 1975, U.S. Supreme Ct. 1982, U.S. Ct. Appeals (6th cir.) 1983, U.S. Ct. Appeals (4th cir.) 1986. Assoc. Metzenbaum, Gaines & Stern (now Gaines & Stern Co. L.P.A.), Cleve., 1975-79; sr. ptnr. Brown & Szaller Co., L.P.A., Cleve., 1979—; lectr. law Cleve. State U., 1978-81. Mem. editorial bd. Cleve. State U. Law Rev., 1973-75.; contbr. articles to profl. jours. Mem. ABA, Fed. Bar Assn., Ohio State Bar Assn., Greater Cleve. Bar Assn., Cleve. Acad. Trial Lawyers, Ohio Acad. Trial Lawyers, Assn. Trial Lawyers Am., Am. Arbitration Assn. (panel arbitrators), Nat. Coll. Advocacy (advocate). Democrat. Roman Catholic. Office: Brown & Szaller Co LPA 14222 Madison Ave Cleveland OH 44107-4510

SZCZUREK, THOMAS EUGENE, marketing executive; b. Chgo., Aug. 29, 1957; s. Eugene and Anne (Potaniec) S.; m. Vickie Lynn Dodds, Oct. 20, 1984. AAS, Morton Coll., 1977; BBA with highest honors, Western Ill. U., 1979; MBA, U. Cin., 1981. Assoc. account mgr. Burroughs Corp., Chgo., 1979-80; sr. mktg. analyst NCR Corp., Dayton, Ohio, 1982-84; mktg. and bus. mgr. Monarch Marking Systems, Dayton, 1984-86; mktg. mgr. Reynolds & Reynolds, Dayton, 1986-87, dir. mktg., 1987-90, dir. product mgmt., dir. nat. accounts mktg., 1990-91; v.p. mktg. Evenflo Juvenile Products Co., Piqua, Ohio, 1991—. Jr. asst. scoutmaster Boy Scouts Am., Cicero, 1972-73; chmn. Cicero Young Adults Assn., 1979-80; mem. St. Mary's Holy Name Soc., 1977-80, planning forum, 1988-89; v.p. Woodview Estates Homeowners Assn., 1988-90, pres., 1990-93. Named one of Outstanding Young Men of Am. U.S. Jaycees, 1986. Mem. Am. Mktg. Assn. (chmn. promotion com. 1978-79), Worldwide Mktg. Leadership Panel, Phi Beta Lambda, Phi Kappa Phi, Beta Gamma Sigma, Alpha Mu Alpha. Home: 3161 Indian Ripple Rd Dayton OH 45440-3608 Office: Evenfo Juvenile Products Co 1801 Commerce Dr Piqua OH 45356-2603

SZIGETI, MICHELLE MARIE, critical care nurse; b. South Bend, Ind., Mar. 21, 1954; d. Eugene Peter and Patricia Joyce (May) S. RN, Meml. Hosp., South Bend, 1976; BS, St. Francis Coll., Joliet, Ill., 1990. Cert. critical care nurse. Charge nurse cardiac intermediate care Meml. Hosp., South Bend, 1976-83, charge nurse cardio vascular intensive care, 1983—; tchr. cardiovasular intensive care Meml. Hosp. of South Bend, 1991—. Mem. AACN. Home: 112 S McCombs St South Bend IN 46637-3330

SZILAGY, ERIC JOSEPH, surgeon; b. Detroit, Dec. 14, 1952. BS, U. Mich., 1975; MD, Wayne State U., 1980. Medical Diplomate. Surg. resident Henry Ford Hosp., Detroit, 1980-85, conol-rectal surgery fellow, 1985-86, sr. staff surgeon, 1986—. Home: 47550 Edinborough Ln Novi MI 48374 Office: Henry Ford Hosp 2799 W Grand Blvd Detroit MI 48202

SZILAGYI-HAWKINS, ELIZABETH MARIA, social services administrator; b. Chgo., Dec. 28, 1949; d. Bernard and Elizabeth (Szombathy) Szilagyi; m. Robert Lee Hawkins. BS in Social Welfare, Olivet Nazarene U., 1973. Lic. social worker, Ill. Social worker Proviso Council on Aging, Bellwood, Ill., 1980-84, dir. sr. citizen services, 1984—; mem. Older Adults Job Fair com. Operation Able, Oak Park, Ill., 1983-86, Gottlieb Hosp. Home Health Adv. Bd., 1988—. Mem. Proviso Coord. Com. (sr. com., pres. 1986-87, 959-96), Family Care Sr. Companion Adv. Coun. (v.p. 1985-86, pres. 1986-87). Office: Proviso Coun on Aging 439 Bohland Ave Bellwood IL 60104-1833

SZOKE, JOSEPH LOUIS, psychologist, mental health facility administrator; b. Rahway, N.J., May 6, 1947; s. Louis Joseph Sr. and Julia Dorothy (Jasa) S.; m. Carolyn Kay Orr, Jan. 13, 1971; children: Elizabeth, Amy. BS, U. Dayton, 1969, MA, 1973. Cert. clin. psychologist, mental health adminstr. Psychologist Dayton (Ohio) Mental Health Ctr., 1969-71; dir. psychol. and social services Dayton Bur. Drug Abuse, 1971-73; assoc. dir. Montgomery County Bd. Mental Health, Dayton, 1973-74; exec. dir. Tri-County Bd. Mental Health, Troy, Ohio, 1974-90; exec. dir. alcohol and drug addiction Mental Health Svcs. Bd. for Montgomery County, Dayton, 1990—; adj. prof. U. Dayton, 1975—, Sinclair Coll., Dayton, 1973-78; cons. Applications Research Corp., Dayton, 1973-74. Treas. Hospice of Miami County, Troy, 1986—, Epilepsy Assn. Miami County, Troy, 1986—. Served to capt. U.S. Army, 1969-72.. Fellow Assn. Mental Health Adminstrs. (pres. 1988, Adminstr. of Yr. 1991); mem. Am. Evaluation Assn., Nat. Assn. Rural Mental Health, Ohio Assn. Community Mental Health Bds. (treas. 1987-89). Roman Catholic. Lodge: Kiwanis (pres. Troy club 1983). Home: 1675 Old School House Rd Troy OH 45373-4435

SZYMANSKI, EDNA MORA, rehabilitation psychology and special education educator; b. Caracas, Venezuela, Mar. 19, 1952; came to U.S., 1952; d. José Angel and Helen Adele (McHugh) Mora; m. Michael Bernard, Mar. 30, 1973. BS, Rensselaer Poly. Inst., 1972; MS, U. Scranton, 1974; PhD, U. Tex., 1988. Cert. rehab. counselor. Vocat. evaluator Mohawk Valley Workshop, Utica, N.Y., 1974-75; vocat. rehab. counselor N.Y. State Office Vocat. Rehab., Utica, N.Y., 1975-80; sr. vocat. rehab. counselor N.Y. State Office Vocat. Rehab., Utica, 1980-87; rsch. assoc. U. Tex., Austin, 1988-89; asst. prof. U. Wis., Madison, 1989-91, assoc. prof., 1991-93, assoc. dean sch. edn., 1993—, dir. rehab. rsch. and tng. ctr., 1993-96, prof. rehab. psychology and spl. edn., 1993—; cons. Rsch. Assocs. Syracuse, N.Y., 1988-90. Co-author various book chpts.; co-editor: Rehabilitation Counseling Basics and Beyond, 1992; co-editor Work and Disability, 1996, Rehabilitation Counseling Bull., 1994—; contbr. articles to profl. jours. Mem. Pres.'s Com. on Employment of People with Disabilities, Washington, 1987—. Recipient Rsch. award Am. Assn. Counselor Edn. and Supr., 1991. Mem. ACA (chair rsch. com. 1992-94, Rsch. awards 1990, 93, 95), Am. Rehab. Counseling Assn. (pres. 1985-86, Rsch. award 1989, 94), Coun. Rehab. Edn. (chair rsch. com. 1990-95, v.p. 1993-95), Nat. Coun. Rehab. Edn. (chair rsch. com. 1992—, Rehab. Edn. Rschr. of Yr. 1993, New Career in Rehab. Edn. award 1990). Office: U Wis Dept Rehab Psychology and Spl Edn 432 N Murray St Madison WI 53706-1407

SZYMONIAK, ELAINE EISFELDER, state senator; b. Boscobel, Wis., May 24, 1920; d. Hugo Adolph and Pauline (Vig) Eisfelder; Casimir Donald Szymoniak, Dec. 7, 1943; children: Kathryn, Peter, John, Mary, Thomas. BS, U. Wis., 1941; MS, Iowa State U., 1977. Speech clinician Waukesha (Wis.) Pub. Sch., 1941-43, Rochester (N.Y.) Pub. Sch., 1943-44; rehab. aide U.S. Army, Chickasha, Okla., 1944-46; audiologist U. Wis., Madison, 1946-48; speech clinician Buffalo Pub. Sch., 1948-49, Sch. for Handicapped, Salina, Kans., 1951-52; speech pathologist, audiologist, counselor, resource mgr. Vocat. Rehab. State Iowa, Des Moines, 1956-85; mem. Iowa Senate, Des Moines, 1989—. Mem. Des Moines City coun., 1978-88; bd. dirs. Nat. League Cities, Wahsington, 1982-84, Girl Scouts U.S., Civic Ctr., House of Mercy, Westminster House, Iowa Leadership Consortium, Coun. on Internat. Understanding, Iowa Commn. on Status of Women, Young Christian Assn.; chairperson Greater Des Moines Coun. for Internat.

Understanding, United Way, 1987-88, Urban Dreams, Iowa Maternal and Child Health com. Named Woman of Achievement YWCA, 1982, Visionary Woman, Young Women's Resource Ctr. Mem. Am. Speech Lang. and Hearing Assn., Iowa Speech Lang. and Hearing Assn. (pres. 1977-78), Nat. Coun. State Legislators (fed. state com. on health, adv. com. on child protection), Women's Polit. Caucus, Nexus (pres. 1981-82). Home: 2116 44th St Des Moines IA 50310-3011 Office: State Senate State Capitol Des Moines IA 50319

TABACZYNSKI, RON, state legislator; m. Mary Tabaczynski. AA, BA, Calumet Coll., St. Joseph. Legis. asst. House Dem. Caucus, 1988-90; mem. from 1st dist. Ind. State Ho. of Reps., 1992—; mem. commerce and econ. devel. com., elections and apportionment com., ins., corps. and small bus. com., environ. affairs com., labor com. Formerly Dem. Precinct Committeeman; del. Dem. State Conv. Mem. N.W. Ind. World Trade Coun., Hammond Mohawks Conservation Club, FDR Club, Elks, KC. Home: 3742 Towle Ave Hammond IN 46327-1146*

TABER, DONALD CHARLES, chemist; b. St. Louis, July 2, 1954; s. Donald Clarence and June Marie (Meyer) T.; m. Christine Juanita Martin, July 2, 1977; children: Christopher Lee, Grace Marie. BGS, U. Mo., 1981. Sr. lab. technician Carboline Co., St. Louis, 1980-85; R & D chemist James River/CZ Inks, St. Louis, 1985—. Contbr. article to profl. jour.; patentee in static dissipative coating. Mem. Am. Chem. Soc., South Side Gamers. Libertarian. Roman Catholic. Office: CZ Inks 4150 Carr Lane Ct Saint Louis MO 63119

TABER, FRANCES KATHRYN, geriatrics nurse, administrator; b. Chattanooga, Dec. 8, 1923; d. Buren M. and Evelyn V. (Keyes) Farr; m. John W. Taber, Dec. 18, 1945; children: Shelley, Jay. Diploma, St. Joseph's Sch. Nursing, Mt. Clemens, Mich., 1945; BSPA, St. Joseph's Coll., Windham, Maine, 1966; Cert. Nursing Home Adminstr., Wayne State U., 1972. RN, Mich.; cert. social worker, Mich. Instr. student nurses St. Joseph's Retreat, Dearborn, Mich., 1946-47; staff nurse Wayne State U., Detroit, 1947-54; dir. nursing Bortz Health Care Facilities, West Bloomfield, Mich., 1966-72, adminstr., v.p., 1972-85; adminstr. Oak Manor, Troy, Mich., 1985—; legal expert for nursing homes Am. Coll. Nursing Home Adminstrs., 1992. With U.S. Navy, 1945. Mem. Oakland County Nursing Home Assn. (past v.p. and pres.). Home: 2536 Robindale Ln Bloomfield Hills MI 48302-0761 Office: 2316 John R Rd Troy MI 48083-2590

TABOR, RANDALL ARDEN, sales executive; b. Durham, N.C., Apr. 9, 1956; s. Thomas Edwin and Marjorie Yvonne (Miller) T.; m. Vicki Ann Gaeth, Aug. 30, 1980; children: Kimberly Erin, Braedon Edwin, Kara Jill. Student, Pa. State U., 1974-75, No. Va. Community Coll., 1976-77. Various sales/clerical positions, 1974-86; police officer State College (Pa.) Bur. of Police Svcs., 1980-82; salesman vacuum cleaners Glickman & Assocs., Altoona, Pa., 1983-86; sole proprietor R.V.T. & Assocs., Charleston, W.Va., 1986-87; product salesman W.Va. dist. div. Ga.-Pacific Corp., Atlanta and Nitro, W.Va., 1987-89; field sales mgr. Mich., No. Ohio & No. Ind. gypsum div. Ga.-Pacific Corp., Atlanta, Grand Rapids, Mich., 1989-95; area mgr. Office Products, Inc./Toledo, Toledo, 1995—. Sgt. USMC, 1976-80. Marksmanship-Bronze medal. Republican. Presbyterian. Home: 3641 Sussex Dr Lambertville MI 48144-9512 Office: Office Products Inc/Toledo Gypsum Div 1915 Monroe St Toledo OH

TABOR, THEODORE EMMETT, chemical company research manager; b. Great Falls, Mont., Dec. 28, 1940; s. John Edward and Alviva Lillian (Thorson) T.; m. Jacqueline Lou Hart, Aug. 5, 1959; children: Lori, John, Lexi. BA, U. Mont., 1962; PhD, Kansas State U., 1967. Various research and devel. positions Dow Chem. Co., Midland, Mich., 1967-81, mgr. coop. research, 1981—; co. rep. to Coun. for Chem. Rsch., 1982—; co. rep. to Indsl. Rsch. Inst., External Rsch. Dirs. Network, 1991—; co. rep. to Am. Chem. Soc., Co. Corp. Assocs., 1993—; program mgr. The Dow Chem. Co. Found., 1989-94. Mem. AAAS, Am. Chem. Soc., Soc. Rsch. Adminstrn., Nat. Coun. Univ. Rsch. Adminstrn. (assoc.), Assn. Univ. Tech. Mgrs. (affiliate), Tech. Transfer Soc. Mem. United Ch. Home: 2712 Mount Vernon Dr Midland MI 48642 Office: Dow Chem Co 1801 Building Midland MI 48674

TABORN, JEANNETTE ANN, real estate investor; b. Cleve., June 9, 1926; d. Ralph Mason and Catherine MArie (Mitchell) Tyler; m. Albert Lorenzo Taborn, Oct. 4, 1947 (dec. 1994); children: Wesley Orren, Annette Loren, KAren Faye, Albert Lorenzo II, Thomas Tyler. Student, Ohio State U., 1944-47. Real estate agt. and investor Cleve., 1947-61; tech. proofreader Sass-Widder Tech Writers, Port Hueneme, Calif., 1961-66, Upjohn Co., Kalamazoo, Mich., 1966-84; mktg. rep. pvt. practice, Kalamazoo, Mich., 1984—; regional mgr. Primerica, 1994; co-facilitator Healing Racism Series. Pres. Kalamazoo County Parent Tchr. Student Assn., 1975; active YWCA, 1981, NAACP, 1983; Kalamazoo Pub. Sch. bd., 1978; Greater Kalamazoo Arts Coun., 1979, Mich. sch. bd. vocat./Edn., Liberty com. C. of Com.; pres. Loy Norrix Trustee Fund, 1983; trustee Kalamazoo Intermediate Sch.; regional mgr. Al Williams. Recipient Cmty. Medal of Arts. Mem. So. West Mich. Alzheimer's Assn. (bd. mem.), Delta Sigma Theta (Mary McLeod Bethune award). Mem. Bahai Faith. Office: PO Box 50853 Kalamazoo MI 49005

TACHA, DEANELL REECE, federal judge; b. Jan. 26, 1946. BA, U. Kans., 1968; JD, U. Mich., 1971. Spl. asst. to U.S. Sec. of Labor, Washington, 1971-72; assoc. Hogan & Hartson, Washington, 1973, Thomas J. Pitner, Concordia, Kans., 1973-74; dir. Douglas County Legal Aid Clinic, Lawrence, Kans., 1974-77; assoc. prof. law U. Kans., Lawrence, 1974-77, prof., 1977-85, assoc. dean, 1977-79, assoc. vice chancellor, 1979-81, vice chancellor, 1981-85; judge U.S. Ct. Appeals (10th cir.), Denver, 1985—. Office: US Ct Appeals 10th Cir 4830 W 15th St Ste 100 Lawrence KS 66049-3846

TACKETT, NATALIE JANE, state administrator; b. Wausau, Wis.; d. Roland Elsworth and Natalie (Zanon) Kannenberg; m. William Marshall Tackett, July 1975 (dec.); children: Roland, Scott, Renee, William. BA in English with highest honors, N.W. Mo. State U., 1966, MA in English, 1968. Instr. English Tarkio (Mo.) Coll., 1968-70, N.W. Mo. State U., Maryville, 1970-78; rsch. dir. Mo. Dept. Revenue, Jefferson City, Mo., 1978-81; rsch. analyst Mo. Ho. of Reps., Jefferson City, 1981-84; dir. oversight div. Mo. Gen. Assembly, Jefferson City, 1984—. Editor various publs.; contbr. articles to profl. jours. Councilman N.W. Mo. Subarea Coun. Area II Health Sys. Agy., 1976-77; bd. dirs. Nodaway County Nursing Svcs. and Health Ctr., pres., 1974-76; gov.'s adv. coun. Comprehensive Health Planning, 1976; chmn. Nodaway County Citizen's Com. for a County Health Ctr., 1972-74; pres. Cole County Hist. Soc., 1996—. Recipient Outstanding Woman award Maryville chpt. Soroptimist Internat. 1975, Joy of Achievement award 1975. Mem. AAUW (legis. com. 1985-87, pres. Mo. div. 1983-85, Woman of Distinction award 1984, Outstanding Contbn. in the Area of Legis., Mo. div. 1987), Legis. Program Evaluation Soc. Office: Mo Gen Assembly Oversight divsn State Capitol Rm 132 Jefferson City MO 65101

TACKI, BERNADETTE SUSAN, principal; b. Kenosha, Wis., Oct. 21, 1913; d. Peter Frank and Anna (Rathke) T. BS in Edn., Dominican Coll., 1952; MA in Edn., Northwestern U., 1958. Tchr. Whitley Sch., Brighton Twp., Wis., 1932-33, Highland Sch., Pleasant Prairie, Wis., 1933-4l, Victory Sch., Pleasant Prairie, 1941-47, Paris (Wis.) Consol. Sch., 1947-53, Southport Sch., Kenosha, 1953-61; prin. Harvey Sch., Kenosha, 1961-80; tchr. St. Casimir, Kenosha, 1983-93, vol. tchr. part-time, 1983—. Pres. Kenosha County Hist. Soc., 1985-89, St. James Parish Coun., Kenosha, 1975-89. Recipient Disting. Svc. award Wis. State Dept., 1980. Mem. AAUW, PTA, Ret. Tchrs. Assn., Kenosha County Tchrs. Assn. (past pres.), Kenosha Edn. Assn. (past pres.), Schubert Club, Quota Club, Delta Kappa Gamma (past pres.). Republican. Roman Catholic. Home: 7527 37th Ave Kenosha WI 53142-7217

TAFELSKI, MICHAEL DENNIS, psychologist; b. Wyandotte, Mich., Apr. 12, 1949; s. Chester John and Veronica (Machcinski) T. BA in Sociology and Psychology, Wayne State U., 1973, MSW, 1975, MEd, 1976. Lic. med. social worker, Mich. Caseworker home attendent div. N.Y.C. Dept. Human Resouces, 1976-78; intake case mgr. Phoenix House Found., Inc., N.Y.C., 1978-81; ptnr. GR Social Svcs., Grand Rapids, Mich., 1982-84; founding ptnr. Tafelski, Tafelski & Gatz and predecessor firm Tafelski, Tafelski, Gatz & Robaskewicz, P.C., Grand Rapids, 1984—. Contbr. to Profl. Jour. of Social Work, 1984-86, DNC, 1992—. State of Mich. Higher Edn. grantee, Lansing, 1969. Mem. Polish Falcons Soc., KC (Grand Knight). Democrat. Roman Catholic. Office: Tafelski Tafelski Gatz 4254 Lamdale Ct SE Ste 9B Grand Rapids MI 49546-2403

TAFT, BOB, state official; b. Jan. 8, 1942; m. Hope Taft; 1 child, Anna. BA, Yale U., 1963; MA, Princeton U., 1967; JD, U. Cin., 1976. Pvt. practice; rep. Ohio Ho. Reps., 1976-80; commr. Hamilton County, Ohio, 1981-90; sec. of state Ohio, 1990—. Office: 30 E Broad St Fl 14 Columbus OH 43266-0418

TAGGART, GARY J., electrical engineer; b. Rolla, Mo., July 2, 1955. BSEE, U. Mo., Rolla, 1978. Co-op student, comm. engr. Mo. Pacific Railroad, St. Louis, 1976-81; R&D project engr. Cardinal Scale Mfg., Webb City, Mo., 1981-85; mfg. mgr. Lynscan Sys., Rolla, 1985-87; sr. engr. Talema Electronics Inc., St. James, Mo., 1987—. Active So. Bapt. Ch., Rolla, 1975—. Mem. IEEE, Kiwanis Internat. Office: Talema Electronics Inc PO Box 306 Saint James MO 65559-0306

TAGGART, RALPH ENOS, botany and geology educator; b. Charlottesville, Va., Aug. 13, 1941; s. Daniel Reeder and Lois (Beatty) T.; m. Alison Louise Lundell, Sept. 14, 1968; children: Jennifer Louise, Heather Beatty, Mary Elizabeth. BA, Rutgers U., 1963; MS, Ohio U., 1967; PhD, Mich. State U., 1971. Rsch. asst. Boyce Thompson Inst., Yonkers, N.Y., 1963-65; instr. Ohio U., Athens, 1967; prof. botany and geology Mich. State U., East Lansing, 1972—. Co-author: Biology - Unity and Diversity of Life, 6th edit., Biology Today, 2d edit. 1975, Slow Scan Television Handbook, 1976; author: Weather Satellite Handbook, 5th edit.; contbr. numerous articles to profl. jours. Trustee, pres. Mason (Mich.) Sch. Bd., 1979-91; trustee, v.p. Ingham Intermediate Sch. Bd., Mason, 1991—. Mem. Bot. Soc. Am., Am. Assn. Stratigraphic Palynologists, Internat. Orgn. Paleobotany, Am. Radio Relay League (tech. advisor), Popular Rotocraft Assn. Presbyterian. Home: 602 S Jefferson Mason MI 48854 Office: Mich State Univ East Lansing MI 48824

TAIVALKOSKI, BRUCE D., electronics engineer; b. Laurium, Mich., Nov. 1, 1954. Drill programmer Calumet (Mich.) Electron, 1972-75; head sayer La. Pacific, Mohawk, Mich., 1978-85; mgr. engring. Calumet Electronic Corp., 1987—. Office: Calumet Electronics Corp 1010 Depot St Calumet MI 49913-1901

TAKAHASHI, FUMIAKI, research mechanical engineer; b. Tokyo, July 9, 1950; came to U.S., 1981; s. Hideo and Fumiko (Kojima) T.; m. Mamiko Niimoto, Sept. 25, 1982; children: Marina, Reina. B Engring., Keio U., Tokyo, 1973, M Engring., 1975, D Engring., 1982. Lectr. Keio U., Tokyo, 1980-81; mem. rsch. staff Princeton (N.J.) U., 1981-88; rsch. engr. U. Dayton, Ohio, 1988—; assoc. prof. U. Dayton, 1996—; vis. rsch. scholar Nat. Inst. for Resources and Environment, Japan, 1995; cons. the BOC Group, Murray Hill, N.J., 1988, MBR Rsch., Inc., Princeton, 1986-88; mem. adv. bd. PneuMotor, Inc., Dayton, 1989-90. Contbg. author: Hydrogen Energy Progress, 1980, Alternative Energy Sources III, 1980, Recent Advances in the Aerospace Sciences, 1985, Dynamics of Heterogeneous Combustion and Reactive Systems, 1993. Predoctoral fellow Japan Scholarship Found., 1975-78; Prof. Rsch. Cert. of Merit, 1994, Wohlleben/Hochwalt Outstanding Profl. Rsch. award, 1995. Mem. ASME, AIAA (Best Paper award Mini-Synposium 1992), The Combustion Inst. (program subcom. 1991-95). Office: U Dayton 300 College Park Ave Dayton OH 45469-0140

TAKAHASHI, JOSEPH S., neuroscientist; b. Tokyo, Dec. 16, 1951; s. Shigeharu and Hiroko (Hara) T.; m. Barbara Pillsbury Snook, June 28, 1985; children: Erika S., Matthew N. BA, Swarthmore (Pa.) Coll., 1974; PhD, U. Oreg., 1981. Pharmacology rsch. assoc. NIMH, NIGMS, Bethesda, Md., 1981-83; asst. prof. Northwestern U., Evanston, Ill., 1983-87; assoc. chmn. Neurobiology and Physiology Northwestern U., Evanston, Ill., 1988—, assoc. prof., 1987-91, prof., 1991-96; Walter and Mary Elizabeth Glass prof. life scis. Northwestern U., Evanston, Ill., 1996—; acting assoc. dir. Inst. for Neuroscience Northwestern U., Evanston, 1988-95; active NIMH Psychobiology and Behavior Rev. Com., 1988-92. Assoc. editor Neuron; mem. adv. bd. Jour. Biol. Rhythms, 1984—; contbr. over 90 articles to profl. jours. Grantee Bristol-Myers Squibb, 1995—; recipient Alfred P. Sloan award A.P. Sloan Found., 1983-85, Searl Scholars award Chgo. Cmty. Trust, 1985-88, Merit award NIMH, 1987, Honma prize in Biol. Rhythms Honma Found., 1986, Presdl. Young Investigator award NSF, 1985-90, 6th C.U. Ariens Kappers award Netherlands Soc. for Advancement Nat. Scis., Medicine and Surgery, 1995. Mem. AAAS, Soc. Neurosci., Assn. for Rsch. in Vision and Ophthalmology, Soc. for Rsch. on Biol. Rhythms (mem. adv. bd. 1986—), Mammalian Genome Soc. Office: Northwestern U Neurobiology 2153 North Campus Dr Evanston IL 60208-3520

TAKAHASHI, LOREY K., psychiatry educator, scientist; b. Honolulu, July 25, 1953; s. George H. and Margie Y. (Yamashita) T.; m. Chintana Yongnorasethkul, Aug. 22, 1982; children: Edwin A., Cyrus G. BA in Psychology, U. Hawaii, 1975, MA in Psychology, 1978; PhD in Psychology, Rutgers U., 1982. Rsch. asst. dept. psychology U. Hawaii, Honolulu, 1976-78; teaching asst. dept. psychology Rutgers U., New Brunswick, 1978-82; asst. scientist dept. psychiatry Med. Sch. U. Wis., Madison, 1986-90, clin. asst. prof., 1989-90, asst. prof. psychiatry, 1990—. Contbr. articles to profl. jours. Japanese Nat. Student Exch. Rsch. fellow Tokyo U. of Edn., 1977; postdoctoral fellow dept. biology Princeton (N.J.) U., 1982-86. Mem. AAAS, APA, Animal Behavior Soc., Internat. Brain Rsch. Orgn., Internat. Soc. for Rsch. on Aggression, Soc. Neurosci., Soc. Study of Reproduction, Sigma Xi (Madison chpt.). Home: 6406 Olympic Dr Madison WI 53705 Office: U Wis Dept Psychiatry Med Sch 600 Highland Ave Madison WI 53792

TAKEN, MAUREEN M., pediatric oncology nurse; b. Beloit, Wis., Feb. 1, 1951; d. Thomas D. and Alice (Graffitt) Laughlin; children: Laura Beth, Brea, Matthew. ADN, Milw. Area Tech. Coll., 1974; BSN cum laude, Cardinal Stritch Coll., 1992. RN, Wis. Staff nurse Milw. Children's Hosp., 1974-78, Children's Hosp. of Wis., Milw., 1992—. Mem. Assn. Pediat. Oncology Nurses, Wis. Assn. Pediat. Oncology Nurses (pres.-elect). Home: 4672 River Vista Dr Cedarburg WI 53012-9132

TALBOT, JOHN DUDLEY, college administrator; b. Summit, N.J., Jan. 12, 1953; s. Jacques and Harriet Talbot; m. Marie Antionette Kehl, Dec. 15, 1975; children: James, Trisha. Student, Ripon Coll., 1985-88. Controls technician Ripon (Wis.) Coll., 1976-81, asst. dir. phys. plant, 1981-91, dir. phys. plant, 1991—. With USN, 1971-75. Mem. IEEE, ASHRAE, Assn. Energy Engrs., Assn. of Phys. Plant Adminstrs., Acoustical Signal Processing Soc., Math. Assn. Am., Wis. Assn. Phys. Plant Adminstrs., Madison Area Safety Coun., Constrn. Specifications Inst. Republican. Home: N7583 Radio Rd Ripon WI 54971-9231 Office: Ripon Coll 300 Seward St Ripon WI 54971

TALBOT-KOEHL, LINDA ANN, dancer, ballet studio owner; b. Fremont, Ohio, July 22, 1956; d. Donald Ray and Doris Ann (Opperman) Talbot; m. James G. Koehl, July 30, 1983. Student, U. Akron, 1974-76; BA in Psychology, Heidelberg Coll., 1984. Owner, instr. BalleTiffin, Inc., Tiffin, Ohio, 1987—; choreographer Heidelberg Summer Theater, Tiffin, 1986, Singing Collegians, 1993; choreographer Calvert H.S. Theater, Tiffin, 1986-88, Swing Choir, 1987-89, 91-92. Appeared (ednl. film) Rights on the Job, State of Ohio Dept. Edn., 1986. Mem. Dance Masters Am., Nat. Multiple Sclerosis Soc., The Ritz Players (choreographer 1985, 88-89, 96, make-up designer, advisor 1989-92, sound booth operator 1993—). Home and Office: BalleTiffin Inc 449 Melmore St Tiffin OH 44883-3628

TALBOTT, KAREN LEE, home health care administrator; b. Martins Ferry, Ohio, Apr. 29, 1947; d. James Arthur and Mildred Leora T. BS in Edn. magna cum laude, Kent State U., 1969, MS in Acctg., 1970. CPA, Ohio. Sr. mgr. Ernst & Young, Akron, Ohio, 1970-79; pres. Vis. Nurse Svc. and Affiliates, Akron, 1979—; bd. dirs. Akron Regional Devel. Bd.; vice-chmn., bd. dirs. BBB; pres. bd. Ctr. for Comty. Based Care, Columbus, 1989-92; sec. bd. Comty. Health Rsch. Group, Akron, 1990—. Chmn. bd. dirs. Portage Path Cmty. Mental Health Ctr., 1992-94, Akron; grad. Leadership Akron, 1990; bd. dirs. Summit County unit Am. Cancer Soc., Akron. Recipient Gov.'s award and Royce award Ohio Coun. Home Care, Columbus, 1990, 94. Mem. AICPAs, Healthcare Fin. Mgmt. Assn. (treas. bd. dirs. N.E. Ohio chpt. 1990-93, Follmer merit award 1985, Reeves merit award 1989, Muncie merit award 1994), Nat. Assn. Home Care (nominating com. 1991, 95), Nat. Health Lawyers Assn. (assoc.), Soc. Ambulatory Care Profls. of Am. Hosp. Assn. (bd. dirs.), Ohio Soc. CPAs, Kent State U. Alumni Assn., Akron City Club. Office: Vis Nurse Svc 1200 Mcarthur Dr Akron OH 44320-3902

TALBOTT, MARY ANN, critical care nurse; b. Adair County, Ky., Dec. 6, 1942; d. Silas Asbury and Nettie Elizabeth (Hamm) Tedder; m. Lionel Talbott, Nov. 2, 1963; children: Jonathan, Timothy. RN, Ky. Bapt. Hosp., Louisville, 1963; student, Georgetown (Ky.) Coll., 1960, Purdue U., Versailles, Ind., 1989-90, Ball State U., Muncie, Ind., 1990—. Staff nurse Ky. Bapt. Hosp., Louisville, 1963; asst. head nurse obstetrics Carter County Meml. Hosp., Elizabethton, Tenn., 1964-67; staff nurse telemetry Harriman (Tenn.) City Hosp., 1970-78; staff nurse ICU/CCU King's Daus. Hosp., Madison, Ind., 1978—. Former chpt. chair membership com. So. Ind. Assn. Critical Care Nurses. Mem. AACN (cert.).

TALCOTT, WESLEY CONRAD, internal revenue agent; b. Barrington, Ill., Jan. 13, 1938; s. Wesley Elwood and Theresa Jane (Rogers) T.; m. Betsy Ruth Moats, Sept. 4, 1960; children: Mark Alan, Robert Daryl, David Edward. BS in Social Sci., Iowa State U., 1960. Dist. scout exec. Piankeshaw Coun. Boy Scouts Am., Danville, Ill., 1961-65; tax auditor Chgo. Dist. IRS, Rock Island, Ill., 1965-69; supr. Chgo. Dist. IRS, Rock Island, Ill., 1971-73; internal revenue agt. Chgo. Dist. IRS, Rockford, Ill., 1969-71; internal revenue agt. Springfield Dist. IRS, Springfield, Ill., 1973-83; internal revenue agt. St. Louis Dist. IRS, St. Louis, 1983—; instr. St. Louis Dist. IRS, 1984-89. Author: (guide) Procedures for Windfall Profit Tax, 1983, Examination of Savings and Loans, 1975. With USAR, 1960-65. Mem. Nat. Treasury Employees Union (steward chpt. 14 1990-93, chief steward 1993-95; exec. v.p. 1993—), Taxtoasters Club 70 (v.p. membership 1988, v.p. edn. 1989, 91, pres. 1990), Toastmasters Internat. (dist. gov. area 16 1990-91, gov. divsn. A 1991-92, dist. sec. 1992-93, dist. pub. rels. officer 1993-94, gov. divsn. D 1994-95, chmn. 1996, internat. conv. host fin. com. 1995-96, Competent award 1991, Able award 1992). Home: 3225 Colgate Pl Granite City IL 62040-3628 Office: IRS Planning Tech Support Br 1222 Spruce St Saint Louis MO 63101

TALEN, WILLIAM CLAIRE, bank executive, financial consultant; b. Ogilvie, Minn., Dec. 28, 1924; s. Clare and Anna (Minnema) T.; m. June Sieswerda (dec.); children: Deborah Ann, William Claire Jr., Julie, Ruth Elizabeth, Mary June; m. Caroline Sarah Hall, July 31, 1982; children: Caroline Rich, Robert Lassiter. BA, Calvin Coll., 1948; student in Banking, U. Wis., 1950; student in Fin. Pub. Rels., Northwestern U., 1955; cert., Am. Inst. Banking, 1961. Pres., bd. dirs. Farmers & Merchants Bank, Watertown, S.D., 1960-62, Univ. State Bank, Green Bay, Wis., 1962-70, New Franken (Wis.) Bank, 1962-70, Algoma (Wis.) Bank, 1962-70; exec. v.p., bd. dirs. Bankers Trust Co., Des Moines, 1970-73; bd. dirs., chair exec. com. First Bank & Trust, Menomonie, Wis., 1973-81; chmn., pres. First State Bank, Edgerton, Wis., 1973-88; pres., bd. dirs. Farmers Savings Bank & Trust, Traer, Iowa, 1974—; pres., chair Talen, Inc.-Bank Holding Co., Traer, Iowa, 1976—, Farmers Savings Bank & Trust, Vinton, Iowa, 1988—; bank cons., Northfield, Minn., 1973—; v.p. Iowa, Am. Bankers Assn., Washington, 1974-76; pres., owner Farmers & Merchant Bank, Greenwood, Wis., 1992-94. Pres. Menomonie (Wis.) C. of C., 1954-55, Green Bay Symphony, 1968-70, Des Moines Symphony, 1972-73; dir. Green Bay YMCA, Jr. Achievement. 1st lt. U.S. Army, 1943-46. Mem. Am. Mgmt. Assn., Am. Consulting League, Nat. Cert. Profl. Mgmt. Cons., Iowa Ind. Bankers, Iowa Bankers Assn., Bank Mktg. Assn., Am. Bankers Assn., Am. Legion, VFW, Toastmasters (pres. 1953-54), Internat. Fellowship Flying Rotarians, Des Moines C. of C. (dir.), Rotary (Paul Harris fellow 1978, 94), 50 Year Club, Wis. Bankers Assn., 50th Yr. Club, Iowa Bankers Assn. Republican. Presbyterian. Office: PO Box 535 Northfield MN 55057-0535

TALENT, JAMES M., congressman, lawyer; b. St. Louis, Mo., Oct. 18, 1956; m. Brenda Lyons, 1984; children: Michael, Kathleen Marie. BA in Polit. Sci., Washington U., 1978; JD, U. Chgo. Law Sch., 1981. Law clk. 7th Ct. Appeals, 1981-82; adj. prof. law, 1982-84; mem. Mo. State Ho. Reps., 1984-93; minority leader, 1989-93; mem. 103rd-104th Congresses from 2nd Mo. Dist., 1993—, mem. econ. & ednl. opportunity com., nat. security com., chmn. small bus. subcom. on regulation and paperwork. Legislative Achievement award Mo. Hosp. Assn., 1989. Mem. Mo. Bar Assn. (Award for significant contbns. to adminstrv. justice 1989), Mo. C. of C. (Spirit of Enterprise award 1990), Order of the Coif. Republican. Office: US Hc Reps 1022 Longworth Office House Members Washington DC 20515-2502*

TALLACKSON, HARVEY DEAN, real estate and insurance salesman; b. Grafton, N.D., May 15, 1925; s. Arthur J. and Mabel R. (McDougald) T.; m. Glenna M. Walstad, Aug. 4, 1946; children: Lynda, Thomas, Debra, Amy, Laura. Grad. h.s., Park River, N.D. Grain and potato farmer Grafton, 1946-68; ins. agt. Tallackson Ins., Grafton, 1968—; mem. N.D. Senate, Grafton, 1976—; real estate salesman Johnson Real Estate, Grafton, 1982—; chmn. appropriation com. N.D. Senate, 1987-93. Bd. dirs. Nodak Rural Electric Coop., Grand Forks, N.D., 1965—; bd. dirs. Minnkota Power Coop., Grand Forks, 1979—, pres., 1990—. Recipient Pub. Svc. award N.D. Lignite Coun., 1989; named Outstanding Young Farmer by Area Chamber of Walsh & Pembina Counties, 1951-52. Mem. Nat. Coun. Ins. Legislatures (mem. exec. com. 1985—, pres. 1996-97), Lions (pres. 1977-79), Masons. Democrat. Lutheran. Office: Tallackson Ins & Real Estate 53 W 5th St Grafton ND 58237-1468

TALLEY, BONNIE EILEEN, city official; b. Cimarron, Kans., Apr. 12, 1928; d. Henry Benton and Edna Catherine (Antenen) Bondurant; m. Don G. Talley, July 9, 1950 (dec. May 1988); children: Ron, Sharon, Jim, Brad. BA, Ottawa (Kans.) U., 1950; postgrad., U. Kans., 1966, Ft. Hays State U., Hays, Kans., 1968. Cert. tchr., real estate salesman and broker, Kans. Salesperson Don Talley, Realtors, Garden City, 1962-74, broker-salesperson, 1974-81, prin. broker, 1981-87; broker-salesperson Sun Country Real Estate, Garden City, 1987-91; commr. City of Garden City, 1983—. Mem. zoning bd. appeals City of Garden City, 1980-83; mem. energy bd., 1979-83, mayor, 1984-85, 89-90, 92-93; Sunday sch. tchr., former trustee 1st Bapt. Ch., Garden City; charter com. mem. Garden City Sister Cities Inc.; charter mem., mem. exec. bd. S.W. Arts and Humanities Coun., 1989-94; pres. Garden City Cmty. Coll. Endowment Assn., 1979; precinct committeewoman Garden City Rep. Com.; charter mem., bd. dirs. Tumbleweed Festival, Inc., 1991—, v.p., 1992—; bd. dirs. Area Mental Health, 1992—, treas., 1993—; bd. dirs. KANZ pub. radio, 1994-96, Sister Cities Internat., 1995—. Named Women of Yr., Garden City Bus. and Profl. Women, 1991, Woman of Distinction, Tumbleweed Girl Scouts, 1995. Mem. League Kans. Municipalities (governing bd. 1988-91), Kans. Assn. Realtors (Hon. Soc. 1986-90, exec. com. 1981-85), Garden City Bd. Realtors (pres. 1978-79, Realtor of Yr. award 1979), Garden City Area C. of C. (Endowment Assn. Outstanding Bd. Mem. 1993), Women's C. of C. (com., bd. dirs.). Home and Office: 1507 Willow Ln Garden City KS 67846-6251

TALLEY, BRIAN CHANDLER, broadcasting executive; b. Litchfield, Ill., May 27, 1955; s. Hayward Leroy and Emma Mae (Chandler) T.; m. Lea Ann Edwards; 1 child, Chandler Paul. BS in Radio-TV Communications, Murray State U., 1977. V.p. engring. ops. Talley Broadcasting Corp., Litchfield, 1977—. Mem. Soc. Broadcast Engrs. (chpt. sec.-treas. 1991-92), Macoupin County Amateur Radio Club. Office: WSMI Radio RR 16 Litchfield IL 62056

TALLMAN, ROBERT HALL, investment company executive; b. Creston, Iowa, Aug. 10, 1915; s. Ralph H. and Hazel Verne (Hall) T.; m. Elizabeth Childs, Sept. 19, 1938; children: Susan, Mary, Timothy. BS, U. Nebr., 1937. Trainee to dist. mgr. Firestone Tire & Rubber Co., Akron, Ohio, 1937-50; pres. Tallman Oil Co., Fargo, N.D., 1950-80; chmn. bd. State Bank of Hawley, Minn., 1966-70, 1st Nat. Bank of Barnesville, Minn., 1965-88; pres. Tallman Investment Ent., Fargo, 1980—; pres., dir. Dak Tech. Inc.; dir. Bell Farms. Past pres. Fargo Bd. Edn., N.D. Petroleum Coun.; past pres. St. Lukes Hosp. Assn.; past chmn. trustees 1st Congl. Ch. of Fargo. Mem.

Fargo C. of C. (past pres.), Am. Assn. Ret. Persons, Nat. Rifle Assn., N.D. State U. Teammakers Club (past pres.), Fargo Country Club, Kiwanis (past pres.), Masons, Shriners, Elks. Republican. Congregationalist. Home: 3201 16th Ave S Fargo ND 58103-8421 Office: Box 9723 2108 S University Dr Fargo ND 58103-5348

TAMBRINO, PAUL AUGUST, college president; m. Faye M. Thompson; children: Paul, Jeffrey, Mark, Lauren. BA, Cen. Coll., Pella, Iowa, 1958; postgrad., Am. Inst. Banking, N.Y.C., 1958-59; MS, Hofstra U., 1966; EdD, Temple U., 1973. Cert. quality transformation cons. Group actuarial supr. N.Y. Life Ins. Co., N.Y.C., 1960-64; tchr. acctg. and bus. N. Babylon (N.Y.) Sr. High Sch., 1964-68; instr. econs. and acctg. coord. Ursinus Coll., Collegeville, Pa., 1968-70; asst. prof. acctg. and edn. Hofstra U., Hempstead, N.Y., 1970-78; dean bus. and art div. Northampton County C.C., Bethlehem, Pa., 1978-83; coll. dean Warren County C.C., Washington, N.J., 1984-91; pres., CEO Iowa Valley C.C. Dist., Marshalltown, 1991—; cons. N.J. Dept. Higher Edn., 1989—, Pfizer, Inc., N.Y.C., 1974-78, John Wiley & Sons, 1984, Union Coll., 1982, Verbatim, Inc.,m 1974-78, McGraw-Hill, 1967-74. Contbr. chpt. to Accountants Encyclopedia, 1978; revised Careers and Opportunities in Accounting, 1978; contbr. articles to profl. jours. 1st lt. USAR, 1959-65. Mem. Rotary Internat., C. of C., Beta Alpha Psi, Delta Pi Epsilon. Home: 2515 Reyclif Dr Marshalltown IA 50158-2351 Office: Iowa Valley CC Dist Marshalltown IA 50158

TAMBURINO, LOUIS ANTHONY, computer scientist, researcher; b. Pitts., May 9, 1936; s. Dominic and Hope (Tedesco) T.; m. Linda Sue Quinlivan, Nov. 8, 1958; 1 child, Linda Athena Tamburino Dershem. BS, Carnegie Mellon U., 1957; PhD, U. Pitts., 1962. Postdoctoral fellow physics dept. Syracuse (N.Y.) U., 1963-64; theoretical physicist gen. physics lab. Aerospace Rsch. Labs., Wright-Patterson AFB, Ohio, 1964-72; sr. scientist Avionics Directorate, Wright Lab., Wright-Patterson AFB, 1972—, Wright Lab. fellow, 1991—; adj. assoc. prof. Wright State U., Fairborn, Ohio, 1988—. Patentee in field; author numerous papers. 1st lt. U.S. Army, 1962-63. Recipient Outstanding Engr. & Scientist award Affiliate Socs. Coun. Engring. & Sci. Found. of Dayton, Ohio, 1991. Mem. IEEE, Soc. Photo-Optical Instrumentation Engrs., Sigma Xi. Office: WL/ACAA Wright Patterson AFB OH 45433

TAMM, ELEANOR RUTH, retired accountant; b. Hansell, Iowa, July 20, 1921; d. Horace Gerald and Sibyl (Armstrong) Wells; m. Roy C. Tamm, Oct. 18, 1941 (dec. Jan. 1980); children: Larry LeRoy, Marilyn Ruth Tamm-Schmitt. Grad., Am. Soc. Travel Agts., Inc., 1970; student, Iowa Cen. C.C., 1983, 85; grad., Inst. Children's Lit., 1994. Tchr. Howard County Rural Sch., Riceville, 1939-41; bookkeeper, cashier Cen. States Power and Light Co., Elma, Iowa, 1941-42; office supr. J.C. Penney Co., Goldsboro, N.C., 1942-44; bookkeeper J.C. Penney Co., West Palm Beach, Fla., 1945; head teller Iowa State Bank, Clarksville, Iowa, 1955-69; office and group mgr. Allen Travel Agy., Charles City, Iowa, 1969-81; tour conductor, tour organizer and planner Allen Travel Agy., Charles City, 1971-81; office mgr. Arora Clinics, P.C., Fonda, Iowa, 1986-90; freelance collaborator on children's books Clarksville, 1989—. Leader Girl Scouts U.S.A., Clarksville, 1946-47; tchr. St. John Luth. Ch., Clarksville, 1946-66, ch. sec., 1954-66, sec.-treas. Altar Guild, 1993-94; United Fund sec.-treas. Clarksville Cmty. Fund, 1956-66; sec.-treas. Clarksville Band Boosters, 1964-66. Lutheran. Home: 408 E 3rd St Fonda IA 50540-0425

TAN, HUI QIAN, computer science and civil engineering educator; b. Tsingtao, China, June 12, 1948; s. Dumen Tan and Ruifan Rao; m. Ren Zhong, June 16, 1994; children: William W., Danny D. BA, Oberlin Coll., 1982; MS, Kent State U., 1984, PhD, 1986. Asst. prof. computer sci. and civil engring. U. Akron, Ohio, 1986-89, assoc., 1990—; rsch. prof. Kent (Ohio) State U., 1987. Contbr. articles to profl. jours. Grantee NASA, 1987—, 91—, NSF, 1988-92. Mem. IEEE Computer Soc., Assn. for Computing Machinery, SIGSAM Assn. for Computing Machinery, Phi Beta Kappa.

TANDON, RAJIV, psychiatrist, educator; b. Kanpur, India, Aug. 3, 1956; came to U.S., 1984; s. Bhagwan Sarup and Usha (Mehrotra) T.; m. Chanchal Nammi Vohra; children: Neeraj, Anisha, Gitanjali. Student, St. Xavier's Coll., Bombay, India, 1974; BS, All India Inst., New Delhi, 1980; MD, Nat. Inst. of MH, India, 1983. Sr. resident Mental Health and Neuro-Scis., India, 1983-84; resident U. Mich. Hosps., Ann Arbor, 1984-87, attending psychiatrist, 1987—; dir. schizophrenia program U. Mich., Ann Arbor, 1987—, assoc. prof., 1993—; cons. Lenawee County Community Mental Health, Adrian, Mich., 1985—. Author: Biochemical Parameters of Mixed Affective States; Negative Schizophrenic Symptoms: Pathophysiology and Clinical Implications; contbr. more than 120 articles to profl. jours. Recipient Young Scientist's award Biennial Winter workshop on Schizophrenia, 1990, 92, Travel award Am. Coll. Neuropsychopharmacology/Mead, 1990, Rsch. Excellence award Am. Assn. Psychiatrists from India, 1993, Sci. award, Best Drs. in Am. award, 1994-95, Gerald Klerman award for outstanding rsch. by a Nat. Alliance for Rsch. in Schizophrenia and Depression young investigator, 1995. Mem. Am. Psychiat. Assn. (Wisniewski Young Psychiatrist Rschr. award 1993), World Fedn. Mental Health, Soc. for Neurosci., N.Y. Acad. Scis., Soc. Biol. Psychiatry, Mich. Psychiat. Soc. Democrat. Hindu. Office: U Mich Med Ctr Dept Psychiatry 1500 E Medical Center Dr # 8D Ann Arbor MI 48109-0999

TANG, GEORGE CHICKCHEE, investment executive; b. Hong Kong, Nov. 8, 1964; came to U.S., 1984; s. George and Margaret Tang. BS, Case Western Res. U., 1987; MS, Northwestern U., 1989. Registered securities rep., commodity rep., ins. agt., Ill. With AT&T Bell Labs., Naperville, Ill., 1989-92; fin. cons. Smith Barney, Oakbrook, Ill., 1992—; spkr., lectr. in field. Contbr. fin. columns to Chgo. Chinese Times, 1993—, Chinese Am. News, 1993—, China Jour., 1994—. Writer ARC, Cleve., 1985-86; spkr. on environ. protection City Coun. Hong Kong, 1982. Recipient Champion of Wildlife Conservation award Hong Kong Std., 1982. Mem. Inst. CFA's, Assn. for Investment and Rsch. (cert. of achievement 1994), Inst. for Investment Mgmt. Cons., Orgn. Chinese Ams. (internal v.p. Chgo. chpt. 1994-95, pres. 1995—). Office: Smith Barney 1 Tower Ln Villa Park IL 60181

TANK, ROBERT T., physical therapist; b. Marshalltown, Iowa, Aug. 25, 1954; s. William McCombs and Avonelle (Tye) T.; m. Amy Irwin, Aug. 28, 1982; children: William, Carrie, Evan. BA, Middlebury (Vt.) Coll., 1976; Cert. in Phys. Therapy, U. Iowa, 1979; MS, Kent (Ohio) State U., 1983. Lic. phys. therapist, Ind. Rsch. asst. U. Iowa, Iowa City, 1978; staff phys. therapist U. Iowa Hosps. and Clinics, Iowa City, 1979; clin. instr. Ohio Coll. Podiatric Medicine, Cleve., 1980-82; phys. therapist Western Res. Therapists, Inc., Chesterland, Ohio, 1979-82; dir. phys. therapy Orthopaedic Assocs. Sports Medicine Ctr., Evansville, Ind., 1982—; adj. faculty sports medicine and joint mobilization U. Evansville, 1982—; cons. U. Evansville, 1983—, U. So. Ind., Evansville, 1983—, Lake Erie Coll., Painesville, Ohio, 1980, athletic trainer 1981-82; athletic trainer Case Western Res. U., Cleve., 1979-81; lectr. in field; sec. All Pro Fitness and Testing, Inc., 1982. Manuscript reviewer Jour. Orthopaedic and Sports Phys. Therapy, 1993—; abstract reviewer Internat. Isokinetic Congress, 1989-92; contbr. articles to profl. jours.; editor, contbg. writer Orthopaedic Assocs. Sports Medicine newsletter. Mem. YMCA Med. Adv. Com., Evansville, 1987—; mem. Phys. Fitness Com. of Nutrtion for Greater Cleve., 1980-82. Mem. Am. Phys. Therapy Assn. (session chair 1992, 93, chmn. nominating com. So. Dist. Ind. 1989, mem. Sports Phys. Therapy sect., Hand Rehab. sect.), Am. Coll. Sports Medicine, Nat. Athletic Trainers Assn. (cert.), Nat. Strength Coaches of Am., Am. Soc. Hand Therapists. Home: 735 Plaza Dr Evansville IN 47715 Office: Orthopaedic Assocs 533 W Columbia Evansville IN 47710

TANNEBAUM, MARILYNN ETTA, elementary education educator; b. N.Y.C., Dec. 29, 1931; d. Jack and Dora B. (Glickman) Barshay; m. Sol Tannebaum; children: Ross, Lisa. BA, Roosevelt Coll., 1953; MA, Roosevelt U., 1957; postgrad., U. Ill., 1960, 85-86, San Diego State Coll., 1965-66, San Francisco State Coll., 1967, No. Ill. U., 1972, Govs. State U., 1980, Nat. Coll. Edn., 1981. Elem. sch. tchr. Park Forest-Chicago Heights Sch. Dist. 163, 1953-59, jr. high tchr. Westwood Jr. H.S., 1959-63, gifted program dir. Lang. Arts Demonstration Ctr., 1965-67, assoc. dir. Ctr. for Ethnic Studies, 1967-71, dir. title IV desegregation program, 1971-73, dir. title III student leadership program, 1972-74, jr. high curriculum coord., 1974-75, elm. prin. primary and intermediate schs., dir. reading, 1975-88, adminstrv. asst. to supt., dir. reading and lang. arts, 1988-89; site coord. reading recovery project Nat. Louis U., Chgo., 1989-91; ednl. cons. strategic reading/tchg. project North Ctrl. Regional Ednl. Labs., Oakbrook, Ill., 1991—; adj. prof. Govs. State U., University Park, Ill.; presenter in field. Bd. dirs. Ill. Philhar. Orch., Park Forest, 1988—, pres. bd. dirs., 1991-93. Mem. ASCD, Ill. ASCD, Nat. Assn. for Tchrs. English, Internat. Reading Assn., Ill. Reading Coun., Ill. State Lang. Arts Adv. Com., Friends of Ill. Philharm. Orch. Home: 2620 Oakwood Dr Olympia Fields IL 60461

TANNEHILL, ROBERT COOPER, theology educator; b. Clay Center, Kans., May 6, 1934; s. Francis Vernon and Cecelia Susan (Cooper) T.; m. Alice Irene Hunter, Aug. 13, 1955; children: Grace, Celia, Paul. BA, Hamline U., 1956; BD, Yale U., 1959, MA, 1960, PhD, 1963. Ordained to ministry United Meth. Ch., 1959. Instr. Oberlin (Ohio) Grad. Sch. Theology, 1963-66; asst. prof. N.T., Meth. Theol. Sch. in Ohio, Delaware, 1966-69, assoc. prof., 1969-74, prof., 1974—, Harold B. Williams prof. Bibl. studies, 1988—; acad. dean, 1994—. Author: Dying and Rising with Christ: A Study in Pauline Theology, 1967, The Sword of His Mouth: Forceful and Imaginative Language in Synoptic Sayings, 1975, A Mirror for Disciples: Following Jesus through Mark, 1977, The Narrative Unity of Luke-Acts: A Literary Interpretation, Vol. 1, The Gospel According to Luke, 1986, Vol. 2, The Acts of the Apostles, 1990; mem. editl. bd. Jour. Bibl. Lit., 1988-93; also numerous articles. Trustee Del-Mor Dwellings, Inc., Delaware, 1990—, chmn., 1995—. Danforth fellow, 1956-63, faculty fellow Assn. Theol. Schs., 1969-70, 75-76, 82, 94. Mem. Soc. Bibl. Lit. (dir. work group on pronouncement story 1975-81, assoc. editor monograph series 1979-85, co-chmn. lit. aspects group 1991—, Claremont fellow 1982), Ea. Great Lakes Bibl. Soc. (pres. 1978-79), Studiorum Novi Testamenti Soc. (presenter Milan 1990). Office: Meth Theol Sch in Ohio 3081 Columbus Pike Delaware OH 43015-3211

TANNENBERG, DIETER E. A., manufacturing company executive; b. Chevy Chase, Md., Nov. 24, 1932; s. E.A. Wilhelm and Margarete Elizabeth (Mundhenk) T.; m. Ruth Hansen, Feb. 6, 1956; 1 child, Diana Tannenberg Collingsworth Cann Marlinski. BSME, Northwestern U., 1959. Registered profl. engr., N.Y., Conn., Ohio, Ill., Ind., Wis., N.J. Supervising engr. Flexonics div. Calumet & Hecla, Inc., Chgo., 1959-61, chief engr., 1961-63, program mgr. advanced space systems, 1963-65, dir. mfg. services, 1965-67; dir. mfg. engring. SCM Corp., Cortland, N.Y., 1967-69; tech. dir. internat. Singer Co., N.Y.C., 1969-71; v.p. ops. internat. div. Addressograph-Multigraph Corp., Cleve., 1971-74; mng. dir. Addressograph Multigraph GmbH, Frankfurt/Main, W. Ger., 1974-78; v.p., gen. mgr. Europe, Middle East, Africa AM Internat. Inc., Chgo., 1978-79; pres. AM Bruning div., 1979-82, AM Multigraphics Div., Mt. Prospect, Ill., 1982-86; corp. v.p. AM Internat., Inc., 1981-83, corp. sr. v.p., 1983-86; chmn. bd. dirs., pres., chief exec. officer Sargent-Welch Sci. Co., Skokie, Ill., 1986-89; pres., CEO ExhibitGroup, Inc., Elk Grove Village, Ill., 1990-91, Bell & Howell Document Mgmt. Products Co., Chgo., 1991-94, Bell & Howell Postal Sys. Inc., Chgo., 1994—; corp. v.p. Bell & Howell Co., Skokie, Ill., 1991—; chmn. AM Internat. GmbH, Frankfurt, 1977-86; bd. dirs. Gerard Daniel & Co., GDC Internat., Inc. Contbr. chpts. to handbooks, articles to tech., trade mags.; patentee in machinery field. Served with M.I., U.S. Army, 1953-56. Named Man of Yr. Quick Print Mag., 1985. Mem. NSPE, ASME, ASCE, Assn. Reprodn. Materials Mfrs. (bd. dirs. 1979-82, v.p. 1980-82), Nat. Assn. Quick Printers (bd. dirs. 1982-84), Nat. Printing Equipment and Supplies Mfg. Assn. (bd. dirs. 1983-86, chmn. govt. affairs com. 1985-86), Computer and Bus. Equipment Mfg. Assn. (bd. dirs. 1983-86, 91-93), Soc. Am. Value Engrs. (hon. v.p. 1985—), Value Found. (trustee 1985—), Chgo. Coun. Fgn. Rels., German-Am. C. of C. (Chgo.), Barrington Hills Country Club, Execs. Club of Chgo., Econ. Club, Pi Tau Sigma. Office: Bell & Howell Co 6800 N McCormick Blvd Chicago IL 60645-2785

TANNER, JUDITH ANN, retired speech-language pathologist; b. Muncie, Ind., Nov. 1, 1934; d. Joseph C. and Anna (Hamming) Silvers; m. John E. Tanner, June 9, 1957; children: Jill A. Tanner Kamman, John Joseph. BS, Ball State U., 1956, MS, 1972. Cert. tchr., Ind. Speech pathologist Howard County Schs., Kokomo, Ind., 1956-57; tchr. hard of hearing Indpls. Schs., 1957-61; speech pathologist Randolph Ctrl. Schs., Winchester, Ind., 1965-92, ret., 1992. Bd. dirs. Community Concert, Randolph County, 1987—. Mem. Ind. Speech, Lang. and Hearing Assn. (sch. svcs. com. 1990—), Speech and Hearing Area Educators (honors and awards com. 1987—), Ind. Lawyers Aux. (chmn. laaw related edn. 1993-94, treas. 1994-95, pres.-elect 1995-96). Republican. Methodist. Home: 400 W Westwood Dr Winchester IN 47394-1933

TANNER, RALPH M., state legislator; m. Judith Tanner. Rep. dist. 10 State of Kans. Republican. Office: Baker Univ Office of the President Baldwin City KS 66006*

TANNER, RICHARD THOMAS, environmental studies educator; b. Hillsboro, Oreg., Nov. 2, 1936; s. Robert Edward and Alba Oleanna (Thompson) T.; m. Sarah Cole Johnson, June 24, 1962; 1 child, Thomas Cole. BS, Oreg. Coll. Edn., 1958; MS, Oreg. State U., 1962; PhD, Stanford U., 1968. Biology tchr. The Dalles (Oreg.) High Sch., 1958-60; traveling sci. tchr. U. Oreg., Eugene, 1960-61; NSF fellow Oreg. State U., Corvallis, 1961-62, vis. asst. prof., 1968-72; Fulbright tchr. Nyakasura Sch., Fort Portal, Uganda, 1962-63; lectr. environ. studies Ctrl. Wash. State U., Ellensburg, 1972-77; prof. Iowa State U., Ames, 1977—; mem. adv. bd. Resource Renewal Inst., San Francisco, 1988—; originator, chair Iowa State U. Aldo Leopold Centennial Celebration, 1986. Contbr. articles and essays to profl. jours.; author: Ecology, Environment and Education, 1974; editor: Aldo Leopold: The Man and His Legacy, 1987; cons. editor: Jour. Environ. Edn., 1978-87. With U.S. Army, 1959. Grantee U.S. Office Environ. Edn., 1971-80. Mem. N.Am. Assn. for Environ. Edn. (bd. dirs. 1974-80), Nature Conservancy, Nat. Audubon Soc., Wilderness Soc., Union Concerned Scientists, So. Utah Wilderness Alliance, Amnesty Internat., Phi Delta Kappa. Home: 1971 205th St Boone IA 50036

TANNER, TERESA L., medical nurse; b. Lancaster, Pa., Nov. 21, 1968; d. Donald G. and Roxie B. Wood. AS, Odessa (Tex.) Coll., 1990, postgrad., 1990—. TN, Tex.; ACLS; advanced EKG cert. Former oncology/telemetry charge nurse; now staff nurse med. floor Akron (Ohio) City Hosp. Vol. ARC, Lancaster.

TANNER-BENDICKSON, MICHELLE KARALYNN, librarian; b. Salt Lake City, June 4, 1957; d. Leslie Russell and Ruby Louise (Reynolds) T.; m. Bob Duane Bendickson, July 9, 1988. BA, Jamestown (N.D.) Coll., 1979. Instr. Steele (N.D.) Pub. Sch., 1980-82; instr. lang. arts Binford (N.D.) Pub. Schs., 1982-88; Title I instr. Cooperstown (N.D.) Pub. Schs., 1989-90; billing clk. Posi Lock Puller Inc., Cooperstown, 1991-95; librn. Griggs County Libr., Cooperstown, 1995—. Co-chair Griggs County Family Farm Safety Fair, 1992-95; svc. unit chair Cooperstown Girl Scouts U.S., 1994—. Elem. edn. fellow Jamestown Coll., 1979. Mem. N.D. Libr. Assn. Methodist. Home: PO Box 239 Cooperstown ND 58425 Office: Griggs County Libr PO Box 546 Cooperstown ND 58425

TANQUARY, OLIVER LEO, minister; b. Springfield, Ill., Nov. 18, 1918; s. Lawrence Henry and Minnie (Potter) T.; m. Winifred Lillian Keen, June 24, 1939; children: Sylvia June, Lowell Emerson. BA, U. Pacific, 1933; MA, Boston U., 1940, STB, 1941; EdD, Fla. State Christian Coll., 1972; postgrad., Walden U., 1977-79. Ordained to ministry United Meth. Ch., 1941; cert. tchr., pub. sch. adminstr., Calif. Min. Hughes Meml. Meth. Ch., Edmonds, Wash., 1941-44; dir. guidance and rsch. County of Humboldt, Calif., 1948-52; min. Union Congl. Ch., Braintree, Mass., 1952-58, Paradise Hills Congl. Ch., San Diego, 1958-62; dir. guidance and counseling Paso Robles (Calif.) City Schs., 1962-68; dir. guidance and vocat. counseling County of Inyo, Calif., 1968-72; min. 1st Congl. Ch., Big Timber, Mont., 1972-77, 1st Meth. Ch., Big Pine, Calif., 1979-84, United Ch. of Christ, Quartz Hill, Calif., 1984-91; chaplain Mayflower Gardens Retirement Cmty., Quartz Hill, 1986-91; dir. vocat. counseling YMCA, San Diego, 1958-68; del. So. Calif. Conf., United Ch. of Christ, Pasadena, Calif., 1984-91, moderator Kern Assn., Calif., 1990; pres. Big Timber Ministerial Assn., 1967. Author: Choosing My Vocation, 1968, Foundations to Fulfillment, 1991, (booklets) At Home in the Universe, 1944, Providential Guidance, 1954; contbr. articles to denominational publs. Mem. Inter-County Libr. Bd. So. Calif., 1982, Inyo County Schs. Adv. Bd., 1982-83, Inyo County Grand Jury, 1983-84. 1st lt., chaplain USAAF, 1944-48. Recipient svc. award Kiwanis Club, Paso Robles, Calif., 1965. Mem. Masons.

TANTRY, SUBHASH BELMAN, computer consultant; b. Udipi, India, May 5, 1953; s. Rama Krishna Belman and Rahna (Achar) T.; m. Manjiri Avadhani, Nov. 25, 1981; children: Sathvik, Kushal. B of Technology, Indian Inst. of Tech., 1975; M in Indsl. Engring., Nitie, Bombay, 1977; M of Mgmt. Sci., Stevens Inst. of Tech., 1981. Tech. advisor to mng. dir. Premier Automobiles, Bombay, 1977-80; dir. product devel. Consilium Inc., Mountain View, Calif., 1981-83; assoc. prof. Andersen Cons., Chgo., 1993—. Patent for Flowstream software, architecture for flowstream. Mem. IEEE, Assn. Computing Machinery. Office: Andersen Cons 7th Fl 100 S Wacker Chicago IL 60610

TAO, RONGJIA, physicist, educator; b. Shanghai, China, Jan. 28, 1947; came to U.S., 1979; s. Yun Tao and Xiao-Mei Zou; m. Weiying Duanmu, Dec. 22, 1976; children: Han, Jing. MA, Columbia U., 1980, PhD, 1982. Rsch. assoc. U. Wash., Seattle, 1982-84; rsch. fellow U. Cambridge, Eng., 1984; rsch. asst. prof. U. So. Calif., L.A., 1984-85; asst. prof. physics Northeastern U., Boston, 1985-89; asst. prof. physics So. Ill. U., Carbondale, 1989-91, assoc. prof. physics, 1991-92; chmn. physics dept., 1994—; prof. physics So. Ill. U., Carbondale, 1993—, chmn. dept. physics, 1994—; cons. UN Developing Program, N.Y. and China, 1992—; chair Internat. Conf. on Electrorheological Fluids, Carbondale, 1991, Feldkirch, Austria, 1993. Editor, author: Electrorheological Fluids, 1992, Electrorheological Fluids, Mechanism, Properties, Materials and Applications, 1994; contbr. articles to profl. p.bls. Office of Naval Rsch. grantee, 1990, 92; recipient award Omni mag., 1987. Mem. Am. Phys. Soc. Office: So Ill U Dept Physics Carbondale IL 62901

TAPLETT, LLOYD MELVIN, human resources management consultant; b. Tyndall, S.D., July 25, 1924; s. Herman Leopold and Emiley (Nedvidek) T.; B.A., Augustana Coll., 1949; M.A., U. Nebr., 1958; postgrad. S.D. State U., U. S.D., U. Iowa, Colo. State U.; m. Patricia Ann Sweeney, Aug. 21, 1958; children: Virginia Ann, Sharon Lorraine, Carla Jo, Carolyn Patricia, Catherine Marie, Colleen Elizabeth. Accredited pers. mgr. Profl. Human Resources. Tchr., Sioux Falls (S.D.) public schs., 1952-69; with All-Am. Transport Co., Sioux Falls, 1969-78, Am. Freight System, Inc., Overland Park, Kans., 1978-79; dir. human resources and public relations, corp. affirmative action compliance ofcl. Chippewa Motor Freight Inc., Sioux Falls, 1979-80; human resource and mgmt. cons., 1980-81; mgr. Sioux Falls Job Svcs. 1981-85, Pioneer Enterprises, Inc., 1985-86; ops. mgr. ATE Environ., Inc., 1986-88, cons. Royal River Casino, 1988-90; acad. dean Huron U., Sioux Falls, 1990-92, instr. econs. Coll. Bus., 1992—; chmn. Chippewa Credit Union; mem. adv. bd. dirs. Nelson Labs., Sioux Falls 1981-82; evening mgmt. instr Nat. Coll., Sioux Falls, 1981-90, chmn. adv. com., 1984—, Huron U., 1990—, S.F. Washington High Sch. Sports Heritage 1899-1989. Past bd. dirs. Jr. Achievement, United Way, Sioux Vocat. Sch. for Handicapped; past mem. Gov.'s Adv. Bd. for Community Adult Manpower Planning; chmn. bus. edn. adv. com. Sioux Falls Public Schs., 1982-85; chmn. adv. com. South East Area Vocat. Sch., 1982-85 ; mem. alumnae bd. Augustana Coll., 1985-88. Capt. USMC, 1943-46, 50-52, Korea. Recipient V.F.W. Commendation award, 1990, Liberty Bell award S.D. Bar Assn., 1967; Sch. Bd. award NEA/Thom McAn Shoe Corp., 1966, S.D. Unsung Heroes Edn. Recognition award 1992; named Boss of Yr., Sioux Falls, 1977; cert. tchr. and counselor, S.D. Mem. Am. Soc. for Personnel Adminstrn. (accredited personnel mgr. life, S.D. dist. dir. 1980-84), Am. Trucking Assn. (mem. pub. rels. coun.), NEA (life mem., Pacemaker award), S.D. Edn. Assn. (life), Sioux Falls Personnel Assn. (past pres.), Sales and Mktg. Club Sioux Falls, Sioux Falls Traffic Club, VFW (life, Nat. Polit. Action Recognition award 1990), Am. Legion. Republican. Roman Catholic. Clubs: Toastmasters (past gov. dist. 41, Disting. Toastmaster award, Outstanding Toastmaster award dist. 41, Hall of Fame 1977), Elks. Contbr. articles to nat. mags. Office: Huron U PO Box 90003 Sioux Falls SD 57105-9060

TARASZKIEWICZ, WALDEMAR, physician; b. Wilno, Poland, July 6, 1936; came to U.S., 1979; s. Michal Taraszkiewicz and Nina (Lutomska) Dylla; m. Teresa Barbara Szwarc, Oct. 15, 1966. MD, Med. Acad., Gdansk, Poland, 1961, internal medicine specialty, 1967, internal medicine specialty II, 1972. Diplomate Am. Bd. Family Practice. Family physician Out Patient Clinic, Sopot, Poland, 1962-64; resident doctor U. Hosp., Gdansk, 1965-71; allergist Clinic of Allergy, Gdansk, 1965-75; physician Cardiology Dept., Gdansk, 1971-75, Hôpital Civil, Telagh, Algeria, 1975-79; surg. asst. Hinsdale (Ill.) Hosp., 1979-82; resident physician St. Mary of Nazareth Hosp., Chgo., 1982-85, emergency room physician, 1984-85; family practice medicine Brookfield, Ill., 1985-88, Westmont, Ill., 1988-89, Chgo., 1987—; med. dir. Winston Manor Nursing Home, Chgo., 1989-90; clin. asst. prof. U. Ill. Med. Coll., 1994—; sr. asst. dept. cardiology Univ. Hosp., Gdansk, 1971-75; mem. adminstrv. com., pres. med. staff Hôpital Civil, Telagh, 1976-79. Contbr. articles to profl. jours. Recipient Bronze medal Polski Zwiazek Wedkarski, 1970, cert. 3d place, 1971. Fellow Am. Acad. Family Practice; mem. AMA (continuing edn. award), Ill. Med. Soc., Chgo. Med. Soc. (practice mgmt. com.), World Med. Assn., Am. Acad. Allergy and Immunology, Am. Coll. Allergy and Immunology, Polish Med. Alliance, N.Y. Acad. Scis. Office: Jefferson Park Med Bldg 4811 N Milwaukee Ave Ste 130 Chicago IL 60630-2103

TARCZAN, HEATHER MARIE, university administrator; b. Lake Forest, Ill., Feb. 8, 1974; d. Leonard Francis and Constance Ann (Tadel) T. BA, U. Dayton, 1996. Enrollment couselor Nat. Louis U., 1993-96; facilitator Jr. Hearing Bd., 1994-96. Health care adminstr. Cystic Fibrosis, Dayton, 1992-94; coord. spl. events Campus Connection, Dayton, 1992-95. Mem. APA, Ohio Acad. Sci. (judge 1992—), Zeta Tau Alpha (alumni-collegiate chair 1994-96). Home: 26708 Jefferson Ct Bay Village OH 44140 Office: Office Student Enrollment 2840 Sheridan Rd Evanston IL 60210

TARLTON, MICHAEL RAY, civil engineer, youth minister; b. Eldorado, Ill., Apr. 11, 1961; s. Virgil Ray and Freda Ellen (Hedger) T.; m. Robin Elaine Osman, Sept. 17, 1993; children: Justin Matthew, Brandon Patrick. BS, So. Ill. U., 1984. Ordained to ministry, So. Bapt. Ch.; cert. engring. technologist. Engr. Brown, Roffmann & Roberts, Harrisburg, Ill., 1982-91; bridge inspection technologist Gallatin County Hwy. Dept., Shawneetown, Ill., 1984—; civil engr. III Ill. Dept. Natural Resources, Marion, 1991—; youth advisor Fairfield Bapt. Assn., McLeansboro, Ill., 1987-89; youth minister First Bapt. Ch., Norris City, Ill., 1989-93; youth pastor First Bapt. Ch., Energy, Ill., 1994—. Village trustee Village of Broughton, Ill., 1982-83. Mem. Nat. Assn. State Land Reclamationists, Christian Coalition. Republican. Home: Rte 3 Box 549 Marion IL 62959 Office: Ill Dept Natural Resources 2001A Industrial Park Dr Marion IL 62959

TASKEY, ROGER L., financial company executive; b. Sault St. Marie, Mich., Jan. 19, 1944. BA in Advt., Mich. State U., 1970. Pres. Tasmac Inc., Kalamazoo, 1974-88, Power Fin. Inc., Kalamazoo, 1987—; cons. recycling project, wholesale electric sales, 1987—. With USAR, 1966-72. Office: Power Fin Inc 5125 Grosse Pointe St Kalamazoo MI 49008-3622

TASSE, MARIE JEANNE, retired art educator; b. Worcester, Mass., Mar. 25, 1925; d. Paul Charles and Marie Antoinette (DesRosiers) T. AB, Anna Maria Coll., 1955; MA, U. Notre Dame, 1962; PhD, Boston U., 1972. Tchr. music., dir. choir St. John's Sch., Newton, Mass., 1945-50, Notre Dame High Sch., Central Falls, R.I., 1950-53; instr. to prof. Anna Maria Coll., Paxton, Mass., 1955-75; from assoc. prof. to prof. Marietta (Ohio) Coll., 1975-92, chmn. art dept., 1977-82, cons. to faculty, 1981-85, dir. Inst. for Learning in Retirement, 1992-95; founder Marietta Calligraphy Soc., 1981—; dir. Letters at an Exhbn., Marietta, 1984, 86, 88, By Women's Hands Exhbn., Marietta, 1989-91. Calligrapher wall hangings, handmade books, broadsides (Merit award 1991). Pres., v.p. bd. The Marietta Chorale, 1978-88; dir. St. Mary's Ch. Choir, Marietta, 1978-88; bd. dirs. Artsbridge, Marietta/Parkersburg, 1981-94; procedural planner The Incredible Community Playground, Marietta, 1992. Recipient Art Educator award Artsbridge, 1991. Mem. Nat. Soc. Arts and Letters (local pres., v.p. bd. 1982—, nat. resolutions chair 1988-90, nat. career liaison 1992-94, nat. editor membership directory 1994—: Career Award Winners; organizer Mus. Showcase 1992, A Showcase of Drawings 1995, A Showcase of the Arts 1997). Roman Catholic.

TAST, ALAN HERBERT, architect; b. Wahoo, Nebr., Mar. 25, 1961; s. Herbert Richard and Patricia Marie (Nietfeld) T.; m. Marci Dawn Wachter, Sept. 11, 1993. BArch, U. Nebr., 1987, MArch, 1989. Registerd architect, Nebr. Archtl. designer Constrn. Midwest, Inc., Omaha, 1989-90; intern architect Archtl. Partnership, Inc., Lincoln, Nebr., 1990-91; architect Tewhill & Kalvelage Assoc., Architects, Omaha, 1991-95, Prochaska & Assocs., Omaha, 1995—. Author: American Classics-Thunderbird, 1955-66, 1996; editor, author mag. Thunderbird Scoop, 1988-94, sr. editor, 1994— (Golden Quill 1992, 93, 94, 95, 96). Mem. AIA, Nebr. chpt. AIA, Classic Thunderbird Club Internat., Vintage Thunderbird Club Internat. (bd. dirs. 1989—, publs. dir.), Ea. Nebr.-Western Iowa Car Coun. (v.p. 1989-91, sec. 1991-93, Outstanding Auto Hobbyist of Yr. 1992). Lutheran. Home: 8711 S Glenview Dr La Vista NE 68128-2005 Office: Prochaska & Assocs 11315 Chicago Cir Omaha NE 68154-2633

TASWELL, HOWARD FILMORE, pathologist, blood bank specialist, educator; b. Paterson, N.J., July 21, 1928; s. Herman Albert and Pauline Ruth (Abels) T.; children: Amy, Carl, Eric, Steven, Laura, Ruth; m. Beryl Byman, May 7, 1989. A.B., Harvard U., 1949; M.D., NYU, 1953; M.S. in Pathology, U. Minn. Mayo Grad. Sch. Medicine, 1961. Diplomate Am. Bd. Pathology; subcert. in clin. and anatomic pathology, blood banking/transfusion medicine. Intern St. Albans Naval Hosp., N.Y., 1953-54; resident in internal medicine Mayo Clinic, Rochester, Minn., 1956-57; resident in anatomical and clin. pathology Mayo Clinic, 1957-61; assoc. pathologist Harrisburg Hosp., Pa.; asst. prof. pathology Hahneman Coll. Medicine, Phila., 1961-63; head sect. blood bank and transfusion services Mayo Clinic; prof. lab. medicine Mayo Med. Sch., Rochester, Minn., 1963-88, Vernon F. and Earlene D. Dale prof. lab. medicine, 1985-93, prof. emeritus, 1993—; fellow Bush Found. of Minn., dept. psychiatry U. Chgo. Hosps., 1993-95; cons. Nat. Heart, Lung, Blood Inst., FDA Bur. Biologics; mem. assoc. faculty Chgo. Ctr. for Family Health, 1995—. Contbr. over 200 articles to med. jours. and textbooks. Served to lt. comdr. USNR, 1953-56. Mem. AMA, Minn. Med. Assn., Ill. State Med. Soc., Am. Assn. Blood Banks (pres. 1978-79), Minn. Assn. Blood Banks (pres. 1969-70), Minn. Soc. Clin. Pathologists (pres. 1972-73), Am. Soc. Clin. Pathology, Am. Soc. Hematology, Coll. Am. Pathologists, Internat. Soc. Blood Transfusion, Am. Family Therapy Acad., Sigma Xi. Home: 2500 N Lakeview Ave Apt 3204 Chicago IL 60614-1829

TATA, PRAKASAM BALA SURYA, utilities research coordinator; b. Vizianagram, Andhra, India, Jan. 5, 1936; came to U.S., 1962; s. Suryanarayana and Narayanamma (Aryasomayajula) T.; married; children: Nagamani, Uma, Narayan. BSc, M.R. Coll., 1953; MSc, Nagpur (India) U., 1955; PhD, Rutgers U., 1966. Asst. rsch. officer All India Inst. of Hygiene and Pub. Health, Calcutta, India, 1955-59; jr. scientific officer Cen. Pub. Health Engring. Rsch. Inst., Nagpur, 1959-62; rsch. asst. Rutgers U., New Brunswick, N.J., 1962-66; rsch. assoc. Cornell U., Ithaca, N.Y., 1966-70, sr. rsch. assoc., lectr., 1970-74; project mgr. Met. Water Reclamation Dist. Greater Chgo., 1974-90, coord. of tech. svcs., 1990-92, coord. of rsch., 1992—; adj. prof. Ill. Inst. of Tech., Chgo., 1990—; cons., advisor NAS, UN, others. Contbr. numerous articles to profl. jours. Mem. Water Environ. Fedn. (arious coms. 1990—), Internat. Assn. for Water Quality, Air and Waste Mgmt. Assn., Toastmasters Power Breakfast Club (v.p. membership com. 1992). Home: 7014 Richmond Ave Darien IL 60561-4017 Office: Met Water Reclamation Dist Of Greater Chgo Chicago IL 60617

TATE, PHIL, state legislator; b. Mar. 21, 1946; m. Nancy Cassity; 1 child, Aaron Phillip. BS, U. Mo. Oil jobber; mem. Mo. Ho. of Reps. from 3d dist.; vice chmn. Misc. Bill and Resolution Com. Mo. Ho. of Reps., mem. Agr., Appropriations, Health and Mental Health, Edn., Legis. Rsch. Coms. Mem. Jaycees, Rotary. Democrat. Home: 901 W Grand St Gallatin MO 64640-1610*

TATGE, MARK W., investigative reporter; b. Harvey, Ill., June 2, 1955; s. Robert Walter and Lucille Harriet Tatge; m. Julie Truck, Sept. 8, 1984. BA, Western Ill. U., Macomb, 1977; postgrad., U. Wis., 1980-82; MA, Ohio State U., 1983; postgrad., U. Md., 1989, Poynter Inst. Media Studies, St. Petersburg, Fla., 1994. Mng. editor Baraboo (Wis.) News Republic, 1978-80; copy editor Wis. State Jour., Madison, 1980-82; staff writer The Denver Post, 1985-89, The Dallas Morning News, 1989-91; investigative reporter The Plain Dealer, Columbus, Ohio, 1991—. Recipient Morton Margolin prize for disting. bus. reporting, 1988, also awards Colo. AP, 1988, Tex. Headliners, 1990, Soc. Profl. Journalists, 1992, 96; Kiplinger fellow in pub. affairs reporting, 1982-83. Mem. Investigative Reporters and Editors (fundraising com. 1995—), Ohio Legis.Corrs. Assn. Office: The Plain Dealer 65 E State St Columbus OH 43215

TATMAN, EDWARD J., entrepreneur, engineer; b. Cleve., Aug. 5, 1949; s. Arthur J. and Mary J. (Sweeny) T.; m. Mary M. Klaus, June 5, 1971; children: Mary A., Edward J. Jr., Ann E., James J., Victoria A. BSEE, Case Inst. Tech., 1971; M Engring. in Electric Power Engring., Rensselaer Poly. Inst., 1972. Registered profl. engr., Ohio, S.C., Utah, Minn. Project engr. S&C Electric Co., Chgo., 1972-74; elec. engr. Arthur Tatman & Assocs., Inc., Cleve., 1974-81; v.p. of engring. Arthur Tatman & Assoc., Inc., Cleve., 1981-86; pres. Tatman Assocs., Inc. (formerly Arthur Tatman & Assocs., Inc.), Cleve., 1986—. Mem. IEEE, Nat. Soc. Profl. Engrs., Ohio Soc. Profl. Engrs., Assn. Energy Engrs., Solon Jaycees (past v.p.), Eta Kappa Nu, Theta Tau, Phi Kappa Tau. Office: Tatman Assocs Inc 29015 Solon Rd Cleveland OH 44139-3440

TAVARES, CHARLETA B., state legislator. Student, Spelman Coll., Ohio State U. Mem. Ohio Ho. of Reps., Columbus, 1993—; mem. Met. Human Svc. Commn. Vol. Huckleberry House, Literacy Initiative. Recipient award Black Students in Comm. Ohio State U., 1992, Ctrl. Comty House award, 1992, Pub. Children's Svc. Assn. award, 1993; named Franklin County Dem. Women's Club Sweetheart, 1993. Mem. LWV, Far East Dem. Women's Club, Columbus Area Women's Polit. Caucus, Coalition of 100 Black Women.

TAVEL, MORTON EDWARD, physician; b. Indpls., June 21, 1932; s. Oscar and Mayme Louise (Dorman) T.; m. Carole Harriet Leve, June 23, 1957; children: Elizabeth, Robert, Michael. AB, Ind. U., Bloomington, 1954; MD, Ind. U., Indpls., 1957. Intern, resident Phila. Gen. Hosp., 1957-60; resident in internal medicine U. Utah, Salt Lake City, 1960-61; clin. cardiologist Northside Cardiology, Indpls., 1987—; prof. Ind. U. Sch. Medicine, Indpls., 1968—. Author: Clinical Phonocardiography, 4th edit., 1985; contbr. numerous articles to profl. jours. Capt. U.S. Army, 1961-63. Fellow ACP, Am. Coll. Cardiology (bd. govs. 1974-76), Am. Coll. Chest Physicians (bd. govs. 1984-86), Am. Heart Assn. (Coun. Clin. Cardiology, pres. Ind. affiliate 1985-87). Jewish. Home: 1139 Frederick Dr S Indianapolis IN 46260 Office: Northside Cardiology 8333 Naab Rd Ste 200 Indianapolis IN 46260

TAYLOR, ANN SIEGRIST, psychologist; b. Lynchburg, Va., Feb. 17, 1953; d. Clifford Joseph Jr. and Bessie Lee (Garbee) Siegrist; m. Allen Richmond Taylor, June 21, 1975. BS with distinction, Va. Poly. Inst., 1975; MA, Cen. Mich. U., 1977; PhD, U. Tenn, 1986. Lic. psychologist, Mich.; cert. employee assistance profl. Psychology asst. Shawnee Mental Health Ctr., Portsmouth, Ohio, 1977-81; behavior specialist Ga. Highlands Ctr., Dalton, 1981-82; psychology intern VA Med. Ctr., Ann Arbor, Mich., 1985-86; adj. faculty Saginaw (Mich.) Valley State U., 1986; psychologist Psych Assocs., Saginaw, 1986-89; employee assistance program specialist Dow N.Am., Midland, Mich., 1989—. Bd. dirs., pers. com. chairperson Big Bros./Big Sisters, Midland, 1986-88. Cen. Mich. U. grad. fellow, 1975. Mem. APA, Soc. for Indsl. and Orgnl. Psychology, Employee Assistance Profls. Assn., Phi Kappa Phi. Office: Dow N Am 2020 Dow Ctr Midland MI 48674

TAYLOR, ANNA DIGGS, federal judge; b. Washington, Dec. 9, 1932; d. Virginius Douglass and Hazel (Bramlette) Johnston; m. S. Martin Taylor, May 22, 1976; children: Douglass Johnston Diggs, Carla Cecile Diggs. BA, Barnard Coll., 1954; LLB, Yale U., 1957. Bar: D.C. 1957, Mich. 1961. Atty. Office Solicitor, Dept. Labor, W, 1957-60; asst. prosecutor Wayne County, Mich., 1961-62; asst. U.S. atty. Eastern Dist. of Mich., 1966; ptnr. Zwerdling, Maurer, Diggs & Papp, Detroit, 1970-75; asst. corp. counsel City of Detroit, 1975-79; U.S. dist. judge Eastern Dist. Mich. Detroit, 1979—. Hon. chair, United Way Cmty. Found., S.E. Mich. Found. Soc., Detroit Inst. Arts, Greater Detroit Health Coun., Eastern Region Henry Ford Health Sys.; co-chair, vol. Leadership Coun. for S.E. Mich. Mem. Fed. Bar Assn., State Bar Mich., Wolverine Bar Assn. (v.p.), Yale Law Assn. Episcopalian. Office: US Dist Ct 740 US Courthouse 231 W Lafayette Blvd Detroit MI 48226-2719

TAYLOR, ARDIS, science educator; b. Lisbon, N.D., July 16, 1934; d. Oscar A. and Magnhild (Johnson) Ringdahl; m. Harvey A. Taylor, Apr. 2, 1962; 1 child, Miles. BS, Colo. State U., 1958; M, N.D. State U., 1980. Tchr. sci. Lisbon (N.D.) Pub. Schs., 1958-63, Sheldon (N.D.) Pub. Schs., 1969-76, Sargent Ctrl. Sch., Forman, N.D., 1976-94; ret., 1994. Author books on pioneer and area history; contbr. articles to profl. jours. and newspapers. Recipient Seim-Forred Soil Stewardship award, 1977, Sargent County Educator of Yr. award, 1994. Mem. Quarter Horse Assn. (founder N.D. chpt., 1960, Founders award 1985). Home: 13532 77th St SE Lisbon ND 58054-9473

TAYLOR, BARBARA ANN, educational consultant; b. St. Louis, Feb. 8, 1933; d. Spencer Truman and Ann Amelia (Whitney) Olin; m. F. Morgan Taylor Jr., Apr. 5, 1954; children: Frederick M. III, Spencer O., James W., John F. AB, Smith Coll., 1954; M of Mgmt., Northwestern U., 1978, PhD, 1984; LHD, U. New Haven, 1995. Mem. faculty Hamden (Conn.) Hall Country Day Sch., 1972-74; cons. Booz, Allen & Hamilton, Inc., Chgo., 1979; program assoc. Northwestern U., Evanston, Ill., 1982; co-founder, exec. dir. Nat. Ctr. Effective Schs. Rsch. & Devel., Okemos, Mich., 1986-89, rsch. assoc., 1987; cons. on effective schs. rsch. and reform Nat. Ctr. Effective Schs. R&D, U. Wis., Madison, 1990-96; pres. Excelsior! Found., Chgo., 1994—; mem. exec. com. Hudson Inst., New Am. Schs. Devel. Corp. Design Team, 1990—; Danforth Disting. lectr. U. Nebr., Omaha, 1993. Co-author: Making School Reform Happen, 1993, Keepers of the Dream, 1994, The Revolution Revisited: Effective Schools and Systemic Reform, 1995; editor: Case Studies in Effective Schools Research, 1990; contbr. articles to profl. jours. Pres. Jr. League of New Haven, 1967-69; pres. NCCJ, New Haven, 1971-73; co-chair Coalition Housing and Human Resources, Hartford-New Haven, 1970-73; co-chair steering com. Day Care Conn., Hartford, 1971-73; bd. dirs. U. New Haven, 1961-71, Smith Coll., Northampton, Mass., 1984-90. Recipient Humanitarian award Mt. Calvary Bapt. Ch., 1988, Outstanding Alumna award John Burroughs Sch., 1994. Mem. ASCD, Nat. Commn. Citizens Edn. (bd. dirs. 1980-86), Nat. Staff Devel. Coun., Phi Delta Kappa. Episcopalian. Office: Nat Ctr Effective Schs Rsch & Devel 222 E Wisconsin Ave Ste 301 Lake Forest IL 60045-1723

TAYLOR, BILLIE WESLEY, retired secondary education educator; b. Charleston, W.Va, Aug. 14, 1940; s. Billie W and Effie (Adams) T.; m. Elisabeth Julia Coler, Jan. 27, 1960; 1 child, Rose Letitia Taylor Allen. BA, Wilmington Coll., 1961; MA, Ohio State U., 1963; PhD, Columbia Pacific U., 1993. Cert. secondary tchr., prin., Ohio. Tchr. Columbus Pub. Schs., Ohio, 1961-64; records, forms, mgnt. officer VI U.S. Army Corps, Battle Creek, Mich., 1964-65; production planner Hoover Ball & Bearing Co., Ann Arbor, Mich., 1965-66; dist. exec. Boy Scouts of Am., Detroit, 1966-72; sales tng. Standard Register Co., Dayton, Ohio, 1972-74; tchr. Dayton Pub. Schs., Dayton, Ohio, 1974—, curriculum specialist for computer tech., 1989-93. Author: History of the D-MC Park District, 1988, Classroom Discipline, 1987. Pres., Johnson Sch. Parent Tchrs. Assoc., Taylor, Mich., 1966-67; dist. chmn., Boy Scouts of Am., Dayton, 1974-79; bd. mem., Southeast Dayton Priority Bd., Dayton, 1976-77. Recipient Pres. trophy Boy's Scouts of Am., 1970; Jenning's scholar Martha Holden Jennings Found., 1980-81. Mem. Nat. Geographic Soc. (life), Nat. Audubon Soc., Smithsonian Nat. Assocs. (charter mem.), Libr. of Congress Assocs. (charter), Nat. Mus. of the Am. Indian (charter), Western Ohio Edn. Assn. (del.), Am. Birding Assn., The Nature Conservancy (life), Am. Assn. Individual Investors (life), Masons. Home: 131 Snow Hill Ave Kettering OH 45429-1705

TAYLOR, BYRON KEITH, industrial engineer; b. Portsmouth, Va., July 9, 1955; s. Robert Lee and Joyce Sue (Cox) T.; m. Barbara Sue Keene, Aug. 27, 1977; l child, Joshua Lee. BS in Indsl. Engring., Va. Poly. Inst. and State U., 1980. Indsl. engr. Deere & Co. (Harvester), East Moline, Ill., 1980-8l, 83-84, product engr., 198l-83, prodn. engr., 1984-90, module owner, 1990-93; sr. engr. new product devel., 1993-95; supr. engring. John Deere, Davenport Works, Moline, 1995—; mem. engring. curriculum devel. panel Black Hawk Coll., Moline, Ill., 1989; tech. del. conf. Citizen's Amb. program Soviet Union, 1990. Program chmn. Meth. Mens Club, Colona, Ill., 1985; advisor Jr. Achievement, East Moline, 1986-87, cons., 1988. Named Young Engr. of Yr. Quad-Cities Engring. and Sci. Coun., 1989-90. Mem. Inst. Indsl. Engrs. (sr., dir. pub. rels. chpt. 46, 1986-87, pres.-elect 1988-89, pres. 1989—). Republican. Home: 3ll0 Halcyon Dr Bettendorf IA 52722 Office: Deere & Co 1100 13th Ave East Moline IL 61244-1455

TAYLOR, CALVIN LEE, public administrator; b. Marietta, Ohio, Dec. 27, 1946; s. Fred O. and Wilma B. Taylor; m. Nancy Downs, Mar. 29, 1969; children: Christina, Matthew. BSc in Natural Resources, Ohio State U., 1969, PhD in Environ. Scis., 1977; MPA, Golden Gate U., 1973. Project officer Corps of Engrs. Sacramento (Calif.) Dist., 1970-73; asst. planning chief Ohio EPA, Columbus, 1973-74; acad. advisor Ohio State U. Sch. of Natural Resources, Columbus, 1974-75; asst. to dir. Ohio Water Resources Ctr., Columbus, 1975-76; adminstr. Ohio Dept. Natural Resources, Columbus, 1976-82; chief of pub. rels. Ohio Adj. Gen.'s Dept., 1982-88; chief ops. and tng. Ohio Emergency Mgmt. Agy., Columbus, 1988-94; chief of emergency planning State of Ohio, Columbus, 1994—; lectr. in field. Contbr. articles to profl. jours. Chmn., mem. Worthington Planning Commn./Archl. Rev. Bd., 1976-82, active coms. Worthington United Meth. Ch., 1980—. Lt. col. U.S. Army Res., 1970—. Named Outstanding Young Man of Am. U.S. Bd. Jaycees, 1981. Mem. Ohi Acad. Sci., Assn. U.S. Army, Ohio State U. Alumni Assn. (pres. natural resources 1979-80), Ohio State U. Army ROTC Alumni Assn. (v.p., pres.), Columbus Acad. Fathers' Assn. Home: 701 Morning St Worthington OH 43085-3772 Office: Ohio Emergency Mgmt Agy 2855 W Granville Rd Columbus OH 43235

TAYLOR, CECELIA MONAT, mental health nurse; b. Bklyn., Nov. 25, 1938; d. Francis Theodore and Rose Helen (Pater) Monat; m. Herbert E. Taylor, Mar. 16, 1968 (div. 1977) 1 child, Corliss Ann. BS, Wagner Luth. Coll., 1959; MA, NYU, 1962; PhD, Syracuse U., 1983. Head nurse Brattleboro (Vt.) Retreat; instr. Bronx (N.Y.) Community Coll., 1962-65; cons. Nat. League Nursing, 1965-68; asst. prof., assoc. dean Downstate Med. Ctr., Bklyn., 1968-70; prof., assoc. dean Syracuse (N.Y.) U., 1970-89; DON Mohawk Valley Psychiat. Ctr., Utica, N.Y., 1989-92; prof., chair dept. nursing. co-chair health sci. div. Coll. St. Scholastica, Duluth, Minn., 1992—. Author: Essentials of Psychiatric Nursing, 14th edit., 1994; also book chpts. and articles to profl. jours. Mem. ANA, Nat. League for Nursing, Soc. for Edn. and Rsch. in Psychiat.-Mental Health Nursing (pres. 1990-92), Sigma Theta Tau, Pi Lambda Theta, Kappa Delta Pi. Home: 1321 E Skyline Pky Duluth MN 55805-1545 Office: Coll of St Scholastica 1200 Kenwood Ave Duluth MN 55811-4199

TAYLOR, CELIANNA ISLEY, information systems specialist; b. Youngstown, Ohio; d. Paul Thornton and Florence (Jacobs) Isley; divorced; children: Polly, Jerry, Jim. BA in Philosophy, Denison U., 1939; MLS, Western Res. U., 1942. Worked in several pub. librs. and univ. librs., 1939-50; head Libr. Cataloging Dept. Battelle Mem. Inst., Columbus, Ohio, 1951-53; head pers. office, assoc. prof. libr. adminstrn. Ohio State U. Librs., Columbus, 1954-65; coord. info. svcs., assoc. prof. libr. adminstrn. Nat. Ctr. for Rsch. in Vocat. Edn., Ohio State U., Columbus, 1966-70; sr. rsch. assoc., adminstrv. assoc., assoc. prof. libr. adminstrn. dept. computer and info. sci. Ohio State U., Columbus, 1970-86; assoc. prof. emeritus Univ. Librs. dept. computer and info. sci. Ohio State U., Columbus, 1986—; mem. Task Force on a Spl. Collections Database, Ohio State U. Librs., Columbus, 1988-89, comm. systems and recs. coord. Ohio State U. Retirees Assn., Columbus, 1992-93; cons. for several profl. orgns. including Ernst & Ernst CPA's and Oreg. State Sys. of Higher Edn., 1961-82. Author: (with J. Magisos) book, Guide for State Voc-Tech Edn. Dissemination Systems 1971, (with A.E. Petrarca, and R.S. Kohn) book, Info. Interaction 1982; several articles for profl. jours.; designer: info. systems, CALL System, 1977-82, Channel 2000 Proj. Home Info. Svc., 1980-81, Continuing Education Info. Ctr., 1989-90, Human Resources (HUR) System, 1976-77,1979-82, DECOS, 1975-86, Computer-asst. libr. System, Optical Scan System, 1972-73, ERIC Clearinghouse for vocat. edn., 1966-70. Bd. dirs. Columbus Reg. Info. Svc., 1974-78, Cmty. Info. Referral Svc., Inc. 1975-81; chmn. subcom. on design, info. and ref. com. Columbus United Cmty. Coun., 1972-73; dir. Computer Utility for Pub. Info. Columbus, 1975-81; acct. coord. Greater Columbus Free-net, 1994—. Mem. ALA, Assn. Computing Machinery (Ctrl. Ohio chpt.), Am. Soc. Info. Sci.,Assn. Faculty and Profl. Women Ohio State U., Columbus Metro Club, Coun. for Ethics in Econs., Olympic Indoor Tennis Club. Home and Office: 3471 Greenbank Ct Columbus OH 43221-4724

TAYLOR, CHARLES EMERY, physics educator; b. White Plains, N.Y., Mar. 2, 1940; s. Francis Emery and Catherine Walton (Hill) T.; m. Catherine Ann Anderson, May 16, 1970; 1 child, Brendan D. BA in Physics, Williams Coll., 1961, MA in Physics, 1963; PhD in Physics, Mich. State U., 1967. Asst. to assoc. prof. physics Antioch Coll., Yellow Springs, Ohio, 1967-79, prof. physics, 1979—; dir. sci. inst. Antioch Coll., Yellow Springs, 1982-86. Dir. Youth Recreational Soccer, Yellow Springs, 1980-85. Fellow NSF, 1975-76; grantee NSF, 1991. Mem. Am. Assn. Physics Tchrs., Am. Solar Energy Assn. Office: Antioch Coll Physics Dept Yellow Springs OH 45387-1697

TAYLOR, CONNIE MARIA, science educator; b. Chgo., May 6, 1952; d. Lonnie Calahoma and Verdenia (Flenoral) T.; children: Rachel, Gabrielle, Paul, Lydia. Student, Moody Bible Inst., 1973-75, Chgo. State U., 1985-87, Ill. Inst. Tech., 1991-95. Adminstr. Christ Acad., Chgo., 1981-85; tchr. 7th and 8th grade Evangelical Sch., Chgo., 1987-89; sci. tchr. St. Sabina, Chgo., 1989-90; tchr. 7th grade Holy Angels, Chgo., 1990-92; sci. tchr. Bethel Christian Sch., Chgo., 1992-96; ret., 1996; writer Urban Ministries, Chgo., 1992—; edn. project dir. Urban Ministries, Chgo. Author: Jumpin' the Broom, 1981; creator (games) Fraperdec, Metric Madness, 1995, Periodical Insanity, 1995. Pprogram dir. Vernon Park Ch. of God, Chgo., 1995—. Named Outstanding Sci./Math. Tchr., Sigma Xi/Argonne Nat. Lab., 1992. Mem. Ill. Sci. Tchrs. Assn. Home: 7714 S Kimbark Ave Chicago IL 60619

TAYLOR, DEBORA DIANNE, home health nurse; b. Canton, Ill., Apr. 5, 1959; d. Richard Jean and Barbara Elaine (Bump) T. AAS, Carl Sandburg Coll., 1980; BSN, U. Ill., Chgo., 1990. Cert. provider BLS, ACLS, Pediatric ALS, Am. Heart Assn. Staff nurse pediatrics St. Mary Med. Ctr., Galesburg, Ill., 1980-94, staff nurse home health, 1994—; clin. instr. LPN program Carl Sandburg Coll., Galesburg, 1990-92; home health nurse UpJohn Healthcare Svcs., Rock Island, Ill., 1990-92; chmn. recruitment and retention com. St. Mary Med. Ctr., 1991-92; mem. nominating com. 5th dist. I.N.A., Moline, Ill., 1990-91; cons. in devel. of parenting programs, 1990. Guest speaker childcare class Galesburg High Sch., 1989; supt. Sunday sch. Henderson (Ill.) United Meth. Ch., 1986-92; active Young Reps., Galesburg, 1990. Mem. ANA, U. Ill. Nursing Alumni Assn. (bd. dirs., award 1990), Sigma Theta Tau. Home: 1713 N Seminary St Galesburg IL 61401-1921 Office: St Mary Med Ctr 3333 N Seminary St Galesburg IL 61401-1251

TAYLOR, DENNIS DEL, marketing executive; b. St. Louis, Oct. 23, 1946; s. James Henry and Helen Ruby (Dell) T.; m. Dorothy June Henthorn, July 26, 1968; 1 child, Keith Gregory. BSBA, U. Mo., 1970; MBA, Fontbonne Coll., 1994. Dept. mgr. Famous-Barr Co., St. Louis, 1965-69; acct. exec. Union Central Life Ins. Co., Cin., 1969-71; dist. sales mgr. Hallmark Cards, Inc., Kansas City, Mo., 1971-80, Steelcase, Inc., Grand Rapids, Mich., 1980-81; v.p. sales and mktg. Holscher-Werning, Inc., St. Louis, 1981-84, Bus. Interiors, Inc., St. Louis, 1984-91; nat. sales mgr. Harvand Inc., St. Louis, 1991-93; v.p. sales and mktg. Tiffany Office Furniture, St. Louis, 1993-94, Berco Industries, St. Louis, 1994—. Mem. exec. coun. Luth. Family and Children's Svcs., 1989. Mem. Nat. Office Products Assn., Downtown St. Louis, Sales and Mktg. Execs. St. Louis, Optimists, Mo. Athletic Club, Hidden Valley Golf Club. Republican. Mem. Assembly of God Ch. Home: 2215 Kehrsglen Ct Chesterfield MO 63005-6518 Office: Berco Industries 1120 Montrose Ave Saint Louis MO 63104-1828

TAYLOR, DONNA BLOYD, vocational rehabilitation consultant; b. Louisville, Ky., July 15, 1958; d. Donald Ray Bloyd and Georgia Carmen (Bryant) Whitehead; 1 child, Stephanie Micah Taylor; m. Douglas A. Garner, June 6, 1992. BS, U. Louisville, 1981, MEd, 1982. Lic. profl. counselor, qualified rehab. provider, Ohio; cert. rehab. counselor U.S. Dept. Labor; qualified rehab. coord., Ky.; cert. disability mgmt. specialist; cert. case mgr., vocat. evaluator, nat. counselor; diplomate Am. Bd. Vocat. Experts; qualified mental retardation profl.; cert. vocat. evaluator, RAS. Program coord. Hazelwood ICF-MR, Louisville, 1981-83; lead vocat. therapist Rehab. Ctr. Southeastern Ind., Clarksville, 1983-85; regional supr., vocat. cons. Rehab. Coords., Inc., Louisville, 1985; asst. mgr., rehab. cons. Nat. Rehab. Cons., Cin., 1985-88; dist. mgr., vocat. cons. Recovery Unlimited, Inc., Cin., 1988-92; pvt. practice, Lawrenceburg, Ind., 1992—; vocat. expert Social Security Adminstrn. Co-author: (with Timothy Field and others) Study Guide to the CIRS Exam, 1992, The St. Thomas Resource on Certification, Ethics and Training for Private Sector Rehabilitation, 1993, CCM Study Guide, 1994. Vol. Am. Cancer Soc., mem. Rape Crisis Intervention Team. Mem. Nat. Assn. Rehab. Profls. in Pvt. Sector (past pres. Ky. chpt., SCRB com., co-chair internat. affairs divsn.), Nat. Rehab. Assn., Nat. Forensic Ctr., Nat. Disting. Svc. Registry, Individual Case Mgmt. Assn., U. Louisville Alumni Assn., Disability Network Ohio-Solidarity, Rehab. Referral Network, Rehab. Internat., Phi Kappa Phi. Democrat. Methodist. Office: 15 Mary St Lawrenceburg IN 47025-1900

TAYLOR, DORIS DENICE, physician, entrepreneur; b. Indpls., Sept. 19, 1955; d. Eugene and Mary Catherine (Ryder) T. BA, U. Minn., 1976, cert. behavior analyst, 1977, MD, 1983; BS, Purdue U., 1979. Diplomate Nat. Bd. Med. Examiners. Pvt. practice Locumtenens, 1989—; mng. dir. Sebree-Watkins-Ovbokhan Meml. Cancer Fund, Indpls.; pres., CEO Taylors of Indy Corp., Indpls.; oncologic svcs. cons. and developer. Lange scholar, U. Minn., 1980, Joseph Collins Found. scholar, 1980-81, Nat. Med. Fellowship scholar, 1980-81. Mem. AMA, Am. Soc. for Therapeutic Radiology and Oncology, Am. Soc. Clin. Oncologists. Office: Taylors of Indy Corp 55 Monument Cir Ste 814 Indianapolis IN 46204

TAYLOR, ELISABETH COLER, secondary school educator; b. N.Y.C., Jan. 24, 1942; d. Gerhard Helmut and Judith (Horowitz) C.; m. Billie Wesley Taylor II, Jan. 27, 1960; children: Letitia Rose, Billie Albert. Student, Wilmington Coll., 1959-60; BS, Wayne State U., Detroit, 1969; MS, The Ohio State U., 1980; postgrad., Wright State U., Dayton, Ohio, 1989—. Cert. home economist. H.s. tchr. home econs., computer sci., lang. arts Dayton (Ohio) City Schs., 1972—. Bd. mem. Camp Fire Girls, 1970-71, vol. Detroit Mus. of Art, 1970-71, group leader Camp Fire Girls, Boy Scouts, Detroit, 1968-74. Mem. AAUW (life), NEA, Ohio Edn. Assn., Dayton Edn. Assn. Home: 131 Snow Hill Ave Dayton OH 45429-1705

TAYLOR, EVA UNIKEL, interior designer; arrived in Can., 1956; came to U.S., 1967; d. Istvan Domolky and Lea Maria (Koszegi) Coan; m. Craig Allan Taylor, Apr. 28, 1972 (div. Feb. 1978); 1 child, Renee Christine; m. June 26, 1993. BS, So. Ill. U., 1972. Dir. mktg. Lococo Design, St. Louis, 1982-83; project mgr., nat. dir. mktg. hosp. div. Hotel Restaurant Planners div. Profl. Interiors, St. Louis, 1983-87; founder Interior Solutions Inc., Hinsdale, Ill., 1987—; mem. adv. com. interior Meramec Community Coll., St. Louis 1985--. Mem. AIA (assoc.), Nat. Assn. Women Bus. Owners, Am. Soc. Interior Design (chairperson 1984-86), Nat. Assn. Indsl. Office Pks., Bldg. Owners and Mgrs. Assn. Roman Catholic. Office: 500 Ravine Rd Hinsdale IL 60521-2449

TAYLOR, FANNIE TURNBULL, social education and arts administration educator; b. Kansas City, Mo., Sept. 11, 1913; d. Henry King and Fannie Elizabeth (Sills) Turnbull; m. Robert Taylor, Dec. 2, 1938 (div. 1974); children: Kathleen Muir Taylor Isaacs, Anne Kingston Taylor Wadsack. BA, U. Wis., 1938; LHD (hon.), Buena Vista Coll., Storm Lake, Iowa, 1975. Mem. faculty U. Wis., Madison, 1941—, prof. social edn., 1949—, emeritus, 1979—, dir. Wis. Union Theater, 1946-66, coord. univ. systems arts council, 1967-70, assoc. dir. Ctr. Arts Adminstrn., 1970-72, coord. Consortium for Arts, 1976-84; cons. in field. Author: The Arts at a New Frontier, Wisconsin Union Theater: Fifty Golden Years; contbr. articles to profl. jours. Program dir. music Nat. Endowment Arts, 1966-67, program info. dir., 1972-76; bd. dirs. Wis. Arts Council, 1964-72, Wis. Found. Arts, 1976-91, Madison Civic Music Assn., 1976-84, Madison Children's Mus., 1983—, Elvehjem Mus. Art Coun., 1976—; chair, 1983-86; Madison Civic Ctr.

Found., 1981-94; hon. chair Wis. Union Theater Program Endowment Fund, 1985—; bd. dirs. Wis. chpt. Nature Conservancy, 1963-84, chmn., 1976-77; bd. dirs. Shorewood Hills Found., 1976—, pres., 1976-81. Recipient Oak Leaf award Nature Conservancy, 1981, Wis. Gov.'s award in Support of the Arts, 1992; named Women of Distinction, Madison YMCA, 1994. Fellow Wis. Acad. Scis., Arts and Letters; mem. Assn. Performing Arts Presenters (founder, exec. dir. 1957-72, Fannie Taylor award 1972), Am. Assn. Dance Cos. (bd. dirs. 1967-72), Nat. Assn. Regional Ballet (bd. dirs. 1975-77), Nat. Guild Community Schs. Arts (bd. dirs. 1977-80), Women in Communications (Writers' Cup 1980), U. Wis. Alumni Assn. (Disting. Svc. award 1979, Madison Civics Club (pres. 1969-70), Madison Club, Univ. Club (pres. 1982-85), Blackhawk Club. Home: 1213 Sweet Briar Rd Madison WI 53705-2227

TAYLOR, GAIL RICHARDSON, university administrator; b. Cleve., July 16, 1949; d. Allen Barnd and Margaret Christine (Thomas) Ricardson; m. William David Taylor, May 16, 1987; 1 child, William Robert. BA, Wellesley Coll., 1971; MS in Journalism, Northwestern U., 1978; JD magna cum laude, Case Western Reserve U., 1993. Bar: Ohio, 1993. Co-editor Time Sharing Today, Phila., 1972-73; reporter Today's Spirit (Montgomery Pub. Co.), Hatboro, Pa., 1973-76, The Argus Leader (Gannett Co.), Sioux Falls, S.D., 1978-82; writer, editor Case Western Res. U., Cleve., 1982-83, sr. writer, editor, 1983-84, dir. news svcs., 1984-87, coord. govt. rels., 1987-90, dir. govt. rels., 1990—. Contbr. articles to newspapers and mags. Chair of the bd. of trustees United Protestant Campus Ministries in Cleve. Mem. Soc. Profl. Journalists. Democrat. Home: 317 Elm St Oberlin OH 44074-1404 Office: Case Western Res U Office of Govt Rels 10900 Euclid Ave Cleveland OH 44106-7024

TAYLOR, GREGORY F., securities broker; b. 1949. BA, Beloit Coll., 1973; MBA, Loyola U., 1975. With Embosograph Display Mfg. Co., Lake Bluff, Ill., 1975-77, Paine Webber, St. Louis, 1977-85; with Stifel nicolaus & Co. Inc., St. Louis, 1985-92, pres., CEO, 1992—. Office: Stifel Nicolaus & Co Inc 500 N Broadway Rm 1700 Saint Louis MO 63102-2110*

TAYLOR, JAMES HARRY, II, management consultant; b. Urbana, Ill., July 10, 1951; s. James Harry and B. June (Collins) T. BS in Biomed. Engring., Rose-Hulman Inst. Tech., Terre Haute, Ind., 1974, postgrad., 1991—. Cons. engr. Taylor and Assocs., New Goshen, Ind., 1974-88; environ. design cons. EPA, Research Triangle Park, N.C., 1984; hazardous materials engr. Newport (Ind.) Army Ammunition Plant, 1984-85; mfg. engr., project cons. Hercules, Inc., Terre Haute, 1985-87; system safety cons. Space div. Morton Thiokol, Brighman City, Utah, 1987; safety and reliability cons. Rocketdyne div. Rockwell Internat., Canoga Park, Calif., 1987-89; v.p. engring. I.S.E., Inc., West Terre Haute, Ind., 1988-91, also chmn. bd. dirs.; system safety/risk assessment cons. LHTEC-T800 Engine Allison Gas Turbine, Indpls., 1989-93; sr. safety engr. T800 program LHTEC/Allison Engine Co., Indpls., 1993-95, reliability and safety project leader various engines, 1994-95; sr. sys. safety/reliability engr. Allison Mobile Power Sys., 1995—. Dem. campaign worker local elections, Terre Haute, 1984; spl. events coord. Ind. Perot for Pres. com., 1992. Recipient Excellence award NASA, Canoga Park, 1987. Mem. Nat. Soc. Profl. Engrs. (assoc.), Ind. Soc. Profl. Engrs., Rose-Hulman Rifles Club (pres. 1971-72). Republican. Home: 4133 Golden Eagle Dr Indianapolis IN 46234 Office: M/C 0-08 2925 W Minnesota St Indianapolis IN 46241

TAYLOR, JANE LUNDEEN, curator; b. New Preston, Conn., Aug. 19, 1935; d. Levi Reinald and Lucy Margaret (Raines) L.; m. James Lee Taylor, Aug. 16, 1958; children: Timothy Dean, Kristin Lee. BA, Marietta (Ohio) Coll., 1957; MS, U. Ill., 1959. Cons. environ. edn. Haslett (Mich.) Pub. Schs., 1970-84; assoc. 4-H Youth Program, adj. faculty Dept. of Hort. Mich. State U., East Lansing, 1985—; curator Mich. 4-H Children's Garden, 1987—; cons., presenter numerous nat. and state orgns., 1970—. Co-author: (extension bull.) Heritage Gardening, Herbs, 1985; author curriculum materials on environ. edn., 1970-84; author numerous bulls. and articles. Recipient Recognition as Educator of Yr., Mich. Environ. Edn. Assn., 1982, award of commendation Am. Assn. for State and Local History, 1976, 85, Silver Seal award Nat. Coun. State Garden Clubs, 1995. Mem. Am. Assn. Bot. Gardens and Arboreta, Am. Hort. Soc., Mich. Bot. Club (pres. 1988-90), Mich. Herb Assocs. (hon. life), Herb Soc. Am., Nat. Jr. Hort. Assn., Royal Hort. Soc. Congregationalist. Home: 6132 Shoeman Rd Haslett MI 48840-9110 Office: Mich 4-H Found 4700 S Hagadorn Rd East Lansing MI 48823-5354

TAYLOR, JEFF, reporter. Reporter Kansas City Star. Recipient Pulitzer Prize for nat. reporting, 1992, Sigma Delta Chi award. Office: Kans City Star 1729 Grand Blvd Kansas City MO 64108-1413

TAYLOR, J(OCELYN) MARY, museum administrator, zoologist, educator; b. Portland, Oreg., May 30, 1931; d. Arnold Llewellyn and Kathleen Mary (Yorke) T.; m. Joseph William Kamp, Mar. 18, 1972 (dec.). B.A., Smith Coll., 1952; M.A., U. Calif., Berkeley, 1953, Ph.D., 1959. Instr. zoology Wellesley Coll., 1959-61, asst. prof. zoology, 1961-65; assoc. prof. zoology U. B.C., 1965-74; dir. Cowan Vertebrate Mus., 1965-82, prof. dept. zoology, 1974-82; collaborative scientist Oreg. Regional Primate Research Ctr., 1983-87; prof. (courtesy) dept. fisheries and wildlife Oreg. State U., 1984—; dir. Cleve. Mus. Nat. History, 1987—; adj. prof. dept. biology Case Western Res. U., 1987—. Assoc. editor Jour. Mammalogy, 1981-82. Contbr. numerous articles to sci. jours. Trustee Benjamin Rose Inst., 1988-93, Western Res. Acad., 1989-94, U. Circle, Inc., 1987—, The Cleve. Aquarium, 1990-93, Cleve. Access to the Arts, 1992—; corp. bd. Holden Arboretum, 1988—. Fulbright scholar, 1954-55; Lalor Found. grantee, 1962-63; NSF grantee, 1963-71; NRC Can. grantee, 1966-84; Killam Sr. Research fellow, 1978-79. Mem. Soc. Women Geographers, Am. Soc. Mammalogists (1st v.p. 1978-82, pres. 1982-84, Hartley T. Jackson award 1993, Lake County environ. award 1996), Australian Mammal Soc., Cooper Ornithol., Assn. Sci. Mus. Dirs. (v.p. 1990-93), Rodent Specialist Group of Species Survival Commn. (chmn. 1989-93), Sigma Xi. Episcopalian. Office: Cleve Mus Natural History 1 Wade Oval Dr Cleveland OH 44106-1701

TAYLOR, JOHN KEMPER, trial judge, retired; b. New Lexington, Ohio, May 19, 1935; s. John W. and Florence E. (Kemper) T.; m. Judith M. Hamilton, Oct. 25, 1958; children: Valerie L., Amy A., John K. Jr., Jocelyn P. BSBA, Ohio State U., 1958; JD, U. Cin., 1963. Bar: Ohio. Law clerk U.S. Dist. Ct., Columbus, Ohio, 1963-64; law dir. City of Heath, Ohio, 1965-74, Village of Granville, Ohio, 1969-71; mcpl. judge Licking County Mcpl. Ct., Newark, Ohio, 1974-83; common pleas judge Perry County, New Lexington, Ohio, 1983-86; v.p., gen. coun. Am. Marietta Corp., Marietta, Ohio, 1990-93; sec., counsel Ideal Sanitation Co., Newark, 1965-74; sec. Environ. Svcs., Inc., Toledo, Ohio, 1967-72. v.p. Perry County C. of C., New Lexington, 1983-90; pres., bd. trustees Southeastern Ohio Regional Coun. on Alcoholism, Athens, 1983-89. With U.S. Army, 1958-60. Recipient Found. award Ohio State Bar Found., 1979. Mem. Rotary Club Marietta (Internat. Svc. award 1995), Marietta Country Club, Masons, Shriners. Methodist. Home: 100 Meadow Ln Marietta OH 45750-1344

TAYLOR, KENARD LYLE, JR., director training; b. Syracuse, N.Y., Dec. 22, 1943; s. Kenard Lyle and Nina T.; m. Sharon Lee Stookey, Dec. 31, 1965; children: Kimberly, Kenard III. BSCE, Ind. Tech. U., 1968; postgrad., Purdue U., 1970-72. Process engr. ARCO, East Chicago, Ind., 1968-71; plant engr. Kiel Chem., Hammond, Ind., 1971-72; mgr. ops. tng. ARCO, 1972-76; dir. Mfg. Tech., St. Louis, 1976—; chmn. bd. dirs. Mfg. Tech., dir. WFI. Author 200 plant tng. workbooks and articles, 1976-95. City coun. mem. City of Valparaiso (Ind.), 1978-83; campaign mgr. Rep. Candidates Porter County, Ind., 1976-95; Center Twp. Rep. chmn., Porter County, Ind., 1993-95; v.p. Ind. JCI Senate, 1978, Ind. Jaycees, 1976; pres. Valparaiso Jaycees, 1974. Mem. Great Lakes API Com. Tng. (assoc.). Republican. Office: Mfg Tech 306 Napoleon St Valparaiso IN 46383-4744

TAYLOR, KOKO, singer. Albums include The Earthshaker, from the Heart of a Woman, I Got What It Takes, Queen of the Blues, 1985, Koko Taylor, 1987, Live From Chicago: An Audience with the Queen, 1987, Teaches Old Standard New Tricks, Jump for Joy, 1990, What It Takes: The Chess Years, 1991, Force of Nature, 1994. Office: Alligator Records care Nora Kinnally PO Box 60234 Chicago IL 60660-0234

TAYLOR, LYNDA DORA, school administrator, principal; b. Chgo., Sept. 11, 1951; d. Dock and Earnestine (Mims) Yancey; m. Robert Taylor, Aug. 4, 1973; children: Robert Jamal, Kyla Nichelle, Shavon Lynn, Lisa Michelle, Joshua Andrew. BS, No. Ill. U., 1973, MS, 1975. Cert. adminstr., elem. tchr., spl. edn. tchr., tchr. of physically handicapped, Ill. Tchr. Ill. Children's Hosp. Sch., 1973; cons., coord. Ill. Office Edn., DeKalb, 1976-77; tchr. Valley View Sch.-Salek Elem., Bolingbrook, Ill., 1980, Mesa (Ariz.) Pub. Schs.; tchr. Valley View Schs.-Northview, Bolingbrook, assoc. prin., 1988-90; assoc. prin. Valley View Schs.-Tibbott, Bolingbrook, 1990-94; prin. Maercker Elem. Sch., Westmont, Ill., 1994—; cons. Knutson Cons. Firm, Chgo., 1988-89. Creator vol. program, writing program, others. Emergency food chair FISH, Bolingbrook, 1989—; leader Girl Scouts U.S., Bolingbrook, 1991—; chair Family Life Conf.-Ill., Little Rock, 1989—. Recipient various awards. Mem. ASCD, Nat. Prins. Assn., Ill. Reading Assn., Ill. Prins. Assn., Phi Delta Kappa, Delta Sigma Theta. Baptist. Office: Valley View Schs-Tibbott 520 Gary Dr Bolingbrook IL 60440-2400

TAYLOR, MARK ALAN, engineering and consulting firm executive; b. St. Clair Shores, Mich., Apr. 19, 1955; m. Vera Angélico; children: Jonathan, Melissa, Daniel. BS in Mgmt. and Computers, Grand Valley State U., 1980. Pres. Taylor Fire Protection Co., Holland, Mich., 1976-77; area sales mgr. Pitney Bowes Inc., Southfield, Mich., 1977-89; v.p., gen. mgr., ptnr. EVCOR of Southeastern Mich., Livonia, 1989—, pres., 1989-90, sec.-treas., 1990—, pres., chief exec. officer, 1991—; tchr. Oakland County Community Coll., Farmington Hills, Mich., 1989-90. Contbr. articles to profl. jours. Bd. dirs. Students Against Suicide, Ann Arbor, 1986. Office: 40800 Five Mile Rd Plymouth MI 48170-2713

TAYLOR, MARY KAY, geriatrics nurse; b. Knoxville, Iowa, Jan. 26, 1954; d. Wendell Shawver and Margery Ethel (Beebe) Kubli; m. Gregory Taylor, Sept. 4, 1993. ADN, Indian Hills Community Coll., 1979; BSN, Teikyo Marycrest U., 1993. RN, Iowa. Staff nurse Mercy Hosp., Des Moines, 1979-81, Knoxville Area Community Hosp., 1981-83, VA Med. Ctr., Knoxville, 1983—. Home: PO Box 646 Knoxville IA 50138-0646

TAYLOR, MAURICE, JR., manufacturing company executive. Student, Mich. Tech. U. Pres., CEO Titan Wheel Internat., Quincy, Ill. Lt. U.S. Army. Office: Titan Wheel Internat 2701 Spruce St Quincy IL 62301-3472

TAYLOR, OWEN EDWIN, manufacturing manager; b. Rockford, Ill., Dec. 22, 1933. Grad. high sch., South Beloit, Ill. Mfg. mgr. Fastener Engrs., Rockford, Ill., 1970-75; gen. mgr. J & M Machine Tool, Rockford, Ill., 1975-79, Flo-Matic Corp., Belvidere, Ill., 1979—. Contbr. articles to profl. jours. Mem. Shriners. Office: Flo Matic Corp 1982 Belford North Dr Belvidere IL 61008-8565

TAYLOR, RALPH ORIEN, JR., real estate developer; b. Kansas City, Mo., Jan. 6, 1919; s. Ralph Orien Sr. and Genevieve (Sturgeon) T.; m. Betty Boswell, Dec. 7, 1940 (dec. Oct. 1959); children: Ralph Bradley, Nancy Virginia Stevens; m. Deborah Rosemary Berger, Oct. 10, 1982. BS in Bus. and Pub. Adminstrn., U. Mo., 1940. Ptnr. Sturgeon & Taylor, Kansas City, Mo., 1940-42; chmn., pres. Sturgeon & Taylor, Inc., Kansas City, Prairie Village (Kans.), 1946-90, Sturgeon & Taylor Devel. Co., Inc., Prarie Village, 1949—, Sturgeon & Taylor, Co., Prarie Village, 1955-90, Roth & Taylor Devel. Co., Inc., Prarie Village, 1989—; ptnr. Script Pro LLC, Mission, Kans., 1994; mem. Johnson County (Kans.) Real Estate Bd., Kansas City Real Estate Bd. Lt. comdr. USNR, 1942-46, PTO, ETO. Decorated Bronze Star. Mem. Nat. Assn. Home Builders (life bd. dirs.), Home Builders Assn. Greater Kansas City (pres. 1951-52, life bd. dirs., Builder of Yr. award 1979), Kans. C. of C., Kansas City C. of C., Olathe C. of C., Indian Hills Country Club (Mission Hills, Kans.), Ft. Lauderdale Country Club, Lauderdale Yacht Club, Phi Delta Theta. Republican. Mem. Christian Ch. Home: 3505 W 71st St Prarie Village KS 66208-3118 Office: Sturgeon & Taylor Devel Co Inc 6909 Nall Ave Prairie Village KS 66208-2061

TAYLOR, RANDALL WILLIAM, quality assurance administrator; b. Paulding, Ohio, Mar. 10, 1948; s. Virgil Myron and Deloris Elizabeth (Myers) T.; m. Patricia Helen Rager, Apr. 29, 1972. AAS in Supervision, Purdue U., Ft. Wayne, 1979, student, 1986-88; BSM, Ind. Wesleyan U., 1989. Broadcaster Radio Sta. WTVB-WANG, Coldwater, Mich., 1969; quality control inspector tire div. B.F. Goodrich, Woodburn, Ind., 1969-74; quality engr. Uniroyal Goodrich Tire Co., Woodburn, Ind., 1987-90; Michelin Americas Small Tires corp. sr. quality engr., 1990-94; gen. mgr. Universal Metalcraft, Inc., Decatur, Ind., 1994-96; client mgr. Brit. Stds. Instn., Inc., 1996—. V.p. Big Bros./Big Sisters, Ft. Wayne, 1982-86. Mem. Ind. State Trapshooting Assn. (bd. dirs. 1984-90). Lodge: Masons.

TAYLOR, RAY, state senator; b. Steamboat Rock, Iowa, June 4, 1923; s. Leonard Allen and Mary Delilah (Huffman) T.; student U. No. Iowa, 1940-41, Baylor U., 1948-49; m. Mary Allen, Aug. 29, 1924; children—Gordon, Laura Rae Taylor Hansmann, Karol Ann Taylor Rogers, Jean Lorraine Taylor Mahl. Farmer, Steamboat Rock, Iowa, 1943—; mem. Iowa Senate, 1973-95; bd. dirs., sec. Am. Legis. Exchange Council, 1979—. Sec., Hardin County Farm Bur., 1970-72; mem. Iowa div. bds. Am. Cancer Soc.; chmn. Am. Revolution Bicentennial Com. Mem. Steamboat Rock Community Sch. Bd., 1955-70; coordinator Republican youth, 1968-72. Chmn. bd. Faith Bapt. Bible Coll.; pres. Am. Council Christian Chs.; chmn. Iowans for Responsible Govt. Named Guardian of Small Bus., NFIB/Iowa, 1989-90, for outstanding support for good govt. and accessible, affordable health care in Iowa, Iowa Physician Assistant Soc., 1991, Ind. Bapt. fellow of the Midwest, Christian Patriots, 1994, Hon. alumnus Faith Bapt. Bible Coll. & Theol. Sem., 1995; recipient Contenders award Am. Coun. Christian Chs., 1991, Legislator of Yr. award Iowa Soc. of Friends, 1991-92. Mem. Wildlife Club. Baptist. Home: 31363 185th St Steamboat Rock IA 50672-8107

TAYLOR, RICHARD L., manufacturing company executive; b. Merrill, Wis., Apr. 21, 1944; s. Donald F. and Eileen M. (Weber) T.; m. Doris R. Carriker, Jan. 30, 1965; children: Richard L. Jr., Patrick Alan, Cynthia Lynn. BBA, Marquette U., 1967. Pres. Merrill (Wis.) Mfg. Corp., 1962—; v.p. Convenience Concepts, Inc., Addison, Ill., 1988—. Bd. dirs. Merrill Area United Way, Sunburst Youth Homes Found., Neillsville, Wis.; pres. Merrill Area C. of C., 1975-76; treas. Merrill Forward Together, 1991—. Rotary (pres. 1983-84). Office: Merrill Mfg Corp 236 S Genesse St Merrill WI 54452

TAYLOR, ROBERT HOMER, quality assurance professional, pilot; b. Rochester, N.Y., Mar. 18, 1922; s. C. Gilbert and Josephine Mary (Woodward) T.; m. Mignon Jane Beight, Aug. 1945; children: Robert Jr., Douglas Beight, Scott Woodward, Sondra Lee. BSME, Case Western Res. U., 1947. Commd. 2d lt. USAF, 1944, advanced through grades to lt. col., 1975; v.p., gen. mgr. Taylor Corp., 1947-53; mgr. quality assurance Spectra Physics Laserplane, Dayton, Ohio, 1976-89; pres., gen. mgr. CON-AV Corp., Tipp City, Ohio, 1989—; chief quality assurance staff on NASA Mercury Booster for USAF, Cape Canaveral, Fla., 1961-63; mgr. nuc. tng. weapons devel. USAF Weapons Lab., 1964-67; CAT I test mgr. F-111, 1967-68; instr. pilot C-7, tng. officer, Vietnam, 1969; project element monitor T-43, attache, A-37, C-130 aircraft, Pentagon, 1970-74; br. chief WPAFB, 1974-75. Advisor Aero Scis. Alternatives, Tipp City, 1990—. Lt. col. CAP. Decorated Air medal with three oak leaf clusters, DFC; named to Aviation Hall of Fame, 1986. Mem. VFW, Exptl. Aircraft Assn., Flying Angels, Inc. (pres. 1991), Masons, Beta Theta Pi (Case chpt. pres. 1942), Theta Tau, Early Birds. Episcopalian. Home: 5855 Us Route 40 Tipp City OH 45371-9419 Office: CON-AV Corp 5855 Us Route 40 Tipp City OH 45371-9419

TAYLOR, ROBERT MILES, police chief; b. Galesburg, Ill., Feb. 22, 1951; s. Miles Thomas and Pearl Violet (Bloom) T.; m. Karen Elizabeth Mustain, Sept. 11, 1971 (div. 1988); children: Angela Kay, John Robert, Rebecca Elizabeth; m. Deanne Jean Vinavich, Sept. 22, 1990; 1 stepchild, Sadie Renee Vinavich. Grad. police tng. inst., U. Ill., 1983. Police officer Villages of Woodhall & Cambridge, Ill., 1980-83; chief of police City of Toulon, Ill., 1983—. ESDA coord. Village of Andover, Ill., 1974-83; vol. Osco-Andover Fire Dept., 1974-83, Henry County (Ill.) Red Cross, 1980-93; mem. exec. com. Ill. Ctrl. Coll. Police Tng. Bd., Peoria, 1988—; mem. 911 adv. bd. Stark County, 1994-95. Mem. Jaycees. Democrat. Methodist. Home: 205 S Union St Toulon IL 61483 Office: Toulon Police Dept 120 N Franklin St Toulon IL 61483

TAYLOR, RONALD DEAN, psychologist, educator; b. Granite, Okla., Sept. 4, 1943; s. Roger Lafayette and Dortha Lee (Snow) T.; m. Joann Edith Irvine (div. Dec. 1984); 1 child, Tracy Kristin; m. Terry Susan Summers, Jan. 3, 1990; 1 child, Brian Sears. BS, Troy State Coll., 1966, MS, 1969; EdD, U. Houston, 1984. Cert. hypnotherapist. Guidance counselor Marathan (Fla.) Schs., 1966-69, Enterprise (Ala.) H.S., 1969-71; adminstr. ednl. programs Tex. Dept. Corrections, Huntsville, 1971-81; tng. cons. Houston, 1981-84; doctoral resident, tchg. asst., rsch. assoc. U. Houston, 1982-84, 86-88; asst. prof. psychology Dickinson (N.D.) State Coll., 1984-86; rsch. assoc. U. Houston, 1986-88; assoc. prof. psychology Columbia (Mo.) Coll., 1988—; vis. lectr. U. Houston, 1984-93, N.D. State U., Dickinson, 1984-86; cons. Priem Group, Dickinson, 1985-86; judge ann. rsch. forum U. Mo., Columbia, 1990, 94—. Author: A Time to Forget--Remembered, 1974; contbr. numerous articles to profl. jours. Named Hon. Lt. Col. Gov. Ala., 1969; recipient Award for Excellence in Tchg. Gov. Mo., 1994. Mem. Internat. Assn. Counselors and Therapists, Am. Ednl. Rsch. Assn., Assn. Tchr. Edn. (Mo. unit), Phi Delta Kappa. Unitarian. Office: Columbia Coll 1001 Rogers Columbia MO 65216

TAYLOR, RONALD LEE, school administrator; b. Urbana, Ill., Nov. 11, 1943; s. Lee R. and Katherine L. (Becker) T.; m. Patricia D. Fitzsimmons, Mar. 10, 1973; children: Jamie, Lara, Meredith, Dana. AB, Harvard U., 1966; MBA, Stanford U., 1971. Asst. contr. Bell & Howell, Chgo., 1971-73; pres. DeVry Inc./Keller Grad. Sch., Chgo., 1973—; bd. dirs. Precision Plastic, Columbia City, Ind., L. Karp & Sons, Elk Grove Village, Ill., Chernin's Shoes, Inc., Chgo. Pres. Hinsdale (Ill.) Sch. Bd., 1983-91; com. chmn. Ill. Bd. Higher Edn., Springfield, 1985—; state chmn. Employer Support of Guard and Res. Mem. Ill. State C. of C. (mem. edn. com. 1987—). Office: DeVry Inc 1 Tower Ln Villa Park IL 60181

TAYLOR, RUSSELL BENTON, mining executive; b. Eskridge, Kans., May 16, 1925; s. Bayard Charles and Eva May (Russell) T.; m. Arlene Marie Krehbiel, Aug. 14, 1959; 1 child, Bruce Charles. BSBA, U. Kans., 1949; JD, U. Kans, 1951. Asst. cashier Eskridge (Kans.) State Bank, 1951-57, cashier, 1957, pres., 1958-69, chmn., 1969-78; v.p., dir South Standard Mining Co., Salt Lake City, 1978—. Mayor City of Eskridge, Kans., 1959. Decorated Purple Heart. Mem. Kans. Bar Assn., Kiwanis, Masonic, Arab Shrine. Republican. Methodist. Home and Office: 6th & Locust Eskridge KS 66423

TAYLOR, SAMUEL DOUGLAS, psychiatrist; b. St. Helens, Ky., Nov. 28, 1924; s. Samuel Bailey and Ethel Marzine (Caudill) T.; m. Etta Lee Bayens, Aug. 1, 1950; children: Deborah Lynn Taylor Morgan, Elizabeth Ann Taylor Payne, Rebecca Leigh Taylor Watson. AB, U. Ky., 1947; MD, U. Louisville, 1951. Diplomate Am. Bd. Psychiatry and Neurology; cert. Am. Bd. Forensic Medicine. Gen. rotating intern St. Anthony's Hosp., Louisville, 1951-52; pvt. practice, Henderson, Ky., 1953-74; dir. lab. svcs. Henderson Clinic, 1958-74; chief staff Meth. Community Hosp., Henderson, 1963-65; resident in psychiatry Mental Health Inst., Cherokee, Iowa, 1976-79, chief adult female svcs., 1980-82, dir. psychiat. tng., 1982-89, dir. clin. svcs., 1989—. With USNR, 1942-45, PTO. Mem. AMA, Am. Psychiat. Assn., Iowa Psychiat. Soc., Alpha Omega Alpha. Democrat. Episcopalian. Home: 1230 W Cedar St Cherokee IA 51012-1511 Office: Mental Health Inst Cherokee IA 51012

TAYLOR, THERESA EVERETH, registered nurse, artist; b. Carthage, N.Y., Aug. 9, 1938; d. Michael Patrick and Angelina (Cerroni) Evereth; m. James Edgar Taylor II, Mar. 12, 1966; children: Britt, Priscilla, Blackwell. Diploma in nursing, House of Good Samaritan Sch. Nursing, Watertown, N.Y., 1959; BFA summa cum laude, Ursuline Coll., 1992, postgrd., 1996—. RN, N.Y., Ohio. Home health nurse DON Brason's Willcare, Cleve., 1995—. Exhbns. in group shows. Pres. Wasmer Gallery Coun., Pepper Pike, Ohio, 1992-96; clk. vestry St. Christophers by the River, Gates Mills, 1979-81; treas. Welcome Wagon, Chesterland, Ohio, 1984-85; vol. artist Cleve. Ctr. Contemporary Art, 1993—; hospice vol.; art therapy intern. Home: 12060 Caves Rd Chesterland OH 44026-2104 Office: 6151 Wilson Mills Highland Heights OH 44143

TAYLOR, THOMAS HUGH, lawyer; b. South Bend, Ind., Apr. 27, 1958; s. Jerome and Carol Ellen (Duthie) T.; m. Alison Kay Handrow, Mar. 11, 1978; children: James Christopher, Pamela Marie. BA, U. Wis., 1980, JD, 1982. Bar: Wis. Judge advocate U.S. Army, Ft. Knox, Ky., 1983-86; assoc. LaFollette & Sinykin, Madison, Wis., 1986-90, ptnr., 1991-93; asst. atty. gen. Wis. Dept. Justice, Madison, 1993-95; exec. asst. and gen. counsel Wis. Dept. Commerce, Madison, 1995, dep. sec. and gen. counsel, 1995—. Mem. Rep. Party, Madison, 1995; dir., coun. mem. Good Shepherd Luth. Ch., Madison, 1988-91, 95—. Decorated Svc. medal U.S. Army. Mem. Wis. Bar Assn. Office: Wis Dept Commerce 123 W Washington Ave Madison WI 53707

TAYLOR, TIMOTHY ALAN, elementary education educator; b. Newark, Ohio, Mar. 19, 1958; s. Elliott Ronald and Betty Lou (Hartsough) T. BS in Edn., Ohio State U., 1979, MS in Natural Resources, 1986, postgrad., 1986—. Cert. elem. tchr., K-12 spl. edn. tchr., Ohio. Learning disabilities resource tchr. Franklin Local Schs., Roseville, Ohio, 1980-86, tchr. gifted edn., 1985-87, elem. tchr., 1986-88, tchr. sci. and outdoor edn., 1988—; facilitator Project Learning Tree, 1982—, Project WILD, 1984—; instr. water safety various pools, Licking County, Ohio, 1982—. Contbr. articles to profl. jours. Fiscal agt. Muskingum County Soil and Water Conservation Dist., 1988-90, chmn., 1990—; bd. dirs. Licking County chpt. ARC, Newark, 1988-90; chmn. Nat. Envirothon Competition, 1989-90, Nat. Envirothon Steering Com., 1990-93. Recipient Conservation Tchr. of Yr. award Muskingum Soil and Water Conservation Dist., 1987, 90, Svc. award Licking County chpt., ARC, 1989, Educators award for disting. svc. Ohio Alliance for Environ., 1990, Friends of Sci. award Sci. Edn. Coun. Ohio, 1996. Home: 397 Myrtle Ave Newark OH 43055-3118 Office: Franklin Local Schs 76 W Athens Rd Roseville OH 43777-1044

TAYLOR, WILLIAM, state legislator. Mem. from dist. 63 Ohio State Ho. of Reps., 1995—. Address: 100 Eastwood Dr Norwalk OH 44857

TAYLOR, WILLIAM LEROY, physical chemist; b. Cin., July 16, 1931; s. William Leroy and Helen Louise (Koch) T.; m. Kathleen Bouchette Nelson, Aug. 23, 1952; children: William, Andrew, Daniel, Robert, Anthony, Thomas. BChemE, U. Cin., 1954, PhD, 1961. Cert. profl. engr., Ohio. Sr. rsch. chemist Monsanto Rsch. Corp.-Mound Lab., Miamisburg, Ohio, 1961-63, group leader, 1963-74, sci. fellow, 1974-88; sci. fellow EG&G Mound Applied Techs., Miamisburg, Ohio, 1988-92, now cons.; prof. chemistry U. Cin., 1984—. Referee Jour. Chem. Physics, The Phys. Rev., Jour. Physics B.; contbr. 75 articles to profl. jours. 1st lt. U.S. Army, 1954-57. Proctor & Gamble fellow, 1960-61. Mem. Am. Phys. Soc., Am. Chem. Soc., Hyde Park Golf and Country Club (gov. 1973, sec. 1974-75), Camargo Racquet Club, Sigma Alpha Epsilon. Presbyterian. Office: EG&G Mound Applied Techs PO Box 3000 Miamisburg OH 45343-3000

TAYLOR, WILLIAM ROBERT, engineer; b. Williamson, W.Va., May 19, 1950; s. Joseph Arthur and Rose (McNeally) T.; m. Janice Louise Taylor, Apr. 16, 1983; children: Patricia Lynn, Gwendolyn Ann, Amy Elizibeth. BSME, U. Cin., 1979. Lic. comml. pilot; cert. energy mgr. With Cin. Milacron, Cin., 1970-76; applications and sales engr. Corp. Equipment Co., Cin., 1976-84; pres. tech. dir. Aetna Equipment Co., Cin., 1984-87; dir. applications engr. Mut. Energy Products, Cin., 1987-91; sales engr. Koolant Koolers, Kalamazoo, Mich., 1991—. Mem. ASHRAE (Energy award 1985), ASME, Assn. Energy Engrs. (cert.), Internat. Aerobatic Assn. Home: 8901 Paw Paw Ln Cincinnati OH 45236-2135 Office: Koolant Koolers Inc 8901 Paw Paw Ln Cincinnati OH 45236-2135

TAYON, JEFFREY EARL, engineering and design executive; b. St. Louis, June 19, 1963; s. James Edward and Frances Kay (Brooks) T.; m. Janna Lynn Burrell, Nov. 2, 1985; children: Jenna Lea, James Earl, Joel Edward. Student, Moberly Area C.C., 1981-92. Apprentice plumber Tayon Plumbers, Inc., St. Louis, 1979-81; tool crib attendant Orbco Mfg. Co., Moberly, Mo., 1981; with Orscheln Co., Moberly, 1981-83, draftsman, 1983-86, R&D engr., 1986, design engr., 1986-88, lead design engr., 1988-90, mgr.

lever design, 1990-94; mgr. advanced cable devel. Dura Automotive Systems, Moberly, 1994—. Patentee brake apparatus with controlled flyback, electro-mechanical park brake, in-line adjuster, non-jamming self-adj pawl and ratchet mech., method and apparatus for terminating wire or other elongated generally rigid elements. Chmn. youth coun. 1st Assembly of God, Moberly, 1982-83; trustee Grace Bapt. Ch., Moberly, 1986—. Republican. Home: RR 2 Box 73A Moberly MO 65270-9605 Office: Dura Automotive Systems Inc 1600A N Morley Moberly MO 65270

TEACHOUT, NOREEN RUTH, writer; b. Oak Park, Ill., July 12, 1939; d. Anselm Uriel and R. Lydia (Bagne) Asp; m. Willem Heyneker, Nov. 20, 1958 (dec. 1968); children: Carolyn Heyneker Fors, Diana Heyneker Olds; m. Richard Kenneth Teachout, Jan. 21, 1966 (div. 1982); children: Jill, Janelle. BS, U. Minn., 1965; postgrad., Am. Inst. Holistic Theology, 1996—. Tchr. Bloomington (Minn.) Pub. Schs., 1965-85; writer, pubr., CEO The Peace Curriculum, Mpls., 1986—; educator Stockton & Franks Chiropractors, Burnsville, Minn., 1986-92; edn. svcs. dept. coord. Dame Comms., Plymouth, Minn., 1990—; cons., workshop leader Dame Comms.; writer U. Calif., Berkeley, 1967, Environ. Sci. Ctr., Mpls., 1968-69; educator, presenter Women's World Peace Conf., Dallas, 1988, World Peace Conf., San Jose, Costa Rica, 1989, 92; sponsor Therapeutic Humor Inst. Minn., Colo., 1996; dir. Wellness NOW, A Learning Place, Colo., 1996. Author curriculum programs, health and revitalization programs.

TEBBE, FRANCIS SYLVESTER, academic administrator; b. Batesville, Ind., Oct. 8, 1948; s. Cleophus William and Mary Elizabeth (Moll) T. BA, Duns Scotus Coll., 1971; MDiv, St. Leonard Sch. Theology, 1975; MEd, Boston Coll., 1982; DD, Andover Newton Theol. Sch., 1986. Ordained priest Roman Cath. Ch., 1975. Assoc. pastor St. Michael Parish, Southfield, Mich., 1975-78; faculty Good Counsel H.S., Chgo., 1978-79; assoc. pastor Holy Family Parish, Albuquerque, 1979; acting pastor St. Teresa Parish, Grants, N.Mex., 1980; dir. adult edn. Archdiocese of Boston, 1980-85; dir. continuing edn. Cath. Theol. Union, Chgo., 1985-90; assoc. dir. Inst. for Ch. Life, Notre Dame, Ind., 1990-93; v.p. Madonna U., Livonia, Mich., 1993—; chairperson Coun. Ongoing Formation Dirs. Franciscan Order, 1991—; priest, cons. Bishops' Com. for Priestly Life and Ministry, 1992—; pres. Nat. Orgn. for Continuing Edn. of Roman Cath. Clergy, 1992—. Editor: Church Divinity 1991-92, 1992, Handbook for Continuing Formation of Priests, 1994; dir. video The Rural Parish: Retrieving Our Future, 1992. Recipient Cmty. Svc. award City of Southfield, Mich., 1978. Mem. Assn. Profs. and Rschrs. in Religious Edn., Religious Edn. Assn., Nat. Assn. Ch. Pers. Adminstrs., Assn. Theol. Field Educators, Nat. Mentoring Assn., Nat. Coalition on Cath. Preaching. Democrat. Office: Madonna Univ 36600 Schoolcraft Rd Livonia MI 48150

TECOS, GEORGE P., engineering executive; b. Trikala, Greece, June 29, 1935; came to U.S., 1960; BS, Tech. Sch. Greece, 1958; MS, Wayne State U., 1978, postgrad. Chief elec. engr. Am. Simflex, Madison Hts., Mich., 1987-90; mgr. Acme Mfg., Madison Hts., 1991—. Contbr. articles to profl. jours. Home: 1237 Balfour St Grosse Pointe MI 48230-1019

TEDESCO, SUSAN MARY, pharmacy technician; b. Chgo., Sept. 22, 1954; d. Edmund L. and Viola M. (Cote) T. BA, U. St. Thomas, Houston, 1976. Cert. pharmacy technician. Sr. pharmacy technician, intravenous specialist Children's Meml. Hosp., Chgo., 1978—; pres., cons. Aseptech, Inc., Chgo., 1989—; instr., pharmacy technician educator South Suburban Coll., 1993—. Mem. Ill. Coun. Health-System Pharmacists (rep. bd. dirs. 1984-88, voting mem. bd. dirs. 1990-92, Pres.'s award 1987). Home: 2245 N Magnolia Ave Chicago IL 60614-3103 Office: Children's Meml Med Ctr 2300 N Childrens Plz Chicago IL 60614-3318

TEEPELL, DAVID G., U.S. airforce firefighter; b. Syracuse, N.Y., Nov. 13, 1955; s. George H. and Marjorie E. (Worden) T.; m. Sandra L. Horan, Jan. 8, 1977; children: Jeffery, Tabatha. BS in Instructional Tech., C.C. of A.F., Scott AFB, Ill. Cert. fire officer II, instr. III. Firefighter USAF, Mt. Laguna, Calif., 1977-79; fire inspector USAF, Spokane, Wash., 1979-83; firefighter, crew chief USAF, Gelena, Alaska, 1983-84; asst. chief for tng. USAF, Colo. Springs, 1984-89; asst. chief for tech. svc. USAF, Iraklion Crete, 1989-91; asst. chief for ops. 375 CES USAF, Scott AFB, Ill., 1991-94, asst. chief for tng. 375 CES, 1994—; safety officer 375 CES, Scott AFB, 1994—, wing evaluator. MSG USAF, 1977—. Mem. Air Force Segents Assn., Vets. of Fgn. Wars. Republican. Roman Catholic. Home: 604 W Jefferson St O'Fallon IL 62269

TEETERS, JOSEPH LEE, mathematician, consultant; b. Caney, Kans., Dec. 10, 1934; s. Jesse L. and Marie (Tapper) T.; m. Janet L. Hamm, June 18, 1984; children: Jeffrey, Susan, Christoper. Student, Colo. Sch. Mines, 1956, U. Kans., 1957; MA in Math., U. No. Colo., 1960, EdD in Math., 1968. Cert. secondary sch. tchr., Colo., Ill., hazard waste profl., OSHA. Exploration geologist Ohio Oil Co., Rawlings, Wyo., 1956-57; instr. Stout State U., Menomonie, Wis., 1960-62; asst. prof. Baker U., Baldwin City, Kans., 1962-65; temp. instr. U. No. Colo., Greeley, 1965-68; asst. prof. Western State Coll., Gunnison, Colo., 1968-69; prof. U. Wis., Eau Claire, 1969-88; cons. assoc. Delphi Data, Corona, Calif., 1989—; land surveying cons. Donaldson Engring., Menomonie, 1960-62; land boundary cons. ACLU, Eau Claire, 1974; lectr., spkr., cons. in field. Author: Creating Escher-Type Drawings, 1977; designer tessellation art; contbr. cover designs for profl. publs. Active Forest Lake (Ill.) Cmty. Assn., 1990—; sr. citizen trainer Marathon Challenge, St. Louis, 1994; mem. Golden Colo. Civic Orch., 1956; unicyclist Kans. State Sunflower State Games. Grantee NSF, 1965, U. New Orleans, 1987. Mem. Internat. Assn. for Math. Geology, Stanton County Kans. Hist. Assn., Santa Fe Trail Assn., Kans. Trails Assn., Am. Volkssport Assn. (triathlete), Colo. Sch. of Mines Assn., Tiblow Trailblazers (sports cons. 1994—), Kappa Kappa Psi, Sigma Gamma Epsilon, Phi Delta Kappa. Home: 21635 W Ravine Rd Lake Zurich IL 60047 Office: Delphi Data 21635 W Ravine Rd Lake Zurich IL 60047

TEETS, JIM, manufcturing executive; b. Loraine, Ohio, Aug. 10, 1954. Tool maker Baver Industries, Loraine, Ohio, 1972-76; dept. supr. Bond Metal Products, Loraine, 1976-79; model shop supr. Ridge Tool Co., Elyria, Ohio, 1979—. Office: Ridge Tool Co 400 Clark St Elyria OH 44035-6108

TEGGE, FRANK ALLEN, stock brokerage company executive; b. Dearborn, Mich., Oct. 29, 1942; s. Frank Alfred and Marjorie Mildred (Allen) T.; 1 child from previous marriage, Kurt Eric; m. Sophia Branoff. BA, Albion Coll., 1964; postgrad., Garrett Theol. Sem., Evanston, Ill., 1965-66, Loyola U., Chgo., 1966-67, Wayne State U., 1967-68; cert. investment mgmt. analyst, U. Pa., 1992. Registered investment advisor. Stock broker Manley, Bennett, McDonald & Co., Lansing, Mich., 1970-73, ltd. ptnr., 1973-75, ptnr., 1975-82, sr. v.p., 1982-84; v.p. Thomson McKinnon Securities, Inc., Lansing, 1984-89; 1st v.p. McDonald and Co. Securities, Inc., East Lansing, Mich., 1989-94, sr. v.p., 1994—; bd. dirs. Manley, Bennett, McDonald, Detroit. Bd. trustees Cen. United Meth. Ch., Lansing, 1985-88, Woldumar Nature Ctr., Lansing, 1986-92, R.E. Olds Mus., Lansing, 1984-86, Chief Okemos Coun., Boy Scouts Am.Trust Fund, Lansing, 1988—, coun. exec. com., 1989—, dist. com., asst. scoutmaster, Wharton Ctr. for Arts, Mich. State U., 1993—; mem. investment com. YMCA, Lansing, 1987-93; bd. dirs. Mid-Mich. chpt. ARC, 1993—; mem. long range planning com. Capital area United Way, 1994—; mem. deans com. coun. Coll. Arts and Letters Mich. State U., 1995—. Decorated Bronze star, Purple Heart, Army Commendation medal with oak leaf cluster; named One of 100 Best New-Style Brokers of 1994, Fin. Planning on Wall St. mag., 1994. Mem. Internat. Assn. Fin. Planners, Investment Mgmt. Cons. Assn., Comdrs. Club of Mich. (pres. 1984), Rotary (bd. dirs. 1989-92, pres. 1992-93). Republican. Home: 1400 Dennison Rd East Lansing MI 48823-2180 Office: McDonald and Co Securities 4660 S Hagadorn Rd Ste 190 East Lansing MI 48823-5353

TEI, TAKURI, accountant; b. Korea, Feb. 25, 1924; s. Gangen and Isun (Song) T.; came to U.S., 1952, naturalized, 1972; diploma Concordia Theol. Sem., 1959; B.D., Eden Theol. Sem., 1965; M.Ed., U. Mo., 1972; m. Maria M. Ottwaska, Dec. 1, 1969; 1 dau., Sun Kyung Lee. Partner, Madeleine Ottwaska & Assos., St. Louis, 1968—; pres. TMS Tei Enterprises Inc., Webster Groves, Mo., 1969—; instr. Forest Park Community Coll. Mem. Am. Coll. Enrolled Agts. (pres. 1976—), Am. Accounting Assn., Am. Taxation Assn., Assn. Asian Studies, NAACP. Republican. Lutheran. Home and Office: 7529 Big Bend Blvd Saint Louis MO 63119-2103

TEITSMA, JACK A., psychologist; b. Grand Rapids, Mich., July 25, 1959; s. Jack E. and Dena (Koenes) T.; m. Doris M. Jabaay-Van Byssum, Nov. 14, 1990; children: Jack Austin, Grant Van Byssum, Jessica Van Byssum, Taylor Van Byssum. MDiv, Western Theol. Sem., 1985; MA, Western Mich. U., 1987; D of Psychology, Ill. Sch. Profl. Psychology, 1994. Lic. psychologist, Ill., Ind. Dir. clin. tng. The Menta Group, Oak Brook, Ill., 1992—; cons. Park Forest (Ill.) Acad., 1992—, deLacey Family Ctr., Carpentersville, Ill., 1993—. Republican.

TEMEYER, TODD JOHN, pizza company executive; b. Waterloo, Iowa, Apr. 28, 1963; s. John Leonard and Louise Adeline (Rhines) T. AA, Ctrl. Coll., 1983. CEO, owner Old Mill Pizza Co., Independence, Iowa, 1988—; CEO, ptnr. Graphic Images and Mississippi Pizza Factory; CEO Mississippi Pizza Pie Factory, 1993-96. Republican. Methodist. Home: 414 1st St W Independence IA 50644 Office: Old Mill Pizza Co 416 1st St W Independence IA 50644-2505

TEMLITZ, SYLVIA (SYLVIA HAAS), gerontology nurse, educator; b. Indpls., May 25, 1947; d. William B. and Ann (Diersman) Jones; children: Sherwin Haas, Scott Haas. AS, Willmar C.C., Worthington, Minn., 1987; BA in Nursing, Metro State U., St. Paul, 1993; postgrad. Sch. Nursing, Augustana Coll., Sioux Falls. Clin. and staff nurse Worthington Med. Ctr.; dir. nursing svcs. Lake Haven Nursing Home, Worthington; insvc. dir., care plan coord., acting DON Colonial Manor Nursing Home, Lakefield, Minn.; pub. health nurse home health sect. Cottonwood Jackson Cmty. Nursing Svc., 1990-95; continuous quality improvement and infection contrl nurse Sogge Good Samaritan Home, Windom, Minn., 1995—; instr. nursing asst. program Southwestern Tech. Coll.; mem. bd. continuous quality improvement and infection control Sogge Good Samaritan Home, Windom, Minn. Office: 705 6th St Windom MN 56101

TEMPLE, DONALD, allergist, dermatologist; b. Chgo., May 21, 1933; s. Samuel Leonard and Matilda Eve (Riff) T.; m. Sarah Rachel Katz, Sept. 29, 1957; children: Michael A., Matthew D., Madeline B. AB in Biology cum laude, Harvard U., 1954; MD, U. Chgo., 1958. Am. Bd. Allergy and Immunology, Am. Bd. Dermatology, Nat. Bd. Med. Examiners; lic. Intern Michael Reese Hosp., Chgo., 1958-59; resident in dermatology U. Chgo. Hosps., 1959-62; clin. asst., dept. dermatology Boston U. Sch. Medicine, 1963-64; clin. instr. dermatology Stanford U. Sch. Medicine, 1965; preceptee in allergy Offices of Leon Unger, M.D., and Donald Unger, M.D., Chgo., 1965-69; practice medicine specializing in allergy and dermatology Des Plaines, Ill., 1969-76; mem. allergy dept. Glen Ellyn (Ill.) Clinic, 1972—; mem. dermatology and allergy staff, Louis A. Weiss Hosp., Chgo., 1965-73, allergy sect. Loyola U. Med. Ctr., Maywood, Ill., 1977-80, exec. and contract medicine coms. Glen Ellyn; clin. asst. prof. dermatology Abraham Lincoln Sch. Medicine, U. Ill., 1972-75; clin. asst. prof. medicine sect. allergy and dermatology, Loyola U., 1977-85; mem. staff Cen. DuPage Hosp., Winfield, Ill., 1973—, Glen Oaks Med. Ctr., Glendale Heights, Ill., Glendale Heights Community Hosp., 1980-92. Contbr. articles to profl. jours. Bd. dirs. Am. Lung Assn., DuPage, McHenry counties, 1980—; chmn. Contract Medicine, HMO Com., Glen Ellyn Clinic, 1985, mem. exec. com., 1988-92. Fellow Am. Coll. Chest Physicians, Am. Assn. Cert. Allergists, Am. Coll. Allergists, Am. Acad. Allergy, Ill. Soc. Allergy and Clin. Immunology, Chgo. Dermatol. Soc.; mem. AMA, Ill. State Med. Soc., DuPage County Med. Soc., Chgo. Med. Soc. Jewish. Home: 110 E Delaware Pl Apt 2004 Chicago IL 60611-1440 Office: Glen Ellyn Clinic 454 Pennsylvania Ave Glen Ellyn IL 60137-4402

TEMPLETON, BARBARA ANN, civil engineering technologist; b. Miller, S.D., Aug. 26, 1954; d. Edward Eugene and Helen Roxanne (Siegling) Labor; m. David James Templeton Jr., Aug. 7, 1976; 1 child, Brian James. AS, U. S.D., 1974. Staff asst. S.D. Dept. Water, Pierre, 1978-81; civil engring. tech. U.S. Army C.E., Pierre, 1981—. Active area PTA. Mem. NOW, Nat. Abortion Rights Action League. Democrat. Lutheran. Home: 1701 Flag Mountain Dr Pierre SD 57501-2811

TEMPLIN, JILL L., physical therapist assistant; b. Olney, Ill., Dec. 9, 1967; d. John Jr. and Rosa Lea (Beaumont) Howard; m. James R. Templin III, July 16, 1994. AS in Phys. Therapy Asst., Vincennes U., 1988. Lic. phys. therapy asst., Ind. Staff phys. therapist asst. Ind. U. Hosp., Indpls., 1988, Deaconess Hosp., Evansville, Ind., 1988—; phys. therapist asst. Riverfront Therapeutics, Vincennes, Ind., 1992—. CPR instr., Am. Heart Assn., 1990—. Mem. Am. Phys. Therapy Assn. Home: PO Box 464 Vincennes IN 47591

TENCZAR, ALAN J., podiatrist, pharmacist; b. Chgo., May 15, 1956; s. Theodore R. and Jean Ann Tenczar. BS in Pharmacy, Drake U., 1979; BS in Biology, DPM, School Coll. Podiatric Medicine, Chgo., 1983. Diplomate Am. Bd. Podiatric Orthopedics, Am. Coll. Foot and Ankle Surgeons, Am. Bd. Podiatric Surgery. Pvt. practice Resurrection Hosp., Chgo., 1983—; mem. staff St. Mary of Hazareth Hosp. Ctr., Oak Park Hosp.; mem. coun. on foot care Am. Diabetes Assn., 1987—; cons. Atlas of Foot Surgery, Vol. 2, 1986. Fellow Am. Coll. Foot Surgeons; mem. Am. Podiatric Med. Assn., Ill. Podiatric Med. Assn., Polish Am. Pharmacists Assn. Office: 1788 Sycamore St Des Plaines IL 60018-2267

TENER, CAROL JOAN, retired secondary education educator; b. Cleve., Feb. 10, 1935; d. Peter Paul and Mamie Christine (Dombrowski) Manusack; m. Dale Keith Tener, Feb. 13, 1958 (div. Aug. 1991); children: Dean Robert, Susan Dawn. Student, Cleve. Mus. Art, 1948-53, Cleve. Art Inst., 1953-54; BS in Edn. cum laude, Kent State U., 1957; MS in Supervision, Akron U., 1974; postgrad., Kent State U., 1964, 81, 88-90, Akron U., 1975, 79, John Carroll U., 1982, 83, 85-86, Ohio U., 1987, Baldwin Wallace Coll., 1989. Cert. permanent K-12 tchr., Ohio. Stenographer Equitable Life Iowa, Cleve., 1953-54; tchr. elem. art Cuyahoga Falls (Ohio) Bd. Edn., 1957-58, 62-63, 1965-68, tchr. jr. h.s., 1968-69; tchr. h.s. Brecksville (Ohio)-Broadview Heights Sch. Dist., 1969-94; chmn. dept. art Brecksville-Broadview Heights (Ohio) H.S., 1979-94; ret., chmn. curriculum devel., 1982, 89; instr. for children Kent State U., 1956; advisor, prodr. cmty. svc. in art Brecksville Broadview Heights Bd. of Edn., 1969-94; former tchr. recreation and adult art edn. 1967-68, City of Cuyahoga Falls, 1967-68; com. mem. North Ctrl. Evaluation Com., Nordonia City, Ohio, 1978, Solon City, Ohio, 1989; chmn. north ctrl. evaluation com. Garfield Heights H.S., 1991; chair pilot program curriculum devel. com. in art/econs. Brecksville-Broadview Heights H.S., 1985, 86. Contbr. articles to newspapers, brochures, mags.; commd. artist for mural Brecksville City's Kids Quarters, 1994, Christopher Columbus/John Glen portraits in relief commemorating Columbus Day, 1961, Wooster (Ohio) Products Co. Chmn. Artmart Invitational Exhibit PTA, 1982-94; active Meals on Wheels, 1995-96, Brecksville Broadview, Cancer, 1993-95, Leukemia, 1995, Heart Disease collection, 1995, Stow-Glen Assisted Living Visitations, 1994-95, NCR Assisted Living transp. provision to hosps. and dr. in neighboring county; trustee Gettysburg Devel. Block Group Parma, 1995-96, Kids Quarters, 1994. Recipient Ohio Coun. on Econ. Edn. award, 1985-86, award for significant svc. to cmty. Retired and Sr. Vol. Program of USA, 1996; Pres.'s scholar Kent State U., 1954-57. Mem. ASCD, Nat. Art Edn. Assn., Ohio Ret. Tchrs. Assn., Internat. Platform Assn., Brecksville Edn. Assn., Acad. Econ. Edn., Cleve. Mus. Art, NAFE, Nat. Mus. Women in Arts, S.W. Area Retired Educators (program chair 1996—), Phi Delta Kappa Pi. Roman Catholic. Home: 7301 Sagamore Rd Parma OH 44134-5732

TENHOUSE, ART, state representative, farmer; b. Dec. 27, 1950; m. Sharon Roberts; children: Kate, Andy, Adam. BS in Agrl. Sci., Econs., U. Ill., 1973, MBA in Fin. Acctg., 1974. CPA, Ill. Cash mgr. DeKalb, Inc., 1973-74; ptnr. Four-Ten Famrs; state rep. 96th dist. State of Ill., 1989—; chmn. pub. safety and infrastructure appropriations com. State of Ill., vice chmn. agr. and conservation coms., transp. and motor vehicles, human svc. and health care, legis. audit commn.; bd. dirs. U. Ill. Coll. Agr. Alumni Assn., Paloma Exch. Bank; instr. agrl. credit and fin. John Wood C.C. Burton Twp. clk., 1981-89; chmn. Adams County Farm Bur. Polit. Involvement Fund, 1988-89; 4-H leader Burton Flyers 4-H Club; state young farmers com. Farm Bur., Adams County, 1979-80, treas., 1983-85, state utility spl. study com., 1986, legis. chmn., 1985-89, past. pres., v.p., 1985-89. Home: PO Box 1161 Quincy IL 62306-1161 Office: Rep Art Tenhouse 640 Maine Quincy IL 62347

TEN HOVEN, JAMES ALAN, project analyst; b. Chgo., May 11, 1951; s. James John and Jeannette (Korte) Ten H.; m. Patricia Ann Harrison, Feb. 5, 1972; children: Angelette, Stephenie. Student, Glendale (Ariz.) C.C., 1970-71; Diploma in Digital Electronics, DeVry Inst., Chgo., 1978; AAS in Elec. Power Tech., Lakeshore Tech. Coll., Cleveland, Wis., 1984; BS in Mgmt., Silver Lake Coll., 1996. Gen. lab technician Kohler (Wis.) Co., 1978-84, CAD analyst, 1984-86, engring. analyst, 1986-93; chmn. elec. power adv. com. Lakeshore Tech. Coll., 1982-90; instr. AutoCAD AME Kohler Co., 1992. Patentee in field. Home: 86 Dewey St Sheboygan Falls WI 53085-1210 Office: Kohler Co 444 Highland Dr Kohler WI 53044-1515

TENNEFOS, JENS JUNIOR, state legislator; b. Fargo, N.D., Feb. 15, 1930; s. Jens Peterson and Iva M. (Gilbraith) T.; m. Jeanne P. Quamme, 1960; children: Daniel J., David A., Judie A., Mary J. Student, N.D. State U., 1947-49. Pres. Tennefos Constrn., 1951-74, Tennefos Enterprises, 1975—; mem. N.D. Ho. of Reps., 1974-76; mem. N.D. Senate, 1977-96, chmn. fin. and taxation com., mem. transp. com., pres. pro tempore, 1995-97; past chmn., bd. trustees Constrn. Employees Pension, Trust and Health and Welfare Plan, capitol ground com., 1976-95. Featured in front page picture and article Modern Hwy. Mag., 1960, Local Guide Mag., 1980. Bd. regents Oak Grove Luth. H.S., 1970—, past pres.; bd. dirs. Friendship. Mem. Assn. Gen. Contractors N.D. (hon., past pres., Disting. Svc. Citation 1969), Elks, Am. Legion, Sons of Norway, Masons, Sigma Alpha Epsilon. Office: 2709 Springfield St Bismarck ND 58501-0965 Home: 310 8th St S Apt 304 Fargo ND 58103-4925*

TENNYSON, JOSEPH ALAN, engineering executive; b. St. Paul, May 28, 1958; s. Walter Arnold and Carol Jean (Hauenstein) T.; m. Patricia Ann Jordan, Aug. 29, 1981; children: Alexa Jordan, Ryley Joseph. BSBA, U. Minn., 1981, AA in Lib. Arts, 1981. Fin. planner K.A. Richard & Assocs., St. Paul, 1981-83; reporting analyst Control Data Corp., Mpls., 1983-84, systems analyst, 1984-85, fin. analyst, 1985-86; dir. ops. Michaud, Cooley, Erickson, Mpls., 1986-89, corp. sec., 1986—, v.p. fin. and adminstrn., 1989-93, prin., exec. v.p., 1993—; bd. dirs. Northwestern Nat. Life Health Network. Mem. Leadership Mpls., 1988-89; bd. dirs. United Arts Partnership Fund, 1996—; mem. assembly com. on intercollegiate athletics U. Minn., 1994—. Mem. Mpls. Club, U. Minn. Alumni Assn. (nat. bd. dirs. 1995—), Sigma Chi (Grand Consul citation 1983, L.G. Balfour award 1981), Omicron Delta Kappa, Order of Omega. Home: 5252 Saint Albans Bay Rd Shorewood MN 55331-8635 Office: Michaud Cooley Erickson 333 S 7th St Ste 1200 Minneapolis MN 55402-2422

TENORIO, RAFAEL ALBERTO, economics educator, researcher; b. Lima, Peru, Nov. 21, 1960; came to U.S., 1984; s. José Enrique and Norma Esther (Coriat) T.; m. Gabriella Amalia Bucci, May 26, 1990; 1 child, Alessandro. BA, U. Lima, 1981; MA, Johns Hopkins U., 1986, PhD, 1990. researcher The World Bank, 1986. Contbr. book chpts. to New Palgrave Dictionary, 1992, International Trade Issues of the Russian Federation, 1995; contbr. articles to Rev. of Econs. and Stats., Managerial and Decision Econs., Jour. of Population Econs., Jour. Internat. Econs. Named Outstanding Scholar, Ctrl. Bank of Peru, Lima, 1982; recipient departmental fellowships Johns Hopkins U., 1985-89; rsch. grantee U. Notre Dame, 1990-95; grantee Lilly Endowment, 1995. Mem. Am. Econ. Assn., Econometric Soc., Royal Econ. Soc., Western Econ. Assn. Office: Dept Fin U Notre Dame Notre Dame IN 46556

TEPE, ANN SILCOTT, library services professional; b. Parkersburg, W.Va., Nov. 7, 1946; d. Jesse Delbert and Imogene Kathryn (Lewis) Silcott; children: Dirk S., Chana B. BA, Marietta (Ohio) Coll., 1968; MEd, Ohio U., 1973. Cert. libr./media, reading, computer and English tchr., Ohio. Tchr. Marietta City Schs., 1968-69, Ft. Frye Schs., Beverly, Ohio, 1969-73; libr. supr. Warren Local Schs., Vincent, Ohio, 1973-75, Fort Frye Schs., 1975-84, Wolf Creek Schs., Waterford, Ohio, 1984-92; mgr. of edn. and tng. Follett Software Co., McHenry, Ill., 1992-96, dir. curriculum resource devel., 1996—; cons. edn. dept. Marietta Coll., 1981-85; del. People to People, People's Republic of China, 1985, People to People, Russia and Poland, 1992; adj. prof. Ashland (Ohio) U., 1988-92; presenter in field. Recipient Merit award Ohio Ednl. Libr. Media, 1991. Mem. ALA, Am. Assn. Sch. Librs., Libr. Media Assn. (pres. 1981-82), Phi Delta Kappa. Office: Follett Software Co 1391 Corporate Dr Mc Henry IL 60050-7040

TERBANC, BARBARA JOYCE, chemical abuse administrator; b. Utahville, Pa., Apr. 16, 1940; d. Frank and Katherine Delores (Poshedley) Lumanick; m. Richard Kralic, Aug. 20, 1960 (dec. Aug. 1974); children: Richard, David; m. Thomas Louis Terbanc, Oct. 10, 1975. Bookkeeper, office mgr. King Floor Coverings, Cleve., 1960-74; ednl. aide Parma (Ohio) City Schs., 1974-76; presch. sorker Bethel Temple Pre-Sch., Parma Heights, Ohio, 1977-79; asst. program mgr. Project CARE (Chem. Abuse Reduced by Edn.), Cleve., 1980—; com. mem. Ohio Goal 6 Subcom., Columbus, 1994—; preceptor, alcohol & drug addiction svcs. bd. Cuyahoga County, Cleve., 1993—. Co-editor: (manuel) Curriculum Recommendations, Alcohol & Druf Prevention: K-8. 1982. Mem. cmty. leadership com. Am. Heart Assn., Brecksville, Ohio, 1994—; vol. Bellflower Agy., Cleve., 1993-94. Home: 14246 Sprague Rd Middleburg Heights OH 44130 Office: Project Care 8001 Brecksville Rd Brecksville OH 44141

TERBIZAN, DONNA JEAN, physiology educator; b. Cleve., Feb. 2, 1953; d. Eugene P. and Evelyn R. (Gauley) T. BS, Cleve. State U., 1976; MA, Ohio State U., 1978, PhD, 1982. Grad. asst. Ohio State U., Columbus, 1978-82; instr. N.D. State U., Fargo, 1982-85, asst. prof., 1986-94, assoc. prof., 1994—; dir. corp./cmty. fitness N.D. State U., 1986—; sports medicine cons. Dakota Clinic, Fargo, 1984—, coord. sports medicine, 1985-86. Contbr. articles to profl. jours. Fellow Am. Coll. Sports Medicine (exercise test technician, pres. Northland chpt. 1989); mem. AAHPERD (Honor award 1995), N.D. Assn. Health, Phys. Edn., Recreation and Dance (pres. 1991, Honor award 1993), Am. Softball Assn., Nat. Strength and Conditioning Assn., Dakota Am. Heart Assn. (pres. Fargo Metro chpt. 1989-91). Office: ND State U Bentson Bunker Fieldhouse Fargo ND 58105

TERKEL, STUDS (LOUIS TERKEL), author, interviewer; b. N.Y.C., May 16, 1912; s. Samuel and Anna (Finkel) T.; m. Ida Goldberg, July 2, 1939; 1 son, Dan. PhB, U. Chgo., 1932, JD, 1934. Stage appearances include Detective Story, 1950, A View From the Bridge, 1958, Light Up the Sky, 1959, The Cave Dwellers, 1960; moderator: (TV program) Studs Place, 1950-53, (radio programs) Wax Museum, 1945— (Ohio State Univ. award 1959, UNESCO Prix Italia award 1962), Studs Terkel Almanac, 1952—, Studs Terkel Show, Sta. WFMT-FM, Chgo.; master of ceremonies Newport Folk Festival, 1959, 60, Ravinia Music Festival, 1959, U. Chgo. Folk Festival, 1961, others; panel moderator, lectr., narrator films; author: (books) Giants of Jazz, 1957, Division Street: America, 1967, Hard Times: An Oral History of the Great Depression, 1970, Working: People Talk About What They Do All Day and How They Feel About What They Do, 1974 (Nat. Book award nomination 1975), Talking to Myself: A Memoir of My Times, 1977, American Dreams: Lost and Found, 1980, The Good War: An Oral History of World War II (Pulitzer prize in nonfiction 1985), Chicago, 1986, The Great Divide: Second Thoughts On The American Dream, 1988, Race: How Blacks and Whites Think and Feel About the American Obsession, 1992, Coming of Age, 1995; (play) Amazing Grace, 1959; also short stories. Named Communicator of Yr. U. Chgo. Alumni Assn., 1969. Office: WFMT Radio 5400 N St Louis Ave Chicago IL 60625

TERMINE, JOHN DAVID, biochemist; b. Bklyn., Sept. 25, 1938; s. Charles Angelo and Mary Rafael (Fiore) T.; m. Virginia Ann Galvin, Dec. 26, 1961; children: Mary, John, Theresa, Anne. BS, St. John's U., N.Y.C., 1960; MS, U. Md., 1963; PhD, Cornell U. Med. Coll., 1966. Asst. rsch. scientist Hosp. Spl. Surgery, N.Y.C., 1966-69, assoc. rsch. scientist, 1969-70; instr. biochemistry Cornell U. Med. Coll., N.Y.C., 1966-69, asst. prof. biochemistry, 1969-70; spl. rsch. fellow NIH, Bethesda, Md., 1970-73, rsch. biochemist, 1973-80, chief skeletal biol. sect., 1980-91, chief bone rsch. br., 1982-91; exec. dir. Eli Lilly and Co., Indpls., 1991-95; v.p. Lilly Rsch. Labs. Eli Lilly & Co., Indpls., 1995—; exec. com., bd. dirs. Internat. Conf. Calcium Regulating Hormones, 1989-95; adj. instr. Ind. U. Sch. Medicine, 1991—. Contbr. 175 articles to profl. jours.. Recipient Dirs. award NIH,

1983, Biol. Mineralization award Internat. Assn. for Dental Rsch., 1987. Mem. Am. Soc. Cell Biology, Am. Soc. Biochemistry and Molecular Biology, Biophys. Soc., Orthoped. Rsch. Soc., Am. Soc. Bone and Mineral Rsch. (councilor 1986-89), Internat. Assn. Dental Rsch. Office: Eli Lilly & Co Lilly Corp Ctr Dept Rsch Labs Indianapolis IN 46285

TERNUS, JEAN ANN, nursing educator; b. Columbus, Nebr., Feb. 29, 1944; d. Maurice Henry and Marcella (Huntemer) T. BS in Nursing, Mt. Marty Coll., 1966; MS, Kans. State U., 1977. RN Kans., Mo., Nebr. Staff nurse Brian Meml. Hosp., Lincoln, Nebr., 1966-67; staff nurse VA Hosp., Milw., 1967-69, Kansas City, Mo., 1969-72; nursing instr. Kansas City (Kans.) Community Coll., 1973—; cardiovascular nurse specialist Meth. Hosp., Houston, 1973. Mem. AAUW, NEA, AACN, Kans. State Nurses Assn. (pres. dist. II 1980-82, chair dist. newsletter 1980—, 2d v.p. 1986-90, 1st v.p. 1990-92, sect. dist. II 1993—, v.p. 1993-95), NLN, Gerontol. Nurses Assn., Kans. Nurses Found. (bd. dirs. 1990-91, sec. 1992—, pres.-elect 1995—), Sigma Theta Tau, Delta Kappa Gamma. Democrat. Roman Catholic. Home: 5342 Juniper Dr Shawnee Mission KS 66205-2225 Office: Kansas City CC 7250 State Ave Kansas City KS 66112-3003

TERP, DANA GEORGE, architect; b. Chgo., Nov. 5, 1953; s. George and June (Hansen) T.; m. Lynn Meyers, May 17, 1975; children: Sophia, Rachel. BA in Architecture, Washington U., St. Louis, 1974; postgrad., Yale U., 1975-76; MArch, Washington U., 1977. Registered architect, Ill., Calif., Fla. Architect Skidmore Owings & Merrill, Chgo., 1976, 1978-84, Terp Meyers Architects, Chgo., 1984—; prin. Arquitectonica Chgo. Inc., 1986—. Exhibited in group shows at Moming Gallery, Chgo., 1980, Printers Row Exhibit, 1980, Frumkin Struve Gallery, Chgo., 1981, Chgo. Art Inst., 1983; pub. in profl jours. including Progressive Architecture, Los Angeles Architect; work featured in various archtl books; exhibited 150 Yrs. of Chgo. Architecture. Bd. dirs. Architecture Soc. Art Inst. Chgo. Recipient hon. mention Chgo. Townhouse Competition, 1978, award Progressive Architecture mag., 1980, Archtl. Record Houses, 1989, GLOBAL Architecture Ga. Houses/26, 1989, Casa Vogue, 1989, 2d place award Burnham Prize Competition, 1991. Office: Terp Meyers Architects 919 N Michigan Ave Ste 2402 Chicago IL 60611-1601

TERPENING, VIRGINIA ANN, artist; b. Lewistown, Mo., July 17, 1917; d. Floyd Raymond and Bertha Edda (Rodifer) Shoup; m. Charles W. Terpening, July 5, 1951; 1 child by previous marriage, V'Ann Baltzelle Dlatrick. Studies with William Woods, Fulton, Mo., 1936-37; student Washington U. Sch. Fine Arts, St. Louis, 1937-40. Exhibited in one-woman shows at Culver-Stockton Coll., Canton, Mo., 1956, Creative Gallery, N.Y.C., 1968, The Breakers, Palm Beach, Fla., 1976; others; exhibited in group shows Mo. Ann., City Art Mus., St. Louis, 1956, 65, Madison Gallery, N.Y.C., 1960; Ligoa Duncan Gallery, N.Y.C., 1964, 78, Two Flags Festival of Art, Douglas, Ariz., 1975, 78-79, Internat. Art Exhibit, El Centro, Calif., 1977, 78, Salon des Nations, Paris, 1985, UN World Conference of Women, Narobi, Kenya, 1985, William Woods Coll., Fulton, Mo., 1992-95, La Junta Coll. Art League Internat., 1992, 94, Coffret Musee, Paris, 1995; represented in permanent collection Nat. Mus. Women in Art., 1990; lectr. on art; jurist for selection of art for exhibits Labelle (Mo.) Centennial, 1972; chmn. Centennial Art Show, Lewiston, 1971, Bicentennial, 1976; dir. exhibit high sch. students for N.E. Mo. State U., 1974; supt. ann. art show Lewis County (Mo.) Fair, 1975-90; executed Mississippi RiverBoat, oil painting presented to Pres. Carter by Lewis County Dem. Com., Canton, 1979. Mem. Lewistown Bicentennial Hist. Soc.; charter mem. Canton Area Arts Coun. N.E. Mo. Recipient cert. of merit Latham Found., 1960-63, Mo. Women's Festival Art, 1974, Bertrand Russell Peace Found., 1973, Gold Medallion award Two Flags Festival Art, 1975, Safeco purchase award El Centro (Calif.) Internat. Art exhibit, 1977, 1st pl. award LaJunta (Colo.) Fine Arts League, 1981, diploma Universita Delle Arti, Parma, Italy, 1981, Purchase award Two Flags Art Festival, 1981, award Assn. Conservation and Mo. Dept. Conservation Art Exhbt., 1982, Purchase award Canton Area Arts Coun., 1988, Colorado Springs Art Festival, 1989; paintings selected for Competition '84 Guide by Nat. Art Appreciation Soc., 1984; 1st pl. award New Orlean Internat. Art Exhibit, 1984, with Am. Women Artists at United Nations Conf. on Women, Nairobi, Kenya, 1985, Two Flags Festival of Art, 1986, Sunflower Judges award Harlin Mus., West Plains, Mo., 1994; named artist laureate, Nepenthe Mondi Soc., 1984, cert. on Arts for the Parks Nat., 1987. Mem. Artist Equity Assn., Inc., Internat. Soc. Artists, Internat. Platform Assn., Nat. Mus. Women in Art (charter), Canton Area Art Coun. (Purchase award 1988), Animal Protection Inst. Mem. Disciples of Christ Ch.

TERRILL, IVAN DALE, accounting educator; b. Cambridge Springs, Pa., Dec. 20, 1936; s. Everett Thomas and Iva Elvirda (Smeltzer) T.; m. Janice Joyce Voge, Aug. 25, 1962; 1 child, Thomas Earl. Student, Ball State U., 1957, 60; BS, Anderson U., Anderson, Ind., 1960; MS, U. Wis., 1968, postgrad., 1970-88; postgrad., No. Ill. U., 1974. Cert. vocat. instr., acctg., related business. Tchr. secondary edn. Alexandria (Ind.) High Sch., 1960-61, Bradford High Sch., Kenosha, Wis., 1962-64, Tremper High Sch., Kenosha, 1964-69; instr. acctg. Gateway Tech. Coll., Kenosha, 1969—; dir. edn. Inst. Mgmt. Accts., Racine, Wis., 1987-88, mem., 1972—; adv. high sch. yearbook "Classic", 1965, 66, 67. Adv. Gateway Chpt. InterVarsity Christian Fellowship, 1982-96; organizer, promoter Crop Walk, Shalom Ctr., Kenosha, 1990, polit. campaigns, 1985-90; officer, elder First Ch. God, Kenosha, 1963-96; mem. promoter Nature Convervancy, Wis. and Washington, 1988-96; state treas. Wis. Assembly of Ch. God., Rock Springs, 1992-96, del., com. mem., counselor, 1975—, Evang. com., 1994-96. With USAR, 1962-68. Recipient Golden Key award Future Bus. Leaders Am., Anderson U., 1960. Mem. NEA, Am. Vocat. Assn. (life), Wis. Vocat. Assn. (Hambrecht award for Excellence 1987), Wis. Edn. Assn., Gateway Vocat. Assn. (treas. social com. 1974-82), Gateway Edn. Assn. (treas. 1972-73), Gideous Internat. (state zone leader 1986-87, various offices 1982-96), Delta Pi Epsilon (Alpha Eta chpt.). Home: 5910 82nd St Kenosha WI 53142-4121 Office: Gateway Tech Coll 3520 30th St Kenosha WI 53144-1610

TERRY, ALLAN KEITH, pharmacist, military officer; b. Aberdeen, S.D., Aug. 21, 1952; s. Wayne Cash and Marjorie Phyllis (Olson) T.; m. Constance Elaine Durocher, June 28, 1986; children: Gordon Edward, James Christopher. BS in Pharmacy, S.D. State U., 1981; MS in Pharmacy, U. Ariz., 1992. Registered pharmacist, S.D. Commd. 2d lt. U.S. Army, 1981, advanced through grades to maj., 1993; staff pharmacist Moncrief Army Hosp., Ft. Jackson, S.C., 1982-85; div. pharmacist 2d Infantry Div., Republic of Korea, 1985-86; pharmacy supr. Womack Army Hosp., Ft. Bragg, N.C., 1987-90; dir. pharmacy Keller Army Hosp., West Point, N.Y., 1992-95; chief pharmacy svc. Irwin Army Cmty. Hosp., Fort Riley, Kans., 1995—; adj. faculty Albany (N.Y.) Coll. Pharmacy, 1992-95. Mem. NRA, Am. Soc. Health Sys. Pharmacists, Ducks Unltd., North Am. Hunting Club (life), Rotary Internat. Republican. Methodist. Office: Irwin Army Cmty Hosp Dept Pharmacy Svc Fort Riley KS 66503

TERRY, RICHARD EDWARD, public utility holding company executive; b. Green Bay, Wis., July 7, 1937; s. Joseph Edward and Arleen (Agamet) T.; m. Catherine Lombardo, Nov. 19, 1966; children—Angela, Edward. BA, St. Norbert's Coll., West DePere, Wis., 1959; LLB, U. Wis., 1964; postgrad., Harvard U., 1986. Assoc. Ross & Hardies, Chgo., 1964-72; atty. Peoples Energy Corp., Chgo., 1972-79, asst. gen. counsel, 1979-81, v.p., gen. counsel, 1981-84; exec. v.p. People's Energy Corp., Peoples Gas Light & Coke Co. and North Shore Gas Co., 1984-87, pres., COO, 1987-90; chair, CEO People's Energy Corp., Peoples Gas Light & Coke Co. and North Shore Gas Co., Chgo., 1990—; bd. dirs. Peoples Energy Corp., Peoples Gas Light, North Shore Gas Co., Harris Bankcorp, Harris Trust & Savs., Amsted Industries. Bd. dirs. Mus. Sci. & Ind., 1991—, Inst. Gas Tech., 1987—, Ill. Coun. on Econ. Edn., 1987—, Big Shoulders, 1991—; mem. Chgo. Area Ctrl. Com., 1991—; mem. bus. adv. coun. Chgo. Urban League, 1991—; prin. Chgo. United, 1991—; trustee St. Xavier U., 1989—, St. Norbert Coll., 1982—, DePaul U., 1992—. 1st lt. U.S. Army, 1959-61. Mem. Am. Gas Assn. (bd. dirs. 1991—), Nat. Petroleum Coun., Chgo. C. of C. (bd. dirs. 1988—), Univ. Club, Mid-Am. Club, Chgo. Club, Econ. Club, Comml. Club Chgo. (mem. civic com. 1991—). Office: Peoples Energy Corp 130 E Randolph St Chicago IL 60601

TERSCHAN, FRANK ROBERT, lawyer; b. Dec. 25, 1949; s. Frank Joseph and Margaret Anna (Heidt) T.; m. Barbara Elizabeth Keily, Dec. 28, 1974; 1 child, Frank Martin. BA, Syracuse U., 1972; JD, U. Wis., 1975. Bar: Wis. 1976, U.S. Dist. Ct. (ea. and we. dists.) Wis. 1976, U.S. Ct. Appeals (7th cir.) 1979, U.S. Ct. Appeals (10th cir.) 1989, U.S. Supreme Ct. 1992. From assoc. to ptnr. Frisch, Dudek & Slattery Ltd., Milw., 1975-88; ptnr. Slattery and Hausman Ltd., Milw., 1988-94, Terschan & Steinle Ltd., Milw., 1994—. Treas., sec. Ville du Park Homeowners Assn., Mequon, Wis., 1985-86; cub scout packmaster pack 3844 Boy Scouts Am., 1989-90, asst. scoutmaster Troop 865, 1991-93. Mem. ABA, Am. Bd. Trial Advocates, Wis. Bar Assn., Milw. Bar Assn., Assn. Trial Lawyers Am., Wis. Assn. Trial Lawyers, 7th Cir. Bar Assn., Order of Coif. Republican. Lutheran. Office: 2600 N Mayfair Rd Ste 700 Milwaukee WI 53226

TERTOCHA, JEAN-PAUL RICHARD, producer; b. Decatur, Ill., Feb. 18, 1955; s. Richard Wayne and Andree Marcelle (Senelle) T.; m. Jennifer Lynn Rhodes, July 7, 1974 (div. July 1984); children: Jessica, Austin, Aubrey. News reporter Sta. WDZ, Decatur, 1973-76; freelance field producer Sta. WCIA-TV, Champaign, Ill., 1979-86; prodn. mgr. H.T.E. Prodns., Decatur, 1979-86, Multi Svc. Ind., Decatur, 1988—; freelance producer Decatur, 1988—; founder Mercury Bros. Audio-Video Prodn. Co., Warrensburg, Ill., 1989-91, Coal Bin Studios, Warrensburg, 1992-93; reporter Pantagraph, Bloomington, Ill., 1993—. Prodr., dir., editor (TV show) O'Glorious Queen, 1982, (TV comml.) Decorteke, 1983, (BBC TV prodn.) Sally Masterson Visit, 1988; prodr., dir. (record) X-static/Troubled Heart, 1986; camera operator, dir. (TV series) Outdoor Illinois, 1987; prodr., dir., co-editor (music video) Breakdown Diesel Blues, 1987; prodr. (tutorial) How to Appear in Court, 1993, How to Tweek Your 80286, 1993, (book) Arny the Storybot, 1994; contbr. articles to profl. jours. Address: PO Box 412 Warrensburg IL 62573-0412

TERWILLEGER, GEORGE E., state legislator; m. Jackie Johnson; children: DeWayne, DeLanna, DeAnna. AA, Xavier Univ. Trustee Hamilton Twp., 1969-74; state rep. Ohio Dist. 2, 1996—; mem. Nat. Land Use com., Nat. Assn. Towns & Townships, County Commn. Assn.; vice chair Clinton Warren Counties Solid Waste Policy com., chair County Reg. Planning Com. Corp. dir. spl. svc. Otterbein Homes, Lebanon, Ohio; treas. Watchdog. Named County Clerk of Yr. Mem. Scottish Rite Club (pres.), County Assn. of Trustees (pres.), Warren County Bd. Realtors (dir., pres.). Home: 10609 Roachester-Cozadale Rd Goshen OH 45122*

TERWILLIGER, ROY W., state legislator; b. June 20, 1937; m. Mary Lou; three children. BS, U. S.D.; MA, U. Iowa. Minn. State sen. Dist. 42, 1992—; banker. Home: 6512 Navaho Trl Edina MN 55439-1138*

TESANOVICH, PAUL, state legislator; b. Jan. 29, 1952. Grad., Mich. Tech. U. Rep. Dist. 110 Mich. Ho. of reps., 1995—, mem. appropriations com.

TESSER, NEIL ANDREW, writer and broadcaster; b. N.Y.C., Sept. 30, 1951; s. Ira and Judith (Posner) T. BS in Journalism, Northwestern U. Asst. editor Down Beat Mag., Chgo., 1973-74; jazz critic Chgo. Reader, 1973—, Chgo. Sun-Times, Daily News, 1973-81; producer, host WNIB-FM Radio, Chgo., 1974-76; media critic, columnist Chgo. Reader, 1978-85; producer, host WBEZ-FM Radio, Chgo., 1980—; jazz critic USA Today, Arlington, Va., 1983-88, Playboy Mag., Chgo., 1991—; mem. founding bd. Jazz Inst., Chgo., 1974. Contbr. articles to profl. publs. Recipient Peter Lisagor award Sigma Delta Chi, Chgo., 1983, Stick-O-Type award Chgo. Newspaper Guild, 1983-84. Mem. Nat. Assn. Recording Arts & Scis. (bd. govs. 1991-95, Grammy awards jazz com. 1992—). Jewish. Office: WBEZ-FM Radio 848 E Grand Chicago IL 60611

TESSING, LOUISE SCIRE, graphic designer; b. Chgo., May 13, 1946; d. Rocco Roy and Ruth Louise (Knueppel) Scire; m. Arvid Victor Tessing, Jan. 18, 1975. BS in Visual Design, Ill. Inst. Tech., Chgo., 1968; MBA in Mktg., Loyola U., Chgo., 1986. Jr. designer Field Mus. of Natural History, Chgo., 1968-69, Charles MacMurray & Assocs., Chgo., 1969-74; designer, art dir. Grant-Jacoby Inc., Chgo., 1974-76, Playboy Enterprises Inc., Chgo., 1976-78, Stevens Biondi Decicco Inc., Chgo., 1978-80; prin., owner Tessing Design Inc., Chgo., 1980—. Lobby treas. Ill. Women's Agenda, Chgo., 1990-92. Mem. Women in Design/Chgo. (founder 1977, pres. 1977-78, 91-93, Friend award 1990), Am. Ctr. for Design (bd. mem. 1971-77, pres. 1976-77), Chgo. Women in Pub., Nat. Assn. Women Bus. Owners. Home and Office: Tessing Design Inc 3822 N Seeley Ave Chicago IL 60618-3912

TESSMANN, CARY ANNETTE, controller; b. Wausau, Wis., Oct. 30, 1956; d. Orin Sidney Olson and Phyllis Olga (Radtke) O. AS, U. Wis., Waukesha, 1986; BBA in Acctg., U. Wis., Whitewater, 1989; MBA in Acctg., U. Wis., 1995. Cert. mgmt. acct.; CPA 1995. Clk.-typist I, II, III Waukesha County Dept. Social Svc., 1974-83; acct. clk. I Northview Nursing Home, Waukesha, 1984; from acct. clk. II, adminstrv. asst.-fiscal mgmt. I, budget technician, sr. fin. analyst to bus. mgr. Waukesha County Health & Human Svcs. Dept., 1984-94; contr. Waukesha County Tech. Coll., Pewaukee, 1994—; mem. acctg. curriculum adv. com. Waukesha County Tech. Coll., 1993—; cons., Sussex, Wis., 1990-93. Vol. Wis. Lutheran Child & Family Svc., Milw., 1989—, Bargain Ctr.-WELS Synod, Milw., 1970-83, Milw. Women's Ctr., 1989-92; vol. tax preparer IRS, Pewaukee, 1989-93; mem. bd. Waukesha County Cmty. Housing Initiatives, 1995—. Recipient Certificate of Spl. Recognition from Christoph Meml. YWCA Women of Distinction Award Program, 1986. Mem. Inst. Mgmt. Accts. (del. Mid-Am. coun. 1992—, chair corp. & acad. devel. 1994-95, co-dir. mem. attendance 1989-90, v.p. comm. 1990-92, v.p. fin. & adminstrn. 1991-92, pres. 1992-93), Southeastern Wis. Fin. Mgrs. Assn. (planning com. 1987-94), Govt. Fin. Officers Assn. (budget reviewer 1994—). Office: Waukesha County Tech Coll 800 Main St Pewaukee WI 53072-4601

TESTERMAN, OPAL MAE, home services administrator; b. Greenfield, Mo., Oct. 25, 1946; d. James Loren and Dorothy Mae (Deckard) Sullivan; m. Leo Gilbert Testerman, Dec. 12, 1964; children: Richard Lee, Leo Douglas, Marjorie Ann, Mark Allen; 1 stepchild, William. AS in Bus. Adminstrn., N.W. Mo. C.C., 1993. Med. technician, asst. adminstr. Allen Home, Mexico, Mo., 1976-80; med. technician Shady Lawn, St. Joseph, Mo., 1992-93, Beverly Manor, St. Joseph, Mo., 1993-94; dir. home svcs. Family First Home Care, Savannah, Mo., 1994—. Chmn. drive Cystic Fibrosis Found., Mexico, 1978-79. Democrat. Baptist. Home: 12511 County Rd 364 Savannah MO 64485

TETERYCZ, BARBARA ANN, entrepreneur, advertising executive; b. Chgo., Jan. 23, 1952; d. Sylvester and Anne (Deutsch) T.; m. Robert Nathan Estes, Oct. 13, 1984. BA, U. Ill., 1974; postgrad. Parkland Coll., 1975-76, U. Ill., 1976-77; grad. Second City Tng. Ctr., 1991. Teller First Fed. of Champaign, Ill., 1974-75; cashier Kroger Co., Champaign, 1975-77; merchandise rep. RustCraft Greeting Cards, Champaign, 1977-78; sales rep. Hockenberg-Rubin, Champaign, 1978, John Morrell & Co., Champaign, 1978-80; account exec. Sta. WICD TV, Champaign, 1981-86; owner Left-Handed Compliments, Champaign; creator 1987, 88 left-handed calendar; now actress, singer/songwriter; active Sta. WEFT Radio Theater, 1991. Contbg. editor mag. Champaign County Bus. Reports, 1986; singer/songwriter I Want to be a Country Music Star, Highway 57; writer, dir. and prodr. Rappin'zel - A 90s Fairy Tale radio Sta. WEFT, 1992, Rumplestiltskin - A Tale of Love and Politics, 1993; inventor Left-Behind Sweat Pants and Shorts. Vol. Am. Cancer Soc., 1985, Ill. Radio Readers for the Visually Impaired, U. Ill. Alumni Assn., 1985-88, Mercy Hosp. Aux., coms. to Elect and Re-elect Beth Beauchamp to City Coun., Champaign, 1984, 87. Ill. State scholar, 1970-74; grad. players workshop of Second City, 1989, grad. Second City Tng. Ctr., 1991. Mem. NAFE, Ad Club of Champaign (finalist several copywriting contests), Internat. Platform Assn., Entrepreneurs Roundtable (founding), Women's Bus. Coun., Urbana C. of C., Champaign C. of C. (pub. rels. com., pres.'s club), Alpha Omega. Roman Catholic. Avocations: reading, writing, bicycling, bodybuilding. Home: 1615 Harbor Point Dr PO Box 873 Champaign IL 61824

TEUSCHLER, MICHAEL ALEXANDER, computer company executive, consultant; b. Chgo., Nov. 30, 1953; s. Edward Michael and Josephine Anastasia (Bien) T. Assoc. editor Peacock N.W. News, Chgo., 1972-74; polit. activist Citizen's Action Program, Chgo., 1974; stockman Cotter & Co., Chgo., 1974-77; asst. mgr. Cloona Health Ctr., Westport, Ireland, 1977-78; computer programmer Sears Roebuck & Co., Chgo., 1978-90; computer cons. Cap Gemini Am., Milw., 1991—. Pres. Old Town Renaissance Consort, Chgo., 1985-89, 2100 N. Albany Block Club, Chgo., 1988-89; vice chmn. fin. com. St. Philomena Parish, Chgo., 1976. Mem. ASPCA, Wis. Assn. Sys. Mgrs., Morning Star Fellowship of Isis (founding mem.), Internat. Platform Assn., Humane Soc. of U.S., Nat. Arbor Day Soc., World Wildlife Fund. Home: 7625 W Wind Lake Rd Wind Lake WI 53185-2253 Office: Cap Gemini Am Plaza East Ste 850 330 E Kilbourn Milwaukee WI 53202

TEUT, KANDI L., emergency medical technician; b. Omaha, Aug. 1, 1949; d. Robert Eugene and Donna Lee (Johnson) Friesz; m. Gary John Teut, Apr. 6, 1974; children: Jason Adam (dec.), Cori Lee, Joshua John, Nathan Andrew. Cert. fire fighter III, II, I, instr. II, I, Iowa State Fire Svc. Inst., Nat. Profl. Qualifications Bd. EMT I State of Iowa, Des Moines, 1994—; hazardous materials technician Waterloo (Iowa) Fire Dept., 1995—; instr. Ind. Instrnl. Svcs., Danbury, Iowa; EMT I Buena Vista County Hosp., Storm Lake, Iowa, 1994—; fire fighter asst. chief Ricketts (Iowa) Vol. Fire Dept., 1987—. Commr. Gov.'s Commn. Emergency Mgmt., Crawford County, Iowa, 1993—. Mem. Iowa Fireman's Assn., Iowa Emergency Med. Svcs. Assn. Home and Office: 1152 C Ave Danbury IA 51019

TEWKSBURY, ROBERT ALAN, professional baseball player; b. Concord, N.H., Nov. 30, 1960. Student, Rutgers U., St. Leo Coll. With N.Y. Yankees, 1981-87, Chgo. Cubs, 1987-88; pitcher St. Louis Cardinals, 1989-94, Tex. Rangers, 1994—; player Nat. League All-Star Game, 1992. Ranked 2d in Nat. League for earned run average, 1992, 3d in Nat. League for wins. *

THACKER, JERRY LYNN, school administrator; b. Mishawaka, Ind., July 7, 1950; s. Burl Willis and Azzie Dell (Davidson) T.; m. Donna Lee, Aug. 11, 1973. BA, Bethel Coll., Mishawaka, Ind., 1972; MS, Ind. U., S. Bend, 1975; EdD, Andrews U., Berrien Springs, Mich., 1987. Tchr., individually guided edn. team leader Penn-Harris Madison Sch. Corp., Osceola, Ind., 1972-85; elem. prin. Twin lakes Sch. Corp., Monticello, Ind., 1985-89, dir. curriculum, 1989-90; dir. curriculum Saginaw (Mich.) Ind. Sch. Dist., 1989-90; dir. elem. edn. MSD Lawrence Twp., Indpl., 1990-96; asst. supt. for Human Resources MSD Lawrence Twp., 1996—. Presenter in field. Recipient various grants; recipient Award for Svc. to Profession, Ind. Assn. Curriculum Devel., others. Mem. ASCD, Nat. Assn. Elem. Prins., IAEMSP (pres.), AASA, Internat Reading Assn., Pi Lambda Theta, Phi Delta Kappa. Home: 759 Buckeye Ct Noblesville IN 46060-9196

THALDEN, BARRY R., architect; b. Chgo., July 5, 1942; s. Joseph and Sibyl (Goodwin) Hechtenthal; m. Irene L. Mittleman, June 23, 1966 (div. 1989); 1 child, Stacey. BArch, U. Ill., 1965; M in Land Architecture, U. Mich., 1969. Landscape architect Hellmuth, Obata, Kassebaum, St. Louis, 1969-70; dir. landscape architecture PGAV Architects, St. Louis, 1970-71; pres. Thalden Corp (formerly Saunders-Thalden & Assocs. Inc.), St. Louis, 1971—. Prin. works include Rock Hill Park, 1975 (AIA award 1977), Wilson Residence, 1983 (AIA award), Nat. Bowling Hall of Fame, 1983 (St. Louis RCGA award 1984), Village Bogey Hills (Home Builders award 1985, St. L. ASLA award 1994), St. Louis U. Campus Mall (St. L. ASLA award 1989), Horizon Casino Resort, Lake Tahoe, Nev., St. Louis Airport's Radisson Hotel, Lady Luck, Treasure Bay, Palace Casinos, Biloxi, Miss., Boomtown Casino, New Orleans, Pres. Casino on the Admiral, St. Louis, Plaza of Champions, Busch Stadium, St. Louis. Bd. dirs. St. Louis Open Space Coun., 1973-83; apptd. Mo. Lands Architect Coun., 1990. Named Architect of Yr. Builder Architect mag., 1986. Fellow Am. Soc. Landscape Architects (nat. v.p. 1979-81, pres. St. Louis chpt. 1975, trustee 1976-79, nat. conv. chair 1991); mem. AIA, World Future Soc. (pres. St. Louis chpt. 1984-94, keynote conf. spkr. 1995). Home: 8 Edgewater Is Saint Louis MO 63105 Office: Thalden Corp 7777 Bonhomme Ave Ste 2200 Saint Louis MO 63105-1911

THANE, RUSSELL T., state legislator; b. Denver, July 14, 1926; s. Joseph and Bernice (Steere) T.; m. Betty Jo Chowning, 1952; children: Ronald, Kathleen. Degree, N.D. State Sch. Sci., 1949, N.D. State U., 1955. Dir. Home Mutual Ins. Co., Wahpeton, 1968—; mem. N.D. Senate, 1971—, asst. majority floor whip, 1981-82, mem. appropriations com., chmn. human svc.; mem. interim adv. com. on intergovt. rels.; farmer; dir. Red River Valley Beet Growers, 1969—. Precinct committeeman 25th dist., N.D., 1964-70; mem. adv. bd. N.D. State Sch. Sci. Drug and Alcohol Prevention, Wahpeton Cmty. Devel. Corp., State Hosp. Mem. N.D. Cattle Feeders Assn. (sec.-treas. 1964-70), Zagal Shrine, Elks, Masons, Eagles, Am. Legion (life), Farm Bur. Office: RR 1 Box 142 Wahpeton ND 58075-9801 Home: 7660 178th Ave SE Wahpeton ND 58075-9615*

THARES, LAURA A., personnel director; b. Ipswich, S.D., Apr. 30, 1968; d. Bernard L. and Deloris A. (Geditz) T. Degree in Mass Comm., Moorhead State U., 1990. Pers. dir. Nat. Crop Ins. Svcs., Overland Park, Kans., 1990—. Mem. Am. Soc. Assn. Execs., Pub. Rels. Soc. Am. Office: Nat Crop Ins Svcs 7201 W 129th St #200 Overland Park KS 66213

THARIN, JAMES COTTER, JR., entrepreneur; b. Champaigne, Ill., Feb. 21, 1959; s. James Cotter and JoAnne Mae (Febel) T.; m. Tarusau Lee Beattie, June 30, 1984; 1 child, Thora-Lee Antoinette. BA, Carleton Coll., 1981. Acct. exec. Merrill Lynch, Wayzata, Minn., 1982-84, Shearson/Lehman, Mpls., 1984-86; v.p. Fossett Corp., Chgo., 1986-90; gen. ptnr. Tharin/Greenwich Trading, Chgo., 1990-93; pres., owner Certificate Clearing Corp., Chgo., 1993—. Home: PO Box 997 Vineyard Haven MA 02568 Office: Certificate Clearing Corp 208 S LaSalle Ste 1414 Chicago IL 60604

THARMAN, MARK RICHARD, quality control technician; b. West Bend, Wis., Apr. 21, 1968; s. Richard Allen and Elaine Dorothea (Hirschmann) T.; m. Lori Anne Zuehls, Sept. 19, 1992; children: Valarie Raquel, Brandon Mark, Lillian Marie. AS in electronics, Moraine Park Tech. Coll., 1988; BS in elec. engring. tech., Devry Inst Tech., 1991. Delivery driver Contel Phone Systems, Waukesha, Wis., 1987-88; factory personnel West Bend Co., 1988; bin filler McMaster Carr Supply, Elmhurst, Ill., 1988-91; field svc. engr. Fanamation, Compton, Calif., 1991-93, Precision Metrology, Milw., 1993; quality control technician Orion Corp., Grafton, Wis., 1994—; inspector Serigraph, West Bend, 1995—. Mem. IEEE (Chgo. sect. scholarship 1992). Home: 1935 Sylvan Way Apt 7 West Bend WI 53095 Office: Orion Corp 1111 Cedar Creek Rd Grafton WI 53024

THARP, EDWARD LEON, civil engineer, consultant; b. Booneville, Mo., June 14, 1943; s. Glenn Edward and Vena Imogene (Jones) T.; m. Sharon Kay Piercy, Mar. 6 1966; children; Shar Susanne, Paul Jason. BS, U. Mo., Rolla, 1965, MS, 1966; PhD, U. Ark., 1971. Registered profl. engr. Asst. prof. U. Mo., Rolla, 1970-74; v.p. Pickett Duncan & Assoc., Inc., Bartow, Fla., 1974-75; asst. prof. U. Mo., Rolla, 1975-77; sr. engr. Zurheide-Hermann, Inc., St. Louis, 1977-80; v.p. Am. Digital Systems, Inc., St. Louis, 1980-81; owner, pres. Edward L. Tharp Consulting, St. Louis, 1981-83; chief engr., assoc. Havens and Emerson, Inc., St. Louis, 1983-93; mgr. St. Louis office Montgomery Watson, 1993—; researcher U.S. Army C.E., Kansas City, Mo., 1972-74, NSF, Rolla, 1972; cons. Peabody Coal Co., St. Louis, 1975-77, Metro. Sanitary Dist., Chgo., 1976. Author, editor (manual) Sewer System Rehab., 1983; reviewer (manual) CSO Pollution Abatement, 1989, Urban Stormwater Mgmt., 1991. Elder St. Mark United Presbyn. Ch., St. Louis, 1981-83; mem. West County Lawnmower Drill Team, Ballwin, Mo., 1987-88. Recipient fellowship NSF, 1966, 67-69. Mem. ASCE (Outstanding Civil Engr. student 1965), Water Environment Fedn., Am. Water Works Assn., Am. Pub. Works Assn., Mo. Soc. Profl. Engrs., Profl. Engrs in Pvt. Practice (sec. treas 1983-86, vice chmn. 1986-90, chmn. 1990-91), Masons, Shriners (Ring candidate 1971). Office: Montgomery Watson 1850 Craigshire Dr Saint Louis MO 63146

THAUER, EDWIN WILLIAM, JR., financial services executive; b. Grand Rapids, Mich., May 24, 1953; s. Edwin William and Lucille Marie (Roy) T.; m. Karen Lee Alberts, Aug. 16, 1973; children: Susan Elizabeth, Angela Marie, Amanda Rose. Grad. high sch., Grand Rapids. Lic. life ins. counselor, Mich. Agt. The Bankers Life Co., Grand Rapids, 1977-80; pres., CEO Design Underwriting, Inc., Grand Rapids, 1980—. Mem. Am. Soc. CLU and Chartered Fin. Cons. (amb. polit. action com.), Nat. Assn. Life Underwriters, Life Ins. Leaders Mich. (life), Cascade Hills Country Club. Mem.

Nazarene Ch. Home: 1875 Wilmont Dr SE Grand Rapids MI 49508-6591 Office: Design Underwriting Inc 985 Parchment Dr SE Grand Rapids MI 49546-3659

THAYER, EDNA LOUISE, medical facility administrator, nurse; b. Madelia, Minn., May 21, 1936; d. Walter William Arthur and Hilda Engel Emily Ann (Geistfeld) Wilke; m. David LeRoy Thayer, Aug. 30, 1958; children: Scott, Tamara, Brenda. Diploma in nursing, Bethesda Luth., 1956; BS in Nursing Edn., U. Minn., 1960; MSN, Washington U., St. Louis, 1966; MS in Counseling, Mankato (Minn.) State U., 1972. Cert. nursing adminstr. advanced ANA. Nurse Bethesda Luth. Hosp., St. Paul, 1956-58, U. Minn. Hosp., Mpls., 1958; from nurse to asst. head nurse supr., edn. dir. Fairmont (Minn.) Community Hosp., 1959-63; instr. Alton (Ill.) Meml. Hosp., 1963-66; from nursing instr. to assoc. prof. and dean Sch. Nursing Mankato State U., 1966-77; asst. adminstr. Rice County Dist. One Hosp., Faribault, Minn., 1977-89; RN, adminstrv. supr. St. Peter (Minn.) Regional Treatment Ctr., 1990—; nurse surveyor Minn. Dept. Tech. Edn., St. Paul, 1980-93; mem. adv. co. LPN and MA programs Tech. Inst., Faribault, 1977—. Mem. Rice County Ext. Bd., Faribault, 1986-91, adult leader 4-H Club, Rice County and St. Paul, 1971—; advisor Med. Explorers, Faribault, 1977-89; mem. Rep. Rodosovich Health Com., Faribault, 1984-94; coun. mem. Our Savior's Luth. Ch., Faribault, 1984-87; mem. Rep. Boudreau Health Care Adv. Com., 1996—. Recipient alumni award Nat. 4-H Club, 1983, Disting. Friend of Nursing award Mankato State U., 1995. Mem. Minn. Orgn. Nurse Execs. (bd. dirs. 1987-89), Dist. F Nursing Svc. Adminstrs. (pres. 1980-82), Minn. Nurses Assn. (bd. dirs. 1982-87, Pres.'s award 1983, pres. 5th dist. 1974, 75, pres. 13th dist. 1984-86), AAUW, Sigma Theta Tau, Delta Kappa Gamma (pres. Pi chptr. 1982-84, Woman of Achievement award 1985), Hosp. Aux. Republican. Home: RR 1 Box 7B Elysian MN 56028-9731 Office: Saint Peter Regional Treatment Ctr 100 Freeman Dr Saint Peter MN 56082-2516

THAYER, RICHARD LEE, small business owner; b. Nelson, Nebr., Aug. 18, 1946; s. Lynn Earl and Patricia Ann (Doher) T.; m. MaryJo Ann Fager, Dec. 6, 1985. BA in Edn., U. Nebr., Kearney, 1969; M in Mgmt., Creighton U., 1993. Tchr. history Holdrege (Nebr.) H.S., 1969-73; salesman Cash-Wa Co., Kearney, 1973-75; from salesman to dist. mgr. Hanes Hosiery Inc., Omaha, 1975-89; owner, mgr. Exec. Mktg., Omaha, 1989—, The Bakery/Deli, Omaha, 1993—. Founder, pres. Constl. Heritage Inst., Omaha, 1993-95. Republican. Baptist.

THEIS, DON LAYNE, research chemist; b. Massillon, Ohio, Mar. 25, 1954; s. John F. and Myrtle E. (Saylor) T.; m. Joan A. Waldecker, 1990; children: Jennifer Paige, Emily Elizabeth. BS, Kent State U., 1976. Clin. chemist Aultman Hosp., Canton, Ohio, 1974-78; chemist, rschr. Pharmacia and Upjohn, Inc. (formerly The Upjohn Co.), Kalamazoo, 1978—. Contbr. articles to Pharm. Rsch., Jour. Pharm. Biomed. Analysis, Jour. Chromatogr. Biomed. Applications, Jour. Labelled Compounds Radiopharm, Jour. Pharm. Sci. Mem. Am. Assn. Clin. Chemistry, Am. Chem. Soc., Am. Soc. Clin. Pathologists, Pi Mu Epsilon. Office: Pharmacia and Upjohn Inc 7000 Portage Rd Kalamazoo MI 49001-0102

THEIS, FRANK GORDON, federal judge; b. Yale, Kans., June 26, 1911; s. Peter F. and Maude (Cook) T.; m. Marjorie Riddle, Feb. 1, 1939 (dec. 1970); children: Franklin, Roger. A.B. cum laude, U. Kans., 1933; J.D., U. Mich., 1936. Bar: Kans. 1937. Since practiced in Arkansas City; sr. mem. firm Frank G. Theis, 1939—; atty. Kans. Tax Commn., 1937-39; chief counsel OPS for Kans., 1951-52; U.S. dist. judge Dist. Kans., 1967—; chief judge, 1977-81, active sr. status, 1981—; Pres. Young Democrats Kan., 1942-46, Kans. Dem. Club, 1944-46; chmn. Kans. Dem. Com., 1955-60; mem. nat. adv. com. polit. orgn. Dem. Nat. Com., 1956-58, nat. committeeman from Kans., 1957-67; chmn. Dem. Midwest Conf., 1959-60; Dem. nominee for Kans., Supreme Ct., 1950, U.S. Senate, 1960. Mem. ABA, Kans. Bar Assn., Kans. Jr. Bar Conf. (pres. 1942), Phi Beta Kappa., Phi Delta Phi, Sachem. Presbyterian. Club: Mason. Office: US Dist Ct 414 US Courthouse 401 N Market St Wichita KS 67202-2000

THEIS, PETER FRANK, engineering executive, inventor; b. Chgo., Mar. 21, 1937; s. Frank Victor and Hazel (Ericsson) T.; m. Jill Anne Pendexter, May 9, 1970; children: Juliana, Ethan. B.E. in Elec. Engring., Yale U., 1958; MBA in Fin., U. Chgo., 1966; JD, Ill. Inst. Tech.-Kent Coll Law, Chgo., 1974; postgrad., U. Stockholm. Bar: Ill. 1975. Engr. ASEA, Ludvika, Sweden, 1959, Signode Corp., Glenview, Ill., 1959-61; importer Internat. Idea, Inc., Chgo., 1961-62; systems analyst Continental Ill. Nat. Bank and Trust, Chgo., 1963-64; sales rep. Honeywell, Inc., Chgo., 1964-68; exec. Morgan Industries, Inc., Chgo., 1968-87; pres. Conversational Voice Technologies Corp., Chgo., Gurnee, Ill., 1973-91, Theis Rsch., Inc., Gurnee, 1991—; cons. Ill. Tech. Transfer LLC, 1994—; cons., mng. mem. Theis Rsch. & Engring. LLC, 1994—. Patentee in field. With Air N.G., 1961-66. Mem. Tech. Exec. Roundtable (bd. dirs. 1992—), Licensing Execs. Soc., Execs. Club of Chgo. (bd. dirs. 1972-74), Intellectual Property Creators (bd. dirs. 1993—). Office: Theis Rsch Inc 4223 Grove Ave Gurnee IL 60031-2134

THEIS, PETER GEORGE, retired classics educator; b. Milw., Dec. 18, 1930; s. Peter Joseph and Laura Gertrude (Kornely) T.; m. Jane Elizabeth Grattan, Aug. 12, 1961; children: Peter Leo, Paul Joseph, Mary Ellen, Thomas George. BA magna cum laude, Marquette U., 1952; AM, U. Chgo., 1957. Part-time instr. U. Wis., Milw., 1956; instr. Rockhurst Coll., Kansas City, Mo., 1960-61; instr., then asst. prof. classics Marquette U., Milw., 1961-90; ret., 1990. Mem. edn. bd. Holy Family Cath. Ch., Whitefish Bay, Wis., 1974-75; troop fundraising chmn. Boy Scouts Am., Whitefish Bay, 1976-77; pres. Post-Polio Resource Group of Southeastern Wis., Wauwatosa, 1987, Milw. Area Latin Tchrs. Assn., 1963-64, Fox River Valley Classical Assn., Milw., 1970-71, Wis. Latin Tchrs. Assn., Milw., 1976-78. Cpl. U.S. Army, 1953-55. NEH grantee, 1973. Mem. AAUP, DAV (life), Am. Classical League, Am. Philological Assn., Classical Assn. of the Mid. West and South, Wis. Assn. Fgn. Lang. Tchrs. (pres. 1980-82, Recognition award 1989), Marquette U. Retirees Assn. Home: 4786 N Woodruff Ave Milwaukee WI 53211-1005

THELEN, BRUCE CYRIL, lawyer; b. St. Johns, Mich., Nov. 24, 1951. BA, Mich. State U., 1973; JD, U. Mich., 1977. Bar: N.Y. 1978, Mich. 1980, Ill. 1992. Assoc. Dewey, Ballantine, Bushby, Palmer & Wood, N.Y.C., 1977-80; assoc. Dickinson, Wright, Moon, Van Dusen & Freeman, Detroit, 1981-83, ptnr., 1984—; mem. U.S. Dept. Commerce-Mich. Dist. Export Coun., 1995—. Contbr. articles to profl. publs. Mem. allocation panel, mem. spkrs. bur., vice chmn. rsch. and tech. com. United Way of Detroit, 1987—; mem. State of Mich. Task Force on Internat. Trade, Lansing, 1990; mem. Detroit Com. on Fgn. Rels., Greater Detroit-Windsor Japan Am. Soc. Mem. N.Y. Bar Assn. (mem. internat. law sect.), Mich. Bar Assn., State Bar Mich. (chmn. internat. law sect. 1990-91), Internat. Bar Assn., Am. Soc. Internat. Law, Ill. Bar Assn. (internat. law sect.), Internat. Law Assn., French-Am. C. of C. of Detroit, German Am. C. of C. of Midwest (bd. dirs. 1992—, pres. Mich. chpt. 1994—), Greater Detroit C. of C. (chmn. European mission com. 1991-92, 95, export com. 1992-95, Leadership Detroit VIII program 1986-87), World Trade Club (exec. com. 1992—). Office: Dickinson Wright Moon Van Dusen & Freeman One Detroit Center 500 Woodward Ave Ste 4000 Detroit MI 48226-3423

THELIN, JOHN ROBERT, academic administrator, education educator, historian; b. West Newton, Mass., Oct. 15, 1947; s. George Willard and Rozalija Katherine (Komarec) T.; m. Anna Sharon Blackburn, June 24, 1978. AB, Brown U., 1969; MA, U. Calif., Berkeley, 1972, PhD, 1973. Rsch. asst. Brown U., Providence, 1968-69; researcher, lectr. U. Calif., Berkeley, 1972-74; asst. prof. U. Ky., Lexington, 1974-77; asst. dean Pomona Coll., Claremont, Calif., 1977-79; from asst. dir. to rsch. dir. Assn. Ind. Calif. Colls. and Univs., Santa Ana, 1979-81; chancellor prof. Coll. William and Mary, Williamsburg, Va., 1981-93, pres. faculty assembly, 1990-91; prof. higher edn. & philanthropy Ind. U., Bloomington, 1993-96; prof. ednl. policy and history U. Ky., Lexington, 1996—; vis. prof. grad. sch. Claremont U., 1978-81; vis. scholar U. Calif., Berkeley, 1995; curator Marquandia Soc., 1971-96; essay rev. editor Rev. of Higher Edn., 1979-91; rsch. cons. NSF, Washington, 1991. Author: Higher Education and Its Useful Past, 1982, The Cultivation of Ivy, 1976, (with others) The Old College Try, 1989, Higher Education and Public Policy, 1991, Games Colleges Plays, 1994; assoc. editor: (jour.) Higher Education: Theory and Research, 1983-91. Pres., bd. dirs. United Way, Williamsburg, 1987-89; pres. Friends of Williamsburg Libr., 1989. Rsch. grantee Spencer Found., 1989-91; Regents fellow U. Calif., 1972. Mem. Assn. for Study of Higher Edn. (bd. dirs. 1988-90, keynote spkr. 1994), History of Edn. Soc. (editl. bd. 1988-91), Phi Beta Kappa. Home: 324 Chinoe Rd Lexington KY 40502 Office: U Ky Edn Policy Studies Lexington KY 40503

THEODORE, ARES NICHOLAS, research chemist; b. Kalamata, Greece, Oct. 28, 1933; came to U.S., 1954; s. Nicholas A. and Angeliki (Myseros) Theodoracopulos; m. Peggy Salvarakis, Sept. 3, 196l; children: Nicholas A., Angie A. BA cum laude, Westminster Coll., Salt Lake City, 1958; MS, U. Utah, 196l; postgrad., Case Western Res. U., 1967-68. Asst. prof. chemistry Westminster Coll., 196l-64; sr. rsch. chemist Diamond Shamrock Corp., Cleve., 1964-69; rsch. scientist Ford Motor Co., Detroit, 1969-73, sr. rsch. scientist, 1973-84, prin. rsch. scientist, 1984—. Contbr. articles to profl. jours.; patentee in field (57). Mem. ch. bd. Holy Cross Greek Orthodox Ch., Farmington Hills, Mich., 1986-88; campaigner Farmington Hills Dem. Com., 1986-88; mem. bus. coun. Boston Dem. Com., 1988—, Nat. Dem. Com., 1988—. U. Utah fellow, 1958-6l, NSF fellow, 1964. Mem. Am. Chem. Soc. (treas. 1967), Ahepa (bd. govs. Dearborn, Mich. 1985-86). Home: 34974 Valley Forge Dr Farmington MI 48331-3210

THERKILDSEN, MARK B., architect; b. Casper, Wyo., July 3, 1959; s. Henry and Marjorie Jeanne (Memmer) T.; m. Vicky Lynn Klein, Oct. 8, 1988; children: Angela Victoria, Edward Taylor, Joseph Thobro. BCE, U. Wyo., 1981. Registered architect, Wyo., S.D. Archtl. designer Henry Therkildsen & Assocs.-Architects, Casper, 1981-89; architect Neumann Monson Wictor Architects, Sioux City, Iowa, 1989—. Mem. coun. Luth. Ch. Mem. AIA (treas. N.W. Iowa chpt. 1991—). Republican. Home: 4111 Ridge Ave Sioux City IA 51106 Office: Neumann Monson Wictor Archs 238 Benson Bldg Sioux City IA 51101

THEUERLING, ANDREW WILLIAM, staff nurse; b. Cin., June 4, 1956; s. Charles Joseph and Elizabeth Margaret (George) T.; m. Lauren Hope Simkin, May 19, 1984; 1 child, Alyssa Marie. Diploma, Jewish Hosp. Sch. Nursing, Cin., 1980-82; student, Xavier U., 1980-84, Coll. Mt. St. Joseph, 1985-88. RN, Ohio. Grad. nurse Daniel Drake Meml. Hosp., Cin., 1982-83; staff nurse St. Elizabeth Med. Ctr., Covington, Ky., 1983-85, The Christ hosp., Cin., 1985-87; transplant coord. Ohio Valley Organ Procurement Ctr., Cin., 1987-89; med. analyst Community Mut. Blue Cross/Blue Shield, Cin., 1989-92; staff nurse Cardiac Cath. Lab. U. Cin. Med. Ctr., 1992—. Co-author abstracts. Co-chair Organ Donor Awareness Coun., Cin., 1987-89; instr. Rite of Christian Initiation for Adults classes, Cin., 1990-92. Mem. ACCN. Roman Catholic. Home: 5149 Leona Dr Cincinnati OH 45238-3725

THIBODEAU, GARY A., academic administrator; b. Sioux City, Iowa, Sept. 26, 1938; m. Emogene J. McCarville, Aug. 1, 1964; children: Douglas James, Beth Ann. BS, Creighton U., 1962; MS, S.D. State U., 1967, S.D. State U., 1970; PhD, S.D. State U., 1971. Profl. service rep. Baxter Lab., Inc., Deerfield, Ill., 1963-65; tchr., researcher dept. biology S.D. State U., Brookings, 1965-76, asst. to v.p. for acad. affairs, 1976-80, v.p. for adminstrn., 1980-85; chancellor U. Wis., River Falls, 1985—; mem. investment com. U. Wis., River Falls Found.; trustee W. Cen. Wis. Consortium U. Wis. System; bd. dirs. U. Wis. at River Falls Found.; mem. Phi Kappa Phi nat. budget rev. and adv. comm., Phi Kappa Phi Found. investment comm., comm. on Agrl. and Rural Devel., steering commn. Coun. of Rural Colls. and Univs., Joint Coun. on Food and Agrl. Scis., USDA. Author: Basic Concepts in Anatomy and Physiology, 1983, Athletic Injury Assessment, 1994, Structure and Function of the Body, 1996, The Human Body in Health and Disease, 1996, Textbook of Anatomy and Physiology, 1996. Mem. AAAS, Sigma Xi, Phi Kappa Phi, Gamma Sigma Delta, Gamma Alpha. Office: U Wis 116 N Hall River Falls WI 54022

THIEBAUTH, BRUCE EDWARD, advertising executive; b. Bronxville, N.Y., Oct. 30, 1947; s. Bruce and Margaret Evelyn (Wiederhold) T.; m. Sherry Ann Proplesch, Aug. 31, 1968; 1 child, Bruce Revere. Student, Colby Coll., Waterville, Maine, 1965-66, Pace Coll., 1971; BA in Bus. Adminstrn. and Sociology magna cum laude, Bellevue Coll., 1972. Mgr. credit GE Credit Corp., Croton Falls, N.Y., 1971; mgr. ops. Bridal Publs., Inc., Omaha, 1972-73; regional mgr. Bridal Fair, Inc., Omaha, 1973-74, sales mgr., 1974-76, chmn. bd., pres., 1976—; bd. dirs. Multi-Media Group, Inc., Fair Communications, Inc. Pub., bd. dirs. Bridal Fair mag. With USAF, 1966-70. Recipient Nat. Def. Svc. medal, Somers (N.Y.) League Citizenship and Pub. Svc. award, 1965. Mem. Mag. Pubs. Assn., Nat. Assn. Broadcasters, Airline Passengers Assn., Bellevue Coll. Alumni Assn., Paso Fino Horse Assn. Republican. Congregationalist. Office: 11248 John Galt Blvd Omaha NE 68137-2320

THIEDE, JANET LYNN, marketing executive; b. Canton, Ohio, Aug. 7, 1958; d. Nelson Clyde and Pearl Marie (Van Voorhis) Graber; m. Robert H. Thiede, Sept. 19, 1987; children: Joshua Robert, Melissa Marie, Taylor Evelyn. BA, Marshall U., 1980, MA, 1988. Producer Sta. WOWK-TV, Huntington, W.Va., 1981-82; reporter Sta. WOWK-TV, Charleston, W.Va., 1982-86; speech instr. U. Charleston, 1985; media and pub. rels. coord. Kent (Ohio) State U., 1986, dir. u. news and info., 1986-90, asst. v.p. mktg. and communications, 1990-92; part-time instr. comm. studies Kent State U., 1990-92; part-time instr. Ohio State U., Marion, 1992—. Chmn. United Way Spl. Events Com., Portage County, Ohio, 1988; pres. Jr. Svc. Guild, 1996, co-chair cmty. needs fundraiser, 1995, co-chair Christmas Clearinghouse, 1995-96, sec. 1996; bd. dirs. Marion YMCA. Recipient Outstanding Reporting award W.Va. Waste Water Treatment Assn., 1985, Outstanding Individual Reporting award UPI, W.Va., 1986.

THIEDE, RICHARD WESLEY, communications educator; b. Detroit, Mar. 30, 1936; s. Harold Victor and Blanche May (Gross) T. BS, Ea. Mich. U., 1961; MA, U. Ill., 1963; PhD, U. Mo., 1977. Teaching asst. U. Ill., Urbana, 1961-62; tchr. Cen. High Sch., Battle Creek, Mich., 1962-63, Shafer High Sch., Southgate, Mich., 1963-64, Chadsey High Sch., Detroit, 1964-68, Stevenson High Sch., Livonia, Mich., 1968-71; part-time instr. Schoolcraft Coll., Livonia, 1969-71; teaching/tech. asst. U. Mo., Columbia, 1971-74; instr. Ottumwa Hts. Coll., Iowa, 1975-76, Midland Luth. Coll., Fremont, Nebr., 1976-77; prof. dept. communication arts The Defiance (Ohio) Coll., 1978—; tchr. summer sch. Southwestern High Sch., Detroit, 1966, Cody High Sch., Detroit, 1967, 68; tchr. evening sch. Chadsey High Sch., 1965-67, Stevenson High Sch., 1969-70. Mem. AAUP, Assn. for Theatre in Higher Edn., Ohio Theatre Alliance, Alpha Psi Omega, Kappa Delta Pi. Democrat. Home: PO Box 1101 Defiance OH 43512-1101 Office: The Defiance Coll 701 N Clinton St Defiance OH 43512-1610

THIEL, BARBARA VOGEL, architect, interior designer; b. Akron, Ohio, Mar. 10, 1953; d. Richard and Helen (Graber) Vogel; m. Friedrich Thiel, Sept. 30, 1978. BFA, Kent State U., 1975; BArch, U. Notre Dame, 1982. Registered architect Nat. Coun. Archtl. Registration Bds.; lic. Nat. Coun. Interior Design Qualifications. Prin. Chagrin Falls, Ohio. Mem. AIA (profl.), Am. Soc. Interior Designers (profl.), Inst. Bus. Designers (profl.). Office: 33 River St Chagrin Falls OH 44022-3020

THIEL, RUTH ELEANOR, real estate broker; b. Chgo., June 11, 1930; d. Frank A. and Lucille L. (Bromm) Dell; m. Joseph Donald Thiel, Sept. 30, 1950; children: Michael F., Jeffrey D., Patti Thiel Pavey, Mary Beth Thiel Davies, Tracy J. Thiel Carroll. Grad. Evanston Twp. Community Coll., 1950, Realtors Inst., 1972. Sales assoc. Indian Hill Realty, Winnetka, Ill., 1967; v.p., mgr. Mitchell Bros. Realtors, Northbrook, Ill., 1972-75; exec. v.p., gen. mgr. Century 21 Mitchell Bros., Evanston, Ill., 1975-82; v.p. Koenig & Strey Realtors, 1982-87; sr. v.p., 1987—. Mem. State of Ill. Real Estate Disciplinary Bd., 1977-95, Evanston Econ. Devel. Com., 1979; treas. North Shore Assn. Retarded, 1977-79; mem. instl. rev. com. St. Francis Hosp., 1981—; mem. Evanston Zoning Bd., 1983-85; pres. Evanston Libr. Friends, 1984-86; alderman 2d Ward, City of Evanston, 1985-86; chmn., bd. trustees Glenview United Meth. Ch. Recipient Ill. Women's Coun. of Realtors Woman of Yr. award, 1979, 93; Svc. award City of Hope, North Shore Assn. for Retarded, 1977. Mem. Nat. Assn. Realtors (bd. dirs. 1978-91), Ill. Assn. Realtors (exec. com. 1979, bd. dirs. 1977-85, Realtor of Yr. award 1984), North Shore Bd. Realtors (dir. 1970-80), Evanston North Shore Bd. Realtors (pres. 1978), Women's Coun. Realtors (state pres. 1977), Women in Real Estate (award 1980). Clubs: Woman of Evanston, Million Dollar, Zonta Club of Evanston (pres. 1995), Kiwanis (pres. Glenview-Northbrook chpts. 1990-91), Rotary Club of Evanston. Office: Koenig & Strey Realtors 2528 Green Bay Rd Evanston IL 60201-2231

THIELEN, JOANNE OLIVIA, day care provider; b. Fargo, N.D., Dec. 8, 1967; d. Joseph Theodore and Doris Susan (Decker) Schwegel; m. Todd Frank Thielen, Aug. 8, 1987; children: Traci Lynn, Julia Grace. Higher Acctg. Degree, St. Cloud (Minn.) Bus. Coll., 1988. Cashier Cash-Wise, Waite Park, Minn., 1985-86; sr. part-timer Little Dukes, St. Cloud, Minn., 1986-87; data entry/acctg. dept. staff Liberty Savs., St. Cloud, 1987-89; acct. Pan-O-Gold Baking Co., St. Cloud, 1989-91; acct., v.p. T&T Floor Covering, Cold Spring, Minn., 1991—; day care provider Cold Spring, 1991—. Office: T&T Floor Covering PO Box 309 Cold Spring MN 56320

THIHER, O. ALLEN, foreign language professional, educator; b. Ft. Worth, Apr. 4, 1941; s. Ottah and Helen (Massey) T.; m. Nancy Thiher, June 1, 1985. BA, U. Tex., 1963; PhD, U. Wis., 1968. Asst. prof. Duke U., Durham, N.C., 1967-69, Middle Coll., Middlebury, Vt., 1969-76; assoc. prof. to prof. U. Mo., Columbia, 1977—; curator's prof. U. Mo., 1989—. Author: (books) Celine: The Novel as Delirium, 1972, The Cinematic Muse: Critical Studies in the History of French Cinema, 1979, Words in Reflection: Modern Language Theory and Postmodern Fiction, 1984, Raymond Queneau, 1985, The Short Stories of Franz Kafka, 1989. Recipient Fulbright grant, Paris, 1966-67, Guggenheim grant, Berlin, 1976-77. Mem. MLA, Am. Assn. Tchrs. French, Soc. for Lit. and Sci., Phi Beta Kappa. Office: U Mo Dept of Romance Langs Columbia MO 65211

THIMESCH, DANIEL J., state legislator; m. Ruth A. Thimesch. Contractor; mem. from dist. 93 Kans. State Ho. of Reps., Topeka. Address: 30121 W 63d St S Cheney KS 67025

THIMSEN, JANICE LORETTA, librarian; b. St. Louis, Jan. 13, 1940; d. Stephen J. and Opal I. (Best) Suyo; m. Richard D. Thimsen, Nov. 19, 1958; children: LeAnn Hoffstot, Lori Petroline, Lanette, Linelle Lyerla, Lorette, Luther, Lorna. Diploma, Mt. Olive (Ill.) H.S., 1958. Sec. Weather-Proof Co., Litchfield, Ill., 1958-59; cashier Mt. Olive (Ill.) Sch. Dist., 1984-89; libr. Mt. Olive Pub. Libr., 1990—; mem. adv. bd. Mt. Olive Sch. Dist., 1972-74, MJM Electric, Carlinville, Ill., 1975-77. Vol. sch. bd. elections Mt. Olive Sch. Dist., 1972, 84; mem. Mt. Olive Band Boosters. Democrat. Lutheran. Home: RR 1 Box 69 Mount Olive IL 62069

THOM, KELSEY C., engineering manager, manufacturing executive; b. Yreka, Calif., May 4, 1951. Tech. degree, Nat. Career Inst., San Francisco, 1972. Designer Calif. Pellet Mill Co., San Francisco, 1974-80, product design mgr., 1980-89; engring. mgr. Reskamp/ Champion, Waterloo, Iowa, 1989—. Inventor: U.S. Patents on Roll Mill, Steam Chamber. Office: Reskamp Champion 2975 Airline Cir Waterloo IA 50703-9631

THOMAN, MARK EDWARD, pediatrician; b. Chgo., Feb. 15, 1936; s. John Charles and Tasula Mark (Petrakis) T.; AA, Graceland Coll., 1956; BA, U. Mo., 1958, MD, 1962; m. Theresa Thompson, 1984; children: Marlisa Rae, Susan Kay, Edward Kim, Nancy Lynn, Janet Lea, David Mark. Intern, U. Mo. at Columbia, 1962-63; resident in pediatrics Blank Meml. Children's Hosp., Des Moines, 1963-65, chief resident, 1964-65; cons. in toxicology, 1966-67; chief dept. pediatrics Shiprock (N.Mex.) Navajo Indian Hosp., dir. N.D. Poison Info. Center, also practice medicine, specializing in pediatrics Quain & Ramstad Clinic, Bismarck, N.D., 1967-69; dir. Iowa Poison Info. Center, Des Moines, 1969—; pvt. solo practice pediatrics, Des Moines, 1969—; sr. aviation med. examiner, accident investigator FAA, 1976—, cons., lectr., 1977—; faculty Iowa State U., U. Iowa, U. Osteo. Sci. and Health; dir. Cystic Fibrosis Clinic, 1973-82; dir. Mid-Iowa Drug Abuse Program, 1972-76; mem. med. adv. bd. La Leche League Internat., 1965—; pres. Medic-Air Ltd., 1976—; aviation seminars lectr. Editor-in-chief AACTION, 1975-90. Bd. dirs. Polk County Pub. Health Nurses Assn., 1969-77, Des Moines Speech and Hearing Center, 1974-79, Ecumenical Coun. of Iowa, 1990—; bd. govs. Mo. U. Sch. Medicine Alumni, 1988—, pres.- elect, 1995. Served with USMCR, 1954-59; lt. comdr. USPHS, 1965-66; capt. USNR, 1993-96, ret. 1996; dir. Dept. Health Svcs. USNR. Recipient N.D. Gov.'s award of merit, 1969; Cystic Fibrosis Rsch. Found. award, 1975, Am. Psychiat. Assn. Thesis award, Diplomate Am. Bd. Pediatrics, Am. Bd. Med. Toxicology (examiner). 1962. Mem. AMA (del. 1970-88), NRA (life), Assn. Am. Physicians & Surgeons, Polk County Med. Soc., Iowa State Med. Assn., Aerospace Med. Assn., Res. Officers Assn., Civil Aviation Med. Assn., Am. Public Health Assn., 1986—, Soc. Adolescent Medicine, Inst. Clin. Toxicology, Internat. Soc. Pediatrics, Am. Acad. Pediatrics (chmn. accident prevention com. Iowa chpt. 1975—), Cystic Fibrosis Club, Am. Acad. Clin. Toxicology (trustee 1969-90, pres. 1982-84), Am. Assn. Poison Control Centers, U.S. Naval Inst. Republican. Elder mem. Reorganized Latter-Day Saints Ch. Clubs: Flying Physicians, Aircraft Owners and Pilots Assn., Nat. Pilots Assn. (Safe Pilot award), Hyperion Field and Country. Editor in chief AACTION, 1976-90. Home: 6896 Trail Ridge Dr Johnston IA 50131-1322 Office: 1426 Woodland Ave Des Moines IA 50309-3204

THOMAS, ALAN, candy company executive; b. Evansburg, Pa., Jan. 1, 1923; s. William Roberts and Letta (Garrett) T.; student Rutgers U., 1941-42, 46-47; B.S., Pa. State U., 1949; M.S., U. Minn., 1950, Ph.D., 1954; m. Marguerite Atria, July 1, 1972; children—Garrett Lee, Michael Alan, Randall Stephen, Brett Eliot. Instr., Temple U., Phila., 1950-51, U. Minn., St. Paul, 1951-54; research asst. Bowman Dairy Co., Chgo., 1954-56; research project mgr. M&M Candies div. Mars, Inc., Hackettstown, N.J., 1956-60, product devel. mgr., 1961-64, chocolate research dir. 1964; v.p. research and devel. Mars Candies, Chgo., 1964-67; v.p. research and devel. M&M/Mars Div., Hackettstown, 1967-77, v.p. sci. affairs, 1977-78; gen. mgr. Ethel M, Las Vegas, 1978-83, cons., 1985; sr. cons. Knechtel Research Scis., Inc., Skokie, Ill., 1984; v.p. tech. Ferrara Pan Candy Co., Forest Park, Ill., 1986-92; cons., 1993—. Chmn. coun. industry liaison panel Food and Nutrition Bd., Nat. Acad. Scis./NRC, 1972-73; adv. U.S. del. Codex Alimentarius Com. on Cocoa and Chocolate Products, 1967-78. Served to 1st lt. inf. AUS, 1942-46. Recipient research award Nat. Confectioners Assn. U.S., 1971. Mem. AAAS, Grocery Mfrs. Am. (chmn. tech. com. 1975-76), Chocolate Mfrs. Assn. (chmn. FDA liaison com. 1975-77), Inst. Food Technologists, Am. Assn. Candy Technologists, Gamma Sigma Delta, Phi Kappa Phi. Home: 2028 Waterbury Ln Las Vegas NV 89134-0384 Office: Ferrara Pan Candy Co 7301 Harrison St Forest Park IL 60130-2016

THOMAS, CAROLYN HARPER, elementary educator; b. Villa Ridge, Ill., June 24, 1950; d. John Nathan Sr and Walterene (Carter) Harper. BS in Edn., Ind. U., Gary, 1977; M in Early Childhood Edn., Edinboro (Pa.) State Coll., 1980. Lic. tchr., Ohio, Ind. Tchr. Ashtabula (Ohio) Area City Schs., 1978-91; program coord. Project Have Hope Mary Chatman Community Ctr., Ashtabula, 1987-90; coord. summer recreation program Ashtabula City Schs. & Job Tng. Partnership Act, summer 1989, 90; tchr. Gary Community Sch. Corp., 1991—; lead tchr. Kids Enrichment Program, Gary, 1992—; program coord. I Can-Tutorial and Enrichment, 1995—; mem. Kneely Mae Fleming Scholarship Selection Com., Ashtabula, 1989-91. Mem. allocations com. United Way, Ashtabula, 1989-90. Mem. Gary Reading Coun., N.W. Ind. Assn. Black Sch. Educators. Pentecostal.

THOMAS, CHRISTOPHER SEAN, information technologies developer; b. Detroit, July 24, 1957; s. Victor J. and Arlene P. (Zurowski) T.; m. Wendy E. Borovich. A of Bus., Henry Ford C.C., Dearborn, Mich., 1977; BBA, Ea. Mich. U., 1981. Cons. Dearborn, 1981-83; project mgr./system analyst ESC Solutions, Southfield, Mich., 1984-86; mgr. application devel. TECH-S Inc., Livonia, Mich., 1986-91; systems mgr./quality assurance mgr. Highland Superstores Inc., Plymouth, Mich., 1991-92; MIS mgr. PlastiPak Corp., Plymouth, 1992-94; mgr. systems devel. Arbor Drugs, Inc., Troy, Mich., 1994—; product & process systems, team leader Chrysler Corp., Auburn Hills, Mich., 1994—. V.p. High Point Estates Assn., Highland, 1994. Mem. Mich. DB2 User Group, Data Processing Mgmt. Assn., Internat. DB2 User Group, Common. Roman Catholic. Home: 2336 Estates Dr Highland MI 48357-4957

THOMAS, CHRISTOPHER YANCEY, III, surgeon, educator; b. Kansas City, Mo., Oct. 27, 1923; s. Christopher Yancey and Dorothea Louise

(Engel) T.; m. Barbara Ann Barcroft, June 27, 1946; children—Christopher, Gregg, Jeffrey, Anne. Student, U. Colo., 1942-44; M.D., U. Kans., 1948. Diplomate Am. Bd. Surgery. Intern U. Utah Hosp., Salt Lake City, 1948-49; resident in surgery Cleve. Clinic Found., 1949-52; pvt. practice specializing in surgery Kansas City, Mo., 1954-89; mem. staff St. Luke's Hosp., chief surgery, 1969-70; mem. staff Children's Mercy Hosp.; prof. surgery U. Mo., Kansas City Med. Sch.; pres. St. Luke's Hosp. Edn. Found., 1977-83, Med. Plaza Corp., 1977-79; pres. Midwest Organ Bank, 1977-82. Editor IMTRAC investment adv. letter, 1978—. Served to capt. M.C., U.S. Army, 1952-54. Fellow ACS; mem. AMA, Southwestern Surg. Congress, Central Surg. Assn., Mo. State Med. Soc., Kansas City Surg. Soc. (pres. 1968), Jackson County Med. Soc. (pres. 1971). Republican. Methodist. Club: Kansas City Country. Home: 5830 Mission Dr Shawnee Mission KS 66208-1139 Office: 4210 Shawnee Mission Pky Mission KS 66205-2506

THOMAS, CRAIG EUGENE, biochemist; b. Clearfield, Pa., Apr. 30, 1958; s. Robert Leonard and Valerie Elva (Yeckley) T.; m. Jean Elaine Cascaddan, July 15, 1959; children: Matthew Craig, Jeffrey Robert. BS, Pa. State U., 1980, MS, 1982; PhD, Mich. State U., 1986. NIEHS postdoctoral fellow Oreg. State U., Corvallis, 1986-88; sr. biochem. toxicologist Rohm & Haas Co., Spring House, Pa., 1988-89; sr. rsch. scientist Marion Merrell Dow Rsch. Inst., Cin., 1989—. Author: Ethel Browning's Toxicity and Metabolism of Industrial Solvents, 1990; contbr. articles to profl. jours. Recipient Meritorious Rsch. in Mechanisms of Toxicity award Soc. of Toxicology, 1986. Mem. The Oxygen Soc., Am. Soc. for Biochemistry and Molecular Biology. Home: 7028 Spruce Hill Cir West Chester OH 45069-3638 Office: Hoechst Marion Roussel 2110 E Galbraith Rd Cincinnati OH 45215

THOMAS, CYNTHIA ELIZABETH, advanced practice nurse; b. Highland, Ind., Sept. 3, 1958; d. James William and Naomi Elizabeth (Rice) T. BS in Animal Sci., Purdue U., 1980; ADN, Purdue U. Calumet, 1986, BSN, 1988, MSN, 1990. RN, Ind.; cert. adult nurse practitioner, family nurse practitioner, clin. specialist in med.-surg. nursing. Med.-surg. open heart ICU/CCU staff nurse, charge nurse Porter Meml. Hosp., Valparaiso, Ind., 1986-94; med.-surg. clin. instr. Purdue U. North Ctrl., Westville, Ind., 1993-94; advanced practice nurse Cmty. Health Ctrs. Koontz Lake, LaCrosse, North Judson, Starke Meml. Hosp., Ind., 1994-95; advanced practice nurse Cmty. Health Ctrs.-Koontz Lake, LaCrosse, North Judson, Ind., 1994-95, Starke Meml. Hosp., Knox, Ind.; nurse practitioner/office coord. Hanna Family Med. Ctr., LaPorte Hosp./Lakeland Area Health Svcs., 1995-96; nursing instr. LaPorte (Ind.) Hosp., Mishawaka, Ind., 1995-96; adult medicine/pulmonary nurse practitioner Arnett Clinic, Lafayette, Ind., 1996—; med.-surg. clin. instr. Purdue U., Westville, Ind., 1993-94; nursing instr. Bethel Coll., Mishawaka, Ind., 1995-96; adult medicine/pulmonary nurse practitioner, Arnett Clinic, Lafayette, Ind., 1996—. Mem. AACN, Am. Acad. Nurse Practitioners, Ceres, Alpha Zeta. Office: Pulmonary Dept Arnett Clinic 1500 Salem St Lafayette IN 47904

THOMAS, CYNTHIA GAIL, public policy research executive; b. Tulsa, Jan. 26, 1956; d. Jack Marcy and Dorothy (Bergfors) T. BS summa cum laude, U. Minn., 1978, MA, 1981. Analyst Met. Coun., St. Paul, 1978; rsch. analyst Common Cause Minn., St. Paul, 1979, lobbyist, 1980, rsch. cons., 1982; adminstr. NBC, N.Y.C., 1980; researcher Minn. State Sen., St. Paul, 1983-85, rsch. dir., 1985-86; owner Thomas Rsch., Dallas and Roseville, Minn., 1986—; pub. policy advisor Rep. Party, St. Paul, 1986—; commr. Roseville Planning Commn., 1991-95. Contbr. articles to profl. publs. Vol. Little Bros. of Poor, Mpls., 1987-94, YWCA, St. Paul, 1989-90; mem. Tex. Pub. Policy Found.; softball coach Girls Age 10-12 team St. Paul, 1988. Mem. Greater Dallas C. of C., Nature Conservancy, Amnesty Internat., Fraser Ins. Republican. Home and Office: Thomas Rsch 1137 Meadow Creek Dr #271 Irving TX 75038

THOMAS, DONNA JOHNS, former hospital administrator; b. Weatherford, Okla., Nov. 19, 1945; d. Doyle D. and Sylvia (Hileman) Johns; m. Charles W. Thomas, June 14, 1964; children: Troy, Kimberly, Kristin. Exec. dir. Nevada (Mo.) Area C. of C., 1974-83; exec. dir. Nevada Econ. Devel. Commn., 1984-88, local program coord., interim exec. dir., 1989; asst. adminstr. Nevada City Hosp., 1991-95; pres., bd. dirs. Mo. Indsl. Devel. Coun., Jefferson City, 1987-88, Mo. C. of C. Execs., 1978-84, Mo. Cmty. Betterment, Jefferson City, 1976-85; vol. mediator, arbitrator Mo. Bar Atty. Fee Dispute Panel, 1991—. Past mem., pres. Nevada Sch. bd. Edn., 1978-91. Named Mo. Community Betterment Amb., 1978. Mem. Mo. Hosp. Assn., Nevada Rotary (bd. dirs. 1988-92, Citizen of Yr. 1980), Assn. Ind. Hosps. (bd. dirs. 1989-92), Vernon County Indsl. Devel. Authority (pres. 1980-92), Nevada Area Econ. Devel. Commn. (bd. dirs., sec. 1984-85, 88-92), Distributive Edn. Clubs Am. (lifetime hon. mem.). Democrat. Baptist.

THOMAS, DOUGLAS ALAN, engineering manager; b. Cedar Rapids, Iowa, Jan. 29, 1961; s. Arthur and Twylla T.; m. Jean, Apr. 27, 1985; children: Alyssa, Derek. B, Northeastern Mo. State U., 1983. Mold designer C.B.M. Tooling, Mt. Vernon, Iowa, 1983-84; tool designer Ledford Engring., Cedar Rapids, Iowa, 1984-86; engring. mgr. J.E. Adams Industries, Cedar Rapids, Iowa, 1986-95; dir. new product devel. Legacy Mfg., Cedar Rapids, Iowa, 1995—. Coach Little League Baseball and Soccer. Mem. Soc. Mfg. Engrs. Office: Legacy Mfg Co 1201 9th St SW Cedar Rapids IA 52404

THOMAS, E.J., state legislator; b. Dec. 7, 1951; s. Eddie James III and Alice (Layne) T. BS, Ohio State Univ.; MA, Ball State Univ. Dep. asst. legis & adminstrn. Gov. James A. Rhodes, Ohio; state rep. Dist. 28, Ohio, 1985-92, Dist. 27, 1993; mem. coord. Am. Legis. Exchange Coun., Ohio, 1996—; Ohio House Rep., 1996—; mem. Ways & Means Ins. Fin. Inst. & Human Resources Com., Select Com. of Child Abuse & Juvenile Justice, Capital Sq. Renovation Hazardous Waste & Landfill Study Com. Indigent Care Task Force; at-large commn. appt. Mayor Moody & Rinehart, Clintonville Area Com.; dir. corp. affairs Security Group; v.p. bus. devel. G.W. Ganning & Assocs.; aviation cons. Treas. Watchdog, 1986, 88, 90. With Ohio Air Nat. Guard, Pub. Affairs officer Air Force, 1976-80. Recipient Vol. of Yr. Columbus Symphony Orchestra, 1988. Mem. Columbus Bd. Realtors, Nat. Guard Assn., Lions, Shriner, Scottish Rite, Am. Legion. Home: 4866 Rustic Bridge Rd Columbus OH 43214*

THOMAS, FAYE EVELYN J., elementary school educator; b. Summerfield, La., Aug. 3, 1933; d. Reginald Felton and Altee (Hunter) Johnson; B.A., So. U., 1954; student Tuskegee Inst., 1958, 69, U. Detroit, summers, 1961, 62, 63, Central Mich. U., summer 1965; M.S., U. Central Ark., 1971; M.S., Cleve. State U., 1979; m. Archie Taylor Thomas, Sept. 8, 1960; 1 son, Dwayne Andre. Tchr., Cullen (La.) Elem. Sch., 1957; tchr. English and social studies Charles Brown High Sch., Springhill, La., 1957-70; tchr. English, Upward Bound Program, Grambling State U., 1968; tchr. English, Springhill (La.) High Sch., 1970; elem. intermediate tchr. Riveredge Elem. Sch., Berea, Ohio, 1971-93; tchr. 7th grade English Ford Middle Sch., 1993-94; tchr. asst. elem. council curriculum and instrn. Berea Sch. Dist., 1984-85. Trustee Charles Brown Soc. Orgn., Christian Forum of N.Y., Inc., 1988—. EPDA grantee, 1970-71; Internat. Paper Found. grantee, summers 1958, 60; NDEA grantee, summer 1965; Martha Holden Jennings scholar, 1984-85. Mem. NEA, Ohio Edn. Assn., Berea Edn. Assn. (2d v.p. 1992-93), N.E. Ohio Tchrs. Assn., Assn. for Supervision and Curriculum Devel., Charles Brown Soc. Orgn. (trustee 1984—), People United to Save Humanity, Black Caucus Nat. Edn. Assn., Ohio Motorists Assn, Order Eastern Star, Midpark Toastmaster Club. Democrat. Baptist. Home: 19353 Bagley Rd Cleveland OH 44130-3319

THOMAS, FRANK, human resources executive, educator; b. Buffalo, Jan. 2, 1948; s. Francis Xavier and Isabel Gateff (Scrivano) T. BSBA, U. Dayton, 1969; M of Mgmt., Northwestern U., 1987. Cons., with dept. corp. recruitment Walgreen Co., Deerfield, Ill., 1977-79; assoc. orgn. planning Baxter Internat. Inc., Deerfield, 1979-84; mgmt. specialist United Airlines Inc., Chgo., 1984-87; cons. William M. Mercer Inc., Columbus, Ohio, 1987-90; prof. Capitol U., Columbus, 1990-91; vis. prof. DePaul U., Chgo., 1991—; mgr. human adminstrn. SAFCO Corp., Chgo., 1992—; mem. adv. bd. Davenport Coll., Grand Rapids, Mich., 1979-83; mem.- pharm. subcom. Midwest Coll. Placement Coun., Chgo., 1983-85; mng. cons. Human Resources Affiliates, Chgo., Columbus, 1990-92. Mem. Electronic Personnel Assn., Employment Mgrs. Assn., Kellogg Alumni Assn., Univ. Dayton Alumni Assn., Norwood Park C. of C. Office: SAFCO Corp 6060 Northwest Hwy Chicago IL 60631

THOMAS, FRANK EDWARD, professional baseball player; b. Columbus, Ga., May 27, 1968. Student, Auburn U. With Chgo. White Sox, 1990—. Named to Sporting News All-Star Coll. All Am. team, 1989; Sporting News All-Star team, 1991, 93-94; recipient Silver Slugger award, 1991, 93, 94; mem. Am. League All-Star Team, 1993-95; recipient Am. League MVP award, 1994; named Major League Player of Yr., Sporting News, 1993. Office: Chgo White Sox Comiskey Park 333 W 35th St Chicago IL 60616-3621*

THOMAS, GEORGE E., engineering executive; b. Chgo., May 28, 1961. BS, U. Ill., 1983. V.p. engring. Bison Gear Engineering Corp., Downers Grove, Ill., 1983—. Mem. Am. Gear Mfrs. Assn. (standards com.). Office: Bison Gear Mfg 2424 Wisconsin Ave Downers Grove IL 60515-4019

THOMAS, GERALD WAYNE, marketing professional; b. Connersville, Ind., Dec. 25, 1954; s. Gerald Wayne and Delores Ann (Smith) T.; m. Susan Jane Million, July 21, 1979; children: Christopher Michael, Benjamin Paul. BS in Ind. Mgmt., Purudue U., 1978. Sales engr. TRW, Lafayette, Ind., 1978-84, sr. sales engr., 1984-87; regional sales mgr. TRW, Sacramento, Calif., 1987-90; sales mgr. major accts. TRW, Lafayette, 1990-93, mgr. mktg., 1993—. Mem. athletic adv. coun. Purdue U., West Lafayette, 1992-96; bd. dirs. Lafayette Civic Theater, 1993—; co-chmn. pub. rels. com. Untied Way, Lafayette, 1995—. Office: TRW Comml Steering Divsn 800 Heath St Lafayette IN 47902-0060

THOMAS, GORDON JEROME, retired municipal official; b. Kansas City, Kans., Feb. 24, 1946; s. Aaron Earl and Edith Wenifred (Record) T.; children: Earl, Stephan, Stephanie, Donna Maxwell, Gordon Jr. Student, Penn Valley Jr. Coll., Kansas City, Mo., 1965-75. With Kansas City (Mo.) Water Dept., 1965-66; drafting aide I Kansas City Dept. Pub. Wks., 1966-67, drafting aide II, 1967-70, drafting aide III, 1970-85, engring. technician, 1985—. Treas., Bethel SDA Ch., Kansas City, Kans., 1974—, tchr., 1972—; treas. V. Lindsay SDA Sch., 1995-96. Mem. Am. Pub. Wks. Assn., Inst. for Engring. Technicians. Democrat. Home: 3612 E Gregory Blvd Kansas City MO 64132 Office: City of Kansas City Dept of Pub Wks 414 E 12th St Kansas City MO 64106

THOMAS, ISIAH LORD, III, former professional basketball player, basketball team executive; b. Chgo., Apr. 30, 1961. Grad. in Criminal Justice, Ind. U., 1987. With Detroit Pistons, 1981-94; v.p. Toronto Raptors, 1994—, now v.p.; mem. U.S. Olympic Basketball Team, 1980, NBA Championship Teams, 1989-90. Named to All-Star team, 1982-93, All NBA First Team, 1984, 85, 86; recipient All-Star team MVP award, 1984, 86, NBA Playoff MVP award, 1990, NBA Finals MVP, 1990. *

THOMAS, JEANETTE ANNE, biology educator; b. LaHarpe, Ill., Mar. 23, 1952; d. L. Keith and Barbara Ann (Ogren) T.; m. Victor Manuel Ramos, Apr. 19, 1984; children: Julienne Thomas-Ramos, Galen Thomas-Ramos. BS, Western Ill. U., 1973; MS, U. Minn., 1977, PhD, 1979. Dir. bioacoustic lab. Hubbs Sea World Rsch. Inst., San Diego, 1980-84; sr. scientist Naval Ocean Systems Ctr., Kailua, Hawaii, 1985-89; prof. biology Western Ill. U., Macomb, 1989—. Editor: Sensory Abilities of Cetaceans, 1990, Marine Mammal Sensory Systems, 1992, Sensory Systems of Aquatic Mammals, 1995. Mem. Soc. for Marine Mammalogy (pres. 1994—). Democrat. Office: Western Ill U Regional Ctr 6502 34th Ave Moline IL 61265

THOMAS, JOHN, mechanical engineer, research and development; b. Tiruvalla, Kerala, India, Jan. 2, 1946; came to U.S., 1974; s. Munnencheril Varghese and Rachel (Mathai) T.; m. Mary Parapat Varghese, Apr. 28, 1975; children: Joel George, Sayana Rachel. BSc in Mech. Engring., Birla Inst. Tech., Ranchi, India, 1969; MA Sc in Mech. Engring., U. Waterloo, Ont., Can., 1974. Registered profl. engr., Wis. Lectr. mech. engring. U. Kerala, India, 1970-71; design engr. Combustion Engring., Inc., Springfield, Ohio, 1974-76; mech. engr. Ingersoll-Rand Co., Painted Post, N.Y., 1977-80; engr. Allis-Chalmers Corp., Milw., 1980-82; pvt. practice engring. cons. Milw., 1982-84; sr. tech. devel. engr. Cross & Trecker divsn. Kearney & Trecker Corp., Milw., 1984-87; prin. John Thomas & Assocs., Brookfield, Wis., 1988—; sr. product engr. N.W. Water Group, Pub. Ltd. Corp., Waukesha, Wis., 1989-94; pres. Thomas Products Co., Brookfield, Wis., 1995—. Patentee in field. Mem. U. Waterloo Alumni Assn. Home: 18330 Benington Brookfield WI 53045-5419 Office: Thomas Products Co PO Box 401 Brookfield WI 53008-0401

THOMAS, JOHN DAVID, musician, composer, arranger, photographer, recording engineer, producer; b. Muncie, Ind., Mar. 30, 1951; s. John Charles and Phyllis Lorraine (Wear) T.; m. Rosalie Faith Baldwin, July 27, 1974 (div. 1991); children: Bethany Carol, Mark David. Student, Purdue U., 1969-71, Jordan Coll. of Music, Indpls., 1961-65; BS in Music Theory and Composition, Ball State U., 1976. Musician, composer, 1955—; cellist The Howe String Quartet (with Ann Pinney, Mary Ann Tilford, Anne Wuster), Indpls., 1967-68; keyboardist, vocalist, cellist Fire and The Rebel Kind rock bands, Indpls., 1967-69, Good Conduct rock band, Muncie, Ind., 1972-73; pianist The Pavillion at Olde Towne, Los Gatos, Calif., 1969; radio announcer John David's Late Night Rock Show WCCR-AM, West Lafayette, Ind., 1969-70; photographer Indpls., 1964-84, 91—; budget analyst Office of Comptr. USAFAC, Indpls., 1976-84; co-leader, keyboardist, composer, arranger, vocalist, sound technician JETSTREAM Band, Indpls., Kokomo, Columbus, Bloomington, Ind., 1979-83; co-leader, keyboardist, vocalist, sound technician The Thomas Bros., King's Crown Inn, Kokomo, 1979; sound/audio visual technician Valley Cathedral Ch., Phoenix, 1987; solo pianist Cascade Club, Everett, Wash., 1990; pianist, synthesist Paul Thomas and Night and Day, The Tim Barnett Band, Indpls. Mus. Art, 1992, Radisson Hotel and Broadmoor Country Club, Indpls., 1991, Highland Country Club, Indpls., The Ritz Charles Hotel and Summertrace, Carmel, Ind., Stonehenge Resort, Bedford, Ind., 1991; solo pianist Terranova Mansion, Paradise Valley, Ariz., 1987, Wrigley Mansion, Phoenix, 1988, Boulders Resort, Carefree, Ariz., 1987, Clarion Inn/McCormick's Ranch Resort, Scottsdale, Ariz., 1986, The Terranova mansion, Paradise Valley, Ariz., 1987, China Gate, Phoenix, 1988, Victor's, Phoenix, 1988; keyboardist, synthesist, key bassist, The Guich Gang, Pinnacle Peak Patio, Scottsdale, 1984, Dee Dee Ryan, The Longhorn Saloon, Apache Junction, Ariz., 1984-86, The Last Straw Band, Country City saloon, Mesa, Ariz., 1986; keyboardist, pianist, vocalist with Peter, Paul and John, Anderson Coll., Anderson, Ind., 1977; CEO, composer, arranger, prodr., musician, engr. John David Thomas Prodns., Indpls., 1993—. Composer, lyricist of over 200 classical, religious, comml., rock, jazz, popular and avante garde/futuristic compositions, including Infinity, 1970-71, Death of Rock and Roll, 1970, Night Visions, 1972, First Things First, 1972, Two Nudes and a Fire Hydrant, 1972-73, Zeitgeist: The Spirit of the Time, 1974, The Little Prince, 1973, When We Dead Awaken, 1973, Pray, 1972, Apogee, 1974, Chinese Baby, 1973, Alabama DA (Top Forty recording), 1973, Angel, 1974, Music for French Horn, Cello, and Piano, 1976, Cruising Beyond, 1979, Jetstream Theme, 1979, Chrissy, 1979, In Your Heart, 1983, Future Music, 1987, The Recurrent New Millenium Orchestral Olympic Disco Festival Dance, 1989, Jubilee in F, 1989, Praise Him, The King Liveth, 1989, Love Flowers: Reflections and Meditations on Beauty and Truth, 1990, Sheena's Theme, 1992, I Want You Forever You're My Miracle, 1992, My Pseudo-Erotic, Sensual, Exotic Musical Fantasy and Romance for Our Heavenly Nocturnal Starry-Skied Carpet Ride to Paradise in Istanbul and Constantinople, 1992, I'm in Love with Someone Beautiful, 1992, Improvisations for Sheena, 1992, Music for Baritone Vocal and String Orch., 1995; (albums) The Journey of Life, Destiny's Calling: Improvisations, 1994, Musical Essences, 1995, Pathway to Love, 1996, (broadcast) Hometown Hour, Sta. WFBQ-FM, Indpls., 1979-80; performed orginal composition, Someday, WFBM-TV, Indpls., 1969; designer automotive concepts and popular fashions; recordings of over 45 original songs and compositions, Ind., Ariz., Wash., 1970—; author (poetry with others) Mind, 1993, 96. Musician, vocalist, composer Downey Ave. Christian Ch., Indpls., 1961-69, Univ. Presbyn. Ch., West Lafayette, Ind., 1969-71, Castleview Bapt. Ch., Indpls., 1974-84, Valley Cathedral CPhoenix, 1986-87, Edmonds (Wash.) Christian Ch., 1988-90, Edmonds United Meth. Ch., 1989-90; page to speaker Ho. of Reps. Ind. State Legislature, 1963; active All Souls Unitarian Ch., Indpls. GM scholar Purdue U., 1969-70, Hoosier scholar, 1969, Palmer Meml. Music scholar Ball State U., 1971-74; named to Ind. All-State Orch. (cellist), 1968; recipient 1st place award (cellist) Ind. State Music Contest, 1968, God and Country award, 1965, Outstanding Musician award Irvington Music Club, Indpls., 1969, Purdue U. Symphonette, 1970, Hometown Hour award WFBQ-FM Radio Sta., Indpls., 1979. Mem. ASCAP, AAAS, Am. Contract Bridge League, Am. Mus. Natural History, U.S. Chess Fedn., Nat. Geographic Soc., World Futurist Soc., World Wildlife Fund, Audubon Engring. Soc., Met. Opera Guild (N.Y.C.), Mus. Modern Art (N.Y.C.), The Guggenheim Mus. (N.Y.C.), Inst. of Noetic Scis., Planetary Soc., Audubon Soc., Mus. Sci. Industry, Met. Mus. Art, La. Societé des Amis du Louvre (Paris), Mensa, Sierra Club, Internat. Amnesty Internat.

THOMAS, JOHN EDWARD, financial services marketing executive; b. Cleve., June 27, 1957; s. Alfred Benjamin and Marian Anne (Ebel) T.; m. Helen Ilic, July 9, 1986; children: Philip, Adam. BA in Psychology, Cleve. State U., 1982. Rsch. project dir. Wyse Advt., Cleve., 1982-85; asst. dir.rsch. Lowe Marschalk, Inc., Cleve., 1985-89; dir. rsch. and planning Griswold, Inc., Cleve., 1989-93; dir. mktg. info. group KeyCorp, Cleve., 1993—. Mem. Am. Mkt. Assn., World Future Soc. Office: KeyCorp 127 Public Sq 3d Fl Cleveland OH 44114

THOMAS, KUDDY SCOTT, auditor; b. West Union, Ohio, Oct. 4, 1960; s. Frank Scott and Nancy Louise (Brooke) T. BS, Ohio State U., 1982; AA, So. State Coll., Hillsborough, Ohio, 1986, AS, 1986; cert. paralegal, Inst. Paralegal Studies, 1990. Farmer Peebles, Ohio, 1978—; lab. technician Ohio State U., Columbus, 1978-82; auditor U.S. Dept. Treasury, Covington, Ky., 1988—; notary pub. State of Ohio, Seaman, 1980—; hon. con. svc. Govt. France, Seaman, 1994—. Presdl. elector Electoral Coll., Washington, 1992. Sgt. USAR, 1982—. Awarded Ky. Col. Commonwealth of Ky., 1985; named hon. sec. of state, Raleigh, N.C., 1995. Mem. MENSA, Loyal Order of the Golden Heart (Master), Sinking Springs Masonic Lodge (sr. warden), York Rite Bodies. Democrat. Home: PO Box 355 6910 Tri-County Rd Seaman OH 45679

THOMAS, LEONA MARLENE, health information educator; b. Rock Springs, Wyo., Jan. 15, 1933; d. Leonard H. and Opal (Wright) Francis; m. Craig L. Thomas, Feb. 22, 1955; (div. Sept. 1978); children: Peter, Paul, Patrick, Alexis. BA, Govs. State U., 1982, MHS, 1986; cert. med. records adminstrn., U. Colo., 1954. Dir. med. records dept. Meml. Hosp. Sweetwater County, Rock Springs, Wyo., 1954-57; staff assoc. Am. Med. Records Assn., Chgo., 1972-77, asst. editor, 1979-81; statistician Westlake Hosp., Melrose Park, Ill., 1982-84; asst. prof. Chgo. State U., 1984—, acting dir. health info. adminstrn. program, 1991-92; acting dir. health info. Internat. Coll., Naples, Fla., 1994; dir. health info. adminstrn. program Chgo. State U., 1994—; chairperson Coll. Allied Health Pers., 1986-88; mem. rev. bd. network Newsletter of Assembly on Edn. Co-pres. Ill. Dist. 60 PTA, Westmont; liaison Ill. Trauma Registry, 1991; mem. adv. com. Health Info. Tech. Program Morraine Valley Cmty. Coll., Palos Hills, Ill., 1995—, Health Info. Tech. Program Robert Morris Coll., Orland Pk., Ill., 1995—, Wellness Ctr., Chgo. State U. Mem. Assembly on Edn., Am. Health Info. Mgmt. Assn., Am. Pub. Health Assn., Ill. Pub. Health Assn., Chgo. and Vicinity Med. Records Assn. (publicity com. 1989-90), Ill. Assn. Allied Health Profls., Gov.'s State Alumni Assn. Democrat. Methodist. Home: 6340 Americana Dr Apt 1101 Clarendon Hills IL 60514-2249 Office: Chgo State U Coll Nursin & Allied Health 95th at King Dr Chicago IL 60628

THOMAS, LEWIS EDWARD, laboratory executive, retired petroleum company executive; b. Lima, Ohio, May 18, 1913; s. Lewis Edward and Ilma Kathryn (Siebert) T.; BS, Ohio No. U., 1935; MS, Purdue U., 1973; m. Elinda Patricia Grafton, Dec. 21, 1939; children: Linda Thomas Collins, Stephanie Thomas Pawuk, Kathryn Thomas Ramsey, Deborah G. Preissler. Asst. prof. chemistry Va. Mil. Inst., 1940-45; devel. engr. Sun Oil Co., Toledo, 1945-49, lab. supr., 1950-69, div. supr., 1969-73, lab. mgr., 1973-78; mgr. Toledo Symphony, 1978-80; mktg. staff Jones & Henry Labs., Toledo, 1980-82; vis. scientist to area high schs. Ohio Acad. Sci., 1960-67; bd. dir. First InternHealth Network, 1990—. Lay reader Episcopal Ch., 1962-89; pres., treas. Harvard Elem. Sch. PTA, 1953-54; mem. Mayor's Indsl. Devel. Com., Toledo, 1963-66; mem. Gov.'s Com. Statewide Health Planning Coun., 1976-82; mem. Lucas County Cen. Com., precinct committeeman Rep. Party, 1958-89; trustee Toledo Public Libr. 1966-70, pres., 1969-70; trustee Toledo Lucas County Pub. Libr., 1970-93, v.p., 1971-72, pres., 1972-75, 85-88; trustee U. Toledo, 1967-76, vice chmn. bd., 1971-75; chmn. adv. bd. St. Charles Hosp., 1990-93; mem. Assn. Governing Bds. Univs. and Colls., 1969-76; trustee Toledo Symphony Orch., 1981-93; mem. governing bd. Northwest Ohio Council Girl Scouts U.S., 1981-89; chmn. Northwest Ohio Easter Seals, 1983. named Chem. Engr. of Year, Toledo Area, 1961, 63, 76; recipient Thanks badge Girl Scouts Am., 1987, 93; registered profl. engr., Ohio. Mem. Nat., Ohio (chmn. state conv. 1975), Toledo (trustee 1974-76) socs. profl. engrs., Am. Inst. Chem. Engrs., Am. Chem. Soc. (pres. Toledo sect. 1960), Nat. Mgmt. Assn. (trustee Toledo chpt. 1962-70, nat. dir. 1968-70), Tech. Soc. Toledo (pres. 1968-69), Explorers Club, Sigma Xi, Pi Kappa Alpha, Tau Beta Pi, Nu Theta Kappa. Club: Toastmasters. Home: 4148 Deepwood Ln Toledo OH 43614-5512 Office: PO Box 920 Toledo OH 43697-0920

THOMAS, LLOYD BREWSTER, economics educator; b. Columbia, Mo., Oct. 22, 1941; s. Lloyd B. and Marianne (Moon) T.; m. Sally Leach, Aug. 11, 1963; 1 child, Elizabeth. AB, U. Mo., 1963, AM, 1964; PhD, Northwestern U., 1970. Instr. Northwestern U., Evanston, Ill., 1966-68; asst. prof. econs. Kan. State U., Manhattan, 1968-72, assoc. prof., 1974-81, prof., 1983—; asst. prof. Fla. State U., Tallahassee, 1973-74; vis. prof. U. Calif., Berkeley, 1981-82, U. Del., 1993; prof., chair dept. econs. U. Idaho, 1989. Author: Money, Banking and Economic Activity, 3d edit., 1986, Principles of Economics, 2d edit, 1993, Principles of Macroeconomics, 2d edit,, 1993, Principles of Microeconomics, 2d edit, 1993, Money, Banking and Monetary Policy, 1996; contbr. articles to profl. jours. Mem. Am. Econs. Assn., Midwest Econs. Assn., So. Econs. Assn., Western Econs. Assn., Phi Kappa Phi. Home: 1501 N 10th Ct Manhattan KS 66502

THOMAS, MARGARET CATHERINE, physical therapist, educator; b. Dubuque, Iowa, June 13, 1959; d. Daniel James and Catherine Ann (Ellerbach) Daly; m. Curtis Darrell Thomas, Nov. 28, 1987; children: Sean Daniel, Katrina Elizabeth. BS, Loras Coll., 1981; cert. in phys. therapy, U. Iowa, 1983, MA, 1991. Staff therapist St. Luke's Hosp., Cedar Rapids, Iowa, 1984-92, neurology supr., 1992-94; PTA program coord. Kirkwood C.C., Cedar Rapids, Iowa, 1994—. PTA program coord. Kirkwood Coll., Cedar Rapids, 1994. Mem. Am. Phys. Therapy Assn., Iowa Phys. Therapy Assn. (sec. 1983-85). Office: PTA Program Kirkwood Cmty Coll PO Box 2068 Cedar Rapids IA 52406

THOMAS, NATHAN, theatre arts educator; b. Jefferson, Iowa, Apr. 27, 1963; s. John E. and Frances J. (Hamsher) T. BA cum laude, Ctrl. State U., Edmond, Okla., 1985; MA in Theatre Arts, Mich. State U., 1993, PhD, 1995. Mem. faculty Ctrl. State U., Edmond, Okla., 1986-87; unit mgr., actor Repertory Theatre of Am., Rockport, Tex., 1987-91; actor Small Change Original Theatre, Mpls., 1995—; guest lectr., 1995—, workshop leader Manhattan Sch. of Music, N.Y., 1994, Lansing (Mich.) Comty. Coll. , 1995. Actor: various stages, 1981—; composer: (incidental music) King Lear and The Seagull, 1986, Beggar on Horseback, 1992; author: (books) Rhythm in Theatrical Art, 1993, Rhythm Training for Actors, 1995. Mem. Delcroze Soc. Am., Masons. Mem. Ch. of the Brethren. Home: 300 E Main St Apt 201 Lansing MI 48933

THOMAS, NED ALBERT, insurance agent; b. Columbus, Ohio, July 15, 1943; s. Hiram Albert and Leona Mary (Hart) T.; m. Marilyn Jane Fedderke, Dec. 2, 1967; children: Amy, Joy, Barrett. BA, Ohio State U., 1968. CLU, ChFC; registered security rep. Ins. agent Mut. Benefit Life, Columbus, Ohio, 1968-74; supr. Mut. Benefit Life, Columbus, 1974-75; pension adminstr. Compensation Underwriting Svcs., Columbus, 1975-79; dir. employee benefits Kientz & Co., Columbus, 1979-82; wholesaler Robert Fulton & Assocs., Columbus, 1982-84; pvt. practice fin. planning Columbus, 1984-86; pres. Compensation Underwriting Svcs., Columbus, 1986-91; estate planning specialist Merrill Lynch, Columbus, 1991—; bd. dirs. Harvest Life Ins. Co., Orlando, Fla.; pres. Ohio Preneed Mktg. Cons., Columbus, 1986;

pension cons., pre-retirement planning cons. Blue Cross Cen. Ohio, Columbus; mktg. cons. Harvest Ins. Agy., Cleve.; pre-retirement planning cons. GE Superabrasives, Worthington, Ohio; lectr. pensions and extended life expectancy, 1977. Cubmaster Westerville area Boy Scouts Am., 1989-91; mem. German Village Soc. 1st lt. Air N.G., 1967-73. Mem. Nat. Assn. Securities Dealers, Columbus Life Underwriters Assn. (past pres.), Ohio State Pres. Club, Westerville C. of C., Internat. Soc. Retirement Planners (trustee 1989-90), Am. Soc. CLU and ChFC, Capitol Club. Republican. Office: Merrill Lynch 65 E State St Columbus OH 43215-4213

THOMAS, NORMAN CARL, political science educator; b. Sioux Falls, S.D., Feb. 16, 1932; s. Russell and Helen Victoria (Matson) T.; m. Marilyn Lou Murphy, Jan. 31, 1953; children—Robert, Margaret, Elizabeth, Anne. B.A., U. Mich., 1953; M.A., Princeton, 1958, Ph.D., 1959. Instr. polit. sci. U. Mich., Ann Arbor, 1959-62; asst. prof. U. Mich., 1962-65, assoc. prof., 1965-69; prof. Duke U., 1969-71; prof. polit. sci. U. Cin., 1971-80, Charles Phelps Taft prof., 1980—, head dept., 1971-76, 81-89, disting. tchg. prof., 1995; cons. Adminstrv. Conf. U.S., 1971-75. Author: Rule 9: Politics, Administration and Civil Rights, 1966, (with Karl A. Lamb) Congress: Politics and Practice, 1964, Education in National Politics, 1975, (with J.A. Pika and R.A. Watson) The Politics of the Presidency, 1983, 2d edit., 1987, 3d edit., 1993, 4th edit., 1996; editor, contbr.: The Presidency in Contemporary Context, 1975; editor: (with A.A. Altshuler) Politics of the Federal Bureaucracy, 1977; contbr. articles to profl. jours. Served to lt. (j.g.) USNR, 1953-56. Recipient Disting. Service award U. Mich. Devel. Council, 1964; Woodrow Wilson fellow, 1956-57. Mem. Am. Polit. Sci. Assn., Am. Soc. Pub. Adminstrn., Kappa Sigma. Democrat. Presbyn. Home: 510 Oliver Ct Cincinnati OH 45215-2505

THOMAS, PAMELA ADRIENNE, special education educator; b. St. Louis, Oct. 28, 1940; d. Charles Seraphin Fernandez and Adrienne Louise (O'Brien) Fernandez Reeg; divorced, 1977; m. Alvertis T. Thomas, July 22, 1981. BA in Spanish and EdS, Maryville Coll., 1962; Cert. EdS, U. Ky., 1966-67; MA in Edn., St. Louis U., 1974. Cert. learning disabilities, behavior disorders, educable mentally retarded, Spanish, Mo. Tchr. Pawnee Rock Kans. Sch., 1963-64; diagnostic tchr. Frankfort State Hosp. Sch., Ky., 1964-67; spl. edn. tchr. St. Louis City Pub. Schs., 1968-71, itinerant tchr., 1971-73, ednl. strategist, 1973-74, elem. level resource tchr., 1974-78, secondary resource tchr., dept. head, 1978—; head dept. spl. edn., 1978—; Co-author: Sophomore English Resource for Credit Curriculum Handbook, 1991. Co-author: Teaching Foreign Language to Handicapped Secondary Students, 1990. Pres. Council for Exceptional Children, local chpt. #103, 1982-83, Mo. Division of Mentally Retarded, 1985-87. Mem. Alpha Delta Kappa (St. Louis chpt. pres. 1982-84). Home: 4534 Ohio Ave Saint Louis MO 63111-1324 Office: Cen VAP High Sch 3616 N Garrison Ave Saint Louis MO 63107-2501

THOMAS, PATRICIA GRAFTON, secondary school educator; b. Michigan City, Ind., Sept. 30, 1921; d. Robert Wadsworth and Elinda (Oppermann) Grafton; student Stephens Coll., 1936-39, Purdue U., summer 1938; BEd magna cum laude, U. Toledo, 1966; postgrad. (fellow) Bowling Green U., 1968; m. Lewis Edward Thomas, Dec. 21, 1939; children: Linda T., Stephanie A. (Mrs. Andrew M. Pawuk), I. Kathryn (Mrs. James N. Ramsey), Deborah (Mrs. Edward Preissler). Lang. art and art tchr. Toledo Bd. Edn., 1959-81, tchr. lang. arts Byrnedale Sch., 1976-81; pres. Jr. High Coun., 1963. Dist. capt. Planned Parenthood, 1952-53, ARC, 1954-55; mem. lang. arts curriculum com. Toledo Bd. Edn., 1969, 73, mem. grammar curriculum com., 1974, pres. Jr. High Coun. Toledo Pub. Schs.; bd. dirs. Anthony Wayne Nursery Sch., 1983—; bd. dirs. Toledo Women's Symphony Orch. League, 1983—, sec., 1985—; co-chmn. Showcase of the Arts, 1990-92. Adolf Dehn fellow, 1939. Mem. AAUW, Toledo Soc. Profl. Engrs. Aux., Helen Kreps Guild, Toledo Artists' Club, Spectrum, Friends of Arts (bd. dirs. 1989—), Phi Kappa Phi, Phi Delta Kappa, Kappa Delta Pi, Pi Lambda Theta (chpt. pres. 1978-80), Delta Kappa Gamma (chpt. pres. 1976-78, area membership chmn. 1978-80, 1st place award for exhbn. 1985). Republican. Episcopalian. Home: 4148 Deepwood Ln Toledo OH 43614-5512

THOMAS, RICHARD LEE, banker; b. Marion, Ohio, Jan. 11, 1931; s. Marvin C. and Irene (Harruff) T.; m. Helen Moore, June 17, 1953; children: Richard L., David Paul, Laura Sue. BA, Kenyon Coll., 1953; postgrad. (Fulbright scholar), U. Copenhagen, Denmark, 1954; MBA (George F. Baker scholar), Harvard U., 1958. With First Nat. Bank Chgo., 1958—, asst. v.p., 1962-63, v.p., 1963-65; v.p., gen. mgr. First Nat. Bank Chgo. (London br.), 1965-66; v.p. term loan divsn. First Nat. Bank, Chgo., 1968; sr. v.p., gen. mgr. First Chgo. Corp., 1969-72, exec. v.p., 1972-73, vice chmn. bd., 1973-75, pres., 1975-92, chmn., pres., CEO, 1992-94; chmn. First Chgo. NBD Corp., 1995-96, ret. chmn., 1996; dir. CNA Fin. Corp., Sara Lee Corp., IMC Global Inc., PMI Mort. Ins. Co. Trustee, past chmn. bd. trustees Kenyon Coll.,Orchestral Assn.; trustee Rush-Presbyn.-St. Luke's Med. Ctr.; trustee Northwestern U. With AUS, 1954-56. Mem. Chgo. Coun. Fgn. Rels., Sunningdale Golf Club (London), Econ. Club (past pres.), Comml. Club (chmn.), Chgo. Club, Casino Club, Mid-Am. Club, Indian Hill Club (Winnetka, Ill.), Old Elm Club (Highland Park, Ill.), Phi Beta Kappa, Beta Theta Pi. Office: First Chgo NBD Corp 1 First Nat Plz Chicago IL 60670

THOMAS, RICHARD STEPHEN, financial executive; b. Mason City, Iowa, June 5, 1949; s. H. Idris and Mildred (Keen) T.; m. Pamela Jane Chipka, Sept. 11, 1982. AA, No. Iowa C.C., 1969; BA, U. No. Iowa, 1971, BLS, 1991; MBA, U. Calif., Berkeley, 1991. Cost acct. Boise Cascade, Mason City, Iowa, 1971-72; cost acct. mgr. Boise Cascade, Shippensburg, Pa., 1973-74; staff acct. Grumman Corp., Williamsport, Pa., 1974-76; acctg. mgr. Pullman Power Products, Williamsport, 1976-79; treas, controller Schweizer Dipple Inc., Cleve., 1979-87; treas., corp. controller Langenau Mfg. Co., Cleve., 1987-92, chief fin. officer, 1987-92; sec.-treas. World Trade Wins Inc., Cleve., 1987-92; v.p. fin. and CFO Norris Bros. Co., Inc., Cleve., 1992—. Mem. employer adv. com. Ohio Job Svc., Greater Cleve. Growth Assn. Mem. Inst. Mgmt. Accts. (contr.'s coun. 1985), Constrn. Fin. Mgmt. Assn. (pres. 1995—, state dir., nat. dir.), Am. Assn. Indsl. Investors, Am. Acctg. Assn. (profl. rels. com. 1986-87), Cleve. Treas.'s Assn., Cleve. Engring. Soc., Associated Builders and Contractors, Constrn. Employers Assn., Econ. Club Indpls., Cleve. World Trade Assn., Masons (local treas. 1984), York Rite Bodies, Phi Beta Lambda. Republican. Home: 1663 Settlers Reserve Way Westlake OH 44145-2042 Office: Norris Bros Co Inc 2138 Davenport Ave Cleveland OH 44114-3724

THOMAS, ROBERT MICHAEL, special education educator; b. Chgo., Mar. 26, 1954; s. John Henry and Jane Eileen (Graff) T.; m. Susan Joan Jans, Oct. 13, 1979. BA, Marquette U., 1976, edn. cert., 1982; postgrad. in urban affairs, U. Wis., Milw., 1977-80; MS in Spl. Edn., U. Wis., LaCrosse, 1987. Cert. secondary social studies tchr., spl. edn. tchr., Wis. Secondary emotionally disturbed program tchr. Norris Sch., Big Bend, Wis., 1983-84; elem. emotionally disturbed program tchr. Tomah (Wis.) Area Sch. Dist., 1984-86; spl. edn. grad. asst. U. Wis., LaCrosse, 1986-87; secondary emotionally disturbed program tchr. Milw. Pub. Schs., 1987-88; secondary emotionally disturbed program tchr. West Allis (Wis.)-West Milw. Schs., 1988-89, collaborative cons. elem. emotionally disturbed program, 1989—; instr exceptional edn. Mt. Mary Coll., Milw., 1993—. Campaign organizer Congressman Jim Moody, Milw., 1982. Bork scholar, 1973. Mem. Wis. Assn. Children with Behavior Disorders, Coun. on Exceptional Children. Home: 1023 S 121st St West Allis WI 53214-2008 Office: Jefferson Sch 7229 W Becher St Milwaukee WI 53219-1217

THOMAS, SUSAN, business executive. Pres. Susan's Spl. Needs, Detroit, 1993—; v.p. Thomas Internat., Detroit, 1985—.

THOMAS, TERRA L., human services institute executive, psychologist; b. Easton, Md., Oct. 16, 1947; d. Clarence S. and Betty (Leatherberry) T.; children: Brooks, Rheaves and Nia (triplets). BS in Exptl. Psychology cum laude, Morgan State U., Balt., 1969; MA in Counselor Edn., NYU, 1971; MA in Clin. Psychology, Adelphi U., 1973, PhD in Clin. and Sch. Psychology, 1982; MBA, Northwestern U., 1991. Acting dean women Bloomingfield (N.J.) Coll., 1969-71; psychol. cons. Brownville Child Devel., Inc., Bklyn., 1972-74, Ebony Mgmt. Assocs., Bklyn., 1976-77; cons., program coord. children's div. Ada S. McKinley, Inc., Bklyn., 1976-78; with Human Resources Devel. Inst., Inc., Chgo., 1978—; v.p. Office Employee Devel., Assistance and Tng. Human Resources Devel. Inst., Inc., 1987-88, sr. v.p. Office Clin. Profl. Svcs., 1988-89, sr. v.p. Office Program Ops., 1989—, sr. v.p. Office Community and Support Svcs., 1990—, exec. v.p. Tech. Resources and Tng. Ctr., Inc., 1984—; assoc. mem. faculty Northwestern U. Med. Sch., Chgo., 1983—; adj. prof. Lewis Natl Coll. Edn., Chgo., 1982-83; mental health specialist Bobby Wright Comprehensive Mental Health Ctr., Chgo., 1975-77; sr. cons. Bakeman and Assoc., Chgo., 1983-87; presenter in field; trainer V.I. Dept. Health, 1988, Nat. Forum for Black Pub. Adminstrs., Chgo., 1990; instr. Jackson (Miss.) State U., summer 1988—; cons. Midwest AIDS Tng. Ctr., U. Ill., Chgo., 1987—, Nat. Inst. on Drug Abuse, 1987—; also others. Bd. dirs.-at-large Nat. Black Alcoholism Coun., 1984—; mem. Ill. Gov.'s Task Force on Consolidation, 1983-84; bd. dirs. Ill. Cert. Bds., Inc., 1985—, AIDS Found. Chgo., 1986-89; co-chmn. internal AIDS adv. panel Chgo. Dept. Health, 1987-88; mem. prevention communication adv. com. Ill. Dept. Alcoholism and Drug Abuse, 1988-89; mem. instl. rev. bd. Addiction Rsch. Inst., 1988—; bd. dirs. Nat. AIDS Network, 1988-90; mem. Ill. AIDS Adv. Coun., 1988—; also others. Recipient mayor's cert. of merit City of Chgo., 1985, Outstanding Alumni award Nat. Assn. for Equal Opportunity in Higher Edn., 1988, recognition award AIDS Found. Chgo., 1989; named One of 10 Outstanding Young Citizens, Chgo. Jr. Assn. Commerce and Industry, 1986. Mem. Assn. Black Psychologists (pres. 1976), Ill. Alcoholism and Drug Dependence Assn. (Prevention Leadership award 1987), NAACP (bd. dirs., edn. com. Chgo. chpt. 1988—), Psi Chi, Alpha Kappa Alpha. Home: 2008 S 7th St Camden NJ 08104-2238

THOMASMA, TIMOTHY DALE, industrial engineer, educator; b. Lakewood, Ohio, July 16, 1954; s. Ronald Arthur and Beatrice Elaine (Cook) T.; m. Teresa Small, Oct. 14, 1989; children: Antwuan, Michael. MS in Math., U. Mich., 1977, PhD in Indsl. and Ops. Engring., 1983. Assoc. prof. indsl. and systems engring. U. Mich., Dearborn, 1990-92, asst. prof., 1987-92; sr. software engr. CDI Computer Svcs., Dearborn, 1992-93; info. systems tech. specialist Ford Motor Co., Dearborn, 1993—; sr. cons. Prodn. Modeling Corp., Dearborn, 1987—. Contbr. articles to profl. jours. Recipient Rinck Meml. award Calvin Coll., Grand Rapids, Mich., 1976; DeVlieg Found fellow, 1980, 81. Mem. Sigma Xi. Office: Fairlane Office Ctr 6 Parklane Blvd Ste 451 Dearborn MI 48126-2618

THOMASON, LARRY, state legislator; b. Jefferson City, Mo., Oct. 31, 1948; m. Diane Bush, 1978; 1 child, Sarah. BS, Ark. State U. Mem. Mo. Ho. of Reps. from 163d dist., 1988—; mem. Agr.-Bus., Appropriations, Comm., Transp. Coms. Mo. Ho. of Reps.; cons. econ. devel.; mem. adv. bd. Internat. Bus. Inst. S.E. Mo. State U., Dyersburg C.C. Assoc. dir. Mo. Indsl. Devel. Commn.; active S.E. Mo. Regional Growth Assn., Hwy. 412 Corridor Assn. Mem. Kennett C. of C. (exec. dir.), Am. Legion, Lions. Democrat. Home: PO Box 523 Kennett MO 63857-0523*

THOMAS TOPP, MARGARET ANN, educational administrator, art educator; b. Waukesha, Wis., June 19, 1951; d. Melvin Michael and Elizabeth (Brewer) T.; 1 child, Michael. BA in Art Edn., Beloit Coll., 1974; MA in Art, U. Wis., Whitewater, 1981, MA in Ednl. Psychology, 1985; MS in Ednl. Adminstrn., U. Wis., 1995, PhD in Ednl. Adminstrn., Ednl. Psychology. Cert. K-12 art tchr., Wis., elem. and H.S. prin., curriculum dir. K-12, supt. Tchr. art Beloit (Wis.) Pub. Schs., 1974—; mem. staff Beloit Coll., 1992-93; muralist instr. Beloit Coll., summers, 1985-91, adj. prof., 1993—; adj. prof. Nat. Louis U., 1994—. Author: Effective Teachers; Effective Schools, 1989; contbr. articles to profl. jours. Bd. dirs. Wis.-Gate Found., 1985-87, Wis. Racquetball Assn., 1986-87, Wis. Future Problem Solving, 1986-87; pres. bd. dirs. YWCA, 1987-91; dir. Beloit and Vicinity Art Show, Beloit Coll., 1982-84, Rock Prairie Showcase Festival; founder Summer Explorers Beloit Coll. Mem. Wis. Coun. for Gifted and Talented (bd. dirs. 1984-87, v.p. 1985-86, pres. 1986-87). Home: 1035 Pleasant #3407 Beloit WI 53571

THOMAS-WILLIAMS, PAMELA RAE, publishing executive; b. La Crosse, Wis., July 30, 1955; d. Dale Richard and Betty Jean (Clark) Thomas; m. Richard G. Williams, Oct. 30, 1987; children: Kim Turpin, Connie Sommers, Rick Williams, Ryan Williams. BA in Journalism, Marquette U., 1977. Pres. Visual Concepts, ltd., La Crosse, 1979-85; v.p. Bridal Guide, Ltd., La Crosse, 1985—; dir. developmental resources Cath. Cmty. Svcs., Las Vegas, Nev., 1990-91; cons., fundraiser Cath. Charities, La Crosse, 1985-91. Author: From My Pallet of Winter, Let Me Paint Your Spring, 1978, Bridal Guide-A Complete Guide on How to Plan Your Wedding, 5th edit., 1988, (Spanish translation Bridal Guide) Guia Nupcial, 1994. Mem. area VFW aux., 1992—. Mem. Pub. Rels. Soc. Am., Fraternal Order of Eagles (aux.), Sigma Delta Chi. Republican. Lutheran. Office: Bridal Guide Ltd 2820 Leonard St La Crosse WI 54601

THOMBRE, MELANIE SUSAN, child psychiatrist; b. Norman, Okla., Dec. 16, 1953. BA, Knox Coll., Galesburg, Ill., 1975; MD, U. Ill., 1979. Diplomate Am. Bd. Psychiatry. Asst. prof. psychiatry Med. Coll. of Ohio, Toledo, 1984-87; med. dir. adolescent psychiat. unit St. Charles Hosp., Oregon, Ohio, 1987-91; pvt. practice Toledo, 1989—. Mem. Am. Orthopsychiat. Assn., Am. Psychiat. Assn., Am. Acad. Child and Adolescent Psychiatry. Office: 2639 Upton Ave Toledo OH 43606

THOMOPULOS, GREGS G., consulting engineering company executive; b. Benin City, Nigeria, May 16, 1942; s. Aristoteles and Christiana E. (Ogiamien) T.; m. Patricia Walker, Sept. 4, 1966 (div. 1974); 1 child, Lisa; m. Mettie L. Williams, May 28, 1976; children: Nicole, Euphemia. BSCE with highest distinction, U. Kans., 1965; MS in Structural Engring., U. Calif., Berkeley, 1966; PhD (hon.), Teikyo Marycrest U., 1996. Sr. v.p. internat. div. Stanley Cons., Inc., Muscatine, Iowa, 1978-84, sr. v.p. project divsn., 1984-87; pres. Stanley Consultants, Inc., Muscatine, Iowa, 1987—; exec. v.p. SC Co., Inc., Muscatine, 1992—, also bd. dirs.; chmn., CEO Stanley Cons. Environ., Inc., Chgo., 1991—, also bd. dirs.; chmn., CEO SC Power Devel., Inc., 1992—; CEO Stanley Design-Build, Inc., Muscatine, 1995—; chmn., CEO Stanley Design-Build, Inc., 1995—; bd. dirs. Stanley Cons., Inc., Muscatine. Bd. dirs. Goodwill Industries Ea. Iowa, 1987—, pres., 1992-94; mem. adv. bd. U. Iowa Coll. Engring., Ctrl. State U. Water Resources Ctr. Fellow ASCE, Am. Cons. Engring. Coun.; mem. NSPE, 33 Club (pres. 1987), Rotary. Presbyterian. Home: 1002 Estron St Iowa City IA 52246-4602 Office: Stanley Cons Inc 225 Iowa Ave Muscatine IA 52761-3730

THOMPSEN, JOYCE ANN, organizational consultant; b. Owatonna, Minn., Mar. 21, 1946; d. Stanley Albert and Elda Margaret Elsie (Buehring) Moeckly; children: James Paul, Matthew John. BS Bus. Edn, Mankato (MN) State U., 1984; MBA, U. St. Thomas, St. Paul, MN, 1988; postgrad., Walden U., 1995—. Exec. sec. Josten's Co., Owatonna, MN, 1964-71; univ. rels. supr. U. Minn., Waseca, 1971-72; v.p. employee and community rels., corp. sec. E.F. Johnson Co., Waseca, 1972—, corp. sec., 1977-81, v.p. adminstrn., corp. sec., 1981-86, v.p. employee and community relations, corp. sec., 1986-88, v.p. human resources, 1988-89, acct. exec., 1989-90; sr. cons. in orgnl. change Devel. Dimensions Internat., 1990—; exec. cons. Zenger Miller, 1995—; mem. rsch. adv. bd., dir. Minn. Coop. Office, Greater Minn. Corp.; asst. prof., adj. lectr. St. Mary's Coll., St. Thomas Coll., U. Minn. Trustee E.F. Johnson Co. Found., Waseca, 1984-89; mem. Gov.'s Computer Edn. Coun., 1984-88; chmn. adv. coun., Mankato (Minn.) State U., 1988-90; mem. adv. coun. grad. mgmt. programs U. St. Thomas, 1987—. Mem. Am. Soc. Tng. and Devel., AAUW, Am. Electronics Assn. (exec. coun. Minn. chpt. 1983-86), Minn. High Tech. Coun. Lutheran. Home: 15143 Patricia Ct Eden Prairie MN 55346 Office: Zenger Miller 3601 Minnesota Dr Ste 880 Minneapolis MN 55435

THOMPSON, BASIL F., ballet master; b. Newcastle-on-Tyne, Eng., 1937; came to U.S., 1958; Grad., Royal Acad. Dance; studies with, David Lichine, Tania Riabouchinska; student, Sch. Classical. Ballet, 1958-60. Dancer Covent Garden Opera Co., Sadler Wells Opera Co., London, 1954-55, Royal Ballet Eng., London, 1955-58; instr. ballet and character Eugene Loring Sch. Ballet, L.A., 1958-60, Al Gilber Sch. Ballet, L.A., 1958-60; instr. ballet Michael Panaieff Sch. Ballet, L.A., 1958-60; soloist Am. Ballet Theatre, N.Y.C., 1960-67; ballet master Joffrey Ballet Co., N.Y.C., 1967-79; ballet master, choreographer N.J. Ballet Co., West Orange, 1979-80; mem. faculty ballet and character N.J. Ballet Sch., Morristown/West Orange, 1979-80; ballet master Milw. Ballet, 1981-86, also artistic head; currently ballet master Pa. and Milw. Ballet; apptd. artistic dir. Milw. Ballet, spring 1995; guest ballet instr. Internat. Ballet Inst., Aix-en-Provence, France, 1980; guest instr. character Am. Ballet Co. Sch., 1981. Roles include (prin.) Billy the Kid, Sleeping Beauty, Graduation Ball, La Sylphide, Moon Reindeer, Peter and The Wolf, Three Cornered Hat, others, (soloist) Rodeo, Fall River Legend, Fire Bird, Coppelia, Swan Lake, Cinderella, La Boutique Fantastic, Undertow, others (opera) Aida; guest appearances include for Dame Margo Fontayne Royal Acad. Gala, Pres. John F. Kennedy, Pres. Lyndon B. Johnson, L.A. Civic Light Opera, Michael Panaieff Ballet Theatre; TV appearances include Bell Telephone Hour Spectacular prodn. Graduation Ball, NBC prodn. Sleeping Beauty and Cinderella; Broadway prodns. On a Clear Day You Can See Forever, Tavarich, Happiest Girl in the World; choreographer La Traviata. Office: Milw Ballet 504 W National Ave Milwaukee WI 53204-1746

THOMPSON, BERTHA BOYA, retired education educator, antique dealer and appraiser; b. New Castle, Pa., Jan. 31, 1917; d. Frank L. and Kathryn Belle (Park) Boya; m. John L. Thompson, Mar. 27, 1942; children: Kay Lynn Thompson Koolage, Scott McClain. BS in Elem. & Secondary Edn., Slippery Rock State Coll., 1940; MA in Geography and History, Miami U., 1954; EdD, Ind. U., 1961. Cert. elem. and secondary edn. tchr. Elem. tchr., reading specialist New Castle (Pa.) Sch. System, 1940-45; tchr., chmn. social studies Talawanda Sch. System, Oxford, Ohio, 1954-63; assoc. prof. psychology and geography, chair edn. dept. Western Coll. for Women, Oxford, 1963-74; assoc. prof. edn., reading clinic Miami U., Oxford, 1974-78, prof. emeritus, 1978—; pvt. antique dealer, appraiser Oxford, 1978—. Contbr. articles to profl. jours. Mem. folk art com. Miami U. Art Mus., Oxford, 1974-76; mem. adv. com. Smith libr., Oxford Pub. Libr., 1978-81. Mem. AAUP, Nat. Coun. Geographic Edn. (exec. bd. dirs. 1966-69), Nat. Soc. for Study Edn., Assn. Am. Geographers, Soc. Women Geographers, Nat. Coun. for the Social Studies, Pi Lambda Theta, Zeta Tau Alpha, Pi Gamma Mu, Gamma Theta Upsilon, Kappa Delta Pi. Home: 6073 Contreras Rd Oxford OH 45056-9708

THOMPSON, BRADLEY MERRILL, lawyer; b. Chgo., Aug. 8, 1961; s. Merrill Sanford and Emma (Lawson) T.; m. Betty Jefvert, Nov. 4, 1989. BA, U. Ill., 1982, MBA, 1983; JD, U. Mich., 1986. Bar: Ind., 1986; bd. cert. regulatory affairs, Ind. Ptnr. Baker & Daniels, Indpls., 1986—; adj. prof. Ind. U. Sch. of Law; bd. dirs. AquaMatic Inc., Rockford, Ill., 1988—, AquaMatic DISC, Inc., Rockford, 1990—. Bd. editors Regulatory Affairs, Med. Device & Diagnostic Industry. Bd. dirs., sec. Indpls. Ambs., Inc., 1988-89, HealthNet, Inc., Indpls., 1990-94; dir. Ind. Health Industry Forum, Inc.; various positions Crossroads of Am. coun. Boy Scouts Am., 1986—. Mem. ABA, Ind. State Bar Assn., Indpls. Bar Assn., Ind. Med. Device Mfrs. Coun., Inc. (sec., gen. counsel 1991), Food and Drug Law Inst., Ind. Bus. Modernization and Technology Corp. (med. tech. com.), Indpls. Athletic Club, Econ. Club of Indpls. Republican. Office: Baker & Daniels 300 N Meridian St Indianapolis IN 46204-1755

THOMPSON, CAROLYN WYNELLE, psychologist, behavioral healthcare executive; b. Birmingham, Ala., Oct. 15, 1939; d. Davis Hunt and Margaret Wynelle (Doggett) T.; m. James Robbin Cochrane (div.). BA, Emory U., 1961; MA, U. Chgo., 1963, PhD, 1968. Lic. psychologist, 1971; diplomate in clin. psychology Am. Bd. Profl. Psychology. Postdoctoral student Gestalt Inst., Chgo., 1970-73; counselor U. Chgo., 1968; acting dir. Am. Inst. for Rsch., Chgo., 1970-71; asst. prof. DePaul U., Chgo., 1968-72; dir. psychol. svcs. Family Svc. Ctrs., Flossmoor, Ill., 1972-78; pres., CEO Family Svc. Ctrs., Matteson, Ill., 1978—; comm. prof. Govs. State U., University Park, Ill., 1973, 75, 76; cons. Met. Sanitary Dist. Chgo., 1969; bd. dirs. Great Lakes Fin. Resources, Inc., First Nat. Bank Blue Island. Contbr. articles to profl. jours. Mem. Ill. Assn. Cmty. Mental Health Agys. (pres. 1994-95, bd. dirs. 1991-95), Rotary Club Chicago Heights. Home: 565 Aberdeen Dr Crete IL 60417-1202 Office: Family Svcs Ctrs 19530 Kedzie Flossmoor IL 60422

THOMPSON, DENNIS RAY, agriculture educator; b. Tuscola, Ill., Aug. 31, 1950; s. Donald Richard and Frances Virginia (Sisk) T.; m. Janet Kay Boyer, June 18, 1971; children: Beth, Diana. BS in Animal Industries, So. Ill. U., 1972, MS in Agrl. Edn. and Mechanization, 1981. Asst. extension adviser agr. U. Ill., Lewistown, 1972-75; assoc. extension adviser agr. U. Ill., Marion, 1975-79; extention adviser agr. U. Ill., Cambridge, 1979-81; sr. I extension adviser U. Ill., East Moline, 1981-88; leader extension unit U. Ill., Champaign, 1992, sr. I extension adviser, 1988-92, extension unit leader, 1992; dir. field svcs. Land of Lincoln Soybean Assn., Bloomington, Ill., 1981-83; adj. prof. Black Hawk Coll., Kewanee, Ill., 1980-81; rsch. extension liaison officer U.S. AID-U. Ill., Zambia, 1985, tech. cons., Pakistan, 1993. Contbg. author: Farm and Ranch Business Management, student and instr. guides, 1985, The Henry County Comprehensive Plan, 1980. Chair task force Cen. Ill. Conf. United Meth. Ch., Springfield, Ill., 1985-88; trustee Village of Cambridge, Ill., 1985-88; mem. Quad City Regional Econ. Econ. Devel. Com., Moline, Ill., 1987. Mem. Nat. Assn. County Agr. Agrs. (chmn. ann. meeting 1990-91), Disting. Svc. award 1989, Rural Devel. award 1986, Environ. Quality award 1976, Livestock award 1987, Ag.Communications-Radio award 1990), Ill. Extension Advisers Assn. (Agronomy award 1987, Disting. Svc. award 1989, v.p. 1990-91), Am. Soc. Agronomy, Phi Kappa Phi. Republican. Home: 1010 N Garden Ct Mahomet IL 61853-9113 Office: Champaign County Coop Ext 1715 W Springfield Ave Champaign IL 61821-3011

THOMPSON, DONALD EUGENE, industrial engineer; b. Harper, Kans., Jan. 13, 1945; s. W.H. and Louise T. BA in Indsl. Arts, Ft. Hays State U., 1968. Engr. Thompson Custom Machine Wks., Ltd., Conway Springs, Kans., 1955—. Patentee on Land-A-Ranger. Asst. chief Fire dept., Conway Springs, 1995—; sponsor Explorer post Boy Scouts Am. Mem. Nat. Fedn. Ind. Bus., N.Am. Hunting Club. Office: Thompson Custom Machine Wks PO Box 528 Conway Springs KS 67031-0528

THOMPSON, DOROTHY DENISE, university administrator; b. Denver, May 19, 1953; d. Charles B. and Margaret A. (Kraska) Turner; m. David Brent Thompson, Mar. 2, 1972; 1 child, Angie. AA, U. Wis., Richland Ctr., 1984; B of Gen. Studies, U. Wis., Green Bay, 1987. Staff writer Spring Green (Wis.) Home News, 1981; free lance writer Richland Observer, Richland Center, 1982-83; co-host, interview coord. Nova Video/Our Town TV, Richland Center, 1987—; assoc. lectr. U. Wis. Ctr., Richland, 1990—, student activities coord., 1988—, pub. info. mgr., 1985—, adminstrv. specialist, 1996—. Contbr. numerous articles to profl. pubs. Home: 878 E Burton St Richland Center WI 53581-2605 Office: U Wis Richland 1200 US Hwy 14 Richland Center WI 53581-1399

THOMPSON, ERIC THOMAS, manufacturing company executive; b. Warren, Ohio, July 19, 1962; s. Thomas Leroy Thompson and Georgia Kay (Rex) Stafani; 1 stepchild, Eugene Stefani; m. Susan E. Robertson, 1988; children: Sara Rebecca, Eric Thomas, Katlyn Grace. Student., Youngstown State U., 1981, 83-84, Kent State U., 1982. Outside sales rep., disc jockey WTCL Radio Sta., Warren, Ohio, 1979-80; disc jockey WOKG, Warren, Ohio, 1981-82, WMGZ, Sharon, Pa., 1982-83; sales rep. Custom Sound Co., Warren, Ohio, 1983-86, Litco Internat., Youngstown, Ohio, 1986-88; admissions rep. Bryant and Stratton Bus. Inst., Cleve., 1988-89; broker Argent Diamond & Gems, Charlotte, N.C., 1983; asst. sales mgr. Gene and Sons Jewelers, Warren, 1986-87; mgr. sales ops. Internat. Graphics Co., Cleve., 1988; network coord. The Ohio Desk Co., Cleve., 1989-90; account executive Alco Office Furniture, Cleve., 1979-81; high sch. admissions rep. Nat. Edn. Ctr., Cleve., 1992-93; small bus. owner, operator, ptnr. Satolli Carpet Floor Covering, Warren, Ohio, 1993—; Cable TV talk show host Falls Focus Cmty. Program, 1995—; disc jockey WSOM-WQXK, Salem, Ohio, 1980-82; host (TV weekly program) Newton Falls Focus, 1995—. Contbr. articles to bus. publs, newspapers and mags. Pres. Brooklyn (Ohio) Rep. club, 1990-93, treas., 1992; team capt. spl. project Am. Heart Assn. N.E. Ohio, 1992; vol. Shoes for Kids, 1991-93, Child Care Task Force, Brooklyn, 1991-93; mem. Greater Cleve. Holiday Lighting Com., 1991-93; st. capt. Mayor's Com. on Recycling, Brooklyn, 1990-93; bd. mem. Trumbull County Govt. Affairs Com., 1996—; cons. Jr. Achievement, Cleve., 1992-93; mem. Rock and Roll Hall of Fame and Mus. Task Force, Clean-Land Ohio Task Force; dir. Broad St. Merchants Group, 1994-95; bd. trustees Newton Falls United Meth. Ch., 1995—; mem. bd. July 4th Com., 1995—; mem. Youngstown-Warren Ohio Better Bus. Bur., 1993—; youth coach Newton Falls (Ohio) Hot Stove Baseball, 1994-95. Recipient Outstanding Leadership award Brooklyn Rep. Club, 1990, Coun. of Sml. Bus. Outstanding Effort award, 1991. Mem. Greater Cleve. Growth Assn. (Outstanding Vol. Svc. award

1991, 93), Greater Cleve. Coun. Smaller Enterprises, Ind. C. of C., Cleve. Zool. Soc., Internat. Customer Svc. Assn., Sale and Mktg. Execs., Eagles Bus. and Profl. Orgn., Internat. Brotherhood Magicians, Soc. Am. Magicians, Fellowship Christian Magicians, Eagles, Newton Falls C. of C. (pres. 1994, 95, 96, bd. dirs. 1993-94, Disting. Svc. Honor Leadership award 1995), N.E. Ohio Floor Covering Assn., Youngstown Warren C. of C., Kiwanis Club (v.p. 1994-95, pres. 1995-96, chmn. program com. Newton Falls chpt. 1993-94, July 4th festivities com. 1995). Methodist. Home: 315 Marshall St Newton Falls OH 44444-1426 Office: 367 High St Warren OH 44481

THOMPSON, GENEVA FLORENCE, medical technologist, cytotechnologist; b. Zionsville, Ind., Apr. 5, 1915; d. Alfred Seymour and Grace Viola (Kutz) T. Cert. in cytotechnology, Ohio State U., 1964; BA, Ind. U./Purdue U., Indpls., 1972. Cert. Am. Soc. Clin. Pathologists. Med. technician Noblesville (Ind.) Hosp., 1948-52; med. technician Riverview Hosp., Noblesville, 1952-56, med. technologist, 1956-60; med. technologist Office of Robert Harris, M.D., Noblesville, 1960-64; cytotechnologist Office of Thornton, Haymond, Costin, Buehl & Bolinger, M.D., Indpls., 1965-78; ret., 1978. Active with local church; served with U.S. Army W.A.C., 1944-46. Mem. AAUW (chmn. literature study group), Ind. U. Women's Club of Indpls., Am. Soc. Clin. Pathologists, Noblesville Tourist Club (sec.), Sr. Citizens Orgn., Inc. Republican.

THOMPSON, GEORGE RICHARD, rheumatologist, educator; b. Ann Arbor, Mich., Apr. 2, 1930; s. Joseph John and Gertrude Dorothy (Flowerday) T.; m. Ruth Marie Payne, Sept. 19, 1957; children: David Edward, Nancy Elizabeth, Susan Alice. BS, U. Mich., 1950, MD, 1954. Intern Ohio State U. Hosp., Columbus, 1954-55; resident U. Mich. Hosp., Ann Arbor, 1955-58; fellow U. Mich. Med. Ctr., Ann Arbor, 1960-62; dir. rheumatology Wayne County Gen. Hosp., Westland, Mich., 1963-84; asst. dir. dept. medicine Wayne County Gen. Hosp., Westland, 1973-84; acting dir. ambulatory care VA Med. Ctr., Ann Arbor, 1984-87; physician clin. svcs. Univ. Health Svc., Ann Arbor, 1987-92; instr. U. Mich. Med. Sch., Ann Arbor, 1962-65; asst. prof., U. Mich. Med. Sch., 1965-69; assoc. prof., U. Mich. Med. Sch., 1969-76; prof., U. Mich. Med. Sch., 1976-92; prof. emeritus, U. Mich. Med. Sch., 1992—. Contbr. articles to profl. jours. Troop Com. Chmn., Boy Scouts Am., Ann Arbor, 1970-73; bd. trustees, Arthritis Found., Southfield, Mich., 1980. Recipient Rheumatology fellowship, USPHS, 1960-62, rsch. grants, NIH, 1965-73. Fellow ACP, Am. Coll. Rheumatology; mem. Am. Fedn. for Clin. Rsch., Ctrl. Soc. for Clin. Rsch., Mich. Rheumatism Soc. (pres. 1971-72, 85-86). Methodist. Office: Rheumatology Divsn U Mich Med Ctr Ann Arbor MI 48109

THOMPSON, HAROLD LEE, lawyer; b. Dayton, Ohio, Feb. 17, 1945; s. Harold Edward Thompson and Johnita Dorothy (Cox) Metcalf; children: Aishah T., Aliya S. BS in Acctg., Cen. State U., Wilberforce, Ohio, 1967; JD, U. Conn., 1972. Bar: Ohio 1975, U.S. Dist. Ct. (so. dist.) Ohio 1975, D.C. 1976, U.S. Ct. Appeals (4th cir.) 1990. Acct. Communication Satellite Corp., 1968-69; atty. Ohio State Legal Service, Columbus, Ohio, 1972-74; of counsel Ohio Indsl. Commn., Columbus, 1974-76; sole practice Columbus, 1976—; ptnr. Jones & Thompson, Columbus, 1984-88; prin. H. Lee Thompson Co. L.P.A., Columbus, 1988—; pres. toys and clothing H. Lee Toy Co., Columbus, 1988—; adj. prof. law Columbus State Coll., 1989; instr. Acad. Ct. Reporting, 1989; adj. prof. tax and prins. of acctg. Bliss Coll., 1990-91; mem. Am. Bd. Forensic Examiners. Reginald Heber Smith fellow U.S. Fed. Ct., 1972. Mem. ATLA (exec. mem. birth trauma litigation group), Ohio Bar Assn., Am. Coll. Legal Medicine, Ohio Acad. Trial Lawyers, Franklin County Trial Lawyers Assn., Univ. Club, Columbus Met. Club. Roman Catholic. Office: 85 E Gay St Ste 810 Columbus OH 43215-3118

THOMPSON, HUGH LEE, academic administrator; b. Martinsburg, W.Va., Mar. 25, 1934; s. Frank Leslie and Althea T.; m. Patricia Smith; children: Cheri, Linda, Tempe, Vicki. B.S., B.A. in English and Secondary Edn, Shepherd Coll., Shepherdstown, W.Va., 1956; MS, Pa. State U., 1958; Ph.D. in Higher Edn. Adminstrn, Case Western Res. U., 1969. Mem. faculty Pa. State U., 1957-60, Akron (Ohio) U., 1960-62; mem. faculty Baldwin-Wallace Coll., Berea, Ohio, 1962-70, asst. to pres., 1966-69, dir. instl. planning, asst. to pres., 1969-70; coordinator Associated Colls., Cleve., 1970-71; pres. Siena Heights Coll., Adrian, Mich., 1971-77, Detroit Inst. Tech., 1977-80; chancellor Ind. U., Kokomo, 1980-90; pres. Washburn U., Topeka, 1990—; mem. president's adv. coun. Assn. Governing Bds. Univs. and Colls. Mem. Am. Assn. State Colls. and Univs. (coun. of state reps., steering com. urban and met. univs. coun.), North Ctrl. Assn. (evaluator, cons.). Home: 3130 SW Shadow Ln Topeka KS 66604-2541 Office: Washburn U Office of Pres Topeka KS 66621

THOMPSON, JACQUELINE KAY, performing company executive, fine arts educator; b. Dayton, Ohio, Jan. 17, 1954; d. Jack Long and Marlien Ann (Vaughn) T.; m. Theodore Lyle Buttel, Aug. 8, 1984. MusB, U. Dayton, 1976; MusM, U. Mo., Kansas City, 1979, D of Mus. Arts, 1984. Cert. profl. tchr., Iowa. Grad. teaching asst. U. Mo., 1976-81; instr. Indian Hills Community Coll., Ottumwa, Iowa, 1981-85; adj. prof. Drake U., Des Moines, 1985—; dir., owner Potpourri Fine Arts Acad., Ottumwa, 1985—. Contbr. articles to profl. jours. Bd. dirs. Ottumwa Community Players, 1982-83; bd. dirs. S.E. Iowa Symphony Orch., 1983, sec., 1985-87, 90-92, v.p. 1992-95; docent P. Buckley Moss Mus.; choreographer Iowa Jr. Miss., Inc., Ottumwa, 1983-89, 92, 94—; dir. music jr. choir camp United Meth. Ch., Cedar Falls, Iowa, 1986-90, Ft. Dodge, 1991-92; bd. dirs. Ottumwa Area Arts Coun., 1990-95; residency roster Iowa Arts Coun., 1991—. Women's Coun. grantee, 1979, 81. Mem. Am. Choral Dirs. Assn., Music Educators Nat. Conf., Iowa Music Educators Assn. (bd. dirs. 1992—), Ottumwa Area C. of C. (bd. dirs. 1991-93), P. Buckley Moss Soc., Sigma Alpha Iowa (life, pres. 1975-76, 77-79, Svc. Leadership award 1976, 79, doctoral grantee 1978). Democrat. Methodist. Home: 122 E Alta Vista Ave Ottumwa IA 52501-1411 Office: Potpourri Fine Arts Acad 116 N Green St Ottumwa IA 52501-3013

THOMPSON, JAMES KENNETH, mechanical engineer; b. Lancaster, Ohio, May 28, 1926; s. John Neil and Helen B. (Vlerebome) T.; m. Barbara Ann McMeans, Oct. 4, 1975. BME, Ohio State U., 1948. Registered profl. engr., Ohio. Rsch. engr. Battelle Meml. Inst., Columbus, Ohio, 1949-52, prin. mech. engr., 1952-71, sr. engr., 1971-81, cons. analyst, 1981-91, project leader, 1991-93, rsch. leader, 1993-95; ret., 1995; mem. energy tech. com. Air Pollution Control Assn., 1974-76, consulting engr., 1996—. Co-author: Energy Research and Development in the USSR, 1986, 3 tech. handbooks; contbr. articles to profl. jours. Fellow AIAA (assoc., sect. chmn. 1981-82, regional dp. dir., 5 states, 1984-85, 50th Anniversary medallion 1983, spl. event award 1982, newsletter award 1991, sect. programs award 1993, regional rep. Columbus sect. 1994-96); mem. Soc. Automotive Engrs. (life). Home: 3347 Kirkham Rd Columbus OH 43221-1313

THOMPSON, JAMES W., JR., state official; b. Sidney, Ohio, Feb. 7, 1948; s. James and Margret Louise (Mote) T.; m. Virginia Ann Wilcoxen, June 11, 1976; 1 child, James W. AAS, Lima (Ohio) Tech. Coll., 1978; student, Wittenberg U., Springfield, Ohio, 1973; grad., FBI Nat. Acad., 1981. Dep. sheriff Shelby County Sheriff's Dept., Sidney, Ohio, 1972-75; chief dep. Shelby County Sheriff's Dept., 1976-83; chief of police Botkins (Ohio) Police Dept., 1975-76; chief criminal investigations Ohio Dept. Agr., Columbus, 1983-88; chief investigations Ohio Vet. Med. Bd., Columbus, 1988—; disaster svcs. coordinator Ohio Dept. Agr., 1983-88. V.p. Ohio Coun. on Welfare Fraud, Columbus, 1988-89; pres. Botkins Village Coun., 1989, 94, 95; councilman, 1986-90, 92-96; pres. Botkins Pub. Libr., 1989-93; mem. Shelby County Regional Planning Commn., 1988-93; treas. bd. dirs. Shelby County Red Cross. With USN, 1968-72. Recipient Combat Action ribbon USN, 1969, Legion of Valor award, Buckeye State Sheriff's Assn., 1977; Disting. Pub. Svc. Hon., Am. Police Officers Hall of Fame, 1980. Mem. Am. Soc. Indsl. Security, Masons. Democrat. Home: PO Box 474 Botkins OH 45306-0474 Office: Ohio Veterinary Med Bd 77 S High St Columbus OH 43266

THOMPSON, JEANNINE LUCILLE, community health nurse; b. Forest City, Iowa, Oct. 1, 1954; d. Kenneth Parr and Janice Lee (Gelner) W.; children: Jill Morehead, Patricia Bitker. ADN, North Iowa Area Community Coll., Mason City, 1975; BSN, Upper Iowa U., 1983; cert. in enterostomal therapy, Abbott N.W. Hosp., 1989. Cert. enterostomal therapy nurse; cert. BLS, breast self-exam. instr. RN St. Joseph Mercy Hosp., Mason City, 1975-83; RN open heart surg. ICU St. Mary's Hosp., Rochester, Minn., 1983-84; health educator North Iowa Med. Ctr., Mason City, 1984-88; enterostomal therapy nurse Amicare Home Healthcare, Mason City, 1988—. Vol. Am. Heart Assn., Am. Cancer Soc. Mem. Wound, Ostomy and Incontinence Soc. Nurses (nat. profl. practice com., regional nomination chairperson, IA govt. affairs chairperson, Nursing in Washington Internship grad., offsite Enterostomal Therapy Nurse Edn. Programs clin. instr.), United Ostomy Assn. (advisor), Iowa Nurses Assn. Home: 201 S Winnebago Lake Mills IA 50450

THOMPSON, JIM D., state legislator. Senator S.D. State Dist. 5; appropriations and laws com. S.D. State Senate. Address: 1016 4th St NW Watertown SD 57201-1310

THOMPSON, JOE E., lawyer; b. Mason City, Iowa, Dec. 3, 1934; s. Ted W. T. and Lucille E. (Atkinson) Lysne; m. Carol R., May 10. 1956 (div. June 1, 1981); children: Laura Ann, Jennifer Grace, Michael William; m. Kay M., Sept. 26, 1981. BA, Hamline U., 1956; BL, William Mitchell Coll. Law, 1958, JD, 1960. Bar: Minn. Ptnr. Schmidt, Thompson, Johnson & Moody Law Firm, Willmar, Minn., 1962—. County lawyer Kandiyoni County, Minn., 1975-78; mem. Willmar (Min.) Utilities Bd., 1980-82. Mem. ABA, An. Coll. Trial Lawyers, Am. Bd. Trial Advocates (pres. Minn. chpt. 1976), Minn. Bar Assn., Kandiyoni Bar Assn. (pres. 1975), Lions (Willmar Moon Lions pres. 1988—), Civil Air Patrol (Wesota sqdn., capt., legal officer, pres. 1990—). Methodist. Home: 6355 24th St NE Willmar MN 56201 Office: Schmidt Thompson Johnson & Moody Box 913 Willmar MN 56201

THOMPSON, JOEL EDWARD, accounting educator; b. Painesville, Ohio, Sept. 8, 1954; s. Ernest Allan and Helen Eleanor (Goos) T.; m. Barbara Joan Lake, June 11, 1977; children: Lisa Anne, Audrey Lynn. BS, Ohio State U., 1976; PhD, Mich. State U., 1982. CPA Ohio. Staff acct. KPMG Peat Marwick, Cleve., 1976-77; grad. asst. Mich. State U., East Lansing, 1978-82; asst. prof. Ohio State U., Columbus, 1982-88; assoc. prof. Northern Mich. U., Marquette, 1988—. Contbr. articles to profl. jours. Deloitte Haskins & Sells fellow, 1981-82. Mem. AICPA, Am. Acctg. Assn., Marquette County Hist. Soc., Acad. Acctg. Historians, Inst. Mgmt. Accts. (bd. dirs. Mich. Upper Peninsula chpt. 1989—). Office: Northern Mich U Dept Acctg & Fin Marquette MI 49855

THOMPSON, JOHN EDWARD, physician, surgeon; b. Blanchardville, Wis., Dec. 30, 1923; s. Edward Bernard and Mary Rosella (Anderson) T.; m. Germaine Marie Kusnierek, Aug. 23, 1947; children: Vicki, Michael, Rebecca, Nancy, Julie. BA, Augsburg Coll., 1947; MD, U. Wis., 1951. Diplomate Am. Bd. Family Practice, Am. Bd. Geriatric Medicine. Capt. USAF, 1942-52; physician USAF, Tex., Fla., 1951-53; surgical resident Gunderson Clinic, Lacrosse, Wis., 1956-57; physician, surgeon Med. Ctr., Nekoosa, Wis., 1957-94; ret., 1994; med. dir. Wood Co. Home, Port Edwards, Wis., 1960-92; pres. hosp. staff Riverview Hosp., Wisconsin Rapids, Wood Med. Soc., Nekoosa Med. Ctr. Contbr. articles to profl. jours. Decorated Air Medal USAF, 1944, Purple Heart, 1944, Prisoner of War medal, 1988. Mem. VFW, AMA, Wis. State Med. Soc., Air Force Assn., Lions, Elks, Alpha Omega Alpha. Home: 705 W 5th St Nekoosa WI 54457 Office: Med Ctr 315 1st St Nekoosa WI 54457

THOMPSON, JOHN HENRY, consulting executive; b. Ute, Iowa, May 15, 1933; s. Frederick Stephen and Georgia (Wilkins) T.; m. Beverly Diane Price, Aug. 25, 1956; 1 child, Jennifer. BA in Psychology, Calif. State U., Fresno, 1960; PhD in Psychology, U. Ill., 1964. Lic. psychologist, Ill., Wash., Calif. Asst. prof. psychology Gonzaga U., Spokane, Wash., 1964-65, chmn. psychology dept., 1965-67; staff psychologist Rohrer, Hibler & Replogle, Portland, Oreg., 1967-69; mng. ptnr. Rohrer, Hibler & Replogle, Seattle, 1969-72; mgr. Rohrer, Hibler & Replogle, L.A., 1972-75; v.p. Rohrer, Hibler & Replogle, 1975-83; exec. v.p. Rohrer, Hibler & Replogle, 1984-85; pres., COO Rohrer, Hibler & Replogle, Chgo., 1985-87; pres., CEO RHR Internat. Co., Wood Dale, Ill., 1987-96, chmn., CEO, 1991-96; chmn., 1996—; bd. dirs. Target Sales, Fresno, Calif., 1978-84. Contbr. articles to profl. jours. and chpts. to books. Mem. State Bd. Med. Quality Assurance, Calif., 1974-77. Sgt. USMC, 1952-55, Korea. Roman Catholic. Office: RHR Internat Co 220 Gerry Dr Wood Dale IL 60191-1139

THOMPSON, JOSEPH WARREN, physician; b. Wichita Falls, Tex., June 27, 1950; s. Allen Dulaney and Norma Helen (Rinabarger) T.; m. Linda K. Sparks, Mar. 19, 1988. BS, S.E. Mo. State U., 1972; DO, U. Health Scis., Coll. Osteo. Medicine, Kansas City, Mo., 1976. Diplomate Am. Coll. Gen. Practitioners, Nat. Bd. Osteo. Med. Examiners. Intern Normandy Hosp., St. Louis, 1976-77, resident in family practice, 1977-79; pvt. practice medicine, St. Louis, 1979—; program dir. family practice residency, 1982-93, chief of staff, Normandy Osteo. Hosps. North and South, 1986-87; pres. of bd. Comprehensive Family Health Plan, Inc., 1987-90; apptd. staff mem. Deaconess Med. Ctr.-West, 1979—, De Paul Health Ctr., St. Louis, 1988—, med. dir. PHO 1995—, Mo. Bapt. Med. Ctr., 1992—, Deaconess Med. Ctr., 1992—; med. dir. DePaul Home Health, 1994—; mem. adv. bd. Olsten Home Health Svcs., 1991-94. Major M.C., USAFR. Mem. Mo. Osteo. Assn. (polit. action com., jud. com. 1986-88, physician licensure com. 1987-90, Young Physician of Yr. 1985), Am. Osteo. Assn. (com. on edn. and evaluation, 1985-86), Nat. Libr. of Medicine, Region IV, (mem. adv. coun. 1987-91), Am. Coll. Osteo. Family Physicians, Mo. Assn. Osteo. Physicians and Surgeons, St. Louis Dist. Assn. Osteo. Physicians and Surgeons, Elks, Masons, Shriners, Phi Theta Kappa. Methodist.

THOMPSON, LAVERNE ELIZABETH THOMAS, education administration educator; b. Bklyn., July 17, 1945; d. Roscoe Lee and Mary Elizabeth (Blackwell) Thomas. BA in English, Bluffton Coll., 1967; MS in Ednl. Adminstrn./Supervision, U. Dayton, 1977; PhD in Higher Edn., U. Toledo, 1991. Cert. sch. prin., Ohio; cert. secondary sch. supr., Ohio; cert. realtor, Ohio; cert. notary public, Ohio. Instr. English, speech Piqua (Ohio) Cen. High Sch., 1967-68; instr. Lima (Ohio) Sr. High Sch., 1968-77, Shawnee High Sch., Lima, 1977-86; grad. asst. U. Toledo, 1986-91, interim counselor/adminstr. Student Support Svcs., 1989, interim adminstrv. asst. Multicultural Student Devel., 1990; dir. urban tchr. program Wayne County C.C., Detroit, $D, 1996—; program dir. urban tchr. program Wayne County C.C., Detroit, 1996—; real estate agt. Alberta Lee Realty, Lima Ohio, 1978-82, Slonaker Realty , Lima, 1982-84, Gooding Co., Lima, 1985-90; former substitute English tchr., Maumee (Ohio) City Schs., 1996; adj. prof., acad. coord. alternative edn. Spring Arbor Coll., Lambertville, Mich., 1995-96. Editor Higher Edn. newsletter, 1987. Bd. dirs. Lima YWCA, 1971; co-chair Brotherhood Dinner Sr. High Sch., Lima, 1976; participant 17th annual Nat. Conf. on Citizenship, Washington, 1962. Mem. NAFE, Va. Assn. New Homemakers Am. (state pres. 1962, nat. pres. 1963), Blackwell Family Assn., Lladro Collectors Soc., Internat. Platform Assn., All God's Children Collectors' Club, Belleek Collectors' Internat. Soc., Sarah's Attic Forever Friends Collectors' Club, Phi Delta Kappa, others. Home: 1038 Valley Grove Dr Maumee OH 43537-3203

THOMPSON, LEIGH LASSITER, psychologist, educator; b. Houston, Jan. 13, 1960; d. Don Raines and Ann Janet (Visintin) Thompson; m. Robert Warner Weeks, June 20, 1992. BS, Northwestern U., 1982, PhD, 1988; MA, U. Calif., Santa Barbara, 1984. Asst. prof. psychology U. Wash., Seattle, 1988-92, assoc. prof., 1992-95; prof. J.L. Kellogg Disting. chair organ. behavior NorthWestern U., Evanston, Ill., 1995—; fellow Ctr. for Advanced Study in the Behavioral Scis., 1994-95. Edtl. bd. Orgnl. Behavior & Human Decision Processes, Internat. Jour. Conflict Mgt., Jour. Exptl. Social Psychology, 1990—; assoc. editor Group Decision Making and Negotiations; contbr. articles to profl. jours. Recipient Presdl. Young Investigator award NSF, 1991, Grad. Rsch. award Sigma Xi Found., 1987; grantee NSF, 1991, 89—, Nat. Inst. Dispute Resolution, 1987, APA, 1989. Mem. APA (S. Rains Wallace Dissertation award 1989), Am. Psychol. Soc., Acad. Mgmt. Office: Northwestern U Kellog Sch Orgn Bevavior Kellogg Sch Evanston IL 60208-2001

THOMPSON, LEONARD ALLEN, insurance sales and marketing specialist, consultant; b. Freeport, Ill., Apr. 1, 1927; s. Allen Marvin and Anna (Baughman) T.; m. Esther Gertrude Johnson, Nov. 4, 1949; children: Daniel J., David C., Deborah D. BTh, No. Bapt. Sem., Chgo., 1949; postgrad., U. Iowa, 1950-53. Salesman Bankers Trust Life, Phoenix, Ariz., 1957-64; nat. sales mgr. Sons of Norway, Mpls., 1964-80, salesman, 1980-87, CEO, 1987-89; cons., 1990—. Mem. Nat. Assn. Life Underwriters, Chartered Life Underwriters, Million Dollar Round Table (life), Fraternal Gield Mgrs. Assn. (bd. dirs., pres. 1965-71), Nat. Assn. Fraternal Ins. Counselors (bd. dirs. 1984—, pres. 1994-95). Republican. Home: 5565 Zachary Ln N Minneapolis MN 55442-3903

THOMPSON, LYNN, state legislator; m. Gloria Thompson; 4 children. Student, Concordia Coll., Aakers Bus. Coll. Farmer pvt. practice, Grafton, N.D., 1952—; mem. N.D. Ho. of Reps., Bismarck, 1990—; mem. Fin., Taxation and Agrl. Coms.

THOMPSON, MICHAEL ALAN, political cartoonist; b. Mankato, Minn., Aug. 3, 1964; s. Orrel Edward and Joan Alice (Hopkins) T.; m. Constance Reneé Gosnell, Oct. 12, 1991. BA in Polit. Sci., U. Wis., Milw. Contbg. cartoonist Milw. Jour., 1988-89; cartoonist St. Louis Sun, 1989-90, State Jour.-Register, Springfield, Ill., 1990—; cartoons syndicated through Copley News Svc. to over 600 newspapers throughout U.S., including Newsweek, Wall Street Jour., N.Y. Times, USA Today, Washington Post, U.S. News & World Report, Nat. Rev. Vol. Big Bros.-Big Sisters, Springfield. Recipient Charles M. Schulz award Scripps Howard Found., 1988, Locher award Assn. Am. Editorial Cartoonists, 1989, Mark of Excellence award Soc. Profl. Journalists, H.L. Mencken Cartooning award, 1994. Office: State Jour-Register 1 Copley Plz Springfield IL 62701-1927

THOMPSON, NANCY JO, special education educator, elementary education educator, consultant; b. Crawfordsville, Ind., Apr. 17, 1950. BE, Manchester Coll., 1971; MEd, Ind. U., South Bend, 1978. Cert. elem. tchr., tchr. emotionally disturbed K-12, Ind. Tchr. 6th grade Boone County Sch. Corp., Dover, Ind., 1971-72; lead tchr. N. Manchester (Ind.) Day Care Ctr., 1972-73; processor H & R Block, Elkhart, Ind., 1973; dept. head, sales Grinnell's Music Store, Elkhart, Ind., 1974-75; administrv. asst. Oaklawn Psychiat. Ctr., Elkhart, 1975-76; tchr. emotionally handicapped Treehouse-Day Treatment Program Oaklawn Psychiat., Elkhart, 1976-78; tchr. emotionally handicapped Elkhart Community Schs., 1978-85, resource team cons., 1985-94; tchr. diagnostic class EH Diagnostic Day Sch., Elkhart, 1994—; state trainer Ind. Dept. Edn., Indpls., 1987-89; bd. dirs. Loveway, Inc., Therapeutic Horseback Riding. Treas. Hively Ave. Nursery Sch., Elkhart, 1974; band mem. Elkhart Mcpl. Band, 1974-77; youth adv. Hively Ave. Mennonite Ch., Elkhart, 1980-84. Mem. NEA, Coun. Exceptional Children (cert. excellence profl. standards, practices Tri-County Coun. 1984), Coun. Children with Behavioral Disorders, Nat. Coun. Autistic Citizens, Ind. State Tchrs. Assn. Office: Elkhart Community Schools Eastwood Elem Sch Dept Diagnostic 53215 (R5) CR 15 N Elkhart IN 46514

THOMPSON, ROBERT DOUGLAS, computer science educator, consultant; b. Van Wert, Ohio, Apr. 2, 1944; s. Ernest Clinton and Gertrude Marcele (McBride) T.; m. Gail Joyce Knudson; children: Linda Marie Temple, Cheryl Elizabeth Christensen, Mark Robert. BS summa cum laude, Huntington Coll., 1966; MA, Mich. State U., East Lansing, 1967; student, Wright State U., 1974-90, Bowling Green State U., 1984, U. Dayton, 1985. Cert. tchr., Ohio. Office sec. United Brethren in Christ Denomination Ch., Huntington, Ind., 1963-66; grad. research asst. Mich. State U., East Lansing, 1966-67; instr. Wright State U. Lake Campus, Celina, Ohio, 1976, 93—, Tri Star Career Compact, Celina, 1984—; ptnr. Thompson Painting and Carpentry, Rockford, Ohio, 1969—; tchr., dept. head, tech. coord. St. Henry (Ohio) Consol. Local Schs., 1967—. Author, photographer numerous newspaper articles, 1974—, Business Professionals of America Ohio Association Handbook, 1989. Bd. dirs., pres., v.p. Oscar Figert Guidance Clinic, 1972-75; pres. Mercer County Mental Health Clinic, 1975; fin. chmn. Coldwater United Meth. Ch., 1982-90, chmn. adminstrv. bd., 1994—; solicitor Coldwater Combined Charities, 1982, 85; PRIDE evaluation svc. rep. State Dept. Edn., 1973, 78; troop treas. Coldwater area Boy Scouts Am., 1989-92; mem. office tech. adv. bd. Wright State U.-Lake Campus, Celina, Ohio, 1991—. Named super advisor Ohio Office Edn. Assn., 1983, 84, 85; recipient proclamation of excellence, Ohio State Dept. Edn. Mem. NEA, Am. Vocat. Assn., Bus. Profl. Am. (advisor 1973—, star advisor and honor advisor award), Ohio Bus. Tchrs. Assn. (state exec. bd. 1976-77, 93-96, state conv. chmn. 1995, Western Ohio Bus. Tchr. of Yr. award 1983, 91, 95, Ohio Bus. Tchr. of Yr. 1995), Ohio Edn. Assn., St. Henry Edn. Assn. (local pres. 1970-72), Wabash Valley Dartball Assn. (sec. 1978-79, 87-88), Delta Pi Epsilon. Republican. Home: 402 E Sycamore St Coldwater OH 45828-1835 Office: St Henry Consol Local Schs 371 E Columbus St Saint Henry OH 45883-9574

THOMPSON, ROLAND, marketing professional; b. Indpls., May 30, 1950; s. William and Violet (Nunn) T.; m. Young Hwa Yang, Sept. 2, 1983 (div. May, 1988); 1 child, Justin Edward. Student, Ind. U., 1968-70. Ordained minister Salvation Ch., 1989; cert. christian counselor; cert. credit cons., 1989. Enlisted USAF, 1970, advanced through grades to E-6, 1990, ret., 1990; network mktg. exec. Thompson and Assocs., Indpls., 1982—. Mem. The Gleanor Soc., Success N Life. Address: 2060 Bellefontaine St Indianapolis IN 46202-1856

THOMPSON, RONELLE KAY HILDEBRANDT, library director; b. Brookings, S.D., Apr. 21, 1954; d. Earl E. and Maxine R. (Taplin) Hildebrandt; m. Harry Floyd Thompson II, Dec. 24, 1976; children: Clarissa, Harry III. BA in Humanities magna cum laude, Houghton Coll., 1976; MLS, Syracuse U., 1976; postgrad., U. Rochester, 1980, 81; cert., Miami U., 1990. Libr. asst. Norwalk (Conn.) Pub. Libr., 1977; elem. libr. Moriah Cen. Schs., Port Henry, N.Y., 1977-78; div. coord. pediatric gastroenterology and nutrition U. Rochester (N.Y.) Med. Ctr., 1978-81, cons., mem. pediatric housestaff libr. com., 1980-81; dir. Medford Libr. U. S.C., Lancaster, 1981-83; dir. Mikkelsen Libr., Libr. Assocs., Ctr. for Western Studies, mem. acad. computing com., libr. com. Augustana Coll., Sioux Falls, S.D., 1983—, mem. adminstrv. pers. coun., 1989-94; presenter in field. Contbr. articles to profl. jours. Mem. adv. com. S.D. Libr. Network, 1986—, chair, 1989-91, 94—; mem. Sioux Falls Community Playhouse, S.D. Symphony, Sioux Falls Civic Fine Arts Assn.; advisor Minnehana County Libr., pers. dept. City of Sioux Falls. Named one of Outstanding Young Women Am., 1983; Syracuse U. Gaylord Co. scholar, 1976; recipient YWCA leader award, 1991. Mem. ALA, AAUW, Assn. Coll. and Rsch. Librs. (nat. adv. coun. coll. librs. sect. 1987—), Mountain Plains Libr. Assn. (chair acad. sect., nominating com. 1988, pres. 1993-94), S.D. Libr. Assn. (chair interlibr. coop. task force 1986-87, pres. 1987-88, chair recommended minimum salary task force 1988, chair local arrangements com. 1989-90), S.D. Libr. Network (adv. coun. 1986—, exec. com. 1992—, chair adv. coun. 1994—). Office: Augustana Coll Mikkelsen Libr 29th & Summit Sioux Falls SD 57197

THOMPSON, ROY LLOYD, agronomist; b. Kensington, Minn., Apr. 29, 1927; s. Arnold Webster and Elsie Agnes (Schultz) T.; m. Blythe Helene Parriott, Feb. 14, 1954; children: Bradley, Barbara Kirkpatrick, Curtis. BS in Agr., U. Minn., 1951, MS, 1959; PhD, Pa. State U., 1967. Cert. profl. agronomist. Crop inspector Minn. Crop Improvement Assn., St. Paul, 1949-51; rsch. fellow U. Minn., St. Paul, 1954-56; agronomist U. Minn., Morris, 1956-67; Rockefeller Found., Cali, Colombia, 1967-72; ext. agronomist U. Minn., St. Paul, 1972-78, asst. dir. agr. expt. sta., 1978-91; agr. cons., U. Minn. Pres. Roseville (Minn.) Luth. Ch., 1992. With U.S. Army, 1951-53, Japan. Recipient Torch and Shield award U. Minn., Crookston, 1991, Merit award Gamma Sigma Delta, 1990, Disting. Svc. award Morris Jaycees; named Minn. Premier Seed Grower. Mem. Am. Soc. Agronomy, Coun. for Agrl. Sci. and Tech., Tropical Root Crop Soc., Crop Sci. Soc., Minn. Crop Improvement Assn., FarmHouse Frat., Phoenix, Alpha Zeta, Phi Epsilon Phi. Home: 2521 Snelling Curve Roseville MN 55113-3111

THOMPSON, SALLY ANN, newspaper editor; b. Hillsboro, N.D., Apr. 10, 1943; d. C. Hilman and Blanche E. (Bjerkan) Swenson; m. Arthur G. Thompson, July 1, 1965 (dec. Mar. 1990); 1 child, Laurie Kate Beth. Student, Concordia Coll., Moorhead, Minn., 1961-65. Reporter The Valley Journal, Halstad, Minn., 1979-84; contbg. editor Prairie West Pubs., Wahpeton, N.D., 1982-84; editor Hillsboro Banner, Hillsboro, N.D., 1984-95, Plymouth Sun-Sailer, Minn. Sun Publs., Minnetonka, Minn., 1995—; lectr. Career Day Mayville State U., N.D., 1985-92. Mem. commns. com. Ea. N.D. Synod ELCA, 1990-93; bd. dirs. Traill County Hist. Soc., 1979-95, Hillsboro Forestry Bd., 1990-93. Recipient numerous journalism awards.

Lutheran. Home: 1805 Hwy 101 N #203 Plymouth MN 55447 Office: Minn Sun Publs 4785 S Hwy 101 Minnetonka MN 55345

THOMPSON, SALLY ENGSTROM, state official; b. Spokane, Wash., Feb. 17, 1940; d. Logan C. and Ava Leigh (Phillips) Engstrom; m. Donald Edward Colcun, 1981; children: Lauri Thompson, Tom Thompson, Tami Thompson, Sheri Colcun Trumpfheller. BS magna cum laude, U. Colo., 1975. CPA, Colo. 1976, Kans. 1986. Audit mgr. and mgmt. cons. Touche Ross & Co., Denver, 1975-82; v.p., mgr. planning and fin. analysis United Bank, Denver, 1982-85; pres., chief oper. officer Shawnee Fed. Svgs., Topeka, 1985-90; treas. State of Kans., 1990—. Past editorial advisor New Accountant mag. Bd. dirs. Everywoman's Resource Ctr., Topeka, 1988-92, Community Svc. Found. Kans., Kids Voting Kans. (hon.); v.p., bd. dirs. Downtown Topeka Inc., YWCA, Topeka, 1986-93, Woman of Achievement award, 1984; mem. fin. com. Girl Scouts U.S., Kaw Valley, various coms., United Way of Greater Topeka; chmn. art auction com. KTWU-TV, summer concert, Topeka Civic Theatre. Recipient Disting. Community Leadership award Topeka Pub. Schs., 1989, Disting. Leadership award Nat. Assn. Community Leadership, 1991, 1991 Class Leadership Kans. Mem. AICPAs, Am. Soc. Women Accts., Kans. Soc. CPAs, Kansas C. of C. and Industry, Greater Topeka C. of C. (bd. dirs. 1989-92), Emporia State U. Bus. Sch. Adv. Bd., Nat. Assn. State Auditors, Controllers and Treas., Nat. Assn. State Treas. (v.p., Midwest regional chair), Women Execs. in Govt., Beta Alpha Psi. Democrat. Offices: Office State Treasurer Landon State Office Bldg 900 SW Jackson St Ste 201N Topeka KS 66612-1220*

THOMPSON, SALLY GAIL, journalist, educator, executive secretary; b. Chgo., June 25, 1938; d. George Donald and Rella Esther (Fox) Sutton; m. Roger James Thompson, Mar. 31, 1957; children: Donald Melzer, Anthony Jay, Stuart Roger. Student, Ill. State U., 1956-57; Assoc., Kankakee Community Coll., 1973; Bachelors, Governors State U., 1975, Masters, 1978. Instr. Kankakee (Ill.) Community Coll., 1975-78, 1987-90; tchr. Grant Park (Ill.) Middle Sch., 1981, Manteno (Ill.) High Sch., 1985-86; editor Grant Park Gazette, 1983-86; reporter Daily Jour., Kankakee, 1986—; exec. sec. Spieth's Market, Inc., Momence, Ill., 1986-95. Ill. State scholar, 1957, PTA scholar, 1957. Mem. Gov. State Alumni Assn., Kankaee Community Coll. Alumni Assn., Ill. Press Assn. Republican. Home: 5514 N 13000E Rd Momence IL 60954-3003

THOMPSON, SETH CHARLES, retired oral and maxillofacial surgeon; b. Whittemore, Mich., Aug. 12, 1927; s. Seth Charles and Annie Ernestine (Washburn) T.; m. Effie Valore Garland, Jan. 20, 1954; children: Seth Charles III, David Garland. BS, Mich. State U., 1949; DDS, U. Mich., 1952, MS, 1959. Pvt. practice oral and maxillofacial surgery Midland, Mich., 1959-95; ret., 1995. Discoverer surgical treatment for trigeminal neuralgia, 1976. Bd. dirs. Midland (Mich.) Christian Sch., 1971-72, Inst. for Achievement of Human Potential, Midland, 1970-71. Served to capt. USAF, 1953-55. Fellow Am. Assn. Oral and Maxillofacial Surgery; mem. ADA, Mich. Dental Assn., Mich. Assn. Oral and Maxillofacial Surgery, Midland County Med. Soc. Republican. Baptist. Lodge: Rotary. Home and Office: 2728 Parrish Rd Midland MI 48642-9601

THOMPSON, STANLEY BURTON, foundation administrator; b. Santo Domingo, Dominican Republic, July 2, 1942; s. William Ralph and Clarible Martha (Hessler) T.; m. Janet Marie Richardson, Oc.t 23, 1942; children: Steven Brian, David Michael, Jill Marie. BA in Lang. Arts, Taylor U., Upland, Ind., 1964; MA in English/Journalism, Ball State U., Muncie, Ind., 1967; EdD in English Edn./Mass Comm., Ind. U., 1972. Adminstrv. asst. to pub. Light & Life Press, Winona Lake, Ind., 1968-70, 72-75; dir. planned giving The Free Meth. Ch. of N.Am., Winona Lake, 1975-81; v.p. instl. advancement Spring Arbor (Mich.) Coll., 1981-87; dir., pres., CEO Free Meth. Found., 1987—; dir., chmn. Christian Stewardship Assn., Mpls., 1988-93. Editor several books Light & Life Press. Trustee Spring Arbor Coll., 1992—. Free Methodist. Home: 227 Wickenham Dr Spring Arbor MI 49283 Office: Free Meth Found PO Box 580 Spring Arbor MI 49283

THOMPSON, THOMAS ADRIAN, secondary school educator; b. Sidney, Mont., Aug. 28, 1944; s. Vernon Eugene and Helen Alice (Torstenson) T.; m. M. Aileen Braun, June 7, 1968; children: Blair C., Meghann C. BA, Concordia Coll., 1966; postgrad., Mich. State U., 1968-69, Oakland U., 1970-72. Art tchr. Carman Ainsworth Sch. Dist., Flint, Mich., 1966—; chmn. Flint Art Curriculum Com., 1980. Mem. NEA, Nat. Art. Edn. Assn., Mich. Art Edn. Assn. (liaison mem.), Internat. Arabian Horse Assn., Arabian Horse Registry. Lutheran. Home: 1120 Old Town Ct Grand Blanc MI 48439-1622 Office: Carman Ainsworth Sch Dist Dept of Art Tchr Flint MI 48501

THOMPSON, THOMAS JAY, association executive; b. Emporia, Kans, Feb. 8, 1969; s. Douglas George Thompson and Mary Beth (Bertwell) Forsythe. BGS, U. Kans., 1991, MA, 1992. Loan analyst Sallie Mae, Lawrence, Kans., 1993-94; assn. exec. Knight Enterprises, Ltd., Lawrence, 1994—; CEO G.R.I., Leawood, Kans., 1991—; cons. in field. Contbr. articles to profl. jours. Mem. NASCAR, Rosicrucians, Assn. Anceint Historians, Libr. Congress, Kans. Sports Hall Fame, Lambda Chi Alpha. Office: Knight Enterprises 4840 W 15th St Ste 1000 Lawrence KS 66049

THOMPSON, TOMMY GEORGE, governor; b. Elroy, Wis., Nov. 19, 1941; s. Allan and Julia (Dutton) T.; m. Sue Ann Mashak, 1969; children: Kelli Sue, Tommi, Jason. BS in Polit. Sci. and History, U. Wis., 1963, JD, 1966. Polit. intern U.S. Rep. Thomson, 1963; legis. messenger Wis. State Senate, 1964-66; sole practice Elroy and Mauston, Wis., 1966-87; mem. Dist. 87 Wis. State Assembly, 1966-87, asst. minority leader, 1972-81, floor leader, 1981-87; self-employed real estate broker Mauston, 1970—; gov. State of Wis., 1987—; alt. del. Rep. Nat. Conv., 1976; chmn. Intergovtl. Policy Adv. Commn. to U.S. Trade Rep.; mem. nat. govs. assn. exec. com.; bd. dirs. AMTRAK. Served with USAR. Recipient med. award for Legis. Wis. Acad. Gen. Practice, Thomas Jefferson Freedon award Am. Legis. Exchange Coun., 1991, Most Valuable Pub. Official award City and State Mag., 1991, Governance award Free Congress Found., 1992. Mem. ABA, Wis. Bar Assn., Rep. Govs. Assn., Phi Delta Phi. Roman Catholic. Office: Office of Gov PO Box 7863 Madison WI 53707-7863

THOMPSON, VERNON, state legislator; b. Tex., Apr. 14, 1943; m. Vernita Thompson; children: Jamil, Dejon, Nathan. Mem. Mo. Ho. of Reps. from 37th dist., 1986—; chmn. Retirement Com. Mo. Ho. of Reps., mem. Budget, Ethics, Transp., Appropriations and Adminstrv. Rules Coms. Active Freedom Inc. Democrat. Home: 1330 Park Ave Kansas City MO 64127-2005*

THOMPSON, WADE FRANCIS BRUCE, manufacturing company executive; b. Wellington, New Zealand, July 23, 1940; came to U.S., 1961, naturalized, 1990.; m. Angela Ellen Barry, Jan. 20, 1967; children: Amanda and Charles (twins). B in Commerce, Cert. Acctg., Victoria U., Wellington, 1961; MSc, NYU, 1963. Dir. diversification Sperry & Hutchinson, N.Y.C., 1967-72; v.p. Textar Corp., N.Y.C., 1972-77; chmn. Hi-Lo Trailer Co., Butler, Ohio, 1977—; chmn., pres., chief exec. officer Thor Industries Inc., Jackson Center, Ohio, 1980—. Trustee Mystic Seaport Mus., Conn., 1984—; trustee Wade F.B. Thompson Charitable Found. Inc., 1985—, N.Y. Studio Sch., 1993—, Mcpl. Art Soc., N.Y.C., 1993—. Mem. Union Club, N.Y. Yacht Club (N.Y.C.). Office: Thor Industries Inc 419 W Pike St Jackson Center OH 45334-9728

THOMPSON, WILLIAM EDWARD, state legislator; b. Lima, Ohio, Apr. 17, 1948; s. Richard Edward and Claudine (Burt) T.; m. Kay Swick, 1974; children; Marshall Burt, Kendra Lea, Parker Sherman. BS, Ohio State Univ., 1972. Ohio State Rep. Dist. 1, 1987—; v.p. Thompson Seed Farm, Inc., 1977; mem. extension adv. com. Mem. Ohio Seed Improvement Assn., Ohio Seed Dealers Assn., Agrl. Genetic Rsch. Assn., Masonic Lodge, Ohio Farm Bureau, Phi Kappa Psi. Home: 4960 Defiance Trail Delphos OH 45833*

THOMS, DAVID MOORE, lawyer; b. N.Y.C., Apr. 28, 1948; s. Theodore Clark and Elizabeth Augusta (Moore) T.; m. Susan Rebecca Stuckey, Dec. 16, 1972. BA, Kalamazoo Coll., 1970; M in Urban Planning, Wayne State U., 1975, LLM in Taxation, 1988; JD, U. Detroit, 1979. Bar: Mich. 1980, N.Y. 1995. Planner City of Detroit, 1971-75; atty. Rockwell and Kotz, P.C., Detroit, 1980-87; pvt. practice David M. Thoms & Assocs., P.C., Detroit, 1987—; adj. assoc. prof. Madonna U., 1993—; presenter NYU Tax Inst. Editor Case and Comment Law Rev., 1978-79. Mem. program com. Fin. and Estate Planning Coun. Detroit, 1980—; mem. adv. bd., chmn. nominating com., mem. exec. com. Met. Detroit Salvation Army, sec.-treas., vice chmn., 1994-95, chmn., 1995-96; bd. dirs. bylaws and property com., mem. nominating com., devel. com., exec. com. Mich. chpt. ARC; bd. dirs., pres. L'Alliance Française de Grosse Pointe, French Festival of Detroit, Inc.; trustee Detroit Symphony Orch. Hall, Inc., Kalamazoo Coll., 1993—, dir., 1995—, exec. com., 1995—; dir. vis. com. European art DIA, 1995—. Recipient Burton scholarship U. Detroit, 1979; Officier dans l'Ordre des Palmes Academiques. Mem. aBA (chmn. subcom. on probate and estate planning, mem. charitable trust com.), Fed. Bar Assn., Oakland County Bar Assn., detroit Bar Assn., State Bar Mich., N.Y. Bar Assn., Bar Assn. of City of N.Y., Fedn. Alliances Françaises-U.S.A. (bd. dirs., treas.), Am. Planning Assn. (Mich. chpt.), Detroit Athletic Club, Renaissance Club. Mem. United Church of Christ. Office: 400 Renaissance Ctr Ste 950 Detroit MI 48243-1509

THOMSEN, PAMELA DEE, long-term care education director; b. Perry, Iowa, July 5, 1948; d. Bernard James and Darlene E. (Workman) Nolan; m. Warren W. Pantier, Aug. 8, 1969 (div. Nov. 1978); m. Terry J. Thomsen, June 20, 1981; 1 child, Bill Pantier Jr. Lic. practical nurse, Des Moines Area Community Coll., 1969, AS with honors, 1988; student, Graceland Coll., 1995—. Nurse Dr. Humphrey, Perry, Iowa, 1981-84; supr. Perry Luth. Home, 1985-89, asst. dir. nursing, 1989-92, dir. nursing, 1992-95; dir. dispensary Perry Iowa Beef Packers, 1992-93; staff IBP, Perry, 1993—; edn. dir. Calvin Manor, Des Moines, 1996—. Mem. AACN, Am. Assn. Occupl. Health Nurses, Nat. Assn. Dirs. of Nursing, Iowa Assn. Assoc. Degree Nurses, Iowa Orgn. Assoc. Degree Nurses, Dallas County Hosp. Aux., Luth. Home Aux., Eastern Star (officer 1986—). Home: 1606 Evelyn St Perry IA 50220-1740

THOMSON, JAMES ADOLPH, medical group practice administrator; b. Kansas City, Mo., Feb. 25, 1924; s. Edward Wilkins and Gladys Lucile (Opperman) T.; m. Patricia Jane Herron, Jan. 24, 1943; children: Linda Lee Thomson Schwartz, Kenneth Leroy, James Howard. BBA, Rockhurst Coll., Kansas City, 1950. Cost acct. Standard Brands, Inc., Kansas City, 1950-52; asst. comptroller Menorah Med. Ctr., Kansas City, 1952-56; comptroller Holzer Hosp. and Clinic, Gallipolis, Ohio, 1956-63; bus. mgr. Oberlin (Ohio) Clinic, Inc., 1963-71; adminstr. and treas. Thompson, Brumm & Knepper Clinic, Inc., St. Joseph, Mo., 1971-80; bus. mgr. Cin. Neurological Assocs., Inc., 1980-89; ret., 1989; cons. med. groups, Ohio, 1968-70. V.p. St. Joseph (Mo.) Area C. of C., 1976-78; pres. Oberlin Health Commn., 1968-69; bd. dirs. St. Joseph Sheltered Workshop, 1978-80. Served with M.C. U.S. Army, 1943-46, ETO. Recipient Disting. Svc. award St. Joseph Area C. of C., 1979. Fellow Am. Coll. Med. Group Adminstrs.; mem. Am. Assn. Hosp. Accts. (charter, pres. 1954-56), Mo. Med. Group Mgmt. Assn. (charter, pres. 1978-79), Med. Group Mgmt. Assn., Ohio Med. Group Mgmt. Assn., Cin. Med. Group Mgmt. Assn. (pres. 1983-84), Rotary (pres. Oberlin and St. Joseph clubs), Lions (pres. 1962-63), KC, Masons, Shriners (clown, asst. circus dir. Syrian Shrine 1993, 94, 95). Republican. Lutheran.

THOMSON, JOHN WANAMAKER, bank executive; b. Sioux Falls, S.D., Oct. 1, 1928; s. John Norman and Muriel Evelyn (Wanamaker) T.; m. Nane A. McConnell, Sept. 16, 1950; children: John L., James R., Ann L. BS in Acctg., U. S.D., 1950; postgrad., U. Wis., 1964. Chmn. First Midwest Bank, Centerville, S.D., 1950—; CEO, pres., chmn. Thomson Holdings, Ind., Centerville, 1986—, Thomson Agy., Inc., Centerville, 1984; chmn. S.D. Banking Commn., Pierre, 1986-95. Mem. S.D. Bankers Assn. (pres. 1980), U. S.D. Found. (bd. dirs.), S.D. Bankers Assn. Found. (chmn. 1990-91), Myrtle Lodge, Masons (treas. 1980-91), Riverview Cemetery Assn., U. S.D. Alumni Assn. (pres. 1990-92). Republican. Office: First Midwest Bank 549 Broadway Centerville SD 57014

THORESON, LAUREL, state legislator; m. Betty Thoreson; 3 children. Rep. N.D. Ho. of Reps., Bismarck, 1994—; mem. human svc. and govt. and vet. affairs com. N.D. Ho. of Reps. Mem. Amvets.

THORN, SCOTT ARON, mechanical engineer; b. Hutnington, Ind., Jan. 2, 1960. Tech. cert. with honors, Ivy Tech. Sch., Ft. Wayne, Ind., 1982. Mgr. engring. svcs. PHD, Inc., Ft. Wayne, 1980—. Vol. local ch. and sch. Mem. ASME, Soc. Mfg. Engrs. Republican. Office: PHD Inc PO Box 9070 Fort Wayne IN 46899-9070

THORNBER, JUDY PAULENE, real estate developer, consultant, lawyer; b. Chgo., May 26, 1941; d. Paul and Irene (Swanson) Davis. BA, U. Chgo., 1963, MBA, 1969; JD, Harvard U., 1966. Bar: Ill. 1967. Vice pres. Rubloff Devel. Corp., Chgo., 1970-72; sr. v.p. Am. INVSCO, Chgo., 1975-76; pres. Thorndev Corp., Chgo., 1978—; v.p. Fogelson Properties, Chgo., 1989-90; adminstrv. v.p. Cen. Sta. Devel. Corp., Chgo., 1990-91; exec. v.p. INVSCO Group, Ltd., 1991-93; pres. Thornber Corp., 1993—. Founding mem. Com. of 200, Chgo.; bd. dirs. Wellspring Wellness Ctr., 1991. Mem. Chgo. Bar Assn., Chgo. Assn. Realtors, U. Chgo. Women's Bus. Group (chmn. entrepreneurship subcom. 1993), Chgo. Fin. Exch. (bd. dirs. 1984), Chgo. Coun. on Fgn. Rels., Harvard Club Chgo., Phi Beta Kappa (exec. com. Chgo. area chpt.). Home: 30 E Huron #1407 Chicago IL 60611

THORNBURGH, DANIEL ESTON, retired university administrator, journalism educator; b. Terre Haute, Ind., Sept. 17, 1930; s. Lester D. and Dorothy (Green) T.; m. M. Adrianne Ames, Aug. 11, 1956; children: Debra Kay Thornburgh Considine, Stewart Beckett, Malcolm Noble. BS, Ind. State U., 1952; MA, U. Iowa, 1957; EdD, Ind. U., 1980. Reporter Terre Haute Star, 1952; publicity dir. Simpson Coll., Indianola, Iowa, 1955-57; info. dir. Marshall U., Huntington, W.Va., 1957-59, Eastern Ill. U., Charleston, 1959-65, chmn., prof. journalism, 1965-84, dir. univ. rels., 1984-92; vis. prof. U. Hawaii, 1982-83, U. Fla. 1993-94; mem. Gov.'s Coun. Health and Phys. Fitness, 1987—; pub. Casey Banner Times, Ill., 1967-69. Editor: (with others) Interpretative Reporting Workbook, 1982. Mem. Charleston City Coun., 1973-77; active Ill. Recreation Coun., Springfield, 1979-85; pres. Coles Hist. Soc., Charleston, 1972-74, 92. Served with U.S. Army, 1952-54. Named Outstanding Advisor, Coun. Coll. Publs. Advisors, 1971. Mem. Charleston C. of C. (area man of yr. award 1971), Assn. Edn. Journalism and Mass Comm., Pub. Rels. Soc. Am., Coun. Advancement and Support Edn. (EIU PRSSA chpt.), Masons, Elks, Rotary (pres. Charleston 1976-77), Sigma Delta Chi. Democrat. Methodist. Avocations: tennis, writing. Home: 1405 Buchanan Ave Charleston IL 61920-2924

THORNBURGH, RON E., state official; b. Burlingame, Kans., Dec. 31, 1962; m. Annette Thornburgh. Student, Washburn U., 1985. Dep. asst. sec. of state, then asst. sec. of state State of Kans., Topeka, 1985-87, sec. of state, 1995—; asst. sec. of state sec. of State's Office, Topeka, 1991-95, sec. of state, 1995—; vice chairperson blue ribbon panel on ethical conduct State of Kans., 1989. Mem. Kids Voting Kans. Exec. Com.; mem. adv. com. United Way. Toll fellow Henry Toll Fellowship Program, 1995. Mem. Washburn U. Alumni Bd., 20/30 Club Internat. Methodist. Office: Sec of State 2d Fl Statehouse 300 SW st Topeka KS 66612*

THORNTON, COLLEEN BRIDGET, investment management executive; b. Tupper Lake, N.Y., Feb. 25, 1948; d. Bernard Cornelius and Carrie Frances (Griffin) Purdy; m. Theodore Kean Thornton, June 23, 1974; children: T. McKinley, Alastair G. B, SUNY, Potsdam, 1970, M, 1971; D, Boston U., 1976. Prof. maths. Kean Coll. N.J., 1978-87; exec. v.p. Marble Corp., Chgo., 1991—. Treas., fin. chmn. LWV, Lake Forest, 1987-91; treas. Women's Rep. Club, Lake Forest, 1991-94, Lake Forest Symphony Guild, 1994—. Home: 885 Maplewood Rd Lake Forest IL 60045-2415 Office: Marble Corp 225 W Washington St Ste 2150 Chicago IL 60606-3418

THORPE, WILLIAM PARR, orthopaedic surgeon; b. Rochester, N.Y., Sept. 14, 1947; s. Ralph Siler and Marilyn (Lawhead) T.; m. Judy Frear, Aug. 15, 1970; children: Jane, Bill. AB, Princeton U., 1969; MD, Harvard U., 1973. Diplomate Am. Bd. Orthopaedic Surgery. Orthop. surgeon Topeka, 1981-82, Orthop. Assocs., P.C., Cape Girardeau, Mo., 1982—. Author: (book chpt.) Arthroscopic Laser Surgery: Clinical Applications, 1995. Deacon, elder 1st Presbyn. Ch., Cape Girardeau; found. dir. S.E. Mo. State U., Cape Girardeau. Mem. Am. Acad. Orthop. Surgeons, Am. Coll. Surgeons, Am. Orthop. Soc. Sports Medicine, Arthroscopy Assn. N.Am., Orthop. Laser Soc. N.Am., Am. Soc. Laser Medicine and Surgery, Inc., Cape Girardeau C. of C. Home: 2418 Brookwood Dr Cape Girardeau MO 63701 Office: Orthop Assocs PC 48 Doctors Park Cape Girardeau MO 63703

THOTTUPURAM, KURIAN CHERIAN, priest, college director, educator; b. Cherianad, Kerala, India; came to U.S., 1971; s. Cherian Koruth and Eliamma (Kandanavila) T.; m. Susan Grace Kompady, Dec. 29, 1969; children: Cherian, Kurian Jr., Theodore-George. BA, St. Joseph's Coll. Lateran U., Alwaye, India, 1970; MA, Karnatak U., 1970, Mundelein Coll., Chgo., 1973; MEd, Loyola U., Chgo., 1979, PhD, 1981; DD, Notre Dame de Lafayette U., 1993. Ordained subdeacon, 1967, deacon, 1970, priest, 1970, chorbishop, 1986. Tchr. Mt. Tabor-Stephen's Coll., Pathanapuram, India, 1966-70; founder Malankarese Orthodox Syrian Ch., 1971—; pastor St. John's Syrian Orthodox Ch., 1971-72; founder, pastor St. Thomas Orthodox Ch., 1972-80, St. Mary's Orthodox Ch., 1982—; counseling psychologist Incentives Inst., Des Plaines, Ill., 1974-76; dir. social svc. Millardogden Ctr., Chgo., 1976-77; ednl. adminstr. ednl. program Chgo. Housing Authority, 1977-81; ecumenical officer Malankarese Orthodox Diocese, Chgo., 1981-85; dir. program planning and devel. Malcolm X Coll., Chgo. City Coll. System, 1985-91; english faculty Truman Coll., 1991-92; exec. dir. International Edn. Cons. and Evaluators of Ill., 1992; dir. curriculum/instrn. S.E.A. Ctr., 1993-94; mem. philosophy faculty Daley Coll., 1993-95, Triton Coll., 1995—; pres. Am. Acad. Comparative-Internat. Edn., Chgo., 1993—; part-time various ednl. founds., 1981—; mem. Sch. Bd. Coun., 1991-93. Author: Dhyanamitram, 1966, Kalari, 1967, Perumpepadam, 1968, Foundations of Kerala Education, 1981, Bible Reading Guide of the Malankara Orthodox Church, Education and Social Change, 1987; chief editor Voice of Orthodoxy, 1986, The Orthodox Christian Priesthood: An Anthology of Patriotic Writings, 1995, Pre-British European Educational Activities in India, 1989. Chmn. social action Diocese of Niraram, India, 1967-71; mem. Zonal coun. Diocese of Am., 1975-78, Diocesan Coun.; bd. regents Lafayette U., Aurora, Colo., 1989—; exec. mem. Alleppey DT Kerala Congress, India, 1967-71; pres. Ecumenical Coun. Kerala Chs. Chgo., 1983—; founder Voice of Orthodox Found., Chgo., 1995. Recipient Taylor award for High Achievement, Greek Orthodox Archdiocese, Schmitt Found. award, 1977, Pub. Svc. award Citizens Cultural Found., 1985. Mem. Am. Ednl. Studies Assn., Midwest History of Edn. Soc., Am. Assn. Biofeedback Clinicians, Internat. Assn. of Mission Studies, Germany. Mem. Eastern Orthodox Ch.

THRASHER, ROSE MARIE, critical care and community health nurse; b. Urbana, Ohio, Jan. 19, 1948; d. Jesse and Anna Frances (Clark) T. Student, Mercy Med. Ctr. Sch. Med. Tech., 1966-67, Wittenberg U., 1969-70; BSN, Ohio State U., 1974, BA in Anthropology, 1994, postgrad., 1994—. RN, Ohio; cert. cmty. health nurse ANA; cert. provider BCLS and ACLS, Am. Heart Assn. Pub. health nurse Columbus (Ohio) Health Dept., 1977-78; critical care nurse VA Med. Ctr., San Francisco, 1981, Staff Builders Health Care Svc., Oakland, Calif., 1975-76, 81-85; supr., case mgr. home health nurse passport program and intermittent care program Interim Health Care (formerly Med. Pers. Pool), Columbus, 1976-77, 85—. Recipient numerous acad. scholarships Wittenberg U. and Ohio State U.; mem. Nat. Women's Hall of Fame. Mem. AACN, ANA (coun. cmty. health nursing), AAUW, Ohio Nurses Assn., Intravenous Nurses Soc., Ohio State U. Alumni Assn., Am. Anthropol. Assn., Ohio Acad. Sci.

THRELKELD, DALE, artist; b. Shelbina, Mo., Apr. 11, 1944; m. Lisa Jayne Willard, June 15, 1985; children: Lisa K., Holly, Alexis, Zachary, Olivia. BS in Art, N.E. Mo. State U., 1966; MA in Drawing, Ball State U., 1970; MFA in Drawing, So. Ill. U., 1975. Art instr. Belleville (Ill.) Area Coll., 1970—. Exhibited in group shows at The Okla. Arts Ctr., Tulsa, 1972, River Rds. Exhbn., St. Louis, 1973, U. N.D. Art Gallery, Minot, 1973, New Horizons Gallery, Chgo., 1973, Purchase Award, Pottsdam, N.Y., 1973, Ark. Arts Ctr., Little Rock, 1973, 74, 75, Krannert Mus., Ill., 1974, 75, Evansville (Ind.) Mus. Art, 1974, Gimpel & Weitzenhoffer Gallery, N.Y.C., 1974, L.A. Print Soc., 1974, Sedona (Ariz.) Art Ctr., 1975, Brooks Meml. Art Gallery, Memphis, 1975, The Dulin Gallery Art, Knoxville, Tenn., 1975, Western Gallery, Bellingham, Wash., 1975, Van Straaten Gallery, Chgo., 1975, Springfield (Mo.) Mus. Art, 1976, Genesis Gallery, N.Y.C., 1976, 78, Azuma Gallery, N.Y.C., 1978, Frank Marino Gallery, N.Y.C., 1978, 79, Prairie House Gallery, Springfield (Ill.), 1979, The Mitchell Mus. Art, 1979, Evanston (Ind.) Arts Ctr., 1980, 82, So. Ill. U. Art Gallery, St. Louis, 1984, Art St. Louis, 1986; one-person shows include Mo. State Libr., Springfield, 1971, The Art Gallery, Tulsa, 1972, The Univ. of South, Sewanee, Tenn., 1973, Wabash (Ind.) Coll., 1974, Roy Boyd Gallery, Chgo., 1977, Ball State U., Muncie, Ind., 1979, Forest Park Contemporary Art Ctr., St. Louis, 1990, Craft Alliance Gallery, St. Louis, 1991, Locust St. Studio, St. Louis, 1991-96, Contemporary Art Ctr., St. Louis, 1996; represented in permanent collections at The Bklyn. Mus. Art, Ill. State Mus., Springfield, The Dulin Gallery Art, Ark. Arts Ctr., The ARCO Collection, L.A., The Boatmen's Bank Collection, St. Louis, St. Lawrence U., Canton, N.Y., Univ. of South, Wabash Coll., Roy Boyd Collection, Cindy Schwab, So. Ill. U. Recipient Purchase award Bklyn. Mus. Art, Ill. State Mus., Ark. Arts Ctr., ARCO Collection, L.A. Office: Belleville Area Coll 2500 Carlyle Rd Belleville IL 62221

THROCKMORTON, PETER EUGENE, organic chemist, consultant; b. St. Paul, Jan. 20, 1927; s. James and Carla Margaret (Strim) T.; m. Phyllis Marie McGrew, June 30, 1948; children: Ann Marie, Carla Louise, Peter Eugene Jr. BSChemE, U. Minn., 1948, MS in Chemistry, 1955; PhD in Organic Chemistry, Kansas State U., 1960. Rsch. engr. Tainton Products Co., Balt., 1948-49; mfg. rsch. engr. Glenn L. Martin Aircraft Co., Middle River, Md., 1949-52; rsch. chemist Gen. Mills Rsch., Inc., Mpls., 1952-56; petroleum fellow Petroleum Rsch. Inst. Kans. State U., Manhattan, 1957-58; assoc. chemist Midwest Rsch. Inst., Kansas City, Mo., 1960-65; sr. rsch. chemist Archer-Daniels-Midland Co., Mpls., 1965-67; sr. rsch. chemist II Ashland Chem. Co. (formerly Archer-Daniels-Midland Co.), Columbus, Ohio, 1967-86; prin. Throckmorton Cons., Plain City, Ohio, 1986-95; cons. Teltech, Inc., Mpls., 1991—; assoc. chmn. 15th Ann. Kansas City Chemistry Conf., 1963; mem. People's Republic China-U.S. Sci. Exchange Program, Beijing and Shanghai, 1984. Contbr. 27 articles to profl. jours., including Modern Plastics, Jour. Am. Chem. Soc., Jour. Elastoplastics, Jour. Am. Oil Chemists Soc., Inorganica Chimica Acta. Recipient Best Paper award Reinforced Plastics Div. of Soc. Plastics Industry, 1963. Fellow Am. Inst. Chemists (bd. dirs. 1987-89); mem. Am. Chem. Soc. (chmn. tech. program Columbus sect. 1979-80), Am. Oil Chemists Soc. (editl. reviewer 1986-91), Sigma Xi, Phi Lambda Upsilon. Democrat. Home and Office: 15943 Hawn Rd Plain City OH 43064-9791

THROGMARTIN, DIANNE, educational foundation administrator; b. Indpls., May 3, 1964; d. Roy Don and Suzzane (Jackson) T. Cert., Landmark Coll., 1988, Motivation Inst., 1991; BS in Edn., Butler U., 1992; cert., Fund Raising Sch., Indpls., 1992-93. Product mgr. H.H. Gregg, Indpls., 1982-85, salesperson, trainer, 1988-90; substitute tchr. Camp Delafield Lakeview Temple, Indpls., 1990-91; gen. asst. Robo Group Internat., Indpls., 1992-93, Indpls. Jaycees, 1993-94; pres., founder Dyslexia Ednl. Found. Am., Indpls., 1994—. Pres. bd. Ind. Hugh O'Brian Youth Found., Indpls., 1992-95, Leadership America, 1996. Recipient Cmty. Svc. award Landmark Coll., 1988, 87. Mem. Jaycees (dir. Indpls. chpt. 1993-95, Mem. of Month 1992, Outstanding Com. chmn. 1993, 94, Dir. of Month 1993, Dir. of Yr. 1994, Mgmt. Devel. award 1994), Indpls. C. of C. Republican. Home: 4625 Sunset Ave Indianapolis IN 46208 Office: Dyslexia Ednl Found Am 4181 E 96th Ste 215 Indianapolis IN 46240

THUEME, WILLIAM HAROLD, educator; b. St. Clair, Mich., Sept. 4, 1945; s. Harold Arthur and Delphine Betty (Buhl) T.; m. Nora Kathleen Koning, May 8, 1971; children: Benjamin William, Rebecca Kathleen, Jeffrey William, Sarah Kathleen. Student Port Huron Jr. Coll., 1963-64; BA, Mich. State U., 1967, MA, 1969; postgrad. Oakland U., 1971, U. Mich., 1971, San Francisco State U., 1975, U. Hawaii, 1975. Cert. tchr., Mich. Tchr. pub. schs., Charlotte, Mich., 1967-69, Ann Arbor, Mich., 1969—; fgn. travel coord.-Ambs. Abroad Program, Amsterdam, Netherlands, 1968—; regional driver coord. for Southeastern Mich., Avis Rent-a-Car, 1983—. Active UN Children's found, Mich. Sheriffs Ednl. Found., Woods Road Assn., Normal Park Neighborhood Assn., U.S. Legal Found., Found. for Nicaraguan Democracy, Nat. Coun. Better Edn., participant Skyhook II Project; elections coord. Eaton County (Mich.) Rep. Party, 1968, mem. nat. com., 1968—, mem. nat. senatorial com.; mem. troop com. Council Boy Scouts Am., Ypsilanti, counselor for reading, 1988-89; cub scout summer camp instr. Wolverine Council, 1987, merit badge counselor, 1988-89; coach of the angels Ypsilanti Am. Little League, 1988; parent adv. bd. The Childrens Devel. Lab. Ea. Mich. U., 1988-89; active Mich. United Conservation Clubs, Big Brothers Am., Charlotte, Mich., Human Rights Watch, Nat. Security Caucus U.S., 1988—, Heritage Found., 1988—, ofcl. sponsor Mandate for Leadership III, Policy Strategies for 1990's Project, Project Save Our Schs., 1988—, Citizens United for Better Edn., World Awareness, Inc., Group 61 Amnesty Internat., Legal Affairs Council, Council for Inter-Am. Security, Nicaraguan Resistance Edn. Found., Nat. Right to Work Legal Def. Found., Citizens Against Govt. Waste, Citizens Commn. for Ethics in Govt., Citizens for Decency Through Law, Inc., Participating Parents For Progress in Ypsilanti Pub. Schs.; parents adv. bd. Chapelle Elem. Sch., Ypsilanti, 1989-90, West Mid. Sch., Ypsilanti, 1991-92, Ypsilanti Pub. Schs., 1990—, Ypsilanti High Sch.; charter sponsor Victory Over Communism Project; nominated charter mem. Presdl. Task Force; participant The Imperial Congress: Crisis in the Separation of Powers Project, line-item veto project The Heritage Found., 1989, campaign to revise medicare catastrophic coverage law project Nat. Assn. for Uniformed Svcs., 1989, repeal of catastrophic coverage act program Conservative Caucus Inc., 1989, Srs. Coalition Against the Tax, 1989; nat. adv. council Citizens Com. for Right to Bear Arms; elders quorum instr., exec. sec. Ch. of Jesus Christ of Latter-day Saints, 1976-81, adult spl. interest coordinator, 1982—, Sunday Sch. sec. Ann Arbor stake, 1983—; mem. Mich. Mormon Concert Choir, 1977—, Ypsilanti Mormon Choir; various polit. and civic orgns. Recipient Spl. Recognition award Richard Nixon, 1968-79, Gerald Ford, 1974-76, Ronald Reagon 1971-88, George Bush, 1989—, Spl. Recognition award Reagan Presdl. Campaign, 1981, Bush Presdl. Campaign, 1988, Citizen of Yr. award Citizens Com. for Right to Bear Arms, 1988, cert. recognition U.S. Justice Found., 1991, Hale Found., Am. Security Council 30th Anniversary Spl. Recognition Cert., Cert. Appreciation award Second Amendment Found., 1988, Appreciation of Devoted and Valuable Svc award Chapelle Elem. Sch., 1988-89, Merit Badge, Wolverine Coun. Mem. NEA, The Lincoln Inst. for Rsch. Edn., United Conservatives of Am. (participant citzens against the catastrophic health act tax 1989), Mich. Edn. Assn., Internat. Reading Assn., Mich. Sheriffs Assn. (assoc.), Police Marksmanship Assn., Washtenaw Reading Council, Southeastern Mich. Reading Assn., Mich. Reading Assn., Mich. Assn. for Supervision and Curriculum Devel., Ann Arbor Edn. Assn., Am. Security Council, Am. Defense Inst., Found. for Christian Living, Am. Family Assn., Nat. Geog. Soc., Am. Film Inst., Taxpayers Edn. Lobby, NRA, Gun Owners Am., Nat. Assn. Federally Lic. Firearms Dealers, Conservative Caucus, Inc., Ams. for Freedom, Tri-County Sportsman LeaguSigma Alpha Eta. Club: Washtenaw Sportsmen's (Ypsilanti). Lodge: Optimist (v.p. and dir. 1975-78) (Ann Arbor). Lutheran. Office: 5187 Palms Rd Casco MI 48064

THULIN, ADELAIDE ANN, design company executive, interior designer; b. Chgo., Nov. 15, 1925; d. Martin Evold and Kathleen Marie (Glennon) Peterson; m. Frederick Adolph Thulin, Jr., Aug. 18, 1945; children: Frederick, Kristin, Mary, Margaret, Francis, Peter, Andrea, Charles, Joseph, Kathleen, James, Suzanne, Patricia. Student Northwestern U., 1943-46; AA in Interior Design, Harper Coll., 1977. Registered interior designer. Asst. production mgr. Cruttenden & Eger, Chgo., 1946; editor Mt. Prospect (Ill.) Independent, 1960; real estate salesperson Homefinders, Northwest Chgo. suburbs, 1965, 69-70; asst. v.p. advt. Littelfuse, Des Plaines, Ill., 1966-67; owner, pres. Applied Design Assocs., Mt. Prospect, 1977—; ptnr., sec. Applied Design Internat. Ltd., Mt. Prospect, 1992—; career day speaker local high schs., 1982—; bd. dirs. Works subs. Pvt. Industry Coun. Author, editor monthly newsletter Women's Archtl. League, 1983-85, The Binnacle, CYC, 1979-81. Organizer, Mother's March of Dimes, Mt. Prospect, 1953-54, Vols. for Stevenson, 1952, 56, Citizens for Douglas, 1954, Citizens for Kennedy, 1960; mem. Fair Review Council, Chgo., 1983-84; mem. 13th Congl. Dist. Dem. Women's Club, publicity chmn. 1957-58; mem. Chgo. Symphony Orchestra Chorus, 1972; del. Ill. Statehouse Conf. on Small Bus., 1984, 85; bd. dirs. Arts Coun. of Mt. Prospect, 1986-93; organizer Mt. Prospect chpt. Internat. Sister Cities Program; chmn. Mt. Prospect Sign Rev. Bd.; mem. renovation com. Mt. Prospect Hist. Soc.; pres. cmty. edn. coun. H.S. Dist. 214; bd. dirs. Cmty. Edn. Found. Mem. AIA (profl. affiliate Chgo. chpt.), Am. Women Internat. Understanding, Nat. Small Bus. United (bd. dirs., v.p. state govt. affairs 1994), Ill. Coalition for N.Am. Free Trade Agreement, Women's Archtl. League (publicity chmn. 1964-65), Mt. Prospect C. of C., Chgo. Women in Arch., Gamma Alpha Chi. Roman Catholic. Avocations: reading for print-handicapped on CRIS radio, 1982-92; choral singing. Home: 4 S Owen St Mount Prospect IL 60056-3309 Office: Applied Design Assocs Ltd 200 E Evergreen Ave Mount Prospect IL 60056-3240

THUNDY, ZACHARIAS PONTIAN, modern language educator; b. Changanacherry, India, Sept. 28, 1936; came to U.S., 1964; s. Joseph Joseph and Mary Joseph (Palakunnez) T.; m. Gina Marie, Dec. 15, 1983; children: Zachary Jospeh, Antonio Joseph. B in Philosophy, Pontificium Athenaeum, Poona, India, 1958, BTh, MTh, 1962; MA, DePaul U., 1965; PhD, U. Notre Dame, 1968. Instr. Dharmaram Coll., Bangalore, India, 1963-64; asst. prof. No. Mich. U., Marquette, 1968-72, assoc. prof., 1972-76, prof., 1976—. Author: Covenant in Anglo-Saxon Thought, 1972, Folktales of Kadar, 1983, Buddha and Christ, 1994; editor: Chaucerian Problems and Perspectives, 1982. Mem. MLA, Mich. Acad., Medieval Acad., Modern Lang. Soc. Roman Catholic. Home: 1420 McClellan Marquette MI 49855 Office: No Mich U 1401 Presque Isle Marquette MI 49855

THUR, MIKE ADAM, SR., product design engineer; b. Cleve., June 12, 1960. CAD mgr. Nook Industries, Beachwood, Ohio, 1990-92; draftsman Famous Supply, Lakewood, Ohio, 1992-93; product design engr. Emerson Electric, Elyria, Ohio, 1993—. Soccer, baseball coach Youth Activities, Maple Heights, Ohio. Office: Emerson Electric Co Ridge Tool Divsn 400 Clark St Elyria OH 44035-6108

THURBER, DALE KING, ornithologist, ecologist and wildlife biologist; b. Idaho Falls, Idaho, Aug. 17, 1962; s. Karl Garner and Viola (Lillywhite) T.; m. Tracey Lee Wilson, Feb. 21, 1987; children: Natasha, Austin, Duncan, Selena. BS in Zoology cum laude, Brigham Young U., 1984, MS in Zoology/Tropical Ecology, 1988; PhD in Forest Resources Sci., W.Va. U., 1992. Grad. teaching/rsch. asst. dept. zoology Brigham Young U., Provo, Utah, 1984-87; field tech. Environ. Labs. Inc., Springville, Utah, 1988; rsch. tech. div. forestry W.Va. U., Morgantown, 1988, grad. teaching asst. dept. biology, 1990-91, instr., 1990-91, grad. rsch. asst., 1988-92; statis. cons. Mylan Pharms., Inc., Morgantown, 1992; rsch. biologist Nat. Biol. Survey, Nat. Mus. Natural History, Washington, 1992-94; rsch. assoc. Ctr. Ecol. Mgmt. of Mil. Lands, Champaign, Ill., 1994—; co-owner and operator Thurber Typing, 1990—; lectr. in field. Contbr. articles to profl. jours. Vol. missionary LDS, Rome, 1981-83. Presdl. scholar Brigham Young U., 1980-87; recipient numerous tuition awards, scholarships. Am. Inst. Biol. Scis., Am. Ornithologists Union (Marcia Brady Tucker travel award 1991), Assn. for Tropical Biology, Assn. Field Ornithologists, Birdlife Internat., Cooper Ornithol. Soc., Nat. Audubon Soc., Nat. Geog. Soc., Nat. Wildlife Fedn., Natural Areas Assn., Nature Conservancy, Soc. for Conservation Biology, Wilderness Soc., Wildlife Conservation Soc., Wilson Ornithol. Soc., World Wildlife Fund. Home: 920 W Beardsley Ave Champaign IL 61821-2559 Office: USA-CERL PO Box 9005 Champaign IL 61826-9005

THURMER, ROBERT, art gallery director; b. Vienna, Austria, Oct. 8, 1953; s. Robert and Helene (Vilim) T.; m. Nancy J. Clark, Aug. 2, 1973 (div. 1988); children: Kate E., Clayton R. BFA, Syracuse U., 1977; MA, U. Nebr., 1979; MFA, RISD, 1981. Instr. SUNY, Oswego, 1982-83; designer Cleve. Mus. Art, 1983-88; curator Everson Mus. Art, Syracuse, N.Y., 1988-90; art gallery dir. Cleve. State U., 1990—; supt. fine arts N.Y. State Fair, Syracuse, 1989-90; asst. dir. CCNY, N.Y.C., 1992-93; visual art review panelist Ohio Arts Coun., Columbus, 1992-95; instr. exhbn. design U. Calif., Berkeley, 1994. Office: Cleve State U Art Gallery 2307 Chester Ave Cleveland OH 44114

THURSWELL, GERALD ELLIOTT, lawyer; b. Detroit, Feb. 4, 1944; s. Harry and Lilyan (Zeitlin) T.; m. Lynn Satovsky, Sept. 17, 1967 (div. Aug. 1978); children: Jennifer, Lawrence; m. Judith Linda Bendix, Sept. 2, 1978; children: Jeremy, Lindsey. LLB with distinction, Wayne State U., 1967. Bar: Mich. 1968, N.Y. 1984, D.C. 1986, Colo. 1990, Ill. 1992, U.S. Dist. Ct. (ea. dist.) Mich. 1968, U.S. Ct. Appeals (7th cir.) 1968, U.S. Supreme Ct., 1994. Student asst. to U.S. atty. Ea. Dist. Mich., Detroit, 1966; assoc. Zwerdling, Miller, Klimist & Maurer, Detroit, 1967-68; sr. ptnr. Thurswell, Chayet & Weiner, Southfield, Mich., 1968—; arbitrator Am. Arbitration Assn., Detroit, 1969—; mediator Wayne County Cir. Ct., Mich., 1983—, Oakland County Cir. Ct. Mich., 1984—, also facilitator, 1991; twp. atty. Royal Oak Twp., Mich., 1982—; lectr. Oakland County Bar Assn. People's Law Sch., 1988. Pres. Powder Horn Estates Subdiv. Assn., West Bloomfield, Mich., 1975, United Fund, West Bloomfield, 1976. Arthur F. Lederle scholar Wayne State U. Law Sch., Detroit, 1964, grad. profl. scholar Wayne State U. Law Sch., 1965, 66. Mem. Mich. Bar Assn. (investigator/arbitrator grievance bd., atty. discipline bd., chmn. hearing panel), Mich. Trial Lawyers Assn. (legis. com. on govtl. immunit, 1984), ATLA (treas. Detroit met. chpt. 1986-87, v.p. 1989-90, pres. 1991-93), Detroit Bar Assn. (lawyer referral com., panel pub. adv. com. judicial candidates), Oakland County Bar Assn. Clubs: Wabeek Country (Bloomfield Hills), Skyline (Southfield, Mich.). Home: 1781 Golf Ridge Dr S Bloomfield Hills MI 48302-1733 Office: Thurswell Chayet & Weiner 1000 Town Ctr Ste 500 Southfield MI 48075-1221

TIBBETTS, GARY GEORGE, research physicist; b. Omaha, Oct. 12, 1939; s. Donald George and Delois Julene (Black) T.; m. Patricia Avis Andreasen, Aug. 1, 1964; children: Margaret Joan, Elizabeth Alison, Katherine Martha. BS in Physics, Calif. Tech. Inst., Pasadena, 1961; MS and PhD in Physics, U. Ill., 1967. Gastforcher Tech. U., Munich, 1967-69; sr. staff rsch. scientist GM Rsch. Labs., Warren, Mich., 1969—. Author: Vapor-Grown Carbon Fibers, 1990; contbr. articles to profl. jours. Mem. Am. Phys. Soc., Am. Carbon Soc., Materials Rsch. Soc. Office: GM R&D Labs Physics & Phys Chem Dept 30500 Mound Rd Warren MI 48090-9055

TIBERI, PAT, state legislator; m. Denice Tiberi. BA, Ohio State Univ. Asst. dist. mgr. Congressman John Kasich; Ohio State Rep. Dist. 26, 1996—; pres. Windsor Terrace Learning Ctr. Active Am. Red Cross, past pres. Forest Park Civic Assn., chmn. Military, Vet. & Cmty. Svc. Com., bd. dirs. Recipient Pres.'s award Northland Cmty. Coun., Vet. Admin Commendation award, Svc. award Am. Red Cross, Watchdog of Treas. award United Conservatives of Ohio. Mem. Sons of Italy. Home: 5208 Honeytree Loop W Columbus OH 43229*

TIBERIO, ANGELA ROSE C., physician; b. Orange, N.J., Feb. 6, 1960; d. Angelo Thomas and RoseMarie (Bifano) T. BS in biology with honors, Lafayette Coll., Easton, 1982; MD, Mich. State U., East Lansing, 1984-88. Diplomate Am. Bd. Internal Medicine. Resident Mich. State U. - Coll. Human Medicine, East Lansing, Mich., 1988-91; chief resident Mich. State U. - Coll. Human Medicine, East Lansing, 1990-91; internal medicine specialist Blodgett Meml. Med. Ctr., Grand Rapids, Mich., 1991—; fellow in primary care Mich. State U. - Coll. of Human Medicine, East Lansing, 1993-95, asst. prof. internal medicine, 1993—; resident in internal medicine, assoc. program dir. Blodgett Meml. Med. Ctr./SMHS/Mich. State U., Grand Rapids, 1994—. Contbr. articles to profl. jours. Mem. med. edn. com. Blodgett Meml. Med. Ctr., 1989—, med. adv. com. Hospice of Greater Grand Rapids, 1995—, Sons & Daughters of Italy, Grand Rapids, 1991—. Recipient W. R. Hunt Prize in Biology Lafayette Coll., 1982. Mem. Am. Medical Women's Assn. (electronic pathways task force), ACP, AMA, Am. Soc. of Internal Medicine, Assn. of Program Dir. in Internal Medicine, Mich. State Med. Soc. (corp. affiliated Physicians com., alt. del.). Office: Blodgett Meml Med Ctr 1840 Wealthy SE Grand Rapids MI 49506

TICE, PATRICIA KAYE, therapist, entrepreneur, educator, trainer; b. Grinnell, Iowa, May 22, 1953; d. Ronald Stephen and Shirley Ann (Arthur) Tice. BS, Iowa State U., 1975, DPhil, 1983; PhD, Oxford U., 1994. Tchr. St. Augustin Sch., Des Moines, 1975-77; tchr. S.E. Polk Schs., Runnells, Iowa, 1977-84, guidance counselor, 1984-86; prevention coordinator Nat. Council on Alcoholism, Des Moines, 1986-87; owner, pres. Tice Assocs., Des Moines, 1987—; bd. dirs. Children's Oncology Svcs. Iowa, Inc., Des Moines, 1986—, pres., 1988—; prof. Am. Inst. Bus.; corp. cons. MidAm. Devel. Group, Inc./Profiles of Iowa. Author: Sources and Effects of Stress in the Workplace, Alpha Delta Pi Pledge Manual, 1975; creator registered svc. Active Des Moines Ronald McDonald House, 1977—. Mem. NAFE, AAUW, Assn. Retarded Persons (human rights commn. 1988-91), Nat. Assn. Women Bus. Owners, Oxford Soc. Scholars, Men's Garden Club, Alpha Delta Pi, Alpha Delta Pi Alumni Assn. Office: Tice Assocs 2800 University West Des Moines IA 50266

TIDWELL, ROY ROBINSON, SR., television producer, consultant; b. Tampa, Fla., Apr. 11, 1953; s. Arthur Kenneth and Alice (Correy) T.; m. Christine Rogers, Aug. 14, 1976; children: Roy Robinson Jr., Heather Christine. BA, Liberty U., Lynchburg, Va., 1976. Cert. broadcast technologist. Prodn. dir. So. Teleprodns., Orlando, Fla., 1976-81; prodr. Liberty Broadcasting Net, Lynchburg, 1981-88; dir. mktg. Freedom Village, USA, Lakemont, N.Y., 1988-91; gen. mgr. Am. Portrait Films, Cleve., 1991—; cons. Save the Manatee Club, Maitland, Fla., 1988—, The Rutherford Inst., Charlottesville, Va., 1990—. Prodr. Jerry Falwell Live, 1987; exec. prodr. videos Child Abuse "Maddness," 1989 (Angel award 1989), The Mountain, 1989 (Angel award 1989). Mem. Soc. Broadcast Engrs. (program chmn. 1987-88, technologist award 1987). Republican. Home: 7205 Jackson St Mentor OH 44060-5027 Office: Am Portrait Films 503 E 200th St Cleveland OH 44119-1545

TIER, CHARLES, applied mathematics educator; b. Albany, N.Y., Sept. 25, 1947; s. David and Freda (Altschuler) T.; m. Beatrice Faye Schreiber, Feb. 17, 1974; children: Jennifer, Matthew. BS, Rensselaer Poly. Inst., 1969, MS, 1971; PhD, NYU, 1976. Asst. prof. U. Ill., Chgo., 1977, assoc. prof., 1982-88, prof., 1988—, assoc. head, 1994—; vis. prof. Northwestern U. dept. engrng. sci. and applied math., Evanston, 1983, 93; cons. NSF, Washington, 1993-95. Contbr. articles to profl. jours. NSF Rsch. grantee, 1986-95, Dept. Energy Rsch. grantee, 1993-95. Mem. Soc. Indsl. and Applied Math., Assn. Computing Machinery, Computer Soc. IEEE. Home: 1635 Linden Ave Highland Park IL 60035-3442 Office: MSCS 851 S Morgan St Chicago IL 60607

TIERNEY, CATHERINE MARIE, librarian; b. Woodbury, N.J., July 11, 1947; d. William John and Marie Cecilia (Oakes) Morgan; m. Phillip A Tierney, Aug. 9, 1969. BA, Cardinal Stritch Coll., 1969; MLS, Kent State U., 1974. Reference libr. Akron (Ohio) Beacon Jour., 1974-76, chief libr., 1976—. Mem. Spl. Librs. Assn. Republican. Episcopalian. Office: Akron Beacon Jour 44 W Exchange St Akron OH 44328-0001

TIERNEY, GORDON PAUL, real estate broker, genealogist; b. Ft. Wayne, Ind., Oct. 17, 1922; s. James Leonard and Ethele Lydia (Brown) T.; m. Carma Lillian Devine, Oct. 17, 1946; 1 child, Paul N. Student, Ind. U., 1940-41, Cath. U. Am., 1941-42; coll. tng. detachment, Clemson U., 1943. Br. mgr. Bartlett-Collins Co., Chgo., 1956-84; prin., broker Kaiser-Tierney Real Estate, Inc., Palatine, Ill., 1984-89; pres. Tierney Real Estate, Newburgh, Ind. Author: Burgess/Bryan Connection, 1978; assoc. editor Colonial Genealogist Jour., 1976-85. Served in USAC, 1943-45, China. Decorated Legion of Honor. Fellow Am. Coll. Genealogists (pres. 1977—); mem. SAR (v.p. gen. 1984-85, genealogist gen. 1981-83, Silver and Bronze medals 1978-80, Patriot medal 1976, Meritorious Svc. award 1983, Minutemen award 1984), Huguenot Soc. Ill. (state pres. 1978-80), Huguenot Soc. S.C., Nat. Huguenot Soc., Huguenot Soc. Ind. (pres. 1993-95), Nat. Geneal. Soc., Ind. Hist. Soc., Soc. Ind. Pioneers, First Families Ohio, Ohio Geneal. Soc., Va. Geneal. Soc., Md. Geneal. Soc., Augustan Soc., Gen. Soc. War 1812 (state pres. 1985), Sons. and Daus. Pilgrims, Descs. Old Plymouth Colony, Mil. Order Stars and Bars, Soc. Descs. Colonial Clergy, Sons of Union Vets., Sons of Confederate Vets., Pioneer Wis. Families, Welcome Soc. Pa., Pa. Geneal. Soc., Nat. Soc. Archivists, Soc. Colonial Wars in Ill., Soc. Colonial Wars in Ind. (gov. 1992-94), Sons of Am. Colonists (nat. v.p. 1971-74), Mil. and Hospitalier Order St. Lazarus of Jerusalem, Order Descs. Ancient Planters, Hump Pilots Assn., Nat. Bd. Realtors, Ill. Bd. Realtors, Sword Bunker Hill, Tri-State Geneal. Soc., Jamestowne Soc., Baronial Order Magna Charta, Masons, Shriners, Rolling Hill Country Club. Republican. Presbyterian. Home and Office: 8766 Hanover Dr Newburgh IN 47630-9327

TIERNEY, JAMES EDWARD, literature educator; b. Newark, Jan. 23, 1935; s. John Thaddeus and Kathryn Marcella (Keogh) T.; m. Susan Marie Schnake, Aug. 9, 1980 (div. 1991); m. Patricia Ann Brunner, May 13, 1995. BA, Seton Hall U., 1956; MA, Fordham U., 1964; PhD, NYU, 1969. Asst. prof. U. Mo., St. Louis, 1968-74, assoc. prof., 1974-87, prof., 1987—. Editor: Correspondence of Robert Dodsley 1733-1764, 1988; contbr. articles to scholarly publs. Fellow NEH, 1974, Am. Coun. Learned Socs., 1978, Huntington Libr., 1977, 90, William Andrews Clark Libr., 1990, Houghton Libr., Harvard U., 1992; grantee Am. Philos. Soc., 1975. Mem. Soc. for History of Authorship, Reading and Publ., Am. Bibliog. Soc., Bibliog. Soc. London, Johnson Soc. Midwest, Assn. for Computers in Humanities, Am. Soc. 18th Century Studies, Midwest Am. Soc. 18th Century Studies, East Ctrl. Am. Soc. for 18th Century Studies. Office: Dept English Univ Mo-Saint Louis Saint Louis MO 63121

TIERNO, EDWARD GREGORY, insurance company executive; b. Latrobe, Pa., Oct. 9, 1948; s. Frank Albert and Mary Christine (Santarelli) T. BA, Youngstown State U., 1970; postgrad. Indiana U. Pa., 1969. Tchr., coach Youngstown (Ohio) Bd. Edn., 1970-74; liability supr., mktg. rep. Underwriters Adjusting Co., Youngstown and Southfield, Mich., 1974-78; ins. risk mgr. McNicholas Transp. Co., Youngstown, 1978-82; pres. Ins. Claim Svc., Youngstown, 1982—; owner Midwest Mobile Testing Svc. Scholar Pa. Higher Edn. Assn., 1966-70, Leadership Youngstown. Mem. Better Bus. Bur.; advisor Jr. Achievement; vol. March of Dimes; corporate chmn. Youngstown Opera Guild. Bd. dirs. Am. Heart Assn.; active Common Carrier Conf. Irregular Route Carriers, Ohio State Claims Assn., Ohio Assn. Ind. Adjusters, Youngstown Claims Assn. (pres., scholarship chmn. 1981-82), Nat. Assn. Ind. Insurance Adjusters, Nat. Italian Am. Sports Hall of Fame (pres.), Italian Scholarship League, Youngstown C. of C., Youngstown State U. Alumni Assn. (bd. dirs., pres.) Penguin Club, Leadership, Order of Ky. Cols., Curbstone Coachs; corp. chair Youngstown Opera guild. Author: Ohio Comparative Negligence, An Overview, 1980. Co-author: How to Collect An Insurance Claim, 1984. Home: 3605 Hummingbird Hill Dr Youngstown OH 44514-5805 Office: PO Box 5375 Youngstown OH 44514-5375

TIERSKY, TERRI S., dentist, lawyer; b. Chgo., July 25, 1959; d. Morris D. and Joan R. (Berets) T.; m. Roland D. Davidson. BA, U. Ill., 1982; DDS, Loyola U., Chgo., 1986; JD, John Marshall Law Sch., 1991. Bar: Ill., 1991. Pvt. practice dentistry Chgo., 1986—; staff mem. Meth. Hosp., Chgo., 1988—. Mem. ABA, ADA, Chgo. Bar Assn., Chgo. Dental Soc., Ill. State Dental Soc.

TIFFEN, NORMAN HERBERT, franchise executive, consultant; b. Chgo., Mar. 22, 1930; s. Herbert Fredrick and Cleo Norma (Nicholson) T.; m. Nancy Lee Scrivner, Sept. 22, 1953 (div. Dec. 1978); children: Scott F., Anne L. Tiffen Taylor; m. Jane Ahlstedt, Mar. 21, 1981. BSBA, Northwestern U., 1951, postgrad., 1951. Mgr. sales ops. H. M. Harper Div. ITT, Morton Grove, Ill., 1955-68; gen. sales mgr. Weatherhead Co., Cleve., 1968-73; v.p. mktg. Rego Corp., Chgo., 1973-77; pres. Rego Distbn. Ctrs., Chgo., 1974-77; pres., chief exec. officer, chief operating officer Mktg. Svcs., Inc., Northbrook, Ill., 1979—; bd. dirs. Mktg. Svcs., Inc. Interviewer Caucus Trustee Selection, Winnetka, Ill., 1975-77, Northbrook, 1990; precinct capt. Rep. Party, Shaker Heights, Ohio, 1969-73; bd. dirs. Normandy Hill Town Home Assn., Northbrook, 1990—. Lt. comdr. USN, 1951-55. Mem. Am. Mktg. Assn., Am. Mgmt. Assn. (seminar leader), Internat. Entrepreneurs Assn., Cleve. Skating Club, Skokie Country Club. Home: 3944 Dundee Rd Northbrook IL 60062-2126 Office: Mktg Svcs Inc 1834 Techny Ct Northbrook IL 60062-5474

TIGGES, JOHN THOMAS, writer, musician, lecturer; b. Dubuque, Iowa, May 16, 1932; s. John George and Madonna Josephine (Heiberger) T.; m. Kathryn Elizabeth Johnson, Apr. 22, 1954; children: Juliana, John, Timothy, Teresa, Jay. Student Loras Coll., 1950-52, 57, U. Dubuque, 1960. Clk. John Deere Tractor Works, Dubuque, 1957-61; agt. Penn Mut. Life Ins. Co., Dubuque, 1961-74; bus. mgr., bd. dirs. Dubuque Symphony Orch., 1960-68, 71-74; v.p., sec. Olson Toy and Hobby Inc., 1964-66; pres. JKT Inc., 1978-82; rsch. specialist Electronic Media Svcs. (Scripp-Howard); violinist. Author: (novels) The Legend of Jean Marie Cardinal, 1976, Garden of the Incubus, 1982, Unto the Altar, 1985, Kiss Not the Child, 1985, Evil Dreams, 1986, The Immortal, 1986, Hands of Lucifer, 1987, As Evil Does, 1987, Pack, 1987, Venom, 1988, Vessel, 1988, Slime, 1988, Book of the Dead, 1989, From Below, 1989, Comes The Wraith, 1990, Breed, 1990, Mountain Massacre, 1990, Blood on the Rails, 1990, One Man Jury, 1991, The Curse, 1993, Milwaukee Road Steam Power, 1994, Monster, 1995, (book of short stories) Nightales, 1990, (plays) No More-No Less, 1983, We Who Are About to Die, 1979; contbg. author: Murder for Father, 1994; radio plays: Valley of Deceit, 1978, Rockville Horror, 1979, The Timid, 1982; TV drama: An Evening with George Wallace Jones, 1983; biographies: George Wallace Jones, 1983, John Plumbe Jr., 1983; producer TV series The Loneliest Job, 1989; co-author: (history) The Milwaukee Road Narrow Gauge: The Bellevue, Cascade & Western, Iowa's Slim Princess, 1985 ; co-author: They came from Dubuque, 1983; co-author, editor: A Cup and a Half of Coffee, 1977; editorial asst. Julien's Jour.; contbg. editor Over 49 News and Views; interviewer, spl. reporter Editorial Assocs., 1982-84; columnist Memory Lane, Remember When...?, What's the Difference, Telegraph Herald; syndicated columnist Tough Trivia Tidbits; tchr. continuing edn. creative writing Northeast Iowa Community Coll.; tchr. writing U. Wis. Outreach Program's Ednl. Teleconference Network, summer writing workshop U. Iowa; cofounder Dubuque Symphony Orch., 1960; founder Julien Strings, 1972, Dubuque Sch. of Novel, 1978, Northeast Iowa Writers Workshop, 1981; cohost Big Broadcast Radio Program, WDBQ Radio, 1979-82; founder Sinipee Writers Workshop, 1985. Founder, bus. mgr. Dubuque Pops Orch., 1957. Recipient Nat. Quality award, 1966-70, Carnegie-Stout Libr. World of Lit. honors award, 1981. Fellow World Lit. Acad.; mem. Nat. Writers Club (profl.), Horror Writers Am., Western Writers Am., Iowa Authors, Internat. Platform Assn., Toy Train Collectors Club, Dubuque Rails Model Railroad (co-founder 1987). Roman Catholic. Office: PO Box 902 Dubuque IA 52004-0902

TIGHE-MOORE, BARBARA JEANNE, electronics executive; b. Wadsworth, Ohio, Jan. 12, 1961; d. Norton Raymond and Laura Alida (Frank) Tighe; m. Derek William Moore, June 26, 1982. AS in Electronic Engring. summa cum laude, Hocking Tech. Coll., 1981; AS in Electronic Data Processing magna cum laude, Sinclair Coll., 1986; BBA Honors Coll. magna cum laude, Kent State U., 1988. Lic. amateur radio operator. Tech. writer computer dept. Sinclair Coll., Dayton, Ohio, 1983; project mgr. O'Neil & Assocs., Dayton, 1983-84; biomed., bio-acoustic real-time flight simulation tempest developer Systems Rsch. Labs., Dayton, 1984-86; owner, pres. Lida Ray Techs., Dayton, 1978—; computer specialist Kent State U. Press, 1987-88; mgmt. analyst Electronic Warfare Frontier Engring. Inc., 1988-89; supr. small computer tech. svcs. Frontier Engring., Inc., 1989-90, project engr., 1990-92; ptnr., bd. dirs. MKCC, Dayton, 1990—; sr. program mgr. C.E.T.A., Dayton, 1992-93; ptnr., bd. dirs. SDCC, Dayton, 1992—; pres. Lida Ray Techs., Dayton; regional mgr. User Tech. Assocs., Dayton, 1993—; mem. graphics steering com., mem. sanctioned UNIX software adv. team Aero. Sys. Divsn.; program chair IEEE Internat. Wireless LAN Conf.; mem. Engring. Application Support Environ. Security Working Group; proceedings chmn. Nat. Aerospace & Electronics Conf., 1995, 96; bd. dirs. MKCC, Dayton, 1993—, SDCC; spkr. Govt. Land Mobile Commn. Conf., 1993, Internat. Engring. Mgmt. Cons., 1994, Wireless '93, Calgary, Alta., Nat. Aeorpace & Electronics Conf., 1995, 96. Author: Job Search Strategies for the 90's, 1993; editor: Graphics Directions, 1990-91; pub. Team Advisor, SDCC Cleaning Times, IEEE Update; contbr. poetry to mags. and anthologies; contbr. papers, articles to profl. jours. Counselor Kwam's Kinder Kamp; tchr. Bible Sch.; cook Meals on Wheels; organizer/cook funeral Svcs. Dinners. Recipient Vol. Citizen award Wadsworth C. of C, 1979, Ohio Essayist award, 1979, Virginia Perryman award, 1979, Disting. Leadership award, 1990, 91. Mem. IEEE (former treas., sec. Dayton sect. 1995-96), Computer Soc. of IEEE (sec. 1991-92, vice chmn. 1992-93, chmn. 1994-95), Engring. Mgmt. Soc. of IEEE, Tech. and Soc. of IEEE, Data Processing Mgmt. Assn., Assn. Computer Machinery, Def. Planning Analysis Soc. (exec. bd.), Assn. Internat. Students Econs. & Commerce (pres. 1986-87), Internat. Film Soc. (pres. 1986-88), Armed Forces Comms. and Electronics Assn. (judge sci. fair western dist. 1992—), Equestrian Team (point rider 1977-87), Fencing Club, Phi Theta Kappa, Mortar Bd., Omicron Delta Kappa, Beta Gamma Sigma. Home: 729 Kyle Drive Tipp City OH 45371

TIGUE, RANDALL DAVIS BRYANT, lawyer; b. Burley, Idaho, Oct. 3, 1948; s. Ralph Louis and Ethel Elsie (Erkkila) T.; m. Josefina Pacquing Ver, July 4, 1976; children: Galadriel, Kristoffer. BA, U. Minn., 1970, JD, 1973. Sole practice, Mpls., 1973-74, 76-80, 81—; legal counsel Minn. Civil Liberties Union, Mpls., 1974-76. Bd. dirs. Minn. Civil Liberties Union, Mpls., 1969—, pres., 1980-81, 88-89; bd. dirs. Ams. for Dem. Action, Washington, 1976, Cultural Soc. Filipino-Ams., Mpls., 1978-82, pres., 1991-93, public rels. officer, 1993—; bd. dirs. Riverview Tower Home Owners' Assn., Mpls., 1979-82 , Minn. Ams. for Dem. Action, Mpls., 1984; mem. rev. bd. Brainerd State Hosp., Minn., 1977—; trustee First Unitarian Soc. Mpls., 1993—. Recipient Kaeder Seal approval, 1988, Defender of Liberty award Minn. Civil Liberties Union, 1995. Mem. Minn. State Bar Assn. (alt. bd. govs. 1978-79), Hennepin County Bar Assn. (vice chmn. individual rights com. 1981-82), First Amendment Lawyers Assn. (sec. 1993-94, 2d v.p. 1994-95, 1st v.p. 1995—), Finnish-Am. Cultural Activities, Inc. Office: 2620 Nicollet Ave Minneapolis MN 55408-1628

TILLEMA, HERBERT KENDALL, political science educator; b. Washington, Apr. 23, 1942; s. John A. and Ruth M. (Kendall) T.; m. Susan H. Murphy, July 11, 1966; children: Anne M., Marie K. BA, Hope Coll., Holland, Mich., 1964; PhD, Harvard U., 1969. Asst. prof. polit. sci. U. Houston, 1968-71; from asst. prof. to prof. polit. sci. U. Mo., Columbia, 1971—; mem. State of Mo. Peace Officer Stds. and Tng. Commn., Jefferson City, 1992-94. Author: Appeal to Force, 1973, International Armed Conflict Since 1945, 1991. Mem. Am. Polit. Sci. Assn., Internat. Studies Assn., Sierra Club (chair Osage Group 1973-74). Home: 306 Westridge Dr Columbia MO 65203-1774 Office: U Mo Dept Polit Sci Columbia MO 65211

TILLESEN, SCOTT ROBERT, gypsum company financial executive; b. Chgo., May 26, 1952; s. Robert Martin and Hannah (Miller) T.; m. Garnet Rae Hoback, Aug. 18, 1979; children: Brian, Matthew, Andrew. BSBA, Roosevelt U., Chgo., 1973, MBA, 1977. Mgr. analytical acctg. U.S. Gypsum Co., Chgo., 1979-81, dir. fin. adminstrn., 1981-82, 88-89, dir. strategic planning, 1983-85; dir. fin. adminstrn. U.S. Gypsum Co., Tarrytown, N.Y., 1985-86, mgr. mktg. svcs., 1986-87; mgr. mktg. policy U.S. Gypsum Co., Atlanta, 1988; dir. credit U.S. Gypsum Co., Chgo., 1989—. Pres. Fox Valley Homeowners Assn., Aurora, Ill., 1981; bd. dirs. Brighton Ridge Property Owners Assn., Naperville, Ill., 1990. Mem. Nat. Assn. Credit Mgmt. (Chgo./Midwest officer 1996), Nat. Bldg. Materials Mfg. Credit Group, Assn. Credit Execs., Credit Rsch. Found. (trustee, author, spkr.). Republican. Presbyterian. Home: 928 W Bailey Rd Naperville IL 60565-4111 Office: US Gypsum Co Dept # 145-10 125 S Franklin St Chicago IL 60606-4605

TILLEY, TERRENCE WILLIAM, religious studies educator; b. Milw., Apr. 19, 1947; s. John C. and Audrey A. (Kau) T.; m. Maureen Antonia Molloy, Dec. 27, 1969; children: Elena, Christine. AB, U. San Francisco, 1970; PhD, Grad. Theol. Union, 1976. Asst. prof. theology Georgetown U., Washington, 1976-79; from asst. to assoc. prof. religious studies St. Michael's Coll., Winooski, Vt., 1979-89; from assoc. prof. to full prof. religion Fla. State U., Tallahassee, 1989-94; chair, dir. grad. studies, prof. religious studies U. Dayton (Ohio), 1994—; dir. seminars NEH, 1987, 90, 94. Author: Talking of God, 1978, Story Theology, 1985 (Book of Yr. Coll. Theology Soc. 1986), The Evils of Theodicy, 1991, The Wisdom of Religious Commitment, 1995, Postmodern Theologies, 1995. NEH fellow, 1987-88. Mem. AAUP, Am. Acad. Religion (co-chair Roman Cath. studies group 1995—), Coll. Theology Soc. (conv. dir. 1988-95, pres. 1996-98), Cath. Theol. Soc. Am. (bd. dirs. 1995-97), Soc. Christian Philosophers, Soc. for Philosophy of Religion. Roman Catholic. Office: U Dayton Religious Studies Dept Dayton OH 45469

TILLMAN, TRACY SALISBURY, professor, consultant; b. Mankato, Minn., Oct. 31, 1956; s. Vincent James and Helen Jane (Salisbury) T.; m. Cheryl Anne Reddy, June 4, 1977 (div. March 1989); m. Lisa Marie Colletti, Sept. 16, 1994; children: Tiffany Anne, Bryce William. BS, Mankato State U., Mankato, 1983, MS, 1986; PhD, Purdue U., West Lafayette, 1989, MS in indsl. engring., 1995. Machinist MICO, Inc., North Mankato, Minn., 1976-83; owner Cloud Nine Sport Aviation, Mankato, 1980-85; engring. mgr. Thin Film Technology, North Mankato, 1983-85; grad. instr. Purdue U., West Lafayette, Ind., 1986-90; employment assessor Jecumseh/Suburu-Isuzu, West Lafayette, 1988-90; cons. Soc. of Mfg. Eng., Dearborn, Mich., 1993—; prof. Eastern Mich. U., Ypsilanti, Mich., 1990—; cons. in field. Recipient Apprentice Faculty Mem. award, Am. Assn. of Engring. Edn., 1989. Mem. Soc. of Mfg. Engr. (certified CMfgE, CEI), Computer and Automated Sys. Assn., Inst. of Indsl. Engrs., Nat. Assn. of Indsl. Tech., Am. Soc. for Quality Control. Office: Eastern Mich Univ 118 S:11 Ypsilanti MI 48197

TILLOTSON, CAROLYN, state legislator; m. John C. Tillotson. Mem. Kans. Senate, 1993—. Republican. Home: 1606 Westwood Dr Leavenworth KS 66048-6622 Office: Kans State Senate State Capitol Topeka KS 66612

TILLSON, JOHN BRADFORD, JR., newspaper publisher; b. Paris, Tex., Dec. 21, 1944; s. John Bradford Sr. and Frances (Ragland) T.; m. Patricia Hunt, June 14, 1966 (div. June 1978); children: John, Karen; m. Cynthia Wornom, Oct. 10, 1981. BA, Denison U., Granville, Ohio, 1966. Reporter Charlotte (N.C.) News, 1969-71; reporter Dayton (Ohio) Daily News, 1971-76, city editor, 1977-80, asst. mng. editor, 1980-82, mng. editor features, 1982-84; editor Dayton Daily News and Jour. Herald, 1984-88, pub., 1988—; lectr. Am. Press Inst., Reston, Va., 1980-84. Exec. com. Vietnam Vets. Meml. Park Fund, Dayton, 1985-86; community bd. advisors Jr. League Dayton, 1986; trustee Dayton Art Inst., 1984—, Victory Theatre, 1986—; trustee Dayton Performing Arts Fund. Mem. Am. Soc. Newspaper Pub. Episcopalian. Home: 4833 Far Hills Ave Dayton OH 45429-2318 Office: Dayton Daily News 45th S Ludlow St Dayton OH 45401

TILOS, GREGORIO SAMAYO, electrical engineer, educator; b. Manila, Philippines, May 9, 1929; s. Anacleto de Jesus and Fidela (Samayo) T.; children: Edwin, Emmanuel. BS in Elec. Engring., Mapua Inst. Tech., Manila, 1954; postgrad., Keio U., Osaka, Japan, 1958, Asian Productivity Ctr., Tokyo, 1970. Lic. prof. engr., Philippines. Staff engr. Radiowealth Inc., Manila, 1954-57; supr. assembly plant Alto Electronics Corp., Manila, 1957-61; head dept. electronics Super Mfg. Inc., Quezon City, Philippines, 1961-64; plant engr., dept. head, tng. officer Philippine Appliance Corp., Manila, 1964-75; sr. assoc. cons. Integrated Manpower Devel. Corp., Manila, 1975-82; tech. coord. Cardinal Trading Corp., Manila, 1975-82; mem. faculty elec./electronics automated systems Joliet (Ill.) Jr. Coll., 1983—; prof. Colls. Engring. U. Santo Tomas and Manuel L. Quezon U., Manila, The Philippines, 1964-82. Mem. Inst. Electronics and Comms. Engrs. of the Philippines, Asian Regional Tng. and Devel. Orgn., Assn. Mgmt. and Indsl. Engrs. of Philippines, Philippine Soc. for Tng. and Devel., Pers. Mgmt. Assn. Philippines. Home: 1710 Glenwood Ave Joliet IL 60435 Office: Joliet Jr Coll 1215 Houbolt Rd Joliet IL 60436

TIMM, MIKE, state legislator; m. Sonia Timm; 4 children. Student, Minot (N.D.) State U. Pres., mgr. Timm Moving & Storage Co.; mem. N.D. Ho. of Reps. from 5th dist., 1973-85, 89—; chmn. Fin. & Taxation Com. N.D. Ho. of Reps., mem. Transp. Com. Named Outstanding Jaycee, 1965. Mem. Elks, Eagles, Moose, Am. Legion, Lions. Republican. Home: PO Box 29 Minot ND 58702-0029*

TIMMER, MARGARET LOUISE (PEG TIMMER), educator; b. Osmond, Nebr., July 4, 1942; d. John Henry and Julia Adeline (Schilling) Borgmann; m. Charles B. Timmer, May 23, 1964 (div. June 1990); children: Jill Marie, Mark Jon. AA, N.E. Community Coll., Norfolk, Nebr., 1987; BA in Edn., K-12 art endorsement, Wayne (Nebr.) State U., 1988; MEd, Bank Street Coll./Parsons Sch. Design, N.Y.C., 1992. Cert. tchr., Nebr. Bookkeeper Goeres Electric, Osmond, 1960-61; tel. operator Northwestern Bell, Norfolk, 1961-64; with want advt. dept. Washington Post, 1964-65; saleswoman Jeannes Fashion Fabrics, Norfolk, 1970-72, Tripps, Norfolk, 1986-87; office and fin. mgr. Tim's Plumbing & Heating Inc., Norfolk, 1972-86; tchr. art Norfolk Cath. Schs., 1988—, mem. bd., 1985-88; instr. art history N.E. Community Coll., 1992—; mem. youth art bd. Norfolk Art Ctr., 1988—. One-woman show Uptown Restaurant, Norfolk, 1993, Norfolk Art Ctr., 1996; exhibited in group shows Sioux City (Iowa) Art Ctr., 1988, Columbus (Nebr.) Art Ctr., 1993. Mem. choir St. Mary's Cath. Ch., Norfolk, 1991—; mem. Norfolk Community Choir, 1991; bd. dirs. Norfolk Community Concerts Assn., 1984-87; treas. Norfolk Cath. Booster Club, 1985-86; leader 4-H, Madison County, 1973-78; judge art show Laurel (Nebr.) Women's Club, 1988. Named outstanding profl. vol. Norfolk Art Ctr., 1996. Mem. Nat. Art Edn. Assn. (presenter 1987), Nebr. Art Edn. Assn. (3d place award 1988). Home: Box 239 83729 Warnerville Dr Norfolk NE 68701-9758 Office: Norfolk Cath Schs 2300 Madison Ave Norfolk NE 68701-4456

TIMMER, STEPHEN BLAINE, lawyer; b. Holland, Mich., May 19, 1962; s. Blaine Edward and Nancy Jean (Mulder) T. BA in Econs., Eckerd Coll., 1984; JD, U. Fla., 1988; LLB (hon.), Kagawa U., Takamatsu, Japan, 1985. Atty. Burditt & Radzius, Chartered, Chgo., 1988—; bd. dirs. The Renaissance Soc. Editor-in-chief Fla. Internat. Law Jour., 1988. Recipient fellowship St. Petersburg, Fla./Takamatsu, Japan Sister City Com., 1986. Mem. ABA, Internat. Young Lawyers Assn., Lawyers for Creative Arts, Chgo. Bar Assn., AIDS Legal Coun. Chgo. (bd. dirs. 1990—), Contemporary Mus. Art, Art Inst. Chgo., Centre du Droit de l'Art (Switzerland). Democrat. Presbyterian. Office: Burditt and Radzius 333 W Wacker Dr Ste 2600 Chicago IL 60606-1227

TIMMERMAN, DORA MAE, community volunteer, art advocate; b. Wichita, Kans., Mar. 28, 1931; d. George M. and Effie (Stevens) Branham; m. Lewin E. Timmerman, Oct. 30, 1949 (dec. 1990); children: Curt E., Kyle A. Student, Wichita State U., 1948-50, 73-75. Legal sec. Wichita, 1948-55; mgr. Wichita Art Mus. Shop, 1977-81; owner, mgr. Rubbing Renaissance, Wichita, 1981—; co-chair Greater Wichita Save Outdoor Sculpture Project Smithsonian Instn.'s Nat. Mus. Am. Art, Nat. Inst. Conservation Cultural Property, 1992—; presenter workshops on brass and stone rubbing, lectr. and program presenter mus., coll., libr. and sch. orgns.; lectr. and tour guide for Wichita's outdoor sculpture and pub. art; developer, dir. Sculpture Appreciation Course, Unified Sch. Dist. 259 Pub. Sch. Sys. Wichita, 1995—. Pres., bd. dirs. Wichita Bar Assn. Aux., 1961-62, Kos Harris PTA, 1963-64, Twentieth Century Cornelias, 1966-68, Met. Arts Bd., 1980, Lands and Peoples Club, 1982-83; bd. dirs. Project Beauty, Inc., 1968—, women's divsn. Inst. Logopedics, YWCA, UNICEF adv. coun., 1985; founding mem. Wichita Pub. Arts Task Force, 1988-90, Wichita Pub. Art Adv. Bd., 1990—, chmn. 1992—; charter and exec. bd. mem. Friends of Campbell Castle, 1993-95; exec. bd. mem. Sedgwick County Cmty. Image Task Force, 1993—; vol. svcs. bd. Wichita Art Mus., 1975-77; active Wichita Ctr. for Arts, Wichita-Sedgwick County Arts and Humanities Coun., Edwin A. Ulrich Mus. Wichita State U., Wichita-Sedgwick County Hist. Mus., Project Concern Internat., 1978-85, various youth and charitable orgns. Recipient many awards from: Project Beauty, Inc., Kans. State Hist. Soc., City of Wichita Pub. Art Adv. Bd., 1996 Good Apple award Wichita Pub. Schs. Mem. Monumental Brass Soc. Eng., Friends of Botanica (charter), Internat. Platform Assn., Stock Markettes Investment Club, Present Day Club. Baptist. Home: 6606 Magill St Wichita KS 67206-1344

TIMMINS, RICHARD HASELTINE, foundation executive, educator; b. Ottumwa, Iowa, Jan. 24, 1924; s. Isaiah Phillip and Nellie Mae (Haseltine) T.; m. Jean Ardelle Moore, Feb. 16, 1946 (dec.); 1 dau., Cynthia Lea (dec.); m. Mischelle Christene Talley Mitchell, Aug. 10, 1983; children: Christene Mitchell, Sam Mitchell. BA, U. Iowa, 1948, MA, 1956; EdD, Columbia U., 1962. Cert. jr. coll. adminstr., Iowa. Vice-pres. Tarkio (Mo.) Coll., 1962-68; pres. Huron (S.D.) Coll., 1968-74; exec. dir. Coun. Chiropractic Edn. and Found. Chiropractic Edn. and Research, Des Moines, 1974-76; pres. Western States Coll., Portland, Oreg., 1976-79; exec. dir. N.D. Cmty. Found., Bismarck, 1979-81, pres., 1981-94, pres. emeritus, bd. emeritus, 1995—; pres. S.D. Assn. Pvt. Colls., 1968-71; chmn. bd. Colls. Mid-Am. Inc., 1972-74; pres. S.D. Edn. Assn. Dept. Higher Edn., 1974; mem. policy adv. com. N.D. Leadership in Edn. Adminstrn., 1987—; mem. state adv. com. Ctr. Continuing Edn., 1985—; mem. planning adv. com. N.D. Higher Edn. Ctr., 1988-89; part time instr. Bismarck State Coll., 1988—; pres. Lib. Found., Bismarck, (bd. dirs., 1992—); pres. libr. bd., 1995—; bd. mem. Bismarck Pub. Libr. (appointed), 1992—; minister, Planned Giving North & South Dakota Conf. United Ch. of Christ, 1992—. Mem. adv. com. higher edn. Midwestern Conf., Council State Govts., 1969-71; Presbyn. lay preacher (commd.), 1980—. Capt. USAF, 1943-45, U.S. Army, 1948-54. Am. Assn. Fund Raising Counsels fellow, 1960-62. Mem. Am. Legion, Air Force Assn., Res. Officers Assn. Ret. Officers Assn., Mil. Order World Wars, Sigma Delta Chi, Kappa Tau Alpha, Kappa Delta Pi, Phi Delta Kappa. Presbyterian. Clubs: Rotary (pres. Bismarck chpt.). Lodges: Masons, Shriners, Elks. Contbr. to books and profl. jours. Home: PO Box 2633 Bismarck ND 58502-2633 Office: PO Box 387 Bismarck ND 58502-0387

TIMMONS, BARBARA ALICE, geriatrics nurse; b. Muncie, Ind., Dec. 11, 1932; d. John and Audrey Muriel (Halleck) Schumacher; m. Jerry Alyn Timmons, Apr. 7, 1951; children: Gary Alyn, Karen, Benjamin. Diploma in nursing, Muncie Sch. Practical Nursing, 1983. LPN. Charge nurse Maple Village Nursing Home, Middletown, Ind., 1983-84, Millers Merry Manor, Middletown, Ind., 1984-85, Sylvesters Nursing Home, Muncie, 1985-87; dir. nursing Countryside Healthcare, Muncie, 1987-90, med. records, 1990-91; nursing adminstrn. Liberty Village, Muncie, 1991—. Mem. Ind. Health Care Assn. Dirs. Nursing (legis. lobbying com. 1989-90).

TIMPE, EUGENE FRANK, German language and literature educator; b. Tacoma, Sept. 24, 1926; s. Charles William Timpe and Olga H. Hordich; m. Sally Ann Madison, Feb. 18, 1950 (dec. Apr. 1990); children: Leslie, Stephen, Kathryn. Student, U. N.Mex., 1944-45; BA, Occidental Coll., 1948; MA, U. So. Calif., 1952, PhD, 1960. Instr. English El Camino Coll., L.A., 1953-66; assoc. prof. German and comparative lit. Pa. State U., State College, 1966-72, vice chmn. program in comparative lit., 1966-70; prof. German dept. fgn. langs. and lits. So. Ill. U., Carbondale, 1972—, chmn., 1972-81, head German sect., spring 1985, dir. fgn. lang. and internat. trade program, 1986—, co-dir. Ctr. for Internat. Bus. and Cultures, 1989-92; Fulbright tchr. Bundesrealgymnasium XVI, Vienna, Austria, 1958-59, Coun. Am. Studies, Magistero U. Rome, 1960-61; lectr. U. Md., Munich, 1963-64; prof. invité U. Neuchatel and U. Fribourg, Switzerland, 1970-71; dir. workshops and seminars U.S. Dept. Ednl. Grants, 1990-91; presenter and lectr. in field. Author: American Literature in Germany, 1861-1872, 1964; editor Thoreau Abroad, 1971; contbr. numerous articles to profl. jours., revs. to books. With USN, 1944-45. Rsch. grantee Am. Philos. Soc., 1970, program devel. grantee NEH, 1983, tng. grantee U.S. Dept. Edn., 1987-90, 89-91, 92-94; Fulbright grantee, Germany, summer 1985. Mem. MLA (pres. Assn. Depts. of Fgn. Lang. 1977, chmn. comparative lit. group I 1974, del. assembly 1973-76, Am. Assn. Tchrs. German, Grillparzer Gesellschaft (bd. dirs.), Ill. Fgn. Lang. Assn. Democrat. Home: 3004 Kent Dr Carbondale IL 62901 Office: So Ill U Dept Fgn Langs Carbondale IL 62901

TIMPE, MICHAEL WAYNE, systems analyst; b. Elkhart, Ind., Jan. 31, 1951; s. Kenneth Lewis and Dona June (Martin) T.; m. Rebecca Susan Lowry, July 22, 1972; children: Scott Michael, Jeffrey Tyler. BA, Western Mich. U., 1973, MBA, 1982. Rte. driver John C. Klosterman Co., Kalamazoo, 1973-74; sales exec. Miller & Boerman, Inc., Kalamazoo, 1974-75, D.L. Gallivan, Inc., Kalamazoo, 1976-78; laborer Kalamazoo Stamping & Die, 1978-80; div. chmn. Davenport Coll., Kalamazoo, 1980-84; chief programmer Allen Test Products, Kalamazoo, 1984-90; dir. software devel. Dynacom, Inc., Lawton, Mich., 1990-94; dir. Greatland Corp., Grand Rapids, 1994—; pres. Data Resources, 1983—; adj. prof. Nazareth Coll. Bd. dirs. Kalamazoo Optimist Hockey Assn., 1986, head coach, 1989-94; coach Eastwood Little League, Kalamazoo, 1985—; co-chmn. Comstock Citizens for Better Edn.; mem. facilities study com. Comstock Schs., 1988-90; mem. 1994 Vicksburg H.S. Project Graduation; mem. Cornstock Pub. Schs. Supts. Adv. Com., 1994-95. Methodist. Home: 3107 East U Ave Vicksburg MI 49097 Office: Greatland Corp 2480 Walker NW Grand Rapids MI 49505

TINCHER, JOHN EVAN, timber company executive, consultant; b. Ishpeming, Mich., Nov. 27, 1961; s. David and Claire Marie (Manley) T. BS, No. Mich. U., 1991. Programmer No. Mich. U., Marquette, 1990-93; personal computer network adminstr. Keweenaw Land Assoc., Ironwood, Mich., 1993—. Mem. Keweenaw Bay Indian Cmty., 1989—. With U.S. Army, 1980-84. Mem. Am. Indian Sci. and Engring. Soc., Am. Legion, Alpha Kappa Psi. Home: PO Box 31 Ironwood MI 49938-0031

TINKER, ROBERT EUGENE, minister, educational consultant; b. Lincoln, Kans., June 10, 1915; s. Eugene F. and Mildred Adelaide (Brown) T.; AB, Am. U., 1937; MDiv, Garrett Theol. Sem., 1942; postgrad. Northwestern U., 1942-46; m. Anne Elizabeth Hall, June 13, 1942; children: Anne Terrill, Robert Bruce, MaryBeth. Ordained to ministry Methodist Ch., 1942, Congregational Ch., 1947-77, United Ch. Christ; minister Oxen Hill, Md., Tuxedo, Md., 1934-37, Evergreen Park, Ill., 1940-41; assoc. minister 1st Presbyterian Ch., Evanston, Ill., 1942-44; minister Glenview Meth. Ch. (Ill.), 1944-46, Broadway Meth. Ch., Chgo., 1946-47; with Chgo. Theol. Sem., 1947-58, asst. sec., asst. treas., bd. dirs., 1947-58, asst. bus. mgr., 1947-50, bus. mgr., 1951-55, dir. devel., 1953-55, v.p. charge devel., 1955-58; assoc. Gonser and Gerber, 1958-64; ptnr. Gonser Gerber Tinker Stuhr, ednl. cons. in devel. and public relations, Chgo., 1964-82, cons., 1982—; pres. Tabco Corp., Chgo., 1983-85; lectr. Creighton U., Omaha, summers 1978-80. N.J. State scholar, 1933; Larry Foster scholar, 1933; Wanamaker scholar Lingnon U., Canton, Republic of China, 1935-36; Howes Meml. scholar, 1939-42. Bd. dirs. Hyde Park YMCA, Chgo., Hyde Park Union Ch., Porter Found., U. Chgo., 1947-58, Bryn Mawr Cmty. Ch., Habitat for Humanity, Tucson, 1992—, Phi Sigma Kappa, Phi Beta Zeta, Pi Gamma Mu. Republican. Contbr. articles to profl. books and jours. Mem. Oro Valley Townhouses Improvement Assn. (bd. dirs. 1993-94, pres. 1994). Home: 63 W Oro Pl Oro Valley AZ 85737-7625

TINNER, FRANZISKA PAULA, social worker, artist, designer, educator; b. Zurich, Switzerland, Sept. 18, 1944; came to U.S., 1969; d. Siegfied Albin and Gertrude Emilie (Sigg) Maier; m. Rolf Christian Tinner, Dec. 19, 1976; 1 child, Eric Francis. Student, U. Del., 1973-74, Va. Commonwealth U., 1974; BFA, U. Tenn., 1984; BA of Arts, U. Ark., Little Rock, 1991, postgrad. Lic. real estate broker. Dominican nun Ilanz, Switzerland, 1961-67; waitress London, 1967-68; governess Bryn Mawr, Pa., 1969; saleswoman, 1970-90, model, 1983; artist, designer Made For You, Kerrville, Tex. and Milw., 1984—; realtor Century 21, Milw., 1987-91; intern Birch Community Ctr., 1992-93. Designer softsculptor doll Texas Cactus Blossom, 1984. Ombudsman Action 10 Consumerline, Knoxville, Tenn., 1983-84; foster mother, Powhatan, Va., 1976-81; vol. ARC, Knoxville, 1979, Va. Home for Permanently Disabled, 1975; vol., counselor Youth For Understanding-Fgn. Exch., Powhatan, Va., 1975-77; tchr. pager/archiving host, mentor, area expert on Am. On Line; vol. Interactive Ednl. Svc. Recipient Art Display award U. Knoxville, 1983, Prof. Choice of Yr. award, 1983, Outstanding Achievemnt award TV Channel 10, Knoxville, 1984, 1st place award for paintings and crafts State Fair Va., Tenn., 1st place award Nat. Dollmakers, 1985, finalist Best of Coll. Photography, 1991, Achievement award Coll. Scholar af Am., 1991, Achievement cert. in technique of anger therapy, 1993, Achievement cert. in crisis response team tng., 1994; named One of Outstanding 1000 Women, 1995, Woman of Yr., 1995. Mem. NASW, NAFE, Milw. Bd. Realtors, Homemakers Club (pres. 1979-80), Newcomers Club, Bowlers Club (v.p.), Internat. Platform Assn.

TINNEY, DEE MELVIN, marketing executive, consultant; b. Muskegon, Mich., Oct. 11, 1940; s. Rodney Melvin Tinney and Katherine Elizabeth (Hollowell) Kunkle; m. Linda Texie Heilig, Apr. 21, 1964; children: Robin E., Christine A. Grad. high sch., Muskegon, Mich.; diploma, McDonald's Mgmt. Sch., 1966; cert.fin. mgmt., Wharton Sch. U. Pa., 1986; cert., U. Denver. Registered fin. broker. Gen. mgr. Millman Broadcasting, St. Petersburg, Fla., 1970-76; pres. Media 1, Inc., Eau Claire, Wis., 1976-81; dir. new bus. Eau Claire Press Co., 1979-81; mgr. new bus. devel. ATC, Englewood, Colo., 1981-86; dir. mktg. SISCOM, Boulder, Colo., 1986-87; mktg. mgr. Digital Equipment Corp., Merrimack, N.H., 1987-92; prin. cons. Bus. Strategy Resource, Maiden Rock, Wis., 1992—. Author: How to Start Your Own Ad Agency, 1979; pub. newsletter, Advertising Ideas, 1978; inventor Still Frame Ad Machine, 1982; contbr. articles in field. Home: N835 190th St Maiden Rock WI 54750-8729

TINOCO, PATRICIA ANN, elementary education educator; b. Belleville, Ill., Dec. 1, 1950; d. Jesse Salvador and Audrey May (Wild) T.; m. Howard Lee Boller, June 14, 1990; 1 stepchild, Kimberly Boller Pope. BSBA in Elem. Edn. and Spanish, So. Ill. U., 1972, MS in Secondary Edn., 1976. Cert. tchr., Ill. 2nd grade tchr. High Mount Sch. 116, Swansea, Ill., 1972-79, 5th grade tchr., 1979-81, jr. high sch. tchr., 1981—, 5th through 8th grade programming instr., 1983-94, speech coach, 1983-94, mem. quality rev. team, 1993-95; mem. sch. improvement team, 1994-95, 95-96; lead tchr. High Mount Sch. 116, Swansea, Ill., 1993-96; mem. collaborative team High Mount Sch. 116, Swansea, 1994—; evaluator Belleville Area Presch. Testing, 1977-80; mem. Belleville Area Effective Teaching Cadre, 1987-88; instr. children's Spanish program Belleville Area Coll., 1991-93; cons. Computer Gender Equity, 1991—. Bd. dirs. Pine Tree, 1983-85, 93, sec.-treas., 1982, v.p., 1987-89. Grantee Women's Action Alliance, Inc., 1991-92, 92-93; recipient Those Who Excel Edn. award State of Ill., 1995-96. Mem. High Mount Fedn. Tchrs. (treas. 1988-89, sec. 1978-80, 89-90, pres. 1980-84, 90-91). Roman Catholic. Office: High Mount Sch 116 1721 Boul Ave Belleville IL 62220-4254

TINSLEY, DIANE JOHNSON, psychologist, educator; b. Hibbing, Minn., Jan. 22, 1944; d. Frank Gustav and Evelyn Loretta (Dahlner) Johnson; m. Howard E.A. Tinsley, Dec. 16, 1967; children: Kelly Anne, Laurel Jeanne. BA, U. Pa., 1966; PhD, U. Minn., 1972. Lic. clin. psychologist; diplomate Am. Bd. Vocat. Experts. Intern Macalester Coll. and U. Minn., Mpls., 1968-70; vocat. counselor, then rsch. psychologist U. Oreg., Eugene, 1972-73; coord. career counseling So. Ill. U., Carbondale, 1973-78, adj. prof. psychology, 1977-94; postdoctoral intern U. Tex., Austin, 1979-80; counseling psychologist So. Ill. U., Carbondale, 1980-94; rsch. psychologist, 1995—; vis. fellow U. Minn., Mpls., 1987-88, U. Wash., Seattle, 1994-95; cons. VA Ill., 1973-78, St. Louis U., 1976, APA, 1976—; edit. cons. ACA, APA, 1976—. Fellow APA (chmn. 1987-89); mem. ACA, Bus. & Profl. Women (chmn. 1985-87, 89-92, State award 1986, 87), Am. Coll. Pers. Assn. (chmn. 1976-78, Rsch. award 1990). Home: 100 S Parrish Ln Carbondale IL 62901-2028 Office: So Ill U Dept Psychology Carbondale IL 62901-6502

TIPP, KAREN LYNN WAGNER, school psychologist; b. Chgo., Feb. 15, 1947; d. Harry and Sarah (Damask) Wagner; m. Michael Harvey, Dec. 30, 1973; children: Brenda Alyse, Brandon Philip. BA in Gen. High Sch. Edn., Roosevelt U., 1971; B of Jewish Studies, Spertus Coll., 1973, cert. in sch. psychology, 1981, MA in Jewish Studies, 1993; MS in Ednl. Theory, Nat. Louis U., 1974, CAS, 1981. Cert. psychologist, Ill.; nat. cert. sch. psychologist. Tchr. Niles Twp. High Sch., Skokie, Ill., 1971-72; mgr. travel agy. Chgo., 1983-85; tchr. spl. edn. No. Cook County, Ill., 1972-90; tchr. Hebrew Chgo. Bd. Jewish Edn., 1969-90, interim prin. religious sch., 1989-90; sch. psychologist Chgo. Pub. Schs., 1990—; ind. ednl. therapist, Chgo., 1973—; contract psychologist N.W. Suburban Chgo., 1981-90; cons. learning disabled Chgo. Bd. Jewish Edn., 1983-90; mem. adv. bd. Tchr.'s Task Force, 1993—. Pres. Truman Coll. (City Coll. Chgo.) Coun., 1985-87, 93-95, nom. chair, 1990—; exec. sec. North Town Cmty. Coun., Chgo., 1984-86, pres., 1989-91, v.p., 1991-93, treas., 1993-96, v.p., 1996—; pres. dist. 2 coun. Chgo. Bd. Edn., 1987-89, spl. edn. chair, 1990-92; exec. sec. North Town Civic League, 1978-80, pres., 1981-84; mem. coop. extension youth coun. U. Ill., sec., 1985-91, exec. coun., 1990-91; charter mem. Hild Culture Ctr., membership chair; beat rep. Chgo. Police Dept.; vice chair Head Start, Salvation Army, Dewey Day Care Evanston, 1972-75, Rogers Park Montessori Sch., 1979-80; corr. sec. Day Care Ctr. Bd.-Evanston, 1978-81, Rogers Park Mental Health Coun.; youth chair Indian Boundary Playground Bldg., 1986-89; mem. steering com. Rogers Park Centennial, 1991-93; mem. state coms. 4-H, 1982-88, Chgo./Cook County 4-H Coun., 1984-95; mem. North Town Post Office Adv. Coun., 1995—. Master Tchr. grantee Jewish Bd. Edn., Chgo., 1981-89, 20 Yr. award, 1990; recipient Cmty. Leadership award Dept. Human Svcs., Chgo., 1985, North Town-Dorothy LeRoy Cmty. Svc. award, 1992. Fellow Am. Orthopsychiat. Assn.; mem. NASP, Coun. Exceptional Children (liaison 1972-86), Assn. Ednl. Therapist, Ill. Psychol. Assn. (Sch. Psychologist of Yr. 1991), Family Resource Ctr. on Disabilities (spl. edn. com. 1990—, bd. dirs. 1993—), Profls. in Learning Disabilities (legis. chair 1987—), Children with Attention Deficit Disorder, Learning Disabilities Assn., Ill. Sch. Psychologists Assn. (Practitioner of Yr. 1991, child study com.), Chgo. Assn. Sch. Psychologists (rec. sec. 1995—, pres.-elect 1996—), Greater Uptown Youth Network, Family Resource Handicapped (spl. edn. com.), Family Resource (bd. dirs. 1993—), Ill. 4-H Found., Edn. Therapists, Samoyed Club Am. (bd. dirs. 1996—), Samoyed Animal Club, Prairieland Samoyed Club (legis. chair 1995—, membership chair). Home: 6730 N Maplewood Ave Chicago IL 60645-4620

TIPTON, JAMES ALVA, real estate agent, farmer; b. Jasper, Mich., May 4, 1931; s. Maurice Emerson and Vera Mildred (Wotring) T.; m. Helen Marie

Carr, Jan. 5, 1952 (div. 1976); children: Roxann Marie, Terrence James, Susan Elaine; m. Mildred Ann Carl, June 27, 1976; children: Amy Ruth, Carrie Lee; 1 stepchild, Kyle C. Doyle. Student, U. Toledo, 1976-77. Master electronics technician RCA Svc. Co., Toledo, 1955-87; master electronics technician Gen. Electric Consumer Svc., Toledo, 1987-91; farm owner, operator Blissfield, Mich., 1948—; sales assoc. Close Realty, Inc., Adrian, Mich., 1986-94; union steward Internat. Brotherhood Elec. Workers, Toledo, 1965-91, nat. contract negotiator, Washington, 1983-89; v.p., pres., bd. dirs. UT/MCO Credit Union, Toledo, 1984-90, mem. supervisory bd., 1990-91. Supr. Twp. Bd. Trustees, Blissfield, 1980-84; deacon United Ch. of Christ, Berkey, Ohio, 1965-75. Mem. Am. Mensa Soc. Home: 12803 Carroll Rd Blissfield MI 49228-9506 Office: First Referral Mich Inc 4415 N Grand River Ave Lansing MI 48906-2614

TIPTON, JON PAUL, allergist; b. Lynchburg, Ohio, Nov. 8, 1934; s. Paul Alvin and Jeanette (Palmer) T.; m. Martha J. Johnson, Dec. 29, 1968; children: Nicole Ann, Paula Michelle. BS, Ohio U., 1956; MD, Ohio State U., 1960. Resident internal medicine Ohio State U. Hosps., Columbus, 1964-66; fellow in allergy and pulmonary disease Duke U. Med. Ctr., Durham, N.C., 1963-64, 66-67; pvt. practice medicine specializing in allergies Athens, Ohio, 1967-74; pvt. practice medicine specializing in allergy Marietta, Ohio, 1974—; dir. cardio respiratory therapy Marietta Meml. Hosp., 1983, med. dir. pulmonary rehab. program, chief of medicine; med. dir. Inhalation Therapy Sch. Wash. State C.C.; cons. Ohio U. Hudson Health Ctr., 1967—, Mariette Coll. Health Ctr., 1974—, United Mine Workers of Am. Funds, 1984—; med. lectr. for physicians groups; med. dir. Washington State C.C. Inhalation Therapy Sch. Vol. Marietta Rep. Hdqrs., 1978—; mem. choir St. Luke's Luth. Ch., Marietta, 1983—. Served to capt. USAF, 1961-63. Mem. Am. Acad. Allergy, Ohio State Med. Assn., Wash. County Med. Soc., Parkersburg Acad. Medicine. Republican. Methodist. Home: 101 Meadow Ln Marietta OH 45750-1345 Office: 100 Front St Marietta OH 45750-3142

TITKEMEIER, DELOY ALLEN, secondary education educator; b. Holdrege, Nebr., Dec. 9, 1944; s. Erwin Karl William and Leona Loretta (Golter) T.; m. Connie Jean Wells, Oct. 25, 1973 (div. July 1981); 1 child, Matthew Wayne. BS in Edn., Kearney (Nebr.) State Coll., 1966, MS in Edn., 1972. Cert. profl. tchr., Nebr. Tchr. Unified Sch. Dist. #237, Smith Ctr., Kans., 1966-67, Ansley (Nebr.) Pub. Sch., 1967-76, 77—; warehouse foreman Sharp Seed Co., Healy, Kans., 1976. Mem. Nebr. Assn. Tchrs. Math., Nebr. Acad. Sci. Lutheran.

TITLEBAUM, RICHARD THEODORE, artist, author; b. Boston, Jan. 26, 1939; s. Max William and Katherine (Kurland) T. BA magna cum laude, Harvard U., 1962, MA in English, 1963, PhD in English, 1969. Libr. Lowell House/Harvard U., Cambridge, Mass., 1962-67; teaching fellow English Harvard U., Cambridge, Mass., 1963-67; asst. prof. rhetoric U. Calif., Berkeley, 1967-69; lectr. English U. Witwatersrand, South Africa, 1975-76; sr. lectr. English U. Haifa, Israel, 1971-72; dir. Titlebaum Art Gallery, Ann Arbor, Mich., 1989—. One-man shows include Alon Gallery, Brookline, Mass., 1986, Winfisky Galler, Mass. St. Coll., Salem, 1987, Cmty. Ctr. for Arts, Michigan City, Ind., 1987, Tennyson Gallery, Provincetown, Mass., 1987, The Mich. Guild, Ann Arbor, 1991; group shows include The Soc. of Four Arts, Palm Beach, Fla., 1981, 82, La. Watercolor Soc., New Orleans, 1983, Harvard U. Sci. Ctr., Cambridge, Mass., 1985, Provincetown Arts Assn. and Mus., 1987, 88, Detroit Artists Market, 1993-95; represented in permanent collections The Jimmy Carter Presdl. Libr., Atlanta, The Fogg Art Mus., Cambridge, Miami City Hall, Art in Pub. Pls., Dade County, Fla., Arvida Corp., Miami, Artine Artinian Collection, Fla. Atlantic U., Boca Raton, Santa Fe C.C., Gainesville, Fla., The Abraham Bornstein Collection, The Hebrew U., Jerusalem, The Robert Todd Collection, Niles, Mich., participant 39 mus. and gallery exhbns., 267 juried art events; author 3 Victorial View of the Italian Renaissance, 1986; contbr. numerous articles to profl. jours. Va. Ctr. for Creative Arts grantee, 1980, Helene Wurlitzer Found. grantee, 1977; recipient 48 awards for painting. Mem. Mich. Guild Artists and Artisans. Home: 3036A South Zeeb Rd Ann Arbor MI 48103-3277

TITUS, ARTHUR LEROY, construction executive; b. Carmichaels, Pa., Aug. 10, 1944; s. Leroy and Mary Jane (Hartley) T.; m. Mary Jo DeHaas, June 3, 1967; children: Timothy, Melissa, Megan. BA, Calif. U. Pa., 1966. Bus. sales rep. Liberty Mut. Ins. Co., Pitts., 1969-70; with Ryan Homes, 1970-95; prodn. supr. Pitts. and Buffalo, 1970-71; div. coordinator Buffalo, 1971-72; mkt. mgr. Rochester, N.Y., 1972-76; regional mgr. Richmond, Va. and Washington, 1976-80; sr. v.p. ops. Mid-Atlantic ops., 1980-85; exec. v.p., chief operating officer Pitts., 1985-95; COO Sundance Homes Inc., Schaumburg, Ill., 1995—. Treas. YMCA Pitts., 1986-87; participant Leadership Pitts. , 1986-87. Served to 1st lt. U.S. Army, 1966-69, Vietnam. Mem. Nat. Assn. Homebuilders. Republican. Presbyterian. Office: Sundance Homes Inc 1375 E Woodfield Rd Schaumburg IL 60173*

TITUS, DAVID KENNETH, county official; b. Morgantown, W.Va., Dec. 17, 1947; s. Albert William Jr. and Marylou (Van Gilder) T.; m. Sharon Lynn Krause, Nov. 15, 1974; children: Allison Blythe, Daniel Kenneth. BA in Sociology, Fairmont State Coll., 1969; MSW, W.Va. U., Morgantown, 1971. Cert. Acad. Cert. Social Workers. Children's probation officer Milw. County Social Svcs., Milw., 1971-74, social work supr., 1974-84, div. mgr. purchase, 1984-91; human svcs. dir. Dodge County, Juneau, Wis., 1991—. Allocation panelist United Way Greater Milw., 1987-91; v.p. Dodge County United Way Bd. Dirs., 1995—. Mem. Nat. Assn. Social Workers, Wis. Counties Human Svcs. Assn. (state com. mem. 1991). Presbyterian. Home: W8840 Burr Oak Dr Beaver Dam WI 53916-9716 Office: Dodge Co Human Svcs 143 E Center St Juneau WI 53039-1330

TITZKOWSKI, ERVIN E., manufacturing company executive; b. Iola, Wis.. Cert. tool and die apprentice, Wis. Pres., owner E.T. Tool, Inc., Racine, Wis., 1983—. Scoutmaster Boy Scouts Am., Racine, 1977-83; adminstr. Soap Box Derby Am., Racine, 1980. Office: E T Tood Inc 1333 23rd St Racine WI 53403-3313

TOADVIN-BESTER, JOSEPHINE VESELLA, academic administrator, educator; b. Toledo, Oct. 22, 1926; d. Albert and Verona Mae (Haynes) Toadvin; m. Raymond Bester, June 18, 1948; children: Michael Bruce, Douglas Alan, Jeffrey Royce. BEd, U. Toledo, 1948, M in Elem. Curriculum, 1970, cert., 1972. Cert. elem. edn. tchr., Ohio. Tchr. Toledo Pub. Schs., 1948-82, cons. tchr., intern intervention program, 1982-85, with career ladder, 1987-88; supr. U. Toledo, 1987—, mem. undergrad. rev. bd.; planner Execellence in Action, Toledo, 1985—; tutor Friend's Ctr., Toledo, 1987—, Toledo Excel Program, 1989—; mem. student devel., honors and awards com. Siena Hghts. Coll.; mem. minorities com. Bishop's Edn. Coun. Mem. adv. bd. Office of Black Caths., Toledo, 1984—, Cen. City Ministries of Toledo, 1984—; trustee Elizabeth A. Zept Mental Health, Toledo, 1984—, Siena Hts. Coll., 1991—; mem. Bishops' Edn. Coun., 1989—; mem. child care adv. com. YMCA, 1990—; chair minorities com. Recipient Sister Thea Bowman medallion, 1994; Martha Holden Jennings Found. scholar, 1975-80; named Outstanding Educator N.W. Ohio, 1985. Mem. Toledo Fedn. Tchrs. (bd. dirs. 1980-87), Top Ladies of Distinction, Negro Bus. and Profl. Women (rec. sec. 1993), Phi Delta Kappa, Kappa Delta Pi, Delta Sigma Theta (sec. 1945), Pi Lambda Theta. Democrat. Home: 817 Keil Rd Toledo OH 43607-2837

TOBECK, DEBORAH ANNE, information systems specialist; b. Ann Arbor, Mich., Nov. 16, 1964; d. Harvey and Susan Louise (Perrett) Sweet; m. Douglas Allen Campbell, Aug. 9, 1989 (div. Mar. 1990); children: Alyssa Anne, Sydney Marie. AAS in Bus. Info. Systems, Parkland Jr. Coll., Champaign, Ill., 1994. Programmer, analyst, mciro computer specialist Carle Clinic Assn., Urbana, Ill., 1989-92; network adminstr. Nat. Coun. Tchrs. English, Urbana, Ill., 1992-94; mgr. info. systems Am. Oil Chemists Soc., Champaign, Ill., 1994—. Mem. East Ctrl. Ill. Netware Users Group (v.p. 1994—). Office: Am Oil Chemists Soc 1608 Broadmoor Champaign IL 61821

TOBIN, BRUCE HOWARD, lawyer; b. Detroit, July 17, 1955; s. Marshall Edward and Rhoda Maureen (Milman) T.; m. Kathleen Tobin; children: Benjamin Stewart, Jenna Rose, Lainie Nicole. BA in Social Sci., Mich. State U., 1978; JD, Detroit Coll. Law, 1982; LLM in Taxation, NYU, 1983. Bar: Mich. 1982, Fla. 1982, Nebr. 1983, U.S. Dist. Ct. (ea. dist.) Mich. 1982, U.S. Tax Ct. 1983. Assoc. Kutak, Rock & Campbell, Omaha, 1983-85; ptnr. Lebow & Tobin, Farmington Hills, Mich., 1985—. V.p. West Bloomfield Sch. Bd., pres. Wards Point Property Owners Assn. Mem. ABA, Fla. Bar Assn., Mich. Bar Assn. (tax com. 1985—), Nebr. Bar Assn., Execs. Club (Bloomfield Hills, Mich.). Jewish. Office: Lebow & Tobin PLLC Ste 120 31420 Northwestern Hwy Farmington Hills MI 48334-2500

TOBIN, CALVIN JAY, architect; b. Boston, Feb. 15, 1927; s. David and Bertha (Tanfield) T.; m. Joan Hope Fink, July 15, 1951; children—Michael Alan, Nancy Ann. B.Arch., U. Mich., 1949. Designer, draftsman Arlen & Lowenfish (architects), N.Y.C., 1949-51; with Samuel Arlen, N.Y.C., 1951-53, Skidmore, Owings & Merrill, N.Y.C., 1953; architect Loebl, Schlossman & Bennett (architects), Chgo., 1953-57, v.p., 1953-57; v.p. Loebl, Schlossman & Hackl, 1957—; Chmn. Jewish United Fund Bldg. Trades Div., 1969; chmn. AIA and Chgo. Hosp. Council Com. of Hosp. Architecture, 1968-76. Archtl. works include Michael Reese Hosp. and Med. Ctr., 1954—, Prairie Shores Apt. Urban Redevel., 1957-62, Louis A. Weiss Meml. Hosp., Chgo., Chgo. State Hosp., Ctrl. Cmty. Hosp., Chgo., Gottlieb Meml. Hosp., Melrose Park, Ill., West Suburban Hosp., Oak Park, Ill., Thorek Hosp. and Med. Ctr., Chgo., Water Power Pl., Chgo., Christ Hosp., Oak Lawn, Greater Balt. Med. Ctr., Shriners Hosp. for Crippled Children, Chgo. Hinsdale (Ill.) Hosp., South Chgo. Cmty. Hosp., Chgo., Mt. Sinai Med. Ctr., Chgo., Alexian Bros. Med. Ctr., Elk Grove Village, Ill., Luth. Gen. Hosp., Park Ridge, Ill., Evanston (Ill.) Hosp., Resurrection Med. Ctr., Chgo., New Cook County Hosp., Chgo., also numerous apt., comml. and cmty. bldgs. Chmn. Highland Park (Ill.) Appearance Rev. Commn., 1972-73; mem. Highland Park Plan Commn., 1973-79; mem. Highland Park City Coun., 1974-89, mayor pro-tem, 1979-89; mem. Highland Park Environ. Control Commn., 1979-84, Highland Park Hist. Preservation Commn., 1982-89; bd. dirs. Highland Park Hist. Soc., Young Men's Jewish Coun., 1953-67, pres., 1967; bd. dirs. Jewish Community Ctrs. Chgo., 1973-78, bd. dirs., 1989-93; Ill. Coun. Against Handgun Violence, 1989-94; trustee Ravinia Festival Assn., 1990—. With USNR, 1945-46. Fellow AIA (2d v.p. Chgo. chpt.); mem. U. Mich. Alumni Soc. Coll. Architecture and Urban Planning (bd. govs. 1989-95), U. Mich. Alumni Assn. (bd. govs. 1990-95, v.p. 1993-95), Std. Club, Ravinia Green Country Club, Pi Lambda Phi. Jewish. Home: 814 Dean Ave Highland Park IL 60035-4749 Office: Loebl Schlossman & Hackl 130 E Randolph St Chicago IL 60601

TOBIN, CHRISTOPHER WARD, computer consulting firm executive; b. Neptune, N.J., Aug. 9, 1957; s. Kenneth Douglas and Carol Ann (Klein) T.; m. Ann McDonald Goss, Aug. 1980 (div. Apr. 1984); m. Lana K. Walker, Oct. 24, 1992; 1 child, Kaelee Elizabeth. BS in Math., U. Vt., 1982; postgrad., U. Dayton, 1988-90. Engr. Veda Inc., Dayton, 1986-88, sr. engr., 1988-90; task leader, info. systems analyst Frontier Engring. Inc., Dayton, 1990-92, project mgr., 1992-96; cons. svcs. mgr. Source Svcs. Corp., Dayton, 1996—. Big bro. Big Bros./Big Sisters of Dayton, 1989—; exec. staff Dayton Area Battle of the Businesses, 1990—; co-coord. Thunder Rd. Bike-A-Thon, Dayton, 1990—; mentor NASA Sharp Plus Program, 1995. Capt. USAF, 1982-86. Mem. Phi Gamma Delta (grad. chpt. pres. 1991-92, grad. chpt. v.p. 1993-94). Home: 6269 Autumn Meadows Dr Dayton OH 45424 Office: Source Svcs Corp One S Main St Ste 1440 Dayton OH 45402

TOBIN, DENNIS MICHAEL, lawyer; b. Chgo., June 3, 1948; s. Thomas Arthur and Lois (O'Connor) T.; m. Sue Wynn Henslee, June 14, 1969 (div. 1977); m. Karen Thompson, Oct. 11, 1980; children: Kyle James, Daniel Patrick. BA with honors, U. Ill., 1971; JD, Loyola U., Chgo., 1976. Bar: Ill 1976, Wis. 1989, U.S. Dist. Ct (no. dist.) Ill. 1976, U.S. Ct. Appeals (7th cir.) 1985, U.S. Supreme Ct. 1985. Trial atty. Cook County Homicide Task Force, Chgo., 1976-84; prin. Dennis M. Tobin & Assocs., Chgo., 1984—; gen. counsel Forest Health Systems and Found., Ill., Miss., Hawaii, 1986—, Manages Behavioral Care Inc., Psychiat. Ins. Co. Am. Dir. Forest Health Systems Found.; mem. Chgo. Coun. on Fgn. Rels. Mem. ABA (forum on health law), Chgo. Bar Assn. (com. on health law), Am. Soc. Law and Medicine, Ill. Assn. Criminal Def. Attys. (v.p. 1984-87), Ill. Attys. for Criminal Justice, Wis. Bar Assn., Ill. Assn. Hosp. Attys., Nat. Health Lawyers Assn., U.S. Sporting Clays Assn., Nat. Sporting Clays Assn., Gateway Gun Club. Roman Catholic. Office: Dennis M Tobin and Assocs 18-3 Dundee Rd Barrington IL 60010

TOBIN, ILONA LINES, psychologist, marriage and family counselor, educator, consultant; b. Trenton, Mich., Apr. 15, 1943; d. Frank John and Marjorie Cathalean (Lines) Kotyuk; m. Roger Lee Tobin, Aug. 20, 1966. BA, Ea. Mich. U., 1965; MA, 1968; MA, Mich. State U., 1975; EdD, Wayne State U., 1978. Diplomate Am. Bd. of Sexology; cert. marriage, family counselor; cert. sex educator and counselor; cert. sex therapist. Tchr., counselor Willow Run Pub. Schs., Ypsilanti, Mich., 1966-72; prof. Macomb County Community Coll., Mt. Clemens, Mich., 1974-79; psychotherapist Identity Ctr., Inc., Mt. Clemens, 1974-79; dir. treatment Alternative Lifestyles, Inc., Orchard Lake, Mich., 1979-80; psychologist Profl. Psychotherapy and Counseling Ctr., Farmington Hills, Mich., 1980-83; pvt. practice clin. psychology, Birmingham, Mich., 1983—; lectr. Wayne State U., Detroit, 1977-88; tchr., lectr. med. edn. St. Joseph's Hosp., Pontiac, Mich., 1993—; recruitment dir. Upward Bound Ea. Mich. U., Ypsilanti, 1969-72. Creator Doc's Dolls. Co-chmn. Birmingham Families in Action, 1982-83; bd. dirs. HAVEN-Oakland County's Phys. and Sexual Abuse Ctr. and Oakland Area Counselors Assn., 1984-85; mem. exec. bd., v.p. pres. Birmingham Community Women's Ctr., 1984-85, also bd. dirs.; mem. adv. bd. Woodside Med. Ctr. for Chemically Dependent Women, 1984-86. NIMH fellow, 1976-78; Wayne State U. scholar, 1976-78. Mem. Am. Psychol. Assn., Mich. Psychol. Assn. (mass media cons. 1983—, mem. crisis intervention network, legis. com. 1992-94), Am. Assn. Sex Educators, Counselors and Therapists, Am. Assn. for Counseling and Devel., Pi Lambda Theta, Phi Delta Kappa. Jewish.

TOBIN, MICHAEL ALAN, architect, real estate developer; b. N.Y.C., Dec. 27, 1952; s. Calvin Jay and Joan Hope (Fink) T.; m. Nancy Jo Liff, Apr. 7, 1979; children: Rebecca Shana, Matthew Kyle. BS, U. Mich., 1974, MArch summa cum laude, 1975. Registered architect, Ill. Sr. architect Skidmore, Owings & Merrill, Chgo., 1975-79; dir. property services Harris Bank, Chgo., 1979-84; real estate exec. Met. Structures, Chgo., 1984-91; pres. Cen. Sta. Devel. Corp., Chgo., 1991—; exec. v.p. Polygon Assoc., LLC, 1995—. Bd. dirs. Young Men's Jewish Coun., Chgo., 1982-84, Greater State St. Coun., 1987, Chgo. Devel. Coun., 1991—; treas. Wacker Dr. Property Owners Assn., 1986-91; pres. Burnham Park Arts Dist., 1993, Mich. Ave. Property Owners Assn.; vice chmn. Near South Planning Bd., 1995—. Named one of 40 bus. leaders under 40 years old Crain's Chgo. Bus., 1992. Mem. AIA, Ill. Coun. Architects, Lambda Alpha. Democrat. Office: Cen Sta Devel Corp 100 S Wacker Ste 850 Chicago IL 60606

TOBLER, WILLIAM JENNINGS, III, farrier; b. Lawrence, Kans., July 5, 1953; s. William J. and Pricella (Price) T.; m. Susan K. Petersen, Jan. 5, 1974; children: Jamie Doris, Brian William. Grad., Johnston County C.C., 1972. Mgr. Toblers Flowers Inc., Kansas City, Mo., 1972-80; delivery driver Coca-Cola Bottling Co., Lenexa, Kans., 1980-90; farrier Drexel, Mo., 1987—. Contbr. articles to profl. jours. Scoutmaster Boy Scout Troop 241, Drexel, 1990-94, com. chmn., 1994-96. Recipient Warrior award Tribe Mic-O-Say, Oceola, Mo., 1968. Mem. Am. Farriers Assn. (cert.), Kans. Farriers Assn. (sec., conv. chmn. 1995-96), Gateway Farriers Assn. (bd. dirs., conv. chmn. 1995-96), Lions Club. Roman Catholic. Home and Office: 33421 McClellan Drexel MO 64742

TODD, CAROL ANN, geriatrics nurse; b. Bellaire, Ohio, Aug. 22, 1955; d. Harold Edwin and Madeline (Pittman) McMahon; m. John A. Todd; children: Michael James, Seana Leigh. LPN, B.M. Spurr Sch. Nursing, 1974; RN, Ohio Valley Gen. Hosp., 1978. Cert. BLS instr., ACLS. Staff nurse critical care unit Reynolds Meml. Hosp., Glendale, W.Va., 1978; charge nurse critical care unit Barnesville (Ohio) Hosp., 1978-80; nurse critical care unit Harrison Community Hosp., Cadiz, Ohio, 1980-83, supr., 1988-91; staff nurse dept. neurology Wheeling (W.Va.) Clinic Found., 1983-87; supr. emergency dept. Twin City Hosp., Dennison, Ohio, 1987-88; staff nurse neuro ICU Bethesda Hosp., Zanesville, Ohio, 1990; nurse surveyor Ohio Dept. Health, Columbus, 1991—. Mem. Order Eastern Stars (past matron 1989). Home: 4484 Hardy Ridge Rd NW Dundee OH 44624 Office: Ohio Dept Health SE Dist Office 107 N 6th St Cambridge OH 43725-2230

TODD, CECIL WILLIAM, ministry director; b. Nashoba, Okla., Oct. 7, 1931; s. Cecil William Sr. and Emily (Cent) T.; m. Barbara Joan Patchin, May 23, 1953 (div. Sept. 1979); children: Janet, Gail, Jon, Tim, Cecil; m. Linda Lorraine Hayden, May 30, 1980. B of Sacred Lit., Ozark Christian Coll., 1954; DDiv, Midwest Christian Coll., 1972. Min. Rinehart Christian Ch., Horton, Mo., 1952-54; sr. min. Albert Pike Christian Ch., Ft. Smith, Ark., 1956-59, Christian Ch., Clayton, Okla., 1960-64; founder, pres., dir. Tide Revival Fires Ministry, Branson and Joplin, Mo., 1964—; spkr. nation wide weekly TV shows Revival Fires, 1965-92. Author: Which Way America-Atheism or Almighty God, 1969, While America Played, 1985, Blue Print for Slavery, 1971; editor Revival Fires Mag., 1964—. Home: PO Box 1060 Kimberling City MO 65686 Office: Revival Fires Ministry PO Box 1008 Branson West MO 65737

TODD, GAYLE LOUISE, telecommunications executive; b. Chgo., Dec. 14, 1956; d. Raymond Walter and Grace Louise (Schlaeger) Garlanger; m. Richard James Todd, June 30, 1979. BS, No. Ill. U., 1978. Mgr. AT&T, West Chicago, Ill., 1979—, instr., 1991-92, asst. staff mgr., 1992—; core team mem. AT&T Benchmarking Team, Parsippany, N.J., 1990-91; instr. John G. Shedd Aquarium, 1989—; lectr. Seaspace, Beneath the Sea, DEMA, Our World Under Water, 1987—. Videographer underwater movies: Dances with Dolphins, 1991, Indonesian Adventure, 1990, Mesmerized - The Red Sea, 1992; underwater photographer: Images - Macro, 1987-91. Bd. dirs. Highlands of Algonquin, Ill., 1989-92. Recipient Award for Outstanding Community Svc. City of Palatine, 1984, Theodore Vail award Ill. Bell, 1985. Mem. Environ. Aware Photographic Image Competition (pres. 1989—, exec. bd.), League of Underwater Photographers, Futures Pioneers (pres. 1979-82), Explorers (pres. 1987, 88, 89). Home: 17675 Riverbend Rd Salinas CA 93908-1421

TODD, JEFFREY WARREN, public health administrator; b. Oak Park, Ill., May 26, 1949. BA, No. Ill. U., 1972; MS, George Williams Coll., 1979. Cert. in principles of epidemiology. Exec. dir. Drug Coordination and Info. Coun., Inc., Joliet, Ill., 1972-74; instr. Ctrl. YMCA C.C., Chgo., 1974; program coord. mental health divsn. Will County Health Dept., Joliet, 1974-76; instr. Coll. of St. Francis, Joliet, 1974-76; dir. mental health divsn. Grundy County Health Dept., Morris, Ill., 1976-79, pub. health adminstr., 1979-84; exec. dir. Ill. Pub. Health Assn., Springfield, 1984-94; adminstr. Stephenson County Health Dept., Freeport, Ill., 1994—; adj. lectr. MPH program U. Ill., Springfield, 1992-94; mem. adj. faculty grad. program in health svcs. adminstrn. Coll. of St. Francis, Joliet, 1982—; instr. Sch. Allied Health Professions, No. Ill. U., DeKalb, 1995—; mentor Ill. Pub. Health Leadership Inst., 1993-94. Contbr. articles to profl. jours. Alderman City of Morris, 1979-83; mem. adv. coun. Region Two Agy. on Aging, 1981-84; bd. dirs. Am. Cancer Soc., 1981-84, Region IX Health Sys. Agy., 1976-81; mem. commn. on future of Springfield, Springfield Urban League, 1993-94; vol. Habitat for Humanity, 1990-94; elder area Presbyn. ch., 1982—, presbytery del., 1991-94. Recipient Outstanding Svc. award Grundy County Bd. Health, 1984, Meritorious Svc. award Ill. Dept. Pub. Health, 1994. Mem. APHA (chairperson membership com. 1993-95, chairperson reference com. and joint policy com. 1994-95, mem. com. on affiliates 1995—), Am. Soc. Assn. Execs. (cert.), Ill. Assn. Pub. Health Adminstrs. (sec.-treas. 1982-83, pres.-elect 1983-84, Spl. Svc. award 1993), Ill. Environ. Health Assn. (Presdl. citation 1988, 91, 92), Ill. Rural Health Assn., Ill. Soc. for Pub. Health Edn., Nat. Assn. County and City Health Ofcls., Lions (bd. dirs. Morris Club 1982-83), Rotary (Freeport Noon chpt.). Home: 1111 Arapaho Dr Freeport IL 61032-7211

TODD, KATHY A., finance company executive; b. Marshall, Mo., Aug. 15, 1962. A in Child Devel., Ctrl. Mo. State Coll., 1982. Sec. Package Express divsn. Fin. Devel., Inc., Marshall, Mo., 1989-95; v.p. Fin. Devel., Inc., Marshall, 1988—. Presbyterian. Office: Capital Fin Devel Inc 868 S Brunswick Ave Marshall MO 65340-2704

TODD, MARY LUDWIG, history educator; b. Berwyn, Ill., Nov. 18, 1947; d. Daniel R. and Minette (Baue) Ludwig; children: Whitney, Jason. BA, Valparaiso U., 1969; postgrad., Ohio State U., 1969; Master of Gen. Studies, Roosevelt U., 1990; PhD, U. Ill., Chgo., 1996. Tchr. River Forest H.S., Hobart Twp., Ind., 1969-70; instr. Roosevelt U., Chgo., 1989—, St. Francis Coll., Joliet, Ill., 1990, Rosary Coll., River Forest, Ill., 1991-93; instr. women's studies program U. Ill., Chgo., 1992-93, asst. to dir. women's studies program, 1993-96, vis. asst. prof. women's studies program, 1996-97. Bd. dirs. Internat. Luth. Women's Missionary League, 1986-91; dir. edn. Nat. Found. March of Dimes, Charlottesville, Va. chpt., 1974-76; religious educator. Mem. Am. Hist. Assn., Orgn. Am. Historians, Nat. Women's Studies Assn., Coord. Coun. for Women in History, Am. Studies Assn. Democrat. Home: 1241 Goldenrod Ln Hoffman Est IL 60195-1176 Office: U Ill Women's Studies Prog 1022 BSB M/C360 1007 W Harrison St Chicago IL 60607-7137

TODD, STEVEN M., mechanical engineer; b. Omaha, Feb. 14, 1957. BSME, U. Nebr., Lincoln, 1979. Cert. fluid power engr. Mech. engr. Internat. Harvester, Hinsdale, Ill., 1980-85, Vicker Corp., Omaha, 1985—. Mem. Fluid Power Soc. Nebr., Pi Tau Sigma.

TODD, ZANE GREY, retired utilities executive; b. Hanson, Ky., Feb. 3, 1924; s. Marshall Elvin and Kate (McCormick) T.; m. Marysnow Stone, Feb. 8, 1950 (dec. 1983); m. Frances Z. Anderson, Jan. 6, 1984. Student, Evansville Coll., 1947-49; BS summa cum laude, Purdue U., 1951, DEng (hon.), 1979; postgrad., U. Mich., 1965; DHL, U. Indpls., 1993. Fingerprint classifier FBI, 1942-43; electric system planning engr. Indpls. Power & Light Co., 1951-56, spl. assignments supr., 1956-60, head elec. system planning, 1960-65, head substation design div., 1965-68, head distbn. engring. dept., 1968-70, asst. to v.p., 1970-72, v.p., 1972-74, exec. v.p., 1974-75, pres., 1975-81, chmn., chief exec. officer, 1976-89, dir., chmn. exec. com., 1989-94, chief exec. officer, 1981-89; chmn., pres. IPALCO Enterprises, Inc., Indpls., 1983-89, dir., chmn. exec. com., 1989-94; chmn. bd., chief exec. officer Mid-Am. Capital Resources, Inc. subs. IPALCO Enterprises, Inc., Indpls., 1984-89, also bd. dirs., 1984-94; gen. mgr. Mooresville (Ind.) Pub. Svc. Co., Inc., 1956-60; bd. dirs. Nat. City Bank Ind. (formerly Mchts. Nat. Corp.), 1975-94, Am. States Ins. Co., 1976-94; hon. dir. 500 Festival Assocs., Inc., pres. 1987. Originator probability analysis of power system reliability; contbr. articles to tech. jours. and mags. Past pres. adv. bd. St. Vincent Hosp.; bd. dirs. Commn. for Downtown, YMCA Found., Crime Stoppers Cen. Ind., Corp. Community Coun.; past chmn., bd. trustees Ind. Cen. U. (now U. Indpls.); bd. govs. Associated Colls. of Ind.; Nat. and Greater Indpls. adv. bds. Salvation Army; mem. adv. bd. Clowes Hall. Sgt. AUS, 1943-47. Recipient William Booth award Salvation Army, 1994; named Disting. Engring. Alumnus Purdue U., 1976, Outstanding Elec. Engr. Purdue U., 1992, Knight of Malta, Order of St. John of Jerusalem, 1986. Fellow IEEE (past chmn. power sys. engring. com.); mem. ASME, NSPE, Power Engring. Soc., Ind. Fiscal Policy Inst. (bd. govs.), Ind. C. of C., Indpls. C. of C., Mooresville C. of C. (past pres.), PGA Nat. Country Club, Ulen Country Club, Columbia Club, Indpls. Athletic Club (past bd. dirs.), Meridian Hills Country Club (past bd. dirs.), Skyline Club (bd. govs.), Newcomen Soc. (past chmn. Ind.), Rotary, Lions (past pres.), Eta Kappa Nu, Tau Beta Pi. Home: 7645 Randue Ct Indianapolis IN 46278-1565

TODOROFF, ALBERT ANDREW, editor, publisher; b. Chgo., May 30, 1912; s. Alexander and ELizabeth (Martin) T.; m. Mary Jane Stangland, Oct. 1, 1938 (div. Apr. 1967); children: Bonnie Sue, Lara; m. Fay Rehn Novakovich, Aug. 25, 1967 (div. Oct. 1990); 1 child, Ann Fay; m. Dorothy Marie Larose, June 13, 1992. AB, DePauw U., 1934. Assoc. editor Grocery Trade Tips, Chgo., 1935-37, The Co-Operative Merchandiser, Chgo., 1937-41; editor Meat Merchandising, St. Louis, 1941-47; editor Meat Plant Mag., St. Louis, 1947-77, publ., 1957-77; editor, publ. Thought-For-The-Week, 1990—. Author: How to Build and Operate a Locker Plant, 1945, Store Tested Ideas for Meat, 1947, How to Wrap Foods for Freezing, 1949. Pres. Upright St. Louis, 1970-90. Recipient Meat Processors Industry award, 1956. Mem. Soc. Bus. Paper Editors, Mason (K.T. Shriner). Republican. Home: Rt 1 Box 13-61 High Hill MO 63350-9801

TOEKES, BARNA, chemical engineer, polymer consultant; b. Budapest, Hungary, Oct. 12, 1923; came to U.S., 1949; s. Barna and Jusztina (Szatmári) Tőkés; m. Ida Maria Kálmán, Aug. 24, 1948 (div. 1966); m. Georgianna D. Doyle, Aug. 26, 1967; 1 child, C. Justin. BS in Engring., UCLA, 1955, postgrad., 1955-57. Rsch. engr. Stauffer Chem. Co., Richmond, Calif., 1955-60; sr. rsch. engr. Rexall Chem. Co., Paramus, N.J., 1960-69, Holyoke, Mass., 1960-69; plant mgr., gen. mgr. Southern Petrochemicals, Channelview, Tex., 1969-73; mgr. process engrng. and devel. Polysar Resins, Inc., Leominster, Mass., 1973-77; system engrng. mgr. Sperry Rsch. Ctr., Sudbury, Mass., 1978-82; prin. process engr. C. F. Braun & Co., Alhambra, Calif., 1982-85; cons. engr. Dart Container Corp., Mason, Mich., 1987—; cons. B. Toekes Cons., Baytown, Tex., 1977-78, Mason, Mich., 1985—. Contbg. author: Aromatic Fluorine Compounds, 1962, Fire Safety Aspects of Polymeric Materials, 1978; editor, co-author: Organic Working Fluid Properties, 1982, System Component Compatibility, 1982; contbr. articles to profl. jours. Mem. AICE, Am. Chem. Soc., Soc. Plastics Engrs. Home: 1148 Okemos Rd Mason MI 48854-9314 Office: Dart Container Corp 432 Hogsback Rd Mason MI 48854-9548

TOELKES, DIXIE E., state legislator; m. Roger Toelkes. Educator; mem. from dist. 53 Kans. State Ho. of Reps., Topeka. Address: 3336 SE Meadowview Dr Topeka KS 66605

TOENISKOETTER, RICHARD HENRY, chemicals executive; b. St. Louis, Mar. 21, 1931; s. Ralph Henry and Marie Loraine (Helfert) T.; m. Jeanne Frances Krill, May 30, 1953; children: David R., Susan M., James B., Richard J., Stephen J., Marian E. BS in Chemistry, St. Louis U., 1952, MS, 1956, PhD, 1958. Rsch. chemist Union Carbide Corp., Parma, Ohio, 1957-63; sr. rsch. chemist Union Carbide Corp., Tarrytown, N.Y., 1963-67; rsch. group leader Ashland Chem. Co., Bloomington, Minn., 1967-71; rsch. sect. mgr. Ashland Chem. Co., Dublin, Ohio, 1971-78; mgr. environ. and occupational safety Ashland Chem. Co., Dublin, 1978-88, dir. health and safety, 1988-91, dir. product safety and health, 1991-93, sr. tech. advisor, 1993; retired, 1993. With U.S. Army, 1953-55. Mem. Am. Chem. Soc., Am. Foundrymen's Soc. (Scientific Merit award 1984, Environ. Div. Svc. award 1993, Silver Anniversary paper Lectr. 1995), Sigma Xi. Home: 6771 Masefield St Worthington OH 43085-3067

TOERNER, DAVID PAUL, architectural engineer; b. Hamilton, Ohio, June 27, 1963; s. Paul Joseph and Mary Ellen (Tegge) T.; m. Mary Elizabeth Thornton, Mar. 21, 1992. A in Architecture, ITT Tech., Dayton, Ohio, 1984. Draftman AWMCO Inc., West Carrolton, Ohio, 1984-85, Kawneer, Harrisonburg, Va., 1985-86, Lorenz & Williams, Dayton, 1986-87; curtainwall engr. Condit Constrn., Columbus, Ohio, 1987-89; curtainwall designer WALTEK, Cin., 1989-93; CAD operator U. Dayton, Ohio, 1993-94; with Harmon Contract W.S.A., Mason, Ohio, 1994—. Mem. AIA, Constrn. Specification Inst. Home: 2016 Oak Tree Dr E Kettering OH 45440-2418

TOFFOLO, DENNIS RAY, retail executive; b. Detroit, Aug. 29, 1946; s. Oswald Peter and Magdalina (Glassi) T.; m. Diana Zampardo, Aug. 9, 1969. AA, St. Clair C.C., Port Huron, Mich., 1967; BA in Bus. Adminstrn., Eastern Mich. U., 1969; MBA in Fin., Ctrl. Mich. U., 1973, D in Bus. Adminstrn., 1994. Econs. tchr. Macomb C.C., Mt. Clemens, Mich., 1977-79; various supervisory positions Hudson's, Detroit, 1969-77; store mgr. Hudson's, Saginaw, Mich., 1977-79, Flint, Mich., 1979-83, Twelve Oaks and Novi, Mich., 1983-84, Northland, Mich., 1984-86; pres. Hudson's, Southfield, Mich., 1990—; group v.p. Dayton's, Mpls., 1986-88, group v.p. Metro stores, 1988-90. Mem. adv. bd. Eastern Mich. U., Ypsilanti, 1969—, Notre Dame Prep H.S., Rochester, Mich., 1995—; bd. dirs. Detroit Renaissance, 1990—, New Detroit, Inc., 1990—, United Way for Southeastern Mich., Detroit, 1990—; mem. master plan task force City of Detroit, 1994. Mem. Greater Detroit C. of C. (bd. dirs. 1990—), Beta Sigma Gamma. Office: Hudsons 21500 Northwestern Hwy Southfield MI 48075-5099

TOFT, BRIAN, mechanical engineer; b. Cin., Nov. 30, 1961. BS in Mech. Engrng., Ohio State U., 1984. Engr.-in-tng. Mech. engr. Rockwell Internat., Columbus, Ohio, 1982, Duluth, Ga., 1984; mech. engr. Xetron, Cin., 1986-87, Cincinnati Electronic, Mason, Ohio, 1988—. Contbr. articles to profl. jours. Mem. SPIE, Soc. Photo-optic Engr. Office: Cincinnati Electronic 7500 Innovation Way Mason OH 45040-9695

TOFTNER, RICHARD ORVILLE, engineering executive; b. Warren, Minn., Mar. 5, 1935; s. Orville Gayhart and Cora Evelyn (Anderson) T.; m. Jeanne Bredine, June 26, 1960; children: Douglas, Scott, Kristine, Kimberly, Brian. BA, U. Minn., 1966; MBA, Xavier U., 1970. Registered environ. assessor, Calif. Sr. economist Federated Dept. Stores, Inc., Cin., 1967-68; dep. dir. EPA, Washington and Cin., 1968-73; mgmt. cons. environ. affairs, products and mktg., 1973-74; prin. PEDCo Environ., Cin., 1974-80; trustee PEDCo trusts, 1974-80; pres. ROTA Mgmt., Inc., Cin., 1980-82; gen. mgr. CECOS, 1982-85, cons., 1985—; v.p. Smith, Stevens & Young, 1985-88; real estate developer, 1980—; pres., CEO Toxitrol Internat., Inc., 1988-89; dir. Environ. Svcs. Belcan Engrng. Group, Inc., Cin., 1989-92; prin. exec. cons. Resource Mgmt. Internat., Inc., 1994—; adj. prof. environ. engrng. U. Cin., 1975-86; lectr. Grad. fellowship rev. panel Office of Edn., 1978-79; advisor, cabinet-level task force Office of Gov. of P.R., 1973; pvt. investor, 1991—; bd. dirs. EnviroAudit Svcs., Inc., pres., CEO, 1992—; mem. legis. com. Ohio Chem. Coun., 1995—; subcom. Nat. Safety Coun., 1972; mem. exec. environ. briefing panels Andersen Consulting, 1991-92; nominee commr. PUCO, Ohio; chmn. Cin. City Waste Task Force, 1987-88; co-chair Hamilton County Resource Recovery Com., 1989—. Contbr. articles on mgmt. planning and environ. to periodicals, chpts. to books; inventor, developer Toxitrol Waste Minimization; inventor EnviroAudit. With AUS, 1954-57. Mem. Nat. Registry Environ. Profl. Rep., Engrng. Soc. Cin., Assn. Corp. Environ. Execs., Cin. C. of C., Global Assn. Corp. Environ. Execs. (charter), Bankers Club. Republican. Lutheran. Home: 9175 Yellowwood Dr Cincinnati OH 45251-1948 Office: 4700 Ashwood Dr Ste 100 Cincinnati OH 45241-2424

TOGNARELLI, RICHARD LEE, lawyer; b. Collinsville, Ill., Aug. 12, 1949; s. Albert John and Rosalie Frances (Brogliatto) T.; m. Gail Marie Culliton, June 11, 1971; children: Michael Anthony, Matthew Paul. AB, St. Louis U., 1971, JD, 1974. Bar: Ill. 1975, U.S. Dist. Ct. (so. dist.) Ill. 1975, U.S. Dist. Ct. (ea. dist.) Ill. 1975, U.S. Ct. Appeals (7th cir.) 1976. Clk., then assoc. firm Dunham, Boman, Leskera & Churchill, East St. Louis, Ill., 1973-78; ptnr. Cadagin, Cain & Tognarelli, Collinsville, 1978-84; ptnr. firm Tognarelli & Mattea, Collinsville, 1984-91, Tognarelli & Levo, P.C., Collinsville, 1992—. Pres. parish coun. Sts. Peter and Paul Roman Cath. Ch., Collinsville, 1988—. Named One of Outstanding Young Men of Am., Collinsville Jaycees, 1981, also recipient Disting. Svc. award, 1984. Mem. ABA (sect. of econs. of law practice com. on lawyer rels. with pub. 1986-87, vice-chair crim. justice com. sec. gen. practice 1990-93, vice-chmn. criminal law com. gen. practice sect. 1990—), Ill. Trail Lawyers Assn. (membership com.), Ill. State Bar Assn. (chmn. jud. adv. polls com. 1986-87, membership and bar activities 1988-93, com. pub. rels.), Collinsville C. of C. (chmn. ambs. 1984-87, v.p. orgn. affairs 1986-88, pres. 1988-90), Rotary (pres. Collinsville 1983-84), KC, Phi Beta Kappa. Democrat. Home: 303 Chesapeake Ln Collinsville IL 62234-4374 Office: Tognarelli & Levo PC PO Box 68 Collinsville IL 62234-0068

TOIRAC, S(ETH) THOMAS, information systems executive, consultant; b. Ft. Wayne, Ind., May 17, 1951; s. Florent D. and Dorothy M. (Lee) T.; m. Martha J. Rife, Dec. 20, 1969 (div. 1979); m. Linda Diane Benecke, Aug. 2, 1987; children: Kristina M., Danielle Shari, Anthony David. Student, Grace Coll., 1970. Computer operator United Telephone Co., Warsaw, 1968-69; programmer-analyst GTE Data Svcs., Ft. Wayne, 1970-76, systems programmer, 1976-79, systems supr., 1979-82; mgr. software N.Am. Van Lines, Ft. Wayne, 1982-84, dir. computing svcs., 1984-90; founder, exec. dir. Pioneer Missionary, Inc., Ft. Wayne, 1990-94; chief fin. officer Pillar Pub., New Carlisle, Ind., 1990-94; exec. v.p. Kessington Network, Indpls., 1990-91; info. mgmt. cons., 1991-95; staff software engr. Lexis-Nexis, Dayton, Ohio, 1995—; chmn. GTE Tech. Adv. Group, 1978-79; cons. in field. Sec.-treas. bd. dirs. Greater Ft. Wayne Crime Stoppers, 1986-91; lay min. Wesleyan Meth. Ch., Ft. Wayne, 1974-75; mem. Share, Inc., 1976-81. Republican. Methodist.

TOLAN, MARY C., pediatric nurse practitioner, educator; b. Mendota, Ill., Apr. 20, 1949; d. Robert John and Anne (Oklesen) T. BSN, U. Ill., Chgo., 1971; postgrad., Ill. Benedictine Coll., 1993—. RN, Ill.; cert. CPR, pediatric nurse practitioner. Staff nurse in surg. ICU U. Ill. Hosp., Chgo., 1971-72; pub. health nurse Mile Sq. Health Ctr., Chgo., 1972-73; PNP DuPage Health Dept., Wheaton, Ill., 1973-78, U. Chgo. Hosp., 1978-80; Sudden Infant Death Syndrome regional cons. Loyola U. Med. Ctr., Maywood, Ill., 1980-82; Apnea clinician Ctrl. DuPage Hosp., Winfield, Ill., 1982-86; PNP Michael Reese HMO, Chgo., 1986-90; Sudden Infant Death Syndrome regional counselor Ill. Dept. Pub. Health, Springfield, Ill., 1990—; cons. Lisle Youth Coun., Lisle, Ill. 1973-78. Fellow Nat. Assn. Pediatric Nurse Assocs. and Practitioners (cert. CPNP); mem. Am. Coll. of Sports Medicine, U.S. Ski Assn., Nordic Fox Ski Club (v.p. 1985-86), Ill. Paddling Coun. Roman Catholic. Home: 3147 Anton Dr Aurora IL 60506 Office: Ill Dept of Pub Health 4212 Saint Charles Rd Bellwood IL 60104-1146

TOLAN, PATRICK HENRY, psychology educator; b. Buffalo, May 30, 1953; s. Francis Henry and Phyllis (Smith) T.; m. M. Ellen Mitchell, Apr. 21, 1984; children: Meredith, Colleen, Kathryn. BA, Temple U., 1978; MA, U. Tenn., 1980, PhD, 1983. Lic. psychologist, cert. sch. psychologist. Psychol. intern Tufts Med. Sch., Boston, 1981-82; postdoctoral fellow U. Chgo. and Michael Reese Hosp., 1983-85; asst. prof. psychology DePaul U., Chgo., 1985-90; assoc. prof. psychology and psychiatry U. Ill.-Chgo., Chgo., 1990—; dir. rsch. Inst. for Juvenile Rsch., Chgo., 1990—; rsch. assoc. dept. psychiatry Michael Reese Hosp., Chgo., 1985-88; cons. dept. pediatrics Cook County Hosp., Chgo., 1984-85. Assoc. editor Jour. Psychotherapy and Family, 1988—; contbr. articles to books and profl. jours. Mem. Am. Psychol. Assn., Am. Assn. for Marital and Family Therapy, Soc. for Research on Child Devel., Am. Soc. Criminology. Office: Inst Juvenile Rsch 907 S Wolcott Ave Chicago IL 60612-7347

TOLAND, CLYDE WILLIAM, lawyer; b. Iola, Kans., Aug. 18, 1947; s. Stanley E. and June E. (Thompson) T.; m. Nancy Ellen Hummel, July 27, 1974; children: David Clyde, Andrew John, Elizabeth Kay. BA, U. Kans., 1969, JD, 1975; MA, U. Wis., 1971. Bar: Kans. 1975, U.S. Dist. Ct. Kans. 1975, U.S. Supreme Ct. 1980. Ptnr. Toland and Thompson, Iola, 1975—. Author: Samuel Franklin Hubbard and Permelia Caroline (Spencer) Hubbard: Pioneer Settlers in 1857 of Allen County, Kansas Territory, and their Descendants, 1985, (with others) Clark and Eliza (Wright) Toland: Their Ancestors and Descendants, 1984, David Wilson and Charlotte Elizabeth (Cooper) Wilson, 1830-1961, and Their Ancestors and Descendants, 1988. Mem. exec. com. Friends of Libr., U. Kans., 1977-92, pres., 1988-91; pres. Allen County Hist. Soc., Inc., 1990-95; founder Annual Buster Keaton Celebration, Iola, Kans., 1993—. Co-recipient with U.S. Sen. Nancy Kassebaum First Alumni Disting. Achievement award Coll. Liberal Arts and Scis. U. Kans., 1996. Fellow Kans. Bar Assn. (Outstanding Svc. award 1988); mem. ABA, Allen County Bar Assn., U. Kans. Alumni Assn. (Strickland award 1969), Phi Beta Kappa, Order of Coif, Omicron Delta Kappa (presdl. plaque 1969). Republican. Prsbyterian. Home: 211 S Colborn St Iola KS 66749-3405 Office: 103 E Madison St Iola KS 66749-3330

TOLAND, JOHN ROBERT, lawyer; b. Iola, Kans., Oct. 7, 1944; s. Stanley E. and June Elizabeth (Thompson) T.; m. Karen Alice Jeffries, Apr. 26, 1980; children: Carol Jane, Mark Charles, Scott Robert, Kent William. BA with highest distinction (Summerfield scholar) U. Kans., 1966, JD, 1969. Bar: Kans. 1969, U.S. Dist. Ct. Kans. 1969, U.S. Ct. Appeals (10th cir.) 1969, U.S. Supreme Ct. 1976. Ptnr. firm Toland and Thompson, Iola, Kans., 1973—; city atty., Yates Center, Kans., 1976-82; spkr. sch. law seminars. Editor-in-chief Kans. Law Rev., 1968-69; mem. bd. editors Kans. Bar Assn. Jour., 1988-92. Trustee Allen County Hosp., Iola, 1979-82; bd. dirs. Iola Pub. Library, 1980-88, pres., 1983-88; bd. dirs. United Fund of Iola Inc., 1975-79, treas., 1975-77; bd. dirs. Iola Area Symphony Orch., 1994—; ruling elder First Presbyn. Ch., Iola, 1983-85; mem. Allen County Hist. Soc., Kansas State Hist. Soc., The Friends of the Eisenhower Found., Univ. Kansas Alumni Assn., mem. com. on ministry John Calvin Presbytery, Presbyn. Ch. (USA), 1986-88. Served as capt. JAGC, U.S. Army, 1969-73; Vietnam. Decorated Bronze Star, Army Commendation medal with oak leaf cluster; recipient John Ise Scholarship Award in Econs; Nat. Merit scholar. Fellow Kansas Bar Foundation; mem. ABA, VFW, Allen County Bar Assn. (pres. 1980-81), Kans. Bar Assn., Kans. Sch. Attys. Assn. (bd. dirs. 1989-93, spkr. at sch. law seminars), Am. Legion, Order of the Coif, Phi Beta Kappa, Phi Delta Phi, Beta Theta Pi, Sigma Pi Sigma. Republican. Lodge: Rotary (pres. Iola chpt. 1980-81, Paul Harris fellow 1986). Home: PO Box 264 Iola KS 66749-0264 Office: Toland and Thompson 103 E Madison St Iola KS 66749-3330

TOLBERT, NATHAN EDWARD, biochemistry educator, plant science researcher; b. Twin Falls, Idaho, May 19, 1919; s. Edward and Helen (Mills) T.; m. Evelynne Cedarlund, June 21, 1952 (dec. Nov. 1963); children—Helen, Carol, James; m. Eleanor Dalgleish, June 22, 1964. BS in Chemistry, U. Calif., Berkeley, 1941; PhD in Biochemistry, U. Wis., 1950. Prof. biochemistry Mich. State U., East Lansing, 1958-89, prof. emeritus, 1989—. Editor: Biochemistry of Plants, Vol. 1, 1980; editor 3 sci. jours.; contbr. numerous papers, revs., abstracts to profl. publs.; patentee in field. Served to capt. USAF, 1943-45, PTO. Named disting. prof. Mich. State U., 1963, Mich. Scientist of Yr., 1985; Fulbright fellow, 1969; grantee NSF, NIH. Mem. Nat. Acad. Sci., Am. Soc. Plant Physiology (pres. 1983-84, Stephen Hale award 1980), Am. Soc. Biol. Chemists, Am. Chem. Soc., Nat. Acad. Sci. Office: Mich State U Dept Biochemistry East Lansing MI 48824

TOLLEFSON, BEN C., retired utility sales manager; b. Minot, N.D., June 14, 1927; s. Ben K. and Hannah G. (Espeseth) T.; m. Lila R. Adams, Apr. 11, 1949; children: Robb, LuAnn, David, Richard. Student, Minot State U., 1946-48. Advt. salesman Minot Daily News, 1956-57; utility salesman No. States Power Co., Minot, 1957-72, sales mgr., 1972-89; retired, 1989; advisor Ctrl. Venture Capital, Minot, 1990-95; state rep. State of N.D., 1984—. Pres. Minot Jaycees, 1957. Served with USN, 1945-47. Recipient Clara Barton Svc. award Am. Red Cross, 1969; named one of Outstanding Young Men Am., Minot Jaycees, 1958, State Ofcl. Yr., Nat. Assn. Home Builders, 1992. Mem. Kiwanis (Minot lt. gov. 1973, Outstanding Lt. Gov. 1973), Elks. Republican. Lutheran. Home: 500 Twenty Fourth St NW Minot ND 58701

TOLLIVER, DAVID JOSEPH, clergyman; b. St. Louis, Feb. 2, 1951; s. Phillip and Wandalee (Payne) T.; m. Myra Lee Crow, June 10, 1972; children: Terra Jo, Adam Leon. B cum laude, Dallas Bapt. U., 1985; MDiv, Midwestern Sem., Kansas City, Mo., 1990, D Ministry, 1995. Ordained to ministry Bapt. Ch., 1986. Pastor Friendship Bapt. Ch., California, Mo., 1986-91, Calvary Bapt. Ch., St. Louis, 1991-95; Oak Hill Bapt. Ch., St. Louis, 1996—; bd. mem. exec. com. So. Bapt. Conv., Nashville, 1992—; bd. mem. Christian Civic Found., St. Louis, 1989-92; bd. mem. Windermere Bd. Advisors, 1990—; v.p. Calif. Ministerial Alliance, 1990-91. Author: Adult Children and Aging Parents—Roles and Responsibilities, 1995. With U.S. Army, 1975-79. Home: 3728 Cranberry Ct Florissant MO 63033-6625 Office: Oak Hill Bapt Ch 3166 Pershall Rd Saint Louis MO 63136

TOLLIVER, KEVIN PAUL, dentist; b. Ft. Wayne, Ind., Mar. 17, 1951; s. Herbert and Norma Jean (Scheele) T.; m. Melanie Beth Johnson, May 5, 1973; children: Chad, Joshua, Jordan, Ashley. BA, Ind. U., 1973; DDS, Ind. U., Indpls., 1977. Lic. dentist, Ind. Gen. practice dentistry Indpls., 1977—. Pres. Williston Green Assn., Indpls., 1983, 85; vol. Pan Am. Games, Indpls., 1986-87; vol., com. mem. Campaing. for Ind. Named one of Outstanding Young Men of Am., 1984. Fellow Acad. Functional Prosthodontics, Acad. Physiologic Dentistry; mem. ADA, Internat. Acad. Laser Dentistry, N.Am. Acad. Laser Dentistry, Acad. Sports Dentistry, Am. Acad. Cosmetic Dentistry, Acad. Gen. Dentistry, Ind. Dental Assn., Indpls. Dist. Dental Soc., Chgo. Dental Soc., Ind. U. Well House Soc., Ind. U. Hoosier Hundred. Home: 648 Suffolk Ln Carmel IN 46032-8660 Office: 3390 W 86th St Ste S-1 Indianapolis IN 46268-1991

TOLLIVER, MARION EUGENE, college administrator; b. Columbus, Ohio, Apr. 21, 1949; s. Marion Eugene and Mary Margaret (Boyhan) T.; m. Evelyn Barlett, Dec. 16, 1981; children: Christine Rene, Cynthia Ann. AS in Engrng. Tech., Franklin U., 1981, BS in Engrng. Tech., 1983; MBA, Ashland U., 1993. Cert. plant engr. Archtl. draftsman Capp Homes, Columbus, Ohio, 1970-74; chief draftsman State of Ohio, Columbus, 1974-77; engrng. technician Ross Labs., Columbus, 1977-84; facilities project engr. Franklin Internat., Columbus, 1984-87; project engr., mgr. Dugan & Meyers Constrn., Cin., 1987-89; facilities mgr. BMY/WVD, Marysville, Ohio, 1989-91; energy and constrn. mgr. Denison U., Granville, 1991-94; dir. facilities mgmt. Augustana Coll., Rock Island, Ill., 1994—. Bd. dirs. Christian Frendliness, Rock Island, 1995; treas., bd. dirs. Lighthouse Mental Health Svc., Reynoldsburg, Ohio, 1987-90; pres. Reynoldsburg APS chpt., 1990-94; chair of counsel of ministry Trinity United Meth. Ch., Pickerington, Ohio, 1985-88. Recipient 1st Pl. Fundraiser League Against Child Abuse, 1986, 88. Mem. Assn. of Higher Edn. Adminstrs., Midwest Assn. of Higher Edn. Adminstrn. (pgram com. 1994-95), Am. Inst. of Plant Engrs., Ill. Phys. Plant Dirs. Assn. Home: 3720 38th Ave Rock Island IL 61201 Office: Augustana Coll 639 38th St Rock Island IL 61201

TOLLIVER, SARAH JAN, writer; b. San Bernardino, Calif., Feb. 15, 1952; d. Marvin M. Van Salter and Gladys Ellen (Klempner) Woodman; m. Bruce Clyde Tolliver, Oct. 23, 1979. BA, U. Calif., Davis, 1977. Office asst. Va. Inst. Tech., Virginia Beach, 1982-87; sec. Hertz Rent A Car, Norfolk, Va., 1987-89, Old Dominion Svcs., Norfolk, 1989-92; coord. Great Neck Writer's Group, Virginia Beach, 1993—. Author: The Cassandra Syndrome, 1993, (screenplay) Sarah's Music, 1992, Happily Ever Aftering in Camelot, 1995, The Man of Words, 1994, Chosen By Lot, 1994, In Black, 1994. Mem. U.S.S. Whidbey Island Support Group, Virginia Beach, 1988—; telecom. rep. Nat. Right to Work, Virginia Beach, 1994. Mem. John F. Kennedy Wives Club (v.p. 1983). Republican. Lutheran.

TOLLMAN, THOMAS ANDREW, librarian; b. Omaha, Mar. 14, 1939; s. James Perry and Elizabeth (McVey) T.; m. Teresa Ramírez, Jan. 4, 1964; children: James Daniel, Lisa Maria. BA, Carleton Coll., 1960; MA, U. Chgo., 1965, U. Minn., 1974; postgrad., U. Ariz., 1977-79. Admissions counselor Carleton Coll., Northfield, Minn., 1960-62; asst. dean of coll. Carleton Coll., Northfield, 1968-73; reference libr. N.W. Mo. State U., Maryville, 1974-77; adj. instr. U. Ariz., Tucson, 1977-79; chair libr. reference dept. U. Nebr., Omaha, 1979-88, assoc. prof., reference libr., 1988—; sr. lectr. Fulbright Commn., Quito, Ecuador, 1991. Contbr. articles to profl. jours. Mem. ALA, Nebr. Libr. Assn., Spl. Librs. Assn., Assn. Coll. and Rsch. Librs., Reference and Adult Svcs. Div., Reforma, Nebr. Libr. Assn. (disting. svc. award, 1995). Mem. ALA, Nebr. Libr. Assn. (Disting. Svc. award 1995), Spl. Librs. Assn., Assn. Coll. and Rsch. Librs., Reference and Adult Svcs. Divsn., Reforma. Home: 2121 S 84th St Omaha NE 68124-2222 Office: Reference Libr U Nebr Omaha NE 68182-0237

TOLLON, WAYNE, engineering manager; b. London, Mar. 27, 1959; came to U.S., 1968; AD, St. Claire Coll., 1982. Design leader dye automation Kinetic Design, Mt Clemens, Mich., 1982-88; fixture design mgr. Lamar Product Devel. Co., Sterling Heights, Mich., 1988-94; engrng. mgr. Weldex Inc., Warren, Mich., 1994—. Coach Soccer, Anchor Bay, Mich., 1984. Home: 27300 Bertrand St Chesterfield MI 48051-1628

TOMAINO, JOSEPH CARMINE, retail executive, retired postal inspector; b. Danbury, Conn., Dec. 12, 1948; s. Joseph and Lena Marie (LaCava) T.; m. Eileen Pulver (div. Nov. 1977); m. Ann C. Underriner, Sept. 20, 1986; children: Joseph Richard, Robert John. BS, Western Conn. State U., 1970; MBA, Roosevelt U., 1978, MS in Acctg., 1986. Cert. fraud examiner. Post office clk. U.S. Postal Svc., Ridgefield, Conn., 1970-71; postal inspector U.S. Postal Svc., Chgo., 1971-80, supervisory postal inspector, 1980-93; mgr. western ops. loss prevention dept. Walgreen Co., Deerfield, Ill. Mem. Am. Soc. Indsl. Security, Fed. Law Enforcement Officers Assn., Nat. Assn. Chiefs Police, Ill. Chiefs Police, Spl. Agts. Assn., Ill. Police Assn., Nat. Soc. Pub. Accts., Assn. Cert. Fraud Examiners. Office: Walgreen Co 300 Wilmot Rd Stop 3153 Deerfield IL 60015-4600

TOMANEK, ROBERT J., anatomy educator; b. Omana, Nebr., Apr. 5, 1937; s. Joseph and Marie (Zatocil) T.; m. Rita R. Svoboda, Aug. 12, 1961; children: Lisa R. Kathe, Paul J., Ann M. Tomanek-Chalkley. BS, U. Omaha, 1959; PhD, U. Iowa, 1967. Asst. prof. Simon Fraser U., Burnaby, B.C., 1967-70; postdoctoral fellow U. Iowa, Iowa City, 1970-72; from asst. prof. to prof. U. Iowa, 1972—; edtl. bd. Circulation Rsch., 1988—, Am. Jour. Physiology, 1993-95, Anatomical Record, 1980—; cons. NIH. Fellow Am. Heart Assn, Am. Physiol. Soc.; mem. Am. Assn. Anatomy, Microcirculatory Soc., Am. Soc. Cell Biology, N.Am. Vascular Biology Orgn. Roman Catholic. Office: Dept Anatomy U Iowa Iowa City IA 52242

TOMASSI, RALPH VINCENT, university administrator; b. Scranton, Pa., Aug. 19, 1954; s. Ralph and Anna C. (Pagnani) T.; m. Betty Jo Slotterbeck, July 18, 1981. BEd, Ashland (Ohio) U., 1977; postgrad., Bowling Green (Ohio) State U., 1977-78. Asst. baseball coach, grad. asst. Heidelberg Coll., Tiffin, Ohio, 1978-79; project coord. Ashland U., 1979-84, dir. transfer admissions, dir. ann. fund, exec. dir. devel., 1987—; cons. Choice Pl. Home, Ashland, 1987; capt. Ohio Found.Ind. Colls., Columbus, 1984-95; advisor Phi Delta Theta, Ashland, 1978-82. Bd. dirs. Ind. Coll. Advancement Assn., Columbus, Ashland Bus. Cmty., 1980-82, United Way campaigns; trustee Ashland County Found., 1995—. Recipient Disting. Svc. award Ashland U. Alumni Assn., 1985. Mem. Young Men's Bus. Club (pres. 1991-92), Ashland Area C. of C. (dir.), Country Club of Ashland (dir. 1992—), Rotary of Ashland, Elks. Republican. Roman Catholic. Office: Ashland U Founders Hall # 301 College Ave Ashland OH 44805

TOMASZEWSKI, KATHLEEN BERNADETTE, social worker, educator; b. Detroit, Jan. 31, 1945; d. Thomas Joseph and Margaret Rice Gilmore; m. Kenneth Patrick Tomaszewski, July 30, 1966; children: Kenneth Anthony, Kara Patricia, Kristyn Alisa, Kraig Matthe. BS, Wayne State U., 1981; MEd, U. Toledo, 1983; MSW, U. Mich., 1984. Cert. social worker, Mich. Social worker hemophilia-obstetrics, child abuse and neglect N.W. Ohio Ctr. for Women & Children, Toledo, 1984-87; social worker nephrology Hosp. for Sick Children, Toronto, Ont., Can., 1987-90; social worker cystic fibrosis and craniofacial Childrens Hosp., Phila., 1990-91; dir. placement svcs. Childrens Bur. of Del., Wilmington, 1991-92; pvt. practice in adoption and counseling Beijing, 1993-94; social worker Crittenton Hosp., Rochester Hills, Mich., 1995—; tchr. NYU, Toronto, 1991; bd. dirs. Nat. Hemophilia Assn., Toledo. Contbr. to profl. pubs. Rsch. grantee Can. Kidney Assn., 1991. Mem. NASW (cert.), Am. Assn. Marriage and Family Therapists (cert., clin. assoc.), Am. Assn. Play Therapists. Home: 2347 Cedar Key Dr Lake Orion MI 48360

TOMAZI, GEORGE DONALD, retired electrical engineer; b. St. Louis, Dec. 27, 1935; s. George and Sophia (Bogovich) T.; m. Lois Marie Partenheimer, Feb. 1, 1958; children: Keith, Kent. BSEE, U. Mo., Rolla, 1958, Profl. EE (hon.), 1970; MBA, St. Louis U., 1965, MSEE, 1971. Registered profl. engr., Mo., Ill., Wash., Ohio, Calif. Project engr. Union Electric Co., 1958-66; dir. corp. planning Gen. Steel Industries, 1966-70; exec. v.p. St. Louis Research Council, 1970-74; exec. v.p. Hercules Constrn. Co., St. Louis, 1974-75; dir. design and constrn. div. Mallinckrodt, Inc., St. Louis, 1975-93; ret., 1993. Author: P-Science: The Role of Science in Society, 1972, The Link of Science and Religion, 1973. Active Nat. Kidney Found.; bd. dirs. U. Mo. Devel. Council, St. Louis Artists Coalition, Citizens for Modern Transit; elder Luth. Ch.; dir. Coun. Luth. Chs., St. Louis; mem. adv. com. grad. sch. U. Mo., Columbia, mem. pres's. role and scope commn.; dir. Coun. Luth. Chs. Greater St. Louis; mem. bldg. com. Humane Soc. Mo.; mem. coun. Luth. Ch. of the Living Christ. Served with U.S. Army, 1959-61. Recipient award Acad. Elec. Engrs., U. Mo., Rolla. Mem. NSPE, IEEE (chmn. state govt. activities com. 1990-93), Japan-Am. Soc., AAAS, AIChE, Profl. Engrs. in Industry, Mo. Soc. Profl. Engrs. (Profl. Engr. in Industry 1989, pres.-elect St. Louis chpt.), Profl. Engrs. and Land Surveyors (chmn. Mo. bd. for architects 1989-95), Am. Def. Preparedness Assn., U. Mo. Alumni Assn. (bd. dirs. 1972-78), Engrs. Club (pres. 1985-86), Mo. Athletic Club, Rotary, Sigma Pi. Office: 12723 Stoneridge Dr Florissant MO 63033-4620

TOMFOHRDE, MITCHELL GERALD, management consultant; b. Marshfield, Wis., Mar. 1, 1962; s. Gilbert Gerald Jr. and Carol Joy (Lubeck) T. BS in Bus., U. Wis., Stevens Point, 1984, BS in Teaching, 1986; MS in Edn., No. Ill. U., 1988. Cert. tchr. Spl. needs asst. Milw. Area Tech. Coll., 1989; mktg. cons. Milw. Symphony Orch., 1989-90; pvt. practice bus. cons. Milw., 1989—; exec. v.p. Unlimited Innovations, Inc., Grafton, Wis., 1992; sr. assoc. World Mktg. Alliance, Brookfield, Wis.; prodn. mgr. Landmark Edn., 1994-96, introduction to the forum leader, 1995—. Author: You're Not Alone, 1995 (Bus. Communicators award 1995); author numerous poems. Vol. money mgmt. program Family Svc., Milw., 1990-95; tchr. YMCA, Milw., 1991-92. Mem. Toastmasters (ednl. v.p. 1990-91, area gov.

1991-92, area speech contest award 1991), Alpha Mu Gamma (fgn. lang. honor soc. 1980-82). Home: 5706A W Vliet St Milwaukee WI 53208-2161

TOMIN, ROBIN KAREN, medical surgical nurse; b. Wilkensburg, Pa., Dec. 12, 1954; d. Robert Bliss and Ella Bernenta (May) House; m. John Joseph Tomin, July 2, 1977; children: John Robert, Christopher, Alison. Diploma, Idabelle Firestone Sch Nursing, Akron, Ohio, 1976; BSN, U. Akron, 1984, MSN, 1988. Staff nurse critical care units Akron City Hosp., 1976-79, staff nurse surg. svcs., 1979-85; staff Aultman Ctr. for One Day Surgery, Canton, Ohio, 1985-86; teaching team mem. nursing dept. nursing U. Tenn., Martin, 1990-92; staff nurse critical care unit Vol. Hosp., Martin, Tenn., 1991-92; staff nurse Hospice Care Ctr., Akron, 1995—; faculty nursing Malone Coll., Canton, Ohio, 1993—; per diem nurse Hospice Care Ctr., 1995; presenter in field. Leader informational and support groups Barberton (Ohio) Free Clinic, 1989; active Barberton Community Edn., 1989, Lifelong Learning Connection, 1989, first aide Canton Montasouri Sch., 1989-90. Grantee Akron Gen. Med. Ctr. Found., 1990, U. Akron Coll. Nursing, 1990, 91. Mem. ANA, Tenn. Nurses Assn., Midwest Nursing Rsch. Soc., Nat. League Nursing, Ohio Citizen League for Nursing, Assn. Operating Rm. Nurses, Sigma Theta Tau. Home: 2830 Aylesbury St NW North Canton OH 44720-4582

TOMITA, TADANORI, neurosurgeon; b. Osaka, Japan, Nov. 19, 1945; s. Tadao and Noriko (Ikeda) T.; m. Kathryn Morley, June 28, 1980; children: Tadaki M., Kenji W., Dan Y. MD, Kobe (Japan) U., 1970. Diplomate Am. Bd. Neurol. Surgery. Attending neurosurgeon Children's Meml. Hosp., Chgo., 1981—, dir. neurosurg. oncology, 1984—; assoc. prof. Northwestern U. Med. Sch. Contbr. articles to profl. jours. Recipient Sherry Kallick award Northwestern Meml. Hosp., 1979, Frank Notides award Children's Meml. Hosp., Chgo., 1980. Fellow ACS, Am. Acad. Pediatrics; mem. Am. Assn. Neurol. Surgeons, Congress Neurorol. Surgeons, Am. Soc. Pediatric Neurosurgery, Soc. Pediatric Neurosurgery. Office: Childrens Meml Hosp 2300 N Childrens Plz Chicago IL 60614-3318

TOMLINSON, GARY EARL, museum curator; b. Yorktown, Ind., June 13, 1951; s. Arthur Earl and J. Irene (Hickman) T.; m. Suzanne Marie Naessens, Dec. 28, 1974; 1 child, James Ronald Earl. BS, Ball State U., 1973; MA, Mich. State U., 1974. Cert. secondary physics and math. tchr., Mich. Assoc. curator Pub. Mus. Grand Rapids, Mich., 1976—; Support Program for Instnl. Competency in Astronomy agt. Harvard/Smithsonian Ctr. Astrophysics, 1990—; coord. astronomy day Astron. League, Washington, 1983—; adv. bd. Regional Math. and Sci. Ctr., Grand Valley State U., Allendale, Mich.; mem. planning team West Mich. Interactive Sci. Ctr. Author and editor: Astronomy Day Handbook, 1988, 2d edit., 1989; editor: Anthology of Astronomical Poetry, 1984, Planetarium Bibliography, 1992; also articles. Crew chief Monogalia County Emergency Med. Svcs., Morgantown, W.Va., 1975-76; advisor Gran Rapids Pub. Sch.'s Spectrum, 1978-80. Recipient Edmund Sci. award, N.J., 1980, Spectrum award Pub. Rels. Soc. Am., 1986, 93, G.R. Wright Svc. award Astron. League, Nat. Svc. award Western Amateur Astronomers, 1992; Hoosier scholar Gov. Ind., 1969. Mem. Am. Astron. Soc., Great Lakes Planetarium Assn. (bd. dirs. 1984—, pres. 1986-87, fellow 1986), Internat. Planetarium Soc. (rep. 1990-92), Sigma Pi Sigma, Sigma Zeta. Office: Pub Mus Grand Rapids 272 Pearl NW Grand Rapids MI 49504

TOMLINSON, JAMES LAWRENCE, mechanical engineer; b. Detroit, Sept. 12, 1935; s. James Emmet and Ethel Pearl (Williams) T.; m. Marilyn Joyce Peterson, Aug. 24, 1957; children: James, Mary, Robert, Susan. BSME, Mich. Tech., 1957. Registered profl. engr., Mich. Design engr. Buick Motor div. GMC, Flint, Mich., 1960-61, project engr., 1961-66, sr. project engr., 1966-71; staff analysis engr. GM Corp., Warren, Mich., 1971-82, sr. staff analysis engr., 1983-88; pres. Eastport (Mich.) Engring., Grand Blanc, Mich., 1989—. Mayor City of Grand Blanc, 1985-89, city councilman, 1969-84, police liaison/commr., 1971-82, planning adv. bd., 1978-80, planning commn., 1985-89; nat. coun. mem. Boy Scouts Am., 1979-90, 93—, regional bd. mem., 1995—, coun. commr., 1979-84, coun. v.p., 1984—, nat. camp sch. staff, 1986-88, regional camp inspector/accreditation team, 1988—; vice chmn. Genesee County Sml. Cities and Villages Assn., 1986, chmn., 1987. Capt. USAF, 1958-60. Recipient Silver Beaver Tail Pine Coun. Boy Scouts Am., 1980, Silver Antelope Ctrl. region, 1996. Mem. NSPE (treas. Flint chpt. 1968-72, Engr. of the Yr. Flint chpt. 1990), SAE (mem. com. 1992-94, 96-98), ASME (exec. bd. Saginaw Valley chpt. 1968-70), Friends of Torch Lake Twp., Inc. (pres. 1994—). United Ch. of Christ. Home: 12077 Harris Beach Rd Eastport MI 49627-0025

TOMLINSON, ROBERT (BOB TOMLINSON), state legislator; m. Carole Tomlinson. Kans. state rep. Dist. 24, 1993—; spl. svc. tchr. Address: 5900 Lamar Mission KS 66202*

TOMLJANOVICH, ESTHER M., judge; b. Galt, Iowa, Nov. 1, 1931; d. Chester William and Thelma L. (Brooks) Moellering; m. William S. Tomljanovich, Dec. 26, 1957; 1 child, William Brooks. AA, Itasca Jr. Coll., 1951; BSL, St. Paul Coll. Law, 1953, LLB, 1955. Bar: Minn. 1955, U.S. Dist. Ct. Minn. 1958. Asst. revisor of statutes State of Minn., St. Paul, 1957-66, revisor of statutes, 1974-77; dist. ct. judge State of Minn., Stillwater, 1977-90; assoc. justice Minn. Supreme Ct., St. Paul, 1990—. Former mem. North St. Paul Bd. Edn., Maplewood Bd. Edn., Lake Elmo Planning Commn; bd. trustees William Mitchell Coll. Law, 1995—. Mem. Minn. State Bar Assn., Bus. and Profl. Women's Assn. St. Paul (former pres.). Office: Supreme Ct MN MN Judicial Ctr Rm 423 25 Constitution Ave Saint Paul MN 55155-1500

TOMPKINS, CURTIS JOHNSTON, academic administrator; b. Roanoke, Va., July 14, 1942; s. Joseph Buford and Rebecca (Johnston) T.; m. Mary Katherine Hasle, Sept. 5, 1964; children: Robert, Joseph, Rebecca. BS, Va. Poly. Inst., 1965, MS, 1967; PhD, Ga. Inst. Tech., 1971. Indsl. engr. E.I. DuPont de Nemours, Richmond, Va., 1965-67; instr. Sch. Indsl. and Systems Engring., Ga. Inst. Tech., Atlanta, 1968-71; assoc. prof. Colgate Darden Grad. Sch. Bus. Adminstrn., U. Va., Charlottesville, 1971-77; prof., chmn. dept. indsl. engring. W.Va. U., Morgantown, 1977-80, dean Coll. Engring., 1980-91; pres. Mich. Tech. U., Houghton, 1991—; mem. engring. accreditation commn. Accreditation Bd. for Engring. and Tech., 1981-86; mem. Commn. on Engring. Edn., Nat. Assn. State Univs. and Land Grant Colls., 1985-90; cons. corps., govt. agys., ednl. instns.; lectr. various univs.; mem. exec. bd. Engring. Deans Coun., 1985-89, vice chmn., 1987-89; mem. engring. adv. com., chmn. of planning com. NSF, 1988-91, chm. Mich. Univs. pres. coun., 1996—, mem. bd. dirs. Oak Ridge Associated Univs., 1996—, Pres. Coun. Assn. Governing bds. 1996—, Gov's. Workforce commn. Author: (with L.E. Grayson) Management of Public Sector and Nonprofit Organizations, 1983, (with others) Maynard's Industrial Engineering Handbook, 1992; contbr. chpt. to Ency. of Profl. Mgmt, 1978, 83. Co-chmn. W.Va. Gov.'s Coun. on Econ. Devel.; bd. dirs. Pub. Land Corp. W.Va., 1980-89; mem. faculty Nat. Acad. Voluntarism, United Way Am., 1976-91; mem. Morgantown Water Commn., 1981-87, Morgantown Utility Bd., 1987-91; mem. steering com. W.Va. Conf. on Environ., 1985-89; chmn. Monogalia County United Way, 1989-90; mem. Mich. Govs. Workforce Commn., 1996—; campaign chmn. Copper Country United Way, 1995-96; mem., bd. dirs. Oak Ridge Associated Univs., 1996—. Fellow Inst. Indsl. Engrs. (life mem., sr. v.p. publs. 1983-85, v.p. edn. and rsch. 1985-87, trustee 1983-90, pres.-elect 1987-88, pres. 1988-89), Am. Soc. Engring. Edn. (chmn. indsl. engring. div. 1981-82, v.p. pub. affairs 1985-87, bd. dirs. 1985-87, 1st v.p., exec. com., fin. com. 1986-87, pres.-elect 1989-90, pres. 1990-91); mem. Am. Assn. Engring. Soc. (bd. govs. 1987-90, exec. com. 1987-90, sec.-treas. 1989-90), Jr. Engring. Tech. Soc. (bd. dirs. 1988-91), Nat. Soc. for Sci., Tech. and Society (bd. dirs. 1991—), Internat. Hall of Fame of Sci. and Engring. (hon. trustee), Sigma Xi, Phi Kappa Phi, Tau Beta Pi, Alpha Pi Mu. Methodist. Home: 2 Woodland Rd Houghton MI 49931-9746 Office: Mich Tech U 1400 Townsend Dr Houghton MI 49931-1200

TOMPKINS, EILEEN, state legislator; m. Patrick Tompkins; 9 children. Attended, Inver Hills C.C., U. Minn., Coll. of St. Thomas. Mem. Minn. Ho. of Reps., 1984—; mem. health and human svcs. com., mem. local govt. com., mem. met. affairs com., mem. transp. and transit com. Home: 7734 133rd St W Apple Valley MN 55124-7623 Office: Minn Ho of Reps State Capital Building Saint Paul MN 55155-1606 also: 245 State Office Bldg Saint Paul MN 55155

TONKENS, REBECCA A., maternal women's health nurse; b. Searcy, Ark., Dec. 17, 1943; d. William T. and Velda M. (Goodloe) McAfee; m. Richard E. Morris, June 24, 1960 (div. Nov. 1980); children: Terri L. Morris Bomar, Toni L. Morris Carroll; m. Solvin W. Tonkens, Dec. 22, 1986. LPN, Area Vocat. Tech. Sch., Kansas City, Kans., 1973; ADN, Kansas City C.C., 1980; BSN, Webster U., 1992. RN, Kans., Mo. Area Vocat. Tech. Sch.; Staff nurse Providence-St. Margaret Hosp., Kansas City, 1973-80; indsl. nurse, office mgr. Kansas City Indsl. Clinic, 1980-81; staff nurse Bethany Med. Ctr., Kansas City, 1981—; active community rels. diabetes unit Bethany Med. Ctr., 1983-86. Officer, v.p., bd. dirs. Cambridge Townhouse Assn., Leawood, Kans., 1989-92; chaperone Rose Bud (Ark.) Band at Presdl. Inauguration, Washington, 1992; mem. adv. bd. Kansas City Kans. C.C. Day Care Ctr.; vol. Habitat for Humanity, Salvation Army, others. Recipient Cert. of Appreciation, Salvation Army, 1994. Mem. ANA, Am. Coll. Occupational and Environ. Medicine (aux.). Episcopalian. Home and Office: 12861 Cambridge Ter Leawood KS 66209-1634

TONN, ROBERT JAMES, entomologist; b. Watertown, Wis., June 23, 1927; s. Harry James and Elise (Foogman) T.; m. Noemi C. Tonn; children: Sigrid M., Monica E. BS, Colo. State U., 1949, MS, 1950; MPH, Okla. Med. Sch., 1963; PhD, Okla. State U., 1959. Rsch. assoc La. State U., Costa Rica/New Orleans, 1961-63; dir. Taunton Field Sta., Taunton, Mass., 1963-65; chief PMO unit WHO, various locations, 1965-87; adj. prof. of parasitology U. Tex.-El Paso, 1988—; cons. USAID/VBC, 1987—. Contbr. numerous articles to profl. jours. Mem. Am. Soc. Tropical Medicine, Soc. Vector Ecology (pres. 1984), Am. Mosquito Control Assn., U.S./Mex. Border Health Assn., Royal Soc. Tropical Medicine and Hygiene, Masons. Congregationalist. Home: RR 3 Box 505 Park Rapids MN 56470-9363

TONNESON, IRENE MARIE, nurse, nutritionist; b. Bottineau, N.D., May 18, 1933; d. Elmer J. and Mildred I. (Torgerson) Lindstrom; m. Maynard I.J. Tonneson, Oct. 29, 1954; children: Michael, Malcolm. Diploma in Nursing, Trinity Hosp., Minot, N.D., 1954. Pediat. supr. Trinity Hosp., Minot, 1954-56; DON St. Andrews Hosp., Minot, 1956-76; home health nurse First Dist. Health Unit, Minot, 1980-82, WIC nutritionist, 1980—; coll. nurse N.D. State U., Bottineau, 1990-92; sec. Immanuel Mission Aide, Bottineau, 1976-80. Mem. Rep. Party, Bottineau County, 1990—. Mem. Stonecroft Ministries (friendship Bible coffee guide/coord. 1976-80). Lutheran. Home: Hc 2 Box 56 Souris ND 58783 Office: WIC Program First Dist Health Unit Dept of Nutritionist Bottineau ND 58318

TOOMEY, JOHN CHRISTOPHER, biologist, research scientist; b. Sewickley, Pa., Nov. 17, 1964; s. William Shenberger and Nancy (Mangin) T.; m. Jennifer Mullen, Nov. 4, 1989; children: Ariel Elizabeth, Chase Evan. BS in Biology, Allegheny Coll., 1987. Assoc. rsch. engr. Medex, Inc., Dublin, Ohio, 1988-89, project engr., 1989-95, sr. project engr., 1995; mem. emergency response team Medex, Inc., Dublin, 1990—. Mem. ASM Internat., Am. Soc. for Microbiology. Office: Medex Inc 6250 Shier Rings Rd Dublin OH 43016-1295

TOOMEY, WILLIAM SHENBERGER, wire manufacturing company executive; b. Windsor, Pa., Feb. 6, 1935; s. Harold DeWitt and Ruth Evelyn Belle (Shenberger) T.; m. Nancy Antoinette Mangin, Oct. 13, 1962; children: William, Michael, John. BS in Metall. Engring., Lehigh U., 1957. Supervising metallurgist primary rolling mills LTV Steel Corp., Aliquippa, Pa., 1972-73, gen. supr. heat treating shipping and invoice, 1973-76, supervising metallurgist rod wire and tubular, 1976-77, mgr. product quality rod and wire, 1977-78, mgr. product quality tubular, 1978-85; mgr. product quality and product devel. Fostoria (Ohio) div. Seneca Wire & Mfg. Co., 1986, plant mgr., 1986, gen. mgr., 1986-87, corp. tech. dir., 1987-91; cons. Am. Spring Wire, Bedford Heights, Ohio, 1991, new product devel. mgr., 1992—. With USN, 1958. Mem. Am. Wire Assn., Am. Soc. Nondestructive Testing. Republican. Home: 280 Ash Grove Cir Aurora OH 44202-8470 Office: Am Spring Wire Dept of Manufacturing Bedford OH 44146

TOOT, JOSEPH F., JR., bearing manufacturing company executive; b. 1935; married. AB, Princeton U., 1957; postgrad., Harvard U. Grad. Sch. Bus. Adminstrn., 1961. With Timken Co., Canton, Ohio, 1962—; dep. mgr. Timken (France) Co., 1965-67; v.p. internat. div. Timken Co., Canton, 1967-68, corp. v.p., then exec. v.p., 1968-79, pres., 1979—, also bd. dirs.; bd. dirs. Rockwell Internat. Mem. Am. Iron and Steel Inst. Office: Timken Co 1835 Dueber Ave SW Canton OH 44706-2728

TOPEY, ISHMAEL ALOYSIUS, urban planner; b. Port Henderson, St. Catherine, Jamaica, Nov. 10, 1926; s. Ferdinand Aloysius and Amy (Brown) T.; m. Dulcie Rose Clarke, Feb. 24, 1960; children: Patrick F., Robert I., Amy L., George A. AA in Bus. Adminstrn., Wayne County C.C., 1983; BBA, U. Detroit, 1985; MA in Labor Rels., Wayne State U., Detroit, 1987. Cert. profl. cons./advisor; cert. adminstrv. mgr. Mgr. Sea Food Club, Jamaica, West Indies, 1960-75; tchr. Detroit Pub. Schs., 1986-87; urban renewal asst. City of Detroit, 1987—; founder Inter-Galactic Enterprises, Inc., Detroit, 1990—; creator of human math.; econ. devel. specialist; cons. in field. Creator Topeyology Sys. of Speedy Learning, 1987; author: Letter to Stephen Hawking, Debunking the Bell Curve, History of Intelligence. Co-recipient Papal Citation for Social Work, 1985; Jesuit Founders scholar U. Detroit, 1984. Mem. Am. Planning Assn., Buckminster Fuller Inst., World Future Soc. Home: 15700 Mapleridge St Detroit MI 48205-3031 Office: City of Detroit City County Bldg Ste 150 Detroit MI 48226

TOPINKA, JUDY BAAR, state official; b. Riverside, Ill., Jan. 16, 1944; d. William Daniel and Lillian Mary (Shuss) Baar; 1 child, Joseph Baar. BS, Northwestern U., 1966. Features editor, reporter, columnist Life Newspapers, Berwyn and LaGrange, Ill., 1966-77; with Forest Park (Ill.) Rev. and Westchester News, 1976-77; coord. spl. events dept. fedn. comm., AMA, 1978-80; rsch. analyst Senator Leonard Becker, 1978-79; mem. Ill. Ho. of Reps., 1981-84; mem. Ill. Senate, 1985-94; treas. State of Ill., Springfield, 1995—; former mem. judiciary com., former chmn. senate health and welfare com.; former mem. fin. instn. com.; former co-chmn. Citizens Coun. on Econ. Devel.; former co-chmn. U.S. Commn. for Preservation of Am.'s Heritage Abroad, serves on legis. ref. bur.; former mem. minority bus. resource ctr. adv. com. U.S. Dept. Transp.; former mem. adv. bd. Nat. Inst. Justice. Founder, pres., bd. dirs. West Suburban Exec. Breakfast Club, from 1976; chmn. Ill. Ethnics for Reagan-Bush, 1984, Bush-Quayle 1988; spokesman Nat. Coun. State Legislatures Health Com.; former mem nat. adv. coun. health professions edn. HHS; mem., GOP chairwoman Legis. Audit Commn. of Cook County; chmn. Riverside Twp. Regular Republican Orgn., 1994—. Recipient Outstanding Civilian Svc. medal, Molly Pitcher award, Abraham Lincoln award, Silver Eagle award U.S. Army and N.G. Office: JR Thompson Ctr 100 W Randolph St Ste 15-600 Chicago IL 60601-3220

TOPLIKAR, JOHN M., state legislator; m. Dianne Lee. Kans. state rep. Dist. 15, 1993—; bus. owner, carpenter. Address: 507 E Spruce Olathe KS 66061*

TOPPER, ROBERT QUINN, theoretical chemist; b. Greeley, Colo., July 1, 1963; s. Paul Quinn Topper and Elizabeth Ann (Roberts) Kingston. BS in Physics and Chemistry, Fla. State U., 1986; MPhil in Phys. Chemistry, Yale U., 1989, PhD in Theoretical Physical Chemistry, 1990. Grad. rsch. asst. Yale U., New Haven, Conn., 1986-90; postdoctoral fellow, Minn. Supercomputing Inst. U. Minn., Mpls., 1990—. Contbr. articles to profl. jours. Robert B. Flint fellow Yale U., 1989, Kent fellow, 1986; recipient Boettcher scholarship, Fla. State U., 1985, Acad. Leadership award, 1986. Mem. Am. Chem. Soc., Am. Physical Soc., Alpha Chi Sigma.

TOPPIN, SCOTT A., agricultural engineer; b. North Adams, Mass., July 14, 1954. BS in Agrl. Engring., Iowa State U., 1977. Registered profl. engr., Iowa. Project engr. John Deere Product Engring. Ctr., Waterloo, Iowa, 1973—. Leader coun. Boy Scouts, Waterloo, 1988—. Mem. Am. Soc. Agrl. Engrs. Office: John Deere Product Engring PO Box 8000 Waterloo IA 50704-8000

TOREN, BRIAN KEITH, futures and research executive; b. St. Paul, Jan. 8, 1935; s. Clarence August and Ann (Penner) T.; divorced; children: Sean Marshall, Kisten Kaye. BBA, U. Minn., 1970. Programmer Sperry Corp., Mpls., 1957-67, sales support staff, 1968-71; site mgr. Sperry Corp., Atlantic City, 1972-76; mktg. cons. Sperry Corp., Mpls., 1976-83, comm. svc. support cons., 1983-86; pres., cons. Internat. Robot, Mpls., 1982—; mgr. quality analysis and support Unisys, Mpls., 1986—, comm. project mgr., 1987-91; v.p. Anticipatory Scis. Inc., St. Paul, 1991—; also bd. dirs.; assoc., workshop guide Fissure Corp., 1994—. Bd. dirs. Minn. Citizens on Line. Mem. Soc. Gen. Systems Rsch. Minn. (contbr. monthly column 1981-88), Minn. Futurists (past pres., 1986-88, contbr. monthly column 1986—, bd. dirs.). Home and Office: 2441 Dupont Ave S Minneapolis MN 55405-2725

TORF, PHILIP R., lawyer, pharmacist; b. Chgo., Aug. 4, 1952; m. Donna Torf; 3 children. BS, U. Ill., 1976; JD, John Marshall Law Sch., 1984. Dem. candidate 10th dist. Ill. U.S. House of Reps., 1996. Jewish. Office: PO Box 7001 Deerfield IL 60015*

TORGERSON, JIM, state legislator; m. Analene Torgerson; 4 children. BS, Minot State U. Operator restaurant and marina Ray, N.D.; mem. from dist. 2 N.D. State Ho. of Reps., Bismarck, 1993—, mem. edn. and natural resources coms. Office: HC 1 Box 22 Ray ND 58849*

TORGERSON, LARRY KEITH, lawyer; b. Albert Lea, Minn., Aug. 25, 1935; s. Fritz G. and Lu (Hillman) T. BA, Drake U., 1958, MA, 1960, LLB, 1963, JD, 1968; MA, Iowa U., 1962; cert., The Hague (The Netherlands) Acad. Internat. Law, 1965, 69; LLM, U. Minn., 1969, Columbia U., 1971, U. Mo., 1976; PMD, Harvard U., 1973, EdM, 1974. Bar: Minn. 1964, Wis. 1970, Iowa 1970, U.S. Tax Ct. 1971, U.S. Supreme Ct. 1972, U.S. Dist. Ct. Minn. 1964, U.S. Dist. Ct. (no. dist.) Iowa 1971, U.S. Dist. Ct. (ea. dist.) Wis. 1981, U.S. Ct. Appeals (8th cir.) 1981. Asst. corp. counsel 1st Bank Stock Corp. (88 Banks) Mpls., 1963-67; asst. corp. counsel 1st. Svc. Corp., (27 ins. agys., computer subs.) Mpls., 1965-67; v.p., trust officer Nat. City Bank, Mpls., 1967-69; sr. mem. Torgerson Law Firm, Northwood, Iowa, 1969-87; trustee, gen. counsel Torgerson Farms, Northwood, 1977—, Redbirch Farms, Kensett, Iowa, 1987—, Sunburst Farms, Grafton, Iowa, 1987—, Gold Dust Farms, Bolan, Iowa, 1988—, Torgerson Grain Storage, Bolan, 1988—, Indian Summer Farms, Bolan, 1991—, Sunset Farms, Bolan, 1992—, Sunrise Farms, Grafton, 1994—; CEO, gen. counsel Internat. Investments, Mpls., 1983-96, Transoceanic, Mpls., 1987-96, Torgerson Capital, Northwood, 1996—, Torgerson Investments, Northwood, 1984—, Torgerson Properties, Northwood, 1987—. Recipient All-Am. Journalism award, Thomas Arkle Clark Outstanding Achievement award, Dennis E. Brumfield Outstanding Achievement award, Johnny B. Guy Outstanding Leadership award, Silver Bullet Outstanding Achievement award Drake ATO; named one of Outstanding Young Men of Am. U.S. Jaycees, Hon. Rotarian; Hagen scholar, Honor Scholarship. Mem. ABA, Am. Judicature Soc., Iowa Bar Assn., Minn. Bar Assn., Wis Bar Assn., Hennepin County Bar Assn., Mensa, Drake Student-Faculty Coun., Drake Student Alumni Coun. (chmn.), Jaycees, Harvard Bus. Sch. Study (pres., exec. com., univ. editor in chief), Psi Chi, Circle K (pres. local chpt.), Phi Alpha Delta, Omicron Delta Kappa (pres. local chpt.), Pi Kappa Delta (pres. local chpt.), Alpha Tau Omega (pres.local chpt., Silver Bullet Outstanding Leadership award), Pi Delta Epsilon (founder, chpt. pres.), Alpha Kappa Delta, Alpha Scholastic Hon. (U. editor-in-chief), Harvard Bus. Sch. Exec. Com. (U. editor-in-chief). Lutheran.

TORGERSON, LINDA MARIE, city clerk, librarian; b. Durand, Wis., June 22, 1960; d. Orville Melvin and Margaret Irene (Lane) T.; m. Neil Ray Loewenhagen, Oct. 28, 1978 (div. Dec. 1988); children: Lucas Ray, Adam Orville. Grad., Durand (Wis.) H.S. Cert. libr., Wis. Dep. city clk., treas. City of Alma, Wis., 1982-88, city clk., treas., 1988—; libr. Alma Pub. Libr., 1982—; bd. dirs. Winding Rivers Libr. Sys. Adv. Bd., Alma. Mem. Wis. Mcpl. Clks. Assn. (Silver award 1995). Lutheran. Office: City of Alma 314 Main St N Alma WI 54610

TORGERSON, THOMAS WAYNE, software developer; b. Phoenix, July 16, 1949; s. Wallace Ben and Esther Louise T.; m. Chris Ann Benson, Jan. 21, 1984; children: Carissa, Kendra. AD, Nicollet Coll. Computer specialist USDA, Missoula, Mont.; programmer NCR, Mpls., Ctrl. Data Corp., Mpls.; owner, software developer Brainwake Devel., Mpls. Author: Visual Basic 3.0 Professional Programming, 1994. Mem. AOL. Home and office: 4749 Georgia Ave N Crystal MN 55428

TORNEDEN, CONNIE JEAN, bank executive; b. Tonganoxie, Kans., Sept. 14, 1955; d. Byron Calvin and Edna Jeannette (Keck) Swain; m. Lawrence Dale Torneden, Sept. 18, 1976; 1 child, James Milton. Bus. cert., Kansas City C.C., Kans., 1974; student, Nat. Compliance Sch., Norman, Okla., 1984. Adminstrv. sec. to chmn. of bd., pres. First State Bank and Trust, Tonganoxie, 1974-80, asst. cashier, 1981-83, asst. v.p. and compliance officer, 1984—, bank security officer, 1989-95. Lobbyist, treas. 24-40 Hwy. Task Force, Leavenworth, Kans., 1989-91; bd. dirs., sec. Reno Cemetery Assn., Tonganoxie, 1986—; co-founder Tonganoxie Days, chmn., 1986, 88-93, 95-96; grad. So. Leavenworth County Leadership Devel., 1991. Mem. Am. Bus. Women's Assn. (treas. 1986-87, Woman of Yr. award Twilight chpt. 1994), Mid-Am. Dairymen Assn. (sec. 1978-80), Nat. Assn. Old West Gunfighter Teams (nat. champions 1989, 90), Linwood Grange (5th and 6th degrees 1978), Tonganoxie C. of C. (sec. 1983-86, 92-93, pres. 1986, 88, 89, 96, v.p. 1995, Mem. of Yr. award 1990, 92), Tonganoxie Jaycees (sec. 1991). Democrat. Mem. Soc. of Friends. Office: First State Bank and Trust 4th and Bury PO Box 219 Tonganoxie KS 66086

TORNO, RANDALL C., engineering executive; b. Detroit, Apr. 26, 1949. AS, Indsl. Tech. Sch., 1978. Tool and dye maker Ford Motor Corp., Dearborn, Mich., 1975-88; product engr. Jenkins Equipment Co., Dexter, Mich., 1988-93, engring. mgr., 1993—. Stage set-up man Cmty. Playhouse, Saline and Ann Arbor, Mich., 1993—. With U.S. Army, 1969-71. Mem. Soc. Mfg. Engring. Home: 4285 Hawthorn Pl Ann Arbor MI 48103-9454

TOROK, JOHN ANTHONY, III, dentist, financial analyst, portfolio manager; b. Cin., July 16, 1952; s. John Anthony Jr. and Anne Champ (Busch) T.; m. Jacquelyn Ann Zeiser, Aug. 26, 1977; children: Amanda, Morgan. BS in Biology with honors, U. Cin., 1974; DDS, Ohio State U., 1977; MBA in Fin., U. Cin., 1986, postgrad. in law, 1986—. Gen. practice dentistry Cin., 1977—; pres. Torok Investment Counsel, 1989—; gen. ptnr. Anthony Alexander and Assocs., 1989—. Cardio Pulmonary Resuscitation instr. Am. Heart Assn., Lake County, Ill., 1977-79. Served to lt. USN, 1977-79. Recipient Disting. Service award Lake County Heart Assn., 1979, Disting. Service award United Appeal Assn, 1981; named one of Outstanding Young Men Am., U.S. Jaycees, Cin., 1983. Mem. ADA, Ohio Dental Assn., Cin. Dental Soc., Assn. Am. Mil. Surgeons, Ohio State U. Alumni Assn. for Dentists, Mensa. Republican. Roman Catholic. Club: U. Cin. Vets. Lodge: KC.

TOROK, RAYMOND PATRICK, aluminum company executive; b. Cleve., Aug. 30, 1946; s. Leonard Jack and Patricia (Harding) T.; m. Kathleen Mary Dunda, July 12, 1975; children: Rebecca, Michael, Melissa. BA, John Carroll U., Cleve., 1969; MBA, Butler U., Indpls., 1980. With Alcoa Corp., 1968—; sales and mktg. mgr. Alcoa Corp., Vancouver, Wash., 1979-81; mktg. mgr. Alcoa Corp., Lafayette, Ind., 1971-83; mktg. and sales mgr. Alcoa Corp., Lafayette, 1983-87, gen. mgr. aerospace and specialty products div., 1987-92, v.p. and gen. mgr. aerospace div., 1992—; pres., CEO Phila. Gear Corp., 1995—. Mem. Lafayette C. of C. (bd. dirs. 1988), Lafayette Country Club (bd. dirs. 1987—). Home: 1210 Hunt Seat Dr Lower Gwynedd PA 19002-1316

TOROK, STEPHEN, information science educator, writer, historian; b. Budapest, Hungary, Aug. 2, 1915; came to U.S., 1951; s. Matthias and Julianna (Sallay) T.; m. Claire Banyay, July 26, 1941; children: Stephen, Andrew, Martin, Leslie, Peter. BEd, State Tchrs. Inst., Budapest, 1934; MS in Libr. Sci., Case Western Res. U., 1960; MA, SUNY, Oswego, 1970; D of Info. Sci., SUNY, Geneseo, 1976; cert. ferrous metallurgy, Pa. State U., 1958; degree in ethnicity edn., Queens Coll., 1975. Cert. electronic data processor; spl. and med. libr. Editor Fiatal Tanító MATOE-Tchr.'s Assn., Budapest, 1936-39; freelance writer Budapest, 1939-42; lit. lector Hungarian Nat. Radio, Budapest, 1942-45; contbr., rschr. Cath. Hungarian Sunday Immigrant's Press, Cleve. and Youngstown, Ohio, 1946-87; instr. Youngstown State U., 1957-63; sci. bibliographer U. Vt. Sch. Medicine, Burlington, 1963-66; coord. spl. projects SUNY, Oswego, 1966-82; cons. Informatics Cons. Ltd., DeKalb and North Port, Ill./Fla., 1987—; adj. prof., lectr. Syracuse

(N.Y.) U., 1969-81; micromedia cons. SUNY, Oswego, 1967-83. Author: History of Hungarian Catholics in U.S., 1978; media reviewer: (filmed media criticism) Libr. Jour., 1970-80. Com. mem. United Univ. Profs., N.Y., 1973—, Nat. Reps., Fla. and nat. brs., 1979—. With Hungarian Army, 1941-44. Recipient literary cultural award Hungarian Min. Pres. Off., 1943, Ethnicity Teaching award Health Ed. Welfare Dept., 1975, Immigration Res. award Am. Hungarian Cath. Soc., 1976; study grantee Spl. Librs. Assn., 1959, fed. grantee, 1975. Mem. Assn. Info. Mgmt., Com. of Active Ret. Academics (del.). Roman Catholic. Office: Informatics Cons Ltd 3303 Greenwood Acres Dr De Kalb IL 60115

TORREGROSA, HECTOR LUIS, JR., state agency adjudicator; b. Ponce, P.R., Aug. 16, 1957; s. Hector Luis and Violeta (Ramos) T.; m. Grisela Margarita Ayala, June 10, 1980; children: Hector Luis III, Violeta M., Victoria M. BA, U. P.R., 1979; postgrad., Sangamon State U., 1979-82; student, Temple U., 1979. Cert. disability examiner. Pres. Internat. Student Assn., Sangamon State U., Springfield, Ill., 1981; acctg. clk. Sangamon State U. Employees Credit Union, Springfield, 1982-85, bd. dirs., 1984-85; disability claims adjudicator II Ill. Dept. Rehab. Svcs., Springfield, 1985—. Editor (newsletter) Ill. Assn. Hispanic State Employees, 1992-94. Mem. Nat. Assn. Disability Examiners, Ill. Assn. Minorities in Govt., Ill. Assn. Hispanic State Employees (bd. dirs. 1991-95), Ill. Union of Social Svc. Employees (profl. rep. local 2000 1991-95, chief steward 1995-96), Springfield Pet Bird Club (recycling coord. 1991-95, v.p. 1993, newsletter editor 1993-95, sec. 1995-96). Roman Catholic.

TORRENS, PEGGY JEAN, technical school coordinator; b. El Dorado, Kans., Oct. 7, 1952; d. Wayne E. and Evelyn M. (Hornbostel) Clark; m. Dennis L. Torrens, May 3, 1975; children: Jason L., Jennifer L. BS in Edn., Emporia State U., 1974, MS, 1975. Cert. secondary tchr., Kans. Instr. reading Burlington (Kans.) High Sch., 1974-75, Lowther Mid. Sch., Emporia, Kans., 1975-76; coord. resouce ctr., tech. prep coord. Flint Hills Tech. Coll., Emporia, Kans., 1976—; TQM team leader Flint Hills Tech. Coll.; mem., chairperson Profl. Devel. Coun., Emporia, Kans., 1990—, applied curriculum inservice presenter; inservice presenter Nat. Tech. Prep., 1996. Author software programs; reviewer workbook Modern Reading, 1982. Community leader Lyon County 4-H, Emporia, 1988—. Mem. NEA, Am. Vocat. Assn. Democrat. Lutheran. Office: Flint Hills Tech Coll 3301 W 18th Ave Emporia KS 66801-5957

TORRISON, WILLIAM RAHR, photographer; b. Two Rivers, Wis., July 27, 1945; s. John William and Mary Elizabeth (Spindler) T.; m. JoAnn Larson, Oct. 14, 1968 (div. July 1970). Student, Bryant & Stratton Bus. Coll., 1964-66, U. So. Calif., L.A., 1981. tchr. Internat. Meditation Soc., Manitowoc, Wis., 1975-80; lectr. Manitowoc Pub. Schs., 1980-85; photographer Project Ocean Search, Maupiti, South Pacific, 1981. Mem. Rep. Presdl. Task Force, Woodland Dunes Nature Ctr., Capital Civic Ctr., Manitowoc Maritime Mus. Sgt. USAF, 1966-70. Mem. Cousteau Soc., Manitowoc County Hist. Soc., Fraternal Order of Eagles.

TORSHEN, JEROME HAROLD, lawyer; b. Chgo., Nov. 27, 1929; s. Jack and Lillian (Futterman) T.; m. Kay Pomerance, June 19, 1966; children: Jonathan, Jacqueline. BS, Northwestern U., 1951; JD, Harvard U., 1955. Bar: Ill. 1955, U.S. Dist. Ct. (no. dist.) Ill. 1955, U.S. Ct. Appeals (7th cir.) 1958, (8th cir.) 1961, (9th and D.C. cirs.) 1972, U.S. Supreme Ct. 1972. Assoc. Clausen, Hirsh & Miller, Chgo., 1955-62; pres. Jerome H. Torshen, Ltd., Chgo., 1963-87, Torshen, Schoenfield & Spreyer Ltd., Chgo., 1987-93, Torshen, Spreyer & Garmisa, Ltd., Chgo., 1994—; spl. asst. atty. gen. Ill., 1965-70; assoc. counsel Spl. Commn. Ill. Supreme Ct., 1969; counsel Ill. Legis. Redistricting Commn., 1971-72; spl. state's atty. Cook County, Ill., 1979-81, 83-86; spl. counsel Met. San. Dist. Greater Chgo., 1977-81, 84-88. Contbr. articles to profl. jours. Counsel Cook County Dem. Cen. Com., Chgo., 1982-87; bd. dirs. Jewish Family and Community Svc., Parents' Coun. Washington U., St. Louis, 1988-92; mem. collectors' group Mus. Contemporary Art; sustaining fellow Art Int. Chgo. Served with U.S. Army, 1951-52. Recipient Torch of Learning award Am. Friends of Hebrew U., 1985, Outstanding Civic Duty award, Union League Club of Chgo., 1967. Fellow Am. Coll. Trial Lawyers; mem. ABA, Chgo. Bar Assn. (commn. on jud. evaluation 1986-90), Bar Assn. 7th Cir. Appellate Lawyers Assn. (founder, pres. 1976-77), Decalogue Soc., Standard Club, Sixty Club of Chgo. Office: 105 W Adams St Ste 3200 Chicago IL 60603-6201

TOSCANO, JAMES VINCENT, medical institute administration; b. Passaic, N.J., Aug. 8, 1937; s. William V. and Mary A. (DeNigris) T.; m. Sharon Lee Bowers; children: Shawn, Lauren, David Brendan, Dania. A.B. summa cum laude, Rutgers U., 1959; M.A., Yale U., 1960. Lectr. Wharton Sch., U. Pa., 1961-64; chief opinion analyst Pa. Opinion Poll, 1962-64; mng. dir. World Press Inst., St. Paul, 1964-68; exec. dir. World Press Inst., 1968-72; dir. devel. Macalester Coll., St. Paul, 1972-74; v.p. resource devel. and public affairs Mpls. Soc. Fine Arts, 1974-79; pres. Minn. Mus. Art, 1979-81; exec. v.p. Park Nicollet Med. Found., 1981-95; corp. sec. Park Nicollet Med. Ctr., 1983-86; sr. v.p. Am. Med. Ctrs., Inc., 1985-87; exec. v.p. Inst. for Rsch. and Edn. Health Sys. Minn., Mpls., 1996—; also bd. dirs. Inst. for Rsch. and Edn., Health Sys. Minn.; adj. prof. sch. of mgmt. U. St. Thomas, 1989—. Author: The Chief Elected Official in the Penjerdel Region, 1964; co-author, co-editor: The Integration of Political Communities, 1964. Bd. dirs., faculty mem. World Press Ins., 1972—; bd. dirs., chmn. Southside Newspaper Mpls., 1975-79; chmn. com. to improve student behavior St. Paul Pub. Schs., 1977-79; bd. dirs. Planned Parenthood St. Paul, 1965-72; emeritus dir. Help Enable Alcoholics Receive Treatment; mem. St. Paul Heritage Preservation Commn., 1979-82, vice chmn., 1981; mem. Citizens Adv. Com. on Cable Comm.; bd. dirs. Citizens League, 1980, Park Nicollet Med. Found., 1981-95, African-Am. Culture Ctr., 1979-82, Minn. Composers Forum, 1981-85, St. Paul Chamber Orch., 1976-80, 83-89, United Theol. Sem., 1985-88; bd. dirs. emeritus, mem. exec. com. Med. Alley Assn., 1986—; mem. task force on tech. assessment Med. Alley, 1992-93; mem. health affairs adv. com. Acad. Health Ctr. U. Minn., 1988-95; bd. dirs. Mother Cabrini House, 1985-92, Minn. Civil Justice Coalition, 1987-91, also chmn.; chmn. Gov.'s Task Force on Health Care Promotion, 1985-86, mem. Gov.'s Com. Promotion Health Care Resources, 1986-87; chmn. bd. Minn. Fin. Counseling Svcs., Inc., 1990-93; mem. task force cost effectiveness Med. Alley, 1994-95. Mem. Minn. Newspaper Found. (bd. dirs. 1987-92), Minn. Coun. Nonprofits (bd. dirs. 1989-95, bd. mem. Plymouth Music series 1993-96, alt. Minn. Healthcare Commn., 1993-95, mem. Minn. Healthcare Commn., 1995—, chair task force on med. edn. and rsch. costs 1994-96; chair com. on med. rsch. and edn. costs, 1996—, liaison health tech. adv. com. 1993), Skylight Club, Informal Club. Address: 1982 Summit Ave Saint Paul MN 55105-1460 Office: Inst for Rsch and Edn Health Sys Minn 3800 Park Nicollet Blvd Minneapolis MN 55416

TOSINO, CLAIR GERARD, nursing administrator; b. Mansfield, Ohio, Oct. 7, 1960; s. Claro T. and Fely Q. Tosino; children: Evan R., Carrington M. BSN, Ohio State U., 1983; MS, Cen. Mich. U., Mt. Pleasant, 1990; postgrad., Union Inst., Cin., 1991—. RN Cert. pediatrics ANA, critical care RN AACN; cert. ACLS Am. Heart Assn., pediatric advanced life support Am. Heart Assn. Staff RN pediatrics Doctors Hosp. North, Columbus, Ohio, 1984-86, staff RN critical care, 1986-88, asst. coord. MICU, 1988-89; nursing instr. Columbus State Community Coll., 1989; dir. patient care activities Doctors Hosp. West, Columbus, 1989-91; asst. prof. Ohio Wesleyan U., Delaware, 1991-93; dir. critical care Columbus (Ohio) Cmty. Hosp., 1993-95; v.p. patient svcs. Columbus Cmty. Hosp., 1995—; adj. faculty Capital U., Columbus, 1991; chmn. recruitment and retetnion com. Doctors Hosp., Columbus, 1991; mem. pediatric liaison group Children's Hosp., Columbus; chmn. quality coun., chmn. nursing quality mgmt. Columbus (Ohio) Cmty. Hosp. Mem. AACN, Am. Assn. for the Care of Children, Ohio Orgn. Nurse Execs., Gestalt Inst. of Ctrl. Ohio, Gestalt Inst. Cleve., Doctors Hosp. Mgmt. Assn., Ohio State U. Alumni Assn., Ctrl. Mich. U. Alumni Assn., Kappa Sigma. Roman Catholic. Office: Columbus Cmty Hosp 1430 S High St Columbus OH 43207

TOSSETT, GLORIA VAY, educator, administrator; b. Hamar, N.D., Jan. 31, 1926; d. Oscar and Lena Bernice (Ellingson) Tossett; m. Arthur Andrew Borstad, Dec. 29, 1946 (div. 1968); children: Stafne Tossett Borstad, Ivy Vay Borstad. BS in Edn. and Religion, Concordia Coll., Moorhead, Minn., 1968; MS in Ednl. Adminstrn., N.D. State U., Fargo, 1972; student, Jamestown (N.D.) Coll., 1981-82. Sch. coord. Harding County Schs., Buffalo, S.D., 1972-73; pub. sch. supt. Balfour (N.D.) Sch., 1975-76, Flaxton (N.D.) Sch., 1978-79; pub. sch. supt., prin. and bus. tchr. Buchanan (N.D.) Pub. Sch., 1981-82; tchr., curriculum coord. Little Hoop C.C., Ft. Totten, N.D., 1983-84; bilingual curriculum coord., adminstr., instr. art and music Trenton, N.D., 1986-89; mem. Spl. Edn. Bd., Burke County, N.D., 1978-79, Stutsman County, N.D., 1981-82. Author: (children's lit.) Angel Album, 1989, Twuddleville Mouse, 1989. Candidate for state supt. of pub. instrn., N.D., 1984. Mem. Am. Assn. Ret. Persons, Order Eastern Star. Home: Box 115 Sheyenne ND 58374 Office: Rainbow Ranch RR 1 Box 77 Warwick ND 58381

TOTZKE, CHRISTOPHER N., supervisor supplier quality; b. Detroit, July 15, 1944. BS in Engring., Mich. Tech. U., 1967. Material engr. Detroit Diesel Corp., 1972-74, supr. supplier quality, 1974—; metallurgist Chrysler Corp., 1974. Mem. Am. Soc. Metals, Am. Soc. Quality Control. Home: 45157 Pinetree Dr Plymouth MI 48170-3842 Office: Detroit Diesel Corp 13400 W Outer Dr Detroit MI 48239-1309

TOTZKE, JAMES RICHARD, accounting and information systems administrator; b. Appleton, Wis., Aug. 22, 1968; s. Eldred Arthur and Marian Bertha (Rohrdanz) T. BBA in Acctg. and MIS, U. Wis., Oshkosh, 1991. CPA, Wis.; cert. internal auditor; cert. mgmt. acct. Acct. Sentry Ins., Stevens Point, Wis., 1991-93; sr. mgmt. cons. Schenck & Assocs. S.C., Appleton, 1993-95; acctg. and MIS mgr. T & J Mfg., Inc., Oshkosh, 1995—. Republican. Roman Catholic. Home: W 6075 Golden Ct Appleton WI 54915

TOUHILL, BLANCHE MARIE, university chancellor, history-education educator; b. St. Louis, Mo., July 1, 1931; d. Robert and Margaret (Walsh) Van Dillen; m. Joseph M. Touhill, Aug. 29, 1959. BA in History, St. Louis U., 1953, MA in Geography, 1954, PhD in History, 1962. Prof. history and edn. U. Mo., St. Louis, 1965-73, assoc. dean faculties, 1974-76, assoc. vice chancellor for acad. affairs, 1976-87, vice chancellor, 1987-90, chancellor, 1991—; bd. dirs. Boatmen's Nat. Bank of St. Louis, Barnes-Jewish Christian Health Hosps. Conglomerate. Author: William Smith O'Brien and His Irish Revolutionary Companions in Penal Exile, 1981, The Emerging University UM-St. Louis, 1963-83, 1985; editor: Readings in American History, 1970, Varieties of Ireland, 1976; adv. editor Victorian Periodicals Rev. Bd. dirs. Sister City Internat., Am. Coun. Fgn. Rels., St. Louis Forum, Network Bd., Mo. State Hist. Soc., 1989—, Mo. Bot. Garden, 1980, St. Louis Symphony Soc., 1993—. Named Outstanding Educator St. Louis chpt. Urban League, 1976; recipient Leadership award St. Louis YWCA, 1986. Mem. Nat. Assn. State Univs. and Land Grant Colls. (exec. com. 1988—), Am. Com. on Irish Studies (pres. 1991—), Phi Kappa Phi, Alpha Sigma Lambda. Office: U Missouri- St Louis Office of the Chancellor 8001 Natural Bridge Rd Saint Louis MO 63121-4499*

TOURTILLOTT, ELEANOR ALICE, nurse, educational consultant; b. North Hampton, N.H., Mar. 28, 1909; d. Herbert Shaw and Sarah (Fife) T. Diploma Melrose Hosp. Sch. Nursing, Melrose, Mass., 1930; BS, Columbia U., 1948, MA, 1949; edn. specialist Wayne State U., 1962. RN. Gen. pvt. duty nurse, Melrose, Mass., 1930-35; obstet. supr. Samaritan Hosp., Troy, N.Y., 1935-36, Meml. Hosp., Niagara Falls, N.Y., 1937-38, Lawrence Meml. Hosp., New London, Conn., 1939-42, New Eng. Hosp. for Women and Children, Boston, 1942-43; dir. H. W. Smith Sch. Practical Nursing, Syracuse, N.Y., 1949-53; founder, dir. assoc. degree nursing program Henry Ford Community Coll., Dearborn, Mich., 1953-74; dir. pioneering use of learning techs. via mixed media USPHS, 1966-71; prin. cons., initial coord. Wayne State U. Coll. Nursing, Detroit, 1975-78; cons. curriculum design, modular devel., instructional media Tourtillott Cons., Inc., Dearborn, Mich., 1974—; condr. numerous workshops on curriculum design, instructional media at various colls., 1966—; mem. Mich. Bd. Nursing, 1966-73, chmn., 1970-72, mem. rev. com. for constrn. nurse tng. facilities, div. nursing USPHS, 1967-70, mem. nat. adv. coun. on nurse tng., Dept. Health Edn. and Welfare, 1972-76. Author: Commitment-A Lost Characteristic, 1982; contbg. co-author: Patient Assessment-History and Physical Examination, 1975-78; contbr. chpts., articles, speeches to profl. pubs. Served to capt. Nurse Corps, U.S. Army, 1943-47; ETO. Recipient Disting. Alumnae award Tchrs. Coll. Columbia U., 1974, Spl. tribute 77th Legislature Mich., 1974, Disting. Alumnae award Wayne State U., 1975, Disting. Service award Henry Ford Community Coll., 1982; established and endowed Eleanor Tourtillott Outstanding Student Nurse of Yr. award at Henry Ford C.C., 1993. Mem. DAR, ANA, Nat. League Nursing (chmn. steering com. dept. assoc. degree programs 1965-67, bd. dirs. 1965-67, 71-73, mem. assembly constituent leagues 1971-73, council assoc. degree programs citation 1974, Mildred Montag Excellence in Leadership award coun. assoc. degree programs 1994), Mich. League for Nursing (pres. 1969-71), Mich. Acad. Sci., Arts and Letters, Am. Legion, Tchrs. Coll. Alumnae Assn., Wayne State U. Alumnae Assn., Phi Lambda Theta, Kappa Delta Pi.

TOURVILLE, JAMES E., writer, automotive worker; b. St. Louis, Aug. 4, 1950; s. Edward Earl and Camille Constance (Wozniak) T. BA in Liberal Arts, Florissant Valley C.C., 1971. Assoc. mgr. Venture Stores, Florissant, Mo., 1968-76; technician Fletcher Reinhardt, Earth City, Mo., 1977-82; machine operator Alco Controls, St. Louis, 1984-95; assembler Chrysler Motors, Fenton, Mo., 1995—. With Mo. Nat. Guard, 1970-76. Mem. Science Fiction Writers of Am., Nat. Space Soc., Nat. Parks Assn., St. Louis Science Ctr., Nature Conservancy, Planetary Soc., Library of Congress. Home: 2260 Derhake Rd Florissant MO 63033

TOVEY, BRAMWELL, conductor, composer; b. London, July 11, 1953; s. Bernard Tovey and Joan Barker Grasham; 1 child, Benjamin Bernard. BMus, London U., 1977; LLD (hon.), U. Winnipeg, Can., 1993. Music dir. Scottish Ballet, Glasgow, 1978-82; prin. conductor Sadler's Wells Royal Ballet, London, 1984-88; artistic dir. New D'Oyly Carte Opera, London, 1987-90, Winnipeg Symphony, 1990-96; founder DuMaurier Arts Ltd. Winnipeg New Music Festival, 1992—; prin. condr. English Sinfonia, 1996—; bd. dirs. Assn. Can. Orch., Tor.; hon. assoc. Royal Acad. Music, London, 1991. Composer (ballet): Cinderella, 1977, The Snow Queen, 1986; composer of orchestral brass and chamber music. Adv. bd. dirs. Salvation Army, Winnipeg, 1992—. Recipient Can. 125 Medal Govt. Can., 1993. Office: Winnipeg Symphony Orch, 555 Main St Rm 101, Winnipeg, MB Canada R3B 1C3

TOWER, MICHAEL J., management consultant; b. Mt. Clare, N.J., Mar. 6, 1959. BA in Acctg., Notre Dame U., 1981; M in Mgmt., Northwestern U., 1987. CPA, Ill. Sr. auditor Arthur Anderson, Chgo., 1981-85; v.p. A.T. Karney, Inc., Chgo., 1987—.

TOWNER, CAROLYN H., political scientist; b. Ravenna, Ohio, Jan. 10, 1948. BA in Polit. Sci., U. Akron, 1974, MA, 1979. Registered lobbyist. Exec. dir. Joint Commn. Agt. Rule Rev. Ohio Gen. Assembly, Columbus, 1979-84; assoc. dir. dept. legislation Ohio State Med. Assn., Columbus, 1984-88; v.p. Ohio Capitol Policy Cons., Columbus, 1988—. Bd. dirs. Ohio Youth and Govt., Columbus, 1993—. Fellow Population Inst., 1974; Louella Haynes Polit. scholar U. Akron, 1973. Mem. Ohio Lobbyist Assn. (bd. dirs. 1992), Little Turtle Country Club, Capital Club. Office: Ohio Capitol Policy Cons 176 E State St Columbus OH 43215-4310

TOWNSEND, EARL CUNNINGHAM, JR., lawyer, writer; b. Indpls., Nov. 9, 1914; s. Earl Cunningham and Besse (Kuhn) T.; m. Emily Macnab, Apr. 3, 1947 (dec. Mar. 1988); children: Starr, Vicki M. (Mrs. Christopher Katterjohn), Julia E. (Mrs. Edward Goodrich Dunn Jr.), Earl Cunningham III, Clyde G. Student, De Pauw U., 1932-34; AB, U. Mich., 1936, JD, 1939. Bar: Ind. 1939, Mich. 1973, U.S. Supreme Ct. 1973, U.S. Ct. Appeals (4th, 5th, 6th, 7th cirs.), U.S. Dist. Ct. (no. and so. dists.) Ind., U.S. Dist. Ct. (ea. dist.) Va., U.S. Dist. Ct. (ea. dist.) Mich. Sr. ptnr. Townsend & Townsend, Indpls., 1941-64, Townsend, Hovde & Townsend, Indpls., 1964-84, Townsend & Townsend, Indpls., 1984—; dep. prosecutor, Marion County, Ind., 1942-44; radio-TV announcer WIRE, WFBM, WFBM-TV, Indpls., 1940-53, 1st TV announcer Indpls. 500 mile race, 1949, 50; Big Ten basketball referee, 1940-47; lectr. trial tactics U. Notre Dame, Ind. U., U. Mich., 1968-79; chmn. faculty seminar on personal injury trials Ind. U. Sch. Law, U. Notre Dame Sch. Law, Valparaiso Sch. Law, 1981; mem. Com. to Revise Ind. Supreme Ct. Pattern Jury Instrns., 1975-83; lectr. Trial Lawyers 30 Yrs. Inst., 1986; counsel atty gen., 1988-92. Author: Birdstones of the North American Indian, 1959; editor: Am. Assn. Trial Lawyers Am. Jour., 1964-88; contbr. articles to legal and archeol. jours.; composer (waltz) Moon of Halloween. Trustee Cathedral High Sch., Indpls., Eiteljorg Mus. Am. Indian and Western Art, Cale J. Holder Scholarship Found. Ind. U. Law Sch.; life trustee, bd. dirs., mem. fin. and bldg. coms. Indpls. Mus. Art; life trustee Ind. State Mus.; founder, dir. Meridian St. Found.; mem. dean's coun. Ind. U.; founder, life fellow Roscoe Pound/Am. Trial Lawyers Found., Harvard U.; fellow Meth. Hosp. Found. Recipient Ind. Univ. Writers Conf. award, 1960, Hanson H. Anderson medal of honor Arsenal Tech. Schs., Indpls., 1971; named to Coun. Sagamores of Wabash, 1969; Rector scholar, 1934, Ind. Basketball Hall of Fame; hon. chief Black River-Swan Creek Saginaw-Chippewa Indian tribe. Fellow Internat. Acad. Trial Lawyers, Internat. Soc. Barristers, Ind. Bar Found. (life trustee, disting. fellow award); mem. ASCAP, ABA (com. on trial techniques 1964-76, aviation and space 1977—), Assn. Trial Lawyers Am. (v.p.), Ind. State Bar Assn. (Golden Career award 1989), Indpls. Bar Found. (disting. charter 1986), Ind. Trial Lawyers Assn. (pres. 1965, pres. Coll. Fellows 1984-90, Lifetime Achievement award 1992), Am. Bd. Trial Advs. (diplomate, pres. Ind. chpt. 1980-86), Am. Arbitration Assn. (nat. arbitrators panel), Am. Judicature Soc., State Bar of Mich. (Champion of Justice award 1989), Roscommon County Bar Assn., 34th Jud. Cir. Bar Assn., Bar Assn. 7th Fed. Cir. (bd. govs. 1966-68), Mich. Trial Lawyers Assn., Soc. Mayflower Descendants (gov. 1947-49), Ind. Hist. Soc., Marion County/Indpls. Hist. Soc. (bd. dirs.), Key Biscayne C. of C., U. Mich. Pres. Club, U. Mich. Victors Club (founder, charter mem.), Trowel and Brush Soc. (hon.), Genuine Indian Relic Soc. (founder, pres., chmn. frauds com.), The Players Club, Key Biscayne Yacht Club, Columbia Club, Indpls. Athletic Club, Masons (33 degree), Shriners, Delta Kappa Epsilon, Phi Kappa Phi. Republican. Methodist. Home: 5008 N Meridian St Indianapolis IN 46208-2624

TOWNSEND, HAROLD GUYON, JR., publishing company executive; b. Chgo., Apr. 11, 1924; s. Harold Guyon and Anne Louise (Robb) T.; AB, Cornell U., 1948; m. Margaret Jeanne Keller, July 28, 1951; children: Jessica, Julie, Harold Guyon III. Advt. salesman Chgo. Tribune, 1948-51; gen. mgr. Keller-Heartt Co., Clarendon Hills, Ill., 1951-62; pub. Santa Clara (Calif.) Jour., 1962-64; chmn. bd. dirs., pub. Dispatch-Tribune newspaper Townsend Communications, Inc., Kansas City, Mo., 1964—. Chmn., Suburban Newspaper Research Commn., 1974—; dir. Certified Audit Bur. of Circulation, 1968-72. del. Rep. Nat. Conv., 1960; chmn. Mission Hills Rep. Com., 1966-77; bd. dirs. Kansas City Jr. Achievement, 1966-68, Kansas City council Girl Scouts U.S.A., 1969-71, Kansas City council Boy Scouts Am., 1974, Kansas City chpt. ARC, 1973-79, Kansas City Starlight Theater, Clay County (Mo.) Indsl. Commn.; treas., trustee Park Coll., Parkville, Mo., 1970-78. Mem. adv. com. North Kansas City Hosp.; bd. dirs. Taxpayers Research of Mo., 1978—, Nelson Gallery Friends of Art, 1980-85. Served with inf. AUS, World War II. Mem. Kansas City Advt. and Sales Club, Kansas City Press Club, Suburban Press Found. (pres. 1969-71), Suburban Newspapers Am. (pres. 1976-77), Kansas City Printing Industries Assn. (pres., dir.), Printing Industries of Am. (pres. non-heatset web sect. 1980-82), North Kansas City C. of C. (dir., pres. 1964-70), Univ. Assocs. (treas. 1977-80), Sigma Delta Chi, Pi Delta Epsilon, Phi Kappa Psi. Clubs: University (treas. 1977); Indian Hills Country; Hinsdale (Ill.) Golf; Field (Sarasota, Fla.). Home: 23 Compton Ct Prairie Village KS 66208 Office: 7007 NE Parvin Rd Kansas City MO 64117-1532

TOWNSEND, JAMES DOUGLAS, accountant; b. Kokomo, Ind., May 20, 1959; s. Lemon Dale and Diamond Sue (Turner) T.; m. Ariane Antonia Atkins, May 7, 1983 (div. July 1992); 1 child, Bradley Alan; m. Mildred Ann Kurtz, Oct. 18, 1992. Student, Ind. U., 1977, Ind. State U., 1977-78; BS in Acctg. summa cum laude, Ball State U., 1980. CPA, Ind.; cert. mgmt. acct. Acctg. intern Chevrolet Motor Div. Gen. Motors Corp., Muncie, Ind., 1979; staff acct. Price Waterhouse, Indpls., 1980-83, sr. acct., 1983-85, mgr., 1985-88, sr. mgr., 1988-89; contr. Raffensperger, Hughes & Co., Inc., Indpls., 1989-92, asst. treas., 1991-95, asst. v.p., 1991-92, v.p. fin., 1992-95; chief adminstrv. officer Nat City Investments, Inc., Indpls., 1995—; coord. Seek Program Ind. U., Indpls., 1985-86; cons. project bus. Jr. Achievement, Indpls., 1986; treas., asst. sec. Sagamore Funds Trust, 1991-94; treas. Raffensberger Hughes Capitol Corp., 1991-94, RHGP, Inc., 1993-95. Baseball coach Pike Twp. (Ind.) Youth League, 1986-87; cubmaster Pike Twp. Coun. Boy Scouts Am., 1987-88; mem. Pike Twp. Sch. Bd., 1988-92, v.p., 1989-90, pres., 1990-92; bd. dirs. Project I-Star, 1992-94. Fellow Life Mgmt. Inst.; mem. AICPA, Nat. Assn. Accts., Ind. CPA Soc. (vice chmn. edn. com. 1988-89, chmn. 1989-90), Indpls. C. of C. (SKLA exec. coun. 1992-94). Republican. Home: 6825 Hollingsworth Dr Indianapolis IN 46268-2789 Office: Nat City Investments Inc 251 N Illinois St Indianapolis IN 46204-3025

TOWNSEND, RICHARD BLEZARD, clinical psychologist; b. Orange, N.J., Nov. 29, 1951; s. Edward Thomas and Thelma Maye (Blezard) T.; m. Marilyn Ruth Lindsay, Dec/ 1. 1973 (div.); children: Donald, Julia, Jessica; m. Deborah Gaye Martin, June 16, 1988; Misty, Jacinda. BS in Psychology, U. Ala., Birmingham, 1974, MA in Counseling, 1976; EdD in Counseling, Psychology, U. Tenn., 1983. lic. psychologist, N.D. Instr. U. Tenn., Knoxville, 1981; coord. program for neglected children U.S. Dept Health and Welfare, Knoxville, 1979-81; asst. prof. psychology Moorhead (Minn.) State U., 1981-86; clin. psychologist and clinic mgr. LifeQuest Mental Health Clinic St. Joseph Hosp., Dickinson, N.D., 1986—; adj. prof. Dickinson State U., 1991—; pres. adv. bd. Dickinson State U. Nursing Program, 1987—. Bd. dirs. Domestic Violence and Rape Crisis Ctr., Dickinson, 1987—, Day Treatment Adv. Bd. Dickinson Schs., 1990. Mem. N.D. Psychol. Assn. (pres.-elect 1995, pres. 1996). Home: 657 Hillside Dr Dickinson ND 58601-3846 Office: St Josephs Hosp LifeQuest Mental Hlth Clin 30 7th St W Dickinson ND 58601-4335

TOWNSLEY-KULICH, LISA GAIL, mathematics educator; b. Honolulu, June 25, 1960; d. Sidney Joseph and Mary Irmhild (Fuss) Townsley; m. James Kulich, Aug. 21, 1983. BS, Santa Clara (Calif.) U., 1981; MS, Northwestern U., 1983, PhD, 1988. Assoc. prof. math. Benedictine U., Lisle, Ill., 1987—; exam. reader, table leader AP/ETS, Clemson, S.C., 1991—. Author: The DERIVE Calculus Workbook, 1994; contbr. articles to profl. jours.; performer Chgo. Festival Ballet Co. Named to Faculty All Stars, Chgo. Tribune, 1994; NSF/ILI grantee, 1993. Mem. Math. Assn. Am., Assn. for Women in Math., Am. Math. Soc., Phi Beta Kappa, Kappa Mu Epsilon, Alpha Sigma Nu. Democrat. Roman Catholic. Office: Benedictine U 5700 College Rd Lisle IL 60532

TOWSLEE, ARTHUR C., electrical engineer; b. Toledo, Ohio, Aug. 27, 1941. BS, U. Toledo, 1965. Sr. elec. engr. Toledo Scale Co., Westerville, wis., 1983—. Contbr. articles to HamRadio Mag. Mem. Amateur TV in Ctrl. Ohio, Inc. (pres. 1992-93). Republican. Lutheran.

TOWSON, THOMAS D., securities trader; b. 1954. Grad., Western Mich. U., 1977. With Pacific Investment, Chgo., 1977-78, Conti Securities, Chgo., 1978-80, Thomson Mc Kinnon Securities, Chgo., 1980-82, Gelber Group Inc., 1982—; exec. v.p. Gelber Group, Chgo., 1986—. Office: Gelber Group 141 W Jackson Blvd Chicago IL 60604*

TOZER, THEODORE WILLIAM, mortgage company executive; b. Bloomington, Ill., Feb. 3, 1957; s. William Thomas and Joan Marie (Heberlein) T.; m. F. Sandra Williams, Mar. 28, 1981. BS, Ind. U., 1978. CPA, Ill., Ohio.; cert. mgmt. acct. Staff acct. Borg-Warner, Chgo., 1978, Armco, Inc., Middletown, Ohio, 1979; v.p., mgr. investment ops. BancOhio Nat. Bank, Columbus, Ohio, 1979-85; contr. BancOhio Mortgage Co., Columbus, 1985-86, CFO, 1986-89; mgr. mortgage trading Nat. City Mortgage Corp., Miamisburg, Ohio, 1989—; mem. adv. bd. Ohio Housing Fin. Agy., Fed. Home Loan Mortgage Corp.; adv. bd. FNMP, 1994-95. Pres. Springboro Jaycees; big brother Big Bros./Big Sisters Warren and Clinton Counties, 1993—; v.p., 1995, pres. 1996; elder, treas. Covenant Presbyn. Ch. Springboro. Mem. AICPA, Inst. Mgmt. Accts., Fed. Home Loan Mortgage Corp. (adv. bd. 1988-89), Ohio Financing Agy. (adv. bd. 1988-89), Fed. Nat. Mortgage Assn. (adv. bd. 1994—). Home: 8494 Innsbrook Ln Springboro OH 45066-9629 Office: Nat City Mortgage Co 3232 New Market Dr Miamisburg OH 45342

TOZZER, JACK CARL, civil engineer, surveyor; b. Marion, Ohio, Jan. 5, 1922; s. Carl Henry and Henrietta (Schellenbaum) T.; children: Brent Jack,

Hal Jack; m. Aleta C. Lehner, July 14, 1974. BCE, Ohio No. U., 1944. Registered profl. engr., Ohio, Fla., registered surveyor, Ohio. Pres. firm Tozzer & Assocs. Inc., Marion, 1948-85; county engr. Marion County, Ohio, 1964—; city engr. Marion, 1959, Galion, Ohio, 1960-85; cons. civil engr. Mem. cons. bd. Coll. Engring. Ohio No. U., 1970; v.p. Marion Community Improvement Corp.; mem. Marion County Regional Planning Commn. Served with USNR, 1944-46. Recipient Order of Engr. Coll. Engring. Ohio No. U., 1971. Fellow ASCE; mem. NSPE, Marion C. of C., Cons. Engrs. Ohio, Profl. Land Surveyors Ohio, Ohio Hist. Soc., Marion County Hist. Soc. (past dir.), Elks, Delta Sigma Phi. Lutheran. Home: 307 Forest Lawn Blvd Marion OH 43302-5523 Office: Courthouse # 1 Marion OH 43302

TRACEY, TERENCE JOHN, psychology educator; b. Washington, Mar. 2, 1952; s. Gerald A. and Virginia R. (Roscoe) T.; m. Cheelan Bo Linn, Aug. 11, 1979 (div. 1990; children: Beilee, Erin, Cameron; m. Cynthia Glidden, Jan. 1, 1995. BA, Cornell U., 1974; MS in Edn., U. Kans., 1977; PhD, U. Md., 1981. Registered psychologist, Ill., N.Y. Psychologist SUNY, Buffalo, 1981-83; prof. ednl. psychology and psychology U. Ill., Champaign, 1983—, acting assoc. chair dept. ednl. psychology, 1986-89, assoc. chair, dept. ednl. psychology, 1995—; therapist Psychol. Clinic, Champaign, 1984—; cons. VA Med. Ctr., Danville, ill., 1985—. Contbr. chpts. to 6 books and over 80 articles to profl. jours. Fellow APA, Am. Psychol. Soc., Am. Assn. Applied and Preventative Psychology; mem. Am. Ednl. Rsch. Assn. (com. chair 1987-89, Outstanding Rsch. award 1989), Soc. Psychotherapist Rsch., Psychometric Soc. Office: Univ Ill 210 Edn 1310 S 6th St Champaign IL 61820-6925

TRACHT, ALLEN ERIC, electronics executive; b. Bethesda, Md., Aug. 14, 1957; s. Myron Edward and Diane Serena (Goldberg) T.; m. Donna June Carothers, Sept. 14, 1986; children: Michael, Diane, Daniel. BS in Physics and Elec. Engring., MIT, 1979; MSEE, Calif. Inst. Tech., 1980. Biomed. researcher Case Western Res. U., Cleve., 1980-85; exec. engr. IOtech. Inc., Cleve., 1985—; cons. engring. Keithley Instruments, Cleve., 1985. Contbr. articles to profl. jours. NIH grantee Case Western Res. U., 1982. Mem. IEEE, Assn. for Computing Machinery, Sigma Xi, Tau Beta Kappa, Eta Kappa Nu. Home: 3066 Scarborough Rd Cleveland OH 44118-4065

TRACY, ALAN THOMAS, government official; b. Janesville, Wis., May 3, 1947; s. Robert Elmer and Frances Dina (Daane) T.; m. Kris Cunningham; children: Chad, Paul, Sarah. B.S. in Agrl. Econs., Cornell U., Ithaca, N.Y., 1969; M.B.A., U. Wis., 1970. With Tracy & Son Farms, Inc., Janesville, Wis., 1970-81, v.p., 1973-76, pres., 1976-81; gen sales mgr., assoc. adminstr. Dept. Agr., Washington, 1981-82, dep. undersec. for internat. affairs and commodity programs, 1982-85, dep. asst. sec. dor mktg. and inspection services, 1985-86; spl. asst. to pres. for agrl. trade and food assistance The White House, 1986-89; spl. asst. to sec. for agrl. promotion Wis. Dept. Agr., Trade & Consumer Protection, Madison, 1989, sec., 1990—; dir. Heritage Bank, Beloit, Janesville, 1978-81. Trustee Beloit Coll., Wis., 1980-83; chmn. Republican party Rock County, 1972-74. Named Outstanding Young Farmer Wis. Wis. Jaycees, 1980; Nat. Merit scholar, 1965. Mem. Janesville C. of C. (chmn. agribus. com. 1978-79). Methodist. Lodge: Rotary-Janesville (dir. 1980-81). Home: 8030 Stagecoach Rd Cross Plains WI 53528-9796 Office: Wis Dept Agr, Trade & Consumer Protection 801 W Badger Rd # 8911 Madison WI 53713-2526

TRACY, JOEL DEAN, marketing researcher; b. Wisconsin Rapids, Wis., Jan. 13, 1961; s. James E. and Betty R. (Sarver) T.; children: Joshua, Matthew. BS, U. Wis., 1985, MS, 1987. Mgr., sales rep. Kirby Co., Schofield, Wis., 1979-82; sales devel. rep. Am. Greetings, Cleve., 1985-86; market rsch. project coord. U. Wis. Hosp., Madison, 1986-87; market intelligence planning mgr. The Upjohn Co., Kalamazoo, Mich., 1987-89, 91—; sr. mktg. rsch. analyst S.C. Johnson and Sons, Racine, Wis., 1989-91. Mem. Am. Mktg. Assn., Beta Gamma Sigma. Home: 4311 Fireside Ave Kalamazoo MI 49002-5841 Office: The Upjohn Co Kalamazoo MI 49001

TRACY, NOEL ADAMS, non destructive evaluation engineer; b. Boston, Mar. 24, 1941; s. Leonard Malcolm and Clara (Adams) T.; m. Judith Francis McNish, Oct. 12, 1968; children: Kyle Evan, Keena Noelle. Bs in Physics, Tufts U., 1962; MS in Engring. Sci., Rensselaer Polytech. Inst., 1967. Engr. Gen. Dynamics Electric Boat, Groton, Conn., 1964-71, Gen. Am. Rsch., Dayton, Ohio, 1971-75; mgr., engr. Universal Tech. Corp., Dayton, 1976—. Mem. Am. Soc. Nondestructive Testing (fellow 1986, tech. editor Liquid Penetrant Vol. of Nondestructive Testing handbook, 1995—, officer Conn. Yankee sect. 1967-71, Miami Valley sect. 1973-77, yearbook editor 1977—). Episcopalian. Home: 3517 Ruby Dr New Carlisle OH 45344 Office: Universal Tech Corp 4031 Col Glenn Hwy Dayton OH 45431-1600

TRACY, THOMAS WILLIAM, insurance company field manager; b. Milw., Sept. 23, 1959; s. William Thomas Tracy and Marguerite Mary (Clark) Dunn; m. Elizabeth Ann Strain, June 30, 1984; children: Patrick Michael, Theresa Elizabeth. BS in Bus. Adminstrn., Marquette U., 1982. Customer svc. rep. Cyganiak Planning, Brookfield, Wis., 1984-89; implementation mgr. Cigna HealthCare, Clayton, Mo., 1989—. Asst. coach Holy Infant 1st Grade Soccer Team, Ballwin, Mo., 1995; treas. Cub Scout Pack #627, Ballwin, 1996—. Mem. Nat. Assn. Health Underwriters, Employee Benefit Assn. Republican. Roman Catholic. Home: 151 Westridge Parc Ln Ballwin MO 63021 Office: Cigna Health Care 8182 Maryland Ave Ste 900 Saint Louis MO 63105

TRADER, JOSEPH EDGAR, orthopedic surgeon; b. Milw., Nov. 2, 1946; s. Edgar Joseph and Dorothy Elizabeth (Senzig) T.; m. Janet Louise Burzycki, Sept. 23, 1972 (div. Nov. 1987); children: James, Jonathan, Ann Elizabeth; m. Rhonda Sue Schultz, May 26, 1990. Student, Marquette U., 1964-67; MD, Med. Coll. Wis., 1971. Diplomate Am. Bd. Orthopaedic Surgery. Emergency rm. physician columbia, St. Joseph's Hosps., Milw., 1972-76; orthopaedic surgeon Orthopaedic Assn., Manitowoc, Wis., 1978—; mem. exec. com. Holy Family Meml. Med. Ctr., Manitowoc, 1985—, chief-of-staff, 1994—, ethics com., 1995, bd. dirs. Chmn. bd. dirs., past pres. Holy Innocents Mens Choir; county del. State Med. Soc. Charitable Sci. and Edn. Found.; mem. adv. bd. Manitowoc Area Cath. Schs. Endowment Fund. Fellow Am. Acad. Orthopaedic Surgeons (orthopaedic rsch. and edn. found. state com.), ACS; mem. AMA, Wis. State Med. Soc. (del. gov. affairs com.), Wis. Orthopaedic Soc., Midwest Orthopaedic Soc., Milw. Orthopaedic Soc., Phi Delta Epsilon, Psi Chi, Crown & Anchor. Roman Catholic. Club: Manitowoc Yacht. Home: 1021 Memorial Dr Manitowoc WI 54220-2242 Office: Orthopaedic Assocs 501 N 10th St Manitowoc WI 54220-4039

TRAEGER, NORMAN, mechanical engineer; b. Wausau, Wis., Jan. 6, 1951. BSME, Milw. Sch. Engring., 1976. Supr. mech. applications Coltec Industries, Beloit, Wis., 1976—. Team mgr. Beloit Area Baseball Assn., 1980; group leader Life Light Bible study St. John's Luth. Ch., Beloit, 1995. Republican. Office: Coltec Industries Dept 985 701 Lawton Ave Dept 985 Beloit WI 53511-5447

TRAFICANT, JAMES A., JR., congressman; b. Youngstown, Ohio, May 8, 1941; s. James A. and Agnes T. Traficant; m. Patricia Coppa; children: Robin, Elizabeth. B.S., U. Pitts., 1963, M.S., 1973; M.S., Youngstown State U., 1976. Exec. dir. Mahoning County Drug Program, Ohio, 1971-81; sheriff Mahoning County, Ohio, 1981-85; mem. 99th-104th Congresses from 17th Ohio dist., Washington, D.C., 1985—; ranking minority mem. transp. and infrastructure subcom. on Coast Guard and maritime transp., mem. sci. com. Office: US House of Reps Office of House Members 2446 Rayburn Bldg Ofc Washington DC 20515-0005

TRAINA, JEFFREY FRANCIS, orthopedic surgeon; b. Nagoya, Japan, Apr. 17, 1956; s. Vincent L. and Carol A. (Anselmo) T.; m. Kathy Traina, Oct. 7, 1981; children: Kristin, Kourtney. B in Gen. Studies, U. Mich., 1975; MD, So. Ill. U., 1978. Intern Emory U./Grady Meml. Hosp., Atlanta, 1978-79; resident Wake Forest U./N.C. Bapt. Hosp., Winston-Salem, N.C., 1979-83; orthopedic instr. Bowman-Gray Med. Sch., Salem, N.C., 1979-83; rsch. fellow Med. Sch. Harvard U., Boston, 1983-84; asst. prof. U. Tex. Med. Sch., Houston, 1984-86; clin. asst. prof. Coll. Medicine U. Ill., Peoria, 1987—; orthopedic surgeon U. Tex. Med. Sch., Houston, 1984-86, Orthopaedic Assocs., Peoria, 1986-89, Heartland Orthopedic Inst., Peoria, 1989-91, Assoc. Orthopaedic Surgeons, Ltd., Peoria, 1992—. Contbr. articles to profl. jours. Recipient Nat. Rsch. Svc. award, 1983; biomed. rsch. support grantee U. Tex., 1985. Mem. AMA, AAAS, N.Y. Acad. Scis., Orthopaedic Rsch. Soc., Peoria Med. Soc., Ill. State Med. Soc., Am. Acad. Orthopaedic Surgeons, Ill. Orthopaedic Soc., Assn. for Arthritic Hip and Knee Surgery, Bowman-Gray Orthopaedic Alumni Assn. Home: 5618 N Prospect Rd Peoria IL 61614-4324 Office: Assoc Orthopaedic Surgeons 2805 N Knoxville Ave Peoria IL 61604-2869

TRAINOR, JOHN FELIX, retired economics educator; b. Mpls., Dec. 1, 1921; s. James Patrick and Myra Catherine (Pauly) T.; m. Margaret Dolores Pudenz, July 3, 1965 (dec. 1977); children: John Anthony, Patrick James. BA cum laude, Coll. St. Thomas, 1943; MA, U. Minn., 1950; PhD, Wash. State U., 1970. Instr. high sch. Mpls., 1946-47; instr. Coll. St. Thomas, 1949-50; v.p. Trainor Candy Co., Mpls., 1949-56; instr., asst. prof. econs. Rockhurst Coll., Kansas City, Mo., 1956-62; instr. Wash. State U., Pullman, 1966-67; asst. prof. Moorhead (Minn.) State U., 1967-70, assoc. prof. econs., 1971-87, prof. econ., 1988-89, chmn. dept. econs., 1981-89; prof. emeritus, 1989—. Author: (with Frank J. Kottke) The Nursing Home Industry in the State of Washington, 1968. Ensign to Lt. (j.g.) USNR, 1943-46, ETO. Mem. Minn. Econs. Assn. (pres. 1976-77), Assn. Social Econs., Omicron Delta Epsilon. Roman Catholic. Home: 1333 4th Ave S Moorhead MN 56560-2971

TRAKAS, DEMETRIUS ALEXANDER, psychiatrist; b. Athens, Greece, May 18, 1932; came to U.S., 1963; s. Alexander Demetrius and Maria (Skordilis) T.; m. Anna Torolopoulos-Trakas, Dec. 27, 1962; children: Alexander, Maria, Anthony. MD, U. Athens, Greece, 1962. Diplomate Am. Bd. Psychiatry and Neurology, added qualifications in geriatric psychiatry. Intern Swedish Covenant Hosp., Chgo., 1963-64; resident Ill. State Psychiat. Inst., Chgo., 1964-67; fellow in psychiatry Ill. State Psychiatric Inst., Chgo., 1967-69; pvt. practice Chgo., 1970—; chief of staff Swedish Covenant Hosp., Chgo., 1980-84, 88-92, chmn. dept. psychiatry, 1988—; asst. prof. psychiatry Rush Med. Sch., Chgo., 1973—. Contbr. articles to profl. jours. Mem. social action com. Hellenic Med. Soc., Chgo., 1976-77. Greek Orthodox. Office: Mental Health Assocs SC 2740 W Foster Ave Ste 409 Chicago IL 60625-3543

TRAMPOSH, ANNE KATHERINE, industrial services executive; b. Belleville, Ill., Feb. 1, 1954; d. Robert A. and Elizabeth (Saffell) Hollis; m. Richard E. Tramposh, May 30, 1975; children: Benjamin, Adam. BS, Kans. U., 1976, MS, 1989. Dir. phys. therapy Wagoner (Okla.) Community Hosp., 1977; staff phys. therapist Muskogee (Okla.) Gen. Hosp., 1977-79; dir. phys. therapy Muskogee Bone & Joint Clinic, 1979-80; owner Muskogee Phys. Therapy & Rehab., 1980-83; dir. phys. therapy Lee's Summit (Mo.) Community Hosp., 1983; co-owner, founder Work Capacities, Inc., Kansas City, Mo., 1984-89, Advantage Health Inc., Kansas City, 1989—; speaker in field; cons. Envelope Mfr.'s Assn. of Am., Alexandria, Va., 1986-89, Comprehensive Loss Mgmt., Inc., Mpls., 1988-89, Motion Analysis Corp., Santa Rosa, Calif., 1989—. Author: Arms, Hands, Fingers & Thumbs, 1988, Avoiding the Cracks: A Guide to Workers Compensation System, 1991, (chpt.) Work Injury, 1988; contbr. numerous articles to profl. jours. Mem. ch. coun. Lenexa (Kans.) Bapt. Ch., 1989—. Mem. Am. Phys. Therapy Assn., Am. Soc. Safety Engrs., Nat. Rehab. Assn., Am. Back Soc. Republican. Office: Advantage Health Inc 920 Main St Ste 700 Kansas City MO 64105-2008

TRAN, NANG TRI, electrical engineer, physicist; b. Binh Dinh, Vietnam, Jan. 2, 1948; came to U.S., 1979, naturalized, 1986; s. Cam Tran and Cuu Thi Nguyen; m. Thu-Huong Thi Tong, Oct. 14, 1982; children: Helen, Florence, Irene, Kenneth. BSEE, Kyushu Inst. Tech., Kitakyushu, Japan, 1973, MSEE, 1975; PhD in Materials Sci., U. of Osaka Prefecture, Sakai, Japan, 1978. Rsch. assoc. U. of Calif.-Irvine, 1979; engr., rsch. scientist Sharp Electronics, Irvine, 1979-80; sr. rsch. scientist Arco Solar Industries, Chatsworth, Calif., 1980-84; sr. rsch. specialist, group leader 3M Co., St. Paul, 1985—; cons., lectr. Japan industry mgmt. Contbr. articles to profl. jours; holder 19 patents in field. Mem. tech. com. various internat. confs. Scholarship fellow Vietnamese Govt., Japan, 1968-73, grad. scholarship fellow Rotary Internat., Japan, 1973-75, predoctoral fellow Japanese Govt., 1975-78. Mem. IEEE, Japan Soc. of Applied Physics. Achievements include research on thin film electroluminescent displays, amorphous silicon solar cells, image sensors, transparent conducting oxide films.

TRANFAGLIA, CHRISTINA MARIE, marketing executive; b. Boston, Mar. 2, 1962; d. George Pasquale and Joan Barbara (Donahue) T. BA in Econs., Harvard U., 1984; M.Mgmt., Northwestern U., 1989. Investment adminstr. First Winthrop Corp., Boston, 1984-85, analyst, 1985-86, assoc., 1986-87; brand asst. Dow Brands div. Dow Chem., Indpls., 1989-90, asst. brand mgr., 1991-92, brand mgr., 1992-93; product mgr. Sara Lee Bakery, Chgo., 1993-94; sr. product mgr. Tenneco Packaging, Deerfield, Ill., 1995—. Tchr., cons. Jr. Achievement, Indpls., 1991-93; alumni recruiter/interviewer for admissions com. J.L. Kellogg Grad. Sch. Mgmt., Northwestern U., 1989—; alumni fundraiser, admissions interviewer Harvard, 1984—. Home: 655 W Irving Park Rd Apt 2301 Chicago IL 60613-3112

TRAPIKAS, BRUNO PETER, city government administrator; b. Chgo., Apr. 26, 1951; s. Henry and Halina (Zukauskas) T.; m. Carol Blyskal, July 4, 1991. BA in Liberal Arts and Scis., U. Ill., Chgo., 1973, MA in Urban and Quantitative Econs., 1974. Computer programmer CNA Ins. Co., Chgo., 1975-76; evaluation specialist City of Chgo. Dept. Human Svcs., 1976-81; city planner City of Chgo. Dept. Planning, 1981-89, dir. community devel., 1989-92; dir. neighborhood planning and devel. City of Chgo. Dept. Planning and Devel., 1992—. Prin. author: (City of Chgo.'s Bid for 1994 World Cup Games) Choose Chicago, 1991. Dep. dir. Midwest region U.S. Amateur Soccer Assn., 1991-96, dir., 1996—, chair rules com., 1992-94; vice chmn. World Cup Chgo., 1987-94. Mem. Nat. Soccer League (pres. 1981-82), Ill. State Soccer Assn. (sec. 1989-92, v.p. 1984-86, 92-94, 96—). Office: City of Chicago 121 N La Salle St Ste 1101 Chicago IL 60602-1209

TRAPP, ROBERT GREIG, rheumatologist; b. Lincoln, Ill., Nov. 7, 1948. BA, Earlham Coll., 1970; MD, Northwestern U., 1974. Resident in internal medicine Evanston (Ill.) Hosp., Northwestern U., 1974-77; fellow in rheumatology U. Cin., 1978-80, U. Manchester, Eng., 1980-81; asst. prof. So. Ill. U. Sch. Medicine, Springfield, 1981-89, chief of divsn. of rheumatology, 1987-89; med. dir. The Arthritis Ctr., Springfield, 1989—. Co-author: Basic and Clinical Biostatistics, 1990. Fellow Am. Coll. Rheumatology; mem. Phi Beta Kappa. Office: The Arthritis Ctr 2528 Farragut Springfield IL 62704

TRAUDT, MARY B., elementary education educator; b. Chgo., Jan. 1, 1930; d. Lloyd Andrews Haldeman and Adele Eleanor (MacKinnon) Haldeman-Oliver; m. Eugene Peter Traudt, Dec. 6, 1952 (dec.); 1 child, Victoria Jean. BS, Cen. Mich. U., 1951; MA, Roosevelt U., 1978; postgrad., U. Ill., 1982. Asst. editor Commerce Clearing House, Chgo., 1951-53; tchr. Cleve. Elem. Sch., 1954-56, Chgo. Sch. System, 1956-57, Community Consolidated # 54, Hoffman Estates, Ill., 1957-64, Avoca Elem. Sch., Wilmette, Ill., 1964—; ret., 1995. Recipient Computer award Apple Computer Co. Mem. Avoca Edn. Assn. (v.p. 1986-91), Alpha Psi Omega. Presbyterian. Home: 107 Lincoln St Glenview IL 60025-4916 Office: Avoca Elem Sch 235 Beech Dr Glenview IL 60025-3274

TRAUGOTT, ARTHUR RICHARD, physician; b. Junction City, Kans., Aug. 27, 1940; s. Arthur Frederick and Laura Marie (Pebler) T.; m. Shirley Ann Cullen Traugott, July 25, 1964; children: David A., Andrea N. BA, U. Kans., Lawrence, 1963; MD, U. Kans. Sch. Medicine, Kansas City, 1967. Head Divsn. Psychiatry Carle Clinic Assn., Urbana, Ill., 1972-92; physician, 1972—, assoc. med. dir. Govt. Affairs, 1992—; clin. asst. prof. U. Ill. Coll. Medicine at Urbana-Champaign, 1972—. Bd. mem. Family Svcs. Champaign Co., 1973-75, Champaign Co. Mental Health Ctr., 1976-84, Mental Health Bd. Champaign County, 1984-87. Fellow Am. Psychiatric Assn., 1980. Mem. AMA (coun. on med. svc.), Ill. State Med. Soc. (pres. 1993-94), Champaign County Med. Soc. Lutheran. Office: Carle Clinic Assn 809 W Church Champaign IL 61820

TRAUNERO, DEBRA ANN, social worker; b. Tiffin, Ohio, July 30, 1959; d. William Louis and Betty Jane (Suttner) T. BS in Social Worker, Ohio State U., 1981, MSW, 1988. Lic. ind. social worker, Ohio. Caseworker Marion County Children Svcs. Bd., Marion, Ohio, 1981-90; therapist Network Enrichment Ctr., Marion, 1990; social worker, adminstr. Delwood, Delaware, Ohio, 1990-92; women's program coord. Turning Point, Marion, Ohio, 1992-93; mental health therapist Sandusky Valley Ctr., Tiffin, Ohio, 1993-95; with Family Resource Ctr., Lima, Ohio, 1995—. Vol. Big Bros.-Big Sisters, 1982. Mem. NASW. Republican. Roman Catholic. Office: Family Resource Ctr 799 S Main St Lima OH

TRAVAGLINI, RAYMOND DOMINIC, corporate executive; b. Greenville, Pa., May 3, 1928; s. Perugino and Mary Ann (DiFalco) T.; children: Alan, Lynne, Debbie, Kimberly, Kristine. LHD (hon.), Youngstown State U., 1993. Mgr. Kroger Co., Meadville, Pa., 1949-62; owner Suburban Water Conditioning, Warren, Ohio, 1962-65; ptnr. Sanray Corp., Meadville, 1965—; bd. dirs. Bank One, Youngstown, Ohio. Bd. dirs. Butler Inst. Am. Art, Youngstown, Mahoning Valley Econ. Devel. Corp.; mem. Base Comty. Coun. Dept. Air Force. Named Man of Yr. Boys' Towns of Italy, 1979, Italian Scholarship League, 1984, Mahoning Valley County Econ. Devel. Corp., 1985, Nat. Italian-Am. Sports Hall of Fame, 1992; recipient Disting. Citizen award Youngstown State U. Alumni Assn., 1993. Office: Sanray Corp 1323 Youngstown Warren Rd Niles OH 44446-4616

TRAVER, NOEL ALLEN, small business owner, creative director; b. New Brunswick, N.J., Nov. 12, 1959; s. Thomas Gordon Sr. and Arline (Yurkunas) T.; m. Jayne Louise Brickner, Mar. 3, 1984. BA, Ohio State U., 1982. Dir. Jeffery Shaw Communications, Columbus, 1982-85; desktop pub. Inacomp Computer Ctrs., Worthington, Ohio, 1985-90; pres., chmn. bd. D'pix, Inc., Columbus, 1990-94, Amber Prodns., Inc., Columbus, 1985—; co-founder, pres., chmn. bd. The Creative Network Inc., Columbus, 1996—; adj. faculty Franklin U., Columbus, 1991—; lectr. Journalism Assn. of Ohio Schs., Broadcast Designers Assn., Nat. Broadcast Promotion Execs., Marion Advt. and Sales Club, Internat. Assn. Bus., Communicators, The Mac Show, numerous others, 1985—. Recipient Honorable Mention Best Resource, MacUser mag., 1991, Honorable Mention Best Logo and two merit awards, How mag., 1992, Best Computer Art and Design award Computer Graphics, 1992; named to Top 10 List, Clip Art Products-MacWorld Mag., 1994. Mem. Nat. Assn. Desktop Pub., Ohio State U. Alumni Assn., Ohio State U. Sch. Journalism Alumni Assn., Advt. Fedn. Columbus, MacDesigner, Columbus Soc. Communicating Arts, Digital Designers Group. Republican. Home: 414 W 4th Ave Columbus OH 43201-3106 Office: Amber Prodns Inc and D'pix 414 West Fourth Ave Columbus OH 43201

TRAVIS, DAVID M., state legislator; b. Pawtucket, R.I., Sept. 21, 1948; s. Gideon and Jessie (Campbell) T.; married. BA, U. Wis., Milw., 1980; MA, U. Wis. Adminstrv. asst. Wis. State Legis., 1971-72; analyst Senate Dem. Caucus, 1972-73, dir., 1973-78; mem. Joint Fin. Com.; Wis. state assemblyman dist. 81, 1978—; majority leader; chmn. rules com.; mem. orgn. com., Joint Com. on Employ Rels. and Spl. Com. on Reapportionment; del. Dem. Nat. Conv., 1980; instr. polit. sci. Mem. Northside Comty. Coun., Eastmorland and Elvehjem Comty. Assn. Home: 4229 Mandrake Rd Madison WI 53704-1653*

TRAVIS, FREDERICK FRANCIS, academic administrator, historian; b. Brookhaven, Miss., Nov. 10, 1942; s. John Alice and Katharine (Brennan) T.; m. Alix Gregory Hallman Travis, May 15, 1971; children: Brennan Nunn, Rachel Frances. BS in Math., U. Miss., Oxford, 1965; MA in History, 1967; PhD in History, Emory U., Atlanta, 1974. Asst. prof. history Fordham U., N.Y.C., 1977-84, assoc. prof. history, 1984-88; assoc. prof. history John Carroll U., Cleve., 1988-92, prof. history, 1992—; dean Coll. of Arts and Scis., 1988-94, acting pres., 1995-96, acad. v.p., 1994—. Author: George Kennan and the American-Russian Relationship, 1865-1924, 1990; contbr. articles to profl. jours. Trustee, v.p. Heights Cmty. Congress, Cleveland Heights, Ohio, 1993—, 1995-97. Named Univ. fellow U. Miss., Oxford, 1965-66, Emory U., Atlanta, 1968-69, vis. scholar Kennan Inst. for Advanced Russian Studies, Washington, 1980; recipient Rsch. Grant Travel to Collections, Nat. Endowment for Humanities, Washington, 1988. Mem. Am. Hist. Assn., Am. Assn. for Advancement of Slavic Studies, Soc. for Historians of Am. Fgn. Rels., Ohio Acad. History, Am. Conf. of Acad. Deans. Home: 2318 Coventry Rd Cleveland Heights OH 44118 Office: John Carroll Univ 20700 N Park Blvd University Heights OH 44118

TRAVIS, LAWRENCE ALLAN, accountant; b. Bloomington, Ill., Sept. 17, 1942; s. Willard Burns and Florence May (Harvey) T.; m. Katy Quinones, Apr. 16, 1965 (div. Feb. 1978); children: Lawrence Allan Jr., Matthew B.; m. Kathleen Lucas, May 20, 1995. BS in Bus. Edn., Ill. State U., 1968; MA in Pub. Adminstrn., Sangamon State U., Springfield, Ill., 1976. CPA, Ill. Staff acct. Alexander Grant & Co., Chgo., 1969; internal auditor State Farm Ins., Bloomington, 1969-73; dep. dir. Ill. Dept. Ins., Springfield, 1973-74; audit mgr. Ill. Auditor Gen., Springfield, 1974-81; pres. Lawrence Travis & Co., P.C., CPAs, Virden, Normal, Springfield, Ill., 1979—; also bd. dirs. Lawrence Travis & Co., P.C., CPAs, Virden, Normal, Springfield; v.p., bd. dirs. Virden Broadcasting Corp., 1986-95; pres., bd. dirs. Travco, Inc., Virden, Ka-Lar Enterprises, Inc., Springfield; v.p., bd. dirs. Carlinville Broadcasting Corp., Miller Comm., Inc.; registered rep. Terra Securities Corp. Mem. Ill. Common Cause, Springfield. Mem. AICPA, Assn. Govt. Accts., Ill. CPA Soc., Internat. Platform Assn., Nat. Space Soc., Smithsonian Assocs., World Future Soc., Internat. Traders. Democrat. Roman Catholic. Home: 2409 Idlewild Dr Springfield IL 62704-5403 Office: 1700 S 1st St Springfield IL 62704

TRAVIS, MARLENE O., healthcare management executive; b. Edmonton, Alta., Can.; Came to U.S. 1959.; d. LeRoy David and Della Jessie (Campbell) T.; m. Gary T. McIlroy, Aug. 20, 1962; children: Jennifer Renee, Montgomery Travis. Student (mass comms.), St. Cloud State U., 1974-76; exec. edn., U. Pa., Stanford U., 1989-92. Cert. exec. edn. Owner Travis Communications, Brainerd, Minn., 1975-77; co-founder, operating officer Midwest Lab. Assoc., Mpls., 1977-80; dir., corp. v.p. Meidinger-HRM (MHRM), Mpls., 1981-83; co-founder, exec. v.p., bd. dirs. Health Risk Mgmt. Inc., Mpls., 1977—, dir., pres., COO, 1986—; chair of bd., CEO HRM Ltd. (Can.), 1989—; founder, chair CEO Inst. Healthcare Quality, Mpls., 1991—; vice-chair Med. Alley, 1994—, bd. dirs. Co-author Self Health Guide to Laboratory Tests, 1982. Chmn. Minn. Task Force on Battered Women, 1977-79; bd. dirs. Minn. Task Force on Sexual Assault, 1974-76; co-founder, chair Mid Minn. Women's Ctr. Brainerd, 1975; founder, chair Crow Wing County Task Force on Sexual Assault, Brainerd, 1974-77; founder Crow Wing County Task Force to Support Battered Women, 1974; mem. Minn. Commr. of Edn.'s Task Force to Eliminate Sexism in Edn., 1973-74; mem. leadership group Amnesty Internat., 1990—, mem. exec. com., 1990—, com. of 200, 1991—. Named Cornerstone Leader in Giving United Way Mpls., 1992, 93. Mem. AAUW, NOW (convenor Marshfield, Wis. chpt. 1972, Brainerd area chpt. 1974), C-200 Found. (mentor contbr.), Can. Coll. Health Svc. Execs., Internat. Platform Assn., Nat. Assn. Corp. Dirs., Toastmasters (sponsor 1988), Phi Beta Gamma. Office: Health Risk Mgmt Inc 8000 W 78th St Minneapolis MN 55439-2534

TRAY, MARIA A., business executive; b. Ashland, Pa., May 25, 1948. BS in Psychology, Pa. State U., 1970. Application programmer Dollar Savs. Bank, Pitts., 1978-83; analyst Comtech Systems, Inc., Columbus, Ohio, 1983-87; pres. Shared Resources, Inc., Dublin, Ohio, 1987—. Bd. dirs. Goodwill Rehab., Columbus, 1984-94. Mem. Data Processing Mgmt. Assn., Dublin C. of C., Columbus C. of C. Republican. Office: Shared Resources Inc 555 Metro Pl N Ste 625 Dublin OH 43017-1375

TREADWAY, DOUGLAS MORSE, academic administrator; b. San Diego, Apr. 23, 1942; s. Thelma Lillian (Lindsay) T.; m. Carole Rae Culp, June 5, 1964; children: Christine, Paul. BA, Calif. Western U., 1964; MT, Claremont Grad. Sch., 1967; PhD, Northwestern U., 1971. Asst. dean students Northwestern U., Evanston, Ill., 1969-71; asst. prof. psychology U.S. Internat. Univ., Maui, Hawaii, 1971-73; dir. coop. edn. Maui Community Coll., 1973-74; dean of students Ea. Oreg. State Coll., La Grande, 1974-79, dean continuing edn., 1979-85; pres. Western Mont. Coll., Dillon, 1985-87, S.W. State U., Marshall, Minn., 1987-91; chancellor N.D. U. System, 1991-94; supt., pres. Shasta Coll., Redding, Calif., 1994—; chmn. Nat. Conf. Rural Edn., Washington, 1987; mem. rsch. coun. USDA. Author: Higher Education in Rural America, 1985; contbr. numerous articles on higher edn. and rural programs to profl. jours. Mem. Big Bros., Maui, 1971-74. Mem. Am. Assn. Higher Edn., Am. Assn. State Colls. and Univs.,

Nat. Univ. Continuing Edn. Assn. Republican. Methodist. Lodge: Rotary. Home: 13310 Pala Mesa Circle Redding CA 96003

TREADWAY, JOSEPH L., state legislator; b. St. Louis, Mar. 23, 1947; m. Marlene Kroeger, 1982; 2 children. Diploma, Forest Pk. C.C. Office mgr., real estate broker; mem. Mo. Ho. of Reps. from 96th dist., 1983—. Mem. C. of C. Democrat. Home: 1456 Telegraph Rd Lemay MO 63125-2532*

TREANOR, JUDITH ANN, writer; b. Ithaca, N.Y., Jan. 31, 1958; d. Harley J. and Sara E. (Kenyon) Otto; m. John F. Petsch (dec.); children: Kindra, Kellie; m. Tad William Treanor, Apr. 19, 1986; children: Alexander, Christopher. Student, U. Colo., 1979, U. Minn., 1982-83, Inver Hills Coll., 1982-83. Group acct. Kaiser Found., Denver, 1979-81; credit corr. Ecolab, Inc., St. Paul, 1981-88; mng. ptnr. Parent Ptnrs. Inc., Bloomington, Minn., 1987-93; spkr., cons. Internat. Nanny Assn., 1993. Author: How to Hire...and Keep Your Nanny, 1991, Triangles, 1995. Union steward Internat. Svc. Workers, Denver, 1979-81; vol. Roseville (Minn.) Pub. Schs., 1993-95; com. chair Boy Scouts Am., St. Paul, 1995—; children's events coord. St. Paul Winter Carnival, 1986; troop leader Girl Scouts U.S., St. Paul, 1984-86; Great Books leader St. Paul Pub. Schs., 1991-93.

TREDWAY, THOMAS, college president; b. North Tonawanda, N.Y., Sept. 4, 1935; s. Harold and Melanya (Scorby) T.; m. Catherine Craft, Jan. 12, 1991; children: Daniel John, Rebecca Elizabeth. BA, Augustana Coll., 1957; MA, U. Ill., 1958; BD, Garrett Theol. Sem., 1961; PhD, Northwestern U., 1964. Instr. history Augustana Coll., Rock Island, Ill., 1964-65, asst. prof., 1965-69, assoc. prof., 1969-71, prof., 1971—, v.p. acad affairs, 1970-75, pres., 1975—; vis. prof. ch. history Waterloo Lutheran Sem., 1967-68. Mem. Am. Hist. Assn., Am. Soc. Ch. History, Phi Beta Kappa, Omicron Delta Kappa. Lutheran. Office: Augustana Coll Office of President 639 38th St Rock Island IL 61201-2210

TREFTS, ALBERT SHARPE, mechanical engineer, consultant; b. Cleve., July 26, 1929; s. George M. and Dorothy (Sharpe) T.; m. Joan Landenberger, June 20, 1952; children: Dorothy E., Albert S. Jr., William G., Deborah C., Elizabeth. BSME, Cornell U., 1953. Registered profl. engr., N.Y., Ohio, Ind. Test eng. Morrison Steel Prod., Inc., Buffalo, 1955-56; sales eng. Worthington Corp., Buffalo, 1956-62; mech. eng. Linde Div. Union Carbide Corp., Tonawanda, N.Y., 1962-64, Davey McKee Corp., Cleve., 1964-82; cons. engr. various firms, Cleve., 1982—, Morrison Knutson Corp., MK Fergusen Group. Lt. USNR, 1953-55. Mem. Nat. Soc. SAR (nat. trustee, pres. Ohio State Soc.), Cleve. Eng. Soc., Cleve. Skating Club, Cleve. Playhouse Club, Union Club Cleve., Western Res. Soc. (pres. 1989), Founders & Patriots (gov. 1984-86), Sons & Daus. Pilgrims (gov. 1986-88), New Eng. Soc. Cleve. (pres. 1986, 88), Mayflower Soc. (gov. 1996—), Barons Magna Carta, Founder Hartford (Conn.), Mayflower Descs. (lt. gov.), Founders Newbury (Mass.), Union Club, Cornell Club N.Y.C., First Families Mass., Clearwater (Fla.) Country Club. Republican. Presbyterian. Home: 20101 Malvern Rd Shaker Hts OH 44122-2825 Office: Morrison Knutson Corp Mk Ferguson Plz Cleveland OH 44113

TREFZGER, RICHARD CHARLES, surgeon; b. Peoria, Ill., Jan. 27, 1948; s. John Dennis and Marilyn Lestilie (Wilson) T.; m. Nancy Ellen Guy, Dec. 19, 1971; children: Emily Jean, Michael Guy. BS, U. Ill., 1970, MD, 1973. Diplomate Am. Bd. Surgery. Intern in surgery Med. Coll. Wis., Milw., 1973-74, resident in surgery, 1974-75; resident in surgery Presbyn.-St. Luke's Hosp., Chgo., 1975-78; instr. surgery Rush Med. Coll., Chgo., 1977-78; med. dir. Westminster Village Retirement Ctr., Bloomington, Ill., 1980-84, St. Joseph's Trauma Ctr., Bloomington, 1986-96, BroMenn Regional Trauma Ctr., Normal, Ill., 1994-96; chief surgery Bromenn Regional Med. Ctr., Normal, Ill., 1987-88, 94-96; chief surgery St. Joseph's Med. Ctr., Bloomington, 1989-91, pres. med. staff, 1991-92; clin. instr. U. Ill. Coll. Medicine, 1980—; chmn. bd. dirs. BroMenn Physician Hosp. Orgn., 1995-96. Mem. Ill. State U. Civic Chorale, Normal, 1991—; bd. dirs. Barton Stone Christian Home, Jacksonville, Ill., 1979-82, Cmty. Cancer Ctr., Bloomington, 1996—. Fellow ACS (councilor Ill chpt. 1986-88); mem. AMA, Ill. Surg. Soc. (gov. 1990-94), Rotary (dir. 1982-85, 94—, sec. 1995-96, v.p. 1996—, mem. bd., Paul Harris fellow 1989), Masons, Scottish Rite, Alpha Omega Alpha. Mem. Christian Ch. Home: 41 Pendleton Way Bloomington IL 61704-6243 Office: Surg Assocs 1404 Eastland Dr Bloomington IL 61701-3517

TREGER, HARVEY, social work educator; b. Chgo., July 5, 1924; s. Sam and Lillian (Ertrachter) T.; m. Shirley G. Feldman, Oct. 24, 1954. BS in Psychology, Roosevelt U., Chgo., 1948; MA, U. Chgo., 1956; cert. in alcohol studies, Yale U., 1957; cert. child care program, Chgo. Inst. for Psychoanalysis, 1963. Caseworker Chgo. Welfare Dept., 1948-50, 51-54; counselor Chgo. Com. on Alcoholism, 1950; probation officer U.S. Dist. Ct. for No. Ill., Chgo., 1957-65; asst. prof. Jane Addams Coll. Social Work, U. Ill., Chgo., 1965-70, assoc. prof., 1970-74, prof., 1974—, prof. criminal justice, 1976—; prof. emeritus social work, 1993—; instr. U. Ind., Gary, fall 1961; article reviewer Fed. Probation Quar., 1978-83; mem. adv. com. on supervision in community Ill. Legis Coun. on Diagnosis and Evaluation Criminal Defendants, 1970-71; presenter in field, 1972—; cons. Wilmette (Ill.) Police Dept., 1978, Park Ridge (Ill.) Police Dept., 1973-74, Elk Grove Village (Ill.) Police Dept., 1972-77, Ministry of Justice Lower Saxony, Fed. Republic of Germany, and German Marshall Fund, 1979, Cook County Jail, 1984—; workshop condr., 1970—. Author: The Police-Social Work Team, 1975; contbr. articles and book revs. to profl. jours., chpts. to books and encys. Mem. Meth. Youth Svc. Bd., 1980—; vice chmn. profl. adv. coun. Safer Found., 1980—; founder, pres. North Shore Chamber Orch. Soc., 1981—; pres. Meth. Youth Svcs., 1984-85; bd. dirs. Chgo. Cello Soc., program chair, 1995—. Recipient Gov.'s Justice Award State of Ill., 1972, John Howard award, 1972, 1st Morris J. Wexler award Ill. Acad. Criminology, 1974, Key to City, Kansas City, Mo., 1976, Social Worker of Yr. Ill. chpt. NASW, 1977, award Meth. Youth Svcs. Bd., 1985; rsch. grantee Village of Niles, Ill., 1973-87, Ill. Law Enforcement Commn., 1970-73, 74-77; recipient Appreciation award Assn. Police Social Workers, 1993. Fellow Am. Orthopsychiat. Assn.; mem. NASW, Acad. Cert. Social Workers. Home: 2320 Central St Apt 301 Evanston IL 60201-1414 Office: U Ill Social Work Jane Addams Coll Chicago IL 60680

TREICHEL, MARY JANE, mathematics and science educator; b. Pitts., Apr. 16, 1940; d. Alexander Joseph and Elizabeth Ann (Kiernan) Polinsky. BA, Carlow Coll., 1962; MSNS, Seattle U., 1969; PhD, Columbia Pacific U., 1993. Lic. profl. counselor, Ohio; cert. tchr., Ohio. Maths., sci. educator Ctrl. cath. H.S., Canton, Ohio, 1962-65, Holy Name H.S., Cleve., 1967-68; maths. educator Cleve. Pub. Schs., 1966-67; chemistry, physics educator St. Ignatius H.S., Cleve., 1968-83; tchr., counselor Painesville (Ohio) Local Schs., 1986—. Author: (pamphlet) Lent '93: A Contemplative View, 1993, Stop! Look! Listen!, 1994, New Life, 1995, Beloved of God, 1995, Ambassadors for Christ, 1996, Live in Joy, 1996. Pastoral min. Cath. Apostolate to the Deaf, Hard-of-Hearing and Blind, Cleve., 1983-86. Mem. NEA, Ohio Ednl. Assn. (del. 1992—), Northeastern Ohio Ednl. Assn. (com. mem. 1986—), Painesville City Tchrs. Assn. (bldg. rep. 1990—), Tri-County Edn. Assn. (sec. 1995). Democrat. Home: 1651 Mentor Ave Apt 3112 Painesville OH 44077 Office: Painesville City Local Sch 58 Jefferson St Painesville OH 44077

TREINAVICZ, KATHRYN MARY, software engineer; b. Brockton, Mass., Nov. 25, 1957; d. Ralph Clement and Frances Elizabeth (O'Leary) T. BS, Salem State Coll., Mass., 1980. Tchr., Brockton Pub. Schs., 1980-81; instr. Quincy CETA Inc., Mass., 1981-82; programmer Systems Architects Inc., Randolph, Mass., 1982, programmer analyst, Dayton, Ohio, 1982-84; sr. programmer analyst System Devel. Corp., Dayton, 1984-86; project mgr. Unisys Inc., Dayton, 1986-87; software engr. Computer Scis. Corp. (formerly Systems and Applied Scis. Corp. 1988), 1987-89, project mgr. Computer Scis Corp. (formerly Atlantic Rsch. Corp. 1994), Fairborn, Ohio, 1989—. Mem. NAFE. Democrat. Roman Catholic. Avocations: Steven King novels, needlepoint, knitting, crocheting.

TRELA, D. J., English language and literature educator, academic administrator; b. Chgo., July 16, 1958; s. Anthony J. and Ruby V. (Andersen) T.; m. Janet L. Boden, May 25, 1986. BA, U. Ill., Chgo., 1980; PhD, U. Edinburgh, Scotland, 1984; postgrad., U. Chgo., 1987-89. Instr. Loop Coll., Chgo., 1985, Pan Am. U., Edinburg, Tex., 1985-87, DePaul U., Chgo., 1987-89, Coll. St. Francis, Joliet, Ill., 1988-89; asst. prof. English Roosevelt U., Chgo., 1989-94, chair dept. English, 1990-93, interm dir. sch. of liberal studies, 1993-94, assoc. prof., dir. sch. liberal studies, 1994—. Author: A History of Carlyle's Cromwell's Letters and Speeches, 1992, Margaret Oliphant: Critical Essays on a Gentle Subversive, 1995, Victorian Urban Settings: Essays on Culture and Society, 1996; assoc. editor Carlyle's Studies Annual; contbr. articles to profl. jours. Mem. AAUP, MLA, Midwest MLA, Carlyle Soc. (Edinburgh), Midwest Victorian Studies Assn. (exec. sec. 1992-96), Rsch. Soc. for Victorian Periodicals. Home: 10608 S Drew St Chicago IL 60643-2922 Office: Roosevelt U Sch Liberal Studies 430 S Michigan Ave Chicago IL 60605-1301

TRELKA, JANICE MARGARET NACE, secondary education educator; b. Cleve., Nov. 9, 1944; d. Allen Samuel and Ethel (Pinhard) Nace; m. Martin Frank Trelka, June 24, 1978. Student, Merrill-Palmer Inst., Detroit, 1965; BE, Ashland Coll., 1966, health tchr. cert., 1985; MEd, Cleve. State U., 1976. Supr. indsl. cafeteria Republic Steel, Cleve., 1967-68; bank teller Cen. Nat. Bank, Cleve., 1968-69; tchr. home econs. Lorain (Ohio) City Schs., 1969—; speaker Cleve. Ctr. for Econ. Edn., 1975, Ohio Home Econs. Conf., 1984, 86, 88, 89, 93, Ohio Edn. Assn., 1985; mem. impact home econs. curriculum guide task force State Dept. Edn., Columbus, Ohio, 1977, mem. mid. sch. resource guide devel., 1988. Tchr. Sunday sch., Cleve., 1967-74; treas. PTA Hawthorne-Boone Sch., Lorain, 1971-74; mem. state bd. Women's Commn., Columbus, 1978-86; mem. bd. Christian edn., Lorain, 1982-88; mem. Sexually Transmitted Disease Task Force, Lorain, 1989-92, Vocat. Task Force, Lorain, 1990-93; mem. choir. State Recognition for Martha Holden Jennings Grant Implementation, 1984; recipient Curriculum Writing Contest 3d Pl. award Ohio Coun. on Econ. Edn., 1984, 1st Pl. award, 1985, Nat. Cert. of Merit award Joint Coun. on Econ. Edn., 1986. Mem. NEA, Am. Vocat. Assn., Am. Home Econs. Assn. (cert.), Ohio Edn. Assn., Ohio Vocat. Assn., Ohio Home Econs. Assn., Lorain Edn. Assn., Lorain County Home Econs. Assn. Home: 2611 Denver Ave Lorain OH 44055-1457 Office: Lorain Mid Sch 602 Washington Ave Lorain OH 44052

TRENARY, MICHAEL, chemistry educator; b. L.A., July 8, 1956; s. Bernard Elroy and Jean Ann (Morris) T.; m. Wendy Greenhouse, June 10, 1984; children: Eleanor Jane, Russell Jack. BS, U. Calif., Berkeley, 1978; PhD, MIT, 1982. rsch. asst. prof. U. Pitts., 1982-84; asst. prof. U. Ill., Chgo., 1984-89, assc. prof., 1989-92, prof., 1992—. Contbr. articles to Jour. of Chem. Physics, Jour. Electron Spectroscopy, Surface Science, Chem. Phys. Letts. Recipient Dreyfus Tchr.-Scholar award Henry and Camille Dreyfus Found., 1989, U.Ill. Scholar award U. Ill. Found., 1990. Member Am. Chem. Soc., Am. Vacuum Soc., Am. Phys. Soc. Office: U Ill at Chgo Dept Chemistry 845 W Taylor St Chicago IL 60607-7001

TRENCHARD, KENNETH ROBERT, auditor; b. Dearborn, Mich., Oct. 31, 1929; s. Robert and Lillian (Livingstone) T.; married, 1955; children: Kenneth Jr., Holly, Randall. BS, Temple U., 1958. CPA, Pa. Acct. Tait, Weller & Baker CPA, Phila., 1958-62; pvt. practice in acctg. Willow Grove, Pa., 1962-64; auditor/regional contr. ARA Svcs., Phila., 1965-84; treas., bd. dirs. Leona's Restaurants, Chgo.; co-trustee Jay Frank Parmly Trust, Chgo., 1977—. With U.S. Army, 1947-52. Mem. DAV, Am. Legion, Ill. Restaurant Risk Mgmt. Assn. Home: 2303 Bartz /Randall Trenchard Rd Valparaiso IN 46383-8350

TRENEFF, CRAIG PAUL, lawyer; b. Columbus, Ohio, July 16, 1952; s. Christ and Marlene Sue (Bach) T.; m. Loraine Marsh Treneff, July 12, 1986. BA, Ohio State U., 1974; JD, Capital U., 1981. Bar: Ohio 1981, U.S. Dist. Ct. (so. dist.) Ohio 1982. Legis. asst. Ohio House Rep., Columbus, 1974-81; law clk. Ohio Supreme Ct., Columbus, 1981-83; assoc. atty. Morrow, Gordon & Byrd, Newark, 1983-84; counsel atty. Teaford, Rich & Dorsey, Columbus, 1984-85; ptnr. Schottenstein, Treneff & Williams, Columbus, 1985—. Del. coord. Gore for Pres., Ohio, 1988; mgr. Franklin County Treas. campaign, 1988; rsch. coord. Brown for Ohio Sec. campaign, 1982, 90, Franklin County Pres. campaign, 1980' treas. Ohioans with Sherrod Brown; pres. bd. trustees Directions for Youth; mem. Zoning Bd. Appeals, Westerville, Ohio. Mem. ABA, Columbus Bar Assn., Ohio Bar Assn. Democrat. Lutheran. Home: 148 Executive Ct Westerville OH 43081-1474 Office: Schottenstein Treneff & Williams 341 S 3rd St Ste 300 Columbus OH 43215-5463

TRENERY, MARY ELLEN, librarian; b. Conran, Mo., Jan. 10, 1939; d. John Herman and Stella Cecelia (Durbin) Hulshof; m. Frank E. Trenery, June 10, 1967. BA in Classics, Coll. New Rochelle, 1962; MALS, Rosary Coll., River Forest, Ill., 1966; postgrad., Fla. Atlantic U., Boca Raton, 1986-89. Tchr. grades 6, 8 Archdiocesan Sch. System, St. Louis, 1962-64; serials and acquisition libr. U. Ill., Chgo., 1966-69; acquisitions, circulation and cataloging libr. Rosary Coll., River Forest, Ill., 1964-66, 70-72; libr. media specialist St. Coleman Cath. Sch., Pompano Beach, Fla., 1973-94; coord. for self study St. Coleman Schs., 1982, 83, 89, 90; cons. Pompano Beach City Libr. Author: Policies and Procedures for School Libraries, 1976, UICC Call Number (founding editor), 1967-68, NIUCLA Newsletter (editor 1969-72). Fed. Funding liaison with Broward County Sch. Bd., 1974-94. Mem. Ill. Libr. Assn. (rsch. and tech. svcs. div. chair 1967-69), Cath. Libr. Assn. (No. Ill. unit chair, sec. 1969-72).

TRENNEL, LAWRENCE WILLIAM, accountant; b. East Cleveland, Ohio, May 21, 1955; s. Anthony John and Jennie (Perko) T.; m. Bette Lou Witherspoon, May 12, 1984; children: Lauren Ivana, Erica Kathleen. BBA, Cleve. State U., 1977; MA in Human Resource Mgmt., Pepperdine U., 1981. CPA, Ohio. Commd. 2d lt. USMC, 1974, advanced through grades to capt., resigned, 1981, active Res., 1981-91; internal auditor USMC, Okinawa, Japan, 1977-78; comptroller, budget officer USMC, New Orleans, 1979-81; internal auditor Med. Mutual div. Blue Shield, Cleve., 1981-82, supr. cost and budget, 1982-84; fin. analyst Cleve. Pneumatic, 1984-85; ptnr. Varner, LaCorte & Trennel, Willoughby, Ohio, 1985-88; pvt. practice acctg. Willoughby, 1988—; instr. Los Angeles Community Coll., Okinawa, 1978, Harding Bus. Coll., Maple Heights, Ohio, 1985-86, MTI Bus. Sch., Cleve., 1987—. Mem. AICPA, NRA, Am. SOc. Mil. Comptrollers, Ohio Soc. CPAs, Am. Legion, Euclid Rifle and Hunting Club (trustee 1985-88, fin. sec. 1988—), Slovene Nat. Benefit Soc. (sec., treas. 1984-88, pres. 1989—, fin. sec. 1990), Amvets. Republican. Episcopalian. Office: Lawrence W Trennel CPA 4139 Erie St Willoughby OH 44094-7806

TRENTMANN, JANET HOLT, corporate human resources consultant; b. Ames, Iowa, Aug. 24, 1951; d. George Lee and Almira Joyce (Olson) Holt; m. Norman Edward Trentmann, Feb. 20, 1982; children: Jonay Lynn, Andrew James. BS in Home Econs. Edn., Iowa State U., 1973; postgrad., U. Nebr., Omaha, 1977-79, Drake U., 1979-80. Customer rep. Iowa Power (now MidAm Energy Co.), Council Bluffs, 1973-79; comm. specialist Iowa Power (now MidAm Energy Co.), Des Moines, 1979-84, coord. pub. rels., 1984, coord. new employee tng., 1984-86, tng. specialist, 1986-91, human resources specialist, 1991-95, mem. employee polit. action com., 1975—; corp. human resources cons. MidAm Energy Co., Des Moines, 1995—; cons. Project Bus., Des Moines, 1982-83. Mem. care rev. com. Bethany Luth. Home, Council Bluffs, 1977-79; bd. dirs., sec. Westfair, Pottawattamie County, Iowa, 1975-79; advisor Jr. Achievement, Omaha, 1975; mem. social ministry com. Grace Luth. Ch., Des Moines, 1980—; mem. human resources coun. Urbandale (Iowa) Schs., 1992-94, mem. supt.'s adv. coun., 1991-94; mem. steering com. Urbandale Bus. Edn. Team, 1990—, chmn., 1991-94; bd. dirs. Des Moines Jr. Women's Club, 1988-94, 1st v.p., 1990-92, pres., 1992-93; mem. Urbandale Civil Svc. Commn.; mem. Greater Des Moines Leadership Inst., 1994-95. Recipient recognition Future Farmers Am., 1985, Woman of Yr. award Des Moines Jr. Women's Club, 1995-96. Mem. ASTD (comm. com. 1990-91, program com. 1991-92), Assn. for Quality and Participation (bd. dirs. 1988-90), Soc. for Human Resources Mgmt. (cert. sr. profl. in human resources, cert. coord., v.p. programs, sec. 1995, state conf. treas.), Urbandale C. of C. Republican. Office: MidAm Energy Co PO Box 657 Des Moines IA 50303-0657

TREPPLER, IRENE ESTHER, state senator; b. St. Louis County, Mo., Oct. 13, 1926; d. Martin H. and Julia C. (Bender) Hagemann; student Meramec Community Coll., 1972; m. Walter J. Treppler, Aug. 18, 1950; children: John M., Steven A., Diane V. Anderson, Walter W. Payroll chief USAF Aero. Chart Plant, 1943-51; enumerator U.S. Census Bur., St. Louis, 1960, crew leader, 1970; mem. Mo. Ho. of Reps., Jefferson City, 1972-84; mem. Mo. Senate, Jefferson City, 1985—; chmn. Minority Caucus, 1991-92. ActiveGravois Twp. Rep. Club, Concord Twp. Rep. Club; alt. del. Rep. Nat. Conv., 1976, 84. Recipient Spirit Enterprise award Mo. C. of C., 1992, Appreciation award Mo. State Med. Assn., Nat. Otto Nuttli Earthquake Hazard Mitigation award, 1993, Disting. Legislator award Cmty. Colls. Mo., 1995; named Concord Twp. Rep. of Yr., 1992. Mem. Nat. Order Women Legislators (rec. sec. 1981-82, pres. 1985), Nat. Fedn. Rep. Women. Mem. Evangelical Ch. Office: Mo State Senate Rm 433 Jefferson City MO 65101

TRETTER, THERESA LYNN, physical therapist; b. Huntingburg, Ind., Mar. 20, 1963; d. Kenneth John and Doris Jean (Olinger) T. BS in Phys. Therapy, St. Louis U., 1985. Lic. phys. therapist, Mo., Ind., Ky. Phys. therapist Bapt. Hosp. East, Louisville, 1985-87, Associated Rehab. Svc., 1989-92, Healthcare Therapy Svc., 1992—. Bd. dirs. Big Sister/Big Bros. of Dubois County, Inc., 1991-92, co-chmn. Superstrikes, 1991, active, 1991—; co-chmn. Huntington Herbsfest, 1992, 93. Mem. Am. Phys. Therapy Assn. Roman Catholic. Home: PO Box 26 706 Orchard Rd Huntingburg IN 47542 Office: St Joseph's Hosp 1900 Medical Arts Dr Huntingburg IN 47542

TREVETHAN, ARTHUR H., insurance company executive; b. Wilkes-Barre, Pa., Nov. 5, 1946; s. George and Elizabeth (Reese) T.; m. Cheryl Ann Lewis, Sept. 2, 1967; children: Arthur R., Elizabeth Ann. BS, Wilkes U., 1968; MBA, U. Dayton, 1981. CPCU; cert. assoc. in reins., Inst. Inst. Dept. mgr. Arlans Dept. Store, Annapolis, Md., 1968-69; ops. mgr. Arthur Cook Supply, Laurel, Md., 1969-71; claims adjuster Royal Ins. Co., Wilkes-Barre, 1971-73, Nationwide Mut. Ins. Co., Wilkes-Barre, 1973-76; claims coord. Nationwide Mut. Ins. Co., Harrisburg, Pa., 1976-77; supr. claim tng. Nationwide Mut. Ins. Co., Columbus, Ohio, 1977-80, product devel. dir., 1980-88; mktg. mgr. Nationwide Mut. Ins. Co., Portland, Oreg., 1988-91; dir. reins. recovery Nationwide Mut. Ins. Co., Columbus, 1991—; mem. property com. N.C. Rate Bur., Raleigh, 1980-88. Mem. Bd. Zoning Appeals, Westerville, Ohio, 1994—. Office: Nationwide Mut Ins 2 Nationwide Plz Columbus OH 43216

TREWIN, REX EDWIN, educational director; b. Waterloo, Iowa, May 11, 1969; s. Arol David and Lynda Rae (Panter) T. Cert. pub. adminstrn., Erasmus U., 1990; BA in Polit. Sci. and Econs., Ind. U., 1991, MA in West European Studies, 1993. Coord. project NW Ind. World Trade Coun., Portage, 1993; job developer Life Skills Found., St. Louis, 1993-94; coord. of job devel. So. Ill. U., Edwardsville, 1994—. Fellow Fgn. Lang. Area Studies U.S. Govt., 1991-92. Mem. Assn. Internat. Educators, Regional Commerce and Growth Assn. (amb.), Ill. Assn. Coop. Edn. and Interns (mktg. chairperson 1995—), Mo. Gov.'s Com. on Employment of People with Disabilites, Engrs. Club St. Louis, World Trade Club St. Louis (seminar com. chair 1993—). Home: 6257 Cates Ave Saint Louis MO 63130-3418

TREYLINEK, DONNA MARIE, physical therapist; b. Library, Pa., Oct. 7, 1966; d. Edward Michael and Helen Lee (Picard) T. BS in Exercise Sci., Pa. State U., 1988; MS in Phys. Therapy, Old Dominion U., 1990. Lic. phys. therapist, Pa., Ind. Staff phys. therapist Indpls. Phys. Therapy and Sports Medicine, Indpls., 1990-91; coord. clin. edn., phys. therapist Meth. Sports Medicine Ctr., Indpls., 1991—; med. staff World Gymnastics Championship, Indpls., 1991. Mem. Am. Phys. Therapy Assn., Ind. Phys. Therapy Assn., Sports Phys. Therapy Sect., Am. Coll. Sports Medicine. Office: Meth Sports Medicine Ctr Ste 200 201 Pennsylvania Pkwy Indianapolis IN 46268

TRICKLER, SALLY JO, technical illustrator; b. Burlington, Iowa, Jan. 7, 1948; d. Frank Joseph and Florence Christina (Hein) Koehler; m. James Edward Trickler, Nov. 4, 1967 (div.); 1 child, Brenda Jo. AA, Southeastern Community Coll., West Burlington, Iowa, 1976; BA, Western Ill. U., 1988. Draftsman Iowa Army Ammunition Plant, Middletown, 1967-73; sr. tech. illustrator J.I. Case Co., Burlington, 1973—; representer tech. illustrating Burlington Community High Sch. Career Day ann. event, 1985-91. Mem. pub. relations com. United Way, Burlington, 1975, chmn. pub. relations 1976-77, art designer, 1987. Mem. Burlington Engrs. Club (v.p. 1974-75, pres. 1975-76, chmn. high sch. counseling com. on career days, 1977-80), Allegro Motor Home Club Iowa, Phi Kappa Phi. Roman Catholic. Club: Good Sam (Big River Sams, Iowa) (sec./treas. 1985-87). Home: 11904 44th St Burlington IA 52601-8966 Office: JI Case Co 1930 Des Moines Ave Burlington IA 52601-4441

TRIGG, TOM, school system administrator; b. Fredonia, Kans., Aug. 13, 1952; s. Dick and Jean (Nuzum) T.; m. Julie Gowen, July 9, 1977; children: Mandy, Whitney, Aaron. BS, Ottawa U., 1974; MS, Emporia State U., 1976; EdD, U. Kans., 1986. Tchr. math. S.M. Northwest H.S., Shawnee, Kans., 1974-79; prin. Gardner (Kans.) Edgerton Antioch Schs., 1979-85, asst. supt., 1985—. Named Outstanding Young Educator Lenexa Jaycees, Kans. 4A Adminstr. of Yr. Kans. Theatre Assn.; recipient Leadership award NSCI. Mem. United Sch. Adminstrs., Am. Assn. Sch. Adminstrs., Kans. Assn. Sch. Adminstrs. Home: 19770 Moonlight Rd Gardner KS 66030 Office: Unified Sch Dist #231 PO Box 97 Gardner KS 66030

TRIMBLE, STEVE, state legislator; b. Dec. 1942; two children. BA, So. Meth. U.; postgrad., U. Chgo. Minn. State rep. Dist. 67B, 1987—; tchr.; vice-chmn. capital investments com.; chmn. regulation of industries and energy; mem. environ. and natural resources, rules and legislation adminstrn., environ. fin. coms. Office: 485 State Office Bldg Saint Paul MN 55155-1298*

TRIOLO, PETER T., dental researcher, educator; b. Rockford, Ill., Jan. 26, 1951; s. Peter Thomas and Angelina Rose (Fiorenza) T.; m. Pamela Ann Klauer, Jan. 6, 1979. BS, U. Iowa, 1983, DDS, 1987, MS, 1991. Recording engr. Source Sound Systems, Iowa City, 1972-93; dentist pvt. practice Iowa City, 1987-93; asst. rsch. scientist ctr. for clin. study U. Iowa, Iowa City, 1988-89, clin. instr. dept. operative dentistry, 1989-93, clin. dir., 1989-93; assoc. prof. operative dentistry Creighton U., Omaha, 1993—; cons. Network Records, Des Moines, 1975-80; reviewer Internat. Assn. Dental Rsch., Jour. Am. Dental Assn., Am. Jour. Dentistry. Contbr. articles to profl. jours. Mem. Dubuque (Iowa) Arts Coun., 1987. Recipient Dean's Leadership award U. Iowa, 1986, 87. Mem. ADA, Internat. Assn. for Dental Rsch. (dental materials program chmn.), Am. Assn. Dental Rsch., Nebr. Dental Assn., Acad. Operative Denistry (sci. sessions com. 1995—, chmn. spl. projects com.), Com. of Operative Dentistry Educators. Office: Crieghton Univ 215 Boyne Sch Dental Sci Omaha NE 68178

TRIPLETT, DOUGLAS ARNOLD, pathologist; b. Lafayette, Ind., Aug. 7, 1943; s. William Arnold and Lorene Virginia (Hafer) T.; m. Lea Nannette Humbert, June 6, 1987; children: Danielle Adrienne, Douglas Alexander. Student, North Park Coll., Chgo., 1961-64; MD, Ind. U., Indpls., 1968. Diplomate Am. Bd. Pathology with spl. qualification in hematology and transfusion medicine. Dir. hematology Ball Meml. Hosp., Muncie, Ind., 1974—, dir. med. edn., 1989—, v.p., 1989—; dir. Muncie Career Med. Edn. Muncie Ctr. Med. Edn. Ind. U. Sch. Medicine, Muncie, 1977—; asst. dean Ind. U. Sch. Medicine, Muncie, 1980—; cons. Nichols Lab., San Juan Capistrano, 1990. Author: Platelet Function, 1976, Hemostasis, 1985. Maj. M.C., U.S. Army, 1972-74. Fellow ACP, Am. Soc. Clin. Pathologists, Coll. Am. Pathologists (com. chair). Home: 3500 E County Road 350 S Muncie IN 47302-9671 Office: Ball Meml Hosp 2401 W University Ave Muncie IN 47303-3428

TRIPLETT, ERIC, fashion coordinator; b. Detroit, July 18, 1960; s. Ulysses and Anna Lenova (Jackson) T. AA, Wayne County C.C., Detroit, 1979; MA in Merchandising, Fashion Inst., L.A., 1981; cert. fashion coord., Paris (France) Fashion Inst., 1981. Chmn. Triplett Corps., Detroit, 1972—; window dresser Himelhochs, Southfield, Mich., 1976; sales assoc. J.L. Hudson, Southfield, 1976; dept. mgr. The Broadway, Culver City, Calif., 1978; intern in merchandising J.W. Robinsons, L.A., 1979; fashion model Kleine-Kinsler, L.A., 1981; presse attache May Co., L.A., 1981; fashion developer Bullocks, Sherman Oaks, Calif., 1980; owner Eric Triplett Inc., Detroit, 1982-83. Paris Fashion Inst. scholar, 1981. Home: 17386 Cherry Lawn Detroit MI 48221 Office: Triplett Corps 5476 W Adams Blvd Los Angeles CA 90016

TRIPLETT, ROBERT JOSEPH, state research analyst; b. Greenfield, Mo., Oct. 28, 1950; s. Elizabeth Triplett; m. Dorothy LaVerne Glover, Dec. 29,

1973 (dec. July 1994). BSBA, Lincoln U., 1974. Sales rep. Met. Life, 1974-75; security profl. Mo. State Senate, 1975-76; rsch. analyst Mo. Ho. of Reps., 1977—, Jefferson City. Chmn. Holts Summit (Mo.) Street Commn., 1979—. Home: PO Box 44 Holts Summit MO 65043

TRIPP, THOMAS NEAL, lawyer, political consultant; b. Evanston, Ill., June 19, 1942; s. Gerald Frederick and Kathryn Ann (Siebold) T.; m. Ellen Marie Larrimer, Apr. 16, 1966; children: David Larrimer, Bradford Douglas, Corinne Catherine. BA cum laude, Mich. State U., 1964; JD, George Washington U., 1967. Bar: Ohio 1967, U.S. Ct. Mil. Appeals 1968, U.S. Supreme Ct. 1968, Wyo. 1991. Pvt. practice law, Columbus, Ohio, 1969—, Wilson, Wyo., 1991—; real estate developer, Columbus, 1969—; chmn. bd. Black Sheep Enterprises, Columbus, 1969—; polit. cons. David A. Keene & Assocs., Washington, 1986—; vice chmn. bd. Sun Valley-Elkhorn Assn., Idaho, 1983-85, chmn. 1986-91; vice chmn. Sawtooth Sports, Ketchum, Idaho, 1983-85; legal counsel Wallace F. Ackley Co., Columbus, 1973—; bd. dirs. KWRP Broadcasting Corp., 1986-91; presiding judge Ohio Mock Trial Competition, 1986-94; bd. dirs. U.S. Master's Swimming, Ohio, 1988-91, 94—; bd. dirs. U.S. Prison Industries (apptd. former pres. Bush 1992), Zero Population Growth, 1993; mem. small bus. adv. coun. FCC (apptd. former pres. Bush 1992); dep. spl. adv. to the pres. North Am. Free Trade Agreement (apptd. Pres. Clinton 1993). Trustee Americans for Responsible Govt., Washington, GOPAC; mem. Peace Corps Adv. Council, 1981-85; mem. U.S. Commn. on Trade Policy and Negotiations, 1985-88; campaign mgr., fin. chmn. Charles Rockwell Saxbe, Ohio Ho. of Reps., 1974, 76, 78, 80; campaign mgr. George Bush for Pres., 1980, nat. dep. field dir., 1980; mem. alumni admissions council Mich. State U., 1984—, George Washington U., 1988—; regional co-chmn. Reagan-Bush, 1984, mem. nat. fin. com., 1984; mem. Victory '84 fin. com.; mem. Victory '88 fin. com. Bush-Quayle; co-chmn. Ohio Lawyers for Bush/Quayle, 1988; Rep. candidate 2d U.S. Congl. Dist., Idaho, 1988; transition dir. Ohio Sec. of State, 1990-91; mem., bd. trustees Columbus Acad. Pvt. Co-ed Secondary Sch., 1991-94; chair bd. dirs. T.R.E.E. Coalition, 1991—. Served to 1st lt. U.S. Army, 1967-69. Fellow Pi Sigma Alpha; Vietnam Vet. Am., Phi Delta Phi. Republican. Avocations: athletics, writing, political essays. Home: 5420 Clark State Rd Columbus OH 43230-1956

TRIST, JAMES E., small business owner, manufacturing engineer; b. Detroit, May 1, 1970. BS, Western Mich. U., 1993. Wood craftsman Select Mill Work, Kalamazoo, Mich., 1991-93; project coord. Plastic Mold Tech., Grand Rapids, Mich., 1993—. Mem. Soc. Plastics Engrs. Office: Plastic Mold Tech 4201 Broadmoor Ave SE Grand Rapids MI 49512-3934

TROJAN, TOM J., mechanical engineer; b. Cleve., Sept. 11, 1954. AD in Engring., Cuyahoga C.C., Cleve., 1976. Mech. designer Stock Equipment Co., Chagrin, Ohio, 1979-81; mech. engr. Lucas Aerospace Inc., Aurora, Ohio, 1981-92, Forry Inc., Cleve., 1992—. Coach, mgr. Lucas Softball, Aurora, ohio, 1983-86. Mem. Am. Metals Assn. Republican. Methodist. Home: 526 Heather Ln Bedford OH 44146-2334 Office: Forry Inc 692 Alpha Dr Cleveland OH 44143-2123

TROMANHAUSER, EDWARD DOWNER, criminologist and political science educator; b. Mpls., Aug. 30, 1932; s. Haver Downer and Lorraine Frances (Rowe) T.; m. Donna Elizabeth Morton, June 5, 1952 (div. Sept., 1957); 1 child, Donna Sharon; m. Mary Lou Mohr, Mar. 13, 1974. BA in Psychology, Chgo. State U., 1973; MA in Criminal Justice, U. Ill., 1975, MA in Polit. Sci., 1980; PhD in Pub. Policy, Union Grad. Sch., Cin., 1990. Writer Ill. Law Enforcement Commn., Chgo., 1970-71; grant writer Chgo. State U., 1971-72, instr., 1972-74, asst. prof., 1974-76, assoc. prof., 1976-78, prof., 1981—; program dir. Chgo. Bd. Edn., 1978-80; chmn. bd. dirs. Ill. Pub. Edn. Assn. Author: (books) An Eye for an Eye, 1970, Schools Under Siege, 1992, A Primer on Gangs, 1995; also articles. Mem. ho. of dels., Am. Correctional Assn., Laurel Park, Md., 1985-88, adv. bd. Salvation Army of Chgo., 1990-95. Mem. Ill. Acad. of Criminology (exec. bd. 1975—, pres. 1975, Hans W. Mattick award 1980), Am. Soc. Criminology, Acad. of Criminal Justice Scis., Midwest Criminal Justice Assn. Office: Chgo State U 9501 S King Dr Chicago IL 60628

TROMBOLD, WALTER STEVENSON, supply company executive; b. Chanute, Kans., June 21, 1910; s. George John and Margaret (Stevenson) T.; m. Charlotte Elizabeth Kaufman, Dec. 28, 1941; children: Joan Benjamin, Lynn Oliphant, Walter Steven, David George, Charles Phillip. BS in Bus., U. Kans., 1932; AA, Iola Jr. Coll., 1930; spl. degree, Balliol Coll., Oxford U., 1943. Pers. worker with evangelist Billy Sunday, 1928; asst. mgr. S.H. Kress & Co., 1932-38; counselor Penn Mut. Life Ins. Co., 1938-41; field mgr. Travelers Ins. Co., Kansas City, 1938-41 with Reid Supply Co., Wichita, Kans., Kansas City, Mo., Topeka, Kans. 1946-86, pres., chmn. bd. Reid Supply Co., Inc., 1954-86, Trombold Consultation Svc., 1986—; bd. dirs., v.p. Nat. Distbrs. Coun. Bd. dirs., officer YMCA, 1922—; merit badge councilor Boy Scouts Am.; bd. dirs. Camp Fire Girls; life mem. PTA, 1953—, pres., 1952; chmn. pers. adv. bd. City of Wichita, Kans., 1956-86; bd. dirs Salvation Army; commr. Gen. Assembly Presbyn. Ch. USA, past deacon, elder, trustee; commr. Synods of Mid-Am., Presbytery of So. Kans.; bd. dirs. Wesley Hosp. Assocs., 1972-82; assoc. chmn. Nat. Laymen's Bible Week, 1972-86; mem. adv. bd. Salvation Army, 1988—; worker with Evangelist Billy Sunday, 1928; mem. Salvation Army Rehab. Ctr., 1988—; mem. Super Sr. Tennis, 1970—; area chmn. Neighbor Watch, 1990—; ofcl. photographer U. Kans. Relays. Lt. comdr. USN, 1942-46. Recipient various awards including Honor Man Wichita Swim Club, 1970, Disting. Svc. award to Youth YMCA, 1970, Svc. award to Swimmers Kans. State High Sch. Activities, 1975, Key Man award Jr. C. of C., 1940, 46; Sr. Olympic State Champion Tennis and Swimming, 1989-90, 91-92; named Outstanding Young Man of Wichita Jr. C. of C., 1940. Mem. Textile Allied Treades Assn. (bd. dirs., dist. chmn. Honor Man 1976), Kans. LST Assn. (charter pres. 1990), Kans. U. Alumni Assn. (life), Kans. C. of C., Wichita C. of C., Sales and Mktg. Execs. (bd. dirs., v.p.), Old Timer Club (sec., treas. 1964-86, Honor Man of Yr. 1977), Wichita Racquet Club, Knife and Fork Internat. Club (bd. dirs., v.p.), Univ. Club (chmn. bd. dirs., v.p.), Rotary (bd. dirs., ofcl. photographer to historian, Disting. Svc. award 1989), Masons (32 deg.), Alpha Tau Omega. Republican. Home: 1401 W River Blvd Wichita KS 67203-3355

TRONVOLD, LINDA JEAN, occupational therapist; b. Yankton, S.D., Dec. 8, 1950; m. Marvis D. Tronvold, July 7, 1976; children: Marcie, Tami, Kristi, Bradley, Cindy. Student, Mt. Marty Coll., 1989; AS, Kirkwood Community Coll., Cedar Rapids, Iowa, 1989; BS, Creighton U., 1991. Registered occupl. therapist, S.D., Neb., Iowa. Psychiatric aide S.D. Human Svcs. Ctr., Yankton, 1969-74, mental health technician, 1974-85, occpul. therapist asst., 1985-89, occupl. therapist, 1991-92; mem. edn. svc. unit Human Svcs. Ctr., Yankton, 1991-93; asst. program dir. occupl. therapy Western Iowa Tech. C.C., Dakota Dunes, S.D., 1993—; dir. occupl. therapy Nova Care, Inc., 1993—; guest speaker Creighton U., Omaha, U. S.D., Vermillion; mem. student staff Upward Bound, Omaha, 1989-91,. Scout leader Boy Scouts Am., Hartington, Nebr., 1977-80, Girl Scouts USA, Yankton, 1986-89; Sunday sch. tchr. United Ch. of Christ, Yankton, 1984-88; mem. spl. populations staff YWCA, Cedar Rapids, Iowa, 1987-88. Mem. Am. Occupl. Therapy Assn., S.D. Occupl. Therapy Assn., Nebr. Occupl. Therapy Assn., Iowa Occupl. Therapy Assn., Creighton U. Student Occupl. Therapy Assn., VFW Aux., Sq. Dance Club (pres. 1979-81), Alpha Tri Ota Club. Home: 705 Broadway St Yankton SD 57078-3923 Office: 350 W Anchor Dr Ste 500 Dakota Dunes SD 57049-5153

TROSKO, JAMES EDWARD, research radiation geneticist; b. Muskegon, Mich., Apr. 2, 1938; s. Andrew and Christina (Nemeth) T.; m. Beverly Kay Dowell, Sept. 3, 1960; 1 chld, Philip Randal. BA, Cen. Mich. U., 1960; MS, Mich. State U., 1962, PhD, 1963. Postdoctoral fellow Oak Ridge (Tenn.) Nat. Lab., 1963-66; asst. prof. Mich. State U., East Lansing, 1966-69, assoc. prof., 1969-74, prof., 1974—; chief of rsch. Radiation Effects Rsch. Found., Hiroshima, Japan, 1990-92; vis. prof. U. Wis., Madison, 1972-73; mem. organ systems com. Nat. Cancer Inst., Bethesda, Md., 1985-87; mem. Critical Materials Registry Adv. Com., Lansing, Mich., 1985-87; mem. adv. com. on health effects of asbestos EPA, Bethesda. Contbr. over 240 sci. and rev. articles, 250 sci. abstracts to profl. jours. Recipient Cancer Devel. award Nat. Cancer Inst., 1972-77, U.K. Environ. Mutagen Soc. award, 1980, Sr. Scientist award Sigma Xi, 1985, Centennial award Ctrl. Mich. U., 1993, Kenneth DuBois Achievement award Midwest Soc. Toxicology, 1995. Mem. Am. Assn. Cancer Rsch., Environ. Mutagen Soc., Toxicology Soc., Genetics Soc. Am. Office: Mich State U Dept Pediatrics Human East Lansing MI 48824

TROTMAN, ALEXANDER J., automobile manufacturing company executive; b. 1933; married. MBA, Mich. State U., 1972. Various positions Ford Motor Co., Europe, 1955-69, Dearborn, Mich., 1969-71, dir. sales and mktg. planning, 1971-72, exec. dir. product planning and research, 1972-75, chief car planning mgr. Car Product Devel. Group, 1975-77, exec. dir. ops. planning, 1977-78, asst. gen. mgr. truck and recreational products ops., 1978-79, corp. v.p., from 1979, mgr. truck ops. Ford of Europe, Inc., then pres. Ford Asia-Pacific Inc., 1983-84, pres., chmn. Ford of Europe, Inc., from 1984, then exec. v.p. No. Am. auto ops., now chmn. bd., pres., CEO, dir. Ford Motor Co., 1993—; bd. dirs. IBM Corp., Armonk, N.Y. Served with RAF, 1951-55. Office: Ford Motor Co The American Rd Dearborn MI 48121*

TROUPE, CHARLES QUINCY, state legislator; b. St. Louis, May 12, 1936. Qiploma, Nat. Inst. Electronics & Tech, Denver. Elec. contrator; mem. Mo. Ho. of Reps. from 63d dist., 1978-82, Mo. Ho. of Reps. from 62d dist., 1982—; chmn. Appropriations, Social Svc. and Corrections Coms. Mo. Ho. of Reps., mem. Budget, Banks & Fin. Instns., Local Govt. Accounts, Ops. and Fin Coms.; mem. Mo. Legis. Black Caucus. V.p. Local 788 ATU. Democrat. Home: 5338 Claxton Ave Saint Louis MO 63120-2537*

TROUT, CALVIN DANIEL, marketing executive; b. Chgo., Aug. 20, 1946; s. Daniel and Theresa (Boudreau) T.; m. Lata Arora Trout, Apr. 14, 1980; children: Victor Kumar, John Kumar. BS in Edn., No. Ill. U., 1969, MS in Edn., 1970. Tchr., prin. Rochelle/Hartsburg/Rockford (Ill.) Schs., 1969-76; Midwest mgr. Harcourt, Brace & Jovanovich, Chgo., 1976-78; pubs. rep. Lyle Hurd's Assocs., Chgo., 1978-79; account exec. P.O.F. Internat. Inc. Co., Chgo., 1979-81; pub. rep. Karaban, Labiner & Assocs., Chgo., 1982-83; dist. mgr. Putman Pub., Chgo., 1983; assoc. sales dir. Inst. Food Technologists, Chgo., 1983-88, dir. mktg. and membership devel., 1988-94; dir. sales and mktg., 1994—. Author: Wealth on Your Paycheck, 1991. Mem. Am. Soc. Assn. Execs. (charter mem. mktg. coun.), Coun. Engring. and Sci. Soc. Execs., Chgo. Soc. Assn. Execs. (founding chmn. mktg./membership spl. interest group, chmn. SIG com., membership com. chmn., adv. bd. mem. Forum Mag.), Soc. of Nat. Assn. Publs. Republican. Baptist. Home: 30 Drexel Ave La Grange IL 60525-5816 Office: Inst Food Technologists 221 N La Salle St Chicago IL 60601-1206

TROUTNER, JOANNE JOHNSON, school technology administrator, educator, consultant; b. Muncie, Ind., Sept. 9, 1952; d. Donal Russel and Lois Vivian (Hicks) Johnson; m. Lary William Troutner, May 17, 1975. BA in Media and English, Purdue U., 1974, MS in Edn., 1976. Media specialist Lafayette (Ind.) Sch. Corp., 1974-77, 81-83, computer resource tchr., 1983-84; media specialist, Tippecanoe Sch. Corp., Lafayette, 1984-85, ednl. computer coord., 1985-87, coord. instrl. support, 1988-94, dir. tech. and media, 1994—; instrnl. specialist edn. IBM, 1987-88; tchr. English, Minot Pub. Schs. (N.D.), 1978-79, media specialist, 1979-81; vis. prof. continuing edn. U. S.C., Columbia, summer 1983; instr. Purdue U., West Lafayette; vis. prof. continuing edn. U. N.D.; bd. dirs. Tippecanoe County Pub. Libr., pres., 1994, 95. Author: The Media Specialist, The Microcomputer and the Curriculum, 1983,; software selector Elementary Sch. Libr. Collection; contbr. materials rev. column Sch. Libr. Media Quar.; computer literacy columnist Jour. Computers in Math. and Sci. Teaching; computer software columnist Emergency Libr., 1989—, internet columnist, 1995—; editor newsletter Indiana Computer Educators. Active Greater Lafayette Leadership Acad. Alumni Group, 1983—; bd. dirs. Lafayette Family Svc. Agy., 1987-89; mem. dean's adv. coun. Sch. Edn. Purdue U. Mem. ALA, Ind. Assn. Media Educators (chmn. computer div. 1982-84), Am. Assn. Sch. Librarians (sec. 1983-84, 2d v.p. 1985-86), Internat. Coun. for Computers in Edn. (interactive video spl. interest group newsletter editor 1986-87), Ind. Computer Educators (bd. dirs. 1986-92, pres. 1990-91), Internat. Soc. Tech. Educators, Assn. Supr. and Curriculum Devel., Phi Beta Kappa, Kappa Delta Gamma, Phi Delta Kappa (v.p. programs 1987-88, v.p. memberships 1988-89, pres. 1989-90). Home: 4001 Penny Packers Mill Rd Lafayette IN 47905-3557 Office: Tippecanoe Sch Corp 21 Elston Rd Lafayette IN 47905-7000

TROWBRIDGE, JEFF, plant engineer; b. Sheboygan, Wis., Jan. 25, 1928. BS, U. Wis., 1950. Plant engr. Benmis Mfg. Co., Sheboygan Falls,, Wis., 1955—; bd. dirs. Bemis Mfg., Sheboygan Falls. Vol. Exptl. Aircraft Assn. Lt. U.S. Navy, 1950-52,. Home: PO Box 181 Sheboygan WI 53082-0181 Office: Bemis Mfg Co PO Box 901 Sheboygan Falls WI 53085-0901

TROY, DANIEL PATRICK, state legislator; b. Cleveland, Ohio, May 6, 1948; s. John Edward and Marjorie (Farrell) T. U. Dayton, 1970. City councilman Ward I, Willowick, Ohio, 1972-77, coun. pres., 1980-82; pres. Lake County Coun. Govt., Ohio, 1975-78; committeeman Lake County Dem. Com., 1976; Ohio State Rep. Dist. 60, 1983-92, Dist. 70, 1993; del. Dem. Nat. Conv., 1984; tech. Kahoe Air Balance Co., 1967-74; prof. Balance Co., 1975-80, proj. engr., 1980. Recipient Legis. Svc. award, 1983-84, Ohio Sea grant Disting. Svc. award, 1988, Legis. Leadership award Ohio Coalition for Edn. Handicapped Children, 1989, 91, Voc. Edn. Person of Yr. award, 1989, Ohio Edn. Broadcasting award, 1983, Friends of Cmty. Coll. Excellence award, 1994. Mem. AFL, East Side Irish-Am. Club. Home: 31600 Lakeshore Blvd Willowick OH 44094*

TROYAN, SCOTT D., communications consultant; b. Akron, Ohio, Oct. 1, 1959; s. David C. and Ellen J. (Oates) T.; m. Marilyn V. Mast, July 10, 1982. BA, U. Akron, 1982, MA, 1985; MA, U. Wis., 1988, PhD, 1991. Teaching asst. U. Akron, 1982-84, U. Wis., Madison, 1987-88; ind. scholar Garland Pub. Inc., N.Y.c., 1991-94; comms. cons. Marschall Products-Rhône-Poulenc, Madison, Wis., 1992-94, Cuna Svc. Group Card Svcs., Madison, 1994-96; sec. Medieval studies program U. Wis., Madison, 1988-91; composition program rep. U. Akron, 1981-82. Author: Textual Decorum, 1994; contbr. articles to profl. jours. Vilas fellow U.Wis., 1987-88. Mem. ASTD, MLA, Phi Sigma Alpha. Republican. Methodist. Home: 3313 Leopold Way # 204 Madison WI 53713

TROYER, DERYL LEE, life sciences educator; b. York, Nebr., May 29, 1947; s. Glenn Titus and Aldene Ethel (Reeb) T.; m Joyce Arlene Larson, May 21, 1972; children: Travis Carl, Darcy Lea. DVM, Kans. State U., 1972, PhD, 1985. Assoc. Arlington Heights (Ill.) Animal Hosp., 1972-73; ptnr. Pawnee City (Nebr.) Animal Hosp., 1973-80; asst. prof. life scis. U. Ill., Urbana, 1985-86; asst. prof. Kans. State U., Manhattan, 1986-90, assoc. prof., 1991-96, prof., 1996—. Contbr. articles to profl. jours. Office: Kans State U 228 Vet Med Scis Bldg Manhattan KS 66506

TROZZOLO, ANTHONY MARION, chemistry educator; b. Chgo., Jan. 11, 1930; s. Pasquale and Francesca (Vercillo) T.; m. Doris C. Stoffregen, Oct. 8, 1955; children: Thomas, Susan, Patricia, Michael, Lisa, Laura. BS, Ill. Inst. Tech., 1950; MS, U. Chgo., 1957, PhD, 1960. Asst. chemist Chgo. Midway Labs., 1952-53; assoc. chemist Armour Rsch. Found., Chgo., 1953-56; mem. tech. staff Bell Labs., Murray Hill, N.J., 1959-75; Charles L. Huisking prof. chemistry U. Notre Dame, 1975-92, Charles L. Huisking prof. emeritus, 1992—, asst. dean Coll. Sci., 1993—, P.C. Reilly lectr., 1972, Hesburgh Alumni lectr., 1986, Disting. lectr. sci., 1986; vis. prof. Columbia U., N.Y.C., 1971, U. Colo., 1981, Katholieke U. Leuven, Belgium, 1983, Max Planck Inst. für Strahlenchemie, Mülheim/Ruhr, Fed. Republic Germany, 1990; vis. lectr. Academia Sinica, 1984, 85; Phillips lectr. U. Okla., 1971; C.L. Brown lectr. Rutgers U., 1975; Sigma Xi lectr. Bowling Green U., 1976, Abbott Labs., 1978; M. Faraday lectr. No. Ill. U., 1976; F.O. Butler lectr. S.D. State U., 1978; Chevron lectr. U. Nev., Reno, 1983; plenary lectr. various internat. confs.; founder, chmn. Gordon Conf. on Organic Photochemistry, 1964; trustee Gordon Rsch. Confs., 1988-92; cons. various chem. cos. Assoc. editor Jour. Am. Chem. Soc., 1975-76; editor Chem. Revs., 1977-84; editorial adv. bd. Accounts of Chem. Rsch., 1977-85; cons. editor Encyclopedia of Science and Technology, 1982-92; contbr. articles to profl. jours.; patentee in field. Fellow AEC, 1951, NSF, 1957-59. Fellow N.Y. Acad. Scis. (chmn. chem. scis. sect. 1969-70, Halpern award in photochemistry 1980), AAAS, Am. Inst. Chemists (Student award 1950); mem. AAUP, Am. Chem. Soc. (Disting. Svc. award St. Joseph Valley sect. 1979, Coronado lectr. 1980, 93, N.Y. state lectr. 1993, Hoosier lectr. 1995, Ozark lectr. 1995), Sigma Xi. Roman Catholic. Home: 1329 E Washington St South Bend IN 46617-3340 Office: U Notre Dame Sch Medicine Notre Dame IN 46556

TRUCKSIS, THERESA A., library director; b. Hubbard, Ohio, Sept. 1, 1924; d. Peter and Carmella (DiSilverio) Pagliasotti; m. Robert C. Trucksis, May 29, 1948 (dec. May 1980); children: M. Laura, Anne, Michele, Patricia, David, Robert, Claire, Peter; m. Philip P. Hickey, Oct. 19, 1985 (dec. May 1993). BS in Edn., Youngstown Coll., 1945; postgrad., Youngstown State U., 1968-71; MLS, Kent State U., 1972. Psychometrist Youngstown (Ohio) Coll., 1946-49; instr. ltd. svc. Youngstown State U., 1968-71; libr. Pub. Libr. Youngstown & Mahoning County, Youngstown, 1972-73, asst. dept. head, 1973-74, asst. dir., 1985-89, dir., 1989—; dir. NOLA Regional Libr. System, Youngstown, 1974-85. Contbr. articles to profl. jours. Mem. bd. Hubbard Sch. Dist., 1980-85. Mem. ALA, Ohio Libr. Assn. (bd. dirs. 1979-81), Pub. Libr. Assn. Office: Pub Libr Youngstown & Mahoning County 305 Wick Ave Youngstown OH 44503-1003

TRUE, RAYMOND STEPHEN, writer, editor, analyst, consultant; b. Lowell, Mass., June 29, 1934; s. Sylvester Raymond and Madeline Rose (Farrell) T.; m. Doreen Therese Jambrosek. BA, U. Chgo., 1961, MBA, 1968, postgrad., 1968-69. Commd. 2nd lt. USAF, 1953, advanced through grades to col., 1980; master navigator U.S. Air Force Reserve, Chgo., 1957-77; regional cons. U.S. Bur. Census, 1970-71; dir. operations U.S. Air Force Reserve, Milw., 1977-80, base civil engr., 1980-87, chief planning analyst, 1987-89; owner Classic Comics Libr., 1990—; fire marshall Milw. County, 1980-87, chmn. membership Reserve Officers Assn., Wash. 1975-78. Editor Classics Newsletter, 1971-75. Campaign mgr. 10th Congressional Dist. Dem. Orgn., Skokie, Ill., 1969. Mem. Air Force Assn., Grad. Sch. Bus. Exec. Council U. Chgo. Roman Catholic. Address: Classic Comics Libr PO Box 784 Libertyville IL 60048-0784

TRUITT, KEVIN, revenue administrator, investment adviser; b. Chgo., Jan. 2, 1953; s. Alfred and Ethel Jane (Gibson) Henry; m. Karen McDowell, May 8, 1993; 1 child, Marissa. Grad., DePaul U., 1977. Registered investment adviser, Ill. Staff auditor Arthur Young and Co., Chgo., 1977-79; sr. fin. analyst Baxter-Travenol, Chgo., 1979-80; corp. banking officer First Chgo. Corp., 1980-87; comml. banking officer Bank Hapoalim, B.M., Chgo., 1988; asst. v.p. Harris Trust and Savs. Bank, Chgo., 1988-89, Bank Hapoalim, B.M., Chgo., 1989-90; dep. dir. Chgo. Dept. Revenue, 1991—. Recipient Pullman scholarship Pullman Edn. Found., 1975, Outstanding Bus. and Profl. award Dollars and Sense Mag., 1993; named one of Outstanding Young Men of Am., 1989. Office: City of Chgo Dept Revenue The DePaul Ctr 333 S State St Ste LL30 Chicago IL 60604

TRUITT, ROBERT LINDELL, immunologist, researcher, pediatrics educator; b. Carbondale, Ill., July 26, 1946; s. Arthur G. and Verna A. (Lingle) T.; m. Dawn M. Kowalkiewicz, Sept. 2, 1967; children: Cabrina M., Valerie L., Tiffany D., Andrea L., Lyndell M. BA, So. Ill. U., 1968, PhD, 1973. Rsch. assoc. Mt. Sinai Med. Ctr., Milw., 1975-77, sr. scientist, 1977-83, assoc. dir. Winter Rsch. Lab., 1983-84; rsch. assoc. prof. Med. Coll. of Wis., Milw., 1984-88, rsch. prof., 1988-91; prof., 1991—; cons. NIH, Bethesda, Md., 1978—, Netherlands Cancer Found., The Hague, VA. Reviewer Blood, Bone Marrow Transplantation, Jour. Immunology; editor: Cellular Immunotherapy of Cancer, 1987. Bd. trustees Leukemia Soc. Am., Wis., 1986-90, 1991—. United Cancer Coun. fellow, 1972-73, Damon Runyon Meml. Fund fellow, 1973-75, Leukemia Soc. Am., Inc. fellow, 1976-78, scholar, 1978-83. Mem. Am. Soc. for Microbiology, Assn. for Gnotobiotics (bd. dirs. 1980-83, 91—, pres. 1981-82), Internat. Soc. for Exptl. Hematology, Am. Assn. Immunologists. Office: Med Coll of Wis Dept of Pediatrics 8701 W Watertown Plank Rd Milwaukee WI 53226-3548

TRUOG, WILLIAM EDWARD, III, pediatrician, educator, researcher; b. Kansas City, Mo., Feb. 5, 1947; s. William E. and Virginia (Sylvester) T.; m. Jill D. Jacobson, July 11, 1992. BA cum laude, Carleton Coll., 1969; MD, U. Chgo., 1973. Intern, resident in pediatrics, chief resident Children's Orthopedic Hosp.-U. Wash., Seattle, 1973-76, research fellow in neonatology, 1976-78; asst. prof. pediatrics U. Wash., 1978-82, assoc. prof., 1982—; med. dir. infant intensive care unit Children's Orthopedic Hosp., Seattle, 1982-91; prof. pediatrics Sch. Medicine UMKC, 1993—; first physician scientist Children's Mercy Hosp., 1993. Author: Critical Care of the Newborn, 1983, 2d edit., 1988; also articles in med. jours. NIH grantee, 1981, 84. Mem. Am. Thoracic Soc. (grantee 1978), Am. Pediatric Soc., Soc. Pediatric Research, Western Soc. for Pediatric Research. Episcopalian. Office: Children's Mercy Hosp 2401 Gillham Rd Kansas City MO 64108

TRURAN, JAMES WELLINGTON, JR., astrophysicist; b. Brewster, N.Y., July 12, 1940; s. James Wellington and Suzanne (Foglesong) T.; m. Carol Kay Dell'Acy, June 26, 1965; children—Elaina Michelle, Diana Lee, Anastasia Elizabeth. B.A. in Physics, Cornell U., 1961; M.S. in Physics, Yale U., 1963, Ph.D. in Physics, 1966. Postdoctoral rsch. assoc. NAS-NRC Goddard Inst. Space Studies, NASA, N.Y.C., 1965-67; asst. prof. physics Belfer Grad. Sch. Sci., Yeshiva U., 1967-70; rsch. fellow in physics Calif. Inst. Tech., 1968-69; assoc. prof. Belfer Grad. Sch. Sci., Yeshiva U., 1970-72, prof., 1972-73; prof. astronomy U. Ill., Urbana, 1973-91; sr. vis. fellow, Guggenheim Meml. Found. fellow Inst. Astronomy, U. Cambridge, Eng., 1979-80; trustee Aspen Ctr. Physics, 1979-85, 91-93, v.p., 1985-88; assoc. U. Ill. Center for Advanced Study, 1979-80, 86-87; prof. astronomy astrophysics U. Chgo., 1991—; Alexander von Humboldt-Stiftung sr. scientist Max-Plank Inst., Munich, Germany, 1986-87, 94. Contbr. articles to profl. jours.; co-editor: Nucleosynthesis, 1968, Nucleosynthesis— Challenges and New Developments, 1985, Nuclear Astrophysics, 1987; editor: Physics Letters B, 1974-80. Co-recipient Yale Sci. and Engring. Assn. annual award for advancement basic or applied sci., 1980. Fellow AAAS, Am. Phys. Soc.; mem. Am. Astron. Soc., Am. Phys. Soc., Internat. Astron. Union. Home: 210 Wysteria Dr Olympia Fields IL 60461-1202 Office: U Chgo Dept Astronomy Astrophysics 5640 S Ellis Ave Chicago IL 60637-1433

TRUSKOWSKI, JOHN BUDD, lawyer; b. Chgo., Dec. 3, 1945; s. Casimer T. and Jewell S. (Kirk) T.; m. Karen Lee Sloss, Mar. 21, 1970; children: Philip K., Jennifer B. BS, U. Ill., 1967; JD, U. Chgo., 1970. Bar: Ill. 1970, U.S. Dist. Ct. (no. dist.) Ill. 1970, U.S. Tax Ct. 1977. Assoc. Keck, Mahin & Cate, Chgo., 1970-71, 74-78, ptnr., 1978—. Author, editor Callaghan's Federal Tax Guide, 1987. Served to lt, USNR, 1971-74. Mem. ABA, Ill. State Bar Assn., Chgo. Bar Assn. Republican. Presbyterian. Home: 251 Kimberly Ln Lake Forest IL 60045-3862 Office: Keck Mahin & Cate 77 W Wacker Dr 49th Fl Chicago IL 60601

TRUTHAN, CHARLES EDWIN, physician; b. Cleve., Mar. 30, 1955; s. Jordan Alexander and Jean Marie (Knoll) T.; m. Joyce Lynn Miller, Dec. 4, 1982; children: Jennifer Ann, Patricia Jean, Kristine Marie. BA in Psychology, U. Toledo, 1979; DO, Ohio U., 1986. Diplomate Nat. Bd. Osteo. Med. Examiners; bd. cert. Am. Coll. Osteo. Family Practitioners. Instr. anatomy and physiology Hocking Tech. Coll., Nelsonville, Ohio, 1980-81; intern Brentwood Osteo. Hosp., Cleve., 1986-87; resident in family practice Davenport (Iowa) Med. Ctr., 1987-88; pvt. practice Wisconsin Dells, Wis., 1989-93; chief med. svcs. Troop Med. Clinic #1, Ft. McCoy, Wis., 1992-93; med. adviser Maple Heights (Ohio) Fire Dept., 1986-87; instr. ACLS, Am. Heart Assn., 1985—; instr. EMT tng. MATC, Madison, Wis., 1989-93; med. dir. Wis. BTLS, 1990-93, bd. dirs., 1992-93; v.p. med. staff Patient Care Specialists, 1994-96, Flight Physician Aeromed., 1994-96. Firefighter, paramedic Willoughby Hills (Ohio) Fire Dept., 1973-84; firefighter Springfield Twp. Vol. Fire Dept., Toledo, 1977-79; EMT instr. Dept. Vocat. Edn., Trade and Indsl. Edn., Ohio, 1976-83; vol. APPAL Corps, Athens, Ohio, 1980; bd. dirs. S.E. Ohio Regional Coun. on Alcoholism, Athens, 1980-81; med. dir. Quad City Air Show, Devenport, 1988. Comdr. USPHS, active duty with U.S. Coast Guard, 1988-89, res., 1989—. Mem. Am. Osteo. Assn., Wis. Assn. Osteo. Physicians and Surgeons (sec.-treas. 1991-92, pres.-elect 1992-93, pres. 1993-94), Wis. Soc. Am. Coll. Osteo. Family Physicians (pres. 1992-93), Mich. Assn. Osteo. Physicians and Surgeons, Mich. Assn. Osteo. Family Physicians, Am. Acad. Family Practitioners, Assn. Mil. Osteo. Physicians and Surgeons, Assn. Mil. Surgeons U.S., Am. Coll. Physician Execs., Aircraft Owners and Pilots Assn., Exptl. Aircraft Assn., Res. Officers Assn. (life). Office: Patient Care Specialists Ste 370 21 Michigan NE Ste 370 Grand Rapids MI 49503

TRUTTER, JOHN THOMAS, consulting company executive; b. Springfield, Ill., Apr. 18, 1920; s. Frank Louis and Frances (Mischler) T.; m. Edith English Woods II, June 17, 1950; children: Edith English II, Jonathan Woods. BA, U. Ill., 1942; postgrad., Northwestern U., 1947-50, U. Chgo., 1947-50; LHD (hon.), Lincoln Coll., 1986. Various positions Ill. Bell, Chgo., 1946-58, gen. traffic mgr., from asst. v.p. pub. rels. to gen. mgr., 1958-69, v.p. pub. rels., 1969-71, v.p. operator svcs., 1971-80, v.p. community affairs, 1980-85; mem. hdqs. staff AT&T, N.Y.C., 1955-57; pres. John T. Trutter Co., Inc., Chgo., 1985—; pres., CEO Chgo. Conv. and Visitors Bur., 1985-88; pres. Chgo. Tourism Coun., 1988-90; mem. adv. bd. The Alford Group, Chgo., 1984—, Bozell-Worldwide, Chgo., 1994-96; chancellor Lincoln Acad. of Ill., 1985—. Co-author: Handling Barriers in Communication, 1957, The Governor Takes a Bride, 1977. Past chmn., life trustee Jane Addams Hull House Assn.; hon. chmn. United Cerebral Palsy Assn. Greater Chgo., chmn. Canal Corridor Assn., 1991—; bd. dirs. Chgo. Crime Commn., Abraham Lincoln Assn., Lyric Opera Chgo.; v.p. English Speaking Union, 1989-91, bd. govs., 1980—; chmn. bd. City Colls. Chgo. Found., 1987-91; past chmn. Children's Home and Aid Soc. Ill.; v.p. City Club Chgo.; treas. Chgo. United, 1970-85; mem. Ill. Econ. Devel. Commn., 1985; past presiding co-chmn. NCCJ; v.p., bd. dirs. Ill. Humane Soc. Found.; numerous others; bd. govs. Northwestern U. Libr. Coun., 1984—; trustee Lincoln (Ill.) Coll., 1987-90, Mundelein Coll., 1988-91; mem. sch. problems coun. State Ill. Assembly, 1985-91, spl. commn. on adminstrn. of justice in Cook County, 1986-92. Lt. col. U.S. Army. Decorated Legion of Merit; recipient Laureate award State of Ill., 1980, Outstanding Exec. Leader award Am. Soc. Fundraisers, Humanitarian of Yr. award, New Directions award SSMD, 1987, Jane Addams award The Hull House Assn., 1991. Mem. Pub. Rels. Soc. Am., Sangamon County Hist. Soc. (founder, past pres.), Ill. State Hist. Soc. (pres. 1985-87), Coun. on Ill. History (chmn. 1991—), U. Ill. Alumni Assn. (bd. dirs. 1990-94), Tavern Club, Econ. Club, Mid-Am. Club, Alpha Sigma Phi (Nat. Merit Achievement award 1994), Phi Delta Phi, founding chm. Evanston Historical Soc. advisory council 1995—.

TRYBER, THOMAS ANTHONY, JR., manufacturing company executive; b. Rapid City, S.D., May 18, 1943; s. Thomas A. and Rose Mary Tryber; student pub. schs., Racine, Wis; m. Kathleen M. Kober, May 25, 1963. Supr. cost and budgets J.I. Case, Racine, 1971-74, mgr. cost and budget control, 1974-77, fin. systems analyst, Wichita, Kans., 1977-78, mgr. systems and data processing, 1978-81; mgr. systems and data processing Steffens Dairy Foods Co., Inc., Wichita, Kans., 1982-87; system mgr. Hay & Forage Industries, 1988—. Mem. Data Processing Mgmt. Assn., Am. Prodn. Inventory Control Soc. Home: 2528 Milro St Wichita KS 67204-2554 Office: Hay & Forage Industries PO Box 4000 Hesston KS 67062-2094

TRYGESTAD, JOANN CAROL, secondary education educator; b. Mpls., Feb. 11, 1950; d. Harvey Oscar and Frances Anne (Libera) T. BS, U. Minn., 1972, MEd, 1983. Cert. tchr. social studies, history, English, Minn. Tchr. Sch. Dist. 742, St. Cloud, Minn., 1973-77, Sch. Dist. 196, Rosemount, Minn., 1977—; grad. asst. U. Minn., Mpls., 1988-90; adj. instr. Hamline U., St. Paul, 1987-90; steering com. mem. Alliance for Geography, St. Paul, 1988—; cons. in field. Contbr. articles to profl. jours. Mem. Nat. Coun. for Social Studies, Nat. Coun. for Geog. Edn., Am. Ednl. Rsch. Assn. Home: 4133 Arbor Ln Eagan MN 55122-2869 Office: Rosemount Sch Dist 14445 Diamond Path W Rosemount MN 55068-4143

TRYTEK, DAVID DOUGLAS, insurance company executive; b. Cleve., Jan. 18, 1955; s. Edmund Trytek and Mary Elaine Salzwedel Blech; m. Lorie Ann Stone, Apr. 10, 1982; children: Dane, Douglas. BS in BA, Bowling Green (Ohio) State U., 1977. Claims adjuster Liberty Mus. Ins. Co., Toledo, 1977-80; claims supr. Liberty Mus. Ins. Co., Milw., 1980-85; spl. claims examiner Liberty Mus. Ins. Co., Boston, 1986-89; claims mgr. Liberty Mus. Ins. Co., Green Bay, Wis., 1989-93; tech. svcs. mgr. Liberty Mut. Ins. Co., Milw., 1993-95; regional field investigations supr. Liberty Mutual Ins. Co., Milw., 1996—; arbitrator Inter-Co. Arbitration Com., Milw., 1984-85. Coach Toledo Optimists Youth Hockey Assn., 1979-80, Wauwatosa (Wis.) Recreation Dept., 1980-85, YMCA Youth Baseball, 1994; alt. Worker's Compensation divsn. Ins. Adv. Com., Madison, Wis., 1994l youth baseball and football coach, Sussex, Wis., 1995. Mem. Exptl. Aircraft Assn., Air Force Assn., Warbirds of Am., USA Hockey Inc. Office: Liberty Mutual Ins PO Box 0915 15700 W Bluemound Rd Brookfield WI 53008

TSAI, TI-DAO, electrophysiologist; b. Shanghai, China, Dec. 17, 1936; s. tong-Yun Cai and Cui-Ying Ma; 1 child, Li Cai. Student, Moscow U., USSR, 1961. From asst. to assoc. prof. Shanghai Inst. of Physiology, Academia Sinica, Shanghai, China, 1961--; electrophysiologist Pharmacia & Upjohn, Kalamazoo, Mich., 1990--; vis. scientist U. of Tex. Med. Branch, Galveston, 1981-82, U. Calgary, Alberta, Canada, 1987-88, U. Alberta, Edmonton, Alberta, Canada, 1989-90, Beckman Rsch. Inst., Duarte, Calif., 1990. Mem. editorial bd. Acta Physiologica Sinica, Shanghai, 1985-87; contbr. articles to profl. jours. Mem. Biophysical Soc., N.Y. Acad. Sci. Office: Upjohn Co 301 Henrietta St Kalamazoo MI 49007-4940

TSENG, JACK C., systems analyst; b. Taiwan, Feb. 2, 1959. BSME, Taipei Inst., Taiwan, 1979; MSME, U. Cin., 1984. Systems analyst M & M Precision Systems, Dayton, Ohio, 1984—. 2d lt. Taiwanese Armed Forces, 1979-81. Mem. Soc. Automotive Engrs., AGMA. Office: M&M Precision Systems 300 Progress Rd Dayton OH 45449-2322

TSUCHIYA, KEN, computer engineer; b. Iiyama, Japan, Dec. 30, 1947; came to U.S., 1967; s. Junzo and Fumi (Shiozaki) T.; m. Viviane M. Clausset, Oct. 6, 1973; 1 child, Aimee. BSEE, U. Minn., 1972. Registered profl. engr., Minn. Design, develop engr. Avionics Honeywell Co., Mpls., 1973-80; sys. design engr. Gen. Mills Co., Mpls., 1980; sr. design engr. Def. Honeywell Co., Mpls., 1980-83; prin. engr., cons. Unisys Co., St. Paul, 1983—. Patentee in field. Mem. IEEE, Minn. Profl. Engring. Soc. Home: 1425 N Innsbuck Dr Fridley MN 55432

TUCKER, BEVERLY SOWERS, information specialist; b. Trenton, N.J., Dec. 1, 1936; d. Eldon Jones and Verbeda Eleanor (Roberts) Sowers; m. Harvey Richard Tucker, Dec. 27, 1958 (div. Nov. 1983); children: Randall Richard, Brian Alan. BS in Chemistry with distinction, Purdue U., 1958; MS in Geology, No. Ill. U., 1985; MA in Library and Info. Sci., Rosary Coll., 1989. Asst. rsch. librarian CPC Internat., Argo, Ill., 1958-62; chem. patent searcher Chgo., 1962-66; info. specialist C. Berger & Co., Wheaton, Ill., 1986, Amoco Corp., Naperville, Ill., 1987—; faculty Coll. Du Page, Glen Ellyn, Ill., 1989—. Mem. Spl. Libraries Assn., Ill. Fedn. Women's Club (treas. 5th dist. 1979-81, Outstanding Jr. Clubwoman award 1979-80), Garden Club Council Wheaton (pres. 1981-82), Wheaton Jr. Woman's Club (pres. 1977-78, Single Parent scholar 1984), Gardens Etc. Club (pres. 1978-79), Alpha Lambda Delta, Delta Rho Kappa, Theta Sigma Phi, Alpha Chi Omega (grantee 1985). Republican. Presbyterian. Home: 1507 Paula Ave Wheaton IL 60187-6135 Office: Amoco Corp PO Box 3083 Warrenville Rd and Mill St Naperville IL 60566

TUCKER, BOWEN HAYWARD, lawyer; b. Providence, Apr. 13, 1938; s. Stuart Hayward and Ardelle Chase (Drabble) T.; m. Jan Louise Brown, Aug. 26, 1961; children: Stefan Kendric Slade, Catherine Kendra Gordon. AB in Math., Brown U., 1959; JD, U. Mich., 1962. Bar: R.I. 1963, Ill. 1967, U.S. Supreme Ct. 1970. Assoc. Hinckley & Allen, Providence, 1962-66; sr. atty. Caterpillar, Inc., Peoria, Ill., 1966-72; counsel FMC Corp., Chgo., 1972-82, sr. litigation counsel, 1982—. Chmn. legal process task force Chgo. Residential Sch. Study Com., 1973-74, mem. Commn. on Children, 1983-85, Ill. Com. on Rights of Minors, 1974-77, Com. on Youth and the Law, 1977-79; mem. White House Conf. on Children, ednl. svcs. subcom., 1979-80; chairperson Youth Employment Task Force, 1982-83; mem. citizens com. on Juvenile Ct. (Cook County), 1978-94, chmn. detention subcom., 1982-94; mem. econ. effects adv. com. Rand Inst. Civil Justice, 1990-92. 1st lt. U.S. Army, 1962-69. Mem. ABA, Am. Law Inst., Ill. State Bar Assn., R.I. Bar Assn., Chgo. (chmn. com. on juvenile law, 1976-77), Engine Mfrs. Assn. (chmn. legal com. 1972), Constrn. Industry Mfrs. Assn. (exec. com. of Lawyers' Coun. 1972, 1975-79, vice chmn. 1977, chmn. 1978-79), Mfrs. Alliance (products liability coun. 1974-95, vice chmn. 1981-83, chmn. 1983-85), Product Liability Adv. Coun. (bd. dirs. 1986—, exec. com. 1990—, vice chmn. 1991-93, chmn. 1993-95), ACLU (bd. dirs. Ill. div. 1970-79, exec. com. 1973-79, sec. 1975-77), Am. Arbitration Assn. (mem panel of arbitrators 1985—), Phi Alph Delta. Club: Brown Univ. of Chgo. (nat. alumni schs. program 1973-85, v.p. 1980-81, pres. 1981-86). Home: 107 W Noyes St Arlington Heights IL 60005-3747 Office: 200 E Randolph St Ste 6700 Chicago IL 60601-6436

TUCKER, DENNIS CARL, library executive; b. St. Louis, Oct. 17, 1945; s. Carl Ernest and Elsa Grace (Witt) T.; m. Maria Teresa Guillermina Castro, Dec. 6, 1975; children: Dennis Andrés, William Alexandro, Eric Scott, Michael Joseph. BS, S.E. Mo. State U., 1967, MAT, 1974; MLS., U. Mo., 1983. Tchr. English, Univ. Autó. de Sinaloa, Culiacán, Mexico, 1971-73, Academia de Idiomas, 1974-76; owner, dir. Academia Logos, Mazatlán, Mexico, 1976-77; tchr. English, U. Américas, Cholula, Mexico, 1977-78; tchr. English and Spanish, Rifle (Colo.) High Sch., 1978-79; libr. Webb Jr. High Sch., East Prairie, Mo., 1980-83; dir. libr. Bethel Coll., Mishawaka, Ind., 1983-87; reference libr. U. Notre Dame, Ind., 1986-87; libr. Mishawaka (Ind.) Pub. Libr., 1988-90; libr. microcomputer specialist Ind. Coop. Libr. Svcs. Authority, 1990-96, dir. project Hi-Net, 1996—. Sec.-treas. S.E. Mo. Dept. Sch. Librs., Cape Girardeau, 1980-82. Author: From Here To There: Moving A Library, 1987, Finding Religion in the Library: A Student Manual for Library Research, 1989, Finding Sociology in the Library, 1990, Finding Nursing in the Library, 1990, Finding Criminal Justice in the Library, 1990; photographer El Periódico del Noroeste, 1975-76. Recipient Kodak Internat. Newspaper Snapshot award, 1975. Mem. ALA, Area Libr. Svcs. Authority (dir. 1983-87), Christian Writers Club Michiana (v.p. 1984, pres. 1985), Sigma Tau Delta. Office: Ind Coop Libr Svcs Authority 6202 Morenci Trail Indianapolis IN 46268

TUCKER, KEITH A., investment company executive; b. 1945. BBA, U. Tex., 1967, JD, 1970. With KPMG Peat Marwick, Dallas, 1970-85, Stephens, Inc., Little Rock, 1985-87, Trivest Inc., Miami, Fla., 1987-91; dir. Waddell & Reed Inc., Shawnee Mission, Kans., 1989—, vice chmn., 1991—, chmn. Office: Waddell & Reed Inc 6300 Lamar Ave Shawnee Mission KS 66202-4247*

TUCKER, MICHAEL J., product marketing manager; b. Warren, Pa., July 21, 1953. BA in English, Pa. State U., 1975. Dir. classified advt. Centre Daily Times, State College, Pa., 1977-81; product mgr. DuPont Printing & Pub., Wilmington, Del., 1981-91; mktg. mgr. Info. Internat. Inc., L.A., 1992-94, Cascade Sys. Inc., Andover, Mass., 1994-95; product mktg. mgr. Gannett Media Techs. Internat., Cin., 1995—. Office: Gannett Media Techs Int Ste 201 151 W 4th St Cincinnati OH 45202

TUCKER, RAY, facilities engineer; b. Port Huron, Mich., July 5, 1956. Apprenticeship degree, St. Claire County C.C., 1980. Apprentice Mueller Brass, Port Huron, 1975-81; indsl. electrician U.S. Mfg., Port Huron, 1985-90; facilities engr. Grace Engring., Memphis, Mich., 1990—. Coach AYSO Soccer, Jr. High Basketball. Office: Grace Engring 81600 Belle River Rd PO Box 202 Memphis MI 48041-4425

TUCKER, THOMAS RANDALL, public relations executive; b. Indpls., Aug. 6, 1931; s. Ovie Allen and Oris Aleen (Robertson) T.; A.B., Franklin Coll., 1953; m. Evelyn Marie Armuth, Aug. 9, 1953; children—Grant, Roger, Richard. Grad. asst. U. Minn., 1953-54; dir. admissions, registrar Franklin Coll., 1954-57; with Cummins Engine Co., Inc., Columbus, Ind., 1957; dir. pub. relations, 1968-88; pub. rels. cons. Mem. Bd. Sch. Trustees Bartholomew County, Ind., 1966-72, pres., 1968-69; mem. Ind. State Bd. Edn., 1977-89; treas. Bartholomew County Rep. Cen. Com., 1960-80; mem. Columbus Area Visitor Info. and Promotion Commn.; chmn. Columbus 2000; trustee, chmn. ednl. policy com. of bd. trustees Franklin Coll.; bd. dirs. The Hoosier Salon. Mem. Pub. Relations Soc. Am., Columbus (Ind.) C. of C. (Community Service award 1986), Kappa Tau Alpha, Phi Delta Theta, Sigma Delta Chi. Lutheran. Lodge: Rotary. Home: 4380 N Riverside Dr Columbus IN 47203-1123 Office: Box 3005 Columbus IN 47202

TUCKER, WILLIAM THOMAS, III, computer software company executive; b. Milw., June 26, 1942; s. William Thomas and Shirley Audrey (Holmes) T.; m. Barbara Ann Granof, Sept. 8, 1965 (dec. Sept. 1982); children: Pamela Ann, Penelope Lynn, Matthew Louis. BS cum laude, U. Wis., 1969. Lic. real estate broker, Wis. Dir. pub. rels. Jr. Achievement S.E. Wis., Milw., 1969-71; exec. dir. Jr. Achievement Fox Valley, Appleton, Wis., 1971-74; mktg. dir. Southridge Mall, Milw., 1974-81; asst. mall mgr. Southridge and Northridge Malls, Milw., 1981-83; pres. Buyer Publs., Inc., San Diego, 1983-86; mall mgr. Mayfair Mall, Milw., 1987-89; pres. CompSys Inc., Milw., 1989—; cons. House Trader mag. Home Buyer Inc., San Diego, 1986—; instr. Waukesha County Tech. Coll. Design engr. computer software Home Search System, 1989. Dep. state dir. Naval Acad. Info. Program, Milw., 1981—; mem. nominating com. Sanator Kasten Acad., Milw., 1990-93, Congressman Kleczka Acad., Milw., 1990-93, Senator Kohn Acad., Milw., 1991—; mem. Naval Recruiting Dist. Coun., 1977—. Capt. USNR. Lutheran. Home: 6065 Doyle St Greendale WI 53129-2215 Office: ML-Asst Inc 6065 Doyle St Greendale WI 53129-2215

TUEL, LARRY LEROY, construction finance executive; b. Spencer, Iowa, Sept. 10, 1951; s. Kenneth Eugene and Evelyn Bernice (Cruse) T.; m. Valerie A. Peterson Tuel, Aug. 5, 1978 (div.); children: Erin Kathleen, Bryant Douglas, Nicole Christina; m. Julie Ranae Ross Tuel, Sept. 16, 1992. BS, Mankato State U., Minn., 1973; JD, Drake U. Law Sch., Des Moines, 1980; MPA, Drake U., 1981. Bar: U.S. Fed. Dist. Cts., Iowa, 1981. Urban planner Northwest Iowa Coun. Govts., Spencer, Iowa, 1973-75; State of Iowa, Des Moines, 1975-78; atty. Diehl & Diehl, Albert City, Iowa, 1981-83; city atty. City of Albert City, 1981-83; gen. counsel Iowa Fin. Authority, Des Moines, 1984-86; exec. dir., 1987-90; pres. Iowa Housing Corp., Des Moines, 1991—; sec. Iowa Assn. Hearing Officers, Des Moines, 1984-85; dir. Iowa Title Guaranty Divsn., 1985-87, Iowa Bus. Devel. Fin. Corp., 1988-90, Des Moines; chair, legal task force Nat. Coun. State Housing Agencies, Washington, 1989. Author and presenter of legal edn. papers. Chief organizer Gov.'s Conf. on Housing and Homelessness, Des Moines, 1989, v.p.Racoon Valley Little League, Des Moines, 1993. Recipient Cert. of Recognition Gov. State of Iowa, 1983, 86. Mem. Iowa State Bar Assn. Home: 21 56th St Des Moines IA 50312 Office: Iowa Housing Corp 100 Court Ave Ste 209 Des Moines IA 50309

TUFT, CAROLYN MARIA, newspaper reporter; b. St. Louis, Apr. 27, 1959; d. Fred Leroy and Alyce LaVerne (Wilson) Garner; m. R. Kevin Tuft. BA, So. Ill. U., 1987. Newseditor The ALESTLE, Edwardsville, Ill., 1986-87; reporter The Belleville (Ill.) News-Democrat, 1987-92; investigative reporter St. Louis Post-Dispatch, 1992—; cons. 60 Minutes, 1993. Contbr. chpt. News Reporting and Writing, 1992. Recipient Paul Tobenkin award Columbia U., 1991, Sweepstakes award AP, 1992, award ACLU, 1992. Mem. Investigative Reporters and Editors (Gold medal 1992). Office: Saint Louis Post-Dispatch 900 N Tucker Blvd Saint Louis MO 63101

TUKUFU, DARRYL SEKOU, social issues advocate, educator; b. Cleve., July 27, 1949; s. Estus Barham and Bernice Starks; m. Myra C. Duncan, July 8, 1988; children: Ricky and Khari. AB in Social Studies, Youngstown U., 1976; MA in Urban Studies, U. Akron, 1977, PhD in Sociology, 1984. Dep. dir Youngstown (Ohio) Urban League, 1971-75; acting dir., EEO officer Youngstown Hometown Plan, 1975-76; EEO officer City of Akron, Ohio, 1977-79; mgr. Akron-Summit Community Action, 1979-80; exec. dir. Fair Housing Contract Svc., Akron, 1980-82; project dir. Vol. & Employment Project, Akron, 1985; asst. prof. African Am. studies Northeastern U., Boston, 1985-86; asst. prof. sociology and social work Memphis State U., 1986-90; asst. prof. social and behavioral scis. LeMonyne-Owen Coll., Memphis, 1990; pres., CEO Urban League Portland, Oreg., 1990-93; dir. divsn. pub. svcs., exec. dir. pub. svc. inst. Lorain County C.C., Elyria, Ohio, 1993—; vis. asst. prof. Kent (Ohio) State U., 1984-85; adj. assoc. prof. Portland State U., mem. pres.'s coun.; commr. Port of Portland, 1991-93; cert. cons. Performax Sys. Internat., Personal Dynamics Inst.; mem. minority affairs rev. bd. NIKE, Inc., 1991-93, Am.-African Trade Rels. Adv. Bd., adv. bd. Oreg. Peace Inst., 1991-93, North/N.E. Econ. Devel. Alliance Bd., 1991-93; presenter various regional and nat. sociol. confs.; rschr. in field. Co-founder, pres. Youngstown Sickle Cell Anemia Found., Inc., 1972-73, Akron Black Leadership Forum, 1980-81; convenor Ohio Coun. Urban Leagues Cmty. Svc. staff, 1973-74; Dem. Precinct Committeeman, 1984-85; local dir. Univ. Area Jaycees, 1987-88; advisor Memphis Urban League Male Connection Program, 1988-90; mem. Mayor's Pub. Works Task Force, 1990-91, exec. com. Leaders Roundtable, 1991-93; bd. dirs. Memphis Urban League, 1989-90, Emanuel Med. Ctr. Found., 1991-93; mem. Lorain County United Way, 1994-95. Recipient Dedicated Svc. Striving for Social Justice award NAACP, 1980, Emerging Leadership award Frontiers Club, 1980, Appreciation award Memphis Edn. Assn., 1991, Gov. Roberts Transition Team, 1991, Youngstown Martin Luther King, Jr. Holiday Com., 1992; named Outstanding Young Man of Am., U.S. Jaycees, 1981. Fellow Am. Leadership Forum (Oreg. chpt.); mem. Am. Sociol. Assn., So. Sociol. Soc., City Club Portland, Kappa Alpha Psi (life, mem. Portland Alumni Chpt. Bd.). Office: Lorain County CC 1005 Abbe Rd N Elyria OH 44035-1613

TULACH, JOHN R., mechanical engineer; b. Western Springs, Ill., July 28, 1930. BS in Mech. Engring., IIT, 1953; postgrad., U. Md., 1955, 56, Art Inst. Chgo., 1957. Project engr. Navistar Internat., Melrose Park, Ill., 1953—. Patentee in field; copywriter various religious songs. Leader Boy Scouts Am., LaGrange, Ill., 1955-70; dir., founder Midwest Ministries, West Chester, Ill., 1993—. Master sgt. U.S. Army, 1955-56. Republican. Home: 2247 Belleview Ave Westchester IL 60154-5207 Office: Navistar Internat 10400 W North Ave Melrose Park IL 60160-1028

TULLIO, JOHN J., electrical engineer; b. 3Chgo., Apr. 20, 2194. BS, Ill. Inst. Tech., 1967. Application engr. Victor Bus. Products, Chgo., 1971-83; engring. mgr. ARC Tronics Inc., Elk Grove Village, Ill., 1983—, also mem. tech. bd. Mem. IEEE, Stock Club. Office: ARC Tronics Inc 1150 Pagni Dr Elk Grove Village IL 60007-6601

TULLIS, CHAILLÉ HANDY, interior designer, volunteer; b. Evanston, Ill., June 16, 1913; d. Jamison Handy and Ethel (Tremaine) Gray; m. Richard Barclay Tullis, Aug. 17, 1935; children: Sarah Gilmore Tullis deBarcza, Barclay Jamison, Garner Handy. BA, Principia Coll., Elsah, Ill., 1935; MA, Case Western Res. U., 1964. Pres., sole owner Chaillé Interiors, Lyndhurst, Ohio, 1983—; trustee Cleve. Inst. Art (hon.), 1984—, Garden Ctr. Greater Cleve., 1975-78, 83-86, Vero Beach (Fla.) Ctr. for the Arts. Pres. Country Garden Club, 1961-63; pres. women's com. Cleve. Orch., 1975-77. Mem. Intown Club, Twentieth Century Club. Home: 1250 W Southwinds Blvd Vero Beach FL 32963 also: 5150 Three Village Dr Cleveland OH 44124-3753

TULLIS, DEAN JAMES, voice products company executive; b. Milw., Feb. 2, 1961; s. James Merle and Margyl Gertrude (Lodes) T.; m. Cynthia Louise Mesa, Mar. 30; children: Trevor Dean, Devin James. Grad., N.W. Glassen H.S., 1979. Sales/mgmt. exec. Dictaphone Corp., Oklahoma City, 1980-88, Al Williams, Wichita, Kans., 1988-89; mgmt. exec., ptnr., owner Electronic Office Sys., Wichita, 1989-90; owner, ptnr. Voice Products, Inc., Wichita, 1990—, Digital Voice Products, Kansas City, Kans., 1993—. Mem. Wichita C. of C. (mem. small bus. coun., pres.' club), Rotary (founder Contact's club). Office: Voice Products Inc 1211 E Douglas Wichita KS 67211

TULLY, THOMAS ALOIS, building materials executive, consultant, educator; b. Dubuque, Iowa, Nov. 11, 1940; s. Thomas Aloysius and Marjorie Mae (Fosselman) T.; m. Joan Vonnetta Dubay, Nov. 30, 1963; children: Thomas Paul, Maureen Elizabeth. BA, Loras Coll., 1962; postgrad., Georgetown U., 1963-66; MPA, Harvard U., 1968. Mgmt. trainee Office of Sec. Def., Washington, 1962-63, fgn. affairs officer, 1963-70; v.p. Dubuque Lumber Co., 1970-84, pres., 1984-91; pres. Tully's, 1991-92, LBM Mktg. Assocs., Inc., 1992—; adj. instr. Divine Word Coll., 1971, Loras Coll., 1972; adj. instr. Clarke Coll., 1987-89, instr., 1989-91, asst. prof., 1992—, chmn. dept. acctg. and bus., 1993—, dir. small bus. inst., 1994—; pres. Hills and Dales Child Devel. Ctr., Inc., 1992—; mem. bd. trustees Alverno Apts., 1995—. Mem. Dubuque Human Rights Commn., 1974-75, chmn., 1975, Iowa State Com. for Employer Support of Guard and Res. Forces, 1988—; city councilman, Dubuque, 1975-79; bd. dirs. League Iowa Municipalites, 1977-79; mayor City of Dubuque, 1978; vice chmn. Iowa Temporary State Land Pres. Policy Com., 1978-79; pres. N.E. Iowa Regional Coordinating Council, 1985-93, East Cen. Intergovtl. Assn. Bus. Growth, Inc., 1987—, chmn., 1993—; bd. dirs. Pvt. Industry Council of Dubuque and Delaware Counties, Inc., 1983-86; trustee Divine Word Coll., 1986—; pres. Barn Community Theatre, 1988-89; chmn. bd. trustees United Way Svcs. of Dubuque, 1990, campaign chmn., 1991, bd. mem., 1980-94. Recipient Meritorious Civilian Svc. award Sec. of Def., 1970, Gov.'s Vol. award, 1989. Mem. Nat. Lumber and Bldg. Material Dealers Assn. (exec. com. 1988-90), Iowa Lumbermen's Assn. (pres. 1984, chmn. legis. com. 1985-90), Northwestern Lumbermen Assn. (bd. dirs. 1984-87, 2d v.p. 1988, 1st v.p. 1989-90, pres. 1990-91). Democrat. Roman Catholic. Home: 838 Stone Ridge Pl Dubuque IA 52001-1362 Office: LBM Mktg Assocs PO Box 771 Dubuque IA 52004-0771

TUMA, JOHN, state legislator, lawyer; b. Sept. 25, 1962; m. Wendy Tuma; 1 child. BA, Mankato State U.; JD, U. Minn. Bar: Minn. Mem. Minn. Ho. of Reps., St. Paul, 1994—. Independent-Republican.

TUNHEIM, JAMES RONALD, state legislator, farmer; b. Drayton, N.Dak., June 6, 1941; s. Olaf and Grace (Doran) T.; m. Diana Lee Rojas, 1964; children: Christopher Alan, Aaron Cory, Nicolle Anne. Student, Thief River Falls Vocat. Sch., 1959-61. Owner, mgr. James Tunheim Farms, Kennedy, Minn., 1964—; mem. Minn. Ho. of Reps., St. Paul, 1982—; vice chmn. commerce and econ. devel. tourism divsn., mem. regulated industry, edn., ethics, and transp. coms. Treas. Kennedy (Minn.) Sch. Dist., 1975; del. Minn. Dem. Conv., 1978; past chmn. Kittson County (Minn.) Dem.-Farmer-Labor Com.; mem. bd. Maria Luth. Ch., 1975. Mem. Nat. Rural Water Assn., Minn. Rural Water Assn. (bd. dirs. 1978), Lions, Masons, Shriners (sec., treas.).

TUNLEY, NAOMI LOUISE, retired nurse administrator; b. Henryretta, Okla., Jan. 10, 1936; d. Alexander and Ludia Bell (Franklin) T. BSN, Dillard U., 1958; MA, U. Mo., Kansas City, 1974. RN, Okla. Staff nurse, assoc. chief nursing svc. Oklahoma City VA Med. Ctr., 1958-65; instr. Iowa Luth. Hosp. Sch. Nursing, Des Moines, 1965-66; charge nurse emergency rm. Mercy Hosp., Iowa City, Iowa, 1966-67; charge nurse, assoc. chief nursing svc. Kansas City (Mo.) VA Med. Ctr., 1967-76, charge nurse neurol. unit, 1976-79, nurse mgr. orthopedic unit, 1979-80, nurse mgr. substance abuse unit, 1980-94; ret., 1994; equal employment opportunity counselor Kansas City (Mo.) VA Med. Ctr., 1976-86; trustee Nat. Coun. Alcohol and Other Drugs, Kansas City, 1986-90. Vol. Am. Cancer Soc., Kansas City, 1971-79, March of Dimes, Kansas City, 1971-79; big sister Big Bros.-Sisters Am., Kansas City, 1974-84. Mem. ARC, Sigma Theta Tau. Home: 3120 Poplar Ave Kansas City MO 64128-1803

TUNNECLIFFE, DANIEL LEE, respiratory care administrator; b. Detroit, Aug. 19, 1953; s. Harold Don Tunnecliffe and Violet Rose (Rumpz) Spearman; m. Carol Lucille Adams, Mar. 2, 1974; children: Angela, Deanna, Jessica. AS, Henry Ford Community Coll., 1982; BS, Senia Heights Coll., 1985. Registered respiratory therapist. Foreman Pacific Coast Inventory, Grass Valley, Calif., 1980-81; respiratory techincian Crittenton Hosp., Rochester, Mich., 1981-82; therapist Crittenton Hosp., Rochester, 1983-86, supr., 1986-87, dir. dept., 1987—. Instr. Am. Heart Assn., Southfield, Mich., 1982; mem. Community Edn. Commn., Rochester, Mich. 1986—; v.p. Clarkston PTO, 1988. Mem. Nat. Bd. Respiratory Care, Am. Assn. Respiratory Care, Mich. Soc. Respiratory Care. Democrat. Methodist. Home: 8656 Shore Dr Davisburg MI 48350-1936 Office: Crittenton Hosp 1101 W University Dr Rochester MI 48307-1863

TUNNEY, GREG ALAN, sales executive; b. Seattle, July 10, 1961; s. Danny Lee and Patricia Ann Tunney; m. Heidi Faye Hansen, Dec. 19, 1985; children: Clayton, Katelin, Chandler, Carson. AA, Phoenix Coll., 1980; BS, Brigham Young U., 1983. Sr. buyer May Corp., St. Louis, 1986-93; nat. sales mgr., v.p. Brown Shoe Corp., St. Louis, 1993—. Pres. Young Men's Program LDS Ch., St. Louis, 1986—, youth basketball coach, 1988-90. Mem. Brigham Young U. Mgmt. Assn. (bd. mem. 1986—, treas. 1990-92), Brigham Young U. Assn. (sec. 1988-90). Republican. Office: Brown Shoe Corp 8300 Maryland Ave Saint Louis MO 63105

TUNNICLIFF, DAVID GEORGE, civil engineer; b. Ord, Nebr., Sept. 18, 1931; s. George Thomas and Ada Ellen (Ward) T.; m. Elaine Jean Interrante, Oct. 17, 1959 (div.); children: Martha Allison Tunnicliff Loeb, Vivian Jean Tunnicliff Perez; m. Joan Elizabeth Duchesneau, Oct. 25, 1975. BS, U. Nebr., 1954; MS, Cornell U., 1958; PhD, U. Mich., 1972. Registered profl.

engr., Nebr., Mass. Engr. Nebr. Dept. Rds., Lincoln, 1954-60; asst. prof., then assoc. prof. Wayne State U., Detroit, 1960-67; chief tech. svcs. Warren Bros. Co., Cambridge, Mass., 1967-79; prin., cons. engr. D.G. Tunnicliff, Cons. Engr., Omaha, 1979—. Contbr. to profl. publs. Rep. precinct del., Detroit, 1965-66. With U.S. Army, 1955-56. Mem. ASTM (chair subcom. 1973-94), ASCE, Assn. Asphalt Paving Tech. (bd. dirs. 1976-78), Transp. Rsch. Bd. (com. chair 1983-89). Mem. Evangel. Covenant Ch. Home & Office: DG Tunnicliff Cons Engr 9624 Larimore Ave Omaha NE 68134-3038

TUONO, ALBERT JOSEPH, physician; b. Phila., Feb. 28, 1964; s. Mario Alfred and Monica Rita (Alessandrini) T.; m. Denise Marie Harnois, Dec. 19, 1992. BA cum laude, Temple U., 1988; DO, Phila. Coll. Osteo. Medicine, 1992. Med. technologist Hosp. of the U. of Pa., Phila., 1989-93; intern Millcreek Community Hosp., Erie, Pa., 1993-94. Mem. Am. Osteo. Assn., Pa. Osteo. Med. Assn. Roman Catholic. Address: 905 W Silver Lake Dr NE Rochester MN 55906-3686

TURCOTTE, TODD WAYNE, controller; b. Dearborn, Mich., Nov. 24, 1963; s. Gerald Wayne and Joan Marie (Tullius) T.; m. Christine Sue Bump, Sept. 20, 1986. BBA magna cum laude, Western Mich. U., 1990. Cert. internal auditor. Internal auditor Whirlpool Corp., Benton Harbor, Mich., 1991-93; sr. internal auditor Dana Corp., Toledo, 1993-95; plant contr. Dana Corp., Richmond, Ind., 1995—. Mem. Inst. Internal Auditors (cert. 2d v.p. 1991-92), Inst. Mgmt. Accts. Republican. Home: 2740 Heathfield Ln Richmond IN 47374 Office: Dana Corp 2175 Williamsburg Ave Richmond IN 47374

TURK, FRANCIS JEROME, writer, editor; b. Cleve., May 20, 1923; s. Frank J. and Louise Marie (Epaves) T.; m. Patricia Dorothea Fashinger, May 5, 1951 (dec. July 1992); children: Patricia Ann Horvath, Francis J., Joel Brian, James Gerard. BA, Baldwin-Wallace Coll., 1963. Sports reporter Cleve. News, 1940-43; combat corr. Press Sect. 103 Infantry Divsn., 1945; copywriter Beaumont & Hohman, Inc., Chgo., 1946-57; broadcast dir. McCann-Erickson Inc., Cleve., 1957-59; pres. Editorial Features, Inc., Cleve., 1959-79; pub. affairs dir., editor AAA-Ohio Motorist, Cleve., 1979-94; pres. Jerome Turk Comm., Inc., Cleve., 1995—. Co-author: (book) Report After ACtion, 1945, Dateline History (2 vols.), 1974-76; originator, producer: (documentary series) On Location, 1961-79; editor Ohio Motorist, 1983-94. Pvt. 1st class Infantry, 1943-45. Decorated Bronze Star; named Man of Yr. Cathedral Latin Alumni Assn., 1990. Mem. Assn. of Ohio Commodores (bd. trustees 1984-92, past grand commodore). Roman Catholic. Office: Jerome Turk Comm Inc 13550 Falling Water Dr Cleveland OH 44136

TURNAGE, JULEEN HOLDERBY, public relations executive; b. Rocks Springs, Wyo., June 15, 1942; d. Robert L. and Sylvia E. (Daley) H.; m. Vance D. Turnage, Aug. 17, 1963; 1 child, Marc V. BA in Writing, S.W. Mo. State U., 1975. Pub. rels. dir. Assemblies of God Headquarters, Springfield, Mo., 1969—; bd. dirs. Berean U., Springfield, 1989—. Editor newsletter On Word; contbr. articles to profl. jours. Mem. nat. prayer breakfast com. City of Springfield, 1990—. Mem. Pub. Rels. Assn. Springfield, Ctrl. Bible Coll. Alumni Assn. (pres. 1980's). Mem. Assembly of God Ch. Office: Assemblies of God Headquarters 1445 Boonville Ave Springfield MO 65802

TURNER, ARTHUR L., state legislator; b. Chgo., Dec. 2, 1950; m. Rosalyn Turner; 2 children. BS, Ill. State U.; MS, Lewis U. Ill. state rep. Dist. 9, 1981—; vice chmn. consumer protection, higher edn. Ill. Ho. Reps., ins., labor and com. revenue, chmn. housing com., health care, ins. com., dep. majority leader; treas. Ill. Minority Caucus, 1987—; exec. com. Nat. Conf. of Black State Legislators, 1987-89; mem. housing com. Nat. Conf. of State Legislators, 1987-89; mem. NCSL, Reapportionment Task Force, 1988—; vice chmn. edn. com., 1989—. Mem. Lawndale Cmty. Econ. Devel. Corp.; active Operation Brotherhood, YMCA. Mem. NAACP, Urban League. Home: 2102 S Avers Ave Chicago IL 60623-2467*

TURNER, DARRELL JOHN, copy editor, writer; b. N.Y.C., Mar. 5, 1949; s. John Darrell and Blanche Florence (Miller) T.; m. Kathleen Marie Frank, June 18, 1983; children: Dawn Marie, Heather Joy. BA, L.I. U., 1970. Prodn. editor Civil Engring. mag., N.Y.C., 1970-72; staff writer, assoc. editor Religious News Svc., N.Y.C., 1972-92; copy editor, religion writer Ft. Wayne (Ind.) Jour. Gazette, 1993—. Contbr. to Ency. Americana Year Book, 1987—, Ency. Brit. Year Book, 1994—. Mem. Soc. Profl. Journalists, Religion Newswriters Assn. Home: 3933 Stanton Dr Fort Wayne IN 46815

TURNER, EVAN HOPKINS, retired art museum director; b. Orono, Maine, Nov. 8, 1927; s. Albert Morton and Percie Trowbridge (Hopkins) T.; m. Brenda Winthrop Bowman, May 12, 1956; children: John, Jennifer. A.B. cum laude, Harvard U., 1949, M.A., 1950, Ph.D., 1954. Head docent svc. Fogg Mus., Cambridge, Mass., 1950-51; curator Robbins Art Collection of Prints, Arlington, Mass., 1951; teaching fellow fine arts Harvard U., 1951-52; lectr., research asst. Frick Collection, N.Y.C., 1953-56; gen. curator, asst. dir. Wadsworth Atheneum, Hartford, Conn., 1956-59; dir. Montreal Mus. Fine Arts, Que., Can., 1959-64, Phila. Mus. Art, 1964-77, Ackland Art Mus., 1978-83, Cleve. Mus. Art, 1983-93; adj. prof. art history U. Pa., U. N.C., Chapel Hill, 1978-83; disting. vis. prof. Oberlin Coll., 1993—. Mem. Assn. Art Mus. Dirs., Coll. Art Assn. Am., Am. Mus. Assn., Century Assn. Club. Home: 3071 N Park Blvd Cleveland OH 44118-4114

TURNER, FRANK ROBIN, tire manufacturing executive; b. Raleigh, N.C., Apr. 3, 1949; s. David Oliver and Edna Margaret (Yow) T.; m. Ruth Mae Eastwood, Nov. 7, 1969: 1 child, Lydia Margaret Turner. BA in Chemistry, Va. Poly. Inst., 1972; MSA in Indsl. Mgmt., George Washington U., 1978. Compounder Goodyear Tire & Rubber Co., Danville, Va., 1973-78; shift mgr. Goodyear Tire & Rubber Co., Lawton, Okla., 1978-81; sr. engr. Goodyear Tire & Rubber Co., Akron, Ohio, 1981-82; dept. mgr., bus. ctr. mgr. Goodyear Tire & Rubber Co., Topeka, Kans., 1982-87; prodn. mgr. Goodyear Tire & Rubber Co., Philippsburg, Germany, 1987-89; plant prodn. mgr. Goodyear Tire & Rubber Co., Wolverhampton, Eng., 1989-92; regional mgr. Europe, facilities planning and opers. analysis Goodyear Tire & Rubber Co., Akron, Ohio, 1992—. Bd. dirs. Boy Scouts Am., Topeka, Kans., 1985-87. Republican. Baptist. Home: 6856 Thornwood St NW Canton OH 44718 Office: Goodyear Tire & Rubber Co 1144 E Market St Akron OH 44316

TURNER, GLENN, fluid power specialist; b. Dover, Ohio, June 23, 1961. Student, Ohio State U., 1979-81, 88-90. Cert. fluid power specialist. Application engr. Rexroth Corp., Wooster, Ohio, 1988—; mem. adv. bd. fluid power curriculum Ohio State U., Wooster. Mem. KP. Presbyterian. Home: 4410 Egypt Rd Smithville OH 44677-9737 Office: Rexroth Corp 1700 Old Mansfield Rd Wooster OH 44691-9050

TURNER, JAMES F., business executive; b. Columbus, Ohio, Aug. 7, 1942. BA, Ohio State U., 1965. Owner, operator Turner Assocs. Inc., Columbus, 1968-80, Bus. Telephone Systems Am., Inc., Columbus, 1973—. Cpl. USMCR, 1960-66. Mem. Rotary. Republican. Office: 400 Dublin Ave Ste 250 Columbus OH 43215-2333

TURNER, JANE ANN, federal agent; b. Rapid City, S.D., Aug. 26, 1951; d. John Owen and Wilma Veona (Thompson) T.; 1 child, Victoria Thompson. BA, Carroll Coll., 1973; student forensic psychology, John Jay Sch. Criminal Justice, N.Y.C., 1985-87. Spl. agt. FBI, Seattle and N.Y.C., 1978-87; sr. resident spl. agt. FBI, Minot, N.D., 1987—; spkr., instr. FBI, Seattle, N.Y.C. and Minot, 1978—, Psychol. Profiler, 1983—. Mem. Minot Commn. on the Status of Women, 1991-93. Mem. Gen. Fedn. Women's Clubs (v.p. 1992-93), Women in Law Enforcement, N.D. Peace Officer Assn., Optimist Club. Office: FBI PO Box 968 Fed Bldg Minot ND 58701

TURNER, JOHN W., state legislator; b. Lincoln, Ill., 1956; m. Kimberly Turner; 1 child, Jack. BA, U. Ill., 1978; JD, DePaul U., 1981. Pub. defender Logan County, 1984-87, state atty., 1988-94; mem. Blue Ribbon Com., Firearm Transfer Inquiry Program, 1992—; Ill. state rep. Dist. 90, 1994—; atty. Kavanagh, Scully Sudow, White & Frederick PC, 1981-82, Turner & Rossi, 1982-87. bd. dirs. Lincoln YMCA, chmn. fin. com.; active Lincoln Jaycees. Mem. Logan County Tri-Police Assn., Elks, Phi Beta Kappa, Phi Kappa Phi. Office: Wallace Computer Svcs Inc 4600 Roosevelt Rd Hillside IL 60162-2034*

TURNER, MILDRED EDITH, day care owner; b. Winnebago, Wis., Jan. 11, 1926; d. Jewett Candfield and Angeline Mary (Long) T. BS, State Tchrs. Coll., 1949; MS of Edn., U. Wis., Milw., 1962; postgrad., U. Wis., Oshkosh, 1965-70. Cert. tchr., Wis. Tchr. Winnebago County, Omro, Wis., 1945-47, Plymouth (Wis.) Pub. Schs., 1949-51, Ripon (Wis.) Pub. Schs., 1951-53, Omro Pub. Schs., 1953-88; instr. U. Wis., Oshkosh, 1971, supervising tchr. of student tchrs., 1970-91; owner, operator Wee Care Children's Ctr., Omro, 1974—. Contbr. articles to newspapers, profl. publs., children's books. Acolyte coord. Algoma Blvd. United Meth. Ch.; supt. Sunday sch., pianist, choir dir., ch. music dir. Eureka/Waukau United Meth. Ch.; sub-dist. children's dir. Watertown sub-dist. United Meth. Ch. Mem. Ret. Tchrs. Assn. Winnebago County, Ret. Tchrs. Assn. Omro, Fox Valley Assn. for Edn. of Young Children, Word and Pen Christian Writers (sec.-treas.), Alumni Assn. U. Wis. Oshkosh), Alumni Assn. Omro (treas.), Odd Fellows (past noble grand Rebekah lodge), Omro Study Club (past pres.). Home and Office: Wee Care Childrens Ctr 305 E Scott St Omro WI 54963-1707

TURNER, PAUL ERIC, state legislator; m. Cyndy Rush. BS, Taylor U., 1975. Pres., CEO Family Sales Co. & T-3 Investments; mem. Ind. State Ho. of Reps. Dist. 32, 1982-86, 1994—, mem. elec. and apportionment com., mem. ways and means com.; former state chmn. Am. Legis. Exch. Coun.; mem. small bus. adv. coun. Fed. Res. Bank. Active State Enterprise Zone. Mem. Am. Pyrotechnics Assn., Taylor U. Trojan Club (bd. mem.), Gas City C. of C. (bd. mem.).

TURNER, ROBERT LLOYD, state legislator; b. Columbus, Miss., Sept. 14, 1947; s. Roosevelt and Beatrice (Hargrove) T.; m. Gloria Harrell; children: Roosevelt, Robert, Ryan. BS, U. Wis., Racine, 1976. Mgr. French Quarter Restaurant, Racine, 1989; legislator Wis. State Assembly, Madison, 1990—, chmn. transp. com. bldg. commn., mem. ways and means com., hwy. com., elections, correction & constitution com., excise fees and license com.; br. sales mgr. ETG Temporaries, Inc., Racine, 1989—; pub. Communicator News, Racine, 1989—; v.p. Racine Raider Football Team. State chmn. Dem. Black Polit. Caucus, Madison; pres. Bd. Health, Racine; chmn. Wis. State Elections Bd., Madison, 1990; alderman Racine City Coun., 1976—; chair Econ. Devel. Com., Racine; regional dir. Badger State Games, Racine; active Pvt. Industry Coun. Southeastern Wis., 1988-89, bd. dirs. Racine County Youth Sports Assn.; active Racine Juneteenth Day Com., bd. advisors Big Bros./Big Sisters. Sgt. USAF, 1967-71, Vietnam. Decorated Commendation medal; named Man of Yr. 2d Missionary Bapt. Ch., 1983. Mem. Urban League (pres. bd. dirs.), NAACP (2d v.p.), VFW, Am. Legion, Masons, Shriners. Home: 36 McKinley Ave Racine WI 53404-3414 Office: Wis Assembly PO Box 8953 Madison WI 53708-8953

TURNER, ROBERT SULLIVAN, consulting company executive; b. Manhasset, N.Y., Apr. 4, 1965; s. Robert Mason and Noreen (Sullivan) T.; m. Monica Lynn Yuhasz, Oct. 21, 1988; children: Alexandra, Erica. BEE, U. Dayton, 1987, M Computer Sci., 1991. Systems programmer U. Dayton Rsch. Inst., Fairborn, Ohio, 1987; grad. asst. U. Dayton, 1987-89, network mgr. and researcher, 1989-92; pres. CommSys, Inc., Dayton, 1991—. Mem. IEEE, Assn. Computing Machinery. Republican. Roman Catholic. Office: CommSys Inc 77 W Elmwood Dr Ste 101 Dayton OH 45459-4263

TURNER, TERRY MADISON, architect; b. Bastrop, La., Apr. 5, 1938; s. Eugene Campbell and Anna Pauline (Terry) T.; m. Mary Alice Fischer, June 20, 1964; children: Mat Madison, Paul Alison, William Terry. BBA, Memphis State U., 1958; BS in Archtl. Scis., Washington U., St. Louis, 1961, BArch, 1963. Registered architect, Mo., N.C.A.R.B. Asst. prof. Sch. Architecture Auburn (Ala.) U., 1965-66, U. Va., Charlottesville, 1966-69; chief architect HUD-FHA, St. Louis, 1969-79; prin. Terry M. Turner, Architect, Clayton, Mo., 1979—; CEO Westminster Apts., Inc., St. Louis, 1993—. Regent Harris-Stowe State Coll., St. Louis, 1992—. 1st lt. USAR, 1963-70. Republican. Episcopalian. Home and Office: 50 Hillvale Dr Clayton MO 63105

TURNER, VERNITA, accountant; b. St. Louis, Jan. 7, 1963; d. Henry Brown Thomas and Miller Murry (Prather) Thomas Naylor; m. Melvin Turner Jr., Aug. 1, 1987; children: Melvin III, Erika Monique, Victoria Elaine. BS in Bus., Kans. State U., 1985; MA in Fin., Webster U., 1989. Mem. accounts receivable staff Am. Dist. Telegraph, St. Louis, 1986-87; mem. accounts payable/taxes staff Nat. Vendors, St. Louis, 1987-89; asst. acctg. mgr. Commerce Bank of Kans. City (Mo.), 1989-92; comml. acct. Resolution Trust Corp., Kansas City, Mo., 1992-93; staff acct. Arthur Andersen, Kansas City, 1993—; registered rep. life, health State of Mo., 1992; project bus. cons. Jr. Achievement, Kansas City, Mo., 1992. Mem. NAFE, Nat. Black MBA Assn. (pres. Kansas City chpt. 1990-92, student affairs com. 1989), Destination MBA, Kans. State U. Alumni Assn. Methodist. Home: 7904 Charlotte St Kansas City MO 64131-2176

TURNLEY, DAVID CARL, photojournalist; b. Fort Wayne, Ind., June 22, 1955; s. William Loyd and Elizabeth Ann (Protsman) T.; m. Karin Nicolette, Apr. 15, 1989. BA in French, U. Mich., 1977; student, Sorbonne, Paris, 1975; DMus (hon.), Keele (Eng.) U., 1991. Staff photogapher Sliger Home Newspapers, Northville, Mich., 1978-80, Detroit Free Press, 1980—; European based photographic corr. Detroit Free Press/Black Star Paris, 1988—. Author: Why Are They Weeping? South Africans under Aparthied, 1988, Beijing Spring, 1989, Moments of Revolution: Eastern Europe, 1990; artist London Decca Records. Recipient Canon essay award for S. African coverage, 1985, World Press Picture of Yr. award for Earthquake in Armenia, 1988, Robert Capa Gold medal for China, Romania coverage, 1990, Pulitzer prize for China, E. Europe coverage, 1990. Office: Detroit Free Press 321 W Lafayette Blvd Detroit MI 48226-2705

TURNS, MARK G., account clerk payment processor; b. Columbus, Ohio, Jan. 11, 1967; s. William E. and Dorothy T. (Banks) T.;. Student, Columbus State U., 1985-86, 93-95. Sales assoc. Nationwise Auto-Parts, Columbus, 1984-85; cashier Sears, Columbus, 1986-87; teller Mid-Am. Fed.-Savings & Loan, Columbus, 1987-89, Banc Ohio Nat. Bank, Columbus, 1989-92; acct. clk. payment processor Franklin County Child Support Enforcement Agy., Columbus, 1992—. Author: (books of poetry) Love, Images-Motional Glass, 1993, Mirror, Moods and Fingers, 1994, Count to Ten, 1995, Waters Path-Solid Ground, 1996. Office: PO Box 13030 Whitehall OH 43213

TURPIN, RICHARD E., sales executive; b. Hamilton, Ohio, Aug. 10, 1950; s. Kenneth and Frances (Parrish) T.; 1 child, Vincent Paul Huntington Turpin. Degree, UCLA, 1972. Dir. sales Pepsico, Hamilton; dir. mktg. Tri-State, Inc., Columbus, Ohio; dir. sales CMR, Inc., Columbus, Ohio, 1985-96; self-employed cons. Turpin Assocs., Cin., 1996—. Vol. Children's Svcs., Columbus, 1994—. Recipient Citizenship award Chgo., 1970. Mem. Columbus C. of C. (com. chmn. 1993-94), Columbus Exec. Sales Assn. Roman Catholic. Home: 3020 Trentwood Rd Columbus OH 43221 Office: Turpin Assocs Shawnay Dr Middletown OH 43202

TURPIN, SAMUEL R., state legislator; m. Amy Traub. Ed., Ind. U. V.p. Turpin Hardware, Inc.; corp. and pub. fin. specialist Traub & Co.; mem. from 40th dist. Ind. State Ho. of Reps., 1985—; mem. pub. health com., chmn. ways and means com. Pres. Brownsburg Multi-sch. Bldg. Corp.; del. Rep. State Conv., 1976-82, 86. Named to Outstanding Young Men of Am., 1984. Mem. Ind. Hardware Assn., Ky. Hardware Assn., Brownsburg C. of C., Masons, Kiwanis. Home: 105 Westbourne Dr Brownsburg IN 46112-1013*

TURSSO, DENNIS JOSEPH, business executive; b. St. Paul, Apr. 13, 1939; s. Joseph Bias and Cecelia Beatrice (Solheid) T.; m. Sharon Ann Benike, June 6, 1964 (div. 1975); 1 child, Jason Bradford; m. Jacqueline Mary Hoffmann, Oct. 19, 1977; children: Shannon, Missey and Michele (twins). Student U. Minn., 1959-61. Sales mgr. Sten-C-Labl Inc., St. Paul, 1958-65; salesman Dymo Industries, Berkeley, Calif., 1965-68; with Dawson Patterson, St. Paul, 1968—; pres., CEO Tursso Cos. holding co., St. Paul, 1980—; dir. Printing Inds. of Minn.; bd. dirs. Northwestern Nat. Bank, St. Paul, HealthEast Found., SBA Adv. Bd. Advisor SBA, St. Paul, 1981-83, Norwest Nat. Bank St. Paul; bd. dirs. Childrens' Home Soc. St. Paul, Family Svc. St. Paul, Dunwoody C.C. Recipient Star Club sales awards Dymo Industries, 1966, 67; named Small Bus. Person of Yr., Small Bus. Adminstrn., 1992. Mem. Nat. Fed. Ind. Bus., Soc. Packaging Engrs., St. Paul C. of C. (bd. dirs., cert. of merit, Outstanding Businessman 1987), Winter Carnival Assn. St. Paul (bd. dirs.), St. Paul Club, Univ. Club, Minnesota Club, Decathlon, Pool and Yacht Club, Town and Country Club. Office: 3540 Midway Blvd Fort Dodge IA 50501-6400 also: Tursso Cos 223 Plato Blvd E Saint Paul MN 55107-1624

TUSCHMAN, JAMES MARSHALL, lawyer; b. Toledo, Nov. 28, 1941; s. Chester and Harriet (Harris) T.; m. Ina S. Cheloff, Sept. 2, 1967; children: Chad Michael, Jon Stephen, Sari Anne. BS in Bus., Miami U., Oxford, Ohio, 1963; JD, Ohio State U., 1966. Bar: Ohio 1966, U.S. Ct. Appeals (6th and 7th cirs.), U.S. Supreme Ct. Assoc. Shumaker, Loop & Kendrick, Toledo, 1966-84, ptnr. 1970-84; co-founder, chmn. ops. com. Jacobson Maynard Tuschman & Kalur, Toledo, Cleve., Cin., Columbus, Youngstown and Dayton, Ohio, Morgantown, W.Va. and Louisville, Kansas City, Mo., Columbia, Md., St. Louis, Phila., 1984—; chmn. bd., sec. Tuschman Steel Co., Toledo, 1969-76; vice chmn. bd. Kripke Tuschman Industries, Inc., 1977-85, dir. 1977-86; chmn. bd., sec. Toledo Steel Supply Co., 1969-86; ptnr. Starr Ave. Co., Toledo, 1969-86; bd. dirs. Capital Holdings Inc., Toledo, Capital Bank, Toledo, Fetal Devel. Eval., Ltd., Toledo. Mem. bd. trustees U. Toledo; past trustee, chmn. fin. com., former treas. Maumee Valley Country Day Sch.; past trustee, v.p., treas. Temple B'nai Israel, 1984-88. Fellow Internat. Soc. Barristers; mem. ABA, Am. Bd. Trial Advocates, Ohio Bar Assn., Toledo Bar Assn., Def. Rsch. and Trial Lawyers Assn., Ohio Civil Trial Lawyers Assn., Toledo Club, Inverness Country Club, Zeta Beta Tau, Phi Delta Phi. Home: 2579 Olde Brookside Rd Toledo OH 43615-2233 Office: 333 N Summit St Toledo OH 43604-2617

TUTTLE, MARTHA BENEDICT, artist; b. Cin., Feb. 4, 1916; d. Harris Miller and Florence Stevens (McCrea) Benedict; m. Richard Salway Tuttle, June 3, 1939; children: Richard, Jr., McCrea Benedict (dec.), Martha (dec.), Elisabeth Hall. Grad. high sch., Cin.; grad., Art Acad. Cin. V.p. Barg Bottling Co., Inc., Cin., 1948-80. One-woman shows include KKAE Gallery, 1963, Univ. Club, 1967, Miller Gallery, 1971, St. Clements, N.Y., 1973, Livingston Lodge, 1974, Holly Hill Antiques, 1979, Peterson Gallery, 1983, Art Acad. Cin., 1984, Closson Gallery, 1986, Camargo Gallery, 1992; represented in permanent collection Cin. Art Mus. Tchr. Sunday sch. Grace Episcopal Ch. and Indian Hill Ch., Cin., 1953-75; shareholder Cin. Art Mus.; founder partnership to save the William and Phebe Betts House; donor with partnership to The Nat. Soc. Colonial Dames of Am. the William and Phebe Betts House for establishing a Rsch. Ctr. Mem. Soc. Colonial Dames Am. (bd. dirs. 1976-89), Camargo Club, Univ. Club. Republican. Home: 5825 Drewry Farm Ln Cincinnati OH 45243-3441

TUXHORN, GARY L., mechanical design engineer; b. Dodge City, Kans., Nov. 20, 1950. Grad., high sch., 1969. Mech. design engr. Crust Buster/ Speed King, Dodge City, Kans., 1978—. Scoutmaster Boy Scouts Am., Kans., 1994-95. Home: 2308 Robin Rd Dodge City KS 67801-2925

TWAY, STEPHEN EDWARD, marketing communications executive, consultant; b. Chillicothe, Ohio, May 13, 1943; s. Rollin E. and Marjorie E. (Householder) T.; children: John Rollin, Matthew James. BS in Bus., Miami U., Oxford, Ohio, 1965. With Marine Midland Grace Trust, 1965-66, Huntington Nat. Bank, 1968-74; ptnr. Tway Lumber Co., 1974-84; owner Indsl. Grade Photography, Columbus, Ohio, 1986—; v.p., creative dir. Veda Gilp Assocs., Columbus, 1984—. Contbr. over 200 articles to profl. jours.; numerous pub. photos. With U.S. Army, 1966-68. Mem. Profl. Photographers Am., Columbus Computer Soc., Sanyo Users of Cen. Ohio. Office: Veda Gilp Assocs 937 S 3rd St Columbus OH 43206-2542

TWEET, ORLANDO A., retired industrial chemist; b. Eleva, Wis., Dec. 22, 1915; s. Andrew N. and Inga Tonetta (Thompson) T.; m. Marion Jeanette Holman, Aug. 9, 1952; children: Victoria Suzanne, Christine Claire, Jean Ellen. BA, St. Olaf Coll., 1939; MS, U. Wis., 1947. Quality control analytical chemist S.C. Johnson Wax Co., Racine, 1947, sr. rsch. chemist in thermal analysis and chromatography; judge S.E. Wis. Sci. and Engring. Fair, Marquette U., Milw., 1972—. Contbr. articles to profl. jours. Life mem. NAACP, Racine, mem. gov. bd., 1970-80; founder US/USSR Friendship Soc., Racine, 1984—; mem. Am. Luth. Ch., Madison, 1982-88; mem. peace and justice bd. dirs. Evang. Luth. Ch., Milw., 1988—; pres. Luth. Human Rels. Assn. Wis., 1978-86, Milw., 1966—. 2d lt. U.S. Army, 1942-45. Recipient Peace Svc. award World Fedn. Assn., 1987, Honor award NAACP, 1979, Peace Pilgrim award Coun. for Internat. Friendship, 1994. Mem. Am. Chem. Soc., Wis. State Hist. Soc., Sons of Norway (Racine). Democrat. Home: 6132 Five Mile Rd Racine WI 53402

TWEITO, ELEANOR MARIE, social services administrator, educator; b. Westgate, Iowa, Dec. 25, 1909; d. Henry Christopher and Amanda Marie (Fink) Frese; m. Thomas E. Tweito, Aug. 26, 1936; children: David Henry, Thomas Elling. Student, Wartburg Coll., 1926-28; BA, Morningside Coll., 1940; MA, U. Mo., 1966. Tchr. Pub. Rural Sch., Waverly, Iowa, 1928-30; pvt. sec. to Frank Gruber, editor, author, TV writer, pub., 1930-31; exec. sec. Century Life Ins. Co., Waverly, 1930-36, State U. Iowa, Iowa City, 1938-40; prof. Tri-State Bus. Coll., Sioux City, Iowa, 1940-42; tchr. Bronson Consolidated High Sch., Bronson, Iowa, 1942-59; founder, prof., chair bus. edn. dept. Mo. Valley Coll., Marshall, 1960-77; adminstr. Sr. Ctr. Dist. III Area Agy. on Aging, Marshall, 1987—; sec. of faculty Mo. Valley Coll., Marshall, 1965-70; lectr. workshop St. Paul's Coll., Concordia, Mo., 1979. Editor, contbr. The Evangel, 1976-86; co-author: Lest We Forget, 1988; contbr. articles to newspapers. Pres. Luth. Daus. of Reformation, Sioux City, 1957-60; sec., fin. sec. Luth. Ch., Marshall, 1976-86; bd. dirs., sec.-treas. Dist. III Area Agy. on Aging, Marshall, 1980—; sec. Saline County Coun. on Aging, 1986—. Recipient several disting. svc. citations Mayor of City of Marshall, 1990, Area Agy. on Aging, 1990, Family div. Mo. Dept. Social Svcs., 1987, resolution Mo. Ho. of Reps., 1990. Fellow AAUW (bd. dirs. Marshall chpt. 1970-90, hon. life); mem. AAUP, AARP (sec.-treas. 1977-88, chpt. 1936 v.p., program chairwoman 1988-92, pres. 1992—), Nat. Assn. Retired Tchrs., Sorosis Club, Faculty Women Club, Pi Gamma Mu, Zeta Sigma, Pi Lambda Theta. Home: 1108 Sunrise Dr Marshall MO 65340-2844

TWESIGYE, EMMANUEL KALENZI, theology educator, clergy member; b. Kambuga, Uganda, May 25, 1948; came to U.S., 1978; s. Blasio and Esther Joy (Katagirwa) Kalenzi; m. Beatrice Joy Tibayungwa, Sept. 4, 1976; children: Joy, Grace, Gloria, Peace. Diploma in theology, U. East Africa, Kampala, Uganda, 1970; BA with honors, Makere U., Kampala, Uganda, 1973, diploma in edn., 1973; MA with honors, Wheaton Grad. Sch., 1978; MST, U. of the South, 1979; MA, Vanderbilt U., 1982, PhD, 1983. Head dept. religious studies Uganda Nat. Tchrs. Coll., Kyambogo, Uganda, 1973-77; dep. adminstr. for Africa Living Bibles, Nairobi, Kenya, 1977-78; dir. black world studies, prof. religion Ohio Wesleyan U., Delaware, Ohio, 1989—; pres. Applied Edn. for Africa, Nashville, 1984-90; sec.-treas. Ohio Acad. Religion, 1992-93, v.p., program chmn. 1993-94, pres., 1994-95. Author: Common Ground: Christianity, African Religion & Philosophy, 1987, The Global Human Problem: Ignorance, Hate, Injustice & Violence, 1988, God, Race, Myth and Power: An Africanist Research Corrective, 1991, African Religion, Philosophy, and Christianity in Logos-Christ: Common Ground Revisited, 1996; editor Zumari, 1993—. Bd. dirs. Global Village, Delaware, 1990-95, v.p., 1994-95; commr. Episcopal Nat. & World Mission, Ohio, 1990—. Princeton U. fellow, 1984, Harvard U. fellow, 1995. Mem. Am. Prof. Assn., Am. Philos. Assn., Am. Acad. Religion, Ohio Acad. Religion. Episcopalian. Home: 651 Governors St Delaware OH 43015 Office: Ohio Wesleyan Univ Dept Religion 62 S Sandusky Delaware OH 43015

TWESTEN, GARY KEITH, science educator; b. Belleville, Ill., Aug. 1, 1941; s. Henry Paul and Cornelia (Bassler) T.; m. Janet Lynn Parsons, Nov. 13, 1976; children: Amanda Parsons-Twesten, Bryce Parsons-Twesten. BA, So. Ill. U., 1966, MS, 1973; student, Kenya Sci. Coll., 1976, Nairobi U., 1976. Tchr. phys. sci. dist. 189 East St. Louis (Ill.) Sr. High Sch., 1966; tchr. biol. sci., photography Dist. 201 Belleville Twp. H.S. West, 1966—, chair biol. sci. dept., 1984—; owner J&G Arts Pub. Co., Belleville, 1973; cons., lectr. various groups and seminars. Author: Wildlife Ecology, 1973, Teaching Photography, 1980 (art book) Mammals of Wild Northwest, Birds of Prey, 1994, others; artist over 100 editions of art prints with Ill. Dept.

Conservation, Ill. State Art Mus., one man shows include Yellowstone Nat. Park. Named Regional Conservation Tchr. of Yr. Agrl. Stabilization Conservation Svc., 1978, 94. Mem. Nat. Wildlife Assn., Nature Conservancy Assn., Sierra Club (cons., guide of nature trail trips), Audubon Soc., Ducks Unltd., St. Louis Artists Guild. Office: Belleville High Sch W Dist 201 2600 W Main St Belleville IL 62223-6651

TWYLA, ROMAN, state legislator; m. John Twyla; children: Lisa, Sheryl. Student, U. Akron. Trustee Springfield Twp., 1981-94; mem. Ohio State Ho. Reps., Columbus, 1994—. Mem. Summit County Emergency Mgmt. Planning and Exec. Commn. Mem. MADD, S.E. Bd. of Trade, Ohio Twp. Assn., Summit County Twp. Assn., Brimfield Meml. House Assn.

TYLER, PRISCILLA, retired English language and education educator; b. Cleve., Oct. 23, 1908; d. Ralph Sargent and Alice Lorraine (Campbell) T. BA in Latin and Greek, Radcliffe Coll., 1932; MA in Edn., Case Western Res. U., 1934, PhD in English, 1953; LLD (hon.), Carleton U., Ottawa, Ont., Can., 1993. Parole officer, case worker Cleve. Sch. for Girls, 1934-35; tchr. English, Latin and French Cleveland Heights (Ohio) Pub. Schs., 1935-45; instr. to asst. prof. English Flora Stone Mather Coll., Cleve., 1945-59, asst. dean, 1957-59; asst. prof. edn., head dept. English Sch. of Edn. Harvard U., Cambridge, Mass., 1959-63; assoc. prof. English, U. Ill., Champaign-Urbana, 1963-67, dir. freshman rhetoric, 1966-67; prof. edn. and English U. Mo., Kansas City, 1967-78, prof. emeritus, 1978—; instr. N.S. (Can.) Dept. Edn., Halifax, summers 1972-73; condr. numerous seminars; former lectr. U. Calif., Berkeley, U. Chgo., Purdue U., U. Mo., Columbia, U. Nebr., Emory U., Fresno State U., Calif. State U., Hayward, San Jose State Coll., Mills Coll., Ala., Tift Coll., Ga., Va. Poly. Inst. and Midwestern U., Tex. Editor: Harpers Modern Classics, 19 vols., 1963, Writers the Other Side of the Horizon, 1964, (with Maree Brooks) Inupiat Paitot, 1974; co-author introduction and co-editor: (with Maree Brooks) Sevukakmet, Ways of Life on St. Lawrence Island (Helen Slwooko Carius), 1979, The Epic of Qayaq, 1995 (Lela Kiana); interviewed authors, Jan Carew, Guyana, George Lamming, Barbados, Christopher Okigbo, Nigeria; also articles. Mem. Ohio Gov.'s Com. on Employment of Physically Handicapped, 1957; mem. Friends of Art of Carleton U., Nelson Atkins Mus. Art, Kansas City, Ottawa (Kans.) Art Gallery, Friends of Libr., Ottawa. Recipient Outstanding Achievement and Contbns. in Field of Edn. award Western Res. U., 1962, Disting. Alumna award Laurel Sch., Cleve., 1994; Priscilla Tyler Endowment Fund named in her honor Case Western Res. U., 1980. Mem. MLA, NEA, Archaeol. Inst. Am., Nat. Coun. Tchrs. English (v.p. 1963, mem. com. on history of the profession 1965-68, Commn. on Composition 1968-71, trustee Rsch. Found. 1970-78, Disting. Svc. award 1978), Conf. on Coll. Composition and Comm. (pres. 1963), Arctic Inst. N.Am., Inuit Art Found., Franklin County Hist. Assn., Calif. Assn. Tchrs. English (hon.. Curriculum Commn. Ctrl. Calif.), Delta Kappa Gamma (pres. Upsilon chpt. 1950-52). Democrat. Presbyterian. Home: 4213 Kentucky Ter Ottawa KS 66067-8715

TYLER, WILLIAM HOWARD, JR., advertising executive, educator; b. Elizabethtown, Tenn., May 21, 1932; s. William Howard and Ethel Margaret (Schueler) T.; m. Margery Moss, Aug. 31, 1957; children: William James, Daniel Moss. Student, Iowa State U., 1950-52, U. Iowa, 1952; AB in Lit., BJ in Advt., U. Mo., 1958, MA in Journalism, 1966. Advt. mgr. Rolla (Mo.) Daily News, 1958-59; instr. sch. journalism U. Mo., Columbia, 1959-61; copy writer, then v.p. copy dir. D'Arcy Advt. Agy., St. Louis, 1961-67; writer, producer, creative supr. Gardner Advt. Co., St. Louis, 1967-69; sr. v.p., creative dir. D'Arcy, McManus, Masius, St. Louis, 1969-77; exec. v.p., creative dir. Larson Bateman Advt. Agy., Santa Barbara, Calif., 1977-80; v.p. advt. Pizza Hut, Inc., Wichita, Kans., 1980-82; v.p., creative dir. Frye-Sills/Y&R, Denver, 1980; exec. v.p., creative dir. Gardner Advt. Co., St. Louis, 1982-88; exec. v.p., ptnr., creative dir. Parker Group, St. Louis, 1988-91; pres. TYLERtoo Advt./Communications, St. Louis, 1991—; assoc. prof. St. Louis U., 1993—. Mng. editor St. Louis Advt. Mag., 1992-95. Trustee Blackburn Coll., Carlinville, Ill., 1983-84; bd. advisors U. Mo. Journalism Sch., 1986-91. 1st lt. USMC, 1952-55, Korea. Mem. St. Louis Advt. and Mktg. Assn. (bd. dirs. 1987-90), U. Mo. Alumni Assn. (bd. dirs. 1969-70, publs. com. 1990-93), St. Louis Ind. Prodn. Profls., St. Louis Radio Profls. Episcopalian. Office: Tylertoo Advt/Communications 13705 Corrington Ct Chesterfield MO 63017

TYLMAN, STANLEY GEORGE, JR., state agency administrator, educator, analyst; b. Houston, July 2, 1945; s. Stanley George Tylman and Betty Louise (Johnsen) Hyndman; m. A. Joanne Hale, June 1, 1968; children: Michelle, Emily. BS in Polit. Sci., Ea. Ill. U., 1969, MA in Polit. Sci., 1974. Instr. Lincoln Land C.C., Springfield, Ill., 1970—; sr. archivist Ill. State Archives, Springfield, 1971-78; dist. mgr. Nat. Fedn. Ind. Bus., Taylorville, Ill., 1978-86; fin. planner Primerica Fin. Svcs., Taylorville, Ill., 1987-88; sr. analyst Ill. Dept. Mental Health and Developmental Disabilities, Springfield, 1988—; dir. PGF Consulting, Inc., Charleston, Ill., 1984—; owner Flashback Photography, Taylorville, 1978-80. Bd. dirs. Taylorville YMCA, 1978-80, Keep Taylorville Beautiful, Inc., 1981-82, Project 29, Inc., 1992—. Sgt. U.S. Army, 1964-67. Grantee NEH, 1976. Republican. Methodist. Home: 225 E North St Taylorville IL 62568 Office: Ill Dept Mental Health 100 N 9th St Rm 308 Springfield IL 62765

TYLUTKI, JOSEPH JOHN, telecommunications industry executive; b. Detroit, Feb. 17, 1947; s. Joseph Albert and Lottie Thresa (Buczek) T.; m. Judith Adele West, May 18, 1974; children: Joseph Patrick, Jennifer Judith, Kimberly Ok. BS, Wayne State U., 1971; MPA, Western Mich. U., 1978; MS in MIS, Ill. Benedictine Coll., 1994. Cert. computing profl. Data systems analyst State of Mich., Lansing, 1971-78; statis. analyst GM, Redford, Mich., 1978-79; bus. systems analyst Fed. Mogul, Southfield, Mich., 1979-80; data processing mgr. Miesel-Sysco, Detroit, 1980-81; comm. systems rep. AT&T Comm., Dearborn, Mich., 1981-88; tech. cons. AT&T Computer Systems, Southfield, 1988-91; project mgr. AT&T Network Systems, Lisle, Ill., 1992—; instr. Lewis U., Romeoville, Ill., 1995, Joliet (Ill.) Jr. Coll., 1994—, Ctrl. Mich. U., Southfield, 1991—, Detroit Coll. Bus., Dearborn, 1989-91. Pres. St. Linus Credit Union, Dearborn Hts., Mich., 1985-91; com. mem. Hawthorne Credit Union, Naperville, Ill., 1993—. With U.S. Army, 1967-68. Mich. Higher Edn. Assistance Authority scholar, 1965. Mem. IEEE (sr. mem.), Assn. for Computing Machinery (chmn. Detroit met. chpt. 1987-88, Svc. award 1988), Assn. Record Mgrs. and Adminstrs. (pres. Mid-Mich. chpt. 1977-78, Svc. award 1978). Roman Catholic. Home: 4525 Shabbona Ln Lisle IL 60532

TYNER, NEAL EDWARD, retired insurance company executive; b. Grand Island, Nebr., Jan. 30, 1930; s. Edward Raymond and Lydia Dorothea (Kruse) T.; children: Karen Tyner Redrow, Morgan. BBA, U. Nebr., 1956. Jr. analyst Bankers Life Nebr., Lincoln, 1956-62, asst. v.p. securities, 1962-67, v.p. securities, treas., 1967-69, fin. v.p., treas., 1970-72, sr. v.p. fin., treas., 1972-83, pres., chief exec. officer, 1983-87, chmn., pres., chief exec. officer, 1987-88, chmn., CEO, 1988-95; bd. dirs. Union Bank & Trust Co., Austins Steaks & Saloon; chmn. emeritus Ameritas Life Ins. Corp. Trustee U. Nebr. Found., Lincoln Found., Investment Banking Inst., NYU; bd. govs. Nebr. Wesleyan U. Capt. USMC, 1950-54, Korea. Fellow CFAs; mem. Omaha/Lincoln Soc. Fin. Analysts, Paradise Valley Country Club. Lutheran. Office: Ameritas Life Ins Corp Ste 324 6940 O St Lincoln NE 68510

TYREE, JAMES C., insurance company executive; b. 1957. Grad., Ill. State U., 1979. With Mesirow Ins. Svcs. Inc., Chgo., 1980—, CEO. Office: Mesirow Ins Svcs Inc 350 N Clark St Chicago IL 60610-4712*

TYRONE, TOMLINSON, designer; b. Huntington, W.Va., Sept. 24, 1948. Designer Nat. Mine Svc. Co., Greenup, Ky., 1980-87, Jeffrey divsn. of Dresser Industries, Columbus, Ohio, 1987-92, J. E. Grote, Blacklick, Ohio, 1992—. Office: J E Grote 1160 Gahanna Pky Blacklick OH 43004-9529

TYSON, JOHN DAVID, JR., public and investor relations executive; b. Lorain, Ohio, 1937; s. John David and Muriel Ruth (Draper) T.; married; children: John, Matthew. BA, Am. U., 1962, JD, 1966; MM, Northwestern U., 1978. Adminstrv. asst. U.S. Congressman C.E. Bennett, Washignton, 1964-68; with Internat. Paper Co., N.Y.C., 1968-74; pub. affairs v.p. Container Corp. of Am., Chgo., 1974-83; corp. affairs v.p. Batus Inc., Louisville, 1983-88; corp. relations v.p. SPX Corp., Muskegon, Mich., 1988—. Bd. dirs. Pub. Affairs Coun., 1983, chmn., 1982; bd. dirs. Opera Grand Rapids, Muskegon Oceana Cmty. Reinvestment Corp., Automotive Industry Pub. Rels. Coun.; chmn. NAIC corp. com. Muskegon Econ. Forum. Mem. Rotary Club Muskegon, Muskegon Country Club. Office: SPX Corp PO Box 3301 700 Terrace Point Dr Muskegon MI 49443

TYSON, MARY P., marketing professional; b. Montoursville, Pa., June 15, 1930. Keypunch operator J&H, inc., Southfield, Mich., 1980-83; travel agt. Travel & Luggage, Troy, Mich., 1983-86; co-owner Tyson Mktg. Inc., Plymouth, Mich., 1987—. Vol. St. Joseph, Mercy Ann Arbor, 1985-87. Republican. Office: Tyson Mktg Inc PO Box 87511 Canton MI 48187-0511

TZAGOURNIS, MANUEL, physician, educator, university administrator; b. Youngstown, Ohio; came to Oct. 20, 1934,; s. Adam and Argiro T.; m. Madeline Jean Kalos, Aug. 30, 1958; children: Adam, Alice, Ellen, Jack George. B.S., Ohio State U., 1956, M.D., 1960, M.S., 1967. Intern Phila. Gen. Hosp., 1960-61; resident Ohio State U., Columbus, 1961-63, chief med. resident, 1966-67, instr., 1967-68, asst. prof., 1968-70, assoc. prof., 1970-74, prof., 1974—, asst. dean Sch. Medicine, 1973-75, assoc. dean, med. dirs. hosps., 1975-80, v.p. health scis., dean of medicine, 1981-95; gen. practice medicine Columbus, 1967—; mem. staff Ohio State U. Hosps./James Cancer Hosp. & Rsch. Ctr.; mem. Coalition for Cost Effective Health Services Edn. and Research Group State of Ohio, 1983. Contbg. author: textbook Endocrinology, 1974, Clinical Diabetes: Modern Management, 1980; co-author: Diabetes Mellitus, 1983, 88. Citation Ohio State Senate Resolution No. 984, 1989. Capt. U.S. Army, 1962-64. Recipient Homeric Order of Ahepa Cleve. chpt., 1976, Phys. of Yr. award Hellenic Med. Soc. N.Y., 1989; citations Ohio State Senate and Ho. of Reps., 1975, 83. Mem. AMA (med. edn. coun. 1993—), Am. Red Cross (vice chair ctrl. Ohio 1996—), Franklin County Acad. Medicine, Assn. Am. Med. Colls., Assn. of Acad. Health Ctrs., Deans' Council. Mem. Greek Orthodox Ch. Home: 4335 Sawmill Rd Columbus OH 43220-2243 Office: Ohio State U Coll Medicine 200 Meiling Hall 370 W 9th Ave Columbus OH 43210-1238

UBBELOHDE, CARL WILLIAM, history educator; b. Waldo, Wis., Nov. 4, 1924; s. Carl William and Carrie (Stratton) U.; m. Mary Jean Tipler, May 31, 1952 (div. 1990); children: Susan, Nell, Libby, Katherine. BS, State Tchrs. Coll., Oskosh, Wis., 1948; MS, U. Wis., 1950, PhD, 1954. From instr. to assoc. prof. U. Colo., Boulder, 1954-65; from assoc. prof. to Henry Eldridge Bourne prof. Case Western Res. U., Cleve., 1965-93, prof. emeritus, 1994—; vis. prof. U. Wis., 1961, U. Tex., 1964, U. Vt. 1966, 67, U. Pa., 1968. Author: Vice Admiralty Courts, 1960, A Colorado History, 7th edit., 1995, The American Colonies, 1968; co-author: Clio's Servant, 1967. Mem. Charter Rev. Commn., Cleve. Hts., Ohio, 1982, Landmark Commn., 1982-87. Recipient Herfurth award U. Wis., 1955. Mem. ACLU (bd. dirs. 1970-73), Am. Hist. Assn., Orgn. Am. Historians, Assn. for Can. Studies in U.S., Ohio Acad. History (pres. 1990-91), Ohio Hist. Soc., Western Res. Hist. Soc. Democrat. Unitarian. Home: 2300 Overlook Rd # 819 Cleveland Hts OH 44106-2346 Office: Case Western Res U Dept History University Cir Cleveland OH 44106-7107

UBEL, JAMES ANDREW, library director; b. St. Paul, Nov. 14, 1937; s. Florian J. and Dorothy Althea (Scott) U.; m. Hiltrud Maria Masuch, Jan. 31, 1959 (div. 1976); children: Mark, Andrea, Clifton; m. Barbara Ann Willis, Apr. 28, 1978. BA, U. Minn., 1959, MA, 1960. City libr. Scottsbluff (Nebr.) Pub. Libr., 1960-62; assoc. dir. Dakota-Scott Regional Libr., West St. Paul, 1962-66; exec. dir. Shawnee Libr. System, Carterville, Ill., 1966—; libr. bldg. and svcs. cons. to numerous pub. and pvt. librs.; mem. Rural Libr. Panel, Ill., 1991-92, Ill. State Libr. Task Force on Rural Libr. Svcs., 1987-88. Mem. Minn. Libr. Assn. (life, pres. 1965-66), ALA, Ill. Libr. Assn. (pres. pub. libr. sect. 1975, chmn., mem. numerous coms.), Beta Phi Mu, Ill. Pub. Employers Labor Rels. Assn. Home: 536 N 15th Murphysboro IL 62966 Office: Shawnee Libr System 511 Greenbriar Rd Carterville IL 62918

UCKO, DAVID ALAN, museum director; b. N.Y.C., July 9, 1948; s. Lawrence L. and Helen H. U.; m. Barbara Alice Clark, Aug. 13, 1977; 1 child, Aaron. BA, Columbia Coll., N.Y.C., 1969; PhD, MIT, 1972. Asst. prof. chemistry Hostos Community Coll., CUNY, Bronx, 1972-76; asst. prof. chemistry Antioch Coll., Yellow Springs, Ohio, 1976-79, assoc. prof. chemistry, 1979; rsch. coord. Mus. Sci. and Industry, Chgo., 1979-80, dir. sci., 1981-87, v.p., 1986-87; dep. dir. Calif. Mus. Sci. and Industry, L.A., 1987-90; pres. Kansas City (Mo.) Mus., 1990—; rsch. assoc. chemistry dept. Columbia U., 1973-76; rsch. assoc., assoc. prof. dept. edn. U. Chgo., 1982-87; adj. staff scientist C.F. Kettering Rsch. Lab., Yellow Springs, 1977-79. Author: (book) Basics for Chemistry, 1982, Living Chemistry, 2d edit., 1986; contbr. articles to profl. jours.; host, producer (radio program) Science Alive!, 1983-87; developer numerous mus. exhibits. V.p., bd. dirs. Heritage League, Greater Kansas City, 1991-92; mem. Mid. Am. Regional Coun., Regional Amenities Task Force, Kansas City, 1990-96; bd. dirs. Cultural Alliance Greater Kansas City, 1995—, Appointed to Nat. Mus. Svcs. Bd.m 1996, Mus. Without Walls, 1996—,. Woodrow Wilson fellow, 1969, NIH postdoctoral fellow, 1972; grantee NSF, NEH, U.S. Dept. Edn., Ill. Humanities Coun., 1976-88; recipient Up and Comers award Jr. Achievement of Mid.-Am., 1992. Fellow AAAS (at large sect. Y 1987-93; mem. Assn Sci. Tech. Ctrs. (publs. com. 1984-94, chmn. 1988-94, ethics com., 1994-95, legis. com., chmn. 1996—, Greater Kansas City C. of C. (edn. com. 1993-96), Alpha Sigma Nu (hon.), Phi Lambda Upsilon, Sigma Xi. Home: 1007 W 66th St Kansas City MO 64113-1815 Office: Kansas City Mus 3218 Gladstone Blvd Kansas City MO 64123-1111

UCKUN, FATIH, research scientist, pediatric medicine educator; b. Istanbul, Turkey, June 12, 1958; came to U.S., 1984.; s. Ilhan A. and Melike R. (Kostem) U.; m. Linda B. Boehner, Apr. 26, 1982. Abitur, German Coll. Sci., Istanbul, 1977; MD, U. Heidelberg, Fed. Republic of Germany, 1982. Postdoctoral assoc. U. Minn., Mpls., 1984-86, asst. prof., 1986-90, assoc. prof., 1990-93, prof., 1993—, dir. tumor immunology lab., 1988—, dir. cancer and leukemia biology sect Dept. Therapeutic Radiology-Radiation-Oncology, 1990—, sci. dir. immunotoxin prodn. facility Bone Marrow Transplant Program, 1990—; attending physician dept. therapeutic radiology/radiation oncology U. Minn., 1992—, dir. children's cancer group acute lymphoblastic leukemia biology ref. lab., 1992—, dir. children's cancer group centralized immunotoxin resource lab., 1992—, dir. and attending physician biotherapy program, 1993—, attending physician bone marrow transplantation program, 1994—, chair leukemia biology program area Cancer Ctr., 1993—, assoc. dir. exptl. therapy and attending physician divsn. pediatric oncology, dept. pediatrics, 1995—, vice chair new agts. com., 1993—, mem. various coms.; tchr., instr. in field. Ad-hoc reviewer for jours.; contbr. articles to profl. jours.; patentee in field. Deutscher Akademischer Austauschdienst scholar U. Heidelberg, 1977-83; recipient New Investigator award NIH, 1986, Spl. Fellowship award Leukemia Soc. Am., 1986, Scholar award, 1989, Stohlman Scholar award, 1992, 3d Pierce Immunotoxin award, 1992, Rsch. award Radiation Rsch. Soc., 1994, Sci. award TUBITAK, the Turkish Nat. Acad. Basic Scis., 1995; recipient numerous rsch. grants and fellowships. Mem. AMA, Am. Assn. Immunologists, Am. Soc. Hematology, Am. Assn. Cancer Rsch., Internat. Soc. Exptl. Hematology, Transplantation Soc. Office: Univ Minn Box 346 UMHC Harvard St at E River Rd Minneapolis MN 55455

UDITSKY, DANIEL NATHAN, dentist; b. Chgo., June 3, 1942; s. Emanual David and Sara (Rose) U.; m. Arlene Sharon Weintraub, Aug. 14, 1966; children: Andrea Susan Uditsky-Nakisher, Jordan Neal. DDS, U. Ill., 1969. Student Loyola U., Chgo.; dentist in pvt. practice Schaumburg, Ill., 1969—; mem. dental staff Alexian Bros. Med. Ctr.; cons. Clin. Rsch. Assocs., Provo, Utah, 1991—, Midwest div. Dentsplty. Corp., Des Plaines, Ill., 1980—. Active Jewish Cmty. Ctrs. of Greater Chgo.; mem. dental divsn. Jewish United Fund of Greater Chgo.; co-chmn. dental divsn. State of Israel Bonds of Ill. Fellow Acad. Gen. Dentistry, Internat. Coll. Dentists; mem. Am. Acd. Cosmetic Dentistry, Am. Equilibration Soc., Ross Taylor Dental Study Club, U. Ill. Coll. Dentistry Alumni Assn. (treas. 1994-95), Chgo. Dental Soc. (br. pres.), Alpha Omega. Office: 650 E Higgins Rd Schaumburg IL 60173

UGGERUD, WARD LEE, electric utility company executive; b. Drayton, N.D., Mar. 28, 1949; s. Edward Rudolph and Lila Marie (Soderfelt) U.; m. Jane Rachelle Triebold, July 26, 1970; children: Mark, Eric. BSEE, N.D. State U., 1971. Registered profl. engr., Minn. Engr. computer svcs. Otter Tail Power Co., Fergus Falls, Minn., 1971-74, system engr., 1974-78, asst. mgr. systems ops., 1978-79, mgr. systems ops., 1979-84, dir. systems ops., 1984-89, v.p. ops., 1989—; vice chmn. oper. com. Mid-Continent Area Power Pool, Mpls., 1984, chmn., 1985; sec. oper. com. N.Am. Electric Reliability Coun., Princeton, N.J., 1986-88, vice chmn. oper. com., 1988-90, chmn. oper. com., 1990-92. Com. mem. Boy Scouts Am., Fergus Falls, 1973-82, cub master, 1983-84; pres. Bethlehem Luth. Ch., Fergus Falls, 1974-75. Mem. IEEE. Lodge: Rotary. Home: 609 W Douglas Ave Fergus Falls MN 56537-3228 Office: Otter Tail Power Co 215 S Cascade St Fergus Falls MN 56537-2801

UHERKA, DAVID JEROME, mathematics educator; b. Wagner, S.D., June 2, 1938; s. Edward L. and Gertrude (Schaefer) U.; m. Dorothy Ann Malouf, Mar. 25, 1965; children: Kara Ann, Michael David. BS in Math., S.D. Sch. Mines and Tech., 1960; MA in Math., U. Utah, 1963, PhD in Math., 1964. Data analysis officer U.S. Army Natick (Mass.) Lab., 1964-66; asst. prof. math. Ariz. State U., Tempe, 1966-68; from assoc. prof. to prof. math. U. N.D., Grand Forks, 1968—; chair math. dept., 1993—; scientist in residence Argonne (Ill.) Nat. Lab., 1981-82, Los Alamos Nat. Lab., 1991-92. Contbr. articles to profl. jours. Capt. U.S. Army, 1964-66. U. N.D. grantee, 1968—; Am. We. Univs. Sabbatical fellow, 1991-92. Mem. AAUP, Math. Assn. Am., Soc. Indsl. and Applied Math., Am. Assn. for Engring. Edn., Nat. Coun. Tchrs. Math., N.D. Ednl. Computing Assn. (sec.-treas., v.p., pres. 1982-84). Office: U ND Dept Math Grand Forks ND 58202-8376

UHLMANSIEK, CHRIS J., automotive engineer; b. Madison, Ind., Nov. 2, 1969. BS, Purdue U., 1992. Engr. Cummins Engine Co., Columbus, Ind., 1993—. Mem. Soc. Automotive Engrs., Pi Tau Sigma, Tau Beta Pi. Republican. Office: Cummins Engine Co PO Box 3005 Columbus IN 47202-3005

ULAKOVICH, RONALD STEPHEN, real estate developer; b. Youngstown, Ohio, Nov. 17, 1942; s. Stephen G. and Anne (Petretich) U. B.S., Indsl. Engring. Coll., 1967; M.S., Method Engring., Ill. Inst. Tech., 1969. Methods engr. Supreme Products, Chgo., 1964-66; pres. Contract Chair, 1966-70; v.p. sales Amrep Corp., Rosemont, Ill., 1970-73; pres. Condo Assoc., Ltd., Arlington Heights, Ill., 1973—, Am. Resorts Internat. Ltd., 1983. Named Employee of Yr., 1965; recipient Nat. Home Builders Grand award, 1977, Million Dollar Circle award Chgo. Tribune, 1978, Cert. of Recognition award Congressional Com., 1982, Cert. of Merit award Pres. Reagan's Task Force, 1984; named to Ky. Col., State of Ky., 1982. Mem. Am. Assn. Investors, Apt. Owners Assn., Real Estate Soc. of Syndicators and Investors, Am. Resort and Resdl. Devel. Assn. Roman Catholic. Avocations: auto racing, golf. Home: 510 N Van Buren St, Dundee IL 60118-1030

ULETT, GEORGE ANDREW, psychiatrist; b. Needham, Mass., Jan. 10, 1918; s. George Andrew and Mabel Elizabeth (Caswell) U.; m. Pearl Carolyn Lawrence; children: Richard Carlton, Judith Anne, Carol Lynn. BA in Psychology, Stanford U., 1940; MS in Anatomy, U. Oreg., 1943, PhD in Anatomy, 1944, MD, 1944. Diplomate Am. Bd. Psychiatry and Neurology. Asst. psychiatrist Barnes Hosp., St. Louis, 1950-64; med. dir. Malcolm Bliss Hosp., St. Louis, 1951-61; dir. Mo. Div. Mental Health, Jefferson City, Mo., 1962-72; prof., chair Mo. Inst. Psychiatry, St. Louis, 1964-73; dir. psychiatry Deaconess Hosp., St. Louis, 1973-94; interim dir. Mo. Inst. of Mental Health, St. Louis, 1990-91; assoc. dir. for policy and ethics Mo. Inst. of Mental Health, 1991-94; clin. prof. dept. family and cmty. medicine St. Louis U. Sch. Medicine, 1995—; mem. adv. coun. Mental Health Assn. St. Louis, 1965-66, 69-70, mem. profl. adv. com., 1965; chair health and hosp. com. Health & Welfare Coun. St. Louis, 1960; mem. alcohol rev. com., psychopharmacology study sect., alcoholism study sect., 1993, grants rev. com. for alternative medicine NIMH, Rockville, Md.; prof. psychiatry Washington U. Sch. Medicine, St. Louis, 1956-61; clin. prof. cmty. and family medicine St. Louis U. Sch. Medicine, 1981-89, U. Mo. Sch. Medicine, 1990—. Author eight books; contbr. over 200 articles to profl. jours. Capt. U.S. Air Force, 1946-47. Recipient Ann. award Mo. Assn. for Mental Health, 1966, Recognition award, 1970, AMA Honorable Mention award Foster Com. Exhibit, 1974, Pax Mundi Fellowship award for profl. excellence, 1989; named hon. mem. Turkish Coll. Neuropharmacology, 1969. Fellow Am. Psychiat. Assn.; mem. Am. Soc. Acupuncture (past pres.), Am. Soc. of Med. Psychiatry (past pres.), Mo. Acad. Psychiatry (past pres.). Office: Mo Inst Mental Health 5247 Fyler Ave Saint Louis MO 63139-1300

ULFERTS, LEON RONALD, trade company executive; b. Slayton, Minn., Aug. 1, 1946; s. Peter and Luella Willhemina (Weiner) U.; m. Rita Ann Miller, Aug. 12, 1972; children: Amy, Eric, Ryan, Todd. Student, Mankato State U., 1971. Mktg. mgr. Philip Morris, Mankato, Minn., 1971-73; mgr. market sales Motorola, Inc., Mankato, 1973-75; mgr. gen. Air Comm., St. Cloud, Minn., 1975-77; exec. v.p. Alpine Windows, Mpls., 1977-85; pres. Tradewinds Internat., Mpls., 1985—. Bd. dirs. Anoka (Minn.)-Hennepin Sch. Bd. Home: 8548 W River Rd Brooklyn Park MN 55444

ULLIAN, JOSEPH SILBERT, philosophy educator; b. Ann Arbor, Mich., Nov. 9, 1930; s. Hyman Benjamin and Frieda G. (Silbert) U. AB, Harvard U., 1952, AM, 1953, PhD, 1957. Instr. philosophy Stanford U., Calif., 1957-58; asst. prof. philosophy Johns Hopkins U., Balt., 1958-60; vis. asst. prof. philosophy U. Pa., Phila., 1959-60, rsch. assoc. in linguistics, 1961-62; vis. asst. prof. philosophy U. Chgo., 1962-63; asst. prof. U. Calif., Santa Barbara, 1964-66; assoc. prof. Washington U., St. Louis, 1965-70, prof., 1970—; lectr. U. Calif., Berkeley, 1961; cons. Rsch. Directorate System Devel. Corp., Santa Monica, Calif., 1962-70. Co-author: The Web of Belief, 1970, 2d edit., 1978; contbr. articles to profl. jours. Mem. Am. Philos. Assn., Assn. for Symbolic Logic (exec. com. 1974-77), Am. Soc. for Aesthetics, Phi Beta Kappa. Democrat. Home: 984 Tornoe Rd Santa Barbara CA 93105-2229 Office: Washington U Dept Philosophy 1 Brookings Dr Saint Louis MO 63130-4899

ULLMAN, FRANK GORDON, electrical engineering educator; b. N.Y.C., Dec. 14, 1926; s. Samuel Robert and Ella (Fischl) U.; m. Deborah Halpern, July 15, 1951; children: Diane Ella, Marian Ruth, Eileen Jane. BA, NYU, 1949; MS, Poly. Inst. Bklyn., 1951, PhD, 1958. Rsch. fellow Poly. Inst. Bklyn., N.Y.C., 1949-51; jr. engr. Sylvania Electric Products, Inc., Mineola, N.Y., 1951-54; rsch. asst. Poly. Inst. Bklyn., N.Y.C., 1954-57, rsch. assoc., 1957-58; sr. rsch. physicist Nat. Cash Register Co., Dayton, Ohio, 1958-66; prof. elec. engring. and physics U. Nebr., Lincoln, 1966-96, prof. emeritus, 1996—, assoc. chmn. dept. elec. engring., 1987-91; instr. U. Dayton, 1960-62; vis. prof. Hebrew U., Jerusalem, 1982; co-dir. Ctr. Laser-Analytical Studies of Trace Gas Dynamics, 1988-96. Mem. editorial bd. Ferroelectrics, Ferroelectrics Letters; contbr. articles in field to profl. jours. With U.S. Army, 1945-46. Mem. AAUP, IEEE (sr. mem.), Am. Phys. Soc., Sigma Xi. Democrat. Jewish. Office: U Nebr Dept Elec Engring Lincoln NE 68588-0511

ULLRICH, ROXIE ANN, special education educator; b. Ft. Dodge, Iowa, Nov. 10, 1951; d. Rocco William and Mary Veronica (Casady) Jackowell; m. Thomas Earl Ullrich, Aug. 10, 1974; children: Holly Ann, Anthony Joseph. BA, Creighton U., 1973; MA in Teaching, Morningside Coll., 1991. Cert. tchr., Iowa. Tchr. Corpus Christi Sch., Ft. Dodge, Iowa, 1973-74, Westwood Community Schs., Sloan, Iowa, 1974-80, Sioux City Community Schs., 1987—. Cert. judge Iowa High Sch. Speech Assn., Des Moines, 1975—. Mem. Am. Paint Horse Assn., Am. Quarter Horse Assn., Sioux City Hist. Assn., M.I. Hummel Club, Phi Delta Kappa. Home: 819 Brown St Sloan IA 51055

ULMER, ANNE CLOSE, foreign language educator; b. Mpls., Sept. 21, 1940; d. Winston Arthur and Elizabeth (Scheu) Close; m. Milton Don Ulmer, Dec. 26, 1966. BA, U. Minn., 1962, MA, 1966; MPhil, Yale U., 1968, PhD, 1973. Lectr. in German U. Minn., Mpls., 1976-78; asst. prof. German Carleton Coll., Northfield, Minn., 1978-86, prof. German, 1986-95, chair German dept., 1987-91, 95—. Translator: (novel) Negatives of my Father (Peter Henisch), 1990. Fulbright grantee Austrian-Am. Ednl. Commn., Vienna, 1962-63. Mem. N.E. MLA, Midwest MLA, German Studies Assn., Women in German, ALTA, ASCAL, Phi Beta Kappa. Office: Carleton Coll 1 N College St Northfield MN 55057-4001

ULRICH, GLADYS MARJORIE, printing company executive; b. Chgo., Dec. 18, 1932; d. Harry Pikal and Rose Barbara (Vojta) Albert; m. William John Ulrich, Dec. 4, 1954; children: Valerie Lynn, Mark Robert, Laura Ann. Student, Gregg Coll., 1950-52. Owner, CEO Insty-Prints, Arlington

Heights, Ill., 1978—; pres., owner Insty-Prints, Elk Grove Village, Ill., 1986—; mem. pres. coun. Insty-Prints, Mpls., 1987-90, nat. adv. governing com., 1987—. Organizer blood drive ARC/Cancer Soc., Elk Grove Village, 1970. Mem. Women's Resource Assn. (pres. 1988-89), Bus. & Profl. Women Assn. Republican. Office: Insty-Prints 2355 E Oakton St Arlington Heights IL 60005-4817

ULSENHEIMER, DEAN, English language educator; b. Cleve., Dec. 20, 1941; s. Lon Sherwood and Mary Dorothy (Kupstas) U.; m. Sharon Lee Williams, Dec. 27, 1963 (div. June 1980); children: Cathi, Chris, Shelley, Scott.; m. Monica Joan Rigo, Aug. 10, 1984. BS in Edn., Ohio U., Athens, 1964; postgrad., John Carroll U., 1969-70, Kent State U., 1979. Cert. secondary sch. tchr. Tchr. English South Amherst (Ohio) Schs., 1964-66; project engr. Otto Konigslow Mfg. Co., Cleve., 1966-67; tchr. English Cardinal Schs., Middlefield, Ohio, 1967-80; owner Burton (Ohio) Washer Sales, 1970—; tchr. English Shaw High Sch., East Cleveland, Ohio, 1980—; instr. English Cuyahoga Community Coll., Cleve., 1980—, Lakeland Community Coll., Mentor, Ohio, 1984—; owner, cons. Profl. Reading, Power Writing; cons. NASA Lewis Rsch. Ctr., The East Ohio Gas Co., Centerior Energy, Owens Corning Inc.; cons. mgmt. devel. program Lubrizol Corp., Wickliffe, Ohio, 1987—; spkr. Lakeland C.C. Spkrs. Bur., Mentor, 1988—; hon. poetry intern NEH, Hiram Coll., 1977. Author: Easy Writing, 1977, Sentence Analysis, 1977, Communication Problems, 1978, Short Story Starters, 1980. Mem. NEA, Am. Cons. League, Ohio Edn. Assn., East Cleveland Edn. Assn., Greater Cleve. Growth Assn., Coun. Smaller Bus. Ent. Roman Catholic. Home and Office: 6691 Morley Rd Concord OH 44077-5924

ULTES, ELIZABETH CUMMINGS BRUCE, artist, retired art historian and librarian; b. Urbana, Ohio, Mar. 27, 1909; d. William Mansfield and Helen Finnette (Cummings) B.; m. William Ultes, Jr., May 2, 1934 (dec. Oct. 1973); 1 child, Elizabeth Cummings Ultes Hoffman. BA in Econs., Hollins Coll., 1930; BFA in History of Art, Wittenberg U., 1979; student painting, Positano, Italy, 1960, San Miguel Allende, Mex., 1980. Instr. art history continuing edn. dept. Wittenberg U., Springfield, Ohio, 1959-80; warder, art libr. Springfield Pub. Libr., 1959-70; ret., 1970; former writer art critiques Springfield Daily News-Sun. Exhibited in 2 one-woman shows, Springfield, group shows in Dayton Art Mus., Springfield Fair, Springfield Mus.; 3 paintings in permanent collection Clark County Hist. Mus. Recipient 1st, 2d and 3d prizes for paintings. Home: 5155 N High St Columbus OH 43214

UMLAND, SAMUEL JOSEPH, English language educator; b. Nebraska City, Nebr., June 22, 1954; s. Lale Edward and Sarah Elizabeth (Witty) U.; m. Linda Ager, Dec. 31, 1982 (div. 1992); children: Lauren Elizabeth, Andrew Allan; m. Rebecca Ann Cochran, Aug. 15, 1992; 1 child, John Lale. BA, U. Nebr., 1979, MA, 1981, PhD, 1987. Instr. English U. Nebr., Lincoln, 1982-86, lectr., 1987-88; asst. prof. U. Nebr., Kearney, 1988-91, assoc. prof. English, 1991—, assoc. dean Coll. of Fine Arts and Humanities, 1994—. Editor Nebr. English Jour., 1988-91; contbr. articles to scholarly books, jour., poetry to jours., book revs. to scholarly books and jours.; author screenplays: The Atomic Man, Sunless Sea, The Fallen Sky, The Ballad of Rachel Goodhart. U. Nebr.-Lincoln Presdl. Grad. fellow, 1986-87. Mem. Assn. Literary Scholars and Critics, Sci. Fiction Rsch. Assn., Philip K. Dick Soc., Internat. Arthurian Soc. Episcopalian. Home: 511 W 35th St Kearney NE 68847-2848 Office: Univ of Nebr Dept English Kearney NE 68849

UMSCHEID, CHRISTINE, medical surgical and oncological nurse; b. Weiden, West Germany, Jan. 28, 1946; d. Barbara Betty; children; Joyelle, Heidi. AD, Meramec Community Coll., St. Louis, 1969, North Cen. Mich. Coll., Petoskey, 1984. Cert. oncology nurse, renal nurse. Primary nurse No. 3 Mich. Hosp., Inc., Petoskey; primary nurse No. 2 Mich. Hosp., Inc., Petroskey. Contbr. poetry to mags. Home: 149 Washington St Petoskey MI 49770-2948

UNDERHEIM, GREGG, state legislator; b. Aug. 22, 1950. BS, U. Wis., La Crosse, 1972. Former mem. Winnebago County Bd.; former congl. aide, Wis. state assemblyman dist. 54, 1987—; former h.s. tchr. Address: 1652 Beech St Oshkosh WI 54901*

UNDERHILL, ROBERT ALAN, consumer products company executive; b. Columbus, Ohio, June 9, 1944; s. Robert Alan and Grace Ruth (Smith) U.; m. Lynn Louise Stentz, Oct. 18, 1963; children: Robert Alan II, Richard Louis. Student, Case Western Res. U., 1962-64, Ohio State U., 1965. With tech. svc. dept. Gen. Tire & Rubber Co., Akron, Ohio, 1966-69; quality control engr. Edmont-Wilson Co., Canton, Ohio, 1969-70; mgr. quality assurance Pharmaseal Labs., Massillon, Ohio, 1970-72; mgr. R&D Internat. Playtex Corp., Paramus, N.J., 1972-78; mgr. R&D Kimberly-Clark Corp., Neenah, Wis., 1978-80, dir. R&D, 1980-83, v.p. R&D, 1983-93, sr. v.p. R&D, sr. tech. officer, 1994—; trustee United Health Group, 1994—, mem. exec. com., 1996—, treas., 1996—, chmn. compensation com., 1994—; trustee Novus Health Group, 1993-94; bd. dirs. Appleton (Wis.) Med. Ctr., 1993—. Patentee (U.S. and fgn.) med. device. Mem. exec. bd. Bay Lakes Coun. Boy Scouts Am., 1988-92; bd. dirs. Outagamie County (Wis.) chpt. ARC, 1993—, chmn. nominations com., 1993—, mem. exec. com., 1994—, sec., 1994—; bd. dirs. Cmty. Blood Ctr., Appleton, Wis., 1996—. Mem. Riverview Country Club, Pi Delta Epsilon. Republican. Home: 1225 W Cedar St Appleton WI 54914-5567 Office: Kimberly-Clark Corp 2100 Winchester Rd Neenah WI 54956-9317 also: 1400 Holcomb Bridge Rd Roswell GA 30076-2190

UNDERLAND-ROSOW, VICKI LOUISE, mediator, publishing executive; b. Moline, Ill., Dec. 4, 1947; d. Arthur and Virginia (Walsh) Underland; m. Richard Rosow, Jan. 15, 1972; children: Michael, Katherine. BS in Corrections, Mankato (Minn.) State U., 1968; MSW, U. Mich., 1977; PhD in Human Sys., Union Inst., Cin., 1992. Youth dir. YMCA, Grand Forks, N.D., 1971-72; mem. faculty U. N.D., Grand Forks, 1972-76; program specialist U. Mich., Ann Arbor, 1976-78; psychotherapist Park Nicollet Clinic, St. Louis Park, Minn., 1978-81; asst. prof. Coll. St. Catherine and St. Thomas, St. Paul, 1981-82; mem. faculty U. Minn., Mpls., 1979-85; pvt. practice facilitator, mediator St. Louis Park, Minn., 1981—; co-dir. Beyond Therapy, Mpls., 1990—; pres. Waterford Publ., Shorewood, Minn., 1994—; facilitator, cons. Anne Wilson Schaef Assn., Boulder, Mont., 1982—; cons. Minn. Dept. Edn., St. Paul, 1981-82. Author: Shame: Spiritual Suicide, 1995. Mem. Midwest Pubs., Coun. Ind. Cons. Home: 19835 Waterford Pl Excelsior MN 55331-7016 Office: 4915 W 35th St Saint Louis Park MN 55416-2643

UNDERWOOD, ROBERT LEIGH, venture capitalist; b. Paducah, Ky., Dec. 31, 1944; s. Robert Humphreys and Nancy Wells (Jessup) U.; BS with gt. distinction (Alcoa scholar), Stanford U., 1965, MS (NASA fellow), 1966, PhD (NSF fellow), 1968; MBA, Santa Clara U., 1970; m. Susan Lynn Doscher, May 22, 1976; children: Elizabeth Leigh, Dana Whitney, George Gregory. Rsch. scientist, project leader Lockheed Missiles & Space Co., Sunnyvale, Calif., 1967-71; spl. asst. for engrng. scis. Office Sec., Dept. Transp., Washington, 1971-73; sr. mgmt. assoc. Office Mgmt. and Budget, Exec. Office Pres., 1973; with TRW Inc., L.A., 1973-79, dir. retail nat. accounts, 1977-78, dir. product planning and devel., 1978-79; pres., CEO OMEX, Santa Clara, Calif., 1980-82; v.p. Heizer Corp., Chgo., 1979-85; v.p. No. Trust Co., pres. No. Capital Corp., Chgo., 1985-86; mng. ptnr. ISSS Ventures, 1986-88; exec. v.p. N.Am. Bus. Devel. Co., Chgo., 1988—; dir. various pvt. and pub. portfolio cos., MECC 1991-96; mem. adv. com. indsl. innovation NSF; mem. sch. bd. Avoca Dist. 37, 1990—; mem. adv. bd. Leavey Sch. Bus. & Adminstrn. Santa Clara U., 1995—. Mem. IEEE, Sigma Xi, Phi Beta Kappa, Tau Beta Pi, Beta Gamma Sigma. Elder, Presbyterian Ch., 1978-79. Clubs: Union League Chgo., Chgo. Club; Manasquan River Yacht (Brielle, N.J.); Indian Hill (Winnetka, Ill.). Contbr. articles to profl. jours. Home: 59 Woodley Rd Winnetka IL 60093-3748 Office: 135 S La Salle St Chicago IL 60603-4105

UNDLIN, CHARLES THOMAS, banker; b. Madison, Minn., Mar. 4, 1928; s. Jennings C. and Alice M. (Berg) U.; m. Lois M. Anderson, June 23, 1953; children: Sarah, Mary Lee, Margaret, Thomas. BA, St. Olaf Coll., 1950. Asst. cashier Northwestern State Bank, Osseo, Minn., 1950-55, N.W. Bancorp., Mpls., 1955-57, Security Bank & Trust Co., Owatonna, Minn., 1957-59, Norwest Bank Black Hills, Rapid City, S.D., 1959-67; pres. and chief exec. officer Norwest Bank S.D., Rapid City, 1967-84, vice-chmn., 1984-85; pres. Norwest Bank Nebr., Omaha, 1985-88, also bd. dirs.; vice-chmn. Rushmore State Bank, Rapid City, 1988—; bd. dirs. Black Hills Corp., Homestake Mining Co. Past bd. dirs. Children's Hosp., Omaha, 1986. Sgt. U.S. Army, 1951-52. Mem. S.D. Bankers Assn. (past pres.), Arrowhead Country Club. Republican. Lutheran. Office: Rushmore State Bank PO Box 2290 Rapid City SD 57709-2290

UNGACTA, MALISSA SUMAGAYSAY, software engineer; b. Agana, Guam, July 3, 1967; d. Renerio Ong and Irene Acfalle (Salas) S. BS in Info. Sci., U. Hawaii, 1989; MS in Info. Tech. Mgmt., Johns Hopkins U., 1992. Cert. power builder developer assoc. Programmer, analyst Facilities Mgmt. Office, Honolulu, 1987-89, Data House Inc., Honolulu, 1989-90, ANSTEC Inc., Fairfax, Md., 1990-93; software specialist, project leader HJ Ford Assocs. Inc., Crystal City, Va., 1993-94; software cons. McDonnell Douglas Tech. Svcs., 1994—. Mem. NAFE. Home: PO Box 1546 Agana GU 96910-1546 Office: McDonnell Douglas 1807 Park 270 Ste 500 Saint Louis MO 63146-4021 also: 4554 Laclede Ave Apt 107 Saint Louis MO 63108-2145

UNGER, ELIZABETH ANN, computer science educator, dean; b. Saginaw, Mich., May 23, 1939; d. Merrill Jacob and Lillian Bawden (Johns) Buschlen; m. Samuel Galen Unger, July 8, 1963; children: Mark Bryan, Michele Elizabeth, Kirsten Ann. BSME, Mich. State U., 1961, MS in Math., 1963; PhD in Computer Sci., U. Kans., 1978. Applied sci. rep. IBM, Lansing, Mich., 1958-62; user svcs. dir. Mich. State U. Computer Ctr., East Lansing, 1963-66; assoc. dir. computing ctr. Kans. State U., Manhattan, 1966-74, asst. prof. computer sci., 1968-78, assoc. prof., 1978-84, prof. computer sci., 1984—, assoc. dean grad. sch., 1990-94, vice provost acad. svcs./technology, dean continuing edn., 1994—. Author 4 books. Named Disting. Alumni Mich. State U., 1972. Mem. IEEE, Assn. for Computing Machinery (chair sig. small/PC 1986—, exec. com. Computer Sci. Accreditation Bd.). Methodist. Home: 3009 Wayne Dr Manhattan KS 66502-1925 Office: Kans State Univ 108 Anderson Hall Manhattan KS 66506-2300

UNGER, GARY A., recording industry executive, singer, lyricist; b. Clinton, Iowa, Aug. 14, 1947; s. Charles Elmer Unger and Lois Grace Brothers; m. Cynthia A. Unger, Aug. 7, 1975 (div. Aug. 1995); m. J. Verna Unger, Jan. 7, 1995; 1 child, Morrision C. Elemy III. Grad. h.s., Ill. Internat. import-export mgr. G & U Enterprises, Clinton, 1968—; mgr., pres. Groove Song Music, Clinton, 1968—, Narrow Rd. Music, Clinton, 1968—; mgr., v.p. AGI Internat. Records, Clinton, 1978-79; mgr., pres. ECI Internat. Records, Clinton, 1980-96, GTM, Clinton, 1973, Music Wave Dist., Nashville, 1981, Sugarvine Music, Chrway Records, 1975-84. Lyricist: I'm Going Home, I Will Always Love You, Southern Rain, I Like It, I Love It, I Write the Songs, Boot Scoffin' Boogie, Thinkin About You, Give Them All to Jesus, Let's Pray Together, Heart to Heart, Maybe I'll Find a Way, 1968, I'm Just a Fool for You, 1968, Maybe, One Day at a Time, 1968, God Bless the U.S.A., 1968-70, Born in the U.S.A., 1968-70,. Mem. ASCAP, BMI, AFM, CMA, AGAC, RIAA, Continental Record Club. Home: PO Box 3169 Clinton IA 52732

UNGER, PAUL A., packaging executive; b. San Diego, Sept. 10, 1914; s. Louis A. and Ray (Seidman) U.; m. Sonja Franz, Jan. 2, 1947; children: Alan, Gerald, Tamara Hyman. AB, Harvard U., 1936. With pub. rels. dept. Works Progress Adminstrn., Washington, 1936-39; with community rels. Dept. U.S. Housing Authority, Washington, 1939-44; relief adminstr. UN Relief and Rehab. Adminstrn., Egypt and Yugoslavia, 1944-47; deputy asst. sec. U.S. Dept. of Interior, Washington, 1947-50, internat. specialist, 1950-53; devel. mgr. The Unger Co., Cleve., 1953-57, pres., 1957-62, 64-88, chmn., 1988-93; sr. advisor, 1994—, The Unger Co., Cleve., 1994—; dep. adminstr. U.S. Dept. Commerce, Washington, 1962-63; mem. U.S. com. Internat. Coun. on Social Welfare; organizer, leader tours to Yugoslavia, Hungary, Austria, Czechoslovakia, East Germany, Poland, USSR, China. Pres. Coun. Internat. Programs; chmn. Cleve. adv. subcom. U.S. Commn. on Civil Rights; chmn. Mayor's Urban Renewal Task Force, Presdl. Campaign Coms. for No. Ohio, Gov.'s Internat. Trade Coun. Recipient Recognition award Rotary, 1974, Neighborhood Ctrs. Assn., 1978, Internat. Exch. award Coun. Internat. Programs, 1985, Hall of Fame award, 1995. Mem. City Club (trustee 1972-75, v.p. 1975), Forum Found. (pres. 1988-91), Cleve. Coun. on World Affairs (program chmn., v.p., mem. exec. com.), English Speaking Union (past pres. Cleve. br., nat. v.p.), Cleve. Skating Club, Cleve. Playhouse Club, Cleve. Blue Book. Home: 13515 Shaker Blvd Ste 2 A Cleveland OH 44120-1671 Office: 13110 Shaker Sq Ste 241 Cleveland OH 44120-2313

UNGERER, WALTER JOHN, minister; b. Bklyn., Nov. 11, 1936; s. Walter and Alice Elizabeth (Fleischmann) U.; m. Janet M. Hagmann, Aug. 25, 1962; children: Cheryl Lyn, Walter J., Brian Alan. BS, Nyack Coll., 1961; DivB, New Brunswick Theol. Sem., 1964; M of Theology, Princeton Theol. Sem., 1965, D of Ministry, 1983. Ordained to ministry, Presbyn. Ch., 1965. Student pastor Olivet Presbyn. Ch., Bklyn., 1958-62; student supply Fairfield (N.J.) Presbyn. Ch., 1964-65; asst. pastor Webster (N.Y.) Presbyn. Ch., 1965-66, assoc. pastor, 1967-71; sr. pastor Northfield (Ohio) Presbyn. Ch., 1972-77, 1st Presbyn. Ch., Kokomo, Ind., 1977—; co-founder, chmn. bd. dirs. Man to Man Internat.; moderator Presbytery Wabash Valley, Ind., 1983; mem. gen. assembly coun. Presbyn. Ch., Louisville, 1991—; pres. bd. dirs. Synod Lincoln Trails, Indpls., 1989-91. Author: Habakkuk, The Man with Honest Questions, 1976, A Look Up, 1992; co-author: Miltenberg Germany to Brooklyn, 1988. Pres. Presbyns. United for Biblical Concerns, 1986-88. Recipient Leadership award Man to Man Assn. Ohio, Columbus, 1977. Mem. Midwest Tool Collectors Assn., Early Am. Indsl. Soc., Elks, Rotary. Democrat. Home: 2808 Locust Ct E Kokomo IN Office: 1st Presbyn Ch 2000 W Jefferson St Kokomo IN 46901

UNIACKE, C(HARLES) ALLYN, optometry educator, consultant; b. Washington, Sept. 21, 1945; s. Charles Lawrence and Nerene Viola (Pickering) U.; m. Nancy Peterson Klein, Sept. 29, 1967 (div. Feb. 1987); children: C. Jeremy, John P.; m. Sue Keifer Hammersmith, Mar. 9, 1988; stepchildren: Emily E. Hammersmith, Marla J. Hammersmith; 1 child, Paula A. BS in Zoology, Ohio State U., 1967, MS in Physiol. Optics and OD, 1971, PhD in Physiol. Optics, 1973. Lic. optomestrist, Ohio, Mich. Asst. prof. Ohio State U., Columbus, 1973-76; assoc. prof. Ferris State U., Big Rapids, Mich., 1976-82, prof., 1982—; asst. to pres. for planning Ferris State U., Big Rapids, pres. acad. senate, 1995-96; bd. trustee Vision Ctr. of Cen. Ohio, Columbus, 1974-77. Author: (rev.) Review of Primary Care of Anterior Segment, 1988. Mem. Coalition for the Elderly Blind, Lansing, Mich., 1988—. Fellow Am. Acad. Optometry; mem. Am. Optometric Assn., Assn. Rsch. in Vision and Ophthalmology, Beta Sigma Kappa (Silver medal 1971), Sigma Xi. Office: Ferris State U Univ Planning 1349 Cramer Cir B15 419 Big Rapids MI 49307-2737

UNKLESBAY, ATHEL GLYDE, geologist, educator; b. Byesville, Ohio, Feb. 11, 1914; s. Howard Ray and Madaline (Archer) U.; m. Wanda Eileen Strauch, Sept. 14, 1940 (dec. 1971); children: Kenneth, Marjorie, Carolyn, Allen; m. Mary Wheeler Myhre, June 8, 1973 (dec. 1980). A.B., Marietta Coll., 1938, D.Sc. (hon.), 1977; M.A., State U. Iowa, 1940, Ph.D., 1942. Geologist U.S. Geol. Survey, 1942-45, Iowa Geol. Survey, 1945-46; asst. prof. Colgate, 1946-47; mem. faculty U. Mo., Columbia, 1947—; prof. geology U. Mo., 1954—, chmn. dept., 1959-67, v.p. adminstrn., 1967-79; exec. dir. Am. Geol. Inst., 1979-85; cons. in field. Author: Geology of Boone County, 1952, Common Fossils of Missouri, 1955, Pennsylvanian Cephalopods of Oklahoma, 1962, Missouri Geology, 1992; also articles. Mem. Columbia Bd. Edn., 1954-70, Columbia Parks and Recreation Commn., 1954-57. Wilton Park fellow, 1968, 72, 76. Mem. Am. Assn. Petroleum Geologists, Paleontol. Soc. Am., Geol. Soc. Am., Nat. Assn. Geology Tchrs., Kiwanis. Methodist. Home: 37 Broadway Village Dr Apt G Columbia MO 65201-8662

UNSWORTH, MICHAEL EDWARD, university librarian; b. Indpls., July 10, 1950; s. Cecil Walker and Dorothy Louise (Wolf) U.; m. Lynn Maria Kaczor, Feb. 12, 1977 (div. Sept. 1981). BA, Ind. U.-Purdue U., Indpls., 1973; MLS, Ind. U., Bloomington, 1974; MA, U. Notre Dame, 1978. Libr. U. Notre Dame, Ind., 1974-79, Colo. State U., Ft. Collins, 1979-84, Mich. State U., East Lansing, 1984—; cons. Chadwyk-Healey, Inc., Alexandria, Va., 1988—; intern Inst. for Editing of Hist. Documents, Madison, Wis., 1993. Co-author: Future War Novels, 1984; editor: Military Periodicals, 1990; mem. editl. bd. Mich. State U. Press, 1994—; contbr. articles to profl. pubis. Mem. faculty coun. U. Notre Dame, 1978; mem. Mich. Freedom of Info. Com.; bd. dirs. Greater Lansing Hist. Soc., 1991-93. Mem. Assn. for Bibliography of History, Soc. for Mil. History, Hist. Soc. Mich., Mich. Oral History Soc. Home: PO Box 6253 East Lansing MI 48826 Office: Mich State Univ Libraries East Lansing MI 48824

UNTERMAN, EUGENE REX, aviation sales and manufacturing company executive; b. Mpls., Sept. 3, 1953; Melvin and Nancy (Wolfson) U.; m. Melanie Wells Munson, July 12, 1980; children: H. Aaron, Jeffery Wells, Julie Ann. Student, Loyola U., Chgo., 1971-73, Northwestern U., 1973-75. Trader Chgo. Mercantile Exchange, 1975-76; pres. Mid-West Aircraft Co., Sandwich, Ill., 1976-89, Heartland Aircraft Group Ltd., Geneva, Ill., 1990—; computer cons. Chgo. Rawhide Corp., Elgin, Ill., 1983. Author: How to Buy A Used Aircraft Without Taking a Dive. Mem. airport adv. bd. City of Geneva, Ill., 1983; alderman 2d ward City of Geneva, 1988-89. Mem. Jaycees (Jaycee of Yr. 1988, 89, 90, pres. 1988-89), St. Charles (Ill.) Sportsman Club (treas. 1985-86, pres. 1987-88, 90—, bd. dirs. 1988-89). Jewish. Office: Heartland Aircraft Group Ltd 530 Lark St Geneva IL 60134-2527

UPTON, FREDERICK STEPHEN, congressman; b. St. Joseph, Mich., Apr. 23, 1953; s. Stephen E. and Elizabeth Brooks (Vial) U.; m. Amey Richmond Rulon-Miller, Nov. 5, 1983; 2 children. BA in Journalism, U. Mich., 1975. Staff asst. to Congressman David A. Stockman, Washington, 1976-81; legis. asst. Office Mgmt. and Budget, Washington, 1981-83, dep. dir. legis. affairs, 1983-84, dir. legis. affairs, 1984-85; mem. 100th-104th Congresses from 4th (now 6th) Mich. dist., Washington, 1986—; mem. commerce com. Field mgr. Stockman for Congress, St. Joseph, 1975; campaign mgr. Globensky for Congress, St. Joseph, 1981. Republican. Office: US House of Reps 2333 Rayburn Bldg Washington DC 20515*

UPTON, RICHARD LEWIS, advertising agency executive; b. St. Louis, Oct. 24, 1950; s. R. Miller and June Yvonne (Gardner) U.; m. Jaye Marion Ince, Aug. 14, 1971; children: Ann, Trevor, Thomas. BA, Beloit (Wis.) Coll., 1973. Pres. Delton Mktg., Walworth, Wis., 1972-76; v.p. Cramer-Krasselt Milw., 1976-89; exec. v.p., gen. mgr. Bender Browning Dolby & Sanderson Advt., Milw., 1989—. Bd. dirs. Ronald McDonald House, Milw., 1996, Friends of Mil. Pub. Mus., 1996, Nat. Childrens Mus. for Performing Arts, 1996. Mem. Milw. Assn. Advt. Agys. (sec., dir. 1995—), Town Club, Milw. Athletic Club. Office: Bender Browning Dolby & Sanderson Advt 1110 N Old World Third St Milwaukee WI 53203

URBAN, FRANK HENRY, retired dermatologist, state legislator; b. St. Louis, May 24, 1930; s. Frank and Helen Gertrude (Zingsheim) U.; m. Lois Elaine Thurwachter, June 18, 1954 (dec. 1991); children: James, Barbara, Michael, Mark, David, Bruce, John; m. Kathryn Calvert Bloomberg, Nov. 28, 1992. BS in Med. Sci., U. Wis., 1951, MD, 1954; MS, U. Minn., 1960. Diplomate Am. Bd. Dermatology. Intern Beaumont Army Hosp., El Paso, 1954-55; resident Mayo Clinic, Rochester, Minn., 1957-60; pvt. practice dermatology Wauwatosa, Wis., 1960-93; asst. clin. prof. Med. Coll. Wis., Wauwatosa, 1964—; mem. Wis. State Assembly, Madison, 1989—. Trustee Village Bd. of Elm Grove, Wis., 1985-87, pres., 1987-89; bd. dirs. ARC of Greater Milw.; pres. Friends U. Wis.-Milw. Sch. Edn., 1995—, bd. dirs.; hon. mem. Potawatomi coun. Boy Scouts Am., pres., 1974-76. Recipient Silver Beaver award East Cen. Region Boy Scouts Am., 1972, Silver Antelope award, 1979, Civic Leadership award State Med. Soc. Wis., 1990, Disting. Svc. award U. Wis. Med. Sch. Alumni Assn., 1991. Fellow Am. Acad. Dermatology; mem. Wis. Dermatol. Soc. (pres. 1969-70), Wis. State Med. Soc. (dir. 1987-92, 93—), Milw. County Med. Soc. (caucus chmn. 1987-92, pres.-elect 1992-93, pres. 1993-94), Brookfield C. of C. (Outstanding Mem. award 1992). Republican. Roman Catholic. Office: State Capitol PO Box 8953 Madison WI 53708-8953

URBAN, PATRICIA A., former elementary school educator; b. Chgo., Oct. 15, 1932; d. Clifford and Caroline (Viegi) Brocken; m. Francis C. Urban, Oct. 20, 1956; children: Jim, David, Anthony, Mary Joan, Barbara, Margaret, Judy, Sharon, Jennifer. BA, Rosary Coll., River Forest, Ill., 1954; MS in Edn., Chgo. State U., 1979; MEd, Loyola U., Chgo., 1986. Cert. tchr., reading tchr., Ill. Tchr. St. Joseph Ch. Sch., Summit, Ill., 1954-56; profl. reading tutor Loyola U., 1987-90; tchr. social studies and reading Dist. 104 Schs., Summit, 1974-94; ret., 1994. Named. Dist. 104 Tchr. of Yr., 1987. Mem. ASCD, Internat. Reading Assn., Am. Fedn. Tchrs., West Suburban Tchrs. Union, Alpha Upsilon Alpha. Home: 1019 Walter St Lemont IL 60439-3290

URBAN, SHARON KAY, elementary school educator; b. Thornton, Iowa; d. Samuel John and Esther Mae (Sorensen) Will.; m. Rudolf John Urban, Aug. 14, 1971 (dec. 1986). BS in Edn., Ill. State U., 1966, MS in Reading, 1969; postgrad., Bradley U., 1983, No. Ill. U., Western Ill. U., 1986, Aurora U., 1991-94. Tchr. Wilson Sch., Pekin, Ill., 1966—. Bd. dirs. Pekin Cmty. Concerts. Assn., 1973—, v.p., 1985-87, pres., 1987-89, sec. 1990—; pres. Tazewell County Med. Aux., Pekin, 1975-76; bd. dirs. YWCA, Pekin, 1987-92. Mem. NEA, AAUW (bd. dirs. Pekin 1973-88, 89—, pres. 1983-85, sec. 1991—, honoree Ednl. Found. 1983), Ill. Edn. Assn., Edn. Assn. Pekin (v.p. 1972-74, 90-91, pres. 1974-76, sec. 1995, del. rep. assembly 1992-95, pres. 1996), Investment Club (bd. dirs.), Alpha Delta Kappa (chpt. pres.-elect 1976-78, pres. 1978-80). Republican. Lutheran. Home: 3 Prestwick Dr Pekin IL 61554-2635 Office: Wilson Sch 900 Koch St Pekin IL 61554-5875

URBOM, WARREN KEITH, federal judge; b. Atlanta, Nebr., Dec. 17, 1925; s. Clarence Andrew and Anna Myrl (Irelan) U.; m. Joyce Marie Crawford, Aug. 19, 1951; children: Kim Marie, Randall Crawford, Allison Lee, Joy Renee. AB with highest distinction, Nebr. Wesleyan U., 1950, LLD (hon.), 1984; JD with distinction, U. Mich., 1953. Bar: Nebr. 1953. Mem. firm Baylor, Evnen, Baylor, Urbom, & Curtiss, Lincoln, Nebr., 1953-70; judge U.S. Dist. Ct. Nebr., 1970—; chief judge U.S. Dist. Ct. Dist. Nebr., 1972-86, sr. judge, 1991—; mem. com. on practice and procedure Nebr. Supreme Ct., 1965-95; mem. subcom. on fed. jurisdiction Jud. Conf. U.S., 1975-83; adj. instr. trial advocacy U. Nebr. Coll. Law, 1979-90; bd. dirs. Fed. Jud. Ctr., 1982-86; chmn. com. on orientation newly apptd. dist. judges Fed. Jud. Ctr., 1986-89; mem. 8th Cir. Com. on Model Criminal and Civil Jury Instrns., 1983—; mem. adv. com. on alternative sentences U.S. Sentencing Com., 1989-91. Contbr. articles to profl. jours. Trustee St. Paul Sch. Theology, Kansas City, Mo., 1986-89; active United Methodist Ch. (bd. mgrs., bd. global ministries 1972-76, gen. com. on status and role of women, 1988—, gen. conf. 1972, 76, 80, 88, 92, 96); pres. Lincoln YMCA, 1965-67; bd. govs. Nebr. Wesleyan U., chmn. 1975-80. With AUS, 1944-46. Recipient Medal of Honor, Nebr. Wesleyan U. Alumni Assn., 1983. Fellow Am. Coll. Trial Lawyers; mem. ABA, Nebr. Bar Assn. (ho. of dels. 1966-70, Outstanding Legal Educator award 1990), Lincoln Bar Assn. (Liberty Bell award 1993, pres. 1968-69), Kiwanis (Disting. Svc. award 1993), Masons (33 deg.), Am. Inns of Ct. (Lewis F. Powell Jr. award for Professionalism and Ethics 1995). Methodist. Home: 4421 Ridgeview Dr Lincoln NE 68516-1516 Office: US Dist Ct 586 Fed Bldg 100 Centennial Mall N Lincoln NE 68508-3804

URHAUSEN, JAMES NICHOLAS, real estate developer, construction executive; b. Berwyn, Ill., Oct. 6, 1943; s. Jack Nicholas and Florence Frances (Stalzer) U.; m. Philomena Anne Malizia, July 16, 1966 (div. 1980); children: Kristen Anne, James Nicholas III; m. Anne Siegert, July 22, 1983; children: Bradley James, Samantha Elise. BA, St. Procopius Coll., Lisle, Ill., 1965. High sch. tchr. Nazareth Acad., LaGrange Park, Ill., 1965-66; asst. village mgr. Village of Hinsdale, Ill., 1966-69; village mgr. Village of Oak Brook, Ill., 1969-73; v.p., sec.-treas. Collins Devel. Corp., St. Charles, Ill., 1973-80; exec. v.p. Westway Constrn. Corp., St. Charles, Ill., 1980-84, pres., chief exec. officer, 1984—; guest lectr. No. Ill. U., Dekalb, 1976—; expert witness Ill. Dept. of Transp., Chgo., 1976—; dir. Harris Bank/St. Charles, Ill., 1992—. Chmn. Hotel Baker Bd. Gov.'s St. Charles, 1982-84, Bd. of Fire and Police Commmrs., St. Charles, 1986—; mem. 708 Comty. Mental Health Bd., St. Charles, 1986—, Kane County Selective Svc. Sys. Bd., St. Charles, 1981—, Kane County Solid Waste Adv. Com., Geneva, 1990—, Metra Citizen's Adv. Bd., 1993—; bd. dirs. Neighborhood Improvement Assn., St. Charles Twp., 1992—, pres., 1996—; bd. dirs. Delnor Comty. Hosp. Found., 1993—, Glenwood Sch. for Boys, 1996—. Mem. Home Bldrs. Assn. Greater Chgo. (dir. 1989—), Nat. Assn. Home Bldrs., No. Ill. Home Bldrs. Assn.,

Fox Valley Polit. Action Group, St. Charles C. of C. (amb. 1988, Community Devel. award 1989, Charlemagne award 1993). Republican. Roman Catholic. Home: 3103 Greenwood Ln Saint Charles IL 60175-5627 Office: Westway Constrn Corp 440 S 3d St Saint Charles IL 60174-5535

URIBE, VICTOR M., psychiatrist, educator; b. Cucuta, Colombia, S.Am., Aug. 23, 1936; came to U.S., 1962; s. Victor M. and Cristina (Castillo) U.; divorced; children: Martha Uribe Scherer, Sonia Uribe McGowan. MD, Universidad Nacional, Bogota, Colombia, 1962. Diplomate Am. Bd. Psychiatry and Neurology. Rotating intern Providence Hosp., Washington, 1964-69; gen. psychiatrist Ill. State. Psychiat. Inst., Chgo., 1969-71; child and adolescent psychiatrist U. Chgo., 1971; asst. prof. psychiatry Loyola U. Med. Sch., Chgo., 1972—; medical dir. adolescent program Mercy Ctr. for Health Care Svcs., Aurora, Fla., 1977-88, chmn. dept. psychiatry, 1980-81; asst. prof. psychiatry Northwestern U. Med. Sch., Chgo., 1983—; profl. lectr. psychiatry U. Chgo., 1986—; dir. Latino-Hispanic program Hartgrove Hosp., Chgo., 1988-90; dir. child and adolescent Univ. Hosp., Chgo., 1990—; cons. psychiatrist Juvenile Ct. Audy Home, Chgo., 1969-72, Chgo. Mental Health Clinics, Chgo., 1969-71, Adolescent and Child Program Tinley Park (Ill.) Inst. Mental Health, 1970-72; advisor, cons. Colegio Colombo-Britanico, Cali, 1973-75, Colegio Nueva Granada, Bogota, 1975-77; pres. Colombian Med. Assn., Chgo., 1990-91; speaker, cons. Wind Radio Sta., Chgo., 1991—. Co-author: Adolescent Sexuality, 1989, (essays) Psychosocial Issues, 1972-80; editor (newsletter) Colmedicas, 1990-91; contbr. articles to med. jours. Fellow Am. Psychiatric Assn., Am. Acad. Psychoanalysis, (cert. 1984) Am. Assn. for Social Psychiatry, Inst. Medicine of Chgo., Am. Soc. Psychoanalytic Physicians (exec. coun.); mem. AMA, Instituto Colombiano del Sistema Nervioso (sec., bd. dirs. 1976-77), Asociacion Psicoanalitica Colombiana (sec., bd. dirs. 1976-77), Internat. Soc. for Adolescent Psychiatry (charter mem., membership and editorial coms.), Am. Soc. Hispanic Psychiatrists (bd. dirs. 1992—).

URICH, JOSEPH JOHN, electrical engineer; b. Iowa City, Iowa, Apr. 21, 1970. BS in Elec. Engring., U. Iowa, 1993. CAD sys. adminstr., elec. engr. Norand, Cedar Rapids, Iowa, 1991—. Mem. IEEE. Republican. Roman Catholic. Office: Norand 550 2nd St SE Cedar Rapids IA 52401-2023

URSCH, RICHARD WAYNE, electrical engineer; b. St. Louis, Apr. 27, 1948; s. Russell J. and Lois E. (Winkler) U.; m. Debra Ann Hromatka, Feb. 1971; children: Matt, Jessica. BSEE, U. Rolla, 1971. Plant engr. Benis Bag Co., St. Louis, 1971-72; quality control mgr. Emerson Electric, St. Louis, 1972-76; test engr. Emerson Electric, Tupelo, Miss., 1976-85; chief engr. Inter Global Inc., St. Louis, 1985—. Capt. U.S. Army, 1971-72. Mem. St. Louis Elec. Bd. Lutheran. Office: Inter Global Inc 3001 Washington Ave Saint Louis MO 63103-1334

USALIS, GEORGE JEROME, metal processing executive; b. Cleve., Aug. 26, 1948; s. George and Amelia (Bugala) U.; m. Marian Elizabeth Dilger, Aug. 29, 1970; children: Mary Beth, Edward. BA, John Carroll U., 1970. Tchr. Gesu Sch., Cleve., 1970-71; asst. dir. admissions John Carroll U., Cleve., 1971-72; gen. supr. materials dept. White Motor Corp., Cleve., 1972-75, materials mgr., 1978-81; materials mgr. indoor lighting div. ITT Corp., Vermillion, Ohio, 1975-78; group mgr. materials and contracts SIFCO Industries Forge Group, Cleve., 1981-94; ptnr., gen. mgr. Accurate Electronics, Inc., Elyria, Ohio, 1994-96; mgr. materials Park Drop Forge, Park Ohio Industries, Cleve., 1996—; assoc. credit com. St. Charles Borromeo Credit Union, Parma, Ohio, 1982-86. Mem. Greater Cleve. Growth Assn., 1981—; cons. Jr. Achievement, Cleve., 1986—; vol. St. John West Shore Hosp., 1986-95, Cleve. Foodbank, 1991. Mem. Purchasing Assn. Cleve., Nat. Assn. Pruchasing Mgmt., Am. Prodn. and Inventory Control Soc., Am. Mgmt. Assn., John Carroll Alumni Assn. (trustee S.W. Cleve. chpt. 1991—), First Friday Club Cleve. Republican. Roman Catholic. Home: 6606 Rockledge Dr Brecksville OH 44141

USELMANN, CATHERINE ROSE (KIT USELMANN), small business owner, network marketer, behavioral researcher, financial independence consultant; b. Madison, Wis., Sept. 17, 1960; d. Richard Lewis and Evelyn Mae (Parr) U. AA, Madison Area Tech. Coll., 1982; BA in Sociology, U. Wis., 1984, MA in Rsch. and Analysis, 1985; DD (hon.), Charter Ecumenical Ministries Internat., 1994. Pub. utility rate analyst Pub. Svc. Commn. Wis., Madison, 1986-89; rsch. mgr. Wis. Lottery, Madison, 1989-90; energy cons. HBRS, Inc., Madison, 1990-91; sr. cons., project mgr. XENERGY, Inc., Burlington, Mass., 1991-93; pres. CRU Prodns., Madison, 1993—; exec. Nutrition For Life Internat., Houston, 1995—, Trudeau Mktg. Group, Chgo., 1995—; team coord. I-Team, Cyberspace, 1996—; Leaders Club, Columbus, Ohio, 1995—; speaker Nat. Assn. Regulatory Utility Commrs., 1987-89; contbg. mem., speaker Assn. for Demand-Side Mgmt. Profls., 1991-93. Univ. rep. operating com. Mall/Concourse, Madison, 1982-84; lobbyist Inst. for Rsch. Poverty, Madison, 1984; activist, mem. People for Ethical Treatment Animals, Washington, 1989—. Mem. Fin. Independence Assn., U. Wis. Alumni Assn., Badger Quarter Horse Assn. (life). Lakota. Home and Office: 3753 Robin Hood Way Madison WI 53704-6243

USHER, MARY MARGARET, special education educator; b. Chgo., July 5, 1949; d. Earl Raymond and Rebecca Patricia (McElroy) Asher; m. James Lee Usher; children: Sherri, Michael, Lori. BS in Edn., U. North Tex., 1971; cert. in behaviorally disorder, Harris Stowe State Coll., 1991. Cert. tchr., Mo.; cert. tchr. learning disabled, mentally handicapped. Substitute tchr. Fox Sch. Dist., Arnold, Mo., 1986-87, 89—, Windsor Sch. Dist., Imperial, Mo., 1985-87, 89—, Spl. Svcs. Co-op., Imperial, 1987, 89—; paraprofessional physically impaired class Pevely Elem., 1992—; juvenile detention ctr. tchr. Jefferson County Children's Home, Mo., 1993—96. Vice pres. bd. dirs. Imperial Khoury Leage, 1987-89, chmn. ways and means com., 1989-90; dist. sec. United Meth. Women, 1993-96, pres. New Hope United Meth. Ch. unit, 1990-91. Mem. Coun. for Exceptional Children (pres. 1991, v.p. Jefferson County chpt. 1994-95, pres. Jefferson County chpt. 1995-96), AAUW, St. Louis Zoo Friends Assn., Kappa Delta. Home: 5125 Darkmoor Ln Imperial MO 63052-3032

UTIGARD, PHILIP RICHARD, real estate executive; b. Indpls., July 18, 1952; s. Richard Charles and Maedell (Hazen) U.; m. Becki A. Elliott, Sept. 27, 1975; children: Emilie, Benjamin, Kevin. BS, Miami U., Oxford, Ohio, 1974. Mktg. rep. IBM Corp., West Lafayette, Ind., 1974-80; regional mktg. rep. IBM Corp., Detroit, 1981; mktg. mgr. IBM Corp., Ft. Wayne, Ind., 1981-85; adminstr. asst. to chmn. IBM Corp., Armonk, N.Y., 1985-86; br. mgr. IBM Corp., N.Y.C., 1986-89; v.p. LaSalle Ptnrs. Ltd., Chgo., 1989-93; v.p. John Buck Co., Chgo., 1993, mng. dir., 1994, prin., 1995—. Fellow Leadership Greater Chgo. Mem. Internat. Devel. Rsch. Coun., Met. Club. Home: 601 North Elm Hinsdale IL 60521 Office: The John Buck Co Sears Tower 5th Flr Chicago IL 60606

UTLEY, ROSE, nursing educator and researcher; b. Broken Arrow, Okla., Aug. 31, 1953; d. Reuben D. and Margie B. (Hudson) U. ADN, Rochester Community Coll., Minn., 1976; BSN, U. Minn., 1981, MS, 1985; postgrad., Wayne State U. RN, N.D., Mich.; CEN. Staff nurse emergency dept. Fairview Community Hosp., Mpls., 1979-86; instr. nursing U. N.D., Grand Forks, 1985-87, U. Mich., Ann Arbor, 1987-91; staff nurse emergency dept. Saratoga Hosp., Detroit, 1991—. Contbr. articles to profl. jours. Mem. AACCN, Emergency Nurses Assn., Sigma Theta. Home: 2700 Shimmons Rd Lot 144 Auburn Hills MI 48326-2047

UWAGIE-ERO, PETER EFOSA, publishing executive; b. Benin City, Nigeria, Sept. 16, 1946; came to the U.S., 1977; s. John Orhue Agbonrobosa and Susanna Amadin (Obayuwana) U.-E.; m. Armatha Assennera Keyes, Oct. 28, 1978. M in Applied Communication Journalism Theory, Cleve. State U., 1993. Pub., editor African Town Crier, Maple Heights, Ohio, 1994—; adviser Cuyahoga C.C., Cleve., 1990-95. Fellow Rosicrucian Order (bd. chmn. 1990-93); mem. Soc. Profl. Journalists. Office: African Town Crier PO Box 370073 Maple Heights OH 44137

VAAL, JOSEPH JOHN, JR., psychologist; b. St. Louis, Nov. 19, 1947; s. Joseph John and Dorothy Jane (Collett) V.; m. Patricia Gail Winkler, Apr. 24, 1982; 1 child, Lauren Elizabeth. BA, Lawrence U., 1969; MA in Psychology, Western Mich. U., 1971; PhD, Columbia Pacific U., 1981. Tchr. spl. edn. KVISD Title VI Program, Kalamazoo, 1970, Mannheim Pub. Schs., Franklin Park, Ill., 1971; sch. psychologist Wheaton (Ill.) Pub. Schs., 1971-79; dir. office continuing edn. Rush-Presbyn.-St. Luke's Med. Ctr., Chgo., 1979-81; adj. instr. Grad. Sch. Nat. Coll. Edn., Evanston, 1972—; spl. edn. due process hearing officer Ill. Bd. Edn., Springfield, 1978—; dir. ednl. svcs. Healthcare Fin. Mgmt. Assn., Oak Brook, Ill., 1981-84; psychologist Sch. Assn. Spl. Edn. in DuPage, Addison, Ill., 1984-87; asst. dir. Sch. Assn. for Spl. Edn. in DuPage, Addison, Ill., 1987-89; dir. planning No. Suburban Spl. Edn. Dist., Highland Park, Ill, 1989-90; sch. psychologist Dept. Pediatrics Luth. Gen. Children's Hosp., Park Ridge, Ill., 1990—. Mem. Ill. Sch. Psychologists Assn., Nat. Assn. Sch. Psychologists. Office: Luth Gen Children's Hosp Yacktman Pavillion 1675 W Dempster Park Ridge IL 60068

VADNER, GREGORY A., state agency administrator; b. Indpls., Mar. 24, 1951; s. Clyde H. and Marilyn (Whickcar) V.; m. Frances A. Woods, May 21, 1983; 1 child, Ariel. BA, DePauw U., 1974; MPA, U. Mo., 1984. Mgr. A&W Root Beer Restaurant, DeSoto, Mo., 1974; photographer Chromalloy Photog. Industries, St. Louis, 1974-75; caseworker Mo. Div. Family Svcs., Hillsboro, 1975-79, income maintenance supr., 1979; county dir. I Mo. Div. Family Svcs., Centerville, 1979-80; county dir. II Mo. Div. Family Svcs., Mexico, 1980-85; county dir. IV Mo. Div. Family Svcs., St. Joseph, 1985-87; income maintenance supr. V Mo. Div. Family Svcs., Kansas City, 1987-88; dep. dir. Mo. Div. Family Svcs., Jefferson City, 1988 . Mem. Am. Pub. Welfare Assn., Nat. Eligibility Workers Assn., Reform Orgn. for Welfare. Lutheran. Home: 1105 Schumate Chapel Rd Jefferson City MO 65109-0585 Office: Mo Div Family Svcs PO Box 88 Broadway State Office Jefferson City MO 65103

VAGNIERES, ROBERT CHARLES, JR., architect; b. Champaign, Ill., Mar. 27, 1954; s. Robert Charles Sr. and Dorothy Lee (Wandrey) V. BArch, U. Ill., 1976; MArch, Washington U., 1980. Architect Eva Maddox & Assoc., Chgo., 1982-83, Solomon Cordwell Buenz & Assoc., Chgo., 1980-82, 83-85; pvt. practice architecture Chgo., 1985—; cons. Mark Shale Hdqrs., Willowbrook, 1990, Mark Shale Expansion, Northbrook, Ill., 1990. Prin. works include renovation of Exec. House Hotel, Chgo., 1987, Amb. West Hotel, Chgo., 1988, Mark Shale Outlet Store, Chgo., 1989, Naperville, 1991, Holiday Inn Chgo. City Ctr. Lobby, 1992, Exec. Plz. Hotel Lobby, 1992, 42-acre Master Plan Kenosha (Wis.) Lakefront, 1992, Ramada Inn exterior renovation and porte-cochere, Lumberton, N.C., 1993, renovation Holiday Inn Chgo. City Ctr., 1995, Szechwan East Restaurant expansion, 1995, McClurg Ct. Sports Ctr. renovation, Chgo., 1996, ballroom renovation Exec. Plaza Hotel, Chgo., 1996, exterior renovation Holiday Inn Midway Airport, Chgo., 1996. Pres. Hawthorne Ct. Townhome Assn., 1990-96, bd. dirs., 1996—. Mem. AIA (vol. advisor Chgo. chpt. student liaison program 1986-95 , vol. Chgo. careers for youth program), French Am. C. of C., Alliance Francaise Chgo. Home: 1148 W School St Chicago IL 60657-2242 Office: Ste 1155 407 S Dearborn Chicago IL 60605

VAGNOZZI, ALDO, editor, newspaper; b. Roseto, Abruzzi, Italy, Oct. 4, 1925; came to U.S., 1933; s. Attilio and Maria Grazia (Sinibaldi) V.; m. Lois Margaret Carl, Jan. 22, 1949; children: Steve, Paul, Nancy, Barbara. BA, Wayne State U., 1948. Asst. editor Mich. CIO News, Detroit, 1948-61; editor Mich. AFL-CIO News, Detroit, 1961-79; editl. cons. Cy Aaron Publs., Detroit, 1979-91, Inland Press, Detroit, 1991-94; editor Detroit Labor News, 1980—; mem. adv. bd. Internat. Visitors Bur., Detroit. Mem. city coun. City of Farmington Hills, Mich., 1987—, mayor, 1991, 95—. With U.S. Army, 1943-46. Democrat. Roman Catholic. Home: 26193 Kiltartan St Farmington Hills MI 48334 Office: Metro Detroit 2550 W Grand Blvd Detroit MI 48208

VAGO, STEVEN, sociology educator, consultant, writer; b. Debrecen, Hungary, June 12, 1937; came to U.S., 1957; s. Joseph and Ibolya (Halasz) V.; m. Kathe Hartley, Feb. 14, 1975. BA, U. Ala., 1961; MA, Wash. U., 1963, PhD, 1967. Prof. St. Louis U., 1967—, dept. chair, 1973-81; program specialist UNESCO, Paris, 1970-73, cons., 1974—; cons. Hungarian Govt., 1987—, St. Louis, 1980—. Author: Law and Society, 5th edit., 1996, Social Change, 3d edit., 1996. Mem. Am. Sociol. Assn., Am. Population Assn., Internat. Sociol. Assn., Law and Soc. Assn., Am. Acad. Arts and Scis. Republican. Office: St Louis U 221 N Grand Blvd Saint Louis MO 63103

VAHLBERG, VIVIAN ELEANOR, philanthropist; b. Oklahoma City, Aug. 12, 1948; d. Charles Julian and Dorothea Vivian (Leavitt) V.; m. Richard Lee Gordon, June 26, 1976; children: Brady Gordon, Ross Gordon, Alexander Gordon. BA in Sociology cum laude, Rice U., 1970. Corr., asst. bur. chief Daily Oklahoman, Washington, 1971-83; v.p. Nat. Press Bldg. Corp., Washington, 1983-84; exec. dir. Soc. Profl. Journalists, Chgo., 1987-90; adj. prof. journalism Northwestern U., Evanston, Ill., 1991; dir. journalism programs Robert R. McCormick Tribune Found., Chgo., 1992—; chmn., CEO Nat. Press Bldg. Corp., Washington, 1982; mem. comms. com. Donors Forum, Chgo., 1994—. Named to Okla. Journalism Hall of Fame, Ctrl. State U., 1983. Mem. Soc. Profl. Journalists, Nat. Press Club (pres. 1982). Office: McCormick Tribune Found 435 N Michigan Ave Chicago IL 60611

VAIL, IRIS JENNINGS, civic worker; b. N.Y.C., July 2, 1928; d. Lawrence K. and Beatrice (Black) Jennings; grad. Miss Porters Sch., Farmington, Conn.; m. Thomas V.H. Vail, Sept. 15, 1951; children: Siri J., Thomas V.H. Jr., Lawrence J.W. Exec. com. Garden Club Cleve., 1962-93; mem. women's coun. Western Res. Hist. Soc., 1960—, Cleve. Mus. Art, 1953—; chmn. Childrens Garden Fair, 1966-75, Public Square Dinner, 1975; bd. dirs. Garden Center Greater Cleve., 1963-77; trustee Cleve. Zool. Soc., 1971—; mem. Ohio Arts Coun., 1974-76, pub. sq. com. Greater Cleve. Growth Assn., 1976-93, pub. sq. preservation and maintenance com. Cleve. Found., 1989-93, chmn. pub. sq. planting com., 1993. Recipient Amy Angell Collier Montague medal Garden Club Am., 1976, Ohio Gov.'s award, 1977. Chagrin Valley Hunt Club, Cypress Point Club, Kirtland Country Club, Colony Club, Women's City of Cleve. Club (Margaret A. Ireland award). Home: 14950 County Line Rd Chagrin Falls OH 44022

VAIL, THOMAS VAN HUSEN, retired newspaper publisher and editor; b. Cleve., June 23, 1926; s. Herman Lansing and Delia (White) V.; m. Iris W. Jennings, Sept. 15, 1951; children: Siri, Thomas Van Husen. A.B. in Politics cum laude, Princeton U., 1949; H.H.D. (hon.), Wilberforce U., 1964; L.H.D., Kenyon Coll., 1969, Cleve. State U., 1973. Reporter Cleve. News, 1949-53, polit. editor, 1953-57; with Cleve. Plain Dealer, 1957—, v.p., 1961-63, pub., editor, 1963-91, pres., 1970-91; dir. AP, 1968-74; ret., 1991. Bd. dirs. Greater Cleve. Growth Assn.; bd. dirs., past pres. Cleve. Conv. and Visitors Bur.; mem. Nat. Adv. Commn. on Health Manpower, U.S. Adv. Commn. on Health Manpower, U.S. Adv. Commn. on Info., Pres.'s Commn. for Observance 25th Anniversay UN; trustee No. Ohio region NCCJ, Nat. Brotherhood Week chmn., 1969; trustee Cleve. Coun. World Affairs, Cleve. Clinic Found.; former Downtown Cleve. Corp.; former mem. distbn. com. Cleve. Found.; chmn., founder New Cleve. Campaign; trustee, founder Cleve. Tomorrow; former trustee Com. Econ. Devel.; former mem. Pres.'s Adv. Coun. on Pvt. Sector Initiatives. Lt. (j.g.) USNR, 1944-46. Recipient Nat. Human Relations award, 1970, Cleve. Man of Year award Sales and Mktg. Execs. Cleve., 1976, Ohio Gov.'s award, 1982, Downtown Bus. Council recognition award Greater Cleve. Growth Assn., 1983. Mem. Am. Newspaper Pubs. Assn., Am. Soc. Newspaper Editors, Soc. Profl. Journalists, Kirtland Country Club (Willoughby, Ohio), Cypress Point Club (Pebble Beach, Calif.), Bohemian Club (San Francisco), Chagrin Valley Hunt Club (Gates Mills, Ohio), Links Club (N.Y.C.), Sigma Delta Chi. Episcopalian. Home: 14950 County Line Rd Hunting Valley Chagrin Falls OH 44022 Office: 29225 Chagrin Blvd #200 Pepper Pike OH 44122

VAINISI, JEROME ROBERT, lawyer, former professional football executive; b. Chgo., Oct. 7, 1941; s. Anthony A. and Marie (Delisi) V.; m. Doris Mary Lane, Nov. 14, 1964; children: Mary Terese, Jerome A., John A., Mark E., Melissa P. B.S. in Bus. Adminstrn., Georgetown U., 1963; postgrad. in law, Loyola U., 1963-64; J.D., Chgo. Kent Coll. Law, 1969. Bar: Ill. 1969, Mich. 1987. News and sports dir. Sta. WRAM, Monmouth, Ill., 1964-65; tax acct., office mgr. Arthur Andersen & Co., Chgo., 1965-72; successively controller, corp. asst. sec., treas. Chgo. Bears Football Club, Inc.; 1972-83, v.p., gen. mgr., 1983-87; gen. counsel Detroit Lions Football Club, Pontiac, Mich., 1987, v.p. player personnel, 1987-90; v.p. football mgmt. World League Am. Football, Irving, Tex., 1990-95; with Hinshaw & Culbertson, Chgo., 1995—; dir., chmn. bd. Forest Park (Ill.) Nat. Bank, 1978—; v.p. NFL Ins. Ltd., 1984-87. Roman Catholic. Office: Hinshaw & Culbertson Ste 300 222 N La Salle St Chicago IL 60601-1081

VAKALO, EMMANUEL-GEORGE, architecture and planning educator, researcher; b. Athens, Greece, May 10, 1946; came to U.S., 1965; s. George Constantine and Eleni (Stavrinou) V.; m. Kathleen Leitgabel, July 20, 1974. BArch, Cornell U., 1969, MArch, 1972, M in Regional Planning, 1977; PhD, U. Mich., 1985. Instr. U. Mich., Ann Arbor, 1975-79, asst. prof., 1979-91, assoc. prof., 1991—, chmn. doctoral program in arch. coll. arch. urban planning, 1994—; cons. JP Industries, Ann Arbor, 1987-88; guest prof. Tech. U. Wien, U. Okla., Carnegie-Mellon U., La. State U., U. Notre Dame, Ryerson Poly. Inst., Calif. State Poly. U., Pomona. Author: Visual Studies, 1983, Visual Syntax: Function and Production of Forms, 1988. Mem. Am. Planning Assn., Environ, Design Rsch. Assn., Nat. Inst. Archtl. Edn., Inst. Math. Geography. Office: U Mich Coll Arch and Urban Planning 2000 Bonisteel Dr Ann Arbor MI 48109-2069

VALANCE, MARSHA JEANNE, library director, story teller; b. Evanston, Ill., Aug. 2, 1946; d. Edward James Jr. and Jeanne Lois (Skinner) Leonard; m. William George Valance, Dec. 27, 1966 (div. 1976); 1 child, Marguerite Jeanne. Student Northwestern U., 1964-66; AB, UCLA, 1968; MLS, U. R.I., 1973; cert. in Profl. Devel., U. Wis., Madison, 1991. Children's libr. trainee N.Y. Pub. Libr., N.Y.C., 1968-69; reference libr. Action Meml. Pub. Libr. (Mass.), 1969-70; mgr. The Footnote, Cedar Rapids, Iowa, 1976-78; assoc. editor William C. Brown, Dubuque, Iowa, 1978-79; dir. Dubuque County Libr., Dubuque, 1979-81, G.B. Dedrick Pub. Libr., Geneseo, Ill., 1981-84, dir. Grand Rapids (Minn.) Pub. Libr., 1984-89; mgmt. libr., Wis. Regional Libr. for Blind and Physically Handicapped, 1989—; workshop coord., participant, sect. chmn. profl. confs.; LSCA grant reviewer U.S. Dept. Edn., 1989-95. Author: (with others) Mystery, Value and Awareness, 1979; Pluralism, Similarities and Contrast, 1979; contbr. articles and book revs. to publs. Troop leader Miss. Valley Coun. Girl Scouts U.S., Cedar Rapids, 1976-78; mem. liturgy com. St. Malachy's Roman Cath. Ch., Geneseo, 1983; com. judging clinic 4-H, Moline, Ill., 1984; trustee KAXE No. Community Radio, 1986-89, ICTV, 1988-90; sec. Grand Rapids Community Svcs. Coun., 1986; coach Itasca County 4-H Horse Bowl Team, 1987; dir. Grand Rapids Storyfest, 1987-89; program chmn. Spotlight on Books Conf., 1989; bd. dirs., trustee Vols. in Svc. to the Visually Handicapped, 1989—; audio describer Artreach, Milw., 1991—. Recipient Weavers award Telephone Pioneers, 1992; Iowa Humanities Bd. grantee, 1981, Minn. Libr. Found. grantee, 1985, 86, 87, Blandin Found. grantee, 1986, Arrowhead Regional Arts Coun. grantee, 1987, 89, Ms. Soc. grantee, 1989. Mem. ALA, Wis. Libr. Assn., Iowa Librs. of Medium Size (sec. 1981), Northlands Storytelling Network (bd. dirs. 1988-94, v.p. 1989, pres. 1990, editor Grapevine, 1991-94), Nat. Assn. Preservation and Perpetuation Storytelling, Alliance Info. and Referral Svcs., DAR (constn. chmn. 1983-84), Miss. Valley Morgan Horse Club, Wis. Morgan Horse Club (newsletter editor 1994-95, sec. 1995), Am. Morgan Horse Assn., Mid States Morgan Horse Club, Geneseo Jr. Women's Club (internat. chmn. 1983-84), UCLA Club Wis. (pres. 1990-91), Alpha Gamma Delta. Home: 6639 W Dodge Pl Milwaukee WI 53220-1329 Office: Wis Regional Libr Blind & Physically Handicapped 813 W Wells St Milwaukee WI 53233-1436

VALANDRA, PAUL, state legislator; m. Cheryl Valandra; four children. Student, Black Hills State U., U. S.D., Oglala Lakota Coll. Former state senator dist. 28 State of S.D., state senator dist. 27, 1993—; mem. com. health and human svcs. S.D. State Senate; tribal adminstr. Democrat. Home: PO Box 909 Rosebud SD 57555-0909*

VALASKOVIC, DAVID WILLIAM, architect, designer; b. Chgo., Apr. 6, 1961; s. William Theodore an Carmella (Stiso) V. BArch, U. Ill., 1986. Registered architect, Ill. Architect Stowell Cook Frolichstein, Inc., Chgo., 1985-86, Skidmore Owings & Merrill, Chgo., 1986—; cons. Philip Kupritz Architects, Chgo. 1987. Mem. AIA, Braidwood Recreation Club. Home: 260 E Chusnut #1610 Chicago IL 60611 Office: Skidmore Owings & Merrill 224 S Michigan Ave Chicago IL 60604-2507

VALDES, ELIZABETH LYNNE, technical writer, editor; b. Alton, Ill., Dec. 13, 1967; d. Lowell Raymond and Vivian Joyce (Shofner) Brosamer; m. Ariel Omar Valdes, May 23, 1992; 1 child, Gabriel Wolfe. BA, U. Ill., 1989. Sr. coord. comms. Skelgas Propane, Inc., Oak Brook, Ill., 1991-94; cons. Brookfield, Ill., 1994—. Mem. Soc. Tech. Comm. Roman Catholic.

VALENCIA, ROGELIO PASCO, electronics engineer; b. Paombong, Bulacan, The Philippines, Mar. 18, 1939; came to U.S., 1959; s. Silvino Carlos and Basilia Galang (Pasco) V.; m. Amelia Almendariz Gomez, May 3l, 1965; children: Zenaida Leticia, Lucinda Amelia, Rogelio Pasco II. Student mech. engring., Mapua Inst. Tech., Manila, 1955-59; student English and math., Coll. William and Mary, 1963-64, numerous USCG tng. schs. Enlisted man USCG, 1959, advanced through grades to chief warrant officer; with USCG cutter Rush, Vietnam, 1970-71; sr. tech. officer USCG Loran Sta., Hokkaido, Japan, 1977-78; exec. officer USCG Loran Sta., Dana, Ind., 1978-79; ret., 1979; computer analyst Wyman & Gordon Co., Danville, Ill., 1979-80; precision measurement electronics lab. technician USAF, Rantoul, Ill., 1980-88, digital computer engr., 1988—. Home: 1303 Bradford Cir Saint Joseph IL 61873-9625 Office: USAF Civil Engring Rantoul IL 61868

VALENSTEIN, ELLIOT SPIRO, psychology educator; b. N.Y.C., Dec. 9, 1923; s. Louis and Helen (Spiro) V.; m. Thelma Lewis, June 15, 1947; children—Paul, Carl. B.S., CCNY, 1949; M.A., U. Kans., 1953, Ph.D., 1954. Chief neuropsychology sect. Walter Reed Inst. Research, 1957-61; Nat. Acad. Sci. fellow USSR, 1961; sr. research assoc. Fels Research Inst., 1961-71; mem. faculty dept. psychology Antioch Coll., 1963-71; faculty mem. U. Mich., Ann Arbor, 1970—, prof. psychology, 1970—, chmn. psychobiology area of dept., 1979—; vis. scientist Oreg. Primate Ctr., 1967; vis. prof. U. Calif.-Berkeley, 1969-70; fellow Ctr. for Advanced Studies in Behavioral Sci., 1976-77; vis. prof. dept. psychology Hebrew U., Jerusalem, 1980; mem. sci. rev. panels NIH, NIMH, NSF, 1964—, chmn., 1971-74; chmn. adv. bd. Wis. Regional Primate Ctr., Madison, 1972-89; disting. sr. lectr. U. Mich. 1992-93. Author: Brain Stimulation and Motivation, 1973, Brain Control, 1973, Psychosurgery Debate, 1980, Great and Desperate Cures, 1986; contbr. articles to profl jours.; cons. editor Jour. Comparative Physiol. Psychology, 1963-75, Brain, Behavior and Evolution, 1967-87; mem. editorial bd. Human Growth and Devel., 1974-89; mem. adv. bd. Internat. Jour. Neurosci., 1974—; mem. editorial and adv. bd. Jour. Law and Human Behavior, 1975-85. Trustee James McKeen Cattel Fund, 1987—; adviser Coun. Internat. Exch. of Fulbright Scholars, 1989-92. With AUS, 1941-45. Decorated Bronze Star medal; James Arthur lectr., 1974; Fulbright fellow, 1980, 95; recipient Kenneth Craik Rsch. award St. John's Coll., Cambridge, Eng., award for Outstanding Achievement in Psychology CCNY, 1989; disting. sr. faculty lectr. U. Mich., 1993; Phi Beta Kappa vis. scholar, 1987-88. Fellow AAAS; mem. APA (pres. divsn. physiology and comparative psychology 1976-77), Internat. Brain Rsch. Orgn., Soc. for Neuroscis., Animal Behavioral Soc., Soc. Exptl. Psychology, Internat. Union Physiol. Scis. (commn. on psychophysiology), Internat. Behavioral Neurosci. Soc. (U.S. coun. rep. 1994—), Mex. Acad. Sci., Phi Beta Kappa. Home: 260 Indian River Pl Ann Arbor MI 48104-1825 Office: U Mich 1103 E Huron St Ann Arbor MI 48104-1630

VALENTA, JANET ANNE, substance abuse professional; b. Cleve., Sept. 22, 1948; d. Frank A. and Ann (Kogoy) Shenk; m. Mario Valenta, May 22, 1971. BA, Cleve. State U., 1970; postgrad., Rutgers U., 1973, U. Cin., 1976-84. Cert. prevention cons., Ohio. Purchasing clk./typist Restaurant div. Stouffer Foods Corp., Cleve., 1967-71; cmty. info. specialist Trumbull Warren Office of Econ. Opportunity, Warren, Ohio, 1972; edn. dir. Trumbull County Coun. on Alcoholism, Warren, 1973-78; rehab. counselor Trumbull County Bur. Vocat. Rehab., Niles, Ohio, 1979-80; owner, operator Ironsmith, Niles, 1978-79; cons., trainer Ohio Network Tng. and Assistance to Schs. and Cmty., Youngstown, Ohio, 1987—; prevention edn. coord. Cmty. Recovery Resource Ctr., Youngstown, 1979-94; prevention coord. Neil Kennedy Recovery Clinic, Youngstown, 1994—; Ohio tng. coord. Babesworld Home, Inc., Detroit, 1986—; nat. chair pub. health caucus Nat. Assn. Prevention Profls., Chgo., 1976-77. Publicity chair Trumbull Art Guild, Warren, 1974-76; bd. dirs. Ebony Life Support Group, Inc., Youngstown, 1992; mem. Policy coun. Youngstown Cmty. Action, Headstart,

1988-90. Named Woman of Yr., Warren Bus. and Profl. Women's Assn., 1978, Tribute in Health Woman of Yr., YWCA, Youngstown, 1987. Mem. Alcohol and Drug Abuse Prevention Assn. Ohio. Office: Neil Kennedy Recovery Clin 2151 Rush Blvd Youngstown OH 44507

VALINE, DELMAR EDMOND, SR., corporate executive; b. Edwardsville, Ill., May 2, 1919; s. Edward and Clara Louise (Schon) V.; m. Geraldine Goley, Aug. 26, 1939; children: Jayne M. Valine Klein, Linda L. Valine Hay, Delmar E. Jr. Student, Summer Bus. Coll., 1939. Purchasing agt. Swift and Co., Nat. Stockyards., Ill., 1937-58; asst. to pres. St. Louis Nat. Stock Yards Co., Nat. Stockyards, Ill., 1958-60; exec. v.p. St. Louis Livestock Mkt. Found., Nat. Stockyards, Ill., 1960-64; exec. sec. Nat. Museum of Transport, St. Louis, Mo.; v.p. First Ill. Bank, East St. Louis, Ill., 1967-81; bd. chairman Southwest Regional Port Dist., Ill., 1961—; bd. dirs. First Ill. Bank, East St. Louis, 1982—, Target 2000, East St. Louis, 1977—, Inland Rivers Port and Terminals 1987—, Port of Metropolitan St. Louis, 1975—, sec., treas. Gateway Ctr. Metropolitan St. Louis, 1976—; exec. v.p. East Side Associated Industries, East St. Louis, 1990—. Mayor village of Dupo, Ill., 1945-49, mem. sch. bd. dist. 193, Dupo, 1955-56, Selective Service bd., East St. Louis, 1950-55; mem. Fed. Agy. Adv. Com., 1964-70; commr. Southwestern Ill. Planning Comm., 1976—. Recipient Medallion award, Boys Club Am., 1969. Mem. U.S. C. of C., Rotary (past pres.), Boys Club, Mo. Athletic Club, Royal Order of Jesters. Republican.

VALINSKY, MARK STEVEN, podiatrist; b. Chgo., May 24, 1951; m. Michelle Susan Morgan; children: Cara Linda, Erin Abra, Noah Allen, Hannah Rae, Arielle Lauren. Student in biology and pre-medicine, Ohio State U., 1969-71, SUNY, Buffalo, 1971-72; BS, D in Podiatric Medicine, Ill. Coll. Podiatric Medicine, 1976; MD (hon.), Inst. Orthopaedics & Traumatology China Acad. Traditonal Medicine, Beijing, 1989. Lic. podiatrist, Ill., Calif., N.Y.; diplomate Am. Bd. Podiatry Examiners, Am. Bd. Ambulatory Foot Surgery; cert. Am. Coun. Cert. Podatric Physicians and Surgeons. Pvt. practice podiatric surgery Oak Park, Ill., 1977—; founder, dir. The Foot Care Ctr., P.C., Oak Park; mem. 1st foot surg. team to China, 1983, also 1987; instr. minimal incision foot surgery to orthopaedic surgeons in China; lectr. 1st Sino N.Am. Treatise of Foot Disorders, Beijing, 1987, vis. prof., 1989; pres., founder Biol. Scis. Rsch. Inst., Inc.; lectr. on minimal incision and radiowave foot surgery in Australia and throughout U.S.; internat. lectr. and tchr. on health care of feet, also radio and TV appearances. Columnist Focus on the Foot; contbr. articles to profl. and popular publs., author video tapes in field. Former mem. Chgo. Mayor's Coun. for Sr. Citizens and Handicapped. Mem. Am. Inst. Foot Medicine (cert.), Ill. Podiatric Soc. (sec. Zone I, 1980-82, zone pres. 1981-82, del. to bd. dirs. 1980-82), Am. Podiatric Soc., Podiatric Med. Assn., Acad. Ambulatory Foot Surgeons (pres. midwest region 1986—), Oak Park-River Forest C. of C. (bd. dirs.), Am. Karate Assn. Office: 163 S Oak Park Ave Oak Park IL 60302-2901

VALLS, ORIOL TOMAS, physicist; b. Barcelona, Catalonia, Spain, Oct. 15, 1947; came to U.S., 1970; citizen, 1978; s. Oriol Subira and Nuria Farell (Tomas) V.; m. Maureen Ellen Doyle, Aug. 31, 1974; Andrew, Anthony. MSc, Brown U., 1972, PhD, 1975. Rsch. assoc. U. Chgo, 1975-77; Miller fellow U. Calif., Berkeley, Calif., 1977-78; asst. prof. U. Minn., Mpls., 1978-93, assoc. prof., 1983-87, prof., 1987—. Contbr. over 100 rsch. papers to sci. and profl. jours. Fellow Minn. Supercomputer Inst.; mem. Am. Phys. Soc., Sigma Chi. Office: U Minn Sch Physics Minneapolis MN 55455

VAMMEN, JAMES OLIVER, human services administrator; b. Green Bay, Wis., June 23, 1932; s. Peter Jens and Olga Christine (Andersen) V.; m. Gladys Bernice Helland, June 17, 1954 (div. Apr. 1974); children: Calvin, Connie, Charlton; m. Jean Brooks, May 5, 1975. BS in Edn., Dana Coll., 1958; postgrad., U. Iowa, 1959, 62, U. Nebr., Omaha, 1962-63, No. Colo. U., 1963, DePauw U., 1961; MEd, Temple U., 1965; postgrad., S.E. Nebr. Community Coll., 1975, DePauw U., 1961. Lic. nursing home adminstr., Nebr. Tchr. Thurston (Nebr.) Pub. Schs., 1958-59, Westside Community Schs., Omaha, 1959-64, Phila. Pub. Schs., 1964-65; exec. dir. Ken-Crest Ctrs., Plymouth Meeting, Pa., 1965-74, Cheyenne Village, Manitou Springs, Colo., 1975-79; exec. v.p. ISS Found., Denver, 1979-83; adminstr. Martin Luther Home, Beatrice, Nebr., 1984-86; pres., CEO North Cen. Human Svcs., Forest City, Iowa, 1987—, Devel. Resources Inc., Forest City, 1992—. Bd. dirs. Forest City 2000. With USN, 1950-54. Recipient award Chapel of Four Chaplains, 1971. Mem. Am. Assn. on Mental Retardation, Am. Network of Cmty. Options and Resources, Rotary Internat. Home: 135 Woodland Dr Forest City IA 50436-2419 Office: North Central Human Svcs 106 E Park St # 368 Forest City IA 50436-2103

VAN ACKEREN, MAURICE EDWARD, college administrator; b. Cedar Rapids, Nebr., Aug. 21, 1911; s. Edward M. and Frances (O'Leary) Van A. B.A. in Chemistry, Creighton U., 1932; M.A. in Edn., St. Louis U., 1946; LL.D. (hon.), Benedictine Coll., 1976. Ordained Jesuit priest Roman Cath. Ch., 1943. Tchr. Campion High Sch., Prairie du Chien, Wis., 1937-40; prin. St. Louis U. High Sch., 1946-51; pres. Rockhurst Coll., Kansas City, Mo., 1951-77, chancellor, 1977—. Recipient Knight of Holy Sepulchre award Catholic Ch., Chgo., 1968, Chancellor's medal U. Mo.-Kansas City, 1981, Mr. Kansas City award Greater Kansas City C. of C., 1983; named to Creighton U. Athletic Hall of Fame, Omaha, 1971; named Mktg. Exec. of Yr., Sales and Mktg. Club Kansas City, 1979. Mem. C. of C. of Greater Kansas City. Lodge: Rotary (Paul Harris fellow 1983). Home and Office: 1100 Rockhurst Rd Kansas City MO 64110-2508

VAN AKEN, WILLIAM J., construction executive; b. 1954. Grad., South Utah State Coll., 1983, Case Western Res. U., Cleve. Pvt. practice as contractor Cedar City, Utah, 1976-83; with Sam W. Emerson Co., Cleve., 1983—, pres., treas., 1990—. Office: Sam W Emerson Co 1621 Euclid Ave Ste 1230 Cleveland OH 44115*

VAN ALLMAN, DON THOMAS, engineering executive; b. Hollidaysburg, Pa., Jan. 23, 1932; s. Thomas Augustus and Dorothy Ellen (Hauser) Van A.; m. Eileen Louise McClintock, Mar. 15, 1952; children: Steven Paul, Linda Jean, Lisa Louise, Scott Thomas, Lora Ann, Samuel Ross. BSBA, Southern Ill. u., 1972. Supt. mfg. Fabricating div. Olin Corp., East Alton, Ill., 1965-68, supt. mfg. Fineweld Tube div., 1969-79, supt. cost engring. Fabricating div., 1980-82, mgr. engring. Ramset div., 1982-86; dir. mktg. ITW Ramset, Rolling Meadows, Ill., 1986-87; dir. engring. ITW Ramset/Red Head, Wood Dale, Ill., 1987—; v.p. Powder Actuated Tool Mfrs. Inst., St. Louis, 1986-89, pres., 1993-94. Contbr. articles to profl. jours.; inventor in field. Mem. bd. edn. Marquette High Sch., Alton, 1982-86. Sgt. USMC, 1950-53. Mem. Am. Soc. Materials, Am. Nat. Stds. Inst. (A10.3 com.), Am. Soc. Test Methods (E6 com.). Republican. Roman Catholic. Home: 807 Sandpiper Ct Palatine IL 60067-7057 Office: ITW Ramset/Red Head 1300 N Michael Dr Wood Dale IL 60191-1009

VAN ANDEL, BETTY JEAN, retired direct selling company executive; b. Mich., Dec. 14, 1921; d. Anthony and Daisy (Van Dyk) Hoekstra; AB, Calvin Coll., 1943; m. Jay Van Andel, Aug. 16, 1952; children—Nan Elizabeth, Stephen Alan, David Lee, Barbara Ann. Elementary sch. tchr., Grand Rapids, Mich., 1943-45; svc. rep. and supr. Mich. Bell Telephone Co., Grand Rapids, 1945-52; bd. dirs. Amway Corp., Grand Rapids, 1972—. Treas., LWV, 1957-60; pres. Eagle Forum, Mich., 1975-91; co-chmn. Mich. Botanic Garden Capital Campaign; former trustee Christian Sch. Internat. Found., Grand Rapids Opera, exec. com.; trustee Pine Rest Christian Hosp.; past pres. La Grave Ave Reformed Ch. Svc. Guild. Mem. Nat. Fedn. Rep. Women, Nat. Trust Hist. Preservation, St. Cecelia Music Soc., Smithsonian Assos., Gerald R. Ford Rep. Women's Club. Home: 7186 Windy Hill Dr SE Grand Rapids MI 49546-9745

VAN ANTWERP, GEORGE B., human services administrator; b. Detroit, Nov. 8, 1927; s. Eugene Ignatius and Mary Frances (McDevitt) Van A.; m. Mary Louise Beale, Oct. 17, 1970; children: George Bernard, Karon Ann, Michael Gerald. BA, Sacred Heart Seminary, Detroit, 1949; MDiv, St. John's Provincial Sem., Plymouth, Mich., 1982. Cert. social worker, Mich. Pastor Archdiocese of Detroit, 1953-70; area dir. U.S. Peace Corps, Brazil, 1970-73; dep. dir. Shar House, Detroit, 1973-80; from dir. employment svcs. to v.p. cmty. rels. Mt. Carmel Mercy Hosp., Detroit, 1981-91; dir. devel. Shar House, 1991-92; pres. Van Antwerp & Assocs., Inc., Royal Oak, Mich., 1992-93; v.p. Nat. Migrant Workers Coun., Farmington Hills, Mich., 1993-94; dir. Boniface Human Svcs., Lincoln Park, Mich., 1994—; pres. Monsignor Clement Kern Found., Detroit, 1985—; bd. dirs., exec. com. Mich. League Human Svcs., Lansing, 1986—; bd. dirs. Gabriel Richard Hist. Soc., 1991—, Latino Pastoral Ctr., 1994—. Named outstanding citizen 12th police precinct, Detroit, 1986; recipient Virginia DeBerry award Northwest Area Bus. Assn., Detroit, 1987. Mem. Nat. Soc. Fund Raising Execs., K. of C. Democrat. Roman Catholic. Home: 2222 Lloyd Royal Oak MI 48073 Office: Boniface Human Svcs 25050 W Outer Dr #201 Lincoln Park MI 48146

VAN APPLEDORN, E(LIZABETH) RUTH, writer; b. Holland, Mich., Dec. 19, 1918; d. John and Elizabeth (Rinck) van A. B of Music, Oberlin Coll., 1940; M of Music, Mich. State U., 1942. Prof. emeritus U. Minn., Duluth, 1946-82; lectr. in field, 1955-70; substitute Ch. organist, 1950-70. Contbr. prose poetry to religious publs. Recipient U. Svc. award, U. Minn., 1983; named Outstanding Educator of Am., 1975. Mem. Internat. Soc. Poets, Mu Phi Epsilon (life). Home: 5120 Norwood St Duluth MN 55804-1149

VANAUKEN, ALAN BRADLEY, greeting card company executive; b. Rochester, N.Y., June 13, 1957; s. Richard Arnold and Roberta May (Ketchell) V. BS, Rensselaer Poly. Inst., 1979; MBA, Harvard U., 1984. Asst. product mgr. Hallmark Cards, Inc., Kansas City, Mo., 1984-86, project mgr., 1986-87, product devel. mgr., 1987-88, sr. new bus. strategist, 1988-90, bus. mktg. mgr., 1990-92, mktg. mgr., food team, 1992-95, dir. product mgmt. and mktg., 1995—; ptnr., co-founder Nadler Assocs., Troy, N.Y., 1978-79; staff cons. Arthur Andersen & Co., N.Y.C., 1979-81, sr. cons., 1981-82; adv. coun. Keller Grad. Sch. Mgmt., Kansas City, 1988—. Product champion (new products) The Birthday Times, 1986, The Anniversay Times, 1987. Mem. adv. com. Arts Ptnrs., Kansas City, 1987-88; mem. exec. com., bd. dirs. Young Audiences, Inc., Kansas City, 1987-90; chmn. RPI Alumni Admissions com., Kansas City, 1984—, alumni admissions steering com., 1988-94, vice-chmn. 1990-92, chmn. 1992-94; dist. activities chmn. Boy Scouts of Am., 1995—; mem. United Way Chmn.'s Club, 1992—. Recipient James E. West Fellowship award 1994. Mem. Renesselaer Alumni Assn. (bd. dirs. 1990—, v.p. 1994—, Dir.'s award 1989, Alumni Key award 1994, Alumni Admissions Recognition of Excellence award 1994), Harvard Club, Lake Stockton Yacht Club. Mem. Christian Ch. Home: 112 W 61st Ter Kansas City MO 64113-1454 Office: Hallmark Cards Inc 2501 Mcgee St Kansas City MO 64108-2615

VANAUKER, LANA LEE, recreational therapist, educator; b. Youngstown, Ohio, Sept. 19, 1949; d. William Marshall and Joanne Norma (Kimmel) Speece; m. Dwight Edward VanAuker, Mar. 16, 1969 (div. 1976); 1 child, Heidi. BS in Edn. cum laude, Kent (Ohio) State U., 1974; MS in Edn., Youngstown (Ohio) U., 1989. Cert. tchr., Ohio; nat. cert. activity cons. Phys. edn. instr. St. Joseph Sch., Campbell, Ohio, 1973-75; program dir. YWCA, Youngstown, 1975-85; exercise technician Youngstown State U., 1985-86; health educator Park Vista Retirement Ctr., Youngstown, 1986-87; sch. tchr. Salem (Ohio) City Sch., 1987-88; recreational therapist Trumbull Meml. Hosp., Warren, Ohio, 1988—; activity cons. Mahoning/Trumbull Nursing Homes, Warren, 1990-92; adv. bd. rep. Ohio State Bur. Health Promotion Phys. Fitness, 1996—; mem. adv. bd. Ohio State Executive Physical Fitness Dept. Health, 1996. Producer chair exercise sr. video Excercise is the Fountain of Youth, 1993; photographer, choreographer. Vol. Am. Cancer Soc., 1980—, Am. Heart Assn., 1986—, Dance for Heart, 1980-86; mem. State of Ohio Phys. Fitness Adv. Bd., 1996. Youngstown State U. scholar, 1986-89. Mem. AAHPERD, Youngstown Camera Club (social chair 1989-90, pres. 1993-95), Resident Activity Profl. Assn. (pres. 1994, 95, 96), Pa. Activity Profl. Assn., Kappa Delta Pi. Democrat. Presbyterian. Home: 385 N Broad St Canfield OH 44406-1256 Office: Trumbull Meml Hosp 1350 E Market St Warren OH 44483-6608

VAN AUSDALL, ROBERT LOREN, association administrator; b. Camden, Ohio, Apr. 22, 1920; s. William Arthur and Elsie Grace (Anderson) Van A.; m. Marilyn Thum, June 13, 1943; children: Robert Jr., Linda, Karen, Dirk. Student, Miami U., Ohio, 1938-40; BA in Chinese Studies, Cornell U., 1948. Col., pilot USAF, 1940-61; mgr. Van Wert (Ohio) C. of C., 1961-65; dist. mgr. U.S. C. of C., Lansing, Mich., 1965-70; regional mgr. U.S. C. of C., Chgo., 1970-82; chmn. Chgo. Inst. Mgmt. Studies, Clarendon Hills, Ill., 1982-93; attache and pilot Am. Embassy, Nanking, China, 1949; lectr. on memory Norwegian Cruise Lines, Miami, Fla., 1980-85; lectr. on time mgmt. Paquet Lines, Miami, 1983; lectr. on memory devel. Cunard Princess, Long Beach, Calif., 1986. Author: (autobiography) Book, 1990. Decorated two Disting. Flying Crosses, two Air medals. Mem. Chgo. Soc. Assn. Execs. (vice chmn. 1980), Chamber Execs. Ohio (cert., bd. dirs. 1964). Home and Office: 435 Traube Ave Clarendon Hills IL 60514-2818

VAN BEEK, DIANNE MARGARET, marketing educator; b. Algoma, Wis., Nov. 6, 1946; d. Frank John and Lillian Anna (Paul) Hucek; m. Lawrence Joseph Van Beek, Apr. 2, 1971. BS magna cum laude, U. Wis., Oshkosh, 1968; MS, U. Wis.-Stout, Menomonie, 1995. Cert. tchr., Wis. Instr. English Seymour (Wis.) Commun. Schs., 1968-75; supr. customer communications Gehl Co., West Bend, Wis., 1976-77; adminstrv. rep. Shade Info. Sys., Green Bay, 1977-79; sr. adminstr. Shade Info. Systems, Green Bay, 1980; instr. mktg. N.E. Wis. Tech. Coll., Green Bay, 1980—; acad. advisor N.E. Wis. Tech. Coll. Advt. Club, 1983-92. Author promotional and mktg. plans. Mem. NEA, Wis. Edn. Assn., N.E. Wis. Vocat. Assn. (pres. 1987-88, Profl. Excellence award 1989), Wis. Vocat. Assn., Am. Vocat. Assn., N.E. Wis. Faculty Assn. (bldg. rep. 1990-91)., Wis. Mktg. Edn. Assn. (bd. dirs. 1993—, Mktg. Educator of Yr. 1995), Am. Advt. Fedn. (Silver medal 1994), Green Bay Advt. Fedn. (bd. dirs. 1985-89). Roman Catholic. Home: 2677 Kathy Dr Green Bay WI 54311-7266 Office: NE Wis Tech Coll 2740 W Mason St Green Bay WI 54307-9042

VAN-BREEMEN, BERTRAM, optical engineer; b. Zion, Ill., May 26, 1919; s. John and Alice Ione (Maltby) Van-B.; m. Pauline Elizabeth Wales, Sept. 1, 1940; children: Dorothy Alice, Charles Anthony, John Leroy, Ellen Kay, Linda Annette. BA, John Fletcher Coll., 1940; postgrad., Drake U., 1947-48, Iowa State Coll., 1948, U. Notre Dame, 1950-51. Sr. engr. Lear Inc., Grand Rapids, 1949-53; optical engr. Goodyear Aircraft, Litchfield, Ariz., 1953-59, Mpls. Honeywell, Duarte, Calif., 1959-62, Perkin Elmer, Costa Mesa, Calif., 1962-65, Hycon, Monrovia, Calif., 1962, 64; sr. engr. Aeronutronic, Newport Beach, Calif., 1965-68; pvt. practice Calif., 1968-75; sr. scientist Mead Digital System, Dayton, Ohio, 1975-81; sr. mem. engring. staff RCA, Indpls., 1981-87; pvt. practice tech. cons. Franklin, Ind., 1988—. Patentee in field. Recipient Technical excellence award, RCA. Home and Office: 498 E Madison St Franklin IN 46131-2527

VANBREMEN, LEE, medical association executive; b. Charleroi, Pa., Mar. 31, 1938; s. Robert and Mildred Geraldine (Frantz) VanB.; m. Jane Reed, June 11, 1960; children: Lynn VanBremen Gilbert, Kara VanBremen Gruver. BA, Pa. State U., 1960; BD, Yale U., 1964; MA, U. Conn., 1971, PhD, 1974. Assoc. pastor Trinity Presbyn. Ch., Cherry Hill, N.J., 1964-67; campus minister New Britain (Conn.) Campus Ministry, 1967-74; dir. membership svcs., asst. exec. dir. Nat. Sch. Bds. Assn., Washington, 1974-83; exec. v.p. Am. Acad. Facial Plastic & Reconstructive Surgery, Washington, 1983-89, Coll. of Am. Pathologists, Northfield, Ill., 1989—. Editor Med. Soc. Execs. publ., 1989-91; mem. editorial bd. Successful Meetings, 1987; author article, book revs., bibliography. Founding pres. Clearview Manor Assn., McLean, Va., 1986; pres. Conn. Bds. Edn., Hartford, 1973-74; elected to New Britain Bd. Edn., 1979-83. Doctoral fellow Danforth Found., 1971-72. Fellow Am. Soc. Assn. Execs. (Key profls. com. 1990—, chmn. Found. 1990-91, bd. dirs. 1993—, Key award 1991); mem. Am. Assn. Med. Soc. Execs. (chmn. ann. meeting 1989, bd. dirs. 1991—, vice chmn. 1996—), Chgo. Soc. Assn. Execs. (CEO com. 1990-92), Greater Washington Soc. Assn. Execs. (Excellence on Comm. award 1985), Northfield C. of C. (bd. dirs. 1991—), Winnetka Tennis Assn. (bd. dirs. 1990-92), Phi Beta Kappa, Phi Delta Kappa, Omicron Delta Kappa. Democrat. Office: Coll Am Pathologists 325 Waukegan Rd Winnetka IL 60093-2719

VAN BRUNT, MARCIA ADELE, social worker; b. Chgo., Oct. 21, 1937; d. Dean Frederick and Faye Lila (Greim) Slauson; student Moline (Ill.) Pub. Hosp. Sch. Nursing, 1955-57; BA with distinguished scholastic record, U. Wis., Madison, 1972, MSW (Fed. tng. grantee), 1973; M.O.E. Bartholomew; children: Suzanne, Christine, David. Social worker div. community services Wis. Dept. Health Social Services, Rhinelander, 1973, regional adoption coordinator, 1973-79, chief adoption and permanent planning no. region, 1979-83, asst. chief direct services and regulation no. region, 1983-84, adminstr., clin. social worker No. Family Services, Inc., 1984—; counselor, psychotherapist, public speaker, cons. in field of clin. social work. Home: 5264 Forest Ln Rt 1 Rhinelander WI 54501 Office: PO Box 237 Rhinelander WI 54501-0237

VAN BUREN, PHYLLIS EILEEN, Spanish and German language educator; b. Montevideo, Minn., June 4, 1947; d. Helge Thorfin and Alice Lillian (Johnsrud) Goulson; m. Barry Redmond Van Buren, Apr. 4, 1970; children: Priscila Victoria Princesa, Barry Redmond Barón. Student, Escuela de Bellas Artes, Guadalajara, Mex., 1968; BS, St. Cloud (Minn.) State U., 1969, MS, 1976; postgrad., Goethe Inst., Mannheim, West Germany, 1984, U. Costa Rica, 1989; PhD, The Union Inst., Cin., 1992. Instr. in Spanish Red Wing (Minn.) Pub. Schs., 1969-70; instr. in Spanish and German St. Cloud Pub. Schs., 1970-80; prof. foreign lang. edn., German and Spanish St. Cloud State U., 1975, 79—; advanced placement reader Ednl. Testing Svcs., Princeton, N.J., 1987—; translator in field; mem. Cen. State Adv. Bd. Contbr. articles to El Noticiero, Minn. Lang. Rev., Hispania; textbook reviewer. Coord. children's programs St. Cloud, 1970—; vol. ELS instr. St. Cloud Community, 1973—; reviewer St. Cloud Pub. Schs., 1985-89. Dept. Def. fellow, 1969, Goethe Inst. fellow, 1983; grantee N.W. Area Found., 1985-86, Bush Found., 1986, Fund for the Improvement of Post-secondary Edn./NEH, 1993—. Mem. AAUW (exec. bd. 1988-92, grantee Minn. Internat. AR 1992), ASCD, MLA, Am. Assn. Tchrs. Spanish and Portuguese, Am. Assn. Tchrs. German, Am. Coun. Tchg. Fgn. Langs. (tester 1989—), Minn. Coun. Tchg. Fgn. Langs. (exec. bd.), Phi Kappa Phi (pres.-elect 1991-92, pres. 1992-93), Sigma Delta Pi, Delta Kappa Gamma, Delta Phi Alpha. Republican. Lutheran. Home: 3001 County Rd # 146 Clearwater MN 55320-1405 Office: St Cloud State U 720 4th Ave S Saint Cloud MN 56301-4442

VANBURKLEO, SANDRA FRANCES, history educator; b. St. Paul, Minn., Oct. 6, 1944; d. Francis Thomas and Gladyce Bessie (Beedle) VanB.; m. Edward Martin Wise, Aug. 19, 1984.; BA in History, Hamline U., 1974; MA in History, U. Minn., 1984, PhD in History, 1988. Instr. U. Minn., Mpls., 1980-82; asst. editor Documentary History of U.S. Supreme Ct., Washington, 1982-83; asst. prof. history Wayne State U., Detroit, 1984-93, assoc. prof. history, 1994—. Bd. editors: Jour. of the Early Republic, 1989-93; bd. advisors Mag. of History, 1993—; contbr. articles to profl. jours. Mem. NOW, ACLU, AAUP, AAUW, NAACP, Am. Soc. for Legal History (bd. dirs. 1995—), Inst. Early Am. History and Culture, Soc. for Historians of Early Am. Republic, Orgn. of Am. Historians, Am. History Assn., others. Democrat. Home: 1176 Bishop Rd Grosse Pointe Park MI 48230-1423 Office: Wayne State Univ Dept of History 3094 FAB Detroit MI 48202

VAN BUSKIRK, JANET LOUISE, library director; b. Pratt, Kans., May 22, 1942; d. Lloyd Ray and Glenda Pearl (Shumway) Ellison; m. Hugh D. Van Buskirk, Dec. 8, 1972; 1 child, Landon Wayne. Chief nuclear medicine St. Josephs Rehab. Hosp., Wichita, Kans., 1962-75; dir. Towanda (Kans.) Pub. Libr., 1990-95; mem. libr. bd. Towanda Pub. Libr., 1979-88. Com. mem. Boy Scouts Am., Towanda, 1989-95; vol. Meals on Wheels, El Dorado, Kans., 1983-95; cmty. advisor Cir. High History Theme, Towanda, 1994, 95. Mem. Am. Registered Radiologic Techs., Am. Soc. Radiologic Techs., Kansas Libr. Assn. Office: Towanda Pub Libr Box 580 Towanda KS 57144

VANCE, DAVID ALVIN, management educator; b. Anchorage, Oct. 5, 1948; s. Alvin Victor and Mary V.; m. Nancy Louise Neimann; children: John Michael, Emily Suzanne. AA, Grossmont Coll., 1976; BBA, Nat. U., 1982, MBA, 1984, postgrad., 1985; postgrad., So. Ill. U., 1994—. Tech. supr. USN, San Diego, 1970-74; engr., project mgr. Wavetek Data Communications, San Diego, 1975-79; v.p. ops. Specialized Systems, Inc., San Diego, 1979-81; prin. Sunhill R&D, San Diego, 1981-84; exec. dir. Brunswick Inst. Tech., San Diego, 1985; tech. staff mem. Veda, Inc., Orlando, Fla. and San Diego, 1985-88; tng. analyst Eagle Tech., Inc., Winter Park, Fla., 1988-89; prof. mgmt. Fla. So. Coll., Orlando, 1991-94; tchr., student mgmt. doctoral program So. Ill. U., Carbondale, 1994—; prin. DA Vance & Assocs., Winter Park, 1986-94; adj. prof. mgmt. Webster U., 1991-94; vis. assoc. prof. So. Ill. U., 1991-94. Author, lectr. on mgmt. and tech. Rep. precinct committeeman, Orange County, Fla., 1988, del. state conv., 1988; chmn. svc. com. CSO, Inc., 1991; tchr. life tng. ctr. Northland Community Ch., 1991. Recipient Achievement award ACCESS, San Diego, 1980; Worthy scholar Woodrow Wilson Found., 1966, Leadership scholar Nat. U., San Diego, 1984. Mem. Am. MENSA, Ltd., Internat. Platform Assn., Acad. of Mgmt., Info. Resources Mgmt. Assn., Computer Profls. for Social Responsibility. Office: So Ill U Dept Mgmt Rehn Hall Rm 214 Carbondale IL 62901

VANCE, DEBBIE DEE, marketing executive; b. Fort Wayne, Ind., May, 1955; d. Kenneth R. and M. Irene Miller; m. Charles D. Lewis (div. 1981); children: David R., Carrie A.; m. R. Dennis Vance, 1995; children: Zachary D., Andrea D. Store activities rep. McDonald's Systems, Newport News, Va., Fort Wayne, Ind., 1978, community relations rep. Fort Wayne, Columbus, Ohio, 1979-81; regional mktg. mgr. Arby's, Inc., Ohio region, 1982-83; mktg. dir. McNeill Enterprises, Inc., Chillicothe, Ohio, 1984-86; project mgr./mktg. dept. Mid-Am. Fed., Columbus, 1987-88; dir. advt. Record Herald, Washington Court House, Ohio, 1988-91; program mgr. Hopewell Jobs for Ohio Grads., Hillsboro, Ohio, 1991-92; acct. exec. Cox. Enterprises/Dayton Daily News, 1993-94; account exec. Ohio Mag., Columbus, 1994-95; trainer regional mktg. mgrs. Arby's, Columbus, 1982-83; mktg. cons. MEI Franchises, 1984-86; mktg. dir. Xenia (Ohio) Daily Gazette. Fund raiser Ronald McDonald House, Columbus, Indpls., 1980-81; pres. Alliance for a Prosperous Downtown Washington Ct. House, 1990. Recipient Best Bets awards McDonald's Indpls. region, 1980, 81, BPW Young Careerist Yr. award, local and regional, 1990-91, Jobs for America's Graduates Phenominal Growth award 1992. Mem. Dayton Advt. Club. Methodist. Avocations: reading, bicycling, crafts. Office: Xenia Daily Gazette 37 S Detroit Xenia OH 45385

VANCE, MICHAEL CHARLES, lawyer; b. Marshalltown, Iowa, May 31, 1951; s. Randall Scott and Irma Mae (Kneeland) V.; m. Bonnie K. Becker, Jan. 1, 1995; children: Thomas Randall, Patrick Michael. BA in Polit. Sci. and Econs., U. Iowa, 1973, JD with distinction, 1976. Bar: Iowa 1976, U.S Dist. Ct. (so. dist.) Iowa 1976, U.S. Tax Ct. 1991. Sole practice Mt. Pleasant, Iowa, 1976—; atty. City of Wayland, Iowa, 1976—; instr. bus. law Iowa Wesleyan Coll., Mt. Pleasant, 1977-78; asst. atty. Henry County, Mt. Pleasant, 1979—. Mem., bd. dirs. Community Mental Health of Henry, Louisa and Jefferson Counties, Mt. Pleasant, 1977-82; chairperson Henry County Dems., Mt. Pleasant, 1978-83; pres. Mt. Pleasant Sesquicentennial Assn., 1984-86, St. Alphonsus Ch. Parish Council (pres. 1983-85), Mt. Pleasant, 1985— (trustee). Mem. ABA, Iowa Bar Assn. (bd. govs. 1996—), Henry County Bar Assn. (sec.-treas. 1977-78, v.p. 1978-79, pres. 1979-80, 88-91), Iowa Trial Lawyers Assn., Iowa Conf. Bar Assn. Presidents (bd. dirs. 1979-81), Mt. Pleasant C. of C. (bd. dirs. 1991-93, named Citizen of Yr. 1985), Mt. Pleasant Jaycees (bd. dirs. 1978-83), Rotary, KC, Omicron Delta Kappa, Omicron Delta Epsilon. Roman Catholic. Home: 19 Bittersweet Cir Westwood Mount Pleasant IA 52641-0469 Office: PO Box 469 101 N Jefferson St Mount Pleasant IA 52641-2039

VAN CLEAVE, WILLIAM ROBERT, international relations educator; b. Kansas City, Mo., Aug. 27, 1935; s. Earl Jr. and Georgiana (Offutt) Van C.; children: William Robert II, Cynthia Kay. B.A. in Polit. Sci. summa cum laude, Calif. State U., Long Beach, 1962; M.A. in Govt. and Internat. Relations, Claremont (Calif.) Grad. Sch., 1964, Ph.D., 1966. Mem. faculty U. So. Calif., 1967-87, prof. internat. rels., 1974-87, dir. def. and strategic studies ctr., 1971-87; prof., dept. head, dir. Ctr. for Def. and Strategic Studies Southwest Mo. State U., 1987—; sr. rsch. fellow Hoover Instn. Stanford U., 1981—; chmn. Strategic Alternatives Team, 1977-90; acting chmn. Pres.'s Gen. Adv. Com. on Arms Control, 1981-82; spl. asst. Office Sec. Def., mem. Strategic Arms Limitation Talks (SALT) delegation, 1969-71; mem. B team on Nat. Intelligence Estimates, 1976; mem. exec. panel, bd. dirs. Com. Present Danger, 1980-93; dir. transition team Dept. Def., 1980-81; sr. nat. security advisor to Ronald Reagan, 1979-80; mem. nat. security affairs adv.

council Republican Nat. Com., 1979—; research council Fgn. Policy Research Inst., Inst. Fgn. Policy Analysis; co-dir. Ann. Internat. Security Summer Seminar, Fed. Republic Germany; trustee Am. com. Internat. Inst. Strategic Studies, 1980—; vis. prof. U.S. Army Advanced Russian Inst., Garmisch, Fed. Republic Germany, 1978-79; chmn. adv. bd. Internat. Security Coun., 1991—; cons. in field, mem. numerous govt. adv. coms. Co-author: Strategic Options for the Early Eighties: What Can Be Done?, 1979, Tactical Nuclear Weapons, 1978, Nuclear Weapons, Policies, and the Test Ban Issue, 1987; author: Fortress USSR, 1986; bd. editors: Global Affairs. Co-chmn. Scholars for Reagan, 1984; mem. exec. coun., dir. for NCAA rels. Haka Bowl, NCAA Postseason Football Bowl. Recipient Freedom Found. award, 1976, Outstanding Contbn. award Air War Coll., 1979, award teaching excellence U. So. Calif., 1980, 86; named Outstanding Prof. U. So. Calif., 1977, Disting. Alumnus Claremont Colls., 1978; Woodrow Wilson fellow, 1962, NDEA fellow, 1963-65. Mem. Internat. Inst. Strategic Studies (U.S. com.). Home: 8226 Panther Hollow Rogersville MO 65742-9126 Office: Ctr for Def and Strategic Studies Southwest Mo State U Springfield MO 65804-0095

VAN CLEVE, SANDRA ROSE, retired nursing educator; b. Olney, Ill., Aug. 31, 1938; d. Muriel William and Marjorie May (Houchin) Cutshall; m. Charles Chadwick, June 14, 1958 (dec. Mar. 1988); children: Rosemarie Finley, Gilbert, Kent. Diploma, Union Hosp. Sch. Nursing, 1960; BA, Ea. Ill. U., 1974; MS in Edn., So. Ill. U., 1980. RN, Ill. Med./surg. staff nurse Good Samaritan Hosp., Mt. Vernon, Ill., 1960-61; staff nurse obstetrics Meml. Hosp., Carbondale, Ill., 1961-62; surg. staff nurse St. Mary's Hosp., Centraila, Ill., 1963-64; staff nurse obstetrics St. Mary's Hosp., Centralia, Ill., 1969-70; nursing asst. instr. Centralia Jr. Coll., 1964-65; practical nursing instr. Mt. Vernon C.C., 1965-69; practical nursing instr. Rend Lake Coll., Ina, Ill., 1970-94, ret., 1994; textbook reviewer W. B. Saunders Co., Orlando, Fla., 1990. Pres. Centralia Bus. and Profl. Woman's Club, 1990-91; mem. Centralia Little Theater Players, Centralia Choral Soc. Recipient Outstanding Faculty award Rend Lake Coll. Found., 1986, Outstanding Community Coll. Faculty Mem. award Ill. Community Coll. Trustees Assn., 1986. Mem. ANA, AAUW, Ill. Nurses Assn. (bd. dirs. 10th dist. 1975-84), Delta Kappa Gamma. Democrat. Methodist. Home: 18 Crestview Dr PO Box 309 Irvington IL 62848

VAN CURA, JOYCE BENNETT, librarian; b. Madison, Wis., Mar. 25, 1944; d. Ralph Eugene and Florence Marie (Cramer) Bennett; m. E. Jay Van Cura, July 5, 1986. BA in Liberal Arts (scholar), Bradley U., 1966; MLS, U. Ill., 1971. Library asst. rsch. library Caterpillar Tractor Co., Peoria, Ill., 1966-67; reference librarian, instr. library tech. Ill. Central Coll., East Peoria, 1967-73; asst. prof. Sangamon State U. (U. Ill.-Springfield), Springfield, Ill., 1973-80, assoc. prof., 1980-86; head library ref. and info. svcs. dept. Ill. Inst. Tech., 1987-90; dir. Learning Resources Ctr. Morton Coll., 1990—; convenor Coun. II, Ill. Clearinghouse for Acad. Library Instrn., 1978; presentor 7th Ann. Conf. Acad. Library Instrn., 1977, Nat. Women's Studies Assn., 1983, others; participant Gt. Lakes Women's Studies Summer Inst., 1981, Nat. Inst. Leadership Devel. seminar, 1995. Dem. precinct Committeewoman, 1982-85 . Pres., Springfield chpt. NOW, 1978-79. Ill. state scholar, 1962-66; recipient Am. Legion citizenship award, 1962; cert. of recognition Ill. Bicentennial Commn., 1974; invited Susan B. Anthony luncheon, 1978, 79, vice-moderator Fourth Presbyn. Women, 1989-90; elder Riverside (Ill.) Presbyn. Ch., 1992—; mem. adv. bd. Suburban Libr. System, 1992-94, Nat. Commn. Learning Resources; v.p. membership Riverside chpt. Lyric Opera Chgo., 1994-96; active Riverside (Ill.) Arts Ctr. Mem. ALA, Assn. Coll. and Rsch. Librs., Libr. Adminstrn. and Mgmt. Assn. (mem. reference and adult svcs. divsn.), Libr. Info. and Tech. Assn., Nat. Assn. Women in C.C., Ill. Library Assn. (presentor 1984) Ill. Assn. Coll. and Rsch. Libraries (bibliog. instrn. com.), Spl. Libraries Assn., No. Ill. Learning Resources Consortium Bd., Am. Mgmt. Assn., Women in Mgmt., AAUW (chmn. standing com. on women Springfield br., mem. com. on women Ill. state divsn., bd. dirs. Riverside br., 1992-94), Nat. Women's Studies Assn. (presentor 1983, 84, 85), No. Ill. Learning Resources Coop. (del. 1990—), Springfield Art Assn., Nat. Trust Historic Preservation, Beta Phi Mu. Reviewer Libr. Jour., Am. Reference Books Ann. Contbr. article in field to publ. Home: 181 Scottswood Rd Riverside IL 60546-2221 Office: Morton Coll Learning Resources Ctr 3801 S Central Ave Chicago IL 60650-4306

VANDAMENT, WILLIAM EUGENE, academic administrator, educator; b. Hannibal, Mo., Sept. 6, 1931; s. Alva E. and Ruth Alice (Mahood) V.; m. Margery Vandament, Feb. 2, 1952; children: Jane Louise, Lisa Ann. BA, Quincy Coll., 1952; MS, So. Ill. U., 1953; MS in Psychology, U. Mass., 1963, PhD, 1964. Psychologist Bacon Clinic, Racine, Wis., 1954-61; NDEA fellow U. Mass., Amherst, 1961-64; asst. prof. SUNY, Binghamton, 1964-69, univ. examiner and dir. instl. research, 1969-73, asst. v.p. planning, instl. research, 1972-76; exec. asst. to pres., dir. budget and resources Ohio State U., Columbus, 1976-79, v.p. fin. and planning, 1979-81; sr. v.p. adminstrn. NYU, N.Y.C., 1981-83; provost, vice chancellor acad. affairs Calif. State U. System, Long Beach, 1983-87; Trustees prof. Calif. State U., Fullerton, 1987-92; pres. No. Mich. U., 1991—. Contbr. articles to psychol. jours. and books on higher edn. Home: 1440 Center St Marquette MI 49855-1625 Office: Northern Michigan U 1401 Presque Isle Ave Marquette MI 49855-5300

VANDEGRIFF, THOMAS HERMAN, employee benefits consultant; b. Zanesville, Ohio, Feb. 6, 1949; s. Charles William and Martha Helen (Vickroy) V.; m. Katrina Lee Watson, Feb. 13, 1982; children: Samantha, Justin, Danielle. BA in Econs., Ohio U., 1971. CLU, Chartered Fin. Cons. Agt. Northwestern Mut. Life., Zanesville, 1971—; co-owner The Forker Co., Zanesville, 1988—. Treas. Muskingum Alcoholism Coun., Zanesville, 1989—; bd. dirs. Zanesville Jaycees, 1973-76; mem. Muskingum County Republican Policy Com., Zanesville. Mem. Zanesville C. of C., Nat. Assn. Life Underwriters, Am. Soc. CLU's, Zanesville Assn. Life Underwriters (pres. 1979, 84, bd. dirs.), Million Dollar Roundtable, Rotary, Masons, Elks. Lutheran. Home: 3295 Buena Vista Cir Zanesville OH 43701-1202 Office: The Forker Co 964 Grove Rd Zanesville OH 43701-1337

VAN DELLEN, CHESTER, JR., environmental consultant, real estate appraiser; b. Grand Rapids, Mich., Nov. 14, 1949; s. Chester and Anne J. (Brouwer) Van D.; m. Judy Ann Tingle, Apr. 13, 1973; children: Matthew Tate, Mark John. Ptnr. C. Van Dellan Oil Co., Cadillac, Mich., 1972-80; pres. PRC Oil & Gas Co., Cadillac, 1980-84, Hope Energy Corp., Cadillac, 1984-90, Cable Classified Corp., Cadillac, 1987-89. Author: Handbook of Common Oil & Gas Terms, 1987. Sgt. U.S. Army, 1969-71, Vietnam. Decorated Bronze Star, Air medal, Commendation fo Heroism; named Outstanding Young Man of Yr. Jaycees, Cadillac, 1978, Lion of Yr. Cadillac Lions Club, 1978-79; recipient Presidents award Cadillac Lions Club, 1978-79, Govs. award Lions Dist. 11-E, 1979. Mem. ASTM (E-50 com.), Nat. Assn. of Environmental Risk Auditors, Nat. Assn. of Realtors, Mich. Assn. of Realtors, Grand Rapid Assn. of Realtors. Republican. Home: 6218 Acropolis Dr SE Grand Rapids MI 49546-7102 Office: Property Profiles Inc 6218 Acropolis Dr SE Grand Rapids MI 49546-7102

VAN DELLEN, H. TODD, state legislator; b. Apr. 24, 1964; m. Dana Lynn; three children. BBA, U. N.D.; JD, U. Minn. Minn. State rep. Dist. 34B, 1993—; corp. counsel EBP Health Plans, Inc. Named Best First Term Mem., State House of Reps., Politics in Minn. newsletter. Home: 14615 43rd Ave N Plymouth MN 55446-2786*

VAN DE MARK, MICHAEL ROY, chemistry educator; b. Pigeon, Mich., May 21, 1950; s. Roy Donald and Alice (Gremel) Van De M.; m. Suzan Elaine Yelek, Nov. 26, 1976; children: Audra, Eric. BS, Saginaw Valley State U., 1972; PhD, Tex. A&M U., 1976. Instr. Blinn Jr. Coll., Bryan, Tex., 1975-76; postdoctoral fellow Colo. State U., 1976-77, U. Minn., Mpls., 1977-78; asst. prof. U. Miami, Coral Gables, 1978-83, assoc. prof., 1983-86; assoc. prof. U. Mo., Rolla, 1986—; dir. Rolla Coatings Inst. U. Mo., 1992—, dir. Rolla Coatings and Polymer Sci. program, 1986—; pres. Rolla Coatings Inc. Contbr. articles to profl. jours. Patentee stripper composition for removal of protective coatings, water borne stripper for protective coatings. Bd. dirs. Mo. Enterprise, Rolla, 1987—. Recipient Westinghouse award, 1984, 3d pl. Best Paper award Fedn. of Coatings, 1991. Mem. Am. Chem. Soc. (pres. Mid-Mo. sect.), Electrochem. Soc., Coatings Fedn. Socs., St. Louis Coatings Tech. Soc. (chmn. tech. com. 1989-92, Merit award 1992-93), Sigma Xi, Phi Lambda Upsilon. Home: RR 4 Box 314A Rolla MO 65401-9319

VANDEMARK, MICHELLE VOLIN, critical care, neuroscience nurse; b. Sioux Falls, S.D., Feb. 14, 1962; d. Verlynne V. and Suzanne (Cronin) Volin; m. Richard E. VanDemark, June 5, 1982; children: Andrew Porter, Hannah Elizabeth. BA in Biology, Lake Forest (Ill.) Coll., 1984; BSN, Northwestern U., Chgo., 1986; MS in Nursing, Loyola U., Chgo., 1990. RN, Ill., S.D.; cert. neurosci. nursing, CNRN, ACLS. Staff nurse neurosci. unit Evanston Hosp., Ill., 1986-90, staff nurse intensive care unit, 1990-93; neurosci. clin. nurse specialist Sioux Valley Hosp., Sioux Falls, S.D., 1995—. Mem. Am. Assn. Neurosci. Nurses (pres. Gt. Plains chpt. 1995—), Sigma Theta Tau, Alpha Sigma Nu.

VAN DEMARK, RUTH ELAINE, lawyer; b. Santa Fe, N. Mex., May 16, 1944; d. Robert Eugene and Bertha Marie (Thompson) Van D.; m. Leland Wilkinson, June 23, 1967; children: Anne Marie, Caroline Cook. AB, Vassar Coll., 1966; MTS, Harvard U., 1969; JD with honors, U. Conn., 1976. Bar: Conn. 1976, U.S. Dist. Ct. Conn. 1976, Ill. 1977, U.S. Dist. Ct. (no. dist.) Ill. 1977, U.S. Supreme Ct. 1983, U.S. Ct. Appeals (7th cir.) 1984. Instr. legal research and writing Loyola U. Sch. Law, Chgo., 1976-79; assoc. Wildman, Harrold, Allen & Dixon, Chgo., 1977-84, ptnr., 1985-94; prin. Law Offices of Ruth E. Van Demark, Chgo., 1995—; bd. dirs., sec. Systat, Inc., Evanston, Ill., 1984-94; mem. Ill. Supreme Ct. Rules com., 1996—. Assoc. editor Conn. Law Rev., 1975-76. Mem. adv. bd. Horizon Hospice, Chgo., 1978—; del.-at-large White House Conf. on Families, Los Angeles, 1980; mem. adv. bd. YWCA Battered Women's Shelter, Evanston, Ill., 1982-86; mem. alumni coun. Harvard Divinity Sch., 1988-91; vol. atty. Pro Bono Advocates, Chgo., 1982-92, bd. dirs. 1993—, chair devel. com., 1993; bd. dirs. Friends of Pro Bono Advocates Orgn., 1987-89, New Voice Prodns., 1984-86, Byrne Piven Theater Workshop, 1987-90; founder, bd. dirs. Friends of Battered Women and their Children, 1986-87; chair 175th Reunion Fund Harvard U. Div. Sch., 1992. Mem. ABA, Ill. Bar Assn., Conn. Bar Assn., Chgo. Bar Assn., Appellate Lawyers Assn. Ill. (bd. dirs. 1985-87, treas. 1989-90, sec. 1990-91, v.p. 1991-92, pres. 1992-93), Women's Bar Assn. Ill., Jr. League Evanston (chair State Pub. Affairs Com. 1987-88, Vol. of Yr. 1983-84). Clubs: Chgo. Vassar (pres. 1979-81), Cosmopolitan (N.Y.C.). Home: 1127 Asbury Ave Evanston IL 60202-1136

VAN DEN AKKER, JOHANNES ARCHIBALD, physicist; b. L.A., Dec. 5, 1904; s. John and Mabel (Freebairn) Van den A.; m. Adelaide H. Carrier, June 20, 1930 (dec. Jan. 1955); 1 child, Valerie; m. Carmen L. Haberman, June 9, 1958 (dec. Mar. 1989); m. Margaret Koller, Jan. 20, 1990. BS in Physics/Engring., Calif. Inst. Tech., 1926, PhD in Physics, 1931. Instr. Washington U., St. Louis, 1930-34; prof. physics Inst. Paper Chemistry, Appleton, Wis., 1935-70; cons. Am. Can Co., Neenah, Wis., 1971-82, James River Corp., Neenah, 1982-85, Appleton, Wis., 1985—; lectr. short courses TAPPI, Atlanta. Co-author 10 books; contbr. Encyclopedia of Physics, 1st and 2d edit. and articles to physics and tech. jours. Named to Paper Industry Hall of Fame, 1995; sr. Fulbright scholar U. Manchester, Eng., 1961-62. Fellow AAAS, TAPPI (gold medal 1968), Am. Phys. Soc.; mem. Am. Inst. Physics, Optical Soc. Am., Am. Assn. Physics Tchrs., Sigma Xi, Tau Beta Pi, Phi Gamma Delta. Home: 1101 E Glendale Ave Appleton WI 54911-3144

VAN DEN BOOM, WAYNE JEROME, industrial engineer; b. Bay City, Mich., Nov. 20, 1953; s. Raymond Francis and Iva Jean (Coupie) Van Den Boom; m. Esperanza Hope Hernandez, Nov. 21, 1981; children: Sean David, Kristine Ashley. B in Indsl. Engring., GM Inst., 1976; MA, Central Mich. U., 1980. Supr. prodn. Chevrolet Co., Bay City, Mich., 1976-78, indsl. engr., 1978-80; engr. material handling Chevrolet Co., Adrian, Mich., 1980-83; sr. project engr. packaging CPC Hdqrs., Warren, Mich., 1983-89, sr. project engr. vehicle program support, 1989-91; mgr. Outside Supplier and Allied Packaging Group, Warren, Mich., 1991-92, NEO Containerization-Gen. Assembly Group, Pontiac, Mich., 1992—. Home: 46347 Franks Ln Shelby Township MI 48315-5309 Office: NAO Containerization MC 483 050 479 One Pontiac Plz Pontiac MI 48340

VANDENBROUCKE, RUSSELL JAMES, theatre director; b. Chgo., Aug. 16, 1948; s. Arthur C. Sr. and Ardelle (Barker) V.; m. Mary Allison Dilg, Sept. 7, 1974; children: Aynsley Louise, Justin Arthur. BA, U. Ill., 1970; MA, U. Warwick, Coventry, Eng., 1975; MFA in Drama, Yale U., 1977, DFA in Drama, 1978. Asst. literary mgr. Yale Repertory Theatre, New Haven, 1977-78; lit. mgr., dramaturg Mark Taper Forum, Los Angeles, 1978-85; assoc. producing dir. Repertory Theatre St. Louis, 1985-87; artistic dir. Northlight Theatre, Evanston, Ill., 1987—; vis. prof. Yale U., 1978, La. State U., 1981, U. Calif.-San Diego, 1983, Middlebury Coll., 1985, Washington U., 1986; adj. assoc. prof. Northwestern U., 1987—; on site evaluator, peer panelist Nat. Endowment for Arts, Washington, 1981—. Author: Truths the Hand Can Tough: The Theatre of Athol Fugard, 1985; adapted play Eleanor: In Her Own Words (for TV), 1985 (Emmy award 1986) (dir. for stage 1990), Los Alamos Revisted (for stage and radio), 1984, 87, Holiday Memories (from Truman Capote), 1991, Atomic Bombers (radio), 1995; adapted, stage dir. Feiffer's America, 1988, Eleanor: In Her Own Words, 1990; adapted An Enemy of the People, 1991; stage dir. Lucky Lindy, Love Letters in Blue Paper, 84 Charing Cross Road, Three Women Talking (also radio), Smoke on the Mountain, The White Rose, Betrayal, My Other Heart, Later Life, Hedda Gabler, Bubbe Meuses, Valley Song; contbr. articles to mags. and newspapers. Recipient L.A. Drama Critics Cir. award, 1984, Spl. Actors Equity Assn. award, 1990; Fulbright sr. scholar, Australia, 1996. Office: Northlight Theatre 600 Davis St Evanston IL 60201-4419

VANDER AARDE, STANLEY BERNARD, retired otolaryngologist; b. Orange City, Iowa, Sept. 26, 1931; s. Bernard John and Christina (Luchtenberg) Vander A.; m. Agnes Darlene De Beer, June 19, 1956; children: Paul, David, Debra, Mary. BA, Hope Coll., 1953; MD, Northwestern U., 1957. Diplomate Am. Bd. Otolaryngology. Intern Cook County Hosp., Chgo., 1957-59; resident in otolaryngology Northwestern U. Hosp., Chgo., 1966-70; mem. staff Mary Lott Lyles Hosp., Madanapalle, India, 1961-66, 71-87; mem. staff Affiliated Med. Clinic, Willmar, Minn., 1987-95, ret., 1995. Served to capt., USAF, 1959-60. Fellow ACS, Am. Bd. Otolaryngology, Am. Acad. Otolaryngology. Republican. Mem. Reformed Church in America. Home: 708 2nd St SE # 112 Orange City IA 51041-2156 Office: Affiliated Med Clinic 101 Willmar Ave SW Willmar MN 56201-3556

VANDERBILT, VERN CROWIN, JR., consulting engineer; b. Indpls., Mar. 29, 1920; s. Vern Corwin and E. Lyne (Connette) V.; m. Gwen C. Curry, Aug. 22, 1942; children: Vern C. III, Burton Lee, Jeffry Neal. BSME, Purdue U., 1942, MS in Aerospace Engring., 1947, PhD in Elec. Engring., 1954. Registered profl. engr. Ind. Assoc. prof. aircraft power plants Purdue U., West Lafayette, Ind., 1946-52; engring. cons., 1952-54; rsch. egnr. GE Elec. Divsn., Syracuse, N.Y., 1954-55; chief rsch. engr. and head rsch. divsn. Perfect Cir. Corp., Hagerstown, Ind., 1956-62, mgr. elecs. divsn., 1962-64; pres., CEO Dynamic Precision Controls, Hagerstown, Ind., 1964-75; owner Vanderbilt Assocs., Hagerstown, Ind., 1975—; adj. prof. Purdue U., Richmond, 1975—. Contbr. articles to profl. jours.; Inventor in field. Coun. v.p. Old Trails coun. Boy Scouts Am., Richmond, Ind., 1958; mem. sch. bd. Nettle Creek Sch. Corp., Hagerstown, 1974-78; mem. adv. bd. Earlham Coll. Inst. Exec. Growth, Richmond, 1964-74, Purdue Programs Eastern Ind., Richmond, 1972-75. Capt. USAF, 1942-46. Mem. NSPE (life), IEEE (life), Am. Soc. Metals (life), Instrument Soc. Am. (life), Ind. Soc. Profl. Engrs. (pres. 1978-79), Soc. Automotive Engrs. (life), Rotary (dist. gov. 1982-83), Sigma Xi, Tau Beta Pi, Eta Kappa Nu, Gamma Alpha Rho. Republican. Home: 9278 Lacy Rd Hagerstown IN 47346 Office: Vanderbilt Assocs PO Box 31 Hagerstown IN 47346

VAN DER BOSCH, SUSAN HARTNETT, real estate broker; b. St. Louis, Mar. 19, 1935; d. Leo Joseph and Mary Julia (O'Neill) Hartnett; m. George Arthur Van Der Bosch, Sept. 10, 1955; children: Mary Jo Van Der Bosch Schauer, Anne, Leo, Ellen, George Jr. Student, Barat Coll., 1953-55. Lic. real estate salesman, real estate broker, Grad Realtor's Inst.; cert. residential specialist. Assoc. broker Covered Bridge Realty, Long Grove, Ill., 1980-83, McKee Real Estate, Long Grove, Ill., 1983—; office mgr. McKee br. office Fields of Long Grove, 1986. Trustee Vernon Pub. Libr., Prairie View, Ill., 1978-84; pres. Villagers, Long Grove, 1986-87; bd. dirs. Citizens' Transp. Coalition, 1988—; dir. Long Grove Open Space Found., 1994—; Long Grove Village rep. Ela Area YMCA Steering Com., 1996—. Mem. N.W. Suburban Bd. Realtors, Barrington Bd. Realtors, North Shore Bd. Realtors, Realtors Inst., Realtors Mktg. Inst., Biohome (bd. dirs. 1989—). Home: Box 3253 RFD Long Grove IL 60047 Office: McKee Real Estate 145 N Old Mchenry Rd Long Grove IL 60047-8860

VANDER GOOT, MARY ELIZABETH, psychologist, educator; b. Orange City, Iowa, Feb. 5, 1947. AB, Calvin Coll., 1968; MA, PhD, Princeton U., 1971. Lic. psychologist, Mich., marriage and family therapist, Mich.; cert. addictions counselor, Mich.; diplomate Am. Bd. Psychotherapy, Am. Bd. Med. Psychotherapists. Psychologist Bd. Edn. for the Borough of North York, Toronto, Ont., Can., 1971-76; prof. psychology Calvin Coll., Grand Rapids, Mich., 1976-87; pvt. practice psychology Grand Rapids, 1978—. Author: A Life Planning Guide for Women, 1982, Piaget as a Visionary Thinker, 1985, Narrating Psychology, 1987, Healthy Emotions, 1987. Bd. dirs. Hope Network, Grand Rapids. Mem. Am. Psychol. Assn., Am. Soc. Clin. Hypnosis. Office: 4477 Cascade Rd SE Grand Rapids MI 49546-3632

VANDERGRAFF, DONNA JEAN, dietitian; b. Milw., Oct. 24, 1956; d. Wayne Eugene and Geraldine Louise (Brever) Zabler; m. Jess Lee Vandergraff, Oct. 11, 1980; children: Daniel Joseph, Joshua David. BS in Dietetics with distinction, Purdue U., 1978, MS in Nutrition, 1990. Registered dietitian. Clin. dietitian Logansport (Ind.) State Hosp., 1979-81, Ind. Vets.' Home, Lafayette, Ind., 1981-84; pvt. practice dietitian West Lafayette, Ind., 1984-90; rsch. asst. foods and nutrition Purdue U., West Lafayette, 1988-90, ext. foods and nutrition asst., 1990-93; acting coord. Expanded Food and Nutrition Edn. Program Purdue U.Food and Nutrition Edn. Program, West Lafayette, 1993-94, coord. Expanded Food and Nutrition Edn. Program, 1994—; cons. dietitian Woodland Manor Nursing Ctr., Attica, Ind., 1985-88; presenter in field. Author: (brochures) Food, Dietary Fiber and You, 1989, Diabetes, Food and You, 1990; co-author: Have a Healthy Baby, 1991, Money Management, 1993. Mem. com. bd. western region Am. Heart Assn., Lafayette, 1985-88; youth advisor Covenant Presbyn. Ch., West Lafayette, 1980-89; active Interagy. Coun. Community Health Edn., Lafayette, 1984-88; mem. Concerned Women for Am., 1985—; pub. rels. com. Greater Lafayette and Tippecanoe County Interagy. Coun. for Community Health Edn., 1984-85, mem. health at worksite com., 1985; weight reduction group leader West Lafayette Parks and Recreation Dept., 1985, YWCA, 1985. Named Outstanding Young Woman of Am., 1984, 86; Lute Troutt fellow Ind. Dietetic Assn., 1989; recipient Mary Hebenstreit Meml. award Ind. Dietetic Assn., 1988; named Recognized Young Dietitian of Yr., Ind. Dietetic Assn., 1987. Mem. APHA, Nat. Perinatal Assn., Am. Dietetic Assn., Soc. for Nutrition Edn., Ind. Dietetic Assn. (chmn. coun. on practice 1987, nominating chmn. 1987-88, continuing edn. chmn. 1988-91, sec. 1991-93), Western Ind. Dist. Dietetic Assn. (co-chmn. cmty. dietetics, chmn. pub. rels., pres. 1983-84, spkrs. bur. chmn. 1985-87, cmty. dietetics chmn. 1987-92, career guidance 1994—), Healthy Mothers, Health Babies Coalition (bd. dirs., breastfeeding task force), Purdue Alumni Assn., Gamma Phi Beta, Gamma Sigma Delta, Kappa Omicron Nu. Republican. Presbyterian. Home: 854 N Salisbury St West Lafayette IN 47906-2764 Office: Purdue Univ Dept Foods and Nutrition 1264 Stone Hall West Lafayette IN 47907-1264

VANDER KOOI, BENJAMIN, JR., lawyer; b. Luverne, Minn., Mar. 3, 1953; s. Benjamin Sr. and Kathryn Cornelia (Kooiman) V K.; m. Debrah K. Ver Hoeven, June 20, 1975; children: William James, Katrina Mae. BA, Calvin Coll., 1975; JD, U. Minn., 1978. Bar: Minn. 1978, U.S. Dist. Ct. Minn. 1979, U.S. Ct. Appeals (8th cir.) 1981. Law clerk Smith, Juster, Feikema, Chartered, Mpls., 1977-78; pvt. practice Luverne, 1978—; city atty. City of Edgerton, Minn., 1982—; pres. 13th Dist. Bar Assn., Luverne, 1986-87; mem. Judicial Merit Adv. Com., St. Paul, Minn., 1987, 89-90. Chair Rock County Dem.-Farmer Labor Party, Luverne, 1980—; pres. Bethesda Christian Counseling Midwest, Inc., Sioux Falls, S.D., 1992-96; trustee Candidate Adv. Coun., St. Paul, 1993—; mem. bd. govs. U. Minn. Health Sys., Mpls., 1994—. Mem. Minn. State Bar Assn. (atty.-coach mock trial program 1990—), Minn. Citizens for Arts (trustee, pres. 1988—), Minn. State Arts Bd. (vice chair 1989-91), Luverne Rotary (pres. 1986-87). Presbyterian. Office: Vander Kooi Law Offices PA 127 E Main PO Box 746 Luverne MN 56156

VANDERLAAN, RICHARD B., marketing company executive; b. Grand Rapids, Mich., Sept. 2, 1931; s. Sieger B. and Helen (Kerr) V.; cert. liberal arts Grand Rapids Jr. Coll., 1952; cert. mech. engring. U. Mich., 1955; cert. indsl. engring. Mich. State U., 1960; cert. Harvard Bus. Sch., 1970; m. Sally E. Conroy, Mar. 26, 1982; children: Sheryl Vanderlaan, Pamella Vanderlaan DeVos, Brenda Vanderlaan Thompson. Tool engr. Four Square Mfg. Co., Grand Rapids, 1950-60; sales engr. Ametek, Lansdale, Pa., 1960-63; br. mgr. J.N. Fauver Co., Grand Rapids, 1964-68; v.p. Fauver Co. subs. Sun Oil Co., Grand Rapids 1968-76, exec. v.p., 1976-80; pres. House of Printers, Inc., 1980-82, also dir.; pres. Richard Vanderlaan Assocs., 1982—. Named eagle scout Boy Scouts Am. Mem. Mfrs. Agts. Nat. Assn., Soc. Automotive Engrs. Republican. Clubs: Birmingham Country, Oakland Hills Country, Economic of Detroit, Detroit Athletic. Avocations: golf, tennis. Office: 22157 Metamora Ln Franklin MI 48025-3609

VAN DER LINDEN, JOHN EDWARD, newspaper broker, consultant; b. Des Moines, Iowa, Aug. 8, 1917; s. John and Kathleen Pomeroy (Gaylord) van der L.; m. Marjorie Rose Wetherbee, Nov. 27, 1948; children: Peter J., Dirk J., Thomas J. BS, Iowa State U., Ames, 1940. Mgr. van der Linden Advt., Ames, 1935-36; farm editor Scott County Tribune, Walcott, Iowa, 1937; reporter Mason City (Iowa) Globe-Gazette, 1940-41; dir. expansion Am. Legion Iowa, Des Moines, 1946-47; editor Marshall (Minn.) Messenger, 1947-48, Northwood (Iowa) Anchor, 1948-60; editor, pub. Sibley (Iowa) Gazette-Tribune, 1960-77; pres. N.W. Pub., Inc., Spirit Lake, Iowa, 1977—; bd. dirs. Nebr.-Iowa Kiwanis Found., Ames.; sec. N.W. Iowa Peach, Inc., Sibley, 1966-87. Editor: (book) Iowa Legion Handbook, 1947, (mag.) Dairymen's Digest, 1970-91. Bd. dirs. Spirit Lake Kiwanis Club, 1984—; lt. gov. Kiwanis Nebr.-Iowa Dist., Spirit Lake, 1980-81; Dem. cand. for Iowa State Senate, 1980; county chmn. Osceola County Dem. Com., Sibley, 1978-80; county ctrl. com. Dickinson County Dem. Com., Spirit Lake, 1980-96; pres. Iowa Sch. Bd. Assn., Des Moines, 1965-66. Lt. col. U.S. Army, 1941-46, PTO. Apptd. to State Ednl. TV Bd. by Gov. of Iowa, Des Moines, 1967-76, State Bd. Pub. Instrn. by Gov. of Iowa, Des Moines, 1970-82; named Disting. Lt. Gov. by N.E. Iowa Kiwanis, Spirit Lake, 1981. Mem. Iowa Newspaper Assn. (Master Editor-Pub. award 1975), Minn. Newspaper Assn., Res. Officers Assn. (50 yr. mem.), Kiwanis, Shriners, Masons, Am. Legion, VFW, Sierra Club. Methodist. Office: Northwest Pub Inc PO Box 275 Spirit Lake IA 51360-0275

VANDER LOOP, WILLIAM N., state legislator; b. Dec. 6, 1932. Grad. h.s. Former alderman City of Kaukauna; former pres. Kaukauna City Coun.; Wis. state assemblyman dist. 5, 1990—; dir. Kaukauna Credit Union. Address: 1908 Parkwood Dr Kaukauna WI 54130*

VAN DER MARCK, JAN, art historian; b. Roermond, The Netherlands, Aug. 19, 1929; s. Everard and Anny (Finken) van der M.; m. Ingeborg Lachmann, Apr. 27, 1961 (dec. Dec. 1988); m. Sheila Stamell, May 24, 1990. BA, U. Nijmegen, The Netherlands, 1952, MA, 1954, PhD in Art History, 1956; postgrad., U. Utrecht, The Netherlands, 1956-57, Columbia U., 1957-59. Curator Gemeentemuseum, Arnhem, The Netherlands, 1959-61; asst. dir. fine arts Seattle World's Fair, 1961-62; curator Walker Art Center, Mpls., 1963-67; dir. Mus. Contemporary Art, Chgo., 1967-70; assoc. prof. art history U. Wash., 1972-74; dir. Dartmouth Coll. Mus. and Galleries, 1974-80, Center for Fine Arts, Miami, 1980-85; curator 20th century art, chief curator Detroit Inst. Arts, 1986-95. Author: Romantische Boekillustratie in Belgie, 1956, George Segal, 1975, Arman, 1984, Bernar Venet, 1988, Decorated Bindings, 1996; contbr. articles to art jours., essays to catalogues. Decorated chevalier Order Arts and Letters; Netherlands Orgn. Pure Rsch. fellow, 1954-55, Rockefeller Found. fellow, 1957-59, Aspen Inst. fellow, 1974, 94; vis. sr. fellow Ctr. for Advanced Study in Visual Arts, Washington, 1986. Mem. Internat. Art Critics Assn., Internat. Coun. Museums.

VANDER MYDE, FRANCES See CECIL, FRANCES

VANDER PAS, WILLIAM T., sales executive; b. Appleton, Wis., Mar. 29, 1962; s. James Anthony and Elizabeth Jane (Poppe) V.P.; m. Lori Lee Kunstman, Dec. 29, 1983; children: Nathan William, Adam Zachary. BSEE, Milw. Sch. Engring., 1984. Engr. in tng., Wis. Field svc. engr. Louis Allis-Drs. & Sys., New Berlin, Wis., 1984-85; commissioning engr. ASEA Indsl. Sys., New Berlin, 1985-88; sr. industry specialist Allen-Bradley Drs. & Sys., Mequon, Wis., 1988-95; regional mgr. Eurotherm Drs., Reston, Va., 1995—. Pres. Lake Erin Estates Homeowners Assn., Erin, Wis., 1995-96. Mem. IEEE, Converting Equipment Mfrs. Assn. (corp. rep. 1991—). Home: 7463 Ireland Dr Hartford WI 53027 Office: Eurotherm Drs 7463 Ireland Dr Hartford WI 53027

VANDERPOOL, WARD MELVIN, management and marketing consultant; b. Oakland, Mo., Jan. 20, 1919; s. Oscar B. and Clara (McGuire) V.; m. Lee Kendall, July 7, 1935. MEE, Tulane U. V.p. charge sales Van Lang Brokerage, Los Angeles, 1934-38; mgr. agrl. div. Dayton Rubber Co., Chgo., 1939-48; pres., gen. mgr. Vee Mac Co., Rockford, Ill., 1948—; pres., dir. Zipout, Inc., Rockford, 1951—, Wife Saver Products, Inc., 1959—; chmn. bd. Zipout Internat., Kenvan Inc., 1952—, Shevan Corp., 1951—, Atlas Internat. Corp.; pres. Global Enterprises Ltd., Global Assos. Ltd.; chmn. bd. dirs. Am. Atlas Corp., Atlas Chem. Corp., Merzat Industries Ltd.; trustee Ice Crafter Trust, 1949—; bd. dirs. Atlas Chem. Internat. Ltd., Kenlee Internat., Ltd., Shrimp Tool Internat. Ltd.; mem. Toronto Bd. Trade; chmn. bd. dirs. Am. Atlas Corp., Am. Packaging Corp. Mem. adv. bd. Nat. Security Council, congl. adv. com. Heritage Found.; mem. Rep. Nat. Com., Presdl. Task Force, Congrl. Adv. Com. Hon. mem. Internat. Swimming Hall of Fame. Mem. Nat. (dir. at large), Rock River (past pres.) sales execs., Sales and Mktg. Execs. Internat. (dir.), Am. Mgmt. Assn., Rockford Engring. Soc., Am. Tool Engrs., Internat. Acad. Aquatic Art (dir.), Am. Inst. Mgmt. (pres. council), Am. Ordnance Assn., Internat. Platform Assn., Heritage Found., Ill. C. of C. Clubs: Jesters, Elks, IAA Swim, Exec., Elmcrest Country, Pyramid, Dolphin, Marlin, Univ., Univ. Athletic, Oxford. Lodges: Masons (consistory), Shriners, Elks. Home: 374 Parkland Dr SE Cedar Rapids IA 52403-2031 also: 40 Richview Rd # 308, Toronto, ON Canada M9A 5C1 also: 704 Park Center Dr Santa Ana CA 92705-3563 Office: PO Box 1972 Cedar Rapids IA 52406-1972 also: 111 Richmond St W Ste 318, Toronto, ON Canada M5H 1T1

VAN DER SLIK, JACK RONALD, academic administrator, political science educator; b. Kalamazoo, Mich., Dec. 14, 1936; s. Julius Henry and Cornelia (Koopsen) Van Der S.; m. Gertrude Jane Bonnema, June 29, 1963; children: Franci Lynn, Gary Jon, Randall Martin. BA, Calvin Coll., 1958; MA, Western Mich. U., 1961; MA, PhD, Mich. State U., 1967. From asst. to assoc. prof., assoc. dean So. Ill. U., Carbondale, 1967-78; polit. sci. rsch. fellow Ill. Legis. Coun., Springfield, 1969-70; acad. dean Trinity Christian Coll., Palos Heights, Ill., 1978-81; prof., dir. U. Ill., Springfield, 1981—; vis. assoc. prof. Calvin Coll., Grand Rapids, Ill., 1972-73; acad. specialist U.S. Info. Agy., Manila, The Philippines, 1993; polit. commentator Ill. Pub. Radio, Springfield, 1982-95; adv. panelist Satellite Ednl. Rsch., Washington, 1993-94; cons. State Bd. Edn., Springfield., 1989-91. Author: One for All and All for Illinois, 1995, Lawmaking in Illinois, 1986, 2d edit., 1989; editor Almanac of Illinois Politics, 1990, 92, 94; contbr. articles to profl. jours. Faculty adv. com. Ill. Bd. Higher Edn., Springfield, 1984-87; active Ill. Redistricting Rev. Commn., Springfield, 1992-95, Task Force on Gov's Veto, Springfield, 1984; bd. dirs. Washington St. Mission, Springfield, 1991-95. Named Ill. Author, Ill. State Libr., 1995; grantee Commn. on Bicentennial, 1990. Mem. Am. Polit. Sci. Assn., Midwest Polit. Sci. Assn. (coun. mem. 1992-95), Ill. Polit. Sci. Assn. (pres. 1988-89), Acad. Polit. Sci., Associated Coll. Chgo. Area (exec. com. 1979-81), Pi Sigma Alpha. Office: Univ Ill Ill Legis Studies Ctr Springfield IL 62793-9243

VANDERVEEN, JOSEPH RICHARD, special education administrator; b. Muskegon, Mich., June 12, 1937; s. J. Barnie and M. Gertrude (Dwyer) V.; m. Hollee Beadle, Feb. 1962 (div. Feb. 1989); children: Joseph, Heather, Patrick. BA, Western Mich. U., 1960, MA, 1965, EdS, 1971. Cert. secondary sch. tchr., sch. psychologist, adminstr., Mich. Tchr., coach Ravenna (Mich.) Schs., 1960-63, Springfield (Mich.) Pub. Schs., 1963-65; sch. psychologist St. Joseph Intermediate Sch. Dist., Centreville, Mich., 1965-67; dir. psychol. svcs. Kent Intermediate Sch. Dist., Grand Rapids, Mich., 1967-76; regional dir. spl. edn. Kent Intermediate Sch. Dist., Grand Rapids, 1984-90; dir. spl. edn. Forest Hills Pub. Schs., Grand Rapids, 1976-84; regional dir. spl. edn. Kentwood (Mich.) Pub. Schs., 1990-96; clin. psychologist Psychiat. Cons. Svcs., Grand Rapids, 1976-85; adj. prof. Mich. State U., Lansing, 1975-77, Grand Valley State U., Allendale, Mich., 1978-90. Author: Handbook for School Psychologists, 1974, also curriculum materials. Mem. exec. bd. Kent County Spl. Olympics, Grand Rapids, 1971-76; advisor Kent County Community Mental Health Bd., Grand Rapids, 1974-76. Mem. Coun. for Exceptional Children (pres. Grand Rapids chpt. 1990-93), West Mich. Pers. and Guidance Assn. (pres. 1980-81), Grand Rapids Area Psychol. Assn. (sec. 1973-79), Mich. Assn. Sch. Psychologists (pres. 1976), Nat. Assn. Sch. Psychologists (del. 1978-81), Mich. Assn. Soc. Spl. Edn. Adminstrs., KC, Phi Delta Kappa (sec. 1991-96). Roman Catholic. Home: 6954 E Springtree Ln SW Grand Rapids MI 49548-7935

VAN DER WERFF, RENEE LYNN, newspaper publisher, journalist; b. Armour, S.D., Feb. 6, 1968; d. Herbert Kenneth and Virginia Ann (Meyer) Harms; m. Scott Lee Van Der Werff, June 8, 1991. BA in English/Journalism, Dakota Wesleyan U., Mitchell, S.D., 1990; grad. studies, Georgetown U., 1989; postgrad., S.D. State U., 1991-92, 96—. Reporter, journalist Douglas County Pub., Corsica, S.D., 1991-92; mng. editor, journalist Douglas County Pub., Armour, 1992; co-owner, pub. Douglas County Pub., Corsica, Armour, Delmont, S.D., 1992—; bd. dirs. Rocket Printing, Inc., Armour. Mem., bd. dirs. Armour Non-Profit Devel. Corp., 1995—; mem. United Ch. of Christ Women's Fellowship, 1993—. Mem. Internat. Soc. Weekly Newspaper Editors (mem. Golden Dozen 1994), Soc. Profl. Journalists, S.D. Newspaper Assn. (1st pl. column, editl., sports story 1995, 1st pl. news story 1994, 1st pl. feature series 1993), Armour Comty. Club. Home: RR 1 Box 84 Armour SD 57313 Office: Douglas County Pub PO Box 129 624 S Main Armour SD 57313

VANDER WIEL, KENNETH CARLTON, computer services company executive; b. Sheldon, Iowa, July 6, 1933; s. Sylvan Vander Wiel and Irene F. (Weekley) Taylor; m. Loretta Marie Smith, Aug. 28, 1969; children: Gretchen G., Alison June, Joseph W., Carol Ann, Andrea., Beth L., David. BA, Bowling Green U., 1955. With mgmt. devel. Dayton (Ohio) Power & Light, 1955-68; cons. G.W. Young & Assocs., Dayton, 1968-69; pres. Datamac Corp., Dayton, 1970-84, Carlton Leasing Co., 1975—, The Carlton Systems Group, Dayton, 1984-89, Carlton Computer Systems, Inc., Dayton, 1989-95; CEO Carlton Computer Systems, Inc., Tampa, Fla., 1993-95; pres. Interlogic Systems of Dayton, Inc., 1995—. Chmn. Montgomery County Data Processing Task Force, Dayton, 1982. With USN, 1955-57. Recipient Commendations, Montgomery County Commn., Dayton, 1982. Mem. Dayton Area C. of C. (nat. affairs com., state legis. com.), Nat. Assn. Mgf. (nat. affairs com.), Dayton Engrs. Club, Dayton Execs. Club (1st lifetime mem. honoree 1995, pres. 1986). Office: Interlogic Systems Inc 1887 Southtown Blvd Dayton OH 45439-1965

VANDEVENDER, BARBARA JEWELL, elementary education educator, farmer; b. Trenton, Mo., Dec. 4, 1929; d. Raleigh Leon and Rose Rea (Dryer) S.; m. Delbert Lyle Vandevender, Aug. 15, 1948; children: Lyle Gail, James R. BS, N.E. Mo. State U., 1971, MA, 1973. Elem. tchr. Williams Sch., Spickard, Mo., 1948-49; reading specialist Spikard R-2 Sch., 1971-74, Princeton (Mo.) R-5 Sch., 1974-89; mem. ad hoc com. State Dept. Edn., Jefferson City, Mo., 1994-95; speaker in field. Pres. Spickard PTA, 1963-64, Women's Ext. Club, Galt, Mo.; foster mother Family Svcs., Trenton, Mi., 1972-79; mem. ad hoc com. State Dept. of Edn., Jefferson City, Mo., 1994-95. Pres. Spickard PTA, 1963-64, Women's Ext. Club, Galt, Mo.; foster mother Family Svcs., Trenton, Mo., 1972-79; mem. ad hoc com. State Dept. Edn., Jefferson City, Mo., 1994-95. Recipient Mo. State Conservation award Goodyear Tire Co., Akron, Ohio, 1972, Balanced Farming award Gulf Oil Co., N.Y.C., 1972, Mo. State Farming award Kansas City C. of C., 1974, FHA State Farming award, Jefferson City, Mo., 1974, Outstanding Leadership Mo. U., Columbia, 1976, Ednl. Leadership award MSTA, Columbia, 1984, Outstanding Contbn. to Internat. Reading Assn., Newark, Del., 1988. Mem. Internat. Reading Assn. (pres. North Ctrl. coun. 1985-86). Republican. Baptist.

VANDEVENDER, DEBORAH ANN, critical care nurse; b. Syracuse, N.Y., Nov. 24, 1954; d. Charles Arthur and Patricia Ann (McGreevy) Kieffer; m. Robert Vandevender II, Sept. 26, 1992. BA in Biology, U. Toledo, 1980, BS in Nursing, 1983. RN, Ohio, N.Y., Pa., Ill., Calif., Iowa; cert. CCRN. Critical care nurse clinician III Toledo Hosp., 1977-89, St. Joseph Hosp., Syracuse, N.Y., 1989-91; critical care nurse II Brandywine Hosp., Coatsville, Pa., 1991; critical care nurse St. Therese Med. Ctr., Waukegan, Ill., 1991-93; sr. clinician Rush Northshore Med. Ctr., Skokie, Ill., 1993-94; critical care nurse St. Lukes Hosp., Davenport, Iowa, 1994, Rush Northshore Med. Ctr., Skokie, Ill., 1994—. Nurse ARC, Toledo, 1988-89. With USN, 1972-77; lt. USNR, 1977—. Mem. AACN, Fractional Currency Collectors Bd., Smithsonian Inst. (assoc.), Nat. Trust for Hist. Preservation. Home and Office: PO Box 4052 Joliet IL 60434-4052

VANDEWALLE, DON MICHAEL, educator, researcher; b. Rock Island, Ill., Jan. 11, 1955; s. Donald B. and Darlene F. (Cotter) V. BA, Park Coll., Parkville, Mo., 1976; MBA, Kansas U., 1982, postgrad studies, 1988-90; PhD, U. Minn., 1995. Dir. athletics, track coach Park Coll., Parkville, Mo., 1976-84; dir. honors program, mem. bus. faculty Kans. C. C., Kansas City, 1983-90; rsch. assoc., instr. U. Minn., Mpls., 1990-94; asst. prof. orgnl. behavior So. Meth. U., Dallas, 1995—; sports info. dir. Nat. Assn. Intercollegiate Athletics, Dist. 16, Kans. City, Mo., 1978-83; bd. dirs. Track and Field Assn. U.S., Kans. City, 1979-81. Pres. Young World Devel., Davenport, Iowa, 1972-73; pub. rels. dir. City of Parkville, Mo., 1977-80; bus. mgr. Atonement Luth. Ch., Overland Park, Kans., 1985-89; pres. Park Coll. Friends of the Libr., Parkville, 1988-90; chmn. subcom. Sch. Employees Credit Union, Kansas City, Kans., 1989-90. Richard D. Irwin Fellow, 1993-94; recipient Excellence award State of Kans. Edn. Dept., 1988, Master Tchr. award NISOD, U. Tex., Austin, 1988, 89, U. Kans. Tchr. Recognition award, 1991; named Coach of Yr. Mo. Track/C.C. Coaches Assn., 1983, Nat. Assn. Intercoll. Athletic, Dist. 16, 1980-84, Journalist of Yr. Mo. Coll. Newspaper Assn., 1976. Mem. Nat. Collegiate Honors Coun. (scholarship com. Great Plains region 1987-90), Coun. Grad. Students U. Minn. (v.p. fin. 1993-94), Nat. Assn. Accts. (bd. dirs.), Am. Acctg. Assn.

VANDEWALLE, GERALD WAYNE, state supreme court chief justice; b. Noonan, N.D., Aug. 15, 1933; s. Jules C. and Blanche Marie (Gits) VandeW. B.Sc., U. N.D., 1955, J.D., 1958. Bar: N.D., U.S. Dist. Ct. N.D. 1959. Spl. asst. atty. gen. State of N.D., Bismarck, 1958-75, 1st asst. atty. gen., 1975-78; justice N.D. Supreme Ct., 1978-92, chief justice, 1993—; mem. faculty Bismarck Jr. Coll., 1972-76. Editor-in-chief N.D. Law Rev, 1957-58. Active Bismarck Meals on Wheels. Recipient Sioux award U. N.D., 1992, Ednl. Law award N.D. Coun. Sch. Attys., 1987, Love Without Fear award Abused Adult Resource Ctr., 1995. Mem. ABA (co-chair bar admissions com.), State Bar Assn. N.D., Burleigh County Bar Assn., Am. Contract Bridge League, Order of Coif, N.D. Jud. Conf. (exec. com.), Phi Eta Sigma, Beta Alpha Psi (Outstanding Alumnus award Zeta chpt. 1995), Beta Gamma Sigma, Phi Alpha Delta. Roman Catholic. Clubs: Elks, K.C. Office: ND Supreme Ct State Capitol 600 E Boulevard Ave Bismarck ND 58505-0660

VAN DIEPENBOS, MARK A., draftsman; b. Goshen, Ind., Feb. 25, 1970. Mfg. engring. technician Behlen Mfg., Universal Mfg. Divsn., Goshen, Ind., 1989—. Mem. Maxwelton Golf Club. Office: Behlen Mfg Universal Mfg Divsn PO Box 115 Goshen IN 46527-0115

VANDIVIER, BLAIR ROBERT, lawyer; b. Rapid City, S.D., Dec. 24, 1955; s. Robert Eugene and Barbara Jean (Kidd) V.; m. Elizabeth Louise Watson, July 26, 1980; children: Jessica Elizabeth, Jennifer Louise. BS magna cum laude, Butler U., 1978; JD cum laude, Ind. U., 1981. Bar: Ind. 1981, U.S. Dist. Ct. (so. dist.) Ind. 1981, U.S. Tax Ct. 1985. Assoc. Henderson, Daily, Withrow, Johnson & Gross, Indpls., 1981-83; assoc., ptnr. Johnson, Gross, Densborn & Wright, Indpls., 1983-85, of counsel, 1985-87; v.p., sec. Benchmark Products, Inc. (formerly Benchmark Chem. Corp.), Indpls., 1985-91, pres., 1991—, also bd. dirs.; ptnr. Gross & Vandivier, Indpls., 1987-89; of counsel Riley, Bennett & Egloff, Indpls., 1990—; mgmt. rep. Pro Com, L.L.C., 1991—; v.p. Seleco Inc., Indpls., 1988-93, pres., 1993—. Mem. com. Conner Prairie Settlement Fund Dr., Indpls., 1983-85, Riley Run, 1987—; mem. regulatory study com. City of Indpls., 1993—. Mem. ABA, Ind. Bar Assn., Indpls. Bar Assn (bd. dirs. young lawyers divsn. 1982-85), Am. Electroplaters & Surface Finisher's Soc. (chmn. nat. law com. 1986—, pres. Indpls. br. 1989, tech. conf. bd. 1991—, chmn. SUR/FIN annual tech. conf. and exhbn. 1994, chmn. SUR/FIN Four Group 1994—, Tech. Conf. Bd. Recognition award 1996), Metal Finishing Suppliers Assn. (spl. projects svcs. com., 1988-93, chmn. 1993—, chmn. hazardous materials br. 1991-93, trustee 1992-95, v.p. 1995—), Highland Golf Club, Highland Country Club (chmn. ins. com. 1989-94, golf. com. 1992-94, bd. dirs. 1995—, chmn. fin. com. 1996), Econ. Club Indpls., Delta Tau Delta (chmn. 1987—, bd. dirs. Beta Zeta Found. 1986, Outstanding Alumnus Beta Zeta chpt. 1986). Republican. Episcopalian. Home: 8927 Woodacre Ln Indianapolis IN 46234-2848 Office: Benchmark Products Inc PO Box 68809 Indianapolis IN 46268-0809

VAN DOREN, RONALD WAYNE, speech communication educator; b. Chgo., Aug. 5, 1942; s. Verne Van Doren and Lecta Corrine Simpson Smith; m. Ellen Louise Wesolowski, Aug. 12, 1989; children from previous marriage: Elizabeth, Mark. BS in Speech Edn., Bob Jones U., Greenville, S.C., 1966; MA in Speech, Northeastern Ill. U., Chgo., 1972, MEd in Lang. Arts, 1982. Tchr. McHenry (Ill.) H.S., 1966-67; asst. mgr. Zayre, Des Plaines, Ill., 1967; ins. agt. Prudential Ins. Co., Chgo., 1967-69; tchr. Ill. State Tng. Sch. for Boys, St. Charles, 1969-72; tchr. speech comms. Triton Coll., River Grove, Ill., 1972—. Dir. Tall Tales Theater, 1994, The Crucible, 1972, God's Trombones, 1974, Thurber Carnival, 1995, Busybody, 1996; storyteller; theater dir. for sch. and ch., 1972—. Mem. Am. Fedn. Tchrs., Ill. Speech and Theater Assn. Office: Triton Coll 2000 5th Ave River Grove IL 60171

VAN DOVER, DONALD, small business owner, consultant; b. St. Louis, Oct. 31, 1932; s. James K. and Ruth Edith (Longnecker) Van D.; m. Gloria Jenna Fahrenkamp, June 21, 1963; 1 child, Victoria Lee. BSBA, Washington U., Clayton, Mo., 1959. Sales rep. Gen. Electric Corp., St. Louis, 1955-60; regional sales mgr. Emerson Electric, St. Louis, 1960-76; dist. mgr. Edwards div. Gen. Signal Corp., Fairfield, Conn., 1976-81; regional mgr. Flintrol, Inc., Jonesboro, Ark., 1981-84; pres. Van Dover & Assoc., Chesterfield, Mo., 1984—; cons. Van Dover & Assocs., 1983—; v.p. Athens Automotive, Falls Church, Va., 1984-87. Mem. Young Reps., Milw., 1965-75. Cpl. U.S. Army, 1953-55. Methodist. Home: 506 Wyncrest Dr Ballwin MO 63011 Office: Van Dover & Assoc PO Box 11673 Saint Louis MO 63105-0473

VANEK, ELIZABETH-ANNE, English language and spirituality educator, minister; b. Hampshire, Eng., Dec. 21, 1951; came to U.S., 1974; d. Alexander and Lilian (Zammit-Tabona) Stewart; m. James Anthony Vanek, Dec. 22, 1973; children: Peter, Alexia. BA with honors, Royal U. of Malta, 1973; MA summa cum laude, DePaul U., 1976; D of Ministry, Grad. Theol. Found., 1989; cert. spiritual direction, Claret Ctr., Chgo., 1989. English instr. DePaul U., Chgo., 1986-90, joint appointment with English Dept. and univ. ministry, 1990-94, joint appointment w/religious studies dept./univ. ministry, 1994—; tchg. fellow Grad. Theol. Found., 1994—; part-time instr. Roosevelt U., Chgo., 1975-79, DePaul U., 1976-80, 82-86; freelance writer, editor, workshop leader, pub. speaker, retreat leader, 1979—; part-time poetry instr. Express-Ways Children's Mus., Chgo., 1984-86; adj. faculty mem. grad. religious studies Mundelein Coll., Chgo., 1986-91; poet cons. liturgical psalter Internat. Commn. on English in the Liturgy, Washington, 1986-92; founder, dir. The Writer's Desk, Chgo., 1979-86. Author: Image Guidance: A Tool for Spiritual Direction, 1992, Image Guidance, Pilgrims at Heart, 1993, Image Guidance and Healing, 1994, (books of poetry) Frost and Fire, 1985, Extraordinary Time, 1988, Woman Dreamer, 1989; contbr. over 60 articles to profl. jours. Recipient Community Svc. award AARP, The Beverly Rev., 1989. Mem. ACA, Spiritual Dirs. Internat. Roman Catholic. Office: DePaul Univ Ministry 248 McGaw Hall 802 W Belden Ave Chicago IL 60614-3214

VAN ENGEN, THOMAS LEE, state legislator; b. Sioux Center, Iowa, Mar. 28, 1953; s. Leo Herman and Dolores (Nelma) Van E.; m. Rosalyn Faye Vander Plaats, 1979; children: Matthew Thomas, David James, Jeremy Lee. BA, Dordt Coll., Sioux Center, 1979. Lic. social worker, Minn. Commd. 2d. lt. U.S. Army, 1972, ret., 1978; state cen., 1989-94; chair dist. 15 Minn. Ho. of Reps., St. Paul, 1992-94; exec. com. chair, 1990-93; mem. Minn. Ho. of Reps., St. Paul, 1994—. Del. Rep. dist. and state convs., 1984—, Minn. Rep. Ctrl. Com., 1989—; chmn. Pipestone County Com., Minn., 1988-89, Kandiyohi County Com., 1991-93; co-chmn. dist. 15 Minn. Senate, 1990-92, chmn., 1992—; candidate for Minn. Ho. of Reps., 1992; chmn. edn. com. Cmty. Christian Sch. Bd., 1990—; elder Christian Reformed Ch., 1985-88, 96—; vol. handicapped children and adults, 1978-82; chem. dependency counselor, 1982. Mem. CAP, Am. Legion. Republican.

VAN ERON, KEVIN J., insurance company executive; b. Hutchinson, Kans., Apr. 9, 1957; s. Kenneth J. and Meriam J. (Buller) Van Eron; m. Ann M. Schwartz, Jan. 1, 1984. B in Gen Studies, U. Md., 1980. Chartered life underwriter. Dist. rep. Aid Assn. for Luths., Appleton, Wis., 1980-83, dist. mgr., 1983-84, gen. agt., 1984-87, gen. mgr., 1987-91, v.p., mem. field svcs., 1992; sr. v.p., mem. field svcs., 1993—. Mem. Nat. Assn. Life Underwriters, Gen. Agts. Mgrs. Conf., Nat. Assn., Fraternal Ins. Counsellors, Am. Soc. Chartered Life Underwriters. Democrat. Lutheran. Home: 1511 N Briarcliff Dr Appleton WI 54915-2840 Office: Aid Assn for Luths 4321 N Ballard Rd Appleton WI 54915-7729

VAN GERPEN, EDWARD E., state legislator. Mem. dist. 19 S.D. Ho. of Reps.; mem. agrl. and natural resources and edn. coms., also farmer. Home: RR 1 Box 57 Avon SD 57315-9742 Address: RR 1 Box EV1 Avon SD 57315-9801*

VAN GINKEL, JAMES CAROL, lawyer; b. Columbus, Ohio, Aug. 20, 1954; s. James and Marvel Jeanette (Crumpacker) Van G.; m. Marci Lou Cohron, May 22, 1982; children: James Cohron, John Cohron. BS, Drake U., 1976, JD, 1979, MBA, 1979. Bar: Iowa 1980, U.S. Dist. Ct. (so. dist.) Iowa 1980. Instr. Drake U., Des Moines, 1979-80; atty. Kluever & Van Ginkel, Atlantic, Iowa, 1979-80; ptnr. Van Ginkel Law Offices, Atlantic, Iowa, 1981—; pres. Cass/Atlantic Devel. Corp., 1995—; dir., sec., v.p. Cass/Atlantic Devel. Corp., 1991-95; chmn., dir. Exch. State Bank, Exita, Iowa, 1991—; pres., dir. Cohron Investment Co., Atlantic, 1986—; chmn. dir. Wireless Comms., Atlantic, 1987—; v.p., sec., dir. Mid-Am. Banks, Inc., Collins, Iowa, 198—. Pres., dir. YMCA, Atlantic, 1981-89; county chmn. Re-elect Senator Grassley, Cass County, Iowa, 1992; del. State Rep. Conf., Iowa, 1980-92; mem. Iowa Rep. Platform Com., 1986; dir. C. of C., Atlantic, 1987-89. Mem. County Bar Assn., Atlantic Rotary (dir., pres. 1984-89), Elks, Atlantic Golf and Country Club (treas. 1993, v.p. 1993-95, pres. 1995—). Republican. Methodist. Home: 202 Crombie St Atlantic IA 50022-2622 Office: Van Ginkel Law Offices 1908 E 7th St Atlantic IA 50022-1915

VAN GORP, GARY WAYNE, clergyman; b. Reasnor, Iowa, July 16, 1953; s. Laverne Leroy Sr. and Emma Jean (Meyers) Van G.; m. Marietta Louise Burns, Dec. 29, 1972; children: Caleb Aaron, Kari Beth, Micah Alan, Faith Elise, Melinda Amy, Joy Annette. Diploma in Pastoral Studies, Bible and Doctrine, Berean Coll., 1975; BS in Pastoral Studies, Religious Edn., North Cen. Bible Coll., Mpls., 1978; Diploma in profl. office mgmt., Alexandria (Minn.) Tech. Sch., 1984; various positions, ADIA Employment, 1993. Ordained to ministry Assembly of God Ch., 1981. Pastor Verndale (Minn.) Assembly of God Ch., 1979-82; asst. mgr., caretaker Lake Geneva Bible Camp, Alexandria, 1982-83; Christian edn. and outreach pastor Alexandria Assembly of God Ch., 1983-84; pastor, adminstrv. asst. Allison Park (Pa.) Assembly God Ch., 1984-90; interim pastor Assembly God Ch., Bklyn. Ctr. and Winona, Minn., 1991; mem. maintenance pers. staff South Fidge Mall, 1991-92; farmhand J&V Van Gorp, Inc., 1992; developer ministry program Berean Assembly of God Ch., Des Moines, Iowa, 1992; founder, owner GW Enterprize, 1993; with ADIA The Employment People, Temporary Svc., 1992-94; pastor Lighthouse Assembly of God, Glencoe, Minn., 1994—; security officer Roland Security, 1995-96; chmn. Glencoe Ministerium, 1995-96; vice prin. Faith Acad. Christian Sch., 1980-82; mgr. book store Gospel Supply Ctr., Minn., 1981-82; pastor Elbow Lake (Minn.) Assembly of God, 1983-84; security officer Rolands Security, 1995-96. Bd. dirs., treas., mem. adv. bd. The DoorWay, Inc., Pitts., 1988-92; mem. adv. bd. Glory Home Sch. Corp., Des Moines, 1994; coord. West League Jr. Bible Oyuiz for State of Minn., 1995-96. Mem. Nat. Assn. Ch. Bus. Adminstrs. (pres. Pitts. chpt. 1987-90). Home and Office: 13849 Lace Ave Glencoe MN 55336-7521

VANHANDEL, RALPH ANTHONY, librarian; b. Appleton, Wis., Jan. 17, 1919; s. Frank Henry and Gertrude Mary (Schmidt) Van H.; m. Alice Catherine Hogan, Oct. 27, 1945; children: William Patrick, Karen Jean, Mary Jo. BA, U. Wis., 1946; AB in Libr. Sci., U. Mich., 1947. Head libr. Lawrence (Kans.) Free Pub. Libr., 1947-51, Hibbing (Minn.) Pub. Libr., 1951-54; libr. dir. Gary (Ind.) Pub. Libr., 1954-74; libr. dir. Wells Meml. Pub. Libr., Lafayette, Ind. (name now Tippecanoe County Pub. Libr.), 1974-84, libr. cons., 1963—; mem. Ind. Library Cert. Bd., 1969-84, Ind. State Library and Hist. Bldg. Expansion Commn., 1973-81. Named Ind. Librarian of Year, 1971, Sagamore of Wabash, 1984. Mem. ALA, KC, Anselm Forum (sec. 1964, v.p. 1965), Ind. Libr. Assn. (pres. 1963-64), Kans. Libr. Assn. (v.p. 1951). Home: 3624 Winter St Lafayette IN 47905-3838

VAN HORN, JOHN KENNETH, health physicist, consultant; b. St. Louis, June 22, 1948; s. Harold E. and Norma L. (Klobe) Van H.; m. Christine A. Lump, Oct. 20, 1995; children: Shawn R., Mark R., Janina. AB in Physics and Math. Edn., Drury Coll., 1971; MS in Instrnl. Tech., No. Ill. U., 1988. Physics, math. tchr. Perryville (Mo.) Pub. Schs., 1971-76; math. dept. head Alden-Hebron (Ill.) Community Schs., 1976-84; program developer prodn. tng. Commonwealth Edison, Braidwood, Ill., 1984-87, health physics instr. prodn. tng., 1987-91; health physicist LaSalle Nuclear Sta. Commonwealth Edison, Marseilles, Ill., 1991—; unit health physicist Commonwealth Edison, Marseilles, Ill., 1993; lead radiation protection instr. LaSalle Nuclear Sta. Commonwealth Edison, Marseilles, Ill., 1995-96, instr. devel. specialist, 1996—. Co-author: New 10CFR20 for HP Technicians, 1992. Mem. Zoning and Planning Bd., Mazon, Ill, 1990-95; First Aid instr. ARC, Morris, Ill., 1986—; merit badge counselor Boy Scouts Am., Morris, 1989-95. Mem. Nat. Soc. Performance and Instrn., Health Physics Soc. (co-chmn. exam. group 1991—, bd. dirs. 1991—, pres.-elect Midwest chpt. 1993, pres. 1994, past pres. 1995, pub. info. com. 1996—), Nat. Health Physics Soc. Kappa Delta Pi. Office: Commonwealth Edison Tng Dept RR1 Box 220 2601 N 21st Rd Marseilles IL 61341

VAN HORN, LECIA JOSEPH, newswriter; b. L.A., Jan. 19, 1963; d. McKinley Joe and Opal Geneva (Ivie) Joseph; m. Philip Dale Van Horn, Apr. 19, 1986; children: Kari Christine, Brandon Joseph. BA in Journalism, U. Southern Calif., 1984. News reporter Sta. KSCR Radio, L.A., 1983; consumer news researcher Sta. KCBS-TV, L.A., 1983, Sta. KABC-TV, L.A., 1983-84; newswriter Headline News, Atlanta, 1984-85; editorial asst., newswriter, field producer Sta. KNBC-TV, Burbank, Calif., 1985-86; newswriter, assoc. producer Sta. WYFF-TV, Greenville, S.C., 1986; freelance newswriter, assoc. producer Sta. WSB-TV, Atlanta, 1987-88; newswriter CNN, Atlanta, 1987-94; freelance newswriter, assoc. producer Sta. KSTP-TV, St. Paul, 1995-96; freelance newswriter Sta. KABC-TV, L.A., 1996—. Author: Thoughts and Inspirational Sayings, 1985; contbr. poetry and articles to newspapers. Mem. U. So. Calif. Alumni. Mem. Science of Mind.

VANHOUTEN, JACOB WESLEY, environmental manager, educator, trainer; b. Grand Rapids, Mich., July 24, 1958; s. Calvin Ross and Lois Mae (Sleight) VanH. AAS, Alpena (Mich.) Community Coll., 1978; BS, Ferris State Coll., 1980; MS, Cen. Mich. U., 1986. Registered environ. property assessor, environ. profl.; cert. environ. trainer. Grad. teaching asst. Cen. Mich. U., Mt. Pleasant, 1982-85; water quality specialist TMI Environ. Svcs., Mt. Pleasant, 1986-88, project mgr., 1988-95; adj. faculty Ctrl. Mich. U., 1986, Saginaw (Mich.) Valley State U., 1988, Delta Coll., Saginaw. Contbr. articles on outdoor and environmental topics to profl. jours. Recipient Beaver Island scholarship Cen. Mich. U., 1982. Mem. ASTM (tech. com., nat. trainer phase I ESA), Nat. Registry Environ. Profls., Nat. Environ. Tng. Assn., Mich. Assn. Environ. Profls., N. Am. Benthol Soc.. Republican. Office: Delta Coll Corp Svcs. 310 Johnson St Saginaw MI 48607

VAN HOUTEN, JAMES FORESTER, insurance company executive; b. Fullerton, Calif., Jan. 13, 1942; s. James Forester and Lois Evangeline (Trout) V.H. children: Kimberly Evangeline, Lori Lynn. BA in English Lit.,

St. Mary's U., 1971; MBA, Ill. State U., 1989. CPCU, CLU. Sales mgr. Canada Motors Ins. Corp. divsn. GM, Detroit, 1963-74; v.p. sales Volkswagen Ins. Group, St. Louis, 1974-78; v.p. personal lines mktg. Wausau Ins. Cos., St. Louis, 1978-80; v.p., chief mktg. officer life and health Wausau Ins. Cos., 1980-84; v.p., chief mktg. officer Country Cos., Bloomington, Ill., 1984-89; pres., CEO Mut. Svc. Ins. Cos., St. Paul, 1989—; prof., mem. grad. faculty in strategic mgmt. Carlson Sch. U. Minn., 1990—. Lectr., program leader Youth Black Achievers, St. Paul; co-chair bus. adv. coun. U.S. 6th Congl. Dist., Minn., 1994; mem. exec. bd. arrowhead coun. Boy Scouts of Am.; mem. bd. advisors CARE, Minn. Assn. Scholars. Mem. Ins. Fedn. Minn. (chmn. bd.), Nat. Coop. Bus. Assn. (bd. dirs. and exec. com., chair fin. com.), Minn. Bus. Partnership (bd. dirs.), Ctr. Am. Experiment (bd. dirs.). Office: Mut Svc Ins Cos 2 Pine Tree Dr Arden Hills MN 55112

VAN HOVEN, MRS. JAY See **VOIGHT, NANCY LEE**

VAN HUIS, PHILIP J., manufacturing executive; b. Holland, Mich., Dec. 31, 1941. Control engr. Ex-Cell-O Micromatic, Holland, Mich., 1966-86; pres. Cardinal Machine Svcs., Holland, 1986—. Contbr. articles to Die Casting Engr. Mag. With USAF, 1960-64. Mem. N. Am. Die Casting Assn. (edn. com., instr.), Holland C. of C. Office: Cardinal Machine Svcs Inc 384 W 24th St Holland MI 49423-4037

VAN KEUREN, ROBERT WILFORD, retired agronomy educator, researcher; b. Virginia, Minn., Jan. 2, 1922; s. Harry Eugene and Cora Marie (Henrichs) Van K.; m. Joyce Elaine Stewart, Aug. 5, 1949; children: Patrice Anne, Jeffrey Robert, James Kenton. BS, U. Wis., River Falls, 1943; MS, U. Wis., Madison, 1952, PhD, 1954. Tchr. vocat. agr. Greenwood (Wis.) Pub. Schs., 1946-49; Wis. Alumni Rsch. Found. rsch. asst. U. Wis., 1951-54; asst. and assoc. agronomist Wash. State U., Pullman, 1954-62; assoc. prof., prof. agronomy Ohio State U., Columbus, 1962-88, prof. emeritus, 1988—; researcher Ohio Agrl. R & D Ctr., Wooster, 1962-88; chmn., mem. several nat. and regional rsch. coms. on forage; mem. U.S.-USSR Agrl. Sci. Exch. Program, 1974; cons. Brazilian Govt. on Forage Rsch., 1978; prin. investigator AID Forage Rsch., Kenya, Peru, 1979-83, mem. survey team for livestock-forage rsch. for S.E. Asia, 1979; prin. investigator USDA-UICD U.S.-Yugoslav Forage Rsch., 1988—; plenary lectr. Internat. Hill Land Congress, 1976, 3d Asian Animal Sci. Congress, 1985; John B. Peters Meml. lectr. U. W.Va., 1987; spkr. internat. grassland congresses, nat. symposia, numerous nat. and regional meetings Am. and Can. sci. and tech. group. Contbg. author: No Tillage Systems, 1986, Forages, The Science of Grassland Agriculture, 1985, Weed Control in Limited Tillage Systems, 1985; contbr. over 350 articles to Agronomy Jour., Jour. Animal Sci., Crop Sci., Jour. Environ. Sci., Ohio Jour. Sci., also others. Lt. (j.g.) USN, 1943-46, ETO, PTO. Grantee EPA, 1979-85. Fellow Am. Soc. Agronomy (editor, editorial com., contbg. author 4 monographs), Crop Sci. Soc. Am. Home: 1497 Morgan Run Wooster OH 44691-1541 Office: Ohio Agrl R & D Ctr 1680 Madison Ave Wooster OH 44691-4114

VAN KIRK, ROBERT JOHN, nursing case manager, educator; b. Jersey City, N.J., Sept. 18, 1944; s. Robert and Doris V.; m. Marjorie Ann Carroll, Mar. 23, 1968 (div. Nov. 30, 1993); children: Walter, Michael, Robert Jr., Peggy. BA cum laude, U. Conn., 1974; MEd, Kent State U., 1983; D of Nursing, Case Western Reserve U., 1986. RN. Sales mgr. Nutmeg Home Protection, Middlebury, Conn., 1972-74; theater mgr. SBC Mgmt. Corp., Boston, 1974; dist. supr. Selected Theatres Mgmt. Corp., Lyndhurst, Ohio, 1974-86; nat. sales mgr. ZBS Video, Inc., Lyndhurst, Ohio, 1981-82; staff nurse Cleve. Clinic Found., 1986-87, clin. instr., 1987-88, head nurse, 1988-93; case mgr., 1993—; asst. clin. prof. Case Western Reserve U., Frances Payne Bolton Sch. Nursing, Cleve., 1990—; case mgr. Cleve. Clin. Home Care, 1993—. Health officer Lake County (Ohio) Bd. Alcohol, Drug Addiction and Mental Health Svcs., 1991—; co-chmn. United Way, Cleve., 1991-93. Staff sgt. U.S. Army, 1964-71, Vietnam. Recipient Achievement award Greater Cleve. Nurses Assn., 1986. Mem. AACN, Am. Assn. Tchrs. German, Am. Assn. Tchrs. Portuguese and Spanish, Assn. Specialists in Aging, Frances Payne Bolton Sch. Nursing Alumni Assn. (pres. 1992-93), Kappa Delta Pi, Sigma Theta Tau. Home: 5011 Nob Hill Dr Apt 9C Chagrin Falls OH 44022 Office: Cleve Clinic Found 9555 Rockside Rd Valley View OH 44125

VANLEER, JAMES G., state legislator; m. Gwendolyn Vanleer. BA, Wilberforce U.; MA, Ball State U. Benefits mgr. New Venture Gear, Inc.; mem. Ind. State Ho. of Reps. Dist. 34, mem. environ. affairs com., mem. pub. policy, ethics and vet. affairs com., mem. roads and transp. com., vice chmn. aged and aging com. Mem. Jr. Achievement Coun.; former mem. Muncie (Ind.) Housing Bd. Mem. C. of C. (mem. advocacy and local govt. com.).

VAN LEUVEN, ROBERT JOSEPH, lawyer; b. Detroit, Apr. 17, 1931; s. Joseph Francis and Olive (Stowell) Van L.; student Albion Coll., 1949-51; BA with distinction Wayne State U., 1953; JD, U. Mich., 1957; children: Joseph Michael, Douglas Robert, Julie Margaret. Bar: Mich. 1957. Since practiced in Muskegon, Mich.; ptnr. Hathaway, Latimer, Clink & Robb, 1957-68, ptnr. McCroskey, Libner & Van Leuven, 1968-81, ptnr. Libner, Van Leuven & Kortering, 1982—; past mem. council negligence law sect. State Bar Mich. Bd. dirs. Muskegon Children's Home, 1965-75. Served with AUS 1953-55. Fellow Mich. Bar Found., Mich. Trial Lawyers Assn., Am. Coll. Trial Lawyers; mem. Assn. Trial Lawyers Am., Delta Sigma Phi. Club: Muskegon Country. Home: 2397 Westwood Muskegon MI 49441 Office: Libner Van Leuven & Kortering Muskegon Mall 400 Comerica Muskegon MI 49443

VAN LUVEN, WILLIAM ROBERT, management consultant; b. Toledo, Feb. 15, 1931; s. Harold Calvin and Ruth Frick (Routson) Van L.; m. Lyda Marie Buchanan Jones, Nov. 15, 1956 (div. Sept. 1960); children: Lynn Chase, Michael Frick; m. Barbara Wilson Ehni, Aug. 17, 1968; children: Eric Finley, Jay Palmer. BBA, U. Toledo, 1957; postgrad., U. Va., 1979. Group gen. mgr. Union Camp Corp., Wayne, N.J., 1961-73, 1979-82; pres.container & carton divs. Clevepak Corp., White Plains, N.Y., 1973-79; v.p., gen. mgr. Jefferson Smurfit Corp., Clayton, Mo., 1982-84; pres. Wm. R. Van Luven & Assocs. Inc., St. Louis, 1984—; exec. dir. Exec. Svcs. Corps of St. Louis; bd. dirs. Smurfit Industries, Alton, Ill., 1982-84, O'Connor Pharm. Corp., Detroit, 1982-84; pres. Mo. Clippers, Inc., 1988—. Cons. United Way of Greater St. Louis, 1987—; chair United Way Mgmt. Assistance Ctr., 1988-90; dir. Combined Health Appeal, Sherwood Forst Camp, Places for People, Inc. With USNR, 1951-53, Korea. Recipient Keyman award Toledo C. of C., 1956. Mem. Fibre Box Assn., Composite Can & Tube Inst. (pres. 1979), Paperboard Packaging Council, U.S. Brewers Assn., Racquet Club (St. Louis), Aspetuch Country Club (Weston, Conn.), Shriner, Sigma Nu. Republican. Episcopalian. Home: 2 Portland Ct Saint Louis MO 63108-1291

VAN MEER, GRETCHEN LEAH, engineering educator; b. Mt. Clemens, Mich., Jan. 1, 1942; d. Leo and Rose Emma (Gulden) Van M.; m. Charles Dallas Sigwart, Oct. 18, 1976; 1 child, Julia Dorothy. BA, Alma Coll., 1963; MS, Northwestern U., 1973, PhD, 1976. Tchr. math. Jefferson Intermediate Sch., Midland, Mich., 1963-65, Nat. Coll. Edn., Evanston, Ill., 1967-69; asst. editor Scott, Foresman & Co., Glenview, Ill., 1965-66; teaching assoc. Northwestern U., Evanston, 1973-75; asst. prof. U. Pitts., 1975-76; sr. rsch. assoc. U. Cin. Med. Ctr., 1976-80; lectr. W.Va. U., Morgantown, 1980-83; asst. prof. Cen. Mich. U., Mt. Pleasant, 1983-88; assoc. prof. computer sci. No. Ill. U., DeKalb, 1988-94; assoc. prof. mech. engring., 1993—; activist in adaptive tech. for persons with disabilities; presenter at profl. confs. Co-author: Fortran Multiple Choice and Programming Exercises, 1982, Software Engineering, 1990; editorial bd. U.S. Women Engr. mag., 1992; contbr. articles to tech. publs. Co-editor newsletter Sierra Club, Ohio, 1976-79; bd. dirs. Coalition Citizens with Disabilities in Ill., DeKalb, 1989—. Grantee NSF, 1985, Benjamin-Cummings Pub. Co., 1986. Mem. Soc. Women Engrs., Sigma Xi. Home: 110 E Sunset Pl De Kalb IL 60115-4424 Office: No Ill U Dept Mechanical Engring De Kalb IL 60115

VAN METER, EROC J., mechanical engineer; b. Pomeroy, Ohio, Oct. 28, 1960. AA in Drafting, Hocking Tech. Coll., 1980; BSME, Ohio U., 1988. Drafter Goodyear Atomic Corp., Piketon, Ohio, 1980-83; design drafter Gerald Hilfrety & Assoc., Inc., Athens, Ohio, 1985-88; project engr. Columbus Industries Inc., Ashville, Ohio, 1989—. Office: Columbus Industries Inc PO Box 257 Ashville OH 43103-0257

VAN MIDDENDORP, JUDY E.S., integrated studies consultant; b. Sussex, N.J., May 19, 1957; d. Tunis and Jennie Elizabeth (Vander Stad) Sweetman; m. Marvin Dale Van Middendorp, Aug. 5, 1983. AA, Orange County Community Coll., Middletown, N.Y., 1978; BA, Northwestern Coll., Orange City, Iowa, 1980; MEd, Sioux Falls Coll., 1987; EdD, U. S.D., 1990. Cert. tchr., Iowa, S.D. 2d grade tchr. Netherlands Reformed Christian Sch., Rock Valley, Iowa, 1980-83; instr., grad. asst. U. S.D., Vermillion, 1988-90; dir. student support svcs. Briar Cliff Coll., Sioux City, Iowa, 1990-91, asst. prof. edn., 1991-93; cons. integrated studies Western Hills AEA, Sioux City, 1993—. Mem. Internat. Reading Assn., Nat. Mid. Sch. Assn., Nat. Coun. for Social Studies, Iowa Coun. for Social Studies, Iowa Reading Assn., Siouxland Artists, Siouxland Reading Assn., Phi Delta Kappa.

VANN, HOWARD D., real estate executive. BS in Avt., Journalism, U. Nebr., 1955. Pres. Vann Realty, Omaha. Chmn. United Cerebral Palsy Campaign, 1961-62, Am. Cancer Soc. Campaign, 1962-63, Nebr. Head Injury Assn. Adv. Bd., 1985-86; vice chmn. Nebr. Bd. Abstract Examiners, 1968-70; pres. Nebr. Epilepsy League, 1962-63; bd. dirs. Nebr. State Bank, 1978-82, Cmty. Svc. Found., 1985-88, Boy Scouts Am. Mid-Am. Coun., 1970-78, v.p., 1978-86; bd. dirs. Omaha Symphony, 1995—; active YMCA, Heart Fund, Arthritis Assn., Rep. Party, Nebr. Gov.'s Traffic Safety Com., and numerous others. Named to Nebr. Jaycees Hall of Fame, 1995. Mem. Rotary Internat. (internat. dir. 1993-95, v.p. 1994-95, Found. Disting. Svc. award 1989, Found. Citation Meritorious Svc. award 1988), Omaha C. of C. (bd. dirs. 1969-73, chmn. Omaha Industry Seekers 1970-71), Oakdale Cmty. Club (pres. 1963-64), Jaycees (Nebr. pres. 1966-67, Omaha pres. 1963-64), U. Nebr. Omaha Alumni Club (pres. 1963-64). Office: Vann Realty Co 4601 S 50th St Omaha NE 68117-1305

VANN, THERESA MARY, historian; b. N.Y.C., Oct. 21, 1962; d. Francis Joseph Sr. and Katherine Blondina (Taylor) V. BA, Fordham U., 1983, MA, 1985, PhD, 1992. Asst. prof. Salem (Mass.) State Coll., 1992-93, U. Minn., Duluth, 1993-95; Malta cataloger Hill Monastic Manuscript Libr. St. John's U., Collegeville, Minn., 1995—. Editor, author: Women of Power, 1992; editor: (series) De re militari, 1994—. Mem. Am. Acad. Rsch. Historians of Medieval Spain (sec.-treas. 1992-96), Medieval Acad. Am., Soc. for Spanish and Portuguese Hist. Studies, Tex. Medieval Assn. (bd. dirs. 1993-95). Office: St John's U Hill Monastic Manuscrp Libr PO Box 7300 Collegeville MN 56321

VAN NIMAN, CYNTHIA MARIE, family physician, artist; b. Cin., Feb. 5, 1958; d. Kempton Charles and Colette Catherine (Ast) Van N.; m. Daniel John Wissel, July 27, 1980 (div. Oct. 1985); children: Catherine Marie, Stephanie Ann; m. David Alan Hart, May 20, 1995; 1 stepchild, Kyle Michael Hart; 1 child, Patrick Matthew. Diploma in German studies, U. Vienna, Ströbl, Austria, 1978; BA summa cum laude, Edgecliff Coll., Cin., 1980; MA in Art Therapy, Wright State U., 1983, MD, 1991. Diplomate Am. Bd. Med. Examiners, Am. Bd. Family Practice; cert. ACLS, PALS, ATR, neonatal resuscitation. Reservationist Gogo Tours, Cin., 1975-81; primary tchr. German, St. Agnes Sch., Cin., 1977-78; asst. counselor Living Arrangements for Developmentally Disabled, Cin., 1977-78; art therapist U. Cin. Med. Ctr., 1983-87, Millcreek Psychiat. Ctr. for Children, Cin., 1987; resident in family practice St. Elizabeth Med. Ctr., Dayton, Ohio, 1991-94, mem. staff, 1994-95; pvt. practice Beavercreek, Ohio, 1995—; pvt. practice Ohio Valley Family Physicians, Hillsboro, Ohio, Sabina, Ohio, 1994-95; keynote speaker Assn. for Edn. Young Children, Cin., 1987. One-woman show Emery Art Gallery, Cin., 1980. Judge Montgomery County Sci. Fair, 1988. Acad. presdl. and German studies scholar, 1976, activity scholar Edgecliff Coll., 1978, grad. scholar Wright State U., 1982, Cornaro scholar, 1990. Mem. Am. Acad. Family Practice, Ohio Med. Assn., Greene County Med. Soc., Chi Sigma Iota, Kappa Gamma Pi, Psi Chi. Roman Catholic. Office: Forest View Family Practice 1911 N Fairfield Rd Dayton OH 45432-2754

VAN NOSTRAND, CATHARINE MARIE HERR, human resources development executive, writer; b. Dubuque, Iowa, June 17, 1937; d. King George and Julia Marie (Hansen) Herr; m. David Michael Van Nostrand, July 16, 1960; children: Laura Susan Van Nostrand Caviani, Catharine Louise, Maren Thyra. Student, Grinnell (Iowa) Coll., 1955-57; BA in Music Edn., U. Iowa, 1959; MA in Human Devel., St. Mary's U. of Minn., Winona, 1989. Music specialist Bound Brook, N.J. and Brookline, Mass., 1959-62; coord. music and worship First United Meth. Ch., St. Cloud, Minn., 1970-75; founder, prin. cons. Catharine Van Nostrand & Assocs., St. Cloud, 1975—; guest lectr., author-in-residence nat. colls. and univs., regional, statewide, nat. and internat. acad. symposia, 1975—; tng. and devel. cons. numerous bus., govt., health and ednl. cons.; keynote spkr. and workshop facilitator regional and nat. confs. and convs., 1987—; cons./featured spkr. on Equal Opportunity for European Union countries, 1995. Author: Gender-Responsible Leadership: Detecting Bias, Implementing Interventions, 1993; contbr. articles to profl. jours. Capt. prof. div. fundraising for area family YMCA, St. Cloud, 1975; founding bd. dirs. St. Cloud Civic Orch.; vol. radio interviewer Minn. Pub. Radio and WJON Radio, Collegeville/St. Cloud, 1976-77. Mem. AAUW, Forum Exec. Women, Nat. Spkrs. Assn., Minn. Spkrs. Assn., St. Cloud Area C. of C. Democrat. Methodist. Home: 36854 Winnebago Rd Saint Cloud MN 56303-9657 Office: 14 7th Ave N Saint Cloud MN 56303-4766

VAN OSTENBURG, DONALD ORA, physics educator; b. East Grand Rapids, Mich., July 19, 1929; s. Arie and Jane (Versluis) Van Oostenbrugge; m. Betty Jean Roskamp, Aug. 31, 1951; children: Suzanne Lynn, Donald Mark. BS, Calvin Coll., 1951; MS, Mich. State U., 1953, PhD, 1956. Assoc. physicist Armour Rsch. Found., Chgo., 1956-59; group leader Argonne (Ill.) Nat. Lab., 1959-70; assoc. prof. DePaul U., Chgo., 1970-74, prof., 1974—; chmn. physics dept. DePaul U., Chgo., 1987-93. Contbr. over 30 articles to profl. jours. Pres. Cen. State Univs., DeKalb, Ill., 1985. Fellow Am. Phys. Soc., Am. Sci. Affiliation. Office: De Paul U 2219 N Kenmore Ave Chicago IL 60614-3504

VAN PATTEN, MARK LEE, newspaper publisher; b. Hillsdale, Mich., Nov. 24, 1947; s. Leon A. and Cass E. (Zeigler) Van P.; m. Nancy J. Reynolds, Aug. 17, 1968; children: Amy J., Rebecca L. BS, Ferris State U., Big Rapids, Mich., 1969. Sales rep. Bay City (Mich.) Times, 1970-74; advt. mgr. Boonville (Mo.) Daily News, 1974-76, asst. pub., 1976-78; pub. Daily Rev. Atlas, Monmouth, Ill., 1978-84, Princeton (Ind.) Pub. Inc., 1985-89; gen. mgr. Oakland Equipment Inc., Evansville, Ind., 1984-85; dir. mktg. Koleszar-Woodruff Advt. Inc., Evansville, 1989-90; pub. Wabash (Ind.) Plain Dealer, 1990-93; gen. mgr. Daily News, Bowling Green, Ky., 1993—; mem. adj. faculty Ind. U., Kokomo, 1992-93. Bd. dirs. United May, Monmouth, 1981, Princeton, 1989, United Way of So. Ky., 1994-95, Warren County Econ. Com., Monmouth, 1980, North Gibson Youth Coalition, Princeton, 1988, Operation PRIDE; mem. steering com. Boonslick Vocat.-Tech. Sch., 1978; chmn. Mo. River Festival, Boonville, 1976; mem. mem. com. YMCA, Monmouth, 1984; v.p. Jr. Achievement, Wabash, 1992, pres. 1993; mem. steering com. Leadership Wabash County, 1992-93; chmn. Leadership Devel. Wabash County. Recipient Disting. Citizen award Boonville Jaycees, 1977, Pub. of Yr. award Brehm Comm., 1988. Mem. Boonville C. of C. (pres. 1976).

VAN PELT, ROBERT IRVING, firefighter; b. Chgo., May 4, 1931; s. Irving Henry and Lillian Christene (Balder) Van P.; m. Donna Arlene Bengtson, Feb. 3, 1962; children: Robert Scott, Barbara Gail, James Arthur. Grad. high sch., Chgo. Fire dept. capt. Chgo. Fire Dept., 1954-89, ret., 1989. Dir. Edgebrook Cmty. Assn., Chgo., 1974-95; dist. vice chmn. programs Chgo. Area coun. Boy Scouts Am., 1985-93; scouting coord. Edgebrook Luth. Ch., Chgo., 1971—; mem. PTA Edgebrook Sch., Taft H.S. Decorated Combat Air Crew Wings, 1951; recipient Award of Merit, Boy Scouts Am., 1982, Silver Beaver award, 1987, Svc. award VFW, 1987; PTA scholar, 1956. Mem. Naval Air Mus. (founding life), Exptl. Aviation Assn., War Birds Am., E.A.A. War Bird Squadron 4, Am. Legion, Order of Arrow, Liberator (San Diego). Home: 6317 N Hiawatha Ave Chicago IL 60646-4219

VAN REGENMORTER, WILLIAM, state legislator; m. Cheryl; four children. Mich. jud. com., econ. devel. com., energy com.; chmn. House Rep. Caucus, 84-90. Commr. Ottawa County Bd. Commrs., 1980-82; rep. Mich. Dist. 55, 1982-90; sen. Mich. Dist. 22, 1995—. Named legis. of yr. 1985 Mich. Sheriff's Assn., Mich. Assn. Police, 1988, Police Officer's Assn. Mich., 1989; recipient Santarelli award Nat. Orgn. for Victim Assistance, 1985, justice award Found. for Improvement of Justice, 1986, leadership award Nat. Sheriff's Assn., 1987. Home: 6293 Springmont Dr Hudsonville MI 49426-8704*

VAN SICKLE, BARBARA ANN, special education educator; b. Dubuque, Iowa, Apr. 29, 1932; d. Ralph and Grace Elizabeth (Dennis) Browne; m. Marvin Allen Van Sickle, June 7, 1953; children: Mark, Lee Ann Van Sickle Back, David, Karen Van Sickle. BA, U. No. Iowa, 1954; MA, Clarke Coll., 1971. Cert. tchr., Iowa. Tchr. remedial reading Dubuque schs., 1967-76; spl. edn. tchr. Indianola (Iowa) schs., 1976-92. Pub. info. chair Nat. Balloon Classic, Indianola, 1990-91, 93-94, 95-96; pres. Warren County Assn. for Children with Learning Disabilities, Indianola, 1978-80. Mem. NEA, AAUW, Iowa State Edn. Assn., Indianola Edn. Assn. (pres. 1988-89, chair govtl. affairs 1990-92), Learning Disabilities Assn. Iowa (chair book room 1978-91, 2d v.p. 1994, 95, 1st v.p. 1996. Appreciation award 1980, Pres. award 1989, Helping Hands award 1993). Democrat.

VAN SICKLE, BRUCE MARION, federal judge; b. Minot, N.D., Feb. 13, 1917; s. Guy Robin and Hilda Alice (Rosenquist) Van S.; m. Dorothy Alfreda Hermann, May 26, 1943; children: Susan Van Sickle Cooper, John Allan, Craig Bruce, David Max. BSL, U. Minn., 1941, JD, 1941. Bar: Minn. 1941, N.D. 1946. Pvt. practice law, Minot, 1947-71; judge U.S. Dist. Ct. N.D., 1971-85, sr. judge, 1985—; mem. N.D. Ho. of Reps., 1957, 59. Served with USMCR, 1941-46. Mem. ABA, N.D. Bar Assn., N.W. Bar Assn., Ward County Bar Assn., Am. Trial Lawyers Assn., Am. Coll. Probate Counsel, Am. Judicature Soc., Bruce M. Van Sickle Inns of Ct., Masons, Shriners, Elks. Office: US Dist Ct 430 US Courthouse PO Box 670 Bismarck ND 58502-0670

VANSTROM, MARILYN JUNE, retired elementary education educator; b. Mpls., June 10, 1924; d. Harry Clifford and Myrtle Agnes (Hagland) Christensen; m. Reginald Earl Vanstrom, Mar. 20, 1948; children: Gary Alan, Kathryn June Vanstrom Marinello. AA, U. Minn., 1943, BS, 1946. Cert. elem. tchr., N.Y., Ill. Tchr. Pub. Sch., St. Louis Park, Minn., 1946-47, Deephaven, Minn., 1947-50, Chicago Heights, Ill., 1950-52, Steger, Ill., 1964; substitute tchr. Pub. Sch., Dobbs Ferry, N.Y., 1965-72, Yonkers, N.Y., 1965-92. Mem. Ch. Women, Christ Meml. Luth. Ch. Mem. AAUW (life, pres. 1988-90, Ednl. Found. award 1990, Morning Book Club, Evening Book Club Met. West br.), Yonkers Fedn. Tchrs. Democrat. Home: 12300 Marion Ln W Apt 2105 Minnetonka MN 55305-1317

VANTINE, BRUCE LYNN, choral conductor; b. Bismarck, N.D., July 21, 1949; s. Thelma J. (Liessman) Vantine; m. Lucinda Reed, June 19, 1971; children: Elizabeth C., Charles R. BM, Concordia Coll., 1971; MM, Mich. State U., 1976; DMA, U. Ill., 1982. Dir. choral music Bismarck Pub. Schs., 1971-72, Pelican Rapids (Minn.) Pub. Schs., 1972-75, Mt. Mercy Coll., Cedar Rapids, Iowa, 1976-78, U. Mo., St. Louis, 1980-93; creator, conductor The Cornerstone Chorale & Brass, St. Louis, 1988—; adv. bd. mem. St. Louis Children's Chorus, 1985—; bd. dirs. Premier Performances, St. Louis, 1985—. Mem. Am. Choral Dirs. Assn. Home: 2685 Woodsage Dr Florissant MO 63033 Office: Cornerstone Chorale & Brass PO Box 4010 Florissant MI 63032

VAN UMMERSEN, CLAIRE A(NN), academic administrator, biologist, educator; b. Chelsea, Mass., July 28, 1935; d. George and Catherine (Courtovich); m. Frank Van Ummersen, June 7, 1958; children: Lynn, Scott. BS, Tufts U., 1957, MS, 1960, PhD, 1963; DSc (hon.), U. Mass., 1988, U. Maine, 1991. Rsch. asst. Tufts U., 1957-60, 60-67, grad. asst. in embryology, 1962, postdoctoral teaching asst., 1963-66, lectr. in biology, 1967-68; asst. prof. biology U. Mass., Boston, 1968-74; assoc. prof. U. Mass., 1974-86, assoc. dean acad. affairs, 1975-76, assoc. vice chancellor acad. affairs, 1976-78, chancellor, 1978-79, dir. Environ. Sci. Ctr., 1980-82; assoc. vice chancellor acad. affairs Mass. Bd. Regents for Higher Edn., 1982-85, vice chancellor for mgmt. systems and telecommunications, 1985-86; chancellor Univ. System N.H., Durham, 1986-92; sr. fellow New Eng. Bd. Higher Edn., 1992-93; sr. fellow New Eng. Resource Ctr. Higher Edn. U. Mass., 1992-93; pres. Cleve. (Ohio) State U., 1993—; cons. Mass. Bd. Regents, 1981-82, AGB, 1992—, Kuwait U., 1992-93; asst. Lancaster Course in Ophthalmology, Mass. Eye. and Ear Infirmary, 1962-69, lectr., 1970-93, also coord.; reviewer HEW; mem. rsch. team which established safety stds. for exposure to microwave radiation, 1958-65; participant Leadership Am. program, 1992-93. Mem. N.H. Ct. Systems Rev. Task Force, 1989-90; mem. New Eng. Bd. Higher Edn., 1986-92, mem. exec. com., 1989-92, N.H. adv. coun., 1990-92; chair Rhodes Scholarship Selection Com., 1986-91; bd. dirs. N.H. Bus. and Industry Assn., 1987-90, 90-93; governing bd. N.H. Math. Coalition, 1991-92; exec. com. 21st Century Learning Community, 1992-93; state panelist N.H. Women in Higher Edn., 1986-93; bd. dirs. Urban League Greater Cleve., 1993—, mem. strategic planning com., chair edn. com., 1996—; bd. dirs. Great Lakes Sci. & Tech. Mus., 1993—, Sci. & Tech. Coun. Cleve. Tomorrow, Ohio Aerospace Inst., 1993—, Northeast Ohio Coun. Higher Edn., 1993—; mem. Leadership Am. Class '93, Leadership Cleve. Class '95. Recipient Disting. Svc. medal U. Mass., 1979, Am. Cancer Soc. grantee Tufts U., 1960. Mem. Am. Coun. on Edn. (com. on self-regulation 1987-91), State Higher Exec. Officers (fed. rels. com., cost accountability task force, exec. com. 1990-92), ACE (com. leadership devel.), Nat. Assn. Sys. Heads (exec. com. 1990-92), Nat. Ctr. for Edn. Stats. (network adv. com. 1989-92, chair accreditation teams 1988—), New Eng. Assn. Schs. and Colls. (commn. on higher edn. 1990-93), North Ctrl. Assn. Schs. and Colls. (evaluator 1993, 95, 96), Soc. Devel. Biology, Greater Cleve. Round Table (bd. dirs. 1993—), Cleve. Playhouse (trustee 1994—), United Way (bd. dirs. 1995—), Nat. Assn. State Univs. and Land Grant Colls. (exec. com. on urban agenda, state rep. AASCU), Phi Beta Kappa, Sigma Xi. Office: Cleve State Univ Rhodes Tower Euclid Ave at E 24th St Cleveland OH 44115

VAN VLEET, WILLIAM BENJAMIN, retired lawyer, life insurance company executive; b. Milw., Dec. 4, 1924; s. William Benjamin and Irene (Peppey) Van V.; m. Marilyn Nilles, Dec. 26, 1946; children: Terese Van Vleet Svetich, Susan Van Vleet Waldo, William Benjamin III, Monica Van Vleet McCarthy, Mark. Student, Marquette U., 1942-43, Lawrence Coll., Appleton, Wis., 1943-44; LLB, JD, Marquette U., 1948. Bar: Wis. 1948, Ill. 1950. Gen. counsel George Rogers Clark Mut. Casualty Co., Rockford, Ill., 1948-59; gen. counsel Pioneer Life Ins. Co. Ill., Rockford, 1950-68, 81-94, v.p., 1959-91, gen. counsel, 1968-91, exec. v.p., 1981-95, also bd. dirs.; exec. v.p., gen. counsel Pioneer Fin. Svcs., Inc., Rockford, 1985-95, gen. counsel emeritus, dir., 1995—; pres. Nat. Group Life Ins. Co., Rockford, 1992-93, exec. v.p., gen. counsel, 1993-94, also bd. dirs.; pres. Western Life Ins. Co. Am., Rockford, 1981-82, Health & Life Ins. Co. Am., Rockford, 1984-92, exec. v.p., gen. counsel, 1993-94; pres. Manhattan Nat. Life Ins. Co., Cin., 1990-92, exec. v.p., gen. counsel, 1993-94, also bd. dirs.; exec. v.p., gen. counsel Continental Life and Accident Co., Boise, Idano, 1993-94, also bd. dirs.; bd. dirs. Nat. Health Svcs. Milw. Mem. adminstrn. Boylan Ctrl. Cath. H.S., Rockford, 1965-72; pres. Diocesan Bd. Edn., Rockford, 1970-78; v.p., pres. Nat. Assn. Bds. Edn., 1972-78; v.p., pres. Nat. Assn. Bds. Edn., 1972-78; v.p., pres. Nat. Assn. Bds. Edn., 1972-78; mem. bd. advisors Marion Coll., 1976-79; mem. adv. bd. St. Anthony's Hosp., Rockford, 1978-91; bd. dirs. Crimestoppers, Rockford, 1982-90; co-chmn. United Cerebral Palsy Telethon, Rockford, 1985-95. Mem. ABA, Ill. Bar Assn., Winnebago County Bar Assn., Forest Hills Country Club, Masons. Office: Pioneer Fin Svcs Inc 303 N Main St Rockford IL 61101

VAN VYVEN, DALE NULSEN, state legislator; b. Cin., Apr. 20, 1935; s. Richard J. and Vera Nulsen Bennett (Plue) Va V.; m. Anne Saterfield, 1952; children: Pamela S. Van Vyven Seils, Stacey C. Van Vyven Petitt, Margo B. Van Vyven Johnson, Eric, Meredith A., Studart D. Student, Univ. Cin., 1953-66. Packaging engr. Avco Corp., Cin., 1955-66; ins. agt. Dale N. Van Vyven, Sharonville, 1967; clk. of coun. Sharonville, Ohio, 1964-65; councilman at large, 1966-75; pres. of coun. Sharonville, Ohio, 1975-78; Ohio state rep. Dist. 32, 1978—; del. Rep. Nat. Conv., 1980; chmn. United Conservatives of Ohio, ALEC. nat. chmn. Named Outstanding Legislator Ohio, 1984, 94, Outstanding ALEC leader, 1989; recipient NFIB Ohio Guardian of

Small Bus. award, 1992. Mem. Cin. Assn. Life Underwriters, Ohio Life Underwriters, Nat. Assn. Life Underwriters, Bus. Assn., Nat. Fedn. Ind. Bus., Kiwanis, Jaycees, Dan Beard Coun. Home: 4799 Fields Ertel Rd Sharonville OH 45241-1759 Office: 11006 Reading Rd Sharon Vine OH 45241-1929 Capitol Office: 910 17th St NW 5th Fl Washington DC 20006*

VAN WAGNER, NANCY LEE, retired educator; b. Bklyn., Aug. 8, 1938; d. Antonio and Julia Kathryn (Frieri) Mercaldo; m. Arthur L. Van Wagner (div. 1979); 1 child, Anthony Burton. Student, Pine Crest Bible Inst., 1959-62; BA, Roberts Wesleyan Coll., 1964; MEd, Mich. State U., 1970; diploma in legal assistance, Oakland U., 1984. Elem. tchr. Holly (Mich.) Sch. Dist., 1966-69; elem. tchr. Clarkston (Mich.) Sch. Dist., 1969-94, ret., 1994; legal asst. intern George Dovas, Southfield, Mich., summer 1984; mem. 1st task force to establish requirements for spl. edn., Mich., 1970-71; mem. sch. improvement com. Pine Knob Elem. Sch., Clarkston, 1994-95; sec. to bd. dirs. WE Restaurant Corp., 1989-90; established Van Wagner Pub. Co., 1992. Precinct del., 1984-92, mem. exec. com. Oakland County Dem. Com., 1986-92, Sunday Sch. leader Brightmoor Tabernacle. Recipient Presdl. Fitness award for walking, 1991. Mem. NEA , Mich. Edn. Assn., Clarkston Edn. Assn. (regional rep. 1988-94, del.-at-large to NEA conf. 1990). Home: 8564 Elzabeth Lake Rd PO Box 402 Union Lake MI 48387

VAN WYK, BETTY VICHA, financial planner, township clerk; b. Berwyn, Ill., Apr. 12, 1939; d. Louis J. and Vlasta Marie (Topinka) Vicha; m. Paul Herbert Van Wyk, June 4, 1960 (div. June 1977); children: Laura Elizabeth, Mark Paul. BA magna cum laude, Hope Coll., 1961; postgrad., No. Ill. U., 1976-80. Cert. fin. planner, Ill. Reporter, columnist Pioneer Press Newspapers, Oak Park, Ill., 1970-75; freelance pub. relations cons. Oak Park, 1975-88; dir. communications Oak Park-River Forest High Sch., Oak Park, 1975-88; fin. planner, investment advisor Van Wyk Fin. Svcs., Oak Park, Ill., 1988—; workshop presenter, panelist speaker Ill. Assn. Sch. Bds.; clk. Oak Park Twp., 1985—. Trustee Oak Park Twp., 1981-85; commr. Oak Park Community Relations Commn., 1979-81. Recipient Faculty Honors Mortar Bd., Hope Coll. Mem. Publicity Club Chgo., Nat. Sch. Pub. Rels. Assn., Ill. Sch. Pub. Rels. Assn. (bd. dirs. 1982-88, various awards), LWV, Oak Park C. of C. (task force 1985-88), Zonta (bd. dirs. Oak Park 1988-91). Unitarian. Office: Van Wyk Fin Svcs 632 Gunderson Ave Oak Park IL 60304-1422

VAN ZANDT, TIM, state legislator. Rep. dist. 38 State of Mo., Kansas City. Office: 3930 Campbell Rm 400 CB Kansas City MO 64110

VARCHETTA, FELIX R., advertising agency executive; b. Chgo., July 11, 1920; s. Vincent and Anne (Allegretti) V. BS in mktg., De Paul U., 1949; MBA, Northwestern U., 1952. Advt. & sales mgr. O-Cedar Corp., Chgo., 1951-62, Strom Becker Corp., Chgo., 1963-67; product mgr. Helene Curtis Industries, Chgo., 1962-63; account exec., owner Phil Varchetta & Assocs., Chgo., 1968—. 1st sgt. U.S. Army, 1942-46. Mem. Assn. Profl. Orchestra Leaders (bd. dirs.), Am. Philatelic Soc. Democrat. Roman Catholic. Home: 5617 N Knox Chicago IL 60646 Office: Phil Varchetta & Assocs 5901 N Cicero Ste 410 Chicago IL 60646

VARDY, ALEXANDER, mathematician, engineer; b. Moscow, Nov. 12, 1963; came to U.S., 1992; s. Aharon Nudelman and Tanya (Peselev) V.; m. Hagit Miriam Itzkowitz, Mar. 10, 1988. BSc, Technion, Haifa, Israel, 1985; PhD, Tel-Aviv U., 1991. Engr. R&D, project mgr. Israeli Air Force, 1985-90; assoc. IBM Sci. and Tech. Ctr., Haifa, Israel, 1991-92; vis. scientist IBM Almaden Rsch. Ctr., San Jose, Calif., 1992-93; asst. prof. U. Ill., Urbana, 1993—; cons. Tadiran Telecomm., Inc., Petah-Tiqua, Israel, 1991-92, AT&T Bell Labs, Murray Hill, N.J., 1996. Assoc. editor: IEEE Transactions on Information Theory, 1995—; patentee in field; contbr. articles to profl. jours. Recipient Career award NSF, 1995, Rsch. Initiation award, 1994, Invention Achievement award IBM Rsch. Divsn., 1993; grantee NSF, 1994-95. Mem. IEEE (sr., assoc. editor, guest editor-in-chief IEEE Transactions and Info. Theory), Am. Math. Soc. Office: Univ Ill 1308 W Main St Urbana IL 61801

VARECKA, CHARLES P., engineering executive; b. Buffalo, N.Y., Sept. 24, 1944; s. Charles and Rosemary (Sharrow) V.; m. Diana R. Can, Aug. 5, 1967; children: Timothy, Andrew. BS in Elec. Engring., SUNY, Buffalo, 1962-66; MS in Elec. Engring., Northeastern U., 1966-68. Chief engr. Honeywell, Mpls., 1980-83, dir. of engring., 1983-86; dir. of programs Honeywell, Edina, Minn., 1986-90; dir. of ops. Alliant Tech. Sys., Edina, 1990-92; v.p. Alliant Tech. Sys., Hopkins, Minn., 1992—. Contbr. numerous articles to profl. pubs. Fellow Assn. of U.S. Army; mem. IEEE, Am. Defense Preparedness Assn. (sr.). Home: 10734 James Cir. S. Bloomington MN 55431-4156

VARGA, CAROLYN ANN, computer company executive; b. Rockford, Ill., Jan. 5, 1950; d. Robert B. and Marie (Pekel) Graff; m. Andrew Varga; children: Charles Kerwin, Robert Kerwin. BS, U. Wis., 1972; MBA, U. Detroit, 1980. Engr. Burroughs, Plymouth, Mich., 1973-81; engring. mgr. Burroughs, Coral Springs, Fla., 1981-84, mgr. product support, 1984-85; mgr. product support Burroughs, Livingston, Scotland, 1985-86; mgr. engring. adminstrn. Unisys, Detroit, 1986-87, mgr. configuration mgmt., 1987-89, mgr. adv. mfg. engring., 1989-90, mgr. new products releases, 1990-93, mgr. media mfg., 1993—. Mem. DAR (regent 1991-92, chmn. state jr. membership 1987-91, chmn. credentials 1991-93, Outstanding Jr. mem. 1983, state vice-regent 1994—), Women in Engring. (guest lectr. 1983-86, OPCON speaker 1994). Roman Catholic. Office: Unisys 13250 N Haggerty Rd Plymouth MI 48170-4206

VARGA, ILONA, state legislator; b. Hungary, Apr. 19, 1951; d. Stephen and Eva (Nagy) Fazekas; children: Laura K., Louis S. JD, Urban Bible Coll., 89. Adminstrv. asst. Spkr. Pro Tem Matthew McNeely; adminstrv. aide House Com. Ins.; state rep. Mich. Dist. 3, 87-94, Mich. Dist. 8, 95—; vice chmn. state affairs com.; mem. Ins. Labor, Liquor Control, Conservation & Environ. & Sr. Citizens & Retirement coms.; Mich. House Rep. Vol. Mich. Metro. Girl Scouts U.S., PTA. Recipient lifetime meml. award Detroit Friends of Headstart, 84, civic award Spkr. Matthew McNeely, 84. Mem. Hungarian Am. Dem. Club, Detroit Improvement Assn., Wayne County Reading Coun., Am. GI Forum. Home: PO Box 30014 Lansing MI 48909-7514 Office: Mich State Senate PO Box 30014 Lansing MI 48909-7514*

VARGA, RICHARD STEVEN, mathematics educator; b. Cleve., Oct. 9, 1928; s. Steven and Ella (Krejcs) V.; m. Esther Marie Pfister, Sept. 22, 1951; 1 dau., Gretchen Marie. BS, Case Inst. Tech. (merged with Case Western Res. U.), 1950; AM, Harvard U., 1951, PhD, 1954; hon. doctorate, U. Karlsruhe, 1991, U. Lille, 1993. With Bettis Atomic Power Lab., Westinghouse Electric Co., 1954-60, adv. mathematician, 1959-60; full prof. math. Case Inst. Tech. (now Case We. Res. U.), 1960-69; univ. prof. Kent (Ohio) State U., 1969—, dir. rsch. Inst. for Computational Math.; Cons. to govt. and industry. Author: Matrix Iterative Analysis, 1962, Functional Analysis and Approximation Theory in Numerical Analysis, 1971, Topics in Polynomial and Rational Interpolation and Approximation, 1982, Zeros of Sections of Power Series, 1983, Scientific Computation on Mathematical Problems and Conjectures, 1990; editor: Numerical Solution of Field Problems in Continuum Physics, 1970, Padé and Rational Approximations: Theory and Applications, 1977, Rational Approximations and Interpolation, 1984, Computational Methods and Function Theory, 1990, Numerical Linear Algebra, 1993; editor-in-chief. Numerische Math., Electronic Transactions Numerical Analysis; mem. editl. bd. Linear Algebra and Applications, Constructive Approximation, Computational Mathematics (China), Utilities Mathematica, Revue Française d'Automatique, Informatique, Recherche Opérationelle, Numerical Algorithms, Analysis. Recipient Rsch. award Sigma Xi, 1965, von Humboldt prize, 1982, Pres.' medal Kent State U., 1981; Guggenheim fellow, 1963; Fairchild scholar, 1974. Home: 7065 Arcadia Dr Cleveland OH 44129-6065 Office: Kent State U Inst Computational Mat Kent OH 44242

VARGAS, PATTIE LEE, author, editor; b. Spencer, S.D., Feb. 4, 1941; d. Gilbert Helmuth and Carol Maxine (Winans) Bohlman; m. Richard D. Gulling Sr., July 17, 1960 (div. 1977); children: Richard D. Jr., David M., Toni C.; m. Allen H. Vargas, May 9, 1979 (dec. 1993). BS in Secondary Edn. cum laude, Miami U., 1969; MA in English, U. Dayton, 1972. Tchr. Kettering (Ohio) City Schs., 1972-83; editor Gurney's Gardening News, Yankton, S.D., 1984-88; dir. pub. relations Gurney Seed and Nursery Co., Yankton, 1985-89; creative supr. catalogs Dakota Advt. div. Gurney Seed and Nursery Co., Yankton, 1986-89; v.p. A.H. Vargas Assocs., Vermillion, S.D., 1987-93; editl. project mgr. Mazer Corp., Dayton, Ohio, 1993—; v.p. A.H. Vargas Assocs. Mktg. and Comm. Cons., Vermillion, S.D., 1987-93; pub. rels. cons. Cath. Conf. of Ohio, Columbus, 1975-76. Author: Country Wines, 1991, Stay Well Without Going Broke, 1993, Cordially Yours, 1996; writer (movie): Planning Cath. Schs. Week, 1975, (multi-media show) Tribute to the Bicentennial, 1976. Mem. Miamisburg (Ohio) Sch. Bond Steering Com., 1980. Mem. Nat. Fedn. of Press Women (recipient Editorial Writing award, 1986, 87, 88), S.D. Press Women (recipient Sweepstakes award 1987, 1988, Catalog award 1988), Nat. Garden Writing Assn.

VARGISH, THOMAS, surgery educator; b. Bklyn., Sept. 23, 1944; s. Jacob Jon and Hildegard Louise (Sack) V.; m. Kathryn Louise Griffin, June 22, 1968; children: Lisa, Jacob Jon. BA, Yale U., 1966; MD, NYU, 1970. Asst. prof. U. Iowa, Iowa City, 1978-82; assoc. prof. W.Va. U., Morgantown, 1982-88; prof. U. Chgo., 1988—. Editor: Pediatric Trauma, 1995. Lt. comdr. USN, 1976-78. Office: U Chgo NC-5036 5841 S Maryland Ave Chicago IL 60637

VARNER, CHARLEEN LAVERNE MCCLANAHAN (MRS. ROBERT B. VARNER), nutritionist, educator, administrator, dietitian; b. Alba, Mo., Aug. 28, 1931; d. Roy Calvin and Lela Ruhama (Smith) McClanahan; student Joplin (Mo.) Jr. Coll., 1949-51; BS in Edn., Kans. State Coll. Pittsburg, 1953; MS, U. Ark., 1958; PhD, Tex. Woman's U. 1966; postgrad. Mich. State U., summer, 1955, U. Mo., summer 1962; m. Robert Bernard Varner, July 4, 1953. Apprentice county home agt. U. Mo., summer 1952; tchr. Ferry Pass Sch., Escambia County, Fla., 1953-54; tchr. biology, home econs. Joplin Sr. H.S., 1954-59; instr. home econs. Kans. State Coll., Pittsburg, 1959-63; lectr. foods, nutrition Coll. Household Arts and Scis., Tex. Woman's U., 1963-64, rsch. asst. NASA grant, 1964-66; assoc. prof. home econs. Central Mo. State U., Warrensburg, 1966-70, adviser to Colhecon, 1966-70, adviser to Alpha Sigma Alpha, 1967-70, 72, mem. bd. advisers Honors Group, 1967-70; prof., head dept. home econs. Kans. State Tchrs. Coll., Emporia, 1970-73; prof., chmn. dept. home econs. Benedictine Coll., Atchison, Kans., 1973-74; prof., chmn. dept. home econs. Baker U., Baldwin City, Kans., 1974-75; owner, operator Diet-Con Dietary Cons. Enterprises, cons. dietitian, 1973—, Home-Con Cons. Enterprises. Mem. Joplin Little Theater, 1956-60. Mem. NEA, Mo., Kans. state tchrs. assns., AAUW, Am., Mo., Kans. dietetics assns., Am., Mo., Kans. home econs. assns., Mo. Acad. Scis., AAUP, U. Ark. Alumni Assn., Alumni Assn. Kans. State Coll. of Pittsburg, Am. Vocat. Assn., Assn. Edn. Young Children, Sigma Xi, Beta Sigma Phi, Beta Beta Beta, Alpha Sigma Alpha, Delta Kappa Gamma, Kappa Kappa Iota, Phi Upsilon Omicron, Theta Alpha Pi, Kappa Phi. Methodist (organist). Home: PO Box 1009 Topeka KS 66601

VARNER, ROBERT BERNARD, counselor, educator; b. Ellsworth, Kans., May 31, 1930; s. Bernard Lafayette and Leota (Campbell) V.; B.S., Kans. State U., Pittsburg, 1952; M.S., U. Ark., 1959; postgrad. Mich. State U., summer 1955, U. Mo., summer 1962, (grantee) U. Kans., 1972-73; m. Charleen LaVerne McClanahan, July 4, 1953. Athletic coach, social sci. tchr. Joplin (Mo.) Sr. High Sch., 1956-63; head social sci. dept. R.L. Turner High Sch., Carrollton, Tex., 1963-66; asst. athletic coach, jr. high sch. social sci. tchr. Warrensburg, Mo., 1966-70; coach, social sci. tchr., Emporia, Kans., 1970-72; asst. cottage dir., counselor Topeka Youth Ctr., 1973—; substitute tchr. Topeka Pub. Schs., 1974—. Recreation dir. Carrollton-Farmers Branch (Tex.) Recreation Center, 1964-66; city recreation dir., Warrensburg, Mo., 1966-68. Served with USN, 1953-54. Mem. NEA, Kans. State U.-Pittsburg Alumni Assn., U. Ark. Alumni Assn., Phi Delta Kappa, Sigma Tau Gamma. Democrat. Methodist. Club: Elks. Address: PO Box 1009 Topeka KS 66601-1009

VARRAN, MIKE J., engineering executive; b. Grand Rapids, Mich., Apr. 23, 1952. BS, Lawrence Inst. Tech., 1976, Lawrence Inst. Tech., 1985. Registered profl. engr., Mich., Ky. Mech. engr. Jervis B. Webb Co., Farmington Hills, Mich., 1980-90; project engr. IDEA Engring. and Fabricating, Detroit, 1990-92, engring. mgr., 1992—. Office: IDEA Engring & Fabricating 13881 Elmira St Detroit MI 48227-3016

VASA, ROHITKUMAR BHUPATRAI, pediatrician, neonatologist; b. Rajula, Gujarat, India, July 26, 1947; came to U.S., 1973; s. Bhupatrai Jayantilal and Vijayalaxmi V.; m. Usha B. Shah, Feb. 26, 1970; children: Falguni, Monisha. MBBS, Med. Coll., Baroda, India, 1970, Diploma Child Health, 1971, MD in Pediatrics, 1973. Diplomate Am. Bd. Pediatrics, Sub-Bd. of Neonatal Perinatal Medicine, Am. Bd. Sports Medicine. Intern, then resident Beth Israel Hosp., N.Y.C., 1973-75; fellow in neonatology Bellvue Hosp. Med. Ctr., N.Y.C., 1975-77; attending pediatrician Gouverneur Hosp., N.Y.C., 1977-79; asst. chief pediatrics U.S. Army Hosp., Fort Campbell, Ky., 1979-81; dir. neonatology Mercy Hosp. and Med. Ctr., Chgo., 1981—. Contbr. articles to profl. jours. Fellow Am. Acad. Pediat.; mem. AMA, Soc. Critical Care Medicine, Am. Coll. Sports Medicine, India Med. Assn. (sec. 1992, pres.-elect 1993, pres. 1994), Indian Acad. Pediat., Ill. State Med. Soc., Chgo. Med. Soc., Chgo. Pediat. Soc., Physicians for Pediat. and Perinatal Care (sec. 1991-93, v.p. 1994). Hindu. Office: Mercy Hosp Dept Pediatrics Stevenson Expy Chicago IL 60616

VASELAAR, MEREDITH STANTON, librarian; b. Tracy, Minn., Sept. 11, 1960; d. Keith Laverne and Lillian Jeanne (Pommier) Stanton; m. Eric David Vaselaar, Sept. 29, 1984; children: Eldon John, Samantha Lynne, Rona Mae. BA in Lit., S.W. State U., Marshall, Minn., 1984. Childen's libr. Redwood Falls (Minn.) Pub. Libr., 1985-88; libr. Adrian (Minn.) Br. Libr., 1990—; storyteller, Nobles County, Minn., 1990—. Tchr. religious edn. St. Adrian's Cath. Ch., Adrian, 1991—; pres. Wee Dragons Presch., Adrian, 1992-93, v.p., 1991-92; tchr. jr. classics Elem. Sch., Redwood Falls, 1986-87. Recipient Good Neighbor award R.E. Miller Home for Mentally Disabled Adults, 1987. Roman Catholic. Office: Adrian Br Libr Box 39 214 Maine Ave Adrian MN 56110

VATCHER, CHERYL ANN, writer, paralegal; b. Woonsocket, R.I., Feb. 5, 1961; d. Edgar Morris Pero and Lorraine Silvia (Gariepy) Branconnier; m. Richard Paul Vatcher, June 27, 1982 (div.); 1 child, Michelle Laura. Student, Worcester State Coll., 1980-81, 87, Assumption Coll., Worcester, Mass., 1981-82, Rivier Coll., Nashua, N.H., 1985-86; AS, Madonna Coll., Westland, Mich., 1990, Vincennes U., 1990; BS, Madonna U., 1991; postgrad., U. Mich., 1993—. Tchr's. asst. Montessouri Preschool, Mew Milford, Conn., 1976; sec. Cin. Milicron, Worcester, 1980-82; sales specialist Avon Products, Mass., N.H., Mich., 1982—; cmty. crier Plymouth Cmty., 1990-95; press, guide Dearborn Press, 1990—; legal clk. N.G., R.I., N.H., Mass., 1979-85, USAR, N.H., Mich., 1986—; asst. mgr. Avon Products, Nashua, 1985-86; leisure time adult edn. tchr., 1994—. Author: poems; editor: Rollin' Times; contbr. articles to profl. jours. With U.S. Army, 1980. Mem. Wilson Quar. Mich. State Bar (legal asst. divsn. 1990—), Byline Mag. Mich. State Rep., Nat. Guard and Army Res., Vietnam Vets. of Am., Disabled Am. Vets., Paralyzed Vets. of Am. Democrat. Roman Catholic. Home and Office: PO Box 85296 Westland MI 48185-0296

VAUGHAN, DAVID JOHN, distribution company executive; b. Detroit, July 17, 1924; s. David Evans and Erma Mildred V.; A.B., U. Ill., 1950; postgrad. U. Chgo., U. Mo.; m. Anne McKeown Miles, Aug. 21, 1975; children by previous marriage: David John, Melissa Ann, Julia Crawford McLaughlin. Chemist, Midland Electric Colleries, 1950-52; pres. Varrco Distbg. Co., Peoria, Ill., 1953—; pres. David Vaughan Investments, Inc., Peoria, 1970—; investment adviser Fundamentalist Fund; instr. Carl Sandburg Coll., Peoria, 1968—; advisor Leelanau Found., Leelanau Meml. Found.; bd. trustees Eureka Coll. Served to lt. USAAF, 1942-46, USAF, 1951-52; Korea. Registered investment adv. Mem. Peoria Country Club, Northport Point Club (Mich.), Peoria Skeet Club, Racquet Club, Naples Club (Fla.), Naples Bath & Tennis Club, Masons, Shriners, Jesters, Alpha Tau Omega, Phi Eta Sigma, Phi Alpha Delta. Republican. Presbyterian. Home: 4413 N Grandview Dr Peoria IL 61614-6628 also: 861 Swallow Pointe Naples FL 33946 Office: 5823 N Forest Park Dr Peoria IL 61614-3559 also: 824 Birchwood Dr North Point MI 49670

VAUGHN, ARTHUR L., electrical engineer; b. Sharon, Pa., Jan. 30, 1948. BSEE, Case Western Res. U., 1970. Sr. devel. engr. Ajax Magnethermic Corp., Warren, Ohio, 1973—. Patentee in field. Office: Ajax Magnethermic Corp 1745 Overland Ave NE Warren OH 44483-2860

VAUGHN, EDWARD, state legislator; b. Abbeville, Ala., July 30, 1934; s. Ivory Vaughn and Posie (White) V.; m. Wilma Jean Lathion, 1957; children: Eric, Randall, Sybil, Attallah. BA, Fisk U., 1955; postgrad., U. Ill., 1955-56. Owner/founder Vaughn's Book Store, 1961—, Langston Hughes Theatre, 1975—; rep. Dist. 8 Mich. Ho. of Reps., 1995—. Contbr. articles to profl. jours. Recipient Hon. Citizenship award Republic of Uganda, East Africa, 1974, African Hist. Club award, Detroit, 1977, Great Contbrs. award Wayne County C.C., 1977, Spirit of Detroit award Detroit Common Coun., 1978. Mem. Pan-African Congress U.S., New Directions Inst., Am. Writers league, The New Pioneers.

VAUGHN, JACKIE, III, state legislator. BA, Hillsdale (Mich.) Coll.; MA, Oberlin (Ohio) Coll.; LittB, Oxford U.; LLD (hon.), Marygrove Coll., Detroit, Shaw Coll., Detroit; HHD (hon.), Highland Park (Mich.) Community Coll. Tchr. U. Detroit, Wayne State U., Detroit, 1963-64; mem. Mich. Ho. of Reps., Lansing, 1966-78; mem. Mich. Senate, Lansing, 1978—, asst. pres. pro tem, 1978-82, pres. pro tem, 1982-86, assoc. pres. pro tem, 1986—. Past pres. Mich. Young Dems.; chmn. Mich. Dr. Martin Luther King Jr. Holiday commn.; exec. bd. dirs. Detroit NAACP. With USN. Fulbright fellow; recipient Frank J. Wieting Meml. Service award, 1977, Focus and Impact award Cotillion Club, 1980, Outstanding Achievement award Booker T. Washington Bus. Assn., Outstanding Community Service award Charles Stewart Mott Community Coll. and Urban Coalition of Greater Flint, Mich., 1981; named Outstanding State Senator of Yr., Detroit Urban League Guild, 1983, Most Outstanding Legislator of Yr., Washburn-Ilene Block Club, 1983, numerous others. Mem. Am. Oxonian Assn., Fulbright Alumni Assn. Baptist. Home: 19930 Roslyn Rd Detroit MI 48221-1853 Office: Mich Senate PO Box 30036 Lansing MI 48909-7536

VAUGHN, JAMES MICHAEL, controller; b. Evansville, Ind., Dec. 21, 1939; s. Ray Chester and Mary Carol (Childress) V.; m. Patricia Rose Morrison, Nov. 10, 1973; 1 child, Annelise Kristin. BSBA, Butler U., 1965; postgrad., Ind. U., Indpls., 1969-71; MA in Bus. Adminstrn., Webster U., 1980; MA in Polit. Sci., Ball State U., 1987. Probate estate adminstr. Mchts. Nat. Bank, Indpls., 1970-71; commd. 2d lt. U.S. Army, 1966, advanced through grades to maj., 1978; fin. and acctg. officer U.S. Army, worldwide, 1974-83; asst. exec. officer Fin. and Acctg. Ctr. U.S. Army, Indpls., 1986-87; ret. U.S. Army, 1988; contr. Ind. Dept. Natural Resources, Indpls., 1988-95; dir. fin. Indpls. Pub. Housing Authority, 1996—; guest speaker on state govt. fin. Ball State U., 1989—. Contbr. to profl. publs. Fin. advisor Ind. Natural Resources Found., Indpls., 1990-95, Ind. Heritage Trust, Indpls., 1992-95. Mem. Govt. Fin. Officers Assn., Assn. Govt. Accts. (cert. govt. fin. mgr.), Ind. Govt. Fin. Mgrs. (chmn. fin. mgmt. steering com. 1993-95), Assn. U.S. Army (treas. local unit 1975-76), Fin. Corps Assn. (Army Regtl. Assn.), Hoosier Buffalo Riders (treas. 1988-95), Hist. Landmarks Found. Ind., Nat. Trust Hist. Preservation, Am. Soc. Mil. Comptrs., Am. Legion, Ind. Hist. Soc., Marion County-Indpls. Hist. Soc. Republican. Methodist. Home: 5221 Hedgerow Dr Indianapolis IN 46226-1621 Office: Ind Dept Natural Resources 402 W Washington St Rm 256W Indianapolis IN 46204-2748 : Indpls Pub Housing Authority 5 Indiana Sq Indianapolis IN 46204

VAUGHN, LISA DAWN, family physician, educator; b. Ashland, Ky., May 10, 1961; d. Charles Clinton and Mildred Darlene (Cantrell) V. AS in Biology, U. Ky., 1981, BS in Zoology, 1983; DO, W.Va. Sch. Osteo. Medicine, 1988. Diplomate Nat. Osteo. Med. Bd. Gen. intern Doctors Hosp. Inc., Massillon, Ohio, 1988-89; family practice resident Doctors Hosp. Inc., Massillon, 1989-91; emergency room physician Coastal Emergency Svcs., Snowpark, Ohio, 1989-90; urgent care physician Acute Care Specialists, Akron, Ohio, 1991; physician Portage Family Practice Clinic, North Canton, Ohio, 1991-95, First Care Family Health & Immediate Care Ctr., Canton, Ohio, 1995-95; dir. occupl. medicine First Care, Canton, 1996—; clin. asst. faculty Ohio U. Coll. Medicine, Athens, 1990-91, adj. clin. faculty, 1992—; asst. dir. family practice residency Ohio U. Coll. Medicine-Doctors Hosp. Inc., Massillon, 1992-95; urgent CARE physician First Care, Canton, Ohio, 1995—; med. dir. family home health svc. Doctors Hosp., 1992-94, chmn. dept. family medicine, 1994-95; med. advisor Boy Scouts Med. Explorers, Massillon, 1989-90; med. career advisor Girl Scouts Career Day, Canton, 1990; affiliate physician Cleve. Clinic, 1991—. Contbr. poems. Col. Ky. Cols. Assn., Ashland, 1989—; vol. United Way of Stark County, 1990-91. Mem. Cleve. Clinic Found. (affiliate physician), AMA, Am. Coll. Gen. Practitioners, Am. Osteo. Assn. (cert.), Ohio State Med. Assn., W.Va. Soc. Osteo. Medicine, Stark County Med. Soc., Sigma Sigma Phi (sec. 1985-86). Democrat. Office: First Care 4612 Tuscarawas St W Canton OH 44708

VAUGHN, NOEL WYANDT, lawyer; b. Chgo., Dec. 15, 1937; d. Owen Heaton and Harriet Christy (Smith) Wyandt; m. David Victor Koch, July 18, 1959 (div.); 1 child, John David; m. Charles George Vaughn, July 9, 1971. BA, DePauw U., 1959; MA, So. Ill. U., 1963; JD, U. Dayton, 1979. Bar: Ohio 1979, U.S. Dist. Ct. (so. dist.) Ohio 1979, U.S. Cir. Ct. (6th cir.) 1987. Communications specialist Charles F. Kettering Found., Dayton, 1968-71; tchr. English Miami Valley Sch., Dayton, 1971-76; law clk. to judge Dayton Mcpl. Ct., 1978-79; coordinator Montgomery County Fair Housing Ctr., Dayton, 1979-81, 85-89; atty. Henley Vaughn Becker & Wald, Dayton, 1981-90; pvt. practice Noel W. Vaughn Law Offices, Dayton, 1990—; lectr. Wright State U., Dayton, 1965-67. Chmn. Dayton Playhouse, Inc., 1981-92; pres. Freedom of Choice Miami Valley, Dayton, 1980-83, 86-87; bd. dirs. ACLU, Dayton, 1982-86; mem. com. Battered Woman Project-YWCA, Dayton, 1983-84; pres. Legal Aid Soc. Dayton, 1983-84; chmn. Artemis House, Inc., 1985-88, bd. dirs., 1988—; bd. dirs. Miami Valley Arts Coun., 1985-86, AIDS Found. Dayton, 1988-90, Miami Valley Fair Housing Ctr., Inc., 1992-94, Human Race Theatre Co., 1995—. Recipient Order of Barristers award U. Dayton, 1979. Mem. ABA, Dayton Bar Assn. (chmn. delivery legal svcs. com. 1983-84, family law com. 1991—), Ohio FAIR Plan Underwriting Assn. (bd. govs. 1986-92). Home: 2230 S Patterson Blvd #101 Dayton OH 45409

VAUGHT, RICHARD LOREN, urologist; b. Ind., Oct. 28, 1933; s. Loren Judson and Bernice Rose (Bridges) V.; widowed, July 1987; children: Megan, Niles, Barbara, Mary; m. Nancy Lee Gusa, Aug. 1992. AB in Anatomy and Physiology, Ind. U., 1955; MD, Ind. U., Indpls., 1958. Diplomate Am. Bd. Urology. Intern, then resident in gen. surgery U.S. Naval Hosp., St. Albans, N.Y., 1958-60, resident in urology, 1960-63; spl. fellow Sloan Kettering Meml. Hosp. for Cancer and Allied Diseases, N.Y.C., 1962; pediatric urology observer Babies Hosp., Columbia-Presbyn. Med. Ctr., N.Y.C., 1962; head urology U.S. Naval Hosp., Beaufort, S.C., 1963-65; asst. chief urology, head pediatric urology U.S. Naval Hosp., San Diego, 1965-68; pvt. practice Plaza Urol., Sioux City; med. dir. dept. hyperbaric medicine St. Luke's Regional Med. Ctr., Sioux City, 1988-95; pres., chmn. bd. dirs. Care Choices of Siouxland, Sioux City, 1987-94; med. dir. Male Impotence Clinic, Marian Health Ctr., Sioux City, 1995—. Organizer telecommunications system for deaf, Siouxland, 1983. Lt. comdr. USN, 1958-68. Fellow ACS, Internat. Soc. Cryosurgery, Am. Acad. Pediat.; mem. Am. Urol. Assn., Soc. Pediatric Urology, European Soc. Pediatric Urology (corr.), Undersea and Hyperbaric Medicine Soc., Am. Coll. Hyperbaric Medicine, Am. Soc. Laser Medicine and Surgery, Am. Lithotripsy Soc., Am. Coll. Physician Execs. (assoc.), Woodbury County Med. Soc. (pres.), Am. Confedn. Urology, Sertoma (Sertoman of Yr. award 1983). Home: 10 Cottonwood Landing South Sioux City NE 68776 Office: Plaza Urol PC 2800 Pierce St Ste 308 Sioux City IA 51104-3759

VAUTIER, JOHN M., sales executive; b. Mt. Claire, N.J., Mar. 18, 1954. BA, Buena Vista Coll., 1976; MA, Bowling Green State U., 1978. Sales rep. UARCO, Inc., Chgo., 1982—; sr. v.p. CommunisPond, inc., Chgo., 1985—. Presenter Arlington Heights (Ill.) Park Dist., 1994—; lector St. Ednas, Arlington Heights, 1988—. Named Citizen of Yr. Village of Saltaire, 1975. Mem. Sales and Mktg. Assn. of Chgo. Republican. Roman Catholic. Home: 1109 Oxford Ln Arlington Heights IL 60004

VAYNMAN, SEMYON, materials scientist; b. Odessa, USSR, Oct. 2, 1949; came to U.S., 1980; s. Kelman and Esther (Potashnik) V.; m. Dora Skladman, Nov. 18, 1977; children: Ethel, Alexander. MS in Chemistry, Odessa U., 1973; PhD in Materials Sci., Northwestern U., 1986. Rsch. scientist Rsch. Inst. Foundry Tech., Odessa, 1973-77, Rsch. Inst. Power

Industry, Lvov, USSR, 1977-80, GARD, Niles, Ill., 1981-84; rsch. scientist, rsch. prof. Northwestern U., Evanston, Ill., 1986—; reviewer Jour. Electronic Packaging, 1989, IEEE publ., 1988—; mem. adv. bd. sci. com. for solder joints reliability Dept. Def., Washington, 1989-90. Contbr. sci. papers to profl. publs., chpts. to books. Mem. Am. Soc. Metals, Mineral, Metals and Materials Soc. (electronic packaging and interconnection materials com. 1989—). Office: Northwestern U 1801 Maple Ave Evanston IL 60201-3135

VAYO, DAVID JOSEPH, composer, music educator; b. New Haven, Mar. 28, 1957; s. Harold Edward and Joan Virginia (Cassidy) V.; m. Margot Ehrlich, May 16, 1981; children: Rebecca Lynne, Gordon Francis. MusB, Ind. U., 1980, MusM, 1982; D of Musical Arts, U. Mich., 1990. Prof. Nat. U., Heredia, Costa Rica, 1982-84, Nat. Symphony Youth Sch., San Jose, Costa Rica, 1982-84; asst. prof. music Conn. Coll., New London, 1988-91; asst. prof. music Ill. Wesleyan U. Sch. Music, Bloomington, 1991-95, assoc. prof., 1995—; resident artist Banff Ctr. for Arts, 1992, 94, Va. Ctr. for Creative Arts, 1994; participating composer Internat. Soc. Contemporary Music-World Music Days, Mexico City, 1993, Internat. Double Reed Festival, Rotterdam, The Netherlands, 1995. Composer chamber composition Poem, 1990 (winner Spectri Sonori Internat. Composition competition Tulane U. 1992), Symphony: Blossoms and Awakenings, 1990 (performer St. Louis Symphony, Leonard Slatkin condr. 1993), Wind Quintet, 1991 (winner Symposium Seven for New Woodwind Quintet Music, U. Ga. 1993), Eight Poems of William Carlos Williams for solo trombonist, 1994 (commd. by St. Louis Symphony); works pub. by MMB Music and A.M. Percussion Publs. Charles E. Ives scholar Am. Acad. and Inst. Arts and Letters, 1988. Mem. ASCAP (awards 1988—), Am. Music Ctr. (copying assistance grantee 1992), Coll. Music Soc. (presenter nat. conf. 1990-94), Soc. for Electro-Acoustic Music in U.S. (presenter nat. conf. 1989), Soc. Composers (membership chmn. 1990—, presenter nat. conf. 1990, 92, 95), Am. Composers Forum. Office: Ill Wesleyan U Sch Music PO Box 2900 Bloomington IL 61702-2900

VAZ, NUNO ARTUR, physicist; b. Uige, Angola, Portugal, Nov. 23, 1951; came to U.S., 1976; s. Nuno and Ilda M. (Pedro) V.; m. Maria Joao, Apr. 16, 1977; children: Ana, Pedro, Bernardo. EE, Tech. U. Lisbon, Portugal, 1975; MA in Physics, Kent (Ohio) State U., 1977, PhD in Physics, 1980. Postdoctoral fellow CFMC, Lisbon, 1981-82; rsch. assoc. Kent State U., 1982-84; sr. rsch. scientist GM Rsch. Labs., Warren, Mich., 1984-86; staff rsch. scientist Tech. Leveraging Office, Warren, Mich., 1992-93, program mgr. govt. partnerships, tech. rsch. partnerships, 1992-93; project mgr. Govt. Leveraging GM Rsch. Labs., Warren, 1993—. Author: (chpt.) Liquid Crystals, 1991; patentee polymer dispersed liquid crystals. Matsumae Internat. Found. fellow, 1983; Nato scholar, 1976-77, Fulbright Hays scholar, 1976-80. Mem. Internat. Soc. Magnetic Resonance, Am. Phys. Soc., Soc. Automotive Engrs., Sigma Xi. Roman Catholic. Office: GM Rsch & Devel Ctr Govt Partnerships Dept 30500 Mound Rd Warren MI 48092-2031

VEACH, DARRELL ALVES, civil engineer, consultant; b. Lexington, Ky., Dec. 21, 1928; s. Darrell Goldman and Gladys Elizabeth (Stanhope) V.; m. Maureen Gay Mefford, July 21, 1932; children: Darrell Charlman, Cynthia Kay Veach Kiesel. BSCE, U. Ky., 1957. Registered profl. engr., Ky.; profl. land surveyor, Ky. Gen. field engr. Portland Cement Assn., 1957-64; v.p. engring. Engr. Assocs. Inc., Evansville, Ind., 1964-83; prin. ptnr. Veach, Nicholson Assoc. Inc., Evansville, 1983—. Pres. Evansville Historic Preservation Commn., 1980—; v.p. Evansville Airport Authority, 1990-93; bd. dirs. Evansville ARC, 1967—; pres. Evansville Rose Soc., 1972-74; mem. adv. com. Deaconess Hosp. Hospice, Evansville, 1988—; pres. Evansville Artists Guild, 1984-88. Recipient Clara Barton Honor award ARC, 1989, Gov.'s Cmty. Svcs. award State of Ind., 1990; named Jr. Engr. of Yr. Ind. Soc. Profl. Engrs., 1963; U. Ky. fellow, 1993. Mem. ASTM, Am. Concrete Inst., Masons (grandmaster 1995-96, Ind. Grand Lodge 1994, 33 degree mason 1989). Episcopalian. Home: 4000 Jennings Ln Evansville IN 47720-2428 Office: Veach Nicholson Assocs 1830 A W Franklin St Evansville IN 47720

VEATCH, JEAN LOUISE CORTY, telemetry nurse; b. Farmer City, Ill., June 4, 1932; d. Eugene Louis and Mary Violette (Mounce) Corty; m. July 23, 1955 (div.); children: Irvin, Ronald, Steven, Julie, James, Jeffery. Diploma, Holy Cross Cen. Sch. Nursing, 1954; BS, Coll. St. Francis, 1984; student, Valparaiso U. Cert. ACLS, coronary, critical care trained IMCU, obstetrics. Obstetrics nurse Holy Family Hosp., LaPorte, Ind., 1954-64; office nurse Dr. McDonald, Gulfport, Miss.; office nurse Dr. Jack Cartwright, LaPorte, Ind., med./telemetry unit nurse, 1977-96; staff nurse level III LaPorte Hosp., 1987-96, charge nurse, preceptor, 1988—. Mem. Am. Heart Assn., 1979-96; mem. Square Dance Club (B&B of Valparaiso, Ind.); organizer yearly square dance Toys for Tots, 1981-89; den mother Cub Scouts, Valparaiso. Mem. Am. Assn. Diabetic Educators. Home: 4409 Campbell St Valparaiso IN 46383-1303

VEAZEY, RICHARD EDWARD, accounting educator; b. Highland Park, Mich., June 20, 1941; s. Earl Leroy Veazey and Laura Louise (Madsen) Gruettner; m. Jeanne Ann Bayak, Aug. 9, 1969 (dec. Dec. 1969). BS, Ferris State U., 1964; MBA, Cen. Mich. U., 1966; PhD, St. Louis U., 1981. Staff acct. Ternstedt div. GM, Warren, Mich.; adminstrv. asst. Homelite div. Textron Corp., Madison Heights, Mich.; instr. acctg. Oakland Community Coll., Bloomfield Hills, Mich., 1966-70, asst. prof., 1970-71; assoc. prof. Walsh Coll., Troy, Mich., 1971-73; grad. fellow St. Louis U., 1973-75, instr., 1975-79; assoc. prof. acctg. Grand Valley State U., Allendale, Mich., 1979-85, 86—; lectr. European div. U. Md., Spain, Fed. Republic Germany, 1985-86; founder, exec. dir. West Mich. PDI, 1987—. Contbr. articles to profl. jours. Mich. Accountancy Found. grantee, 1973-76; Price Waterhouse scholar, 1975-76. Mem. Inst. Mgmt. Accts., Am. Acctg. Assn., Midwest Acctg. Soc. (pres. 1990-91), Masons, Shriners, Beta Alpha Psi, Sigma Phi Epsilon. Home: 2651 Westbrook Dr NW Grand Rapids MI 49504-2346 Office: Grand Valley State U 241 Lake Huron Hall Allendale MI 49401

VEBURG, RONALD NEIL, speech and theater educator; b. Hordville, Nebr., Apr. 20, 1930; s. John Emil and Emily Clarissa (Bengtson) V.; m. Darlene Bernice Prante, Oct. 4, 1959; children: Susan Jean, Anne Christine. AA, Luther Jr. Coll., Wahoo, Nebr., 1949; BA, Augustana Coll., Rock Island, Ill., 1951; MA, U. N. Colo., 1958. Instr. St. Paul (Nebr.) High Sch., 1951-58; instr., theater dir. Hastings (Nebr.) Sr. High Sch., 1958-92; ret., 1992; speech instr. Central Community Coll., Hastings, 1968; actor, technician Little Theatre of Rockies, Greeley, Colo., summer 1959. Concert mgr. Hastings Community Concert Assn., 1958-70, pres., 1970-72. Mem. Hastings Edn. Assn., Howard County Edn. Assn. (pres. 1956-58), NEA (life), Nebr. Speech Communication Assn. (sec. 1966-70), Nebr. State Edn. Assn., Internat. Thespian Soc., Lions, Kiwanis, Phi Delta Kappa (mem. 1956—, chpt. found. rep. 1984-87). Republican. Lutheran. Home: 901 Brentwood Ave Hastings NE 68901-3308

VECCHIO, ROBERT PETER, business management educator; b. Chgo., June 29, 1950; s. Dominick C. and Angeline V.; m. Betty Ann Vecchio; Aug. 21, 1974; children: Julie, Mark. BS summa cum laude, DePaul U., 1972; MA, U. Ill., 1974, PhD, 1976. Instr. U. Ill., Urbana, 1973-76; mem. faculty dept. mgmt. U. Notre Dame, 1976-86, dept. chmn., 1983-90, Franklin D. Schurz Prof. Mgmt., 1986—. Editor Jour. of Mgmt., 1995—. Mem. Acad. Mtm., Am. Psychol. Assn., Assn. Consumer Rsch., Am. Inst. Decision Scis., Midwest Acad. Mgmt., Midwest Psychol. Assn., Phi Kappa Phi, Delta Epsilon Sigma, Phi Eta Sigma, Psi Chi. Home: 16856 Hampton Dr Granger IN 46530-6907 Office: U Notre Dame Dept Mgmt Notre Dame IN 46556

VECOLI, RUDOLPH JOHN, history educator; b. Wallingford, Conn., Mar. 2, 1927; s. Giovanni Battista and Settima Maria (Palmerini) V.; m. Jill Cherrington, June 27, 1959; children: Christopher, Lisa, Jeremy. BA, U. Conn., 1950; MA, U. Pa., 1951; PhD, U. Wis., 1963. Fgn. affairs officer Dept. State, 1951-54; instr. history Ohio State U., 1957-59, Pa. State U., 1960-61; asst. prof. Rutgers U., 1961-65; assoc. prof. U. Ill., Champaign, 1965-67; prof. history, dir. Immigration History Research Center, U. Minn., Mpls., 1967—; vis. prof. U. Uppsala, Sweden, 1970, U. Amsterdam, The Netherlands, 1988, Maria Curie-Sklodowsk U., Lublin, Poland, 1992. Author: The People of New Jersey, 1965, Foreword to Marie Hall Ets, Rosa: The Story of an Italian Immigrant, 1970, (with Joy Lintelman) A Century of American Immigration, 1884-1984, (with others) The Invention of Ethnicity, 1990; contbg. author: Encyclopedia of the United States in the Twentieth Century, (1996), The Cambridge Survey of World Migration, (1995); Gil italiani fuori d'Italia, 1983, They Chose Minnesota: A Survey of the State's Ethnic Groups, 1981, Pane e Lavoro: The Italian American Working Class, 1980, Perspectives in Italian Immigration and Ethnicity, 1977, Immigrants and Religion in Urban America, 1977, The State of American History, 1970, The Reinterpretation of American History and Culture, 1973, Failure of a Dream, Essays in the History of American Socialism, 1984, Italian Americans: New Perspectives, 1985, May Day Celebration, 1988, In the Shadow of the Statue of Liberty, 1988, From Melting Pot to Multiculturalism, 1990, Studi Sull' Emigrazione, 1991, The Lebanese in the World, 1992, Swedes in America: New Perspectives, 1993, The Statue of Liberty Revisited, 1994, La Riscoperta delle Americhe, 1994, The Encyclopedia of Twentieth Century America, 1995, The Cambridge Survey of World Migration, 1995; editor, contbg. author: The Other Catholics, 1978, Italian Immigrants in Rural and Small Town America, 1987, The Gale Encyclopedia of Multicultural America, 1994; mem. editl. bd. Jour. Am. Ethnic History, Studi Emigrazione, America: History and Life Mid-America, Internat. Migration Rev., Estudios Migratorios Latino Americanos, Altreitalie; co-editor (with Suzanne Sinke) A Century of European Migrations, 1830-1930, 1991; contbr. articles to profl. jours. Chair history com. Statue of Liberty-Ellis Island Centennial Commn., 1983-90. With USNR, 1945-46. Decorated Knight Officer, Order of Merit (Italy); recipient Am. Philos. Soc. grantee, 1970; Newberry Libr. fellow, 1964, Am.-Scandinavian Found. fellow, 1970, NEH fellow, 1985-86; Fulbright-Hays sr. rsch. scholar Italy, 1973-74; Am. Coun. Learned Soc. grantee, 1974, 86, U.S. Dept. State Travel grantee, 1977, Acad. Specialist, U.S. Info. Agy., Brazil, 1993. Mem. Am. Italian Hist. Assn. (pres., mem. exec. council), Am. Hist. Assn., Orgn. Am. Historians, AAUP, Immigration History Soc. (pres., exec. council). Home: 610 E 58th St Minneapolis MN 55417-2426

VEENHUIS, MARK EDWARD, optometrist; b. Ann Arbor, Mich., 1960. BS in Psychology, U. Wis., Madison, 1984; MS in Physiol. Optics, U. Ala., 1986; OD, U. Mo., St. Louis, 1990. Pvt. practice. Mem. Am. Optometric Assn. Home: 2564 Pheasant Run Maryland Heights MO 63043-1480

VEGA, FRANK J., newspaper publishing executive. Pres., CEO Detroit Newspapers. Office: 615 W Lafayette Blvd Detroit MI 48226-3124*

VEGA, STEVE, probation officer, poet; b. N.Y.C., Nov. 13, 1949; s. Exio Ocasio Vega; m. Veronica Gonzalez, Jan. 3, 1971; children: Katherine, James-Paul Christian, Diamond Zhane. Cert. in bus. mgmt., Marion Bus. Coll., 1973; cert., John Marshall Law Sch., 1977; cert. in corrections and probations svcs., Chgo. Loop Coll., 1986; BA, Coll. of Commr. Sci., 1995. Adult probation officer Cook County, Ill.; union chief steward Cook County Adult Probation Dept., AFSCME, 1989-91; 1st v.p. AFSCME local 3486 APD officers, Chgo., 1991-92; cons. Chgo. Police Dept., FBI, U.S. Secret Svc. Contbr. poetry to over 20 anthologies worldwide, 1974—; appeared in films Only the Lonely, Music Box, Gladiator, Mo' Money, Hero, Hoffa, Natural Born Killers, others. Vol., mem. com. City of Chgo. Health Systems Agy., 1981-85; asst. scoutmaster Boy Scouts Am. Troop # 935, Chgo. 1993, Owasippe, Mich., 1994; unit commr. Boy Scouts Am. Troop # 978, Chgo., 1994. With USAF, 1970. Decorated USAF Commendation medal, 1969, knight comdr. (Italy); recipient Presdl. Commendations, Pres. Ronald Reagan, George Bush, 1987, 88, 90. Mem. ASCAP (composer, writer), Fraternal Order of Police (officer 1988), Sovereign, Military and Hospitaller Order of St. George in Karinthia (titular head). Roman Catholic. Address: PO Box 18-096 Chicago IL 60618-0096

VEINERMAN, ELLIOT, chemical process engineer; b. Shanghai, Jan. 4, 1947; came to U.S., 1960; s. Manasy J. and Michaella (Kraslavsky) V. BSChemE, Polytech. Inst., N.Y.C., 1970. Registered profl. engr., Ill., Ohio. Sr. process engr. UOP Inc., Chgo., 1970-1978, Brown & Root Inc., Chgo., 1978-1980, Sohio Oil Co., Cleve., 1980-1985; engring. cons. BP Oil Co., Cleve., 1985-92; process cons. Middough Assn. Inc., Cleve., 1992—. Patentee hydrocarbon processing. Mem. Cleve. Mus. Art, 1980—. Mem. AIChE, Musical Arts Assn., Musart Assn. Home: 6653 Duneden Ave Solon OH 44139

VEIT, WERNER, newspaper executive; b. Stuttgart, Federal Republic Germany, July 31, 1929; came to U.S., 1940, naturalized, 1948; s. Konrad David and Ida Sophie (Wolber) V.; m. Marianne DeWeese, Dec. 24, 1958; children—Anthony, Tamilyn, Andrea. Student, U. Md. With Grand Rapids (Mich.) Herald, 1949-59, mng. editor, 1958-59; Sunday editor Grand Rapids Press, 1959-63, mng. editor, 1963-66, editor, 1966-78; pres. Booth Newspapers, Inc., Grand Rapids, 1978—. Served with AUS, 1948-49. Mem. Am. Newspaper Pubs. Assn., Am. Soc. Newspaper Editors. Club: Kent Peninsular Torch (Grand Rapids). Home: 7361 Graeden Dr SE Grand Rapids MI 49546-9713 Office: Booth Newspapers Inc PO Box 1147 Ann Arbor MI 48106-1147 also: Booth Newspapers Inc 155 Michigan St NW Grand Rapids MI 49503-2302

VELARDO, JOSEPH THOMAS, molecular biology and endocrinology educator; b. Newark, Jan. 27, 1923; s. Michael Arthur and Antoinette (Iaculo) V.; m. Forresta M. Monica Power, Aug. 12, 1948 (dec. July 1976). AB, U. No. Colo., 1948; SM, Miami U., 1949; PhD, Harvard U., 1952. Rsch. fellow in biology and endocrinology Harvard U., Cambridge, Mass., 1952-53; rsch. assoc. in pathology, ob-gyn. and surgery Sch. Medicine Harvard U., Boston, 1953-55; asst. in surgery Peter Bent Brigham and Women's Hosp., Boston, 1954-55; asst. prof. anatomy and endocrinology Sch. Medicine, Yale U., New Haven, 1955-61; prof. anatomy, chmn. dept. N.Y. Med. Coll., N.Y.C., 1961-62; cons. N.Y. Fertility Inst., 1961-62; dir. Inst. for Study Human Reprodn., Cleve., 1962-67; prof. biology John Carroll U., Cleve., 1962-67; mem. rsch. and edn. divs. Saint Ann Obstetric and Gynecologic Hosp., Cleve., 1962-67; head dept. rsch. Saint Ann Hosp., Cleve., 1964-67; prof. anatomy Stritch Sch. Medicine Loyola U., Chgo., 1967-88, chmn. dept. anatomy Stritch Sch. of Medicine, 1967-73; pres. Internat. Basic and Biol.-Biomed. Curricula, Lombard, Ill., 1979—; course moderator laparoscopy Brazil-Israel Congress on Fertility and Sterility, and Brazil Soc. of Human Reproduction, Rio de Janeiro, 1973; organizer, chmn. symposia in field. Author, contbr.: (with others) Annual Reviews Physiology, Reproduction, 1961, Histochemistry of Enzymes in the Female Genital System, 1963, The Ovary, 1963, The Ureter, 1967, rev. edit., 1981; editor, contbr.: Endocrinology of Reproduction, 1958, The Essentials of Human reproduction, 1958; cons. editor, co-author: The Uterus, 1959; contbr. Progestational Substances, 1958, Trophoblast and Its Tumors, 1959, The Vagina, 1959, Hormonal Steroids, Biochemistry, Pharmacology and Therapeutics, 1964, Human Reproduction, 1973; co-editor, contbr.: Biology of Reproduction, Basic and Clinical Studies, 1973; contbr. articles to profl. jours.; live broadcasts on major radio and TV networks on subjects of bioscis., biomed. careers, biomed. subjects; co-author movie on human reprodn. The Soft Anvil. Apptd. U.S. del. to Vatican, 1964; charter mem. U.S. Rep. Presdl. Task Force, 1988—; rep. U.S. Senate Inner Circle, 1988—, U.S. Rep. Senatorial Commn., 1991—. With USAAF, 1943-45. Decorated Presdl. Unit citation, 2 Bronze Stars; recipient award Lederle Med. Faculty Awards Com., 1955-58; named hon. citizen City of Sao Paulo, Brazil, 1972; U.S. del. to Vatican, 1964. Fellow AAAS, N.Y. Acad. Scis. (co-organizer, chmn., consulting editor internat. symposium The Uterus), Gerontol. Soc., Pacific Coast Fertility Soc. (hon.); mem. Am. Assn. Anatomists, Am. Soc. Zoologists (organizer symposium The Uterus 1973), Am. Physiol. Soc. (vis. prof. 1962), Endocrine Soc., Soc. Endocrinology (Gt. Britain), Soc. Exptl. Biology and Medicine, Am. Soc. Study Sterility (Rubin award 1954), Internat. Fertility Assn., Pan Am. Assn. Anatomy (co-organizer symposium Reproduction 1972), Midwestern Soc. Anatomists (pres. 1973-74), Mexican Soc. Anatomy (hon.), Harvard Club, Sigma Xi, Kappa Delta Pi, Phi Sigma, Gamma Alpha, Alpha Epsilon Delta. Office: 607 E Wilson Ave Lombard IL 60148-4062

VELASCO, ESDA NURY, speech and language professional; b. Cali, Colombia, Oct. 1, 1953; d. Florentino and Dominga (Castro) Rivera; m. William Lubin Velasco, July 29, 1972; children: Martin Hernando, Monica Marie, Jaime Mauricio, Christopher Michael. BA in Psychology and Spanish cum laude, Cleve. State U., 1989, MEd. Spanish tchr. Berlitz Sch. of Langs., Cleve., 1979-85; interpreter Fed. Ct., Cleve., 1980-87; founder, pres. ENV Global Comm. Inc., Cleve., 1987—, Spanish instr., interpreter, translator, 1987—; interpreter various orgns., 1980-87. Mem. MLA, N.E. Ohio Translators Assn., Am. Translators Assn. (cert.). Roman Catholic. Office: ENV Global Comm 5005 Rockside Rd Ste 600 Cleveland OH 44136

VELDKAMP, BRENT M., engineering executive; b. Linden, Wash., Sept. 22, 1961. BS, Dordt Coll., Sioux Center, Iowa, 1984; MS, Iowa State U., 1993. Registered engr. and land surveyor, Iowa. Engr. Escon Tool, Escondido, Calif., 1985-86, Silent Drive, Inc., Orange, Iowa, 1987-91; project engr. Townsend Engring., Des Moines, 1992—. Christian Ref. Co. Office: Townsend Engring PO Box 1433 Des Moines IA 50305-1433

VELICER, JANET SCHAFBUCH, elementary school educator; b. Cedar Rapids, Iowa, Aug. 27, 1941; d. Allan J. and Geraldine Frances (Stuart) Schafbuch; m. Leland Frank Velicer, Aug. 17, 1963; children: Mark Allan, Gregory Jon, Daniel James. BS, Iowa State U., 1963, MS, 1966; cert. Elem. Edn., Mich. State U., 1976. Tchr. chemistry Prendergast High Sch., Upper Darby, Pa., 1964-65; tchr. home econs. Cardinal O'Hara High Sch., Springfield, Pa., 1965-66; substitute tchr. Pa., Mich., 1967-76; elem. tchr. Winans Elem. Sch., Waverly, Mich., 1976-78, Wardcliff Elem. Sch., Okemos, Mich., 1978-94; tchr. gifted and talented alternative program grades 4 and 5 Hiawatha Elem. Sch., Okemos, 1994-95; tchr. grade 4 Wardcliff Elem. Sch., 1995—; computer coord., Great Books coord.; dist. com. mem. math, computer, substance abuse, cable TV, evaluation revision Okemos Pub. Schs., Instructional Coun. Author: (video) Wardcliff School Documentary, 1982, The Integrated Arts Program of the Okemos Elementary Schools, 1983. Citizens adv. com. to develop a five-yr. plan, 1982-83, Bldg. utilization adv. com., 1983-84, Community use of schs. adv. com., 1984-85, Strategic planning steering com., 1989-90, Taking our schs. into tomorrow com., 1990-91, Bonding election steering com., 1991; chmn. wellness com. Okemos Pub. Schs., 1993-95. Recipient Classrooms of Tomorrow Tchr. award Mich. Dept. Edn., 1990. Mem. NEA, NAFE, Mich. Edn. Assn., Inst. Noetic Scis., Okemos Edn. Assn., Phi Kappa Phi, Mich. Coun. Tchrs. Math., Omicron Nu, Iota Sigma Pi. Democrat. Home: 2678 Blue Haven Ct East Lansing MI 48823-3804 Office: Okemos Pub Schs 4406 Okemos Rd Okemos MI 48864-2553

VELISARIS, CHRIS NICHOLAS, financial analyst; b. Berwyn, Ill., June 2, 1961; s. Nicholas Chris and Panagiota Nicholas (Georgiou) V.; m. Mary Elizabeth Vlahos, July 23, 1994. BS, U. Ill., 1983; MS, U. Wash., 1985; MBA, Dartmouth Coll., 1990; postgrad., U. Naples, Italy, 1991-94. Rsch. engr. Amoco Chem. Co., Naperville, Ill., 1983, 85-94; cons. Orco Ltd., Athens, 1989; rsch. mgr. U. Wash., Seattle, 1990-94; staff analyst fin. United Airlines, Chgo., Ill., 1994—; founder, prin. officer Velisaris Investment Cons. Svcs., Inc., Brookfield, Ill., 1994—; cons. in field. Author: Proc. 31st Ann. Nat. Sampe Symp., 1986, Polymer Engring. and Sci., 1986, 88, Proc. of the 5th European Conf. on Comp. Materials, 1992. Counselor Valleyview Correctional Ctr., Ill. Benedictine Coll., St. Charles, 1988; advisor Jr. Achievement of Chgo., Naperville, 1987-88. Mem. Tri-Orgn. of Amoco Corp. (bd. dirs. 1987-88). Greek Orthodox. Home: 59 N Drexel Ave La Grange IL 60525 Office: United Airlines World Hdqs WHQCJ PO Box 66100 Chicago IL 60666

VENERE, AL H., manufacturing company executive; b. Elmhurse, Ill., Nov. 23, 1957. Assoc. Bus., Coll. of DuPage, 1976. Mech. engr. Snow Mfg., Bellwood, Ill., 1978-85, Calif. Feeders, Anaheim, 1986-88; pres. Ragsdale Feeder Sys. Inc., Itasca, Ill., 1989—. Mem. C. of C. Roman Catholic. Office: Ragsdale Feeder Sys Inc 1371 Industrial Dr Itasca IL 60143-1856

VENEZIA, JOHN CARL, insurance company executive; b. Saint Joseph, Mo., June 24, 1947; s. V.A. and Katherine (Manger) V.; m. Peggy Ann Lindsey, Aug. 15, 1970; children: Anthony J., Christopher G. BS, Mo. Valley Coll., Marshall, 1969. CLU, ChFC. Agent, sales mgr. Aetna Life & Casualty, Champaign, Ill., 1973-79; rep. Northwestern Nat., Champaign, 1979-80; gen. agent, owner Venezia Ins. Brokerage, Champaign, 1980—; mem. chmn. Champaign Area Life Underwriters, 1986-87, treas. 1987-88, pres. 1988-89. Campaign worker Rick Winkel Campaign for State Representative, Champaign County, 1994; amb. Champaign C. of C., 1996. With USAF 1969-73. Recipient Membership award Ill. Life Underwriters, 1987. Mem. Am. Soc. Chartered Life Underwriters & Chartered Fin. Cons. (mem. Golden Key Soc.), Nat. Assn. Life Underwriters, Ea. Ill. Estate Planning Coun., Assn. Health Ins. Agents (charter), Champaign-Urbana Kiwanis (mem. chair 1995-96). Republican. Baptist. Home: 2310 Sumac Ct S Champaign IL 61821 Office: Venezia Ins Brokerage 1906 Fox Dr Champaign IL 61820

VENIT, WILLIAM BENNETT, electrical products company executive, consultant; b. Chgo., May 28, 1931; s. George Bernard and Ida (Schaffel) V.; m. Nancy Jean Carlson, Jan. 28, 1956; children: Steven Louis, Aprilann. Student U. Ill., Champaign, 1949. Sales mgr. Coronet, Inc., Chgo., 1952-63, pres., chmn. bd. dirs., 1963-74, Roma Wire Inc., Chgo., 1971-74; chmn. bd. dirs. Swing Time # 2, 1988-89; pres. Wm. Allen Inc., Chgo., 1972-74; pres., chmn. bd. dirs. Wraprama Inc., 1988-95, Swag Lite, Inc., 1989—; pres. William Lamp Co., Inc., 1993, William Wire Co., Inc., 1974-76; chmn. bd. dirs. MSWV, Inc., 1978—, pres. bd. dirs. 1985—; pres. Trio Steel Inc., Chgo., 1987-90; chmn. bd. Chgo. Lamp Works LLB, 1995; spl. cons. Hamilton Lamp Corp. div. Roadmaster Corp.; cons. Nu Style Lamp Shade. Patentee Printed-Cir., 1964. With QMC AUS, 1949-52. Mem. Mfr. Agt. Club, Chgo. Lamp and Shade Inst. (bd. dirs.). Avocation: bicycling. Home: 323 Suwanee Ave Sarasota FL 34243-1930 Office: MSWV Inc 2620 W Fletcher St Chicago IL 60618-7110

VENO, GLEN COREY, management consultant; b. Montreal, Que., Can., Sept. 5, 1951; came to U.S., 1953; s. Corey Elroy and Elsie Milly (Munro) V. BS in Aviation Tech. and Mgmt., Western Mich. U., 1976. Cert. mgmt. cons. Project mgr. The ASIST Corp., Oak Park, Mich., 1978-83; mgr. tech. support J.B. Systems, Inc., Woodland Hills, Calif., 1984-85; mgr. cons. svcs. Mgmt. Tech., Inc., Troy, Mich., 1985-88; v.p. Mgmt. Support Svcs., Inc., Southfield, Mich., 1989-90; owner Maintenance Mgmt. Support Svcs., Brighton, Mich., 1990—. With U.S. Army, 1969-72, Vietnam. Mem. ASTD, VFW (life), Inst. Mgmt. Cons. (treas. Detroit chpt.), Soc. Mfg. Engrs. (sr.), Am. Prodn. and Inventory Control Soc., Inst. Indsl. Engrs., Project Mgmt. Inst., Am. Mgmt. Assn., Am. Soc. Quality Control, Am. Inst. for Total Productive Maintenance. Home: 6397 Kinyon Dr Brighton MI 48116 Office: PO Box 605 Brighton MI 48116-0605

VENTO, BRUCE FRANK, congressman; b. St. Paul, Oct. 7, 1940; s. Frank A. and Ann (Sauer) V.; children: Michael, Peter, John. AA, U. Minn., 1961; BS, Wis. State U., River Falls, 1965. Tchr. sci., social studies Mpls. Pub. Schs.; mem. Minn. Ho. of Reps., 1971—; asst. majority leader 95th-103rd Congresses from 4th Minn. Dist., 1974-76; chmn. Ramsey County del., gen. legis. and vet. affairs com.; vice-chmn. jud. com.; chmn. natural resources subcom. on nat. parks, forests and pub. lands, 1985-94; mem. resource com. and subcoms; mem. banking and fin. svcs. com., ranking mem. subcom. on fin. instns. and consumer credit; mem. housing and devel. subcom.; chmn. speaker's task force on homelessness 103d Congress. Mem. legis. rev. com. Minn. Commn. on Future Del.; Democratic Farmer Labor party Central com., 1972; chmn. Ramsey County com., 1972. Recipient numerous awards including Ansel Adams award Wilderness Soc.; NSF scholar, 1966-70. Mem. Minn. Fedn. Tchrs., Beta Beta Beta, Kappa Delta Phi. Office: US House of Reps 2304 Rayburn Bldg Washington DC 20515-0005

VENTRES, JUDITH MARTIN, lawyer; b. Ann Arbor, Mich., Feb. 10, 1943; d. D. Lawrence and Donna E. (Webb) Moran; children: Laura C. Martin, Paul M. Martin, A. Lindsay Martin; m. Daniel B. Ventres Jr., Dec. 27, 1984. BA, U. Mich., 1963; postgrad., Universite de Jean Moulin, Institut du Droit, Lyon, France, 1981; JD, U. Minn., 1982. Bar: Minn. 1982, Fla. 1991, Colo. 1994, U.S. Tax Ct. 1989, U.S. Dist. Ct. Minn. 1989, U.S. Ct. Appeals (8th cir.) 1989. Tax supr., dir. fin. planning, asst. nat. dir. Coopers & Lybrand, Mpls., 1981-84; dir. fin. planning Investors Diversified Services subs. Am. Express, Mpls. and N.Y.C., 1984-85; sr. tax mgr., dir. fin. planning KPMG Peat Marwick Main & Co., Mpls., 1985-89; prin. Martin & Assocs., P.A., Mpls., Minn., 1989—; faculty Minn. CLE, 1994; mem. adv. bd. Nicollet/Ebenezer, 1996. owner Alternatax, Inc. Mem. Mpls. C. of C. Campaign, Downtown Coun. Coms., Mpls., 1982-84, Metro Tax Planning Group, 1984-86, Mpls. Estate Planning Coun., 1985—, Nicollet Good Samaritan Adv. Bd., 1996—, Planned Giving Coun.; class chmn. fundraising campaign U. Minn. Law Sch., Mpls., 1985; usher Christ Presbyn. Ch.,

Edina, Minn., 1983—; mem. adv. coun. on planned giving ARC. Mem. ABA (task force on legal fin. planning), Minn. Bar Assn., Hennepin County Bar Assn., Fla. Bar Assn., Colo. Bar Assn., Minn. Soc. CPAs (instr. continuing legal edn. 1983-84, continuing profl. edn. 1982-86, individual, trust and estate provisions Tax Reform Act 1986, continuing legal edn. -estate planning 1994), Minn. Planned Giving Coun., Am. Assn. Ind. Investors (speaker), Am. Soc. CLUs, Minn. Soc. CLUs, Minn. Women Lawyers, Fla. Women Lawyers, Lex Alumnae, U. Mich. Alumni Assn. (coun. govs. 1989—, pres.-elect, scholarship chmn.), U. Minn. Alumni Club (bd. dirs. 1996, coun. govs. 1988—, pres., treas. mem. com.), Minn. World Trade Assn., Internat. Assn. Fin. Planners, Edina C. of C., Interlachen Clubb, Athletic Club, Lafayette Club, U. Minn. Alumni Assn. Bd. (mem. univ. issues com.). Home: 1355 Vine Pl Mound MN 55364-9635 Office: Martin & Assocs PA 1650 W 82nd St Ste 1460 Minneapolis MN 55431-1466

VENTRESCA, JOSEPH ANTHONY, energy coordinator; b. Lancaster, Ohio, Feb. 5, 1949; s. Giuseppe Attilio and Maria Artemia (Ciamacco) V.; m. Barbara Welling Hall, Dec. 18, 1982. BS in Math., Ohio U., 1971; MS in Environ. Sci., Miami U., Oxford, Ohio, 1978. Quality assurance insp. Phillips Roxanne Labs., Columbus, Ohio, 1972-74; teaching asst. Miami U., 1974-77; solar engr. Spectrum Solar Systems, Columbus, 1977; energy specialist State of Ohio, Columbus, 1977-79; energy coord. City of Columbus, 1979—, project dir. DOE funded rsch., 1989—; adj. tchr. architecture Miami U., 1988; mem. Columbus Weatherization Task Force, Renewable Energy Sources Fedn. Author: Budget Incentives for Municipal Energy Management, 1984, Before Ohio P.U.C., 1984; author peer reviewed papers on energy mgmt. and indoor air quality; reviewer: The Columbus Energy Plan, 1981. Judge State Sci. Fair, Columbus, 1986-87; participant 1st U.S.-USSR Emerging Leaders Summit, 1988. Charles Kilbarger scholar, 1968-71; citation of Recognition Mayor of Columbus, 1988. Mem. Am. Soc. of Heating, Refrigeration, Airconditioning Engrs., Ohio Assn. of Energy Engrs. (bd. dirs. 1988), Nat. Assn. of Energy Engrs., Ohio Pub. Facilities Maintenance Assn. (bd. dirs. 1988), Ohio Solar Energy Assn. (mem. steering com. 1980). Home: 1640 W 3rd Ave Columbus OH 43212-2734 Office: City of Columbus Facilities 90 W Broad St Columbus OH 43215-9000

VENTURA, ROBIN MARK, professional baseball player; b. Santa Maria, Calif., July 14, 1967. Student, Oklahoma State U. Mem. U.S. Olympic Baseball Team, Seoul, South Korea, 1988; with Chgo. White Sox, 1988—. Recipient Golden Glove award, 1991-93, Golden Spikes award USA Baseball, 1988; named Sporting News Coll. Player of Yr., 1987-88, Third Basemen Sporting News All-Am. team, 1987-88; named to Am. League All-Star team, 1992. Office: Chgo White Sox 333 W 35th St Chicago IL 60616-3621*

VENUS, SUSAN M., legal assistant, director corporate pro bono program. BA, Northwestern U., Ill., 1972, MA, 1979; PhD, Loyola U., Chgo., 1984. Paralegal Holstein Mack & Klein, Chgo., 1988-92, Baxter Healthcare, McGaw Park, Ill., 1992—; English instr. Oakton Cmty. Coll., Des Plaines, Ill., 1996—, Coll. of Lake Co., Grayslake, Ill., 1995—. Editor, Poetry and Philosophy of Good, Practice and Procedure in Labor Arbitration; author, Midwest Anthology of Poetry; development writer, Modern Real Estate Practice in Pennsylvania; contributing articles to professional journals. mentor Project Succeed, 1996. Dir. Corporate Pro Bono Prog. Lake Co. Bar Assn. Waukegan, Ill., 1994; Individual Pro Bono Award, Volunteer Lawyers Prog., 1995. Ill. Teachers of English to Speakers of Other Languages, Inst. for Entrepreneurship Ed., Lake Co. Bar Assn. Volunteer Lawyers Prog. Office: Baxter Healthcare Corp 1450 Waukegan Rd Highland Park IL 60035

VERBA, BETTY LOU, real estate executive; b. Cleve., Sept. 22, 1933; d. Albert Roy and Philomena (Weigel) Short; m. James Richard Verba, Sept. 11, 1954; children: Marilyn Danko, Christine Adkins, Patricia Zore. Student, Miami U., Oxford, Ohio, 1952, Bowling Green State U., 1953. Lic. realtor, Ohio. Owner B&J Properties, 1963—; trustee Holiday Lakes Property Owners Assn., Willard, Ohio, 1973-77; realtor Realty One (formerly HGM/Hilltop), Parma Heights, Ohio, 1977-94, Century 21 DePiero & Assocs., 1994—. Geneaologist (family history book) Short Family History, 1823-1973, Update, 1974-85. Mem. grand jury Cuyahoga County, 1990. Mem. Parma Genealogy Club (v.p.). Democrat. Roman Catholic. Home: 8800 Banner Ln Parma OH 44129-6072 Office: Century 21 De Piero and Assoc 5581 Ridge Parma OH 44130

VERCH, RICHARD LEE, biology educator; b. Wakefield, Mich., Feb. 15, 1937; s. Louis Charles and Helen Madeline (Benedict) V.; m. Mary Mona Hunt, June 27, 1968; children: Christopher Louis, Matthew Aaron. BS, Northland Coll., 1962; MA, No. Mich. U., 1966; ArtsD, U. N.D., 1971. Biology tchr. Duluth (Minn.) East H.S., 1962-63, Ashland (Wis.) H.S., 1964-65, Bay de Noc C.C., Escanaba, Mich., 1965-69; prof. biology Northland Coll., Ashland, Wis., 1971—; dept. chair Northland Coll., Ashland, 1971-74, 83—, divsn. head, 1974-80; former v.p. and pres. Wis. Soc. for Ornithology. Author: Chequamegon Bay Birds, 1988, Birds of Wisconsin and Tabaseo, 1989. Park bd. chairperson City of Ashland, Wis., 1990-94, planning commn., 1991-94. Airman 1st USAF, 1955-58. Mem. Nat. Assn. Biology Tchrs., Wilson Ornithol. Soc., Lake Superior Biology Assn. Home: 906 Ellis Ave Ashland WI 54806

VERDIER, QUENTIN ROOSEVELT, human resources consultant; b. Mancelona, Mich., Mar. 19, 1921; s. John Walter and Louise (Hills) V.; m. Margaret Elizabeth Wells, Nov. 13, 1943; children: Margaret Louise, Quentin Wells, Nanette Marie Bloom. AB in Pub. Adminstrn., Kalamazoo Coll., 1943, MA in Pub. Adminstrn., 1947; postgrad., Am. U., 1948-51; PhD in Human Resource Devel., Columbia Pacific U., 1985. Diplomate Am. Bd. Forensic Medicine; bd. cert. forensic examiner; cert. employment cons., pers. cons., forensic examiner, forensic vocat. expert; registered employment agt., Wis. Asst. pers. officer U.S. Savs. Bonds div. U.S. Treasury Dept., Washington, 1951-58; div. chief office of pers. Internat. Coop. Adminstrn./Agy. for Internat. Devel., Washington, 1959-63; dep. chief pub. adminstrn. div. U.S. Ops. Mission/Agy. for Internat. Devel., Saigon, South Vietnam, 1963-65; asst. dir. tng. Inst. Govt. Affairs U. Wis. Extension, Madison, 1966-67; pres., chief ops. officer AvailAbility of Madison, Inc., 1967—, also chmn. bd. dirs.; mem. adv. panel Nat. Forensic Ctr., Princeton, 1983—; intern Group XIV, Nat. Inst. Pub. Affairs, 1948-49. Author City Employee Handbook-Better Pub. Service, 1947; editor hist. pamphlet series Understanding Backgrounds, 1964; contbr. articles to profl. jours. Bd. dirs. Friendship Force of Wis., 1991-95, West Side Sr. Ctr., Madison, Westside Coalition for Older Adults, 1992-93; pres. Zor Shrine Clown Unit, 1992-93; mem. Madison Symphony Chorus. With U.S. Army Air Corps, 1943-46. Decorated Republic of Vietnam Merit medal 1st class, 1965; recipient Wm G. Howard prize in polit. sci., 1946, Suggestion awards U.S. Treasury Dept., 1949; Upjohn fellow Kalamazoo Coll., 1946-47. Fellow Am. Coll. Forensic Examiners; mem. Am. Arbitration Assn. (arbitrator mem. panel Chgo. regional office), Am. Assn. Retired Persons, Nat. Forensic Ctr., Wis. Acad. Scis., Arts and Letters, Wis. Regional Writers Assn., Nat. Geographic Soc., Smithsonian Instn., Nat. Assn. Retired Credit Union People, Nat. Wildlife Assn., World Future Soc., Internat. Exec. Svc. Corps, Plato, Friendship Force, Internat. Shrine Clown Assn., Sun Valley Health Club, Toastmasters (dist. 36 gov.), Masons (32 degree), Shriners, Rotary (bd. dirs. Madison-West-Town-Middleton club 1988-92), Plato (Madison).

VEREBELYI, ERNEST RAYMOND, manufacturing company executive; b. Northampton, Pa., Nov. 17, 1947; s. Julius Ernest and Hermina Carolyn (Simon) V.; m. Linda Ann Million, Dec. 19, 1970; children: Michael, David, Jenny. BS in Engring., U. Mo., Rolla, 1969; grad. gen. electric mfg. mgmt. program, U. Louisville, 1972. Registered profl. engr., Mo. Various managerial positions Gen. Electric, Louisville (Ky.) and Columbia (Md.), 1969-83; v.p. mfg. Goodman Mfg., Houston, 1983-84; dir. strategic planning Hussmann Corp., St. Louis, 1984-85, group v.p. mfg., 1985-89, corp. v.p. quality, 1989-91; div. v.p. ops. Emerson Electric Co., St. Louis, 1991-93, exec. v.p., 1994—; VIP chmn. Gen. Electric, Columbia, 1975-76; also jr. achievement advisor. Tutor Dyslexic Children De Paul Sch., Louisville, 1980; coach Holy Trinity Basketball, Louisville, 1982, Ascension Baseball, St. Louis, 1986, 87. Mem. Am. Ceramic Soc., Am. Soc. Quality Control, Internat. Platform Assn., Keramos (treas. 1968-69), Sigma Nu, KC. Republican. Roman Catholic. Home: 15875 Lymington Common Chesterfield MO 63005-4725 Office: Emerson Electric Co 8400 Pershall Rd Hazelwood MO 63042-3075

VERGIN, TIMOTHY LYNN, commercial real estate appraiser and broker; b. Watertown, Minn., Nov. 13, 1962; s. William Alfred and Carol Mae (Strecker) V.; m. Randi Noelle Spencer, May 9, 1987. AA in Bus. Adminstrn., North Hennepin Community Coll., Brooklyn Park, Minn., 1983; BS in Real Estate, St. Cloud State U., 1985. Lic. real estate broker, Minn.; cert. gen. real property appraiser, Minn. Appraiser Newcombe & Hansen Appraisals, Inc., Mpls., 1985-92, Diversified Real Estate Svcs., Inc., Mpls., 1992—; broker Realty World-Vergin, Buffalo, Minn., 1985-94; CFO, prin. Diversified Real Estate Svcs., Inc., Mpls., 1992—; bd. dirs. Realty World-Vergin Corp.; ptnr. Waverly Properties, LLP, Vandalia Assocs., LLP, 1993—; CEO Diversified Realty Corp., 1994—, LDU Inc.; real estae investor and cons. Scholar, Minn. Right of Way Appraisers, Mpls., 1985. Mem. Appraisal Inst. Chgo., Minn. Assn. Realtors, Cloud State Real Estate Alumni (mem. exec. com. 1985, scholarship com. chmn. 1991-96), Phi Theta Kappa. Republican. Lutheran. Home: 3115 Cahill Ave SE Buffalo MN 55313-5302 Office: Diversified Real Estate Svc Ste 520 12 S 6th St Minneapolis MN 55402-1504

VERHESEN, ANNA MARIA HUBERTINA, counselor; b. Heerenveen, Friesland, Netherland, Dec. 6, 1932; came to U.S., 1968; d. Hendrikus H. and Henrika C. (Kluessjen) V. BS, Mercy Coll. of Detroit, 1981; MA, Sienna Height, Adrian, Mich., 1992. Childcare worker Schiedam, Netherland, 1952-54; social worker Rotterdam Halfweg, Netherland, 1954-59; childcare worker Mt. St. Ann's Home, Worcester and Lawrence, Mass., 1968-70; chem. dependency social worker St. Vincent Med. Ctr., Toledo, Ohio, 1970-75; social worker St. Joseph Hosp., Nashua, N.H., 1975-78; vocation dir. Grey Nuns, Lexington, Mass., 1978-79; coord. community svcs. St. Vincents Med. Ctr., Toledo, 1981-91; pvt. practice clin. therapist Sylvania, Ohio, 1992—; alcohol/drug addiction/mental health counselor for ex-prisoners; founder St. Vincent Med. Ctr. Alcoholism Detox and Rehab. Unit, Toledo, 1970-75. Co-founder Transitional Residences for the Homeless, Toledo, 1981-90, Ohio Coalition for the Homeless, Columbus, 1982-89; co-founder of a home for persons with AIDS; co-chair City of Toledo Housing Policy, 1985-90; coord. Housing Now, Toledo, 1988-90. Recipient Woman of Achievement award Women in Communication, Toledo, 1986, Spirit of '87 award N.W. Ordinance and U.S. Constn. Bicentennial Commn., Toledo, 1987, Gov.'s Spl. Recognition award, 1988, Man for Others award St. John's High Sch., 1991; named Woman of Toledo, St. Vincent Med. Ctr. Aux., 1988, Ohio Ho. of Reps., 1987; featured in various mags. Roman Catholic. Home: 219 Page St Toledo OH 43620-1430 Office: Elliott and Assocs Inc 5600 Monroe St Sylvania OH 43560-2701

VERICH, MICHAEL GREGORY, state legislator; b. Warren, Ohio, Dec. 30, 1953; s. Alex and Dolores (Kudrich) V.; m. Aliza Wallace. BA magna cum laude, Bowling Green State Univ., 1976; JD, Univ. Akron, 1981; MPA, Harvard Univ., 1985. Cong. intern U.S. House Rep., Washington, 1987, cong. aide, 1976-77; State rep. Dist 59 Ohio, 1983-92, Dist 66, 1993—; chmn. aging & housing com. Ohio House Rep.; lawyer Wiener, Orkin, Abbate & Suit, 1984—; acad. hist. asst. Bowling Green State Univ., 1975-76. Named Outstanding Young Man of Yr., Edn. Excellence award, Disting. Disabled Vet. award, Legislator of Yr. award. Mem. MENSA, KC, Phi Alpha Theta, ABA, Ohio Bar Assn., Trumbull County Bar Assn. Home: 1460 Central Parkway Ave SE Warren OH 44484-4457*

VERMA, KRISHNANAND, mathematics educator, researcher, administrator, consultant; b. Muzaffarpur, Bihar, India, Aug. 1, 1946; came to U.S., 1984; s. Raisaheb Brinda Prasad Varma and Ramjyoti (kuar) Varma; m. Sushma Verma, Feb. 25, 1975; children: Kaninika, Samarth. BS in Math. (hons.), Physics and Chemistry, U. Bihar, 1964, MS in Math., 1966, MA in Econs., 1971, PhD in Math., 1973; BA in Lit., Orisa Rashtra Bhasha Parisad, 1980; MA in Lit., Bombai Hindi Vidya Pith, Bombay, 1980; MBBS, U. Bihar, 1983; student, U. Nev., Las Vegas, 1984. Hon. lectr. U. Bihar, 1966-68; asst. prof. M.I.T., Bihar, India, 1968-76; prof., coord. and planner rsch. divsn. Fed. U. Brazil, Joao Pessoa, 1976-78; sr. faculty mem. MIT, Bihar, India, 1978-84; dir., pres. S.V. Coll. India, 1980-84, founder mem. governing body, bd. regents, 1973-84; assoc. prof. U. Nevada, Las Vegas, 1984-87, U. Minn., Duluth, 1987-89; assoc. prof. U. Wis., Whitewater, 1989-92, prof., 1992—; specialist in field of numerical analysis, optimization techniques, math. modeling, biomechanics, algebra, econ. planning and devel., fed. fin., pub. fin. and Indian lit.; propounder, discoverer of numerical quadratures and a variety of math. postulates, theorems, formulae, and identities; supr. and examiner of PhD and MS theses; tech. adv. manuscript examiner for more than 25 grad. and undergrad. upper-divsn. textbooks; cons., tech. adv. biomed. human subject com. U. Nev.-Reno, 1987—, Neurol. Inst. Nev., Sparks, 1987—, Am. Med. Laser, Inc., Dallas, 1988—, dept. math. Aichi U. Edn., Japan, 1986—, Med. Intelcom., Inc., Las Vegas, 1987—; judge Internat. Sci. and Engring. Fair, U.S. Naval Rsch., 1991, 92; referee 7 math. jours.; invited speaker profl. instns. worldwide. Contbr. over 100 articles to profl. jours. Troup sgt. Nat. Cadet Corps, India, 1957-59; active numerous rsch. oriented cmty. svc. projects, com. works at internat., nat. and local levels, and univs.; visited all leading countries in sci. and tech. Recipient Best Sportsman award, Excellence in Teaching and Rsch. award, nat. and merit scholarships for outstanding acad. results, variety of medals and prizes for best sportsman, debator, essay writer, musician; math. postulates, theorems, formulae and identities named after her. Mem. Am. Math. Soc., Math. Assn. Am., Can. Math Soc., Indian Math Soc. Home: 274 N Esterly Ave Whitewater WI 53190-1315 Office: U Wis 800 W Main St Whitewater WI 53190-1705

VEROSKI, JOSEPH DAMIAN, electrical engineer; b. Barberton, Ohio, Sept. 3, 1970; s. William and Dolores Veroski. BSEE summa cum laude, Ohio U., 1992. Product engr., sr. design engr. Comml. (Motors) Products Group Rockwell Automation, Gallipolis, Ohio, 1992—. Water polo coach Ohio U. Mem. Moose Lodge, Tau Beta Pi, Eta Kappa Nu.

VERSIC, LINDA JOAN, nurse educator, research company executive; b. Grove City, Pa., Aug. 27, 1944; d. Robert and Kathryn I. (Fagird) Davies; m. Ronald James Versic, June 11, 1966; children: Kathryn Clara, Paul Joseph. RN, Johns Hopkins Sch. of Nursing, 1965; BS in Health Edn., Ctrl. State U., 1980. Asst. head nurse Johns Hopkins Hosp., Balt., 1965-67; staff Nurse Registry Miami Valley Hosp., Dayton, Ohio, 1973-90; instr. Miami Jacobs Jr. Coll. Bus., Dayton, 1977-79; pres. Ronald T. Dodge Co., Dayton, 1979-86, chmn. bd., 1987—; chmn. bd. dirs. A-1 Travel, Inc. instr. Warren County (Ohio) Career Ctr., 1980-84, coord. diversified health occupations, 1984—. Coord. youth activities, mem. steering com. Queen of Apostles Cmty. Recipient Excellence in Tchg. award, 1992, award for Project Excellence, 1992. Active Miami Valley Mil. Affairs Assn., Glen Helen, Friends of Dayton Ballet, Dayton Art Inst., Cin. Art Mus. Mem. Ohio Vocat. Assn., Am. Vocat. Assn., Vocat. Indsl. Clubs Am. (chpt. advisor 1982—). Roman Catholic. Club: Johns Hopkins, Yugoslav of Greater Dayton. Home: 1601 Shafor Blvd Dayton OH 45419-3103 Office: Ronald T Dodge Co PO Box 630 Dayton OH 45459-0630

VER STEEG, CLARENCE LESTER, historian, educator; b. Orange City, Iowa, Dec. 28, 1922; s. John A. and Annie (Vischer) Ver S.; m. Dorothy Ann De Vries, Dec. 24, 1943; 1 child, John Charles. AB, Morningside Coll., Sioux City, Iowa, 1943, MA, Columbia U., 1946, PhD, 1950; LHD, Morningside Coll., 1988. Lectr., then instr. history Columbia U., N.Y.C., 1946-50; mem. faculty Northwestern U., Evanston, Ill., 1950—, prof. history, 1959—, dean grad. sch., 1975-86; vis. lectr. Harvard U., 1959-60; mem. council Inst. Early Am. History and Culture, Williamsburg, Va., 1961-64, 68-72, chmn. exec. com., 1970-72; vis. mem. Inst. Advanced Study, Princeton, N.J., 1967-68; chmn. faculty com. to recommend Master Plan Higher Edn. in Ill., 1962-64; mem. Grad. Record Exam. Bd., 1981-86, chmn., 1984-86; bd. dirs. Ctr. for Research Libraries, 1980-85, Council Grad. Schs. in U.S., 1983-87; pres. Assn. Grad. Schs., 1984-85; mem. steering com. Grad. Research Project, Consortium on Financing Higher Edn., 1981-85; mem. working group on talent Nat. Acad. Scis., 1984-87; mem. Higher Edn. Policy Adv. Com. to OCLC, Online Computer Library Ctr., 1984-87. Author: Robert Morris, Revolutionary Financier, 1954, A True and Historical Narraative of the Colony of Georgia, 1960, The American People: Their Historical, 1961, The Formative Years, 1607-1763, 1964 (Brit. edit.), 1965, The Story of Our Country, 1965, (with others) Investigating Man's World, 6 vols., 1970, A People and a Nation, 1971, The Origins of a Southern Mosaic: Studies of Early Carolina and Georgia, 1975, World Cultures, 1977, American Spirit, 1982, rev. edit., 1990; sr. author: Health Social Studies, 7 Vols., 1991, Planning at Northwestern University in the 1960s, 1993; editor: Great Issues in American History, From Settlement to Revolution 1584-1776, 1969; editl. cons.: Papers of Robert Morris, vols. I-VIII, 1973—; contbr. articles to profl. jours. Served with USAAF, 1942-45. Decorated Air medal with 3 oak leaf clusters; 5 Battle Stars; Social Sci. Research Council fellow, 1948-49, George A. and Eliza Gardner Howard Found. fellow, 1954-55, Huntington Library research fellow, 1955, Am. Council Learned Socs. sr. fellow, 1958-59, Guggenheim fellow, 1964-65, NEH sr. fellow, 1973. Mem. AAUP, Am. Hist. Assn. (nominating com. 1965-68, chmn. 1967-68, Albert J. Beveridge prize 1952, hon. mention 1991 Eugene Asher Disting. Teaching award), Orgn. Am. Historians (editorial bd. Jour. Am. History 1968-72), So. Hist. Assn. (nominating com. 1970-72). Presbyterian. Home: 2619 Ridge Ave Evanston IL 60201-1717 Office: Northwestern Univ Dean Grad Sch Evanston IL 60208

VERZAR, CHRISTINE BEATRICE, art historian, educator; b. Basel, Switzerland, Sept. 5, 1940; came to U.S., 1966; d. Fritz and Edith Jean (McDougall) V.; m. George Bornstein, Dec. 21, 1967 (div.); 1 child, Benjamin Jay; m. Daniel N. Fader, Oct. 15, 1988. Cert., U. Geneva, 1960; PhD, Basel U., Switzerland, 1966. Asst. prof. history of art Boston U., 1966-69; lectr. Princeton (N.J.) U., 1969-70; asst. prof. U. Mich., Ann Arbor, 1973-84, assoc. dir. Medieval and Renaissance Collegium, 1975-76; assoc. prof., chmn. Ohio State U., Columbus, 1984-89, prof., chair, 1989-95; prof., 1995—; chairperson The Ohio State U. Dept. History of Art, Columbus, 1984-95. Author: Portals and Politics in the Early Italian City-State, 1988, The Meeting of Two Worlds, 1981, Die Romanischen Skulpturen der Abtei Sagra di San Michele, 1968. Mem. Coll. Art Assn., Internat. Ctr. for Medieval Art (bd. dirs. 1985-88, 94—), Medieval Acad. Am. Office: The Ohio State U Dept Art History Columbus OH 43210

VESCOVI, SELVI, pharmaceutical company executive; b. N.Y.C., June 14, 1930; s. Antonio and Desolina V.; BS, Coll. William and Mary, 1951; m. Elma Pasquinelli, Oct. 16, 1954; children: Mark, James, Anne. Salesman, Upjohn Co., N.Y.C., 1954-59, sales supr.,1959-62, product mgr. U.S. domestic pharm. dir., 1962-65, mgr. mktg. planning internat. div., 1965-71, v.p. Europe, 1971-74, group v.p. Europe, 1975-77, exec. v.p. Upjohn Internat., Inc., Kalamazoo, Mich., 1978-85, pres., gen. mgr., 1975-88, v.p. parent co., 1978-88; adj. prof. mgmt. Western Mich. U., Kalamazoo, 1988-92; chmn. bd. Carrington Labs; bd. dirs. Cytrx Pharms. Corp. 2d lt. M.C., U.S. Army, 1951-53. Mem. Internat. Pharm. Mfrs. Assn., NYAC (N.Y.). Republican. Roman Catholic. Office: Upjon Internat Co 7000 Portage Rd Kalamazoo MI 49001-0102

VESPER, ROSE, state legislator; m. Lee Vesper; children: Stephanie, Jennifer, Jessica. BA, Xavier U., 1960; MA, Midwestern U., 1967. Vice chairwoman Ohio Valley Regional Devel. Commn., Ohio Water and Sewer Rotary Commn., Ohio Clermont County Farm Bur.; rep. Ohio State Ho. Reps. Dist. 72; mem. Nat. Fedn. Rep. Women; chmn. Clermont County Rep. Party, 1990—, Southwestern Ohio Rep. Leadership; owner, operator beef cattle/crop farm. Named Clermont County Farm Woman of Yr., 1988; recipient Disting. Svc. award Ohio Med. Polit. Action Com., 1988, Coop. Ext. Agts. Assn. award, 1990, Frances Boltom award Ohio League Young Reps., 1990. Mem. Richmond Hist. Soc., Clermont, Brown and Clinton County C. of C., State Med. Assn., Farm Bur., Farmers Union. Home: 1174 Watkins Hill Rd New Richmond OH 45157-9504 Office: Ohio Ho of Reps State House Columbus OH 43215*

VETERE, COLLEEN MARIE, nurse; b. Washington, Sept. 10, 1957; d. Alphonse Louis and Margaret Hilda (Nolan) V. BA in Biology, U. Tex., 1980, BS in Nursing, 1982; MPH, U. Tex., Houston, 1993. RN, Tex. Nurse intensive care unit Brackenridge Hosp., Austin, Tex., 1983, nurse emergency room, 1984; quality rev. supr. Tex. Med. Found., Austin, 1985-86; asst. dir. Peer Rev. Orgn. Tex., Austin, 1986-87, asst. to exec. dir., 1987-88, dir. quality rev. statewide, 1988-90; nurse emergency rm. St. Luke's Hosp., Houston, 1990-91; nurse emergency room Brackenridge Hosp., 1991; clin. rsch. monitor Pharmaco, Austin, 1992-93; v.p. Peer Rev. Orgn. Ind., Terre Haute, 1993-94; area support team mgr., decision support cons. VHA, Inc., Indpls., 1994-95, area support team mgr., 1995—. Med. support organizer Area 13 Tex. Spl. Olympics, Austin, 1985-89, vol. support Area 4, Houston, 1990-91. 1st lt. Nurse Corps, USAR, 1983-93. Recipient Army Achievement medal USAR-ANC, 1986. Mem. NAFE, Tex. Nurses Assn. Democrat. Roman Catholic. Office: 8900 Keystone Crossing Ste 480 Indianapolis IN 46240-2146

VETTE, JOHN LYLE, III, manufacturing specialist; b. Phila., Dec. 19, 1937; s. John Lyle, Jr. and Janet Elsa (Wolfermen) V.; m. Susan Maria Thomson, Feb. 6, 1966; children: Susanne, Lucinda, Jonelle. BA, Bowdoin Coll., 1960; BFT, Am. Grad. Sch. Internat., Mgmt., Phoenix, 1964. Export salesperson Morton Salt Co., San Juan, P.R., 1964-66; mfg. tech. rep. Black & Decker Mfg. Co., San Salvador, 1967-68; asst. to the pres. SNC Mfg. Co., Inc., Oshkosh, Wis., 1968-77, pres., 1978—; bd. dirs. M&I Bank, Oshkosh, United Fund of Oshkosh, Pub. Expenditure Survey of Wis.; bd. dirs., pres. The Hooper Cmty. Ctr., Inc.; dir. Telecomm. Industries Assn., 1994—. Bd. trustees The Paine Art Ctr. and Arboretum, 1984-91, Lourdes Acad.; bd. dirs. U.S. Telecomms. Suppliers Assn. 1984-88, Salvation Army, Oshkosh Citadel, Oshkosh chpt. ARC, Wis. Found. of Ind. Colls.; del. White House Conf. on Sml. Bus., 1986, others. 1st lt. U.S. Army, 1961-63.

VETTER, JAMES LOU, international marketing executive; b. New London, Wis., Feb. 13, 1965; s. Raymond Carl Vetter and Diana Marie (Titterud) Vetter Ravey; m. Kathleen Rosemary Little, Oct. 5, 1985. Grad. high sch., Waupaca, Wis. Lic. ins. agt., Wis. V.p. ops. Gemini Investments, Inc., Waupaca, 1983-85; pres. The Capret Medix, Ltd., Neenah, Wis., 1985-90, Capital Mktg. Assocs., Menasha, Wis., 1990-95; pres., CEO Team Internat., Menasha, Wis., 1995—; pres. Team Travel, Menasha, Wis., 1995—. With USAR, 1982—. Recipient Internat. Sponsorship award Nat. Safety Assocs., 1992; decorated Army Achievment medal. Mem. Nat. Assn. Self Employed, Direct Sales Assn. Office: Team Internat PO Box 654 Menasha WI 54952

VETTER, WILLIAM MAX, government information technology administrator; b. Springfield, Ill., June 30, 1931; s. William M. Sr. and Catherine Marie (Kornfeld) V.; m. Marian Jane Edwards, Feb. 14, 1953; children: Gary Allen, Kevin William, Carrie Lynn. AA, Springfield Coll., 1951; BS, U. Ill., 1955. CLU; cert. data processor. Equipment control mgr. Hayes Freight Lines, Springfield, 1955-58; sr. systems analyst Franklin Life Ins. Co., Springfield, 1958-69, R&D mgr., 1969-74; sr. acct. exec. Franklin Data Svcs., Springfield, 1974-81; exec. dep. dir. State of Ill., Springfield, 1981-82, computer sci. exec., 1982-92, sr. pub. svc. adminstr., 1993—; mem. adv. bd. Lincolnland C.C., Springfield, 1991—; advisor Distance Learning Found., Springfield, 1993—. Band dir. 144th Army Band (N.G.), 1960-77; trustee Village of Buffalo, Ill., 1965—; pres. Mechanicsburg (Ill.) Cemetery, 1994—; treas. Scott Crown for Svc. Com., Mechanicsburg, 1994—; chmn. Buffalo Tree Com., 1984—. Served with U.S. Army, 1949-53. Fellow Life Mgmt. Inst.; mem. Am. Mgmt. Assn. (tech. coun. 1994—), Data Processing Mgmt. Assn. (internat. v.p. 1983-84), Elks, Lions (chpt. pres. 1988-89), Albert Hall Steering Com. (chmn. 1985—), Ill. Distance Learning Found. Republican. Roman Catholic. Home: PO Box 65 Buffalo IL 62515 Office: Ill Bur of Comm & Computer Svcs 120 W Jefferson Springfield IL 62702

VICK, ROD RYAN, secondary education educator, writer; b. Waukesha, Wis., Feb. 18, 1955; s. Gordon C. nad Beulah M. (Holsinger) V.; m. Marsha E. Dilley, Aug. 27, 1988; children: Haley Marie, Joshua Ryan. BSE, U. Wis., Whitewater, 1977. Cert. journalism tchr., Wis. Tchr. English and journalism Mukwonago (Wis.) Schs., 1977—; cross country coach Mukwonago H.S., 1978—, publs. adviser, 1977—. Author short stories. Recipient Outstanding Young Educator award Jaycees, Mukwonago, 1983. Mem. Wis. Cross County Coaches Assn. (State Coach of Yr. 1994, Dist. Coach of Yr. 1987, 93). Mem. United Ch. of Christ. Office: Mukwonago HS 605 W School St Mukwonago WI 53149

VICKERMAN, BARB, state legislator; m. Gerald Vickerman; four children. Minn. State Rep. Dist. 23A, 1992—; retail sales profl.; mem. health and human svc. com./fin. divsn., labor-mgmt. rels. com., regulated industry and engery com. Home: 325 E Oak St Redwood Falls MN 56283-1146*

VICKERMAN, JIM, state legislator; b. May 1, 1931; m. Wava; six children. County commr.; Minn. State Sen. Dist. 22; chmn. vet. and gen. legis. com.; vice-chmn. health and human svc. com., agr. and rural devel. com., local and urban govt. com, transp. com., vet. and mi. affairs com., health care com., health care and family svc. fin. divsn. com., rules and adminstrn. com., transp. com. and transp. fin. divsn. com.; farmer. Office: RR 2 Box 134 Tracy MN 56175-9430 also: State Senate State Capitol Building Saint Paul MN 55155-1606*

VICKERS, DAVID S., physicist; b. Cleve., Mar. 30, 1951; s. Paul Orland and Margaret Corrine (Wolfe) V.; m. Kathleen Heller, Sept. 5, 1981; children: Erin Patricia, Monica Jean, Alexander Patrick. BS in Physics, Rensselaer Poly. Inst., 1973; MBA, John Carroll U., 1988. Rsch. engr. Am. Gas Assn., Independence, Ohio, 1973-76; group leader, clin. rsch. Technicare Corp., Solon, Ohio, 1976-86; mgr. advanced devel. Innovative Imaging Syss., Solon, Ohio, 1986-89; assoc. Plexar Assocs., Solon, Ohio, 1989-91; project mgr. SMV Am., Twinsburg, Ohio, 1991-95. Inventor 3-D CT scanner, new gamma camera, gamma camera. Deacon, Presbyn. Ch., 1976. Mem. IEEE, Beta Gamma Sigma. Republican. Presbyterian. Home: 9020 Bramley Dr Cleveland OH 44131 Office: SMV Am Inc 8383 Darrow Rd Twinsburg OH 44087

VICKERY, MILLIE MARGARET, photographer, journalist; b. Clinton County, Ind., Apr. 29, 1920; d. Walter L. and Opal M. (Small) Cox; m. Eugene Livingstone Vickery, Dec. 21, 1941; children: Douglas Eugene, Constance Michelle Suski, Anita Sue Ramsey, Jon Livingstone. Student Ind. U., 1938-42, U. Toledo, 1944. Writer, Sheridan News (Ind.), 1937-38; floor mgr. Lamsons Dept. Store, Toledo, 1943-45; receptionist, bookkeeper Office E.L. Vickery, M.D., Lena, Ill., 1946-85; freelance writer-photographer, Lena, 1964—. Author: P.S. I Love You, 1983; editor Pulse of the Doctor's Wife mag., 1966-78; contbg. editor MD's Wife mag., 1964-74; contbr. articles and photographs to various newspapers and mags. Bd. dirs. Highland Coll. Found., Freeport, Ill., 1970—; columnist Cooking with Millie, N.W. Ill. Farmer Newspaper, 1991—. Recipient Pacesetter award Highland C.C., Freeport, 1978; Sweepstake award, several 1st trophies Rockford Cooking Contests (Ill.), 1979-81; Disting. Alumnae award Marion-Adams High Sch., Sheridan, Ind., 1981. Mem. Ill. Woman's Press Assn. (pres. 1971-73, over 46 writing awards, Woman of Achievement award 1984), Nat. Fedn. Press Women (dir. 1971-73, Nat. Woman of Achievement nominee 1984), Ill. State Med. Soc. Aux. (state pres. 1975-76, Ill. Humanitarian of the Yr. award 1984), Ill. Acad. Family Physicians Aux. (state pres. 1976-77), Ill. Press Photographers Assn., Women in Communications, Mortar Board, Delta Delta Delta, Beta Sigma Phi (pres. chpt. 1950, 72, 91-92, Order of Rose award 1981, internat. award of Distinction 1982, photography award 1982-90), Beta Sigma Phi (editor Straight from the Bucket for Highland Coll. Found., BUZZ newsletter for PEO, 1990-91, 1st Beta Sigma Phi Internat. Founder's award 1990, Golden Circle award, 1994). Republican. Mem. Evangel. Free Church. Clubs: Lena Women's, Lena Golf. Lodges: Order Eastern Star, PEO. Home: 115 Grove St Lena IL 61048

VICKREY, JENE, state legislator; m. Teresa Vickrey. Kans. state rep. Dist. 6, 1993—; carpet layer. Address: 6740 W 263rd Louisburg KS 66053*

VICKROY, WILLIAM REES, II, civic volunteer, investor; b. St. Louis, Dec. 28, 1929; s. Theodore Sessinghaus and Helen Harwood (Southern) V.; m. Margaret Doolittle Vickroy, Dec. 5, 1953; children: Theodore Sears, William Rees III, Nancy Doolittle. BS, Cornell U., Ithaca, N.Y., 1952. Lt. gunnery officer USN Atlantic Fleet, 1952-55; elec. data processing sales IBM, N.Y.C., 1955-66; v.p., gen. mgr. McDonnell Douglas Automation Internat., St. Louis, 1966-84; v.p. mktg. McDonnell Douglas Info. Sys. Group, St. Louis, 1984-87; pres. Clark Holdings Inc., St. Louis, 1987-91. Chmn. YMCA Greater Needs, St. Louis, 1980—; Data Sys. More Grace Hill Settlement House, St. Louis, 1991—; treas. Haven of Grace, St. Louis, 1994-96; chmn. Cmty. Comn., St. Peter's Episc. Ch., Ladue, Mo., 1990—. Republican. Episcopalian. Home: 12329 Boothbay Ct Saint Louis MO 63141-8119

VICTOR, LORRAINE CAROL, critical care nurse; b. Duluth, Minn., June 14, 1953; d. George E. and Phyllis M. (Pierce) Drimel; m. Robert G. Victor. BA in Nursing, Coll. St. Scholastica, 1975; MS in Nursing, U. Minn., 1984. Cert. regional trainer for neonatal resuscitation program. Staff nurse St. Mary's Hosp., Rochester, Minn., 1975-79, 80-81, U. Wis. Hosp., Madison, 1979-80, U. Minn. Hosps., Mpls., 1981-84, 85-86; clin. instr. neonatal ICU, Children's Hosp. Inc., St. Paul, 1984-86; clin. nurse specialist neonatal ICU, Orlando (Fla.) Regional Med. Ctr., 1986-88, Children's Hosp. St. Paul, 1988—. Mem. AACN (Critical Care Nurse of Yr. award Greater Twin Cities chpt. 1992), Nat. Cert. Corp. (cert. in neonatal intensive care nursing), Nat. Assn. Neonatal Nurses, Sigma Theta Tau. Office: Children's Health Care St Paul Birth Ctr 345 N Smith Ave Saint Paul MN 55102-2392

VICTORINE, JOHN WILLIAM, card company executive; b. Chgo., Apr. 30, 1964; s. Arthur George and Margrete Agnus (Kline) V.; m. Cynthia Anette Plomin, Mar. 31, 1990. Grad. H.S., Chgo. Plant mgr. Custom Card Co., Chgo., 1982-94, v.p., 1994—. Home: 234 Skylark Bartlett IL 60103 Office: Custom Card Co 4201 N Honore Chicago IL 60103

VIDOLOFF, JOHN CLARENCE, physiatrist; b. Chgo., Jan. 17, 1941; s. Victor Zaprian and Ruth Ann (Gilmore) V.; m. Mary Roberta Michiels, May 2, 1970; children: Ann, Michael, Robert, Kathleen. BS, Loyola U., Chgo., 1963, MD, 1966. Rotating intern Great Lakes Naval Hosp., Waukegan, Ill., 1966-67; resident Northwestern, Chgo., 1969-73; staff physiatrist Rockford (Ill.) Meml. Hosp., 1973-80, Cox Med. Ctr., Springfield, Mo., 1980-87; assoc. dir. Madonna Ctr., Lincoln, Nebr., 1987-88; cons. Rio Vista Hosp., El Paso, Tex., 1988-89; dir. rehab. St. Lukes Hosp., Aberdeen, S.D., 1989—; cons. S.D. Devel. Disability Ctr., Redfield, S.D., 1989-95. Pres. Med. and Dental Staff of Hosp., Aberdeen, 1995. Lt. comdr. USN, 1967-69. Fellow Acad. Phys. Medicine and Rehab.; mem. AMA, S.D. State Med. Assn. Republican. Roman Catholic. Home: 1403 Squire Ln Aberdeen SD 57401 Office: 1440 15th Ave NW Aberdeen SD 57401

VIDRICKSEN, BEN EUGENE, food service executive, state legislator; b. Salina, Kans., June 11, 1927; s. Henry and Ruby Mae Vidricksen; m. Lola Mae Nienke, Jan. 20, 1950; children: Nancy, Janice, Ben, Penelope, Jeffery. AB, Kans. Wesleyan U., 1951. Field supt. Harding Creamery div. Nat. Dairy Products, Kearney, Kans., 1951-52; plant mgr. Kraft divsn. Nat. Dairy Products, O'Neill, Nebr., 1952-59; owner Vidricksen's Food Service, Salina, 1959—; cons. in field; mem. Kansas Senate, 1979—, asst. majority leader; chmn. joint bldg. constrn. com., legis. and congressional apportionment com., legis. post audit,econ. devel., transp. and utilities, pub. health and welfare, fed. and state affairs, govtl. orgn., spl. interim com. on efficiency in state govt., 1983; del. White House Conf. Small Bus., 1995, White House Conf. on Tourism and Travel, 1995; mem. Hennessy/USAF Worldwide Food Service Evaluation Team, 1978, 79. Mem. Salina Airport Authority, 1972-84, chmn., 1976-77; chmn. Republican Central Com., County of Saline, Kans., 1974-79; adv. council SBA, 1982—, chmn. adv. coun. small bus. devel. ctr.; mem. adv. bd. Salvation Army; past chmn. Salina Convention and Tourism Bur.; vice chmn. Kans. Turnpike Authority, 1995—. Served with USN, 1945-46. Recipient Salut au Restaurateur award Fla. State U., 1974, Gov.'s Spl. award Kans. Assn. Broadcasters, Guardian award Nat. Fedn. Indep. Bus., 1989, Promotion of Tourism and Travel award Travel Ind. Assn. Kans., 1989, Support of Kans. Nat. Guard award Kans. Adjutant Gen., 1990, Good Citizenship award Kans. Engring. Soc., 1991, 92, Freedom award NRA, 1994; named Nat. Rep. Legislator of Yr., Nat. Rep. Legislators Assn., 1991, Assoc. of Yr., Am. Womens Bus. Assn., 1992. Mem. USAF Assn., Assn. U.S. Army, Nat. Rep. Legislators Assn., Am. Legis Exch. Coun., Pan Am. Hwy. Assn. (Internat. Achievement award 1992, Road Builders award 1995), North Salina Bus. Assn. (past pres.), Internat. Bridge, Tunnel and Tpke. Assn., Kans. Restaurant Assn. (past pres., Restauranteur of Yr. 1973), Kans. Tourism and Travel Commn., Kans. Film Commn., Nat. Restaurant Assn. (dir. 1977—), Travel Industry Assn. Kans. (dir.) VFW (life), Salina C. of C. (past bd. dirs.), Am. Legion, Optimists, North Salina Lions Club, Elks, Moose, Eagles, Masons (knight commdr. Scottish rite, 1994), Shriners. Office: State Senate State Capitol Topeka KS 66612

VIEHLAND, LARRY ALAN, chemist, educator; b. St. Louis, Apr. 30, 1947; s. Harold Henry and Beulah Fay (Allensworth) V.; m. Claudia Kimberling Winters, Aug. 28, 1969; children: Jeremy Scott, Brian Daniel. BS, MIT, 1969; PhD, U. Wis., 1973. Rsch. asst. Los Alamos (N.Mex.) Sci. Labs., 1969; rsch. assoc. Brown U., Providence, R.I., 1973-76, asst. prof., 1976-77; asst. prof. Parks Coll. St. Louis U., Cahokia, Ill., 1977-79, assoc. prof., 1979-83, prof., 1983—; vis. prof. U. B.C., Vancouver, Can., 1987, Leiden (The Netherlands) U., 1991. Contbr. articles to profl. jours. including Jour. Chem. Physics, Jour. Physics B, Annals of Physics, Physics of Fluids, Atomic Data and Nuclear Data Tables, Internat. Jour. Mass Spectrometry and Ion Processes, Chem. Physics, Chem. Physics Letters. Scoutmaster Boy Scouts Am., St. Louis, 1987-94, cubmaster 1985-87; treas. Normandy United Meth. Ch., St. Louis, 1987—. Recipient equipment grant Pitts. Conf. Applied Spectography, 1978, rsch. grants NSF, 1980, 83, 89, 92, Rsch. Corp., 1980; Fulbright sr. scholar Australian Nat. U., 1988. Mem. Am. Phys. Soc., Am. Assn. Univ. Profs. (chpt. pres.), Sigma Xi. Home: 19 Bellerive Acres Saint Louis MO 63121-4328 Office: Parks Coll St Louis Univ Cahokia IL 62206

VIELEHR, BYRON COVENEY, mutual fund executive; b. Kanpur, India, Nov. 25, 1963; arrived in U.S., 1967; s. Jerome E. Vielehr and Patricia W. Driscoll. BS, Drexel U., 1987; MBA, U. Pa., 1994. Asst. v.p. Aid Assn. Luth. CMC, Appleton, Wis.; gen. mgr. Systems & Software Tech., Milw.; founding ptnr. Real Land Mgmt. Systems, Elkton, Md. Mem. MENSA, Soc. Info. Mgmt., Leadership Fox Cities, John Holland Soc. Republican. Presbyterian. Office: AAL CMC 222 W College Ave Appleton WI 54711

VIETS, ROBERT O., utilities executive; b. Girard, Kans., Dec. 8, 1943; s. Willard O. and Caroline L. (Bollwinkel) V.; m. Karen M. Kreiter, June 13, 1980. BA in Econs., Washburn U., 1965; JD, Washington U., 1969. Bar: Kans. 1966, Mo. 1969, Ill. 1975; CPA, Kans. Auditor Arthur Andersen & Co., St. Louis, 1969-73; mgr. spl. studies Cen. Ill. Light Co., Peoria, 1973-76, mgr. rates and regulatory affairs, 1976-80, asst. v.p., regulatory affairs, 1980-81, v.p. fin. services, 1981-83, v.p. fin. group, 1983-86, sr. v.p., 1988—; sr. v.p. Cilcorp, Inc., Peoria, 1986-88; pres., chief exec. officer, chmn. bd. Cilcorp, Inc. and Cen. Ill. Light Co., Peoria, 1988—; bd. dirs. First of Am. Bank, N.A., Ill., Lincoln Office Supply, Inc., RLI Corp., Environ. Sci. and Engring., Inc., Peoria. Bd. dirs. Meth. Health Svcs., Inc.; trustee Bradley U. Mem. ABA, Ill. Bar Assn., Peoria County Bar Assn., AICPA, Ill. Soc. CPAs. Republican. Lutheran. Lodge: Rotary (bd. dirs. 1985—, pres. 1986-87). Home: 11305 N Pawnee Rd Peoria IL 61615-9796 Office: Cilcorp Inc Hamilton Blvd Peoria IL 61602

VIEWEG, BRUCE WAYNE, mental health researcher; b. Westminster, Mass., July 30, 1947; s. Herman C. and Ardath (Woollacott) V.; m. JoAnne Rawlings, Dec. 19, 1970; children: Emily, Anna. BMus Ed, U. Lowell, 1969; MSEd, So. Ill. U., 1975. Tchr. Hampshire Country Sch., Rindge, N.H., 1969-71; rsch. technician U. Mo. Inst. Psychiatry, Columbia, 1972-75, rsch. specialist, 1975-80, rsch. asst., 1980-84, rsch. assoc., 1984-94, dir. computer lab., 1987-94; dep. dir. for quality of treatment Mo. Dept. of Mental Health, Jefferson City, 1994-95, dir. of office of info. systems, 1995—. Author: (with others) several sci. books; contbr. articles profl. jours. Treas. Hand in Hand Presch., St. Charles, Mo., 1980; pres. Becky-David Elem. Sch. PTO, St. Charles, 1988, 89; long-range planning coun. Francis Howell Sch. Dist., 1988-94, long-range study com. on tech.,1990, long range task force on faculty compensation, 1990, mem. bd. edn., 1992-94, pres. 1993; steering com. Knights of Excellence North H.S., 1990. Recipient Howell of Fame award Francis Howell Sch. Dist., 1990. Mem. Silver Key. Home: 1017 Mayfair Rd Saint Charles MO 63303-4024 Office: Mo Dept Mental Health 1706 E Elm St Jefferson City MO 65102

VIG, PRADEEP KUMAR, geophysics educator; b. Kanpur, India, July 6, 1954; came to U.S., 1985; s. Girdhari Lal and Usha Rani (Raghubir Lamba) V.; m. Neelu Kumar Mahindru, June 24, 1981; children: Sanjana, Dhruv. BS, Meerut (India) U., 1972; MTech, U. Roorkee, India, 1975; M. in Profl., St. Louis U., 1988, PhD, 1989. Sr. geophysicist Oil India Ltd., Duliajan, Assam, 1976-82; geophysicist Seiscom Delta United, Inc., Singapore, 1982-83, Oceaneering Internat., Inc., Singapore, 1983, Geomex Surveys Ltd., Hong Kong, 1983-85; rsch. asst. St. Louis U., 1986-89; assoc. prof. sci. and math. Louisburg (N.C.) Coll., 1989-94; earth sci. instr. Central Lakes Coll., 1994—. Contbr. articles to profl. jours. Merit scholar Univ. Grants Commn., U. Roorkee, 1972-75, Soc. Exploration Geophysicists, 1986-89. Mem. Alpha Sigma Nu. Home: 516 College Dr # 101 Brainerd MN 56401-9999 Office: Central Lakes Coll 501 W College Dr Brainerd MN 56401-3904

VIGEN, KATHRYN L. VOSS, nursing administrator, educator; b. Lakefield, Minn., Sept. 24, 1934; d. Edward Stanley and Bertha C. (Richter) Voss; m. David C. Vigen, June 23, 1956 (div. 1977); children: Eric. E., Amy Vigen Hemstad, Aana Marie. BS in Nursing magna cum laude, St. Olaf Coll., 1956; MEd, S.D. State U., 1975; MS, Rush U., 1980; PhD, U. Minn., 1987. RN. Staff nurse various hosps., Mpls, Boston, Chgo., 1956-68; nursing instr. S.E.A. Sch. Practical Nursing, Sioux Falls, S.D., 1969-74; statewide coord. upward mobility in nursing Augustana Coll., Sioux Falls, S.D., 1974-78; cons./researcher S.D. Commn. Higher Edn., 1974-79; gov. appointed bd. mem. S.D. Bd. Nursing, 1975-79; RN upward mobility project dir., chair/dir. div. of nursing Huron Coll. S.D. State U., 1978-79, mobility project dir., 1980-84; head dept. nursing, assoc. prof. Luther Coll., Decorah, Iowa, 1984-94; prof. nursing Graceland Coll., Independence, Mo., 1994—; cons. in field; developer outreach MSN programs Graceland Coll.; governing bd. mem. Midwest Alliance in Nursing, 1984-92; founder Soc. for Advancement of Nursing, Malta, 1992; developer Health Care in the Mediterranean Study Abroad Program, Greece and Malta, 1994, 96; developer summer internship for Maltese nursing students Mayo Med. Ctr. and Luther Coll. Author: Role of a Dean in a Private Liberal Arts College, 1992; devel. and initiated 3 nursing programs in S.D., 1974-84 (named Women of Yr., 1982). Lobbyist Nursing Schs. in S.D., 1974-79; task force mem. Sen. Tom Harkin's Nurse's Adv. Com., 1986-94. Fellow to rep. U.S.A. ANA cand. in internat. coun. nursing 3M, St. Paul, 1978; recipient Leadership award Bush Found., St. Paul, 1979; tenure Luther Coll., 1986; Faculty fellow Minn. Area Geriatric Edn. Ctr. U. Minn., 1990-91; recipient Fulbright award Malta Coun. Internat. Exch. of Scholars, Washington, 1992—. Mem. AAUW, ANA, Am. Assn. Colls. Nursing (exec. devel. subcom. 1990—), Internat. Assn. Human Caring, Iowa Nurse's Assn. (bd. dirs. 1989-92, mem. nursing edn. com. 1989—, co-pres. 1989—), Midwest Alliance in Nursing (gov. bd. rep. Iowa 1989-92, chair membership com. 1989-92, S.D. gov. bd. rep. 1984-86, Rozella Schlotfeldt Leadership award 1993), Iowa Acad. Sci., Iowa Assn. Colls. Nursing Soc., Gerontol. Soc. Am., Rotary, Sigma Theta Tau. Democrat. Lutheran. Home: 4316 Northern Ave Apt 2633 Kansas City MO 64133-7249 Office: Graceland Coll Divsn Nursing 221 W Lexington Ave Independence MO 64050-3707

VILIM, JOHN ROBERT, social services administrator; b. Chgo., July 4, 1922; s. Herbert William and Loretta May (Stapleton) V.; m. Rosemary Susan Malpede, Jan. 15, 1949; children: John Jr., Nancy Catherine, Vilim-Horner, Peter M. BA, St. Joseph's Coll., 1943; postgrad., La Verne U., 1978-79. Salesman Armour Leather Co., Chgo., 1946-57; gen. agt. Consolidated Am. Life Ins. Co., Chgo., 1957-60; treas. Forestry Rsch. Corp., Arlington Heights, Ill., 1960-68; gen. mgr. Lilton Typing Svc., Chgo.; registered rep. Union Securities Co., Chgo., 1956-76; securities custodian La Salle Nat. Bank, Chgo., 1974-79; alcoholism counselor Rush Presbyn. St. Lukes Hosp., Chgo., 1979-82; exec. dir. Way Back Inn, Maywood, Ill., 1982-85; asst. dir. Guildhaus, Blue Island, Ill., 1985—. Lt. USNR, 1942-46. Mem. Ill. Alcoholism Counselors Alliance Inc., KC. Home: 5041 N Nagle Ave Chicago IL 60630-1814 Office: Guildhaus 2413 Canal St Blue Island IL 60406-2926

VILLALON, DALISAY MANUEL, nurse, real estate broker; b. Angat, Bulacan, Philippines, Apr. 27, 1941; came to U.S., 1967; d. Federico Manuel and Librada (Garcia) Manuel; divorced; children: Ricky, May, Liberty, Derrick, Dolly Rose. BS in Nursing, Manila Cen. U., 1961; postgrad. in nursing, U. Ill., Chgo., 1972-74. RN, Ill. Instr. nursing Cen. Luzon Sch. Nursing, Philippines, 1966-67; staff nurse St. Alexis Hosp., Cleve., 1968-70, Augustana Hosp., Chgo., 1972-74; nurse mgr. Holy Child Med. Clinic, Chgo., 1976-80; nurse auditor 1st Health Care, Rosemont, Ill., 1982-83; dir. nurses North Shore Terr., Waukegan, Ill., 1983-90, Carlton House, 1991-94. Columnist Philippine News. Bd. dirs. Filipino Am. Coun., Chgo., 1978-80, v.p., 1980-82; bd. dirs. Asian Human Svcs., Chgo.; pres. Am.-Filipino Profl. Civic Alliance, Chgo., 1984-90, Philipino-Am. United for Svc.-Oriental Objective, 1991—; chmn. Philippine Week Com., 1979; past v.p. Filipino Ams. Concerned for Elderly; trustee Rizal-MacArthur Found.; past v.p. Filipino Svc. League, 1989-91; past exec. v.p. Asian Festival, Inc.; past chmn. various civic coms.; mem. Asian-Am. Adv. Coun. Mayor Daley, 1989-97. Recipient Cert. Appreciation Rizal-MacArthur Found., 1977, Most Outstanding Filipino in Midwest award Cavite Assn. Am., 1980, Outstanding Community Svc. Appreciation award Filipino Am. Coun., 1981, 89, NGHIA Sinh Internat., Inc., 1989, Outstanding Svc. award Asian-Am. Coaliton, 1989, Outstanding Contrn. award Dirs. Nursing and Adminstrs. Conf., 1988; named to Filipino Hall of Fame for comty. svc., 1996 Phil Reports TV. Mem. Ill. Nurses Assn. (bd. dirs., dist. senator 1989-91, human rights and ethics commn. 1990-91), Philippine Med. Assn. Aux. (pres. 1980, Outstanding Leadership award 19891), Chgo. Med. Soc. Aus. (v.p. 1980), Chgo. Philippine Lioness Club (pres. 1983-84, Outstanding Svc. award 1985), Filipino Woman's Club Chgo. (Outstanding Woman in Leadership 1992, Chgo. Filipino Hall of Fame award), Filipino Am. Polit. Assn. Democrat. Roman Catholic. Home: 1070 Sanders Rd Northbrook IL 60062 Office: Vitas Health Care Corp Vitas Innovative Care 5215 Old Orchard Rd Skokie IL 60077

VILLALPANDO, JESSE MICHAEL, state legislator; b. East Chicago, Ind., July 4, 1959; s. Jesse and Rose (Oria) V.; m. Elizabeth Villalpando. BA, Ind. U., 1981, JD, 1984. Bar: Ind. 1984. Atty. Lesniak & Ruff, East Chicago; mem. from 12th dist. Ind. State Ho. of Reps., 1982—; co-chmn. cts. com.; mem. criminal code, ins. and corps. com., judiciary com., pub. safety com., pub. policy com., ethcis com., vets. affairs com. Named to Ind. State AFL-CIO Honor Roll, 1984. Mem. Ind. State Bar Assn., Griffith Dem. Club, Hammond FDR Club, South Hammond Dem. Club, Mutualista of Gary, Phi Delta Theta. Home: 956 N Griffith Blvd Griffith IN 46319-1514*

VILLARRUEL, MAYOLA LARA, medical surgical nurse, administrator; b. East Chicago, Ind., Mar. 4, 1956; d. Arturo and Natalia Lara Villaruel. ADN, Ind. U. N.W., Gary, 1977, BSN, 1987; MSN, Ind. U., Indpls., 1991. cert. nursing adminstrn. ANCC. Staff nurse, critical care St. Margaret Hosp., Hammond, Ind., 1977-78; staff nurse, progressive care unit Ind. U. Hosp., Indpls., 1978-79; staff nurse ICU-CCU Community Hosp., Munster, Ind., 1979-84, supr. nursing svc., 1984-87, head nurse, 1987-90; nurse mgr. South Suburban Hosp., Hazel Crest, Ill., 1990-91; clin. faculty Ind. U. Sch. Nursing, Gary, Ind., 1991—, Methodist Hosp., Gary, Ind., 1991-94; cons. Sylvia Rayfield & Assocs., Shreveport, La., 1993—; bd. dirs. Indian med. Edn. Bd., 1993—. Mem. Nat. Assn. Hispanic Nurses (pres. elect, bd. dirs. N.W. Ind. chpt.), Ind. State Nurses Assn., Consortium Ind. Nursing Orgns. (vice chair 1993—). Home: 1923 Springvale Dr Crown Point IN 46307-1030

VILLARS, HORACE SUMNER, food company executive, marketing professional; b. San Francisco, Mar. 15, 1931; s. Horace Sumner and Alice Emily (Stacy) V.; m. Patricia Ann Adams, June 15, 1951; children: Rebecca, Thomas, Constance, Laura, Russell. BS, Northwestern U., 1952. With Armour Co., Chgo., 1952-54, Durkee Foods, Chgo., 1954-65; mgr. indsl. sales McCormick & Co., Balt., 1965-68; exec. v.p. Kraft Sesame Corp., Paris, Tex., 1968-71; pres. Food Ingredients, Inc., Elk Grove, Ill., 1971—; chmn. Sycamore Foods, Inc., Elk Grove, 1987—. Contbg. author: Encyclopedia of Food Technology, 1974, Elements of Food Technology, 1977. Mem. Inst. Food Technologists (exec. com. Chgo. sect. 1974—), Am. Assn. Cereal Chemists, Am. Oil Chemists Soc., Am. Assn. Candy Technologists (chmn. Chgo. sect. 1964-65), Am. Soc. Bakery Engrs. Republican. Home: 820 Acorn Dr Dundee IL 60118-2659 Office: Food Ingredients Inc 215 Industrial Dr Unit D Hampshire IL 60140*

VINEYARD, JERRY D., geologist; b. Dixon, Mo., Mar. 26, 1935; s. Henry and Bessie Florence (Geisler) V.; m. Helen Louise Anderson, Nov. 24, 1960; children: Monica Lynne, Vanessa Anne. BA, U. Mo., 1960, MA, 1963. Registered profl. geologist, Ark., Mo. Lectr. in geology and geography Kansas City (Mo.) Met. Coll., 1961-63; chief publs. and info. Mo. Geol. Survey, Rolla, 1963-79; asst. state geologist Mo. Dept. Natural Resources, Rolla, 1979-89, dep. state geologist, 1989—; mem. adv. bd. U. Mo., Columbia, 1982-91. Author: Springs of Missouri, 1978; co-author: Geologic Wonders and Curiosities of Missouri, 1979, Missouri Geology, 1992. Lt. (j.g.) USN, 1958-60. Fellow Geol. Soc. Am. (Disting. Hydrogeologist 1989); mem. Nat. Speleological Soc. (hon. life mem., bd. dirs., editor jour. 1973), Mo. Speleological Soc. (hon. life mem., founder 1955—), Mo. Acad. Sci. (pres. 1996—), Sigma Xi (pres. Mo. chpt. 1974—). Baptist. Home: 1524 Lola Ln Saint James MO 65559 Office: Mo Dept Natural Resources 111 Fairgrounds Rd Rolla MO 65402

VINING, JOHN KENDALL, performing arts company administrator, composer; b. Grand Rapids, Mich., Dec. 10, 1953; s. Keats Kendall and Janet Ethel (Bird) V.; m. Sharon Elaine Forrester, Jan, 6, 1979 (div. Nov. 1983); m. Linda Louise Renicky, May 31, 1986; children: Elizabeth Kendall, Grace Eastin. Student, Grand Valley State Coll., 1972-74, U. Mich., Interlochen, 1973; MusB, Cleve. Inst. Music, 1980. Freelance music theater with numerous cos. including Cleve. Opera, Pitts. Opera, Santa Fe Opera, Eugene Opera, Chamber Opera Theater N.Y., Chgo. Opera Theatre, Ill. Opera Theatre, Glimmerglass Opera, Picolo Teatre, 1978-87, Opera Memphis, Music Theatre Group N.Y.C., 1978-87; founder, dir. Magic Lantern Opera Co., N.Y.C., 1980-82; asst. dir. No. Westchester Ctr. for the Arts, Goldens Bridge, N.Y., 1986-87; pres. Pearl Spring Enterprises, Inc., Mt. Vernon, Ohio, 1987—; dir. Pearl Spring Ctr. for Am. Folksong, 1993—. Composer, performer: (rec.) Treasures of the Heart, 1989, Before the Winter, 1992; performer (music theater) The Mother of Us All, 1983 (Obie award 1983). Bd. dirs. Knox County Visitors Bur., Mt. Vernon, 1989-91, Knox County Symphony, Mt. Vernon, 1989-91; v.p., bd. dirs. Knox County Renaissance Found., Mt. Vernon, 1988-90; chair Mt. Vernon Christmas Carol Sing, 1989-91; mem. Commn. on Ministry Episcopal Diocese of Ohio, Cleve., 1991-95; elected lay deputy to the 1994 Gen. Convention of the Episcopal Ch., 1992. Singer's Club Cleve. scholar, 1976-78. Mem. Am. Guild Mus. Artists, Actor's Equity Assn., Ohio Arts Presenter's Network, Mt. Vernon Rotary (bd. dirs. 1992-95, pres. 1995-96), Knox County Pilot's Assn., Magna Carta Barons (Somerset chpt.). Republican. Office: Pearl Spring Enterprises 18359 Coshocton Rd Mount Vernon OH 43050-9218

VINING, (GEORGE) JOSEPH, law educator; b. Fulton, Mo., Mar. 3, 1938; s. D. Rutledge and Margaret (McClanahan) V.; m. Alice Marshall Williams, Sept. 18, 1965; children: George Joseph IV, Spencer Carter. BA, Yale U., 1959, Cambridge U., 1961; MA, Cambridge U., 1970; JD, Harvard U., 1964. Bar: D.C. 1965. Atty. Office Dep. Atty. Gen., Dept. Justice, Washington, 1965; asst. to exec. dir. Nat. Crime Commn., 1966; assoc. Covington and Burling, Washington, 1966-69; asst. prof. law U. Mich., 1969-72, assoc. prof., 1972-74, prof., 1974-85, Hutchins prof., 1985—. Author: Legal Identity, 1978, The Authoritative and the Authoritarian, 1986, From Newton's Sleep, 1995. Bd. dirs. Am. Friends of Cambridge U. NEH sr. fellow, 1982-83. Fellow Am. Acad. Arts and Scis.; mem. ABA, D.C. Bar Assn. Am. Law Inst., Century Assn. Office: U Mich 432 Hutchins Hall Ann Arbor MI 48109-1215

VINSON, JAMES SPANGLER, academic administrator; b. Chambersburg, Pa., May 17, 1941; s. Wilbur S. and Anna M. (Spangler) V.; m. Susan Alexander, Apr. 8, 1967; children: Suzannah, Elizabeth. B.A., Gettysburg Coll., 1963; M.S., U. Va., 1965, Ph.D., 1967. Asst. prof. physics MacMurray Coll., Jacksonville, Ill., 1967-71; asso. prof. physics U. N.C., Asheville, 1971-78; prof. physics U. N.C., 1974-78, chmn. dept. physics, dir. acad. computing, 1974-78; prof. physics, dean Coll. Arts and Scis. U. Hartford (Conn.), 1978-83; v.p. acad. affairs Trinity U., San Antonio, 1983-87; pres. U. Evansville, Ind., 1987—; computer cons. Contbr. articles to profl. jours. Mem. Am. Phys. Soc., World Future Soc., AAAS, Am. Assn. for Advancement of Humanities, Am. Assn. for Higher Edn., Am. Assn. Physics Tchrs., Phi Beta Kappa, Sigma Xi, Phi Sigma Kappa. Methodist. Office: U Evansville 1800 Lincoln Ave Evansville IN 47722-0001

VIOLET, RON J., electrical engineer; b. South Milwaukee, Wis., Jan. 25, 1944. BSEE, Marquette U., 1966; MSEE, Stanford U., 1967. Mem. design devel. staff Bell Labs., Denver, 1967-71, GTE Lankurt, San Carlos, Calif., 1971-76; mem. sci. staff Square D. Co., Milw., 1985—. Patentee for adaptive modem. percentage amplifier. Republican. Roman Catholic. Office: Square D Co 4080 N 1st St Milwaukee WI 53212-1239

VIRGO, JOHN MICHAEL, economist, researcher, educator; b. Pressburry, Eng., Mar. 11, 1943; s. John Joseph and Muriel Agnes (Franks) V.; m. Katherine Sue Ulmrich, Sept. 6, 1980 (div. 1979); 1 child, Debra Marie. BA, Calif. State U., Fullerton, 1967, MA, 1969; MA, Claremont Grad. Sch., 1971, PhD, 1972. Instr. econs. Whittier (Calif.) Coll., 1970-71, Calif. State U., Fullerton and Long Beach, 1971-72, Claremont (Calif.) Grad. Sch., 1971-72; asst. prof. econs. Va. Commonwealth U., Richmond, 1972-74; assoc. prof. mgmt. So. Ill. U., Edwardsville, 1975-83, prof., 1984—; bd. dirs., founder Internat. Health Econ. & Mgmt. Inst., Edwardsville, 1983-87. Author: Legal & Illegal California Farmworkers, 1974; author, editor: Health Care: An International Perspective, 1984, Exploring New Vistas in Health Care, 1985, Restructuring Health Policy, 1986; founder, editor-in-chief Internat. Advances in Econ. Rsch. Served with USN, 1965-68. Mem. Internat. Hosp. Fedn., Am. Econ. Assn., Am. Hosp. Assn., Am. Soc. Assn. Execs., Royal Econ. Soc., Atlantic Econ. Soc. (founder, exec. v.p., mng. editor jour. 1973—), Allied Social Scis. Assn. (chmn. exec. confs. 1982-84), AMA, So. Econs. Assn., Sunset Hills Club (Edwardsville). Democrat. Roman Catholic. Home: 5277 Lindell Blvd Saint Louis MO 63108-1223 Office: So Ill U Atlantic Econ Soc PO Box 1101 Edwardsville IL 62026

VIRKHAUS, TAAVO, symphony orchestra conductor; b. Tartu, Estonia, June 29, 1934; came to U.S., 1949; s. Adalbert August and Helene Marie (Sild) V.; m. Nancy Ellen Herman, Mar. 29, 1969. MusB U. Miami, 1955; MusM Eastman Sch. of Music, Rochester, 1957, DMA, 1967. Dir. music U. Rochester (N.Y.), also assoc. prof. Eastman Sch., Rochester, 1967-77; music dir., condr. Duluth (Minn.) Superior Symphony Orch., 1977-94; guest condr. Rochester Philharm., Minn. Orch., Balt. Symphony, Vancouver Symphony and others, 1972—; music dir., condr. Hunstville (Ala.) Symphony Orch., 1989—; guest condr. at Tallinn, Estonia, 1978, 88, 90, 92, 93, 94; lectr. U. Minn.-Duluth, U. of Wis.-Superior. With U.S. Army, 1957-58, USAR, 1957-61. Recipient Howard Hanson Composition award, 1966, Am. Heritage award JFK Libr. for Minorities, 1974; Fulbright scholar, Musickhochschule, Cologne, 1963. Mem. Am. Symphony Orch. League, Condrs. Guild, Am. Fedn. of Musicians. Composer: Violin Concerto, 1966, Symphony No. 1, 1976, Symphony No. 2, 1979, Symphony No. 3, 1984, Symphony No. 4, 1989, Symphony No. 5, 1994. Republican. Lutheran.

VIRTUE, JACK DOWN, engineer, consultant; b. Sioux City, Iowa, July 23, 1930; s. William Wayne and Ariel M. (Moore). B.S.E., Iowa State U., 1952. Registered profl. engr., Iowa. Ptnr., Virtue & Virtue, Onawa, Iowa, 1960-74; pres. Virtue Engr. P.C., Onawa, 1974—; dir. Pioneer Valley Bank. Pres. Prairie Gold council Boy Scouts Am., 1976-79, mem. central regional bd., 1982—. Mem. Monona County Planning and Zoning Com., 1972—; trustee Onawa Pub. Library, 1969-92 Mem. Iowa Engring. Soc. (N.W. chpt. pres. 1974), Nat. Soc. Profl. Engrs., Soc. Land Surveyors Iowa (dir. 1972-80), Am. Congress Surveying and Mapping. Congregationalist. Lodge: Masons (33 degree). Home: 1004 15th St Onawa IA 51040-1517 Office: Virtue Engr PC PO Box 297 Onawa IA 51040-0099

VISCI, JOSEPH MICHAEL, newspaper editor; b. Delaware, Ohio, Oct. 8, 1953; s. Leonard Albert and Alice Mary (Buzzelli) V. B.A., Ohio Wesleyan U., 1975; M.A., Ohio State U., 1977. Reporter Naples Daily News, Fla., 1975-76; editor Columbus Citizen-Jour., Ohio, 1977-78, Detroit Free Press, 1978—. Office: Detroit Free Press 321 W Lafayette Blvd Detroit MI 48226-2705

VISCLOSKY, PETER JOHN, congressman, lawyer; b. Gary, Ind., Aug. 13, 1949; s. John and Helen (Kauzlaric) V. B.S. in Acctg., Ind. U.-Indpls., 1970; J.D., U. Notre Dame, 1973; LL.M. in Internat. and Comparative Law, Georgetown U., 1983. Bar: Ind., D.C., U.S. Supreme Court. Legal asst. Dist. Atty.'s Office, N.Y.C., 1972; assoc. Benjamin, Greco & Gouveia, Merrillville, Ind., 1973-76, Greco, Gouveia, Miller, Pera & Bishop, Merrillville, Ind., 1982-84; assoc. staff appropriations com. U.S. Ho. of Reps., Washington, 1976-80, assoc. staff budget com., 1980-82; mem. 99th-104th Congresses from 1st dist. Ind., 1985—; mem. Appropriations com., subcoms. treasury, postal svc., gen. govt. and military constrn. Democrat. Roman Catholic. Office: US House of Reps 2464 Rayburn Bldg Washington DC 20515-1401*

VISKANTA, RAYMOND, mechanical engineering educator; b. Lithuania, July 16, 1931; came to U.S., 1949, naturalized, 1955; s. Vincas and Genovaite (Vinickas) V.; m. Birute Barbara Barpsys, Oct. 13, 1956; children: Renata, Vitas, Tadas. BSME, U. Ill., 1955; MSME, Purdue U., 1956, PhD, 1960; DEng (hon.), Tech. U. Munich, 1994. Registered profl. engr., Ill. Asst. mech. engr. Argonne (Ill.) Nat. Lab., 1956-59, student rsch. assoc., 1959-60, assoc. mech. engr., 1960-62; assoc. prof. mech. engring. Purdue U., West Lafayette, Ind., 1962-66, prof. mech. engring., 1966-86, Gross disting. prof. engring., 1986—; guest prof. Tech. U. Munich, Germany, 1976-77, U. Karlsruhe, Germany, 1987; vis. prof. Tokyo Inst. Tech., 1983. Contbr. over 400 tech. articles to profl. jours. Recipient Sr. U.S. Scientist award Alexander von Humboldt Found., 1975, Sr. Rsch. award Am. Soc. Engring. Edn., 1984, Nusselt-Reynolds prize, 1991, Thermal Engring. award for Internat. Activity, Japan Soc. Mech. Engrs., 1994; Japan Soc. for Promotion of Sci. fellow, 1983. Fellow ASME (Heat Transfer Meml. award 1976, Max Jakob Meml. award 1986, Melville medal 1988), AIAA (Thermophysics award 1979); mem. AAUP, AAAS, NAE, Acad. Engring. Scis. Russian Fedn. (fgn.), Sigma Xi, Pi Tau Sigma, Tau Beta Pi. Home: 3631 Chancellor Way West Lafayette IN 47906-8809 Office: Purdue Univ 1288 Mechanical Engring Bui West Lafayette IN 47907

VISKANTA, TADAS EDMUND, bank officer, investment analyst; b. Lafayette, Ind., Oct. 15, 1967; s. Raymond and Barbara (Barpsys) V. BA with highest distinction, Ind. U., 1989; MBA with honors, U. Chgo., 1992. First scholar 1st Nat. Bank Chgo., 1989-92, investment officer, 1992-94, asst. v.p., 1994-95, v.p., 1996—. Contbr. articles to profl. jours. Mem. Chgo. Quantitative Alliance, Investment Analysts Soc. Chgo. (affiliate), Cato Inst., Ind. U. Alumni Assn., Chgo. GSB Club, Nat. Assn. Scholars, Heritage Found., Golden Key, Phi Beta Kappa, Beta Gamma Sigma. Republican. Roman Catholic.

VISSER, JENNIFER LYNNE, sales executive; b. St. Louis, Dec. 18, 1964; d. Earl Wayne Visser and Mary Jane Heinrichs. Student, Graceland Coll., Lamoni, Iowa, 1983-85; BA in Sociology and Bus. Adminstrn., U. Nebr., 1987. Mem. food svc. staff adv. bd. Graceland Coll., Lamoni, 1985; mem. account receivables/payable staff Johnson Venetian Blind, Kansas City, Mo., 1984; sales assoc. Miller/Paine (now Dillards), Lincoln, Nebr., 1985-86; records processor Union Ins., Lincoln, Nebr., 1986-88; amb. Conv. and Vis. Bur., Lincoln, Nebr., 1984-85; banquet attendant Hillcrest Country Club, Lincoln, Nebr., 1987-88; apparel sales mgr. Montgomery Ward, Lincoln, Nebr., 1988-90; telemarketer, sales exec. Today's Temporary, Lincoln, Nebr., 1990-94; telemarket, telemktg. dir. Modern Methods Inc., Lincoln, Nebr., 1990-93; mgr., office mgr. Midwest Venetian Blind Office, Lincoln, 1993; sales assoc. Dillards Dept. Store, Lincoln, 1993-94; dist. supr. Omaha World Herald, 1994-96; customer svc. rep. Pioneering Svcs.- Mutual Funds, Omaha, 1996—; apartment mgr. 6 plex, 1987-90. Mem. Jr. C. of C. (individual devel. v.p. 1990-91, new mem. orientations dir. and state program mgr. 1991-92, trainer, spkr. 1994—, mem. devel. v.p. 1992-93, treas. 1993-94, pub. rels. dir. Millard 1994-95, dist. dir. east region 1995-96, vrious project planning awards 1989—), Nebr. Jaycees (Bronze Key Svc. award 1990, 92, Program Mgr. of Yr. 1992), Waverly Jaycees (v.p., dir. 1991, Brownfield award 1990, Jaycee of Yr. 1992-93, exec. bd. 1993-94), Women in Sales (Outstanding Young Women of Am. award 1991). Home: 3490 S 82d St # 2 Omaha NE 68124

VISWANATH, DABIR SRIKANTIAH, chemical engineer; b. Bangalore, India, Aug. 5, 1934; s. Srikantiah and Kamalamma Viswanath; m. Pramila Viswanath, Jan. 5, 1967; 1 child, Arvind. BS, Mysore U., Bangalore, 1953; DIIS, Indian Inst. of Sci., Bangalore, 1956; MS, U. Rochester, 1960, PhD, 1962. Chemist Essen & Co., Bangalore, 1953-54; chem. engr. Sarabhai Chems., Bangalore, 1956-57; asst. prof. to prof., chmn. Indian Inst. of Sci., Barda, 1965-78; vis. prof. Tex. A&M, College Station, 1978-79; prof. U. Mo., Columbia, 1979-90, prof., chmn., 1990—. Co-author: Data Book on Viscosity of Liquids, 1989; contbr. articles to profl. jours. Pari Hargovandas fellowship Indian Inst. of Sci., Lever Bros. fellowship U. Rochester; recipient Halliburton Travel awards, Mo; grantee NSF, 1985, 1990-91, U. Wis., 1982-83, IBM Corp., 1988-91, USEPA-Kans. State, 1988-91, Waste Mgmt. of N.Am., 1992-93. Fellow AIChE, Am. Inst. Chemists; mem. AAAS, Am. Chem. Soc., Indian Inst. Chem. Engrs., Catalyst Soc. India, Rotary. Home: 507 Onofrio Ct Columbia MO 65203-0318 Office: U Mo Dept Chem Engring Columbia MO 65211

VITALE, DAVID J., banker; b. 1946. With First Nat. Bank of Chgo. subs. First Chgo. NBD Corp., 1968—, exec. v.p., 1986—; exec. v.p. First Chgo. NBD Corp., 1986—, also bd. dirs., 1992—, vice chmn., 1995—. Office: First Chgo NBD Corp 1 First National Plz Chicago IL 60670*

VITALE, GERALD LEE, credit union executive; b. Chgo., Apr. 3, 1950; s. Le Roy Allen and Gilda Leanora (Rasori) V. BS in Psychology, Loyola U., Chgo., 1972, MS in Fin., 1982, MBA in Fin., 1982. Credit mgr. Mellon Fin., Chgo., 1973-76, Kemper Ins. Co., Chgo., 1976-78; pres., CEO Tribune Employees Credit Union, Chgo., 1978—; pres. NCR Credit Union User Group, Dayton, Ohio, 1984-91, Garfield Enterprise Redevel. Corp., 1995—; mem. adv. bd. Ill. Gov.'s Credit Union, 1993—. Co-host Chicagoland Cable (CLTV) TV Fin. Reports, Tribune Broadcasting. Counselor youth motivation Chgo. C. of C. and Industry, 1980—, mem. adv. bd., 1996—; counselor Hire the Future, 1988; vol. Red Cloud Athletic Assn., 1993—, Friends of Providence-St. Mel, 1993—; mem. Chgo. Coun. Fgn. Rels., Nat. Italian Am. Found., Coun. of 1000, 1995—; active Rep. Nat. Com., GOP Action Com., 42d Ward Regular Reps.; mem. Ctr. for Study of Presidency; dep. gov. Am. Biog. Inst., 1993—, Filene Inst., 1992—. Mem. Midwest Assn. Credit Unions (bd. dirs. 1992—), Pres. Assn. Credit Union Exec. Soc., Am. Mgmt. Assn., Nat. Assn. State Chartered Credit Unions (region V dir., bd. dirs. 1995—), Greater Garfield C. of C. (bd. dirs., pres. 1992—), Monroe Club (bd. dirs. 1995—), Sky Line Club, Nat. Assn. Cubs, Ill. Arts Alliance, RNC's Pres. Club, Exec. Club. Roman Catholic. Home: 1636 N Wells St Apt 2410 Chicago IL 60614-6020 Office: Tribune Credit Union 435 N Michigan Ave Chicago IL 60611-4001

VITE, FRANK ANTHONY, realtor; b. Aurora, Ill., Feb. 9, 1930; s. Frank A. and Rose (Cosentino) V.; grad. Marmion Mil. Acad., 1948; student Sch. Mgmt., U. Notre Dame, 1958; D.B.A. (hon.), Hillsdale Coll., 1972; m. Barbara Ann Decio, Oct. 23, 1954; children: Bradley Scott, Mark Steven, Michael Lee, Leslie Ann, Lisa Ann. Plant engr. Lyon Metal Products, Aurora, 1951-52, purchasing agt., 1953-54; became sales mgr., exec. v.p., owner, dir. Skyline Homes, Inc., Elkhart, Ind., 1954; pres., owner B&F Realty, Inc., No. Ind. Appraisal Co., Golden Falcon Homes, Inc.; real estate broker; dir. 1st Nat. Bank, Elkhart, Ind. Trustee Hillsdale (Mich.) Coll., Holy Cross Coll., South Bend, Ind.; bd. dirs. Ind. Commn. Higher Edn. Served with AUS, 1952-53, Korea. Mem. Elkhart Bd. Realtors, Nat. Sales Execs. Assn., Ind. Real Estate Assn., Nat. Inst. Real Estate Brokers, Holy Name Soc. Republican. Clubs: K.C. (4 deg.), Knight of Malta, Elks. Home: 23236 Shorelane Elkhart IN 46514-4560 Office: 1300 Cassopolis St Elkhart IN 46514-3248

VIVERITO, LOUIS S., state legislator; m. Carolyn Strobl; children: Dean, Diane, Marianne. Mem. Ill. State Senate, 1995—. Mem. Stickney Twp. Dem. Com., 1969—; del. Dem. Nat. Conv., 1972; commr. Met. Sanitary Dist. Greater Chgo., 1980-86; mem. Cook County Zoning Bd. Appeals, 1987-95; local chmn. Chgo. Lung Assn., 1973—. Named Man of Yr., Joint Civic Com. Italian-Am., 1980; inductee Hall of Fame, Valentine Boys & Girls Club, 198. Mem. VFW (life), Am. Legion (life), Burbank C. of C., Burbank Sertoma Club (founder).

VIVONA, DANIEL NICHOLAS, chemist; b. Chgo., Apr. 13, 1924; s. Daniel and Mary Rose (Lomonico) V.; student Chgo. City Coll., 1941-42, 46; BA, U. Maine, 1951; MS, Pa. State U., 1953; postgrad. Purdue U., 1953-56; m. Helen Mary Belanger, Sept. 14, 1950; 1 son, Daniel Maurice. Instr. chemistry Purdue U., Lafayette, Ind., 1955-56; with Minn. Mining and Mfg. Co., St. Paul, 1956-86, sr. chemist, 1969-79, info. scientist, 1979-81, quality assurance sr. chemist, 1981-86; cons., 1986—. With USAAF, 1943-45. Decorated Air medal with oak leaf clusters, DFC. Dow Corning fellow, 1952-53. Mem. Am. Chem. Soc., Phi Beta Kappa. Roman Catholic. Home: 3253 Kraft Cir N Lake Elmo MN 55042-9720 Office: Beta of Dan Vivona PO Box 128 Lake Elmo MN 55042-0128

VLACH, JEFFREY ALLEN, environmental specialist; b. Detroit, May 18, 1953; s. Robert Allen and Virginia Mae (Melton) V.; m. Diane Kay Daugherty, Oct. 27, 1984; children: Elizabeth Daugherty, Meredith Anna. BS, Purdue U., 1975. Cert. asbestos bldg. inspector, mgmt. planner. Environ. specialist D.E. McGillem and Assocs., Inc., Indpls., 1975-80, United Cons. Engrs., Inc., Indpls., 1980-88, Beam, Longest & Neff, Inc., Indpls., 1988—; asbestos bldg. inspector, mgmt. planner EPA, 1989. Conservation coord. Amos Butler chpt. Nat. Audubon Soc., Indpls., 1980-82. Named Eagle Scout Boy Scouts Am., 1969. Mem. ASCE (affiliate), Nat. Wildlife Fedn., Natural Resources Def. Coun., Nat. Assn. Environ. Profls. Office: Beam Longest & Neff Inc 8126 Castleton Rd Indianapolis IN 46250-2007

VLCEK, DONALD JOSEPH, JR., food distribution company executive, consultant; b. Chgo., Oct. 30, 1949; s. Donald Joseph and Rosemarie (Krizek) V.; m. Claudia Germain Meyer, July 22, 1978 (div. 1983); 1 child, Suzanne Mae; m. Valeria Olive Russell, Nov. 11, 1989; children: James Donald, Victoria Rose. BBA, U. Mich., 1971. Gen. mgr. Popps, Inc., Hamtramck, Mich., 1969-76; pres. Domino's Pizza Distbn. Corp., Ann Arbor, Mich., 1978-93, chmn., 1993-94, also bd. dirs.; pres. Don Vlcek & Assocs., Ltd., Plymouth, Mich., 1994—; trustee Domino's Pizza Ptnrs. Found.; bd. dirs. RPM Pizza Inc., Gulfport, Miss., Dimango Corp., South Lyon, Mich.; sr. v.p. distbn. and tech. Domino's Ohio Commissary, Zanesville; pres. Morel Mountain Corp.; judge 1994 Duck Stamp contest U.S. Dept. Interior, Jr. Fed. Duck Stamp Contest, 1995. Author: The Domino Effect, 1991 (Best of Bus. award ALA 1992, Soundview's Top 30 Business books of 1993); contbr. articles to profl. jours. Bd. dirs. Men's Hockey League of Oak Park, Mich., 1973-78. Named Person of Yr. Bd. Franchises, Boston, 1981; recipient Teal award Ducks Unltd., 1992, State Major Gifts Chmn. award, 1992, 93, State Chmn.'s award, 1992, State Major Gifts award, 1994. Mem. Mich. Steelheaders Assn. (life), Ducks Unltd. (life, Domino's Pizza chpt. treas., sponsor, chmn. 1988—, Mich. state bd. dirs., life sponsor, chmn. 1989, 91-92, state trustee 1992—, chmn. exec. com. 1992-94, major gifts chmn. 1993—, chmn. strategic devel. com. 1994, sponsor in perpetuity Grand Slam Life), Mich. United Conservation Club (life), Whitetails Unltd. (life), Pheasants Forever (life), Midstates Masters Bowling Assn. (bd. dirs. 1976-85), Barton Hills Country Club (golf com., capt. dist. team), U. Mich. Alumni Assn. (life), Domino's Lodge/Drummond Island Wildlife Habitat Found. (pres., chmn. bd.), Vlcek Family Wildlife Found. (pres., chmn. bd.), Elks (life), Die Hard Cubs Fan Club. Republican. Roman Catholic. Home: 9251 Beck Rd N Plymouth MI 48170-3336 Office: Don Vlcek & Assoc Ltd PO Box 701353 Plymouth MI 48170-0963

VLEISIDES, GREGORY WILLIAM, lawyer; b. Kansas City, Mo., June 17, 1950; s. William Chris and Irene Helen (Karos) V. BA, U. Kans., 1972; JD, U. Mo., Kansas City, 1976. Bar: Mo. 1977, U.S. Dist. Ct. (Mo.) 1977, U.S. Ct. Appeals (8th cir.) 1977. Law clk. presiding justice Circuit Ct. of Jackson County, Kansas City, 1976-78; assoc. Tierney & Ernst, Kansas City, 1978-86; of counsel Law Office of F. Lee Bailey, Boston, 1982-88; assoc. Turner & Boisseau, Kansas City, 1986-89; mng. ptnr. Vlesides, Donnelly & O'Leary, Kansas City, 1989—; regional counsel Video Software Dealers Assn., Overland Park, Kans., 1986-89. Author: (with others) Challenges to Court Action in Child Abuse and Neglect Cases, 1976, Opening Statements by Julien, 1994, Stein on Closing Arguments, 1994. Mem. ABA, ATLA, Mo. Assn. Trial Lawyers, Kansas City Bar Assn. Republican. Greek Orthodox. Home: 3008 W 84th Pl Leawood KS 66206-1309 Office: Vlesides Donnelly & OLeary One Ward Pky Ste 249 Kansas City MO 64112

VOCHT, MICHELLE ELISE, lawyer; b. Detroit, Sept. 27, 1956. BA with honors, U. Mich., 1978; JD, Wayne State U., 1981. Bar: Mich., U.S. Dist. Ct. (ea. and we. dist.) Mich., U.S. Ct. Appeals (6th cir.), 1981. V.p., treas. Roy, Shecter, Mirer & Vocht PC, Detroit, Bloomfield Hills, Mich., 1981—; mem. pro bono teaching faculty Detroit chpt. Fed. Bar Assn.; mediator Mediation Tribunal Wayne County Cir. Ct., 1989—; pre-sentencing probation officer 48th Dist. Ct., 1989-90. Mem. com. for re-election of current Mich. Supreme Ct. Justice, 1986; mem. Rep. Assembly, Oak County, 1992—; exec. bd. Birmingham Women's Community Ctr., 1987-88; bd. dirs. Community Adv. Bd.-Arbor Clin. Group, Inc., 1989-91; mem. drug and alcohol abuse spl. task force County of Oakland, 1989—. Mem. Assn. Trial Lawyers Am., Am. Inns of Ct. (barrister 1984-87), Mich. Trial Lawyers Assn., Women Lawyers Assn. (exec. bd. dirs. 1982-84, 88—, sec. 1990—, v.p. 1991-92, pres. 1992-95), State Bar Assn. Mich. (chmn. gen. practice sect. 1984-86, sec. 1982-83, vice chmn. 1983-84, mem. civil procedure com. 1982-84, assoc. mem. lawyers and judges assistance com. 1988-89, hearing and panelist atty. discipline bd. 1982—, labor and employment sect., domestic rels. sect., rep. 6th judge cir. 1993—, chair drafting com., chair com. on state regulation, com. on state trial ct. adminstrn.), Mich. Employment Law Assn., Interna. Platform Assn., Indsl. Rels. Rsch. Assn. Roman Catholic. Home: 901 N Adams Rd Birmingham MI 48009-5646 Office: Roy Shecter Mirer & Vocht 1400 Woodward Ave Ste 205 Bloomfield Hills MI 48304-3972 also: 2715 Cadillac Tower Detroit MI 48226

VOELKER, ROBERT HETH, electrical engineering educator. BSEE, U. Mich., 1982, MSEE, 1983, PhD in Elec. Engring., 1989. Asst. prof. U. Nebr., Lincoln, 1990—. Contbr. articles to profl. jours. Mem. IEEE (sr.), Am. Soc. Engring. Edn. Office: Univ Nebr Dept Elec Engring 209 N WSEC Lincoln NE 68588-0511

VOELZ, JAMES WILLIAM, theology educator, pastor; b. Milw., June 18, 1945; s. Roy Alfred and Coraine Margaret (Dambruch) V.; m. Judy Annette Hayes, Apr. 2, 1977; 1 child, Jonathan James. AA, Concordia Coll., Milw., 1965; BA, Concordia Sr. Coll., Ft. Wayne, Ind., 1967; MDiv, Concordia Sem., St. Louis, 1971; PhD, Cambridge (Eng.) U., 1978. Asst. prof. Concordia Theol. Sem., Springfield, Ill., 1975-76; asst. prof. Concordia Theol. Sem., Ft. Wayne, 1976-82, assoc. prof., 1982-89; assoc. prof. Concordia Sem., St. Louis, 1989-93, prof., 1993—; pastoral asst. Zion Luth. Ch., Fort Wayne, 1984-88; mem. Commn. on Theology and Ch. Rels., Luth. Ch.-Mo. Synod, St. Louis, 1992—. Author: Fundamental Greek Grammar, 1986, 2d edit., 1993, What Does This Mean? Principles of Biblical Interpretation in the Post-Modern World, 1995; contbr. articles to profl. jours. John W. Behnken postdoctoral fellow Aid Assn. for Luths. Ins. Co., 1982. Mem. Internat. Orgn. for Septuagint and Cognate Studies, Soc. Biblical Lit., Studiorum Novi Testamenti Societas. Home: 466 Elm Crossing Ct Ballwin MO 63021-7476 Office: Concordia Seminary 801 De Mun Ave Saint Louis MO 63105-3168

VOGEL, ARTHUR ANTON, clergyman; b. Milw., Feb. 24, 1924; s. Arthur Louis and Gladys Eirene (Larson) V.; m. Katharine Louise Nunn, Dec. 29, 1947; children: John Nunn, Arthur Anton, Katharine Ann. Student, U. of South, 1942-43, Carroll Coll., 1943-44; B.D., Nashotah House Theol. Sem., 1946; M.A., U. Chgo., 1948; Ph.D., Harvard, 1952; S.T.D., Gen. Theol. Sem., 1969; D.C.L., Nashotah House, 1969; D.D., U. of South, 1971. Ordained deacon Episcopal Ch., 1946, priest, 1948; teaching asst. philosophy Harvard, Cambridge, Mass., 1949-50; instr. Trinity Coll., Hartford, Conn., 1950-52; mem. faculty Nashotah House Theol. Sem., Nashotah, Wis., 1952-71; asso. prof. Nashotah House Theol. Sem., 1954-56, William Adams prof. philosophical and systematic theology, 1956-71, sub-dean Sem., 1964-71; bishop coadjutor Diocese of West Mo., Kansas City, 1971-72; bishop Diocese of West Mo., 1972-89; rector Ch. St. John Chrysostom, Delafield, Wis., 1952-56; dir. Anglican Theol. Rev., Evanston, Ill., 1964-69; mem. Internat. Anglican-Roman Cath. Consultation, 1970-90; mem. Nat. Anglican-Roman Catholic Consultation, 1965-84, Anglican chmn., 1973-84; mem. Standing Commn. on Ecumenical Relations of Episcopal Ch., 1957-79; mem. gen. bd. examining chaplains Episcopal Ch., 1971-72; del. Episcopal Ch., 4th Assembly World Council Chruches, Uppsala, Sweden, 1968, and others. Author: Reality, Reason and Religion, 1957, The Gift of Grace, 1958, The Christian Person, 1963, The Next Christian Epoch, 1966, Is the Last Supper Finished?, 1968, Body Theology, 1973, The Power of His Resurrection, 1976, Proclamation 2: Easter, 1980, The Jesus Prayer for Today, 1982, I Know God Better Than I Know Myself, 1989, Christ in His Time and Ours, 1982, God, Prayer and Healing, 1995, Radical Christianity and the Flesh of Jesus, 1995; editor: Theology in Anglicanism, 1985; contbr. articles to profl. jours. Vice chmn. bd. dirs. St. Luke's Hosp., Kansas City, Mo., 1971, chmn., 1973-89. Research fellow Harvard, 1950. Mem. Am. Philos. Assn., Metaphys. Soc. Am., Soc. Existential and Phenomenological Philosophy, Catholic Theol. Soc. Am. Home: 524 W 119th Ter Kansas City MO 64145-1043

VOGEL, CARL M., state legislator. Mem. Mo. Ho. of Reps. from 114th dist. Republican. Home: 311 Constitution Dr Jefferson City MO 65109-5723*

VOGEL, CEDRIC WAKELEE, lawyer; b. Cin., June 4, 1946; s. Cedric and Patricia (Woodruff) V. BA, Yale U., 1968; JD, Harvard U., 1971. Bar: Ohio 1972, Fla. 1973, U.S. Tax Ct. 1972, U.S. Supreme Ct. 1975. Ptnr. Vogel, Heis, Wenstrup & Cameron, Cin., 1972—; bd. dirs. Pro Srs., 1994—. Chmn. mem.'s com. Cin. Art Mus., 1987-88; chmn. auction Cin. Hist. Soc., 1985; local pres. English Speaking Union, 1979-81, nat. bd. dirs., 1981; chmn. Keep Cin. Beautiful, Inc., 1994—; active Bravo! Cin. Ballet, 1989; chmn. Act II Nutcracker Ball, 1987-88; bd. dirs. Merc Libr., 1991—; bd. dirs. Cin. Preservation Assn., 1990-93; vice chmn. Children's Heart Assn. Reds Rally, 1989; bd. dirs. Cin. Country Day Sch., 1983; pres. Alumni Coun. and Ann. Fund, 1983. Mem. Cin. Bar Assn., Fla. Bar Assn., Harvard Law Sch. Assn. Cin., Heimlich Inst. (trustee 1987—), Yale Alumni Assn. (del. 1984-87), Cin. Yale Club (pres. 1980, 96). Republican. Home: 2270 Madison Rd Cincinnati OH 45208-2659 Office: Vogel Heis Wenstrup & Cameron 524 Walnut St Cincinnati OH 45202-3114

VOGEL, SARAH, state agency administrator, lawyer; b. Bismarck, N.D., May 3, 1946; d. Robert and Elsa Marie (Mork) V.; 1 child, Andrew. BA, U. N.D., 1967; JD, NYU, 1970. Bar: N.Y. 1970, N.D. 1982. Commr. N.D. Agrl. Dept., Bismarck, N.D. Office: ND Agrl Dept 600 E Boulevard Ave Bismarck ND 58505-0660

VOGELZANG, JEANNE MARIE, professional association executive, lawyer; b. Hammond, Ind., Apr. 15, 1950; d. Richard and Laura Ann (Vanderaa) Jabaay; m. Nicholas John Vogelzang, May 17, 1971; children: Nick, Adam, Tim. BA, Trinity Christian Coll., Palos Heights, Ill., 1972; MBA, U. Minn., 1981; JD, U. Chgo., 1987. Bar: Ill. 1987; CPA, Ill. Tchr. Timothy Christian H.S., Elmhurst, Ill., 1972-74; tchg. assoc. in fin. U. Minn., Mpls., 1980-81; fin. analyst Quaker Oats Co., Chgo., 1982-84; atty. Baker & McKenzie, Chgo., 1987-89, Jenner & Block, Chgo., 1989-91; pres., owner J.M. Vogelzang & Assocs., Western Springs, Ill., 1991—; exec. dir. Structural Engrs. Assn. Ill., Chgo., 1992—, Nat. Coun. Structural Engrs. Assns., 1996—. Mem. jud. code com. Christian Reformed Ch. N.Am., Grand Rapids, Mich., 1991—; bd. dirs. Austin Christian Law Ctr., Chgo., 1989-92, Barnabas Found., Palos Heights, 1989-95, Trinity Christian Coll., Palos Heights, 1992—; com. mem. Western Springs Planning Commn., 1991-95, village trustee, 1995—, chmn. fin. com., mem. gen. govt. com. Mem. ABA, Am. Soc. Assn. Execs., Nat. Coun. Structural Engrs. Assn. (exec. dir. 1996—), Ill. State Bar Assn., Chgo. Bar Assn. Mem. Christian Reformed Ch. Home: 5108 Fair Elms Ave Western Springs IL 60558-1808 Office: 203 N Wabash Ave Ste 1000 Chicago IL 60601-2412

VOIGHT, JACK C., state official; b. New London, Wis., Dec. 17, 1945; s. Oscar C. and Thelma J. (Hamm) V.; m. Martha J. Wolfe, July 14, 1973; children: Carly, Emily. BS, U. Wis., Oshkosh, 1971. Claims adjuster U.S. F&G Ins. Co., Appleton, Wis., 1971-74; ins. agy. owner Voight Ins. Agy., Appleton, 1974—; state treas. State of Wis., Madison, 1995—; bank organizer Am. Nat. Bank, Appleton, 1992-94; real estate broker Voight Realty & Ins., Appleton, 1977-92. Pres. Appleton Northside Bus. Assn., 1982; alderman City Coun., City of Appleton, 1983-83, pres., 1992-93. Sgt. U.S. Army, 1968-70. Decorated Bronze Star; named Citizen of Yr., Appleton Northside Bus. Assn., 1990. Mem. Nat. Assn. State Treas., Appleton Noon Optimist Club (pres. 1980). Republican. Presbyterian. Office: State Treas Wis PO Box 7871 Madison WI 53707-7871

VOIGHT, NANCY LEE (MRS. JAY VAN HOVEN), counseling psychologist; b. Kansas City, Mo., Nov. 24, 1945; d. Paul and Leona Alvina (Schultz) V.; m. Jay Van Hoven, June 27, 1975; children: Joshua, Janna, Lydia. BA, Wittenberg U., 1967; MA, Ball State U., 1971; PhD, Mich. State U., 1975. Tchr. lang. arts Ashland (Ohio) City Schs., 1967-68; tchr. English,

Speedway (Ind.) City Schs., 1969; basic literacy instr. Army Edn. Ctr., Gelnhausen, W. Ger., 1969-70; individual assistance Bethel Home for Boys, Gaston, Ind., 1970-71; counselor Wittenberg U. Ohio, 1971-72; staff psychologist Ingham County Probate Ct., Lansing, Mich., 1972-74; asst. prof. U. N.C., Chapel Hill, 1975-79, counseling psychologist, 1976-79; psychologist for employee devel. Gen. Telephone Electronics, No. Region Hdqrs., Indpls., 1979-80; behavioral sci. coord. Family Practice Ctr., Community Hosp., Indpls., 1980-82; media psychologist Sta. WIFE, Indpls., 1981-82; asst. dir. Chapel Hill Counseling Ctr., 1980-86; dir. Behavior Therapy Ctr., Indpls., 1982-86; treas. Med. Specialty Disability Ins. Corp., Indpls., 1982-86; psychologist Alternatives to Boys Sch., 1983-85, Mich. Dept. Corrections, Kincheloe, 1986-88, Wasilewski & Assocs., Monroe, Mich., 1994—, Elliott and Assocs., Toledo, 1995—; staff psychologist Meth. Hosp. Ind., 1985-86; assoc. prof. psychology Lake Superior State U., Sault St. Marie, Mich., 1988-95; psychologist VIII Mich. Dept. of Mental Health Huron Valley Ctr., 1995—; advisor Sex Info. and Counseling Ctr., Chapel Hill, 1977-79. Chmn. housing bd. U. N.C., 1976-79. Office Edn. grantee, 1977-78, 78-80; Spencer Found. young scholars grantee. Mem. Am. Psychol. Assn., Ind. Psychol. Assn., Mich. Psychol. Assn., Assn. Advancement Behavior Therapy, Inst. Rational Living, Soc. Behavioral Medicine, Am. Assn. Marriage and Family Therapists. Lutheran. Author: Becoming, 1978; Becoming: Leader's Guide, 1978; Becoming Aware, 1979; Becoming Informed, 1979; Becoming Strong, 1979; also articles. Home: 12270 N Suder Rd Erie MI 48133-9724 Office: Huron Valley Ctr 3511 Bemis Rd Ypsilanti MI 48197

VOINOVICH, GEORGE V., governor; b. Cleve., July 15, 1936; m. Janet Voinovich; 3 children. B.A., Ohio U., 1958; J.D., Ohio State U., 1961; LL.D. (hon.), Ohio U., 1981. Bar: Ohio 1961, U.S. Supreme Ct. 1968. Asst. atty. gen. State of Ohio, 1963-64; mem. Ohio Ho. of Reps., 1967-71; auditor Cuyahoga County, Ohio, 1971-76; commr., 1976-78; lt. gov. State of Ohio, 1979; mayor City of Cleve., 1979-90; gov. State of Ohio, 1991—; 1st v.p. Nat. League Cities, 1984-85, pres., 1985; trustee U.S. Conf. Mayors; chmn. Midwestern Govs. Conf., 1991-92, Coun. Gt. Lakes Govs., 1992-94. Recipient cert. of Merit award Ohio U., Humanitarian award NCCJ, 1986; named one of Outstanding Young Men in Ohio Ohio Jaycees, 1970; one of Outstanding Young Men in Greater Cleve. Cleve. Jaycees; Disting. Urban Mayor award Nat. Urban Coalition, 1987; named to All-Pro City Mgmt. team City & State Mag., 1987. Mem. Rep. Govs. Assn. (vice chmn. 1991-92, chmn. 1992-93), Nat. Govs. Assn. (chmn. edn. action team on sch. readiness 1991, chmn. child support enforcement work group 1991-92, mem. strategic planning task force 1991-92, mem. human resources com. 1991—, co-chmn. task force on edn. 1992-93, mem. exec. com. 1993—, co-lead gov. on fed. mandates 1993—), Omicron Delta Kappa, Phi Alpha Theta, Phi Delta Phi. Republican. Office: Office of Gov 77 S High St 30th fl Columbus OH 43266-0601

VOJCAK, EDWARD DANIEL, metallurgist; b. Chgo., Mar. 15, 1960; s. Edward Donald and Joyce Denise (Dibiase) V. BS, U. Ill., Chgo., 1983. Engr. in tng., Ill. Metallurgist Bliss & Laughlin Steel, Harvey, Ill., 1984-87, mgr. quality enging., 1989-92; supr. heat treat Brad Foote Gear Works, Cicero, Ill., 1987-89; plant metallurgist LaSalle Steel, Hammond, Ind., 1992—. Author symposia procs., 1992. Mem. ASTM (com. mem. 1984-89), Am. Soc. Metals, The Metall. Soc., Math. Assn. Am., U. Ill. Alumni Assn. Office: 1412 150th St Hammond IN 46327-1743

VOLESKY, RON JAMES, state legislator; b. Bullhead, S.D., July 13, 1954; s. Leonard and Louise (Kleinsasser) V. BA in Govt., Harvard Coll., 1976; MS in Journalism and Mass Communication, S.D. State U., 1977; postgrad., U. S.D. Sch. Law, 1980. Prodr. bicentennial programming S.D. Pub. TV, 1975; news dir., anchorman S.D. Pub. Radio Network, 1976-77; real estate salesman Montgomery Agy., 1978-79; pvt. practice as atty.; ptnr. Churchill, Manolis, Freeman & Volesky; bd. dirs. Bank Wessington. Co-author: Who's Who Among the Sioux, 1977. Del. Rep. State Conv., 1978; chmn. Beadle County Rep. Ctrl. Com., S.D., 1979-80; state rep. dist. 23 State of S.D., majority whip, 1983-84, dist. 21, 1993—, mem. judiciary and transp. coms. S.D. Ho. of Reps. Recipient Citizenship award Huron Am. Legion, 1972; scholar Harvard Club N.Y., 1972-76, Sarah and Pauline Maier scholar Harvard Coll., 1972-76. Mem. Soc. Profl. Journalists, S.D. Trial Lawyers Assn., ABA, Jaycees. Democrat. Home: 592 Dakota Ave S Huron SD 57350-2858*

VOLIVA, SHARON LEE (GROSSMAN), community volunteer, child and education advocate; b. Chgo., Feb. 27, 1944; d. Andrew Edward Grossman and Gertrude Rose (Mallory) Grossman Kvasnicka; m. Benjamin Harrison Voliva Jr., July 23, 1966; children: Annette L. Voliva DeLaCroix, Alan L., Andrea E. Voliva Krainik, Cheryl L. Voliva Merritt, Benjamin H. III. Contbr. articles to profl. jours. Bd. edn. Thornton Twp. High Schs. Dist. 205, 1985, 89, 93; bd. dirs. Dolton-Riverdale United Way, Ill. Learning Partnership; v.p. Coalition for Ednl. Rights; trustee Ivanhoe United Meth. Ch.; dist. 19 legis. asst. Ill. PTA; state bd. mgrs. Ill. Congress Parents and Tchrs., legislation chmn./lobbyist; mem. exec. bd. dirs. South Met. Assn. for Low Incidence Handicapped; chmn. Parents March for Sch. Funding. Recipient Appreciation award South Cook County Girl Scouts, 1977, Thanks Badge award, 1980, Outstanding Community Svc. award Riverdale-Dolton Jaycees, 1978, WTTW Svc. Appreciation plaque, 1975, 76, 77, WTTW Chmn.'s Gavel award, 1978, Pres.'s award for Svc. United Way, 1989. Methodist. Home: 10 W Sibley Blvd Dolton IL 60419-1513

VOLK, JOHN M., electrical engineer; b. South Bend, Ind., May 16, 1955. BSEE, Perdue U., 1979. Controls engr. K & E Mfg., Granger, Ind., 1988-89, Weldun Internat., Bridgman, Mich., 1989-92; engr. Trinetics Inc., Mishawaka, Ind., 1992—. Office: Trinetics Inc 55807 Currant Rd Mishawaka IN 46545-4805

VOLKERS, BURTON JAY, electrical engineer; b. Brookings, S.D., Mar. 16, 1957; s. Barteld and Johanna Dorothy (Walburg) V.; m. June Lynn Dahl, Aug. 8, 1981; children: Mischele, Justine, Nathan. BEE, S.D. State U., 1981; MS in Engrin. Mgmt. with honors, U. Kans., 1992. Registered profl. engr., Kans.; cert. plant engr. Elec. engr. Kans. facilities Hercules Inc., Radford, Va., 1981-84; sr. elec. engr. Hercules Inc., DeSoto, Kans., 1984-87, supt. maintenance and utilities, 1987-95; mgr. maintenance and utilities Alliant Tech Systems, DeSoto, Kans., 1995—. Cmty. svc. vol. Jr. Achievement, 1993, 94; chmn. Elem. Sch. Site Coun., 1993-95. Mem. Am. Ins. Profl. Engrs., Toastmasters (treas. Radford, Va. chpt. 1982-83). Republican. Lutheran. Home: 2829 Missouri St Lawrence KS 66046-4557 Office: Alliant Tech Systems Inc 35425 W 103rd St De Soto KS 66018

VOLKMER, HAROLD L., congressman; b. Jefferson City, Mo., Apr. 4, 1931; m. Shirley Ruth Braskett; children: Jerry Wayne, John Paul, Elizabeth Ann. Student, Jefferson City Jr. Coll., 1949-51, St. Louis U. Sch. Commerce and Finance, 1951-52; LL.B., U. Mo., 1955. Bar: Mo. 1955. Individual practice law Hannibal, 1958—; asst. atty. gen. Mo., 1955; pros. atty. Marion County, 1960-66; mem. Mo. Ho. of Reps., 1966-76; chmn. judiciary com., mem. revenue and econs. com.; mem. 95th-104th Congresses from 9th Mo. Dist., 1977—; ranking minority mem. agr. subcom. livestock, dairy, & poultry. Served with U.S. Army, 1955-57. Recipient award for meritorious pub. service in Gen. Assembly St. Louis Globe-Democrat, 1972-74. Mem. Mo. 10th Jud. Circuit bar assns. Roman Catholic. Clubs: KC, Hannibal Lions. Office: US House of Reps 2409 Rayburn House Bldg Washington DC 20515*

VOLLMER, HOWARD ROBERT, artist, photographer; b. St. Paul, Dec. 16, 1930; s. Herbert Lenard and Elfreida Wilhelmena Elizabeth (Rubbert) V.; m. Velma Martin, Feb. 10, 1951; children: Mark David, Lori Lynn. BA, Hamline U., 1957; MA, Ariz. State U., 1968; postgrad., U. Minn., 1970-85. Screen print tech. developer 3M Co., St. Paul, 1948-51; tchr. art ESL, St. Paul Pub. Schs., 1957-87; corp. product analyst, treas. Gateway Labs., Golden Valley, Minn., 1975-78; owner, photographer, artist Remember Art and Photog. Svcs., White Bear Lake, Minn., 1980—; creator, co-presenter TV program Crafts in Edn., Sta. KTCA-TV, St. Paul, 1959. Author, illustrator: Chipmunk Children's Book, 1995. Chmn. White Bear Arts Coun., 1975-80; elected bd. dirs. Florence Gardens Mobil Home Assn. Sgt. USAF, 1951-52. Nat. Experienced Tchrs. Art fellow, 1967-68. Mem. Nat. Art Edn. Assn., St. Paul Fedn. Tchrs. Democrat-Farmer-Labor Party. Lutheran.

VOLPERT, MARY KATHERINE, administrative assistant, revenue specialist; b. Topeka, May 4, 1959; d. Fredrick Harvey and Mary Alice (Conroy) Lewis; m. Jeffrey Jay Volpert, June 6, 1981 (div. Oct. 1990); 1 child, Anissa Marie. From acctg. clk. to acct. adminstr. Vol. Shoe Corp., Topeka, 1978-88; office mgr., cons. Lewis Repair Svc., Topeka, 1985—; adminstrv. mgr., cons. Lewis Auto, Truck & Elec. Repair Svc., Topeka, 1994—; adminstrv. asst., devel. technician Hill's Pet Products, Topeka, 1988-94; revenue specialist Western Resources, Inc., Topeka. Assoc. mem. Spl. Olympics, 1983—, United Way, 1981—; mem., advisor Jr. Achievement, 1990—. Mem. Am. Bus. Women's Assn. (Kan-Kan chpt. 1979--81, exec. chpt. 1992—), Nat. 600 Bowling Club, Inc. Republican. Roman Catholic. Home: 6123 SW 27th St Apt 3 Topeka KS 66614 Office: Lewis Auto Truck & Elec Repair Svc 114 NW Van Buren St Topeka KS 66603-3316 also: Western Resources Inc 818 Kansas Ave Topeka KS 66603

VONDERHEIDE, RICHARD SCOTT, insurance executive; b. Batesville, Ind., Nov. 18, 1953; s. Watler Leo and Janet Lee (McCool) V.; m. Dala Ann Vonderheide, Nov. 23, 1953; children: Amy Michelle, Jon David, Jennifer Rebecca, Keevan Bryant. BS, Marion Coll., Indpls., 1976. Tchr. Franklin County Sch. Corp., Brookville, Ind., 1976-78; ins. salesperson Kirschman Vonderheide & Assocs., Inc., Batesville, 1978-86; regional mgr. Consol. Nat. Life, Lake Charles, La., 1986-89; pres. Am. Venture Capital Corp., Batesville, 1989—; dir. United Life Ins. Co., Cin. Dir. sch. bd. Batesville Cmty. Sch. Corp., 1992—; mem. park bd. City of Batesville, 1992—. Home and Office: 313 N Elm St Batesville IN 47006

VONDRUSKA, ELOISE MARIE, librarian; b. Chgo., Sept. 13, 1950; d. George A. and Irene L. (Pionke) Klebba; m. Richard J. Vondruska, Aug. 11, 1972. BA, Loyola U., Chgo., 1972; MS, U. Ill., 1973. Acquisitions librarian Parkland Coll., Champaign, Ill., 1973-79, tech. svcs. librarian, 1979-83; serials cataloger Arlington Heights (Ill.) Meml. Library, 1983-85; authorities librarian Northwestern U., Evanston, Ill., 1985-87; rsch. adminstr. Dastrup/Vondruska Assocs., Chgo., 1987-91; head catalog dept. Northwestern U. Sch. Law Libr., 1989—; cons. Catalist, Champaign, 1983-85. Editor: The Micocomputer, 1983, jour. issue Ill. Libraries, 1983. Ill. State scholar, 1968-72, DePaul U. scholar, 1968; Katharine L. Sharp fellow, 1972. Mem. AALL, ALA, CALL, Ill. Libr. Assn. (bd. dirs. 1983, 85-86), Beta Phi Mu. Office: 357 E Chicago Ave Chicago IL 60611-3008

VON HEIMBURG, ROGER LYLE, surgeon; b. Chgo., Feb. 5, 1931; s. Franklin Dederick and Alice Julia (Zebuhr) von H.; m. Mary Ellen Janson, July 12, 1952; children: Mary Deborah, Donald Franklin. AB, Johns Hopkins U., 1951, MD, 1955; MS in Surgery, U. Minn., Rochester, 1964. Diplomate Am. Bd. Surgery. Intern Johns Hopkins Hosp., Balt., 1955-56; resident in surgery Mayo Clinic, Rochester, 1958-62, chief resident in surgery, 1962, asst. to staff in surgery, 1962-64; practice medicine specializing in surgery Green Bay, Wis., 1964-94; staff St. Vincent Hosp., Green Bay, 1964-94, Bellin Meml. Hosp., Green Bay, 1964-94; ret., 1994. Contbr. articles to profl. jours. Mem. state Bd. of Health Care Info., 1988-91; reapptd., 1991-95. Lt. USNR, 1956-58. Fellow ACS; mem. State Med. Soc. Wis. (bd. dirs. 1980-89, vice-chmn. 1983-87, chmn. 1987-89, pres.-elect 1989-90, pres. 1990-91), Wis. Chpt. ACS (v.p. 1985-86, pres.-elect 1986-88, pres. 1988-90), Brown County Med. Soc. (pres. 1986), Wis. Surg. Soc. (coun. mem. 1987-90). Republican. Methodist. Home: 344 Terraview Dr Green Bay WI 54301-1523

VONIER, SPRAGUE, retired broadcast executive; b. Mpls., Feb. 28, 1918; s. Chester William and Esther Elizabeth (Bril) V.; m. Mary-Jo Maurina, Aug. 2, 1947 (dec. July 1994); children: Thomas, Victoria, Jeanna. BA, U. Hawaii, 1946. Copy editor Milw. Sentinel, 1946-47; press sec. to mayor City of Milw., 1947-48; promotion mgr. Jour. Broadcasting, Milw., 1948-50; prodr.- dir. Sta. WTMJ-TV, Milw., 1950-55, chief prodr., 1956-58, program mgr., 1958-62, mgr., 1963-77; v.p. devel. Midwestern Relay, Milw., Chgo., 1977-83; v.p. electronic info. svcs. Tectron, Inc., Milw., 1983-87; cons. electronic media, Milw., 1987-92; adjunct lectr. mass communications, U. Wis., Milw., 1962-93. Author: Edward R. Murrow, 1989; contbr. articles and poems to profl. jours. Bd. dirs. LaBelle Industries, Inc., Oconomowoc, Wis., 1959-92; founder, dir. Skylight Opera Theatre, Milw., 1959-80; bd. dirs. Bookfellows-Friends of Milw. Pub. Libr., 1968-89, Sta. WVWM-FM, 1975-90; mem. task force for Wis. Ice Age Trail, 1996. Capt. AUS, 1941-45. Mem. Soc. Profl. Journalists, Milw. Press Club, Milw. Ad Club (pres.). Home: 2921 N Lake Dr Milwaukee WI 53211

VON LANG, FREDERICK WILLIAM, librarian, genealogist; b. Scranton, Pa., May 6, 1929; s. Frederick William and Carrie Della (Brundage) von L.; m. Ilsabe von Wackerbarth, July 12, 1960; children: Christoph, Karl Philipp. B.S., Kutztown U., 1951; M.L.S., Syracuse U., 1955. Libr. Broughal Jr. High Sch., Bethlehem, Pa., 1951-52; asst. libr. Bethlehem Pub. Libr., 1952-55, Enoch Pratt Free Libr., Balt., 1956-66; dir. Lehigh County Community Coll. Libr., Allentown, Pa., 1966-73, Auburn (Maine) Pub. Libr., 1973-77, St. Joseph (Mo.) Pub. Libr., 1977-79, Hibbing (Minn.) Pub. Libr., 1980—. Assoc. editor: Genealogisches Handbuch des in Bayern immatrikulierten Adels, Vol. 4, 1954. Treas., mem. exec. bd. Friends of Bethlehem Pub. Library; treas., mem. steering com. Auburn City Bicentennial Com.; mem. exec. bd. Northampton County Assn. for Blind, Pa.; ofcl. del. Mo. Gov.'s Conf. on Libraries and Info. Scis. Mem. ALA (councilor from Maine Libr. Assn. 1974-77), Maine Library Assn. (fed. coord. A.L.A.), S.A.R., Maine Soc. Mayflower Descendents, Soc. Colonial Wars in Maine, Huguenot Soc. Maine, Bradford Family Compact., Beta Phi Mu. Lutheran. Clubs: Masons (32 deg.), KT, Shriners, Order Eastern Star, Elks, Rotary. Home: 2129 3rd Ave W Hibbing MN 55746-1509 Office: 2020 Fifth Ave E Hibbing MN 55746-1702

VON RIEMER, DAVID WILHELM KARL (GENERAL), retired real estate representative, author; b. Milw., July 21, 1929; s. William Frank and Anna Marie (Hunsicker) Riemer; m. Arlene J. Pierzchalski, Dec. 23, 1964. Student, U. Wis., Milw., 1949-51. Lic. real estate broker. Real estate rep. Milwaukee County Pub. Works Dept., Milw., 1960-90. Author: Phonics In Your Face, 1996, Military Day, 1996. Served with U.S. Army, 1947-49. Mem. South Shore Yacht Club (life). Lutheran. Home: 6319 W Allerton Ave Greenfield WI 53220-3410

VON ROENN, KELVIN ALEXANDER, neurosurgeon; b. Louisville, Dec. 5, 1949; s. Warren George and Catherine Jean (Bauer) Von R.; m. Jamie Hayden, June 24, 1979; children: Erika Marie, Lisa J., Alexander H., Karl G. BS, Xavier U., 1971; MD, U. Ky., 1975. Diplomate Am. Bd. Neurol. Surgery. Instr. neurosurgery Rush-Presbyn. St. Luke's Med. Ctr., Chgo., 1980-83, asst. prof. neurosurgery, 1983—; cons. neurosurgery Shriner's Hosp. for Crippled Children, Chgo., 1988—, attending neurosurgeon, 1990—; lectr. sect. of neurosurgery U. Ill. Coll. Med., 1996. Named one of Outstanding Young Men of Am., 1986. Fellow ACS; mem. Congress Neurologic Surgeons, Am. Assn. Neurol. Surgeons, Ill. Neurosurg. Soc. (v.p. 1994-95, pres. 1995-96), Alpha Sigma Nu, Alpha Omega Alpha. Office: Assocs in Neurol Surgery 1725 W Harrison St # 1117 Chicago IL 60612-3828

VON STOCKHAUSEN, RON J., mechanical designer; b. Milw., July 21, 1956. AD in Drafting, United Tech. Inst., 1975. Mech. designer Louis Allis Co., Milw., 1975%. Republican. Roman Catholic. Office: Louis Allis Co PO Box 2020 Milwaukee WI 53201-2020

VOORHEES, HAROLD J., SR., state legislator; s. John and Helena V.; m. Joanne Land; children: Harold Jr., Nancy Baker Voorhees, Karla Vereecken Voorhees. Grand Rapids (Mich.) Jr. Coll. Councilman-at-large Wyoming (Mich.) City Coun.; mayor Wyoming, Mich.; state rep. Dist. 77 Mich. Ho. of Reps., 1993—; owner, pres. Serv-U-Sweets, Inc., Grandville, Mich., 1996—; vice chair Local Govt. Com., Mich. Ho. of Reps., 1993—; mem. Ins., Mil. & Vets. Affairs, State Affairs & Transp. Coms., 1993—. V.p. Grandville Srs. Housing Facility, 1996—. Mem. Rotary Club. Home: 5380 Kenowa Ave SW Grandville MI 49418-9501*

VORA, MANU KISHANDAS, chemical engineer, quality consultant; b. Bombay, India, Oct. 31, 1945; s. Kishandas Narandas and Shantaben K. (Valia) V., m. Nila Narotamdas Kothari, June 16, 1974; children: Ashish, Anand. BSChemE, Banaras (India) Hindu U., 1968; MSChemE, Ill. Inst. Tech., Chgo., 1970, PhD in ChemE, 1975; MBA, Keller Grad. Sch. Mgmt., Chgo., 1985. Grad. asst. Ill. Inst. Tech., 1969-74; rsch. assoc. Inst. Gas Tech., Chgo., 1976-77, chem. engr., 1977-79, engring. supr., 1979-82; mem. tech. staff AT&T Bell Labs. (now Lucent Techs.), Holmdel, N.J., 1983-84, Naperville, Ill., 1984—; mgr. customer satisfaction AT&T Bell Labs. (now Lucent Techs.), Naperville and Milw., 1990—; mem. faculty Ill. Inst. Tech., Chgo., part-time, 1993—; spkr. in field. Invited editor Internat. Petroleum Encyclopedia, 1980. Chmn. Save the Children Holiday Fund Drive, 1986—; trustee Avery Coonley Sch., Downers Grove, Ill., 1987-91; pres., dir. Blind Found. for India, Naperville, 1989—; dir. Nat. Ednl. Quality Initiatives, Inc., Milw., 1991—, fellow, 1992. Recipient Non-Supervisory AA award Affirmative Actions Adv. Com., 1987, 92, Outstanding Contbn. award Asian Am. for Affirmative Actions, 1989, Disting. Svc. award Save the Children, 1990. Fellow Am. Soc. Quality Control (standing rev. bd. 1988—, editl. re. bd. 1989, tech. media com. 1989, mixed media rev. bd. 1994, nat. quality month regional planning com. 1989-94, nat. cert. com. 1989-94, chmn. cert. process improvements subcom. 1990-94, testimonial awards 1996, exec. bd. Chgo. sect., vice chmn. sect. affairs 1993-94, sect. chmn. 1994-95, spl. award 1991, Century Club award 1992, Founders' award 1993, Joe Lisy Quality award 1994); mem. Chgo. Assn. Tech. Socs. (ann. merit award 1992), Ill. Team Excellence (chief judge 1993—, steering com. 1993—, award). Hindu. Home: 1256 Hamilton Ln Naperville IL 60540-8373 Office: Lucent Techs 2000 N Naperville Rd Naperville IL 60566-7033

VORCE, TIMOTHY C., systems engineer; b. Ypsilanti, Mich., May 2, 1951; s. Raymond H. and Marian E. (Carr) V.; m. Marilyn A. Edwards, May 13, 1978; children: Jennifer, Emily, Brian, Amanda. BS, Mich. State U., 1973; MS, Okla. State U., 1976. Registered profl. engr., Mich. Process control computer programmer Ford Motor Co., Flat Rock, Mich., 1973-74; rsch. analyst TVA, Chattanooga, 1976-78; engr. Detroit Edison Co., 1978-84; sys. analyst Tektronix, Inc., Farmington, Mich., 1984-86; sys. engr. SysScan Inc., Dearborn, Mich., 1986; network mgr. on contract to Chrysler Auburn Hills, Mich., 1986-90; tech. cons. on contract to Ford Dearborn, Mich., 1990; sys. engr. Electronic Data Sys., Milford, Mich., 1990—; vol. spkr. Mich. Future, Inc., Birmingham, 1994-95. Chair strategic planning com. City of Wixom, Mich., 1992, vol. water com., 1989-93; vol. outcome bd. edn. Walled Lake (Mich.) Schs., 1992-93, instrnl. applications team leader, 1993. Named one of Outstanding Young Men in Am., Jaycees, 1982. Home: 1366 Bishops Ter Wixom MI 48393

VOROUS, PATRICIA ANN MARIE, elementary school educator; b. Cleve., Sept. 12, 1951; d. Leon Jr. and Margaret (Cotter) V. BS Edn. in Elem. Edn., St. John Coll., Cleve., 1973; postgrad., Notre Dame Coll., Cleve., 1988, Baldwin-Wallace Coll., Berea, Ohio, summer 1979, 91; Ashland Coll., 1995. Cert. tchr., Ohio. Intermediate tchr. lang. arts, social studies St. Mel Sch., Cleve., 1973-74; grade 6 tchr. lang. arts, social studies and religion St. James Sch., Lakewood, Ohio, 1975-80; tchr. grades 5 and 6 Our Lady of the Angels Schs., Cleve., 1980—; supervisory tchr. for elem. edn. students Cleve. State U.; from asst. dir. to dir. Lakewood Recreation Dept. Summer Play Ctr., 1973-94, summer 1995; safety patrol coord. Our Lady of Angels, Cleve., 1985—. Craftsman animals, dolls, 3-D scenes for fall festivals and gifts. Roman Catholic.

VORPAHL, JEFF, computer company executive; b. 1954. Audit mgr. Touche Ross & Co., Milw., 1975-84; with Kemper Clearing Corp., Milw., 1985—; CFO Beta Systems Inc., Brookfield, Wis. Office: Beta Systems Inc 350 N Sunny Slope Rd Brookfield WI 53005*

VORST, GERRY D., agricultural engineer; b. Lima, Ohio, Oct. 14, 1962. BS in Agrl. Engring., Ohio State U., 1986. Product engr. Universal Co-op, Goshen, Ind., 1987-88; project engr. Cadillac Gage Textron Co., Greenville, Ohio, 1989—. Mem. Soc. Agrl. Engrs. Office: Cadillac Gage Textron Co 5963 Jaysville-St John Greenville OH 45331

VOSS, ANNE COBLE, nutritional biochemist; b. Richmond, Ind., Aug. 22, 1946; d. James Richard and Helen Lucille (Hoyt) Coble; m. Harold Lloyd Voss, July 20, 1969; children: Daniel, Jordan Matthew, Sarah Georgette. BS, Ohio State U., 1968, PhD, 1984. Registered dietitian. Therapeutic dietitian Johns Hopkins Hosp., Balt., 1968-69; clin. instr. Ohio State U. Hosps., Columbus, 1969-70; clin. dietitian U.S. Army Med. Clinic, Rothwesten, Fed. Republic Germany, 1970-72; clin. rsch. monitor Ross Labs., Columbus, 1978-79; rsch. asst. Ohio State U., Columbus, 1979-84, rsch. assoc., lectr., 1985-91; mgr. outcomes rsch. Ross Products divsn. Abbott Labs., Columbus, Ohio, 1992—; adj. asst. prof. Otterbein Coll., Westerville, Ohio, 1990-93; nutrition advisor Ohio Dental Assn., Columbus, 1977-93, ADA, Chgo., 1987-93; cons. Ohio Bd. Dietetics, Columbus, 1989-93; vis. scientist Rikshospitalet, Oslo, Norway, 1992. Author: Polyunsaturated Fatty Acids and Eicosanoids, 1987; author, editor: Nutrition Perspectives, 1990, 91, 2d edit., 1993; contbr. articles to profl. jours. Mem. exec. bd. Aux. to Ohio Dental Assn., Columbus, 1979-95; bd. dirs. Ohio Dental Polit. Action Com., Columbus, 1989-92, YWCA, Columbus, 1990-93; Gov.'s appointee, chmn. Ohio Bd. Dietetics. Recipient award Clement Found., Westerville, 1991, Nutrition Edn. in Tng. grant Ohio Dept. Edn., Columbus, 1978. Mem. Am. Dietetic Assn., Ohio Dietetic Assn., Med. Dietetics Assn. (founding mem., pres., v.p., sec. 1978—), Ohio Coun. Against Health Fraud (founding mem., bd. govs. 1987—), Ohio Nutrition Coun. (exec. bd. 1987-94), Columbus Dietetic Assn., Sigma Xi, Sigma Delta Epsilon (sec. 1985—). Methodist. Home: 1526 Bridgeton Dr Columbus OH 43220-3908 Office: Abbott Labs Ross Products Divsn 625 Cleveland Ave Columbus OH 43215-1724

VOSS, MICHAEL J., product manager electronics company; b. La Crosse, Wis., Dec. 5, 1962. BS, U. Wis., 1986. R&D staff Allied Signal, La Crosse, Richmond, Wis., Va., 1986-94; product mgr. GE Co., Coshocton, Ohio, 1994—. Contbr. articles to circuitry mags. Vol. Big Brother/Big Sister, YMCA. Mem. I.P.C. Office: GE Company 1350 S 2nd St Coshocton OH 43812-1980

VOTAVA, THOMAS ANTHONY, real estate and insurance professional; b. Chgo., Nov. 11, 1925; s. Joseph Patrick and Anna Rose (Novak) V. BSc, DePaul U., 1953; postgrad., Loyola U., Chgo., 1954, U. Chgo., 1955, St. Francis Coll., Lockport, Ill., 1972. Indsl. engr. Inland Steel Co., Indiana Harbor, Ind., 1953-55; field auditor GM Corp., Detroit, 1955-57; bus. mgr. various GM automobile agys., Chgo., 1957-68; asst. prin. Chgo. Archdiocese schs., 1969-72, curriculum chmn., 1969-79; investment councilor Bus. Techniques, Inc., Westchester, Ill., 1962—; broker Assurance Ins. and Real Estate, Berwyn, Ill., 1972—; bd. dirs., Polyurethane Enging. Co., Inc., Lake Forest, Ill.; tchr., lectr., elem. and high schs., Ill. and Fla., 1968—. Bd. dirs., Boys Club, Cicero, Ill., 1956—; scoutmaster, Cicero area Boy Scouts Am., 1957-65; pres., Cicero Youth Commn., 1961-63; trustee, mem. exec. bd., Cicero Assn. Recreation, 1963-65; advisor Order of the Arrow, 1956-65. Sgt. maj. U.S. Army, 1945-51, World War II and Korea. Decorated Various campaign medals in Asiatic-Pacific Campaign in WWII & Korean Wars; recipient Silver Beaver award Chgo. Coun. Boy Scouts Am., 1962, Ill. PTO award, 1965, Boys Club Am. award, 1965, Longest Tenured bd. dirs. mem., award for achievement with youth Gov. of Ill., 1962-63, Outstanding Svc. to Cmty. award Boys Club, 1965. Mem. VFW (comdr. Cicero post 1956-58), United Vets. Coun. (comdr. 1967-69), Am. Legion (sr. vice-comdr. Berkeley post 1967-69, councilor Berkeley post youth program 1968-71). Republican. Roman Catholic.

VRAKAS, DANIEL P., state legislator; b. Oct. 31, 1955. BA, U. Wis., Stevens Point. Wis. state assemblyman dist. 33, 1990—; vice chmn. Rep. Caucus; former restaurant owner. Mem. Waukesha Meml. Hosp. Found., Am. Cancer Soc. Named Friend of Agr., Wis. Farm Bur., 1992—, Champion of Commerce, Milw. Met. Area C. of C., 1992. Mem. Hartland and Delafield C. of C., Lake Country Rotary. Address: N 45 W 28912 Capital Dr Hartland WI 53029*

VRANA, VERLON KENNETH, professional society administrator, conservationist; b. Seward, Nebr., June 25, 1925; s. Anton and Florence (Walker) V.; m. Elaine Janet Flowerday, June 5, 1949; children: Verlon Rodney, Timothy James, Carolyn Elaine, Jon David. Student, U. Nebr., 1959-62; BBA, George Washington U., 1967, MBA, 1970; mgmt. course, Harvard U., 1979. Field technician Soil Conservation Svc., USDA, Seward, 1948-58; watershed planner, cons. Soil Conservation Svc., USDA, Lincoln, Nebr., 1958-62; mem. pers. staff Soil Conservation Svc., USDA, Washington,

1962-72, dir. pers. div., 1972-76, asst. adminstr. for mgmt., 1976-79, assoc. dep. chief for adminstrn., 1979-80; chief planning div. Nebr. Natural Resources Com., Lincoln, 1980-88; owner-farmer Blue Ridge Farm, Seward, 1980-89; exec. v.p. Soil and Water Conservation Soc., Ankeny, Iowa, 1989-91; pres. Vrana Assocs., Seward, Nebr., 1992—; bd. dirs., sec. N.E. Natural Resources Dist., York, Nebr., 1988-89; bd. dirs. Watershed Coalition, Denver, Groundwater Policy Edn. Project, Mpls., Cattle Nat. Bank, Seward; alt. dir. Renewable Natural Resources Foun., Washington, 1989-91. Contbr. articles to jours. in field. Mem. Com. on Ministry Presbyn. Ch. U.S.A., 1986-89, elder, 1970—; vice moderator Homestead Presbytery, 1989; treas. Nebr. Soil and Water Conservation Found., 1992—. Recipient N.E. Centennial Grass Seeding award N.E. Centennial Commn., Lincoln, 1967, N.E. Soil Steward award N.E. Natural Resources Commn., Lincoln, 1986. Fellow Soil and Water Conservation Soc. (pres. N.E. Coun. 1986, Presdl. citation 1989), Isaac Walton League (dir. Seward chpt. 1984-89), Nat. Wildlife Fedn. (soil conservationist of yr. award 1987), Seward Grange (officer 1984-89, 92—), Shriner. Home and Office: Vrana Assocs 131 N 1st St Seward NE 68434-2130

VRATIL, KATHRYN HOEFER, federal judge; b. Manhattan, Kans., Apr. 21, 1949; d. John J. and Kathryn Ruth (Fryer) Hoefer; children: Alison K., John A., Ashley A. BA, U. Kans., 1971, JD, 1975; postgrad., Exeter U., 1971-72. Bar: Kans. 1975, Mo. 1978, U.S. Dist. Ct. Kans. 1975, U.S. Dist. Ct. (we. dist.) Mo. 1978, U.S. Dist. Ct. (ea. dist.) Mo. 1985, U.S. Ct. Appeals (8th cir.) 1978, U.S. Ct. Appeals (10th cir.) 1980, U.S. Ct. Appeals (11th dist.) 1983, U.S. Supreme Ct., 1995. Law clk. U.S. Dist. Ct., Kansas City, Kans., 1975-78; assoc. Lathrop Koontz & Norquist, Kansas City, Mo., 1978-83; ptnr. Lathrop & Norquist, Kansas City, 1984-92; judge City of Prairie Village, Kans., 1991-92; bd. dirs. Kans. Legal Svcs. Bd. editors Kans. Law Rev., 1974-75, Jour. Kans. Bar Assn., 1992—. Mem. Kansas City Tomorrow (XIV); bd. trustees, shepherd-deacon Village Presbyn. Ch.; nat. adv. bd. U. Kans. Ctr. for Environ. Edn. and Tng., 1993-95. Fellow Kans. Bar Foun., Am. Bar Found.; mem. ABA, Am. Judicature Soc., Nat. Assn. Judges, Fed. Judges Assn., Kans. Bar Assn., Mo. Bar Assn., Kansas City Met. Area Bar Assn., Wyandotte County Bar Assn., Johnson Coutny Bar Assn., Assn. Women Lawyers, Lawyers Assn. Kansas City, Supreme Ct. Hist. Soc., Kans. State Hist. Soc., U. Kans. Law Soc. (bd. govs. 1978-81), Kans. U. Alumni Assn. (mem. devel. com. 1985—, mem. Kansas City chpt. alumni bd. 1990-92, nat. bd. dirs. 1991—, bd. govs. Adams alumni ctr. 1992—, pres. 1985-86, membership chair 1983-84, mem. learned club 1992ú, mem. chancellor's club 1993—, mem. Williams ednl. fund 1993—, mem. Jayhawks for higher edn. 1993—), Homestead Country Club Prairie Village (pres.), Sons and Daus of Kans. (life), Rotary, Jr. League Wyandotte and Johnson Counties, Kans. State Hist. Soc., Order of Coif, Kans. Inn of Ct. (master 1993—), Overland Park Rotary, Univ. Club, Phi Kappa Phi. Republican. Presbyterian. Office: US Courthouse 511 500 State Ave Kansas City KS 66101-2403

VRBANCIC, JOHN EMERICK, engineering consultant; b. East Chgo., Ind., Sept. 10, 1955; s. George Emerick and Corrine E. (Miterko) V.; m. Ann Carole Del Giorno, May 22, 1982. BS, Loyola U., 1977, MBA, 1985; postgrad, De Paul U., 1988. Sr. systems analyst Northwestern Meml. Hosp., Chgo., 1980-82; pres. Vrbancic and Assocs. Inc., Evanston, Ill., 1982-87, The Hannibal Group, Evanston, 1987-93; cons. engr. The CS Group, Inc., Mundelein, Ill., 1993—; cons. engr. Program Power II, Chgo., 1986-93. Author: Expert Ease-Minerals, 1987 Expert Ease-Trees, 1988. Mem. Computing Machinery Assn., Am. Artifical Intelligence Assn., Ind. Computer Cons. Assn., Certified Computer Profls. Assn. (cert. award 1984, cert. data profls. award 1985), US Chess Fedn. Home: 1717 Oakton St Evanston IL 60202-2763

VROMAN, BARBARA FITZ, writer, educator; b. Chgo., Mar. 31, 1933; d. William Edwin and Pearl Asenith (Coombs) Fitz; m. Dale Duane Vroman, June 30, 1951; children: Guy, Kim, Marc, Ryan. Grad. high sch., Plainfield, Wis. News editor Waushara Argus Newspaper, Wautoma, Wis., 1966-72; pub. Pearl-Win Pub. Co., Hancock, Wis., 1981-91; tchr. summer sessions The Clearing, Ellison Bay, Wis., 1989—; presenter pvt. seminars Rhinelander Sch. of Arts, U. Wis., 1975—. Novelist: Sons of Thunder, 1981, Linger Not at Chebar, 1992; co-author: Tomorrow is a River, 1977. Home: RR 1 Box 300 Hancock WI 54943-9775

VRTISKA, FLOYD P., state legislator; b. Oct. 12, 1926; m. Doris Vrtiska; children: Terri Jo, Lori Ann, Kim R. Grad., Table Rock H.S. Commr., chmn. Pawnee County, Nebr., 1973-92; mem. from dist. 1 Nebr. State Senate, Lincoln, 1992—, mem. agr., health and human svc. coms., vice chmn. bus. and labor com. Recipient Ak-Sar-Ben Agr. Achievement award, Outstanding Cmty. Svc. award Peru State Coll., Ak-Sar-Ben Nebr. Farm Bur. award, Appreciation award Table Rock Devel. Corp., County Ofcl. of Yr. award and Pres.'s award Nebr. Assn. County Ofcls., Spl. Svc. award Table Rock Vol. Fire Dept. Office: State Capitol Rm 350 Lincoln NE 68509*

VUCOVICH, DONN TIMOTHY, insurance executive; b. Des Plaines, Ill., Aug. 9, 1963; s. Emil Daniel and Jean Elizabeth (Killeen) V.; m. Carol Ann Bethell, May 25, 1988; children: Matthew Timothy, Emily Elizabeth. BS, Ill. State U., 1985; MBA, U. Chgo., 1990. Sr. mgr. Anderson Consulting, Chgo., 1985-91; prin. Ky. Enterprises, Inc., Chgo., 1991-92; mng. assoc. Coopers & Lybrand, Chgo., 1992-93; v.p. CNA Ins. Co., Chgo., 1993—. Mem. Coun. on Fgn. Rels. Home: 711 Wood Creek Ct Island Lake IL 60042 Office: CNA Ins 711 Wood Creek Ct Island Lake IL 60042-9590

VUKOVICH, JOSEPH JOHN, state legislator, lawyer; b. Youngstown, Ohio, Sept. 29, 1945; s. Joseph J. and Josephine (Kurdowski) V.; m. Patricia D. Matthews, 1988; children: Andrew Jospeh, Joseph John. BA, Youngstown State U., 1968; JD, U. Akron, 1973. Bar: Ohio. Asst. atty gen. State of Ohio, 1973-77; dep. dir. law City of Youngstown, Ohio, 1978—; rep. dist. 52 Ohio Ho. Reps., Columbus, 1978-92; senator Ohio State Senate, Columbus, 1993—; atty., sole practice, Canfield, Ohio; mem. civil and comml. law commn., 1982-84, Ohio Ho. Reps., chmn. ethics com. 1980-82, 88-92. Mem. Easter Seal Soc. Decorated Bronze star U.S. Army; recipient Meritorious Svc. award Ohio Acad. Trial Lawyers, 1981, 87, Commdrs. award Nat. Amvets 1983, Resolution of Merit, Ohio Prosecuting Attys., 1984, Meritorius Service medal U.S. Selective Svc. System, 1986. Mem. ABA, VFW (Legislator of Yr. Ohio 1982), Ohio State Bar Assn., Mahoning County Bar Assn., Cath. War Vets. Am. (Disting. Legislator Ohio 1988), Conf. Ins. Legislators, Am. Legion.

VUKOVICH, THOMAS WALTER, architect; b. Chgo., Aug. 21, 1952; s. Walter and Sonia (Bogich) V. AA, Lincoln Jr. Coll., 1972; BS cum laude, Kans. State U., 1975, BArch, 1980. Contractor Bldg. Log Home, Mound City, Kans., 1975; with Spring Factory, Chgo., 1976-77; component fabricators Pre-Fab Roof Trusses, Manhattan, Kans., 1977; architects Maan & Co., Hutchinson, Kans., 1977-81; urban planners Trkla, Pettigrew, Allan & Payne, Chgo., 1981-82; architect Gresham Smith & Ptnrs., Dallas, 1982-83, RGA Architects, Dallas, 1983, Corgan Assoc. Architecture, Dallas, 1983-85, Perkins & Will, Chgo., 1985-92; city architect City of Chgo., 1992—. Contbr. articles to profl. jours. Mem. Serbian Orthodox Ch., Chgo., 1988--. Mem. Environ. Design & Rsch. Assn., Phi Kappa Phi.

VULGAMORE, MELVIN L., college president; b. Springfield, Ohio, July 19, 1935; s. Leo Beeman and Della Marie (McCoy) V.; m. Ethelanne Oyer, Feb. 17, 1957; children: Allison Beth, Sarah Faith Vulgamore Evans. B.A. with honors, Ohio Wesleyan U., 1957; B.D., Harvard U., 1960; Ph.D., Boston U., 1963. Chmn., prof. religion Ohio Wesleyan U., Delaware, 1962-78, assoc. dean faculty, 1972-73, dean acad. affairs, 1973-78; v.p., provost U. Richmond, Va., 1978-83; pres. Albion Coll., Mich., 1983—; vis. prof. Am. U. Beirut, 1971-72; dir. Chem. Bank; vis. scholar Harvard U., 1995. Contbr. articles to profl. jours. Trustee Howe Mil. Sch., Ind., 1984—; mem. Mich. Coun. for Humanities, 1985-89, 96-97. Mem. Am. Acad. Religion, Tillich Soc. N.Am., Univ. Club N.Y., Detroit Athletic's Club, Rotary, Univ. Club. N.Y., Phi Beta Kappa, Omicron Delta Kappa, Delta Sigma Rho, Pi Sigma Alpha. Lodge: Rotary. Club: Univ. Club. N.Y. Home: 1620 Van Wert Rd Albion MI 49224-9743 Office: Albion Coll Office of Pres Albion MI 49224

VYBORNY, CARL JOSEPH, radiologist; b. Oak Park, Ill., Nov. 23, 1950; s. Ernest Joseph and Praxedes Felicia (Nowinski) V.; m. Terrieann Susin, Nov. 28, 1975; 1 child, Margaret. BS with highest distinc., U. Ill., Chgo., 1972; MS, U. Ill., Urbana, 1973; PhD, U. Chgo., 1976, MD with hons., 1980. Diplomate Am. Bd. Radiology. Fellow dept. physics U. Ill., Urbana, 1972-73; fellow dept. radiology U. Chgo., 1973-76, resident in radiology, 1980-84, asst. prof. radiology, 1984-85, clin. assoc. prof. radiology, 1985—; attending radiologist La Grange (Ill.) Meml. Hosp., 1985—; bd. physicians practice group LaGrange Meml. Hosp., 1991—; mem. institutional rev. bd. LaGrange Meml. Hosp., 1994—; chmn. mammography com. Ill. Radiol. Soc., 1990—; mem. early detection com. Am. Cancer Soc., Ill., 1986—; mem. clin. rev. tng. com. Ctr. for Disease Control/Am. Coll. Radiology, 1991—; spl. reviewer diagnostic radiology study sect. NIH, 1993; bd. dirs. Acad. of Radiology Rsch.; radiation protection adv. coun. State of Ill., 1994—. Contbr. articles to profl. jours. Recipient Eastman Kodak Sci. award, 1976, Itek award, Soc. Photographic Scientists and Engrs., 1979, Nels Stranford Meml. award, U. Chgo., 1980; Andrew W. Mellon Found. fellow, 1984. Fellow Soc. for Breast Imaging, Am. Coll. Radiology (mem. mammography accrditation com.); mem. AMA, Radiol. Soc. N.Am., Am. Assn. Physicists in Medicine, Chgo. Radiol. Soc. (pres., resident sect. 1983-84). Roman Catholic. Home: 171 Michaux Rd Riverside IL 60546-1827 Office: La Grange Meml Hosp 5101 Willow Springs Rd La Grange IL 60525-2600

VYVERBERG, ROBERT WILLIAM, mental health facility administrator; b. Dubuque, Iowa, Dec. 23, 1940; s. William Pifer and Virginia Thelma (Rutger) V.; m. Mari Ann Jacobs, Nov. 6, 1982; children by previous marriage: Robert William, Benjamin Rutger. BEd, Ill. Wesleyan U., 1963; MS, Ill. State U., 1964; EdD, No. Ill. U., 1972. Dir. counseling services Crown High Sch., Carpentersville, Ill., 1964-67; dir. outcare services, children and adolescent unit H. Douglas Singer Mental Health Center, Rockford, Ill., 1969-72, dir. psychiat. rehab. and extended care services, 1972-82; region coordinator Services to Elderly, 1978-83; clin. dir. Children's and Adolescent Services, 1982-84, adminstrv. dir., 1982-84; supt. Zeller Mental Health Ctr., 1984—; lectr. crisis theory and crisis intervention No. Ill. U., 1970-84, instr. group counseling and psychotherapy, 1973; cons. Juvenile Justice Personnel Devel. Center, U. Wis., 1977. Mem. Nat. Rehab. Assn., Am. Assn. Counseling and Devel., Am. Rehab. Counselors Assn., Am. Mental Health Counselors Assn., Internat. Assn. Psycho-Social Rehab. Services, Assn. Mental Health Adminstrs. Methodist. Home: 4420 W Lynnhurst Dr Peoria IL 61615-2365 Office: Zeller Mental Health Ctr 5407 N University St Peoria IL 61614-4736

WAALER, JACK, lawyer; b. Chgo., May 22, 1934; s. George Richard and Josephine (Dittrich) W.; m. Virginia Baker, Jan. 30, 1965; children: Christopher, Luke, Grant. AB, U. Ill., 1956, LLB, 1959. Bar: Ill. Asst. states atty. Champaign County, Urbana, Ill., 1962-64, pub. defender, 1965-69; city atty. City of Urbana, 1969—; ptnr. Waaler & Evans, Urbana, 1969-90. Contbr. chpt. to legal handbook. Capt. U.S. Army, 1959-62, lt. comdr. USN, 1969-78. Mem. Phi Beta Kappa.

WAARA, MARIA ESTHER, artist; b. Menahga, Minn., June 16, 1930; d. William Matt and Maria Matilda (Alajoki) Haataja; m. Hubert Frank Waara, Dec. 25, 1954. Student, U. Calif., 1975, Gogebic Coll., Ewen, Mich., 1976. Freelance artist Bruce-Crossing, Mich. Home: RR 2 Box 31 Bruce Crossing MI 49912-9707

WACHTMAN, LYNN R., state legislator; m. Trudy Wachtman; children: Cory, Aaron. Student, Four County Joint Vocat. Sch. Plant mgr. Culligan Water Conditioning, Napoleon, Ohio; pres. Maumee Valley Bottlers, Inc.; city councilman City of Napoleon, Ohio; dist. 80 rep. Ohio Ho. of Reps., Columbus, 1985-92, dist. 83 rep., 1993—. Recipient Legislator's award Am. Legion Commdrs. Ohio. Mem. Ohio Right to Life, Gideons Internat., Ohio Farm Bur., Ducks Unlimited.

WACKER, FREDERICK GLADE, JR., manufacturing company executive; b. Chgo., July 10, 1918; s. Frederick Glade Wacker and Grace Cook Jennings; m. Ursula Comandatore, Apr. 26, 1958; children: Frederick Glade III, Wendy, Joseph Comandatore. BA, Yale U., 1940; student, Gen. Motors Inst. Tech., 1940-42; LLD (hon.), Northwood U., 1989, GMI Engring. and Mgmt. Inst., 1996. Efficiency engr. AC Spark Plug divsn. Gen. Motors Corp., 1940-43; with Ammco Tools, Inc., North Chicago, Ill., 1947-87, pres., 1948-87, chmn. bd., 1948-87; founder, pres. Liquid Controls Corp., North Chicago, 1954-87, chmn. bd., 1954—; chmn. bd. Liquid Controls Europe, Zurich, Switzerland, 1985-87; ltd. ptnr. Francis I. DuPont & Co., N.Y.C., 1954-70; mem. exec. coun. Conf. Bd., 1971-92, chmn., 1977. Condr. Freddie Wacker and His Orch., 1955-69, orch. has appeared on TV and radio, recs. for Dolphin and Cadet records. Bd. govs. United Rep. Fund Ill., Art Inst. Chgo., 1984—; trustee Lake Forest Acad., 1956-71, life trustee, 1992—; trustee Warren Wilson Coll., 1973-81, Chgo. chpt. Multiple Sclerosis Soc.; bd. govs. Lyric Opera Chgo., 1963-66; bd. advisers Nat. Schs. Com., 1966-88; adv. coun. Trinity Evang. Div. Sch., 1977-87; adv. bd. Internat. Coun. Biblical Inerrancy, 1981-88; bd. dirs., vice chmn. Rockford Inst., 1983-91; bd. govs. GMI Engring. and Mgmt. Inst., 1983-91; bd. regents Milw. Sch. Engring., 1981-91; mem. pres.'s coun. Ligonier Ministries, 1989—. Lt. (j.g.) USNR, 1943-45, PTO. Recipient Outstanding Bus. Leader award, Northwood, 1994; named to Hall of Fame Lake Forest Acad., 1987. Mem. Chief Execs. Forum, Young Pres. Orgn. (chmn. Chgo. chpt. 1965-66), Sports Car Club Am. (founder Chgo. region 1949, pres. 1952-53), Ill. Mfrs. Assn. (bd. dirs. 1966-91, chmn. bd. 1975), Chgo. Pres. Orgn. (pres. 1972-73), Automotive Hall of Fame (life, bd. dirs. 1976-88, v.p. 1980-81, sec. 1981-88, Disting. Svc. Citation 1989, Chief Exec. Forum 1967-89), Soc. Automotive Engrs., World Bus. Coun., Waukegan C. of C. (bd. dirs. 1965-68), Art Inst. Chgo. (gov.), Chgo. Fedn. Musicians (life), Am. Motorcycle Assn. (life), Living Desert (life), Racquet Club (pres. 1960-61), Shoreacres Club, Onwentsia Club, Vintage Club, Conway Farms Golf Club, The Quarry. Presbyterian. Home: 1600 Green Bay Rd Lake Bluff IL 60044-2306 Office: Liquid Controls Corp 105 Albrecht Dr Lake Bluff IL 60044-2252

WACKER, THOMAS J., management executive, outplacement consultant; b. Milw., Aug. 2, 1949. BA in Sociology, U. Wis., 1971. Gen. mgr. Graebel/St. Louis Movers, Inc., 1983-85; v.p. Challenger, Gray & Christmas, Inc., Brookfield, Wis., 1985—. Mem. Soc. for Human Resource Mgmt. Office: Challenger Gray & Christmas Inc 250 N Sunny Slope Rd Brookfield WI 53005-4809

WADE, SUSAN KAYE, elementary education educator; b. East St. Louis, Ill., Nov. 29, 1956; d. Floyd Robert and Rosemary (Reichert) W. Postgrad., Ill. State U., 1981, 82. Cert. in elem. edn., elem. reading, teaching visually impaired, Ill. Resource tchr. visually impaired Alta Sita Elem. Sch., East St. Louis, 1978-79; tchr. 3d grade St. Catherine Laboure Sch., Cahokia, Ill., 1979-95; tchr. 2d grade Holy Family Sch., Cahokia, 1995—; curriculum writer, textbook reviewer St. Catherine Laboure Sch., 1979-95. Mem. Nat. Cath. Edn. Assn., Coun. for Exceptional Children, Assn. for Edn. and Rehab. Blind and Visually Impaired, Tchrs. Applying Whole Lang. Republican. Roman Catholic. Home: 806 St Thomas Ln Cahokia IL 62206-1811 Office: Holy Family Sch 116 E 1st St Cahokia IL 62206

WADEMAN, PATSY ANN, psychiatric, geriatrics nurse; b. Atlantic, Iowa, Nov. 20, 1943; d. Willie Hollesen and Annie Mae (Lewis) Hollesen Bennet; m. Fredrick N. Wademan, Sept. 11, 1966; children: Stephen, Linnea, Bethany. Diploma, Mercy Hosp., Council Bluffs, Iowa, 1966; BGS in Gerontology, U. Nebr., Omaha. Cert. psychiat. mental health nurse, gerontol. nurse. Nurse Nebraska City (Nebr.) Pub. Schs., 1966-68, St. Mary's Hosp., Nebraska City, 1973-74, 76-78; staff nurse Duffs Friendship Villa Nursing Home, Nebraska City, 1986-88; dir. nursing Nebraska City Manor, 1988-89; staff nurse Med. Ctr. U. Nebr. Med. Ctr., Omaha, 1989-95; health coord. Head Start, Tecumseh, Nebr., 1984-86; rsch. nurse intern I U. Nebr. Med. Ctr., Omaha, 1995-96, rsch. nurse intern II, 1996—; instr. Southeast C.C., Lincoln, Nebr., 1976-84; mem. Nat. Coun. on Aging. Mem. Am. Psychiat. Nurses Assn., Am. Gerontol. Nurses Assn., Nebr. Gerontol. Nurses Assn., Golden Key Nat. Honor Soc.

WADSWORTH, THOMAS P., manufacturing manager; b. Sandusky, Ohio, June 26, 1943. Sec. corp. Clyde (Ohio) Welding Inc., 1965-76; plant mgr. Cal-Van Tools, Fremont, Ohio, 1976—. Patentee in field. Republican. Office: Cal Van Tools 1500 Walter Ave Fremont OH 43420-1449

WAGENAAR, DOREEN DAWN, marketing professional; b. Rock Rapids, Iowa, Feb. 17, 1961; d. Enno and Harriet Elizabeth Wagenaar. AA in Bus., Freeman (S.D.) Jr. Coll., 1981; BS, U. Nebr., 1991. Pers. asst. pers. dept. Back to the Bible, Lincoln, 1981-86; adminstrv. asst. Tompsett Ins., Lincoln, 1987-91; devel. asst. pub. rels. and mktg. dept. Back to the Bible, Lincoln, 1992—; vol. coord. Tabitha, Lincoln, 1990. Staffing coord. Haven Manor. Mem. Phi Upsilon Omnicron, Omnicron Nu. Republican. Home: 1024 E St #4 Lincoln NE 68508

WAGENAAR, LARRY JOHN, archivist; b. Grand Rapids, Mich., June 11, 1962; s. Cornelius and Mary (Blom) W., m. Sarah, 1 child, Amy. BA in History and Religion cum laude, Hope Coll., 1987; MA, Kent State U., 1989—. With customer service dept. Eberhard Foods Inc., Grand Rapids, 1978-81; ops. mgr. Video Today Inc., Holland, Mich., 1981-85; collection organizer, developer computer programs, museum interpreter Netherlands Museum, 1987; supplies mngr. Hope-Geneva Bookstore-Hope Coll., 1985-87; hist. researcher Kent State U., 1987-88; archivist, assoc. prof. Joint Archives Holland (Mich.) Hope Coll., 1988—; consultant Amway, Inc., 1996—. Author: Guide to the Collections of the Joint Archives of Holland, 1989, Supplement to the Guide to the Collections, 1991; columnist for News From Hope Coll. and others, speaker in field. Grantee DeWitt Conduit Found. 1990, Natl. Historical Publications and Records Commn. 1990, 1992, Mich. Coun. for the Humanities, 1991, Crystal Cathedral Ministries, 1993, 1994—, Amway Intl., 1996—. Mem. Assn. for Advancement of Dutch-Am. Studies (pres.), Am. Assn. of State and Local History, Orgn. Am. Historians, Soc. Am. Archivists, Mich. Archival Assn. (pres. v.p. sec.), Midwest Archives Conf., Mich. Alliance for Conservation of Cultural Heritage (bd. dirs.), Historical Soc. Mich (v.p., bd. dirs.), Mich. St. Records Advisory Bd., Holland Sesquicentennial Commn., Dutch Am. Historical Soc. (bd. dirs.), Holland Area Historical Soc. (sec. treas.), Zeeland Historical Soc. (bd. dirs.). Home: 3403 Starflower Ct Holland MI 49424 Office: Hope Coll Joint Archives Holland MI 49423

WAGENER, DONNA LYNN, real estate company official; b. Chgo., Oct. 15, 1959; d. James Robert and Faith Josephine (Jackson) Michalak; m. Thomas Peter Wagener, Sept. 26, 1987; 1 child, Trevor Michael. BS in Fin., U. Ill., Chgo., 1985. Sales mgr., advt. mgr. Menconi Co., Chgo., 1979-81; asst. v.p. constrn. Jupiter Realty Corp., Chgo., 1985—; cons. Captive Audience, Chgo., 1988—. Mem. AAUW, NAFE. Home: 1911 N Mohawk St Unit A Chicago IL 60614-5219 Office: Jupiter Realty Corp 919 N Michigan Ave Chicago IL 60611

WAGER, PAULA JEAN, artist; b. Lansing, Mich., Dec. 19, 1929; d. Mervin Elihu and Cora Della (Raymer) Fowler; m. William Douglas Wager, May 4, 1952; children: Pamela Ann, Scott Alan. Student, Mich. State U., 1949-52. Music tchr. Toledo, Ohio, 1968-72, Union Lake, Mich., 1972-76; tchr. art, artist Paula Wager's Art Studio, Commerce Twp., Mich., 1984—; hostess Artistic Touch with Paula, Cable Comcast channel 44, Waterford, Mich., TCI West Oakland, Walled Lake, Mich., Channel 10, 1991-94. Exhibited in group shows including Village Art Supplies, 1982-88, Pontiac Oakland Soc. Artists, 1983—, Pontiac Galleria, 1983, Oakland C.C., Commerce Twp., 1985, Red Piano Gallery, Hilton Head, S.C., 1985-89, Mich. State U., East Lansing, 1986, Silver Pencil Gallery, Pontiac, 1987-89, Wooden Sleight, Vestaburg, Mich., 1988-93, Art Pad, Keego Harbor, Mich., 1990-93, Local Color Gallery, Union Pier, Mich., 1992-94, Mich. Assn. Artists, Southfield Civ. Ctr. Mich. 1995; Waterford Public Lib., Solo Exhibit, 1996; Swann Gallery, Detroit, 1995—, Millers Artist Supplies, Ferndale, Mich., 1996; one-woman shows include Waterford (Mich.) Pub. Libr., 1996; represented in pvt. collections. Recipient Outstanding Achievement award in instructional programming Comcast Cable TV, Waterford, 1992, 1st place, Waterford Friends of the Arts Art Show, 1988, Pontiac Oakland Soc. Artists Cmty. Rm., 1990, Am. Biog. Inst. Woman of Yr. Commemorative medal, 1995; Waterford Cable Commn. grantee, 1991, 93, Charter Twp. of Waterford grantee, 1991-94. Mem. Nat. Assn. Female Exec. Pontiac Oakland Soc. Artists, Waterford Friends of the Arts, Mich. Watercolor Soc., Birmingham Bloomfield Art Assn., Colored Pencil Soc. Am., Colored Pencil Soc. Detroit, Village Fine Arts Assn. Home and Studio: 3316 Greenlawn Ave Commerce Township MI 48382-4629

WAGGONER, DANIEL LEROY, hobby industry executive; b. Lawrence County, Ind., Apr. 29, 1934; s. Roger and Virginia Mary (Thomas) W.; m. Barbara Faith Bowman, Sept. 26, 1952; 1 child, Dennis L. Office clk. Wheeler Foutch Co., Bedford, Ind., 1952-59; in house sales Central Ind. Distbr. Corp., Indpls., 1959-60; v.p. Wacker Distbr. Corp., Indpls., 1960-79; sr. v.p. merchandising United Model Distbr. Inc., Wheeling, Ill., 1979-91; nat. sales mgr. LGB products M.W. Kasch Co., Mequon, Wis., 1991-92; nat. sales mgr. William K. Walthers Inc., Milw., 1992-96; cons. Cave Creek, Ariz., 1996—. With U.S. Army, 1956-59, West Germany. Republican. Home and Office: 28831 N 45th St Cave Creek AZ 85331

WAGGONER, DORIS EVON See **WENZEL, DORIS JEAN REPLOGLE**

WAGGONER, SUSAN MARIE, electronics engineer; b. East Chicago, Ind., Sept. 1, 1952; d. Joseph John and Elizabeth Vasilak; m. Steven Richard Waggoner, July 31, 1976; children: Kenneth David, Michael Christopher. AS, Ind. U., 1975, BA in Journalism, 1976, BS in Physics, 1982, M in Pub. Affairs, 1991. Engring. technician Naval Surface Warfare Ctr., Crane, Ind., 1978-82, electronics engr. test and measurement equipment, 1982-91, electronics engr. batteries, 1991—. Mem. Am. Soc. Naval Engrs., Fed. Mgrs. Assn., Federally Employed Women, Am. Rose Soc., Am. Hort. Soc., Mensa, Theatre Circle Ind. U., Sigma Pi Sigma. Home: RR 5 Box 387 Loogootee IN 47553-9337 Office: Naval Surface Warfare Ctr 300 Hwy 361 Crane IN 47522-5001

WAGLE, SUSAN, state legislator, small business owner; b. Allentown, Pa., Sept. 27, 1953; m. John Thomas Wagle, Apr. 3, 1980; children: Julia Marie, Andrea Elizabeth, John Timothy, Paul Thomas. BA in Elem. Edn. cum laude, Wichita State U., 1979, post grad., 1979-82. Tchr. Chisholm Trail Elem., Kans., 1979-80; tchr. emotionally disturbed, special edn. Price Elem., Kans., 1980-82; real estate investor Kans., 1980—; prin. Wichita Bus. Inc., Kans., 1983—; mem. Kansas Ho. Reps., 1990, 92, 94—, speaker pro tem, 1994—. Mem. Am. Legis. Exchange Coun. (Outstanding Legis. of the Yr. 1994), Farm Bur., Nat. Fedn. Ind. Bus., Nat. Restaurant Assn., Wichita Ind. Bus. Assn. Home: 14 N Sandalwood St Wichita KS 67230-6612 Office: Kans Ho of Reps Rm 330 N State Capitol Topeka KS 66612-1504

WAGNER, BILL PETER, writer; b. Watertown, S.D., Oct. 4, 1940; s. Walter and Emma Jane (Donkersgoed) W. BA, U. St. Thomas, St. Paul, 1963. Account mgr. Dun & Bradstreet, Mpls., 1963-65; reporter Watertown (S.D.) Pub. Opinion, 1966-67, Rapid City (S.D.) Jour., 1967-69; editor S.D. Farmers Union, Huron, 1970; aide Sen. George McGovern, Washington, 1971-72; press sec. Atty. Gen. Kermit Sande, Pierre, S.D., 1972-74; comm. coord. Nat. Farmers Union, Denver, 1977-78; Washington corr. NRECA, Washington, 1978-79; dir. comms. NFO, Corning, Iowa, 1979-81; writer, 1981—; mem. Codington County Bd. Edn., Watertown, 1967; sec. Rural Electric Press Assn., Washington, 1978-79; mem. Farmers Union Press Assn., Denver, 1977-78. Contbr. articles to profl. jours. Active in state, local and nat. Dem. campaigns and fundraising. Recipient Disting. Reporting of Pub. Affairs award Am. Polit. Sci. Assn., Washington, 1970; named Best Newspaper article Am. Optometric Assn., St. Louis, 1970. Mem. S.D. Hist. Soc. Home: 45 S Lexington Pkwy St Paul MN 55105

WAGNER, BRETT ALAN, biologist; b. Waterloo, Iowa, Apr. 19, 1959; s. Larry Gene and Karen Kay (Mitchell) W.; m. Pamela Sue Morehead, Aug. 10, 1991. BA, U. No. Iowa, 1983, MA, 1987. Rsch. asst. III U. Iowa Hosps. and Clinics, Iowa City, 1987—. Contbr. articles to Biochemistry, Med. Oncology and Tumor Pharmacotherapy, Jour. Lipid Rsch., Cancer Rsch. Mem. Sigma Xi (assoc.). Office: U Iowa 357 MRF Dept of Bio Iowa City IA 52242

WAGNER, CHARLES ALAN, librarian; b. Elkhart, Ind., Apr. 27, 1948; s. C. Arthur and Lydia M. (Stump) W.; BA, Manchester (Ind.) Coll., 1970; MLS, Ind. U., 1973; m. Marilynn B. Dray, Aug. 17, 1971; children: Sarah, Wendy. Libr. dir. Peru (Ind.) Pub. Libr., 1973—. With USAR, ret.

Decorated Oak Leaf Cluster. Mem. Ind. Library Assn., Plymouth Club Am. Lodge: Rotary. Contbr. articles in field. Cartoons appear in comic books, newspapers, mags. Address: 102 E Main St Peru IN 46970-2338

WAGNER, CINDY KAY, college administrator; b. Buffalo, Mar. 17, 1956; d. Edward and Yolanda (LaBruna) Hawes; children: Marcus, Lance, Chris, Kent. BS, Houghton (N.Y.) Coll., 1976; MA, Ball State U., 1980; postgrad., U. Notre Dame, 1990. Counselor Twin Pines Camp, Stroudsburg, Pa., 1975-79; family svcs. dir. Salvation Army, Munster, Ind., 1980-81; exec. dir. Greater Hammond (Ind.) Community Svcs., 1981-84; pvt. practice counseling, 1984-87; devel. officer Calument Coll. of St. Joseph, Whiting, Ind., 1987-89, dir. admissions and fin. aid, 1989-91, v.p. enrollment mgmt., 1991-95, dir. divsn. of continnuing edn., 1995—; mem. pres. adminstrv. coun., instr. orgn. mgmt. Calumet Coll., Whiting, 1989—. Named Cindy Mola day Mayor of Hammond, 1984; recipient Community Svcs. Leadership award Greater Hammond Community Svcs. 1984, Community Excellence award Hammond Jaycees, 1983, Govs. Cmty Svc. award, 1994. Mem. Ind. Assn. of Admissions and Registrars, Ind. Assn. of Fin. Aid, Nat. Assn. of Fin. Aid, Ins. State Fin. Aid Adminstrs. Office: Calumet Coll St Joseph 2400 New York Ave Whiting IN 46394-2146

WAGNER, HELEN ADEENE, elementary education educator; b. Burlington, Kans., Mar. 9, 1931; d. John Floyd and Clara Myrtle (Jasper) Stone; m. Kenneth Edward Wagner, Sept. 20, 1949; children: Karen, Kent, Kirk. BS, Kans. State Tchrs. Coll., 1964; MS, Emporia (Kans.) State U., 1968, postgrad., 1983, 88-90; postgrad., Ft. Hays (Kans.) State Coll., 1978, 1983-84, Kans. State U., 1979-80, Butler County Community Coll., 1983. Cert. master tchr., Kans. Tchr. Sunnyside Rural Sch., Gridley, Kans., 1948-50; tchr. spl. reading Haviland (Kans.) Grade Sch., 1958-60, tchr. grade 8, 1960-61; edn. sec. Skelly-Jefferson Elem. Sch., El Dorado, Kans., 1962-64; tchr. Skelly Elem. Sch., El Dorado, 1964-81, El Dorado Mid. Sch., 1981-91; ret., 1991; chmn. social studies elem. schs. El Dorado Unified Sch. Dist. 490, 1978-82; chmn. lang. arts dept. El Dorado Mid. Sch., 1987-91; mem. profl. teaching practices commn. Kans. State Bd. Edn., 1976-82, mem. bd. dirs., 1975-80; tchr. edn. teams Nat. Coun. Accreditation, 1974-86; presenter seminars Brooks Jr. H.S., Wichita, 1990; supr. student tchrs.; tchr. mentor El Dorado Pub. Schs., 1991—; mem. Kans. Found. for Excellence in Edn., 1992-95; mem. Kans. Tchr. of Yr. Steering Com., 1992-95. Instr. CPR ARC, 1977-86; vol. El Dorado Helpline, 1972; ruling elder, 1984-86. Named Kans. Tchr. of Yr. Dept. Edn., 1981, Outstanding History Tchr. DAR, 1983, Kans. Outstanding History Tchr. Daus. Colonial Wars, 1983; named to Kans. Tchr. Hall of Fame, 1991; recipient Kans. Master Tchr. award, 1991. Mem. AAUW (chair future astronaut tng. program com. 1991-93), NEA (rep. various confs.), Nat. Assn. Mid. Level Educators, Nat. State Tchr. of Yr. Assn. (del. state conf., steering com. 1989-90), Kans. Edn. Assn., Kans. Assn. Mid. Level Educators (presenter 1987, 91), Kans. Tchr. of the Yr. Assn. (v.p. 1989-91, pres. 1992-95, 2d v.p. 1995—, organizer, presenter celebration of teaching 1989, 95), Kans. Tchr. of Yr. Congl. Dist. 4 (co-chair 1992-95, mem. steering com. 1992-95), El Dorado Edn. Assn. (pres. 1970-71, chmn., mem. various coms. 1964-91), Order Ea. Star (sec. 1960-62), Chelsea Swingin' Sq. Dance Club (bd. dirs., sec.-treas. 1972-94), El Dorado C. of C. (sr. ambs. 1988—), Phi Delta Kappa (coop. learning presenter conf. 1989). Presbyterian.

WAGNER, JON A., computer programmer; b. Cuyahoga Falls, Ohio, Oct. 25, 1969; s. Frank and Darlene W. BA, Kent State, 1993. Material handler Matrix Essentials, Solon, Ohio, 1990; warehouse asst. lead Sea World, Aurora, Ohio, 1991-92, adminstrv. rec. asst. lead, 1992-94, adminstrv. rec. lead, 1994-95; programmer Information Access, Independence, Ohio, 1995; cons. Match King, Akron, Ohio, 1990-95; data analyst Infocision, Akron, 1996. Mem. Kent State Alumni Assn. Home: 5271 Newton Falls Ravenna OH 44266

WAGNER, JOSEPH CRIDER, retired university administrator; b. North Manchester, Ind., Feb. 19, 1907; s. Arthur Augustus and Grace (Crider) W.; A.B., Manchester Coll., 1929, LL.D., 1961; M.A. in Econs., U. Mich., 1936; postgrad. U. Wis., 1930, U. Chgo., 1931-32, Columbia, 1935; m. Geraldine B. Garber, June 30, 1933; 1 dau., Joene Henning. Tchr. Hartford City (Ind.) High Schs., 1929-35, prin., 1936-37, supt. schs., 1937-45; supt. schs., Crawfordsville, Ind., 1946; bus. mgr., treas. Ball State U., Muncie, Ind., 1946-61, v.p. for bus. affairs, 1961-73, v.p. emeritus, 1973—, treas., prof., gen. bus. adminstrn.; nat. chmn., 1976 Annual Fund. Drive; lectr. Mem. Ind. Common Sch. Bldg. Commn., 1960—. Active United Fund of Delaware County. Trustee Ind. Heart Found., Manchester Coll.; mem. ins. trust of Am. Assn. Ret. Persons and Nat. Ret. Tchrs. Assn.; bd. dirs. Muncie YMCA, Ind. State Tchrs. Retirement Fund. Mem. gen. bd. edn., nat. cons. in fin. Methodist Ch. in U.S. Paul Harris fellow Rotary; named Sagamore of the Wabash State of Ind. Gov's. Bowen and Orr, 1976, 88; recipient Friend of Journalism award, Friend of Music Citation, Retiree Recognition award Ball State U., 1992. Mem. Ind. Schoolmen's Club (pres. 1949), Ind. State Tchrs. Retirement Fund (bd. trustees 1975, pres. 1987-88), Retired Sch. Supt. Assn. Ind., Internat. Platform Assn., Am. Assn. Ret. Persons (ins. trust, Retiree Recognition award), Tau Kappa Alpha, Delta Pi Epsilon, Phi Delta Kappa (Cert. of Recognition), Sigma Alpha Epsilon. Mason, Rotarian (past pres.). Contbr. articles to profl. and religious jours. Home: 629 N Forest Ave Muncie IN 47304-3818

WAGNER, MARION KATHRYN, social work educator; b. Oil City, Pa., June 14, 1943; d. Harry Clifford and Reba Estella (Tobin) W. BA in Govt., Calif. State U., L.A., 1965; MSW, San Diego State U., 1969; PhD in Social Work, U. Ill., 1992. CCSW, Ind. Social worker Orange County Welfare Dept., Santa Ana, Calif., 1965-70, San Diego County Welfare Dept., 1970-71; employment counselor, social worker children's svcs. divsn. State of Oreg., La Grande, 1971-75; supr. Children's Bur. Indpls., 1975-82; tchr. Ind. U. Sch. Social Work, Indpls., 1982-83, vis. asst. prof., 1984-86, dir. weekend/work study program, 1986-91, dir. MSW programs, 1991—; polit. asst. to pres. NOW, Washington, 1983; mem. Ind. State Domestic Violence Prevention and Treatment Coun., Indpls., 1991—; chair social/psychol. svcs. subcom. Indpls Commn. on Domestic Violence, 1992—; pres. sojourner commn. Julian Ctr., Indpls., 1980-82. Mem. NASW (Social Worker of Yr. 1984), Coun. on Social Work Edn., Ind. Assn. Social Work Educators, Assn. for Women in Social Work, NOW (regional dir. Gt. Lakes region 1994—, nat. bd. dirs. 1992—), Ind. NOW (pres. 1991-94, state coord. 1978-81, Woman of Yr. 1991), NAACP. Office: Ind U Sch Social Work 902 W New York St E/S 4138J Indianapolis IN 46202-5156

WAGNER, MARK ANTHONY, videotape editor; b. Bethlehem, Pa., Mar. 15, 1958; s. Harry Paul and Theresa Marie (Spadaccia) W.; m. Nancy Susan Davis, Sept. 8, 1984. BA in Comm., Temple U., 1980. Videotape operator Swell Pictures, Chgo., 1983-85; asst. editor Post Pro Video, Chgo., 1985-88; sr. editor Ave. Edit, Chgo., 1988-91; editor/post-prodn. supr. WMX Techs., Chgo., 1992—. Dir. exptl. film Guernica, 1980; dir. video Amusement Park, 1987. Recipient R.L. Jacobs Meml. award Boys' Clubs Am., 1976. Mem. Soc. Motion Picture and TV Engrs., Nat. Amusement Park Hist. Assn., Soc. Comml. Archaeology. Office: 720 Butterfield Rd Lombard IL 60148

WAGNER, MARY ANN, human resources executive; b. St. Louis, May 24, 1947; d. John Gerard and Carmela Lucy (Cozza) Blethroad; 1 child, John Patrick. BA, Webster U., St. Louis, 1979, MA, 1982. Tchr. Our Lady of Fatima, St. Louis, Wetterau, St. Louis; personnel mgr. Venture, St. Louis, 1979-81; customer svc. coord. Venture, O'Fallon, Mo., 1981-84, personnel mgr., 1984-86; regional personnel mgr., 1986-88, dir. tng. and devel., 1988-92; divsn. v.p. dir. of assoc. rels. May Merchandising, St. Louis, 1995—; adj. prof. Webster U., 1990-95, divisional v.p. tng. and devel., 1992—. Chmn. United Way, O'Fallon, 1985, bd. dirs. Mem. AAIM Mgmt. Assn., Am. Soc. Tng. and Devel., Am. Mgmt. Assn. Roman Catholic. Home: 15525 Debridge Way Florissant MO 63034-3456

WAGNER, MARY ANTHONY, theology educator, writer, editor; b. Miesvillle, Minn., Dec. 5, 1916; d. Anton M. and Marie (Wagner) W. BA, St. Louis U., 1945; MA, Cath. U. Am., 1948; PhD, St. Mary's Notre Dame, 1957. Joined Benedictine Sisters, Roman Cath. Ch., 1936. Elem. sch. tchr. various schs., Buckman, Minn., 1936-39, Farmington, Minn., 1939-43; tchr. St. Benedict's High Sch., St. Joseph, Minn., 1945-48, high sch. prin., 1950-54, 62-64; tchr. Coll. of St. Benedict, St. Joseph, 1948-91; prof. emerita Coll. St. Benedict, St. Joseph, 1986—; dean grad. sch. and asst. dean St. John's U., Collegeville, Minn., 1957-78; editor The Liturgical Press, Sisters Today, Collegeville, 1979—; retreat dir. Religious women and priests in midwest; lecturer at various parishes for men, women, and youth groups, 1960—. Author: The Sacred World of the Christian: Sensed in Faith, 1993; contbr. articles to profl. jours. Fellow Danforth Found. Democrat. Home: St Benedicts Monastery 104 Chapel Ln Saint Joseph MN 56374 Office: Sisters Today Liturgical Press Collegeville MN 56321

WAGNER, MARY KATHRYN, sociology educator, former state legislator; b. Madison, S.D., June 19, 1932; d. Irving Macaulay and Mary Browning (Wines) Mumford; m. Robert Todd Wagner, June 23, 1954; children: Christopher John, Andrea Browning. BA, U. S.D., 1954; MEd, S.D. State U., 1974, PhD, 1978. Sec. R.A. Burleigh & Assocs., Evanston, Ill., 1954-57; dir. resource ctr. Watertown (S.D.) Sr. High Sch., 1969-71, Brookings (S.D.) High Sch., 1971-74; asst. dir. S.D. Com. on the Humanities, Brookings, 1976-90; asst. prof. rural sociology S.D. State U., 1990—; mem. S.D. Ho. of Reps., 1981-88, S.D. Senate, 1988-92. Mem., pres. Brookings Sch. Bd., 1975-81; chair fund dr. Brookings United Way, 1985; bd. dirs. Brookings Chamber music Soc., 1981—, Advance and Career Learning Ctr. Named Woman of Yr., Bus. and Profl. Women, 1981, Legislator Conservationist of Yr., Nat. and S.D. Wildlife Fedn., 1988. Mem. Population Assn. Am., Midwest Sociol. Soc., Rural Sociol. Soc., Brookings C. of C. (mem. indsl. devel. com. 1988—), PEO, Rotary. Republican. Episcopalian. Home: 929 Harvey Dunn St Brookings SD 57006-1347

WAGNER, MICHAEL DICKMAN, state representative; b. Omaha, Sept. 24, 1957; s. Loyd R. and Donna (Dickman) W.; m. Paula Spriggs, Oct. 11, 1975; children: Jeremiah, Stephanie, Joshua. AAS in Bus. Mgmt., Kilian C.C., Sioux Falls, S.D., 1984, cert. computer programming, 1984; postgrad., Harvard U., 1995—. From mouldings worker to inventory database coord. Jordan Millwork Co., 1975-84; from dir. ops. info. systems to mgr. Austad's, 1984-93; owner grocery store, entertainment arcade, cons. svc., 1993-94; mayor Baltic, S.D., 1986-92; state rep. State of S.D., Pierre, 1988—, asst. majority leader, 1993-94, mem. legis. exec. bd., 1994—; instr. Kilian C.C., Sioux Falls, 1984-86. Del. leader Am. Coun. Young Polit. Leaders 1992 Exch. to China, del. 1990 Exch. to Japan; exec. dir. Habitat for Humanity, 1994-95; Bus. Leadership fellow, 1995. Bus. Leadership fellow, 1995. Mem. Nat. League of Cities (small cities coun., comty. and econ. devel. policy com. 1989-92), S.D. Mcpl. League (1st and 2d v.p. 1987-89, state exec. bd. trustee 1984-87, dist. chmn. S.E. S.D. 1984, legis. policy com., chmn. mcpl. computerization task force), Nat. Conf. State Legislature (vice chair fiscal oversight and intergovtl. affairs com.), S.E. Coun. Govts. (exec. bd.), Rotary Internat., Minehaha County Rural Mayors Assn., Minnehaha County Centennial Commn., Baltic Area Cub Scouts (past chmn.), Baltic Area Jaycees, Baltic Comty. Club, Baltic Athletic Assn. Home: PO Box 308 Baltic SD 57003-0308

WAGNER, MURIEL GINSBERG, nutrition therapist; b. N.Y.C., Apr. 6, 1926; d. Irving A. and Anna Ginsberg; divorced; 1 child, Emily Lucinda Faith. BA, Wayne State U., 1948, MS, 1951; PhD, U. Mich., 1982. Registered dietitian. Nutritionist Merrill-Palmer Inst., Detroit, 1951-74; pvt. practice, nutritional therapist Southfield, Mich., 1976—; cons. select com. on nutrition U.S. Senate, 1973-74, Ford Motor Co., Dearborn, Mich., 1975-78, Detroit Dept. Consumer Affairs, 1979—; adj. faculty mem. Wayne State U., Detroit, 1970-80, U. Mich., Dearborn, 1974-79. Author: (cookbook) Tun...ahhh, 1993; contbr. articles to profl. publs. Vol. Am. Heart Assn. of Mich.; also various local and nat. govtl. groups. Recipient Outstanding Cmty. Svc. award Am. Heart Assn., 1990; named Outstanding Profl., Mich. Dietetic Assn., 1974. Fellow Am. Dietetic Assn. (organizer Dial-A-Dietitian); mem. Soc. Nutrition Edn., Am. Diabetes Assn. Office: 4400 Town Ctr Ste 275 Southfield MI 48075

WAGNER, NANCY JO, extension educator; b. Brazil, Ind., Oct. 21, 1946; d. George Rex and Erma Lorine (Spelbring) Stearley; m. Paul Wagner, Dec. 29, 1979. BS, Ind. State U., 1970, MS, 1971. Sec., bookkeeper Farm Bur. Co-op, Brazil, 1964-66; tchr. Bloomfield (Ind.) Sch. Dist., 1971-77; coop. ext. svc. educator Purdue U., Covington, Ind., 1977—; project coord. Fountain County Mural Restoration, Covington, Ind., 1981-82; arts coord. Wabash Valley Arts Festival, Covington, 1983—; county ext. dir. Purdue Ext.-Fountain County, 1986—; mem. Fountain County Park Bd., 1994—; chair Fountain County Step Ahead Coun., 1993—; mem. Nat. Ext. Leadership Devel. n. ctrl. region, 1993-94; presenter in field. Bd. dirs. Fountain County divsn. Am. Heart Assn., 1993—; active Covington Community Tree Project, 1992; initiator, advisor Recycling Project, Covington and Veedersburg, Ind., 1989; organist United Meth. Ch., Covington, 1979—, trustee 1992—; organist Attica United Meth. Ch., 1989-92. Rural Energy Conservation grantee Ind. Dept. Energy, Indpls., 1982. Mem. Nat. Assn. Ext. Home Economists (Disting. Svc. award 1995, Continued Excellence award 1996), Ind. Ext. Agts. Assn. (bd. dirs., Comm. award 1981, Innovator award 1990, Sr. Cmty. Devel. award 1995), Kappa Kappa Kappa (pres. 1991-93), Epsilon Sigma Phi. Office: Purdue Ext-Fountain County Courthouse 301 4th St Covington IN 47932-1237

WAGNER, PAUL DEAN, oral and maxillofacial surgeon; b. Mankato, Kans., Dec. 24, 1937; s. Oral Harlan and Mary Belle (Amis) W.; m. Sharon Kay, July 17, 1960; children: Anne, Mary Beth, Paul Jr. BS in Pharmacy, Kans. U., 1961; DDS, U. Tenn., 1968. Diplomate Am. Bd. Oral and Maxillofacial Surgery. Resident in oral and maxillofacial surgery Harrisburg (Pa.) Hosp., 1968-71; practice dentistry specializing in oral and maxillofacial surgery Hershey, Pa., 1971-75, Hays, Kans., 1975—; chief of staff Hays Med. Ctr., 1991—. Pres. Hays Area Rd. Runners, 1975-85. Mem. ADA, Kans. Dental Assn., Am. Soc. Oral and Maxillofacial Surgery, Kans. Soc. Oral and Maxillofacial Surgery (pres. 1984-85), Oil Belt Dental Soc. (pres. 1977-78), Kans. Dental Specialty Bd. (examiner), Hays Area C. of C., Kans. C. of C., Sierra Club. Republican. Unitarian. Home: 2746 Thunderbird Cir Hays KS 67601-1425 Office: 2501 Canterbury Dr Hays KS 67601-2233

WAGNER, ROBERT TODD, university president, sociology educator; b. Sioux Falls, S.D., Oct. 30, 1932; s. Hans Herman and Helen Emilie (Castle) W.; m. Mary Kathryn Mumford, June 23, 1954; children: Christopher, Andrea. BA, Augustana Coll., Sioux Falls, 1954; MDiv, Seabury Western Theol. Sem., 1957, STM, 1970; PhD, S.D. State U., 1972; DHL, Augustana Coll., 1994. Ordained to ministry Episc. Ch., 1957. Staff analyst AMA, Chgo., 1954-57; vicar Ch. of Holy Apostles, Sioux Falls, 1957-64; chaplain All Saints Sch., Sioux Falls, 1962-64; rector Trinity Episcopal Ch., Watertown, S.D., 1964-69; prof. sociology S.D. State U., Brookings, 1971—, acting head dept. sociology, 1978, asst. to v.p. for acad. affairs, 1980-84, pres., 1985—; v.p. Dakota State U., Madison, S.D., 1984-85; cons. sociologist Devel. Planning and Research, Manhattan, Kans., 1976-85; bd. dirs. Deuel County Nat. Bank, Clear Lake, S.D., Found. Seed Stock. Bd. dirs. Karl Mundt Found., Prairie Repertory Theatre, REACH, S.D. 4-H Found., S.D. State U. Found., SA Found., Griffith Charitable Trust, F.O. Butler Found., Christian Edn. Camp and Conf. of Episcopal Dioceses of S.D. Arthur Vinning Davis Found. fellow, 1969-70, Episcopal Ch. Found. fellow, 1969-71, Augustana Coll. fellow, 1977. Mem. Nat. Assn. State Univs. and Land Grant Colls., Brookings C. of C., Phi Kappa Phi, Phi Kappa Delta, Pi Gamma Mu, Alpha Kappa Delta, Alpha Lambda Delta, Sigma Gamma Delta. Republican. Lodges: Elks, Rotary. Home: 929 Harvey Dunn St Brookings SD 57006-1347 Office: SD State U Adminstrn Bldg 222 Office of Pres Brookings SD 57007-2298

WAGNER, THOMAS EDWARD, academic administrator, educator; b. Lexington, Ky., Dec. 6, 1937; s. Thomas Caney and Gaynell (Waggoner) W.; m. Susan Adell Brant, Sept. 3, 1960; children: Brant, Brian, Jennifer. BS, U. Cin., 1962; MA, Miami U., Oxford, Ohio, 1967; EdD, U. Cin., 1973. Tchr. Finneytown Sch. Dist., Cin., 1962-67; admissions officer U. Cin., 1967-70, summer sch. dean, 1970-73, asst. to pres., 1973-74, asst. v.p., 1974-77, vice provost faculty affairs, 1977-85, sr. vice provost, 1985-91, univ. dean for undergrad. and student affairs, 1987-91, v.p. student affairs and svcs., 1991-94, univ. prof. planning, 1983—; mem. adv. com. The Collegeboard, N.Y.C., 1989-91. Contbr. articles to profl. jours and chpts. to books. Bd. dirs. Charter Com., Cin., 1985-88, Inroads, Cin., 1990—, Presbyn. Child Welfare Agy., 1992—, Buckhorn Children's Ctr., 1992—; mem. steering com. Cin. Youth Collaborative, 1988-91; active Fernald Citizens Task Force, 1993—. With USAFR, 1955-63. Fulbright fellow, 1992. Fellow Ctr. for Dispute Resolution, Soc. for Values in Higher Edn. Presbyterian. Home: 1086 W Galbraith Rd Cincinnati OH 45231-5612 Office: Univ Cin Sch of Planning PO Box 210073 Cincinnati OH 45221

WAGNON, JOAN, former state legislator, association executive; b. Texarkana, Ark., Oct. 17, 1940; d. Jack and Louise (lucas) D.; m. William O. Wagnon Jr., June 4, 1964; children: Jack, William O. III. BA in Biology, Hendrix Coll., Conway, Ark., 1962; MEd in Guidance and Counseling, U. Mo., 1968. Sr. research technician U. Ark. Med. Sch., Little Rock, 1962-64; sr. research asst. U. Ark. Med. Sch., Columbia, Mo., 1964-68; tchr. No. Hills Jr. High Sch., Topeka, 1968-69, J.S. Kendall Sch., Boston, 1970-71; counselor Neighborhood Youth Corps, Topeka, 1973-74; exec. dir. Topeka YWCA, 1977-93; mem. Kans. Legislature, 1983-94. Mem. Health Planning Rev. Commn., Topeka, 1984-85. Recipient Service to Edn. award, Topeka NEA, 1979, Outstanding Achievement award, Kans. Home Econs. Assn., 1985; named Woman of Yr. Mayors Council Status of Women, 1983; named one of Top Ten Legislators Kans. Mag., Wichita, 1986. Mem. Topeka Assn. Human Svc. Execs. (pres. 1981-83), Topekans for Ednl. Involvement (pres. 1979-82), Women's Polit. Caucus (state chair). Democrat. Methodist. Lodge: Rotary. Home: 1606 SW Boswell Ave Topeka KS 66604-2729 Office: Kans Families for Kids 2209 SW 29th St Topeka KS 66611-1908

WAGONER, RALPH HOWARD, academic administrator, educator; b. Pitts., May 30, 1938; s. Richard Henry and Charlotte (Stevenson) W.; m. Wilma Jo Staup, Dec. 21, 1961; children: Amanda Jane, Joseph Ryan. AB in Biology, Gettysburg Coll., 1960; MS in Ednl. Adminstrn., Westminster Coll., 1963; PhD, Kent State U., 1967; postgrad., MIT, 1973, Dartmouth Coll., 1979. Prin., tchr., coach Williamsfield (Ohio) Elem. and Jr. High Sch., 1960-62; dir. elem. edn. Pymatuning Valley (Ohio) Local Schs., 1962-64, asst. supt. instrn., 1964-65; acad. counselor, asst. to dean coll. edn. Kent (Ohio) State U., 1965-66, instr. edn., 1966-67; asst. prof. Drake U., Des Moines, Iowa, 1967-70, assoc. prof., 1970-71, chmn. dept. elem. edn., 1968-70, chmn. dept. tchr. edn., 1970-71, acad. adminstrn. intern Am. Council Edn., Office of Pres., 1971-72, asst. to pres., 1972-77, dir. devel., 1975-77; v.p. pub. affairs and devel., prof. Western Ill. U., Macomb, 1977-87, pres., 1987-93; pres. Augustana Coll., Sioux Falls, S.D., 1993—; adj. prof. San Francisco Theol. Sem., 1971; mem. senate Drake U., 1968-77; sponsor interhall council Western Ill. U., 197893, mem. BOG/UPI task force on incentives for faculty excellence, co-chmn., faculty mentor, 1985-93; cons. in field. Co-author: (with L. Wayne Bryan) Societal Crises and Educational Response: A Book of Readings, 1969, (with Robert L. Evans) The Emerging Teacher, 1970, (with William R. Abell) The Instructional Module Package System, 1971, Writing Behavioral Objectives or How Do I Know When He Knows, 1971; contbr. articles to profl. jours. Chmn. Mid-Ill. Computer Consortium, 1980, 85, Western Ill. Corridor of Opportunity, 1987-93; mem. Pres.' Regional Adv. Coun., 1977-87; mem. investments com. McDonough County YMCA; mem. exec. com. Macomb Area Indsl. Corp.; trustee Robert Morris Coll., 1983-88, Chgo. and Carthage, Ill., 1983-88; bd. dirs. Ill. Coun. Econ. Edn., 1987-93, McDonough County United Way Dr., 1980-82; bd. trustees The Cornerstone Found. LSS of Ill., 1990-96; mem. Sioux Falls Tomorrow Task Force, 1993-94; bd. dirs. S.D. Symphony, 1993—, Edn. Telecomms. State of S.D., 1993—, Sioux Falls Devel. Found., 1993—, Children's Inn, 1993—, Sioux Valley Physicians Alliance, 1995—, LECNA, 1996—; life trustee Lutheran Social Svcs., 1996—. Recipient Man of Yr. award Andover Rotary Club, 1964, Quax Honor award, 1969-70, Disting. Alumni award Gettysburg (Pa.) Coll., 1991; named McDonough County Citizen of Yr., Elks, 1982. Fellow Am. Coun. Edn. (cons. fund raising 1984-87); mem. Am. Assn. State Colls. and Univs. (com. econ. devel. 1988, com. on athletics 1987), Ednl. Computing Network (chmn. policy bd. 1985-87), Assn. Midcontinent Univs. (coun. dels. 1987-93), Gateway Conf. (coun. dels. 1987-93), Coun. for Advancement and Support of Edn. (discussion leader, speaker, 1975, 77, 80, 84, 86, 91, 92, 93, 94, Citation award 1981, 83, Grand award 1982, Bronze award 1985, Silver award 1986), Macomb C. of C. (exec. com., bd. dirs.), Ill. Chamber Econ. Devel. Policy Task Force, Blue Key (hon.), Omicron Delta Kappa, Phi Eta Sigma (hon.), Phi Mu Alpha. Lutheran. Lodge: Rotary. Home: 2817 S Grange Ave Sioux Falls SD 57105-4616 Office: Augustana Coll 29th and Summit Sioux Falls SD 57197

WAGONER, WILLIAM DOUGLAS, public administrator, urban/regional planner; b. Detroit, Jan. 20, 1947; s. Bernard Leo and Ruby (Duckett) W.; Terry Ann Tolaro, Dec. 17, 1971; children: Melissa Ann, Emily Marie. BS in Edn., Wayne State U., 1971, MA in Urban Planning and Pub. Adminstrn., 1980; D in Pub. Adminstrn., Nova U., 1982; AA in Liberal Arts, U. State of N.Y., 1987, BA in Liberal Studies, 1988; BS in Emergency Disaster Mgmt./Human Svc, Thomas A. Edison State Coll., 1993. Instr. Clarkston (Mich.) Pub. Sch. Dist., 1972-74; city planner City of Berkley, Mich., 1974-80; dir. community devel., planning and rsch. City of Berkley, 1980-92, asst. city mgr., 1978-92; cons. community mgmt. Wagoner and Assocs., Royal Oak, Mich., 1985—; dir. planning and emergency mgmt. Livingston County, Mich., 1992—; adj. prof. Cen. Mich. U., Mt. Pleasant, 1985—, Mich. State Police div. Emergency Mgmt., 1989—; bd. registration Profl. Emergency Mgrs., 1990—; bd. dirs., treas. Berkley-LaSalette Credit Union, Oakland Family Svcs.; chair, bd. visitors Emergency Mgmt. Inst., FEMA; mem. coord. coun. Livingston County Human Svcs., 1992—. Editorial auditor jour. Transp. and Distbn., 1987-92; bd. editors jour. World Safety Orgn., 1987-92; contbr. articles to profl. jours. Tech. chmn. Northwestern Hwy. Impact Study Com., Oakland County, Mich., 1975-77, tech. advisor Traffic Engrng. Coordination Group, Oakland County, 1976-88, mem. adv. coun. Community Devel., Oakland County, 1985—; apptd. ofcl. S.E. Mich. Coun. Govts.; coun. on Environ. Strategy, Detroit, 1975-92; mem. Nat. Def. Exec. Res., Washington, 1986—; resource rep. Oakland County Cultural coun., 1975-92; mem. Task Force on Land Use Guidelines, 1992—. With U.S. Army, 1964-66. Fellow Brit. Inst. Mgmt., Inst. Transp. Engrs.; mem. ASPA (pres. 1988-90), Am. Arbitration Assn. (arbitrator 1983—), Southeastern Emergency Mgrs. Assn. (pres. 1986-88), Southeastern Oakland County Water Authority (chmn. 1988-90), Can. Inst. Mgmt., U.S. Jaycees (hon.), Wayne State U. Alumni Assn. (pres. 1987-88), Am. Legion, KC (Columbian award 1984), Lions (pres. 1983-85), Shrine Dad's Club. Roman Catholic. Home: 2332 Hawkins Ave Royal Oak MI 48073-4803 Office: Livingston County 304 E Grand River Ave Howell MI 48843-2323

WAICKMAN, FRANCIS JOSEPH, physician; b. Akron, Ohio, Apr. 22, 1923; s. Leo A. and Kathryn M. (Gillooly) W.; m. Marie Martin; children: Leo Anthony, Francis J., Ann Marie, Mark, William, Michael, Kathryn. AB, Holy Cross Coll., 1945; MD, St. Louis U., 1948, M in Pediat., 1952. Diplomate Am. Bd. Pediat., Am. Bd. Allergy and Immunology, Am. Bd. Quality Assurance and Utilization Review, Am. Bd. Environ. Medicine. Rotating intern St. Louis U., 1948-49, pediatric resident, 1949-52; instr. pediat. St. Louis U. Med. Sch., 1952-53; pvt. practice Akron, 1955—; assoc. clin. prof. pediat. Northeastern Ohio Univs. Coll. of Medicine, 1982—; sr. staff Children's Hops. Med. Ctr. of Akron, 1960—; consulting staff allergey/clin. immunology and pediat. St. Thomas Hops., Akron Gen. Med. Ctr., Akron City Hosp.; co-dir. allergy clinic Children's Hops. Med. Ctr. of Akron, chmn. multiple coms. Contbr. articles to prof. jours. Served to capt. USAF, 1953-55. Recipient Rinkel award for excellence in teaching Am. Acad. Environ. Medicine, Johnathan Forman Gold medal for meritorious contbns. in environ. medicine. Mem. Am. Acad. Environ. Medicine (pres. 1981, asst. dir. med. edn. 1982-83, dir. med. edn. 1984-90), Summit County Med. Soc. (chmn. multiple coms., del. or alt. del. 1972—). Home: 2377 Thurmont Rd Akron OH 44313 Office: Francis J Waickman MD & Assocs Inc 544B White Pond Dr Akron OH 44320

WAINWRIGHT, WILLIAM JUDSON, philosophy educator; b. Kokomo, Ind., Feb. 14, 1935; s. Francis Jack and Marian Meredith (Martin) W.; m. Eleanor Collier Skinner, June 28, 1958; children: Rebecca Pickard, Sarah Martin. BA, Kenyon Coll., 1957; MA, U. Mich., 1959, PhD, 1961. Instr. Dartmouth Coll., 1960-62; instr., asst. prof. U. Ill., Urbana, 1962-68; assoc., full prof. U. Wis., Milw., 1968—. Author: Philosophy of Religion, 1976, Mysticism, 1981, Philosophy of Religion, 1988, Reason and the Heart, 1995; editor: (jour.) Faith and Philosophy; contbr. articles to profl. jours. fellow NEH, 1976, 84, 89; recipient Rsch. award U. Wis., Milw., 1988, Undergraduate Teaching award U. Wis., Milw., 1990. Mem. Am. Philos. Assn., Am. Acad. Religion, Soc. Christian Philosophers, Soc. for Philosophy of Religion. Episcopalian. Office: University of Wisconsin Dept of Philosophy Milwaukee WI 53201

WAIT, RONALD A., state legislator; b. Apr. 15, 1944; m. Jody Wait, 1989. BS, Drake U., JD; MBS, No. Ill. U., MS in Spl. Edn. Farm mgr.; mem. Ill. State Ho. of Reps. Dist. 64, 1983-93, Ill. State Ho. of Reps. Dist. 68, 1995—. bd. dirs. Highland Hosp., Boone County Housing Authority Bd., Janet Wattles Mental Health Bd., United Givers Bd.

WAITE, DARVIN DANNY, accountant; b. Holdenville, Okla.; s. Delmer Charles and Lorraine (Young) W. BSBA, U. Ark., 1954. CPA, Ill. Auditor USDA, N.Y.C., New Orleans, 1963-69; auditor Commodity Exchange Authority USDA, Chgo., 1969-75; sr. auditor U.S. Commodity Futures Trading Commn., Chgo., 1975—. With U.S. Army, 1948-51, Ark. Air N.G. Mem. Am. Inst. CPA's, Assn. Govt. Accts. (Chgo. chpt.), Ill. CPA Soc., Chgo. Met. CPA. Chpt. Republican. Lutheran. Home: 230 Springhill Dr Roselle IL 60172-2400 Office: US Commodity Futures Trading Commn 300 S Riverside Plz Chicago IL 60606-6613

WAITE, DONALD EUGENE, medical educator, consultant; b. Columbus, Ohio, Aug. 25, 1925; s. Sidney B. and Louise Alice (Lipsey) W.; children: David L., Larry R., James A., Steve C., Debra J., Julie A., Craig D., Tracy E., Christopher R. D in Osteopathic Medicine, U. Osteo. Medicine and Health Scis., 1955; MPH, U. Calif., Berkeley, 1989. Intern Doctors Hosp., Columbus, Ohio, 1955-56; pvt. practice Columbus, 1956-72; prof. family medicine Mich. State U., East Lansing, 1972-90, prof. emeritus, 1990—; cons. Environ. Health Conss., Columbus, East Lansing, 1990—. Author: Your Environment, Your Health and You, 1991, Environmental Health Hazards, 1994. Med. examiner FAA, East Lansing, 1964-90; asst. scoutmaster Boy Scouts Am., East Lansing, 1980-83. With USN, 1943-45. Mem. Am. Osteo. Assn., Am. Coll. Occupl. Medicine, Aerospace Med. Assn., Ohio Osteo. Assn., Mich. Assn. Osteo. Physicians. Home: 117 Agate Way Williamston MI 48895 Office: Mich State U Dept Family Medicine East Lansing MI 48824

WAITE, JAMES LEROY, political science and geography educator; b. Murray, Utah, Sept. 26, 1940; s. Jack Elbert and Mary A. (White) W.; m. Susan Mary Fechser, Aug. 20, 1964; children: Peter, Andrew, Phillip, Jaimie, Paul. BA, Brigham Young U., 1968, MA, 1969; PhD, So. Ill. U., 1971; Phil Mag, U. Stockholm, 1971. Asst. prof. Iowa Wesleyan Coll., Mt. Pleasant, Iowa, 1971-72, Southeastern Iowa Community Coll., Burlington, 1971-72; asst. prof. Ctrl. Mo. State U., Warrensburg, 1972-80, assoc. prof., 1980-86, prof. polit. sci. and geography, 1986—, chair dept., 1989—; dir. Mo. London Program, 1989; exch. prof. Växjö (Sweden) U., 1987, vis. prof. 1995-96; vis. prof. Skoude U., 1995. Co-author: The Other Western Europe, 1983; author: George Gideon Hendricks, 1980, The Intelligence Analyst, 1980; contbr. articles to profl. jours. High councilman LDS Ch., Kansas City, 1985-91, bishop, Warrensburg, 1991—. Comdr. USNR, 1974—. Fulbright-Hays scholar U.S. State Dept., Sweden, 1970-71; NEH grantee Smith Coll., 1979; diplomat exch. scholar U.S. State Dept., Washington, 1981; instl. grantee Ctrl. Mo. State U., Sweden, London, 1987-89. Mem. Am. Polit. Sci. Assn., Naval Res. Assn., Mo. Polit. Sci. Assn. Home: 755 S Main St Warrensburg MO 64093-2239 Office: Ctrl Mo State U Dept Polit Sci & Geography Wood 8 Warrensburg MO 64093

WAITE, LAWRENCE WESLEY, osteopathic physician; b. Chgo., June 27, 1951; s. Paul J. and Margaret E. (Cresson) W.; m. Courtnay M. Snyder, Nov. 1, 1974; children: Colleen Alexis, Rebecca Maureen, Alexander Quin. BA, Drake U., 1972; DO, Coll. Osteo. Medicine and Surgery, Des Moines, 1975; MPH, U. Mich., 1981. Diplomate Nat. Bd. Osteo. Examiners. Intern Garden City Osteo. Hosp., Mich., 1975-76; practice gen. osteo. medicine, Garden City, 1979-82, Battle Creek, 1982-96, Onalaska, 1996—; assoc. clin. prof. Mich. State U. Coll. Osteo. Medicine, East Lansing, 1979—; dir. med. edn. Lakeview Gen. Osteo. Hosp., Battle Creek, Mich., 1983-87; cons. Nat. Bd. Examiners Osteo. Physicians and Surgeons, 1981-88; chief med. examiner Calhoun County, 1991-93. Writer TV program Cross Currents Ecology, 1971; editor radio series Friendship Hour, 1971-72. Bd. dirs., instr. Hospice Support Services, Inc., Westland, Mich., 1981-86; mem. profl. adv. council Good Samaritan Hosp., Battle Creek, 1982-83; bd. dirs. Neighborhood Planning Council 11, Battle Creek, 1982-92; mem. population action council Population Inst., 1984—; exec. bd. officer Battle Creek Area Urban League, 1987-91; vestryman St. Thomas Episcopal Ch., 1990-93; leader Boy Scouts Am. Served to lt. comdr. USN, 1976-79. State of Iowa scholar, 1969. Mem. AMA, APHA, Aerospace Med. Assn., Nat. Eagle Scouts Assn. (life), Am. Osteo. Assn., S. Cen. Osteo. Assn. (officer, state del. 1983-96), Am. Acad. Osteopathy, Bermuda Hist. Soc. (life). Avocations: geography, medieval history, genealogy. Home: 2110 Evenson Dr Onalaska WI 54650 Office: Gunderson Clinic Ltd 1836 South Ave La Crosse WI 54601

WAITE, ROBERT ALLAN, clergyman; b. Watertown, S.D., Nov. 15, 1949; s. Ellsworth William and Astrid Harriet (Rorvick) W.; m. Susan Kay Guddal, Feb. 24, 1970; children: Jessie Nicole, Casey Elena, Lindsay Katherine. BSBA, U. S.D., 1972; MDiv, Luther N.W. Sem., St. Paul, 1984. Ordained to ministry Luth. Ch. Terminal ops. mgr. Roadway Express Inc., St. Paul, 1973-78; terminal mgr. Glendenning Motorways Inc., Sioux Falls, S.D., 1978-80; pastor Luth. Ch. France, Bethoncourt, France, 1984; prof. theology Luth. Theol. Sem., Baboua, Ctrl. African Republic, 1985-89; missionary in residence S.D. Synod, Evang. Luth. Ch. Am., Watertown, 1989-90; assoc. pastor Grace Luth. Ch., Evang. Luth. Ch. Am., Watertown, 1990-93; pastor Florence (S.D.) Luth. Parish, 1993—; cons. mem. Bd. for World and Am. Missions, S.D. Synod, Evang. Luth. Ch. Am., Sioux Falls, 1990—; mission rep. Div. Global Mission Evang. Luth. Ch. Am., Baboua, Ctrl. African Republic, 1988-89. Capt. U.S. Army, 1972-78. Mem. Watertown Ministerial Assn., U. S.D. Alumni Assn., Luther Northwestern Sem. Alumni Assn., Delta Tau Delta Alumni Assn. Home: 538 N Lake Dr Watertown SD 57201-5514 Office: PO Box 5 Florence SD 57235-0005

WAITE, RUTH IRENE, electrical and computer engineering educator; b. Fargo, N.D., Jan. 25, 1957; d. Robert Vernon Duckett and Dorothy Alice Williams Miller; m. Lee R. Waite, July 2, 1977; children: Sarah Ruth, William Robert. BS, Iowa State U., 1980, MS, 1985, PhD, 1987. Faculty Rose-Hulman Inst. Tech., Terre Haute, Ind., 1987—; rsch. fellow NASA Goddard Space Flight Ctr., Greenbelt, Md., 1992; vis. prof. Kanazawa (Japan) Inst. Tech., 1993-94; reviewer West Ednl. Pub., John Wiley & Sons, NSF, Washington, 1992. Contbr. articles to profl. jours. Youth leader United Meth. Ch., Terre Haute, 1991-92, mem. choir, 1988-96. Hewlett Packard Faculty fellow Iowa State U., 1983-87. Mem. IEEE, Am. Soc. Engring. Edn., Soc. Women Engrs., Sigma Xi. Office: Rose-Hulman Inst Tech 5500 Wabash Ave Terre Haute IN 47803-3920

WAITS, GARY LEE, sales manager; b. Cin., Dec. 3, 1953; s. Bernard Leeroy and Gloria Mae (Bronniman) W.; m. Susan Kathleen Ernest, Aug. 31, 1974; children: Gary Jr., Joseph, Michael, Matthew, Jonathan. AS in Mktg., So. Ohio Coll., 1979; BS, Urbana U., 1982. Cert. contact lens optician, Ohio. Aerospace med. technician USCG, Elizabeth City, N.C., 1972-76; dir. internal ops. York Optometrists, Cin., 1976-82; sales rep. Procter & Gamble, Cin., 1982-84, dist. field rep., 1984-85, unit mgr., 1985-87, assoc. mgr. sales merchandising, 1987-90; mgr. regulatory svcs. Procter & Gamble Paper Divsn., Cin., 1990-94; sales mgr. managed care Procter & Gamble Pharm., Cin., 1994-96; mgr. tele-mktg. programs, patient care products Procter & Gamble Health Care, Cin., 1996—; presenter in field; bd. dirs. Cin. Area Sr. Svcs., 1987-92. Bd. dirs. Loveland (Ohio) City Sch. Bd., 1993—; adv. com. Tri-State White House Conf. on Aging, Cin., 1994—; medicaid adv. com. Ohio Legislature, Columbus, Ohio, 1994—. 2d class petty officer USCG, 1972-76. Recipient Honor Man Aerospace Med. Technician Class award USN, 1974. Mem. Am. Soc. on Aging (chair bus. forum 1992-94, bd. dirs. San Francisco 1992-94), Ohio Sch. Bd. Assn., Nat. Sch. Bd. Assn. Republican. Ch. of Christ. Home: 6561 Clearfield Ct Loveland OH 45140 Office: Procter & Gamble Health Care One Procter & Gamble Plz Cincinnati OH 45201

WAJER, RONALD EDWARD, management consultant; b. Chgo., Aug. 31, 1943; s. Edward Joseph and Gertrude Catherine (Rytelny) W.; m. Mary Earlene Hagan, July 5, 1969; children: Catherine, Michael. BSIE, Northwestern U., 1966; MBA, Loyola U., Chgo., 1970. Cert. mgmt. cons. Project engring. mgr. Procter & Gamble, Chgo., 1966-67; indsl. engring. mgr. Johnson & Johnson, Bedford Park, Ill., 1967-71; project mgr. Jewel Cos., Franklin Park, Ill., 1971-73; div. engring. mgr. Abbott Labs., North Chicago, Ill., 1973-79; pres. Bus. Engring. div. R.E. Wajer & Assocs., Northbrook, Ill., 1979—. Contbr. articles to profl. jours. Sec. Downtown Redevel. Commn., Mt. Prospect, Ill., 1977-78; fundraising vol. Maryville Acad., Des Plaines, 1985—; bd. dirs. Lattof YMCA, Des Plaines, 1984-95; profl. advisor Sch. for New Learning, DePaul U., 1994—. Recipient Cmty. Svc. award Chgo. Lighthouse for the Blind, 1989, Cert. of Merit, Village of Mt. Prospect, 1978. Mem. Inst. Indsl. Engrs. (community svc. chmn. 1984), Inst. Mgmt. Cons. (exec. v.p., bd. dirs. 1987-94), Assn. Mgmt. Cons. (ctrl. regional v.p. 1985-87), Midwest Soc. Profl. Cons., Northwestern Club Chgo. Roman Catholic. Office: Bus Engring 5 Revere Dr Ste 200 Northbrook IL 60062-8000

WAKS, AMIR, medical equipment development manager; b. Tel Aviv, Israel, Sept. 3, 1953; came to U.S., 1986; m. Gershon and Irena (Kriger) W.; m. Leah Lapidot, Feb. 7, 1978; children: Zeev, Eitan. BS, Technion Israel Inst. Tech., 1975; MS, Drexel U., 1987, PhD, 1991. Project mgr. Tadiran Industries, Holon, Israel, 1980-84; product mgr. Scitex, Herzeliah, Israel, 1985-86; rsch. specialist Drexel U., Phila., 1986-90; rsch. supr. Amoco Tech., Naperville, Ill., 1991-94; program mgr. Mennen Med., Clarence, N.Y., 1995—; cons. KOY, Nashua, N.H., 1991—, U. Pa., Phila., 1990-91. Editor: Image Acquisition and Scientific Imaging Systems, 1994; contbr. articles to profl. jours. Mem. IEEE, IEEE Computer Soc., SPIE (chmn. 1994). Home: 874 Shambliss Ln Buffalo Grove IL 60089 Office: Mennen Med 10123 Main St Clarence NY 14031

WALBERG, TIMOTHY LEE, state legislator; b. Chgo., Apr. 12, 1951; s. John Andrew and Alice (Wilcox) W.; m. Susan Gail Polensky, 1973; children: Matthew Lee, Heidi Gail, Caleb Paul. Grad., Western Ill. U., 1970; Diploma, Summit Christian Coll., 1973; BS, Ft. Wayne Bible Coll., 1975; MA with hons., Wheaton Coll. Grad. Sch., 1978. Pastor New Haven (Ind.) Bapt. Ch., 1973-77, Union Gospel Ch., Tipton, Mich., 1978-83; state rep. Dist. 40 Mich. Ho. of Reps., 1995—; asst. minority whip Mich. Ho. of Reps., vice chmn. Corrections Com., mem. Agriculture, Forestry & Minerals, Edn. Econ. Devel. & Energy Coms., Prison Reform & Children at Risk Task Force. Mem. Tecumseh Kiwanis Club, Lenawee County Riding for the Handicapped, Lenawee County Basic Human Needs Task Force. Home: 6769 Teachout Rd Tipton MI 49287-9781*

WALBRIDGE, JOHN, foreign language educator; b. Lake Forest, Ill., Apr. 28, 1950; s. John T. Jr. and Mary Lou (Sailor) W.; m. Linda Strickland, May 27, 1972; children: John, Nathaniel. BA, Yale U., 1973; PhD in Near Eastern Langs., Harvard U., 1983. V.p. No. Land and Lumber Co., Escanaba, Mich., 1980-87; gen. editor Bahai Ency. Project, Wilmette, Ill., 1987-91; asst. editor Ctr. for Iranian Studies, Columbia U., N.Y.C., 1991-93; assoc. prof. Near Eastern langs. Ind. U., Bloomington, 1993—; dir. No. Land and Lumber Co., Escanaba. Author: The Science of Mystic Lights, 1992; translator (books): The Storm, by Kahlil Gibran, 1993, The Beloved, by Kahlil Gibran, 1994; mng. editor Bibliotheca Persian, N.Y.C., 1993-96; editl. bd. Bahai Ency., 1984-95. Baha'i. Home: 3125 S Snoddy Rd Bloomington IN 47401

WALBURN, JOHN CLIFFORD, mental health services professional; b. Marion, Ind., Apr. 6, 1945; s. Rex Raymond and Norma Jane (Clifford) W.; m. Linda Sue Spall, Sept. 21, 1968 (div. Dec. 1987); 1 child, Geoffrey Jacob; m. Mitzi Lynn Johnson, June 20, 1992; 1 child, Abigail Rae. BS, Ball State U., 1969, MA, 1975; JD, I.U., Indpls., 1991. Bar: Ind. 1992. Planner Metro. Planning Commn., Muncie, Ind., 1970-72; dir. adult svcs. Del. County Assn. for Retarded, Muncie, Ind., 1972-76; exec. dir. Fayette-Union Assn. for Retarded, Connersville, Ind., 1976-83; cons. Ind. Protection and Advocacy, Indpls., 1984-86; case mgr. Ind. Dept. Mental Health, Indpls., 1986-87; v.p. Cardinal Svc. Mgmt., New Castle, Ind., 1987—; ofcl. Ind. Spl. Olympics, 1973—; chmn. Ind. Residential Mgmt. Com., 1991—; cons. DLG Cons. and Mktg. Svc., Ind., 1992. Co-author: Feldman/Walburn Habilitation System, 1988; phote, drawing artist, 1978—. With USN, 1965-67. Named Ky. Col., Commonwealth of Ky., 1978. Mem. Am. Assn. Mental Retardation (bd. dirs. 1991—). Home: 1121 Indiana Ave New Castle IN 47362-4620 Office: Cardinal Svc Mgmt Inc PO Box 505 New Castle IN 47362-0505

WALCH, TIMOTHY GEORGE, library administrator; b. Detroit, Dec. 6, 1947; s. George Louis Walch and Margaret Mary (Shields) DeSchryver; m. Victoria Irons, June 24, 1978; children: Thomas Emmet, Brian Edward. BA, U. Notre Dame, 1970; PhD, Northwestern U., 1975. Assoc. dir. Soc. Am. Archivists, Chgo., 1975-79; grants analyst Nat. Hist. Publ. Commn., Washington, 1979-81; budget analyst Nat. Archives, Washington, 1981-82, editor Prologue, 1982-88; asst. dir. Hoover Presdl. Libr., West Branch, Iowa, 1988-93, dir., 1993—. Author: Catholicism in America, 1989, Pope John Paul II, 1989, Parish School, 1996, others; editor: Farewell to the Chief, 1990, Herbert Hoover & Harry S Truman, 1992, Immigrant America, 1994, and others; assoc. editor: U.S. Cath. Historian, 1983—; mem. editl. bd. Soc. Am. Archivists, 1982-86; series editor: Garland Pub. Co., 1988-92; contbr. articles to profl. jours. Recipient Achievement and Svc. awards Nat. Archives, 1980, 83, 87, 89, 93, Journalism awards U.S. Cath. Press Assn., 1986-91, 1st place publ. award Nat. Assn. Govt. Communicators, 1988. Mem. Soc. Am. Archivists, Orgn. Am. Historians, U.S. Cath. Hist. Soc., Rotary Internat. Home: 65 N Westminster St Iowa City IA 52245-3833 Office: Hoover Presdl Libr PO Box 488 West Branch IA 52358-0488

WALCOTT, DELORES DEBORAH, psychologist, educator. BA in Psychology, Chgo. State U., 1976, MS in Corrections, 1978; cert. group treatment with adolescents, Youth Guidance Tng. Inst., 1981; cert. law program for cmty. developers and social workers, John Marshall Law Sch., 1982; cert. MMPI-2 and MMPI-A clin. workshops, Western Mich. Psychol. Assn., 1992; PhD in Clin. Psychology, Ill. Sch. Profl. Psychology, Chgo., 1993. Cert. in sex edn.; cert. family life edn. tng.; licensed clin. psychologist, Ill., Mich. Psychologist, correction specialist, alcohol youth prevention specialist Bobby E. Wright Comprehension Inc., Chgo., 1978-84; child welfare worker Habilitative Sys., Inc., Chgo., 1984-85; program coord. Brass Found., Essence House, Chgo., 1985-86; social worker Kaleidoscope, Inc., Chgo., 1986-87; psychology extern, adult unit Ill. State Psychiat. Inst., Chgo., 1990-91; coord. family life edn. program Nia Comprehensive Ctr. for Developmental Disabilities, Inc., Chgo., 1987-92; clin. psychology intern Western Mich. U., Kalamazoo, 1992-93; clin. psychologist Onarga (Ill.) Acad.-Nexus Inc., 1993-95; asst. prof. Counseling Ctr. Western Mich. U., Kalamazoo, Mich., 1995—. Mem. APA, Am. Profl. Soc. Abuse of Children, Nat. Black Alcoholism Coun., Nat. Black Psychol. Assn., Western Mich. Psychol. Assn., Chem. People Task Force, Human Resource Devel. Inst. (Vol. award), Westside Youth Booster (bd. dirs. 1983-84), Alumni Assn. The Family Inst. Home: 8122 South Green Chicago IL 60620 Office: Western Mich U Counseling Ctr Kalamazoo MI 49008

WALD, BRUCE LEWIS, lawyer; b. Chgo., Feb. 6, 1946; s. Jerome Solomon and Bernyce (Rubin) W.; m. Carol; children: Daniel, Lauren. BA cum laude, U. Wis., 1968; JD, Northwestern U., Chgo., 1972. Bar: Ill. 1972. Assoc. Brown, Fox & Blumberg, Chgo., 1972-74, Ressman & Tishler, Chgo., 1974-76; ptnr. Wald & Wald, Chgo., 1976-80, Tishler & Wald, Ltd., Chgo., 1980—; lectr. IICLE, Chgo., 1987-90, Ctr. for Profl. Edn., Phila., 1991—. Contbg. editor/author: IICLE Handbook on Bankruptcy, 1991, editor supplement, 1995. Campaign mgr. Com. to Elect James T. Arvey to 13th Congl. Dist., Chgo., 1974. Sgt. USAF, 1968-74. Mem. Chgo. Bar Assn. (Cert. Appreciation lawyers com. 1982, 96), Phi Kappa Phi. Office: Tishler & Wald Ltd 200 S Wacker Dr Ste 2600 Chicago IL 60606-5802

WALD, FRANCIS JOHN, state legislator; b. N.D., Apr. 8, 1935; s. Anton S. and Magdelena (Borsch) W.; m. Sharon Kay Mischel, 1961; children: Kirk James, Mark Allen, Jo Lynn, Laura, Cara, Maria, Michael, Jay. BSBA, U. N.D., 1959. Pres., ins. broker Wald Agy. Inc., Dickinson, N.D., 1973—; mem. from dist. 37 N.D. State Ho. of Reps., Bismarck, 1979-83, 85—, chmn. appropriations, edn. and environ. coms.; chmn. Am. Legis. Exch. Coun. Mem. exec. com. Conf. of Ins. Legislators. Recipient Korean Occupation award. Mem. Dickenson C. of C. (past pres.), N.D. Profl. Ins. Agts., Am. Legion, Rotary, KC, Elks, Alpha Tau Omega. Office: PO Box 330 Dickinson ND 58601*

WALDBAUM, JANE COHN, art history educator; b. N.Y.C., Jan. 28, 1940; d. Max Arthur and Sarah (Waldstein) Cohn. BA, Brandeis U., 1962; MA, Harvard U., 1964, PhD, 1968. Rsch. fellow in classical archaeology Harvard U., Cambridge, Mass., 1968-70, 72-73; asst. prof. U. Wis.-Milw., 1973-78, assoc. prof., 1978-84, prof. art history, 1984—, chmn. dept., 1982-85, 86-89, 91-92; Dorot rsch. prof. W.F. Albright Inst. Archaeol. Rsch., Jerusalem, 1990-91. Author: From Bronze to Iron, 1978; Metalwork from Sardis, 1983; author (with others), editor Sardis Report I, 1975; mem. editorial bd. Bull. Am. Schs. Oriental Rsch., 1994—; contbr. numerous articles to profl. jours. Bd. dirs. Milw. Soc. of Archaeol. Inst., 1973—, pres., 1983-85, 91-95. Woodrow Wilson Found. fellow, dissertation fellow, 1962-63, 65-66, NEH post-doctoral rsch., Jerusalem, 1989-90; grantee Am. Philos. Soc., 1972, NEH, summer 1975, U. Wis.-Milw. Found., 1983. Mem. Am. Schs. Oriental Research, Soc. for Archaeol. Sci., Archaeol. Inst. Am. (exec. com. 1975-77, chmn. com. on membership programs 1977-81, nominating com. 1984, chmn. com. on lecture program 1985-87, acad. trustee 1993—, com. profl. responsibilities 1993—, fellowships com. 1993—, gold medal com. 1993—, Ancient Near East com. 1993—, chair 1996—), W.F. Albright Inst. Archaeol. Rsch. (bd. trustees 1996—, mem. governance com. 1996—), Phi Beta Kappa. Office: U Wis Dept Art History PO Box 413 Milwaukee WI 53201-0413

WALDECK, JOHN WALTER, JR., lawyer; b. Cleve., Sept. 10, 1949; s. John Walter Sr. and Marjorie Ruth (Palenschat) W.; m. Cheryl Gene Cutter, Sept. 10, 1977; children: John III, Matthew, Rebecca. BS, John Carroll U., 1973; JD, Cleve. State U., 1977. Bar: Ohio 1977. Product applications chemist Synthetic Products Co., Cleve., 1969-76; assoc. Arter & Hadden, Cleve., 1977-85, ptnr., 1986-88; ptnr. Porter, Wright, Morris and Arthur, Cleve., 1988-90, ptnr. in charge, 1990-96; ptnr. Walter & Haverfield, Cleve., 1996—. Chmn. Bainbridge Twp. Bd. Zoning Appeals, Chagrin Falls, Ohio, 1981-94; trustee Greater Cleve. chpt. Lupus Found. Am., 1978-91, sec., 1979-86; trustee LeBlond Housing Corp., Cleve., 1990—, sec., 1996—, Univ. Circle, Inc., 1993—, Fairmount Ctr. for Performing and Fine Arts, Novelty, Ohio, 1993—, sect., 1994—; bd. dirs. Geauga County Mental Health Alcohol and Drug Addiction Svc. Bd., Chardon, Ohio, 1988—, treas., 1991-93, vice chmn., 1993-95, chmn., 1995—; mem. bd. advisors Palliative Care Svcs., Cleve. Clinic Cancer Ctr., 1989-91. Mem. ABA (real property sect.), Ohio State Bar Assn. (real property sect. bd. govs. 1992), Greater Cleve. Bar Assn. (real property, corp. banking sect., co-chair real estate law inst. 1990, 95, 96), The Union Club, Chagrin Valley Athletic Club. Democrat. Roman Catholic. Home: 18814 Rivers Edge Dr W Chagrin Falls OH 44023-4968 Office: Walter & Haverfield 1300 Terminal Tower 50 Public Sq Cleveland OH 44113

WALDECKER, THOMAS RAYMOND, social worker; b. Monroe, Mich., Sept. 4, 1950; s. Henry Stephen and Martha Louise (Skinner) W.; m. Lilian Marlene Ames, Nov. 19, 1983; 1 child, Sean. AA, Monroe County C.C., 1970; BS, Ea. Mich. U., 1973; MSW, U. Mich., 1977. Cert. social worker. Tng. and vol. coord. Monroe County (Mich.) Helpline, 1970-74; substance abuse and employee assistance svcs. coord. Monroe County, Monroe, 1978-81; employee counselor Kelsey Hayes Co., Romulus, Mich., 1981-82; outreach counselor Flower Meml. Hosp., Sylvania, Ohio, 1983-86; regional mgr. Managed Health Network, Inc., Dearborn, Mich., 1986—; bd. dirs. Southeastern Mich. Substance Abuse, 1981—; mktg. cons. Counseling Assocs., Southfield, 1985—. Vice chmn. bd. dirs. Monroe County C.C.;bd. dirs. Monroe County Mental Health Bd., 1986-91. Mem. NASW, Employee Assistance Soc. N.Am. (pres. Mich. chpt.), Am. Coll. Mental Health Adminstrn., Dearborn C. of C. Democrat. Home: 634 W 9th St Monroe MI 48161-4004 Office: Managed Health Network 23400 Michigan Ave Dearborn MI 48124-1915

WALDEN, JAMES WILLIAM, accountant, educator; b. Jellico, Tenn., Mar. 5, 1936; s. William Evert and Bertha L. (Faulkner) W.; m. Eva June Selvia, Jan. 16, 1957 (dec. Aug. 1988); 1 child, James William; m. Hattie Nan Lamb, Jan. 6, 1990 (div. June 1992); m. Janet Faulkner, Aug. 12, 1993. BS, Miami U., Oxford, Ohio, 1963; MBA, Xavier U., Cin., 1966. CPA, Ohio. Tchr. math. Middletown (Ohio) City Sch. Dist., 1963-67, Fairfield (Ohio) High Sch., 1967-69; instr. accounting Sinclair Community Coll., Dayton, Ohio, 1969-72, asst. prof., 1972-75, assoc. prof., 1975-78, prof., 1978-89, prof. emeritus, 1991—; cons., public acct. Group comdr. Ohio Wing, CAP. Served with USAF, 1954-59. Mem. Butler County Torch Club, Pub. Accts. Soc. Ohio (pres. S.W. chpt. 1985-86), Inst. Mgmt. Accts., Nat. Soc. Pub. Accts., Greater Hamilton Estate Planning Coun., Ohio Soc. CPAs, Beta Alpha Psi. Home: PO Box 469 Springboro OH 45066-0469 Office: Sinclair C C 444 W 3rd St Dayton OH 45402-1421

WALDERA, WAYNE EUGENE, crisis management specialist; b. Cayuga, N.D., Mar. 23, 1930; s. Bernard Cyril and Eleanor Nee (Kugler) W.; m. Eva Jenzene Personius, Jan. 13, 1958; children: Anthony, Lori, Mia, Shauna. BSBA, N.D. State U., 1952. With Gamble-Skogmo, 1954-88; pres. Gamble div. Gamble-Skogmo, Mpls., 1972-88; pres., CEO Retail Resource Co., Mpls., 1988-89; pres., CEO Amdura Corp., Denver, 1989-92, also bd. dirs.; chmn. Sullivan Waldera, Inc., Mpls., 1992-93; prin., CEO Waldera & Co. Inc., Mpls., 1993—. 1st lt. USAF, 1952-54. Home: 12125 62nd St Waconia MN 55387-9411 Office: Waldera & Co Inc 15500 Wayzata Blvd Ste 604-208 Wayzata MN 55391-1435

WALDERBACH, KURT MICHAEL, physical therapist; b. Cedar Rapids, Iowa, Nov. 20, 1960; s. Charles Richard and JoAnne (Driscoll) W.; m. Kristi Kay Toresdahl, Sept. 10, 1991; 1 child, Blake Michael. BS, U. Iowa, 1983, M.Phys. Therapy, 1986. Registered phys. therapist, Iowa; cert. athletic trainer, Iowa. Staff therapist U. Iowa Hosps., Iowa City, 1986-88, team trainer, 1984-88; asst. dir. North Iowa Med. Ctr., Mason City, 1988-92; clinic mgr. St. Joseph Mercy Hosp., Mason City, 1992-95; dept. dir. North Iowa Mercy Health Sys., Mason City, 1995—; guest lectr. U. Iowa, Iowa City, 1987-88; faculty North Iowa Area C.C., Mason City, 1990-95. Mem. Am. Phys. Therapy Assn., Am. Bd. Phys. Therapy Specialties (com. mem.), Iowa H.S. Athletic Assn. Democrat. Roman Catholic. Home: 16763 290th St Mason City IA 50401 Office: North Iowa Mercy Health Sys 84 Beaumont Dr Mason City IA 50401

WALDO, CHRISTINE B., marketing promotions specialist; b. Peoria, Ill., Sept. 19, 1972; d. Terry Wayne and Diane Elaine (James) W. AAS, Ill. Ctrl. Coll., East Peoria, 1992; BS, Bradley U., 1994, postgrad., 1996—. Floor dir., sales asst. WEEK-TV, East Peoria, 1992-95; mktg. promotions specialist Citizens Equity Fed. Credit Union, Peoria, 1995—. Mem. com., promotions specialist Ptnrs. In Peace Ctr. for Prevention of Abuse, Peoria, 1995—. Mem. Soc. Profl. Journalists. Office: Citizens Equity Fed Credit Union PO Box 1715 Peoria IL 61656-1715

WALDREP, CHRISTOPHER REEF, historian; b. Oak Ridge, Tenn., Nov. 19, 1951; s. Reef Vuin and Ella Christine (Yates) W.; m. Pamela Jean Heiney, Aug. 15, 1976; children: Janelle Christine, Andrea Jean. BS in Edn., Eastern Ill. U., 1973; MA, Purdue U., 1974; PhD, Ohio State U., 1990. Tchr. Washington (Ohio) City Schs., 1974-90; asst. prof. Eastern Ill. U., Charleston, 1990-94, assoc. prof., 1994—. Author: Night Riders: Defending Community, 1993; contbr. articles to profl. jours. NEH fellow, 1995, Am. Philosophical Soc. fellow, 1994, Am. Coun. Learned Socs. fellow, 1993. Mem. Am. Hist. Assn., Am. Soc. Legal History, Orgn. Am. Hists., So. Hist. Assn. Democrat. Methodist. Office: Ea Ill U Dept History 600 Lincoln Ave Charleston IL 61920

WALENGA, JEANINE MARIE, medical educator, researcher; b. Evergreen Park, Ill., Nov. 21, 1955; d. Eugene Adam and Therese Marie (Podsiadlik) W. BS, U. Ill., Chgo., 1978; Diplome d'Etudes Approfondies, U. Paris VI, 1984, PhD, 1987; postgrad., Loyola U., Maywood, Ill., 1981-84. Cert. med. technologist. Med. technologist MacNeal Hosp., Berwyn, Ill., 1978-79; rsch. asst. Loyola U. Med. Ctr., Maywood, 1979-80, hemostasis rsch. lab. supr., 1980-87, co-dir. hemostasis rsch. lab., 1987—, asst. prof. thoracic/cardiovascular surgery/pathology, 1988-94, assoc. prof., 1994—; mem. Cardiovascular Inst., Loyola U., 1995—; cons. in field; lectr. in field; observer Nat. Com. for Clin. Lab. Stds., 1988—; del. US Pharmacopeia, 1990—. Contbr. articles to profl. jours. Named Alumnus of Yr., U. Ill., 1990; NHLBI rsch. grantee, 1989—; recipient Investigator Recognition award, 1993. Fellow Am. Coll. Angiology; mem. Internat. Inst. for Thrombotic Diseases (sec. 1989—), Am. Assn. Pathologists, Am. Soc. Hematology, Internat. Soc. Thrombosis and Hemostasis (sci. and standardization subcom. on heparin

1990-93), Am. Soc. Clin. Pathologists, Am. Heart Assn., Am. Soc. Med. Tech.

WALES, M. ELIZABETH, psychologist; b. Wichita, Kans., Dec. 5, 1932; d. Jesse Lee and Olive F. (Bryant) Moore; children: Dirk O., Jessica W., Stacey E. PhD, U. Cin., 1967. Diplomate Am. Bd. Profl. Psychology. With U. Cin. Sch. Medicine, 1967-71; U. Cin., 1971-76, Wright State U. Sch. Medicine, Dayton, Ohio, 1976-82; acad. dean Calif. Sch. Profl. Psychology, L.A., 1982-84; dir. UCS Univ. Counseling Svcs., Mpls., 1984-92; pvt. practice Cin., 1992—; cons., 1967—; bd. dirs. Nat. Tng. Labs., Washington, 1983-87. Bd. dirs. ARC, Dayton, 1980, Lifespring, L.A., 1982, Hamilton County Mental Health Bd., 1994—. Cin. Acad. Profl. Psychology, 1994—; pres. Soc. Psychologists in Mgmt., Tampa, Fla., 1988-89. Named Tchr. of Yr., Wright State U. Sch. Medicine, 1973. Mem. APA, Sigma Xi. Episcopalian. Home: 1071 Celestial St Apt 2105 Cincinnati OH 45202-1653

WALGREEN, CHARLES RUDOLPH, III, retail store executive; b. Chgo., Nov. 11, 1935; s. Charles Rudolph and Mary Ann (Leslie) W.; m. Kathleen Bonsignore Allen, Jan. 23, 1977; children: Charles Richard, Tad Alexander, Kevin Patrick, Leslie Ray, Chris Patrick; stepchildren—Carleton A. Allen Jr., Jorie L. Allen Grassie. B.S. in Pharmacy, U. Mich., 1958. With Walgreen Co., Chgo., 1952—, adminstrv. asst. to v.p. store ops., 1963-65, 65-66, dist. mgr., 1966-69, regional dir., 1968-69, v.p., pres., 1969-71, pres., chief exec. officer, 1971-76, chmn., chief exec. officer, 1976—, also bd. dirs. Mem. bus. adv. coun. Chgo. Urban League; bd. dirs. Jr. Achievement Chgo. Mem. Nat. Assn. Chain Drug Stores (bd. dirs.), Ill. Retail Mchts. Assn. (bd. dirs. 1966—), Am. Pharm. Assn., Ill. Pharm. Assn., Comml. Club of Chgo., Great Lakes Cruising Club, Exmoor Country Club (Highland Park, Ill.), Key Largo (Fla.) Anglers Club, Sailfish Point Club (Stuart, Fla.), Conway Farms Golf Club (Lake Forest, Ill.), Delta Sigma Phi. Office: Walgreen Co 200 Wilmot Rd Deerfield IL 60015-4620

WALHOUT, JUSTINE SIMON, chemistry educator; b. Aberdeen, S.D., Dec. 11, 1930; d. Otto August and Mabel Ida (Tews) S.; m. Donald Walhout, Feb. 1, 1958; children: Mark, Timothy, Lynne, Peter. BS, Wheaton Coll., 1952; PhD, Northwestern U., 1956. Instr. Wright City Community Coll., Chgo., 1955-56; asst. prof. Rockford (Ill.) Coll., 1956-59, assoc. prof., 1959-66, 81-89, prof., 1989—, dept. chmn., 1987-95; cons. Pierce Chem. Co., Rockford, 1968-69; trustee Rockford (Ill.) Coll., 1987-91. Contbr. articles to profl. jours. Mem. Ill. Bd. Edn., 1974-81. Mem. AAUW (Ill. bd. mem. 1985-87), Am. Chem. Soc. (councilor 1993—), Rockford LWV (bd. dirs. 1983-85), Sigma Xi. Presbyterian. Home: 320 N Rockford Ave Rockford IL 61107-4547 Office: Rockford Coll 5050 E State St Rockford IL 61108-2311

WALKER, BILLY CUMMINS, minister, evangelist; b. Detroit, Dec. 28, 1937; s. William Burgess and Pearl Marie (Cummins) W.; m. Sharon Anne Harris, Sept. 26, 1958; children: Billy Harris, Craig David. BA, Wayne State U., 1964. Ordained to ministry Bapt. Ch., 1959. Evangelist Billy Walker Evangelistic Assn., Southgate, Mich., 1955—; camp dir. Hiawatha Youth Camp, Eckerman, Mich., 1964—; pastor Calvary Bapt. Ch., Southgate, 1974—; dir. Billy Walker Presents, weekly TV program. Author: Billy Walker Talks with Teens, 1967; contbr. articles to religious jour. Mem. Southgate Schs.. Adv. Com., Southgate Compensation Commn., Southgate Nativity Scene Com. Recipient Peace Oratory award Wayne State U., 1958, Community Svc. award City of Southgate; grantee Kresge Found., 1973. Mem. Detroit Econ. Club. Office: PO Box 1456 Southgate MI 48195-0456

WALKER, BRUCE F., state legislator; m. Agnes Walker; three children. Student, Minot State U. Ins. agt., small bus. owner pvt. practice, Minot, N.D.; city councilman City of Minot; rep. N.D. Ho. of Reps., Bismarck; mem. human svc. and polit. subdivsn. coms., N.D. Ho. of Reps. Mem. N.D. Profl. Ins. Agts. (Ins. Agt. of Yr.), N.D. League Cities (past pres.), Minot Elks, Kiwanis. Office: ND Ho of Reps Capitol Bldg Bismarck ND

WALKER, DAVID FRANCIS, social services administrator; b. Chgo.; s. Gerald Francis and Kathleen Mary (Redlich) W.; m. Judith Ann Masterson, Dec. 12, 1970; children: Amy Susan, Melissa Kathleen, David Gerald Francis. BA, U. Ill., 1973; MA, No. Ill. U., 1981; PhD, U. Ill., 1995. Securities trader F.S. Moseley & Co., Chgo., 1968-69; br. mgr. Beneficial Mgmt. Corp., Chgo., 1969-71; planning & rsch. cons. Ill. Dept. Corrections, Springfield, Ill., 1973; caseworker Ill. Dept. Pub. Aid, Chgo., 1974-76; exec. dir. Edgewater Cmty. Coun., Chgo., 1976-79, No. Ill. Law Enforcement & Criminal Justice Commn., Rockford, Ill., 1979-82, Child Abuse Prevention Svcs., Chgo., 1982—; asst. prof. No. Ill. U., De Kalb, 1985—; adj. faculty Roosevelt U., Chgo., 1988—; appt. mem. Citizen's Com. on Child Abuse & Neglect, Chgo., 1987—. Bd. edn. River Forest (Ill.) Sch. Dist., 1986-90; mem. River Forest Mental Health Com., 1984-86, River Forest Youth Commn., 1985-87. Named outstanding young alumni No. Ill. U., 1988. Mem. Am. Soc. Pub. Adminstrn. (exec. coun. 1994—), Execs. Club Chgo., Assn. for Rsch. in Nonprofit & Vol. Action, Internat. Soc. 3d Sect. Rsch., Southwestern Polit. Sci. Assn., Sierra Club. Democrat. Roman Catholic. Home: 915 William St River Forest IL 60305

WALKER, DEBRA MAY, marketing professional; b. Flint, Mich., May 11, 1956; d. Vern Luke and Rosemary (Deanhofer) W.; m. Stephen Robert Strong, Aug. 14, 1982; 1 child, Evan Walker Strong. BA in Advt., Mich. State U., 1978, MA in Advt., 1979. Sr. bus. analyst Goodyear Tire & Rubber Co., Akron, Ohio, 1979-81, mgr. advt. rsch., 1981-82, mgr. market planning systems, 1982-85; mktg. strategy mgr. Europe Goodyear Tire & Rubber Co., Brussels, 1985-89; mktg. strategy mgr. U.S. Goodyear Tire & Rubber Co., Akron, 1989-90, mktg. mgr. retail stores div., 1990-91, gen. mktg. mgr. retail, 1991-92; mktg. mgr. auto tires Goodyear Tire & Rubber Co., 1992-94; mgr. dealer sales San Leandro, Calif., 1994-95; dir. retail sys. Goodyear Tire & Rubber Co., Akron, 1995-96, v.p. retail systems, 1996—; speaker on mktg. and distbn. topics. Contbr. articles to various publs. Mem. Am. Mgmt. Assn. Office: Goodyear Tire & Rubber Co 1144 E Market St Dept 704 Akron OH 44316

WALKER, DEWAYNE FRED, design engineer; b. Hastings, Nebr., Mar. 28, 1942; s. Fred K. and Waunita M. W. BA in Math. and Physics, Hastings Coll., 1965. Design engr. Ingersoll Rand, Hastings, 1963-79; mech. design engr. Data Sys., Denver, 1979-83, Eaton Corp., Riverton, Wyo., 1983-88; sr. mech. design engr. Data South Computer Corp., Charlotte, N.C., 1988-90; sr. design and materials engr. Frigidaire, Webster City, Iowa, 1990—. Mem. ASTM, Soc. Plastics Engrs., Am. Soc. Quality Control. Home: 1305 Locust St Webster City IA 50595-2652

WALKER, DONALD ROBERT, JR., minister; b. Leavenworth, Kans., Oct. 24, 1955; s. Donald Robert and Norma Elizabeth (Wagner) W.; m. June Marie Chinn, Jan. 1, 1976; children: Heather Renee, Eric David, Michelle Renee. Student, Kans. City Kans. Community Coll., 1973-75, Full Faith Bible Coll., 1977-79. Ordained minister, 1979. Sr. pastor Abundant Life Fellowship, Leavenworth, 1978-82; assoc. pastor Full Faith Ch. of Love, Shawnee, Kans., 1982-84; sr. pastor Full Faith Ch. of Love East, Kans. City, Mo., 1984-94; pastor Christ Covenant Ch., Kansas City, Mo., 1995—; exec. coun. Nat. Leadership Conf., Montreat, N.C., 1988-90, bd. dirs., 1990—; mem. adv. bd. World Indigenous Missions, New Braunfels, Tex., 1990-95. Pres. Found. for the Family, Overland Park, Kans., 1989—. Mem. Internat. Churchill Soc. Republican.

WALKER, DORIS ANN, education educator; b. Oxford, Miss., Aug. 6, 1950; d. Earnest Jr. and Mildred (Blackmon) McEwen; m. Grady Walker Jr., June 19, 1971 (div. Aug. 1990); children: Maleika Rene, Cheo Da'Mu. BS, No. Mich. U., 1971; MS, Mich. State U., 1975, PhD, 1981. Cert. tchr. 7-12, secondary adminstr. 5-12, supt. endorsement, Mich.; tchr., adminstr., Nev.; secondary adminstr., supt., Ind. Tchr. Flint (Mich.) Sch. Dist., 1972; tchr., sch. adminstr. Lansing (Mich.) Sch. Dist., 1973-86; prof. U. Nev., Reno, 1986-88; asst. prin. Waverly H.S., Lansing, 1988-91; prin. East Lansing (Mich.) H.S., 1991-94; assoc. prof. Ind. U., South Bend, 1994—; edn. cons. Nev. State Dept. Edn., Carson City, 1986-88. Contbr. articles to profl. jours. Bd. dirs. Lansing Art Gallery; past advisor Boy Scouts Am.; cadette leader Mich. Capitol Girl Scouts; mem. nominating bd. YWCA; trustee meml. Hosp.; mem. urban youth adv. bd. YMCA. Mem. ASCD, NAACP, Nat. Assn. Secondary Sch. Prins., Nat. Alliance Black Sch. Educators, Am. Assn. Sch. Adminstrs., Mich. Assn. Secondary Sch. Prins., Ind. Assn. Secondary Sch. Prins., Optimist Club, Phi Delta Kappa, Delta Sigma Theta. Home: 5227 Finch Dr South Bend IN 46614

WALKER, DOUG, state legislator; m. Diana Walker. Kans. state sen. Dist. 12; former tchr.; self-employed. Address: 212 1st St Osawatomie KS 66064*

WALKER, EDWIN HOCKADAY, IV, alcohol and drug abuse services professional; b. Richmond, Ky., Mar. 17, 1932; s. Edwin Hockaday and Maria Lynn (Evans) W. AB magna cum laude, Centre Coll. of Ky., 1954; MDiv, Nashotah House Sem., Wis., 1971. Curate St. Mary's Ch., Denver, 1971-73; rector All Saint's Ch., San Francisco, 1973-78; chaplain and coord. social svcs. St. Augustine's Ctr. for Am. Indians, Chgo., 1978-83; gen. mgr. Chgo. Chamber Choir, 1984; exec. dir. Lake View Citizens Coun., Chgo., 1984-86, The Way Back Inn, Inc., Maywood, Ill., 1987—. Choirmaster Christ the Redeemer Byzantine Cath. Ch., 1988—. Maj. USMC, 1956-68. Decorated Bronze Star with combat V, Vietnamese Silver Star with oak leaf cluster; recipient Exec. Dir. of Yr. award United Way of Suburban Chgo., 1995; Fulbright scholar U. Heidelberg, Germany, 1954-55; commd. Ky. Col. by Gov. of Ky., 1992. Mem. Ill. Assn. Residential Extended Care Programs (pres. 1995-96), Maywood C. of C. (pres. 1989-93), West Surburban Addictions Resource Consortium (pres. 1990-93), Kiwanis Club of Lake View (pres. 1987-88, lt. gov. divsn. 1 1990-92). Republican. Home: 209 S 3rd Ave Maywood IL 60153-1637

WALKER, ELVA MAE DAWSON, health consultant; b. Everett, Mass., June 29, 1914; d. Charles Edward and Mary Elizabeth (Livingston) Dawson; m. John J. Spillane Jr. R.N., Peter Bent Brigham Hosp., Boston, 1937; student Simmons Coll., 1935, U. Minn., 1945-48; m. Walter Willard Walker, Dec. 16, 1939 (div. 1969). Supr. nursery Wesson Maternity Hosp., Springfield, Mass., 1937-38; asst. supr. out-patient dept. Peter Bent Brigham Hosp., Boston, 1938-40; supr. surgery and out-patient dept. Univ. Hosps., Mpls., 1945. Chmn. Gov.'s Citizens Coun. on Aging, Minn., 1960-68, acting dir., 1962-66, Econ. Opportunity Com. Hennepin County, 1964-69; v.p., treas. Nat. Purity Soap & Chem. Co., 1968-69, pres., 1969-76, chmn. bd., 1976—, co. exec. officer, 1993—; cons. on aging to Minn. Dept. Pub. Welfare, 1962-67; mem. nat. adv. Coun. for Nurse Tng. Act, 1965-69, Com. Status on Women in Armed Svcs., 1967-70; dir. Nat. Coun. on the Aging, 1963-67, sec., 1965-67, 1986-88, chairperson, 1988-91; chmn. Minn. Bd. on Aging, 1982-91, Nat. Retiree Vol. Ctr., 1982-89; dir. Planning Agy. for Hosps. of Met. Mpls., 1963-67, United Hosp. Fund of Hennepin County, 1955-60, Nat. Coun. Social Work Edn., 1966-68; vice chmn. Hennepin County Gen. Hosp. Adv. Bd., 1965-68; sec. Hennepin County Health Coalition, 1973; chmn. bd. dirs. Am. Rehab. Found, 1962-68, vice chmn., 1968-70, chmn. Minn. Bd. On Aging, 1988-91, Sr. Resources, 1985-87, Older Persons Vision Coun., United Way, 1995—; pres. bd. trustees Northwestern Hosp., 1956-59, Children's Hosp. Mpls., 1961-65; dir. Twin Cities Internat. Program for Youth Leaders and Social Workers, Inc., 1965-67; mem. community adv. coun. United Cmty. Funds and Coun. Am., Inc., 1968, Nat. Assembly Social Policy and Devel., Inc., 1968-74, Minn. Action for Children Commn., 1989—, mem., 1991—; mem. priorities determination com. United Fund Mpls., 1971; vice chmn. govt. specifications com. Soap and Detergent Assn., 1972-76, vice-chmn. indsl. and instn. com., 1974-76, chmn., 1976-78, bd. dirs., 1974—; candidate for Congress, 3d Minn. Dist., 1966; trustee Macalester Coll., Archie D. and Bertha H. Walker Found.; chmn. St. Mary's Jr. Coll. Bd., 1970-74, 78-80, Older Persons vis. com. coun. United Way, 1996—; pres. U. Minn. Sch. Nursing Found., 1958-70; pres. Minn. Gerontological Soc., 1994-95; sec. Metro Area Agy. Aging Minn., 1995—. Mem. Am. Pub. Welfare Assn., Minn. Gerontol. Soc. (pres. 1994—), Mpls. Med. Research Found., Minn. League Nursing (pres. 1971-73), Jr. League Mpls. Democrat. Presbyterian. Home: 3655 Northome Rd Wayzata MN 55391-3020 Office: Nat Purity Soap & Chem Co 434 Lakeside Ave Minneapolis MN 55405-1529

WALKER, FRANK BANGHART, pathologist; b. Detroit, June 14, 1931; s. Roger Venning and Helen Frances (Reade) W.; m. Phyllis Childs; children: Nancy Anne, David Carl, Roger Osborne, Mark Andrew. BS, Union Coll., N.Y., 1951; MD, Wayne State U., 1955, MS, 1962. Diplomate Am. Bd. Pathology (trustee 1982-94, treas. 1984-91, v.p. 1991-92, pres. 1993-94). Intern Detroit Meml. Hosp., 1955-56; resident Wayne State U. and affiliated hosps., Detroit, 1958-62; pathologist, 1962-93; dir. labs. Detroit Meml. Hosp., 1984-87, Cottage Hosp., Grosse Pointe, Mich., 1984-93; pathologist, dir. labs. Macomb Hosp Ctr. (formerly South Macomb Hosp.), Warren, Mich., 1966-93, Jennings Meml. Hosp., Detroit, 1971-79, Alexander Blain Hosp., Detroit, 1971-85; ptnr. Langston, Walker & Assocs., P.C., Grosse Pointe, 1968-93; instr. pathology Wayne State U. Med. Sch., Detroit, 1962-72, asst. clin. prof., 1972-94, assoc. clin. prof., 1994—. Pres. Mich. Assn. Blood Banks, 1969-70; mem. med. adv. com. ARC, 1972-83; mem. Mich. Higher Edn. Assistance Authority, 1975-77; trustee Alexander Blain Meml. Hosp., Detroit, 1974-83, Detroit-Macomb Hosp. Corp., 1974-93, 95—; bd. dirs. Wayne State Fund, 1971-83. Capt. M.C., U.S. Army, 1956-58. Recipient Disting. Svc. award Wayne State U. Med. Sch., 1990. Fellow Detroit Acad. Medicine (pres.-elect 1995-96); mem. AMA (coun. on long-range planning and devel. 1982-88, vice chmn. 1985-87, chmn. 1987-88, trustee 1988—), Coll. Am. Pathologists (Disting. Svc. award 1989), Am. Soc. Clin. Pathologists (sec. 1971-77, pres. 1979-80, Disting. Svc. award 1989), Mich. Soc. Pathologists (pres. 1980-81), Wayne County Med. Soc. (pres. 1984-85, trustee 1986-91, chmn. 1990-91), Mich. Med. Soc. (bd. dirs. 1981-90, vice chmn. 1985-88, chmn. 1988-90), Am. Assn. Blood Banks, Mich. Assn. Blood Banks, Wayne State U. Alumni Assn. (bd. govs. 1968-71), Wayne State U. Med. Alumni Assn. (pres. 1969, trustee 1970-85, Disting. Alumni award 1974), Econ. Club Detroit, Detroit Athletic Club, Lochmoor Club, Mid-Am. Club, Alpha Omega Alpha, Phi Gamma Delta, Nu Sigma Nu. Republican. Episcopalian. Home and Office: 14004 Harbor Place Dr Saint Clair Shores MI 48080-1528

WALKER, GAYLORD THOMPSON, non-profit organization administrator; b. Winston Salem, N.C., Sept. 7, 1935; s. Gaylord Thompson and Margaret Elizabeth (Crouse) W.; m. Nancy Jean Krul, June30, 1950; children: David Scott, Robin Vanessa. Student, Davidson Coll., 1953-56. Owner, mgr. GRW Travel, Rye, N.Y., 1965-75; self-employed Jackson, Mich., 1975-83; dir. pub. affairs Nat. Child Safety Coun., Jackson, 1983-90, 1993—; exec. dir. Mich. Head Injury Alliance, Brighton, 1990-93; pres., vol. Mich. Coun. Injury Control, Lansing, 1990—. With U.S. Army, 1956-59. Office: Nat Child Safety Coun 4065 Page Ave Jackson MI 49204

WALKER, GEORGE HERBERT, III, investment banking company executive, lawyer; b. St. Louis, Mar. 16, 1931; s. George H. and Mary (Carter) W.; m. Sandra E. Canning, Dec. 23, 1955 (div. Oct. 1962); children: Mary Elizabeth, Wendy, Isabelle; m. Kimberly Gedge, July 27, 1968 (div. Jan. 1977); children: George H. IV, Carter; m. Carol Banta, Feb. 21, 1987. B.A., Yale U., 1953; LL.B., Harvard U., 1956. Bar: Conn. 1956. Gen. ptnr. G.H. Walker & Co. (later G.H. Walker, Laird Inc.), 1961-74; sr. v.p., also bd. dirs. White, Weld & Co. Inc., 1974-75; chmn. bd. dirs. G.H. Walker & Co., 1973-74; exec. v.p. Stifel Nicolaus & Co., 1976-78, pres., CEO, 1978-92, chmn., 1982—, also bd. dirs.; civilian aide to sec. U.S. Army for Ea. Mo., 1973-80; bd. dirs. Laidlaw Corp., Laclede Steel Co., Eck-Adams Corp.; bd. govs. Midwest Stock Exch., 1982-88. Bd. dirs. Downtown St. Louis Inc., 1975-90, chmn., 1984-86; bd. dirs. Webster U., chmn. bd., 1987-92; trustee Mo. Hist. Soc., St. Louis Children's Hosp., 1972-92, Jefferson Nat. Expansion Meml. Assn., 1992; vestryman St. Ann's Ch., Kennebunkport, Maine; mem. Mo. Rep. Ctrl. Com., 1983—; adv. bd. St. Louis Area coun. Boy Scouts Am., 1989—; trustee investment trust Episcopal Diocese of Mo.; hon. bd. dirs. Anti-Drug Abuse Edn. Fund, Inc., 1990—; bd. dirs. St. Louis Zoo, 1992. With USAF, 1956-58. Mem. Rotary (St. Louis club). Home: 136 S Price Rd Saint Louis MO 63124-1858 Office: Stifel Fin Corp 500 N Broadway Rm 1700 Saint Louis MO 63102-2110*

WALKER, JEWEL LEE, health facility administrator, consultant; b. Columbus, Ohio, Jan. 4, 1950; d. Zerold and Frieda Arlene (Tolliver) Sizemore; m. David Walker (div. Sept. 1984). AS, Mt. Vernon (Ohio) Nazarene Coll., 1970; diploma in Nursing, Mansfield (Ohio) Gen. Hosp., 1974; BSBA summa cum laude, Franklin U., 1983; postgrad., U. Dayton, 1985; MSA in Health Care Adminstrn., Cen. Mich. U., 1991. RN Ohio. Nurse Martin Meml. Hosp., Mt. Vernon, 1974-75, Ohio State U. Hosp., Columbus, 1974-78; chief registrar Nurses Profl. Registry, Columbus, 1978-82, cons., 1982-84; dir. nurses Bryden Manor Nursing Home, Columbus, 1982-83; health svcs. coord. Nat. Nursing Corp., Columbus, 1983-86, corp. dir. nursing svcs., 1986-88; pvt. practice nursing cons. Columbus, 1988—; shift dir. Columbus Community Hosp., 1991-95; clin. svcs. coord. Care Connections Inc., Columbus, 1995—; clin. svcs. dir. Care Connections, Inc., Columbus. Callvac, Columbus, 1988, Columbus Arthritis Found., 1988. Mem. NOW, ANA (cert. in nursing adminstrn. 1989), NAFE. Democrat. Home and Office: 1407 Royston Dr Columbus OH 43204-1532

WALKER, JOHN PATRICK, theater producer, actor; b. Elgin, Ill., Apr. 21, 1956; s. John Patrick and Ruth Ellen (Borror) W.; m. Pamela Jean Gay, Dec. 5, 1981; children: Miranda, Caitlin. BA, Notre Dame U., 1978; cert., Am. Conservatory Theatre, San Francisco, 1980. Actor Peninsula Players, Door County, Wis., 1978-84, gen. mgr., 1984-86; house mgr. Civic Ctr. Performing Arts, Chgo., 1984-86; gen. mgr. Royal George Theater, Chgo., 1986-89, Cullen, Henaghan, Platt, Chgo., 1989-91; mng. dir. Victory Gardens Theater, Chgo., 1991—; pres. League of Chgo. Theaters. Office: Victory Gardens Theater 2257 N Lincoln Ave Chicago IL 60614-3717

WALKER, JONATHAN ALAN, steelworker; b. Alton, Ill., July 8, 1958; s. Donald Eugene and Patricia Louise (Ford) W.; m. Angelica del Pilar Gemma Infante, Nov. 17, 1978; children: Jonathan Patrick, Jacqueline Sue, Joseph Daniel. Student, St. Louis Coll. Pharmacy, 1976-77; AS with honors, Lewis & Clark Community Coll., Godfrey, Ill., 1990. Attendant gas sta. Flash Oil Co., Alton, Ill., 1976-77; stockboy-cashier Venture Store # 4, Alton, 1977-78; laborer, hydrostatic test operator, galvanizer-crew leader Laclede Steel Co., Alton, 1978-90, plant joint safety commr., 1990-92; mem. Tube Mill Safety Com., sec., 1989; union steward local 3643 AFL-CIO, 1989, 90; mem. United Steelworkers Am., treas. local 3643 1991-94, fin. sec., 1994—, cmty. svcs. chmn., 1993-96, union counselor, 1994—, local 3643 21st dist. COPE chmn., 1995—. Mem. Sch. to Work Opportunities Task Force, 1994-95. Mem. Lewis and Clark Alumni Assn. Mem. Assemblies of God Ch. Home: 3733 Berkeley Ave Alton IL 62002-3112

WALKER, JONATHAN LEE, lawyer; b. Kalamazoo, Mar. 8, 1948; s. Harvey E. and Olivia M. (Estrada) W. BA, U. Mich., 1969; JD, Wayne State U., 1977. Bar: Mich. 1977, U.S. Dist. Ct. (ea. dist.) Mich. 1983. Assoc. Moore, Barr & Kerwin, Detroit, 1977-79; ptnr. firm Barr & Walker, Detroit, 1979-82; assoc. firm Richard M. Goodman, P.C., Detroit, 1983-87; hearing officer Mich. Civil Rights Commn., Detroit, 1983-86; pvt. practice, Detroit, 1988-89, Birmingham, 1990—; participant Detroit Bar Assn. Vol. Lawyer Program. Bd. dirs. Community Treatment Ctr.-Project Rehab., Detroit, 1983-89; mem. scholarship com. Latino en Marcha Scholarship Fund, Detroit, 1984; treas. youth assistance program Citizens Adv. Coun., 1987. Mem. State Bar Mich. Found., Wayne County Mediation Tribunal, Inc. (mediator), Am. Arbitration Assn. (arbitrator), Nat. Lawyers Guild (exec. bd. Detroit chpt. 1988-92, pres. Detroit chpt. 1988-90), Mich. Trial Lawyers Assn. (co-chmn. coalition com. 1988-89, 89-90, exec. bd. 1988-96, co-chair pro-bono com. 1991-96), Assn. Trial Lawyers Am., State Bar Mich. (mem. com. on underrepresented groups in law 1980-92, chmn. 1983-85, mem. com. jud. qualifications 1985-86, mem. Latin Am. affairs coun. 1978-96), Legal Aid and Def. Assn. (bd. dirs. 1990-95), Hispanic Bar Assn., Trial Lawyers for Pub. Justice (founder 1981, mem. Amicus com. 1985-86, state capt. 1991-95), Ctr. for Auto Safety, Washtenaw County Bar Assn.. Office: 118 Maincentre Ste 305 Northville MI 48167

WALKER, KATHRINE L., museum educational administrator, educator; b. San Jose, Calif., Mar. 12, 1962; d. Paul D. and Barbara (White) W. BA with honors, Stanford U., 1984; MA, Coll. William and Mary, 1985; cert. mus. mgmt., U. Colo., 1996. Archaeologist Va. Rsch. Ctr. for Archaeology, Newport, 1984-85; curatorial asst. Colonial Williamsburg Found., Va., 1985-86; asst. curator, coord. edn. Nantucket (Mass.) Historical Assn., 1986-88; dir. edn. Webb-Deane-Stevens Mus., Wethersfield, Conn., 1988-91, Lyman Allyn Art Mus., New London, Conn., 1991-94, Beach Mus. Art, Kans. State U., Manhattan, 1994—; mem. Mass. Arts Lottery Coun., Nantucket, 1988-89; chair diversity subcom. Regional Adv. Com. on Edn. Reform, 1994; adv. bd. Manhattan Arts Coun., 1995-96; panelist Kans. Arts Commn., 1995. Author: (curriculum) The Outsiders, 1990, The Face in Art, 1994, (gallery guide) From Distaff Side, 1992; author: (with others) Cultural Diversity in Literature, Art and Music, 1992, The American Collection 1620-1920: Guide to the Palmer Gallery, 1994. Vol. tchr. Nantucket Learning & Resource Ctr., 1988; mem. New London Culture and Tourism Alliance, 1991—; Manhattan C. of C. Edn. com., 1996; Big Brothers, Big Sisters, 1996. Grantee Inst. Mus. Svcs., Nantucket, 1987, 88, Rockefeller Found./Conn. Humanities Coun., New London, 1991-92; scholar Conn. Humanities Coun., 1989—. Mem. Am. Assn. Mus. (rep. bd. 1990-93, 95—, edn. com. 1988—, Excellence and Equity award) Nat. Art Edn. Assn., New Eng. Mus. Assn. (edn. com. 1988-94, chair 1991-94), Mountain Plains Mus. Assn. (chair edn. com. 1995—), Conn. Art Docents Network (bd. dirs. 1991—), Alliance of Cultural Educators of Hartford, Nat. Art Edn. Assn., Kans. Art Edn. Assn., Manhattan C. of C. (edn. com. 1996). Office: Beach Art Mus 2323 Anderson Ave Ste 151 Manhattan KS 66502-2912

WALKER, MICHAEL CLAUDE, finance educator; b. Sherman, Tex., June 8, 1940; s. Andrew Jackson and Alice Lorene (Curry) W.; m. Martha Ellen Hindman, Sept. 10, 1966; children: Stephanie Elizabeth, Rebecca Elaine, Priscilla Eileen. BA, Austin Coll., 1965; MA, Ohio State U., 1966; PhD, U. Houston, 1971. Instr. U. Houston, 1969-70; asst. prof. Ga. State U., Atlanta, 1971-75; assoc. prof. U. Okla., Norman, 1975-78; prof., head dept. fin., ins. and real estate North Tex. State U., Denton, 1978-85; prof. U. Cin., 1985-88, dept. head, 1985—, Virgil M. Schwarm prof. fin. and investments, 1988—. Co-editor: Cases in Financial Institutions, 1979; contbr. articles to profl. jours. Served with AUS, 1958-61. Recipient Leonard P. Ayers fellowship award, 1973. Mem. Am. Fin. Assn., Fin. Execs. Inst., Fin. Mgmt. Assn., So. Fin. Assn. (bd. dirs. 1983-85, sec.-treas. 1986-88, v.p. 1988-89, pres. 1989-90), Southwestern Fin. Assn. (bd. dirs. 1986-88), Ea. Fin. Assn., Midwest Fin. Assn., Beta Gamma Sigma, Omicron Delta Epsilon. Methodist. Office: U Cin Fin Dept Mail Location 195 Cincinnati OH 45221-0195

WALKER, PAUL DAVID, newspaper publisher; b. Upland, Calif., July 26, 1934; s. Paul David and Laura Frances (Wilcox) W.; m. Barbara White, June 22, 1957; children: Kathrine L., Michael P., Caroline D., Christopher W. AB, Stanford U., 1956; MBA, Harvard U., 1961; EdD, Columbia U., 1976. Asst. rsch. adminstr. Stanford (Calif.) U., 1961-63; bus. mgr. Stanford U. Librs., 1963-66; bus. mgr., comptroller Elmira (N.Y.) Coll., 1966-67; dir. spl. programs Colby Coll., Waterville, Maine, 1970-72; pubr. The Emporia (Kans.) Gazette, 1972—. Bd. dirs. Presbyn. Manors, Wichita, Kans., 1989—, Bethany Coll., Lindsborg, Kans., 1988-95, chmn., 1992-95; with Kans. Humanities Coun., Topeka, 1984-90, chmn., 1987-89; pres. William Allen White Found., Lawrence, Kans., 1982-84, Big Bros./Big Sisters, Emporia, 1984-89, pres., 1989. 1st lt. USAF, 1957-59. Mem. Emporia C. of C. (dir. 1974-77). Episcopalian. Home: 1732 Hammond Dr Emporia KS 66801-5313 Office: The Emporia Gazette 517 Merchant St Emporia KS 66801-7215

WALKER, (GALE) RICHARD, state agency staff; b. Stockport, Ohio, Nov. 28, 1948; s. Earl Eugene and Grace Lydia (Kirkbride) W.; m. Lori Joan Beaver, Aug. 28, 1976; children: R. Dougal, Daniel Earl. BA with honors, Marietta Coll., 1972; MA, Purdue U., 1974, PhD, 1976. Asst. prof. Muhlenberg Coll., Allentown, Pa., 1976-78; prof. Blackburn Coll., Carlinville, Ill., 1978-85; sr. policy analyst Ill. Dept. Nuc. Safety, Springfield, 1985-89; sci. assessment cons. Ill. State Bd. Edn., Springfield, 1989—; spkr. in field. Author: Wolf Creek & the Muskingum, 1996, Running Dogs of Loyalty, 1995. Mem. Ill. Fedn. State Office Educators (chair 1992—), Morgan County Hist. Soc., Skeptics Soc., Phi Beta Kappa. Home: 28 Providence Ln Springfield IL 62707 Office: Ill State Bd Edn 100 N First St Springfield IL 62777

WALKER, RONALD F., corporate executive; b. Cin., Apr. 9, 1938; married. BBA, U. Cin., 1961. V.p. Kroger Co., Cin., 1962-72; with Am. Fin. Corp., Cin., 1972—, exec. v.p., 1978-84, pres., COO, bd. dirs., 1984-95; exec. v.p. Gt. Am. Ins., Cin., 1972-80, pres., 1980-87, vice chmn., 1987—; pres., COO Penn Cen. Corp., 1987-92, COO, 1987-92; pres., CEO Gen. Cable Corp., 1992-94; also bd. dirs.; bd. dirs. Chiquita Brands Internat., Cin., Am.

Fin. Enterprises, Cin., Am. Annuity Gruop, Inc., Tejas Gas Corp. Office: Gt Am Ins Co 580 Walnut St Cincinnati OH 45202-3110 also: Am Fin Corp 1 E 4th St Cincinnati OH 45202-3717

WALKER, SCOTT KEVIN, state legislator; b. Colorado Springs, Nov. 2, 1967; s. Llewellyn Scott and Patricia Ann (Fitch) W.; m. Tonette Marie Tarantino; 1 child, Matthew David. Grad., Marquette U., 1990. Acct. adminstr. IBM, 1988-90; chmn. 5th congl. dist. Wis. State Rep. Party, 1991-93; assemblyman Wis. State Dist. 14, 1993—; exec. com. Wis. State Rep. Party, 1991—; chmn. com. elections and constnl. law, Wis. State Assembly, 1995—. Fin. devel. specialist ARC, 1990-93; coun. mem. Milw. County Boy Scouts Am. Mem. Wauwatosa Hist. Soc., Wauwatosa Area C. of C. Address: PO Box 8953 Madison WI 53708

WALKER, THOMAS H., federal agency administrator; b. Hattiesburg, Miss., Nov. 11, 1950; s. Thomas Ray and Mary Ella (Bennett) W.; m. Cynthia Kay Sherer, June 5, 1993; children: Ty, Kelly, Rachel, Stacey. BS in Engring., Miss. State U., 1972; MBA, U. West Fla., 1982; postgrad., Nat. Def. U., 1987-88, Harvard U., 1990, Fed. Exec. Inst., 1992. Registered profl. engr., Va. Indsl. engr. Navy Pub. Works Ctr., Norfolk, Va., 1973-75, Atlantic Divsn. Naval Facility Engring. Commn., Norfolk, Va., 1975-76; supervisory gen. engr. Naval Comm. Sta., Exmouth, Australia, 1976-78; indsl. engr. Western Divsn. Naval Facility Engring. Commn., San Bruno, Calif., 1978-79; head facilities mgmt. Navy Pub. Works Ctr., Pensacola, Fla., 1979-82, Subic Bay, The Philippines, 1982-85; dep. dir. facilities mgmt. USMC, Washington, 1985-89; asst. commr. GSA, Washington, 1989-92, dep. asst. regional adminstr., 1992-93; asst. regional adminstr. pub. bldgs. GSA, Kansas City, Mo., 1993—; bd. dirs. Kansas City BOMA. Coach Little League Baseball, Fairfax, Va., 1986-92, Girls Softball Team, Lees Summit, Va., 1995. cub scout den father Boy Scouts Am., Fairfax, 1987-88. Miss. State U. Disting. Engring. fellow, 1992; recipient Arthur S. Fleming award Washington Jaycees, 1989. Mem. NSPE, Va. Soc. Profl. Engrs., Bldg. Owners and Mgrs. Assn. (mem. govt. bldgs. com. 1991—, chmn. 1993—, mem. corp. facilities com. 1991—, nat. adv. coun. 1995—), Internat. Facilities Mgmt. Assn. (mem. pub. sector com. 1991—, Golden Cir. award 1994), Sr. Execs. Assn., Phi Kappa Phi, Alpha Pi Mu, Gamma Beta Phi. Methodist. Home: 328 NE Sunderland Ct Lees Summit MO 64064-1610 Office: GSA 1500 E Bannister Rd Kansas City MO 64131-3009

WALKER, TRACEY LYNN, editor; b. Cleve., Mar. 2, 1966; d. Gilbert Wayne and Judith Mae (Enderlein) Batdorf; m. David Alter Walker, Jr., Oct. 20, 1990; children: Kaila Jerica Nicole, Somer Allyson Rose. BS in Journalism, Bowling Green State U. Contbg. editor Advanstar Comm., Cleve., 1988-89, asst. editor Food & Drug Packaging, 1989-90, assoc. editor Beverage Industry, 1990-94, assoc. editor Dermatology Times, Urology Times, Ophthalmology Times, 1995, asst. mng. editor Dermatology Times, Urology Times, Relax, 1995-96; mng. editor Dermatology Times, 1996—. Home: 3645 Rockport Ave Cleveland OH 44111 Office: Advanstar Comm 7500 Old Oak Blvd Cleveland OH 44130

WALKER, TREVOR JOE, computer network engineer; b. Lincoln, Ill., Mar. 5, 1971; s. Terry Joe and Sandra Lou (Hines) Thompson; m. Sandra Kay Absher, Oct. 9, 1993; 1 child, Prescott. Student, So. Ill. U., Edwardsville, 1989-91, So. Ill. U., Carbondale, 1991-92, Sangamon State U., 1992-95. Computer oper., network adminstr. United Cmty. Bank, Pawnee, Ill., 1993-94; mgmt. analyst programmer, network adminstr. U. Ill., Springfield, 1994—. Home: PO Box 373 Williamsville IL 62693 Office: UIC-DSCC 2815 W Washington Ste 300 Springfield IL 62794

WALKER, WALTER WILLARD, real estate and investments executive; b. Mpls., Dec. 4, 1911; s. Archie Dean and Bertha Willard (Hudson) W.; BA, Princeton U., 1935; MD, Harvard U., 1940; postgrad. U. Minn., 1942-48; m. Elva Mae Dawson, Dec. 16, 1939 (div. Oct. 1969); m. Elaine Barbatsis, Mar. 17, 1972; stepchildren: Nicholas K. Barbatsis, Marianna Barbatsis Priest, Becka Barbatsis Mourmouras, Christian Barbatsis Dayton. Teaching fellow pathology U. Minn., 1942-48; left medicine, went into bus., 1948; dir. Shasta Forest Co., Redding, Calif., 1951-71, treas., 1954-66, v.p., 1966-71; sec., dir. Barlow Realty Co., Mpls., 1954-67, pres., 1967-77, chmn., 1977-80, sec., 1980-83, v.p., 1983-88; ptnr. Barlow Assocs., 1988—; sec., bd. dir. Walker Pence Co., 1950-72; sec. Penwalk Investment Co., 1958-72, bd. dir., 1943-72; bd. dir. Craig-Hallum Corp., Mpls., 1954-92; adv. bd. Lincoln office Northwestern Nat. Bank, Mpls., 1957-74. Bd. dirs. T.B. Walker Found., 1953-76, v.p., 1954-76; bd. dirs. Minn. Opera Co., 1968-73, Archie D. and Bertha H. Walker Found., 1953—, Mpls. Found., 1962-79, Walker Art Ctr, 1954-76, United Fund, 1966-72; trustee Abbott-Northwestern Hosp., 1969-77; trustee Children's Health Ctr., Inc., 1968-73, treas., 1969-73; pres. Found. Services, 1967-73; bd. dirs., exec. com. Minn. Charities Review Council, 1965-74; mem. Hennepin County Capital Budgeting Task Force, 1973-74. Mem. Sigma Xi, Nu Sigma Nu, Mpls. Club, Princeton Club (N.Y.C.), U. Minn. Alumni Club. Methodist. Home: 1900 Knox Ave S Minneapolis MN 55403-2839 also: 4143 W Gulf Dr Sanibel FL 33957-5101 Office: 1121 Hennepin Ave Minneapolis MN 55403-1785

WALKER, WILLIE MARK, electronics engineering executive; b. Bessemer, Ala., Aug. 18, 1929; s. Johnnie and Annie Maimie (Thompson) W.; m. Mae Ruth Fulton, Apr. 28, 1952; children—Patricia Ann, Mark William, Karen Marie. BEE, Marquette U., 1958; MS in Elec. Engring., U. Wis., 1965. Registered profl. engr., Wis. Devel. technician AC Spark Plug, Milw., 1953-56, project engr., 1956-60, engring. supr., 1960-65; sr. devel. engr. AC Electronics, Milw., 1965-71; sr. prodn. engr. Delco Electronics, Oak Creek, Wis., 1971-94; chmn. occupl. adv. bd. on computer sci. Milw. Area Tech. Coll., 1983-86; owner, prin. Walker Engring., 1994—. Author various proprietary reports. Pres., Potawatomi Area coun. Boy Scouts Am., Waukesha, Wis., 1982-84, chief camp inspector area 1, east ctrl. region, 1987, v.p. program area 1, 1988-93, v.p. area 3 ctrl. region, 1993—; loaned exec. United Way of Greater Milw., 1983; usher, minister of communion St. Mary Cath. Ch., Menomonee Falls, Wis., 1967—; internat. commr. Ctrl. Region Boy Scouts Am. Scout Jamboree, 1993. Served with USAF, 1949-53. Elected to Black Achievers in Bus. and Industry, Milw. Met. YMCA, 1984; recipient Civic Svc. award Rotary Club, 1983; GM award for Excellence, 1980; St. George award Milw. Archidiocese, 1975; Silver Beaver award Boy Scouts Am., 1973, Silver Antelope award Boy Scouts Am., 1987; Black Achiever in Bus. and Industry award YMCA Greater Milw., 1984. Mem. IEEE (computer soc., sr. mem.), Computer Automated Sys. Assn., Soc. Mfg. Engrs., Wis. Soc. Profl. Engrs., Inst. Indsl. Engrs. (sr. mem., cert. sys. integrator), Lions (chpt. pres. 1979-80, sec. 1974-75), K.C. (recorder 1966-67, advocate 1975-76). Office: GM Corp Delco Electronics Div 7929 S Howell Ave Oak Creek WI 53154-2931

WALKOWICZ, TED H., manager special engineering; b. Chgo., May 27, 1948. BBA, Aurora (Ill.) U., 1991, BS in Engring., 1993. Mgr. spl. engring. Rapistian, Oak Brook, Ill., 1984-91; design engr. Pulver Systems, Chgo. Ridge, Ill., 1991-93; project engr. Alloyd, DeKalb, Ill., 1993; mgr. spl. engring. Automotion, Inc., Worth, Ill., 1993—. With USMC, 1967-69, Vietnam. Office: Automotion Inc 11743 S Mayfield Ave Worth IL 60482-2427

WALL, DOUGLAS FOSTER, mathematics educator; b. Red Bank, N.J., Nov. 22, 1965; s. William Foster and Priscilla (Roberts) W.; m. Claudia Anne-Elisabeth Childs, Nov. 24, 1990. BS in Math., Wheaton Coll., 1988; MS in Edn., No. Ill. U., 1993. Tchr. math. Naperville (Ill.) North High Sch., 1988—. Football, basketball and softball coach Naperville North H.S. Mem. Nat. Edn. Assn. Republican. Office: Naperville North High Sch 899 N Mill St Naperville IL 60563-2909

WALL, JEFFREY LYNN, intravenous nurse, educator; b. Dayton, Ohio, July 2, 1954; s. Ollie Tilden and Almeda (Alford) W.; m. Jane Ann Coppess, June 4, 1977; 1 child, Alexander Perry. Student, Ohio State U., 1972-73; ADN, Sinclair Commun. Coll., Dayton, 1976. RN, Ohio; cert. intravenous nurse. Staff nurse Good Samaritan Hosp., Dayton, 1976-77; paramedic, nurse Fontana-Taylor Ambulance Svc., Ann Arbor, Mich., 1977-80; nurse, tng. officer Greenville County Emergency Med. Svcs., Greenville, S.C., 1980-83; intravenous therapy nurse St. Francis Commun. Hosp., Greenville, 1981-83; relief charge nurse Greenville (S.C.) Meml. Hosp., 1983; ICU staff nurse Wayne Hosp., Greenville, Ohio, 1982-83; intravenous therapy nurse Children's Med. Ctr., Dayton, 1984—; ednl. cons., 1991—. Contbr. chpt. to book. Recipient Appreciation award Dayton Area Candlelighters, Am. Cancer Soc., 1988. Mem. Intravenous Nurses Soc., Nat. Assn. Vascular Access Networks. Home: 101 N Diamond Mill Rd Clayton OH 45315-9766 Office: Children's Med Ctr 1 Childrens Plz Dayton OH 45404-1898

WALL, JOHN H., electrical engineer; b. Ft. Wayne, Ind., Sept. 2, 1965. BSEE, Purdue U., 1988. Tech. mgr. Alcoils - Dana Corp., Columbia City, Ind., 1987—. Patentee clutch controller, encapulation plastic and electromagnetic coils, winding machine, resistance bonding machine.

WALL, RONALD RAE, public school superintendent; b. Hampton, Nebr., Oct. 4, 1941; s. Raymond A. and Donna (Bagby) W.; m. Jane Louise Boeka, June 10, 1967; 1 child, Megan Elizabeth. BA, U. Nebr., Kearney, 1964, MS, 1970; EdS, U. Nebr., Lincoln, 1973, EdD, 1991. Cert. profl. adminstr., Nebr. Tchr. Aurora (Nebr.) Pub. Schs., 1966-71; supt. Farnam (Nebr.) Pub. Schs., 1971-74, Medicine Valley Pub. Schs., Curtis, Nebr., 1974-85, Sutton (Nebr.) Pub. Schs., 1985-90, Central City (Nebr.) Pub. Schs., 1990—. Mem. ASCD, Am. Assn. Sch. Adminstrs., Nebr. Coun. Sch. Adminstrs. Office: Central City Pub Schs 1804 14th Ave Central City NE 68826-2017

WALLACE, BARBARA RAE, library director; b. Detroit, Mich., Sept. 22, 1941; d. Raymond W. and Dorothy M. (Pickett) Suchner; m. William Donald Wallace, May 9, 1981; children from previous marriage: Michael R. Yanko, David M. Yanko. BA in French, Mich. State U., 1961; MA in Libr. Sci., U. Mich., 1966, MBA, 1988. Cert. tchr., ctrl. adminstr., libr., Mich. Elem. libr. Livonia (Mich.) Pub. Schs., 1967-69; libr. Friends Sch., Detroit, 1969-74, Carol Morgan Sch., Santo Domingo, Dominican Republic, 1974-77; asst. to pres. asst. Cement divsn. Nat. Gypsum, Detroit, 1977-80; adminstrv. asst. Cellar Book Shop, Detroit, 1980-82; lower sch. libr. Am. Sch. Paris, France, 1982-84; dir. libr. svcs. Wyandotte (Mich.) Pub. Schs., 1985-94; dir. Bacon Meml. Dist. Libr., Wyandotte, 1985—; regional rep. Am. Assn. Sch. Librs., Region III-Midwest, 1993-95. Columnist Bacon Bits, News Herald, 1987—; contbr. articles to profl. jours. Adv. coun. mem. Salvation Army, Wyandotte, 1993—. Recipient Alumni Disting. scholarship Mich. State U., 1958. Mem. Internat. Assn. Sch. Librs., Am. Libr. Assn., Mich. Libr. Assn., Mich. Assn. Media In Edn. (pres. 1992, Pres. award 1993), Women's Nat. Book Assn. (Detroit chpt., pres. 1990-92), Detroit Suburban Librs. Roundtable (chair 1995—), Detroit Story League (corr. sec. 1994—), Kiwanis, Soroptimist Internat. Unitarian Universalist. Office: Bacon Meml Dist Libr 45 Vinewood Wyandotte MI 48192

WALLACE, DOROTHY ALENE, special education administrator; b. Wright County, Mo., Sept. 11, 1942; d. Stephen Foster and Lois Alene (Breman) Dudley; widowed; children: Michael Dean Huckaby, David Lee. BS in Edn., Drury Coll., 1975, MS in Edn., 1978; Specialist in Ednl. Adminstrn., Southwest Mo. State U., 1988. Cert. tchr. and adminstr., Mo. Tchr. 3rd grade Mansfield (Mo.) R-IV Schs., 1975-78, tchr. 1st grade, 1978-85, tchr. learning disabled, 1985-89, adminstr. spl. edn., 1989-92, adminstr. spl. svcs., 1992—; active sch. coms. on curriculum and nutrition Mansfield R-IV Schs., mem. sch./cmty. adv. coun., 1992—. Mem. Am. Salers Assn., Mo. State Tchrs. Assn., Mo. Coun. Adminstrs. of Spl. Edn., Coun. for Exceptional Children, Coun. Adminstrs. of Spl. Edn., Local Adminstrs. of Spl. Edn., Cmty. Tchrs. Assn. Home: 3489 Jerico Rd Seymour MO 65746

WALLACE, FRANKLIN SHERWOOD, lawyer; b. Bklyn., Nov. 24, 1927; s. Abraham Charles and Jennie (Etkin) Wolowitz; student U. Wis., 1943-45; BS cum laude, U.S. Mcht. Marine Acad., 1950; LLB, JD, U. Mich., 1953; m. Eleanor Ruth Pope, Aug. 23, 1953; children: Julia Diane, Charles Andrew. Bar: 1954. Practiced in Rock Island; ptnr. firm Winstein, Kavensky & Wallace; asst. state's atty. Rock Island County, 1967-68; local counsel UAW at John Deere-J.I. Case Plants. Former bd. dirs. Tri City Jewish Ctr.; former trustee United Jewish Charities of Quad Cities; bd. dirs. Blackhawk Coll. Found. Mem. ABA, Ill. Bar Assn. (chmn. jud. adv. polls com. 1979-84), Rock Island County Bar Assn., Am. Trial Lawyers Assn., Ill. Trial Lawyers Assn., Nat. Assn. Criminal Def. Lawyers, Ill. Appellate Lawyers Assn., Am. Orthopsychiat. Assn., Am. Judicature Soc., Blackhawk Coll. Found. Democrat. Jewish. Home: 3405 20th Street Ct Rock Island IL 61201-6201 Office: Rock Island Bank Bldg Rock Island IL 61201

WALLACE, JACK HAROLD, employee development specialist, educator; b. Pleasant Ridge, Mich., Dec. 3, 1950; s. Jack Alfred and Mary Hilda (Hemming) W.; m. Laura Jeannine Placer, May 20, 1978. AA, Oakland Community Coll., 1972; BA, Oakland U., 1974; postgrad., Cen. Mich. U., 1984; MeD, Wayne State U., 1986, postgrad., 1988—. Cert. secondary tchr., Mich. Supply systems analyst TACOM, Warren, Mich., 1979-84; employee devel. specialist Army Tank Automotive Command, Tng. and Dev. Div., Warren, 1985—; site coord. TA COM long distance learning program Nat. Tech. U., Warren, 1993—; v.p. acad. affairs Virtual U., Bloomfield Hills, Mich., 1994—; instr. Ferndale (Mich.) Bd. of Edn., 1976-86; instr., cons. Jordan Coll., Detroit, 1986—, Detroit Coll. Bus., Dearborn, Mich., 1986—; trainer, instr. govt. agys. Co-author: (book) Balancing the Scales of Justice, 1986, (cable TV prodn.) A Course in Law and Application in Everyday Living, 1989. Mem. Am. Soc. for Tng. and Devel., Assn. for Ednl. Comm. and Tech., Fed. Mgrs. Assn., Mich. Soc. Instructional Tech., Phi Delta Kappa. Lutheran. Home: 3005 Kenmore Rd Berkley MI 48072-1684 Office: TACOM AMSTA-RM-PRT Warren MI 48397-5000

WALLACE, KIMBERLEE BELLE, pharmacy educator, consultant; b. Santa Barbara, Calif., June 19, 1965; d. Ronald David Wallace and Ardith Kay (Welch) Schwendeman. BS, U. Wash., 1990, Doctorate, 1993. Cert. pharmacy. Pharmacy intern U. Wash. Med. Ctr., Seattle, 1987-90, Evergreen Med. Ctr., Kirkland, Wash., 1989-90; pharmacist U. Wash. Med. Ctr., Seattle, 1990-91, Evergreen Med. Ctr., Kirkland, 1990-91; asst. prof. pharmacy Ferris State U., Big Rapids, Mich., 1993—. Mem. Am. Pharm. Assn., Am. Soc. Hosp. Pharmacists, Mich. Pharmacists Assn., West Mich. Soc. Hosp. Pharmacists, Kappa Psi (treas. 1988). Home: 11747 Stebbins NW Sparta MI 49345

WALLACE, LOUISE MARGARET, clinical coordinator; b. Norwich, Conn., June 15, 1942; d. Irving Clifford and Helen Lucille (Fain) Hayden; m. R.D. Wallace, Dec. 2, 1967; 1 child, Donald Orville. Grad., Joseph Lawrence Sch. Nursing, Conn., 1963; student, Miami-Dade (Fla.) Jr. Coll., 1966-67, Yavapai Coll., 1970. RN, Ariz., Mo., D.C., Fla., Conn., New Zealand; ACLS, ABLS. Nurse ICU and ob-gyn. dept. George Washington U. Hosp., Washington, 1964-65; nurse pediatrics dept. Jackson Meml. Hosp., Miami, Fla., 1965-66; nurse ICU Bapt. Hosp., Miami, 1966-67; nurse ICU and CCU N. Shore Hosp., Miami, 1967-71; nurse ICU and CCU VA Med. Ctr., Prescott, Ariz., 1971-84; nurse ICU and CCU VA Med. Ctr., Poplar Bluff, Mo., 1984-93, relief clin. coord., 1991-92; clin. coord., 1993—; instr. nursing Miami-Dade Jr. Coll., 1968-69; instr. basic CPR, Prescott, 1975-81. Mem. Am. Diabetes Assn. Home: HC 1 Box 76 Grandin MO 63943-9602

WALLACE, RALPH EUGENE, automotive and mechanical engineer; b. Bement, Ill., Nov. 27, 1923; s. Ralph Thomas and Lydia Jane (Fisher) W.; m. Marjorie Lefftas; children: Thomas, Roger, Phillip, Lawrence. BS in Engring., U. Ill., 1944. Registered profl. engr., Ill. Material handling engr. Internat. Harvester, Chgo., 1944-49, test engr., 1949-56, rsch. engr., 1956-65; mgr. applied rsch. Internat. Harvester, Hinsdale, Ill., 1965-80, acting mgr. Computer Tech. Ctr., 1980-84; mgr. computer aided engring. J.I. Case, Hinsdale, 1984-89; affiliate engr., cons. Gear Rsch. Inst., Evanston, Ill., 1990—. Contbr. articles to profl. jours. Scoutmaster Boy Scouts Am., Elmhurst, Ill., 1964-68. Comdr. USN, 1943-44. Mem. ASME, Soc. Automotive Engrs. (mem. auto emissions com. 1976-79, bd. dirs. Chgo. sect.). Home: 29 Mockingbird Ln Oak Brook IL 60521-1751

WALLACE, ROBERT LUTHER, II, engineer; b. Ronceverte, W.Va., Jan. 27, 1949; s. Robert Luther and Eloise Virginia (Houck) W.; m. Dorothy James, May 1970 (div. 1979); m. Lucy Alice Frazier, June 13, 1981; children: Sheena Rene, Lacey Christina. BS in Aerospace Engring., W.Va. U., 1970, MS in Indsl. Engring., 1973. Project engr. Naval Air Systems Commd., Washington, 1972-78, Air Force Logistics Command, Wright Patterson AFB, Ohio, 1978-81; engring. work leader Air Force Logistics Command, 1981-84; logistics mgmt. specialist Mil. Airlift Commd., Scott AFB, Ill., 1984-86; program mgr. Air Force Logistics Commd., Wright-Patterson AFB, 1986-91; chief mission requirements unit Edn. and Tng. Flight 88th Support Group, Wright-Patterson AFB, Ohio, 1991-95; chief ops. edn. and tng. office Mission Support Squadron, Wright-Patterson AFB, 1995—. Trustee Idle Hour Swim Club, Beavercreek, Ohio, 1990—; mem. Beavercreek Schs. Strategic Planning Com., 1990; asst. lay minister Peace Evang. Luth. Ch., Beavercreek, 1987—, asst. dir. evang., 1987-89, v.p. for ministries, 1992-96. Mem. ASTD, AIAA, Soc. Logistics Engrs., Fed. Mgrs. Assn. (pres. chpt. 271 1994), Inst. Indsl. Engrs. (chpt. v.p. 1983-84). Republican. Home: 3755 Olde Willow Dr Beavercreek OH 45431-2469 Office: 88 MSS/DPEO Ste 4 5215 Thorlow St Ste 4 Wright Patterson AFB OH 45433

WALLACE, ROBERT WELDON, classicist, educator; b. Balt., Mar. 20, 1950; s. Weldon and Flora C.C. (Murray) W.; m. Caroline Astrid Bruzelius, May 15, 1982 (div. Aug. 1994); 1 child, Anders. BA, Columbia U., 1972; MA, Oxford (Eng.) U., 1977; PhD, Harvard U., 1984. Asst. prof. N.C. State U., Raleigh, 1982-87; from asst. prof. to assoc. prof. Johns Hopkins U., Balt., 1987-91; assoc. prof. Greek, Latin & ancient history Northwestern U., Evanston, Ill., 1991—; vis. prof. U. Siena, Italy, 1992; master Chapin Coll., Northwestern U., Evanston, 1995—. Author: The Areopagos Council, to 307, 1989; editor: Harmonia Mundi, 1991. Recipient NEH award, 1991-92, award Consilio Nazionale, Italy, 1993—. Mem. Am. Philol. Assn. (monograph com. 1993—). Office: Northwestern U Dept Classics Evanston IL 60208

WALLACE, SAMUEL TAYLOR, hospital administrator; b. Blytheville, Ark., Sept. 2, 1943; s. Samuel Edward and Minnie (Taylor) W.; m. Sara Billow, Apr. 30, 1992. B.S., U. Mo., 1965; M.H.A., Washington U., St. Louis, 1970. Asst. adminstr. Hillcrest Med. Ctr., Tulsa, 1969-75; adminstr. St. Luke's Meth. Hosp., Cedar Rapids, Iowa, 1975-81, pres., 1981-95; pres. Iowa Health Sys., Des Moines, 1995—. Bd. dirs. Vol. Hosp. Am., Dallas, 1982-94; Cedar Rapids Symphony, 1993—; chmn. bd. dirs. Vol. Hosp. Iowa, Cedar Rapids, 1983—; bd. dirs. Cedar Rapids Pub. Libr., 1983; pres. bd. Cedar Rapids Community Theatre, 1983, Cedar Rapids coun. Boy Scouts Am., 1983. Served to capt. M.S.C. U.S. Amry, 1965-68, Vietnam. Recipient Silver Beaver award Boy Scouts Am., 1979, Silver Antelope award, 1992. Fellow Am. Coll. Healthcare Execs. (Iowa bd. regents 1982-85, 88—); mem. Iowa Hosp. Assn. (dir. 1982-85). Republican. Methodist. Lodge: Rotary (pres.-elect Cedar Rapids 1985, pres. 1986—). Office: Iowa Health Sys 1200 Pleasant Des Moines IA 50309-1453

WALLACE, SHAWN PATRICK, sales professional; b. Moline, Ill., Nov. 30, 1963; s. Robert David and Gretchen Joy (Wonderlich) W.; m. Pamela Sue Shorb, June 15, 1985; children: Ryan Scott, Paige Lynn. AS, Hamilton Tech. Coll., 1986. Warehouse night supr. Flick's, Moline, 1981-84; lawn specialist Chemlawn, Davenport, Iowa, 1984-85; midwest dist. mgr. Atlas Roofing Corp., East Moline, Ill., 1985—.

WALLACE, THEODORE CALVIN, state legislator; b. Kimball, W.Va., Dec. 31, 1941; s. Theodore Calvin Sr. and Bonnie (Goddard) W.; m. Bernice Marie Jones, 1987; children: Audrey Diane, Theodore C., III, Michael Scott Paritee. BS, Wright State U., 1973; JD, U. Mich., 1979. Atty. pvt. practice; state rep. Dist. 5 Mich. Ho. of Reps., 1988—, asst. minority floor leader, 1989—; vice chmn. Judiciary & Civil Rights Com. Mich. Ho. of Reps. Mem. issues com. Mich. NAACP; parliamentarian Nat. Black Caucus of State Legislators. Chief warrant officer Mich. Nat. Guard. Mem. Mich. Law Revision Commn., Mich. NAACP, Urban League. Home: 20500 Goddard St Apt 106 Detroit MI 48234-1352*

WALLACE, THOMAS PATRICK, university administrator; b. Washington, Apr. 11, 1935; 4 children. BS, SUNY, Potsdam, 1958; MS, Syracuse U., 1961, St. Lawrence U., 1964; PhD in Physical Chemistry, Clarkson U., 1968. Asst. prof. chemistry SUNY, Potsdam, 1961-67; Mellon Inst. fellow Carnegie-Mellon Inst., 1967-68; mem. faculty Rochester (N.Y.) Inst. Tech., 1968-78, assoc. prof., 1970-78, head dept. chemistry, 1970-72, assoc. dean, 1972-73, dean, 1973-78; prof. chem. scis. Old Dominion U., Norfolk, Va., 1978-86, dean sci. and health professions, 1978-83, v.p. acad. affairs, 1983-86; chancellor Ind. U.-Purdue U., Ft. Wayne, 1986-88; pres. Ill. State U., Normal, 1988—. Contbr. articles to profl. jours. Mem. Am. Chem. Soc. Office: Ill State U Office of Pres Normal IL 61761*

WALLACH, BARBARA PRICE, classicist, educator; b. Roanoke, Va., Aug. 31, 1946; d. Benjamin Thomas and Geneva Mae (Bittinger) Price; m. Luitpold Wallach, Aug. 22, 1970 (dec. Nov. 1986). BA in Latin, Mary Washington Coll., 1968; MA in Classics, U. Ill., 1970, PhD in Classical Philology, 1974. Summer vis. lectr. U. Ill., Urbana, 1977; vis. asst. prof. U. Pitts., 1979-80; asst. prof. U. Mo., Columbia, 1980-85, assoc. prof., 1985—. Author: Lucretius and the Diatribe, 1976; contbr. articles to profl. jours. Mem. Am. Philol. Assn., Classical Assn. Middle West and South, Internat. Soc. for the History of Rhetoric, Soc. for Ancient Greek Philosophy, Vergilian Soc., Internat. Plutarch Soc., Phi Beta Kappa. Democrat. Office: U Mo Dept Classical Studies Columbia MO 65211

WALLACH, JOHN S(IDNEY), library administrator; b. Toronto, Ohio, Jan. 6, 1939; s. Arthur M. and Alice I. (Smith) W.; children: John Michael, Wendy Anne, Bethany Lynne, Kristen Michele; m. Joyce Bapst. B.S. in Edn, Kent State U., 1963; M.L.S., U. R.I., 1968; M.P.A., U. Dayton, 1977. Dir. Mercer County (Ohio) Library, 1968-70, Greene County (Ohio) Library, 1970-77; asso. dir. Dayton and Montgomery County (Ohio) Library, 1978, dir., 1979—. Bd. dirs. Dayton Mus. Natrual History, Family Svc. Assn., Dayton, Technology Resource Ctr. Served with USN, 1963-68, capt. ret. Mem. ALA, Ohio Libr. Assn. Office: Dayton & Montgomery County Pub Libr 215 E 3rd St Dayton OH 45402-2103

WALLE, JAMES PAUL, lawyer; b. Detroit, Sept. 4, 1956; s. Leonard Julius and Mary Frances (Baigent) W.; m. Joanne Marie Albert, Aug. 23, 1986; children: Patrick Joseph, Michael James, Mary Elizabeth, Peter Richard. Honors BA summa cum laude, U. Detroit, 1977, JD- MBA cum laude, 1979; LLM, Wayne State U., 1986. Bar: Mich. 1980, U.S. Dist. Ct. (ea. and we. dists.) Mich. 1980, U.S. Ct. Appeals (6th cir.) 1980, U.S. Ct. Appeals (D.C. cir.) 1982, U.S. Supreme Ct. 1983. Law clk. to assoc. justice Mich. Supreme Ct., Detroit, 1980-82; atty. environ. law GM, Detroit, 1982—; teaching fellow Detroit Coll. Law, 1980-81; adj. prof. law U. Detroit, 1981-82, mem. planning com. environ. law seminar, U. Detroit Mercy Law Sch. Continuing Legal Edn., 1991; speaker in field U. Mo. Kansas City Sch. Law, 1991. Case and comment editor U. Detroit Law Rev., 1979-80; mem. editorial bd. Mich. Corp. Fin. and Bus. Law Jour. Vol. 3. Vol. legal services St. Benedict Cath. Ch., Highland Park, Mich., 1983-85. Mem. State Bar Mich. (environ. and energy law sect., subcom. 1983—, speaker young lawyers sect. 1983-86), Detroit Bar Assn. (pro bono atty. 1985-87, 89-91, 94—). Office: Office Gen Counsel GM Corp GM Bldg 3044 W Grand Blvd Rm 12-140 Detroit MI 48202

WALLEN, MARTHA LOUISE, foreign language educator; b. Mpls., Aug. 13, 1946; d. Clarence Melvin and Myrthel Evangeline (Nelson) W. BA summa cum laude, St. Olaf Coll., 1968; MA, U. Wis., 1969, PhD, 1972; MA, Middlebury Coll., 1976. From asst. prof. to prof. fgn. lang., fgn. lang. coordinator U. Wis.-Stout, Menomonie, 1972—. Contbr. articles to profl. jours.; asst. editor: Annals of Tourism Research, 1976—. Faculty grantee U. Wis., 1984-85, 90-95. Mem. Internat. Arthurian Soc., Am. Assn. Tchrs. French, Phi Beta Kappa. Lutheran. Office: U Wis-Stout Dept of Fgn Lang Menomonie WI 54751

WALLEN, RICHARD LEE, transportation executive; b. Omaha, Feb. 25, 1953; s. Eber and Darlena Mae (Stienblock) W.; m. Cecily Lucia Caniglia, July 15, 1972 (div. July 1976); 1 child, Nicole Ann; m. Kerrie Lynn Sedwick, Jan. 18, 1994; 1 stepchild, Annajo Marie. Grad. high sch., Omaha. Dir. safety ARA Transp., Omaha, 1976-84, Watts Trucking Service Nebr., Omaha, 1984; corp. dir. safety Watts Trucking Service, Inc., Rock Island, Ill., 1984—; instr. Level I State of Nebr., Omaha, 1982-83, Nat. Solid Waste Inst., Rock Island, 1986—. Mem. Assoc. Employers Quad City Accident Prevention Coun., Davenport, 1986-90; mem. Vol. Emergency Fire Search and Rescue, 1987-92; chief Scott County Rescue, Davenport, 1990-92; aux. police officer City of Milan, Ill., 1993—. Mem. Nat. Safety Mgmt. Soc. (cert. 1985), Am. Soc. Safety Engrs. (cert. 1988). Republican. Baptist. Office: Watts Trucking Svc Inc 525 17th St PO Box 5410 Rock Island IL 61204-5410

WALLENHORST, THOMAS, electrical engineer; b. Cin., Feb. 17, 1957. BSEE, Ohio State U., 1982. Customer mgr. Wren, Cin., 1982-88; elec. engr. Am. Laundry Machinery, Cin., 1988-92, Bus. Systems, Cin., 1992-94, LeBlond Makino Machine Tool Co., Mason, Ohio, 1994—; adv. bd. Cin. State Cmty. and Tech. Coll., 1995. Pres. Assumption Parish Credit Union, Cin., 1995. Office: LeBlond Makino Machine & Tool Co 7680 Innovation Way Mason OH 45040

WALLENHORST, TIMOTHY JAMES, newspaper executive; b. Berea, Ohio, Nov. 18, 1954; s. Albert John and Mary Louise (Lorig) W. BSBA, John Carroll U., 1976; M of Labor Rels. and Human Resources, Cleve. State U., 1992. Warehouse mgr. Manco Tape Co., Cleve., 1972-78; cost acct. Kirkwood Industries, Cleve., 1978-80; dist. mgr. Cleve. Plain Dealer, 1980—. Mem. John Carroll U. Alumni Assn., Cleve. State Alumni Assn., St. Edward High Sch. Alumni Assn., Cleve. West Road Runners Club, Iota Phi Theta. Democrat. Roman Catholic. Office: Cleve Plain Dealer 1801 Superior Ave E Cleveland OH 44114-2107

WALLER, ARLOU GILL, retired mental health specialist; b. Galatia, Ill., July 8, 1922; d. Palmer and Ethel Grace (Lewis) Brown; m. Lee Roy Gill, Oct. 9, 1943 (div. Sept. 1973); 1 child, Joan Ellen; m. Ira J. Waller, Jan. 30, 1976 (dec. Nov. 1986). Student, So. Ill. U., 1970-74; BA, Lewis and Clark U., 1977. Registered social worker; cert. tax. rep. Mental health specialist Ill. Dept. Mental Health, Alton, 1950-83; vol. tax instr. and preparer IRS and Am. Assn. Ret. Persons, Alton, 1985—. Author therapy program Deconfusion Therapy, 1971. Tax advisor Vita Sr. Svcs. Plus, Alton, 1985—; mem. People, Springfield, Ill., 1968—. Recipient award Nat. Psychiat. Assn., 1959. Mem. Am. Fedn. State, County and Mcpl. Employees (treas.), Metro East Retirees (pres. 1989-92), Nat. Assn. Tax Profls., Madison County Mental Health Assn. Democrat. Baptist. Home: 3432 1/2 Thomas Ave Alton IL 62002-4119

WALLER, DAVID T., engineering company executive; b. Sommerville, Mass., May 28, 1940. BS, U. Evansville, 1964; student, AT&T Data Comm. Tng. Ctr., Cooperstown, N.Y., 1966. Account specialist for data/voice Ind. Bell Tel. Co., Indpls., 1964-67; corp. data comm. mgr. Continental Tel. Corp., St. Louis, 1967-70; sales mgr. Western Union Data Svcs., Detroit, 1970-72; account exec. MCI Telecom., Detroit, 1973; pres. WALLCOMM Industries, Inc., Troy, Mich., 1973—. Mem. Troy Planning commn.; mem. president's adv. coun. Walsh Coll., Troy; mem. adv. bd. Met. Ctr. for High Tech., Detroit; mem. adv. com. Leadership Oakland, Oakland County, Mich.; mem. strategic planning com. Leadership Troy; bd. dirs. Troy Boys and Girls Club; mem. tech. coun. Seaholm H.S., Birmingham, Mich.; com. exec. troop 1034 Boy Scouts Am., Birmingham. Mem. Troy C. of C. (bd. dirs. 1988-94, Vol. of Yr. award 1994). Home: 2921 Townhill Dr Troy MI 48084-1053 Office: WALLCOMM Industries Inc 1760 Maplelawn Dr Troy MI 48084-4604

WALLER, ELAINE LOUISE, retired music materials librarian; b. New Cristobal, Panama Canal Zone, Aug. 29, 1918; parents Am. citizens; d. Ernest Roy and Irma Edna (Lewis) Johnson; m. John Oscar Waller, Jan. 6, 1946. BA, Pacific Union Coll., Angwin, Calif., 1942; MS in LS, U. Ill., 1970. Libr. paraprofl. James White Libr., Andrews U., Berrien Springs, Mich., 1960-70, cataloger, 1970-75, music materials libr., 1975-93. Mem. Libr. of Congress Assocs. (charter), Music OCLC Users Group (charter), Music Libr. Assn. Home: 8886 George Ave Berrien Springs MI 49103

WALLER, EPHRAIM EVERETT, retired professional association executive; b. Sioux City, Iowa, Aug. 10, 1928; s. Everett and Ruth Emma (Little) W.; m. Virginia Louise Harper, Oct. 3, 1959. BA, U. Iowa, 1951, MA, 1959; grad. with honors, Comd. and Gen. Staff Coll., 1966, State Dept. Fgn. Svc. Inst., 1967, Turkish Lang. Sch., 1968; EdD, U. S.D., 1981. Cert. fgn. area specialist, cryptologist. Commd. 2d lt. U.S. Army, 1951, advanced through grades to lt. col., 1967, retired, 1979; exec. dir. Midwest Agrl. Chems. Assn., Sioux City, Iowa, 1981-95; cons., 1996—; mem. sci. and regulatory oversight coun. Am. Crop Protection Assn., Washington, 1990-95; mem. interregional coord. coun. Joint Body U.S. Regional Agrl. Assns., Dawson, Ga., 1991-95. Contbr. numerous articles to profl. jours. Mem. coms. 1st Congrl. Ch., Sioux City, 1937—. Decorated Bronze Star, Cross of Gallantry with Silver Star, Legion of Merit with Oak Leaf Cluster, Chinese and Vietnamese Honor medals. Mem. Retired Officers Assn., Siouxland C. of C. (com. mem. 1981-95), Scottish Rite, Masons, Phi Delta Kappa, Delta Sigma Rho.

WALLER, KELLY SUE, investment broker; b. Monticello, Ill., May 25, 1969. BA, U. Ill., 1991. Investment broker A. G. Edwards & Sons Inc., Belleville, Ill., 1991—. Office: A G Edwards & Sons Inc PO Box 23918 3601 N Belt W Belleville IL 62223

WALLER, ROBERT REX, ophthalmologist, educator, foundation executive; b. N.Y.C., Feb. 19, 1937; s. Madison Rex and Sally Elizabeth (Pearce) W.; m. Sarah Elizabeth Pickens, Dec. 27, 1963; children: Elizabeth, Katherine, Robert Jr. BA, Duke U., 1958; MD, U. Tenn., 1963. Diplomate Am. Bd. Ophthalmology (dir. 1982—, vice chmn. 1988-89, chmn. 1989—). Intern City of Memphis Hosps., 1963-64; resident internal medicine Mayo Grad. Sch. Medicine, Rochester, Minn., 1966-67, resident in ophthalmology, 1967-70, mem. faculty, 1970—; assoc. prof. ophthalmology Mayo Clinic, Rochester, Minn., 1974-78, prof., 1978—; chmn. dept. ophthalmology Mayo Med. Sch., Rochester, Minn., 1974-84, cons., 1970—, mem. bd. govs., 1978-93, chmn., 1988-93; trustee Mayo Found., Rochester, 1978—, pres., chief exec. officer, 1988—. Contbr. chpts. to books, articles to profl. jours. Elder 1st Presbyn. Ch., Rochester, 1975-78; mem. Rochester Task Force on Pub. Assembly Facilities, 1983-84. Sr. asst. surgeon USPHS, 1964-66. Ocuplastic surgery fellow U. Calif. San Francisco, 1973. Mem. AMA, Minn. State Med. Assn., Zumbro Valley Med. Assn., Am. Acad. Ophthalmology, Am. Ophthalmol. Soc., Am. Soc. Plastic and Reconstructive Surgery, Orbital Soc., Am. Soc. Ophthalmic Plastic and Reconstructive Surgery, Minn. Acad. Ophthalmology and Otolaryngology, Rochester Golf and Country Club, Augusta Nat. Golf Club, Alpha Omega Alpha, Delta Tau Delta. Presbyterian. Home: 800 12th Ave SW Rochester MN 55902-2071

WALLESTAD, PHILIP WESTON, retired business owner; b. Madison, Wis., May 14, 1922; s. John Oscar and Dorothy Francis (White) W.; BA, U. Wis., 1947, MD, 1954; m. Edith Stolle, Jan. 15, 1949 (div. Mar. 1967); children: Kristin Eve, Ingrid Birgitta, Erika Ann; m. 2d, Muriel Annette Moen, June 22, 1968; children: Thomas John, Scott Philip. Intern, Calif. Luth. Hosp., L.A., 1954, resident in surgery, 1955-56; pvt. practice medicine, Fredonia and Port Washington Wis., 1957-72, Libby, Mont., 1972-74; staff physician VA Hosp., Fort Harrison, Mont., 1974-77, Tomah, Wis., 1977-78, VA Hosp., Iron Mountain, Mich., 1978-88, ret., 1989; owner Wallestad's Arms, mil. antique collectables store, Sturgeon Bay, Wis., 1989-95, ret., 1995. Mem. Conservative Caucus. Served with AUS, 1943-46; ETO; lt. col. USAF Res., 1979-82. Mem. NRA, DAV, VFW, Am. Legion, Air Force Assn., Conservative Caucus, Res. Officers Assn., Sons of Norway, Coun. for Inter-Am. Security, U. Wis. Alumni Assn., Nat. W Club, Rotary. Republican. Presbyterian Ch. (elder). Home: 443 N 12th Ave Sturgeon Bay WI 54235-1313

WALLINGFORD, ANNE, writer, marketing consultant; b. Chgo., June 29, 1949; d. Lester Arlyn and Roseanne (Jones) W. BS in Edn., Chgo. State U., 1975. Cert. elem. and mid. sch. tchr., Ill. Profl. dressmaker Annie's Original's, Chgo., 1968-72; instr., asst. prin., St. Bonaventure Sch., Chgo., 1972-81; instr., chairperson sci. dept. Our Lady of Lourdes Sch., Chgo., 1981-88; product designer, catalog mgr. FSC Ednl., Inc., Mansfield, Ohio, 1988-91; founder, dir. The Wordsmiths, Chgo., 1992—. Contbr. bus. profiles to profl. publs., 1990—. Active The Vol. Ctr., Mansfield, 1992-93, steering com. Wright Community Ctr., 1991; treas. Wolfram St. Block Club, Chgo., 1975-78. Recipient Gold award Adler Planetarium, Chgo., 1985. Mem. Nat. Writers's Union, Chgo., Women in Pub. (Individual Excellence in Prodn., 1994, 95), Soc. Tech. Communicators, Profl. Freelance Assn. (founder, pres., 1991-92), Mensa. Office: 6155 N Moody Ave Chicago IL 60646-3806

WALLIS, ELIZABETH SUSAN, air traffic control specialist; b. Tulsa, Dec. 20, 1953; d. Ralph David and Margaret Ella (Nolen) W. Student, Drury Coll., 1972-73; BS, U. Ark., 1976. Placement interviewer Okla. Employment Svc., Tulsa, 1977-78; air traffic control specialist FAA Houston, 1978-84, regional staff specialist, L.A., 1984-85, plans and programs specialist, Olathe, Kans., 1985, supervisory air traffic control specialist, 1985-87; Cen. Region quality assurance specialist FAA, 1987-89, Cen. Region NAS implementation specialist, 1989-91; asst. air traffic mgr. Kansas City (Mo.) Internat. Air Traffic Control Tower, 1991-93; Cen. Region resource mgmt. br. mgr., 1993-95, asst. mgr. for tng., Olathe, 1995—. Bd. dirs. Westmont Homes Assn., 1987-89. Mem. Profl. Women Controllers (charter, cen. regional area dir. 1985-86, nat. sec. 1987-89), Air Traffic Control Assn., Women's Leadership Inst. Avocation: travel, quilting. Office: FAA ACE-520 601 E 12th St Kansas City MO 64106-2808

WALLIS, LLOYD RANDALL, accountant; b. Princeton, Ind., Aug. 6, 1954; s. Randall R. and Gladys V. (Husk) W.; m. Linda K. White, June 14, 1975; 1 child, Chad. BS in Acctg., U. Evansville, 1977. CPA, Ind. Contr. Home Fed. Savs. & Loan, Evansville, Ind., 1973-77; ptnr. Gaither Rutherford & Co., Evansville, Ind., 1977—. Pres. S.W. Ind. Easter Seals Soc., Evansville, 1985-86; allocations cabinet mem. S.W. Ind. United Way, 1993-95. Named Exec. of Yr. Evansville chpt. Profl. Secs. Internat., 1989. Mem. Inst. Mgmt. Accts. (bd. dirs. Evansville chpt. 1978-91, pres. 1990-91), Ind. CPA Soc. (fin. instns. com. chmn. 1988-89, pres. Evansville chpt. 1988-89, quality rev. com. 1989-91, chmn. 1991-93, bd. dirs. 1993—), Northside Kiwanis (pres. 1984-85, bd. dirs. 1993-95), Inst. Mgmt. Acct. Ednl. Found. (bd. dirs. Evansville chpt. 1993).

WALLIS, MICHAEL VAN, manufacturing manager; b. Galesburg, Ill., Sept. 4, 1961; s. Raymond Albert Wallis and Marelyn Mae (Vander Wert) Verner; 1 child, Alexander Joel. BS in Adminstrv. Scis., So. Ill. U., Carbondale, 1983. Ops. supr., acct. rep., terminal mgr. Roadway Express, Inc., St. Louis, Ill., 1983-94; branch mgr. The Fruehauf Trailer Corp., St. Louis, 1994—. Mem. U.S. Parachute Assn., Am. Assn. Indsl. Mgmt., Aircraft Owners and Pilots Assn., World Trade Club St. Louis. Republican. Methodist. Home: 1001 Oak Glen Cir Ballwin MO 63021-7481 Office: 3944 Duncan Ave Saint Louis MO 63110

WALLIS, WALTER DENIS, mathematician, researcher; b. Sydney, NSW, Australia, June 26, 1941; came to U.S., 1985; s. Walter Edwin and Olive May (Roche) W.; m. Denise Alice Nisbet, Aug. 25, 1984. BSc, U. Sydney, 1963, PhD, 1968. Lectr. math. Latrobe U., Melbourne, Australia, 1967-70; sr. lectr., assoc. prof. U. Newcastle, Australia, 1970-85; prof. U. So. Ill., Carbondale, 1985—. Author: Combinatorial Designs, 1988; co-author: Combinatorics-Room Squares; Sum-free Sets; Hadamard Matrices, 1972, Combinatorial Theory-An Introduction, 1977, Combinatorics-A First Course, 1985; editor: Computational and Constructive Design Theory, 1996; editor Jour. Combinatorial Math. and Combinatorial Computing. Fellow Inst. of Combinatorics and Its Applications (founding fellow); mem. Am. Math. Soc., Math. Assn. Am., Combinatorial Math. soc. of Australasia. Office: So Ill U Dept of Math Research Carbondale IL 62901

WALLJASPER, DAVE LEROY, fender engineer; b. Burlington, Iowa, Apr. 11, 1959. BS in Mech. Engring, Iowa State U., 1988. Engring. mgr. Trellex Morese, Keokuk, Iowa, 1988-94; fender engr. Trellex Morese, Keokuk, 1995—; field specialist Iowa State U. Extension Svcs., Davenport, Iowa, 1994-95. Mem. ASME. Office: Trellex Morse 3588 Main St Keokuk IA 42632

WALLMAN, CHARLES JAMES, historian; b. Kiel, Wis., Feb. 19, 1924; s. Charles A. and Mary Ann (Loftus) W.; m. Charline Marie Moore, June 14, 1952; children: Stephen, Jeffrey, Susan, Patricia, Andrew. Student Marquette U., 1942-43, Tex. Coll. Mines, 1943-44; BBA, U. Wis., 1949. Sales promotion mgr. Brandt, Inc., Watertown, Wis., 1949-65, v.p., 1960-70, exec. v.p., 1970-80, v.p. corp. devel., 1980-83, past dir.; written formal paper to the inst. "The 48ers of Watertown", presented orally at Symposium U. Wis.-Madison (Inst. for German-Am. Studies), 1986, written formal paper "Business, Industry and the German Press in Early Watertown, Wis., 1853-65", presented orally at symposium U. Wis.-Madison Inst. for German-Am. Studies, 1987; guest speaker dept. German, U. Wis.-Madison, 1987; dir., sec. The Friends of the Max Kade Inst. for German Am. Studies U. Wis.-Madison. Author: Edward J. Brandt, Inventor, 1984, Pioneer Memoirs of Early Watertown, 1986, The Joe Davies Scholars, 1988, The German-Speaking Forty-Eighters: Builders of Watertown, Wisconsin, 1990, Built on Irish Faith, 150 Years at St. Bernard's, 1994, (with others) The Prisoners of War of the 12th Armored Division, 1988. Former mem. exec. bd. Potawatomi council Boy Scouts Am., also former v.p. council; former bd. dirs., former pres. Earl and Eugenia Quirk Found., Inc. Trustee, mem. Joe Davies Scholarship Found.; former bd. dirs., former exec. com. mem. Watertown Meml. Hosp., dir. emeritus. Served with armored inf. AUS, 1943-45; ETO. Decorated Bronze Star; recipient Local History Award of Merit, State Hist. Soc. Wis., 1994. Mem. Am. Legion, E. Central Golf Assn. (past pres.), Wis. Alumni Assn. (local pres. 1950-52, 89-91, bd. dirs. nat. orgn. 1989-91), 12th Armored Div. Assn., Watertown Hist. Soc. (bd. dirs.), Am. Ex-Prisoners of War, Inc., Phi Delta Theta. Republican. Roman Catholic. Club: Watertown County (past dir.). Lodges: Rotary (past pres., former bd. dirs., Paul Harris fellow), Elks (past officer). Home: 604 Votech Dr Watertown WI 53098-1124

WALLS, LARRY E., design engineer; b. Niles, Mich., Mar. 3, 1969; s. Floyd Earl and Darla Jean (Klute) W.; m. Cheryl Ann Hurley Walls, Sept. 3, 1994. AA in Tool Engring. Tech., ITT Inst., 1989. Design draftsman Able Engring. Inc., South Bend, Ind., 1989—. Home: 1434 Marion St Niles MI 49120-3861 Office: Able Engring 3605 Gagnon St South Bend IN 46628-4366

WALLS, THOMAS FRANCIS, management consultant; b. Phila., June 4, 1947; s. Thomas Francis and Margaret Mary (Whalen) W.; m. Kathleen Cecilia Lyons, Dec. 7, 1968; children: Thomas, James, Eleanor. ABA in Econs., U. Pa., 1974, BBA in Mgmt., 1977. Cert. practitioner inventory mgmt. Programmer Gen. Elec. Re-entry Systems, King of Prussia, Pa., 1965-69; mgr. Keane Assocs., Paoli, Pa., 1969-73, Alco Standard Corp., Valley Forge, Pa., 1973-80, Comserv Corp., Mendota Heights, Minn., 1980-88; mgr. Andersen Cons., Chgo., 1988-89, Phila., 1989-95; with Andersen Cons., St. Charles, Ill., 1995—. Contbg. author: APICS Dictionary. With USNR, 1967-68, Vietnam. Mem. Am. Prodn. and Inventory Control Soc. Roman Catholic. Office: Andersen Cons 1405 N Fifth Ave Saint Charles IL 60174

WALLSCHLAEGER, JOSEPHINE INGEBORG, mental health nurse; b. Montevideo, Minn., Nov. 20, 1942; d. Carl J. and Gertrude G. (Qualley) Nerison; m. Joseph F. Wallschlaeger, Aug. 6, 1967; children: Joseph, Melanie. BSN, Augustana Coll., Sioux Falls, S.D., 1965. Cert. psychiat.-mental health nurse, ANA. Staff nurse U.S. Army Nurse Corps, Washington, 1965; asst. head nurse U.S. Army Nurse Corps, Vung Tau, Vietnam, 1966; recruiter U.S. Army Nurse Corps, Indpls., 1967; dir. nursing Granite Falls (Minn.) Hosp., 1968; staff nurse Mankato (Minn.) House Nursing Home, 1973; staff nurse, access Immanuel-St. Joseph's Hosp., Mankato, 1974-92; night supr. St. Peter (Minn.) Regional Treatment Ctr., 1992—; instr. Mankato State U., 1991-94. Leader Cub Scouts Boy Scouts Am, Mankato, 1975-86; leader Girl Scouts U.S.A., 1977-80; v.p. PTA, Washington Sch., Mankato, 1975-78; vol. ARC, Makato, 1971—; mem. State Adv. Coun. for Mental Health, 1992-96. Recipient Amb. award City of Mankato, 1991. Mem. ANA, Minn. Nurses Assn. (pracice com., del., Excellence award 1991), Sigma Theta Tau. Lutheran.

WALNER, ROBERT JOEL, lawyer; b. Chgo., Dec. 22, 1946; s. Wallace and Elsie W.; m. Charlene Walner; children: Marci, Lisa. BA, U. Ill., 1968; JD, De Paul U., 1972; M in Mgmt. with distinction, Northwestern U., 1991. Bar: Ill. 1972, U.S. Dist. Ct. (no. dist.) Ill. 1972, U.S. Ct. Appeals (7th cir.) 1972, Fla. 1973. Atty. SEC, Chgo., 1972-73; pvt. practice Chgo., 1973—; adminstrv. law judge Ill. Commerce Commn., Chgo., 1973-76; atty. Allied Van Lines, Inc., Broadview, Ill., 1976-79; sr. v.p., gen. counsel, sec. The Balcor Co., Skokie, Ill., 1979-92; prin. fin. ops. Balcor Securities divsn. The Balcor Co., Skokie, 1984-92, pres., 1989-92; of counsel Lawrence, Walner & Assocs., Ltd., Chgo., 1992-93; sr. v.p., gen. counsel, sec. Grubb & Ellis Co., San Francisco, 1994—; mem. securities adv. com. to Ill. Sec. of State, 1984-94; mem. editl. bd. Real Estate Securities Jour., Real Estate Securities and Capital Markets; program chmn. Regulators and You seminar. Contbr. chpts. to books, articles on real estate and securities law to profl. jours.; assoc. editor De Paul U. Law Rev. Mem. Kellogg Career Devel. Com., 1992—, Kellogg Bus. Adv. Com., 1992—; mem. enterprise forum MIT, 1992—, mem. exec. com., 1993-94. With USAR, 1968-73. Mem. ABA, Ill. Bar Assn., Chgo. Bar Assn., Am. Real Estate Com. (pres. com. 1985-90), Real Estate Syndication Com. (chmn. 1982-85), Ill. Inst. Continuing Legal Edn., N.Am. Securities Adminstrs. Assn. Inc. (industry adv. com. to real estate com., 1987-89), Real Estate Securities and Syndication Inst. of Nat. Assn. Realtors (chmn. regulatory and legis. com., 1984, 87, specialist, real estate investment, group v.p., 1987, exec. com. 1987-90), Nat. Real Estate Investment Forum (chmn. 1985, 88), Real Estate Investment Assn. (founder, exec. com. 1990-92), Beta Gamma Sigma.

WALRATH, JOE BILL, secondary education educator; b. Gainesville, Mo., Dec. 14, 1967; s. Pawnee Bill and Mary Francis (Harley) W.; m. Pamela Denise Davis, Mar. 28, 1992. BS in social studies, Coll. Ozarks, 1991, teaching cert., 1991. Mgr. Western Auto., Gainesville, 1991—; tchr. history, softball coach Lutie RVI Sch. Dist., 1995—. Sch. bd. mem. Gainesville R-V Sch. Bd., Gainesville, 1993—. Recipient Lion's Club scholarship, 1986, Luna Tchr.'s scholarship Gainesville H.S., 1986, Murray Diplomatic Hist. award Coll. Ozarks, 1990. Republican. Home: HCR-4 Box 180-2 Gainesville MO 65655

WALSH, ALAN JOHN, architect; b. Milan, Ind., Mar. 14, 1947; s. John Leslie and Ruth Marie (Brower) W.; m. Brenda Jean Zehner, Oct. 27, 1967 (div. Oct. 1987); children: Jeffrey Alan, Anthony Brett; m. Arlene B. Thayer, June 12, 1993. Student, Vincennes (Ind.) U., 1965-67, Oakland City (Ind.) Coll., 1967. Prin. architect Walsh Architects, Bloomington, Ind., 1979—, Schick-Walsh Architects, Bloomington, 1979-82; owner Walsh Properties, Nashville, Ind., 1983-93, Keystone Devel., Bloomington, 1988-93; mktg. exec. Melaleuca, Inc., 1991—. Mem. Nat. Coun. Archtl. Registration Bds. Home: 2471S Scarce-O-Fat Ridge Rd Nashville IN 47448 Office: Walsh Architects 2471 S Scarce Fat Ridge Rd Nashville IN 47448

WALSH, JOSEPH, policy analyst, educator, social worker; b. Evanston, Ill., Dec. 27, 1961; m. Laura Jo; 3 children. BA, U. Iowa, 1985; MA, U. Chgo., 1991. Rep. candidate 9th dist. Ill. U.S. House of Reps., 1996. Roman Catholic. Office: 1311 Livingston Evanston IL 60201*

WALSH, JOSEPH LEO, III, lawyer; b. St. Louis, Dec. 7, 1954; s. Joseph Leo and Joan Marie (Bocklage) W.; m. Eileen Rose Boland, June 11, 1982; children: Katie Rose, Joseph L. IV, Brian James, John Patrick. BS cum laude, Loras Coll., 1977; JD, St. Mary's U., 1984. Bar: Tex. 1984, U.S. Dist. Ct. (so. dist.) Tex. 1985, Mo. 1986, U.S. Dist. Ct. (ea. dist.) Mo. 1989, U.S. Ct. Appeals (8th cir.) 1989, U.S. Supreme Ct. 1991. Assoc. Chamberlain, Hrdlicka, White, Johnson & Williams, Houston, 1984-86; atty. Haley, Fredrickson & Walsh, St. Louis, 1986-88; assoc. Gray & Ritter, St. Louis, 1988-95; sole practitioner St. Louis, 1995—; pro bono legal clinic St. Patrick Ctr., 1991—; jud. clk. U.S. Dist. Ct. (we. dist.) Tex., 1984. Co-author: Missouri Bar CLE Treatise on Torts, 2d edit., 1990; sr. assoc. editor St. Mary's U. Sch. Law Jour., 1983-84. Mem. Holly Hills Neighborhood Assn., 1991-93. Recipient Torts and Evidence award Lawyers' Co-op Pub. Co., 1982; named to Nat. Order Barristers, 1984. Mem. ABA (litigation sect., tort and ins. sect.), Assn. Trial Lawyers Am., Mo. Assn. Trial Attys., Bar Assn. Met. St. Louis, Lawyers Assn. St. Louis, St. Louis County Bar Assn., Phi Delta Phi (pres. 1984). Roman Catholic. Home: 10469 White Bridge Ln Saint Louis MO 63141 Office: Joseph L Walsh PC 10829 Olive Blvd Ste 202 Saint Louis MO 63141

WALSH, THOMAS JAMES, state senator; b. Chgo., July 4, 1960; s. William Dowdle and Barbara Ann (Kennedy) W. BBA, Loras Coll., 1982. Lic. real estate salesperson. From sales rep. to pub. rels. mgr. Binks Mfg. Co., Franklin Park, Ill., 1982—; state rep. State of Ill., Springfield, 1992—; state senator, 1994—. Commr. Met. Water Reclamation Dist. of Greater Chgo., 1988-90, chmn. Engring. com., Health and Pub. Welfare com.; active LaGrange Park Caucus, LaGrange Park Libr., St. Francis Xavier Ch., LaGrange. Mem. Irish Fellowship Club Chgo., Phoenix Soc. of Community Family Svc. and Mental Health Assn., LaGrange Kiwanis, Loras Coll. Alumni Club Chgo. Office: State of Ill 10544 W Cermak Rd Westchester IL 60154-5202

WALSTAD, JOHN MICHAEL, lawyer, code revisor; b. Minot, N.D., June 23, 1952; s. Harris O. and Alyce D. (Cuffe) W.; m. Jeanne L. Albrecht, Aug. 28, 1981; children: Jesse, Daniel, Matthew. Student, N.D. State U., Fargo, 1970-72; BA, Minot State Coll., 1975; JD, U. N.D., 1978. Bar: N.D., 1978. Atty. pvt. practice Bismarck, N.D., 1978-80; atty. State Bar Assn., Bismarck, 1980-81; atty N.D. Legislative Coun., Bismarck, 1981—, code revisor, 1993—. Office: ND Legislative Coun 600 E Boulevard Ave Bismarck ND 58505

WALSTON, LOLA INGE, dietitian; b. Chgo., Jan. 26, 1943; d. Willy and Ingeborg (Smith) Neumann; m. Steven Ward Walston, Aug. 5, 1967; children: Bradley, Scott. BS, No. Ill. U., 1965; MS, U. Iowa, 1967. Registered, lic. dietitian. Asst. dietary dir. Alaska Hosp. Med. Ctr., Anchorage, 1975-78; cons. dietitian Mercer County Hosp., Coldwater, Ohio, 1979; profl. service cons. Health Care and Retirement Corp. Am., Lima, Ohio, 1981-84; dietary dir. Estes Health Care Ctr., Montgomery, Ala., 1979-80, Mercy Meml. Hosp., Urbana, Ohio, 1984-86, Dairy & Nutrition Council Mid East, Dayton, Ohio, 1987-89; cons. Sharonview Nursing Home, South Vienna, Ohio, 1987—; Miami Health Care Ctr., Troy, Ohio, Columbia House, Springfield, Ohio, SCOPE Nutrition Program for the elderly, Fairborn, Ohio, CLS Nutrition Program, Bellefontaine, Ohio, 1987-90, Westview Acres Care Ctr., Eaton, Ohio, 1988—, St. John's Nursing Home, Springfield, 1989—, Oakwood Village, Springfield, 1989—, Villa Springfield, Springfield, Ohio, 1990—, Covington (Ohio) Care Ctr., 1990-91, Champaign Nursing Home, 1993—, Covenant House, 1993. Mem. com. Tecumseh council Boy Scouts Am., 1984—, Tri-County Community Action Commn./CLS Nutrition, Bellefontaine, Ohio, 1987-90. Mem. Am. Dietetic Assn., Ohio Dietetic Assn., Ohio Cons. Dietitians Health Care Facilities (chmn. 1982-84), Dayton Dietetic Assn., AAUW. Club: Hilltoppers (Fairborn, Ohio) (pres. 1982-83). Avocations: camping, sewing, knitting, crocheting, cooking.

WALTER, JAMES SMILEY, physiologist, researcher; b. Charleston, W.Va., Dec. 12, 1946; s. Andrew Tainter and Jane (Smiley) W.; m. Carolyn Calhoun, Aug. 4, 1979; children: James Calhoun, Claire Jane. BS, Chgo. State U., 1972, MS, 1976; PhD, Chgo. Med. Sch., 1982. Postdoctoral fellow Chgo. Med. Sch., North Chicago, Ill., 1983-85; rsch. physiologist Hines (Ill.) VA Hosp., 1985—; adj. assoc. prof. urology Loyola U. Med. Sch., Maywood, Ill., 1989—. Contbr. articles to Am. Jour. Physiology, Jour. Urology, Neurology and Urodynamic. Bd. dirs., bd. trustees Unitarian Universalist Ch., Oak Park, Ill., 1990-93. VA grantee 1988—. Mem. IEEE Engring. in Medicine and Biology Assn., Neurosci. Assn., Am. Urological Assn. Home: 124 S Grove Ave Oak Park IL 60302-2806

WALTERMAN, SCOTT A., mechanical engineer; b. Menomonee, Wis., June 21, 1966. BSME, U. Milw., 1988. Design engr. Marquette Electronics, Milw., 1989-92, O & S Designs, Menomonee, 1993—; applications engr. Profl. Control Corp., Germantown, Wis., 1992-93. Home: 2748 N Hackett Ave Milwaukee WI 53211-3856 Office: O & S Designs W 146 N9362 Held Dr Menomonee Falls WI 53051-1643

WALTERS, D. ERIC, biochemistry educator; b. Circleville, Ohio, Jan. 20, 1951; s. David E. and Sarah G. (Riley) W.; m. Gale Climenson, 1994; children: Abigail Lee, Matthew Steven. BS in Pharmacy, U. Wis., 1974; PhD in Medicinal Chemistry, U. Kans., 1978. Postdoctoral researcher Ind. U., Bloomington, 1978-79; rsch. scientist Kraft Foods, Glenview, Ill., 1979-82, Searle Pharm. Co., Skokie, Ill., 1982-85; group leader NutraSweet Co., Mount Prospect, Ill., 1985-91; assoc. prof. Chgo. Med. Sch., North Chicago, Ill., 1991—; adj. asst. prof. U. Ill., Chgo., 1987-91; cons. pharm., food, software cos.; mem. spl. study sects. NSF, Washington, 1983-84. Author: Opiates, 1986; editor: Sweeteners: Discovery, Molecular Design, Chemoreception, 1991; referee Jour. Medicinal Chemistry, Chem. Senses; contbr. articles to profl. jours. Mem. Am. Chem. Soc. (Agr. and Food Chemistry Divsn. Platinum award 1994), Bread for the World, Woodstock Inst. for Sci. and Humanitites. Lutheran. Office: Chgo Med Sch Dept Biol Chemistry 3333 Green Bay Rd North Chicago IL 60064-3037

WALTERS, GWENDOLYN MAE (WALLACE), nursing educator, clinical specialist; b. Northville, Mich., Feb. 15, 1943; d. Leo William and Marian Ruth (Lamb) Wallace; m. John Patrick Walters, Aug. 3, 1968; children: Daniel, Debra, David, Douglas. BSN, Mercy Coll. Detroit, 1971; MSN, Madonna U., 1992. RN, Mich., Ohio. Practical nurse New Grace Hosp., Detroit, 1970-71, RN, 1971; RN in-house contingent staff St. Mary Hosp., Livonia, 1972-73; primary care nurse critical care unit Met. West Hosp., Westland, Mich., 1974-79, newspaper reporter, chairperson nursing care rev., peer rev. and coronary care coms., 1975-81, pharmacy nurse IV ad mixture and acute care, 1979-80, team leader Outpatient Clinic, 1980-81; contingent staffing SRT Med-Staff Internat., 1981-83; staff nurse, team leader, charge nurse critical care div. Saratoga Hosp., Detroit, 1981-83; staff nurse critical care div. Providence Hosp., 1983-84; nursing faculty ADN program Henry Ford Community Coll., Dearborn, Mich., 1984-91; RN in-house contingent staffing and med./surg. units U. Mich. Med. Ctr., 1988-90; nurse Favorite Nurses, Southfield, Mich., 1990-91, Nurses, Inc., Southfield, Mich., 1990-92, STAT Health Svcs., Inc., Southfield, Mich., 1992—; nursing instr. staff devel. VA Med. Ctr., Allen Park, Mich., 1992-93; nursing faculty Med. Coll. Ohio Sch. Nursing, Toledo, 1994—. Vol. adult leader Sr. Assistance Program, Detroit, 1986—, Appalachia Svc. Project, Johnson City, Tenn., 1986—; vol. leader Care for the Homeless, Detroit, 1984—; vol. med. staff nurse UAW Black Lake Camp and Conference Ctr., Detroit, 1977-81;vol. Focus Hope-Assistance to the Elderly, Pontiac, 1980—; mem. Am. Heart Assn.; mentor nursing career Girl Scouts U.S., Livonia, 1990—. Mem. ANA (cert. continuing edn. and staff devel., del. conv. Houston chpt. 1980), AACN, Acad. Med.-Surg. Nurses, Mich. Nurses Assn., Detroit Dist. Nurses Assn. (bd. dirs. 1978, 79, med./surg. membership com.), Mich. League for Nursing (nurse practice com.), Sigma Theta Tau (Kappa Iota and Zeta Theta chpts.). Mem. United Methodist Ch. Home: 34415 Wallace Ct Livonia MI 48150-2692 Office: Med Coll Ohio Sch Nursing 3355 Glendale Ave Toledo OH 43699

WALTERS, JEFFERSON BROOKS, musician, retired real estate broker; b. Dayton, Ohio, Jan. 20, 1922; s. Jefferson Brooks and Mildred Frances (Smith) W.; m. Mary Elizabeth Espey, Apr. 6, 1963 (dec. July 22, 1983); children: Dinah Christine Basson, Jefferson Brooks; m. Carol Elaine Clayton Gillette, Feb. 19, 1984. Student, U. Dayton, 1947. Composer, cornetist Dayton, 1934—, real estate broker, 1948-88; ret., 1988. Condr., composer choral, solo voice settings of psalms and poetry Alfred Lord Tennyson; composer Crossing the Bar (meml. performances U.S. Navy band), 1961; composer The Yorktown Grand March (Good Citizenship medal SAR, 1988). Founder Am. Psalm Choir, 1965; apptd. deferred giving officer Kettering (Ohio) Med. Ctr., 1982-85. Served with USCGR, 1942-45, PTO, ETO. Mem. SAR, Greater Dayton Antique Study Club (past pres.), Dayton Art Inst., Montgomery County Hist. Soc., Masons (32d deg.). Brethren Ch. Home: 4113 Roman Dr Dayton OH 45415-2423

WALTERS, JOE ALDRICH, lawyer; b. Youngstown, Ohio, Jan. 28, 1920; m. Lois Pratt; children: Susan Holmes, William Walters, Ann Walters. BA, U. Minn., 1946, LLB, 1947. Bar: Minn. 1947, U.S. Dist. Ct. 1948, U.S. Ct. Appeals (8th cir.) 1951, D.C. 1964, U.S. Supreme Ct. 1967; cert. civil trial specialist. Ptnr. O'Connor & Hannan, Mpls., 1958—; bd. dirs. Possis Corp., Mpls. With U.S. Army, 1943-46. Mem. ABA, Minn. Bar Assn., D.C. Bar Assn., Mpls. Club, Univ. Club (Washington). Office: O'Connor & Hannan 700 Baker Bldg 706 2nd Ave S Minneapolis MN 55402

WALTERS, JOEL M., school system administrator; b. Detroit Lakes, Minn., Jan. 2, 1945; s. Ernie and Vivian (Thomsen) W.; m. Ruth ann Winemiller, Aug. 7, 1966; children: Kimberly Jo Walters Steger, Jeffrey Bryan. BA, Wayne State Coll., 1967; MS in Edn., Ctrl. Mo. State U., 1974, EdS, 1980. Bus. edn. tchr., coach ALC Cmty. Sch. Dist., Lineville, Iowa, 1967-68, Fairfax (Mo.) H.S., 1972-75; prin. South Iron H.S., Annapolis, Md., 1975-78; asst. to dean continuing edn. Ctrl. Mo. State U., Warrensburg, 1978-80, asst. dir. placement, 1980-82; asst. exec. dir. Pub. Sch. Retirement Sys., Jefferson City, Mo., 1982—; pres. Mo. Assn. Pub. Employment Retirement Sys., Jefferson City, 1994—. With U.S. Army, 1968-72, Vietnam. Home: 2015 Sandra Ln Jefferson City MO 65101 Office: Pub Sch Retirement Mo PO Box 268 Jefferson City MO 65102-0268

WALTERS, MICHAEL S., mechanical engineer; b. Cin., Mar. 9, 1968. BSME, U. Dayton, Ohio, 1990; postgrad., Ashland (Ohio) U. Product engr. DC Enterprises, Cin., 1990-94; design engr. Nordson Advanced Gasketing Tech., Cleve., 1994—; adv. bd. CE Cert. Bd., Cleve., 1994—. Mem. Ross Hawks Semi-pro baseball, Cinn., 1992-93, J.C.'s Semi-pro baseball, Cleve., 1994—. Mem. ASME. Roman Catholic. Office: Nordson AGT 28601 Clemens Rd Cleveland OH 44145-1148

WALTERS, NANCY LU, medical services educator; b. Luverne, Minn., Sept. 25, 1938; d. H. Calvin and Bijou (Stockton) Knock; divorced; children: Mary Patricia, Anthony Thomas, Deborah Kay. AB, Lindenwood Coll., 1960. Med. technologist St. Joseph Hosp., Kirkwood, Mo., 1960-63, Good Samaritan Hosp., Vincennes, Ind., 1963-65; chief med. technologist Johnson County Meml. Hosp., Franklin, Ind., 1965-68; health occupations coord. Ind. Vocat. Tech. Coll., Tippewa Tech. Inst., Lafayette, Ind., 1968-70; head allied health dept. Cin. Tech. Coll., 1970-76, coord. med. assts., 1976—. Mem. profl. edn. com. Am. Cancer Soc., Cin., 1976-82; bd. dirs. ACLU, Cin., 1988—; bd. dirs. ACLU Ohio, 1992, sec. exec. com., 1993-95, pres., 1995—; bd. dirs. Cin. chpt. Ind. Voters Ohio, 1975-77, Cin. Women's Polit. Caucus, 1994—; mem. various coms. Hyde Park Cmty. United Meth. Ch., Cin., 1986—, chmn. singles com., 1983-86, chmn. stewardship com., 1983-86, chmn. coun. on ministries, 1987-90, lay del. to ann. conf., 1992—, chmn. adminstrv. bd., 1994—. Recipient Drummer's award Cin. Conv. and Vis. Bur., 1978. Mem. Am. Soc. Allied Health Professions (bd. dirs. 1976-79), Am. Assn. Med. Assts. (curriculum rev. bd. 1993—, vice chmn. 1994—), Ohio Soc. Allied Health Professions (pres. 1981-82), Ohio Soc. Med. Assts. (sec. 1993-94), Ohio Soc. Med. Technologists, Woman's City Club (women's com. 1993—), Single Parent Ctr. Club (group leader). Democrat. Home: 1317 Grace Ave Cincinnati OH 45208-2427 Office: Cin Tech Coll 3520 Central Pky Cincinnati OH 45223-2612

WALTERS, TOM FREDERICK, manufacturing company official; b. Des Moines, Oct. 18, 1931; s. Basil Leon and Reah E. (Handy) W.; m. Mary Katherine Russell, Dec. 8, 1956; children: Karen E., Juliet M., Thomas R., Alexandra K., Suzanne C. BA, Beloit Coll., 1953; postgrad., Northwestern U., 1962-66. Sales and advt. staff Eaton, Yale & Towne, Chgo., 1956-62, prodn. mgr., 1962-65; sr. cons. Cresap, McCormick & Paget, Chgo., 1965-67; materials mgr. Joy Mfg. Co., Michigan City, Ind. 1967-73, gen. mgr., Elk Grove Village, Ill., 1973-87, mktg. mgr. Cooper Industries, 1987—; lectr. Contbr. articles to profl. jours. Pres. LaPorte County Young Reps., Ind., 1970-71; dist. chmn. Boy Scouts Am., 1972; elder, trustee 1st Presbyn. Ch., Libertyville, Ill., 1980-83; mem. village bd. Village of Long Beach, Ind., 1969. Served to lt. (j.g.) USNR, 1953-56, Far East. Mem. Indsl. Compressor Distbrs. Assn. (chmn. com. 1979-84), Constrn. Industry Mfrs. Assn. (bd. dirs., com. chmn. 1975-82), Am. Prodn. and Inventory Control Soc. (chpt. pres. 1970-71), Greater O'Hare Assn. Commerce and Industry, Quincy Hist. Soc., U.S. Power Squadrons, Abbey Yacht Club, Michigan City Yacht Club, Spring Lake Country Club, Phi Kappa Psi, Omicron Delta Kappa. Republican. Presbyterian. Avocations: boating, fishing, skiing, swimming. Home: 56 Spring Lake Est Quincy IL 62301-8749 Office: Cooper Industries 1800 Gardner Expy Quincy IL 62301-9464

WALTHER, ERNEST EUGENE, farmer; b. Boonville, Mo., Jan. 24, 1948; s. Jacob Edward and Leola Frances (King) W.; m. Sharon Kay Mochel, Oct. 16, 1971; children: Ernest Eugene Jr., Sondra Kay, Susan Elizabeth. Diploma, Boonville R-I H.S., 1966. Dir. Cooper County Pork Prodrs., Boonville, 1976—, treas., 1977—, pres., 1990—. Mem. Boonville R-I Sch. Bd., 1992—; mem. West Boonville Evang. Ch., 1962, Sunday sch. tchr., 1978—; mem. Cooper County Youth Fair Bd., Boonville, 1989—; v.p. Cooper County Pub. Water Supply Dist. # 2, 1993—. Recipient Feeder Pig award Mo. Pork Prodrs. Assn., 1973, Master Pork Prodr. Dist. 6, Dist. 6 Pork Prodrs., Mo., 1985, County Membership award Cooper County Pork Prodrs., 1985, Mo. State Fair Farm Family award State of Mo., 1988, Master Pork Prodr. award Cooper County Pork Prodrs., 1980, 85, Livestock Prodn. award Boonville C. of C., 1986. Home: 11500 Blackbird Ln Boonville MO 65233

WALTMAN, ALFRED A., state legislator; m. Sally Waltman; ten children. Grad. high sch. Former state rep. dist. 2 State of S.D., state rep. dist. 3, 1993—; mem. local govt. and taxation coms. S.D. Ho. of Reps.; farmer, rancher. Democrat. Home: RR 2 Box 524 Aberdeen SD 57401-9802*

WALTNER, JOHN RANDOLPH, banker; b. San Diego, Dec. 11, 1938; s. Glenn H. and Pauline B. (Hoffman) W.; m. Janice L. McNamara, Nov. 23, 1963; children: Mary E., Ann L. BSBA, U. S.D., 1961, MBA, 1989. Trainee 1st Nat. Bank, Freeman, S.D., 1961-62, v.p., cashier and bd. dirs., 1968-87, pres., CEO and bd. dirs., 1988—; ops. officer Wells Fargo Bank, Monterey, Calif., 1964-67; bd. dirs. S.D. Blue Shield; mem. faculty U. S.D., Vermillion, 1990—, bus. adv. coun. Sch. of Bus., 1985—, chmn., 1992; mem. S.D. Investment Coun., 1994—, S.D. Lottery Commn., 1996—. Mem. S.D. Lottery Commn., 1996—; mem. Freeman Cmty. Devel. Corp., 1967—, past pres.; pres. Freeman Sch. Bd., 1981-84; treas. City of Freeman, 1961-62. With U.S. Army, 1962-64. Mem. Am. Bankers Assn. (govt. rels. coun. 1995—), S.D. Bankers Assn. (bd. dirs., v.p. 1991, pres.-elect 1992, pres. 1993-94), Freeman C. of C. (past sec.-treas.), Beta Gamma Sigma. Republican. Mennonite. Home: 541 S Poplar St PO Box 566 Freeman SD 57029 Office: 1st National Bank PO Box H Freeman SD 57029

WALTON, FRANK T., engineering executive; b. Des Moines, Iowa, May 6, 1939. Dir. advanced planning Emerson Elec., Pitts., 1958-80; v.p. engring. and quality assurance Wellman Automotive Products, Shelbyville, Ind., 1980—. Patentee electrical heating applications. Sgt. U.S. Army, 1962-68. Mem. Elks. Office: Wellman Automotive Products 1 Progress Rd Shelbyville IN 46176-1837

WALTON, RALPH GERALD, psychiatrist, educator; b. Darlington, Eng., Aug. 18, 1942; came to U.S., 1950; s. Kenneth and Paula (Weissman) W.; m. Ellen Paula Liebling, Feb. 15, 1970 (div. 1980); children: Deborah, Rachel; m. Mary Elaine Hultburg, Sept. 27, 1981; children: Lisa, Jonathan. AB, U. Rochester, 1963; MD, SUNY, Syracuse, 1967. Diplomate Am. Bd. Psychiatry and Neurology. Intern Strong Meml. Hosp., Rochester, N.Y., 1967-68, resident in psychiatry, 1968-71; asst. prof. psychiatry Sch. Medicine U. Rochester, N.Y., 1973-76; chief psychiatry Jamestown (N.Y.) Gen. Hosp., 1976-88; commr. mental health Chautauqua County, Jamestown, 1985-88; chmn. dept. psychiatry Western Res. Care System, Youngstown, Ohio, 1988—; prof. psychiatry N.E. Ohio Univs. Coll. of Medicine, Rootstown, Ohio, 1988—; med. dir. Profl. Recovery Plus Alcoholic Clinic, Youngstown, 1992—. Contbr. chpt. to: Dietary Phenylalanine and Brain Function, 1988; contbr. foreword to: Katherine It's Time, 1989; contbr. articles to profl. jours., 1972—. Maj. U.S. Army, 1971-73, Panama. Fellow Am. Psychiat. Assn. Jewish. Office: 725 Boardman Canfield Rd Youngstown OH 44512-4380

WALTZ, RICHARD W., electrical engineer; b. Milw., Wis., May 23, 1939. BSEE, U. Wis., 1961. Registered profl. engr., Wis. Sr. project engr. Allen-Bradley Co., Milw., 1961—; cons. Madison Kipp, Madison, Wis., 1980-82, T.C.T. Ltd., Milw., 1984—. Achievements include 6 patents for electronic control devices. Republican. Methodist. Home: 7398 Williams Ct Hales Corners WI 53132

WALTZ, ROBERT DEAN, entomologist, state agency administrator; b. Richmond, Ind., Nov. 12, 1953; s. Charles Robert and Betty Eloise (Richardson) W.; m. Nancy Ellen Campbell, Jan. 7, 1978; children: Daniel, Ellen. BS, Purdue U., 1976, MS, 1982, PhD, 1986. Sr. resident naturalist Hayes Regional Arboretum, Richmond, 1977-80; resident Purdue U., West Lafayette, Ind., 1980-86; mus. svcs. coord. Thames Sci. Ctr., New London, Conn., 1987-88; state entomologist, dir. div. entomology/plant pathology Ind. Dept. Natural Resources, Indpls., 1988—; Mem. Pesticide Rev. Bd., Indpls., 1989—, Cen. Plant Bd., Indpls., 1988—; sect. editor Ind. Acad. Scis., Indpls., 1990—. Contbr. over 50 articles to profl. jours. Mem. N.Am. Benthological Soc., Am. Entomol. Soc., Entomol. Soc. Am. (R.E. Snodgrass award 1986), Entomol. Soc. Wash., N.Y. Entomol. Soc. Mem. Ch. of Christ. Office: Ind Dept Natural Resources Div Entomol/Plant Pathology 402 W Washington St Rm 290W Indianapolis IN 46204-2739

WALTZER, HERBERT, political science educator; b. Bklyn., May 29, 1930; s. Samuel and Pearl (Bernstein) W.; m. Marilyn L. Fishchvogt, June 11, 1962 (dec.); children: Adam Koehler, Sarah Lee, Samuel John; m. Miriam B. Grobman, 1992. B.A., NYU, 1951, M.A. (Penfield fellow), 1954, Ph.D., 1959. Program prodn. coord. Radio Free Europe, 1951; instr. polit. sci. N.Y. U., 1954-55; faculty polit. sci. Miami U., Oxford, Ohio, 1957—; prof. Miami U., 1966—, chmn. dept., 1970-82, dean grad. sch. and rsch., 1983-84; assoc. provost, dean Grad. Sch. Miami U., Oxford, Ohio, 1994-95. Author: American Government: Principles, Institutions and Processes, 1962, 5th edit., 1991, (with others) Ideologies and Modern Politics, 3d edit., 1981, Values and Interests in Public Administration: The Linkages of Influence, 1979, The Job of Academic Department Chairmen, 1975; contbr. to Politics Of Reapportionment, 1963, New Structures of Campus Power, 1978; also articles to Midwest Rev. Pub. Adminstrn., Western Polit. Quar., Pub. Opinion, Change, Publius, Cities and Villages, Rural Devel. Perspectives, Pub. Rels. Rev. Vice chmn. Oxford Village Planning Commn., 1962-64; Bd. advisers Ohio Ctr. Edn. in Politics, 1958-64, 72-74; dir. S.W. Ohio Ctr. for Edn. in Politics, 1972-74. Served to capt. USAF, 1955-57. Faculty rsch. fellow Rockefeller Found. Project on Constl. Democracy, 1964-65; Social Sci. Rsch. Coun. Faculty fellow, 1968; Nat. Conv. Faculty fellow, 1964. Mem. Am. Polit. Sci. Assn., Midwest Polit. Sci. Assn. (exec. council 1977-80), Ohio Assn. Polit. Scientists and Economists (v.p. 1971-72, pres. 1972-73), Internat. Communicaton Assn. Home: 2444 Madison Rd #1703 Cincinnati OH 45208

WALVOORD, BARBARA ELLEN, faculty development director; b. Monmouth, N.J., May 30, 1941; d. Christian Herman and Marie Jeanette (Verduin) W.; m. Albert William Fassler, Jr., Dec. 30, 1964; children: Lisa Katherine Fassler Warner, Brian Albert Fassler; m. Hoke LaFollette Smith, June 30, 1979. BS, Hope Coll., 1963; MA, Ohio State U., 1964; PhD, U. Iowa, 1976; HHD (hon.), Phillips U., 1991. Instr. of English U. Del., Newark, 1964-65; instr. asst. prof. English Ctrl. Coll., Pella, Iowa, 1965-79, head divsn. humanities, 1976-79, assoc. prof. English, 1976-79; co-dir. Md. Writing Project, Balt., 1980-83; prof. English Loyola Coll., Balt., 1979-91; prof. English, dir. Writing Across the Curriculum U. Cin., 1991-96, prof. English, dir. Kaneb Ctr. for Tchg. and Learning, 1996—; cons. on teaching for instns. of higher learning, 1976—; chair Hist. Commn. of Reformed Ch. in America, New Brunswick, N.J., 1977-83; coord. Balt. Area Consortium for Writing Across the Curriculum, 1980-84. Author: (book) Helping Students Write Well, 1986, Thinking and Writing in College, 1991; contbr. articles to profl. jours. and chpts. to books. Dir. Iowa Impact Project for Women, Marion County, Iowa, 1974-76, Pella, Iowa chpt. of Project on Equal Edn. Rights, 1978; co-dir. for conf. program Nat. Women's Studies Assn., 1980. Named Danforth Assoc., Danforth Found., 1979; recipient Tchr. of Yr. for Higher Edn. award Md. Coun. Tchrs. of English Lang. arts, 1987. Mem. MLA, Am. Assn. for Higher Edn., Assn. for Study of Higher Edn., Conf. on Coll. Composition and Comm. Home: 10 W Burke Ave Towson MD 21204 Office: U Cincinnati ML 0069 Cincinnati OH 45221

WALWORTH, SANDRA MARIE, educator; b. Aberdeen, S.D., Mar. 31, 1948; d. Wilfred Simon and Rozella Marie (Roggenbuck) Parrow; m. Gary Lee Walworth, Nov. 5, 1971; children: James Darin, David Joseph. BS in edn., Northern State U., 1966; postgrad., Mankato State U., 1989. cert. tchr. art and social studies, Minn.; cert. CPR instr. Art tchr. Monroe Jr. High, Aberdeen, 1970-71, Waubay (S.D.) Pub. Sch., 1971-72; art tchr. Cedar Mountain Schs., Morgan, Minn., 1979-93, art, social studies tchr., 1993-94, social studies tchr., 1994—; curriculum cons. Redwood River Edn. Dist., Redwood Falls, Minn., 1993-94; rep. Brown County Prairie Lakes Regional Arts Coun., Waseca, Minn., 1993—;rep. Brown County Region 9 Arts Adv. Coun., 1985-93, chair., 1990-91, vice chair, 1988-90. Emergency med. technician Springfield (Minn.) Ambulance Svc., 1991—; mem., lobbyist Minn. Citizens for the Arts, 1993; mem. pool planning and constrn. com. Springfield Swimming Pool, 1989-92; mem. exec. com., sec., troop asst., camp leader Springfield Boy Scouts, 1980-93; mem. Prairie Lakes Regional Arts Coun., Brown County rep., 1993—, vice chair, 1994-95. Mem. Minn. EMT Assn., Minn. Fedn. Tchrs. Home: 420 South Paffrath Ave Springfield MN 56087

WALZ, BRUCE JAMES, radiation oncologist; b. Waterloo, Ill., Sept. 18, 1940; s. George Frederick and Alberta Emma (Heyl) W.; m. Renata T. Jaeger, Mar. 8, 1970; children: Jennifer Mara Walz Kuhn, Rachel Elizabeth. A.B., Washington U., 1962, M.D., 1966. Diplomate Am. Bd. Radiology Therapy. Intern, St. Luke's Hosp., St. Louis, 1966-67; resident Washington U. St. Louis, 1969-72; instr. Harvard Med. Sch., Boston, 1972-74; asst. prof. Washington U., 1974-82, assoc. prof., 1982-86, clin. assoc. prof., 1986—; dir. radiation therapy St. Anthony's Med. Ctr., St. Louis, 1986—. Contbr. articles to profl. jours. Active med. adv. com. Medicare, 1992—. Served to lt. comdr. USNR, 1967-69, Vietnam. Harvard Med. Sch. fellow, 1972-73. Fellow Am. Coll. Radiology; mem. AMA, Am. Cancer Soc. (bd. dirs. Mo. divsn. 1992-96), Mo. Med. Soc. (ho. of dels. 1975—), Mo. State Radiol. Soc. (bd. dirs. 1982-87, sec.-treas. 1987-90, v.p. 1990-91, pres. 1991-92, ACR counselor 1995—), St. Louis Metro Med. Assn. (councilor 1987-89), Greater St. Louis Soc. Radiologists (chair therapy sect. 1985, sec.-treas. 1988-89, pres. elect 1989-90, pres. 1990-91), Am. Soc. Therapeutic Radiologists and Oncologists, Am. Coll. Radiology, Am. Soc. Clin. Oncologists, Arab-Am. Med. Soc. Presbyterian. Clubs: Whittemore House (Clayton, Mo.). Avocations: gardening, travelling, scuba diving. Office: St Anthony's Med Ctr Div Radiation Therapy Saint Louis MO 63128

WALZ, ROBERT DEHAVEN, retired military officer, teacher; b. Great Falls, Mont., May 15, 1944; s. Robert Chaussee and Jean (DeHaven) W.; m. Merrill Ann Martin, Jan. 25, 1967; 1 child, Juli Ann. BA, U. S.D., 1966, MA, 1968. Battery officer, 3d bn., 320th arty. U.S. Army, Ft. Bragg, N.C., 1968-69; fire support officer, 2d bn., 320th arty. U.S. Army, Gia Le, Viet Nam, 1969-70; battery comdr., battery A, 1st bn., 17th arty. U.S. Army, Ft. Sill., Okla., 1971-72; asst. prof. mil. sci. U. Vt., Burlington, 1972-74; staff officer, 1st bn., 38th field arty. U.S. Army, Camp Stanley, Korea, 1974-75; area comdr., recruiting area U.S. Army, Mason City, Iowa, 1976-77; fgn. area officer trainee Nat. U. of Singapore, 1980-81; chief new systems, div. target acquisition dept. U.S. Army, Ft. Sill, Okla., 1982-84; author instr. (China) U.S. Army Command and Gen. Staff Coll., Ft. Leavenworth, Kans., 1984-89; staff officer strategy and Pacific policy issues Office of Dep. Chief of Staff for Ops. and Plans Dept. Army, Washington, 1989-91; instr. strategy U.S. Army Command and Gen. Staff Coll., Ft. Leavenworth, 1992—. Contbr. articles to profl. publs. Decorated Legion of Merit, Bronze Star, Meritorious Service medal, Commendation medals, Air medals. Mem. Santa Fe Railway Hist. and Modeling Soc., Nat. Railway Hist. Soc.

WALZER, NORMAN CHARLES, economics educator; b. Mendota, Ill., Mar. 17, 1943; s. Elmer J. and Anna L. (Johnston) W.; m. Dona Lee Maurer, Aug. 22, 1970; children: Steven, Mark. BS, Ill. State U., Normal, 1966; MA, U. Ill., 1969, PhD, 1970. Rsch. dir. Cities and Villages Mcpl. Problems Com., Springfield, Ill., 1974-84; vis. prof. U. Ill., Urbana, 1977-78; prof. econs. Western Ill. U., Macomb, 1978—, chmn. dept. econs., 1980-89, dir. Ill. Inst. Rural Affairs, 1988—, interim dean coll. bus. and tech., 1993-95. Author: Cities, Suburbs and Property Tax, 1981; Government Structure and Public Finance, 1984; editor: Financing State and Local Governments, 1981, Rural Community Economic Development, 1991; co-editor: Financing Local Infrastructure in Non Metro Areas, 1986, Financing Economic Development in The 1980s, 1986, Financing Rural Health Care, 1988, Rural Health Care, 1992, Rural Community Economic Development, 1992, Local Economic Development: International Trends and Issues, 1995, Community Visioning Programs: Practice and Principles, 1996. Mem. Am. Econs. Assn., Ill. Econs. Assn. (pres. 1979-80), Mid-Continent Regional Sci. Assn. (pres. 1985-86). Lodge: K.C. Home: 727 Auburn Dr Macomb IL 61455-3002 Office: Western Ill U Ill Inst Rural Affairs 518 Stipes Hall Macomb IL 61455

WAMBLES, LYNDA ENGLAND, educational sales consultant, retired; b. Nashville, Dec. 30, 1937; d. Henry Russell and Doris Olivia (Stuart) England; m. Byron Adolph Wambles, Sept. 3, 1965; 1 child, Teri Leigh Moore Wambles Taylor. Student, U. Tenn., 1964-65, 73-74, Washington U., St. Louis, 1984-86. Cert. profl. sec. Exec. sec. Gen. Truck Sales, Knoxville, Tenn., 1972-74; asst. to dean Coll. Law U. Tenn., Knoxville, 1974-76; office mgr. Washington U. Sch. Bus., St. Louis, 1977-78, registrar, dir. info. systems, 1978-83, asst. dean for faculty and adminstrn. services, 1983-86; cons. in field St. Louis, 1978-86, Overland Park, Kans., 1986—; acct. rep. Met. Life and Affiliated Cos., Shawnee Mission, Kans., 1992-94; retired, 1996; cons. in field St. Louis, 1978; lectr. divsn. continuing edn. Washington U., St. Louis, 1978-80. Author: (with others) Procedures Manual and Information for State Guaranty Associations, 1987. Active United Way of Greater Knoxville, 1973-74; leader lunch participant YWCA, St. Louis, 1981-83. Fellow Acad. Cert. Profl. Secs.; mem. Prof. Secs. Internat., Nat. Secs. Assn. (Sec. of the Yr. 1975). Republican. Presbyterian. Home and Office: 8425 W 113th St Shawnee Mission KS 66210-2437

WAMBSGANSS, JACOB ROY, accounting educator, small business consultant; b. Hillsboro, Kans., Nov. 9, 1950; s. Eldor Jacob and Betty Maxine (Wait) W.; m. Dona Kay Koby, May 22, 1971; children: Warren Jacob, Jay Roy. BA in History, Wichita State U., 1973; Emporia State U., Emporia (Kans.) State U., 1981; PhD in Bus. and Acctg., U. Nebr., 1985. CPA, N.D.; cert. govt. fin. mgr. Owner Wagon Wheel Restaurant, Strong City, Kans., 1975-76; mgmt. instr. Minot (N.D.) State U., 1981-83; asst. prof. U. S.D., Vermillion, 1985-88; assoc. prof. Emporia (Kans.) State U., 1988-92, U. N.D., Grand Forks, 1992—. Contbr. articles to profl. jours. Past treas. coun. Pleasant Valley Ch., 1986-88; mem., bell choir dir. Walle Luth. Ch., treas., Greater Grand Forks Sr. Citizens Ctr., Grand Forks Rural Luth. Parish. Grantee Bush Found., 1987; recipient Rsch. award Assn. Govt. Accts., 1990. Mem. Inst. Mgmt. Accts., Am. Acctg. Assn., N.D. Soc. CPAs, Decision Sci. Inst., Midwest Acctg. Soc. (treas. 1991-93, program chair/pres.-elect 1994-95), Assn. Govt. Accts. Republican. Lutheran. Home: RR 1 Box 17A Thompson ND 58278-9718 Office: U ND PO Box 8097 Grand Forks ND 58202-8097

WANDLING, MARILYN ELIZABETH BRANSON, artist, art educator; b. Alton, Ill., May 16, 1932; d. Ralph Marion and Mary Mildred (Branson) W.; children: Jeffrey, Douglas, Pamela. Student, Monticello Coll., Godfrey, Ill, 1950-51, U. Ill. U-C Sch. Fine Arts, 1951-53; BA in Art, Webster U., St. Louis, 1968; MA Edn. in Art Edn., Washington U., St. Louis, 1975. Cert. tchr. art Kindergarten-Grade 12, Mo. 4th grade tchr. Alton (Ill.) Pub. Schs., 1961-62; art. buuying dept. Gardner Advt. Co. Inc., St. Louis, 1962-63; art tchr. mid. sch. Lindbergh Sch. Dist., St. Louis, 1968-75; cons., designer V.P. Fair, Inc., St. Louis, 1982; adminstrv. asst. to headmaster, coll. counseling dept. John Burroughs Sch., St. Louis, 1979-82; dir. pub. rels. and advt. Dance St. Louis, 1983-85; freelance art and design St. Louis, 1970—; art tchr. mid. sch. St. Louis Pub. Schs., 1987-90, art tchr. Elem. Magnet Sch. for Visual & Performing Arts, 1990—; tchr. drawing and painting Summer Arts Inst., St. Louis Pub. Schs., 1992, graphic arts designer, cons. comty. affairs divsn., 1985—, sch. vol. divsn., 1990-92, Webster Groves (Mo.) Sch. Dist., 1989-90, Pub. Sch. Retirement Sys., St. Louis, 1991; implementer classroom multi-cultural art edn. projects, 1987—; summer participant Improving Visual Arts Edn., Getty Ctr. for Edn. in Arts, 1990; book illustrator-McGraw Hill Inter-Americana de Mexico, Mexico City, 1994-95. Designer Centennial Logo for St. Louis Pub. Schs. Sesquicentennial, 1988; painter, designer murals for Ctrl. Presbyn. Ch. Nursery, 1978-79, St. Nicholas Greek Orthodox Ch., 1980; designer two outdoor villages VP Fair, Arch Grounds, St. Louis, 1982. Recipient merit and honor awards Nat. Sch. Pub. Rels. Assn., 1990, 91, 92, 93, Mo. Sch. Pub. Rels. Assn., 1989-90, 91, 92, 93. Mem. Nat. Art Edn. Assn., St. Louis Art Mus., PEO Sisterhood, Nat. Soc. DAR, Chi Omega Alumnae. Office: Ames Visual & Performing Arts Center Admin Office 2900 Hadley St Saint Louis MO 63107-3911

WANDOVER, GEORGE, engineering consultant; b. Ft. Belvoir, Va., Apr. 3, 1959; s. Alonzo Jerome and Jean Marie (Eaton) Moon; 1 child from previous marriage, Kimberleigh; m. Christy-Lee Waugh, Oct. 22, 1988.; s. Alonzo Jerome and Jean Marie (Eaton) Moon; m. Virginia Peterson (div.) 1 child, Kimberleigh; m. Christy-Lee Waugh, Oct. 22, 1988. BS in Petroleum Engring., U. Alaska, 1985, MSME, 1990. Rsch. engr. State of Alaska, Faribanks, 1985-87; resident engr. Griener Engrs., Utica, N.Y., 1987-88; project engr. W-M Engrs., Syracuse, N.Y., 1988-91; utilities engr. City of Adrain, Mich., 1991-92; project mgr. Feller Finch & Assoc., Maumee, Ohio, 1992-94; owner Wandovers Engrs., Toledo, Ohio, 1994—. Author: End Station, 1995. Sgt. U.S. Army, 1977-81. Mem. ASCE. Republican. Buddist. Home: PO Box 2021 Toledo OH 43603

WANEK, RONALD MELVIN, orthodontist; b. Richland Center, Wis., Nov. 3, 1938; s. Melvin Leo and Mary Esther (Picha) W.; m. Janet Eleanor Lundquist, June 22, 1974; children: Lynn Ann, Mark Ronald. Student, U. Wis., 1956-60; DDS, Marquette U., 1964, MS, 1969. Practice dentistry specializing in orthodontics Madison, Wis., 1969—. Served to lt. USNR, 1964-67, Vietnam. Mem. ADA, Wis. Dental Assn., Dane County Dental Assn., Am. Assn. Orthodontists, Wis. Soc. Orthodontists, Midwest Soc. Orthodontists, Omicron Kappa Upsilon. Republican. Methodist. Office: 4915 Monona Dr Madison WI 53716-2665

WANG, GUNG H., management consultant; b. Ningpo, Zhejiang, China, Feb. 3, 1909; s. Cheng V. and Zhao S. (Zhu) W.; m. Gladys Chen Wang, Sept. 10, 1938; children: Edward, Jo-Ann, Nancy, James. BA, U. Shanghai, China, 1928; MA, Tulane U., New Orleans, 1952; LLD (hon.), Loyola U., Chgo., 1989. Staff officer Mil. Fgn. Affairs, Nanking, China, 1928-30; vice cons. Consulate Gen. China, Chgo., 1930-38; cons. Consulate of China, New Orleans, 1938-50; exec. dir. Chinese Am. Civic Council, Chgo.; mng. dir. Chinatown Devel. Inc., Chgo., 1960-64; asst. dir. Chgo. Dwellings Assn., 1964-69; housing specialist Model Cities Program, Chgo., 1969-73; dir. Neighborhood Housing Services, Dept. Human Services, 1973-76; owner G.H. Wang Assocs., Chgo., 1976-; sec. Chinese Del. UN Gen. Assembly, Lake Success, N.Y., 1946-47; alt. del. UN Temporary Commn. on Korea, Seoul and Paris, 1948; pres. Neighborhood Redevel. Assn. Inc., Chgo., 1972—; exec. dir. South Side Planning Bd., 1977; adminstr. fund for intercultural edn. NRAI, 1989—. Author: The Chinese Mind 1946, Kinsiskt Tankande, 1948; contbr. articles to profl. jours. 1948-51. Mem. Nat. Assn. Housing and Redevel. Ofcls., Am. Planning Assn., Rotary Club Chgo., Phi Sigma Alpha. Presbyterian. Home: 8200 S Indiana Ave Chicago IL 60619-4725

WANG, HENGTAO (HANK T. WANG), lawyer; b. Tianjin, China, Apr. 8, 1953; came to U.S., 1989; s. Shiying and Yungqiu W.; m. Shenzhong L. Wang, June 5, 1978; 1 child, Lenny. BA in English Lit. with honor, Normal U., Dalian, China, 1974, MA in English Lit., 1977; JD, St. Louis U., 1992. Bar: Mo. 1992, Ill. 1993, U.S. Dist. Ct. (ea. dist.) Mo. Prof., vice chair dept. langs. and internat. studies Dalian Naval Acad., China, 1985-88; mem. Chinese Nat. Linguistic Profs. Soc., China, 1985-88; atty. Mcpl. Fgn. Bus. Legal Office, Dalian, China, 1988-89; assoc. Armstrong, Teasdale, Schlafly & Davis, St. Louis, 1992-96, Bryan Cave, LLP, St. Louis, 1996—. Co-author: Maritime English Textbook Series, 1985-87; author: U.S. Naval Training & Educational System, 1987; contbr. essays to profl. jours. Advisor, bd. dirs. Asian Am. Coalition, Mo., Ill., 1991, Orgn. Chinese Ams. St. Louis Chpt., 1990—; mem. World Affairs Coun., St. Louis, 1993—, St. Louis-Nanjing Sister City Com., 1993—. Comdr. Navy, 1969-88, China. Recipient Acad. Achievements award St. Louis U., 1991, Best Author of Yr. award Navy Mag., 1986. Mem. ABA (bus. law com., internat. law assn.), Am. Immigration Lawyers Assn., Asian-Am. Lawyers Assn., Mo. Bar Assn., Bar Assn. of Met. St. Louis, Ill. Bar Assn., Alpha Sigma Nu. Home: 15641 Clayton Rd Ballwin MO 63011-2363 Office: Bryan Cave LLP One Metropolitan Sq Saint Louis MO 63102-2740

WANG, RICHARD LIQUN, molecular biologist; b. Shanghai, Peoples Republic of China, Dec. 7, 1959; came to the U.S., 1983; s. Kexiang and Fenzhu (Zhang) W.; m. Menyan Cheng, July 11, 1985; children: Charlie, Stephanie. BS, U. Sci. and Tech. China, 1983; PhD, U. Md., 1990. Teaching asst. U. Md., Balt., 1985-88, rsch. asst., 1988-90; postdoctoral fellow NIH, Balt., 1990-93, staff fellow, 1993-94; rsch. scientist Procter & Gamble Pharms., Cin., 1994—. Contbr. articles to profl. jours. Home: 5860 Hazeltine Blvd West Chester OH 45069-1963 Office: Procter & Gamble Miami Valley Labs PO Box 398707 Cincinnati OH 45239-8707

WANG, STUART SUI-SHENG, mathematics educator; b. Canton, Kwangtung, China, July 28, 1946; came to U.S., 1969; s. Man-Po and Chin-Feng (Yin) W.; m. Margaret Mou-Yi Kuo, July 22, 1972; children: Elizabeth, Diana, Sarah. BS, Nat. Taiwan U., 1968; PhD, Cornell U., 1975. Instr. U. Okla., Norman, 1975-76; vis. lectr. Tex. Tech U., Lubbock, 1976-78; vis. asst. prof. Oakland U., Rochester, Mich., 1978-79, asst. prof., 1979-83, assoc. prof., 1983-91, prof., 1991—; vis. assoc. prof. Purdue U., West Lafayette, Ind., 1984-86, Cornell U., Ithaca, N.Y., 1988-89; vis. scholar U. Mich., Ann Arbor, 1994-96. Mem. Am. Math. Soc., Math. Assn. Am. Home: 630 Sorbonne Dr Rochester Hills MI 48309-2311 Office: Oakland U Dept of Math Rochester MI 48309-4401

WANG, VINCENT TSAN-LEUN, food service executive; b. Taipei, Republic of China, Oct. 18, 1953; came to U.S., 1978.; s. Chen-Tong and Chen Chin-Lien Wang. BS, Fu Jen Cath. U., Republic of China, 1976; MS, U. Fla., 1980. Pres., chief exec. officer Dr. Wang Restaurant, Inc., Vincent Wang Inc., Mankato, Minn., 1982—; also chmn. bd. dirs. Dr. Wang Restaurant, Inc., Mankato, Minn.; cons. Tien Hsiang Co., Republic of China, 1974-78; pres., chmn., bd. dirs. Eastland Corp., Mankato, 1988. Named Minn. Minority Small Bus. Person of Yr., 1995. Office: 818 S Front St Mankato MN 56001-2401

WANGLER, MARK ADRIAN, anesthesiologist; b. Coldwater, Ohio, Sept. 29, 1955; s. William Henry and Rita Francis (Vielkind) W.; m. Kathleen Sara Schlarman, May 6, 1977; children: Nathan, Aaron. BS in Biology, Wright State U., 1977; MD, Ohio State U., 1981. Diplomate Am. Bd. Anesthesiology. Intern Ohio State U., Columbus, 1981-82, resident, 1982-84, chief resident, 1983-84; asst. prof. anesthesiology Northeastern Ohio Coll. Medicine, Canton, 1984-86; dir. anesthesiology Mercer County Joint Twp. Community Hosp., Coldwater, 1987-90; ptnr. Anesthesia Assocs. of Lima, Inc., 1990—; dir. rsch. Northeastern Ohio Coll. Medicine, Canton, 1985-86, dir. pain clinic, 1985-86; dir. pain clinic Mercer County Cmty. Hosp., Coldwater, 1986-90, St. Rita's Med. Ctr., 1994—. Contbr. articles to numerous profl. jours. Mem. Mercer County Hist. Soc., Celina, Ohio, 1988; patron Lighthouse Ministries, Celina, 1988. Grantee, NIH, Bethesda, Md., 1978. Mem. AMA, Internat. Anesthesia Rsch. Soc., Am. Soc. Anesthesiologists, Ohio Med. Assn., Ohio Soc. Anesthesiologists, Allen County Acad. of Medicine. Republican. Home: 860 Yorkshire Dr Lima OH 45804-3300 Office: 1103 Bank One Twr Lima OH 45801

WANGSNESS, WAYNE ROGER, economics educator; b. Decorah, Iowa, June 20, 1941; s. Elmer Melvin and Hazel Orleans (Lee) WW.; m. Cheryl Ann Lee, Feb. 9, 1974; children: Amy, Ryan, Karin, Philip. Degree in tech. agriculture, Iowa State U., 1965; BA in Econs., Luther Coll., 1968; MA in Econs., U. Iowa, 1971. Teaching asst. U. Iowa, Iowa City, 1970-71; instr. agriculture N.E. Iowa C.C., Calmar, 1972-78, instr. computers, 1982-84, instr. econs., 1990-91, 95—; vis. asst. prof. econs. Luther Coll., Decorah, Iowa, 1986-91; econs. faculty Upper Iowa U., 1996—; cons. Small Bus. Devel. Corp., Dubuque, Iowa, 1988—. Contbr. articles to profl. jours. Bd. dirs. N.E. Iowa Rsch. Ctr., Nashua, 1980-83. With U.S. Army, 1961-64. Mem. Nat. Corn Growers Assn. (bd. dirs. Washington and St. Louis 1980-83), Rotary (bd. dirs. Decorah 1986-89). Republican. Lutheran. Home: 1869 Middle Ossian Rd Decorah IA 52101-7542

WANNENMACHER, PHILIP, state legislator; b. Rochester, N.Y., Oct. 19, 1960. BS, Evangel Coll., 1982. Tchr.; mem. Mo. Ho. of Reps. from 139th dist. Mem. Jaycees. Office: Assemblies of God 1445 N Boonville Ave Springfield MO 65802-1894*

WANTLAND, WILLIAM CHARLES, bishop, lawyer; b. Edmond, Okla., Apr. 14, 1934; s. William Lindsay and Edna Louise (Yost) W. BA, U. Hawaii, 1957; JD, Okla. City U., 1967; D in Religion, Geneva Theol. Coll., Knoxville, Tenn., 1976; DD (hon.), Nashotah House, Wis., 1983, Seabury-Western Sem., Evanston, Ill., 1983. With FBI, various locations, 1954-59, Ins. Co. of N.Am., Oklahoma City, 1960-62; law clk.-atty. Bishop & Wantland, Seminole, Okla., 1962-77; vicar St. Mark's Ch., Seminole, 1963-77, St. Paul's Ch., Holdenville, Okla., 1974-77; presiding judge Seminole Mcpl. Ct., 1970-77; atty. gen. Seminole Nation of Okla., 1969-72, 75-77; exec. dir. Okla. Indian Rights Assn., Norman, 1972-73; rector St. John's Ch., Oklahoma City, 1977-80; bishop Episcopal Diocese of Eau Claire, Wis., 1980—; interim bishop of Navajoland, 1993-94; adj. prof. Law Sch. U. Okla., Norman, 1970-78; instr. canon law Nashotah House, 1983—; mem. nat. coun. Evang. & Cath. Mission, Chgo., 1977-90; co-chmn. Luth.-Anglican Roman Cath. Commn. of Wis., 1987-95; mem. Episcopal Commn. on Racism, 1990-92, Episcopal Coun. Indian Ministries, 1990-95, Standing Commn. on Constitution and Canons, 1992-95. Author: Foundations of the Faith, 1982, Canon Law of the Episcopal Church, 1984, The Prayer Book and the Catholic Faith, 1994; co-author: Oklahoma Probate Forms, 1971; contbr. articles to profl. jours. Pres. Okla. Conf. Mcpl. Judges, 1973; v.p. South African Ch. Union, 1985-95; trustee Nashotah House, Wis., 1981—, chmn., 1992—; bd. dirs. SPEAK, Eureka Springs, Ark., 1983-89; mem. Wis. adv. com. U.S. Civil Rights Commn., 1990-91; mem. support com. Native Am. Rights Fund, 1990—; co-chmn. Luth.-Anglican-Roman Cath. Commn. of Wis., 1989-95; pres. Wis. Episc. Conf., 1995—. Recipient Most Outstanding Contbn. to Law and Order award Okla. Supreme Ct., 1975, Outstanding Alumnus award Okla. City U., 1980, Wis. Equal Rights Coun. award, 1986, Manitou Ikwe award Indian Alcoholism Coun., 1988, Episcopal Synod Pres.'s award, 1995. Mem. Okla. Bar Assn., Okla. Indian Bar Assn., Living Ch. Found., Oklahoma City Law Sch. Alumni Assn. (pres. 1968), Wis. Conf. Chs. (pres. 1985-86), Wis. Episcopal Conf. (pres. 1995—). Democrat. Home: 145 Marston Ave Eau Claire WI 54701-3911 Office: Diocese of Eau Claire 510 S Farwell St Eau Claire WI 54701-3723

WANZEK, TERRY M., state legislator; m. Janice Wanzek; 2 children. Farmer, rancher Cleveland, N.D.; mem. from dist. 29 N.D. State Senate, Bismarck, 1995—, mem. edn. com., 1995—, vice chmn. agr. com., 1995—. Pres. Stutsman County Farm Bur. Fellow Jamestown Coll.; recipient Agriculturist award Pres.' Agr. Club N.D. State U. Mem. Stutsman County Agrl. Improvement Assn. (pres.), KC. Office: ND State Senate 3877 68th Ave SE Cleveland ND 58424*

WARADY, JOEL DAVID, consumer products company executive; b. Chgo., Nov. 4, 1956; s. John Seymour and Betty Norrine (Hochman) W.; m. Heidi Kanter, Sept. 9, 1990. BA in History, U. Ill., 1979. V.p. The Fellinger Corp., Chgo., 1980-85; field dir. Northwestern Mut. Life, Dallas, 1985-88; v.p. sales and mktg. Wisdom Toothbrush Co., Chgo., 1988-90; pres. Wisdom Toothbrush Co., Deerfield, Ill., 1990—. Mem. Sigma Alpha Mu (leadership chmn. 1989). Republican. Jewish. Office: Wisdom Toothbrush Co 151 S Pfingsten Rd Deerfield IL 60015-4934

WARAKOMSKI, ALPHONSE WALTER JOSEPH, JR., sales executive; b. N.Y.C., Apr. 1, 1943; s. Alphonse Walter and Mary (Dupnock) W. BS in Chemistry, St. Bonaventure, Allegheny, N.Y., 1968; MBA in Mktg., Keller Grad. Sch., Chgo., 1981. Chemist, lab. mgr. Purification Scis., Geneva, N.Y., 1968-73; applications engr. Pollution Control Industries, Stamford, Conn., 1973; sales mgr. Kopper's Environ. Elements, Baltimore, 1974; mktg. specialist, regional mgr. Union Carbide Linde, Chgo., 1975-79; sales engr. Dorr Oliver, Chgo., 1980-81; regional mgr. Linde AG Lotepro, Glen Ellyn, Ill., 1981—; Contbr. articles to profl. jours. Mem. Am. Chem. Soc., Am. Inst. Chem. Engrs. Home: 5830 Oakwood Dr Apt 4H Lisle IL 60532-2964 Office: Linde AG Lotepro 800 Roosevelt Rd Glen Ellyn IL 60137-5839

WARANIUS-VASS, ROSALIE JEAN, artist; b. Fond du Lac, Wis., Dec. 10, 1938; d. John Stanley and Anna Francis (Jonaitis) Waranius; m. Kenneth James Vass, June 11, 1960; children: Kealie, Ross, Kenlyn, Jason. BA, Alverno Coll., 1960; postgrad., Madonna Coll., 1967-68, Blackhawk Tech., 1974, U. No. Iowa, 1976. Cert. art tchr., Ill. One-woman shows include Alverno Coll., Milw., 1991, Roberta Campbell Art Gallery, Geneva, Ill., 1991, 95, St. Charles (Ill.) Libr. Art Gallery, 1989, Bellarmine Coll. Art Gallery, Louisville, 1989, Aurora (Ill.) U. Art Gallery, 1989, Jesse Besser Mus., Alpena, Mich., 1993, Beacon Street Gallery, Geneva, 1995; exhibited in group shows San Diego Watercolor Soc., 1992, Norris Cultural Arts Ctr., St. Charles, 1989-96, Nat. Watercolor Soc., 1988-89, 94, Neville Mus., Green Bay, Wis., 1988, Houston Internat. Watercolor Soc., 1993, 94, Watercolor Masters, Lincolnwood, Ill., 1995, Youngstown, Ohio, 1994, Aurora, 1994; represented in permanent collections Jesse Besser Mus., Kane County Courthouse, Delnor-Cmty. Hos., Alverno Coll., St. Francis Hosp., also corp. collections. Mem. Nat. Watercolor Soc. (life), Chgo. Artist's Coalition, Nat. Mus. Women in Arts, Art Inst. Chgo., Valley Art Ctr., Batavia Artists Guild. Home and Studio: Thistle Hill Farm Studio OS 888 Wenmoth Rd Batavia IL 60510-9711

WARBASSE, LAWRENCE HILL, III, physician, educator; b. N.Y.C., July 5, 1955; s. Lawrence Hill Warbasse Jr. and Anne (Fredrick) deGersdorff; m. Jamie Ann Kalil, Oct. 16, 1987; children: Alexandra Anne, Larry Kalil, Elizabeth Ashley. AB, Dartmouth Coll., 1978; MD, Wayne State U., 1982; MS, U. Mich., 1989. Diplomate Am. Bd. Internal Medicine. Intern Wayne State U. Affiliated Hosps., Detroit, 1982-83, resident, 1983-85, chief med. resident, 1985-86; instr. Wayne State U. Sch. Medicine, Detroit, 1986-90, asst. prof., 1990—. Contbr. articles to profl. jours. Mem. Soc. Gen. Internal Medicine, ACP, Soc. Med. Decision Making, Am. Assn. Med. Informatics, Am. Pub. Health Assn. Office: Wayne State Univ Univ Health Ctr 5C 4201 Saint Antoine St Detroit MI 48201-2153

WARCH, RICHARD, academic administrator; b. Hackensack, N.J., Aug. 4, 1939; s. George William and Helen Anna (Hansen) W.; m. Margot Lynn Moses, Sept. 8, 1962; children: Stephen Knud, David Preston, Karin Joy. B.A., Williams Coll., 1961; B.D., Yale Div. Sch., 1964; Ph.D., Yale U., 1969; postgrad., U. Edinburgh, 1962-63; H.H.D., Ripon Coll., 1980. Asst. prof. history and Am. studies Yale U., 1968-73, asso. prof., 1973-77; asso. dean Yale Coll.; dir. summer plans Yale U., 1976-77; asso. dir. Nat. Humanities Inst., New Haven, 1975-76; v.p. acad. affairs Lawrence U., Appleton, Wis., 1977-79; pres. Lawrence U., 1979—; cons. Nat. Humanities Faculty; ordained to ministry United Presbyn. Ch. in U.S.A., 1968; dir. Bank One of Appleton. Author: School of the Prophets, Yale College, 1701-1740, 1973; editor: John Brown, 1973. Rockefeller Bros. Theol. fellow, 1961-62. Mem. Am. Studies Assn., Soc. for Values in Higher Edn., Winnebago Presbytery. Club: Rotary. Home: 229 N Park Ave Appleton WI 54911-5414 Office: Lawrence U PO Box 599 Appleton WI 54912-0599

WARD, CAROL BUHNER, textile artist, educator; b. Sullivan, Ind., Apr. 13, 1947; d. John Colin and Betty (Bevis) Buhner; m. Charles Wesley Ward, Aug. 22, 1969. Student, U. Bologna, 1967-68, Ind. U., 1969-70; BA, Ind. U., 1970. Lectr. Herron sch. art Ind. U., Indpls., 1970-72, 78-81, 87; artist-in-residence Indpls. Parks Dept., 1975-77; instr. Indpls. Arts League, 1976-78, 82-85; artist-in-residence St. Mary-of-the-Woods Coll., Terre Haute, Ind., 1977; artist-in-service Met. Arts Council, Indpls., 1978-79; owner Carol Ward Tours, Indpls., 1980—; pvt. practice textile artist Indpls., 1981—; participating artist Ind. Arts Commn., Indpls., 1975-85; curator craft exhbn. Indpls. Art League, 1979, 81, 83, 85; rschr., art historian legal firm, Indpls., 1980-87; judge art exhbns. throughout Midwest, 1978—; lectr. art history Franklin (Ind.) Coll., 1990—; artist in residence Sprillmill Sch., Indpls., 1992; acad. escort Guatemala study tour San Jose (Calif.) State U., 1992, Cote d'Azur Study Tour, 1995, Women's Issues in China 4th UN Conf. on Women, Bejing; NGO participant San Jose State U., 1995. V.p. edn. Indpls. Art League, 1978-80; pres. bd. dirs. visual arts orgn. Art Net, Indpls., 1985-86; sec. bd. dirs. Arts Insight, 1979-82; bd. dirs. Friends of Planned Parenthood, Indpls. Mem. Nat. Soc. Colonial Dames, Mayflower Soc., Indpls. Women's Club, Rotary Club (Scholarship 1967). Home and Office: 21 W 59th St Indianapolis IN 46208-1512

WARD, DAVID W., state legislator; b. Ft. Atkinson, Wis., Apr. 29, 1953; m. Jean M. Ward, 1975; 1 child, Kevin. BA, U. Wis., Platteville. Past mem. Wis. Milk Mktg. Bd., Ft. Atkinson Sch. Bd.; Wis. state assembly man dist. 37, 1992—; farmer. Mem. Jefferson County Farm Bur., pres. Address: 3401 County Rd G Fort Atkinson WI 53538*

WARD, DEAN MORRIS, appliance manufacturing executive; b. Ladora, Iowa, Dec. 30, 1925; s. Andrew Morris and Bess (Balmer) W.; m. Elizabeth Slings, July 22, 1948; children: Mary Elizabeth Ward Ahrenholz, Mark Dean. Student, Drake U., 1962-70. Optician B.C. Jensen, Optometrist, Newton, Iowa, 1942-44, 46-54; with Maytag Corp., Newton, 1954—, asst. dir. purchases, 1977, dir. purchases, 1977-90; pvt. practice purchasing cons. Newton, 1991—; mem. Svc. Corps of Ret. Execs.; adj. instr. Des Moines Area C.C.-Newton Campus, 1993; cons. in field. Precinct chmn. Rep. Party, Newton, 1960-68; industry chmn. United Way, Newton, 1962; chmn. Key 73 Evangelistic Program, Newton, 1973; mem. denominational bd. Christian Reformed Ch., del. Nat. Synod, 1993. Sgt. U.S. Army, 1944-46, PTO, 1950-51. Mem. Nat. Assn. Purchasing Mgmt. (pres. 1980, sec.-treas. exec. steel buyers sect. 1989, cert. purchasing mgr., Joseph P. Stagg award for purchasing excellence 1990), Nat. Mgmt. Assn., Am. Prodn. and Inventory Control Soc. (pres. 1966—). Home: 308 E 28th St S Newton IA 50208-2714

WARD, JAMES FRANK, pension fund administrator; b. Chgo., May 29, 1938; s. Frank William and Josephine (Calderone) W.; m. Judith Evelyn Drake, Nov. 22, 1957 (dec. Sept. 1981); children: Jeffrey Thomas, Jason Banning. BEd in Acctg., Ill. State U.; MBA, DePaul U., 1967. Chartered fin. analyst. Asst. traffic mgr. Witco Chem. Co., Stickney, Ill., 1958-59; office mgr. R.E. Chatterton Indsl. Diamonds, Chgo., 1960-62; acctg. tchr. Chgo. Bd. Edn., 1963-66; asst. exec. dir. Chgo. Tchrs. Pension Fund, 1967-76, exec. dir., 1977—. Author, editor numerous newsletters, bulletins. Speaker on pension topics various civic & tchr. orgns. Mem. Nat. Coun. on Tchr. Retirement, Nat. Conf. Pub. Employee Retirement Systems, Govt. Fin. Officers Assn. U.S. & Canada (cert. of excellence in achievement for fin. acctg. & disclosures 1989, 90), Investment Analysts Soc. Chgo., Assn. for Investment Mgmt. & Rsch. Home: 300 N State St Apt 5233 Chicago IL 60610-4808 Office: Chgo Tchrs Pension Fund 55 W Wacker Dr Chicago IL 60601

WARD, JAMES GORDON, education administration educator; b. Auburn, N.Y., June 28, 1944; s. Gordon J. and Alice A. Ward; m. Lynn Elizabeth Harmon, Jan. 19, 1981; children: Heather Anne, James Thomas, Audrey Lynn. BA, SUNY, Albany, 1966, MPA, 1975, MA, 1968; EdD, Va. Poltechnic Inst., 1984. Tchr. social studies Waterloo (N.Y.) Central Schs., 1967-72; policy analyst N.Y. State United Tchrs., Albany, 1972-77; dir. rsch. Am. Fedn. Tchrs., Washington, 1977-85; asst. prof. U. Ill., Champaign, 1985-89, assoc. prof. edn. adminstrn., 1989-93, prof. ednl. adminstrn., 1993, assoc. dean edn., 1990-95; cons. in field; mem. Urbana Bd. Edn., 1991—. Contbr. over 80 chpts. to books and articles to profl. jours. Mem. Am. Soc. Pub. Administrn., Am. Edn. Fin. Assn. (bd. dirs. 1980-86, pres. 1986-87), Am. Ednl. Rsch. Assn. Home: 703 W Iowa St Urbana IL 61801-4037 Office: Univ Ill 1310 S 6th St Champaign IL 61820-6925

WARD, JAMES K., engineering administrator; b. Beloit, Wis., May 12, 1961. Project mgr. Rockford (Ill.) Automation, 1980-87; engring. mgr. Inta-Roto, Richmond, Va., 1987-89; divsn. mgr. Martin Automatic, Inc., Rockford, 1989—. Coach Little League Baseball, Rockford.

WARD, MARCIA BALMUT, secondary education educator; b. Springfield, Ohio, Aug. 5, 1946; d. Henry and Margery Louise (Zerkle) B.; m. Gregory Dow Ward, July 26, 1969; children: Katherine, Vincent, Anthony. BS in Edn., Wittenberg U., 1968; postgrad., U. Dayton, 1991—, Wright State U., 1996. Tchr. Georgesville Sch. Emotionally Disturbed, Columbus, Ohio, 1968-69, Miami East Jr. High Sch., Conover, Ohio, 1969-74, Graham High Sch., St. Paris, Ohio, 1974-76; tchr. gifted edn. and gifted enrichment Graham Schs., St. Paris, 1980-84, 84-92; substance abuse coord., coord. title one programs Graham Schs., St. Paris, Ohio, 1990—; nat. pres. Internat. Sch.-to-Sch. Experience, Urbana, Ohio, 1982-87, internat. bd., 1977-87; USA del. Children's Internat. Summer Village, Hexham, Eng., 1971. Author: Do's and Dont's in CISV, 1982. Pres. St. Paris Antique Study Club, 1980, St. Paris Pub. Libr., 1992; chmn. Champaign County Heart Drive, Urbana, 1981; tchr. jr. ch. 1st Christian Ch., Urbana, 1983-92; Sunday sch. tchr., jr. choir leader Westville United Meth.; chair St. Paris Pub. Libr. Levy Com. and Expansion Program; advisor Champaign County Teen Age Sexuality and Pregnancy Prevention Advisor, Teens Opposed to Premarital Sex; del. World PRIDE Conv. and N.W. Tobacco Coalition, Nat. Sch. Bd. Conv., San Francisco. KTH Edn. grantee, 1981, Martha Holden Jennings Scholar grantee, 1995-96. Mem. 4-H Clubs Am. (leader). Home: 156 Eris Rd Urbana OH 43078-9662 Office: Graham Schs 104 W Main St Saint Paris OH 43072-9703

WARD, MARIA FRANCES, community relations manager; b. Cleve., Aug. 14, 1949; d. Frank K. and Mary (Crawford) Ward. BA magna cum laude, U. Detroit, 1971, MA, 1974, postgrad. Sch. Law., 1971-72. Cert. tchr. Grants rsch. analyst City of Southfield, Mich., 1974-78, community devel. coordinator, 1978-80, dir. legis. svcs., 1980-87, asst. city adminstr., 1987-90; exec. dir. Southfield Community Found., 1989-90; mgr. community rels., midwest, state and local govt. affairs Consol. Rail Corp., Dearborn, Mich., 1990—; instr. Henry Ford Community Coll., 1977-80; researcher, labor union arbitrator, Warren, Mich., 1974. Author: Glossary of Terms, 1981; Southfield Auto Insurance Report, 1986; editor: Southfield 2001, 1983. Mem. Zoning Bd. of Appeal, City of Berkley, Mich., 1987—; charter mem. Hist. Commn., Berkley, 1977—. Recipient Distng. Woman in Govt. award, 1991. Mem. Am. Coun. Railroad Women, Mich. Community Devel. Dirs. Assn. (sec. 1978-79, pres. 1979-80), Am. Soc. for Pub. Adminstrn. (pres. 1986-88), Mich. City Mgmt. Assn., Women's Econ. Club, Rotary, Alpha Sigma Nu, Delta Zeta. Roman Catholic. Home: 1838 Rosemont Rd Berkley MI 48072-1846 Office: Consol Rail Corp 17301 Michigan Ave Dearborn MI 48126-2700

WARD, MICHAEL JAMES, sales executive; b. St. Louis, Aug. 3, 1959; s. James Curtis and Karen Ann (Meyer) W.; m. Kim Louise Beyatte, Oct. 8, 1982; children: Zack, Kelly. BSBA, S.E. Mo. State U., 1981. Sales rep. Beecham Products, St. Louis, 1981-83; key account mgr. Beecham Products, Chgo., 1983-84, dist. supr., 1984, dist. mgr., 1984-88; dist. mgr. Johnson & Johnson, Chgo., 1988-90; field mgr. key accounts Johnson & Johnson, St. Louis, 1990-91, mgr. nat. accounts, 1991—. Fireman Lake Forest (Mo.) Vol. Fire Dept., 1992—. Mem. Lake Forest Community Assn., Jaycees, Ste. Genevieve Golf Assn. Roman Catholic. Home and Office: 109 Lake Forest Est Lot 392 Sainte Genevieve MO 63670-9202

WARD, OLLIE TUCKER, counselor, educator; b. St. Louis, June 14, 1930; d. George Thomas and Luevenia (Casey) Stewart; m. George O. Tucker, Dec. 25, 1950 (div. Apr. 1969); children: George Stewart, Jeffrey Terrance; m. John Henry Ward, 1974 (dec. Sept. 1995). Student, Stowe Tchrs. Coll., 1946-50; MA, Washington U., St. Louis, 1958; postgrad., Webster U., 1972, U. Mo., 1973. From reading instr. to mid. sch. counselor St. Louis Pub. Schs., 1950-90; substitute tchr. Maplewood-Richmond Heights, 1990—; adj. faculty Harris Stowe State Coll., St. Louis, 1974, 84, 90; field rep. Tucker Bus. Coll., St. Louis, 1950-66, Tucker Bus. Coll. Alumni Assn., 1987—. Trustee, usher Missionary. Recipient Disting. Svc. award Iota Phi Lambda, 1988, award Nat. Bd. for Cert. Counselors; named Coro finalist, Class 30, 1994. Mem. NAACP (life, 1st v.p. St. Louis County br. 1988-89), CORE (So. Christian Leadership award St. Louis br. 1986), St. Louis Pers. and Guidance Assn. (pres.-elect 1984), St. Louis Sch. Counselors Assn. (pres. 1987-88, Svc. award 1990), Coalition 100 Black Women (charter mem., ad hoc chmn. 1984-85), Am. Cancer Assn. Abarasque (pres. 1977-78), Jack and Jill Am. (1st v.p., pres.-elect, assoc. 1968-91), Nat. Coun. of Negro Women (assoc.), Nat. Cert. Coun., Optimist Club (v.p. Mid County), Alpha Kappa Alpha. Democrat. Baptist. Home: 1513 Bredell Ave Richmond Heights MO 63117-2110

WARD, PATRICIA ELAINE, geriatrics nurse; b. McAndrews, Ky., Nov. 10, 1948; d. Buddy and Martha Alice (Leedy) Ball; divorced; children: Angela, Kevin, Jason. ADN, Shawnee State U., 1979. Supr. Heartland, Portsmouth, Ohio, 1984-86; staff nurse Scioto Meml., Portsmouth, 1986-88; supr. Hempstead Manor, Portsmouth, 1988-89, DON, 1989—. Mem. Ohio Dirs. Nursing Adminstrn. in Long Term Care. Democrat. Home: 1645 7th St Portsmouth OH 45662-4549 Office: Hempstead Manor PO Box 911 Portsmouth OH 45662-0911

WARD, PHILLIP CHARLES, physical education educator; b. Brisbane, Queensland, Australia, Sept. 14, 1957; m. Marie C. Cull, Dec. 17, 1992; 1 child, Robert Nathan. Diploma in tchg., North Brisbane Coll. of Edn., Australia, 1987; grad. diploma Sports Sci., Victoria Coll., Australia, 1988; BE, Deakin U., Australia, 1989; MEd, Victoria Coll., Australia, 1991; PhD, Ohio State U., 1993. Cert. tchr., Australia. Phys. edn. tchr. Victorian Edn. Dept., Australia, 1984-87, tchg. cons., 1988-90; grad. asst. Ohio State U., 1990-93; vis. prof. Wilmington (Ohio) Coll., 1993-94, Ill. State U., 1994-95; asst. prof. health and human performance U. Nebr., 1995—; cons. Dublen Sch. Dist., Columbus, Ohio, 1992, Lincoln Pub. Schs., Nebr., 1995. Author: Teaching Children Tumbling, 1996; contbr. articles to profl. jours. including Jour. of Tchg. in Phys. Edn., The Phys. Educator, also others. Recipient Frank Vig Trophy for Sportsmanship Queensland Gymnastic Assn., 1979, Cooper Siedentop award Ohio State U., 1992; Vance Cotter fellow, 1993. Mem. Am. Edn. Rsch. Assn., Assn. for Behavior Analysis, Nat. Assn. for

Sport and Phys. Edn., Am. Alliance for Phys. Edn., Recreation and Dance, Nebr. Assn. for Phys. Edn., Recreation and Dance, Phi Kappa Phi. Office: U Nebr Dept Health & Human 247 Mabel Lee Hall Lincoln NE 68588

WARD, RICHARD C., advertising executive; b. 1933. BA, Mich. State U., 1960. With Kenyon & Eckhardt, Detroit, Mich., 1954-73; dir. mktg. Monroe (Mich.) Auto Equipment, 1973-78; with Ross Roy, Inc., Bloomfield Hills, Mich., 1978-94, former pres.; vice chmn. Roy Ross Comm., Inc., Bloomfield Hills, Mich., 1994—. Office: Roy Ross Comm Inc 100 Bloomfield Hills Pky Bloomfield Hills MI 48304-2949*

WARD, RICHARD COMPTON, management consultant; b. Washington, Sept. 14, 1941; s. Truman and Gladys (Nutt) W.; m. Sally Ingham Sweet, June 20, 1964; children: David Truman, Jonathan Reid, Owen William. BArch, Va. Poly. Inst. and State U., 1964, M in Urban & Regional Planning, 1965; MArch in Urban Design, Washington U., St. Louis, 1968; MBA, Washington U., 1991. Lic. real estate broker, Mo. Prin., founder, pres. Team Four, Inc., St. Louis, 1968-88; pres. Team Four Rsch., 1984-88; pres., founder Devel. Strategies, Inc., St. Louis, 1988; bd. dirs. Nat. Coun. for Urban Econ. Devel., Washington. Contbr. articles to profl. jours. Active Leadership St. Louis, 1981-82; adv. coun. Coll. Arch. and Urban Studies Va. Poly. Inst. and State U., 1987—; bd. dirs. Downtown St. Louis, 1990—; chmn., bd. dirs. Redevel. Authority University City, Mo., 1978-86, Indsl. Devel. Authority, 1980-86; bd. dirs. Boys Town Mo., St. James and St. Louis, 1980—, Confluence St. Louis, 1986-92. Grad. fellow HUD, 1967-68; recipient Prticipant award Leadership St. Louis, 1981-82. Mem. Am. Inst. Cert. Planners (cert.), Am. Planning Assn. (pres. Mo. chpt. 1973-75, Grad. Student award 1965), Urban Land Inst., Phi Kappa Phi (Acad. Excellence award 1964). Home: 6370 Waterman Ave Saint Louis MO 63130-4707 Office: Devel Strategies Inc 10 S Broadway Ste 1640 Saint Louis MO 63102-1712

WARD, RICHARD EUGENE, civil engineering technician; b. Marion, Ohio, Nov. 29, 1931; s. Joseph Clyde and Ivanell M. (Pace) W.; m. Donna Belle Rosebrough, June 30, 1950; children: Sheri, Michael, Richard, David, Susan. Student, Ohio No. U., 1950-51. Telegraph operator Erie-Lackawanna R.R., Marion, 1951-71; engring. technician City of Springfield, Ohio, 1964-81, sr. design technician, 1981-89, design supr., 1989-94; ret. Mem. Clark County Bicentennial Com., Springfield, 1979-80; fair master Fair at New Boston, Springfield, 1982-88; chmn. issue 2 com. Clark County Park Dist., 1984; trustee George Rogers Clark Heritage Assn., Springfield, 1979-88, pres., 1985-88. Mem. Nat. Inst. for Cert. Engring Techs., 1st Am. Regt. (Esplanade com. 1991). Republican. Home: 358 S Greenmount Ave Springfield OH 45505-2214

WARD, RICHARD HURLEY, university administrator, writer; b. N.Y.C., Sept. 2, 1939; s. Hurley and Anna C. (Mittasch) W.; children from a previous marriage: Jeanne M., Jonathan B.; m. Michelle Pierczynski, June 15, 1987. BS, John Jay Coll. Criminal Justice, 1968; M in Crim., U. Calif.-Berkeley, 1969, D in Crim., 1971. Detective, N.Y.C. Police Dept., 1962-70; coord. student activities John Jay Coll., N.Y.C., 1970-71, dean students, 1971-75, v.p., 1975-77; vice chancellor, prof. internat. criminology U. Ill., Chgo., 1977-93; assoc. chancellor and prof. internat. criminology U. Ill., Chgo., 1993—; exec. dir. Office Internat. Criminal Justice, 1985—; vis. prof. Zagazig U., Egypt, Egyptian Police Acad., 1986, East China Inst. Politics and Law, Shanghai, 1990-91; lecturer, various conferences in China, Egypt, Russia, Italy, England, Peru, Germany, Vietnam and the U.S., 1983—. Author: (with others) Police Robbery Control Manual, 1975; Introduction to Criminal Investigation, 1975, An Anti-Corruption Manual for Administrators in Law Enforcement, 1979; (with Robert McCormack) Quest for Quality, 1984; gen. editor Foundations of Criminal Justice, 46 vols., 1972-75; editor: (with Austin Fowler) Police and Law Enforcement, Vol. I, 1972; Police and Law Enforcement, Vol. II, 1975; (with Harold Smith) International Terrorism: The Domestic Response, 1982, International Terrorism: Operational Issues, 1988; co-author: (with James Osterburg) Criminal Investigation: A Method for Reconstructing the Past, 1992. Mem. Near West Side Community Conservation Council, 1982—; varsity baseball coach U. Ill., Chgo., 1980-82; varsity baseball coach John Jay Coll. Criminal Justice, N.Y.C., 1971-72. Served to cpl. USMC, 1957-61. Recipient Leonard Reisman award John Jay Coll. Criminal Justice, 1968, Alumni Achievement award, 1978, Richard McGee award U. Calif.-Berkeley Sch. Criminology, 1971, Friendship medal Peoples Republic of China, 1994; Justice Dept. fellow U. Calif.-Berkeley, 1968-69; Danforth Found. fellow, 1971. Mem. Acad. Criminal Justice Scis. (pres. 1977-78, Founder's award 1985), Am. Soc. Pub. Adminstrn., Internat. Assn. Chiefs of Police (chmn. edn. and tng. sect. 1974-75), Am. Assn. for Higher Edn., Am. Acad. for Profl. Law Enforcement (nat. bd. dirs. 1978-84), Sigma Delta Chi. Office: U Ill at Chicago 1033 W Van Buren St Chicago IL 60607

WARD, ROBERT D., state legislator; b. Desloge, Mo., July 3, 1940; s. Harry G. and Scbeulah (Weitzel) W.; m. Joy V. Vincent, 1962; children: Kevin, Shannon. BS, Murray State Coll. Fee agt. Mo. Dept. Revenue; owner R.D. Ward Land & Rental Co., Desloge; mem. Mo. Ho. of Reps. from 151st dist., 1983-93, Mo. Ho. of Reps. from 107th dist., 1993—; majority whip Mo. Ho. of Reps., 1985-88. Mem. St. Francois County Dem. Club. Mem. Elks, Eagles. Home: RR 2 Box 127F Bonne Terre MO 63628-9508*

WARD, ROBERT JACKSON, American literature educator; b. Akron, Ohio, July 17, 1926; s. Lester Larry and Rebecca L. (Atkinson) W.; m. Catherine Balaj, June 18, 1951; children: Sean Lester, Sari Catherine. BA, U. Akron, 1951; MA, Ohio State U., 1952; PhD, U. Mo., 1967. Instr. U. Mo., Columbia, 1952-58; asst. prof. U. No. Ill., DeKalb, 1958-63; prof. U. No. Iowa, Cedar Falls, 1963—; Fulbright lectr. U. Timisoara, Romania, 1981, 85; exch. prof. U. No. Iowa/ U. Extremadura, Spain, 1992. Author: Seven Masters of American Poetry, 1979, Eight Masters of American Poetry from Edgar Allen Poe to James S. Hearst, 1991, Romania, A Land of Lowering Darkness: Poems of Romania Under Ceausescu's Tyranny, 1991, Poems for Our Winter Seasons, 1993; editor: A Country Man: Posthumous Poems of James Hearst, 1993, co-editor/translator: Seleccion de Poemas de James Hearst, 1993. With USN, 1944-46. NFH Summer fellow Stanford U., 1980. Mem. Soc. Study Midwestern Literature. Office: U No Iowa Dept of Am Ed Cedar Falls IA 50614

WARD, SHERMAN CARL, III (BUZZ WARD), theater manager; b. Camden, N.J., Apr. 21, 1958; s. Sherman Carl Jr. and Ann Laura (Bodie) W. BA, Princeton U., 1980; MBA, Harvard U., 1986. Contr.'s asst. McCarter Theatre Co., Princeton, N.J., 1977-80; spl. projects analyst Madison Fin. Corp., Nashville, 1980-81, dir. client svcs., 1981-83; tchr. English, vol. tchr. Nan, Thailand, 1983-84; studio ops. Walt Disney Pictures, Burbank, Calif., summer 1985; contr. Coconut Grove Playhouse, Miami, Fla., 1986-87, dir. ops., 1987-88; gen. mgr. Yale Sch. Drama, Yale Repertory Theatre, New Haven, Conn., 1988-92; exec. dir. Cin. Playhouse in the Park, 1992—. Recipient Letter of Appreciation, King of Thailand, 1984. Mem. Actor's Equity Assn. Office: Cin Playhouse in the Park 962 Mount Adams Cir Cincinnati OH 45202-6023

WARD, TODD POPE, consultant; b. Mount Vernon, Ill., Nov. 14, 1938; s. George F.M. and D'Ella (Williams) W.; m. Rita Epperson, Aug. 29, 1959; children: Christina Lee, Julie Ann, Todd P. III. Student, Westminster Coll., 1956-58, So. Ill. U., 1958-59. Pres. Lincoln Trial Bank, Fairview Heights, Ill., 1964-75; exec. v.p. Security Bank, Mankato, Minn., 1975-76; pres. Village Bank, Oklahoma City, 1976-80, First City Bank, Oklahoma City, 1980-81, Rolling Hills Bank, Oklahoma City, 1981-84, US Capital Corp., North Kansas City, Mo., 1984-90; cons. Ward Assocs., Kansas City, Mo., 1990—. Pres. United Way, Fairview Heights, 1972. Mem. ASTD (pres.-elect Kansas City chpt. 1996), Soc. for Human Resource Mgmt., Rotary Internat. Republican. Home: 7803 N Lydia Ave Kansas City MO 64118-1961 Office: PO Box 28881 7803 N Lydia Ave Kansas City MO 64118-1961

WARD, VERNON GRAVES, internist; b. Palisade, Nebr., Mar. 5, 1928; s. Charles Bennett and Mildred Belle (Graves) W.; m. Eleanore Mae Farstveet, Aug. 28, 1952; children: Margo, Alison, Barry. BA, Nebr. Wesleyan U., 1948; MD cum laude, U. Nebr., Omaha, 1954. Diplomate Am. Bd. Internal Medicine. Instr. in anatomy Columbia U., N.Y.C., 1948-50; intern U. Wis., Madison, 1954-55, resident internal medicine, 1955-58, chief resident, physician, 1957-58; fellow in neurophysiology and psychosomatic medicine U. Okla., Oklahoma City, 1960-61; asst. clin. prof. medicine U. Wis., Madison, 1961-62; pvt. practice internal medicine Kearney, Nebr., 1962-67; asst. prof. U. Nebr. Coll. Medicine, Omaha, 1967-69; assoc. clin. prof. medicine U. Nebr., Omaha, 1969—; pvt. practice internal medicine Omaha, Nebr., 1969—; chmn. dept. internal medicine Clarkson Hosp., Omaha, 1996—. Contbr. articles to profl. jours. including JAMA, Nebr. State Med. Jour., Wis. State Med. Jour., Am. Heart Jour., Postgrad. Medicine. Pres. Nebr. chpt. Arthritis Found., 1969-71. Lt. Commdr. USNR, 1958-60. Named Hutton Traveling Scholar Coll. of Physicians, 1965. Fellow ACP, Am. Coll. Rheumatology; mem. AMA, Nebr. State Med. Soc., Omaha Med. Soc., Am. Soc. Internal Medicine, Am. Psychosomatic Soc., Nebr. Soc. Internal Medicine (pres. 1980-82, Disting. Internist award 1990), Phi Kappa Phi, Alpha Omega Alpha (pres. Nebr. chpt. 1984-85), Phi Chi (grand sec.-treas. 1986—, co-chmn. nat. conv. Omaha 1953), Phi Kappa Tau. Republican. Lutheran. Home: 302 N 54th St Omaha NE 68132-2813 Office: 201 S Doctor's Bldg Omaha NE 68131

WARD, WILLIAM EDWARD, museum exhibition designer; b. Cleve., Apr. 4, 1922; s. Edward and Lura Dell (Eckelberry) W.; BS, Western Res. U., 1947, MA, 1948; diploma Cleve. Inst. Art, 1947; postgrad. Columbia U., 1950; m. Evelyn Svec, Nov. 12, 1952; 1 dau., Pamela. Mem. staff edn., Oriental depts. Cleve. Mus. Art, 1947—, designer, 1957—, retired chief designer; prof. calligraphy and watercolor Cleve. Inst. Art, 1960—, after 1960, now prof. cons. graphic and installation exhbn, design cons. Egyptian Mus. Cairo 1995-96. Exhibited in numerous exhbns. including (with Evelyn Svec Ward) Oaxacan Inspirations: An Exhbn. of Collage and Watercolor, 1986, Valley of Oaxaca: Exhibition of Watercolors and Photographs, Folk Art Gallery, Cleve., 1992; Cleve. Playhouse Gallery, 1984; designer George Gund Collection of Western Art Mus., 1972; Firemen's Meml., Cleve., sculpture design, 1968; designer ofcl. seals Case Western Res. U., also Sch. Medicine, 1969; curator Culcon exhbn. Masterpieces of World Art from Am. Museums, Tokyo and Kyoto, Japan, 1976; co-author (catalogue, exhibition) Folk Art of Oaxaca: The Ward Collection, Cleve. Inst. Art, 1987. Mem. Internat. Design Conf., Aspen, 1959—; mem. The Trideca Soc. (trustee); mem. Fine Arts Adv. Com. City Cleve., 1966-90; mem. mayor's com. for selection of ofcl. seal City of Cleve., 1973, mem. design rev. com., 1991-92. Served with Terrain Intelligence, AUS, 1942-45, Southeast Asia Command. Recipient commn. award City Canvas competition Cleve. Area Arts Coun., 1975, No. Ohio LIVE Achievement award Cleve. Mus. Art, 1987. Mem. Cleve. Soc. Contemporary Art, Print Club Cleve., Rowfant Club, Women's City Club Cleve. (Arts Prize Spl. citation 1988). Home: 27045 Solon Rd Cleveland OH 44139-3452 Office: Cleve Mus Art 11150 East Blvd Cleveland OH 44106-1711

WARD, WILLIAM SCOTT, II, economic development specialist; b. Detroit, Jan. 7, 1953; s. Robert George and Helen Blanche (White) W.; m. Michele Marie Duffey, Oct. 12, 1985 (dec. Apr. 1988). BA, Western Mich. U., 1977. Registered social worker, Mich. Curator Kalamazoo (Mich.) Pub. Mus., 1977-78; writer Kalamazoo, 1977—; asst. dir. New Eng. Residential Svcs., Hubbardston, Mass., 1985-87; dir. New Eng. Residential Svcs., Hubbardstrom, Mass., 1987-89; social worker Cmty. Mental Health, Sault St. Marie, Mich., 1989-91; econ. devel. specialist Inter. Tribal Coun. Mich., Sault St. Marie, Mich., 1992—; chairperson Bay Mills Planning Coun., Brimley, Mich., 1994—; Industrial Devel. Commn., Barre, Mass., 1986-89, Industrial Devel. Fin. Authority, Barre, 1986-89. Candidate for register of deeds Chippewa County, Mich., 1992, Kalamazoo County, 1980; chairperson Mich. Com. Dem. Alt., Mich., 1979; mem. Barre Thief and Rogue Detecting Soc., 1986—; mem. Mich. Rural Devel. Coun., 1993—, Econ. Devel. Work Group Operation Action, 1994—. Democrat. Home: Rte 1 Box 262 Brimley MI 49715 Office: Inter Tribal Coun Mich 405 E Easterday Ave Sault Sainte Marie MI 49783

WARDER, MICHAEL YOUNG, think tank executive; b. Buffalo, June 29, 1946; s. Thomas Grayston and Norma A. (Young) W.; m. Cheryl Lynn Gilkerson, Feb. 8, 1975; children: Maureen, Amy, Michael Jr. BA, Stanford U., 1968. Tchr. Drew Sch., San Francisco, 1968-69; pres. Internat. Re-edn. Found., San Francisco, 1970-73; sec.-gen. Internat. Conf. on the Unity of Scis., N.Y.C., 1974-79; pres., pub. Newsworld Comm., N.Y.C., 1976-69; dir. adminstrn. Heritage Found., Washington, 1980-83; exec. v.p. Ethics and Pub. Policy Ctr., Washington, 1983-84, The Rockford (Ill.) Inst., 1985-95; v.p. devel. The Claremont (Calif.) Inst., 1995—; radio commentator (bi-weekly) Sta. WNIJ-FM NPR Affiliate, DeKalb, Ill., 1991-95; del. leader People to People, USSR, 1991, Rockford Inst., Lithuania, Latvia, Estonia, 1994; spkr. in field. Op-ed columnist The Wall Street Jour., USA Today, The Chgo. Tribune, Chgo. Sun Times, San Francisco Chronicle, St. Louis Post Dispatch, Indpls. Star, 1985—; host/prodr. (TV weekly public affairs show) Stateline Newsmakers, 1990-92; columnist (weekly) Rockford Register Star, 1991-92. Recipient Silver Dome award Ill. Broadcasters Assn., 1993, 95; grantee Earhart Found., 1988. Mem. Nat. Strategy Forum (mem. rsch. comm.), Phila. Soc., Chgo. Coun. Fgn. Rels., Chgo. Pub. Affairs Coun., Rockford Rotary Club (past bd. dirs.), Sigma Delta Chi. Republican. Office: The Claremont Inst 250 W 1st St Ste 330 Claremont CA 91711

WARD-MCDUFFIE, KAY FRANCES, elementary education educator, paralegal; b. Chgo., Aug. 10, 1947; d. Thomas David and James Ola (Suddoth) Ward; (div.); 1 child, Angela Catherine. BS in Edn., Chgo. State U., 1971, MS in Edn., 1977; cert. paralegal, Roosevelt U., Chgo., 1987. Cert. tchr. sci., lang. arts, social studies, K-9, Ill. Lab. asst. Field Mus. Nat. History, Chgo., 1965-66; tel. operator Ill. Bell Tel. Co., Chgo., 1966-68; waitress Charles A. Stevens, Chgo., 1968-69; data entry clk. Credit Bur. Cook County, Chgo., 1969-71; tchr. Chgo. Pub. Schs., 1971—, paralegal, summer 1987; adj. prof. Chgo. State U., Nat.-Louis U.; instr. staff devel. Chgo. Pub. Sch. Assn., 1979, coord. Elem. and Secondary Edn. Act, 1977-78. Author parent handbook, 1977; editor: Basal Reader, 1993. V.p., mem. Calumet Sch. Dist. #132, Calumet Pk., Ill., 1992—; mem., sec. Morgan Pk. Civic League, Chgo., 1979-82; mem. NAACP, Chgo., 1983—, Nat. Coun. Negro Women, Chgo., 1983—, Operation Push, Chgo., 1983—. Recipient Disting. Svc. Scroll Scanlon Sch. PTA, 1972, Honorary Life Membership Grissom Sch. PTA, 1992. Mem. Beth Eden Bapt. Ch. (trustee, club pres., tchr. Sunday Sch.), Phi Delta Kappa. Office: Chgo Pub Schs 12810 S Escanaba Chicago IL 60633

WARDNER, RICH, state legislator; m. Kayleen Wardner; children: Brant, Cory. Math. and chemistry tchr., football coach Dickinson (N.D.) H.S.; mem. from dist. 37 N.D. State Ho. of Reps., Bismarck, 1991—, former mem. state and fed. govt. com., former vice chmn., chmn. govt. and vet. affairs com., now mem. fin. and taxation com. Office: 1042 12th Ave W Dickinson ND 58601*

WARE, GEORGE HENRY, botanist; b. Avery, Okla., Apr. 27, 1924; s. Charles and Mildred (Eshelman) W.; BS, U. Okla., 1945, MS, 1948; PhD, U. Wis., 1955; m. June Marie Gleason, Dec. 21, 1955; children: David, Daniel, Patrick, John. Asst. prof. Northwestern State U. of La., Natchitoches, 1948-56, assoc. prof., 1956-62, prof., 1962-67; dir. Conservation Sect., No. La. Supplementary Edn. Ctr., Natchitoches, 1967-68; dendrologist Morton Arboretum, Lisle, Ill., 1968-92, adminstr. rsch. group, 1976-93, adminstr. Urban Vegetation Lab., 1986-92, rsch. fellow in dendrology, 1992-94, rsch. assoc., 1995—; vis. prof. U. Okla., Norman, summers, 1957, 61, 63, 64; adj. prof. Western Ill. U., 1972-85; mem. extension faculty George Williams Coll., Downers Grove, Ill., 1969-76, Nat. Coll. Edn., Evanston, Ill., 1972-76. Trustee nomination caucus Coll. of DuPage, Glen Ellyn, Ill., 1974-78; bd. dirs. Kane-DuPage Soil and Water Conservation Dist., 1969-81; pres. La. Acad. Scis., 1966-67; dir. La. State Sci. Fair, 1966. With USN, 1942-46. Recipient Gold Seal award Nat. Coun. State Gardens Club, 1991, Am. Forests Urban Forestry Rsch. medal, 1994, Lifetime Svc. award Nat. Urban and Cmty. Forestry Adv. Coun., 1995. Mem. Southwestern Assn. Naturalists (treas. 1963-69), Internat. Soc. Arboriculture, Ill. Arborist Assn. (pres. 1987-88). Home: 573 59th St Lisle IL 60532-3102 Office: Morton Arboretum Lisle IL 60532-1293

WAREHAM, JERRY, broadcast executive; b. 1948. With Greater Dayton Pub. TV, Ohio, 1985-93; pres. Sta. WVIZ-TV, Cleve., 1993—. Office: Sta WVIZ-TV 4300 Brookpark Rd Cleveland OH 44134*

WAREN, ALLAN DAVID, computer information scientist, educator; b. Toronto, Ontario, Can., Nov. 23, 1935; s. David and Sirkka Siiri (Kahara) W.; m. Marion Veronica Halligan, Jan. 25, 1962; children: David, Melissa, Melanie, Jessica. BASc, U. Toronto, 1960; MSEE, Case Inst. Tech., Cleve., 1962, PhD, 1964. Profl. engr., Ontario. Staff engr. Clevite Electronics Research Div., Cleve., 1963-66; assoc. prof. Cleve. State U., 1966-69, prof., 1971-93, prof. emeritus, 1993—, interim dean Coll. Bus. Adminstrn., 1990-91; pres. Com-Share Ltd., Toronto, 1969-71; cons. Gould, Cleve., 1974-84, Texaco, Houston, 1987-88, PPG Industries, Cleve., 1988-92, LTV Steel, 1993—; v.p. Optimal Methods, Austin, Tex., 1993—; expert witness Rose Law Firm, 1993-95. Co-author: Modeling and Optimization with Gino, 1986, Optimization with the IBM Optimization Subroutine Library, 1994, Handbook for IBM OSL, 1994; co-developer computer software GRG2, 1973, What-If-Solver, 1988, Excel Solver, 1991, Borland Quatro Pro Solver, 1991; co-author case study, 1985 (runner-up best case 1985); contbr. articles to profl. jours. Recipient Disting. Faculty Rsch. award, Cleve. State U., 1979, First Annual Faculty Rsch. award, Nance Coll. of Bus. Adminstrn., 1993, grant in Ohio Rsch. Challenge Program, State of Ohio, 1988, various other rsch. grants, 1973-84. Mem. IEEE (sr.), Assn. Computing Machinery, Ops. Rsch. Soc. Am., Math. Programming Soc. Home: 9155 Woodsway Dr Willoughby OH 44094-9370 Office: Cleve State U E 24th and Euclid Ave Cleveland OH 44115

WARFIELD, ROBERT N., management executive; b. Guthrie, Ky., Nov. 29, 1948. BA in Speech and English, East Ky. U., 1970; M in Comm., Columbia U., 1974. V.p., sta. mgr. Sta. WDIV-TV, Detroit, 1979-91; exec. v.p., treas. Alpha Capital Mgmt. Inc., Detroit, 1991—. Producer (T.V. Spl./Video) Mandela's U.S. Visitacian, 1990 (6 Emmy's), Never Lose Your Hope, 1991 (Telly award). Bd. dirs. Red Cross of Mich., Detroit, 1982—, Big Bros./Big Sisters, Detroit, 1987—; exec. mem. bd. trustees Mary Grove Coll., Detroit, 1990—;. Mem. Renassance Club of Detroit, NAACP (life), Omega Phi Psi. Baptist. Office: 600 W Lafayette Blvd Detroit MI 48226-3125

WARGOWSKY, FREDERICK AUGUST, retired draftsman; b. Oak Harbor, Ohio, May 7, 1925; s. Paul Martin and Wanda Pauline Rosena (Harder) W.; m. Mary Carolyn Cross Roller, Apr. 30, 1948 (div. July 1970); children: Patricia Anne, Paul George; m. Fayma Dorothy Labredee Clark, June 9, 1984. Diploma, No. Tech. Inst., 1971, Chgo. Tech. Coll., 1977. Farmer Oak Harbor and Lindsey, 1942-58; agrl. fieldman No. Ohio Sugar Co., Fremont, Ohio, 1958-67; mech design draftsman various locations, Oak Harbor and Williston, No. Ohio, 1968-89. Mem. Ottawa County Geneal. Soc., Lucas County Geneal. Soc., Genealogy by Computer Soc. Republican. Lutheran. Home: PO Box 338 21090 Oak St Williston OH 43468-0338

WARLICK, DENNIS P., company executive. MBA, U. Mich. Pres. Autovision Inc., Columbus, Ohio, 1992—. Mem. U. Mich. Alumni.

WARMAN, RICHARD STANLEY, retired statistician; b. Columbus, Ohio, Sept. 30, 1920; s. Aaron Stanley and Stella Esmeralda (Deupree) W.; m. Dolores Hummel, June 12, 1951 (dec. Apr. 1992); 1 child, Robert Frederick. AB, Kenyon Coll., 1941; BS in Edn., Ohio State U., 1951. Tchr. govt. and Am. history Lebanon (Oho) Sch. Dist., 1951-52; med. libr. White Cross Hosp., Columbus, 1952-54; cataloguer Enging. Libr. N.Am. Aviation, Columbus, 1955-56; statistician Ohio Bur. Employment Svcs., Columbus, 1956-79, chief labor force reports, 1979-87; pres. Ohio Civil Svc. Employees Assn., 1972-74. Sgt. Med. Dept., U.S. Army, 1942-46, PTO. Mem. Am. Statis. Assn. (pres. Columbus chpt. 1971).

WARMBROD, CATHARINE PHELPS, educational researcher, consultant; b. Lost Nation, Iowa, July 2, 1929; d. Paul Edward and Ruth Dorthea (Langhorst) Phelps; m. J. Robert Warmbrod, Jan. 30, 1965. BA, U. Iowa, 1952; MS, U. Ill., 1965, advanced cert. in edn., 1967. Head supr. student tchrs. in bus. edn. U. Ill., Urbana, 1966-67; chmn. office adminstrn. Columbus (Ohio) State Community Coll., 1970-77; rsch. specialist NCRVE Ohio State U., Columbus, 1977-88, rsch. specialist emeritus, 1988—; prin. Warmbrod Ednl. Svcs., Columbus, 1988—; bd. dirs. Nat. Assn. Industry/Edn. Cooperation, Buffalo, 1980-88. Author: Retraining and Upgrading Workers, 1983; contbr. to profl. publs.; editor: VocEd Insider for Tech. Edn., 1981. Bd. dirs. Ohio Women, Inc., Columbus, 1986-92, Friendship Village, Dublin, Columbus, 1990—. Mem. Am. Vocat. Assn. (policy com. 1980-83), Assn. Faculty and Profl. Women Ohio State U. (pres. 1984-85), Am. Assn. Community and Jr. Colls., Am. Tech. Edn. Assn., Delta Pi Epsilon. Presbyterian. Office: Warmbrod Ednl Svcs 3853 Surrey Hill Pl Columbus OH 43220-4778

WARNER, JAMES JOHN, small business owner; b. Paw Paw, Mich., Feb. 22, 1942; s. James Kelley and Arleta Alice (Turner) W.; m. Lynne Ann McGuire, June 19, 1965 (div. Apr. 4, 1994); children: Todd M., Kirk T., Beth K. BA, Mich. State U., 1965; postgrad., Western Mich. U., 1968-72. Sales rep. Warner Vineyards, Paw Paw, 1965-70, gen. mgr., 1970-73, v.p., 1973-75, pres., 1976—, also bd. dirs.; bd. dirs. Peninsular Products Co., Lansing, Mich., 1975—. Chmn. Lakeview Found., Paw Paw, Mich., 1978, Van Buren County Econ. Devel. Corp., Paw Paw, 1977; dir. Van Buren Emergency Med. Svcs., Paw Paw; 1982, Hospice of Van Buren and Kalamazoo, 1988. With U.S. Army, 1966-68, Vietnam. Decorated Bronze Star. Mem. Am. Mktg. Assn. (Man of Yr. 1978), Am. Assn. Vintners (dir. 1981—), Young Pres.' Orgn. (chmn. 1982-83), Mich. Grape and Wine Industry Coun. Episcopalian. Home: 304 S Kalamazoo St Paw Paw MI 49079-1528 Office: Warner Vineyards 706 S Kalamazoo St Paw Paw MI 49079-1558

WARNER, JEROME, state legislator; b. Waverly, Nebr., Nov. 23, 1927; s. Charles J. Warner and Esther Anderson Warner; m. Betty Person; children: Jamie, Elizabeth. BS, U. Nebr., 1952. Mem. Nebr. State Senate, 1962—, sprk., 1969-71, vice chair edn. com., 1962-65, 73-75, chmn. govt. & mil. affairs com., 1965-67, mem. legis. coun. exec. bd., 1967-69, appropriations com., 1977-91, exec. bd., com. on coms. Mem. Lancaster County Extension Bd., Lincoln-Lancaster County Planning Commn., Nebr. State Agr. Bd., Lancaster County Com. Reorganization Sch. Dist. Mem. Lancaster County Agr. Soc. (treas.), Nebr. State Grange, Order Eastern Star, Scottish Rite, Alpha Zeta, Gamma Sigma Delta. Home: RR 1 Box 100A Waverly NE 68462-9801 Office: State Legislature State Capitol Lincoln NE 68516*

WARNER, JUDITH KAY, elementary education educator; b. Detroit, Jan. 5, 1940; d. James Alfred and Marjorie Katherine (Lickfelt) White; m. Charles Harold Warner, Jr., Oct. 14, 1967; 1 child, Curtis Charles. BS, No. Mich. U., 1967, MA, 1970, postgrad., 1976-92. Bookkeeper Can. Life Assurance Co., Detroit, 1959-61; with R.L. Polk Co., Detroit, 1961-62; substitute tchr., phys. edn. tchr. Lincoln Park (Mich.) Pub. Schs., 1962-65; tchr. 2nd grade Taylor (Mich.) Pub. Schs., 1967, Fisher Elem. Sch., Marquette, Mich., 1973-74; tchr. 3rd grade Am. Sch. Found., Monterrey, Mex., 1974-76; tchr. 2nd grade Whitman Elem. Sch., Marquette, 1967-70, 73-74, tchr. 1st grade, 1976—; accreditation climate com. Whitman Elem. Sch., Marquette, 1994—, mem. AIMS Day, 1994—, Field Day, 1994. Hostess chmn. Campaign for Bob Anderson, Mich. Senate, Marquette, 1988; mem. field svc. com. No. Mich. U., 1989-91; sec. World Svc. Guild, 1992—; mem. com. Federated Women's Club, 1990—, corr. sec., 1994—; mem. Federated Women's House Com., 1992—. Mem. NEA (life), AAUW (life, edn. chmn. 1990—, v.p. membership 1994—, gift from Marquette br. to Eleanor Roosevelt Fund for Women and Girls given in her name 1993), Mich. Reading Assn., Mich. Coun. for the Social Studies (pres. dist. 1 1986-88), Marquette-Alger Reading Coun. (treas. 1988-90), Marquette-Alger Young Authors (mem. steering com. 1977-89), Marquette-Alger Coun., Marquette County Hist. Soc., Marquette County Humane Soc., Marquette Women's Ctr., Marquette Maritime Mus., Marquette Area Edn. Assn. (Whitman Elem. Sch. bldg. rep. 1990—).

WARNER, PHILIP T., state legislator; b. Goshen, Ind., Jan. 13, 1931; s. DeMain and Hazel F. (Kein) W.; m. Susie Warner; children: Stephen, Jennifer, Nancy. BS, Purdue U. Owner Warner Farms; mem. from 49th dist. Ind. Ho. of Reps., 1970—, chmn. edn. com., mem. agr. and rural devel., aging, ways and means coms., also mem. fin. instns./families, children/human affairs coms; bd. dirs. First Nat. Bank; mem. adv. bd. Ind. Vocat. and Tech. Coll., 1968—. Recipient Master Farmer award, 1968, Lorin A. Burt award, 1978, Outstanding Govt. Leader award Assn.Disabled, 1978;

named Outstanding Young Farmer Ind., 1960. Mem. Farm Bur., Ind. Farm Policy Study Group, Am. Legion, Rotary, Delta Upsilon. Home: 17607 State Road 4 Goshen IN 46526-6670*

WARNER, (ROBERT) STEPHEN, sociologist, educator; b. Oakland, Calif., Dec. 7, 1941; s. Robert Michael and Ethelyn (Seeman) W.; m. Patricia Barrett, Sept. 11, 1960 (div. 1967); 1 child, John; m. Anne Harrington Heider, Dec. 29, 1979; 1 child, Dove. BA, U. Calif., Berkeley, 1963, MA, 1966, PhD, 1972. Asst. prof. sociology Sonoma (Calif.) State Coll., 1967-68; acting asst. prof. U. Calif., Berkeley, 1969-70; asst. prof. Yale U., New Haven, 1970-76; from asst. prof. to prof. U. Ill., Chgo., 1977—; mem. Inst. for Advanced Study, 1988-89. Author: New Wine in Old Wineskins, 1988. Woodrow Wilson fellow, 1963, Guggenheim fellow, 1974-75, NEH fellow, 1991-92. Mem. Phi Beta Kappa. Democrat. Presbyterian. Office: U Ill Dept Sociology Chicago IL 60607-7140

WARREN, BARBARA JONES, nursing researcher, educator; b. Maysville, Ky., Sept. 22, 1944; d. James Martin and Virginia Lee (Haley) Jones; m. Stephen D. Warren, June 1, 1968; children: James Eric, Heather Nicole. G-rad., Mt. Carmel Coll. Nursing, Columbus, Ohio, 1965; BSN, Ottrbein Coll., 1989; MSN, Ohio State U., 1990, PhD, 1995. RN, Ohio. Psychiat. nurse insvc. coord. Mt. Carmel Med. Ctr., 1965-68; adminstr. nursing svcs. Tng. Ctr. for Youth/Ohio Youth Svcs., Columbus, 1968-70; supr. geriatric patients Resthaven Convalescent Ctr., Columbus, 1971-72; chmn. edn. div. CACE/Lamaze, Columbus, 1974-79; adminstr. health care Franklin County Bd. Mental Retardation-Devel. Disabilities, Columbus, 1982-86; grad. nurse intern Harding Hosp., Worthington, Ohio, 1987, 89-90; grad. rsch. assoc. Coll. Nursing Ohio State U., Columbus, 1989—; liaison rsch. mgr. U. Cin., 1993—; rsch. assoc. Ohio State U. Coll. Nursing, 1990—; mem. Nat. Black Women's Health Project. Mem. Worthington Alliance Black Parents, 1987—. Ohio Dept. Mental Health grantee, 1993—. Mem. ANA (fellow 1991), Am. Psychiat. Nurses Assn., Ohio Psychiat. Nurses Network, Nat. Black Nurses Assn., Soc. for Edn. and Rsch. in Psychiat. Nursing (presenter 1991), Otterbein Coll. Nursing Alumni Assn. (pres. 1990—), Torch and Key, Sigma Theta Tau (chair nominating com. Epsilon chpt.). Office: Ohio State U Coll Nursing 1585 Neil Ave Columbus OH 43210-1216

WARREN, JANET ELAINE, librarian; b. Lindsborg, Kans., Sept. 19, 1951; d. Jack Edward and Mildred Louise (Ahlstedt) Beebe; m. Perry DeLong Warren, July 6, 1974; children: Emily Louise, Britta Elizabeth. Student Stephens Women's Coll., 1969-70; BS in Edn., U. Kans., 1973; MLS, Emporia State U., 1974. Asst. dir. Goodland Pub. Library (Kans.), 1974-75, libr. dir., 1975—. Bd. dirs. Sherman County Jr. Miss Program, 1979; mem. exec. com. N.W. Kans. Library System, 1988—; pres. Chpt. Philantropic Edn. Orgn., 1992-94. Mem. ALA, Kans. Libr. Assn., Mountain Plains Libr. Assn., AAUW. Republican. Club: Thalia Women's (pres. 1982-83, 90-91). Home: PO Box 185 Goodland KS 67735-0185 Office: Goodland Pub Libr 812 Broadway Goodland KS 67735-3037

WARREN, KENNETH JOHN, transit system executive; b. Milw., Nov. 19, 1948; s. Robert Francis Warren and Marion Irene (Heyer) Simmons; m. Mary Catherine Steinmetz, July 1, 1994; children: Nathan, Michael. BA in Math., Ripon Coll., 1969; MS in Urban and Regional Planning, U. Wis., 1973. Transportation planner Dane County Regional Planning Commn., Madison, Wis., 1971-73; exec. asst. Milw. Transp. Services, 1976-81; asst. mgr. ops. Milw. Transport Services, 1981-83, dir. ops., 1983-93, v.p.-dep. dir., 1993—, also bd. dirs. Mem. Inst. Transp. Engrs. (assoc.), Transp. Research Bd., Transp. Devel. Assn. (bd. dirs. 1984—), Transp. Employees Mut. Benefit Assn., Wis. Urban Transit Assn. (past chmn.). Office: Milw Transport Services Inc 1942 N 17th St Milwaukee WI 53205-1652

WARREN, RICHARD M., experimental psychologist, educator; b. N.Y.C., Apr. 8, 1925; s. Morris and Rae (Greenberg) W.; m. Roslyn Pauker, Mar. 31, 1950. BS in Chemistry, CCNY, 1946; PhD in Organic Chemistry, N.Y. U., 1951. Flavor chemist Gen. Foods Co., Hoboken, N.J., 1951-53; rsch. assoc. psychology Brown U., Providence, 1954-56; Carnegie sr. rsch. fellow Coll. Medicine NYU, 1956-57; Carnegie sr. rsch. fellow Cambridge (Eng.) U., 1957-58, rsch. psychologist applied psychology Rsch. Unit, 1958-59; rsch. psychologist NIMH, Bethesda, Md., 1959-61; chmn. psychology Shimer Coll., Mt. Carroll, Ill., 1961-64; assoc. prof. psychology U. Wis., Milw., 1964-66, prof., 1966-73, rsch. prof., 1973-75, disting. prof., 1975-95, adj. disting. prof., 1995—; vis. scientist Inst. Exptl. Psychology, Oxford (Eng.) U., 1969-70, 77-78. Author: (with Roslyn Warren) Helmholtz on Perception: Its Physiology and Development, 1968, Auditory Perception: A New Synthesis, 1982; contbr. articles on sensation and perception to profl. jours. Fellow APA, Am. Psychol. Soc.; mem. AAAS, Acoustical Soc. Am., Am. Chem. Soc., Am. Speech and Hearing Assn., Sigma Xi. Office: U Wis Dept Psychology Milwaukee WI 53201

WARREN, SANDRA KAY, writer; b. Grand Rapids, Mich., Oct. 17, 1944; d. Marinus Dieleman and Adrianne Jeanne (Mol) Dieleman-Sjoerdsma; m. Roger Dennis Warren, Sept. 10, 1966; children: Kerri Sue, Leslie Ann, Michelle Lynn. A in Home Econs. Edn., Grand Rapids Jr. Coll., 1964; BS in Home Econs. Edn., Mich. State U., 1966; postgrad., Merrill Palmer Inst., 1967. Writer Trillum Press Royal Fireworks, Unionville, N.Y., 1986—, Mind Play/Methods & Solutions, Tucson, 1988—, Pieces of Learning, Beavercreek, Ohio, 1992-95, Kane Press, N.Y.C., 1994; editor Creative Leaning Conss., Beavercreek, 1992-93, cons., writer, mem. sales dept., 1992-95; sales rep. Synergetics, East Windsor Hill, Conn., 1992—; owner, writer Arlie Enterprises, Strongsville, Ohio, 1992—. Author: Being Gifted: Because You're Special From the Rest, 1987, If I Were a Road, 1987, If I Were a Road, 1987, If I Were a Table, 1987, The Great Bridge Lowering, 187, (book, audio tape, puppet) Arlie the Alligator, 1992, (booklet) Kwanzaa, 1994; author Pieces Ednl. Newsletter, 1993, Nat. State Leadership Tng. Bull., 1978; author, prodr.: (video study kit) Being Gifted: The Gift, 1990; editor Nat. Assn. Gifted Children Parent-Cmty. Newsletter, 1996—. Named Hon. Life mem. Strongsville PTA, 1991. Mem. Mid-Am. Pubs. Assn., Nat. Assn. Gifted Children, Pubs. Mktg. Assn., North East Ohio Pubs. Group (bd. dirs. 1992—), Strongsville Assn., Gifted/Talented Children (founder, past pres., bd. dirs. 1977—), Strongsville C. of C., Ohio assn. Gifted Children (Civic Leadership award 1983), Soc. Children's Book Writers and Illustrators, Great Lakes Booksellers Assn., No. Ohio Pubs. Assn. (v.p. 1995-96), Ohio Libr. Assn., World Coun. Gifted and Talented Children. Office: Arlie Enterprises PO Box 360933 Cleveland OH 44136

WARREN, STEVEN DEAN, ecologist, researcher; b. Joplin, Mo., Oct. 12, 1955; s. Donald Eugene and Hilda Lorelei (Altom) W.; m. Heather Long, Aug. 23, 1980; children: Micah Nicholas, Alyssa Nicole, Jonas Benjamin, Leah Alexandra. BS, Brigham Young U., 1980, MS, 1982; PhD, Tex. A&M U., 1985. Cert. profl. soil erosion and sediment control specialist. Ecologist U.S. Army Constrn. Engring. Rsch. Lab., Champaign, Ill., 1985—; vis. grad. faculty Tex. A&M U., College Station, 1986—, N.Mex. State U., 1994—. Contbr. numerous reports and articles to profl. jours. Scoutmaster Boy Scouts Am., Champaign, 1989-91, troop com. chmn., 1991-94, 96—, dist. com., 1994—, cubmaster, Mahomet, Ill., 1991-93. Mem. Soil and Water Conservation Soc., Alpha Zeta. Mem. LDS Ch. Office: USACERL-LL-R PO Box 9005 Champaign IL 61826-9005

WARRENE, KEVIN CHARLES, sales executive; b. Pitts., June 10, 1961; s. Charles Raymond Sr. and Janet Audry (Bryson) W.; m. W. Sue Bier, Feb. 29, 1992; children: Joshua James, Cynthia Carol. Grad. H.S., Massillon, Ohio. Night chef Shady Hollow Country Club, Massillon, Ohio, 1977-81; exec. chef Holiday Inn, New Philadelphia, Ohio, 1981-85; distbr. sales Dover (Ohio) Foods Co., 1985-87, Abbott Foods Co., Columbus, Ohio, 1987—; adv. bd. mem. Buckeye Career Ctr., New Philadelphia, 1987—; distributor sales rep. adv. coun. I.D. Mag., N.Y.C., 1993. Chairperson New Philadelphia (Ohio) Levy City Schs., 1994. Republican.

WARSHAW, ROBERTA SUE, lawyer, financial specialist; b. Chgo., July 10, 1934; d. Charles and Frieda (Feldman) Weiner; m. Lawrence Warshaw, July 5, 1959 (div. June 1978); children: Nan R., Adam; m. Paul A. Heise, Apr. 2, 1994. Student, U. Ill., 1952-55; BFA, U. So. Calif., 1956; JD, Northwestern U., 1980. Bar: Ill. 1980. Atty., fin. specialist Housing Svcs. Ctr., Chgo., 1980-84, Chgo. Rehab. Network, 1985-91, 92-95; dir. housing State Treas., State of Ill., Chgo., 1991; sole practitioner, 1995—; legal worker Sch. of Law, Northwestern U. Legal Clinic, Chgo., 1977-80; real estate developer, mgr., marketer, Chgo., 1961-77; bd. dirs. Single Room Housing Assistance Corp. Co-author: (manual) The Cook County Scavenger Sale Program and The City of Chicago Reactivation Program, 1991, (booklet) Fix the Worst First, 1989; co-editor: The Caring Contract, Voices of American Leaders, 1996. Alderman 9th ward City of Evanston, Ill., 1985-93, mem. planning and devel., rules com., unified budget com., chair flood and pollution control com.; pres. Sister Cities Found.; mem. cmty. and econ. devel. policy Nat. League Cities, 1990-93; mem. Dem. Nat. Com.; bd. dirs. Dem. Ctrl. Com. Evanston, 1973—; elected committeeman Evanston Twp. Dem. Com., 1994—; del. Dem. Nat. Conv., 1996. Mem. ABA (affordable housing com.), Ill. State Bar Assn., Chgo. Bar Assn. (real estate coms.), Decalogue Soc. Lawyers, Chgo. Coun. Lawyers (housing com.). Home: 550 Sheridan Sq # 5G Evanston IL 60202-3169

WARSHAWSKY, ISIDORE, physicist, consultant; b. N.Y.C., May 27, 1911; s. Morris and Esther (Sherman) W. BS, CCNY, 1930. Physicist Nat. Adv. Com. Aeronautics, Langley Field, Va., 1930-42; chief instrumentation sect. Nat. Adv. Com. Aeronautics, Cleve., 1942-50; chief instrument rsch. br. Nat. Adv. Com. Aeronautics/ NASA, Cleve., 1950-72; instrumentation cons. NASA, Cleve., 1972-90, ret., 1990, disting. rsch. cons. (unsalaried), 1990-95. Author: (textbook) Foundations of Measurement and Instrumentation, 1990; contbr. 10 NACA/NASA tech. report, 20 articles to sci. jours. and books. Fellow Instrument Soc. Am., Am. Phys. Soc., Combustion Inst., Am. Vacuum Soc.

WASCHER, JAMES DEGEN, lawyer; b. Chgo., Aug. 4, 1953; s. Gilbert Arthur and Virginia Ellen (Bowen) W.; m. Sally Lynn Goldman, Oct. 6, 1990; children: Jack Gilbert, Matthew James. BA, Stanford U., 1975; JD cum laude, Northwestern U., 1978. Bar: Ill. 1978, U.S. Dist. Ct. (no. dist.) Ill. 1978, U.S. Ct. Appeals (7th cir.) 1981, U.S. Supreme Ct. 1981. Atty. James P. Chapman & Assocs., Chgo., 1978-82, Phelan, Pope & John Ltd., Chgo., 1982-85; exec. dir. Mayor Washington Fund, Chgo., 1985-87; deputy gen. atty. Chgo. Park Dist., 1988-91; atty. Friedman & Holtz, P.C., Chgo., 1991—. Bd. dirs. Legal Assistance Found. Chgo., 1989—; inquiry bd. panel chair Atty. Registration and Disciplinary Commn., Chgo., 1992-96. Recipient Disting. PILI Alumni award Pub. Interest Law Initiative, Chgo., 1993. Mem. ABA, Am. Judicature Soc., Chgo. Bar Assn., Chgo. Coun. Lawyers (pres. 1990-91). Office: Friedman & Holtz 11 E Adams St Chicago IL 60603-6301

WASFIE, TARIK JAWAD, surgeon, educator; b. Baghdad, Iraq, July 1, 1946; m. Barina Y. Wasfie, Mar. 11, 1975; children: Giselle, Nissan. BS, Central U., Iraq, 1964; MD, Baghdad Med. Sch., 1970. Cert. gen. surgeon. Surg. rsch. assoc. Sinai Hosp. of Detroit/Wayne State U., 1981-85; clin. fellow Coll. Phys. & Surg., Columbia U., N.Y.C., 1985-91, postdoctoral rsch. scientist, 1987-91; attending surgeon Mich. State U./McLaren Hosp., Flint, 1991—. Contbr. articles to profl. jours. NIH grantee, 1984. Fellow ACS (assoc.), Internat. Coll. Surgeons; mem. AMA, Mich. State Med. Soc., Flint Acad. Surgeons, Am. Soc. Artificial Internal Organs, Internat. Soc. Artificial Organs, Soc. Am. Gast. Endoscopic Surgeons. Home: 1125 Kings Carriage Rd Grand Blanc MI 48439-8715

WASHBURN, JOHN JAMES, lawyer, financial services company executive; b. Chelsea, Mass., Sept. 15, 1956; s. Frank Eugene and Kathryn Lorraine (Webster) W. BSBA cum laude, Suffolk U., Boston, 1978; MBA, Suffolk U., 1983; JD, New Eng. Sch. Law, 1987; LLM in Taxation, Boston U., 1989. Bar: Mass. 1987, Ill. 1996, U.S. Dist. Ct. Mass. 1988, U.S. Ct. Appeals (1st, 3d and 4th cirs.) 1988, U.S. Tax Ct. 1989, U.S. Ct. Claims 1991, U.S. Ct. Appeals (D.C. cir.) 1992, U.S. Ct. Appeals (7th cir.) 1996, U.S. Supreme Ct. 1996, U.S. Dist. Ct. (no. and ctrl. dists.) Ill. 1996. Intern Boston Mcpl. Ct., Suffolk County Dist. Atty.'s Office; assoc. Boxer & Assocs., Boston, 1987-88; pvt. practice North Reading, Mass., 1988—, Westchester, Ill., 1996—; v.p. legal Nat. Translink Corp., Westchester, Ill., 1995—; cons. FGL Commodity Svcs. New England, 1988-92. Editor Confinement jour., 1986-87, B.U. Taxation jour., 1988-89; contbr. articles to profl. jours. Mem. North Reading Rep. Town Com., 1989-95, vice chmn., 1992-95; del. Mass. Rep. State Conv., 1990, 94; selectman North Reading, 1991-94, chmn., 1993-94, fin. com., 1994-95, clk., 1995; bd. dirs. Essex-Middlesex Sanitary Dist., 1991-95; Mass. Justice of Peace. Mem. ATLA, Ill. State Bar Assn., DuPage County Bar Assn., Chgo. Bar Assn., Am. Soc. Notaries, Phi Alpha Delta, Delta Sigma Pi. Republican. Office: Nat Translink Corp 1127 S Mannheim Rd Ste 103 Westchester IL 60154 also: PO Box 264 4 Dodge Rd North Reading MA 01864

WASHINGTON, ADRIENNE MARIE, elementary school educator; b. Chgo., June 26, 1950; d. Henry and Emily Marguerite (Sims) Robertson; m. Gregory Blake, Mar. 26, 1967 (div.); children: Emily M., Gregory D.; m. Donald Booker Washington, Apr. 18, 1990. BA, U. Mich., 1976, MA, 1977; Specialist in Arts, Ea. Mich. U., 1991. Cert. tchr., Mich. Head tchr. Second Bapt. Day Care, Ann Arbor, Mich., 1977; tchr. Willow Run Pub. Schs., Ypsilanti, 1977—; workshop presenter Nat. Black Child Devel. Inst., detroit, 1984; pub. rels./crisis chair WREA; founder What Black History Means to Me essay contest. Youth leader NAACP, Ypsilanti, 1980's; campaign asst. Dem. orgn., Ypsilanti, 1988, 91; canvasser Mar. Dimes; corr. sec. Brown Chapel A.M.E. Ch., tchr. Bible sch., co-chair sesquencentinnel anniversary. Hon. Citizen City of Nashville, 1992, State of Tenn., 1992. Mem. Nat. Assn. Black Bus. and Profl. Women's Clubs (pres. 1984-86), Tenn. Black Caucus of State Legislators (hon. mem.), Elks (pres. PSP Club of Mich. 1988-95, fin. sec. Anna G. Parker Temple No. 1283). Home: 1835 Manchester Dr Ypsilanti MI 48198-3646

WASHINGTON, CASSANDRA, elementary education educator; b. Chgo., Jan. 4, 1962; d. Robert and Bobbie (Hill) W. BA in Polit. Sci., Rockford Coll., 1983; MA in Tchg., Nat. Louis U., 1992. Gentil organizer Club Mediteranee, Montrouis, Haiti, 1984-85; rsch. asst. DDB Neddham Worldwide, Chgo., 1986-87; info. specialist Burrell Advt., Chgo., 1987-91; instr. U. Ill., Chgo., 1992—; tchr. Chgo. Pub. Schs., 1992—. Author: (comic book) Sustah-Girl Queen of Black Age, 1993; author, pub.: The Grammar Patrol, 1994. Mem. Am. Booksellers Assn., Soc. Childrens Writers & Illustrators, African-Am. Lang. Club (pres. 1992-94). Methodist. Home: 9534 S Bishop Chicago IL 60643

WASHINGTON, MARILYN GARRISON, health care educator; b. Bloomington, Ill., Nov. 21, 1943; d. Louis Arthur and Carrie (Winston) Garrison; m. René André Perry, May 25, 1968 (div. June 1982); children: Wendi Lynn, René André II; m. Lawrence Wendell Washington, 1992. AAS, Ill. Ctrl. Coll., 1973; BA, SUNY, Albany, 1987; MS, Nat. Louis U., 1991. RN; cert. tchr., Ill. RN, physicians asst. Xerox Corp., Webster, N.Y., 1977-82; trauma nurse Hermann Hosp., Houston, 1984-86; critical care, trauma and emergency rm. RN Nurse Finders, St. Louis and Houston, 1986-88; critical care/emergency rm. nurse St. Elizabeth Hosp., Granite City, Ill., 1989—; H.S. allied health instr. Granite City Schs., 1991—; allied health instr. Belleville Area Coll., Granite City, 1992—; owner, futurist, cons. Garrison Prodn. and Assocs., Edwardsville, Ill., 1990—. Author: Skills Lab, 1994. Choir dir. Mt. Joy Missionary Bapt. Ch., Edwardsville; mem. Lillian E. Campbell Choral, 1990. Recipient Achievement and Professionalism award Am. Soc. Profl. and Exec. Women, 1987. Mem. NAFE, Metro East Profl. Women. Home: 608 Chestnut St Edwardsville IL 62025 Office: Granite City Sr HS 3101 Madison Ave Granite City IL 62040

WASHINGTON, WILMA JEANNE, business executive; b. Magnolia, Miss., Oct. 14, 1949; d. Melvin and Wilma Magee; m. Michael Washington, Dec. 18, 1971 (div. 1978); children: Charisse, Jay. Student, Ind. U., 1973-80. Adminstrv. asst. Fred Harvey, Inc., Chgo., 1970-72; office mgr. Model Cities Agy., Gary, Ind., 1972-76; adminstrv. mgr. Med. Ctr. of Gary, 1976-81; events coord. Genesis Convention Ctr., Gary, 1981-83, exec. mgr., 1983-85; mgr. corp. devel. Dimensions Unltd., Inc., Chgo., 1985-87, v.p., 1987-92; owner Splty. Promotions, Gary, 1992—; booking agt. New Regal Theater, Chgo., 1995—. Mem. Miller Citizens Orgn., 1976—. Recipient appreciation cert. Northwest in Black Expo, 1985. Mem. NAFE, Gary C. of C. Baptist. Home & Office: 7741 Oak Ave Gary IN 46403-1364

WASICK, MARY ANN, librarian; b. Milw., July 19, 1946; d. Julius John and Florence Elizabeth (Brockway) W. BS in Edn., U. Wis., Milw., 1969; MA in Libr. Sci., U. Wis., Oshkosh, 1972; postgrad., U. Wis., 1969—. Tchr., libr. Milw. Pub. Schs., 1969-71; adminstrv. grad. asst. U. Wis., Oshkosh, 1971-72; libr. West Allis (Wis.) Pub. Libr., 1972—; reviewer in field. Bd. dirs. West Allis Hist. Soc., 1991-93; publicity chair Fountain Art Fair West Allis Art Alliance, 1991. Mem. ALA, Am. Classical League, Embroiderer's Guild Am (program chmn. 1989-90), Wis. Libr. Assn., Wis. Quilters Inc., U. Wis.-Oshkosh Alumni Assn. (life), U. Wis. Milw. Alumni Assn. (life). Home: 1310 S 98th St West Allis WI 53214-2641 Office: West Allis Pub Libr 7421 W National Ave West Allis WI 53214-4699

WASINGER, KRISTI LYNN, marketing professional, advertising consultant; b. Caldwell, Kans., Dec. 29, 1967; d. Richard Leon and Norma Lee (Fast) W. BS in Mktg., Kans. State U., 1990. Mgr. sect. sales Procter & Gamble, Overland Park, Kans., 1990-92; mktg./media planner Sullivan Higdon & Sink Advt., Wichita, Kans., 1992—. Mem. PEO-Women's Ednl. Orgn., Am. Mktg. Assn., Advt. Fedn.

WASMUND, MICHAEL CHARLES, aerospace engineering company administrator; b. Red Wing, Minn., Nov. 13, 1952. B, U. Minn., Duluth, 1976; M, U. Wis.-Stout, Menomonie, 1982. Group leader Woodland Hills Treatment Ctr., Duluth, Minn., 1976-78; machinist Ctrl. Rsch. Labs., Red Wing, 1978-80; gen. mgr. Aerospace Systems Co., Fairmont, Minn., 1982—. Mem. Exptl. Aircraft Assn. Office: Aerospace Systems Co 1007 E 10th St Fairmont MN 56031-3728

WASSELL, LOREN W., public affairs administrator, writer; b. Chgo., July 15, 1948; s. H. W. and Bernice (Kramer) W.; m. Rhonda Rothballer, Sept. 29, 1979; 1 daughter, Courtney C. BA, Lakeland Coll., 1969; postgrad., Ill. Cen. Coll., 1981-83. Reporter, anchorman Stas. WXCL and WZRO, Peoria, Ill., 1970-73; reporter Journal Star, Peoria, Ill., 1973-82; publs. editor Cen. Ill. Light co., Peoria, Ill., 1982-84; exec. communications writer Caterpillar Tractor Co., Peoria, Ill., 1984-85; mgr. editorial services Monsanto Co., St. Louis, 1985-90, pub. affairs dir., 1990-95; dir. pub. affairs Monsanto Chem. Co., St. Louis, 1995—. Mem. Peoria Pub. Bldg. Commn., 1982-85; trustee Orchard Lakes Subdiv., 1988—. Recipient Enterprise Reporting award Ill. Valley Press Club, 1974, Spot News Reporting award Ill. Valley Press Club, 1974. Mem. Internat. Assn. Bus. Communicators, Pub. Rels. Soc. Am., Coun. Communication Mgmt. Home: 12017 Lake Meade Dr Saint Louis MO 63146-4828

WASSER, FREDERICK ANTHONY, communications educator, writer; b. N.Y.C., June 30, 1953; s. Henry Hirsch and Solidelle Wasser. BA with honors, U. Chgo., 1975; MFA, Columbia U., 1981. Film editor Salt Lake City, 1983-84; critic The Event, Salt Lake City, 1983-84; journalist Sun & Moon Press, Salem Press et al, L.A., 1984-91; sound editor Hollywood Film Industry, L.A., 1984-91; instr. comms. Temple U., Phila., 1991-92, U. Ill., Champaign, 1992—; invited participant Media Studies Conf./Freedom Forum, N.Y.C., 1995. Producer, dir. film documentary Paterson 1979, 1980; producer, dir. comedy New Amsterdam New Amsterdam, 1981; film editor, 1984-91; set designer Hellbent, 1987; translator The Bird Lovers, 1994. Recipient Rsch. award Norway-Am. Assn., 1994; dissertation grantee U. Ill., 1995. Mem. Soc. for Cinema Studies, Univ. Film and Video Assn., Am. Studies Assn., Henry Adams Soc., Assn. for Edn. in Journalism and Mass Comm., Internat. Assn.Theatre and Stage Employees. Office: Inst for Comms Rsch 505 E Armory Rm 222B Champaign IL 61820

WASSERMAN, SHELDON A., state legislator; b. Milw., Aug. 15, 1961; m. Wendy Jo Wolfman; children: Joseph, Lauren. BS, U. Wis., 1983; MD, Med. Coll. Wis., 1987. Assemblyman Wis. State Dist. 22, 1993—; staff physician St. Mary's Hosp., Milw., 1991—, Columbia Hosp., Milw., 1991—, Sinai Samaritan Hosp., Milw., 1991—, Northwest Gen. Hosp., Milw., 1991—. Fellow AGOG; mem. AMA, Wis. Med. Soc., Milw. County Med. Soc., Phi Beta Kappa, Phi Kappa Phi. Address: 3487 N Lake Dr Milwaukee WI 53211

WASSON, BARBARA HICKAM, music educator; b. Spencer, Ind., Feb. 12, 1918. Student, DePauw U., 1937-38; BA, Vassar Coll., 1939; MusM, Chgo. Mus. Coll., 1944; postgrad., Ind. U., 1962-63. Founder, co-dir. Wasson Piano Studios, Dayton, 1946—; instr. Cedarville (Ohio) Coll., Dayton, 1970-72; adj. prof. Wright State U., Dayton, 1973-78; asst. prof. U. Cin., 1982-87. Mem. Ohio Music Tchrs. Assn. (pres. 1980-82), Dayton Music Club (pres. 1989-91), Mu Phi Epsilon (pres. Dayton alumnae chpt. 1986-88). Home: 5797 Paddington Rd Dayton OH 45459-1749

WASSON, JAMES WALTER, aircraft manufacturing company executive; b. Pitts., Dec. 9, 1951; s. George Fredrick and Dolores Helen (Weurl) W.; m. Evelyn Fay Gonzales, Dec. 28, 1974; children: Robert, Brian. AST, Pitts. Inst. Aeronautics, 1972; BSET, Northrop U., Inglewood, Calif., 1981; MBA, U. Phoenix, 1988, govt. contracts mgmt. cert., 1989. Avionics technician various cos., 1972-74; electronics prodn. mgr. Ostgaard Industries, Gardena, Calif., 1974-75; sr. avionics design engr. Allied Signal Garrett Airesearch Aviation Co., L.A., 1975-81; v.p. engring., co-founder Avionics Engring. Svcs., Inc., Tucson, 1980-81; sr. tech. specialist Northrop Aircraft Div., Hawthorne, Calif., 1981-84; prog. mgr. McDonnell Douglas Helicopter Co., Mesa, Ariz., 1984-86; tech. devel. mgr. McDonnell Douglas Helicopter Co., 1986-93; exec. v.p., co-founder Leading Edge Technologies, Inc., Mesa, 1991-95; mgr. bus. devel. McDonnell Douglas Helicopter Sys., Mesa, 1993-95; dir. tech. mktg. Smiths Aerospace, Grand Rapids, Mich., 1995—; adj. prof. govt. contract mgmt., program mgmt., proposal devel., strategic mktg., tech. mgmt., rsch. projects U. Phoenix, 1990—; cons. in field. Author: Avionics Systems Operation and Maintenance, 1993, Business Opportunities in Artificial Intelligence, 1988; contbr. articles to profl. jours. Inventor in field. Com. chmn. industry adv. bd. Northrop U., 1981; chmn. bd. dirs., pres. Alta Mesa Community Assn., 1989; organizer Boy Scouts Am., Mesa, 1988. Named Engr. of Yr., Northrop U., 1980; recipient Disting. Alumnus award Pitts. Inst. Aeronautics, 1981, U. Phoenix, 1996; named to Hall of Fame, Career Colls. Assn., 1991. Mem. IEEE, NSPE, Assn. Avionics Educators, Soc. Automotive Engrs., Army Aviation Assn. (chpt. sr. v.p. 1988-91, treas. 1993—), Am. Def. Preparedness Assn., Am. Helicopter Soc. (chmn. avionics com. 1990), Assn. Avionics Educators. Republican. Roman Catholic.

WASSON, RICHARD LEE, organic chemistry consultant; b. Farmington, Ill., May 19, 1932; s. Clair Wayne and Clarinda Maude Haines Wasson; m. Neva Joan Adams, June 25, 1955; children: Sue Anne Wasson Bohm, Nancy Jo. BS in Chemistry, U. Ill., 1953; PhD, MIT, 1956. Rsch. scientist Monsanto Co., St. Louis, 1956-65, rsch. group leader, 1965-71, mgr. flavor and fragrance rsch., 1971-76, mgr. new product rsch. and comml. devel., 1976-78, dir. tech., 1978-84; cons. on rsch. info. systems Monsanto Co., 1980-85; dir. devel. G.D. Searle div. Monsanto Co., St. Louis, 1984-89; ret., 1989, sci. cons., 1990—; lectr. on mgmt. process, 1975—. Contbr. articles to profl. jours., chpt. to Ency. Chem. Process and Design. Naturalist Mo. Dept. Conservation; elder Presbyn. Ch. U.S.A. Fellow Am. Inst. Chemists; mem. Am. Chem. Soc., N.Y. Acad. Scis., St. Louis Acad. Scis., Sigma Xi, Phi Eta Sigma, Phi Kappa Phi, Phi Lambda Upsilon, Alpha Kappa Lambda (Alumni award 1965). Home and Office: 8821 Hemingway Dr Saint Louis MO 63126-1929

WASYLIK, KENNETH EDWARD, business development manager; b. Chgo., Apr. 29, 1957; s. Edward Marion and Dolores Elizabeth (Lewandowski) W.; m. Dolores Maria Eykmans, Sept. 15, 1984; children: Amanda Maria, Lucas Kenneth, Leah Danielle. BS in Acctg. and Fin., Marquette U., 1979; M. Internat. Mgmt., Am. Grad. Sch. Internat. Mgmt., 1983. CPA. Sr. comml. loan analyst officer First Wis. Nat. Bank, Milw., 1979-82; mgr. sales/fin., bus. devel. Harris Corp., Rochester, N.Y., 1984-89; mgr. sales, fin. & bus. devel. Harris Corp., Quincy, Ill., 1989—; lectr. SUNY, Brockport, 1985-88, John Wood C.C., Quincy, 1989—. Exec. v.p. Rochester (N.Y.) Internat. Bus. Coun., 1986-89; dir. Harris Credit Union, Quincy, 1992-95. Mem. AICPAs. Office: Harris Corp 3200 Wisman Ln Quincy IL 62301-1252

WASYLKOWSKI, STEVE EUGENE, brokerage house executive; b. Dover, Del., July 3, 1941; s. John and Helen (Chike) W.; m. Charlotte Ann Ziaya, Dec. 24, 1974. BS, Fla. State U., 1969, MBA, 1970. Lic. gen. securities prin. Broker Paine Webber Jackson & Co., Denver, 1970-75; broker, asst. v.p. A.G. Edwards & Sons, Denver, 1975-81; v.p. Drexel Burnham Lambert, Denver, 1981-85; pres. Integrated Fin. Securities Inc., Denver, 1985-87,

Comml. Fed. Investment Svcs. Corp., Omaha, 1987-90; pres., CEO FMB Brokerage Svcs., Inc., Holland, Mich., 1990-93, also dir.; sole proprietor, mng. dir. Securities Am., Inc., Holland, 1993—. Vice consul U.S. Dept. State, 1965-68; fundraiser Herrick Pub. Libr., Holland, 1992. With USCG, 1959-63. Mem. Macatawa Bay Yacht Club (bd. dirs.). Republican. Home: 1242 Oak Hampton St Holland MI 49424-2625

WATERMAN, JOHN M., state legislator; m. Cheryl Lynn Waterman. Sheriff Sullivan County; mem. Ind. State Senate Dist. 39, mem. agr. and small bus. com., mem. corrections, criminal and civil procedures com., mem. natural resources com., mem. pub. policy com. Mem. NRA.

WATERS, DONALD EUGENE, academic administrator; b. Muncie, Ind., Mar. 28, 1941; s. William James and Mary Harriet (Peare) W.; m. Kathryn Elaine Small, Aug. 17, 1963; children: Jill Maras, Janet Schulenburg. BS in Social Studies and English, Ball State U., 1963, MS in Guidance, 1964; EdD in Adminstrn. and Higher Edn., U. Mo., 1973. Dir. residence hall Ball State U., Muncie, 1964-66; asst. dean of students U. No. Iowa, Cedar Falls, 1966-70; with U. Mo., Columbia, 1970-73; dir. community edn. Muscatine (Iowa) Community Coll., 1973-75, dean arts and scis., 1975-77; asst. to pres. Elgin (Ill.) Community Coll., 1977-88, v.p. corp. devel., 1988—. Councilman City of Elgin, 1980-87; mem. policy steering com. Nat. League of Cities, Washington, 1986-87; v.p., bd. dirs. United Way of Elgin, 1986-94, chair, bd. dirs. Golden Corridor Steering Com., Ill., 1986-90. Mem. Nat. Coun. Resource Devel. (pres. 1993, treas., bd. dirs. 1986-90, Lifetime Svc. award 1994), Ill. Resource Devel. Commn. (pres. 1986-87), Kiwanis (dist. pres. 1983-84). Methodist. Office: Elgin Community Coll 1700 Spartan Dr Elgin IL 60123-7189

WATERS, ELLEN MAUREEN, publishing executive, writer; b. Liberty, Ill., Aug. 19, 1938; d. Charles Francis and Virginia Elizabeth (Robinson) Linker; m. Gerald Louis Waters, Jan. 18, 1957 (div. 1990); children: Tamara, Gerri-Layne, Christina, Andrea. Student, Baker U., 1977-82, 88—; grad. Women's Leadership Inst., Avila Coll., 1990, grad. Women's Entrepreneur Program, 1990. Typesetter, reporter Baldwin (Kans.) Ledger, 1967-73; editor Wellsville (Kans.) Globe, 1973-74; asst. registrar Baker U., Baldwin City, 1975-77, registrar, 1977-82; mng. editor Mag. Design and Prodn., editor Pre mag. Southwind Pub. Co., Prairie Village, Kans., 1985-92; editor Signature mag., 1992-94; freelance writer, Baldwin City, 1974—, Overland Park, 1984—; owner, operator Mentor Editl. Svc., Overland Park; lectr., cons. on mentoring. Editor, publ. Mentor newsletter. Mentor, Women's Network for Entrepreneurial Tng., SBA. Mem. Internat. Mentoring Assn., Nat. Spkrs. Assn. (v.p. profl. devel. Kansas City chpt.). Office: PO Box 4382 Overland Park KS 66204-0382

WATERS, GARY L., poultry scientist. Pres. DeKalb Poultry Rsch. Inc. Office: DeKalb Poultry Rsch Inc PO Box 926 De Kalb IL 60115*

WATERS, GWENDOLYN, human services administrator; b. Columbus, Ohio, Jan. 10, 1954; d. Harry Amos and Bertha Beatrice (Meadows) W.; 1 child, Harry B. BA, Holy Cross Coll., 1976; postgrad., Capital Law Sch., 1977-79. Income maintenance worker Franklin County Dept. Human Svcs., Columbus, 1977-79; accounts payable clk. Assn. for Developmentally Disabled, Columbus, 1979-80, cmty. aide, 1980-84; mgmt. evaluation reviewer Ohio Dept. Human Svcs., Cleve., 1985-89, pub. assistance coord., 1989—. Violinist Heights Civic Orch., Cleveland Heights, Ohio, 1985-90, pres. bd. dirs., 1990; mem. Libr. of Congress, African Am. Mus. Recipient Blue Ribbon, Ohio State Fair, 1978-84, Cuyahoga County Fair, 1985-95, Grand prize Ohio State Fair, 1989-90. Mem. Assn. for Study of African-Am. Life and History, Smithsonian Instn. Office: Ohio Dept Human Svcs 615 W Superior Ave Ste 990 Cleveland OH 44113-1801

WATERS, HAROLD ARTHUR, veterinarian; b. Denver, May 19, 1928; s. Arthur Bryan and Viola Johanna (Johnson) W.; m. Margaret Evangeline Zylstra, June 22, 1952; children: Paul Harold, David Lloyd, Mary Margaret. DVM, Colo. State U., 1952. Cert. veterinarian, Kans. Veterinarian USDA, Washington, 1953-82; pres. Animal Health Internat., Inc., Topeka, 1982—. Mem. Am. Vet. Med. Assn., Nat. Assn. Fed. Veterinarians, Animal Transp. Assn. (bd. mem. 1980-89), Kans. Vet. Med. Assn. Democrat. Methodist. Home and Office: Animal Health Internat 2912 SW Cedar Cove Ct Topeka KS 66614

WATERS, STEPHEN RUSSELL, state agency administrator; b. Quincy, Ill., Jan. 9, 1954; s. Russell O. and Dorothy Ann (Bartz) W.; m. Nancy K. Morris, Aug. 31, 1974; children: Leslie Ann, Ryan Patrick. BS in Law Enforcement, N.E. Mo. State, 1976. Police officer City of Kirksville, Mo., 1975; adminstrv. asst. to speaker pro-tem Mo. House of Reps., Jefferson City, 1976; investment counselor IDS Mktg., Dubuque, Iowa, 1977-78; dir. legal svcs. Mark Twain Legal Svcs., Canton, Mo., 1978-80; probation and parole officer State of Mo., Hannibal, 1980-84; juvenile officer 2d Jud. Cir., Edina, Mo., 1984-86; rep. Mo. Ho. of Reps., Canton, 1987-94; dir. Mo. Divsn. Transp. Dept. Econ. Devel., Jefferson City, 1994—. Chmn. parks City of Canton, 1980-82; alderman City of Canton, 1980-84. Mem. Am. Corrections Assn., Mo. Corrections Assn., N.E. Mo. Peace Officers, Moose, Kiwanis (bd. dirs. Canton chpt. 1979-80), Canton C. of C. (pres. 1979-82). Democrat. Mem. Christian Ch. Office: Mo Divsn Transp Dept Econ Devel PO Box 1216 Jefferson City MO 65101

WATERS, THOMAS ALFRED, political science educator; b. Harlingen, Tex., Nov. 16, 1940; s. Cecil Daniel and Lexie Ruth (Dunagin) W. BA, Pan Am. U., 1963; AM, The George Washington U., 1966; doctoral candidate, The Ohio State U., 1972. Assoc. prof. U. Wis., Platteville, 1966—, chmn. social scis. dept., 1995. Supr., elected ofcl. Grant County Bd. of Suprs., Lancaster, Wis., 1978—; chair employee rels. Grant County Bd., 1988-94, chair fin. com., 1994—, vice chair county bd., 1994—. Mem. Am. Polit. Sci. Assn., Internat. Studies Assn., Midwest Polit. Sci. Assn. Home: 335 Southwest Rd Platteville WI 53818 Office: U Wis Platteville 1 University Plz Platteville WI 53818

WATERS, WAYNE ARTHUR, conference and travel service agency executive; b. Ft. Wayne, Ind., Mar. 9, 1929; s. Roy Edwin and Mary Catherine (Housel) W. m. Helen Marie Gump, Nov. 18, 1950; children: Bradley Wayne, Jeffry Scott, Ann Kathryn. Owner, mgr. Grain and Dairy Farm, Ft. Wayne, 1947-54; auto salesman Haynes & Potter, Auburn, Ind., 1956-58; asst. v.p. Lincoln Nat. Life, Ft. Wayne, 1958-83; pres. Conf. and Travel Svcs. Inc., Ft. Wayne, 1983-93; chmn., CEO Conf. and Trafel Svcs. Inc., 1993—; bd. dirs. Meeting World, 1979-81, 87; mem. adv. coun. United Airlines Travel Agy. Contbr. articles to Best Ins. Guide, Meetings and Conventions, Green Book of Convention Planning, Ins. Conf. Planners Mag., others. With U.S. Army, 1954-56. Fellow Internat. Biog. Assn.; named Boss of Yr. Am. Bus. Women Assn., 1972, Boss of Yr. Ft. Wayne Jaycees, 1987, Small Bus. Person of April 1991. Mem. Soc. Co. Meeting Planners (bd. dirs. 1973-74, pres. 1975-76, Leadership award 1974), Ins. Conf. Planners (bd. dirs. 1979-81, pres. 1982), Am. Soc. Travel Agts., Soc. Incentive Travel Execs., Cruise Line Internat. Assn., Meeting Planners Internat., The Travel Coun., Ft. Wayne C. of C. (air svc. coun. 1984—, Sml. Bus. Person of May 1984), Ind. C. of C., Ft. Wayne Air Svc. Coun., Sml. Bus. Coun. Republican. Mem. Ch. of the Brethren. Clubs: Orchard Ridge Country (Ft. Wayne), Summit. Office: Conf & Travel Svcs Inc 5681 Coventry Ln Fort Wayne IN 46804-7145

WATHEN, KAREN DENISE, home health care nurse; b. Shelbyville, Ind., Oct. 12, 1953; d. James and Patsy Ruth (Bowman) Francis; m. Michael Joseph Wathen, Aug. 17, 1974; children: Christopher Michael, David Andrew. BSN, Ball State U., 1975. RN, Ind.; cert. home health nurse ANCC. Nurse ICU, critical care unit, med.-surg., obstetrics Greene County Gen. Hosp., Linton, Ind., 1976-79; nurse emergency rm. Greene County Gen. Hosp., Linton, 1979-85, relief evening supr., 1983-85; dir. Greene County Gen. Hosp. Home Care, Linton, 1985—; CPR instr. Am. Heart Assn., Linton, 1985—. Com. mem. Boy Scouts Am. Troop 450 and Pack 453, Linton. Named Young Careerist, Bus. and Profl. Women's Club, Linton, 1982. Mem. Ind. Assn. Home Health Agys. (ethics com., pub. rels. com., medicare com., program chmn.). Roman Catholic. Office: Green County Gen Hosp RR 1 Box 555 Linton IN 47441

WATKINS, CHERYL DENISE, newspaper editor; b. Cleve., July 29, 1966; d. Edward Watkins and Joeann Patton Carter; 1 child, Tonya Monique Merchant. Grad. h.s., Cleve. With USN, 1985-93. Baptist.

WATKINS, HORTENSE CATHERINE, middle school educator; b. St. Louis, Nov. 29, 1924; d. Isaiah S. and Katie M. (Phelps) W. BA, Harris-Stowe State Coll., St. Louis, 1946; MEd, U. Ill., 1953; postgrad. U. Chgo., InterAm. U., Saltillo, Coahuila, Mex.; postgrad., U. Seville, Spain, Webster U., St. Louis. Cert. life tchr., reading specialist, Mo. Coord. urban rural programs Carver-Dunbar Schs., St. Louis, 1975-76; adminstrv. asst. Shaw Visual Performing Arts Sch., St. Louis, 1978-82; team IV leader Woerner IGE, St. Louis, 1982-87; tchr., head lang. arts dept. Nottingham Mid. Sch., St. Louis, 1987-92; tutor fgn.-speaking religious, presenter, lectr. numerous workshops; curriculum advisor St. Louis Pub. Schs. Active numerous comty. orgns.; bd. dirs. St. Louis Cathedral Sch., St. Louis Metro Singers, Concert Series of St. Louis Cathedral. Mem. ASCD, Nat. Coun. Tchrs. English, Mo. State Tchrs. Assn., Greater St. Louis Coun. Social Studies, Delta Sigma Theta (Golden life), Delta Kappa Gamma. Home: 5070A Enright Ave Saint Louis MO 63108-1008

WATKINS, MICHAEL JAMES, real estate broker; b. Crawfordsville, Ind., Dec. 18, 1945; s. James H. Gordon and Mary Jane Harlson; m. Jeanne Watkins, Apr. 3, 1971; children: Patrick, christopher. BS, U. Indpls., 1968; MS, Butler U., 1972. Tchr., coach New Palestine (Ind.) High Sch., 1968-69, Franklin (Ind.) High Sch., 1969-72; admissions counselor U. Indpls., 1972-73, dir. fin. aid, 1973-76, dean of students, 1975-78; owner Michael J. Realty, Indpls., 1978-80; sales mgr. Credence Contractors, Greenwood, Ind., 1980-83; broker, assoc. Tomlin Realtors, Greenwood, 1983-95; pres. Mike Watkins Real Estate Group, Greenwood, 1995—. Mem. Pres.'s Club, U. Indpls., 1984—; trustee Marian Coll., Indpls., 1989-92, U. Indpls., 1992—. Named to Outstanding Young Men of Am., 1974, 76. Mem. Met. Bd. Realtors (named Southside Realtor of Yr. 1984), Nat. Assn. Realtors, U. Indpls. Alumni Varsity Club (Alumnus of Yr. 1986). Republican. Roman Catholic. Home: 3696 Saddle Club Rd Greenwood IN 46143-9230 Office: Mike Watkins Real Estate 633 Library Park Ste J Greenwood IN 46142

WATKINS, SHERRY LYNNE, elementary school educator; b. Bloomington, Ind., Oct. 13, 1944; d. Quentin Odell and Velma Ruth W. BSEd, Ind. U., 1966, MSEd, 1968. Tchr. 4th grade North Grove Elem. Sch., Ctr. Grove Sch. Dist., Greenwood, Ind., 1966-68; tchr. 4th and 6th grades John Strange Sch., Met. Dist. of Wash. Twp., Indpls., 1968-91; tchr. 4th grade Allisonville Sch. Met. Sch. Dist. of Wash. Twp., Indpls., 1991—. Mem. People for Ethical Treatment of Animals. Mem. NEA (nat. del. 1978—), ACLU, AAUW, Ind. Tchrs. Assn. (state del. 1966—), Washington Twp. Edn. Assn. (pres. 1986-89), World Confedn. Orgn. of Tchg. Profls. (del. Costa Rica 1990), Delta Kappa Gamma (chpt. pres. 1992-94, chmn. coord. coun. Indpls. area 1994-96), Alpha Omicron Pi. Office: Allisonville Sch 4920 E 79th St Indianapolis IN 46250-1615

WATLINGTON, SARAH JANE, community volunteer, retired military officer; b. Denver, May 6, 1938; d. William Thomas and Margaret (Stewart) W. BS, Purdue U., 1960; MA, Naval Post Grad. Sch., 1970. Commd. ensign USN, 1960, advanced through grades to capt., 1979; social sec. Chief of Naval Operations, Washington, 1966-69; exec. officer Recruit Tng. Command, Bainbridge, Md., 1971-73; head officer student placement Bur. Naval Personnel, Washington, 1973-75; exec. officer NROTC Unit, Purdue U., West Lafayette, Ind., 1976-79; commanding officer Navy Manpower and Material Analysis Ctr., San Diego, 1979-82; dep. dir. manpower & tng. Office Chief of Naval Ops., Washington, 1982-83; ret., 1984; sec. Cmty. and Family Resource Ctr., Lafayette, Ind., 1990-91; mem. dean of liberal arts adv. coun., 1992—. Vol. YWCA, Lafayette, 1984—, bd. dirs., 1985-91, pres., 1988-90, v.p., 1994-95, sec., 1995-96; bd. dirs. YWCA Found., Lafayette, 1988-90, 94—, Greater Lafayette Mus. Art, 1984-85; pres. Greater Lafayette Cmty. Found., 1996—; mem. nat. nominating com. YWCA U.S.A., 1991-94; trustee, sec.-treas. Alpha Chi Omega Found., 1996; pres. Ind. Coun. YMCAs, 1994—, Cmty. Health Clinic, 1995-96. Decorated Legion of Merit with gold star; recipient Jefferson award, 1989, Disting. Alumna award Purdue Sch. Liberal Arts, 1990, Grand Marquis de Lafayette award for Cmty. Svc., 1995, Mortar Bd. award of achievement, 1995, Sagamore of the Wabash award Ind. Gov., 1995. Mem. Purdue U. Sch. Liberal Arts Alumni Assn. (pres. 1991-92), Purdue Pres. Coun., John Purdue Club, Gold Block Booster Club (sec. 1986-87, Girl Scout Woman of Distinction 1992), Boilermaker Network Booster Club (sec. 1991-94), Alpha Chi Omega (Disting. Alumna award 1980, Golden Gavel Woman of Distinction award 1994). Congregational. Home: 9 Elvernan Dr West Lafayette IN 47906-9424

WATNE, DARLENE CLAIRE, state legislator; b. Minot, N.D., Feb. 11, 1935; d. Charles and Anna (Fjeld) Widdel; m. Clair A. Watne, 1954; children: Carmen (Watne) Hadreas, Steven, Nancy (Watne) Mitchell, Matthew. Cert. ct. reporting, Minot Bus. Coll., 1975. Assoc. broker; cert. residential specialist; grad. Real Estate Inst.; residential mktg. master. Senator N.D. State Senate, Bismarck, 1994—; bd. dirs. Minot Bd. Realtors, 1993, No. States Power, 1995—; vice chmn. judiciary com. polit. subdivsn. com. N.D. State Senate. Bd. dirs. Minot YWCA, 1989-92, Minot Symphony Assn., 1986-91, 95—; mem. Minot Area Coun. Arts, 1995—. Named Woman of Distinction in Bus. and Industry, Minot YWCA, 1993. Mem. Nat. Bd. Realtors, N.D. Realtors Assn. (vice chmn. com., 1990—), N.D. Shorthand Reporters Assn. (pres. 1984-85), Rotary. Home: 520 28th Ave SW Minot ND 58701 Office: 408 N Broadway Bismarck ND 58703

WATSON, ANDREW SAMUEL, psychiatry and law educator; b. Highland Park, Mich., May 2, 1920; s. Andrew Nicol and Eva Arvel (Barnes) W.; m. Catherine Mary Osborne, Sept. 1942; children: Andrew Nicol, John Lewis, David Winfield, Steven; m. Joyce Lynn Goldstein, July 21, 1967. BS in Zoology, U. Mich., 1942; MD, Temple U., 1950, M in Med. Sci., 1954. Intern, U. Pa. Grad. Hosp., 1950-51; resident in psychiatry Temple U., Phila., 1951-54; spl. lectr. Sch. Social Work, Bryn Mawr Coll., 1955-59; mem. med. faculty U. Pa., 1954-59, law faculty, 1955-59; prof. psychiatry U. Mich., Ann Arbor, 1959-80, mem. law faculty, 1959-90, prof. emeritus psychiatry and of law, 1990; pvt. practice medicine, specializing in psychiatry, Ann Arbor, 1959—. Mem. Mich. Law Enforcement and Criminal Justice Commn., 1968-72. Served to capt. Med. Service Corps, AUS, 1942-46. Recipient Issac Ray award Am. Psychiat. Assn., 1978. Mem. Am. Psychiat. Assn., Am. Coll. Psychiatry, ABA (assoc.). Democrat. Unitarian. Author: Psychiatry for Lawyers, rev. edit., 1978; The Lawyer in the Interviewing and Counseling Process, 1976; others. Home: 21 Ridgeway St Ann Arbor MI 48104-1739 Office: 555 E William St Apt 21D Ann Arbor MI 48104-2427

WATSON, DAVID BRUCE, civil, structural engineer; b. Yuma, Colo., Aug. 5, 1955; s. Eldon Glen and Patricia Ruth (Hartwell) W.; m. Sheila Christine Most-Watson; children: Amber Ann, Alicia Dawn. BSCE, U. Nebr., 1980. Registered profl. engr., Kans., Nebr., Colo., Mo., Tenn., Iowa, Ohio, Oreg., Ark.; pvt. pilot. Structural engr. Howard-Needles-Tammen & Bergendoff, Overland Park, Kans., 1980-81; project engr. Butler Mfg. Inc., Kansas City, Mo., 1981-82; civil design mgr. Payless Cashways, Inc., Kansas City, 1982-88, design mgr., 1992—; chief engr. Oppenheimer Design/Build, Kansas City, 1988-90; civil/structural engr. Lutz, Daily & Brian, Overland Park, 1990; prin. Watson & Assocs., Shawnee, Kans., 1990-92; v.p. Facility Design, Inc., Overland Park, Kans., 1994—. Scholarship Bd. Regents, 1976. Mem. ASCE (program com. 1987—), Am. Concrete Inst., Aircraft Owners and Pilots Assn., Exptl. Aircraft Assn. Republican. Lutheran. Home: 6721 Earnshaw St Shawnee KS 66216-2847 Office: Facility Design Inc 8500 W 110th Ste 525 Overland Park KS 66210

WATSON, DEBRAHA KAFI, respiratory therapist; b. Detroit, Aug. 23, 1951; d. John and Gerri (Cox) Smith; children: Yohanis, Jamila. BA in Allied Health, Siena Heights, 1987; MS, Ctrl. Mich. U., 1992; MEd, Morehead State U., 1994. Reg. respiratory therapist. Respiratory therapist Detroit Osteo., Highland Park, Mich., 1980-81; respiratory supr. Annapolis Hosp., Wayne, Mich., 1980-89; asst. dir. Detroit Receiving Hosp., 1989-93; tchr. Highland Park (Mich.) Schs., 1994-95; respiratory therapist Grace Hosp., Detroit, 1995—; mgmt. cons. Enlightenment Inc., Detroit, 1995—; mem. adv. bd. Marygrove Allied Health, Detroit, 1992-93. Author: Revelations, 1993, (poetry collection) Good Hair, 1995. Active Penn Ctr., Detroit, Black Women's Health Project, Atlanta. Mem. Am. Assn. Respiratory Care, African Am. Women's Network (chair 1993—), Nat. Black Grad. Assn. Home: 15048 Whitcomb Detroit MI 48227

WATSON, DUANE FREDERICK, religious studies educator; b. Watertown, N.Y., May 15, 1956; s. Frederick Halsted and Beverley Alice (Taylor) W.; m. JoAnn Christine Ford, June 2, 1984; 1 child, Christina Lucille. BA, Houghton (N.Y.) Coll., 1978; MDiv, Princeton Theol. Sem., 1981; PhD, Duke U., 1986. Ordained to ministry Meth. U., 1980. Asst. prof. biblical studies Ashland (Ohio) Theol. Sem., 1984-86; pastor Northwestern (N.Y.) United Meth. Ch., 1987-89; asst. prof. N.T. studies, chair dept. religion & philosophy Malone Coll., Canton, Ohio, 1989-92, assoc. prof., 1992-96, prof., 1996—, chair dept. religion & philosophy, 1993—. Author: Invention, Arrangement and Style, 1988, Persuasive Artistry, 1991, Rhetorical Criticism of The Bible, 1994; contbr. articles to profl. jours.; mem. editl. bd. Proceedings, Ea. Gt. Lakes and Midwest Bibl. Socs., 1993-95. Recipient Excellence in Bibl. studies award Am. Bible Soc., Houghton Coll., 1978. Mem. Studiorum Novi Testamenti Societas, Soc. Bibl. Lit. (steering com. rhetoric sect. 1990-95), Cath. Bibl. Assn., Internat. Soc. for History of Rhetoric, Rhetoric Soc. Am., Inst. Bibl. Rsch., Ea. Great Lakes Bibl. Soc. Republican. Office: Malone Coll 515 25th St NW Canton OH 44709

WATSON, FRANK CHARLES, state legislator; b. St. Louis, July 26, 1945; s. Charles I. and Pauline (Logsdon) W.; m. Susan DeAnn Rasler, 1969; children: Charles Adam, Kathry Melissa. BPharm, Purdue U., 1968. Trustee and supr. Bond County Ctrl. Twp., Greenville, Ill., 1973-77, bd. suprs.; Ill. state rep., 1979-82; mem. Ill. State Senate, Dist. 55, 1983—, minority spokesman, mem. transp. appropriations II, elem. and secondary edn., mem. Ill. adv. coun. on alcoholism and drug abuse, legis. printing unit coms., joint com. on regulation of professions and occupation, citizens assembly coun. on energy resources, agrl. and conservations and revenue coms., asst. majority leader; owner The Corner Clothing Store, Greenville, Ill., 1971—, Watson Drug Store, 1972—; bd. dirs. Hillview Manor Nursing Home, First Nat. Bank, Salem Nat. Bank; pharmacist. Mem. Phi Gamma Delta. Republican. Office: RR 4 Box 24B Greenville IL 62246-9405*

WATSON, JAMES ROBERT, design educator; b. New Orleans, July 27, 1950; s. James Webster and Loraine Ruth (Remmel) W. BS, U. Tex., 1979; MEd, U. North Tex., 1982, PhD, 1987. Cert. tchr., Tex. Designer Richland Coll., Dallas, 1982-87; freelance designer Dallas, 1984-87; instr. design Brookhaven Coll., Dallas, 1984-87; prof. U. Ctrl. Okla., Edmond, 1987—. Home: 424 E 4th Edmond OK 73034-9999 Office: Univ Ctrl Okla Art Dept Art Dept Edmond OK 73034

WATSON, JOANN FORD, theology educator; b. Ashland, Ohio, Apr. 11, 1956; d. Laurence Wesley and Edna Lucille (Garber) F.; m Duane Frederick Watson, June 2, 1984; 1 child, Christina Lucille. BA, DePauw U., 1978; MDiv, Princeton Theol. Sem., 1981; PhD, Northwestern U., 1984. Ordained to ministry, Presbyn. Ch. Asst. prof. hist. theology Ashland Theol. Sem., 1984-86, assoc. prof. theology, chair dept. ch. history and theology, 1989-95, H.R. Gill Prof. of theology, 1996—; chaplain Grady Meml. Hosp., Atlanta, 1986-87; co-pastor Tri-Ch. Parish United Meth. Chs. Northwestern, N.Y., 1987-89; pastor Camroden Presbyn. Ch., Rome, N.Y., 1987-89; clergy commr. del. Gen. Assembly of Presbyn. Ch., 1995. Author: Manna for Sisters in Christ, 1989, Mutuality in Christ, 1991, Meditations on Suffering, 1993, Study of Karl Barth's Doctrine of Man and Woman, 1995. Missionary vol. Mother Teresa's Missionaries of Charity, Calcutta, 1988; mem. Hospice Ashland County chpt., 1989-93; assoc. mem. Women's Symphony League, Ashland Symphony Orch., 1989-94. Doctoral fellowship Northwestern U., 1982-84. Mem. Internat. Assn. of Women Mins. (exec. bd., trustee 1990-95), Presbyn. Women in Leadership, Nat. Assn. of Presbyn. Clergywomen, Soc. of Biblical Lit., Am. Acad. of Religion, Alpha Lambda Delta, Phi Beta Kappa. Republican. Office: Ashland Theolog Sem 910 Center St Ashland OH 44805

WATSON, JOHN CECIL, insurance company executive; b. Riverton, Ill., Dec. 10, 1932; s. Clarence C. and Isabel H. Watson; m. Nancy J. Walker, June 17, 1958; children: Troy, Tracey. BS, Ill. State U., 1954; MBA, So. Ill. U., 1957. CLU. Mgmt. trainee Franklin Life Ins. Co., Springfield, Ill., 1957-66, asst. v.p., 1966-69, v.p., 1969-73, consumer affairs officer, 1973-74, sr. v.p., consumer affairs officer, 1974-82, sr. v.p. mktg., 1982-85, exec. v.p., 1985-88, exec. v.p., chief operating officer, 1988-90, pres., chief operating officer, 1990—, also bd. dirs.; chmn., CEO Midland Nat. Life Ins. Co., Sioux Falls, S.D., 1992—; chmn., CEO, pres. Sammons Fin. Holdings, Dallas, 1996—; bd. dirs. Franklin United Life of N.Y., Franklin Fin. Svcs. Corp., Am. Franklin Life Ins. Co. Gen. chmn. Springfield Meml. Med. Ctr. Found. Mem. Life Office Mgmt. Assn. (cert.), Am. Coll. Life Underwriters, Life Ins. Mktg. Rsch. Assn., Springfield C. of C. (bd. dirs.). Office: Midland Nat Life Ins Co 1 Midland Plz Sioux Falls SD 57193-0001

WATSON, JOYCE ANN, foundation administrator; b. Rockford, Ill., June 2, 1946; d. Sumner I. and Mildred H. (Doeden) Ranken; m. Allan Watson, June 17, 1967; 1 child, Ty. BS in Edn., Western Ill. U., 1968, postgrad., 1971. Home econs. instr. Avon (Ill.) Jr. High Sch., 1968-72; dir. consumer edn. Ill. Beef Industry Coun., Macomb, 1973-80; food svc. mgmt. instr. Robert Morris Coll., Carthage, Ill., 1981; acting exec. dir. Ill. Agrl. Leadership Found., Macomb, 1980-82, exec. dir., 1982-94; pres., 1994—. Editor, designer: Kitchen Economy: Cut Your Own Beef, 1976, Kitchen Economy: Beef in the Microwave, 1977; co-editor: Basics About Beef, 1975. Bd. dirs. Salvation Army, Macomb, 1982—, Rural Ptnrs., 1993—. Mem. Nat. Soc. Fund Raising Execs., Chgo. Soc. Assn. Execs. (mem. chief exec. officer com. 1988-91, edn. com. 1992, spl. events com. 1993-94, A Better Chicagoland com. 1994-95, exec. profile task force com. 1995—), Chgo. Soc. Fund Raising Execs. (mem. cert. com. 1988), Ill. Leadership Coun. for Agr. Edn. (v.p. 1988), Macomb Country Club (bd. dirs. 1982-92). Office: Ill Agrl Leadership Found PO Box 160 100 S Campbell Macomb IL 61455-0160

WATSON, LYNN R., executive; b. Minot, N.D., May 19, 1954. BS and BA, U. N.D., 1981. Stock broker Dean Witter, Billings, Mont., 1983-91; v.p. acquisitions Odell-Wentz and Assocs. LLC, Minot, N.D., 1991—. Mem. Kiwanis Club. Mem. NRA. Republican. Methodist. Office: Odell-Wentz and Assoc LLC 12 Main St S Minot ND 58701-3835

WATSON, RICHARD THOMAS, lawyer; b. Lakewood, Ohio, Aug. 21, 1933; s. Thomas Earl Watson and Sara Lucille (Whapham) Hadfield; m. Judith C. Briggs, Aug. 6, 1960; children: David, Andrew, Susan (dec.). AB, Harvard U., 1954, JD, 1960. Bar: Ohio 1960. Assoc. Spieth, Bell, McCurdy & Newell, Cleve., 1960, ptnr., 1965, mng. ptnr., 1987—; bd. dirs. numerous corps. Chancellor Episcopal Diocese of Ohio, Cleve., 1986—; mem. Harvard U. Univ. Resources, 1992—; v.p. bd. trustees Cleve. Mus. Art, 1991—; trustee Case Western Res. U., 1993—. Mem. Union Club Cleve. Office: Spieth Bell McCurdy & Newell 925 Euclid Ave Cleveland OH 44115

WATSON, STEPHEN ALLISON, III, lawyer; b. Spokane, Wash., Aug. 17, 1957; s. Stephen Allison Jr. and Joan (Sauter) W. BA in Polit. Sci., Northwestern U., 1979; JD, Case We. U., 1982. Bar: Ohio 1983, U.S. Dist. (no. dist.) Ohio 1983. Counsel, environ. claims mgr. Argonaut Ins. Co., Cleve., 1982-86; mgr. hazardous waste unit Zurich Ins. Co., Schaumburg, Ill., 1989-91; mgr. environ. line bus. Zurich Ins. Co., Schaumburg, 1991-94; dir. regulatory svcs. Foster Wheeler Environ. Corp., Lyndhurst, N.J., 1995—; cons. Office Spl. Dep., Chgo., 1995—; lectr. in field. Contbr. articles to profl. jours. Mem. ABA (natural resource, energy and environ. law sect.), Def. Rsch. Inst. (environ. law com.). Republican. Office: Foster Wheeler Environ Corp 1290 Wall St W Lyndhurst NJ 07071

WATT, JEFFREY XAVIER, mathematics sciences educator, researcher; b. Indpls., July 14, 1961; s. John Hayden and Beverly Ann (Schneider) W. BS in Geophysics, Mich. Technol. U., 1983; MS in Geology, Emory U., 1984; MS in Applied Math., Purdue U., 1986; PhD in Math., Ind. U., 1990. Lectr. Ind. U.-Purdue U., Indpls., 1988-90; asst. prof. math. scis. Purdue U. Sch. Sci., Indpls., 1990—; cons. Park Tutor High Sch., Indpls., 1990—. Eucharistic min. St. Albert the Gt. Ch., Mich., 1982; referee Ind. High Sch. Athletic Assn., 1983—. NSF rsch. grantee, 1992—. Mem. Indpls. Hockey Ofcls. Assn. (exec. bd. 1986—). Home: PO Box 2813 Indianapolis IN 46206-2813

WATT, JOHN HAYDEN, pharmacist; b. Indpls., Aug. 2, 1938; s. William Roy Jr. and Flora Marie (Altemeyer) W.; m. Beverly Ann Schnedier, Dec. 26, 1960 (div. Mar. 1972); children: Jeffery X., Frederick K., Christopher J.; m. Nina Jo Dean, Apr. 6, 1973. BS in Pharmacy, Butler U., 1960, MS in Clin. Pharmacy, 1988. Registered pharmacist, Ind. Asst. mgr., chief pharmacist Jordan Pharmacy, Indpls., 1960-61, 62-64; mgr., chief pharmacist Hooks Drugs, Indpls., 1961; owner, mgr., chief pharmacist Ind. Cen. Pharmacy, Indpls., 1964-87; clin. staff pharmacist Wishard Meml. Hosp., Indpls., 1988—; vis. scholar WHO pilot program in palliative care Cleve. Clinic, 1993; part-time clin. pharmacist Marion County Health Care Ctr., Indpls., 1989-95; instr. U. Indpls., 1975-79, Ind. U.-Purdue U., Indpls., 1995—; cons. in field. Block capt. Marion County Rep. Party, Indpls., 1969-72, committeeman, 1976—; del. Ind. Rep. Conv., Indpls., 1988, 90, 96; usher St. Jude Roman Cath. Ch., Indpls., 1989—; sponsor Ind. Cen. Little League, 1965-87. Mem. Am. Soc. Hosp. Pharmacists, Ind. Soc. Hosp. Pharmacists, Indpls. Assn. Pharmacists (chmn. profl. rels. com. 1968-73, exec. com. 1991—), Ind. Acad. Pharmacists (exec. sec. 1963-69), KC, Rho Chi. Home: 2404 Depauw Rd Indianapolis IN 46227-4403 Office: Wishard Meml Hosp Pharm Dpt 1001 W 10th St Indianapolis IN 46202-2859

WATTERSON, JOYCE GRANDE, editor, publisher; b. Cleve., May 15, 1937; d. Anthony John Sr. and Helen Bernice (Kramer) Grande; m. Thomas Batchelor, Sept. 27, 1968; children: Sean Anthony, William Grande. BA, Notre Dame Ohio, 1960; Cert. Pratique, U. Paris, 1964; MA, Case Western Res., 1967. Cert. sales profl.; cert. tchr., Ohio. Tchr. Cleve. Bd. Edn., 1960-63, 64-65; asst. pers. dir. Cleve., Ohio Retail, 1965-66; tchr. Shaker Hieghts (Ohio) Bd. Edn., 1966-69, 71-72, 1983-85; lectr. Cleve. State U., 1987-88, Notre Dame Coll. Ohio, Cleve., 1990-91; adminstrv. dir. No. Ohio Acad. Pharmacy, Cleve., 1991-94; editor, pub. Concord Gazette GrandeLine Custom Comms., 1994—. Author, editor, pub.; Cascade Valley Soups, 1989, Cascade Valley Beans, 1992; editor/pub. Concord Gazette, 1994—. Advisor Alateens, Cleve., 1970-73; pres. Parents of U. Sch., Hunting Valley, Ohio, 1986-87; mem. adv. com. Painesville Adult Basic and Literacy Edn. Project, 1995—; mem. 50th anniversary com. Lake County Soil and Water Conservation Dist. Mem. Lake County Soil and Water Conservation Dist. (50th Ann. Com.), Le Cercle des Conferences Francaises of Cleve. (pres. 1986-88, life). Republican. Roman Catholic. Home: 7067 Cascade Rd Concord OH 44077-9509 Office: GrandeLine Custom Comm 7067 Cascade Rd Concord OH 44077-9509

WATTERSON, THOMAS BATCHELOR, investment executive; b. Cleve., July 11, 1938; s. William Herbert and Mercedes (Rendall) W.; m. Joyce Marie Grande, Sept. 27, 1968; children: Sean Anthony, William Grande. BA, William Coll., 1962. Loan officer Cleveland Trust Co., Cleve., 1962-65; v.p. Merrill, Turben and Co., Cleve., 1965-70, Prescott, Merrill Turben, Cleve., 1970-75; ptnr. Ball, Burge and Krause, Cleve., 1975-78; sr. ptnr. Prescott, Ball and Turben, Cleve., 1978-79; exec. v.p. McCloy, Watterson and Co., Cleve., 1974-79; spl. ltd. ptnr. Cowen and Co., Cleve., 1979-94. Trustee Univ. Sch., Cleve., 1988—, Greater Cleve. Garden Ctr., 1989-92; pres. men's coun. St. Paul's Episcopal Ch., Cleve., 1978-81; chmn. stewardship com. Cottonwood Hollow-Cleve. Natural History Mus. Mem. Nat. Assn. Security Dealers (regional bus. conduct com. 1989-92), Cleve. Bond Club (bd. govs. 1992—), Ohio Mcpl. Adv. Coun. (pres. bd. govs. 1972-74, 94-96), Univ. Sch. Alumni Assn. (pres. 1987), Williams Club. Republican. Episcopalian. Home: 7067 Cascade Rd Painesville OH 44077-9509 Office: Cowen and Co 1400 E 9th St Cleveland OH 44114-1727

WATTONVILLE, JASON D., agricultural engineer; b. Ames, Iowa, June 27, 1967. BS in Agrl. Engring., Iowa State U., 1990. Agrl. engr. John Deere Davenport Works, Dubuque, Iowa, 1990—. Lutheran. Office: John Deere Davenport Works Hwy 386 SW John Deere Dubuque IA 52001

WATTS, DEY WADSWORTH, retired lawyer; b. Chgo., Jan. 8, 1923; s. Amos Holston and Lida Cremora (Hough) W.; m. Faith Whittemore Weis, June 28, 1951; children—William, D. Whittemore, John, Judson, Merideth. A.B., Princeton U., 1947; LL.B., Harvard U., 1949. Bar: Ill. 1950. Assoc. Chapman and Cutler, Chgo., 1949-63; ptnr. Chapman and Cutler, 1963-91, retired, 1991. Pres. Glencoe Cmty. Chest, Ill., 1959-60; arbitrator Am. Arbitration Assn., Chgo., 1965-91; treas. Little House of Glencoe, 1966-80; chmn. adv. coun. Glencoe Caucus Plan, 1985-87. Capt. AUS, 1943-46, PTO. Fellow Am. Coll. Investment Counsel; mem. ABA, Ill. Bar Assn. (chmn. corp. and securities law com. 1961-62), Chgo. Bar Assn. (chmn. ethics com. 1974-75, chmn. legal econs. com. 1978-79), Legal Club Chgo. (exec. com. 1978-79), Law Club Chgo., Univ. Club, Mid Day Club, Skokie Country Club (sec. 1980-82), Royal Poinciana Country Club (Naples, Fla.), Harbour Town Yacht Club (Hilton Head, S.C.). Home: 684 Greenleaf Ave Glencoe IL 60022-1765 Office: care Chapman and Cutler 111 W Monroe St Chicago IL 60603-4003

WATTS, EMILY STIPES, English language educator; b. Urbana, Ill., Mar. 16, 1936; d. Royal Arthur and Virginia Louise (Schenck) Stipes; m. Robert Allan Watts, Aug. 30, 1958; children: Benjamin, Edward, Thomas. Student, Smith Coll., 1954-56; A.B., U. Ill., 1958, M.A. (Woodrow Wilson Nat. fellow), 1959, Ph.D., 1963. Instr. English U. Ill., Urbana, 1963-67, asst. prof., 1967-73, assoc. prof., 1973-77, prof., dir. grad. studies dept. English, 1977—; bd. dirs. U. Ill. Athletic Assn., chmn., 1981-83; mem. faculty adv. com. Ill. Bd. Higher Edn., 1984—, vice chmn., 1986-87, chmn., 1987-88. Author: Ernest Hemingway and The Arts, 1971, The Poetry of American Women from 1632 to 1945, 1977, The Businessman in American Literature, 1982; contbg. editor: English Women Writers from the Middle Ages to the Present, 1990; contbr. articles on Jonathan Edwards, Anne Bradstreet to lit. jours. John Simon Guggenheim Meml. Found. fellow, 1973-74. Mem. MLA, AAUP, Midwest MLA, Am. Inst. Archaeology, Authors Build, Ill. Hist. Soc., Phi Beta Kappa, Phi Kappa Phi. Presbyterian. Home: 1009 W University Ave Champaign IL 61821-3317 Office: U Ill 208 English Urbana IL 61801

WATTS, EUGENE J., state legislator; b. St. Louis, Oct. 17, 1942; s. Eugene H. and Norma (Shaughnessy) W.; children: Julia Brianne, Mackenzie Mulrane. AB, Knox Coll., 1964; MA, Emory U., 1965, PhD, 1969. Senator Ohio State Senate Dist. 16, 1985—, asst. pres. pro temp, chmn. reference and oversight, fin. subcom. on edn., mem. rules, edn., retirement & aging com., mem. fin. inst. and ins. com.; assoc. prof. history, rsch. asst. Ohio State U., 1972—; rsch. fellow Am. Coun. Learned Soc., 1975—. Author: The Social Basis of City Politics, 1978. Decorated Bronze star, Vietnam Campaign ribbon, Vietnam Svc. ribbon; State and Local Govt. fellow NEH, 1978; Fulbright fellow Internat. Exch. of Scholar, 1981; recipient Humanitarian Achievement award Columbia Dispatch Cmty. Svc. award, 1984; named Outstanding Legislator, Am. Legion, Amvets, Cath. War Vets., Disabled Am. Vets., Ohio State Coun. Vietnam Vets. Am., Ohio VFW, Vet. Assn. State Comdrs. and Adjutants, Ohio Assn. Chiefs of Police, Ohio Crime Prevention Assn., Ohio Prosecutors Assn. Mem. Vietnam Vet. Leadership Program (state chmn. 1982-85), Am. Legion, VFW, Fraternal Order of Police Assn., Orgn. Am. Historians, AMVETS. Office: 100 Galloway Rd Galloway OH 43119-9248 also: State Senate State Capital Columbus OH 43215*

WATTS, JOHN RANSFORD, university administrator; b. Boston, Feb. 9, 1930; s. Henry Fowler Ransford and Mary Marion (Macdonald) W.; m. Joyce Lannon, Dec. 20, 1975; 1 child, David Allister. AB, Boston Coll., 1950, MEd, 1965; MFA, Yale U., 1953; PhD, Union Grad. Sch., 1978.Prof., asst. dean Boston U., 1958-74; prof., dean of fine arts Calif. State U., Long Beach, 1974-79; dean and artistic dir. The Theatre Sch. (Goodman Sch. of Drama), DePaul U., Chgo., 1979—; mng. dir. DePaul U. Blackstone Theatre, 1988—; gen. mgr. Boston Arts Festivals, 1955-64; adminstr. Arts Programs at Tanglewood, 1966-69; producing dir. Theatre Co. of Boston, 1973-75. Chmn., Mass. Council on Arts and Humanities, 1968-72; dir., v.p. Long Beach (Calif.) Pub. Corp. for the Arts, 1975-79; mem. theatre panel, Ill. Arts Council, 1981-90. Served with U.S. Army, 1953-55. Mem. Mass. Ednl. Communications Commn., Am. Theatre Assn., Nat. Council on Arts in Edn., Met. Cultural Alliance, U.S. Inst. Theatre Tech., League Chgo. Theatres, Chgo. Internat. Theatre Festival, Phi Beta Kappa, Phi Kappa Phi. Clubs: St. Botolph (Boston); University (Chgo.). Office: De Paul U The Theatre Sch 2135 N Kenmore Ave Chicago IL 60614-4111

WATTS, ROBERT ALLAN, publisher, lawyer; b. Adrain, Mich., July 4, 1936; s. Richard P. and Florence (Hooker) W.; m. Emily Stipes, Aug. 30, 1958; children: Benjamin H., Edward S., Thomas J. Student DePauw U., 1954-55; BA, U. Ill., 1959, JD, 1961. Bar: Ill. 1961. Assoc. Stipes Publishing Co., Champaign, Ill., 1962-67, ptnr., editor, 1967—. Treas., Planned Parenthood, 1976-80; mem. Pres.'s Council, U. Ill.; pres. Friends of Library, U. Ill., 1980-82; bd. dirs. local United Way, 1972-81, City of Champaion Libr. Found., 1993—. Mem. Ill. Bar Assn., U. Ill. Found., Nat. Acad. Arts (bd. dirs. 1983-89). Republican. Clubs: Champaign Country; Saugatuck Yacht (commodore); Lake Shore Bath & Tennis (pres. 1983-85). Home: 1009 W University Ave Champaign IL 61821-3317 Office: Stipes Publishing Co 10-12 Chester St Champaign IL 61820

WATTSON, PETER STRAND, lawyer; b. Rice Lake, Wis., Aug. 2, 1944; m. Jo M. Berger, July 23, 1973; children: Daniel A., Kathryn E. BA in Govt., Harvard U., 1966; JD, U. Minn., 1969. VISTA atty. Mpls. Legal Aid Soc., Mpls., 1969-70; sen. counsel Minn. Senate, St. Paul, 1971—. Mem. Minn. Yacht Club (commodore 1979-80), Lake Minn. Sailing Sch. (pres. 1991, sec. 1992-94, v.p. 1995). Office: Senate Counsel & Rsch 17 Capitol Saint Paul MN 55155

WAUGH, JOANNA, electric utility employee; b. Gary, Ind., June 16, 1948; d. Joseph and Shirley M. (Caplinger) Rinkovsky; m. Raymond G. Waugh, Jul. 19, 1975; 1 child, Todd M. Student, Chgo. Acad. Fine Art, 1966-67, Ind. U., 1985-86. Journeyman elec. meterman Northern Ind. Pub. Svc., Michigan City, Mich., 1967—; NIPSCOfolks reporter, pub. rels. dept. No. Ind. Pub. Svc., Hobart, 1975-77, Conduit newsletter reporter, Michigan City, 1991—. Contbr. articles to profl. jours. Sec. Stop Taking Our Property, 1990—, Land Rights Found., 1994—; state coord. Alliance for Am., 1994—; Hoosier Network, 1993-95. Republican. Lutheran. Home: 500 Pottowatomi Trail Porter IN 46304-1838 Office: Stop Taking Our Property P O Box 599 Chesterton IN 46304

WAWRO, GEOFFREY DWIGHT WINSLOW, history educator; b. Hartford, Conn., Oct. 3, 1960; s. Nestor William and Judith Aileen (Stoughton) W.; m. Cecilia Schilling, June 10, 1995. BA magna cum laude, Brown U., 1983; MPhil, Yale U., 1989, PhD, 1992. Asst. prof. Oakland U., Rochester, Mich., 1992—. Author: The Austro-Prussian War, 1996. Recipient Austrian cultural Inst. prize, 1994, Moncado prize Am. Mil. Inst., 1996; Fulbright scholar, 1989-91. Mem. Phi Beta Kappa. Republican. Office: Oakland U History Dept Rochester MI 48309

WAX, NADINE VIRGINIA, retired banker; b. Van Horne, Iowa, Dec. 7, 1927; d. Laurel Lloyd and Viola Henrietta (Schrader) Bobzien; divorced; 1 child, Sharlyn K. Wax Munns. Student, U. Iowa, 1970-71; grad. Nat. Sch. Real Estate and Fin., Ohio State U., 1980-81. Jr. acct. McGladrey, Hansen, Dunn (now McGladrey-Pullen Co., CPAs), Cedar Rapids, Iowa, 1944-47; office mgr. Iowa Securities Co. (now Norwest Mortgage Co.), Cedar Rapids, 1954-55; asst. cashier Mchts. Nat. Bank, Cedar Rapids, 1956-75, asst. v.p., 1976-78, v.p., 1979-91; ret., 1991. Bd. dirs., v.p. Kirkwood C.C. Facilities Found., Cedar Rapids, 1970-96; bd. dirs., treas. Kirkwood C.C., 1984-91; trustee Indian Creek Nature Ctr., Cedar Rapids, 1974—, pres., 1980-81; vol. St. Luke's Hosp. Aux., Cedar Rapids, 1981-85; mem. Linn County Regional Planning Commn., 1982-92, Cedar Rapids-Marion Fine Arts Coun., 1994—; bd. suprs. Compensation Commn. for Condemnation, 1987-92; bd. dirs. Am. Heart Assn., Cedar Rapids, 1983-94; mem. Iowa Employment and Tng. Coun., Des Moines, 1982-83. Recipient Outstanding Woman award Cedar Rapids Tribute to Women and Industry, 1984. Mem. Fin. Women Internat. (state edn. chmn. 1982-83), Am. Inst. Banking (bd. dirs. 1968-70), Soc. Real Estate Appraisers (treas. 1978-80), Linn County Bankers Assn. (pres. 1979-80), Cedar Rapids Bd. Realtors, Cedar Rapids C. of C. (bus.-edn. com. 1986-91), Cedar Rapids Country Club. Republican. Lutheran. Home: 147 Ashcombe SE Cedar Rapids IA 52403-1700

WAXSE, DAVID JOHN, lawyer; b. Oswego, Kans., June 29, 1945; s. I. Joseph and Mary (Poole) W.; m. Linda Schilling (div.); children: Rachel, Ryan, Rebecca; m. Judy Pfannenstiel, May 29, 1982; 1 child, Elayna. BA, U. Kans., 1967; teaching cert., Columbia U., 1968, JD, 1971. Bar: Kans. 1971, U.S. Ct. Appeals (10th cir.) 1971, U.S. Supreme Ct. 1975. Dean of students Intermediate Sch. 88, N.Y.C., 1968-70; spl. edn. tchr. Peter Cooper Sch., N.Y.C., 1970-71; assoc. Payne & Jones, Olathe, Kans., 1971-74, ptnr., 1974-84; of counsel Shook, Hardy & Bacon, Overland Park, Kans., 1984-86, ptnr., 1986-95; ptnr. Shook, Hardy & Bacon L.L.P., Overland Park, Kans., 1995—; shareholder Shook, Hardy & Bacon P.C., Overland Park, 1993-95, v.p., asst. gen. counsel, 1995—; mcpl. judge City of Shawnee, Kans., 1974-80; atty. City of DeSoto, Kans., 1972-79; adj. prof. U. Kans. Sch. Law, Lawrence, 1981-82; mem. juv. code adv. com. Kans. Jud. Coun., 1979-83, guardianship adv. com., 1982-83, atty. fees adv. com., 1986-87; mem. Civil Justice Reform Act Adv. Com., U.S. Dist. Ct. for Dist. Kans., 1991—; mem. Kans. Commn. on Jud. Qualifications, 1992-94, vice-chmn. 1994—; v.p. Kans. Legal Svcs., Inc., 1980-82, pres., 1985-87; bd. advisors Kans. Coll. Advocacy, 1979-80. Author: (with others) Kansas Employment Law, 1985, Litigating Employment Law Cases, 1987, Kansas Employment Law Handbook, 1991, supplements, 1992, 95, Kansas Annual Survey, 1990—. Mem. Kan. Gov.'s Adv. Com. on Criminal Justice, 1974-77; gen. counsel Western Mo. Dist. ACLU, 1976-78, 86—, v.p., 1983-86, nat. bd. dirs., 1979-86, 91—, chmn. children's rights com., 1980-86; mem. AIDS Pol. Network, 1987—, med. treatment issues com., 1991—, constn. com., 1991—; mem. med./tech. com. AIDS Coun. Greater Kans. City, 1986—, ethics com. consortium Midwest Bioethics Ctr., 1990—; bd. dirs. Parents Anonymous Kans., 1978-83, pres., 1979; bd. dirs., mem. fin. com. Kans. Com. for Prevention Child Abuse, 1980-83. Mem. ABA (chmn. children's rights com. and family law sects. 1985-86), Am. Employment Law Coun., Kans. Bar Assn. (chmn. legal aid com. 1978-83, bd. govs. 1988—, v.p. 1996—, Pres.' Outstanding Svc. award 1982), Johnson County Bar Assn. (chmn. legal aid com. 1975-82, 92—), Amnesty Internat. (legal com. Kansas City chpt.), Common Cause, Sierra Club. Home: 9976 Hemlock Dr Shawnee Mission KS 66212-3447 Office: Shook Hardy and Bacon LLP 40 Corporate Woods 6th flr 9401 Indian Creek Pky Overland Park KS 66210-2005

WAY, KENNETH L., seat company executive; b. 1939. BS, Mich. State U., 1961, MBA, 1971. V.p. Lear Siegler, Inc., Southfield, Mich., 1966-88; chmn., chief exec. officer Lear Seating Co., Southfield, Mich., 1988—. With USAF, 1962-66. Office: Lear Seating 21557 Telegraph Rd Southfield MI 48034

WAYMAN, DAVID ANTHONY, state agency administrator; b. Feb. 8, 1950. BA in Psychology, Sangamon State U., 1980; MA in Psychology, U. Tex., 1983. Devel. dir. Travis Assn., Austin, Tex., 1980-83; market researcher Support Svcs., Springfield, Ill., 1983-85; devel. dir. Ill. Issues mag., Springfield, 1985-92; exec. dir. Ill. Coalition to End Homeless, Springfield, 1992-94, Ill. Coalition to End Homelessness, Springfield, 1992-94; prin. D. Anthony Wayman Consulting, Springfield, 1994—; cons. Ill. Alcoholism and Drug Dependence Assn., 1976; evaluator, expert witness various Springfield law firms, 1983-84; fundraising cons., devel. assoc. Sta. WSSU-FM Sangamon State U., Springfield, 1989-91; area rep. Aspect Found., 1991-92. Organizer presdl. campaigns of Eugene McCarthy, Springfield, 1964, George McGovern, Chgo., 1968, John Anderson, Springfield, 1980, Paul Simon, Iowa, Springfield, 1988; organizer Paul Simon for U.S. Senate campaign, 1990; organizer Ill. gubenatorial campaign for Neil Hartigan, 1990; coach, organizer Ill. Spl. Olympics, Springfield and Chgo., 1971-73. Democrat. Address: 1325 S Wabash Ave Ste 204 & 2 Chicago IL 60605-2504

WAYMIRE, DAVID DEAN, public affairs consultant; b. Indpls., Sept. 9, 1956; s. Lester Dean and Barbara Anne (Wilson) W.; m. Marsha Lee Lantz, Jan. 16, 1982; 1 child, Emily Allison. BS in Journalism, Northwestern U., 1978. Reporter Belleville (Ill.) News-Democrat, 1978-80, Flint (Mich.) Jour., 1980-82; reporter Lansing (Mich.) Bur. Booth Newspapers, 1982-88, chief corr., 1988-90; v.p. Mktg. Resource Group, Lansing, 1990—; host Mich. Agenda With Gov. John Engler, Lansing, 1992-94. Sr. editor The Secchia Commission Report on Government Efficiency, 1995; prodr. The Business Page. Recipient 1st Place Breaking News award AP of Mich., 1981, Morgan O'Leary award for Polit. Reporting, U. Mich., 1986. Home: 4557 Otto Rd Charlotte MI 48813-9723 Office: Mktg Resource Group 225 Washington Sq S Lansing MI 48933-1807

WAYMIRE, JOHN THOMAS, principal; b. Rensselaer, Ind., June 10, 1949; s. John Frederick and Elizabeth Ann (Pettet) W.; m. Kristi Antoinette Cerny, Oct. 4, 1975; children: John Johanson, Thomas Joseph. BS, St. Joseph's Coll., 1971; MS, Ind. U., Gary, 1976; postgrad., U. Iowa, 1978-82. Cert. tchr., adminstr., Ind., Iowa, S.D. Tchr. Kankakee Valley Schs., DeMotte, Ind., 1971-73, South Ctrl. Schs., Union Mills, Ind., 1973-78; grad. asst. U. Iowa, Iowa City, 1978-79; tchr. sci. Lincoln Community Schs., Mechanicsville, Ind., 1979-80; test editorial asst. Riverside Pub. Co., Iowa City, 1980-82; prin. elem. edn. Sully Buttes Schs., Onida, S.D., 1982-86; asst. prin. Tippecanoe Valley Schs., Mentone, Ind., 1986-90; prin. Pioneer Regional Schs., Royal Center, Ind., 1990-94, Granville Wells Sch., Jamestown, Ind., 1994—. Mem. ASCD, NAESP, S.D. Assn. Elem. Sch. Prins. (dist. rep. 1985), Ind. Assn. Sch. Prins. (charter 1992), Ind. Prin.'s Acad. (grad.), Royal Center Lions (pres. 1992-94), Phi Delta Kappa (pres. 1989-90). Home: 217 E Main St Jamestown IN 46147-9742 Office: 5046 S State Road 75 Jamestown IN 46147-9294

WAYNE, LISLE, II, plastic surgeon; b. N.Y.C., Feb. 9, 1936; s. Ernest Lisle and Teresa (Garcia) W.; m. Martha Weatherford, Jan. 4, 1964 (div. July 1977); children: Teresa, Lisle III; m. Sheila Ann Adkins, Sept. 10, 1977; children: Todd, Kyle. BS, Tex. A&M U., 1957; MD, U. Tenn., 1962. Diplomate Am. Bd. Plastic Surgery. Intern Jackson Meml. Hosp., Miami, Fla., 1962-63; resident in gen. surgery VA Hosp., Memphis, 1963-68; resident in plastic surgery Duke U. Med. Ctr., Durham, N.C., 1970-73; chief plastic surgery Trover Clinic & Hopkins Co. Hosp., Madisonville, Ky., 1973-77; clin. instr. surgery U. Louisville, 1976-77; att. phys. St. Mary's Med. Ctr., Evansville, Ind., 1977—, Deaconess Hosp., Evansville, 1977—, Welborn Bapt. Hosp., Evansville, 1977—. Contbr. articles to profl. jours. Maj. USAF, 1968-70. Fellow ACS; mem. AMA, Ind. Med. Soc., Vanderburgh County Med. Soc., Am. Soc. Plastic and Reconstructive Surgeons, Am. Soc. for Aesthetic Plastic Surgery, Southeastern Soc. for Plastic and Reconstructive Surgeons, Ohio Valley Soc. Plastic and Reconstructive Surgeons, Bowers Surgical Soc. Republican. Methodist. Club: Petroleum (Evansville). Home: 807 Canterbury Dr Evansville IN 47715-4231 Office: Evansville Plastic Surgery Assoc 3700 Bellemeade Ave Ste 105 Evansville IN 47714-0106

WAZIR, TADAR JIHAD, chaplain, small business owner; b. Kansas City, Mo., Dec. 28, 1944; s. Roosevelt and Osceola (Moore) Byers; m. Kay Frances Kyle-Byers, May 17, 1969; children: Tarik, Ibrahim; 1 adopted child, Ajamu. AA in Adminstrn. of Justice, Penn Valley Community Coll., Kansas City, 1977. Ins. salesperson Western & So. Life Ins. Co., Kansas City, 1968-69, N.Y. Life Ins. Co., Kansas City, 1969; supr. check transit dept. First Nat. Bank, Kansas City, 1969-70, methods analyst, 1971-72; paramedic St. Joseph's Hosp., Kansas City, 1974-77; owner W. K. Enterprises, Kansas City, 1977-79; ins. salesperson Roosevelt Nat. Life, Independence, Mo., 1978-79; pvt. mcht., Kansas City, 1980-81, Marshall, Mo., 1989—; bd. dirs. Welcome Home, Inc. 1994—; real estate salesperson Mid-Western Realty, Kansas City, 1980-86; chaplain, hostage negotiator, Mo. Dept. of Corrections, Jefferson City, 1982—; speaker, cons. Masjid Omar, Inc., Kansas City, 1977-92, Islamic Life Mission, 1992—; contract chaplain, cons. U.S. Med. Ctr. Fed. Prison, Springfield, Mo., 1979—; co-chmn. report the drug pusher Ad-Hoc Group Against Crime, Kansas City, 1978-82, pres. A.U. (African Unity, Inc.) 1994—, (Qadi) spl. master of the Jackson County, Mo. cir. ct., 1992. Chaplain chpt. 393, Vietnam Vets. Assn. Am. Jefferson City, 1991; Mo. st. coun. of the Vietnam Vets. of Am. co-chaplain 1991, treas. 1992-94; With USMC, 1962-66; mem. U.S. affiliate Islamic African Relief Agy. Mem. Am. Corrections Assn., Mo. Corrections Assn., Mo. Assn. Social Welfare, Nat. Assn. Muslim Chaplains, NAACP (pres. Marshall-Saline chpt. 1989-90, v.p., 1990-91, polit. action com. chmn. 1994—), Mid.-Am. Coun. Imams, Islamic Soc. N.Am., Optimists (chaplain Marshall 1990-91, chmn. community svcs. 1991-92, co-organizer ROTC program Ark. AM&N Coll.). Home: 456 W Porter St Marshall MO 65340-1358 Office: Mo Dept of Corrections 2729 Plaza Dr Jefferson City MO 65109-1146

WEAKLAND, REMBERT G., archbishop; b. Patton, Pa., Apr. 2, 1927; s. Basil and Mary (Kane) W. AB, St. Vincent Coll., Latrobe, Pa., 1948, DD (hon.), 1963, LHD (hon.), 1987; MS in Piano, Juilliard Sch. Music, 1954; grad. studies sch. music, Columbia U., 1954-56; LHD (hon.), Duquesne U., 1964, Belmont Coll., 1964, Cath. U. Am., 1975, Loyola U., Chgo., 1986, Xavier U., Cin., 1988, DePaul U., 1989, Loyola U., New orleans, 1992, Dayton U., 1993, Villanova U., Fond du Lac, 1992, Marian Coll., Fond du Lac, Wis., 1995; HHD (hon.), St. Ambrose U., Davenport, 1990, Aquinas Inst. Theology, St. Louis, 1991, St Mary's Coll., Notre Dame, Ind., 1994; LLD (hon.), Cardinal Stritch Coll., Milw., 1978, Marquette U., 1981, U. Notre Dame, 1987, Mt. Mary Coll., Milw., 1989, John Carroll U., Cleve., 1992, Fairfield U., 1994; D of Sacred Music (hon.), St. Joseph's Coll., Rensselaer, Ind., 1979; DST (hon.), Jesuit Sch. Theology, Berkeley, Calif., 1989, St. John's U., Collegeville, Minn., 1991, Santa Clara U., 1991, Yale U., 1993; DD (hon.), Lakeland Coll., Sheboygan, 1991, Ill. Benedictine Coll., Lisle, Ill., 1992, Regis Coll., Toronto, 1993. Joined Benedictines, Roman Cath. Ch., 1945, ordained priest, 1951. Mem. faculty music dept. St. Vincent Coll., 1957-63, chmn., 1961-63, chancellor chmn. of bd. of Coll., 1963-67; elected co-adjutor archabbot, 1963; abbot primate Benedictine Confederation, 1967-77; archbishop of Milw., 1977—. Mem. Ch. Music Assn. Am. (pres. 1964-66), Am. Guild Organists. Office: PO Box 07912 Milwaukee WI 53207-0912

WEALE, JOHN JOSEPH, veterinarian; b. Passaic, N.J., May 30, 1959; s. Gerald Ralph and Theresa Ann Weale; m. Debra Ann Black, June 19, 1982; children: Jason, Kathryn, Debra. BS, Vanderbilt U., 1981, MS, 1983; DVM, Ohio State U., 1987. Biomed. engr. VA Hosp., Nashville, 1981-83; computer programmer in pvt. practice Columbus, Ohio, 1982—; veterinarian Knapp Vet. Hosp., Columbus, 1987-90, Suburban Animal Clinic, Columbus, 1990—. Sec. Worthington (Ohio) Green Civic Assn., 1989, pres., 1995; mem. animal care com. Capital Area Humane Soc., Columbus, 1994. Vanderbilt U. scholar, 1979-81, grad. fellow, 1981-83, Ohio State U. scholar, 1983-87. Mem. Columbus Acad. of Vet. Medicine (westside rep. 1992, treas. 1993-95, pres.-elect 1996), Ohio Vet. Med. Assn. (com. chair newsletter 1991—), Am. Vet. Med. Assn., Am. Vet. Computer Soc., KC. Office: Suburban Animal Clinic 640 N Wilson Rd Columbus OH 43204

WEAN, BLANCHE MCNEELY, accountant; b. Monroe County, Ind., Jan. 28, 1901; d. Homer Clark and Ruth Jane (Tutterrow) McNeely; m. Francis Willard Wean, June 16, 1926 (dec.); children: Jane, Doris, Ruth. BA, Ind. U., 1923, MA, 1932, postgrad., 1945-46. CPA, Ind. Tchr. Mt. Carroll (Ill.) High Sch., 1918-19, Bloomington (Ind.) High Sch., 1923-26, Jefferson High Sch., Lafayette, Ind., 1923-26; head bus. dept. Cen. Normal Coll., Danville, Ind., 1931-47; acct. Wean Acctg., Danville, 1947-80, Wean, Andrews & Co., Danville, 1980—. Author; Blanche Accented, 1996. Mem. Danville Pub. Libr. Bd., 1969-82, treas. Recipient John F. Jenner III Citizenship award, 1972. Mem. Nat. Assn. Pub. Accts., Ind. Pub. Accts. Assn. (pres. 1977-78, 89, Hall of Fame), Danville C. of C. (sec. 1950-75), Bus. and Profl. Womens Assn., Beta Gamma Sigma. Republican. Home and Office: PO Box 128 Danville IN 46122-0128

WEATHERFORD, GEORGE EDWARD, civil engineer; b. Oakdale, Tenn., Jan. 8, 1932; s. Walter Clyde and Kathleen (Hinds) W.; m. Martha Jeannette Beck, July 9, 1960; children: Kathleen Jeannette Weatherford-Hommeltoft, Elizabeth Lynn. BSCE, Ind. Inst. Tech., Fort Wayne, 1957; BS Engr. in Constrn., U. Mich., 1959; MSBA, St. Francis Coll., 1975. Registered profl. engr., Ind., Ga., Ohio, Minn., Iowa, S.C., Pa., Ky., Ill., Md., La., Tenn., Mich. Plant engr. Cen. Soya Co., Inc., Decatur, Ind., 1959; civil engr. Cen. Soya Co., Inc., Decatur, 1959-64; county hwy. engr. Allen County Ind. Govt., Ft. Wayne, 1964-66; sr. civil engr. Cen. Soya Co., Inc., Fort Wayne, 1966-69, engring. mgr., 1969-77, prin. engr., 1977—; ind. cons. 1964—. Author book chpts.; contbr. articles to profl. jours. Trustee Ft. Wayne YWCA, 1973-76, North Christian Ch. and Endowment Trust. Sgt. USMC, 1950-54. Mem. ASCE (state treas. 1957), NSPE, Am. Concrete Inst., Am. Inst. Steel Constrn., Nat. Grain and Feed Assn. (fire and explosion rsch. and edn. com.), Ill. Assn. Structural Engrs., Grain Elevator and Processing Soc. (edn. programming com.). Republican. Home: 3617 Delray Dr Fort Wayne IN 46815-6012

WEATHERHEAD, ALBERT JOHN, III, business executive; b. Cleve., Feb. 17, 1925; s. Albert J. and Dorothy (Jones) W.; m. Celia Scott, Jan. 1, 1975; children: Dwight S., Michael H., Mary H. AB, Harvard U., 1950, postgrad., 1951. Prodn. mgr. Yale & Towne, Stamford, Conn., 1951-54, Blaw-Knox, Pitts., 1954-56; plant mgr. Weatherhead Co., Cleve., 1957-59, gen. mgr., 1959-61, v.p., gen. mgr., 1962-66, gen. sales mgr., 1962-63, v.p. mfg., 1964-66; v.p., dir. Weatherhead Co. of Can., Ltd. 1960-63, pres., chief exec. officer, dir., 1964-66; treas. Weatherchem Corp., 1971-82, pres., dir., 1971—; pres. Weatherhead Industries, 1987—, also bd. dirs., 1987—; bd. dirs. Weatherhead Co., Protane Corp., L.P.G. Leasing Corp., Leasepac Corp., Leasepac Can., Ltd., Creative Resources, Inc. Author: The New Age of Business, 1965. Mem. Harvard U. com. on univ. resources; trustee Case Western Res. U., mem. resources com., council on research involving human subjects, trustee Michelson-Morley Centennial Celebration; mem. Univ. Sch. alumni council, trustee Univ. Sch., hon. trustee for life Univ. Sch., Cleve., 1988—; trustee, adv. bd. Egyptian Studies Assn., U. S.C.; mem. vis. com. Ohio U., Athens; v.p. nat. adv. com. Rollins Coll., Winter Park, Fla.; adv. trustee Pinecrest Sch., Ft. Lauderdale, Fla.; mem. capital campaign steering com. Laurel Sch.; trustee Vocat. Guidance and Rehab. Services, Hwy. Safety Found., Arthritis Found.; v.p. Weatherhead Found., 1953-86, pres. 1987—; bd. dirs. New Directions Inc., Glenwillow, Ohio; col. CAF. With USAAF, 1943-46Patentee in field. Mem. Am. Newcomen Soc., Beta Gamma Sigma (hon.). Clubs: Union (Cleve.); Country (Shaker Heights, Ohio); Ottawa Shooting (Freemont, Ohio); Ocean (Delray, Fla.); Everglades (Palm Beach, Fla); Codrington (Oxford, Eng.). Home: 19601 Shelburne Rd Cleveland OH 44118-4957 Office: 25825 Science Park Dr Beachwood OH 44122-7315

WEATHERWAX, THOMAS K., state legislator; b. Cedar Rapids, Iowa, Oct. 22, 1942; s. Richard G. and Alyce (Kelly) W.; m. Kay A. Weatherwax, 1972; children: Michelle, Kris Chauncey, Kevin, Steve, David, Craig. AA, Cedar Rapids Bus. Coll., 1962; student, ICS Correspondence Sch., 1963-64, U. Ky. From cost acct. to sec.-contr. Wilson & Co., Oklahoma City, 1961-78; sec.-contr. Erny's Fertilizer Svc., Waiton, Ind., 1978—; bus. chmn. LEDC Indsl. Park; mem. Ind. Ho. of Reps., 1984-88; mem. Ind. State Senate, 1988—, chmn. transp. & interstate coop. com., local govt. financing subcom., mem. agr. & small bus. com., commerce & consumer affairs com. Sec. Logansport Area Devel. Corp., 1979-85; gen. chmn. United Way, 1979; mem. Hosp. Cmty. Rels. Bd., pres., 1981-83; Iron Horse Fetival gen. chmn. C. of C., 1983; mem. 21st Century com. Coun. State Govts., Nat. Conf. State Legislatures, Energy & Transp.; bd. dirs. Logansport Econ. Devel. Found., Logansport Area Devel. Corp.; mem. Grissom Cmty. Coun.; advisor Ind. Acad. Competitions Excellence; former pres. Meml. Hosp. Cmty. Rels. Bd., bd. dirs. Sangralea Valley Boys' Home; mem. steering com. Hoosier Heartland Corridor. Recipient John Tipton award Cass County Commrs., 1979, Ind. Small Bus. Champion award, Merit award Ind. Assn. Nurserymen, Guardian award Nat. Fedn. Ind. Bus., 1992, Small Bus. Champion award Ind. State C. of C., 1993, Frank M. McHale Econ. Devel. award, 1995, Nat. Rep. Legis. of Yr. award Nat. Rep. Legs. Assn., 1995, Govt. Leader of Yr. Ind. C. of C., 1995; named Outstanding Freshman Legislator, 10th Gen. Assembly, 1985. Mem. Masons (32 deg.), Shriners. Home: 3012 Woodland Dr Logansport IN 46947-1357*

WEAVER, ARTHUR ADOLPH, physician; b. Omaha, Nebr., Sept. 12, 1952; s. Arthur James and Gwendolyn Ruth (Sachs) W.; m. Bobbett Ann Torrison, May 25, 1974; 1 child, Arthur Robert. Diploma, USAF Air Univ., 1979; BS, U. Nebr., 1976; DO, Mich. State U., 1984. Cert. advanced trauma life support, advanced cardiac life support. Intern Lansing (Mich.) Gen. Hosp., 1984-85; clinic physician Heartland Corp., Omaha, 1985—; med. staff Edmundson Meml. Hosp., Council Bluffs, Iowa, 1986-89, St. Joseph Hosp., Omaha, 1988—; clinic physician U. Nebr., Omaha, 1992—; mem. Nebr. State Bd. Health, Lincoln, 1989—, chmn., 1991—; vol. physician Indian-Chicano Health Ctr., Omaha, 1991-94. Contbr. articles to profl. jours. Squadron comdr. Civil Air Patrol, Nebr. and Mich., 1974-82 (Unit Citation award 1975); instr. ARC, Nebr. and Mich., 1976-88. Recipient scholarship Nebr. Heart Assn., 1970, Physicians Recognition award AMA, 1987, 90; named Nebr. State Navy Admiral, 1995. Mem. Nebr. Assn. Osteopathic Physicians and Surgeons (sec. 1987—), Omaha Country Club, Sigma Nu. Home: 16556 Dorcas St Omaha NE 68130-1649 Office: 8552 Cass St Omaha NE 68114-3567

WEAVER, ARTHUR LAWRENCE, physician; b. Lincoln, Nebr., Sept. 3, 1936; s. Arthur J. and Harriet Elizabeth (Walt) W.; BS (Regents scholar) with distinction, U. Nebr., 1958; MD, Northwestern U., 1962; MS in Medicine, U. Minn., 1966; m. JoAnn Versemann, July 6, 1980; children: Arthur Jensen, Anne Christine. Intern U. Mich. Hosps., Ann Arbor, 1962-63; resident Mayo Grad. Sch. Medicine, Rochester, Minn., 1963-66; practice medicine specializing in rheumatology and internal medicine, Lincoln, 1968—; mem. staff Bryan Meml. Hosp., chmn. dept. rheumatology, 1976-78, 82-85, 89-91, vice-chief staff, 1984-87; bd. dirs. Bryancare (PHO), 1995—, chmn. fin. com., 1995—; mem. courtesy staff St. Elizabeths Hosp., Lincoln Gen. Hosp.; mem. cons. staff VA Hosp.; chmn. Juvenile Rheumatoid Arthritis Clinic, 1970-88; assoc. prof. dept. internal medicine U. Nebr., Omaha, 1976-88, assoc. prof., 1988-95, prof., 1995—; med. dir. Lincoln Benefit Life Ins. Co., Nebr., 1972-90; bd. dirs. Lincoln Mutual Life Ins., Co., 1994—, med. dir., 1995—; mem. exam. bd. Nat. Assn. Retail Druggists; mem. adv. com. Coop. Systematic Studies in Rheumatic Diseases III. Bd. dirs. Nebr. chpt. Arthritis Found., 1969—; mem. tech. cons. panel for rheumatology Harvard Resource Based Relative Value Study; trustee U. Nebr. Found., 1974—. Served to capt., M.C., U.S. Army, 1966-68. Recipient Outstanding Nebraskan award U. Nebr., 1958, also C.W. Boucher award; Philip S. Hench award Rheumatology, Mayo Grad. Sch. Medicine, 1966. Diplomate Am. Bd. Internal Medicine, Am. Bd. Rheumatology. Fellow ACP (Nebr. council 1983—), Am. Rheumatism Assn. (com. on rheumatologic practice 1983-87, pres.-elect Cen. region 1983-84, pres. Cen. region 1984-85); mem. AMA, Am. Coll. Rheumatology (sec. 1991-93, 1st Paulding Phelps award, bd. dirs. 1985—, planning com. 1987—, exec. com. 1991—, sec. 1991-93, pres. rsch. and edn. found. 1991-93, 2nd v.p. 1993-94, 1st. v.p., pres. elect. 1994-95, pres. 1995-96), Am. Soc. Internal Medicine (coord. com. physician payment svcs. 1988-93), Nebr. Soc. Internal Medicine (Internist of Yr., 1988), Nebraska Rheumatism Assn., Nebr. Med. Assn., Lancaster County Med. Soc., Mayo Grad. Sch. Medicine Alumni Assn., Arthritis Health Professions Assn. (com. on practice 1984-87), Nat. Soc. Clin. Rheumatology (program chairperson 1986-87, 88, exec. com. 1987-92), Midwest Cooperative Rheumatic Disease Study Group, (chmn. exec. com. 1986—), Arthritis Found. (profl. del.-at-large 1987-88, 89, 90, 96, Nat. Vol. Svc. citation, 1988, blue ribbon rsch. com. 1996—), Phi Beta Kappa, Sigma Xi, Alpha Omega Alpha, Pi Kappa Epsilon, Phi Rho Sigma. Republican. Presbyterian. Editorial bd. Nebr. Med. Jour., 1982—; contbr. articles to med. jours. Home: 4239 Calvert Pl Lincoln NE 68506-4252 Office: 2121 S 56th St Lincoln NE 68506-2111

WEAVER, CHARLES LYNDELL, JR., educational administrator; b. Canonsburg, Pa., July 5, 1945; s. Charles Lyndell and Georgia Lavelle (Gardner) W.; m. Ruth Marguerite Uxa, Feb. 27, 1982; children: Charles Lyndell III, John Francis. BArch, Pa. State U., 1969; cert. in assoc. studies U. Florence (Italy), 1968. Registered architect, Pa., Md., Mo., Va., Mass., Ky. With Celento & Edson, Canonsburg, Pa., part-time 1966-71; project architect Meyers & D'Aleo, Balt., 1971-76, corp. dir., v.p., 1974-76; ptnr. Borrow Assocs.-Developers, Balt., 1976-79, Crowley/Weaver Constrn. Mgmt., Balt., 1976-79; pvt. practice architecture, Balt., 1976-79; cons., project mgr. U. Md., College Park, 1979-80; corp. cons. architect Bank Bldg. & Equipment Corp., Am., St. Louis, 1980-83; dir. archtl. and engrng. svcs. Ladue Bldg. & Engring. Inc., St. Louis, 1983-84; v.p., sec. Graphic Products Corp.; pres. CWCM Inc. Internat., 1987—; dir. K-12 Edn. Market Ctr. and sr. program mgr., Sverdrup Corp., 1989-95; prin. Benham Internat. Eurasia, 1995; v.p., dir. mktg. and bus. devel. The Benham Group, St. Louis, 1995—; vis. Alpha Rho Chi lectr. Pa. State U., 1983; vis. lectr. Washington U. Lindenwood Coll., 1987, Wentworth Inst., Boston, Am. Assn. Cost Engrs., So. Fla., 1994; panel mem. Assn. Univ. Architects Conv., 1983. Project bus. cons. Jr. Achievement, 1982-85; mem. cluster com., advisor Explorer Program, 1982-85. Recipient 5 brochure and graphic awards Nat. Assn. Indsl. Artists, 1973; 1st award Profl. Builder/Am. Plywood Assn., 1974; Honor award, 2 articles Balt. chpt. AIA, 1974; Better Homes and Gardens award Sensible Growth, Nat. Assn. Home Builders, 1975; winner Ridgely's Delight Competition, Balt., 1976. Mem. ASCD, BBC Credit Union (bd. dirs. 1983-85), AACE (conv. speaker So. Fla. sect. 1994), Vitruvius Alumni Assn., Penn State Alumni Assn., BOCA, NFPA, Am. Assn. Sch. Administrs. (nat. coun., panel moderator 1994), Coun. Ednl. Facilities Planners, Assn. Sch. Bus. Officials (Mehlville Mo. schs. program mgmt. 1992-94, Chelsea, Mass., 1993-95. Orange County, Fla., 1994-95), Alpha Rho Chi (nat. treas. 1980-82, dir. nat. found. treas. 1989—). Office: 1318 Shenandoah Saint Louis MO 63104

WEAVER, CHARLIE, state legislator; b. Sept. 14, 1957; m. Julie; two children. BS, U. Oreg.; JD, U. Minn. Atty.; Minn. State rep. Dist. 49A, 1988—; asst. minority leader; mem. edn., environ. and natural resources, ways and means, local govt. and met. affairs com. Home: 440 Rice St Anoka MN 55303-2128*

WEAVER, DONNA RAE, company executive; b. Chgo., Oct. 15, 1945; d. Albert Louis and Gloria Elaine (Graffis) Florence; m. Clifford L. Weaver, Aug. 20, 1966; 1 child, Megan Rae. BS in Edn., No. Ill. U., 1966, EdD, 1977; MEd, De Paul U., 1974. Tchr. H.L. Richards High Sch., Oak Lawn, Ill., 1966-71, Sawyer Coll. Bus., Evanston, Ill., 1971-72; asst. prof. Oakton Community Coll., Morton Grove, Ill., 1972-75; vis. prof. U. Ill., Chgo., 1977-78; dir. devel. Mallinckrodt Coll., Wilmette, Ill., 1978-80, dean, 1980-83; campus dir. Nat.-Louis U., Chgo., 1983-90, dean div. applied behavioral scis., 1985-89; dean Coll. Mgmt. and Bus., 1989-90; pres. The Oliver Group, Inc., Kenilworth, Ill., 1993—; cons. Nancy Lovely and Assocs., Wilmette, 1981-84, North Ctrl. Assn., Chgo., 1982-90; ptnr. Le Miccine, Gaiole-in-Chianti, Italy. Contbr. articles to Am. Vocat. Jour., Ill. Bus. Edn. Assn. Monograph, Nat. Coll. Edn.'s ABS Rev., Nat. View. Mem. Ill. Quality of Work Life Coun., 1987-90, New Trier Twp. Health and Human Svcs. Adv. Bd., Winnetka, Ill., 1985-88; bd. dirs. Open Lands Project, 1985-87, Kenilworth (Ill.) Village House, 1986-87. Recipient Achievement award Women in Mgmt., 1981; Am. Bd. Master Educators charter disting. fellow, 1986. Mem. Nat. Bus. Edn. Assn., Delta Pi Epsilon (past pres.). Office: 505 N Lake Shore Dr Ste 4010 Chicago IL 60611-3408

WEAVER, JANET, newspaper editor. Mng. editor The Wichita (Kans.) Eagle. Office: The Wichita Eagle 825 E Douglas Ave PO Box 820 Wichita KS 67201-0820*

WEAVER, LEAH ANN, journalist, speech writer; b. Galion, Ohio, May 4, 1958; d. William Hiram and Virginia Louise (Reif) Weaver; m. Charles Lamont Hall, Jr., Apr. 14, 1990. BA, Malone Coll., Canton, Ohio, 1980; MA, Ohio State U., 1989. Program coord. editorial projects Ohio State U. Office of the Pres., Columbus, 1989-92, editorial coord., 1992—; English tutor Creative Living, Columbus, 1987, 88. Author: (plays) Wilber and Wife, 1989, Dora Dodd, 1991; contbg. writer Univ. Comms., Columbus, 1993—; spl. assignment reporter The Lantern, Columbus, 1987-88; freelance scriptwriter Ctr. for Teaching Excellence, Columbus, 1989; contbr. articles to jours. Mem. Soc. Profl. Journalists, N.Y. Dramatists Guild (playwright and assoc. mem.), Authors League Am., Coun. for Advancement and Support of Edn., Kappa Tau Alpha, Phi Kappa Phi. Home: 4077 Bimini Ct Columbus OH 43230

WEAVER, MICHAEL L., state legislator; b. Freeport, Ill., Oct. 9, 1946; 1 child. BS, Ea. State U., MS, MBA. Ill. state rep. Dist. 106, 1985—; mem. appropriations II, elem. and secondar edn. com. Ill. Ho. Reps., higher edn., human svcs., labor and com. housing, ins. econ. devel., scholastic excellence and extracurricular activities com., edn. fin. and transp. and motor vehicles coms.; instr. in field. Home: 915 S Iowa St Ashmore IL 61912-9543*

WEAVER, MICHAEL GLENN, pharmacist; b. Tuscola, Ill., Sept. 11, 1955; s. Glen H. and Margaret I. (Long) W.; m. Catherine A. (Paynic), Sept. 30, 1978; children: Jennifer L., Michelle R., Gregory M. BS, St. Louis Coll. of Pharmacy, 1978; MBA, So. Ill. U., 1989. Registered pharmacist. Clin. coordinator, staff pharmacist St. Elizabeth Med. Ctr., Granite City, Ill., 1975-87; dir. pharmacy Freeport (Ill.) Meml. Hosp., 1987-92, dir. pharmacy and info. systems, 1992—; dir. Ill. State Bd. Pharmacy, 1995—. Am. Soc. Hosp. Pharmacists, Ill. Pharm. Assn., Am. Soc. Parenteral and Enteral Nutrition, Ill. Coun. Hosp. Pharmacists (dir. ednl. affairs 1991-94), Am. Coll. Healthcare Execs., Phi Kappa Phi, Beta Gamma Sigma, Delta Sigma Theta. Republican. Mem. United Church of Christ. Home: 1346 Carriage Hill Ln Freeport IL 61032-6168 Office: Freeport Meml Hosp 1045 W Stephenson St Freeport IL 61032-4864

WEAVER, RICHARD L., II, writer, educator; b. Hanover, N.H., Dec. 5, 1941; s. Richard L. and Florence B. (Grow) W.; m. Andrea A. Willis; children: R. Scott, Jacquelynn Michelle, Anthony Keith, Joanna Corinne. AB, U. Mich., 1964, MA, 1965; PhD, Ind. U., 1969. Asst. prof. U. Mass., 1968-74; assoc. prof. speech communication Bowling Green State U., 1974-79, prof., 1979-96, dir., basic speech communication course, 1974-96; vis. prof. U. Hawaii-Manoa, 1981-82, Bond U., Queensland, Australia, 1990, St. Albans, Melbourne, Australia, 1990, Western Inst., Perth, Australia, 1990. Author: (with Saundra Hybels) Speech/Communication, 1974, 2d edit., 1979, Speech/Communication: A Reader, 1975, 2d edit., 1979, Speech/Communication: A Student Manual, 1976, 2d edit., 1979, Understanding Interpersonal Communication, 1978, 2d edit., 1981, 3d edit., 1984, 4th edit., 1987, 5th edit., 1990, 6th edit., 1993, 7th edit., 1996, (with Raymond K. Tucker, Cynthia Berryman-Fink) Research in Speech Communication, 1981, Foundations of Speech Communication: Perspectives of a Discipline, 1982, Speech Communication Skills, 1982, Understanding Public Communication, 1983, Understanding Business Communication, 1985, Understanding Speech Communication Skills, 1985, Readings in Speech Communication, 1985, (with Saundra Hybels) Communicating Effectively, 1986, 2d edit., 1989, 3d edit., 1992, 4th edit., 1995, Skills for Communicating Effectively, 1985, 2d edit., 1988, 3d edit., 1991, 4th edit., 1993, rev. edit., 1995, (with Howard W. Cotrell) Innovative Instructional Strategies, 1987, 2d edit., 1988, 3d edit., 1989, 4th edit., 1990, 5th edit., 1992, 6th edit., 1993, (with Curt Bechler) Listen to Win: A Guide to Effective Listening, 1994, Study Guide to Accompany Communicating Effectively, 1995, Essentials of Public Speaking, 1996. Mem. Internat. Comm. Assn., Internat. Soc. Gen. Semantics, Speech Comm. Assn., World Comm. Assn., Ctrl. States Speech Assn., Ohio Speech Assn., Internat. Listening Assn., Midwest Basic Course Dirs. Conf., Golden Key, Phi Kappa Phi (Bowling Green Faculty Excellence award 1989). Home and Office: 9583 Woodleigh Ct Perrysburg OH 43551-2669

WEAVER, SHARON B., educator; b. Chgo., Apr. 8, 1942; d. Raymond William and Bertha Elsie (Lawrence) Bagus; m. Hoyt Eugene Weaver, May 16, 1964; children: Sheryl D. Reynolds, Jeff. AAS in Computer Programming with honors, Ind. Vocat. Tech. Coll., 1987; BS Computer Info. Sys. with distinction, Calumet Coll. St. Joseph, 1992. Data entry instr. Ross Twp. Assessor, Merrillville, Ind., 1987-89; instr. computer info. sys. Ind. Vocat. Tech. Coll., Gary, 1988-93; lectr. mgmt. info. sys. Calumet Coll., Whiting, Ind., 1992-93; instr. mgmt. info. sys./supervisory mgmt. techniques Lincoln Land C.C. at Graham Correctional, Hillsboro, Ill., 1994-95; instr. bus. mgmt. Lincoln Land C.C., Taylorville, Ill., 1995—. Mem. Correctional Educators Assn. (adv. bd. Ill.). Home: 465 Fox Hunt Trail Hillsboro IL 62049

WEAVER, WILLIAM CLAIR, JR. (MIKE WEAVER), human resources development executive; b. Indiana, Pa., Apr. 11, 1936; s. William Clair and Zaida (Bley) W.; m. Janet Marcelle Boyd, Sept. 18, 1963 (div. 1978); 1 child, William Michael; m. Donna June Hubbuch, Feb. 10, 1984. B Aero Engring., Rensselaer Poly. Inst., 1958; MBA, Washington U., St. Louis, 1971; postgrad., Rutgers U.; grad., Armed Forces Indsl. Coll. Registered profl. engr. Engr. aerodynamics N.Am. Aviation, Los Angeles, 1959-60; engr. flight test ops. Boeing/Vertol, Phila., 1963-66; engr. flight test project Lockhead Electronics, Plainfield, N.J., 1966-69; project engr. advanced systems, sr. staff engr. Emerson Electric Co., St. Louis, 1969-72; pres. Achievement Assocs., Inc., St. Louis, 1972—; founder, charter mem. Catalyst, 1978—; speaker in field. Contbr. articles to profl. jours.; author: Winning Selling, 1983, Winning Manager, 1990. Mem. adv. com. Boy Scouts Am., Bridgeton, Mo., 1974. Served to capt. USAF, 1960-63, USAFR. Mem. Nat. Soc. Profl. Engrs.,Am. Soc. Bus. and Mgmt. Cons., Am. Ordnance Soc., Am. Inst. Aeronautics and Astrounautics, Assn. MBA Execs., Air Force Assn., Am. Helicopter Soc., Acacia Frat., St. Louis C. of C., Mensa, Beta Gamma Sigma. Republican. Lutheran. Home and Office: 13018 Ray Trog Ct Saint Louis MO 63146-1802

WEBB, CHARLES HAIZLIP, JR., university dean; b. Dallas, Feb. 14, 1933; s. Charles Haizlip and Marion (Gilker) W.; m. Kenda McGibbon, June 21, 1958; children: Mark, Kent, Malcolm, Charles Haizlip III. AB, So. Meth. U., 1955, MMus, 1955; DMus, Ind. U., 1964; DMus (hon.), Anderson. Coll., 1979. Asst. to dean Sch. Music, So. Meth. U., 1957-58; mem. faculty Sch. Music, Ind. U., 1960—, dean, 1973—. dir. Indpls. Symphony Choir, 1967-81; guest condr. chorus and orch. festivals throughout U.S.; duo-pianist with Wallace Hornibrook in U.S. and Australian tour, 1973; organist First Meth. Ch., Bloomington, 1961—, mem. hymnal revision com. Meth. Ch.; mem. jury Chopin competition; mem. jury internat. piano competitions in Munich, Budapest, South Africa, Paris, Chile, Warsaw, Bolzano, London, Cologne, Japan. Chmn. adv. bd. Internat. Music Festivals, Inc.; mem. Ind. Arts Commn., 1975-83, U.S.-USSR Commn. on Music Performance Edn., Am. Coun. Learned Socs./USSR Ministry of Culture; mem. adv. panel The Music Found.; mem. recommendation bd. Avery Fisher Prize Program; bd. dirs. Busoni Found.; mem. bd. advisors Van Cliburn Internat. Piano Competition; mem. nat. adv. bd. Am. Guild Organists; trustee Indpls. Symphony Orch. With U.S. Army, 1955-57. Decorated D.S.M.; recipient Disting. Alumni award So. Meth. U., 1980, Sagamore of Wabash Gov. award, 1987, 89, Thomas Hart Benton medal Ind. U., 1987, Disting. Alumni award Highland Park High Sch., Dallas, 1989, Ind. Gov. award for arts, 1989. Mem. Ind. Acad., Century Assn. of N.Y., Pi Kappa Lambda, Phi Mu Alpha, Phi Delta Theta. Home: 648 S Woodcrest Dr Bloomington IN 47401-5417 Office: Ind U Sch Music Bloomington IN 47405

WEBB, MARVIN RUSSELL, former state agency director; b. Dodge City, Kans., Sept. 15, 1918; s. Loris Everett and Clara Mae (Crotinger) W.; m. Dorothy Daugherty, Feb. 15, 1948 (div. Mar. 1963); m. Betty Louise McDonald, Jan. 15, 1966, (div. Apr. 1983); m. Georgina M. Haydon, June 5, 1983; 1 child, Walter Loris. Student, U. Nebr., 1937-39, U. Mo., 1964. Warehouse examiner Kans. State Grain Inspection Dept., Topeka, 1959-61, dir., 1981-87; warehouse examiner Argl. Stabilization and Conservation Svc., USDA, Kansas City, Mo., 1962-66; warehouse cert. examiner Argl. Stabilization and Conservation Svc., USDA, Camphill, Pa., 1966-73; conservation specialist U.S. Dept. Energy, Kansas City, 1973-79; real estate developer, pres. Webb Assoc. Cons. firm, Topeka, 1987—; pres. Southboro Estate Devel. Pres. Kans. Dem. Vets. Club, 1990—; mem. Kans. Dem. Party Exec. Com., 1994—. Mem. Am. Legion (chmn. state energy commn. 1976-81), U.S. Army Assn., Home Builders Assn. Kans. (bd. dirs. 1992-93), Topeka Home Builders Assn. (sec., bd. dirs.). Methodist. Home: 4240 SE Wisconsin Ave Topeka KS 66609-1708 Office: Webb & Assocs Jayhawk Towers 700 SW Jackson St Topeka KS 66603-3731

WEBB, ROBERT DONALD, JR., financial executive; b. Chgo., Apr. 23, 1943; s. Robert D. and Marjorie (Hoffman) W.; m. Linda Dale Wasserman, June 25, 1967; children: Lauren, Robyn. BSBA, No. Ill. U., 1965. C.P.A., Ill. From auditor to audit mgr. Arthur Andersen & Co., Chgo., 1965-78; dir. corp. fin. CF Industries, Inc., Long Grove, Ill., 1978-79, corp. controller, 1980-87, v.p. planning and control, 1987—; v.p. fin. Valley Nitrogen Producers, Fresno, Calif., 1979-80. Served as staff sgt. USAFR, 1965-71. Named Outstanding Acctg. Alumnus, No. Ill. U., 1982. Mem. Fin. Execs. Inst., Am. Inst. CPA's, Ill. Soc. CPA's, Beta Alpha Psi (Gamma Pi chpt.). Lutheran. Office: CF Industries Inc Salem Lake Dr Lake Zurich IL 60047

WEBB, RONALD C., engineering manager; b. Fayette, Iowa, Apr. 19, 1943. Owner Mfrs. Rep., Mpls., 1985-89; gen. mgr. Solder Clade, Inc., Mpls., 1989; mgr. engrng. Graphic Circuits Corp., Cedar Rapids, Iowa, 1990—. Office: Graphic Circuits Corp 818 Dows Rd SE Cedar Rapids IA 52403-7010

WEBB, RUTH CAMERON, retired educator; b. Honolulu, June 1, 1923; d. William Henry and Ruth Gray (Cameron) W. AB, Drew U., 1948, DHL, 1972; MA, Syracuse U., 1949; PhD, U. Ill., 1963. Nursery sch. cons. Swarthmore, Pa., 1953-55; with Jewish Vocat. Soc., Milw., 1963-66, Hamburg (Pa.) Hosp. Sch., 1966-87, Glenwood (Iowa) State Sch., 1989—. Author: Journey into Personhood, 1994. Home: 619 Park St Apt B104 Grinnell IA 50112-2269

WEBB, THOMAS IRWIN, JR., lawyer; b. Toledo, Sept. 16, 1948; s. Thomas Irwin and Marcia Davis (Winters) W.; m. Polly S. DeWitt, Oct. 11, 1986; 1 child, Elisabeth Hurst. BA, Williams Coll., 1970; postgrad., Boston U., 1970-71; JD, Case Western Res. U., 1973. Bar: Ohio. Assoc. Shumaker, Loop & Kendrick, Toledo, 1973-79, ptnr., 1979—, chmn. corp. law dept., 1992-94, mgmt. com., 1994—; dir. Comml. Aluminum Cookware Co., York Oldsmobile, Inc. Coun. mem. Village of Ottawa Hills, Ohio, Divsn. Securities, 1979—, adv. com.; trustee Kiwanis Youth Found. of Toledo, 1982—; dir. Toledo Area Regional Transit Authority, 1989-91; trustee Arts Commn. Greater Toledo, 1993—, exec. com., 1994—, v.p., 1994-96, pres., 1996—; trustee Jr. Achievement of Northwestern Ohio, Inc., 1992—, Lourdes Coll. Found., 1995—. Mem. ABA, Ohio Bar Assn. (corp. law com. 1989—), Toledo Bar Assn., Northwestern Ohio Alumni Assn. of Williams Coll. (pres. 1974-83), Toledo-Rowing Found. (trustee 1985—), Toledo Area C. of C. (trustee 1991—, exec. com. 1993—), Order of Coif, Crystal Downs Country Club, Toledo Country Club, The Toledo Club (trustee 1984-90, pres. 1987-90), Williams Club N.Y. Republican. Episcopalian. Office: Shumaker Loop & Kendrick 1000 Jackson St Toledo OH 43624-1515

WEBBER, ROLLAND LLOYD, state legislator; b. Doylestown, Ohio, Apr. 28, 1932; s. Leland Leon and Stella (Fielder) W.; m. Betty Barbara Ball, 1952; children: Rickey Leon, Jeffrey Allen. Grad., Anderson H.S., 1950. Formerly rep. employee health and safety Delco-Remy divsn. GMC; mem. from 37th dist. Ind. Ho. of Reps., 1984—; chmn. labor com.; mem. elections and apportionment, ethics, pub. policy, vet. affairs, urban affairs, aged and aging coms. Dem. precinct committeeman, Anderson, Ind., 1974—; ward chmn. Anderson City Dem. Com., 1982-84. Mem. Eagles, Am. Legion, Amvets. Home: 32 South Dr Anderson IN 46013-4140*

WEBB-GROE, MARY CHRISTINE, special education educator; b. Ames, Iowa, Jan. 3, 1947; d. Howard Darrell and Lorena Faye (North) Webb; m. Harlen DuWayne Groe, Dec. 29, 1989. BS in Elem. Edn., Iowa State U., 1969, MS in Emotional Disabilities, 1980, MEd in Learning Disabilities, 1986. Cert. tchr. K-9, learning disabilities, behavioral disabilities, multicategorical, cons., Iowa. 1st grade tchr. Holy Spirit Sch., Carroll, Iowa, 1970; severe behavior disabilities tchr. Area Edn. Agy 7, Waterloo, Iowa, 1979-85; teaching and rsch. assistantship Iowa State U., Ames, 1985-86; multicategorical 3-8 self contained with integration tchr. Madrid Elem. and Jr. High Sch., 1986-87; behavior disability self contained with integration tchr. Des Moines Pub. Schs., 1987-88, resource rm. tchr., 1988-95; multicategorical self contained with integration tchr., 1995—. mem. People to People Spl. Edn. Delegation to Mainland China, 1993. Mem. ASCD, NEA, Des Moines Edn. Assn., Iowa State Edn. Assn., Coun. for Exceptional Children. Office: Perkins Elem School 4301 College Ave Des Moines IA 50311-2454

WEBECK, ALFRED STANLEY, management consultant, financial analyst; b. Kewanee, Ill., Nov. 10, 1913; s. Edward Nels and Anna Louise (Ericson) W.; m. Phyllis Cotton, June 18, 1935; children: Carole Webeck Miller, Beth Webeck Wilfong. BSEE, U. Ill., 1935. Cert. mfg. engr., Ill. Research engr. Barber Colman Co., Rockford, Ill., 1935-40; mfg. mgr. of motors Barber Colman Co., Rockford, 1962-75; v.p. works mgr. Sampsel Time Control, Inc., Sring Valley, Ill., 1940-47; works mgr. Victor Animatograph Corp., Davenport, Iowa, 1947-51; v.p. gen. mgr. Ind. Gen. Corp., Oglesby, Ill., 1951-61; indsl., comml. sales mgr. Hart Realtors, Rockford, Ill., 1975-85; cons. fin. analysis Rockford, 1983—. Mem. Ill. Mfrs. Assn. (bd. dirs. 1962), Ill. Valley Mfg. Club LaSalle (pres. 1955-61). Presbyterian. Home and Office: 1514 Comanche Dr Rockford IL 61107-2224

WEBER, ARNOLD R., academic administrator; b. N.Y.C., Sept. 20, 1929; s. Jack and Lena (Smith) W.; m. Edna M. Files, Feb. 7, 1954; children: David, Paul, Robert. B.A., U. Ill., 1951; M.A., MIT, 1958, Ph.D. in Econs., 1958. Instr., then asst. prof. econs. MIT, 1955-58; faculty U. Chgo. Grad. Sch. Bus., 1958-69, prof. indsl. relations, 1963-69; asst. sec. for manpower Dept. Labor, 1969-70; exec. dir. Cost of Living Council; also spl. asst. to Pres. Nixon, 1971; Gladys C. and Isidore Brown prof. urban and labor econs. U. Chgo., 1971-73; former provost Carnegie-Mellon U.; dean Carnegie-Mellon U. (Grad. Sch. Indsl. Adminstrn.), prof. labor econs. and pub. policy, 1973-80; pres. U. Colo., Boulder, 1980-85; pres. Northwestern U., Evanston, Ill., 1985-95, chancellor, 1995—; vis. prof. Stanford U., 1966; cons. union, mgmt. and govt. agys., 1960—, Dept. Labor, 1965; mem. Pres.'s Adv. Com. Labor Mgmt. Policy, 1964, Orgn. Econ. Coop. and Devel., 1987;

vice chmn. Sec. Labor Task Force Improving Employment Svcs., 1965; chmn. rsch. adv. com. U.S. Employment Svc., 1966; assoc. dir. OMB, Exec. Office of Pres., 1970-71; chmn. Presdl. R.R. Emergency Bd., 1982; trustee Com. for Econ. Devel.; bd. dirs. Aon Corp., Burlington No., Inc., Inland Steel Co., Pepsico Inc., Tribune Corp., Deere & Co. Author: Strategies for the Displaced Worker, 1966; Contbr. articles to profl. jours. Trustee com. econ. devel., U. Notre Dame; bd. dirs. Chgo. Coun. Fgn. Rels., Eurasia Found. Lt. (j.g.) USCGR, 1952-54. Laureate, Lincoln Acad. Ill.; Ford Found. Faculty Rsch. fellow, 1964-65. Mem. Am. Acad. Arts and Scis., Indsl. Rels. Rsch. Assn. (bus.-higher edn. forum), Nat. Acad. Pub. Adminstrn., Comml. Club Chgo. (pres., civic com.), Econ. Club Chgo. (pres.), Phi Beta Kappa. Jewish. Office: Northwestern U Office of Chancellor 555 Clark St Evanston IL 60208-0805

WEBER, DELBERT DEAN, academic administrator; b. Columbus, Nebr., July 23, 1932; s. Charles and Ella M. (Hueschen) W.; m. Lou Ann Ross, Dec. 29, 1954; children: William, Bethany, Kelly. BA, Midland Coll., Fremont, Nebr., 1954; MEd, U. Nebr., 1958, EdD, 1962; LittD (hon.), Shizuoka (Japan) U., 1982; LLD (hon.), U. City of Manila, 1984. Tchr. social studies and English, prin. Creston (Nebr.) High Sch., 1956-58; instr. ednl. founds. U. Nebr., Lincoln, 1958-60, instr. and coord. jr. high lab. sch., 1960-62; chancellor U. Nebr., Omaha, 1977—; from asst. to assoc. prof. edn. Ariz. State U., Tempe, 1962-65, dean and prof. edn., 1969-77; asst. to pres. and sec. to trustees Cleve. State U., 1965-69; chmn. commn. on culture and edn. to Pakistan, U.S. Dept. of State, 1984; bd. dirs. Norwest Bank, Omaha. Author: (with N.L. Haggerson, L.H. Griffith) Secondary Education Today, 1968; contbr. articles to profl. jours. trustee Nebr. Meth. Hosp., Omaha Home for Boys, Nebr. Meth. Hosp., 1980—; bd. dirs. Midlands region NCCJ, Omaha Community Playhouse, numerous others; gen. campaign chmn. United Way of Midlands, 1983; chmn. midlands region Nat. Conf. Christians and Jews, 1989-92; mem. consultation com. Strategic Command, 1988—, adv. bd. Salvation Army, 1991—, Nebr. state exec. bd. U.S. West Comm., Inc., 1992—, merit selection panel for Magistrate Judge, 1992. With U.S. Army, 1954-56. Named Citizen of Yr., United Way of Midlands, 1984, Disting. Educator N. Cen. Region Bosy Scouts Am., 1989, Outstanding Citizen, Woodmen of the World, 1990, King of Ak-Sar-Ben, 1990, Man of Yr. Omaha Club 1992, Merry Makers 1992; recipient Vision award Soc. Prevention of Blindness, 1991, Svc. to Mankind award Sertoma Club, 1994. Mem. Am. Assn. Colls. for Tchr. Edn. (bd. dirs. 1976-79, chmn. ann. conv. 1975, appeals bd. 1984-85, task force 1984-85), Am. Assn. State Colls. and Univs. (task force on excellence in edn. 1982-84, bd. dirs., exec. com. 1983-86, com. communications tech. 1984-86, resource ctr. bd. liaison 1985, com. acad. affairs, com. on internat. programs 1987, com. on urban affairs 1987), Assn. Urban Univs. (bd. dirs. 1980-85), Nat. Assn. State Univs. and Land Grant Colls. (mem. exec. com. 1982-83, chmn. urban affairs div. 1982-83), Nat. Assn. Colls. and Schs. of Edn. in State Univs. and Land Grant Colls. (bd. dirs. 1974-77, pres. 1977-78), Nat. Collegiate Athletic Assn. (pres. commn. 1984-89), Nat. Coun. for Accreditation of Tchr. Edn. (appeals bd. 1983), Omaha C. of C., Strategic Air Command (bd. dir. consultation com.). Lutheran. Home: 1816 N 132nd Avenue Cir Omaha NE 68154-3898 Office: U Nebr Eppley 201 Omaha NE 68182

WEBER, DICK A., bowler; b. Indpls., Dec. 23, 1929; s. Carl John and Marjorie Amelia (Dunn) W.; m. Juanita Delk, Dec. 23, 1948; children: Richard Jr., Paula Kae, Carl John, Peter David. Address: 1305 Arlington Dr Florissant MO 63033

WEBER, GLORIA RICHIE, minister, retired state representative; married; 4 children. BA, Washington U., St. Louis; MA, MDiv, Eden Theol. Sem., Webster Groves, Mo. Ordained to ministry Evang. Luth. Ch. Am., St. Louis, 1974;. Min. Am. Luth. Ch., St. Louis, 1974; family life educator Luth. Family & Children's Svcs. Mo.; state representative State of Mo., 1993-94; Mo. state organizer, dir. comm. Mainstream Voters C.A.R.E., 1995. Exec. dir. Older Women's League, 1990-95; Dem. candidate for Mo. State Senate, 1996. Recipient Woman of Achievement award St. Louis Globe-Dem., 1977, Unselfish Cmty. Svc. award St. Louis Sentinel Newspaper, 1985, Faith in Action award Luth. Svcs. St. Louis, 1994, Outstanding Woman award Coalition of St. Louis Labor Women, 1994; named Woman of Yr., Variety Club, 1978, Woman of Worth, Older Women's League, 1993. Democrat. Home and Office: 4910 Valley Crest Dr Saint Louis MO 63128-1829

WEBER, GRETCHEN AGGERTT, speech communication educator; b. Albion, Mich., Sept. 20, 1951; d. Otis J. and Lucile (Larson) Aggertt; m. Michael Lee Weber, Feb. 5, 1972; 1 child, Amy Lee. BS, Ind. State U., 1975, MS, 1996. Tchr. Carmel (Ind.) Jr. H.S., 1975-76; broker Hallmark Agts., Inc., Plainfield, Ind., 1979-80; caseworker Hendricks County Dept. Children and Families, Danville, Ind., 1980-90; supr. Boone County Dept. Children and Families, Lebanon, Ind., 1990; grad. teaching asst. speech comm. Ind. State U., Terre Haute, 1993-96; instr. comm. Hazard (Ky.) C.C., 1996—; judge Gov.'s Cup Debate, Rose-Hulman Inst. Tech., Terre Haute, 1995. Pres. Danville Cmty. Bd. Sch. Trustees, 1990-91, sec., 1989-90; mem., sec. Redevel. Commn., Danville, 1991-92. Recipient Disting. Svc. award Danville Cmty. Sch. Bd. Trustees, 1993, Ednl. Excellence award Ind. State U., 1995, Instrs. Materials award, 1994. Mem. Speech Comm. Assn., Ctrl. States Speech Comm. Assn., Phi Kappa Phi. Home: 448 E Mill St Danville IN 46122 Office: Hazard C.C. Dept Comm Hazard KY 41701

WEBER, HERMAN JACOB, federal judge; b. Lima, Ohio, May 20, 1927; s. Herman Jacob and Ada Minola (Esterly) W.; m. Barbara L. Rice, May 22, 1948; children: Clayton, Deborah. BA, Otterbein Coll., 1949; JD summa cum laude, Ohio State U., 1951. Bar: Ohio 1952, U.S. Dist. Ct. (so. dist.) Ohio 1954. Ptnr. Weber & Hogue, Fairborn, Ohio, 1952-61; judge Fairborn Mayor's Ct., 1956-58; acting judge Fairborn Mcpl. Ct., 1958-60; judge Greene County Common Pleas Ct., Xenia, Ohio, 1961-82, Ohio Ct. Appeals (2d dist.), Dayton, 1982-85, U.S. Dist. Ct. (so. dist.) Ohio, Cin., 1985—; chmn. Ohio Jud. Conf., Columbus, 1980-82; pres. Ohio Common Pleas Judges Assn., Columbus, 1975. Vice mayor City of Fairborn, 1955-57, council mem., 1955-59. Served with USNR, 1945-46. Office: US Dist Ct 801 Potter Stewart US Courthse 5th & Walnut Sts Cincinnati OH 45202

WEBER, JACK BERNARR, sales executive; b. Highland Park, Mich., Apr. 13, 1937; s. Jack William and Gertrude May (Weinberg) W.; m. Karen L. White, Dec. 12, 1963; children: Brooks B., Stephen C., John W. Grad., U.S. Army Lang. Sch., Monterey, Calif., 1958; BA, Mich. State U., 1961. Salesman La Driere Studios, Inc., Bloomfield Hills, Mich., 1961-63; sales and mktg. Ford Motor Co., Dearborn, Mich., 1963-66; salesman McWilliams Irwin Studios, Detroit, 1966-67, Al Hutt Studios, Detroit, 1967-68, New Ctr. Studios, Detroit, 1968-71; salesman, owner and ptnr. Blvd. Photographic, Highland Park, 1971—. Cpl. U.S. Army, 1957-60. Mem. Adcraft Club. Office: Blvd Photographic 18161 E 8 Mile Rd East Detroit MI 48021-3219

WEBER, JEFFERY A., advertising executive; b. 1953. With Griswold-Eshleman Co., Cleve., 1977—, now exec. v.p. *

WEBER, JEFFREY WILLIAM, public affairs professional; b. Akron, Ohio, Nov. 21, 1953; s. Carl William and Ellen Ann (Evans) W.; m. Kittie Michelle VanArsdel, Apr. 28, 1979; children: Graham, Emily. BS, Ind. State U., 1975. News reporter Sta. WTWO, Terre Haute, Ind., 1972-75; asst. news dir. Sta. WTHI, Terre Haute, 1975-78; pub. rels. coord. Amax Coal Co., Indpls., 1978-79; supr. community/media rels. Amax Coal Co., Springfield, Ill., 1979-81, Evansville, Ind., 1981-83; mgr. community/media rels. Amax Coal Industries, Indpls., 1983-89; dir. pub. affairs Champion Internat. Corp., Norway, Mich., 1989-91; regional dir. pub. affairs Champion Internat. Corp., Hamilton, Ohio, 1991—; co-founder Ohio Paper Info. com., Columbus, Ohio, 1992—. Author: Illinois Coal Facts, 1989; editor: Indiana Coal Facts, 1989; writer/producer (documentary) Juvenile Justice, 1977. Chmn. Hamilton Cmty. Leadership Award Com., 1992; mem. Accent Hamilton, 1992; sponsor Adopt-A-Sch. Program, Hamilton, 1991—, Miami U. Charity Points, Oxford, Ohio, 1991; bd. trustees Hamilton C. of C. and Econ devel. corp., vice chmn. Butler County Transp. Improvement Dist. Commn.; bd. dirs. Fitton Ctr. for Creative Arts, Hamilton Futures Forum, Shared Harvest Foodbank; mem. task force Cin. Regional Stadium Public Opinion Subcom., Butler County United Way Mktg. Com., chmn. Am. Forest and Paper Assn. Mich. Legis. com., exec. bd. Ohio C. of C. Environ. and Energy Com., Pub. Affairs Com.; adv. Iron Mountain Sch. Corp., Mich. Named Hon. deputy Marion County Sheriffs Dept., 1989. Mem. Hamilton City Club, U. Club, Chippewa Club, Kiwanis, Southwestern Ohio Pub. Affairs Group. Office: Champion Internat Corp 101 Knightsbridge Dr Hamilton OH 45011-3166

WEBER, JOHN BERTRAM, architect; b. Evanston, Ill., Oct. 15, 1930; s. Bertram Anton and Dorothea Hennecke (Brammer) W.; m. Sally Ann French; children: Suzanne French Weber Roulston, Jane Marie Weber McCarthy, Patricia Ann Weber Blodgett, Nancy Brammer. AB in Architecture, Princeton U., 1953; postgrad., Ill. Inst. Tech., 1959. Lic. architect. Field engr. United Constrn. Co., Riverdale, N.D., 1952; draftsman Bertram A. Weber Architect, Chgo., 1947- 53, architect, 1958-1973; field engr. Atkinson United Constrn. Co., Greenup and Ashland, Ky., 1956-58; ptnr., proprietor Weber & Weber Architects, Chgo., Northbrook and Winnetka, Ill., 1973—; Mem. Ill. Architecture Act Revision task force, 1982-89. Prin. works include Prestwick Country Club, the 3175 Commercial Ave. Bldg., Northbrook, med. office bldg. and additions to Bi-county hospital, Warren, Mich., additions and alterations to Detroit Osteopathic Hosp., addition to Duraclean Internat. Bldg., Deerfield, additions to The Admiral (a retirement home in Chgo.), and numerous pvt. residences, churches, comml., ednl., and recreational bldgs. Active Winnetka (Ill.) Cmty. Caucus, 1965, 74; mem. Mayor's adv. com. on bldg. codes, Chgo., 1975-80; chmn. bldg. com. Winnetka Cmty. House, 1977-81; mem. Winnetka Zoning Bd. Appeals, 1983-88, chmn., 1987-88; mem. Winnetka Ad Hoc Zoning Com., 1995-96; deacon, elder Winnetka Presbyn. Ch. With USN, 1953-56. Fellow Ill. Soc. Architects (bd. dirs. 1969-84, 91—, pres. 1976-78); mem. AIA (health com. 1969-76), Ill. Architect-Engr. Coun. (chmn. 1981-82, del. 1976-87, 92—), Northbrook C. of C., Architects Club Chgo. (pres. 1981, bd. dirs. 1976-86, 94), Builders Club Chgo. (bd. dirs. 1986—, pres. 1973-74), Am. Legion, Old Willow Club, Mchts. and Mfrs. Club, Dairymen's Country Club. Home: 415 Berkeley Ave Winnetka IL 60093-2109 Office: Weber & Weber Architects 415 Berkeley Ave Winnetka IL 60093-2109 also: 464 Central Ave Northfield IL 60093-3040

WEBER, MARGARET LAURA JANE, accountant; b. Fairview, Mo., Jan. 4, 1933; d. Mert James and Margaret Orr (Mortensen) Joel; m. James E. Jennings, Mar. 1953 (div.); children: James Edward Jennings, Janie Lea Franks, David Alan Jennings; m. Albert H. Weber, June 1956; children: Luhwanna Stonecipher, Margaret Anne Shadwick. AA, Crowder Coll., Mo., 1972; postgrad. Mo. So. Coll., 1988. Teller, First State Bank, Joplin, Mo., 1951-53; clk. Mo. Lic. Dept., Joplin, 1954-57, U. Mo. Ext. Dept., Neosho, 1967-68; cashier Crowder Coll., Neosho, Mo., 1968-83, acct., 1983—. Mem., Newton County Welfare Com., 1984—. Mem. Am. Bus. Women's Assn. (Woman of Yr. 1982, Bus. Assoc. of Yr. 1987), Nat. Assn. Female Execs., Mo. Assn. Community Jr. Colls. (bd. dirs. 1978-82). Republican. Baptist. Home: RR 6 Box 197 Neosho MO 64850-9135 Office: Crowder Coll 601 Laclede Ave Neosho MO 64850-9165

WEBER, MICHAEL JAMES, retail executive; b. Troy, N.Y., Oct. 14, 1962; s. William Frank and Patricia Ann (Ireland) W. BS in Prodn. and Ops. Mgmt., Miami U., Oxford, Ohio, 1985. Cert. prodn. and inventory mgmt. Product cons. Pansophic Sys., Chgo., 1985-87; sr. cons. Deloitte & Touche, Cin., 1987-90; dir. corp. sys. U.S. Shoe Corp., Cin., 1990-93, dir. retail sys., 1993-95; mgr. sys. planning Nationwide Ins. Co., Columbus, Ohio, 1995—. Mem. Am. Prodn. and Inventory Control Soc. Home: 1911 Fulton Dr Coshocton OH 43812

WEBER, MILAN GEORGE, retired army officer, management consultant; b. Milw., Oct. 15, 1908; s. Adam George and Frances (Lehrbaumer) W.; B.S., U.S. Mil. Acad., 1931; grad. Coast Arty. and Air Def. Sch., 1938, Nat. War Coll., 1952; m. Mary Agnes Keller, Sept. 2, 1931; 1 son, Milan George. Commd. 2d lt. U.S. Army, 1931, advanced through grades to col., 1944; various army command and staff exec. positions, Philippine Islands, 1932-36, Hawaii, 1938-41, Ft. Monroe, Va., 1936-38; anti-aircraft exec., hdqrs. 3d and 9th armies, U.S., Europe, 1943-45; mem. Gen. Patton's staff, 1944, War Dept. Gen. Staff, 1945-48; mil. adviser to Argentine govt., 1949-51; global strategic planner Joint Chiefs of Staff, 1952-54; comdr. Missile Defense of Norfolk and Hampton Roads, 1954-55; chief of staff advisory group, Japan, 1955-58; dept. comdr. Air Def. Region, Ft. Meade, Md., 1958-60, ret., 1960; mgr. electronic counter measures Loral Electronics Corp., N.Y.C., 1960-62; product mgr. electronic counter measures Hallicrafters Corp. (name changed to Northrop Corp.), Chgo., 1962-64; partner Weber Assos., Mgmt. Cons., Deerfield, Ill., 1964-69; pres. dir. Milan G. Weber Associates, Inc., Deerfield, 1969—; mgmt. cons. to various bus. firms, 1964—; acquisitions and mergers cons. to various corps., 1969—. Chmn. Great Lakes Ecology Assn. Ill., 1974—; chmn. Citizens Com. Honesty in Govt., 1969—; mem. Ill. Drivers Safety Adv. Com., 1975—, Deerfield Library Bd., 1976—, Deerfield Caucus Com., 1978—, Deerfield Energy Adv. Council, 1981—. Decorated Legion of Merit, Bronze Star, Commendation medal with oak leaf cluster. Mem. Assn. Old Crows, West Point Soc. Chgo., Internat. Platform Assn., Assn. Grads. U.S. Mil. Acad., Electronic Counter Measures Assn., Great Lakes Ecology Assn. of the Mil. Clubs: Army Navy, Army Navy Country. Contbr. articles on anti-aircraft arty., air def. and mil. strategy to profl. publs.; author of joint strategic capabilities plan; author weekly column on environment, 1977—. Home: 611 Colwyn Ter Deerfield IL 60015-3109 Office: PO Box 81 Deerfield IL 60015-0081

WEBER, NICHOLAS NOEL, physicist, researcher; b. Breckenridge, Minn., Dec. 25, 1957; s. Jerome P. and Jewel (Fangsrud) W. BS in Physics, Mont. State U., 1979; MS in Physics, U. Ill., 1986. Rsch. physicist U. Ill., Urbana. Mem. Internat. Soc. for Philos. Enquiry, Illini Space Devel. Soc. Home: 105 S 4th St #204 Champaign IL 61820 Office: Dept Physics Loomis Lab 1110 W Green St Urbana IL 61801-3003

WEBER, PATRICIA LOUISE BRADEN, marketing educator; b. Ft. Wayne, Ind., Oct. 31, 1945; d. Walter Frederick and Margaret June (Houk) Nagel, Jr.; m. Joseph Lou Braden, Aug. 23, 1969 (div. Feb. 1975); m. 2d, Walter Jacob Weber, Jr., July 20, 1981 (div. July 1988). B.S. in Bus. Adminstrn. with distinction, Ind. U., 1967, M.B.A., 1969, D.Bus.Adminstrn., 1973. Staff research assoc. div. research Sch. Bus. Adminstrn., Ind. U., Bloomington, 1967-70; adj. asst. prof. mktg. Coll. Bus., Eastern Mich. U., Ypsilanti, 1970, assoc. dean Coll. Bus., 1981-87; dir. Ctr. for Entrepreneurship, 1987-95, assoc. prof. mktg., 1995—; mem. research faculty Grad. Sch. Bus. Adminstrn., U. Mich., Ann Arbor, 1970-81, asst. dir. div. research, 1980-81, adj. assoc. prof. mktg., 1974-81; subprogram coordinator Coastal Zone research Mich. Sea Grant Program, Ann Arbor, 1977-86; mem. steering com. Minority Tech. Council Mich., Ann Arbor, 1982-83; mem. resource adv. com. Mich. changing economy program Mich. Dept. Commerce, Lansing, 1975-76; mem. subcoms. on competitive position, econ. growth and diversification, and statis. data Mich. Econ. Action Council, Lansing, 1975-76; dir. many sponsored research projects, cons. to govt., industry, bus. firms and profl. groups, 1970—; mem. bd. trustees Eastern Mich. U. Found., 1991-95. Author: Technological Entrepreneurship, 1977; (with Ramesh Gurnani) Data Processing in the Tax Function, 1980; also numerous tech. reports and articles in profl. jours. Program advisor Mich. Council for Arts, Detroit, 1978; bd. dirs. Child and Family Services of Washtenaw, Ann Arbor, 1983—, sec. of the bd., 1992—, chmn. devel. com., 1984—. Mem. AAAS, Am. Inst. for Decision Scis. (chmn. Mktg. Track, Midwest AIDS), Am. Mktg. Assn. (chpt. v.p., dir. 1976-80, chmn. program com. 1977-78, editor chpt. membership directory 1977, Marketeer 1975-77; chpt. cert. of recognition 1976-79, Best Competitive Paper, Educators Conf., San Diego, 1991), Am. Statis. Assn., Internat. Council for Small Bus. (research adv. com. 1974-75), Mich. Tech. Council (mem. state bd. dirs, chmn. bd. dirs. so. cen. 1986-90, research adv. bd. 1982-84, chmn. state bd. dirs., 1990-94), Soc. Automotive Engrs. (assoc. mem.; co-chmn. socio-tech. com. 1982-94, chmn., 1994—, sessions chmn. internat. congress 1982), Greater Detroit C. of C. (econ. devel. strategic planning com. 1982-92), Eastern Mich. U. Women's Assn. (pres.-elect 1983, pres. 1984), Mich. Hist. Soc., Ann Arbor Art Assn. (dir., treas. 1980-85), DAR, Alpha Gamma Delta, Beta Gamma Sigma, Omicron Delta, Alpha Lambda Delta. Home: 6750 Bethel Church Rd Saline MI 48176-9731 Office: Ea Mich U 543 Owen Coll Bus Bldg 300 W Michigan Ave Ypsilanti MI 48197-5443

WEBER, ROBERT R., state legislator; b. Nov. 19, 1925; m. Shirley V. Roe, 1948; children: Mary, Anthony, Kathleen, William. State rep. dist. 6 State of S.D., state rep. dist. 4, 1993—; mem. agriculture and natural resources and local govt. coms. S.D. Ho. of Reps.; farmer, rancher. Supr. Twp. Sch. Bd. Mem. S.D. Farmer's Union (state dir.), Nat. Farmers Orgn., Am. Agriculture Assn., K.C. Republican. Home: RR 1 Box 111 Strandburg SD 57265-9679*

WEBER, SHARI, state legislator; m. Mervin E. Weber. Program dir. Main St., Herington, Kans.; mem. from dist. 68 Kans. State Ho. of Reps., Topeka. Address: 934 Union Rd Herington KS 67449

WEBER, STEPHEN ALEX, computer-aided designer; b. Hartford, Wis., Dec. 15, 1967. Assoc. degree, Moraine Park Coll., 1988. Designer Coll. Rsch. Corp., Germantown, Wis., 1988, Micromange Display Corp., Hartford, 1990, Eye Comms., Hartford, 1992, Leeson Electric Corp., Grafton, Wis., 1994—. Home: 919 N Main St Hartford WI 53027-1201 Office: Leeson Electric Corp 2100 Washington St Grafton WI 53024-9540

WEBER, WILLIAM BRAMAN, JR., mathematician, educator; b. Toledo, Nov. 19, 1957; s. William Braman and Mary Jane (Ray) W.; m. Kristina Marie Ford, Sept. 19, 1987; children: Andrew James, Adam Kristian. BE, U. Toledo, 1980, MEd, 1986; EdD, U. Mich., 1994. Tchr. Northwood (Ohio) Local Schs., 1980-93; asst. prof. maths. edn. U. Toledo, 1993—; instr. Detroit Area Pre-Coll. Engring. Program, 1990-95; cons. several sch. dists. in Ohio, Mich. Mem. Am. Ednl. Rsch. Assn., Nat. Coun. Tchrs. Math. (Greater Toledo chpt. pres. 1996-98), Ohio Math. Edn. Leadership Coun., Fraternal Order Eagles Aerie # 2322, Alpha Sigma Phi (faculty advisor 1994—), Phi Kappa Phi, Kappa Delta Pi. Office: Univ Toledo Toledo OH 43606

WEBSTER, DOUGLAS PETER, emergency physician; b. Chgo., July 4, 1957; s. David Ferguson and Margaret Webster; m. Mariruth K. Burkhart, Sept. 25, 1989. BA in Chemistry, BS in Psychology, Loyola U., Chgo., 1978; MS in Chem. Physics, Wayne State U., 1980; DO, Chgo. Coll. Osteo. Medicine, 1985. Diplomate in emergency medicine Am. Osteo. Bd. Emergency Medicine, Am. Bd. Forensic Examiners. Intern Chgo. Coll. Osteo Medicine, 1985-86; resident in gen. surgery Sinai Hosp. Detroit, 1986-87; resident in emergency medicine Chgo. Coll. Osteo Medicine, 1988-90; clin. asst. prof. emergency medicine Chgo. Coll. Osteo. Medicine, 1990-93, clin. assoc. prof., 1993—; assoc. chmn. dept. emergency medicine, 1995—; assoc. chmn. emergency medicine Chgo. Coll. Osteo. Medicine, 1995—; assoc. dir. emergency svcs. Olympia Fields (Ill.) Osteo Med./Trauma Ctr., 1990-91; dir. emergency svcs. St. Anthony Hosp., Chgo., 1991-93; sr. ptnr. Med. Rev. Assocs., S.C., 1992—; chmn., med. dir. emergency medicine Little Co. of Mary Hosp., Evergreen Park, Ill., 1993-95; med. dir. Trauma Ctr. Columbia Olympia Fields (Ill.) Osteo. Med. Ctr., 1996—; assoc. clin. coord., cons. Crescent Counties Found. for Med. Care, 1992—; speaker in field. Diplomate in emergency medicine Am. Osteo. Bd. Emergency Medicine, Am. Bd. Forensic Examiners, Am. Bd. Forensic Medicine. Recipient award Disting. Physicians Am., 1991, Family Medicine award Lemmon Pharm. Found., 1985, others; Univ. Grad. fellow Wayne State U., 1979. Fellow Am. Coll. Osteo. Emergency Physicians; mem. Am. Bd. Forensic Examiners, Am. Bd. Forensic Medicine, Am. Coll. Emergency Physicians, Am. Osteo. Assn., Phi Lambda Upsilon, Alpha Epsilon Delta. Home: 4439 Cascara Ln Lisle IL 60532-4368 Office: Columbia Olympia Fields Osteo Med Ctr 20201 S Crawford Olympia Fields IL 60461

WEBSTER, JEFFREY LEON, graphic designer; b. Idaho Falls, Idaho, Nov. 23, 1941; s. Leon A. and Marjory M. (McAllister) W.; student Sch. Associated Arts, St. Paul, 1962; m. Judith Kess, Apr. 17, 1965; children: Eric J., Marjorie P. Sci. illustrator Mayo Clinic, Rochester, Minn., 1963-66; layout artist Brown & Bigelow, St. Paul, 1966; graphic designer U. Minn., Mpls., 1966-67, U. Calgary (Alta., Can.), 1967-68; sr. artist Control Data Corp., St. Paul, 1968-70; mem. Idaho State U. Meml. Lectureship Com.; graphic designer Idaho State U., 1970-78; owner, operator studio, Harmony, Minn.; mktg. and advt. cons. to 45 regional and nat. firms, 1978—. Mem. Idaho Civic Symphony Bd. Chairperson rub. rels. Unitarian Ch. Rochester, 1991—; bd. dirs. Gift of Life Transplant House, Rochester, Minn. 1996, Rochester Orch. and Chorale, 1996. Recipient Profl. citation Libr. Congress, 1976; 1st Pl. Best Trucking ad, Overdrive Mag., 1990. Artist pub. ednl. exhibits. Home and Office: RR 1 Harmony MN 55939-9801

WEBSTER, SUSAN VERDI, art history educator; b. Lafayette, Ind., Dec. 4, 1959; d. Grady Linder and Barbara Ann (Donahue) Webster. BA, Reed Coll., Portland, Oreg., 1982; MA, Williams Coll., Williamstown, Mass., 1986; PhD, U. Tex., 1992. Instr. U. Tex., Austin, 1991; asst. prof. art history U. St. Thomas, St. Paul, 1992—; scholar/cons. Yellowcat Prodns., Washington, 1993-94. Contbr. articles to profl. jours. U. Tex.-Austin fellow, 1986-87; Grantee Mex. Rsch. Program for Cultural Coop., 1989, 93, Tinker Found., 1989, Soc. for Hispanic Art, 1991, NEH, 1995, Spain '92 Found., 1995. Mem. Coll. Art Assn., Renaissance Soc., Soc. for Confraternity Studies, L.Am. Studies Assn., Am. Soc. Hispanic Hist. Studies, Assn. for L.Am. Art. Office: Univ of Saint Thomas Dept Art History 2115 Summit Ave Saint Paul MN 55105

WECHSLER, SERGIO, automotive executive, consultant; b. Rio de Janeiro, Aug. 10, 1944; came to U.S., 1965; s. Michael and Gertrud (Putziger) W.; m. Renate Schuler, June 26, 1969; children: Mark, Andrew. Student, Mackenzie U., 1962, Gen. Motors Inst. Engring., 1967; MBA in Internat. Bus., NYU, 1974. Quality supr. GM do Brasil, Sao Paulo, 1963-65, quality control supt., 1967-70; quality control mgr. Gillette Corp., Berlin, 1970-71; project mgr. GM, N.Y.C., 1971-76; plant mgr. GM de Portugal, Lisbon, 1976-79; project mgr. Adam Opel AG, Russelheim, Fed. Republic of Germany, 1979-81; quality dir. GM, Linden, N.J., 1981-85; dir. ops. and quality control GM, Warren, Mich., 1985-93, mgr. internat. programs, 1985-95; program mgr. Cadillac Luxury Car divsn. GM, Flint, Mich., 1993—; pres. Marswex Global Enterprises, St. Petersburg, Fla., 1982—, Hudson (Fla.) Pla., 1984—. V.P. Temple Beth Jacob, Pontiac, Mich., 1986, pres., 1987-89. Mem. Am. Soc. Quality Control (cert. quality engr. 1992), Radio Club. Republican. Office: Marswex Global Enterprises # 220 100 Carillon Pkwy Saint Petersburg FL 33716

WECHTER, CLARI ANN, paint manufacturing company executive; b. Chgo., June 1, 1953; d. Norman Robert and Harriet Beverly (Golub) W.; m. Gordon Jay Siegel, Feb. 10, 1980; 1 child, Alix Jessica. BA, U. Ariz., 1975; BE, Loyola U., Chgo., 1977. Cert. tchr., Ill. Saleswoman, v.p. sales Federated Paint Mfg. Co., Chgo., 1979—. Republican. Jewish. Home: 25 E Cedar St Chicago IL 60611-1151 Office: Federated Paint Mfg Co 1882 S Normal Ave Chicago IL 60616-1013

WECK, KRISTIN WILLA, savings bank executive; b. Elgin, Ill., Nov. 5, 1959; d. John Francis and Florence Elaine (Ebel) W. BBA, Augustana Coll., Rock Island, Ill., 1981. Lic. real estate broker, Ill., life/health ins. producer; registered securities rep. (series 7 and series 24). Intern with investment banking group First Chgo. Bank, London, 1980; intern Prudential-Bache Co., Ft. Lauderdale, Fla., 1981; residential appraiser Fox Valley Appraisal Counselors, Ltd., West Dundee, Ill., 1982-84; asst. real estate loan officer First Nat. Bank, Barrington, Ill., 1982-84; savs. and loan field examiner III Office of Thrift Supervision, Chgo., 1984-90; mng. agt. Resolution Trust Corp., Elk Grove Village, Ill., 1990-91; sr. v.p., treas., bd. dirs. Cardunal Savs. Bank, West Dundee, Ill., 1991—. Vice pres. Brandywine Condo Assn., Crystal Lake, Ill., 1983; Project Bus. cons. Jr. Achievement, 1992—. Recipient Outstanding Achievement award Fed. Home Loan Bank Bd., 1985. Mem. Nat. Assn. Securities Dealers (registered rep., registered prin.). Republican. Lutheran. Home: PO Box 930 Dundee IL 60118-0930 Office: Cardunal Savs Bank FSB 704 W Main St # 97 Dundee IL 60118-2028

WEDDELL, LINDA ANNE, speech and language pathologist; b. Pitts., Nov. 21, 1946; d. Gilbert Eugene and Anna Margaret (Duffer) Everett; m. Charles Michael Weddell, Aug. 7, 1971; children: Michael Everett, Allison Joanne. BS, Purdue U., 1970; postgrad., Butler U., 1987. Speech pathologist Clermont County Sch. System, Batavia, Ohio, 1970-71, MSD Decatur Twp., Indpls., 1971-76; asst. dir. Mom's Day Out program Calvary United Meth. Ch., Brownsburg, Ind., 1983-86; speech pathologist Brownsburg Community Schs., 1989—. Vol. Am. Heart Assn., Indpls., 1988; com. mem. Calvary United Meth. Ch., Brosnwburg, 1976—; dir. Brownsburg Tennis Tournament, 1988; leader Girl Scouts U.S.A., Brownsburg, 1987-89. Continuing edn. grantee Brownsburg Fellowship, 1990. Mem. Ind. Speech & Hearing Assn., Purdue Alumni Assn. (life). Home: 3115 N 950th E Brownsburg IN 46112

WEDDIGE, EMIL ALBERT, lithographer, art educator; b. Sandwich, Ont., Can., Dec. 23, 1907; came to U.S., 1909; s. Carl Albert and Marie Emma (Boismier) W.; m. Juanita Gertrude Pardon, Aug. 18, 1919. BS (hon.), Ea. Mich. U., 1934, DFA (hon.), 1973; student, Art Students League, N.Y.C.; studies with Emil Ganso, Woodstock, N.Y.; M of Design, U. Mich., 1937; Dr. Fine Arts (hon.), Ea. Mich. U., 1973; D (hon.), Cleary Coll., 1992. Tchr. Dearborn (Mich.) Pub. Schs., 1934-35; supr. art Dearborn Sch. System, 1935-37; from instr. to prof. art Univ. Mich., Ann Arbor, 1937-73, ret., apptd. prof. emeritus, 1974; owner pvt. studio Paris, 1949—, Ann Arbor; Cons. to John Weiss, Detroit, 1969—, to Louis G. Basso, West Bloomfield Hills, Mich., 1980—. One-man shows include Fishy Whale Studio, 1975, Washtenaw Community Coll., Ann Arbor, Tokyo, Japan, numerous others; exhibited in Paris, 1986, 87, T'Marra Gallery, Japan, 1991, U. Mich. Mus. of Art, Tokyo, Japan, 1993; permanent collections at Met. Mus. Art, N.Y.C., Libr. of Congress, Washington, Bibliotheque Nationale, Paris, Nat. Gallery of Art, Washington, various worldwide U.S. Embassies, many colls. and univs., many others; commd. by Parke Davis & Co., Chrysler Corp., Dow Chem. Co., United Nergo S. F.; designer Mich. Artain; contbr. articles to profl. jours. Pres. Izaack Walton League, Ann Arbor, 1945—. Recipient Philip and Ester Klein prize Am. Color Print Soc., 1965, Print award Libr. of Congress, 1951, Print of Yr. award The Print Club, Phila., 1957, Eugene Power award for art work done for United Negro Found., 1993, United Meml. Coll. Found. award, numerous other awards. Mem. Internat. Soc. Appraisers, Mich. Water Color Soc. (founder, pres., charter organizer), Mich. Printmakers (founder, pres.), Ann Arbor Art Assn. (exhbn. dir. 1943-55). Republican. Congregational. Home and Studio: 870 Stein Rd Ann Arbor MI 48105-9216

WEDE, RICHARD J., school superintendent; b. Cherokee, Iowa, Nov. 11, 1949; s. Robert C. and Beatrice I. (Albers) W.; m. Carol E. Teeter, Dec. 22, 1969; 1 child, Robert D.R. BA, U. No. Iowa, 1971; MS, Iowa State U., 1979; EdS, N.W. Mo. State U., 1985. Drivers' edn. tchr. N.W. Webster Community Sch. Dist., Barnum, Iowa, 1971, Everly (Iowa) Community Sch. Dist., 1974-75; jr. high math tchr. Blessed Sacrament Sch., Waterloo, Iowa, 1973-75; high sch. math tchr. Council Bluffs (Iowa) Community Sch. Dist., 1975-80; assoc. mid. sch. prin. Lewis Cen. Community Sch. Dist., Council Bluffs, 1980-83; sec. prin. Bedford (Iowa) Community Sch. Dist., 1983-86; supt. schs. Everly Community Sch. Dist., 1986-89, Everly & Clay Cen. Community Sch. Dists., 1989-91, Prairie Community Sch. Dist., Gowrie, Iowa, 1991-93, Cedar Valley Community Sch. Dist., 1991-93, Praire Valley Community Sch. Dist., Gowrie, Iowa, 1993-94; supt. Dunkerton (Iowa) Cmty. Sch. Dist., 1994—. Bd. dirs. Regional Transit Authority, Spencer, Iowa, 1990-91. Mem. Am. Assn. Sch. Adminstrs., Sch. Adminstrs. Iowa, Am. Legion, Westend Optimists of Council Bluffs, Ruritan, Phi Delta Kappa. Roman Catholic. Home: Box 67 207 E Sycamore Dunkerton IA 50626 Office: Dunkerton Cmty Sch Dist PO Box 308 509 S Canfield Dunkerton IA 50626

WEDIN, CAROLYN E., English educator; b. Frederic, Wis., Oct. 2, 1939; d. Reuben Peter and Ruth Elizabeth (Hane) W.; m. Stefan O. Sylvander, Aug. 26, 1961 (div. Feb. 3, 1987); children: Monika Ruth Creden, Mario K. Sylvander, Brendan A. Sylvander; m. Anthony A. Rolloff, Dec. 31, 1989. BA, Gustavus Adolphus Coll., 1961; MA, U. Kans., 1964; PhD, U. Wis., 1976. Teaching asst., editorial asst. Modern Drama Mag. U. Kans., Lawrence, 1961-64; instr. Shaw U., Raleigh, N.C., 1964-66; prof. U. Wis., Whitewater, 1966—; instr. AT&T State U., U. N.C., Greensboro, summers 1966-69; interim appointments U. Wis. System Adminstrn., Madison, 1974-75, 80, 81, U. Gothenburg, Sweden, 1985-86; Fulbright lectr. U. Silesia, Poland, 1991-92; Fulbright roving scholar, Norway, 1996—. Author: Jessie Redmond Fauset, 1981, James Baldwin, 1980, Wisconsin: A Year, 1985, Letters and Reflections from Poland, 1993; contbr. articles to profl. jours., newspapers, encys.; co-author books. Treas. Alternative Directions, Inc., Whitewater, 1973—; sr. rsch. assoc. U. Wis. System Inst. on Race and Ethnicity, 1992-93. Woodrow Wilson fellow Woodrow Wilson Found., 1961-63, Woodrow Wilson Dissertation fellow Woodrow Wilson Found., 1975-76, fellow Inst. for Rsch. in the Humanities, U. Wis., Madison, 1988-89; named one of Wis. Women Leaders AAUW, 1987. Mem. Phi Beta Kappa. Democrat. Lutheran. Home: N7559 E Lakeshore Dr Whitewater WI 53190-4347

WEDNER, H. JAMES, physician, researcher; b. Pitts., May 12, 1941; s. Benjamin Mayer and Lucille Ruth (Jacobs) W.; m. Maureen Patricia Martin, June 18, 1978; children: Bryna Kimberly, Jason Oliver. BS, Cornell U., 1963; MD, Cornell Med. Coll., N.Y.C., 1967. Intern Barnes Hosp., St. Louis, 1867-68; resident internal medicine Washington U. Med. Sch., St. Louis, 1970-71; fellow allergy and immunology Wash. U. Med. Sch., 1971-73; lt. comdr. USPHS, Govenor's Island, N.Y., 1968-70; dir. tng. program allergy and immunology Washington U. Med. Sch., St. Louis, 1986-95, chief clin. allergy and immunology, 1988—, prof. medicine, 1990—; vis. prof. Am. Coll. of Allergy and Immunology, Little Rock, Ark., 1991; prin. investigator psychosocial aspects of asthma, St. Louis Asthma Study Unit; chmn. steering com. Nat. Coop. Inner City Asthma Study. Editor: Allergy: Theory and Practice, 1984, 2d rev. edit., 1991; mem. editl. bd. Jour. Immunology, 1980-82, Jour. Allergy and Clin. Immunology, 1991-96. Fellow Am. Acad. Allergy Asthma Immunology; mem. Internat. Soc. Immunopharmacology, Am. Coll. Allergy Asthma Immunology, Am. Ass. Immunology. Office: Washington U Med Sch Campus Box 8122 600 S Euclid Ave Saint Louis MO 63110-1010

WEED, MELVIN L., retired railroad conductor, small business owner; b. Detroit, Jan. 25, 1947; s. Merrill L. and Flora McMillan Galbraith (Thornton) W.; m. Malinda D. Ward-Corey, Jan. 29, 1966 (div. Feb. 1994). Railroad condr. Pennsylvania Railroad, Melvindale, Mich., 1966-68, Pen Cen. Railroad, Detroit, 1968-76, ConRail, Detroit, 1976-86, Amtrack, Detroit, 1986-88; proprietor Mel's Snow Removal, Madison Heights, Mich., 1978-84, Mel's Bldg. and Landscape Supply, Madison Heights, 1979-84; local chmn., union steward United Transp. Union, Detroit, 1967-69, local v.p., 1970-76. Author: (books) Do You Feel Like Me?, 1991; contbg. poet: (anthology) Reflections of Light, 1995; singer/songwriter/composer: Cloud Nine With an Angel, 1993. Guardianship/foster parent State of Mich., Oakland County, 1985. Recipient citation for citizen arrest, City of Madison Heights, 1987. Office: Earnest Stone Publs PO Box 1288 Sterling Heights MI 48311-1288

WEEDEN, TIMOTHY L., state legislator; b. Beloit, Wis., Nov. 13, 1951; s. Loren G. and Edythe M. (Soderberg) W.; m. Sandra J. Thorpe, June 18, 1977; 1 child, Blake A. BA in Polit. Sci., Wheaton Coll., 1973; MBA, U. Wis., Whitewater, 1982. Expeditor Revere Electric Supply Co., Chgo., 1973-77; buyer Fairbanks-Morse Engine div. Colt Industries, Beloit, 1977-79; sr. buyer Warner Electric Brake & Clutch Co., South Beloit, Ill., 1979-85; state rep. Wis. State Assembly, Madison, 1985-87; state senator Wis. State Senate, Madison, 1987—. Mem. Beloit Bd. Edn., 1983-85, Beloit Econ. Devel. Corp., 1984—, Rock County Rep. Party, Wis., 1984—. Mem. Beloit Jaycees (Disting. Svc. award 1986). Home: 1821 Sherwood Dr SW Beloit WI 53511-5657

WEEKLY, JOHN WILLIAM, insurance company executive; b. Sioux City, Iowa, June 21, 1931; s. John E. Weekly and Alyce Beatrice (Preble) Nichols; m. Bette Lou Thomas, Dec. 31, 1949; children: John William Jr., Thomas Patrick, Michael Craig, James Mathew, Daniel Kevin. Grad. high sch., Omaha. V.p. First Data Resources, Inc., Omaha, 1969-74; v.p. Mut. of Omaha/United of Omaha Ins. Co., Omaha, 1974-81, sr. exec. v.p., 1981-87, pres., COO, 1987-95, vice chmn., pres., COO, 1995—, vice chmn., pres., CEO, 1996—; CEO Mutual of Omaha Ins. Co., 1996—; also bd. dirs. Mut. of Omaha/United of Omaha Ins. Co., Omaha, 1996—; bd. dirs. KPM Investment Mgmt., Midwest Express Airlines, Inc., Harbor Holdings, Inc., Companion Life Ins. Co., Kirkpatrick, Pettis, Smith, Polian, Inc., Tele-Trip Co., Inc., Omaha Property and Casualty Co., United World Life Ins., Mut. Asset Mgmt. Co., Norwest Bank Nebr., N.A., Omaha Airport Authority, Mut. of Omaha Investor Svcs., Preferred HealthAlliance, Inc. Bd. dirs. Bellevue (Nebr.) U., 1986—. Mem. Health Ins. Assn. Am. (chmn. of bd. 1996), Am. Coun. Life Ins. (bd. dirs. 1995—), Greater Omaha C. of C. (bd. dirs. 1991—). Office: Mut Omaha Ins Co Mutual Omaha Plz Omaha NE 68175

WEEKS, LLOYD F., state legislator; b. Cheboygan, Mich., June 9, 1932; m. Gracy; children: Mitzi, Dan, Don, Lorrie, Peter, Gregg, Lisa, Jim, Lynda.; Maycomb C.C., God's Bible Coll., Cin., Wayne State U. Various positions, 1965-81; asst. to v.p. bus. & dir. purchasing Macomb C.C., 1981-83; state rep. Dist. 70 Mich. Ho. of Reps., 1983-94, 95—. Mem. Warren City Coun., 1977-82. Mem. Mich. Pub. Purchasing Officers Assn., Macomb County Schs. Bus. Officers Assn., Warren Police Res. Home: 11337 Jonas Ave Warren MI 48089-1061*

WEEKS, M. J., international management consultant; b. N.Y.C., June 12, 1942; d. Kenneth James and Annette Jude (Williams) Altman; m. Robert S. Weeks, June 15, 1960; children: Sean Robert, Megan Elizabeth. BA cum laude, U. S.D., 1967, MA, 1969. Tchr. high sch. Orono Schs., Long Lake, Minn., 1970-74; mem. faculty Winona (Minn.) State U., 1976-82; mem. faculty Sioux Falls (S.D.) Coll., 1982—, dir. Ctr. Mgmt., 1985-89; pres. M.J. Weeks Seminars, Sioux Falls, 1982—; cons. to numerous Fortune 500 orgns.; mgmt. cons., Sioux Falls, 1982—; speaker at numerous nat. assns., seminars, workshops, and convs. throughout U.S., S.Am., Can., and Mexico. Author: Taking Control with Time Management, rev. edit., (cassette tapes) Listening: The Quiet Side of Communication, How To Deliver Unpopular Information; also videos on strategic communication. Bd. dirs. League of Women Voters, Sioux Falls, 1983-85; mem. Women's Network, S.D., 1984-86, Peace and Justice Ctr., 1984-86, Sioux Falls Leadership II. Mem. AAUW (bd. dirs. 1983-84), ASTD, Internat. Platform Assn., Nat. Coun. Tchrs. of English, Nat. Am. Soc. Tng., Sioux Falls Pers. Assn. Home and Office: 3505 Spencer Blvd Sioux Falls SD 57103-4654

WEEKS, ROBERT EARL, advertising executive; b. Yazoo City, Miss., Sept. 17, 1925; s. Dennis H. and Mamie O. (Randolph) W.; children: Suzanne Lynn, Robin Denise, Linda, Robert Earl II, Lisa Ann. Student, Wilson Jr. Coll., 1947, Latin Am. Inst. Pub. Relations, 1950, DePaul U., 1952. Br. mgr. King Records Inc., Chgo., 1948-50; assoc. Pursell Pub. Relations, Chgo., 1950-65; insp. Chgo. Bd. Health, 1965-66; adminstrv. asst. to Alderman Robert H. Miller, Chgo., 1966-69; coordinator task force for community broadcasting Chgo. Digest mag., 1969-76; pres. Troubadour & Assocs., Ltd., Chgo., 1969—; pub. Troubadour Digest mag., 1976—; writer Cablecommunications Resource Ctr., Washington, 1972—; cons. New Regal Theatre, Chgo, 1990; program specialist City of Chgo., 1990. Author: Cable TV in Chicago, 1976; editor Chgo. Radio Guide, 1985. Active with South Side Community Art Ctr., Hyde Park Improvement Assn.; pres. Hyde Park West Tenant Assn., 1992. Served with USAAF, 1944-46. Mem. Black Media Reps. (v.p. 1976), Ill. Arts Assn., Am. Soc. Profl. Cons., Pub. Relations Soc. Am. Democrat. Roman Catholic. Clubs: Clef Social, Publicity of Chgo. Home and Office: Apt 517 5307 S Hyde Park Blvd Chicago IL 60615-5744

WEERTS, RICHARD KENNETH, music educator; b. Peoria, Ill., Oct. 7, 1928; s. Gerhard Nicholas and Ellen Marie (Lindeburg) W. BS, U. Ill., 1951; MA, Columbia U., 1956, EdD, 1960; MA, N.E. Mo. State U., 1973. Tchr. Lyndhurst (N.J.) Pub. Schs., 1956-57; dir. instrumental music Scotch Plains (N.J.) Pub. Schs., 1957-61; prof. music Truman State U. (formerly N.E. Mo. State U.), Kirksville, 1961—, chair dept. music, 1994—. Author: Handbook for Woodwinds, 1965, Developing Individual Skills for the High School Band, 1969, How to Develop and Maintain a Successful Woodwind Section, 1972, Original Manuscript Music, 1973, Handbook of Rehearsal Techniques for Band, 1976; numerous papers and monographs; nat. bd. editors The Quarterly, jour. of Ctr. for Rsch. in Music Learning and Teaching, 1989. Dir. music First United Meth. Ch., Kirksville, 1970—. Served with U.S. Army, 1951-55. Mem. Coun. for Rsch. in Music Edn., Nat. Assn. Coll. Wind and Percussion Instrs. (nat. exec. sec./treas. 1971—, editor jour. 1968—), Music Educators Nat. Conf., Phi Delta Kappa. Office: NACWPI Northeast Mo State U Divsn Fine Arts Kirksville MO 63501

WEFLER, WILSON DANIEL, publisher, editor, management consultant; b. Rocky River, Ohio, Feb. 27, 1927; s. Wilson Daniel and Myra (Johns) W.; m. Bonnie Kistner, Feb. 9, 1952; children: Wendy, Nancy, Bonnie, Susan, John. BS in Journalism, Northwestern U., 1950. Asst. editor, writer Standard Oil Co., Chgo., 1951-55; asst. editor Keeney Pub. Co., Chgo., 1955-56; pub. rep. Urban Farley & Co., Chgo., 1957-61; dir. alumni relations Northwestern U., Evanston, Ill., 1961-65; pres. Com. for Middle Western Bus. Devel., Inc., Chgo., 1965-75; sr. v.p. Unimark Internat., 1975-79; pres. Wefler & Assocs., Inc., Evanston, 1979—; past pres. Assn. Profl. Design Firms, Cambridge, Mass., 1985-88, chmn. founding com., 1984; pub. Design Firm Directory, 1979—. Editor Design Firm Mgmt., 1980—. Bd. commrs. Lighthouse Park Dist., Evanston, 1992—. Recipient Service award Northwestern U. Alumni Assn., 1966. Mem. Am. Ctr. Design, Internat. Interior Design Assn., John Evans Club. Home: 6 Milburn Park Evanston IL 60201-1744 Office: Wefler & Assocs Inc PO Box 1167 Evanston IL 60204-1167

WEGENER, KRISTY ANN, medical surgical nurse, homecare nurse; b. Greenville, S.C., Dec. 3, 1954; d. Gordon Wayne and Beverly Ann (Lewis) W. Lic. practical nurse diploma, 1975; ADN, North Iowa Area Community Coll., 1979; BSN, Buena Vista Coll., Ft. Dodge, Iowa, 1987. RN, Iowa, Minn., Colo., Calif. Nurse emergency room Boone County Hosp., Boone, Iowa; team nurse Wyo. Family Clinic, Casper; nursing assoc. Universal Nursing Svc., Des Moines; dir. nursing Cen. Iowa for Home Care, Colo.; asst. DON Ft. Dodge (Iowa) Villa Care Ctr.; home care nurse Cross County Nursing, 1992-93; adminstr. home care agy. Nurses House Call, Iowa City, Iowa, 1993-94; home care nurses IMMC, Des Moines, 1995—; hightech. pediatrics home care Cross Country Nursing, Tucson, 1992. Founding mem. Am. Air Mus. in Eng. Capt. USAR. Mem. ANA, Smithsonian Soc., Ducks Unltd. (ladies com.).

WEGENKE, GARY L., school systems administrator; b. South Bend, Ind., Feb. 28, 1938; s. Edward and Blanche Wegenke; m. Sandra S. Gard, Aug. 17, 1963; children: Bart and Bret (twins), Blake. BA, DePauw U., 1961; MS, Ind. U., 1964; PhD, Ohio State U., 1971. Secondary tchr. South Bend (Ind.) Cmty. Sch. Corp., 1961-69; grad. rsch. assoc. Coll. Edn. Ohio State U., Columbus, 1969-71; prin. Hill H.S., Lansing, Mich., 1972-76; dir. adminstrvs. svcs. Lansing Sch. Dist., 1976-78, asst. supt. Fiscal and Adminstrv. Svcs., 1979-81, dep. supt., 1981-83; supt. schs. Waterloo (Iowa) Cmty. Sch. Dist., 1983-88, Des Moines Ind. Cmty. Sch. Dist., 1988—; adj. asst. prof. Ohio State U., Columbus, 1971-72; adj. prof. Mich. State U., East Lansing, 1980-84, U. Northern Iowa, Cedar Falls, 1984—, Drake U., 1991; nat. adv. panel chairperson Ctr. for Rsch. on Ednl. Accountability and Tchr. Evaluation, Western Mich. U., Kalamazoo, 1990—, Danforth Found. Leadership Initiative, 1994—; chairperson state outcomes and assessment Iowa State Dept. Edn., 1992-93; project dir. Statewide Libr. Planning and Evaluation, Ohio State U., 1971-72; lectr. various symposia. Contbr. articles to profl. jours. Bd. dirs. Cedar Valley United Way, 1985-88, Leadership Investment for Tomorrow, Waterloo/Cedar Falls, 1986-88, HMO Iowa, 1990-92, Boy Scouts Am., 1991—, Jr. Achievement, Des Moines, 1988—, Polk County United Way, 1989—, Community Focus, 1992—; chairperson Urban Edn. Network, 1987. Named Exec. Educator 100 Best Sch. Execs., 1993, Iowa Supt. of Yr., 1993-94; recipient Lansing Concerned Citizen award Jr. C. of C., 1972. Mem. Am. Assn. Sch. Adminstrs. (finalist Supt. of Yr. 1994), Sch. Adminstrs. Iowa, Des Moines Sch. Adminstrs. Assn., Des Moines C. of C. (bd. dirs. 1990), Waterloo C. of C. (bd. dirs. 1985-87, Pub. Servant of Yr. award 1985), Phi Delta Kappa (v.p. U. No. Iowa chpt., Des Moines area Outstanding Educator of Yr. award 1992). Office: Des Moines Pub School 1800 Grand Ave Des Moines IA 50309-3310

WEGNER, WALDO WILBERT, retirement community and health care facility executive; b. Clay County, Iowa, Jan. 17, 1913. BSCE, Iowa State U., 1935. Registered profl. engr., Iowa, Minn. CIRAS Iowa State U., Ames, 1963-78; civil engr. Stenberg Concrete, Ames, 1978-90; chmn. Green Hills Residents Assn., Ames, 1988-95. Capt. U.S. Navy Res., 1941-78. Mem. NSPE (v.p. 1935—), Iowa Engring. Soc. (pres. 1956, Herbert Hoover award 1994), Ctr. for Indsl. Rsch. and Svc. (founding dir.). Republican. Home and Office: 2200 Hamilton Dr Apt 401 Ames IA 50014-8274

WEHDE, ROGER ALLAN, secondary education educator; b. Sioux Falls, S.D., Feb. 14, 1951; s. Raymond John and Violet Elizabeth (Kram) W.; m. Janet Mae Glaus, Sept. 29, 1984; 1 child, Kelsey Ann. BS in Agrl. Edn., S.D. State U., 1973. Agrl. tchr. Menno (S.D.) High Sch., 1973-80, Dell Rapids (S.D.) High Sch., 1980—; mem. Modernization Com. for the Dell Rapids Sch. Dist.; pres. local tchrs. orgn., 1994-95. Vice pres. S.D. Jaycees, Menno, 1973-80; coun. pres. Dell Rapids Luth. Ch., 1988-90, Sunday sch. tchr., mem. choir, 1980—; advisor Future Farmers Am. Recipient Am. Hon. Deg., Hon. State Deg., Future Farmers Am., 1990. Mem. NEA, Am. Vocat. Assn., S.D. Vocat. Assn. (exec. com. 1989-90), S.D. Edn. Assn. (state negotiations com. 1979-80), S.C. Vocat. Agr. Tchrs. Assn. (pres. 1989-90, award 1990), Nat. Vocat. Agr. Tchrs. Assn. (state officer, exec. com. 1987-90), Dell Rapids Edn. Assn. (head negotiations com., pres. 1994—, mem. sch. improvement local modernization com. for edn. 1993—). Republican. Home: 713 Iowa Ave Dell Rapids SD 57022-1227 Office: Dell Rapids H S 1216 Garfield Ave Dell Rapids SD 57022-1036

WEHLING, ROBERT LOUIS, household products company executive; b. Chgo., Nov. 27, 1938; s. Ralph Joseph and Rita Helen (Casey) W.; m. Carolyn Thierry Harmon, July 5, 1958; children: Susan, Mary, Jennifer, Linda, Karen, Sandra. BA magna cum laude, Denison U., 1960. Brand asst. Procter & Gamble Co., Cin., 1960, 63-64, asst. brand mgr., 1964-66, br. mgr., 1966-70, assoc. advt. mgr., 1970-74, advt. mgr. bar soap and household cleaning products div., 1974-77, div. mgr. gen. advt., 1977-84, assoc. gen. advt. mgr., 1984-87, gen. mktg. svcs. mgr., 1987-88, v.p. mktg. svcs., 1988-90, v.p. pub. affairs, 1990-94, sr. v.p. advt., market rsch. and pub. affairs, 1994—, 1994—; mem. edn. task force Bus. Roundtable, 1990—. Pres. March of Dimes, Cin., 1981-84; mem. allocations com. Fine Arts Fund, Cin., 1987—; bd. dirs. Just Say No Internat., 1991-93; co-founder with USA Today, Coalition on Edn. Initiatives, 1991—; mem. Mayor's Commn. on Children, 1992—; vice chmn. Downtown Cin., Inc.; exec. com. Cin. Youth Collaborative; trustee United Way Cin., Ohio Schs. Devel. Corp.; bd. dirs. Edn. Excellence Partnership; participant Gov.'s Edn. Mgmt. Coun.; mem. Hamilton county Family and Children First Coun. Named One of 200 Greater Cincinnatians, Cin. Bicentennial Commn., 1988. Mem. Assn. Nat. Advertisers, Advt. Coun. (campaign dir. 1988—), Greater Cin. C. of C. (trustee, exec. com.), Queen City Club, Commonwealth Club, Phi Beta Kappa. Republican. Methodist. Office: Procter & Gamble Co 1 Procter Gamble Plz Cincinnati OH 45202

WEHLING, WAYNE F., entomologist; b. Denver, Sept. 15, 1957; s. Herman F. and Nina Wehling; m. Donna L. Wehling; 1 child. BS in Zoology and Entomology, Colo. State U., 1980; MS, Wash. State U., 1984, PhD in Zoology, 1994. Rsch. asst. Wash. State U., Pullman, 1980-84, agrl. rsch. technologist, 1985-87, rsch. asst. II, 1987-94; vis. rsch. assoc. Mich. State U., East Lansing, 1994—. Mem. Ecol. Soc. Am., Entomol. Soc. Am., Soc. for Study of Evolution, Xerces Soc., Lepidopterists Soc., Lepidopterists Rsch. Found., Evergreen Aurelians. Office: Mich State U Dept Entomology 243 Natural Sci East Lansing MI 48824

WEHRBEIN, ROGER RALPH, state senator; b. Lincoln, Nebr., Aug. 18, 1938; s. Ralph Jennings and Vivian Lucille (Johns) W.; m. Jeanene Arlene Markussen, Oct. 7, 1961; children: Douglas, David. BS in Animal Scis., U. Nebr., 1960. Farmer, livestock feeder Breeze Valley Farms Inc., Plattsmouth, Nebr., 1962—; Nebr. state sen. Lincoln, 1987—; chairperson appropriations com. 1995-96; bd. dirs. Lincoln Fed. Land Bank Assn. Bd. dirs. Leadership-Edn.-Action-Devel. (LEAD), Lincoln, 1988-94. Capt. U.S. Army, 1961-62. Named to Nebr. Hall of Agrl. Achievement, 1988; U. Nebr. Block and Bridle Club honoree, 1993. Mem. Nebr. Cattlemen's Assn. (pres. 1985), Nebr. Pork Producers, Ag-Bldrs. Nebr., Toastmasters (pres. Plattsmouth chpt. 1983), Am. Legion, Nebr. Farm Bur., Rotary (pres. Plattsmouth chpt. 1983), Masons, Kiwanis (Outstanding Farmer Omaha 1985). Republican. Presbyterian. Home: 5812 Highway 66 Plattsmouth NE 68048-7488

WEHRLE, DAVID S., engineer; b. Euclid, Ohio, May 20, 1969; s. Robert King and Cheryl Ilone (Raber) W.; m. Lisa May Bockmiller, Sept. 19, 1992; 1 child, Micah. BSEE, Cleve. State U., 1992; postgrad., Case Western Res. U., 1994. Engr.-in-tng., Ohio. F/W engr. Allen Bradley Control, Cleve., 1992—. Mem. IEEE. Republican. Baptist. Office: Allen Bradley 747 Alpha Dr Cleveland OH 44143-2124

WEHRWEIN, AUSTIN CARL, newspaper reporter, editor, writer; b. Austin, Tex., Jan. 12, 1916; s. George S. and Anna (Ruby) W.; m. Judith Oakes, 1950; children: Sven Austin, Paul, Peter, Joanna Judith. A.B., U. Wis., 1937; LL.B., Columbia U., 1940; student, London Sch. Econs., 1948. Reporter Washington Bur., UP, 1941-43, 46-48; information specialist E.C.A., London, Copenhagen, Oslo, Stockholm, 1948-51; financial writer Milw. Jour., 1951-53; staff corr. Time, Inc., Chgo., 1953-55; reporter Chgo. Sun-Times, 1955-56, fin. editor, 1956-57; chief Chgo. bur. N.Y. Times, 1957-66; editorial writer Mpls. Star, 1966-82; contbr. London Economist, Collier's Year Book; corr. Chronicle of Higher Edn., Edn. Week. Editor The Observer, 1984-87. Served with USAAF, 1943-45; mem. staff Stars and Stripes 1945-46, Shanghai, China. Recipient Pulitzer prize for internat. reporting, 1953; Disting. Journalism award U. Wis., 1963; cert. of merit ABA Gavel competition, 1968, 80; Gavel award, 1969, 71. Home and Office: 2309 Carter Ave Saint Paul MN 55108-1640

WEI, LESTER YEEHOW, research chemist; b. Foochow, Fukien, People's Republic of China, Sept. 4, 1944; came to U.S., 1968; s. Do Yuen and Show Chin (Chen) W.; m. Karen Tongli Chen, Aug. 19, 1972; children: Michael C., Melissa Y. BSE, Taiwan Cheng Kung U., 1967; MS, East Tex. State U., 1970, EdD, 1974. Postdoctoral rsch. assoc. Emory U., Atlanta, 1974-76; spl. rsch. assoc. Ill. Geol. Survey, Champaign, Ill., 1976-77; rsch. chemist Ill. Natural History Survey, Champaign, Ill., 1977-92; sr. scientist Sandoz Agro, Inc., Des Plaines, Ill., 1992—. Contbr. articles to Jour. Environ. Sci. Health, Pesticide Sci., Bull. Environ. Contamination Toxicol., Phytochemistry, Jour. Assn. Ofcl. Analytical Chemists, Jour. Agrl. Food Chem. Mem. AAAS, Am. Chem. Soc. Home: 110 W Mchenry St Urbana IL 61801-6636 Office: Sandoz Agro Inc 1300 E Touhy Ave Des Plaines IL 60018-3304

WEI, WILLIAM L., marketing professional, consultant; b. Oct. 17, 1960; s. Chi-Min and Tina (Liang) W. Student, U. Pa., 1978-79; BBA, Bernard Baruch Coll., N.Y.C., 1985; postgrad., Keller Grad. Sch., Kansas City, Mo., 1989-92. Clearance acctg. Chem. Corp., N.Y.C., 1981-83; assoc. sales mgr. Macy's N.Y., N.Y.C., 1983-84; mktg. rep. IBM Corp., N.Y.C., 1984-86; staff analyst, instr. Nynex Corp., Atlanta, 1986-88; br. mgr. Nynex Corp., Kansas City, Mo., 1988-90; dir. mktg. ISI-Integrated Support, Inc., Kansas City, 1990; product mgr. Sprint Corp., Kansas City, 1991-93; owner Weicorp, Overland Park, Kans., 1990—; pres. Epley Kansas City Group Inc., Overland Park, 1993-94; program mgr. Sprint Multimedia, Overland Park, 1994—. Treas. Turnberry Ln. Homeowners Assn., Marietta, Ga., 1987-88; bus. cons. Jr. Achievment, Kansas City, 1991; youth leader Colonial Presbyn. Ch., Kansas City, 1992—; active Big Bros., 1995—. Mem. Soc. of Competitive Intelligence Profls., Am. Mktg. Assn., Am. Mgmt. Assn., Overland Park C. of C., Kansas City C. of C., Healthcare Info. and Mgmt. Sys. Soc. Home: # 83 8908 W 124th St Overland Park KS 66213-1730 Office: Sprint Multimedia 4th Fl 8330 Ward Pkwy Kansas City MO 64114

WEIBL, RICHARD A., educational researcher; b. Mansfield, Ohio, Apr. 7, 1956; s. Anton and Shirley (Mitsch) W. BS in Edn., Bowling Green State U., 1979; MEd, U. Ga., 1981; postgrad., Ohio State U. Resident dir. Marquette U., Milw., 1981-83; rsch. asst. Ctr. for Tchg. Excellence, Columbua, Ohio, 1990-92, Ctr. Collaborative Studies in Tchr. Edn., Columbus, 1992-93; with Office Instnl. Rsch. Antioch Coll., Yellow Springs, Ohio, 1993—. Office: Office Instnl Rsch Antioch Coll Yellow Springs OH 45387

WEICKER, JACK EDWARD, educational administrator; b. Woodburn, Ind., June 23, 1924; s. Monald Henry and Helen Mae (Miller) W.; m. Janet Kathryn Thompson, May 29, 1946; children: John H., Kathryn Ann, Jane Elizabeth, Emily Jo. AB, Ind. U., 1947, MA, 1950. James Albert Woodburn fellow, All-Univ. fellow; tchr. history and English, Harrison Hill Sch., Ft. Wayne, Ind., 1947-48, South Side High Sch., Ft. Wayne, 1951-61; counselor, asst. prin. South Side High Sch., 1961-63, prin., 1963-90. Mem. Ind. State Scholarship Commn., 1969-77; mem. exec. com. Midwest regional assembly

Coll. Entrance Exam. Bd., 1974-77, chmn. nominating com., 1976-77, mem. nat. nominating com., 1979; mem. Midwest Regional Coll. Access Svcs. Com., 1982-84. Chmn., Easter Seal Telethon, Allen County Soc. Crippled Children and Adults, 1982, 83. Recipient award for meritorious svc. Ball State U., 1980; Outstanding Prin. of Yr. award Ind. Secondary Sch. Adminstrs. Assn., 1981, Ind. Prin. Yr., Ind. Assn. Ednl. Secs., 1986, Disting. Service award Midwestern Regional Assembly of Coll. Entrance Examination Bd., 1987, Sagamore of the Wabash award Ind. Gov. Evan Bayh, 1989; Rotary Paul Harris fellow, 1985; South side High Sch. Prin. Emeritus,1996. Mem. Ft. Wayne Prins. Assn., Nat. Assn. Secondary Sch. Prins. (conf. speaker New Orleans 1985, 89), Ind. Secondary Sch. Adminstrs., PTA (life), Phi Beta Kappa, Phi Delta Kappa, Phi Alpha Theta. Mem. Christian Ch. (Disciples of Christ) (moderator of bd. trustees 1975-79). Clubs: Ft. Wayne Rotary (dir. 1973-76, 79-82, pres.-elect 1981-82, pres. 1982-83), Quest (dir. 1979-81, v.p. 1988-89, pres. 1989-90), Fortnightly (v.p. 1984-85, pres. 1985-86, 91-92). Author: (with others) Indiana: The Hoosier State, 1959, 63; (monographs) Due Process and Student Rights/Responsibilities: Two Points of View, 1975; Back to Basics: Language Arts, 1976; College Entrance Exams—Friend or Foe?, 1981; How the Effective Principal Communicates, 1983; Readin', Writin', and Other Stuff, 1984, The Last 25 Years in Education: One Educator's Perspective, 1988, The Power of Poetry: A Muse for All Seasons, 1988, American Political Humor: Mark Twain to Mark Russell, 1992. Home: 5200 N Washington Rd Fort Wayne IN 46804-1844

WEIDENBRUCH, ANNA MAE, nurse; b. Owosso, Mich., July 26, 1926; d. Robert Harry and Della Jane (Gander) Thompson; m. Manley Lavern Nixon, Aug. 3, 1946 (div. 1961); children: Terry Lee, Douglas Kent, LaVerna Ann, Norma Jean; m. Donald F. Clewley, Aug. 27, 1961 (dec. 1973); m. Heinz Weidenbruch, 1984. ADN, Lansing (Mich.) C.C., 1983; BS in Health Studies, Western Mich. U., Kalamazoo, 1993. RN, Mich. Staff nurse Sparrow Hosp., Lansing, 1958-62, Ingham Med. Hosp., Lansing, 1962-64, Lansing Gen. Hosp., 1964-66, 77-88, Hazel I. Findlay Country Manor, St. Johns, Mich., 1987-89, Staff Builders, Okemos, Mich., 1990—. Democrat. Home: 2123 Northwest Ave Lansing MI 48906-3653

WEIDLICK, MICHAEL JOSEPH, information systems specialist; b. St. Louis, Mar. 1, 1967; s. Joseph John and Mary Catherine (Dunne) W.; m. Theresa Ann Ewing, July 21, 1990. Software devel. mgr. Delta Log, St. Louis, 1992; dir. info. sys. Airmax, Inc., St. Louis, 1992-96; Lotus notes adminstr. MEMC, Inc., St. Louis, 1996—. Mem. KC. Republican. Roman Catholic. Home: 1209 Whispering Pines Ct. Creve Coeur MO 63146

WEIDNER, ROBERT WRIGHT, music educator; b. Brookfield, Wis., Oct. 21, 1923; s. Oswald Frederick and Minnie Marie (Giencke) W.; m. Jean Dionne Rockwell; children: Robert Rockwell Weidner, Diane Jean Weidner. BS, Milw. State Tchrs. Coll., 1949; MA, Eastman Sch. of Music U. R.I., 1951, PhD, 1960. Band dir., tchr. history North Divsn. H.S., Milw., 1949-50; music dir. Oostburg (Wis.) Pub. Schs., 1951-52; band dir., music prof. Ohio No. U., Ada, 1952-55; band dir., prof. music Tex. Luth. Coll., Seguin, 1953-56; dir. music Abbotsford (Wis.) Pub. Schs./Dorchester (Wis.) Pub. Schs., 1956-58; prof. music, dir. orchestra Nebr. Wesleyan U., Lincoln, 1959-62; prof. music, dept. head U. Dubuque (Iowa), 1962-65; prof. music Ea. Ill. U., Charleston, 1965-93, retired, 1994. Composer Tex. Luth. Coll. alma mater, 1956; editor (book) Christopher Tye: The Instrumental Music, 1965, Tye's Actes of the Apostles, 1970. Bd. dirs. Charleston Civic Assn., Charleston, 1991—. With U.S. Army, 1943-46, ETO. Mem. Am. Musicol. Soc. Mem. Dem. Socialists of Am. Home: 1620 Douglas Charleston IL 61920

WEIDNER, THEODORE JOHN, university administrator, architect, engineer; b. Cleve., Dec. 13, 1954; s. Ebert and Harriet (Billman) W.; m. Marilyn E. Barnes, July 9, 1986. BS in Bldg. Sci., Rensselaer Poly. Inst., Troy, N.Y., 1977, MArch, 1979, MS in Engring., 1980. Registered architect, Ill.; registered profl. engr., Ill. Mgr. facilities planning Rensselaer Poly. Inst., Troy, 1988-89; asst. dir. phys. plant Ill. State U., Normal, 1989-93; dir. phys. plant Ea. Ill. U., Charleston, 1993—; judge for FAME awards Am. Inst. Plant Engrs., 1991. Contbr. articles to profl. jours. Trustee Trinity United Meth. Ch., Albany, N.Y., 1988-89; mem. Charleston Tomorrow Com., 1995. Mem. ASCE, AIA, NSPE, Constrn. Specifications Inst., Assn. of Higher Edn. Facilities Officers, Assn. Univ. Architects, Rensselaer Poly. Inst. Alumni Assn. (Alumni Key 1982). Office: Eastern Illinois Univ Physical Plant Charleston IL 61920

WEIGAND, ROBERT EUGENE, university educator; b. Terre Haute, Ind., Aug. 13, 1930; s. Arthur A. and Nora L. (Epler) W. Student, Eastern Ill. State Coll., 1948-50; BS in Commerce, U. Notre Dame, 1952; MS in Mktg., U. Ill., 1956, PhD in Bus., 1961. From instr. to assoc. prof. mktg. De Paul U., Chgo., 1959-67, chmn. dept., 1960-65, prof., 1967-69; head dept. mktg. U. Ill., Chgo., 1969-78, prof., 1969—; vis. assoc. prof. bus. adminstrn. Grad. Sch. Bus., U. Ill., Urbana, 1967-68, lectr. mgmt. devel. program, 1970-75; com. mem. Am. Assembly Collegiate Schs. Bus. Adminstrn; external examiner, faculty Bus. Adminstrn. U. Lagos, Nigeria, 1976, 77, 78; internat. speaker, cons. in field; radio and TV guest. Co-author: Basic Retailing, 1976, rev. ed. 1982 with accompanying manual and workbook; editor Resource Book, 1974, Doing Business in Japan, 1963, Doing Business in France, 1964; cons. editor Review of Business and Economic Research, 1971—; contbr. book reviews, articles to profl. jours., chpts. to books. Served to cpl. U.S. Army, 1952-54, res. 1954-60. Am. Assn. Advt. Agys. fellow, 1964, Ford Found. fellow, 1965. Mem. AAUP, Am. Mktg. Assn. (internat. mktg. teaching com. 1960-61, social concerns com. 1970-71, v.p. mktg. edn. Chgo. chpt. 1973-74), So. Mktg. Assn., Acad. Internat. Bus., Am. Econ. Assn., Am. Acad. Advt., Chgo. Council Fgn. Relations. Roman Catholic. Home: 5455 N Sheridan Rd Chicago IL 60640-1958 Office: U Ill PO Box 802451 Chicago IL 60680-2451

WEIGEL, LUCINDA MAE, legislative staff member; b. Aberdeen, S.D., Mar. 2, 1965; d. Peter A. and Janet Mae (Cowle) W. BS in Psychology, No. State U., 1986. Copywriter, traffic mgr. Sta. KKAA/KQ95 Radio, Aberdeen, 1983-86; mem. Congl. staff U.S. Senator Tom Dashle, U.S. Congressman Tim Johnson, Aberdeen, 1986—; cons. Jim Lawler for State Senate, S.D., Paul Dennert for State House, S.D. Campaign mgr. Rep. Craig Schaunaman, S.D., 1988-94; vice chair Brown County Dem. Cen. Com., Aberdeen, 1991-92. Recipient Addy award Black Hills Advt. Fedn., 1984, Richard F. Kneip Young Leader award, S.D. Dem. Party, 1993. Home: PO Box 335 Aberdeen SD 57402-0335

WEIGEL, OLLIE J., dentist, former mayor; b. Guthrie County, Iowa, Sept. 29, 1922; s. Verne Noble and Ethel Rebecca (Johnson) W.; m. Mary Kathryn Finnegan, June 3, 1944; children: John, Marilyn, Larry, Susan. DDS, U. Iowa, 1951. Practice dentistry Ankeny, 1951-94; mayor City of Ankeny, 1974-93; mem. Metro Planning Orgn., 1995—; bd. dirs. Brenton Bank of Ankeny, Neveln Resource Ctr. Mem. Ankeny City Coun., 1966-73, Des Moines Area C.C. Found. Bd., 1993—, Des Moines Area Metro Forum, 1985-93, found. bd. On With Life, 1994—; life mem. Ankeny Indsl. Devel. Corp. 2d lt. USAAF, 1943-45, ETO. Mem. ADA (life), Iowa Dental Assn. (life), Des Moines Dist. Dental Assn., Ankeny C. of C. (life, pres., Outstanding Citizen 1976, 93), Mid Iowa Assn. Local Govts. (chmn. 1983), League of Iowa Municipalities (pres. 1976-77), Ctrl. Iowa Regional Govts. (pres. 1978), Am. Legion, Lions. Republican. Methodist. Home and Office: 2506 NW 4th St Ankeny IA 50021-1002

WEIGERT, ANDREW JOSEPH, sociology educator; b. N.Y.C., Apr. 8, 1934; s. Andrew Joseph and Marie Teresa (Kollmer) W.; m. Kathleen Rose Maas, Aug. 31, 1967; children: Karen Rose, Sheila Marie. BA, St. Louis U., 1958, PhL, 1959, MA, 1960; BTh, Woodstock (Md.) Coll., 1964; PhD, U. Minn., 1968. NIMH trainee U. Minn., Mpls., 1965-67; asst. prof. sociology U. Notre Dame, Ind., 1968-72, assoc. prof., 1972-76, prof., 1976—, chmn. dept., 1980-84, 88-89; vis. assoc. prof. Yale U., New Haven, 1973-74; participant nat. and regional profl. meetings. Co-author: Family Socialization, 1974, Interpretive Sociology, 1978, Society and Identity, 1986; author: Everyday Life, 1981, Social Psychology, 1983, Life and Society, 1983, Mixed Emotions, 1991; adv. editor various sociology jours.; contbr. over 50 articles to profl. jours., chpts. to books. Grantee NSF, 1969. Mem. Soc. for Study Symbolic Interaction, Soc. for Sci. Study Religion, Assn. for Sociology Religion. Office: U Notre Dame Dept Sociology Notre Dame IN 46556

WEIHING, JOHN LAWSON, plant pathologist, state senator; b. Rocky Ford, Colo., Feb. 26, 1921; s. Henry John and Clara Adele (Krull) W.; m. Shirley Ruth Wilkerson, Aug. 18, 1948; children: Lawson James, Martin Roy, Adell Ann, Warren John. BS in Agronomy, Colo. State U., 1942; MSc in Agronomy, U. Nebr., 1949, PhD in Botany and Plant Pathology, 1954. Instr. plant pathology U. Nebr., Lincoln, 1950-54, asst. prof., 1954-56, assoc. prof., 1956-60, prof., 1960-61, 62-64, 66-71, prof., interim chmn. plant pathology dept., 1961-62; prof., dir. Panhandle Rsch. and Extension Ctr. U. Nebr., Scottsbluff, 1971-84; with Alumni Office, Panhandle Found. U. Nebr., Scottsbluf, 1984-86; prof., chmn. plant sci. dept. Ataturk U., Erzurum, Turkey, 1964-66; mem. dist. 48 Nebr. Legislature, Lincoln, 1987-91; cons. Am. Hydrponics Systems, Inc., Grapevine, Tex., 1969-72. Creator U. Nebr. TV series Backyard Farmer, The Equation of Nature, 1959-60. Campaign chmn. United Way, Scottsbluff and Gering, Nebr., 1978. Lt. U.S. Army, 1942-46. Recipient Honor award Soil Conservation Soc. Am., 1982, Merit award Gamma Sigma Delta, 1977, Disting. Svc. award Nebr. Turfgrass Found., 1982, Nebr. Coop. Extension, 1970; named to Nebr. Hall Agrl. Achievement, 1987. Mem. Am. Phytopathol. Soc. (chmn. nat. extension com. 1963, pres. north cen. dir. 1971-72), AAAS, Am. Inst. Biol. Scis., Scottsbluff/Gering United C. of C. (pres. 1980-81), Rotary (bd. dirs. 1977-80), Elks. Republican. Presbyterian. Home: 1605 Holly Dr Gering NE 69341-1954

WEIL, IRWIN, Slavic languages and literature educator; b. Cin., Apr. 16, 1928; s. Sidney and Florence (Levy) W.; m. Vivian Weil, Dec. 27, 1950; children: Martin, Alice, Daniel. A.B., U. Chgo., 1948, M.A., 1951; Ph.D., Harvard U., 1960. Sr. social sci. research analyst Library of Congress, 1951-54; teaching fellow Harvard U., 1956-58; mem. faculty Brandeis U., 1958-65; mem. faculty dept. Slavic langs. and lit. Northwestern U., Evanston, Ill., 1966—; chmn. dept. Northwestern U., 1976-82; vis. prof. U. Moscow, Soviet Acad. Scis.; set up series of internat. symposia between Am. scholars and USSR Acad. Scis.; founder 1st Soviet-Am. TV Student Competition in Lit., 1988-89. Author books and articles pub. in field, pub. in U.S.A. and Russia. Recipient Pushkin Internat. gold medal for outstanding teaching and research, 1984, Outstanding Teaching award Northwestern U. Alumni Assn., 1987, Tempo All-Professor Team, Humanities, Chicago Tribune, 1993; Ford Found. fellow, 1954-55. Mem. Am. Assn. Tchrs. Slavic and East European Langs. (exec. sec. 1962-68, Excellence in Teaching award 1993), Am. Coun. Tchrs. Russian (v.p. 1975-79, pres. 1980-84), Internat. Assn. Profs. Russian (founding U.S. mem.). Jewish. Office: Northwestern U Slavic Dept Evanston IL 60208

WEIL, ROLF ALFRED, economist, university president emeritus; b. Pforzheim, Germany, Oct. 29, 1921; came to U.S., 1936, naturalized, 1944; s. Henry and Lina (Landauer) W.; m. Leni Metzger, Nov. 3, 1945; children: Susan Linda, Ronald Alan. B.A., U. Chgo., 1942, Ph.D., 1950; D. Hebrew Letters, Coll. Jewish Studies, 1967; L.H.D., Loyola U., 1970; D.H.L., Bowling Green State U., Ohio, 1986; LHD, Roosevelt U., 1988. Rsch. asst. Cowles Commn. for Rsch. in Econs., 1942-44; rsch. analyst Ill. Dept. Revenue, 1944-46; mem. faculty Roosevelt U., Chgo., 1946—, prof. fin. and econs., also chmn. dept. fin., 1954-65, dean Coll. Bus. Adminstrn., 1957-64, acting pres., 1965-66, pres., 1966-88, pres. emeritus, 1988—; past pres. Selfhelp Home for the Aged, Chgo.; cons. to non-profit orgns., 1988—. Author: Through these Portals-from Immigrant to College President, 1991; contbr. articles on fin. Bd. dirs. trustees Roosevelt U., Selfhelp of Chgo., Inc. Mem. Am. Econ. Assn., Cliff Dwellers Club.

WEIL, VIVIAN, philosophy educator; b. Cin.; d. Morris Max and Rose Chasi (Alter) Max-Finkelstein; m. Irwin Weil, Dec. 27, 1950; children: Martin, Alice, Daniel. AB, U. Chgo., 1949, MA in Philosophy, 1953; PhD in Philosophy, U. Ill., Chgo., 1972. Instr. gen. edn. Boston U., 1964-66; asst. prof. Ill. Inst. Tech., Chgo., 1972-78, sr. rsch. assoc. Ctr. Study Ethics in Professions, 1978-86, acting. dir., 1986-87, dir., 1987—, assoc. prof. ethics, 1988-95, prof. ethics, 1995—; dir. ethics & values studies NSF, Washington, 1990-91. Editor: Beyond Whistleblowing, 1983, Owning Scientific and Technical Information, 1989; mem. adv. bd. Teaching Philosophy, Sci. Tech. & Human Values, Profl. Ethics, Sci. & Engring. Ethics, Sci. Comm., Internat. Jour. Applied Philosophy. Fellow AAAS (nominating com. 1993-95), Am. Philos. Assn. (com. computer use in philosophy 1992-95). Home: 1049 Michigan Ave Evanston IL 60202 Office: Ill Inst Tech Ctr Study Ethics in Professions 3101 S Dearborn Chicago IL 60616

WEILAND, GALEN FRANKLIN, state legislator; s. Joseph Franklin and Ida Lucille (Dunn) W.; m. Ruth Arlene Howland; children: Teresa Jean and Terry Dean. Student, Highland C.C., 1957-58. Kans. state rep. Dist. 49, 1991—; asst. mgr. Bendena Grain Co. Mem. Elks, Masons. Address: PO Box 217 Bendena KS 66008*

WEILAND, RICHARD PAUL, political scientist; b. Madison, S.D., July 26, 1958; s. Donald Peter Sr. and Thorine Elaine (Mellom) W.; m. Stacy Lee Newcomb, June 6, 1981; children: Nicholas, Adam, Carter, Taylor. BS in Comm. and Polit. Sci., U. S.D.; postgrad., Dakota State Coll. Campaign coord. U.S. Congl. candidate Tom Daschle, Aberdeen, S.D., 1978; campaign mgr., field rep. U.S. Congressman Tom Daschle, Sioux Falls, S.D., 1980-83; field dir. U.S. Congressman Tom Daschle, Rapid City, S.D., 1983-85; fin. dir., sr. advisor U.S. Senator Tom Daschle, Washington, 1985-89; state dir. U.S. Senator Tom Daschle, Sioux Falls, 1989-95; candidate for U.S. Congress People for Weiland, Sioux Falls, 1995—; advisor Dem. candidates, S.D., 1989—. Author: (software) Prospector, 1995. Bd. dirs. Carroll Inst., Sioux Falls; musician St. Marys Ch., Sioux Falls, 1989—; vol. Emersons Elem. Sch., Sioux Falls, 1995—. Award Crow Circle Sioux Tribe, 1992. Mem. Rotary Club Sioux Falls. Roman Catholic. Home: 326 E 21st St Sioux Falls SD 57105 Office: People for Weiland PO Box 761 Sioux Falls SD 57101

WEILER, SCOTT MICHAEL, machine tool manufacturing company executive; b. Fargo, N.D., Jan. 9, 1952; s. F.S. and Lorraine M. (Kopach) W.; m. Sandra L. Meyer, Aug. 28, 1971 (div. July 1986); 1 child, Kimberly. Application engr. Devlieg Machine Co., Royal Oak, Mich., 1973-84; project mgr. Devlieg Machine Co., 1984-89, Giddings & Lewis, Fraser, Mich., 1989-94, Ingersoll CM Systems, Midland, Mich., 1994—. Mem. Soc. Mfg. Engrs., Am. Mgmt. Assn., Project Mgmt. Inst. Office: Ingersoll CM Systems Midland MI 48642

WEIMER, FERNE LAURAINE, librarian; b. Valparaiso, Ind., May 28, 1950; d. John Junior and Helen Lorraine (Dillingham) W. AB in History, Wheaton Coll., 1972; MA in Libr. Sci., No. Ill. U., 1974. Cataloger, Lake County Pub. Library, Merrillville, Ind., 1974-77, Billy Graham Ctr. Libr., Wheaton (Ill.) Coll., 1977-79, dir., 1979— . Mem. ALA, Am. Theol. Libr. Assn. (chairperson bibliographic systems com. 1988-89), Assn. Christian Librs. (dir. at large 1991-92, treas. 1992—), Chgo. Area Theol. Libr. Assn. (v.p. 1985-86, pres. 1986-87), DuPage Libr. Assn. (sec. 1981-82, pres. 1982-83), Evang. Ch. Libr. Assn. (v.p. 1991—). Office: Wheaton Coll Billy Graham Ctr Libr Wheaton IL 60187

WEIMER, GARY W., academic administrator, consultant; b. Louisville, Mar. 28, 1944; s. G. Wilfred and Wanda Ruth (Green) W.; m. M. Elizabeth Enterline, Aug. 29, 1966; children: Inga Elizabeth, Kirk Ayleston. AB, Princeton U., 1966; M.T.S., Harvard U., 1971. Reporter, copy editor The Vindicator, Youngstown, Ohio, 1970; dir. devel. programs Oberlin (Ohio) Coll., 1971-78; dir. devel. U. Calif., Santa Barbara, 1978-82; v.p. Hiram (Ohio) Coll., 1982-87; sr. devel. officer Case Western Res. U., Cleve., 1987-90; dir. devel. U. Hosps. of Cleve., 1991—. Contbr. articles to profl. jours. Trustee U. Calif. Santa Barbara Found., 1979-82, Robert Maynard Hutchins Ctr. for the Study of Dem. Insts., Santa Barbara, 1979-81. With U.S. Army, 1968-69, Vietnam. James A. Garfield fellow Hiram Coll., 1982, Rockefeller Bros. Theol. fellow Rockefeller and Booth-Ferris Founds., Harvard Divinity Sch., 1966-67; decorated Bronze Star, Air medal, U.S. Army Am. Spirit Honor medal. Mem. Princeton Club N.Y.

WEINBERG, HELEN ARNSTEIN, American art and literature educator; b. Orange, N.J., June 17, 1927; d. Morris Jerome and Jeannette (Tepperman) Arnstein; m. Kenneth Gene Weinberg, Sept. 12, 1949; children: Janet Sue Weinberg Strassner, Hugh Benjamin, John Arnstein. BA in English Lit., Wellesley Coll., 1949; MA in English Lit., Western Res. U., 1953, PhD in English Lit., 1966. Teaching fellow Ohio State U., Columbus, 1949-51, Western Res. U., Cleve., 1953-57; instr. to prof. Cleve. (Ohio) Inst. Art, 1958—; standing officer Coll. English Assn. Ohio, 1987-90; vis. tchr. NYU, 1985, Sch. Visual Art's, 1981; lecture tours Israel, 1968, 70, 71. Author: The New Novel in America: The Kafkan Mode in Contemporary Fiction, 1970. Recipient fellowship in art history NEH, Columbia U., N.Y.C., 1977-78; Recipient Am. Culture grantee NEH/Vassar Coll., 1993. Mem. AAUP, Modern Lang. Assn., Coll. Art Assn. Democrat. Jewish. Home: 3015 Huntington Rd Shaker Hts OH 44120-2407 Office: Cleve Inst Art 11141 East Blvd Cleveland OH 44106-1710

WEINBERG, MILTON, JR., cardiovascular-thoracic surgeon; b. Sumter, S.C., Aug. 8, 1824; s. Milton and Ethel (Harper) W.; m. Joan Ehrenstrom, Nov. 24, 1956; children: Caryl, Susan, Amy. Student, Duke U., 1941-43, MD, 1947. Diplomate Am. Bd. Surgery, Am. Bd. Thoracic Surgery. Attending surgeon Rush Presbyn.-St. Luke's Med. Ctr., Chgo., 1957-90, emeritus attending, 1990—; attending surgeon Cook County Hosp., Chgo., 1956—, Luth. Gen. Hosp., Park Ridge, Ill., 1986—; mem. governing coun., 1996—; assoc. prof. Rush Med. Coll., Chgo., 1969-78, prof. surgery, 1978-90, emeritus prof., 1990—; clin. prof. U. Chgo., 1990—; chmn. dept. surgery Luth. Gen. Hosp., Park Ridge, 1988-94, vice-chmn. dept. surgery, 1994—; pres. med. staff Rush Med. Ctr., Chgo., 1977-79; presenter movies at mtgs. ACS. Mem. editorial bd. Annals of Thoracic Surgery, 1968-79; contbr. articles to profl. jours., chpts. to surg. textbooks. Trustee The Presbyn. Home, Evanston, Ill., 1984-94; bd. dirs. Chgo. Symphony Orch., 1985-95; adv. Charitable Found., 1996—. Maj. U.S. Army, 1951-53. Decorated Bronze Star. Fellow ACS, Am. Coll. Chest Physicians, Am. Coll. Cardiology; mem. Am. Assn. Thoracic Surgery, Soc. Thoracic Surgeons, Soc. Vascular Surgery, Internat. Cardiovascular Soc., Ctrl. Surg. Soc. Home: 2550 Princeton Ave Evanston IL 60201-4941 Office: Luth Gen Hosp 1775 Dempster St Park Ridge IL 60068-1143

WEINBERG, ROBERT L., management consultant; b. N.Y.C., Feb. 4, 1947; s. Alfred J. and Ruth R. (Stern) W.; m. Joyce K. Widland, Oct. 20, 1968; children: Deborah L., Mark T. BSBA, Boston U., 1967; MBA, U. Chgo., 1971. adj. prof. direct mktg. Medill Sch., Northwestern U., 1993—. V.p., dir. Kestnbaum & Co., Chgo., 1972-88; sr. mgr. Andersen Consulting, Chgo., 1988-91; pres. Kobs, Gregory, Passavant, Chgo., 1991-95, RW Consulting, Northfield, Ill., 1996—. Mem. rev. com. United Way, Chgo., 1976-82, bd. dirs., Northfield, ill., 1984-86. Mem. Chgo. Assn. Direct Mktg. (bd. dirs. 1976-84, 93-95, pres. 1982-83), Chgo. Assn. Direct Mktg. Edn. Found. (bd. dirs. 1994—), Inst. Mgmt. Cons.

WEINBERGER, SETH JAY, lawyer; b. Jersey City, Mar. 8, 1955; s. Martin I. and Shirley (Epstein) W.; m. Barbara L. Goodman, Aug. 21, 1983; 1 child, Ian Fredric. BA, U. Mich., 1977, JD, 1979. Bar: N.J. 1980, Ill. 1982. Assoc. Pitney, Hardin, Kipp & Szuch, Morristown, N.J., 1980-82; assoc., then ptnr. Mayer, Brown & Platt, Chgo., 1982—. Office: Mayer Brown & Platt 190 S La Salle St Chicago IL 60603-3410

WEINBLATT, CHARLES SAMUEL, university administrator, employment consultant; b. Toledo, Dec. 23, 1952; s. Morris and Clara (Volk) W.; m. Frances Barbara Auslander, Aug. 12, 1973; children: Brian J., Lauren M. BA, U. Toledo, 1974. Cert. edn. and tng. counselor, Ohio. Psychiat. counselor St. Vincent Hosp., Toledo, 1974-77; vocat., rehab. counselor Goodwill Industries, Toledo, 1977-85; employment cons., pvt. practice Toledo, 1985—; tng. counselor UAW Chrysler, Perrysburg, Ohio, 1987; dir. divsn. orgnl. devel. U. Toledo, 1988—; employment svcs. cons. Employers' Assn. Toledo, 1985-90; outplacement cons. Toledo Pub. Schs., 1986. Author: Job Seeking Skills for Students, 1987. Mem. Toledo Vision Com., 1989-90. Recipient Quality Improvement award Chrysler, 1987, cert. Am. Inst. Banking, 1989. Mem. ASTD, Ohio Continuing Higher Edn. Assn. Jewish. Home: 5118 Brenden Way Sylvania OH 43560-2223 Office: U Toledo Seagate Campus 401 Jefferson Ave Toledo OH 43604-1063

WEINER, ESTHER RIZA, clinical psychologist; b. Cleve., Mar. 16, 1938; d. Abraham Isaac and Gizella Gertrude (Pollack) Blankfeld; m. Henry Weiner, June 11, 1960; children: Suzanna Lynn, Alexander James. BA, Antioch Coll., 1961; MS, Purdue U., 1963, PhD, 1970. Diplomate Am. Bd. Sexology; lic. health svc. provider in psychology. Psychologist, family life educator Family Svc. Agy., Lafayette, Ind., 1970-75; dir. cons. and edn. Wabash Valley Hosp./Mental Health Ctr., West Lafayette, Ind., 1975-77; dir. profession svcs. Family Svc. Agy., Lafayette, 1977-79; pvt. practice clin./counseling psychology West Lafayette, 1977—. Fellow Am. Acad. Clin. Sexologists; mem. APA, Am. Assn. Sex Educators, Counselors and Therapists, Ind. Psychol. Assn.

WEINER, GERALD ARNE, stockbroker; b. Chgo., Dec. 20, 1941; s. Irwin S. and Lilyan (Stock) W.; m. Barbara I. Allen, June 18, 1967; children—Rachel Anne, Sara Naomi. BSS, Loyola U., Chgo., 1964; student U. Vienna, Austria, 1962-63; MS, Georgetown U., 1966; postgrad. Ind. U., 1966-72, S.E. Asian Areas cert., 1967. Pacification specialist AID, Laos, 1965; instr. polit. sci. Loyola U.-Chgo., 1970-72; asst. v.p. A.G. Becker & Co., Chgo., 1973-78; sr. v.p. Oppenheimer & Co., Chgo., 1978-83; sr. v.p. J. David Securities, Inc., Chgo., 1983-84; sr. v.p. Dean Witter Reynolds, Chgo., 1984—; exec. edn. for securities industry Wharton Sch. Bus. U. Pa., 1988-90. Trustee Highland Pk. Police Pension Fund. Mucia fellow, 1969. Mem. Midwest Bonsai Soc., Elgin Bonsai Group. Democrat. Jewish. Club: Multiplex Club. Office: Dean Witter Reynolds 70 W Madison St Chicago IL 60602-4205

WEINER, GERSHON RALPH, physician; b. Detroit, Apr. 12, 1935; s. Morris and Phyllis (Lemberg) W.; m. Myra H. Levenson, July 1956 (div. May 1972); children: Bruce J., Sandra C. Mishory, Stuart J. (dec.); m. M. Jean (Jeannie) Mann, Dec. 31, 1975; 1 child, Joel Edward Jackson. BS, Wayne State U., 1955; DO, Coll. Osteopathic Medicine and Surgery, 1963. Diplomate Nat. Bd. Examiners, Am. Osteo Bd. Rehab. Medicine (bd. examiner 1982-91). Intern Mt. Clemens (Mich.) Gen. Hosp., 1963-64; family practice Detroit and Warren, Mich., 1964-71; practice in emergency medicine Macomb (Mich.) County hosps., 1964-73; dep. med. examiner Macomb County, 1965-74; resident, fellow in physical medicine and rehab. Wayne State U. Sch. Medicine, Detroit, 1971-74; practice medicine specializing in physical medicine and rehab. Wayne and Macomb Counties, 1974—; team physician wheelchair basketball team Detroit Sparks, 1971-72; rehab. med. cons. Detroit League Handicapped Goodwill Industries, 1972-76; lectr. phys. therapy Wayne State U., 1972-74; postgrad. trainer, lectr., cons., staff psychiatrist BiCounty Cmty. Hosp., Warren, Riverside Osteo. Hosp., Trenton, Mich., 1974—; spkr. in field. Contbr. articles to profl. jours. Served to capt. USAF, 1955-58. Fellow Am. Osteo. Coll. Rehab. Medicine (trustee 1982-89, pres. 1984-85); mem. Am. Osteo. Assn., Am. Congress Rehab. Medicine, Macomb County Osteo. Assn. Jewish.

WEINER, LYNN YVETTE, history educator; b. Detroit, Feb. 8, 1951; d. Charles Mendel and Audrey (Allen) W.; m. Thomas Glenn Moher, May 5, 1974; children: Andrew Allen, Jeffrey Stephen. AB, U. Mich., 1972; MA, Boston U., 1975, PhD, 1981. Rsch. assoc. Jane Addams papers project U. Ill., Chgo., 1983-84; vis. asst. prof. Northwestern U., Evanston, Ill., 1990-91; instr., lectr. history Roosevelt U., Chgo., 1985-90, assoc. prof., 1991—, assoc. dean Arts and Scis., 1993—; exec. dir. Coordinating Com. on Women in Hist. Profession/Conf. Group on Women's History, 1989-91. Author: From Working Girl to Working Mother: The Female Labor Force in the U.S., 1820-1980, 1985 (nominated for Pulitzer prize 1985); also articles and book revs. Fellow NEH, 1988. Mem. Am. Hist. Assn., Orgn. Am. Historians (Binkley-Stephenson prize 1995), Am. Studies Assn., Chgo. Area Women's History Assn., LWV, NOW. Democrat. Jewish. Home: 527 Clinton Ave Oak Park IL 60304-1110 Office: Roosevelt U History Dept 430 S Michigan Ave Chicago IL 60605-1301

WEINER, STUART EARL, economist; b. St. Louis, Apr. 1, 1955; s. Earl Louis and Lela Elizabeth (Barton) W.; m. Martha Bruening, Aug. 5, 1978; children: Matthew Stuart, Sarah Elizabeth. BA with distinction, Cornell U., 1977; MA, Northwestern U., 1980, PhD, 1982. Economist Fed. Reserve Bank, Kansas City, Mo., 1982-85, sr. economist, 1985-87, rsch. officer, economist, 1988-89, asst. v.p., economist, 1990-94; vis. assoc. prof. econs. Dartmouth Coll., Hanover, N.H., 1992; v.p., economist Fed. Reserve Bank, Kansas City, 1995—. Contbr. articles to profl. jours. Mem. Am. Econ. Assn., Phi Beta Kappa. Office: Fed Reserve Bank 925 Grand Ave Kansas City MO 64198

WEINGARDT, JOHN W., accountant; b. Indpls., Oct. 22, 1961; s. Jake E. and Betty J. (Crouch) W.; m. Kristina L. Gullion, Aug. 31, 1985; children: Ashley, Abigail, John Robert. BS in Acctg. and Econs., U. Indpls., 1984. CPA, Ind. Tax sr. Ernst & Young, Indpls., 1984-87; tax mgr. Laventhol & Horwath, Indpls., 1987-89; pres. John W. Weingardt CPA, PC, Indpls., 1989-92; mng. ptnr. Peachin, Schwartz & Weingardt, PC, Indpls., 1992—; instr. Ind. U.-Purdue U., Indpls., 1986-93. Treas. Geist Christian Ch., Indpls., 1994, 95. Mem. AICPA, Ind. CPA Soc. (fed. tax com.). Home: 7983 Destry Pl Fishers IN 46038-1246 Office: Peachin Schwartz Weingardt 8555 River Rd Ste 470 Indianapolis IN 46240-4306

WEINGARTEN, JOSEPH LEONARD, aerospace engineer; b. N.Y.C., June 5, 1944; s. Herman H. and Irene Jane (Binzer) W.; 1 child, Toby. B of Mech. Engring., NYU, 1966; postgrad., Air War Coll., 1976. Chief engr. Air Transportability Test Loading Agy. Wright-Patterson AFB, Wright-Patterson AFB, Ohio, 1972-74; project engr. dept. engring. USAF, Wright-Patterson AFB, 1966-72, sr. project engr. dept. engring., 1974-76, planning and project engr. dept. engring., 1976-81, chief mgmt. ops. dept. engring., 1981-83, sr. tech. planner dept. engring., 1983-92; tech. asst. DCS Engring. and Tech. Mgmt. Air Force Material Command, Wright-Patterson AFB, 1992-93; founder, CEO Huffman Wright Inst., 1993—; CEO Weingarten Gallery, Dayton, Ohio, 1967—; v.p., sec., treas., bd. dirs. Ohio Designer Craftsmen, Columbus; sec. Ohio Designer Craftsmen Enterprise, Columbus, 1982—; chmn. continuing edn. design dept. Affiliate Socs. Coun., Dayton, 1971-74, chmn. edn. coord. com. Kettering Inst., Wright State U., 1974-76, chmn. scientist and engr. awards panel, 1990-91, mem., 1992-94. Contbr. articles on systems engring. to Aeronautical Sys. divsn. Mech. Engring. Jour. (1st place award nat. contest 1970), Procs. 4th Intersoc. Conf. on Transp., Air Force Sys. Command, USAF Spl. Purpose Report, Gems and Minerals, Friends Jour. USAF Mus., Ceramics Monthly, The Crafts Report, Macintosh Software. Scoutmaster Troop 81 Boy Scouts Am., Kettering, Ohio, 1985-91, com. mem., 1991-93, dist. chmn. Sequoia Dist. Miami Valley Coun., 1991-93, asst. coun. commr., 1993—; pres. Friends of Montessori Sch. South Dayton, 1978-94. Capt. USAF, 1967-71. Named Eagle Scout Boy Scouts Am., 1962; recipient Disting. Eagle award Boy Scouts Am., 1992, Silver Beaver award Boy Scouts Am., 1995. Mem. AIAA (sr. mem., air transport systems tech. com. 1976-78, 80-82, Lawrence Sperry award 1977), ASME (sr. mem.), Am. Nat. Standards Inst. (materials handling 5 com. 1968-70), Soc. Automotive Engrs. (aircraft ground support equiment com. 1969-75).

WEINGARTNER, GERARD JOHN, dentist; b. Jamaica, N.Y., Jan. 4, 1949; s. Gerard John and Evelyn Alice (Donelan) W.; m. Susan Mary Cromer (div. Aug. 1995); children: Caryn, Lauren. BA in biology, St. Thomas Coll., 970; DDS, Creighton U., 1974. Resident St. Mary's Hosp., Waterbury, Conn., 1974-75; dentist Dr. Steven Nielsen, Leadville, Colo., 1975-76; prin. Gerard Weingartner, DDS, Cottage Grove, Minn., 1976—. Mem. Afton Planning Commn., Afton, 1983-88; secy. Econ. Dev. Authority, Cottage Grove, 1986—. Fellow Acad. of Gen. Denistry; mem. Am. Orthodontic Soc., ADA, Cottage Grove C. of C. (pres. 1987-88, bd. dirs. 1981—). Home: 8991 Hidden Meadow Rd Woodbury MN 55125 Office: Gerard Weingartner DDS PA 7501 80th St S Cottage Grove MN 55016

WEINGARTNER, JANE ELLEN, college administrator; b. St. Louis, July 5, 1943; d. H. Kurt and Mary C. (Beresford) Vahle; m. James J. Weingartner, Aug. 20, 1966; children: Kirsten, Mary. BA, U. Wis., 1965, MA, 1969. Tchr. Lincoln Jr. High Sch., Madison, Wis., 1966-67, Berlitz Sch. Langs., St. Charles, Mo., 1980-81; program dir. Berlitz Sch. Langs., Lebanon, Ill., 1981-83; alumni dir. McKendree Coll., Lebanon, 1983-88, dir. devel., 1988-95, dir. major and planned gifts, 1995—. Mem. Nat. Soc. Fund Raising Execs. Office: McKendree Coll 701 College Rd Lebanon IL 62254-1212

WEINHOEFT, JOHN JOSEPH, data processing executive; b. Springfield, Ill., Nov. 23, 1952; s. Henry and Mary F. Weinhoeft; m. Kerry D. McKean, May 19, 1984; children: Bryan, Bill (dec.). Assoc., Springfield Coll., 1972. Lead operator fin. dept. State of Ill., Springfield, 1970-72, shift supr. fin. dept., 1973-77, tech. asst. to ops. mgr., 1977-78, system coordinator adminstrv. services, 1978-84, sr. systems architect resource mgmt. cen. mgmt. services, 1984-93; sr. pub. svc. adminstr., 1993—. Author: SNA: An IBM Standard, 1986, rev. edit., 1987, Capacity Management for IBM Mainframes, 1987, SAA: IBM's Master Plan, 1988, ESA/370: IBM's Architecture for the 1990s, 1989, IBM 3390 Disk Technology, 1990, The System/390 Report, 1991, Downsizing for Cost-Effective Enterprise Computing, 1993; editor: IBM 4381 Processors, 1987, Inside Sierra, 1988, The 3990/3390 Disk Report, 1990. Webelos den leader Boy Scouts Am., 1995—. Mem. Data Processing Mgrs. Assn., Nat. Systems Programmer Assn., Computer Measurement Group, Cen. Ill. Personal Computer Users Group (v.p. 1987-88, pres. 1988-89), ComputerFest Inc. (founding mem., bd. dirs., sec. 1987-90), Tandy Computer Club. Home: 2525 S Glenwood Ave Springfield IL 62704-4535 Office: Cen Mgmt Svcs 201 W Adams St Springfield IL 62704-1874

WEINLANDER, MAX MARTIN, retired psychologist; b. Ann Arbor, Mich., Sept. 9, 1917; s. Paul and Emma Carol (Lindemann) W.; BA, Ea. Mich. Coll., 1940; MA, U. Mich., 1942, PhD, 1955; M.A., Wayne U., 1951; m. Albertina Adelheit Abrams, June 4, 1946; children: Bruce, Annette. Psychometrist, VA Hosp., Dearborn, Mich., 1947-51; sr. staff psychologist Ohio Div. Corrections, London, 1954-55; lectr. Dayton and Piqua Centers, Miami U., Oxford, Ohio, 1955-62; chief clin. psychologist Child Guidance Clinic, Springfield, Ohio, 1956-61, acting dir., 1961-65; clin. psychologist VA Center, Dayton, Ohio, 1964-79; cons. Ohio Divsn. Mental Hygiene; summer guest prof. Miami U., 1957, 58, Wittenberg U., 1958; adj. prof. Wright State U., Dayton, 1975-76; cons. State Ohio Bur. Vocat. Rehab., Oesterlen Home Emotionally Disturbed Children. Pres. Clark County Mental Health Assn., 1960, Clark County Health and Welfare Club, 1961; mem. Community Welfare Coun. Clark County, 1964; chmn. Comprehensive Mental Health Planning Com. Clark County, 1964; trustee United Appeals Fund, 1960. Mem. citizens adv. coun. Columbus Psychiat. Inst., Ohio State U. Served as sgt. AUS, 1942-46. Fellow Ohio Psychol. Assn. (chmn. com. on utilization of psychologists; treas., exec. bd. 1968-71); mem. Am. Psychol. Assn., Ohio Psychol Assn., Mich. Psychol. Assn., DAV, U. Mich. Pres. Club, Pi Kappa Delta, Pi Gamma Mu, Phi Delta Kappa. Republican. Lutheran. Lodge: Kiwanis. Contbr. 18 articles to psychology jours. Home: 17185 Valley Dr Big Rapids MI 49307-9523

WEINMAN, STEVEN ALAN, emergency nurse, researcher, writer, educator; b. St. Louis, July 17, 1962; s. Stanley I. Weinman and Diana Raye (Kessler) Schrader; m. Carol Angela Daiber, July 27, 1986; children: Erin Elizabeth, Sarah Katherine. Diploma in Nursing, Jewish Hosp. of St. Louis, 1986; BSN, Webster U., Kansas City, 1996. RN, Mo.; cert. emergency nurse. Staff nurse Jewish Hosp. of St. Louis, 1986-87, Truman Med. Ctr.-West, Kansas City, Mo., 1987-93; clin. educator, 1993-95; clin. nurse mgr. Truman Med. Ctr.-West, Kansas City, Mo., 1987-93; staff nurse St. Luke's Northland Hosp., Kansas City, Mo., 1996—; ptnr. Emergency Care Cons., Overland Park, Kans., 1996—; clin. rsch. assoc. Clin. Multiphase Rsch., Wilton, Conn., 1991-93, nurse rschr., 1991—; coord. emergency dept. study Truman Med. Ctr., Kansas City, 1991-95. Contbg. author to books and book chpts; contbr. articles to profl. jours. Mem. adv. bd. Kansas City chpt. ARC, 1991-94; chief nurse first aid KansasCity Spiritfest, 1989-95. Recipient staff recognition award Truman Med. Ctr.-West, 1991. Mem. Emergency Nurses Assn. (treas. Greater Kansas City chpt. 1989-91, pres. 1994, state coun. exec. com. 1993-95, sec. 1991, state del. 1991-95, Recognition award 1991, 93, 94, Edn. award 1993, Educator of Yr. 1994), Am. Trauma Soc., Soc. Trauma Nurses, Internat. Assn. Forensic Nurses. Home: 8498 Carter St Overland Park KS 66212-4417 Office: St Luke's Northland Hosp 5820 NW Barry Rd Kansas City MO 65138

WEINSTEIN, BARRY ALAN, architect; b. Chgo., Oct. 31, 1943; s. Reuben and Dorothy (Weiss) W.; m. Margery Gail Spector, June 12, 1966; children: Scott Howard, Allison Beth. BArch, U. Ill., 1967. Architect-in-tng. C.F. Murphy Assocs., Chgo., 1967-69, Norman A. Koglin Assocs., Chgo., 1969-71; project mgr., tech. dir. R.M.M. Inc., Chgo., 1971-74; ptnr. Berger-Weinstein Assocs., Chgo., 1974-81; owner B. Weinstein Assocs., Chgo., 1981—; instr. Harrington Inst. of Interior Design, Chgo., 1972-74; adj. prof. Triton Coll., 1988. Recipient Hon. award Am. Architecture State of the Art in the '80s, 1985. Mem. Nat. Council Archtl. Registration Bds., AIA. Home and Office: 1166 Wade St Highland Park IL 60035-3451

WEINSTEIN, WILLIAM JOSEPH, lawyer; b. Detroit, Dec. 9, 1917; s. Joseph and Bessie (Abromovitch) W.; m. Evelyn Ross, Apr. 5, 1942 (dec.); children: Patricia, Michael; m. 2d, Rose Sokolsky, Oct. 25, 1972. LL.B., Wayne State U., 1940. Bar: Mich. 1940, U.S. Dist. Ct. (ea. and so. dists.) Mich. 1940, U.S. Ct. Appeals (6th cir.) 1951, U.S. Ct. Appeals (9th cir.) 1972. Ptnr. Charfoos, Gussin & Weinstein, Southfield, Mich., 1951-54, Charfoos, Gussin, Weinstein & Kroll, Detroit, 1955-59, Gussin, Weinstein & Kroll, Detroit, 1959-65, Weinstein & Kroll, P.C., Detroit, 1965-73, Weinstein, Kroll & Gordon, P.C., Detroit, 1973-85; pvt. practice, Southfield, 1985—; apptd. to standard jury instrn. com. Mich. Supreme Ct. 1965-72. Maj. gen. USMCR, 1941-75. Decorated Bronze Star with Combat V, Legion of Merit (2), Purple Heart (2). Recipient Disting. Alumnus award Wayne State U., 1973. Mem. Mich. Bar Assn. (chmn. negligence sect. 1962-63), Am. Coll. Trial Lawyers, Internat. Acad. Trial Lawyers, USN League (nat. v.p. 1971-72), Tam-o-Shanter Club (Orchard Lake, Mich.), St. Andrews Country Club (Boca Raton, Fla.). Contbr. articles to legal jours. Home and Office: 3922 Wabeek Lake Dr E Bloomfield Hills MI 48302-1261

WEINSTOCK, GRACE EVANGELINE, librarian, retired educator; b. Currie, Minn., Dec. 16, 1904; d. Charles Clementine and Lydia Hannah (Halland) O'Neill; m. Joseph Marshall Weinstock, Sept. 1, 1945 (dec. July 1973). BA, Hamline U., 1925; AAS in Libr. Sci. Tech., Coll. Lake County, 1988. High sch. tchr. Latin, history, phys. edn. Bd. Edn., Grafton, N.D., 1925-27; high sch. tchr. Latin, history, phys. edn. Bd. Edn., Norwood, Minn., 1928-32; high sch. tchr. Latin, English, libr. Bd. Edn., Wells, Minn., 1932-38; interviewer I Minn. State Employment Svc., Redwood Falls, Minn., 1938-45; interviewer II U.S. Employment Svc., Mpls., 1938-45; substitute tchr. English and bus. depts. North Chicago (Ill.) High Sch. Dist. 123, 1956-72; contractual employment instr. typing U.S. Dept. Army 5th U.S. Army Edn. Ctr., Ft. Sheridan, Ill., 1959-71; mil. personnel clk. Dept. Def., USN, Great Lakes, Ill., 1972-86; part-time libr. Outboard Marine Corp., Waukegan, Ill., 1988-90; part-time clerical worker Highland Park (Ill.) Hosp., 1990-91. bd. dirs. Lake County Community Concert Orgn., Waukegan, 1990. Grantee Waukegan br. Ednl. Found., 1993. Mem. AAUW (program chmn. Waukegan br. 1960), Navy League U.S., Phi Theta Kappa, Alpha Kappa Delta, Pi Gamma Mu. Home: 450 Pine Ct Lake Bluff IL 60044-2433

WEINSTOCK, KENNETH MARTIN, judge; b. Chgo., Nov. 13, 1928; s. Alexander Simon and Gertrude Victoria Weinstock; m. Marilyn Joan Vogelsang, Sept. 11, 1955; children: Amy Victoria Lowry, Charles William. AB, U. Mo., 1952; JD, St. Louis U., 1956. Bar: Mo., 1956. Ins. adjuster Safeco, St. Louis, 1952-58; pvt. practice various law firms, St. Louis, 1958-60; assoc. Markus and Maue, St. Louis, 1960-61, Dagem, Doasey and Gray, St. Louis, 1961-62; ptnr. Feigenbaum & Weinstock, St. Louis, 1962-65; assoc. James F. Koester, St. Louis, 1965-72; ptnr. Saitz and Weinstock, St. Louis, 1972-81, Kenneth Weinstock, St. Louis, 1982-84; judge St. Louis County Ct., Clayton, Mo., 1984—. Bd. dirs. Friendship Villages West and South, St. Louis County, 1980-84. With U.S. Army, 1946-47. Mem. Am. Judges Assn., Am. Judicature Soc., Mo. Bar Assn., Mo. Assn. Trial Lawyers, Lawyers Assn. St. Louis, St. Louis Met. Bar Assn., St. Louis County Bar Assn., Gideons Internat. (sec. St. Louis-Florissant chpt. 1995—). Baptist. Home: 11103 Queensway Dr Saint Louis County MO 63146 Office: St Louis County Courthouse 7900 Carondelet Clayton MO 63105

WEINZAPFEL, JONATHAN, public relations executive, congressional aide; b. Evansville, Ill., Nov. 16, 1965. BA, Ind. U., 1988; MA, Georgetown U., 1993. Dem. candidate 8th dist. Ind. U.S. House of Reps., 1996. Roman Catholic. Office: Weinzapfel for Congress PO Box 6893 Evansville IN 47719*

WEINZETL, LAWRENCE MARTIN, architect; b. St. Paul, Apr. 5, 1943. BA, U. Minn., 1970, BArch, 1972. Draftsman Conkey and Assocs., Mpls., 1973-77; architect several architectural firms, Mpls., 1977-79; project architect Ellerbe Assocs., Bloomington, 1979-84; architect and constrn. mgr. Nat. Car Rental System, Edina, 1984-87; assoc. 3M, 1988, RC Consultants, 1994. Home: PO Box 580350 Minneapolis MN 55458-0350

WEINZIERL, THOMAS ALLEN, data processing and data communications manager; b. Pitts., Sept. 5, 1951; s. George William and Genevieve Blanche (Nyga) W.; m. Elizabeth Katherine Yost, Dec. 16, 1972; children: Cynthia Ann, Cheryl Lynn, Thomas Michael. BS in Engring., U. Ill., Chgo., 1972; MBA, DePaul U., 1975. Cert. data processor. Data processing specialist Internat. Harvester, Chgo., 1972-77; supr. data communications, Milw., 1978-79, planning mgr., Chgo., 1980; cons. Blue Cross Blue Shield Milw., 1981-85; network control, contingency planning and data security officer, Marine Bank Svcs. Corp., Milw., 1986-89; contingency planner Deluxe Data Systems and sr. telecom. cons., New Berlin, Wis., 1990—. James scholar U. Ill., 1969-72. Mem. Soc. Mfg. Engrs., Phi Kappa Phi, Delta Mu Delta. Roman Catholic. Home: 3004 N Fairwood Ct Milwaukee WI 53222-4020 Office: Deluxe Data Systems 16363 W Ryerson Rd New Berlin WI 53151-3629

WEIR, EDWARD KENNETH, cardiologist; b. Belfast, No. Ireland, Jan. 7, 1943; came to U.S. 1973; s. Thomas Kenneth and Violet Hilda (ffrench) W.; m. Elizabeth Vincent Pearman, May 29, 1971; children: Fergus G., Conor K. BA, U. Oxford, U.K., 1964; MA, BM, BCh, U. Oxford, 1967, DM, 1976. Diplomate Am. Bd. Internal Medicine. Sr. house physician Nuffield Dept. Medicine, Radcliffe Infirmary, Oxford, 1970-71; registrar in cardiology Groote Schuur Hosp., Cape Town, South Africa, 1971-73; postdoctoral rsch. fellow U. Colo., Denver, 1973-75; cons. pediatric cardiologist U. Cape Town Med. Sch., 1975-76; cons. cardiologist U. Natal Med. Sch., Durban, South Africa, 1976-77; assoc. prof. medicine U. Minn., Mpls., 1978-85, prof. medicine, 1985—; staff physician Va. Med. Ctr., Mpls., 1978—; dir. Grover Confs. on Pulmonary Circulation, 1984—. Co-editor: Pulmonary Hypertension, 1984, The Pulmonary Circulation in Health and Disease, 1987, Pulmonary Vascular Physiology and Pathophysiology, 1989, The Diagnosis and Treatment of Pulmonary Hypertension, 1992, Ion Flux in Pulmonary Vascular Control, 1993, The Pulmonary Circulation and Gas Exchange, 1994, Nitric Oxide and Radicals in the Pulmonary Vasculature, 1996. Fulbright scholar, 1973-75; Sr. Internat. Fogarty fellow, 1993. Fellow Am. Coll. Cardiology, Royal Coll. Physicians London; mem. Am. Heart Assn. (Minn. affiliate bd. dirs. 1989-93, Nat. Cardiopulmonary Coun. (exec. com. 1992—), Pulmonary Circulation Found. (treas. 1985—). Office: VA Med Ctr 1 Veterans Dr # 111C Minneapolis MN 55417-2300

WEIR, MORTON WEBSTER, retired academic administrator, educator; b. Canton, Ill., July 18, 1934; s. James and Frances Mary (Johnson) W.; m. Cecelia Ann Rumler, June 23, 1956; children: Deborah, Kevin, Mark. AB, Knox Coll., 1955; MA, U. Tex., 1958, PhD, 1959. Rsch. assoc., asst. prof. child devel. U. Minn., Mpls., 1959; asst. prof. child devel. U. Ill., Urbana, 1960-64, assoc. prof., 1964-68, prof., 1968-93, prof. emeritus, 1993—, head dept. psychology, 1969-71, vice chancellor acad. affairs, 1971-79, v.p. acad. affairs, 1982-88, chancellor, 1988-93, chancellor emeritus, 1993—, sr. found. rep., 1993—; dir. Boys Town Center Study Youth Development, 1979-80. Contbr. numerous articles to profl. jours. Chmn. bd. trustees Knox Coll., 1995—. With AUS, 1960. NSF Predoctoral fellow, 1957-59. Fellow AAAS; mem. Soc. Rsch. in Child Devel. (chmn. bd. publs. 1971, chmn. fin. com. 1993-95), Sigma Xi, Phi Beta Kappa, Phi Kappa Phi. Office: U Ill Found Harker Hall 1305 W Green St Urbana IL 61801-2919

WEIS, LAWRENCE FREDERICK, city official; b. Highland Park, Mich., Aug. 26, 1939; s. Howard Emanuel and Amelia Lanson (Morell) W. BS, Purdue U., West Lafayette, Ind., 1962; MA, Wayne State U., Detroit, 1984. Hockey referee Detroit, 1956—; gen. mgr. Detroit Jr. Wings Hockey Club, 1970-72; ops. mgr. data processing Federal-Mogul Corp., Southfield, Mich., 1963-70; tchr. polit. sci. Bishop Gallagher H.S., Harper Woods, Mich., 1983-88; baseball mgr. ITM Corp., Detroit, 1969-87; referee-in-chief Internat. Hockey Referee Assn., Detroit, 1974—; cross country coach Wayne State U., Detroit, 1988-94; pres. World Pancratium Fedn., Detroit, 1989—; arena mgr. City of St. Clair Shores, Mich., 1988—. Author/editor: Cross Country Guide, 1994, Baseball Guide, 1985. Pres., chmn. bd. Mich. Amateur Sports Hall of Fame, Detroit, 1974—; mem. ground observers corp U.S. Dept. of Def., Detroit, 1953-56. Named U.S. Amateur Mgr. of Yr., Soc. Baseball Friends, 1973. Lutheran. Home: 560 Cook Rd Grosse Pointe Woods MI 48236 Office: City of St Clair Shores 20000 Stephens Saint Clair Shores MI 48080

WEIS, RICHARD C., mayor; b. Milw., Apr. 27, 1936; s. Richard Albert and Dorothy (Hammer) W.; m. Carolyn Ann Mitton, Nov. 24, 1956; children: Sandy, Sherrie, Debbie, Dawn, Lori. BS, Wis. U., 1976. Reporter Northwest Reporter, Milw., 1956-59; publisher Teen Beat, Milw., 1959-61; account exec. W-RIT Radio, Milw., 1961-63; sales mgr. WYLO Radio, Milw., 1963-65, WUTU Channel 18, Milw., 1965-70; v.p. gen. mgr. Schlitz Broadcast, Milw., 1970-78, Channel 24 WCGV, Milw., 1978-81; owner Weis Inc., Freeport, Ill., 1981-89; mayor City of Freeport, Ill., 1984—. Pres., Crime Stoppers, Freeport, Ill., 1984, Muscular Dystrophy, Milw., 1974, Greater Downtown Freeport, 1985; vol. VietNow, Freeport, 1990. Named Vol. of Year, Martin Luther King Cmty. Svcs., 1990, Outstanding Citizen, Freepert Internation Fellowship, 1992. Mem. Am. Leadership (bd. mem. 1994), Ill. Mcpl. League (bd. mem. 1989-90), Major League Baseball Players Assn., Freeport C. of C. (past pres. 1986), Rotary (past pres., noon). Republican. Lutheran. Office: City Hall Mayor's Office 230 W Stephenson Freeport IL 61032

WEIS, TIMOTHY CHARLES, healthcare executive, consultant; b. Burlington, Wis., Sept. 19, 1958; s. Charles William and Marlene Mary (Scherrer) W.; m. Tracy Lynn Lohrey, June 6, 1981; children: Stephanie Lohrey Weis, Curtis Timothy Weis. BBA, U. Wis., Whitewater, 1978. CPA, Tex. Audit staff acct. Arthur Andersen & Co., Milw., 1978-81; sr. staff Arthur Andersen & Co., Dallas, 1981-83, mgr., 1983-88; sr. mgr. Arthur Andersen & Co., San Francisco, 1988-90; contr. Macneal Hosp., Chgo., 1990-92; v.p. Quorum Health Resources, Inc., Nashville, 1992—; cons. Kaufmann, Hall & Assocs., Northbrook, Ill., 1992. Trustee Lisle (Ill.) Congl. Ch., 1990-92; long range plannign bd. mem. Naperville (Ill.) Congl. Ch., 1994. Fellow Healthcare Fin. Mgmt. Assn. Home and Office: 2779 Shellingham Dr Lisle IL 60532

WEISBERG, LEONARD R., retired research and engineering executive; b. N.Y.C., Oct. 17, 1929; s. Emanuel E. and Esther (Raynes) W.; m. Frances Simon, Mar. 23, 1980; children: Glenna Weisberg Andersen, Orren Weisberg Falk, Frances Weisberg Brookner. BA magna cum laude, Clark U., 1950; MA, Columbia U., 1952. Rsch. asst. Watson Labs. IBM, N.Y.C., 1953-55; with RCA Labs., Princeton, N.J., 1955-71; mem. tech. staff RCA Labs., 1955-66, head rsch. group, 1966-69, dir. semicondr. device rsch. lab., 1969-71; dir. materials rsch. lab. Itek Corp., Lexington, Mass., 1972-74; v.p., dir. ctrl. rsch. lab. Itek Corp., 1974-75; dir. electronics tech U.S. Dept. Def., Washington, 1975-79; v.p. rsch. and engring. Honeywell Inc., Mpls., 1980-94, ret., 1994; mem. adv. group on electron devices U.S. Dept. Def.; bd. dirs. SubMicron Sys. Corp., XLI Corp. Contbr. articles to profl. jours. Recipient award for initiating VHSIC program U.S. Dept. Def., 1979. Fellow IEEE; mem. Am. Phys. Soc., Sigma Xi. Home: 1225 Lasalle Ave Apt 1407 Minneapolis MN 55403-2331

WEISBERG, SEYMOUR WILLIAM, physician; b. Chgo., Aug. 5, 1910; s. Isaac and Eda (Provus) W.; B.S., U. Chgo., 1932; M.D., Rush Med. Coll., 1936; m. Ella Sperling, Oct. 16, 1949; children—Gerald, Louise. Intern Michael Reese Hosp.; resident Cook County Hosp., Chgo.; practice medicine specializing in internal medicine, Chgo., 1940—; asso. prof. medicine U. Ill. Coll. Medicine, Chgo.; asso. attending physician Cook County Hosp., 1940-44; chief resident tng. unit Chgo. Regional Office VA; mem. attending staff Michael Reese Hosp., Chgo., Louis A. Weiss Meml. Hosp., Chgo., St. Joseph Hosp. Served with AUS, 1944-47. Diplomate Am. Bd. Internal Medicine. Mem. AMA, Ill. Med. Soc., Phi Beta Kappa, Alpha Omega Alpha. Office: 5801 N Sheridan Rd Chicago IL 60660

WEISBROD, RITA ROFFERS, sociologist, educator; b. Marshfield, Wis., June 28, 1933; d. Anton Henry and Irene Ina (Erickson) R.; m. Alan Richard Weisbrod, Sept. 10, 1960; children: Anne Victoria, Margaret Alexandra. PhD, Cornell U., 1971. Rsch. assoc. div of epidemology Sch. Pub. Health U. Minn., Mpls., 1986-89; asst. prof. Augsburg Coll., Mpls., 1991—. Co-editor (with William Lambert) Cross Cultural Perspectives on Social Psychology, 1972; contbr. articles to profl. jours. Chair adv. com. Washington County Dept. Pub. Health, Minn., 1993-96. Mem. APHA, Am. Sociol. Assn., Nat. Coun. on Family Rels. Home: 14866 Old Marine Trl N Marine Saint Crx MN 55047-9781 Office: Augsburg Coll Dept Sociology 2211 Riverside Ave Minneapolis MN 55454-1338

WEISBROT, MARVIN MYRON, retired health care administrator, consultant; b. Phila., Oct. 20, 1928; s. Lewis Harold Weisbrot and Rose (Horn) Weisbrot/Abel; m. Jan Levin, Feb. 14, 1954; 1 child, Michele Ann. BA, U. Pa., 1950; BS, Phila. Coll. Pharmacy, 1959; MBA, Temple U., 1973. Registered pharmacist, N.J. Pres. Drug Ctrs., Inc., Burlington, N.J., 1956-71; adminstrv. officer VA Med. Ctr., Tampa, Fla., 1973-74; adminstrv. officer, clin. studies coord. Drug Dependence Treatment Ctr. VA Med. Ctr., Phila., 1974-80; lectr. psychiatry Sch. Medicine U. Pa., Phila., 1974-93; adminstrv. officer, co-investigator, coord. Psychiatry Svc. VA Med. Ctr., Phila., 1980-90, clin. rsch. Med. Rsch. Svc., 1990-93; cons. on addictive disease Roxane Labs., Columbus, Ohio, 1995—; bd. dirs. Comty. Nursing Svcs., Mt. Holly, N.J., 1986-88; bd. trustees Meml. Health Alliance, Mt. Holly, 1988—; cons. addictive disease Bio Devel. Corp., McLean, Va., 1993-95; cons. health edn. Evesham (N.J.) sch. dists., 1995. Author: Comparison of Modalities of Treatment for Narcotic Addiction, 1973;; contbr. papers and monographs to profl. jours. Mem., cons. Mcpl. Alliance for Drug and Alcohol Awareness and Edn. (DARE), Mt. Laurel, N.J., 1993—; mem. Legion of Honor, Chapel of Four Chaplains, Phila., 1977. 1st lt. U.S. Army, 1951-54. Named Outstanding Young Man of Yr., Jaycees, 1962, 64. Fellow Am. Coll. Apothecaries. Jewish. Home: 327 Carleton Ln Mount Laurel NJ 08054

WEISER, IRVING, financial services company executive; b. Munich, Dec. 4, 1947; s. Siegfried and Paula (Lederman) W.; m. Marjorie Lee Dicker, Mar. 29, 1970; children: Jennifer Suh, Dana Park. BA, SUNY, Buffalo, 1969; JD cum laude, Brooklyn Law Sch., 1973. Bar: Minn., 1973. Assoc. Dorsey & Whitney, Mpls., 1973-78, ptnr., 1979-85; pres. Inter-Regional Fin. Group, Inc., Mpls., 1985-89, pres., CEO, 1990—, also bd. dirs.; pres., CEO Dain Bosworth Inc., Mpls., 1990—; adj. prof. William Mitchell Coll. Law, St. Paul, 1974-81; bd. dirs. Dain Bosworth Inc., Rauscher Pierce Refsnes, Inc. Trustee Guthrie Theater Found., Mpls., 1983-90; bd. dirs. Temple Israel, 1989—, Children's Home Soc. of Minn., Mpls., 1988—, Minn. Wellspring, Mpls., 1986-88, Legal Rights Ctr., Mpls., 1978-81. Mem. Am. Mgmt. Assn. (mem. pres. assn. 1985—), Young Pres.'s Orgn. Jewish. Club: Mpls. *

WEISMAN, HERBERT NEAL, dentist, financial planner; b. Mpls., Mar. 12, 1940; s. Sholem and Katherine (Fink) W.; m. Doris Sue Epstein, Dec. 27, 1964; children: David Nathan, Marna Faye. BS, U. Minn., 1962, DDS, 1964; cert. in real estate, LaSalle U., Chgo., 1969; cert., Coll. for Fin. Planning, Denver, 1989. Pvt. practice, St. Louis Park, Minn., 1966—; pres. Miller Supply Co., St. Paul, 1976-77/ v.p. Lebewitz, Weisman, Greene, Mpls., 1982-86; dental ins. cons. Prudential Ins. Co., Mpls., 1988-89; forensic cons. Hennepin County Med. Examiners Office, Mpls., 1988—. Author: So You Want to be Rich, 1994; assoc. editor N.W. Dentistry, 1974-75; contbr. articles to profl. jours. Mem. exec. bd. Jewish Family and Childrens Svc., Mpls., 1982-87; bd. dirs. Adath Jeshuran Synagogue, Mpls., 1983. Capt. USAF, 1964-66. Fellow Acad. Gen. Dentistry (state pres. 1969-70), Royal Soc. Health (Eng.); mem. ADA, Minn. Dental Assn., Mpls. Dental Soc., Inst. Cert. Fin. Planners. Office: 5407 Excelsior Blvd Saint Louis Park MN 55416-2929

WEISMANTEL, GREGORY NELSON, management consultant and software executive; b. Houston, Sept. 8, 1940; s. Leo Joseph and Ellen Elizabeth (Zudis) W.; m. Marilyn Ann Fanger, June 18, 1966; children: Guy Gregory, Christopher Gregory, Andrea Rose. BA in English, U. Notre Dame, 1962; MBA in Internat. Bus., Loyola U., Chgo., 1979. With mgmt. staff Gen. Foods Corp., White Plains, N.Y., 1966-80; pres., chief exec. officer Manor House Foods, Inc., Addison, Ill., 1980-82, Weismantel & Assocs., Downers Grove, Ill., 1982-84; v.p. perishable div. Profl. Marketers, Inc., Lombard, Ill., 1984-86; group v.p. sales and mktg. services, dir. corp. strategy Profl. Marketers, Inc., Lombard, 1986-87; v.p. mng. prin. CPG Industry, Louis A. Allen Assoc. Inc., Palo Alto, Calif., 1987-88; pres., chief exec. officer The Vista Group, St. Charles, Ill., 1989—; bd. dirs. Epicurean Foods, Ltd., Chgo.; pres., CEO The Vista Tech. Group, Ltd., The Vista Mgmt. Group. Chmn. fin. St. Edward's High Sch. Jubilee, Elgin, Ill., 1982-85; bd. dirs. Dist. 301 Sch. Bd., Burlington, Ill., 1980-84, St. Edward's Found., Elgin, 1982—. Capt. U.S. Army, 1962-66. Recipient ICP/Chgo. Software Assoc. Re-Engring. award, 1994; State of Ill. grantee, 1989, Build Ill. Investment Fund. Mem. Grocery Mfg. Sales Execs., Chgo. Software Assn., Chg. C. of C. (small bus. com.). Roman Catholic. Clubs: Merchandising Execs., Food Products, Am. Mktg. (Chgo.).

WEISPFENNING, CURTIS, design technician; b. Clinton, Iowa, Mar. 30, 1957. AAS, Ea. Iowa C.C., 1987. Design technician Genesis Sys., Davenport, Iowa, 1982—. Pres. Mobil Meals, Clinton, Iowa, 1980-86. With U.S. Army, 1975-78. Scholar Ea. Iowa C.C., 1986. Republican. Lutheran. Office: Genesis Systems 4821 Tremont Ave Davenport IA 52807-1010

WEISPFENNING, JOHN THOMAS, communications educator; b. Cooperstown, N.D., July 30, 1960; s. Walter William and Edna Margaret (Gums) W.; m. Christine M. Kelly, June 15, 1991. BS, Moorhead State U., 1982; MS, N.D. State U., 1985; PhD, Purdue U., 1992. Asst. program dir. Sta. KVOX, Moorhead, Minn., 1981-82; announcer Sta. KQWB, Fargo, N.D., 1982-84; sta. mgr. Sta. KCSD, Sioux Falls, S.D., 1985-88; instr. mass communications Sioux Falls Coll., 1985-88; instr. interviewing Purdue U., West Lafayette, Ind., 1988-91; vis. lectr. Ind. U., Indpls., 1991-92; asst. prof. U. Maine, Orono, 1992-95, Otterbein Coll., Westerville, Ohio, 1995—. Producer, host (radio program) South Dakota Focus, 1985-88. Mem. Speech Communication Assn., Assn. Edn. in Journalism and Mass Communication, Broadcast Edn. Assn., Ctrl. States Comm. Assn. Democrat. Presbyterian.

WEISS, BENTON HERBERT, broadcast engineer; b. Ottawa, Kans., Sept. 14, 1942; s. Herbert John and Coralee (McCrary) W.; m. Patty Sue Rule, June 6, 1964; children: Sarah Catherine, Timothy Alan, Peter Herbert. BA in Speech/Drama, Ottawa (Kans.) U., 1965. FCC 1st class lic.; profl. broadcast engr. cert. Ops. mgr., chief engr. KJRG and KOEZ Radio Stas., Newton, Kans., 1965-71, KCCV Radio Sta., Independence, Mo., 1972-75; chief engr. KJLA Radio Sta., Kansas City, Mo., 1975-90; mem. engring. staff KCTV-TV, Kansas City, 1977-78; chief engr. KSAS and KLDY Radio Stas., Liberty, Mo., 1978-82; dir. engring. Sta. KMXV-KUDL, Kansas City, 1982—; owner Weiss Enterprises, Raytown, Mo., 1972—. Contbr. articles to profl. jours. Mem. Soc. Broadcast Engrs. (sec.-treas. Kansas City chpt. 1982—), Kansas City Amateur Radio Club. Republican. Mem. Assembly of God Ch. Office: Regent Comms of Kansas City 3101 Broadway St Ste 460 Kansas City MO 64111-2416

WEISS, DEBRA S., customer service officer; b. Three Rivers, Mich., Dec. 4, 1953; d. Harold E. and Winifred (Dunn) W. Student Albion Coll., 1972-73, Lake Superior State Coll., 1974-76; cert. Industrialized Housing Inst., Wausau, Wis., 1975. Lic. builder and mech. contractor, Mich. Sales mgr. Weiss Constrn., Inc., Alanson, Mich., 1976-80; owner, chmn. bd. dirs. Weiss Constrn., St. Ignace, Mich., 1980-91; corp. sec., supr. spl. projects Weiss Corp., St. Ignace, 1984; mktg. dir. First Nat. Bank of Gaylord, Mich., 1992—. Bd. dirs. Ea. Upper Peninsula Pvt. Industry Council, Sault Ste. Marie, Mich., 1984-92, treas., 1985-87, pres. 1987-89; mem. Downtown Devel. Authority, Mackinaw City, Mich., 1985-87; mem. St. Ignace Zoning Bd., 1984-92, vice chmn., 1990-92; mem. St. Ignace City Coun., 1985-92; chmn. Utility Authority Task Force; conv. chmn. designate, 1993; pres., bd. dirs. Otsego County/Gaylord Friendship Shelter for Homeless, 1992-94. Recipient Ruth Huston Whipple award, 1986, Garden City award, 1986, Athena award Ostego C. of C., 1995. Mem. NAFE, NOW, St. Ignace Bus. and Profl. Women (pres. 1980-81; Woman of Yr. 1980, Anna Howard Shaw award 1981, 82), Mich. Fedn. Bus. and Profl. Women (mem. strategic long range planning com. 1985-87, chmn. issues mgmt. com., named Outstanding Young Career Woman 1982, Woman of Achievement award 1987), Nat. Fedn. Bus. and Profl. Women (long range strategic planning comm., 1987-89), Silver Mountain Ski Assn. (bd. dirs. 1982-85), Mich. Fedn. of Bus. and Profl. Women, St. Ignace C. of C., Gaylord C. of C., St. Ignace Tourist Assn., Upper Peninsula Tourist and Recreation Assn., Silver Mountain Cross Country Club. Avocations: skiing, reading, water sports. Office: 1st Nat Bank Gaylord PO Box 310 Gaylord MI 49735-0310

WEISS, MAREDA RUTH, dean; b. Chgo., Sept. 23, 1941; d. William Arthur and Ruth Emily (Schauble) W. BBA, U. Wis., 1963. Acct., then supr. rsch. adminstrn./fin. U. Wis. System, Madison, 1964-69; specialist, asst. dean, now assoc. dean, dir. rsch. svcs. U. Wis., Madison, 1969—; univ. chair State Employees Combined Campaign, Madison, 1986. Treas. Wis. Cen. Ctr. Aux., Madison, 1971-73, 75-77, 79-81, Frineds of WHA-TV pub. tv, Madison, 1989-91; chair nominating com. U. Wis. Credit Union, 1982-88. Mem. Nat. Coun. Univ. Rsch. Adminstrs. (presenter workshops, sec.-treas. 1980-83, chair, vice-chair mid-Am. region 1989-91, Disting. Svc. award 1989), Univ. Ins. Assn. (bd. dirs. 1982—). Office: U Wis Grad Sch 500 Lincoln Dr Madison WI 53706-1314

WEISS, MARK LAWRENCE, anthropology educator; b. Bklyn., Nov. 1, 1945; s. Arthur A. and Ruth E. Heilbrunn W.; m. Linda K. Spangler, July 31, 1993; children: Evan M., Emily C. BA, SUNY, Binghamton, 1966; MA, U. Calif., Berkeley, 1968, PhD, 1969. Asst. prof. anthropology Wayne State U., Detroit, 1969-73, assoc. prof., 1973-87, prof., 1987—; program dir. phys. anthropology NSF, Washington, 1990-92, 95—. Co-author: Human Biology and Behavior, 1975; contbr. articles to Nature, Am. Jour. Primatology, Yearbook, Phys. Anthropology, Jour. Molecular Biology; mem. editorial bd. Human Biology, 1988—, Yearbook of Phys. Anthropology, 1992—, Jour. Human Evolution, 1994—. Recipient award in excellence in teaching and rsch. Probus Club, 1973. Fellow Am. Anthrop. Assn., Am. Assn. Phys. Anthropologists (exec. com. 1993-96). Jewish. Office: Dept Anthropology Wayne State Univ. Detroit MI 48202

WEISS, SUSAN CHRISTINE, nuclear medicine-radiation technologist, educator; b. Mpls., June 14, 1944; d. Frank and Leila Mae Andersen; m. Stephen Weiss. Student, U. Minn., 1962-65; BA, Roosevelt U., Chgo., 1974. Cert. nuclear medicine technologist. Staff technologist U. Minn. Hosps., Mpls., 1965-67, Manchester (Conn.) Meml. Hosp., 1967-69, Albert Einstein Med. Ctr., Phila., 1969-71; staff technologist Children's Meml. Hosp., Chgo., 1971-74, chief technologist, 1974-96, radiation safety officer, 1978—; clin. instr. Northwestern Meml. Hosp., Chgo., 1972-75, Triton Coll., River Grove, Ill., 1974—; numerous presentations on nuclear medicine, 1974—. Editor Jour. Nuclear Medicine Tech.; contbr. articles and abstracts to med. jours. Recipient best paper award Jour. Nuclear Medicine Tech., 1974. Mem. Soc. Nuclear Medicine (hon. life technologist sect. N.Y. chpt.; pres. technologist sect. Ctrl. chpt., bd. govs. 1992—, Presdl. award 1980, del. nat. coun., mem. exec. com., bd. dirs.-adminstrv. dir. Edn. and Rsch. Found.), Assoc. and Tech. Affiliates Chgo. Area, P.R. Soc. Nuclear Medicine (hon.). Office: Children's Meml Hosp 2300 N Childrens Plz Chicago IL 60614-3318

WEISSENBURGER, FRED ELMER, school system administrator; b. Moline, Ill.; m. Jacalyn Wright, May 16, 1981; children: Kimberly, Kurtis, Derek. MA, U. Iowa, 1972, PhD, 1987. Cert. dir. spl. edn. and sch. psychologist, Iowa, Minn., Wis. Sch. psychologist Miss. Bend Area Edn. Agy., Bettendorf, Iowa, 1975-77, head psychologist, 1977-78, supr. sch. psychology, 1978-90, coord. spl. edn., 1990-93; exec. dir. student svcs. Eau Claire (Wis.) Area Sch. Dist., 1993—; adj. prof. U. Wis., Eau Claire, 1993—; spkr. numerous local, state and nat. meetings and convs. Contbr. articles to profl. jours. Bd. dirs. Coun. on Children at Risk, Moline, 1988-92. Recipient Golden Achievement award Nat. Sch. Pub. Rels. Assn., 1987. Fellow Am. Orthopsychiatry Assn.; mem. NASP, Iowa Sch. Psychologists Assn. (pres. 1989-90), Coun. for Exceptional Children. Office: Eau Claire Area Sch Dist 500 Main St Eau Claire WI 54701-3770

WEISSMAN, JAMES K., tax specialist. BS in Acctg., U. Park Forrest South, 1975; BA, Govs. Park U., 1989; M in Taxation Law, Washington Sch. Law, 1993. CPA, Ill.; cert. tax profl. Owner Heritage Glenwood (Ill.) Mobile, 1976-79; pres. Weisco, Inc., Chicago Heights, Ill., 1980—. Treas. Boy Scouts Am., Country Club Hills, Ill., 1970-79, Girl Scouts Am., Country Club Hills, 1970-79. Served to sgt. U.S. Army, 1971-73. Mem. Am. Soc. Notarys, Ind. Accts. Assn. Ill., Nat. Soc. Pub. Accts., Country Club Hills C. of C. (co-founder, past bd. dirs. 1982—). Republican. Jewish. Office: Weisco Inc 445 S Halsted St Chicago Heights IL 60411-1212

WEISZHAAR, DOUGLAS JAMES, civil engineer; b. Mobridge, S.D., July 2, 1949; s. Henry George and Doris Isabel (Himrich) W.; m. Nancy Kay Johnson, Aug. 12, 1972; children: Nicholas Jon, Sarah Beth. BSCE, S.D. State U., 1972. Registered profl. engr., Minn. Project engr. Kans. Dept. Transp., Topeka, 1972-76; asst. county engr. Otter Tail County Hwy. Dept., Fergus Falls, Minn., 1976-81; county engr. Chisago County Hwy. Dept., Center City, Minn., 1981-87, Stearns County Hwy. Dept., St. Cloud, Minn., 1987—; chmn. Minn. Local Rd. Rsch. bd., St. Paul, 1984-89; pres. Minn. Transp. Alliance, St. Paul, 1992-94; chmn. Coun. on Transp. Infrastructure, St. Paul, 1989—. V.p. Trinity Luth. Ch. Coun., Lindstrom, Minn., 1986; pres. Resurrection Luth. Ch. Coun., St. Joseph, Minn., 1995. Mem. Minn. County Engrs. Assn. (pres. 1981—, Engr. of Yr. 1992), Minn. Engrs. and Surveyors Soc., Eagles Club. Lutheran. Home: 29290 Kraemer Lake Rd Saint Joseph MN 56374 Office: Stearns County Hwy Dept PO Box 246 Saint Cloud MN 56302

WEIXLMANN, JOSEPH NORMAN, JR., English educator, dean; b. Buffalo, N.Y., Dec. 16, 1946; s. Joseph Norman and Mary C. (Degenhart) W.; m. Sharron Pollack, Mar. 14, 1982; children: Seth Jacob, Adira Jenna, Benjamin Ari. AB, Canisius Coll., 1968; MA, Kans. State U., 1970, PhD, 1973. Instr. U. Okla., Norman, 1973-74; asst. prof. Tex. Tech U., Lubbock, 1974-76; from asst. prof. to prof. Ind. State U., Terre Haute, 1976—, assoc. dean, 1987-92, acting dean, 1992-94, dean, 1994—. Author: John Barth, 1976, American Short-Fiction Criticism, 1982; co-editor: Black American Prose Theory, 1984, Belief vs. Theory in Black American Literary Criticism, 1986, Black Feminist Criticism, 1988, Studies in Black Am. Lit. Ann., 1984-88; editor African Am. Rev. jour., 1976—; contbg. editor High Plains Lit. Rev., 1987—; adv. editor Langston Hughes Rev., 1982—. Fellow NDEA, 1970-72, NEH, 1980; Nat. Endowment for Arts grantee, 1988-95. Mem. MLA (exec. com. divsn. Black Am. Lit. and Culture 1985—), Coll. Lang. Assn., Langston Hughes Soc., Zora Neale Hurston Soc., Coun. Colls. Arts and Scis., Coun. Lit. Mags. and Presses (grantee 1977-96, Editor's grantee 1986), Coun. Editors Learned Jours. Home: 1601 S 6th St Terre Haute IN 47802-1608 Office: Ind State Univ Stalker Hall # 213 Terre Haute IN 47809

WEJCMAN, LINDA, state legislator; b. Dec. 1939; m. Jim. Student, Iowa State U. Minn. State rep. Dist. 61B, 1991—; cons.; mem. local govt. and met. affairs com., energy, health and human svcs., housing and judiciary coms. Home: 3203 5th Ave S Minneapolis MN 55408-3248 Office: Minn Ho of Reps State Capital Building Saint Paul MN 55155-1606*

WEKENBORG, CONNIE LOUISE, retail administrator; b. Jefferson, Mo., Oct. 17, 1959; d. Lonnie James and Alice Ann (Schepker) W. Student, S.W. Mo. State U., Springfield, 1978-81. Intern, mdse. mgr. trainee J.C. Penney Co., Jefferson City, Mo., 1980-83, sr. mdse. mgr., 1983-85; sr. mdse. mgr. J.C. Penney Co., Kansas City, Mo., 1985-89; internal staff auditor J.C. Penney Co., Overland Park, Kans., 1989-90; sr. mdse. mgr. J.C. Penney Co., Inc., Chgo., 1990-92; sr. mdse. mgr. J.C. Penney Co., Inc., Overland Park, Kans., 1992. Mem. NAFE, Inst. Internal Auditors. Roman Catholic. Home: 10585 Goddard St Apt 431 Overland Park KS 66214-3729

WELCH, DAVID WILLIAM, lawyer; b. St. Louis, Feb. 26, 1941; s. Claude LeRoy Welch and Mary Eleanor (Peggs) Penney; m. Candace Lee Capages, June 5, 1971; children: Joseph Peggs, Heather Elizabeth, Katherine Laura. BSBA, Washington U., St. Louis, 1963; JD, U. Tulsa, 1971. Bar: Okla. 1972, Mo. 1973, U.S. Dist. Ct. (we. dist.) Mo. 1973, U.S. Dist. Ct. (ea. dist.) Mo. 1974, U.S. Ct. Appeals (8th cir.) 1977, U.S. Ct. Appeals (7th cir.) 1991. Contract adminstr. McDonnell Aircraft Corp., St. Louis, 1965-66; bus. analyst Dun & Bradstreet Inc., Los Angeles, 1967-68; atty. U.S. Dept. Labor, Washington, 1972-73; ptnr. Moller Talent, Kuelthau & Welch, St. Louis, 1973-88, Lashly & Baer, St. Louis, 1988-96, Armstrong, Teasdale, Schlafly & Davis, St. Louis, 1996—. Author: (handbook) Missouri Employment Law, 1988; contbr. book chpts. Missouri Bar Employer-Employee Law, 1985, 87, 89, 92, 94; co-editor: Occupational Safety and Health Law, 1996. Mem. City of Creve Coeur Ethics Commn., 1987-88, Planning and Zoning Commn., 1988—; bd. dirs. Camp Wyman, Eureka, Mo., 1982—, sec., 1987-88, 2nd v.p. 1988-89, 1st v.p. 1990-92, pres., 1992-94. Mem. ABA, Fed. Bar Assn., Mo. Bar Assn., Okla. Bar Assn., St. Louis Bar Assn., Tulsa County Bar Assn., Kiwanis (bd. dirs. St. Louis 1979—, sec. 1982-83, 93-94, v.p. 1983-84, 88-90, 92-93, Man of Yr. award 1985). Democrat. Mem. Christian Ch. (Disciples of Christ). Home: 536 N Mosley Rd Saint Louis MO 63141-7633 Office: Armstrong Teasdale Schlafly & Davis 1 Metropolitan Sq 2600 Saint Louis MO 63102

WELCH, JOHN FRANCIS, violin and viola manufacturing company executive; b. Chgo., Aug. 1, 1934; s. Lourde J. and Regina (Delire) W.; married Mary Dittmer, Mar. 3, 1961; children: Daniel, Douglas, Gregory, Edith. Student, N.Y. State U., Buffalo, 1953-58, Chgo. Musical Coll.; student of, Aaron Copland. Asst. gen. mgr. Chgo. Symphony Orch., 1964—; gen. sales mgr. Alfred Publs., Port Washington, N.Y., 1971—; exec. v.p. Studio P/R Publs., Lebanon, Ind., 1974—; pres., CEO Consort Internat., Indpls., 1984—, Consort Internat. B.G., Sofia, Bulgaria, 1984—; chmn. Internat. Consortia, Inc., Indpls., 1984—; bd. dirs. U.S. Dept. Commerce Dist. Export Coun., Indpls., 1984-85; mem. adv. bd. Small Bus. Devel. Ctrs., Indpls., 1994—. Composer, editor: (with Charles Schultz) Peanuts Piano Book, 1993. Served with U.S. Army, 1958-64. Mem. Ind. World Trade Club (pres. 1984-85), Ind. Venture Capital Club. Office: Consort Internat 429 E Vermont St Indianapolis IN 46202

WELCH, JOSEPH DANIEL, lawyer; b. University City, Mo., Feb. 1, 1952; s. Robert Joseph and Mary Virginia (Church) W.; m. Sharon Susan Filipek, Mar. 16, 1973; children: Eric Ryan, Christopher Joseph, Colin Andrew, Maria Nicole, Theresa Katherine. BA cum laude, St. Louis U., 1974, JD, 1977. Bar: Mo. 1977, U.S. Dist. Ct. (ea. and we. dists.) Mo. 1977, U.S. Ct. Appeals (8th cir.) 1984, U.S. Supreme Ct. 1994. Assoc. Ely & Cary, Hannibal, Mo., 1977-79; ptnr. Ely, Cary & Welch, Hannibal, Mo., 1979-82, Ely, Cary, Welch & Hickman, Hannibal, Mo., 1982—; mem. Mississippi River Pky. Commn., St. Paul, 1988—, head Mo. del., 1988; mem. Nat. Heritage Corridor Comml., Washington, 1990—; prof. bus. law Hannibal-LaGrange Coll.; speaker various orgns. Editor: Year in Review-Bankruptcy, 1991-94, co-author, 1988-90; speaker various profl. orgns.; contbr. articles to profl. jours. Bd. dirs. Mark Twain Area Physician's Recruitment Assn., Hannibal, 1984-85, Hannibal Free Pub. Libr., 1980-82, Hannibal C. of C., 1978-80; pres. Hannibal Ctrl. Bus. Devel., Inc., 1982-85; mem. Mo. Right-to-Life, 1977—; community adv. bd. St. Elizabeth Hosp., 1985-86; Birthright of Hannibal, Inc., 1980—, Holy Family Sch. Bd., 1990-95. Recipient acad. scholarship St. Louis U., 1970-74, recognition for Significant Contribution to Bush Administrn., Dept. Interior, 1993. Mem. ATLA, Mo. Assn. Trial Lawyers., Mark Twain Astron. Soc. (co-founder). Roman Catholic. Home: 601 Country Club Dr Hannibal MO 63401-3033 Office: Ely Cary Welch and Hickman 1000 Center St Hannibal MO 63401-3449

WELCH, PATRICK DANIEL, state senator; b. Chgo., Dec. 12, 1948; s. William C. and Alice W. Student, So. Ill. U., 1970; JD, Chgo. Kent Coll. Law, 1974. Bar: Ill. 1974. Pvt. practice, Peru, Ill., 1974—; mem. Ill. Senate, 1983—; asst. minority leader, 1993—; former chmn. energy and environ. comm.; nat. Del., mem. credentials com. Dem. Nat. Conv., 1976, del., 1980, 84, 88, 92; precinct committeeman Peru Dem. Party, 1976-86; del. Dem. Nat. Mid-Term Conf., 1978, 82; committeeman Ill. Dem. Cen. Com., 1978—, mem. exec. com., 1983—; mem. Peru Citizens' Svc. Orgn.; vice-chmn. Ill. Dem. Party, 1990-94, chmn. party platform com., 1994. Recipient Disting. Svc. award Ill. Bicentennial Commn., 1976. Mem. Ill. Bar Assn., La Salle County Bar Assn. Office: State Senate State Capitol Springfield IL 62706

WELCH, PATRICK JAMES, economics educator, author, consultant; b. Chgo., Feb. 8, 1944; s. Lourde John and Regina Frances W.; m. Geraldine Frances Nasiatka, Apr. 15, 1968. BSBA, Marquette U., 1966, MA in Econs., 1968; PhD in Econs., U. Pitts., 1974. Instr. econs. St. Ambrose Coll., Davenport, Iowa, 1968-70; asst. prof. St. Louis U., 1974-78, assoc. prof., 1978-83, prof., 1983—, prof. sch. pub. health, 1985—, prof. pub. policy studies, 1987—; vis. economist Fed. Res. Bank St. Louis, 1982; spl. asst. dir. strategic planning Ralston Purina Agri-Prod Group, St. Louis, 1983; cons. competitive analysis Monsanto Co., St. Louis, 1984-86; cons. antitrust and competitive analysis various clients, 1988—. Co-author: Economics: Theory and Practice, 1982, rev. 5th edit., 1995; editor: Forum for Social Economics, 1995—; contbr. articles to profl. jours. chpts. in books. Mem. Human Rights Commn., Archdiocese of St. Louis, 1992—. Grantee NSF, 1973. Mem. Nat. Assn. Bus. Economists (pres. St. Louis chpt. 1992-93), Assn. Social Econs. (bd. dirs. 1989-91). Home: 320 S Gray Ave Saint Louis MO 63119-3608 Office: St Louis U Dept Econs 3674 Lindell Blvd Saint Louis MO 63108-3302

WELCH, ROBERT DINWIDDIE, retired school administrator; b. Chgo., July 19, 1925; s. Ira Hubert Reginald and Ella Sarah (Dinwiddie) W.; m. June 18, 1955; children: Robert Dean, Richard Allen. BA summa cum laude, Dartmouth Coll., Hanover, N.H., 1948; MA in English Lit., U. Chgo., 1952; postgrad., New Sch. Social Rsch., N.Y.C., 1948-52, Wayne State U., Detroit, 1952-60. Lic. tchr., adminstr., Mich. Instr. St. Paul's Sch., Garden City, N.Y., 1948-52; instr. English/social studies Pierce Jr. H.S., Grosse Pointe, Mich., 1952-59; instr. English Grosse Pointe H.S. South, 1959-62, libr. coord., 1962-64, asst. prin. curriculum, 1964-68; asst. prin. curriculum Grosse Point H.S. North, 1968-75; dir. curriculum Grosse Point Pub. Schs., 1975-92; ret.; part-time master tchr. English Harvard U., Cambridge, Mass., summers 1958-66; part-time English instr., supr. Wayne County C.C., Detroit, 1970-80; evaluator, writer North Ctrl. Assn., Detroit area, 1975-85; dir. Dept. Secondary Curriculum, Grosse Pointe Pub. Schs., 1980-92. Book reviewer Libr. Jour., 1972-83; author (curriculum books) in reading, composition, literature, grammar, 1965. Adv. bd. Grosse Point Found. Acad. Enrichment, 1983-90; chmn. social responsibilities com. Grosse Pointe Unitarian Ch., 1965, mem. bldg. com., 1960; chmn. of recorders ct. study Detroit Riots Com., 1966; advisor, spkr. Native Am. Program, East Detroit, 1978-83. Lt. (j.g.) USNR, 1942-46. Mem. Detroit Inst. Arts, Nat. Coun. Tchrs. English, U.S. Naval Res. Assn., Greenfield Village/Henry Ford Mus., Phi Beta Kappa, Phi Delta Kappa. Democrat. Home: 23313 Greencrest Dr Saint Clair Shores MI 48080

WELDON, THEODORE TEFFT, JR., retail company executive; b. Evanston, Ill., July 19, 1932; s. Theodore Tefft and Dorothe Galbraith (Stover) W.; m. Barbara Ann Eskilson, Aug. 17, 1957; children: Lisa Courtney Weldon LeFevre, Theodore Tefft III, Margaret Helen. BA, Dartmouth Coll., 1954. Retail store salesman Sears Roebuck & Co., Gary, Ind., 1954-58; retail store mgr. Sears Roebuck & Co., Kankakee, Ill., 1958-62; sales mgr. Craftsman Sears Roebuck & Co., Chgo., 1962-69, advt. mgr. Craftsman, 1969-70, mktg. mgr. tires, 1970-81, sr. buyer sporting goods, 1981-82, nat. gen. catalog mgr., 1982-86; dir. home TV shopping Sears/QVC, Chgo., 1986-92; cons. Drake, Beam, Morin, Inc., Chgo., 1992-94, Focus Media, Inc., L.A., 1993—, Std. Mktg. Corp., Naperville, Ill., 1993—, King World Direct, L.A., 1993—. Mem. Jr. Achievemnt, Chgo., 1966-68; rep. Winnetka (Ill.) Village Caucus, 1972-74; advisor Children's Theatre of Winnetka, 1972—; pres. Sunset Improvement Assn., Winnetka, 1975—. Home: 426 Sunset Rd Winnetka IL 60093-4232

WELDON-LINNE, C. MICHAEL, pathologist, microbiologist; b. Danville, Ill., Dec. 25, 1953; s. Curtis Lane and A. Charline Linne; m. Madeleine Marie Weldon, Dec. 27, 1976; children: Aleksandra Patrice, Mariel Charline, Alyssa Faith. BS, Northwestern U., 1977, MD, 1978. Diplomate Am. Bd. Pathology, Am. Bd. Med. Examiners. Resident in pathology Evanston (Ill.) Hosp.-Northwestern McGaw Med. Ctr., 1978-81, chief resident in pathology, 1981-82; staff pathologist, dir. microbiology and virology Ill. Masonic Med. Ctr., Chgo., 1982—, assoc. chmn., chief divsn. clin. pathology, 1994—; clin. asst. prof. U. Ill., Chgo., 1984—; mem. faculty Nat. Ctr. Advanced Med. Edn., Chgo., 1983—. Contbr. chpts. to books, articles to profl. jours. Fellow Am. Soc. Clin. Pathologists, Coll. Am. Pathologists, Am. Soc. Microbiology, Inst. Medicine Chgo.; mem. AMA, Ill. Soc. Pathologists (sec., treas., bd. dirs. 1986-92), Alpha Omega Alpha. Roman Catholic. Office: Ill Masonic Med Ctr 836 W Wellington Ave Chicago IL 60657-5147

WELGE, DONALD EDWARD, food manufacturing executive; b. St. Louis, July 11, 1935; s. William H. and Rudelle (Fritze) W.; m. Mary Alice Childers, Aug. 4, 1962; children: Robert, Tom. B.S., La. State U., 1957. With Gilster-Mary Lee Corp., Chester, Ill., 1957—, pres., gen. mgr., 1965—; dir. Buena Vista Bank of Chester; pres. Buena Vista Bankcorp. Former chmn. St. John's Luth. Bd. Edn. 1st lt. Transp. Corp, U.S. Army, 1958-63. Named So. Ill. Bus. Leader of Yr. So. Ill. U., 1988. Mem. Perryville C. of C. (pres. 1989), Chester, Ill. C. of C. (past pres.), Alpha Zeta, Phi Kappa Phi. Republican. Lutheran. Home: 5 Knollwood Dr Chester IL 62233-1416 Office: Gilster Mary Lee Co 1037 State St Chester IL 62233-1657

WELKE, ROBERT A., state official. Dir. Transp. Dept., Lansing, Mich. Office: Transp Dept Box 30050 Lansing MI 48909*

WELLER, CHARLES DAVID, lawyer; b. Hartford, Conn., Oct. 19, 1944; s. Harry Deets and Betty Jane (Allenbaugh) W. BA, Yale U., 1966; JD, Case Western Res. U., 1973. Bar: Ohio 1973, U.S. Dist. Ct. (so. dist.) Ohio 1974, U.S. Dist. Ct. (no. dist.) Ohio 1976, U.S. Ct. Appeals (6th cir.) 1987, U.S. Ct. Appeals (4th cir.) 1994, U.S. Supreme Ct. 1978. Math tchr. U.S. Peace Corps, Johore Bahru, Malaysia, 1966-68; spl. asst. U.S. Peace Corps, Washington, 1969; dep. dir. so. region U.S. Peace Corps, Atlanta, 1969-70; asst. atty. gen. antitrust sect. Ohio Atty.'s Gen. Office, Columbus and Cleve., Ohio, 1973-82; of counsel Jones, Day, Reavis & Pogue, Cleve., 1982-94; ptnr. Baker & Hostetler, Cleve., 1994—; trustee Health Action Coun., Cleve., 1982-95, Health Sys. Agy. of North, 1983-92, Cleve. Health Edn. Mus., 1991—. Mem. ABA (antitrust sect. and forum com. on health law). Home: 12521 Lake Shore Blvd Cleveland OH 44108-1134 Office: Baker and Hostetler 3200 National City Ctr Cleveland OH 44114

WELLER, CHARLES WESTON, insurance executive; b. New Brunswick, N.J., Mar. 24, 1948; s. Fredrick Charles and Janet Evelyn (Pack) W.; m. Carol Joyce, May 28, 1971; children: Nathanael Weston, Sarah Elizabeth. BA, Thiel Coll., 1970; Masters, Moody Bible Inst., 1989; ThD, Fla. Theol. Sem., 1995. Ins. agt. Multi-Line Cos., 1972-77; pres. Multi-Line Cos., St. Joseph, Mo., 1977-89; life mktg. specialist Farmers Ins. Group Regional Office, Columbus, Ohio, 1994—; v.p. regional Fla. Theol. Sem., Orlando, 1994—; dist. mgr. Modern Woodmen of Am., St. Joseph, 1987-94. Editor Restoration Ministries, 1972-94. Pres. Not I But Christ, Hilliard, Ohio. Fellow Fraternal Inc. Counselors; mem. Nat. Assn. Life Underwriters. Home and Office: PO Box 532 Hilliard OH 43026-0532

WELLES, GEORGE WILLIAM, III, electronic imaging specialist; b. Duluth, Minn., July 9, 1940; s. George William Jr. and Leslie Elizabeth (Griggs) W.; m. Maren Keith Kinney, July 27, 1963. Student, Macalester Coll., 1958-60, U. Minn., Duluth, 1961-63; BA in Journalism, U. Minn., Mpls., 1972. News photographer Sta. KDAL-TV, Duluth, 1962-63; news, documentary photographer Hubbard Broadcasting, St. Paul, 1963-74; mgr. audio visual and employee info. Northwestern Bell (name changed to U.S. West Comm.), Mpls., 1974-87, mgr. broadband applications COMPASS, 1987—; instr. electronic imaging Winona Internat. Sch. Profl. Photography, Jerusalem and Arles, France, 1992, Singapore and Dublin, Ireland, 1995; keynote spkr. ACUTA Nat. Conf., San Francisco, 1992; seminar leader USAF Acad., 1994-95. Dir., editor (film) Who's Responsible (award of Merit Chgo. Internat. Film and Video Festival, 1984); co-dir., spl. effects (video) Escape from Ubadistan, 1985 (Silver Screen award U.S. Indsl. Film Festival, 1986, Best Interactive Video of 1986 Videotape Prodn. Assn.), producer, dir. (video) Techno-Shock! (Gold medal Internat. Film and Video Festival N.Y., 1986, Gold Hugo INTERCOM '86 Chgo. Film Fest., 1986). Mem. Mpls. Found. Itasca Conf., 1980-94. With U.S. Air N.G., 1960-66. Recipient Silver award of achievement Internat. Teleconferencing Assn., 1986. Mem. Comm. Media Mgmt. Assn. (pres. 1983-85). Congregationalist. Office: US WEST Comm 200 S 5th St Ste 1500 Minneapolis MN 55402-4200

WELLINGTON, ROBERT HALL, manufacturing company executive; b. Atlanta, July 4, 1922; s. Robert H. and Ernestine V. (Vossbrinck) W.; m. Marjorie Jarchow, Nov. 15, 1947; children: Charles R., Robert H., Christian J., Jeanne L. BS, McCormack Sch. of Engring. and Applied Scis. (formerly Northwestern Tech. Inst.), 1944; MSBA, MBA, U. Chgo., 1958. With Griffin Wheel Co., 1946-61; v.p. parent co. Amsted Industries, Inc., Chgo., 1961-74, exec. v.p., 1974-80, pres., chief exec. officer, 1981-88, chmn. bd., chief exec. officer, 1988-90; bd. dirs. Prudential Money Market Assets, Prudential Intermediate Income Fund, Inc. Served to lt. USN, 1943-46. Mem. Chgo. Athletic Club, Mid-Am. Club. Office: Amsted Industries Inc 205 N Michigan Ave Fl 44 Chicago IL 60601-5925

WELLIVER, ROSE M., healthcare information company executive; b. Owosso, Mich., June 25, 1958; d. Bernard George and Mary Lou (Oates) Odette; m. David Elden Welliver, Dec. 22, 1979; children: David R., Brian, Kaitlin. BS in packaging engring., Mich. State U., E. Lansing, 1980. Packaging engr. IBM, Rochester, Minn., 1980-81, Tucson, 1981-83; acctg. systems engr. IBM, Grand Rapids, Mich., 1983-85; adv. systems engr. IBM, Traverse City, Mich., 1985-93; pres. BlueWare, Cadillac, Mich., 1993—; adv. bd. mem. Northwestern Mich. Coll., Cadillac, 1990-93. V.p. PTO, Cadillac, 1992; program mgr. COMMON, 1993—. Mem. Healthcare Info. & Mgmt. Systems Soc., Cadillac C. of C. Roman Catholic. Office: BlueWare 601A 13th St PO Box 329 Cadillac MI 49601

WELLIVER, WARREN DEE, lawyer, retired state supreme court justice; b. Butler, Mo., Feb. 24, 1920; s. Carl Winfield and Burdee Marie (Wolfe) W.; m. Ruth Rose Galey, Dec. 25, 1942; children: Gale Dee (Mrs. William B. Stone), Carla Camile (Mrs. Dayton Stone), Christy Marie. BA, U. Mo., 1945; JD, U. Mo., 1948. Bar: Mo. 1948. Asst. pros. atty. Boone County, Columbia, 1948-54; sr. ptnr. Welliver, Atkinson and Eng, Columbia, 1960-79; tchr. law Law Sch. U. Mo., 1948-49; mem. Mo. Senate, 1977-79; justice Supreme Ct. Mo., Jefferson City, 1979-89; mem. Gov. Mo. Adv. Coun. Alcoholism and Drug Abuse, chmn. drug coun., 1970-72; chmn. Task Force Revision Mo. Drug Laws, 1970-71; liaison mem. coun. Nat. Inst. Alcoholism and Alcohol Abuse, 1973-76; mem. Cen. Regional Adv. Coun. Comprehensive Psychiat. Svcs., 1990-92. Bd. dirs. Nat. Assn. Mental Health, 1970-76, regional v.p., 1973-76; pres. Mo. Assn. Mental Health, 1968-69, Stephens Coll. Assocs., 1965-79; pres. Friends of Libr., U. Mo., 1976, bd. dirs., 1979-92; chmn. Dem. Com., 1954-64; hon. fellow Harry S. Truman Libr. Inst., 1979—; bd. dirs. Supreme Ct. Hist. Soc., 1982—; vice chair adv. bd. U. Mo. Multiple Sclerosis Inst., 1992—; bd. curators Stephen's Coll., 1980-92. With USNR, 1941-45. Recipient Disting. Alumni medal and award U. Mo., 1994. Fellow Am. Coll. Trial Lawyers, Am. Bar Found.; mem. ABA, Mo. Bar Assn. (pres. 1967-68), Boone County Bar Assn. (pres. 1970), Am. Judicature Soc., Am. Legion (past post comdr.), Multiple Sclerosis Soc. (Gateway chpt. bd. dirs. 1986-92), Order of Coif, Country Club of Mo., Columbia Country Club (past pres.). Home: 3430 Woodrail Ter Columbia MO 65203-0926

WELLMAN, BILLY LEE, pastor; b. Kenova, W.Va., Sept. 23, 1950; s. Eddie J. and Irene (Osborne) W.; m. Emily Catheryn Sprott, Mar. 3, 1973; children: Christy Lee, Vicky Lee, Allison Lee. Student, Ashland (Ky.) C.C., 1970-71; BS in History & Religion, Belmont Bapt. Coll., 1973; MDiv, So. Bapt. Theol. Sem., 1976. Pastor Westford Bapt. Ch., Madison, Ind., 1974-76, Grace Bapt. Chapel, Flatwoods, Ky., 1976-80, Burlington Bapt. Ch., South Point, Ohio, 1980-84, First Bapt. Ch., Athens, Ohio, 1984—; chaplain USAFR, Denver, 1986—; state exec. bd. State Conv. Bapt., Columbus, Ohio, 1988-91, trustee Bapt. Found., 1994—; regional coord. Sunday Sch. State Conv. Bapt., Columbus, 1994—. Contbr. articles to profl. jours. Pres. PTO, Burlington, Ohio, 1980-82; mem. Band Boosters, Athens, 1988-93. Mem. Res. Officers Assn., Scioto Valley Bapt. Assn. (dir. seminary ext., moderator 1985-87, Honor award for 10 yrs. faithful svc. 1990). Home: 37 Euclid Dr Athens OH 45701 Office: First Bapt Ch 336 E State St Athens OH 45701

WELLMAN, GERALD EDWIN, JR., safety and fire inspector; b. Steubenville, Ohio, Feb. 27, 1948; s. Gerald Edwin Sr. and Rose Marie (Bonacci) W.; 1 child, Jerad Anthony. AS Data Processing, West Liberty State Coll., 1974, BSBA, 1974; MS in Safety Mgmt., W.Va. U., 1991, cert. of advanced study, 1995. With production, mechanical Wheeling and Pitts. Steel Corp., Beech Bottom, W.Va., 1966-76; with production, mechanical, safety Wheeling and Pitts. Steel Corp., Steubenville, Ohio, 1976—, also safety and fire insp., safety coord.;, 1993, 95; mem. wellness com. Wheeling and Pitts. Steel Plant; safety coord. Wheeling and Pitts. Steel Corp. Hazardous Material Team; safety chmn., trustee local 1190 United Steel Workers Am.; mem. Am. Iron and Steel Inst. R.R. Com. Contbr. articles to profl. jours. With U.S. Army, 1967-69, Vietnam. Mem. Am. Iron and Steel Inst. (railroad com.), West Liberty State Coll. Alumni Club, West Liberty State Coll Hilltops Club, W.Va. U. Alumni Club, Mountaineer Athletic Club, Dapper Dan Club Upper Ohio Valley, Brooke High Sch. Boosters Club, W.Va. Sheriffs Assn., Follansbee Blue Waves Boosters Club, Nat. Fire Protection Assn., Nat. Safety Coun., W.Va. Safety Coun., Western Pa. Safety Coun., U.S. Steel Workers Am., Eagles Club, Am. Soc. Safety Engrs. (nominating com. 1989—), Alpha Kappa Psi. Home: 311 Hillcrest Dr Wellsburg WV 26070-1943

WELLNITZ, CRAIG OTTO, lawyer, English language educator; b. Elwood, Ind., Dec. 5, 1946; s. Frank Otto and Jeanne (Albright) W.; m. Karen Sue Thomas, Apr. 13, 1974 (div. Sept. 1987); children: Jennifer Suzanne, Anne Katherine; m. Carol L. Hinesley, Jan. 23, 1988. BA, Purdue U., 1969; MA, Ind. U., 1972; JD, Ind. U.-Indpls., 1978. Bar: Ind. 1978, U.S. Dist. Ct. (so. dist.) Ind. 1978, U.S. Supreme Ct. 1983, U.S. Ct. Appeals (7th and Fed. cirs.) 1984, U.S. Dist. Ct. (no. dist.) 1990. Instr. Danville Jr. Coll., Ill., 1972-74, S.W. Mo. State U., Springfield, Mo., 1974-75; ptnr. Coates, Hatfield, Calkins & Wellnitz, Indpls., 1978—; pub. defender criminal div. Marion Superior Ct., Marion County, 1979-88, master commr. criminal div., 1988—; instr. U. Indpls., 1981-82; mem. adj. faculty dept. English Butler U., Indpls., 1982—; instr. English Ind. U.-Purdue U., Indpls., 1987-90; pres. Ind. Account Mgmt., Inspls., 1985-94; v.p. Carol Craig Assocs., Indpls., 1987—; lectr. in field. Columnist A Jury of Your Peers, 1984-86. Vice committeeman Indpls. Rep. precinct, 1978; chmn. fin. com. St. Luke's United Meth. Ch., 1985-87; sponsor Christian Children's Fund, 1990—; active Am. Mus. Nat. History, Indpls. Zoo, Children's Mus. Indpls. Post-grad. study grantee S.W. Mo. State U., Springfield, 1975. Mem. ABA, AAUP, MLA, ATLA, Nat. Lawyers Assn., Nat. Assn. Retail Collection Attys., Am. Collectors Assn., Ind. Bar Assn., Ind. Trial Lawyers Assn., Indpls. Bar Assn., Nat. Coun. Tchrs. English, Smithsonian Assocs., Libr. Congress Assocs., Internat. Platform Assn., Nat. Spkrs. Assn., Spkrs. U.S.A., Internat. Spkrs. Network, Broad Ripple Village Assn., Columbia Club, Rivera Club Indpls., Elks. Home: 6248 N Meridian St Indianapolis IN 46260-4226 Office: 1 Indiana Sq Ste 2335 Indianapolis IN 46204-2004

WELLS, BYRON KEITH, sales executive; b. Indpls., Dec. 18, 1948; s. Kenneth Warren and Lettie Rose (Goebbel) W.; m. Pepper Lynn Herron, Oct. 21, 1972. BA, Purdue U. Regional sales mgr. Burroughs/Unisys, Rochester, N.Y., 1973-86; nat. retail sales mgr. ITEK Graphic Corp., Rochester, 1986-89; v.p. ops. Time Tech. Svcs., Ft. Wayne, 1990; nat. sales mgr. Arvey Paper/Internat. Paper, Chgo., 1990—; cons. Rochester (N.Y.) Travel Network Assn., 1984-86. Author: (sales tng. seminar book) Professional Development Seminar, 1985, 94 (Mktg. Excellence award 1994). With U.S. Army N.G., 1971-77. Home: 2960 Roslyn Ln Buffalo Grove IL 60089 Office: Arvey Paper/Resource Net Divsn Internat Paper 3351 W Addison Chicago IL 60618

WELLS, CAROLYN CRESSY, social work educator; b. Boston, July 26, 1943; d. Harris Shipman Wells and Marianne Elizabeth (Monroe) Glazier; m. Dale Reed Konle, Oct. 11, 1970 (div. Sept. 3, 1982); m. Dennis Alan Loefler, Sept. 29, 1990. BA, U. Calif., Berkeley, 1965; MSW, U. Wis., 1968, PhD, 1973. Cert. ind. clin. social worker, marriage and family therapist. Vol. VISTA, Espanola, N.Mex., 1965-66; social worker Project Six Cen. Wis. Colony, Madison, 1968, Milw. Dept. Pub. Welfare, 1969, Shorewood (Wis.) Manor Nursing Home, 1972; sch. social worker Jefferson (Wis.) County Spl. Edn., 1977-78; lectr. sociology and social work Marquette U., Milw., 1972-73, dir. social work program, 1973-90, 93—, assoc. prof. social work, 1981-94, prof. social work, 1994—; social work therapist Lighthouse Counseling Assocs., Racine, Wis., 1989-91, The Cambridge Group, 1991-92; Achievement Assocs., 1992-95; vis. lectr. social work U. Canterbury, Christchurch, N.Z., 1983. Author: Social Work Day to Day, 1982, rev. edit., 1988, Social Work Ethics Day to Day, 1986; co-author: The Social Work Experience, 1991, rev. edit., 1996. Mem. Wis. Coun. on Social Work Edn., pres., 1980-82, sec., 1985-87, mem. exec. com., 1993—. Mem. NASW, Am. Assn. Profl. Hypnotherapists, Coun. on Social Work Edn. (mem. publs. and media com. 1989-91, site visitor for accreditation 1987—), Acad. Cert. Social Workers, Assn. Baccalaureate Program Dirs. Democrat. Home: 4173 Sleeping Dragon Rd West Bend WI 53095-9296 Office: Marquette U Social Work Program 526 N 14th St Milwaukee WI 53233-2211

WELLS, CHARLENA RENEE, editor, writer; b. Cleve., Oct. 2, 1964. BA in Comm., Cleve. State U., 1988. Libr. asst./typist John Carroll U., University Heights, Ohio, summer 1982; asst. sociology dept., registration asst. Cleve. State U., 1985-88; project asst. Jones, Day, Reavis & Pogue, Cleve., 1988-94; asst. writer Righteousness Newsletter, Cleve., 1990—; editor-in-chief, writer Holiness Inc., Cleve., 1993—; project asst. Jones, Day, Reavis & Pogue, 1988-94; adminstrv. exec. USA Mobile Comms., 1994; law clk. Pioneer Stds. Electronics Inc., 1994; mktg. rep. APT Publs., 1996—; adminstrv./registration asst. MBA degree program Case Western Res. U., Cleve., 1996—; radio asst. Sta. WABQ, Cleve., spring 1987. Nursing asst. St. Vincent Charity Hosp., Cleve., 1987; co-hostess Sta. WCIN, Cin., 1991; guest speaker AME Zion Ch., Cleve., 1993, Assembly Missionary Bapt. Ch., Cleve., 1994; facilitator/exhibit guide Cleve. Children's Mus., summer 1986. Acad. scholar John Carroll U., 1982. Office: Case Western Res U Enterprise Hall # 310 10900 Euclid Ave Cleveland OH 44106-7235

WELLS, JONATHAN, state legislator; m. Justina Wells. Kans. state rep. Dist. 84, 1993—. Address: 830 N Madison Wichita KS 67214*

WELLS, MELANIE GAIL, pediatric physical therapist, educator; b. South Bend, Ind., Feb. 11, 1966; d. Leslie Edwin and Elizabeth June (Sanford) W. BS in Phys. Therapy, U. Evansville, 1988; MS in Phys. Therapy, U. Indpls., 1993. Phys. therapist Frazier Rehab. Ctr., Louisville, 1988-89; dir. phys. therapy ROD Spl. Edn. Coop., Sunman, Ind., 1989-93; phys. therapist Clermont County MR/DD, Owensville, Ohio, 1993-95; pvt. practice Wells Pediatric Alternative Phys. Therapy, Cin., 1994—; coord. S.W. Dist. Pediatric Study Group, Cin., 1994—; adj. faculty U. Cin., 1995—. Mem. Columbia-Tusculum Neighborhood Assn., Cin., 1994—, Updowntowners, Cin., 1995—. Mem. Am. Phys. Therapy Assn., Cin. Sport and Social Club; charter mem. Am. Bus. Clubs. Home and Office: Wells Ped Alt Phys Therapy 3607 Morris Pl Cincinnati OH 45226

WELLS, RANDY LEE, policy analyst; b. Ife, Nigeria, July 29, 1961; s. Delbert Lee and Beverly Ceclia (Helms-Goode) W.; m. Ann Swords Freeman, June 22, 1991; children: Ashley, Alexis. AAS, Colby C.C., 1990; BA, Sangamon State U., 1993. Legis. asst. ACLU, Springfield, Ill., 1993-94; sr. policy analyst Ill. Assistive Tech. Project, Springfield, 1994—; steering com. ACLU, 1994—. Mem. Ill. Rehab. Assn. (bd. dirs. cen. chpt. 1995—, chair legis. com. 1994—), Phi Sigma Alpha. Office: Ill Assistive Tech Project Ste 100 528 South Fifth Springfield IL 62701

WELLSTONE, PAUL, senator; b. Washington, July 21, 1944; s. Leon and Minnie W.; m. Sheila Wellstone, 1963; children: David, Marcia, Mark. BA, U. N.C., 1965, PhD Polit. Sci., 1969. Tchr. Carleton Coll., Minn.; U.S. senator from Minn., 1991—, mem. coms. on small bus., energy and natural resources, Indian affairs, labor and human resources, sen. dem. policy com., chmn. subcom. rural economy and family farming. Author: How the Rural Poor Got Power, Powerline. Dir. Minn. Community Energy Program. Office: US Senate 717 Hart Senate Office Bldg Washington DC 20510*

WELSH, JOHN ROBERT, musician; b. Seward, Nebr., Oct. 27, 1924; s. Frank Harrison and Ethel Mae (Steele) W.; children: Maxine, Fred, John, Richard. MMus, Cin. Conservatory of Music, 1946. Ptnr. Welsh, Hamilton & Ford, Deerfield, Ill., 1954-58; owner Hampshire House Gallery, Muskegon, Mich., 1976-89; ret., 1989; ednl. clinician Orff-Kodaly, 1975—. Author: Making Music at the Keyboard, 1979. Dir. Port City Playhouse, Muskegon, 1979-83. With U.S. Army, 1941-42. Democrat. Episcopalian. Home: 487 W Webster Ave Muskegon MI 49440-1047

WELSHIMER, GWEN R., state legislator, real estate broker, appraiser, tax consultant; b. Poughkeepsie, N.Y., Nov. 5, 1935; d. Freanor Ralph and Beulah M. (Reedy) Grant; m. Billy L. Blake (div. 1979); children: Donald E., Jerry A.; m. Robert E. Welshimer. Student, Kans. State U., 1953-54; cert., Jones Real Estate Coll., Colorado Springs, Colo., 1975. Cert. real estate appraiser, 1993. Exec. sec. Coll. Bd. Trustees, Bellevue, Wash., 1967-69; exec. sec. to chmn. bd. dirs. Garvey Industries, Wichita, Kans., 1969-73, adminstrv. asst. pers. and pub. affairs, 1969-73; copywriter Walter Drake & Sons, Colorado Springs, 1973-75; real estate agt. UTE Realty, Colorado Springs, 1975-76; newspaper pub., owner Black Forrest News, Colorado Springs, 1976-79; real estate broker, appraiser Gwen Welshimer Real Estate, Wichita, 1979—; coord. Epic Real Estate Sch., Wichita, 1988—; legislator Kans. Ho. of Reps., Topeka, 1990—; mem. taxation com., mem. banking and ins. com. Kans. Ho. or Reps., Topeka, 1991-96; minority leader local govt. and joint com. adminstrv. rules regulations Kans. Ho. of Reps., Topeka, 1994-96. Dem. precinct committeewomen, Wichita; bd. dirs. United Meth. Urban Ministries, Wichita, 1990—. Mem. NOW, Nat. Women's Polit. Caucus, Nat. Order Women Legislators (state dir. 1994-96), Nat. Conf. State Legislators (Kans. mem. Art and Tourism Ctr.). Democrat. Methodist. Home: 6103 Castle Dr Wichita KS 67218-3601 Office: Kans Ho of Reps State Capitol Topeka KS 66612

WEMPE, ERIC T., design engineer; b. Kansas City, Kans., Aug. 7, 1962. BS in Drafting Tech., Ctrl. Mo. State U., 1985. Sr. engr./product engr. HES Internat., Inc., Kansas City, 1986—. Capt., Volleyball team, Kansas City, Mo. Roman Catholic. Office: HES Internat Inc 1851 Merriam Ln Kansas City KS 66106-4713

WEMPE, JACK, state legislator; b. Aug. 23, 1934; m. Vicky Wempe. BS, Rockhurst; MA, U. Kans. Kans. state rep. Dist. 113; dir. Econ. Devel. Address: PO Box 187 895 Main Little River KS 67457*

WENDELL, BARBARA TAYLOR, retired real estate agent; b. Ames, Iowa, Jan. 30, 1920; d. Harvey Nelson and Ruby (Britten) Taylor; m. Donald Thomas Davidson Sr., May 22, 1942 (dec. Oct. 1962); children: Donald Thomas Jr., John Taylor, Ann Elizabeth Davidson Costanzo; m. Connell S. Wendell, Oct. 10, 1992 (dec. Sept. 1995). BS in Home Econs. Sci., Iowa State U., 1943. Assoc. tchr. Ames (Iowa) Pub. Schs., 1970-73; retail mgr. Gen. Nutrition Ctr., Ames, 1974-77; sales assoc. Century 21 Real Estate, Ames, 1978-82, Friedrich Realty, Ames, 1982-89. Pres. Ames City PTA Coun., 1950; leader, advisor Boy Scouts Am., Ames, 1952-58; chmn. Campfire Leaders' Assn., Ames, 1959-61; sec. bd. dirs. Campfire Girls, Ames, 1964-66; property com. United Meth. Ch., Ames, 1964-67; vol. Para-Legal Svcs. for Elderly; active Octagon for the Arts, Brunier Gallery, Med. Ctr. Aux., Art Gallery Com. Mem. Nat. Home Econs. in Homemaking (chmn. fgn. student rels. com.), Internat. Orch. Assn., Iowa State U. Meml. Union (life), Iowa State U. Alumni Assn. (life), Ames Community Arts Coun. Republican. Home: 1110 Johnson St Ames IA 50010-4206

WENDELL, DAVID V., historian, public relations consultant; b. Cedar Rapids, Iowa, Mar. 18, 1967; s. Kenneth M. and Marlene J. (Erickson) W. Grad., Linn-Mar Cmty. Schs., 1985. Coord. Louis Sullivan Archtl. Symposium, Cedar Rapids, Iowa, 1986; dir. Garden Ch. Hist. Preservation Project, Marshalltown, Iowa, 1987-89; sr. hist. interpreter Mus. of Prairie Pioneer, Grand Island, Nebr., 1991; tour interpreter Chgo. Motorcoach Co., 1992; historian/archivist Rosehill Cemetery, Chgo., 1993—; dir. Rosehill Cemetery Civil War Mus., Chgo., 1994—; founder, coord. Save Our Station Orgn., Marion, Iowa; hist. cons., bd. advisors Discovery Channel "Death in America", 1996. Author: The Civil War at Rosehill, 1993, Rosehill: Monument to the Past, 1994, Appomattox: End of an Era, 1995. Vol. coord. Congl. Campaign, 2d Dist., Iowa, 1984, 86; site contact Presdl. Campaign, 2d Dist., 1988; chmn. Marion (Iowa) Bicentennial Com., 1987-90. Mem. U.S. Capitol Hist. Soc., Iowa State Hist. Soc., Nebr. State Hist. Soc., Chgo. Conv. and Tourism Bur., Linn County Hist. Assn. (bd. dirs.). Republican. Lutheran. Office: Rosehill Cemetery & Civil War Mus 5800 N Ravenswood Ave Chicago IL 60660

WENDELN, DARLENE DORIS, English language educator; b. Indpls., July 18, 1956; d. Robert Edward and Doris Mae (Brabender) W. BS, U. Indpls., 1978; MS, Ind. U., 1986. Lic. tchr., Ind. Secondary English tchr., coach Centerville (Ind.)-Abington Sch. Corp., 1978—; coach girls' tennis regional and sectional championships. Mem. NEA, Nat. Coun. Tchrs. English, Ind. H.S. Tennis Coaches Assn., U.S. Tennis Assn. Lutheran. Office: Centerville High Sch Willow Grove Rd Centerville IN 47330

WENDT, CHRISTOPHER HAROLD, physicist; b. Mainz, Germany, May 28, 1959; s. Hans Werner and Martha Anne (Linger) Arthur; m. Amy Eileen Fearing, Sept. 1, 1979. BS in Physics, Calif. Inst. Tech., Pasadena, 1981; PhD in Physics, Stanford U., 1988. Asst. scientist U. Wis., Madison, 1988—; cons. Los Alamos (N.Mex.) Nat. Lab., 1993—. Contbr. articles to profl. jours. NSF fellow, 1981. Home: 31 Bagley Ct Madison WI 53705

WENDT, ELIZABETH WARCZAK, retired insurance company executive; b. Chgo., Aug. 27, 1931; d. John George and Elizabeth Marion (Jankowski) Warczak; m. John Edward Wendt, Oct. 31, 1953 (div.); children: John Alan, Brian Arthur, James Michael. Student Loyola U., Chgo., 1951-52; BSBA, St. Mary-of-the-Woods Coll., 1980; postgrad. Chgo. Kent Coll. Law, 1981-82. Asst. to actuary Globe Life Ins. Co., Chgo., 1970-74; asst. compliance officer Globe Life/Ryan Ins. Group, Chgo., 1974-86; mgr. credit product devel., 1986-96; ret. 1996; mem. FLMI Soc. Chgo., 1983—; co. rep. Consumer Credit Ins. Assn., Chgo., 1983-89; co. rep., mem. Handout Com. Life & Health Compliance Assn., 1979—. Election judge, 1984—. Mem. United Farm Workers Support Com., Chgo. Fellow Life Mgmt. Inst. Democrat. Roman Catholic.

WENDT, HANS W(ERNER), life scientist, educator; b. Berlin, July 25, 1923; s. Hans O. and Alice (Creutzburg) W.; m. Martha A. Linger, Dec. 23, 1956 (div. 1979); children: Alexander, Christopher, Sandra; m. Judith A. Hammer, June 25, 1988. MSc, U. Hamburg, Germany, 1949; PhD in Psychopharmacology, U. Marburg, Germany, 1953. Diplomate in psychology. Rsch. asst. U. Marburg, 1949-53; rsch. assoc. Wesleyan U. and Office Naval Rsch., Middletown, Conn., 1952-53; asst. prof., field dir. internat. project U. Mainz, Germany, 1955-59; engring. psychologist to prin. human factors scientist Link Aviation, Apollo Simulator Systems, Binghamton, N.Y., 1959-61; assoc. to prof. psychology Valparaiso (Ind.) U., 1961-68; prof. psychology Macalester Coll., St. Paul, 1968-93; sr. rsch. fellow Chronobiology Labs. U. Minn., 1980—; prin. investigator Behavioral Geomedicine Collaboration Minn. Br., 1994—; cons. and reviewer, 1961—; hon. prof. sci. U. Marburg, Germany, 1971—; vis. prof. U. Victoria, B.C., Can., U. Marburg, U. Bochum, U. Bielefeld, U. Goettingen, all Germany, 1966-89. Contbr. articles to profl. jours., chpts. to books. Recipient Disting. Sr. Scientist award, Alexander von Humboldt Found., 1976. Mem. Internat. Soc. Biometeorology, Internat. Soc. Chronobiology, Bioelectromagnetics Soc., Soc. Sci. Exploration, Planetary Soc., others. Home: 2180 Lower Saint Dennis Rd Saint Paul MN 55116-2831

WENDT, THOMAS GENE, controller; b. Watertown, Wis., May 14, 1951; s. Walter Harry and Gladys Florence (Munzel) W. BBA, U. Wis., Whitewater, 1973. CPA, Wis. Auditor Coopers & Lybrand, Milw., 1973-75; supr. Conley, McDonald, Sprague & Co., Milw., 1975-80; dir. fin. E. Cen./Select Sires, Waupun, Wis., 1981—, also rec. sec., bd. dirs.; bd. dirs. Moravian Homes Inc., Mueller Apts., Inc., Marquardt Meml. Manor, Inc., Watertown, Wis., 1985—, sec. and treas. bd. dirs., 1986—. Mem. Marquardt Found., 1988—; bd. dirs. Zinsendorf Hall, 1989—, sec., treas., 1989, forward campaign chmn., 1988; pres. bd. trustees Watertown Moravian Ch., 1981-84, bd. elders, 1990-93; adv. del. Western Dist. Synod, Wis., 1982, 86, 90, 96; bd. dirs. Moravian Homes of Sturgeon Bay, 1991—; bd. dirs. Hus Apts., Inc., 1993—, sec., treas., 1993—. Mem. AICPA, Wis. Inst. CPAs, Milw. Art Mus. Office: E Central/Select Sires PO Box 191 Waupun WI 53963-0191

WENINGER, ROBERT KARL, foreign literature educator; b. Hitchin, Eng., Oct. 9, 1954. PhD, U. Frankfurt, Germany, 1982. Lectr. U. Frankfurt, 1982-85; asst. prof. U. Tex., Arlington, 1985-88; asst. prof. Washington U., St. Louis, 1988-92, assoc. prof. German and comparative lit., 1992—. Author: Arno Schmidts Joyce Rezeption, 1982, The Mookse and The Gripes, 1984, Literarische Konventionen, 1994, Arno Schmidt Bibliographie, 1995, Framing a Novelist, 1995. Hamburger Stiftung Rsch. grantee, 1993. Mem. MLA, James Joyce Found., German Studies Assn., Am. Assn. Tchrs. German, Am. Comparative Lit. Assn. Office: Washington Univ Box 1104 One Brookings Dr Saint Louis MO 63130

WENK, DANIEL N., landmark site administrator. Supt. Mt. Rushmore Nat. Meml., Keystone, S.D. Office: Mt Rushmore Nat Meml PO Box 268 Keystone SD 57751-0268

WENK, PHILIP ANDREW, foundation administrator, consultant; b. Cleve., May 19, 1963; s. Philip S. and Joan (Paciotti) W.; m. Amy M. Rowen (div. Dec. 1992); 1 child, Lindsay (dec.); m. Marsha Ann Gulas, Mar. 18, 1995. BSBA, Xavier Univ., 1984, MBA, 1985; interventionalist (hon.), Johnson Inst., Mpls., 1993; postgrad., Cleve. State U., 1995. Sales rep. Blue Cross/Shield of Ohio, Cleve., 1985-86; v.p. mktg., cmty. rels. Creative Playrooms Inc., Solon, Ohio, 1986-89; co-founder O.H.I.O. Found., Cleve., 1987-93, also bd. dirs.; dir. cmty. rels. E.J. DeBartolo Corp., Youngstown, Ohio, 1989-91; exec. v.p. K.J. Majcen & Assoc., Cleve., 1991-93; co-founder, CEO Lindsay Rowen Wenk Found., Cleve., 1993—, also bd. dirs.; preferred cons. HUD, Washington, 1992—; com. mem. various city task forces, Cleve. Author: 14 Ways to Buy a Business, 1985. Campaign coord., speechwriter, scheduler various polit. candidates/lobbying initiatives, 1980-94, activity coord., vol. numerous agys., 1987-93. Recipient Point of Light award Pres. Bush, 1992, Citation, Pres. Clinton, 1994, Hometown Hero award, 1994; named Entrepreneur of Yr. Nat. Assn. Entrepreneurs, 1985. Republican. Home and Office: 13944 Cedar Rd # 284 University Heights OH 44118

WENNLUND, LARRY, state legislator; b. DeKalb, Ill., Oct. 31, 1941; s. Donald F. and Gertrude Wennlund; m. Shirley Ann Major, 1963; children: Jayna, Donald Cass, Joelle, Kara. BA, U. Ill., 1964; JD, John Marshall Law Sch., 1968. Ill. state rep. Dist. 38, 1987—; mem. transp. and motor vehicles, jud. I, jud. II Ill. Ho. Reps., registration and regulation, labor and commerce coms., elections com., spl. com., conflicts of interest, asst. fl. leader, mem. joint com. on adminstrv. rules, asst. majority leader; pvt. practice law. Named Legislator of Yr. Ill. State Attys. Assn., 1988, Ill. Environ. Coun., 1987-89, Ill. Hosp. Assn., 1988, Friend of Agrl. award Agrl. Assn. Activator, 1988, 89; recipient Legislative award Ill. Assn. of Ophthalmology, 1989, Legislative Leadership award Ill. Assn. Recyclers. Mem. Lenox Lions Club, New Lenox C. of C., Mokena C. of C., Frankfort C. of C. Home: Regan Rd New Lenox IL 60451*

WENTE, PATRICIA ANN, radio executive; 1 child, Jessica. BA in Communications, Sangamon State U., 1978, MA in Communications, 1981. Vol. coord. Sta. WSSR-FM, Springfield, Ill., 1977-79; sta. mgr. Stas. WRRS, KMUW, Wichita, Kans., 1979-85; gen. mgr. Sta. KGOU, Norman, Okla., 1985-87; mgr. sta. grant programs Corp. for Pub. Broadcasting, Washington, 1987-89; dir., gen. mgr. Sta. KWMU-FM, St. Louis, 1989—; participant NPR Pub. Radio Conf., 1979-90, Pub. Broadcasting Svc. Conf., 1987-89, Corp. for Pub. Broadcasting Conf., 1977-80, Rocky Mountain Pub. Radio Meetings, 1987-89, SECA Meetings, 1987-89; bd. dirs. Pub. Radio in Mid-Am. Conf., 1986-88; mem. gerontology faculty Wichita State u., 1983-84; promotion & pub. svc. announcer Sta. KPTS-TV, Wichita, 1979-80; judge coord. Ohio State Awards, 1986-87. Mem. adv. com. for handicapped svcs. Wichita State U., 1980-82. Mem. Pub. Telecommunication Fin. Mgmt. Assn. (bd. dirs. 1990—), Alpha Epsilon Rho (pres. 1979-84, advisor 1990). Office: Sta KWMU-FM Univ Mo-St Louis 8001 Natural Bridge Rd Saint Louis MO 63121-4401

WENTZ, JANET MARIE, state legislator; b. McClusky, N.D., July 21, 1937; d. Charles G. and Martha (Schindler) Neff; m. Thomas Arthur Wentz, 1957; children: Elizabeth, Karin, Thomas. Student, Westmar Coll., 1955-57, U. Minn., 1960-62, Minot State Coll., 1967-70. Registered securities rep.; mem. from dist. 3 N.D. State Ho. of Reps., Bismarck, 1975—, vice chmn., then chmn. appropriations com. Bd. dirs. Ind. Peace Gardens; mem. Commn. on Status of Women in N.D. United Meth. Ch., rep. N.D. Conf. Chs., 1973—; mem. Ct. Svc. Adminstrn. Com.; mem. N.D. Displaced Homemaker Program, Souris Valley Humane Soc. Mem. LWV, PEO, Orgn. Women Legislators, Nat. Assn. Securities Dealers, Minot C. of C. Office: 505 8th Ave SE Minot ND 58701 Office: ND House of Reps Office Of House Mems Bismarck ND 58505*

WENTZ, WENDELL FRANKLIN, columnist, writer; b. Eufaula, Ala., Mar. 24, 1939; s. Hermann Wendell and Johnnie Mae (Jones) W.; m. Corrine Hansel Reeves, July 3, 1965; 1 child, Hermann Wendell II. AB, Mercer U., Macon, Ga., 1961. Pastor Liberty Bapt. Ch., Georgetown, Ga., 1956-57, Mitchell (Ga.) Bapt. Ch., 1957-70, Benton (Ala.) Bapt. Ch., 1970-77, First Bapt. Ch., Lowry City, Mo., 1977-79, Lakeland Bapt. Ch., Clinton, Mo.,

1979-80; with material svcs. Kansas City Power & Light Co., Clinton, 1979—; columnist Clinton Daily Dem., 1989—; freelance writer. Home: 1402 S Main St Ste A Clinton MO 64735-2730 Office: Kansas City Power & Light 400 SW Highway P Clinton MO 64735

WENZ, THOMAS WILLIAM, computer services executive, government administrator; b. May 19, 1944; m. Rosemary F. Voyles, Sept. 23, 1972; children: Christopher Thomas, Katherine Elizabeth. BBA, U. Cin., 1967. Asst. dir. rsch., evaluation and budget City of Cin., 1969-80, asst. dir. econ. devel., 1976-80, dir. rsch., evaluation and budget, 1980-87; county adminstr. Hamilton County, Cin., 1987-91; mgr. computer svcs. Regional Computer Ctr., Cin., 1991—, chmn. control bd., 1989, 90. Contbr. articles to profl. jours. Trustee Cin. Natural History Mus., 1988-91, Drake Meml. Hosp., Cin., 1987-91. Named Pub. Adminstr. of Yr., Am. Soc. Pub. Adminstrn., Cin., 1987, recipient Spl. Recognition, 1990; recipient Mgr. award HUD, Cin., 1983. Mem. Cincinnatus Assn. Home: 7175 Regiment Dr Cincinnati OH 45244 Office: Regional Computer Ctr 138 E Court St Cincinnati OH 45202

WENZEL, ANN MARIE PRICE, women's health nurse; b. Chgo., Nov. 5, 1966; d. John Vincent and Charlene Ann (Staerk) Price; m. James J. Wenzel Jr. Cert. in cardiac exercise tech., Harper Coll., Palatine, Ill., 1989; ADN, Elgin Community Coll., Elgin, Ill., 1993. EKG technician Hoffman Estates (Ill.) Med. Ctr., 1989-92, RN telemetry unit, 1993—; lab. technician Crossroads Clinic, Palatine, 1992—, women's health nurse practitioner; women's health nurse practitioner Planned Parenthood, 1995. Roman Catholic. Home: 225A Chesterfield Ct Schaumburg IL 60193

WENZEL, DORIS JEAN REPLOGLE (DORIS EVON WAGGONER), publisher; b. Mattoon, Ill., Feb. 11, 1940; adopted d. Forest Dale Replogle and Sarah Amanda (Thompson) Redburn; m. Jerry L. Porter, June 9, 1957 (div. Dec. 1983); children: Brian H., Todd M., Teresa Porter Hackler, Cullen J., Aaron M., Quintin M., Michelle Porter Scott; m. Harry George Wenzel Jr., May 28, 1988; 1 stepchild, Kenneth F. BA, North Ctrl. Coll., 1981; postgrad., Northwestern U., 1982; MS, Ill. State U., 1988. Writer freelance Chgo., 1978—; researcher Leo Burnett Advt., Chgo., 1966-70; instr. Coll. of DuPage, 1984-85; actress Chgo., 1977-86; instr. Parkland Coll., Champaign, Ill., 1986-87, Lincoln (Ill.) Coll., 1986-87; comms. cons. Champion Fed., Bloomington, Ill., 1987-90; instr. U. Ill., Urbana, 1986-91; owner, editor Mayhaven Pub., Mahomet, 1990—. Contbr. articles to newspapers, mags., and profl. jours. Recipient Richter fellowship North Ctrl. Coll., 1980. Home: PO Box 557 Mahomet IL 61853-0557 Office: Mayhaven Pub PO Box 557 Mahomet IL 61853-0557

WENZEL, STEPHEN G., state legislator; b. Little Falls, Minn., Dec. 7, 1946; s. Mr. and Mrs. Anthony W. BS, St. Cloud State U. Congrl. intern Sen. Walter F. Mondale, 1967—; pres. St. Cloud State YDFL; chmn. Morrison County Dem.-Farm-Labor Com., 1968-70; Minn. State rep. Dist. 13B, 1972, 74, 76—; mem. 7th Dist. and Minn. Dem. Farmer-Labor Party; chmn. agr. com.; mem. edn., ins. labor mgmt. rels., environ., nat. resources coms.; del. Dem. Nat. Mid-Term Conf., 1978—; adj. instr. polit. sci. Brainerd C.C., Minn. Active Minn. Citizens Concerned for Life, Morrison County Farmers Union. Mem. K.C., Jaycees. Office: 487 State Office Bldg Saint Paul MN 55155*

WENZLER, EDWARD WILLIAM, architect; b. Milw., Feb. 17, 1954; s. William Paul and Dolores Ann (Rahn) W.; m. Georgine Marie Eggert, Apr. 3, 1976; children: Christopher E., Michael E. BArch, U. Milw., 1978. Registered architect Wis., 1981. Architect Gordon Sibeck, Dallas, 1978-79; assoc. Wenzler and Assocs., Milw., 1979-84, ptnr., 1984—. Prin. works include Oak Hill Terr, Waukesha, Wis., The Student Ctr. Addition at U. Wis.-Whitewater, Laurel Oaks Retirement Cmty, Glendale, Wis., Ctr. for the Arts at U. Wis.-Whitewater, Seven Oaks Skilled Care Facility, Glendale. Mem. AIA, Nat. Coun. Archtl. Registration Bds., Constrn. Specification Inst. Home: 19600 Gebhardt Rd Brookfield WI 53045-4823

WEPPLER, ROBERT CHARLES, electrical engineer; b. Cleve., May 19, 1951; s. Charles G. and Arline H. Weppler. BS in Elec. Engring., Case Wstern Res. U., 1973. Project engr. Gilford Instrument Lab., Cleve., 1973-78; engring. specialist Bausch & Lomb, Rochester, N.Y., 1978-82; project engr. Allen-Bradley Co., Cleve., 1982—. Patentee in field. Methodist. Home: 6747 Larchmont Dr Mayfield Hts OH 44124-3638 Office: Allen Bradley Co Allen Bradley Dr Cleveland OH 44124

WERBEL, JAMES DAVID, management educator; b. Elkhorn, Wis., Nov. 26, 1949; s. Harold Jerome and Muriel (Wilson) W.; m. Kathryn Marlett, June 26, 1972 (div. June 1978); m. Delphine Douglass, June 29, 1985. BA, U. Wis., 1971, MS, 1974; PhD, Northwestern U., 1980. Dir. fin. aid Cin. Tech. Coll., 1974-76; asst. prof. U. Tex., San Antonio, 1980-84; asst. prof. mgmt. La. State U., Baton Rouge, 1984-86, assoc. prof., 1986-94; assoc. prof., dept. exec. officer Iowa State U., Ames, 1994—. Contbr. articles to profl. jours., chpt. to book. Mem. Acad. Mgmt. (div. chmn. 1989-90), So. Mgmt. Assn. Democrat. Jewish. Home: 2871 Torrey Pines Ames IA 50014 Office: Iowa State University College of Business Ames IA 50011

WERLICH, DAVID PATRICK, history educator; b. Mpls., Nov. 2, 1941; s. Eugene Gordon and Mary Ellen (Doran) W.; m. Sandra Cecilia Januszewski, Dec. 28, 1960; children: David A., Thomas G., Susan E. BA, U. Minn., 1963, MA, 1967, PhD, 1968. Lectr. history U. Minn., Mpls., 1966-67; asst. prof. history So. Ill. U., Carbondale, 1968-78, assoc. prof., 1978-84, prof., 1984—, chmn. dept. history, 1988—. Author: Peru: A Short History, 1978, Research Tools for Latin American Historians, 1980, Admiral of the Amazon, 1990. Recipient Delta award Friends of Morris Libr., So. Ill. U., 1991. Mem. Conf. of L.Am. History, Midwest Assn. for L.Am. Studies. Office: Southern Illinois Univ Dept of History Carbondale IL 62901-4519

WERMUTH, JEROME FRANCIS, academic administrator; b. Madison, Wis., Oct. 19, 1936; s. Louis Francis and Frances Mary (Kalscheur) W. m. Alice Elizabeth Riney, July 18, 1964; children: Sarah, Mary, Alison, Anneliese, Leah. BS, U. Wis., 1957, MS, 1960; PhD, Ind. U., 1968. Instr. Rockhurst Coll., Kansas City, Mo., 1961-64; asst. prof. St. Joseph Coll., Rensselaer, Ind., 1965-66; asst. prof. Purdue U., Hammond, Ind., 1969-78, assoc. prof., 1978—, asst. dean, 1982-87, exec. asst. to chancellor, 1987—; postdoctoral rsch. asst. U. Notre Dame (Ind.), 1968-69; vis. Ind. U., Bloomington, 1975-78. Eigenmann fellow Ind. U., Bloomington, 1967-68, Nat. Cancer Inst. Spl. Rsch. fellow, 1972-73. Home: 8007 Spruce St Highland IN 46322 Office: Purdue U Calumet Hammond IN 46323

WERMUTH, MARY LOUELLA, secondary education educator; b. Oakland County, Mich., May 2, 1943; d. Burt and Ila A. (Cole) W.; m. David J. Kohne, Dec. 28, 1975; 1 child, John B. BA, Oakland U., 1965, MA, 1969, 81. Tchr. Rochester Cmty. Schs., Rochester Hills, Mich., 1965-96; instr., counselor Internat. Acad., Bloomfield Hills, Mich., 1996—; farmer, 1964—; presenter various English confs., 1982, 84, 87; mem. bd. dirs. Mich. Future Problem Solving, 1992—; exchange tchr. New South Wales, Australia, 1996. Author: Images of Michigan, 1981, Michigan Centennial Farm History, 1986. Pres. Horizons Residential Ctrs., Inc., New Baltimore, Mich., 1984—. Recipient Disting. Alumni award Oakland U., 1976. Mem. NEA, Rochestern Edn. Assn., Mich. Edn. Assn., Mich. Coun. Tchrs. English (coms. 1985, 87), Oakland U. Alumni Assn. (pres. 1971-73), Mich. Centennial Farm Assn. (bd. dirs. 1979—), Mich. Assn. Gifted Edn. (v.p. 1991-93), Oakland County Tchrs. English (coms. 1985-93), Internat. Acad. (faculty, chmn. English dept. 1996—). Office: Rochester Sch 180 S Livernois Rd Rochester MI 48307-1840

WERNECKE, HEINZ, die cast manufacturer, mechanical engineer; b. Stendal, Fed. Republic of Germany, Oct. 8, 1922; came to U.S., 1925; s. William and Mary (Schultz) W.; m. Dorothy Robinson, March 3, 1945; children: Robert, Ann, Thomas, John. BS, Alma Coll., Mich., 1945. Registered profl. engr., Wis. Chief die cast engr. Mercury Outboards Div., Ceaderburg, Wis., 1961-66; gen. mgr. Continental Die Casting Div., Detroit, 1969-72; pres., founder Liberty Die Casting Ltd., Detroit, 1972—; founder, pres. Werco Engring., Southfieldd, 1949—; instr. die design Oakland U., Rochester, Mich., 1989—; co-owner Double Diamond Bldg. Systems, Detroit, 1988—. Co-author: Die Cast Die Design, 1971. Councilor, leader Boy Scouts Am., Saginaw, Mich. and Grafton, Wis., 1946-66. With U.S. Navy, 1942-46, PTO. Recipient Vol. award, Nat. Ind. for the Severly Handicaped, San Francisco, 1983. Mem. North Am. Die Cast Assn., (dir. 1971—, chmn. chpt. 1 1978-79), Soc. of Die Cast Engr. (disting. life mem., 1987). Lutheran. Home: 30375 Woodgate Dr Southfield MI 48076-1064

WERNER, ARNOLD, psychiatrist; b. Bklyn., June 8, 1938; m. Elizabeth A. Rederer; 2 children. BS cum laude, Bklyn. Coll., 1959; MD, U. Rochester, 1963. Diplomate Am. Bd. Psychiatry and Neurology in Psychiatry. Intern Vanderbilt U., Nashville, 1964; resident in psychiatry U. Rochester, N.Y., 1964-67, instr. psychiatry, 1966-67; instr. psychiatry Temple U., Phila., 1967-69; asst. prof. Mich. State U., East Lansing, Mich., 1969-72, assoc. prof., 1972-78, prof., 1978—; residency trainer Mich. State U., East Lansing, 1986-92; coord. Psychosocial Curriculum, 1986-95; gen. practice psychiatry Temple U., 1967-69, Mich. State U., 1969—; dir. home vis. svc. Temple U., 1967-69, psychiat. svcs. Mich. State U. Health Ctr., 1969-78; dir. consultation liaison psychiatry Ingham Med. Ctr., Lansing, 1983-85. Contbr. numerous articles and book reviews to profl. jours., syndicated newspaper columnist, 1969-76. Research grantee NIMH, 1970-71, undergrad. grant, 1980, psychiat. edn. grants. 1982-85; recipient Outstanding Faculty award Sr. Class Council Mich. State U., 1971. Fellow Am. Psychiat. Assn. (com. on pub. info. 1972-75, chmn. 1974-75, peer rev. com. 1975-76, joint commn. on pub. affairs 1976-82, com. on med. student edn. 1982-89, sci. program com. 1988-94); mem. Am. Psychosomatic Soc. Office: Mich State U A 228 E Fee Hall East Lansing MI 48824-1316

WERNER, CHRISTIAN THOR, retired engineer, consultant; b. Chgo., Mar. 25, 1916; s. Thor Christian and Anna Hedvig (Engstrom) Rothstein; m. Barbara Ruth Shneck, July 20, 1957 (div. 1974); 1 child, Diane Lynn Werner Zink. BS in Aero. Engring., Aero. U., 1937. Aero. engr. Boeing Aircraft Co., Seattle, 1938-43; aerodynamicist Republic Aviation Corp., Farmingdale, N.Y., 1944-46; sr. aerodynamicist Rep. Aviation Corp., Farmingdale, N.Y., 1946-48; contract aerodyns. cons. U.S. Naval Air Devel. Ctr., Johnsville, Pa., 1949-50; systems engr. Bendix Missile Systems Div., Mishawaka, Ind., 1951-57, sr. systems engr., 1958-67; sr. mech. engr. Sparton Electronics Div., Jackson, Mich., 1968, prin. mech. engr., 1969, mgr. fluid mechanics analysis and design lab., 1970-71, staff engr., 1972-86, engring. cons., 1987-95; instr. Swedish Jackson (Mich.) Community Coll., 1976-80. Fellow AIAA (assoc.); mem. Marine Tech. Soc., Am. Def. Preparedness Assn. Home: 9660 Myers Rd Clark Lake MI 49234-9642

WERNER, DAVID J., personnel administrator; b. Alpena, Mich., Sept. 18, 1948; s. Theodor H. and Eileen F. (Koehler) W.; m. Claudia J. Paad; children: Sarah, Aaron. BA, Mich. State U., 1971; MA, Ctrl. Mich. U., 1975. Cert. tchr., cert. prin., cert. supt., Mich. Tchr. Alcona Cmty. Schs., Lincoln, Mich., 1971-76; prin. Hillman (Mich.) Cmty. Schs., 1976-90; tchr. Alpena Pub. Schs., 1970-71, prin., 1990-95, dir. personnel, 1995—. Contbr. articles to ednl. publs. Bd. dirs. Child and Family Svcs., Alpena, 1995—, Boy Scouts Am., Alpena, 1989-95; mem. DARE (Drug Abuse Resistance Edn.) adv. bd. Montmorency County, Atlanta, Mich., 1979-90; chairperson, bd. dirs. Regional Edn. Media Ctr., Indian River, Mich., 1976-90; chairperson Montmorency County Child Abuse Prevention Coun., Atlanta, 1982-90; mem. exec. com., precinct del. Alpena County Rep. Party, 1973-75. Mem. Mich. Assn. Sch. Pers. Dirs., Alpena Exch. Club (treas., sec., pres., v.p. 1975-90, Exchangite of Yr. 1985). Lutheran. Home: 1240 Crestview Dr Alpena MI 49707 Office: Alpena Pub Schs 2373 Gordon Rd Alpena MI 49707

WERNER, EDWARD GEORGE, research consultant state legislature; b. Mountain Lake, Minn., Nov. 21, 1949; s. William George and Ruby Overa (Nelson) W.; m. Rebecca Jeanne Christensen, Sept. 27, 1972 (div. Nov., 1982); children: Candice Jeanne, Carrrie Lea; m. Joani Temple Rice, Apr. 4, 1987; 1 child, Courtney June. BS, Mankato State U., 1972, MA in Pub. Adminstrn., 1990. Bus., sales mgr. Lagers, Inc., St. Peter, Minn., 1976-87; rsch. cons. III Minn. Ho. of Reps. IR Caucus, St. Paul, Minn., 1991-96. Republican. Lutheran. Home: 1758 Crystal Ave Arden Hills MN 55112-2859 Office: Ho Reps Rep Caucus State Office Bldg Rm 222 Saint Paul MN 55155

WERNER, GARY M., JR. (GERHARD), manager systems engineering; b. Detroit, June 10, 1955. B, Mich. State U., 1977. Mgr. system engring. Unisys ISD, Plymouth, Mich., 1977—. Patentee in field. Troop leader Boy Scouts Am., 1989—. Roman Catholic.

WERNER, GLENN ALLEN, psychologist, administrator; b. Mpls., June 11, 1955; s. James Allen Werner and Barbara Jean (Prigmeier) Risdall; m. Beth Ann Michnowski, Oct. 1, 1988; children: Brianna Charlene, Brittany Jean. AA in Psychology, Normandale C.C., 1975; BA in Psychology and Speech with honors, St. Cloud (Minn.) State U., 1977, MA in Counseling Psychology and Vocat. Rehab., 1979, B in Elective Studies cum laude, 1982; cert. adult psychiatry, U. Minn., 1984, cert. in indsl. rels., 1989. Lic. psychologist, Minn. Counselor M&R Inc., Mpls., 1974-79; employment placement specialist St. Paul Rehab. Ctr., 1979; sr. vocat. rehab. counselor Minn. Correctional Facility, St. Cloud, 1979-81; psychologist Minn. Security Hosp., St. Peter, 1981-83; clin. psychologist Anoka (Minn.)-Metro Regional Treatment Ctr., 1983-89; psychologist Stillwater Prison, 1989-91; psychologist supr. Cambridge (Minn.) Regional Treatment Ctr., 1991—. Author, illustrator: How to Land A Job- A Guide for Ex-Offenders, 1979. Recipient Exceptional Performance award State of Minn., 1982, 83, 85, 86, 87, 88, 89, 96; nominee for 1st Annual Mo. awards for Health Excellence award, 1989. Mem. Mensa, Psi Chi. Home: 12020 Isanti St NE Blaine MN 55449-7915 Office: care Oakview Cambridge Regional Treatment Ctr 1235 Highway 293 S Cambridge MN 55008-9002

WERNER, NANCY DARLINGTON, university development researcher; b. Charleston, W.Va., June 26, 1942; d. Kenneth L. and Rosalie K. (Fravel) Darlington; m. James Grierson Werner, II, Dec. 22, 1964; children: Thomas Joseph, James G. III. AA, So. Va. Coll. for Women, 1963; postgrad., Marshall U., 1963-64. Sec. accounts receivable Ind. U. Found., Bloomington, 1977-79, pub. rels. staff, 1979-84, rsch. asst., 1984-89, mgr. devel. rsch. dept., 1989-91, sr. rsch. assoc., 1991—. Contbr. articles to profl. jours. Mayors ednl. task force, mayors com. to organize and identify funding prospects for Bloomington Cmty. Found., City of Bloomington, 1990-91; trustee, endowment devel. com., mktg. com., publicity com. Bloomington Cmty. Found., 1990-95, adv. bd., 1996—; bd. dirs. Tulip Trace coun. Girl Scouts Am. U.S., 1995—, Panthers for Better Edn., 1993—, sec., 1993-95, chmn. bd. 1996—, chmn. mktg. com.; active Bloomington Arts Coun. Mem. Am. Prospect Rsch. Assn. (bd. dirs. Ind. chpt. 1988-92), Coun. for Advancement and Support of Edn., Local Coun. Women, Network Career Women, Nat. Soc. Fund Raising Execs. (bd. dirs. Ind. chpt. 1992-95, chmn. found. devel. com. 1992-94), Bloomington C. of C. (edn. com. 1992—), Smithsonian Assocs., Bloomington Press Club, Psi Iota Xi. Republican. Mem. Christian Ch. Home: 1517 E Elliston Dr Bloomington IN 47401-8746 Office: Ind Univ Found N State Rd 46 Byp Bloomington IN 47408

WERT, CHARLES ALLEN, metallurgical and mining engineering educator; b. Battle Creek, Iowa, Dec. 31, 1919; s. John Henry and Anna (Spotts) W.; m. Lucille Vivian Mathena, Sept. 5, 1943; children: John Arthur, Sara Ann. B.A., Morningside Coll., Sioux City, 1941; M.S., State U. Iowa, 1943, Ph.D., 1948. Mem. staff Radiation Lab., Mass. Inst. Tech., 1943-45; instr. physics U. Chgo., 1948-50; mem. faculty U. Ill. at Urbana, 1950—, prof., 1955, head dept. metall. and mining engring., 1967-86, prof. emeritus, 1989; cons. to industry. Author: Physics of Metals, 1970, Opportunities in Materials Science and Engineering, 1977; also articles.; Cons. editor, McGraw Hill Book Co. Recipient sr. scientist award von Humboldt-Stiftung. Fellow Am. Phys. Soc., Am. Soc. Metals, AAAS, AIME; mem. Sigma Xi. Home: 1708 W Green St Champaign IL 61821-3721 Office: U Ill Metallurgy & Mining Bldg Urbana IL 61801

WERTS, MERRILL HARMON, management consultant; b. Smith Center, Kans., Nov. 17, 1922; s. Mack Allen and Ruth Martha (Badger) W.; BS, Kans. State U., 1947; MS, Cornell U., 1948; m. Dorothy Wilson, Mar. 22, 1946; children: Stephen M., Riley J., Todd J., Kelly M. Beef sales mgr. John Morrell & Co., Topeka and Memphis, 1948-53; dir. mktg. Kans. Dept. Agr., Topeka, 1953-55; sec.-treas. Falley's Markets, Inc., Topeka, 1955-58; v.p. S.W. State Bank, Topeka, 1958-65; pres. First Nat. Bank, Junction City, Kans., 1965-78; pvt. practice mgmt. cons., Junction City, 1978—; mem. Kans. Senate, 1978-88; mem. Kans. Pub. Employee Rels. Bd., 1989-94, Kans. Comsn. on Future of Health Care, 1991-94; chmn. Kans. WWII Commemoration Com. 1995—, Kans. Commn. on Vets. Affairs, 1995—; chmn. Geary County Pub. Bldg. Commn., 1996—; dir. Stockgrowers State Bank, Maple Hill, Kans., J.C. Housing & Devel., Inc., Kans. State Hist. Soc., Transformer Disposal Specialists, Inc. Mem. Kans. Bank Mgmt. Commn., 1967-71; mem. adv. com. U.S. Comptroller of Currency, 1971-72. Mem. Topeka Bd. Edn., 1957-61; pres. Junction City-Geary County United Fund, 1967-68; pres. Junction City Indsl. Devel., Inc., 1966-72. Trustee Kans. State U. Endowment Assn., Kans. Synod Presbyn. Westminster Found., 1965-72. 1st lt., inf., AUS, 1943-46. Decorated Bronze Star medal, Purple Heart, Combat Inf. badge; named to Inf. Officer Candidate Hall Fame, 1981, Civilian Aide to Sec. of Army for Kans., 1991-95; named Outstanding State Legis. Am. Legis. Exchange Coun., 1988. Mem. Kans. State U. Alumni Assn. (pres. 1957), Am. Legion, VFW, Kans. Bankers Assn., Assn. U.S. Army, U.S., Kans. (bd. dirs., v.p. 1979-84), Junction City (pres. 1975-76) chambers commerce, Kans. Farm Bur., Kans. Livestock Assn., DAV, Junction City Country Club (past pres.), Masons, Shriners, Jesters, Rotary (dist. gov. 1973-74), Sigma Phi Epsilon. Republican. Presbyterian. Address: 1228 Miller Dr Junction City KS 66441-3312

WERTZ, JOHN ALAN, secondary school educator; b. Mpls., May 28, 1945; s. John Edward and Florence (Carlson) W.; m. Margaret M. Schlangen, 1993. BS, Hamline U., 1967; MS, St. Cloud State Coll., 1973; postgrad., George Washington U., 1985. Tchr. social sci. St. Cloud (Minn.) Community Schs., 1967—; trainer and field rep. New Games Found., San Francisco, 1980-83; tchr.-coach Apollo H.S. Mock Trial team, 1987—. Mem. com. social action Minn. Synod, Luth. Ch. Am., 1971-74; chair social action com. Salem Luth. Ch. Coun., St. Cloud, 1974-76; mem. affirmative action com. St. Cloud Cmty. Schs., 1975-78, co-chair student assistance com., 1982-83, mem. site coun. Apollo H.S., 1994-96, co-chair site coun. Apollo H.S., 1995-96; chair St. Cloud Human Rights Commn., 1979-86; adv. Ctrl. Minn. Sexual Assault Ctr., 1981-83; bd. dirs. St. Cloud Area Tenants' Assn., 1975-77, St. Cloud Area Spl. Olympics, 1982-83, United Way St. Cloud Area, 1996, Minn. Edn. Assn., 1996. Recipient Merit award St. Cloud Area Coun. for Handicapped, 1976; grad. St. Cloud Area Leadership Program, 1995. Mem. ASCD, NEA, Minn. Edn. Assn. (bd. dirs. 1996), St. Cloud Edn. Assn. (chair govtl. rels. coun. 1978-83, 88-96), Am. Hist. Soc. of Germans from Russia, St. Cloud Area C. of C. (edn. divsn. 1992—, vice-chmn. PreK-12 com. 1993-94, chair edn. recognition com. 1994-96). Home: 816 Rilla Rd Saint Cloud MN 56303-1037 Office: Apollo High Sch 1000 44th Ave N Saint Cloud MN 56303

WESELI, ROGER WILLIAM, lawyer; b. Cin., Dec. 23, 1932; s. William Henry and Margaret Antoinette (Hoffman) W.; m. Sue Ann Daggett, Sept. 1, 1956; children: Erin, Stacey, Vincent. BA in Polit. Sci, U. Cin., 1955; MS in Hosp. Adminstrn, Northwestern U., 1959; D Tech. Letters (hon.), Cin. Tech. Coll., 1985; JD, No. Ky. U., 1995. Bar: Ky. 1995. Adminstrv. asst. Good Samaritan Hosp., Cin., 1959-61, asst. adminstr., 1961-70, assoc. adminstr., 1970-75, v.p., adminstr., 1975-78, exec. v.p., adminstr., 1978-79, pres., 1979-91, cons., 1991-93; cons. healthcare practice Deloitte & Touche, Cin., 1991-93; sec. Greater Cin. Hosp. Council, 1978-80, chmn. bd., 1983-84; assoc. Copeland & Brown Co., L.P.A., Cin., 1995—. Chmn. legis. com. health dept. Ohio Cath. Conf., 1978-83, 86; bd. dirs. Friars Boys Club, 1978-94. Recipient Praestans Inter Omnes award Purcell High Sch., 1984, Laura Jackson award Northwestern U. Program in Health Svcs. Mgmt., 1987, Preceptor of Yr. award Xavier U. Program Hosp. and Health Svcs. Adminstrn., 1990. Fellow Am. Coll. Healthcare Execs. (regent for Ohio 1983-90, bd. govs. 1990-94); mem. ABA, Am. Hosp. Assn. (coun. on fedn. rels. 1983-84, coun. on patient svcs. 1984-86, ho. of dels. 1989-91), Ohio Bar Assn., Cin. Bar Assn., Ohio League for Nursing (v.p. 1977-79, cert. of appreciation 1978), Ohio Hosp. Assn. (chmn. govt. liaison com. 1978-83, 86, trustee 1981-83, sec.-treas. 1987, chmn.-elect 1988, chmn. 1989), Cath. Health Assn. (trustee 1983-86), Alpha Mu Sigma. Democrat. Roman Catholic. Home: 3615 Clifton Ave Cincinnati OH 45220-1703

WESELY, DONALD RAYMOND, state senator; b. David City, Nebr., Mar. 30, 1954; s. Raymond Ely and Irene (Sabata) W.; m. Geri Williams, 1982; children: Sarah, Amanda, Andrew. BA, U. Nebr., 1977; LLD (hon.), Kirksville Coll. Osteopathic Medicine, 1989. Mem. Nebr. Legislature, Lincoln, 1978—; exec. assoc. Selection Rsch., Inc., Lincoln, 1984-86; sr. rsch. assoc. Lincoln Telephone Co., 1985—. Del., Dem. Nat. Conv., 1984, 88, 92, 96; chair Assembly on Legislature, Nat. Conf. State Legislatures., 1992-93, exec. com., 1993-96; del. Am. Coun. Young Polit. Leaders, 1993. Recipient Friend of Edn. award Nebr. State Edn. Assn., 1982, Disting. Svc. award Nebr. Pub. Health Assn., 1984, Disting. Alumni award Lincoln Northeast High Sch., 1991, Disting. Health Care award Nebr. Nurse Anesthetists Assn., 1992, Leadership award for Quality in Health Care, Nebr. League Nursing, 1992, Pres.'s award Nebr. Acad. Physicians Assts., 1993, U. Nebr.-Lincoln Outstanding Young Alumni award, 1994; named Mental Health Citizen of Yr., Nebr. Mental Health Assn., 1984, Outstanding Young Man, Nebr. Jaycees, 1985, Pub. Official of Yr., Nebr. Assn. Retarded Citizens, 1992, Advocate of Yr, Nebr. Family Day Care Assn., 1993. Roman Catholic. Office: State Capitol Lincoln NE 68509

WESENER, BARBARA ANN, trade association executive; b. Sheboygan, Wis., Oct. 16, 1948; d. Melvin Rudolph and Delores Angeline (Wagner) W.; m. Clinton Lee Toms, June 27, 1981. BA cum laude, Alverno Coll., 1970. Cert. secondary tchr., Wis. Tchr. English Pius High Sch., Milw., 1970-72; tchr. Journalism Divine Savior Holy Angels, Milw., 1972-75; teaching asst. U. Wis., Milw., 1975-76; asst. dir. continuing edn. dept. Marquette U., Milw., 1976-79; assoc. dir. pub. relations Internat. Found. Employee Benefits, Milw., 1979-86; exec. dir. Wis. Ready Mixed Concrete Assn., Milw., 1986—. Bd. dirs. St. Mary's Acad., Milw., 1983-89, pres., 1986-89. Mem. Women in Comm. Inc. (v.p. nat. bd. 1981-85), Pub. Rels. Soc. Am. (bd. dirs. Milw. chpt. 1987-95, pres. 1994, accredited in pub. rels.), Am. Soc. Assn. Execs. (bd. dirs. Wis. chpt. 1995-98, cert. assn. exec.), Internat. Coun. Execs. (bd. dirs. pres. 1991-92). Office: Wis Ready Mixed Concrete 9415 W Forest Home Ave Hales Corners WI 53130-1680

WESLEY, RUBY LAVERNE, nursing educator, administrator, researcher; b. Detroit, Nov. 25, 1949; d. David Williams and Leatrice (Gragg) Williams; 1 child, Nathaniel Rogers Wesley III. Diploma, Providence Hosp. Sch. Nursing, Southfield, Mich., 1971; BS in Nursing, Wayne State U., Detroit, 1974, MEd, 1977; PhD, U. Md., Balt., 1987. Clin. instr. U. Tenn. Sch. Nursing, 1978-79; community health nursing instr. U. Md., Balt., 1984-85; assoc. prof. Bowie State U., 1985-89; asst. dean Coppin State Coll., Balt., 1989-90; asst. prof. Wayne State U., 1991—; nurse researcher Rehab. Inst. Mich., 1992; dir. nursing practice Rehab. Inst. Mich., Detroit, 1992-93, dir. nursing, 1993-96; asst. v.p. med./surg. rehab. nursing Sinai Hosp., Detroit, 1996—. Henry C. Welcome fellow, 1986-87; Nat. Inst. Disability and Rehab. rsch. fellow, 1991-92. Mem. Am. Assn. Spinal Cord Injury Nurses (chair rsch. com.). Home: 2146 Bryanston Crescent St Detroit MI 48207-3818

WESSE, DAVID JOSEPH, academic administrator; b. Chgo., May 5, 1951; s. Herman Theodore and Lorraine Joan (Holland) W.; m. Deborah Lynn Smith, Oct. 11, 1975; children: Jason David, Eric Joseph. AA, South Suburban Coll., 1971; postgrad., Purdue U., 1971-72; BEd, Ill. State U., 1973; MS, Loyola U., 1983. Adminstr. Don Tech, Inc., Chgo., 1974-76; adminstrv. mgr. Loyola U., Chgo., 1976-79, Joint Commn. on Accreditation of Healthcare Orgns., Oak Brook Terrace, Ill., 1979-81; adminstrv. dir., asst. sec. Northwestern U., Evanston, Ill., 1981—. Pres., bd. dirs. Riverdale (Ill.) Libr. Dist., 1975, Riverdale Youth Commn., 1975; bd. dirs. Better Bus. Bur. Chgo. and No. Ill., 1991—. Recipient Svc. Recognition award Riverdale Libr. Dist., 1975, Excellence in Journalism award Nat. Assn. Coll. Aux. Svcs., 1989. Mem. Adminstrv. Mgmt. Soc. (bd. dirs. Chgo. chpt. 1983-88, pres. 1986-87, bd. regents 1986-88), Acad. Adminstrv. Mgmt. (bd. regents 1992-94), Profl. Office Mgmt. Assn. Chgo. (bd. dirs. 1992-93, sec. 1993-95, pres. 1995), Nat. Mgmt. Assn. (chpt. pres. 1995), Nat. Assn. Coll. and Univ. Bus. Officers (com. mem. 1986-87, 89-90, cost reduction awards 1986-88, 90, 92), Midwest Higher Edn. Commn. (com. mem. 1996—), Assn. Coll. Adminstrn. Profls. (seminar leader 1995), Chgo. Area Bus. and Support Svc. Adminstrs. (founder), Big Ten Bus. and Support Svc. Adminstrs. (founder),

Lambda Epsilon. Lutheran. Home: 207 S Washington St Wheaton IL 60187-5429 Office: Northwestern U 633 Clark St Evanston IL 60208-1121

WESSEL, DENNIS JAMES, mechanical engineering administrator; b. Pitts., Mar. 31, 1949; s. Elmer Herman and Fern (Staley) W.; m. Karen Dudziak, Jan. 1970; children: Eric, Heidi, Dana. BME, Cleve. State U., 1972. Registered profl. engr., Ohio, Pa., N.Y., Calif. Designer Avery Engring., Cleve., 1968-71; sales engr. Met-Chem Inc., Cleve., 1971-73; engr. Byers Engring., Cleve., 1973-78; assoc. URS Corp., Cleve., 1978-87; v.p. Bacik, Karpinski Assocs., Cleve., 1987—; instr. continuing edn. bldg. maintenance, Cleve. State U., 1982-84. Chmn. Hudson (Ohio) H.S. Career Night Com., 1987-91; mem. fin. com. St. Marys Ch., Hudson, 1986—, bdlg. com. 1986-95. With USAR, 1972-78. Mem. ASHRAE (local pres. 1984-85, regional vice chmn. 1986-90, tech. com. chmn. 1991-93, vice chmn. task group 1989-93, 94-96, handbook com. 1993—, chmn. 1996-2000, Region V Energy award 1983, 86, Merit award 1990), Am. Cons. Engrs. Assn., Nat. Fire Protection Assn., Bldg. Ofcls. and Code Adminstrs. Roman Catholic. Office: Bacik Karpinski Assocs 3135 Euclid Ave Cleveland OH 44115-2524

WESSELER, DAVID, agricultural engineer; b. Ellsworth, Kans., Aug. 14, 1962; s. Delmar Louis and Thelea (Schroeder) W. BBA, Baylor U., 1984, MBA, 1986; MS in Agrl. Engring., Kans. State U., 1992. Lic. health, property, and casualty ins. agt., Kans. Econs. lectr. Baylor U., Waco, Tex., 1984-85; dept. head mgmt. info. analysis Plantation Foods, Waco, Tex., 1986-87; tchg. asst. econs. Kans. U., Lawrence, 1987-88; auditor for ticket sales Breckenridge (Colo.) Ski Corp., 1991; tchg. asst. agrl. engring. Kans. State U., Manhattan, 1990; mgr. Wesseler Farms, Lorraine, Kans., 1988—; vol. economist Citizens Network for Fgn. Affairs, Belaya Kalitua, Russia, 1994; mem. Kans. Agrl. and Rural Leadership Seminars, 1993-95; bd. dirs. Lorraine Grain Fuel and Stock. Mem. Ellsworth County Econ. Devel. Com., 1994-95; del. Kans. State Bd. Agr., Topeka, 1993; membership com. Kans. Farm Bur., 1993-95; pres. Ellsworth County Farm Bur., 1994; trustee, treas. Lorraine Bapt. Ch., 1990—. Named Kans. state scholar. Mem. Fin. Mgmt. Assn., Omicron Delta Epsilon, Beta Gamma Sigma, Sigma Iota Epsilon. Home and Office: PO Box 19 Lorraine KS 67458

WESSELMANN, GLENN ALLEN, hospital executive; b. Cleve., Mar. 21, 1932; s. Roy Arthur and Dorothy (Oakes) W.; m. Genevieve De Witt, Sept. 6, 1958; children: Debbie, Scott, Janet. A.B., Dartmouth, 1954; M.B.A. with distinction, Cornell U., 1959. Research aide Cornell U., Ithaca, N.Y., 1958-59; adminstrv. resident Meml. Hosp., N.Y.C., 1957-58; adminstrv. asst. Meml. Hosp., 1959-61, asst. adminstr., 1961-65, asst. v.p., 1965-68; v.p. for adminstrn. Meml. Hosp. for Cancer and Allied Diseases, N.Y.C., 1968-79; exec. v.p., chief operating officer St. John Hosp., Detroit, 1979-84; pres., CEO St. John Health System, 1984-95—, vice chmn., 1995—; chmn., pres., CEO St. John Hosp. & Med. Ctr., 1984-94; mem. bus. adv. bd. City of Detroit, 1991-95, chmn., 1993-94; mem. exec. com. Greater Detroit Area Health Coun.; bd. dirs. Caymich Ins. Co. Ltd., Mich. Health Care Alliance, SelectCare, Detroit Econ. Growth Corp. Trustee Sisters of St. Joseph Health System 1981-94, Sisters of St. Joseph Health Svc., 1983—, St. John Hosp. and Med. Ctr., 1979-95, St. John Health System, 1984—, The Oxford Inst., 1984-95, Eastwood Clinics, 1992-95; mem. bus. adv. bd., City of Detroit, 1991—, chmn. 1993-94. Served with MC AUS, 1955-57. Fellow ACHE; mem. Am. Hosp. Assn., Internat. Hosp. Fedn., Mich. Hosp. Assn. (trustee, chmn. 1994—, mem. exec. com.), Assn. Am. Med. Colls. (Coth rep.), Am. Cancer Soc. (regional adv. bd. 1994—), Med. Group Mgmt. Assn., Soc. Health Service Adminstrs., Sigma Phi Epsilon. Home: 63 Big Woods Dr Hilton Head Island SC 29926 Office: St John Health Sys Office of the Pres 22101 Moross Rd Detroit MI 48236-2148

WESSELS, JON J., insurance executive; b. Cedar Falls, Iowa, June 20, 1968. V.p. Generations Fin. Group, Cedar Falls, Iowa, 1991-94, Life Brokers Resource, Inc., Des Moines, 1992—. Republican. Baptist. Office: Generations Fin Group PO Box 530 Cedar Falls IA 50613-0530

WEST, GENE A., electrical engineer; b. Watertown, Wis., Nov. 15, 1933. B, Milw. Sch. Engring., 1958; M, U. Wis., 1966. Elec. engr. Delco Elecs., Kokomo, Ind., 1958—. Tutor Kokomo High Sch., 1970—. With U.S. Army, 1954-56. Recipient GM Kettering award, Kokomo, 1992.

WEST, HUGH BRIAN, business owner; b. Akron, Ohio, Jan. 23, 1939; s. Glen W. and Carrie (Merkle) W.; m. Phyllis A. Behrle, Dec. 27, 1969; children: Tara M., Todd B. BS in Bus. Adminstrn., Kent State Univ., 1961. V.p. West Chevrolet, Inc., Mogadore, Tallmadge, Ohio, 1957-88, pres., 1988—; pres. West Agy, Inc., Tallmadge, 1962-88; v.p., pres. West's Investments, Inc., Akron, 1964-90, pres., 1990—; pres., CEO West Leasing, Inc., Akron, 1978—; dir., ptnrs. Investors Fidelity Life Assurance, Co., Columbus, Ohio, 1977-90. Pres. Cuyahoga Falls Music Assn., 1975-76; treas., pres., chmn. Akron Community Hall Found.-Akron Civic Theater, 1966-76; trustee, dir. Stan Hywet Hall & Garden Found., Inc., Akron, 1976-92; deacon Fairlawn West Ch. of Christ, Akron, 1988—; dir., officer All Am. Soap Box Derby Com. Mem. Sales and Mktg. Execs. Akron (bd. dirs. 1990-95, dir. 1996—), Phi Delta Theta (pres. N.E. Ohio alumni 1980-95, treas. 1995—, W. Richard Wright-Phi Delta Theta Svc. award 1989). Republican. Congregationalist. Home: 287 Ely Rd Akron OH 44313-4563 Office: West Leasing Inc 287 Ely Rd Akron OH 44313

WEST, KRISTA ANN, political science educator; b. Bountiful, Utah, Feb. 22, 1962; d. Robert Davenport and Gayno Shirley W. BA, Brigham Young U., 1985, MPA, 1987; PhD, Va. Poly. Inst. and State U., 1996. Instr. Hollins Coll., Roanoke, Va., 1990-92; asst. prof. No. Mich. U., Marquette, 1993—. Mem. Bd. of Health, Marquette County, 1996—; co-chair Green Ribbon Com., Marquette City, 1994-95. Mem. ASPA, Internat. Pers. Mgmt. Assn., Beta Gamma Sigma, Phi Kappa Phi. Republican. Mormon. Office: No Mich U Dept Pol Sci 1401 Presque Isle Ave Marquette MI 49855

WEST, MARK ALLEN, librarian, educator; b. Chgo., Mar. 22, 1950; s. John Charles and Virginia Delphine (Dirks) W.; m. Michelle Bucheck, June 6, 1970 (div. 1973); m. Barbara Elizabeth Grant, June 10, 1977. BS, Bradley U., 1971; MLS, Rosary Coll., 1978. Sales rep. Jack West Mfrs. Rep., Chgo., 1972-74, Kinney Printing Co., Chgo., 1978-80; libr. asst. Elk Grove Village (Ill.) Pub. Libr., 1974-75, adminstrv. libr., 1987—; adminstr. libr. Rickton Park (Ill.) Pub. Libr., 1976-78, Chicago Ridge (Ill.) Pub. Libr., 1980-87; instr. Coll. of DuPage, Glen Ellyn, Ill., 1993—. Contbg. author: Insiders Guide to Library Automation, 1993. Trustee/treas. Grande Prairie Pub. Libr. Dist., Hazel Crest, Ill., 1979-86. Mem. ALA, Ill. Libr. Assn., Bay Shore Yacht Club (commodore 1995—). Republican. Roman Catholic. Office: Elk Grove Village Pub Libr 1001 Wellington Ave Elk Grove Village IL 60007

WEST, MICHAEL ALAN, hospital administrator; b. Waseca, Minn., Aug. 4, 1938; s. Ralph Lel and Elizabeth Mary (Brann) W.; m. Mary Thissen, Jan. 21, 1961; children—Anne, Nancy, Douglas. B.A., U. Minn., 1961, M.H.A., 1963. Sales corr. Physicians and Hosps. Supply Co., Mpls., 1959-60; adminstrv. resident R.I. Hosp., Providence, 1962-63; adminstrv. asst. R.I. Hosp., 1963-65, asst. dir., 1965-68; exec. asst. dir. Med. Center U. Mo., Columbia, 1968-70; assoc. dir. Med. Center U. Mo., 1970-74, asst. prof. community health and med. practice, 1968-74; v.p. for adminstrn. Luth. Gen. Hosp., Park Ridge, Ill., 1974-80; exec. v.p. Luth. Gen. Hosp., 1980-84; pres., CEO Akron Gen. Med. Ctr., Ohio, 1984—; bd. dirs. Vol. Hosps. Am. Inc.; chair VHA-Ctrl., Inc. Mem. Am. Coll. Healthcare Execs., Akron Regional Hosp. Assn. (chmn.), Portage Country Club, Akron City Club, Rotary. Home: 495 Woodbury Dr Akron OH 44333-2780 Office: Akron Gen Med Ctr 400 Wabash Ave Akron OH 44307-2433

WEST, ROBERT ALLAN, engineer; b. Parsons, Kans., Nov. 2, 1957; s. Donald E. and Doris M. (Hamm) W.; m. Karen J. Wilson, Apr. 18, 1981; 1 child, Curtis. BS in Edn., Ctrl. Mo. State U., 1979; BS in Bus. Adminstrn., Columbia Coll., 1994. Tchr. Renick (Mo.) Elem. Jr. High, 1979-81; engr. Toastmaster, Boonville, Mo., 1981-95; prodn. supr., engr. INDEECO, Boonville, Mo., 1995—. Editor Nat. Antique Truck Newsletter; contbr. articles to profl. jours. Mem., song leader Ch. of Christ, Boonville; asst. T-Ball League, Boonville. Mem. Am. Electro Platers an dSurface Finishers Soc., Alpha Chi Nat. Coll. Honor Soc. Office: INDEECO 2301 Boonslick Dr Boonville MO 65233

WEST, ROBERT CULBERTSON, chemistry educator; b. Glen Ridge, N.J., Mar. 18, 1928; s. Robert C. and Constance (MacKinnon) W.; children: David Russell, Arthur Scott, Derek. B.A., Cornell U., 1950; A.M., Harvard U., 1952, Ph.D., 1954; ScD (hon.), G. Asachi Tech. U., Iasi, Romania, 1995. Asst. prof. Lehigh U., 1954-56; mem. faculty U. Wis.-Madison, 1956—, prof. chemistry, 1963—, Eugene G. Rochow prof., 1980; indsl. and govt. cons., 1961—; Fulbright lectr. Kyoto and Osaka U., 1964-65; vis. prof. U. Würzburg, 1968-69, Haile Selassie I U., 1972, U. Calif.-Santa Cruz, 1977, U. Utah, 1981, Inst. Chem. Physics Chinese Acad. Sci., 1984, Justus Liebigs U., Giessen, Fed. Republic Germany, U. Estadual de Campinas, Brazil, 1989; Abbott lectr. U. N.D., 1964, Seydel-Wooley lectr. Ga. Inst. Tech., 1970, Sun Oil lectr. Ohio U., 1971, Edgar C. Britton lectr. Dow, Midland, Mich., 1971, Jean Day Meml. lectr. Rutgers U., 1973; Japan Soc. for Promotion Sci. vis. prof. Tohoku U., 1976, Gunma U., 1987; Lady Davis vis. prof. Hebrew U., 1979; Cecil and Ida Green honors prof. Tex. Christian U., 1983; Karcher lectr. U. Okla., 1986; Broberg lectr. N.D. State U., 1986; Xerox lectr. U. B.C., 1986, McGregory lectr. Colgate U., 1988; Lady Davis vis. prof. Technion Israel Inst. Tech., 1990; Humboldt prof. Tech. U. Munich, Fed. Republic Germany, 1990; George W. Watt lectr. U. Tex., Austin, 1992; vis. prof. U. Estadual de Campinas, Brazil, 1993; Dozor vis. fellow Ben Gurion U. of the Negev, Israel, 1993. Co-editor: Advances in Organometallic Chemistry, Vols. I-XXXVI, 1964—, Organometallic Chemistry--A Monograph Series, 1968—; contbr. articles to profl. jours. Pres. Madison Community Sch., 1970-81; founder, bd. dirs. Women's Med. Fund, 1971—; nat. bd. dirs. Zero Population Growth, 1980-86; bd. dirs., v.p. Protect Abortion Rights Inc., 1980; lay minister Prairie Unitarian Universalist Soc., 1982. Recipient F.S. Kipling award, 1970, Outstanding Sci. Innovator award Sci. Digest, 1985, Chem. Pioneering award Am. Inst. Chemists, 1988, Wacker Silicon prize, 1989, Humboldt U.S. Scientist award, 1990. Mem. Am. Chem. Soc., Chem. Soc. (London), Japan Chem. Soc., AAAS, Wis. Acad. Sci. Home: 305 Nautilus Dr Madison WI 53705-4333

WEST, ROBERTA BERTHA, writer; b. Saline County, Mo., Sept. 7, 1904; d. Robert and Amanda Melvina (Driver) Baur; m. Harold Clinton West, Aug. 27, 1932; children: Arle Faith W. Lohof, Lydia Ann (Lyda) F H. Hyde, Danna Rose F H. Burns. AB, William Jewell Coll., 1928; AM, U. Mo., 1930. Cert. tchr., Mo., Mont. Elem. and secondary sch. tchr. Mo. and Mont. Schs., 1922-47; supt. schs. Hogeland (Mont.) Schs., 1947-48, 55; prof. fgn. langs. Will Mayfield Coll., Marble Hill, Mo., 1930; columnist Quad County Star, Viburnum, Mo., 1982—; writer and researcher ch. history, 1964-91; cons. hist. com. Yellowstone Conf. Meth. Ch., 1971-84; compiler Mont. list of Meth. Mins. 1784-1984. Author: Northern Montana Methodist History, 3 vols., 1974, Faith, Hope and Love in the West, 1971; editor: Brother Van by Those Who Knew Him, 1975, reprinted, 1989,; also contbr. articles. Recipient 1st John M. Templeton prize, 1959. Mem. Alpha Zeta Pi. Democrat. Home: PO Box 583 Viburnum MO 65566-0583 Office: Quad County Star Viburnum MO 65566

WEST, THOMAS MEADE, financial services strategic consultant; b. Owensboro, Ky., Aug. 15, 1940; s. Frank Thomas and Vivian (Brown) W.; children: Thomas Meade, Alexandra, Theodora. B.A. cum laude, Vanderbilt U., 1962; M.A. magna cum laude, U. Mich., 1964. Various mgmt. positions Lincoln Nat. Life Ins. Co., Fort Wayne, Ind., 1964-75, v.p., 1975-78, sr. v.p., 1978-81, exec. v.p., 1981-94; pres., CEO Lincoln Nat Reins. Cos.; prin. West Cons. Corp.; bd. dirs. Union Fed. Savs. Bank of Indpls., Union Acceptance Corp. Area pres. Boy Scouts Am., Ind.; dir. Jr. Achievement, Ft. Wayne. With U.S. Army, 1964-66. Fellow Soc. of Actuaries; mem. Am. Acad. Actuaries, Fort Wayne C. of C. (bd. dirs.). Presbyterian. Home: 2201 Turnberry Ln Fort Wayne IN 46804-2827

WESTENBARGER, DON EDWARD, retired association executive; b. Wadsworth, Ohio, July 23, 1928; s. Worth D. and Alma M. (Beck) W.; m. Barbara Ann Halstead, May 11, 1957; children: Susan Jane, Donna Lee, Heidi Ann. BA in Journalism, Ohio State U., 1950; postgrad., Kent State U., 1955-56. Announcer WHKK Radio, Akron, Ohio, 1950-52; 1st lt. USAF, Dayton, Ohio, 1952-53; news dir. WHKK Radio, Akron, 1953-54; news reporter, TV anchor WKBN Radio and TV, Youngstown, Ohio, 1954-56; asst. dir. Indsl. Info. Inst., Inc., Youngstown, 1956-66; acct. exec. R.J. McCallister Co., Youngstown, 1966-70; sta. mgr. WTCL Radio, Warren, Ohio, 1970-73; dir. Indsl. Info. Inst., Inc., Youngstown, 1973-93; ret., 1993. Trustee Youngstown Com. on Alcholism, Boardman Civic Assn., pres., 1988. 1st Lt. USAF, 1952-53, Japan. Recipient Career Educator award Career Edn.Assn., 1990, Community Svc. award Boardman Civic Assn., 1990. Mem. Soc. Profl. Journalists, Nat. Assn. Industry-Edn. Cooperation, Rotary Club Boardman (Paul Harris Fellow 1986). Republican. Methodist. Home: 681 Forest Ridge Dr Youngstown OH 44512-3514

WESTENDORF, ROBERT GEORGE, chemist; b. Cin., Nov. 5, 1959; s. George Bernard and Maria (Bauke) Bambach; m. Roxanne Drago, Mar. 8, 1959. BS, Xavier U., 1979. Dir. rsch. & devel. Tekmar Co., Cin., 1979-90; leader air devel. Internat. Tech., Cin., 1990-91; leader air quality O I Analytical, College Station, Tex., 1991-92; pres. RGW Consulting Svcs., Cin., 1992—; cons. Cargill, Inc., Mpls., 1994-95. Contbr. papers to profl. publs.; inventor in field. Mem. ASTM, Am. Chem. Soc., Cin. Velo Club (pres. 1985-95), Queen City Wheels (dir. 1987-95, Tim Gehling award 1994).

WESTERFIELD, DONALD LEE, economics educator; b. Newport, Ark., Sept. 6, 1935; s. Matthew Hayden and Ella Maude (Jones) W.; m. Mary Louise Cotton, June 14, 1958; children: Ronald Henry, Douglas Lee. BBA, U. Miami, 1959, MA, 1960; PhD, St. Louis U., 1984. Assoc. prof. U. S.W. La., Lafayette, 1970-72; econometrician Southwestern Bell Telephone, St. Louis, 1972-84; assoc. prof. Webster U., St. Louis, 1984-89, prof. economics, 1989—; dir. London Campus Webster U., 1989; vis. prof. Webster U. in Leiden, Netherlands, 1986, Leiden and Geneva, 1987, Geneva, 1988; cons. to various firms, St. Louis, 1972—; founder, adv. dir. Alpha Kappa Psi, St. Louis, 1985—. Author: Mandated Health Care: Issues and Strategies, 1991, National Health Care: Law, Policy, Strategy, 1993, War Powers: The President, The Congress, and The Question of War, 1996, (with Thomas Curtis) Congressional Intent, 1992; referee/reviewer Jour. Econs. and Fin., Jour. Bus. and Econ. Perspectives; author more than 100 articles, scholarly papers and presentations. Mem. adv. group Joint Legis. D.P. Com., State of La., 1970-72; bd. dirs. Met. Symphony Orch., St. Louis, 1986-89; interpreter for deaf, U. So. La., 1970-72. With USCG, 1952-56. Mem. AAUP (sec. 1962-64, exec. com. 1995), Am. Econ. Assn., Midwest Econs. Assn., Bus. and Health Adminstrn. Assn., Sigma Xi. Republican. Baptist. Office: Webster U 470 E Lockwood Saint Louis MO 63119

WESTERHAUS, CATHERINE K., social worker; b. Corydon, Ind., Oct. 13, 1910; d. Anthony Joseph and Permelia Ann (Mathes) Kannapel; m. George Henry Westerhaus, Apr. 15, 1950. BEd in Music, Kans. U., 1934; MSW, Loyola U., Chgo., 1949. Cert. Acad. Cert. Social Workers. Clin. social worker Friendly Acres Home of Aged, Newton, Kans.; county welfare dir., state adult svcs. supr. Newton-Harvey County, State of Kans.; vol. cert. social worker Newton. Project dir.: Memories of War Years, 1995, The War Years Including Veterans of Harvey County, Kansas, 1995; contbr. articles to profl. jours. With USNR, 1945-46. Named Kans. Social Worker of Yr., 1975. Mem. NASW (cert.), Kans. Soc. Cert. Social Work, Am. Legion (comdr. Wayne G. Austin post 1981-82). Home: 313 W Broadway St Newton KS 67114-2631

WESTERMAN, PHILIP WILLIAM, biomedical researcher, medical educator; b. Brisbane, Australia, June 16, 1945; came to U.S., 1971; s. Stephen Edward and Jeanne Minta (Parish) W.; m. Janice Mary Carson, Jan. 10, 1970; children: Natasha Ann, Karen Lynn. BSc, U. Sydney, Australia, 1967, PhD, 1971. Post-doctoral fellow Case Western Res. U., Cleve., 1971-73; rsch. assoc. Australian Nat. U., Canberra, 1974-75, Calif. Inst. Tech., Pasadena, 1975-76; asst. prof. Northeastern Ohio U. Coll. Medicine, Rootstown, 1976-82, assoc. prof., 1982-88, prof., 1988—; mem. Liquid Crystal Inst., Kent (Ohio) State U., 1980—, adj. prof. chemistry, 1982—, full grad. faculty mem. Sch. Biomedical Scis., 1981—. Contbr. over 90 articles to profl. jours. Treas. Am. Field Svc. (exchange student orgn.), Kent, 1990-92. Recipient Student Teaching award Northeastern Ohio U. Coll. Medicine, 1979, 82, 89, Rsch. award NIH, 1980-87, Rsch. Challenge award Bd. Regents State of Ohio, 1988-91, Grant-in-Aid Am. Heart Assn., 1992-96. Mem. Am. Chem. Soc., Biophys. Soc., Am. Soc. Biochemistry and Molecular Biology, Internat. Liquid Crystal Soc., N.Y. Acad. Scis., Internat. Soc. Magnetic Resonance, Sigma Xi (pres. Kent State U. chpt. 1990-92). Home: 343 Burr Oak Dr Kent OH 44240 Office: Northeastern Ohio Univ Coll Medicine PO Box 95 Rootstown OH 44272-0095

WESTFALL, MORRIS, state legislator; b. Apr. 5, 1939; s. Raymond Earl and Ethel Faye (Neill) W.; m. Sharon Kay Douglas, Dec. 19, 1964; children: Craig Lin, Christi Dawn. BS, U. Mo., 1962. Rep. State of Mo., 1971-81; asst. minority floor leader, minority whip Mo. Ho. of Reps., 1995—; senator dist. 28 State of Mo.; state exec. dir. agrl. stabilization conservation svc. USDA, Mo., 1981-93. Bd. dirs. Polk County Fair, 1967-71, Polk Soil and Water, 1970-71. Mem. S.E. Lions Club, Mo. Vocation Assn., U. Mo. Alumni Assn., Saddle Club. Office: State Capitol Bldg Jefferson MO 65101

WESTFALL, WAYNE LYNN, chemical engineer; b. Mechanicsburg, Pa., Jan. 9, 1941; s. Karl H. and Mae L. (Conrad) W.; m. Sharon L. Hillis, Aug. 10, 1966; children: Amy, Wendy, Danielle, Kristian. AS, York (Pa.) Jr. Coll., 1960; BS in Chem. Engring., Pa. State U., 1965. Project engr. Avon Products, Inc., Suffern, N.Y., 1971-74; sr. project engr. H.J. Heinz Co., Pitts., 1974-77; plant engr. Witco Corp., Petrolia, Pa., 1977-79, mgr. ops., 1979-84; mgr. mfg. Witco Corp., Indpls., 1984-86; area supr Witco Corp., Blue Island, Ill., 1989-91; maintenance mgr. Witco Corp., Chgo., 1991-94; ins. agt., registered rep. Prudential Ins. Co., Lewistown, Pa., 1986-87; ops. mgr. Envirotrol, Inc., Sewickley, Pa., 1987-88; pres. Westfall Cons., Joliet, Ill., 1994—. With U.S. Army, 1960-63. Mem. AIChE, AAAS. Office: Inolex Chem Co 4200 S Hermitage Chicago IL 60609

WESTLAKE, PAUL EDWARD, JR., architect, educator; b. Wheeling, W.Va., July 3, 1952; s. Paul Edward Sr. and Kathryn Ann (Steinhilber) W.; m. Suzanne E. Grima, June 28, 1976; children: Carrie Kieffer, Emily Hart, Elizabeth Fox. BA, U. Pa., 1974, BS, 1974; MArch, Harvard U., 1978. Designer Louis Sauer Architect, Phila., 1979-80; assoc. William B. Morris Architect, Cleve., 1980-81; prin. Van Dijk Pace Westlake & Archs., Cleve., 1981—; assoc. prof. Kent (Ohio) State U. Sch. Architecture and Environ. Design. Co-founder, editor Harvard Architecture Rev. Regional chmn. alumni coun. Harvard U. Grad Sch. Design; vice chmn. Flats Osbow Design Rev. Com.; mem. corp. Hathaway Brown Sch.; trustee Cleve. Ctr. for Contemporary Art, Com. for Pub. Art, Ohio Preservation Alliance. Recipient Cleve. Arts prize for architecture, 1995. Fellow AIA. Office: Van Dijk Pace Westlake & Ptnrs 700 W Saint Clair Ave Cleveland OH 44113-1298

WESTLIE, MARGARET ANNE, nurse, writer; b. Halifax, N.S., Can., Apr. 21, 1947; d. Charles Reginald and Hazel Christena (MacKinnon) MacLeod; m. John David Westlie, Apr. 21, 1984. BSN, Dalhousie U., Halifax, N.S., 1972; student, William Jewell Coll., Liberty, Mo., 1988-94; MA in English, U. Mo., Kansas City, 1996. Family life cons. Dept. Health and Social Svcs., Charlottetown, PEI, Can., 1979-81; inservice edn. coord. Sarcee Hosp., Calgary, Alta., Can., 1981-82; nursing supr. Mid-Maine Med. Ctr., Waterville, Maine, 1983-84; charge nurse Liberty (Mo.) Hosp., 1987-88. Violin player Philharmonia of Kansas City. Mem. AAUW. Baptist.

WESTLY, KENNETH, engineering manager; b. Edgerton, Wis., Sept. 26, 1955. Engring. foreman Schleter Co., Jonesville, Wis., 1973-84; sr. engr. Sani-matic Systems, Madison, Wis., 1984-94; engring. mgr. Johnson/Nelles Corp., Windsor, Wis., 1994—. Patentee in field. Lutheran. Office: Johnson/Nelles Corp 6391 Lake Rd Windsor WI 53598-9708

WESTMAN, ALIDA SPAANS, psychology educator; b. The Hague, The Netherlands, Oct. 16, 1944; came to U.S., 1958, naturalized 1963; d. Adrian David and Alida H. (Hooft) Spaans; m. Ronald S. Westman, Sept. 28, 1971; 1 child, Christopher. BS, Wash. State U., 1966, MS, 1968; PhD, Cornell U., 1971. Rsch. assoc. Ctrl. Inst. for The Deaf, St. Louis, 1971-72; asst. prof. Ea. Mich. U., Ypsilanti, 1972-76, assoc. prof., 1976-81, prof. psychology, 1981—. cons. book cos. and jours.; contbr. articles to profl. jours. Pack and den leader Cub Scouts Am., Ypsilanti, 1988-92; sec. then pres. parent adv. bd. East Mid. Sch., Ypsilanti, 1993-95. Mem. APA, Am. Psychol. Soc., Soc. Rsch. Child Devel., Soc. Sci. Study Religion, Phi Beta Kappa, Phi Kappa Phi, Sigma Xi, Sigma Delta Epsilon, Psi Chi. Office: Ea Mich U Psychology Dept Ypsilanti MI 48197

WESTMAN, ROBERT ALLAN, management consultant; b. Marbleton, Que., Can., Feb. 22, 1926; s. James Amon and Flora Gladys (Gilbert) W.; m. Esther Florence Renshaw, July 2, 1949; children: Michael, Joel, Robin, Andrew. Student Chemistry, Physics, U. Bishop's Coll., Que., Can., 1942-43; BASc, U. Toronto, 1949; postgrad. Bus. Adminstrn., U. Pa., 1955-56. V.p. spl. projects Ogden Metals, Inc., Cleve., 1970-74; chmn. Warren (Ohio) Fabricating Corp., 1974-78; v.p., gen. mgr. C-L Metals, Niles (Ohio), Inc., 1978-79; pres. Inred Iron, Inc., Roseland, N.J., 1981-85, R.A. Westman & Assoc., Warren, 1979—; bd. dirs., cons. Felber Studios, Inc., Ardmore, Pa., 1984—. Patentee cast clad steel plate. Rep. ward leader, Sunnyvale, Ca., 1961-62. Served with RCAF, 1943-45. Mem. Assn. Iron and Steel Engrs. (assoc.), Am. Iron and Steel Inst. (assoc.). Presbyterian. Clubs: Duquesne (Pitts.). Home and Office: 359 Quarry Ln NE Apt F Warren OH 44483-4554

WESTON, JAMES RANDALL, state legislator; b. Marion, Ohio, May 2, 1958; s. James Edson and Geraldine (Gibb) W.; m. Carolyn Fabey, 1984; children: J.R., Patrick. BS, Stetson U., 1981. Rep. Ohio State Ho. Reps. Dist. 90, 1991-92, 1993—; grain farmer, 1974—; tchr., 1983—. Named Legis. of Yr., Ohio Jewelers Assn., 1992, 93. Mem. Fraternal Order Police (assoc.), Marion County Trustees (assoc.), Farmers Union, Farm Bur., Marion County Dem. Club. *

WESTON, PHYLLIS JEAN, art gallery director; b. Cleve.; d. Armin and Wilma H. (Wasserman) Hornstein; m. Leo F. Weston, Oct. 18, 1963; children: H. Todd Cobey, John Cobey. Ed., Yale U., 1949-50. v.p., dir. AB Closson Jr. Co. Art Gallery, Cin., 1964—; art cons. Proctor & Gamble Co., Cin., 1983—; cons., lectr. in art. Named Woman of the Yr. Cin. Enquirer, 1987; recipient Post Corbett award, 1989. Chmn., founder Enjoy the Arts; founder Cin. Commn. on the Arts, The Post Corbett awards; bd. dirs., mem. numerous arts and civic orgns. including Internation Visitors Ctr., Inc., Friends of Cin. Parks, Cinn. Chamber Orch., C.A.S.A.; adv. judge Congl. Art Competition Sch. Creative and Performing Arts; mem. Citizens Against Substance Abuse, Internat. Visitors Ctr., Japan Am. Soc. Home: 4 Taft Road Ln Cincinnati OH 45206-1805 Office: 401 Race St Cincinnati OH 45202-2804

WESTON, ROY B., anesthesiologist; b. Port-of-Spain, Trinidad, May 9, 1929; came to U.S., 1977; s. Bertrand H. and Doris (Pantin) W.; m. Elizabeth C. McLaughlin, Oct. 7, 1961; children: Shiobhan R., Brian R. MB, nat. U. Ireland, Dublin, 1956. Cert. anesthesiologist, Fellow Royal Can. Physicians, 1966. Staff anesthesiologist Humber Meml. Hosp., Weston, Ont., Can., 1962-77, Park City Hosp., Bridgeport, Conn., 1977-88; chief anesthesiology Huntington (Ind.) Meml. Hosp., 1988—. Fellow Am. Coll. Anesthesiologists; mem. Am. Soc. Anesthesiologists, Royal Soc. Medicine, Ind. Med. Assn., Ind. State Soc. Anesthesiologists, Acad. Medicine, Am. Soc. Regional Anesthesia. Roman Catholic. Home and Office: 3293 N Rangeline Rd Huntington IN 46750

WESTPHAL, LEONARD WYRICK, health care executive, consultant; b. Kansas City, Mo., Sept. 28, 1946; s. Leonard Henry and Elizabeth (Wyrick) W.; m. Sandra Sanders, Aug. 13, 1972; children: Michael Weston, Margaret Elizabeth. BFA, So. Meth. U., 1969; MA, S.W. Mo. State U., 1972; postgrad., U. Mich., Cen. Mo. State U., Lincoln U. of Mo., Century U. Lic. nursing home adminstr., Mo., Ark. Exec. dir. Dist. III Area Agy. on Aging, Warrensburg, 1972-83; state dir. Mo. Div. of Aging, Jefferson City, Mo., 83-85; spl. asst. to dir. Mo. Dept. Mental Health, Jefferson City, 1985-86; exec. dir. Missouri River Health Care, Jefferson City, 1986-88; health care adminstr., cons., 1988—; continuing edn. instr., mem. adv. coun. continuing edn. SW Mo. State U., 1993—; adj. instr., internship supr. Cen. Mo. State U., Warrensburg, 1974-83; mem. rev. panel State of Mo., 1974-76, HHS, 1984-85; cons. Adminstrn. on Aging, Fed. Emergency Mgmt. Agy., 1977-83; bd. dirs. Mid-Am. Congress on Aging, 1975; chmn. Mo. Gov.'s Task Force, Hearings and Conf. on Alternative Care for Elderly, 1982-83; mem. Mo. Bd. Nursing Home Adminstrs., 1983-85; founder, coord. Older Missourians Craft Festival, 1978-83; pres., v.p. Mo. Alliance Area Agys. on Aging, 1974-76;

host radio programs Sta. Kmos-TV, Sta. KCMW-FM, Sta. KWTO, 1993—; mem. adv. com. health care adm. program S.W. Mo. State U.; presenter in field. Author articles in disaster assistance. Mem. Mo. Rep. Com., 1970—, rev. panel United Way, Warrensburg, 1978; mem. coun. ministries lst United Meth. Ch., Warrensburg, 1979-83, mem. adminstrv. coun., 1981-83, pres. Meth. Men, 1982-83; mem. commn. on missions, Wesley United Meth. Ch., Jefferson City, 1984-86, liturgist, 1985-89; mem. ch. and soc. commn. Wesley United Methodist Ch., Springfield, 1989—; pres. PTA, Warrensburg, 1982; coach Little League Football and Basketball, Warrensburg, 1981-82; bd. dirs. Warrensburg Community Betterment, 1976-78; mem. adminstrv. coun., mem. chancel choir Grace United Meth. Ch., Springfield, 1993—. Recipient Boss of Yr. award Warrensburg Jaycees, 1976, svc. recognition Mo. Office Aging, 1977, Mo. Alliance Area Agys. on Aging, 1977, Older Adult Transp. Svc., Columbia, Mo., 1983, Mo. State Fair, 1983, Mo. Dept. Mental Health, 1986; Exceptional Svc. in Disaster Assistance award City of Sedalia, 1977, 80; Outstanding Contbns. award Ret. Sr. Vol. Programs, 1977, 79, Excellence in Adminstrn. award Mo. Office Aging, 1977, Outstanding Svcs. award Hickory County, Mo., 1984, also others. Fellow Am. Coll. Healthcare Adminstrs. (cert.); mem. Am. Coll. Healthcare Execs., Gerontol. Soc. Am., Am. Soc. Pub. Adminstrn., Mo. Alliance for Homecare, Mo. League Nursing Home Adminstrs., Am. Coll. Healthcare Profls., Jefferson City C. of C., Springfield C. of C. (mem. retirement and devel. coms.), Optimists (v.p. Warrensburg 1979-81), Rotary, Elks, Delta Sigma Rho-Tau Kappa Alpha, Delta Chi (alumni advisor, alumni bd. trustees, achievement award). Home: 1420 S Lovers Ln Springfield MO 65804-2123

WETHINGTON, NORBERT ANTHONY, college administrator; b. Dayton, Ohio, Sept. 14, 1943; s. Norbert and Sophie Lillian W.; m. Martha M. Vannice, Aug. 13, 1966; children: Paula, Mark, Eric, Kristen, Rebecca, Lisa, Bethany. BA, U. Dayton, 1965; MA, John Carroll U., 1967; postgrad. Baldwin Wallace Coll., 1968-70, U. Toledo, 1990—. Grad. asst., teaching assoc. John Carroll U., Cleve., 1965-67; English tchr. Padua Franciscan High Sch., Parma, Ohio, 1967-70; instr., chmn. dept. tech. writing and speech N. Central Tech. Coll., Mansfield, Ohio, 1970-74; dir. evening div. Terra Tech. Coll., Fremont, Ohio, 1974-80, dir. public and cmty. svc. technologies, 1980-94; dir. humanities Terra State C.C., 1994—; cons. several profl. assns. and non-profit groups. Vice pres. Sandusky County Bd. Health, 1979-80. Mem. Am. Vocat. Assn., Ohio Vocat. Assn. (pres. tech. edn. div. 1985-86, Disting. Svc. award 1987), Nat. Council Tchrs. English. Democrat. Roman Catholic. Contbr. articles to profl. jours. Home: 1036 Hazel St Fremont OH 43420-2115 Office: Terra State Cmty Coll 2830 Napoleon Rd Fremont OH 43420-9670

WETTERS, HOWARD, state legislator; b. Bay City, Mich., June 2, 1952; s. Howard and Helen W.; m. Juliann Chamberlain, 1991; 1 child, Hanna. AA, Delta Coll., 1972; BS, Mich. State U., 1975. Owner, operator Howard Wetters Farms, 1977-88; agrl. agt. Bay County ext. Mich. State U., 1983-87; com. aide Agriculture & Forestry com. Mich. Ho. of Rep., 1987-88; adv. Agriculture & Natural Resources Mich. Gov.'s Office, 1988-90; state rep. Dist. 97 Mich. Ho. of Reps., 1993—; mem. Agriculture & Forestry Com., Conservation, Environment, Great Lakes & Tax Policy coms. Mich. Ho. Reps. Home: 1866 Wetters Rd Kawkawlin MI 48631-9429*

WETZEL, KARL H., computer programmer; b. Mineral Wells, Tex., Apr. 21, 1951. BA, Morningside Coll., 1973. Libertarian candidate for Clay County Commr., 1994, for U.S. House 6th Dist., Mo., 1996; treas. Mo. Libertarian Party, 1994—. Office: 210 NE 58th St # 19 Gladstone MO 64118*

WEXMAN, VIRGINIA WRIGHT, English language educator; b. Winnipeg, Man., Can., Apr. 2, 1941; d. Douglas Wright and Jean Swinton Hine; m. Todd Ellis Wexman, July 25, 1960 (div. 1979); children: Kimberly, Todd; m. John W. Huntington, Jr., Aug. 28, 1982. BA, U. Chgo., 1970, MA, 1971, PhD, 1976. Producer Office of Radio-TV, U. Chgo., 1971-75; asst. prof. U. Ill., Chgo., 1975-82, assoc. prof., 1982-92, prof. dept. English, 1992—; vis. assoc. prof. U. Chgo., 1990; seminar leader Lilly Endowment Workshop on Liberal Arts, Colorado Springs, 1988-94. Editor: Cinema Jour., 1982-87; editl. bd. U. Ill. Press, 1991-94; author: Creating the Couple, 1993, Roman Polanski, 1984; co-editor: Letter from an Unknown Woman, 1986; co-author: Robert Altman, 1984; contbr. articles to profl. jours. Mem. MLA (chair film divsn. 1981-82), Soc. for Cinema Studies (pres. 1993-95). Democrat. Home: 711 S Dearborn St Apt 808 Chicago IL 60605-1827 Office: Univ Ill at Chgo Dept English # 162 601 S Morgan St Chicago IL 60607-7120

WEYL, TOM F., advertising executive; b. 1943. Creative dir. Am. Acad. Art, 1963-68; with Campbell-Mithun Inc., Mpls., 1968-73; pres., sec., CCO Martin-Williams Inc., Mpls., 1973—. Office: Martin Williams Advt Inc 60 S 6th St Ste 2800 Minneapolis MN 55402-1012*

WEYMER, PATRICK TIMOTHY, mechanical engineer; b. Chgo., Apr. 24, 1969. BSME, Milw. Sch. Engring., 1992. Engr.-in-tng., Wis. Applications engr. Indsl. Heat Enterprises Internat., Inc., Franklin, Wis., 1991-93, Lindberg Co., Watertown, Wis., 1994—. Mem. Advanced Soc. for Metals. Republican. Home: 2102 Mac Arthur Rd Waukesha WI 53188-5648 Office: 304 Hart St Watertown WI 53094-6616

WHALEN, PATRICIA THERESE, marketing professional; b. Columbus, Ohio, June 26, 1955; d. Daniel Edward and Rose Eileen (Callahan) W. BA in English, Ohio State U., 1977; MS in Bus. Adminstrn., Ind. U., 1981; postgrad. in mass media, Mich. State U., 1994—. Sales promotion specialist Clark Components Div., Buchanan, Mich., 1978-81, supr., advt. and pub. rels., 1981-82; mgr. corp. comm. Clark Equipment Co., Buchanan, Mich., 1982-84; dir. govt. affairs Clark Equipment Co., South Bend, Ind., 1984-86; dir. pub. rels. COMSAT World Systems Div., Clarksburg, Md., 1986-87; dir. mktg. communications COMSAT World Systems Div., Washington, 1987-90; dir. mktg. COMSAT Mobile Comm., Washington, 1990-94; instr. dept. advt., mktg. cons. Miss. State U., 1995—; seminar speaker in field. Bd. dirs. Tri-county Pvt. Industry Coun., St. Joseph County, Mich., 1983-85, Jr. Achievement, Niles, Mich. and South Bend, Ind., 1982-86; chmn. Clark PAC Polit. Action Com., South Bend, 1984-86. Mem. Pub. Rels. Soc. Am. (tech. com. 1982—, Silver Anvil award 1982), Internat. Assn. Bus. Communicators, Bus. and Profl. Advertisers Assn., Soc. Satellite Profls. (bd. dirs. 1990-93). Roman Catholic. Home: 1747 Mapleridge Rd Apt 13 Haslett MI 48840-8648

WHALEN, ROBERT JAMES, business consultant; b. Dayton, Ohio, Feb. 17, 1953; s. James Daniel and Jean Katherine Whalen; married, 1986; 2 children. BSBA, Miami U. of Ohio, 1975; MBA, U. Pa., 1979. CPA, Ohio; cert. mgmt. acct., Inst. Mgmt. Accts. Asst. bank examiner FDIC, Chgo., 1975-77; fin. mgr. AT&T Global Info. Solutions, Dayton, Ohio, 1979-92; bus. cons. Oakwood Assocs., Dayton, Ohio, 1992—. Mem. AICPA, Inst. Mgmt. Accts. (dir. CPE programs 1994-95), Ohio Soc. CPAs, Planning Forum (co-chair programs 1992-93). Office: Oakwood Assocs PO Box 712WBB Dayton OH 45409

WHALEN, VERMEL M., state legislator; b. Portageville, Mo.. Student, Cleve. State U., U. Ga., Cuyahoga C.C. Mem. Ohio Ho. Reps., 1993—, vice chair interstate coop com., mem. children & youth subcom., edn. select com., human resources com., health & retirement com., mem. local govt. & transp. com., urban affairs com., vice chair econ. devel. & small bus. com. Trustee United Black Fund. Recipient Physicians for Better Govt. award. Home: 16804 Glendale Ave Cleveland OH 44128-1454*

WHALEY-BUCKEL, MARNIE, social service administrator; b. Madison County, Ohio, July 16, 1946; d. H. John and Frances (Kramer) Hostetler; m. John Benjamin Whaley, Sept. 14, 1974 (wid. Mar. 1977); 1 child, Monica Anne; m. Raymond J. Buckel, May 17, 1991; 1 adopted child, Dimitri R.A. Buckel. BA in Social Work, Bluffton Coll., 1969; MSW, Ohio State U., 1983. Lic. ind. social worker, Ohio. Counselor Family Counseling, Lima, Ohio, 1969-70; social worker psychiat. unit St. Rita's Hosp., Lima, 1970-74; emergency counselor Northwest Ctr. for Human Resources, Lima, 1975-78, outpatient therapist, 1977-80, coord. emergency svcs., 1979-82; intern coord. pub. rels. Northwest Couseling, Columbus, Ohio, 1982-83; coord. community rels. Madison County Hosp., London, Ohio, 1983-85; assoc. dir. Madison County Health Ctr Inc., London, 1985-89; exec. dir. Bd. Alcohol, Drug Addiction and Mental Health Svcs., London, 1989-94; chmn. Allen County Welfare Adv. Bd., Lima, 1979-82; vice chmn. Act. Inc., Columbus, 1989-91, chmn., 1991-93; Ohio Hospice Adv. Bd., London, 1990-91, pvt. cons., agy. adminstrn., mediation, 1995—. Chmn. bd. ch. edn. Big Darby Bapt. Ch., Plain City, Ohio, 1987, clk., 1989—, sec.-treas., 1988, 89,, chmn. constitution com., 1990. Mem. NASW, Mental Health Adminstrs., Phi Kappa Phi, Delta Sigma Mu.

WHALLON, ROBERT EDWARD, anthropology educator; b. Boston, Apr. 23, 1940; s. Robert E. and Dorothy J. (Curme) W.; m. Nadine Rose DeVries, Jan. 1, 1962 (dec.); 1 child, Saskia Olga; m. Barbara Abbott Segraves, Apr. 29, 1978 (div. May 1983); m. Nada Rakic, Jan. 16, 1990; children: Vuk Novak, Nikola Lazar. B.A. summa cum laude, Harvard U., 1961; M.A., U. Chgo., 1963, Ph.D., 1966. Teaching asst. dept anthropology, Chgo., 1965; curator mediterranean prehistory, asst. prof. U. Mich., Ann Arbor, 1966-71, curator, assoc. prof., 1971-77, curator, prof., 1977—, acting dir. Mus. Anthropology, 1978-79; fellow Netherlands Inst. for Advanced Studies, 1971-72; mem. NSF adv. panel for anthropology, 1976-77. Editor: Jour. Anthrop. Archaeology, 1981-94, Mich. Archaeologist, 1969-70; author monographs, essays; contbr. numerous articles on anthropology and archaeology to profl. jours. NSF grantee, 1967—; Woodrow Wilson fellow, 1965; NDEA fellow, 1961-64. Fellow AAAS, Current Anthrpology; mem. Soc. for Am. Archaeology (exec. com. 1981-82, com. on archaeologist-Native Am. rels. 1982), Internat. Union for Prehist. and Protohist. Scis. (Commn. 4 sec. 1976-81, pres. 1981-87, permanent coun. 1987—), Sigma Xi, Phi Beta Kappa. Home: 1704 Baldwin Pl Ann Arbor MI 48104-3509 Office: U Mich Mus Anthropology Ann Arbor MI 48109-1079

WHANG, UN-YOUNG, music educator; b. Seoul, Korea, Feb. 22, 1954; came to U.S., 1968; parents Sung Soo and Kewha (Kim) W. MusB, The Juilliard Sch., 1978, MusM, 1978; MEd, Columbia U., 1984, EdD, 1986. Ch. pianist Manhattan Korean Ch., N.Y.C., 1972-74, Full Gospel Korean Ch., N.Y.C., 1976-79; pianist, organist Trinity Korean Presbyn. Ch., Woodside, N.Y., 1981-83, Hudson Korean Presbyn. Ch., Jersey City, 1983-86; ch. pianist The Korean Ch. of Queens, Jackson Heights, N.Y., 1986-87; piano tchr. Tchrs. Coll. Community Music Ctr., N.Y.C., 1984-87; piano instr. Columbia U., N.Y.C., 1985-87; ch. pianist Korean Cen. Covenant Ch., Northbrook, Ill., 1989-91; asst. prof. Moody Bible Inst., Chgo., 1987-93, assoc. prof., 1993-95, prof., 1995—; soloist, chamber musician of sacred and classical music. Recipient Presdl. Award for Excellence in Piano Korean Govt., 1968, Competition Winner and scholarship The Juilliard Sch., 1970. Mem. Coll. Music Soc., Music Tchrs. Nat. Assn. (cert.). Presbyterian. Office: Moody Bible Inst 820 N La Salle Dr Chicago IL 60610-3214

WHARTON, JOHN JAMES, JR., management consultant, physicist; b. Warrensburg, Mo., May 28, 1949; s. John James and Carol Jean (West) W.; m. Anne Elizabeth Connolly, Sept. 21, 1985; children: Elizabeth, Angela, J.J., Eric. BSEE, U. Mo., 1971; MS, Air Force Inst. Tech., 1977; PhD, U. Ariz., 1984. Asst. prof. physics U.S. Air Force Acad., Colorado Springs, Colo., 1978-80; assoc. prof. physics, dep. dept. head Air Force Inst. Tech., Dayton, 1983-87; program mgr. Def. Advanced Rsch. Projects Agy., Rosslyn, Va., 1987-91; dir. info. mgmt. Environ. Rsch. Inst. Mich., Ann Arbor, 1991—; adj. assoc. prof. Coll. Engring., U. Mich., 1996—. Mem. IEEE, Optical Soc. Am. (bd. dirs. 1990-92), Am. Phys. Soc., Mensa, Tau Beta Pi. Home: 7409 Steeplechase Ct Saline MI 48176 Office: Environ Rsch Inst Mich PO Box 134001 Ann Arbor MI 48113-4001

WHARTON, MELANIE L., business executive; b. Wooster, Ohio, Sept. 18, 1963. Student, Akron U., 1981. Copy prep. clk. Bell and Howell, Wooster, 1985-90; pres. Agri-Industries Corp., Big Prairie, Ohio, 1990—. Republican. Office: Agri Industries Corp 11671 Township Road 506 Big Prairie OH 44611-9656

WHEALEY, LOIS DEIMEL, humanities scholar; b. N.Y.C., June 20, 1932; d. Edgar Bertram Deimel and Lois Elizabeth (Hatch) Washburn; m. Robert Howard Whealey, July 2, 1954; children: Richard William, David John, Alice Ann Whealey Dediu. BA in History, Stanford U., 1951; MA in Edn., U. Mich., 1955; MA in Polit. Sci., Ohio U., 1975. Tchr. 5th grade Swayne Sch., Owyhee, Nev., 1952-53; tchr. 7th grade Ft. Knox (Ky.) Dependent's Sch., 1955-56; tchr. adult basic edn. USAF, Oxford, 1956-57; tchr. 6th grade Amerman Sch., Northville, Mich., 1957-58; tchr. 8th grade English, social studies Slauson Jr. High Sch., Ann Arbor, Mich., 1958-59; adminstrv. asst. humanities conf. Ohio U., Athens, 1974-76, 83; part-time instr. Ohio U., Athens, 1966-68, 75. Contbr. articles to profl. jours. Mem. Athens County Regional Planning Commn., 1974-78, treas., 1976-78; bd. dirs. Ohio Meadville Dist. Unitarian-Universalist Assn., 1975-81, Ohio Women Inc., 1995—; mem. Ohio coord. com. Internat. Women's Yr., 1977; v.p. Black Diamond Girl Scout Coun., 1980-86; chair New Day for Equal Rights Amendment, 1982; mem. Athens City Bd. Edn., 1984-90, v.p., 1984, pres., 1985; mem. Tri-County Vocat. Sch. Bd., Nelsonville, Ohio, 1984-90, v.p., 1988-89; mem. adv. com. Ohio River Valley Water Sanitation Commn., 1986-95; bd. dirs. Ohio Environ. Coun., 1984-90, sec., 1986-90; bd. dirs. Ohio Alliance for Environ., 1993—; coord. Southeast Ohio Collaborative on Women and Children, Ohio Dept. Edn., 1994—. Recipient Unsung UU award Ohio-Meadville Dist. Unitarian Universalist Assn., 1984, Thanks badge Black Diamond Girl Scout Coun., 1986, How to award Ednl. Press Assn. Am., 1990, Donna Chen Women's Equity award Ohio U., 1994; named Woman of Achievement, Black Diamond Girl Scout Coun., 1987. Mem. AAUW (pres. Athens br. 1969-70, 89-90, 93—, nat. pub. policy chair AAUW/Ohio 1995—), LWV (pres. 1975-77), Phi Lambda Theta (life). Democrat. Home: 14 Oak St Athens OH 45701-2605

WHEALLER, SUSAN CORNELIA, college dean, educator; b. Atlanta, June 5, 1953; d. John Anson and Ora Cornelia (Cordell) W. BA in English lit. summa cum laude, Rollins Coll., Winter Park, Fla., 1975; MA in English lit., Purdue U., 1978, PhD in English lit., 1982. ESL instr. Orange County Adult Edn., Orlando, Fla., 1975-76; grad. instr. Purdue U., West Lafayette, Ind., 1976-82; dir. devel. composition Purdue U., West Lafayette, 1981-82; mem. faculty English Rockford (Ill.) Coll., 1982—, chmn. dept. English, 1987-91, assoc. dean, 1989—; assoc. dean Regent's Coll., London, 1995-96; writing cons. various bus. and industries, Rockford, 1983—; acad. adv. bd. European Bus. Sch., London, 1995-96. Editl. reviewer MacMillan Pub., 1988-89. Bd. dirs. YWCA, Rockford, 1992-95, ARC, Rockford, 1991-95. NEH summer seminar Harvard U., 1990; recipient Svc. award ARC, Rockford, 1995. Mem. MLA, Nat. Coun. Tchrs. English, Jane Austen Soc. N.Am. Office: Rockford Coll 5050 E State St Rockford IL 61108-2393

WHEAT, CHRISTOPHER JOHN, SR., broadcast executive; b. Boston, Dec. 22, 1950; s. Robert Haase Wheat and Florence Edith (Potter) Wiley; m. Becky Ann Renshaw, June 3, 1972; children: Christopher John Jr., Colan Michael. BE, U. Cin., 1972; postgrad., U. Pa., 1978. Account exec. Sta. WKRQ-FM, Cin., 1972-76; account exec. Sta. WKRC-AM, Cin., 1976-78, mgr. local sales, 1978-80, gen. mgr. sales, 1980-82; v.p., gen. mgr. Sta. WYNF-FM, Tampa, Fla., 1982-83, Sta. WFBQ-FM, Indpls., 1983-87, Sta. WNDE-AM, Indpls., 1987—. Mem. Little Red Door, Indpls. Cancer Soc. Named one of Outstanding Young Men of Am., 1982. Mem. Radio Broadcasters of Indpls. (v.p., pres. 1988—), U. Cin. Alumni Club, Beta Theta Pi Alumni Club, Indpls. C. of C. (ptnrs. in edn. com., Ambassadors sect.). Republican. Methodist. Club: Indpls. Athletic. Home: 10723 Seascape Ct Indianapolis IN 46256-9529 Office: Sta WFBQ-FM 6161 Fall Creek Rd Indianapolis IN 46220-5032*

WHEATON, SHARON A., designer; b. Charles City, Iowa, Nov. 1, 1938; d. Gordon Bernard and Gertrude Marie (O'Harrow) Atherton; m. Darrell Dean Wheaton, Apr. 4, 1959; children: Douglas, David, Patrick. BA, U. Iowa, 1973; MA, U. Nebr., 1976. Prodn. mgr. Sta. KTVT, Salt Lake City, 1959-61; promotion mgr. Sta. KWWL-TV, Waterloo, Iowa, 1961-63; writer instrnl. TV Nebr. Coun. Higher Edn., 1969-74; ednl. tech. specialist U. Mid-Am., Lincoln, Nebr., 1975-82; ednl. tech. Modular Computer Systems, Fort Lauderdale, Fla., 1982-84; v.p. creative svcs. E.T. Interactive Multimedia, Lincoln, 1985—; new media cons. Ctr. for Ednl. Media, Richmond, Ind., 1991—; cons. Ctr. for Ednl. Media, Richmond, 1991—, Asia Soc., N.Y.C., 1993—; assoc. Media Prodn. Group, Vt., Japan, 1990—; vis. rschr. Nat. Inst. Multimedia Edn., Chiba, Japan, 1990-91; nat. conf. presenter Midwest Conf. on Asian Affairs, Macomb, Ill., 1994, Soc. for Applied Learning, Orlando, Fla., 1990. Editor: (video) Fit Surroundings, 1994; contbr. chpt. to books; assoc. producer (TV series) Japan: The Changing Tradition, 1976-77. Active Mayor's Friendship Com., Lincoln, Host Family Assn., Lincoln. Mem. Assn. for Asian Studies, Assn. for Tng. and Devel. Home: 400 N 73d St Lincoln NE 68505

WHEELER, DAVID LEE, theology educator; b. Louisville, Dec. 8, 1946; s. Robert Lee and Maureen Reid (Mosby) W.; m. Betty Davis, Feb. 2, 1974 (div. July 1988); children: Clare, Micah; m. Carol A. Allen, Oct. 12, 1990. BA, Georgetown Coll., 1968; MDiv, Yale Divinity Sch., 1971; ThD, Grad. Theol. Union, 1984. Ordained to ministry Bapt. Ch., 1971. Youth dir. Leitchfield (Ky.) Bapt. Ch., 1967-68; pastor Utopia Pkwy. Bapt. Chapel, Flushing, N.Y., 1971-73, Portola Bapt.Ch., San Francisco, 1978-82, Central Bapt. Ch., Elizabeth, N.J., 1984-85; prof. theology Central Bapt. Theol. Sem., Kansas City, Kans., 1985—; adj. prof. philosophy St. Mary Coll., Leavenworth, Kans., 1990—; faculty rep. Central Bapt. Sem., Kans. City Assn. Theol. Schs., Kansas City, Kans./Mo., 1987—. Author: A Relational View of the Atonement, 1989; contbr. articles to profl. jours. Bd. dirs. Kansas City Hispanic Ministries, 1985-91; bd. dirs., sec. Kaw Valley Habitat for Humanity, Kansas City, Kans., 1988—; bd. dirs. edn. com. chair Kansas City (Mo.) Interfaith Peace Alliance, 1989-93. Luther Wesley Smith citation Christian Higher Edn. Bd. Ednl. Ministries, Am. Bapt. Chs. in the USA, 1989. Mem. Am. Acad. Religion, Assn. Christian Philosophers, Bapt. Assn. Philosophy Tchrs., Nat. Assn. Bapt. Profs. Religion. Democrat. Office: Central Bapt Theol Sem 741 N 31st St Kansas City KS 66102-3984

WHEELER, DOUGLAS WALTER, executive; b. Elmhurst, Ill., May 26, 1956. BS in Polit. Sci. and BA in History, U. Wis., Oshkosh, 1979. Buyer Aldens Catalog, Chgo., 1983-85; v.p. Std. Mktg. Corp., Hinsdale, Ill., 1985-89, Consolidated Incentive Corp., Itaska, Ill., 1989—. Republican. Roman Catholic. Office: Consolidated Incentive Corp 650 E Devon Ave Ste 120 Itasca IL 60143-3115

WHEELER, OTIS V., JR., public school principal; b. Silex, Mo., Oct. 1, 1925; s. Otis V. and Pearla F. (Howell) W.; m. Virginia Rogers, June 7, 1947; children: Jan Leigh, Mark Patrick. BBA, U. Mo., 1948, MEd, 1965, EdD, 1971. USN, 1948-52, Bus. mgr., 1952-61; sci. tchr. Columbia (Mo.) Pub. Schs., 1961-63, principal, 1963-91; supt. Boone County Sch. Dist., Mo., 1971; instr. U. Mo., Columbia, 1970-72, asst. prof. 1972-75, 78-79; cons. Midwest Ctr for Equal Ednl. Opportunities, 1972-75. Served to lt. USNR, 1943-85, World War II, Korea. Mem. Nat. Assn. Elem. Sch. Prins. (U.S. Dept. Edn., Nat. Disting. Prin. award 1985, Excellence in Edn. award 1986), Mo. Assn. Elem. Sch. Prins. (Disting. Service award 1984, editor jours. 1967-88), Mo. State Tchrs. Assn., Retired Officers Assn., U. Mo. Columbia Coll. Edn. Alumni (Citation of Merit award 1987), Phi Delta Kappa, Phi Delta Theta, Kappa Delta Pi. Methodist. Club: Lake Ozark Yachting Assn. (Mo.). Home: 916 W Ash St Columbia MO 65203-2636 Office: Ridgeway IGE Sch 107 E Sexton Rd Columbia MO 65203-4082

WHEELER, PAUL LEONARD, retired transportation executive; b. Ashland, Ky., Apr. 23, 1926; s. Ora Y. and Norma L. (Murry) W.; m. Alice Kathryn Ritchie, June 8, 1947; children: Paul Allison, David Ritchie. Student, U. Ky. Designer Refinery Engring. Co., 1943; asst. signalman C&O Rwy. Co., 1944-46; various positions leading to signal engr. C&O/B&O R.R., 1948-73; various mgmt. positions leading to pres. and chief exec. officer Safetran Systems Corp., Mpls., 1973-91, also bd. dirs. Served to 2d lt. U.S. Army, 1944-46. Mem. Assn. Am. R.R.'s (communication and signals sect.), Rwy. Progress Inst. (bd. govs., mem. exec. com.). Republican. Baptist.

WHEELER, TOM CARL, seminary dean; b. Seminole, Okla., May 3, 1954; s. Carl Theron and Gloria Ruth (Durham) W.; m. Rebecca Jane Phillips, June 25, 1983; children: Daniel Paul, Nathan Thomas, Elisabeth Ruth. BA in Bible, Bob Jones U., 1976, MA, 1978, PhD in Theology, 1984. Grad. asst. Bob Jones U., Greenville, S.C., 1979-81; shipping floor coord. Bob Jones U. Press Warehouse, Greenville, 1981-85; dir. Tri-City Bible Coll., Kansas City, Mo., 1985—. Author: American Christian Civics, 1996. Organizer Neighborhood Watch, Independence, Mo., 1989; bd. dirs. Family Forum Coalition Group, Kansas City, 1991-94; polit. campaign helper. Home: 9012 E 32d St Independence MO 64052 Office: Tri-City Ministries 4500 Selsa Rd Blue Springs MO 64015

WHEELER, WILMOT FITCH, III, automotive industry executive; b. N.Y.C., July 15, 1945; s. Wilmot Fitch and Barbara (Rutherfurd) W.; m. Wanda Lee Presnell, Dec. 2, 1981. BA, Lake Forest Coll., 1969. Pres., COO Acco Controls Group FKI Babcock Inc., Adrian, Mich., 1971-87; pres. Wheeler Cons., Jerome, Mich., 1987-88; pres., CEO PBM Industries, Mt. Clemens, Mich., 1988-92, Batten Design & Engring., Romulus, Mich., 1989-92; exec. v.p. Hi-Lex Corp., Bloomfield Hills, Mich., 1992—; bd. dirs. Ohio Fabricators Inc., Coshocton, Ohio. Vice chmn. St. Christopher House, Detroit, 1990—. Episcopalian. Home: 54344 Starlite Dr Shelby Township MI 48316

WHEELOCK, LARRY ARTHUR, engineer, consultant; b. Chgo., Nov. 20, 1938; s. Preston J. and Rozella (Schonert) W.; m. Ruth E. Pruess (div. Sept. 1975); children: John P., J. Robert, William D., Thomas K.; m. Norma Jane Fair, Oct. 22, 1984. BSEE, U. Evansville, 1962. Registered profl. engr., Ind.; cert. instrument rated comml. pilot, airframe and powerplant mechanic, FAA. Co-op student engr. Naval Avionics Facility, Indpls., 1958-59; co-op student engr. Naval Weapons Support Ctr., Crane, Ind., 1959-62, elec. engr., 1963-78; elec. engr. Delco Electronics, Kokomo, Ind., 1962-63; sr. mfg. eng. Ford Aerospace & Comm., Bedford, Ind., 1979-80; plant engr. Ethyl Corp., Terre Haute, Ind., 1980-81; plant mgr. Tredegar Industries/Ethyl Corp., Terre Haute, 1981-91. Patentee in field. Bd. dirs. Hulman Regional Airport Authority, 1991-95, pres., 1992; pres. Greene County Airport Bd. Commrs., Bloomfield, Ind., 1972-81. Mem. IEEE, NSPE, Aircraft Owners & Pilots Assn., Exptl. Aircraft Assn., Antique Aircraft Assn., Internat. Flying Farmers, Flying Engrs. Internat. (pres. 1994, 95), Mensa, Internat. Assn. Flying Rotarians, Rotary Internat. Home: 7480 State Road 42 Terre Haute IN 47803-9778 also: PO Box 309 Raymondville TX 78580

WHELAN, DONALD JOSEPH, fundraising executive; b. Omaha, Nov. 8, 1934; s. Edward Charles and Mary Margaret (Weppner) W.; m. Patricia Jean McCabe, Oct. 1, 1960; children—Donald Joseph, Jr., Timothy, Michael, Mary, Kathryn, Theresa, Joseph. B.S. in Journalism, Creighton U., 1957; L.H.D., Duchesne Coll., 1968. Dir. devel. Duchesne Coll. and Acad., Omaha, 1965-68, John Burroughs Sch., St. Louis, 1968—; cons. The Latin Sch. of Chgo., 1986-88, others; workshop leader. Author, editor: Handbook for Development Officers at Independent Schools, 1979, 2d edit., 1982. Pres. sch. bd. St. Joseph Cath. Ch., Manchester, Mo., 1970-71; pres. parish council St. Clare Cath. Ch., Mo., 1973-75; bd. dirs. Campbell House Found., 1987-90. Served to 1st lt., U.S. Army, 1957-59. Mem. Council Advancement and Support of Edn. (nat. chmn. ind. sch. sect. 1978-81, trustee 1978-81; recipient Steel award 1974, 83, Exceptional Achievement award 1980, Disting. Service award 1980, Robert Bell Crow award 1982). Republican. Lodge: Rotary. Home: 907 Clayworth Dr Ballwin MO 63011-3522 Office: John Burroughs Sch 755 S Price Rd Saint Louis MO 63124-1866

WHELAN, JOSEPH L., neurologist; b. Chisholm, Minn., Aug. 13, 1917; s. James Gorman and Johanna (Quilty) W.; m. Gloria Ann Rewoldt, June 12, 1948; children: Joe, Jennifer. Student, Hibbing Jr. Coll., 1935-38; BS, U. Minn., 1940, MB, 1942, MD, 1943. Diplomate Am. Bd. Psychiatry and Neurology. Intern Detroit Receiving Hosp., 1942-43; fellow neurology U. Pa. Hosp., Phila., 1946-47; resident neurology U. Minn. Hosps., Mpls., 1947-49; chief neurology svc. VA Hosp., Mpls., 1949; spl. fellow electroencephalography Mayo Clinic, Rochester, Minn., 1951; practice medicine specializing in neurology Detroit, 1949-73, Petoskey and Gaylord, Mich., 1973-87; asst. prof. Wayne State U., 1957-63; chief neurology svcs. Grace Hosp., St. John's Hosp., Bon Secour Hosp., Detroit; cons. neurologist No. Mich. Hosps., Charlevoix Area Hosp.; instr. Med. Sch. U. Minn., 1949; cons. USPHS, Detroit Bd. Edn. Contbr. articles to profl. jours. Founder, mem. ad hoc Com. to Force Lawyers Out of Govt. Fellow Am. Acad. Neurology (treas. 1955-57), Am. Electroencephalography Soc.; mem. AMA, AAAS, Assn. Rsch. Nervous and Mental Diseases, Soc. Clin. Neurologists, Mich. Neurol. Assn. (sec.-treas. 1967-76, Disting. Physician award 1988), Mich. Med. Soc., No. Mich. Med. Soc., Grosse Pointe (Mich.) Club. Address: 9797 N Twin Lake Rd Mancelona MI 49659-9203

WHINNA, GEORGE WALTMAN ROPER, III, secondary education educator; b. Chgo., Oct. 22, 1941; s. George Waltman Roper Jr. and Roseanna (Kepner) W. AA, Wilson Jr. Coll., Chgo., 1961; BA in History, Wartburg Coll., 1963. Cert. secondary tchr., Ill. Tchr. Roosevelt Jr. H.S., Rockford, Ill., 1963-69, West Sr. H.S., Rockford, 1969-89, Auburn Sr. H.S., Rockford, 1989—. Co-chmn. Bicentennial Sch.'s Com., Rockford, 1975-76. Recipient Am. History award DAR, 1980, Rotary award Rockford Rotary, 1989. Republican. Lutheran. Home: 2535 Halsted Rd # 5 Rockford IL 61101 Office: Auburn HS 5110 Auburn St Rockford IL 61101

WHIPPLE, HARRY M., newspaper publishing executive; b. Tulsa, June 30, 1947; m. Mary Jane Whipple; children: Garth, Erin. Student, Ind. U., 1965-68; U. Evansville, 1965-68, Ark Poly. Coll., 1965-68. Gen. mgr. Mt. Vernon (Ind.) Pub. Co., 1972-75; asst. pub. Pioneer Newspapers (formerly Scripps League Newspapers), Monongahela, Pa., 1975-77; advt. dir. Rockford (Ill.) Morning Star and Register Republic, 1977-81; pres., pub. Valley News Dispatch, The Herald, North Hills News Record, Tarentum, Pa., 1981-84; v.p., regional mgr. Midwest Gannett Media Sales/Gannett Nat. Sales, Chgo., 1984-87; pres. TNI Ptnrs., Tucson, 1987-92; pres., pub. The Cincinnati Enquirer, 1992—. Bd. trustees Cin. Symphony Orch., Jewish Hosp. Cin., Zool. Soc. Cin., NCCJ, Greater Cin. Region; co-chair, steering com. Nat. Underground R.R. Freedom Ctr.; bd. dirs. Greater Cin. Ctr. for Econ. Edn., Downtown Cin., Inc. Mem. Greater Cin. C. of C. (bd. trustees). Office: Cincinnati Enquirer 312 Elm St Cincinnati OH 45202-2739

WHIPPLE, WILLIAM PERRY, foundation administrator; b. Cedar Rapids, Iowa, Nov. 1, 1913; s. Robert Milo and Jeanette (Fry) W.; m. Gayle Schroeder, Sept. 18, 1937; children: John William, Robert Milo. BA, Coe Coll., 1935, hon. doctorate, 1996. Prin. Whipple Ins. Agy., Cedar Rapids, 1935-57; pres. Whipple and Winterberg, Cedar Rapids, 1957-71; chmn. Frank B. Hall of Iowa, Inc., Cedar Rapids, 1971-74; pres. Hall Found., Inc., Cedar Rapids, 1974-95, also bd. dirs.; chair Hall-Perrine Found., Cedar Rapids, 1995—; exec. in residence Colo. State U., Fort Collins, 1973; bd. dirs. Fire Mark Cir. of Ams., Chamblee, Ga., Interocean Reins. Corp., Cedar Rapids, 1st Fed. Savs. and Loan, Cedar Rapids, Nissen Corp., Cedar Rapids, 1966-72, Banks of Iowa, Inc., Des Moines, 1982-85. Trustee Cedar Rapids Pub. Library, Coe Coll., chmn.; hon. bd. dirs. Methwick Manor, Cedar Rapids, Linn County ARC. Recipient Outstanding Layman award YMCA, Cedar Rapids, 1986, Alumni Achievement award, Coe Coll., 1990, First Community Svc. award, Cedar Rapids Rotary, 1993. Mem. Rotary (Paul Harris fellow 1987), Elks. Republican. Presbyterian. Home: 1224 13th St NW Cedar Rapids IA 52405-2404 Office: Hall-Perrine Found 115 3d St SE Cedar Rapids IA 52401-1222

WHIPPS, EDWARD FRANKLIN, lawyer; b. Columbus, Ohio, Dec. 17, 1936; s. Rusk Henry and Agnes Lucille (Green) W.; children: Edward Scott, Rusk Huot, Sylvia Louise, Rudyard Christian. B.A., Ohio Wesleyan U., 1958; J.D., Ohio State U., 1961. Bar: Ohio 1961, U.S. Dist. Ct. (so. dist.) Ohio 1962, U.S. Dist. Ct. (no. dist.) Ohio 1964, U.S. Ct. Claims 1963, U.S. Supreme Ct. 1963, Miss. 1965, U.S. Ct. Appeals (6th cir.) 1980. Assoc. George, Greek, King & McMahon, Columbus, 1961-66; ptnr. George, Greek, King, McMahon & McConnaughey, Columbus, 1966-79, McConnaughey, Stradley, Mone & Moul, Columbus, 1979-81, Thompson, Hine & Flory, Columbus, 1981-93; prin. Edward F. Whipps & Assocs., Columbus, 1993-94; ptnr. Whipps & Wistner, Columbus, 1995—; founder, trustee Creative Living, Inc., 1969—; trustee, v.p. Unverferth House, Inc., 1989. Host: TV programs Upper Arlington Plain Talk, 1979-82; TV program Briding Disability, 1981-82, Lawyers on Call, 1982—, U.A. Today, 1982-86, The Ohio Wesleyan Experience, 1984—. Mem. Ohio Bd. Psychology, 1992—; mem. Upper Arlington (Ohio) Bd. Edn., 1971-80, pres., 1978-79; mem. bd. alumni dirs. Ohio Wesleyan U., 1975-79; trustee Walden Ravines Assn., 1992—, pres. 1993—. Mem. ABA, Columbus Bar Assn., Ohio State Bar Assn., Assn. Trial Lawyers Am., Ohio Acad. Trial Lawyers, Franklin County Trial Lawyers Assn., Am. Judicature Soc., Columbus Bar Found., Ohio Bd. Psychology, Columbus C. of C., Upper Arlington Area C. of C. (trustee 1978—), Lawyers Club, Barrister Club, Columbus Athletic Club, Columbus Touchdown Club, Downtown Quarterback Club, Ohio State U. Faculty (Columbus) Club, Ohio State U. Golf Club, Highlands Country Club, Delta Tau Delta (nat. v.p. 1976-78). Republican. Home: 3111 Walden Ravines Columbus OH 43221-4640 Office: Whipps & Wistner 500 S Front St Columbus OH 43215-7619

WHITAKER, AUDIE DALE, hospital laboratory medical technologist; b. Cin., Jan. 19, 1949; s. Audie and Wanda Edith (Weaver) W.; m. Sandra Sue McPhail, Aug. 22, 1970; children: Audie David Nathaniel, Andrea Grace, Alexandra Christine. BA, Olivet Nazarene U., 1971; Degree in Med. Tech., Silver Cross Hosp., Joliet, Ill., 1972. Med. tech. Riverside Hosp., Kankakee, 1971-72, Silver Cross Hosp., Joliet, 1972-77; lab. mgr. Lakeshore Community Hosp., 1977-90; evening lab. supr. Community Hosp., Anderson, Ind., 1990-93; med. technologist Community Hosp. of Anderson, 1990—; lectr. in field. Health care rep. Local Emergency Preparedness Com., Hart, Mich., 1988-90; sec., deacon, bd. dirs. West Shore Christian Fellowship, Muskegon, 1987-90, vice chmn. edn. com., 1988-90; mem. Rep. Nat. Com. S.W. Nazarene Ch. Dist. grantee, 1967, Directed Study grantee, 1970-71, rsch. grantee Sigma Xi, 1993, 95; grad. rsch. grantee Ball State U., 1994, 95. Mem. Am. Soc. Clin. Pathologists. Republican. Home: 1705 N Tillotson Muncie IN 47304-4337 Office: Community Hosp 1515 N Madison Ave Anderson IN 46011-3453

WHITAKER, CHARLES, state official. Now adjutant gen. State of Ind., Indpls. Office: 2002 Holt Rd Indianapolis IN 46241-4839

WHITAKER, ROBERT JOHN, physics educator; b. Cheyenne, Wyo., Dec. 19, 1936; s. Reginald Ormerod and Dorothy (Hopkins) W.; m. Eleanor Mannlein, Aug. 11, 1962; children: John Robert, Patrick Michael. BS, Creighton U., 1958; MS, St. Louis U., 1961; PhD, U. Okla., 1972. Instr. in physics Creighton U., Omaha, 1959-60, Regis Coll., Denver, 1961-63; program devel. specialist U. Okla., Norman, 1963-74; asst. prof. physics S.W. Mo. State U., Springfield, 1974-79, assoc. prof., 1979-84, prof., 1984—. Author: An Inquiry Into Physics, 1995, Physics 123 Laboratory, 1995; contbr. articles to profl. jours. Mem. AAAS, Am. Assn. Physics Tchrs. (pres. Mo. sect. 1986-87), Nat. Assn. Rsch. in Sci. Teaching, Sch. Sci. and Math. Assn., Assn. for Edn. of Tchrs. of Sci., Nat. Sci. Tchrs. Assn., Phi Delta Kappa. Roman Catholic. Home: 1818 E Richmond Pl Springfield MO 65804-7544 Office: SW Mo State U Dept Physics and Astronomy 901 S National Ave Springfield MO 65804-0027

WHITBURN, GERALD, state agency administrator; b. Wakefield, Mich., July 12, 1944; s. Donald and Ruby E. (Nichols) W.; m. Charmaine M. Heise, May 3, 1969; children: Bree, Luke. BS, U. Wis., Oshkosh, 1966; MA, U. Wis., Madison, 1968; postgrad., Harvard U., 1988. Aide Gov. Warren P. Knowles, Wis., 1966-69; personal asst. USN sec. John H. Chafee, Washington, 1969-72; automobile dealer, real estate developer Merrill, Wis., 1973-80; exec. asst. to Senator Robert W. Kasten U.S. Senate, Washington, 1981-87; dep. sec. Wis. Dept. Adminstrn., Madison, 1987-89; sec. Wis. Dept. Industry, Labor and Human Rels., Madison, 1989-91, Wis. Dept. Health and Social Svcs., Madison, 1991-95; sec. exec. office of health and human svcs. Commonwealth of Mass., 1995—; Mem. U.S. Labor Sec.'s Commn. on Achieving Necessary Skills, Washington, 1990-92. Contbr. articles to newspapers. Del. Rep. Nat. Conv., 1988, 92. Recipient Disting. Alumni award U. Wis., Oshkosh, 1991. Home: 390 Main St Lynnfield MA 01940 Office: MA Exec Office Hlth & Human Svc 1 Ashburton Pl Rm 1109 Boston MA 02108

WHITE, CATHARINE BOSWELL (C.B. WHITE), composer; b. Omaha, Mar. 21, 1958; d. A. Wray and Charlotte (Gaylor) W. MusB, U. Cin., 1982, MusM, 1989; cert. publishing mags., U. Chgo, 1993; MAT in elem. edn., Nat. Louis U., 1996. Gen. mgr., editor Internat. Soc. Bassists, 1990-91; freelance composer, editor, pub., tchr. Evanston, Evanston, Ill., 1991—; owner, pub. English Plus, 1994—. Composer various chamber, choral and orchestral works performed largely in the Cin. area (copying grant 1986). V.p. concerts Cinn. Composers' Guild, 1988-90, directory editor, 1987-89, dir. pub. rels., 1986. Recipient Rosenberger Meml. Music Commissioning Competition award, 1988, ASCAP award 1990, 91, 92, 93, 94, 95, 96; Ohio Arts Coun. fellow, 1990. Mem. ASCAP, Soc. Composers, Pi Kappa Lambda. Home: 545 Sheridan Rd Apt 2W Evanston IL 60202-3130

WHITE, CHRISTOPHER W., sales professional; b. Cleve., Sept. 8, 1964; s. Ralph F. and Anna May (Glaeser) W.; m. Tammy Katherine Drozdz, Sept. 23, 1989; children: Taylor Kaitlin, Carly Alexandra. BBA, Cleve. State U., 1988; MBA with distinction, DePaul U., 1995. Mgmt. assoc. USS-Lorain (Ohio) Works, 1988, account mgr., 1988-89; regional sales rep. USS/Kobe Steel Co., Cin., 1989-92; regional sales mgr. USS/Kobe Steel Co., Chgo., 1992—; cons. Flower Shop, Shaker Heights, Ohio, 1988—. Mem. Beta Gamma Sigma, Delta Mu Delta. Office: 1807 E 28th St Lorain OH 44055-1803

WHITE, DAVID DWAYNE, government tax lawyer; b. Greenville, Tex., Dec. 26, 1967; s. Thomas Easter and June Linda (Wallace) Pickens. BBA in Acctg., U. Tex., 1990; JD, Thomas M. Cooley Law Sch., 1993. Bar: Tex. 1994, Mich. 1994, Washington 1995; CPA, Tex. Sr. law clk. Mich. Tax Tribunal, Lansing, 1991-93; taxation counsel Mich. Ho. of Reps., Lansing, 1993—; mem. taxation counsel, taxation com. Mich. Ho. of Reps., 1993—. Active Rep. Party, Mich., 1993—. Mem. Tex. Soc. CPAs, Mich. Assn. CPAs, Tex. Bar Assn., Mich. Bar Assn. (taxation sect. 1994—), D.C. Bar Assn. Methodist. Office: Mich Ho of Reps Rm 518 Olds Plaza Bldg Lansing MI 48909

WHITE, DOUG, state legislator; m. Shirley White; children: Steve, Jenny. BS, Ohio State U. Commr. Adams County, 1985-90; former rep. Ohio State Rep. Dist. 77; rep. Ohio State Rep. Dist. 88, 1993—; owner, operator livestock and crop farm. Mem. Ohio Cattlemen's Assn. (pres.), Ohio Beef Coun. (former treas.), Adams County Rep. Club, Ohio 4-H Found., Manchester Lions, Ohio Farm Bur. Home: 3830 Old Dutch Rd Manchester OH 45144-9714*

WHITE, EUGENE A., physician, neuroradiologist; b. Birmingham, Ala., Oct. 29, 1935; s. Roger O. and Gregory C. (Durr) W.; m. June Ardis Johnson, Feb. 6, 1965; children: Theodore O., Forrest E., Darlene E. BA summa cum laude, Fisk U., 1956; MD, Case Western Res. U., 1964. Diplomate Am. Bd. Radiology. Postdoctoral fellow dept. neuroradiology Karolinska Hosp., Stockholm, 1969-70; radiologist Forest City Hosp., Cleve., 1970-72, Luth. Hosp., Cleve., 1972-73; from instr. to asst. prof. radiology Case Western Res. Med. Sch., Cleve., 1973-77, asst. clin. prof. radiology, 1977—; neuroradiologist in pvt. practice Drs. Hill & Thomas Inc., Beachwood, Ohio, 1977—, ptnr., v.p. neuroradiology svcs., 1988—, also bd. dirs.; mng. dir. Assoc. Med. Enterprises, Beachwood, 1980-87; clin. cons. Technicare Corp., Solon, Ohio, 1984-86. Contbr. articles to profl. jours. Bd. dirs. League Park Ctr., Cleve., 1976-82, Murtis Taylor Cmty. Ctr., 1986-92, Fisk U., Nashville, 1988—, Adrienne Kennedy Soc., 1989—, Great Lakes Theatre Festival, Cleve., 1992—, Cleve Internat. Program, 1994—. Mem. NAACP, Am. Coll. Radiology, Am. Soc. Neuroradiology, Am. Roentgen Ray Soc., Internat. Symposium Neuroradiology, Cleveland Skating Club, Pasteur Club, Phi Beta Kappa, Alpha Phi Alpha (life). Home: 3199 Van Aken Blvd Shaker Heights OH 44120 Office: 3355 Richmond Rd Beachwood OH 44122

WHITE, GARY R., automotive executive; b. Grand Island, Nebr., Feb. 24, 1943. Designer Tool & Dye Design, Grand Island, Nebr., 1971-74; project mgr. Chief Automotive Systems, Grand Island, Nebr., 1974-84, engring. mgr., v.p., 1984—. Mem. ASME, SAE, Welding Soc. Office: Chief Automotive Systems 1924 E 4th St Grand Island NE 68801-3008

WHITE, HARRY E., company executive, retired. Supr. prodn. Mesta Machine Co., West Homestead, Pa., 1940-63; mfg. mgr. Treadwell Corp., Easton, Pa., 1966-70; v.p., gen. mgr. Prodn. Machine Corp., Mentor, Ohio, 1973-79; pres. W.I.S. Inc., Waterville, Ohio, 1980—; sec., treas. Toledo Small Bus. Assn., 1974-91; mem. exec. com. Edison Indsl. Systems Ctr., Toledo, 1988-93. Mem. Gov.'s Small Bus. Venture to China, Columbus to Beijing, 1988; citizen amb. U.S. Govt., Beijing, 1988. Recipient Man of Yr. award Small Bus. Assn., 1992. Mem. Masons. Democrat. Home: 710 Village Pky Waterville OH 43566-1368

WHITE, JAMES, JR., psychiatric, mental health nurse, consultant; b. Muskogee, Okla., Nov. 24, 1944; s. James Sr. and Mary Bd. (Brassfield) W.; children: Stacie R., Stephen W. BA, Northeastern State U., 1969; MS, Pittsburg State U., 1972, BSN, 1982; PhD, Columbia Pacific U., 1984. Diplomate Am. Bd. Forensic Examiners, Soc. for Study of Neuronal Regulation; CSW, advance register nurse practitioner, cert. rehab. counselor, limited license psychologist, nationally bd. cer. counselor. Exec. dir. Sanilac County Mental Health, Sandusky, Mich., 1975-78, Crawford County Mental Health, Pittsburg, 1978-80; psychologist Psychol. and Ednl. Svcs., Pittsburg, 1980-81; dialysis nurse St. John Med. Ctr., Joplin, Mo., 1982-84; psychiatric practitioner Family Counseling and Resource Ctr., Joplin, 1983-86; pvt. practice Joplin, 1986-88; med. sociologist Mich. Health Ctr., Detroit, 1988-91; psychiatric practitioner Wayne County Sheriff and Sinai Hosp. Psychiatry, Detroit, 1990—; clin. coord. Detroit Health Care for Homeless, 1991—; chmn. recipient right com. Lafayette Clinic, Detroit, 1991—, coun. mem., 1990—. Lt. U.S. Army, 1969-82. Mem. ANA for Nurses in Advanced Practice, Am. Psychatric Nurses Assn., Am. Acad. Nurse Practitioners (Mich. State Rep. 1991—), Am. Bd. Med. Psychotherapists (cert., clin. assoc.), Coun. Psychaitric and Mental Health Nursing, Am. Acad. Pain Mgmt. Home: 42029 Utah Dr Sterling Heights MI 48313 Office: Inst for Inner Resource 75 W Square Lake Rd Troy MI 48098

WHITE, JAMES FLOYD, theology educator; b. Boston, Jan. 23, 1932; s. Edwin Turner and Madeline (Rinker) W.; m. Marilyn Atkinson, Aug. 23, 1959 (div. 1982); children: Louise, Robert, Ellen, Laura, Martin; m. Susan Jan Waller, Oct. 28, 1982 (div. 1993). Grad., Phillips Acad., Andover, Mass., 1949; AB, Harvard U., 1953; BD, Union Theol. Sem., 1956; PhD, Duke U., 1960. Ordained to ministry United Meth. Ch., 1955. Instr. Ohio Wesleyan U., Delaware, 1959-61, Meth. Theol. Sch. in Ohio, Delaware, 1960-61; prof. Perkins Sch. Theology, So. Meth. U., Dallas, 1961-83, U. Notre Dame, Ind., 1983—. Author: Cambridge Movement, 1962, New Forms of Worship, 1971, Introduction to Christian Worship, 1980, Protestant Worship, 1989, Roman Catholic Worship (1st place award Cath. Press Asasn. 1995), also others; mem. editl. bd. Religious Book Club, 1980-93. Named one of 100 Most Influential People in Am. Religion, Christian Century mag., 1982; honored by book published in his honor: The Sunday Service of the Methodists: Studies in Honor of James F. White, 1996. Mem. N.Am. Acad. Liturgy (pres. 1979, Berakah award 1983), Am. Soc. Ch. History, Liturgical Conf., Societas Liturgica. Office: U Notre Dame Dept Theology Notre Dame IN 46556

WHITE, JEFFERY, emergency medical services executive; b. Brunswick, Ga., Sept. 11, 1961; s. Mell Robert and Barbara Jo (Glover) W.; m. Mary Katherine Deslippe, Aug. 16, 1986; children: Lindsay Tate, Samantha Kay, Morgan Pauline. Cert., Wayne County C.C., Oakland C.C. Dir. ops. Mich. Ambulance Inc., Detroit, 1980-89; pres. Richmond (Mich.) Lenox Ambulance Authority, 1989—; bd. dirs. St. Clair County Med. Adv., Port Huron, Mich.; mem. paramedic com. Macomb County Med. Coun., 1995—. Mem. Memphis (Mich.) Bd. Edn., 1993-95; commr. Riley Twp. Planning Commn., Mich., 1992-95. Paul Harris fellow Richmond Rotary Club, 1994. Mem. Memphis C. of C., Richmond C. of C. Republican. Methodist. Office: Richmond Lenox Ambulance 34505 32 Mile Rd Richmond MI 48062

WHITE, JEFFREY PAUL, lawyer; b. Farmington, Maine, Apr. 5, 1955; s. Calvin Coolidge and Dorothy Louise (Barker) W.; m. Cynthia June Daugherty, May 24, 1986; children: McKenzie Sara, Hilary Ann. BA, U. Maine, Orono, 1977; JD, Suffolk U., 1981. Bar: Mass. 1981, Ill. 1982, U.S. Dist. Ct. (no. dist.) Ill., 1982, U.S. Dist. Ct. (no. dist.) N.Y., 1983, Wis. 1986, U.S. Dist. Ct. (ea. dist.) Wis., 1986, U.S. Dist. Ct. (we. dist.) Wis., 1986, Maine 1988, U.S. Dis.t Ct. Nebr. Assoc. William L. Needler & Assocs., Chgo., 1981-83; pvt. prctice Chgo. and Barrington, 1983—; pres. Jeffrey White, P.C., Chgo. and Barrington, 1985—; real estate broker Hopscotch Realty, Chgo., 1985—; ptnr. Bosworth Real Estate Assocs., Chgo., 1985—. V.p. Lake Acres Property Owners Assn., 1990-91, pres., 1992-93. Mem. Am. Agrl. Law Assn., Am. Bankruptcy Inst., Ill. Bar Assn., Mass. Bar Assn., Wis. Bar Assn. (mem. bankruptcy sect. 1988—), Maine Bar Assn., Chgo. Bar Assn. (mem. bankruptcy com. 1982—, chmn. agrl. law com. 1987-88). Office: 400 E Main St Barrington IL 60010-3219

WHITE, JOE LLOYD, soil scientist, educator; b. Pierce, Okla., Nov. 8, 1921; s. Claud Amos and Alta Maurice (Denney) W.; m. Wanita Irene Robertson, May 29, 1945; children—Lerrill, Darla, Ronna, Bren, Janeil. Student, Connors State Agrl. Coll., 1940-42; B.S., Okla. State U., 1944, M.S., 1945; Ph.D., U. Wis., 1947. Asst. prof. agronomy Purdue U., West Lafayette, Ind., 1947-51, assoc. prof., 1951-57, prof., 1957-88; cons. Bancroft Co., William H. Rorer Co., Chattem Chem. Co., Merck Sharp & Dohme Rsch. Lab. Patentee in field. Fellow NSF, 1965-66, Guggenheim Found., 1972-73; Fulbright scholar, 1973; recipient Sr. U.S. Scientist award Alexander von Humboldt Found., 1980-81. Fellow AAAS, Am. Soc. Agronomy, Am. Inst. Chemists, Soil Sci. Soc. Am., Mineral Soc. Am., Royal Soc. Chemistry; mem. Am. Chem. Soc., Clay Minerals Soc. (disting.), Am. Pharm. Assn., Coblentz Soc., Geochem. Soc., Internat. Soil Sci. Soc., Internat. Assn. Colloid and Interface Scientists, N.Y. Acad. Sci., Royal Soc. Chemists (chartered chemist), Soc. Petroleum Engrs. of AIME, Internat. Zeolite Assn., Soc. Applied Spectroscopy, Sigma Xi, Phi Kappa Phi, Phi Lambda Upsilon. Mem. Ch. of Christ. Home: 2505 Roselawn Ave Lafayette IN 47904-2319 Office: Purdue U Dept Agronomy West Lafayette IN 47907

WHITE, JOHN ABIATHAR, pilot, consultant; b. Chgo., May 29, 1948; s. Abiathar Jr. and Gretchen Elizabeth (Zuber) W.; m. Therese Ann Denz, June 21, 1980; children: Kathryn Ann, Laura Ellen. Student, Art Ctr. Coll. of Design, 1969-70, Calif. Inst. Tech., 1966-67; BArch, U. Ill., 1972. Archtl. apprentice Farner Und Gründer Industriearchitekten, Zürich, Switzerland, 1972; archtl. draftsman Walter Carlson Assocs., Elk Grove, Ill., 1973; architectural job capt. Unteed Assocs., Palatine, Ill., 1974-75; flight instr. Planemasters, Inc., West Chicago, Ill., 1976; pilot Aero Am. Aviation, West Chicago, 1977, Beckett Aviation, Cleve., 1978; pilot Am. Airlines, Chgo. and L.A., 1979—, capt., 1988—; archtl. cons. Nat. Accelerator Lab., Batavia, Ill., 1980, Constrn. Collaborative, Park Ridge, Ill., 1982, L.K. White Assocs., San Diego, 1988-92. Nat. Coun. Tchrs. of English scholar, 1966. Mem. Nat. Assn. Flight Instrs. Unitarian.

WHITE, JOHN HENRY, photojournalist; b. Lexington, N.C., Mar. 18, 1945; s. Reid R. and Ruby M. (Leverette) W.; m. Emily L. Miller, May 29, 1966 (dec.); children: Deborah, Angela, Ruby, John Henry. A.A.S., Central Piedmont Community Coll. Photographer U.S. Marine Corps., Quantico, Va., 1966-68, Tom Walters Photograpahy, Charlotte, N.C., 1968-69; photojournalist Chgo. Daily News, 1969-78, Chgo. Sun-Times, 1978—; instr. photojournalism Columbia Coll., Chgo., 1978—; lectr. in field. Mem. Blackwell Meml. A.M.E. Zion Ch., Chgo., 1972—, steward, 1979—, supt. Sunday Sch. Recipient over 200 photography in journalism awards; recipient Pulitzer prize, 1982. Mem. Nat. Press Photograhers Assn., Ill. Press Photographers Assn. (photographer of yr. award 1971, 79, 82), Chgo. Press Photographers Assn. (pres. 1977-78 photographer of yr. award), Chgo. Assn. Black Journalists. Office: Chicago Sun Times 401 N Wabash Ave Chicago IL 60611-3532

WHITE, LAWRENCE TODD, psychology educator; b. San Rafael, Calif., Oct. 25, 1953; s. James Harold and Bette Norene (Breid) W.; m. Hester Ann Dinwiddie, May 27, 1983; children: Catherine Elizabeth, Peter James. BA, Whittier Coll., 1975; MA, Calif. State U., 1979; PhD, U. Calif., Santa Cruz, 1984. Prof. Beloit (Wis.) Coll., 1984—; rsch. assoc. East-West Ctr., Honolulu, 1990; vis. prof. Portland (Oreg.) State U., 1987, Calif. Sch. of Profl. Psychology, Fresno, 1990; legal cons., 1987—. Contbr. articles to profl. jours. Rsch. grantee NIMH, 1987. Mem. Am. Psychol. Soc., Am. Psychology/Law Soc., Soc. for Psychol. Study of Social Issues, Soc. for Advancement of Social Psychology (mem. steering com. 1991-95), Contemporary Social Psychology (editl. bd. 1986—). Office: Beloit Coll Dept Psychology 700 College St Beloit WI 53511-5595

WHITE, LINDA SUE, cardiology technician; b. Gary, Ind., Apr. 14, 1964; d. Ralph Warren and Anna Elizabeth (Chadourne) W. Cert., Ill. Med. Tng. Ctr., 1986, Commonwealth Coll., Merrillville, Ind., 1988; student, Internat. Corr. Schs., 1991-93. With Video King, Merrillville, 1983-85, Olan Mills, Portage, Ind., 1984-85; EKG tech. Porter Meml. Hosp., Valparaiso, Ind., 1986-87; med. asst. Dr. Brown, Crown Point, Ind., 1988-89; office mgr., med. asst., office nurse Dr. Pargaonker, Merrillville, 1989-92; med. asst. Dr. J. Timothy Ames, Valparaiso, 1992—. Mem. Contact Cares of N.E. Ind. Democrat. Baptist. Home: 399 Keystone Dr Valparaiso IN 46383-8829 Office: Dr J Timothy Ames 1101 Glendale Blvd Valparaiso IN 46383-3724

WHITE, MICHAEL ERNEST, animal scientist; b. Ames, Iowa, Feb. 5, 1958; s. Donald Benjamin and Jean (Grove) W.; m. Susan Kay Swanson, June 19, 1982; children: Sarah Elizabeth, Eric Michael. BS, U. Minn., 1980, PhD, 1986. Lab. technician trainee U. Minn., St. Paul, 1977-81, rsch. asst., 1981-84, doctoral fellow, 1984-86; asst. prof. animal sci. Ohio State U., Columbus, 1986-91; asst. prof. animal sci. U. Minn., St. Paul, 1992-93, assoc. prof., 1993—; univ. senator, 1994—; reviewer grant proposals U.S. Dept. Agr., NSF, NIH, BARD, 1987—. Reviewer Jour. Animal Sci., Jour. Nutrition, Transgenic Rsch., 1987—; mem. editl. bd. Jour. Animal Sci., Jour. Domestic Animal Endocrinology; contbr. articles to profl. jours. Cantor St. Judes Cath. Ch., 1980-82. USDA grantee, 1986-98; U. Minn. grad. scholar, 1982. Mem. AAAS, Am. Soc. Animal Sci. (chmn. Midwestern sect. com. on growth, devel., muscle biology and meat sci. 1990-91, chmn. grad. competition com. 1993-96, invited symposium spkr. 1995, chmn. coll. faculty consultative com. 1995-96), Ohio Acad. Sci., sigma Xi, Phi Kappa Phi (award for acad. excellence 1980—), Gamma Sigma Delta. Roman Catholic. Office: U Minn 1354 Eckles Ave Saint Paul MN 55108-6003

WHITE, MICHAEL REED, mayor; b. Cleve., Aug. 13, 1951; s. Robert and Audrey (Silver) W. BA, Ohio State U., 1973, MPA, 1974. Spl. asst. Columbus (Ohio) Mayor's Office, 1974-76; adminstrv. asst. Cleve. City Coun., 1976-77; sales mgr. Burks Electric Co., Cleve., 1978-84; state senator Ohio Senate, Columbus, 1984-89; mayor Cleve., 1990—; minority whip Ohio Senate Dems., 1987-89. City councilman City of Cleve., 1978-84; bd. dirs. Glenville Devel. Corp., Cleve., 1978—, Glenville Festival Found., Cleve., 1978—, United Black Fund, Cleve., 1986, Greater Cleve. Dome Corp., 1986. Named one of Outstanding Young Men Am., 1985, Outstanding Svc. award Cleve. chpt. Nat. Assn. Black Vets., 1985, Cmty. Svcs. award East Side Jaycees, Pres.'s award, 1993, named Black Profl. of Yr., 1993, Humanitarian award, 1994. Democrat. Home: 1057 East Blvd Cleveland OH 44108-2972 Office: Office of Mayor 601 Lakeside Ave E Cleveland OH 44114-1015

WHITE, PAUL DUNBAR, lawyer; b. LaGrange, Ky., Oct. 20, 1917; s. Isham Forrest and Florence (Harris) W.; m. Marion Loutenas Stallworth, Sept. 2, 1949; children: Paulette, Ronald. A.B., Ky. State Coll., 1940; LL.B., Western Res. U., 1950. Bar: Ohio 1950, U.S. Supreme Ct. 1972. Supr. Ind. State Boys Sch., 1940-41; group worker spl. projects Karamu, Cleve., 1941-43; visitor Cuyahoga County Agy., 1946-47; individual practice law Cleve., 1950-51; police prosecutor City of Cleve., 1951-59, 1st asst. prosecutor, 1960-63, dir. law, 1967-68; judge Cleve. Mcpl. Ct., 1964-67; assoc. Baker & Hostetler, Cleve., 1968-70; ptnr. Baker & Hostetler, 1970—; mem. State of Ohio Bd. Examiners, 1972-78. Trustee NCCJ, Cleve., 1972-86; trustee Ohio Law Opportunity Fund, 1975-87, Cleve. Urban League, 1975-78, Dyke Coll., Cleve., 1976-86; bd. commrs. Cleve. Met. Park, 1975-78. Served with U.S. Army, 1943-46. Mem. ABA, Ohio Bar Assn., Greater Cleve. Bar Assn. (trustee 1976-79, del. 8th Jud. Dist. Ohio conf. 1985—), Nat. Bar Assn., Soc. Benchers (Case Western Res. U.), Norman S. Minor Bar Assn. Home: 16210 Telfair Ave Cleveland OH 44128-3736 Office: Baker & Hostetler 3200 National City Ctr 1900 E 9th St Cleveland OH 44114-3401

WHITE, POLLY SEARS, religious organization administrator; b. Phila., Jan. 29, 1931; d. W. Heyward and Emily P. (Welsh) Myers; m. Peter White, June 13, 1953; children: Katharine, Peter, Jennifer, Jeffrey. AB, Smith Coll., 1953. Adminstrv. aide Inst. Local and State Govt., U. Pa., Phila., 1953-55; parish sec. St. Mary's Episcopal Ch., Wayne, Pa., 1977-85; program dir. Metro Toledo Chs. United, 1987—. Sec., treas. Friends Radnor Twp. Meml. Libr., Wayne, 1978-80; pres. Presbyn. Hosp. Med. Aux., Phila., 1983-85; bd. dirs. Wood County Planned Parenthood Coun., Bowling Green, Ohio, 1985-86, Perrysburg (Ohio) LWV, 1986-88, pres. 1995-97; oper. com. 1st Call for Help of United Way, Toledo, vice chair, 1993—; mem. altar guild, flower guild St. Timothy's Episc. Ch., vestry, 1993—; trustee Hist. Perrysburg, 1990, bd. dirs., 1990—; mem. Perrysburg Landmarks Commn., 1992—.

Democrat. Home: 525 E 6th St Perrysburg OH 43551-2223 Office: Metro Toledo Chs United 444 Floyd St Toledo OH 43620-1735

WHITE, RAY LEWIS, education educator; b. Abingdon, Va., Aug. 11, 1941; s. Benjamin Wesley and Maude (Patterson) W. BA, Emory and Henry, 1962, LittD (hon.), 1990; MA, U. Ark., 1963, PhD, 1971. Instr. N.C. State U., Raleigh, 1965-68; asst. prof. Ill. State U., Normal, 1968-71, assoc. prof., 1971-73, prof., 1973-85, Disting. prof., 1985—; sr. prof. U. Munich, 1979. Author numerous books including: Winesburg, Ohio: Critical Edition, 1996, Sherwood Anderson's Secret Love Letters: For Eleanor A Letter a Day, 1991, Winesburg, Ohio: An Exploration, 1990, Sherwood Anderson: Early Writings, 1989, Indec to Best American Short Stories and O. Henry Prize Stories, 1988, Arnold Zweig in the USA, 1986, Certrude Stein and Alice B. Toklas: A Reference Guide, 1984, R.K. Narayan: The American Reception, 1953-70, 83, others. Named Disting. Alumnus, Emory and Henry Coll., Emory, Va., 1979. Mem. Am. Lit. Assn., Sherwood Anderson Soc., Assn. Study Midwestern Lit. (Disting. Svc. award 1985). Libertarian. Home: 29990 White Oak Dr Mackinaw IL 61755-8980 Office: 4240 Dept English Ill State Univ Normal IL 61761

WHITE, REGGIE (REGINALD HOWARD WHITE), professional football player; b. Chattanooga, Dec. 19, 1961; m. Sara Copeland; children: Jeremy, Jecolia. Student, U. Tenn. With Memphis Showboats, 1984-85, Phila. Eagles, 1985-93, Green Bay Packers, 1993—. Named to Sporting News Coll. All-Am. team, 1983, Sporting News United States Football League All-Star team, 1985, Pro Bowl team, 1986-95, Sporting News All-Pro team, 1987, 88, 91, 93. Office: Green Bay Packers 1265 Lombardi Ave Green Bay WI 54307-0628*

WHITE, REGINALD WESLEY, computer educator; b. Stillwater, Okla., Oct. 7, 1951; s. Richard C. and Pauline (Drabek) W.; m. Dinana M. Brown, May 28, 1994. BS in Math., Western Ill. U., 1973; AAS in Data Processing, Black Hawk Coll., 1984; MS in Computer Sci., Teikyo Marycrest U., 1992. Substitute tchr. Davenport (Iowa) Pub. Schs., 1978-82; mgr. night kitchen Bringer Inn, Milan, Ill., 1982-84; tchr. computers St. Mary's Sch., East Moline, Ill., 1983-84; instr. Coll. St. Francis, Joliet, Ill., 1991; programmer CDS/Wordworks, Davenport, 1984-88; prof. Black Hawk Coll., Moline, Ill., 1984—; chmn. data processing dept. Black Hawk Coll.,1987-90, bus. info. sys. dept., 1995—. Mem. Math. Assn. Am., Data Processing Mgmt. Assn. (awards chmn. 1985-86). Roman Catholic. Office: Black Hawk Coll 6600 34th Ave Moline IL 61265

WHITE, ROBERT JAMES, newspaper columnist; b. Mpls., Nov. 6, 1927; s. Robert Howard and Claire Lillian (Horner) W.; m. Adrienne Hoffman, Sept. 24, 1955; children: Claire, Pamela, Sarah. BS, U.S. Naval Acad., 1950. V.p. White Investment Co., Mpls., 1957-67; editl. writer Mpls. Tribune, 1967-73, assoc. editor, 1973-82; editor editl. pages Mpls. Star Tribune, 1982-93, columnist, 1993-95, contbg. columnist, 1996—. Recipient cert. of excellence Overseas Press Club, 1981. Mem. Coun. Fgn. Rels., Refugee Policy Group (mem. bd. trustees), Mpls. Club. Presbyterian. Home: 4721 Girard Ave S Minneapolis MN 55409-2212

WHITE, STEPHEN EDWARD, geography educator; b. Frankfort, Ky., Apr. 15, 1947; s. Edward Earl and Doris June (Oliver) W.; m. Susan Mary Lockhorn, Oct. 4, 1969; children: Eric Stephen, Benjamin Nathan. BS, U. Ky., 1969, MA, 1972, PhD, 1974. Planner Ky. Dept. Trans., Frankfort, 1969; sect. mgr. Ky. Dept. Trans., 1975; asst. prof. Kans. State U., Manhattan, 1975-80; dept. head geography Kans. State U., 1979-87, 94—, assoc. prof. geography, 1980-85, prof. geography, 1985—; lectr. in field. Contbr. articles to profl. jours. and books. Pres. Tatarrax Homeowners Assn., Manhattan, 1990, bd. dirs., 1988-90; youth baseball coach Manhattan Recreation Dept., 1977-88 (Coach of the Yr. 1988). 1st lt. U.S. Army, 1969-71. Recipient Disting. Teaching Ach. award Nat. Coun. Geographic Edn, 1991, William L. Stamey Teaching award, Kans. State U., 1989, Outstanding Undergrad. Teaching award, 1988. Mem. Assn. Am. Geographers (pres. population specialty grp. 1985-86, exec. bd. 1982-87), Population Assn. Am., Nat. Coun. for Geographic Edn. (awds. com. 1989). Democrat. Roman Catholic. Home: 3002 Tomahawk Cir Manhattan KS 66502-1974 Office: Kansas State U Geography De 201C Dickens Hall Manhattan KS 66506-0800

WHITE, SYLVIA FRANCES, gerontology home care nurse, consultant; b. Dayton, Ohio, May 2, 1952; d. Arthur Francis and Eleanor Ida (Beach) Scarpelli; m. Alan Bruce White, Nov. 28, 1981. BSN, Loyola U., 1975; MPH, U. Ill., Chgo., 1984. Cert. gerontol. nurse; lic. nursing home adminstrn., Ill. Staff nurse Vis. Nurse Assn., Chgo., 1975-80, team leader, 1980-81, supr., 1981-83, dist. adminstr., 1984-86, mgr. North side, 1986-87, dir. patient svcs., 1987; dir. clin. svcs. Kimberly Quality Care, Evanston, Ill., 1987-89; pub. health nurse City of Evanston, Ill., 1989-90; geriatric nurse assoc. City of Evanston, 1990—; cons. surveyor Joint Commn. on Accreditation of Healthcare Orgns., Oakbrook Terrace, Ill., 1988—; vol. Hospice, literacy. Trainer The Arthritis Found., Chgo., 1991-92; mem. Panel Rev. State of Ill. Continuing Edn.; mem. profl. edn. com. Arthritis Found.; hospice vol. Mem. APHA, Ill. Pub. Health Assn., Ill. Home Health Coun., Ill. Alliance for Aging, Zonta, Arthritis Profl. Edn. Com., Nat. Assn. Home Care. Roman Catholic. Home: 222 Sunset Dr Wilmette IL 60091 Office: Evanston Health Dept 2100 Ridge Ave Evanston IL 60201-2796

WHITE, VICKI LEE, bank service representative; b. Steubenville, Ohio, Feb. 18, 1960; d. Paul W.H. and Norma Jean (Thomas) Oxier; m. John Robert White, Apr. 12, 1980. Diploma, Am. Inst. Banking, 1986, Am. Banker's Assn., 1987; AS in Banking and Fin., Jefferson County Tech. Coll., 1991. Teller Miners and Mechs. Savs. and Trust Co., Steubenville, 1979-85, mgr. cen. reference files, 1985-91, fedline coord., security adminstr., 1992-94; br. svc. rep. Nat. City Bank N.E., Steubenville, 1994—; adv. bd. mem. Jefferson Tech. Coll., 1988—. Active Foster Parents Plan, Steubenville Urban Mission, People for the Ethical Treatment Animals; adminstrv. bd. mem. Richmond United Meth. Ch., 1987—. Mem. Am. Inst. Banking (sec. Steubenville chpt. 1985-93), Steubenville Art Assn., Order Eastern Star, Rosicrucians. Republican. Methodist. Home: PO Box 51 654 County Hwy 54 Richmond OH 43944-0051 Office: Nat City Bank NE 124 N 4th St Steubenville OH 43952-2132

WHITE, WILLIAM JAMES, information management and services company executive; b. Kenosha, Wis., May 30, 1938; s. William H. and Dorothy Caroline White; m. Jane Schulte, Aug. 13, 1960; children: James N., Thomas G., Maria, Gretchen S. BS, Northwestern U., 1961; MBA, Harvard U., 1963. Mech. planning engr. Procter & Gamble Corp., 1961-62; bd. dirs. TJ Internat., Boise, Idaho; corp. v.p. Hartmarx Corp., Chgo., 1963-74; group v.p. Mead Corp., Dayton, Ohio, 1974-81; pres., chief oper. officer, dir. Masonite Corp., Chgo., 1981-85; exec. v.p. and dir. USG Corp., 1985-88, pres., chief exec. officer Whitestar Enterprises, Inc., 1989-90; chmn., pres., chief exec. officer Bell & Howell Co., 1990-95; chmn. CEO Bell & Howell Holdings Co., 1995—. Author: (with Henderson et al) Creative Collective Bargaining, 1965. Vice chmn. adv. coun. McCormick Sch. Engring. and Applied Scis.; mem. bus. adv. coun. U. Ill., Chgo., 1981—; bd. dirs. TJ Internat., IMSA Fund for Advancement Edn., Aurora; past chmn. bd. Ill. div. Am. Cancer Soc. Mem. Econ. Club, The Chgo. Com., Chgo. Club, Glen View Country Club. Office: Bell & Howell Co 5215 Old Orchard Rd Skokie IL 60077-1035

WHITE, WILLIS SHERIDAN, JR., retired utilities company executive; b. nr. Portsmouth, Va., Dec. 17, 1926; s. Willis Sheridan and Carrie (Culpepper) W.; m. LaVerne Behrends, Oct. 8, 1949; children: Willis Sheridan III, Marguerite Louise White Spangler, Cynthia D.W. Haight. B.S., Va. Poly. Inst., 1948; M.S., Mass. Inst. Tech., 1958. With Am. Electric Power Co. Inc., 1948-91; chmn., chief exec. officer Am. Electric Power Co., Inc. and its subs., N.Y.C., 1976-90, chmn., 1991, mem. bd. dirs., 1972-92; pres., bd. dirs. Ohio Valley Electric Corp., Ind.-KTV Electric Corp., 1977-91; bd. dirs. Bank of N.Y. Trustee Battelle Meml. Inst., Grant/Riverside Meth. Hosp., Columbus. With USNR, 1945-46. Sloan fellow, 1957-58. Mem. IEEE, NAE, Eta Kappa Nu, Omicron Delta Kappa. Methodist.

WHITEFACE, CHARMAINE FRANCINE, freelance writer; b. Deadwood, S.D., Mar. 12, 1947; d. Frederick Philip and Margaret Pearl (Brewer) W.; m. Varick F. Cutler; children: Michael, Marc, Mara, Mitchell. BS in Edn., Black Hills State U., 1973. Tchr. Little Wound High Sch., Kyle, S.D., 1975-76; news reporter Sta. KEVN-TV, Rapid City, S.D., 1979; tchr., counselor Standing Rock Coll., Fort Yates, N.D., 1980-82, instr., 1990-92; sr. specialist Oglala Sioux Tribe, Manderson, S.D., 1982-83; transp. dir. Oglala Sioux Tribe, Pine Ridge, S.D., 1984-88; copy editor, staff writer Lakota Times, Rapid City, 1989-90; freelance writer Manderson, 1992—; advisor ecology club Standing Rock Coll., 1990-92. V.p. Wounded Knee Dist. Coun., Manderson, 1982-83; bd. mem. N.D. Indian Edn. Assn., 1981-82, S.D. Indian Edn. Assn., 1974-77; with S.D. Day Care Adv. Com., Pierre, 1974-76, S.D. Equal Opportunities Adv. Com., Pierre, 1974-76. Named Vol. of Yr. Summer Youth Program Pine Ridge Reservation, 1982, one of Outstanding Young Women Am., 1982. Home: PO Box 194 Manderson SD 57756

WHITEHEAD, NEIL LANCELOT, anthropologist; b. London, Mar. 19, 1956; came to U.S., 1993; s. Kenneth Lancelot and Irene Winifred (Dormer) W.; m. Theresa Margaret Murphy, June 7, 1986; children: Luke, Florence, Rose. BA, Oxford U., 1977, MA, 1978; MA, Oxford U., 1986, DPhil, 1984. Fellow U. London, 1979-80, Ecole de Haute Etudes, Paris, 1980-81, Guggenheim Found., N.Y.C., 1985-90; tutor Oxford U., England, 1990-92; prof. U. Wis., Madison, 1993—. Author: Lords of the Tiger Spirit, 1988; co-author: Wild Majesty, 1992; editor: Wolves From the Sea, 1995; co-editor: War in the Tribal Zone, 1992. Fellow Royal Anthropol. Inst.; mem. Am. Anthropol. Assn., Koningslisk Inst., Hakluyt Soc. Office: U Wis 1180 Observatory Dr Madison WI 53706

WHITEHORN, KENNETH LEE, county official; b. Ridgecrest, Calif., Sept. 14, 1947; s. Howard and June L. (Leff) W. BS, U. Minn., Mpls., 1988. Lic. land surveyor, Minn. Survey technician Michael Baker, Jr. Inc., Jackson, Miss., 1966; survey technician, photogrammetrist L. Robert Kimball, Engrs., Ebensburg, Pa., 1970-72; survey technician Harry S. Johnson Cos., Lakeville, Minn., 1973-74, Minn. Dept. Natural Resources, St. Paul, 1974-78; computer drafter M. J. Weber Co., Howard Lake, Minn., 1978-80; zone surveyor U.S. Forest Svc., Chippewa Nat. Forest, Deer River, Minn., 1981-86; county surveyor Itasca County, Grand Rapids, Minn., 1986—; adj. instr. Bemidji (Minn.) State U., 1991; instr. Minn. Dept. Natural Resources, Grand Rapids, 1987-90, com. mem., St. Paul, 1987-88; mem. Minn. Gov.'s Coun. on Geog. Info., St. Paul, 1992-94. Tech. prodn. Grand Rapids Player Cmty. Theater, 1988-92. Mem. Minn. Assn. County Surveyors (pres. 1993), Minn. Soc. Profl. Surveyors (bd. dirs. 1989-92, del. 1992-94, chpt. 4 pres. 1987, treas. 1996—). Office: Itasca Co Dept Survey & Map 123 NE 4th St Rm 220 Grand Rapids MN 55744-2600

WHITEHOUSE, FRANK, JR., microbiologist; b. Ann Arbor, Mich., Nov. 20, 1924; s. Frank and May Belle (MacIntire) W.; m. Helen Alice Schimkat Whitehouse; children: Lynne, Beth Ann, Frank Scott, Kim Elaine. BA, U. Mich., Ann Arbor, 1949; MD, 1953. Faculty U. Mich., Ann Arbor, 1954-95. Contbr. over 65 articles and abstracts to profl. jours. 1st Lt. USAF, 1942-46. Decorated Air medal, 1945; recipient Univ. Hopwood Literary award, Ann Arbor, 1947; Sr. Fulbright lectr. Bahrain, 1979-80. Mem. Am. Soc. Microbiology. Home: 3411 Woodland Rd Ann Arbor MI 48104-4257 Office: Dept Microbiology Univ Michigan Box 0620 Med Sci II Ann Arbor MI 48109-0620

WHITEHOUSE, JOHN HARLAN, JR., systems software consultant, diagnostician; b. Lakewood, Ohio, Sept. 12, 1951; s. John Harlan and Frances Elizabeth (Nation) W.; divorced; 1 child, John Harlan III. BA magna cum laude, Ohio Wesleyan U., 1973; MBA, Cleve. State U., 1976; PhD, Columbia Pacific U., San Rafael, Calif., 1988; postgrad., U. Chgo., 1974. Cert. computing profl.; cert. info. sys. auditor. Programmer San Antonio Express-News, 1977; programming mgr. S.W. Info. Mgmt. Systems, San Antonio, 1977, Utility Data Corp., Houston, 1978; sr. data systems auditor Nat. City Corp., Cleve., 1978-81; sys. programmer Standard Oil Co., Cleve., 1981-84; adv. systems engr. IBM, Cleve., 1984-92; pres. Semiotica Corp., 1992—; mem. exams. editorial coun. Inst. for Cert. Computer Profls., Des Plaines, 1990—. Author: CICS Problem Determination Workshop, 1990; co-author: ICCP Guidelines for Recertification, 1990, ICCP Official Study Guide, 1991-95; also numerous articles, columnist. Mem. Assn. for Computing Machinery (chmn. Greater Cleve. chpt. 1982-83, Svc. Recognition award 1984), Assn. of Inst. for Cert. Computer Profls. (regional dir. 1989-93, nominating com. 1991), Masons, Phillethes Soc., Scottish Rite, Phi Beta Kappa. Unitarian. Home: 22291 Berry Dr Rocky River OH 44116-2013 Office: Semiotica Corp 25935 Detroit Rd Ste 241 Westlake OH 44145-2426

WHITESELL, PATRICIA S., academic administrator; b. Ann Arbor, Mich., Mar. 22, 1950; d. Don McKinstry and Patricia Jane (Smith) W.; m. John R. Wolfe, Sept. 7, 1990. BA, Olivet Coll., 1972; MA, U. Mich., 1980, PhD, 1994. Fin. aid officer U. Mich., Ann Arbor, 1973-80; dir. fin. aid U. Mich. Law Sch., Ann Arbor, 1980-86; adminstrv. mgr. U. Mich. offfice of v.p. rsch., Ann Arbor, 1986-94, asst. to v.p., 1994—. Contbr. article to profl. jour. Chair adv. com. Detroit Observatory, U. Mich., 1994—; bd. dirs., curator Kempf House Ctr. for Local History, 1995—. Mem. Washtenaw County Hist. Soc. Office: Office VP Rsch Univ Mich 503 Thompson St Ann Arbor MI 48109-1340

WHITESIDE, DALE, state legislator; b. Chillicothe, Mo., Oct. 19, 1930; m. Marilou Reed, 1953; children: Zoann, Jeffrey, Bruce, Steven. BS with honors, Mo. U. Coll. Agr. Farmer; pres. Whiteside Hog Farms, Inc.; mem. Mo. Ho. of Reps. from 7th dist.; mem. Agr. Com. Mo. Ho. of Reps., mem. Correctional Instns. Com., Appropriations Com., Edn. and Pub. Safety Com., Pub. Health and Safety Com., Joint Com. Corrections. Active youth work; tchr. Sunday Sch. Mem. Farm Bur., Cattlemen Assn., Soybean Assn., Corn Growers Assn., Nat. Ole Time Fiddlers Assn., Am. Legion. Republican. Home: RR 2 Box 80 Chillicothe MO 64601-9578*

WHITING, FRED C., state legislator. State rep. State of S.D., 1993-94; state senator dist. 33 S.D. State Senate, 1995—; mem. judiciary state affairs and transp. coms. Republican. Home: 7573 Crossbill Cir Rapid City SD 57702-9026*

WHITMAN, ANDREW FRANKLIN, management educator, insurance-legal consultant; b. Phila., May 28, 1938; s. Russell Wilson Whitman and Amelia Richard; children: David B., Scott M., Andrew Franklin Jr., Zachary B.; m. Susan J. Draheim, Nov. 3, 1981. BS, Pa. State U., 1960, MBA, 1962; PhD, U. Wis., 1966; JD, U. Minn., 1968. CPCU, CLU, Cert. Fin. Planner. Instr. U. Wis., Madison, 1965-66; rschr. Wis. Ins. Dept., Madison, 1966; prof. mgmt. U. Minn., Mpls., 1966—; dep. commr., acting chief counsel Pa. Ins. Dept., Harrisburg, 1971-72; pres., cons. Risk Mgmt., Inc., Maple Grove, Minn., 1978—. Author: Index and Summary Statements of Wisconsin Attorney Gener's Opinions on Insurance, 1965, (with W.T. Hold) Agent's Education and Training Manual on Principles of Property and Casualty Insurance, 1965, (with R.M. Hein and W.T. Hold) Study Guide for the Text Book Risk Management and Insurance, 1967, Risk Management Administration Manual, 1978, Insurance Producer Liability: In Plain Language, 1991; co-author: Minnesota Insurance Law, 1995, Stay Out of Court and Stay in Business, 1995; contbr. articles to profl. publs. With Air ROTC, 1960-62. Home: 6969 Carey Ln Maple Grove MN 55369-5409

WHITMAN, GAYLE RUTH, nursing administrator, educator; b. Erie, Pa., Jan. 21, 1952; d. Robert Edwin and Georgalee (Jackson) W. BSN, U. Pitts., 1974; MS in Nursing, Case Western Res. U., 1978. RN, Ohio. Staff nurse Cleve. Clinic Hosp., 1974-76, asst. head nurse, 1976-77, head nurse CT ICU, 1977-80, clin. nurse specialist, 1980-85, dept. chmn., 1985-87, dir. cardiac nursing, 1987-95; vice chair nursing PT Care OP/Don, 1995—; staff nurse Med. Pers. Pool, Cleve., 1974-76; co-owner Critical Care Educators, 1976-85; instr., lectr. Cleve. State U., 1976-83; clin. instr. Case Western Res. U., Cleve., 1986—; bd. dirs. Frances Payne Boston Sch. Nursing, Cleve., 1989-92. Editor Nursing Scan in Critical Care, 1991—; contbr. articles to nursing jours., chpts. to books. Recipient Career Woman of Achievement award YWCA, Cleve., 1985. Fellow Am. Acad. Nursing, Am. Heart Assn.; mem. ANA, AACCN (bd. dirs. 1985-88, chmn. bd. dirs. 1992-94), Soc. Critical Care Medicine, Am. Heart Assn. (del. ann. assembly 1982-83, vice chmn. program com. 1990-91, chmn. 1991-94, mem. sci. sessions planning 1990-94, vice chmn. coun. CVN 1995—), Sigma Theta Tau. Office: Cleve Clinic Found 9500 Euclid Ave Cleveland OH 44195-0001

WHITMAN, ROBERT LESLIE, acoustic and optic engineer; b. Kansas City, Mo., Aug. 8, 1933; s. Leslie Rodman and Laura (Arey) W.; m. Marjorie Lassen, May 29, 1958; 1 child, Julie. BSEE, U. Ill., 1954. Microwave engr. Motorola, Inc., Chgo., 1954-60, Raytheon, Santa Barbara, Calif., 1960-61; elec. engr., then mgr. light modulation Zenith Electronics, Chgo., 1961-78; mgr. R & D Extel, Northbrook, Ill., 1978-84; mgr. acoustic R & D Zenith Electronics, Glenview, Ill., 1984-87; dir. R & D Intra Action, Bellwood, Ill., 1988-91; pres. Whitman Cons., Northbrook, Ill., 1991—; referee for tech. jour., 1969-78; mem. Internat. Video Disc Standards Com., Chgo., 1973-75; organizing chmn. Soc. Photographic and Instructional Engring., Chgo., 1977. Contbr. to profl. publs. Vice-pres. sch. PTA, Oak Park, Ill., 1971. Mem. IEEE, Optical Soc. Am., Tau Beta Pi. Home: 3904 Oak Ave Northbrook IL 60062-4923 Office: Whitman Cons 3904 Oak Ave Northbrook IL 60062-4923

WHITMER, MELVIN HOWARD, technician, educator; b. Mpls., Jan. 20, 1928; m. Sophia Ubert, Nov. 8, 1948 (div. 1982); children: Christine, Kathleen; m. Connie Elizabeth Oldham, May 3, 1985; stepchildren: Denise, Paul, Rick, James. Student, U. Chgo., 1950; certificate, Alexander Hamilton, N.Y., 1960-63. With TV Svc. Admiral Corp., Chgo., 1949-55; instr. Devry Inst., Chgo., 1955-58; writer, contract adminstr. Admiral Corp., Chgo., 1958-64; sales promotor Dynapar Corp., Gurnee, Ill., 1964-71; pres. AdTech Printing Co., Gurnee, Ill., 1971-77; instr. Lake County Area Vocational Ctr., Grayslake, Ill., 1977-85; tech. instr. Allen Bradley Co., Milw., 1985—. Author: Service Industrial Control, 1962, Service Closed-Circuit TV, 1964; contbr. articles to profl. jours. With USN, 1946-48. Mem. IEEE (sub-chpt. pres. 1960-61), Instrument Soc. Am. Mormon. Home: 153 Flagstaf Bolingbrook IL 60440 Office: Allen Bradley 7055 High Grove Blvd Burr Ridge IL 60521

WHITMORE, ANDREW, business owner, sales professional; b. Paw Paw, Mich., Sept. 26, 1969; s. Thomas Alva Whitmore Jr. and Rose M. Brondyke. Grad. H.S., Holland, Mich. Info. sys. mgr. Fort's Candies, Holland, 1988-92; owner, salesman Whitmore & Assocs., Holland, 1992—. Office: Whitmore & Assocs 369 W 35th St Holland MI 49423-4609

WHITNEY, BARRY LYN, religious studies educator; b. Cornwall, Ont., Can., Dec. 10, 1947; s. Earl Stanley Whitney and Gwendolyn Grace (Meldrum) Whitney. BA with honors, Carleton U., 1971; PhD in Religious Studies, McMaster U., Hamilton, Ont., 1977. Prof. religious studies U. Windsor, Ont., 1976—, rsch. prof., 1992-93; prof. pastoral edn. Southwestern Regional Ctr., Cedar Springs, Ont., 1977-79; mem. Anglican commn. Canterbury Coll., London and Windsor, 1977-79, tutor of admissions, Windsor, 1979-82, fellow, 1979-82; regional coord. Ctr. for Process Studies, 1979—. Author: Evil and the Process God, 1985, What are They Saying About God and Evil?, 1989, Theodicy, 1993; contbr. articles to profl. jours. Scholar Carleton U., 1967-71, McMaster U., 1971-76, Can. Coun. scholar McMaster, U., 1972-75; rsch. grantee Social Scis. and Humanities Rsch. Coun., 1988-90. Mem. Soc. for Study Process Philosophies, Coll. Theology, Soc. Am. Acad. Religion, Coun. for Study Religion, others. Home: 601-1385 Riverside Dr W, Windsor, ON Canada N9B3R9 Office: U Windsor Religious Studies, 401 Sunset Ave, Windsor, ON Canada N9B 3P4

WHITNEY, DONALD STEPHEN, pastor, writer; b. Memphis, Feb. 14, 1954; s. Donald Walker and Dollie Faye (Roper) W.; m. Caffy Irene Cox, Jan. 8, 1977; 1 child, Laurelen Christiana. BA, Ark. State U., 1975; MDiv, Southwestern Bapt. Theol. Sem., Ft. Worth, 1979; D of Ministry, Trinity Evang. Div. Sch., Deerfield, Ill., 1987. Assoc. pastor Pioneer Dr. Bapt. Ch., Irving, Tex., 1977-80; pastor Cedar Grove Bapt. Ch., Arkadelphia, Ark., 1980-81, Glenfield Bapt. Ch., Glen Ellyn, Ill., 1981-95; asst. prof. spiritual formation Midwestern Bapt. Theol. Sem., Kansas City, 1995—. Author: Spiritual Disciplines for the Christian Life, 1991, Spiritual Disciplines for the Christian Life Study Guide, 1994; How Can I Be Sure I'm a Christian, 1994, Spiritual Disciplines Within the Church, 1996. Office: Midwestern Bapt Theol Sem 5001 N Oak St Trfy Kansas City MO 64118

WHITNEY, GWIN RICHARD, brick distribution company executive; b. N.Y.C., Sept. 3, 1932; s. Gwin Allison and Charlotte (Wilson) W.; m. Marjorie Joan Turnbloom, Dec. 26, 1954; children: Gregg Richard, Laura Ann, Jane Louise, Eric Gwin. BA, Stanford U., 1954; postgrad., Brick Inst. Am., 1979. Asst. mgr. Whitney's, Duluth, Minn., 1958-70; adminstrn. mgr. Thomas and Vecchi Architects, Duluth, 1970-75; owner, pres. Standard Brick and Supply Inc., Duluth, 1975-89; gen. mgr. Standard Brick (div. Brock White), Duluth, 1989-92; mem. exec. com. Brock White, St. Paul, 1992—. Trustee Pilgrim Congl. Ch., Duluth, 1980-82; bd. dirs. Woodland Hills Juvenile Residential Treatment Home, 1993—. Mem. ASTM, Arrowhead Builder Assn. (bd. dirs. 1976-85), Nat. Assn. Brick Distbrs. (chmn. 1990-92, bd. dirs. 1982-93), Duluth Builders Exch. (bd. dirs., pres. 1988-89), Minn. Brick Distbrs. (bd. dirs. 1980—, pres. 1993-95), Duluth C. of C., Rotary, Northland Club, Kitchi Gammi. Republican. Office: Standard Brick PO Box 16507 4231 W 1st St Duluth MN 55816

WHITSEL, ROBERT MALCOLM, retired insurance company executive; b. Lafayette, Ind., Dec. 30, 1929; s. Earl Newton and Elizabeth (Bader) W.; m. Marilyn Katherine House, Oct. 15, 1955; children—Rebecca Sue, Cynthia Ann. BS, Ind. U., 1951, MBA, 1954; hon. D of Mgmt., Purdue U. With Lafayette Life Ins. Co., 1954-95, mem. exec. com., 1968-95, exec. v.p., 1973, pres., 1973-95, also bd. dirs., ret., 1995; mem. adv. bd. NBD, Bank. Elder, trustee, deacon Presbyn. Ch., 1965-74; dir., past pres. Jr. Achievement Greater Lafayette, Inc., 1976-77, Ctrl. Presbyn. Found., Edgelea PTA; past pres., bd. dirs., past campaign chmn. United Way Greater Lafayette; past v.p., bd. dirs. Wabash Sch. for Mentally Retarded; past mem. adv. bd. Purdue Ctr. for Econ. Edn.; past pres., bd. dirs. Capital Funds Found. Greater Lafayette; bd. dirs. Lafayette Home Hosp., 1972—, mem. fin. com., 1976—, past pres.; trustee YWCA Found.; past chmn. Greater Lafayette Progress Inc., North Ctrl. Health Svcs., Inc.; chmn. West Lafayette Found., Inc., Westminster Village Retirement Ctr.; past pres. Greater Lafayette Cmty. Found.; bd. dirs., mem. exec. com. purdue Rsch. Found. 1st lt. USAF, 1951-53. Recipient Nat. Bus. Leadership award Jr. Achievement, 1977. Mem. Soc. Residential Appraisers, Ind. Mortgage Bankers Assn. (past pres.), Am. Coun. Life Ins. (bd. dirs., chmn. Forum 500 sect.), Soc. Fin. Analysts, Assn. Ind. Life Ins. Cos. (past pres.), Ind. C. of C. (past dir.), Greater Lafayette C. of C. (past pres.), Ind. Soc. of Chgo., Lafayette Country Club (past pres., dir.), Sagamore of the Wabash (designated), Town and Gown Club, Masons, Beta Gamma Sigma. Republican. Home: 541 Old Farm Rd Lafayette IN 47905-3515 Office: Lafayette Life Ins Co 1905 Teal Rd # 7007 Lafayette IN 47905-2225

WHITSELL, DORIS BENNER, retired educator; b. Poplar Grove, Ill., Mar. 17, 1923; d. Ralph Erwin and Sarah McKay (Mulligan) Wheeler; m. Robert M. Benner, Dec. 1945 (div. 1955); 1 child, Geoffrey Mark Benner (dec.); m. Eugene B. Whitsell, Feb. 1969 (dec. 1972). BS, No. Ill. U., 1944, MS in Edn., 1967; postgrad., Rockford Coll., 1964. Tchr. English and home econs. Lee (Ill.) High Sch., 1944-45; tchr. English Ashton (Ill.) Community High Sch., 1945-46; tchr. Morris Kennedy Sch., Rockford, Ill., 1952-55, William Nashold Sch., Rockford, 1955-56; tchr. English, drama Jefferson Jr. High Sch., Rockford, 1956-69; tchr. English Richwoods High Sch., Peoria, Ill., 1969-71; tchr. Calvin Coolidge Sch., Peoria, 1972-81; mem. textbook selection com. Dist. 150, Peoria, 1973-75, curriculum planning com., 1974-75, tutor for homebound, 1982-83, cons. competency test seminar; cons. textbook divsn. Harcourt, Brace, Jovanovich, 1981-83; evaluator North Ctrl. Accreditation Team, Jefferson H.S., Rockford, 1980. Counselor Operation Sr. Security, Peoria, 1986-89; treas. Rockford Women's Club Fortnighty Dept., 1961-62; past deaconess 1st Federated Ch., Peoria; pres. Willow Heights Homeowner's Assn., Peoria, 1979-81; bldg. rep. Rockford Edn. Assn., 1954-56, 3d v.p., 1968-70; vol. Rockford Midway Village and Mus. Ctr., 1992, 95-96; bd. dirs. Forest Vale Estate Condominiums, Meadows Assn., Rockford, 1994, treas., 1995-96. Named for Significant Svc. to the Community, Ret. Sr. Vol. Program, Peoria, 1986. Mem. Ill. Ret. Tchrs. Assn. (life, sec. 1982-90, bd. dirs. Found. Inc., 1985-93, moderator conv. panel 1990, Outstanding Svc. award 1989), Peoria Area Ret. Tchrs. Assn. (2d v.p. 1987-88, pres. 1989-90, chmn. state bldg. fund. com. 1987-88), AAUW (program v.p. 1988-89), Nat. Ret. Tchrs. Assn. (life), No. Ill. U. Alumni Assn., Delta Kappa Gamma (chmn. ins. com. Beta Gamma chpt. 1956-60, v.p. 1962-64, pres. 1964-66, profl. affairs com. 1992-96, chmn. personal growth and svc. com. Nu chpt. 1988-90, program com. Lambda chpt. 1978-80, Winnabego County ret. tchrs. unit 1992-96). Home: 1283 Aarons Ct Rockford IL 61108-1536

WHITT, DIXIE DAILEY, microbiology educator; b. Longmont, Colo., Mar. 9, 1939; d. Herman Eden and Helen Lurissia (Stanton) Dailey; m. Gregory Sidney Whitt, Aug. 25, 1963. BS, Colo. State U., 1961, PhD, 1965. Postdoctoral trainee Yale U., New Haven, Conn., 1965-68; rsch. biologist, lectr. Yale U., 1968-69; rsch. assoc. U. Ill., Urbana, 1969-87; lectr. basic scis. U. Ill. Coll. Medicine, 1987—. Co-author: (lab. manual) Properties of Bacterial Pathogens, 1990, (textbook) Bacterial Pathogenesis: A Molecular Approach, 1994; contbr. articles to profl. jours. NDEA Title IV fellow, 1961-64, NIH fellow, 1964-65. Fellow Am. Acad. Microbiology; mem. AAAS, Am. Soc. Microbiology (chair membership com. 1995—). Home: 1510 Trails Dr Urbana IL 61801-7052 Office: U Ill Dept Microbiology 407 S Goodwin Ave Urbana IL 61801-3704

WHITT, LINDA L., health facility administrator; b. Cin., May 31, 1958. With accounts payable dept. Uniroyal-Goodrich Tire, Mason, Ohio, 1984-87; admissions rep. S.W. Coll. Bus., Middletown, Ohio, 1987-91; supr. patient svcs. Physicians Billing Com., Middletown, 1991—. Baptist. Office: Ancillary Svcs Middletown 1533 Central Ave Middletown OH 45044-3401

WHITTEMORE, ALAN THOMAS, plant taxonomist; b. Redwood City, Calif., May 16, 1957; s. Thomas Edwin and Evelyn Anne (Fawcett) W. BS in chemistry, botany, U. Calif., Davis, 1978; MA in biology, Humboldt State U., 1982; PhD in botany, U. Tex., 1987. Tchg. asst. Humboldt State U., Arcata, Calif., 1979-80; chemist Peninsula Labs., Belmont, Calif., 1980-81; tchg. asst. U. Tex., Austin, 1982-87; postdoctoral rschr. Washington U., St. Louis, 1988-90, U.S. Dept. Agriculture, Griffin, Ga., 1990-91; asst. curator Mo. Botanical Garden, St. Louis, 1991—; part-time lectr. Washington U., 1993—. Contbr. articles to profl. jours. Postdoctoral fellowship Alfred P. Sloan Found., 1988-90. Mem. AAAS, Am. Bryological Soc., Am. Soc. Plant Taxonomists, Botanical Soc. Am., Calif. Botanical Soc., Soc for Study Evolution. Home: 5047 Waterman Apt 309 Saint Louis MO 63108 Office: Mo Botanical Garden PO Box 299 Saint Louis MO 63166

WHITTEMORE, DONALD OSGOOD, geochemist, hydrogeochemistry educator; b. Pitts., May 4, 1944; s. Osgood James and Barbara Estelle (Greenwood) W.; m. Andrea Ann Yaswinski, Sept. 11, 1971; children: Luke Andrew, Paul James, Mark Donald. BS in Chemistry, U. N.H., 1966; PhD in Geochemistry, Pa. State U., 1973. Asst. prof. dept. geology Kans. State U., Manhattan, 1972-78; assoc. scientist Kans. Geol. Survey, Lawrence, 1978-95, sr. scientist, 1995—; chief geohydrology sect., 1996—; courtesy assoc. prof. dept. geology U. Kans., 1988—. Author chpts. in books; contbr. articles to profl. jours. Mem. Am. Geophys. Union, Soil Sci. Soc. Am., Internat. Assn. Geochemistry and Cosmochemistry, Assn. Ground Water Scientists and Engrs., Kans. Acad. Sci. (coun. 1986-88, v.p. 1989, pres. 1991). Office: Kans Geol Survey Campus W/KU 1930 Constant Ave Lawrence KS 66047-3724

WHITTEN, DORIS JEAN, professional speaker; b. Ashland, Ky., Nov. 28; d. Isom Richard Gillum and Blanche Elizabeth (Horton) Boyer; m. Chester Burdette Whitten (dec. Sept. 1993); children: Montel Ackerman, Tammy McGinnis. Grad. h.s., Portsmouth, Ohio. Author: Happy Homemaking, 1972. Singer Pasadena (Calif.) Civic Chorus, 1944-68; chmn. Salem (Ill.) Tourism Coun., 1989-94, Salem Hist. Commn., 1974-96. Named to Nat. Women's Wall of Fame, 1993. Republican. Home: PO Box 1321 Salem IL 62881

WHITTER, PAMELA LETHA, journalist; b. Gary, Ind., Mar. 24, 1962; d. Walter Raleigh and Frances Jean (Renwick) Somerville; m. Herman Whitter, May 27, 1995. BS, Va. State U., 1985; MEd, Harvard U., 1986; MBA, Georgetown U., 1991. Mgr. Reliable References, Rockville, Md., 1992-93; mktg. asst. Prudential Securities, Pitts., 1993-94; journalist Herald-Star, Steubenville, Ohio, 1994—. Recipient Dedication and Vol. Svc. award Family House, 1995. Mem. Cmty. Jr. League Pitts (assessment devel. com.), Soc. Profl. Journalists.

WHITTINGTON, JEREMIAH, physician; b. Eagle Mills, Ark., Jan. 25, 1946; s. George Washington Jr. and Lula (Brooks) W.; m. Mary Ellen Branch, July 1, 1972 (div. July 1976); 1 child, Carrie Kenyatta; m. Kaye Francis Atkinson, June 18, 1977; 1 child, Christopher Jerome. Student, Calvin Coll., 1969; MA, U. Mich., 1970, postgrad., 1971-72; MD, Mich. State U., 1979. Diplomate Am. Bd. Ob-Gyn.; ordained to ministry Ch. of God in Christ, 1992. Intern, resident ob/gyn intern, resident ob-gyn, Youngstown, Ohio, 1979-83; physician Planned Parenthood of Mahoning County, Youngstown, 1980-83, Ashtabula (Ohio) County Commn. Action Agy., 1981-83; practice medicine specializing in ob-gyn Grand Rapids, Mich., 1984-89; attending physician City of Faith Med. and Research Ctr., Tulsa, 1985-89; clin. asst. prof. UCLA, Sylmar; physician specialist dept. ob-gyn L.A. County Hosp., Olive Med. Ctr., Sylmar, 1989-90; ob-gyn physician So. Calif. Permanente Med. Group, Panorama City, Calif., 1990-93, Providence Hosp. Med. Ctrs., Southfield, Mich., 1993—; physician Ambulatory Gynecology, Infertility and Obstetrics, Claremore, Okla., 1983-86; staff physician USPHS and Claremore Indian Hosp. 1983-86; asst. prof. dept. ob-gyn. Oral Roberts U. Sch. Medicine, Tulsa, 1985-89; cons., physician Rogers County Health Dept., Claremore, 1983-86; mem. People to People delegation Citizens Amb. program to Finland, 1987; tchr., spkr. Sch. Medicine U. Zambia, Lusaka, 1990; spkr. Victory Celebrations, Zambia, 1988, 90, 91, 93, 95. Contbr. articles to hosp. jour. Mem. Okla. Med. Polit. Action Com., Oklahoma City, 1986. Pub. health service scholar U.S. Pub. Health Service, 1976. Fellow Am. Coll. Ob-Gyn.; mem. AMA, Calif. Med. Assn., L.A. County Med. Assn., L.A. Ob-Gyn. Soc. Democrat. Home: 22450 Eaton Ct Novi MI 48375-3813 Office: Providence Med Ctr N Woodward-OB/GYN 2575 N Woodward Ave Ste 210 Royal Oak MI 48073

WHITWAM, DAVID RAY, appliance manufacturing company executive; b. Stanley, Wis., Jan. 30, 1942; s. Donald R. and Lorraine (Stoye) W.; m. Barbara Lynne Peterson, Apr. 13, 1963; children: Mark, Laura, Thomas. B.S., U. Wis., 1967. Gen. mgr. sales So. Calif. div. Whirlpool Corp., Los Angeles, 1975-77; mdse. mgr. ranges Whirlpool Corp., Benton Harbor, Mich., 1977-79, dir. builder mktg., 1979-80, v.p. builder mktg., 1980-83, v.p. whirlpool sales, 1983-85, vice chmn., chief mktg. officer, 1985-87, chmn., pres., chief exec. officer, 1987—, also bd. dirs.; bd. dirs. Combustion Engring. Inc., Stamford, Conn. Pres. bd. dirs. The Soup Kitchen, Benton Harbor, 1980—; mem. Nat. Council Housing Industry, Washington. Served to capt. U.S. Army. Fellow Aspen Inst. Republican. Lutheran. Club: Point O'Woods (Benton Harbor). Office: Whirlpool Corp 2000 M63 North Benton Harbor MI 49022*

WHYMAN, DEBORAH, state legislator; b. St. Louis, July 1, 1958. BSBA, Ctrl. Mich. U., MSA. Rep. State of Mich., Lansing, vice chair edn. com., mem. taxation, human svcs. & children com., house ethics & oversight com. Home: 44446 Newburyport Dr Canton MI 48187-2509 Office: Mich Ho of Reps PO Box 30014 Lansing MI 48909-7514*

WIATR, CHRISTOPHER L., microbiologist; b. Chgo., Jan. 5, 1948; s. Joseph Thomas and Beatrice Harriet (Kaminski) Wiatr; m. Jeanne Lynn Malecki, Oct. 20, 1978; children: Kelli Jean, Christopher Joseph, Kaycee Lynn, Kirby Ann, Nicholas Aloysius. BS, Ill. Benedictine Coll., 1969; MS, IIT, 1974; PhD, U. Ill., Chgo., 1985. Cert. tchr. Tchr., coach St. Rita High Sch., Chgo., 1969-74; rsch. microbiologist Swift & Co./Esmark/Beatrice Foods, Chgo., 1974-75, lab. mgr., 1975-76, tech. dir. rsch. and quality assurance, 1976-79; sr. microbiologist Nalco Chem. Co. Water and Waste Treatment R & D, Naperville, Ill., 1985-87, sr. rsch. microbiologist, 1988, group leader water rsch., 1989-91; group leader Pulp & Paper Chems. R & D, Naperville, Ill., 1991-94; mgr. microbiology and biochemistry R&D Calgon Corp.-ECCI, Pitts., 1994—; reviewer Nat. Assn. Corrosion Engrs; chmn. biocide session Internat. Water Conf., 1996. Co-author: (book chpt.) Food Preservation by Irradiation, 1978; contbr. articles to profl. jours. Com. Maplebrook I Swim Club, Naperville, 1990-94; Eagle scout, merit badge counselor Boy Scouts Am., 1963—. Named Researcher of Yr., Nalco Chem. Co., 1987. Mem. TAPPI (microbiology and microbiol tech. and water quality com. 1993—), Am. Chem. Soc., Nat. Assn. Corrosion Engrs., Soc. Indsl. Microbiology, Am. Soc. for Microbiology, Sigma Xi (pres. Nalco chpt. 1991-92, session chair microbiology internat. water conf. 1996). Roman Catholic.

WICAL, GREGG THOMAS, mechanical engineer; b. Dayton, Ohio, Apr. 19, 1970; s. Richard Lee and Judith Carol (Ball) W. BSME, Purdue U., West Lafayette, Ind., 1992. Project engr. Fujitec Am., Lebanon, Ohio, 1992—. Office: Fujitec America Inc MDD 401 Fujitec Dr Lebanon OH 45036-9691

WICE, PAUL CLINTON, news director, educator; b. West Branch, Mich., Sept. 30, 1944; s. Clinton Harold and Viola Ruth (Potratz) W.; m. Dolores Ann Janovec, Sept. 30, 1967. BA, Kearney State Coll., 1966; MA, U. Nebr., Kearney, 1989. News anchor Sta. KHGI-TV, Kearney, Nebr., 1965-66; news editor Sta. KWBE Radio, Beatrice, Nebr., 1966-67; city editor Kearney Hub, 1968-69; news dir. Sta. KGFW-AM, Kearney, 1967-68, 69—; adj. faculty speech communication U. Nebr., Kearney, 1981—. Bd. dirs. Buffalo County Crimestoppers, Kearny Area Habitat for Humanity, Luth. Family Svcs. of Nebr.; bd. dirs., patron chair Community Concert Assn. Mem. Soc. Profl. Jours. (bd. dirs. Nebr. chpt.). Home: Box 1754 #2 Sycamore Pl Kearney NE 68848-1754 Office: Sta KGFW-AM PO Box 666 Kearney NE 68848-0666

WICK, HAL GERARD, state legislator; b. New Ulm, Minn., Oct. 31, 1944; s. Roland Theodore and Esther Marie La Fontaine W.; m. Jane Dorothy Rance, 1965; children: Anne Marie, Paula Jo, Betsey Jane, Ross Anthony. Student, Exec. Air Travel Flight Sch., Sioux Falls, S.D., 1966-68; BS, S.D. State U., Brookings, 1967. Flight instr. Snediger Flying Svc., Rapid City, S.D., 1968, Airways Svc., Sioux City, Iowa, 1968-70; pilot Iowa Air Nat. Guard, Sioux City, 1970-75; chief pilot, flight instr. Soo Flying, Sioux City, 1971-72; pilot NW Airlines, Mpls., 1972—; S.D. state rep. Dist. 11, 1977-80; now S.D. state rep. Dist. 12; also S.D. House rep.; chmn. Minnehaha County Rep. Party Victory Squad, S.D., 1974-76; chmn. Minnehaha County Citizens for Reagan, 1976; del. Rep. Nat. Conv., 1976; mem. Legis. Rsch. Coun., State of S.D., 1977-78, mem. Edn. and Transp. Coms.; former chmn., coord. People for Alternative to McGovern, Nat. Conservative Polit. Action Com. Named Top Gun, Sioux City, 1974, Outstanding Optimist, Morning Optimist Club, 1975. Mem. Am. Legion, NG Assn., Air Line Pilots Assn., Hartford Lions. Home: 3009 Danahue Dr Sioux Falls SD 57105-0153*

WICKER, ELMUS ROGERS, economics educator; b. Lake Charles, La., Sept. 13, 1926; s. Elmus Rogers and Georgia Mary (Moss) Wicker; m. Carolyn Braswell, Sept. 18, 1948; children: Vanessa Louise, Roger Andrew. BA, La. State U., 1945, MA, 1948; MPhil, Oxford (Eng.) U., 1951; PhD, Duke U., 1956. Prof. econs. Ind. U., Bloomington, 1955-92, prof. emeritus, 1992—. Author: Federal Reserve Monetary Policy, 1966; co-author: Principles of Monetary Economics, 1975, The Banking Panics of the Great Depression, 1996. With USN, 1945-46. Rhodes scholar, 1948. Mem. Am. Econ. Assn., Econ. History Assn. Democrat. Roman Catholic. Home: 1315 S Nancy St Bloomington IN 47401-6041

WICKER, NANCY LYNN, art history educator; b. Shelbyville, Ind., Sept. 27, 1953; d. Gene Gray and Mary Myrtle (Stewart) W.; m. Matthew Leigh Murray, May 17, 1991. BA in Art History and Art Studio, Ea. Ill. U., 1975; MA in Art History, U. Minn., 1979, PhD in Ancient Studies, 1990. Adj. instr.. Mankato (Minn.) State U., 1986, asst. prof., 1990-95, assoc. prof., 1995—; adminstr. asst. U. Minn., Mpls., 1986-90. Contbr. articles to profl. jours. Birka Internat. scholar, 1992; Am.-Scandinavian Found. fellow, 1982; grantee Am. Coun. Learned Soc., 1990, Am-Numismatic Soc., 1994. Mem. European Assn. Archaeologists, Soc. Am. Archaeology, Archaeol. Inst. Am., Medieval Acad. Am., Internat. Ctr. Medieval Art, Coll. Art Assn. Office: Mankato State U Art Dept PO Box 8400 Mankato MN 56002-8400

WICKERSHAM, WILLIAM R., state legislator; b. Lusk, Wyo., Oct. 22, 1948. BSBA, Creighton U.; JD, U. Nebr. Mem. from dist. 49 Nebr. State Senate, Omaha, 1992—, mem. edn., revenue coms., 1994—, chmn. retirement sys., 1994—. Mem. ABA, Nebr. State Bar Assn., Sioux City Hist. Soc., Siouc County Agr. Soc., Elks. Office: State Capitol Rm 2017 Lincoln NE 68509*

WICKHAM-ST. GERMAIN, MARGARET EDNA, mass spectrometrist; b. Kansas City, Mo., June 7, 1956; d. Ronald Lee and Mary Ann (Nicholas) Wickham; m. Christopher Newman St. Germain, June 11, 1988; 1 child, Mark Anthony. BS in Chemistry, St. Mary Coll., Leavenworth, Kans., 1978; student, U. Mo., 1979-80, 1994—. Lab. technician VA Hosp., Kansas City, 1977; jr. chemist Midwest Rsch. Inst., Kansas City, 1978-80, jr. mass spectrometrist, 1980-81, asst. mass spectrometrist, 1981-85, assoc. mass spectrometrist, 1985-86, mass spectrometrist, 1986-90, sr. mass spectrometrist, 1990-94; owner Wickham Sci. Svcs., 1994—; chemist EPA Region 7, Kansas City, Kans., 1994—. Co-author: Priority Pollutants, 1983; author: Method Development for VOST Fractionator, 1994. Active Mid-Continent coun. Girl Scouts U.S., 1962—, St. Bernadette's Ch., Kansas City, 1986—. Mem. Am. Chem. Soc. (mem. nat. younger chemist com. 1988-91, chair memberships com. Kansas City chpt. 1979-80, sec. 1984, chair-elect 1985, chair 1986, past chair 1987, chair chemistry conf. 1989, founding mem. regional younger chemist com. 1990—, Chemagro Essay award 1977, 78), Am. Soc. for Mass Spectrometry, Soc. for Applied Spectroscopy, Air & Waste Mgmt. Assn., Kappa Gamma Pi (Excellence award 1978), Delta Epsilon Sigma (Excellence award 1978). Office: Wickham Sci Svcs 9102 E 50th Ter Kansas City MO 64133-2120

WICKLOW, DONALD THOMAS, mycologist; b. San Francisco, June 22, 1940; s. Thomas Paton and Willa (Cope) W.; m. Constance Sue Kirchhoff, Dec. 20, 1970 (div. Apr. 1983); children: Cameron Kirk, Brandon James. BA, San Francisco State Coll., 1962, MA, 1964; PhD, U. Wis., 1971. Instr. biology U. Wis., Waukesha, 1969-70; asst. prof. U. Pitts., 1970-77; rsch. microbiologist Nat. Ctr. for Agrl. and Utilization Rsch., Peoria, Ill., 1977—; lead scientist Nat. Ctr. for Agrl. and Utilization Rsch., Peoria, 1984—; mem. adv. panel ecology NSF, Washington, 1979-81, adv. panel biolog. control NRC, Washington, 1988, adv. panel fermentations NCI Cancer Rsch., Frederick, Md., 1991; organizing com. 3d Internat. Microbial Ecology Symposium, East Lansing, Mich., 1983. Editor: (book) The Fungal Community, 1981, 2d rev. edit. 1992; contbr. articles to Mycologia, Canadian Jour. Of Botany, Phytopathology, Ecology, Mycological Rsch. and others, 1966—. Grantee NSF, Washington, 1973—. Fellow Am. Acad. Microbiology, Ecolog. Soc. Am., Mycolog. Soc. Am. Brit. Mycolog. Soc. Office: Nat Ctr for Agrl & Utilization Rsch 1815 N University St Peoria IL 61604-3902

WICKMAN, JOHN EDWARD, librarian, historian; b. Villa Park, Ill., May 24, 1929; s. John Edward and Elsie (Voss) W.; m. Shirley Jean Swanson, Mar. 17, 1951; children—Lisa Annette, Eric John. A.B., Elmhurst Coll., 1953; A.M., Ind. U., 1958, Ph.D., 1964; LL.D., Lincoln Coll., 1973. Instr. history Hanover (Ind.) Coll., 1959-62, Southeast Campus, Ind. U., Jeffersonville, 1962; asst. prof. history Northwest Mo. State Coll., Maryville, 1962-64; asst. to Gov. William H. Avery of Kans., Topeka, 1964-65; asst. prof. history Regional Campus, Purdue U., Fort Wayne, Ind., 1965-66; dir. Dwight D. Eisenhower Libr., Abilene, Kans., 1966-89; ret., 1989. Contbr. articles on Am. West, archival mgmt., adminstrv. history, oral history to profl. publs. Served with U.S. Army, 1953-55. Nat. Ctr. for Edn. in Politics faculty fellow, 1964-65; Am. Polit. Sci. Assn. Congl. fellow, 1975-76. Mem. Oral History Assn. (v.p. 1971-72, pres. 1972-73), Western History Assn. (coun. 1972-75), Kans. Hist. Soc. (2d v.p. 1974-75, pres. 1976-77, dir.). Home: PO Box 325 Enterprise KS 67441-0325

WICKSTROM, LAWRENCE LEE, manufacturing company executive, consultant; b. Lander, Wyo., Feb. 7, 1947; s. Lee Worth and Emma Edith (Krone) W.; m. Connie Lynette Burroughs, May 19, 1979; 1 child, Phillip Everett. BS, U. Wyo., 1970; MS, Wichita State U., 1980; MBA, U. Chgo., 1984. Registered prof. engr., Ala., Calif., Mich., Mo., Colo., Ill., Ind., Iowa, Kans., Nebr., Ohio, Wyo. Product engr. Full Vision, Inc., Newton, Kans., 1973-74; project engr. Farmland Industries SPP, Hutchinson, Kans., 1974-79; chief engr. Superior Equipment Mfg. Co., Mattoon, Ill., 1979-80; dir. engring. Agrl. Bldg. Co., Mendota, Ill., 1980-82; chief engr. Chgo. Eastern Corp., Marengo, Ill., 1982-85; mgr. Engring. and Constrn. Farmland Industries SPP, Hutchinson, Kans., 1985-86; dir. customer svc. Behlen Mfg. Co., Columbus, Nebr., 1986-87; pres. Wickstrom, PE, MBA & Assoc., Blair, Nebr., 1987—; chief engr. Concrete Equipment Co., Inc., Blair, 1988—. Served to 1st lt. U.S. Army, 1970-72. Decorated Bronze Star. Mem. NSPE. Office: Concrete Equipment Co Inc 237 N 13th St Blair NE 68008-1673

WIDELL, LARRY RICHARD, plant ecologist; b. Rockford, Ill., May 24, 1950; s. Clarence Albert and Doris Vivian (Johnson) W.; m. Sarah Satorius, May 31, 1975 (div. Dec. 1984); 1 child, Christopher Matthew. BA, MacMurray Coll., 1972; MS, No. Ill. U., 1975; PhD, Duke U., 1981. Cert. arborist; cert. pesticide applicator, Ohio. Lab. technician USDA Forest Svc., Research Triangle Park, N.C., 1978-79; biologist N.C. State U., Raleigh, 1979-80; adj. prof. sci. Urbana Coll., London, Ohio, 1982-85; environ. advisor O.M. Scott and Sons, Marysville, Ohio, 1981-82, sr. project leader, 1982-89; nat. dir. ops. Barefoot Grass, Worthington, Ohio, 1989-95; founder, owner PhD Landscapes, Rockford, Ill., 1995—. Mem. Internat. Soc. Arboriculture, Nat. Wildflower Rsch. Ctr., No. Ill. Bot. Soc., Am. Soc. Landscape Architects, The Cousteau Soc., Nat. Arbor Day Found., Duke Alumni Assn. Home: 1314 Bolenhill Ct Columbus OH 43229

WIDELL, THOMAS ALAN, emergency physician; b. Rockford, Ill., Mar. 10, 1953; s. Stig Eric Einer and Elaine Shirley (Pearson) W.; m. Susan Kay Isely; children: Stig Erik, Christine Nichole, Aaron Kai. BA in Biochemistry and Molecular Biology, Northwestern U., 1976; MD, U. Ill., 1988. Orderly Evanston (Ill.) Hosp., 1973-74; EMT LaSalle Ambulance, Chgo., 1976-77; clin. biochemist CliniTec Lab., Winnetka, Ill., 1977-80; supr., clin. instr. Michael Reese Med. Ctr., Chgo., 1981-84; intern St. Francis Hosp., Evanston, 1988-89; resident Beth Israel, Elmhurst, N.Y.C., 1989-92; dir., attending physician Mt. Sinai Hosp. Med. Ctr., Chgo., 1992—. Mem. Am. Coll. Emergency Physicians, Emergency Medicine Residents Assn. (chair 1989-92), Ill. Coll. Emergency Physicians, N.Y. Coll. Emergency Physicians, Emergency Medicine Residents Assn. N.Y. (bd. dirs., sec., pres. 1989-92). Home: 2212 Pioneer Rd Evanston IL 60201-2517 Office: Mt Sinai Hosp Med Ctr California at 15th Chicago IL 60608

WIDIN, GREGORY PETER, biomedical development administrator; b. Plainfield, N.J., Apr. 2, 1952; m. Katharine D. Dawson, May 25, 1974. AB, Kenyon Coll., 1974; PhD, U. Minn., 1979, MS in Mgmt. of Tech., 1992. Postdoctoral fellow Rsch. Lab. Electronics, Cambridge, Mass., 1979-82; supr. 3M, St. Paul, 1982—. Contbr. articles to profl. jours. on aspects of hearing and digital hearing aids. Mem. IEEE, MOT Alumni Assn. (pres. 1994-95). Office: 3M Bldg 270-2N-05 Saint Paul MN 55144

WIDMAN, ELIZABETH ANN, educator; b. Pukwana, S.D., Apr. 12, 1937; d. Emmett John and DeLonde (Svoboda) Healy; m. Paul Joseph Widman, July 30, 1959; children: Cynthia, Susan, Shelly, Richard, Mark. BS in Home Econs. Edn., S.D. State U., 1959. Ext. home economist Kingsbury County, Desmet, S.D., summer 1957-58; home econs. educator Gen. Beadle Campus High Sch., Madison, S.D., 1959-60; kindergarten tchr. Henry (S.D.) Grade Sch., 1962-64; home econs. tchr. Custer (S.D.) High Sch., 1964-66, Mitchell (S.D.) High Sch., 1966-67, Mitchell Middle Sch. and High Sch., 1976—; lectr. Weight Watchers, Mitchell, Plankinton and Kimball, S.D., 1991-93; mem. adv. bd. S.D. State U. Coll. Home Econs., 1982-85. Mem. precinct com. Davison County Dem. Com., Mitchell, 1992; leader 4-H, 1969-81; mem. alumni coun. S.D. State U., 1974-84. Named Outstanding 4-H Alumni, S.D. 4-H Leaders, 1979, Outstanding Tchr., Mitchell Schs., 1981, Master Advisor, Future Homemakers Am., 1988, Advisor Mentor, 1992. Mem. Nat. Assn. Vocat. Home Econs. Tchrs. (legis. chmn. 1992), S.D. Vocat. Home Econs. Tchrs. (pres. 1988, Outstanding Educator award 1990, Arch of Fame award 1991, Carl Perkins Humanitarian award 1993, Outstanding Svc. to Vocat. Edn. award 1996), Am. Home Econs. Assn., S.D. Home Econs. Assn., Am. Vocat. Assn., S.D. Vocat. Assn. (pres.-elect 1993-94, pres. 1994-95, past pres. 1995-96), S.D. State U. Alumni Assn. (pres. 1983-84, Outstanding Alumni Leadership award 1984, Disting. Alumnus Svc. to Alumni award 1993). Roman Catholic.

WIDMAN, PAUL JOSEPH, insurance agent; b. DeSmet, S.D., Dec. 18, 1936; s. Warren Clay and Lorraine (Coughlin) W.; m. Elizabeth Ann Healy, July 30, 1959; children: Cynthia, Susan, Shelly, Richard, Mark. BS, Dakota State Coll., Madison, 1959; M in Comm., S.D. State U., 1968. Tchr. Clark (S.D.) Pub. Sch., 1959-60, Henry (S.D.) Pub. Sch., 1960-64, Custer (S.D.) Pub. Sch., 1964-66; ins. agt. Horace Mann Ins., Mitchell, S.D., 1966-77, Universal Underwriters, Mitchell, S.D., 1980-87, NGM Ins. Assn., Mitchell, S.D., 1987-91, Reginald Martin Agy., Mitchell, S.D., 1991—; state rep. State of S.D., 1993—. City coun. mem. Mitchell City Coun., 1972-76; state legislator S.D. Ho. of Reps., 1993-94. Sgt. U.S. Army N.G., 1955-61. Mem. Elks, Mitchell Jaycees (pres., v.p. 1968-70, Outstanding Jaycee 1970), S.D. Jaycees (v.p., regional dir. 1969-70). Democrat. Roman Catholic. Office: Reginald Martin Agy 510 W Havens St Mitchell SD 57301-3935

WIDMER, LAURA BETH, mass communication educator; b. Moberly, Mo., May 6, 1956; d. John Richard and Gertrude (Roling) Widmer. B.S., Northwest Mo. State U., 1979; M.S., Iowa State U., 1983. Media asst. Earle Palmer Brown Advt. Agy., Washington, 1980; photo lab. instr. Iowa State U., Ames, 1981, instr. yearbook workshop, 1981—; publs. coordinator Clinton Sch. Dist. (Mo.), 1982-83; publs. dir., asst. prof. Northwest Mo. State U., Maryville, 1983—, dir. summer publs. workshop, 1978—; instr. yearbook workshop Drake U., Des Moines, 1983, U. Mo., 1984—. Nominee Case Prof. of Yr. Mem. Nat. Press Photographers Assn., Soc. Profl. Journalists, Mo. Press Women's Fedn., Coll. Media Advisers (pres. 1991-93). Roman Catholic. Home: 206 Alco Maryville MO 64468 Office: Northwest Mo State U 4 Wells Hall Maryville MO 64468

WIDMER, MARK STEVEN, school administrator; b. Oshkosh, Wis., Aug. 1, 1957; s. Ronald Lee and Blanche Marie (O'Keefe) W.; m. Naomi Ruth Nelson, July 9, 1976; children: Carissa, Caleb, Joel, Ashley. ThG, Bapt. Bible Coll., Springfield, Mo., 1978. Youth pastor, sch. tchr. Sheboygan (Wis.) County Bapt. Ch., 1978-79, Bible Bapt. Ch., Quincy, Ill., 1979-83; sch. adminstr., tchr. Bible Bapt. Ch., Quincy, 1983-89, Faith Christian Sch., Coleman, Wis., 1989—. Trustee First Bapt. Ch., 1991—; mcpl. judge Village of Coleman, Wis., 1993—. Baptist. Home: 147 N Franklin St Coleman WI 54112

WIEBER, DAVID JOHN, physical therapist, athletic trainer, business owner; b. St. Joseph, Minn., July 24, 1963; s. John Paul and Ethel Catherine (Meller) W. BS in Biology, St. Cloud (Minn.) State U., 1985. Cert. phys. therapist, cert. athletic trainer. Staff phys. therapist Merle West Med. Ctr., Klamath Falls, Oreg., 1987-92; traveling therapist Q Resources, Indpls., 1992-93; cons. in phys. therapy Naeve Health, Albert Lea, Minn., 1993—. Republican. Christian.

WIECHERS, JAMES DAVID, data processing executive, electronic data processing auditor; b. Racine, Wis., Apr. 23, 1937; s. James Leonard and Edna May (Davidson) W.; m. Carol Jean Hlavka, July 16, 1959; children: James, Susan, Matthew. BA in Philosophy, U. Wis., 1960. Cert. data processing auditor. Systems analyst Walker Mfg. Co., Racine, Wis., 1962-71; mgr. data processing Hamlin, Inc., Lake Mills, Wis., 1971-74; v.p. Menco Corp., Springfield, Ill., 1974-77; EDP audit mgr. Western Pub. Co., Racine, 1978-81; EDP sr. auditor JI Case Co., Racine, 1981-84; pres. Logical Technologies, Racine, 1984—, also chmn. bd. V.p. Council-Trinity Luth. Ch., Lake Mills, Wis., 1972-74, pres. Racine, 1981-85. Mem. Data Processing Auditors Assn., Data Processing Mgrs. Assn. Republican. Lutheran. Club: US Senatorial (Washington). Lodge: Lions. Home: 2324 Kinzie Ave Racine WI 53405-2643 Office: JI Case Co 700 State St Racine WI 53404-3343

WIECHERT, ALLEN LEROY, educational planning consultant, architect; b. Independence, Kans., Oct. 25, 1938; s. Norman Henry and Serena Johanna (Steinke) W.; BArch, Kans. State U., 1962; m. Sandra Swanson, Aug. 19, 1961; children: Kirstin Nan, Brendan Swanson, Megan Ann. Architect in tng. McVey, Peddie, Schmidt & Allen, Wichita, Kans., 1962-63; architect Kivett & Myers, Kansas City, Mo., 1963-68; asst. to vice chancellor plant planning and devel. U. Kans., Lawrence, 1968-74, asso. dir. facilities planning, 1974-78, univ. dir. facilities planning, 1978-92; univ. architect, 1993-95; campus planner Gould Evans Assocs., Lawrence, Kans., 1995-96;

mem. long range phys. planning com. Kans. Bd. Regents, 1971-95; designer, archtl. programmer of ednl. facilities; bd. dirs. Kans. U. Fed. Credit Union, 1972-81, pres. bd., 1974. Chmn. horizons com. Lawrence Bicentennial Commn.; designer Kaw River Trail, 1976; mem. Action 80 Com., 1980-81, Lawrence-Douglas County Horizon 2020 Task Group, 1993-95; mem. standing com. Kans. Episcopal Diocese, 1976-80, pres. com., 1981, mem. diocesan council, 1982-84, chmn. coll. work com., 1982-84, commn. on ch. architecture and allied arts, 1986—, long range planning com., 1988; sr. warden Trinity Episc. Ch., Lawrence, 1978-80; trustee Kans. Sch. Religion, 1973-80, 82-95, v.p., 1984-85, pres., 1986-92, trustee friends of the dept. of relig. studies, 1995—; mem. adv. bd. Salvation Army, 1990—; bd. dirs. Trinity Group Care Home, 1973-79; advancement chmn. troop com. Boy Scouts Am., 1981-87, dist. com. Pelathe dist., 1984—, vice chmn., 1984; chmn., 1985-87, exec. bd. Heart of Am. council, 1985-87. Recipient Dist. Award of Merit Boy Scouts Am., 1988, Silver Beaver award, 1991. 1st lt. Kans. Air N.G., 1961-67. Lic. architect, Kans.; cert. Nat. Council Archtl. Registration Bds. Mem. AIA, Assn. Univ. Architects (sec./treas. 1986-87, v.p. 1987-88, pres. 1988-89), Nat. Hist. Trust, Kans. U. Endowment Assn. (sec. 1981-85, founder, exec. bd. Hist. Mt. Oread Fund. div.), Nat. Cathedral Assn. (regional co-chairperson 1993—). Editor, contbr. to Physical Development Planning Work Book, 1973. Home: 813 Highland Dr Lawrence KS 66044-2431 Office: U Kans Office Of Capital Prog Lawrence KS 66045

WIED, GEORGE LUDWIG, physician; b. Carlsbad, Czechoslovakia, Feb. 7, 1921; came to U.S., 1953, naturalized, 1960; s. Ernst George and Anna (Travnicek) W.; m. Daga M. Graaz, Mar. 19, 1949 (dec. Aug. 1977); m. Kayoko Y. Yamauchi, Nov. 1, 1990. MD, Charles U., Prague, 1945, Hon. Med. Degree, 1995. Intern County Hosp., Carlsbad, Czechoslovakia, 1945; intern U. Chgo. Hosps., 1955; resident in ob-gyn U. Munich, Fed. Republic Germany, 1946-48; practice medicine specializing in ob-gyn West Berlin, 1948-53; asst. ob-gyn Free U., West Berlin, 1948-52; assoc. chmn. dept. ob-gyn Moabit Hosp., Free U., West Berlin, 1953; asst. prof., dir. cytology U. Chgo., 1954-59, assoc. prof., 1959-65, prof., 1965-91, mem. bd. adult edn., 1964-68, prof. pathology, 1967-91, Blum-Riese prof. ob-gyn, 1968-91, acting chmn. dept. ob-gyn, 1974-75. Editor-in-chief Jour. Reproductive Medicine, Acta Cytologica, Analytical and Quantitative Cytology, Clinical Cytology; editor: Introduction to Quantitative Cytochemistry, Automated Cell Identification and Cell Sorting, Compendium on Clinical Cytology, Compendium on the Computerized Cytology and Histology Laboratory, Compendium on Quality Assurance in Clinical Cytology; sr. editor Gen. and Diagnostic Pathology. Hon. dir. Chgo. Cancer Prevention Ctr., 1959-83; chmn. jury Maurice Goldblatt Cytology award, 1963-92. Recipient Cert. of Merit, U.S. Surgeon Gen., 1952, Maurice Goldblatt Cytology award, 1961, George N. Papanicolaou Cytology award, 1970. Mem. Am. Soc. Cytology (pres. 1965-66), Mex. Soc. Cytology (hon.), Spanish Soc. Cytology (hon.), Brazilian Soc. Cytology (fgn. corr.), Indian Acad. Cytology (hon.), Latin-Am. Soc. Cytology (hon.), Japanese Soc. Cytology (hon.), German Soc. Cytology (pres. 1977-80), Ctrl. Soc. Clin. Rsch., Chgo. Path. Soc., Chgo. Gynecol. Soc. (hon.), Am. Soc. Cell Biology, German Soc. Ob-Gyn, Bavarian Soc. Ob-Gyn, German Soc. Endocrinology, Russian Assn. Cytologists (hon.), Swedish Soc. Medicine (hon.), Austrian Soc. Clin. Cytology (hon.), Sigma Xi. Home and Office: 1640 E 50th St Chicago IL 60615-3161

WIEGAND, JAMES RICHARD, association executive; b. Chgo., Oct. 22, 1928; s. Herman Richard and Thea (Parker) W.; m. Betty Elaine Kirby, Feb. 7, 1953; children: Mark Richard, Mary Jennifer. BA summa cum laude, U. Iowa, 1953; MA magna cum laude, Yale U., 1954. Managerial positions Kimberly Clark Corp., 1955-64, Universal Oil Products Co., 1968-74; cons. indsl. rels. Brookfield, Wis., 1974—; dir. Employee Rels. Svcs. MRA The Mgmt. Assn., Brookfield, 1981—; lectr. in field; bd. dirs. Employers Nat. Job Svc. Coun., 1992—. Editor: Employee Relations, Law for Wisconsin Employers. Pres. Heart of North Safety Coun., 1956; active Boy Scouts Am., United Fund; vol. tchr. Project Bus.; arbitrator Better Bus. Bur.; citizen amb. to USSR, April 1992. Mem. ASTD, Am. Mgmt. Assn., Indsl. Rels. Assn., Wis. Soc. Tech. Writers and Pubs., Am. Ordnance Assn., Dayton C. of C., Wilderness Soc., Employers Nat. Job Svc. Coun. (bd. dirs. 1992—), Soc. Human Resource Mgmt. Episcopalian. Home: 3835 Klondike Ct Unit A Brookfield WI 53045-2030 Office: MRA Mgmt Assn 235 N Executive Dr Brookfield WI 53005-6004

WIEGAND, KENNETH ALLAN, marketing professional; b. Sheboygan, Wis., Aug. 24, 1947; s. Arno A. and Marion D. (Janisse) W.; m. Sandra A. Blaudzuhn, Nov. 7, 1970; children: Jessica L., Kimberly D. BSEE, U. Wis., 1970; MBA, Xavier U., 1975. Devel. engr. AT&T, Columbus, Ohio, 1970-75; mgr. sys. N.Am. Van Lines, Ft. Wayne, Ind., 1975-80; dir. sys. Hammermill Paper, Erie, Pa., 1980-82, Colgate-Palmolive, Boston, 1982-86, Burlington No. RR, St. Paul, 1986-87, Burger King Corp., Miami, Fla., 1987-89; CFO Rotocast Plastics, Inc., Miami, 1989-92; dir. mktg. Macwhyte Co., divsn. Amsted Industries, Kenosha, Wis., 1992-96; v.p. sales/mktg. and engring. Poly Vinyl Co., Sheboygan Falls, Wis., 1996—. Advisor Jr. Achievement, Kenosha, 1992—. Mem. IEEE. Home: 2229 Henry St Sheboygan WI 53081 Office: Poly Vinyl Co PO Drawer 300 Sheboygan Falls WI 53085

WIELAND, KATHERINE COLLEEN, government official; b. Oxford, Nebr., May 28, 1953; d. Myrl Wesley and Virginia Lea (Morse) W. BA in Edn., Kearney (Nebr.) State Coll., 1974; postgrad., U. Nebr., 1976, 77, Wichita State U., 1979-92; computer applications mgmt. cert., Wichita State U., 1992; postgrad., Butler County Community Coll., 1992; CIS degree with honors, Friends U., Wichita, 1994. K-12 librarian Mullen (Nebr.) Pub. Schs., 1974-76, Hamburg (Iowa) Schs., 1976-78; case adminstrv. support specialist U.S. Trustee, Wichita, Kans., 1980—; sec. Mid-Range Computer Users, Wichita, 1989-95; recorder Tech. Assistance Group, Eoust, Washington, 1988-91; chmn. Region 20 Tech. Computer Group, 1992—. Deacon First Presbyn. Ch., 1994, computer com., 1996—. Mem. NAFE, Midrange Computer Users Group, Data Processing Mgmt. Assn., Phi Alpha Theta. Office: US Trustee 500 Epic Ctr 301 N Main St Wichita KS 67202-2000

WIELAND, PAUL JOSEPH, state legislator. Rep. dist. 101 State of Mo., Imperial. Office: State Capitol 201 W Capital Ave Rm 155-I Jefferson City MO 65101

WIEMANN, MARION RUSSELL, JR. (BARON OF CAMSTER), biologist, microscopist; b. Chesterton, Ind., Sept. 7, 1929; s. Marion Russell and Verda (Peek) W.; 1 child from previous marriage, Tamara Lee (Mrs. Donald D. Kelley). BS, Ind. U., 1959; PhD (hon.), World U. Roundtable, 1991; ScD (hon.), The London Inst. for Applied Rsch., England, 1994, World Academy Germany, 1995. Histo-rsch. technician U. Chgo., 1959, rsch. asst., 1959-62, rsch. technician, 1962-64; tchr. sci. Westchester Twp. Sch., Chesterton, Ind., 1964-66; with U. Chgo., 1965-79, sr. rsch. technician, 1967-70, rsch. technologist, 1970-79; prin. Marion Wiemann & Assocs., cons. R&D, Chesterton, Ind., 1979-89; consultive faculty World U., 1991—, SkyWarn, Nat. Weather Svc., 1993—. Author: Tooth Decay, Its Cause and Prevention Through Controlled Soil Composition, 1985, The Mechanism of Tooth Decay, 1985; contbr. articles to profl. jours. and newspapers. Vice-chmn. The Duneland 4th of July Com., 1987-91; v.p. State Microscopical Soc. Ill., 1969-70, pres., 1970-71. With USN, 1951-53. Recipient Disting. Tech. Communicator award Soc. for Tech. Communication, 1974, Internat. Order Merit (Eng.), 1991; ennobled Royal Coll. Heraldry, Australia, 1991, Highland Laird, Scotland, 1995; named Sagamore of the Wabash Gov. Ind., 1985; McCrone Rsch. Inst. scholar, 1968; named Prof. of Sci. Australian Inst. for Co-Ordinated Rsch., Australia, 1995, knight corps Diplomatique The Sovereign Military Templar Order, 1994; recipient Scouters Key award Boy Scouts Am., 1968, Arrowhead honor, 1968, Albert Einstein Silver medal, Huguenin, Le Locke, Switzerland, Henri Dunant Silver medal with silver bars, 1995, Henri Dunant Silver medal, 1995. Fellow World Lit. Acad.; mem. Internat. Soc. Soil Sci., Order Internat. Fellowship, Internat. Graphoanalysis Soc., Maison Internat. des Intellectuels and Akademie MIDI, VFW (charter mem., bd. dirs., post judge adv. 1986—, apptd. post adj. 1986—, Cross of Malta 1986), Govs. Club. Address: PO Box 532 Chesterton IN 46304-0532

WIENER, DANIEL NORMAN, psychologist; b. Duluth, Minn., Feb. 6, 1921; s. Joseph Baxter and Fannie (Winer) W.; m. Phyllis Eileen Zager, Dec. 9, 1971; children: Jonathan Marc, Paul Aaron, Sara Ruth Wiener Pearson. BA, U. Minn., 1941, MA, 1942, PhD, 1950. Diplomate in Clin. Psychology Am. Bd. Profl. Psychology; lic. psychologist, Minn. Psychologist State of Conn., Hartford, 1943-44; chief psychologist VA Rehab. and Mental Hygiene Clinic, St. Paul and Mpls., 1944-76; Comty. Clinic, Two Harbors, Minn., 1968-89; pvt. practice psychology Mpls., 1952—; clin. prof. psychiatry and psychology U. Minn., Mpls., 1952—; cons. Hennepin County Dist. Ct., Mpls., 1982—. Author: Discipline, Achievement and Mental Health, 1960, Dimensions of Psychotherapy, 1965, Short-Term Psychotherapy and Structured Behavior Change, 1966, Training Children, 1968, Practical Guide to Psychotherapy, 1968, Classroom Management, 1972, Consumers Guide to Psychotherapy, 1975, Albert Ellis: Passionate Skeptic, 1988, B.F. Skinner: Benign Anarchist, 1996; book reviewer: Star-Tribune, Mpls. With USAF, 1942-43. Mem. Fellow APA, Am. Psychol. Soc.; mem. PEN, Minn. Psychol. Assn. (life, exec. coun.), Nat. Book Critics Cir. Home and Office: 1225 Lasalle Ave Apt 801 Minneapolis MN 55403-2329

WIENER, DEANNA, state legislator; m. Jim Tilsen; three children. RN, St. Mary's Jr. Coll. Minn. State sen., 1993—, real estate profl. Home: 1238 Balsam Trl E Saint Paul MN 55123-1706 Office: Minn State Senate State Capital Building Saint Paul MN 55155-1606*

WIENER, MORRY, food broker executive; b. Wurtzburg, Fed. Republic Germany, June 10, 1948; came to U.S., 1956; s. Jacob and Rose W.; m. Michele Lynn Fox, June 30, 1974; children: Alison Nicole, Melanie Rachel, Seth Adam. BA, U. Cin., 1970. V.p. Budget Rent A Car, Cin., 1972-74; sales cons. Esco Disposables, Cin., 1974-77; sales exec. Mailender-Barnett Inc., Cin., 1977-82; exec. Victory Wholesale Grocers, Springboro, Ohio, 1982—. Mem. exec. bd. dirs. Jewish Cmty. Ctr., Cin., 1973-82; bd. dirs. Hillel, U. Cin., 1974-76; vol. Jewish Welfare Fund Campaign, 1988—; coach youth sports; v.p. Adath Israel Men's Club, 1991—; bd. dirs. Adath Israel, 1995—. Recipient Greater Cin. Human Relations award, 1975, Kovod award Jewish Community Ctr., 1978, Svc. award Big Bros. Am., 1979; winner Gold medal Pan-Am Maccabiah Games, 1966. Mem. Investors Assn. Ohio (pres. 1984-86). Office: Victory Wholesale Grocers 400 Victory Ln Springboro OH 45066-3046

WIENKEN, RITA MAE, farmer; b. Lima, Ohio, Nov. 11, 1950; d. Leon J. and Rovena R. (Schwinnen) W. BS in Edn., Ohio State U.; cert. in pastoral studies, Cath. Theol. Union; MA in Pastoral Ministry, St. Thomas U. Elem. tchr. Miller City (Ohio) Elem. Sch., 1974-77, St. Mary's Sch., Edgerton, Ohio, 1977-79; gardener, asst. maintenance mgr. St. Francis Convent, Tiffin, Ohio, 1980-86; CCD coord. St. Joseph and St. Pius Chs., Tiffin, 1980-82; asst. coord. hort. program Meadowcreek Project, Fox, Ark., 1988-91; dir. earth literacy office Sisters of St. Francis, Tiffin, Ohio, 1993—. Dist. coord. Network Religious Lobby, N.W. Ohio, 1978-85; coord. nuclear freeze zone, N.W. Ohio, 1982-84. Mem. Ohio Ecol. Food and Farm Assn. Roman Catholic. Office: Sisters of Saint Francis 200 Saint Francis Ave Tiffin OH 44883

WIER, PATRICIA ANN, publishing executive, consultant; b. Coal Hill, Ark., Nov. 10, 1937; d. Horace L. and Bridget B. (McMahon) Norton; m. Richard A. Wier, Feb. 24, 1962; 1 child, Rebecca Ann. B.A., U. Mo., Kansas City, 1964; M.B.A., U. Chgo., 1978. Computer programmer AT&T, 1960-62; lead programmer City of Kansas City, Mo., 1963-65; with Playboy Enterprises, Chgo., 1965-71; mgr. systems and programming Playboy Enterprises, 1971; with Ency. Britannica, Inc., Chgo., 1971—; v.p. mgmt. svcs. Ency. Britannica USA, 1975-83, exec. v.p. adminstrn., 1983-84; v.p. planning and devel. Ency. Britannica, Inc., 1985, pres. Compton's Learning Co. div., 1985; pres. Ency. Britannica (USA), 1986-91, Ency. Britannica N.A., 1991-92; exec. v.p. Ency. Britannica, Inc., 1986-94; pres. Ency. Britannica N.Am., 1991-94; mgmt. cons. pvt. practice, Chgo., 1994—; lectr. mktg. U. Chgo. Grad. Sch. Bus., 1995—; cons. pvt. practice, Chgo., 1994—; bd. dirs. NICOR, Inc., Golden Rule Ins., Alcas Corp.; mem. coun. Northwestern U. Assocs. Mem. fin. Coun. Archdiocese of Chgo., Coun. of Grad. Sch. of Bus. U. of Chgo. Mem. Direct Selling Assn. (bd. dirs. 1984-93, chmn. 1987-88, named to Hall of Fame 1991), Women's Coun. U. Mo. Kansas City (hon. life) Com. 200, The Chgo. Network. Roman Catholic. Office: Patricia A Wier Inc 175 E Delaware Pl Apt 8305 Chicago IL 60611-1732

WIERZBICKI, JACEK GABRIEL, physicist, researcher; b. Lódz, Poland, Oct. 27, 1948; came to U.S., 1986; s. Gabriel Wiktor and Jadwiga Krystyna (Skarzynska) W.; m. Grazyna Maria Chawrona, Aug. 31, 1974; children: Grazyna, Przemystaw, Danuta, Kinga. MS in Physics, U. Lódz, 1971, MS in Math., 1973, PhD in Physics, 1981. Researcher U. Lódz, 1971-75; reseacher Joint Inst. for Nuclear Rsch., Dubna, USSR, 1975-79; med. physicist Oncological Ctr., Lódz, 1980-83; lectr. Fed. U. Tech., Bauchi, Nigeria, 1983-86; rsch. fellow Ohio U., Athens, 1986-88; asst. prof. U. Ky., Lexington, 1988-92; assoc. prof. Wayne State U., Detroit, 1993—; Russian translator Am. Inst. Physics, N.Y., 1987. Contbr. over 100 articles to sci. jours. Mem. Am. Phys. Soc., Am. Assn. Physicists in Medicine, Radiation Rsch. Soc., Sigma Xi. Roman Catholic. Home: 3422 Shakespeare Dr Troy MI 48084-1489 Office: Wayne State U Radiation Oncology Ctr 3990 John R St Detroit MI 48201-2018

WIESE, DOROTHY JEAN, business educator; b. Chgo., Sept. 20, 1940; d. Charles Ennis Chapman and Evelyn Catherine Flizikowski; m. Wallace Jon Wiese, Oct. 10, 1959; children: Elizabeth Jean Wiese Christensen, Jonathan Charles. BS in Edn., No. Ill. U., 1970, MS in Edn., 1976, EdD, 1994. Tchr. bus. Hampshire (Ill.) High Sch., 1970-78; prof. bus. Elgin (Ill.) C.C., 1978—; cons. Gould, Inc., Rolling Meadows, Ill., 1984; instr. vocat. practicum McDonald's Hamburger U., Ofcl. Airline Guides, Oak Brook, Ill., 1986; spkr. SIEC, Sweden and Austria, 1987-88, Czech Republic, 1995, North Ctrl. Bus. Edn. Assn./Wis. Bus. Edn. Assn. Conv., 1992, Chgo. Ara Bus. Edn. Assn., 1992, AAUW, Batavia and Geneva, 1993, Elgin, 1996; 1995 Internat. Bus. Inst. for Cmty. Coll. faculty Mich. State U., 1995. Presented paper 34th annual Adult Edn. Rsch. Conf., Pa. State U., 1993. Mem., sec. N.W. Kane County (Ill.) Airport Authority, 1987-94; bd. dirs. St. Joseph Hosp. Found., 1995—, mem. adv. bd. Cancer Wellness and Resource Ctr., 1995—; host family Am. Intercultural Student Exch., 1989-90; presenter women's seminar Trinity Luth. Ch., Roselle, Ill., 1992. Mem. AAUW, Am. Women of Internat. Understanding (bd. dirs.), Nat. Bus. Edn. Assn. (internat. task force), Internat. Soc. Bus. Edn. (North Ctrl. Bus. Edn. Assn. rep. 1989-90, rep.-elect 1996), Societe Internat. pour l'Ensignment Commercial, Ill. Bus. Edn. Assn., Ill. Vocat. Assn., Women in Mgmt. (spkr. No. Fox Valley chpt. 1996), Delta Pi Epsilon (past historian Alpha Phi chpt.), Kappa Delta Pi. Lutheran. Office: Elgin CC 1700 Spartan Dr Elgin IL 60123-7189

WIESNER, DALLAS CHARLES, immunologist, researcher; b. Brookings, S.D., Mar. 19, 1959; s. Charles Howard Wiesner and Coleen Marie (Hendrickson) Bailey; m. Priscilla Anne Semon, 1992. BS in Microbiology with high honors, S.D. State U., 1982. HIV product devel. tech. Abbott Labs., Diagnostic Div., Abbott Park, Ill., 1985-87; HIV retrocell product mgr. Abbott Labs., Diagnostic Div., North Chicago, Ill., 1987-88; sect. mgr. infectious disease and immunology Abbott Labs., Diagnostic Div., Abbott Park, Ill., 1988-90; mgr. sexually transmitted diseases tech. product devel. Diagnostic div. Abbott Labs., Abbott Park, Ill., 1990-91, sect. mgr. retrovirus tech. product devel., 1991—. Mem. Am. Biog. Inst. Rsch. Assn. (dep. gov.), Am. Soc. for Microbiology, Phi Kappa Phi. Republican. Lutheran. Home: 8716 1st Ave Kenosha WI 53143-6508 Office: Abbott Labs 1 Abbott Park Rd North Chicago IL 60064-3500

WIFF, DONALD RAY, polymer physicist, manager, researcher; b. Youngstown, Ohio, Feb. 19, 1936; s. Ernest and Mildred Bietta (Kreps) W.; m. Carol June Skipper, Aug. 25, 1962; children: David S., Devin D., Daniel D. BS in Physics, Capital U., 1958; MA in Physics, Kent (Ohio) State U., 1960; PhD in Physics, Tex. A&M U., 1967; MBA in Bus., U. Dayton, Ohio, 1981. Rsch. assoc. U. Dayton Rsch. Inst., 1967-72, prin. investigator, 1972-85; sect. head Gencorp Inc./Corp. Rsch., Akron, Ohio, 1985-94, sr. technologist, 1994—; mem. Akron Polymer Lecture Group, 1985—, chmn. conf., 1993. Author: Electronic Energy Band Cubic BN-Calculation, 1967, Mathematically Ill Posed Problems, 1970, Molecular Weight Distribution and Relaxation Spectra, 1974, Molecular Composites, 1980, In-Situ Composites, 1986, Nonlinear Optical Polymers, 1990, Molecular Modeling, 1992. Chmn. edn. com. Luth. Ch., Huber Heights, Ohio, 1970-76, pres., 1976-78. Mem. SAMPE, Am. Phys. Soc., Am. Mgmt. Assn., Brit. Inst. Physics, European Phys. Soc., Soc. Rheology, Soc. Plastics Engrs., Am. Crystallographic Assn., Sigma Pi Sigma, Pi Mu Epsilon. Office: Gencorp Inc/Corp Technology Ctr 2990 Gilchrist Rd Akron OH 44305-4489

WIGG, RITA AGNES, writer, public relations consultant; b. Milw., June 14, 1946; d. Frank P. and Claudia E. (Diel) Lesar; m. Larry W. Wigg, June 15, 1968; children: Morgan, Laura, Charles, Lawrence. BA in Journalism, Marquette U., 1968. Staff writer Wauwatosa (Wis.) News-Times, 1982-85; corr. Sheboygan (Wis.) Press, 1986-91; cons. pub. rels. Rehab. Ctr., Sheboygan, 1986-91; asst. to pres. Leadership Dynamics, Sheboygan, 1989-90; comms. asst. Lakeland Coll., Sheboygan, 1991-92, comms. coord., 1992-93, communications dir., 1993—. Contbr. articles to various newspapers. Mem., scholarship chair Wauwatosa Jr. Women's Club, 1984-85; mem., pub. rels. cons. TOSA-FEST Com., Wauwatosa, 1984-86. Recipient Cert. Appreciation St. Bernard's Parish, 1984, Cub Pack #3804, 1987, Lakeland Coll. chpt. Students in Free Enterprise, 1994; named Jr. of Month, Wauwatosa Jr. Women's Club, 1984. Mem. Bus. and Profl. Women of Wis. (bd. dirs. Sheboygan chpt.), Wis. Pubs. Prodn. Club, Wis. Regional Writer's Club. Roman Catholic. Home: 1214 N 4th St Sheboygan WI 53081-3538 Office: Lakeland Coll PO Box 359 Sheboygan WI 53082-0359

WIGGINS, GARY, state legislator. Mem. Mo. Ho. of Reps. from 8th dist. Democrat. Home: RR 1 Box 12 New Cambria MO 63558-9707*

WIGGINS, HARRY, state senator, lawyer; b. Kansas City, Mo., Aug. 1, 1934; s. John M. and Helen F. (Murphy) W. BA, Rockhurst Coll.; JD, St. Louis U. Bar: Mo. 1957, U.S. Dist. Ct. (we. dist.) Mo. 1959, U.S. Ct. Appeals (8th cir.) 1962, U.S. Supreme Ct. 1963. Asst. U.S. atty. U.S. Dist. Ct. (we. dist.) Mo., Kansas City, 1961-67; supr. liquor control State of Mo., Jefferson City, 1967-70, gen. counsel dept. pub. svcs., 1973-74; western judge Jackson County Ct., Kansas City, 1971-73; state senator Mo. 10th Dist., Kansas City, 1974—. Mem. Alpha Delta Gamma (past nat. pres.), Alpha Sigma Nu. Democrat. Roman Catholic. Home: 7817 Terrace St Kansas City MO 64114-1672 Office: Mo Senate The Capitol Rm 423 Jefferson City MO 65101

WIGGINS, LAURENCE EUGENE, sales executive; b. Enid, Okla., Jan. 8, 1935; s. Laurence Eugene and Fern S. (Potter) W.; m. Mary K. Irwin, June 5, 1960; children: Michael L., David W. AB in Econs., Drury Coll., 1959. Sales rep. Pillsbury Co., Mpls., 1963-68; ptnr. Greer-Carver, Inc., Shawnee Mission, Kans., 1968-82; cons. Davis Mktg., Shawnee Mission, 1982-90; sales mgr. Faultless Starch Co., Kansas City, Mo., 1990—; pres. Allied Food Club, Kansas City, 1975. With U.S. Army, 1955-57. Republican. Episcopalian. Home: 4507 W 66th Terrace Prairie Village KS 66208 Office: Faultless Starch/Bon Ami Co 510 Walnut Kansas City MO 64106

WIGHT, DARLENE, retired speech educator; b. Andover, Kans., Jan. 5, 1926; d. Everett John and Claudia (Jennings) Van Biber; m. Lester Delin, Jan. 21, 1950; children: Lester Delin II, Claudia Leigh. AA, Graceland Coll., 1945; BA, U. Kans., 1948, MA, 1952. Permanent profl. cert., Iowa; life tchr.'s cert., Mo. Instr. U. Kans., Lawrence, 1949-50; instr. overseas program U. Md., Munich, 1954; speech pathologist Independence (Mo.) Pub. Sch. Dist., 1958-61; assoc. prof. Graceland Coll., Lamoni, Iowa, 1961-87; cons. Quad-County Sch. Dist., Leon, Iowa, 1966-67, Mt. Ayr (Iowa) Cmty. Sch. Dist., 1967-70; cons. Head Start program SCIAP, Leon, 1972-75, MATURA, Bedford, Iowa, 1973-75. Co-author: Speech Communication Handbook, 1979. Mem. Common Cause, 1989, Friends of Art, Nelson-Atkins Mus. Art, Planned Parenthood, U.S. English, Inc., Habitat for Humanity, Nat. Mus. Women in Arts, Am. Craft Coun. Recipient Award of Merit U. Kans., 1982, Award of Distinction U. Kans., 1947-48. Mem. AAUW, Am. Speech, Lang. and Hearing Assn. (speech pathology clin. competency), Coun. Exceptional Children. Democrat. Mem. Reorganized Latter Day Saints Ch. Office: Graceland Coll Speech Dept Lamoni IA 50140

WIGHTMAN, DORIS STEPHENSON, library director, city collector; b. Bosworth, Mo., May 27, 1927; d. Frank Audsley and Junie Ethel (Patton) Stephenson; m. Buford Earl Wightman, June 18, 1951; children: John Buford, Nancy Jo. Student, Mo. State Libr. Summer Sch., Columbia, Mo., 1964, 65, 66. Dir. Norborne (Mo.) Pub. Libr., 1969—. Picture editor: (book) Centennial History of Norborne, 1968. Mem. PTA Norborne, 1958-72. Republican. Methodist. Office: Norborne Pub Libr 109 E 2nd Norborne MO 64668

WIGODNER, BYRON I., pharmaceutical executive; b. Chgo., Ill., Nov. 16, 1952; s. Jerome and Shirley (Simon) W.; m. Ellen Lois Dennen, July 27, 1980; 1 child, Michael. BS in Biology, No. Ill. U., 1974; MBA with distinction, DePaul Grad. Sch., 1979. Profl. sales rep. Sanofi Winthrop Pharms. divsn. Sanofi Winthrop Inc., N.Y.C., 1974-76, regional accounts mgr., 1976-78, med. ctr. rep., 1978-87, divsn. mgr., 1987-94, nat. account mgr., 1994-95, nat. account dir., 1995—; assoc. prof. mktg. Mundelein Coll., Chgo., 1980-91, Webster U., 1993—, Lake Forest Grad. Sch., 1996—; instr. mktg. Coll. of Lake County, 1991-93, Harper Coll., 1992—; adj. instr. Northeastern Ill. Univ., 1981-90. Health bd. commr. Buffalo Grove (Ill.) Bd. Health, 1985—. Mem. Am. Mgmt. Assn., Am. Mktg. Assn., Acad. Health Svcs. Mktg. Home: 2094 Sheridan Rd Buffalo Grove IL 60089-8009

WIK, JEAN MARIE (JEAN MARIE BECK), librarian, media specialist; b. Aitkin, Minn., Feb. 10, 1938; d. Herman Otto Beck and Ferdina Mathilda (Petersen) Kalt; m. Richard Lyle Wik, Aug. 17, 1958; children: Steven L., Lori Jo. BS, No. State U., Aberdeen S.D., 1963; MA, U. Minn., 1972; cert. in media arts, Mankato State U., 1974. Elem. tchr. Howard Hedger Sch., Aberdeen, S.D., 1958-62; tchr. spl. edn. Westwood Sch., Bloomington, Minn., 1963-64; elem. tchr. Washburn Sch., 1964-71; media generalist elem. elem. and secondary schs., 1972-85; media generalist Kennedy High Sch., Bloomington, 1985-96; fashion coord. Weekender Casual Wear, 1993—; dir. Annehurst Curriculum Classifications System project Bloomington Schs., 1976-85, dist. media leadership position, 1990-92. Chmn. Christian Women's Club, 1972-74, area rep., 1981-85. Mem. NEA, Minn. Edn. Assn., Minn. Ednl. Media Assn. Office: Kennedy High Sch 9701 Nicollet Ave Minneapolis MN 55420-4448

WIKANDER, MATTHEW HAYS, English language educator; b. Phila., Mar. 21, 1950; s. Lawrence Einar and Ethel Marie (Whitlow) W.; m. Kathryn Adisman, Jan. 30, 1971 (div. Oct. 1979); m. Christine Anne Child, July 31, 1980. BA, Williams Coll., 1970, Cambridge (Eng.) U., 1972; MA, Cambridge (Eng.) U., 1979; PhD, U. Mich., 1975. Lectr. in drama Residential Coll. U. Mich., Ann Arbor, 1975-78; asst. prof. English Columbia U., N.Y.C., 1978-87; assoc. prof. English U. Toledo, 1987-90, prof. English, 1990—, dir. Master Liberal Studies program, 1992—. Author: The Play of Truth and State, 1986 (Choice Outstanding Book award 1986-87), Princes to Act, 1993; contbr. articles to profl. publs. Marshall Aid Commemoration Commn. scholar, 1970-72; grantee Am. Coun. Learned Socs., 1989, NEH, 1990. Mem. MLA, Shakespeare Assn. Am. Office: U Toledo Master Liberal Studies Program Toledo OH 43606

WIKARSKI, NANCY SUSAN, information technology consultant; b. Chgo., Jan. 26, 1954; d. Walter Alexander and Emily Regina (Wejnerowski) W.; m. Michael F. Maciekowich, Dec. 5, 1976 (div. Feb. 1985). BA, Loyola U., Chgo., 1976, MA, 1978; PhD, U. Chgo., 1990. Paralegal Winston & Strawn, Chgo., 1978-79; real estate analyst Continental Bank, Chgo., 1979-84, systems analyst, 1984-88, ops. officer, 1988-89, automation cons., 1989-92; systems mgr. PNC Mortgage Co. of Am., Vernon Hills, Ill., 1992-94; ind. cons. Lake Bluff, Ill., 1994—. Author: German Expressionist Film, 1990. Fellow U. Chgo., 1987-90. Mem. NAFE, Am. Mensa, Chgo. Computer Soc., Alpha Sigma Nu.

WILCOX, BEVERLY JOAN, school nurse; b. Scottsbluff, Nebr., Dec. 23, 1940; d. John F. and Edna (Buxman) Meller; m. Marlyn D. Wilcox, Oct. 7, 1962; 1 child, Judi K. RN, West Nebr. Gen. Hosp., Scottsbluff, 1962; BSN, U. Nebr., 1982; MS in Edn., U. Nebr., Kearney, 1986. Staff nurse med./CCU West Nebr. Gen. Hosp., Scottsbluff, 1962-70; clin. instr. West Nebr. Gen. Hosp. Sch. Nursing, 1970-75; sch. nurse North Platte (Nebr.) pub. schs., 1977—; CPR instr. Mid-Plains Community Coll., North Platte, 1982-90. Mem. Nebr. Interagy. Planning Region 27, 1986—; mem. emergency cardiac care com. Nebr. affiliate Am. Heart Assn.; chmn. Nebr. West Ctrl.

BLS Task Force, 1991—; mem. sch. health adv. com. Nebr. Dept. Health, 1992-95; mem. Nebr. Dept. Edn. HIV/AIDS Rev. Panel, 1995—. Mem. NEA, Nebr. Edn. Assn., North Platte Edn. Assn. (sec. 1995), Nat. Assn. Sch. Nurses, Nebr. Sch. Nurse Assn. (bd. dirs., tri-valley rep. 1992-95). Home: 2221 W C St North Platte NE 69101-4547 Office: North Platte Pub Schs PO Box 1557 North Platte NE 69103-1557

WILCOX, DONALD ALAN, lawyer; b. Grantsburg, Wis., July 18, 1951; s. John Charles and Lois Margaret (Finch) W.; m. Rachel Ann Johnson, Dec. 28, 1973; children: Benjamin Ray, Joseph Charles (dec.), Sara Johanna. BS, USAF Acad., 1973; JD, Georgetown U., 1979. Bar: Minn. 1979. Commd. 2d lt. USAF, 1973, advanced through grades to capt., resigned, 1979; assoc Holmquist & Holmquist, Benson, Minn., 1979-81; ptnr. Holmquist & Wilcox, 1981-90; shareholder Wilcox, Erhardt & Spates, P.A., Benson, 1990-91; pvt. practice Benson, 1991—; gen. counsel Swift County-Benson Hosp., 1981—, Farmer;s Mut. Coop., Bellingham, Minn., 1986—, Agralite Coop., Benson, 1986—, Kandiyohi County Coop., 1995—; atty. City of Benson, 1985—; examiner of titles, Swift County, Benson, 1986—, Federated Tel. Coop., Chokio, Minn., 1988—. Mem. Benson Planning Commn., 1979—; pres. Our Redeemer's Luth. Ch., Benson, 1985-86, 93-94; pres., bd. dirs. Swift County Homes, Inc., Benson, 1984-92. Recipient Lawyers Coop. Pub. award Lawyers Coop. Pub. Co., 1979. Mem. Minn. Bar Assn., Twelfth Dist. Bar Assn. (pres. 1995—), Benson C. of C. (bd. dirs. 1981-84), Kiwanis (treas. Benson 1982-84). Home: 604 13th St S Benson MN 56215-2017 Office: 1150 Wisconsin Ave Benson MN 56215-1841

WILCOX, JEFFREY SCOTT, instrument company executive; b. Moorhead, Minn., Aug. 16, 1956. Student, Alexandria Tech. Coll. Machinist Versatile, Fargo, N.D., 1977-86, Superior Equipment, Morris, Minn., 1986—; pres. Wilco Precision Inc., Morris, Minn., 1986—. Republican. Lutheran. Office: Wilco Precision Inc RR 3 Box 275 Morris MN 56267-9400

WILCOX, JON P., justice; b. Berlin, Wis., Sept. 5, 1936; m. Jane Ann; children: Jeffrey, Jennifer. AB in Polit. Sci., Ripon Coll., 1958; JD, U. Wis., 1965. Pvt. practice Steele, Smyth, Klos and Flynn, LaCrosse, Wis., 1965-66, Hacker and Wilcox, Wautoma, Wis., 1966-69, Wilcox, Rudolph, Kubasta & Rathjen, Wautoma, 1969-79; elected judge Waushara County Cir. Ct., 1979-92; apptd. justice Wis. Supreme Ct., 1992—; commr. Family Ct., Waushara County, 1977-79; vice chmn., chmn. Wis. Sentencing Commn., 1984-92; chief judge 6th Jud. Dist., 1985-92; co-chair State-Fed. Jud. Coun., 1992, Jud. Coun. Wis., 1993; mem. Prison Overcrowding Task Force, 1988-90; mem. numerous coms. Wis. Judiciary; mem. faculty Wis. Jud. Coll., 1986—; chmn. Wis. Chief Judges Com., 1990-92; co-chair comm. on judiciary as co-equal br. of govt. Wis. State Bar; lectr. in field. Co-author: Wisconsin News Reporter's Legal Handbook: Wisconsin Courts and Court Procedures, 1987. Bd. visitors U. Wis. Law Sch, 1970-76. Lt. U.S. Army, 1959-61. Named Outstanding Jaycee Wautoma, 1974; recipient Disting. Alumni award Ripon Coll., 1993. Fellow Am. Bar Found.; mem. ABA (com. on continuing appellate edn.), Nat. Coun. Juvenile and Family Ct. Judges, Wis. Bar Assn. (bench bar com.), Wis. Law Found., Tri-County Bar Assn., Dane County Bar Assn., Trout Unltd., Ruffed Grouse Soc., Ducks Unltd., Rotary, Phi Alpha Delta. Office: Supreme Court State Capitol PO Box 1688 Madison WI 53701-1688

WILCOX, LAIRD MAURICE, researcher, writer, carpenter; b. San Francisco, Nov. 28, 1942; s. Laird and AuDeene Helen (Stromer) W.; student Washburn U., 1961-62, U. Kans., 1963-65; m. EilcolmMaddocks, 1962 (div. 1967); children: Laird Anthony IV, Elizabeth Leone; m. Diana Brown, 1978; 1 child, Carrie Lynn. With Fluor Corp., Ltd., 1960-62; mgr. office supply store U. Kans., 1963; editor Kans. Free Press, 1963-66; owner, operator Maury Wilcox Constrn. Co., Kansas City, Mo., 1967-70; carpenter foreman various employers, 1974-87; semi-profl. genealogist, 1975-78; chief investigator Editorial Rsch. Svc., Kansas City, Mo., 1977—; assoc. faculty Baker U., 1986—; lectr. various fields. Dep. sheriff Wyandotte County, Kans., 1971-75. Fellow Augustan Soc., Acad. Police Sci.; mem. Internat. Brotherhood of Carpenters and Joiners of Am. (officer 1975-82, condr. carpenter's local 61 1977-82), NRA, Mensa, ACLU, Internat. Legion of Intelligence, Amnesty Internat., Nat. Coalition Against Censorship, Free Press Assn., SAR, Soc. Mayflower Descs., Mil. Order Loyal Legion źf U.S., Nat. Soc. Old Plymouth Colony Descs., St. Andrew Soc., Bertrand Russell Soc. Author: Guide To The American Left, 1970, Guide to The American Right, 1970, Psychological Uses of Genealogy, 1976, Astrology, Directory of the Occult and Paranormal, 1981, Guide to the American Right, 1991, Guide to the American Left, 1991, Nazi's Communists, Klansmen, and Others on the Fringe, 1992; editor Wilcox Report, 1979—, Civil Liberties Rev., 1986—, Master Bibliography on Terrorism, Assassination, Espionage and Propaganda, 1988, Selected Quotations for the Ideological Skeptic, 1988, What Is Political Ertremism?, 1989, Be Reasonable: Selected Quotations for Inquiring Minds, 1993, Crying Wolf, 1994. Recipient award Kansas City Archivists Assc., 1989. Founder Wilcox Collection on Contemporary Polit. Movements, U. Kans. Libraries; benefactor Kans. U. Friends of Libr. Home and Office: PO Box 2047 Olathe KS 66051-2047

WILCOX, SHEILA MAUREEN, music educator; b. St. Paul, Jan. 12, 1965; d. Leonard Reuben and Bethel Elaine (Cottrell) Anderson; m. Mark Stephen Wilcox, July 11, 1992. BM, U. Wis., Superior, 1987; MM, U. Wis., Madison, 1992. Lic. tchr., Minn. Orch. tchr. Sch. Dist. of Superior (Wis.), 1987-88, Ind. Sch. Dist. #706, Virginia, Minn., 1988—; section violinist Duluth Superior Symphony Orch., 1984—. Mem. Minn. Music Educators Assn., Music Educators Nat. Conf., Minn. Edn. Assn., Nat. Sch. Orch. Assn. (Minn. chpt.). Democrat. Swedish Baptist. Office: Ind Sch Dist 706 Technical Bldg Virginia MN 55792

WILCOX, WINTON WILFRED, JR., computer specialist, consultant; b. Independence, Mo., Aug. 24, 1945; s. Winton Wilfred Wilcox Sr. and LaPreal (Adams) Craig; m. Kathy Postell, July 4, 1990; children: Steven Michael, Jake Anders. BS, U. Nev., 1973. Nat. product dir. Am. Photography Corp., N.Y.C., 1974-77; gen. mgr. Golden Valley (Minn.) Coffee, 1977-80; div. mgr. Cable Data, Sacramento, 1981-84; v.p., chief fin. officer Cultch Enterprises, Inc., Sacramento, 1980-86; v.p. mktg. div. Parallex, Winston-Salem, N.C., 1985-88; owner IK & Cons., Sacramento, 1990-94; pres. Broadcast Comm. Sys. Inc., New Glarus, Wis., 1995—; instr. Heald Bus. Coll., 1990-94. Author: How to Create Computer Entertainment, 1985; contbg. author: Apple Fun & Games, 1986. With USAF, 1966-70. Mem. Cable TV Adminstrn. and Mktg. (pay view com. Washington chpt. 1985-87, SE chpt. formation com. Tampa, Fla. chpt. 1986-87), Entelec. Republican. Home: 1310 17th Ave Monroe WI 53566 Office: Broadcast Comm Sys Inc PO Box 730 New Glarus WI 53560

WILD, STEPHEN LLOYD, computer scientist; b. Detroit, Jan. 6, 1957; s. Lloyd William Wild and Barbara Maie (Owen) W.; m. Margaret Ellen Schlosser, July 31, 1982; 1 child, Carolyn Ruth. BS in Computer and Info. Sci., Cleve. State U., 1981, MBA, 1993. Computer application programmer Diamond Shamrock, Cleve., 1981-83; sr. computer programmer/analyst Gen. Tire, Akron, Ohio, 1983-89; computer sys. project leader Reliance Electric, Cleve., 1989—. Republican. Baptist. Home: 35 Houghton Rd Northfield OH 44067 Office: Reliance Electric 24701 Euclid Ave Cleveland OH 44117

WILDE, WILLIAM JAMES, printing company executive; b. Milw., Sept. 13, 1927; s. Henry H. and Anna M. (Lamp) W.; m. Jeanne G. Cearhard, June 14, 1952 (dec.); children: James, Anne, Joan, Charles, Denise, Daniel, Mary, Mark. PhB, Marquette U., 1951. Mem. sales staff Gillfoy Printing Co., Milw., 1951-70, pres., 1970—; pres. Williston-Wilde Graphics, Milw., 1970—. Capt. Thiensville (Wis.) Rescue Squad, 1960-71. With U.S. Army, 1945-47. Republican. Roman Catholic.

WILDE, WILLIAM RICHARD, lawyer; b. Markesan, Wis., Mar. 1, 1953; s. Leslie Maurice and Elaine Margaret (Schweder) W.; m. Carolyn Margaret Zieman, July 17, 1981 (div. 1987); 1 child, Leah Marie; m. Barbara Joan Rohlf, Jan. 6, 1990. BA, U. Wis., Milw., 1975; JD, Marquette U., 1980. Bar: Wis. 1980, U.S. Dist. Ct. (ea. and we. dists.) Wis. 1980. Dist. atty. Green Lake County, Green Lake, Wis., 1980-83, corp.counsel, 1981; ptnr. Curtis, Wilde and Neal, Oshkosh, Wis., 1983—. Mem. Assn. Trial Lawyers Am., Wis. Bar Assn., Wis. Acad. Trial Lawyers (Amicus Curiae Brief com. 1987-92, bd. dirs., assoc. editor The Verdict, treas. 1993, sec. 1994, v.p. 1995, pres.-elect 1996), Wis. Assn. Criminal Def. Lawyers (bd. dirs. 1987-91), Winnebbago County Bar Assn., Green Lake County Bar Assn., Lions. Home: PO Box 282 Markesan WI 53946-0282 Office: Curtis Wilde & Neal 1010 W 20th Ave Oshkosh WI 54901-6618

WILDER, DELLA JUANITA, librarian, secondary education educator; b. Jane, Mo., July 3, 1941; d. Clifford Glen and Eileen Mabel (Horton) Akehurst; m. Ivan C. Wilder, Feb. 23, 1963 (div. May 1985); children: Leslie Glen, Leah Gene. BA, Ctrl. Mich. U., 1963; MLIS, Wayne State U., 1994. Cert. elem. tchr., sch. libr. media specialist, Mich. Libr. Freeland (Mich.) H.S., 1963-66, Freeland Elem. and Mid. Sch., 1966-68, Douglas MacArthur H.S., Saginaw, Mich., 1968-88; tchr. 1st grade Arrowwood Elem. Sch., Saginaw, 1989-90; libr. media specialist Heritage H.S., Saginaw, 1988—. Mem. AAUW, Mich. Assn. Media in Edn., Alpha Xi Delta. Methodist. Home: 6130 Garfield Rd Freeland MI 48623

WILDER, MICHAEL O., state legislator; b. Nov. 10, 1941. Wis. state assemblyman dist. 67, 1993—; owner printing bus. Mem. Chippewa Area United Way, pres., 1989-90. Mem. Kiwanis (pres. 1990), Chippewa Lions, Chippewa Falls Optimists. *

WILDERMUTH, GORDON LEE, architect; b. Lima, Ohio, Nov. 13, 1937; s. Oliver and Margery (Mason) W.; B.S. in Architecture, U. Cin., 1961; m. Patricia Williams, June 1, 1963 (dec. 1983); m. Hannelore Brauning, Aug. 10, 1993. With Skidmore, Owings & Merrill, Architects/Engrs., 1963—, assoc., 1967-70, assoc. ptnr., 1970-73, ptnr., 1973-87, ret. ptnr., 1987-90, cons. ptnr., 1991—. Bd. dirs. Police Athletic League N.Y., 1974-81, N.Y. Poly. Inst., 1975-77, Founders Council, Field Mus. Natural History. Served with Spl. Forces, U.S. Army, 1962-1963. Recipient Aga Khan award for architecture, 1983. Fellow AIA. Home: 175 E Delaware Pl Chicago IL 60611-1739 Office: Skidmore Owings & Merrill 224 S Michigan Ave Chicago IL 60604-2507

WILDHABER, MARK LEE, fish ecologist, ecotoxicologist; b. St. Louis, Jan. 21, 1959; s. Rainey A. and Velma A. (Kloeppel) W.; m. Vickie Elaine Wildhaber, Aug. 1, 1981; children: Eric Lee, Rachel Elaine. BS in Math. and Zoology magna cum laude, S.E. Mo. State U., 1981; MS in Wildlife and Fish Sci., Tex. A&M U., 1985; PhD in Zoology, N.C. State U., 1989. Lab. asst. S.E. Mo. State U., Cape Girardeau, 1979; teaching and rsch. asst. Tex. A&M U., College Station, 1981-83; rsch. asst. N.C. State U., Raleigh, 1983-86, teaching asst., 1986, rsch. asst., 1987-89, tutor, rsch. assoc., 1990-91; quantitative ecologist Nat. Fisheries Contaminant Rsch. Ctr. U.S. Fish and Wildlife Svc., Columbia, Mo., 1991-93; quantitative ecologist Midwest Sci. Ctr. Nat. Biol. Svc., Columbia, 1993—; Lucas Meml. asst. N.C. State U., 1983, 84. Pres.'s scholar S.E. Mo. State U., 1977. Mem. Am. Soc. Ichthyologists and Herpetologists, Am. Fisheries Soc., Animal Behaviour Soc. Office: Midwest Sci Ctr Rsch Ctr 4200 E New Haven Rd Columbia MO 65201-8709

WILDHABER, MICHAEL RENE, accountant; b. Jefferson City, Mo., Aug. 4, 1952; s. Rainey A. and Velma W.; m. Paula M. Wildhaber, Sept. 28, 1974; 1 child, Wendy. AA, Florissant Valley Coll., 1972; BS, U. Mo., 1974. CPA, Mo.; cert. info. sys. auditor, cert. internal auditor, cert. tax preparer, assoc. ins. acctg. and fin., enrolled agt. Sr. auditor I.T.T. Fin., St. Louis, 1974-79; audit mgr. Navco, St. Louis, 1980-85; contr. Millers mutual, Alton, Ill., 1985-88; pres. R&M Tax and Acctg., St. Louis, 1988—. Tchr. Jr. Achievement, St. Louis, 1993-94; vol. Olympic Festival, St. Louis, 1994, 100 Neediest Cases, St. Louis, 1990-94, Old News Boy, St. Louis, 1992-94. Mem. AICPA, Mo. Soc. CPAs, Inst. Internal Auditors. Office: R&M Tax and Acctg 3805 S Kings Hwy Saint Louis MO 63109

WILDUNG, WENDY JO, lawyer; b. Luverne, Minn., July 2, 1954. BA magna cum laude, U. Minn., 1976; JD, Harvard U., 1979. Bar: Minn. 1979, U.S. Dist. Ct. Minn. 1979, U.S. Supreme Ct. 1983, U.S. Ct. Appeals (8th cir.) 1991, U.S. Ct. Appeals (fed. cir.) 1992. Assoc. Faegre & Benson, Mpls., 1979-86, ptnr., 1987—. contbr. articles to profl. jours. Mem. Harvard Law Sch. Coun., 1995—. Mem. ABA, Fed. Bar Assn., Minn. Bar Assn., Harvard Law Sch. Assoc. Alumni Coun., Harvard Law Sch. Assn. Minn. (pres. 1991-95), U. Minn. Alumni Assn., Mpls. Athletic Club. Office: Faegre & Benson 2200 Norwest Ctr 90 S 7th St Minneapolis MN 55402-3903

WILEY, JACK CLEVELAND, mechanical engineer; b. Evansville, Ind., Mar. 17, 1940; s. Paul and Louise (Cleveland) W.; m. Joyce Hale, Jan. 26, 1965; children: Jason, Alice. BS, Purdue U., 1962; MS in Theoretical and Applied Mechanics, U. Ill., 1964; PhD in Engring. Sci., Purdue U., 1967. Asst. prof. theoretical and applied mechanics U. Ill., Urbana, 1967-72; prin. engr. Deere & Co. Tech. Ctr., Moline, Ill., 1972—. Pantentee in field. Named Presdl. Exchange Exec., U.S. Dept. Commerce, 1979-80. Mem. ASME (local pres. 1978), Am. Soc. Agrl. Engrs., Soc. Mfg. Engrs. Home: 3732 40th Street Ct Moline IL 61265-5410 Office: Deere & Co Tech Ctr 3300 River Dr Moline IL 61265-1746

WILFONG, BRENDA A., telecommunications executive; b. Ashland, Ohio, Jan. 2, 1963; d. Edward Eugene and Barbara Ann (Butterfield) Bush; m. Duane Hubert Wilfong, Oct. 22, 1984 (dec. Sept. 1994); children: Jessie Leona, Christina Elizabeth. BBA, Kent State U., 1989. Asst. editor Ohio dir. Harris Pub. Co., Twinsburg, Ohio, 1983-84; accounts payable clerk M. O'Neil's Co., Akron, Ohio, 1984-85; network mgmt. asst. Alltel Corp., Hudson, Ohio, 1985-86, treasury asst., 1986-87, assoc. analyst treasury, 1987-92, carrier svcs. coord., 1992-93; sr. staff asst. Alltel Corp., Twinsburg, 1993-95, adminstr. carrier svcs., 1995—; contracts adminstr. Alltel Corp., Hudson, Ohio, 1995—. Recipient Brownie Mother Vol. award Girl Scouts Am., Akron, 1994. Mem. Inst. Mgmt. Accts. (editor newsletter 1990-92, dir. ins. 1992-94). Baptist. Home: 1630 Goodyear Blvd Akron OH 44305-3505

WILFRED, ERNEST PRABHAKAR, electrical engineer; b. Bangalore, India, May 14, 1940; came to U.S., 1988; BS in Physics and Chemistry, Mysore U., Bangalore, India, 1959, BSEE, 1963. Divsn. mgr. designs NGEF Ltd., Bangalore, India, 1964-88; sr. design engr. ABB Power T & D, St. Louis, 1988—. Home: 12609 Glen Lea Dr Saint Louis MO 63043 Office: ABB Power T & D 4350 Semple Ave Saint Louis MO 63120-2241

WILGUS, JOHN WILLIAM, company executive; b. Pataskala, Ohio, Mar. 30, 1964; s. Alan Lee and Patricia Ann (Brown) W.; m. Karen Marie Richey, Sept. 10, 1988 (div. 1991); m. Cliflean Lorraine Wantland, Sept. 20, 1991; stepchildren: Matthew William Hayes, David Allen Hayes; 1 child, Cameron James Wilgus. Grad., Trotwood Sr. High Sch., Ohio, 1982. Sta. agt. Piedmont Airlines, Inc., Dayton, Ohio, 1983-87, tng. coord., 1987-89; supr. USAir, Inc., Dayton, Ohio, 1989-92; pres., treas. ProVest Multisvcs., Inc., St. Louis, 1991—; sta. agt. USAir, Inc., Dayton, Ohio, 1992-93; lead negotiator ProVest Assocs., St. Louis, 1992—. Libertarian. Office: ProVest Multisvcs Inc 2953 Trapper Tr Wentzville MO 63385

WILHELMI, SANDRA G., health facility administrator; b. Trenton, Mich., Dec. 2, 1949; d. Lester T. and Joycelyn C. (Spencer) Oyler; m. Darrell J. Wilhelmi, Nov. 29, 1975. BSN, The Ohio State U., 1972. Cert. profl. in utilization rev. Night house supr. Meml. Gen. Hosp., Las Cruces, N.Mex.; staff nurse, med./surgical unit, staff devel. coord. USAF Hosp., Grand Forks AFB, N.D.; staff devel. coord. 857th Strategic Hosp., Minot AFB, N.D.; charge nurse, med./surgical unit. asst. chief nurse USAF Hosp., Laughlin AFB, Tex.; chief med. svcs. flight 319th Med. Group, Grand Forks AFB, N.D. Mem. ANA, Am. Assn. Utilization Mgmt. Nurses, N.D. Nurses Assn. Home: RR 1 Box 57-b Manvel ND 58256-9775

WILK, KENNY A., state legislator. Kans. state rep. Dist. 42, 1993—; mgr. Hallmark Cards. Address: 701 S DeSoto Rd Lansing MI 66043*

WILKE, DUANE ANDREW, educator; b. Chgo., July 2, 1948; s. Joseph V. and Helena (Komulainen) W.; m. Sue Rowley, Oct. 9, 1970; children: Mya, Kira, Noah. BS, Ill. State U., Normal, 1970; MS in Edn., No. Ill. U., 1978. Cert. tchr., Ill. Tchr. Glencoe (Ill.) Pub. Schs., 1970-71; English tchr. middle sch. U.S. Peace Corps, Daegu, S. Korea, 1971-73; tchr. tng. coord U.S. Peace Corps, S. Korea, 1973-74; diagnostician, tchr. Singer Mental Health Ctr., Rockford, Ill., 1974-78; spl. edn. cons., diagnostician Rockford Pub. Schs., 1978-90; edn. instrn. specialist EduQuest/IBM, Rockford, 1992-93; math, computer specialist title 1 Rockford Pub. Schs., 1993—; adj. instr. No. Ill. U., De Kalb, 1980-90; presenter Closing the Gap Conf., Bloomington, Minn., 1989; evaluator North Cen. Evaluation Team, Ottawa, Ill., 1989; instr. coord. St. Xavier U., Internat. Renewal Inst., Chgo., Rockford, 1990-94; featured spkr. 1991 conv. Coun. for Exceptional Children. Co-author: (assessment instrument) Task Asessment for Prescriptive Teaching, 1979. Presenter, vol. Parent Action Network, Winnebago County, Ill., 1989-91; pres. bd. trustees Unitarian Ch., Rockford, 1991-93. Named Svc. Personnel of Yr., Those Who Excel, Rockford, Ill., 1987. Mem. ASCD, Phi Delta Kappa. Home: 1419 Post Ave Rockford IL 61103-6222

WILKEN, CAROLINE DOANE, critical care, emergency, recovery room, and medical/surgical nurse; b. Watseka, Ill., Jan. 4, 1962; d. Robert Charles and Barbara Jane (Perkinson) W. BSN, Rush U., Chgo., 1984. RN, Ill., Calif., Del., Mass., Md., N.J., Ariz., Conn., Va., Ga., U.K.; cert. ACLS. Travel nurse AMN, San Diego, Nurses Across Am., Boynton Beach, Fla., HSSI, Ft. Lauderdale, Fla.; staff nurse Rush-Presbyn.-St. Luke's Med. Ctr., Chgo., UCLA Med. Ctr.; travel nurse Travcorps, Malden, Mass.; staff nurse Riverside Med. Ctr., Kankakee, Ill. Mem. Emergency Nurses Assn. Home: PO Box 51 Onarga IL 60955

WILKENS, ROBERT ALLEN, utilities executive, electrical engineer; b. Esmond, S.D., Jan. 3, 1929; s. William J. and Hazel C. (Girch) W.; m. Barbara M. Davis, Apr. 15, 1952; children—Bradley Alan, Beth Ann, Bonnie Sue, William Frank. B.S.E.E., S.D. State U., 1951. Dispatcher, engr. G.O., Northwestern Pub. Service Co., Huron, 1953-55, div. engr., Huron 1955-58, div. elec. supt., 1958-59, div. mgr., 1959-66, asst. to pres., 1966-69, vice pres. ops., G.O., 1969-80, pres., chief operating officer, 1980-90, pres., chief exec. officer, 1990-94, chmn. bd. dirs. 1994—, also dir.; v.p., past pres. N. Cen. Electric Assn., past dir. Midwest Gas Assn.; dir. Farmers & Mchts. Bank Huron; past adminstrv. chmn., treas. Mid-Continent Area Power Pool. Mem. Salvation Army Adv. Bd., 1962-87; S.D. State R.R. Bd., 1982-87; past pres. Huron United Way. Served to capt. USAF, 1951-53. Named Disting. Engr., S.D. State U., 1977. Mem. North Central Elec. Assn., Midwest Gas Assn., S.D. Engring. Soc., Huron C. of C. (pres. 1963). Republican. Methodist. Lodges: Kiwanis, Masons, Shriners. Office: Northwestern Pub Svc Co 33 3rd St SE Huron SD 57350-2015

WILKERSON, RITA LYNN, special education educator, consultant; b. Crescent, Okla., Apr. 22; Mem. ASCD, Coun. for Exceptional Children, OARC, OACLD, Phi Delta Kappa, Kappa Delta Pi. BA, Cen. State U., Edmond, Okla., 1963; MEd, Cen. State U., 1969; postgrad., U. Okla., 1975. Elem. tchr. music Hillsdale (Okla.) Pub. Sch., 1963-64; jr. high sch. music and spl. edn. Okarche (Okla.) Pub. Sch., 1965-71; cons. Title III Project, Woodward, Okla., 1971-72; dir. Regional Edn. Svc. Ctr., Guymon, Okla., 1972-81; dir., psychologist Project W.O.R.K., Guymon, 1981-90; tchr. behavioral disorders Unified Sch. Dist. 480, Liberal, Kans., 1990—; sch. psychologist Hardesty (Okla.) Schs., 1994; cons. Optima (Okla.) Pub. Schs., 1990, Felt (Okla.) Pub. Schs., 1990, Texhoma (Okla.) Schs., 1994, Balko (Okla.) Pub. Schs., 1996; spl. edn. cons. Optima Pub. Schs., 1992—, Goodwell (Okla.) Pub. Schs., 1992—; diagnostician Tyrone, Okla. Pub. Schs., 1992-95; home svcs. provider Dept. Human Svcs., Guymon, 1990; active Kans. Dept. Social and Rehab. Svcs., 1993—; adj. tchr. Seward County C.C., 1994—. Grantee Cen. State U., 1968-69, Oklahoma City Dept. Edn., 1988-89. Mem. ASCD, NAFE, NEA (liberal Kans. chpt.), AAUW, Coun. Exceptional Children, Okla. Assn. Retarded Citizens, Okla. Assn. for Children with Learning Disabilities, Phi Delta Kappa. Republican. Home: 616 N Crumley St Guymon OK 73942-4341 Office: Unified Sch Dist 480 7th And Western Liberal KS 67901

WILKIE, GERRY L., state legislator; m. Kathy Wilkie; 3 children. BS, N.D. State U. Supr. soil conservation dist. Rolette County; mem. from dist. 9 N.D. State Assembly, Bismarck, 1987—, mem. appropriations, edn. and environ. coms. Bd. dirs. Mt. Pleasant Sch. Dist. Found.; past mem. Water Mgmt. Bd. Mem. Rolette County Agrl. Improvement Assn. (past chmn. bd. dirs.), Farmers Union, Nat. Food Orgn., Rolla Jaycees (past pres.). Office: PO Box 1140 Rolla ND 58367*

WILKIE, NANCY CLAUSEN, classics and archaeology educator; b. Milw., Dec. 27, 1942; d. Harry H. and Teresa (D.) Clausen; m. Robert J. D. Wilkie, May 9, 1964 (div. 1974); m. Craig H. Anderson, Sept. 27, 1975. AB, Stanford U., 1964; MA, U. Minn., 1967, PhD, 1975. Instr. Macalester Coll., St. Paul, 1972-75; instr. Carleton Coll., Northfield, Minn., 1974-75, from asst. prof. to assoc. prof., 1975-93, prof., 1993—, chair dept. classical langs., 1991-96; Parker vis. scholar Brown U., Providence, 1983; Fulbright lectr. Tribhuvan U., Kathmandu, Nepal, 1988; trustee Archaeol. Inst. Am., Boston, 1989-94, 1st v.p., 1994—; mem. exec. com. Ctr. for Ancient Studies, U. Minn., Mpls., 1990-93; mem. exec. bd. Soc. Profl. Archaeologists, Fresno, Calif., 1991-93, 95—. Editor: Contributions to Aegean Archaeology, 1985, The Great Isthmus Corridor Route, Vol. I, 1991; author, editor: Excavations at Nichoria in SW Greece, Vol. II, 1992. Mem. Assn. Ancient Historians, Am. Philol. Assn., Soc. for Am. Archaeology, Women's Classical Caucus. Home: 6504 Shawnee Cir Edina MN 55439-1154 Office: Dept Classical Lang Carleton College Northfield MN 55057

WILKINS, ARTHUR NORMAN, retired college administrator; b. Kansas City, Mo., Sept. 24, 1925; s. Arthur Miller and Jean (DeWitt) W.; AA, Jr. Coll. of Kansas City, 1947; MA, U. Chgo., 1950; PhD, Washington U., 1953. Grad. asst. Washington U., St. Louis, 1950-52; instr. English, La. State U., Baton Rouge, 1953-56; instr. English, Jr. Coll. of Kansas City, 1956-64, chmn. Dept. English, 1961-64; instr. English, Met. Jr. Coll., Kansas City, Mo., 1964-69, chmn. Dept. English, 1964-68, chmn. Div. Humanities, 1968-69; instr. English, Longview C.C., Lee's Summit, Mo., 1969-70, chmn. dept. humanities, 1969-70, dean instrn., 1970-84; dir. acad. affairs Met. C.C.s, Kansas City, Mo., 1984-90. Mem. Mo. State Libr. planning com., 1980-83. Served with U.S. Army, 1943-46. Washington U. fellow, 1952-53. Mem. Bookmark Soc., U. Chgo. Libr. Soc. Author: Mortal Taste, 1965; High Seriousness, 1971; The Leonore Overtures, 1975; Attic Salt, 1984, Dirt Behind Our Ears, 1995; contbr. articles to profl. jours. Home: 210 W 100th Ter Apt 202 Kansas City MO 64114-4431

WILKINS, DANIEL CHAIM, physicist, educator; b. N.Y.C., Apr. 28, 1947; s. Alvin Francis Meyer and Sophie Clara (Prombaum) W. BA, Amherst Coll., 1967; MS, Stanford U., 1968, PhD, 1972. Postdoctoral fellow, vis. asst. prof. U. Calif. Santa Barbara, 1972-75; postdoctoral fellow Tata Inst. Fund Rsch., Bombay, 1975-77, U. Bonn, Germany, 1978-80, Inst. Astrophys. and Space Sci., Frascati, Italy, 1980-81; vis. asst. prof. Oakland U., Rochester, Mich., 1981-83; asst. prof., assoc. prof. U. Nebr., Omaha, 1983—. Contbr. articles to profl. jours. Judge Met. Sci. and Engring. Fair, Omaha, 1984—. Fellow NASA-ASEE, 1985-86, Jove fellow NASA, 1991-94. Mem. Am. Assn. Physics Tchrs., Sigma Xi. Office: U Nebr Dept Physics 60th and Dodge Omaha NE 68182-0266

WILKINSON, ALFRED E., engineering executive; b. Caro, Mich., June 1, 1927. AS, R.E.T.S., Detroit, 1952. Design engr. Bryant Computer Products, Walled Lake, Mich., 1962-72, I.D.S. Corp., West Bloomfield, Mich., 1972-77, Automatic Parking, Farmington, Mich., 1977-80; pres., prin. Wilkinson Engring., Inc., Commerce Twp., Mich., 1980—. With U.S. Army, 1945-56. Mem. Am. Legion. Office: Wilkinson Engring Inc 3070 Glengary Rd Commerce Township MI 48382-2143

WILKINSON, CONNIE MARIE, early childhood education director; b. Jefferson City, Mo., Feb. 11, 1965; d. Martin Herman and Mary Antonio (Muenks) Brandt; m. Dale Lee Wilkinson, Aug. 5, 1989; children: Elizabeth Marie, Phillip Vincent. BS in Elem. Edn., BS in Spl. Edn., Cen. Mo. State U., 1987, MS in Spl. Edn., 1988. Life cert. elem. tchr., K-12 tchr. educable mentally retarded, K-12 learning disabilities tchr., sch. psychol. examiner, early childhood spl. edn. tchr., Mo.; cert. early childhood spl. edn. tchr., Kans. Clk.-typist Mo. Dept. Health and Mo. Dept. Nursing, Jefferson City, 1983-85; grad. asst. Ward Edwards Libr. Cen. Mo. State U., Warrensburg, 1987-88; tchr. learning disabilities Sedalia (Mo.) Unified Sch. Dist. 200, 1988-89; tchr. early childhood spl. edn. North Ctrl. Kans. Spl. Edn. Coop., Glade, 1989-90; tchr. educable mentally handicapped Cassville (Mo.) High Sch., 1990-91; tchr. summer studies enrichment program Monett (Mo.) Elem. Sch., 1990-91, tchr. early childhood spl. edn./Chpt. 1, early childhood dir, 1991-92; supr. div. spl. edn. Mo. State Dept. Elem. and Secondary Edn., 1992-94; dir. Wilkinson Early Childhood Programs, 1994—. Mem. Parish Coun. Cath. Women, Monett, 1991; mem. Ladies Aux. Sts. Peter and Paul

Ch., Boonville, Mo. Regents scholar Cen. Mo. State U, 1983-88, Don Rice scholar, 1986, Leroy Barrows scholar, 1986. Mem. AAUW, Coun. for Exceptional Children (pres.-elect divsn. for learning disabilities, state membership chmn. divsn. for early childhood 1991-93, pres.-elect 1993-94, v.p. 1994-95, state pres. DEC 1995-96), Mo. Tchrs. Assn., Kappa Delta Pi, Pi Omicron Delta. Home and Office: 17 Riverside Dr Boonville MO 65233-1344

WILKINSON, TODD THOMAS, project engineer; b. Mitchell, S.D., June 23, 1959; s. Ralph W. and Margret Jean (Kent) W. BSME, S.D. Sch. Mines and Tech., 1981; MS in Applied Mech., U. Cin., 1984. Registered profl. engr., Ohio. Pilot Singleton/Shea Spray Svc., Pierre, S.D., 1977-80; program engr. GE Aircraft Engines, Cin., 1981-85; field rep. naval air propulsion ctr. GE Aircraft Engines, Trenton, N.J., 1985-86; field rep. Grumman F-14 flight test GE Aircraft Engines, Calverton, N.Y., 1986-88; project engr. MATV flight demonstration GE Aircraft Engines, Cin., 1989-95; field engr. Midwest Tech. Svcs., Inc., Pierre, S.D., 1996—. Tech. illustrator: (book) The Instrument Pilot Handbook, 1980. Recipient Kelly Johnson award Soc. Flight Test Engrs., 1994. Mem. AIAA. Roman Catholic.

WILKS, R(ALPH) KENNETH, JR., government planner; b. Springfield, Mo., Sept. 25, 1956; s. Ralph Kenneth and Virginia Lacy (Phillips) W.; s. Melinda Sue Maxwell, July 21, 1984. BA, Evangel Coll., 1978; MPA, U. Mo., Kansas City, 1980. Adminstrv. aide City of Leawood (Kans.), 1979-80; theater mgr. Crown Cinema Corp., Jefferson City, Mo., 1981-84; rsch. analyst II Mo. Dept. Social Svcs., Jefferson City, 1984-86, planner II, 1986-93; planner III Mo. Dept. Corrections, Jefferson City, 1993—; legis. intern U.S. Sen. Robert Dole, Washington, 1978; lectr. in field. Contbr. articles to profl. jours. Mem. Am. Soc. Pub. Adminstrn., Am. Corrections Assn., Mo. Inst. Pub. Adminstrn., Social Sci. Honor Soc. (life). Home: 4802 Rainbow Hills Rd Jefferson City MO 65109

WILKS, STEPHEN L., manufacturing company executive; b. Dayton, Ohio, Dec. 12, 1958. AS in Tooling, ITT Dayton, 1979. Draftsman Indsl. Design Concepts, Dayton, 1978-81, Prototype Tech., Troy, Ohio, 1982, Chemineer Inc., Dayton, 1982-83, Futura Design, Dayton, 1983-84; contract designer Sasco Corp., Dayton, 1985; design drafter Whirlpool Corp., Dayton, 1989—. Pentecostal Ch. Office: Whirlpool Dayton Tech Ctr 3800 Space Dr Dayton OH 45414-2565

WILL, ERIC JOHN, state senator; b. Omaha, Nebr., Apr. 16, 1959; s. John Babcock and Patricia Elaine (Propst) W. BA in Polit. Sci., U. So. Calif., 1981; postgrad., Creighton U., 1993—. Legis. researcher Nebr. State Legis., Omaha, 1981-90, senator, 1991—; chmn. enrollment and rev. com., 1991-93, rules com., 1993—; vice chmn. gen. affairs com., 1991—; mem. revenue and urban affairs com., 1991—. Mem. Phi Beta Kappa. Democrat. Presbyterian. Home: 6029 Pinkney St Omaha NE 68104-4333 Office: Nebr State Capitol District 8 Lincoln NE 68509

WILL, JAMES ARTHUR, pharmaceutical executive, educator; b. Wauwatosa, Wis., Nov. 2, 1930; s. Arthur Julius and Anne Amalia (Kranz) W.; m. Lorna Ruth Smithyman, June 27, 1953; children: Lorna Ruth, Leslie Ann, James. BS, U. Wis., 1952, MS, 1953, PhD, 1967; DVM, Kans. State U., 1960. Lic. vet., Wis. Veterinarian Columbus (Wis.) Vet. Hosp., 1960-64; asst. prof. U. Wis., Madison, 1967-71, assoc. prof., 1971-73, prof., 1974—, grad. sch. dir. Rsch. Animal Resources, 1981-90; v.p. Clarion Pharms., Inc., Madison, 1994—. Editor: The Pulmonary Circulation in Health and Diseases, 1987. 1st lt. U.S. Army, 1954-56. Fellow Royal Soc. Medicine, Am. Physiol. Soc.; mem. Am. Vet Med. Assn., Assn. Am. Vet. Med. Colls. (pres. 1975-76), Wis. Vet. Med. Assn. Home: 344 S Charles St Columbis WI 53925 Office: Dept Animal & Biomed Scis 1655 Linden Dr Madison WI 53706 also: Clarion Pharm Inc 585 Science Dr Madison WI 53711

WILL, JANE ANNE, psychologist; b. Evansville, Ind., Feb. 6, 1945; d. Edwin Francis and Frances Elizabeth (Patry) W. BA in Edn., St. Benedict's Coll., Ferdinand, Ind., 1968; MA in Edn., MS in Clin. Psychology, U. Evansville, 1973, 1987; MA in Christian Spirituality, Creighton U., 1979; D Psychology, Fla. Tech., Melbourne, 1991. Lic. psychologist, Ind.; joined Sisters of St. Benedict, Inc., Roman Cath. Ch. Tchr. Ireland (Ind.) Jr. H.S., 1969-76, Meml. H.S., Evansville, Ind., 1976-77; dir. recruitment and tng. Sisters of St. Benedict, Inc., Ferdinand, Ind., 1978-84, cons. admissions bd., 1984—; tchr. Mater Dei H.S., Evansville, 1984-88; therapist Osceola Ctr., Kissimme, Fla., 1989-90, Charter Hosp., Kissimme, Fla., 1989-90; intern VA Med. Ctr., St. Louis, 1990-91; clin. psychologist St. Mary's Health Care Svcs., Evansville, 1991—; adj. prof. Bresica Coll., Owensboro, Ky., 1978-80, St. Mary's of the Woods Coll., Terre Haute, Ind., 1980-84. Author jour. Ind. Reading Quarterly, 1973. Bd. dirs. Nat. Formation Dirs., Washington, 1982-84; chairperson region VII Formation Conf., Mich. and Ind., 1982-84. Luise Whiting Bell scholar, 1986. Mem. APA, Ind. Psychol. Assn., Southwestern Ind. Psychol. Assn. (treas. 1992, sec. 1993, v.p. 1994, pres. 1995), Vanderburgh County Mental Health Assn. (bd. dirs. 1994—, v.p. 1996). Roman Catholic. Home: 725 Wedeking Ave Evansville IN 47711-3861

WILL, ROLAND TRACY, II, writer, editor; b. Schenectady, N.Y., May 18, 1954; s. Albert Roland and Constance Mary (Headley) W.; m. Gay Adair Strandemo, July 1, 1989; children: Roland Leigh Leonard, Glenn Tracy. BA, U. Wis., 1988. Pol. sci., comm. arts editor, pub., journalist Wis. Health Policy Report, Madison, Wis., 1994—. Author: (Compass Am. Guide) Wisconsin, 1994; (plays) Packer Glory, 1984, Fatal Time to Final End, 1986. Bus. mem. Dane County Hist. Soc., Madison, 1995; sec. bd. dirs. Broom St. Theater, Madison, 1984—. Episcopalian. Office: Wis Health Policy Report Press Rm/State Capitol Madison WI 53703

WILL, THOMAS ERIC, psychologist; b. Feb. 28, 1949. BA in Edn., Concordia Coll., St. Paul, 1972; MPH, U. Minn., 1980, postgrad. in epidemiology, 1980-81; PsyD with distinction, Forest Inst. Profl. Psychology, Des Plaines, Ill., 1986. Lic. psychologist. Rsch. asst. dept. epidemiology Nat. Cancer Inst. U. Minn., Mpls., 1980-81; mem. crisis intervention staff Forest Psychiat. Hosp., Des Plaines, 1982-83; psychiat. researcher Ill. State Psychiat. Inst., Chgo., 1983-84; psychometrician Evaluation Ctr./U. Chgo. Med. Ctr., 1983-84; health psychologist Group Health, Inc. Mental Health Ctr., Mpls., 1986—; assoc. core faculty Minn. Sch. Profl. Psychology, Mpls., 1988—; adj. asst. prof. Forest Inst. Profl. Psychology, Des Plaines, 1983-85; regional faculty The Fielding Inst., Santa Barbara, Calif., 1991—. Contbr. articles to profl. jours. Recipient grants, Group Health, Inc., 1988. Mem. APA, Nat. Acad. Neuropsychology, Nat. Register of Health Svc. Providers in Psychology, Psi Chi. Office: Health Ptnrs Univ Ave Clinic 2701 University Ave SE Minneapolis MN 55414-3233

WILLADSEN, MICHAEL CHRIS, marketing professional, sales executive; b. Cheboygan, Mich., Sept. 18, 1946; s. Chris Jens and Helen Margaret (Barr) W.; m. Kay Ann Brooks, Dec. 10, 1964 (div. Dec. 10, 1989); children: Michael Jr., Erik; m. Linda Sue Degroff, Apr. 4, 1992; children: Stephanie, Gretchen, Ross. Student, Delta Coll., 1964-66; A in Bus. Mgmt., Northwood Inst., 1968, BA in Bus. Mgmt., 1969. Mktg. rep. Detroit dist. Petemco, Inc., 1970-73, mktg. rep. Indpls. Dist., 1973-74; dist. mgr. Petemco Inc.-Ind. Ohio Mich., Ind., Ohio, Mich., 1974-76, Consolidated Stas. Marathon Oil, Oshkosh, Wis., 1976-79; sales mgr. Champaign (Ill.) Dist. Marathon Oil, 1981-82; supr. Credit Card Ctr. Marathon Oil, Findlay, Ohio, 1982-84; wholesale mktg. profl. Marathon Brand Mktg./Ohio, Mich., Ky., 1982-84; jobber sales Marathon Oil/Ohio, Pa., W.Va., Ohio, Pa., W. Va., 1984-92, Marathon Oil/Ill., Wisc., Chgo., Chgo., 1992—. Named to Nat. Assn. Intercollegiate Athletes Sml. Coll. All-State Football Team/Dist. 23, 1968. Mem. Cleve. Petroleum Club (v.p. 1988-91), Chgo. Oilmens. Republican. Presbyterian. Office: Marathon Oil Co P O Box 1635 Bolingbrook IL 60440

WILLARD, KAREN, state legislator. BS, Eastern Mich. U.; JD, U. Detroit. Ethics prosecutor Mich. Atty. Grievance Commn.; state rep. Dist. 82 Mich. Ho. of Reps., 1993—; atty.; vice-chmn. Tourism & Recration Com., 1993—; mem. Agriculture & Forestry, Mil. & Vets. Affairs, Sr. Citizens Coms., 1993—; prof. legal writing Law Sch. U. Detroit. *

WILLARD, TIMOTHY J., higher education executive, consultant; b. Denver, June 24, 1943; m. Carmen A. McCanna, June 10, 1967; children: Anna, Adam, Elizabeth. BA, Regis Coll., Denver, 1965; MA, U. Colo., 1970, PhD, 1984. Instr. English Regis H.S., Denver, 1965-73, chmn. dept. English, 1973-74, asst. to prin., 1974-75, asst. to headmaster, 1975-77, dir. devel., 1977; dir. devel. Regis Coll., 1977-80; dir. devel. U. San Diego, 1980-86, capital campaign dir., 1986-92; v.p. univ. advancement Millikin U., Decatur, Ill., 1992-95; v.p. devel. and instl. advancement Fontbonne Coll., St. Louis, 1996—; cons. U. Dallas, 1994; mem. devel. com. Assoc. Colls. Ill., Chgo., 1995; speaker in field. Author articles. Chair pub. svc. and edn. United Way of Decatur and Macon County, Ill., 1994-95; bd. dirs. Gallery 510, Decatur, 1994-95, Family Svc. Assn., San Diego, 1984-92, ARC; mem. strategic planning com. Holy Family Sch. Recipient Bd. Trustees commendation U. San Diego, 1992, Outstanding Leadership award Kiwanis Club of San Diego Found., 1991. Mem. Coun. for Advancement and Support of Edn., Nat. Soc. Fund Raising Execs., Ptnrs. in Edn. (FirstGrant adv. bd.), Metro Decatur C. of C.

WILLEY, JAMES LEE, dentist; b. Colorado Springs, Colo., Oct. 26, 1953; s. Elwood James and Dorothy Jean (Norton) W.; m. Catherine Margaret Whitmer, Aug. 23, 1975; children: Andrew James and David Lee (twins). BA, So. Ill. U., 1975; BS in Dentistry, U. Ill., Chgo., 1977, DDS, 1979; MBA, No. Ill. U., 1986. Pvt. practice dentistry Elburn, Ill., 1979—; lectr. Dental Arts Labs., Peoria, Ill., 1981-90. Trustee Paul W. Clopper Meml. Found., 1989—, chmn. fund raising com., 1991—, treas., 1992—; mem. adminstrv. bd. Geneva United Meth. Ch., 1991-92; asst. scoutmaster Boy Scouts Am., Elburn, 1995—; spokesperson Prevent Abuse and Neglect Through Dental Awareness, 1995—; village trustee Village of Elburn, 1995—, mem. fin. com., 1995-96, mem. police com., 1995, mem. pub. works com., 1996. Recipient Certificate of Merit, Swissedent Found., Glendale, Calif., 1983; fellow Clopper Found., 1992. Fellow Am. Endodontic Soc.; mem. ADA (Outstanding Young Dentist Leader award 1992), Ill. State Dental Soc. (alt. del. 1990, spokesperson 1990—, del. 1991-92, dental edn. com. 1991-93, chmn. 1994—, vice speaker ho. of dels. 1992-93), Fox River Valley Dental Soc. (bd. dirs. 1988-93, sec. 1989, treas. 1990, v.p. 1991,pres. 1992), Legis. Interest Com. Ill. Dentists (bd. dirs. 1988—, exec. com. 1989—, 2d v.p. 1991-92, 1st v.p. 1993-94, pres. 1995-96). Home: 711 N 3rd St Elburn IL 60119-9018 Office: 135 S Main St # 7G Elburn IL 60119-9142

WILLEY, KEVIN CHARLES, systems engineer; b. Flint, Mich., Mar. 14, 1968. BS in Mech. Engring., GMI Engr. and Mgmt. Inst., Flint, Mich., 1991. Sys. engr. Perot Systems, Romulus, Mich., 1992—. Mem. ASME. Office: Perot Systems 38481 W Huron River Dr Romulus MI 48174-1158

WILLHITE, LEE A., human resources administrator; b. Seoul, Jan. 2, 1963; (parents Am. citizens); d. Frank J. Nixon and Yun C. (Yi) Huffman; m. Eddie D. Willhite, Nov. 16, 1986. Adminstrv. asst. Northco Corp., Mpls., 1983, office mgr., investor rels. rep., mgr. human resources, 1983—, benefits coord., 1984—. Vol. Minn. Korean Women's Assn., Mpls., 1990. Mem. Am. Bus. Women's Assn. Mem. Dem. Farmer Labor Party. Methodist. Office: Northco Corp 1201 Marquette Ave Minneapolis MN 55403

WILLHOIT, JIM, minister; b. Springfield, Ill., June 25, 1943; s. Richard and Virginia (Hampton) W.; m. Karen Huddleston, June 19, 1966; children: Amy Lynn, Todd Christopher. BA, Lincoln Christian Coll., 1969; MDiv., Lincoln Christian Sem., 1974, MA, 1975. Ordained to ministry Ch. of Christ, 1971. Minister Salisbury (Ill.) Christian Ch., 1964-72, Walnut Grove Christian Ch., Arcola, Ill., 1972-81; sr. minister First Ch. Christ, Highland, Ind., 1981—; mem. site com. Project 300, Lincoln, Ill., 1979-81; bd. dirs. Onesimus Ministries, 1978-81; chaplain Lake County Police Dept., Crown Point, Ind., 1982-83, Glenwood (Ill.) Police Dept., 1986—. Mem. sch. bd. Unit Dist. 306, Arcola, 1978-81; chaplain South Suburban (Ill.) Emergency Response Team, 1992—. Mem. Soc. Bibl. Lit., Am. Sci. Affiliation (assoc.), Chgo. Dist. Minister's Assn. (sec.-treas. 1982—). Home: 8936 Schneider Ave Highland IN 46322-1841 Office: First Ch Christ 2420 Lincoln St Highland IN 46322-1876

WILLIAM, WILLIAM H.A., professor; b. Phila., Feb. 10, 1937; s. William H.A. and Evelyn (Hamm) W.; m. Leslie Ann Dec. 15, 1941; children: William H.A. III, L. Lavinia Kate. BA, Lafayette Coll., 1959; MA, Johns Hopkins U., 1962, PhD, 1971; MLS, Ind. U., 1965. Instr. So. Ill. U., Carbondale, 1965-66; coll. lectr. U. Coll., Dublin, Ireland, 1966-72; vis. prof. U. Glesson, Germany, 1972-74, Ariz. State U., Tempe, 1975-78; dir. Linkage, Inc., Phoenix, 1980-83; proj. dir. Orgn. Am. Historians, Bloomington, Ind., 1985-87; prof. The Union Inst., Cin., 1987—. Author: H.L. Mencken, 1977, 'Twas Only an Irishman: Dream, 1996. 1st lt. inf. U.S. Army, 1963-65. John Noble Leadership fellow Lafayette Coll., 1959-62, Woodrow Wilson fellow Johns Hopkins U., 1962-63. Mem. Orgn. Am. Historians, Am. Conf. Irish Studies, Polanyi Soc., Irish Am. Cultural Inst. (Four Masters 1992), Wash. Evolutionary Sys. Soc. Mem. Soc. of Friends. Office: The Union Inst 440 E McMillan St Cincinnati OH 45206-1947

WILLIAMS, ANDREW PHILIP, agricultural management consultant; b. Davenport, IA; s. Philip Gary and Celia Anne (Weaver) W. Student, U. Nebr., 1986-90. Cons. William Logistics Mgmt. Svcs., Bonner Springs, Kans., 1991—; pres. Williams Landscaping & Nursery Co., Bonner Springs, Kans., 1987—; founder, co-dir., Baltic Agri. Ptnrs., Kans., Latvia, 1994—; adv. Latvian Ministry of Agri., Riga, Catuia, 1992—. Firefighter, EMT Bonner Springs Fire Dept., 1991; mem. St. Andrew's Soc. K.S., 1992, Nelson Atkins Art Soc., 1994. Decorated Admiral Nebr. Navy Gov. Ben Nelson, 1993; named Hero of Yr., Nebr. Rescue & Emer. Care Assn., 1986, Hon. mem. Rep. of Latvia Olympic Team, Riga, Latvia, 1992, Outstanding Youth of Yr. Fremont Rotary Club, 1986. Mem. Bonner Springs Edwardsville Jaycees, Bonner Springs C. of C., NFPA, Kans. State Firefighters Assn. Home: 13121 Richland Ave No 10 Bonner Springs KS 66012 Office: Williams Logistics Mgmt Svcs P O Box 454 Bonner Springs KS 66012

WILLIAMS, ANGIE, journalism educator; b. Augsburg, West Germany, Nov. 23, 1966; d. Thomas and Addie Mae (Williams) W. BA, Mt. St. Joseph Coll., Cin., 1989; MA, Wright State U., Dayton, 1994; cert. in deaf studies, Sinclair C.C., Dayton, 1996. Reporter Bristol (Conn.) Press, 1989-90, Poughkeepsie (N.Y.) Jour., 1990; stringer Dayton (Ohio) Daily News, 1990-91; pub. rels. specialist City of Trotwood, Ohio, 1991; promotion specialist Mead Fine Paper Divsn., Dayton, 1992-93; instr. Internat. Coll. Broadcasting, Dayton, 1992-93; instr., faculty advisor Clark State Comty. Coll., Springfield, Ohio, 1994—. Editor: (books) Order Out of Chaos, 1995, Faith That Works, 1995; author: (annual) Shades of Gray, 1995. Recipient Scripps Howard Jr. Colls. scholarship Mt. St. Joseph Coll., Cin., 1990, 91, Presdl. cert. appreciation, Clark State, 1996. Office: Clark State Comty Coll 570 E Leffel Ln Springfield OH 45501

WILLIAMS, ANNETTE POLLY, state legislator; b. Belzoni, Miss., Jan. 10, 1937. Student, Milw. Area Tech. Coll.; BS, U. Wis. Mem. Wis. State Assembly, Milw., 1980—; attendee African-Am. Leadership summit, New Orleans; organizer Com. 21, 1985, Black Ribbon Commn. to study forced busing, Milw., 1989; panelist Nat. Conf. State Legislators, 1989; active parental sch. choice legislation; lectr. numerous colls. and univs. T.V. appearances include 60 Minutes, ABC World News, This Week with David Brinkley, McNeil Lehrer Report, The British Broadcasting Company, Great Lakes Watch on Washington, CBS This Morning, Both Sides with Rev. Jesse Jackson, CNN News; contbr. articles to profl. jours. Dem. adminstrv. and exec. com.; state chairperson Wis. Jesse Jackson for Pres. campaign; del. Nat. Dem. Conv., 1984, 88; mem. Nat. Dem. Platform Com., 1984; bd. dirs. Rainbow Coalition; founder, chmn. bd. dirs. Milw. Parental Assistance Ctr. Recipient Carrie Chapman Catt award as Nat. Women's Bus. Advocate of Yr., Outstanding Leadership award Dem. party Wis., Harambee Martin Luther King Jr. award for Outstanding Accomplishment and Svc. Am. Legis. Exchange Coun., 1991, Nat. Human Rights award Nat. Cath. Ednl. Assn., 1992, Seton award Career Youth Devel., 1992, Image award for Excellence in Community Svc. and Love of Youth Gamma Phi Delta, 1992, Community Leadership award Libertarian Party Wis., 1992, Liberty award, 1993, Martin Luther King Jr. Community Svc. award Lydell Comm., 1994; named Legislator of Yr. Freedom Mag., 1992; vis. fellow Auckland (New Zealand) Inst. Tech., 1993. Mem. Nat. Black Caucus State Legislators (bd. dirs.). Home: 3927 N 16th St Milwaukee WI 53206-2918 Office: Wis State Assembly State Capital Madison WI 53702

WILLIAMS, BOBBY See EVERHART, ROBERT PHILLIP

WILLIAMS, CALVIN, librarian, consultant; b. Hogansville, Ga., Jan. 29, 1946; s. Azell and Lella (Mullins) W.; m. Delores Hayes, June 23, 1973; children: Sheniqua LaToya, Calvin Mikkel. BA, Morris Brown Coll., 1969; MS in Library Sci., Atlanta U., 1973; MSA, Cen. Mich. U., 1979. Librarian assoc. Atlanta Pub. Library, 1972-73, community analyst, 1973; head librarian Morris Brown Coll., Atlanta, 1971-73; br. librarian Saginaw (Mich.) Pub. Library, 1973-75; acad. librarian Saginaw Valley State Coll., University Center, Mich., 1975-87; librarian Oakland Community Coll., Auburn Hills, Mich., 1987—, dept. chmn., 1989—; Mem. Bridgeport (Mich.) Library Commn., 1981-88, pres. 1985-86; library cons. Saginaw County Mental Health Ctr., 1984-86. Editor Great Lakes and Finger Lakes newsletter, 1981-88, Bethel AME Ch. newsletter, 1989-90. Pres. Bridgeport (Mich.) Library Commn., 1985-88. Served to U.S. Army, 1969-71. Atlanta U. fellow, 1971-73; recipient Community Service awards Saginaw Pub. Schs., 1975-85. Mem. ALA, NAACP, Mich. Acad. Sci. and Arts (GODORT), Mich. Libr. Assn. (docus chmn. 1981-82, Cert. 1980—), Acad. Polit. Sci., Atlanta U. Alumni Assn., Ctrl. Mich. U. Alumni Assn. (life), Saginaw Alumni Chpt. (treas. 1984-92), Kappa Alpha Psi (life, Outstanding Alumni 1982). Democrat. Methodist. Home: 3286 Southfield Dr Saginaw MI 48601-5642 Office: Oakland Community Coll 2900 Featherstone Rd Auburn Hills MI 48326-2817

WILLIAMS, CLAY RULE, lawyer; b. Milw., Sept. 25, 1935; s. George Laverne and Marguerite Mae (Rule) W.; m. Jeanne Lee Huber, Jan. 18, 1986; children: Gwynne, Amy, Daniel, Sarah. BA, Lawrence U., 1957; LLB, U. Mich., 1960. Bar: Wis. 1960, U.S. Dist. Ct. (ea. and we. dists.) Wis. 1964, U.S. Ct. Appeals (7th cir.) 1965, U.S. Ct. Mil. Appeals 1963, U.S. Supreme Ct. 1963. Assoc. Gibbs, Roper & Fifield, Milw., 1963-67; ptnr. Von Briesen, Purtell & Roper, Milw., 1967—; mem. Gov.'s Task Force Creation Bus. Ct., 1994—; instr. profl. seminars. Author: Berry, Davis, Deguire and Williams, Wisconsin Business Corporation Law, 1992; contbr. articles to profl. publs. Mem. Shorewood (Wis.) Sch. Bd., 1976-79. Capt. USAF, Judge Adv. Corps., 1960-63. Mem. ABA (sect. antitrust law, corp. counseling com., task force on Uniform Securities Act, com. on securities litigation), Wis. Bar Assn. (co-chmn. com. to revise corp. laws 1986-90, chmn. standing com. on bus. corp. law 1990—, Pres.'s Award of Excellence 1990), Milw. Bar Assn. (probate and real property sect., joint bench-bar com. Ct. Appeals, 1986-88, long-range planning com. 1987), 7th Cir. Bar Assn., Fedn. Ins. and Corp. Counsel, Def. Rsch. Inst., Am. Law Inst., Assn. Bar City N.Y., Wis. Bar Found., Milw. Club, Univ. Club, Milw. Athletic Club. Republican. Episcopalian. Office: Gibbs Roper Loots & Williams 735 N Water St Milwaukee WI 53202-4100

WILLIAMS, CLIFFORD EMMETT, philosophy educator; b. Chgo., Dec. 7, 1943; s. Henry Fortson and Ruth Edna (Veerman) W.; m. Linda Wallace, Aug. 21, 1965; 1 child, Laura. BA magna cum laude, Wheaton (Ill.) Coll., 1964; PhD, Ind. U., 1972. Teaching assoc. Ind. U., Bloomington, 1967-68; from instr. to assoc. prof. philosophy St. John Fisher Coll., Rochester, N.Y., 1968-82; assoc. prof. philosophy Trinity Coll., Deerfield, Ill., 1982—, chmn. dept. philosophy, 1982—; vis. assoc. prof. philosophy Houghton (N.Y.) Coll., spring 1980; lectr. in field. Author: Free Will and Determinism: A Dialogue, 1980, Singleness of Heart, 1994, On Love and Friendship: Philosophical Readings, 1995; contbr. articles to profl. jours. including The Personalist, The Philos. Forum, So. Jour. Philosophy, Christian Scholar's Review, Australiasian Jour. Philosophy, Religious Studies, Internat. Jour. Philosophy Religion, The Philosophical Quarterly, Christianity Today. Recipient award for teaching excellence and campus leadership Sears Roebuck Found., 1989, award for best sermons competition Harper/San Francisco Pub. Co., 1990; Ind. U. fellow, 1965-66, 67. Mem. Philosophy of Time Soc., Soc. of Christian Philosophers. Office: Trinity College Dept Philosophy Deerfield IL 60015

WILLIAMS, DAVID ALLAN, dentist, educator; b. Dayton, Ohio, June 30, 1949; s. Robert Eugene and Mary Ellen (Moore) W.; m. Diane Elizabeth Costello, Nov. 12, 1993. BS, Mich. State U., 1971; DDS, Case Western Res. U., 1975. Clin. assoc. prof. Northwestern U. Dental Sch., Chgo., 1978—; gen. practice dentistry Northbrook, Ill., 1979—, Chgo., 1980-96. Bd. dirs. United Way of Northbrook. With USN, 1975-78. Armed Forces Health Profls. Scholar, 1972-75. Fellow Acad. Gen. Dentistry; mem. ADA (commn. on dental accreditation), Ill. Dental Soc., Chgo. Dental Soc., Acad. Operative Dentistry, Northbrook Rotary, Delta Tau Delta. Lutheran. Office: Ste 801 666 Dundee Rd Northbrook IL 60062-2734

WILLIAMS, DEBRA ARNEICE, computer engineer; b. Toledo, July 14, 1953; d. Albert M. and Doretha (Walls) Carter; m. Clarence Williams, Jr., Feb. 5, 1988; children: Latisha Doretha, El Christopher. Cert. Computer Sci., Davis Bus. Coll., Toledo; Cert. Computer Technology, Control Data Inst., Toledo. Clk. Toledo County Pub. Libr., 1979-85; computer engr. IBM/TSS, Toledo, 1988—. Methodist. Office: DC Enterprise Ste 103 39 W Alexis Rd Toledo OH 43612-3601

WILLIAMS, DELETA, state legislator. BS, Ctrl. Mo. State U. Mem. Mo. Ho. of Reps. from 121st dist., 1993—. Mem. Citizens for Drug Free Environment, Inc. Mem. Bus. and Profl. Women, C. of C., Women's Dem. Club, Mo. Fedn. Dem. Women's Club. Address: 713 Tyler Warrensburg MO 64093 Office: Mo Ho of Reps State Capitol Building Jefferson City MO 65101-1556*

WILLIAMS, DONALD MACE, newswriter, educator; b. Abilene, Tex., Oct. 24, 1929; s. Robert H. and Betty Lou (Montgomery) W.; m. Nell Osborne, Oct. 22, 1956; children: Andrew Montgomery, Elizabeth. BA, Tex. Tech. U., 1969, MA, 1970; PhD, U. Tex., 1975. Asst. city editor Fort Worth Star-Telegram, 1956-63; city editor Amarillo (Tex.) Globe-News, 1965-68; assoc. prof. Baylor U., Waco, Tex., 1976-80; co-owner The Miami (Tex.) Chief, 1981-82; exec. editor Pine Bluff (Ark.) Comml., 1984-87; spl. writer Newsday, Melville, N.Y., 1987-89; writing coach The Wichita (Kans.) Eagle, 1989—. Author: Interlude in Umbarger, 1992. Sgt. Army, 1948-49. Recipient 2nd place Ernie Pyle award Scripps-Howard Found., 1981. Presbyterian. Home: 6420 E Murdock Wichita KS 67206 Office: The Wichita Eagle 825 E Douglas Wichita KS 67202

WILLIAMS, EDSON POE, retired automotive company executive; b. Mpls., July 31, 1923; s. Homer A. and Florence C. Williams; m. Irene Mae Streed, June 16, 1950; children: Thomas, Louise, Steven, Linnea, Elisa. B.S.M.E. cum laude, U. Minn., 1950. Spl. purpose machinery operator, 1946-50; mfg. mgr., project engr. Crestliner div. Bigelow Sanford Inc., 1950-53, v.p., mgr. mfg. and engring., 1953-58, pres., 1958-63; with Ford Motor Co., 1963-87, mgr. customer svc. div., 1973; gen. mgr. Ford Motor Co. (Ford Mexico), 1973-75; pres. Ford Motor Co. (Ford Mid-East & Africa), 1975-79, Ford Motor Co. (Ford Asia-Pacific Inc.), 1979-87; v.p. Ford Motor Co., 1979-82, v.p.-gen. mgr. N.Am. truck ops., 1982-86, v.p. Ford Diversified Products ops., 1986-87. Served with USAAF, 1942-46. Mem. Naples Yacht and Sailing Club. Home: 688 21st Ave S Naples FL 33940-7610

WILLIAMS, ELEANOR JOYCE, government air traffic control specialist; b. College Station, Tex., Dec. 21, 1936; d. Robert Ira and Viola (Ford) Toliver; m. Tollie Williams, Dec. 30, 1955 (div. July 1978); children: Rodrick, Viola Williams Smith, Darryl, Eric, Dana Williams Jones, Sheila Williams Watkins, Kenneth. Student Prairie View A&M Coll., 1955-56, Anchorage Community Coll., 1964-65, U. Alaska-Anchorage, 1976. Clk./stenographer FAA, Anchorage, 1965-66, adminstrv. clk., 1966-67, pers. staffing asst., 1967-68, air traffic control specialist, 1968-79, air traffic contr. supr., San Juan, P.R., 1979-80, Anchorage, 1983-85, airspace specialist, Atlanta, 1980-83 ; with FAA, Washington, 1985-87; area mgr. Kansas City Air Rt. Traffic Control Ctr., Olathe, Kans., 1987-89, asst. mgr. quality Assurance, 1989-91, supr. traffic mgmt., 1991, supr. system effectiveness section, 1991-93, asst. air traffic mgr., 1993-94, air traffic mgr. Cleve. Air Route Traffic Control Ctr., Oberlin, Ohio, 1994—, acting mgr. sys. mgmt. br., Des Plaines, Ill., 1995-96, mem. human resource reform team task force, Washington, 1996—. Sec. Fairview Neighborhood Coun., Anchorage, 1967-69; mem. Anchorage Bicentennial Commn., 1975-76; bd. dirs. Mt. Patmos Youth Dept., Decatur, Ga., 1981-82; mem. NAACP; del. to USSR Women in Mgmt., 1990; mem. citizens amb. program People to People Internat.

Recipient Mary K. Goddard award Anchorage Fed. Exec. Assn. and Fed. Women's Program, 1985, Sec.'s award Dept. transp., 1985, Pres. VIP award, 1988, C. Alfred Anderson award, 1991, Disting. Svc. award Nat. Black Coalition of Fed. Aviation Employees, 1991, Paul K. Bohr award FAA, 1994, Nat. Performance Rev. Hammer award from V.P. Al Gore, 1996; A salute to Her Name in the Congl. Record 104th Congress, 1995. Mem. Nat. Assn Negro Bus. and Profl, Women (North to the Future club, charter pres. 1975-76), Blacks in Govt., Nat. Black Coalition of Fed. Aviation Employees (pres. cen. region chpt. 1987-92, Over Achievers award, 1987, Disting. Svc. award 1988), Profl. Women Contrs. Orgn., Air Traffic Contrs. Assn., Fed. Mgrs. Assn., Internat. Platform Assn., Women in Mgmt. (del. Soviet Union), Gamma Phi Delta. Democrat. Baptist. Avocations: singing; sewing. Home: 5770-D2 Great Northern Blvd North Olmsted OH 44070 Office: FAA 326 E Lorain St Oberlin OH 44074-1216

WILLIAMS, ELIZABETH EVENSON, writer; b. Sioux Falls, S.D., Sept. 25, 1940; d. A. Duane and Eleanor (Kelton) Evenson; m. Louis P. Williams Jr., Aug. 31, 1968; 1 child, Katherine. BS, S.D. State U., 1962; MA, U. Wis., 1964; postgrad., U. Minn., 1969-70; MA, S.D. State U., 1983, postgrad., 1992—. Dir. pubs. No. State Coll., Aberdeen, S.D., 1965-68; instr. journalism S.D. State U., Brookings, 1968-69, 85—; asst. editor Journalism Quar., Mpls., 1969-70; pub. info. specialist S.D. Com. on Humanities, Brookings, 1975-78; asst. and instr. speech dept. S.D. State U., Brookings, 1981-92; part-time dir. Women's Ctr., Brookings, 1988-90; reading series coord. S.D. Com. on Humanities, Brookings, 1986-91. Author: Emil Loriks: Builder of a New Economic Order, 1987, More Reflections of a Prairie Daughter, 1993; weekly columnist Brookings Daily Register, 1985-92, RFD News, 1992-95; contbr. articles to profl. jours. Vestry mem. St. Paul's Ch., Brookings, 1975-76, 84-86, 92—, sr. warden, 1995—; pres. LWV of S.D., 1985-89, treas., 1990-92. S.D. Humanities Com. grantee, 1984, 87, 90. Mem. Nat. Fedn. Press Women (1st place nat. writing contest 1977), Phi Kappa Phi, Pi Kappa Delta, Alpha Kappa Delta. Episcopalian. Home: 1103 3rd St Brookings SD 57006-2230 Office: SD State U Journalism Dept Brookings SD 57007

WILLIAMS, GALE R., realtor; b. Ava, Ill., Aug. 3, 1922; s. Denton Hubert and Bertha Mae (Lively) W.; m. Helen R. Falkenheim, Dec. 9, 1947. Student, So. Ill. U., John Logan Jr. Coll. Elected Jackson County Coroner, Springfield, Ill., 1956-60; state rep. State of Ill, Springfield, 1960-70; mobile home sales Springfield, 1960—. With USMC, 1945-46. Mem. Elks, Am. Legion, Masons, Mississippi Valley Consistory, Murphysboro C. of C. Republican. Baptist. Home: 1408 Roberta Dr Murphysboro IL 62966

WILLIAMS, GILBERT THOMAS, systems engineer, consultant; b. New Bern, N.C., Dec. 29, 1956; s. Clayton Olan and Dawn Vernice (Hart) W. BS, Jacksonville State U., 1977; postgrad., Case Western Res. U., 1990—. Programmer Computer Sci. Corp., Huntsville, Ala., 1978-81; engr. Nat. Aeronautics & Space Adminstrn., Huntsville, 1981-83, Honeywell, Inc., Hopkins, Minn., 1983-86; systems engr. Westinghouse Electric Co., Cleve., 1986-95; founder 4C cons., Richmond Heights, Ohio, 1994—; propr. Williams Oil and Gas, Richmond Heights, 1989—. Inventor in field; contvr. articles to profl. jours. Mem. Heritage Found., Wilderness Soc. Recipient Snoopy award NASA, Huntsville, 1980, cert. of appreciation NASA, 1983. Mem. AAAS, IEEE, Am. Motorcycle Assn., Assn. for Computing Machinery. Office: 4C Cons 25101 Chardon Rd Richmond Heights OH 44143

WILLIAMS, GLEN E., small business owner; b. Broken Bow, Nebr., July 31, 1954; s. Ray E. and Gertrude C. (Fehr) W.; m. Beth E. Williams, Jan. 4, 1974; children: Emily, Joseph, Meridith. BS in Edn., U. Nebr., 1977; MS in Edn., Ctrl. States U., Edmond, Okla., 1986. Tchr. Tekamah Pub. Sch., Nebr., 1977-78; asst. zone svc. mgr. motor divsn. Chevrolet, Omaha, 1978-1987, Houston, 1978-1987, Oklahoma City, 1978-1987, Kansas City, Mo., 1978-1987; svc. mgr. Classic Cadillac, Omaha, 1987-89; owner operator Williams Sales Svc., Ashland, Nebr., 1989—. Bd. dirs. Nebr. Assn. Sch. Bd., Lincoln, 1990-91; mem. sch. bd. Ashland Greenwood Schs., 1988—. Republican. Home: 401 N 12th Ashland NE 68003-1338 Office: Williams Sales Svc Inc 204 S 23d St Ashland NE 68003

WILLIAMS, HOPE DENISE, academic administrator, business consultant; b. Chgo., Dec. 24, 1952; d. Welmon and Mary Ann (Brefford) Walker; children: Albert Lee, Ebony Emani Denise. Student Ill. State U., 1971-72. BA in Psychology, St. Ambrose Coll., 1975, postgrad. bus. adminstrn. 1985—; postgrad. Harvard U. Grad. Sch. Design, summer 1981, Nat. Assn. Collegiate Athletic Adminstrs./Higher Edn. Resources Summer Inst., 1995. Social svc. dir. Friendly House, Davenport, Iowa, 1977-78; data collector, cons., 1978; supr. CETA/Summer Youth Employment Program, Davenport, 1978; lead organizer Central and Western Neighborhood Devel. Corp., Davenport, 1978-79; exec. dir. Inner City Devel. Corp., Davenport, 1980-83; owner Midwestern Internat. Mktg. Assocs., San Francisco, 1983; ops. mgr. Dramatic Mktg. Assn., San Francisco, 1983-85; adminstrv. asst. Parker Ross Assocs., 1984-85; crisis intervention counselor Cath. Social Svcs., 1985-86; adminstrv. intern Scott County Iowa, 1985-87; counselor Marycrest Coll., Davenport, 1986-87, asst. dean, 1987-90, dir. of advising, 1989-90; dir. spl. svcs. Augustana Coll., Rock Island, Ill., 1990, asst. dean of students svcs., 1991—; bus. cons. Incorporator, sec. bd. dirs. United Neighbors Inc., 1980; bd. dirs. Community Health Care, 1978-80; v.p., treas. Athletes Say More Edn., 1980; treas., exec. com. F&A Community Warehouse, 1982—; bd. dirs. HELP Legal Aid, 1987—, v.p., 1990, pres., 1991, allocations panel United Way, 1987—. Recipient cert. of appreciation Palmer Jr. Coll., Davenport, 1979, Personal Dedication plaque Jr. Achievement, 1988, 89, 90; cert. of merit Ch. Women United, 1983; NEH grantee, 1979; presdl. grantee Palmer Jr. Coll., 1978. Mem. NAFE, Assn. Black Women Higher Edn., Nat. Assn. Women Edn. (nat. treas. 1993, Dorothy Truex award for Emerging Profls. 1994), Quad Cities Career Womens Network (treas., exec. com.), Assn. Acad. Affairs Adminstrs. (bd. dirs. 1989—, award for new profls. 1989, treas. 1992—), Nat. Assn. for Blacks at Predominately White Instns. (v.p. fin.), Nat. Acad. Advisors Assn., Nat. Assn. Acad. Advisors (bd. dirs. 1988), Quad Cities Assn. Black Sch. Educators (founding, charter, treas. 1993), Quad City Negro Heritage Soc., Assn. Black Profls. (chairperson), Nat. Assn. Black MBAs, Alpha Kappa Alpha (chair connection com. Xi Eta Omega chpt. 1989, pres. 1990—, mem. internat. stds. com. 1994—), Quad Cities Strivers Inc. (bd. dirs.). Author narrative and final report for oral history project, 1979. Home: 1217 Ripley St Davenport IA 52803 Office: 639 38th St Rock Island IL 61201-2210

WILLIAMS, JACK RAYMOND, civil engineer; b. Barberton, Ohio, Mar. 14, 1923; s. Charles Baird and Mary (Dean) W.; m. Mary Berneice Jones, Mar. 5, 1947 (dec.); children: Jacqueline Rae, Drew Alan; m. Betty Ruth Scholfield, Nov. 9, 1990. Student Colo. Sch. Mines, 1942-43, Purdue U., 1944-45; BS, U. Colo., 1946. Gravity and seismograph engr. Carter Oil Co., Western U.S. and Venezuela, 1946-50; with Rock Island R.R., Chgo., 1950-80, structural designer, asst. to engr. bridges, asst. engr. bridges, 1950-63, engr. bridges system, 1963-80; sr. bridge engr. Thomas K. Dyer Inc., 1980-82; v.p. Alfred Benesch & Co., 1982-96. Served with USMCR, 1943-45. Fellow ASCE; mem. Am. Concrete Inst., Am. Ry. Bridge and Bldg. Assn. (past pres.), Am. Ry. Engring. Assn. (past chmn. com. 8, Concrete and Foundations). Home: 293 Minocqua St Park Forest IL 60466-1942

WILLIAMS, JACKSON JAY, education consultant; b. Mitchell, Ind., Sept. 14, 1961; s. Jackie Eugene and Judith Ann (Chastain) W. Student, Drake U., 1979-80, 81-84, George Williams Coll., 1984-85; BS in Leisure and Environ. Resource Adm., Aurora U., 1986; MS in Experiential Edn., Mankato (Minn.) State U., 1990; postgrad., U. Ky., 1992—. Course instr., coord. George Williams Coll., Williams Bay, Wis., 1984-86; course dir. Inner Quest Inc., Leesburg, Va., 1986-88; instr. Voyager Outward Bound Sch., Ely, Minn., 1989; challenge course coord., Outdoor Edn. Inst. Tex. A&M U., Coll. Sta., 1990-91; substitute tchr. Mitchell (Ind.) H.S., 1994-95; grad. asst., dept. ednl. policy studies U. Ky., Lexington, 1995—; cons. Ednl. Consultants, Mitchell, 1990—; cons. Chgo. Area Girl Scout Coun., 1985. CPR instr. ARC, Ill., Iowa 1980-88. Ill. State Scholar, 1979; recipient Vigil Honor, Order of the Arrow, Boy Scouts Am., 1979. Mem. Assn. Experiential Edn., Assn. for Challenge Course Tech., Ohio Valley Philosophy of Edn. Soc., Nat. Eagle Scout Assn., Mitchell (Ind.) C. of C., Loyal Order of Moose. Home: 516 Marion St Mitchell IN 47446 Office: Univ Kentucky Dept Ednl Policy Studies 134 Taylor Education Bldg Lexington KY 40506

WILLIAMS, JACKSON TAYLOR, legislative director, lawyer; b. Chgo., Sept. 4, 1963; s. John Taylor and Sheila Ann (Morris) W. BA, U. Ill., Chgo., 1985; JD, Loyola U., Chgo., 1988. Bar: Ill. 1988, U.S. Supreme Ct. Asst. state's atty. Sangamon County, Springfield, Ill., 1989-90; assoc. Choi & Schugg, Chgo., 1990-92; legis. dir. Def. Rsch. Inst., Chgo., 1993—. Editor Chgo. Bar Record, 1995; contbr. articles to profl. jours. Bd. dirs. Edgewater Cmty. Coun., Chgo., 1990-92, Ind. Voters of Ill., 1990-91, Young Dems. of Cook County, Chgo., 1985-88. Recipient Disting. Svc. award Chgo. Vol. Legal Svcs., 1995; named Young Dem. of Yr., Young Dems. of Cook County, 1987. Mem. Chgo. Bar Assn. (chair bench-bar com. 1993-94). Office: The Def Rsch Inst 750 N Lake Shore Dr Ste 5 Chicago IL 60611-4403

WILLIAMS, JEFFRY CEPHAS, business executive; b. Streator, Ill., Jan. 3, 1960; s. Kenneth Joseph Williams and Betty Patricia (Brooks) Brassfield; m. Linda Ann Danko, Oct. 1, 1993. B of Fin., Ill. State U., Normal, 1982, B of Econs., 1982. Corp. sec. Westgate, Inc., Streator, 1977—, Chris' Flower Shop, Inc., Streator, 1985—, Wilfield, Inc., Streator, 1986—. Sec. Streator Police Pension Bd., 1992—; co-chair KEEP Com., Streator, 1992; mem. budget com. United Way, Streator. Mem. Masons. Office: Westgate Inc 116 S 1st St PO Box 942 Streator IL 61364-0942

WILLIAMS, JOHN ALBERT, developmental disabilities agency director; b. Terre Haute, Ind., Aug. 6, 1941; s. Ralph and Hazel Isabella (Kane) W.; m. Phyllis Jean Cooper, Aug. 15, 1959 (div. 1969); children: Sherri, John, David, Michael; m. Sandra Adair Smedley Hobson, Oct. 6, 1973; stepchildren: Scott Hobson, Laura Rude, Elizabeth Watters. BS Therapeutic Recreation, Ind. U., 1969. Lic. health facility adminstr., Ind. Dir. recreation therapy dept. Larue D. Carter Meml. Hosp., Indpls., 1960-72; coord. activity therapy Quinco Consulting Ctr., Columbus, Ind., 1972-74; regional dir. Mental Health Assn. in Ind., Indpls., 1974-76; exec. dir. Johnson County Assn. for Retarded Citizens, Franklin, Ind., 1976-78; adminstr. Fountainview Place of Indpls., 1978-80; mgr. youth employment and tng. program Occupational Devel. Ctr. Area J, Madison, Ind., 1980-82; adminstr. Columbus Nursing Home, 1982-83; dir. staff devel./quality assurance Muscatatuck State Devel. Ctr., Butlerville, Ind., 1983-87; co-exec. dir. Archer Consultation Svcs., Inc., North Vernon, Ind., 1986—; chief cons. Leo Consultation Svcs.; cons., instr. Indiana Health Care Assn.; tchr. geriatric programming corr. course, ind. study div. Ind. U.; exec. dir. Arrow Consultation Svcs., Inc., On Target, Inc. Former pres. Ind. Soc. Health Facility Adminstrs. Named Ky. Col., Gov. of Ky., 1987; recipient Little Buck of Muscatatuck citation, 1987. Mem. Lions (pres. North Vernon chpt.), Phi Epsilon Kappa, Sigma Lamda Sigma. Home: 4102 Ridgeway Ave Columbus IN 47203-1145 Office: Archer Consultation Svcs PO Box 947 North Vernon IN 47265-0947

WILLIAMS, JOHN LOUIS, principal; b. Toledo, Ohio, June 6, 1948; s. Paul Anthony and Lillian Rose (Antesberger) W.; m. Susan Elizabeth Lane, Aug. 7, 1970; children: Elizabeth, Melissa, Rebecca. BA in Edn., U. Mich., 1971, MA in Edn., 1973. Cert. tchr. Mich.; cert. secondary adminstr. Mich. Tchr. English and psychology Howell (Mich.) High Sch., 1971-74, dean students, 1974-75; asst. prin. Indian Hills High Sch., Cin., 1975-77; prin. Chelsea (Mich.) High Sch., 1977-89, Capital Area Career Ctr., Ingham Ind. Sch. Dist., Mason, Mich., 1989—; charter mem. Adminstr. Cert. Commn., State of Mich., 1989-92, periodic rev. commn., 1993—. Contbg. author handbook: The Principalship, 1988. Active Chelsea Area Players, 1982—. Mem. Mich. Occup. Edn. Assn. (bd. dirs. 1991—), Mich. ASCD, Mich. Assn. Secondary Sch. Prins. (exec. bd. 1986-89, 93-95), Area Career-Tech. Adminstrs. (pres. 1992—), Re-Thinking Edn. K-16 State of Mich., Mich. Congress Vocat. Adminstrn. (pres.-elect 1995-96). Home: 750 Darwin Dr Chelsea MI 48118-1152 Office: Capital Area Career Ctr Ingham Ind Sch Dist 611 Hagadorn Rd Mason MI 48854-9357

WILLIAMS, JOHN MICHAEL, physical therapist, sports medicine educator; b. Columbus, Ohio, Oct. 19, 1951; s. James Hutchison and Helen Lucille (Knight) W.; m. Karen Sue Eaglen, June 23, 1973; children: Michelle Rene, Elizabeth Ann. BS in Phys. Therapy, Ohio State U., 1975, MS in Allied Medicine, 1983. Lic. phys. therapist, Ohio. Asst. dir. phys. therapy Licking Meml. Hosp., Newark, Ohio, 1978-80; pvt. practice phys. therapy Westerville, Ohio, 1977-80; asst. dir. rehab. St. Anthony Hosp., Columbus, 1980-88; chief phys. therpist St. Ann's Sports Medicine, Westerville, 1988-90, dir., 1990-92, dir. phys. and sports medicine, 1992-95; mgr. Nova Care Rehab., 1995—; clin. instr. Ohio State U., Columbus, 1984—; adj. faculty sports medicine Otterbein Coll., Westerville, 1989—; cons. Licking County Arthritis Found., Newark, 1978-80; mem. phys. therapy adv. bd. Ctrl. Ohio Tech. Coll., Newark, 1978—; bd. dirs. SAHCU Credit Union, Westerville, 1989—. Author monograph. Med. team capt. Columbus Marathon, 1989—, U.S. Men's Olympic Marathon Trials, Columbus, 1992. Lt. col. USAR, 1969—. Decorated Army Commendation medal; recipient Mayor's award for vol. svc. City of Columbus, 1993. Mem. Am. Acad. Med. Adminstrs., Am. Phys. Therapy Assn. (rep. to state assembly 1987—), Rotary Internat. Episcopalian. Home: 132 Ormsbee Ave Westerville OH 43081

WILLIAMS, JOHN TROY, librarian, educator; b. Oak Park, Ill., Mar. 11, 1924; s. Michael Daniel and Donna Marie (Shaffer) W.; B.A., Central Mich. U., 1949; M.A. in Libr. Sci., U. Mich., 1951, M.A., 1954; Ph.D., Mich. State U., 1973. Reference libr. U. Mich., Ann Arbor, 1955-59; instr. Bowling Green (Ohio) State U., 1959-60; reference librarian Mich. State U., East Lansing, 1960-62; 1st asst. reference dept. Flint (Mich.) Pub. Library, 1962-65; head reference svcs., Purdue U., West Lafayette, Ind., 1965-72; head pub. svcs. No. Ill. U., Dekalb, 1972-75; asst. dean, asst. univ. libr. Wright State U., Dayton, Ohio, 1975-80; vis. scholar U. Mich., Ann Arbor, 1980—; cons. in field. Served with U.S. Army, 1943-46. Mich. State fellow, 1963-64; HEW fellow, 1971-72. Mem. Am. Libr. Assn., Spl. Libraries Assn., Am. Soc. for Info. Scis., Am. Sociol. Assn., AAUP, Coun. on Fgn. Rels. Contbr. articles to profl. jours. Home: PO Box 7531 Ann Arbor MI 48107-7531

WILLIAMS, JULIE BELLE, psychiatric social worker; b. Algona, Iowa, July 29, 1950; d. George Howard and Leta Maribelle (Durschmidt) W. BA, U. Iowa, 1972, MSW, 1973. Lic. psychologist, ind. clin. social worker, marriage and family therapist, Minn.; lic. social worker, Iowa. Social worker Psychopathic Hosp., Iowa City, 1971-72; OEO counselor YOUR, Webster City, Iowa, 1972; social worker Child Devel. Clinic, Iowa City, 1973; therapist Mid-Eastern Iowa Community Mental Health Ctr., Iowa City, 1973; psychiat. social worker Mental Health Ctr. No. Iowa, Mason City, 1974-79, chief psychiat. social worker, 1979-80; asst. dir. Community Counseling Ctr., White Bear Lake, Minn., 1980-85, dir., 1985—; lectr., cons. in field. NIMH grantee, 1972-73. Mem. NASW (Acad. Cert. Social Workers, Qualified Clin. Social Workers, diplomate), NOW, Am. Orthopsychiat. Assn., Am. Assn. Sex Educators, Counselors and Therapists, Minn. Women Psychologists, Minn. Lic. Psychologists, Phi Beta Kappa. Democrat. Office: 1280 N Birch Lake Blvd White Bear Lake MN 55110

WILLIAMS, KENNETH EUGENE, advertising specialist; b. Weyburn, Sask., Can., July 17, 1955; came to U.S., 1960; s. Claude Dennis and Audrey (Ireland) W.; m. Kelly Sue Minton, Aug. 13, 1988; 1 child, Megan Ann. BS in Radio, TV and Film, N.W. Mo. State U., 1977; MBA, Calif. Coast U., 1992. With pub. rels. dept. Reorganized Ch. of Jesus Christ of Latter-day Saints, Independence, Mo., 1977-83; account exec. Mast Advt. and Pub., Overland Park, Kans., 1983-84, Kansas City (Mo.) Star Newspaper, 1984-86, Christenson, Barclay & Shaw, Overland Park, 1986-87; regional account supr. Young & Rubicam, N.Y.C., 1987-92; in-store adv. mgr. Associated Wholesale Grocers, 1992—. Named one of Outstanding Young Men of Am., 1986. Democrat. Home: 3712 NE Beechwood Dr Lees Summit MO 64064-1895

WILLIAMS, LESLIE ANN, art historian; b. Allentown, Pa., Dec. 15, 1941; d. Edgar Daniel and Merle Leslie (Williamson) Leibensperger; m. William H.A. Williams, June 27, 1964; children: Bill, Lavinia. BA, U. Pa. Coll. for Women, 1963; MA (hon.), U. Ireland, Dublin, 1971; PhD, Ind. U., Blomington, 1990. Lectr. Gesamt Hoch Schule Kassel, Kassel, Germany, 1972-74; curator Phoneix Art Mus., 1974-76; producer, writer Young & Rubicam, Bozell & Jacobs, Phoenix, 1977-80; officer Ariz. State Govt., Phoenix, 1980-81; grant writer, curator Ariz. State U., Phoenix, 1982-83; Kress fellow Samuel Kress Found., London, 1985-86; asst. dir. Collins Living Learning Ctr., Bloomington, Ind., 1986-87; vis. asst. prof. Ohio U., Athens, 1988-89; assoc. prof. U. Cin., 1989—, head humanities and social scis., 1996—; consulting curator Handicapped Artists of Ariz., Phoenix, 1979. Author: A Bear in the Air, 1976, What's Behind That Tree, 1982, What is Work?, 1969; author, producer Infrared Reflectoraphy, 1984, Africans in Western Art, 1993. Pres. Ariz. Women's Caucus for Art, Phoenix, 1978; liaison officer McCluskey for Cong., Bloomington, Ind., 1986. Recipient Ariz. Humanities Coun. award NEH, 1981-83, IBM Multicultural Humanities, IBM, 1992, Lily Lecture prize Ind. U., Bloomington; fellow Samuel Kress Found., London, 1985-86. Mem. Medieval Acad. Ireland, Coll. Art Assn., Victorian Inst., Midwest Victorian Studies Assn., Midwestern Art History Soc., Sixteenth Century Studies Assn. Democrat. Office: Univ Cin M L # 206 Cincinnati OH 45221

WILLIAMS, LYNN ROY, mathematics and statistics educator, consultant; b. Detroit, Apr. 23, 1945; s. John Thomas and Elsie Loraine (Rowland) W.; m. Cynthia Sue Cardea, June 24, 1967 (div. June 1983); children: Delania Kathryn, Kristina Lynn; m. Julie Marie Jenkins, May 18, 1984; 1 child, Matthew Thomas. BA, King Coll., Bristol, Tenn., 1967; MS, U. Ky., 1968, PhD, 1971. Asst. prof. La. State U., Baton Rouge, 1971-75; asst. prof. math. Ind. U., South Bend, 1975-77, assoc. prof., 1977-88, prof., 1988—, assoc. dean Coll. Liberal Arts and Scis., 1992—, acting dean Coll. Liberal Arts, 1995-97; vis. scientist Oak Ridge Nat. Lab., 1987-88, cons., 1979—; vis. scholar U. N.C., Chapel Hill, 1980-81. Author: Embeddings and Extensions in Analysis, 1975. NSF grantee, 1973, 80, Martin Marietta Corp. grantee, 1987. Mem. Am. Math. Soc. Office: Ind U South Bend PO Box 7111 South Bend IN 46634-7111

WILLIAMS, MARILYN, state legislator. Mem. Mo. Ho. of Reps. from 159th dist., 1993—. Democrat. Address: Rte 1 Box 98 Dudley MO 63936 Office: Mo Ho of Reps State Capitol Building Jefferson City MO 65101-1556*

WILLIAMS, MARK ALLEN, secondary education educator; b. Gallipolis, Ohio, Apr. 18, 1959; s. Bertha Maxine (West) Williams; m. Carol Ann Wagner, June 20, 1987; 1 child, Andrew James. Vocat. cert., Gallia-Jackson-Vinton Joint Vocat. Sch., Rio Grande, Ohio, 1977; BS, Rio Grande Coll., 1981; MEd, Bowling Green State U., 1983; postgrad., Ohio State Univ. Cert. vocat. supr., dir. and high sch./vocat. bus. and mktg. edn. tchr. Bus. tchr. New Boston (Ohio) Local Schs., 1980-82; med. secretarial coord. 4 County Joint Vocat. Sch. Dist., Archbold, Ohio, 1983; instr. clerical svcs. Pickaway-Ross Joint Vocat. Sch. Dist., Chillicothe, Ohio, 1983-85, instr. stenography, 1986-90; curriculum cons. Ohio Dept. Edn., Columbus, 1985-86; bus. and comm. instr. Hayes Tech. High Sch., Grove City, Ohio, 1990—; adj. instr. Ohio U., Chillicothe, 1985-88; editor Instrnl. Materials Lab., Columbus, 1985-86; participant, spkr., counselor Bus. Leadership Inst. Bowling Green U., 1993-94, Captial U., 1995-96; mem., auditing chairperson Nat. Policies Commn. for Bus. and Econ. Edn., 1992, auditing chair, 1993-94. Contbr. articles to profl. jours.; co-author curricular supplements. Active St. Thomas R. More Cath. Newman Ctr., Columbus, 1987—; trustee Rio Grande Coll., 1987-89; chmn. endorsement and nominating com. Franklin County Dem., 4th ward committeeman Grove City; mem. Grove City and Jackson Twp. Dems. Club, 1989—, Kellar Farms Civic Assn., 1987-95; past officer Jaycees, Chillicothe, 1983-88; mem. Our Lady of Perpetual Help parish, Grove City, sch. bd., tuition com., chair nominating com. and elections com.; del. Am.-Russian Exch. for Vocat. Edn., 1996; participant and peer assistance leader South-Western City Schs. Future Leaders, 1995-97. Merit scholar Bus. Profls. Am., 1986, 90; recipient Super Advisor award Office Edn. Assn., 1984, Bus. Edn. New Profl. award Ohio Vocat. Assn., 1987, 88. Mem. NEA, Nat. Bus. Edn. Assn., North Ctrl. Bus. Edn. Assn. (Secondary Tchr. of Yr. 1991), Nat. Assn. Classroom Educators Bus. Edn. Assn. (nominating com. chair 1993, 94, 95), Am. Vocat. Assn., Bus. Profls. Am. (nat. pres. alumni divsn. 1993-94), Ohio Vocat. Assn. (bus. edn. membership chair 1992-95, Tchr. of Yr. 1993), Ohio Bus. Tchrs. Assn. (advt. mgr. 1987-90, exec. bd. 1987-90, Tchr. of Yr. 1990), Ctrl. Ohio Bus. Tchrs. Assn. (chair 1992, 93), Alpha Sigma Phi (grand councilor 1994-96, nat. dir. scholarship 1990—, grand province chief 1990-94, Milestone Svc. award 1991), Delta Beta Xi (award 1990), Delta Pi Epsilon, Pi Omega Pi. Democrat. Roman Catholic. Home: 3600 Sterling Park Cir G Grove City OH 43123-2982 Office: Hayes Tech High Sch 4436 Haughn Rd Grove City OH 43123-3219

WILLIAMS, MARTHA ETHELYN, information science educator; b. Chgo., Sept. 21, 1934; d. Harold Milton and Alice Rosemond (Fox) W. B.A., Barat Coll., 1955; M.A., Loyola U., 1957. With IIT Rsch.Inst., Chgo., 1957-72, mgr. info. scis., 1962-72, mgr. computer search ctr., 1968-72; adj. assoc. prof. sci. info. Ill. Inst. Tech., Chgo., 1965-73, lectr. chemistry dept., 1968-70, rsch. prof. info. sci., coordinated sci. lab. Coll. engring.; also dir. info. retrieval research lab. U. Ill., Urbana, 1972—, prof. info. sci. grad. sch. of libr. info. sci., 1974—, affiliate, computer sci. dept., 1979—; chmn. large data base conf. Nat. Acad. Sci./NRC, 1974, mem. ad hoc panel on info. storage and retrieval, 1977, numerical data adv. bd., 1979-82, computer sci. and tech. bd., nat. rsch. network rev. com., 1987-88, chmn. utility subcom., 1987-88; mem. task force on sci. info. activities NSF, 1977; U.S. rep. review com. for project on broad system of ordering, UNESCO, Hague, Netherlands, 1974; vice chmn. Gordon Rshc. Conf. on Sci. Info. Problems in Rsch., 1978, chmn., 1980; mem. panel on intellectual property rights in age of electronics and info. U.S. Congress, Office of Tech. Assessment; program chmn. Nat. Online Meeting, 1980—; cons. to numerous cos., govt. agys. and rsch. founds.; invited lectr. Commn. European Communities, Industrial R&D adv. com., Brussels, 1992. Editor in chief Computer-Readable Databases Directory and Data Sourcebook, 1976-89, founding editor, 1989-92; editor Ann. Rev. Info. Sci. and Tech., 1976—, Online Rev., 1979-92, Online and CDROM Rev., 1993—, procs. nat. online meeting, 1981—; contbg. editor column on databases to Bull. Am. Soc. Info. Sci., 1974-78; mem. editorial adv. bd. Database, 1978-88; mem. editorial bd. Info. Processing and Mgmt., 1982-89, The Reference Libr.; contbr. more than 200 articles to profl. jours. Trustee Engirng. Info., Inc., 1974-87, bd. dirs., 1976-91, chmn. bd. dirs., 1982-91, v.p., 1978-79, pres., 1980-81; regent Nat. Libr. Medicine, 1978-82, chmn. bd. regents, 1981; mem. task force on sci. info. activities NSF, 1977-78; mem. nat. adv. com. ACCESS ERIC, 1989-91. Recipient best paper of year award H. W. Wilson Co., 1975; NSF travel grantee Luxembourg, 1972; NSF travel grantee Honolulu, 1973; NSF travel grantee Tokyo, 1973; NSF travel grantee Mexico City, 1975; NSF travel grantee Scotland, 1976. Fellow AAAS (computers, info. and comm. mem.-at-large 1978-81, nominating com. 1983, 85), Inst. Info. Sci. (hon.); mem. NAS (joint com. with NRC on chem. info. 1971-73), Am. Chem. Soc., Am. Soc. Info. Sci. (councilor 1971-72, 87-89, chmn. networks com. 1973-74, spl. interest group of SDI 1974-75, pres.-elect 1986-87, pres. 1987-88, past pres., mem. planning com. 1988-89, publs. com. 1974—, chmn. 1989, mem. nominations com. 1989, chmn. budget and fin. com. 1987-89, award of merit 1984, Pioneer Info. Sci. award 1987, Watson Davis award 1995), Assn. for Computing Machinery (pub. bd. 1972-76), Assn. Sci. Info. Dissemination Ctrs. (v.p. 1971-73, pres. 1975-77), Internat. Fedn. for Documentation (U.S. nat. com.). Home: 2134 Sandra Ln Monticello IL 61856-9801 Office: U Ill 1308 W Main St Urbana IL 61801-2307

WILLIAMS, MARY ALICE BALDWIN, retired home economist, volunteer consultant; b. St. Louis, Mar. 24, 1928; d. Ulysses Grant and Irene (Jenkins) Gray; m. Earl Randolph Baldwin, June 28, 1952 (div. 1973); 1 child, Arlene Denise; m. Robert Williams Jr., Dec. 21, 1985. BS, Lincoln U., 1952; MA, Webster U., 1971; postgrad., Harris Stowe Tchrs. Coll., 1976-78, Cen. Mo. State U., 1979-80, U. Mo., 1981-82. Cert. home economist, Mo. Tchr. home econs. Cen. High Sch., Hayti, Mo., 1952-53, Cleve. Pub. Schs., 1953-56; tchr. elem. sch. St. Louis Pub. Schs., 1958-67, tchr. home econs., 1968-83, curriculum supr. home econs., 1984-93, cons. home econs. and character edn., 1993—; presenter workshops. Author curriculum materials in home econs. and character edn. Fund raising com. Annie Malone Children's Home, St. Louis, 1987-90; 75th anniversary com. YYWCA Phyllis Wheatley, St. Louis, 1988. Mem. Nat. Assn. Univ. Women (del. 1992), Am. Home Econs. Assn. (ethics com. 1990-92, population com. 1990-91), Mo. Home Econs. Assn. (tchr. rep. 1988-90), Am. Vocat. Assn., Mo. Vocat. Assn. (legis. com.), St. Louis Home Econs. Tchrs. Assn. (founder, adviser), Lincoln Univ. Alumni Assn. (chair founders day), Delta Sigma Theta. Home: 4910 Maffitt Pl Saint Louis MO 63113-1727

WILLIAMS, MAXINE ELEANOR, retired elementary education educator; b. Birmingham, Ala., Nov. 8, 1940; d. Ocie and Annie Bell (McCants)

Easter; m. Ardre Dell Williams, Aug. 3, 1968 (div. 1988); children: Andrea Babett, Roxanne Denise, John Ashley. BS, Tuskegee Inst., 1963; MA, Mich. State U., 1970. Elem. tchr. Chester A. Moore Elem. Sch., Ft. Pierce, Fla., 1963-64, R.J. Wallis Elem. Sch., Kincheloe AFB, Mich., 1964-66, Alexander Elem. Sch., Grand Rapids, Mich., 1966-67, Brown St. Elem. Sch., Milw., 1967-68, Jefferson T.P.L.L., Milw., 1968-78; team leader Twenty First Sch., Milw., 1978-80; reading tchr. Bryant & Parkview Sch., Milw., 1980-81; reading resource tchr. Morse Mid. Sch., Milw., 1981-93, Parkman Mid. Sch., 1993—. Census ctr. vol. Morse Mid. Sch., 1990. Recipient Excellence Pin Milw. Pub. Schs., 1983. Mem. ACA, NAACP, Milw. Tchrs. Edn. Assn., Wis. State Reading Assn. Democrat. Home: 11706 N Silver Ave Thiensville WI 53097-3025

WILLIAMS, MELVIN DONALD, anthropologist, educator; b. Pitts., Feb. 3, 1933; s. Aaron and Gladys Virginia (Barnes) W.; m. Faye Wanda Strawder, June 20, 1958; children: Aaron Ellsworth, Steven Rodney, Craig Haywood. A.B., U. Pitts., 1955, M.A., 1969, Ph.D., 1973. Owner, operator Wholesale Periodical Distbn. Co., Pitts., 1955-66; instr. dept. sociology and anthropology Carlow Coll., 1969-71, asst. prof., 1971-75, chmn. dept. sociology and anthropology, 1973-75; assoc. prof. anthropology U. Pitts., 1976-79, adj. prof., 1979-82; prof. anthropology Purdue U., 1979-83, U. Md., College Park, 1983-88, U. Mich., Ann Arbor, 1988—; Olie B. O'Connor prof. Am. instns. Colgate U., 1976-77. Author: On the Street Where I Lived, Community in a Black Pentecostal Church, The Human Dilemma, The Black Middle Class, An Academic Village, Race for Theory; editor: Selected Readings in Afro-American Anthropology; contbr. articles to profl. publs. Co-chmn. project area com. Urban Redevel. Authority, Pitts., 1972—; co-dir. interdisciplinary family community project Western Psychiat. Inst. and Clinic, 1973-76; bd. dirs. Cath. Social Svc. of Allegheny County, Pa., 1973-76; coll. ombudsman, 1991-93, faculty senate, 1993-96. NSF field tng. fellow in anthropology, 1967; grantee, 1969-72; Community Action Pitts. grantee, 1969-71; Social Sci. Research Council grantee, 1974-75; Lilly Endowment grantee, 1980-83, 85-86; NDEA Title IV fellow, 1969. Fellow Am. Anthrop. Assn.; mem. African Studies Assn., AAAS, AAUP, Am. Sociol. Assn., Assn. Study Afro-Am. Life and History, Soc. for Psychol. Anthropology. Home: 520 W Washington St Ann Arbor MI 48103-4232

WILLIAMS, MICHAEL ALAN, psychologist; b. Cin., May 20, 1948; s. Chester and Gentry Mae (Canada) W.; m. Linda Ann Presswood, Aug. 8, 1970; children: Michael Alan II, Derrick Alexander. BA, U. Cin., 1970, MA, 1971, EdD, 1980. Instr. U. Cin., 1972-75; sch. psychologist Dayton Bd. Edn., Ohio, 1975-78; assoc. prof. Wright State U., Dayton, 1978—, coord. spl. edn. program, 1992—; clin. psychologist Profl. Psychol. Services, Dayton, 1981—; psychol. services coordinator Montgomery County Children's Services, Dayton, 1983-88; psychol. cons. Diversion Alternative for Youth, Dayton, 1990—; program mgr. Head Start Supplementary Tng. Program, Cin., 1973-74; cons. Ohio Luth. Synod, Dayton, 1981-83, Blacks in Govt., Dayton, 1982-85, Montgomery County, Stillwater Health Ctr., Dayton, 1982-86. Co-editor (book): Teaching in a Multicultural Pluralistic Society, 1982, 2d edit., 1987. Treas. Dayton Free Clinic and Counseling Ctr., Dayton, 1983; bd. dirs. Planned Parenthood Assn., Dayton, 1983, Miami Valley Literacy Coun., Dayton, 1990—, Dayton Mediation Ctr., 1995—. Named Outstanding Young Man Am., Jaycees, 1984, Top Ten African-Am. Males, Dayton chpt. Urban League, 1995; McCall Scholarship, 1966-70. Mem. Am. Psychol. Assn., Nat. Assn. Black Psychologists, Nat. Assn. Sch. Psychologists, Dayton Assn. Black Psychologists (v.p. 1986-88, pres. 1988-89), Mental Health Assn. (bd. dirs. 1985), Assn. Tchr. Educators. Home: 4830 Old Hickory Pl Dayton OH 45426-2149 Office: Wright State U 373 Millett Hall Dayton OH 45435

WILLIAMS, MICHAEL K., agricultural production educator; b. Buffalo, Sept. 11, 1947; s. Walter K. and Della M. (Murphy) W.; m. Donna F. Wissel, Sept. 5, 1969; children: Nathan S., Mandi A. BA, Hastings Coll., 1970. Tchr. Fremont (Nebr.) Pub. Schs., 1972-79; owner Archeles Greenhouses, Fremont, 1979-86; cons. ECO-Soils Sys. Inc., Lincoln, Nebr., 1986-88; owner, pres. PMC Inc., Fremont, 1989—. Mem. devel. and funding staff Camp Calvin Crest, Saunders County, 1983-85; dir. West African Corn Growers Project, USDA, Nebr. and Iowa, 1988-89. 1st lt. Nebr. N.G., 1969-75. Mem. Nat. Alliance Ind. Crop Cons., Nebr. Ind. Crop Cons. Assn. (bd. dirs. 1992-94, chair polit. com. 1994—). Home: 1143 Pebble Fremont NE 68025

WILLIAMS, MYRON DAVID, dean; b. Advance, Ind., July 28, 1947; s. David James and Margret (Stone) W.; m. B. Sue Wolfe, May 24, 1969; children: Noel David, Sara Renee. BA, Ky. Christian Coll., 1969; MRE, Lincoln Christian Sem., 1983; PhD, Mich. State U., 1989. Asst. min. to youth Indianola Ch. of Christ, Columbus, Ohio, 1969-70; youth min. 2d Ch. of Christ, Danville, Ill., 1971-74; min. youth and edn. Ctrl. Christian Ch., Ironton, Ohio, 1974-77; instr. N.Y. Christian Inst., Clarence, 1978-81; prof. Great Lakes Christian Coll., Lansing, Mich., 1981-91; prof. Cin. Bible Coll. & Sem., 1991-95, asst. dean, 1995-96, acad. dean, 1996—. Chmn. leadership bd. First Ch. of Christ, Florence, Ky., 1995-96. Mem. ASCD, Profl. Assn. Christian Educators, Phi Kappa Phi, Delta Epsilon Chi. Office: Cin Bible Coll & Sem 2700 Glenway Ave Cincinnati OH 45204

WILLIAMS, PAUL LEON, psychologist; b. Friendly, W.Va., Feb. 12, 1929; s. James Blaine and Katheryn Esther (Tennant) W.; m. Maryalice Walsh, Aug. 21, 1948; children: Patricia Mary, Robert James, Paul Leon Jr., Aaron Blaine. BS, Northwestern U., 1951; MS in Psychology, Ill. Inst. Tech., 1953, PhD in Psychology, 1966. Lic. psychologist, Wis., Ill. Staff psychologist Vernon Psychol. Lab., Chgo., 1951-54; testing adminstr. RR Donnelly & Sons, Chgo., 1954-56; cons., staff psychologist Booz Allen & Hamilton, Chgo., 1956-58; dir. employee rels. Chgo. Aerial Industries, Barrington, Ill., 1958-60; orgn. devel. assoc. Mead Johnson & Co., Evansville, Ind., 1960-62; from asst. prof. to assoc. prof., head dept. psychology S.D. State U., Brookings, 1962-67; prof. psychology, exec. v.p., dean Yankton (S.D.) Coll., 1967-71; from v.p. to pres. Vernon, Roache, Hodgson, Williams, Chgo. and Milw., 1971-81; pres. Paul L. Williams & Assocs., Waukesha, Wis., 1981—; adj. faculty Cardinal Stritch Coll., Milw., 1975&; bd. dirs. Wis. Sch. Profl. Psychology, 1995—. Co-author: (with Kenneth Krause) Study of Characteristics of Farm Manager Couples in South Dakota, 1967. With USN, 1946-48. Mem. Sigma Xi, Psi Chi, Pi Gamma Mu. Home and Office: 1931 A Springbrook N Waukesha WI 53186

WILLIAMS, PETER WILLIAM, religion educator; b. Hollywood, Fla., Aug. 8, 1944; s. William John and Harriet Elizabeth (Stacey) W.; m. Ruth Ann Alban, June 1, 1980; children: Jonathan A. Schneider, Dana A. Schneider. AB, Harvard U., 1965; MA, Yale U., 1967, M. Philosophy, 1968, PhD, 1970. Prof. religion Miami U., Oxford, Ohio, 1970—; disting. prof. Religion and Am. Studies, 1994—; dir. Program in Am. Studies. Author: America's Religions, 1990, Popular Religion in America, 1980; editor: Encyclopedia of the American Religious Experience, 1988, Encyclopedia of America Social History, 1993, Studies in Anglican History; mem. editorial bd. Anglican and Episcopal History, 1990—. Lay reader Episc. Diocese of So. Ohio. Mem. Am. Soc. Ch. History (coun. 1989-91), Am. Acad. Religion. Democrat. Episcopalian. Home: 206 Oakhill Dr Oxford OH 45056-2710 Office: Miami U Dept Religion The Old Manse Oxford OH 45056

WILLIAMS, PHILIP COPELAIN, gynecologist, obstetrician; b. Vicksburg, Miss., Dec. 9, 1917; s. John Oliver and Eva (Copelain) W.; B.S. magna cum laude, Morehouse Coll., 1937; M.D., U. Ill., 1941; m. Constance Shielda Rhetta, May 29, 1943; children—Philip, Susan Carol, Paul Rhetta. Intern, Cook County Hosp., Chgo., 1942-43, resident in ob-gyn, 1946-48; resident in gynecology U. Ill., 1948-49; practice medicine specializing in ob-gyn, Chgo., 1949—; mem. staff St. Joseph Hosp., Ill. Masonic Hosp., Cook County Hosp., McGaw Hosp.; clin. prof. Med. Sch. Northwestern U., Chgo. Bd. dirs. Am. Cancer Soc. Chgo. unit and Ill. div. Served with U.S. Army, 1943-45. Recipient Civic award Loyola U., 1970; Edwin S. Hamilton Interstate Teaching award, 1984; diplomate Am. Bd. Ob-Gyn, Fellow ACS, Internat. Coll. Surgeons; mem. AMA, Chgo., Ill. med. socs., AMA, Chgo. Gynecol. Soc. (treas. 1975-78, pres. 1980-81), Am. Fertility Soc., Inst. Medicine, N.Y. Acad. Scis., AAAS. Presbyn. Clubs: Barclay, Carlton, Plaza. Contbr. articles to profl. jours. Home: 1040 N Lake Shore Dr Chicago IL 60611-1165 Office: 200 E 75th St Chicago IL 60619-2249

WILLIAMS, REG ARTHUR, nursing educator, software programmer; b. Price, Utah, Mar. 8, 1944; s. Reginald Charles and Edna Katherine (Toson) W.; m. Cynthia Cook, Mar. 18, 1969 (div. 1986); 1 child, Bryan Kelly; m. Yvonne Marie Abdoo, Dec. 20, 1987; 1 child, Christina Marie. AS, Coll. Ea. Utah, 1964; BSN, U. Utah, 1968; M of Nursing, U. Wash., 1972, PhD, 1980. Cert. clin. specialit in psychiat. mental health nursing AACN. Commd. ensign USN, 1967, advanced through grades to capt., 1992; charge nurse Pensacola Naval Hosp., 1968-69, St. Albans Naval Hosp., 1969-71; nurse educator, asst. prof. U. Wash., 1973-78; chairperson psychiat.-mental health nursing U. Mich., Ann Arbor, 1980-84, 89-91, nurse educator, assoc. prof. Sch. Nursing, 1980—; mem. planning com. NIMH, Mich., 1989-92; mem. rsch. com. Mich. Dept. Mental Health, 1991—; reviewer Tri-Svcs. Nursing Rsch. Program, 1992-93, chairperson, 1994. Coll. Ea. Utah scholar, 1962-63, Shriners scholar, 1964-65; recipient Nat. Rsch. Svc. award NIH, 1978-80. Fellow Am. Acad. Nursing (nominations com. 1989-90); mem. Sigma Theta Tau (counselor 1991-93). Home: 2028 Collegewood St Ypsilanti MI 48197-1714 Office: U Mich School Nursing 400 N Ingalls St Ann Arbor MI 48109-2003

WILLIAMS, ROGER, academic administrator. Dir. Art Acad. Cin. Office: Art Acad of Cincinnati Office of Director 1125 Saint Gregory St Cincinnati OH 45202-1734

WILLIAMS, ROSS ARNOLD, computer systems engineer; b. Canton, Ohio, Feb. 28, 1953; s. Nick P. Williams and Dolores M. (Gilson) Kobzowicz; m. Kimberly Ann Werner, June 25, 1983; children: Michael, Emily. Student, Ohio State U., 1970-73; BA, U. Akron, 1977, MS, 1980; MA, Kent State U., 1994. Cert. computing profl. Computer sys. analyst Goodyear Tire and Rubber Co., Akron, Ohio, 1979-92, sr. computer applications analyst, 1992-95, sys. engr., 1995—; lectr. U. Akron, 1979-84. Mem. Assn. for Computing Machinery, Kappa Kappa Psi, Pi Mu Epsilon. Lutheran.

WILLIAMS, SHERDA KAYE, landscape architect; b. Berkeley, Calif., June 20, 1954; d. Cleo M. and Maudine (Bastin) W. BS in Forestry, Purdue U., 1976; M in Landscape Architecture, Ball State U., 1992. Registered forester, Ark. Unit forester Internat. Paper Co., Arkadelphia, Ark., 1977-86; grad. asst. Ball State U., Muncie, Ind., 1988-91; intern U.S. Nat. Pk. Svc., Washington, 1990; hist. landscape architect U.S. Nat. Pk. Svc., Omaha, 1992—. Co-author: (booklets) Oral History Guide for Landscape Historians, 1990, Landscape Development Plan-Morris Butler House, 1991. Recipient Honor award Am. Soc. Landscape Architects, 1991; scholarship recipient Garden Club Ind., 1991. Mem. Am. Hort. Soc., Alliance for Hist. Landscape Preservation, Bus. and Profl. Women (chairperson com. Ark. chpt. 1983, pres. Arkadelphia chpt. 1984), Sigma Lambda Alpha. Mem. Unitarian Universalist Ch. Office: US Nat Pk Svc 1709 Jackson St Omaha NE 68102-2513

WILLIAMS, SHIRLEY JEAN OOSTENBROEK AKERS, daycare provider, educator, writer; b. Kansas City, Kans., Feb. 18, 1931; d. James Ralph and Florence (Snodgrass) Akers; m. Raymond Gale Williams, Feb. 17, 1949; children: David Ray, James Ronald, Vickie Sue, Richard Gene, Randy Wayne. Tchr. Su-Z-Lu Ceramics, Kansas City, 1957-70, 78, 79; sch. bus. driver Argentine Transit Lines, Kansas City, 1959-69; ceramic tchr., owner Su-Z-Lu Ceramics, Tonganoxie, Kans., 1972-78; tchr. Ft. Leavenworth Army Post, Leavenworth, Kans., 1979-85; pres. Wagonettes Extension Homemakers Club, Forsyth, Mo., 1987-88; ceramic tchr. Crystal's Creations and Ceramic Shop, Drexel, Mo., 1996—; day-care provider for the elderly, 1990-93, 95—. Den mother Boy Scouts Am., Kansas City and Tonganoxie, 1955-66, instr., 1961; driver ARC, Kansas City, 1958-63, canteen chmn., campfire leader, 1961-64; contbr. Taney County Rep. newspaper, Forsyth, 1986-87, bd. dirs., 1987-91; mem. Univ.-Extension Coun. bd., 1988-91; vol., supt. ceramic divsn. Leavenworth County Fair, 1974-84; vol. tchr. Kester Found., 1956-57. Recipient 4-H Gold Clover, Taney County 4-H, 1987. Democrat. Home: PO Box 705 203 Willetta Drexel MO 64742-9110

WILLIAMS, THEODORE JOSEPH, JR., lawyer; b. Pitts., July 23, 1947; s. Theodore Joseph and Isabel (McAnulty) W.; m. Sherri Lynne Foust, July 4, 1970; children: Kelley Shields, Jonathan Stewart, Jordan Fuller. BA, Purdue U., 1969; JD, U. Tulsa, 1974. Bar: Ill. 1975, Mo. 1978, D.C. 1981, U.S. Ct. Appeals (7th cir.) 1975, U.S. Ct. Appeals (8th cir.) 1978, U.S. Ct. Appeals (D.C. cir.) 1988, U.S. Dist Ct. (ea. and we. dists.) Mo. 1978, U.S. Dist. Ct. (no., so. and cen. dists.) Ill. 1975, U.S. Dist. Ct. D.C. 1988, U.S. Ct. Mil. Appeals 1991, U.S. Supreme Ct. 1978. Asst. city prosecutor City of Tulsa, 1974; trial atty., law dept. Chgo. and North Western R.R., Chgo., 1975-78; assoc. Thompson and Mitchell, St. Louis, 1978-81; assoc. Shepherd, Sandberg & Phoenix, P.C., St. Louis, 1981-84, ptnr., 1984-88; ptnr., chmn. transp. law dept. Armstrong, Teasdale, Schlafly & Davis, St. Louis, 1988—. Assoc. editor Law. Jour., U. Tulsa, 1974. Treas. sch. bd. Mary Queen of Peace Sch., Webster Groves, Mo., 1986, v.p., 1987. Major U.S. Army Res., 1991—. Mem. ABA (vice chmn. rail and motor carrier law com., torts and ins. practice law sect. 1989-90, chair-elect 1990-91, chair 1991-92), Ill. Bar Assn., Mo. Bar Assn., Def. Rsch. Inst. (chair, railroad law commn. 1996—), Nat. Assn. R.R. Coun., We. Conf. Ry. Coun., Assn. ICC Practitioners, Maritime Law Assn., Internat. Assn. Def. Coun., Transp. Lawyers Assn., Assn. Transp. Practitioners. Republican. Roman Catholic. Office: Armstrong Teasdale Schlafly & Davis One Metropolitan Sq Saint Louis MO 63102

WILLIAMS, TONY (JOHN), English educator; b. Swansea, U.K., Jan. 11, 1946; came to U.S., 1984; s. Glyn and Margaret (Cunnick) W.; m. Kathleen Ensor, June 1, 1990. Tchrs. cert., Swansea (U.K.) Coll. Edn., 1967; BA with first class honors, Manchester (U.K.) U., 1970, PhD in Theology, 1974; MA in Film Studies, Warwick (U.K.) U., 1977. Tchr. Gravesend (U.K.) Sch. for Boys, Kent, 1974-77; rschr. in entertainment Bury (U.K.) Met. Coun., 1979-80; adminstr. No. Black Light Theatre, York, Eng., 1980-81; lectr. Coll. of Adult Edn., Manchester, 1981-84, Manchester (U.K.) U., 1981-84; assoc. prof. So. Ill. U., Carbondale, 1984—; cons. Jack London Rsch. Ctr., Sonoma, Calif., 1988—; adv. bd. Jack London Found., Sonoma, 1989—, Jack London Soc., France, 1994—; reviewer Cinema Jour., 1993—. Author: Jack London: The Movies, 1992, Hearths of Darkness, 1996; co-author: Italian Western, 1975; co-editor: Vietnam War Films, 1994; contbg. editor Viet Nam Generation, 1991—; editl. bd. mem. Jour. of Film and Philosophy, 1993—; contbr. articles to profl. jours. Named Jack London Man of Yr., Jack London Rsch. Ctr., Sonoma, 1989. Mem. Popular Culture Assn. (area chair 1989), Soc. for Cinema Studies, Manchester U. Film Soc. (life; v.p. 1972-73), Assn. Cinema and TV Technicians, Emile Zola Soc. (mem. editorial com. Excavatio 1992—). Office: Dept English So Ill Univ Carbondale IL 62901

WILLIAMS, VERNON J., JR., historian, educator, writer; b. Marshall, Tex., Apr. 25, 1948; s. Vernon J. Sr. and Vella D. (Roland) W.; m. Beverly Lynn Brown, Apr. 26, 1986 children: Vella L., Alexander M. BA in History, U. Tex., 1969; AM in Am. Civilization, Brown U., 1973, PhD in Am. Civilization, 1977. Instr. U. R.I., Kingstown, 1978; lectr. Clark U., Worcester, Mass., 1978-79; editor Edit, Inc., Chgo., 1979-80; lectr. Elmhurst Coll., Chgo., 1981-82; asst. prof. U. Iowa, Iowa City, 1985, R.I. Coll., Providence, 1985-90; lectr. Boston U., 1989-90; assoc. prof. Purdue U., West Lafayette, Ind., 1990—; rsch. assoc. William Monroe Trotter Inst., Boston, 1987, Boston U., 1989; archives cons. Boston Anthenaeum, 1989; cons. Henry Rasof Lit. Agy., Boston, 1989-90. Author: From a Caste to a Minority, 1989, Rethinking Race, 1996; editor New England Jour. Black Studies, 1990-94. Recipient Grant-in-Aid, Am. Coun. of Learned Socs., 1990; Clio grantee Ind. Hist. Soc., 1994. Mem. Nat. Assn. Ethnic Studies, Orgn. Am. Historians, So. Hist. Assn., Immigration History Soc. Office: Purdue Univ Dept History Lafayette IN 47907

WILLIAMS, W. VAIL, psychologist; b. Denver, Apr. 13, 1940; s. Warren J. and Edna M. (Follen) W.; m. Sandra M. Eisenrich (div. 1972); 1 child, Jason; m. Linda Lou Fain, Dec. 27, 1975; children: Ken, Dan, Davis, Jeremiah. BS, Bradley U., 1963, MA, 1964; PhD, U. Okla., 1968. Lic. psychologist, S.D., Colo., Calif. Owner Social Systems Devel., 1970-78; sr. psychologist Ft. Logan Mental Health Ctr., Denver, 1968-74; sr. rsch. assoc. Mental Rsch. Inst., Palo Alto, Calif., 1974-78; assoc. prof. Med. Sch. U. S. D., Sioux Falls, 1978—; chmn. curriculum and evaluation com. Sch. Medicine U. S.D., Sioux Falls, 1989-92; bd. dirs. Univ. Physicians, U. S.D. Sch. Medicine; cons. Charter Hosp., Sioux Falls, 1989-94; clin. dir. Psychiatry Assocs., 1989—. Contbr. to books and articles to profl. jours. Bd. dirs. S.D. Jr. Football Assn., Sioux Falls, 1988-92, Citizens Against Rape and Violence, Sioux Falls, 1988-89. Fellow Am. Orthopsychiat. Assn.; mem. APA, AAAS, S.D. Psychol. Assn. (pres. Div. 1 1993-94), Woodlake Athletic Club. Office: Psychiatry Assoc 4009 W 49th St Ste 308 Sioux Falls SD 57106-5221

WILLIAMS, WALKER RICHARD, JR., social services administrator; b. Dayton, Ohio, July 11, 1928; s. Walker Richard Sr. and Addie Mary (Smith) W.; m. Eddora L. Saunders, Aug. 6, 1949 (dec. Sept. 1966); 1 child, Yvette R.; m. Emma Jean Griffin, Sept. 4, 1971; children: Timotny E., Walker R. III. Student, U. Dayton, 1946-48. Commd. 2d lt. U.S. Army, 1952; advanced through grades to capt. USAF, Wright Patterson AFB, Ohio, 1963, employee rels. specialist, pers. mgmt. specialist, 1966-71; EEO investigator and grievance examiner Army and Air N.G., Wright Patterson AFB, Ohio, 1971-88; retired USAR, 1988; program dir. Youth Svc. U.S.A.-Dayton, 1988-89; pvt. contractor Dayton, 1989—. Mem. Adjutant Gen. Ohio Minority Recruiting Adv. Com., 1988—; bd. dirs. Dayton Opportunities Industrialization Ctr., 1976—, Wright Patterson Domestic Action Programs, Inc., 1984—; pres. Jefferson Twp. Bd. Edn., 1980—; mem. Nat. Black Caucus of Black Sch. Bd. Mems., 1980—, Nat. Black Caucus Local Elected Officials, Gov.'s Com. to Preserve Statue of Liberty, 1987, Citywide Vocat. Ednl. Com., 1986—, adv. com. Dayton Bd. Edn., 1980—. Recipient Air Force Civilian Svc. award, Dayton C. of C., Internat. Personnel Mgmt. Assn. Employee of the Yr., Blacks in Govt. Pres.'s award, Federally Employed Women's Supr. of the Yr. runner up, Hispanic Heritage Wk. Spl. award, NAACP Humanitarian award, Community Svc. award, Dayton Bd. Edn., James W. Cisco award , Vocat. Ednl. award Wilberforce U., Urban League Humanitarian award, Svc. to Youth award Girl Scouts U.S., Spl. award United Negro Coll. Fund, Jack & Jill, 7 Air Force Logistics Command Significant Achievement awards, AG of Ohio award, Ohio State U. award, Black Studies Group award, Russell Lyle award Wright Patterson AFB Quarter Century Club, Student Intervention Program Radcliff Sch., others; a day named in his honor, Dayton, 1987, 88. Mem. Miami Valley Pers. Assn., Internat. Pers. Mgmt. Assn., Retired Officers Assn., Air Force Assn., NAACP, Urban League, Blacks in Govt., Dayton Intergovt. EEO Coun. (chmn., historian 1967—), Miami Valley Mil. Affairs Assn., Wright Patterson Quarter Century Club (past pres.). Democrat. Home: 5050 Fortman Dr Dayton OH 45418-2233

WILLIAMSON, GLENNA SUE, physical therapist; b. Huntsville, Ala., Oct. 26, 1959; d. Arnold G. and Alda A. (Schmutz) Hildebrand; m. Gary Lee Williamson, May 22, 1981; children: Carrie LeAnn, Calvin Ross. BS, Wichita State U., 1982. Cert. by Kans. State Bd. of Healing Arts. Phys. therapist SW Kans. Area Coop. Dist. 613, Dodge City, Kans., 1982—, KiCom Spl. Svcs., Coldwater, Kans., 1993—, Arrowhead West, Inc., Dodge City, 1992—; mem. Head Start Adv. Bd., Dodge City, 1985-87; clin. edn. instr. Colby (Kans.) Cmty. Coll., 1983—, Wichita (Kans.) State U., 1992—; coord. Disability Awareness Program, 1991-95. Dir. Kans. Twirling Championship, Nat. Baton Twirling Assn., Wis., 1981, 86, 89, 92, 95; pres. Nazarene mission soc. Dodge City Nazarene Ch., 1991-93, children's dept. dir., 1993-95, coach Bible quiz team, 1993-95. Named Therapist of the Yr., AMBUCS, 1993. Mem. Am. Phys. Therapy Assn., (pediatric sect. 1989-95), Kans. Phys. Therapy Assn. (pediatric com. 1982-95). Republican. Nazarene. Home: 1104 Greenwood Dodge City KS 67801

WILLIAMSON, HAROLD E., pharmacologist, educator; b. Racine, Wis., Aug. 8, 1930; s. Harold E. and Grace Mae (McIntyre) W.; m. Joan Louise Chase, Apr. 26, 1957; children: Timothy, Julie, Eric. BS, U. Wis., 1953, PhD, 1959. Project assoc. U. Wis., Madison, 1959-60; from instr. to assoc. prof. U. Iowa, Iowa City, 1960-70, prof., 1970—; vis. scientist U. Bergen, Norway, 1988-89; grant reviewer Am. Heart Assn., St. Louis, 1974-78, Am. Scandinavian Found., N.Y.C., 1988—. Contbr. articles to profl. jours. Grantee NIH, 1961-75, Iowa Heart Assn., 1965-83, 3M, 1986—. Fellow Am. Coll. Clin. Pharmacology; mem. Am. Soc. Pharmacology and Exptl. Therapeutics, Am. Soc. Nephrology, Soc. Exptl. Biology and Medicine, Internat. Soc. Nephrology. Home: 131 S Mt Vernon Dr Iowa City IA 52245-4821 Office: U Iowa 2-252 Bsb Iowa City IA 52242

WILLIAMSON, JOHN MAURICE, accountant; b. Maroa, Ill., July 23, 1938; s. Richard and Margaret Alice (Thrift) W.; m. Donna I. Smith, Dec. 28, 1957; children: Robert, Susan, Sally, John II. BSBA in Accountancy, Bradley U., 1965. CPA, Ill.; CVA. Systems analyst P & PU RY Co., Peoria, Ill., 1963-65; staff acct. Clifton Gunderson & Co., Peoria, 1965-68; controller C. Iber & Sons, Inc., Peoria, 1968-72; ptnr. John Dobson & Co., South Bend, Ind., 1973-79; controller E.H. Tepe Co., Inc., South Bend, 1979-82; dir. gift adminstrn., asst. treas. U. Ill. Found., Urbana, 1982—. Mem. Am. Inst. CPA's, Ill. CPA Soc. Home: 204 S Meadowhill Ln Mahomet IL 61853-8521 Office: U Ill Found Harker Hall 1305 W Green St Urbana IL 61801-2919

WILLIAMSON, JOHN PRITCHARD, utility executive; b. Cleve., Feb. 22, 1922; s. John and Jane (Pritchard) W.; m. Helen Morgan, Aug. 3, 1945; children: John Morgan, James Russell, Wayne Arthur. BBA, Kent State U., 1945; postgrad., U. Toledo, 1953-56, U. Mich., 1956. CPA, Ohio. Sr. acct. Arthur Andersen & Co., Detroit and Cleve., 1945-51; dir. methods and procs. Toledo Edison Co., 1951-59, asst. treas., 1959-60, sec., 1960-62, sec.-treas., 1962-65, v.p. finance, 1965-68, sr. v.p., 1968-72, pres., chief exec. officer, 1972-79, chmn., chief exec. officer, 1979-86; chmn. Centerior Energy Corp., 1985-86; chmn. emeritus Toledo Edison Co., Centerior Energy Corp., 1986—; dir. emeritus, chmn. 1st Nat. Bank of Toledo, 1974-75; chmn. N.Am. Electric Reliability Coun., 1984-87; founder, chmn. Nat. Electric Security Com., 1987-88. Pres. Ohio Electric Utility Inst., 1972; chmn. East Cen. Area Power Coordination Pool, 1971-72, mem. exec. com. Edison Electric Inst., 1981-85; trustee Assn. Edison Illuminating Cos., 1982-84; pres. Toledo C. of C., 1970; chmn. Ohio C. of C., 1979-81, life dir.; trustee Toledo Symphony Orch., pres., 1985-86; hon. trustee Toledo Mus. Art, Toledo Hosp.; trustee U. Toledo Found., 1980-87, Kent State U. Found.; vice chmn. Greater Toledo Corp., 1984-86; trustee, treas. Rio Verde Cmty. Ch., 1989-92; elder Presbyn. Ch.; pres. Toledo Cmty. Chest, 1972; chmn. Greater Toledo Area United Way, 1971. Named Toledo Outstanding Citizen, 1976; recipient Kent State U. medallion, 1992;Williamson Alumni Ctr. named in his honor, 1991. Mem. Fin. Analysts Soc. Toledo (pres. 1968-69), Systems and Procs. Assn. (internat. treas. 1960), Inst. Pub. Utilities (chmn. exec. com. 1969-70), Toledo Boys Club (Echo award 1974), Kent State U. Alumni Assn. (pres. 1971-72, Outstanding Alumnus 1974), Belmont Country Club, Rio Verde Country Club, Inverness Club (gov. 1967-76), Rio Verde Saddle Club (past pres.), Kiwanis (past pres. Toledo, Disting. Svc. award 1977), Blue Key, Delta Sigma Pi, Beta Alpha Psi, Delta Upsilon. Republican. Home: 10661 Cardiff Rd Perrysburg OH 43551-3404 also: 18524 E Poco Vista Rio Verde AZ 85263-7125

WILLIAMSON, VIKKI LYN, financial executive; b. Huntington, W.Va., June 30, 1956; d. Ernest E. and Wanda C. (Cole) W. BA in Secondary Edn., English, Temple U., 1978; postgrad. in Acctg. and Fin., U. Cin., 1984-86. CPA, Ohio; cert. tchr., Tenn., Ohio. Tchr. Springfield Christian Acad., Tenn., 1978-79; acctg. asst. Children's Hosp. Med. Ctr., Cin., 1979-84; asst. dir. fin. svcs. U. Cin. Med. Ctr., 1984-85, dir. fin. svcs., 1985-88, dir. fin. and adminstrn., 1988-91, dep. dir., 1991—; bd. dirs. Contemporary Dance Theatre, 1987-90. Bd. dirs. Habitat for Humanity-Hamilton, 1991—, v.p., 1991, pres., 1992. Mem. AICPA, Healthcare Fin. Mgmt. Assn., Am. Assn. Blood Banks, Ohio Assn. Blood Banks (fin. co. 1986-90, treas. 1991—), Coun. Community Blood Ctrs. (fin. com. 1991—, alt. trustee 1991—), Assn. Women Adminstrs. (fin. com. 1987-90), Assn. Mid-Level Adminstrs. (bd. dirs. 1987-90), Alpha Epsilon Theta, Beta Gamma Sigma, Delta Mu Delta. Office: Hoxworth Blood Ctr Univ Cin Med Ctr 3130 Highland Ave ML 55 Cincinnati OH 45267

WILLIAMSON-STOUTENBURG, JANE SUE, nurse practitioner; b. Davenport, Iowa, Mar. 10, 1949; d. George Baker and Hazel Elaine (Kline) W.; m. Noel Wayne Stoutenburg, Aug. 25, 1979 (div. July 1996); 1 child, Karen. AS, Black Hawk Jr. Coll., East Moline, Ill., 1970; BA, BS, Augustana Coll., 1973, 75; Cert. in Fire Sci., Harper Coll., Palatine, Ill., 1982; AS in Nursing with high honors, Elgin Community Coll., 1987. EMT; cert. paramedic. Srsch. technologist Rush-Presbyn. St. Luke's Med. Ctr., Chgo., 1974-75; acct. supr., pvt. investigator Per Mar Security Inc., Davenport,

Iowa, 1975-77; pre-trial release investigator 7th Jud. Ct. Dist., Davenport, Iowa, 1976-77; pharm. rep. Bristol Labs., Syracuse, N.Y., 1977-80; dir. safety tng. Zee Med., Irvine, Calif., 1981-83; tng. specialist ARC, Chgo., 1983-86, Lake County Fire Rescue, Barrington, Ill., 1981—; nurse practitioner Boy Scouts of Am., St. Charles, Ill., 1990—; nurse trainer Buehler YMCA, Palatine, Ill., 1990-92; emergency med. svc. coord. Robbins (Ill.) Fire Dept., 1985—; bd. dirs. Barrington Area Devel. Coun., 1981-90. Author: Academy of Science, 1967, (poetry), 1970. Troop leader Girl Scouts, Barrington, 1990-95; book fair chmn. Lines Sch. PTO, Barrington, 1991-94; camp nurse Boy Scouts Am., Camp Big Timber, Ill., YMCA Camp Duncan, Fox Lake, Ill. Recipient Ill. EMT of the Yr. award, 1989-90, Disting. Svc. award ARC, 1989, Disting. Svc. key Alpha Phi Omega, 1989, Key, Phi Theta Kappa, 1989, Vol. of the Yr. award Chgo. Vol. Bur., 1993, J.C. Penney Golden Flame award, 1993. Mem. Am. Soc. Safety Engrs., Am. Trauma Soc., Am. Acad. Sci., Internat. Soc. Fire Sci. Instrs., Prehosp. Care Providers of Ill., Alpha Phi Omega (mem. bd. dirs. 1995—, publicity com.), P.E.O. Sisterhood. Episcopalian. Office: Lake County Fire Rescue 618 S Northwest Hwy Ste 213 Barrington IL 60010

WILLIFORD, EDWARD ALLAN, III, software consultant; b. Danville, Pa., Jan. 24, 1946; s. Edward Allan Jr. and Myriam Francine (Davenport) W.; m. Robin Gentry, June 16, 1966 (div. Nov. 1977); m. Catherine Louise Kujat, Mar. 20, 1988; children: Edward Allan IV, Lon Davenport, James Travis. AS, Del Mar Coll., Corpus Christi, Tex., 1966; B in Bus., Southwestern U., 1968; postgrad., U. Tex., 1970. Salesman NCR Corp., Austin, 1969-72; comptroller U. Co-op, Austin, 1973-75; software cons. Austin, 1976-94, Grosse Pointe, Mich., 1994—. Chmn. troop com. Boy Scouts Am., Austin, 1983-91, 95, cubmaster, 1992-94; coach, mgr. Little League, Austin, 1988-92; mem. ski patrol Alpine Valley, Highland, Mich., 1995—. Named Sertoma of Yr., Austin Sertoma, 1983-84, Dist. Sertoma of Yr., 1983-84. Office: Amicus Software 470 Madison Ave Grosse Pointe MI 48236

WILLIG, LESLIE AUGUST, photography equipment manufacturing company executive; b. Ft. Wayne, Ind., Jan. 29, 1926; s. August Aloysius and Laura Elizabeth Willig; children: Constance J. Willig Hansen, Diana K. Willig Osborne, Larry A., Rosanne M. Willig Johnson, Laura L. Willig Wells. BS, Purdue U., 1947; MA, U. Louisville, 1951; PhD, U. Iowa, 1956. Asst. dean of men U. Iowa, Iowa City, 1954-56; asst. dir., assoc. prof. Purdue U., Ft. Wayne, 1956-60; exec. v.p. Tri-State U., Angola, Ind., 1960-70; v.p., bd. dirs. Bankers Investment Corp., Ft. Wayne, 1966-75; chmn. bd. dirs., chief exec. officer, pres. Photo Control Corp., Mpls., 1974—; bus. broker and cons. mgmt., Ft. Wayne, 1970—; sec., bd. dirs. North Snow Bay, Inc. Chmn. Internat. Sci. Fair Council, 1967; co-founder, bd. dirs. Sci. Edn. Found. Ind., 1963—, chmn., 1986-88. Served to capt. USNR, 1944-47, 51-53. Recipient Disting. Pub. Service award Navy Dept., 1973. Mem. Am. Psychol. Assn., Midwest Psychol. Assn., Naval Res. Assn. (nat. pres. 1971-73, Merit award 1974). Roman Catholic. Club: Summit (Ft. Wayne). Home: 135 Lane 780 Snow Lk Fremont IN 46737-9473 Office: Photo Control Corp 4800 Quebec Ave N Minneapolis MN 55428-4520

WILLING, KATHERINE, state legislator; m. Donald Willing. BS, Purdue U. Formerly tchr.; mem. from 39th dist. Ind. Ho. of Reps., 1992—, mem. aged and aging, agr., edn., ways and means coms. Mem. Boone County Coun., 1988-92; bd. govs. Boone County Jr. Achievement; v.p. Boone County Leadership; bd. dirs., formerly treas. Witham Meml. Hosp. Found. Recipient Richard G. Lugar Excellence in Svc. award. Mem. Boone County Rep. Women's Club (pres.), Boone County and Carmel Clay County C. of C., Farm Bur., Zonta, Tri Kappa, Alpha Chi Omega. Home: 2309 Ulen Overlook Lebanon IN 46052-1146 Office: Ind Ho of Reps State Capitol Indianapolis IN 46204*

WILLIS, DOUGLAS ALAN, lawyer; b. Taylorville, Ill., Feb. 22, 1963; s. Roy Willis and Sharon (Peel) Boaden. BA, Ill. Coll., 1985; JD, DePaul Coll. of Law, 1988. Bar: Ill. 1988, U.S. Dist. Ct. (no. dist.) Ill. 1988, U.S. Ct. Appeals (7th cir.) 1992. Intern BBC, Dallas, 1984, Ill. Dept. Registration/Edn., Springfield, 1983, Ill. State Senate Staff, Springfield, 1982, 84; rsch. asst. M.C. Bassiouni, Chgo., 1986-87; summer clk. Hon. Richard Mills, U.S. Dist. Judge, Springfield, 1987; asst. corp. sec. Profl. Svc. Industries, Inc., Lombard, Ill., 1991—, assoc. corp. counsel, 1989—. Intern U.S. House Minority Leader Robert Michel, Jacksonville, Ill., 1983. Named to Order of the Barrister, 1988, DePaul Exec. Moot Ct. Bd., 1988. Mem. Ill. State Bar Assn., Delta Theta Phi. Republican. Methodist. Home: 1510 Lakeview Dr # 145 Darien IL 60561 Office: Profl Svc Industries Inc 510 E 22nd St Lombard IL 60148-6110

WILLIS, JACK, broadcasting executive; b. 1934. Exec. prodr. Nat. Ednl. TV, N.Y.C., 1966-71; v.p. programming Ednl. Broadcasting Corp., N.Y.C., 1971-74; prodr. CBS, Inc., N.Y.C., 1974-75, v.p. programming and prodns., 1980-83; exec. prodr. Cinelit Prodns., Inc., N.Y.C., 1975-80; exec. dir. programming Metromedia Prodns. Corp., N.Y.C., 1983-84; exec. prodr. Multimedia Entertainment, N.Y.C., 1984-87; pres. The Willis Group, Inc., N.Y.C., 1987-90; pres., CEO Sta. KTCA-TV, St. Paul, 1990—. Office: Sta KTCA-TV 172 E 4th St Saint Paul MN 55101*

WILLIS, JOAN ELLEN, nurse; b. Wheaton, Kans., Sept. 6, 1931; d. Henry Michael and Nelle Gerva (Keating) Horgan; m. Bernard Edward Willis, Nov. 10, 1956; children: Patricia, Mary, Eileen, Maureen, Mike, Tim. Diploma in nursing, St. Francis Hosp., Topeka, 1953. Staff nurse St. Francis Hosp., Topeka, 1953-56; staff nurse RN, CPR instr. Community Hosp., Onaga, Kans., 1956-92. Recipient Nursing Heart of Healthcare award Kans. U. Med. Ctr., Kansas City, 1991. Home: RR 1 216 Lincoln Wheaton KS 66551

WILLIS, ROBERT ADDISON, dentist; b. Wichita, Kans., Apr. 27, 1949; s. Everett Clayton and Mary Ann (Rohlin) W.; m. Janet Sue Jones, Jan. 21, 1968 (div. Dec. 1986); children: Gregory, Jeffrey; m. Sherryl Ann Galloway, Apr. 26, 1991; children: Wes Misak, Wendy Misak. Student, Okaloosa Walton Jr. Coll., Niceville, Fla., 1970-71, Wichita State U., 1972-74; DDS, U. Mo., 1978. Dentist Wellington, Kans., 1978—; cons. Sumner County Regional Hosp., 1980—, Lakeside Lodge Nursing Home, Wellington, 1980—. Bd. dirs. Kans. Babe Ruth Leagues, Inc., dist. commr., 1990—; bd. of elders Calvary Luth. Ch., 1989-94. With USAF, 1968-71. Mem. ADA, Acad. Gen. Dentistry, So. Dist. Dental Soc. (pres. 1980), Kans. Dental Assn. (coun. on peer rev. 1988-89), Wellington Dental Soc. (treas. 1981—), Optimist CLub, Wellington Area C. of C. (com. on indsl. devel. 1992), Am. Legion, Xi Psi Psi. Republican. Home: 620 Circle Dr Wellington KS 67152-3206 Office: 204 E Lincoln Ave Wellington KS 67152-3061

WILLIS, SUSAN JEANETTE, library director; b. Chanute, Kans., June 20, 1956; d. John Merrill and Wanda (Bagby) Gorton; m. Gordon R. Willis, July 26, 1981; 1 child, Matthew. BS, Pittsburg (Kans.) State U., 1978; MLS, Emporia (Kans.) State U., 1991. Real estate broker Gorton Realty, Chanute, 1978-86; dir. Chanute Pub. Libr., 1987—. Bd. dirs. Chanute Tourism Bd., 1993—, Main St. Chanute, 1994—. Mem. ALA, Kans. Libr. Assn. (1st v.p.). Methodist. Office: Chanute Public Libr 111 N Lincoln Chanute KS 66720

WILLNOW, RONALD DALE, editor; b. Adrian, Mich., Mar. 12, 1933; s. Wilbur A. and Irene L. (Sword) W.; m. Onnalee Thompson, Aug. 24, 1957; childrn: Lindle, Randall, Evan. AB, Adrian Coll., 1954; MA, U. Mich., 1959. Reporter St. Louis Post-Dispatch, 1959-66, asst. city editor, 1966-71, city editor, 1971-76, news editor, 1976-81, asst. mng. editor, 1981-90, dep. mng. editor, 1990—. With U.S. Army, 1954-56. Mem. Mid-Am. Press Inst. (bd. dirs. 1978—, past pres.), Mo. Associated Press Editors Assn. (pres. 1995—), St. Louis Journalism Found. (chmn. 1973-79), Press Club St. Louis (pres. 1983-86). Unitarian. Home: 7432 Cornell Saint Louis MO 63130 Office: St Louis Post-Dispatch 900 N Tucker Saint Louis MO 63101

WILLON, MYCHAEL COLE, school system administrator; b. Cambridge, Md., Apr. 1, 1955; s. Wallace Edwin and Iris Mary (Slacum). BS, U. Md., 1973-77, MEd, 1984; PhD, LaSalle U., 1992. Notary pub., Kans. Tchr. Charles Co. Bd. of Edn., Pomfret, Md., 1977-78; tchr. Howard Co. Bd. of Edn., Columbia, Md., 1978-85, gifted and talented resource tchr., 1985-86; asst. prin. Frederick County Bd. Edn., Md., 1986-88, gifted and talented coord., 1987; prin. McCollom Elem. Sch., Wichita, Kans., 1988-89, coord. spl. projects in curriculum, 1989-90, coord. elem. social studies, 1990-91, dir. elem. programs, 1991-93, asst. to supt., 1993-95; dir. Horace Mann/Irving/Park Complex, 1995—. Recipient MATE Cooperating Teacher of the Year. Md. Assoc. of Teacher Education, 1984, Excellence in Teaching award Howard County C. of C., Columbia, Md. 1984. Mem. Wichita Reading Assn., Am. Numismatic Soc., U. Md. Alumni Assn., Assn. Tchr. Educators. Republican. Home: 1249 N Saint Francis Wichita KS 67214-2838 Office: Unified Sch Dist # 259 Adminstrv Ctr 1243 N Market St Wichita KS 67214

WILLOUGHBY, BRUCE EDWARD, managing editor; b. Newark, Ohio, Nov. 8, 1948; s. Harry Allen and Sue Marie (Johnson) W.; m. Tracy Blotner; children: David Bruce, Jamin Andrew. BA, David Lipscomb Coll., 1970; MA, Abilene Christian U., 1977; ABD, U. Mich., 1981. Prodn. mgr., mng. editor Am. Schs. of Oriental Rsch., Ann Arbor, Mich., 1978-82; mng. editor Ctr. for Japanese Studies U. Mich., Ann Arbor, 1982—. Contbr. articles to Mysteries of the Bible, 1988, Books of the Bible, 1989, Theological Dictionary of the Old Testament, 1995. Vol. local Humane Soc. Recipient Honor award Chgo. Book Clinic, 1990, also numerous scholarships. Mem. Soc. Scholarly Pub. Home: 11 N Wallace Blvd Ypsilanti MI 48197-4663 Office: U Mich Ctr Japanese Studies 108 Lane Hall Ann Arbor MI 48109

WILLOUGHBY, DAVID CHARLES, photographer, forensics illustrator; b. Indpls., Nov. 16, 1940; s. Charles C. and Mabelle L. (Haller) W.; student Ind. U., 1958-62, Butler U., 1962-64; m. Victoria LaMarre, Mar. 6, 1971; children: Brian D., Kara L. Med. photographer Ind. U. Sch. Medicine, Indpls., 1962-68; dir. med. media prodns. Meth. Hosp. of Indpls., 1968-85; owner, operator BioMed. Photography, Indpls., 1985— ; forensic illustrator Indpls.-Marion County Forensic Svcs. Agy., Indpl., 1986—. Registered biol. photographer. Fellow Biol. Photog. Assn. (dir. 1978-80, exec. sec. bd. of registry 1981-85); mem. Profl. Photographers Am., Midwestern Assn. Forensic Scientists, Inc., Internat. Assn. Identification, Ind. Ofcls. Assn., Masons, Shriners, Order of Eastern Star. Republican. Methodist. Home: 6711 Studebaker Ct Indianapolis IN 46214-1918 Office: 40 S Alabama St Indianapolis IN 46204-3635

WILLS, BART FRANCIS, insurance company executive; b. Champaign, Ill., Jan. 22, 1955; s. Creed A. and Betty L. (Reifsteck) W. AAS, Parkland Coll., 1975; BS, So. Ill. U., 1977. Coord. Program Runaway Youth U. Ill. (YMCA), Champaign, 1978; caseworker Survival Skills Program (YMCA), Champaign, 1978-79, dir., 1979-80; dir. Champaign County Youth Svcs., 1980-82; ins. agt., registered rep. Prudential Ins. Co., Champaign, 1982-95; with 1st Alliance Fin. Group, Inc., Champaign. Adv. bd. Ill. Children's Home and Aid Roundhouse Program, 1980; treas. Ill. Youth Svc. Bur., 1981-82. Mem. Champaign Area Assn. Life Underwriters (chmn. legis. com. 1984-93, pub. rels. chmn. 1995-96, membership chmn. 1996—), Assn. Health Ins. Agts., Life Underwriters Polit. Action Com. (regional chmn. 1989—), Ill. Life Underwriters Assn. (nat. quality award 1984-89, 91-92), Champaign County C. of C. (govt. affairs com. 1994—), Champaign C. of C. (legis. com. 1988-93, environ subcom. 1993—). Republican. Methodist. Home: 4202 Ironwood Ln Champaign IL 61821-3322 Office: 1st Alliance Fin Group Inc 206 N Randolph St Ste 400 Champaign IL 61820-3978

WILLS, GARRY, journalist, educator; b. Atlanta, May 22, 1934; s. John and Mayno (Collins) W.; m. Natalie Cavallo, May 30, 1959; children: John, Garry, Lydia. BA, St. Louis U., 1957; MA, Xavier U., Cin., 1958, Yale U., 1959; PhD, Yale U., 1961; LittD (hon.), Coll. Holy Cross, 1982, Columbia Coll., 1982, Beloit Coll., 1988, Xavier U., 1993, St. Xavier U., 1993, Union Coll., 1993, Macalester Coll., 1995, Bates Coll., 1995. Fellow Center Hellenic Studies, 1961-62; assoc. prof. classics Johns Hopkins U., 1962-67, adj. prof., 1968-80; Henry R. Luce prof. Am. culture and public policy Northwestern U., 1980-88, adj. prof., 1988—; newspaper columnist Universal Press Syndicate, 1970—; mem. adv. com. Internat. Ctr. Jefferson Studies; mem. Historians' adv. bd., Mt. Vernon. Author: Chesterton, 1961, Politics and Catholic Freedom, 1964, Roman Culture, 1966, Jack Ruby, 1967, Second Civil War, 1968, Nixon Agonistes, 1970, Bare Ruined Choirs, 1972, Inventing America, 1978, At Button's, 1979, Confessions of a Conservative, 1979, Explaining America, 1980, The Kennedy Imprisonment, 1982, Lead Time, 1983, Cincinnatus, 1984, Reagan's America, 1987, Under God, 1990, Lincoln at Gettysburg, 1992 (Pulitzer Prize for gen. non-fiction 1993), Certain Trumpets: The Call of Leaders, 1994, Witches and Jesuits: Shakespeare's Macbeth, 1994. Recipient Pulitzer prize, 1993, Merle Curti award Orgn. Am. Historians, Nat. Book Critics Circle award (2), Wilbur Cross medal Yale U., Peabody award. Mem. AAAL, Am. Acad. Arts and Scis., Am. Antiquarian Soc., Mass. Hist. Soc. Roman Catholic. Office: Northwestern U Dept History Evanston IL 60201

WILLS, JOHN CLIFTON, insurance agent; b. Kirksville, Md., Nov. 3, 1954; s. John William and Dorothy Winifred (Gruber) W.; m. Patricia Lynn Stiles, May 24, 1975; children: Matthew William, Kimberly Ellen. BS, Ctrl. Mo. State U., 1976. Sales rep. Ctrl. Soya, Kansas City, Mo., 1976-77, Isis Foods, Kansas City, Mo., 1977-78, Oscar Mayer, Kansas City, Mo., 1978-82; dist. sales mgr. Orvil Kent, Kansas City, Mo., 1982-83; agent State Farm Ins., Kansas City, Mo., 1983-88; agy. mgr. State Farm Ins., Kansas City, 1988-95, agy. field exec., 1995—. Deacon chmn. Emmanuel Presbyn. Ch., 1994-95; vol. State Farm Spkrs. Bur., Columbia, Mo., 1995; coord. polling dist. Talent for U.S. Congress, St. Louis, 1995; mem. West County Cmty. Ch., 1995—. Mem. Nat. Assn. Life Underwriters, Toastmasters, Jaycees (pres. 1980-81). Republican. Home: 34 Grand Isle Ct Grover MO 63040 Office: State Farm Ins Ste 139 502 Earth City Expy Bridgeton MO 63045

WILLS, ROBERT HAMILTON, retired newspaper executive; b. Colfax, Ill., June 21, 1926; s. Robert Orson and Ressie Mae (Hamilton) W.; m. Sherilyn Lou Nierstheimer, Jan. 16, 1949; children: Robert L., Michael H., Kendall J. B.S., M.S., Northwestern U., 1950. Reporter Duluth (Minn.) Herald & News-Tribune, 1950-51; reporter Milw. Jour., 1951-59, asst. city editor, 1959-62; city editor Milw. Sentinel, 1962-75, editor, 1975-91; exec. v.p. Jour./Sentinel, Inc., Milw., 1991-92, pres., 1992-93; vice-chmn., 1993; also bd. dirs. Jour./Sentinel, Inc., Milw.; pub. Milw. Jour.; sr. v.p., bd. dirs. Jour. Communications; pres. Wis. Freedom of Info. Council, 1979-86; Pulitzer Prize juror, 1982, 83, 90. Mem. media-law rels. com. State Bar Wis.; mem. privacy coun. Wis. Pub. Svc. Commn., 1996, chmn., 1994-95, vice-chmn. Recipient Leadership award Women's Ct. and Civic Conf. Greater Milw., 1987, Freedom of Info. award, 1988; named Wis. Newsman of Yr. Milw. chpt., 1973. Mem. Wis. Newspaper Assn. (pres. 1985-86, Disting. Svc. award 1992), Wis. AP (pres. 1975-76, Dion Henderson award Svc. 1993), Am. Soc. Newspaper Editors, Internat. Press Inst., Milw. Press Club (Media Hall Fame 1993), Soc. Profl. Journalists (prs. Milw. chpt. 1979-80, nat. pres. 1986-87), Sigma Delta Chi Found. (bd. dirs. 1993—). Home: 2030 Allen Blvd Apt 3 Middleton WI 53562-3469

WILMOTT, ROBERT WILLIAM, pediatrician, educator; b. London, Sept. 12, 1948; came to U.S., 1982; s. William Walter Charles and Rosemary (Moore) W.; m. Susan Jennifer Pitcher; m. Cathryn Maria Clark, Dec. 12, 1981; children: Jennifer, Francesca, Gina, Annabelle. BS, U. Coll. London, 1970, MB, 1973; MD, U. London, 1984. Diplomate Am. Bd. Pediatrics, Pediatric Pulmonary. Clin. dir. pulmonology Children's Hosp. Phila., 1982-86; dir. pulmonary medicine Children's Hosp. Mich., Detroit, 1986-89, Children's Hosp. Med. Ctr., Cin., 1989—; asst. prof. pediatrics U. Pa., Phila., 1981-86; assoc. prof. pediatrics Wayne State U., Detroit, 1986-89, assoc. immunology, 1987-89; assoc. prof. pediatrics U. Cin., 1989—. Editor: Pediatric Clinics of North America, 1994, assoc. editor, Journal of Pediatrics, 1995—; contbr. articles to profl. jours. Bd. trustees Cystic Fybrosis Found., Cin., 1990—, ctr. com., Bethesda, Md., 1990-95, Appreciation award, 1987, 95. Fellow Royal Coll. Physicians, Am. Coll. Chest Physicians, Am. Acad. Pediatrics; mem. AAAS, Am. Thoracic Soc. Office: Children's Hosp Med Ctr 3333 Burnet Ave Cincinnati OH 45229

WILNER, FREEMAN MARVIN, hematologist, oncologist; b. Detroit, June 14, 1926; s. Jack Burton W. and Belle Gertrude (Goldberg) Weeks; m. Marjorie Louise Tewkesbury, Aug. 29, 1948; children: Jeffrey, Robert, Paul, Laura. BS with honors, Wayne State U., 1950, MD, 1953. Diplomate Am. Bd. Internal Medicine, Am. Bd. Hematology, Am. Bd. Oncology. Intern Detroit Receiving Hosp., Detroit, 1953-54, resident, 1954-57, chief med. resident, 1956; pres. Hematology/Oncology Assocs., Royal Oak, Mich., 1974-86, Hematology/Oncology Cons., Mich., 1986—; med. dir. Rose Cance Inst., chief sect. hematology-oncology Rose Cancer Ctr.-William Beaumont Hosp., Royal Oak, Mich., 1972—; presenter, with others, numerous med. seminars; clin. assoc. prof. medicine Wayne State U. Co-author: (with Schneider, John R., Bedell, and Archie) Bleeding and Clotting Disorders, 1981; contbr. articles to profl. jours., case reports and other publs. Bd. dirs. Red Cross Southeastern Mich. Blood Bank, 1991, Karmamous Cancer Inst., 1993. Sgt. USAAF, 1944-47. Recipient Disting. Service Award, School of Medicine , Alumni of Wayne State U., Detroit, 1985; named Tchr. of Yr., House Staff, William Beaumont Hosp., 1969-70, Providence Hosp., 1971. Fellow ACP (Laureate award 1993), Internat. Soc. Hematology, Detroit Acad. Medicine; mem. AMA, Am. Soc. Hematology, Am. Soc. Clin. Oncology, Mich. State Med. Soc., Oakland County Med. Soc., Leukemia Found. Mich. (adv. bd. 1958-79), World Fedn. Hemophilia. Office: Hematology Oncology Cons PC 3601 W 13 Mile Rd Royal Oak MI 48073-6712

WILSDON, THOMAS ARTHUR, product development engineer, administrator; b. Waterbury, Conn., Aug. 18, 1942; s. Arthur and Ruth (Wellington) W.; m. Yvonne Jeanne Pettit, June 19, 1964 (div. Apr. 1986); children: Thomas Charles, Beth Jeanne; m. Sharon Diann Culbertson, Feb. 14, 1988; children: Vandee Hyder, Jacklynn Hyder. BSEE, U. Conn., 1964; MBA, SUNY, Buffalo, 1978. Product design engr. Westinghouse Gen. Control Divsn., Buffalo, 1964-78; mgr. product devel. Westinghouse Control Divsn., Asheville, N.C., 1978-87; mgr. Advantage engrng. Westinghouse Elec. Components Divsn., Asheville, 1987-94; mgr. logic control products devel. engrng. Eaton/Cutler Hammer, Milw., 1994—. Mem. IEEE, NSPE, Am. Mgmt. Assn. Methodist. Home: PO Box 250 Pewaukee WI 53072-0250 Office: Eaton/Cutler Hammer 4201 N 27th St Milwaukee WI 53216-1807

WILSON, BENJAMIN CALVIN, Black American studies educator; b. Tampa, Fla., Mar. 30, 1947; s. Benjamin Calvin Sr. and Winifred Jean (Jefferson) W.; divorced; children: Nikki Kai, Ayanna Tene, Danya Aisha. BA in History, Benedictine Coll., 1969; MA in African History, Mich. State U., 1972, PhD in Am. History, 1974. From instr. to assoc. prof. GM Inst., Flint, Mich., 1970-75; from asst. prof. to prof. Black Am. studies Western Mich. U., Kalamazoo, 1975—; instr. human rels. Kalamazoo Regional Police Tng. Acad., 1977-80; instr. Comstock Pub. Sch. System, 1988; cons. and lectr. in field. Author: Rural Black Heritage Between Chicago and Detroit, 1985; producer audio visual including Idlewild: The Apollo of Michigan, 1984 (Philo award), and many more; contbr. articles to profl. jours. Football coach Milwood Jr. High Sch., 1978-80; basketball coach Comstock Youth Athletic Assn. Young Ladies, 1980-87; mem. revenue sharing bd. City of Kalamazoo, 1984-86; bd. dirs. New Vic Theater, 1980-82. Grantee NEH, 1979-80, Mich. Coun. Humanities, 1981-82, and 17 others. Mem. NAACP (1st v.p. 1976-78, exec. bd. dirs. 1979—, historian 1979-88). Baptist. Home: 2229 Clark Ave Kalamazoo MI 49004-1815 Office: Western Mich Univ Black Am Studies 818 S Kalamazoo MI 49008

WILSON, CHARLES DOUGLAS, public affairs executive; b. Cleve., Feb. 28, 1945; s. Charles Schaffner and Isabelle Irene (Foote) W.; m. Carolyn Flowers; 1 child, Suzanne Flowers. BAE, U. Fla., 1966; diploma, N.Y. Inst. Fin., 1969. Asst. nat. dir. Chi Phi Frat., Atlanta, 1966-68; stockbroker White, Weld and Co., Atlanta, 1968-69; legis. aide Congressman Lou Frey, Washington, 1970; fed. affairs rep. Commonwealth of Va., Richmond, 1970-72; chief of staff Congressman M. Caldwell Butler, Washington, 1972-77; dir. legis. affairs Am. Paper Inst., Washington, 1977-79; dir. pub. affairs Union Camp Corp., Washington, 1979-87; dir. govt. affairs Ft. Howard Corp., Green Bay, Wis., 1987-94, v.p. pub. affairs, 1994—; chmn. Water Com. Nat. Assn. Mfrs., Washington, 1993-94, Govt. Affairs Com. Polystyrene Packaging Coun., Washington, 1988-89, Am. Forest Paper Assn., Washington, 1987, 92-93. Founder, vice chmn. Christmas in April, Green Bay, 1993-94; trustee Union Congl. Ch., Green Bay, 1989-91; bd. dirs. Pub. Affairs Coun., Washington, exec. com. 1985-87. Mem. Univ. Club (Washington), Capitol Hill Club (Washington), Chi Phi Frat. (mem. nat. coun. 1982-85, Alumnus of Yr. 1987). Republican. Home: 3301 Delahaut St Green Bay WI 54301 Office: Ft Howard Corp PO Box 19130 Green Bay WI 54307

WILSON, CLARENCE SYLVESTER, JR., lawyer, educator; b. Bklyn., Oct. 22, 1945; s. Clarence Sylvester and Thelma Louise (Richards) W.; m. Helena Chapellin Iribarren, Jan. 26, 1972. BA, Williams Coll., 1967; JD, Northwestern U., 1974. Bar: Ill., 1975; U.S. Supreme Ct., 1985. Vice consul, 3d sec. U.S. Dept. State, Washington, 1969-74; adj. prof. law Kent Coll. of Law, Ill. Inst. Tech., Chgo., 1981-94; mem. vis. com. music dept. U. Chgo., 1991—; mem. bd. govs. Sch. of Art Inst. of Chgo., 1994—; bd. dirs. Jazz Musicians of Chgo., 1994—; Fgn. Svc. Res. officer U.S. Dept. of State, 1969-74; vice consul, third sec. Am. Embassy, Caracas, Venezuela, 1969-71. Trustee Chgo. Symphony Orch., 1987—, Art Inst. Chgo., 1990—, Jazz Mus. Chgo., 1994—; mem. adv. bd. Chgo. Dept. Cultural Affiars, 1988—; bd. dirs. Arts Midwest, Mpls., 1985-89, Harold Washington Found., Chgo., 1989-91; mem. MERIT Music Program, 1991-96, Ill. Arts Coun., 1984-89; project mgr. Dept. Justice Task Force, The Pres.'s Pvt. Sector Survey on Cost Control in the Fed. Govt., 1982-84. Mem. Lawyers for the Creative Arts (pres. 1987-88). Republican. Episcopalian. Home: 5555 S Everett Ave Chicago IL 60637-1968 Office: 25 E Washington St Ste 1500 Chicago IL 60602-1804

WILSON, DARRELL GLENN, investment banker, software developer; b. Eden, N.C., July 2, 1939; s. Walter Glenn and Bonnie Edna (Riddle) W.; m. Sandra Lee Walton, Sept. 2, 1967; 1 child, Walton Glenn. Registered securities prin., investment advisor. Field engr. Nuclear Chgo. Corp., 1964-67; pres. Nelson Wilson Enterprises, Kansas City, Mo., 1967-73; v.p. Prudential Bache Securities, N.Y.C., 1973-83, Butcher & Singer Inc., Phila., 1983-84; pres. Overland Investments Inc., Overland Park, Kans., 1984-91, Federated Deposit Recovery, Overland Park, 1988-91; mng. ptnr. Fin. Mgmt. Group, Shawnee Mission, Kans., 1991-94; dir. R&D Aegis Consumer Funding, Merriam, Kans., 1994-96; pres. Stonewood Systems Devel., 1996—. Author: Ginnie Mae, 1985, Net Present Value Hedging, 1986 (computer software) Snapshot, 1987, Interest and Term Reduction, 1991, Artificial Intelligence Trading System Software, 1993. With USN, 1958-64. Republican. Home: 9059 Overhill Cir De Soto KS 66018-9171

WILSON, DENNIS M., state legislator; m. Vickie Wilson. Mem. from dist. 29 Kans. State Ho. of Reps., Topeka. Address: 11545 Carter Overland Park KS 66210

WILSON, DIANNE CAROL, nurse; b. Kansas City, Mo., May 17, 1951; d. Lawrence Edward and Jacqueline Jeanene (Bolton) McElyea; m. Abdullah H. Al-Rubaie, Jan. 24, 1970 (div. Mar. 1974); 1 child, Jamal A.; m. Michael Harold Wilson, Jan. 24, 1976. BSN, BA in Sociology, Avila Coll., 1984; MA in Sociology, U. Mo., Kansas City, 1991; MSN, Fort Hays State U., Hays, Kans., 1994; cert. Family Nurse Practitioner, 1994. RN, Mo., Kans., Nebr. Cardiac care nurse Kansas City (Mo.) Area Hosps., 1984-88; home health nurse Kansas City, 1987—; RN cons., med. case mgr. Jewish Vocat. Svcs., Kansas City, 1988-89, Kansas City, 1989-91; faculty Penn Valley Coll., Kansas City, 1991-92, Park Coll., Parkville, Mo., 1993; prin. Avisa Rehab. Case Mgmt., 1989-93; adj. prof. dept. sociology Fort Hays State U., Hays, Kans., 1994; family nurse practitioner Northwest Health Svc., Mound City, Mo., 1995-96; family nurse practitioner Sch. Nursing U. Kans., 1996—; tchr. childbirth edn. rsch. project HCFA, 1988. Vol. Lakeside Nature Ctr., Kansas City, 1990; pres. mother's coun. Boy Scouts Am., Kansas City, 1979-84; originator nursing radio program Sta. KKFI-FM, Kansas City, 1989-90. Mem. Kans. Anthrop. Soc., Great Plains Nurse Practitioner Soc. Mona, KSNA, Mo. Coalition of Nurse Practitioners Kans. Alliance of Nurse Pactitioners. Home and Office: PO Box 18443 Kansas City MO 64133-8443

WILSON, DON WHITMAN, archivist, historian; b. Clay Center, Kans., Dec. 17, 1942; s. Donald J. Wilson and Lois M. (Sutton) Walker; m. Patricia Ann Sherrod, July 9, 1983; children—Todd, Jeffrey, Michael, Denise. AB, Washburn U., Topeka, 1964; MA, U. Cin., 1965, PhD, 1972, LittD (hon.), 1988. Archivist Kans. State Hist. Soc., Topeka, 1967-69; instr. history Washburn U., 1967-69; historian, dept. dir. Dwight D. Eisenhower Library, Abilene, Kans., 1969-78; assoc. dir. State Hist. Soc. Wis., Madison, 1978-81; dir. Gerald R. Ford Library and Mus., Ann Arbor, Mich., 1981-87; lectr. history U. Mich., 1982-87; Archivist of the U.S. Washington, 1987-93; rsch. prof. Tex. A&M U., College Station, 1993—, exec. dir. George Bush libr. ctr., 1993—. Author: Governor Charles Robinson of Kansas, 1975; editor:

D-Day: The Normandy Invasion, 1971. Mem. Abilene Library Bd., 1973-76; mem. Abilene City Commn., 1976-78; pres. Dickinson County Hist. Soc., Abilene, 1976-77. NDEA fellow, 1964-67; recipient Pub. Service award Gen. Services Adminstrn., 1973. Mem. Am. Hist. Assn. (mem. Beveridge Book Prize com. 1979-82), Am. Assn. State and Local History, Kans. Hist. Soc. (bd. dirs. 1987—), Am. Antiquarian Soc. Republican. Baptist. Home: 209 Chimney Hill Cir College Station TX 77840-1829 Office: Tex A&M U George Bush Libr Ctr College Station TX 77843-1145

WILSON, DONALD WALLIN, academic administrator, communications educator; b. Poona, India, Jan. 9, 1938; s. Nathaniel Carter and Hannah Myrtle Wilson; m. Kathleen, Dec. 28, 1965; children: Carrie, Jennifer, Gregory, Andrew. B.A., So. Missionary Coll., 1959; M.A., Andrews U., 1961; Ph.D., Mich. State U., 1966. Dean applied arts and tech. Ont. (Can.) Colls., North Bay, 1968-73; acad. dean Olivet Coll., 1973-76; pres. Castleton State Coll., 1976-79; pres. Southampton Coll., 1979-83, prof. communications and history, 1973-83; pres., prof. Pittsburg State U. (Kans.), 1983-95; pres. Kilang Nusantara Pacific, 1995—. Author: The Untapped Source of Power in the Church, 1961, Long Range Planning, 1979, The Long Road From Turmoil to Self Sufficiency, 1989, The Next Twenty-Five Years: Indonesias Journey Into The Future, 1992, The Indispensable Man: Sudomo, 1992. Mem. Kans. Adv. Coun. of C.C.'s; bd. dirs. Internat. U. Thailand; pres. Internat. Univ. Found. Named Alumnus of Achievement Andrews U., 1981; recipient Outstanding Alumni award Mich. State U., 1984. Mem. Speech Communication Assn., Assn. Asian Studies, Internat. Univ. Found. (pres.), Rotary. Methodist. Home: 824-B Hugh St Frontenac KS 66763 Office: Kilang Nusantara Pacific Office of Pres Frontenac KS 66763

WILSON, DOUGLAS R., science foundation executive. Pres. 21st Century Genetics Cooperative. *

WILSON, DUANE ISAAC, executive search consultant; b. Westmore, Vt., Nov. 9, 1920; s. Isaac Allen and Ina Elizabeth (Hinton) W.; m. Helen Viola Henrickson, Apr. 25, 1943 (dec. 1985); 1 child, Keith Duane; m. Ellen Merrette Clarke, Apr. 13, 1995. BS, Trinity Coll., Hartford, Conn., 1949. Regional mgr. Roerig div. Charles Pfizer & Co., 1950-61; div. mgr. Hoechst Roussel Inc. (formerly Lloyd Bros.), Mich.,Ohio, 1961-63; pres., owner Duane I. Wilson Assocs., Birmingham, Mich., 1963—. Cpl. U.S. Army, 1942-43. Paul Harris fellow Rotary Internat., 1989. Mem. Rotary Internat. (pres. chpt. 1986-87), Masons-York Rite-KT (pres. Detroit Temple 1989-90, Order of Purple Cross 1992). Republican. Home: 3133 Myddleton Dr Troy MI 48084-1224 Office: Duane Wilson Assocs Inc Veritas-Truth Capabilities 3133 Myddleton Dr Troy MI 48084-1224

WILSON, ESTHER ELINORE, technical college educator; b. Uehling, Nebr., Nov. 4, 1921; d. Lorenz John and Dorothea Emma Rosena (Schmidt) Paulsen; m. Billy LeRoy Wilson, Nov. 14, 1919; 1 child, Frances Ann Wilson Dellar. BS, Morningside Coll., 1950; postgrad., U. Nebr., 1947-80, U. S.D., 1954-83; MS, U. Minn., 1963. Cert. postsecondary tchr., Iowa. Tchr. Irvington (Nebr.) Pub. Schs., 1942-44, Immanuel Luth. Schs., Wichita, Kans., 1944-45, Winnebago (Nebr.) Pub. Schs., 1946-50, Nat. Bus. Coll., Sioux City, Iowa, 1950-51; tchr., asst. prin. Liberty Consol. Sch., Merrill, Iowa, 1951-55; mktg. tchr. coord. South Sioux City (Nebr.) Community Schs., 1955-86; adj. faculty prof. adult basic edn. Western Iowa Tech. Coll., Sioux City, 1989-94; mgr. rental properties Sioux City, 1950—; real estate assoc. State Nat., Dakota City, Nebr., 1988-92, Century 21 Marketplace, Sioux City, 1987-88; advt. sales mgr. Auto Hotline, South Sioux City, 1986-87. Author: I Said I Would, 1995. Vol. tchr. N.E. Nebr. C.C., South Sioux City, 1987-90; supt. St. Paul's Luth. Sunday Sch., Sioux City, 1972-76; treas. Hope Luth. Ch., 1989-95; SBA counselor SCORE, 1995—; co-pres. Friends of Libr., South Sioux City, 1986-88; fundraiser South Sioux City Pub. Libr., 1984-85; pres. Am. Cancer Soc., Dakota County, Nebr., 1979-88; state pres. Nebr. Bus. Edn. Assn., 1979, Distributive Edn. Tchrs. Assn., 1980. Recipient Outstanding Svc. to State Orgns., Nebr. Vocat. Edn. Assn., 1976, Woman of the Yr. Am. Bus. Women Assn., 1972. Mem. Nebr. State Edn. Assn. (sec., treas., v.p., pres., Dedicated Svc. award 1986), NEA, South Sioux City Chamberettes (sec., v.p., pres. 1972-89), Am. Federated Women's Club (sec., v.p., pres.). Home and Office: 435 Dixon Path South Sioux City NE 68776

WILSON, ESTHER MARIE, state legislator; b. Gary, Ind., Jan. 4, 1932; d. John and Mary (Groza) Bulza; m. Cortie L. Wilson, 1922; children: Cynthia Lynn, Cortie Lee, Jr., Tammy Irene. BS, Moody Bible Inst., 1953; MA, Valparaiso U., 1965, LS, 1970. Mem. Ind. Ho. of Reps., 1976-80, 82—; asst. majority whip, vice chmn. human affairs com.; mem. environ. affairs com., roads and transp. com., ways & means com.; bookkeeper Carpets by C.W. Former reading specialist Portage Twp. Sch. Mem. Am. Fedn. Teachers, Nat. Fedn. Bus. and Profl. Women, League Women Voters, Internat. Reading Assn., Ind. State Tchrs. Assn., Portage Democrats Club. Home: 2727 Poplar St Portage IN 46368-2942 Office: Ind State Senate State Capitol Indianapolis IN 46204*

WILSON, FRANCES EDNA, protective services official; b. Keokuk, Iowa, Aug. 4, 1955; d. David Eugene and Anna Bell (Hootman) W. BA, St. Ambrose Coll., 1982; MA, Western Ill., 1990; cert. massage therapist, Shocks Ctr. for Edn., Moline, Ill., 1993. Lic. massage therapist, Iowa. Trainer, defensive tactics Davenport (Iowa) Police, 1990—, police corporal, 1985-94; police sgt. Iowa Assn. Women Police, Davenport, 1994—, apptd. recs. bur. comdr., 1996—, pres., 1989-92; cons., def. tactics Scott C.C., Bettendorf, Iowa, 1993—; owner Wilson Enterprises Ltd., Davenport, 1995—; spkr. workshops. Bd. dirs. Scott County Family YMCA, Davenport, 1990-95, instr., 1989—, The Family Connection, Ltd.; instr. Davenport Cmty. Adult Edn., 1991-94; mem. Iowa SAFE KIDS Coalition, 1992—; mem. First Presbyn. Ch., Davenport, 1986—, bd. deacons, 1995; vol. asst. Davenport Police Dept.'s Sgts. Planning Com. on Tng., 1991, K-9 Unit, 1990-94. Mem. Am. Soc. Law Enforcement Trainers, Law Enforcement Alliance Am., Am. Women Self Def. Assn., Iowa Assn. Women Police (pres. 1989-92, Officer of Yr. 1995), Iowa State Police Assn., Internat. Platform Assn., Internat. Assn. Women Police. Office: Davenport Police Dept 420 N Harrison st Davenport IA 52801-1310

WILSON, FRANCIS MARION, public health services officer; b. Kahoka, Mo., Sept. 7, 1934; s. Francis M. and Florence (Busse) W.; m. Linda Inman, Feb. 16, 1957; children: Gerald, Randall. BS, Culver Stockton Coll., Canton, Mo., 1956; student, U. Mo. Child welfare worker State of Mo., Moberly, 1959-63; counselor Family Svc. Adams Co., Quincy, Ill., 1963-69; exec. dir. Family Svc. Adams Co., Quincy, 1969-73, Schuyler County Mental Health Adminstrn., Rushville, Ill., 1973—; adminstr. Schuyler County Pub. Mental Health, Rushville, 1983—. with U.S. Army, 1956-62. Mem. NASW, Assn. Mental Health Adminstr. (cert.), Am. Orthopsychiatric Assn., Ill. Pub. Health Assn., Masons.

WILSON, FRANKLIN LEONDUS, III, political science educator; b. L.A., Feb. 7, 1941; s. Franklin Leondus II and Ruth (Elieson) W.; m. Carol Ann West, Feb. 16, 1968; children: Erin, Sara, John, Marc. BA in Internat. Rels., UCLA, 1964, MA in Polit. Sci., 1965, PhD in Polit. Sci., 1969; postgrad., Harvard U., 1996. Teaching asst. UCLA, 1966-67, lect., 1969-70; asst. prof. Iowa State U., Ames, 1970-71; assoc. prof. Purdue U., West Lafayette, Ind., 1971-83, prof., head dept. polit. sci., 1987—; vis. scholar Ctr. for European Studies, Harvard U., 1993; vis. asst. prof. Calif. State Coll., Long Beach, 1969-70; vis. prof. UCLA, summers 1984-86, Brigham Young U., Provo, Utah, 1986; chmn. advanced placement test devel. in govt. and politics Coll. Bd., N.Y.C., 1988-93. Author: French Political Parties under the Fifth Republic, 1982, Interest Group Politics in France, 1987, (co-author) Comparative Politics, 1986, 3rd edit., 1995, The Failure of West European Communism, 1993, West European Politics Today, 2nd edit., 1994, Concepts and Issues in Comparative Politics, 1995. Ct. apptd. spl. advocate Tippecanoe County Superior Ct. No. 3, Lafayette, Ind., 1988—&. Named Frederick Hovde Outstanding Faculty Fellow, Purdue U., 1989; Spencer Found. grantee, Chgo., 1989; Japan Found. grantee, N.Y.C., 1990-93. Fellow Am. Philos. Soc.; mem. Am. Polit. Sci. Assn., Midwest Polit. Sci. Assn., French Politics and Soc. (exec. com.), Coun. European Studies, Phi Beta Kappa (pres. Purdue chpt. 1991-92). Home: 423 Jennings St West Lafayette IN 47906-1147 Office: Purdue U Dept Polit Sci 1363 LAEB West Lafayette IN 47907-1363

WILSON, FREDERIC SANDFORD, pharmaceutical company executive; b. Schenectady, NY, Mar. 28, 1944; s. Robert Omer and Isabel May (Sandford) W.; children: Amy Kathleen, Adrienne Ann; m. Judith Ann Goettsche, Feb. 7, 1973; children: Marla Ann, Brian Bennett, Jessica Lea, Jennifer Lynn. BS, Syracuse U., 1968. Acct. exec. Mastropaul Design Inc., Syracuse, N.Y., 1969-70; copy editor Norwich Eaton Pharms., Norwich, N.Y., 1970-72; sales rep. Norwich Eaton Pharms., Gary, Ind., 1972-73; asst. product mgr. Norwich Eaton Pharms., Norwich, 1974-75, mktg. svcs. mgr., 1975-76, product mgr., 1977-81, bus. devel. mgr., 1981-83, sr. product mgr., 1983-85, mgr. med. foods, 1986-89; assoc. mktg. mgr. P&G Pharms., Norwich, 1989-92; dir. profl. rels. P & G Pharms., Cin., 1993—; cons. Sandoz Nutrition Corp., Mpls., 1992. Inventor Jejunostomy Kit, 1981, Vivonex T.E.N. med. food, 1983, Tolerex med. food, 1987. Bd. dirs. Syracuse U. Minority Access Program, 1989-91, Nat. Osteo. Found.; mem. Physician Asst. Found. Mem. Am. Acad. Nurse Practitioners (corp. adv. coun., healthcare industry adv. coun.), Pharms. Assn. for Continuing Med. Edn. (treas., membership chmn.), Am. Acad. of Family Physicians (corp. adv. coun.). Office: P&G Pharms Sharon Woods Tech Ctr 11520 Reed Hartman Hwy Cincinnati OH 45241-2422

WILSON, HAROLD H., executive; b. Jacksonville, Fla., Dec. 17, 1946. BS, Lincoln U., 1968; BS in Personnel Mgmt., Tampa (Fla.) Coll., 1978. Personnel mgr. Fla. Steel Corp., Tampa, 1973-78; tng. and devel., plant safety mgr. Proctor & Gamble, Dallas, 1978-83; cons. Barnhill-Hayes, Milw., 1983-86; nat. tng. mgr. Discover Card, Riverwoods, Ill., 1986-89; affirmative action officer Dean Witter, Riverwoods, Ill., 1989-91; pres. Wilson Group, Inc., Barrington, Ill., 1993—. Co-founder Trinity Baptist Cmty. Ch, Carey, Fla., 1991—. With U.S. Army, 1969-73. Mem. Am. Mgmt. Assn., Am. Compensation Assn., Safety Mgrs. Assn., Nat. Safety Engrs. (sec. 1980), Toastmasters Internat. (pres. 1979-80), Alpha Phi Omega. Office: Wilson Group Inc 26290 W Glenbarr Ln Barrington IL 60010-2863

WILSON, JAMES P., computer consultant; b. Cleve., June 30, 1950; s. John A. and Ruth (Amos) W.; m. Susan Marie Amann, June 26, 1971; children: Mary Patricia, James P. Jr., Richard P. BA, Yale U., 1972; MBA, U. Dayton, 1977. Project coord. Gem City Savs., Dayton, 1972-78; sys. engr. IBM Corp., Dayton, 1978-93; computer cons. Tech. and Telecom Sys., Dayton, 1993—. Mem. Oakwood City Sch. Bd., Dayton, 1981—.

WILSON, JAMES RODNEY, air equipment company executive; b. Kalamazoo, Oct. 5, 1937; s. Orton James and F. Magdalene (Critchelow) W. BA in Psychology, Kalamazoo Coll., 1960. Musician Kalamazoo, Mich., 1955-60; music tchr. Kalamazoo, 1958-60; capt. U.S. Army, 1960-68; sales rep. Wilson Air Equipment Co., Kalamazoo, 1962-70, v.p. mktg., 1970-91, pres., 1991—; cons. in field. Co-founder Rep. Presdl. Task Force, Washington, 1981—, life mem., 1990—; vol. probation officer Kalamazoo County Juv. Ct., Kalamazoo, 1971—; big bro. Mich. Dept. Social Svcs., Kalamazoo, 1987—; mem. steering com. U.S. Senatorial Bus. Adv. Bd., Washington, 1981-88; bd. dirs. Girl Scouts Am., 1995—, Kalamazoo Pub. Edn. Found., 1995—. Recipient Presdl. citation Vols. in Juvenile and Criminal Justice, 1984, Cert. of Merit, Mich. Dept. Social Svcs., 1988, Points of Light award Pres. Bush, 1992, Disting. Svc. award Kalamazoo Coll., 1989. Mem. Chief Engrs. Club Kalamazoo, Kalamazoo Coll. Alumni Assn. (pres. 1984-86), Cathedral Canyon Country Club (Palm Springs, Calif., sec./treas., bd. dirs. 1994—). Republican. Roman Catholic. Office: Wilson Air Equipment Co PO Box 2620 Kalamazoo MI 49003-2620

WILSON, JANET LYNN, broadcast executive; b. Milw., Aug. 24, 1959; d. Raymond George and Rose Marie (Grycowski) W. BA in Radio-TV and Film, U. Wis., 1981. Mem. floor crew and reception dept. Sta. WKOW-TV, Madison, Wis., 1981-82, program asst., 1981-83, program mgr., 1983-86; program coord. Sta. KOTV, Tulsa, 1986-90; program and pub. affairs dir. Sta. WLUK-TV, Green Bay, Wis., 1990-94; mgr. TCI Cable Market Place, Madison, 1994-96; sales rep. WISC 2, Madison, 1996—. Com. mem. Celebrate Americafest, Green Bay, 1990—, com. mem. celebrity auction Muscular Dystrophy Assn., Green Bay, 1990—; sta. chmn. United Way Green Bay, 1990—. Named Media Crimestopper of Yr., Madison Area Crimestoppers Assn., 1994. Office: TCI Cable Advt 7617 Mineral Point Rd Madison WI 53717

WILSON, JANICE L., hydraulic engineer; b. St. Paul, June 2, 1966. BS in Mech. Engring., U. Minn., 1989. Hydraulic engr. Amclyde Engineered Products, St. Paul, 1990—.

WILSON, JANIS KAY, marketing executive; b. Anamosa, Iowa, Dec. 28, 1939; d. Clyde S. and Irma L. (Davis) W. B.F.A., Drake U., 1962. Copywriter, Chase Manhattan Bank, N.Y.C., 1962-66; presentation mgr. Newspaper Advt. Bur., N.Y.C., 1966-71; mktg./promotion mgr. Metromedia, N.Y.C., 1971-74; sr. promotion writer N.Y. Times, 1974-78; dir. mktg. svc. Crain Communications, N.Y.C., 1978-83; promotion dir., Standard Rate & Data Svc. div. Macmillan Pub., Wilmette, Ill., 1984-88, circulation dir., 1988-89; copy supr. The Bradford Exchange, Niles, Ill., 1989—. Mem. Direct Mktg. Assn. Republican. Roman Catholic. Home: 927 Suffolk Ct Libertyville IL 60048-5218 Office: The Bradford Exch 9333 N Milwaukee Ave Niles IL 60714-1303

WILSON, JEAN GADDY, journalism educator, think-tank administrator; b. Lawton, Okla., Feb. 21, 1944; d. Herschel Jamison and Dona (Stiles) Gaddy; m. Rick R. Wilson, Aug. 28, 1966; children: Lindsay Jeanne, Leigh Denise. BJ, U. Mo., 1966. Dir. pub. rels. Columbia (Mo.) Coll., 1967-70, cons., 1970—; dir. pub. rels. Missouri Valley Coll., Marshall, Mo., 1973-74, mem. faculty, 1978-84; dir. devel. U. Mo., Columbia, 1985-86, instr. journalism, 1984-93, exec. dir. New Directions for News, 1987—; pub. rels. cons., 1970-84; dir. Nat. Women and Media Collection, Columbia, 1987--; rsch. cons. Internat. Women's Media Project, Washington, 1987; adj. assoc. prof. U. Mo., Columbia, 1993—. Contbr. articles to various publs., chpts. in books. Bd. dirs. Mo. Sch. Bd. Assn., 1976-82, Marshall Philharm. Orch., 1976-92, Arrow Rock (Mo.) Lyceum Theatre, 1986-92, Journalism and Women Symposium Exec., 1991—; pres. Marshall Sch. Dist., 1981-82. Rsch. grantee Gannett Found., 1981, 84, Knight Found., 1982, AAUW Ednl. Found., 1982, Women in Communications, 1983, Am. Newspaper Pubs. Assn. Found., 1983, Nat. Fedn. Press Women, 1983, U. Mo., 1985, 1993, Robert R. McCormick Tribune Found., 1992—, The Freedom Forum, 1993. Mem. Assn. for Edn. in Journalism and Mass Communications, Women in Communications (student chpt. advisor 1984-90, nat. recognition awrd 1983), AAUW, PEO. Democrat. Presbyterian. Home: Rte 1 Box 198 Marshall MO 65340 Office: New Directions for News 9th And Elm Sts 76G Ga Columbia MO 65201

WILSON, KAREN LEE, museum director; b. Somerville, N.J., Apr. 2, 1949; d. Jon Milton and Laura Virginia (Van Dyke) W.; m. Paul Ernest Walker, 1980; 1 child, Jeremy Nathaniel. AB, Harvard U., 1971; MA, NYU, 1973, PhD, 1985. Rsch. assoc., dir. excavation at Mendes, Egypt Inst. Fine Arts, NYU, 1979-81; coord. exhbn. The Jewish Mus., N.Y.C., 1981-82, adminstrv. cataloguer, 1982-83, coord. curatorial affairs, 1984-86; curator Oriental Inst. Mus. U. Chgo., 1988-96, mus. dir., 1996—. Author, editor: Mendes, 1982; contbr. articles to profl. jours. Mem. Am. Oriental Soc., Am. Rsch. Ctr. in Egypt. Office: Oriental Institute Museum 1155 E 58th St Chicago IL 60637-1540

WILSON, KATHRYN TERESE, food service director; b. Milw., Mar. 7, 1959; d. George Charles and Mary Kathryn (Fink) Schuld; m. Russel Harold Wilson, Dec. 21, 1985; children: Thomas Lawrence, James Charles. BS in Dietetics, U. Wis.-Stout, Menomonie, 1981, MS in Food Sci. and Nutrition, 1984. Lic. food svc. dir./adminstr. Resident housing-bldg. dir. U. Wis.-Stout, Menomonie, 1983-85, substitute teaching staff, 1984-85; asst. food svc. dir. Onalaska (Wis.) Pub. Schs., 1987-90; food svc. dir. West Salem (Wis.) Schs., 1990—; cons. outreach Wis. Dept. Pub. Instrn., Madison, 1993—. Recipient Silver Penguin award Nat. Frozen Food Assn., 1995-96; named Dir. of Yr., Wis. Sch. Food Svc., 1995-96; nutriton edn. grantee Wis. Dept. Pub. Instrn., Madison, 1992. Mem. Am. Sch. Food Svc. Assn. (legis. del. 1991-92, 93, 94, 95, midwest rep. dirs./suprs. com. 1995-98), Wis. Sch. Food Svc. Assn. (chpt. pres. 1991-93, v.p. 1992-93, pres.-elect 1993-94, state pres. 1994-95, legis. com., dist. rep. 1990-93, cons. program of excellence 1992—, legis. com. chair 1996-98, Gold awards 1991-93). Home: N2130 Sunset Ln Rt 2 La Crosse WI 54601

WILSON, KATHY KAY, foundation executive; b. Monticello, Ind., Jan. 25, 1961; d. Kenneth L. and Janet I. (Linback) Kruger; m. Kenneth Culp III, June 18, 1983 (div. Jan. 1986); m. Douglas M. Wilson, July 20, 1991. AS, Ball State U., 1981; BS, Ind. Wesleyan U., 1989. Legal sec. Nesbitt Law Firm, Rensselaer, Ind., 1981-84; asst. to dir. Office of Patents and Copyrights Purdue Rsch. Found., West Lafayette, Ind., 1984-86; legal sec. Barnes & Thornburg, Indpls., 1986-87; rsch. and info. specialist Ind. U. Found., Indpls., 1987-91; dir. prospect rsch. Ind. U. Found., Bloomington, 1991—; cons. Prospect Rsch., Indpls., 1991—; mem. faculty Fund Raising Sch., 1988—. Mem. adv. coun. Bloomington Hosp., 1992—. Mem. NAFE, Am. Prospect Rsch. Assn. (v.p. bd. dirs. 1991, pres. 1992, Ind. chpt. pres. 1988-90), Phi Gamma Nu, Delta Delta Delta. Home: 1225 Pickwick Pt Bloomington IN 47401-6118 Office: Ind U Found PO Box 500 Bloomington IN 47402-0500

WILSON, KAY ARLENE, artist; b. Pemberville, Ohio, Dec. 1, 1937; d. Edwin Thomas and Clarice Kathryn (Reimund) Ridenour; m. David L. Wilson, Aug. 31, 1957; children: Leslie, Julianne, Rhonda. Student, Miami U., Oxford, Ohio, 1956-57; BS in Art Edn., Youngstown State U., 1959. Tchr. adult oil painting Butler Inst. Am. Art, Youngstown, Ohio, Trumbull Art Guild, Warren, Ohio, 1970s and 1980s; owner pvt. home studio, Canfield, Ohio; judge for area shows; speaker, demonstrator for art and civic groups. Exhibited in solo shows at Youngstown Playhouse, 1964, 74, 79, Trumbull br. Kent State U., 1968, Jewish Cmty. Ctr., Youngstown, 1969, Malone Coll., Canton, Ohio, 1970, Trumbull Art Gallery, Warren, Ohio, 1972, 83, 93, Apple Gallery, Boardman, Ohio, 1986, Valley Arts Guild, Sharon, Pa., 1996; affiliated with galleries in Ohio, Pa. and N.Y.C. Recipient Boston Mills Invitational Honor awrd, 1974, Women Artists: A Celebration Body of Work award and First Oil, 1989, 92, Margaret Evans award Body of Work, 1994, The Artist's Mag. Goldern Gallery of Winners, 1995; named Youngstown's (Ohio) YWCA's Woman fo the Year, 1987. Home: 330 Verdant Ln Canfield OH 44406-1134

WILSON, KEN, electrical engineer; b. Logansport, Ind., Oct. 4, 1950. A in Elec. Engring., Purdue U., 1983, BSEE, 1986; MS in Mfg., Boston U., 1992. Software engr. Boxburo, Plymouth, Mass., 1986-87; diagnostic engr. Prime Computer, Framingham, Mass., 1987-89; sr. diagnostic engr. Stratis Computer, Marburo, Mass., 1990-92; owner Real Time Engr., Nashua, N.H., 1993-94; project engr. Bowmar Technologies, Ft. Wayne, Ind., 1994—; owner, cons. Real Time Engr., Ft. Wayne, 1993—. Mem. Optimist Club, Warsaw, Ind.,1995. Recipient Outstanding Grad. award Purdue U., 1986, Alumni award Purdue U., 1986. Office: Bowmar Technologies PO Box 9088 Fort Wayne IN 46899

WILSON, KENNETH GEDDES, physics research administrator, educator; b. Waltham, Mass., June 8, 1936; s. E. Bright and Emily Fisher (Buckingham) W.; m. Alison Brown, 1982. A.B., Harvard U., 1956, DSc hon., 1981; Ph.D., Calif. Tech. Inst., 1961; Ph.D. (hon.), U. Chgo., 1976. From asst. prof. to prof. physics Cornell U., Ithaca, N.Y., 1963-88, James A. Weeks prof. in phys. sci., 1974-87; Hazel C. Youngberg Trustees Disting prof. The Ohio State U., Columbus, 1988—. Co-author: Redesigning Education, 1974. Recipient Nobel prize in physics, 1982, Dannie Heinemann prize, 1973, Boltzmann medal, 1975, Wolf prize, 1980, A.C. Eringen medal, 1984, Franklin medal, 1982, Aneesur Rahman prize, 1993. Mem. NAS, Am. Philos. Soc., Am. Phys. Soc., Am. Acad. Arts and Scis.

WILSON, LOIS ANN, journalist; b. Akron, Ohio, Sept. 27, 1969; d. Edwin and Glenda Louise (Brant) W.; m. Eric Alan Banks, Aug. 12, 1995. BA, Kent State U., 1991. Reporter Palladium-Item, Richmond, Ind., 1991—. Recipient 1st place in-depth bus./econs. news coverage divsn. IV Hoosier State Press Assn., 1995, 1st place best innovation divsn. IV Hoosier State Press Assn., 1995. Mem. Soc. Profl. Journalists. Office: Palladium-Item 1175 N A St Richmond IN 47374

WILSON, LORRAINE M., medical and surgical nurse, nursing educator; b. Mich., Nov. 18, 1931; d. Bert and Frances Fern (White) McCarty; m. Harold A. Wilson, June 9, 1953; children: David Scott, Ann Elizabeth. Diploma in Nursing, Bronson Meth. Sch. Nursing, Kalamazoo, Mich., 1953; BS in Chemistry, Siena Heights Coll., 1969; MSN, U. Mich., 1972; PhD, Wayne State U., Detroit, 1985. RN, Mich. Staff nurse U. Mich. Med. Ctr., Ann Arbor, 1953-54, Herrick Meml. Hosp., Tecumseh, Mich., 1954-69; asst. prof. nursing U. Mich., Ann Arbor, 1972-78, Wayne State U., Detroit, 1978-79; assoc. prof. nursing Sch. of Nursing Oakland U., Rochester, Mich., 1986-89; prof. nursing Ea. Mich. U., Ypsilanti, Mich., 1989—; researcher in field; bd. advs. Profl. Fitness Systems, Warren, Mich., 1986—; cons. wellness and exercise program General Motors CPC Hdqs., Warren, 1986; cons. and faculty liaison nurse extern program in critical care Ea. Mich. U. Catherine McAuley Health Ctr., 1989—. Co-author: (with Sylvia Price) Pathophysiology: Clinical Concepts of Disease Processes, 5th edit., 1986; contbr. articles to profl. jours. Vol. Community Health Screening Drives, Tecumseh, 1960-70, leader Girl Scouts U.S., Tecumseh, 1960; sunday sch. tchr. Gloria Dei Luth. Ch., Tecumseh, 1960; mem. PTA. Grantee Mich. Heart Assn., 1984, 88, R.C. Mahon Found., 1988. Mem. ANA (various offices and com. chairs), Midwest Nursing Rsch. Soc. (v.p., sec.-treas., bd. dirs.), Mich. Nurses Assn. (del.), Nat. League Nursing, Nat. Orgn. Women, Sigma Theta Tau. Lutheran. Home: 1010 Red Mill Dr Tecumseh MI 49286-1145 Office: Ea Mich U 53 W Michigan Ave Ypsilanti MI 48197-5436

WILSON, MARC FRASER, art museum administrator and curator; b. Akron, Ohio, Sept. 12, 1941; s. Fraser Eugene and Pauline Christine (Hoff) W.; m. Elizabeth Marie Fulder, Aug. 2, 1975. BA, Yale U., 1963, MA, 1967. Departmental asst. Cleve. Mus. Art, 1964; translator, project cons. Nat. Palace Mus., Taipei, Taiwan, 1968-71; assoc. curator of Chinese art Nelson Gallery-Atkins Mus., Kansas City, Mo., 1971-73, curator of Oriental art, 1973—, interim dir., 1982, dir. and curator Oriental art, 1982—; mem., rapporteur Indo-US Subcom. on Edn. and Culture, Washington, 1976-79; mem. adv. com. Asia Soc. Galleries, N.Y.C., 1984—, China Inst. in Am., 1985—. Mem. adv. com. Muni-Art Commn. on Urban Sculpture, Kansas City, 1984-87; com. mem. Kansas City-Xi'an, China, Sister City program, 1986—; mem. humanities coun. Joynson County Cmty. Coll., 1976-79; commr. Japan-U.S. Friendship Commn., Washington, 1986-88; panelist Japan-U.S. Cultural and Edn. Cooperation, Washington, 1986-88; mem. mayor's task force on race relations, 1996—; mem. indemnity adv. panel, 1995—; v.p. Brush Creek Ptnrs. 1995—. Recipient The William Yates Medallion Civic Svc. award William Jewell Coll., 1995. Mem. Assn. Art Mus. Dirs. (treas., trustee 1988-90, chmn. works of art com. 1986-90), Mo. China Coun., Fed. Coun. Arts and Humanities (chmn. arts and artifacts indemnity adv. panel 1986-89). Office: Nelson-Atkins Mus Art 4525 Oak St Kansas City MO 64111-1818

WILSON, MARY LOUISE, psychiatric nurse; b. Detroit, Aug. 23, 1954; d. Percy Brown and Willie Margaret (McClellan) Booker; m. Loyall E. Wilson Jr., Nov. 11, 1995; children: Anjeanetta, Anitra, Brandi. Diploma, LPN, Manpower Devel. Tng. Act Sch. Practical Nursing, 1976; AAS in Nursing, Southwestern Mich. Coll., 1993. RN, Mich., Ind. Staff nurse Henry Ford Hosp., Detroit, 1976-84, Detroit (Mich.) Receiving Hosp., 1984-86, Northville Regional Psychiat. Hosp., Northville, Mich., 1986-90, York Woods Ctr., Ypsilanti, Mich., 1986-90; staff nurse Med. Pers. Pool Interim Health Care, South Bend, Ind., 1992—, Nathrup Village, Mich., 1992—; staff nurse Lakeview Community Hosp., Paw Paw, Mich., 1993-95, South Bend (Ind.) Sch. Corp., 1993-95, Meriman Ctr. Westland, Mich., 1995—; nurse cons. Aetna, Southfield, Mich., 1995; cons. Mary Kay Cosmetics. Mem. Phi Theta Kappa. Democrat. Home: 24810 Rensselaer Oak Park MI 48237-1771 Office: Oakland Gen Home Health Agy 27351 Dequindie Madison Heights MI 48071

WILSON, MELODIE J., broadcast journalist; b. Oakland, Calif., July 13, 1950; d. Floyd Brandt Wilson and Muriel June Olson Baumgart; m. Wayne Chalres Oldenburg, June 26, 1982; children: Morgan, Courtney, Lauren, Ryan. BA in Journalism and Mass Comm., U. Minn., 1972; Hon. Doctorate, Lakeland Coll., Plymouth, Wis., 1991. Reporter Mesabi Daily News, Virginia, Minn., 1972-73; reporter/anchor WDIO-TV, Duluth, Minn., 1973-74, WTMJ-TV, Milw., 1974-91; reporter/anchor, polit. analyst WITI-TV, Milw., 1992—; v.p. Milw. Forum, 1988-91; mem. edn. and outreach com. Glass Ceiling Commn., Wis., 1995—. Mem. Child Abuse Prevention Bd., Wis., 1989-92; bd. dirs. Children's Mus., S.E. Wis., 1992—, YWCA,

Milw., 1993—; founding chair Cancer Ctr. Adv. Bd., Med. Coll. Wis., 1995—; mem. Task Force on Battered Women, 1992; bd. trustees Med. Coll. Wis., 1996—. Recipient Legal Reporting award Bar Assn. 7th Cir., 1978, Edn. Reporting award Wis. Edn. Assn., 1979, Reporting award Am. Women in Radio and TV, 1980, Excellence in Journalism award Sigma Delta Chi, 1989. Mem. TEMPO (pres. 1993-94, 96—), Milw. Press Club, Knights of the Golden Quill. Office: WITI TV 9001 N Green Bay Rd Milwaukee WI 53209

WILSON, NIXON ALBERT, biologist, educator; b. Litchfield, Ill., May 20, 1930; s. Benezette Nixon and Adrian Pauline (Barnes) W.; m. Flora Nell Hines, June 15, 1963; children: Stephen Nixon, David Stewart. AB, Earlham Coll., 1952; M in Wildlife Mgmt., U. Mich., 1954; PhD, Purdue U., 1961. Ecologist Hawaii State Dept. Health, Honokaa, 1961-62; acarologist Bernice P. Bishop Mus., Honolulu, 1962-69; prof. biology U. No. Iowa, Cedar Falls, 1969—. Contbr. articles to profl. jours. With U.S. Army, 1954-56. Mem. Iowa Acad. Sci. (zoology editor 1976-91), Iowa Natural History Assn. (sec. 1981-92, hon. mem. 1995), Am. Soc. Mammalogists, Acarological Soc. Am., Am. Soc. Parasitologists, Entomol. Soc. Washington. Office: U No Iowa Dept Biology Cedar Falls IA 50614-0421

WILSON, NORMA CLARK, English language educator; b. Clarksville, Tenn., Jan. 30, 1946; d. James Page and Gertrude Laura (Barton) Clark; m. Larry Newton Wilson, Dec. 27, 1966 (div. Sept. 1970); m. Jerry Wayne Wilson, Nov. 20, 1973; children: Walter Clark, Laura Grace. BA in English, Tenn. Technol. U., 1968; MA in English, Austin Peay State U., 1970; PhD in English, U. Okla., 1978. Tchr. of English Ft. Campbell (Ky.) Mid. Sch., 1968-69; grad. asst. Austin Peay State U., Clarksville, Tenn., 1969-70; tchr. of English Montgomery Cen. High Sch., Cunningham, Tenn., 1970-71; teaching assoc. U. Okla., Norman, 1971-77; English instr. Western Okla. State Coll., Altus, 1977-78; prof. English U. S.D., Vermillion, 1978—; mem. S.D. Humanities Coun., Brookings, 1992—, v.p., 1995-96; vis. prof. Native Am. Lit., Oldenburg U., Germany, 1986. Author: (poetry book) Wild Iris, 1978, (study guide) The Fictional Eye of Eudora Welty, 1991; co-author: (with Jerry Wilson, film script) South Dakota: A Meeting of Cultures, 1985; contbr. articles to profl. jours. Del. Witness for Peace, Nicaragua, 1987, Mexico and Guatemala, 1992; bd. dirs. Clay County Coun. for Recycling and Conservation, Vermillion, S.D., 1992; mem. S.D. Peace and Justice Ctr., Watertown, S.D., 1980—. Symposium grantee Bush Found., 1984, rsch. grantee, 1985; artist's grantee S.D. Arts Coun., 1985. Mem. NEA (mem. pub. rels. com. 1989), MLA (mem. exec. com. of Am. Indian Lit. discussion group 1982-86), Coun. Higher Edn. (pres. U. S.D. chpt. 1993-94), Students for a Just and Dem. Soc. (faculty advisor 1987-91, Environ. award 1991), Voters for Control of Nuclear Waste (faculty advisor 1983-87). Democrat. Home: RR 1 Box 104 Vermillion SD 57069-9737 Office: U SD English Dept Vermillion SD 57069

WILSON, OTIS GARFIELD, appliance dealership executive, commissioner; b. Kenbridge, Va., Dec. 2, 1934; s. Kermit Allen and Lucille Rozelia (Blackwell) W.; m. Carole Lee Swansey, Apr. 15, 1960; children: John Leroy Kovach, Scott Craig, Charles Garfield II. BS, Va. State U., 1957; MS, Fla. Inst. Tech., 1974. Commd. 2d lt. U.S. Army, 1957, advanced through grades to col.; ret., 1985, v.p. Midland (Mich.) Electric Co., 1985—; commr. Midland County, 1991—; mem. bus. adv. bd. Northwood U., Midland, 1992—. Pres. Assn. for Retarded Citizens, Midland, 1988-89; treas. Midland County Child Protection Coun., 1989-90; chmn. Midland County Social Svcs. Bd., 1989; co-chmn. ad hoc com. on delivery of children's svcs. in Mich., Midland County Social Svcs. Agy. Brig. gen. Militia, 1985—. Mem. Midland C. of C. (vice chmn. bd. dirs., chmn. Found. 1993), Elks, Rotary (sgt.-at-arms Midland 1993-94). Republican. Home: 6917 Eastman Ave Midland MI 48640 Office: Midland Electric 6911 Eastman Ave Midland MI 48640

WILSON, PATRICIA MARIE, reading education educator; b. Indpls., Apr. 17, 1942; d. Ezra Lewis and Bertha Ella (Jennison) Moore; m. Daniel Pittman, June 13, 1965; children: Catharine Lynn, Sarah Elizabeth, Kent Daniel. AB, Wheaton Coll., 1964; MA, Mich. State U., 1977, PhD, 1983. Dir. acad. program Grand Rapids (Mich.) Bapt. Coll., 1974-79; adminstr. Calvin Coll., Grand Rapids, 1979-82; asst. prof. Gordon Coll., Wenham, Mass., 1982-86; assoc. prof. Bethel Coll., Mishawaka, Ind., 1987-91; prin. Imlay City (Mich.) Christian Sch., Imlay City, 1991-92; assoc. prof. edn. Taylor U., Upland, Ind., 1992-94, Bethel Coll., Mishawaka, Ind., 1994—. Recipient Excellence in Teaching and Campus Leadership award Sears Roebuck Found., 1989. Mem. ASCD, Internat. Reading Assn., Ind. Reading Profs., Ind. Reading Assn., Ind. Assn. Tchr. Edn. Office: Bethel Coll 1001 W Mckinley Ave Mishawaka IN 46545-5509

WILSON, RAYMOND GALE, physics educator; b. Oak Park, Ill., Jan. 26, 1932; s. Frank Benjamin and Mathilda Dorothy (Havemann) W.; m. Carolyn Curtis, Aug. 1956; children: Laura, Timothy, David; m. Akiko Omoto, Dec. 20, 1985; children: Aya Liann, Taiyo Jon. BS, U. Ill., 1958, MS, 1960; PhD, U. Ariz., 1970. Assoc. prof. physics Ill. Wesleyan U., Bloomington, 1962—; vis. scholar Hiroshima (Japan) Jogakuin U., summers 1983, 86, 89, 92, 95. Author: Fourier Series and Optical Transform Techniques in Contemporary Optics, 1995. Co-dir. Hiroshima Panorama Project, 1988—. With U.S. Army, 1952-54. Sci. faculty fellow NSF, 1966-68, rach. grantee, 1979. Mem. Am. Assn. Physics Tchrs., Optical Soc. Am., Internat. Peace Rsch. Assn., Peace Studies Assn. of Japan. Office: Ill Wesleyan U Bloomington IL 61702

WILSON, ROBERT BYRON, manufacturing executive; b. Flint, Mich., Sept. 13, 1936; s. Hershal B. and Rita M. (Shelton) W.; m. Heide H. Metz, Apr. 13, 1965; children: Martina, Michael, Natalie. BA, U. Chgo., 1959, postgrad., 1960; postgrad., U. Heidelberg, Fed. Republic Germany, 1962. Mgr. market rsch. Westvaco Internat. Div., N.Y.C., 1965-68; various positions Internat. Paper, N.Y.C., 1968-81; pres., chief exec. officer Elgin (Ill.) Corrugated Box Co., 1981—. Home: 711 Council Hill Rd Dundee IL 60118-1008 Office: Elgin Corrugated Box Co 824 Raymond St Elgin IL 60120-8340

WILSON, ROBERT CHARLES, JR., secondary education educator, consultant; b. Trenton, N.J., May 12, 1953; s. Robert Charles and Joan Helen (Graham) W.; m. Pamela Dawn Reinholt, July 9, 1977; 1 child, Brook Douglas. BS in Biology, Baldwin-Wallace Coll., 1975; MA in Sci. Edn., Ohio State U., 1990. Tchr. mid. sch. sci. Lakewood (Ohio) City Schs., 1975-76; high sch. sci. tchr. Reynoldsburg (Ohio) City Schs., 1976—; cons. N.E. Regional Ctr. for Drug-Free Schs. and Communities, U.S. Dept. Edn.; cons. Drug-Free Schs., Consortium of Franklin County, Ohio; co-dir. Reaching Into Student Kliques, 1982—; clin. educator visiting scholar Ohio State U. and Reynoldsburg High Sch.; author, designer peer leadership program Prevention Is the Key, 1990—; mem. Ohio Re-Learning faculty for the Coalition of Essential Schs. of Brown U. and the Dept. of Edn., State of Ohio. Co-author: Global Connections, article in Ednl. Leadership, Jour. of ASCD, 1993. instr. CPR and first aid ARC, Columbus, 1983—. Mem. NEA, Nat. Athletic Trainers Assn. (cert.), Ohio Athletic Trainers Assn., Assn. for Supervision and Curriculum Devel. Home: 7753 Featherleaf Ct Reynoldsburg OH 43068-3172 Office: Reynoldsburg High Sch 6699 E Livingston Ave Reynoldsburg OH 43068-3688

WILSON, ROBERT FOSTER, lawyer; b. Windsor, Colo., Apr. 6, 1926; s. Foster W. and Anne Lucille (Svedman) W.; m. Mary Elizabeth Clark, Mar. 4, 1951 (div. Feb. 1972); children: Robert F., Katharine A.; m. Sally Anne Nemec, June 8, 1982. BA in Econs., U. Iowa, 1950, JD, 1951. Bar: Iowa 1951, U.S. Dist. Ct. (no. and so. dists.) Iowa 1956, U.S. Ct. Appeals (8th cir.) 1967. Atty., FTC, Chgo., 1951-55; sole practice, Cedar Rapids, Iowa, 1955—; pres. Lawyer Forms, Inc.; dir. Lawyers Forms, Inc. Democratic state rep. Iowa Legislature, Linn County, 1959-60; mem. Iowa Reapportionment Com., 1968; pres. Linn County Day Care, Cedar Rapids, 1968-70; del. to U.S. and Japan Bilateral Session on Legal and Econ. Rels. Conf., Tokyo, 1988, Moscow Conf. on Law and Bilateral Rels., Moscow, 1990; U.S. del. to Moscow conf. on legal and econ. rels., 1990. Served to sgt. U.S. Army, 1944-46. Mem. ATLA, Am. Arbitration Assn. (panel arbitrators), Am. Legion (judge advocate 1970-75, 1987-93), Iowa Trial Lawyers Assn., Iowa Bar Assn., Linn County Bar Assn., Delta Theta Phi. Club: Cedar View Country. Lodges: Elks, Eagles. Home: 100 1st Ave NE Cedar Rapids IA 52401

WILSON, ROBERT M., financial executive; b. St. Louis, Aug. 10, 1952; s. William H. and Mary E. (Sacksteder) W.; m. Joli S. Schneeberger, Oct. 7, 1978; 1 child, William Wilcox. BS, Miami U., Oxford, Ohio, 1974; JD, Cleve. State U., 1977. Bar: Ohio; CPA, Ohio. Ptnr. Touche Ross & Co., Dayton, Ohio, 1972-88; exec. v.p. Roberds, Inc., Dayton, 1988—. Chmn. Dayton Ballet Assn., 1979-91; trustee Carillon Park, Dayton, 1988-94, City-Wide Devl. Corp., 1991—; assoc. bd. Dayton Art Inst., 1989-95. Mem. ABA (com. chmn. 1990-92), Ohio Soc. CPAs (pres. 1985-86). Republican. Roman Catholic. Office: Roberds Inc 1100 E Central Ave Dayton OH 45449-1812

WILSON, ROGER B., lieutenant governor, school administrator; b. Columbia, Mo., Oct. 10, 1948; m. Patricia O' Brien; children: Erin, Drew. BA, Ctrl. Methodist Coll.; MA in Edn., U. Mo.; grad., Harvard U., 1990. Asst. prin. Russell Blvd. Elem. Sch., Columbia, Mo.; real estate broker; collector Boone County, Mo., 1976-79; mem. Mo. State Senate from Dist. 19, 1979-92; lt. gov. State of Mo., 1993—; chmn. senate appropriations com., apportionment com., vice chmn. tourism commn.; mem. Mo. bus. and edn. partnership commn., transportation devel. commn., gov.'s adv. coun. physical fitness. Bd. dirs. United Way, Columbia; mem. Mo. Assn. Community Arts Agencies, Boone County Hist. Soc.; mem. com. Mo. Parents as Tchrs. Recipient Everett award MSTA, Boss of the Yr. award Am. Businesswomen's Assn., Disting. Legis. award NCSL, Horace Mann award MNEA, Outstanding Legis. of Yr. award MSTA, 1991 Pub. Official of Yr. award Mo. Assn. Homes for Aging, M.U. Alumni award, 1991. Mem. Columbia C. of C., Cosmopolitan Internat. Office: State Capitol Bldg # 121 Jefferson City MO 65101

WILSON, RONALD J., marriage and family therapist, educator; b. Bismarck, N.D., July 6, 1962; s. Billy E. and Della I. (Olson) W. BS, Ga. State U., Atlanta, 1988, MA, 1990; PhD, U. Ga., 1993. Rsch. asst. Ga. State U., 1989-90, rsch. cons., 1990-93; asst. prof. dept. consumer sci. We. Mich. U., Kalamazoo, 1993—; marriage and family therapist. We. Mich. U. grantee, 1993, 94, 95. Mem. Nat. Coun. on Family Rels., Am. Assn. for Marriage and Family Therapy, So. Sociol.Soc., Am. Orthopsychiat. Assn. Office: We Mich U 3022 Kohrman Hall Kalamazoo MI 49008-5067

WILSON, SAMUEL JOSEPH, historian, educator; b. Gary, Ind., Feb. 19, 1956; s. Charles Wayne and Rose Mary (Odar) W.; 1 child, Rose Mary. BA in History, Ind. U., Gary, 1981; PhD in History, Ind. U., 1991; MA in History, U. Ill., Chgo., 1985. Cert. Kossuth Lajos Tudomanyegyetem, Hungary, 1984. Teaching asst. U. Ill., Chgo., 1981-82; instr. Ind. U., Bloomington, 1984-89; assoc. prof. U. Rio Grande, Ohio, 1991—; mem. editorial adv. bd. Collegiate Press, Alta Loma, Calif. Author: Oszkár Jászi and the Danubian Confederation, 1994, Hungarian Plans..., 1991, books revs.; contbr. articles to profl. jours. Analyst In Focus radio show, Gallipolis, Ohio, 1992; lectr. Rotary, Gallipolis, 1992; active Gallipolis Big Bros./Big Sisters. Grantee Hungarian Ministry of Edn. Rsch. 1984. Mem. SAR, Galla County Hist. Soc., Great War Soc., Hungarian Cultural Assn. (treas. 1984-85), Ohio Acad. History, Ind. U. Alumni Assn., U. Ill. Alumni Assn., Ariel Players, Amnesty Internat., Civil War Trust, Sons Civil War Vets, Kiwanis Gallipolis, Phi Delta Gamma (historian 1991), Phi Alpha Theta. Office: U Rio Grande Wood Hall 216 Rio Grande OH 45674

WILSON, SUSAN BERNADETTE, psychologist; b. Pitts., May 3, 1954; d. Booker Talifero and Edna Jean (Marconi) W.; m. John C. Scott Jr., Feb. 1975 (div.); children: Sharmel D., Justin. BS cum laude, U. Pitts., 1974, MS, 1981, PhD, 1985. Lic. clin. psychologist, Mo. Teaching asst., fellow U. Pitts., 1979-81; intern VA Med. Ctr., Pitts., 1983-84; staff psychologist, fellow Menninger Found., Topeka, 1984-89; clin. dir. Crittenton Kansas City (Mo.) Clinic, 1989-90; asst. prof. Med. Sch. U. Mo., Kansas City, 1990—; cons. The Kaufmann Found., Kansas City, 1990; mem. faculty Karl Menninger Sch. Psychiatry, Topeka, 1986-89; asst. prof. Sch. Medicine, U. Mo., Kansas City, 1990—. Creator workshop: Being the Best You Can Be: A Psychoeducational Program for an Urban Workforce, 1989. Commr. Mayor's Commn. on Human Rights, Kansas City, 1992—; regional adv. com. Dept. Mental Health, Alcohol and Drug Abuse, 1992. Provost Devel. Fund fellow U. Pitts., 1977-79. Mem. Am. Psychol. Assn., Am. Group Psychotherapy, Jack and Jill of Am., Delta Sigma Theta. Democrat. Roman Catholic. Home: 7223 E 134th Cir Grandview MO 64030-3343 Office: Crittenton Kansas City 10918 Elm Ave Kansas City MO 64134-4108

WILSON, THOMAS, draftsman; b. Sarnia, Ont., Can., Apr. 16, 1967; came to U.S., 1967; AD, St. Clair County C.C., Port Huron, Mich., 1989, St. Clair County C.C., Port Huron, Mich., 1992. Draftsman Empire Tool Co., Memphis, Mich., 1990—. Office: Empire Tool Co 11500 Lambs Rd Memphis MI 48041-3106

WILSON, WALTER LEROY, architect; b. Pitts., Aug. 2, 1942; s. Walter Clarence and Marie Zella (Wilcox) W.; m. Maxine Davis, June 4, 1968 (div. 1970); m. Lois Mary McCollum, Mar. 24, 1984; 1 child, Hilary Ann. Student, Altus (Okla.) Jr. Coll., 1961, Cen. State U., 1964-67; BArch, B Archtl. Engring., Okla. State U., 1971. Registered architect, Ohio, Tex., Ark., Wis. Architect, intern Trott & Bean Assocs., Columbus, Ohio, 1971-73; mgr. architecture Southwestern Bell, Little Rock, Houston and St. Louis, 1973-80; prin., ptnr. Caradine & Wilson Assocs., North Little Rock, Ark., 1980-82; office mgr., divsn. mgr. Polytech Inc., Milw., 1982-85; prin., owner The Wilson Firm, Milw., 1985-92; pvt. practice architecture, Wauwatosa, Wis., 1992—; bd. dirs. Milw. Area Tech. Ctr. Archtl. Program; mgr. archtl. and engring. svcs. Housing Authority Dept. City Devel.; co-chairperson Wis. AIA Diversity in Architecture Com.; guest lectr. architectural design solutions to urban design problems U. Wis.-Milw. Sch. Architecture and Planning. Mem. Coalition for Econ. Devel. and Justice, Milw., 1986, State Capitol and Exec. Residence Bd., State of Wis., 1986—; del. state Dem. conv., Milw., 1986; apptd. State Com. Ct.-Related Needs of Elderly and Persons with Disabilities; bd. dirs. Schroeder YMCA, Brown Deer, Wis., 1993—. Served with USAF, 1960-64. Recipient Catalyst for Future Success award Milw. Sch. Engring. Mem. AIA, Am. Solar Energy Soc., Wis. Soc. Architects (sec., treas. S.E. chpt. 1990, v.p., pres.-elect 1991, pres. 1992, past pres., co-chair Architecture Awareness Week 1992), Constrn. Specifications Inst. (pub. rels. chmn. 1986, membership com.). Democrat. Presbyterian. Home and Office: 7601 Harwood Ave Milwaukee WI 53213-2608

WILSON, WILLIAM MICHAEL, JR., theatre educator, director, choreographer; b. Pitts., Sept. 29, 1963; s. William Michael and Patricia Ann Wilson. BFA, We. Mich. U., Kalamazoo, 1987; MFA, Wayne State U., 1992. Asst. prof., assoc. dir. theatre Moorhead (Minn.) State U., 1993—; freelance dir. and choreographer, 1982—; judge Minn. State H.S. League, 1994—. Dir. plays Red Hot and Cole, 1994, Play it Again Sam, 1995, Dames at Sea, 1995. Waldo Sangren rsch. grantee, 1987. Mem. Minn. Comm. and Threatre Assn., Soc. for Stage Dirs. and Choreographers. Office: Moorhead State U Dept Theatre Moorhead MN 56563

WILSTED, JOY, elementary education educator, reading specialist, parenting consultant; b. St. Marys, Pa., Aug. 12, 1935; d. Wayne and Carrie (Neiger) Furman; m. Richard William Wilsted, Feb. 14, 1982; 2 children. BA, Fla. Atlantic U., 1970; MS in Edn., Old Dominion U., Norfolk, Va., 1975. Cert. reading specialist, elem. tchr., Mo.; cert. permanent tchr., N.Y. Tchr. creative dramatics Hillsboro Country Day Sch., Pompano Beach, Fla., 1966-68; tchr. PTA Kindergarten, Boca Raton, Fla., 1968-69; tchr. creative dramatics Wee-Wisdom Montessori Sch., Delray Beach, Fla., 1969-70; elem. tchr. Birmingham (Mich.) Pub. Schs., 1970-72; classroom and reading resource tchr. Chesapeake (Va.) Pub. Schs., 1972-79; reading coord. Harrisonville (Mo.) Pub. Schs., 1979-81; Chpt. I reading tchr., reading improvement tchr. North Kansas City Pub. Schs., Kansas City, Mo., 1981-96; instr. continuing edn. U. Mo., Kansas City, 1980-87, Ottawa U., Overland Park, Kans., 1990—; cons. Young Authors' Conf., Oakland U., Rochester, Mich., 1971; coord. fine arts Alpha Phi Alpha Tutorial Project, Chesapeake, 1973-75; presenter Chpt. I Summer Inst., Tech. Asistance Ctr., Mo., 1984; cons. on parenting Reading Success Unltd., Gallatin, Mo., 1987—; mem. adv. bd. Parents & Children Together, Ind. U. Family Literacy Ctr., Bloomington, 1990-93; keynote speaker ann conf. Nat. Coalition of Chapter I Parents. Author: Dramatics for Self-Expression, 1967, Now Johnny CAN Learn to Read, 1987, Reading Songs and Poems of Joy, 1987, Character-Building Poems for Young People. Mem. Internat. Reading Assn. (mem. coun., pres. local coun. 1986-88, state chmn. parents and reading com. 1988-89, mem. nat. parents and reading com. 1989-92, keynote spkr. IRA Conf. Inst. 1990, local coun., Literacy award 1989). Office: Reading SUCCESS Unltd PO Box 215 Gallatin MO 64640-0215

WILTSE, RICHARD ALLAN, school system official; b. Grand Rapids, Mich., May 10, 1951; s. Eugene William and Ardath Aileen (Johnson) W.; m. Stephanie Ann Wolf, June 7, 1975; children: Jacob Vaughan, Joseph Robert. BS in Edn., Cen. Mich. U., 1973; Masters in Librarianship, Western Mich. U., 1979, postgrad., 1979—. Cert. secondary edn. Media specialist Allegan (Mich.) High Sch., 1974-81; media dir. Northview High Schs., Grand Rapids, Mich., 1981-82; dir. tech. East Grand Rapids Pub. Schs., 1992—. Mem., sect. leader Grand Rapids Chamber Choir, 1984—; chmn. Festival of Music , Grand Rapids, 1985. Recipient Outstanding Tchr. award Northview High Sch., Grand Rapids, 1983, 84, 87, 89, 90, 92, Bus. Week Mag. award for Instructional Innovation, 1990. Mem. Mich. Assn. Media in Edn. (Pub. Rels. award), Mich. Assn. Computer Users in Learning (columnist), Beta Phi Mu. Methodist. Home: 1046 San Juan SE Grand Rapids MI 49506 Office: East Grand Rapids Pub Schs 2915 Hall St SE Grand Rapids MI 49506-3111

WINANS, ANNA JANE, dietitian; b. Freeport, Ill., June 13, 1939; d. Leo Dale and Gwendolyn Jane White; m. Roger Eugene Winans, Aug. 26, 1967; children: Robert, Jonathan. BS in Dietetics, Iowa State U., 1962. Registered dietitian. Clin. dietitian VA Hosp., Madison, Wis., 1963-67; coord. U. Wis. Hosp., Madison, 1967-69; instr. nutrition Madison Gen. Hosp., 1969-75, Madison Area Coll., 1976-81; nutritionist Women, Infants and Children Nutrition Program, USDA, Fremont, Nebr., 1981—; nutrition cons. area health care facilities, Madison, 1976-81, Nebr., 1985—; food svc. auditor, 1995—. Sec. Chapel Hill Pool Bd., Elkhorn, Nebr., 1987-89; bd. dirs. Homeowner's Assn., Elkhorn, 1989-93; active Elkhorn Woman's Club, 1982—; pres. Elkhorn Libr. Bd., 1989-91, 94. Mem. Am. Dietetic Assn. (registered), Nebr. Dietetic Assn., Omaha Dietetic Assn., PEO, Omicron Nu, Psi Chi. Methodist. Home: 910 S 218th St Elkhorn NE 68022-1938 Office: WIC 626 N D St Fremont NE 68025-5054

WINCEL, JEFFREY P., material management professional; b. Dearborn, Mich., Mar. 23, 1963; s. Ralph Dale and Judith Mae W.; children Emily Nicole, Matthew Henry, Alison Lindsey. BS in Labor Relations, Mich. State U., East Lansing, 1986, MBA in Ops. Mgmt., 1988. Purchasing specialist Ford Motor Co., Dearborn, Mich., 1989-94; dir. purchasing, supplier quality assurance ASC Inc., Southgate, Mich., 1994-96; dir. corp. materials Donnelly Corp., Holland, Mich., 1996—. Home: 1323 Steaders Pass Zeeland MI 49464

WINCHELL, GEORGE WILLIAM, curriculum and technology educator; b. Coldwater, Mich., Nov. 12, 1948; s. Elwood F. and Ethel L. (DeBray) W.; m. Marcia A. Hersh, June 7, 1969 (dec.); 1 child, Paul Michael. BA, Mich. State U., 1969; diploma, Leningrad (USSR) State U., 1967; MA, Mich. State U., 1973; EdS, Cen. Mich. U., 1982. Cert. elem., secondary, Russian, lang. arts and social sci. tchr.; cert. adminstr., supt., elem. prin. Elem. tchr. Silverton (Colo.) Pub. Schs.; tech. edn. cons. Stanton, Mich.; off-campus instr. Cen. Mich. U., Mt. Pleasant; profl. devel. coord., facilitator strategic planning, dir. instrn. Ctrl. Montcalm Pub. Sch., Stanton; dir. tech. edn. Cen. Montcalm Pub. Sch., Stanton. Mem. ASCD, Internat. Soc. Tech. Edn., Mich. Assn. Computer Users in Learning, Nat. Staff Devel. Coun. Office: Ctrl Montcalm Pub Sch PO Box 9 Stanton MI 48888-0009

WINCHELL, MARGARET WEBSTER ST. CLAIR, realtor; b. Clinton, Tenn., Jan. 26, 1923; d. Robert Love and Mayme Jane (Warwick) Webster; student Denison U., 1940, Miami U., Oxford (Ohio), 1947, 48; m. Charles M. Winchell, June 7, 1941; children—David Alan (dec.), Margaret Winchell Boyle; m. 2d, Robert George Sterrett, July 15, 1977 (dec. 1982). Saleswoman Fred K.A. Schmidt & Shirmer real estate, Cin., 1960-66, Cline Realtors, Cin., 1966-70; owner, broker Winchell's Showplace Realtors, Cin., 1972—; ins. agt. United Liberty Life Ins. Co., 1966—, dist. mgr., 1967-70, 77-82, regional mgr., 1982—; stockbroker Waddell & Reed, Columbus, Ohio, 1972—, Security Counselors; ins. broker, 1984, gen. agent; dir. Fin. Consultants, 1984, 85, 86, 87, owner; instr. evening coll. Treas., v.p. Parents without Partners, 1969, sec., 1968; pres. PTA; dir. Children's Bible Fellowship Ohio, 1953-76; dir. Child Evangelism Cin.; nat. speaker Child Evangelism Fellowship and Nat. Sunday Sch. Convs., 1955-57; pres. Christian Solos, 1974, Hamilton Fairfield Singles; chaplain Bethesda N. Hosp.; leader singles groups Hyde Park Community United Meth. Ch.; dir. Financial Cons., Sr. Ctr. Dance Leader and Coord. Mem. Nat. Assn. Real Estate Bds. West Shell Realtors (v.p.), Womens Council Real Estate Bd. (treas.). Clubs: Alfonta, Travel go go, Guys and Gals Singles (founder, 1st pres.), Hamilton Singles (pres.). Home and Office: 8221 Margaret Ln Cincinnati OH 45242-5309

WIND, BARRY, art history educator; b. N.Y.C., May 29, 1942; s. Fred and Minnie (Unger) Wind; m. Geraldine Dunphy; children: James Gardner, Clifford Dunphy. BA, CCNY, 1962; MA, NYU, 1964, PhD, 1973. Instr. Rutgers U., New Brunswick, N.J., 1965-66; asst. prof. U. Ga., Athens, 1967-71; from asst. prof. to assoc. prof. U. Wis., Milw., 1971-87, prof., 1987—. Author: Velazquez's Bodegones: A Study in 17th Century Genre, 1987, Genre in the Age of the Baroque, 1991; contbr. articles and revs. to profl. jours. Inst. Fine Arts fellow, 1964-65, NEH fellow Brit. Arts Ctr., Yale U., 1984, Brown U., 1992; Wis. Cook Travel grantee Inst. Fine Arts, 1965.

WINDSOR, MARGARET EDEN, writer; b. Flemington, Mo., Aug. 10, 1917; d. John Denny and Rhoda Belle (Morgan) Head; m. Eugene B. Windsor, Jan. 10, 1987. Ret. med. technologist, 1982. Author: Murder in St. James, 1990, The Outhouse, 1996; editor: From Pandora's Box, 1993. Cpl. USAF, 1944-45. Mem. Columbia Chpt. Mo. Writers Guild (v.p. 1989-90). Democrat. Roman Catholic. Home: 2404 Iris Dr Columbia MO 65202-1265

WINEGAR, LUCIA SPENCER, retired secondary school administrator; b. Fargo, N.D., Mar. 10, 1931; d. Langford and Lucia (Keller) Spencer; children: Lucia Anne Blackwell, William L. BA with high honors, MA, U. Idaho, 1951; postgrad., U. Minn. Cert. French tchr., English 7-12 tchr., secondary prin., dist. supt., Minn. Tchr. Cascade (Mont.) High Sch., 1951-52, St. Margaret's Acad., Mpls., 1952-53; with Carmelite Home, Duluth, 1954-60; dir. Nat. Conf. Christians and Jews, Duluth, 1955-59; tchr. East Side High Sch. Dist., San Jose, Calif., 1966-68, Sunrise Park, White Bear Lake, Minn., 1968-75; assoc. prin. White Bear High Sch., 1975-93. Mem. NEA, Minn. Edn. Assn., NASSP, Minn. Prins. Assn., Phi Beta Kappa, Pi Delta Phi, Delta Kappa Gamma. Roman Catholic.

WINEGARDNER, ROSE MARY, special education educator; b. Granite City, Ill., Feb. 4, 1933; d. Arthur Udell and Margaret Helen (Brown) Barco; m. Carl Norman Winegardner, July 23, 1954; children: Laura Helen, Thelma Rose Winegardner Czajkowski, Jacob Harrison (dec.). BS in Edn., Mo. U., Columbia, 1954; MA in Ednl. Adminstrn., Wyo. U., 1977; edn. specialist, Nebr. U., 1988. Cert. tchr., Nebr., Iowa, Mo. Tchr. Elem. Sch. Grandview & Belton, Mo., 1957-64; tchr. mid. sch. Schleswig (Iowa) Community Schs., 1978-82; spl. edn. resource tchr. Ednl. Svc. Unit #4, Auburn, Nebr., 1982-94, Kans. U. Inst. Rsch. Learning trainer strategy implementation model, 1989—; spl. edn. resource tchr. Dawson-Verdon Consol. Schs., 1990—. Grantee Nebr. Dept. Edn., 1990-93. Mem. Internat. Reading Assn., Coun. for Exceptional Children (v.p. S.E. Nebr. chpt. 1990-92, pres. 1992-94, 94-96), DAR, Phi Delta Kappa, Zeta Tau Alpha. Lutheran. Home: 2100 23rd St Auburn NE 68305-2400

WINEKE, JOSEPH STEVEN, state legislator; b. Madison, Wis., Jan. 5, 1957; s. Edward and Jennie Lanigan Wineke; m. Debora Howe, 1980; children: Scott, Brian. BA, U. Wis., 1980. Alderman Verona, Wis., 1980-83; Wis. state assemblyman dist. 79, 1982-92; former mem. joint fin. com. Wis. State Assembly; legislator dist. 27 Wis. State Senate, 1993—; rsch. assoc. Pub. Expenditure Survey of Wis., Madison, 1980-83; real estate agt. Address: Box 7882 Madison WI 53707*

WINEMILLER, JAMES D., accountant; b. Sullivan, Ind., July 22, 1944; s. Floyd Maurice and Doris Marie (Lone) W.; m. Nancy Kay Walters, Aug. 10, 1963; 1 child, Nancy Marie. AS, Vincennes U., 1964; BS, Ind. U., 1966,

MBA, 1967. With Peat, Marwick, Mitchell & Co., CPAs, Honolulu, 1967-71, with Blue & Co., CPAs, Indpls., 1971-93, ptnr.-in-charge, 1974-92, mng. ptnr., 1977-93. Grad. teaching asst. dept. acctg. Ind. U., Bloomington, 1966-67; instr. acctg. Coll. Gen. Studies, U. Hawaii, Honolulu, 1968-69; dir. Poland State Bank (Ind.), 1974-75. Mem. bd. dirs. Vincennes U. Found., 1992—; dir. Marion County Health Care Ctr., 1988-95. Recipient Elizah Watt Sells Nat. Honorable Mention award, 1966. Vincennes U. Found. fellow. Mem. AICPA (com. mem. 1985—, coun. mem. 1985-96), Ind. CPA Soc. (dir. 1980-86, treas. 1981-82, exec. com. 1983-86, pres. 1985-86, Outstanding Svc. award 1994), Ind. CPA Ednl. Found. (life), Hawaii Soc. CPAs, Continental Assn. CPA Firms (dir. 1978-92, v.p. 1982-83, pres. 1983-84), Nat. Inst. Mgmt. Accts., Ind. U. Well House Soc., Ind. U. Bus. Sch. Deans Assoc. (sr), Ind. U. Alumni Assn. (life), Ind. U. Varsity-Hoosier Hundred, Vincennes U. Alumni Assn. (life, bd. dirs., Pres. award 1994), Rotary (dir. 1973-75, 84-87, 92—, v.p. 1984-86, pres. 1974-75, 87-88, Paul Harris fellow), Econ. Club of Indpls., Hillcrest Country Club. Methodist. Home: 8084 River Bay Dr W Indianapolis IN 46240-2988 Office: 11460 N Meridian St PO Box 80069 Indianapolis IN 46280

WINER, JEROME ALLEN, psychoanalyst, educator; b. Rochester, N.Y., Mar. 19, 1938; s. Lewis and Jean (Shulman) W.; m. Inge Krarup, Sept. 5, 1965; children: Rebecca, Elizabeth, Eric Samuel. AB, U. Rochester, 1959; MD, Yale U., 1963; cert., Chgo. Inst. Psychoanalysis, 1979. Diplomate Am. Bd. Psychiatry and Neurology. Resident in psychiatry Yale U., New Haven, Conn., 1964-67; instr. U. Chgo., 1969-71, asst. prof. coll. medicine, 1971-75; assoc. prof. U. Ill., Chgo., 1976-88, prof. coll. medicine, 1988—; tng. and supervisory analyst Chgo. Inst. for Psychoanalysis, 1986—. Editor: Ann. Psychoanalysis, 1991—; contbr. articles and revs. to profl. jours. Lt. comdr. USNR, 1967. Fellow Am. Coll. Psychoanalysts, Am. Psychiat. Assn.; mem. Am. Coll. Psychiatrists, Ctr. Advanced Psychoanalytic Studies, Internat. Psychoanalytic Assn., Am. Psychoanalytic Assn., Internat. Soc. Polit. Psychology. Jewish. Office: U Ill Med Ctr Dept Psychiatry M/C 913 912 S Wood St Chicago IL 60612-7325

WINES, LAWRENCE EUGENE, lawyer, corporate executive; b. St. Louis, Jan. 17, 1957; s. Frank Peter and Audrey Margret (Murphy) W. BA, U. Mo., 1984; JD, St. Louis U., 1987. Bar: Mo., U.S. Dist. Ct. (we. dist.) Mo. Mem. staff Gephardt for President, Washington, 1987-88; sole practice Ferguson, Mo., 1989-90; ptnr. Progressive Consulting, Ferguson, 1988-93, Wines & Stein attys., P.C., Ferguson, 1990-95; Wines Law Office, L.C., 1995—; pres. Catewood Industries, Inc., Wines Properties, Inc., Wines Enterprises, Inc.; prin. Wines Law Offices, L.C., 1995—. Cons. fundraising Missourias for Mike Wolff, St. Louis, 1988-92, John Shear Election Com., St. Louis, 1988-95, Congresswoman Joan Kelly Horn, St. Louis, 1990-92, Quinn for Sec. State, St. Louis, 1991-92; Ferguson Com. man St. Louis County Dem. Com., 1987-92; vol. Congressman Richard Gephardt, St. Louis and Washington, 1984—. Recipient: Presdl. Svc. award U. Mo. St. Louis Alumni Assn., 1989-90, Disting. Svc. award Disabled Student Union, 1991, Disting. Vol. award U. Mo. St. Louis, 1987; named Outstanding Male Young Dem. Mo. Young Dems., 1986. Mem. Mo. Bar Assn., Mo. Assn. Trial Attys. Roman Catholic. Office: 111 Church St Ste 214 Saint Louis MO 63135-2458

WINFIELD, DAVID MARK, former professional baseball player, commentator; b. St. Paul, Oct. 3, 1951. Student, U. Minn.; LL.D.(hon.), Syracuse U., 1987. Player San Diego Padres (Nat. League), 1973-80, N.Y. Yankees (Am. League), 1980-90, Calif. Angels (Am. League), 1990-91; with Toronto Blue Jays (Am. League), 1991-92, Minnesota Twins (Am. League), 1992-94, Cleve. Indians, 1995; commentator Fox Broadcasting Co., Beverly Hills, Calif., 1996—; mem. Nat. League All-Star team, 1977-80, Am. League All-Star team, 1981-88; led Nat. League in total bases, 1979; played in World Series, 1981. Author (with Tom Parker) autobiography Winfield: A Player's Life, 1988. Recipient Golden glove, 1979-80, 82-85, 87, Silver Slugger award, 1981-85, 92; named top Sporting News All-Star Team, 1979, 82-84, 92; named Sporting News Am. League Comeback Player of Yr., 1990. Office: Fox Broadcasting Co PO Box 900 Beverly Hills CA 90213*

WINFREY, OPRAH, television talk show host, actress, producer; b. Kosciusko, Miss., Jan. 29, 1954; d. Vernon Winfrey and Vernita Lee. BA in Speech and Drama, Tenn. State U. News reporter Sta. WVOL Radio, Nashville, 1971-72; reporter, news anchorperson Sta. WTVF-TV, Nashville, 1973-76; news anchorperson Sta. WJZ-TV, Balt., 1976-77, host morning talk show People Are Talking, 1977-83; host talk show A.M. Chgo. Sta. WLS-TV, 1984; host The Oprah Winfrey Show, Chgo., 1985—; nationally syndicated, 1986—; host series of celebrity interview spls. Oprah: Behind the Scenes, 1992—; owner, prodr. Harpo Prodns., 1986—. Appeared in films The Color Purple, 1985 (nominated Acad. award and Golden Globe award), Native Son, 1986, Throw Momma From the Train, 1988, Listen Up: The Lives of Quincy Jones, 1990; prodr., actress ABC-TV mini-series The Women of Brewster Place, 1989, also series Brewster Place, 1990, movie There Are No Children Here, 1993; exec. prodr. (ABC Movie of the Week) Overexposed, 1992; host, supervising prodr. celebrity interview series Oprah: Behind the Scenes, 1992, ABC Aftersch. Spls., 1991-93; host, exec. prodr. Michael Jackson Talks...to Oprah-90 Prime-Time Minutes with the King of Pop, 1993. Recipient Woman of Achievement award NOW, 1986, Emmy award for Best Daytime Talk Show Host, 1987, 91, 92, 94, 95, America's Hope award, 1990, Industry Achievement award Broadcast Promotion Mktg. Execs./Broadcast Design Assn., 1991, Image awards NAACP, 1989, 90, 91, 92, Entertainer of the Yr. award NAACP, 1989, CEBA awads, 1989, 90, 91, George Foster Peabody's Individual Achievement award, Gold Medal award IRTS; named Broadcaster of Yr. Internat. Radio and TV Soc., 1988; r ecognized as America's 25 Most Influential People Time mag. Office: Harpo Prodns 110 N Carpenter St Chicago IL 60607-2101

WING, ADRIEN KATHERINE, law educator; b. Oceanside, Calif., Aug. 7, 1956; d. John Ellison and Katherine (Pruitt) Wing; children: Che-Cabral, Nolan Felipe. A.B. magna cum laude, Princeton U., 1978; M.A., UCLA, 1979; J.D., Stanford Law Sch., 1982. Bar: N.Y. 1983, U.S. Dist. Ct. (so. and ea. dists.) N.Y. 1983, U.S. Ct. Appeals (5th and 9th cirs.). Assoc. Curtis, Mallet-Prevost, Colt & Mosle, N.Y.C., 1982-86, Rabinowitz, Boudin, Standard, Krinsky & Lieberman, 1986-87; assoc. prof. law U. Iowa, Iowa City, 1987-93, prof. law, 1993—; mem. alumni council Princeton U., 1983-85, trustee Class of '78 Alumni Found., 1984-87, v.p. Princeton Class of 1978 Alumni, 1993—; mem. bd. visitors Stanford Law Sch., 1993-96. Mem. bd. editors Am. Jour. Comp. Law, 1993—. Mem. ABA (exec. com. young lawyers sect. 1985-87), Nat. Conf. Black Lawyers (UN rep., chmn. internat. affairs sect. 1982-95), Internat. Assn. Dem. Lawyers (UN rep. 1984-87), Am. Soc. Internat. Law (exec. council 1986-89, group chair S. Africa 1996—, nom. com. 1991, 93), Black Alumni of Princeton U. (bd. dirs. 1982-87), Transafrica Scholars Forum Coun. (bd. dirs 1993—), Iowa City Foreign Rels. Coun. (bd. dirs. 1989-94), Iowa Peace Inst. (bd. dirs. 1993-95), Council on Fgn. Rels., Internat. Third World Legal Studies Assn. (bd. dirs. 1996—). Democrat. Avocations: photography, jogging, writing, poetry. Office: U Iowa Sch Law Boyd Law Bldg Iowa City IA 52242

WING, JOHN ADAMS, financial services executive; b. Elmira, N.Y., Nov. 9, 1935; s. Herbert Charles and Clara Louise (Stewart) W.; m. Joan Cook Montgomery, June 19, 1964; children: Lloyd Montgomery, Elizabeth Montgomery, Mary Ellen. B.A. in Econs., Union Coll., 1958; LL.B., George Washington U., 1963. Bar: Va. 1963, D.C. 1965, Ill. 1968. Fin. analyst SEC, Washington, 1960-63; trial atty. SEC, 1963-66; asst. to pres. Investors Diversified Services, Inc., Mpls., 1966-67; v.p., gen. counsel A.G. Becker & Co., Chgo., 1968-71, sr. v.p., 1971-74, pres., 1974-80, also dir.; pres., chief exec. officer Chgo. Corp., 1981—, now chmn. bd. dirs.; bd. dirs. Chgo. Bd. Options Exch., Am. Mut. Life. Bd. dirs. Ill. Inst. Tech., Risk Mgmt. Ctr. Chgo. With U.S. Army, 1958-60. Mem. Ill. Bar Assn., Va. Bar Assn., Ill. State C. of C. (bd. dirs. capital fund). Episcopalian. Clubs: Chgo., Economics, Civic, Mid-Day, Bond, Saddle & Cycle. Office: Chgo Corp 208 S La Salle St Chicago IL 60604-1003

WINGFIELD, LAURA ALLISON ROSS, fraternal organization executive; b. Kansas City, Mo., June 8, 1954; d. John Joseph and Jean Marie Ross; m. Wesley Hughes Wingfield, May 13, 1989. BFA, William Woods Coll., 1972-76. Div. chmn. Beta Sigma Phi Sorority div. Walter W. Ross and Co., Inc., Kansas City, 1979-80, dir. rushing, v.p. and asst. dir. service, 1986—; dir. svc., 1991—. Pub. chmn. Kansas City Am. Diabetes Assn., 1985-87, pres., 1986-87; bd. dirs., mem. exec. com. Heart of Am. affiliate, 1986-87, sec. state bd., chmn. pub. rels. com. Mo. state affiliate, 1993-94, bd. dirs. Kansas City chpt., 1993 pub. chmn. Walk fest; reading tutor Project Literacy, 1986, Penn Valley C.C. Republican. Office: 1800 W 91st Pl Kansas City MO 64114-3243

WINITZ, HARRIS, pyschology educator; b. White Plains, N.Y., Mar. 4, 1933; s. Israel and Ann (Weinshank) W.; m. Shevie Winitz; children: Flora, Simeon, Jennifer. BA, Univ. Vt., 1954; MA, Univ. Iowa, 1956, PhD, 1959. Rsch. assoc. Univ. Kansas, Lawrence, 1959-63; asst prof. Case Western Reserve, Cleve., 1963-65; prof. Univ. Mo., Kansas City, 1965—. Author: Articulatory Acquisition and Behavior, 1959; editor: Comprehension Approach to Foreign Language Instruction, 1981, Human Communication and Its Disorders, 1995. City Mental Health, 1987-91. Recipient Career Devel. award NIH, 1968-73. Mem. APA, Linguistic Soc. Am., Acoustical Soc. Am., Child Devel. Office: U Mo 5100 Rockhill Rd Kansas City MO 64110-2446

WINKEL, RICHARD J., state legislator; b. Kankalee, Ill., Sept. 25, 1956; m. Debra Winkel; children: Meghan, David. Ptnr. Harrington, Porter & Winkel, Champaign, Ill.; bd. mem. Champaign County, 1992-94; Ill. state rep. Dist. 103, 1995—; mem. Appropriations-Edn., Higher Edn., Agrl. & Conservation & Judiciary-Civil Law Coms., Ill. House, 1995—. Office: Huntington Towers PO Box 1736 201 W Springfield Ave Ste 205 Champaign IL 61824-1736*

WINKLE, WILLIAM ALLAN, music educator; b. Rapid City, S.D., Oct. 10, 1940; s. Curis Powell and June Ada (Alexander) W.; m. Carola Kay Croll, June 16, 1968; children: Brenda, Rachelle. MusB, Huron U., 1962; MA, U. Vt., 1971; ArtsD, U. Northern Colo., 1976; postgrad., North Tex. State U. Dir. choral and band Arlington (S.D.) High Sch., 1962-64; band dir. DeSmet (S.D.) High Sch., 1964-67; coord. music Huron (S.D.) Pub. Schs., 1967-69; head of instrumental music Huron Coll., 1969-71; dir. bands, prof. music Chadron (Nebr.) State Coll., 1971—; instr. tuba music camp S.D. State U., Brooking, 1969-71, Internat. Music Camp, Dunseith, Nebr., 1977—, high sch. sessions U. Vt., Burlington, 1964-71; tubist, bassoonist Huron Symphony/Huron Mcpl., 1957-69, Nebr. Panhandle Symphony & Symphonia, Chadron, 1971—; tubist Blue Jean Philharmonic, Estes Park, Colo., 1960-64, Internat. Brass Quintet, 1985—; conductor, tour dir. Am. Youth Symphony and Chorus, European Tours, 1967-78; performing artist, clinician Yamaha Music Corp. USA, 1977—. Author: List of Tuba/Euphonium Solos, 1984; co-author: Art of Tuba, 1992; contbr. articles to mags. Moderator, trustee, deacon, conf. bd. dirs. United Ch. of Christ, 1974-90. Recipient Freedom Found. award, 1972, Chadron State Coll. Rsch. Inst. 5 awards, 1974-78. Mem. Chadron C. of C., Nebr. State Bandmasters (dist. VI and coll. rep. 1978-84), Internat. Music Camp (bd. dirs. 1980-86, Disting. Svc. award 1987), Tubist Universal Brotherhood Assn. (internat. rep. 1971—, Nat. Sem. award 1975, 77), Music Educators Nat. Conf., Internat. Assn. Jazz Educators, Concert Bands Am., Nat. Band Assn., Coll. Band Dirs. Nat. Assn., Phi Beta Mu, Kappa Kappa Psi, Kappa Delta Pi. Republican. Home: 318 Ann St Chadron NE 69337-2412 Office: Chadron State Coll 10th Main Chadron NE 69337

WINKLER, ANNE E., economics educator; b. Boston, Oct. 10, 1961. BA in Econs., Wesleyan U., Middletown, Conn., 1983; MS in Econs., U. Ill., 1986; PhD in Economics, Univ. Ill, 1989. Rsch. asst. U. Ill, Urbana, 1986-89; asst. prof. econs. U. Mo., St. Louis, 1989-95, assoc. prof. econs., 1995—. Contbr. articles to profl. jours. Mem. Nat. Assn. Bus. Econs. (sec. St. Louis chpt. 1994-95, treas. 1995-96), Am. Econ. Assn., Population Assn. Am., Midwest Econ. Assn. Office: U Mo Dept Econs 8001 Natural Bridge Saint Louis MO 63121

WINKLER, CHERYL J., state legislator; m. Ralph Winkler; children: Robert C., Ralph E. Student, U. Cin. Clk. Green Twp., 1984-85, trustee, 1986-90; former rep. Ohio State Ho. Reps. Dist. 20; rep. Ohio State Ho. Reps. Dist. 34, 1993—, mem. interstate coop. com., children and youth com., mem. reference, edn. and state govt. com., mem. select com. on tech., mem. joint com. on juvenile corrections & overcrowding. Mem. Cin. Bar Assn. Aux., Green Twp. and Bridgetown Civic Clubs, Western Hamilton County Econ. Coun. Home: 5355 Boomer Rd Cincinnati OH 45247-7926*

WINKLER, DOLORES EUGENIA, retired hospital administrator; b. Milw., Aug. 10, 1929; d. Charles Peter and Eugenia Anne (Zamka) Kowalski; m. Donald James Winkler, Aug. 18, 1951; 1 child, David John. Grad., Milw. Bus. Inst., 1949. Acct. Curative Rehab. Ctr., Milw., 1949-60; staff acct. West Allis (Wis.) Meml. Hosp., 1968-70, chief acct., 1970-78, reimbursement analyst, 1978-85, dir. budgets and reimbursement, 1985-95; ret., 1995; mem. adv. coun./fin. com. Tau Home Health Care Agy., Milw., 1981-83. Mem. Healthcare Fin. Mgmt. Assn. (pres. 1989-90, Follmer Bronze award 1980, Reeves Silver award 1986, Muncie Gold award 1989, medal of honor 1993), Inst. Mgmt. Accts. (pres. 1983-84, nat. dir. 1986-88, pres. Mid Am. Regional Coun. 1988-89, award of excellence 1989), Beta Chi Rho (pres. 1948). Home: 12805 W Honey Ln New Berlin WI 53151-2652

WINKLER, MARGARET ANN, geriatrics nurse, nursing administrator; b. Mo., June 6, 1957; d. John Harvey and Mary Ann (Honigfort) Stark; m. Karl H. Winkler, Mar. 25, 1979; children: Karyl, Kim, Karl. Diploma, Deaconess Hosp., 1978. RN, Mo.; cert. gerontol. nurse; lic. nursing home adminstr. Asst. dir. nursing Masonic Home, St. Louis, 1984-86; dir. nursing Grand Manor, St. Louis, 1986-88; dir. nursing, asst. adminstr. Gravois Health Care, St. Louis, 1988-90; asst. dir. nursing Sherbrook Village, St. Louis, 1990; adminstr. South County Manor, Arnold, Mo., 1990-91, St. Louis Hills Retirement Ctr., St. Louis, 1991-93, Birchway Health Care, St. Louis, 1993—. Mem. Mo. Assn. Dirs. Nursing Adminstrn. (past pres., founding mem.), Long Term Care Dirs. Nursing Assn. St. Louis (past pres.), Nat. Assn. Dirs. Nursing Adminstrn. (founding mem.).

WINN, HUNG NGUYEN, obstetrician, gynecologist, maternal-fetal medicine physician; b. Thanh Hoa, Vietnam, Feb. 11, 1953; came to U.S., 1975; s. Su Cong Nguyen and Diep Thi Truong; m. Lee Nguyen Winn, Aug. 8, 1975; children: John, Jessica, Justin. BA in Biology and Chemistry, Greenville Coll., 1977; MD, U. Ill., Chgo., 1982. Resident in ob-gyn. U. Ill. Peoria, 1982-86, teaching assoc. coll. medicine, 1983-86; fellow in maternal-fetal medicine Yale U. Sch. Medicine, New Haven, 1986-88, instr., 1986-88; asst. prof. ob-gyn Wash. U. Sch. Medicine, St. Louis, 1988-90, maternal-fetal medicine physician Barnes Hosp., St. Louis, 1988-90; dir. maternal-fetal medicine div. St. Louis U., 1990—, assoc. prof. ob-gyn., 1993—. Editor St. Louis Gynecological Soc., 1993—; co-editor: (also co-founder) Jour. of Maternal-Fetal Medicine, (textbook) Clinical Maternal-Fetal Medicine; contbr. articles to profl. jours., chpts. to med. textbooks. Mem. Am. Coll. Obstetricians and Gynecologists, Soc. Perinatologists and Obstetricians. Roman Catholic. Office: St Louis U Sch Medicine St Mary's Health Ctr 6420 Clayton Rd Saint Louis MO 63117-1811

WINN, JILL KANAGA KLINE, management executive; b. Oakland, Calif., Jan. 20, 1944; d. Lawrence Wesley and Virginia Louise (Honold) Kanaga; m. Donald Gene Kline, May 30, 1964 (div. 1979); children: Christian Lawrence, Kirsten Michael. Student, Northwestern U., 1961-63, Stella Adler Theater Studio, N.Y.C., 1963-64, Columbia Coll., Chgo., 1970-71. Comml. actress N.Y.C., 1964-77; v.p. Mid-Continent Agys., Inc., Glenview, Ill., 1980-92, mgr. accouts receivable portfolio program, 1983-92, cons., 1985-92, v.p. ednl. svcs., 1987-92, dir. seminars, 1987-92; dir. mktg. S.E. Collection Co., Glenview, Ill., 1992-93; founder, mng. mem. Vivendi, L.L.C., Northbrook, Ill., 1994—. Recipient CLIO award Am. TV Comml. Festival, 1966. Mem. Kappa Kappa Gamma (v.p. Westport, Conn. chpt. 1996). Democrat. Home: 2050 Valencia Dr Northbrook IL 60062-7057

WINN, KENNETH HUGH, archivist, historian; b. Seattle, June 27, 1953; s. John Hugh and Elaine (Spoor) W.; m. Karen Anderson, June 13, 1981; children: Alice Anderson, David Dysart. BA, Colo. State U., 1975, MA, 1977; AM, Washington U., 1979, PhD, 1985. Resident historian Mo. Hist. Soc., St. Louis, 1987-90, jour. editor, 1987-91, dir. publications, 1989-91; state archivist Sec. State, Jefferson City, Mo., 1991—; vis. asst. prof. Washington U., St. Louis, 1984-87, adj. asst. prof., 1987-90, adj. prof., 1991—; cons. St. Louis Art Mus., 1989-90; dep. coord. Mo. Hist. Records adv. bd., 1991—; adv. bd. Mo. Ctr. for Book, 1993—; bd. dirs. Mo. Conf. History, 1991—, pres., 1994-95; vice chair Mo. Bd. Geog. Place Names, 1995—. Author: Exiles in a Land of Liberty, 1989; co-author Differing Visions, 1994; contbr. chpt. to ency. Charlotte W. Newcombe fellow Woodrow Wilson Found., 1981-82; grantee Richard S. Brownlee Fund, 1992-93, 93-94. Mem. Nat. Assn. Govt. Archives and Records Adminstrs. (pubs. com. 1996—), Am. Hist. Assn., Orgn. Am. Historians, Coun. State Hist. Records Coords. (steering com. 1996—), Soc. Historians Early Am. Republic. Home: 814 Primrose Ln Jefferson City MO 65109-1888 Office: Mo State Archives 600 W Main St Jefferson City MO 65101-1532

WINN, ROBERT CHEEVER, rehabilitation services professional; b. N.Y.C., Apr. 11, 1939; s. Richard Wilkens and Ella Jane (Mackenzie) W.; m. Margery Ellen Irwin (div. Sept. 1983); children: Elizabeth Jane, Margaret Ruth, Nancy Louise; m. Susan Elizabeth Gengler, June 4, 1988. BA, U. Bridgeport, 1962; MA, Ball State U., 1975. Advanced through grades to maj. USAF, 1963-83; customer support rep. Boeing Mil. Airplanes, Wichita, Kans., 1983-89; counselor Wichita Counseling Ctr., 1988; vocat. rehab. counselor Kans. Rehab. Svcs., Wellington, 1989—. Mem. Sumner County ADA Accsssibility Adv. Bd., 1994—; deacon Hillside Christian Ch., 1991-94, elder, 1995—. Mem. Nat. Rehab. Assn., Kans. Rehab. Assn., Kans. Head Injury Assn., Lions (pres. 1994-95, zone chmn. 1991-92, 94-95), VFW (jr. vice comdr. Derby, Kans. chpt. 1989, adj. 1988), Kans. Rehab. Couselors Assn. (sec., treas. 1994-96). Republican. Home: 924 Bristol Ter Wichita KS 67207-4306 Office: Kans Rehab Svcs 1116 W 8th St Wellington KS 67152-0248

WINNING, JOHN PATRICK, lawyer; b. Murphysboro, Ill., Oct. 29, 1952; s. William T. Jr. and Lillian (Albers) W.; m. Jessica Anne Yoder, June 17, 1978; children: Erika Anne, Brian Patrick, Derek Matthew. AB with distinction, Mo. Bapt. Coll., 1974; JD, St. Louis U., 1979. Bar: Mo. 1979, U.S. Dist. Ct. (ea. dist.) Mo. 1979, U.S. Ct. Appeals (8th cir.) 1979, U.S. Dist. Ct. (so. dist.) Tex. 1985, U.S. Ct. Appeals (5th cir.) 1987, U.S. Dist. Ct. (we. dist.) Tex. 1988, Tex. 1989. Assoc. Chused, Strauss, Chorlins, Goldfarb, Bini & Kohn, St. Louis, 1979-81; assoc. counsel Mfrs. Hanover Fin. Services, Phila., 1981-83; corp. counsel Cessna Fin. Corp., Wichita, Kans., 1983-85; atty. Southwestern Bell Publs., Inc., St. Louis, 1985-90; pvt. practice St. Louis, 1990—; pres. Butler Hill Investments, Inc., St. Louis, 1990-91; prin. Success Mgmt. Group, 1991—; sec., bd. dirs. Winning Equipment Co.; asst. prof. bus. adminstn. Mo. Bapt. Coll., 1986-91. Treas. Concerned Citizens of Chesterfield, 1989-91; deacon, mem. fin. com. 1st Bapt. Ch., Ellisville, Mo., 1992-93, vice chmn. fin. com., 1993-94, chmn. fin. com., 1994-95, vice chmn. deacons, 1993-95, dir. Sunday sch., 1993-94; bd. trustees, chmn. athletic com., chmn. by-laws com. Mo. Bapt. Coll., 1992—, sec. presdl. search com., 1994, mem. exec. com., bd. trustees, 1994—; mgr. St. Louis Flames Youth Baseball, 1992-95; mgr. St. Louis Thunder Youth Baseball, 1995—. Named one of Outstanding Young Men of Am., 1987, Outstanding Alumnus Mo. Bapt. Coll., 1987-88, Athletic Hall of Fame, Mo. Bapt. Coll., 1989. Mem. Nat. Lawyers Assn., Eagle Scouts Assn., Met. St. Louis Bar Assn., Christian Legal Soc., Acad. Family Mediators, Assn. Family and Conciliation Cts., Mo. Bapt. Coll. Alumni Assn. (pres. 1980-81, 88-90), St. Louis Assn., Christian Attys., West County C. of C., Chesterfield C. of C. Republican. Southern Baptist. Home: 13261 Romany Way Ct Saint Louis MO 63131-1610 Office: Ste 107 12855 Flushing Meadow Dr Saint Louis MO 63131

WINSEY, GREG JAMES, project engineer; b. Milw., Apr. 17, 1962. Degree in electronics servicing, Waukesha County Tech. Coll., 1983, Assoc. in PCB Tech., 1995. Circuir bd. design engr. Quad Graphics, Pewaukee, Wis., 1985-87; CAD CAM mgr. Cornell Comms., Inc., Milw., 1989—. Merit badge counselor Boy Scouts Am., Milw., 1992-86. Methodist. Home: 115 Concord Pl Apt 8 Thiensville WI 53092-1244 Office: Cornell Comms Inc 4911 W Good Hope Rd Milwaukee WI 53223-4840

WINSHIP, DANIEL HOLCOMB, medicine educator, university dean; b. Houston, July 4, 1933; m. Winnifred Jeneanne Rowold; children: Charles Dwayne, Nancy Ellen, David Rhoads, Rebecca Susan, Molly Beth. BA, Rice U., 1954; MD, U. Tex., Galveston, 1958. Diplomate Am. Bd. Internal Medicine. Intern in internal medicine Ochsner Found. Hosp., New Orleans, 1958-59; asst. resident U. Utah Coll. Medicine, Salt Lake City, 1959-61; fellow in gastroenterology Yale U. Sch. Medicine, New Haven, 1961-63; rsch. fellow med. ethics, fellow law, sci.-medicine program Yale U. Divinity Sch., Yale U. Law Sch., New Haven, 1977; asst. prof., then assoc. prof. medicine Marquette U. Sch. Medicine, Milw., 1963-69; assoc. prof., then prof. U. Mo. Sch. Medicine, Columbia, 1969-84, assoc. dean for VA affairs, 1982-84; prof. U. Kans. Sch. Medicine, Kansas City, 1984-87; assoc. dep. chief med. dir. dept. medicine and surgery VA Ctrl. Office, Washington, 1987-90; prof. medicine, dean Loyola U. Stritch Sch. Medicine, Maywood, Ill., 1990—; gastroenterologist Harry S. Truman Meml. Vets. Hosp., Columbia, 1974-79, chief med. svc., 1979-82, chief staff, 1982-84; chief staff VA Med. Ctr., Kansas City, 1984-86, dir., 1986-87; attending physician Loyola U. Med. Ctr., 1990—, Edward Hines (Ill.) Med. Ctr., 1990—; mem. adv. bd. Greater Chgo. Alliance for Mentally Ill, 1991; pres., bd. dirs. gastroenterology adv. com. VA, 1982-85, chmn. clin. and programs adv. coun., 1988-90; mem. rev. com. Mo. Dept. Mental Health, 1981-82; numerous others. Mem. editl. bd. Clin. Rsch., 1970-73, Annals Clin. Gastroenterology, 1978-83, Gastroenterology: A Weekly Update, 1978-81; assoc. editor Jour. Lab. and Clin. Medicine, 1980-83; contbr. numerous articles and abstracts to med. jours. Bd. dirs. John H. Walters Hospice Ctrl. Mo., 1982-84, chmn., 1983-84. Recipient Outstanding Clin. Tchr. in Medicine award Milwaukee County Hosp. Housestaff, 1964, Golden Apple award Student AMA, 1972, Disting. Svc. medal and award VA, 1990, Ashbel Smith Disting. Alumnus award U. Tex. Med. Br., 1992. Mem. Am. Gastroent. Assn. (com. on rsch. 1975-78, com. on tng. and edn. 1978-81, dir. clin. tchg. project 1990-82, program chmn. motility sect. 1987), Gastroenterology Rsch. Group, Ctrl. Soc. for Clin. Rsch., So. Soc. for Clin. Investigation, Am. Fedn. for Clin. Rsch., Midwest Gut Club (presiding pres. 1980-83), Soc. for Health and Human Values, Inst. Society, Ethics and Life Scis., Sigma Xi, Alpha Omega Alpha (vis. prof. U. Mo. Sch. Medicine 1991, Med. Coll. Wis. 1993). Office: Loyola U Med Ctr 2160 S 1st Ave Maywood IL 60153-3304

WINSHIP, MYRON JAY, physician, microbiologist; b. Casper, Wyo., July 21, 1941; s. Myron Glenn and Betty Jo (Harrington) W.; m. Marilynn Diane Louquet, Sept. 9, 1961; children: Rebecca Lynn, Amy Kathleen. Student, U. Mont., 1959-61, Mont. State U., 1961-62; BS, Northwestern U., 1964, MD, 1966. Diplomate Am. Bd. Internal Medicine, Am. Bd. Infectious Diseases, Am. Bd. Med. Microbiology, Am. Bd. Geriatric Medicine; cert. in infection control. Intern Riverside (Calif.) Gen. Hosp., 1961-67, resident, 1969-71; fellow in infectious disease U. Calif. Davis, Sacramento, 1971-72; practice medicine Missoula, Mont., 1972-89; cons. Mont. Dept. Health, Helena, 1981-89; cons. infectious disease Vets. Hosp., Ft. Harrison, Mont., 1976-89; clin. asst. prof. U. Wash., Seattle, 1974-86, clin. assoc. prof., 1987-89; adj. assoc. prof. Mont. State U.; faculty affiliate in microbiology and pharmacy U. Mont., Missoula, 1976-89; clin. assoc. prof., dept. medicine U. Kans. Med. Ctr., 1994—. Contbr. articles to profl. jours. Mem. adv. com. Missoula C. of C., 1985; trustee Missoula Community Hosp., 1985-86; mem. Mont. Adv. Com. Biotech., Helena. Served to capt. USAF, 1967-69. Fellow ACP, Am. Acad. Microbiology; mem. Am. Soc. Internal Medicine, Am. Soc. Microbiology, Infectious Disease Soc. Office: Hoechst Marion Roussel Inc 10236 Marion Park Drive Kansas City MO 64137

WINSTON, HAROLD RONALD, lawyer; b. Atlantic, Iowa, Feb. 7, 1932; s. Louis D. and Leta B. (Carter) W.; m. Carol J. Sundeen, June 11, 1955; children: Leslie Winston Yannetti, Lisa, Laura L. BA, U. Iowa, 1954, JD, 1958. Bar: Iowa 1958, U.S. District Ct. (no. and so. dists.) Iowa 1962, U.S. Tax Ct. 1962, U.S. Ct. Appeals (8th cir.) 1970, U.S. Supreme Ct. 1969. Trust Officer United Home Bank & Trust Co., Mason City, Iowa, 1958-59; mem. Breese & Cornwell, 1960-62, Breese, Cornwell, Winston & Reuber, 1963-73, Winston, Schroeder & Reuber, 1974-79, Winston, Reuber, Swanson & Byrne, P.C., Mason City, 1980-92, Winston, Reuber & Byrne, 1992-96. Police judge, Mason City, 1961-73. Contbr. articles to profl. publs. Past pres. Family YMCA, Mason City, Cerro Gordo County Estate Planning Coun.; active numerous local charitable orgns. Capt. USAF, 1955-57. Fellow Am. Coll. Trust and Estate Counsel, Am. Bar Found. (life), Iowa Bar Found. (life); mem. ABA, Iowa Bar Assn. (gov., lectr. ann. meeting 1977, 78, 79), 2d Jud. Dist. Bar Assn. (lectr. meeting 1981, 82), Cerro Gordo County Bar Assn. (past pres.), Am. Judicature Soc., Assn. Trial Lawyers Am., Euchre and Cycle Club, Mason City Country Club, Kiwanis, Masons. Republican. Presbyterian (elder). Office: Winston Reuber & Byrne 119 2nd St NW Mason City IA 50401-3105

WINSTON, MAXINE SPEARS, social worker; b. New Orleans, Feb. 12, 1954; d. Thomas Lee and Lovie (Clipps) Spears; m. Joseph M. Winston, July 16, 1983. BS, Southern U., 1975; MSW, U. Wis., Milw., 1985. Genetic counselor sickle cell ctr. Deaconess Hosp., Milw., 1976-77; mental health asst. Milw. County Mental Health Ctr., Milw., 1977-83; social worker adolescent health care MCCH Teach Program, Milw., 1986-88; social worker United Meth. Children's Svcs., 1988-93; social worker, case mgr. Milw. Pub. Schs., 1993—. Recipient Helen Carey Award for Acad. Excellence. Mem. NASW, Wis. Assn. Black Social Workers (treas.), Pi Gamma Mu. Home: 3291 N 36th St Milwaukee WI 53216-3715

WINSTON, ROLAND, physicist, educator; b. Moscow, USSR, Feb. 12, 1936; s. Joseph and Claudia (Goretskaya) W.; m. Patricia Louise LeGette, June 10, 1957; children—Joseph, John, Gregory. A.B., Shimer Coll., 1953; B.S., U. Chgo., 1956, M.S., 1957, Ph.D., 1963. Asst. prof. physics U. Pa., 1963-64; mem. faculty U. Chgo., 1964—, prof. physics, 1975-95, chmn. physics dept., 1989-95. Recipient Kraus medal Franklin Inst., 1996. Fellow AAAS, Am. Phys. Soc., Am. Optical Soc.; mem. Internat. Solar Energy Soc. (Abbot award 1987). Home: 5217 S University Ave # C Chicago IL 60615-4405 Office: Physics Dept U Chgo 5630 S Ellis Ave Chicago IL 60637-1433

WINT, DENNIS MICHAEL, museum director; b. Macon, Ga., Mar. 17, 1943; s. Paul Kenneth and Mary (McClure) W.; m. Patricia McLaughlin, Dec. 27, 1970; 1 child, Laurel Julia. B.S., U. Mich., 1965; tchr.'s cert., Lake Erie Coll., 1970; Ph.D., Case Western Res. U., 1977. Dir. environ. edn. Wiloughby Eastlake City Schs., 1968-70; dir. Ctr. Devel. Environment Curiculum, 1970-75; cons. Ohio Dept. Edn., 1975-77; dir. mus. and edn. Acad. Natural Scis., Phila., 1977-79; v.p., dir. natural history mus. Acad. Natural Scis., 1979-82; dir. Cranbrook Inst. Sci., Bloomfield Hills, Mich., 1982-86; pres. St. Louis Sci. Ctr., 1986-95; pres., CEO The Franklin Inst., Phila., 1995—; adj. asst. prof. Temple U.; past chmn. edn. and human resources adv. com. NSF, 1991-92; past pres. St. Louis Area Mus. Collaborative, 1991-92, mem. exec. com. Grantee in field. Mem. Am. Assn. Mus., Assn. Sci.-Tech. Ctrs. (mem. nominating com., v.p. 1993-95, pres. 1995—), Greater Phila. Cultural Alliance. Home: 8205 Ardmore Ave Wyndmoor PA 19038

WINTER, DALE G., manufacturing executive; b. Sibley, Iowa, Nov. 21, 1956. AS, N.W. Iowa Tech. Coll., Sheldon, Iowa, 1979. Product mgr. Sudenga Industries, Inc., George, Iowa, 1979—; mem. adv. bd. N.C.C. Mem. Luth. Ch. Coun., Boyden, Iowa. Home: PO Box 254 Boyden IA 51234-0254 Office: Sudenga Industries Inc Milling Divsn PO Box 8 George IA 51237-0008

WINTER, KENNETH MICHAEL, editor; b. Lansing, Mich., Aug. 7, 1950; s. Richard G. and Beverly (Radcliff) W.; m. Kay M. Leviere, Aug. 20, 1982; 1 child, Michael. Student, Adrian Coll., 1968-69, Am. U., 1970; BA, Mich. State U., 1972; fellow in journalism, U. Mich., 1979. Youth beat writer Lansing State Jour., 1964-72, reporter, 1972-73, pub. svc. dir., 1973; editor Charlevoix (Mich.) Courier, 1974-76; reporter Petoskey (Mich.) News-Rev., 1973-74, asst. gen. mgr., spl. projects editor, 1976-79, editor, gen. mgr., 1979—; sec., bd. dirs. Otsego Herald Times Inc., Gaylor, MIch., Rev. Dirs. Inc., Petoskey; v.p. No. Mich. Rev. Inc., Petoskey, 1994—. Author: (chpt. in book) Historical Glimpses - Petoskey, 1986; contbr. articles to profl. jours. Pres. Litle Traverse Hist. Soc., Petoskey, 1977-82, United Way Emmet County, Petoskey, 1982; trustee Hist. Soc. Mich., 1979-85; trustee, vice chair Little Traverse Conservancy, Harbor Springs, Mich., 1982—; v.p. Crooked Tree Arts Coun., Petoskey, 1979-86. Nat. journalism fellow U. Mich., 1978-79; numerous journalism awards Nat. Newspaper Assn. Mem. Mich. Press Assn. (bd. dirs. 1992—, numerous journalism awards), Mich.AP Edit. Assn. (bd. dirs. 1992—, pres. 1995—), Am. Soc. Newspaper Editors, Kiwanis (pres. Petoskey chpt. 1983-84). Home: 702 Karamol Ct Petoskey MI 49770-3237 Office: Petoskey News-Rev PO Box 528 319 State St Petoskey MI 49770-2746

WINTER, RICHARD LAWRENCE, financial and health care consulting company executive; b. St. Louis, Dec. 17, 1945; s. Melvin Lawrence and Kathleen Jane (O'Leary) W.; children from previous marriage: Leigh Ellen, Jessica Marie, George Bradford; m. Kathryn Ann Geppert, Dec. 4, 1993. B.S. in Math., St. Louis U., 1967, M.S. in Math. (fellow), 1969; M.B.A., U. Mo., St. Louis, 1976. Rsch. analyst Mo. Pacific R.R., St. Louis, 1971-73; dir. fin. relations Linclay Corp., St. Louis, 1973-74; asst. v.p. 1st Nat. Bank in St. Louis (name now Centerre Bank, N.A.) subs. Boatmen's Nat. Bank, 1974-79; v.p. fin. UDE Corp., St. Louis, 1979-81; pres. Health Care Investments, Ltd., St. Louis, 1981—, Larus Corp., St. Louis, 1981—, Garden View Care Ctr., Inc., O'Fallon, Mo., 1987—; mem. exec. bd. Duchesne Bank, St. Peters, Mo., 1989—; lectr. math. U. Mo.-St. Louis, 1972-74, St. Louis U., 1982-90. Active various fund raising activities including St. Louis Symphony, Jr. Achievement, United Way St. Louis, Arts and Edn. Fund, St. Louis, 1974-79. Served with U.S. Army, 1969-71. Mem. Nat. Health Lawyers Assn., Pi Mu Epsilon. Roman Catholic. Club: Mo. Athletic (St. Louis). Home: 1321 Green Tree Ln Saint Louis MO 63122-4744 Office: Ste 175 12412 Powerscourt Dr Saint Louis MO 63131

WINTER, THEODORE, state legislator; b. Slayton, Minn., Nov. 26, 1949; s. Alphonse and Josephine Schettler W.; m. Marge Meier, 1969; children: Jason, Nathan, Shannon, Brent. AA, Worthington C.C., Minn., 1970. Farmer, 1968—; Minn. State rep. Dist. 22A, 1987—; vice-chmn. ins. and tax coms.; mem. agr. econ. develop., environ. and natural resources, govt. ops. and fin. inst. coms. Mem. Minn. Jaycees (Minn. Statesman award 1983, JCI senatorship 1983—, reg. dir. 1983, dist. dir. 1982), Fulda Area Jaycees (pres. 1981, treas. 1980), Nat. Farmer's Orgn., Fulda Area Comm. Club. Home: RR 2 Box 23 Fulda MN 56131-9503*

WINTER, THOMAS, history educator; b. Bremen, Germany, July 20, 1961; came to U.S., 1988; s. Rolf and Ingeborg (Fehr) W. BA, U. Hamburg, Germany, 1987; MA, U. Cin., 1990; PhD, U. Cinn., 1994. Lectr. Xavier U., Cin., 1994—; adj. asst. prof. U. Cin., 1994-96, No. Ky. U., 1994—; steering com. Soc. History Conf., Cin. 1992-93, co-chair, 1991. Contbr. book rev. to profl. jours., 1994, 95. Rsch. grantee study of philanthropy Ctr. Philanthropy Ind. U., Indpls., 1993; Newberry Libr. Short-Term fellow, 1993, Charles Phelps Taft fellow U. Cin., 1992-93. Mem. Am. Hist. Assn. (Albert J. Beveridge grantee 1996), Am. Studies Assn., Orgn. Am. Historians, So. Historian Assn., Phi Alpha Theta.

WINTER, WINTON ALLEN, JR., lawyer, state senator; b. Ft. Knox, Ky., Apr. 19, 1953; s. Winton A. and Nancy (Morsbach) W.; m. Mary Boyd, July 28, 1978; children: Katie, Molly, Elizabeth. BA, U. Kans., 1975, JD, 1978. Bar: Kans. 1978. Ptnr. law firm Stevens, Brand, Golden, Winter & Skepnek, Lawrence, Kans., 1978—; pres. Corp. for Change; mem. Kans. Senate, 1982-92. Bd. dirs. Lawrence United Fund, Boys Club of Lawrence. Mem. ABA, Kans. Bar Assn., Douglas County Bar Assn. Kans. U. Law Soc. Republican. Roman Catholic. Club: Rotary. Note and comment editor Kans. Law Rev., 1977-78. Office: PO Box 189 502 Mercantile Bank Tower Lawrence KS 66044-0189

WINTERNITZ, FELIX THOMAS, editor, educator; b. Wichita Falls, Tex., Sept. 15, 1958; s. Walter Hines and Josephine (Thomas) W.; m. Connie Yeager, May 28, 1988; 1 child: Kathryn Ann. Attended, Temple U., 1978-81. Police reporter Wilmington (Del.) News-Jour., 1981-83; Sunday editor Savannah (Ga.) News-Press, 1983-85; asst. features editor Rochester (N.Y.) Times-Union, 1985-86; dep. features editor Cin. Enquirer, 1986-89; editorial dir. Cin. mag., 1989-96; spl. projects editor Cin. City Beat, 1996—; adj. prof. journalism U. Cin., 1991—; fellow Poynter Inst. Media Studies, St. Petersburg, Fla., 1991, Knight Ctr. for Specialized Journalism, U. Md., College Park, 1993. Contbr. articles to profl. jours. Mem. Cin. Soc. Profl. Journalists (pres. 1995—). Office: 23 East Seventh St Cincinnati OH 45202

WINTERS, BRENT ALLAN, headmaster, writer, geologist; b. Terre Haute, Ind., Oct. 14, 1954; s. Fredrick Douglas and Wanda Mae (Hudson) W.; m. Susan Kay Armstrong, Oct. 14, 1977; children: Caleb Allan, Jeremiah Brent, Cacey Ariana, Jennifer Beth, Christy Autumn. BS, Ea. Ill. U., 1981; MDiv., Biola U., 1984, ThM, 1987; postgrad., U. Mo., 1988—. Ordained to ministry Christian Ch., 1988. Pastor New Life Bible Fellowship, Terre Haute, Ind., 1988-90; headmaster C.M. Hudson Acad., Martinsville, Ill., 1985—; geologist Sunburst Gold Mining Project, Weaver, Ariz., 1990—, also bd. dirs. Author: Book by Book, 1990, Educate for Freedom, 1991. Speech writer Rep. congl. primary, Ill., 1987. With USN, 1975-85.Rep cand. for U.S. House 19th District, I.L., 1996. Office: C M Hudson Acad PO Box 41 Martinsville IL 62442-0041*

WINTERS, DAVID FORREST, state legislator; b. Springfield, Ill., June 30, 1952; s. Robert Winters Jr. and Helen (Steele) W.; m. Kathleen Wise, 1975; children: Colin, Theresa. BA, Dartmouth Coll., 1974; MS, U. Ill., 1976. Farmer Winnebago County, Ill., 1976-94; commr. Winnebago County, 1986-92; mem. Ill. State Ho. of Reps. Dist. 69, 1995—. dir. Winnebago County Farm Bur., 1993—.

WINTERS, DONNA MAE, writer; b. Rochester, N.Y., Nov. 19, 1949; d. Donald Wansey and Frances Elizabeth (Patte) Rogers; m. Frederick Harvey Winters, Dec. 27, 1971. BS in Mus. Edn., Potsdam State Coll., 1971. Music tchr. pub. sch. Hancock, N.Y., 1971, Caledonia, Mich., 1971—; proofreader Lear/Siegler Inc., 1978-84; freelance writer Caledonia, Mich., 1982—. Author: For the Love of Roses, 1985, Elizabeth of Saginaw Bay, 1986, Jenny of L'Anse Bay, 1988, Mackinac, 1989, The Captain and the Widow, 1990, Sweethearts of Sleeping Bear Bay, 1991, Charlotte of South Manitou Island, 1992, Aurora of North Manitou Island, 1993, Bridget of Cat's Head Point, 1994, Rosalie of Grand Traverse Bay, 1996. Office: Bigwater Publishing PO Box 177 Caledonia MI 49316-0177

WINTERS, PETER L., dermatologist; b. Lockport, N.Y., Dec. 19, 1938; s. Earl Lloyd and Ruby Josephine (Gilmer) W.; m. Judith Barbara Amenta, June 17, 1965 (div. June 1974); children: Christopher Lee, Jonathan Bright; m. Diana Louise bucher, Nov. 27, 1993. BS, Allegheny Coll., Meadville, Pa., 1960; MD, Temple U., 1965. Diplomate Am. Bd. Dermatology, Nat. Bd. Med. Examiners. Pvt. practice dermatology Indpls. Lt. USNR, 1966-68. Fellow Am. Soc. Dermatology (pres. 1992-93), Am. Assn. Dermatology (mem. adv. bd.); mem. AMA, Ind. Med. Soc., Indpls. Med. Soc. (pres. 1989-90, chmn. bd. 1991-92, speaker ho. of dels. 1993-96), Meth. Hosp. Alumni (pres. 1992-94), Ind. Dermatol. Soc. (pres. 1989-90), Highland Country Club, Columbia Club. Republican. Methodist. Home: 1591 Preston Trail Carmel IN 46032 Office: 8402 Harcourt Rd # 620 Indianapolis IN 46260

WINTERS, STEVE G., business executive; b. Oklahoma City, Dec. 22, 1955. Grad., high sch., 1974. Machinist Parts and Equipment, Wichita, Kans., 1975-80; pres. ARE Industries, Wichita, 1980—; speaker in field. Author articles. Office: ARE Industries PO Box 16537 Wichita KS 67216-0537

WINTERSMITH, DEBORAH SUE, drug abuse services professional; b. Tucson, Apr. 11, 1955; d. Howard A. and Lorraine E. (Walker) Stephens; m. Daniel E. Knakiewicz, June 3, 1973 (div. Aug. 1982); children: Sean M., Dani Leigh; m. William H. Wintersmith, Oct. 15, 1983. Tech. degree, Durham Bus. Sch., Phoenix, 1972; computer technician, Midwest Data, Columbus, Ohio, 1984-85; student, Lourdes Coll., 1993—. Counselor substance abuse St. Vincent's Hosp., Toledo, 1992-94, St. Anthony's Villa, Toledo, 1993-95; mgr. Battered Women's Shelter YWCA, Toledo, 1995—. Vol. St. Vincent's Hosp., 1992-93, St. Vincent's Tennyson Ctr., 1991-93. Mem. Zonta Internat. Maumee River Valley chpt. Democrat. Baptist. Office: YWCA 1018 Jefferson Ave Toledo OH 43624

WINTERSTEIN, JAMES FREDRICK, academic administrator; b. Copperas Cove, Tex., Apr. 8, 1943; s. Arno Fredrick Herman and Ada Amanda Johanna (Wagnr) W.; m. Diane Marie Bochmann, July 13, 1963; children: Russell, Lisa, Steven, Amy. Student, U. N.M., 1962; D of Chiropractic cum laude, Nat. Coll. Chiropractic, 1968; cert., Harvard Inst. for Ednl. Mgmt., 1988. Diplomate Am. Chiropractic Bd. Radiology; lic. chiropractic, Ill., Fla., S.D., Md. Night supr. x-ray dept. DuPage Meml. Hosp., Elmhurst, Ill., 1964-66; x-ray technologist Lombard (Ill.) Chiropractic Clinic, 1966-68, asst. dir., 1968-71; chmn. dept. diagnostic imaging Nat. Coll. Chiropractic, Lombard, Ill., 1971-73, chief of staff, 1985-86, pres., 1986—; pvt. practice West Chicago, Ill., 1968-73, Fla., 1973-85; faculty Nat.-Lincoln Sch. Post-grad. Edn., 1967—; chmn. x-ray test com. Nat. Bd. Chiropractic Examiners, 1971-73; govs. adv. panel on coal worker's pneumoconiosis and chiropractic State of Pa., 1979; v.p. Am. Chiropractic Coll. Radiology, 1981-83; mem. adv. coun. on radiation protection Dept. Health and Rehabilitative Svcs. State of Fla., 1984-85; cons. to bd. examiners State of S.C., 1983-84, State of Fla., 1980-85; cons. to peer review bd. State of Fla., 1980-84; trustee Chiropractic Centennial Found., 1989-90; speaker in field. Pub. Outreach, monthly Nat. Coll. Chiropractic; author numerous monographs on chiropractic edn. and practice; inventor composite shielding and mounting means for x-ray machines; contbr. articles to profl. jours. Chmn., bd. dirs. Trinity Luth. Ch., West Chgo., 1970-72, Luth. High Sch., Pinellas County, Fla., 1979-82, St. John Luth. Ch., Lombard, 1988; chmn. bd. edn. First Luth. Sch., 1975-79; chmn. First Luth. Congregation, Clearwater, Fla., 1979-82; chmn. bldg. planning com. Grace Luth. Ch. and Sch., St. Petersburg, Fla., 1984-85; bldg. planning com. ch. expansion, new elem. sch., First Luth. Sch., 1975-79; stewardship adv. coun. Fla./Ga. dist. Luth. Ch. Mo. Synod, 1983-85; trustee West Suburban Regional Acad. Consortium, 1993—. With U.S. Army, 1961-64. Recipient Cert. Meritorious Svc. Am. Chiropractic Registry of Radiologic Technologists, Cert. Recognition for Inspiration, Guidance, and Support Delta Tau Alpha, 1989, Cert. Appreciation Chiropractic Assn. South Africa, 1988. Mem. Am. Chiropractic Assn., Am. Chiropractic Coll. Radiology (pres. 1983-85, exec. com. 1985-86), Am. Chiropractic Coun. on Diagnostic Imaging, Am. Chiropractic Coun. on Diagnosis and Internal Disorders, Am. Chiropractic Coun. on Nutrition, Nat. Coll. Alumni Assn., Am. Pub. Health Assn., Assn. Chiropractic Colls. (sec.-treas. 1986-91), Coun. Chiropractic Edn. (sec.-treas. 1988-90, v.p. 1990-92, pres. 1992-94, immediate past pres. 1994), Fla. Chiropractic Assn. (chmn. radiol. health com. 1977-. Republican. Lutheran. Home: 276 E Edward St Lombard IL 60148-3905

WIRCH, ROBERT W., state legislator; b. Nov. 16, 1943. BA, U. Wis., Parkside. State assemblyman Wis. State Assembly, Dist. 65, 1992—. Mem. Kenosha (Wis.) County Bd. Mem. Polish Legion Am. Vets., Danish Am. Club. Address: 3007 Springbrook Rd Kenosha WI 53142-5701*

WIRKKULA, GEORGE L., investment company executive; b. 1937. With IDS Fin. Svcs., Mpls., 1968-71, Teig-Ross, Mpls., 1971-73; regional sales v.p. Waddell & Reed Inc., Shawnee Mission, Kans., divsnl. sales mgr., exec. v.p. Office: Waddell & Reed Inc 6300 Lamar Ave Shawnee Mission KS 66202*

WIRSCHING, CHARLES PHILIPP, JR., brokerage house executive, investor; b. Chgo., Oct. 26, 1935; s. Charles Philipp and Mamie Ethel (York) W.; m. Beverly Ann Bryan, May 28, 1966. BA, U. N.C., 1957. Sales rep. Adams-Millis Corp., Chgo., 1963-67; ptnr. Schwartz-Wirsching, Chgo., 1968-70; sec., dir. Edwin H. Mann, Inc., Chgo., 1971-74; stockbroker Paine Webber, Inc., Chgo., 1975-85, account v.p., 1986-95; ret., 1995; ind. cons. Paine Webber, Inc., Chgo., 1996—. Mem. adv. coun. John Nuveen & Co., Inc., 1993-95; trustee Wirsching Charitable Trust, 1987—. Republican. Episcopalian. Home and Office: 434 Clinton Pl River Forest IL 60305-2249

WIRSING, DAVID A., state legislator. Commr. Coon Creek Drainage Dist. Ill.; chmn. Syramore Youth Coun.; mem. Sycamore Sch. Bd.; chmn. Sch. Bd. LINK Advt. Com.; Ill. state rep. Dist. 70; pres. Pork Prodrs. Exec. Bd., DeKalb Area Pork Prodrs. Bd. Mem. DeKalb County Farm Bur., Western Ill. U. Swine Rsch. Com., Sycamore Agrl. Advt. Com. Republican. Home: 402 Somonauk St # B Sycamore IL 60178-2249*

WISDOM, BILLIE JOE, state legislator; b. Apr. 11, 1932; m. Joann Wisdom; 2 children. AA, Kansas City C.C. With GM, now ret.; mem. from dist. 6 Kans. State Senate, Topeka, 1993—. Mem. Caw Valley Arts and Humanities. Mem. Masons. Address: 915 S 29th St Ct Kansas City KS 66106

WISE, KENNETH LLOYD, political science, international studies educator; b. Youngstown, Ohio, Aug. 31, 1939; s. William Gilbert and Margaret Irene W.; m. Kay Ann Harris, June 1, 1962; children: Kristl, Kenton. BA, Midland Luth. Coll., 1961; MA, Am.U., 1965, PhD, 1967. Agrl. editor Hastings (Nebr.) Daily Tribune, 1961-63; assoc. prof. polit. sci. Creighton U., Omaha, 1967—, dir. Internat. Rels. Grad. Program, 1981—; v.p. The Wise Choice, Cons., Omaha, 1988—; pres. InterChange Internat., Inc., Omaha, 1976—; cons. North Atlantic Treaty Assn., Brussels, 1987—; coun. mem. InterUniv. Ctr., Dubrovnik, Yugoslavia, 1988-91, 96—. Editor, author: German Unification and All-European Security, 1991; author: Crisis Decisionmaking, 1991. Dir. Omaha Com. on Fgn. Rels., 1968-96. Mem. Nebr. UN Assn. (pres.), Omaha UN Assn. (pres.), Am. Soc. Internat. Law, Global Edn. Assocs., Internat. Studies Assn., Atlantic Coun. of the U.S. (acad. assoc.), Pi Sigma Alpha, Pi Epsilon, Alpha Sigma Nu, Phi Beta Delta. Lutheran. Office: Creighton U Polit Sci & Internat Studies Dept 2500 California Plz Omaha NE 68178-0113

WISE, KEVIN ANDREW, aerospace engineer; b. Champaign, Ill., Nov. 10, 1956; s. Clark Edward Jr. and Mary Julia W.; m. Dana Lynne Thomure; children: Tara Lynne, Ashley Daniel, Nicole Deanne, Jordan Alexandra. BSME, U. Ill., 1980, MSME, 1982, PhD, 1987. Assoc. prof. elec. engring. U. Mo., Rolla, 1990—, So. Ill. U., Edwardsville, 1987—; aerospace engr. McDonnell Douglas, St. Louis, 1982—; owner Inncon Software, Champaign, Ill., 1980-85. Mem. AIAA (assoc. fellow), IEEE, Soc. for Indsl. and Applied Maths. Republican. Roman Catholic.

WISE, LAWRENCE ALLEN, computer analyst; b. Champaign, Ill., Mar. 9, 1964; s. Nelson Ivan and Janice Ruth (Allen) W. BS in Physics, Jacksonville (Fla.) U., 1986. Cert. NetWare engr. Rschr. U. Dayton, Ohio, 1990-91; LAN mgr. Ctrl. Res. Life Ins., Strongsville, Ohio, 1991-94; LAN analyst GTE Mobilnet, Independence, Ohio, 1994—. Lt. comdr. USN, 1986-90. Mem. IEEE, Optical Soc. Am., Soc. Photo-Instrumentation Engrs., Am. Legion, Res. Officer Assn. (jr. v.p. naval svcs. 1993—), Naval Res. Assn., Navy League. Republican. Lutheran. Home: 16400 Heather Ln # 303 Middleburg Heights OH 44130 Office: GTE Mobilnet 6060 Rockside Woods Blvd Independence OH 44131

WISE, MICHAEL STEPHEN, hospice director; b. Jefferson City, Tenn., Feb. 14, 1954; s. Frank W. and Myrtle M. (Newman) W.; m. Adrianne M. Hill, Feb. 28, 1976; children: Stacey L. Wise Mapes, Tammy L. Wise LeClair, Wesley S. AS in Indsl. Safety, Walters State C.C., 1982; BA in Sociology, Carson-Newman Coll., 1987. Asst. safety dir. U.S. Steel Zinc Mines, Jefferson City, Tenn., 1977-85; pastor Mullins Bapt. Ch., Dandridge, Tenn., 1985-87, Rivertown Bapt. Ch., Cheboygan, Mich., 1987-91; dir. Hospice of the Straits, Cheboygan, Mich., 1991—. Bd. dirs. Salvation Army, Cheboygan, Mich., 1994. With USN, 1972-75. Mem. Nat. Hospice Orgn., Mich. Hospice Orgn., Cheboygan County Habitat for Humanity (bd. dirs. 1994-95), Cheboygan Area Ministerial Assn. (sec., v.p. 1989-95). Republican. Baptist. Office: Hospice of the Straits 520 N Main Ste 102 Cheboygan MI 49721

WISE, RITA J., writer, poet; b. Indpls., June 8, 1954; d. Arlessie T. Byrd; children: Chajuana Marita, Russell Aaron. BGS, Purdue U., Indpls., 1995. Cert. beauty/image cons. Office mgr. State Atty. Gen.'s Office, Indpls., 1973-81; adminstrv. sec. student affairs Ind. U., Indpls., 1980-90; part-time bus. instr. Ind. U.-Purdue U., Indpls., 1993-95; loaned assoc. United Way Ctrl. Ind., Indpls., 1995; adminstrv. sec. materials engring. dept. Kelly Svcs./Allison Gas Turbine, 1991-93; outplacement career cons. Outplacement Internat., Indpls., 1996—. Author: (poetry) Relief, 1995, Windows of the World, 1991, What Shall I Tell My Children, 1994, A Mothers' Pay Message, 1989. Mem. Ind. U.-Purdue U. Sch. of Bus. Alumni. Home: 3319 Manor Ct Indianapolis IN 46218

WISE, ROBERT NORMAN, JR., comedian, actor; b. Hinsdale, Ill., June 22, 1949; s. Robert Norman and Rose Marie (Benes) W.; m. Vicki Susan Harland, Aug. 21, 1971. BS in Speech, Ill. State U., 1972. Announcer WIOK/WAKC Radio, Normal, Ill., 1969-76, Keed Radio, Eugene, Oreg., 1976-78, WFMS Radio, Indpls., 1978-80, WIRE Radio, Indpls., 1980-85; stand up comedian US, Can., Caribbean, 1985—. Mem. Assembly of God. Named Air Personality of the Year, Billboard Magazine, 1973. Mem. Masons (North Park lodge). Republican.

WISECARVER, RON B., association executive, consultant; b. Des Moines, Nov. 6, 1939; s. Wendell B. and Eliene D. (Husted) W.; m. Terry J. Coberley, Aug. 25, 1962; children: Kara Eileen, Andrew. BA, Augustana Coll., 1961; MDiv, Luth. Theol. Seminary, 1965. Pastor, campus chaplain Luth. Ch. in Am., Rockland and Bangor, Me., 1965-70; pastor Luth. Ch. in Am., Port Byron, Ill., 1970-72; program dir. Assn. Retarded Citizens, Moline, Ill., 1972-78; exec. dir. McClean County Assn. for Retarded, Bloomington, Ill., 1978-79; dep. dir. Ill. Planning Coun. Developmental Disabilities, Springfield, 1979-81; pres., CEO PARC, Peoria, Ill., 1981—; bd. dirs. CARF, Tucson; bd. reps. ANCOR, Annandale, Va.; cons. cmty. non profit agys., state coms.; pres. Ill. Conf. Execs. of Assns. Retarded Citizens. Contbr. articles to profl. jours. Mem. bd. Office Econ. Opportunity, Rockland, Me., 1965-68; chmn. bd., Bangor-Brewer Mobil Ministry, Me., 1968-70. Recipient Disting. Svc. award, Pine Tree Legal Assistance, 1968, Cert. of Appreciation, PACT, 1987. Mem. Am. Assn. Mental Retardation, ANC. Lutheran. Home: 202 E Miller Rd Edelstein IL 61526 Office: PARC P O Box 3418 Peoria IL 61612

WISEMAN, C. MARVIN (MARV WISEMAN), marriage and family therapist; b. Topeka, Feb. 26, 1938; s. Chester Howard and Frances Lenore (Dick) W.; m. Shirley Joan Stidham, June 16, 1961. BS, Ball State U., 1979, MA, 1979, PhD, 1982. With campus ministries Youth for Christ Internat., various cities, 1956-75; grad. asst., doctoral fellow Ball State Univ., Muncie, Ind., 1976-81; dir. Westminster Counseling Svcs., Marion, Ind., 1979—; instr. Ind. Wesleyan Univ., Marion, 1983-86; presenter/group leader Marion Gen. Hosp., 1987-89. V.p. Marion Urban League, 1981-83; pres. bd. dirs. Marion Philharm. Orch., 1989-92, Family Svc. Soc., Inc., 1993-94; pres. bd. dirs. Habitat for Humanity of Grant County, marion, 1995—. Recipient Citizen Acclaim award Grant County C. of C., 1985, Svc. to Arts award Marion Philharm. Orch., 1991, Vision award Family Svc. Soc., Inc., 1994. Mem. Marion Rotary Club (program chmn. 1992-93). Presbyterian. Home: 4025 N Willow Dr Marion IN 46952 Office: Westminster Counseling Svcs 1100 Jeffras Ave at F/Briarwood Marion IN 46952

WISH, JAY BARRY, nephrologist, specialist; b. Hartford, Mar. 30, 1950; s. Martin and Evelyn Lillian (Lassman) W.; m. Linda Kristina Hansen, June 29, 1971; (div. 1980); children: Allen Jeremy, Robin Lindsey; m. Diane Elizabeth Perkins, June 5, 1983; children: Jeffrey Bryan, David Phillip. BA, Wesleyan U., 1970; MD, Tufts U., 1974. Diplomate Am. Bd. Internal Medicine, Am. Bd. Nephrology. Resident in medicine New England Med. Ctr., Boston, 1974-79; instr. in medicine Tufts U., Boston, 1978-79; lectr. in health sci. Northeastern U., Boston, 1978-79; asst. prof. of medicine Case Western Res. U., Cleve., 1979-85, assoc. prof. of medicine, 1985-96; prof. medicine U. Cleve., Cleve., 1996—; dir. hemodialysis U. Hosps. of Cleve., 1980—, dir. continuing edn., 1987-95; chmn. Med. Adv. Bd. Kidney Found. of Ohio, Cleve., 1985-88. Author: Renal Disease and Hypertension, 1982, Disorders of Potassium, 1984, Metabolic Diseases, 1986, Rheumatic Diseases of the Kidney, 1993, Acid-Base and Electrolyte Disorders in the Critically Ill Patient, 1993, Assuring Quality of Care in Dialysis Patients, 1994; contbr. articles to med. jours. Chmn. med. rev. bd. End-Stage Renal Disease Network #22, Pitts., 1982-87, End-State Renal Disease Network #9, Indpls., 1992—; mem. exec. com. Forum of End-Stage Renal Disease Networks, 1992—; bd. dirs. Renal Phys. Assn., 1993—, sec. 1996—; mem. Nat. Kidney Found. Fellow Am. Coll. of Physicians; mem. Cleve. Restoration Soc., Am. Soc. of Nephrology, Internat. Soc. of Nephrology, Alpha Omega Alpha. Democrat. Jewish. Office: U Hosps Cleve 11100 Euclid Ave Cleveland OH 44106-2602

WISHARD, DELLA MAE, state legislator; b. Bison, S.D., Oct. 21, 1934; d. Ervin E. and Alma J. (Albertson) Preszler; m. Glenn L. Wishard, Oct. 18, 1953; children: Glenda Lee, Pamela A., Glen Ervin. Grad. high sch., Bison. Mem. S.D. Ho. of Reps., Pierre, 1984—. Columnist County Farm Bur., 1970—. Committeewoman state Rep. Cen. Com., Perkins County, S.D., 1980-84. Mem. Am. Legis. Exch. Coun. (state coord. 1985-91, state chmn.

1991—), Fed. Rep. Women (chmn. Perkins County chpt. 1978-84), S.D. Farm Bur. (state officer 1982). Lutheran. Home and office: HC 1 Box 139 Prairie City SD 57649-9714

WISNIEWSKI, SHEILA LOUISE, physical therapist; b. Coldwater, Ohio, June 7, 1965; d. Virgil Lawrence and Alice Ann (Hartings) Moorman; m. Geoffrey Robert Wisniewski, Nov. 3, 1990; 1 child, Kyle. Student, Bowling Green State U., 1983-85; BS in Allied Health, Ohio State U., 1987. Lic. phys. therapist. Phys. therapist, staff supr. Mercy Hosp., Fairfield, Ohio, 1987-89, Advanced Phys. Therapy, Indpls., 1989-93; phys. therapist, supr. Outpatient Rehab. Svcs., Newark, Ohio, 1993—. Mem. Am. Phys. Therapy Assn. Home: 5756 Running Brook Dr Westerville OH 43081

WITCHER, DANIEL DOUGHERTY, retired pharmaceutical company executive; b. Atlanta, May 17, 1924; s. Julius Gordon and Myrtice Eleanor (Daniel) W.; divorced; children: Beth S., Daniel Dougherty Jr., J. Wright, Benjamin G.; m. Betty Lou Middaugh, Oct. 30, 1982. Student, Mercer U., 1946-47, Am. Grad. Sch. Internat. Mgmt., 1949-50. Regional dir. Sterling Drug Co., Rio de Janeiro and Sao Paulo, Brazil, 1951-56; gen. mgr. Mead Johnson & Co., Sao Paulo, 1956-60; area mgr. Upjohn Internat., Inc., Sao Paulo, 1960-64; v.p. Upjohn Internat., Inc., Kalamazoo, 1964-70, group v.p., 1970-73; pres., gen. mgr. Upjohn Internat., 1973-86; v.p. Upjohn Co., 1973-86, sr. v.p., 1986-89, asst. to pres., 1988-89; chmn. Upjohn Healthcare Svcs., 1982-87; ret., 1989; bd. dirs. Upjohn Co.; trustee Am. Grad. Sch. Internat. Mgmt., 1981—. With USNR, 1943-46. Mem. Pharm. Mfrs. Assn. (chmn. internat. sect. 1981-82, 85-86), Am. Grad. Sch. Internat. Mgmt. Alumni Assn. (pres. 1989-91). Republican. Episcopalian.

WITCHER, GARY ROYAL, minister, educator; b. Clinton, Okla., July 4, 1950; s. Alton Gale and Frances Loraine (Royal) W.; m. Victoria Amy Waddington, June 6, 1970; children: Jessica, Toni, Monica. BA in Art, Southwestern Okla. State U., 1973, BA in Art Edn., 1975, MEd in Art, 1978. Minister, 1979. Tchr. Window Rock Sch. Dist., Ft. Defiance, Ariz., 1973-76, Western Heights (Okla.) Sch. Dist., Oklahoma City, 1976-77, Mustang (Okla.) Sch. Dist., 1977-79; minister Ch. of Christ, Cervignano, Italy, 1979-86, Watertown, S.D., 1986—; instr. Harmony Hill Coll., Watertown, 1987—; part-time tchr. Watertown Sch. Dist., 1987—; bd. dirs. East River Bible Camp, 1988—. Recipient 1st Place Slide Program Competition prize Am. Fedn. Mineralogical Socs., 1993, 95. Mem. Coteau des Plains Gem and Mineral Soc. (pres. 1991-92, 95). Republican. Home: PO Box 1622 1105 4th St NE Watertown SD 57201 Office: Ch of Christ 1103 4th St NE Watertown SD 57201-1202

WITEK, KATE, state senator, trucking company executive; b. Detroit, Oct. 22, 1954; m. Charles Wite, 1974; children: Thomas Charles, Kimberly Rose. Student, Ea. Mich. U. Owner, mgr. Witek Trucking Co.; mem. Nebr. Senate, Lincoln, 1992—; mem. commerce and ins. com., govt., mil. and vet. affairs com. Mem. Nat. Small Bus. United, Nebr. Motor Carriers, Millard Jaycees. Republican. Home: 5179 S 147th St Omaha NE 68137-1439*

WITHEM, RONALD E., state senator, trade association executive; b. Logan, Iowa, June 9, 1946; m. Diane Weinstein, 1973; children: Susanne, Justin. BA, Wayne State Coll., 1968; MS, U. Nebr., Omaha, 1975. Tchr. Papillion (Nebr.) H.S.; exec. v.p. Mech. Constructors Assn. Omaha; mem. Nebr. Senate, Lincoln, 1983—; chmn. edn. com., mem. rules com., revenue com., former mem. govt., mil. and vet. affairs coms. Former chmn. Edn. Commn. of States; former office mgr. U.S. Rep. John J. Cavanaugh. Mem. Papillion C. of C., LaVista C. of C., Omaha C. of C. Democrat. Home: 719 Donegal Dr Papillion NE 68046-2101 also: Nebr State Legislature State Capital Lincoln NE 68516*

WITHERSPOON, WILLIAM, investment economist; b. St. Louis, Nov. 21, 1909; s. William Conner and Mary Louise (Houston) W.; student Washington U. Evening Sch., 1928-47; m. Margaret Telford Johanson, June 25, 1938; children: James Tomlin, Jane Telford, Elizabeth Witherspoon Vodra. Rsch. dept. A. G. Edwards & Sons, 1928-31; pres. Witherspoon Investment Co., 1931-34; head rsch. dept. Newhard Cook & Co., 1934-43; chief price analysis St. Louis Ordnance Dist., 1943-45; head rsch. dept. Newhard Cook & Co., 1945-53; owner Witherspoon Investment Counsel, 1953-64; ltd. ptnr. Newhard Cook & Co., economist, investment analyst, 1965-68; v.p. rsch. Stifel, Nicolaus & Co., 1968-81; lectr. on investments Washington U., 1948-67. Mem. Clayton Bd. of Edn., 1955-68, treas., 1956-68, pres., 1966-67; mem. Clayton Park and Recreation Commn., 1959-60; trustee Ednl. TV, KETC, 1963-64; mem. investment com. Gen. Assembly Mission Bd. Presbyn. Ch. (USA), Atlanta, 1976-79, mem. permanent com. ordination exams, 1979-85; cons. to investment com. Ctr. Theol. Inquiry, Princeton, N.J., 1995—. Served as civilian Ordnance Dept., AUS, 1943-45. Chartered fin. analyst. Mem. St. Louis Soc. Fin. Analysts (pres. 1949-50). Club: Mo. Athletic (St. Louis). Home: 6401 Ellenwood Ave Saint Louis MO 63105-2228

WITHROW, MARY ELLEN, treasurer of United States; b. Marion, Ohio, Oct. 2, 1930; d. Clyde Welsh and Mildred (Stump) Hinamon; m. Norman David Withrow, Sept. 4, 1948; children: Linda Rizzo, Leslie Legge, Norma, Rebecca. Mem. Elgin Local Bd. Edn., Marion, Ohio, 1969-73, pres., 1972; safety programs dir. ARC, Marion, 1968-72; dep. registrar State of Ohio, Marion, 1972-75; dep. county auditor Marion County, Ohio, 1975-77, county treas., 1977-83; treas. State of Ohio, Columbus, 1983-94; treas. of the U.S. Dept. Treasury, Washington, 1994—; chmn. Ohio Bd. Deposits, 1983—, Anthony Commn. on Pub. Fin. Mem. exec. com. Ohio Dem. Com., mem. exec. com. women's caucus; mem. Dem. Nat. Com.; mem. Met. Women's Ctr.; pres. Marion County Dem. Club, 1976; participant Harvard U. Strategic Leadership Conf., 1990.; mem. Dem. Leadership Coun. Recipient Donald L. Scantlebury Meml. award, 1991, Women of Achievement award YWCA of Met. Columbus, 1993, Outstanding Govt. Svc. award Am. Numis. Assn., 1995; inducted Ohio Women's Hall of Fame, 1986; named Outstanding Elected Dem. Woman Holding Pub. Office, Nat. Fedn. Dem. Women, 1987, Advocate of Yr., SBA, 1988, Most Valuable State Pub. Ofcl., City and State newspaper, 1990; Women Execs. in State Govt. fellow Harvard U., 1987. Mem. LWV (dem. leadership coun.), State Assn. County Treas. (legis. com. 1979-83, treas. 1982), Nat. Assn. State Treas. (pres. 1992, Jesse Unruh award 1993, chair long range planning com., mem. exec. com.), Nat. Assn. State Auditors Comtps. and Treas. (pres. 1990, strategic planning com., intergov. rels. com., chair state and mcpl. bonds com.), Coun. State Govts. (exec. com., internat. affairs com., orgnl. planning and coord. com., strategic planning task force), Women Execs. in State Govt. (chair fund devel. com.). Club: Bus. and Profl. Women's. Office: Dept Treasury 1500 Pennsylvania Ave NW Washington DC 20005-1007

WITHROW, SHEILA KAY, school nurse; b. Dayton, Ohio, Oct. 13, 1959; d. Robert and Shirley Elaine (McGuire) H.; m. James Laurence Withrow, Jr., Aug. 7, 1982; 1 child, Robert Laurence. AAS in Nursing, Miami U., Oxford, Ohio, 1982, BS in Nursing, 1987. RN, Ohio. Staff nurse Children's Hosp. Med. Ctr., Cin., 1982-84; staff nurse Middletown (Ohio) Regional Hosp., 1984-87, adminstrv. clin. coord., 1987-90; clin. coord. Middletown Regional Hosp., 1990-91; sch. nurse Franklin (Ohio) City Schs., 1991—; participant Nursing Grand Rounds The Total Hip Patient, 1986; mem. Patient Care task force, 1988. Mem. Nat. Assn. Sch. Nurses, Ohio Assn. Sch. Nurses. Democrat. Baptist. Home: 205 Leland Ct Middletown OH 45042-3915 Office: Franklin City Schs 150 E 6th St Franklin OH 45005-2555

WITT, CAROLYN M., library director, educator; b. St. Louis, Nov. 25, 1949; d. Clyde Max and Jane (Hawman) W. BA, William Woods Coll., 1972; MA in History, St. Louis U., 1974; MLS, U. Mo., 1976. Tchg. cert. grades 7-12 social studies, libr. cert grades K-12, Mo. Sch. libr. New Haven (Mo.) Sch. Dist., 1976-81; dir. Washington (Mo.) Pub. Libr., 1981—; part-time prof. East Ctrl. Coll., Union, Mo., 1987—. Sec. United Fund, Washington, 1990-91. Recipient Literacy award Moremac Valley Coun. IRA, 1992. Mem. ALA, Pub. Libr. Assn., Mo. Libr. Assn. (sec. 1993-94), Mo. Pub. Libr. Dirs. (pres. 1995—). Office: Washington Pub Libr 415 Jefferson Washington MO 63090

WITT, GARY DEAN, state legislator; b. Smithville, Mo., Feb. 2, 1965; s. Donald Audon and Jo Ellen Witt. BA in Comm., William Jewel Coll., 1987; JD, U. Mo., Columbia, 1990. Bar: Mo. 1990, Kans. 1992. Assoc. Witt & Hicklin, Platte City, Mo., 1990—; mem. Mo. Ho. of Reps., Jefferson City, 1990-96, chmn. judiciary and ethics com., 1993-96. Named one of Ten Outstanding Young Missourians, Mo. Jaycees, 1993, Outstanding Legislator, Mo. Bar Assn., 1993; recipient Outstanding Contbn. to Adminstrn. of Justice award Mo. Jud. Conf., 1991, 92, 93, 94, 95; Walter Pope Binns pus. svc. fellow, 1993. Mem. Mo. Assn. Trial Attys. (Outstanding Legislator 1991-92, 93), Platte County Mech. and Agrl. Soc. (bd. dirs. 1992-94), Delta Theta Phi, Kappa Alpha Order. Democrat. Baptist. Office: Mo Ho of Reps 100 E Capitol Ave Jefferson City MO 65101-3029

WITT, MERLE DEAN, agronomist; b. Dighton, Kans., Sept. 25, 1944; s. Arthur W. and Ruth M. (Schlick) W.; m. Polly A. Geyer, Sept. 5, 1973; children: William, Jay, Lee. MS, Kans. State U., 1969; PhD, U. Nebr., 1981. Range mgmt. technician Kans. State U., Manhattan, 1966-67, grad. rsch. asst., 1967-68, NDEA fellow, 1968-69; rsch. assoc. U. Nebr., Lincoln, 1979-80; temporary asst. prof. Garden City (Kans.) Experiment Sta., 1969-71, asst. prof., 1971-84; assoc. prof. S.W. Rsch.-Extension Ctr., Garden City, 1984—; germplasm devel. Milkweek Prodn. Adv., Ogallah, Nebr., 1988—. Contbr. articles to profl. jours. Recipient Meritorious Grad. stipend, 1981, NDEA fellowship, 1968; named Rsch. Leader of the Yr., 1982. Mem. Am. Soc. Agronomy, Crop Sci. Soc. Am., Delta Tau Alpha, Gamma Sigma Delta. Office: Kans State U 4500 E Mary St Garden City KS 67846-9132

WITTBRODT, FREDERICK JOSEPH, JR., automotive designer; b. Detroit, Feb. 6, 1955; s. Frederick Joseph Sr. and Hilda Lottie (Neubert) W.; m. Deborah Carrie Kay, Apr. 11, 1992; stepchildren: Angela Defer, Michael Defer II; children from previous marriage: Robin Lynn, Daniel Joseph. Grad., Philpot Sch. Automotive Body Drafting, Royal Oak, Mich., 1977, Entech. Engring., Troy, Mich., 1984. Designer Modern Engring Co.-Design, Troy, Mich., 1977-78, Detroit Indsl. engring., Troy, Mich., 1978-80, Engring Tech., Ltd., Troy, Mich., 1980-86, Pioneer Engring., Dearborn, Mich., 1986, APD, Dearborn, Mich., 1988-89, Mega-Tech. Engring., Warren, Mich., 1989-90, Uni-Tech, Madison Heights, Mich., 1990-91, Harman at Harvard, Southfield, Mich., 1991; sr. automotive designer Lincoln Tech. at Schlegel, Madison Heights, 1991-92; sr. designer, surface devel. specialist Resource Techs. at Harvard Industries, Farmington Hills, Mich., 1992-95; sr. designer, surface devel. specialist, resource tech. Brytax-Rainford, Inc., Marysville, Mich., 1996—; owner Wittbrodt Design Co., Chesterfield, Mich. Mem. NRA, Internat. Platform Soc. Home: 52286 Lexington Ln Chesterfield MI 48051-2182

WITTE, JEFFREY ROBERT, physical therapist assistant; b. Ft. Lauderdale, Fla., Oct. 25, 1963; s. Robert William and Joyce Lee (Niemeier) W.; m. Samantha Jolene Elwood, Aug. 24, 1985; children: Lauren Elizabeth, Cameron Robert. AS, U. Evansville (Ind.), 1985; student dept. health svcs., U. So. Ind., 1987—. Lic. physical therapist asst., Ind., Ky. Phys. therapist asst. Am. Phys. Therapy, Lexington, Ky., 1985-86, Pro-Care Home Health, Hartford, Ky., 1986-87, Manina Charnes, phys. therapist, Henderson, Ky., 1987-88; phys. therapist asst. Associated Rehab., Evansville, 1988-91, Henderson, 1991-93; phys. therapist asst. CMS Therapies Inc., Evansville, 1993-94, MedRehab Inc., Evansville, 1994, Preferred Rehab., Evansville, 1994—. Chmn. spiritual growth, music and worship St. John's East United Ch. of Christ, Evansville, 1994. Anna and Benjamin Bosse scholar, 1982. Mem. Am. Phys. Therapy Assn., Ind. Phys. Therapy Assn. Home: 2721 Autumnwood Way Evansville IN 47715 Office: Preferred Rehab 1300 Professional Blvd Evansville IN 47714

WITTENBERG, MERLE EUGENE, management consultant; b. LaCrosse, Wis., Feb. 3, 1929; s. Roy and Gertrude (Renner) W.; m. Joan McHaffey, Apr. 20, 1952; children: Roy, Heidi, Lisa, Kurt. Sales rep. Container Corp. Am., Chgo., 1954-58; rsch. assoc. Northwestern U., Evanston, Ill., 1958-61; project dir. Kielty, Dechert & Hampe, Chgo., 1961-65; v.p. Beldo & Willmarth, Chgo., 1965-69; chmn. Dechert-Hampe & Co., Northbrook, Ill., 1969-95. Author: The Lifeline of America: A History of the Food Industry, 1965, How Salesman Are Compensated, 1964, SalesExpense Practices, 1967. Cpl. U.S. Army, 1951-53.

WITTENBORN, VERNON DUANE, civil engineer; b. Sparta, Ill., Oct. 9, 1944; s. Charles Roger and Mary Doralee (Scott) W.; m. Diane Elaine Elliot, June 28, 1968; children: Amy Jo Pisoni, Molly Beth, Chad Elliot, Cassie Luanne. BS in Engring. Tech., So. Ill. U., 1967. Registered profl. engr., Ill. Asst. resident engr. Ill. Dept. Transp., Carbondale, 1967-69, resident engr., 1969-81; supt. hwys./county engr. Williamson County, Marion, Ill., 1981—. Chmn. Williamson County Soil and Water Conservation Dist., Marion, 1979; pres. Herrin (Ill.) Youth Sports, Inc., 1983-84, coach flag football, basketball, 1979-90; pres. Herrin Booster Club, 1991-92. Mem. Ill. Assn. County Engrs. (sec. 1995, dir. 1989-94, v.p. 1996), Dist. 9 Assn. County Supts. of Hwys. (pres. 1984), Ill. Assn. County Supts. Hwys. (chmn. various coms.). Baptist. Office: Williamson County Hwy Dept 1817 N Court St Marion IL 62959

WITTENBRINK, BONIFACE LEO, priest; b. Evansville, Ill., June 30, 1914; s. Max C. and Catherine Rose (Pautler) W. PhL, Gregorian U., Rome, 1939; STL, Ottawa (Can.) U., 1943; MA, Cath. U. Am., 1947. Ordained priest Oblates of Mary Immaculate, Roman Cath. Ch., 1941. Instr. Latin, logic, history and religion St. Henry's Coll., Belleville, Ill., 1943-48; instr., registrar, prin. high sch. dept. Coll. of Our Lady of the Ozarks, Carthage, Mo., 1948-52; founding dir. King's House of Retreats, Buffalo, Minn., 1952-53; mission procurator Roman Cath. Ch., St. Paul, 1955-56, 59-62; prin. Alemany High Sch. for Boys, Oblate Western Province, San Fernando, Calif., 1956-59; permanent sec. Conf. Maj. Superiors of Men, Washington, 1963-69; exec. dir., sec. Found. for Community Creativity, Washington, 1970-71; founder, dir., then dir. devel. Radio Info. Svc. for Blind and Handicapped, Belleville, 1972-84; pres., then local dir. Friends of Eye Rsch., Boston, 1983-87; exec. v.p. Citizens for Eye Rsch., Belleville, 1987—; pres. Oblate Ednl. Assn., St. Paul, 1961-62; sci. adv. bd. Nat. Acad. Child Devel., 1984-86; mem. com. Eye Experience St. Louis, 1984; adv. bd. Welfare of the Blind, Inc., 1984—; adv. coun. svcs. for print-handicapped Nat. Pub. Radio, 1976-77; active Internat. Christian Leadership, 1968-72; bd. dirs. LOGOS Translators. Bd. dirs. Technoserve, 1968-72, Internat. Book Svc., 1969-72; vol. Ill. Literacy Project, 1989-90; founding charter mem., bd. dirs. Washington Workshops Found. Mem. Madison County Assn. Blind, Mo. Coun. Blind, Am. Coun. of Blind (ednl. radio com. 1974-76), Am. Found. for Blind (radio talking book com. 1973-76), Inst. for Study of Econ. Systems (bd. dirs. 1971-72), Ednl. Communications Assn., Coun. for Dept. of Peace, Wycliffe Bible Translators Assn., Vols. for Internat. Tech. Assistance, Ill. Radio Info. Svc., Soc. Internat. Devel., UN Assn., Rotary Internat., Belleville Econ. Progress, Eagles, KC, Press Club St. Louis, Am. Assn. Ret. Persons. Home: 9500 W State Rt 15 Belleville IL 62223-1013

WITTMEYER, RONALD F., managing partner; b. Chgo., Apr. 3, 1931; s. Wm. F. and Elizabeth F. W.; m. Dea A., Aug. 21, 1954; children: Ron Jr., Ward W., Jena, Bruce C. BS, U. Ill., 1953, MS, 1955; postgrad., No. Ill. Law Sch., 1970-72. Sales adminstrn. Allstate Ins. Co., Northbrook, Ill., 1960-66; mng. ptnr. Hatfield-Wittmeyer Ins.-Investment, Prospect Heights, Ill., 1993—, Subway of Arlington Inc., Arlington Hgts., Ill., 1985-93; adv. bd. Village of Palatine, 1991—. Bd. dirs. Lattoff Y.M.C.A., Desplaines, Ill., 1970-85; bd. dirs. C. of C., Arlington Hgts., 1994—; adv. com. edn. Lt. Gov.'s Office, Springfield, Ill., 1994-95. With U.S. Army, 1955-57, Germany. Mem. U. Ill.-Chgo. Alumni Club (founder 1958-59, pres. 1959). Office: Subway of Arlington Hgts 35 W Golf Rd Arlington Heights IL 60005

WITWER, SAMUEL WEILER, JR., lawyer; b. Chgo., Aug. 5, 1941; s. Samuel Weiler and Ethyl Loraine (Wilkins) W.; m. Susan P. Stewart, Sept. 18, 1971; children: Samuel Stewart, Michael Douglas. AB with honors, Dickinson Coll., 1963; JD, U. Mich., 1966. Bar: Ill. 1967, U.S. Dist. Ct. (no. dist.) Ill. 1967, U.S. Ct. Appeals (7th cir.) 1972, U.S. Supreme Ct. 1973, U.S. Ct. Appeals (6th cir.) 1985, U.S. Dist. Ct. (ea. dist.) Mich., 1987. Assoc. Witwer, Moran, Burlage & Atkinson, Chgo., 1967-74, ptnr., 1974—; mem. Fed. Trial Bar Admissions Com. No. Dist. Ill., 1982—. Governing mem. Chgo. Zool. Soc., 1986-90; trustee United Meth. Homes and Services, Chgo., 1974—, Dickinson Coll., Carlisle, Pa., 1976—; mem. Cook County Home Rule Commn., Chgo., 1974-75; chmn. Agy. Appeals Com. Chgo., 1975-78; atty. Glenview Park Dist., 1982—; spl. asst. atty. gen. Auditor Gen. Ill., 1984-92. Mem. ABA, Meth. Bar Assn. (pres. 1972-73), Chgo. Bar Assn., Ill. Bar Assn., Law Club of Chgo., Sigma Chi, Phi Delta Phi. Republican. Methodist. Club: Union League. Home: 1330 Overlook Dr Glenview IL 60025-5166 Office: Witwer Poltrock & Giampletro 125 S Wacker Dr Chicago IL 60606-4402

WIXTROM, DONALD JOSEPH, translator; b. Republic, Mich., Oct. 14, 1928; s. Joseph Albert and Edith (Johnson) W.; m. Marilyn Jean Sjoquist, Oct. 14, 1961; children: Joe Alan, Lorna Jean, Aaron Matthew. Free lance translator Republic, 1966—. Mem. Am. Translators Assn. Baptist. Home and Office: RR 1 Box 98 Republic MI 49879-9726

WODOSLAWSKY, THEODORE STEVEN, advertising executive; b. Johnstown, Pa., Sept. 1, 1957; s. Theodore Francis and Alice Joann (Stupi) W.; m. Lorraine Rose Messina, Sept. 29, 1984; children: Leah Christine, Ava Michelle. Tech. Dipl., Ohio Inst. Tech., Columbus, 1977; Tech. Cert. with hons., Admiral Perry Vo-Tech, Ebensburg, Pa., 1975; BA, Malone Coll., Canton, Ohio, 1992. Electronics technician Allen-Bradley Co., Programmable Controller div., Highland Hts., Ohio, 1977-79; sales technician Allen-Bradley Co., Programmable Controller div., 1979-80, sales coord., 1980-81, group leader order svcs., 1981-84, supr. order svcs., 1984-85; distbr. mktg. specialist Allen-Bradley Co., Indsl. Computer div., 1985-87, comml. mktg. specialist, 1987-88; mgr. comml. progs. mgr. comml. progs., 1988-90; mgr. distbr. progs. Allen-Bradley Co., Indsl. Computer/Communications Group, 1990-92; mgr. program devel. distbn. systems Allen-Bradley Co., Cleve., 1992-93; product mktg. mgr. Rockwell Automatron, Allen-Bradley Co. Automation Group, Cleve., 1993-96; account supr. Saifman, Richards and Assocs., Beachwood, Ohio, 1996—; bus. cons. Jr. Achievement project, 1995. Mng. editor/author Between the Shelves, 1990-92; contbg. editor/author Allen Bradley Network for Distbn., 1993-94. Employee campaign mgr. Allen-Bradley United Community Fund United Way, 1991-93. Mem. Internat. Platform Assn., Amnesty Internat. (Ptnr. of Conscience). Libertarian. Home: 8390 Paddock Ct Mentor OH 44060-7649 Office: Allen Bradley Co 1 Allen-Bradley Dr Mayfield Heights OH 44124

WOEHRLEN, ARTHUR EDWARD, JR., dentist; b. Detroit, Dec. 9, 1947; s. Arthur Edward and Olga (Hewka) W.; m. Sara Elizabeth Heikoff, Aug. 13, 1972; 1 child, Tess Helena. DDS, U. Mich., 1973. Resident in gen. dentistry USAF, 1973-74; gen. practice dentistry Redwood Dental Group, Warren, Mich., 1976—; instr. Sinai Hosp., Detroit, 1977—; chief of dentistry St. John's Hosp., Macomb Ctr., Mt. Clemens, Mich., 1982—; mem. dentistry staff Hutzel Hosp., Warren; reviewer Chubb Ins. Co. (malpractice claims), 1978-89; bd. mem. Mich. Acad. Gen. Dentistry (chmn. State of Mich. Continuing Dental Edn. Accreditation). Contbr. articles on dentistry to profl. jours. Served to capt. USAF, 1973-76. Fellow Internat. Coll. of Oral Implantologists; mem. ADA, Acad. Gen. Dentistry (Master), Mich. Dental Assn., Acad. Gen. Dentistry, Am. Acad. Oral Medicine, Fedn. Dentaire Internationale, Acad. Dentistry for the Handicapped, Am. Acad. Oral Implantologists, Internat. Coll. Oral Implantologists, Macomb Dist. Dental Soc.; panel mem. Am. Arbitration Assn. Republican. Home: 25460 Dundee Rd Royal Oak MI 48067-3018 Office: Redwood Dental Group 13403 E 13 Mile Rd Warren MI 48093-3188

WOGAMAN, GEORGE ELSWORTH, insurance executive; b. Mikado, Mich., May 29, 1937; s. Edgar R. and Leah Katherine (McGuire) W.; m. Sandra Lee Jensen, Apr. 10, 1965; children: Jennifer, Christopher. Grad. various ins. courses. CLU; chartered fin. cons. With Blair Transit Co., Dun & Bradstreet, Chrysler Engring. Co., 1955-61; exec. chef Westward Ho!, 1961-68; owner, mgr. George Wogaman Ins. Agy., Grand Forks, N.D., 1969—; mem. pres. coun. Farmers Ins. Group, 1988; alderman East Grand Forks (Minn.) City Coun., 1979—, v.p., 1982—. Corp. mem. United Hosp., Grand Forks, 1982—; mem. East Grand Forks Area Emergency Med. Svcs. adv. com., Grand Forks- East Grand Forks Bus Com., Met. Planning Coun.; chmn. pub. safety com. police and fire City of East Grand Forks; mem. Nat. Rep. Congl. Com., Rep. Presdl. Task Force; mem. Wesley United Meth. Ch., Grand Forks; mem. econ. devel. authority, East Grand Forks, Minn. Recipient Pub. Service award East Grand Forks City Coun., 1979. Mem. North Valley Life Underwriters Assn. (Life Underwriter of Yr. 1988), Am. Soc. CLU's, Farmers Ins. Group Pres.'s. Coun., Elks. Home: 1703 20th St NW East Grand Forks MN 56721-1013 Office: 2612 Gateway Dr Grand Forks ND 58203-1406

WOIT, KATHLEEN E., fund developer; b. Madison, Wis., Mar. 25, 1947; d. James Frances and Ellen Julia (Fahey) Green; m. Thomas Herbert Woit, Feb. 21, 1979; 1 child, Katherine Keeley. BE in Edn., U. Wis., Whitewater, 1969; MS in Edn., U. Wis., 1982, PhD in Edn., 1991. Reading-lang. coord. Middleton (Wis.) Cross Plains Sch. Dist., 1977-80; coord. U. Wis., Madison, 1980-82; dir. Centennial Ariz. State U., Tempe, 1982-84; devel. dir. Edgewood Coll., Madison, 1984-85; ast. chancellor U. Wis., Whitewater, 1985-88, Milw., 1988-90; v.p. Meriter Health Svcs., Madison, 1990—; reading and lang. tchr. Alexandria (Va.) Pub. Schs., 1974-76; elem. tchr. Madison Met. Sch. Dist., 1969-74; lead tchr. inst. U. Wis., Madison, 1971. V.p. bd. Jr. League Madison, 1993-94; trustee Edgewood H.S., 1992-95. Recipient Fellowship Healthcare Forum, Calif., 1994; named Know Your Madisonian, Wis. State Jour., Madison, 1994. Mem. Tempo for Exec. Women, Madison Club, Downtown Rotary. Roman Catholic. Home: 5897 Schuman Dr Madison WI 53711 Office: Meriter Health Svcs 309 W Washington Madison WI 53703

WOJCICKI, ANDREW ADALBERT, chemist, educator; b. Warsaw, Poland, May 5, 1935; s. Franciszek Wojcicki and Janina (Kozlowa) Hoskins; m. Marba L. Hart, Dec. 21, 1968; children: Katherine, Christina. BS, Brown U., 1956; PhD, Northwestern U., 1960; postdoctoral fellow, U. Nottingham, Eng., 1960-61. Asst. prof. chemistry Ohio State U., Columbus, 1961-66, assoc. prof., 1966-69, prof., 1969—, acting chmn., 1981-82; assoc. chmn. Ohio State U., 1982-83, 84-86; vis. prof. Case Western Res. U., 1967, U. Bologna, Italy, 1988; vis. researcher U. Coll. London, 1969; sr. U.S. scientist Alexander von Humboldt Found., Mulheim/Ruhr, Germany, 1975-76; vis. scholar U. Calif.-Berkeley, 1984. Contbr. articles to profl. and scholarly jours. Guggenheim fellow U. Cambridge (Eng.), 1976; recipient Disting. Teaching award Ohio State U., 1968, Humboldt Sr. award Humboldt Found., 1975, 76. Mem. Am. Chem. Soc. (Columbus sect. award 1992), Royal Chem. Soc., Sigma Xi, Phi Lambda Upsilon. Home: 825 Greenridge Rd Columbus OH 43235-3411 Office: Ohio State U 120 W 18th Ave Columbus OH 43210-1106

WOJTAK, ROGER C., electrical engineer; b. Kenosha, Wis., Aug. 25, 1962. BSEE, U. Wis. Parkside, Kenosha, 1985. Elec. engr. Square D Co., Milw., 1985-89, Jordan Controls Inc., Milw., 1989—. Patentee for phase loss relay, solid state overload relay. Roman Catholic. Office: Jordan Controls Inc 5607 W Douglas Ave Milwaukee WI 53218-1613

WOJTANEK, GUY ANDREW, mechanical engineer; b. Chgo., Dec. 26, 1954; s. Edmund A. and Beatrice Marie (Saugling) W.; m. Jean Marie Sylwestrak, May 19, 1979; 1 child, Devin Charles. BSME, U. Ill., 1977; MBA, Roosevelt U., 1982. Registered profl. engr., Ill. Design/product engr. Littelfuse, Inc., Des Plaines, Ill., 1977-78; project engr. Controls div. Singer Co., Schiller Park, Ill., 1979-84, sr. project engr. Controls div., 1984-87; sr. project engr. Controls div. Eaton Corp., Carol Stream, Ill., 1987—; cons. Non-Destructive Engring. Instruments Inc., Boulder, Colo., 1989—. Patentee in field. Mem. Nat. Soc. Profl. Engrs., Am. Soc. Mech. Engrs. (assoc.). Home: 3N 244 Valewood Dr West Chicago IL 60185 Office: Eaton Controls Div 191 E North Ave Carol Stream IL 60188-2019

WOJTAS, THOMAS GERARD, art historian, consultant; b. Detroit, Nov. 7, 1955. BA, Wayne State U., 1979; MA, U. Mich., 1984; MPhil, CUNY, 1988, postgrad., 1988—. Rschr. dept. European art Detroit (Mich.) Inst. Arts, 1977-79, cons. to dir., 1980-84; rsch. fellow art history CUNY, N.Y.C., 1985-90; asst. dir. Barbara Fendrick Gallery, N.Y.C., 1989-90; cons. art appraiser O'Toole-Edwald Art Assocs., N.Y.C., 1991-93; ind. art historian/cons. Detroit and N.Y.C., 1993—; bd. dirs. Detroit Focus Gallery. Contbg. author: Gods, Saints, Heros: Painting in the Age of Rembrandt, 1981; copy editor Detroit Focus Quar., 1993—; contbr. articles to profl. jours. Presdl. merit scholar Wyne State U., 1974-79, GM scholar Wayne State U., 1984-89; Art History Dept. Travel grantee U. Mich., 1983; Art History Dissertation fellow CUNY, 1989. Mem. Am. Assn. Mus., Coll. Art Assn. Am., Founders Soc. Home: 15 E Kirby Detroit MI 48202

WOLANDE, CHARLES SANFORD, corporate executive; b. Chgo., July 25, 1954; s. Sam C. and Marie Helene (Riccio) W.; m. Marian Helene Gillespie, Nov. 10, 1985; children: Eric, Jill, Patrick. B, St. Mary's Coll., Winona, Minn., 1976. Lab. tech. Jefferson Electric, Bellwood, Ill., 1976-73; pres. Comark, Inc., Glendale Heights, Ill., 1978--; also CFO Comark, Inc., Bloomingdale, Ill. Named High Tech. Entrepreneur of the year Peat, Marwick, Mitchell, Chgo., 1987. Mem. C. of C. Glendale Heights. Republican. Roman Catholic. Home: 937 Fox Glen Dr Saint Charles IL 60174-8808 Office: Comark Inc 471 Brighton Dr # 600 Bloomingdale IL 60108-3102

WOLANIN, JOHN CHARLES, realtor; b. Spangler, Pa., Jan. 8, 1957; s. George M. and Ellen (Chigas) W.; m. Andrea Katrina Donato, Oct. 21, 1978; children: Tricia Ann, John Paul. AA, Cuyahoga C.C., 1979; BA, Hiram Coll., 1981. Mail clk. Republic Steel, Cleve., 1975-79; payroll acct. LTV Steel, Cleve., 1979-89; regional credit mgr. Republic Engineered Steel, Missillon, Ohio, 1989-90; realtor Bob Princelon Realty, Massillon, Ohio, 1991-93, Re/Max Ptnrs., Canton, Ohio, 1993—; prof. devel. com. Stark County Bd. Realtors, Canton, 1994-95; mktg. exec. Wolanin Enterprises, Cleve., 1979-89. Coach basketball Boys and Girls Club, Massillon, 1991—; parish coun. mem. St. Marys Ch., Massillon, 1991—. Mem. KC. Republican. Roman Catholic. Home: 314 Sheffield Ave NE Massillon OH 44646 Office: Re/Max Ptnrs 4535 Dressler Rd NW Canton OH 44718

WOLANIN, SOPHIE MAE, civic worker, tutor, scholar, lecturer; b. Alton, Ill., June 11, 1915; d. Stephen and Mary (Fijalka) W. Student Pa. State Coll., 1943-44; cert. secretarial sci. U. S.C., 1946, BSBA cum laude, 1948; PhD (hon.), Colo. State Christian Coll., 1972. Clk., stenographer, sec. Mercer County (Pa.) Tax Collector's Office, Sharon, 1932-34; receptionist, social sec., nurse-technician to doctor, N.Y.C., 1934-37; coil winder, assembler Westinghouse Electric Corp., Sharon, 1937-39, duplicator operator, typist, stenographer, 1939-44, confidential sec., Pitts., 1949-54; exec. sec., charter mem. Westinghouse Credit Corp., Pitts., 1954-72, hdqrs. sr. sec., 1972-80, reporter WCC News, 1967-68, asst. editor, 1968-71, asso. editor, 1971-76; student office sec. to dean U. S.C. Sch. Commerce, 1944-46, instr. math., bus. adminstrn., secretarial sci., 1946-48. Publicity and pub. relations chmn., corr. sec. South Oakland Rehab. Council, 1967-69; U. S.C. official del. Univ. Pitts. 200th Anniversary Bicentennial Convocation, 1986; mem. nat. adv. bd. Am. Security Council; mem. Friends Winston Churchill Meml. and Library, Westminster Coll., Fulton, Mo.; active U. S.C. Ednl. Found. Fellow; charter mem. Rep. Presdl. Task Force, trustee; sustaining mem. Rep. Nat. Com.; permanent mem. Nat. Rep. Senatorial Com.; patron Inst. Community Service (life), U. S.C. Alumni Assn. (Pa. state fund chmn. 1967-68, pres. council 1972-76, ofcl. del. rep. inauguration Bethany Coll. pres. 1973); mem. Allegheny County Scholarship Assn. (life), Allegheny County League Women voters, AAUW (life), Internat. Fedn. U. Women, N.E. Historic Geneal. Soc. (life), Hypatian Lit. Soc. (hon.), Acad. Polit. Sci. (Columbia) (life), Bus. and Profl. Women's Club Pitts. (bd. dirs. 1963-80, editor Bull. 1963-65, treas. 1965-66, historian 1969-70, pub. relations 1971-76, Woman of Year 1972), Met. Opera Guild, Nat. Arbor Day Found., Kosciuszko Found. (assoc.), World Literary Acad., Missionary Assn. Mary Immaculate Nat. Shrine of Our Lady of Snows; charter mem. Nat. Mus. Women in Arts, Statue Liberty Ellis Island Found. Inc., Shenago Conservancy (life); supporting mem. Nat. Woman's Hall of Fame; Recipient numerous prizes Allegheny County Fair, 1951-56; citation Congl. Record, 1969; medal of Merit, Pres. Reagan, 1982; named WPIC Sweetheart-of-the-Day Mercer County's Info. and Entertainment Radio Sta. 790, 1991. Fellow Internat. Inst. Community Service (founder); mem. World Inst. Achievement (rep.), Liturgical Conf. N. Am. (life), Westinghouse Vet. Employees Assn., Nat. Soc. Lit. and Arts, Early Am. Soc., Am. Acad. Social and Polit. Sci., Societe Commemorative de Femmes Celebres, Nat. Trust Historic Preservation, Am. Counselors Soc. (life), Am. Mus. Natural History (asso.), Nat. Hist. Soc. (founding mem.), Anglo-Am. Hist. Soc. (charter), Nat. Assn. Exec. Secs., Internat. Platform Assn., Smithsonian Assos., Asso. Nat. Archives, Nat., Pa., Fed. bus. and profl. women's clubs, Mercer County Hist. Soc. (life), Am. Bible Soc., Polish Am. Numismatic Assn., Polonus Philatelic Soc., UN Assn. U.S., Polish Inst. Arts and Scis. Am. Inc. (assoc.), N.Y. Acad. Scis. (assoc.), Am. Council Polish Cultural Clubs Inc. Roman Catholic (mem. St. Paul Cathedral Altar Soc., patron organ recitals). Clubs: Jonathan Maxcy of U. S.C. (charter); Univ. Catholic of Pitts.; Key of Pa., Fedn. Bus. and Profl. Women (hon.); Coll. (hon.) (Sharon). Contbr. articles to newspapers. Home: 5223 Smith Stewart Rd Girard OH 44420-1341

WOLBER, WILLIAM GEORGE, retired instrument engineer; b. Detroit, Feb. 19, 1927; s. Joseph Gregory and Therese Wolber; m. Velma Faye Campbell, June 17, 1950; children: Paul K., William G., Teresa Ann Eustis, Andrew J., Robert A. BSChemE, U. Mich., 1949, BS in Engring. Math., 1949, MS in Physics, 1950. Registered profl. engr., Ind., Mich. Group leader Uniroyal Tire Div. Process Devel., Detroit, 1950-54; project engr. Bendix Rsch. Labs., Southfield, Mich., 1954-81; sr. tech. advisor Cummins Electronics, Columbus, Ind., 1981-85, exec. engr., 1985-95; peer grant reviewer NSF, 1982—; mem. Fleetguard Tech. Coun., 1988-93, Ingersoll-Rand Electronics Tech. Coun., 1991-95; cons., lectr. in field. Contbr. tech. papers to profl. publs. With USN, 1945-46. Recipient Chmn.'s Tech. award Bendix Corp., 1975. Mem. Soc. Automotive Engrs. (seminar instr., design revs. :985—), Instrument Soc. Am. (organizer, chmn. symposium 1979-80). Roman Catholic. Home: 3151 Sumac Ct Columbus IN 47203-2745

WOLF, ANDREW, food manufacturing company executive; b. Budapest, Hungary, May 20, 1927; came to U.S., 1947, naturalized, 1952; s. Alfred and Magda Farkas. Diploma, Baking Inst. Tech., Budapest, 1942-45; B.S. in Mech. Engring., CCNY, 1955-62; postgrad. Ill. Inst. Tech., Chgo., 1962-64; M.B.A., U. Chgo., 1973. Pres., owner, Mignon Pastry Shops, N.Y.C., 1948-51, 1952-54; cons. Hanscom Bakeries, N.Y.C., 1954-55; dir. new products Arnold Bakers, N.Y. and Conn., 1955-60; dir. new products research and devel. Kitchens of Sara Lee, Deerfield, Ill., 1960-71, v.p. research and devel., 1971-89, spl. asst. to pres., 1989—; rep. Sara Lee Corp., Grocery Mfrs. Am. Tech. Com. for Food Protection, 1975—; spokesman Frozen Food Action Communications Team, Inc., radio and TV, 1982—. Contbr. articles to profl. jours. Patentee bakery equipment and methods. Served with U.S. Army, 1947-48, 1951-52. Recipient Hon. Tex. Citizenship award State of Tex., 1969; Bishop award Tex. Dept. Mental Health, 1972. Mem. White House Conf. on Food and Nutrition, 1959, Pres. Reagan's Task Force on Phys. Fitness and Nutrition, 1983. Mem. Am. Frozen Food Inst. (research and tech. services council, quality maintenance task force council), Am. Bakers Assn. (liaison com. U.S. Dept. Agr.), Inst. Food Technologists, Am. Soc. Bakery Engrs., Sr. Rsch. Execs. Round Table, Tau Beta Pi, Pi Tau Sigma. Home: 2785 Daiquiri Dr Deerfield IL 60015-3805

WOLF, GEORGE FRANK, JR., program director; b. N.Y.C., Mar. 30, 1963; s. George F. and Elizabeth (Eberhardt) W.; m. Yvonne L. Benham, Nov. 8, 1966. BA, Ky. Wesleyan U., 1986; postgrad., Siena Heights Coll., 1994—. Admissions counselor Ky. Wesleyan U., Owensboro, 1986-87, asst. dir. admissions, 1987-88, assoc. dir. admissions, 1988-89, interim dir. admissions, 1989-90; dir. admissions Adrian (Mich.) Coll., 1990—, asst. v.p. enrollment mgmt., 1993—; del. Coll. Bd., Chgo., 1993—; presenter conf. workshops, 1993, 94. Mem. Nat. Assn. Coll. Admissions Counselors, Mich. Assn. Coll. Admissions Counselors (exec. coun.), Ind. Assn. Coll. Admissions Counselors, Am. Assn. Coll. Admissions/Registrat Officers. Republican. Methodist. Office: Adrian Coll 110 S Madison Adrian MI 49221

WOLF, JOAN MANGON, health occupations instructor, nursing educator; b. Dover, Ohio, June 25, 1936; d. William James and Ruth (Metcalf) M.; m. Robert Charles Wolf. Diploma in Nursing, St. Luke's Sch. Nursing, 1957; Bachelor, Kent State U., 1978; MS, U. Dayton, 1979. RN; cert. secondary tchr., Ohio, Fla., sch. nurse, sch. guidance counselor. Charge nurse St. Luke's Hosp., Cleve., 1957-58; staff nurse Union Hosp., Dover, Ohio, 1959-64; sch. nurse Buckeye Career Ctr., New Philadelphia, Ohio, 1980-82, health occupational instr., 1982—; adult edn. coord. nurse aid tng. program Buckeye J.V.S., New Philadelphia, Ohio, 1991—. Co-author Diversified Health Occupation Lab Mmgmt Guide, 1992. Lay del. East Ohio conf. of Gnadenhutten United Meth. Ch., Lakeside, Ohio, 1991—, Order of St. Luke; vol. Am. Cancer Soc., New Philadelphia, 1960—, Am. Heart Assn., New Philadelphia, 1960—, Cmty. Bloodmobile Program, Canton, Ohio, 1980—. Recipient Rockefeller Found. grant Ohio State U., 1959. Mem. Buckeye Edn. Assn. (chmn., founder scholarship com. 1986), Ohio Edn. Assn., Nat. Edn. Assn., Am. Vocat. Assn., Ohio Vocat. Assn. (Disting. Svc. award 1992, Pacesetter award 1995), Alpha Tau Delta (Jennings scholar 1996-97). Office: Buckeye Career Ctr 545 University Dr NE New Philadelphia OH 44663-9450

WOLF, KEN, state legislator; b. Dec. 30, 1937; m. Mary; three children. BA, U. St. Thomas. Minn. State rep. Dist. 41B, 1993—; computer cons. Home: 13319 Morgan Ave S Burnsville MN 55337-2095*

WOLF, MARGARET A., computer programmer; b. Chgo.. BS, U. Ill., 1977; MS, Knowledge Systems Inst., 1993. Dir. music Paylos Elem. Schs., Paylos Hills, Ill., 1982-84; info. systems mgr. Paragon Automation, Elk Grove Village, Ill., 1984-95; sr. programmer Info. Resources Inc., Chgo., 1995—. Dir. Our World Underwater. Mem. Nicol. Mem. Evanston Meeting of Freinds Ch. Home: 5531 N Mcvicker Ave Chicago IL 60630-1111

WOLF, MARGARET LOUISE, sales support information administrator, marketing; b. Rochester, Pa., Oct. 23, 1947; d. Fred Herbert and Mary Louise (Arnold) W.; m. Fouad R. Marina, Aug. 1, 1970 (div. July 1974). Cert. Med. Sec., Md. Med. Secretarial Sch., 1967; AAS, Youngstown State U., 1990, BS in Applied Sci., 1993. Cert. nurses asst., Ohio. Med. sec. U. Md., Balt., 1967-68; blue print machine operator NRM Corp., Columbiana, Ohio, 1969-70; legal sec. Youngstown, Ohio, 1970; ward sec. Lakewood (Ohio) Hosp., 1970-72; office coord. Drs. Bell, Pardee, Chapman, Lakewood, 1972-74; outside sales/adminstrv. asst. Hattenbach Co., Cleve., 1974-79; tech. instr. Unico/Adam, Eatontown, N.J., 1979-81; nurses asst. Windsor Manor Nursing Home, Lisbon, Ohio, 1982-84; clerical asst. Reliable Source of Metalwork, Youngstown, 1987-89; sales support info. mgr. Store Systems and Svcs., Youngstown, 1989—; mem. adv. bd. Ohio State Ext. Dept. Agr., Canfield, 1992—. Stephen min. Pleasant Grove Presbyn. Ch., USA, Youngstown, 1992—; mem. Young Men's Christian Assn., Youngstown, 1987—. Recipient Wall of Fame Achievement award Kent State U., 1993. Mem. Am. Legion Aux. Home: 3531 Hillman St Apt 422 Youngstown OH 44507 Office: Store Systems and Svcs 52 E Myrtle St Youngstown OH 44507

WOLF, NEAL LLOYD, lawyer; b. Chgo., Feb. 8, 1949; s. Ira and Bettye (Brainin) W.; m. Caren Ellen Mirsky, June 11, 1972 (div. Apr., 1995); children: Michael Elliot, Brian Martin. AB magna cum laude, Princeton U., 1970; JD, U. Chgo., 1974. Bar: Ariz. 1974, U.S. Dist. Ct. Ariz. 1974, U.S. Ct. Appeals (9th cir.) 1975, Ill. 1983, U.S. Dist. Ct. (no. dist.) Ill. 1983, U.S. Ct. Appeals (7th cir.) 1983, U.S. Ct. Appeals (8th cir.) 1985, U.S. Supreme Ct., 1985, U.S. Dist. Ct. (no. dist.) Tex., 1990. Ptnr. Lewis and Roca, Phoenix, 1974-83, Winston & Strawn, Chgo., 1983-86, 89—, Ross & Hardies, Chgo., 1986-89. Mem. ABA. Office: Winston & Strawn 35 W Wacker Dr Chicago IL 60601-1614

WOLF, RICHARD ALAN, investment executive; b. Lake Odessa, Mich., June 20, 1935; s. Harry and Gladys (Gross) W.; m. Judith Ann Schreiner, Oct. 13, 1962; 1 child, Erik Alan. BBA, U. Mich., 1957, MBA, 1958. Chartered fin. analyst. Security analyst Colo. Nat. Bank, Denver, 1958-60; v.p., portfolio mgr. Commerce Bank, Kans. City, Mo., 1960-66; v.p., trust investment dept. head Omaha Nat. Bank, 1967-77; treas., sr. v.p. fixed income research and trading Citizens & So. Investment Advisors, Inc., Atlanta, 1977-91; mng. dir. fixed income First Am. Investment Corp., 1991-92, pres., CEO, chief investment officer, 1992—. Mem. Inst. Chartered Fin. Analyst, We. Mich. Soc. Fin. Analysts, Assn. Investment Mgmt. & Rsch. Republican. Episcopalian. Avocations: philately, golfing. Home: 1526 Edgeridge Cir Kalamazoo MI 49008-2245 Office: First of Am Investment Corp 303 N Rose St Ste 500 Kalamazoo MI 49007-3850

WOLF, RONALD CLARENCE, information systems manager; b. Sheboygan, Wis., May 14, 1949; s. Clarence Arthur and Agnes Clara (Bogenschuetz) W.; m. Joyce Lela Heincke, Aug. 14, 1971; children: Rebecca Jean, Matthew Thomas. BS, U. Wis., Milw., 1972; MBA, U. Wis., Oshkosh, 1980. Cert. prodn. & inventory mgmt. Programmer Kohler Co., Kohler, Wis., 1972-74, systems analyst, 1974-79, supr. tech. support, 1979-82; supr. mfg. systems A.O. Smith Data Systems, Milw., 1982-85, mgr. mfg. systems, 1985-86; mgr. bus. application systems A.O. Smith Automotive Products Co., Milw., 1986—; seminar instr. Marquette U., Milw. 1982-85. Mem. Am. Prodn. and Inventory Control Soc. Home: 6120 W Floral Ln Brown Deer WI 53223-1245 Office: A O Smith Automotive Prods Co 3533 N 27th St Milwaukee WI 53216-2663

WOLF, THOMAS PHILLIP, political science educator, consultant; b. Norton County, Kans., Sept. 27, 1933; s. Theodore Phillip and Elizabeth Grantham (Bosley) W.; m. Ella Nora Weigand, July 14, 1953; children: Heather Lynn Carlisle, Lance Alan, Tracy Renee Simkins. AB in Polit. Sci., Wichita (Kans.) State U., 1959; AM in Polit. Sci., Stanford (Calif.) U., 1961, PhD in Polit. Sci., 1967. Data processor Beech Aircraft, Wichita, 1954-57; asst. prof. polit. sci. U. N.Mex., Albuquerque, 1963-70, assoc. prof. polit. sci., 1970; assoc. prof. polit. sci. Ind. U. S.E., New Albany, 1970-75, chair social scis., 1971-80, 84-85, prof. polit. sci., 1975—, dean social scis., 1992—. Author: Bibliography, N.Mex. Politics, 1974, (with others) chpt. Pols in the American West, 1969; editor: Brit. Politics Group Newsletter, 1994—. Mem. Leadership So. Ind., 1985—; exec. dir. Ind. Consortium for Internat. Programs, 1993—; mem. Louisville Com. on Fgn. Rels., 1986—; pres. Legal Aid Bd., So. Ind., 1979—. Sgt. USMC, 1951-54, Korea. Woodrow Wilson Found. fellow, 1959-60, NEH fellow, 1976-77, 87, Joseph J. Malone fellow Nat. Coun. U.S.-Arab Rels., 1986. Mem. Am. Polit. Sci. Assn. (dept. svcs. com. 1978-81), Hansard Soc. for Parliamentary Govt., Western Social Sci. Assn. (pres. 1970-71), Am. Soc. for Pub. Adminstrs. (state pres. 1967-68), Cherokee Roadrunners. Democrat. Methodist. Office: Ind U SE 4201 Grant Line Rd New Albany IN 47150-2158

WOLFE, ARTHUR LLEWELLYN, chemical executive; b. Lehighton, Pa., May 11, 1930; s. Charles William and Alverta Matrona (Bauer) W.; m. Marcelline Grace Moyer (div. 1966); children: Richard A., Ruth Ann Valentino, Charles G., Keith A. Student, Muhlenberg Coll., 1953-56, Drexel U., 1958; Bs in chemistry, Lehigh U., 1958. Chemist Trojan Powder Co., Allentown, Pa., 1949-57; rsch. chemist Rohm & Haas Co., Phila., 1958-65, Diamond Shamrock Corp., Painesville, Ohio, 1966-81; mgr., cons. Internat. Sci. Svcs., Mentor, Ohio, 1982-84; sr. rsch. cons. Quantum Techs. Inc., Twinsburg, Ohio, 1985-91; pres., cons. Internat. Sci. Svcs., Mentor, 1991—; radiation safety officer Diamond Shamrock Corp., 1972-80. Author: Millions by Mail, 1949; inventor in field; contbr. articles to profl. jours. Pres. Southwest Civic Assn., Mentor, 1973-80; coord. Common Cause, Ohio, 1973-76; bd. dirs. Harbor Credit Union, Fairport Harbor, Ohio, 1975—, Mentor Pub. Libr., 1977—. Recipient Nat. Honors award Nat. Honor Soc., Lehighton, 1947. Mem. Am. Chem. Soc. Democrat. Humanist. Office: Internat Sci Svc PO Box 581 Willoughby OH 44094

WOLFE, BARBARA L., economics educator, researcher; b. Phila., Feb. 15, 1943; d. Manfred and Edith (Heimann) Kingshoff; m. Stanley R. Wolfe, Mar. 20, 1965 (div. Mar. 1978); m. Robert H. Haveman, July 29, 1983; children: Jennifer Ann Wolfe, Ari Michael Wolfe. BA, Cornell U., Ithaca, N.Y., 1965; MA, U. Pa., 1971; PhD, U Pa., 1973. Asst. prof. Bryn Mawr (Pa.) Coll., 1973-76; rsch. assoc. Inst. Rsch. on Poverty, Madison, 1976-77, dir., 1994—; from asst. prof. to assoc. prof. U. Wis., Madison, 1977-88; prof., 1988—; resident scholar NIAS, Wassenear, The Netherlands, 1984-85; vis. scholar Russell Sage Found., N.Y., 1991-92. Co-author: Succeeding Generations, 1994; editor: (book) Role of Budgetary Policy in Demographic Transitions, 1994, contbr. articles to profl. jours. Active Commn. on Children with Disabilities, Washington 1994-95, Tech. Adv. Panel Social Security, Washington, 1994-95. Recipient Best Article of Yr. award Rev. Income and Wealth, 1992, Fulbright award Coun. Internat. Exch. of Scholars, 1984. Mem. Am. Econ. Assn. (bd. com. 1989-92, exec. bd. 1996—). Office: U Wis Inst Rsch on Poverty 1180 Observatory Dr Madison WI 53706

WOLFE, CARL DEAN, electrical engineer; b. La Salle, Ill., May 13, 1957; s. Jerry Lee and Rose Marie (Geraci) W.; m. Ruth Christine Hoelzer, Sept. 13, 1980; children: Kyle Ryan, Kristin Bryce, Kara Nicole. AS, Ill. Valley Community Coll., 1977; BSEE, U. Ill., 1979; MSEE, Ill. Inst. Tech., 1988. Applications engr. Harris Semicondr., Melbourne, Fla., 1979-84; mgr. component engring. Rockwell Telecommunications, Downers Grove, Ill., 1984-93; field application engr. Burr Brown Corp., Tucson, Ariz., 1993—. Office: Burr Brown Corp 85 W Algonquin Rd Ste 310 Arlington Heights IL 60005-4423

WOLFE, GAIL SOMMERS, veterinarian; b. Balt., June 11, 1947; d. Abraham William and Helen (Meyers) Sommers; m. Alan Jay Wolfe, June 18, 1967; children: Rustin, Kyle, Lauren, Kami. BS, Mich. State U., 1969, DVM, 1970. Pvt. practice Okemos, Mich., 1971—; relief veterinarian, Mich., 1970-78. Vol. pet-a-pet program Burcham Hills Retirement Ctr., East Lansing, Mich., 1985-96, Tender Care South Retirement, East Lansing, 1994—; charter mem. Orgn. for Rehab. Through Tng., East Lansing, 1985—; fin. sec., treas. B'nai B'rith Women, Lansing, 1975, 89-92; chair youth scholarship Shaarey Zedek Sisterhood, East Lansing, 1988-92, v.p. Judaism, 1991-96; chair mem. Hadassah, Lansing, 1987, chair blue box, 1988—, chair Hadassah Camp Young Judaea, 1991—. Mem. Am. Vet. Med. Assn., Mid. State Vet. Med. Assn., Mich. Vet. Med. Assn. (Award for Highest Scholastic Standing), Mensa, Phi Zeta. Home: 2298 Bennett Rd Okemos MI 48864-3233 Office: Bennett Rd Animal Clinic 2298 Bennett Rd Okemos MI 48864-3233

WOLFE, MARGARET ETHEL (VANCE), nurse; b. Lexington, Nebr., Aug. 19, 1931; d. Ira Dell and Georgia Francis (Oliver) Vance; m. Ronald Eugene Wolfe; children: Robert E., Katherine I., Jerrie D., Richard B., Mitchel E. Cert., Grand Island Bus. Coll., 1955, Cen. Community Coll., Kearney, Nebr., 1982. Practical nurse Luth./Grand Island (Nebr.) Meml. Hosp., 1983-87; practical nurse hospice Grand Island Meml. Hosp., 1983-87; practical nurse St. Francis Med., Grand Island, 1987—; facilitator Make Today Count, Grand Island, 1978-86; coord. I Can Cope, Grand Island, 1981-82. Contbr. articles to profl. jours. Vol. ARC, Grand Island, 1987-92; instr. HIV and AIDS, 1991-93; vol. Birthright, 1987-92; mem. Nat. Right to Life, 1990-96, Presbyn. Pro-Life, Christian Women, After 5 Group; advisor, decoration and Bible study chmn. HIV and AIDS Support Group, 1990-92; elder Presbyn. Ch.; speaker on HIV and AIDS. Named Extra Ordinary Person Grand Island Ind. Newspaper, 1989. Mem. Am. Heart Assn., Nebr. Hospice Assn. Home: 608 W Charles St Grand Island NE 68801-6526

WOLFE, MARTHA, elementary education educator; b. Centralia, Ill., Apr. 16, 1944; d. Elmer A. and Dorothy L. (Stonecipher) Krietemeyer; children: Kimberly S., Debora L. BS, So. Ill. U., 1967, MS, 1973, adminstrv. cert., 1987. Cert. elem. tchr., K-12 adminstrn., Ill. Tchr. Title I reading, dir. Cobden (Ill.) Unit Sch. Dist.; presenter in field. Recipient Master Tchr. award Gov. of Ill., 1984. Mem. NEA, Internat. Reading Assn., So. Ill. Reading Assn. (pres., v.p., bd. dirs.), Delta Kappa Gamma (Lambda State scholar 1986). Home: 301 South St Anna IL 62906-1528

WOLFE, PETER, educator, author; b. N.Y.C., Aug. 25, 1933; s. Milton Berlinger and Mae (Salius) W.; m. Marie Paley, Dec. 22, 1962 (div. 1969); children: Philip Graham, John Bennett. BA, CCNY, 1955; MA, Lehigh U., 1957; PhD, U. Wis., 1965. Asst. prof. English U. Nebr., Lincoln, 1964-67; prof. English U. Mo., St. Louis, 1967—; vis. prof. U. Windsor, Ont., 1971, U. Waikato, Hamilton, New Zealand, 1980, U. Queensland, Brisbane, Australia, 1980, Nat. Taiwan Normal U., Taipei, Republic of China, 1982, Moscow State U., 1984, U. Karnataka, Dharwad, India, 1987, Cath. U. Lublin, Poland, 1991, U. Szczecin, 1992, Flinders U., South Australia, 1995. Pub. Lucas Hall Press, St. Louis, 1992—; author: A Vision of His Own: William Gaddis, 1996, Alarms & Epitaphs, Eric Ambler, 1993, Yukio Mishima, 1989, Corridors of Deceit: John le Carré, 1987, Raymond Chandler, 1985, Laden Choirs: Patrick White, 1983, Beams Falling: Dashiell Hammett, 1980, Jean Rhys, 1980, Dreamers Who Live Their Dreams: Ross Macdonald, 1977, John Fowles, 1976, Graham Greene, 1972, Rebecca West, 1971, Mary Renault, 1969, Iris Murdoch, 1966. With U.S. Army, 1957-59. Recipient Armchair Detective award, 1994, U. Mo. Presdl. award for rsch. and creativity, 1995. Democrat. Home: 4466 W Pine Blvd Apt 18B Saint Louis MO 63108-2340 Office: U Mo St Louis Dept English 8001 Natural Bridge Rd Saint Louis MO 63121-4401

WOLFE, RALPH STONER, microbiology educator; b. Windsor, Md., July 18, 1921; s. Marshall Richard and Jennie Naomi (Weybright) W.; m. Gretka Margaret Young, Sept. 9, 1950; children: Daniel Binns, Jon Marshall, Sylvia Suzanne. Mem. faculty U. Ill., Urbana, 1953—, prof. microbiology, 1961—; cons. USPHS, Nat. Inst. Gen. Med. Scis. Contbr. microbial physiology rsch. papers to profl. jours. Guggenheim fellow, 1961, 75, USPHS spl. postdoctoral fellow, 1967; recipient Pasteur award Ill. Soc. for Microbiology, 1974, Selman A Waksman Award in Microbiology Nat. Acad. of Sciences, 1995. Mem. NAS (Selman Waksman award in microbiology 1995), Am. Acad. Arts and Scis., Am. Soc. Microbiology (Carski Disting. Teaching award 1971, Abbott Lifetime Achievement award 1996, hon. mem.), Am. Soc. Biol. Chemists. Office: U Ill Dept Microbiology 335 Burrill Hall Urbana IL 61801

WOLFF, EDWIN RAY, construction engineer; b. Continental, Ohio, Mar. 24, 1933; s. Ray Simeon and Datha Ruth (Donaldson) W.; m. Elizabeth I. Sutterlin, Feb. 16, 1963; children: Sandra Jean, Donald Scott. BSME, U. Toledo, 1969. Registered profl. engr., Ohio. Mem. design staff City of Ft. Lauderdale, Fla., 1965-67; mem. design/spl. orders staff Devilbiss Co., Toledo, 1967-69; engineer, mem. R & D staff Toledo Scale, 1969-70; design/constrn. engr. Lucas County Engr., Toledo, 1970—; cons. G.A.F., Inc., Oregon, Ohio, 1980—. Vol. Spl. Olympics, Lucas County, 1989—; trustee, bd. elders Fairgreen Ch., Toledo, 1975—; trustee Beneficial Union Pittsburg, 1986—. With Combat Engrs. Corps, 1956-58. Mem. Phi Kappa Chi, Pi Kappa Alpha. Democrat. Presbyterian. Home: 4312 Grantley Toledo OH 43613

WOLFF, GUNTHER ARTHUR, physical chemist; b. Essen, Germany, Mar. 31, 1918; came to U.S., 1953; s. Joseph and Anna (Breidecker) W.; m. Gertrude Anna Stolte, Feb. 27, 1945; children: Christine, Francis. B.S., Berlin U., 1944, M.S., 1945; Sc.D., Berlin Tech. U., 1948. Research assoc. Fritz Haber Inst., Berlin, 1944-50, sci. head, dep. chief crystal kinetics dept., 1950-53; cons. sr. scientist, team leader Signal Corps Research and Devel. Lab. U.S. Army, Fort Monmouth, N.J., 1953-60; sr. group leader material research Harshaw Chem. Co., Cleve., 1960-63; dir. material research Erie Tech. Products Co., Pa., 1963-64; prin. scientist Tyco Labs., Inc., Waltham, Mass., 1964-70; cons. chemist Lamp Phenomena Research Lab., Lamp Envelope Materials Research Lab. Gen. Electric Co., Cleve., 1970-77; sr. staff engr. Nat. Semicondr. Corp., Hawthorne, Calif., 1977-81, indsl. cons., 1981-83; indsl. cons. G.A. Cons. NPO, 1983—; chmn. Gordon Research Conf. on Chemistry and Metallurgy of Semicondrs., 1965; mem. crystal growth com. Internat. Union Crystallography, 1967-75; mem. Am. com. for crystal growth, 1967-72. Fellow Am. Inst. Chemists, Mineral Soc. Am.; mem. N.Y. Acad. Sci., Am. Chem. Soc., Electrochem. Soc., Am. Crystallographic Assn., Am. Ceramic Soc., Am. Assn. for Crystal Growth, AAAS. Home and Office: 3776 Northampton Rd Cleveland OH 44121-2027

WOLFF, THOMAS WILLIAM, manufacturing executive; b. Milw., Oct. 28, 1964; s. Jerome R. and Sandra A. (Dunn) W.; m. Joanne Marie Hosni, Aug. 13, 1988; children: Ryan Thomas, Ashley Marie. BBA in Mktg., U. Wis., Milw., 1987, BBA in Fin., 1987, MBA in Orgn. Devel., 1992. Sales rep. Uarco Bus. Forms, Milw., 1987-90; mktg. mgr. Lifestyle Svcs., Milw., 1989-90; field sales asst. Schwaab Inc., Milw., 1990-91, Ga. regional mgr., 1991-92, So. Ill. regional mgr., 1992-93, Wis. regional mgr., 1993-94, ctrl. divsn. mgr., 1994—. Tchr., cons. Jr. Achievement, Milw., 1986-92. Republican. Roman Catholic. Home: W165 N8654 Dardis Ave Meno Falls WI 53051 Office: Schwaab Inc 11415 W Burleigh St Milwaukee WI 53226

WOLFORD, JOHN BRENTON, anthropologist, educator; b. Louisville, Ky., July 13, 1952; s. Thorp Lanier W. and Evelyn Regina (Cox) W.; m. Mary Lewis Walters, May 24, 1980; children: George Walters, Charles Sumner. BA magna cum laude, U. Louisville, 1979; MA with distinction, Ind. U., 1982, PhD, 1992. Assoc. instr. Ind. U., Bloomington, 1982-84, oral historian, 1983-93, instr., 1984-86; folklife slide archivist Ind. U., 1988-91; instr. Ind. U.-Purdue U., Indpls., 1993; asst. prof. anthropology U. Mo., St. Louis, 1993—; urban anthropologist Mo. Hist. Soc., St. Louis, 1993—; cons. Kyiana Blues Soc., Louisville, Ky., 1991. Author (short story) Still Life Disturbed, 1978. Grants rev. panelist Ind. Arts Commn., Indpls., 1989-91; mem. adv. bd. Mo. Folk Arts, Columbia, Mo., 1993—. Recipient Thomas fellow, 1979, Ind. U. dissertation fellow, 1987-88; Ind. U. grantee, 1987-88. Mem. Am. Folklore Soc., Am. Studies Assn., Am. Anthropological Assn., Mo. Hist. Soc., Orgn. Am. Historians, Oral History Assn., Pi Lambda Theta. Office: U Mo 8001 Natural Bridge Rd Saint Louis MO 63121-4499 also: Mo Hist Soc PO Box 11940 Saint Louis MO 63112-0040

WOLFSON, LESTER MARVIN, former university chancellor; b. Evansville, Ind., Sept. 13, 1923; s. William and Bess (Silverman) W.; m. Esther Evans, July 3, 1949; children: Alice Jeanette, Margaret Gail, George Stephen. AB, U. Mich., 1945, AM., 1946, PhD, 1954; LHD, Ind. U., 1988. Instr. English Wayne State U., Detroit, 1950-53; asst. prof. English and speech U. Houston, 1953-55; asst. prof. English Ind. U. N.W., Gary, 1955-61, assoc. prof., 1961-64; assoc. prof. Ind. U., South Bend, 1964-67, prof., 1967-87, prof. emeritus, 1987—, dir., asst. dean, 1964-66, dean, 1966-68, dean, acting chancellor, 1968-69, chancellor, 1969-87, chancellor emeritus, 1987—; vis. asst. prof. English U. Calif., Santa Barbara, 1958-59. Contbr. articles to profl. jours. Horace H. Rackham fellow, 1948-50. Mem. Phi Beta Kappa, Phi Kappa Phi, Phi Eta Sigma. Office: Ind U South Bend 1700 Mishawaka Ave South Bend IN 46615-1408

WOLK, HOWARD MARVIN, poet, retired theatre equipment company executive; b. Chgo., Apr. 20, 1920; s. Edward H. and Adele (Marks) W.; m. Sylvia Grade. Grad., Wright Jr. Coll., 1939. With Edward H. Wolk, Inc., Chgo., 1939-80, v.p., 1950-80. Contbr. to over 35 poetry books including My Favorite Poems, Anthology of Verse, Search for the Soul, A Vision of Verse, Lyrical Voices, Our Worlds's Most Beloved Poems, World Poetry Anthology, Great American Poetry Anthology, American Poetry Anthology, Vols. 1 and 2, A Time to Be Free, Impressions, Peoples Bible '83-'84, New Poets One/Anthology, New Poets Three/Anthology, Select American Poetry, Vol. 1, Am. Poetry Showcase, New Morning Anthology, Poets '88, Lyrical Voices, Dreams and Visions, Poems of the Century, Anthology of Midwestern Poetry, American Poetry Annual, National Poetry Anthology, Themes, Thoughts and Treasures, Vol. 1, Satori, Vol. 1, Tapestry of Word, A Composition on Verse, others, also poems have appeared in various mags. and papers including All Around the Editor's Desk, Black Creek Rev. mag., Poetry mag. (Calif.), Chgo. Sheets, Lerner News, Canvas Quar., Reflections, Poetry Magic, Bristol House Rev., Venus Publs.; also chpts. to books. Recipient award Longfellow Poetry Contest, 1980, poetry award Nashville News Letter, 1982, certs. merit, 1984, 87, Golden Poet award World of Poetry, 1985, 90, 3d place Hermu Competition, 1986, 2d place, 1988, 4th place award New Am. Poets Contest, 1988, 3d place poetry competition N.Am. Open Nat. Libr. Poetry, 1988, 3d place Psych It Contest, 1989, Silver Poet award World of Poetry, 1989, others. Mem. Am. Philatelic Soc., Acad. Am. Poets, Variety Club. Home: 6007 N Sheridan Rd Chicago IL 60660-3039

WOLKINS, DAVID A., state legislator; b. Warsaw, Ind., June 2, 1943; S. Merrille Otis and Mary Catherine (Roe) W.; m. Candace Jeanne Endicott, 1965; 1 child, Matthew David. BS, Greenville Coll., Ill., 1966; MS, St. Francis Coll., Ft. Wayne, Ind., 1973. Mem. Ind. Ho. of Reps., Indpls., 1988—, chmn. environ. affiars com., mem. labor & employment and ways & means coms. Former pres., v.p. Winona Lake Town Bd., 1969-88. Mem. Optimists Club. Republican. Home: 501 Pierceton Rd Winona Lake IN 46590-1550*

WOLLE, CHARLES ROBERT, federal judge; b. Sioux City, Iowa, Oct. 16, 1935; s. William Carl and Vivian (Down) W.; m. Kerstin Birgitta Wennerstrom, June 26, 1961; children: Karl Johan Knut, Erik Vernon, Thomas Dag, Aaron Charles. AB, Harvard U., 1959; JD, Iowa Law Sch., 1961. Bar: Iowa 1961. Assoc. Shull, Marshall & Marks, Sioux City, 1961-67, ptnr., 1968-80; judge Dist. Ct. Iowa, Sioux City, 1981-83; justice Iowa Supreme Ct., Sioux City and Des Moines, 1983-87; chief judge, 1992—; judge U.S. Dist. Ct. (so. dist.) Iowa, Des Moines, 1987-92, chief judge, 1992—; faculty Nat. Jud. Coll., Reno, 1983—, chief judge 1992—. Editor Iowa Law Rev., 1960-61. Vice pres. bd. dirs. Sioux City Symphony, 1972-77; sec., bd. dirs. Morningside Coll., Sioux City, 1977-81. Fellow Am. Coll. Trial Lawyers; mem. ABA, Iowa Bar Assn., Sioux City C. of C. (bd. dirs. 1977-78). Home: 1601 Pleasant View Dr Des Moines IA 50315-2129 Office: US Dist Judge 103 US Courthouse 123 E Walnut St Des Moines IA 50309-2035

WOLLERT, GERALD DALE, retired food company executive, investor; b. LaPorte, Ind., Jan. 21, 1935; s. Delmar Everette and Esther Mae W.; m. Carol Jean Burchby, Jan. 26, 1957; children—Karen Lynn, Edwin Del. B.S., Purdue U., 1957. With Gen. Foods Corp., 1959-89; dir. consumer affairs Gen. Foods Corp., White Plains, N.Y., 1973-74; mng. dir. Cottee Foods div. Gen. Foods Corp., Sydney, Australia, 1974-76; gen. mgr. Mexico div. Gen. Foods Corp., Mexico City, 1978-79; pres. Asia/Pacific ops. Gen. Foods Corp., Honolulu, corp. v.p. worldwide coffee and internat. div., 1979-89; ret., 1989; dir. Gen. Foods cos., Japan, Peoples Republic China, Korea, India, Taiwan, Singapore, Philippines. Webelos leader Boy Scouts Am., Mexico City, 1978-79; co. gen. chmn. United Fund campaign, Battle Creek, Mich., 1964-65, White Plains, N.Y., 1972-73. Served with U.S. Army, 1958. Mem. Asian-U.S. Bus. Coun., Oahu Country Club (Hawaii), Venice Golf and Country Club (Fla.), Beacon Hills and Beechwood (Ind.) Club.

WOLOSHEN, JEFFERY LAWRENCE, automobile executive, consultant, accountant; b. Highland Park, Mich., July 4, 1949; s. Michael and Virginia May (Rosenaw) W.; m. Catherine Ann Nowakowski, June 24, 1972; children: Matthew, Veronica. BSBA with distinction, Wayne State U., 1971. CPA, Mich., Ill., Cert. Mgmt. Acct. Auditor Plante & Moran, CPAs, Southfield, Mich., 1986-74; mgmt. acct. Caterpillar Tractor Co., Peoria, Ill., 1974-77; div. controller Household Mfg., Freeport, Ill., 1977-80, SPX Corp., Muskegon, Mich., 1980-85; fin. exec. Chrysler Corp., Auburn Hills, Mich., 1985—. Treas. United Way Fund, Aurora, Ill., 1976-77; century mem. Boy Scouts Am., Detroit, 1988—. Mem. AICPAs, Nat. Assn. Accts., Inst. Cert. Mgmt. Accts. Republican. Roman Catholic.

WOLT, JEFFREY DUAINE, environmental chemist, researcher; b. Grand Forks, N.D., Oct. 18, 1951; s. Myron Duaine and June Agnes (Coulter) W.; m. Evelyn Elvira Richmond, Aug. 16, 1980; children: Kathryn Elvira, Raymond Jeffrey. Student, Case Western Res. U., 1969-71; BS in Bioagrl. Scis., Colo. State U., 1973; MS in Agronomy, Auburn U., 1976, PhD in Soil Chemistry, 1979. Cert. profl. soil scientist/agronomist. Asst. prof. U. Tenn., Knoxville, 1979-84, assoc. prof., 1984-88; project leader Dow Chem., Midland, Mich., 1988-89; tech. leader DowElanco, Midland, 1990-95, sr. scientist, 1991-93; rsch. scientist DowElanco, Indpls., 1994—, environ. issues mgr., 1995—; vis. scientist U. Hawaii, Honolulu, 1988-89; pvt. cons. Jeffrey D. Wolt, Cons., Seymour, Tenn., 1983-90; adj. prof. agronomy Purdue U., 1993—. Author: Soil Solution Chemistry, 1994; contbr. articles to profl. jours. Mem. AAAS, Am. Soc. Agronomy (Vis. Scientist award 1988), Soil Sci. Soc. Am., Am. Chem. Soc., Coun. Agrl. Sci. and Tech., Sigma Xi, Phi Kappa Phi, Gamma Sigma Delta. Office: DowElanco Environ Chemistry Lab Indianapolis IN 46268-1053

WOMACK, DOUG C., labor union representative; b. Marshalltown, Iowa, Dec. 7, 1950; s. Robert J. and Mildred R. (Woods) W.; m. Paulette A. Junge, June 4, 1971. Grad. high sch., Garwin, Iowa. Steward local #893 UAW, Marshalltown, 1976-77, recording sec., 1977-82, chairperson consumer affairs dept., 1981-84, chairperson Lennox unit, 1982-86, v.p., 1983-85, pres., 1985-94; mem. region 4 exec. bd. UAW, Chgo., 1985-94, mem. UAW internat. staff, 1994—. Active Marshall County Dem. Com., 1984-93; co-chmn. Labor/Mgmt. Coun.; mem. City Econ. Devel. Commn., 1986-92; bd. dirs., local United Way, 1985-92; apptd. by gov. Iowa State Labor-Mgmt. Coop. Coun., 1990-93; participant Young Trade Union Leaders Exch. Program, Tokyo, 1988. Named to Top 25 Up and Coming Young State Leaders Des Moines Register, 1987. Office: UAW Sub-Region Office 2525 E Euclid Ave Ste 201 Des Moines IA 50317

WOMACKS, MARTHA A., state legislator. BS, Valparaiso U.; MPA, Ind. U. Auditor Marion County; city councilman Valparaiso, Ind., 1976-78; assessor Porter County, 1979-87; mem. Ind. State Ho. of Reps. Dist. 100, mem. aged and aging com., mem. natural resources com., mem. pub. health com., vice chmn. local govt. com. Bd. dirs. Greater Ind. Rep. Women's Club; v.p. East Ctr. Twp. GOP club.

WONG, KENNETH K., education educator; b. Hong Kong, May 11, 1955; s. H.C. Wong and C.K. Man; m. Michelle A. Chu, 1979; 1 child, Ellen E. BA with honors, U. Chgo., 1977, MA, 1980, PhD, 1983. Asst. prof. U. Oreg., Eugene, 1983-88; asst. prof. dept. edn. U. Chgo., 1988-93, assoc. prof., 1993—; cons. Nat. Commn. for Employment Policy, 1990, U.S. Dept. Edn., 1988, Edn. Devel. Ctr. and NSF, 1994-96. Author: City Choices, 1990; co-author: When Federalism Works, 1986; editor: Politics of Policy Innovation, 1992, Rethinking School Reform in Chicago, 1996, Rethinking Policy for At-Risk Students, 1994; co-editor: Politics of Urban Education, 1992; mem. editl. bd. Am. Ednl. Rsch. Jour., 1992—; series editor Advances in Ednl. Policy, 1995—. Mem. rsch. adv. com. Chgo. Urban League, 1988—; mem. human capital devel. com. United Way of Chgo., 1990—. Spencer fellow Nat. Acad. Edn., 1989-90; rsch. grantee Inst. Poverty Rsch., Madison, 1990-91, Benton Ctr., Chgo., 1990-93, Spencer Found., Chgo., 1992-93, Nat. Ctr. on Edn. in Inner Cities, 1993-95, Joyce Found., Chgo., 1993-95, U.S. Dept. Edn., 1994-95, 95-97. Mem. Am. Ednl. Rsch. Assn., Am. Polit. Sci. Assn., Assn. for Policy Analysis and Mgmt., Midwest Polit. Sci. Assn. Office: U Chgo Dept Edn 5835 S Kimbark Ave Chicago IL 60637-1608

WONG, THOMAS TANG YUM, engineering educator; b. Hong Kong, July 27, 1952; came to U.S., 1976; s. Kwai Sun and Yee Yuen (Fung) W.; m. Mini-i Lee, June 9, 1984; children: Clara Joyce, Lillian Denise. BSc in Engrng., U. Hong Kong, 1975; MS, Northwestern U., Evanston, Ill., 1978, PhD, 1981. Product engr. Motorola Semiconductor, Inc., Hong Kong, 1975-76; teaching asst. Northwestern U., 1976-78, rsch. asst., 1978-80, postdoctoral fellow, 1980-81; asst. prof. Ill. Inst. Tech., Chgo., 1981-86, assoc. prof., 1986-96, prof., 1996—, dir. grad. program dept. elec. engring., 1987-95; dir. rsch. and devel. Telecomm. Equipment Corp., Chgo., 1994—; chmn. Chicagoland Microwave Symposium, 1988; cons. to pvt. industry, 1981—. Author: Fundamentals of Distributed Amplification, 1993; contbr. articles to profl. jours.; book reviewer tech. publs. GE fellow, 1983; rsch. grantee NASA, 1989-91, U.S. Dept. Energy, 1992—, pvt. industry, 1993—. Mem. IEEE (chmn. joint Chgo. chpt. Antenna Propagation and Microwave Theory Techniques Soc. 1987-88, mem. steering com. joint symposium Antennas Propagation Soc./Internat. Union of Radio Sci./Nuclear Electromagnetic Pulse 1992), AAUP, Am. Phys. Soc., Tau Beta Pi, Eta Kappa Nu. Office: Ill Inst Tech Dept Elec/Computer Engring Chicago IL 60616

WOO, PETER WING KEE, organic chemist; b. Canton, China, June 22, 1934; came to U.S., 1950; s. Yu Chang and Lim Tsing (Poon) W.; m. Katherine Liang, Aug. 27, 1966; children: Karen H.W., Lena H.A., Nelson H.Y. BS with great distinction, Stanford U., 1955; PhD, U. Ill., 1958. From assoc. rsch. chemist to sr. rsch. chemist Parke Davis & Co., Detroit, 1958-71; from rsch. scientist to sr. rsch. assoc. Parke Davis Pharm. Rsch. (divsn. Warner-Lambert Co.), Ann Arbor, Mich., 1971—. Co-inventor antileukemia drug; patentee in field; reviewer in field; contbr. articles to profl. jours. Mem. Am. Chem. Soc. (excellence in indsl. chem. rsch. award 1983, Huron Valley sect.), Internat. Isotope Soc., Sigma Xi, Phi Beta Kappa. Office: Parke-Davis Pharm Rsch 2800 Plymouth Rd Ann Arbor MI 48105

WOO, WILLIAM FRANKLIN, newspaper editor; b. Shanghai, China, Oct. 4, 1936; came to U.S., 1946; s. Kyatang and Elizabeth Louise (Hart) W.; m. Patricia Ernst, Dec. 18, 1964 (div. June 1980); m. Martha Richards Shirk, Sept. 15, 1981; children—Thomas Shenton, Bennett Richards, Peter Snowdon. B.A., U. Kans., 1960. Reporter Kansas City Star, Mo., 1957-62; feature writer St. Louis Post-Dispatch, 1962-68, editorial writer, 1968-73, asst. editor, 1973-74, editorial page editor, 1974-86, editor, 1986—. Served to staff sgt. USAFR, 1962. Nieman fellow Harvard U., 1966-67. Mem. Am. Soc. Newspaper Editors (bd. dirs. 1993—), Am. Press Inst. (bd. dirs. 1995). Home: 156 S Gray Ave Saint Louis MO 63119-2914 Office: Pulitzer Pub Co 900 N Tucker Blvd Saint Louis MO 63101-1069*

WOOD, ALLISON LORRAINE, lawyer; b. N.Y.C., May 30, 1962; d. Walter C. and Joan T. Wood. BA, Pace U., 1984; JD, DePaul U., 1987; postgrad., Northwestern U. Bar: Ill. 1987, U.S. Dist. Ct. (no. dist.) Ill. 1989, Fed. Trial Bar 1990. Judicial extern U.S. Bankruptcy Ct., Chgo., 1987; pub. defender, Office of Pub. Defender Cook County, Ill., 1987-89; counsel The Peoples Gas Light and Coke Co., Chgo., 1989-93; assoc Albert, Bates, Whitehead & McGaugh, Chgo., 1993—; adj. prof. DePaul U. Coll. Law, 1992—. Tutor, lectr. Minority Legal Edn. Resources, Inc., Chgo.; bd. dirs., sec. Ctrs. for New Horizons; mem. Target Hope-Mentor. Mem. ABA, Ill. State Bar Assn., Chgo. Bar Assn., Cook County Bar Assn., DePaul U. Coll. of Law Alumni Bd. Office: Albert Bates Whitehead & McGaugh One S Wacker Dr Ste 1990 Chicago IL 60603

WOOD, BARBARA ANN, financial executive; b. Davisburg, Mich., June 15, 1945; d. John Eakers and Florence Fay (Adams) Carter; m. Bruce Michael Wood, Nov. 21, 1964; children: Christine Ann Wood-Wall, Michael Nolan. Student, Oakland C.C., Rochester, Mich., 1970. Owner, pres. Keys Tax Svc., Auburn Hills, Mich., 1980-90; divsn. mgr. Advantage Capital Corp., Houston, 1984—, CEO, mem. coun., 1993—; bd. dirs. Chief Pontiac Fed. Credit Union; mem. prodr.'s adv. coun. Advantage Capital Corp. Mem. Internat. Assn. Fin. Planning, Am. Bus. Womens Assn. Republican. Office: Comprehensive Investment Sv Ste 102 1899 Orchard Lake Rd Sylvan Lake MI 48320-1775

WOOD, DIRK GREGORY, surgeon, physician; b. Springfield, Ohio, Sept. 19, 1953; s. Carlos Paul and Evelyn Cecelia (Bird) W. BA magna cum laude, Urbana (Ohio) U., 1973; MD, UAG Facultad de Medicina, Guadalajara, Mexico, 1980; JD, Capital Law Sch., Columbus, Ohio, 1991. Diplomate Am. Bd. Ob-Gyn, Am. Bd. Forensic Medicine. Intern Bronx (N.Y.) Lebanon Hosp., 1981-82; resident William Beaumont Hosp., Royal Oak, Mich., 1982-86; physician, surgeon Her Care, Inc., Springfield, 1986—; CEO Just What the Doctor Ordered, Springfield, 1992. Coroner Clark County, Ohio, 1991—. Fellow ACS, Am. Coll. Ob-gyn., Internat. Coll. Surgeons, Am. Coll. Legal Medicine, Royal Soc. Medicine (London). Republican. Home: 202 Tuttle Rd Springfield OH 45503-5236 Office: Her Care Inc 2029 E High St Springfield OH 45505-1315

WOOD, HARLINGTON, JR., federal judge; b. Springfield, Ill., Apr. 17, 1920; s. Harlington and Marie (Green) W. A.B., U. Ill., 1942, J.D., 1948. Bar: Ill. 1948. Practiced in Springfield, 1948-69; U.S. atty. So. Dist. Ill., 1958-61; mem. firm Wood & Wood, 1961-69; assoc. dep. atty. gen. for U.S. attys. U.S. dept. Justice, 1969-70; assoc. dep. atty. gen. Justice Dept., Washington, 1970-72; asst. atty. gen. civil div. Justice Dept., 1972-73; U.S. dist. judge So. Dist. Ill., Springfield, 1973-76; judge U.S. Ct. Appeals (7th cir.), 1976—; adj. prof. Sch. Law, U. Ill., Champaign, 1993; disting. vis. prof. St. Louis U. Law Sch., 1996. Chmn. Adminstrv. Office Oversight Com., 1988-90; mem. Long Range Planning Com., 1991-96. Office: US Ct Appeals PO Box 299 600 E Monroe St Springfield IL 62701-0299

WOOD, JAMES NOWELL, museum director and executive; b. Boston, Mar. 20, 1941; s. Charles H. and Helen N. (Nowell) W.; m. Emese Forizs, Dec. 30, 1966; children: Lenke Hancock, Rebecca Nowell. Diploma, Universita per Stranieri, Perugia, Italy, 1962; B.A., Williams Coll., Williamstown, Mass., 1963; M.A. (Ford Mus. Tng. fellow), NYU, 1966. Asst. to dir. Met. Mus., N.Y.C., 1967-68, asst. curator dept. 20th century art, 1968-70; curator Albright-Knox Art Gallery, Buffalo, 1970-73, assoc. dir., 1973-75; dir. St. Louis Art Mus., 1975-80, Art Inst. Chgo., 1980—; vis. com. visual arts U. Chgo., 1980-94; head com. Nat. Endowment Arts. Mem. Intermuseum Conservation Assn. (past pres.), Assn. Art Mus. Dirs. Office: Art Inst Chgo 111 S Michigan Ave Chicago IL 60603-6110

WOOD, KATHLEEN OLIVER, writer, editor; b. Mt. Kisco, N.Y., Sept. 17, 1921; d. Eli Leslie and Melba Antoinette (Gislason) Oliver; m. John Thornton Wood, June 1941 (div. 1947); children: Mark Thornton, Jonna Hinkle; m. Clifford Emanuel Huff, June 1948 (div. 1955); 1 child, Karen Weston. Student Swarthmore Coll., 1938-39, Antioch Coll., 1940-41, U. N.Mex., 1949, Cleve. Coll., 1960-61. Tech. sec. Gray Iron Founders Soc., Cleve., 1955-57; tchr. Whiting Bus. Coll., Cleve., 1957-62; editorial asst. Chem. Rubber Co., Cleve., 1966; editor, writer Jefferson Ency., World Pub. Co., Cleve., 1967-68; disc jockey, announcer Sta. WCLV-FM, Cleve., 1968-69; communications coord., writer, editor Highlights newsletter University Circle, Inc., Cleve., 1971-81; talk-show hostess, announcer Sta. WERE-AM, Cleve., 1972-73; tele-cons. Mktg. Programs, Inc., 1995—; free-lance writer, editor, cons., 1981—; editor Insideout Magazine, 1994—, editor Riveting News, 1996—, Hard Hatted Women, 1996; publicity specialist Am. Assn. Retired Persons, Ohio, 1987-88; tchr. Project LEARN; tutor VIP program. Author: Greenwood, 1967; editor, pub. Frog in the Milk Pan (Marie Wallace), 1963; editor Graffiti Mag., 1967, Office Gal Mag., 1962-63, Smorgasbrain Mag., 1968. Hostess weekly radio show, CRRS, Cleve. Soc. for Blind; taper books for Libr. of Congress Svc. for Visually Handicapped; treas. Cleve. Beautiful Com., 1980, sec., 1982; v.p. Cleve. Cultural Garden Fedn., exec. sec. 1989-90, 90-91, acting pres., 1989—; trustee E. Cleve. Community Theatre. Mem. Pub. Rels. Soc. Am., Internat. Assn. Bus. Communicators, Advt. Women of Cleve. (past pres., editor Weathervane 1982-83), Women in Communication (editor Write-Up 1989—), World Assn. Women Journalists and Writers (congress coordinator 1982-83, v.p. U.S. chpt. 1988—), Mensa, Early Settlers. Quaker. Clubs: Zonta Internat. (pres. Cleve. chpt. 1991—, dir. Area 3 Dist. V, 1984-86), Women's City, Esperanto League of N.Am., Universal Esperanto Assn. Home: 3118 E Overlook Rd Cleveland OH 44118-2440 Office: PO Box 5612 Cleveland OH 44101-0612

WOOD, LEONARD EARLE, III, managed health care executive; b. San Francisco, Jan. 27, 1942; s. Leonard Earle Jr. and Elizabeth (Fleager) W.; m. Stephanie Ann English, Oct. 16, 1993; children: Margery, April, Adam. AA, Menlo Coll., Menlo Park, Calif., 1963, BSBA, 1965. Sales rep. Del Monte Corp., San Francisco, 1965-67; asst. v.p., mgr. Chubb Group Ins. Cos., Warren, N.J., 1967-75; v.p. Marsh & McLennan Cos., Chgo., 1975-84; exec. v.p., COO, Blue Cross-Blue Shield Nebr., Omaha, 1984-87; sr. v.p. nat. mktg. Blue Cross-Blue Shield Assn., Chgo., 1987-91; pres., CEO, Gallagher Bassett Benefit Adminstrs., Itasca, Ill., 1991—; trustee Mktg. Sci. Inst., Boston, 1991. Contbg. author: Health Care Handbook, 1991; also articles. Mem. coun. Luth. Ch. of Ascension, Northfield, Ill., 1984; chmn. Nebr. Comprehensive Health Ins. Pool, Lincoln, 1986; mem. alumni com. Menlo Coll., 1991. Staff sgt. U.S. Army, 1966-71. Named col., gov.'s staff State of Tenn., 1989; Alfred P. Sloan scholar Sloan Found., 1962. Mem. Am. Mgmt. Assn. (trustee 1991—, chmn. investment com. 1992), Conway Farms Golf Club. Office: 1581 Asbury Ave Winnetka IL 60093-1303

WOOD, LESLIE ANN, retail administrator; b. Chgo., Apr. 9, 1957; d. Howard Arnold and Anita Eleanor (Andler) W. AA, Harper Coll., 1977; BS in Communication Scis., Ill. State U., 1979; postgrad., Olivet Nazarene U. Advt. asst. Harry Alter Co., Chgo., 1979-80; clk. typist Career Guild, Evanston, Ill., 1980-81; reporter Aparacor, Evanston, Ill., 1981-82; sales mgmt. trainee Prudential Ins. Co. Am., Millburn, N.J., 1983-84; fin. cons. Summit Fin. Resources, Livingston, N.J., 1984; mgr. Chgo. area Renault Inc. div. AMC/Jeep/Renault, Elk Grove Village, Ill., 1985-87; customer relations specialist Chrysler Motors, Lisle, Ill., 1987-88; dist. svc. and parts mgr. Chrysler, Lisle; dist. parts mgr. Subaru of Am., Addison, Ill., 1989-91, dist. fixed ops. mgr., 1992-95; univ. rep. Olivet Nazarene Coll., 1996—. Sunday sch. tchr., mem. ch. choir, rainbows co-coord. First Presbyn. Ch., Libertyville, Ill. Mem. NAFE. Home and Office: 230 Brett Cir Unit D Wauconda IL 60084-1587

WOOD, LEWIS, agricultural products supplier, farmer; b. 1928. Farner Marked Tree, Ark., 1950—; pres. Marked Tree (Ark.) Coop., Inc. Office: Marked Tree Coop Inc 110 W 2d St Marked Tree AR 72365*

WOOD, LINDA SUSAN, molecular biologist, researcher; b. Kans. City, Mo., Dec. 1, 1959; d. Roger Allen and Anna Lou (Haskamp) W. BS, U. Mo., Kans. City, 1982, MS, 1984; BBA in Mgmt., Davenport Coll., 1994. Rschr. VA, Long Beach, Calif., 1984-85; rsch. biochemist Upjohn Co., Kalamazoo, 1985—. Contbr. articles to profl. jours. Vol., Clinton/Gore Campaign, Kalamazoo, 1992. Mem. Cath. Alumni Club (treas. 1990-94), Phi Kappa Phi. Office: Upjohn Co 301 Henrietta St Kalamazoo MI 49007-4940

WOOD, MARGARET A., accountant; b. Crown Point, Ind., May 21, 1962; d. James A. and Marjorie I. (Wylie) Forsythe; m. James Barry Wood, Sept. 1, 1990; 1 child, Michael. BS in Acctg. with highest distinction, Purdue U., 1984. CPA. Staff acct. Arthur Andersen & Co., Indpls., 1984-86, sr. acct., 1986-88; instr., course developer Chgo., 1987-88; contr. The Bodner Cos., Indpls., 1989-90, v.p. acctg., treas., 1990-93, sr. v.p., 1993-95; sr. v.p. S.C. Bodner Co., Inc., Indpls., 1996—. Speaker in field. Vol. Indpls. Ambs., 1989-91, election bd. Marion County Rep. Party, Indpls., 1984—; bd. dirs. Heritage Place, 1992—, pres., 1995—. Recipient Svc. award Indpls. Ambassadors, 1991. Mem. Ind. CPA Soc., Columbia Club (jr. exec. bd., mag./mktg. com.). Republican. United Methodist. Office: SC Bodner Co Inc Ste 120 8500 Keystone Crossing Indianapolis IN 46240

WOOD, MARLENE ANN, nursing administrator; b. St. Paul, Jan. 16, 1951; d. Timothy Joseph and Dorothy A. Kehl (Getter) W.; m. Joseph Carl Wood, Nov. 6, 1971; children: Rachel, Martin, Theresa, Joseph. Diploma, Andker Sch. Nursing, St. Paul, 1972; BS, St. Francis Coll., Joliet, Ill., 1988. Staff RN CCU St. Paul Ramsey Med. Ctr., 1972, Cloquet (Minn.) Meml. Hosp., 1973, St. Lukes Hosp., Duluth, Minn., 1973-78, Itasca Meml. Hosp., Grand Rapids, Minn., 1978-80; staff RN ICU/CCU St. Lukes Hosp., Duluth, Minn., 1980-88; nurse mgr. Itasca Med. Ctr., Grand Rapids, Minn., 1988—; bd. mem. Minn. Orgn. Leaders in Nursing, 1993-95. Bd. mem. Campfire Boys and Girls, Grand Rapids, Minn., 1991-95. Mem. AACCN. Home: 3120 Winnebago Dr Grand Rapids MN 55744 Office: Itasca Medical Center 126 SE 1st Ave Grand Rapids MN 55744

WOOD, MICHAEL ALLEN, health care executive; b. Mpls., Apr. 4, 1956; s. Lloyd Allen and Mary Frances (Devereaux) W.; m. Jane Mary Selzer, June 5, 1976; children: Jennifer Elizabeth, Jessica Marie. AAS in Cardiopulmonary Tech., Maryville Coll., St. Louis, 1976; BSBA in Fin., Lindenwood Coll., St. Charles, Mo., 1981, MS in Fin., 1982, MBA in Mktg., 1983. Dir. clin. svcs. Health Cons., Inc., St. Louis, 1976-78; adminstrv. dir. Clasen Home Health Care, St. Louis, 1978-83; v.p. mktg. Biomed. Systems Corp., St. Louis, 1983-84; dir. fin. ARA Med. Rehab. Svcs., St. Louis, 1984-85; pres., CEO St. Louis Mgmt. Group, Inc., 1985—, Physicians Healthcare Network, Inc., 1992—; assoc. prof. Lindenwood Coll., 1984—. Contbr. articles to profl. jours. Bd. dirs. Lindenwood Coll. Bd. Overseers, 1988—; bd. dirs. Lindenwood Coll. Alumni Bd., 1986-90; corp. com. Juvenile Diabetes Found., St. Louis, 1989. Mem. St. Louis Soc. Healthcare Planning and Mktg., Med. Group Mgmt. Assn., Mo. Athletic Club, Alpha Sigma Tau. Roman Catholic. Office: St Louis Mgmt Group Inc 1023 Executive Pky Dr Saint Louis MO 63141-6323

WOOD, RICHARD J., academic administrator. A.B., Duke U., 1959; B.D., Union Theol. Sem., 1962; M.A., Yale U., 1963, Ph.D., 1965. Pres. Earlham Coll., Richmond, Ind., 1985—. Office: Earlham Coll Office of President Richmond IN 47374

WOOD, RUTH DIEHM, artist, design consultant; b. Cleve., July 31, 1916; d. Ellis Raymond and Frances Helen (Peshek) Diehm; m. Kenneth Anderson Wood, Sept. 14, 1937. Student, Spencerian Bus. Coll., 1935-36, John Huntington Inst., 1936, Cleve. Inst. Art, 1934-37, 45. Legal sec. Klein, Diehm & Farber, Attys., Cleve., 1936-37; freelance graphic designer Bailey Meter Co., Wickliffe, Ohio, 1967; interior design cons., lectr. One-woman shows include Artist & Craftsmen Assn., Cleve., 1949, Art Colony, Cleve., 1953, Women's City Club, Cleve., 1955, Cleve. Inst. Art Alumni, 1954, Malvina Freedson Gallery, Lakewood, Ohio, 1965, Intown Club, Cleve., 1953, Studio Inn, Painesville, Ohio, 1955, Little Gallery, Chesterland, Ohio, 1961, Hospitality Inn, Willoughby, Ohio, 1965, Coll. Club Cleve., 1965, Lakeland Community Coll., Mentor, Ohio, 1979, Holden Arboretum, Mentor, 1981, Fairmount Fine Arts Ctr., Russell, Ohio, 1992; represented in 12 nat. juried shows, 28 regional and local mus., many pvt. collections. Recipient 1st prize Oil Still Life, Cleve. Mus. Art, 1945, Grumbacher Merit award Lakeland Fla. Internat., 1952, Artistic Achievement award Gates Mills, 1973, numerous other awards; certs. of award in Nyumon and Shoden, Ikenobo Sch. Floral Art, Kyoto, Japan. Mem. Cleve. Inst. Art Alumni, Artists and Craftsmen, Geauga Artists, Women in the Arts. Republican. Mem. Seventh-Day Adventist. Home and Studio: Kenwood Designers 11950 Sperry Rd Chesterland OH 44026-2225

WOOD, SAMUEL EUGENE, college administrator, psychology educator; b. Brotherton, Tenn., Aug. 16, 1934; s. Samuel Ernest and Daisy J. (Jernigan) W.; m. Helen J. Walker, June 2, 1956; children: Liane Wood Kelly,

Susan Wood Benson, Alan Richard; m. Ellen Rosenthal Green, Sept. 8, 1977; stepchildren: Bart M. Green, Julie Alice Green. BS in English and Music, Tenn. Tech. U., 1961; M in Edn. Adminstrn., U. Fla., 1967, D in Edn., 1969. Asst. prof. edn. W.Va. U., 1968-70; asst. prof. edn. U. Mo., St. Louis, 1970-75, mem. doctoral faculty, 1973-75; dir. rsch. Ednl. Devel. Ctr., Belleville, Ill., 1976-81; prof. psychology Meramec Coll., St. Louis, 1981-94; pres. Higher Edn. Ctr., St. Louis, 1985—; prof. psychology Lindenwood Coll., 1995—; exec. dir. Edn. Opportunity Ctrs., St. Louis, 1985—, Project Talent Search, St. Louis, 1991—; bd. commrs. Pub. TV Com., St. Louis, 1985—; planning com. St. Louis Schs., 1985-90; adminstr. German-Am. student exch. program Internat. Bus. Students, 1985—; sponsor Higher Edn. Ctr. Internat. Edn. Coun., 1985—; co-founder, pres. Higher Edn. Cen. Cable TV Channel, Sta. HEC-TV, St. Louis, 1986; v.p. St. Louis County Cable TV Commn., 1991—. Musician, composer with USN Band, 1956-59; composer A Nautical Musical Comedy, A Child's Garden of Verses in Song, 1979; numerous poems set to music; co-author: (with Ellen Green Wood) (textbook) The World of Psychology, 1993, 2d edit., 1996, Can. edit., 1996; contbr. articles to ednl. and sci. jours. Served with USN, 1955-59. US Office Edn. grantee 1976-81, 85—. Mem. Internat. Edn. Consortium (bd. dirs. 1985-91), Phi Kappa Phi. Democrat. Baptist. Home: 5 Sona Ln Saint Louis MO 63141-7742 Office: Higher Edn Ctr 8420 Delmar Blvd Ste 504 Saint Louis MO 63124-2180

WOOD, SUSAN ELLIOTT, art history educator; b. Mt. Holly, N.J., Nov. 13, 1951; d. Alexander Cooper and Evaline (Smyth) W. AB, Bryn Mawr Coll., 1973; MA, Columbia U., 1975, PhD, 1979. Mellon postdoctoral teaching fellow Case-Western Res. U., Cleve., 1979-81; asst. prof. Harvard U., Cambridge, Mass., 1981-87; assoc. prof. Oakland U., Rochester, Mich., 1987—. Author: Roman Portrait Sculpture, 218-260, 1986; editor (newsletter) Classical Soc. Am. Acad. Rome; contbr. articles to profl. jours. Grantee in aid for seminar Am. Numismatic Soc., 1976, univ. grantee Harvard U., 1982-83; fellow classical archaeology Am. Acad. in Rome, 1977-78. Mem. Archaeological Inst. Am., Coll. Art Assn., Women's Classical Caucus, Detroit Classical Assn. Democrat. Office: Oakland U Art History Dept Rochester MI 48309-4401

WOOD, SUSANNE GRIFFITHS, environmental chemist, microbiologist; b. Buffalo, N.Y., Dec. 28, 1933; d. John Arnold and Alice Fredericka (Wiede) Griffiths; m. Richard Bruce Wood, Aug. 8, 1970. BA in Biology, SUNY, Buffalo, 1954, MA in Biology, 1957; PhD in Plant Pathology, U. Ill., 1976. Asst. cancer rsch. scientist Roswell Park Meml. Inst., Buffalo, 1957-59, 64-66; clin. microbiologist Deaconess Hosp., Buffalo, 1959-64; teaching and rsch. asst. U. Ill., Urbana-Champaign, 1966-75, rsch. assoc., 1975-80; asst. profl. scientist Ill. Natural History Survey, Champaign, 1980-83, assoc. profl. scientist, 1983-92; lab. supv. Northern Ill. Water Corp., Champaign, Ill., 1993-94; lab mgr. Integrated Analytical, Clinton, Ill., 1995—. Contbr. articles on microbial physiology and environ. chemistry to profl. jours. Assoc. chimesmaster U. Ill., carillonneur U. Luth. Ch., Champaign, 1968—; organist Philo (Ill.) Presbyn. Ch., 1987—; mem. libr. U. Ill. Russian Folk Orch., 1974-92. Mem. AAAS, Am. Chem. Soc., Soc. for Environ. Toxicology and Chemistry, Am. Indsl. Hygiene Assn., Guild for Carillonneurs in N.Am., Am. Acad. Microbiology (reg. microbiologist). Home: PO Box 437 207 S Hayes St Philo IL 61864 Office: Integrated Analytical Rte 54 East PO Box 678 T-33 Clinton IL 61727

WOOD, VIRGINIA ANN, educator; b. Petoskey, Mich., June 24, 1936; d. William Nelson and Mildred Alice (Cope) Reed; m. Frederick Lee Wood, Sept. 28, 1970 (dec. Apr. 1971); 1 child, Frederick Lee. BS, Ferris State U., 1957. Tchr. Reese (Mich.) Schs., 1957-59, Utica (Mich.) Schs., 1963-64, Richmond (Mich.) Cmty. Schs., 1959-63, 64—; coach Sci. Olympiad, Richmond H.S., 1984—. Contbr. software revs. to Sci. Tchr. mag., 1987. Trustee Pub. Libr. Bd., 1980—; mem. Richmond Cmty. Theatre, 1965-71; organist United Ch. of Christ. NSF grantee in chemistry and project physics, 1962-68. Mem. NEA, Nat. Sci. Tchrs. Assn., Mich. Edn. Assn., Mich. Sci. Tchrs. Assn. (sec., bd. dirs. 1961-70), Richmond Edn. Assn. (pres. 1966-67, sec. 1984-94), Alpha Delta Kappa (pres. 1968-70). Republican. Home: 70109 Karen St Richmond MI 48062-1098 Office: Richmond High Sch 35320 Division Rd Richmond MI 48062-1378

WOOD, WAYNE W., state legislator; b. Janesville, Wis., Jan. 21, 1930. Grad. high sch., Janesville. Formerly builder, contractor, factory worker; mem. Janesville City Coun., 1972-76, pres., 1974-75; mem. Wis. Ho. of Reps., Madison, 1976—; mem. criminal justice and corrections com., rules com., ways and means com., 1985—, vice chmn., 1989-95, mem. state affairs com., 1987—. Mem. State VTAE Bd., 1975-76; mem. Coun. of State Govts. Legis. Oversight Task Force, 1983, Janesville Housing Authority, 1971-77; former mem. Children's Svc. Soc. Adv. Bd., Rock County Sr. 4-H Coun., Sinnissippi Coun. Boy Scouts Am. Mem. UAW. Home: 2429 Rockport Rd Janesville WI 53545-4445

WOOD, WELLINGTON GIBSON, III, biochemistry educator; b. Balt., Dec. 29, 1945; s. Wellington Gibson Jr. and Elsie Bernice (Johnson) W.; m. Beverly Jean Beaver, Feb. 8, 1969; children: Wellington Gibson IV, Katherine Brittingham. BA, Tex. Tech U., 1971, PhD, 1976. Postdoctoral fellow Syracuse (N.Y.) U., 1976-77; staff scientist Bangor (Maine) Mental Health Inst., 1978-80; evaluation coord. VA Med. Ctr., St. Louis, 1980-89; assoc. dir. for edn. and evaluation VA Med. Ctr., Mpls., 1989—; asst. prof. St. Louis U. Sch. Medicine, 1982-87, assoc. prof., 1987-89; assoc. prof. dept. pharmacology U. Minn. Sch. Medicine, Mpls., 1990-96, prof. dept. pharmacology, 1996—; mem. sci. editorial bd. Alcoholism and Drug Rsch. Comm. Ctr., Austin, Tex., 1990—; mem. biochemistry, physiology and medicine study sect. NIH-Nat. Inst. Alcohol Abuse and Alcoholism, 1992-96. Assoc. editor Exptl. Aging Rsch., 1977-82; contbr. numerous articles to profl. jours. Nat. Inst. on Alcohol Abuse and Alcoholism postdoctoral fellow, 1976-77; grantee Nat. Inst. on Alcohol Abuse and Alcoholism, 1987—, Nat. Inst. on Aging, 1993—, Dept. Vets. Affairs, 1981—. Mem. Am. Aging Assn. (bd. dirs. 1984-87), Rsch. Soc. on Alcoholism (chmn. membership com. 1988-91), Internat. Soc. for Biomed. Rsch. on Alcoholism, Am. Soc. for Neurochemistry, Internat. Soc. for Neurochemistry. Home: 16091 Huron Path Lakeville MN 55044-8874 Office: VA Med Ctr GRECC 11G Minneapolis MN 55417

WOOD, WILLIAM J., real estate consultant; b. Cook County, Ill., Mar. 19. Student, Miami U., Oxford, Ohio, 1971. Pres. Omega Studios, Ltd., Chgo., 1971-76; divsn. mgr. NRC Inc., Detroit, 1976, Triad Mgmt. Corp., Ann Arbor, Mich., 1981-83; fin. analyst Feasibility Rsch. Group, Ann Arbor, 1982-91; COO Tri Corp. Securities, Ltd., Ann Arbor, 1982-91; assoc. Triad Mortgage, Ann Arbor, 1983-91, Triad Corp., Ann Arbor, 1988—, McKinley Assocs., Ann Arbor, 1991; cons. Real Estate Acctg. SRU, Ann Arbor, 1991—. Home: 314 Pauline Ann Arbor MI 48103 Office: Triad Corp 335 E Liberty Ann Arbor MI 48104

WOODBURY, PETER MICHAEL, airline pilot; b. Boston, Nov. 29, 1958; s. Paul Wilhelm and Gloria (Mackey) W.; m. Brandelyn Lee Wellendorf, Oct. 26, 1990; children: Matthew, Christopher, Chelsea, Benjamin. BS in Math., U. Wyo., 1980. Cert. pilot single engine land, multi-engine land, comml. pilot, instrument, flight engr. Commd. USAF, advanced through grades to capt., 1985; A-10 operational fighter pilot USAF, RAF Bentwaters, U.K., 1982-84; A-10 instr. pilot USAF, RAF Bentwaters, Eng., 1984-85; air liaison officer, jump qualified 3/325 Airborne Bn. Combat Team, Vicenza, Italy, 1985-87; F-16 fighter trainer USAF MacDill AFB, Tempa, Fla., 1987; F-16 operational fighter pilot USAF Hill AFB, Layton, Utah, 1989-89; comml. airline pilot N.W. Airlines, St. Paul, 1989—. Dist. commr. Boy Scouts Am., Ogden, Utah, 1988-89. Maj. Minn. Air Nat. Guard, 1990—. Mem. Air Line Pilot's Assn., Air Force Assn., Nat. Eagle Scout Assn., Nat. Guard Officer's Assn. Republican. Mem. Covenant Ch. Home: 1816 Trail Dr Duluth MN 55803

WOODBURY, STEPHEN ABBOTT, economics educator; b. Beverly, Mass., Oct. 25, 1952; s. Stephen E. and Barbara (Sandberg) W.; m. Susan Pozo, May 29, 1982 (div. June 1992); 1 child, Ricardo Pozo. AB, Middlebury (Vt.) Coll., 1975; MS, U. Wis., 1977, PhD, 1981. Asst. prof. of econs. Pa. State U., University Park, 1979-82; asst. prof. of econs. Mich. State U., East Lansing, 1982-88, assoc. prof. econs., 1988-94; prof. econs., 1994—; sr. economist W.E. Upjohn Inst., Kalamazoo, Mich., 1984—; dep. dir. Fed. Adv. Coun. on Unemployment Compensation, Washington, 1993-94, cons., 1994-96; cons. U. Hawaii/State of Hawaii, Honolulu, 1991—, State of Mich. Task Force, Lansing, 1989-90, U.S. Dept. Labor, Washington, 1988, European Communities Commn., Brussels, 1987-88; vis. prof. U. Stirling, Scotland, 1992; vis. scholar Fed. Res. Bd., Washington, 1992. Author: Tax Treatment of Benefits, 1991; (with others) Access to Health Care, 1992; editor Rsch. in Employment Policy; contbr. articles to profl. jours. Recipient Rsch. grants William H. Donner Found., 1991, U.S. Dept. Health and Human Svcs., 1985, and U.S. Dept. Labor, 1995. Mem. Am. Econ. Assn., Am. Statis. Assn., Assn. for Evolutionary Econs., Econometric Soc., Indsl. Rels. Rsch. Assn., Midwest Econs. Assn. (1st v.p. 1993-94), Ea. Econ. Assn., Soc. Labor Economists, Am. Law and Econs. Assn. Office: Dept Econs Marshall Hall Mich State U East Lansing MI 48824 also: WE Upjohn Inst 300 S Westnedge Ave Kalamazoo MI 49007

WOODCOCK, RICHARD L., engineer executive; b. Salina, Kans., June 2, 1950. Sys. adminstr. Marlin Rsch. Corp., Overland Park, Kans., 1992-93; CAD mgr. R & D Tool and Engring., Lee's Summit, Mo., 1993—; cons. Tech. Cons. Co., Belton, Mo., 1995. Sgt. U.S. Army, 1970-72, Vietnam. Republican. Baptist. Home: 15711 Vicie Ave Belton MO 64012

WOODEN, JULIE, critical care nurse; b. Joplin, Mo., Sept. 13, 1957; d. J. Sheldon and Barbaline (Mathews) Dudley; children: April, Kent. LPN, Sch. Dist. Joplin, 1982; BSN, BA, William Jewell Coll., 1989; postgrad., U. Mo., Kansas City. CCRN, RNC. EMT S. Barry County Ambulance, Cassville, Mo., 1978-80; CNA Aurora (Mo.) Nursing Ctr., 1980-82, charge nurse, 1982-83; staff practical nurse St. Vincent's Hosp., Monett, Mo., 1982-83; charge nurse Lacoba Homes, Monett, 1983; prin. nurse Truman Med. Ctr. East, Kansas City, Mo., 1984-85, sr. nurse, 1985-89, staff nurse, 1989; emergency nurse critical care Mid Am. Heart Inst. St. Luke's Hosp., Kansas City, 1989—; staff nurse level III ICU Bapt. Med. Ctr., Kansas City, 1989—; ptnr.-cons. Health Care Resource Assocs., Kansas City, 1992—. Mem. adv. bd. organ tissue ARC, Kansas City, 1993-94. Mem. ANA (RN med./surg.), AACN (NTI proposal rev. panel), Mo. Nurses Assn. (bd. dirs. dist. 2 1991—, program chair 1992-93, state govt. mental affairs com., state coun. nursing practice, state med./surg. Spl. Interest Group- chair), ANA Congress of Nursing Practice, Greater Kansas City Assn. Critical Care Nurses (treas. 1991-92, mktg. Spring Symposium 1993-95, scholarship chair 1994, rsch. chair 1995, registration chair 1996), Sigma Theta Tau (Mu Mu chpt.). Democrat. Methodist. Home: 4011 Harrison St Kansas City MO 64110-1207

WOODEN, REBA FAYE BOYD, guidance counselor; b. Washington, Ind., Sept. 21, 1940; d. Lester E. and Opal M. (Burch) Boyd; m. N. Nuel Wooden, Jr., Dec. 23, 1962 (div. 1993); children: Jeffrey Nuel, Cynthia Faye. BA, U. Indpls., 1962; MS, Butler U., 1968, Ind. U., 1990. Cert. tchr., counselor, Ind. Tchr. Mooresville (Ind.) High Sch., 1962-66; tchr. Perry Meridian High Sch., Indpls., 1974-92, counselor, 1992—; part-time instr. Ind. U.-Purdue U. at Indpls., 1994-95. Named Outstanding High Sch. Psychology tchr. APA, 1987. Mem. NEA, Ind. State Tchrs. Assn., Perry Edn. Assn. Methodist. Home: 113 Severn Dr Greenwood IN 46142-1880 Office: Perry Meridian High Sch 401 W Meridian School Rd Indianapolis IN 46217-4215

WOODFORD, MARK M., laboratory automation specialist, computer system project administrator; b. Chgo., Dec. 17, 1957; s. Charles Walter and Barbara Jean (Johnson) W.; m. Thanh-Van Phan, August 1, 1992; children: Ian, Sean. BS in Biology with distinction, U. Va., 1979; MS in Bioengring., U. Ill., Chgo., 1984. Cons. Yale U., New Haven, Conn., 1984; project leader Searle Pharmaceuticals, Skokie, Ill., 1985—. Contbr. articles to jours in field. Mem. IEEE. Home: 4549 N Harding Chicago IL 60625 Office: Searle R&D 4901 Searle Pky Skokie IL 60077

WOODIN, CHARLES P., engineering director; b. Waukesha, Wis., May 24, 1947. AS, Milw. Sch. Engineering, 1968, BS, 1971. Product engr. Husco, Waukesha, 1972-75; mfg. engr. Oil Gear, Milw., 1975-76; dir. engring. Versa Techs., Inc., Cudahy, Wis., 1976—. Office: Versa Techs Inc 5877 S Pennsylvania Ave Cudahy WI 53110-2456

WOODLE, ROBERT M., mathematics educator; b. Omaha, Nebr., Dec. 4, 1954; s. Robert F. and Harriet M. (Nevitt) W.; m. Katherine M. Kraft, Oct. 11, 1986. BA in Math., U. Nebr., 1976, MA in Math., 1978. Instr. math. Benedictine Coll., Atchison, Kans., 1978-79, Davis and Elkins Coll., Elkins, W.Va., 1979-82, No. Ariz. U., Flagstaff, 1982-86; asst. prof. math. Jamestown (N.D.) Coll., 1986—, chmn. dept. math., 1986—. Mem. Math. Assn. Am., Am. Statis. Assn., Nat. Coun. Tchrs. Math. Democrat. Presbyterian. Office: Jamestown College 6034 College Ln Jamestown ND 58405

WOODMAN, ELLEN ARMSTRONG, nurse educator; b. Chardon, Ohio, Sept. 17, 1937; d. John Jacob and Martha (Armstrong) Kulp; children: John Warren, Andrew James. BSN, U. Cin., 1959; MS, U. Mich., 1966, PhD, 1994. Staff nurse Cin. Gen. Hosp., 1959-60, Cleve. Met. Hosp., 1960-61; staff nurse U. Mich. Hosp., Ann Arbor, 1961-62, supr. adminstrv. nursing, 1962-63; faculty mgr. U. Mich. Sch. Nursing, Ann Arbor, 1963-64; clin. specialist, supr. William Beaumont Hosp., Royal Oak, Mich., 1966-68; asst. prof. U. Mich. Sch. Nursing, Ann Arbor, 1969-70; asst. dir. Mansfield (Ohio) Gen. Hosp. Sch. Nursing, 1971-76; asst. prof. and dir. dept. nursing U. Mich., Flint, 1976—; mem. Genesee County Cmty. Mental Health Svc. Bd., 1983—, chmn., 1991-92, cons. on nursing and legal matters, 1987—. Contbr. articles to profl. jours. Mem. ANA, Mich. Nurses Assn., GLS Dist. Nurses Assn. (bd. dirs. 1987-92, Profl. Nurse of Yr.), Mich. Statewide Coord. Coun. (adv. bd. to Dept. Pub. Health 1986-89). Home: 8254 Creekwood Dr Grand Blanc MI 48439-9311 Office: U Mich-Flint 516 Crob Flint MI 48502

WOODMAN, GREY MUSGRAVE, psychiatrist; b. Birmingham, Eng., Jan. 26, 1922; came to U.S., 1959, naturalized, 1963; s. Edward Musgrave and Ida (Cullen) W.; m. Bette Woodman; children: Sheila, Shonagh. BA, U. Oxford (Eng.), 1943, MA, BM, BCh, 1945. Ship's surgeon, 1946-48; intern Whipps Cross Hosp., London, 1948-49, med. registrar, 1951-54, also Newcastle-on-Tyne, Eng., 1951-54; resident in Psychiatry U. Okla. Med. Ctr., 1959-62; staff psychiatrist Western Mo. Mental Health Ctr., Kansas City, 1962-76; med. dir. Mental Health Ctr. Clinton County, Clinton, Iowa, 1976-87; pvt. practice, Clinton, 1976—; founder, dir. Lincolnshire Clinic; mem. staff Jane Lamb Health Ctr., Mercy Hosp. (now Samaritan Health System); staff mem. Comphealth; cons. Mufon. Served with Brit. Merc. Marines, 1946-48. Fellow Royal Soc. Medicine (London, life); mem. AMA (life), Am. Psychiat. Assn. (life), Am. Acad. Med. Hypoanalysts (assoc.), Brit. Med. Assn., World Fedn. Mental Health, Iowa Med. Soc. (past chmn. hospice com.), Internat. Assn. Social Psychiatry, Am. Assn. Hypoanalysts. Republican. Episcopalian. Home: 515 N 13th St Clinton IA 52732-4816 Office: Lincolnshire Clinic 223 Wilson Bldg Clinton IA 52732

WOODRUFF, DAVID P., journalist; b. Pitts., Mar. 3, 1957; s. Neal Jr. and Christine (Lipps) W. BA in Comparative Lit., Beloit Coll., 1979; MS in Journalism, Northwestern U., 1983. Staff writer Kalamazoo (Mich.) Gazette, 1984-89; corr. Bus. Week, Detroit, 1989—. Dir. Literacy Vol. Am., Detroit, 1991—. Recipient 2nd Place award Natl. Newspaper Assoc., 1988, Overseas Press Club Am., 1992, Detroit Press Club Found., 1992. Mem. Investigative Reporters and Editors, Inc. Office: Business Week 407 E Fort St Ste 108 Detroit MI 48226

WOODRUFF, JANE, sales executive; b. Derby, Eng., July 20, 1945; d. George John Schwaegerman and Joyce (Robinson) Turnock; m. Charles Walter Woodruff, Aug. 1, 1964 (div. 1976); 1 child, Jon Bradley. BA, Purdue U., 1967, MS, 1968, MA, 1970. Tchr. Kansas City (Mo.) Schs., 1970-73; asst. dir. communicatons Skyline Corp., Elkart, Ind., 1974-77; market analyst Motor Wheel Corp. subs. Goodyear Tire and Rubber Co., Lansing, Mich., 1977-80, mgr. planning and research, 1980-82, mgr. car and light truck mktg., 1982-84; account exec. Motor Wheel Corp., Farmington Hills, Mich., 1984—. Chmn. Motor Wheel Savs. Bond Drive, Lansing, 1980; fundraiser Capital Area United Way, Lansing, 1981; cons. bus. projects Jr. Achievement, Lansing, 1981-82. NDEA scholar U.S. Dept. Edn., 1967-68; teaching fellow Purdue U., 1968-70; recipient Cert. Achievement YWCA, Lansing, 1980. Mem. Indsl. Mktg. Group Am. Mktg. Assn. (treas.), Automotive Market Research Council, Soc. Automotive Engrs. Office: Motor Wheel Corp 28295 Bayberry Rd Farmington MI 48331-3317

WOODS, BRUCE WALTER, editor, poet; b. Dunkirk, N.Y., Apr. 13, 1947; s. Walter Gerald Woods and Alma (Johnson) Rice. B.A., SUNY-Fredonia, 1969. Assoc. editor Dirt Rider, Canoga Park, Calif., 1972, editor, 1972-75; exec. editor Dirt Bike, Encino, Calif., 1975-76, editor, 1976; asst. editorial dir. Daisey Pub., Encino, Calif., 1976-78; editor The Mother Earth News, Hendersonville, N.C., 1978-87; editor-in-chief The Mother Earth News and Am. Country, Hendersonville, N.C., 1987-94; assoc. publ. Writer's Digest, Cin., 1994-95; editor Writer's Yearbook, Cin.; assoc. pub. Writer's Digest; editl. dir. Popular Woodworking. Author: From the Carp of Good Hope, 1970, How Far?, 1971, Food, 1973, Fieldbook, 1976; editor: Back Country Handbook, 1989, Chui! A Guide to the African Leopard, 1994. Office: F&W Pubs Writer's Digest 1507 Dana Ave Cincinnati OH 45207-1056

WOODS, DONALD DEWAYNE, advertising materials designer/manufacturer; b. Chattanooga, June 17, 1942; s. Wilburn William and Stella Elizabeth (Hooks) W.; m. Wanda Louise Hines, May 29, 1974 (div. Oct. 1989); m. Donna Maria Spanier, Feb. 21, 1992. GED (Gen. Ednl. Devel.), Tex. Camera/reprodn. mgr. Benco Plastics Inc., Knoxville, Tenn., 1964-69; sous chef Cherokee Country Club, Knoxville, 1967-69; auto/screen pressman Gibson Greeting Cards Inc., Cin., 1973-80; plant mgr. Am. Sign Co., Florence, Ky., 1984-86; gen. mgr., co-owner Trans-Acc Graphics, Cin., 1986; owner D & D Enterprises, Cin., 1986—; cons. screen printing Levi Strauss, Cin., 1975-76, Journey Electronics Inc., Mason, Ohio, 1992; designer Screen Printed Products, 1986-89. Author: Screen Printing: Techniques for Point of Sale Merchandise, 1984; co-patentee utilization of night vision device in processing film. Cons., v.p. 7th Step Found., Cin., 1973-78; cons. Cin. Coalition for Homeless, 1992. With U.S. Army, 1960-64, Germany. Recipient Update award Printers Week/Cin. Enquirer, 1989. Mem. Profl. Photographers Assn., Advt. Specialties Assn. (imprinter 1986—), The Planetary Soc., Midwest Screen Printers Assn. (cons. 1978—), Civil War Soc. (participant drama reenactment 1974—). Republican. Mem. Ch. of God. Home and Office: 3300 Gamble Ave Cincinnati OH 45211-5616

WOODS, ELSWORTH PETER, educator, dean, retired; b. Estherville, Iowa, Aug. 4, 1912; s. Robert Elsworth and Elsie Elizabeth (Einsele) W.; m. Sylvia Curry, Aug. 19, 1936; children: Joan, Carmen, Elizabeth. BA, U. Iowa, 1936, MA, 1939, PhD, 1949. High sch. tchr. Sr. High Schs., Iowa and Ill., 1936-43; instr. Drake U., Des Moines, Iowa, 1946-47, dean liberal arts, 1955-72, prof. polit. sci., 1971-82; instr. U. Iowa, Iowa City, 1947-49; from asst. prof. to prof. Western Mich. U., Kalamazoo, 1949-55. Pres., charter mem. Golden K. Kiwanis, Des Moines. Carnegie Teaching fellow Harvard U., 1953-54, Fulbright Teaching fellow U. Papua, New Guinea, 1970. Mem. Torch Club (charter, pres. 1993-94). Presbyterian. Home: Calvin West 4210 Hickman Rd Des Moines IA 50310

WOODS, GWENDOLYN LENAR, parole program administrator; b. Cin., Jan. 6, 1962; d. Ike and Jessie L. (Warren) Everson; m. Robert Anthony Woods, Aug. 19, 1961; 1 child, Brandon Antohio. BA, Ohio U., 1984; MS, Xavier U., Cin., 1986. Cert. fitness instr. Receptionist, adminstrv. asst. Chester C. Pryor II, MD, Cin., 1978-86; diversion officer Montgomery County Prosecutor, Dayton, Ohio, 1986-91; mediator Cin. Prosecutor's Office, 1984-86; fitness instr. Holiday/Bally's Fitness, Dayton and Columbus, Ohio, 1989—; instr. Sinclair C.C., Dayton, 1989-91; supr. U.S. Census Bur., Dayton, 1990; parole officer Ohio Dept. Rehab. and Corrections, Columbus, 1992-93, parole program specialist, 1993-95, dep. superintendent, 1995—. Mem. Am. Fitness Assn., Am. Probation/Parole Assn., Am. Correctional Assn., Nat. Coun. Negro Women, Alliance of Women in Cmty. Rels., Delta Sigma Theta. Office: Ohio Dept Rehab/Corrections 1050 Freeway Dr N Columbus OH 43229

WOODS, LAWRENCE ALAN, librarian; b. Springfield, Vt., Mar. 27, 1939; s. Percival Bugbee and Alice Millicent (White) W.; m. Kathleen Anne Hazen, Aug. 27, 1960; children: Timothy Alan, Peter Kevin, Stephen Jeffrey. Diploma, Ea. Bible Inst., Green Lane, Pa., 1959; BA, Ea. Nazarene Coll., 1968; postgrad., Dartmouth Coll., 1964-68, 68-70; MLS, Simmons Coll., 1972. Chief libr. automation Dartmouth Coll., Hanover, N.H., 1972-77; head R&D Purdue U., West Lafayette, Ind., 1977-82; asst. dir. librs. U. Notre Dame, Ind., 1982-85; mgr. libr. systems McDonnell Douglas Computer Sys., Newport Beach, Calif., 1985-87; v.p. RMG Cons., Irvine, Calif., 1987-91; dir. info. systems and tech. U. Iowa, Iowa City, 1991—. Author: Librarians Guide to Microcomputer Technology and Applications, 1983. Mem. ALA, Am. Soc. Info. Sci. (Watson Davis award 1985). Home: 606 S Johnson St Iowa City IA 52240-4839 Office: U Iowa Librs Iowa City IA 52242

WOODS, WARREN CHIP, civil engineer; b. Kansas City, Mo., Apr. 26, 1948; s. Russell McDonald and Sadie Maxine (Peatling) W.; m. Marie Annette Weyer, Aug. 22, 1970; children: Erica Grayce, Jenessa Marie. BSCE, U. Mo., Rolla, 1970, MSCE, 1972. Registered profl. engr., Kans.; registered land surveyor, Kans. Rd. supr. Marshall County, Marysville, Kans., 1970-76, county engr., 1976-80; project engr./project surveyor BG Cons., Inc., Manhattan, Kans., 1980-88; county engr. Lyon County, Emporia, Kans., 1988—. Mem. NSPE, Nat. Soc. Profl. Surveyors, Kans. Engring. Soc., Am. Congress on Surveying and Mapping, Kans. County Hwy. Assn. (sec.-treas. 1992, pres. 1994), Profl. Surveyors of the 6th P.M. (life), Kans. Soc. Land Surveyors (pres. 1991-93). Republican. Lutheran. Home: 1730 Thompson St Emporia KS 66801-6082 Office: Lyon County Hwy Dept 500 S Prairie St Emporia KS 66801-9478

WOODSON, DONNA MARIE, physical therapist, Franciscan sister; b. Omaha, July 10, 1934; d. Cleo Eugene and Josephine Mary (Hoban) W. BS in Phys. Therapy, St. Louis U., 1957; MA in Franciscan Studies, St. Bonaventure U., 1980. Lic. phys. therapist, Ill., Wis. Phys. therapist to supr. rehab. St. John's Hosp., Springfield, Ill., 1962-71; supr. phys. therapy Sacred Heart Hosp., Eau Clair, Wis., 1971-73; mem. faculty Chgo. Med. Sch., 1973-75; phys. therapy cons. Edgewater Rehab. Assoc., Northbrook, Ill., 1973-80; phys. therapist St. Elizabeth Hosp., Belleville, Ill., 1957-60, 80-82; missionary, tchr. English and Franciscan spirituality Med. Sisters of St. Francis, Anjali, Niketan, India, 1982-83; co-founder med. mission for leprosy and polio Med. Sisters of St. Francis, Bihar, India, 1984; pres. Assisi Bhawan Med. Sisters of St. Francis, Ramgarh Cantt, Bihar, India, 1984-91; phys. therapist Edgewater Rehab. Assoc., Northbrook, 1992—; adj. faculty Franciscan Inst. Spirituality of India, 1988-91; spiritual asst. Secular Franciscan Order Groups, Belleville, 1980-82, Granite City, Ill., 1980-82, Chgo., 1993—. Contbr. articles to profl. publs. Chmn. St. Louis Metro Franciscan Coun., 1981-82; co-chmn. Chgo. Francis 800 Celebration, 1975-76. Mem. Am. Phys. Therapy Assn. (vice chmn. Ill. Ctrl. dist. chpg. 1968-71), Franciscan Fedn., Fedn. Returned Overseas Missionaries. Roman Catholic. Home: 11923 S Ridgeway Apt 10 Alsip IL 60658

WOODSON, SHAWN HAROLD, aerospace company executive; b. Buffalo, June 18, 1960; s. Richard Hilton and Maureen Mary (Graham) W. BS, N.C. State U., 1983, MS, 1985, PhD, 1988. Rsch. assoc. NASA Langley Rsch. Ctr., Hampton, Va., 1988-89; sr. engr. Gen. Dynamics Corp., Ft. Worth, 1989-91, Cessna Aircraft Co., Wichita, Kans., 1991—; postdoctoral rsch. assoc. NRC, Hampton, 1988-89. Contbr. articles to profl. publs. Vol. Spl. Olympics, Charlotte, N.C., 1988, 89, Ft. Worth, 1990, Wichita, 1992, 93, Habitat for Humanity, Hampton, 1989. Mem. AIAA (sr. mem., judging chmn. region IV student paper competition 1990, sec. Wichita sect. 1993, mem. applied aerodynamics tech. com. 1993-95), Royal Aeronautical Soc. Republican. Office: Cessna Aircraft Co PO Box 7704 Wichita KS 67277-7704

WOODWARD, KEVIN DALE, writer; b. Quincy, Ill., Dec. 18, 1963; s. Marion Dale Woodward and Leta Irene (Garnett) Dodd. BS in advt., So. Ill. U., 1987; MA in journalism, U. Iowa, 1991. Writer Chgo., 1992—; mktg. coord. Smith, Bucklin & Assocs., Chgo., 1993-94. Editor: Urban Romantic: Paul Gapp, 1994. Scripps Howard scholar Scripps Howard Found, Carbondale, Ill., 1987, Murray scholar U. Iowa, Iowa City, 1991; Murray Rsch. grantee, U. Iowa, 1991.

WOODWARD, ROBERT SIMPSON, IV, economics educator; b. Easton, Pa., May 7, 1943; s. Robert Simpson and Esther Evans (Thomas) W.; B.A., Haverford Coll., 1965; Ph.D., Washington U., St. Louis, 1972; m. Mary P. Hutton, Feb. 15, 1969; children—Christopher Thomas, Rebecca Marie. B-rookings Econ. Policy fellow HEW, Washington, 1975-76; asst. prof. U.

Western Ont. (Can.), London, 1972-77; asst. prof. Sch. Medicine, Washington U., St. Louis, 1978-86, assoc. prof., 1986—; pres. Writing Assessment Software, Inc., 1987-91. Mem. adv. council Mo. Kidney Program, 1980-86, vice-chmn., 1983, chmn. 1984-85; coop. mem. Haverford Coll., 1968-90. NDEA fellow, 1968-71; Kellogg Nat. fellow, 1981-84. Mem. Am. Econs. Assn., Am. Statis. Assn. Contbr. articles to profl. jours. Home: 7050 Westmoreland Dr Saint Louis MO 63130-4421 Office: 4547 Clayton Ave Saint Louis MO 63110-1501

WOODWORTH, MARY ESTHER, microbiology educator, consultant; b. Grand Rapids, Mich.; d. Irving and Doris Gertrude (Linsenmeyer) W. BS summa cum laude, U. Mich., 1957; MS, Temple U., 1965, PhD, 1968. Postdoctoral fellow U. Mich., Ann Arbor, 1968-72; rsch. assoc. Syracuse (N.Y.) U., 1972-73; rsch. scientist Johns Hopkins U. Sch. Medicine, Balt., 1973-76; cancer rsch. scientist Roswell Park Meml. Inst., Buffalo, N.Y., 1977-89, acting chair, 1983-84; asst. prof. Roswell Park div. SUNY, Buffalo, 1977-86, assoc. prof., 1986-89; prof. microbiology, dept. chmn. Miami U., Oxford, Ohio, 1989—; bd. dirs. Health Rsch., Inc., Buffalo, 1984-87. Contbr. articles to profl. jours. including Jour. Virology, Jour. Molecular Biology, Molecular Cell Biology, Nucleic Acids Rsch., Biophysics Jour., Jour. Molecular Applied Genetics, Jour. Biol. Chemistry. Recipient Rsch. Career Devel. award NIH, 1978-83. Fellow Am. Acad. Microbiology; mem. AAAS, AAUW, Am. Soc. Microbiology (lectr. 1989-90, com. mem. for genetic and molecular microbiology 1990, chair com. for genetic and molecular microbiology 1992—), Am. Soc. Biochemistry and Molecular Biology, Am. Soc. Virology, Am. Women in Sci., Sigma Xi, Phi Beta Kappa, Phi Kappa Phi. Home: 6313 Bigwood Cir Oxford OH 45056-9271 Office: Miami U Dept Microbiology Oxford OH 45056

WOODWORTH, ROBERT C., newspaper executive. Pres., gen. mgr. Kansas City (Mo.) Star. Office: Kansas City Star 1729 Grand Blvd Kansas City MO 64108-1413*

WOODY, JOHN FREDERICK, secondary education educator; b. Indpls., Apr. 27, 1941; s. Ralph Edwin and Crystal Oleta (Thomas) W.; m. Nancy Ann Henry, July 7, 1963; children: Michael, Laura. BS in Secondary Sch. Teaching, Butler U., 1963, MS in Edn., 1967, adminstrn. lic., 1979, postgrad., 1991—; postgrad., UCLA, 1980-82, Ind. U., 1990, U. Amsterdam, The Netherlands, 1985, Mont. State U., 1993, Purdue U., 1994. Tchr. Pub. Sch. 90, Indpls., 1963-66, Broad Ripple High Sch., Indpls., 1966-89; tchr., head social studies dept. Arlington H.S., Indpls., 1989—. Author: (resource kits for hist. events) Cram, Inc., 1976-81, (filmstrips) Lowe Sheldrew, 1976-81; contbr. articles to profl. jours. and sch. materials. Sponsor Rep. Nat. Com., 1982—; deacon Heritage Bapt. Ch., 1983—; mem. U.S. Congress German Bundestag Select Com. Ind., 1986-93. Fulbright scholar U.S. Info. Agy., 1985. Mem. ASCD, Nat. Coun. Social Studies, Ind. Coun. Social Studies, Arlington Acad. Com. Home: 7362 Woodside Dr Indianapolis IN 46260-3137 Office: Arlington High Sch 4825 N Arlington Ave Indianapolis IN 46226-2401

WOODYARD, HARRY, state legislator; b. Danville, Ill., Dec. 3, 1930; s. Lewis J. and Lucile (Holden) W.; m. Mary D. Hester, 1952; children: Leslie, Kirk. Student, Wesleyan U. State rep. Dist. 106, 1979-87; Ill. state senator Dist. 53, 1987—; mem. agrl. and conserv. Ill. State Senate, internat. trade and port promotion coms., joint coms. on adminstrn. rules, local govt., revenue coms., state employees suggestion award bd. coms., appropriations I & II, com. econ. devel. coms.; chmn. bd. Ridgefarm State Bank; farmer. Named Outstanding Legislator for Cmty. Colls.; recipient John M. Lewis Outstanding Legislator award Ill. Cmty. Coll. Trustees Assn., 1982, Svc. award Ill. Land Improvement Contractors Assn., 1983, Meritorious Svc. award Ill. Cmty. Coll. Trustees Assn., 1987. Mem. VFW, Kiwanis, Shriners, Farm Bur., Masons, Am. Legion (life mem.), Sigma Chi. Republican. Home: 104 W Washington Ave Chrisman IL 61924-1141*

WOOLARD, LARRY, state legislator; s. Bertus and Vera Woolard; m. Mary Ann Switzer; children: Laurie Matson, Scott, Machelle, Jason. Commr. Williamson County, 1984-90; mem. Ill. Ho. Reps., Springfield, 1989—, mgm. agr. com., appropriations com., elections law com., elem. & secondary edn. com., mental health com., pub. health & infrastructure appropriations. Mem. Carterville C. of C. (chmn.), Herrin C. of C. (chmn.), Lions, Masons, Moose. Address: 840 Terminal Dr Ste 106 Marion IL 62959*

WOOLF, STEVEN MICHAEL, artistic director; b. Milw., Dec. 23, 1947; s. Raleigh and Lenore (Shurman) W. BA in Theatre, U. Wis., 1968, MFA, 1971; D of Fine Arts (hon.), U. Mo., 1993. Prodn. stage mgr. The Juilliard Sch. Drama, N.Y.C., 1973-75; project producer Musical Theatre Lab., N.Y.C., 1974-75; prodn. stage mgr. Barter Theatre, Abingdon, Va., 1976-79, Stagewest, Springfield, Mass., 1976-79; prodn. mgr. Repertory Theatre of St. Louis, 1980-83, acting artistic dir., mng. dir., 1983-85, mng. dir., 1985-86, artistic dir., 1986—; adj. faculty Webster U., St. Louis, 1982—; mem. nat. negotiating coms. League of Resident Theatres, N.Y.C., 1986—; on-site evaluator Nat. Endowment for the Arts, 1985. Dir. plays A Life in the Theatre, 1982, the Crucible, 1986, Company, 1987, The Voice of the Prairie, 1988, 90, The Boys Next Door, 1989, Dog Logic, 1990, Born Yesterday, 1990, Terra Nova, 1991, The Diary of Anne Frank, 1991, Other Peoples Money, 1991, Six Degrees of Separation, 1992, Sight Unseen, 1993, Lion in Winter, 1993, Death and the Maiden, 1993, The Living, 1994, Wait Until Dark, 1994, The Caine Mutiny Court Martial, 1994. Mem. ad hoc coms. for funding Mo. Arts Coun., St. Louis, 1988; chair citizen rev. panel Reg. Arts Commn., St. Louis, 1986; bd. dirs. Mo. Citizens for the Arts, 1990—; exec. com. League of Resident Theatres, 1990—. Recipient award Mo. Citizens for the Arts, 1992, Women's Polit. Caucus, 1993, award for Individual Excellence in the Arts, Arts Edn. Coun., 1993. Mem. AFTRA, Soc. of Stage Dirs. and Choreographers, Actors Equity Assn. Office: Repertory Theatre St Louis 20 Kingshighway Blvd Saint Louis MO 63108

WOOLLACOTT, ANGELA MARY, historian; b. Adelaide, Australia, July 16, 1955; came to U.S., 1982; d. Lloyd Smith and Mollie Gwenneth (Scales) W.; m. Carroll Wirth Pursell, Dec. 20, 1986. BA, Australian Nat. U., 1978; BA in History (hon.), Adelaide U., 1979; MA, U. Calif., Santa Barbara, 1984, PhD, 1988. Rsch. historian Constl. Mus. of South Australia, Adelaide, 1979-82; asst. prof. history Case Western Res. U., Cleve., 1988-94, assoc. prof. history, 1994—. Author: On Her Their Lives Depend: Munitions Workers in the Great War, 1994; editor: (with Miriam Cooke) Gendering War Talk, 1993. Fellow Rsch. Inst. on Gender and War, Dartmouth Coll., 1990; NEH grantee, 1991. Fellow Royal Hist. Soc. (U.K.); mem. N.Am. Conf. on Brit. Studies, Am. Hist. Assn., Nat. Women's Studies Assn. Office: Case Western Res Univ Euclid Ave Cleveland OH 44106

WOOLLING, KENNETH RAU, internist; b. Indpls., Mar. 6, 1918; s. Kenneth Kaarta and Marie May (Rau) W.; m. Catherine Margaret McColl, Mar. 20, 1948; children: Kenneth Rau Jr., Mary Catherine. BA magna cum laude, Butler U., 1939; postgrad., Harvard U., 1939-40; MD, Ind. U., 1943; MS in Medicine, U. Minn., 1951. Diplomate Nat. Bd. Med. Examiners, Am. Bd. Internal Medicine, Am. Bd. Cardiovascular Disease. Intern Indpls. City Hosp. (now Wishard Meml.), Indpls., 1943-44; resident in internal medicine Marion County Gen. Hosp., Indpls., 1947; fellow, first asst. internal medicine Mayo Found., Rochester, Minn., 1948-52; mem. med. staff, mem. tchg. staff postgrad. med. edn. Marion County Gen. Hosp. (name now Wishard Meml. Hosp.), Indpls., 1952—; founder, dir., peripheral vascular diseases clinic Indpls City & Marion County Gen. Hosp. (now Wishard Meml.), Indpls., 1952-68; pvt. practice internal medicine and cardiovascular diseases Indpls, 1952—; founder, dir. peripheral vascular diseases clinic, 1967-72; founder, dir. vascular lab. Meth. Hosp., Indpls., 1970-73, mem. med. staff, tchr. staff postgrad. med. edn., 1952—; mem. staff St. Vincent Hosp., St. Francis Hosp. and Winona Meml. Hosp., Indpls., 1952—; charter mem. med. adv. com. Butler U., Indpls, 1956—. Contbr. articles to profl. jours., 1950—. Capt. Med. Corps U.S. Army, 1944-46. Fellow Am. Coll. Chest Physicians, Coun. on Clin. Cardiology Am. Heart Assn., 1963. Fellow ACP, Am. Coll. Angiology (gov. state of Ind. 1979-80); mem. AMA (50 Yr. award 1993), SAR, Am. Soc. Internal Medicine, Am. Diabetes Assn., Ind. Diabetes Assn., Am. Fedn. for Clin. Rsch., N.Y. Acad. Med. Scis., North Ctrl. Clin. Soc., Mayo Cardiovascular Soc., Ind. Hist. Soc., Res. Officers Assn., Am. Legion, Shriners, Masons (Scottish Rite), Contemporary Club of Indpls., Indpls. Athletic Club, Highland Golf and Country Club, Phi Delta Theta (50 yr. award 1985), Phi Kappa Phi, Phi Chi. Presbyterian. Office: PO Box 80192 Indianapolis IN 46280-0192

WOOTEN, CHARLES (CHUCK), state legislator; b. Springfield, Mo., July 14, 1927; m. Joan M. Davidson, 1979; children: Charles Jr., Janet (twins), Mary, Terry. Diploma, U. Md., 1960, Northwestern U., Evanston, Ill., 1973, U. Tenn., 1981. With U.S. Postal Svc.; mem. Mo. Ho. of Reps. from 137th dist.; mem. Labor, Retirement, Retirement Statutory Tourism, Elem. and Secondary Edn. Coms. Mo. Ho. of Reps. Mem. Springfield (Mo.) City Coun., 1983-88. Mem. AARP, Am. Legion, Elks, Gate Temple Lodge. Republican. Address: 2146 N Broadway Springfield MO 65803*

WORACHEK, SUSAN HANLIN, music educator; b. Bloomington, Ind., Feb. 18, 1952; d. Charles Harold and Kathryn M. Hanlin; m. James Allen Worachek, July, 1978; children: Jennifer Ann, Sarah Elizabeth. BS, Miami U., 1974; MEd, Xavier U., 1981. Cert. tchr., Ohio. Music educator Norwood (Ohio) Pub. Schs., 1974-85; gifted students educator P.A.G.E., Inc., Cin., 1992-94; coord. musical arts Cin. Hills Christian Acad., 1995—. Dist. chmn. cultural arts contest Valley Area Coun. PTA, Cin, 1990-93, advisor, 1990-91; chmn. bd. Christian edn. Messiah Luth. Ch., Cin., 1993—; mem. supt.'s adv. coun. Princeton Bd. Edn., Cin., 1993—; mem. bus. adv. com. Glendale Elem. Sch., Cin., 1993—, pres. No. Hills Piano Tchr's. Forum, 1991-93, Glendale PTA, 1993-95; judge Ohio Fedn. Music Clubs, Cin., 1986-94. Mem. Glendale Lyceum, Village Gardeners, Delta Omicron. Office: Cin Hills Christian Acad 11300 Snider Rd Cincinnati OH 45249

WORDEN, DOUGLAS JAMES, city official; b. Burlington, Iowa, Apr. 5, 1955; s. Hersel Lewis and Mary Irene (St. Clair) W.; m. Jan Lynette Wafefield, Apr. 4, 1992; 1 child, Nicholas Allen. BBA in Acctg., U. Iowa, 1977. CPA, Iowa. Fin. commr. City of Burlington (Iowa), 1978-82, fin. dir., 1982—. Pres. S.E. Iowa coun. Boy Scouts Am., Burlington, 1987-90, Miss. Valley coun., 1993; v.p., pres. Burlington Steamboat Days, 1984—; treas. Burlington Conv./Tourism Bur., Burlington, 1985-91. Recipient Dist. Merit award Blackhawk Dist. Boy Scouts Am., 1985, Silver Beaver award S.E. Iowa Coun., 1989. Mem. Iowa Mcpl. Fin. Officers Assn. (bd. dirs. 1990-94, pres. 1994—), Govt. Fin. Officers Assn., Masons (Malta 318 chpt.). Home: 609 S Starr Ave Burlington IA 52601

WORK, MITCHELL ROBERT, healthcare marketing professional; b. Vienna, Austria, Mar. 17, 1947; came to U.S., 1947; s. Robert E. and Rosalyn Joy (Mitchell) W.; m. Susan M. Intveldt, Mar. 10, 1979; children: Jessica, Emily. BA, Pa. State U., 1969; MPA, Am. U., 1971. Prof. sociology Luther Rice Coll., Springfield, Va., 1970-71; sr. trainer Pa. Health Rsch. Inst., Harrisburg, 1971-73; v.p. edn. and drug abuse prevention Adapt, Inc., Des Moines, 1973-75, pres., 1975-76; exec. dir. drug and alcohol treatment program ADASI, Inc., Des Moines, 1976-78; dir. mktg. and sales IMS Am., Ltd., Ambler, Pa., 1978-86; sr. v.p., ptnr. Sheldon I. Dorenfest Assocs., Chgo., 1986—; cons. Spl. Action Office Drug Prevention, White House, Washington, 1974, Nat. Inst. Drug Abuse, Washington, 1975, Pan Am. Health Orgn., Washington, 1979-81; presenter at profl. confs. Mem. Biomed. Mktg. Assn., Ctr. Health Info. Mgmt. (chair industry rsch. com. 1992, networking com. 1995). Home: 2936 Grant St Evanston IL 60201-2059 Office: Sheldon I Dorenfest Assocs 515 N State St Chicago IL 60610-4320

WORKE, GARY D., state legislator; b. Mankato, Minn., Jan. 20, 1949; m. Kathy; four children. BS, Mankato State U.; postgrad., St. Johns Coll. Minn. State rep. Dist. 28A, 1993—; owner Residential Care Home. Home: 6 Knoll Dr Waseca MN 56093-9003*

WORKMAN, GAYLE JEAN, physical education educator; b. Mt. Vernon, Ohio, Sept. 26, 1959; d. Willard L. Workman and Joyce (Pealer) Workman-Garvic. BS in Phys. Edn., Bowling Green State U., 1982; MS in Sport Studies, Slippery Rock U., 1991; PhD, Ohio State U., 1995. presenter in field, 1992—. Elem. phys. edn. tchr., coach East Knox Sch. Dist., Howard, Ohio, 1983-89; teaching asst. Slippery Rock (Pa.) U., 1989-91; adj. prof. Butler (Pa.) C.C., 1991; prof. Kutztown (Pa.) U., 1992; teaching asst. Ohio State U., Columbus, 1992-95; asst. prof. U. Akron, Ohio, 1995—; presenter Midwest Conv. of Adult Edn., Columbus, 1993. Mem. AAHPERD (presenter at nat. convs.). Home: 1250 Weathervane Ln Akron OH 44313

WORKMAN, JOHN MITCHELL, chemist; b. Uniontown, Pa., Oct. 25, 1949; s. Hugh Lawrence and Mary Louise (Mitchell) W.; m. Gayle Sue Zappin, Nov. 20, 1987. BA in Psychology, Miami U., Oxford, Ohio, 1971; MS in Edn., Kans. State U., 1976; MS in Chemistry, U. Cin., 1985, PhD in Chemistry, 1987; MBA in Fin., Wright State U., Dayton, Ohio, 1995. Teaching and rsch. asst. dept. chemistry Wright State U., Dayton, Ohio, 1977-81; grad. teaching asst. U. Cin., 1982-83, grad. rsch. asst., 1983-86; sr. scientist Chemsys Inc., Fairborn, Ohio, 1986-89, dir. elemental analysis, 1989—; lab. dir., 1994—. Contbr. articles to jours. Analytical Chemistry, Applied Spectroscopy. Sgt. U.S. Army, 1972-75. Mem. Am. Chem. Soc., Am. Phys. Soc., Soc. Applied Spectroscopy, Am. Mgmt. Assn., Sigma Xi, Sigma Pi Sigma, Sigma Iota Epsilon. Roman Catholic. Home: 1379 Sunset Dr Fairborn OH 45324-5649 Office: Chemsys Inc PO Box 1649 Fairborn OH 45324-7649

WORKMAN, ROBERT PETER, artist, cartoonist; b. Chgo., Jan. 27, 1961; s. Tom Okko and Virginia (Martin) W. Freelance artist Chgo.; artist Villager Newspaper, Chgo., 1991—; instr. St. Xavier Coll., Chgo., 1985; cartoonist Bridge View News, Oak Lawn, Ill., 1983-89, Village View Pubs., Oak Lawn, 1989; artist Villager News, 1991; TV art dir. Media-In-Action, Oak Lawn; lectr. Oxford U., Eng.; substitute tchr. Morgan Pk. Acad., Chgo.; artist-in-residence Chgo. Pub. Libr.; featured voice Am. Radio, 1992; exhibitor Seville Spain Am. Pavilion, Expo 92, Seville, 1992, Royal Acad. Arts Exhbn., 1995. Author: (cartoon strip) Cypher, 1983-89; Sesqui Squirrel Coloring Book, 1982, Sesqui Squirrel History of Chicago, 1983, (artists' books) Sesqui Squirrel History of the Constitution, Sesqui Squirrel Presents How Columbus Discovered America; author: (novel) Angels of Doom; artworks and books in collections of 87 mus. and librs. and pvt. collections, including Smithsonian, Art Inst. Chgo., Daley Br. Libr., Chgo., Ill. Exec. Mansion Mus., Sesquicentennial Archives Chgo. Pub. Libr. (awards and honors), The Vatican Libr., Rome, Bodleian Libr. U. Oxford, Eng., Mt. Greenwood Br. Pub. Libr. Chgo., Ill. Collection, Libr. Nat. Mus. Am. Art, Nat. Portrait Gallery. Mem. nat. adv. bd. Am. Security Coun., Boston, Va.; originator Kennedy Pk. Libr., Chgo. Featured in Artist's mag., 1990; recipient Resolution City Coun. Chgo., 1992. Mem. Am. Watercolor Soc., No. Ill. Newspaper Assn., Art Inst. Chgo. (freelancer 1991), Artists' Resource Trust Ft. Wayne Mus. Art, Ridge Art Assn., VFW, S.W. Archdiocesan Singles, Friends Oxford U., Alumni Sch. Art Inst. Chgo., KC. Roman Catholic. Home and Office: 2509 W 111th St # 2E Chicago IL 60655-1325

WORKMAN, THOMAS ELDON, lawyer; b. Galion, Ohio, Apr. 3, 1944; s. Eldon Barger and Mary Magdalene (Holcker) W.; m. Pamela Ann Mulbarger, Sept. 4, 1965; children: Thomas Christian, Sarah Christian. BSBA, Ohio State U., 1966, JD, 1969. Bar: Ohio 1969, U.S. Dist. Ct. (so. dist.) 1974, U.S. Ct. Mil. Appeals 1970, U.S. Supreme Ct. 1985. Assoc. Bricker & Eckler, Columbus, Ohio, 1973-76, ptnr., 1976—; trustee Griffith Found. on Ins., Columbus, 1990—; legis. counsel Assn. Ohio Life Ins. Cos., Columbus, 1973—; bd. dirs. Fedn. Regulatory Counsel, Denver, 1991—, chair; bd. dirs. Ohio Farmers Ins. Co. Contbr. articles to profl. jours. Ctrl. committeeman Franklin County Rep. Orgn., Columbus, 1988—; bd. trustees Ohio Hunger Task Force; treas. Ohio pub. expenditure coun. Mem. ABA, (past chair life ins. law com. 1992-93), Ohio State Bar Assn., Columbus Bar Assn., Masons (33rd degree AASR), Shrine (Aladdin), Columbus Country Club, Crichton Club, Delta Tau Delta. Republican. Home: 134 Ashbourne Rd Bexley OH 43209-1451 Office: Bricker & Eckler 100 S 3rd St Columbus OH 43215-4236

WORKMAN, TOM, state legislator; b. Sept. 1959; m. Carolyn; three children. BA, St. Cloud State U. Mo. State rep. Dist. 43A, 1993—; ins. agt. Home: 181 S Shore Ct Chanhassen MN 55317-9318*

WORLEY, MARVIN GEORGE, JR., architect; b. Oak Park, Ill., Oct. 10, 1934; s. Marvin George and Marie Hyancinth (Donahue) W.; B.Arch., U. Ill., 1958; m. Maryalice Ryan, July 11, 1959; children—Michael Craig, Carrie Ann, Alissa Maria. Project engr. St. Louis area Nike missile bases U.S. Army C.E., Granite City, Ill., 1958-59, architect N.Cen. div. U.S. Army C.E., Chgo., 1960; architect Yerkes & Grunsfeld, architects, Chgo., 1961-65, asso., 1965; asso. Grunsfeld & Assos., architects, Chgo., 1966-85.; prin. Marvin Worley Architects, Oak Park, Ill., 1985—. Dist. architect Oak Park Elementary Schs., Dist. 97, 1973-80. Mem. Oak Park Community Improvement Commn., 1973-75; mem. exec. bd. Oak Park Council PTA, 1970-73, pres., 1971-72. Served with AUS, 1959. Mem. AIA (corporate), Chgo. Assn. Commerce and Industry, Oak Park-River Forest C. of C. Office: 37 South Blvd Oak Park IL 60302-2777

WORLEY, MICHAEL PRESTON, art historian; b. Wichita, Kans., June 25, 1950; s. Robert Warren and Peggy Joyce (Lancaster) W. BA, Wichita State U., 1972; MA, U. Chgo., 1976, PhD, 1986. Lectr. European divsn. U. Md., Heidelberg/Mannheim, Germany, 1979-80; lectr. Northeastern Ill. U., Chgo., 1986; assoc. libr. Nat. Opinion Rsch. Ctr., Chgo., 1981-94; rschr. Smart Mus. of Art, U. Chgo., 1992-94; art rschr., libr. R. H. Love Galleries, Chgo., 1996—. Author: (with others) David & Alfred Smart Museum of Art Catalogue, 1990; contbr. articles to profl. jours. Scholar French Govt., 1972-73, 78-79; fellow U. Chgo., 1977. Mem. Alliance Française Chgo.

WORMAN, RICHARD W., insurance company executive, state senator; b. Noble County, Ind., July 3, 1933; s. William D. and Leah M. W.; m. Marna Jo Neuhouser, Sept. 29, 1951; children—Terry Jo, Renny, Denny, Rex, Tammy. Buyer, Neuhouser Poultry, Leo, Ind., 1951-53; salesman Allen Dairy, Ft. Wayne, Ind., 1953-57; with Nationwide Ins. Co., Columbus, Ohio, 1951-88, dist. sales mgr.; owner Securance Ins., 1990—; mem. Ind. Ho. of Reps., 1972-76, Ind. Senate, 1978—; trustee, assessor County of Allen, Ind., 1970-72. C.L.U. Mem. Life Underwriters Assn., Republican. United Methodist. Clubs: Lions (past pres.), Mason (past master), Shriner, Elks, Optimist. Office: PO Box 320 Leo IN 46765-0320

WORNER, JENNIFER KATHRYN, legislative liaison; b. Lewiston, N.Y., Sept. 1, 1967; d. Gary Allen and Penny Ann (Peterson) W. BS in Bus., Ohio State U., 1990. Mktg. intern Ohio State U. Hosps., Columbus, 1989-90; cons. Gillmor for Congress, Columbus, 1989-90; dist. campaign coord. Gillmor for Congress, Port Clinton, Ohio, 1990-93; dist. aide U.S. Congressman Paul E. Gillmor, Port Clinton, 1990-93; legis. aide Senator Karen Gillmor, Columbus, 1993-95; fed. liaison Ohio Atty. Gen.'s Office, 1995—; mgr. Karen Gillmor for State Senate, Old Fort, Ohio, 1992-96; vol. Dutch Schultz for Twp. Trustee, Port Clinton, 1991. Trustee, Port Clinton, 1991; vol. Thurber House, 1996—, ARC, Columbus and Port Clinton, 1988—; pub. policy bd. dirs. Am. Heart Assn., 1995—. Mem. Am. Mktg. Assn., Jr. Women's Club, Ohio State U. Alumni Assn., Phi Mu. Republican. Roman Catholic. Home: 193 Nerger Alleyw Dr Columbus OH 43206 Office: 30 E Broad 17th Fl Columbus OH 43215

WOROBEC, CHRISTINE DIANE, history educator; b. Toronto, July 30, 1955; d. Nicholas and Olga Maria (Romanko) W.; m. David Edward Kyvig, Oct. 15, 1988. BA, U. Toronto, 1977, MA, 1978, PhD, 1984. Asst. prof. Kent (Ohio) State U., 1984-92, assoc. prof., 1992—. Author: Peasant Russia, 1991; co-editor: Russia's Women, 1991; assoc. editor: Canadian Slavonic Papers, 1988-91; contbr. articles to profl. jours. Mem. Assn. for Women in Slavic Studies (v.p. 1993-95, pres. 1995—), Am. Assn. for Advancement of Slavic Studies, Am. Hist. Assn., Canadian Assn. Slavists, Ohio Acad. History, Ukrainian Hist. Assn., Phi Alpha Theta. Office: Kent State U Dept History PO Box 5190 Kent OH 44242

WORONOFF, ISRAEL, retired psychology educator; b. Bklyn., Dec. 30, 1926; s. Samuel and Lena (Silberman) W.; m. Fay Goldberg, Feb. 11, 1950; 1 child, Gary. AB in Psychology, U. Mich., 1949, MA in Sociology, 1952, PhD in Edn., 1954. Lic. psychologist, Mich. Instr. Flint (Mich.) Jr. Coll., 1953-54; asst. prof. St. Cloud (Minn.) State Coll., 1954-56; asst. prof. Ea. Mich. U., Ypsilanti, 1956-59, assoc. prof., 1959-62, prof., 1962-92; cons. psychologist Midwest Mental Health Clinic, Dearborn, Mich., 1978-83, Orchard Hills Psychiat. Ctr., Novi, Mich., 1983—. Author: Educator's Guide to Stress Management, 1986. Mem. bd. Jewish Family Svc. of Ann Arbor, 1996—; mem. cmty. rels. com. Jewish Cmty. Assn., Ann Arbor, Mich., 1990-92; v.p. edn. Beth Israel Congregation, Ann Arbor, 1985-87; mem. adv. bd. Mich. Anti-Defamation League of B'nai B'rith, 1958—. Mem. APA, Mich. Psychol. Assn., Am. Ednl. Rsch. Assn. Democrat. Home: 2519 Londonderry Rd Ann Arbor MI 48104-4017

WORSECK, RAYMOND ADAMS, economist; b. Providence, Mar. 25, 1937; s. Wilford Howe and Florence Marie (Dillmann) W.; m. Mary Elizabeth Lottes, July 15, 1972; children: Andrew Wilford, David Edward. BS in Math., St. Louis U., 1959, MA in Econs., 1970. Registered rep. N.Y. Stock Exchange. Commodity analyst Longstreet-Abbott & Co., St. Louis, 1959-65, dir. basic rsch., 1965-67; sr. price analyst Doane Agrl. Svc., St. Louis, 1967-69; dir. commodity rsch. A.G. Edwards & Sons, Inc., St. Louis, 1969-85, mgr. econ. rsch., 1985—, chief economist, 1989—. Mem. Am. Econs. Assn., Nat. Assn. Bus. Economists (chpt. pres. 1984-85), Fin. Analysts Soc. (bd. govs. St. Louis chpt. 1994-95), St. Louis Com. on Fgn. Rels., Futures Industry Assn. (nat. pres. rsch. divsn. 1983-84), Pub. Securities Assn. (econs. adv. com.), St. Louis Soc. Fin. Analysts (bd. govs.). Home: 331 Elm Valley Dr Saint Louis MO 63119-4574 Office: AG Edwards & Sons Inc 1 N Jefferson Ave Saint Louis MO 63103-2205

WORSTER, DONALD EUGENE, history educator; b. Needles, Calif., Nov. 14, 1941; s. Winfred Delbert and Bonnie Pauline (Ball) W.; m. Beverly Joan Marshall, Aug. 23, 1964; children: William Thomas, Catherine Anne. BA, U. Kans., 1963, MA, 1964; MPhil, Yale U., 1970, PhD, 1971. Asst. prof. Am. studies Brandeis U., Waltham, Mass., 1971-74; Meyerhoff prof. Am. environ. studies Brandeis U., Waltham, 1985-89; from assoc. prof. to prof. Am. studies U. Hawaii, Honolulu, 1975-85; Hall Disting. prof. Am. history U. Kans., Lawrence, 1989—; bd. dirs. Land Inst., Salina, Kans., 1989—, Kans. Land Trust, Lawrence, 1990-92. Author: Nature's Economy, 1977, 2d rev. edit., 1994, Dust Bowl, 1979 (Bancroft prize 1980), Rivers of Empire, 1985, Under Western Skies, 1992, The Wealth of Nature, 1993, An Unsettled Country, 1994. Mem. Orgn. Am. Historians, Western History Assn., Am. Soc. for Environ. History (pres. 1983-84). Home: 1034 E 450 Rd Lawrence KS 66047-9311 Office: U Kans Wescoe # 2017 Lawrence KS 66045

WORTHAM, JAMES CALVIN, retired mathematics educator; b. Oconee County, Ga., Sept. 12, 1928; s. James Notley and Effie (Cross) W.; B.A., U. Akron, 1957; M.A. (NSF Scholar), Ohio State U., 1969; m. Mary Helena Shelley, Dec. 23, 1953; children: Sharon Elaine, Marilyn Kay, Deborah Louise, James Donald. Tchr. high sch. Akron Pub. Schs., 1956-62, tchr. sr. high sch., 1962-66; math. curriculum specialist Akron (Ohio) Pub. Schs., 1966-90; instr. math. U. Akron, 1966—, ret., 1990. Served with USAF, 1951-55. Mem. NEA, Ohio Edn. Assn., Math. Assn. Am., Nat., Ohio councils tchrs. of math., Nat. Council Suprs. of Math., Greater Akron Math. Educators Soc. (pres. 1984-86), Pi Mu Epsilon. Republican. Mem. Ch. of Nazarene. Home: 229 Sand Run Rd Akron OH 44313-5364

WORTHEN, JOHN EDWARD, academic administrator; b. Carbondale, Ill., July 15, 1933; s. Dewey and Annis Burr (Williams) W.; m. Sandra Damewood, Feb. 27, 1960; children: Samantha Jane, Bradley Edward. BS in Psychology (Univ. Acad. scholar), Northwestern U., 1954; MA in Student Pers. Adminstrn., Columbia U., 1955; EdD in Adminstrn. in Higher Edn. (Coll. Entrance Exam. Bd. fellow), Harvard U., 1964; PhD (hon.), Yeungnam U., Daegu, Korea, 1986. Dean of men Am. U., 1959-61; dir. counseling and testing and asst. prof. edn., 1963-66, asst. to provost and asst. prof., 1966-68, acting provost and v.p. acad. affairs, 1968, assoc. provost for instrn., 1969, v.p. student affairs, 1970-75, v.p. student affairs and adminstrn., 1976-79; pres. Ind. U. of Pa., 1979-84, Ball State U., Muncie, Ind., 1984—; cons. to public schs. Aviator USN, 1955-59. Mem. Am. Assn. Counseling and Devel., Rotary Internat., Phi Delta Kappa, Kappa Delta Pi, Ind. C. of C., Ind. Bus. Modernization and Tech. Corp.

WORTHING, CAROL MARIE, minister; b. Duluth, Minn., Dec. 27, 1934; d. Truman James and Helga Maria (Bolander) W.; children: Gregory Alan Beatty, Graydon Ernest Beatty. BS, U. Minn., 1965; Master of Divinity, Northwestern Theol. Seminary, 1982; D of Ministry, Grad. Theol. Found.,

Notre Dame, Ind., 1988; MBA in Ch. Mgmt., Grad. Theol. Found., Donaldson, Ind., 1993. Secondary educator Ind. (Minn.) Sch. Dist., 1965-78; teaching fellow U. Minn., 1968-70; contract counselor Luth. Social Svc., Duluth, 1976-78; media cons. Luth. Media Svcs., St. Paul, 1978-80; asst. pastor Messiah Luth. Ch., Fargo, N.D., 1982-83; vice pastor Messiah Luth. Ch., Fargo, 1983-84; assoc. editor Luth. Ch. Am. Ptnrs., Phila., 1982-84; editorial assoc. Luth. Ptnrs. Evang. Luth. Ch. Am., Phila. and Mpls., 1984—; parish pastor Resurrection Luth. Ch., Pierre, S.D., 1984-89; assoc. pastor Bethlehem Luth. Ch., Cedar Falls, Iowa, 1989-90; exec. dir. Ill. Conf. Chs., Springfield, 1990-96, Tex. Conf. of Chs., 1996—; mem. pub. rels. and interpretation com. Red River Valley Synod, Fargo, 1984-86, mem. ch. devel., Pierre, 1986-87; mem. mgmt. com. office comm. Luth. Ch. in Am., N.Y.C., Phila., 1984-88; mem. mission ptnrs. S.D. Synod, 1988, chmn. assembly resolutions com., 1988; mem. pre-assembly planning com., ecumenics com., chmn. resolutions com. N.E. Iowa Synod, 1989-90; mem. ch. and society com., 1990-96; ecumenical com., 1995-96; Luth. Ecumenical Rep. Network, 1995-96; Cen. and So. Ill. Synod,; nat. edn. cons. Am. Film Inst., Washington, 1967-70; chaplain state legis. bodies, Pierre, 1984-89. Author: Cinematics and English, 1967, Peer Counseling, 1977, Tischrede Lexegete, 1986, 88, 90, Way of the Cross, Way of Justice Walk, 1987, Introducing Collaboration as a Leadership Stance and Style in an Established Statewide Conference of Churches, 1993. Co-facilitator Parents of Retarded Children, 1985; bd. dirs. Countryside Hospice, 1985; cons. to adminstrv. bd. Mo. Shores Women's Ctr., 1986. Mem. NAFE, Nat. Assn. Ecumenical Staff (chair of site selection com. 1991-92, chair of scholarship com. 1993-94, mem. profl. devel. com. 1993-94, chair program planning com. 1996, bd. dirs. 1995-96), Pierre-Ft. Pierre Ministerium (v.p. 1986-87, pres. 1987-88). Democrat. Home: 3816 S Lamar Blvd #3816 Austin TX 78704 Office: Tex Conf Chs 6633 Hwy 290 E Ste 200 Austin TX 78723-1157

WORTHINGTON, PATRICIA, elementary education educator; b. Mineola, N.Y., Sept. 25, 1948; d. George Edward and Thelma (Carson) Donnelly; m. Michael Worthington, July 16, 1977. BS, Parsons Coll., Fairfield, Iowa, 1970; postgrad., Morningside Coll., Davenport, Iowa, Drake U. Cert. tchr., Iowa. Elem. tchr. Gilmore City (Iowa) Bradgate Comunity Sch., 1970—; co-chmn. Phase III, Iowa Dept. Edn.; chairperson for Cmty. Svc. Grant, 1996. Career edn. grantee, 1977, Roy J. Carver grantee Nat. Geog. Kids Network, 1990. Mem. Iowa Edn. Assn. (past sec.-treas., pres.). Home: 2014 W River Dr Humboldt IA 50548-2634 Office: 412 S E Ave Gilmore City IA 50541

WORTHY, JAMES CARSON, management educator; b. Midland, Tex., Jan. 8, 1910; s. James Arthur and Minnie (Gressett) W.; m. Mildred Leritz, June 20, 1934; 1 dau., Joan (Mrs. Robert Wood Tullis). Student, Northwestern U., 1929-33; AB, Lake Forest Coll., 1952, LLD (hon.), 1961; LLD, Chgo. Theol. Sem., 1960; LittD (hon.), Sangamon State U., 1991. Employment mgr. Schuster & Co., Milw., 1936-38; mem. personnel staff Sears, Roebuck & Co., Chgo., 1938-50; dir. employee relations Sears, Roebuck & Co., 1950-53, asst. to chmn. bd., 1955, vice pres. pub. relations, 1956-61; v.p. Cresap, McCormick & Paget, 1962-72; prof. Sangamon State U., Springfield, Ill., 1972-78, J.L. Kellogg Grad. Sch. Mgmt. Northwestern U., Evanston, Ill., 1978—; asst. dep. adminstr. NRA, Washington, 1933-36; asst. sec. commerce, 1953-55; Industry mem. spl. panel WSB, 1952; mem. President's Com. on Govt. Contracts, 1953-55, President's Commn. on Campaign Costs, 1961-62; Mem. Ill. Bd. of Higher Edn., 1967-69. Bd. dirs. Nat. Merit Scholarship Corp., 1958-63; mem. exec. bd. Indsl. Relations Research Assn., 1952-54; pres. Sears-Roebuck Found., 1956-61; trustee Latin Sch. Chgo., 1968-72, Chgo. Theol. Sem., 1953-73; dir. Selected Am. Shares, 1961-79,Comml. Credit Co., 1975-81, Control Data Corp., 1979-87, William C. Norris Inst., 1987—; co-chmn. Ill. Citizens for Eisenhower-Nixon, 1952; v.p. United Rep. Fund of Ill., 1955-59, pres., 1959-60, exec. com., 1961-72; mem. Nat. Rep. Finance Com., 1958-60; del. Rep. Nat. Conv., 1960; pres. Republican Citizens League Ill., 1961-62. Fellow Acad. Mgmt. (Dean of Fellows 1987-90), Internat. Acad. Mgmt.; mem. Commercial Club, Univ. Club (Chgo.), Indian Hill Club (Winnetka, Ill.). Congregationalist. Home: 23 Calvin Cir Evanston IL 60201-1911 Office: Northwestern U JL Kellogg Grad Sch Mgmt Evanston IL 60201

WOS, CAROL ELAINE, small business owner; b. Bremerton, Wash., Apr. 21, 1957; d. Standley Ralph and Janet Estele (Galber) Stocker; m. George Joseph Wos; children: Samuel Harrison, Bridget Monique. BS in Chem., Wash. State U., 1979. Mfg. engr. Internat. Bus. Machines, E. Fishkill, N.Y., 1979-80; process devel. engr. Sperry Corp., Eagan, Minn., 1980-83; sr. process devel. engr. Cray Rsch. Inc., Chippewa Falls, Wis., 1983-90, mem. cleanroom design and constrn. team, 1991-92, bump/tab process engr., 1993-94; owner, mgr. The Nature of Things, Eau Claire, Wis., 1995—. Bd. dirs. Eau Claire Regional Arts Coun.

WOYTHAL, CONSTANCE LEE, psychologist; b. Milw., Nov. 6, 1954; d. Gerald Clarence and Shirley Estelle (Gross) W.; m. John Francis Neisius, Mar. 20, 1982; children: Adam, Abby. BS, U. Wis., Milw., 1976; MS in Edn., U. Wis., River Falls, 1978; postgrad., Alfred Adler Inst., Chgo., 1980, George Williams Coll., 1984, Marquette U., 1984, Cardinal Stritch Coll., 1987, Wis. Sch. Profl. Psychology, 1990. Lic. sch. psychologist, Wis.; nat. cert. sch. psychologist. Psychologist Sch. Dist. of Marshfield, Wis., 1978-81, Sheboygan County Handicapped Children's Edn. Bd., Sheboygan Falls, Wis., 1981-91; devel. coord. wellness program Sheboygan County Handicapped Children's Edn. Bd., Plymouth, Wis., 1984—; psychologist Plymouth (Wis.) Joint Sch. Dist., Plymouth, Wis., 1991—; workshop facilitator Marshfield Clinic, 1981; cons. wellness lifestyle program Sch. of Sheboygan County, 1985—; lectr. profl. groups; mem. profl. adv. bd. Children with Attention Deficit Disorder (ChADD), 1992-93. Bd. dirs. Family Connections, 1988-90. Mem. APA (student affiliate), NASP, Nat. Wellness Assn., N.Am. Soc. Adlerian Psychologists, Wis. Sch. Psychology Assn., Sheboygan Wellness Assn. (bd. dirs. 1982-88), Mental Health Assn. Home: 859 Chaplin Ct Plymouth WI 53073-1012 Office: Riverview Mid Sch Riverview Cir Plymouth WI 53073

WOZENCRAFT, SHARON ANNE, minister; b. Lubbock, Tex., Apr. 19, 1945; d. W. T. and Frances Geraldine (Ball) W.; m. Gary Lynn Ries, July 4, 1963 (div. Apr. 1974); children: Krista Lynn Buster, Tanya Michele Bouwman; m. George Nelson Thompson, Nov. 19, 1989. AA in Design, Chgo. Sch. of Design, 1968; MTh, Rhema Bible Tng. Ctr., 1984; BA in Sociology summa cum laude, Northwestern State U., Tahlequah, Okla., 1986; MDiv, Boston U., 1989. Ordained to ministry, Christian Ch., 1984, Meth. Ch., 1985; lic. minister, 1982. News reporter Reporter-Telegraph & Avalanche Jour., Lubbock and Midland, Tex., 1962-65; adminstr. Heritage Acad., Midland, 1965-67; news dir. Sta. KKKK, Midland, 1967-68; owner, designer Total Interiors of Tex., Lubbock, 1969-75; dir. Manasseh Mission, Lubbock, 1972-79; assoc. pastor Our Lord's Bible Ch., Oklahoma City, 1979-82; pastor Maranatha Fellowship, Broken Arrow, Okla., 1982-84, United Meth. Ch., Porter, Okay and Hulbert, Okla., 1984-86, East Natick United Meth. Ch., Natick, Mass., 1987-93; sr. min. Mayflower Congl. Ch., Lansing, Mich., 1993—; prof. Trinity Bible Inst., Lubbock, 1976-80, Faith Bible Inst., Oklahoma City, 1981-82; ministerial mem. Natick Alcohol and Drug Adv. Coun., 1990-93; trustee Bright Beginnings Day Care, Natick, 1990-93; mem. steering com. Mich. Religious Coalition for Reproductive Choice, 1993—; bd. dirs. Congregational Found. for Theological Studies. Author: The Way of Truth, 1970, God's Grace & Human Will, 1989; contbr. articles to profl. jours. Active Citizens' Com. on Housing, Midland, 1975, Task Force on Flood Relief, Okay, Okla., 1986, Alliance for the Mentally Ill, Mass., 1987-89; bd. dirs. Arthritis Found., Midland, 1969-79. Okla. State Regents scholar Tulsa State Coll., 1984, Northeastern State U., 1985-87, Wesley scholar Boston U., 1987-90, Warren Found. scholar, 1989-90. Mem. AAUW, Natick Clergy Assn. (chair 1990-93, co-host TV show 1988-93), Am. Assn. Ret. Persons, Evang. Women's Caucus, Am. Acad. of Ministry, The Congregationalist (mem. editor's roundtable), Alpha Chi. Democrat. Home: 2525 Barstow Rd Lansing MI 48906 Office: Mayflower Congl Ch 2901 W Mount Hope Ave Lansing MI 48911

WOZNIAK, RICHARD MICHAEL, SR., city and regional planner; b. rural Fullerton, Nebr., Nov. 28, 1928; s. Theo Charles and Monica (Lesiak) W.; m. Evalyn Louise Pickett, Sept. 9, 1951; children: Debra, Karen, Richard Michael, Steve. BS, Iowa State U., 1954. Cert. landscape architect. Landscape architect Rockford (Ill.) Nurseries, 1954-55; landscape architect, city planner Harland Bartholomew & Assocs., St. Louis, 1955-58; sr. planner Springfield/Sangamon County Regional Planning Commn., Springfield, Ill., 1958-60; city planner City of Omaha, 1960-64; owner, cons. Richard M. Wozniak & Assocs., Fremont, Nebr., 1964-74; exec. v.p. Mits Kawamoto & Aassocs., Omaha, 1974-76; owner, planning cons., racher Richard M. Wozniak & Assocs., Long Pine, Nebr., 1976-84; dir. planning and community devel. City of Norfolk (Nebr.)/Madison County, 1984—; cons. to more than 45 cities and counties in Ill., Mich. and Nebr., 1955-84; v.p., pres. Nebr. State Bd. Landscape Architects, Lincoln, 1967-84; treas. Nat. Coun. Landscape Architecture Bds., 1976. Author numerous studies and reports, comprehensive plans; designer land planning for parks and subdivs. With U.S. Army, 1946-49, USAFR, 1954-68. Recipient numerous awards. Mem. Am. Planning Assn. (charter), Am. Inst. Cert. Planners (charter), Nebr. Assn. County Ofcls. (v.p., pres. 1985-91), Am. Legion, Nebr. Planning and Zoning Assn. Home: RR 1 Box 410 Madison NE 68748-9746 Office: Madison County Dept Planning and Zoning PO Box 864 Norfolk NE 68702

WOZNIAK, WAYNE THEODORE, physical chemist; b. Chgo., Oct. 13, 1945; s. Theodore Clements Wozniak and Victoria (Goleb) Biernacik; m. Susan Marie Chester, June 19, 1971; children: Justin, Ethan, Darren. BS, Ill. Benedictine Coll., Lisle, 1967; PhD, Fla. State U., 1971. Rsch. assoc. ADA, Chgo., 1975-78, head physics lab., 1978-79, asst. sec. coun. on dental materials, 1979-89, dir. cert. lab., 1989-94; dir. eval. criteria, 1994—; cons. U. Fla., Gainesville, 1989—; mem. editorial bd. Jour. Clin. Dentistry, Yardley, Pa., 1990—. Contbr. numerous articles to profl. jours. Commr., Hoffman Estates (Ill.) Park Dist., 1979-83. Mem. Am. Chem. Soc., Am. Assn. for Dental Rsch., Inter-Soc. Color Coun., Soc. Sigma Xi. Office: ADA 211 E Chicago Ave Chicago IL 60611-2616

WRAY, DAVID LYNN, association executive; b. Denver, July 15, 1947; s. H. Lynn and Elizabeth Jane (Park) W.; m. Judy Ann Haley, Jan. 25, 1969; children: Amy Lynne, Nathan Frederick, Keriann Elizabeth. BA, Creighton U., 1969; MA, U. Colo., 1971. Reading clk. Colo. Ho. of Reps., Denver, 1970-73; instr. in polit. sci. U. Colo., Boulder, 1972-73, Met. State Coll., Denver, 1973, Drake U., Des Moines, Iowa, 1973-75; chief clk. Iowa Ho. of Reps., Des Moines, Iowa, 1975-80; v.p., sec. Alliance Am. Insurers, Schaumburg, Ill., 1980-87; pres. Profit Sharing 401(k) Coun. Am., Chgo., 1987—; exec. dir. Profit Sharing 401(k) Edn. Found., Chgo.; spkr. in field. Contbr. articles in field to profl. jours. Mem. AMA, ASAE, CSAE, Am. Soc., U.S. C. of C. (health and benefit com.), Internat. Assn. for Fin. Participation (pres.). Office: Profit Sharing Coun Am 10 S Riverside Plz Ste 1460 Chicago IL 60606-3802

WRAY, GAIL MILLER, environmentalist, government agency administrator; b. Milw., Feb. 23, 1939; d. Frederic C. Miller and Adele E. (Kanaley) O'Shaughnessy; children: Jennifer, Edward, Hillary. BA in Polit. Sci., Trinity Coll., Washington, 1961; spl. degree, Montessori Soc., Chgo., 1963. Office mgr., asst. plant mgr. Americology Can Co., 1978-81; recycling dir. Village of Shorewood, Wis., 1981-89; recycling coord. U.S. EPA, Washington, 1989-91; chair Presidential Coun. on Fed. Recycling and Procurement Policy, Washington, 1991-94; apptd. by gov. Wis. as exec. dir. Wis. Recycling Market Devel. Bd., 1994—. Polit. affairs chair Jr. League of Am., 1976-77; founder Shorewood (Wis.) Conservation Com., 1980; chair LWV Nat. Resources Portfolio, 1987-86, pres. Greater Milw. LWV, 1980-82; mem. program com. Pub. Policy Forum, Milw., 1985-89; founder and pres. Associated Recyclers of Wis., 1987-89; bd. dirs. Midwest Recycling Coalition. Recipient Cert. Appreciation Am. Field Svc. Internat./Inter-cultural., People on the Move award, Milw. Bus. Jour., 1988, Nat. Govs. Assn. Recognition award, 1990; Named to Most Interesting People, Milw. Mag., 1990. Mem. Worldwide Women in the Environment (chair EPA Forum 1989-94, bd. dirs.), Friends of UN Environment Program, Nat. Recycling Coalition (market devel. com.). Roman Catholic. Home: 12144 N Ridge Rd Mequon WI 53092-1025

WREN, MORRIS LEE, minister; b. Houston, May 29, 1935; s. Horace L. and Etha Lee (Johnson) W. BA, Oakwood Coll., 1963; MDiv, Andrews U., 1968; postgrad., U. Bibl. Studies, 1996. Prin. Beren Acad., Houston, 1963-64; tng. instr. Poston (Ariz.) Job Corp. Fed. Govt., 1964-66; tchr. Benton Harbor (Mich.) Pub. Sch., 1967-68; min., instr. Lake Region Conf. Seventh-Day Adventist, Chgo., 1968—; pres. Ministerial Seminar, Huntsville, Ala., 1956-58, Metro Bible & Health Ctr., Evansville, Ind., 1972—. Author: Remedies for Remnant-Daylife Maximizer, 1994; inventor universal cam wrench. With U.S. Army, 1958-60, 62-64. Office: Metro Bible & Health Ctr 1710 E English St Dept 7A Danville IL 61832-3453

WRENN, WALTER BRUCE, marketing educator, consultant; b. Mobile, Ala., Nov. 9, 1950; s. Walter P. and Winona A. (Jeffrey) W.; m. Jan F. Carmichael, June 12, 1971. BS, Auburn U., 1973; M of Mgmt., Northwestern U., 1974, PhD, 1989. Market analyst The UpJohn Co., Kalamazoo, Mich., 1974-78; asst. prof. mktg. Andrews U., Berrien Springs, Mich., 1978-89; assoc. prof. Ind. U., South Bend, 1995—; cons. The UpJohn Co., Kalamazoo, 1982, N.Am. Div. SDA, Washington, 1983, Worthington (Ohio) Foods, 1985—, Adventist Health System, Austin, Tex., 1986, Leco, 1991, Bio-Met, 1991. Author: (instr. manuals) Principles of Marketing, 1983, 86, Marketing Management, 1984, 88, 91, 94; co-author: Marketing for Congregations, 1993, The Marketing Research Guide, 1996, Marketing Planning Guide, 1997; contbr. articles to profl. jours. Dir. University Press, Berrien Springs, 1986-89, Sta. WAUS, Berrien Springs, 1987—. Named Outstanding Young Man of Am. Jr. C. of C., 1980; univ. scholar Northwestern U., 1980-83. Mem. Am. Mktg. Assn. (Outstanding Mktg. Student 1973), Acad. Mktg. Sci., Phi Kappa Phi, Alpha Mu Alpha, Omicron Delta Epsilon, Delta Sigma Pi, Delta Mu Delta. Seventh Day Adventist. Home: 5027 E Bluffview Dr Berrien Springs MI 49103-1435 Office: Ind Univ 1700 Mishawaka Ave South Bend IN 46634-7111

WRIGHT, ARTHUR FRANKLIN, transportation executive, municipal official; b. Monroe, Mich., Apr. 5, 1950; s. Leslie Arthur and Dorothy Esther (Brammer) W.; m. Karen Louis Kelly, Apr. 2, 1983; children: David, Daniel, Andrew. BA, Mich. State U., 1972; MBA, Ea. Mich. U., 1978. With Detroit, Toledo & Ironton R.R., Dearborn, Mich., 1973-80, yardmaster, 1973-77, mgr. indsl. engring., 1977-79, mgr. cost analysis, 1979-80; with Grand Trunk Western R.R., Detroit, 1980—, mgr. fin., 1980-84, dir. fin., 1984-91, equipment dir., 1991—. Elected treas. Brownstown Twp., 1992—, elected trustee, 1991-92, chmn. planning commn., 1990-92, chmn. zoning bd. appeals, 1990-91. Recipient Investment Excellence award Mcpl. Treas.'s Assn. U.S. and Can. Mem. Brownstown Kiwanis, Brownstown Good Fellows. Democrat. Roman Catholic. Office: GTW RR Co 24002 Vreeland Rd Flat Rock MI 48134-9999 also: Brownstown Twp 21313 Telegraph Rd Trenton MI 48183-1314

WRIGHT, CHARLES SPAULDING, II, writer, communications consultant; b. Traverse, Mich., Apr. 13, 1955; s. Charles Spaulding and Carol (McManus) W.; m. Debra Lynn Memmer, June 20, 1981; children: Katherine, Sarah, Zachary. AA, Northwestern Mich. Coll., Traverse City, Mich., 1981; BS, Western Mich. U., 1983. Coord. supr. Traverse Bay Area Sch. Dist., 1977; announcer, producer Interlochen (Mich.) Arts Acad., 1977; gen. mgr. Sta. WNMC-AM and FM, Traverse City, 1977-79; archtl. news reporter McGraw-Hill, Dearborn, Mich., 1985-86; community editor Pioneer Publs., Big Rapids, Mich., 1987-88; freelance writer North Channel, Southfield, Mich., 1988-91; pres. Northwind Cons., Southfield, Mich., 1991-92; writer, cons. CSW Enterprises, Traverse City, 1991-95; cons. Spec Assocs., 1996—; cons. McCann-Dumont & Assocs., Ferndale, Mich., 1990-96; reporter numerous articles on constrn., design, police beat, human interest, 1985-88; rep. Com. for a Responsible Fed. Budget, Southfield, Mich., 1995. Author: Public Affairs in N.W. Michigan, 1980. Pub. affairs dir. Blue Star Found., Birmingham, Mich., 1990-91; philanthropist Children's Make-A-Wish Found., Village Assn., Southfield, 1990—; del-at-large Rep. Party Planning Com., 1996. Recipient Cert. Appreciation Pres. of U.S., 1980, HHS, 1980, scholarship Western Mich. U., 1983. Mem. Smithsonian Inst. Roman Catholic.

WRIGHT, CREIGHTON BOLTER, cardiovascular surgeon, educator; b. Washington, Jan. 29, 1939; s. Benjamin Washington and Catherine Adele (Bolter) W.; m. Carolyn Eleanor Craver, Jan. 29, 1966; children: Creighton Bolter, Benson, Kathryn, Elizabeth. BA, Duke U., 1961, MD, 1965; MBA, Xavier U., 1995. Diplomate Am. Bd. Thoracic Surgery, Am. Bd. Surgery, subbd. Gen. Vascular Surgery. Intern, Duke U., Durham, N.C., 1965-66; resident in surgery U. Va., Charlottesville, 1966-71; from asst. prof. to assoc. prof. George Washington U., 1974-76; assoc. prof., then prof. surgery U. Iowa, 1976-81; prof. clin. surgery U. Cin., 1982-89, also clin. prof. surgery Uniformed Services U., 1989—; dir. Dept. of Surgery Jewish Hosp., Cin. Col. USAR, 1966-93; ret., 1993. Decorated Bronze star, Meritorious Svc. medals; recipient Kindred Resident Teaching award, 1967, Golden Apple Teaching award, 1975. Mem. Assn. Acad. Surgery (pres. 1980), Central Surg. Assn., Soc. Univ. Surgeons, Soc. Vascular Surgery, Internat. Soc. Cardiovascular Surgery, Muller Surg. Soc. (pres. 1985-87), Am. Assn. Thoracic Surgery, Soc. Thoracic Surgery, So. Thoracic Surg. Assn., Midwestern Vascular Surg. Soc., Cardiovascular and Thoracic Surgeons, Cin. Surg. Soc. (pres. 1996), Comml. Club, Alpha Omega Alpha, Sigma Chi (Significant Sig award 1993). Editor: Vascular Grafting, 1983; (with others) Venous Trauma, 1983; contbr. articles to profl. jours., chpts. to books. Home: 312 E Second St Covington KY 41011 Office: Cardiovascular & Thoracic Surgeons 2123 Auburn Ave Cincinnati OH 45219

WRIGHT, DAVID L., electrical design engineer; b. Youngstown, Ohio, Feb. 26, 1962. BSEE, Youngstown State U., 1984. Sr. design engr. Taylor Winfield Corp., Brookfield, Ohio, 1984—. Republican.

WRIGHT, DIANA KRENZEL, client support supervisor, computer consultant; b. Salzburg, Austria, Dec. 19, 1951; came to U.S., 1953; d. Thomas P. and Margaret (Stiegler) Krenzel; m. William J. Wright, Mar. 20, 1982; 1 child, Erica Roberts. BS in mgmt. info. sys., Kennedy-Western U., 1996. Rsch. assoc. Gould, Inc., Rolling Meadows, Ill., 1979-82; owner DKW Assocs., Palatine, Ill., 1982-88, DKW Consulting, Milw., 1990—; CEO Accudata Techs., Milw., 1988-90; client support supr. Froedtert Hosp., Milw., 1992—; cons. AEC, Inc., Woodale, Ill., 1984-86, Wisc. Bell, Brookfield, Ill., 1988-89. Leader Girl Scouts Am., Palatine, 1986-87, coun. cookie com., Elk Grove Village, Ill., 1987. Bus. devel. initiative grantee State Wis., 1990; named Mrs. Brookfield, 1996. Mem. Computer Security Inst. Office: Froedtert Meml Luth Hosp 9200 W Wisconsin Milwaukee WI 53226

WRIGHT, ELIZABETH ANNE, foundation administrator; b. Kokomo, Ind., Jan. 5, 1947; d. Raymond Edward and Josephine Rosemary (Dudley) Schrader; m. Frank D. Wright, Oct. 29, 1977; stepchildren: Troy Martin, Brad Allen. Degree in bus. adminstrn., Ind. Wesleyan U., Marion, 1987. Exec. officer Bd. of Realtors, Marion, 1984-91; exec. dir. Cmty. Found., Marion, 1991—; chmn. State Exec. Officers, Indpls., 1986-88; mem. Ind. Donors Alliance, Indpls., 1991—, East Ctrl. Cmty. Found., Muncie, 1991—. Councilwoman Grant County Govt., 1986-94; mem. policy panel Ind. Govs. Initiative Econ. Devel., 1990; cmmr. Conv. and Visitors Com., Marion, 1983—. Recipient Dick Snyder Svc. award Ind. Assn. Realtors, 1989. Mem. Marion C. of C. (bd. dir. 1986—, Athena award 1988), Rotary Club (rotarion asst. treas. 1991—), Career Womens Coun. Democrat. Roman Catholic.

WRIGHT, EMMETT LEE, science educator; b. Winchester, Kans., Oct. 13, 1940; s. Enoch Emmett and Helen Irene (Hawk) W.; m. Mary Jane Jackson, June 5, 1961; children: David Andrew, Cynthia Lynn. BS, U. Kans., 1963; MA, Wichita State U., 1968; PhD, Pa. State U., 1974. Tchr. math. and sci. Rossville (Kans.) High Sch., 1963-65; dir. Kans. Health Mus., Halstead, 1965-68; instr. biology and sci. edn. Dept. Biology Pittsburg (Kans.) State U., 1968-72; asst. prof., coord. conservation and resource devel. U. Md., College Park, 1974-79, assoc. prof., dir. sci. teaching ctr., 1979-84; prof., dir. Ctr. for Sci. Edn. Coll. of Edn., Kans. State U., Manhattan, 1984-87, head dept. Curriculum and Instrn., 1986-90, head Div. Tchr. Edn., 1988-90, assoc. dean, 1990—; bd. dirs., chmn. rsch. com. Brown Found. for Equity, Excellence and Rsch., Topeka, 1988—; dir. Kans. Jr. Acad. Sci., 1985-90; dir., pres. ARIOS-Kansas, 1994—; pres., coord. Russian-Am. Educators Project, 1994—; cons. numerous schs., univs., govt. and profl. orgns. Cons. editor Sci. Activities Jour., 1983—; mem. editorial rev. bd. Jour. Rsch. in Sci. Teaching, 1986-89; contbr. numerous articles to profl. jours. Mem. Nat. Sci. Tchr. Assn. (bd. dirs. 1984-87, 91-93), Nat. Assn. Rsch. in Sci. Teaching (bd. dirs. 1986-89, pres.-elect 1991, pres. 1992-93, best article award 1990), Sch. Sci. and Math. Assn. (assoc. jour. editor 1988-93), Md. Assn. Sci. Teaching (past pres.), Kans, Adv. Coun. Environ. Edn. (pres. 1987-89), Nat. Assn. Biology Tchrs. (book rev. editor 1982-88). Democrat. Methodist. Office: Kans State U 1100 Mid Campus Dr 237 Bluemont Hall Manhattan KS 66506-5300

WRIGHT, (JAMES) GARLAND, artistic director; b. Midland, Tex., Apr. 18, 1946; s. Joe Bailey and Flora Gladys (Milstead) W. BFA, So. Meth. U., 1969; LittD (hon.), St. John's U., 1991. Freelance dir., 1970—; assoc. dir. Am. Shakespeare Theatre, Stratford, Conn., 1970-73; artistic dir. Lion Theatre Co., N.Y.C., 1974-77; assoc. artistic dir. The Guthrie Theater, Mpls., 1980-83; artistic assoc. Arena Stage, Washington, 1985-86; artistic dir. The Guthrie Theater, 1986—; adj. prof. U. Minn., Mpls., 1987—. Dir. (plays) Vanities, 1976, "K"Impressions of KAFKA'S The Trial, 1977 (Obie award), Imaginary Invalid, 1982, Moliere's The Misanthrope, 1984, Happy End & Good Person of Sechuan, 1984, 85, Don Juan, 1985 (Denver Critics award), On The Verge, 1986 (Obie award), Cherry Orchard, 1986 (Denver Critics award), Richard III, 1987, Hamlet, 1988, History Cycle: Richard II, Henry IV & Henry V, 1990, The Clytemnestra Project (Iphegenia in Aulis, Agamemnon, Electra), 1992, The Seagull, 1992. Co-founder Arts over AIDS, Mpls., 1988—; bd. dirs. Theater Communications Group, N.Y.C., 1986-88; panel mem. N.E.A Profl. Theaters Co., Washington, 1990—. Winston Churchill fellow English Speaking Union, Eng., 1972. Democrat. Office: Guthrie Theater 725 Vineland Pl Minneapolis MN 55403-1139*

WRIGHT, GLADYS STONE, music educator, composer, writer; b. Wasco, Oreg., Mar. 8, 1925; d. Murvel Stuart and Daisy Violet (Warren) Stone; m. Alfred George Wright, June 28, 1953. BS, U. Oreg., 1948, MS, 1953. Dir. bands Elmira (Oreg.) U-4 High Sch., 1948-53, Otterbein (Ind.) High Sch., 1954-61, Klondike High Sch., West Lafayette, Ind., 1962-70, Harrison High Sch., West Lafayette, 1970-84; organizer, condr. Musical Friendship Tours, Cen. Am., 1967-79; v.p., condr. U.S. Collegiate Wind Band, 1975—; bd. dirs. John Philip Sousa Found. 1984—; chmn. Sudler Cup, 1986—, Sudler Flag, 1982; pres. Internat. Music Tours, 1984—, Key to the City, Taxco, Mex., 1975. Editor: Woman Conductor, 1986—; composer: marches Big Bowl and Trumpets and Tabards, 1987; contbg. editor: Informusica (Spain). Bd. dirs. N. Am. Wildlife Park, Battleground, Ind. 1985. Recipient Medal of the order John Philip Sousa Found., 1988, Star of Order, 1991; 1st woman guest conductor U.S. Navy Band, Washington D.C., 1961, Goldman Band, N.Y.C., 1958, Kneller Hall Band, London, 1975, Tri-State Music Festival Massed Orch., Band, Choir, 1985; elected to Women Bd. Dirs. Hall of Fame of Disting. Women Conductor, 1994. Mem. Am. Bandmasters Assn. (bd. dirs. 1993, 1st woman mem.), Women Band Dirs. Nat. Assn. (founding pres. 1967, sec. 1985, recipient Silver Baton 1974, Golden Rose 1990, Hall of Fame 1995), Am. Sch. Band Dirs. Assn., Nat. Band Assn. (Citation excellence 1970), Tippecanoe Arts Fedn. (bd. dirs. 1986-90), Tippecanoe Fife and Drum Corps. (bd. dirs. 1984), Daughters of Am. Revolution, Col. Dames-Pre Quitanen Chpt., New England Women, Tau Beta Sigma (Outstanding Svc. to Music award 1970), Phi Beta Mu (1st hon. women mem. 1972), North Am. Wildlife Park (bd dirs, 1990—).

WRIGHT, GREG ALAN AUGUST, mechanical engineer; b. Santa Ana, Calif., June 7, 1958. B, Bringham Young U., 1983. Design engr. Eder Industries, Oak Creek, Wis., 1983-85; devel. engr. Beloit (Wis.) Corp., 1985-87; controls mgr. Taylor Co., Rockton, Ill., 1987—. Patentee in field. Cub master Weeblos coun. Boy Scouts Am., 1994, den leader, 1994—; bishop local ch., 1994—. Mormon. Office: Taylor Co 750 N Blackhawk Blvd Rockton IL 61072-2104

WRIGHT, GWEN SLOAS, college administrator; b. Dayton, Ohio, Aug. 31, 1960; d. Glennis Erma and Patsy Pauline (Goodwin) Sloas; children: Paula Greer, Timothy Evan. BA, Transylvania U., Lexington, Ky., 1981; MA, Ohio State U., 1983; student, Nova Southeastern U. Asst. residence hall dir. Ohio State U., Columbus, 1981-83; residence hall dir. Xavier U., Cin., 1983-84, Morehead (Ky.) State U., 1984-85; asst. dean students Hanover (Ind.) Coll., 1985-88; dir. student and alumni affairs Miami Valley Sch. Nursing, Wright State U., Dayton, 1988-90; dir. ops. Ivy Tech.-S.E., Lawrenceburg, Ind., 1990—. Sunday sch. tchr., mem. long range planning Hamline Chapel United Meth. Ch., Lawrenceburg, 1991; VBS dir. Tyson United Meth. Ch., 1994-95. Recipient Merit award S.E. Assn. Coll. and Univ. Housing Officers, 1981. Mem. Ind. Assn. Women in Edn. (state membership chair 1990-92, state conf. coord. 1992-93, v.p. 1992-93, pres.-elect 1993-94, pres. 1994-95), Kiwanis (bd. dirs. Lawrenceburg 1990-95, chair young children priority one com. 1992-93, pres. 1993-94), Habitat for Humanity (Dearborn and Ohio counties family sect. com., steering com. 1993—), Omicron Delta Kappa. Democrat. Office: Ivy Tech State Coll 575 Main St Lawrenceburg IN 47025-1661

WRIGHT, HELEN KENNEDY, professional association administrator, publisher, editor, librarian; b. Indpls., Sept. 23, 1927; d. William Henry and Ida Louise (Crosby) Kennedy; m. Samuel A. Wright, Sept. 5, 1970; 1 child, Carl F. Prince II (dec.). BA, Butler U., 1945, MS, 1950; MS, Columbia U., 1952. Reference libr. N.Y. Pub. Libr., N.Y.C., 1952-53, Bklyn. Pub. Libr., 1953-54; reference libr., cataloger U. Utah, 1954-57; libr. Chgo. Pub. Libr.; asst. dir. pub. dept. ALA, Chgo., 1958-62, edit. Reference Books Bull., 1962-85, asst. dir. for new product planning, pub. svcs., 1985—, dir. office for libr. outreach svcs., 1987-90, mng. editor yearbook, 1988—. Contbr. to Ency. of Careers, Ency. of Libr. and Info. Sci., New Book of Knowledge Ency., Bulletin of Bibliography, New Golden Book Ency. Recipient Louis Shores/Oryx Pr. award, 1991. Mem. Phi Kappa Phi, Kappa Delta Pi, Sigma Gamma Rho. Roman Catholic. Home: 1138 W 111th St Chicago IL 60643-4508 Office: ALA 50 E Huron St Chicago IL 60611-2729

WRIGHT, JUDITH RAE, retired accountant; b. Paoli, Ind., Feb. 16, 1929; d. Samuel Earl and Bernice Louise (Lomax) Hudelson; m. James Edward Walters, July 11, 1947 (div. June 1971); children: Jamie Jo, Jennifer Rae; m. 2d, George Ralph Wright, Feb. 20, 1972 (dec. Apr. 1977). Student Northwood Inst., West Baden, Ind., 1968-69, Ind.-U.-Purdue U., Indpls., 1972-77. Acct., Ind. Hwy. Commn., Indpls., 1969-75, Ind. Dept. Correction, Indpls., 1975-76, Ind. Dept. Pub. Welfare, Indpls., 1976-78, Ind. Office Social Services, Indpls., 1978-79; acct. supr. Ind. Dept. Pub. Welfare, Indpls., 1979-92, ret. 1992. Recipient Gov.'s Spl. Achievement award, 1992; Mem. Assn. Govt. Accts., Am. Legion Aux., Order of the Eastern Star, Kappa Kappa Kappa. Republican. Mem. First Christian Ch.

WRIGHT, LEE ALFRED, language educator; b. Cleve., Feb. 19, 1951; s. Lee Ardie and Dolores Claire (Carroll) W.; m. Beth Ann Nancarrow, Aug. 17, 1984; children: Amy Jennifer, Brittany Lee, Caitlin Ann. BS in Biology, Bowling Green (Ohio) State U., 1973; MA in English Lit., U. Toledo, Ohio, 1977, PhD in English Lit., 1992. Med. technologist various hosps.; instr. English lit. U. Toledo, 1991—. Author: Identity, Family and Folklore in African American Literature, 1995; assoc. editor Literary Anthology, Glass Review, 1992, 93, Mark, 1994. Chmn. Libr. Village Coalition, Toledo, 1994—; pres. Libr. Village Assn., Toledo, 1993-94, v.p., 1992-93, bd. dirs., 1991—. Mem. MLA, Nat. Coun. Tchrs. English. Home: 1322 Pingree Toledo OH 43612 Office: Univ of Toledo Dept of English 2801 W Bancroft St Toledo OH 43606

WRIGHT, LISA ANN, legal assistant; b. Kansas City, Mo., Oct. 2, 1965; d. Kenneth H. and Joan L. (Green) W. BA in French and Communications, U. Mo., Kansas City, 1988. With customer svc. dept. Delta Airlines, Kansas City, 1988-90; radio producer Sta. KCUR-FM, Kansas City, 1990; office mgr. Nat. Reporting Co., Kansas City, 1990-91; legal asst. Shook, Hardy & Bacon, L.L.P., Kansas City, Mo. Roman Catholic.

WRIGHT, LLOYD JAMES, JR., broadcast executive, educator, announcer; b. San Benito, Tex., Dec. 28, 1949; s. Lloyd James Sr. and Lillian (Hemmerling) W. BA in Mass Communication, Pan Am. U., 1976; MA in Speech Communication, U. Houston, 1983. Lic. FCC restricted radiotelephone operator. Announcer Sta. KRYS, Corpus Christi, Tex., 1973-74, Sta. KZFM-FM, Corpus Christi, 1974-75, Sta. KRGV, Weslaco, Tex., 1975-76, Sta. KULF, Houston, 1976-77; instr. broadcasting Elkins Inst., Houston, 1976-77; announcer Sta. KBFM-FM, Edinburg, Tex., 1977-78; instr. radio Houston Ind. Sch. Dist., 1978-83; gen. mgr. Sta. KTAI-FM Tex. A&I U., Kingsville, 1983—; cons. Stas. KINE, KDUV-FM, Kingsville, 1985—, weekend reporter Sta. KRIS-TV, Corpus Christi, 1987—. Producer: (documentaries) Kerrville Folk Festival, 1984, Texas Border Patrol, 1987. Served with Tex. NG, 1970-76. Mem. Nat. Assn. Broadcasters, Broadcast Edn. Assn., Tex. Assn. Broadcasters, Tex. Assn. Broadcast Educators, Tex. Speech Communication Assn. Democrat. Methodist. Lodges: Lions (chmn. publicity), Elks. also: WFYI-FM 1401 N Meridian St Indianapolis IN 46202-2304*

WRIGHT, MICHAEL WILLIAM, wholesale distribution, retailing executive; b. Mpls., June 13, 1938; s. Thomas W. and Winifred M. Wright. B.A., U. Minn., 1961, J.D. with honors, 1963. Ptnr. Dorsey & Whitney, Mpls., 1966-77; sr. v.p. Supervalu Inc., Mpls., 1977-78; pres., chief operating officer Super Valu Stores, Inc., Mpls., 1978—, chief exec. officer, 1981—, chmn., 1982—; bd. dirs., past chmn. Fed. Res. Bank, Mpls.; bd. dirs. Norwest Corp., Honeywell, Inc., The Musicland Group, Shopko, Inc., S.C. Johnson & Co., Inc., Cargill, Inc., Internat. Ctr. for Cos. of the Food Trade and Industry, Food Mktg. Inst., Nat. Am. Wholesale Grocers Assn., Inc.; vice chmn. Food Mktg. Inst. 1st lt. U.S. Army, 1964-66. Office: Supervalu Inc PO Box 990 Minneapolis MN 55440

WRIGHT, PATRICIA DONOVAN, communications executive; b. Rhinelander, Wis., Mar. 10, 1952; d. Stanley Timothy and Evelyn Mae (Smith) Donovan; m. Larry James Wright, May 17, 1980; children: Lindsay Mae, Molly Donovan. BS, U. Wis., 1974. Writer Amoco Corp., Chgo., 1974-77; rep. pub., community rels. Amoco Oil, Texas City, 1977-81; sr. pub. affairs advisor Amoco Corp., Kansas City, Mo., 1981-84; supr. media relations Amoco Corp., Chgo., 1984-86; dir. pub., govt. affairs Amoco Oil Co., Chgo., 1986-89; regional dir. pub. & govt. affairs Midwest Amoco Corp., Chgo., 1989-91, dir. corp. media rels., 1991-92; exec. dir., mgr. corp. rels Amoco Found., Chgo., 1992—. Recipient Award of Excellence Internat. Assn. Bus. Communicators, 1992, honors Arthur Page Soc., 1992. Mem. Women In Communications (bd. dirs. Chgo. chpt., chmn. 1985-86, regional meeting chmn.; Clarion award 1977, Cub's Cup award 1977), Publicity Club of Chgo. (Silver Trumpet 1992). Home: 30 Citation Cir Wheaton IL 60187-1117 Office: Amoco Corp 200 E Randolph St # 3707 Chicago IL 60601-6436

WRIGHT, PEGGY ANN, artificial intelligence specialist; b. Kansas City, Mo., Sept. 7, 1947; d. Denfred Ola and Margaret Florence (Hughes) Watskey; m. Clyde Stephen Wright, June 8, 1968; children: Diana Jill, Jennifer Ann. BA in Math., Washington U., St. Louis, 1968; BS in Computer Sci., Wichita State U., 1982, MS in Computer Sci., 1984. Instr. computer sci. U. Nebr., Omaha, 1984-86, Wichita State U., 1986-88; artificial intelligence specialist The Boeing Co., Wichita, 1988—; vis. scientist Software Engrng. Inst., Pitts., 1986. Contbr. articles to profl. jours. Office: Boeing Product Support PO Box 7730 M/S K82-71 Wichita KS 67277-7730

WRIGHT, RICHARD ALLEN, journalist, educator; b. East Liverpool, Ohio, Oct. 15, 1933; s. Orrin Bennett and Dorothy Louise (Marquette) W.; m. Joan Margaret Puchalski, June 21, 1959 (div. 1981); children: Douglas R., Judith A., Deborah E. BA, Wayne State U., 1959, JD, 1965. Bar: Mich. 1966, U.S. Fed. Bar, 1966. Reporter, copy editor Detroit Free Press, 1956-61, reporter, 1968-69; reporter, editor Automotive News, Detroit, 1961-68, editor, 1970-84; film writer Chrysler Corp., Center Line, Mich., 1969-70; reporter, editor Detroit News, 1984-88; prof. Wayne State U., Detroit, 1985—. Author: Love and Revolution, 1987, Detroit Inc., 1995; editor: Reuther: A Daughter Strikes, 1991. With U.S. Army, 1953-56. Episcopal. Home: 1384 Beaconsfield Grosse Pointe Park MI 48230 Office: Wayne State U 199 Manoogian Detroit MI 48202

WRIGHT, ROY DEAN, sociologist, educator, association executive; b. Stroud, Okla., Sept. 12, 1938; s. Leland and Ella (Murray) W.; m. Susan E. Walker; 1 child, Ehren Dean. B.S., Pitts. State U., 1960, M.S., 1961; Ph.D., U. Mo., 1970. Asst. prof. Va. Poly. Inst., Blacksburg, 1968-71; vis. prof. Meml. U. Nfld., St. John's, 1971; prof. Drake U., Des Moines, 1971—, chmn. dept. sociology, 1978-81. Author: Marginality and Identity, 1973; Alternatives to Prison. Issues and Options, 1979. Contbr. articles to profl. jours. Chmn., Adult Instnl. Commn., State of Iowa, 1980-81, Iowa Criminal and Juvenile Justice Council, 1982-95; active Community-Based Corrections Council, State of Iowa, 1983-84, Classification Com., State of Iowa, 1984—; chair Gov.'s Task Force on the Homeless, 1991; chair atty. Gens.' Blue Ribbon Panel on Sentencing. Chair bd. dirs. Greater Des Moines Salvation Army, Urban Dreams; v.p. Des Moines Coalition for the Homeless. Served to capt. U.S. Army, 1954-66. Fulbright grantee, 1963-64; NSF grantee, 1967; Univ. House fellow U. Iowa, 1979; named Outstanding Ptnr. in Action, Iowa Cmty. Action Assn., 1993, recipient Maddie Levitt Disting. Cmty. Svc. award, 1995, Outstanding Pub. Svc. award Iowa Corrections Assn., 1995. Mem. Midwest Sociology Soc. (bd. dirs. 1980-88, co-editor Newsletter, Disting. Svc. award 1993, pres. elect, 1996—). Home: 920 45th St West Des Moines IA 50265-3034

WRIGHT, SCOTT OLIN, federal judge; b. Haigler, Nebr., Jan. 15, 1923; s. Jesse H. and Martha I. Wright; m. Shirley Frances Young, Aug. 25, 1972. Student, Central Coll., Fayette, Mo., 1940-42; LLB, U. Mo., Columbia, 1950. Bar: Mo. 1950. City atty. Columbia, 1951-53; pros. atty. Boone County, Mo., 1954-58; practice of law Columbia, 1958-79; U.S. dist. judge Western Dist. Mo., Kansas City, from 1979. Pres. Young Democrats Boone County, 1950, United Fund Columbia, 1965. Served with USN, 1942-43; as aviator USMC, 1943-46. Decorated Air medal. Mem. ABA, Am. Trial Lawyers Assn., Mo. Bar Assn., Mo. Trial Lawyers Assn., Boone County Bar Assn. Unitarian. Clubs: Rockhill Tennis, Woodside Racquet. Lodge: Rotary (pres. Columbia 1965). Office: US Dist Ct US Courthouse 811 Grand Blvd Ste 741 Kansas City MO 64106-1909

WRIGHT, STEVEN LEE, reporter; b. Wadsworth, Ohio, Oct. 22, 1964; s. Kenneth Lee and June Evelyn (Persons) W.; m. Heidi Johnson, June 11, 1988. BA in Journalism, Kent State U., 1987. Reporter Columbus (Ohio) Dispatch, 1987—; featured columnist Handicapped Travel newsletter, 1993—, Chariot mag., U.K., 1995—; featured writer Arthritis Today, 1994—; lectr. in field. Co-author: Ideas for Easy Traveling, 1994; contbr. articles to profl. jours. Recipient First Amendment award, 1990; Lectr. grantee Poets and Writers, 1994. Mem. Soc. Profl. Journalists. Office: Columbus Dispatch 34 S 3d St Columbus OH 43221

WRIGHT, SUE ELLEN, translator, educator; b. Joliet, Ill., Oct. 26, 1943; d. Leonard Edwin and Enid Emily (Shipley) Shupe; m. Leland Duane Wright, Jr., July 7, 1942; 1 child, Elena Marguerite. BA, Simpson Coll., 1965; MA, Wash. U., St. Louis, 1966; PhD, Wash. U., 1971. Accredited translator, Am. Translators Assn. Adj. prof. Baldwin Wallace Coll., Berea, Ohio, 1976-80, Cleve. State U., 1978-80; in-house translator LuK, Inc., Wooster, Ohio, 1981-86; freelance translator LIS, Berea, 1986—, Wright & Assocs., Kent, Ohio, 1986—; asst., assoc. prof. Kent State U., 1991—; adv. bd. Infoterm, Vienna, Austria, 1992—; exec. bd. TermNet, Vienna, 1994—. Co-Author: (with Leland D. Wright, Jr.) Scientific and Technical Translation, 1993; (with Strehlow) Standardizing Terminology for Better Communication: Practice, Applied Theory, and Results, 1993, Standardizing and Harmonizing Terminology: Theory and Practice, 1995. Contbr. articles to profl. jours. Grantee rsch. and sponsored programs Kent State U., 1993, 95. Mem. Am. Translators Assn. (com. chair, series adv. bd.), Gesellschaft für Terminologie und Wissenstransfer, Internationales Institut für Terminologie Forschung, Internat. Orgn. Standardization (U.S. tech. adv. group), Am. Soc. Testing and Materials. Episcopalian. Office: Kent State U MCLS 109 Satterfield Hall Kent OH 44242

WRIGHTON, MARK STEPHEN, chemistry educator; b. Jacksonville, Fla., June 11, 1949; s. Robert D. and Doris (Cutler) W.; children: James Joseph, Rebecca Ann. BS, Fla. State U., 1969; PhD, Calif. Inst. Tech., 1972; DSc (hon.), U. West Fla., 1983. Asst. prof. chemistry MIT, Cambridge, 1972-76, assoc. prof., 1976-77, prof., 1977-95, Frederick G. Keyes prof. chemistry, 1981-89, head dept. chemistry, 1987-90, Ciba-Geigy prof. chemistry, 1989-95, provost, 1990-95; prof., chancellor Washington U., St. Louis, 1995—; bd. dirs. Ionics, Inc., Helix Tech. Corp., OIS (Optical Imaging Sys.), Inc. Author: Organometallic Photochemistry, 1979; editor books in field; cons. editor, Houghton-Mifflin. Trustee Mo. Bot. Garden, St. Louis Symphony. Recipient Herbert Newby McCoy award Calif. Inst. Tech., 1972, Disting. Alumni award, 1992, E.O. Lawrence award Dept. Energy, 1983, Halpern award in photochemistry, N.Y. Acad. Scis., 1983, Fresenius award Phi Lambda Upsilon, 1984, Dreyfus tchr.-scholar, 1975-80; Alfred P. Sloan fellow, 1974-76, MacArthur fellow, 1983-88. Fellow AAAS; mem. Am. Acad. Arts and Scis., Am. Chem. Soc. (award in pure chemistry 1981, award in inorganic chemistry 1988), Electrochem. Soc. Office: Washington Univ Office of Chancellor 1 Brookings Dr Box 1192 Saint Louis MO 63130

WRIGLEY, ROBERT ERNEST, museum director, ecologist; b. Buenos Aires, Argentina, May 2, 1943; s. Ernest and Eva (Muir) W.; m. Gail Trueman, May 20, 1967 (dec. 1984); children: Mark E., Robert A.; m. Arlene Dahl, May 24, 1986. BS, McGill U., Montreal, Que., Can., 1965; MS, McGill U., 1967; PhD, U. Ill., 1970. Curator Man. (Can.) Mus. of Man and Nature, Winnipeg, 1970-80; mus. dir. Man. (Can.) Mus. of Man and Nature, 1980-86, dir. rsch. and collections, 1986-88; assoc. prof. Natural Resources Ins. U. Man., 1988-89; dir. Oak Hammock Marsh Interpretive Ctr., Stonewall, MB, Can., 1989-95; curator Assiniboine Park Zoo, Winnipeg, Can., 1996—; bd. dirs. Ft. Whyte Centre, Winnipeg, 1983-90, Friends of Assiniboine Park Conservatory, 1988—. Author: 12 books including Reptiles and Amphibians, 1989, Mammals in North America , 1986, Large Mammals, 1984 (Gold award 1984), Manitoba's Big Cat, 1982; mng. editor Manitoba Nature, 1972-82; contbr. articles to profl. jours. Mem. Manitoba Conservation Awards, Ecological Res. and Endangered Species Coms., 1982-91. Mem. Am. Soc. Mammalogists, The Can. Field-Naturalist, Ducks Unlimited Can., Cactus and Succulent Soc. Am., Manitoba Naturalists Soc., Zool. Soc. Manitoba. Home: 505 Boreham Blvd, Winnipeg, MB Canada R3P 0K2 Office: Assiniboine Park Zoo, 2355 Corydon Ave, Winnipeg, MB Canada R3P 0R5

WRONSKI, STANLEY PAUL, education educator; b. Mpls., Apr. 8, 1919; s. John and Katherine (Kotvis) W.; m. Geraldine Breslin, May 27, 1943; children: Linda A., Mary Jo Twinkel, Sandra J., John S., Paul S. BS in Edn., U. Minn., 1942, MA, 1947, PhD, 1950. Counselor Bur. Vet. Affairs U. Minn., Mpls., 1946-47, instr. Coll. Edn., 1948-49; tchr. Marshall High Sch., Mpls., 1947-48; asst. prof. Ctrl. Wash. Coll., Ellensburg, 1950-51; from asst. to assoc. prof. Boston U., 1951-57; from assoc. prof. to prof. Mich. State U., East Lansing, 1957-84, prof. emeritus, 1984—; advisor Ministry of Edn., Bangkok, Thailand, 1964-66; pres. New Eng. Assn. Social Studies Tchrs., Boston, 1955-56, Mich. Coun. for Social Studies, 1960-61, Nat. Coun. for Social Studies, 1974. Co-author: Teaching Social Studies in High School, 1958, 73, Modern Economics, 1964, School and Society, 1964, Social Studies and Social Sciences, 1986. Active U.S. Nat. Commn. for UNESCO, Washington, 1974-76, mil. adv. coun. Ctr. for Def. Info., Washington, 1988—; pres. Greater Lansing UN Assn., 1986-88, chair Mich. UN at Fifty Planning Com., 1995. Comdr. USN, 1942-64. Recipient Internat. Educator award Pacific Rim Consortium, 1992, Glen Taggart award Mich. State U., 1995; named Outstanding Social Studies Educator, Social Studies Tchr. Jour., 1981. Mem. NEA (life), Nat. Peace Found. (charter), Univ. Club (charter), Mich. U. Nat. Fifty com. (chair, 1995). Home: 4520 Chippewa Dr Okemos MI 48864-2008 Office: Mich State U Sch of Edu Erickson Hall East Lansing MI 48824

WRZESINSKI, ELIZABETH JANE, university official; b. Chgo., July 8, 1938; d. Edward P. and Mildred (Kotenski) Waner; m. Alvin John Wrzesinski, Aug. 18, 1962. Diploma, Fox Coll., 1957. Sr. adminstrv. coord. USG Corp., Chgo., 1965-95; spl. asst. for acad. affairs U. Chgo., 1996—. Mem. Archer Heights Civic Assn., Chgo.; deacon Chgo. United. Mem. Profl. Secs. Internat. (pres. 1986-87, v.p. 1985-86, treas. 1984-85), Exec. Women Internat. (sec. 1992, v.p. 1993, pres. 1994), Lourdes Alumnae Assn. (Outstanding Alumna Bus. award 1987).

WU, HAI, mechanical engineer; b. Tunghai, Kiangsu, China, Aug. 22, 1937; came to U.S., 1961; s. Shan-san and Aei-feng (Chen) W.; m. Grace Hsiao-lee Ma, Dec. 17, 1966; children: Frank, Carson, Nelson. BSME, Nat. Cheng Kang U., Tainan, Republic of China, 1958; MSME, U. Iowa, 1963; PhD, Case Western Res. U., 1969. Mech. engr. Syska and Hennessy Engrs., N.Y.C., 1963-65; rsch. asst. Case Inst. Tech., Cleve., 1965-69; sr. rsch. engr. Ford Motor Co., Dearborn, Mich., 1969-76, prin. engr., 1976-81, prin. staff engr., 1981-85, prin. rsch. engr., 1985-88, mgr. crash analysis dept., 1988-93, mgr. safety and NVH analysis, 1993-95, mgr. chassis engrng. Core Tech. Group III, 1995—, mgr. brake tech. & chassis CAE Group; lectr. Detroit Inst. Tech., 1974. Contbr. articles to profl. jours. Advisor Ford Chinese Club, Dearborn, 1988—. Taiwan Cement Co. fellow Nat. Cheng Kung U., Tainan, 1954-58; Internat. scholar U. Iowa, Iowa City, 1961-63. Mem. ASME. Home: 50150 Hanford Rd Canton MI 48187-4609 Office: Ford Motor Co 20000 Rotunda Dr Dearborn MI 48124-3958

WU, HARRY PAO-TUNG, librarian; b. Jinan, Shandong, China, May 1, 1932; came to U.S., 1960; s. James Ching-Mei and Elizabeth Hsiao (Lu) W.; m. Irene I-Len Sun, June 23, 1961; children: Eva Pei-Chen, Walter Pei-Liang. BA, Nat. Taiwan U., Taipei, 1959; student Ohio State U., 1962; MLS, Kent State U., 1966.. Archive and library asst. Taiwan Handicraft Promotion Center, Taipei, 1959-60; student asst. Kent State U. Library, 1960-61; reference librarian Massillon (Ohio) Pub. Library, 1964-65, acting asst. dir., 1965, asst. dir., head adult services, 1966; dir. Flesh Pub. Library, Piqua, Ohio, 1966-68; dir. St. Clair County Library System, Port Huron, Mich., 1968—; founder and dir. Blue Water Library Fedn., Port Huron, 1974—; pres. Mich. Library Film Circuit, Lansing, 1977-79; mem. St. Clair County Literacy Project Com., 1986—; bd. dirs. Blue Water Reading Coun., 1987-88, Mich. Waterways council Girl Scouts U.S.A., Port Huron, 1985-86; bd. dirs. United Way St. Clair County, Mich., 1990-91; bd. trustees Libr. Mich., 1992—. Mem. Am., Mich. (chmn. library systems roundtable 1974-75) library assns., Am. Mgmt. Assn., Assn. Ednl. Communications and Tech., Detroit Suburban Librarians Roundtable, Chinese-Am. Librarians Assn. Clubs: Port Huron Internat. (pres. 1988), Rotary (dir. 1972-74, 88-90, Paul Harris fellow 1988). Home: 1518 Holland Ave Port Huron MI 48060-1511 Office: 210 Mcmorran Blvd Port Huron MI 48060-4001

WU, NELSON IKON, art history educator, author, artist; b. Peking, China, June 9, 1919; came to U.S., 1945, naturalized, 1956; s. Aitchen K. and Lu-Yü (Yang) W.; m. Mu-lien Hsüeh, Dec. 1, 1951; children: Chao-ming, Chao-ting, Chao-ping, Chao-ying. B.A., Nat. Southwest Asso. U., Kunming, China, 1942; M.A., Yale U., 1949, Ph.D., 1954. Instr. Nat. S.W. Asso. U. Kunming, China, 1942-43; asst. prof. history of art San Francisco State Coll., 1954-55; instr. Yale U., 1955-59, asst. prof., 1959-65; prof. history of art and Chinese culture Washington U., St. Louis, 1965-68, Edward Mallinckrodt Disting. Univ. prof., 1968-84, emeritus, 1984—, chmn. dept. art and archaeology, 1969-70; founder-adviser Asian Art Soc. Washington U., St. Louis, 1972—; fellow Davenport Coll., Yale, 1956-65; vis. prof. Tokyo U., 1972; Founder art festivals Yenling Yeyuan Picnic, 1952-65, Ashiya Seminar, Japan, 1966-67. Cinematographer, assoc. dir., editor motion picture The Flop, 1952; dir., writer music The Finger Painting of Wu Tsai-yen, 1955; author: (pseudonym Lu-ch'iao): Wei-yang Ko (Song Never to End, voted Most Profoundly Influential Book of 1950's by readers of China Times, 1991), 1959 (over 50 printings), Tung Ch'i-ch'ang: Apathy in Government and Fervor in Art, 1962, Chinese and Indian Architecture: City of Man, Mountain of God, and Realm of Immortals, 1963 (Italian and German transls.), Jen-tzu Tales, 1974, over 20 printings, Ch'an-ch'ing-shu, 1975, over 10 printings; contbg. author: Renditions, 1976, (with Kohara and Ch'en) Hsu/Wei and Tung Ch'i-ch'ang, Tokyo, 1978, Chinese garden design Yanling Yeyuan, 1951—; contbr. to Artibus Asiae, 1966, River Styx, 1980, 81, 82, St. Louis Post-Dispatch, 1988, China Times, 1988, 89, 92, 95, China Times Weekly, 1992, United Daily News, 1995, 96; adv. editor Tsing-hua Jour. Chinese Studies, 1982—; exhibited at Faculty Show, Washington U., 1985, St. Louis Art Mus., 1985; featured on PBS show Living Treasures, 1987. Trustee Yale-in-China Assn., 1959-65; hon. trustee Nankai Sch., Tientsin, China, 1993. Tsing-hua Research fellow, 1954-55; Morse fellow Yale, 1958-59; Am. Council Learned Socs. fellow, 1958-59; Guggenheim Found. fellow, 1965-66; Fulbright research scholar, 1965-67; research scholar Kyoto U., Japan, 1965-67; Nat. Endowment for Humanities sr. fellow, 1972; New Haven Art Festival Lit. award, 1960; Calligraphy prize Ashiya, Japan, 1966; Living Treasures plaque St. Louis Older Adult Services and Info. System, 1985; hon. in Taipei, Taiwan at a conf. on contemporary Chinese lit., 1990. Mem. St. Louis Chinese Soc. (pres. 1969-70), League of Chinese Americans (dir. 1974-77). Home: 6306 Waterman Ave Saint Louis MO 63130-4707 also: 1530 Notch Rd Cheshire CT 06410-1970

WUEBBLES, DONALD JAMES, atmospheric scientist; b. Breese, Ill., Jan. 28, 1948; s. James Edward and Helen (Isaac) W.; m. Barbara J. Yaley, June 12, 1970; children: Ryan, Kevin, Alan. BS, U. Ill., 1970, MS, 1972; PhD, U. Calif. Davis, 1983. Atmospheric scientist Nat. Oceanic and Atmospheric Adminstrn., Boulder, Colo., 1972-73; atmospheric scientist Lawrence Livermore (Calif.) Nat. Lab., 1973-94, group leader, 1987-94; head dept. atmospheric scis. U. Ill., Urbana, 1994—. Author: Primer on Greenhouse Gases, 1991 (Spl. Achievement award 1991); co-author: Scientific Assessment of Ozone Depletion, 1994, Climate Change 1994: Radiative Forcing of Climate Change, 1994, Climate Change 1995: The Science of Climate Change, 1995; contbr. articles to profl. jours. Chairperson, mem. sch. site coun., Livermore, 1985-90. Mem. AAAS, Am. Geophys. Union, Am. Meteorol. Soc. Home: 3405 S Persimmon Cir Urbana IL 61801-7128 Office: U Ill Dept Atmospheric Scis 105 S Gregory St Urbana IL 61801-3070

WUEBKER, COLLEEN MARIE, librarian; b. LaCrosse, Wis., June 22, 1943; d. Harris M. and Mary Frances (Collins) Gruber; m. William Joseph Wuebker, Aug. 14, 1965; children: Jon Paul, Timothy William, Maree Jean. BA, Mount Mercy Coll., 1965; MS, Mankato State U., 1975. Cert. permanent profl. media specialist, tchr., Iowa. Secondary tchr. Luverne Community Sch., Minn., 1965-66; tchr. St. Mary's Sch., Larchwood, Iowa, 1966; secondary tchr. SEMCO Community Sch., Gilman, Iowa, 1966-67; substitute tchr. West Bend (Iowa) Community Schs., 1968-74, sch. media specialist, 1975—; tchr., libr. Mallard Community Schs. (Iowa), 1974-75; mem. selection com. Lakeland Area Edn. Agy., Cylinder, Iowa, 1977—; mem. Gov.'s Sch. Efficiency Task Force, West Bend, 1987; mem. sch. evaluation team Dept. Pub. Instrn., Des Moines, 1986. Mem. Sts. Peter and Paul Parish Coun., West Bend, 1987—, music coord., song leader, 1987—; speaker Marriage Encounter Movement, Sioux City Diocese, 1985—, Pre-Cana Workshops, Emmetsburg, 1985—; chmn. Parish Liturgy Com., West Bend, 1987—. Mem. NEA, Iowa Edn. Assn., Iowa Ednl. Media Assn., Cath. Daus. Am. (past v.p. West Bend). Roman Catholic. Home: Box 426 11 1st Ave NE West Bend IA 50597-5036 Office: West Bend Community Sch 3 D Ave W West Bend IA 50597

WUEHLE, EDWIN EVERETT, association executive; b. Hettinger, N.D., Aug. 24, 1925; s. Edwin Herman and Alma Charlotte (Buehler) W.; m. Helen Jean, Aug. 21, 1971; children: Michele, Martin. BSE, Concordia Coll., River Forest, Ill., 1948; MA, DePaul U., 1952. Cert. elem., secondary sch. tchr. Tchr. St. John's Luth. Sch., Ventura, Iowa, 1943-44, Walz, Mich., 1944-45; tchr. Morton Grove (Ill.) Pub. Schs., 1949-53, prin., 1954-57; tchr. Lake Zurich (Ill.) Pub. Schs., 1953-54; supt. Bark River-Harris (Mich.) Schs., 1957-71, Manistique (Mich.) Area Schs., 1968-71; pres. Bay of Noc Community Com., Escanaba, Mich., 1971-85, Internat. Home and Pvt. Poker Player's Assn., Manistique, 1985—. Author: Poker Small Limit Game, 1980, Poker Record System, 1983. Mem. Rotary (past pres.), Elks. Lutheran. Home and Office: IH3PA 220 E Flamingo Rd Ste 127 Las Vegas NV 89109

WUNDERLIN, CLARENCE EDWARD, JR., historian, editor; b. Pitts., Mar. 9, 1951; s. Clarence Edward Sr. and Lorraine Mabel (Herbold) W.; m. Anita Marie Weber, May 19, 1981. BA, Pa. State U., 1976; MA, No. Ill. U., 1979, PhD, 1987. Asst. editor George C. Marshall Papers Project Marshall Found., Lexington, Va., 1983-87; staff historian Naval Hist. Ctr. USN, Washington, 1987-88; asst. prof. history Kent (Ohio) State U., 1988-93, assoc. prof. history, 1993—. Author: Visions of a New Industrial Order, 1992; author, reviewer Jour. Mil. History, 1988—; editor The Papers of Robert A. Taft, 1988—. Vol. campaign staff McGovern Presdl. Campaign, Lawrence County, Pa., 1972. Served to sgt. U.S. Army, 1969-72, Vietnam. Decorated Bronze Star with oak leaf cluster, Air medal, Combat Infantry badge; recipient fellowship Nat. Hist. Publs. and Records Commn., 1982-83, Hoover scholar Hoover Presdl. Libr., 1987-88. Fellow Inst. for Bibliography and Editing; mem. Orgn. Am. Historians, Soc. for Historians of Am. Fgn. Rels., Soc. for Mil. History. Office: Kent State Univ Dept History 305 Bowman Hall Kent OH 44242

WUNDERMAN, LORNA ELLEN, healthcare strategic planner, biostatistician; b. Hollywood, Calif., Mar. 23, 1954; d. Irwin and Gilda Shirley (Margulies) Wunderman; m. Kenneth E. Monroe, Feb. 27, 1987; 1 child, Katie. AA, Foothill Coll., 1972; BS, U. Calif., Berkeley, 1976, MPH, 1978. Cert. Community Coll. tchr., Calif. Research asst. AMA, Chgo., 1978-79, research assoc., 1978-81, dir. dept., cons., 1981-86, exec. asst. to v.p., 1986—, dir. corp. planning, 1987—. Editor: Characteristics of Physicians, 1979,

Contbr. articles to med. jours. Grantee Dept. Health and Human Services, Washington, 1979-80, 82, scholar Washington, 1976-78. Mem. The Planning Forum, Am. Statis. Assn., Am. Mktg. Assn., Am. Pub. Health Assn. Avocations: tennis, swimming, traveling. Home: 22299 N Saddle Tree Ln Barrington IL 60010-2428 Office: Joint Commn on Accreditation 1 Renaissance Blvd Villa Park IL 60181-4294

WUNSCH, MARIE ANN, provost, vice chancellor; b. Harrisburg, Pa., Feb. 19, 1944; d. Vincent Anthony and Catherine (Tomec) Drobniak; m. Aaron Wunsch, Oct. 26, 1967. BA in English, Coll. Misercordia, 1960; MA, Loyola U., 1964; MEd in Adminstrn., U. Hawaii, 1973, PhD in Am. Studies, 1978. Asst. prof. English Loyola U., Chgo., 1964-66, U. Hawaii, Honolulu, 1968-71; prof., dept. chair Leeward Coll., Pearl City, Hawaii, 1971-80; asst. to chancellor U. Hawaii, Honolulu, 1981-85, dean instructional support, 1985-89, dir. faculty devel., 1989-92; vice chancellor U. Wis. Ctrs., Madison, 1993, provost, 1994—. Editor: Mentoring Revisited, 1994; contbr. articles to profl. jours. Bd. dirs. YWCA, Hololulu, 1987-92, Profl. and Organizational Devel. Network in Higher Edn. Fulbright lecturship British Fulbright Assn., 1992; recipient Rsch. Scholar award USAID, 1990; Woodrow Wilson fellowship U.S. Dept. Edn., 1966. Home: 5959 Woodcreek Ln Middleton WI 53562 Office: Univ Wis Ctrs 780 Regent St Madison WI 53708

WURDEMAN, LEW EDWARD, data processing corporation consultant; b. Colorado Springs, Colo., Oct. 31, 1949; s. Robert Martin and Shirley Gladys (Reetz) W. Student U. Tex., El Paso, 1967-69, U. Minn., 1969-72. Adminstr. Control Data Corp., Bloomington, Minn., 1969-81, product specialist, 1981-83, systems mgr., 1983-84, cons., 1984-89; mgr. The Roach Orgn., Inc., Mpls., 1989-90; computer cons. Wurdeman Enterprises, Inc., Farmington, Minn., 1991-93; network cons. Connect Computer Co., Edina, Minn., 1993—. Mem. German Shepherd Dog Club of Mpls., German Shepherd Dog Club of Am., Twin Cities Personal Computer Users Group, Minn. Purebred Dog Breeders Assn., Minn. River Valley Kennel Club. Republican. Lutheran. Avocations: dog breeding and training, computers, photography. Office: Connect Computer Co 7101 Metro Blvd Edina MN 55439-2113

WURSCHMIDT, TODD NEIL, association executive; b. Chico, Calif., Oct. 29, 1950; s. Leo Clifford and Patsey (Stampfli) W.; m. Suzanne Youmans, July 3, 1971; children: Mitchell Todd, Austin Todd. BS, Ohio State U., 1975, M, 1980, PhD, 1992. Rsch. assoc. Nat. Rural Crime Prevention Ctr., Columbus, Ohio, 1978-80; exec. dir. Ohio Crime Prevention Assn., Columbus, 1980-84, Ohio Crime Prevention Edn. Found., Columbus, 1980-86, Ohio Assn. Chiefs Police, Columbus, 1985—; pres. Law Enforcement Found., Columbus, 1986—; exec. dir. Ohio DARE Officers Assn., Columbus, 1989—, Law Enforcement Found. Ill., Joliet, 1989-92; adj. asst. prof. Ohio State U., 1995—; chmn. Constitutional Com. Co-editor: Rural Crime, 1982. Councilman Village of Plain City, Ohio, 1988-91. With USAF, 1971-73. Mem. Am. Soc. Assn. Execs. (CEO mentor, mgmt. evaluator, commn. 1995-97), Am. Sociol. Assn., Assn. Applied Sociology, Nat. Soc. Fundraising Execs., Internat. Assn. Chiefs Police (chmn. exec. dirs. com. 1988-89), Ohio Soc. Assn. Execs. (exec. com. 1988-91). Office: Ohio Assn Chiefs Police 6277 Riverside Dr Dublin OH 43017-5067

WURSTER, DALE ERWIN, pharmacy educator, university dean emeritus; b. Sparta, Wis., Apr. 10, 1918; s. Edward Emil and Emma Sophia (Steingraeber) W.; m. June Margaret Peterson, June 16, 1944; children: Dale Eric, Susan Gay. BS, U. Wis., 1942, PhD, 1947. With faculty U. Wis. Sch. Pharmacy, 1947-71, prof., 1958-71; prof., dean N.D. State U. Coll. Pharmacy, 1971-72, U. Iowa Coll. Pharmacy, Iowa City, 1972-84, prof., 1972—, interim dean, 1991-92, dean emeritus, 1984—; George B. Kaufman Meml. lectr. Ohio State U., 1968; cons. in field; phys. sci. adminstr. U.S. Navy, 1960-63; sci. adv. Wis. Alumni Rsch. Found., 1968-72; mem. revision com. U.S. Pharmacopoeia, 1961-70, pharmacy rev. com. USPHS, 1966-72. Contbr. articles to profl. jours., chpts. to books; patentee in field. With USNR, 1944-46. Recipient Superior Achievement citation Navy Dept., 1964, merit citation U. Wis., 1976; named Hancher Finkbine Medallion Prof. U. Iowa, 1984; recipient Disting. Alumni award U. Wis. Sch. Pharmacy, 1984. Fellow Am. Assn. Pharm. Scientists (founder, sponsor Dale E. Wurster Rsch. award 1990—, Disting. Pharm. Sci. award 1991); mem. Am. Assn. Colls. Pharmacy (exec. com. 1964-66, chmn. conf. tchrs. 1960-61, vis. scientist 1963-70, recipient Disting. Educator award 1983), Acad. Pharm. Scis. (exec. com. 1967-70, chmn. basic pharmaceutics sect. 1965-67, pres. 1975, Indsl. Pharm. Tech. award 1980), Am. Pharm. Assn. (chmn. sci. sect. 1964-65, Rsch. Achievement award 1965), Wis. (Disting. Service award 1971), Iowa Pharmacists Assn. (Robert G. Gibbs award 1983), Wis. Acad. Scis., Arts and Letters, Soc. Investigative Dermatology, Rumanian Soc. Med. Sci. (hon.), Am. Found. Pharm. Edn. (bd. grants 1987-92), Ea. Va. Med. Sch. Contraceptive Rsch. and Devel. Program (tech. adv. com. 1989—), Am. Assn. Pharm. Scientists (Disting. Scientist award 1991), Sigma Xi, Kappa Psi (past officer), Rho Chi, Phi Lambda Upsilon, Phi Sigma. Home: 16 Brickwood Knls NE Iowa City IA 52240-9144

WURTZ, CARL JOSEPH, financial company executive, management consultant; b. Cin., Oct. 16, 1936; s. Carl Henry and Marian Elizabeth (Keckels) W.; m. Joan Rita Overberg, June 7, 1958; children: Mary Joanna, Carl Edward, Lora Ann, Matthew Wayne. BSBA, Xavier U., 1958. CPA, Ill. V.p., contr. Swedlow, Inc., Garden Grove, Calif., 1969-74; CFO Alexander-Patterson Assoc., Cin., 1974-82; pvt. practice Cin., 1982-85; CFO Davey Compressor Co., Cin., 1985-94, exec. v.p., 1991-94; pvt. practice mgmt. cons. Cin., 1992-95; staff exec. Geo. S. May Internat. Co., Park Ridge, Ill., 1995—; bd. dirs. Cin. Hydraulics. Treas. Valley Inter-Faith Charities, Cin., 1984. Republican. Roman Catholic. Home: 4099 Sharon Park Ln # 8 Cincinnati OH 45241

WUSTENBERG, WENDY WIBERG, public affairs specialist, consultant; b. Faribault, Minn., Sept. 30, 1958; d. George Lyman and Ruth Elizabeth (Morris) Wiberg; m. William Wustenberg, Nov. 11, 1989; children: Russell Morris, Lauren Ruth. BA in Journalism, U. Minn., 1977-83. Dir. comms., press sec. Office Gov. Quie, St. Paul, 1980-83; sr. prodr. news and pub. affairs Twin Cities Pub. TV, St. Paul, 1983-88; chief of staff Minn. House Reps., St. Paul, 1990; CFO, mng. ptnr. Issue Strategies Group, St. Paul, 1988-92; cons. Wustenberg and Assocs., Farmington, MN, 1992—; trustee Farmington Sch. Bd., 1993—; dir. Cmty. Action Coun., Apple Valley, Minn., 1991-93; pres. SOAR, Inc., Rosemount, Minn., 1990—; adj. prof. Metro. State U., St. Paul, 1986—; lobbyist State of Minn., St. Paul, 1992—. Author: Families and Sexuality, 1983; creative dir.: (avt. campaign) Environmental Trust Fund, 1988 (Assn. Trends award 1988); contbr. articles to profl. jours. Minn. exec. dir. Bush/Quayle Campaign, Bloomington, 1992; instr. Courage Ctr. Alpine Skiers, Welch, Minn., 1988; trustee The Carpenter Found. and Carpenter Nature Ctr., 1995—. Recipient Nat. Promotion award Corp. for Pub. Broadcasting, Washington, 1986, 87, Local Documentary and Outreach award, 1987, J.C. Penney award U. Mo. Journalism Sch., 1987; finalist TV Acad. awards Nat. Acad. TV Arts and Scis., N.Y.C., 1986; named Adult Educator of Yr., Mo. Valley Assn. Adult Edn., 1986; named Disting. Alumni, U. Minn., 1994. Mem. Minn. Sch. Bds. Assn. (del.), Minn. Alumni Assn., Order Eastern Star. Republican.

WYATT, ROSE MARIE, clinical social worker; b. San Angelo, Tex., Feb. 16; d. James Odis and Anne LaVernia (Lott) W. BA, Fisk U., 1957; MS, U. So. Calif., 1963; MA, MSW, U. Chgo., 1972; postgrad., Ill. Inst. Tech., 1976—. Elem. tchr. Chgo. Bd. Edn., 1959-63, clin. social worker, 1979—; adult program dir. Chgo. YWCA, 1963-64; youth counselor Chgo. Commn. on Youth Welfare, 1964-66; supervising social worker for Head Start, Chgo. Com. on Urban Opportunity, 1966; social worker Chgo. Commn. on Youth Welfare, 1966-68, Jewish Vocat. Svc., 1968; social worker Sch. Community Rels., Detroit Pub. Schs., 1968-70; social worker United Charities, 1972-74; clin. social worker Rosman-Wyatt and Assocs., Chgo., 1980—, pres., 1981—; instr. dept. corrections Chgo. State U., 1972—. Adv. bd. United Charities, Calumet area, program com. chmn., 1974-80; vol. Assn. of Community Agts. 1968-70, Southside Sr. Citizens Coalition, Chgo., 1963-66, Roseland Health Planning Com., 1974-76, Teen Pregnancy Caucus, 1978-82; mem. social work adv. coun. Chgo. Bd. Edn., 1976. Recipient Outstanding Employee award for med.-social work svcs. Maternal and Child Health Svcs. div. HEW; 1971; Ford Found. scholar Fisk U., 1953-57, U. Chgo. scholar, 1970-72, United Charities scholar, 1970-72. Mem. Nat. Assn. Social Workers, Acad. Cert. Social Workers, Ill. Cert. Social Workers, Chgo. Psychol. Club, Ill Acad. Criminology, NEA, Ill. Assn. Sch. Social Workers, Am. Assn. Mental Deficiency, Qualified Mental Retardation Profls., Fisk U. Alumni Assn., Am. Bridge Assn., Civenos Bridge Club, Alpha Kappa Alpha.

WYDRA, FRANK THOMAS, healthcare executive; b. Republic, Pa., May 11, 1939; s. Frank T. and Anne M. (Kois) W.; m. Karen Branch, June 24, 1961; children: Denise Lee, Sheryl Lynn, Frank Thomas III. BS in Mgmt., U. Ill., 1961. V.p. Allied Supermarkets, Inc., Detroit, 1967-75; sr. v.p. HGH Health System, Detroit, 1975-85; pres. Radius Health Care Sysytems, Inc., Detroit, 1983-85; cons. Birmingham, Mich., 1985-88; exec. v.p. The Chi Group, Ann Arbor, Mich., 1988-91; cons. Indsl. Rels. Inc., Detroit, 1991—; lectr. various profl. groups; bd. dirs. Mich. Health Systems Inc., Saber-Salisbury Assocs. Inc., Midwestern Health Ctr., MultiCare Med. Inc., RHS Inc. Author: Learner Controlled Instruction, 1980, (with others) Hospital Survival Guide, 1984, The Cure, 1992; creator 2 mgmt. games Performulations, 1978, The Dynamics of Power and Authority, 1981; contbr. articles to profl. jours. Personnel program advisor Mich. State U. Sch. Labor Relations, 1979-83; chmn. new programs Wayne County Community Coll., Detroit, 1979-80; bd. dirs. Detroit Metro Youth Found., 1980-83, State Mich. Health Occupations Council, Lansing, 1982-85. Capt. U.S. Army, 1961-63. Recipient numerous awards ASTD, Nat. Soc. Performance and Instrn., Mich. SOc. Instructional Tech., Supermarket Inst. Mem. Am. Hosp. Assn., Planning Soc. of Am. Hosp. Assn., Hosp. Personnel Adminstrs. Assn. (pres. 1981-82, numerous awards), Am. Mgmt. Assn., Am. Soc. Hosp. Pers.Adminstrs. (bd. dirs. 1981-83), Mich. Soc. Instrnl. Tech. (life, pres. 1973-74), Mich. Hosp. Assn., Employers Assn. Detroit (bd. dirs. 1982-85), Detroit Athletic Club. Home: 1001 W Glengarry Cir Bloomfield Hills MI 48301-2223

WYLER, KATHRYN KISHPAUGH, vocational evaluator; b. Blissfield, Mich., July 5, 1937; d. G. Charles and Mildred I. (Foltz) Kishpaugh; m. John G. Wyler, Mar. 21, 1959; children: Linda L., Karen L. Zantopulos, John F. BA, Adrian (Mich.) Coll., 1959. Cert. vocat. assessment/evaluation coord., elem. tchr., Ohio. Libr. aide Lenawee County Libr., Adrian, 1955-57; sch. libr. Adrian Pub. Schs., 1959-60, Croswell (Mich.)-Lexington Schs., 1961-63; vocat. evaluation asst. Canton (Ohio) City Schs., 1975-78, vocat. evaluator, 1978-95. Curator Book of Golden Memories, Adrian Coll., 1992—, mem. alumni bd. dirs., 1986-92, sec., 1987-89, chair awards, nominations and scholarship coms., 1990-92; libr. Westbrook Park United Meth. Ch., 1968-94. Mem. NEA, Am. Vocat. Assn., Ohio Vocat. Assn. (Disting. Svc. award 1995), OhioEdn. Assn., Ohio Assn. Vocat. Edn. Spl. Needs Pers. (pres. 1990-92, conf. chair 1990), Canton Orgn. Vocat. Educators (sec. 1985, pres. 1986-88). Republican. Home: 2502 41st St NE Canton OH 44705-2808 Office: Canton City Schs 521 Tuscarawas St W Canton OH 44702-2019

WYMAN, BOSTWICK FRAMPTON, mathematics educator; b. Aiken, S.C., Aug. 22, 1941; s. Bostwick F. and Myra (Faust) W.; m. Lockhart Moore, Oct. 28, 1967 (dec. Nov. 1973); m. Linda Curtis, Nov. 29, 1975; children: Tracy L. and John G. SB, MIT, 1962; MA, U. Calif., Berkeley, 1964, PhD, 1966. Instr. Princeton (N.J.) U., 1966-68; asst. prof. Stanford U., Palo Alto, Calif., 1968-72; from assoc. prof. to prof. math. Ohio State U., Columbus, 1972—, vice chmn. dept., 1995—; vis. asst. prof. U. Oslo, Norway, 1970-71, U. Notre Dame, South Bend, Ind., 1979-80. Editor: New Trends in System Theory, 1991; contbr. articles to profl. jours. Grantee NSF 1975—. Mem. IEEE (sr.), Soc. Indsl. and Applied Math., Am. Math. Soc., Math. Assn. Am. Episcopalian. Office: Ohio State U Math Dept 231 W 18th Ave Columbus OH 43210-1101

WYMAN, PAUL K., human resources consultant; b. Mpls., Sept. 23, 1945; s. Vernon and Jacqueline (Bender) W.; children: Nicole, Andrew. AA, Acad. Acctg., 1967. Personnel mgr. Gen. Mills, Mpls., 1965-77; mgr. corp. personnel Henkel Corp., Mpls., 1977-87; pres. Primentor Corp., Mpls., 1987—. With U.S. Army, 1968-69, Korea. Home: 15900 N Hillcrest Ct Eden Prairie MN 55346-3714

WYMORE, LUANN COURTNEY, education educator; b. Kansas City, Mo., Feb. 22, 1942; d. Clifford Willis and Lola (Moore) Courtney; m. George Philip Wymore, Dec. 27, 1964; children: Courtney, Kristin, Ryan. BA, William Jewell Coll., 1964; MA, U. Mo., Kansas City, 1969; PhD, Mo. U., 1989. Cert. elem., biology, Englisy tchr., Mo. Elem. tchr. Sch. Dist. North Kansas City, Mo., 1964-69; assoc. prof. elem. edn. Mo. Valley Coll., Marshall, 1989—; presenter in field. Contbr. articles to profl. jours. Leader Girl Scouts U.S.A., Slater, Mo., 1980's, 4-H Club, Orearville, Mo., 1980's. Mem. ASCD, PEO, Internat. Reading Assn. Democrat. Home: 820 Rich St Slater MO 65349-1258 Office: Mo Valley Coll 500 E College St Marshall MO 65340-3109

WYRSCH, JAMES ROBERT, lawyer, educator, author; b. Springfield, Mo., Feb. 23, 1942; s. Louis Joseph and Jane Elizabeth (Welsh) W.; m. B. Darlene Wyrsch, Oct. 18, 1975; children: Scott, Keith, Mark, Brian, Marcia. BA, U. Notre Dame, 1963; JD, Georgetown U., 1966; LLM, U. Mo., Kansas City, 1972. Bar: Mo. 1966, U.S. Ct. Appeals (8th cir.) 1971, U.S. Supreme Ct. 1972, U.S. Ct. Appeals (10th cir.) 1974, U.S. Ct. Appeals (5th cir.) 1974, U.S. Ct. Mil. & Appeals 1978, U.S. Ct. Appeals (6th cir.) 1982, U.S. Ct. Appeals (11th cir.) 1984, U.S. Ct. Appeals (7th cir.) 1986, U.S. Ct. Appeals (4th cir.) 1990. Assoc. Wyrsch, Atwell, Mirakian, Lee and Hobbs, P.C. and predecessors, Kansas City, Mo., 1970-71, of counsel, 1972-77, ptnr., 1978—, pres., shareholder, 1988—; adj. prof. U. Mo., 1981—; mem. com. instrns. Mo. Supreme Ct., 1983—. Capt. U.S. Army, 1966-69; named to Who's Who in Kansas City Law, Kansas City Bus. Jour., 1991, 1994; recipient Joint Svcs. Commendation medal U.S. Army, 1969, U. Mo. Kansas City Svc. award Law Found., 1991-92. Fellow Am. Coll. Trial Lawyers, Am. Bar Found.; mem. ABA, Am. Arbitration Assn. (panel arbitrators), Mo. Bar Assn. (vice chmn. criminal law com. 1978-79), Kansas City Bar Assn. (chmn. anti-trust com. 1981), Assn. Trial Lawyers Am., Am. Bd. of Trial Advocates (adv.), Nat. Assn. Criminal Def. Attys., Mo. Assn. Criminal Def. Attys. (sec. 1982), Phi Delta Phi, Country Club of Blue Springs. Democrat. Roman Catholic. Co-author: Missouri Criminal Trial Practice, 1994; contbr. articles to profl. jours. Home: 1501 Sunnycreek Ln Blue Springs MO 64014 Office: Wyrsch Atwell Mirakian Lee & Hobbs PC 1101 Walnut St Fl 13 Kansas City MO 64106-2122

WYSE, LOIS, advertising executive, author; b. Cleve., 1928; d. Roy B. Wohlgemuth and Rose (Schwartz) Weisman; m. Marc Wyse (div. 1980); m. Lee Guber (dec. 1988). Pres. Wyse Advt. Inc., N.Y.C., 1951—; bd. dirs. Consol. Natural Gas, Pitts.; ptnr. City & Co. Author 56 books; contbg. editor Good Housekeeping; syndicated columnist Wyse Words. Trustee Beth Israel Med. Ctr., N.Y.C. Mem. Woman's Forum (bd. dirs.), PEN. Office: Wyse Advt Inc 24 Public Sq Cleveland OH 44113-2201*

WYSE, MARC A., advertising agency executive; b. 1925. BA in English, Western Res. U., Cleve., 1946. With Smith and Ross, Cleve., 1946-48; advt. mgr. Gottfried Co., Cleve., 1948-51; sole owner Wyse Advt., Cleve., 1951-55; chmn. bd. dirs., formerly pres., gen. mgr. Cleveland office Wyse Advt. Inc., Cleve. Office: Wyse Advt Inc 24 Public Sq Cleveland OH 44113-2201*

WYSOCKI, THEODORE JOSEPH, JR., non-profit organization executive; b. Chgo., Dec. 28, 1949; s. Theodore Joseph Sr. and Daisy (Faulkner) W.; m. Lynne Marie Cunningham, July 21, 1979; 1 child, Theodore Joseph III. BA, Providence Coll., 1971; MA, U. Chgo., 1973. Dir. reinvestment Nat. Tng. and Info. Ctr., Chgo., 1974-84; exec. dir. Chgo. Assn. Neighborhood Devel. Orgns. (CANDO), 1984—; sec. Nat. Cmty. Reinvestment Coalition, Washington, 1992; mem. Harris Trust Neighborhood Lending Rev. Bd., Chgo., 1984—; mem. consumer adv. coun. Fed. Res. Bd., 1996—; mem. empowerment zone coordinating coun. City of Chgo., 1996—. Founding editor Disclosure, 1974-84; pub. Cando Quarterly, 1984—. Roman Catholic. Office: Chgo Assn Neighborhood Devl Orgns 343 S Dearborn St Ste 910 Chicago IL 60604-3808

WYSONG, LINDA MARIE, career center administrator; b. Oakland, Calif., Sept. 20, 1950; d. Earl W. and Melva (Baldwin) Wright; m. Dennis Wysong, Aug. 24, 1974 (div. Feb. 1991); children: Daniel, Melissa. BA, Pacific Union Coll., 1972; MAT, Andrews U., 1974. Tchr. Monterey Bay Acad., Watsonville, Calif., 1973-74, Loma Linda (Calif.) Acad., 1974-75, Salt Pond Elem. Sch., Newfoundland, Can., 1976-77, Wenatchee (Wash.) Valley Coll., 1980-85; prin. Kailua (Hawaii) Mission Sch., 1985-86; dir. quality mgmt. Castle Med Ctr., Kailua, 1989-93; dir. Career Ctr. Union Coll., Lincoln, Nebr., 1993—. Mem. Am. Soc. Quality Control. Mem. Seventh-Day Adventist Ch. Office: Union Coll 3800 S 48th St Lincoln NE 68516

WYSS, THOMAS JOHN, state senator; b. Ft. Wayne, Ind., Oct. 24, 1942; s. John Paul and Winifred Ann (Ebersole) W.; m. Shirley Dawn Pabst, Jan. 16, 1965; children: Tamara, Angela. B in Indsl. Supervision, Purdue U., 1975. Apprentice GE, Ft. Wayne, 1961-65, mem. mfg. mgmt. staff, 1965-71, mem. mktg. mgmt. staff, 1971—; senator Ind. State Senate, Ft. Wayne, 1985—. Councilman Allen County Coun., Ft. Wayne, 1976-85; chmn., founder Ind. State Crimestoppers, Indpls., 1988—. Lt. col. Ind. Air N.G., 1966—. Recipient Ind. NFIB Guardian of Small Bus. award, 1994; named Outstanding Legislator Ind. State Dental Soc., Indpls., 1987, Outstanding Legislator Ind. Dept. Bldg. Svcs., Indpls., 1987. Mem. Ind. Soc. Chgo., N.G. Assn. (Charles Dick award 1994), Ft. Wayne Jaycees (v.p. 1971-72, Key Man of Ind. and Outstanding Young Man Am. 1971), Am. Legis. Exch. Coun. (state chmn.). Home: 5820 W Wallen Rd Fort Wayne IN 46818-9408 also: State Senate State Capital Indianapolis IN 46204

WYSZYNSKI, JAMES EDWARD, JR., lawyer, state government; b. Elyria, Ohio, Nov. 16, 1950; s. James Edward and June Eleanor (Coe) W.; m. Kay Boston, Nov. 17, 1979; 1 child, James Edward III. A in Gen. Studies, Macomb Cmty. Coll., 1981; B of Accountancy, Walsh Coll., 1983; JD, Detroit Coll. of Law, 1989. Bar: Mich. 1989. Controller Metro-East Drug Treatment Corp., Detroit, 1984-87; chief acct. Cmty. Case Mgmt., Inc., Detroit, 1987-89; rsch. atty. Mich. Ct. of Appeals, Lansing, 1989-90; law clk. Appeals Judge Donald Holbrook, Lansing, 1990-91; commr. Workers Compensation Appellate Commn., Lansing, 1991-93, 95—, chmn., 1993-95. Contbr. articles to profl. jours. Chmn. Eaton County Hist. Commn., Charlotte, Mich., 1993-94, Eaton County Rep. Party, 1995-96; trustee Greater Lansing Cath. Edn. Found., 1995—, Eaton Area Habitat for Humanity, 1995—. Recipient Employee of Yr. award Metro-East Drug Treatment Corp., 1985, Scroll of Appreciation, Macomb Cmty. Coll., 1986, Recognition certificate Detroit Coll. of Law Rev., 1989, Top Paper award 21st Ann. Internat. Workers Compensation Coll., 1994. Mem. ABA, State Bar of Mich., Advocates Polish Am. Bar Assn., Mich. Polit. History Soc., DCL Alumni Assn. (bd. dirs. 1994-97), KC. Republican. Roman Catholic. Home: 912 Cedar St Grand Ledge MI 48837 Office: Workers Compensation Appellate Commn 201 N Washington St Lansing MI 48933

XU, CHARLIE YUPING, geochemist; b. Shanghai, Apr. 2, 1964; m. Yangzhen Xin, May 19, 1990; 1 child, Joshua. BS, U. Sci. and Tech. China, 1986; MS, Ohio State U., 1990, PhD, 1994. Rsch. asst. Chinese Acad. Sci., Guiyang, 1986-87; mgr. asst. Nanhai Geochem. Co., Guangzhou, Peoples Republic of China, 1987-88; asst. prof. U. Ill., Chgo., 1994—. Presdl. fellow Ohio State U., 1993. Mem. Am. Chem. Soc., Am. Geophys. Union, Geochem. Soc., Clay Mineral Soc. Office: U Ill Chgo 845 W Taylor St M/C 186 Chicago IL 60607

YACKEL, JAMES WILLIAM, mathematician, academic administrator; b. Sanborn, Minn., Mar. 6, 1936; s. Ewald W. and Marie E. (Heydlauff) Y.; m. Erna Beth Seecamp, Aug. 20, 1960; children: Jonathan, Juliet, Carolyn. BA, U. Minn., 1958, MA, 1960, PhD, 1964. Rsch. instr. dept. math. Dartmouth Coll., Hanover, N.H., 1964-66; asst. prof. dept. stats. Purdue U., West Lafayette, Ind., 1966-69, from assoc. prof. to prof., 1969-76, assoc. dean sci., 1976-87; vice chancellor acad. affairs Purdue U. Calumet, Hammond, Ind., 1987-90, chancellor, 1990—; rsch. mathematician Inst. Def. Analysis, Washington, 1969. Author: Applicable Finite Mathematics, 1974; editor Statistical Decision Theory, 1971; contbr. articles to profl. jours. Fellow AAAS; mem. Am. Math. Soc., Math. Assn. Am., Inst. Math. Stats. Office: Purdue U Calumet Office of Chancellor Hammond IN 46323

YACONETTI, DIANNE MARY, business executive; b. Chgo., Dec. 16, 1946; d. Anthony and Dora Marie (Mazzoni) Pontillo. Student, Mallinckrodt Coll., 1984-85; Advanced Mgmt. Program, Harvard U., 1990. Various positions Brunswick Corp., Skokie, Ill., 1964-80, mgr. legal support services, 1980-83, asst. sec., 1984-86, corp. sec., 1986-88, v.p. adminstrn., corp. sec., 1988—; bd. dirs. The Lambs, Libertyville, Ill. Mem. Am. Soc. Corp. Secs. Roman Catholic. Office: Brunswick Corp 1 N Field Ct Lake Forest IL 60045-4811

YAEGER, THERESE FRANCIS, management consultant; b. Chgo., 1955; d. Walter W. and Eileen Bronson; m. Paul Alan Yaeger, 1975; 4 children. AA in English, Coll. DuPage, 1993; BA in Lit. and Comm. magna cum laude, Ill. Benedictine, 1995; MS in Mgmt. & Orgnl. Behavior, Benedictine U., 1996. Gen. mgr. Bestway Carpeting Inc., Naperville, Ill., 1976—; asst. PhD dept. Orgn. Devel. Benedictine U., Lisle, 1995—. Editor (mag.) DuPage Arts Life, 1995, 96; asst. editor (newsletter) Lit/Com Chronicles, 1995. Mem. Chgo. Orgn. Devel. Inst. Chpt. (adminstr. 1995), Soc. Profl. Journalists, Phi Theta Kappa. Roman Catholic.

YAGEL, RONI, computer science educator, consultant; b. Sau Paulo, Brazil, Jan. 5, 1959; came to U.S., 1987; s. Joseph and Vera (Treibitch) Feigelstock; m. Miri Sircovich, Aug. 13, 1984; children: Chay, Hane, Gal, Tal. BSc, Ben Gurion U., Israel, 1986, MSc, 1987; PhD, SUNY, Stony Brook, 1991. Rschr. SUNY, Stony Brook, 1987-91; asst. prof. Ohio State U., Columbus, 1991-95. Patentee in field; contbr. papers to profl. jours. Sgt. Israeli Army, 1979-82. Recipient Rsch. Initiation award NSF, 1992. Mem. IEEE, Assn. Computer Machinery. Jewish. Office: Ohio State U 2015 Neil Ave Columbus OH 43210

YAKES, BARBARA LEE, occupational and preventive medicine physician, former nurse; b. Detroit; d. Glen Wendel and Marie Louise (Jock) Y.; m. Richard Allen Jankowics, Sept. 12, 1984; 1 child, Allen Glen. BA, Wayne State Univ., 1973, BS in Nursing, 1978; D in Osteopathic medicine, Mich. State Univ., 1986; M in Occupational Health, Harvard Sch. Pub. Health, 1988. Diplomate Am. Bd. Preventive Medicine, Occupational Medicine, Nat. Bd. Osteopathic Medical Examiners. Registered nurse Lafayette Clinic Grace Hosp., Oakwood Hosp., Detroit, 1978-83; internship Mich. Health Ctr., Detroit, 1986-87; resident Harvard Sch. Pub. Health, Boston, 1987-89; plant medical dir. General Motors Corp., Warren, Mich., 1989—. Contbr. articles to profl. jours. Bd. Govs. Acad. scholar Wayne State U., 1969-73; recipient Bubeck OB/GYN award Mich. State U., 1984, Mead-Johnson rsch. award Mead-Johnson Pharm., 1987-88. Fellow Am. Coll. Preventive Medicine; mem. Am. Osteo. Assn., Am. Coll. Occupational and Environ. Medicine, Mich. Assn. Osteo. Physicians and Surgeons, Mich. Occupational Med. Assn., Detroit Inst. Arts Founders Soc., Harvard Club Eastern Mich., Phi Beta Kappa, Sigma Sigma Phi. Office: General Motors Corp Mfg B Bldg Medical Dept 30300 Mound Rd Warren MI 48092-2027

YAKURA, THELMA PAULINE, retired library director, consultant, writer; b. Wilmington, Del.; d. Michael J. and Bertha (Blanchfield) Masticola; m. James N. Yakura, Nov. 18, 1950 (dec. 1974); children: James Peter, Kristie. BA, U. Del., 1945; BLS, Drexel Inst. Tech., 1946. Reference asst. U. Pitts. Library, 1946; head engring. library Carnegie Mellon U. (formerly Carnegie Inst. Tech.), 1947-51; children's librarian, head adult bookmobile Cuyahoga County Pub. Library, Cleve., 1952-55; asst. head bookmobile dept. Westwood Br. Dayton (Ohio) Pub. Library, 1956-57, head librarian, 1957-64; dir. Wright Mem. Pub. Library, Dayton, 1964-89; libr. cons., freelance writer, 1989—; County rep. Miami Valley Libr. Orgn., Dayton; mem. creative writer's group Miamisburg (Ohio) Sr. Ctr. Active in Oakwood Hist. Soc. Mem. ALA, Ohio Library Assn., Oakwood Hist. Soc. (life). Home and Office: 1327 Carlwood Dr Miamisburg OH 45342-3517

YAMAKAWA, ALLAN HITOSHI, academic administrator; b. San Francisco, Oct. 18, 1938; s. Victor Tadashi and Alice Tsugie (Sato) Y.; m. Nancy Ann Habel, Apr.17, 1977 (div. Mar 1987); children: Bryan Allan, David Scott. BS, Roosevelt U., 1962, MEd, 1970. Tech. svcs. dir. audio visual libr. Roosevelt U., Chgo., 1958-60; dean, exec. dir. Ency. Britannica Schs., Inc., Chgo., 1960-67; curriculum svcs. dir. Field Enterprises Newspaper Div., Chgo., 1967-70; edn. svcs. dir. Chgo. Tribune Co., 1970-76; tng. svcs. dir. Dialogue Systems Inc., N.Y.C., 1976-79; orgn. devel. dir. U. Ill.,

Chgo., 1979—; cons., trainer Can. Daily Newspaper Pub. Assn., Toronto, 1973-84, Am. Newspaper Pub. Found., Reston, Va., 1972-80, Gifted Students Found. Dallas, 1974-75; cons. Cedars Sinai Med. Ctr., Beverly Hills, Calif., 1983—, W. K. Kellogg Found., 1987—. Author: Handbooks of Teaching Methods, 1974, Communicate, 1975, Catalysts For Change, 1976, Evaluation of Senior Administrators, 1994; patentee experiential learning method. Instr. ARC, Chgo., 1954-85; bd. dirs. Edison Regional Gifted Ctr. Sch., Chgo., pres., 1989-93; dist. program chmn. Boy Scouts Am., 1985—. Mem. ASTD, ASCD, Soc. Programmed and Automated Learning, Toastmasters (pres. 1974-76). Office: Univ Ill 1524(G) W Pratt Blvd Chicago IL 60626

YAMAUCHI, EDWIN MASAO, history educator; b. Hilo, Hawaii, Feb. 1, 1937; s. Shokyo Yamauchi and Haruko (Owan) Yamauchi Higa; m. Kimie Honda, Aug. 31, 1962; children: Brian, Gail. Student, U. Hawaii, 1957-58; BA, Shelton Coll., 1960; MA, Brandeis U., 1962, PhD, 1964. Instr. Greek lang. Shelton Coll., Ringwood, N.J., 1960-61; grad. asst. Brandeis U., Waltham, Mass., 1962-63; asst. prof. Rutgers U., New Brunswick, N.J., 1964-69; assoc. prof. Miami U., Oxford, Ohio, 1969-73, prof. dept. history, 1973—, dir. grad. studies, 1978-82. Author: Pre-Christian Gnosticism, 1973, World of the First Christians, 1981, Foes from the North Frontier, 1982, Persia and the Bible, 1990, 7 other books, 1992-94; sr. editor Christianity Today, 1992—. Fellow NEH, 1968, Inst. for Holy Land Studies, Jerusalem, 1968, Inst. for Advanced Christian Studies, 1974-75; grantee Am. Philos. Soc., 1970. Fellow Am. Sci. Affiliation (pres. 1983), Inst. Bibl. Rsch. (chair 1984-86, pres. 1987-89); mem. Conf. on Faith and History (pres. 1974-76), Near East Archaeol. Soc. (v.p. 1978-79), Archaeol. Inst. Am. (chpt. pres. 1973-74), Evang. Theol. Soc. (chair ea. sect. 1965-66). Office: Miami Univ Dept History Dept History Oxford OH 45056

YAMIN, JOSEPH FRANCIS, lawyer, counselor; b. Detroit, Mar. 12, 1956; s. Raymond Samuel and Sadie Ann (John) Y. 1975; BA, U. Mich., 1978; J.D., London Sch. Econs., 1981; JD, Detroit Coll. Law, 1982. Bar: U.S. Ct. Appeals (6th cir.) 1982, U.S. Dist. Ct. (ea. dist.) Mich. 1982. Atty. Alan R. Miller, P.C., Birmingham, Mich., 1981-93; ptnr. Beier Howlett PC, Bloomfield Hills, Mich., 1993—; bd. dir. Am. Wash Systems, Birmingham, 1979—; instr. Detroit Coll. Law Rev., 1984-86; mediator Wayne County, Oakland County. Recipient Am. Jurisprudence Book award Am. Jurisprudence Soc., 1981. Mem. ABA, Oakland County Bar Assn., Oakland County Mediation, Wayne County Mediator Comml. Litigation Panel, State of Mich. Bar Assn., Chi Phi, Oakland County Real Property Sect. Roman Catholic. Office: Beir Howlett PC 200 E Long Lake Rd Ste 110 Bloomfield Hills MI 48304-2361

YAMMINE, MICHAEL RIAD, electrical engineering; b. Findlay, Ohio, Aug. 11, 1965; s. Riad Nassib and Beverly Ann (Hosack) Y.; m. Laurie Nicole Mullen, Dec. 1, 1990. BA in Elec. Engring., Ohio No. U. Project engr. Marathon Pipe Line Co., Martinsville, Ill., 1989-94; engr. info. svcs. Marathon Oil Co., Houston, 1994; elec. engr. TRW-Transp. Electronics, Marshall, Ill., 1994; mgr. application engring. Northwest Controls, Holland, Ohio, 1994—. Mem. IEEE, Instrument Soc. Am., Ohio Soc. Prof. Engrs., Findlay Amatuer Radio Club. Home: PO Box 527 681 N Main St Arlington OH 45814 Office: Northwest Controls 1142 Corp Dr Holland OH 43528

YAMOOR, MOHAMMED YOUNIS, livestock and agricultural development consultant; b. Mosul, Iraq, July 7, 1941; s. Younis Yousif and Sabiha Ziyada (Husein) Y.; m. Catherine Marie Hagen, Sept. 11, 1965; children: Nadia Marie, Omar Wayne. BS, U. Baghdad, 1962; MS, U. Minn., 1967, PhD, 1971. Prof., head dept. animal prodn. U. Tripoli, Libya, 1972-78; FAO-UN expert, Rome, 1978-79; Mid-East cons. agrl. devel. projects, 1979-83; FAO-UN livestock officer, Rome, Saudi Arabia, 1983-89, FAO-UN chief tech. advisor livestock devel., Yemen, 1989-93; FAO-UN cons. livestock devel., Somalia, 1993; cons. UNDP, N.Y., 1995. Mem. U. Minn. Alumni Assn., Sigma Xi.

YAN, HONG-CHENG, electrical engineering educator; b. Fuzhou, Fujian, China, May 28, 1947; came to U.S., 1983; s. Ziqi Yan and Ruiting Xu; divorced; 1 child, Qijia. BSin Elec. Phys. Engring., Harbin Poly. U., China, 1970; MSc in Engring. in Control Theory, Chinese Acad. Scis. Grad. Sch., 1981; PhD in Engring. Sci., Clarkson U., 1985; PhD in Elec. Engring., Purdue U., 1989. Cert. of tng. for patent examiner World Intellectual Property Orgn., UN, 1981. Elec. engr. Fujian Longyan Iron and Steel Co., 1970-82; trainee, practitioner U.K. Patent Office, London, 1980-81; applied software engr. Inst. Petroleum Exploration and Devel., Beijing, 1982-83; tchg. asst. Clarkson U., Potsdam, N.Y., 1983-85; rsch. asst. Purdue U., West Lafayette, Ind., 1986-88; asst. prof. elec. engring. Mo. Western State Coll., St. Joseph, 1989-94, assoc. prof., 1994—. Contbr. articles to profl. jours. Fellow World Intellectual Property Orgn., 1980. Mem. IEEE, Mo. Vocat. Assn. Home: 3029 Bristol St Saint Joseph MO 64506-1159 Office: Mo Western State Coll 4525 Downs Dr ET 189 Saint Joseph MO 64507-2294

YANCURA, ANN JOYCE, library director; b. Ft. Smith, Ark., Oct. 1, 1943; d. John Michael and Elizabeth Ann (Grcevic) Traub; m. Nicholas Daniel Yancura, Dec. 26, 1966; children: Daniel, Elizabeth. BA, U. Akron, 1965; MLS, Kent (Ohio) State U., 1982. Tchr. Akron Pub. Schs., 1966-70; mgr. SCM Corp., Strongsville, Ohio, 1982-85; exec. dir. Nola Regional Libr., Youngstown, Ohio, 1985-90, McKinley Meml. Libr., Niles, Ohio, 1990—. Bd. dirs. Info. Access, Foster City, Calif., 1993—; mem. Niles Hist. Soc., 1990—. Named Outstanding Grad., Kent State U./Crawford Bindery, 1982, Boss of the Yr., Am. Bus. Women, 1992, Outstanding Cmty. Leader, Youngstown Vidicator, 1993; recipient Recognition award Friends of Libr., Niles, 1992. Mem. ALA (mem. coms.), Ohio Libr. Assn. (bd. dirs., mem. coun.), Ohio Mus. Assn., Pub. Libr. Assn. (mem. coms.), Niles C. of C. (bd. dirs. 1991-94), Niles Rotary (bd. dirs. 1990—, Outstanding Svc. award 1992, 93, 94), Beta Phi Mu. Republican. Roman Catholic. Home: 2180 Brittainy Oaks Trail Warren OH 44484 Office: McKinley Meml Libr 40 N Main Niles OH 44446

YANG, HENRY T., university chancellor, educator; b. Chungking, China, Nov. 29, 1940; s. Chen Pei and Wei Gen Yang; m. Dilling Tsui, Sept. 2, 1966; children: Maria, Martha. BSCE, Nat. Taiwan U., 1962; MSCE, W.Va. U., 1965; PhD, Cornell U., 1968; Doctorate (hon.), Purdue U., 1996. Rsch. engr. Gilbert Assocs., Reading, Pa., 1968-69; asst. prof. Sch. Aeros. and Astronautics, Purdue U., West Lafayette, Ind., 1969-72, assoc. prof., 1972-76, prof., 1976-94, Neil A. Armstrong Disting. prof., 1988-94, sch. head, 1979-84; dean engring. Purdue U., 1984-94; chancellor U. Calif., Santa Barbara, 1994—; mem. sci. adv. bd. USAF, 1985-89; mem. aero. adv. com. NASA, 1985-89; mem. engring. adv. com. NSF, 1988-91; mem. mechanics bd. visitors ONR, 1990-93; mem. def. mfg. bd. DOD, 1988-89, def. sci. bd., 1989-91; mem. acad. adv. bd. Nat. Acad. Engring., 1991-94; mem. tech. adv. com. Pratt & Whitney, 1993-95; bd. dirs. Space Industries Internat., 1993-95; mem. Naval Rsch. Adv. Com., 1996—. Recipient 12 Best Tchg. awards Purdue U., 1971-94, Centennial medal Am. Soc. Engring. Edn., 1993. Fellow AIAA, ASEE; mem. NAE, Academia Sinica. Home: University House University Calif Santa Barbara CA 93106 Office: Chancellor's Office U California Santa Barbara CA 93106

YANG, RALPH TZU-BOW, chemical engineering educator, researcher; b. Chung King, China, Sept. 18, 1942; came to U.S., 1965, naturalized, 1976; s. Chen Pei and Wei (Gee) Y.; m. Frances H. Chang, Dec. 23, 1972; children—Michael, Robert. BS, Nat. Taiwan U., 1964; MS, Yale U., 1968, PhD, 1971. Rsch. assoc. Argonne Nat. Lab., Ill., 1972-73; sci. Aluminum Co. of Am., Pitts., 1973-74; group leader Brookhaven Nat. Lab., Upton, N.Y., 1974-78; assoc. prof. SUNY-Buffalo, 1978-82, prof., 1982—, chmn. chem. engring. dept., 1990-95; Praxair prof. chem. engring., chair, 1993-95, prof., chmn. chem. engring. dept. U. Mich., 1995—; cons. in field. Author: Gas Separation by Adsorption Processes, 1987. Contbr. articles to profl. jours. Patentee in field. Research grantee NSF, 1980—, Dept. Energy, 1980—, Alcoa Found., 1979-81. Fellow Am. Inst. Chem. Engring. (William H. Walker award for excellence in contbn. to chem. engring. lit., 1991); mem. Am. Chem. Soc. (Ind. Engring. Chem. Rsch. jour. adv. bd. 1991-93), Am. Carbon Soc. (adv. bd. 1985—), Am. Soc. Engring. Edn., Internat. Adsorption Soc. (adv. bd. Jour. of Adsorption 1993—), Adsorption Sci. and Tech. (adv. bd. 1986—). Office: U Mich Dept Chem Engring Ann Arbor MI 48109

YANIKOSKI, RICHARD ALAN, university president; b. Chicago Heights, Ill., Nov. 30, 1946; s. Florian Felix and Julia Gertrude (Smith) Y.; m. Wendy Kay Towner, June 25, 1977; children: Laura, Catherine, Kristin. BA, Stonehill Coll., 1968; PhD, U. Chgo., 1987. Evaluation coordinator DePaul U., Chgo., 1975-77; rsch. asst. Spencer Found., Chgo., 1977-78; dir. inst. planning and research DePaul U., Chgo., 1978-82, assoc. v.p. acad. affairs, 1983-91; assoc. prof., dir. Mgmt. Pub. Svcs. Program, 1991-94; dir. Chaddick Inst., 1993-94; pres. St. Xavier U., Chgo., 1994—. Contbg. author: Values in Conflict, 1986, Education in Massachusetts, 1989, Survey of Social Sciences: Government and Politics, 1995; mem. editl. bd. Jour. Mktg. in Higher Edn.; contbr. articles to profl. jours. Mem. Univ.-City Edn. Group, Chgo., 1986-87, Ill. Export Devel. Internship Com., 1985-88; mem. exec. com. Ill. Consortium Ednl. Opportunity, 1986-88; mem. adv. bd. St. Joseph Sch., La Porte, Ind., 1990-93; trustee Stonehill Coll., North Easton, Mass., 1995—; mem. exec. com. Fedn. Ind. Ill. Colls. and Univs., 1995—; chmn. Metro S.W. Alliance, 1996—. Research grantee Exxon Edn. Found., 1985. Mem. Assn. Instl. Rsch., Assn. Study Higher Edn., Am. Ednl. Rsch. Assn. Roman Catholic. Office: Saint Xavier Univ 3700 W 103rd St Chicago IL 60655-3105

YANKAITIS, MICHAEL JAMES, manufacturing engineer; b. Rockford, Ill., Sept. 7, 1962. B, U. Wis., 1986. Engring. mgr. Rockford Mfg., Roscoe, Ill., 1987-92, project engr., 1993—. Patentee in field (3). Fredine scholar. Mem. S.A.E., Pi Tau Sigma.

YANOS, J. EDWARD, farmer; b. Reading, Pa., Apr. 19, 1955; s. Joseph E. and Anna L. (Angstadt) Y.; m. Susan B. Rihm; children: Katherine, Allison. Attended, Purdue U., 1973-74. Owner, operator Yanos Farms, Cambridge City, Ind., 1975—; dir. Farmers Grain Co., Pershing, Ind., 1988—, Ind. Young Farmers Assn., Indpls., 1984, Ind. Corn Growers Assn., 1988—; pres. Ind. Corn Growers Assn., 1991-93. Mem. bd. trustees S. Henry Sch. Bd., Straughn, Ind., 1990-96, pres. 1993. Mem. Nat. Corn Growers Assn., Ind. Farm Bur. (county pres. 1989-91), Ind. Soybean Growers Assn., Optimists Internat.

YANOSKO, RAYMOND ANTHONY, retired educator, game company executive; b. Cleve., Sept. 25, 1929; s. Matthew and Veronica Marie (Mellicant) Y.; m. Anne Marie Dockendorf, June 23, 1956; children: Cecilia, Juanita, Michele, Jerome, Kevin, Mark, Peter, Clifford. Student, Benedictine U., Lisle, Ill., 1947-49; BA, St. John's U., 1952; A.Y.I., U. Minn., 1960; MA, Columbia Pacific U., 1979. Math. tchr. Benedictine High Sch., Cleve., 1952-55, Cathedral Latin Sch., Cleve., 1957-62, St. Joseph High Sch., Cleve., 1962-64, 67-69, Lake Catholic High Sch., Mentor, Ohio, 1974-88; printer, linotypist William J. Gall Printing Co., Cleve., 1945-62; sales mgr. World Book Ency., Cleve., 1964-67; office mgr. Plumbers Pipe & Supply Inc., Brooklyn Heights, Ohio, 1969-74; gen. mgr. Worlds Unlimited, Inc., Lakeline, Ohio, 1988-91; ret.; lectr. in field. Cpl. U.S. Army, 1955-62. Martha Holden Jennings Found. grantee, 1979, 80, 81. Democrat. Roman Catholic. Home: 18105 Windward Rd Cleveland OH 44119-1752

YANTIS, RICHARD PERRY, mathematics educator, consultant; b. Westerville, Ohio, July 1, 1932; s. Samuel Perry and Mabel Martha (Snook) Yantis; m. Jane McAllister, Oct. 10, 1959; children: John Perry, James Theodore. BS, U.S. Naval Acad., 1954; MA, U. N.C., 1962; PhD, Ohio State U., 1966. Commd. 2d lt. USAF, 1954, advanced thorugh grades to lt. col., 1969, served as transport navigator military air transp. service, 1956-57; instr., navigator USAF, McGuire AFB, N.J., 1957-60; instr. maths. USAF Acad., Colorado Springs, Colo., 1962-64, asst. to assoc. prof. maths., 1966-68, dep. chief enrichment br., dept math., 1968-69, chief advanced br. dept. math., 1969-70; reconnaissance navigator 553 Recon Squad, personnel officer USAF, Korat, Thailand, 1970-71; assoc. prof. ops. research AFIT USAF, Wright-Patterson AFB, Ohio, 1971-74; retired USAF, 1974; prin. systems analyst Battelle Research, Columbus, Ohio, 1974-75; instr. math. Columbus Acad., 1975-76; assoc. prof. Otterbein Coll., Westerville, Ohio, 1976-87, prof., 1987—; cons. actuarial dept. Nationwide Ins. Co., Columbus, 1965-66, asst. chief staff Studies and Analysis, Pentagon, 1967, USAF dir. Personnel Plans, Pentagon, 1972-73, OSD Manpower and Res. Affairs, Pentagon, 1973-74, Chas E Merrill Publ. Co., Westerville, Ohio, 1985-86. Co-author: Elementary Matrix Algebra with Linear Programming, 1971, Matrix Algebra with Applications, 1977; co-editor: Westerville, Ohio 1910 Census and Genealogical Data, 1985, Blendon Township, Ohio 1880 Census and Genealogical Data, 1987. Trustee Westerville Hist. Soc., 1985-86, 2d v.p., 1989-93. Mem. Nat. Coun. Tchrs. Math., Ret. Officers Assn., Westerville Internat. Rels. Club (pres. 1987-88, 89-90), Nat. Geneal. Soc., Franklin County Geneal. Soc., Ohio His. Soc., Md. Hist. Soc., Palatines to Am. Presbyterian. Home: 265 Storington Rd Westerville OH 43081-1318 Office: Otterbein Coll Math Dept Westerville OH 43081

YAPOUJIAN, NERSES NICK, manufacturing executive; b. Yerevan, Armenia, USSR, June 19, 1950; came to U.S., 1975; s. John and Sandought (Chekijian) Y. BSEE, BS in Physics, Yerevan Poly. Inst., Armenia, 1971; MSEE, MS in Physics, Yerevan Poly Inst., Armenia; B in English, Harvard U., 1973; postgrad. in engring., Northeastern U., Mass., 1978, Marquette U., 1980. Assoc. prof. physics Electrotech Coll., Yerevan, 1973-74; chief engr. Electric Light Corp., Yerevan, 1974-75; quality control specialist E.G. & G. Corp., Waltham, Mass., 1975-78; project leader Gen. Instrument Corp., Chgo., 1978-83; pres., chief exec. officer Gen. Protection Corp., Chgo., 1983—; internat. engring. cons Protel, Paris, 1986—, chmn., CEO Stress Mgmt. Group, Chgo., 1987—; chmn. bd. dirs. Employment Application Svc., Chgo., 1991—; translator/interpreter Cosmopolitan Trans. Bur., Inc., Chgo., 1983—. Sr. contbg. editor NBC Defense & Technolgy, 1985-87; contbr. articles to profl. jours.; patentee in field. Com. chmn. St. James Presbyn. Ch., 1988—. Sr. lt. Russian Army, 1973. Republican. Office: Gen Protection Corp PO Box 597631 Chicago IL 60659-7631

YARGER, LEROY ALLEN, minister; b. Starbuck, Minn., Feb. 25, 1942; s. Edwin James and Clarice Percile (Stenson) Y.; m. Janice Jeanette mcDowell, Aug. 29, 1964; children: Jonathan, Christopher. BA, St. Olaf Coll., 1964; BD, Luther Theol. Seminary, St. Paul, Minn., 1968. Pastor Calvary Luth. Ch., Orr, Minn., 1968-70, Camp Vermilion, Cook, Minn., 1968-70, Atonement Luth. Ch., Overland Park, Kans., 1970-75, Calvary Luth. Ch., Grand Forks, N.D., 1975-88, First Luth. Ch., Minot, N.D., 1988—; regent Concordia Coll., Moorhead, Minn., 1992—. Recipient Bush fellowship Bush Found., Mpls., 1984. Home: 515 Walders St Minot ND 58703

YARKONY, GARY MICHAEL, physician, researcher; b. N.Y.C., May 22, 1953; m. Kirsten Kohlmeyer; children: Judith, Rachel, Seth, Lauren. BA in Biology, SUNY, Buffalo, 1974; MD, SUNY, Syracuse, 1978; Master in Mgmt., Northwestern U., 1994. ;. Intern, then resident in physical medicine, rehab. Northwestern U., Chgo., 1978-81, chief resident dept. rehab. medicine, 1980; asst. dir. head trauma program Rehab. Inc. Chgo., 1981-84, attending staff, 1981-94; v.p. clin. program devel. Schwab Rehab. Hosp., Chgo., 1994—; clin. prof. sect. orthopaedic surgery and rehab. medicine U. Chgo. Med. Ctr., 1995—, clin. prof. dept. surgery and neurology, 1995—; attending physician Northwestern Meml. Hosp., Chgo., 1984-94; assoc. prof. dept. rehab. medicine Northwestern U. Med. Sch., 1985-94; adj. prof. Pritzker Inst. for Med. Engring., Ill. Inst. Tech., 1991—; dir. rehab. Midwest Regional Spinal Cord Injury Care Svs., Chgo., 1984-94. Contbr. articles to profl. jours. and chpts. to book. Fellow Am. Acad. Physical Medicine and Rehab.; mem. Assn. Academic Physiatrists, Am. Spinal Injury Assn., Internat. Med. Soc. Paraplegia, Internal Rehab. Medicine Assn., Phi Beta Kappa, Phi Eta Sigma. Office: Schwab Rehab Hosp 1401 S California Ave Chicago IL 60608-1612

YARNELL, JEFFREY ALAN, regional credit executive; b. Columbus, Ohio, Oct. 23, 1941; s. Russell Lester and Grace Wilma (Adams) Y.; m. Carroll Ginevra Meier, July 6, 1982; children: Natalie, Brian. Student, Ohio State U., 1963. Cert. credit exec. Nat. Assn. Credit Mgmt. Teller Huntington Nat. Bank, Columbus, Ohio, 1965-66; credit mgr. janitrol divsn. Midland Ross, Columbus, 1966-68; asst. credit mgr. Marlite divsn. Masonite, Dover, Ohio, 1968-72; v.p., gen. credit mgr. wholesale fl. coverings Carson Pirie Scott, Chgo., 1972-88; regional credit mgr. Ga.-Pacific Corp., Des Plaines, Ill., 1988—; bd. dirs. Chgo.-Midwest Credit Mgmt. Assn., 1991-94. Author: Credit Manual, 1978. Advisor Jr. Achievement, Dover, Ohio, 1969-70; mem. Toastmasters Internat., Columbus, Ohio, 1965-67; councilor Boy Scouts Am., Palos Heights, Ill., 1980-81. With USNR, 1963-65. Mem. Chgo.-Midwest Credit Mgmt. Assn. (bd. dirs. 1991-94). Republican. Lutheran. Office: Ga Pacific Corp 2300 Windy Ridge Pkwy SE Atlanta GA 30339

YARRINGTON, HOLLIS ROGER, communications administrator, editor; b. Des Moines, Oct. 17, 1931; s. Byron Odell and Leta Berniece (Winans) Y.; m. Lynda Carol Andersen, Aug. 11, 1957; children: Byron Peter, Douglas Kent, Jeffrey Scott. AA, Graceland Coll., 1951; BS, U. Kans., 1953; MA, U. Ia., 1956; Phd, U. Md., 1970. Editor Herald Pub. House, Independence, Mo., 1955-62; v.p. Am. Assn. of Community and Jr. Colleges, Washington D.C., 1963-82; assoc. dean College of Journalism, U. Md., College Park, Md., 1982-84; communications dir. Reorganized Church of Jesus Christ of Latter Day Saints, Independence, Mo., 1985-96. Author Community Relations Handbook, 1983. Bd. dirs. Independence Rotary Club, pres., 1996—; bd. dirs. Uptown Independence Inc., Independence Cmty. Found., Comprehensive Mental Health Svcs. Found.; chmn. Tourism Adv. Bd., 1990, 91. Mem. Pub. Rels. Soc. Am. (coll. of fellows; pres. Greater Kansas City chpt.), Independence C. of C. (chmn. 1993, bd. dirs., Disting. Citizen award 1995). Mem. Reorganized LDS Ch. Office: Herald Pub House 3225 S Noland Rd Independence MO 64055

YASENKA, DEBRA ANN, software consulting company executive; b. Plainfield, N.J., June 16, 1950; d. Ronald Howard and Irene Quadt; m. Robert Charles Yasenka, Mar. 17, 1973; children: Nancy, Robby. BBA, Kent State U., 1972. Asst. supr. Ea. Air Lines, N.Y.C., 1972-77; account exec. Sales Cons., Inc., Southfield, Mich., 1985-86; br. mgr. Analytical Techs., Inc., St. Paul, 1986-88, regional mgr., 1988-90; v.p. Analytical Techs., Inc., Bingham Farms, Mich., 1990-94; pres. Visual Sys. Devel. Group, Troy, Mich., 1994-96; dist. mgr. PowerCerv Corp., Tampa, Fla., 1996—; cons., trainer in field. Com. chair Jr. Woman's League, Canfield, Ohio, 1984-85. Athena award finalist, 1992; named Profl. Woman of Yr. St. Paul Area C. of C. Mem. NAFE, Data Processing Mgmt. Assn., Forest Lake Country Club, Dellwood Hills Golf Club (social chmn. 1989-90). Home: 4611 Brightmore Rd Bloomfield Hills MI 48302-2123 Office: PowerCerv Corp 1301 West Lone Lake Rd Ste 236 Troy MI 48084

YATES, DAN CHARLES, insurance company official; b. Spring Valley, Ill., Oct. 14, 1952; s. Earl John Jr. and Charlotte Elaine (Sandberg) Y.; m. Margaret Mary McBride, Mar. 1, 1980; 1 child, Keith. B Bus. in Fin., Western Ill. U., 1977. CPCU. Claims adjuster G.A.B. Bus. Svcs., Kansas City, Mo., 1978-80; claims mgr. Dodson Group, Kansas City, 1980—; mem. conf. com. Property Loss Rsch. Bur., Schaumburg, Ill., 1994-96, vice chair, 1994-95, chair, 1995-96; adv. coun. midwest region Nat. Assn. Ind. Ins. Adjusters, 1986-89, mem. Credit Com. for Bee Dee Co. Credit Union, 1992— (pres., chair 1994—). Vol. Jr. Achievement. With U.S. Army, 1972-74. Mem. Kansas City Property Claims Assn. (pres. 1992). Office: Dodson Group 9201 State Line Rd Kansas City MO 64114

YATES, ROBERT ALLEN, English language educator; b. Berwyn, Ill., Feb. 4, 1950; s. Jesse Howard Yates and Charlotte Rose (Vavrik) Gettman; m. Maria Jeanne Gerdes, May 10, 1970 (div. Oct. 1975); m. Karin Christa Mühlnickel, June 18, 1982. BS in Comm. Studies, Northwestern U., 1982; MA in TESL, U. Ill., Chgo., 1982; PhD in Applied Linguistics, U. Ill., Urbana, 1990. Teaching asst. U. Ill., Champaign-Urbana, 1984; assoc. prof. English Ctrl. Mo. State U., Warrensburg, 1990—; adj. instr. Nat.-Louis U., Chgo., 1982-84; mem. ESL Facilitators for State of Mo., Jefferson City, 1992—. Contbr. articles and revs. to profl. jours. Mem. adv. bd. West Ctrl. Citizens for Choice, Warrensburg, 1991—. Mem. Mid Am. TESOL (pres. 1995-96), Assembly for the Teaching of English Grammar (v.p. 1995—), Linguistics Soc. Am., TESOL, Nat. Coun. Tchrs. of English, Mo. Philological Assn. (treas. 1992—). Democrat. Office: Ctrl Mo State U Dept English Warrensburg MO 64093

YATES, SIDNEY RICHARD, congressman, lawyer; b. Chicago, Ill., Aug. 27, 1909; s. Louis and Ida (Siegel) Y.; m. Adeline Holleb, June 24, 1935; 1 child, Stephen R. Ph.B., U. Chgo., 1931, J.D., 1933. Bar: Ill. bar 1933. Practiced as sr. mem. Yates & Holleb; asst. atty. Ill. State Bank Receiver, 1935-37; asst. atty. gen. attached as traction atty. Ill. Commerce Commn., 1937-40; mem. 80th-87th, 89th-104th Congresses from 9th Dist. Ill., 1949-62, 1965—; ranking minority mem. Appropriations subcoms. on the Interior; U.S. del. UN Trusteeship Council with rank of ambassador. Served to lt. USN, 1944-46. Recipient Joseph Henry medal Smithsonian Instn., 1995. Mem. Am., Ill. State, Chgo. bar assns., Am. Vets. Com., Chgo. Council Fgn. Relations, Decalogue Soc. Lawyers. Democrat. Jewish. Clubs: City, Bryn Mawr Country. Office: US House of Reps 2109 Rayburn House Bldg Washington DC 20515-1309*

YATES, VIVIAN MARIE, nurse educator; b. Elyria, Ohio, July 15, 1952; d. James William and Nellie Sue (Corn) Shores; children: Andre, Eric and Leslie Board; m. Edward William Yates, Mar. 17, 1990. ADN, Lorain County Community Coll., 1980; BSN, U. Akron, 1987; MSN, Kent State U., 1994. Staff nurse, float nurse Elyria (Ohio) Meml. Hosp., 1980-87; nurse mgr. Lorain (Ohio) Community Hosp., 1987-88, nurse case coord., 1988-89; faculty practical nursing Lorain County C.C., 1989—; occupational health nurse GM Corp., Elyria, 1983-84. Mem. ANA, Nat. League Nursing (coun. of practical nursing programs), Ohio Nurses Assn., Midwest Nurses Rsch. Soc., Ohio Orgn. Practical Nurse Educators, Sigma Theta Tau. Democrat. Office: Lorain County CC 1005 Abbe Rd N Elyria OH 44035-1613

YEAGER, ANSON ANDERS, columnist, former newspaper editor; b. Salt Lake City, June 5, 1919; s. Charles Franklin and Elise Marie (Thingelstad) Y.; m. Ada May Bidwell, Sept. 10, 1944; children: Karen Ann, Anson Anders, Harry H., Terry Douglas, Ellen Elise. BS, S.D. State U., Brookings, 1947; LLD, Dakota State Coll., Madison, S.D., 1972; D of Pub. Svc. (hon.) S.D. State U., 1991. Printer's devil, linotype operator Faith Ind. and Gazette (S.D.), 1935-38; printer S.D. State U., 1940-41; staff writer Argus Leader, Sioux Falls, S.D., 1947-55, Sunday editor, 1955-60, exec. editor, 1961-77, assoc. editor, 1978-84, editor editorial page, 1961-84, columnist, 1984—, author Travel articles and commentary; lectr. dept. journalism U. S.D., 1953-55. Contbr. World Book Ency., 1966-84. Bd. dirs. Sioux Falls Devel. Found., 1967; bd. dirs. S.D. State U. Found., 1987—, chmn., 1988-89; dir. Sioux council Boy Scouts Am., Sioux Falls, 1967-72, v.p., 1970-72; bd. dirs. Boys' Club of Sioux Falls, 1966-68. Capt. U.S. Army, 1942-46, 50-52; lt. col. Res. (ret.). Decorated Army Commendation medal; recipient Editorial Excellence award William Allen White Found., 1976; Disting. Alumni award S.D. State U., 1980; Friend of Augustana Coll. award Augustana Coll. Alumni Assn., 1980; Ralph D. Casey Minn. award for Disting. Svc. in Journalism U. Minn., 1981, Eminent Service award East River Elec. Power Coop., 1984, Mass Communications award S.D. State U., 1985, Disting. Svc. award S.D. Press Assn., 1988, Les Helgeland Community Svc. award S.D. AP Mng. Editors, 1985, named Newsman of Yr., 1978, South Dakota A.H. Pankow award, 1995; named to S.D. Newspaper Hall of Fame, 1994. Mem. Sioux Falls Area C. of C. (dir. 1967-70), Am. Soc. Newspaper Editors, Soc. Profl. Journalists, Rotary. Republican. Methodist.

YEAGER, DAVID LEROY, utility company executive; b. Youngstown, Ohio, Feb. 12, 1935; s. LeRoy and Marjorie (Ballington) Y.; m. Margaret Scott; children: David, Karen Fetterhoff, Ellen. BEME, Youngstown State U., 1959. Registered profl. engr., Ohio. Superintendent of electric and steam sales Ohio Edison Co., Youngstown, 1968-70; dir. comml. indsl. mktg. Ohio Edison Co., Akron, Ohio, 1971-76, project coordination mgr., 1976-78, asst. to exec. v.p., 1978-79, asst. to pres., 1980-85, v.p., 1985—. Active Summit County unit Am. Cancer Soc., Akron, v.p., 1979-81, pres., 1981-83, bd. dirs., trustee Ohio divsn., 1991—, chmn. bd. trustees, 1994—; trustee Healthaven Nursing Home, 1984—. Mem. ASME, NSPE, ASHRAE, Akron City Club, Harvard Bus. Sch. Club. Office: Ohio Edison Co 76 S Main St Akron OH 44308

YEAGER, JOSEPH HEIZER, JR., lawyer; b. Indpls., Jan. 8, 1957; s. Joseph Heizer and Marilyn Virginia (Hillyard) Y.; m. Candance A. Grass, June 2, 1984; children: Samuel, Henry. AB cum laude, Harvard U., 1979; JD cum laude, Ind. U., 1983. Bar: Ind. 1983, U.S. Dist. Ct., (so. and no. dist.) Ind. 1983, U.S. Ct. Appeals (7th cir.) 1986, U.S. Supreme Ct. 1996. Dir. ops. Penn and Schoen Assocs., N.Y.C., 1979-80; assoc. Baker & Daniels, Indpls., 1983-89, ptnr., 1990—. Pres. Indpls. Legal Aid Soc., 1992-94; chmn. Indpls. Com. for UNICEF, 1986-91; mem. Indpls. Com. for Fgn. Affairs, 1986-91. Mem. Ind. Bar Assn., Indpls. Bar Assn. (litigation sect.

exec. com. 1985-86, 1996—). Democrat. Office: Baker & Daniels 300 N Meridian St # 2700 Indianapolis IN 46204-1755

YEAMANS, GEORGE THOMAS, librarian, educator; b. Richmond, Va., Nov. 7, 1929; s. James Norman and Dolphine Sophia (Manhart) Y.; m. Mary Ann Seng, Feb. 1, 1958; children: Debra, Susan, Julia. AB, U. Va., 1950; MLS, U. Ky., 1955; EdD, Ind. U., 1965. Asst. audio-visual dir. Ind. State U., Terre Haute, 1957-58; asst. film librarian Ball State U., Muncie, Ind., 1958-61, film librarian, 1961-69, assoc. prof. libr. sci., 1969-72, prof., 1972-95; prof. emeritus, 1995—; cons. Pendleton (Ind.) Sch. Corp., 1962, 67, Captioned Films for the Deaf Workshop, Muncie, Ind., 1963, 64, 65, Decatur (Ind.) Sch. System, 1978; adjudicator Ind. Media Fair, 1979-93, David Letterman Scholarship Program, 1993. Author: Projectionists' Programmed Primer, 1969, rev. edit., 1982; Mounting and Preserving Pictorial Materials, 1976; Tape Recording, 1978; Transparency Making, 1977; Photographic Principles, 1981; Computer Literacy—A Programmed Primer, 1985; songwriter Branson Bound, 1996; contbr. articles to profl. jours. Campaign worker Wilson for Mayor, Muncie, Ind., 1979. Served with USMC, 1950-52. Recipient Citations of Achievement, Internat. Biog. Assn., Cambridge, Eng., 1973, Am. Biog. Assn., 1976, Mayor James P. Carey award for achievement for disting. contbns. to Ball State U. and City of Muncie, 1988; Video Information Systems grantee Ball State U., 1993. Mem. NEA (del. assembly dept. audiovisual instrn. 1967), Audio-Visual Instrn. Dirs. Ind. (exec. bd. 1962-68, pres. 1966-67), Ind. Assn. Ednl. Communications and Tech. (dist. dir. 1972-75), Assn. Ind. Media Educators (chmn. auditing com. 1979-81), Am. Film Inst., Autism Soc. Am., Assn. Ednl. Comm. & Tech., Phi Delta Kappa. Republican. Unitarian. Home: 4507 W Burton Dr Muncie IN 47304-3575

YEAZEL, KEITH ARTHUR, lawyer; b. Fayetteville, N.C., Feb. 14, 1956; s. Russell E. and Barbara E. (Weaver) Y.; m. Deborah M. MacDonald, Aug. 30, 1986. BA, Ohio State U., 1983; JD, Capital U., 1989. Bar: Ohio 1989, U.S. Dist. Ct. (so. dist.) Ohio 1989, U.S. Ct. Appeals (6th cir.) 1990, U.S. Supreme Ct. 1992. Law clk. to judge George C. Smith U.S. Dist. Ct., Columbus, Ohio, 1988-89; prin. Keith A. Yeazel, Atty. at Law, Columbus, 1989—. Mem. ABA, Ohio Bar Assn., Columbus Bar Assn., Nat. Assn. Criminal Def. Lawyers, Ohio Assn. Criminal Def. Lawyers, Order of Curia. Republican. Lutheran. Office: 65 S 5th St Columbus OH 43215-4353

YELON, WILLIAM B., physicist, researcher; b. Brooklyn, N.Y., Aug. 23, 1944; s. Martin and Fanny (Salzman) Y.; m. Harriet Gale Most, July 16, 1978; children: Joshua Michael, Rachel Samara, Sasha Max (dec.), Jessica Leigh. BA, Haverford Coll., 1965; MS, Carnegie-Mellon, 1967, PhD, 1970. Physicist Institut Lave-Langevin, Grenoble, France, 1972-75; group leader crystal and magnetic structures U. Mo. Rsch. Reactor, Columbia, 1975—; group leader neutron scattering, 1975—; assoc. prof. U. Mo., Columbia, 1984—; cons. GM Rsch., Warren, Mich., 1980-92, Ovonic Synthetic Materials, Troy, Mich., 1987-94; investigator U. Mo., Rolla, 1992—. Editor Jour. Applied Physics; contbr. more than 200 articles to profl. jours. Grantee Dept. of Energy, NSF, NATO; recipient award Sigma Xi, 1984, Chancellors award 1986. Mem. Am. Phys. Soc., Materials Rsch. Soc. (steering com., publ. chair ann. conf. on magnetism and magnetic materials 1988-94, treas. ann. conf. on magnetism and magnetic materials 1995—). Jewish. Home: 1309 Overhill Ct Columbia MO 65203-1521 Office: U Mo Rsch Reactor Physics Dept Columbia MO 65211

YELTON, STEVEN JOHN, electronics educator; b. Ft. Thomas, Ky., July 16, 1957. AAS, Cin. Tech. Coll., 1977; BSEE, Ohio State U., 1982. Registered profl. engr., Ohio. Design engr. Foster Transformer Co., Cin., 1977-82; rsch. asst. dept. chemistry Ohio State U., Columbus, 1978-82; program chmn. Cin. (Ohio) Tech. Coll., 1982—; cons. Work Place, Inc., Cin., 1984—; advisor No. Ky. U., Highland Heights, 1992—. Mem. IEEE, Assn. for the Advancement Med. Instrumentation, Am. Soc. Engring. Educators. Office: Cin State Tech and CC 3520 Central Pky Cincinnati OH 45223-2690

YEN, DAVID CHI-CHUNG, management information systems educator; b. Tai-Chung, Taiwan, Republic of China, Nov. 15, 1953; s. I-King and Chi-Ann (Ro) Y.; m. Wendy Wen-Yawn Ding, July 4, 1981; children: Keeley Ju, Caspar Lung, Christopher Jai. MBA in Gen. Bus., Cen. State U., Edmond, Okla., 1981, BS in Computer Sci., 1982; MS in Computer Sci., PhD in Mgmt. Info. Systems, U. Nebr., 1985. Asst. prof. Miami U., Oxford, Ohio, 1985-89, assoc. prof., 1989-93, prof., 1994—, MIS advisor computer study com., 1986—; asst. chmn., 1993-95; chmn. Miami U., Oxford, Ohio, 1995—; sr. faculty teaching excellence, 1994; chmn., mem. computer policy com. Miami U., 1991-94, computer adv. group, 1993-94, com. evaluation adminstrs., 1993, conf. and session chair, seminar dir., Smucker prof. internship. Contbr. articles to profl. jours. Served to 2d lt., Rep. China Navy. Alumni teaching scholar Miami U., 1987-88; named Prof. of Yr. Delta Sigma Pi, 1993; GE grantee, Cleve. Found. grantee. Mem. IEEE, Soc. Info. Mgmt., Internat. Sch. Bus. Computer User Group (chair conf., proceedings editor 1988), Assn. Computing Machinery, Ohio Mgmt. Info. System Assn., Decision Sci. Inst., Soc. Data Educators. Office: Miami U 309 Upham Hall Oxford OH 45056

YEN, YI-MEI, clinic nurse; b. Kaohsiung, Taiwan, Republic of China, May 11, 1962; d. Chin-Chang Yen and Ai-Kuei Tsai; children: Gabriel Chou, Raphael Chou. BSN, Taipei (Taiwan) Med. Coll., 1985; MSN, U. Mo., 1993. Charge nurse Cathay Gen. Hosp., Taipei, 1985-87; clin. instr. Mei-Ho Jr. Coll. Nursing, Pingtung, Taiwan, 1987-88; clinic nurse Clark County Health Dept., Jeffersonville, Ind., 1993—; teaching asst. U. Mo., 1992. Baptist. Home: 107 Fenley Ave Apt G5 Louisville KY 40207-2516

YESILADA, BIROL ALI, political science educator; b. Nicosia, Cyprus, Aug. 12, 1956; came to U.S., 1971; s. Ali and Sermin (Mustafa) Y.; m. Susan Diana Lesea, Aug. 20, 1980; children: Sermin, Selin. AB, U. Calif., Berkeley, 1977; MA, San Francisco State U., 1979; PhD, U. Mich., 1984. Vis. asst. prof. U. Mo., Columbia, 1984-85, asst. prof., 1985-91; vis. asst. prof. Middle East Tech. U., Ankara, Turkey, 1987-88; vis. rsch. specialist State Planning Orgn., Ankara, Turkey, 1987-88; assoc. prof. U. Mo., Columbia, 1991—, chair dept. polit. sci., 1994—; pres. Oceania Corp., 1992—; cons. State Planning Orgn., Ankara, 1987-88, Libr. of Congress, Washington, 1988-92, Coun. on Fgn. Rels., N.Y.C., 1990-91, U.S. State Dept. Fgn. Svc. Inst., 1995—, Nat. Intelligence Coun., Washington, 1996, U.S. Inst. Peace, 1996; chair internat. studies adv. com. U. Mo., Columbia, 1992-94. Author, co-editor: Agrarian Reform in Reverse: The Food Crisis in the Third World, 1987, The Political and Socioeconomic Transformation of Turkey, 1993; co-author: The Emerging European Union, 1995; mem. editl. bd. Cyprus Rev. Jour., 1987—, New Perspectives on Turkey, 1987-95; contbr. articles to profl. jours. Bd. dir. U. Mo. Peace Studies, Columbia, 1988-92. Rsch. fellow Am. Coun. Learned Socs. and Social Sci. Rsch. Coun., 1987, Fulbright-Hays, 1982, Turkish Econ. and Social Studies Found. of Eczacibasi Holding, 1995, William T. Kemper fellow for tchng. excellence U. Mo. and Commerce Bank, 1996; recipient Purple Chalk Teaching Excellence award U. Mo., Columbia Arts and Scis. Coll., 1991; rsch. bd. grantee U. Mo., 1996. Mem. Am. Polit. Sci. Assn., European Community Studies Assn., Middle East Studies Assn., Columbia Rotary Club. Muslim. Home: 1700 Princeton Dr Columbia MO 65203-1851

YETMAN, NORMAN ROGER, sociology educator; b. N.Y.C., Jan. 10, 1938; s. Norman Charles and Lucile (Darling) Y.; m. Anne Steuer Bishop, July 25, 1964; children: Barbara Jill, Norman Douglas. BA, U. Redlands, Calif., 1960; MA, U. Pa., 1961, PhD, 1969. Instr. sociology U. Redlands, 1962-63; asst. prof. Am. studies and sociology U. Kans., Lawrence, 1966-71, assoc. prof., 1971-77, prof., 1977-92, Chancellors Club teaching prof., 1992—, chair Am. Studies Program, 1973-81, 93-96, chair dept. sociology, 1986-89; sr. rsch. fellow Johns Hopkins U., Balt., 1972-73; Fulbright prof. Odense U., U. Copenhagen, 1981-82. Editor: Life Under the "Peculiar Institution," 1970, 76, Majority and Minority, 1971, 75, 82, 85, 91; co-author: Sociology, 1979, 6th editor., 1995. Democrat. Methodist. Home: 1637 Louisiana St Lawrence KS 66044-4053 Office: U Kans Dept Sociology Lawrence KS 66045

YFF, PETER, mathematics educator; b. Chgo., Mar. 8, 1924; s. Nicholas and Agnes (Ooms) Y.; m. Ellen Prodan, Feb. 10, 1951 (div. May 1979); children: Catherine, Philip, David, Eric; m. Juliette Haddad, July 7, 1979. BS, Roosevelt Coll., 1947; MS, U. Chgo., 1948; PhD, U. Ill., 1957. Instr. Roosevelt Coll., Chgo., 1948-50; asst. prof. Am. U., Beirut, Lebanon, 1951-55, Fresno (Calif.) State Coll., 1957-58; assoc. prof. Am. U., Beirut, 1958-64; rsch. fellow U. Toronto, 1964-65; prof. Am. U., Beirut, 1964-88; vis. lectr. U. Louisville, 1987-88; vis. prof. Ball State U., Muncie, Ind., 1988—. Contbr. articles to profl. jours. Lt. (j.g.) USNR, 1943-46. Mem. AAUP, Am. Math. Soc., Math. Assn. Am., Iranian Math. Soc., Edinburgh Math. Soc. Home: 3109 W Riggin Rd Muncie IN 47304-1030 Office: Ball State Univ Math Dept Muncie IN 47306

YIANNIAS, NANCY MAGAS, municipal official; b. Kalamazoo, Feb. 1, 1936; d. George A. and Irene (Callas) Magas; m. Andrew Chris Yiannias, Oct. 20, 1968; 1 child, Chris Andrew. BA, Western Mich. U., 1957; MPH, U. Mich., 1963. Registered sanitarian, Ill. Health educator Stickney Pub. Health Dist., Burbank, Ill., 1966-72, Chgo. Heart Assn., 1972-73; health coord. Village of Elk Grove, Ill., 1974—. Bd. counselors Alexian Bros. Med. Ctr., Elk Grove Village, 1977-93. Mem. Am. Pub. Health Assn., Ill. Pub. Health Assn. (sec. 1981), Soc. Pub. Health Educators, Ill. Soc. Pub. Health Educators (program planning com. 1966), Ill. Environ. Health Assn., N.W. Suburban Access to Care Assn. Home: 1521 Manor Ln Park Ridge IL 60068-1541 Office: Elk Grove Village Dept Health 901 Wellington Ave Elk Grove Village IL 60007

YIH, CHIA-SHUN, fluid mechanics educator; b. Kweiyang, Kweichow, China, July 25, 1918; s. Ting-Jian and Wan-Lan (Shiao) Y.; m. Shirley Gladys Ashman, Feb. 17, 1949; children: Yiu-Yo, Yuen-Ming David, Weiling Katherine. BS, Nat. Central U., 1942; MS, U. Iowa, 1947, PhD, 1948. Instr. Nat. Kweichow U., 1944-45; instr. math. U. Wis., 1948-49; lectr. U. B.C., 1949-50; assoc. prof. Colo. State U., 1950-52; rsch. engr. U. Iowa, 1952-54, assoc. prof., 1954-56; assoc. prof. U. Mich., Ann Arbor, 1956-58; prof. U. Mich., 1958-68, Stephen P. Timoshenko Disting. univ. prof. fluid mechanics, 1968-88, S.P. Timoshenko Disting. univ. prof. emeritus, 1988—; grad. rsch. prof. U. Fla., 1987-90, grad. rsch. prof. emeritus, 1990—; vis. prof. U. Paris, U. Grenoble, France, 1970-71; Henry Russel lectr. U. Mich., 1974; lectr. Chinese Acad. Sci., Beijing, 1981, von Kármán Inst., Brussels, 1981, Internat. Ctr. of Theoretical Physics, Trieste, Italy, 1994, Cheng Kung U., Tainan, Taiwan, 1995; G.I. Taylor lectr. U. Fla., 1992; hon. prof. U. Hong Kong, 1996—; cons. Huyck Felt Co., 1960-64; trustee Rocky Mountain Hydraulic Lab., 1976-85; attachè de recherche in math. French Govt., 1951-52. Author: Dynamics of Nonhomogeneous Fluids, 1965, Fluid Mechanics, An Introduction to the Theory, 1969, 79, 88, Stratified Flows, 1980; editor: Advances in Applied Mechanics, 1970-82; mem. editl. bd. Advances in Applied Mechanics, Physics of Fluids, 1969-72, SIAM Jour. Applied Math., 1971-72, Ann. Revs. of Fluid Mechanics, 1969-72, Advances in Mechanics of China, Acta Mechanica Sinica, Applied Math. and Mechanics, to 1989, Jour. Hydrodynamics, to 1989; contbr. articles to profl. jours. Recipient Achievement award Chinese Inst. Engrs. N.Y., 1968, Achievement award Chinese Engrs. and Scientists Assn. So. Calif., 1973, Sr. Scientist award Humboldt Found., Fed. Republic Germany, 1977-78, Theodore von Kármán medal ASCE, 1981, Stephen S. Attwood award U. Mich., 1984; sr. postdoctoral fellow NSF, 1959-60, Guggenheim fellow, 1964. Fellow Am. Phys. Soc. (chmn. exec. com. fluid dynamics divsn. 1973-74, Fluid Dynamics prize 1985, Otto Laporte award 1989); mem. U.S. Nat. Acad. Engring., Academia Sinica, Sigma Xi, Pi Mu Epsilon, Tau Beta Pi, Phi Kappa Phi. Home: 3530 W Huron River Dr Ann Arbor MI 48103-9417 Home (winter): 4084 NW 23d Cir Gainesville FL 32605

YIN, PHILIPPA BROWN, Spanish language and literature educator; b. San Antonio, Tex., Nov. 7, 1942; d. Alvin George and Margaret Lorena (Finch) Brown; m. Khin Maung Yin, Oct. 12, 1964; children: Jordan Shein, Lorena Elizabeth. BA, Oberlin (Ohio) Coll., 1964; MA, Pa. State U., 1968; PhD, Case Western Reserve U., 1978. Lectr. Cleve. State U., 1972-78, asst. prof., 1978—; faculty cons. advanced placement Ednl. Testing Svc. Princeton, N.J., 1992-96. Editor: (book) Studies in Honor of Donald W. Bleznick, 1995; contbr. chpts. to. Dictionary of Mexican Literature, 1993 (Best Reference award 1994), El Teatro Español del Siglo XX, De lo Particular al Universal, 1994, Creative Approaches to Foreign Language Teaching, 1992. Prin. violist, Cleve. Philharmonic Orch., 1993—; trustee Cleve. Chamber Music Soc., 1992—. Mem. Am. Assn. Tchrs. of Spanish and Portugese, Ohio Fgn. Lang. Tchrs. Assn., Sigma Delta Pi. Office: Cleve State Univ Dept Modern Langs Cleveland OH 44115

YIN, RAYMOND WAH, radiologist; b. Canton, Republic of China, July 2, 1938; came to U.S., 1972; m. Jean Youe Mok, Jan. 29, 1967; children: Linda, Dany, Judy. MD, Sun Yat Sen U., Canton, 1961, Nat. Taiwan U., 1965. Diplomate Am. Bd. Radiology, Am. Bd. Nuclear Medicine. Intern Victoria Gen. Hosp., Dalhausie U., Halifax, Nova Scotia, Can., 1967-68; resident Royal Victoria Hosp., McGill U., Montreal, Que., 1968-72; staff radiologist St. Francis Hosp., Hartford, 1972-75; radiologist St. Joseph Hosp., Bloomington, Ill., 1975-89, Menonnite Brakaw Hosp., Normal, Ill., 1975—; practice medicine specializing in radiology Bloomington, 1975—; asst. prof. radiology U. Ill., Peoria, 1980—, So. Ill. U., 1988—. Fellow Royal Coll. Physicians of Can. Home: 4210 E Quail Ave Las Vegas NV 89120

YING, JOHN L., manufacturing executive; b. Shanghai, Chiang-Su, People's Republic of China, June 15, 1948; came to U.S., 1970; s. D.C. and W.T. (Ma) Y.; m. Cynthia C. Chen, Apr. 7, 1981; children: Janice, Jonathan. BS, Tatung Inst. Tech., Taipei, Taiwan, 1969; MS, Poly. Inst. Bklyn., 1972; Profl. Engrs. Degree, Columbia U., N.Y.C., 1974. Application engr. Summit Engring Co., Taipei, 1969-70; asst. to pres. James Betesh Import Co., N.Y.C., 1972-73; strategic planner GM, Detroit, 1973-79; asst. to pres. Lawless Detroit Diesel Corp., City of Industry, Calif., 1979-81; pres., chief exec. officer Cen. Power Products, Inc., Liberty, Mo., 1981—, also bd. dirs.; bd. dirs. Cen. Mfg., Inc., Grandview, Mo., USA-China C. of C. Dir. adv. bd. Mark Twin Banks, Kansas City, Mo.; mem. Clay County (Mo.) Econ. Devel. Coun., 1984—; mem. Rep. Senatorial Inner Circle, Washington, 1985—. Recipient Outstanding Minority Bus. Enterprise award Minority Bus. Devel. Agy., Kansas City/Washington, 1986. Mem. USA-China C. of C., Kansas City Club, Hallbrook Country Club.

YINGER, MARY ANN, neonatology nurse; b. Zanesville, Ohio, Mar. 13, 1958; d. Raphael J. and Verna S. (Crock) Y. BSN, Capital U., 1982. Staff nurse Children's Hosp., Columbus, Ohio, 1982-90, clin. nurse III, 1990—; creator, chairperson Cost Awareness Com., Columbus, 1985—; cert. counselor Bereavement Com., Columbus, 1991—. Residential crusader Am. Cancer Soc., Columbus, 1987—. Mem. Nat. Assn. Neonatal Nurses, Ctrl. Ohio Assn. Neonatal Nurses (sec. 1993—, chair comms. com.). Democrat. Roman Catholic. Home: 5405 Paladim Rd Columbus OH 43232-5442

YOAKAM, MARVIN C., telephone company executive; b. Mt. Vernon, Ohio, Mar. 6, 1948; s. Carroll Cunningham and Edna Monima (Cochran) Y, .; m. Linda Jane Rafert, May 25, 1980; 1 child, William Edward. BA, Western Ky. U., 1970; MS, Purdue U., 1973, PhD, 1983. Grad. teaching asst. Purdue U., W. Lafayette, Ind., 1973-83; vis. asst. prof. physics Wabash Coll., Crawfordsville, Ind., 1983; software engr. AT&T Bell Labs., Naperville, Ill., 1985-89; staff engr. Gen. Systems Group Motorola, Inc., Arlington Heights, Ill., 1989-91; owner, mgr. Konnections Cons. Svcs., Naperville, 1991—; owner, mgr. Konnections Cons. Svcs., Naperville. Contbr. articles to profl. jours. Mem. Am. Inst. Physics, Sigma Pi Sigma. Office: Konnections Cons Svcs 5S 786 Timberlane Dr Naperville IL 60563

YOCKIM, JAMES CRAIG, state senator, oil and gas executive; b. Williston, N.D., Feb. 13, 1953; s. Daniel and Doris (Erickson) Y.; m. Donna Jean Erickson, Apr. 21, 1985; children: Jenna, Ericka. BSW, Pacific Luth. U., 1975; MSW, San Diego State U., 1979. Caseworker Dyslin Boys Ranch, Tacoma, 1975-77; landman Fayette Oil & Gas, Williston, 1980-82; head caseworker, program dir. Pyslin Boys Ranch, 1979-80; owner Hy-Plains Energy, Williston, 1982-87; city fin. commr. City of Williston, 1984-88; therapist Luth. Social Svcs., Williston, 1983-95; senator N.C. State Senate, 1986—; owner James C. Yockim Resources, Williston, 1987—. Dir. Bethel Luth. Found., 1993—; del. N.D. Dem. Conv., 1984, 86, 88, 90, 92, 94, 96; dist. chmn. Dem. Party, Williston, 1988; caucus chmn. Dem. Caucus N.D. State Senate. Recipient Ruth Meiers award N.D. Mental Health Assn., 1989, Legislator of Yr. award N.D. Children's Caucus, 1989; named Outstanding Young North Dakotan N.D. Jaycees, 1988. Mem. NASW. Home: 1123 2nd Ave E Williston ND 58801 Office: 322 Main Ste 202 PO Box 2344 Williston ND 58802-2344

YODER, ANNA A., elementary school educator; b. Beach City, Ohio, Sept. 5, 1934; d. Abram J. and Barbara D. (Miller) Y. BS, Ea. Mennonite Coll., 1966; MEd, Frostburg State Coll., 1974. Cert. elem. tchr., Ohio, recreational leader. Tchr. Garrett County Schs., Oakland, Md., 1966-70; prin. elem. sch. Garrett County Schs., 1970-74; tchr. E. Holmes Local Schs., Berlin, Ohio, 1974—; chairperson edn. com. German Culture Mus., Berlin, Ohio, 1987-90; cons. bilingual edn. E. Holmes Local Schs., Berlin, Ohio, 1982—. Supporting mem. German Culture Mus., Berlin, Ohio, 1983—; mem. Killbuck (Ohio) Valley mus., 1988—, Holmes County Hist. Soc., Millersburg, Ohio, 1989—; life mem. Mennonite Info. Ctr., Berlin, Ohio, 1985—; sustaining mem. The Wilderness Ctr., Wilmot, Ohio, 1974—. Jennings scholar Martha Holden Jennings Found., 1983-84; Silver Poet award World of Poetry, 1986. Mem. AAUW (v.p. Holmes County chpt. 1994), Creative Arts Soc. (sec.-treas. 1987-89), Delta Kappa Gamma (sec. Beta Iota chpt. 1987-90, pres. 1990-92). Mennonite. Home: 6583 State Route 241 Millersburg OH 44654-8824

YODER, BRUCE ALAN, chemist; b. Seward, Nebr., Apr. 29, 1962; s. Elwood John and Elda Raye (Stutzman) Y. BS in Chemistry, Wayne State Coll., 1983. Lab. technician Wayne (Nebr.) State Coll., 1982-83; lab. technician Harris Labs., Lincoln, Nebr., 1984, chemist, 1984; scientist Dorsey Labs., Lincoln, 1984-86, scientist A, 1986-88; product stability analyst Sandoz Pharms., Lincoln, 1988-89, Sandoz Rsch. Inst., Lincoln, 1989-91; mgr. lab. computer ops. Sandoz Pharms., Lincoln, 1991—. Mem. Lancaster County Young Reps., Lincoln, 1988—, co-chmn., 1990-91, pres., 1991-93; mem. Nebr. Fedn. Young Reps., 1988—, mem. exec. com., 1990—; mem. exec. com. Lancaster County Rep. Party, 1990—; mem. Def. Adv. Com. Lancaster County, 1992—; mem. Lincoln Mayor's Cmty. Cabinet, 1992-93; mem. Lincoln City Charter Revision Commn., 1994—; trustee Wayne State Coll. Found., 1991—; advisor Jr. Achievement, 1993—. Recipient Dwight M. Frost, MD award for Overcoming a Phys. Disability Immanuel Rehab. Ctr., 1993, Verdi Smith award for outstanding voluntary contbns. to Lancaster County Rep. Party, 1995-96. Mem. Am. Inst. Chemists, Am. Chem. Soc., Jaycees. Mennonite. Home: 2240 Winding Way Lincoln NE 68506-2846 Office: Sandoz Pharms 10401 Highway 6 Lincoln NE 68517-9704

YODER, HAROLD ELIAS, small business owner; b. Huntertown, Ind., Feb. 18, 1913; s. Albert and Edith E. (Garman) Y.; m. Dorothy Grant, Nov. 9, 1940; 1 child: Milton Grant. Student, Walton Sch. Commerce, Chgo., 1933. Mgr. Cooperative Mills, Auburn, Ind., 1933-45; v.p., treas. Trenton (Ill.) Milling Co., 1946-62; v.p. Shiloh Co., Martel, Ohio, 1963-69; controller Midwest Constructors, Mansfield, Ohio, 1969-96; founder, chief exec. officer Herald Inventory, Inc., Mansfield, 1974—; mem. wage and hour div. U.S. Dept. Labor, Washington, 1942, nat. industry adv. bds. War Foods Adminstrn., 1942-45, FDA, Dept. Health and Edn., 1955-57, advisor Office Price Adminstrn., Washington, 1943-45; mem. Standards and Ethics for N.Am. Creator Food Packaging Artistic Design 1948 (Nat. Outstanding award). Pres. Wesclin Community Sch. Dist., Trenton, 1957-62. Mem. N. Am. Assn. Inventory Svcs. (chmn. standards and ethics com. 1987—, bd. dirs. 1988—) Worldwide Inventory Network (treas. 1991—), Trenton C. of C. (pres. 1953), Masons (Worshipful Master 1942-56), Shriner. Republican. Presbyterian. Home: 660 Dirlam Ln Mansfield OH 44904-1744

YODER, JOHN CLIFFORD, producer, consultant; b. Orrville, Ohio, Jan. 30, 1927; s. Ray Aquila Yoder and Dorothy Mildred (Hostetler) Yoder Hake; m. Alice Vigger Andersen, Mar. 2, 1963 (div. Nov. 1992); children: Gorm Clifford, Mark Edward. BA in Philosophy and Polit. Sci., Ohio Wesleyan U., 1951. Prodn. supr. Sta. WFMJ-TV, Youngstown, Ohio, 1954-62; producer Sta. NBC-TV, Chgo., 1964-72; ind. producer cons. Evanston, Ill., 1972—. Producer radio program Conversations From Wingspread, 1972-90 (George Foster Peabody Broadcasting award 1974, Ohio State award 1978, Freedoms Found. Honor medal 1978); appeared in film The Untouchables, 1994, TV program Missing Persons, 1993. Pub. rels. and pub. info. com. Chgo. Heart Assn. (Meritorious Svc. award 1978); electronic media advisor The White House, Washington, 1972; bd. dirs. Youngstown (Ohio) Sumphony Soc., 1959-63, Bensenville (Ill.) Home Soc. 1985-89. With USAF, 1945-47 PTO. Recipient Disting. Svc. award Inst. Medicine of Chgo. 1971. Mem. Nat. Acad. TV Arts and Scis., Midwest Pioneer Broadcasters, Soc. Profl. Journalists, Mus. Broadcast Comms., Masons, Am. Legion, Chgo. Headline Club. Home: 720 Noyes St Apt D 2 Evanston IL 60201

YODER, JOHN-DAVID SAMUEL, mechanical engineer; b. Elkhart, Ind., Apr. 27, 1969; s. John Howard and Ann Marie (Guth) Y.; m. Lynda Deanne Nyce, July 28, 1991. BSME, U. Notre Dame, 1991, MSME, 1994, PhD, 1996. Software engr. SMI, Elkhart, 1986-90; pres. Yoder Software, Inc., Elkhart, 1991—. Mem. IEEE, Sigma Xi, Tau Beta Pi. Democrat. Mem. Mennonite Ch.

YODER, LARRY DAVID, industrial designer; b. Kalona, Iowa, Apr. 8, 1940. BA in Arts, U. Iowa, 1964, MA in Indsl. Design, 1967. Sr. indsl. designer Amana (Iowa) Refrigeration, 1966—. Patentee in field. Mem. Color Mktg. Group. Methodist. Home: 2421 160th St Marengo IA 52301-8574 Office: Amana Refrigeration 2800 220th Trail Amana IA 52204

YODER, SUSAN FISCHER, tourist agency executive; b. St. Louis, Mar. 25, 1938; d. Arthur Harry Louis and Virginia Jane (Christen) Fischer; m. Bruce Richard Yoder, June 15, 1959; 1 child, Virginia Christen. BS, Washington U., St. Louis, 1961. Tchr. 3d grade Ferguson-Florissant Sch. Dist., Saint Louis County, Mo., 1961-62; tour guide St. Louis Scene, Inc., 1978—, account exec., 1987—. Bd. dirs. Women's Exch. of St. Louis; trustee Washington Nat. Cathedral. Episcopalian. Home: 4534 Pershing Pl Saint Louis MO 63108

YODER-GAGNON, PAMALA S., orthopedic nurse; b. Portage, Mich., Aug. 7, 1952; d. Jacob L. and Florence M. (Van Dommelen) Yoder; m. Georges Gagnon, July 3, 1982; children: Brianna Kay Marie, Garrett Patrick Antoine, Cameron Michael André. AAS, Kalamazoo Valley C.C., 1974, AAS in Nursing, 1975; BSN magna cum laude, Nazareth Coll., 1991. Staff nurse Borgess Med. Ctr., Kalamazoo, 1976-77, dept. dir. orthopedic/trauma unit, dept. dir. renal transplant, med. surgery unit, 1992-94. Mem. Nat. Assn. Orthopedic Nurses (v.p. local chpt. 1986-89, pres.-elect 1990-91, pres. 1991-92). Home: 6856 Towhee Ct Portage MI 49002-3181

YOGEV, SARA, psychologist; b. Tel Aviv, May 23, 1946; came to U.S., 1975; d. Israel and Cila (Fink) Frankel; m. Ram Yogev, Oct. 2, 1967; children: Eldad, Shelly, Tomer. BA, Hebrew U., 1965-69, MA, 1970-73; PhD, Northwestern U., Evanston, Ill., 1976-79. Cert. clin. psychologist, Ill. Clin. experience dist. sch. psychologist Office Edn. and Culture, Jerusalem, Israel, 1968-71; intern. Beer Yaakov Psychiatric Hosp., Israel, 1971-72; asst. dir. Dept. Psychology, Hebrew U., Jerusalem, Israel, 1972-73; psychotherapist Mental Health Ctr., Hebrew U., Jerusalem, Israel; clin. psychologist Inst. Psychoanalysis, Jerusalem, Israel, 1973-75; psychotherapist, supr. Youth and Family Services, Ill., 1977-80; pvt. practice psychology Skokie, Ill., 1981—; academic experience instr. counseling psychology, 1977-79, asst. prof., Northwestern U., 1979-82, research psychologist at the rank asst. prof., 1983-86, visiting scholar, Ctr. Urban Affairs and Policy Research, 1987. Contbr. articles to profl. jours. and books. Mem. American Assn. for Marriage and Family Therapy, American Psychological Assn., Nat. Register Health Service. Jewish. Office: # 32 5225 Old Orchard Rd Skokie IL 60077-1027

YOGGERST, JAMES PAUL, journalist, educator, public relations consultant; b. Springfield, Ill., Oct. 9, 1924; s. Paul Anthony and Helen (Ford) Y.; m. Norma Jean White, Nov. 25, 1948 (dec. Aug. 1976); children: Maureen, Karen, Dianne, Patricia, Paul, Steven. BS in Journalism, U. Ill., 1949; MA in English, 1950, postgrad. Reporter, Ill. State Register, Springfield, 1950-51; asst. editor Austin News, Chgo., 1951-55; tchr. journalism and English, Waukegan East High Sch., 1956-85; part-time lectr. Roosevelt U., Chgo., 1971-85; instr. Coll. of Lake County, Grayslake, 1965-72; part-time reporter News-Sun, Waukegan, Ill., 1956-70; contbg. editor La Montage Mag., Lake Bluff, Ill., 1977; dir. J. P. Yoggerst and Assoc., Pub. Relations and Writing Cons., Waukegan; lectr. in field, leader seminars; writing cons. Cherry Electric Co., Waukegan, 1971-72; pub. relations dir. Lake County Contractors Assn., Waukegan, 1973-74; pub. affairs cons. Social Security Adminstrn., Chgo., 1973-74. Author weekly column "Our

Prairie States", Waukegan News-Sun, 1977-79, Copley News Service, 1985—; contbr. articles and short stories to newspapers and mags. Pub. relations dir. Ray Bradbury Soc., Waukegan, 1978, Stonebridge Priory, Servite Fathers, Lake Bluff, Ill., 1971. Served with AUS, 1943-46; PTO. Recipient Pres.'s Coun. award Ill. Regional Tourism Coun., 1988. Democrat. Roman Catholic. Home: 2528 N Jackson St Waukegan IL 60087-3131 Office: JP Yoggerst and Assocs 2528 N Jackson St Waukegan IL 60087-3131

YOH, DONNA (DEE), state legislator. Mem. from dist. 2 Kans. State Ho. of Reps., Topeka.

YOKE, CARL BERNARD, English language educator, critic; b. Clarksburg, W.Va., Mar. 23, 1937; s. John Bernard and Doris Elma (Groghan) Y.; m. Beverly Jean Crow, Oct. 26, 1962 (div. 1968); 1 child, Christopher Carl; m. Sherry Elizabeth Gray, Oct. 6, 1973; children: Alexander Adam Gray (dec.), Andrea Elizabeth. BS, Kent State U., 1959, MA, 1961; postgrad., U. Wis., 1961-62, Case Western Res. U., 1962-68. Instr. English, Kent (Ohio) State U., 1962-68, asst. prof., 1968-74, assoc. prof., 1974—, dir. Euclid Acad. Ctr., 1965-66, various mid. level acad. positions, 1966-80, asst. to v.p. regional campuses, 1980-87. Author: (criticism) Readers Guide-Zelazny, 1979; author, co-editor: Death and the Serpent, 1985; author, editor: Phoenix from the Ashes, 1988; assoc. editor Extrapolation, 1978-86; contbr. over 100 articles, book revs. and radio shows to profl. publs. Ohio Wesleyan U. scholar, 1955; U. Wis. fellow, 1961. Mem. Internat. Assn. for Fantastic in Arts (v.p. 1985-89, bd. dirs. 1985—, exec. editor, founder, pub. JFA Jour. 1987—). Office: Kent State U Trumbull 4313 Mahoning Ave NW Warren OH 44483

YOKICH, TRACEY A., state legislator; 02251960; BA, Mich. State U., 1982; JD, U. Detroit Law Sch., 1985. Law clk. for Hon. George Clifton Edwards, Jr. 6th Cir. U.S. Ct. Appeals, 1985-86; asst. prosecuting atty. Macomb County, 1986-89, asst. corp. counsel, 1989-90; state rep. Dist. 26 Mich. Ho. of Reps., 1991—; vice-chmn. Election Com.; mem. Pub. Health, Environment, Great Lakes, Consumer, Judiciary & Conservation Coms.; chmn. Tourism & Recreation Com. Commr. Macomb County Criminal Justice Bldg. Authority. Mem. Mich. Bar Assn., Macomb County Bar Assn., Clair Shores Dem. Club. Home: 22710 Gordon Switch St Saint Clair Shores MI 48081-1308 Office: Mich Ho of Reps State Capitol Lansing MI 48909*

YONKER, JOHN F., engineering executive; b. Mich., Mar. 30, 1939. BA, Mich. Tech. U., 1963. Mech. engr. GM Corp., Saginaw, Mich., 1963-92; chief engr. Advance Vehicle Concepts, Grand Blanc, Mich., 1992—. Inventor: holds patents in automotive field. Mem. Soc. Automotive Engrs. Home: 5130 Churchgrove Rd Frankenmuth MI 48734-9793 Office: Advanced Vehicle Concepts 4000 E Baldwin PO Box 654 Grand Blanc MI 48439-9336

YOPP, JOHN HERMAN, dean of graduate school, plant biology educator; b. Paducah, Ky., Nov. 13, 1940; s. Herman John and Sarah Virginia (Bean) Y.; m. Donna Marie Denton, June 10, 1965; children: John Michael, Joseph Patrick, Anne-Marie. BS in Biology, Georgetown U., 1962; PhD in Biology, U. Lousville, 1969; post-doctoral fellow, NASA Ames Rsch. Ctr., 1969-70. Lectr. Spalding Coll., Louisville, 1963-64; asst. prof. So. Ill. U., Carbondale, 1970-74, assoc. prof., 1974-79, prof., 1979—, assoc. dean of sci., 1984-86, assoc. v.p. rsch., dean grad. sch., 1986—; cons. Corn Products Corp., Summit, Ill., 1985, Coun. of Grad. Schs., Washington, 1987, 92, Abbott Labs., Chgo., 1989; chmn. internat. com. Oak Ridge (Tenn.) Associated Univs., 1994-96, TOEFL Policy Bd. of Ednl. Testing Svc., Princeton, N.J., 1994-95, Inst., for Energy Analysis, Oak Ridge, 1988, Coun. Rsch. Policy and Grad. Edn., Washington, 1987-90, Ill. Assn. Grad. Schs., 1989-90; mem. Gov.'s Bd. Natural Resources and Conservation, Springfield, Ill., 1989-90; vice chmn., mem. of bd. Ill. Resource Network, Chgo., 1987-88; mem. evaluation panel Ford Found. Doctoral Fellowships for Minorities, 1987-90, exec. com. of Grad. Deans of African-Am. Inst., N.Y.C., 1989-97, Gov.'s Rural Affairs Coun., Ill., 1991—, adv. com. on minorities Coun. of Grad. Schs., Washington, 1993-96, minority grad. edn. com. Ednl. Testing Svc., Princeton, N.J., 1993-96; senator Nat. Assn. of State Univs. and Land Grant Colls., Washington, 1989-90; bd. mem. grad. record exam., Coun. Ednl. Testing Svcs., Princeton, 1993-97, Coun. Grad. Schs. U.S. and Can. and others. Author, coeditor: Bioassays and Other Special Techniques for Plant Hormones, 1986; co-author: A Laboratory Manual for General Biology, 1974, Determination of Maximal Permissible Levels of Selected Chemicals That Exert Toxic Effects on Plants of Economic Importance in Illinois, 1974; co-editor: Symmetries in Sci. IV Biological and Biophysical Systems, 1990; contbr. chpt to Encyclopedia Brittanica, 1991, The Global Sulfur Cycle, 1985; contbr. about 30 articles to profl. jours. including Plant Physiology, Phycologia, Archives of Microbiology, Jour. of Phycology, Botanica Marina, Phytochem, and others; inventor patented method for regulating plant growth, 1988. Recipient Outstanding Tchg. award AMOCO Found., 1981; inductee Am. Men and Women of Sci., 1986. Mem. Soc. for Rsch. Administrs., Ill. Assn. Grad. Schs. (pres. 1989-90), Internat. Soc. for the Study of the Origin of Life, Sigma Xi (Kaplan award 1986). Roman Catholic. Office: So Ill Univ Grad Sch Woody Hall B 120 Carbondale IL 62901

YORK, JOHN C(HRISTOPHER), lawyer, investment banker; b. Evansville, Ind., Apr. 27, 1946; s. James Edward and Madge (Wease) Y.; m. Judith Anne Carmack, Aug. 24, 1968; children: George Edward Carmack, Charlotte Bayley, Alice Mercer. BA, Vanderbilt U., 1968; JD, Harvard U., 1971. Bar: Ill. 1971, U.S. Dist. Ct. (no. dist.) Ill. 1971. Assoc. firm Mayer Brown & Platt, Chgo., 1971-74; sr. v.p., sec., prin. JMB Realty Corp., Chgo., 1974-84; pres. Robert E. Lend Co. Inc., 1984—, Packard Properties Inc., 1984—; counsel Bell, Boyd & Lloyd, Chgo., 1986—; bd. dirs. McKeever Electric Supply Co., Columbus, 1984—. Bd. dirs. Landmarks Preservation Coun. of Ill., 1972-92, Streeterville Corp., 1986-87, Washington Sq. Health Found., 1985—, Henrotin Hosp., 1976-89; mem. vestry St. Chrysosotom's Ch., 1980-92; mem. alumni bd. dirs. Vanderbilt U., 1994—. Mem. ABA, Chgo. Bar Assn., Lambda Alpha Internat., Chgo. Club, Casino Club, Racquet Club. Republican. Episcopalian. Home: 1242 N Lake Shore Dr Chicago IL 60610-2361 Office: Robert E Lend Co Inc 3 First Nat Plz Chicago IL 60602

YORK, JOSEPH RUSSELL, media production technician; b. Royal Center, Ind., Oct. 19, 1940; s. William Russell and Naomi (Wellman) Y.; Student Olivet Nazarene Coll., until 1965; BS, Ball State U. student, 1980, MS, 1982; m. Teresa Luanne Ping, June 15, 1963; children: Sherra JoAnn, Kerra SuzAnn, Darren Joseph, Terra LeAnn. Photojournalist, Danville (Ill.) Comml. News, 1961-62, Kankakee (Ill.) Daily Jour., 1963; motion picture dir., editor Calvin Prodns., Inc., Kansas City, Mo., 1965-71, Communico, Inc., St. Louis, 1971-73; editing supr. Premier Film & Rec. Co., Inc., St. Louis, 1973—; producer, dir. TV programming Kans. Fish and Game Commn., 1983—; owner, operator Trinity Prodns., St. Louis, 1963-83; pres. York's Foto Express, Inc., 1986—; asst. libr., prof. humanities and lit. Pratt C.C., 1988—; dir. med. svcs. audio support systems and spl. events Olivet Nazarene U., Bourbonnais. Ill., 1990—; owner, pres. EQ Audio, 1996—, J. York-Wooden Games & Recreation, 1996—. Pastor Ch. of the Nazarene, Selma, Ind. Recipient 1st Pl. award U.S. Indsl. Film Festival, 1972; 2d Pl. award Festival of Ams.-V.I., 1977. Mem. Profl. Photographers Am., Photomarketing Assn. Internat.; Golden Key Nat. Honor Soc. Home: 140 S Country Ct Bourbonnais IL 60914-2113 Office: Olivet Nazarene U 240 E Marsile St Bourbonnais IL 60914-1926

YORK, LINDA NATTKEMPER, clinical nurse specialist. BS, Ind. State U., 1970; MSN, Ind. U., 1978; postgrad., Ind. State U., 1979-84, St. Louis U., 1989—. RN, Mo., Ind. Concurrent rev. coord., staff nurse Katherine Hamilton Mental Health Ctr., Terre Haute, Ind., 1974-75; asst. prof. nursing Ind. State U., Terre Haute, 1978-85; psychiat./mental health adminstr. La. State U. Med. Ctr., Shreveport, 1985-87; instr. Barnes Hosp. Sch. Nursing, St. Louis, 1987-90; assoc. prof. Barnes Coll., 1990-94; instr. U. Mo.-St. Louis, 1994-95; clin. nurse specialist chem. dependency Barnes Hosp., St. Louis, 1996—; mental health nursing specialist Terre Haute Regional Hosp., 1980-85. Vol. fund raising activities Sierra Club; mem. Greenpeace; mem. St. Louis chpt. Nat. Alliance for the Mentally Ill. Capt. U.S. Army nurse Corps, 1970-73. Mem. ANA, Mo. Nurses Assn. (govtl. affairs com., exec. bd. dirs.), Psychiat. Spl. Interest Group, Sigma Theta Tau, Phi Delta Kappa. Home: 873 Fuhrmann Ter Saint Louis MO 63122-3221

YORK-BERIAULT, ANN JANE, advertising executive; b. Trenton, Mich., July 31, 1961; d. Leon Gerad and Margaret Mary (Cousineau) Y. MS in Advt., Northwestern U., Evanston, Ill., 1989; BS in Communications, Eastern Mich. U., 1984. Adminstr. Soc. Mfg. Engrs., Dearborn, Mich., 1986-87; acct. exec. Young & Rubicam, Chgo., 1987-90; from sr. acct. exec. to v.p. dir. ops. Lou Beres & Assocs., Chgo., 1990-92, sr. v.p., dir. ops. and svcs., 1992-93, exec. v.p., 1993-95; v.p., account supr. Blaising St. Claire Assocs., Carmel, Ind., 1995-96; account supr. Montgomery, Zukerman, Davis, Indpls., 1996—. Democrat. Roman Catholic. Home: 3110 Amherst St Indianapolis IN 46268 Office: Montgomery, Zukerman, Davis 1800 N Meridian St Indianapolis IN 46202

YOST, NANCY RUNYON, artist, designer, art educator; b. Eaton, Ohio, July 16, 1933; d. Stanley Everett and Treva (Geeting) Runyon; m. Kenneth John Yost, Aug. 17, 1952 (div. Dec. 1962); 1 child, Debra Colleen Yost Mayne. BS in Art Edn., Miami U., Oxford, Ohio, 1966, MEd in Art, 1970. Cert. profl. permanent tchr., Ohio. Sec. N.Am. Aircraft, Columbus, Ohio, 1957; sec. Miami U., Oxford, 1957-61, textile instr., 1978; textile instr. Living Arts Ctr., Dayton, Ohio, 1972-73; coord. art, music and phys. edn. Stewart Jr. High Sch., Oxford, 1981-86; art instr. Talawanda Sch. System, Oxford, 1965-90, dist. coord., 1986-90; owner, creator Allegro Adornments Bus., 1988—; postgrad. Sem. Charles Jeffrey, Cleve., Inst. Art, Miami U., 1973, David Van Dommelen Penn State at U. Tenn., 1975, Bill Helwig, N.Y., 1975, Nik Krevitsky, N.Y., 1976, Tom Shafer, Columbus, Ohio, 1982; mem. curriculum coun. Talawanda Sch. Dist., 1982—; rep. Amway Corp., 1980-81, World Book Co., Chgo., 1986-88; lectr. Miami U., 1986; invited workshop speaker, presenter Nat. Art Edn. Assn. Conv., Phoenix, 1992. Contbg. artist: Wall Hangings, 1971, Knotting, 1973; One-woman exhibit at Creative Fibers Studio, Buffalo, 1974; exhibited group show Dayton Art Inst., Invitational Fiber Artists Am., Ball State U., 1974, Christkindl Markt, Canton Art Inst. 1994 (hon. mention); designer Oxford Bicentennial Calender, 1976; guest jewelry designer Saks 5th Avenue. Supr. Community Artworks, 1986; mem. adv. bd. Miami U. Summer Theatre, 1991-93; mem. spl. events planning com. Miami U. Art Mus., 1993—. Recipient Winner Most Creative Costume Ohio Mart, 1992, 93, First Pl. awards Community Photo Contest, 3d Pl. and Hon. Mention award Oxford Audubon Photo Show, 1994, 1st Pl. 3D Design, Greater Hamilton Art Exhibit at Fitton Ctr, Cash award ribbon and Purchase award Wyo. Art Show, 1996. Mem. Southwestern Art Edn. Assn., Ohio Art Edn. Assn., Ohio Edn. Assn., Talawanda Edn. Assn., Ohio Designer Craftsmen, Ohio Arts and Crafts Guild, Oxford Arts Club, Kappa Delta Pi. Home and Studio: 6674 Fairfield Rd Oxford OH 45056-9707

YOST, ROBERT BYRON, insurance company executive; b. Zanesville, Ohio, July 15, 1958; s. Robert Byron and Norma Jean (Sherbs) Y.; m. Lynne Cunningham, Dec. 3, 1977 (div. Apr. 1980); m. Christine Marie Boyles, May 8, 1982; 1 child, Robert Byron III. AA, Essex C.C., Balt., 1981; BA in Bus. Mgmt., Fairmont (W.Va.) State Coll., 1982. Owner dry cleaning bus., Balt., 1979-81; with Kaiser Aluminum, Balt., 1980-81; ins. agt. Prudential Ins., Fairmont, 1982-84; ins. sales Prudential Ins., Bridgeport, W.Va., 1984-89; ins. asst. v.p. Prudential Ins., Jacksonville, Fla., 1989; gen. mgr. Prudential Ins., Steubenville, Ohio, 1989-93, sales mgr., 1993—; owner, mgr. Robert B. Yost II Cons., Steubenville, 1992—. Contbr. articles to profl. jours. Bd. dirs. Wintersville (Ohio) Baseball Assocs., 1994-95, River Valley Cruisers, Wintersville, 1993-95. Served with U.S. Army, 1976-79, Okinawa. Mem. Nat. Assn. Life Underwriters. Democrat. Methodist. Home: 2718 Iva Way Steubenville OH 43952 Office: Prudential Ins 2228 Sunset Blvd Steubenville OH 43952

YOUKILIS, TOM FISHEL, purchasing agent; b. Cin., May 1, 1954; s. Alvin and Sara (Mostow) Y.; m. Alison Maddux, Dec. 29, 1983; children: Ashley, Jordan. BA, U. Cin., 1976. Mem. Glendale Lyceum, Juvenile Diabetes Found. (bd. dirs., pres. 1982-85). Home: 185 E Fountain Cincinnati OH 45246

YOUNG, ARTHUR PRICE, librarian, educator; b. Boston, July 29, 1940; s. Arthur Price and Marion (Freeman) Y.; m. Patricia Dorothy Foss, June 26, 1965; children: John Marshall, Christopher Price. B.A., Tufts U., 1962; M.A.T., U. Mass., 1964; M.S. in L.S., Syracuse U., 1969; Ph.D., U. Ill., 1976. Head reader services, social sci. bibliographer SUNY-Cortland, 1969-72; rsch. assoc. U. Ill. Libr. Rsch. Ctr., Urbana, 1972-75; asst. dean pub. services, assoc. prof. U. Ala., Tuscaloosa, 1976-81; dean librs., prof. U. R.I., Kingston, 1981-89; dir. Thomas Cooper Libr., U. S.C., Columbia, 1989-93; sr. fellow UCLA, 1991; dir. librs. No. Ill. U., DeKalb, 1993—; mem. adj. faculty Syracuse (N.Y.) U., 1970-71, Rosary Coll., River Forest, Ill., 1994—; pres. Consortium R.I. Acad. and Rsch. Librs., 1983-85; bd. govs. Univ. Press New Eng., 1987-89; mem. exec. bd. Ill. Libr. Computer Sys. Orgn., 1995—; chair Coun. Dirs. State Univ. Librs., 1994-95. Author: Books for Sammies: American Library Association and World War I, 1981, American Library History: A Bibliography of Dissertations and Theses, 1988, Higher Education in American Life, 1636-1986: A Bibliography of Dissertations and Theses, 1988, Cities and Towns in American History: A Bibliography of Doctoral Dissertations, 1989, Academic Libraries: Research Perspectives, 1990, Religion and the American Experience, 1620-1900: A Bibliography of Doctoral Dissertations, 1992, Religion and the American Experience, the Twentieth Century: A Bibliography of Doctoral Dissertations, 1994; editl. bd. various jours. Chair Coun. of Dirs. Ill. State Univ. Librs., 1994-95. Served to capt. USAF, 1964-68. Recipient Berner Nash award U. Ill., 1976. Mem. ALA (chmn. editorial bd.), Assn. Coll. and Rsch. Librs. (publs. in librarianship 1982-88, chmn. Jesse H. Shera Endowment Fund com. 1991-94), S.C. Libr. Assn. (chmn. libr. adminstrn. sect. 1991-92), Assn. Rsch. Librs. (scholarly commn. com. 1991-93), Orgn. Am. Historians, Am. Hist. Assn., Phi Kappa Phi, Beta Phi Mu, Phi Delta Kappa. Episcopalian. Home: 912 Borden Ave Sycamore IL 60178-3200

YOUNG, BING-LIN, physics educator and researcher; b. Louyang, Henan, China, Feb. 3, 1937; came to U.S., 1961; s. Tseng and Suying Young; m. Theresa Fo-Ying Chen, Sept. 12, 1964; 1 child, Rowena Ya-Han. BS, Nat. Taiwan U., 1959; PhD, U. Minn., 1966. Postdoctoral fellow U. Ind., Bloomington, 1966-68; rsch. assoc. Brookhaven Nat. Lab., Upton, N.Y., 1968-70; asst. prof. Iowa State U., Ames, 1970-74, assoc. prof., 1974-79, prof., 1979—; assoc. physicist dept. energy Ames (Iowa) Lab., 1970-74; physicist Ames (Iowa) Lab., DOE, 1974-79, sr. physicist, 1979-94, sect. chief theoretical high energy physics, 1984-94; dir. Henan Fundamental and Applied Sci. Rsch. Inst., Zhengzhou, Henan, China, 1988—. Author: Introduction to Quantum Field Theory, 1987; editor Beyond the Standard Model, 1988; editl. bd. mem. High Energy and Nuclear Physics, 1994—; contbr. articles to profl. jours. Mem. Am. Phys. Soc., Overseas Chinese Physics Assn. (exec. coun. 1990—, vice chair 1990-92, chair 1993-94). Home: 4520 Westbend Dr Ames IA 50014 Office: Dept Physics & Astronomy Iowa State Univ Ames IA 50011

YOUNG, DALE, business manager; b. Zanesville, Ohio, June 28, 1938. BS, Ohio U., 1963. Gen. mgr. Custom Bobbin Windings, Zanesville, 1964—. Office: Custom Bobbin Windings 2920 Newark Rd PO Box 2369 Zanesville OH 43702-2369

YOUNG, DEAN A., state legislator. BA, Purdue U.; JD, Valprasio U. Mem. Ho. of Reps., Indpls., 1992—, mem. judiciary, labor & employment, pub. health coms.; pros. atty. Blackford County. Mem. Hartford City econ. devel. com., 1985—, pres. 1989-90; mem. Blackford County Cmty. Corrections Bd., 1990—. Republican. *

YOUNG, DONALD EDWARD, retired physicist, science company executive; b. Lake Zurich, Ill., June 13, 1922; s. Edward Frederick and Gertrude Dorothy (Scholz) Y.; m. Bille Grace Hooper, Sept. 13, 1947; children: Lynda Ayres, Patricia Ellis, Phillip Young. AB, Ripon Coll., 1946; MS, U. Minn., 1951, PhD, 1959. Rsch. asst. U. Minn., Mpls., 1949-53; head dept. physics Gen. Mills Rsch. Lab., Mpls., 1953-59; physicist Midwestern Rsch. Assn., Stoughton, Wis., 1959-67, head physics divsn., 1964-67; prof. dept. nuclear engring. U. Wis., Madison, 1967-68; leader Linac sect. Fermi Nat. Accelerator Lab., Batavia, Ill., 1967-71, leader accelerator ops. sect., 1971-77, head colliding beams dept., 1977-81, dep. head accelerator divsn., 1978-81, dep. project mgr. Tevatron 1 sect., 1981-86, head Linac dept., 1986-89, scientist emeritus, 1989—; pres. Particle Accelerator Corp., Downers Grove, Ill., 1990—; cons. G.H. Gillespie Assocs., Del Mar, Calif., 1988-94; co-chair 1989 Particle Accelerator Conf., 1987-89; chmn. 1970 Proton Linac Conf., 1969-70. Mem. editl. adv. bd. Particle Acceleration Jour., 1987-90. 1st lt. inf. AUS, 1943-46, ETO. Fellow Am. Phys. Soc.; mem. AAAS, Kiwanis Internat. (treas. 1991—), Sigma Xi. Home: 4513 Cornell Ave Downers Grove IL 60515

YOUNG, FREDERIC HISGIN, information systems executive, data processing consultant; b. Boston, Sept. 7, 1936; s. Ralph Randel Jr. and Wilhelmina Amalia (Imberger) Y.; m. Carol Joan Costello, Sept. 7, 1963 (div. Dec. 1971); children: Tracy Jean, Jodi Ann; m. Kathleen Paula Thorne, Dec. 1, 1984. BBA, U. Mass., 1961; JD, Suffolk U., 1966. Mgr. systems and programs Matrix Corp., Burlington, Mass., 1968-69; sr. cons. Programming Dimensions, Inc., Burlington, 1969-70; bus. mgr. JTB Rehab. Ctr., North Reding, Mass., 1970-75; regional bus. mgr. Mass. Dept. Mental Health, Waltham, 1975-78; dir. personnel mgmt. Mass. Dept. Mental Health, Boston, 1978-81; prin. cons. Lafayette Assocs., Chelsea, Mass., 1980-81; asst. regional dir. Corp. for Applied Systems, Indpls., 1982-84; v.p. cons. svcs. HAS, Inc., Carmel, Ind., 1984-88; v.p. info. sytems Ind. Fed. Credit Union, Anderson, Ind., 1988-95; sys. cons. AIC, Inc., Indpls., 1995—. With USN, 1954-56. Republican. Home: 20447 State Rd 37 N Noblesville IN 46060-6814

YOUNG, JACK ALLISON, financial executive; b. Aurora, Ill., Dec. 31, 1931; s. Neal A. and Gladys W. Young; m. Virginia Dawson, Jan. 24, 1959; children: Amy D., Andrew A. BS in Journalism, U. Ill., 1954. CLU; chartered fin. cons.; registered security rep. Advt. writer Caterpillar Tractor Co., 1956-58; ins. agent Equitable Life Assurance Soc., St. Geneva, Ill., 1958—, ins. broker, 1972—; pres. Jack A. Young and Assocs., 1978—; pres. Creative Brokerage, Inc., 1982—; pres., gen. securities prin. Chartered Planning, Ltd.; past trustee Equitable CLU Assn.; past chmn. Equitable Nat. Agents Forum. Bd. dirs. Tri-City Family Services, 1975-83, pres., 1979-81; trustee Delnor-Community Health System, 1985—, chmn., 1988-91; bd. dirs. St. Charles Ctr. Phys. Rehab., 1991—; chmn., pres. Delnor-Community Health Care Found., 1986-88. Served to lt. (j.g.), USN, 1954-56. Named to Equitable Hall of Fame, 1978. Mem. Million Dollar Round Table (life), Am. Soc. C.L.U.s, Am. Coll. C.L.U. Golden Key Soc., Fox Valley Estate Planning Council, Internat. Assn. for Fin. Planning, Inc., Aurora Assn. Life Underwriters (past pres., nat. committeeman), Nat. Assn. Securities Dealers (registered prin.). Club: Geneva Golf (pres. 1994). Home: 18 Campbell St Geneva IL 60134-2732 Office: 28 N Bennett St Geneva IL 60134-2207

YOUNG, JAMES E., company executive; b. Celina, Ohio, Sept. 1, 1941; s. Thomas D. and Margaret E. (Flora) Y.; m. Patricia C. Teare, June 13, 1964; children: Kathleen M., Peter C. BSME, Rose-Hulman Inst. of Technology, 1963; MBA, Ind. U., 1965. V.p. Citicorp, N.Y.C., 1965-73; pres. James E. Young & Assoc., Inc., Indpls., 1974-91; vis. prof. guest lectr. Purdue U., Lafayette, Ind., 1986—; adv. bd. Purdue-Anderson, Inc., 1985—, Rsch. Inst. for Devel. of Interactive Learning Sys., Terre Haute, Ind., 1986—; pres. Remote Equipment Corp., Indpls., 1988-90; pres. Forum for Internat. Profl. Svcs., Inc., 1988-91, bd. dirs., 1988—; chmn. bd. WKJM, Inc., 1989-90; chmn. World Competitiveness Conf., 1990—; pres. G & G Angola, Inc., 1991—; pres. Rainco of Ind., 1992—. Co-founder and bd. chmn. Ind. Amateur Baseball Assn., Inc., 1982—; mktg. chmn. Ind. Major League Baseball Commn., Indpls., 1982-86. Mem. ASME, Soc. Mfg. Engrs., Bus. Modernization and Tech. Corp. (chmn. telecomm. 1984—), Rotary Club. Home: 406 Inglenook Pl Angola IN 46703 Office: 301 Growth Pky Angola IN 46703

YOUNG, JAMES V., political science educator; b. Waterloo, Iowa, June 12, 1936; s. Robert Arthur and Edith M (Van Houten) Y.; m. Virginia Ann Hudson, June 11, 1959; children: Ann Elizabeth Young Anderson, James Hudson. BA, U. Iowa, 1958, JD, 1960, PhD, 1964. Instr. U. Iowa, Iowa City, 1964; asst. prof. polit. sci. St. Olaf Coll., Northfield, Minn., 1964-68, chmn. dept. polit. sci., 1965-68; from. asst. prof. to assoc. prof. polit. sci. Ctrl. Mo. State Coll., Warrensburg, 1968-75, chmn. dept. polit. sci., 1971-82, prof., 1975—; bd. advisors Heartland Inst., Chgo., 1990—. Author: Judges and Science: The Case Law on Atomic Energy, 1979, Landmark Constitutional Law Decisions, 1993; co-author: Remembering Their Glory: Sports Heroes of the 1940s, 1977. Mem. adv. com. citizenship edn. Mo. Bar, 1989-95, cmty. maintenance and improvement adv. bd. City of Warrensburg, 1992-94, Citizens Task Force, Warrensburg, 1991—. Named All-Am. Masters Track and Field USA Track and Field, 1991-92, 94-95. Mem. Am. Polit. Sci. Assn., Mo. Polit. Sci. Assn. (sec. 1988-91), Supreme Ct. Hist. Soc., Midwest Polit. Sci. Assn., Johnson County Hist. Soc., Phi Beta Kappa. Home: 320 Goodrich Dr Warrensburg MO 64093-2219 Office: Ctrl Mo State U Dept Polit Sci 8C Wood Hall Warrensburg MO 64093-5059

YOUNG, JAMES WILLIAM, health science association administrator; b. West Union, Ohio, Mar. 13, 1961; s. Donald James and Dorothy Mae (Holliday) Y.; m. Carrie Marie Carnahan, July 14, 1984; children: Katie Marie, Julie Ann. BS in Journalism, Bowling Green State U., Ohio, 1982, MA in Speech Comms., 1984. Legis. asst. Ohio Senate, Columbus, 1984-85; legis. liaison Ohio Dept. of Health, Columbus, 1985-90, chief of staff, 1990-91; dir. state socs. & govt. rels. Assn. of Community Cancer Ctrs., Columbus, 1991—. Office: Assn Community Cancer Ctrs Ste 125 445 Hutchinson Ave Columbus OH 43235

YOUNG, JOHN WESLEY, political science educator; b. Richmond, Va., Oct. 29, 1951; s. Frank Wesley and Kathleen (Jones) Y. BA, Columbia Union Coll., 1973; MA, U. Va., 1980, PhD, 1987. Editl. asst. Papers of George Washington, Charlottesville, Va., 1980-85; asst. prof. polit. sci. Andrews U., Berrien Springs, Mich., 1985-91, assoc. prof. polit. sci., 1991-96, prof., 1996—. Author: Totalitarian Language: Orwell's Newspeak and Its Nazi and Communist Antecedents, 1991, (with others) American Conservative Opinion Leaders, 1990. Bradley fellow Lynde and Harry Bradley Found., 1987. Mem. Phi Kappa Phi, Pi Sigma Alpha, Phi Alpha Theta. Republican. Office: Andrews U Dept History and Polit Sci Berrien Springs MI 49104-0010

YOUNG, JOSEPH FLOYD, JR., state legislator; b. Detroit, Nov. 4, 1950; m. Mary J. Gerbe; children: Kimberly Ann, Kerry Marie, Joe, III, Brooke Melinda. Mich. State U., Cooley Law Sch., Western Mich. U., Urban Bible Inst., Detroit. Com. analyst House Spkr. William Ryan; adminstrv. asst.; legis. asst. State Rep. Alma Stallworth; com. adminstr., legis. asst. Sen. Dale Kildee; state rep. Dist. 4 Mich. Ho. of Reps., 1978-94; senator Mich. State Sen., 1994—; chnn. State Affairs Com.; mem. Standing Coms. on Conservation, Environment & Great Lakes, Econ. Devel., Edn. & Tourism & Recreation Mich. Ho. of Reps.; mem. Families, Mental Health & Human Svc. & Judiciary Coms., Mich. State Senate, vice chmn. Local Urban & State Affairs Com. Mem. NAACP, KC, YMCA, Block Clubs. Home: 8570 E Outer Dr Detroit MI 48213-1420*

YOUNG, JOYCE C., municipal official; b. Springfield, Mass., Sept. 27, 1934; d. George Gridley and Ruth Gardener (Kempton) Canney; m. Frederick Nevin Young, Aug. 27, 1955; children: Margaret Ruth Wilson, Shirley Kathryn Spelman, Nancy Elisabeth, Mary Rachel Lundergan. Student, Mount Holyoke Coll., 1952-55, Radcliffe, 1955-56; BA, Wright State U., 1975. Assoc. dir. devel., dir. sch. medicine found. Wright State, Dayton, Ohio, 1978-80; pub. affairs mgr. Met. Ins. Cos., Dayton, Ohio, 1980-83; assoc. Kettering Found., Dayton, Ohio, 1983-93; mgr. Child Care Clearinghouse, Dayton, Ohio, 1988-91; township trustee Washington Twp., Dayton, Ohio, 1995—; cons. in fund raising, devel., pub. rels. and cmty. orgn., 1983-88; pres. Ergonomics, Inc. Chmn. Ohio State Use Com., Columbus, 1991—; trustee Sinclair C.C., Dayton, 1994—; mem. Pres.'s Com. for Purchase from People Who are Blind or Severely Disabled, 1976-95; vol. for various orgns. Recipient Legion of Honor award Pres.'s Club, Miami Valley, Ohio, 1991, award Nat. Assn. Social Workers, Altrusa Vol. of Yr. award, Evangeline Lindsley award for svc. to youth, 1992, others. Republican. Episcopal. Home: 6058 Mad River Rd Dayton OH 45459

YOUNG, KATHLEEN MARIE, special education educator; b. Anchorage, July 29, 1953. BS in Spl. Edn., Ill. State U., 1975; MS in Spl. Edn., No. Ill. U., 1981; student, Concordia U., 1994. Cert. learning disabilities, EMH, elem., blind and visual impaired, adminstrn. and supervision, Ill. Learning disabled/visually impaired tchr. St. Joseph (Ill.) Sch. Dist., 1975-78; learning disabilities resource tchr. Sch. Dist. # 300, West Dundee, Ill., 1978-81, Sch. Dist. # 102, Buffalo Grove, Ill., 1981—; adj. faculty mem. Govs. State U., Univ. Park, Ill., 1988—. Founder of Lambda Delta Fraternity, nat.

recognized orgn. for successful people with learning disabilites. P. Buckley Moss Learning Disabled Tchr. of Yr. 2d place winner, 1994. Mem. Orton Dyslexia Soc. (pubs. chmn. 1987-90, tchr. trainer pres. 1991-94, v.p. 1992-94), Learning Disabilities Assn. (conf. com. 1994), Lioness Club, Delta Kappa Gamma (literacy com. 1991). Home: 355 High Rd Cary IL 60013 Office: Meridian Mid Sch 2195 Brandywyn Ln Buffalo Grove IL 60089

YOUNG, KEITH LAWRENCE, lawyer; b. Chgo., Jan. 15, 1953; s. Lawrence E. and June E. (Verboomen) Y.; m. Wendy A. Kollross; children: Kyle W., Lauren E., Taylor E. BS, Iowa State U., 1974; JD, Ill. Inst. Tech., 1977. Bar: Ill. 1977, U.S. Dist. Ct. (no. dist.) Ill. 1977, U.S. Ct. Appeals (7th cir.) 1977. Pvt. practice law Chgo., 1977—; assoc. Anesi, Ozmon & Lewin, Chgo., 1977-79, James Demos Ltd., Chgo., 1979-80; ptnr. Lambruschi Young & Assocs., Chgo., 1980-87. Mem. Ill. Bar Assn., Chgo. Bar Assn., Ill. Trial Lawyers Assn., Assn. Trial Lawyers of Am. Office: 333 W Wacker Dr Chicago IL 60606-1218

YOUNG, KENNETH D., company executive; b. Davenport, Iowa, May 1, 1943. Owner PGK Unltd., Davenport, 1978—. Republican. Office: PKG Unltd 736 Federal St Davenport IA 52803-5753

YOUNG, LARRY JOE, insurance agent; b. Chanute, Kans., July 19, 1958; s. Larry Louis and Judith Ann (Leslie) Y.; m. Vickie Lea Everhart; children: Tyler Jay, Joseph Michael, Katherine LeAnn, Hayleigh Imogene, Larry Joe Jr. Student, Kans. City (Kans.) Community Coll., 1976-78; BGS in Meterology, Kans. U., 1980. Reg. rep., FDIC. Sales rep. Met. Life, Overland Park, Kans., 1981-86, Union Cen. Life, Overland Park, 1986—; pres. Young & Assocs., Overland Park, Kans., 1988-95; Young & Assocs. Inc. (now incorporated), 1995—; broker 1st Nat. CD Exch., 1996—. Coach Shawnee (Kans.) Soccer Club, 1986. Fellow, Life Underwriting Tng. Coun. Mem. Nat. Assn. Securities Dealers, Profl. Ind. Ins. Agts. Kans. Office: 6333 Long Ste 224 Shawnee Mission KS 66216

YOUNG, LEON D., state legislator; b. July 4, 1957. Degree in police sci., Milw. Area Tech. Coll.; student, U. Wis., Milw. Police officer; mem. Social Devel. Commn. Minority Male Forum on Corrections. Mem. NAACP, Urban League. Home: 2351 N Richards St Milwaukee WI 53212-3321*

YOUNG, MARGARET ANNE, elementary educator; b. Evergreen Park, Ill., Aug. 5, 1951; d. Dennis James and Elenore Louise (Fraser) Y. BA in Edn., U. Ill., Chgo., 1975; MS in Edn., U. Ill., 1991. Elem. tchr. St. Pius V Sch., Chgo., 1980-82, Holy Family Sch., Chgo., 1982-86; elem. tchr. Wilkins Sch., Justice, Ill., 1986-95, title I reading tchr., 1995—; pres. Tng. Wheels, Inc., Northbrook, Ill., 1995—. Author: Training Wheels for Reading and Spelling, 1995.

YOUNG, PHILIP GILMER, policy analyst; b. Asheville, N.C., May 27, 1957; s. Philip Hobart and Betty Jean (Gilmer) Y. BA in Polit. Sci., Carleton Coll., 1979; MA in Tech. and Pub. Policy, Washington U., St. Louis, 1982. Rsch. analyst Minn. Dept. Natural Resources, St. Paul, 1983-87; dir. Office of Sci. and Tech. Minn. Dept. Trade and Econ. Devel., St. Paul, 1987-91; rsch. mgr. Minn. Tech., Mpls., 1991—; advisor Coun. Great Lakes Govs., Chgo., 1988—; agrl. and econ. devel. bd. mem. Minn. Dept. Trade and Econ. Devel., St. Paul, 1991—; adv. coun. mem. Coll. Biol. Scis. U. Minn., St. Paul, 1990—; mem. Tech. Transfer Adv. Coun. Minn. Project Innovation, Mpls., 1991—. Mem. USA Volleyball. Office: Minn Tech Inc 400 Mill Pl 111 3d Ave S Minneapolis MN 55401

YOUNG, R. MICHAEL, state legislator. BA, Ind. U. Mem. Ind. Ho. of Reps., Indpls., 1986—, mem. ins. corps. and small bus. com., govt. affairs com.; real estate developer; polit. cons.; mng. ptnr. Phoenix Devel. Mem. Marion County Bd. Zoning Appeals, Wayne Twp. Rep. Com., Pike Twp. Rep. Com., Eagle Creek Rep. Com.; precinct committeeman. Republican. Home: 3102 Columbine Ct Indianapolis IN 46224-2021*

YOUNG, REBECCA LEE, special education educator; b. Muncie, Ind., June 22, 1950; d. Norman Lee and Evelyn Faye (Mann) Hofherr; m. James Paul Young, Feb. 21, 1974; children: Evelyn Kaye, Jason Paul. BS, Ball State U., 1975; MS, St. Francis Coll., Ft. Wayne, Ind., 1985. Cert. screener for scotopic sensivity syndrome. Tchr. severe and profound Carlin Park Elem. Sch., Angola, Ind., 1975-80; tchr. learning disabled Lakeland High Sch., La Grange, Ind., 1980—; tchr.-multi-categorical class Parkside Elem. Sch., La Grange, 1991—; tchr. presch. handicapped Sch. Opportunity, LaGrange, summer 1987; insvc. presenter, 1987—; mem. Lakeland Tech. Com., 1992-95, Parkside Tech. Com., 1992—. Vol. instr. Lakeland Band Camp, 1986-88; bd. dirs. Lakeland Band Boosters, 1986-89, Human Rights Com., La Grange, 1987—; mem. Lakeland Tech. Com., 1992—. Mem. ASCD, Coun. for Exceptional Children, Ind. Tchrs. Assn., Ind. Computer Educators, Lakeland Edn. Assn. (tech. com. 1992), Delta Kappa Gamma (chmn. scholarship com. 1985—), Sigma Alpha Iota, Learning Disabilities Assn. (Parkside child study team 1990—). Home: 353 Parkway St Lagrange IN 46761-1603 Office: Parkside Elem Sch 1 LeMaster Cir Lagrange IN 46761

YOUNG, REBECCA MARY CONRAD, state legislator; b. Clairton, Pa., Feb. 28, 1934; d. Walter Emerson and Harriet Averill (Colcord) Conrad; m. Merwin Crawford Young, Aug. 17, 1957; children: Eve, Louise, Estelle, Emily. BA, U. Mich., 1955; MA in Teaching, Harvard U., 1963; JD, U. Wis., 1983. Bar: Wis. 1983. Commr. State Hwy. Commn., Madison, Wis., 1974-76; dep. sec. Wis. Dept. of Adminstrn., Madison, 1976-77; assoc. Wadsack, Julian & Lawton, Madison, 1983-84; elected rep. Wis. State Assembly, Madison, 1985—. Translator: Katanga Secession, 1966. Supr. Dane County Bd., Madison, 1970-74; mem. Madison Sch. Bd., 1979-85. Recipient Wis. Register Deeds Assn. Cert. of Appreciation for Leadership, 1995, Wis. NOW Feminist of Yr. award, 1996. Mem. LWV. Democrat. Home: 639 Crandall St Madison WI 53711-1836 Office: State Legislature-Assembly PO Box 8953 Madison WI 53708-8953

YOUNG, RICHARD D., state legislator; b. Dec. 2, 1942; m. Elaine Young; 5 children. BA, Vincennes U. U.S. senator from Ind., 1988—, mem. agr., small bus., edn., fin. and natural resource coms.; farmer. Mem. Farm Bur., Crawford County C. of C., Lions.' Democrat. Home: RR 1 Box 106-c Milltown IN 47145-9720*

YOUNG, ROBERT DONALD, physicist, educator; b. Chgo., Apr. 20, 1940; s. Robert Joseph and Nellie (Krik) Y.; children: Robert Gerald, Jennifer Ann Young Rolinski; m. BJ Marymont, Feb. 14, 1981; 1 child, Emily Marymont. BS in Physics, Ill. Inst. Technology, 1962; MS in Physics, Purdue U., 1965, PhD in Physics, 1967. Devel. engr. Western Elec., Cicero, Ill., 1962; process engr. Nat. Video Corp., Chgo., 1963; asst. prof. physics Ill. State U., Normal, 1967-73, assoc. prof., 1974-78, prof., 1979—, dir. rsch. Coll. Arts and Scis., 1994-95, assoc. v.p. for rsch., dean grad. studies, 1995—; adj. prof. physics U. Ill., Urbana, 1986—. Contbr. articles to Proceedings Nat. Acad. Sci., Ann. Rev. Biophysics, Phys. Rev. Letters, Chemica Scripta, Jour. Phys. Chemistry, Jour. Chem. Physics, Computers in Physics, Physical Rev., Biophysical Jour. Named Researcher of Yr., Ill. State U., 1989. Mem. Am. Phys. Soc., Am. Chem. Soc., Biophys. Soc., Am. Assn. Physics Tchrs. Home: 4 Turner Rd Normal IL 61761-4218 Office: Grad Sch Ill State Univ Normal IL 61790-4040

YOUNG, VERNON LEWIS, lawyer; b. Seaman, Ohio, Oct. 13, 1919; s. Ezra S. and Anna (Bloom) Y.; m. Eileen Humble, Sept. 20, 1941; children: Robert, Loretta, Bettie Jo., Jon W., Denise L. Student Alfred Holbrook Coll., 1938-39; JD, Ohio No. U., 1942. Bar: Ohio 1942. Sole practice, West Union, Ohio, 1942-50, 78-81; ptnr. Young & Young, West Union, 1959-78, Young & Young, 1978-81, Young-Caldwell & BUBP, West Union, 1981—; spl. counsel Office of Atty. Gen., State of Ohio, West Union, solicitor Cities of Jamestown, Seaman, Winchester, Manchester, Ohio; pros. atty. Adams County, Ohio, 1952-56, acting county judge, 1968-79. Mayor City of Seaman, 1944-46; mem. Adams County Health Bd., West Union, 1968-75; chmn. membership com. Eastern Shore Inst. Lifelong Learning, Fairhope, Ala., 1983-84; mem. Republican Presdl. Task Force, 1980-94. Mem. Ohio State Bar Assn., Adams County Bar Assn. (former pres.), Masons, Lions (pres. 1950-51, dist. gov. 1951-52), Sigma Delta Kappa (chancellor 1940). Avocations: fishing, hunting, gardening. Home: 10 Hickory Dr Seaman OH 45679-9762 Office: 225 N Cross St West Union OH 45693

YOUNGBERG, CHARLOTTE ANNE, education specialist; b. Hampton, Iowa, May 8, 1937; d. Sebo and Marion Bradford (Boutin-Clock) Reysack; m. Paul Gordon Neal, Mar. 29, 1969 (div. Jan. 1984); children: Rachel Elizabeth, Kory Bradford; m. Lyle Edwin Youngberg, June 30, 1990; children: Lynn Eugene Youngberg, Lori Ann Youngberg Dodson. BA, U. No. Iowa, 1958; MEd, DePaul U., 1966; postgrad. No. Ill. U. Tchr., 4th grade, Des Moines Ind. Sch. Dist., 1958-59; tchr., 3d grade Glenview (Ill.) Pub. Schs., 1959-61, tchr. 3d grade, psychol. ednl. diagnostic Schaumburg Dist. Schs., Hoffman Estates, Ill., 1961-69; supr. learning disabilities and behavior disorders Springfield (Ill.) Pub. Schs., 1969-73; psycho-ednl. diagnostician Barrington (Ill.) Sch. Dist. 220, 1973-77; ednl. strategist Area Edn. Agy. 7, Cedar Falls, Iowa, 1978-90; dir. spl. edn. Verona, Mo., 1992-95, spl. edn. tchr. Verona, Mo., 1990—, testing evaluator Verona, Mo., 1990—; ednl. cons. Spl. Edn. Dist. Lake County, Gurnee, Ill., summer, 1968. Certified K-14 teaching and supervising in guidance, counseling, elementary supervisory K-9, elementary K-9 teaching, spl. K-12 learning disabilities. Mem. NEA, Iowa Edn. Assn., Phi Delta Kappa. Home: PO Box 147 Verona MO 65769-0147 Office: Verona R7 Sch Dist PO Box 98 Verona MO 65769-0098

YOUNGBLOOD, JAMES ROBERT, information systems executive; b. Avon, Ohio, Oct. 20, 1939; s. Irving George Youngblood and Regina (Schneider) Dea; m. Barbara Ann Hoover, Oct. 21, 1961; children: Craig, Lynne. Student, Am. U., Washington, 1963, 64. Cert. systems profl. Programmer Nat. Security Agy., Ft. Mead, Md., 1962-68; programmer/analyst Cuyahoga County Data Ctr., Cleve., 1968-69, mgr. systems, 1969-71; assoc. dir., cons. Cuyhoga County Welfare Dept., Cleve., 1971-78; asst. v.p. systems Cuyahoga County Hosp., Cleve., 1978-83; sr. v.p., chief info. officer Iowa Meth. Med. Ctr., Des Moines, 1983—. Advisor Boy Scouts Am., Avon Lake, Ohio, 1983. Served with U.S. Army, 1958-61. Mem. Ohio Info. Systems Soc. (pres. 1981-82), Assn. Systems Mgmt. (cert.), Iowa Hosp. Assn., ECHO, Am. Coll. Healthcare Execs. Roman Catholic. Home: 7009 NW Coburn Ln Johnston IA 50131-1253 Office: Iowa Meth Med Ctr 1200 Pleasant St Des Moines IA 50309-1406

YOUNGE, WYVETTER HOOVER, state legislator; b. St. Louis, Aug. 23, 1930; s. Ernest Jack and Annie (Jordan) H.; m. Richard G. Younge, 1958; children: Ruth F., Torque E., Margrett H. BS, Hampton Inst., 1951; JD, St. Louis U., 1955; LLM, Wash. U., 1972. Ill. state rep. Dist. 114, 1975—; mem. appropriation II com., chmn. urban redevel. com. Ill. Ho. Reps., labor and com., vice chmn. energy, environ. and natural resources com., aging, edn. appropriations, human svc., reappointment coms., chmn. higher edn. com.; asst. circuit atty. City of St. Louis; pvt. practice, 1955—; exec. dir. Neighborhood Ctrs. War on Poverty, 1965-68; East St. Louis adv. and devel. nonprofit housing corp., 1968—. Author: The Implementation of Old Man River, 1972. Recipient Humanity award Project Upgrade, 1969, Citizen of Yr. award Monitor Newspaper, Cert. of Recognition Black Heritage Com. Mem. Alpha Kappa Alpha. Democrat. Address: 1617 N 46th St East Saint Louis IL 62204-1919*

YOUNGER, BETTY NICHOLS, social worker; b. Cleve., 1927; d. Manson E. and Esther L. (McDonald) Nichols; m. Paul A. Younger, 1952 (dec. Mar. 1969); children: Deborah, Rebekah, Sarah, Martha. BA, Otterbein Coll., 1949; MS in Social Adminstrn., Western Res. U., 1951. Cert. social worker, Mich.; diplomate Am. Bd. Examiners in Clin. Social Work. Family and youth worker East Harlem Protestant Parish, N.Y.C., 1951-52; organizer, parent worker Fidelity Presch., Cleve., 1955, 58-60; community worker YWCA, Cleve., 1966-67; organizer, dir. Community United Headstart, Cleve., 1965; social worker Children's Hosp., Columbus, Ohio, 1968, Mt. Sinai Hosp., Chgo., 1972-73, Billings Hosp. U. Chgo., 1973; supr. Ill. Masonic Med. Ctr., Chgo., 1974-79; counselor Barry County Substance Abuse, Hastings, Mich., 1981-82; organizer, dir. Love, Inc., Barry County, Mich., 1983-84; therapist Family & Child Svcs., Jackson, Mich., 1986, Livonia (Mich.) Counseling Ctr., 1986-89; pvt. practice Shumard Counseling, Livonia, 1988-91, Cambridge Counseling, Livonia, 1991-93, Tapestry Counseling, Ann Arbor, 1991-93; tchr. Schoolcraft Coll., Livonia, 1989—; bus. ptnr. Creating Results, Ann Arbor, Mich., 1990—. Mem. ACLU, NOW, Women's Internat. League Peace and Freedom, Sierra Club.

YOUNGER, ROBERT JOSEPH, human resource management specialist; b. Brunswick, Md., June 29, 1943; s. Harry Leonard and Elizabeth Marguerite (Potter) Y.; m. Elsibeth Semone Heimlid, Mar. 3, 1966 (div. May 1984); children; Marlena, Harry Gregory, Robert Viking, Heidi Beth, Benita Renee, Trixy Marie; m. Marjorie Lee Boettcher, Apr. 2, 1985. BSBA, Southwest Mo. State U., 1978; MS in Edn., Kans. State U., 1988. Enlisted U.S. Army, 1965, commd. 2d lt. adj. gen. corps, 1969, advanced through grades to maj., 1980, retired, 1985; mgr. tng. and devel. Kans. State U., Manhattan, 1985-92, coord. employee asst. program, 1986-92, mgr. benefits counseling and comm., 1993—; instr. U. for Man, 1985—. Commdr. Royal Rangers Assemblies of God, Junction City, Kans., 1982-84; assoc. United Way Campaign, Manhattan, Kans., 1985—. Mem. Am. Soc. Tng. and Devel., Employee Assistance Soc. N.Am. Republican. Mem. Ch. of the Brethern. Home: 1122 Claflin Rd # 108 Manhattan KS 66502-4641 Office: Kans State U Human Resources 103 Edwards Hall Manhattan KS 66506-0100

YOUNG LIVELY, SANDRA LEE, nurse; b. Rockport, Ind., Dec. 31, 1943; d. William Cody and Flora Juanita (Carver) Thorpe; m. Kenneth Leon Doom, May 4, 1962 (div. 1975); children: Patricia, Anita, Elizabeth, Melissa, Kenny. AS, Vincennes U., 1979, student, U. So. Ind., 1987—. Nursing aide, nurse Forest Del Nursing Home, Princeton, Ind., 1975-80; charge nurse Welborn Bapt. Hosp., Evansville, Ind., 1979-80, 82-83; staff nurse Longview Regional Hosp., Tex., 1980-82; dir. home health Roy H. Laird Meml. Hosp., Kilgore, Tex., 1984-86; med. post-coronary nurse Mercy Hosp., Owensboro, Ky., 1987, Dept. of Corrections charge nurse, Branchville Tng. Ctr., Tell City, Ind, 1987-90; charge nurse dept. mental health Evansville (Ind.) State Hosp., 1990—; staff nurse, asst. dir. Leisure Lodge Home Health, Overton, Tex., 1983-84. Grantee Roy H. Laird Meml. Hosp., 1986. Mem. NAFE, Menniger Found., Vincennes U. Alumni Assn., Internat. Platform Assn. Avocations: writing, research, cake decorating, house plants. Home: 614 Gilmer Rd Apt 251 Longview TX 75604 Office: Evansville State Hosp 3400 Lincoln Ave Evansville IN 47714-0147

YOUNGS, CURTIS R., animal science educator; b. Columbus, Ohio, Nov. 10, 1960; s. James E. and Nancy L. (Thomson) Y.; m. Linda L. Miller, Sept. 12, 1981; children: Matthew C., Adam J., Darren E. AAS, U. Minn., Waseca, 1980; BS, U. Minn., St. Paul, 1981, PhD in Animal Sci., 1985. Postdoctoral rschr. La. State U., Baton Rouge, 1985-86; asst. prof. animal sci. U. Idaho, Moscow, 1986-89; asst. prof. animal sci. Iowa State U., Ames, 1989-94, assoc. prof., 1994—. Contbr. chpt. to book, articles to profl. jours. Named Outstanding Alumnus Under Age 40, U. Minn., 1987; named to Outstanding Young Men of Am., 1988. Mem. Soc. for Study of Reprodn., Internat. Embryo Transfer Soc. (import-export com. 1990—), Am. Soc. Animal Sci., Nat. Assn. Colls. and Tchrs. of Agr., Block and Bridle Club (hon.), Gamma Sigma Delta. Office: Iowa State U 11 Kildee Hall Ames IA 50011

YOUNGS, DIANE CAMPFIELD, learning disabilities specialist, educator; b. Margaretville, N.Y., Feb. 16, 1954; d. Richard Maxwell and Charlotte June (Rickard) Campfield; m. William H. Youngs, June 30, 1984. BS in Edn., SUNY, Geneseo, 1976, MS in Edn., 1977. Tchr. educable mentally retarded Tompkins-Seneca-Tioga Bd. Coop. Ednl. Svcs., Ithaca, N.Y., 1978-80; tchr. learning disabled Joint Svcs. for Spl. Edn., Mishawaka, Ind., 1980—; mem. Task Force for Reorgn. Spl. Edn., Mishawaka, 1990-91; coord. Tiny Talkers Summer Speech/Lang. Camp, 1994—. Mem. Coun. for Exceptional Children, Learning Disabilities Assn., Coun. for Learning Disabilities, Kappa Delta Pi, Psi Iota Xi. Republican. Office: Walt Disney Sch 4015 Filbert Rd Mishawaka IN 46545-4072

YOUNIS, MAHMOUD RACHID, business owner, electrical engineer; b. Majdel Tarchich, El-Metn, Lebanon, Jan. 4, 1948; came to U.S., 1972; s. Rachid Abdallah Younis and Jamileh (Khalil) Damen; m. Jouhaina Maleh Yountis, Apr. 22, 1982; children: Waseemn, Maya. BSEE, Detroit Inst. Tech., 1976; MSEE, Wayne State U., 1981. Registered profl. engr., Mich. Field installation rep. Staff Industries, Detroit, 1974-76; elec. engr. K-R Automation, Madison Heights, Mich., 1976-77; jr. elec. engr., cons. Gussow & Dean Engring. Cons., Dearborn, Mich., 1977-78; sr. elec. engring. designer Ford Motor Co., Dearborn, 1978-82; founder, chief exec. officer T.M.A. Travel & Tours, Dearborn, 1981—, Travel Tng. Ctr., Inc., Dearborn, 1986—. Author, editor: catalog Travel School, 1987. Founder, chief exec. officerTakaddom Athletic and Social Club, Majdel-Tarchich, 1970; chmn. bd. Rabitat Al-Kalam, Dearborn, 1995. Mem. Am. Translators Assn. (Cert. 1981), Pan Am World Club (cert.), Internat. Airlines Travel Assn. (Cert. 1981). Office: TMA Travel & Tours 13234 Michigan Ave Dearborn MI 48126-3539

YOUNT, DAVID B., business executive; b. Franklin, Ind., Feb. 4, 1962. BA in Journalism/Polit. Sci., Ind. U., 1984. Community devel. specialist Ind. Dept. of Commerce, Indpls., 1985-87; pres. Logansport (Ind.) Econ. Devel. Found., 1987-91, Columbus (Ind.) Enterprise Devel. Corp., 1991—; adv. bd. mem. Ind. Small Bus. Devel. Ctr., Indpls., 1987—. Pres., bd. dirs. United Way of Cass Co., Logansport, 1987-91. Mem. Nat. Bus. Incubator Assn. Republican. Office: Columbus Small Bus Devel 4920 N Warren Dr Columbus IN 47203-1705

YOUNT, KIM ALLEN, dentist; b. Leavenworth, Kans., Apr. 30, 1954; s. Robert Eugene and Barbara Jean (Gee) Y.; m. Debra Jo Walker, Feb. 20, 1990; children: Jacob Allen, Lucas Arthur, Kimberly Ann. AA, Johnson County C.C., 1974; BS in Biology, U. Mo., 1976, DDS, 1981. Lic. Practitioner Dental Bd., Kans., Mo. Landscape designer Rieke Nursery, Shawnee, Kans., 1974-80; clin. dentistry instr. U. Mo., Kansas City, 1981; gen. practice dentistry Rolling Fork, Miss., 1982-83, Liberal, Kans., 1983—. Mem. Profl. Devel. Coun., Liberal, 1995. Mem. ADA, Miss. Dental Assn., Ducks Unltd., S.W. Dental Study Club, Psi Omega. Republican. Home: 2300 S Holly Dr Liberal KS 67901-2085 Office: 1411 W 15th St Ste 301 Liberal KS 67901-2285

YOURZAK, ROBERT JOSEPH, management consultant, engineer, educator; b. Mpls., Aug. 27, 1947; s. Ruth Phyllis Sorenson. BCE, U. Minn., 1969; MSCE, U. Wash., 1971, MBA, 1975. Registered profl. engr., Wash., Minn. Surveyor N.C. Hoium & Assocs., Mpls., 1965-68, Lot Surveys Co., Mpls., 1968-69; site layout engr. Sheehy Constrn. Co., St. Paul, 1968; structural engring. aide Dunham Assocs., Mpls., 1969; aircraft and aerospace structural engr., program rep. Boeing Co., Seattle, 1969-75; engr., estimator Howard S. Wright Constrn. Co., Seattle, 1976-77; dir. project devel. and adminstrn. DeLeuw Cather & Co., Seattle, 1977-78; sr. mgmt. cons. Alexander Grant & Co., Mpls., 1978-79; mgr. project systems dept., project mgr. Henningson, Durham & Richardson, Mpls., 1979-80; dir. project mgmt., regional offices Ellerbe Assocs., Inc., Mpls., 1980-81; pres. Robert Yourzak & Assocs., Inc. Mpls., 1982—; lectr. engring. mgmt. U. Wash., 1977-78; lectr., adj. asst. prof. dept. civil and mineral engring. and mech./indsl. engring. Ctr. For Devel. of Tech. Leadership, Inst. Tech.; mgmt. scis. dept. Sch. Mgmt. U. Minn., 1979-90, bd. adv. inst. tech., 1989-93; founding mem., membership com., mem. Univ. of Minn. com. Minn. High Tech. Coun., 1983-95; speaker in field. Author: Project Management and Motivating and Managing the Project Team, 1984. Chmn. regional art group experience Seattle Art Mus., 1975-78; mem. Pacific N.W. Arts Council, 1977-78, ex-officio adviser Mus. Week, 1976; bd. dirs. Friends of the Rep. Seattle Repertory Theatre, 1973-77; mem. Symphonics Seattle Symphony Orch., 1975-78. Scholar Boeing Co., 1967-68, Sheehy Constrn. Co., summer 1967. Named An Outstanding Young Man of Am., U.S. Jaycees, 1978. Fellow Project Mgmt. Inst. (cert. project mgmt. profl., speaker, founding pres. 1985, chmn., adv. com. 1987-89, bd. dirs. 1984-86, program com. chmn. and organizing com. mem. Minn. chpt. 1984, speaker, project mgr. internat. mktg. program 1985-86, chmn. internat. mktg. standing com. 1986, long range and strategic planning com. 1988-93, chmn., 1992, v.p. pub. rels. 1987-88, ex-officio dir. 1989, 1992, internat. pres. 1990, chmn. bd. 1991, ex-officio chmn. 1992, internat. bd. dirs., chmn. nominating com. 1992); mem. ASTD (So. Minn. chpt.), Am. Cons. Engrs. Coun. (peer reviewer 1986-89), Am. Arbitration Assn. (mem. Mpls. panel of constrn. arbitrators), Minn. Surveyors and Engrs. Soc., ASCE (chmn. continuing edn. subcom. Seattle chpt. 1976-79, chmn. program com. 1978, mem. transp. and urban planning tech. group 1978, Edmund Friedman Young Engr. award 1979, chmn. continuing edn. subcom. 1979-80, chmn. energy com. Minn. chpt. 1980-81, bd. dir. 1981-89, sec. 1981-83, v.p. profl. svcs. 1983-84, v.p. info. svcs. 1984-85, pres. 1986-87, past pres. 1987-89, fellow 1988—, speaker), Inst. Indsl. Engrs. (pres. Twin Cities chpt. 1985-86, chmn. program com. 1983-84, bd. dirs. 1985-88, awards com., chmn. 1984-89, speaker), Cons. Engrs. Council Minn. (chmn. pub. rels. com. 1983-85, vice chmn., 1988, chmn., 1989, program com. chmn. Midwest engrs. conf. and exposition 1985-90, speaker, Honor award 1992), Inst. Mgmt. Cons. (cert. mgmt. cons.), Mpls. Soc. Fine Arts, Internat. Facility Mgmt. Assn., Am. Soc. Engring. Edn., Rainer Club (co-chmn. Oktoberfest), Sierra Club, Chowder Soc., Mountaineers, North Star Ski Touring, Chi Epsilon (life). Office: 7320 Gallagher Dr Ste 325 Minneapolis MN 55435-4510

YU, CLEMENT TAK, educator, researcher, consultant; b. Hong Kong, Aug. 31, 1948; came to U.S., 1967; s. Ching Hang and Chen-Chun (Sheit) Y.; m. Teresa Yuen-Ling Chan, May, 2, 1950; children: Victor Kar-Yun, Christine Mei-Yun. BSc, Columbia U., 1970; PhD, Cornell U., 1973. Asst. prof. U. Alberta, Edmunton, Can., 1973-77, assoc. prof., 1977-78; assoc. prof. U. Ill., Chgo., 1978-84, prof., 1984—; cons. System Devel. Corp., MCC, Shell Oil, Amoco Oil, Argonne Nat. Lab., Trilogy, Info. Arts., Fla. Internat. U. Contbr. more than 100 article to profl. jours. Mem. IEEE (assoc. editor 1994—), Assn. for Computing Machinery (chmn. 1985-87), Distributed and Parallel Databases (mem. editl. bd. 1992—). Office: U Ill Dept EECS Chicago IL 60607-7053

YU, FU-LI, biochemistry educator, cancer researcher; b. Beijing, May 2, 1934; came to U.S., 1958; s. Ling-Ko and Ying (Chang) Y.; m. Jie Feng, Apr. 20, 1980; children: Jimmy Chan-Ching, Chan-Mei. MS, U. Ala., 1962; PhD, U. Calif., San Francisco, 1965. Asst. prof. biochemistry Jefferson Med. Coll., Phila., 1973-79; asst. prof. biomed. scis. U. Ill. Coll. Medicine, Rockford, 1979-80, assoc. prof., 1980-85, prof., 1985—, head dept., 1988—. Contbr. articles to Proc. NAS, Nature, Jour. Biol. Chemistry, Carcinogenesis. Rsch. grantee NIH, 1974-77, 78-80, 81-90, Am. Cancer Soc., 1978-81, 95—. Mem. Am. Soc. Biochem. and Molecular Biology, Am. Assn. for Cancer Rsch., Am. Chem. Soc. Office: U Ill Coll Medicine 1601 Parkview Ave Rockford IL 61107-1822

YU-LEE, REGINALD TOMAS, engineering educator; b. Dayton, Ohio, May 3, 1964; s. Rudolph Mario and Winifred Earline (Webster) Lee; m. Mi Hwa Yu, Nov. 10, 1990; 1 child, Erin Jeong Mi. B in engring., U. Dayton, 1987, M in engring., 1994, postgrad., 1995—. Staff engr. Montgomery County, Dayton, 1987; devel. engr. IBM, Dayton, 1987-91; pres., chief oper. officer Bus. Dynamics & Rsch., Dayton, 1994—; from asst. prof. to assoc. prof. Sinclair Coll., Dayton, 1991—; cons. Sinclair Coll., 1991-94; mentor underpriviledged minority students; cons. Dayton Daily News, 1993-94. Contbr. articles to profl. jours. Mem. Parity 2000 Econ. Devel., Dayton, 1995. Mem. Soc. Mfg. Engrs., Am. Prodn. and Inventory Control Soc., Omega Psi Phi (editor 1991-94, Brotherhood award 1991). Home: 5201 Birdland Ave Dayton OH 45427 Office: Sinclair Coll 444 W Third St Dayton OH 45402

YUNE, HEUN YUNG, radiologist, educator; b. Seoul, Korea, Feb. 1, 1929; came to U.S., 1966; s. Sun Wook and Won Eun (Lee) Y.; m. Kay Kim, Apr. 12, 1956; children: Jeanny Kim, Helen Kay, Marc Eany. MD, Severance Med. Coll., Seoul, 1956. Lic. physician, Republic of Korea, Ind.; diplomate Am. Bd. Radiology, Korean Bd. Radiology. Intern Presbyn. Med. Ctr., Chonju, Korea, 1956-57, resident in surgery, 1957-60; resident in radiology Vanderbilt U. Hosp., Nashville, 1960-63, instr. radiology, 1962-64; chief radiology Presbyn. Med. Ctr., Chonju, Korea, 1964-66; from asst. to assoc. prof. radiology Vanderbilt U. Med. Sch., Nashville, 1966-71; prof. radiology Ind. U. Sch. Medicine, Indpls., 1971—; John A. Campbell prof. of radiology, 1991—; dir. residency program Ind. U. Sch. Medicine, Indpls., 1985—; prof. otolaryngology, head and neck surgery, 1992—; vis. prof. Yonsei U. Coll. Medicine, Seoul, 1985; active staff Ind. U. Hosps., 1971—, Indpls. VA Hosp., 1971—, Wishard Meml. Hosp., 1971—. Editorial reviewer Am. Jour. Roentgenology, 1975—, Radiology, 1985—, Jour. Vascular and Interventional Radiology, 1989—; contbr. articles to profl. jours. Capt. Rep. of

Korea Army, 1951-55. Decorated Bronze Star, U.S. Army, Wharang medal for meritorious mil. svc., Rep. of Korea Army. Fellow Am. Coll. Radiology; mem Assn. Univ. Radiologists, Radiol. Soc. N.Am., Am. Roentgen Ray Soc., Alpha Omega Alpha, others. Presbyterian. Home: 2887 Brook Vista Carmel IN 46032 Office: Ind U Med Ctr 926 W Michigan St Indianapolis IN 46202-5203

YURKO, JOSEPH ANDREW, chemical engineer; b. Youngstown, Ohio, Mar. 30, 1955; s. Joseph George and Virginia Mary (Cossentino) Y.; m. Valerie Ann Congdon, Sept. 9, 1992; children: Andrew Dale, Laura Ann. B in BioEngring. Sci., Cleve. State U., 1981, B in Chem. Engring., 1981. Lic. profl. engr. Tex. Structural draftsperson HK Ferguson Co., Cleve., 1974-76, architectural draftsperson, 1976-77, process design engr., 1981-84; chem. engr. Chemical Data Systems, Inc., Oxford, Pa., 1984-85; tech. sales engr. Autoclave Data Systems, Inc., Erie, Pa., 1985-86; sr. process design engr. Morrison Knudsen Corp., Cleve., 1987—, process start up engr., 1988-95; cons. EI Dupont de Nemours and Co., Wilmington, Del., 1985-86, Mobil Oil Rsch. Ctr., Princeton, N.J., 1985-86, SmithKline French Labs., Phila., 1985-86, Anheuser-Busch Cos., St. Louis, Dow Corning, Midland Mich., 1996; spkr. in field. Author: (manuals) Aseptic Filtration Tech. Operating Procedure, 1990, Waste Stream Evaporator Tech. Operating Procedure, 1991, Clean-in-Place Process Tech. Operating Procedure, 1992, Viobin Sci. Proten Labs. Pancreatin, Heparin and Blood Processes, 1995; editor: (manual) Natural Water Carbonation Tech. Ops., 1992. Coach track Cath. Youth Orgn. St. Bridgets Cath. Ch., Parma, Ohio, 1977; campaigner Multiple Sclerosis Soc., Cleve., 1978; counselor Soc. Cripplied Children Cuyahoga County, Strongsville, 1979. Mem. Am. Inst. Chem. Engrs. (sec. Cleve. chpt. 1988-89, vice chair Del. Valley chpt. 1986-87), Food Pharm. and Bioengring. Div., Am. Chem. Soc, Cleve. Engring. Soc., Internat. Soc. Pharm. Engring. Republican. Methodist. Home: 19099 Hunt Rd Strongsville OH 44136-8415 Office: Morrison Knudsen Corp MK Ferguson Plaza 1500 W 3rd St Cleveland OH 44113-1453

YUSSOUFF, MOHAMMED, physicist, educator; b. Cuttack, India, Aug. 14, 1942; came to U.S., 1991; s. Haji and Nurunnisa Fakhruddin; m. Farhana Begum, Apr. 6, 1969; children: Ashraf, Zeenat, Mustafa. MSc, Delhi U., 1963; PhD, Indian Inst. Tech., Kanpur, 1967. Prof. physics Indian Inst. Tech., Kanpur, 1967-90; vis. prof. physics Mich. State U., East Lansing, 1991—; vis. scientist U. Köln, Germany, 1972-74, U. Western Ont., London, Can., 1990-91; Humboldt scientist Atomic Energy Agy, Jülich, Germany, 1979-81; vis. prof. U. Konstanz, Germany, 1986-89; guest scientist Ford Rsch., Dearborn, Mich., 1991—; mem. com. physics examination Pub. Svc. Commn., Delhi, India, 1976-86, rsch. grants Univ. Grants Commn., Delhi, 1985-90; bd. dirs. Aligarh (India) Muslim U., 1989-90; dir. Internat. Sch. on Band Structure, Indian Inst. Tech., 1986. Editor: Electronic Band Structure and Its Applications, 1987, The Physics of Materials, 1987; developer of Slow Pace program for teaching sci. and engring. to deficient students with poor social, econ. or sch. backgrounds; patentee for monitoring the catalytic converters in cars, U.S., 1996. Mem. Am. Phys. Soc., Internat. Ctr. Theoretical Physics (assoc.). Islam. Home: 31011 Grandview Westland MI 48186 Office: Mich State Univ Dept Physics East Lansing MI 48824-1116 also: Ford Motor Co Scientific Rsch Lab Dearborn MI 48121-2053

YZERMAN, STEVE, professional hockey player; b. Cranbrook, B.C., Can., May 9, 1965. With Detroit Red Wings, 1983—. Recipient Lester B. Pearson award, 1988-89; named Sporting News NHL Rookie of Yr., NHL All-Rookie Team, 1983-84, 1988-93. Office: Detroit Red Wings 600 Civic Center Dr Detroit MI 48226-4408*

ZABEL, LYNDON ROY, minister; b. Mpls., June 13, 1955; s. Kenneth George and Marlene Lyda (Webster) Z.; m. Judith Kreager; children: Benjamin, Brian, Elizabeth. BS, Moorhead State U., 1979; MDiv, United Theol. Sem. Twin Cities, 1985. Min. Rosemount (Minn.) United Meth. Ch., 1985-90, Gethsemane United Meth. Ch., Lino Lakes, Minn., 1990-93, Woodbury (Minn.) United Meth., 1993—; pres. Jumpin Jehoshaphats, Minn., 1986—; vice-chair Operation Classroom, Minn., 1987—. Office: Woodbury United Meth Ch 7465 Steepleview Rd Woodbury MN 55125

ZABROCK, EDWARD JOSEPH, state legislator.

ZACCONE, SUZANNE MARIA, sales executive; b. Chgo., Oct. 23, 1957; d. Dominic Robert and Lorretta F. (Urban) Z. Grad. high sch., Downers Grove, Ill. Sales sec. Brookeridge Realty, Downers Grove, 1975-76; sales cons. Kafka Estates Inc., Downers Grove, 1975-76; adminstrv. asst. Chem. Dist., Inc., Oak Brook, Ill., 1976-77; sales rep., mgr. Anographics Corp., Burr Ridge, Ill., 1977-85; pres., owner Graphic Solutions, Inc., Burr Ridge, 1985—. Recipient Supplier Mem. award Internat. Bottled Water Assn., 1987-88, Supplier award for excellence, 1990, Adminstrs. award for excellence U.S. SBA, 1990, Eugene Singer award for best managed co. in small bus. category Graphic Solutions, 1992, Top Performer Supplied award Cutler Hammer Westinghouse Divsn., 1993, 94, Blue Chip Enterprise Initiative award, 1994; named Supplied of Yr. Through Preferred Supplied, Gen. Binding Corp., 1988. Mem. NAFE, Tag and Label Mfrs. Inst. (chmn. pub. rels. and mktg. com., bd. dirs. Best Managed Co. award 1993, 1st place award in U.S. for screen printing 1994), Women Entrepreneurs DuPage County (past pres.), Inst. Packaging Profls., Women in Packaging (exec. bd.), World Label Assn. (1st place in world championship awards 1994, 95). Office: Graphic Solutions Inc 150 Shore Dr Hinsdale IL 60521-5819

ZACHERY-HOPKINS, DONNA S., government tax examiner; b. Kansas City, Kans., Apr. 6, 1952; d. Jerome and Mabel Lee (Gooden) Zachery; m. John Wesley Hopkins, Dec. 22, 1979; children: Carlos and Christopher (twins). BA in Speech, Drama and English, Benedictine Coll., 1974; postgrad., U. Mo., Kans. City, 1975, U. N.Mex., 1976, U. Kans., 1979, Ctrl. Mich. U., 1992—. Libr. clk. Kansas City (Mo.) Pub. Libr., 1974, substitute acting libr., 1975; substitute tchr. Kansas City (Mo.) Sch. Dist., 1974-76, tchr., 1976-87; tchr. Hope Day Sch., Independence, Mo., 1987-89; tax examiner U.S. Dept. Treasury, Kansas City, Mo., 1989—; Libr. Kiddie Coll., Kansas City, Kans., 1986-88; creative dramatics Happy Heart Montessori Pre-Sch., Kansas City, 1972-74. Vol. religious edn. tchr. St. Mary's Cath. Ch., Independence, 1987-91. Recipient Mt. St. Scholastica award, 1974. Mem. Nat. Coun. Tchrs. English, Nat. Assn. Negro Bus. and Profl. Women (chaplain 1980-81, treas. 1981-82), NAACP (entertainment and tourism planner nat. conv., recognition award 1988), Assn. for Improvement Minorities in IRS, Nat. Coun. Accreditation Tchr. Edn. (life, award), Independence Neighborhood Couns.-Clermont Neighborhood Coun. (treas. 1983-88).

ZACKERY, ROBERT THOMPSON, health facility administrator; b. Champaign, Ill., Aug. 22, 1951; s. Robert Lee and Julia Ann (Thompson) Z.; m. DeBorah Pearl Green, Mar. 15, 1975; children: Paul, Bryce, Lauren. B in Social Work, Wartburg Coll., 1973; M in Social Work, U. Ill., 1974. Psychiat. social worker, supr. mental health program Olmsted County Social Svcs., Rochester, Minn., 1975-79; psychiat. svcs. adminstr., dir. psychiat. social svcs. Mayo Med. Ctr., Rochester, 1979—; bd. dirs. Olmsted County Social Svcs. Adv. Bd., Rochester, 1993-94. Football coach Rochester Youth, 1975—, baseball coach, 1989—; mem. alumni bd. Wartburg Coll., 1982-92, bd. regents, 1982—, bd. regents exec. com., 1994—, chmn. minority adv. com., 1989-93; mem. Assn. Governing Bds. Univs. and Colls., 1982—. Named one of Outstanding Young Men of Am., 1983; recipient Alumni citation Wartburg Coll., 1995. Mem. Am. Hosp. Assn. Soc. Social Work Adminstrs. in Health Care (social health policy com. 1995—), Nat. Assn. Social Workers (Minn. chpt. 1979—). Office: Mayo Med Ctr-St Marys Hosp Generose Bldg # 3-110A 1216 2nd St SW Rochester MN 55902

ZACKS, JOELLEN, public affairs executive; b. Tomah, Wis., Nov. 29, 1958; d. John R. and Carol Geane (Nahley) B. BA, U. Wis., 1981; JD, John Marshall Law Sch., 1987. Bar: Ill. 1987, U.S. Dist. Ct. (no. dist.) Ill. 1987. Promotion coord. Playboy Enterprises, Inc., Chgo., 1981-83; dir. pub. rels. ABA, Chgo., 1984—. Mem. ABA, Chgo. Bar Assn., Chgo. Coun. Lawyers, Infant Welfare Chgo. Near North Ctr. (pres.), Achievement Rewards for Coll. Scientists.

ZAFREN, HERBERT CECIL, librarian, educator; b. Balt., Aug. 25, 1925; s. Morris and Sadie Mildred (Edlavitch) Z.; m. Miriam Koenigsberg, Feb. 11, 1951; children: Ken, Edie. A.B., Johns Hopkins U., 1944, postgrad., 1946-49; diploma, Balt. Hebrew Coll., 1944, Litt.D. (hon.), 1969; A.M. in Library Sci, U. Mich., 1950. Jr. instr. Johns Hopkins U., Balt., 1947-49; bibliog. searcher Law Libr. U. Mich., Ann Arbor, 1949-50; libr. Hebrew Union Coll.-Jewish Inst. Religion, Cin., 1950-91, prof. Jewish bibliography, 1968-95; prof. emeritus, 1996—; exec. dir. Am. Jewish Periodical Ctr., Cin., 1956-80, co-dir., 1980-96, dir., 1996—; dir., 1966—; dir. librs. Cin., L.A., N.Y.C., Jerusalem, 1966-94; dir. emeritus librs. Hebrew Union Coll., Jewish Inst. Religion, Cin., 1994—; mem. exec. bd. Jewish Book Council Am., 1979—. Editor Studies in Bibliography and Booklore, 1953—, Bibliographica Judaica, 1969—; compiler: A Gathering of Broadsides, 1967. Served with USN, 1944-46. Mem. Ala, Assn. Jewish Librs. (founder, nat. pres. 1965-66), World Coun. on Jewish Archives (v.p. 1977-81), Assn. Jewish Studies, Spl. Librs. Assn. (pres. Cin. chpt. 1953-54), Coun. Archives and Rsch. Librs. in Jewish Studies (pres. 1974-78, 89-91), Am. Hist. Assn., Israel Bibliophiles, World Union Jewish Studies, AAUP (chpt. pres. 1964-68), Grolier Club (N.Y.C.), Phi Beta Kappa, Beta Phi Mu. Office: Hebrew Union Coll Jewish Inst Religion 3101 Clifton Ave Cincinnati OH 45220-2404

ZAGOREN, ALLEN JEFFREY, surgeon; b. Bklyn., May 17, 1947; s. Max and Harriett (Feldman) Z.; m. Gail Marie Sarcinella, Feb. 20, 1977. BA in Biology, Hofstra U., 1969; DO, Phila. Coll. Osteo. Medicine, 1975. Diplomate Am. Bd. Osteo. Surgery, Nat. Bd. Examiners Osteo.-Med. Surgery. Intern Stratford (N.J.) div. John F. Kennedy Meml. Hosp., 1975-76; resident Cherry Hill (N.J.) Med. Ctr., 1976-80; assoc. prof. surgery U. Medicine and Dentistry, Piscataway, N.J., 1980-82; practice osteo. medicine specializing in surgery Rose Clinic, Des Moines, 1982-94, Capitol Hill Surgery, Des Moines, 1994—; mem. staff Mercy Hosp. Med. Ctr., Des Moines; practice osteo. medicine specializing in surgery Capitol Hill Surgery, Des Moines; chmn. dept. surgery Des Moines Gen. Hosp., 1985-91, Madison County Meml. Hosp., Winterset, Iowa; adj. prof. surgery and nutrition U. Osteo. Medicine; assoc. prof. pharmacy Drake U.; lectr. in field; mem. Nat. Bd. Examiners in Osteo. Medicine and Surgery; mem. surg. rev. com. Bd. Med. Examiners of Iowa, 1996—; med. dir. Wound Care Ctr., 1996, program dir. gen. surgery residency, 1993—. Contbr. articles to profl. jours.; creator videotapes (with others). Bd. dirs. Des Moines Gen. Hosp. Found., sec., 1986—; active Iowa Found. for Med. Care, Nutritional Coun. Iowa; chmn. bd. dirs. Des Moines Gen. Found., 1991-94; trustee Tiffereth Israel Synagogue, 1992. Grantee SKF Labs., Phila., 1986, Norwich (N.Y.) Eaton Labs., 1986, Ross Labs., 1995. Fellow Am. Coll. Osteo. Surgeons (rsch., nutritional support, visual aids coms., chair rsch. com. 1991-92, 1st Prize awards 1982, 83), Am. Coll. Nutrition, Internat. Coll. Surgeons; mem. Am. Osteo. Soc., Am. Soc. Gastrointestinal Endoscopy, Iowa Osteo. Med. Assn. (pres. 1994-95, chmn. constrn. and v.p. bylaws coms. 1992, trustee), Polk County Med. Soc. (treas. 1991-93), Am. Soc. Parenteral and Enteral Nutrition (bd. dirs. 1986, chmn. various coms.), Iowa and Nebr. Soc. Parenteral and Enteral Nutrition (pres. 1990-92), Nat. Wildlife Fedn. (chair com. postgrad. edn. Iowa Health Reform Project 1993), Iowa Health Leadership Consortium (CEO com.), Smithsonian Instn., Airplane Owners and Pilots Assn., Iowa Nebr. Nutrition Soc. (pres. 1990-92). Jewish. Office: Capitol Hill Surgery 1300 Des Moines St Des Moines IA 50309

ZAHN, ANDREW JOSEPH, food company executive; b. Chgo., May 22, 1963; s. Melvyn Herschel and Judith Carol (Cohon) Z.; m. Sandee Lee Castle, Sept. 24, 1989; children: Samantha Lynn, Jacob Louis. Prin. Louis Zahn Drug Co., Melrose Park, Ill., 1986-88; pres. Zahn Investment Group, Chgo., 1988-89, Mama Tish's Internat Foods, Chgo., 1989—. Charity fundraiser Families' and Children's AIDS Network, Chgo., 1992. Mem. Northmoore Country Club, Standard Club. Republican. Jewish. Office: Mama Tishs Internat Foods Ste 640 1111 W 22nd St Hinsdale IL 60521

ZAHNER, MARY ANNE, art educator; b. Dover, Ohio, Mar. 30, 1938; d. Alfred James and Anna Elizabeth (Stewart) Riggle; m. Gordon Dean Zahner, Aug. 27, 1960 (dec. Mar. 1967); 1 child, Anne Colette; m. John Charles Opalek, Aug. 21, 1982. BFA, Ohio U., 1960, MA, 1969; PhD, Ohio State U., 1987. Cert. tchr., Ohio. Instr. art Springfield Twp. Schs., Akron, Ohio, 1960-61, Logan (Ohio) High Sch., 1961-62; instr. art Dover High Sch., 1967-68, chair art dept., 1969-71; teaching asst. Ohio State U., Columbus, 1980-82; from instr. art edn. to asst. prof. U. Dayton, 1971-80, asst. prof., 1982-91, assoc. prof., 1991—; mem. faculty rights, governance and svc. com. U. Dayton, 1992-93, mem. arts series com., 1995—; reviewer Harcourt, Brace, 1993-94. Author: (chpt.) The History of ARt Education: Proceedings from the Second Pa. State Conference, 1989; group exhibn. includes Westpeth Gallery, N.Y., 1995. Sec. Kettering (Ohio) Arts Coun., 1990, mem., 1988—; mem. discretionary support com. Miami Valley Arts Coun., Dayton, 1992; coord. 3d congl. art contest sponsored by Tony P. Hall, Dayton, 1993, 94, 95. Recipient Best of Show award Canton Art Inst., 1969, Inst. Faculty award The Ohio Partnership for the Visual Arts, 1989. Fellow Ohio Art Edn. Assn. (mem. editl. bd. Ohio Art Edn. Jour. 1986—, editor newsletter Artline 1988, workshop coord. 1992, cons. tchr. insvc. for Dayton Pub. Schs. 1995, Outstanding Art Tchr. western dist. 1992); mem. ASCD, Nat. Art Edn. Assn., Assn. Tchr. Educators, Ohio Alliance for Arts Edn. (bd. dirs.), Univ. Coun. for Art Edn., Phi Delta Kappa, Phi Kappa Phi, Delta Kappa Gamma. Democrat. Presbyterian. Home: 4429 Wilmington Pike Kettering OH 45440-1934 Office: U Dayton 114 Rike Ctr Dayton OH 45489-1690

ZAHORSKI, KENNETH JAMES, English language educator, college administrator; b. Cedarville, Ind., Oct. 23, 1939; s. Joseph Antone and Catherine (Romanowski) Z.; m. Marijean Allen, Aug. 18, 1962; children: Twila Michelle Meo, Alison Dawn Hoffman. BS, U. Wis., River Falls, 1961; MA, Ariz. State U., 1963; PhD, U. Wis., 1967. Asst. prof. English U. Wis., Eau Claire, 1967-68; prof. English St. Norbert Coll., De Pere, Wis., 1968—; dir. faculty devel. St. Norbert Coll., De Pere, 1984—. Author: Fantasy Literature: A Core Collection and Reference Guide, 1979 (ALA Outstanding Ref. Book 1979), Lloyd Alexander, Evangeline Walton Ensley, Kenneth Morris: A Primary and Secondary Bibliography, 1981, Peter S. Beagle, 1988, The Sabbatical Mentor: A Practical Guide to Successful Sabbaticals, 1994; editor: The Fantastic Imagination, vol. I, 1977, Dark Imaginings, 1978, The Fantastic Imagination, vol. II, 1978, The Phoenix Tree, 1980, Visions of Wonder, 1981, Fantasists on Fantasy, 1984, Visions and Imaginings, 1992. Recipient Outstanding Alumnus award, U. Wis., River Falls, 1975, Mythopoeic Soc. Spl. award, 1985, Sears Roebuck Found. Teaching Excellence and Campus Leadership award, 1991; Named Outstnding Tchr., 1974, Disting. Scholar, 1987, St. Norbert Coll., De Pere. Mem. Am. Assn. Higher Edn., Assn. Am. Colls., Nat. Coun. Tchrs. of English, Profl. and Organizational Devel. in Higher Edn., Coun. Ind. Colls. (sr. staff assoc.). Office: St Norbert Coll English Dept De Pere WI 54115

ZAHRLY, JANICE HONEA, management educator; b. Ft. Payne, Ala., Sept. 27, 1943; d. John Wiley and Lillian (McKown) Honea. BA, U. Fla., 1964; MBA, U. Ctrl. Fla., 1980; PhD, U. Fla., 1984. Tchr. Hope Mills (N.C.) H.S., 1964-65, Satellite Beach (Fla.) H.S., 1965-69; realtor-assoc. WD Webb Realty, Melbourne, Fla., 1969-70; realtor Aero Realty, Melbourne, 1970-72, Albert J. Tuttle, Realtor, Melbourne, 1972-74; mktg. mgr. Cypress Woods Devel., Orlando, Fla., 1974-76; regional campaign mgr. Pres. Ford Com., 1976; ednl. researcher Peace Corps, Korea, 1976-78; rsch. analyst, tech. writer Rsch. Sys. Inc., Orlando, 1979-80; rsch. asst., lectr. U. Fla., Gainesville, 1980-84; asst. prof. Wayne State U., Detroit, 1984-89; assoc. prof. Old Dominion U., Norfolk, Va., 1989-94, U. N.D., Grand Forks, 1994—; mem. Melbourne Bd. Realtors, 1969-76, orientation chair, 1972, pub. rels. chair, 1973, civic affairs chair, 1973, grievance com., 1975; cons. Wayne County Retarded Persons Assn., Detroit, 1985, Gov.'s Conf. on Women Entrepreneurs, Mich., 1986, Oakland County AAUW Conf. on Women, Mich., 1987, 88, Coll. Bus. and Pub. Adminstrn. Inst. of Mgmt., Old Dominion U., Norfolk, 1990, U.S. Army Corps Engrs., Norfolk, 1990; presenter in field. Contbr. chpts. to books, articles to profl. jours. and procs. Vol. Tidewater AIDS Crisis Task Force, Norfolk, 1990-93, bd. dirs., 1990-92, v.p., 1991, rec. sec., 1992; mem. occupational adv. com. Brevard County Mental Health Ctr., Fla., 1973-74; mem. Brevard County Libr. Bd., 1973-74; bd. dirs. Fla. Dist. 12 Mental Health Bd., 1973-74, sec. 1973-74; bd. dirs. Alachua County Crisis Ctr., Gainesville, 1982-84, chair, 1983-84; vol. Open Door, Detroit, 1986-89; bd. dirs. United Way Grand Forks area, 1996—. Recipient Best Paper award Midwest Soc. for Human Resources/Indsl. Rels., 1989; rsch. fellow Fed. Mogul Corp., 1987-88; rsch. grantee Wayne State U., 1985-89, Old Dominion U., 1990, U. N.D., 1995, 96. Mem. AAUW (bd. dirs. 1974-75), Acad. Mgmt., Assn. for Rsch. on Nonprofit Orgns./Vols., So. Mgmt. Assn., Hampton Rds. Gator Club (co-founder, treas. 1989-91), Alpha Omicron Pi (bd. dirs. alumnae chpt. 1969-73, v.p. 1969-73). Home: 3424 Cherry St Apt A1 Grand Forks ND 58201-7692

ZAIKOW, LARRY J., painter; b. Red Lake, Ont., Can., Dec. 25, 1951; s. Jim DeMetor and Alice Helen (Dutka) Z. Grad., Red Lake H.S. With Poetry Co., Sacramento, Calif., 1987-92. Author: Who's Who in Poetry, 1992. Home: 334 Howey St, Red Lake, ON Canada

ZAIMAN, K. ROBERT, dentist; b. Cin., Oct. 19, 1944; s. Noboru Gary and Toshiko (Matsuyama) Z.; m. Kimberly Ann Sass, Nov. 6, 1976; children: Kara Jean, Matthew Robert. Student, Creighton U., Omaha, 1962-64, DDS, 1968. Asst. prof. Creighton U. Sch. Dentistry, Omaha, 1971-73, assoc. prof., 1973-75; pvt. practice dentistry Omaha, 1971—. Past v.p., bd. dirs. Japanese-Am. Citizens League, Omaha, 1977-86; bd. elders King of Kings Luth. Ch., 1990—. Lt. comdr. USN, 1964-71. Fellow Acad. Gen. Dentistry (pres. 1976-77, nat. del. 1971-76), Acad. Continuing Edn.; mem. ADA, Omaha Dist. Dental Soc. (treas. 1980-85, bd. dirs. 1968—), Nebr. Dental Assn. (del. 1971—), Omaha Study Club (pres.), Delta Sigma Delta (pres. 1973-74). Office: 10841 Q St Ste 109 Omaha NE 68137-3701

ZAJICEK, LYNN ENGELBRECHT, educational administrator; b. Newport News, Va., Mar. 25, 1950; d. Herbert Charles and Lois (Kohler) Engelbrecht; m. Jon M. Zajicek, June 6, 1970; children: Carlye Lynn, Kate Elizabeth. BA, Kearney State Coll., 1971; MEd, U. Nebr., 1973, EdS, 1988. Cert. profl. adminstr./supr., Nebr. Tchr. Lincoln (Nebr.) Pub. Schs., 1971-73; instr. U.S. Army PREP Program, Crailsheim, Fed. Republic of Germany, 1974-76; subs. tchr. Grand Island (Nebr.) Pub. Schs., 1976-77; mgr., owner rental property Grand Island, 1978—; asst. on survey project U. Nebr., Lincoln, 1987-88; adminstr., ednl. diagnostician Nebr. Ctr. for Evaluation of Devel. and Learning, Inc., Grand Island, 1988—; bd. dirs. Reorganized Mark V Mortgage Corp. Bd. mem. PTA, Grand Island, 1980—; supt. Bible Sch. St. Stephen's Ch., Grand Island, 1984-85; mem. Christian edn. com. St. Stephen's, 1985—, subcom. for adult and continuing edn. of strategic planning com. Grand Island Pub. Schs., 1987; coach Odyssey of the Mind Grand Island Pub. Schs., 1986—; active in heart and cancer funds in Grand Island; bd. dirs. Episc. Ch. Women; candidate cmpaign mgr. Rep. Women, 1978; bd. dirs., exec. com. Marque of Nebr., 1989—. Recipient Gen. Arnold scholarship USAF, 1967. Mem. AAUW, Assn. Supervision and Curriculum Devel., Nat. Assn. Secondary Sch. Prins., Nebr. Coun. Sch. Adminstrs., Nebr. Assn. Elem. Sch. Prins., Nebr. Dental Assn. Aux. (numerous offices including pres. 1981-82), Hall County Dental Aux. (sec., treas. 1976—), St. Francis Med. Aux., Nebr. Assn. for Children and Adults with Learning Disabilities, Phi Delta Kappa, Pi Delta Phi, Alpha Mu Gamma, Sigma Tau Delta, Xi Phi. Home: 1618 S Harrison St Grand Island NE 68803-6359 Office: Nebr Ctr for Evaluation of Devel and Learning Inc 2121 N Webb Rd Ste 305 Grand Island NE 68803-1751

ZAKAS, JOSEPH C., state legislator; b. Chgo., Nov. 4, 1950; s, Anthony and Ann (Phillips) Z.; m. Margaret Anne Kaiser, 1978; children: Mary Sarah, Katherine Grace, Stephen John. BA, U. Ill., 1972; JD, MBA, U. Notre Dame, 1980. U.S. senator from Ind., 1982—; assoc. Thorne, Grodnik & Ransel, South Bend, Ind., 1980—; chmn. admin. rules oversight commn., govt. affairs and transactions com., chmn. civil law divsn. judiciary com.; mem. natural resources com., ethics com. taxation divsn., finance and public policy com., govt. and regulatory affairs coms. bd. dirs. REAL Serv, Michiana Arts & Sci. Coun.; active Blue Ribbon Commn. Against Domestic Violence. Mem. Am. Bar Assn., Ind. Bar. Assn., St. Joseph County Bar Assn., Knights of Columbus. Republican. Office: 16372 Wild Cherry Dr Granger IN 46530-8544 also: State Senate State Capital Indianapolis IN 46204*

ZAKER, GREGORY ALLEN, electronics engineer; b. Cleve., May 28, 1948; s. Vito and Carol Lilian (Peters) Z.; m. Kathleen Alice Gogerty, Nov. 28, 1970. BSEE, Case Western Res. U. Chief engr. WIXZ Radio, McKeesport, Pa., 1970-72, Shepard Broadcasting WLYV Radio, Fort Wayne, Ind., 1972-74; devel. engr. Zipcor Inc., Ft. Wayne, 1974-77; engr. Gould Ocean Systems Divsn., Cleve., 1977-78; electronics engr. LXD Operation, Gen. Electric, Beachwood, Ohio, 1978-82; prin. engr. Technicare Corp., Solon, Ohio, 1982-86, ABL Engring. Inc., Mentor, Ohio, 1986—; cons. Inovative Imaging Inc., Solon, 1986, Orion Inc., Cleve., 1986-87. Mem. IEEE, Audio Engring. Soc. Office: ABL Engring Inc 6111 Heisley Rd Mentor OH 44060

ZAKSHESKE, MARK RICHARD, treasurer; b. Erie, Pa., Apr. 16, 1956; s. Vernon F. and Ruth M. (Merski) Z.; m. Heidi Widmar, July 18, 1981; children: Jennifer, Joseph, Julia. BS, John Caroll U., 1978; MBA, Loyola Coll., 1993. CPA, Ohio. Internal auditor Ameritrust, Cleve., 1978-79, Eaton Corp., Cleve., 1979-80; sr. internal auditor Marshall Field, Cleve., 1980-81; contr. Standard Products Co., Goldsboro, N.C., 1981-88, Haskell of Pitts., Verona, Pa., 1988-90, Stone Indsl., College Park, Md., 1990-95; treasurer Precision Products Group, Inc., Rockford, Ill., 1995—; bd. dirs. Kingship Fed. Credit Union, Balt. Mem. Fin. Mgmt. Assn., KC (warden 1988-94). Republican. Roman Catholic. Home: 7241 Sentinel Rd Rockford IL 61107-5503 Office: Precision Products Group 4205 Galleria Dr Rockford IL 61111

ZAMECNIK, PAUL ARTHUR, medical device manufacturing company executive; b. East Cleveland, Ohio, Apr. 19, 1960; s. Norman A. and L. Jean (Treter) Z.; m. Susan M. Griffin, June 19, 1987; children: Julia Lynn, Brian Griffin. BSEE, Purdue U., 1982; MBA, Harvard U., 1987. Project engr. Welch Allyn, Skaneateles Falls, N.Y., 1982-85; cons. McKinsey & Co., Cleve., 1987-92; dir. mktg. STERIS Corp., Mentor, Ohio, 1992-93; v.p. Steris Corp., Mentor, Ohio, 1993—. Home: 9450 Highbridge Ct Mentor OH 44060 Office: STERIS Corp. 5960 Heisley Rd Mentor OH 44060

ZAMMIT, JOHN P., financial planner; b. N.Y.C., May 11, 1942; s. John G. and Farla (Rudolph) Z.; m. Linda Zammit, Jan. 24, 1992; children from previous marriage: Karen M., Christine B. BA, Hunter Coll., 1972; MS, L.I. U., 1976; adminstrn. cert., Emporia U., 1979. Investigator Equifax, N.Y.C., 1965-67; agent N.Y. Life Ins. Co., N.Y.C., 1967-76; elem. sch. tchr. L.I., N.Y., 1976-77; elem. prin. Olpe, Kans., 1977-78, Buffalo, Minn., 1978-79; mgr. Kraun & Assocs., St. Paul, 1978-79; pres., owner Midwest Adv. Svc. Inc., St. Paul, 1979—. Contbr. articles to profl. jours. With USMC, 1960-64. Home and Office: Midwest Advisory Ser-Kramer 104 N Main St Geneva NY 14456-1604

ZANDER, GAILLIENNE GLASHOW, psychologist; b. Bklyn., Apr. 7, 1932; d. Saul and Anna (Karasik) G.; m. A.J. Zander, Aug. 5, 1952; children: Elizabeth L., Caroline M., Catherine A. MusB, U. Wis., 1953, MS, 1970; PhD, Marquette U., 1984. Diplomate Bd. Forensic Examiners. Music tchr. Wis. Sch. Systems, 1953-65; psychol. asst. Vernon Psychol. Labs., Chgo., 1965-70; psychologist Milw. Pub. Schs., 1970-92, CESA 19, Kenosha, Wis., 1977-78; pvt. practice psychology Milw., 1980—. Fellow Am. Orthopsychiat. Assn.; mem. APA, Wis. Psychol. Assn., Psychologists Assn. in Milw. Pub. Schs. (rep., v.p., pres.), Am. Acad. Pain Mgmt. (diplomate). Home: 13750 Carson Ct Brookfield WI 53005-4989 also: Cooper Resource Ctr 20860 Watertown Rd Waukesha WI 52186-1872

ZANDER, SIDNEY G., manufacturing executive; b. Toledo, Oct. 10, 1923. Pres. Indsl. Enterprises, Inc., Toledo, 1976-92, chmn., 1992—. With USN, 1943-46. Republican. Office: Indsl Enterprises Inc 324 W Laskey Rd Toledo OH 43612-3433

ZANEVSKY, ANDREW, computer consulting company executive; b. Minsk, Belarus, Apr. 27, 1964; came to U.S., 1991; s. Anatoli and Galina (Urieva) Z.; divorced; 1 child, Nikkie; m. Katrin Ofitserova, Sept. 14, 1994; 1 child, Anthony. BS in Computer Sci. cum laude, Minsk U. Info. Systems, 1986, MS in Computer Sci., 1990. Programmer, analyst Minsk U. Info. Systems, 1983-88; dir. software dept. DIA, Minsk, 1988-90; project leader Centaurus, Minsk, 1990-91; cons. BEZ Systems, Inc., Deerfield, Ill., 1991-94; pres. AZ Databases, Inc., Buffalo Grove, Ill., 1994—. Contbr. articles to profl. jours. and newsletters. Mem. Great Lakes SQL Server Users Group (v.p. programs 1993-94, pres. 1994—). Office: AZ Databases Inc 89 Manchester Dr Buffalo Grove IL 60089

ZANG, DEBRA JEAN, librarian; b. Pratt, Kans., June 3, 1953; d. Robert Lee and Mary Joan (Stephenson) Greenstreet; m. Ray Gene Zang, July 18, 1981; children: Jennifer Annette Glenn Zang. AS, Pratt (Kans.) C.C., 1973; BS, Northwestern Okla. State U., 1975. Cert. in libr. sci., K-12, Kans. K-12 libr. Unified Sch. Dist. #332, Cunningham, Kans., 1975-81; h.s. libr. Unified Sch. Dist. #254, Medicine Lodge, Kans., 1981-91; mid. sch. libr. Unified Sch. Dist. #382, Pratt, Kans., 1991—. Mem. NEA, Kans. Edn. Assn., Pratt Edn. Assn., Kans. Assn. of Sch. Librs., Delta Kappa Gamma (Beta Psi).

ZANGER, LARRY MARTIN, lawyer, partner; b. Bklyn., July 10, 1946; s. Mark H. and Lillian (Cohen) A.; m. Bonnie Agnes Zanger, June 8, 1975; children: Laura, Eric. BS, BA, Northwestern U., 1967, JD, 1970. CPA, Ill. Assoc. McDermott, Will & Emery, Chgo., 1970-72; adj. prof. U. Ill., Chgo., 1972-75; ptnr. Zanger, Lang & Heftman, Chgo., 1972-83, Martin, Craig, Chester & Sonnenschein, Chgo., 1983-90, McBride Baker & Coles, Chgo., 1990—. Columnist Chgo. Computer Guide, 1989—; contbr. articles to profl. jours. Treas. Elmhurst (Ill.) Baseball Leagues, 1990—. Recipient Elijah Watts Sells award, Am. Inst. CPA, 1968. Mem. Chgo. Bar Assn., 1989— (chmn. computer law com., 1994-95). Office: McBride Baker & Coles 500 W Madison St Chicago IL 60661

ZANGGER, RUSSELL GEORGE, organization executive, flying school executive; b. Larchwood, Iowa, Feb. 22, 1922; s. Charlie and Lina Bell (Sharp) Zangger; m. Marie Unruh, May 24, 1944; 1 child, James Russell. Student pub. schs., Larchwood; DD (hon.), Ch. Gospel Ministries, Chula Vista, Calif., 1981. Farmer, Larchwood, 1944-79; owner, operator Zangger Flying Svc., Larchwood, 1949—; founder, dir. The Remain Intact ORGANization, Larchwood, 1980—. Spokesperson against infant circumcision. Home and Office: The Remain Intact Organization RR 2 Box 86 1917 135th St Larchwood IA 51241-7712

ZANGRANDO, ROBERT LEWIS, historian educator; b. Albany, N.Y., May 16, 1932; s. Silvio John and Margaret (Troestler) Z.; m. Irma Ann Comeau, Dec. 30, 1954 (div. Mar. 1969); children: Lisa Marie (Zangrando) Van Vechten, David Duane; m. Joanna Elizabeth Schneider, Mar. 29, 1969 (div. Dec. 1992). BA, Union Coll., 1958; MA, U. Pa., 1960, PhD, 1963. Asst. prof of history Rutgers U., Camden, N.J., 1963-65; asst. exec. sec. Am. Hist. Assn., Washington, 1965-69; editor Yale Univ. Press, New Haven, Conn., 1969-71; assoc. prof. history U. Akron, Ohio, 1971-81; prof. history U. Akron, 1981-94, prof. emeritus history, 1994—; program coord. State of N.J. OEO, Trenton, 1965; lectr. Yale U., New Haven, Conn., 1969-71. Co-editor: (with Albert Blaustein) Civil Rights and the Black American, 1970, with new Introduction Civil Rights and African Americans, 1991; author: NAACP Crusade Against Lynching, 1909-1950, 1980; contbr. articles to profl. jours. V.p., bd. dirs. Akron Rape Crisis Ctr., 1979-81; sec. Ohio-Chgo. Art Project, 1980-83; bd. dirs. Planned Parenthood of Summit County, Ohio, 1980-83; mem. Akron Human Relations Commn., 1981. Recipient Grants in Aid Am. Coun. Learned Socs., 1969, Eleanor Roosvelt Inst., 1974-75, Harry S. Truman Libr. Inst., 1983. Mem. Am. Hist. Assn., Ohio Acad. History, Orgn. Am. Historians, Coordinating Coun. for Women in History. Democrat. Home: 2067-B Higby Dr Stow OH 44224 Office: Univ Akron History Dept History Dept Akron OH 44325-1902

ZANOT, CRAIG ALLEN, lawyer; b. Wyandotte, Mich., Nov. 15, 1955; s. Thomas and Faye Blanch (Sperry) Z. AB with distinction, U. Mich., 1977; JD cum laude, Ind. U., 1980. Bar: Ind. 1980, U.S. Dist. Ct. (so. dist.) Ind. 1980, Mich. 1981, U.S. Dist. Ct. (no. dist.) Ind. 1981, U.S. Ct. Appeals (6th cir.) 1985, U.S. Dist. Ct. (ea. dist.) Mich. 1987. Law clk. to presiding justice Allen County Superior Ct, Ft. Wayne, 1980-81; ptnr. Davidson, Breen & Doud P.C., Saginaw, Mich., 1981—. Mem. ABA, Mich. Bar Assn., Ind. Bar Assn., Saginaw County Bar Assn. Roman Catholic. Home: 547 S Linwood Beach Rd Linwood MI 48634-9432 Office: Davidson Breen & Doud PC 1121 N Michigan Ave Saginaw MI 48602-4762

ZANOW, LEROY, manufacturing company technician; b. Milw., Nov. 5, 1939. Assoc. Mech. Design, Milw. Area Tech. Coll., 1990. Machinist Evinrude Motors, Milw., 1970-90; CAD technician Milsco Mfg. Co., Milw., 1990—. Office: Milsco Mfg Co 9009 N 51st St Milwaukee WI 53223-2403

ZAPKE, CLIFFORD F., secondary education educator; b. N.Y.C., Dec. 28, 1946; s. Edward and Edith (Bellion) Z.; m. Sue Gebhart, Aug. 16, 1969; children: Heather, Allison. BA, U. Dubuque, 1969; MA, No. Ill. U., 1974. Cert. social studies and English tchr., adminstr., Ill. Tchr. social studies Machesney Park (Ill.) Schs., 1969—; chief negotiator Harlem Fedn. Tchrs., Machesney Park, 1984-88; founder Project Ill. Future, Harlem Schs., Machesney Park, 1987-95, gifted cons., 1984-89. Mem. blue print commn. Rockford (Ill.) Cmty., 1994. Named Econs. Tchr. of Yr., Jr. Achievement, Rock River Valley, 1990. Mem. Nat. Coun. Scoial Studies, Ill. Coun. on Teaching Econs. Edn. (award for excellence in teaching 1995), Ill. Fedn. Tchrs., C. of C. (ednl. com. 1995). Home: 3648 Doreen Roscoe IL 61073

ZAPP, DAVID EDWIN, infosystems specialist, investment consultant; b. Columbus, Ohio, Dec. 6, 1950; s. Robert Louis and Harriet (Miller) Z.; divorced; 1 child, Heather; m. Grace Lynn Spidell, Apr. 28, 1978. Road freight conductor N&W Ry., Columbus, 1971-77; with Franklin County Welfare, Columbus, 1977-78; income tax preparer J.E. Wiggins Co., Columbus, 1978-81; pub. inquiry asst. Ohio Bur. Workers Compensation, Columbus, 1978-80, auditor, 1980-82, programmer, analyst, 1982-88, infosystems analyst, 1988-94; investment cons. Montano Securities Corp., Columbus, 1994; ind. registered rep. Quest Capital Strategies, Inc., Columbus, 1995—. Council mem. Southside Orgns., Columbus, 1985-86; mem. Gates Street Block Watch, Columbus, 1986. Mem. Nat. Assn. Investors Corp., Am. Assn. Individual Investors, Assn. Sys. Mgrs., Ohio Jaycees (program mgr. 1984-85, #1 individual devel. v.p. 1983-84, dist. dir. 1986—, named Outstanding Dist. Dir. 1986), Southside Columbus Jaycees (mgmt. v.p. 1984-85, pres. 1985-86, senator 1989), Employee Mgmt. Participation (chmn. 1985-86). Home: 299 E Gates St Columbus OH 43206-3627 Office: Quest Capital Strategies Inc P O Box 077680 Columbus OH 43207-7680

ZAPP, ROBERT LOUIS, electronic test engineer; b. Columbus, Ohio, Apr. 19, 1946; s. Robert Louis and Harriet Evelyn (Miller) Z.; m. Mary Louise Appl, May 1, 1971; children: Christine, Robert. AD in Electronic Engring. Tech., DeVry Inst., 1974; BS in Electronic Engring. Tech., Franklin U., 1984. Electronic technician Battelle Meml. Inst., Columbus, 1973-84; quality control test engr. Liebert Corp., Worthington, Ohio, 1984-87, quality control engr., 1987-94, electronics test engr., 1994—. Big brother Big Bro. Assn., 1968-74. With USAF, 1965-69. Mem. Am. Soc. Quality Control, Am. Legion. Roman Catholic. Home: 322 Demorest Rd Columbus OH 43204-1125

ZAR, JERROLD H(OWARD), academic administrator, biology educator, statistician; b. Chgo., June 28, 1941; s. Max and Sarah (Brody) Z.; m. Carol Bachenheimer, Jan. 15, 1967; children: David Michael, Adam Joseph. BS, No. Ill. U., 1962; MS, U. Ill., Urbana, 1964, PhD, 1967. NSF fellow marine sci. Duke U. Marine Lab., Beaufort, N.C., 1965; research assoc. dept. zoology U. Ill., Urbana, 1967-68; asst. prof. dept. biol. scis. No. Ill. U., DeKalb, 1968-71; assoc. prof. No. Ill. U., 1971-78, prof., 1978—, chmn. dept. biol. scis., 1978-84, assoc. provost grad. studies and research, dean Grad. Sch., 1984—; vis. scientist Argonne Nat. Lab., 1974; cons. EPA, also other govt. agys. and industries; founder, dir. ENCAP, Inc., 1974-93. Author: Biostatistical Analysis, 1974, 2d edit., 1984, 3d edit., 1996. NIH fellow U. Ill. Urbana, 1965-67. Fellow AAAS; mem. Am. Inst. Biol. Scis., Am. Ornithologists Union, Am. Physiol. Soc., Am. Statis. Assn., Biometric Soc., Cooper Ornithol. Soc., Am. Soc. Zoologists, Ecol. Soc. Am. (cert. sr. ecologist), Nat. Assn. Biol. Tchrs., Nat. Assn. Environ. Profls. (cert. environ. profl.), Wilson Ornithol. Soc. Office: No Ill U Off Dean Grad Sch De Kalb IL 60115-2864

ZAREFSKY, DAVID HARRIS, academic administrator, communication studies educator; b. Washington, June 20, 1946; s. Joseph Leon and Miriam Ethel (Lewis) Z.; m. Nikki Sheryl Martin, Dec. 23. 1970; children: Beth Ellen, Marc Philip. BS, Northwestern U., 1968, MA, 1969, PhD, 1974. Instr. communication studies Northwestern U., Evanston, Ill., 1968-73, asst. prof., 1974-77, assoc. prof., 1977-82, prof., 1982—, chmn. dept., 1975-83, assoc. dean Sch. Speech, 1983-88, dean, 1988—. Author: President Johnson's War on Poverty, 1986 (Winans-Wichelns award 1986), Lincoln, Douglas and Slavery, 1990 (Winans-Wichelns award 1991), Public Speaking: Strategies for Success, 1996; co-author: Contemporary Debate, 1983; editor: Rhetorical Movement, 1993; co-editor: American Voices, 1989, Contemporary American Voices, 1992; contbr. articles to profl. jours. Recipient Best Article award So. Speech Communication Assn., 1985, Midwest Forensic Assn., 1988; named Debate Coach of the Year Georgetown U., 1973, Emory U., 1972. Mem. AAUP, Speech Comm. Assn. (pres. 1993, dist. scholar award 1994), Ctrl. State Comm. Assn. (pres. 1986-87), Am. Forensic Assn. (Svc. award 1989), Delta Sigma Rho-Tau Kappa Alpha (Svc. award 1986), others. Democrat. Jewish. Office: Northwestern U 1905 Sheridan Rd Evanston IL 60208-2260

ZARICZNYJ, BASILIUS, orthopedic surgeon; b. Ukraine, Aug. 31, 1924; came to U.S., 1951; s. Alex and Maria (Kostiw) Z.; m. Stefania Pidburny, Aug. 21, 1954; children: Marta, Stephanie Christine, Andrea Maria, Mark B. MD, U. Bonn, Germany, 1951. Diplomate Am. Bd. Orthopedic Surgery. Resident St. Luke's Hosp., Chgo., 1954-56, Univ. Hosps., Oklahoma City, 1955-56; fellow in orthopedics Northwestern U., Chgo., 1957; asst. prof. Sch. Medicine U. Okla., Oklahoma City, 1957-58; orthopedic surgeon Springfield, Ill., 1958—; clin. prof. Sch. Medicine So. Ill. U., Springfield, Ill., 1973-85, acting chmn. divsn. orthopedic surgery, 1972-75, chief sports medicine sect., 1975-82, program chmn. sports injury symposium, 1977-79, 82, 83; mem. sports medicine com. Ill. State Med. Soc., 1979-80; chmn. dept. orthopedic surgery St. John's and Meml. Hosps., Springfield, 1970-79; program chmn. Med. Congress of World Fedn. of Ukrainian Med. Assn., Dniepropetrovsk, 1994, Odessa, Ukraine, 1996; presenter Am. Acad. Orthopedic Surgeons, Miami, Fla., 1961, N.Y., 1969, San Francisco, 1971, Washington, 1972, Las Vegas, 1973, 77, Anaheim, Calif., 1983, Chgo. Orthopedic Soc., 1967, 76, O'Donoghue Okla. Orthopedic Alumni Assn., Oklahoma City, 1972, 75, 78, Internat. Soc. for Orthopedic Surgery and Traumatology, XII World Congress, Tel Aviv, 1972, Copenhagen, 1975, Kyoto, Japan, 1978, So. Ill U. Sch. Medicine, Springfield, 1977, 79, 80, 82, Ill. State Orthopedic Soc., Chgo., 1978, ACS, Chgo., 1979, Am. Orthopedic Soc. for Sports Medicine, Atlanta, 1980, Big Sky, Mont., 1980,, Lake Tahoe, Nev., 1981, Clin. Orthopedic Soc., Chgo., 1987, World Fedn. Ukrainian Med. Assn., Kiev, Ukraine, 1990, U. Lviv, Ukraine, 1990, 11th Congress of Orthopedic Surgeons of Ukraine, Kharkiv, 1991, 4th Congress of World Fedn. of Ukrainian Med. Assn., Kharkiv, 1992, among others. Mem. editl. bd. Jour. Ukrainan Med. Assn. N.Am., 1977-95; contbr. articles to profl. jours. Fellow Am. Acad. Orthopedic Surgery; mem. AMA, Ill. Orthopedic Soc., Internat. Soc. Orthopedic Surgery and Traumatology, Am. Orthopedic Soc. for Sports Medicine, Internat. Soc. of the Knee, Mid-Am. Orthopedic Assn., Ukrainian Acad. and Profl. Assn. Pres. 1985-89), Sangamon County Med. Soc., Chgo. Orthopedic Soc. Home and Office: 125 Oakmont Dr Springfield IL 62704

ZARRELLI, MARGARET COTT, community action agency administrator; b. Boonville, Mo., Aug. 17, 1946; d. Lawrence William and Hazel Agnes (Hugg) Cott; m. Charles L. Stouffer; children by previous marriage: Jennifer M., Anne-Marie. Student, U. Ibero-Americana, Mexico City, 1968; BA, U. Chgo., 1969. Rsch. asst. Dr. Alice Rossi, Chgo., 1964-66, Nick Ardito, Sec. Agr. in Panama, Chgo., 1966-67; cmty. vol. VISTA, Brownsville, Tex., 1969; county coord. Mo. Valley Human Resource Cmty. Action Agy., Marshall, Mo., 1980-82, housing inspector, 1982-86, asst. dir. cmty. svc., 1986-90, spl. projects coord., 1990-93, exec. asst., 1993—; mem. adv. bd. Fitzgibbon Hosp., Marshall, 1993—; mem., past officer Saline County Inter-Agy. Coun., Marshall, 1984—. Creator emergency program AWARE, 1983—. Mem. city coun., Miami, Mo., 1985-90; chair bd. ARC, Marshall, 1988—; mem. Friends of Miami, 1993—. Recipient Proclamation of Recognition Mo. Legislature, 1985. Mem. Mo. Assn. Cmty. Action, Mo. Assn. Social Welfare, Com. to Keep Missourians Warm, Marshall C. of C. Democrat. Baptist. Home: PO Box 36 Miami MO 65344 Office: Mo Valley Human Resource Cmty Action Agy PO Box 550 Marshall MO 65340

ZARRETT, MARY ANN, mental health professional, educator, consultant; b. Big Clifty, Ky., July 8, 1949; d. Julius Forest and Gladys Mae (Hawkins) Duvall; m. Robert Warren Zarrett, Dec. 27, 1969 (div. Aug. 1983); children: Rob Warren, Elizabeth Duvall. BSN, U. Ky., 1971; MS in Counseling, Ctrl. Mo. State U., 1977; MA in Human and Orgnl. Devel., The Fielding Inst., 1994, PhD in Human and Orgnl. Systems, 1996. RN, N.D.; nat. cert. counselor. Rsch., cataloging and circulation asst. U. Ky. Med. Ctr. Library, Lexington, 1969-71; nurse aide Taylor Manor Nursing Home, Versailles, Ky., 1970; self-employed Burlington, Vt., 1971-74; per diem nurse psychiat. ward St. Luke's Hosp., Fargo, N.D., 1988-92; counselor, instr. Moorhead State U., Fargo, 1985-89, asst. prof., 1990—, dir. tng. Counseling Ctr., 1987-90, outreach coord., 1989-90, affirmative action officer, 1992; cons. Minn. Army N.G. through Met. State U., 1987; cons. Pathways/U.S. West, 1990—; orgnl. cons., 1990—. Adv. bd. mem. Compassionate Friends Fargo, N.D., 1986—; chmn. music Plymouth Congregational Ch., Fargo, 1986-88; chmn. Fargo Clinic Art Gallery, 1982-84. Mem. ACA, Minn. Assn. Specialists in Group Work, Am. Mental Health Counselors Assn., Nat. Orgnl. Devel. Network, Phi Kappa Phi. Republican. Congregationalist. Office: Moorhead State U Counseling Ctr Counseling Ctr Moorhead MN 56560

ZASADIL, JEANNE, management consultant; b. Oak Park, Ill., Dec. 28, 1940; d. Rudolph John and Elizabeth (Voldrich) Z. AA, Morton Coll., 1960; BS in Communications cum laude, U. Ill., 1962. Assoc. pub. rels. dir. United Way/Crusade of Mercy, Chgo., 1969-82; v.p. not-for-profit devel./pub. rels. Focus on Fundraising, Inc., Chgo., 1983-84; exec. search profl., v.p., gen. mgr. The Cantor Concern, Chgo., 1985-86; prin. Zasadil & Assocs., Chgo., 1982—. Bd. dirs. The Anixter Ctr., Greater Chgo. Food Depository, Primitive Art Soc. Chgo. Recipient Disting. Svc. award Women in Communications, Inc. Mem. Pub. Rels. Soc. Am. (pres. Chgo. chpt. 1984-85), Women in Comm., Inc. (pres. Chgo. chpt. 1977-78), Internat. Assn. Bus. Communicators (pres. Chgo. chpt. 1972-73). Office: 175 E Delaware Pl Chicago IL 60611-1739

ZAUDTKE, GARY ARNOLD, college dean, quality consultant; b. Mission Creek, Minn., Feb. 4, 1948; s. Arnold Albert and Sylvia Ann (Spinler) W.; m. Karen Ann Maack, July 10, 1970 (div. 1985); 1 child, Kelly; m. Joan Elaine Bianchet, Dec. 31, 1985; children: Bryan, Brenda. BA in Indsl. Edn., U. Minn., Duluth, 1966, MEd, 1975. Instr. Duluth Tech. Coll., 1970-94; dean indsl. div. Lake Superior Coll., Duluth, 1994—; mgr. Minn. Tech. Coll. System, St. Paul, 1986-92; prin. Quality Tng. for Quality Award, Mpls., 1992-94; pres. Customized Bus. and Industry Tng. Svcs., 1991-93, treas., 1989-90. Mem. Am. Soc. for Quality Control. Democrat. Roman Catholic. Home: 3232 Piedmont Ave Duluth MN 55811-2840 Office: Lake Superior Coll 2101 Trinity Rd Duluth MN 55811

ZAVACKY, LYNETTE MICHELE, women's health nurse; b. Wheeling, W.Va., Feb. 2, 1966; d. Sam J. and Linda L. (Cheroka) Z. ADN, Belmont Tech. Coll., 1986; BSN, Ohio U., 1989; MSN, W.Va. U., 1990. RN, Ohio; cert. child birth tchr., inpatient obstetric nurse. Staff nurse obstetrics Bellaire (Ohio) City Hosp.; part-time clin. instr. W.Va. No. Community Coll., Wheeling. Home: 67561 Elizabeth St Saint Clairsville OH 43950-9127

ZAWADA, EDWARD THADDEUS, JR., physician, educator; b. Chgo., Oct. 3, 1947; s. Edward Thaddeus and Evelyn Mary (Kovarek) Z.; m. Nancy Ann Stephen, Mar. 26, 1977; children: Elizabeth, Nicholas, Victoria, Alexandra. BS summa cum laude, Loyola U., Chgo., 1969; MD summa cum laude, Loyola-Stritch Sch. Medicine, 1973. Diplomate Am. Bd. Internal Medicine, Am. Bd. Nephrology, Am. Bd. Nutrition, Am. Bd. Critical Care, Am. Bd. Geriatrics, Am. Bd. Clin. Pharm. Intern UCLA Hosp., 1973, resident, 1974-76; asst. prof. medicine UCLA, 1978-79, U. Utah, Salt Lake City, 1979-81; assoc. prof. medicine Med. Coll. Va., Richmond, 1981-83; assoc. prof. medicine, physiology & pharmacology U. S.D. Sch. Medicine, Sioux Falls, 1983-86, Freeman prof., chmn. dept. Internal Medicine, 1987—, chief div. nephrology and hypertension, 1983-88, pres. univ. physician's practice plan, 1992—; chief renal sect. Salt Lake VA Med. Ctr., 1980-81; asst. chief med. service McGuire VA Med. Ctr., Richmond, 1981-83. Editor: Geriatric Nephrology and Urology, 1984; contbr. articles to profl. publs. Pres. Minnehaha div. Am. Heart Assn., 1984-87, pres. Dakota affiliate Am. Heart Assn., 1989-91. VA Hosp. System grantee, 1981-85, 85-88; Health and Human Svcs. grantee Pub. Health Scvs. Rsch. Adminstrn. Bureau Health Profl., 1993—. Fellow ACP, Am. Coll. Chest Physicians, Am. Coll. Nutrition, Am. Coll. Clin. Pharmacology, Internat. Coll. Angiology, Am. Coll. Angiology, Am. Coll. Clin. Pharmacology, Royal Soc. Medicine; mem. Internat. Soc. Nephrology, Am. Soc. Nephrology, Am. Soc. Pharmacology and Exptl. Therapeutics, Am. Physiol. Soc., Am. Inst. Nutrition, Am. Soc. Clin. Nutrition, Am. Geriatric Soc., Westward Ho Country Club. Democrat. Roman Catholic. Home: 2908 S Duchess Ave Sioux Falls SD 57103-4826 Office: U SD Sch Medicine 1400 W 22nd St Sioux Falls SD 57105-1505

ZAWADZKI, DOLORES JOAN, adult education educator; b. Chgo., Oct. 22, 1949; d. Anthony William and Josephine Frances (Mancuso) Arena; m. Joseph Zawadzki, July 14, 1973; children: Joseph Michael, Alice Louise. BA, Northeastern Ill. U., 1980, MA in Ednl. Adminstrn., 1993. Substitute tchr. Chgo. Archdiocese, 1980-85; adult educator Wright C.C., Chgo., 1985-86, ESL coord., 1986—; ESL tchr. St. Patrick's H.S., 1989—; bd. mem. Pow Wow Comm.; adv. bd. Northeastern Ill. U., Chgo., 1993—. Campaign Aid Democratic Orgn., Chgo., 1995. Recipient cert. appreciation Native Am. Ednl. Svcs. Coll., 1995; Excellence in Academic Leadership-Wright Coll. 1991. Mem. Ill. Teachers of English to Speakers of Other Languages, Native Am. Ed. Svcs. Coll. Powwow Com. Home: 5908 W Warwick Chicago IL 60634 Office: Wright Cmty Coll 3400 N Austin Ave Chicago IL 60634

ZEHNDER, FREDERICK JOHN, retired automotive executive; b. Detroit, Feb. 11, 1926; s. Frederick Ernest and Katherine Josephine (Raymann) Z.; m. Yvonne Knox, June 25, 1951 (div. Aug. 1957); 1 child, Frederick J. Jr.; m. Adele Louise Leslie, May 15, 1970; children: Leslie, John, Linda. BS, U.S. Merchant Marine Acad., 1947; MBA, U. Mich., 1951. Credit analyst Comerica Bank, Detroit, 1951-53; with Ford Motor Co., Detroit, 1953—, budget analyst, 1953-64, with sales promotion and tng., 1964-76, used vehicle mgr. truck ops., 1976-80; ops. mgr. Ford Dealer Ops. div. Ford Motor Co., Detroit, 1980-90, ret., 1990. Served to lt. USNR, 1947-67. Mem. U. Mich. Club, Delta Sigma Pi. Republican. Lutheran.

ZEHR, ERIC WAYNE, healthcare administrator; b. Pontiac, Ill., July 9, 1962; s. Kendall W. and Iris Irene (Ragon) Z.; m. Jennifer S. Clyatt, Mar. 4, 1994. BA in Psychology, Ea. Ill. U., Charleston, 1984; MS in Clin. Psychology, Ill. State U., Normal, 1987. Cert. supr. alcohol and other drug counselors, Ill. Counselor, chem. dependence ctr. Proctor Hosp., Peoria, Ill., 1987-89, coord. outpatient svcs., 1989-92, exec. dir. addiction and behavioral svcs., 1992—; mem. adv. bd. Teens Need Teens Crisis Hotline, Peoria, 1992—; bd. dirs. Ill. Coun. on Problem and Compulsive Gambling, Evanston, 1992-95, Ill. Hosp. Addiction Treatment Adminstrs. Forum, Naperville, 1995—; pathol. gambling cons. Proctor Hosp., 1993—, chair continuous improvement bd., 1993—. Mem. com. Heart of Ill. United Fund, Peoria, 1993-94. Office: Proctor Hosp 5409 N Knoxville Peoria IL 61614

ZEID, PAULA KLEIN, metals broker; b. Chgo., Oct. 16, 1941; d. Arthur A. and Rosalyn (Davidson) Schwartz; student Mich. State U., 1959-60; B.A., Governors State U., 1974, M.A., 1975; m. Sanford David Klein, Dec. 18, 1960 (div. 1981); children—Gregory Scott, Julie Ann. Mem. editorial staff Okinawa Morning Star, Machinato, 1960-63; exec. dir. Bloom Twp. Com. on Youth, Chicago Heights, Ill., 1975-81; dir. fund devel. and pub. relations South Chgo. Community Hosp., 1981-84; v.p. South Chgo. Health Care Found., 1982-84; dir. devel. and pub. relations Chgo. Crime Commn., 1985-88; broker Universal Metals, Chgo., 1988—. Mem. Calumet Area Indsl. Commn. Mem. Nat. Soc. Fund Raising Profls., Nat. Assn. Prevention Profls., So. Suburban Youth Service Alliance, Criminal Def. Consortium, Nat. Assn. Hosp. Devel., Twp. Ofcls. Ill., Youth Network Council, Sierra Club. Jewish. Home: 1908 N Dayton St Chicago IL 60614-5029 Office: Universal Scrap Metals 2201 W Fulton St Chicago IL 60612-2205 also: Klein Trading Co 2500 W Fulton Chicago IL 60612

ZELENAK, BONNIE SUSAN, director; b. Trenton, N.J., Feb. 15, 1948; d. Charles Anthony and Ruth Anna (Greenwood) McKnight; m. Melchior Jimmie Zelenak, Aug. 24, 1968; children: Melchior Charles, Lindsey Kaitlin. BA, Trenton State Coll., 1970, MA, 1972; EdS, U. Iowa, 1973; PhD, Kans. State U., 1976. Cert. tchr., N.J. Tchr. Ewing Township Pub. Schs., Trenton, 1970-72; tchr. Univ. Lab. Sch. Univ. Iowa, Iowa City, 1972-73; coord. fin. aid Calif. State U. Long Beach, 1973-74; dir. Learning Ctr., Columbia, Mo., 1976—; asst. prof. U. Mo. Columbia, 1977—; adv. mem. Adult Edn. Bd. Columbia Pub. Schs., 1986—; vis. scholar U. Western Cape, South Africa, 1989. Contbr. chpts. in books and articles to profl. jours. Mem. Am. Assn. for Adult and Continuing Edn., Am. Assn. Higher Edn., Mo. Assn. for Adult Continuing and Cmty. Edn., Mo. Valley Assn. Adult Edn., Midwest Assn. for Remedial and Devel. Edn. Methodist. Office: Learning Ctr 231 Arts and Science Columbia MO 65211

ZELENAK, EDWARD MICHAEL, lawyer, musician; b. Dearborn, Mich., Aug. 26, 1953; s. Edward Patrick and Irene Elaine (Maruska) Z.; m. Angline Rose Cianfarani, May 24, 1986; children: Amelia Mary Rose and Edward Patrick (twins), Elliott William. BA, Wayne State U., 1975, JD, 1977. Bar: Mich. 1977, U.S. Dist. Ct. (ea. dist.) Mich. 1977, 6th Cir. Ct. of Appeals 1987. Leader Ed Zelenak Orch., Lincoln Park, Mich., 1971—; dir. pub. affairs Sta. WDRQ, Southfield, Mich., 1977-83, host talk show, 1978-83; instr. Wayne State Univ., Detroit, 1977-84; sole practice Lincoln Park, 1977—; atty. Cities of Lincoln Park and Southgate (Mich.), 1978—; host talk show United Cable TV of Mich., Woodhaven, 1980—; guest host talk show Sta. WXYT, 1988—; guest host Sta. WXYT talk shows, 1988; corr. RKO Network, 1980-83. Composer, performer (album) C. B. Polka, 1977. Alt. del. Dem. Nat. Conv., Miami, Fla., 1972, mem. staff Dem. Nat. Conv., N.Y.C., 1976; mem. exec. bd. 16th Dist. Dems., Dearborn, 1975-87; gen. counsel First Cath. Slovak Union U.S. and Can., 1988—; spl. counsel City of Ecorse, Mich., 1989—; bd. dirs. People's Community Svcs. of Detroit, 1992—. Recipient Commendation Mich. State Senate, 1982; named One of Five Outstanding Young Michiganders, Mich. Jaycees, 1990. Mem. Am. Fedn. Musicians, State Bar Mich., Downriver Bar Assn., Slovak League Am. (nat. dir. 1985—, del. meeting with Vaclav Havel and Alexander Dubcek conf. in Czecho-Slovakia 1990), Slovak Cath. Sokol Club, Slovak Jednota Club, KC (fin. com. Robert Jones chpt. 1987—), Kiwanis (pres. local chpt. 1981-82). Home: 957 Emmons Blvd Lincoln Park MI 48146-4238 Office: 2933 Fort St Lincoln Park MI 48146-2425

ZELEVAS, SHARON ROSE, art history educator, lawyer; b. Chgo., Aug. 1; d. John Andrew and Stella Regina (Swik) Z. BS with honors in Psychology, Loyola U., Chgo., 1975; MA in Museology, No. Ill. U., 1977; MA in History of Art and Culture, Rosary Coll., Florence, Italy, 1981; JD, John Marshall Law Sch., Chgo., 1986. Mgmt. cons. Hartford (Conn.) Ins. Group, 1977-79; archivist, curator mus. and hist. collection ADA, Chgo., 1981-83; mus. intern Nat. Gallery of London, 1987; tax specialist Coopers and Lybrand, Chgo., 1987-89; rsch. assoc. Uffizi Gallery and Bargello Mus., Florence, 1989; prof. law St. Xavier U., Chgo., 1990-91; prof. art history Triton Coll., River Grove, Ill., 1990—; pres. ZeLeVas & Assocs., Internat. and Domestic Tax Counsel, Chgo., 1993—; cons. Abrams Pub., N.Y.C., 1993—; reviewer, critic Blackwell Pubs., London, 1991—, McGraw-Hill, Inc., N.Y.C., 1995—. Author: Giovanni Domenico Tiepolo's Divertimenti Per Li Regazzi, 1981; curator (Pfaelzer Collection Exhibit) Form and Unform: A Search for Unity, 1976. Harvard U. Ctr. for Renaissance Studies vis. fellow Villa I Tatti, Florence, 1979, 80, 89; Anabel Mack Taylor scholar, 1979, 80. Mem. Coll. Art Assn., Internat. Ctr. of Medieval Art, Advocates Soc., Phi Alpha Delta (vice-justice 1985-86). Roman Catholic. Home: 4858 S Kildare Ave Chicago IL 60632 Office: Triton Coll Dept Fine Arts 2000 5th Ave River Grove IL 60171

ZELKO, FRANK ANTHONY, neuropsychologist, educator; b. Cleve., July 6, 1955; s. Frank Anthony and Constance (Turk) Z.; m. Maria Isabel Ferrera, Oct. 17, 1981; 1 child, Elizabeth. BA summa cum laude, Case Western Res. U., 1977; MA, U. Minn., 1980, PhD, 1985. Lic. clin. psychologist, Ill., Ky. Psychology intern Judge Baker Guidance Ctr., Boston, 1981-82; psychiatry fellow Harvard U. Med. Sch., Boston, 1982-84; staff psychologist Douglas Thom Clinic, Boston, 1983-86; asst. prof. pediat. U. Louisville Sch. Medicine., 1986-90; asst. prof. psychiatry U. Chgo. Med. Sch., 1990-93, Northwestern U. Sch. Medicine, Chgo., 1994—. Mem. APA, Internat. Neuropsychol. Soc., Soc. for Rsch. in Child Devel., Phi Beta Kappa. Office:

Childrens Meml Hosp Dept Psychiatry 2300 Childrens Plaza Chicago IL 60614

ZELL, BLAIR PAUL, systems engineer; b. Waterloo, Iowa, Mar. 11, 1942; s. Harold Lewis and Ruth Anna (Palmer) Z.; m. Elizabeth Carol Stenzel, June 10, 1961; children: Jeffrey Scott, Deborah Ruth. BSBA, Roosevelt U., 1970. Indsl. engr. assoc. Western Electric, Cicero, Ill., 1970-71; field svc. engr. Teledyne Pines, Aurora, Ill., 1971-72; mainenance tech. Chgo. Circuit Drilling, Alsip, Ill., 1973-74; from systems engr. to dir. systems rsch. & devel. Aurora Pump, North Aurora, Ill., 1974-90; product mgr. Aurora Pump, North Aurora, 1991-92; sr. systems engr. Aurora/Hydromatic Pumps, North Aurora, 1992-93; automation engr. TetraPak Plant Engring. N.Am., Pleasant Prairie, Wis., 1993—. Contbr. articles to profl. jours. With USN, 1962-70. Mem. Assembly of God Ch. Office: Tetra Pak Inc PO Box 179 Ste 500 8400 Lakeview Pkwy Pleasant Prairie WI 53158

ZELLE, JOSEPH FRANK, radio engineer, physics and electronics educator; b. Cleve., Ohio, Feb. 25, 1912; s. Michael and Jennie (Tekavec) Z. BA magna cum laude, John Carroll U., 1939; MA, Western Res. U., 1942. Registered profl. engr., Ohio. Radio technician Columbia Broadcasting System, N.Y.C., 1941-44; radio engr. Office of War Info., N.Y.C., Ohio, 1944-45; cons. radio engr. Max Hayes Trade Sch., Cleve., 1946—; tech. writer electronics Cleve. Inst. Radio Electronics, 1946-47; radio announcer Sta. WERE-FM, Cleve., 1947-51, Sta. WCLV, Cleve., 1974-86, Sta. WCVJ, Jefferson, Ohio, 1946-47; cons. radio engr. Sta. WERE-FM, Cleve., 1946—; radio engr. various stas. Sta. WCLV, Ohio, 1947-72; radio announcer Sta. WCVJ, Jefferson, Ohio; instr. electronics, physics Cuyahoga C.C., Cleve., 1974-86, Cleve. Technicians Sch.; instr. electronics Max Hayes Trade Sch., Cleve.; instr. Slovenian Cleve. State U. Author several poems; editor St. Vitus Holy Name News, 1934, Am. Home, 1939-41; contbr. numerous articles to profl. jours.; producer (documentaries) including A Slovenian Main Street: Saint Clair, Slovenian Cultural Garden, Little Miss Telban: An Angel (honorable mention), Baragaland, Baragaland Revisited. Mem. St. Vitus Holy Name Soc., St. Vitus Alumni (honoree 1991), Am. Slovenian Cath. Union #172, Friends the Slovenian Nat. Home Inc., Slovenian Rsch. Ctr.; stage mgr. St. Vitus Theater Guild, 1936-41, 46-49. Recipient Edison Radio Amateur award, 1957, Citation award Nat. Acad. Scis., Honor Citation award Nat. Religious Broadcasters, 1979. Mem. AAAS, AIEE, IEEE (sr.), Am. Radio Relay League (life), Am. Phys. Soc., Am. Astron. Soc., Am. Math. Soc., Math. Assn. Am., Ohio Acad. Sci. (emeritus), N.Y. Acad. Scis., Ohio Ret. Tchrs. Assn. (life), N.E. Ohio Commodore User's Group, Inst. Radio Engrs., Quarter Century Wireless Assn. (life, editor Chpt. I newsletter 1992—, Golden Anniversary award 1989), Radio Amateur Corp. (life), North Shore Animal League, 700 Club. Home: 24124 Glenbrook Blvd Euclid OH 44117-1971

ZELLER, FRANCIS JOSEPH, dean; b. Chgo., July 31, 1943; s. Charles Joseph and Erma J. (Kile) Z.; m. Frances Joan McGrath, Aug. 3, 1968; children: Patrick, Brian. BA in English, Lewis U., 1967; MA in Edn. Adminstrn., No. Ill. U., 1970, EdD in Edn. Adminstrn., 1983. Chmn. Robert Frost Jr. High Sch., Schaumburg, Ill., 1967-69; asst. bus. mgr. Park Ridge (Ill.) Elem. Sch., 1970-71; bus. mgr. Barrington (Ill.) High Sch., 1971-73; dean bus. svcs. Illinois Valley Community Coll., Oglesby, Ill., 1973—. Contbr. articles to profl. jours. Mem. adv. com. state Univ. Retirement System, Champaign, Ill., 1983-90. Named Outstanding Life Rotarian La Salle (Ill.) Rotary Club, 1976. Mem. NEA, Ill. C.C. Chief Fin. Officers (bd. dirs. 1984-87, chair 1993-95), Ill. Assn. Sch. Bus. Ofcls. (past pres., life mem. 1972—). Internat. Assn. Sch. Bus. Ofcls. (chair comm. col. com.), Ottawa C. of C., Golden Triangle Club, Art Inst. Chgo., Delta Sigma Pi. Office: Ill Valley Cmty Coll 815 N Orlando Smith Ave Oglesby IL 61348-9692

ZELLER, KENNETH J., state official. Commr. Dept. Labor, Indpls. Office: Rm W195 402 W Washington St Indianapolis IN 46204

ZELLIOT, ELEANOR MAE, history educator; b. Des Moines, Oct. 7, 1926; d. Ernest A. and Minnie (Hadley) Z. BA, William Penn Coll., 1948; MA, Bryn Mawr (Pa.) Coll., 1949; PhD, U. Pa., 1969. Assoc. editor The Am. Friend, Richmond, Iowa, 1950-58; tchr. Scattergood Sch., West Branch, Iowa, 1958-60; editor Pendle Hill Pubs., Wallingford, Pa., 1960-62; acting instr., asst. prof. U. Minn., Mpls., 1966-69; researcher South Asia Hist. Atlas, Mpls., 1966-69; from asst. prof. to assoc. prof. Carleton Coll., Northfield, Minn., 1969-79; prof. Carleton Coll., Northfield, 1979—, dept. chair, 1989-92, Laird Bell prof., 1993—; v.p. Midwest Conf. on Asian Affairs, 1994—. Author: From Untouchable to Dalit, 1992, 96; editor: Experience of Hinduism, 1988, (jour. issue) Marathi Sampler, 1982; contbr. articles to profl. jours. Mem. Dem. Farmer Labor Party, Minn., LWV. Fellowship NEH, 1987, Fulbright, 1992. Mem. Minn. Consortium for South Asia, Am. Inst. of Indian Studies (v.p. 1994—, bd. trustees, fellowship 1985, 89), Assoc. Colls. of Midwest, India Studies, Assn. of Asian Studies, Asia Network (exec. com.). Mem. Soc. of Friends. Office: Carleton Coll Northfield MN 55057

ZEMAITIS, CONSUELO IRENE, mathematics educator; b. Laredo, Tex., Mar. 27, 1936; d. Guillermo P. and Matilde (Millareal) Martinez; m. John J. Zemaitis, June 22, 1959; 1 child, Rachel. BA in Math., Incarnate Word Coll., 1959; postgrad., Concordia U., River Forest, Ill., 1964. Pers. advisor Standard Kollsman, Melrose Park, Ill., 1960-62; tchr. Archdioces of Chgo., Chgo., 1963-68, La Grange Park, Ill., 1966-69; onwer Adorno Imports, Melrose Park, 1975-79; tchr. Archdiocese of Chgo., Franklin Park, 1975-80, Mother Guerin H.S., River Grove, Ill., 1980-89; tchr., tutor Triton Coll., River Grove, Ill., 1990-94, 94—; exec. asst. State Treasurer, Chgo., 1991-94; mem. adv. bd. Triton Coll. C.C., Melrose Park, 1990—, mem. multicultural task force, 1991-92. Bd. dirs. League of Women Pres. Proviso Twp., Maywood, Ill., 1990; chair Ill. Hispanic Coun., Cook County, 1990—; treas., mem. Hispanic Fest Com., Melrose Park, 1992—; mem. sch. bd. Proviso Twp. H.S. Dist. 109, Maywood, 1994—. Recipient Citizenship award Triton Coll., 1993. Mem. AAUW, LWV, Ill. Assn. Sch. Bds., Nat. Assn. Sch. Bds. Democrat. Roman Catholic. Home: 1204 Hirsch Melrose Park IL 60160-2229

ZEMAN, MICHAEL, advertising executive. Pres. Collins Rapp Agy. Group, Inc., Mpls. Office: Collins Rapp Agy Group Inc 901 Marquette Ave Minneapolis MN 55402*

ZEMEL, DAVID MICHAEL, charitable organization administrator, human services educator; b. St. Louis, Feb. 16, 1949; s. Jack and Delores Mae (Aubuchon) Z.; m. Jane Mary Sandler, Jan. 14, 1973; children: Abby Sandler, Rebecca Clare. BS in Edn., U. Mo., 1971; MSW, Washington U., St. Louis, 1975. Tchr. Title I, St. James Schs., Mo., 1971-72; social worker II Boys Town Mo., St. James, 1972-75; program dir. St. Louis County Juvenile Court, 1975-79; dir. devel. Providence Program, Inc., St. Louis, 1979-80; devel. officer United Way Greater St. Louis, 1980-82, v.p., 1982-88; exec. officer United Way Bartholomew County, Ind., 1988—; assoc. prof. human services St. Louis Community Coll., 1975-88; lectr. George Warren Brown Sch. Social Work, Washington U., 1987-88; cons. in field. Author tng. manuals on fundraising. Mem. com. alternative edn. University City Schs., 1979-85; trainer United Way Mgmt. Assistance Ctr., St. Louis, 1980-88; mem. nat. profl. adv. com. Strategic Planning and Market Research, Nat. Acad. for Volunteerism, United Way Am., 1986—; bd. dirs. Confluence St. Louis, 1983-84, Boys Town Mo., St. Louis, 1977-79; participant Leadership St. Louis, 1987-88, Leadership Bartholomew County, 1989—. Mem. Nat. Soc. Fund Raising Execs. (chmn. legis. 1982-83), Washington U. Alumni Assn. (ann. program com.). Jewish. Home: 5510 E 110th Pl Tulsa OK 74137-7256 Office: United Way Bartholomew County 522 Franklin St Columbus IN 47201-6214

ZEMKE, ROBERT LOWELL, family practice physician; b. Fairmont, Minn., Apr. 1, 1935; m. Joan Louise Belk, June 3, 1960; children: Stephen, Daniel, Jonathan. BA, St. Olaf Coll., 1957; BS, MD, U. Minn., 1961. Diplomate Am. Bd. Family Practice. Intern Santa Clara County Hosp., San Jose, Calif., 1961-62; resident Stanislaus County Hosp., Modesto, Calif., 1962-64; family practice physician Fairmont (Minn.) Med. Clinic, 1971—. Address: 800 Clinic Cir Fairmont MN 56031-4428

ZEMKE, WILLIAM A., farm management educator; b. Pulcifer, Wis., Nov. 26, 1938; s. Alfred E. and Geneva A. (Bergner) Z.; m. Sharon Joy Anderson, Dec. 2, 1961; 1 child, William A. Jr. BS in Agrl. Edn., U. Wis., River Falls, 1960, MS in Agrl. Edn., 1972. Artificial inseminator Badger Breeders, Shawano, Wis., 1960-62; farm loan officer Prodn. Credit Assn., Antigo, Wis., 1965-66; vocat. agrl. Lake Holcombe, Wis., 1966-71; teaching asst. U. Wis., River Falls, 1971-72; instr. farm mgmt. Northeast Wis. Tech. Coll., Green Bay, 1972—; dir. State Bank Kewaunee (Wis.), 1987—, Kewaunee Area Scholars Inc., 1989—. Author: Farm Business Analysis, 1975, Financial Management Tools, 1993, Feed Economics and Dairy Decision Making Tools, 1996, 300 Farm Business Management Computer Spreadsheet Programs, 1986-96. Sec. Kewaunee Lions, 1991; mem. Am. Legion, Kewaunee, 1972-92. With U.S. Army, 1962-65. Mem. NAt. Vocat. Agrl. Tchrs. Assn., NAt. Farm Ranch Bus. Mgmt. Edn. Assn., Wis. Assn. Vocat. Agrl. Instrs., Wis. Vocat. Assn., Wis. Edn. Assn. Lutheran. Home: N1302 Lakeshore Rd Kewaunee WI 54216-9584 Office: Northeast Wis Tech Coll PO Boc 19042 2740 W Mason St Green Bay WI 54307

ZENO, JO ANN, sales executive; b. Akron, Ohio, Sept. 25, 1952; d. Ross and Mary Francis (Gerbec) Z. BA in French and Edn., BS in Spanish, U. Akron, 1975. Tchr. French, Spanish S.E. Local, Ravenna, Ohio, 1975-77, Akron Pub. Schs., 1977-80; sales rep. Xerox Corp., Akron, Cleve., 1980-83; cert. stapling technician U.S. Surg. Corp., Norwalk, Conn., 1983-88; rep. cardiovascular surg. products Medtronic Inc., 1988-95; sales rep. Karl Storz Endoscopy-Am. Inc., Culver City, Calif., 1995—. Home: 272 Somerset Rd Akron OH 44313-4533

ZEPF, THOMAS HERMAN, physics educator, researcher; b. Cin., Feb. 13, 1935; s. Paul A. and Agnes J. (Schulz) Z. BS summa cum laude, Xavier U., 1957; MS, St. Louis U., 1960, PhD, 1963. Asst. prof. physics Creighton U., Omaha, 1962-67, assoc. prof., 1967-75, prof., 1975—, acting chmn. dept. physics, 1963-66, chmn., 1966-73, 81-93, coord. allied health programs, 1975-76, coord. pre-health scis. advising, 1976-81; cons. physicist VA Hosp., Omaha, 1966-71; vis. prof. physics St. Louis U., 1973-74; program evaluator Am. Coun. on Edn., 1988—. Contbr. articles and abstracts to Surface Sci., Bull. Am. Phys. Soc., Proceedings Nebr. Acad. Sci., The Physics Tchr. jour., others. Chmn. physics judging com. Greater Nebr. Sci. and Engring. Fair, 1973-85. Recipient Cert. Recognition award Phi Beta Kappa U. Cin. chpt., 1953, Disting. Faculty Svc. award Creighton U., 1987. Mem. AAAS, Am. Phys. Soc., Am. Assn. Physics Tchrs. (pres. Nebr. sect. 1978), Nebr. Acad. Sci. (life, chmn. physics sect. 1985—), Internat. Brotherhood Magicians, Soc. Am. Magicians (pres. assembly #7, 1964-65), KC, Sigma Xi (Achievement award for rsch. St. Louis chpt. 1963, pres. Omaha chpt. 1993-94), Sigma Pi Sigma. Roman Catholic. Office: Creighton U Dept Physics Omaha NE 68178

ZERBE, JOHN IRWIN, forest products technologist, researcher; b. Hegins, Pa., June 4, 1926; s. Allen and Rosa Jane (Miller) Z.; m. Ruby June Deitrich, Sept. 1, 1951; children: Lynne Diane, Eric Alan, Donna Lee. BS, Pa. State U., 1951; MS in Wood Tech., N.Y. State Coll., Syracuse, 1953, PhD in environ. sci. and forestry, 1956. Asst. rsch. prof. U. Ill., Utbana, 1956-58; mgr. Nat. Forest Products Assn., Washington, 1958-65, asst. v.p., 1965-70; rsch. dir. forest svc. USDA, Washington, 1970-76; program mgr. USDA, Madison, Wis., 1976-91; program mgr. Energy Global Change Forest Products Lab., Madison, 1990—. Editor: UNICOM Method of House Construction, 1965. With USNR, 1944-46. Recipient merit award Forest Svc., USDA, 1990. Mem. ASTM, Forest Products Rsch. Soc. (bd. dirs. 1974-76), Soc. Wood Sci. and Tech. (trustee 1959-62), Biomass Energy Rsch. Assn., Xi Sigma Pi. Lutheran. Home: 3310 Heatherdell Ln Madison WI 53713-3446 Office: USDA Forest Products Lab 1 Gifford Pinchot Dr Madison WI 53705-2398

ZERBS, STEPHEN TAYLOR, telecommunications development engineer; b. Churdan, Iowa, May 5, 1946; s. Hobert Frank and LaVon Monica (Mantz) Z.; m. Patricia Lynn Tvrdik, Mar. 28, 1976; children: Rick Andrew, Steve Matthew. AAS in Electronics Tech., Iowa State U., 1967; BS, U. Nebr., 1984. Engring. assoc. Western Elec., Omaha, Nebr., 1967-82; planning engr. Western Elec./AT&T, Omaha, 1983-91; sr. engr. AT&T/Lucent Technologies, Omaha, 1992—. Inventor and patentee in field with numerous U.S. and Fgn. Patents. Elected mem. Sanitary Improvement Dist. 29, Gretna, Nebr., 1980-82. Recipient Outstanding Recognition Jr. Achievement Omaha, 1969. Mem. IEEE, Tel. Pioneers Am., Am. Legion (assoc.). Office: AT&T 120th and I Streets Omaha NE 68137

ZERR, FRANK MICHAEL, city clerk, treasurer; b. Shelbyville, Ind., Feb. 13, 1949; s. Paul Anthony and Audrey Bonaventura (Dill) Z.; m. Phyllis Jean Jenkins, Mar. 24, 1984. BA, Purdue U., 1971. Tchr. Shelbyville High Sch., 1971-72; br. mgr. Shelby Nat. Bank, Shelbyville, 1973-78; county treas. Shelby County, Shelbyville, 1979-86; customer svc. rep. Bank One, Shelbyville, 1987; clk.-treas. City of Shelbyville, 1988—; one of 3 exec. dirs. representing third class cities Ind. League of Mcpl. Clks. and Treas., 1992-93, state treas., 1993-94, state v.p., 1994-95, state pres. 1995-96; arrangements chmn. ann. State Bd. Accounts Sch., Indpls., 1992, 93. Treas. Shelby County Heart Assn., 1973-88, Shelby Dem. Ctrl. Com., 1975-80, St. Joseph Parish Coun., Shelbyville, 1980-82; mem. adv. bd. Salvation Army, 1988—. Recipient Ind. Accredited Mcpl. Clk. award, 1992. Mem. Shelby County C. of C. (bd. dirs. 1980-83), KC, Ind. Assn. Cities & Towns (exec. com. 1995-96), Internat. Inst. Mcpl. Clerks. Roman Catholic. Home: 1031 W Mckay Rd Shelbyville IN 46176-3204 Office: Clk-Treas Office 44 W Washington St Shelbyville IN 46176-1247

ZEYEN, RICHARD JOHN, plant pathology educator; b. Mankato, Minn., Jan. 17, 1943; s. Clifford John and Eleanor Otilla (Laase) Z.; m. Anita Kozan, June 25, 1967 (div. 1971); m. Carol Breese Van Why, Dec. 10, 1984. Dir. EM facility Minn. Agrl. Exptl. Sta., St. Paul, 1971—; asst. prof. plant pathology U. Minn., St. Paul, 1973-75, assoc. prof., 1976-83, prof., 1983—; cons. Minn. Pollution Control Agy. Contbr. articles to profl. jours. Underwood fellow Agr., Food and Rsch. Coun., U.K., 1993; NATO Scientific Exch. Program fellow, Wales, U.K., 1990-95. Mem. AAAS, Am. Phytopathol. Soc. (chmn. various coms. 1967—), Microscopy Soc. Am., Minn. Microscopy Soc. (past officer, bd. dirs., pres. 1981-82), Mankato State U. Alumni Assn. (bd. dirs. 1974-77), Sigma Xi. Office: U Minn Dept Plant Pathology 495 Borlaug Hall Buford Cir Saint Paul MN 55108

ZHANG, CHARLES CHENG, financial planner; b. Shanghai. M in Econs., Western Mich. U., 1991; PhD candidate, LaSalle U. ChFC; CFP; CLU. Sr. fin. advisor Am. Express Fin. Advisors, Inc., Kalamazoo, 1991—. Mem. Am. Soc. CLU and ChFC, Inst. cert. Fin. Planners, Internat. Assn. Fin. Planning. Office: Am Express Fin Advisors Inc 5136 Lovers Ln Ste 200 Kalamazoo MI 49002

ZHAO, MEISHAN, chemical physics educator, researcher; b. Shanxian, Shandong, People's Republic of China, Nov. 5, 1958; came to U.S., 1984; s. Zhong Chen Zhao and Ming Rong Zhang; m. Linlin Cai, Sept. 2, 1983; children: Fang, Yuan, Nan. MS in Physics, U. Minn., 1986, PhD in Chem. Physics, 1989. Lectr. physics S.E. U. China, Nanjing, 1982-84; teaching asst., rsch. asst. U. Minn., Mpls., 1984-89; rschr. James Franck Inst. U. Chgo., 1990—. Contbr. articles to profl. jours. Mem. AAAS, Am. Phys. Soc. (internat. editl. bd. Internal. Physics Edn., Chinese ed., 1991-92), N.Y. Acad. Sci. Home: 5642 S Drexel Ave Chicago IL 60637-1418 Office: Univ Chgo James Franck Inst 5640 S Ellis Ave Chicago IL 60637-1433

ZHAO, YUQI, molecular geneticist, educator; b. Qingdao, Shandong, China, May 20, 1957; came to U.S., 1983; s. Fenghe and Guizhen (Ma) Z.; m. Sharon Chen; children: Jennie Jingyi, Andrew Zhongming, Adam Chen. BS, Shandong Coll. Oceanography, Qingdao, 1981; MS, Oreg. State U., 1985, PhD, 1991; postgrad., Columbia U., 1991-92. Grad. teaching asst. Oreg. State U., Corvallis, 1984-86, 88-89, grad. rsch. asst. dept. zoology, 1984-86, grad. rsch. asst. genetics program, 1986-90, rsch. asst./cons. Ctr. for Gene Rsch. and Biotech., 1989; postdoctoral rsch. scientist dept. radiation oncology Ctr. Radiol. Rsch. Coll. Physicians and Surgeons Columbia U., N.Y.C., 1991-92, assoc. rsch. scientist/rsch. asst. prof., 1992-94; asst. prof. dept. pediatrics Med. Sch. Northwestern U., Chgo., 1994—; dir. Molecular Diagnostics Lab. Meml. Children's Hosp., Chgo., 1994—; mgr. radiation rsch. facility Columbia-Presbyn. Cancer Ctr., Columbia U., 1994; mem. Nat. AIDS Clin. Trial Groups; invitd lectr. in field. Editor: (with Y. Li) Practical Protocols in Molecular Biology, 1995; contbr. chpt. (with others) to Molecular Genetics of Plant-microbe Interactions, 1988, Molecular Strategies of Pathogens and Host Plants, 1991; co-contbr. articles to sci. publs.; editor Jour. Current Agrl. Scis. and Techs., 1990-94, Jour. Biol Sci. and Tech., 1993-94, Clin. Immunol. Newsletter, 1994—. Rsch. grantee Am. Chem. Soc., 1994, Chgo. Pediat. Faculty Found., 1994-97; govtl. scholar China, 1983-85; NAS rsch. fellow, 1985. Mem. AAAS, Am. Soc. Microbiology, Am. Radiation Rsch. Soc. (travel award 1992), Chinese Agriculture Assn. Students and Scholars (pres. 1989-90, chmn. organizing com. 2nd nat. conf. 1990, chmn. fund raising com. 1989-90, chmn. com. pub. rels. 1990-91), bd. dirs. exec. com. 1990-91), Assn. Chinese Biologists in N.Am. Home: 1550 E Castle Ct Palatine IL 60067-4195 Office: Meml Childrens Hosp Molecular Diagnostics Lab 2300 N Childrens Plz Chicago IL 60614-3318

ZHENG, LISA LIQING, computer programmer; b. Xian, China, May 11, 1966; came to U.S., 1990; d. Youzhong Zheng and Siuping Huang. BSEE, Huazhong U. Sci. & Tech., 1988; MSEE, Purdue U., 1992. Asst. engr. Inst. Electronics Chinese Acad. Scis., Beijing, 1988-90; electronics engr., systems programmer Computer Graphics, Corp., Indpls., 1992-94; programmer Bertelsmann Music Group, Inc., Indpls., 1994—. Office: Bertlesmann Music Group Inc 6550 E 30th St Indianapolis IN 46219-1102

ZHUO, MIN, neurobiology educator; b. Xia Pu, People's Republic of China, Nov. 25, 1964; came to U.S., 1988; s. Zi-Jing and Wan-Ru (Huang) Z.; m. Kelly Bin Wei, Apr. 27, 1993. BS, Chinese Inst. Sci. Tech., 1985; MS, Shanghai Inst. Physiology, 1987; PhD, U. Iowa, 1992. Vis. scientist U. Iowa, 1988-89; postdoctoral fellow Columbia U., N.Y.C., 1992-93; rsch. assoc. Howard Hughes Med. Inst. Columbia U., 1993-95, Stanford U., 1995-96; asst. prof. dept. anesthesiology Washington U., St. Louis, 1996—. Contbr. articles and abstracts to profl. jours. Mem. Soc. for Neurosci., Internat. Assn. for Study of Pain (Travel award 1990), Am. Pain Soc. (Travel awards 1990, 91, 92), AAAS. Office: Washington U Dept Anesthesiology Saint Louis MO 63110-1093

ZICHEK, MELVIN EDDIE, retired clergyman, educator; b. Lincoln, Nebr., May 5, 1918; s. Eddie and Agnes (Varga) Z.; A.B., Nebr. Central Coll., 1942; M.A., U. Nebr., 1953; D.Litt., McKinley-Roosevelt Ednl. Inst., 1955; m. Dorothy Virginia Patrick, May 28, 1942; 1 dau., Shannon Elaine. Ordained to ministry Christian Ch., 1942; minister Christian chs., Brock, Nebr., 1941, Ulysses, Nebr., 1942-43, Elmwood, Nebr., 1943-47, Central City, Nebr., 1947-83, ret., 1983; rural tchr., Merrick County, Nebr., 1937-40; prin. Alvo (Nebr.) Consol. High Sch., 1943-47; supt. Archer (Nebr.) Pub. Schs., 1948-57; head dept. English and speech Central City (Nebr.) High Sch., 1957-63; supt. Marquette (Nebr.) Consol. Schs., 1963-79. Served as chaplain's asst. AUS, 1942. Mem. Grand Island Ret. Tchrs. Assn. Republican. Home: 2730 N North Rd Grand Island NE 68803-1143

ZICHEK, SHANNON ELAINE, secondary school educator; b. Lincoln, Nebr., May 29, 1944; d. Melvin Eddie and Dorothy Virginia (Patrick) Z. AA, York (Nebr.) Coll., 1965; BA, U. Nebr., Kearney, 1968; postgrad., U. Okla., Edmond, 1970, 71, 72, 73, 74, 75, U. Nebr., Kearney, 1980, 81, 82, 89, 92. Tchr. history and English, NW High Sch., Grand Island, Nebr., 1948—. Republican. Christian. Home: 2730 N North Rd Grand Island NE 68803-1143

ZICKLER, LEONARD LOUIS, exhibit company executive; b. Indpls., July 28, 1943; s. Louis Leonard and Mary Louise (Walsman) Z.; m. Victoria Kay Dargitz; children: Michael Johnathan, Matthew Leonard. BBA, Ind. U., 1965; postgrad., Ball State U., 1967-68. Acct. Western Electric Co., Indpls., 1965; with mgmt. tng. Ford Motor Co., Chgo., 1965-70; v.p. sales Hamilton Display Mfg. Co., Indpls., 1970—. Office: Hamilton Display Mfg Co 9150 E 33rd St Indianapolis IN 46236-3605

ZICKUS, ANNE, state legislator; b. Apr. 6, 1939; m. Charles Zickus, 1958; children: Kathy, Chuck. State rep. Dist. 48, 1992—; pres. Re/Max S.W. Mem. Suburban Assn. Realtors, Nat. Assn. Realtors. Republican. Home: 7909 W 112th St Palos Hills IL 60465-2731 Office: Ill Ho of Reps State Capitol Springfield IL 62706*

ZIEGELBAUER, ROBERT F., state legislator; b. Aug. 26, 1951. BA, Notre Dame; MS, U. Pa. Mem. Manitowoc County Bd.; mem. City Coun., fin. dir.; now mem. dist. 25 Wis. State Assembly, 1992—; owner of retial music shop. Home: 1213 S 8th St Manitowoc WI 54220-5311 Address: PO Box 8953 Madison WI 53708*

ZIEGENHORN, ERIC HOWARD, lawyer, legal writer; b. Independence, Mo., Oct. 17, 1957. AB in Econs. with honors, U. Mo., 1979; JD, U. Calif., Berkeley, 1983. Bar: Calif. 1983, Kans. 1986, Mo. 1987. Atty. Law Offices of Richard A. Goodman, Oakland, Calif., 1983-86, Lewis, Rice & Fingersh, Overland Park, Kans., 1986-87; sole practitioner, legal writer Kansas City, Mo., 1987-91; sr. staff atty. Midland Loan Svcs., 1991-96. Author: (3-vol. set) Missouri Legal Forms, 1992. Mem. Mo. Bar Assn., Calif. Bar Assn. Office: Courtyard Ste 104 W 42d St Kansas City MO 64111

ZIEGLER, CHARLES LOUIS, retired dentist; b. Milw., Oct. 8, 1926; s. Walter F. and Ruth Elizabeth (Bernatz) Z.; m. Ingeborg Dorothy Kummerteldt, Sept. 12, 1953; children: Ann E. (dec.), Kay L., Charles L. Jr., Nancy E., James W. DDS, Marquette U., 1951. Gen. practice dentistry Milw., 1951-92; ret., 1992; adj. prof. Marquette U. Sch. Dentistry, Milw., 1953—. V.p. Library Bd., Hales Corners, Wis., 1976-78. Served to cpl. USAF, 1944-45. Named Disting. Alumnus Marquette U. Sch. Dentistry, 1980. Fellow Internat. Coll. Dentists (Regent 1987-93), Am. Coll. Dentists; mem. ADA, Am. Acad. Restorative Dentistry, Internat. Coll. Dentists (vice regent 1983-86, regent 1987-93), Am. Acad. Crown and Bridge Prosthodontics (pres. 1975-76), Wis. Dental Assn. (pres. 1980-81), Milw. Dental Forum (pres. 1969-70), Wis. Gnathological Soc. (pres. 1971-72), Omicron Kappa Upsilon (pres. 1967-68). Roman Catholic. Home: 2329 N 100th St Milwaukee WI 53226-1637

ZIEGLER, CHARLES LOUIS, JR., architect; b. Wauwatosa, Wis., Apr. 11, 1957; s. Charles Louis and Ingeborg Dorothy (Kummerfeldt) Z.; m. Jamie Goodrich, Apr. 12, 1986; children: Nicholas, Christina. BArch, U. Minn., 1980; MS in Architecture, Columbia U., 1982. Registered architect, Ill. Architect Kober Belluschi Architects, Chgo., 1982-84, Fujikawa, Johnson & Assocs., Chgo., 1984-86; project mgr. Hyatt Hotels & Resorts, Chgo., 1986-88, dir. project and planning, 1988-91; sr. project mgr., dir. ops., v.p. Lieber Architects Inc., Chgo., 1991—. Mem. AIA, IDRC, Heartland Alliance. Home: 825 Greenleaf Ave Wilmette IL 60091-2702 Office: Lieber Architects Inc 444 N Michigan Ave Chicago IL 60611-3903

ZIEGLER, EARL KELLER, minister; b. Sheridan, Pa., Mar. 4, 1929; s. Abraham Hoffman and Rhoda Bucher (Keller) Z.; m. Vivian Zug Snyder, Aug. 12, 1951; children: Karen Louise Miller, Randall Earl, Doreen Kay Creighton, Michael Wayne, Konnae Ziegler Berces, Sulien Nicodemus. BA, Elizabethtown (Pa.) Coll., 1951; MDiv, Bethany Theol. Sem., Chgo., 1954; DDiv, Lancaster (Pa.) Theol. Sem., 1982. Ordained to ministry Ch. of the Brethren, 1950. Pastor Woodbury (Pa.) Congregation, Pa., 1954-60, Black Rock Ch. of Brethren, Brodbecks, Pa., 1960-70, Mechanic Grove Ch. of Brethren, Quarryville, Pa., 1970-83, Atlantic N.E. Dist. Exec., Harrisburg, Pa., 1983-89, Lampeter (Pa.) Ch. of the Brethren, 1989—; moderator Ch. of the Brethren, Elgin, Ill., 1993-94; moderator various dists., Pa., 1959—; mem. Gen. Bd., Ch. of Brethren, 1975-80; chmn. Parish Ministerial Commn., 1979-80; dir. Family Life Inst., 1961, 64, mem. Nat. Korean Cons. Com., 1988-91, Denominational Structure Com., 1990-91, others; adj. prof. ch. history Evang. Sem., Myerstown, Pa., 1988—. Author: Divorce Among the Church of the Brethren Clergy, 1981; contbr. articles to profl. jours. Pres. Manheim Elem. PTA, 1964-65; trustee Elizabethtown Coll., 1965-83; dir. Community Choir, Lineboro, Md., 1966-70; dir. Solanco Community Men's Chorus, Quarryville, 1976-83. Recipient Alumni citation, Elizabethtown Coll. Alumni Assn., 1964, award for Outstanding Ch. Planting in Azua Province of Dominican Republic, 1990, Award of Appreciation, Germantown Ch. of Brethren, 1990. Mem. Lampeter Willow St. Ministerium (pres. 1989-91). Republican. Office: Ch of the Brethren Gen Offices 1451 Dundee Ave Elgin IL 60120-1674

ZIELINSKI, ROBERT S., multi media desinger; b. Cin., Ohio, July 15, 1965. BS, Ea. Ky. U., 1986; MLA, Ohio State U., 1989. Instructional design Authorware, Mpls., 1989-91; v.p. Turn-Key Tng. Techs., Grand Rapids, Mich., 1991-92; pres. The Human Element, Mpls., 1992—; Spkr. in field. Author: Software Macrain Barrell, 1989; contbr. articles to profl. jour. Mem. Nat. Soc. Instrn. Performance, Interactive Info. Comms. Soc. Evangelical. Office: The Human Element Inc 8120 Penn Ave S Ste 433 Minneapolis MN 55431

ZIELKE, WILLIAM ARTHUR, telecommunications company executive; b. Chgo., Sept. 18, 1946; s. Arthur Henry and Arlene Bernice (Rieker) Z.; m. Pamela Sue Gross, Mar. 29, 1969; children: John, Jennifer. BA, No. Ill. U., 1971. Comml. rep. Contel of Ill., Dekalb, 1972-73; personnel supr. Contel Svc. Corp., St. Louis, 1973-76, indsl. rels. mgr., 1976-79; dir. human resources Contel-South Ctrl. Div., Wentzville, Mo., 1979-81; asst. v.p. human resources Contel Svc. Corp., Dulles, Va., 1981-85; v.p. human resources Contel Hdqrs., Atlanta, 1985-88; div. pres. Contel of Ind. & Ills., Seymour, 1988-91; regional v.p., gen. mgr. GTE North-Ind., Ft. Wayne, 1991-93; region v.p. gen. mgr. for Ind. and Mich., 1993, regional pres. North, 1994—. Chmn. United Way-Allen County, Ft. Wayne; bd. dirs. Jr. Achievement, Ind., Telecomms. Assn. (chmn.), Ind. C. of C., Ft. Wayne C. of C., Ft. Wayne Corp. Coun., Norwest Bank. Office: GTE North Ind 8001 W Jefferson Blvd Fort Wayne IN 46804-4141

ZIEMAN, MARK, newspaper editor. Mng. editor Kansas City (Mo.) Star. Office: The Kansas City Star 1729 Grand Blvd Kansas City MO 64108*

ZIEMANN, EDWARD FRANCES, food service company executive, sales and marketing professional; b. Chgo., July 3, 1944; s. Edward F. and Ethyle (Ruthenbeck) Z.; m. Linda Magarethe Nakamichi Sowka, July 14, 1952; children: Russell, Jeffrey, Robert, Christina. BA, U. Ill., Chgo., 1967. Cert. foodservice profl. Reservations freight clk. Milw. Road. R.R., Chgo., 1965-66; sales adminstr. Robertson Photo Mechanic, Des Plaines, Ill., 1966-68; v.p. and officer Anetsberger Bros., Inc., Northbrook, Ill., 1968—; mem. Tech. Liaison Com., Chgo., 1990-91. Bd. dirs. Village Improvement Com., Round Lake, Ill.; asst. Catholic Charities, Waukegan, Ill., 1990-91. Mem. Am. Mktg. Assn., Nat. Assn. Food Equipment Manufacture, Bakers Club (century mem.), Moose. Republican. Roman Catholic. Office: Anetsberger Bros Inc 180 Anets Dr Northbrook IL 60062-5452

ZIEMER, JOHN ROBERT, software engineer; b. Berkley, N.J., Jan. 25, 1939; s. John Ziemer Jr. and Doris Catherine (Taylor) Rife; m. Patricia Ann Gable, June 29, 1963 (div. Nov. 1979); children: Brian A., Gary R., Wendy S; m. L. Sue Hayden Boggess, Dec. 29, 1979; stepchildren: Loretta Sue Boggess, Tim Kent Boggess. Student, Trenton (N.J.) State U., 1964-65, Memphis State U., 1965, U. Mo., 1971, Florissant Valley (Mo.) U., 1973-78. Enlisted USN, 1957, resigned, 1967; simulation engr. Link-Flight Simulation, Binghamton, N.Y., 1967-69, Conductron Electronics, St. Louis, 1969-72; rsch. programmer MacDonnal Douglas Rsch. Lab, St. Louis, 1972-81; software engr. Mastercard Internat., St. Louis, 1981—. Designer antisubmarine warfare tactics trainer, rsch. computer and test facilities. Mem. exec. coun. Boy Scouts Am., St. Louis, 1976-77. Mem. St. Louis Area Computer Club. Home: 1285 Swallow Ln Florissant MO 63031-3326

ZIENTY, FERDINAND BENJAMIN, chemical company research executive, consultant; b. Chgo., Mar. 21, 1915; s. Albert Frank and Rose Cecelia (Przypyszny) Z.; BS, U. Ill., 1935; MS, U. Mich., 1936, PhD, 1938; m. Claylain Lorraine Cawiezell, Apr. 14, 1945; children: Jane Zienty Wheeler, Donald Ferd. Research chemist organic chems. div. Monsanto Co., St. Louis, 1938-40, research group leader, 1940-47, asst. dir. research, 1947-50, asso. dir. research, 1950-56, dir. research, 1956-60, dir. advanced organic chems. research, 1960-64, mgr. research and devel., 1964-79, dir. chemistry bio med program, 1979-83, dir. research Health Care div., 1983, cons., 1983—, v.p. research George Lueders & Co. subs. Monsanto Co., St. Louis, 1968-70. Recipient Hodel, Saltiel, Hodel prize for scholarship, 1935, Sesquicentennial award U. Mich., 1967; Disting. Alumnus award U. Mich. Coll. Pharmacy, 1981. Fairchild scholar, 1935, Frederick Stearns fellow, 1936-37. Fellow AAAS, N.Y. Acad. Scis., Acad. Scis. of St. Louis (trustee); mem. Am. Chem. Soc., Am. Inst. Chem. Engrs., Am. Pharm. Assn., Inst. Food Technologists, Mo. Acad. Sci., Soc. Chem. Industry (London). Clubs: Triple A Country, Univ. Club. St. Louis. Contbr. articles to profl. jours. Patentee in field. Home and Office: 850 Rampart Dr Saint Louis MO 63122-1644

ZIEROLF, MARY LOUISE, nurse anesthetist; b. Lima, Ohio, Dec. 12, 1946; d. Charles Peter and Agatha Cecilia (Jackman) Z. Diploma in nursing, St. Rita's Sch. Nursing, Lima, Ohio, 1967; diploma in anesthesia, Cin. Gen. Hosp., 1971; BS in Edn., U. Cin., 1974. RN, Ohio; cert. nurse anesthetist; cert. CPR instr., neonatal resuscitation. Staff nurse operating rm. St. Rita's Hosp., Lima, 1967-69; staff anesthetist, insvc. coord. Mercy Anesthesia Assocs Inc/Anesthesia & Intensive Care Cons, Cin., 1971—; vis. lectr. Coll. Nursing, U. Cin., 1990-92; lectr. anesthesia in 3d world countries, 1992. Author papers. Mem. anniversary program to Russia, People to People/Citizen Amb. Program, Seattle, 1991, participant in 1st CRNA anesthesia exch. of tech. and sci. info. in China, 1989; active taking monthly blood pressures Fairfax (Ohio) Sr. Citizens, 1988—. Named one of Outstanding Young Women of Am., 1976. Mem. Am. Assn. Nurse Anesthetists, Ohio State Assn. Nurse Anesthetists (bd. dirs. 1981-83, 92—, pres. Greater Cin. Ednl. Dist. 1991—, chair fall Osana meeting 1995—), Am. Bus. Woman's Assn. (pres. 7 Hills chpt. 1982—, Woman of Yr. 1982), U. Cin. Alumni Assn., Gen. Hosp. Sch. Nurse Anesthesia Alumni. Roman Catholic. Home: 120 Prevalent Dr Oxford OH 45056-9756 Office: Mercy Hosp Anderson 7500 State Rd Cincinnati OH 45255-2439

ZIESE, NANCYLEE HANSON, social worker; b. Sioux City, Iowa, July 26, 1938. BA in Sociology, Morningside Coll., 1960; MSW, U. Iowa, 1982, cert. in aging studies, 1986. Social worker Florence Crittenton Home, Sioux City, 1960-65, L.A. County, 1965; social worker, supr. Polk County Dept. Social Welfare, Des Moines, 1966-69; social worker, community liaison Tommy Dale Meml., Sioux City, Iowa, 1977-79; dir. internships Briar Cliff Coll., Sioux City, 1981-83; dir. continuing edn. Coe Coll., Cedar Rapids, Iowa, 1983-85; exec. dir. Profl. Women's Network, Cedar Rapids, 1985-87; pvt. practice WOMANPLACE Counseling, Cedar Rapids, 1985-87; adoption coord. Hillcrest Family Svcs., Cedar Rapids, 1987—; bd. dirs. Young Parent's Network M.E.L.D., Cedar Rapids, 1988—, pres., 1994-96; cons. projects related to community improvement, recycling. Contbr. articles to newspapers. Bd. mem., v.p. Sioux City Sch. Bd., 1978-83; bd. mem., pres. Friends of Iowa Pub. TV, 1978-88, Family Svc., Boys and Girls Home, Sioux City, 1973-81; steering bd. Iowa Women's Polit. Caucus, 1987-93, pres., 1992-93; chair Iowa Women's Caucus Rsch. and Edn. Ctr., 1994; bd. dirs. commn. mem. Episcopal Diocese Iowa-Human Needs; chair Birth Defects Inst. Adv. Com., Iowa Inter-Agy. Adoption Coalition; bd. mem. Linn County Adolescent Pregnancy Prevention Coalition, treas. 1992-96, Young Parents Network, 1988—, pres. 1994-96, Friends of Iowa Commn. on Status of Women; mem. steering com. ERA Iowa 1992, 1991—; mem. gov.'s com. adoption reform in Iowa, 1993, 94, lt. gov.'s com. spl. needs adoption in Iowa, 1994; bd. dirs., pub. policy chair AAUW, 1995—; mem. Breast Cancer Advocacy Group, Cedar Rapids, Iowa, 1995—; cons. med. ethics com. U. Iowa, 1995. Recipient Outstanding Svc. awards Sioux City C. of C., 1976, Siouxland Arts Coun., 1977; named Woman of the Yr., Linn County, Cedar Rapids, Iowa, 1995. Mem. NASW, Profl. Women's Network Cedar Rapids (bd. mem.). Republican. Episcopalian. Office: Hillcrest Family Svcs 205 12th St SE Cedar Rapids IA 52403-4028

ZIETZ, LONNY E., oral and maxillofacial surgeon; s. Edward H. and Vera E. (Veitengruber); m. Sanda J. Zietz, May 11, 1968; children: Jeffrey, Patrick, Gregory. BS, U. Mich., 1965, DDS, 1969, MS, 1973. Diplomate Am. Bd. Oral and Maxillofacial Surgery. Rotating dental intern VA Hosp., U. Fla., Gainesville, 1970; oral surgery resident U. Mich.; active staff Blodgett Meml. Med. Ctr., Butterworth Hosp., St. Mary's Hosp., libr. com. 1983, 94, operating rm. and patient care com., 1984-89, cosmetic and reconstructive surgery task force, 1985-86; mem. cons. staff Met. Hosp., mem. West Mich. Ambulatory Surg. Ctr.; tchr. Grand Rapids Jr. Coll. Dental Asst. Program, 1978, 79. Contbr. numerous articles to profl. jours. Mem. dental adv. com. Grand Rapids Jr. Coll., 1980-82. Fellow Am. Assn. Oral and Maxillofacial Surgeons (del.); mem. ADA, Internat. Assn. Oral and Maxillofacial Surgeons, Chalmers J. Lyons Acad. Oral Surgery (pres. 1990-91), Gt. Lakes Soc. Oral and Maxillofacial Surgeons, Mich. Soc. Oral and Maxillofacial Surgeons (pres. 1993-95), Am. Dental Soc. Anesthesiology, PICOM Dental Adv. Com., Mich. Dental Assn. (del., mem. various coms.), West Mich. Dental Found. (bd. dirs. 1995), West Mich. Dental Soc. (chmn. emergency svc. com. 1977-88), Kent County Dental Soc. (pres. 1980), Omicron Kappa Upsilon, Phi Kappa Alpha. Home: 1111 Cramton NE Ada MI 49301 Office: 2140 Lake Michigan Dr NW Grand Rapids MI 49504

ZILVERSMIT, ARTHUR, history educator; b. The Hague, The Netherlands, July 5, 1932; came to U.S., 1939; s. Marcus and Marianne (de Korte) Z.; m. Charlotte Perlman, Dec. 26, 1955; children: Marc Jonathan, Karen Golden. BA, Cornell U., 1954; AM, Harvard U., 1955; PhD, U. Calif., Berkeley, 1962. From instr. to assoc. prof. Williams Coll., Williamstown, Mass., 1961-66; prof. History Lake Forest (Ill.) Coll., 1966—; acad. dir. Nat. Coun. for History Edn. History Acad., Columbus, Ohio, 1992-93. Author: Changing Schools, 1993, First Emancipation, 1967. Mem. Am. Hist. Assn., Orgn. of Am. Historians. Office: Lake Forest Coll. 555 N Sheridan Rd Lake Forest IL 60045-2338

ZIMMER, ANNE FERN YOUNG, educator, researcher, administrator; b. Detroit, Dec. 19, 1920; d. Arthur Frederick and Jessie (Clements) Young; m. D. Robert Stewart, Oct. 3, 1942 (dec. July 1944); 1 child, Robert Arthur; m. Arnold Earnest Zimmer, Apr. 7, 1951; 1 child, Kathleen Anne (dec.). BS, Wayne State U., 1962, MA, 1964, PhD, 1966. With pers. dept. Standard Accident Ins. Co., Detroit, 1944-46, bond underwriter, 1946-52; part-time med. sec. various drs. and hosps. Detroit, 1955-59; instr. Wayne State U., Detroit, 1966-67, asst. prof., 1967, asst. prof., adminstr. grad. program, 1967-75, assoc. prof., 1976—, ret., 1986; sec., treas. bicentennial com. Wayne State U., 1973-75, chmn., 1976. Author: (biography) Jonathan Boucher, Loyalist in Exile, 1978 (Ella V. Dobbs award 1979); contbr. articles to profl. jours. Initiator Citizens for Advanced Life Support, Grosse Pointe Woods (Mich.) Emergency Med. Svc., 1981, 83; founder Cass Assn. of Cass Tech. High Sch., Detroit. Wayne State U. fellow, 1962-64, scholar, 1959-62; recipient Colonial Dames award DAR, 1965. Mem. AAUW (chair ad hoc com. for emergency med. svcs. Grosse Pointe br. 1984-92, area rep. and bd. mem. 1992—), So. Assn. Women Historians, So. Hist. Assn. (membership com. 1974-75, chair nominating com. 1979-80, Francis Simkins award com. 1980-81, Green award com. 1976-78), Inst. Early Am. History, Smithsonian, Nat. Trust for Hist. Preservation, Grosse Pointe Woman's Club. Home: 813 Anita Ave Grosse Pointe MI 48236-1414

ZIMMER, DONALD WILLIAM, coach professional athletics, former professional baseball manager; b. Cin., Jan. 17, 1931; s. Harold Lesley and Lorraine Bertha (Ernst) Z.; m. Jean Carol Bauerle, Aug. 16, 1951; children: Thomas Jeffrey, Donna Jean. Student pub. schs., Cin. Baseball player Dodger Farm Clubs, 1949-54, Bklyn. Dodgers, 1954-57, Los Angeles Dodgers, 1958-59, Chgo. Cubs, 1960-61, N.Y. Mets, 1962, Cin. Reds, 1962, Los Angeles Dodgers, 1963, Washington Senators, 1963-65, Toei Flyers, Tokyo, 1966; mgr. Cin. Reds Farm Clubs, Knoxville and Buffalo, 1967, Indpls., 1968; mgr. San Diego Padre Farm Clubs, Key West, Fla., 1969, Padre Farm Club, Salt Lake City, 1970; coach Montreal Expos, Que., Can., 1971; mgr. San Diego Padres, 1972-73; coach Boston Red Sox, 1974-76, mgr., 1976-80; mgr. Tex. Rangers, 1981, 82; coach N.Y. Yankees, 1983, 86, 96, Chgo. Cubs, 1984, 85, 86, San Francisco Giants, 1987; mgr. Chgo. Cubs, 1988-91; coach Boston Red Sox, 1992, Colo. Rockies, Denver, 1993-95, N.Y. Yankees, 1996—; mem. minor league All-Star Teams, Hornell, N.Y., 1950, Elmira, N.Y., 1951, Mobile, Ala., 1952, St. Paul, 1953; player World Series teams 1955, 56, 59, coach 1975. Recipient Bill Stern award NBC, 1949; named St. Paul Rookie of Yr., 1953; mem. All Star Team, 1961, 78, 81, 90; named Nat. League Mgr. of Yr. 1989. Mem. Profl. Baseball Players Am. (life), Old Time Ball Players Wis. Office: c/o N.Y. Yankees Yankees Stadium Bronx NY 10451

ZIMMER, JOHN HERMAN, lawyer; b. Sioux Falls, S.D., Dec. 30, 1922; s. John Francis and Veronica (Berke) Z.; student Augustana Coll., Sioux Falls, 1941-42, Mont. State Coll., 1943; LLB, U. S.D., 1948; m. Deanna Langner, 1976; children by previous marriage: Mary Zimmer Quinlin, Robert Joseph, Judith Maureen Zimmer Rose. Bar: S.D. 1948. Pvt. practice law, Turner County, S.D., 1948—; of counsel Zimmer & Duncan, Parker, S.D., 1992—; states atty. Turner County, 1955-58, 62-64; asst. prof. med. jurisprudence U. S.D.; minority counsel U.S. Senate Armed Services Com. on Strategic and Critical Materials Investigation, 1962-63; chmn. Southeastern Council Govts., 1973-75; mem. U. S.D. Law Sch. adv. council, 1973-74. Chmn. Turner County Rep. Com., 1955-56; mem. S.D. Rep. adv. com., 1959-60; alt. del. Rep. Nat. Conv., 1968; pres. S.D. Easter Seal Soc., 1986-87. Served with AUS, 1943-46; PTO. Decorated Bronze Star, Philippine Liberation ribbon. Mem. ABA, Fed., S.D. (commr. 1954-57) Bar Assns., Assn. Trial Lawyers Am., S.D. Trial Lawyers Assn. (pres. 1967-68), VFW, Am. Legion, Phi Delta Phi. Lodges: Elks, Shriners. Home: RRI PO Box 640 Parker SD 57053 Office: Zimmer & Duncan Law Bldg PO Box 550 Parker SD 57053-0547

ZIMMERMAN, CHERYL LEA, pharmacy educator; b. Chippewa Falls, Wis., May 2, 1953; d. Robert Herman and Lucille May (Jennings) Z.; m. Rory Patrick Remmel, June 25, 1983. BS, U. Wis., 1976; PhD, U. Wash., 1983. Registered pharmacist, Wis. Rsch. asst. U. Wash., Seattle, 1978-83; asst. prof. U. Minn., Mpls., 1983-90, assoc. prof., 1990—. Recipient Horace T. Morse Alumni Award U. Minn., 1989. Mem. AAAS (nominations com. 1991-92, mem.-at-large 1996—), Am. Assn. Pharm. Scientists (com. chair, sect. sec. 1996), Am. Assn. Colls. Pharmacy. Democrat. Roman Catholic. Office: U Minn Coll Pharmacy 308 Harvard St SE Minneapolis MN 55455-0353

ZIMMERMAN, DEAN ARTHUR, polymer engineer; b. Danville, Ky., Oct. 31, 1967; s. Craig Arthur and Jane Z.; m. Elizabeth Weed Zimmerman, Aug. 17, 1991. BS in Chem. Engring., Case Western Reserve, 1989; MS in Polymer Sci., 1992, PhD in Polymer Sci., 1995. Rsch. intern Amoco Chemical, Naperville, Ill., 1988; rsch. asst. Dow Chemical, Midland, Mich., 1989, Case Western Reserve, Cleve., 1989-94; sr. rsch. engr. Quantum Chemical, Cin., 1995—. Contbr. articles to profl. jours. Dir. Case Western Reserve Alumni, Cleve., 1991—; vol. New Life Cmty., Cleve., 1994. Recipient A.W. Smith award 1989, Instrnl. Excellence award 1994, Case Western Reserve. Mem. Soc. Plastic Engrs., Mortar Bd., Tau Beta Pi. Home: 8925 Keehner Dr West Chester OH 45069

ZIMMERMAN, DELANO ELMER, physician; b. Fond du Lac, Wis., Mar. 21, 1933; s. Elmer Herbert and Agatha Angeline (Freund) Z.; m. Nancy Margaret Garry, Aug. 13, 1966; children: Kate Zimmerman Lennard, Joseph, Nick. BS, U. Wis., 1961, MD, 1965. Diplomate Am. Soc. Profl. Disability Cons. Intern, Hennepin County Hosp., Mpls., 1965,; physician, surgeon Winnebago (Wis.) State Hosp., 1966-67; gen. practice medicine, Neenah, Wis., 1967-73; emergency room physician Community Emergency Svcs. , Appleton, 1973-77, Meml. Med. Center, Springfield, Ill., 1977-92; faculty So. Ill. U. Sch. Medicine, Springfield, 1977—; past bd. dirs. nominating com. Sangamon Valley chpt. ARC. With USN, 1951-56. Mem. Am. Coll. Emergency Physicians, Ill. Coll. Emergency Physicians (bd. dirs., awards com., fin. com., mem.-at-large, govt. affairs com.), Soc. for Acad. Emergency Medicine. Roman Catholic. Home: The Cottage 1467 Cowling Bay Rd Neenah WI 54956-9205

ZIMMERMAN, DORIS LUCILE, chemist; b. L.A., July 30, 1942; d. Walter Merritt and Letta Minnie (Reese) Briggs; m. Christopher Scott Zimmerman, June 5, 1964; children: Susan Christina, David Scott, Brian Allan. BS in Chemistry, Carnegie Mellon U., 1964; MS in Chemistry, Youngstown State U., 1989, MS in Materials Engring., 1992; postgrad., Kent (Ohio) State U. High sch. tchr. Ohio County Schs., Vienna and Campbell, 1983-87; sr. chemist Konwal, Warren, Ohio, 1988-91; limited faculty mem. Kent (Ohio) State U., 1991-95; temp. full-time instr. dept. chemistry Edinboro U. Pa., 1995—; substitute tchr. County Schs. of Ohio, Warren, 1972-82; tutor, 1965—. Instr. water safety ARC, Warren, 1965—; chmn. Trumbull Mobile Meals, Warren, 1977-92, Pink Thumb Garden Club, Warren, 1965—. Recipient Svc. award ARD, 1981, Trumbull Mobile Meals, 1985. Mem. Materials Info. Soc., Soc. for the Advancement of Material and Process Engring., Am. Chem. Soc. (sec. 1985-90, chmn. elect 1990, chmn. 1991, alternate councilor 1992—, Commendation award 1990), Carnegie Mellon Alumni Assn. (admissions councilor, Svc. award 1981), Phi Lambda Upsilon, Phi Kappa Phi, Sigma Xi. Republican. Methodist. Home and Office: 1390 Waverly Dr NW Warren OH 44483-1718

ZIMMERMAN, HAROLD SEYMOUR, elementary school educator; b. Bklyn., June 3, 1928. BA, Bklyn. Coll., 1950; MA, So. Ill. U., Edwardsville, 1970; postgrad., various, 1950-90. 8th grade English, Social Studies, Reading tchr. Sherwood Day Sch., Chesterfield, Mo., 1956-64; 7th grade core curriculum, English, Social Studies tchr. Nipher Jr. High Sch., Kirkwood, Mo., 1964-70; 7th grade Social Studies, team teaching tchr. Brittany Woods Sch., University City, Mo., 1971-91; tchr. Russian lit. OASIS, 1995; tchr. Russian Art Oasis, 1996; adj. prof. Russian studies Lindenwood Coll., St. Charles, Mo., 1975—, Washington U., 1972-91; participant 1st U.S./Russia Joint Conf. on Edn., 1994; cons. in field. Author: Facing Issues of Family Living; contbr. articles to profl. jours. Chairperson bd. trustees Indian Meadows subdivsn., Olivette, Mo.; chairperson Youth Commn., Olivette; vol. OASIS, St. Louis Zoo. Mem. NEA, ASCD, Mo. Edn. Assn., Nat. Coun. Social Studies (spl. interest groups psychology, tchr. edn., religion in schs.), Mo. Geog. Alliance Tchr. Cons., People to People, World Coun. of Affairs, Bus. for Russia. Home: 450 E Lockwood Webster Groves MO 63119

ZIMMERMAN, HOWARD ELLIOT, chemist, educator; b. N.Y.C., July 5, 1926; s. Charles and May (Cohen) Z.; m. Jane Kirschenheiter, June 3, 1950 (dec. Jan. 1975); children: Robert, Steven, James; m. Martha L. Bailey Kaufman, Nov. 7, 1975 (div. Oct. 1990); m. Peggy J. Vick, Oct. 1991; stepchildren: Peter and Tanya Kaufman. B.S., Yale U., 1950, Ph.D., 1953. NRC fellow Harvard U., 1953-54; faculty Northwestern U., 1954-60, asst. prof., 1955-60; assoc. prof. U. Wis., Madison, 1960-61; prof. chemistry U. Wis., 1961—, Arthur C. Cope and Hilldale prof. chemistry, 1975—; chmn. 4th Internat. Union Pure and Applied Chemistry Symposium on Photochemistry, 1972; organizer, chmn. Organic Photochemistry Symposium at Pacifichem 95, Honolulu, 1995. Author: Quantum Mechanics for Organic Chemists, 1975; mem. editorial bd.: Jour. Organic Chemistry, 1967-71, Molecular Photochemistry, 1969-75, Jour. Am. Chem. Soc., 1982-85, Revs. Reactive Intermediates, 1984-89; contbr. articles to profl. jours. Recipient Halpern award for photochemistry N.Y. Acad. Scis., 1979, Chem. Pioneer award Am. Inst. Chemists, 1986, Sr. Alexander von Humboldt award, 1988, Hilldale award U. Wis., 1988-89, 90. Mem. NAS, Am. Chem. Soc. (James Flack Norris award 1976, Arthur C. Cope Scholar award 1991), Chem. Soc. London, German Chem. Soc., Inter-Am. Photochemistry Assn. (co-chmn. organic div. 1977-79, exec. com. 1979-86), Phi Beta Kappa, Sigma Xi. Home: 1 Oconto Ct Madison WI 53705-4925 Office: U Wis Chemistry Dept 1101 University Ave Madison WI 53706-1322

ZIMMERMAN, JO ANN, health services and educational consultant, former lieutenant governor; b. Van Buren County, Iowa, Dec. 24, 1936; d. Russell and Hazel (Ward) McIntosh; m. A. Tom Zimmerman, Aug. 26, 1956; children: Andrew, Lisa, Don and Ron (twins), Beth. Diploma, Broadlawns Sch. of Nursing, Des Moines, 1958; BA with honors, Drake U., 1973; postgrad., Iowa State U., 1973-75. RN, Iowa. Asst. head nurse maternity dept. Broadlawns Med. Ctr., Des Moines, 1958-59, weekend supr. nursing svcs., 1960-61, supr. maternity dept., 1966-68; instr. maternity nursing Broadlawns Sch. Nursing, 1968-71; health planner, community rels. assoc. Iowa Health Systems Agy., Des Moines, 1978-82; mem. Iowa Ho. Reps., 1982-86; lt. gov., Senate pres. State of Iowa, 1987-91; cons. health svcs., grant writing and continuing edn. Zimmerman & Assocs., Des Moines, 1991—; dir. patient care svcs. Nursing Svcs. of Iowa, 1996—; ops. dir. Medlink Svcs., Inc., Des Moines, 1992-96; dir. nurses Nursing Svcs. of Iowa, 1996—. Contbr. articles to profl. jours. Mem. advanced registered nurse practioner task force on cert. nurse mid-wives Iowa Bd. Nursing, 1980-81, Waukee, Polk County, Iowa Health Edn. Coord. Coun., Iowa Women's Polit. Caucus, Dallas County Women's Polit. Caucus; chmn. Des Moines Area Maternity Nursing Conf. Group, 1969-70, task force on sch. health svcs. Iowa Dept. Health, 1982, task force health edn. Iowa Dept. Pub. Instruction, 1979, adv. com. health edn. assessment tool, 1980-81, Nat. Lt. Govs., chair com. on Agrl. and Rural Devel., 1989; Dallas County Dem. Cen. Com., 1972-84; bd. dirs. Waukee Cmty. Sch. Bd., 1976-79, pres. 1978-79; bd. dirs. Iowa PTA, 1979-83, chairperson Health Com., 1980-84; mem. steering com. ERA, Iowa, 1991-92; founder Dem. Activist Women's Network (DAWN), 1992. Mem. ANA, LWV (health chmn. met. Des Moines chpt.), Iowa Nurses Assn., Iowa League for Nursing (bd. dirs. 1979-83), Family Centered Childbirth Edn. Assn. (childbirth instr., advisor), Iowa Cattleman's Assn., Am. Lung Assn. (bd. dirs. Iowa 1988-92), Dem. Activist Women's Network (founder 1992). Mem. Christian Ch. Office: Zimmerman & Assocs 7630 Ashworth Rd West Des Moines IA 50266-5859

ZIMMERMAN, JUDITH ROSE, elementary art educator; b. Youngstown, Ohio, Jan. 17, 1945; d. Emery and Josephine Leona (Terlecki) Ference; m. William Carl Zimmerman, Jr., Nov 27, 1965; children: Shawn, William III. BFA in Art Edn., Kent State U., 1977, MEd in Curriculum and Instruction, 1992. Cert. art tchr., Ohio. Elem. art tchr. Sandy Valley Sch. Dist., Magnolia, Ohio, 1977—; instr. art Massillon (Ohio) Art Mus. Adv. com. Edn. Enhancement Partnership Coun., Canton, Ohio, 1992; active Little Art Gallery, 1992, Massillon Art Mus. Mem. NEA, Nat. Art Edn. Assn., Ohio Edn. Assn., Ohio Art Edn. Assn. (chairperson east cen. divsn. 1985-90, elem. divsn. 1989-91, Art Educator of Yr. 1983, Featured Art Tchr. of Month 1990), Ohio Alliance for Art Edn., Canton Art Inst. (Art Educator of Yr. 1992), Phi Delta Kappa (newsletter editor McKinley chpt.). Roman Catholic. Home: 802 Lucille Ave SW North Canton OH 44720-2820 Office: Sandy Valley Sch Dist RR 2 Magnolia OH 44643-9802

ZIMMERMAN, SHIRLEY LEE, family social science educator, researcher; b. Mpls., Nov. 23, 1925; m. Peter David Zimmerman, Aug. 3, 1947; children: Michael, Daniel, Kevin, Julie. BA in Sociology, U. Minn., 1947, MSW, 1977, PhD, 1977, postgrad., 1977-78. Social worker Hennepin County Dept. Pub. Welfare, Mpls., 1947-49; child welfare cons. Minn. Dept. Pub. Welfare, St. Paul, 1967-69; planner United Way, St. Paul, 1969-70; asst. dir.continuing edn. U. Minn., Mpls., 1970-84, prof. family social sci., 1984—; cons. Northstar Rsch. Inst., Mpls., 1969, Interstudy, Mpls., 1973-76. Author: Understanding Family Policy, 1988, Family Policies and Family Well-Being: The Role of Political Culture, 1992, Understanding Family Policy: Theories and Applications, 1995; contbr. numerous articles to profl. jours. NIMH fellow, 1977-78. Mem. NASW, Am. Pub. Welfare Assn., Nat. Coun. on Family Rels. (chair, bd. dirs. family policy sect. 1989—, guest editor family rels. jours. 1990, program v.p. 1995-96), Policy Studies Orgn. Democrat. Home: 3843 Glenhurst Ave Minneapolis MN 55416-4915

ZIMMERMAN, SUSAN G., sales executive; b. Lincoln, Nebr., Aug. 3, 1952; d. Robert Loyal and Marion Lucille (Brown) Mueller; m. Steven D. Zimmerman, Jan., 1988; children: Kathryn, Jamison, Sari, Desiree. BS, U. Minn., 1974. ChFC, CLU. Traffic coord. Barrickman Red Barron Advt., Mpls., 1974-75; high sch. tchr. Robbinsdale, Osseo and Blaine Schs., Mpls., 1974-83; adult edn. instr. Osseo, Robbinsdale Sch. Dist., Mpls., 1983; conf. coord. Lakewood Pub./Tng. Mag., Mpls., 1983-84; from project mgr. to dir. sales Cardinal Health Systems, Mpls., 1984-87, exec. dir. sales, 1987-88; registered rep./trainer Equitable Fin. Cos., St. Paul, 1987—; with Zimmerman Fin. Group, Mpls., 1987—; pres. Mgmt. Edn. Cons. Corp. of Am., Mpls., 1984—. Free-lance writer Mpls. Star & Tribune, 1982-83. Mem. NAFE, ASTD, Nat. Assn. Profl. Saleswomen (pres. local chpt., chmn. women's leads exch.), Internat. Assn. Fin. Planners, Nat. Assn. Life Underwriters, Minn. Alumni Assn., Cmty. Edn. Assn., Am. Mgmt. Assn., Flagship Club (Eden Prairie, Minn.). Presbyterian. Home: 14530 Pennock Ave Saint Paul MN 55124-7395 Office: 8400 Normandale Blvd Ste 1700 Minneapolis MN 55437

ZIMMERMANN, DAVID SCOTT, advertising sales executive; b. Cape Gireadeau, Mo., June 14, 1955; s. Russell Robert and Dolores Marie (Muetze) Z.; m. Stephanie Ann Rice, Aug. 6, 1976; children: Ashley Rice, Alexandra Rice. Student, U. Mo., 1973-76, Gov. State U., 1985-88. Mgr. div. Asch Advt., Chgo., 1978-81; field svc. rep. Brown-Forman Media Svcs., Chgo., 1981-85; mgr. Chgo. sales Gateway Outdoor Advt., Chgo., 1985-87, nat. sales mgr., 1987-89, gen. mgr., v.p., 1989; nat. sales mgr., media dir. Universal Outdoor Advt., Chgo., 1989-91, v.p. nat. sales, 1991-92, v.p. nat. and intermarket sales mgr., 1992, dir. midwest outdoor mgmt., 1992-93; v.p. sales, mktg. Universal Eight Outdoor Advt., Chgo., 1993-94, gen. mgr., 1994—. Mem. Eight St. ADv. Assn. Am. (sec./treas. 1994), Chgo. ADvt.

Club, Alhambra. Roman Catholic. Office: Universal Outdoor Advt 321 N Clark St Ste 1010 Chicago IL 60610-4715

ZIMMERMANN, ROBERT LAURENCE, marketing professional; b. Mpls., Jan. 1, 1932; s. Lawrence and Bertha Mabel (Foss) Z. BA, U. Minn., 1954, MA, 1965, PhD, 1970. Asst. prof. psychology U. Winnepeg, Man., Can., 1968-69; research assoc. psychiatry research unit U. Minn., Mpls., 1969-75; sr. scientist biometrics lab. George Washington U., Washington, 1975-76; pvt. cons. research design and data analysis Mpls., 1976-84; sr. research mgr. Maritz Market Rsch., Mpls., 1984—; clin. asst. prof. psychiatry dept. U. Minn., Mpls., 1976—; external rev. officer FDA, Washington, 1974-77. Contbr. numerous articles to profl. jours. Fellow NIMH, 1958, 61, 69-71; merit fellow State of Minn. Mem. AAAS. Democrat. Home: 1920 S 1st St Apt 1104 Minneapolis MN 55454-1048 Office: Maritz Market Rsch Inc 1650 W 82nd St Minneapolis MN 55431-1419

ZIMNY, ROBERT WALTER, metal processing executive; b. Chgo., June 7, 1937; s. Walter William and Francis Clara (Greskowiak) Z.; m. Patrisia S. Tillema, June 6, 1964; children: Brian Walter, Douglas Robert, Russell Patrick. BS in Vocat. Edn., Chgo. State U., 1971; MA in Adminstn. and Supervision, Govs. State U., Park Forest, Ill., 1976. Cert. welding educator. Welding leadman Elkay Mfg. Co., Broadview, Ill., 1955-63; plant foreman Stembridge Mfg. Co., Addison, Ill., 1963-65; welding dir. Am. Inst. Engring., Chgo., 1964-66; welding instr., chmn. dept. Chgo. Vocat. H.S., 1965-70, Washburn Trade Sch., Chgo., 1970-79; welding instr. Triton Coll., Rivergrove, Ill., 1968-72; tech. cons. Met. Sanitary Dist. of Chgo., 1970-90; owner, pres. Zimny Welding Svc., Chgo., 1978—; owner Weldors Unltd.; cons. H.K. Porter Elec., Lynchburg, Va., 1968-80, Delta Unibus, Franklin Park, Ill., 1981—, Miner Enterprise, Geneva, Ill., 1978—, Ryerson Steel, Chgo., 1984—; chmn. bd. dirs. Airolen Capital Ventures, 1988—; officer adv. coun. Washburne Trade Sch. Author: Welding Instructor's Handbook, 1971. Alderman Ind. Party, Hickory Hills, Ill., 1981. Sgt. U.S. Army, 1959-61. Mem. Am. Welding Soc. (cert. weld insp., cert. welding educator, 1993), Southern Shore Yacht Club (commodore 1989-91), Chgo. Yachting Assn. (bd. dirs.), Salmon Unltd. Republican. Roman Catholic. Home: 16818 S Spicebush Ln Orland Park IL 60462-8474 Office: Zimny Welding Svc 3314 W 47th St Chicago IL 60632-2915

ZIMOSTRAD, SCOTT WILLIAM, psychologist; b. Bay City, Mich., Feb. 14, 1956; m. Christine; children: Emily, Abbey. BS, Western Mich. U., 1978, MA, 1979; PhD, Ball State U., 1987. Outpatient therapist Ausable Valley CMH, Tawas City, Mich., 1980-84; staff neuropsychologist Mid Michigan Regional Med. Ctr., Center Midland, Mich., 1987-94; pvt. practice Midland, Mich., 1994—. Leader Girl Scouts U.S., Midland, 1995—; mem. Midland Safe Bike Coalition, 1990—, Optomist Club, Midland, 1995—. Mem. APA, Nat. Acad. Neuropsychology, Internat. Acad. Neuropsychology, Mich. Psychological Assn. (reg. rep. to exec. council, Youth Advocacy com.). Home: 1880 E Chippewa River Rd Midland MI 48640 Office: 2708 N Saginaw Rd Midland MI 48640

ZIMOV, BRUCE STEVEN, software engineer; b. Cin., Oct. 16, 1953; s. Sherman and Sylvia Zimov; m. Ruth Ellen Zimov, Sept. 7, 1974 (div. 1981); 1 child, Sarah Eleanor. BS in Physics, U. Cin., 1975, MA in Philosophy, 1979. Physicist Kornylak Corp., Hamilton, Ohio, 1982-83; software engr. Entek Sci. Corp., Cin., 1983-89, project mgr., 1989—. Inventor chess variants, table tennis variant. Mem. IEEE, Internat. Neural Network Soc., Tri-State Online Philosophy SIG (founder). Home: 5 Woodsview Ln Cincinnati OH 45241-2173 Office: Entek Sci Corp 4480 Lake Forest Dr Cincinnati OH 45242-3740

ZINDEL, JON WALTER, financial services consultant; b. Decatur, Ill., June 9, 1967; s. James Walter and Helen Ann (Johno) Z.; m. Jennifer Lynn Blum, Aug. 5, 1989; children: Carolynn Christina, Ellie Grace. BS in Acctg. and Fin., Loyola U., New Orleans, 1989. CPA, La., Nebr., Mo. Audit cons. Price Waterhouse LLP, New Orleans, 1989-92; tax cons. Price Waterhouse LLP, Omaha, 1992-94; fin. svcs. tax mgr. Price Waterhouse LLP, Kansas City, Mo., 1994—. Bd. dirs. Ronald McDonald House, Kansas City, Mo.; mem. fin. and planning coms. Arthritis Found., Kansas City; active Project Bus., Jr. Achievement, New Orleans, 1991, Omaha, 1993. Mem. AICPA, Nat. Soc. Accts. for Coops., Nebr. Soc. CPAs, K.C. (treas. 1995, 3 deg.), Jesuit Honor Soc., Beta Alpha Psi. Democrat. Roman Catholic. Home: 12512 W 101st Terr Lenexa KS 66215 Office: Price Waterhouse LLP 1055 Broadway St Kansas City MO 64105

ZINKE, MICHAEL DUANE, finance and accountancy manager; b. Mendota, Ill., Oct. 13, 1954; s. Elmer H. and Barbara A. (Williams) Z.; m. Cathy L. Myers, July 22, 1978; children: Duane M., Brian M. AA cum laude, Ill. Valley Community Coll., 1974; BS, No. Ill. U., 1976; MBA, Cen. State U., Edmond, Okla., 1988. Comptr. Office World, Oklahoma City, 1977-79; credit analyst C.I.T. Corp., Oklahoma City, 1979-80, sr. credit analyst, 1980-81, dist. credit mgr., 1982-84; credit mgr. Macklanburg-Duncan Co., Oklahoma City, 1984-87, mgr. credit, payroll, accounts payable, gen. acctg., 1987-90; credit mgr. N.Am. Chem. Co., Mission, Kans., 1991-92, N.Am. Salt Co. and N.Am. Chem. Co., Overland Park, Kans., 1992—; chmn. unsecured creditors com. H.E. Leonhardt Lumber, Oklahoma City, 1989-90; mem. unsecured creditors com. O'Hommel Co., Overland Park, Kans., 1991—. Author rsch. papers. Membership drive vol. Oklahoma City C. of C., 1989; rep. Napco Constrn. to Oklahoma City C. of C., 1990-91; dist. sec.-treas. Am. Bus. Clubs, Oklahoma City, 1985-86; bearer of U.S. Olympic Festival Torch, 1989. Mem. Nat. Assn. Credit Mgmt., Nat. Chem. Creditors Assn., Fin. Credit and Internat. Bus. Assn., Internat. Trade Club of Greater Kansas City. Democrat. Lutheran. Home: 8800 Candlelight Ln Lenexa KS 66215-3432 Office: NAm Salt Co 8300 College Blvd Overland Park KS 66210-1841

ZINKON, LANA SUE, occupational health nurse; b. Dover, Ohio, Oct. 19, 1954; d. Jack Eugene and Virginia Louise (Brown) Z.; divorced; children: Amanda Elyse and Emily Suzanne (twins). Diploma, Grant Hosp. Sch. Nursing, Columbus, Ohio, 1976; student, Ashland U., 1991—. RN, Ohio. Supr. med. Cedar Point Amusement Park, Sandusky, Ohio, 1977-82; shift supr. Nursing Home, Port Clinton, Ohio, 1978-82; staff nurse Flying Nurses, Calif. La., 1982-83; camp nurse Camp Blue Star, Hendersonville, N.C., summer 1983; staff nurse Med. Pers. Pool, Hendersonville, 1983; occupl. health nurse Rockwell Internat., Fletcher, N.C., 1984-88; staff/charge nurse Joel Pomerene Hosp., Millersburg, Ohio, 1988-89, off-shift supr., 1989-93, dir. occupl. health, 1990-94; occupl. health nurse The Timken Co., New Philadelphia, Ohio, 1989—; coord. on-site svc. for occupl. medcine Ctr. of Tuscarawas County, New Philadelphia, 1995—; dir., creator On-the-Job Occupational Program, Joel Pomerene Meml. Hosp., Millersburg, 1990. Mem. Am. Assn. Occupational Health Nurses, Ohio Assn. Occupational Health Nurses, Stark Assn. Occupational Health Nurses, Am. Legion Aux., Ohio Eastern Star. Democrat. Methodist. Office: Med Ctr Tuscarawas County 306 W High Ave New Philadelphia OH 44663-2134

ZIOMEK, JONATHAN S., journalist, educator; b. Newport News, Va., July 28, 1947; s. Stanley Walter and Joy Carmen (Schmidt) Z.; m. Rosalie Ziomek, Aug. 14, 1977; children: Joseph, Jennifer; 1 stepchild, Daniel. BA in Sociology, U. Ill., 1970, MS in Journalism, 1982. Reporter, feature writer, Sun. fin. editor Chgo. Sun-Times, 1970-78; press sec. Robert Ash Wallace for U.S. Senate campaign, Chgo., 1979-80; asst. prof. Medill Sch. Journalism, Northwestern U., Evanston, Ill., 1983-88; dir. grad. editl. programs Medill Sch. Journalism/Northwestern U., Evanston, Ill., 1988—, asst. dean, assoc. prof., 1994—; presenter writing workshops. Contbr. articles to various mags.; editor: Chgo. Journalist Newsletter, 1991-93. Participant Internat. Visitors Ctr., Chgo., 1988—; fact-finder USIA, Bulgaria and Yugoslavia, 1990. Mem. Assn. for Edn. in Journalism and Mass Communications, Soc. Profl. Journalists, Nat. Assn. Sci. Writers, Headline Club. Home: 2149 Hartrey Ave Evanston IL 60201-2571 Office: Northwestern Univ Medill Sch Journalism Evanston IL 60208

ZIPF, WILLIAM BYRON, pediatric endocrinologist, educator; b. Dayton, Ohio, Mar. 20, 1946; s. Robert Eugene and Merium (Murr) Z.; m. Joanne Fisher, Sept. 20, 1969; children: William Byron Jr., Thanda Lynn, Robert E. II. BA, Denison U., 1968; MD, Ohio State U., 1972. Diplomate Nat. Bd. Med. Examiners, Am. Bd. Pediatrics, Am. Bd. Pediatric Endocrinology. Intern in pediatrics Mott Children's Hosp./U. Mich., Ann Arbor, 1972-73, resident in pediatrics, 1973-75, clin. fellow in pediatric endocrinology, 1975-76, rsch. fellow, 1976-78; asst. prof. dept. pediatrics and physiology Ohio State U., Columbus, 1978-83, assoc. prof., 1983-89, prof., 1989—; dir. clin. study ctr. Children's Hosp./Ohio State U., Columbus, 1982—, vice-chmn. dept. pediatrics, 1989—, dir. pediatric endocrinology, 1990—. Contbr. chpts. on endocrine diseases of children to books, articles to profl. jours. Grantee NIH, 1980-84, Cystic Fibrosis Found., 1987-92. Fellow Am. Acad. Pediatrics, Nat. Med. Bd.; mem. Soc. Pediatric Rsch., Endocrine Soc., Lawson Wilkins Soc. Pediatric Endocrinolgoy. Office: Childrens Hosp 700 Childrens Dr Columbus OH 43205-2666

ZIRBES, MARY KENNETH, social justice ministry coordinator; b. Melrose, Minn., Sept. 4, 1926; d. Joseph Louis and Clara Bernadine (Petermeier) Z. BA in History and Edn., Coll. St. Catherine, 1960; MA in Applied Theology, Sch. Applied Theology, Berkeley, Calif., 1976. Joined Order of St. Francis, Roman Cath. Ch., 1945. Tchr. Pub. Grade Sch., St. Nicholas, Minn., 1947-52; prin. Holy Spirit Grade Sch., St. Cloud, Minn., 1953-59, St. Mary's Jr. High Sch., Morris, Minn., 1960-62; coord. Franciscan Mission Team, Peru, South America, 1962-67, Franciscan Missions, Little Falls, Minn., 1967-70; dir. St. Richard's Social Ministry, Richfield, Minn., 1971-80, Parish Community Devel., St. Paul, Mpls., Minn., 1980-85; councillor gen. Franciscan Sisters of Little Falls, 1960-62, 67-70; asst. dir. Renew-Archdiocese of St. Paul-Mpls., 1986-89; coord. Parish Social Justice Ministry-Archdiocese of St. Paul-Mpls., 1990-93; minister Franciscan Assocs., 1993—; leader of team on evangelical life Franciscan Sisters of Little Falls, 1994—; co-developer Assn. of Pastoral Ministers, Mpls., St. Paul, 1979-81, Compañeros/Sister Parishes-Minn. and Nicaragua, 1984-89, Minn. Interfaith Ecology Coalition, 1989-92. Author: Parish Social Ministry, 1985, (manual) Acting for Justice, 1992. Organizer Twin Cities Orgn., Mpls., 1979-80; bd. dirs. Franciscan Sisters Health Care, Inc., Little Falls, 1990-93, Rice-Marion Residents Assn., St. Paul, 1991-92. Named Outstanding chair Assn. Pastoral Ministers, 1981; recipient Five Yrs. of Outstanding Svc. award Companeros, 1989. Mem. Assn. Pastoral Ministers (chair 1979), Amnesty Internat., Voices for Justice-Legis. Lobby, Audubon Soc., Network, Minn. Interfaith Ecology Coalition, Franciscan Sisters of Little Falls. Office: Franciscan Sisters 116-8th Ave SE Little Falls MN 56345

ZITNY, RUSSELL JAMES, telecommunications executive; b. Oak Lawn, Ill., Apr. 6, 1956; s. Roy Stanley and Vlasta (Linhart) Z.; m. Kathryn Marie Hynek, Aug. 4, 1979; children: Eric, Kelly. BA, We. Ill. U., 1978, MBA, 1979. Dir. mktg. Marie's Food Svc., Hinsdale, Ill., 1979-82; sr. mktg. rep. Pansophic, Oak Brook, Ill., 1982-83; regional dir. Ztel, Chgo., 1983-86, Telenova, Schaumburg, Ill., 1986-90; v.p. Monterey Techs., Chgo., 1991-93, dir. mktg. and sales BPSI, 1993-95, gen. mgr. mobilcom., 1995—. Author: (play) The Son, 1987. Mem. Am. Sokol Orgn., Sigma Theta Epsilon. Mem. Am. Sokol Orgn., Darien Lions Club, Sigma Theta Epsilon. Office: Monterey Techs 8721 Lake Ridge Dr Darien IL 60561-8429

ZITTO, RICHARD JOSEPH, physics educator; b. Lisbon, Ohio, Sept. 1, 1945; s. Tony Joseph and Olive Lucille (Davison) Z.; m. Pamela Daryl Irons, July 22, 1967; children: Angela Marie, Elena Michelle. BS in Sci. Edn., Ohio State U., 1968, MA in Phys. Sci. Edn., 1978. Tchr. sci. Kenton (Ohio) Jr. H.S., 1968-70; tchr. physics and sci. Kenton Sr. H.S., 1970-76; tchr. physics Boardman H.S., Youngstown, Ohio, 1976—; physics educator Youngstown State U., 1981—, coord. Physics Olympics, 1994—; dir. Youngstown Area Physics Alliance, 1987—. Trustee Hardin Meml. Hosp., Kenton, 1971-76; bd. dirs. Blue Cross of Lima, Ohio, 1973-76, Nat. Multiple Sclerosis Soc. N.E. Ohio, 1981-91; trustee Columbiana Pub. Libr., 1990—, pres., 1993-95. Recipient Outstanding Young Educator award Kenton Jaycees, 1972, Outstanding Sci. Tchr. Youngstown State U. Sigma Xi, 1980. Mem. ASCD, Am. Assn. Physics Tchrs. (physics teaching resource agt. 1986—, pres. Ohio sect. 1989-90, mem. physics in high schs. com. 1991—), Ont. Assn. Physics Tchrs., Nat. Sci. Tchrs. Assn., N.E. Tchrs. Assn. (co-chmn. sci. workshop 1979—), Ohio Acad. Sci., Sci. Edn. Coun. Ohio, United Teaching Profession, Lions, Rotary (sec. 1978-79), Elks. Republican. Presbyterian. Home: 332 W Park Ave Columbiana OH 44408-1242 Office: Boardman High Sch 7777 Glenwood Ave Youngstown OH 44512-5824

ZLATIC, THOMAS DAVID, English literature educator; b. St. Louis, Apr. 15, 1947; s. Thomas F. and Rose (Stilinovic) Z.; m. Mary L. Leahy, Aug. 14, 1969; children: Rebecca, Daniel, Joseph. BA in English, U. Mo., St. Louis, 1969; PhD, St. Louis U., 1974. Instr. St. Louis U., 1973-74; prof. English Cardinal Glennon Coll., St. Louis, 1975-87, St. Louis Coll. Pharmacy, 1987—; prof. Maryville Coll., Parks Coll., Jefferson Coll.; writing cons. McBride & Son, St. Louis, 1988; writer, facilitator, rschr. Synod 10-Archdiocese St. Louis, 1988-89, Irvington (Ill.) Med. Ctr., 1977-81; local coord. Found. for Improvement of Post-Secondary Edn. Grant, 1993—. Contbr. articles to profl. jours. Co-recipient Norman Foerster prize MLA, 1981; NEH grantee, 1979; GAPS grantee Am. Assn. Colls. Pharmacy, 1992. Home: 1680 Blakefield Ter Manchester MO 63021-7102 Office: St Louis Coll Pharmacy 4588 Parkview Pl Saint Louis MO 63110-1029

ZLATIN, LARION Y., mechanical engineer; b. Odessa, USSR, June 3, 1945. MME, Poly. Tech. Inst., Odessa, Russia, 1968. Project engr. Miles Inc. TY, Westchester, Ill., 1984—. Mem. Soc. Mech. Engrs. Office: Miles Inc TY 9855 Derby Ln Westchester IL 60154-3765

ZOBEL, ROBERT LEONARD, state government official; b. Reedsburg, Wis., July 28, 1935; s. Leonard Walter and Kathryn Jennifer (Cleveland) Z.; m. Faith Minnie Weatherwax, Aug. 5, 1961; children: Karl, Paul, Mary. BS in Fin., U. N.D., 1961. Investment banker Loewi & Co., Milw., 1961-65; bank examiner State of Wis., Madison, 1965-68, dir. investment bd., 1968—; mem. adv. bd. Merrill Lynch Capital, N.Y.C., Madison Fund, Boston, Zell/Chillmack, Chgo., Hancock Internat., Boston, Horizon Ptnrs., Milw.; mem. stockholder rep. bd. Burdick, Milton/Madison, A.C. Equipment, Milw.; bd. dirs. Trak Internat., Port Washington, Pa Vera, Madison; presenter nat. and internat. profl. assns., seminars, others. Mem. owners' com. Olympia Resort, Oconomowoc, Wis.; coach youth soccer, Baseball and basketball orgns.; lay min. area United Meth. Ch.; participant mission projects, including ch. bldg., Vulcain, Costa Rica, Rio Claro, Costa Rica, Prince Town, Trinidad, Portsmouth, Dominica, hosp. and sch. rehab., Bo, Sierra Leone, Maua, Kenya, Santa Cruz, Bolivia, Cochabamba, Bolivia, Gomay, St. Vincent; vol. Salvation Army. With USN, 1956-58. Mem. Elks. Home: 5312 Healy Ln Monona WI 53716-2519 Office: Wis Investment Bd 121 E Wilson St Madison WI 53703-3455

ZOBERI, NADIM BIN-ASAD, management consultant; b. Karachi, Pakistan, July 20, 1951; came to U.S., 1973; s. Asad Ahmad and Nawab Bano Zoberi; m. Samira Khalid, Mar. 24, 1989; 1 child, Noor Jehan. BS in Math., Physics and Chemistry, U. Karachi, 1971; B in Computer Sci., U. Wis., River Falls, 1981, BBA, 1980. Indsl., project engr. ADC Telecommunications, Mpls., 1979-84, supr. prodn. and inventory control, 1984-87; cons. Coopers & Lybrand, Mpls., 1988-89; dir. mfg. Daig Corp., Minnetonka, Minn., 1989-90; dir. quality internat. op. N.W. Airlines, St. Paul, 1990-92; mgmt. cons. KPMG Peat Marwick, Mpls., 1992—. Exec. advisor Jr. Achievement, Mpls., 1985-87. Mem. Assn. Mfg. Excellence, Inst. of Indsl. Engrs. Muslim. Home: 1550 Murphy Pky Saint Paul MN 55122-1753 Office: KPMG Peat Marwick 4200 Norwest Ctr 90 S 7th St Minneapolis MN 55402-3903

ZOBRIST, BENEDICT KARL, library director, historian; b. Moline, Ill., Aug. 21, 1921; s. Benedict and Lila Agnas (Colson) Z.; m. Donna Mae Anderson, Oct. 23, 1948; children: Benedict Karl II, Markham Lee, Erik Christian. AB, Augustana Coll., Rock Island, Ill., 1946; postgrad., Stanford U., 1946-47; MA, Northwestern U., 1948, PhD, 1953; postgrad., U. Ill., 1961, Tunghai U., Taiwan, 1962, Columbia U., 1962-63, Fed. Exec. Inst., Charlottesville, Va., 1974, Hebrew U., Israel, 1978; LHD, Avila Coll., 1995. Manuscript specialist in recent Am. history Library of Congress, Washington, 1952-53; asst. reference librarian Newberry Library, Chgo., 1953-54; command historian Ordnance Weapons Command, Rock Island Arsenal, 1954-60; prof. history, chmn. dept. Augustana Coll., 1960-69, asst. dean faculty, 1964-69, asso. dean, dir. grad. studies, 1969; asst. dir. Harry S. Truman Libr., Independence, Mo., 1969-71; dir. Harry S. Truman Libr., 1971-94; exec. sec. Harry S. Truman Libr. Inst., Independence, 1971-94; mem. steering com. Harry S. Truman Statue Com., Independence, 1973-76; dir., regent Harry S. Truman Good Neighbor Award Found., 1974—; mem. Independence Truman Award Commn., 1975-94, Mo. Hist. Records Adv. Bd., 1978—; adj. prof. history U. Mo.-Kansas City, 1975—, Ottawa U., Kansas City, 1977-94, U. Mo. St. Louis, 1987-94; chmn. Independence Commn. Bicentennial of U.S. Constitution, 1987, Uptown Independence, Inc., 1989-94; mem. adv. coun. Truman Little White House State Historic Site, Key West, Fla., 1987-94. Contbr. articles, revs. to profl. jours. Trustee Heritage League of Greater Kansas City, 1981—, Liberty Meml. Assn., Kansas City, Mo., 1990—, Black Archives Mid-Am., Inc., Kansas City, 1992-94; mem. Truman Nat. Centennial Com., 1982-84. Served with AUS, 1942-46. Recipient Outstanding Alumni Achievement award Augustana Coll., 1975, Bronze Good Citizenship medal Kans. SAR, 1986, People's Choice award Independence (Mo.) Neighborhood Councils, 1987, Mid-Am. Regional Council award for contbns. to met. community, 1987, Citizen Achievement award Black Archives of Mid-Am., 1988, Silver Good Citizenship medal Mo. SAR, 1988, Special Recognition award City of Independence, 1988, Outstanding Civic Leader in Independence, 1989, Gold Medal of Honor DAR, 1990, Spl. Commendation award Nat. Park Svc., 1993; named World Citizen of Yr. by Kans. City Mayor's UN Day Com., 1994. Mem. AAUP, Am. Hist. Assn., Jackson County (Mo.) Hist. Soc. (v.p. 1972-82, 93-95), Orgn. Am. Historians, Assn. Asian Studies, Am. Assn. State, Local History, Soc. Am. Archivists, U.S. Power Squadron, Am. Legion, La Societe des 40 Hommes et 8 Chevaux, VFW. Home: 71B T St Lake Lotawana MO 64086-9728

ZOBRIST, GEORGE WINSTON, computer scientist, educator; b. Highland, Ill., Feb. 13, 1934; s. George H. and Lillie C. (Augustin) Z.; m. Freida Groverlyn Rich, Mar. 29, 1955; children: Barbara Jayne, George William, Jean Anne. B.S., U. Mo., 1958, Ph.D., 1965; M.S., Wichita State U., 1961. Registered profl. engr., Mo., Fla. Electronic scientist U.S. Naval Ordnance Test Sta., China Lake, Calif., 1958-59; research engr. Boeing Co., Wichita, 1959-60; instr. Wichita State U., 1960-61; assoc. prof. U. Mo., Columbia, 1961-69, U. So. Fla., Tampa, 1969-70; chmn. elec. engring. dept. U. Miami, Coral Gables, Fla., 1970-71; prof. U. South Fla., Tampa, 1971-72, 73-76; prof., chmn. dept. elec. engring. U. Toledo, 1976-79; dir. computer sci. and engring. Samborn, Steketee, Otis, Evans, Inc., Toledo, 1979-82; prof. computer sci. Grad. Engring. Ctr. U. Mo.-Rolla, St. Louis, 1982-85; prof. computer sci. U. Mo., Rolla, 1985—, chmn. dept., 1994—; rsch. prof. U. Edinburgh, Scotland, 1972-73; lectr. U. Western Cape, South Africa, 1995 summer; cons. Wilcox Electric Co., Bendix Corp., both Kansas City, Mo., 1966-68, ICC, Miami, 1970-71, Def. Comm. Agy., Washington, 1971, 72, U.S. Naval Rsch. Labs., Washington, 1971, Med. Svc. Bur., Miami, 1970-71, NASA, Kennedy Space Ctr., Fla., 1973-76, 88, 89, 93, 94, Prestolite Corp., Toledo, 1977-79, IBM, Lexington, Ky., 1983-86, Wright-Patterson AFB, Ohio, 1986, PAFB, Fla., 1987, McDonnell Douglas, Mo., 1989, Digital Systems Cons., Mo., 1989, Oak Ridge Nat. Labs., 1992. Author: Network Computer Analysis, 1969, Progress in Computer Aided VLSI Design, 1988-90; editor: Internat. Jour. Computer Aided VLSI Design, 1989-91, Object Oriented Simulation IEEE Press, 1996, Computer Sci. and Computer Engring. Monograph series, 1989-91, Internat. Jour. of Computer Simulation, 1990—, VLSI Design, 1992—; contbr. articles to profl. jours. Served with USAF, 1951-55. Named Young Engr. of Yr. ctrl. chpt. Mo. Soc. Profl. Engrs., 1967; NSF summer fellow, 1962, 64; NASA, IBM, DOE, UES/AFOSR, McDonnell Douglas rsch. grantee, 1967-88. Mem. IEEE (sr.), Soc. Computer Simulation, Am. Legion, Rotary, Sigma Xi, Tau Beta Pi, Phi Eta Sigma, Eta Kappa Nu, Pi Mu Epsilon, Upsilon Pi Epsilon. Home: 12030 Country Club Dr Rolla MO 65401-7469 Office: U Mo-Rolla Dept Computer Sci Rolla MO 65409

ZOLOTO, JERROLD ALBERT, psychologist, consultant; b. Chgo., Jan. 1, 1944; s. Ben and Marian Idele (Cohen) Z.; m. Angela Nijole Yurkus, Sept. 27, 1981; children: Jill, Lydia, Alexandra. BS, U. Ill., 1966; MS, Wayne State U., 1972, PhD, 1979. Dir. DuPage Mental Health, Wheaton, Ill., 1973-81; dir. dept. psychiatry St. Joseph's Hosp., Chgo., 1981-82; cons. Rohrer, Hibler, Replogle, Chgo., 1982-84; v.p. Vici Internat., San Francisco, 1984-85; prse. Anova, Inc., Chgo., 1985—; adj. faculty Coll. of DuPage, Glen Ellyn, Ill., 1974-80; faculty Police Tng. Inst., Lisle, Ill., 1974-78; internship supr. numerous students at univs., 1983—; spkr. numerous orgns., 1973—. Author, inventor: (software) Listen: The Leadership Information System, 1990. Pres., bd. dirs. Mental Health Assn., Ill., 1987-89, Du Page County, 1983-86; v.p. Breckenridge Homeowners Assn., Naperville, Ill., 1994-95; mem., bd. dirs. Girl Scouts USA, Lisle, 1984-86. Office: Anova Inc 3 First National Plz 70 W Madison St Ste 1400 Chicago IL 60602

ZONKA, CONSTANCE Z., educational organization administrator; b. Evanston, Ill.; d. Herbert Edward and Agnes Irene (Turpin) Zipprodt; m. Robert F. Zonka, Aug. 5, 1970; children: Heidi Zapanta, Milo Matthew. BA, U. Fla., 1958; postgrad., U. Chgo., 1960. Account exec. Daniel J. Edelman, Inc., Chgo., 1964-68; pres. Connie Zonka Assocs., Chgo., 1974-89; dir. coll. rels. Columbia Coll., Chgo., 1970-89; sr. dir. univ. rels. Roosevelt U., Chgo., 1990-93; dir. office pub. affairs Gov.'s State U., University Park, Ill., 1993—. Mem. NAFE, Pub. Rels. Soc. Am., Publicity Club Chgo., Nat. Assn. Women Bus. Owners, Friends of WFMT (sec. 1989—), Friends of Downtown, Friends of the Parks. Democrat. Home: 901 S Plymouth Ct Apt 1205 Chicago IL 60605-2053

ZONNEVILLE, ROBERT E., trucking company executive; b. Williamson, N.Y., Jan. 23, 1925; s. Adrian J. and Matie L. Z.; student U. Buffalo, 1949-52; m. Carol A. Alliger, June 7, 1947; children—Bethann, Robin, Kim, David. Dock worker Associated Transport, Buffalo, 1952-53, terminal mgr., 1960-66; terminal mgr. Spector Redball, Cleve., 1966-68, regional mgr., Wis., Minn. and Ill., 1968-71, v.p. central area, Northfield, Ohio, 1971-82; regional mgr., Inway Nationwide, 1982-87, v.p. 1987-89, pres., chief exec. officer, 1989—; v.p. nat. accounts, Landstar, 1995—. Pres. local Presbyn. Ch., Home Owners Assn., Mentor Gardens Home Owners Assn., 1987—; mem. golf com. City of Euclid, Ohio, 1975, com. to elect mayor of Euclid, 1979; sec., bd. dirs. Deercreek Time Share Owners, 1986-87. Served with U.S. Army, 1943-45. Decorated Purple Heart with oak leaf cluster, Bronze Star. Recipient awards for community activities, K.C., 1979. Mem. Western Res. Traffic Club. Clubs: Elks, Masons, Scottish Rite, Shriners. Home: 5803 Mallard Ct Mentor OH 44060-1811 Office: 7350 Palisades Pky Ste 34 Mentor OH 44060-5302

ZORN, ROBERT LYNN, education educator; b. Youngstown, Ohio, Mar. 22, 1938; s. Robert S. and Frances L. Zorn; B.S. Ed., Kent State U., 1959; M.Ed., Westminster Coll., 1964; Ph.D., U. Pitts., 1970; m. Joan M. Wilkos, Apr. 26, 1957; children: Deborah Lynn, Patricia Lynn. Tchr., West Branch (Ohio) Schs., 1961-62; elem. prin. Poland (Ohio) Schs., 1962-67, supt. schs., 1976—; high sch. unit prin. Boardman (Ohio) Schs., 1967-70; dir. adminstrv. services Mahoning County (Ohio) Schs., 1970-73, asst. supt., 1973-76; adj. prof. edn. Westminister Coll., 1985—; chmn. Ohi Adv. Com. to State Dept. Edn.; chmn. McGuffey Hist. Soc. Nat. Educator's Hall of Fame. Chmn. Mahoning County chpt. Am. Cancer Soc.; pres. bd. trustees Poland Methodist Ch.; trustee Mahoning County chpt. Am. Heart Assn. Served to lt. USAF, 1959-61. Mem. Doctoral Assn. Educators (life), Am. Assn. Sch. Adminstrs., Ohio PTA (life; Educator of Yr. 1980-81), Phi Delta Kappa. Republican. Clubs: Fonderlac County, Rotary, Protestant Men's. Author numerous books including Speed Reading, 1989, rev. edit., 1994; contbr. articles to profl. jours. Office: 30 Riverside Dr Youngstown OH 44514-2008

ZORNOW, WILLIAM FRANK, historian, educator; b. Cleve., Aug. 13, 1920; s. William Frederick Emil and Viola (Schulz) Z. A.B., Western Res. U., 1942, A.M., 1944, Ph.D., 1952. Vice pres., treas. Glenville Coal & Supply Co., Real Value Coal Corp., Zornow Coal Corp., 1941-45; dep. clk. Probate Ct., Cuyahoga County, Ohio, 1941-43; prodn. planning engr. Hickok Elec. Instrument Co., Cleve., 1943-46; teaching asst. Western Res. U., 1944-47; instr. U. Akron, 1946-47, Case Inst. Tech., 1947-50, Washburn U., 1950-51; lectr. Cleve. Coll., 1948-49; asst. prof. Kans. State U., 1951-58; asst. prof. history Kent (Ohio) State U., 1958-61, asso. prof., 1961-66, prof. history, 1966—; perpetual hon. fellow Harry S. Truman Libr. Inst., Independence, Mo.; collection corr. Berkshire Loan and Fin. Co., Painesville (Ohio) Security Credit Acceptance Corp., Mentor, Ohio, 1951-60; cons. Karl E. Mundt Library, Dakota State Coll., Madison, S.D.; presenter 1st coll. arts and scis. faculty lecture series Kent State U., 1962. Author: Lincoln and the Party Divided, 1954, rev. edit., 1972, Kansas: A History of the Jayhawk State, 1957, America at Mid-Century, 1959; author: (with others) Abraham Lincoln: A New Portrait, 1959, Kansas: The First Century, 1956; contbr.

articles to encys. and profl. jours.; editor: Shawnee County (Kans.) Hist. Bull, 1950-51; abstractor: America: History and Life: Historical Abstracts, 1964—. Mem. Dir.'s Circle Cleve. Mus. Art, 1989—, Cleve. Clin. Found., 1992—, Soc. Fellows. Faculty rsch. grantee Kans. State U., 1955-57, Kent State U., 1960-64. Mem. AAAS, AAUP, Soc. Fellow of Cleve. Clinic Found., Am. Acad. Polit. and Social Sci., Am. Assn. State and Local History (award of merit 1958), Am. Hist. Assn., Orgn. Am. historians, Ohio Acad. History (chmn. awards com.), Ohio Hist. Soc. (libr. adv. com. 1969—), Ohio Soc. N.Y., Ctr. Study of Presidency, Acad. Polit. Sci., Lincoln Fellowship of Wis., Sierra Club San Francisco, Delta Tau Delta (4-star coun. 1992—), Pi Gamma Mu, Phi Alpha Theta, Phi Beta Kappa. Home: 7893 Middlesex Rd Mentor OH 44060-7617 Office: Kent State U 305 Bowman Dr Kent OH 44240-4507

ZOUBAREFF, OLGA KATARINA (KATHY BAREOFF), accounting adminstrative assistant; b. Hassalt, Belgium; d. Vladimir F. and Kataryna (Sarcov) Z. BA in Polit. Sci., Wayne State U.; postgrad., Ann Parsley Sch. Dance, Clinton Twp., Mich., 1990-95, Mary Skiba Sch. Dance, 1995—; A in Gen. Studies, Drama, Macomb Community Coll.; fitness and nutrition cert., Internat. Corr. Schs. Ctr., Detroit; voice studies, Ctr. for Creative Studies, Detroit, 1994—; drama studies, Wayne State U., 1994—. Acct./adminstrv. asst. Univ. Orthopaedic Assocs. Detroit, P.C., 1990—; mem. Charles J. Givens Orgn., 1991-96; actress, dancer, fashion, TV comml. and photgraphic model/film screen extra. Model, Renaissance Ctr. Fashion Panel, Detroit, 1989-91; rsch. bd. advisors Am. Biog. Inst.; mem. Internat. Biog. Centre Adv. Coun., 1992. Home: 38579 Delta Dr Clinton Township MI 48036-1711 Office: Univ Orthopaedic Assocs Detroit PC 4707 Saint Antoine St Detroit MI 48201-1427

ZRULL, JOEL PETER, psychiatry educator; b. Detroit, Jan. 10, 1932; s. Arthur Benjamin and Mildred (Bazy) Z.; m. Nancy Jane Eichenlaub, June 19, 1954; children: Mark Christian, Lisa Carol. BA with honors, U. Mich., 1953, MD, 1957. Diplomate Am. Bd. Psychiatry, Am. Bd. Child Psychiatry. From instr. to assoc. prof. psychiatry U. Mich. Med. Sch., Ann Arbor, 1962-73; prof., chief child psychiatry Med. Coll. Ohio, Toledo, 1973-75, prof., chmn. dept. psychiatry, 1975—; cons. Monroe (mich.) County Intermediate Sch. Dist., 1961—; pres. Associated Physicians MCO, Inc., Toledo, 1983-84, 87-90; chief of staff Med. Coll. Hosps., Toledo, 1984-86; mem. com. on cert. in child psychiatry Am. Bd. Psychiatry and Neurology, 1986-91, chmn. 1990-91. Editor: Adult Psychiatry: New Directions in Therapy, 1983; contbr. articles to profl. jours. Grantee NIMH, 1974-76, Ohio Dept. Mental Health, 1978-86. Fellow Am. Psychiat. Assn. (life), Am. Acad. Child and Adolescent Psychiatry (chmn. com. tng. 1984-87, chmn. comm. memls. and awards 1992-95), Am. Coll. Psychiatrists, Am. Ortho-Psychiat. Assn.; mem. AMA, Soc. Profs. of Child and Adolescent Psychiatry (sec. treas. 1989-92, pres.-elect 1992-94, pres. 1994-96). Roman Catholic. Home: 6133 W Wyandotte Rd Maumee OH 43537-1334 Office: Med Coll Ohio PO Box 10008 Toledo OH 43699

ZUBROFF, LEONARD SAUL, surgeon; b. Minersville, Pa., Mar. 27, 1925; s. Abe and Fannie (Freedline) Z.; BA, Wayne State U., 1945, MD, 1949. Diplomate Am. Bd. Surgery. Intern Garfield Hosp., Washington, 1949-50, resident in surgery, 1951-55, chief resident surgery, 1954-55; pvt. practice medicine specializing in surgery, 1958-76; med. dir. Chevrolet Gear and Axle Plant, Chevrolet Forge Plant, GM, Detroit, 1977-78, divisional med. dir. Detroit Diesel Allison div., 1978-87, regional med. dir. GM, 1987-89; ret., 1989; bd. trustees LeVine Found.; mem. staff Hutzel Hosp., Detroit Meml. Hosp.; chief of surgery, chief profl. svcs. N.E. Air Command, Pepperell AFB, Newfoundland. With USAF, 1956-58. Fellow ACS; mem. Acad. Surgery Detroit, Coll. Occupational and Environ. Medicine, Mich. Occupational Med. Assn. (pres. 1990-91), Detroit Occupational Physicians Assn. (former pres.), Masons (33 degree), Phi Lambda Kappa. Home and Office: 22511 Bellwood Dr South Southfield MI 48034

ZUCARO, ALDO CHARLES, insurance company executive; b. Grenoble, France, Apr. 2, 1939; s. Louis and Lucy Zucaro; m. Gloria J. Ward, Oct. 12, 1963; children: Lucy, Louis, Faye. BS in Acctg, Queens Coll., N.Y.C., 1962. C.P.A., N.Y., Ill. Ptnr. Coopers & Lybrand (and predecessor), Chgo. and N.Y.C., 1962-76; exec. v.p., chief fin. officer Old Republic Internat. Corp., Chgo., 1976-81, pres., 1981—, chief exec. officer, 1990—, also chmn. bd. dirs., 1993—, chmn. of the bd., 1993—; pres., bd. dirs. Old Republic Life Ins. Co., Old Republic Life of N.Y., Old Republic Ins. Co., Internat. Bus. and Merc. Reassurance Co., Republic Mortgage Ins. Co., Old Republic Nat. Title Ins. Co., Home Owners Life Ins. Co. Editor: Financial Accounting Practices of the Insurance Industry, 1975, 76. Mem. AICPAs. Roman Catholic. Office: Old Republic Internat Corp 307 N Michigan Ave Chicago IL 60601

ZUCCHERO, ROCCO, communications specialist; b. Chgo., Dec. 19, 1956; s. Rocco and Rosaria Francesca (Patellaro) Z.; m. Patricia Anne Howard, May 19, 1990. AA, U. Ill., Chgo., 1977. Outside plant tech. Ameritech, Chgo., 1981—. Home: 8107 Leawood Ln Woodridge IL 60517-4125

ZUCHOWSKI, BEVERLY JEAN, chemistry educator; b. Toledo, Ohio, Jan. 11, 1950; d. Frank I. and Esther C. (Steinke) Patronik; m. Mark G. Zuchowski, May 21, 1971; children: Caroline H., Mark J., Gregory S., Beverly A. BS in Edn., Bowling Green State U., 1974, MAT in Chemistry, 1989. Cert. tchr. physics, chemistry and math. 7-12, Ohio. Instr. chemistry and physics Eastwood Schs., Luckey, Ohio, 1974-77, Perrysburg (Ohio) Pub. Schs., 1978-88, Owens Tech. Coll., Perrysburg, 1981-88; grad. asst. Bowling Green (Ohio) State U., 1988-89; chemistry instr. Perrysburg Pub. Schs., 1989—; mem. Ohio Dept. Edn. Sci. Proficiency Content Com., 1995—; tchr. intern Ctr. of Sci. and Industry, Columbus, Ohio, 1987; mem. Rossford (Ohio) Bd. Edn., 1988—; tchr. chaperone, Young Exptl. Scientist, Columbus, 1988—, Women in Sci., Bowling Green, 1989—. Mem. Rossford (Ohio) Bd. Edn., 1988—, v.p., 1991-92; mem. Penta County Vocat. Sch. Bd. Edn., 1994-95; leader Girl Scouts U.S., Rossford, 1978—; precinct worker Wood County Bd. of Elections, 1982-87. Mem. NEA, Ohio Edn. Assn., Nat. Sci. Tchrs. Assn., Ohio Coun. Tchrs. Math., Ohio Acad. Sci., Sch. Edn. Coun. Ohio, Perrysburg Edn. Assn. (treas. 1981), Rossford Community Svc. League (sec. 1992), Ohio Womens Caucus, Rossford Lions Club (charter), Toledo Mothers of Twins Club, Penta County Vocational Sch. Bd. of Edn. Democrat. Lutheran. Home: 3 Riverside Dr Rossford OH 43460 Office: Perrysburg High Sch 550 E South Boundary St Perrysburg OH 43551-2501

ZUCKER, ROBERT A(LPERT), psychologist; b. N.Y.C., Dec. 9, 1935; s. Morris and Sophie (Alpert) Z.; m. Martine Latil; children: Lisa, Alex, Eleanor; m. Kristine Ellen Freeark, Mar. 10, 1979; 1 child, Katherine. B.C.E., CCNY, 1956; postgrad., UCLA, 1956-58; Ph.D., Harvard U., 1966. Lic. psychologist, Mich. From instr. to asst. prof. psychology Rutgers U., 1963-68; from asst. prof. to assoc. prof. to prof. Mich. State U., 1968-94; prof. psychology in psychiatry and psychology U. Mich., 1994—, dir. Alcohol Rsch. Ctr., 1994—, dir. substance abuse divsn. dept. psychiatry, 1994—; vis. prof. U. Tex., Austin, 1975; vis. rsch. prof. psychology in psychiatry U. Mich., 1990-91; vis. scholar Nat. Inst. Alcohol Abuse and Alcoholism, 1980; dir. clin. tng. Mich. State U., 1982-94; lectr. Nebr. Symposium on Motivation, 1986; cons. in field. Editor: Further Explorations in Personality, 1981, Personality and the Prediction of Behavior, 1984, The Emergence of Personality, 1987, Studying Persons and Lives, 1990, Personality Structure in the Life Course, 1992, The Development of Alcohol Problems: Exploring the Biopsychosocial Matrix of Risk, 1994, Alcohol Problems Among Adolescents: Current Directions in Prevention Research, 1995; contbr. chpts. and articles to profl. publs. Bd. dirs. Nat. Coun. on Alcoholism-Mich., 1978-82; mem. Psychosocial Initial Rev. Group, Nat. Inst. Alcohol Abuse and Alcoholism, 1989-92. Fellow AAAS, APA, APS, Am. Orthopsychiat. Assn.; mem. Midwestern Psychol. Assn., Ea. Psychol. Assn., Soc. Personology, Soc. Life History Rsch. in Psychopathology. Office: Univ Mich 400 E Eisenhower Pky Ann Arbor MI 48108-3318

ZUCKERMAN, RICHARD ENGLE, lawyer, law educator; b. Yonkers, N.Y., Aug. 2, 1945; s. Julius and Roslyn (Ehrlich) Z.; m. Denise Ellen Spoon, July 14, 1968; children: Julie Ann, Lindsay Beth. BA, U. Mich., 1967; JD cum laude, Southwestern U., 1974. Bar: Calif. 1974, Mich. 1976, Nev. 1986, U.S. Dist. Ct. (ea. and we. dists.) Mich. 1977, U.S. Ct. Appeals (6th cir.) 1977, U.S. Ct. Appeals (9th cir.) 1982, U.S. Ct. Appeals 2d and 7th cirs.) 1994, U.S. Tax Ct. 1980, U.S. Supreme Ct. 1985. Spl. atty. organized crime and racketeering sect. U.S. Dept. Justice, Detroit, 1974-77; sr. ptnr. Raymond, Rupp, Wienberg, Stone & Zuckerman, P.C., Troy, Mich., 1977-87; chair litigation dept. Honigman, Miller, Schwartz & Cohn, Detroit, 1996—; adj. prof. Detroit Coll. Law, 1978—; mem. Mich. Atty. Grievance Commn., 1995—. Served to lt. USN, 1967-71, Vietnam. Mem. ABA (grand jury com. criminal justice sect.), Mich. Atty. Grievance Commn. (supreme ct. nominee 1995—), Fed. Bar Assn. (chmn. criminal law sect. Detroit chpt. 1985-90, bd. dirs. 1985-94, co-chair criminal def. atty. com. 1955—), Knollwood Country Club (West Bloomfield, Mich.), Std. Club, Am. Inns Ct. (master of bench 1995—). Republican. Jewish. Office: Honigman Miller Schwartz & Cohn 2290 First National Bldg Detroit MI 48226

ZUERLEIN, DAMIAN JOSEPH, priest; b. Norfolk, Neb., May 28, 1955; s. Victor Damian and Elizabeth P. (Wegener) Z. BA, U. St. Thomas, St. Paul, 1977; MDiv, St. Paul Sem., 1981. Ordained priest Roman Cath. Ch., 1981. Tchr. Norfolk Cath. High Sch., 1981-85; asst. pastor Sacred Heart/St. Mary's Parish, Norfolk, 1981-85; assoc. pastor St. Pius X Cath. Ch., Omaha, 1985-88, Mary Our Queen Cath. Ch., Omaha, 1988-90; pastor Our Lady of Guadalupe Parish, Omaha, 1990—; cons. Archdiocesan Vocations Office, Omaha, 1985-95; bd. dirs. Juan Diego Ctr., Omaha, 1990—; chmn., co-founder Omaha Together One Cmty., 1991-95; co-founder Weaving, Women's Advocacy Group, Omaha, 1988—. Presenter (video) Loving Your Marriage, 1990, El Matrimonio: Una Jornada Para Todo Una Vida, 1995; co-author: (manual) Hispanic Pastoral Plan, 1991. Bd. dirs. United Cath. Social Svcs., Omaha, 1990—, Chicano Awareness Ctr., Omaha, 1991—; bd. dirs. Omaha 100 Inc., 1991-96, chair, 1991-93; advisor Mayor P.J. Morgan, Omaha, 1991-95; mem. Gov. Nelson's Urban Adv. Task Force, 1994; mem. Douglas County Commn. on Domestic Violence, 1996—. Mem. Pax Cristi, Amnesty Internat., Fontenelle Forest Assn., Priests for Equality, Greater Omaha Clergy Assn. (pres. 1987-88), South Omaha Neighborhood Assn. (bd. dirs. 1992, pres. 1994—). Home and Office: 2310 O St Omaha NE 68107-2837

ZUERN, ROSEMARY LUCILE, manufacturing executive, treasurer; b. Eureka, Wis., May 28, 1934; d. Kenneth Arthur and Vera Christine (Barnett) George; m. David Lee Zuern, June 30, 1956. Student, U. Wis., 1954-56. With Kimberly-Clark Corp., Neenah, Wis., 1956-78, sales promotion specialist, 1969-71, trade show adminstr., 1971-78; conv. mgr. Smith Bucklin & Assocs., Chgo., 1979-84, account exec., 1984—; exec. dir. Bakery Equipment Mfrs. Assn., Chgo., 1984-96, Soc. Gynecologic Oncologists, Chgo., 1984-96; assoc. sec., treas. Internat. Baking & Industry Exposition, Chgo., 1986—; consumer cons. Kimberly-Clark Corp., Neenah, 1969. Mem. Internat. Assn. Exposition Mgrs. (Midwest chpt.), Am. Soc. Assn. Execs., Exptl. Aircraft Assn., Charles A. Lindbergh Collectors Soc. (pres.). Home: 913 Wylde Oak Dr Oshkosh WI 54904-7633 Office: Smith-Bucklin Assocs 420 N Michigan Ave Chicago IL 60611-4006

ZUGER, WILLIAM PETER, lawyer; b. Bismarck, N.D., Sept. 16, 1946; s. John A. and Irene (Kolb) Z.; children: Peter William, Jack Everett. BA, U. Minn., 1969, JD, 1972. Bar: N.D. 1972, U.S. Dist. Ct. N.D. 1972, U.S. Ct. Appeals (8th cir.) 1972, Minn. 1985; diplomate Nat. Bd. Trial Advocacy, recert. 1986. Ptnr. Zuger & Bucklin, Bismarck, 1972-84, sr. ptnr. Zuger Kapsner & Blazer, 1984-87; pvt. practice, 1987-96; ret. 1996; lectr. various med. groups, nursing schs., physician groups. Mem. ABA (nat. affiliate rep. young lawyers sect. 1975-76), ATLA, N.D. Bar Assn. (chmn. law office mgmt. and procedures com. 1974-77, pres. young lawyers sect. 1975-76, sec.-treas. 1975-76), Burleigh County Bar Assn., 4th Dist. Bar Assn. (v.p. 1976), Am. Soc. Law and Medicine, Def. Rsch. Inst., Am. Bd. Profl. Liability Attys. Contbr. articles to legal jours. Home: 615 W Thayer Bismarck ND 58501

ZUHLKE, MARYBETH, elementary school curriculum consultant, educator; b. Kenosha, Wis., Jan. 16, 1946; d. Charles Casmir and Elizabeth (Mulich) Safransky; m. Lee VanLunduyt, Aug. 24, 1968 (div. 1985); children: Kyle, Ravi; m. Tom Zuhlke, Sept. 9, 1990. Student, U. Dallas, 1965-67; BS, U. Wis., Whitewater, 1968; MS, U. Wis., Milw., 1973, postgrad., 1988-89; postgrad., Marquette U., 1978-81. Cert. elem. tchr., prin., coord. instruction, Wis. Tchr. second grade Kenosha Unified Sch. Dist., 1968-70, community liaison tchr., 1974-79, dissemination specialist, 1979-82, curriculum cons., 1982—; cons. Conn. Facilitator, North Haven, 1984-86, South Ocean Internat. Sch., Datong, China, 1995-96; prin. McKinley Elem. Sch., Kenosha, 1988-89. Co-author: Kenosha Model Kindergarten Manual, 1985, Kenosha Model Math. Manual, 1986; editor: Kenosha Model Language Experience, 1979. Mem. Racine (Wis.) Arts Coun., 1980—. Mem. ASCD, Internat. Reading Assn., Parent Edn. and Childhood Assn. (exec. bd. 1976-83), Inst. of World Affairs, Wis. State and Fed. Specialists (newsletter editor 1986-87), Assn. Wis. Sch. Administrs., Phi Delta Kappa. Home: 1419 Crabapple Dr Racine WI 53405-1703 Office: Kenosha Unified Sch Dist Parkside Kenosha WI 53142

ZUIDERVAART, LAMBERT PAUL, philosophy educator; b. Modesto, Calif., Aug. 1, 1950; s. Martin and Tena (Beuving) Z.; m. Joyce Alene Recker, Jan. 8, 1977. BA, Dordt Coll., 1972; MPhil, Inst. Christian Studies, Toronto, Ont., Can., 1975; postgrad., Free U. Berlin, 1977-80; PhD, Free U. Amsterdam, The Netherlands, 1981. Asst. prof. philosophy The King's Coll., Edmonton, Alta., Can., 1981-85, chmn., divsn. humanities, 1982-85; assoc. prof. philosophy Calvin Coll., Grand Rapids, Mich., 1985-89, prof. philosophy, 1989—, chairperson, dept. philosophy, 1991—; vis. prof. Inst. for Christian Studies, Toronto, Ont., Can., 1991, mem. senate, 1993—; treas. bd. dirs. The King's Coll. Found., U.S., Grand Rapids, Mich., 1989-95; pres., bd. dirs. Urban Inst. for Contemporary Arts, Grand Rapids, 1994—; conf. dir. Calvin Coll., 1995; pub. lectr. Kendall Coll. Art and Design, 1993. Author: Adorno's Aesthetic Theory, 1991; co-author: Dancing in the Dark, 1991; co-editor: Pledges of the Jubilee, 1995, The Semblance of Subjectivity, 1996; contrib. articles to profl. jours. Pres. bd. dirs. Inn Roads Housing Coop., Edmonton, Alta., Can., 1982-85; mem. Politics Meaning Discussion Group, Grand Rapids, 1994—; workshop leader Leadership Grand Rapids, Mich., 1993, 94. Grantee STEP Prov. Alberta., Can., 1984, 85, Travel grant Am. Coun. Learned Socs., 1988, Rsch. Visit grant German Acad. Exch. Svc., 1994; Calvin Coll. Rsch. fellow, 1990, 93, 94. mem. Am. Philosophical Assn., Am. Soc. Aesthetics, Can. Philosophical Assn., Can. Soc. Aesthetics, Internat. Assn. Aesthetics, Soc. Phenomenology and Existential Philosophy. Democrat. Office: Calvin College Department of Philosophy Grand Rapids MI 49546

ZUKOWSKI, ROBERT K., state legislator; b. Apr. 24, 1930; m. Dolores; 4 children. Student, U. Md. State assemblyman Wis. State Assembly, Dist. 69. Mem. Thorp Sch. Bd. Named Thorp Farmer of Yr., 1968, Chap Farmer Future Farmers Am., 1972. Mem. Wis. State Assn. County Vets. Svc. Commn. (pres.). Home: W9884 County Road Mm Thorp WI 54771-8106*

ZÚÑIGA, JOSÉ GUADALUPE, minister; b. Delicias, Mex., Dec. 12, 1953; arrived in U.S., 1958; s. Román Tarín and Raquel (Luján) Z.; m. Febe Montes, July 25, 1981; children: Eric Jonathan, Ariel Mark. Diploma in bib. studies, Nat. Apostolic Bible Coll., Hayward, Calif., 1975; BA in Bus. Adminstrn. with honors, Loyola U., 1995. Ordained to ministry Apostolic Ch., 1974. Pastor Apostolic Assembly, Silver City, N.Mex., 1977-79; dean, tchr. Apostolic Faith Bible Inst., Chgo., 1979-81; asst. pastor Apostolic Faith Tabernacle, Chgo., 1981-91; tchr. Apostolic Christian Acad., Chgo., 1983-91; pastor Apostolic Assembly, Melrose Park, Ill., 1991—; dist. treas. Midwest dist. Apostolic Assembly, Chgo., 1995—, dist. elder, 1993-95, dir. Christian edn., 1985-94. Mem. Clergy of Melrose Park, 1995. Mem. Religious Conf. Mgmt. Assn., Alpha Sigma Lambda. Office: Apostolic Asssembly 2337 N Mannheim Melrose Park IL 60160

ZUPANCIC, ANTHONY, English and communication educator; b. Cleve., July 20, 1949; s. Anthony and Angela Ann (Zugel) Z.; m. Jane Van Bergen, Dec. 15, 1984; children: Anthony Robert, Grace Mae. BA in English, Cleve. State U., 1970; MA in Speech and Drama, North Tex. State U., 1973; postgrad., Kent State U., 1977-88. Counsellor, coach Police Athletic League, Cleve., 1967-70; grad. asst. N. Tex. State U., Denton, 1972-73; dir., actor Bizerko Improvisational Theatre Ensembe, Cleve., 1973-78; tchr. Cleve. Bd. Edn.; coord., cons. Comprehensive Youth Svcs. Program, Cleve., 1977-83; instr., teaching fellow Kent (Ohio) State U., 1977-81; dir. theatre, assoc. prof. English, communication Notre Dame Coll. Ohio, South Euclid, 1981—; cons. State Barricading Co., 1973-91; mem. instrnl. tech. com. N.E. Ohio Commn. on Higher Edn., 1987—; advisor, bd. dirs. Benedictine H.S., Cleve., Diocese of Cleve. Comm. Dept., 1985-87; cons. Ednl. Testing Svcs., Princeton, N.J., 1988—. Cons. to the Coll. Bd., 1993—, Cleve. Heights Cable TV Commn., 1994—; candidate City Coun., Cleve., 1981. Mem. Am. Fed. TV and Radio Artists, Speech Comm. Assn., Nat. Coun. Tchrs. English, Catholic Order of Foresters (treas. 1976-86), Soc. Prof. Journalists; Alpha Psi Omega (faculty advisor 1982—). Democrat. Roman Catholic. Home: 3115 Lincoln Blvd Cleveland OH 44118-2035 Office: Notre Dame Coll 4545 College Rd Cleveland OH 44121-4228

ZURAW, KATHLEEN ANN, special education and physical education educator; b. Bay City, Mich., Sept. 29, 1960; d. John Luke and Clara Josephine (Kilian) Z. AA with high honors, Delta Community Coll., 1980; BS with high honors, Mich. State U., 1984, MA, 1987. Cert. spl. edn., mentally impaired phys. edn. grade K-12, adaptive phys. edn. tchr., Mich. Summer water safety instr. Camp Midicha, Columbia, Mich., 1982, Bay Cliff Health Camp, Big Bay, Mich., 1983; summer spl. edn. tchr. Jefferson Orthopedic Sch., Honolulu, 1984, 85, 86, Ingham Intermediate Sch. Dist., Mason, Mich., 1987; spl. edn. tchr. Bay Arenac Intermediate Sch. Dist., Bay City, 1985-87, Berrien County Intermediate Sch. Dist., Berrien Springs, Mich., 1987—; mem. citizen amb program fitness delegation People's Republic China, 1991. Area 17 coach Mich. Spl. Olympics, Berrien Springs, 1987—; mem. YMCA, St. Joseph, Mich., 1987—, Y-Ptnrs., 1989, Coun. Exceptional Children; participant Citizen Ambassador Delegation to People's Republic of China, 1991. Mem. Am. Alliance Health, Phys. Edn., Recreation and Dance, Phi Theta Kappa, Phi Kappa Phi, Phi Delta Kappa. Roman Catholic. Home: 7306 W S Saginaw Rd Bay City MI 48706

ZWEBEN, STUART HARVEY, information scientist, educator; b. Bronx, N.Y., Apr. 21, 1948; s. Max D. and Ruth (Schwartz) Z.; m. Rochelle T. Small, June 13, 1971; 1 child, Naomi. BS, CUNY, 1968; MS, Purdue U., 1971, PhD, 1974. Systems analyst IBM Corp., Kingston, N.Y., 1969-70; asst. prof. Ohio State U., Columbus, 1974-80, from vice chmn. to acting chmn. computer sci. dept., 1982-84, assoc. prof., 1980-92, prof., 1992—; chmn. Ohio State U., 1994—; pres. Computing Scis. Accreditation Bd., Stamford, Conn., 1989-91, v.p. 1987-89, sec.-treas. 1986-87; sec.-treas. Fedn. on Computing in the U.S., Washington, 1992. Contbr. articles to profl. jours. Rsch. grantee NSF, 1981-83, 88-90, 91-93, 93-96, Army Rsch. Office, 1980-83, Dept. Edn., 1983-85, Applied Info. Tech. Rsch. Ctr., 1990-91; equipment grantee AT&T Bell Labs, 1984, 86-88. Mem. AAUP, IEEE Computer Soc. (assoc. editor 1990—), Assn. for Computing Machinery (pres. 1994-96, v.p. 1992-94, coun. mem. 1982-88, chpt. bd. chmn. 1982-85, publications bd. 1988-92, fin. com. 1990-92, constn. and bylaws chmn. 1988-92, Recognition of Svc. award 1980, 85, 87, 88). Office: Ohio State U Computer Scis 2015 Neil Ave Columbus OH 43210-1210

ZWECKER, WILLIAM RENE, JR., newspaper columnist, television reporter; b. Chgo., Dec. 25, 1949; s. William Rene and Margaret Rishel (Bushee) Z.; m. Deborah Heidrich Bunn Alley, Sept. 1, 1973 (div. July 1977); 1 child, Brayton. AB in History cum laude, Princeton U., 1971. Legis. asst. U.S. Senator Charles Percy, Washington, 1971-73; asst. officer First Nat. Bank of Chgo., 1973-75; adminstrv. v.p. Krancer & Frank, Inc., Chgo., 1975-77; pres. Animal Accents, Inc., Chgo., 1977-83; mgr. Saks Fifth Ave, Chgo. and Oak Brook, Ill., 1983-86; regional v.p. BMW (N) Holding Corp., Chgo., 1986-87; assoc. editor, columnist Lerner Newspapers, Chgo., 1987-92; columnist Chgo. Sun-Times, 1992—; corr. The Joan Rivers Show, N.Y.C., 1990-94; host, producer Cast of Characters, Group W Cable TV, Chgo., 1988-90; celebrity reporter WMAQ-TV, NBC, Chgo., 1994—, WPNT-FM Radio, Chgo., 1993-95. Author numerous articles on lifestyle, fashion, travel in Chgo. Daily News, Crain's Chgo. Bus., Town and Country, Chgo., others. Bd. dirs. Greater N. Michigan Ave Assn., Chgo., 1980-85, Mental Health Assn. Greater Chgo., 1983-88; founding bd. dirs. Aux. bd. Lincoln Park Zoo, Chgo., 1979-89. Recipient Tradition of Excellence alumni awrd Oak Park-River Forest H.S., 1995. Mem. Sco. Profl. Journalists (bd. dirs. 1992-94), North Dearborn Assn. (bd. dirs. 1993—), Rotary Club of Chgo. Episcopalian. Office: Chgo Sun-Times 401 N Wabash Chicago IL 60611

ZWICKE, DIANNE LYNN, internist, cardiologist, educator; b. Marshfield, Wis., Oct. 27, 1952; d. Edward Raymond and Donna Mae (Erickson) Z. Diploma in nursing, St. Joseph's Hosp., Marshfield, 1973; BS in Nursing, Marquette U., 1975; MD, U. N.C., 1982. Diplomate Am. Bd. Internal Medicine, subspecialty cert. in cardiovascular diseases. Resident in internal medicine U. Wis.-Marshfield Clinic-St. Joseph's Hosp., 1982-84, chief resident, 1984-85; fellow in cardiology U. Wis. Clin. Campus-Sinai Samaritan Med. Ctr., Milw., 1985-87, assoc. prof. medicine, 1987—; mem. active staff in cardiology and emergency medicine U. Wis. Clin. Campus-Sinai Samaritan Med. Ctr., Milw., 1987—; clin. instr. surgery emergency-trauma svcs. Med. Coll. Wis., Milw; attending staff St. Luke's Hosp., St. Francis Hisp., St. Michael's Hosp., West Allis Meml. Hosp., Milw.; bd. govs., mem. State Wis. Nat. Faculty Am. Heart Assn.; presenter in field. Contbr. articles and abstracts to med. jours. Fellow ACP, Am. Coll. Cardiology, Am. Coll. Chest Physicians; mem. Soc. Critical Care Medicine, Wis. Med. Soc. (chmn. on continuing med. edn. 1987), Milw. County Med. Soc. (med. dir. cardiovascular fellowship tng. program, med. dir. women's heart care program and pulmonary hypertension program), Sigma Theta Tau. Democrat. Lutheran. Office: U Wis Clin Campus 950 N 12th St Milwaukee WI 53233-1306

Professional Index

AGRICULTURE

UNITED STATES

ARKANSAS

Marked Tree
Simpson, Art *agricultural products supplier*
Wood, Lewis *agricultural products supplier, farmer*

ILLINOIS

Auburn
Burtle, Paul Walter *farmer*

Bloomington
McMillan, Kenneth Gordon *farm organization executive*

Breese
Kennedy, Gary L. *agricultural organization administrator*

Champaign
Thompson, Dennis Ray *agriculture educator*

Danville
Konsis, Kenneth Frank *forester, educator*

De Kalb
Poage, Roy L. *animal breeder*

Freeport
Mann, Donna Marie *extension educator*

Griggsville
Bradshaw, Philip E. *farmer, consultant*

Harvel
Folkerts, Kenneth Lee *farmer, educator*

Jacksonville
Randall, Robert Quentin *nursery executive*

Kenilworth
Clary, Rosalie Brandon Stanton *timber farm executive*

Mendota
Stamberger, Edwin Henry *farmer, civic leader*

Nashville
Peithman, Marvin H. *retired farmer, income tax practitioner*

Pontiac
Cutter, Gary Lee *corn breeder, researcher*

Urbana
Courson, Roger Lee *agricultural educator*

INDIANA

Hanover
Heck, Richard T. *tree farmer*

IOWA

Akron
Hultgren, Dennis Eugene *farmer, management consultant*

Anita
Bailey, Varel G. *farmer*

Charles City
McCartney, Rhoda Huxsol *farm manager*

Des Moines
Mertz, Dolores Mary *farmer, legislator*

Indianola
Mapel, Patricia Jolene *farmer, consultant*

Mason City
Kuhlman, James Weldon *county extension education director*

Muscatine
Kautz, Richard Carl *chemical and feed company executive*

Postville
Kozelka, Edward William *seed and feed company executive*

Vinton
Jorgensen, Ann *farmer*

Wilton
Lenker, Floyd William *farmer*

KANSAS

Bonner Springs
Williams, Andrew Philip *agricultural management consultant*

Brookville
Bohata, Emil Anton *rancher*

Claflin
Burmeister, Paul Frederick *farmer*

Garden City
Reeve, Lee M. *farmer*

Inman
Schroeder, Donald Lee *farm manager*

MICHIGAN

Howell
Cotton, Larry *ranching executive*

Pigeon
Maust, Joseph J. *agricultural products supplier*

MINNESOTA

Ada
Ogaard, Donald Harvey *farmer*

Finlayson
Luoma, Judy *ranching executive*

Saint Paul
Dille, Stephen Everett *farmer, state legislator, veterinarian*

MISSOURI

Boonville
Walther, Ernest Eugene *farmer*

Cabool
Durnell, Earl *rancher*

Rogersville
Marsden, Stephen James *agricultural consulting company executive*

Springfield
Strickler, Ivan K. *dairy farmer*

Sturgeon
Fashing, Edward Michael *ranch owner, physical sciences educator*

NEBRASKA

Broken Bow
Koepke, Lonnie Dean *agricultural studies educator*

Elm Creek
Anderson, Donald Carney *farmer*

Funk
Sjogren, Donald Ernest *farmer*

Lincoln
Sheffield, Leslie Floyd *retired agricultural educator*

Republican City
Bugbee, E. Eugene *farmer, stockman*

NORTH DAKOTA

Amidon
Bergquist, Gene Alfred *farmer, rancher*

Bismarck
Carlisle, Ronald Dwight *nursery owner*

Jamestown
Legler, Victor W. *retired farmer*

Lefor
Martin, Clarence F. *farmer, state legislator*

Medina
Kirschenmann, Frederick Ludwig *farmer*

Regent
Krauter, Aaron Joseph *farmer, state senator*

Sanborn
Gerntholz, Gereld Felix *farmer, state representative*

Stanley
Piepkorn, Evonne A. *farming operation administrator*

Tappen
DeKrey, Duane Lee *farmer, rancher*

Turtle Lake
Lindteigen, Susanna *rancher, state official*

Wahpeton
Osborn, Larry Lee *farmer, county official*

Williston
Rennerfeldt, Earl Ronald *farmer, rancher*

OHIO

Tiffin
Wienken, Rita Mae *farmer*

Xenia
Steele, Hilda Berneice Hodgson *farm manager, retired home economics supervisor*

SOUTH DAKOTA

Elk Point
Chicoine, Roland Alvin *farmer, state official*

Hot Springs
Lambeth, Clayton Lee *agricultural company executive*

Wessington
Lockner, Vera Joanne *farmer, rancher, legislator*

WISCONSIN

Baldwin
Rudesill, Matilda *retired farm wife*

Green Bay
Zemke, William A. *farm management educator*

Madison
Felstehausen, Herman Henry *natural resources-land planning educator*

ADDRESS UNPUBLISHED

Champlin, Mike *rancher, former county commissioner*
Hameister, Lavon Louetta *farm manager, social worker*
Heberer, Amy Sue *farm office manager*
Inbody, Dale Dewayne *farmer*
Yanos, J. Edward *farmer*

ARCHITECTURE AND DESIGN

UNITED STATES

FLORIDA

Vero Beach
Tullis, Chaillé Handy *interior designer, volunteer*

ILLINOIS

Barrington
Coffin, Robert Parker *architect, engineer*

Bloomington
Switzer, Jon Rex *architect*

Champaign
Anthony, Kathryn Harriet *architecture educator*
Baker, Jack Sherman *architect, designer, educator*
Bognar, Botond *architecture educator*
Selby, Robert Irwin *architect, educator*

Chicago
Allen, Janice Mandabach *interior designer, nurse, office manager, actress, model*
Beach, David Duncan *naval architect*
Clark, John W. *architect*
Flom, Mark Alan *architect*
Fowler, George Selton, Jr. *architect*
Gardano, Joseph *landscaping company executive*
Gin, Jackson *architect*
Hackl, Donald John *architect*
Holabird, John Augur, Jr. *retired architect*
Jahn, Helmut *architect*
Kerbis, Gertrude Lempp *architect*
Kurtich, John William *architect, film-maker, educator*
Legge Kemp, Diane *architect, landscape architect*
Mack, Alan Wayne *interior designer*
McCullagh, Grant Gibson *architect*
McCurry, Margaret Irene *architect, educator*
Meyers, Lynn Betty *architect*
Murrie, Herbert Lee *package design executive, consultant*
Phillips, Frederick Falley *architect*
Pratt, Susan G. *architect*
Rugo, Steven Alfred *architect*
Simovic, Laszlo *architect*
Smith, Craig Malcolm *architect, consultant*
Terp, Dana George *architect*
Tobin, Calvin Jay *architect*
Tobin, Michael Alan *architect, real estate developer*
Vagnieres, Robert Charles, Jr. *architect*
Valaskovic, David William *architect, designer*
Wildermuth, Gordon Lee *architect*
Ziegler, Charles Louis, Jr. *architect*

Evanston
Schneider-Criezis, Susan Marie *architect*

Highland Park
Weinstein, Barry Alan *architect*

Hinsdale
Taylor, Eva Unikel *interior designer*

Lake Forest
Moylan, Stephen Craig *architect*

Marengo
Grover, Karen A. *designer*

Mount Prospect
Thulin, Adelaide Ann *design company executive, interior designer*

Normal
Appel, Susan Kay *architecture and art historian, educator*

Northbrook
Dobrin, Sheldon L. *architect*

Northfield
Bunce, Jayne *interior designer*
Roupp, Albert Allen *architect*

Oak Park
Katz, Richard *architect, lawyer*
Worley, Marvin George, Jr. *architect*

Plainfield
Hofer, Thomas W. *landscape company executive*

Rockford
Seehausen, Richard Ferdinand *architect*

Waukegan
Bleck, Thomas Frank *architect*

Wheeling
Klumpp, Stephen Paul *architect*

Wilmette
Siegel, Jeanne Beryl *furniture appraiser*

Winnetka
Weber, John Bertram *architect*

INDIANA

Fort Wayne
Hill, David William *design company executive*
Park, Steven Lynn *architect*

Indianapolis
Conly, Michael Frederick *architect*
Florestano, Dana Joseph *architect*
Hess, Jonathan Robert *architect*
LoTurco, Raymond Andrew *industrial designer, consultant*
Mair, Bruce Logan *interior designer, company executive*
Patton, James Elliott *architectural technology educator*

Nashville
Walsh, Alan John *architect*

South Bend
Mroczkiewicz, Kenneth J. *design draftsman*

IOWA

Amana
Yoder, Larry David *industrial designer*

Cedar Rapids
Healey, Edward Hopkins *architect*

Davenport
Monty, Mitchell *landscape company executive*
Weispfenning, Curtis *design technician*

Des Moines
DeAngelo, Anthony James *architect*

Fairfield
Clark, Henry Ogden *architect*
Lipman, Jonathan *architect, historic preservationist*

Red Oak
Lantz, Eric A. *design engineer manager*

Sioux City
Therkildsen, Mark B. *architect*

Webster City
Follett, Jeff L. *design engineer*

KANSAS

Hutchinson
Haag, Joel Edward *architect*

Leavenworth
Still, Christopher Gene *industrial designer*

Moundridge
Parker, Alan Leslie, II (Chip Parker) *architect*

Pittsburg
Fish, David Carlton *architect*

Shawnee Mission
Colgrove, Thomas Michael *landscape architect*

Topeka
Slemmons, Robert Sheldon *architect*

Wichita
Ellington, Howard Wesley *architect*
Kruse, Wilbur Ferdinand *architect*

MICHIGAN

Ann Arbor
Flowers, Damon Bryant *architect, facility planner*
Groat, Linda Noel *architectural educator*
Metcalf, Robert Clarence *architect, educator*
Sutton, Sharon Egretta *architect, educator, artist*
Vakalo, Emmanuel-George *architecture and planning educator, researcher*

Big Rapids
Samson, Joseph Michael *architect, educator*

Chesterfield
Wittbrodt, Frederick Joseph, Jr. *automotive designer*

Farmington
Reddig, Walter Eduard *architect, master cabinet maker*

Ferndale
Chambers, Donald H. *industrial designer*

Grand Rapids
Dickerson, Allen Bruce *interior designer, consultant*
Mathison, Thomas Richard *architect*

Grosse Pointe Woods
McCafferty, Charles Terrence *architect*

Jackson
Kendall, Kay Lynn *interior designer*

Kalamazoo
Hamann, Norman Lee, Sr. *architect*

Kentwood
Clark, James Robert *architect*

Romulus
Steele, Charles Edward *industrial designer*

Saint Joseph
Keech, Elowyn Ann *interior designer*

Troy
Hankis, Roy Allen *interior designer*

MINNESOTA

Chaska
James, Allen Dewayne *designer*

Hector
Rieke, Tom James *mechanical draftsman*

Minneapolis
Chilton, William David *architect*
Eyberg, Donald Theodore, Jr. *architect*
Helmes, Leslie Scott *architect*
Meese, Robert Allen *architect*
Weinzetl, Lawrence Martin *architect*
Zielinski, Robert S. *multi media desinger*

Minnetonka
Rasche, J. David *retired architect*

Saint Paul
Gray, Carl Thomas *architect*
Stewart, Bruce Edmund, Sr. *retired mechanical designer, writer*

MISSOURI

Ballwin
Kern, Gary L. *golf course architect*

Cassville
Pueppke, Darrell E. *design draftsman*

Clayton
Turner, Terry Madison *architect*

Columbia
Brent, Ruth Stumpe *design educator, researcher, educator*

Florissant
Counts, Donald R. *furniture maker*

Foristell
Heinrich, James K. *designer*

Kansas City
Shoemaker, Robert Shern *architect*

Saint Louis
Beuc, Rudolph, Jr. *architect, real estate broker*
Bovary, Thomas Dean *design draftsman*
Cameron, Paul Scott *architect*
Haggans, James Michael *architect, university planning services director*
Krebs, Carol Marie *architect, psychiatric therapist*
Lickhalter, Merlin Eugene *architect*
Macon, Irene Elizabeth *interior designer, consultant*
Thalden, Barry R. *architect*

Springfield
Liu, Yuan Hsiung *drafting and design educator*

Washington
Alfermann, Gary L. *industrial designer*

Weatherby Lake
Hawkins, Geri Sue *interior designer, jewelry designer, realtor*

NEBRASKA

Lincoln
Berggren, Jerry Lee *architect, consultant*

Omaha
Minor, Hugh David *draftsman*
Ryan, Mark Anthony *architect*
Tast, Alan Herbert *architect*
Williams, Sherda Kaye *landscape architect*

OHIO

Akron
Castronovo, Thomas Paul *architect, consultant*
Howe, Joseph A. *mechanical designer*

Berea
Pattison, Robert Maynicke *architect*

Celina
Fanning, Ronald Heath *architect, engineer*

Chagrin Falls
Thiel, Barbara Vogel *architect, interior designer*

Cincinnati
Cole, Thomas Ferguson *architect*
Gosling, David *architect, urban design educator*
Levinson, Charles Bernard *architect*
Luckner, Herman Richard, III *interior designer*

Cleveland
Akins, Jacqueline Van Auken *architect*
Bowen, Richard Lee *architect*
Eberhard, William Thomas *architect*
Hancock, James Beaty *interior designer*
Hunter, Sally Irene *interior designer*
Kucinski, Richard J. *product designer*
Sourbrine, Richard Don, II *architect*
Westlake, Paul Edward, Jr. *architect, educator*

Columbiana
Richman, John Emmett *architect*

Columbus
Ford, Thomas Brady *architect, consultant*
Howell, Norbert Allen *architect*
Patton, William E. *designer*

Dover
Jackson, Martin A. *industrial designer*

Dublin
Cornwell, Paul M., Jr. *architect*

Hamden
McWhorter, Lawrence James *design draftsman, township trustee*

Hudson
Isabel, Robert Stephen *interior designer*

Kent
Flanigan, Alan Wayne *designer*
Sommers, David Lynn *architect*

Kinsman
Alfonsi, William E. *interior designer, funeral industry consultant*

Lorain
Finkel, Warren Edward *architect*

Medina
Haugh, Jeffrey L. *electronic draftsman*

Mount Vernon
Heebsh, Saundra L. *interior designer*

Novelty
Phelps, G. Robert *retired architect*

Pepper Pike
Bowles, John L. *industrial designer*

Toledo
Martin, Robert Edward *architect*
Smith, Robert Franklin *mechanical designer*

Wauseon
Boyers, Janeth Mauree *interior designer*

Westerville
Serraglio, Mario *architect*

Williston
Wargowsky, Frederick August *retired draftsman*

Wright Patterson AFB
Brinkley, James Wiley *industrial designer, bioengineering consultant*

Youngstown
Mastriana, Robert Alan *architect*
Murcko, Donald Leroy *architect*
Simpkins, John Robert *machine designer*

SOUTH DAKOTA

Rapid City
Pearson, Louis W. *architect*

WISCONSIN

Beloit
Driscoll, Mark *draftsman*

Brookfield
Wenzler, Edward William *architect*

Delevan
Boutelle, Edward W. *industrial designer*

Elkhorn
Henry, William Robert *architect, engineer*

Kenosha
Potente, Eugene, Jr. *interior designer*

Madison
Alanen, Arnold Robert *landscape architecture educator*
Norlin, Erl E. *drafter*

Milwaukee
Dumas, Tyrone Pierre *architect, construction manager, consultant*
Greenstreet, Robert Charles *architect, educator*
Herche, Marvin C. *mechanical designer*
Krenz, James T. *product designer*
Nwagbara, Chibu Isaac *industrial designer, consultant*
Prem, Gregory A. *mechanical designer*
Savarino, Ronald R. *die designer*
Wilson, Walter Leroy *architect*

Pewaukee
Kube, James A. *draftsman*

Racine
Meilicke, Warren A. *mechanical designer*

Waukesha
Leatherberry, Anne Knox Clark *interior designer, architectural designer*

ADDRESS UNPUBLISHED

Bauman, Robert Gene *architect*
Beight, Janice Marie *interior designer*
Brattain, Arlene Jane Clark *interior designer*
DiNardo, Russell Anthony *architect*
Euans, Robert Earl *architect*
Hutchins, Robert Ayer *architectural consultant*
Jobin, Kenneth Joseph *robotic applications designer*
Kern, Ron Lee *golf course architect, photographer*
Kiewel, Harold Dean *architect*
Kotz, George J. *industrial designer*
Kucharik, Kay E. *industrial designer*
Leaman, Jack Ervin *landscape architect, community/regional planner*
Loss, John C. *architect, retired educator*
Munson, Virginia Aldrich *interior designer, decorator*
Nederlander, Marjorie Smith *retired interior designer and decorator*
Neimark, Vassa *interior architect*
Ries, Donald *industrial designer*
Ryan, John Michael *landscape architect*
Sorgen, Richard Jesse *architect*
Stearns, Carol Keiser *architect*
Vukovich, Thomas Walter *architect*

ARTS: LITERARY. *See also* COMMUNICATIONS MEDIA.

UNITED STATES

CALIFORNIA

Fremont
Maloney, Cheryl Ann *author, photographer*

Newport Beach
Dovring, Karin Elsa Ingeborg *author, poet, playwright, communication analyst*

ILLINOIS

Argonne
McGrath, John Julian *writer, communication consultant*

Batavia
Dowd, James Patrick *bookseller, writer*

Champaign
Wasser, Frederick Anthony *communications educator, writer*

Chicago
Birch, John Edward, Jr. *publisher, retired military officer*
Brooks, Gwendolyn *writer, poet*
Buehler, Evelyn Judy *poet*
Curry, David Lee *writer*
Edwards-Kulikowski, Ernestine Vivian *writer*
Fremon, David Kent *writer, consultant*
Furnweger, Karen *science and environmental writer, editor*
Kolkey, Eric Samuel *screenwriter*
Lach, Alma Elizabeth *food and cooking writer, consultant*
Madsen, Dorothy Louise (Meg Madsen) *writer*
Nelson, Marcus Thomas *playwright, producer*
Rivers, Jessie Mae *writer*
Schandelmeier, Cathleen Ann *playwright, poet*
Terkel, Studs (Louis Terkel) *author, interviewer*
Wallingford, Anne *writer, marketing consultant*
Wolk, Howard Marvin *poet, retired theatre equipment company executive*

Deerfield
Aitchison, Robert Snyder *writer, publishing company executive*

Des Plaines
Kudenholdt, Sharon Sue *freelance author*

Evanston
Burket, Gail Brook *author*
Kleinman, Susan Phyllis *travel writer, photographer, insurance salesperson*
Knight, Louise Wilby *writer*
Mitchell, Kendall *writer, literary critic*
Oleksy, Walter George *author*

Galesburg
Litvin, Martin Jay *author, lecturer*

Gurnee
Anderson, Leo Sheridan *writer*

Henry
Raffensperger, Helen Elizabeth *writer*

Highland Park
Feldman, Ruth Duskin *writer*

Jacksonville
Seator, Lynette Hubbard *freelance writer*

La Salle
Miller, Kristie *writer*

Lake Bluff
Chapman, Fern Schumer *freelance writer*

Lake Forest
Swanton, Virginia Lee *author, publisher, bookseller*

Marion
Lindsey, Anne West *writer*

Moline
Skromme, Arnold Burton *educational writer, engineering consultant*

Morton
Olsen, Theresa Marie Grimaldi *freelance writer, educator*

Mount Prospect
Bueschel, Richard Martin *writer*

Naperville
Belford, Virginia Helen Wisdom *freelance writer*
Schanstra, Carla Ross *technical writer*

Niles
Kramer, Marilyn Koll *technical writer, small business owner*

North Riverside
Sedlak, S(hirley) A(gnes) *freelance writer*

Skokie
Gershon, William I. *copywriter, voiceover actor, communications executive*
Lieberman, Douglas Lionel *scriptwriter, software writer*
Parker, Ann E. *writer, astrologer*

South Barrington
Kissane, Sharon Florence *writer, consultant*

Sparland
Deffenbaugh, David Paul, Sr. *writer, artist*

Waukegan
Hughes, Katherine Dodson *technical writer, editor, developmental scientist*
Marks, Martha Alford *author*

Western Springs
Glanz, Barbara Anne *author, speaker, consultant*

Zion
Gay, Kathlyn Ruth *author*

INDIANA

Bloomington
Dorr, James Suhrer *writer*
Kibbey, Hal Stephen *science writer*

Brownsburg
Drozda, Joseph Michael *author*

Crown Point
Palmeri, Sharon Elizabeth *freelance writer, community educator*

Fort Wayne
Lair, Helen May *poet*
Turner, Darrell John *copy editor, writer*

Highland
Goldman, Dona Lu *writer, retired educator*

Indianapolis
Fish, George *writer*
Wise, Rita J. *writer, poet*

Monticello
Berry, Michael John *author, medical/dental management consultant*

South Bend
Black, Virginia Morrow *writer*
Collins, Walton Robert *writer, educator*

IOWA

Ames
Smiley, Jane Graves *author, educator*

Des Moines
Davidson, Sol M. *author, management consultant*
Hunter, Linda Mason *author*
Schauberger, Amanda Louise *freelance writer*

Dubuque
Tigges, John Thomas *writer, musician*

Iowa City
Davidson, Osha Gray *writer*
Rodnitzky, Donna Joy *author*

Montezuma
Gregor, Wilbur Ray *writer*

KANSAS

Carbondale
Rogers, Vivian Kommedahl *writer, homemaker*

Lawrence
Irby, Kenneth Lee *poet, English language educator*

Manhattan
Andrews, Emmett Lynn (Rusty Andrews) *promotional writer, consultant*
Cokinos, Christopher Andrew *writer, educator, environmental activist*

Olathe
Wilcox, Laird Maurice *researcher, writer, carpenter*

Shawnee Mission
Keach, Margaret Sally *writer, lecturer*
Levin, Marian Sunie *author*

KENTUCKY

Burlington
Burleigh, Anne Husted *freelance writer*

MICHIGAN

Ann Arbor
Attarian, John Charles *writer*

Battle Creek
Cline, Charles William *poet, pianist, rhetoric and literature educator*

Bay City
Kuerbitz, Patricia Ann *writer, poet, artist*

Bloomfield Hills
Goldwasser, Judith Wax *writer*

Caledonia
Winters, Donna Mae *writer*

Detroit
Johnson, Reginald Amin *writer*

Dorr
Berg, Melody G. *author*

Harbert
McKelvy, Natalie Ann *writer, novelist, poet*

Kalamazoo
Johnston, William Arnold *playwright*
Light, Christopher Upjohn *writer, computer musician*

Keego Harbor
Kienzle, William Xavier *author*

Laingsburg
Burns, Virginia Law *writer*

Lansing
Carlson, Ann Marie *poet*
Klunzinger, Thomas Edward *writer, actor, director, reappointment specialist, consultant*

Lincoln Park
Heck-Rabi, Louise Evelyn *writer*

Niles
Curtis, Elaine Rose *environmental writer, consultant*

Republic
Wixtrom, Donald Joseph *translator*

Southfield
Socolow, Elizabeth Anne *poet, educator, artist, writer*

Sunfield
Huggler, Tom *freelance writer, photographer*

Traverse City
Evancho, Joseph Andrew *writer*

West Bloomfield
Cohassey, John Fredrick *writer*
Kowalski, Kathleen Patricia *reporter, publishing executive*

Westland
Vatcher, Cheryl Ann *writer, paralegal*

Williamsburg
Ketchum, Sally DeBolt *writer*

MINNESOTA

Collegeville
Hassler, Jon Francis *novelist*

Duluth
van Appledorn, E(lizabeth) Ruth *writer*

Edina
Schwarzrock, Shirley Pratt *author, lecturer, educator*

Eveleth
Moffatt, David Robert *freelance writer*

Forest Lake
Loquasto, Klaus Wolfgang *writer, editor*

Hovland
Drabik, Harry Francis *writer*

Minneapolis
Baker, John Stevenson (Michael Dyregrov) *writer*
Boylan, Brian Richard *author, producer, photographer, director, literary agent*
Curry, Jane Anne *writer, educator, performer*
Korotkin, Fred *writer, philatelist*
Lange, Katherine JoAnn *writer*

Saint Louis Park
Beck, Jules Karroll *technical writer*

Saint Paul
Cowan, John Willard *writer, management consultant, priest*
Cutler, (Robert) Bruce *author*
Lambert, LeClair Grier *writer, lecturer, state government public information administrator*
Wagner, Bill Peter *writer*

MISSOURI

Berkeley
Johnson, John Lee *retired civil servant, writer*

Bloomfield
Ferrell, Paul Cleveland *author*

Breckenridge
Barry, Aileen Ella (Alisa Barry) *poet, songwriter, retired practical nurse*

Columbia
Diamond, Deborah Beroset *writer*
Windsor, Margaret Eden *writer*

Florissant
Basler, Theodore Eugene *poet*
Tourville, James E. *writer, automotive worker*

Joplin
Jones, Veda Rae Boyd *author*

Kansas City
Kirchner, L.R. (Larry) *writer, publishing executive*
Martin-Bowen, (Carole) Lindsey *freelance writer*

Moscow Mills
Castle, Diana Christine *poet*

O'Fallon
Otti, Robert F. *author, retired soldier*

Saint Louis
Corbett, Suzanne Elaine *food writer, film producer, marketing executive, food historian*
Linville, Judith Ann *writer*
Lubbock, James Edward *retired writer, photographer, publicity consultant*

Springfield
Brown, Michael H. *freelance writer*
Harris, Bruce Wayne *writer, gold mining consultant*
Hickory, Betty May *songwriter, writer*

Viburnum
West, Roberta Bertha *writer*

NEBRASKA

Norfolk
Scheve, Addie R. *author*

NEW YORK

New York
Bloomingdale, Teresa Burrowes

OHIO

Canton
Sowd, David Howard *writer*

Chillicothe
Reitz, Barbara Maurer *poet, freelance writer*

Cincinnati
Braman, Heather Ruth *technical writer, editor, consultant, antiques dealer*
Oden, Fay Giles *author, educator*

Circleville
Mytinger, Geoffrey James *writer, antiques and arts dealer*

Cleveland
Turk, Francis Jerome *writer, editor*
Warren, Sandra Kay *writer*
Wood, Kathleen Oliver *writer, editor*

Columbus
Kass, Linda S. *writer, communications consultant, child advocate*

Dayton
Hayes, Stephen Kurtz *author*
Heath, Mariwyn Dwyer *writer, legislative issues consultant*

Eastlake
Kurtz, William Alan *writer*

Highland Heights
Covington, Edward James *author, retired physicist*

Highland Hills
Badal, James Jessen, Jr. *writer, educator*

Lakewood
Koco, Linda Gale *writer*

Milford
Banks, Michael Alan *freelance writer*

Napoleon
Meekison, MaryFran *writer, photographer*

Oxford
Branch, Edgar Marquess *American literature researcher, writer*

Perrysburg
Weaver, Richard L., II *writer, educator*

Shaker Heights
Pavlovich, Donald *technical writer*

Springfield
Fickert, Kurt Jon *writer, retired language educator*

Toledo
Bleznick, Susan Risa *writer, journalist*

SOUTH DAKOTA

Brookings
Williams, Elizabeth Evenson *writer*

Manderson
Whiteface, Charmaine Francine *freelance writer*

Sioux Falls
Reynolds, William James *writer*

Vermillion
Green, Vincent Scott *writer*

WISCONSIN

Argyle
Daley, Ronald Eugene *playwright, poet, director, producer*

Hancock
Vroman, Barbara Fitz *writer, educator*

Kenosha
Carroll, Richard *novelist, researcher*

Little Chute
Rice, Ferill Jeane *writer, civic worker*

Madison
K-Turkel, Judith Leah Rosenthal (Judi K-Turkel) *writer, editor, publisher*
Stone, John Timothy, Jr. *writer*
Will, Roland Tracy, II *writer, editor*

Milwaukee
Grade, Lorna J(ean) *medical writer & editor, medical business manager*
Parnell, Charles L. *speechwriter*

New Berlin
Lowder, James Daniel *writer, editor, educator*

West Bend
Scribbins, Jim *writer*

ADDRESS UNPUBLISHED

Bauman, Andrew William *author*
Beck, E. Lee *writer*
Bellow, Saul C. *writer*
Boss, Judith Carol *writer, consultant*
Brennan, T. Casey *writer*
Cohen, Richard Lawrence *writer*
Devine, Mary Virginia *author, researcher*
Eisenstein, Phyllis Leah *writer, writing educator*
Featherston, James William *freelance writer*
Frencl, Rebecca Lynn *writer*
Greb, Richard Harold *writer*
Horning, Andrew Michael *technical writer and illustrator*
Jacobowitz, Ruth Scherr *writer, public relations consultant, lecturer*
Knoepfle, John *writer*
Kurtz, Karen Barbara *writer, editor, administrator, consultant*
Laycock, George Edwin *author, journalist*
Lockwood, Walter Lee *screenwriter, English language educator*
Lohmann, Joan Gardner Jenkins *writer*
Maddox, Linda Gay Nelson *freelance writer*
Manchester, Diana *writer*
Neely, Mark Edward, Jr. *writer*
Neidorf, Robin Mara *writer, magazine*
Page, Thomas Leslie *poet, writer*
Quay, Joyce Crosby *writer*
Rickerl, Susan Marie *writer*
Sass, Mary Martha *freelance writer, artist*
Sears, Donna Mae *technical writer and illustrator*
Shepley, Carol Ferring *writer, art critic, magazine editor*
Smith, Marya Jean *writer*
Sundeen, Ann Lowry *writer, community volunteer*
Teachout, Noreen Ruth *writer*
Tolliver, Sarah Jan *writer*
Treanor, Judith Ann *writer*
Valdes, Elizabeth Lynne *technical writer, editor*
Woodward, Kevin Dale *writer*
Wright, Charles Spaulding, II *writer, communications consultant*

ARTS: PERFORMING

UNITED STATES

CALIFORNIA

Los Angeles
Jackson, Isaiah *conductor*

ILLINOIS

Bloomington
Vayo, David Joseph *composer, music educator*

Bourbonnais
York, Joseph Russell *media production technician, & film*

Charleston
Weidner, Robert Wright *music educator*

Chicago
Arney, Randall *artistic director*
Axelrod, Bernadette Bonner *television director, producer*
Brockmeier, Matthew George *arts administrator*
Conte, Lou *artistic director, choreographer*
Dabrowski, Edward John *television technical director*
DeWeese, Keith Patrick *cinematology researcher*
Duell, Daniel Paul *artistic director, choreographer, lecturer*
Harvey, Roy James *television producer*
Hays, Nancy *entertainment executive, entertainer*
Higgins, Ruth Ellen *theatre producer*
Krainik, Ardis *opera company executive*
Maggio, Michael John *artistic director*
McCarter, William J., Jr. *broadcasting executive*
Mellema, Donald Eugene *radio news reporter and anchor*
Neal, Jeff *stage director*
Padberg, Helen Swan *violinist*
Pokorni, Orysia *musician*
Ran, Shulamit *composer*
Renard, Paul Steven *music educator*
Rich, J. Dennis *performing arts educator*
Robinson, Martin *television and radio broadcaster, media consultant*
Schulfer, Roche Edward *theater executive director*
Scogin, Robert Erwin *actor*
Scott, Stephen Brinsley *theater producer*
Solti, Sir Georg *conductor*
Taylor, Koko *singer*
Walker, John Patrick *theater producer, actor*
Whang, Un-Young *music educator*
Winfrey, Oprah *television talk show host, actress, producer*

Coal City
Major, Mary Jo *dance school artistic director*

Crystal Lake
Meter, Karen Shelley *music educator, veterans advocate*

De Kalb
Gallagher, Kent Grey *theater arts educator, real estate developer*

Downers Grove
Humphreys, David Leroy *musician*

Edwardsville
Haley, Johnetta Randolph *musician, educator, university administrator*

Elgin
Bishop, Ruth Ann *coloratura soprano, voice educator*
Dodohara, Jean Noton *music educator*

Evanston
Eberley, Helen-Kay *opera singer, classical record company executive, poet*
Kaiserman, David Norman *music educator*
Vandenbroucke, Russell James *theatre director*
White, Catharine Boswell (C.B. White) *composer*
Yoder, John Clifford *producer, consultant*

Galesburg
Polay, Bruce *music director, music eductor*

Grayslake
Paxton, Joan Susan *vocalist*

Lake Forest
Kirby, Frank Eugene *musicology educator, author, editor*

Lombard
Wagner, Mark Anthony *videotape editor*

Northbrook
Janello, David A. *music composer, computer scientist*

Oak Park
Northway, Dennis Edward *conductor*

Park Forest
Billig, Etel Jewel *theater director, actress*

Rockford
Larsen, Steven *orchestra conductor*
Robinson, Donald Peter *musician, retired electrical engineer*

Shorewood
Lombardo, David Albert *actor, writer, speaker, aviation educator*

Skokie
Childers, John Henry *talent company executive, personality representative*

Springfield
Ellis, Michael Eugene *documentary film producer, writer, director*

Warrensburg
Tertocha, Jean-Paul Richard *producer*

Wheaton
Edwards, Karin Redekopp *piano educator*

Wheeling
Saltzman, Barry *actor*

Wilmette
Merrier, Helen *actress, writer*

INDIANA

Bloomington
Burkholder, James Peter *music educator*
Sharrow, Leonard *musician, educator*

Carmel
Conrad, Charles Phillip *musician, educator*

Chesterton
Musgrave, Charles Edward *retired music director, correctional official*

Fort Wayne
Sack, James McDonald, Jr. *radio and television producer, marketing executive*
Stovall, Doris Grace *performing arts association executive*

Greencastle
Irwin, Stanley Roy *music educator, singer, conductor*

Huntingburg
Palmer, Curtis Ray *video company executive*

Indianapolis
Alvarez, Thomas *film and video producer, director*
Johnson, David Allen *singer, songwriter, investor, minister*
Lord, William Herman *performing arts educator, theatre consultant*
Schellen, Nando *opera director*
Wheat, Christopher John, Sr. *broadcast executive*

Kokomo
Highlen, Larry Wade *music educator, piano rebuilder, tuner*

Marion
McPhail Whitaker, Sandra Sue *vocalist, educator*

Muncie
Betancourt, Cindy Alyce *music educator*
Mackey, Elizabeth Jocelyn *music educator*

Terre Haute
Damer, Linda K. *music educator*

Vincennes
Spurrier, James Joseph *theater educator*

IOWA

Clinton
Unger, Gary A. *recording industry executive, singer, lyricist*

Des Moines
Giunta, Joseph *conductor, music director*
McElroy, Laurince Dean (Larry McElroy) *theater director, educator, consultant*

Dyersville
Ambrose, Thomas William *broadcasting executive*

Iowa City
Mather, Roger Frederick *music educator, freelance technical writer*

Marion
McDonald, Carolyn Ann *dance educator, choreographer*

Mount Etna
Sparks, (Theo) Merrill *entertainer, translator, poet*

Mount Vernon
Sannerud, Paul David *theater design educator*

Ottumwa
Thompson, Jacqueline Kay *performing company executive, fine arts educator*

Walnut
Everhart, Robert Phillip (Bobby Williams) *entertainer, songwriter, recording artist*

KANSAS

Emporia
Miller, Marie Catherine *music educator*

Hays
Murphy, James Lawson *music educator*

Hutchinson
Smith, Delos V., Jr. *actor, producer, director*

Iola
Chrisenberry, Carol Ann *music educator*

Lawrence
Priestman, Brian *classical musician*

Manhattan
Sutton, Mary Ellen *organist, educator*

Pittsburg
Dannessa, Karen Lynn *musician, professor*

Shawnee Mission
Asner, Marie A. *musician, classical*
Craighead, Wendel Lee *film and video producer, director*

Wichita
Bryan, Wayne *producer*
Johnson, Guy Charles *music educator, musician*

KENTUCKY

Louisville
Hedges, John Kim *actor, performing arts administrator, consultant*

MICHIGAN

Ann Arbor
Austerlitz, Paul *ethnomusicologist, jazz musician*
Bolcom, William Elden *musician, composer, educator, pianist*
Huttar Bailey, Julia Ruth *music director, educator*
King, Lee Ann *ballet instructor, choreographer*
Scharp-Radovic, Carol Ann *choreographer, classical ballet educator, artistic director*
Smith, Virginia Brown *classical musician*

Bloomfield Hills
Haidostian, Alice Berberian *concert pianist, civic volunteer and fundraiser*

Dearborn
Manfro, Patrick James (Patrick James Holiday) *radio artist*

Detroit
Calarco, N. Joseph *theater educator*
Di Chiera, David *performing arts impresario*
Jarvi, Neeme *conductor*
Stroud, Bradley Lyn *ballet company executive*

Florissant
Vantine, Bruce Lynn *choral conductor*

Grand Rapids
Arthur Estner, Charthel *artistic director*
Brink, Norma S. *performing arts educator, actress*
Smith, Peter Wilson *symphony orchestra administrator*

Grandville
Coffield, Curtis Steven *music director*

Kalamazoo
Roederer, Silvia *concert pianist, educator*

Lansing
Kluge, Len H. *director, actor, theater educator*
Thomas, Nathan *theatre arts educator*

Mount Pleasant
Craig, John Robert *broadcast and cinematic arts educator, researcher*

Muskegon
Welsh, John Robert *musician*

Oak Park
Spradley, David Lee *music producer*

Redford
Goslin, Gerald Hugh *concert pianist, teacher*

Rochester
Bajor, James Henry *musician, jazz pianist*
Daniels, David Wilder *conductor, music educator*

Saginaw
Najar, Leo Michael *conductor, arranger, educator*

Westland
Harris, Frances Alvord (Mrs. Hugh W. Harris) *retired radio and television broadcaster, consultant*

Ypsilanti
McGuire, Michael G. *music therapist, educator*

MINNESOTA

Bloomington
Smith, Henry Charles, III *symphony orchestra conductor*

Golden Valley
Strand, Dean Paul *disc jockey, audio engineer*

Litchfield
Snelling, Norma June *retired music educator, English educator*

Mankato
Hustoles, Paul John *theater educator*

Minneapolis
Anderson, Clyde Bailey *musician, educator*
Hyslop, David Johnson *arts administrator*
Martenson, Edward Allen *theater manager*
Patrow, Kristine Lydal *television news anchor, reporter, producer*
Price, Henry Escoe *broadcast executive*
Welles, George William, III *electronic imaging specialist*
Wright, (James) Garland *artistic director*

Moorhead
Revzen, Joel *conductor*
Rothlisberger, Rodney John *music educator*
Wilson, William Michael, Jr. *theatre educator, director, choreographer*

Northfield
Ferguson, John Allen *organist, church musician, music educator*

Saint Paul
Edwards, J. Michele *conductor, educator*
Nice, Pamela Michele *theatre director*

Shoreview
Olsen, Gerald James *art industry executive*

Virginia
Wilcox, Sheila Maureen *music educator*

MISSOURI

Branson
Bradley, Leon Charles *musician, educator*

Canton
Mathieson, Carol Ann Fisher *music educator*

Columbia
Sims, Wendy L. *music educator*

Kansas City
Bolender, Todd *choreographer*
Costin, James D. *performing arts company executive*
Franaho, Susan M. *theater administrator*
Keathley, George *performing arts executive*
Moore, Larry Emmett *television news reporter, horse breeder*
Patterson, Russell *conductor, opera executive*

Kirksville
Weerts, Richard Kenneth *music educator*

Liberty
Harriman, Richard Lee *performing arts administrator, educator*

Saint Louis
Bernstein, Mark D. *theater director*
DuMaine, Daniel Jerome *musician, composer, musical director*
Eichhorn, Arthur David *music director*
Geiger, Harold Stephen *television producer*
Goldenhersh, Lauri Davidian *musician, educator*
McDonald, Hal Mark *music educator, pianist*
Slatkin, Leonard Edward *conductor, music director, pianist*
Woolf, Steven Michael *artistic director*

Springfield
Moulder, T. Earline *musician*
Orms, Howard Raymond *drama educator*

Warrensburg
Smith, Dolores Maxine Plunk *dancer, educator*

NEBRASKA

Chadron
Winkle, William Allan *music educator*

Kearney
Nichols, Harold James *theatre educator*

Lincoln
Collier, Nathan Morris *musician, educator*
Miller, Tice Lewis *theatre educator*

Omaha
Bounds, Nancy *modeling and talent company executive*
Brothen, Jeffrey Peter *theatre, speech educator*
Saker, James Robert *music educator*

NEW YORK

New York
Leppard, Raymond John *conductor, harpsichordist*

NORTH DAKOTA

Fargo
Fornes, Candace Rae *professional violist*

Grand Forks
Jacobson, Daniel Christopher *music educator*

Valley City
Starke, Shirley Diana *composer, harpist*

OHIO

Akron
Guegold, William Kent *music educator*
Poll, Heinz *choreographer, artistic director*

Ashtabula
Sebell, Tellervo Maria *musician*

Athens
Conaty-Cooley, Donna Marie *music educator, oboist*

Bowling Green
Lee, Briant Hamor *theatre educator*

Bratenahl
Drichta, Clarence James *music educator, conductor, violinist*

Cincinnati
Alexander, Jeffrey *performing company executive*
Couch, Leon Wheland, III *music educator, performer*
Ferguson, Robert P. (H-Bomb) *musician, songwriter*
Harbison, Patrick Lewis *music educator*
James, Jefferson Ann *performing company executive, choreographer*
Lopez-Cobos, Jesus *conductor*
Pridonoff, Eugene Alexander *music educator*
Stern, Edward *performing company executive*
Ward, Sherman Carl, III (Buzz Ward) *theater manager*
Worachek, Susan Hanlin *music educator*

Cleveland
Bamberger, David *opera company executive*
Ciarlillo, Marjorie Ann *musician, educator*
DesRosiers, Anne Booke *performing arts administrator*
Dohnányi, Christoph von *musician, conductor*
Gladden, Dean Robert *arts administrator, educator, consultant*
Nahat, Dennis F. *artistic director, choreographer*
Pettijohn, William Lee *singer, poet*
Strekal, Debra Joan *producer, writer, director, actress*
Tidwell, Roy Robinson, Sr. *television producer, consultant*

Columbus
Allen, Lois Arlene Height (Mrs. James Pierpont Allen) *musician*
Bennett, Sharon Kay *music educator*
Fisher, Mary Bucher *technical editor*
Harper, Nelson Owen *pianist, educator*
Lowe, Clayton Kent *visual imagery, cinema, and video educator*
Pierson, Margaret Rosalind *dance educator, choreographer*
Rice, John Robin *music educator, singer*

Dayton
Burke, Dermot *artistic director*
Hanna, Marsha L. *artistic director*
Swanson, Roy Andrew *music educator*
Walters, Jefferson Brooks *musician, retired real estate broker*
Wasson, Barbara Hickam *music educator*

Delaware
Jamison, Roger W. *pianist, piano educator*

Delta
Monahan, Leonard Francis *musician, composer*

Findlay
Anders, Micheal Fred *vocal music educator*

Kent
Albrecht, Theodore John *conductor, music historian*

Milford
Kibby, Arthur Stephen *video and film producer, director of photography*

Mount Vernon
Vining, John Kendall *performing arts company administrator, composer*

New Concord
Brown, Karen Rima *orchestra manager, Spanish language educator*

Novelty
Miller, Dwight Richard *cosmetologist, corporate executive, hair designer*

Poland
Perlozzi, Darla Rae *musician, composer*

Tiffin
Talbot-Koehl, Linda Ann *dancer, ballet studio owner*

Toledo
Bennett, Elizabeth Ann *elementary education educator, music specialist*
Knorr, John Christian *entertainment agency executive, bandleader, producer*
Kuhn, John Stephen *drama educator*
Massey, Andrew John *conductor, composer*
Schleuter, Lois Jean *music educator*

Wilberforce
Smith, James E. *music educator, jazz guitarist*

Willoughby
Harris, Robert Edward *comedian, history educator*

SOUTH DAKOTA

Mitchell
Skelly, Joseph Patrick *radio personality*

Rapid City
Brennan, Ruth Anne *arts administrator*
Lockhart, Gemma *producer, writer*

Yankton
Stastny, Charles Joseph *musician*

VIRGINIA

Norfolk
Mark, Peter *director, conductor*

WASHINGTON

Seattle
Jenkins, Speight *opera company executive, writer*

WISCONSIN

Appleton
Below, Robert Claude *music educator*
Meidl, Kevin *music educator*

La Crosse
Hindson, Harry Burdette, III *music educator*
Rusterholz, Paul Oliver *conductor*

Madison
Burns, Elizabeth Murphy *media executive*
Kryn, Jeannette Miriam *music educator, retired research botanist*
Rosser, Annetta Hamilton *composer*

Milwaukee
Cook, Wayne Evans *music educator*
Devlin, John Paul *performing arts educator*
Downey, John Wilham *composer, pianist, conductor, educator*
Grange, William Marshall *actor, educator*
Hanreddy, Joseph *stage director*
Hansen-Rachor, Sharon Ann *conductor, choral music educator*
Hanthorn, Dennis Wayne *performing arts association administrator*
Lafontsee, Dane *ballet company artistic director*
O'Connor, Sara Andrews *theater director*
Ovitsky, Steven Alan *musician, symphony orchestra executive*
Schneider, John David *theatre director, playwright, actor, jazz singer*
Thompson, Basil F. *ballet master*

Oshkosh
Pensis, Henri Bram *music educator, conductor*

Solon Springs
Giesen, Mary Margaret *performing arts company administrator*

Stevens Point
Larrick, Geary Henderson *composer*

CANADA

MANITOBA

Winnipeg
Lewis, Andre Leon *artistic director*
Tovey, Bramwell *conductor, composer*

ONTARIO

Kitchener
Coles, Graham *conductor, composer*

Mississauga
Peterson, Oscar Emmanuel *pianist*

THE NETHERLANDS

Hilversum
De Waart, Edo *conductor*

SWITZERLAND

Geneva
Barenboim, Daniel *conductor, pianist*

ADDRESS UNPUBLISHED

Arenz, Mark Wesley *video editor*
Arnold, Robert Jeffrey *musician*
Balter, Alan *conductor, music director*
Birkett, Cynthia Anne *theater company executive*
Burns, Jeffrey Phillips *music theorist, composer*
Caldwell, Sarah *opera producer, conductor, stage director and administrator*
Chummers, Paul *performing company executive*
de Blasis, James Michael *artistic director, producer, stage director*
Harris, Robert A. *retired music educator*
Havener, Neal Steven *filmmaker, musician*
Hopkins, Robert Elliott *music educator*
Horisberger, Don Hans *conductor, musician*
Korinke, James Levine, Jr. *actor*
Lamb, Gordon Howard *music educator*
Macaulay, Allen F. *radio broadcasting executive*
Marth, Mary Ellen (Kim Martin) *entertainer*
MernaLyn *actress, writer, producer*
Opelka, Gregory P. *composer, lyricist, conductor*
Ortmann, Jeffrey *theater producer, director*
Pope, Durand L. *opera manager*
Shockley, Earl McCoy (Coy Shockley) *jazz musician, educator*
Skowronski, Vincent Paul *concert violinist, recording artist, executive producer, producer classical recordings*
Thomas, John David *musician, composer, arranger, photographer, recording engineer, producer*
Virkhaus, Taavo *symphony orchestra conductor*
Wise, Robert Norman, Jr. *comedian, actor*
Wright, Gladys Stone *music educator, composer, writer*

ARTS: VISUAL

UNITED STATES

CALIFORNIA

Beverly Hills
Barrett, James Allan *photographer, author, lyricist, business owner*

ILLINOIS

Batavia
Waranius-Vass, Rosalie Jean *artist*

Belleville
Threlkeld, Dale *artist*

Bloomington
Gregor, Harold Laurence *artist, educator*

Chicago
Bender, Janet Pines *artist*
Berdich, Vera *artist, educator*
Boggess, Thomas Phillip, III *graphic arts company executive*
Castillo, Mario Enrique *artist, educator*
Desiderio-Bucci, John *designer and developer of custom exhibits*
Dompke, Norbert Frank *retired photography studio executive*
Kolkey, Gilda P. *artist*
Marino Angstadt, Marlene *fine artist, artist agent*
Mendenhall, Hans *graphic designer*
Mosak, Barbara Marcia *designer*
Rosenthal, John W. *art slides producer*
Smith, Harry Buchanan, Jr. *graphic designer, painter, photographer, writer*
Sorell-Jensen, Inez Marie *photography studio executive*
Tessing, Louise Scire *graphic designer*
Workman, Robert Peter *artist, cartoonist*

Crystal Lake
Salvesen, B(onnie) Forbes *artist*

Des Plaines
Banach, Art John *graphic artist*

Edwardsville
Harroff, William Charles Brent *artist*

Evanston
Rasco, Kay Frances *antique dealer*

Glencoe
Grabosky, Terri Jo *artist*

Glenview
Hough, Winston *artist*

Jacksonville
Calhoun, Larry Darryl *art educator*

Lake Forest
Pudles, Lynne *art historian*

Lena
Vickery, Millie Margaret *photographer, journalist*

Lisle
Barrows, Scott Thorn *medical illustrator*

Mc Henry
Siebert, Theodore Brian *sculptor*

Naperville
Fleming, Scott Thomas *commercial artist*

Normal
Kukla, Cynthia Mary *artist*

Northbrook
Farber, Phil A. *photographer, lecturer*

Onarga
Lockhart, Lisa Holmstrom *artist, librarian*

Park Ridge
Charewicz, David Michael *photographer*
Lesiak, Lucille Ann *graphic designer*

River Forest
Balgemann, Lee Alan *photographer*
Sloan, Jeanette Pasin *artist*

Rolling Meadows
Rebbeck, Lester James, Jr. *artist*

South Holland
Fota, Frank George *artist*

Villa Park
Hoegler, Jean Sandberg *artist, art educator, computer programmer, analyst*

Waukegan
Bleck, Virginia Eleanore *illustrator*

Westchester
Chukman, L(ouis) D. *artist, illustrator*

Wheaton
Lowrie, Pamela Burt *artist, educator*

Winnetka
Sharboneau, Lorna Rosina *artist, educator, author, poet, illustrator*

Zion
Hettich, Paul Joseph *theatre designer, military officer*

INDIANA

Anderson
Case, Hank *retired art educator, photographer, wine importer*
Jackson, Dennis R. *auctioneer*

Beverly Shores
Collins, Moira Ann *graphics and communications company executive, calligrapher*

Evansville
Roth, Carolyn Louise *art educator*

Fort Wayne
Lytal, Patricia Lou *art educator*

Indianapolis
Hayes, Brenda Sue Nelson *artist*
Shuck, D(ee) R(oss) *industrial exhibit designer*
Ward, Carol Buhner *textile artist, educator*
Willoughby, David Charles *photographer, forensics illustrator*

Muncie
Connally, Sandra Jane Oppy *art educator*
Jeroski, Anthony Joseph, Jr. *artist, designer*

Notre Dame
Lauck, Anthony Joseph *artist, retired art educator, priest*

Terre Haute
McDaniel, Craig Milton *art educator*

Valparaiso
Olson, Lynn *sculptor, painter, writer*

Westfield
Spurgeon, Katherine J. *library director, consultant*

Whiting
Fies, Ruth Elaine *media specialist*

IOWA

Albia
Caskey, Bethany Anne *artist*

Bettendorf
Bartels, Susan Herdman *art educator, artist*

Burlington
Trickler, Sally Jo *technical illustrator*

Davenport
Jecklin, Lois Underwood *art corporation executive, consultant*

Eldridge
Christison, Judy Ann *graphic arts trainer*

Mallard
Grethen, Cheryl Ann *artist*

Mount Pleasant
Scarff, Hope Dyall *photographer*

Oxford
Andrews, John Gerard *artist*

Waverly
Frick, Arthur Charles *art educator*

KANSAS

Hays
Kuchar, Kathleen Ann *art educator, artist*

Lawrence
Hermes, Marjory Ruth *machine embroidery and arts educator*

Leavenworth
Crary, Sharon Anne *needlework designer*

Leawood
Blitt, Rita Lea *artist*

Liberal
Rosel, Carol Ann *artist*

Ottawa
Howe, William Hugh *artist*

Wichita
Smith, Patrick S. *art history educator*

MICHIGAN

Ann Arbor
Cervenka, Barbara *art educator, artist*
Lee, Denis C. *medical sculptor and illustrator, educator*
Titlebaum, Richard Theodore *artist, author*
Weddige, Emil Albert *lithographer, art educator*

Battle Creek
Cramer, Janis R. *educational art specialist, artist*

Bruce Crossing
Waara, Maria Esther *artist*

Carleton
Falls, Kathleene Joyce *photographer*

Commerce Township
Wager, Paula Jean *artist*

Farmington Hills
Donald, Edward Milton, Jr. *graphic designer*

Glen Arbor
Hurlin, Kristin J. *illustrator*

Glenn
Rizzolo, Louis B. M. *artist, educator*

Grand Rapids
Becherer, Joseph Paul *art educator*
Blovits, Larry John *retired art educator*
Bolt, Eunice Mildred DeVries *artist*

Harsens Island
Slade, Roy *artist, college president, museum director*

Jackson
Abbott, Mary Elaine *photographer, lecturer, researcher*

Mount Pleasant
Born, James E. *art educator, sculptor*

Port Huron
Rowark, Maureen *fine arts photographer*

Roseville
Geck, Francis Joseph *furniture designer, educator, author*

Royal Oak
Eisner, Gail Ann *artist, educator*
Fredericks, Marshall Maynard *sculptor*

Saginaw
Niven, Norma Jean *artist*

Skandia
Johnson, Judy M. *artist, writer*

Southfield
Stein, Myron Sanford *art educator, social worker*

Traverse City
Hibbard, Eugene Joseph *graphic illustrator, photographer*

Troy
Corey, Glenn Michael *artist, educator*

MINNESOTA

Arden Hills
Alexander, Marjorie Anne *artist, hand papermaker, consultant*

Duluth
Ojard, Bruce Allen *photographer, educator*

Harmony
Webster, Jeffrey Leon *graphic designer*

Mankato
Frink, Brian Lee *artist, educator*

Minneapolis
Bratnober, Patricia Ray *artist*
Joseph, René Michele *artist, painter*
Preuss, Roger E(mil) *artist*

Minnetonka
La Liberte, Ann Gillis *graphic artist, consultant, designer, educator*

Monticello
Ingeman, Jerry Andrew *artist*

Saint Paul
Berg-Johnson, Karen Ann *photographer, art educator*
Godollei, Ruthann *artist, educator*
Matteson, Clarice Chris *artist, educator*
Redmond, Patrick Michael *graphic designer, art director, author, poet*

Springfield
Walworth, Sandra Marie *educator*

MISSOURI

Ballwin
Stout, Frederick Hubbell *artist*

Bridgeton
Phipps, Mark *technical illustrator*

Des Peres
Smith, Barbara Martin *art educator*

Kansas City
Eaton, Thomas Newton *cartoonist*
Lee, Margaret Norma *artist*
Mast, Kande White *artist*

Kimberling City
Greenwald, Dorothy I. *art educator*

Parkville
Bachmann, Donna Grace *painter, art educator*
Pettes, Robert Carlton *artist*

Rockaway Beach
Alkire, Betty Jo *artist, commercial real estate broker, marketing consultant*

Rogersville
Davis, Evelyn Marguerite Bailey *artist, organist, pianist*

Saint Louis
Bohan, Ruth Louise *art educator*
Dunivent, John Thomas *artist, educator*
Huffington, Rose *artist, consultant*
Kodner, Martin *art dealer, consultant*
Sauer, Jane Gottlieb *artist, educator*
Sutter, Jane Elizabeth *artist, educator*
Wandling, Marilyn Elizabeth Branson *artist, art educator*

Springfield
Delaney, Jean Marie *art educator*
King, (Jack) Weldon *photographer*

Valley Park
Sagan, Sandra Joyce *artist, educator*

Versailles
Reynolds, Sallie Blackburn *artist, civic volunteer*

NEBRASKA

Amelia
Jellico, Nancy Rose *painter, sculptor*

Dannebrog
Lamberson, Mary Jane *artist, educator*

Kearney
Hoffman, M. Kathy *graphic designer, packaging designer*

Lincoln
Wheaton, Sharon A. *designer*

North Platte
Kirk, Flora Kay Stude *artist, accountant, insurance company official*

Omaha
Bradshaw, Laurence James *artist, educator*

Wellfleet
Hughes, Michele Evalinde *artist, design company executive*

NORTH CAROLINA

Lewisville
Desley, John Whitney *medical illustrator*

Tryon
Jeanson, John Bouduin *clothing designer*

OHIO

Akron
Keener, Polly Leonard *illustrator*
Lawrence, Alice Lauffer *artist, educator*
Smith, Waring Grant *graphic arts designer, advertising executive*

Canfield
Wilson, Kay Arlene *artist*

Canton
Cavender, Jeanne McLaren *artist*

Chagrin Falls
Ross, Sally Price *artist, mural painter*

Chesterland
Wood, Ruth Diehm *artist, design consultant*

Cincinnati
Albert, Gregory Charles *artist, book editor*
Cleveland, Robert Harold *artist, designer*
Strohmaier, Thomas Edward *designer, educator, photographer*
Sullivan, Connie Castleberry *artist, photographer*
Tuttle, Martha Benedict *artist*
Weston, Phyllis Jean *art gallery director*

Cleveland
Boyer, Robert Lewis *photographer*
Brouillard, William Craig *artist, art educator*
Draznin, Wayne Michael *artist, educator*
Shoemaker, Diane Marie *goldsmith, designer*
Sloane, Phyllis Lester *artist*

Columbus
Collings, Betty *artist, curator, writer*
Fernández, Oscar A. *designer, graphic*
Goff, Wilmer Scott *photographer*
Gruliow, Agnes Forrest *artist, educator*
Sunami, John Soichi *designer*
Ultes, Elizabeth Cummings Bruce *artist, retired art historian and librarian*

Dayton
Myers, Jack Fredrick *artist, educator, author*
Schorgl, Thomas Barry *arts administrator*
Zahner, Mary Anne *art educator*

Euclid
Hill, Robyn Lesley *artist, designer*

Galion
Drake, Michael W. *designer*

Mount Gilead
Fitzpatrick, Valda *artist*

Oberlin
Lermond, Charles Afton *artist, educator*
Reinoehl, Richard Louis *artist*

Oxford
Dietrich, Linnea Sandberg Stonesifer *art educator*
Yost, Nancy Runyon *artist, designer, art educator*

Pepper Pike
Rule-Hoffman, Richard Carl *art therapist, educator, counselor*

Perrysburg
Autry, Carolyn *artist, art history educator*

Reynoldsburg
Boiman, Donna Rae *artist, art academy executive*

Shaker Heights
McKenna, Kathleen Kwasnik *artist*

Springfield
Patterson, Martha Ellen *artist, art educator*

Toledo
Brower, James Calvin *graphic artist, painter*
Jenkins, George Henry *photographer, educator, writer*
Orloff, Deborah Beth *art educator, photography program director*

West Alexandria
Sappington, Lynda Louisa Burton *sculptor, freelance writer, photographer*

OKLAHOMA

Edmond
Watson, James Robert *design educator*

OREGON

Eugene
Stafford, Joyce Ruth *artist*

SOUTH DAKOTA

Sioux Falls
DeGeus, Wendell Ray *photographer*

WISCONSIN

Fish Creek
Butler, Geraldine Heiskell (Gerri Butler) *designer, artist*

Gleason
Raash, Kathleen Forecki *artist*

Iola
Rosenberger, Carolyn A. *art educator*

Kenosha
Michetti, Susan Jane *media relations director, video producer, communications consultant*

Madison
Launder, Yolanda Marie *graphic design director*

Mequon
Smith, Leila Hentzen *artist*

Milwaukee
Klein, Wolfgang *art educator*
Poczos, Gary Michael (A.B. Seymore) *author, illustrator*

Oshkosh
Smith, Merilyn Roberta *art educator*

Princeton
Sylke, Loretta Clara *artist*

Sturgeon Bay
Becker, Bettie Geraldine *artist*

Verona
Handler, Audrey Solomon *artist, educator*

Wausau
Fleming, Thomas Michael *artist, educator*

West Allis
Porter, Russell Dennis *marine and railroad artist and historian*

Whitewater
Gauger, Michele Roberta *photographer, studio administrator, corporate executive*

Winneconne
Gust, Joyce Jane *artist*

CANADA

ONTARIO

Red Lake
Zaikow, Larry J. *painter*

ADDRESS UNPUBLISHED

August, Robert William *designer*
Benzle, Curtis Munhall *artist, art educator*
Bradley, Marilynne Gail *advertising executive, advertising educator*
Bunnell, Sandra Jean *jewelry designer*
Carson, Gail Maria *fashion designer, marketing consultant*
Evens, Michelle Jeanette *photographer*
Havens, Keith Cornell *artist*
Jordan, Sharie Cecilia *industrial artist*
Kawer, Dina Rochelle *artist*
Kohn, Karen Josephine *graphic and exhibition designer*
Kyle, Gene Magerl *merchandise presentation artist*
Lekan, Briana Marker *photographer*
Lustig, Edith Perkins *freelance photographer*
Mason, Robert Thomas *theatrical lighting designer, writer*
Matlow, Linda Monique *photographic agency executive, publishing executive*
Maxwell, Ruth Elaine *artist, interior designer, decorative painter*
Ostlund, Richard Allen *designer*
Pettit, Sue *artist*
Rankin, Scott David *artist, educator*
Rataj, Elizabeth Ann *artist*
Reid, Geraldine Wold (Geraldine Reid Skjervold) *artist*
Schoene, Mary Patricia *artist*
Schultz, Gerald A. (Jerry Schultz) *graphic designer*
Slaughter, James Luther, III *graphic designer*
Tasse, Marie Jeanne *retired art educator*
Terpening, Virginia Ann *artist*
Torrison, William Rahr *photographer*
Vollmer, Howard Robert *artist, photographer*

ASSOCIATIONS AND ORGANIZATIONS. *See also* specific fields.

UNITED STATES

ARIZONA

Fountain Hills
Deutsch, William Reaugh *trade association executive*

Scottsdale
Muller, H(enry) Nicholas, III *foundation executive*

CALIFORNIA

Claremont
Warder, Michael Young *think tank executive*

Newport Beach
Maxwell, Patricia Joy *fund raising executive*

Palm Desert
O'Rourke, Joan B. Doty Werthman *educational administrator*

DISTRICT OF COLUMBIA

Washington
Hudnut, William Herbert, III *senior resident fellow, political scientist*

ILLINOIS

Altamont
Davis, Cornelia Haven Casey *civic leader*

Belleville
Brian, Patricia Ann *social services administrator*
Harper, Joseph J. *social welfare specialist*
McNeill, Donald Aubrey *labor union administrator*

Bellwood
Szilagyi-Hawkins, Elizabeth Maria *social services administrator*

Belvidere
Luhman, William Simon *community development administrator*

Blue Island
Vilim, John Robert *social services administrator*

Carlinville
Goudy, Josephine Gray *social services administrator*

Channatton
Hensley, Leo Basil *foundation administrator*

Chicago
Allen, Lynn Elizabeth *foundation director*
Boyke, Paul William *association executive*
Braden, William Lou *non-profit agency manager*
Chacko, Samuel *association official*
Connelly, John Dooley *social service organization executive*
Cyr, Arthur *professional society administrator*
Feldstein, Charles Robert *fund raising consultant*
Fetridge, Bonnie-Jean Clark (Mrs. William Harrison Fetridge) *civic volunteer*
Ford, Mary Alice *city employee*
Harris, Joan White *foundation officer, arts administrator*
Harris, John Chester *educational charity administrator, book editor, screen writer, movie script writer*
Harvey, Katherine Abler *civic worker*
Hendrickson, John Edward *social services association executive*
Hersh, William *social services administrator*
Hess, G(eorge) Alfred, Jr. *non-profit educational association administrator*
Hurley, John G. *foundation executive*
Kelly, Jerry Bob *social services administrator*
Klaus, Joan McAdams *association administrator*
Knezovich, Jeffrey Paul *professional association executive*
Leff, Deborah *foundation executive*
Lingenfelter, Paul Eugene *foundation administrator*
McLin, Nathaniel, Jr. *civic worker*
Mercer, David Robinson *cultural organization administrator*
Milstein, Robert Arlen *fund development administrator, consultant*
Murstein, Denis *human services administrator*
Psiharis, John Peter *community services executive*
Scalish, Frank Anthony *labor union administrator*
Schaefer, Helene G(eraldine) *social services professional*
Schimberg, Barbara Hodes *organizational development consultant*
Sigmon, Joyce Elizabeth *professional society administrator*
Stanton, Janet Lyn *social service administrator*
Sullivan, James Michael *association executive*
Vogelzang, Jeanne Marie *professional association executive, lawyer*
Wray, David Lynn *association executive*
Wright, Helen Kennedy *professional association administrator, publisher, editor, librarian*
Wysocki, Theodore Joseph, Jr. *non-profit organization executive*

Clarendon Hills
Van Ausdall, Robert Loren *association administrator*

Crystal Lake
Linklater, Isabelle Stanislawa Yarosh-Galazka (Lee Linklater) *foundation administrator*

Decatur
Outcalt, Merlin Brewer *child care center administrator, consultant*

Deerfield
Stavropoulos, Rose Mary Grant *community activist, volunteer*

Des Plaines
Pannke, Peggy M. *insurance agency executive*
Quellmalz, Frederick *foundation executive, editor*

Dolton
Voliva, Sharon Lee (Grossman) *community volunteer, child and education advocate*

Evanston
Circle, Lilias Wagner *honor society administrator*
Kreml, Franklin Martin *educational administrator, association executive*

Frankfort
Glatz, Christine Elizabeth *association administrator*

Glen Ellyn
Jens, Elizabeth Lee Shafer (Mrs. Arthur M. Jens, Jr.) *civic worker*

Godfrey
Hutchinson-Gross, Dorothy A. *non-profit organization administrator*
Sheppard, Joan Locker *activist*

Grayslake
Edwards, Charles Arthur *fundraising consultant*

Hoffman Estates
Rowe, Donald Eugene *fundraising consultant*

Homewood
Barsuk, Sidney Alan *fundraising executive*

Kankakee
Gurney, Pamela Kay *social services official*

Lake Forest
Smith, Wendy L. *foundation executive*
Taylor, Barbara Ann *educational consultant*

Lake Villa
Powers, Kathryn Dolores *social services administrator*

Macomb
Watson, Joyce Ann *foundation administrator*

Mascoutah
Richter, Mary Kaye *foundation director*

Mattoon
Foster, David Raymond *economic development organization administrator*

Mooseheart
Ross, Donald Hugh *fraternal organization executive*

Naperville
L'Allier, James Joseph *educational multimedia company executive, instructional designer*

Palatine
Bassi, Suzanne H. *volunteer*

Park Ridge
Bailey, Marianne Therese *social service administrator*
Ewald, Robert Frederick *insurance association executive*
Howlett, Phyllis Lou *athletics conference administrator*

Pekin
McDonnell, Rosemary Cynthia *special populations programmer*

Peoria
Wisecarver, Ron B. *association executive, consultant*

Percy
Rice, Charles Dale *labor relations specialist, writer*

River Forest
Walker, David Francis *social services administrator*

Riverside
Dengler, Robert Anthony *professional association executive*

Rock Falls
Julifs, Sandra Jean *community action agency executive*

Rock Island
Fainter, Lynda Jean *organization executive*

Skokie
Peurye-Hissong, Celene Nan *foundation executive*

Springfield
Barton, Florin Edward *retired social services administrator*
Blaauw, Russell Wayne *legislative liaison*
Blackman, Jeanne A. *policy advisor*
Flickinger, Theodore Blair *association administrator*
Kempiners, William Lee *professional association executive*
Knoepfle, Margaret Sower *community organizer, educator, writer*
Puckett, Carlissa Roseann *non-profit association executive*
Ramey, Karen Marie *political organization consultant*
Sheriff, Kenneth Wayne *social services administrator*

Urbana
Hubbard, Frances Pauline Leonhardt *bowling executive*
Sturtevant, William T. *fundraising executive, consultant*

Wilmette
Brink, Marion Francis *trade association administrator*

Winnetka
Owens, Luvie Moore *association executive*

INDIANA

Bloomington
Wilson, Kathy Kay *foundation executive*

Columbus
Zemel, David Michael *charitable organization adminstrator, human services educator*

Crown Point
Moreno, Susan Jayne *foundation adminstrator*

Evansville
Early, Judith K. *program evaluation director*
Halterman, Martha Lee *social services administrator, counselor*

Fort Wayne
Chapman, Paula Anne *cultural organization administrator*

Greenwood
Means, George Robert *organization executive*

Hanna
Stephenson, Dorothy Maxine *volunteer*

Indianapolis
Barcus, Robert Gene *educational association administrator*
Braun, Robert Clare *retired association and advertising executive*
Burnett, Judith Jane *foundation administrator, consultant*
Dennis, William Cullen *foundation officer*
Dickeson, Ludmila Weir *organization administrator*
Earnhart, Don Brady *retired charitable foundation executive*
Hammock, Perry T. *foundation executive*
Harbron, Garrett Lee *educational association executive*
Holland, Richard Manson *educational foundation executive*
Honor, Noël Evans *social services supervisor*
Kolda, Thomas Joseph *non-profit organization executive*
Kreegar, Phillip Keith *educational administrator*
Maxwell, Florence Hinshaw *civic worker*
Plotinsky, Anita H. *research organization executive*
Powers, James Stevenson *state adjutant*
Sweezy, John William *political party official*
Throgmartin, Dianne *educational foundation administrator*

Lafayette
Scaletta, Helen Marguerite *volunteer*

Monroeville
Howard, Stephen Raymond *apartment project manager*

Muncie
Bakken, Douglas Adair *foundation executive*

North Vernon
Williams, John Albert *developmental disabilities agency director*

Plainfield
Christopher, Gregory Alan *professional society executive*

Portage
Paugh, C(harles) Michael *political activist*

Santa Claus
Platthy, Jeno *cultural association executive*

South Bend
Hunt, Mary Reilly *organization executive*

Terre Haute
Aldridge, Sandra *civic volunteer*

Valparaiso
Bourdelais, Alfred Arthur *social services administrator*

West Lafayette
Watlington, Sarah Jane *community volunteer, retired military officer*

IOWA

Cedar Rapids
Berry, Roberta Mildred *civic worker*
Brandt, John Edward *human services administrator*
Huber, Rita Norma *civic worker*
Whipple, William Perry *foundation administrator*

Center Point
Neenan, Thomas Francis *association executive, consultant*

Clive
Barnes, Ernie L. *fundraiser*

Council Bluffs
Slevin, Tara Margaruite *volunteer coordinator*

Davenport
Campagna, Timothy Nicholas *institute executive*

Des Moines
Blake, Darlene Evelyn *political worker, consultant, educator, author*
Daggett, Horace Clinton *retired state legislator*
Hutchison, Charlotte Pancoast (Sherry Hutchison) *civic worker*
Mulqueen, Robert Edward *public policy analyst*
Sutton, James Hercules *educational association administrator*
Womack, Doug C. *labor union representative*

Dubuque
Sheehy, Patrick David *organizational and fundraising consultant*

Kellogg
Anderson, Dale C. *scouting executive, travel consultant*

Larchwood
Zangger, Russell George *organization executive, flying school executive*

West Branch
Forsythe, Patricia Hays *development professional*

KANSAS

Junction City
Nelson, Steven Frank *social services administrator*

Kansas City
Steineger, Margaret Leisy *non-profit organization officer*

Larned
Hewson, Mary McDonald *civic volunteer*

Lawrence
Thompson, Thomas Jay *association executive*

North Kansas City
Burger, Stephen E. *religious organization executive*

Overland Park
Gale, Pamela Lynn Beckman *organization executive*
Green, John Lafayette, Jr. *education executive*
Smith, Phyllis Elizabeth *community volunteer*

Prairie Village
Richards, Karen Kirk *association executive*

Rose Hill
Morrison, Carole Lynne *community volunteer*

Topeka
Hayashi, Eric *art association administrator*
Menninger, Roy Wright *medical foundation executive, psychiatrist*
Palace, Thomas Michael *trade association executive*

Wichita
Myers, John Moore *fraternal organization administrator*
Timmerman, Dora Mae *community volunteer, art advocate*

MICHIGAN

Adrian
Henricks, Roger Lee *social services administrator*

Alma
Kinkead, Verda Christine *non-profit organization executive, consultant*

Ann Arbor
Porter, John Wilson *education executive*

Bay City
Grew, Kimberly Ann *social service administrator*

Brighton
Darlington, Judith Mabel *clinical social worker, Christian counselor*

Canton
Porter, Karen Collins *non-profit organization administrator, counselor*

Detroit
Knight, Catherine O'Connor *developer, fundraiser*
Noland, Mariam Charl *foundation executive*
Proctor, Valerie Floyd *educational administrator*
Reid, Baxter Ellis, Jr. *labor union representative*

East Lansing
Mitstifer, Dorothy Irwin *honor society administrator*

Flint
Belcher, Max *social services administrator*

Grosse Pointe Shores
Smith, Frank Earl *retired association executive*

Jackson
Courtney, Jerry L. *social welfare administrator*
Walker, Gaylord Thompson *non-profit organization administrator*

Lansing
Harbage, Peter Todd *political organization worker*

Oak Park
Piper, Annette Cleone *social services administrator, researcher*

Okemos
Luecke, Eleanor Virginia Rohrbacher *civic volunteer*

Pontiac
Laing, James Thomas *charitable association administrator*

Rochester
Davis, Kathryn Ward *fundraising executive*

Saint Joseph
Phenix, Gloria Gayle *educational association administrator*

Southgate
Jacob, Robert Edward *small business and non-profit tax consultant*

Spring Arbor
Thompson, Stanley Burton *foundation administrator*

Sylvan Lake
Davison, Luella May *organization executive, retired writer*

Troy
Dunlap, Richard Lowell *foundation administrator, church organist*

Ypsilanti
Barr, Marlene Joy *volunteer*

MINNESOTA

Britt
Grubich, Donald Nicholas *retired association administrator*

Minneapolis
Blake, John Emerson *youth organization administrator*
Casselman, Barry *political correspondent, nonprofit administrator, author*
Ericson, Richard Charles *social service agency executive*
Halfhill, Robert Wakefield *volunteer association executive*
Herbison, Priscilla Joan *public policy and law educator, consultant*
Schanfield, Fannie Schwartz *community volunteer*
Schroeder, Jon Henry *public affairs professional*
Speer, Nancy Girouard *educational administrator*

Minnetonka
Fogelberg, Paul Alan *continuing education company executive*

Rochester
Kaskubar, Bruce Edward *foundation executive*
Lawrence, David Wilson *foundation executive*

Roseville
Hughes, Jerome Michael *education foundation executive*

Saint Paul
Archabal, Nina M(archetti) *historical society director*
Bethke, Jesse *non-profit organization executive*
Calvin, Rochelle Ann *development association adminstrator*
Dixon, Sally Foy *arts administrator*
Doermann, Humphrey *foundation administrator*
Fesler, David Richard *foundation director*
Papas, Robert Felton *fraternal organization administrator*
Parsons, Mark Frederick *fundraiser*
Pruzan, Irene *arts administrator, music educator, flutist, marketing and public relations specialist*

Spicer
Jacobson, Phyllis Mae *development resource director*

MISSOURI

Ballwin
Horn, Joan Kelly *political research and consulting firm executive*

Bolivar
Rice, Cindy G. *foundation development director*

Bridgeton
Kenison, Raymond Robert *fraternal organization administrator, director*
Martin, Russell Lee *social service executive*

Bucklin
Payne, Flora Fern *retired social service administrator*

Columbia
Lang, Mary Lou *educational administrator*

Elkland
Hoag, Edwin *advocate for the disabled*

Hallsville
McFate, Kenneth Leverne *trade association administrator*

Independence
Hettrick, Richard Harry *community organizer*
Potts, Barbara Joyce *historical society executive*

Ironton
Douma, Harry Hein *social service agency administrator*

Jefferson City
Fine, Dwight Lyle *lobbyist*
Goller, Sue Lynne *government consultant, researcher*

Kansas City
Burt, Robert Eugene *civic organization administrator*
Dickenson, H. H. *professional society administrator*
Slater, William Adcock *social services organization executive*
Switzer, Samuel Thomas *non-profit administrator*
Wingfield, Laura Allison Ross *fraternal organization executive*

Kimberling City
Stott, Diana Ellen *social services advocate*

Marshall
Tweito, Eleanor Marie *social services administrator, educator*
Zarrelli, Margaret Cott *community action agency administrator*

Maysville
Bram, Isabelle Mary Rickey McDonough (Mrs. John Bram) *civic worker*

Osage Beach
CasaSanta, Joseph John, III *association director*

Richmond Heights
Chandler, James Barton *international education consultant*

Saint Joseph
Beatty, Judy Iola Spencer *educational specialist*

Saint Louis
Crosslin, Anna Eriko *association executive*
Duhme, Carol McCarthy *civic worker*
McKenzie, Andrew *union administrator*
Rich, Patricia *non-profit executive*
Robins, Marjorie McCarthy (Mrs. George Kenneth Robins) *civic worker*
Schulte, William Paul *religious fund raiser*
Strutz, Thomas Edward *association administrator*
Sutter, Elizabeth Henby (Mrs. Richard A. Sutter) *civic leader, management company executive*
Vickroy, William Rees, II *civic volunteer, investor*
Whelan, Donald Joseph *fundraising executive*

Springfield
Himstedt, Ronald Eugene *union official*
Morris, Ann Haseltine Jones *social welfare administrator*
Sable, Louis Anthony *trade association executive*

Webster Groves
Johnson, Leif O. *political activist*

NEBRASKA

Bancroft
Neihardt, Hilda *foundation administrator, writer*

Bellevue
Leach, Christine Elaine *technical support executive*

Cozad
Roberts, Judith Virginia *social worker*

Grand Island
Miller, Thomas B. *educational administrator*

Harrison
Coffee, Virginia Claire *civic worker, former mayor*

Lincoln
Crosby, LaVon Kehoe Stuart *civic leader*
Swartz, Jack *fraternal organization administrator*

Omaha
Ansorge, Luella M. *retired association administrator*
Flanery, Gail Linden *administrator*
Moore, Terry Lee *organized labor administrator*
Prince, Frances Anne Kiely *civic worker*

Seward
Vrana, Verlon Kenneth *professional society administrator, conservationist*

NEVADA

Las Vegas
Wuehle, Edwin Everett *association executive*

NORTH CAROLINA

Montreat
Robinson, Spencer, Jr. *retired service club executive, accountant*

NORTH DAKOTA

Bismarck
Atkinson, Patrick John *foundation executive, educator*
Murry, Barbara R. *social services administrator, public administrator*
Timmins, Richard Haseltine *foundation executive, educator*

Fargo
Barlow, Howard C. *social services administrator*

Minot
Moe, Vida Delores *civic worker*

OHIO

Akron
Frank, John V. *foundation executive*

Canal Winchester
Bacus, Terrence Lee *labor relations consultant*

Canton
Schreiber, Barbara Louise *civic worker*

Chagrin Falls
Vail, Iris Jennings *civic worker*

Cincinnati
Day, Lyn Tibbits *fundraising consultant*
Hiatt, Marjorie McCullough *service organization executive*
Norman, Peter Minert *fundraising consulting company executive*
Ruehlmann, Virginia Juergens *foundation administrator, writer*
Sowder, Fred Allen *foundation administrator, alphabet specialist*

Cleveland
Buescher, Thomas Paul *labor market analyst*
Calabrese, Leonard M. *social services administrator*
Cook, Anda Suna *civil rights advocate*
Cooper, James Clinton *social services administrator, consultant*
Garrison, William Lloyd *cemetery executive*
Joseph, Charles Homer, III *emergency services director*
Kittredge, Marie *non-profit housing development manager*
Lord, James Gregory *marketing and fundraising consultant*
Russell, Valerie Eileen *social service executive*

College Corner
Gilmore, Robert Witter *foundation administrator*

Columbus
Barker, Judy *foundation executive*
Benton-Borghi, Beatrice Hope *educational consultant, author, publisher*
Blair, William Travis (Bud Blair) *retired organization executive*
Dukas, Philip Alexander *association executive*
O'Sullivan, Michael David *foundation executive*
Patrick, Jane Austin *association executive*
Sharp, Paul David *institute administrator*
Woods, Gwendolyn Lenar *parole program administrator*

Dayton
Briggs, James Stemen, Jr. *association executive*
Crowe, Shelby *educational specialist, consultant*
Daley, Robert Emmett *foundation executive, retired*
McDonald, Bronce William *community activist, advocate*
Williams, Walker Richard, Jr. *social services administrator*

Dublin
Wurschmidt, Todd Neil *association executive*

Elyria
Tukufu, Darryl Sekou *social issues advocate, educator*

Girard
Wolanin, Sophie Mae *civic worker, tutor, scholar, lecturer*

Lakewood
Macfarlane, William Noble, Jr. *foundation executive*

Lima
Lauer, Ann Riley *community volunteer*

Medina
Giebner, Cara Rae *trade association administrator*

Oberlin
Ramp, Marjorie Jean Sumerwell *civic worker*

Shaker Heights
Brucken, Lois Gilbert *volunteer*

University Heights
Wenk, Philip Andrew *foundation administrator, consultant*

Westerville
Maxwell, Richard Eugene *educational association administrator*

Westlake
Murphy, Michele Susan *non-profit agency executive*

Willoughby
Bromelmeier, Gale Marie *retired nursing association administrator*

Worthington
Suber, Tommie Lee *union organizer, writer*

Youngstown
Westenbarger, Don Edward *retired association executive*

SOUTH DAKOTA

Pierre
Lewis, Lona Lee *association executive, educator*
Schumacher, Ervin *retired social services administrator*

TEXAS

Houston
Bush, Barbara Pierce *volunteer, wife of former President of the United States*

WISCONSIN

Balsam Lake
Mattson, Carol Linnette *social services administrator*

Beloit
Thomas Topp, Margaret Ann *educational administrator, art educator*

Brookfield
Wiegand, James Richard *association executive*

Custer
Spencer, John Robert *social service administrator*

Fond Du Lac
Reitemeier, Joseph Richard *municipal association executive*

Hales Corners
Wesener, Barbara Ann *trade association executive*

Janesville
Posner, Linda Rosanne *charity volunteer, educator*

Kenosha
Adler, Seymour Jack *social services administrator*

Madison
Brennan, Robert Walter *association executive*
Collins, Richard Ward *labor union administrator, secondary education educator*
Woit, Kathleen E. *fund developer*

Mequon
Ambelang, Joel Raymond *social worker*

Milwaukee
Hutchings, S. Douglas *financial development professional*
Joyce, Michael Stewart *foundation executive, political science educator*

Monroe
Brown, Sandra Lee *educational consultant, watercolorist*

Oconomowoc
Kaye, Gerard W. *association executive*

Shawano
Lyon, Thomas L. *agricultural organization administrator*

Stoughton
Sundling, Mary Jo *community volunteer*

Wausau
Connor, Mary Roddis *foundation administrator*

Wisconsin Dells
Laatsch, Audrey Frieda *volunteer, consultant*

ADDRESS UNPUBLISHED

Albrecht, Diane D. *fundraiser*
Bay, Thomas Robert *clinical social worker*
Beatty, Frances *civic worker*
Chernish, Lelia Margaret *developer, fundraiser*
Corderman, Douglas George *retired non-profit organization executive*
Deinzer, George William *public welfare organization administrator*
Flapan, Jan *civic worker*
Florian, Marianna Bolognesi *civic leader*
Foley, Casey Charles *non-profit executive*
Franklin, Margaret Lavona Barnum (Mrs. C. Benjamin Franklin) *civic leader*
Gendreau, Margot Lynn *lobbyist*
Gilchrest, Thornton Charles *retired association executive*
Goldman, Rachel Bok *civic volunteer*
Hadas, Julia Ann *social services administrator*
Haessly, Jacqueline *peace and family life education specialist, writer, consultant*
Hardin, Martha Love Wood *civic leader*
Heitzman, Lynn Needham *labor relations consultant, educator*
Jost, Lee Fred *employee benefits consultant*
Kabat, Linda Georgette *civic leader*
Ketchum, Irene Frances *library trustee*
Koller, Karen Kathryn *social services administrator*
Laird, Bradley Duane *social services administrator, psychotherapist*
Meek, Forrest Burns *educational administrator, trading company executive*
Palmer, Jocelyn Beth *civic worker*
Saario, Terry Natalie Tinson *foundation executive*
Schulz, Kraig Franklyn *Peace Corps volunteer*
Sebela, Vicki D. *association executive, freelance writer*
Stephens, Gay *public administrator*
Stuever, Anita Carol *trade association executive*
Waller, Ephraim Everett *retired professional association executive*
Wright, Elizabeth Anne *foundation administrator*

ATHLETICS

UNITED STATES

ALABAMA

Mobile
Jackson, Bo (Vincent Edward Jackson) *professional baseball, former football player*

CALIFORNIA

Beverly Hills
Winfield, David Mark *former professional baseball player, commentator*

El Segundo
Ball, Jerry Lee *professional football player*

Los Angeles
Kelly, Roberto Conrado (Bobby Kelly) *professional baseball player*

COLORADO

Colorado Springs
Schultz, Richard Dale *national athletic organizations executive*

Englewood
Perry, Michael Dean *professional football player*

GEORGIA

Atlanta
Laettner, Christian Donald *professional basketball player*

ILLINOIS

Alsip
Hammer, Patrick *scuba diving educator*

Charleston
Ankenbrand, Larry Joseph *physical education educator*

Chicago
Abbott, Jim (James Anthony Abbott) *baseball player*
Belfour, Ed *professional hockey player*
Cannon, Bennie Marvin *physical education educator*
Einhorn, Edward Martin (Eddie Einhorn) *professional baseball team executive*
Grace, Mark Eugene *professional baseball player*
Johnson, Howard Michael *professional baseball player*
Jordan, Michael Jeffery *professional basketball player, retired baseball player*
Krause, Jerry (Jerome Richard Krause) *professional basketball team executive*
Lee, Marva Jean *physical education educator, counseling administrator, family life education consultant*
Pippen, Scottie *professional basketball player*
Reinsdorf, Jerry Michael *professional sports teams executive, real estate executive, lawyer, accountant*
Riggleman, James David *professional baseball team manager*
Thomas, Frank Edward *professional baseball player*
Ventura, Robin Mark *professional baseball player*

Highland Park
Mordini, Marilyn Heuer *physical education educator*

Lake Forest
McCaskey, Michael B. *professional football team executive*

Lincolnshire
Schauble, John Eugene *physical education educator*

Mundelein
Carr, Bonnie Jean *professional ice skater*

Sterling
Moran, Joan Jensen *physical education and health educator*

Urbana
Sydnor, Synthia *kinesiology educator*

INDIANA

Bloomington
Knight, Bob *college basketball coach*

Indianapolis
Irsay, James Steven *professional football team executive*

Muncie
Shondell, Donald Stuart *physical education educator*

Notre Dame
Holtz, Louis Leo *college football coach*

IOWA

Des Moines
Foster, James Franklin *professional sports management executive*

KANSAS

Lawrence
Green, Diana Beesley *athletic company executive*

Mission Woods
Bork, Tricia *athletics association administrator*

North Newton
Rogers, George, III *college dean, athletic director, educator*

Shawnee Mission
Brown, Arnold Harris *professional athlete management executive*

MARYLAND

Baltimore
Johnson, Davey (David Allen Johnson) *baseball team manager*

MICHIGAN

Auburn Hills
Robertson, Alvin Cyrrale *professional basketball player*

Detroit
Bowman, Scotty *professional hockey coach*
Coffey, Paul *professional hockey player*
Fielder, Cecil Grant *professional baseball player*
Fryman, David Travis *professional baseball player*
Ilitch, Marian *professional hockey team executive*
Roberts, Peter Allen *physical education educator*
Yzerman, Steve *professional hockey player*

East Lansing
Perles, George Julius *coach, educator*

Mount Pleasant
Kirchner, Richard Jay *retired physical education educator*

Pontiac
Blades, Horatio Benedict (Bennie Blades) *professional football player*
Brown, Lomas, Jr. *professional football player*
Fontes, Wayne *professional football team head coach*
Gray, Mel *professional football player*
Sanders, Barry *football player*
Spielman, Chris *professional football player*

MINNESOTA

Bloomington
Allen, Mary Louise Hook *physical education educator*
MacLean, Hugh Cameron *bridge professional, international bridge master*

Coon Rapids
Schommer, Dennis Harold *physical education educator*

Duluth
McLeod, Bruce M. *sports association executive*

Eden Prairie
Headrick, Roger Lewis *professional sports executive*
McDaniel, Randall Cornell *professional football player*

Minneapolis
Kelly, Tom (Jay Thomas Kelly) *major league baseball club manager*
Mack, Shane Lee *professional baseball player, olympic athlete*
Pohlad, Carl R. *professional baseball team executive, bottling company executive*

Saint Louis Park
Ratner, Harvey *health club owner, operator*

Saint Paul
Foster, Pamela Anne *adapted physical education educator*

MISSOURI

Florissant
Weber, Dick A. *bowler*

Kansas City
Appier, (Robert) Kevin *professional baseball player*
Brett, George Howard *baseball executive, former professional baseball player*
Hanover, R(aymond) Scott *physical education trainer*
Hunt, Lamar *professional football team executive*
Montgomery, Jeffrey Thomas *professional baseball player*
Robinson, Spencer T. (Herk Robinson) *professional baseball team executive*
Smith, Neil *professional football player*
Steadman, Jack W. *professional football team executive*

Lees Summit
Ferguson, Julie Ann *physical education educator*

Maryville
Mull, Sandra Sue *health, physical education and recreation educator*

Saint Louis
Caron, Ronald Jacques *professional sports team executive*
Cooper, Scott Kendrick *professional baseball player*
Keough, Ty *soccer coach*
Quinn, Jack J. *professional hockey team executive*
Smith, Ozzie (Osborne Earl Smith) *professional baseball player*

NEBRASKA

Lincoln
Ward, Phillip Charles *physical education educator*

Norfolk
Masteller, Bruce Allen *exercise specialist*

Omaha
Gottschalk, John E. *newspaper publishing executive*

NEW YORK

Bronx
Zimmer, Donald William *coach professional athletics, former professional baseball manager*

OHIO

Akron
Workman, Gayle Jean *physical education educator*

Berea
Byner, Earnest Alexander *professional football player*
Rypien, Mark Robert *professional football player*

Cadiz
Hoffman, Barbara Jo *health and physical education educator, home economist*

Canton
Elliott, Peter R. *athletic organization executive*

Cincinnati
Gant, Ron (Ronald Edwin Gant) *professional baseball player*
Larkin, Barry Louis *professional baseball player*
Schott, Marge *professional baseball team executive*

Cleveland
Alomar, Sandy, Jr. (Santos Velazquez Alomar) *professional baseball player*
Baerga, Carlos Obed Ortiz *professional baseball player*
Belle, Albert Jojuan *professional baseball player*
Gordon, Larry David *professional sports team owner, broadcast executive*
Hargrove, Mike (Dudley Michael Hargrove) *professional baseball team manager*
Hershiser, Orel Leonard, IV *professional baseball player*
McDowell, Jack Burns *professional baseball player*
Murray, Eddie Clarence *professional baseball player*

Delaware
Snouffer, Chet Alan *coach, manufacturing executive*

New Concord
Goodwin, Charles Pemberton *athletic trainer*

Shaker Heights
Morgan, Jerry *physical education educator, consultant*

Youngstown
DeBartolo, Edward John, Jr. *professional football team owner, real estate developer*

PENNSYLVANIA

Philadelphia
Cheveldae, Tim *professional hockey player*
Jefferies, Gregory Scott *professional baseball player*

SOUTH DAKOTA

Sioux Falls
Oakland, Carol Jean *athletic development administrator*

WISCONSIN

Coon Valley
Riness, Clay Morgan *fishing guide, educator*

Green Bay
Holmgren, Mike *professional football coach*
Parins, Robert James *professional football team executive, judge*
White, Reggie (Reginald Howard White) *professional* football player

Milwaukee
Selig, Allan H. (Bud Selig) *professional baseball team executive*
Steinmiller, John F. *professional basketball team executive*

Stevens Point
Garber, David J. *sports association executive, marketing consultant*

ADDRESS UNPUBLISHED

Bevington, Terry Paul *professional baseball manager*
Carrier, Mark Anthony *professional football player*
Davidson, Bonnie Jean *gymnastics educator, sports management consultant*
Dent, Richard Lamar *professional football player*
Doleman, Christopher John *professional football player*
Herman, Wayne Delton *rodeo entertainer*
Mason, Linda *physical education educator, basketball coach*
Modano, Michael *professional hockey player*
Paddock, John *professional hockey team head coach*
Pierce, Ricky Charles *professional basketball player*
Price, (William) Mark *professional basketball player*
Stark, Rohn Taylor *professional football player*
Tewksbury, Robert Alan *professional baseball player*
Thomas, Isiah Lord, III *former professional basketball player, basketball team executive*

BUSINESS. *See* **FINANCE; INDUSTRY.**

COMMUNICATIONS. *See* **COMMUNICATIONS MEDIA; INDUSTRY: SERVICE.**

COMMUNICATIONS MEDIA. *See also* ARTS: LITERARY.

UNITED STATES

COLORADO

Dillon
Follett, Robert John Richard *publisher*

ILLINOIS

Alton
Hillig, Terry Thomas *journalist*

Arlington Heights
Baumann, Daniel E. *newspaper executive*
Becker, Gerald Arthur *publisher*
Lampinen, John A. *newspaper editor*
Paddock, Stuart R., Jr. *publishing executive*
Ray, Douglas *newspaper editor*

Bloomington
Cheever, Raymond Craig *publisher, editor*

Brookfield
Hansen, Donald Marty *journalist, accountant*

Burr Ridge
Sund, Jeffrey Owen *publishing company executive*

Carbondale
Paddon, Anna Ruth Olsen *journalist, educator*
Spellman, Robert Luther *journalism educator*

Champaign
Foreman, John Richard *newspaper editor*
Strang, Philip Andrew *recording company executive*
Watts, Robert Allan *publisher, lawyer*

Chicago
Anderson, Karl Stephen *newspaper executive*
Andries, Linda J. *publishing director*
Barks, Horace Bushnell *publisher, editor*
Barr, James, IV *publishing executive, book*
Beck, Joan Wagner *journalist*
Berry, J(ames) Christopher *journalist, radio station executive*
Botts, Elizabeth Doris *newspaper editor*
Britton, Dennis A. *newspaper editor, newspaper executive*
Brumback, Charles Tiedtke *retired newpaper executive*
Brummel, Mark Joseph *magazine editor*
Callaway, Karen A(lice) *journalist*
Cameron, William Johnson *broadcasting executive*
Camp, Paul Allen *publisher, consultant, writer*
Campbell, Michelle Dawn Clara *journalist*
Camper, John Jacob *writer, university administrator*
Cappo, Joseph C. *publisher*
Ciccone, Richard *newspaper editor*
Cohn, Scott Howard *television and radio news correspondent*
Corfman, Thomas A. *editor, newspaper*
Daume, Daphne Marie *editor*
Dee, Ivan Richard *book publisher*
Dodds, Claudette La Vonn *radio executive and consultant*
Dold, Robert Bruce *journalist*
Downey, Joseph Francis *publishing executive*
Eady, Lydia Davis *publishing executive*
Ebert, Roger Joseph *film critic*
Elitzik, Paul *publishing executive*
Fair, Hudson Randolph *recording company executive*
Fetridge, Clark Worthington *publisher*
Field, Edward *journalist*
Freeman, Sandra Marlene *publishing executive*
Frisbie, Richard Patrick *communications consultant, author*
Fuller, Jack William *writer, newspaper executive*
Gaines, William Chester *journalist*
Garbo, Bernard *publisher, fiduciary consultant*
Garza, Melita Marie *journalist*
Gilbert, Vincent Newton *publisher*
Golin, Milton *editor, publisher, writer*
Green, Dennis S. *broadcast executive*
Higgins, Jack *editorial cartoonist*
Husar, John Paul *newspaper columnist, television panelist*
Iglauer, Bruce *record company executive*
Jansson, John Fredrick *journalist*
Joyce, Emmett Michael *radio broadcaster*
Judge, Bernard Martin *law bulletin editor, publisher*
Juliusson, Marguerite *sales executive*
Kazik, John Stanley *newspaper executive*
Kelley, Michael John *newspaper editor*
Kisor, Henry Du Bois *newspaper editor, critic, columnist*
Klaviter, Helen Lothrop *magazine editor*
Kniffel, Leonard John *editor, librarian*
Kotulak, Ronald *newspaper science writer*
Krejcsi, Cynthia Ann *textbook editor*
Krueger, Bonnie Lee *editor, writer*
Kupcinet, Irv *columnist*
Larson, Keith Donald *magazine editor*
Leckey, Andrew A. *financial columnist*
Lenehan, Michael Daniel *editor, writer*
Levine, Jane *newspaper publisher*
Lind, Rebecca Ann *mass communication educator*
Lipinski, Ann Marie *newspaper editor*
Loesch, Katharine Taylor (Mrs. John George Loesch) *communication and theatre educator*
Lyon, Jeffrey *journalist, author*
Madigan, John William *publishing executive*
Matanky, Arnie *publisher*
McCarron, John Francis *columnist*
McDaniel, Charles-Gene *journalism educator, writer*
McDougal, Alfred Leroy *publishing executive*
Migala, George Wesly *broadcast executive*
Migala, Lucyna Jozefa *broadcast journalist, arts administrator, radio station executive*
Miller, Mark *newspaper editor*
Moberg, David Forrest *journalist*
Nash, Jessie Madeleine *journalist, science writer*
Nebenzahl, Paul *broadcast executive*
Nolan, Carole Rita *broadcasting executive*
Norton, Peter Bowes *publishing company executive*
Page, Terry *publishing executive*
Perrotto, Larry J. *newspaper executive*
Petacque, Arthur M. *journalist*
Pitt, Judson Hamilton *publisher*
Pruter, Margaret Franson *encyclopedia editor*
Pruter, Robert Douglas *editor*
Puckorius, Philip Michael *editor*
Quaal, Ward Louis *broadcast executive*
Reardon, Patrick Thomas *newspaper reporter*
Reese, Nancy Irene Zander *journalist*
Richter, Elizabeth Dunlop *television executive*
Rodenkirk, Robert Francis, Jr. *journalist*
Rodenkirk, Robert Francis, Jr. *journalist*
Rodgers, Johnathan *broadcast executive*
Ross, Michael Neil *publishing executive*
Schmeltzer, John Charles *financial writer*
Sengstacke, Frederick D. *newspaper publishing executive*
Sengstacke, John Herman Henry *publishing company executive*
Siwicki, Bill *journalist*
Skolnick, Andrew Abraham *science and medical journalist, photographer*
Smarte, Charlotte Elizabeth *educator, journalist*
Tesser, Neil Andrew *writer and broadcaster*
White, John Henry *photojournalist*
Wier, Patricia Ann *publishing executive, consultant*
Zwecker, William Rene, Jr. *newspaper columnist, television reporter*

De Kalb
Burns, Gary Curtis *communications educator*

Decatur
Brooks, Randy Mark *technical communication educator, computer publishing consultant*

Deerfield
Scholl, Marilyn Darby *publishing company executive*
Smith, Carole Dianne *legal editor, writer*

Des Plaines
Caudill, Charlotte *publishing executive*
Foszcz, Joseph L. *editor*
Harrington, Richard J. *newspaper publishing executive*
Katzel, Jeanine Alma *journalist*

Edwardsville
Regnell, Barbara Caramella *media educator*

Elgin
Alft, E. C. (Mike) *columnist, retired secondary education educator*

Elmwood Park
Forst, Edmund Charles, Jr. *communications educator, consultant*

Evanston
Abrahamson, David Stephen Rodler *journalism educator, writer*
Gold, Don *magazine editor, author*
Henry, (Mary) Catherine *publications director*
Kelly, Tony S. *publisher*
Lund, Eric Rudolph *journalist, educator*
Nelson, Ronald William *journalist*
Schwarzlose, Richard Allen *journalism educator*
Wefler, Wilson Daniel *publisher, editor, management consultant*
Wills, Garry *journalist, educator*
Ziomek, Jonathan S. *journalist, educator*

Flossmoor
Fabian, Heather Lynn *journalist*

Franklin Park
Duncanson, Donald George *retired encyclopedia editor*

Glen Ellyn
Lundin, Robert King *freelance journalist, photographer*

Highland Park
Kramer, Laura Jane *journalist, touring company executive*
Rutenberg-Rosenberg, Sharon Leslie *journalist*

Hinsdale
Carlman, Susan Frick *reporter*
Dussman, Judith Ann *publishing executive*

Homewood
Grunwald, Arnold Paul *communications executive, engineer*

Joliet
Schatz, Jonathan Harry *journalist*

Lake Forest
Mc Cutcheon, John Tinney, Jr. *journalist*

Lebanon
Church, Harrison Leon *publishing executive, newspaper*

Libertyville
True, Raymond Stephen *writer, editor, analyst, consultant*

Lincolnwood
Pattis, S. William *publisher*

Litchfield
Jackson, David A. *retired newspaper editor*
Talley, Brian Chandler *broadcasting executive*

Mahomet
Wenzel, Doris Jean Replogle (Doris Evon Waggoner) *publisher*

Mattoon
Heldebrandt, Beth Marie *newspaper editor*

Mount Prospect
Cromer, Earle George Hayward, Jr. *editor, electrical and chemical engineer, consultant*

Northbrook
Roloff, Karen Marie *communication educator*

Oak Brook
Nelson-Walker, Roberta *company executive*

Oak Park
Knight, Robert Milton *journalist, educator*
Lyles, Jean Elizabeth Caffey *journalist, church worker*

Palatine
Lindberg, Richard Carl *editor, author, historian*
Perez, Gerard Vincent *art publishing company executive*

Park Ridge
Johnson, Kenneth Stuart *publisher, printer*
Koren, Jerome Quentin *publishing executive*
Peterson, Richard Elton *publisher*

Peoria
Booth, Sara Daniel *editor*
Duncan, Royal Robert *publisher*
Harkrader, Alan Dale, Jr. *photojournalist*
Kenyon, Theo Jean *reporter*
McConnell, John Thomas *newspaper executive, publisher*
Russell, Julie Rapp *broadcast executive*

Plainfield
Diercks, Eileen Kay *educational media coordinator, elementary school educator*

Plano
Booth, Douglas Alan *news director*

Quincy
Baker, Mark *television newscaster*

Riverside
Finnegan, James John, Jr. *editor, publisher*
Gwinn, Robert P. *publishing executive*
Nieuwsma, Milton John *newspaper syndicate executive*

Rockford
McAley, David William *broadcasting executive*

Savoy
Smiley, Wynn Ray *director of communications*

Schaumburg
Schlossberg, Howard Barry *editor, freelance writer*

Skokie
McNally, Andrew, IV *publishing executive*

Springfield
Heinecke, Burnell A. *retired newspaper reporter*
St. Louis, Paula Marie *journalist*
Schoenburg, Bernard Alan *reporter, columnist*
Thompson, Michael Alan *political cartoonist*

Stockton
Miccolis, Dominic Jon *publishing advisor, consultant*

Urbana
Duffy, Norman Vincent, III *news director*
Duvall, Darin Lee *electronic publishing specialist, educator*
Hansen, Kathryn Gertrude *editor, former state official*
Liebovich, Louis William *journalist, educator*
Meyer, Eric Kent *journalism educator and consultant*

Waukegan
Yoggerst, James Paul *journalist, educator, public relations consultant*

Westchester
Shabel, Dennis Joseph *printing executive*

Wheaton
Beers, V(ictor) Gilbert *publishing executive*

Wheeling
Anderson, Sandra Florence *publishing executive*

Wilmette
Klein, Robert Edward *publishing company executive*

INDIANA

Anderson
Bivens, Paula Sue *journalist*

Bedford
Himebaugh, Eleanor Schmedel *editor*

Bloomington
Jacobi, Peter Paul *journalism educator, author*
Lee, Don Yoon *publisher, academic researcher and writer*

Boonville
Johnson, Charles Richard *publisher*

Cicero
Poindexter, Beverly Kay *media and communications professional*

Crawfordsville
Karg, Thelma Aileen *writer, retired educator*

Crown Point
Suttinger, Mary Catherine *media specialist*

Elkhart
Moore, Rich Blaise *radio station official, music researcher*

Evansville
Jackson, Bill D. *newspaper editor*

Fort Wayne
Klugman, Stephan Craig *newspaper editor*
Lawson, Jerry Marshall *journalist*
Oxley, Ann *television executive*
Pellegrene, Thomas James, Jr. *editor, researcher*

Franklin
Jacobs, Harvey Collins *newspaper editor, writer*
Meadows, Amy Lynn *newspaper copy chief*

Gary
Richards, Rick A. *newswriter*

Hammond
Neff, Bonita Dostal *communication developmental facilitator*

Huntingburg
Matthews, William Edmund *newspaper and travel magazine publisher*

Huntington
Clark, Lance David *communications educator*
Lindsey, Jacquelyn Maria *editor*

Indianapolis
Applegate, Malcolm W. *newspaper executive*
Caperton, Albert Franklin *newspaper editor*
Caudill, Dorene Jackson *editor*
Cohen, Gabriel Murrel *editor, publisher*
Comiskey, Nancy *publishing executive*
Corcoran, Kevin Michael *newspaper reporter*
Koenig, William Joseph *reporter*
McConnell, Joseph Fredrick *sportscaster*
McKeand, Patrick Joseph *newspaper publisher, educator*
Medland, Timothy Joseph *broadcast executive*
Owen, Kenneth Alan *reporter*
Price, (John) Nelson *journalist*
Pulliam, Eugene Smith *newspaper publisher*
Rice, William Ross *media specialist*
Wright, Lloyd James, Jr. *broadcast executive, educator, announcer*

Kokomo
Follick, Joseph Howard *journalist*

Lafayette
Finch, Robert Jonathan *communications engineering consultant*

Lebanon
Hansen, Owen Peter *newspaper editor*

Martinsville
Kendall, Robert Stanton *newspaper editor, journalist*

Mishawaka
Hodges, Lydia Rose *journalist, reporter*

Muncie
Needham, James Robert *television station executive, producer, telecommunications educator*
Sumner, David Edward *journalist, educator*
Swingley, Sheryl Ann *journalism educator, consultant*

Munster
Moore, Carolyn Lannin *video specialist*

Richmond
Fessler, Joyce Ann *journalist*
Jose, Victor Rudolph *publishing executive, editor*
Muzzillo, Rachel Evelyn Sheeley *reporter*
Wilson, Lois Ann *journalist*

Rushville
Moore, Helen Elizabeth *reporter*

Saint Meinrad
Cody, Aelred Joseph *editor, priest*

South Bend
Doyle, Joseph Arthur *freelance sports writer*
Smith, E. Berry *television and radio executive*

Terre Haute
Chesebro, James William *communications educator*

Vincennes
Chattin, Duane Herbert *director of media relations*

West Harrison
Ellison, David Walter *editor*

West Lafayette
King, Margaret Ann *communications educator*

IOWA

Ames
Gartner, Michael Gay *editor, television executive*

Cedar Rapids
Hladky, Joseph F., Jr. *newspaper publisher, broadcasting executive*
Jandik, Linda Jean *studio executive*

Davenport
Brocka, Bruce *editor, educator, software engineer*

Des Moines
Edwards, Charles C., Jr. *newspaper publisher*
Graham, Diane E. *newspaper editor*
Henry, Barbara A. *publishing executive*
Kruidenier, David *newspaper executive*
Leach, Dave Francis *editor, musician*
Peterson, David Charles *photojournalist*

Dubuque
Kolz, Beverly Anne *publishing executive*

Fort Dodge
Johnson, Larry W. *newspaper editor, educator*

Iowa City
Keller, Eliot Aaron *broadcasting executive*
Sinicropi, Stephen Anthony *radio station executive*

Mason City
Etzen, Jason A. *journalism and mass communication educator*

Mount Vernon
Rexroat, Dee Ann *publicist*

Spirit Lake
Kannenberg, Kenneth Karl *media center administrator*
van der Linden, John Edward *newspaper broker, consultant*

West Des Moines
Soth, Lauren Kephart *journalist, economist*

Zearing
Britten, William Harry *editor, publisher*

KANSAS

Dodge City
Muncy, Martha Elizabeth *retired newspaper publisher*

Ellsworth
Gaston, Karl Kuntis *newspaper publisher*

Emporia
Walker, Paul David *newspaper publisher*

Fairway
Jones, Philip Alan *broadcasting executive*

Fort Leavenworth
Neeld, Vaughn DeLeath *technical publications editor*

Fort Scott
Emery, Frank Eugene *publishing executive*

Hays
Foster, Tonya Lea *journalist*

Junction City
Montgomery, John Grey *publisher, television executive*

Lake Quivira
Cuniberti, Betty Alena *journalist*

Lawrence
Newton, Robert George *radio station executive*
Orel, Harold *literary critic, educator*

Manhattan
Kruh, Janet Jackson *telecommunications consultant*
Morgan, Stephen Carl *communications educator*
Schenck-Hamlin, William Joseph *rhetoric and communications educator*
Schofield, Eileen Kathryn *editor*

Mankato
Boyd, Mary Dexter *newspaper editor*

Overland Park
Anderson, Mark Curtis *newspaper editor*
Caterer, Claire Mildred *editor, writer*
Giannetto-Adams, Judy Maria Teresa *magazine editor*
Hinthorn, Aletha Sue *editor, writer*
Waters, Ellen Maureen *publishing executive, writer*

Parsons
Charles, Ann Kennett *editor, publisher*

Prairie Village
Franking, Holly Mae *software publisher*
Jacobs, Vernon Kenneth *publisher*

Saint Marys
Latham, Dudley Eugene, III (Del Latham) *printing and paper converting executive*

Salina
Entriken, Robert Kersey, Jr. *retired newspaper editor, freelance, motorsport writer*
Pyle, George Bower *newspaper editor, columnist*

Shawnee Mission
Matchette, Phyllis Lee *editor*

Sublette
Horinek, Charity Ann *editor*

Topeka
Stauffer, Stanley Howard *newspaper and broadcasting executive*

Wichita
Ashe, Reid *publishing executive*
Chaffin, Leslie Renée *corporate communications administrator, writer*
Claassen, Sherida Dill *newspaper executive*
Curtright, Robert Eugene *newspaper critic and columnist*
Lilly, George David *broadcasting executive*
Mc Cray, Billy Quincy *newspaper owner, former state senator, real estate agent*
McMillin, Molly Odiorne *reporter*
Weaver, Janet *newspaper editor*
Williams, Donald Mace *newswriter, educator*

KENTUCKY

Hazard
Weber, Gretchen Aggertt *speech communication educator*

MICHIGAN

Ada
Engle, Paul E. *book editor, educator*

Adrian
Goldsen, Bruce I. *radio executive*
Goldsen, Susan Eva *radio station executive*
Quigley, Samantha Leigh *journalist, photographer*

Ann Arbor
Fitzsimmons, Joseph John *publishing executive*
Semion, A. Kay *editor*
Veit, Werner *newspaper executive*
Willoughby, Bruce Edward *managing editor*

Birmingham
Moss, Charles Joseph, III (Chuck Moss) *writer, broadcaster*
Robinson, Peter Eliot *cable television executive*
Simmons, Ethel Loretta *journalist*

Bloomfield Hills
Brown, Lynette Ralya *journalist, publicist*
Mead Rosen, Clare *journalist, consultant*

Cedar Springs
Andersen, Niels Toft *publisher, writer*

Dearborn
Rink, Jim *editor, columnist*
Semion, William Alexander *magazine editor*

Detroit
Akre, Brian Scott *journalist*
Bradford, Christina *newspaper editor*
Castronova, Frank Vincent *editor*
Cockburn, Eve Gillian *newsletter editor*
DeVine, (Joseph) Lawrence *drama critic*
Giles, Robert Hartmann *newspaper editor*
Hannington, Mary Lee *production company executive*
McGruder, Robert *newspaper publishing executive*
McTyre, Robert Earl *publishing executive*
Meriwether, Heath J. *newspaper publisher*
Turnley, David Carl *photojournalist*
Vagnozzi, Aldo *editor, newspaper*
Vega, Frank J. *newspaper publishing executive*
Visci, Joseph Michael *newspaper editor*
Woodruff, David P. *journalist*
Wright, Richard Allen *journalist, educator*

East Lansing
Alvarado, Yolanda *journalist, editor, minority outreach consultant*
Freedman, Eric *journalist*
Mitzelfeld, Jim *lawyer, journalist*
Ralph, David Clinton *communications educator*

Escanaba
Jacobs, Donald Phillip *telecommunications technician*

Flint
Samuel, Roger D. *newspaper publishing executive*
Simms, Amelia Moss *publishing executive*

Grand Rapids
Baker, Richard Lee *book publishing company executive*
DeWitt, Michelle Lynn *media company administrator*

Holland
Herrick, James Allen *communications educator*

Kalamazoo
Jamison, Frank Raymond *communications educator*

Lansing
Maran, Michael Joseph *publisher, writer, lawyer*
McCoy, Bernard Rogers *television anchor*

Livonia
Burke, Paul Norman *publishing executive, toy manufacturing executive*

Marquette
Manning, Robert Hendrick *development director*

Midland
Messing, Carol Sue *communications educator*

Monroe
Gray, Stephen Thomas *newspaper editor*

Mount Pleasant
Housley-Anthony, Mary Pat *community relations administrator*
Hughes, James *radio station official*
Murray, Christine J. *managing editor*

Northville
Gesler, Donna Marie *newsletter editor, consultant*

Oak Park
McClellan, Keith *editor, writer*

Ontonagon
Hauswirth, Sandra Fay Marie *newspaper editor*

Otsego
Lawson, Anita Jean *media specialist*

Petoskey
Schaller, Doris Gladys *writer*
Winter, Kenneth Michael *editor*

Rochester
Davio, John Joseph *publishing executive*

Royal Oak
Davis, Michael Warren Rees *journalist, public relations executive*

Saginaw
Avery, William Barton *broadcast executive*
Chaffee, Paul Charles *newspaper editor*
Puravs, John Andris *journalist*
Socier, Michael James *television executive*

Saint Clair Shores
Shine, Neal James *journalism educator, former newspaper editor, publisher*

Southfield
Crump, Constance Louise *journalist*
Nadel, Roger *radio executive*
Osborne, John Hampton *publishing company executive*

Spring Arbor
Stone, Michelle Yvonne *broadcast executive*

Sturgis
Hair, Robert Eugene *editor, writer, historian*

Traverse City
Hacker, David Willson *newspaper correspondent and staff writer*

Troy
Fritz, Jock Thane *radio executive*

MINNESOTA

Center City
Odegard, Daniel James *publisher, bookselling and publishing consultant*

Duluth
Kelly, Joe F. *publisher, editor*

Edina
King, Heather Ann *freelance journalist*

Excelsior
Kaufman, Jeffrey Allen *publisher*

Lakeville
Godwin, David Frank *editor*

Mankato
Larson, Michael Len *newspaper editor*

Maple Grove
Pederson, Jay Porter *editor, writer*

Maple Lake
Andrus, Theresa Kester *photojournalist, communications specialist*
Nelson, Lucille Bonevieve Lewis *journalist*

Minneapolis
Bartz, Paul Alan *editor*
Diaz, Kevin Bruce *journalist*
Hill, Gary Dean *journalist*
Huntzicker, William Edward *journalism educator*
Kramer, Joel Roy *journalist, newspaper executive*
Nelson, Margaret Mogensen *journalist*
Omdahl, Becky Lynn *communications educator*
Scallen, Thomas Kaine *broadcasting executive*
Seaman, William Casper *retired news photographer*
White, Robert James *newspaper columnist*

Minnetonka
Thompson, Sally Ann *newspaper editor*

Moorhead
Gunaratne, Dhavalasri Shelton Abeywickreme *communications educator, journalist*

Saint Joseph
Rowland, Howard Ray *mass communications educator*

Saint Louis Park
Harstad, Carl Leslie *consultant, writer*

Saint Paul
Bree, Marlin Duane *publisher, author*
Doctor, Kenneth Jay *editor*
Gurak, Laura Jean *communication educator, computer consultant*
Hecker, Mel Jason *publishing company executive*
Henry, John Thomas *retired newspaper executive*
Hubbard, Stanley Stub *broadcast executive*
Karnath, Joan Edna *editor*
Kling, William Hugh *broadcasting executive*
Neuzil, Mark Riley *journalism educator*
Ridder, Peter B. *publishing executive*
Stauffer, Kathleen *editor, author*
Wehrwein, Austin Carl *newspaper reporter, editor, writer*
Willis, Jack *broadcasting executive*

Shevlin
Coronato, James Allen *publishing executive, author*

South Saint Paul
Miller, Robert Michael *publishing executive*

Waseca
Larson, Keith Wayne *printing company executive, industrial engineer*

West Saint Paul
Cento, William Francis *retired newspaper editor*

MISSOURI

Aurora
Donley, Paul E. *newspaper publisher*

Buffalo
Hamilton, James Eugene *publishing executive, writer*

Cape Girardeau
Mosley, Jean Bell *columnist*

Chesterfield
Gill, Suzanne *software publisher*

Clinton
Wentz, Wendell Franklin *columnist, writer*

Columbia
Fears, Lillie Mae *journalism educator, mass media researcher*
Hager, Henry Brandebury *journalism educator*
Wilson, Jean Gaddy *journalism educator, think-tank administrator*

Farmington
Firebaugh, Emily Roulette *newspaper editor, publisher*

Fayette
Davis, H(umphrey) Denny *publisher*

Hannibal
Hefley, James Carl *publisher*

Higginsville
Rhodes, Robert Charles *cable company executive, consultant*

High Hill
Todoroff, Albert Andrew *editor, publisher*

Independence
Buttram, James David *publishing company executive*
Clemons, Ronald Dale *journalism educator*
Fortman, Richard Allen *publishing executive*
Francis, Paul William *retired broadcast executive*

Jefferson City
Ahrens, Steven N(orman) *publisher*
Hughes, Mark Douglas *journalist, communications director*
Priddy, Robert Allen (Bob) *news director*

Kansas City
Brisbane, Arthur Seward *newspaper editor*
Cahill, Patricia Deal *radio station executive*
De Mott, John Edward *journalist*
Frauens, Marie *editor, researcher*
McKean, Meryl Lin *television news reporter*
Meiners, Phyllis Henri *publisher, training consultant, author*
Piette, Edward James *television executive*
Reed, William T. *broadcasting executive*
Scott, James White *newspaper editor*
Taylor, Jeff *reporter*
Townsend, Harold Guyon, Jr. *publishing company executive*
Weiss, Benton Herbert *broadcast engineer*
Woodworth, Robert C. *newspaper executive*
Zieman, Mark *newspaper editor*

Liguori
O'Connor, Francine Marie *magazine editor*

Maryville
Widmer, Laura Beth *mass communications specialist*

Saint Joseph
Jackson, James T. *operations manager*

Saint Louis
Baker, Barry *broadcast executive*
Beckner, Jeffery Edward *periodical editor*
Davis, Foster *editor*
Domjan, Laszlo Karoly *newspaper executive*
Elkins, Ken Joe *broadcasting executive*
Freeman, Gregory Bruce *newspaper columnist*
Goldberg, Norman Albert *music publisher, writer*
Graham, Lester Lynn *radio executive*
Green, Joyce *book publishing company executive*
Hunt, Robert G. *film critic, educator*
Lipman, David *multimedia company executive*
Marcus, Larry David *broadcasting executive*
Norman, Charles Henry *broadcasting executive*
O'Day, John Hervey, Jr. *broadcast journalist*
Penniman, Nicholas Griffith, IV *newspaper publisher*
Perkins, Norris Lynwood, III *newspaper columnist and writer*
Pollack, Joe *retired newspaper critic and columnist, writer*
Pulitzer, Michael Edgar *publishing executive*
Richmond, Richard Thomas *journalist*
Rosner, Patrice Lynn *editor*
Staake, Bob Ted *cartoonist, writer*
Tuft, Carolyn Maria *newspaper reporter*
Wente, Patricia Ann *radio executive*
Willnow, Ronald Dale *editor*
Woo, William Franklin *newspaper editor*

Seymour
Sosniecki, Gary Stuart *newspaper editor, publisher*
Sosniecki, Helen Louise Stephens *newspaper editor, publisher*

Springfield
Champion, Norma Jean *communications educator, state legislator*
Jacobi, Fredrick Thomas *newspaper publisher*
Leger, Robert David *newspaper editor*
Sawyer, Jim Charles *journalist*

University City
Benson, Joseph Fred *journalist, legal historian*

NEBRASKA

Cozad
Peterson, Marilyn Ann Whitney *journalism educator*

Hartington
Burney, Joan Rossiter *columnist, counselor, public speaker*

Hastings
Powell, John Wilmer *retired broadcast consultant*
Stofer, Kathryn Tamara *communication arts educator*

Kearney
Wice, Paul Clinton *news director, educator*

Lincoln
Dyer, William Earl, Jr. *retired newspaper editor*
Ebel, A. James *broadcasting consultant*
Spence, Michele Jeanne *editor, writer*

Norfolk
Huse, Eugene Franklin *newspaper publisher*

Omaha
Andersen, Harold Wayne *contributing editor, newspaper executive*
Batchelder, Anne Stuart *former publisher, political party official*
Derrick, Deborah Ball *communications specialist*
Frolio, Jeffrey Lynn *photojournalist, musician*
Johansen, Bruce Elliott *communication and Native American studies educator*
Lipschultz, Jeremy Harris *communication educator*
Sands, Deanna *editor*

NEW YORK

Bronxville
Lombardo, Philip Joseph *broadcasting company executive*

Liverpool
Mitchell, John David *journalism educator*

New York
Fornay, Alfred Richard *publishing executive, editor*
Gissler, Sigvard Gunnar, Jr. *journalism educator, former newspaper editor*
Johnson, John H. *publisher, consumer products executive, chairman*
Litke, James Allan *columnist*
Mauldin, William Henry (Bill Mauldin) *cartoonist*

NORTH DAKOTA

Devils Lake
Aman, Terry J. *editor*

Fargo
Collins, Ross Francis *communications educator*
DeVine, Terry Michael *newspaper editor*
Dill, William Joseph *newspaper editor*
Marcil, William Christ, Sr. *publisher, broadcast executive*

Grand Forks
Austin, Alvin Easton *retired journalism educator*
McCutchan, Neil J. *communications educator*

OHIO

Akron
Allen, William Dale *newspaper editor*
Dotson, John Louis, Jr. *newspaper executive*
Endres, Kathleen Lillian *journalism educator*
Herman, Roger Eliot *professional speaker, consultant, futurist, writer*

Athens
Alsbrook, James Eldridge *journalist, educator*
Bush, Gordon Kenner, Jr. *newspaper publisher*
Metters, Thomas Waddell *sports writer*

Berea
Harf, Patricia Jean Kole *syndicated columnist, educational consultant, lecturer*

Bucyrus
Moore, Thomas Paul *broadcast executive*

Carrollton
Strawder, Jimmy Lee *publisher, author*

Chagrin Falls
Lange, David Charles *journalist*

Cincinnati
Beaupre, Lawrence Kenneth *newspaper editor*
Blake, George Rowell *newspaper executive*
Borgman, James Mark *editorial cartoonist*
Canaan, Don *journalist*
Feister, John Bookser *editor, journalist*
Knue, Paul Frederick *newspaper editor*
Leach, Janet C. *publishing executive*
Liss, Herbert Myron *newspaper publisher, communications company executive*
Marques, José D., Sr. *communications specialist*
Moll, William Gene *broadcasting company executive*
Roman, John Charles *retired publishing company executive*
Santen, Ann Hortenstine *broadcasting executive*
Schottelkotte, Albert Joseph *broadcasting executive*
Whipple, Harry M. *newspaper publishing executive*
Winternitz, Felix Thomas *editor, educator*
Woods, Bruce Walter *editor, poet*

Cleveland
Bingham, Richard Donnelly *journal editor, director, educator*
Bluhm, Gene Elwood *trade journal editor and publisher*
Clapp, Betty S. *journalism educator*
Clark, Gary R. *newspaper editor*
Cooper, Carolyn Annette *proofreader, journalist*
Gilbert, Harold Frederick *publishing executive, art lecturer*
Greer, Thomas H. *newspaper executive*
Gudgeon, Richard Gene *assistant translation editor*
Hamilton, Thomas Woolman *publishing company executive*
Jeffres, Leo Wayne *communication educator*
Jensen, Kathryn Patricia *public broadcaster*
Kanzeg, David George *radio programming director*
Kovacs, Rosemary *newpaper editor*
Lowry, Joan Marie Dondrea *broadcaster*
Machaskee, Alex *newspaper publishing company executive*
Robinson, John William *broadcasting professional*
Walker, Tracey Lynn *editor*
Wallenhorst, Timothy James *newspaper executive*
Wareham, Jerry *broadcast executive*
Wells, Charlena Renee *editor, writer*

Columbus
Barry, James P(otvin) *writer, editor*
Becker, Lee Bernard *journalism educator*
DeVassie, Terry Lee *publishing executive*
Flanagan, Harry Paul *publishing executive*
Fornshell, Dave Lee *educational broadcasting executive*
Gruliow, Leo *journalist, translator, educator*
Kiefer, Gary *newspaper editor*
Langholz, Armin Paul *communications educator*
Murphy, Andrew J. *managing news editor*
Nordstrom, Mark Allen *journalist*
Ouzts, Dale Keith *broadcast executive*
Sherrill, Thomas Boykin, III *newspaper publishing executive*
Simon, Robert H., Jr. *journalist*
Smith, Robert Burns *newspaper magazine executive*
Tatge, Mark W. *investigative reporter*
Weaver, Leah Ann *journalist, speech writer*
Wright, Steven Lee *reporter*

Concord
Watterson, Joyce Grande *editor, publisher*

Dayton
Cawood, Albert McLaurin (Hap Cawood) *newspaper editor*
Franklin, Douglas E. *publishing executive*
Hamlin, Tom *radio and television sportscaster, realtor*
Minnich, Daniel Harold *television news reporter*
Tillson, John Bradford, Jr. *newspaper publisher*

Defiance
Thiede, Richard Wesley *communications educator*

Elyria
Miller, Arnold *newspaper editor*

Fairborn
Leger, Dawn Elizabeth *newspaper reporter*

Findlay
Little, Carol Elizabeth *journalism consultant*

Gates Mills
Baker, Charles B. *publishing executive*

Hilliard
Douglas, David Wayne *mechanical design consultant*

London
McVicar, Richard Lee *journalist*

Loveland
Curliss, James Andrew *journalist*

Lyndhurst
Kastner, Christine Kriha *newspaper correspondent*

Marysville
Behrens, Daniel Eckert *newspaper editor, lawyer*

Maumee
Schwier, Priscilla Lamb Guyton *television broadcasting company executive*

Oxford
Sanders, Gerald Hollie *communications educator*

Pepper Pike
O'Neill, Katherine Templeton *journalist, museum administrator, former nursing educator*
Vail, Thomas Van Husen *retired newspaper publisher and editor*

Reynoldsburg
Powell, Edward Lee *broadcasting company executive*

Salem
Sommers, Bambi Vail *radio executive*

Springfield
Williams, Angie *journalism educator*

Steubenville
Nicholson, Joyce Elaine *radio station official*

Sunbury
Jinks-Weidner, Janie *editor*

Tallmadge
Peterson, David Glenn *service center mangager communicatons company*

Toledo
Block, William K., Jr. *newspaper executive*
Royhab, Ronald *journalist, newspaper editor*

Warren
Svihlik, Susan Jessup *editor*

Westlake
Sowa, Julie Holmes *journalist*

Willoughby
Green, Jerie Ireland *editor, reporter, freelance writer*
O'Toole, Joanne Rose *journalist*

Xenia
Louderback, Jeffrey Dale *journalist, publishing executive*

OREGON

Portland
Banaszynski, Jacqueline Marie *newspaper reporter*

PENNSYLVANIA

Scranton
Lynett, William Ruddy *publishing, broadcasting company executive*

SOUTH DAKOTA

Armour
Van Der Werff, Renee Lynn *newspaper publisher, journalist*

Sioux Falls
Ellis, Peter *editor*

Spearfish
Diamond, David (Sid I., Jr. Davison) *communications educator*

Wilmot
Rondeau-Bassett, Cheryl MaryAnn *publisher, editor*

TEXAS

Dallas
Fiddick, Paul William *broadcasting company executive*

San Antonio
Mays, Lester Lowry *broadcast executive*

WISCONSIN

Beloit
Barth, William R. *editor*

Black River Falls
Michaels, Marion Cecelia *writer, editor, news syndicate executive*

Cedarburg
Hurt, Jeanette Clarice *city reporter, educator*
Paige, Philip Harold *publishing executive, newspaper*

Chippewa Falls
Baker, Mark Joseph *editor*

Eau Claire
Stein, Timothy Andrew *copy editor*

Edgerton
Everson, Diane Louise *publishing executive*

Fort Atkinson
Sager, Donald Jack *publisher, former librarian*

Greendale
Curl, Thomas Leonard *magazine editor*
Pohl, Kathleen Sharon *editor*

Hartland
Peterson, Scott Brian *journalist*

Iola
Cuhaj, George *publishing executive*
Krause, Chester Lee *publishing company executive*

Janesville
Fitzgerald, James Francis *cable television executive*

Kenosha
Rushing, James Taylor *journalist*

La Crosse
Stoeffler, David Bruce *newspaper editor*
Thomas-Williams, Pamela Rae *publishing executive*

Madison
Blake, Philip Edward *newspaper executive*
Brann, Edward R(ommel) *editor*
Burgess, James Edward *newspaper publisher, executive*
Evanson, Elizabeth Moss *editor*
Gillan, Jeffrey Scott *news anchor*
Miller, Frederick William *publisher, lawyer*
Troyan, Scott D. *communications consultant*
Wilson, Janet Lynn *broadcast executive*

Menomonee Falls
Sauer, Michael Richard *editor*

Middleton
Wills, Robert Hamilton *retired newspaper executive*

Milwaukee
Backes, David James *communications educator*
Behrendt, David Frogner *journalist*
Berkman, Dave *mass communications educator*
Enk, Scott *editor*
Hinkley, Gerry *newspaper editor*
Hoffmann, Gregg J. *journalist, author*
Kaiser, Martin *newspaper editor*
Levine, Gail Janice *publisher*

Meisner, Mary Jo *editor*
Santapoalo, Julie Ann *media production professional*
Spore, Keith Kent *newspaper executive*
Stevens, Joan D. *design company executive*
Vonier, Sprague *retired broadcast executive*
Wilson, Melodie J. *broadcast journalist*

Mineral Point
Jett, Frank Hubert *broadcast executive*

Montello
Burns, Robert Edward *editor, publisher*

Neenah
Langel, Ann Elizabeth *journalist*

New Glarus
Marsh, Robert Charles *writer, music critic*

Oconomowoc
Dahms, William Lauritz *broadcasting executive*

Oshkosh
Cowling, Michael Ray *communications educator*
Cox, Justin B. *editor*

Racine
Scolaro, Joseph Alan *journalist*

Saint Francis
Gintoft, Ethel Margaret *journalist*

Saint James
Giesen, Francis Gregory *newspaper editor*

Schofield
Burns, James Timothy *communications company executive*

Sheboygan
Wigg, Rita Agnes *writer, public relations consultant*

Stevens Point
Bednarz, Shirley Diane *publishing company executive*

Stoughton
Brenz, Gary Jay *publishing executive*

Sun Prairie
Kay, Alan Edward *editor*
Mertes, Christopher Patrick *newspaper editor*

Verona
Schroeder, Henry William *publisher*

Waterloo
Kay, Dennis Matthew *publishing company official*

Waukesha
Gruber, John Edward *editor, railroad historian, photographer*

CANADA

ONTARIO

Kitchener
Rittinger, Carolyne June *newspaper editor*

London
Bembridge, John Anthony *newspaper editor*
McLeod, Philip Robert *publishing executive*

ADDRESS UNPUBLISHED

Abellera, Thomas, Jr. *cartoonist*
Agarwal, Suman Kumar *editor*
Barlow, Thomas Reed *broadcast executive*
Bellamy, Gail Anne Ghetia *magazine editor, author, speaker*
Biles, Janice Marie *journalist*
Borysewicz, Mary Louise *editor*
Brekke, Gail Louise *broadcasting administrator*
Carrillo, Carmel J. *journalist*
Cassin, James Richard *broadcast educator*
Clery, Roger G. *communications educator, telecommunications consultant*
Cohen, Allan Richard *broadcasting executive*
Cook, Stanton R. *media company executive*
Cowles, John, Jr. *publisher, women's sports promoter*
Disbrow, Lynn Marie *communication educator*
Ewing, Raymond Peyton *educator, author, management consultant*
Fink, John Francis *newspaper editor*
Forcinio, Hallie Eunice *editor*
Gillmor, Verla Jane *communication consultant*
Griggs, Ruth Marie *retired journalism educator, writer, publications consultant*
Hawkins, Phelps Stokes *broadcast news executive, consultant, journalist*
Honeywell, Larry Gene *retired publishing company executive, retired travel company executive*
Hurd, Byron Thomas *newspaper executive, retired*
Jansky, Larry Richard *communication specialist*
Jennings, Mary Ellen *journalist*
Johgart, Steve R. *index editor*
John, Erwin Ernest *editor*
John, Mertis, Jr. *record company executive*
Justice, Phyllis C. *newspaper editor*
Katz, Amy Beth *editor, magazine*
Krueger, Donald Alvin *publishing executive*
Lake, Charles William, Jr. *retired printing company executive*
Larson, Robert Frederick *public broadcasting company executive*
Leventhal, Aaron J. *travel writer, fundraiser, publisher*
Lewin, Rhoda Greene *editor, historian, columnist*
Locher, Richard Earl *editorial cartoonist*
McGarry, Kevin Vincent *retired magazine executive*
McGrail, Michael Joseph *communications specialist*
McInnis, James Milton *publishing company executive*
McManus, Jane H. *reporter*
Moore, Steven Dana *editor, publisher, critic*
Neeson, Peg *broadcast executive*
Neitzel, Lisa Ann *newscaster, reporter*
Newcom, H. Lee *communications consultant*
Paine, Richard Earl *communication educator*
Penkoff, Diane Witmer *communication educator*
Potamianos, Peter G. *editor, educator*
Prady, Norman *journalist, advertising executive, writer, marketing consultant*
Pratt, Richard Alan *newspaper editor*
Ramsay, Karin Kinsey *publisher, educator*
Rhodes, Steve Neil *journalist*
Roberts, Nancy Lee *journalism educator*
Schrand, Richard Henry *broadcaster*
Simpson, Howard Matthew *textbook publisher*
Stewart, Barbara Ellen *media specialist*
Van Horn, Lecia Joseph *newswriter*
Van Patten, Mark Lee *newspaper publisher*
Vargas, Pattie Lee *author, editor*
Watkins, Cheryl Denise *newspaper editor*
Whitter, Pamela Letha *journalist*
Yeager, Anson Anders *columnist, former newspaper editor*

EDUCATION. For postsecondary education, *See also* specific fields.

UNITED STATES

ARKANSAS

Conway
Holmes, Barbara Deveaux *college president*

CALIFORNIA

Carlsbad
McLevie, John Gilwell *education educator*

Long Beach
McDonough, Patrick Dennis *academic administrator*

Redding
Treadway, Douglas Morse *academic administrator*

Santa Barbara
Yang, Henry T. *university chancellor, educator*

COLORADO

Denver
Halgren, Lee A. *academic administrator*

Littleton
Rychecky, Helen Rose *private school system administrator*

DISTRICT OF COLUMBIA

Washington
Starr, Stephen Frederick *academic administrator, historian*

FLORIDA

Boca Raton
Miller, Eugene *university official, business executive*

ILLINOIS

Alexis
Nelson, Janice Elizabeth *educator*

Alton
Hamelmann, Norma Ruth *secondary education educator*

Andover
Anderson, Ruth Carrington *retired secondary education educator*

Anna
McMahan, Gale Ann Scivally *school system administrator*
Wolfe, Martha *elementary education educator*

Arlington Heights
Brod, Catherine Marie *college director*
Placek-Zimmerman, Ellyn Clare *school system administrator, educator, consultant*

Aurora
Colosimo, Karen Elizabeth *academic administrator*

Barrington
Scranton, Lynda Kay *secondary education educator*

Belleville
Ellis, Nanette C. *home-based specialist*
Tinoco, Patricia Ann *elementary education educator*
Twesten, Gary Keith *science educator*

Bethalto
Gallinot, Ruth Maxine *educational consultant*

Bethany
Syfert, Samuel Ray *retired librarian*

Bloomington
Gregor, Marlene Pierce *primary education educator, elementary science consultant*
Lovell, Harry Rhys *university administrator*
Myers, Minor, Jr. *academic administrator, political science educator*

Bolingbrook
Taylor, Lynda Dora *school administrator, principal*

Braceville
Rutzky, Ronald *school district superintendent*

Bradley
Anderson, Janice Lee Ator *secondary education mathematics educator*

Brownstown
Jones, Betty Jeanne *school superintendent*

Buffalo Grove
Boesch, Deborah Ann *elementary education educator*
Young, Kathleen Marie *special education educator*

Cahokia
Wade, Susan Kaye *elementary education educator*

Calumet City
Butler, James Martin *science educator*
Jandes, Kenneth Michael *superintendent*
Palagi, Robert Gene *college administrator*

Cambridge
Frisk, Ruth Davis *retired educator*

Carbondale
Clarke, Ingrid Gadway *academic ombudsman, consultant*
Cordoni, Barbara Keene *special education educator*
Covington, Patricia Ann *university administrator*
Guyon, John Carl *university administrator*
Snyder, Carolyn Ann *university dean, librarian*
Yopp, John Herman *dean of graduate school, plant biology educator*

Carterville
Legan, Gregory Mark *university development administrator*

Champaign
Asaad, Kolleen Joyce *special education educator*
Creamer, Bruce Cunningham *retired safety educator, property manager*
Kollar, Karen L. *university administrator*
Levy, Stanley Roy *educational administrator*
Ward, James Gordon *education administration educator*

Charleston
Buckellew, William Franklin *retired education educator*
Moler, Donald Lewis *educational psychology educator*
Rinefort, Foster Christian, Jr. *business management educator*
Rives, Stanley Gene *university president emeritus*
Thornburgh, Daniel Eston *retired university administrator, journalism educator*
Weidner, Theodore John *university administrator, architect, engineer*

Chicago
Alexandroff, Mirron (Mike Alexandroff) *academic administrator*
Anderson, Rudolph Valentino, Jr. *principal*
Beck, Frances Josephine Mottey (Mrs. John Matthew Beck) *secondary education educator*
Beck, Irene Clare *educational consultant, writer*
Beckwith, John Adams *school superintendent*
Bernadetta, Sister Maria *special education educator*
Brusky, Linda L. *middle school mathematics and science educator*
Celic, Lillian Christina *consciousness and growth techniques educator*
Coleman, Roy Everett *secondary education educator, computer programmer*
Collens, Lewis Morton *university president, legal educator*
Coy, Patricia Ann *special education director, consultant*
Crockett, George Ephriam *secondary education educator*
Cross, Dolores Evelyn *university administrator, educator*
Culverwell, Rosemary Jean *principal, elementary education educator*
Cummings, Maxine Gibson *elementary school educator*
Dempsey, James Randall *academic administrator*
Einoder, Camille Elizabeth *secondary education educator*
Elwin, James William, Jr. *dean, lawyer*
Fontánez-Phelan, Sandra Maria *special education director, consultant*
Fowler, Carl *retired educator, boxing statistician*
Fruchter, Rosalie Klausner *elementary school educator*
Furlong, Patrick David *educator, researcher*
Gantz, Suzi Grahn *special education educator*
Greenberg, Patricia Thomas *educational administrator*
Gross, Theodore Lawrence *university administrator, author*
Harris, Shirley *elementary, secondary and adult education educator*
Hart, Mary *educator*
Hawkins, Loretta Ann *secondary school educator, playwright*
Hawley, Warren John *private school educator*
Hirsch, Arlene Sharon *career counselor*
Iaquinta, Leonard Phillip *university development and alumni official*
Iwanski, Mary *parochial school educator*
Jordan, Mark D. *school administrator*
Kane, Michael J. *dean*
Kirshbaum, Jon Alan *educational administrator*
Kloc, Emily Alvina *retired elementary school principal*
Kubistal, Patricia Bernice *educational consultant*
Lester, Robin Dale *educator, author, former headmaster*
Lindahl, Wesley E. *academic administrator*
Linnerud, Mark Alan *secondary education educator*
Martin, Barbara Jean *elementary school principal*
McIntyre, Michael Truett *university administrator*
Minogue, John P. *academic administrator, priest, educator*
Monaghan, M. Patricia *university administrator, writer, poet*
Moss, Gerald S. *dean, medical educator*
Murray, Robb *software educator*
Pate, Clara Hairston *education director*
Petitan, Debra Ann Burke *educator, education counselor, design engineer, writer, author*
Piderit, John J. *university educator*
Pollack, Erwin Wilburt *adult education educator, reseacher, writer*
Poskanzer, Steven Gary *university administrator, lawyer*
Reyes, Jesus Emmanuel *university dean*
Reynolds, Ruth Carmen *school administrator, secondary school educator*
Richardson, John Thomas *academic administrator, clergyman*
Rosenbluth, Marion Helen *educator, consultant, psychotherapist*
Schubert, William Henry *curriculum studies educator*
Schwarzkopf, Gloria A. *education educator, psychotherapist*
Snodgrass, Klyne Ryland *seminary educator*
Spearman, David Leroy *elementary education educator, administrator*
Standberry, Herman Lee *school system administrator, consultant*
Stelmack, Gloria Joy *elementary education educator*
Strong, Dorothy Swearengen *educational administrator*
Stukel, James Joseph *academic administrator, mechanical engineering educator*
Sulkin, Howard Allen *college president*
Ward, Richard Hurley *university administrator, educator, writer*
Ward-McDuffie, Kay Frances *elementary education educator, paralegal*
Washington, Cassandra *elementary education educator*
Watts, John Ransford *university administrator*
Wong, Kenneth K. *education educator*
Yamakawa, Allan Hitoshi *academic administrator*
Yanikoski, Richard Alan *university president*
Yu, Clement Tak *educator, researcher, consultant*
Zawadzki, Dolores Joan *adult education educator*
Zonka, Constance Z. *educational organization administrator*

Collinsville
Leyda, Margaret Larue *retired educator, bed and breakfast owner*

Country Club Hills
McClelland, Helen *music educator*
Scherer, George Robert *retired secondary education educator*

Crystal Lake
Abbate, Dee *college administrator*

Danville
Rogers, Gary C. *educational administrator*

Darien
Meyer, James Philip *secondary education social studies educator*

De Kalb
Carp, Richard Merchant *educational administrator*
Healey, Robert William *school system administrator*
James, Marilyn Shaw *secondary education educator, social service worker*
King, Kenneth Paul *secondary education educator*
La Tourette, John Ernest *academic administrator*
Simmons, Deborah Anne *education educator*
Zar, Jerrold H(oward) *academic administrator, biology educator, statistician*

Decatur
Peters, Connie Jane *secondary education media specialist*

Deerfield
Graddy, William Edward *English professor*
Jennetten, John Peter *higher education executive*

Des Plaines
McClure, Matthew K. *secondary education educator*

Downers Grove
DeJulio, Ellen Louise *special education administrator*
Dodd, James Michael *secondary education educator*
Gomberg, Samuel Harris *social studies educator*
Hlavacek, Paula Jean *educational administrator*
LaRocca, Patricia Darlene McAleer *middle school mathematics educator*
Punt, Leonard Cornelis *educational services company executive*

Edgewood
Lewis, Linda Sue *elementary education educator*

Edwardsville
Lazerson, Earl Edwin *academic administrator emeritus*

Effingham
Pickett, Steven Harold *elementary education educator*

Elgin
Waters, Donald Eugene *academic administrator*

Erie
Latham, LaVonne Marlys *physical education educator*

Evanston
DeLong, Mark Randall *English language educator, director*
Herron, Orley R. *college president*
Shanafield, Harold Arthur *school system administrator*
Tarczan, Heather Marie *university administrator*
Weber, Arnold R. *academic administrator*
Wesse, David Joseph *academic administrator*
Worthy, James Carson *management educator*
Zarefsky, David Harris *academic administrator, communication studies educator*

Flossmoor
Ferreira, Daniel Alves *secondary education Spanish language educator*

Fox Lake
Galitz, Laura Maria *secondary education educator*

Frankfort
Shultz, Kenneth Lowell *athletic director*

Freeport
Baumgartner, Reuben Albert *retired school administrator*

Galesburg
Kilpatrick, Jean Ann *elementary education educator*

Glen Ellyn
Patten, Ronald James *university dean*
Sobie, Robert Fransis *educator*

Glenview
Corley, Jenny Lynd Wertheim *elementary education educator*
Traudt, Mary B. *elementary education educator*

Granite City
Eftimoff, Anita Kendall *educational consultant*

Grayslake
Harold, Kathleen T. *elementary education educator*

Harvard
Boese, Kathleen Carol *principal*

Hillsboro
McCafferty, Marlyn Jeanette *elementary education educator*
Weaver, Sharon B. *educator*

Hillside
Kirchhoff, W. James *school district administrator*

Hoffman Estates
Starzynski, Christine Joy *secondary educator*

Homer
Gilhaus, Barbara Jean *secondary education home economics educator*

Homewood
Awe, Clara *academic administrator*

Ingleside
Krentz, Eugene Leo *university president, educator, minister*

Jacksonville
Hansmeier, Barbara Jo *elementary education educator*
Johns, Beverly Anne Holden *special education administrator*
Jones-Grooms, Rebecca S. *deaf education educator, consultant*
Pfau, Nancy Ann *secondary education educator*
Schmidt, Alvin J. *educator*

Jerseyville
Phillips, Howard R. *adult education educator, director*

Joliet
Carpanzano, Christina Steitz *college administrator*
Hodgman, Vicki Jean *retired school system administrator*
Murphy, Jo Anne *data processing administrator*
Scott, Linda Ann *assistant principal, elementary education educator*

Kewanee
Lee, Paula Dea *business education educator*

La Grange
Jaffe-Notier, Peter Andrew *secondary education educator*

Lake Forest
Adelman, Pamela Bernice Kozoll *education educator*
Hotchkiss, Eugene, III *college president emeritus*

Lansing
Guzak, Debra Ann *special education educator*

Lebanon
Weingartner, Jane Ellen *college administrator*

Lemont
Urban, Patricia A. *former elementary school educator*

Lincolnwood
Greenblatt, Deana Charlene *elementary education educator*

Lombard
Winterstein, James Fredrick *academic administrator*

London Mills
McKinley Balfour, Stephanie Ann *learning resources director, librarian*

Macomb
Espahbodi, Hassanali *educator*

Madison
Pope, Sarah Ann *elementary education educator*

Martinsville
Winters, Brent Allan *headmaster, writer, geologist*

Mason City
Breedlove, Jimmie Dale, Jr. *elementary education educator*

Maywood
Crane, Jerome Calvin, Jr. *college, university administrator*

Mc Leansboro
Brinkley, William John *secondary education educator*

Metamora
Crow, Mary Jo Ann *elementary education educator*

Moline
Acuff, John Thomas *technology educator*
Cubbage, Diana *school system administrator*
Schauenberg, Susan Kay *educational counselor, educator*

Morton
Corey, Judith Ann *educator*

Morton Grove
Blockinger, James Anson *superintendent of schools*
Di Prima, Stephanie Marie *educational administrator*

Mundelein
Anderson, John McNeill *secondary education educator*
Shisler, Sister Mary Paul *elementary school administrator, educator*

Murphysboro
Brewer, Donald Louis *school superintendent*
Hall, James Robert *secondary education educator*

Naperville
Hicks, Amelia Marie *secondary educator, consultant*
Johnson, Herman *secondary education educator*
Knuckles, Barbara Miller *academic administrator*
Loscheider, Paul Henry *academic administrator*
Rosenthal, Edward Leonard *secondary school educator*
Wall, Douglas Foster *mathematics educator*

New Lenox
Mostyn, Marge Lois Irwin *secondary school educator*

Normal
Hickrod, George Alan Karnes Wallis *educational administration educator*
Wallace, Thomas Patrick *university administrator*
White, Ray Lewis *education educator*

North Chicago
Booden, Theodore *dean*

Northfield
Fodrea, Carolyn Wrobel *educational researcher, publisher, consultant*
Hestad, Marsha Anne *educational administrator*

O Fallon
Bradley, Thomas Michael *school system administrator*

Oak Brook
Baar, John Greenfield, II *secondary school educator*

Oak Forest
Hull, Charles William *special education educator*

Oak Park
Davis, Christine Eurich *elementary education educator*
Patricks, Edward J *elementary education educator*

Oglesby
Zeller, Francis Joseph *dean*

Olney
Saul, Barbara Ann *English studies educator*

Olympia Fields
Tannebaum, Marilynn Etta *elementary education educator*

Orland Park
Bucinski, Janice Kay *secondary education educator*

Palatine
Chapman, Gerald D. *school superintendent*
Stowe, Carol Ann *education educator*

Palos Hills
Keogh, Laurence D. *educator, gerontology consultant*

Paris
Essinger, Susan Jane *special education educator*

Patoka
Borgmann, Norma Lee *school superintendent*

Pekin
Herbstreith, Yvonne Mae *primary education educator*
Urban, Sharon Kay *elementary school educator*

Peoria
Brazil, John Russell *academic administrator*
Hartnett, Barbara Mary *college program director*
Keim, Barbara Howell *university administrator, biology educator, association administrator*
McMullen, David Wayne *education educator*
Sisson, Mary Winifred *retired elementary education educator*

Pontiac
Burnett, Eugene Allen *secondary education educator*

Prospect Heights
Silver, Bella Wolfson *daycare center executive, educator*

River Forest
McDonald, Glena June *elementary education educator*
Smith, Curtis Alfonso, Jr. *university administrator*

River Grove
Stein, Thomas Henry *social science educator*

Van Doren, Ronald Wayne *speech communication educator*

Rock Island
Tolliver, Marion Eugene *college administrator*
Tredway, Thomas *college president*
Williams, Hope Denise *academic administrator, business consultant*

Rockford
Hart, Elsie Faye *elementary education educator*
McConville, Lynn Cuppini *school system director*
Steele, Carl Lavern *academic administrator*
Whealler, Susan Cornelia *college dean, educator*
Whinna, George Waltman Roper, III *secondary education educator*
Whitsell, Doris Benner *retired educator*
Wilke, Duane Andrew *educator*

Romeoville
Rusnak, Martha Hendrick *reading education educator*

Roscoe
Zapke, Clifford F. *secondary education educator*

Rosemont
Baldwin, Robert Thomas *school superintendent*

Saint Joseph
McDade, Linna Springer *retired academic program administrator*

Schaumburg
Roderick, William Rodney *academic administrator*

Seneca
Jones, Lee A. *school system administrator, consultant, small business owner*

Shelbyville
Storm, Sandy Lamm *secondary education educator*

Shorewood
Hall, Patricia Marie *special education administrator*

Skokie
Cerveny, Kathryn M. *educational administrator*
Goldberg, Vicki Comm *employment services executive*
Savage, Patrick Joseph *secondary education educator*

South Holland
Larsen, Mary Ann Indovina *counselor, English educator*

Springfield
Bretz, William Franklin *retired elementary and secondary education educator*
Cowles, Ernest Lee *academic administrator, educator, consultant, researcher*
Johnson-Leeson, Charleen Ann *former elementary school educator, insurance agent, insurance consultant*
Koschmann, Timothy Durant *educational researcher*
McCabe, Gene Jerome *dean*
Phillips, John Robert *college dean, political scientist*
Schroeder, Raymond Ernest *educational administrator*
Van Der Slik, Jack Ronald *academic administrator, political science educator*

Sterling
Albrecht, Beverly Jean *special education educator*
Donahue, Shirley Ohnstad *elementary education educator*

Streamwood
Polkowski, Delphine Theresa *elementary education educator, speech therapist*

Sycamore
Johnson, Yvonne Amalia *elementary education educator, science consultant*

Urbana
Aiken, Michael Thomas *academic administrator*
Ikenberry, Stanley Oliver *education educator, former university president*
Rogers, Paula Ann *secondary school educator*
Schoell, Richard Martin *university administrator*
Skirvin, Robert Michael *college professor*
Weir, Morton Webster *retired academic administrator, educator*

Venice
Purdes, Alice Marie *adult education educator*

Villa Park
Peterson, Elaine Grace *technology director*
Smith, Barbara Ann *gifted education coordinator*
Taylor, Ronald Lee *school administrator*

Virden
Rohrer, Susan Jane *principal*

Washington
McKinney-Keller, Margaret Frances *retired special education educator*

Waukegan
Edwards, David B. *education coordinator*
Robinson, Georgia May *education educator*
Stone, Barbara Suzanne *educator, dean*

Wilmette
Smutny, Joan Franklin *academic director, educator*
Sprague, Donald Eugene *educational administrator*

Wilmington
Clardy, Mary Joanne *gifted education educator*

Winnetka
Bundy, Blakely Fetridge *early childhood educator, advocate*
Huggins, Charlotte Susan Harrison *secondary education educator, author, travel specialist*
Rhoad, Richard Arthur *secondary school educator, writer*

Woodstock
Levandowski, Barbara Sue *educational administrator*

Worth
Droel, William Louis *educator*

INDIANA

Alexandria
Erwin, Linda L. *college administrator*

Bainbridge
Pride, Murray Franklin *school system administrator*

Bloomington
Brand, Myles *academic administrator*
Brescia, William Fred, Jr. *development officer*
Bull, Barry Leonard *education educator*
Gros Louis, Kenneth Richard Russell *university chancellor*
Hill, Howard Darnell *fraternal organization executive, educator*
Hopkins, Jack Walker *former university administrator, environmental educator*
Mehlinger, Howard Dean *education educator*
Motsinger, Linda Sue *university official*
Webb, Charles Haizlip, Jr. *university dean*
Werner, Nancy Darlington *university development researcher*

Brownsburg
Hays Butler, Holly Lynn *university youth extension educator*

Carmel
Garretson, James DeHart *secondary education educator*

Covington
Wagner, Nancy Jo *extension educator*

Crawfordsville
Day, Joseph William *educator*
Spurgeon, Nannette SuAnn (Susie Spurgeon) *special education educator*

Crown Point
Bryan, Shirley Winifred *education educator*
Jones, Walter Dean *community program director*
Nikolich, Michel Miro *retired secondary education educator*

Dale
Hayes, Mary Joanne *special education educator*

East Chicago
Platis, James G. *secondary school educator*

Elkhart
Thompson, Nancy Jo *special education educator, elementary education educator, consultant*

Elwood
Barnett, Marilyn Doan *secondary education business educator*

Evansville
Aucoin, Paul *registrar, consultant*
Davies, Sara Beth *educator, writer*
Vinson, James Spangler *academic administrator*

Fort Branch
Bertram, Michael Wayne *secondary education educator*

Fort Wayne
Balthaser, Linda Irene *academic administrator*
Daniels, Mark Lee *secondary education educator*
Guse, Carol Ann *educational consultant*
Lewark, Carol Ann *special education educator*
Pease, Ella Louise *elementary education educator*
Phinney, Nathan *college administrator*
Souers, Marjorie Elaine *education educator*
Weicker, Jack Edward *educational administrator*

Franklin
Bender, Larry Wayne *vocational educator*

Gary
Hales, Patricia Louise *secondary education educator*
Richards, Hilda *academic administrator*
Schwartz, Joel Barry *psychologist, educational researcher*
Smith, Vernon G. *education educator, state representative*

Granger
Early, Thomas Michael *educator*
Klem, Lynne Ellen *developmental disabilities consultant, educator*

Greencastle
Bottoms, Robert Garvin *academic administrator*
Houck, Carolyn Marie Kumpf *special education educator*
Lord, Stuart C. *dean*

Hammond
Servies, Carol *academic program director*
Singer, Sandra Manes *university administrator*
Wermuth, Jerome Francis *academic administrator*

Highland
Gregory, Marian Frances *educator, counselor*

Indianapolis
Barcus, Mary Evelyn *primary school educator*
Bepko, Gerald Lewis *university administrator, law educator, lecturer, consultant, lawyer*
Brooks, Patricia Scott *principal*
Brown, Freezell, Jr. *private school educator*
Eikenberry, Kevin Leon *training consultant*
Evenbeck, Scott Edward *university official, psychologist*
Fadely, James Philip *admissions director, educator, writer*
Fox, Patricia Sain *academic administrator*

Gooldy, Patricia Alice *elementary education educator*
Guffin, Jan Arlen *secondary education educator*
Hefler, William Louis *elementary education educator*
Huffman-Hine, Ruth Carson *adult education administrator, educator*
Klinker, Sheila Ann J. *middle school educator, state legislator*
Kultgen, Kimberly Jo *university administrator, graphic artist*
Livesay, Robin Rucker *university dean*
Mendenhall, Gordon Lee *secondary school educator*
Metzner, Barbara Stone *university counselor*
Nelson, Carl Vincent *secondary education educator*
Ney, Michael Vincent *university administrator*
Segrest, Katrina Ann Wordlaw *academic administrator*
Solomon, Marilyn Kay *educator, consultant*
Speth, Gerald Lennus *education and business consultant*
Watkins, Sherry Lynne *elementary school educator*
Wooden, Reba Faye Boyd *guidance counselor*
Woody, John Frederick *secondary education educator*

Jamestown
Waymire, John Thomas *principal*

Kokomo
Daniels, Doral Lee *education educator*
Hill, Emita Brady *academic administrator*
Kirkpatrick, Holly Jean *elementary education educator, special education educator*

Lafayette
Schramm, Beatrice G. *retired teacher*
Troutner, Joanne Johnson *school technology administrator, educator, administrator, consultant*

Lagrange
Schmidt, David Joseph *special education educator, consultant*
Young, Rebecca Lee *special education educator*

Lakeville
Morgan, Ardys Nord *superintendent of schools*

Lawrenceburg
Wright, Gwen Sloas *college administrator*

Madison
Hill, Paul Richard *financial aid director, educator*

Martinsville
Bastin, Catherine Jean *elementary education educator*

Milton
Schwartz, Susan Lynn Hill *principal*

Mishawaka
Wilson, Patricia Marie *reading education educator*
Youngs, Diane Campfield *learning disabilities specialist, educator*

Monroeville
Geldien, Judith Ruth Motter *elementary educator*

Muncie
Alford, Jeffrey W. *university administrator*
Linson, Robert Edward *university administrator emeritus*
McLaughlin, Charles Hugh, Jr. *technolgy educator*
Richmond, DeWayne *secondary school educator*
Stainbrook, James Ralph, Jr. *educator*
Stroud, James Clyde *early childhood educator*
Wagner, Joseph Crider *retired academic administrator*

Munster
Fies, James David *elementary education educator*
Platis, Chris Steven *educator*
Sherman, Mona Diane *school system administrator*

New Albany
Rand, Leon *academic administrator*

New Carlisle
Serpe-Schroeder, Patricia L. *elementary education educator*

New Harmony
Rice, David Lee *university president emeritus*

Newburgh
Brown, Rhonda Marie *secondary education educator*

Noblesville
Thacker, Jerry Lynn *school administrator*

North Manchester
Hunt, Luke Leland *secondary education educator*

Pittsboro
Hassfurder, Leslie Jean *principal*

Plymouth
Cardinal, Shirley Mae *education educator*
Jurkiewicz, Margaret Joy Gommel *secondary education educator*

Richmond
Robinson, Dixie Faye *school system administrator*
Ronald, Pauline Carol *school system administrator*
Wood, Richard J. *academic administrator*

Schererville
Griffin, Anita Jane *elementary education educator*

Seymour
Ozinga, Connie Jo *library director*

South Bend
Frick, James William *university administrator, consultant*
Ganaway, Norma Jean *vocational counselor*
Mills, Nancy Anne *elementary education educator*
Walker, Doris Ann *education educator*
Wolfson, Lester Marvin *former university chancellor*

Terre Haute
Hulbert, Samuel Foster *college president*
Landini, Richard George *university president, emeritus English educator*
Moore, John W. *academic administrator*

Upland
Harbin, Michael Allen *religion educator, writer*

Valparaiso
Chupp, Diana Lynn *textiles and needlework educator*
Harre, Alan Frederick *university president*

Vincennes
Nead, Karen L. *university professor*

Wakarusa
Anglemyer, Roma Kathleen *elementary school educator*

Waterloo
Gearhart, Marilyn Kaye *mathematics and biology educator*

West Lafayette
Beering, Steven Claus *academic administrator, medical educator*
Feldhusen, Hazel J. *elementary education educator*
Ford, Frederick Ross *university official*
Frick, Gene Armin *university administrator*
Gappa, Judith M. *university administrator*
Ringel, Robert Lewis *university administrator*
Rud, Anthony Gordon, Jr. *university administrator*
Shepardson, Daniel Philip *science education educator*

Westville
Alspaugh, Dale William *university administrator, aeronautics and astronautics educator*
Duttlinger, Linda M. *education educator*

Whiting
Wagner, Cindy Kay *college administrator*

IOWA

Adair
Johnson, Joyce Marie *school system administrator*

Ames
Hughes, Ruth Pierce *retired educator*
Jischke, Martin C. *academic administrator*
Mattila, Mary Jo Kalsem *elementary and art educator*
Snow, Joel Alan *research director*

Andrew
Burrow, John Randolph *secondary education educator, writer, editor*

Burlington
Brocket, Judith Ann *elementary education mathematics educator*

Cedar Falls
Schneider, Melvin Frederick *retired secondary music educator*

Cedar Rapids
Stirler, Karen Sue *special education educator, adult education educator*

Clarence
Stonerook, Eleanor Rae *librarian*

Davenport
Garfield, Phyllis H. *international program administrator, educational consultant*
Hudson, Celeste Nutting *education educator, reading clinic administrator, consultant*
Mortiboy, Clara Louise Beck *educator*

Des Moines
Boren, Donna *primary school educator*
Carrigan, Pamela Sue *new resident administrator*
Ferrari, Michael Richard, Jr. *university administrator*
Hetzler, Susan Elizabeth Savage *educational administrator*
Koons, Susan Ann *school guidance counselor*
Strentz, Herbert J. *educator, journalist*
Webb-Groe, Mary Christine *special education educator*
Wegenke, Gary L. *school systems administrator*

Dubuque
Peterson, Walter Fritiof *academic administrator*

Dunkerton
Wede, Richard J. *school superintendent*

Estherville
Cook, Judith Ann *academic program director*

Fairfield
Pearson, Craig Alan *academic administrator, educator, author*

Fayette
Stinson, Karen *education educator*

Fort Dodge
Pratt, Diane Adele *elementary education educator*

Fort Madison
Carroll, Melody J. *educator, writer*
Scott, Craig *superintendent*

Garner
Mestad, Gary Allen *education educator*

Gilmore City
Worthington, Patricia *elementary education educator*

Grinnell
Webb, Ruth Cameron *retired educator*

Indianola
Jennings, Stephen Grant *academic administrator*

Iowa City
Barkan, Sandra Lynn *dean, literature educator*
Duffy, William Edward, Jr. *retired education educator*
Flaherty, Susan Sweeney *university educational foundation administrator*
Henry, Joseph King *university administrator*
Johnson, William Bruce *university dean*
Retish, Esther Shifra *elementary educator*
Seavy, Mary Ethel Ingle *art educator*

Iowa Falls
Sessler, Donna Jean Hotz *secondary education educator*

Jefferson
Said, Clifford Everett *seminar company executive, speaker*

Marshalltown
Tambrino, Paul August *college president*

Mason City
Olson, Paul Buxton *retired social studies, marketing, and business educator*

Mount Vernon
Dendurent, Sharon Drwall *university administrator*

Muscatine
Miller, Suzanne Kay *corporate educator*

Nevada
Carlson, Russell Busby *media specialist*

Norwalk
Christowski, Henry Franklin *school system administrator*

Onawa
Petersen, Joan Marie *talented and gifted education coordinator, educator, florist*

Orient
Lane, Steven Joseph *middle and high school principal, physical education educator*

Oskaloosa
Eliason, Larry Elmer *education educator*

Primghar
Schnoes, Mark Allan *middle school educator, baseball coach*

Sioux Center
DeHoogh, Noreen Beth *secondary education educator, school system administrator*

Sioux City
Green, Ruth Milton *retired college administrator, consultant*
Nichols, Roger Sabin *school counselor*

Sloan
Ullrich, Roxie Ann *special education educator*

Story City
Kruger, Vicki Henry *elementary education educator*

Urbandale
Hewitt (Ver Hoef), Lisa Carol *elementary education educator*

Walnut
Madson, Paulette Kay *home economics educator*
Myers, Gloria J. *elementary education educator*

Waterloo
Alfrey, Marian Antoinette *retired education educator*
Hasek, Jane Ellen *chancellor*
Kober, Arletta Refshauge (Mrs. Kay L. Kober) *educational administrator*

KANSAS

Anthony
Carr, Cynda Annette *elementary education educator*

Bonner Springs
Jarrett, Gracie Mae *junior high school guidance counselor*

Downs
La Barge, William Joseph *tutor, researcher*

El Dorado
Hilyard, Janice Elaine *college administrator*

Emporia
Figgs, Linda Sue *principal*
Glennen, Robert Eugene, Jr. *university president*
McGlone, Edward Leon *dean, consultant, academic administrator*
Torrens, Peggy Jean *technical school coordinator*

Frontenac
Wilson, Donald Wallin *academic administrator, communications educator*

Garden City
Garrier, Jo Ann Ross *college program administrator*
Jarmer, Gary Edward *dean*

Gardner
Trigg, Tom *school system administrator*

Goddard
Kastens, Beverly Ann *special and elementary education educator*

Goodland
Sharp, Glenn (Skip Sharp) *vocational education administrator*

Great Bend
Rittenhouse, Nancy Carol *elementary education educator*

Hays
Davidson, Mary Theresa *educational administrator*
Hammond, Edward H. *university president*
Ross, John Allan *university director*

Hiawatha
Pennel, Marie Lucille Hunziger *elementary education educator*

Hutchinson
Stevens, Leota Mae *retired elementary education educator*

Kansas City
Clifford, Rita Kay *nursing school administrator*
Powell, Nancy Egan *elementary education educator*

Lawrence
Gracy, Janine Louise *director health education, educator*
Wiechert, Allen LeRoy *educational planning consultant, architect*

Liberal
Wilkerson, Rita Lynn *special education educator, consultant*

Manhattan
Budke, Camilla Eunice *secondary education educator*
Davis, Freeman Milton, II *university adminstrator, educator, consultant, per*
Muir, William Lloyd, III *academic administrator*
Troyer, Deryl Lee *life sciences educator*

Mc Pherson
Mason, Stephen Olin *academic administrator*

Mulvane
George, Donald Richard *retired principal*

Olathe
Booth, Jody Shelton *educational executive director*

Overland Park
Speer, Hugh W. *education educator*

Pittsburg
Huddleston, Michael Ray *counseling administrator, consultant, educator*
Smoot, Joseph Grady *academic administrator*
Sullivan, F(rank) Victor *retired dean*

Saint Marys
Steele, David Frank *elementary education educator*

Shawnee Mission
Koster-Peterson, Lois Mae *educational administrator*
Wambles, Lynda England *educational sales consultant, retired*

Topeka
Anderson, C. Wilson, Jr. *learning specialist*
Bruno-Stanley, Melinda Ann *technology facilitator*
Jennings, Nancy Ann *retired elementary education educator*
Sheley, Wayne McDowell *academic administrator*
Thompson, Hugh Lee *academic administrator*
Varner, Robert Bernard *counselor, educator*

University Of Kansas
Hemenway, Robert E. *university administrator, language educator*

Westwood Hills
Ehrlich, Larry G. *educator*

Wichita
Andrews, Bettyo *early childhood educator*
Cooper, John Wesley *school system administrator*
Groff, Susan Carole *elementary education educator*
Jantze, R. Dale *retired educator*
Link, Gary D. *university director*
Maurer, Michael Dean *secondary school educator*
Platt, George Milo *university administrator*
Rager, Kathleen Byrne *academic administrator*
Spears, Laura Elizabeth *special education educator*
Willon, Mychael Cole *school system administrator*

KENTUCKY

Lexington
Flynn, Peter Francis *superintendent of schools*
Thelin, John Robert *academic administrator, education educator, historian*
Williams, Jackson Jay *education consultant*

MARYLAND

Rockville
Larsen, Max D. *survey researcher*

MASSACHUSETTS

Boston
Robinson, Sumner Martin *college administrator*

MICHIGAN

Adrian
Wolf, George Frank, Jr. *program director*

Albion
Campbell, Catherine Mary *school system administrator*

Vulgamore, Melvin L. *college president*

Allendale
Lubbers, Arend Donselaar *academic administrator*

Alma
Moerdyk, Charles Conrad *school system administrator*
Seveland, John Wallace *college administrator*
Stone, Alan Jay *college administrator*

Almont
Ferzacca, Pamela Ann *elementary education educator*

Alpena
Authier, Gail Judith *preschool consultant*

Ann Arbor
Brighton, Marcella Ann *academic administrator*
Byrd, Mark Alan *institutional researcher, educator*
Duderstadt, James Johnson *university president*
Porretta, Louis Paul *education educator*
Rose, Homer Cameron, Jr. *dean*
Simoni, Mary Hope *university official*
Stark, Joan Scism *education educator*
Whitesell, Patricia S. *academic administrator*

Battle Creek
Dryer, Shawn Peter *secondary education educator*
Stilwell, Martha Ann *academic administrator*

Bay City
Zuraw, Kathleen Ann *special education and physical education educator*

Beverly Hills
Faxon, Jack *headmaster*

Birch Run
Radwick, Melissa Jane *elementary counselor*

Birmingham
Aginian, Diana Carol *child development specialist*

Bloomfield Hills
Fulton-Calkins, Patsy Jo *educational administrator, writer*

Burton
Jackson, Garnet Nelson *elementary education educator, writer*

Cadillac
McKay, Laurie Marie *special education educator*

Carsonville
Mueller, Don Sheridan *retired school administrator*

Casco
Thueme, William Harold *educator*

Cheboygan
Patterson, Deborah Mae *educator, researcher*

Clarkston
Mousseau, Doris Naomi Barton *retired elementary school principal*

Clio
McCabe, Donald James *educational research director*

De Tour Village
Kemp, Patricia Ann *principal*

Detroit
Boykin, Nancy Merritt *academic administrator*
Burnside, Wanda Jacqueline *elementary school educator*
Cox, Clifford Ernest *deputy superintendent, chief information officer*
Fay, Sister Maureen A. *university president*
Hagman, Harlan Lawrence *education educator*
Hough, Leslie Seldon *educational administrator*
Kline, Mable Cornelia Page *retired secondary school educator*
Lee, James Edward, Jr. *educational administrator*
Paul, Rhonda Elizabeth *university program director, career development counselor*
Pietrofesa, John Joseph *education educator*
Rogers, Richard Lee *educator*
Semanik, Anthony James *university program administrator*
Syropoulos, Mike *school system director*

Dowagiac
Mulder, Patricia Marie *education educator*

East China
Hillier, Charles Frederick *elementary school educator*

East Lansing
Abramson, Janet Carolyn *communicty college educator*
Barbatis, Gretchen Lynda *telecommunications educator*
Hungiville, Maurice Neill *educator*
McPherson, Melville Peter *academic administrator, former government official*
Unsworth, Michael Edward *university librarian*
Wronski, Stanley Paul *education educator*

Escanaba
Ling, Robert William, Jr. *academic director*

Farmington Hills
Hartman-Abramson, Ilene *adult education educator*

Flint
Duckett, Bernadine Johnal *retired elementary principal*
Green, Allison Anne *retired secondary education educator*
Nelms, Charlie *academic administrator*
Reska-Hadden, Marcia Ann *special education educator*
Silkwood-Sherer, Deborah Jo *dean*
Thompson, Thomas Adrian *secondary school educator*

Flushing
Barnes, Robert Vincent *elementary and secondary school art educator*

Fruitport
Collier, Beverly Joanne *elementary education educator*

Gaylord
Magsig, Judith Anne *early childhood education educator*

Grand Haven
Beekman, Lloyd George *retired education educator*

Grand Rapids
Barkema, David Victor *secondary education educator*
Flory, Betsy J. *educator*
Leavenworth, Paul Stephen, Jr. *secondary school educator*
Montgomery, Marianne Beatty *primary education educator*
Roels, Shirley Jean *academic administrator*
VanderVeen, Joseph Richard *special education administrator*
Wiltse, Richard Allan *school system official*

Grosse Pointe
Dupuis, Robert *retired principal*
Gruenwald, Barbara Savage *secondary school art educator, art coordinator*
Morlan, Gordon Elliott *secondary school educator*
Zimmer, Anne Fern Young *educator, researcher, administrator*

Gwinn
Lasich, Vivian Esther Layne *secondary education educator*

Harrison Township
Cobb, Cecelia Annette *counselor*
Suchecki, Lucy Anne *elementary education educator*

Haslett
Hotaling, Robert Bachman *community planner, educator*

Hillsdale
Kline, Faith Elizabeth *college administrator*

Holland
Hill, JoAnne Francis *elementary education educator*
Jacobson, John Howard, Jr. *college president*
Nyenhuis, Jacob Eugene *college official*

Houghton
Tompkins, Curtis Johnston *academic administrator*

Huntington Woods
Logan, Linda Mary *art education educator*

Ironwood
Sobolewski, Jane Ann *business educator*

Ithaca
Mayes, Bill Edwin *educational administrator*

Jackson
Haglund, Bernice Marion *elementary school educator*

Jenison
Headley, Kathryn Wilma *secondary education educator*

Kalamazoo
Badra, Robert George *philosophy, religion and humanities educator*
Brashear, Robert Marion *retired education educator, consultant*
Cline, Sandra Williamson *elementary education educator*
De Graffenried, Micheal *public service educator*
Gordon, Alice Jeannette Irwin *secondary and elementary education educator*
Gray, Audrey Nesbitt *elementary education educator*
Haenicke, Diether Hans *university president*
McGaghie, Thomas James *adult educator*
Muncey, Barbara Deane *university official, consultant*

Kentwood
Pappas, William John *principal, educator*

Lansing
Carter, Pamela Lee *school system administrator*
Cunningham, Paula Diane *community college administrator*
Marazita, Eleanor Marie Harmon *secondary education educator*
Piveronus, Peter John, Jr. *education educator*
Small, Roger Steven *middle school educator*

Lawrence
Fudge, Mary Ann *vocational school educator*

Livonia
Tebbe, Francis Sylvester *academic administrator*

Macomb
Farmakis, George Leonard *education educator*
Skavery, Stanley *school system administrator*

Madison Heights
Pricer, Wayne Francis *counseling administrator*
Smith, David E. *secondary education educator, English*

Marquette
Harrington, Lucia Marie *elementary education educator*
Heldreth, Leonard Guy *university administrator*
Magnaghi, Russell Mario *education educator*
Suomi, Paul Neil *alumni association director*
Vandament, William Eugene *academic administrator, educator*

Mason
Williams, John Louis *principal*

Midland
Barker, Nancy Lepard *university official*

Milford
Black, Denise Louise *secondary school educator*

Monroe
Siciliano, Elizabeth Marie *secondary education educator*

Mount Pleasant
Carlson, Charles Evans *university official*
Cook, Wells Franklin *education educator*
Cooley, Nancy Jo *university administrator*
Lippert, Robert J. *administrator and culinary arts educator, consultant*
Plachta, Leonard E. *academic administrator*
Radell, Karen Marguerite *educator*
Rapaport, Ross Jay *counseling administrator, educator*

Okemos
Velicer, Janet Schafbuch *elementary school educator*

Ontonagon
Clark, Raymond John *Academic Administrator*

Oscoda
Lee, Patsy Ruth *retired elementary education educator*

Plainwell
Barton, Edward Read *educator*
Sanders, James Richard *education educator, consultant, researcher*

Pleasant Ridge
Sneed, Marie Eleanor Wilkey *retired secondary education educator*

Pontiac
Decker, Peter William *academic administrator*

Port Huron
Gall, Helen Louise *elementary education educator, retired*
McDaniels, Peggy Ellen *special education educator*

Richmond
Wood, Virginia Ann *educator*

River Rouge
Benford, Rosa Wright *special education administrator*

Rochester
Packard, Sandra Podolin *education educator, consultant*
Polis, Michael Philip *university dean*
Russi, Gary D. *academic administrator*
Splete, Howard Henry, Jr. *counselor educator*
Wermuth, Mary Louella *secondary education educator*

Roseville
Ruehle, Dianne Marie *retired elementary education educator*

Saginaw
Blue, Robert Lee *secondary education educator*

Saint Clair Shores
Doutt, Geraldine Moffatt *retired educational administrator*
Welch, Robert Dinwiddie *retired school administrator*

Saint Joseph
Hall, Patricia Ann *educational administrator*

Sault Sainte Marie
Arbuckle, Robert Dean *university administrator*
Coffing, Janet S. *principal, special education educator*
Money, Margaret Sarah *primary education educator*

South Lyon
DeNoyer, Georgia Ann *consultant, educator*

Stanton
Winchell, George William *curriculum and technology educator*

Sterling Heights
Cutter, Jeffrey S. *secondary education educator, music educator*
Lancour, Karen Louise *secondary education educator*

Tawas City
Jacob, Elizabeth Ann *elementary education educator*

Traverse City
Edson, Daniel Charles *educational administrator*
Halsted, Judith Ann Wynn *educational consultant*
Stepnitz, Susan Stephanie *special education educator*

Trenton
Shaw, Danny Wayne *secondary education educator*

University Center
Gilbertson, Eric Raymond *academic administrator, lawyer*

Warren
Mignacca, Egidio Carmen *principal*

Watervliet
Peal, Christopher John *educational administrator*

White Lake
Grant, Phyllis Moore *elementary education educator*

Wixom
Boynton, Irvin Parker *educational administrator*

Ypsilanti
Allen, Janet Louise *school system administrator*
Blair, John Raymond *educational psychology educator*
Gwaltney, Thomas Marion *education educator, researcher*
Lee, Benjamin Ling-Hsiao *industrial technology educator, consultant*
Sullivan, Thomas Patrick *academic administrator*
Tillman, Tracy Salisbury *professor, consultant*
Washington, Adrienne Marie *elementary school educator*

MINNESOTA

Albert Lea
Rechtzigel, Sue Marie (Suzanne Rechtzigel) *child care center executive*

Annandale
Schilplin, Yvonne Winter *educational administrator*

Bemidji
Martel, Petra Jean Hegstad *elementary school educator*
McDonald, Judith Louise *dean*

Cold Spring
Thielen, JoAnne Olivia *day care provider*

Collegeville
Kellom, Gar E. *university official*

Duluth
Ianni, Lawrence Albert *university administrator, English language educator*
Pilon, Daniel Henry *academic administrator*
Ranta Aho, Martha Helen *retired elementary education educator*
Zaudtke, Gary Arnold *college dean, quality consultant*

Grand Rapids
King, Sheryl Jayne *secondary education educator, counselor*

Lakeville
Royse, Sue Marion *special education educator*

Mankato
Rush, Richard R. *academic administrator*

Maple Grove
Gall, Patience Beth *elementary education educator*

Marshall
Curtler, Hugh Mercer, Jr. *educator*

Minneapolis
Buggey, Lesley JoAnne *education educator, consultant*
Hansen, Lorraine Sunny Sundal (Sunny Hansen) *counselor, educator*
Kirschner, Ruth Brin *elementary education educator*
Lowthian, Petrena *college president*
Matson, Wesley Jennings *educational administrator*
Nolting, Earl *academic administrator*
Schmit, David Michael *retired secondary education educator, artist, designer*

Minnetonka
Vanstrom, Marilyn June *retired elementary education educator*

Moorhead
Barden, Roland Eugene *university administrator*
Dahlquist, Joel Powell *university administrator*
Dille, Roland Paul *college president*
Myrvik, Donald Arthur *college administrator*
Nicholson, Lawrence Alvin *university administrator*

Moose Lake
Jensen, Gwendolynn Marie *special education educator*

Morris
Johnson, David Chester *university chancellor, sociology educator*

Northfield
Campbell, Carol Norton *college official*
Eckdahl, Wendy Ann *research officer*
Jorgensen, Daniel Fred *academic director*
Larson, Emilie Gustava *retired school counselor*
Schmidt, Debra Jean *college official*

Ortonville
Schrom, Elizabeth Ann *educator*

Osseo
Hersch, Russell LeRoy *secondary education educator*

Preston
Hokenson, David Leonard *secondary school educator*

Remer
McNulty-Majors, Susan Rose *special education administrator*

Rochester
Loutzenhiser, Carolyn Ann *elementary education educator*
Sherman, Thomas Francis *education educator*

Rosemount
Griffith, Denise Irene *school administrator*
Staloch, James Edward, Jr. *vocational educator*
Trygestad, JoAnn Carol *secondary education educator*

Saginaw
Stauber, Marilyn Jean *secondary and elementary school*

Saint Cloud
Bates, Margaret Helena *special education educator*
Murray, Richard Edward *university administrator, career consultant*
Wertz, John Alan *secondary school educator*

Saint James
Jones, Patricia Louise *elementary counselor*

Saint Paul
Calvin, Stafford Richard *academic administrator*
Cameron, Jean Elizabeth *academic dean*
Dykstra, Robert *retired education educator*
McLean, Gary Neil *educator, management consultant*
Pappenfus, Mabel Louise *retired educator*
Peterson, Harry Leroy *academic administrator*

Walnut Grove
Nordstrom, Grace Irene *retired elementary educator*

White Bear Lake
Gabrick, Robert William *secondary education educator*

Winona
Beyer, Mary Edel *primary education educator*
Boseker, Barbara Jean *education educator*
Breitlow, John Richard *retired speech communication educator*
DeThomasis, Brother Louis *college president*
Haugh, Joyce Eileen Gallagher *education educator*
Krueger, Darrell W. *university president*
Nasstrom, Roy Richard *education educator, academic administrator*
Preska, Margaret Louise Robinson *education educator, district service professional*

MISSOURI

Ballwin
Guinther, Christine Louise *special educator education*

Blue Springs
Hatley, Patricia Ruth *school system administrator*
Wheeler, Tom Carl *seminary dean*

Boonville
Cline, Dorothy May Stammerjohn (Mrs. Edward Wilburn Cline) *educator*
Wilkinson, Connie Marie *early childhood education director*

Camdenton
Hosman, Sharon *elementary education educator*

Cape Girardeau
Keys, Paul Ross *university dean*
Kupchella, Charles Edward *academic administrator, author, educator*
Stroup, Kala Mays *state education official*

Centralia
Fashing, Annette Louise *elementary education educator, reading specialist*

Clinton
Carter, Sally Packlett *elementary education educator*

Columbia
Brown, Mary Ellen *educator*
Brown, Tracy Elizabeth *elementary education educator*
Curby, Vicki Morgan *academic program director*
Fiene, Jeanne Rae *education educator*
Fluharty, Charles William *policy research institute director, consultant, researcher*
Hatley, Richard V(on) *education educator*
McCampbell, Wanda Mae Hennecke *vocational school administrator*
McGill, James Terry *academic administrator*
Monroe, Haskell M., Jr. *university educator*
Russell, George Albert *university president*
Staley, Marsha Lynn *elementary school educator*
Wheeler, Otis V., Jr. *public school principal*
Zelenak, Bonnie Susan *director*

Delta
Burton, Drenna Lee O'Reilly *kindergarten educator*

Drexel
Williams, Shirley Jean Oostenbroek Akers *daycare provider, educator, writer*

Fayette
Inman, Marianne Elizabeth *college administrator*

Fenton
Korn, Irene Elizabeth *elementary education educator, consultant*

Florissant
Payuk, Edward William *elementary education educator*

Fulton
Staley, R(obert) Eric *academic administrator*

Gainesville
Walrath, Joe Bill *secondary education educator*

Gallatin
Wilsted, Joy *elementary education educator, reading specialist, parenting consultant*

Hannibal
Carty, Raymond Wesley *academic administrator*

Hazelwood
Bennett, Thomas Mitchell *secondary education educator*

Houston
Ruckert, Rita E. *elementary education educator*

Imperial
Usher, Mary Margaret *special education educator*

Independence
Henley, Robert Lee *school system administrator*
Melton, Jean Edith *retired elementary education educator*
Smith, Joseph W. *elementary education educator*

Jefferson City
Brandt, William Edmund *school system administrator*
Gonder, Sharon *special education educator*
Heldenbrand, Lois Elaine *academic administrator*
Walters, Joel M. *school system administrator*

Jennings
Robards, Bourne Rogers *elementary education educator*

Joplin
Allman, Margaret Ann Lowrance *counselor*
Freeman, Catherine Elaine *educator*
Horvath, Juliana *special education educator*
Pulliam, Frederick Cameron *educational administrator*

Kansas City
Audley, Thomas Joseph *educational administrator, consultant*
Caulfield, Joan *academic relations coordinator, educator*
Doyle, Wendell E. *retired band director, educator*
Gibbons, Dona Lee *principal*
Hamilton, Richard Alfred *university administrator, marketing educator*
Henry, Gloria Jean Mullins *secondary education educator*
Hulett, Barbara June *elementary and special education educator*
McKnight, Susan Coleman *dean, academic director*
Powell-Brown, Ann *special education educator, public relations executive*
Roos, Kathleen Marie *special education educator*
Sturges, Gloria June *learning disabilities educator*
Van Ackeren, Maurice Edward *college administrator*
Wilkins, Arthur Norman *retired college administrator*

Kirksville
Gaber, Elsie Jean Kins *university counselor*
Haxton, Lori Ann *university administrator*
Koutstaal, Cornelis W. *university administrator*
Smith, Dwyane *university administrator*

Lees Summit
Boehm, Toni Georgene *seminary dean, nurse*

Liberty
Campbell, Joyce Marie *elementary education educator*

Linn
Gove, Peter Charles *special education educator*

Marionville
Estep, Mark Randall *secondary education educator, dairy farmer*

Marshall
Wymore, Luann Courtney *education educator*

Maryville
Hubbard, Dean Leon *university president*
Mauzey, Elizabeth Mowry *technical education educator*

Point Lookout
Howell, Camille Fly *university public relations administrator*

Richmond Heights
Ward, Ollie Tucker *counselor, educator*

Rolla
Deering, Thomas Edwin *academic administrator*

Saint Charles
Cassy, Catherine Mary *elementary school educator*
Huckshold, Wayne William *elementary education educator*

Saint Joseph
Murphy, Janet Gorman *college president*

Saint Louis
Bartlett, Frank Walter *university administrator*
Biondi, Lawrence *university administrator, priest*
Bloomberg, Terry *early childhood education administrator*
Bohne, Jeanette Kathryn *mathematics and science educator*
Brennan, Donald George *university dean, research administrator*
Bubash, Patricia Jane *special education educator*
Conaway, Mary Ann *dean*
Cook, Jeannine Harriss *educational administrator, educator*
Danforth, William Henry *retired academic administrator, physician*
Downey, Norma Jean *special education educator*
Earle, James A. *educational administrator*
Ferzacca, William *education educator, consultant*
Fortus, Janet Anne *special education educator*
Friedel, Helen Brangenberg *counselor, therapist*
Gerdine, Leigh *retired academic administrator*
Gocial, Tammy Marie *educational administrator*
Gregory, Patricia Jeanne *corporate relations director*
Hackel, Mary Roeper *counselor, placement coordinator*
Hall, Homer L. *journalism educator*
Jacobi, Jan de Greeff *school administrator*
Kelly, Ann Terese *elementary education educator*
Lacey, R. Alton *academic administrator*
Martens, Patricia Frances *adult education educator*
McFarland, Mary A. *elementary and secondary school educator, administrator*
McGannon, John Barry *university administrator*
Nikolai, Robert Joseph *dean, biomechanics in orthodontics educator*
Peak-Hoffmann, Cynthia Sue *academic administrator*
Pfefferkorn, Michael Gene, Sr. *secondary school educator, writer*
Pflueger, M(elba) Lee *academic administrator*
Ramming, Michael Alexander *school system administrator*
Reed, Sheila Kaye *program coordinator*
Russell, Mary Elizabeth *admissions director*
Schmidt, Victoria *educator, author, consultant*
Schoeneberg, Joyce Eileen *secondary school biology educator*
Thomas, Pamela Adrienne *special education educator*
Touhill, Blanche Marie *university chancellor, history-education educator*
Trewin, Rex Edwin *educational director*
Watkins, Hortense Catherine *middle school educator*
Wood, Samuel Eugene *college administrator, psychology educator*

Sainte Genevieve
Cantu, Dino Antonio *secondary education history educator*

Salem
Dent, Catherine Gale *secondary education educator*

Sedalia
Noland, Gary Lloyd *vocation educational administrator*

Seymour
Wallace, Dorothy Alene *special education administrator*

Springfield
Ames, Jimmy Ray *education educator*
Bamberger, Ruth *educator*
Bentley, Roseann *educational consultant, state senator*
Groves, Sharon Sue *elementary education educator*
Rademacher, Gary Edward *secondary school educator*
Stovall, Richard L. *academic administrator*
Summers, Patsy Jo *educator*

Verona
Youngberg, Charlotte Anne *education specialist*

Warrensburg
Albright, Dianne Elizabeth *counseling educator*
Alewel, Teresa Fine *university director*
Elliott, Eddie Mayes *academic administrator*
Ramsey, Allen R. *educator*
Sterling, Duane Ray *university administrator*

Washington
Chambers, Jerry Ray *school system administrator*

Webster Groves
Zimmerman, Harold Seymour *elementary school educator*

West Plains
Asberry, Henry Anthony *vocational school educator*

Windyville
Clark, Laurel Jan *adult education educator, author, editor, minister*
Condron, Daniel Ralph *academic administrator, metaphysics educator*

Winfield
Laughman, Lyle William *school superintendent*

NEBRASKA

Auburn
Winegardner, Rose Mary *special education educator*

Blair
Christopherson, Myrvin Frederick *college president*
Penna, Nancy Sue *dean, registrar*

Callaway
Lofquist, James Wallace *school system administrator*

Central City
Wall, Ronald Rae *public school superintendent*

Chadron
Green, Donald Edward *dean*

Columbus
Rieck, Janet Rae *special education educator*

Grand Island
Zajicek, Lynn Engelbrecht *educational administrator*
Zichek, Shannon Elaine *secondary school educator*

Hastings
Veburg, Ronald Neil *speech and theater educator*

Kearney
Johnston, Gladys Styles *university official*
Smith, Ronald Noel *facilities manager*

Lincoln
Edmunds, Niel Arthur *vocational education educator, consultant, researcher*
Gates, Charles R. *college administrator*
Harris, Marilyn Louise *educator*
Hermance, Lyle Herbert *college official*
Houtz, Lynne Elaine *education educator*
Liggett, Twila Marie Christensen *academic administrator, public television company executive*
Lingle, Muriel Ellen *elementary education educator*
Omtvedt, Irvin Thomas *academic administrator, educator*
Powers, David Richard *educational administrator*
Wysong, Linda Marie *career center administrator*

Madison
Mortensen-Say, Marlys (Mrs. John Theodore Say) *school system administrator*

Mc Cook
Creasman, Virena Welborn (Rene Creasman) *retired elementary and secondary school educator, genealogist, researcher*
Koetter, Leila Lynette *college administrator*

Morrill
Steele, Sarah Jane *elementary school educator*

Newcastle
Myers, Kenneth L(eRoy) *secondary education educator*

Norfolk
Marshall, Dallas Ray *college marketing agent*
Timmer, Margaret Louise (Peg Timmer) *educator*

Omaha
Bednarz, Susan Clare *educational administrator*
Bruce, Willa Marie *education educator*
Callahan, Dorothy Mott *educational program director*
Coyne, Ann *social work educator*
Denton, Joan Cameron *reading educator*
Dickel, Charles Timothy *education educator*
Dixon, Terry Phillip *academic administrator, educational consultant*
Hall, William Edward *educator*
Hill, John Wallace *special education educator*
Jacobs, Henrietta Marie *early childhood educator, consultant*
Kuhlman, Thomas Ashford *American studies educator, writer*
McEniry, Robert Francis *education educator*
Morrison, Michael Gordon *university president, clergyman, history educator*
Peck, Ernest James, Jr. *academic administrator*
Saunders, Lucille Mae *elementary education educator, librarian*
Schuerman, Norbert Joel *school superintendent*
Schulze, Mark Howard *secondary school educator*
Stohs, Sidney John *dean*
Weber, Delbert Dean *academic administrator*

Plainview
Mauch, Jeannine Ann *elementary education educator*

South Sioux City
Moseman, Mildred Mae *retired elementary school educator and principal*
Wilson, Esther Elinore *technical college educator*

York
Niemann, Birgie Ann *college official*

NEW YORK

Ithaca
Rawlings, Hunter Ripley, III *university president*

NORTH DAKOTA

Bismarck
Evanson, Barbara Jean *middle school education educator*
Laches, Robert Duane *vocational educator*

Dickinson
Conn, Philip Wesley *university president*

Fargo
Ozbun, Jim L. *academic administrator*

Grand Forks
Baker, Kendall L. *academic administrator*
Jentz, Jeff J. *multicultural educator*
Lindquist, Mary Louise *special education educator*
Page, Sally Jacquelyn *academic administrator*
Prigge, Glenn Russell *educator*
Sand, Phyllis Sue Newnam (Phyllis Sue Newnam) *retired special education educator*

Minot
Jermiason, John Lynn *elementary school educator, farmer, rancher*
Shaar, H. Erik *academic administrator*

Minot AFB
Pederson, Kathryn Marie *college administrator*

Warwick
Tossett, Gloria Vay *educator, administrator*

OHIO

Ada
Perusek, Wesley *educational program developer, administrator*

Akron
Auburn, Norman Paul *university president*
Becker, Mary Julia *secondary education educator, writer*
Dietz, Margaret Jane *retired public information director*
Elliott, Peggy Gordon *university president*
Saccone, Vivian Rich *retired elementary educator, author, illustrator*

Alliance
Dunagan, Gwendolyn Ann *special education educator*
Sheetz, Ernest Austin *academic administrator, educator*

Andover
Mathay, John Preston *elementary education educator*

Ansonia
Spencer, Rex LeRoy *secondary education educator*

Ashland
McKinley, Norma Elizabeth *education educator*
Piirto, Jane Marie *education educator, creativity educator*

Tomassi, Ralph Vincent *university administrator*

Ashtabula
Pizor, Raymond Francis *secondary educator, guidance counselor, school psy*

Athens
Carr, Jacquelyn *university administrator*
Denbow, Carl Jón *university official*
Harrison, Richard Paul, Jr. *university program administrator*
Honerkamp, Frank W. *university administrator*
Johnson, Jeannette Selby *vocational education educator*
Kelley, Charles Aaron *dean*

Barberton
Samples, Iris Lynette *elementary school educator*

Batavia
Nichols, Marci Lynne *gifted education coordinator, educator, consultant*

Beachwood
Sneiderman, Marilyn Singer *secondary and elementary school educator*

Berea
Hairston, Jay Timothy *college administrator*

Bergholz
Goddard, Sandra Kay *elementary education educator*

Bloomingburg
Lester, Richard Lee *elementary education educator, consultant*

Bloomingdale
Martin, Clara Rita *elementary education educator*

Bluffton
Keeney, William Echard *educator, minister*

Bowling Green
Campbell, Malcolm Byron *educator*
Gehring, Donald D. *education educator*
Olscamp, Paul James *academic administrator*
Petersen, George James *education educator*

Brecksville
Johnson, L. Neil *school system administrator*

Brooklyn
Middleton, Mary *secondary education educator*

Bucyrus
Frey, Judith Lynn *elementary education educator*

Burton
Latimore, Ritchie R. *computer technology educator, consultant*

Cambridge
Dray, Dwight Leroy *retired school system administrator*
Greenwood, David Wilbur *elementary education educator*

Canton
Herritt, David R. *elementary education educator*
Nwa, Willia L. *special education educator*
Wyler, Kathryn Kishpaugh *vocational evaluator*

Celina
Grapner-Mitchell, Pamela Kay *primary education educator*

Chagrin Falls
Phillips, Dorothy Ormes *elementary education educator*

Chesapeake
Harris, Bob L(ee) *educational administrator*

Chillicothe
New, Eloise Ophelia *special education educator*

Cincinnati
Bell, Howard Wesley, Jr. *educational administrator*
Campbell, Patricia Elaine *elementary education educator*
Clifton, Audrienne Kay *education educator, sociologist*
De Courten-Myers, Gabrielle Marguerite *education educator, researcher*
Fischer, Patricia Ann *middle school educator*
Gottschalk, Alfred *college chancellor*
Greengus, Samuel *academic administrator, religion educator*
Heideman, Renita Kay *school district technology coordinator*
Hoke, Eugena Louise *special education educator*
Johnson, Betty Lou *secondary education educator*
Jordan, Mary Lee *retired elementary education educator*
Kukulinsky, Nancy Elaine *academic administrator*
Meyer, Paul S. *counselor*
Nester, William Raymond, Jr. *retired academic administrator and educator*
Newman, Mary Alice *academic administrator*
Prior, Joseph LaFayette *counseling administrator*
Ragland, Anna Mae *educator*
Sanford, Wilbur Lee *elementary education educator*
Skilbeck, Carol Lynn Marie *elementary educator and small business owner*
Steger, Joseph A. *university president*
Sweeney, Dennis Joseph *educator, author*
Wagner, Thomas Edward *academic administrator, educator*
Walvoord, Barbara Ellen *faculty development director*
William, William H.A. *professor*
Williams, Myron David *dean*
Williams, Roger *academic administrator*

Cleveland
Boyatzis, Richard Eleftherios *academic administrator*
Callesen-Gyorgak, Jan Elaine *special education educator*
Comienski, James Sigmon *secondary education educator, planetarium director*
Conrad, Loretta Jane *educational administrator*
Goll, Paulette Susan *secondary education educator*
Gronick, Patricia Ann Jacobsen *school system administrator*
Jirkans, Maribeth Joie *school counselor*
Jones, Rosemary *education director*
Kay, Irene Pramisloff *school system administrator*
Lundstrom, William John *academic administrator*
Mayer, Robert Anthony *college president*
Nickerson, Gary Lee *secondary education educator*
Pinchot, Sister Miriam Fidelis *elementary education educator*
Pytte, Agnar *academic administrator*
Sachs, Marjorie Bell *vocational and educational counselor*
Taylor, Gail Richardson *university administrator*
Thomas, Faye Evelyn J. *elementary school educator*
Van Ummersen, Claire A(nn) *academic administrator, biologist, educator*

Columbia Station
Schuckman, Barbara Anne *psychology instructor*

Columbus
Armes, Walter Scott *vocational school administrator*
Baughman, George Washington, III *retired university official, financial consultant*
Beller, Stephen Mark *university administrator*
Cormanick, Rosa-Maria Moreno *academic program coordinator*
Cunningham, Patricia Anne *costume and textiles educator*
Ellinger, John Michael *university administrator*
Gee, Elwood Gordon *university administrator*
Hairston, Elaine Hayden *state college and university board of regents*
Hamersley, Sharon Lee *academic advisor, church musician*
Hart, Mildred *counselor*
Heinlen, Daniel Lee *alumni organization administrator*
Heron, Timothy Edward *special education educator, consultant*
Jackson, John Charles *retired secondary education educator, writer*
Magliocca, Larry Anthony *education educator*
Mathis, Lois Reno *retired elementary education educator*
McCoy, Terry *educator, community activist*
Miller, Wayne Clayton *student services assistant director*
Oxley, Margaret Carolyn Stewart *elementary education educator*
Paul, Peter Vincent *special education educator*
Riedinger, Edward Anthony *international educator, Brazilianist*
Singer, Norman Marvin *international education consultant*
Warmbrod, Catharine Phelps *educational researcher, consultant*

Cortland
Piros, Michael George *adult education director*

Coshocton
Havelka, Thomas Edward *secondary education educator*

Dayton
Delgado, Clara Sue *university administrator*
Fitz, Brother Raymond L. *university president*
Gies, Frederick John *education educator*
Heft, James Lewis *academic administrator, theology educator*
Hoffman, Sue Ellen *elementary education educator*
Lasley, Thomas J. *education educator*
Ponitz, David H. *academic administrator*
Raynor, Denise Marie *educational consultant*
Taylor, Elisabeth Coler *secondary school educator*

Delaware
Bettac, Teresa Forsythe *secondary education educator*
Huckabee, Colleen J. *school system administrator*

Dublin
Keck, David Michael *school administrator*

Eaton
Rinehart, Kathryn Ann *principal*

Elyria
Skillicorn, Judy Pettibone *gifted and talented education coordinator*

Euclid
Clements, Mary Margaret *retired educator*
Hoffert, Frank, Jr. *secondary education educator*

Fairborn
Russell-Rader, Kathleen *secondary school educator*

Findlay
Badertscher, Mark Allen *vocational educator*
Draper, David Eugene *seminary president*
Goedde, Tony G. *registrar*
Recker, Dennis L. *school superintendent*
Sipes, Theodore Lee *educator*

Forest Park
Ashley, Lynn *educator, consultant, administrator*

Fremont
Sattler, Nancy Joan *curriculum chair*
Wethington, Norbert Anthony *college administrator*

Gahanna
Ellsworth, Cynthia Ann *counseling administrator*

Granville
Bennett, Paul Lewis *retired educator, writer*
Myers, Michele Tolela *university president*

Grove City
Williams, Mark Allen *secondary education educator*

Hartville
Pettigrew, Frank Edwin, Jr. *assistant dean, physical education educator*

Hiram
Oliver, G(eorge) Benjamin *academic administrator, philosophy educator*

Hudson
Breuker, John *private school educator*
Goheen, Janet Moore *counselor, sales professional*
Kennedy, Frederick Morgan *secondary education educator*

Jamestown
Liem, Darlene Marie *secondary education educator*

Kent
Cartwright, Carol Ann *university president*
Fultz, John Howard *elementary school educator*
Schwartz, Michael *university president, sociology educator*

Kettering
Taylor, Billie Wesley *retired secondary education educator*

Kingston
Mathew, Martha Sue Cryder *retired education educator*

Lima
Meek, Violet Imhof *dean*

Logan
Donahey, Beverly Ellinger *elementary education educator*

Lorain
Strick, Cynthia Lee *elementary education educator*
Trelka, Janice Margaret Nace *secondary education educator*

Louisville
Shade, Donna A. Francis *principal*

Magnolia
Zimmerman, Judith Rose *elementary art educator*

Mansfield
Ogden, William Michael *school system administrator*
Riedl, John Orth *university dean*

Marietta
Ray, R. Glenn *education and business director*

Maumee
Thompson, LaVerne Elizabeth Thomas *education administration educator*

Mc Connelsville
Retton, Sandra Jo *physical education educator, coach*

Mechanicsburg
Maynard, Joan *education educator*

Medina
Kiefer, Jacqueline Lorraine *special education educator, consultant*

Millersburg
Childers, Lawrence Jeffrey *superintendent of schools*
Yoder, Anna A. *elementary school educator*

Morrow
Carey, Christopher John *outdoor education specialist, consultant*

New Middletown
Ade, Barbara Jean *secondary education educator*

New Philadelphia
Doughten, Mary Katherine (Molly Doughten) *retired secondary education educator*
Goforth, Mary Elaine Davey *secondary education educator*

North Olmsted
Hughes, Kenneth G. *elementary school educator*
Smolen, Cheryl Hosaka *special education educator*

Norton
Kun, Joyce Anne *secondary education educator, small business owner*

Oregon
Crain, John Kip *school system administrator*

Oxford
Bacon, Betty J. *school administrator*
Davis, Sherie Kay *special education educator*
Dizney, Robert Edward *retired secondary education educator*
Hanger, William Sherwood *university administrator*
Kelly, James Stewart *associate professor, associate director*
Pearson, Paul Guy *academic administrator emeritus*
Thompson, Bertha Boya *retired education educator, antique dealer and appraiser*

Painesville
Blyth, Ann Marie *secondary education educator*

Parma
Eustache, Daniel Lee *secondary education educator*
Humphrey, Ronald Murray *educator, publisher*
McFadden, Nadine Lynn *secondary education Spanish educator*
Nemeth, Dian Jean *secondary school educator*
Tener, Carol Joan *retired secondary education educator*

Pepper Pike
Diederich, Anne Marie *college president*

Perrysburg
Zuchowski, Beverly Jean *chemistry educator*

Plain City
Brown, D. Robin *elementary educator*

Port Clinton
Ewersen, Mary Virginia *retired secondary educator*

Powell
Becker, Karen Ann *academic program director*
Ehlert, Nancy Lynne *elementary education educator*
Montenaro, Regina Lynne *secondary education educator*

Put In Bay
Isaly, Edwin Robert *principal, curator*

Reynoldsburg
Wilson, Robert Charles, Jr. *secondary education educator, consultant*

Rio Grande
Shibley, Ralph Edwin, Jr. *special education educator*

Roseville
Taylor, Timothy Alan *elementary education educator*

Saint Paris
Ward, Marcia Balmut *secondary education educator*

Sharonville
Horn, Stanley Dale *automotive technology educator*

Sheffield Lake
McHenry, Timothy Howard *elementary education educator*

Sidney
Seitz, James Eugene *retired academic administrator, freelance writer*

Smithville
Finley, Dennis Howard *vocational education educator*

South Euclid
Conrad, Sister Linda *elementary school educator*

Springboro
Ramey, Rebecca Ann *elementary education educator*

Springfield
Cantrell, John L. *secondary education educator*
Kinnison, William Andrew *retired university president*

Streetsboro
Drugan, Cornelius Bernard *school administrator, psychologist, musician*

Sylvania
Sampson, Earldine Robison *education educator*

Tiffin
Davis, C(laud) Neal *academic administrator, educator, service club executive, fund development specialist*

Toledo
Binkley, Jonathan Andrew *secondary education educator, government educator*
Cole, Jeffrey Clark *college development professional*
Flaskamp, Ruth Ehmen Staack *retired elementary education educator*
Hanncken Henry, Judith Curtis *education educator*
Horton, Frank Elba *university official, geography educator*
Kozbial, Richard James *elementary education educator*
Romanoff, Marjorie Reinwald *education educator*
Ruma, Jan Lynne *college alumni administrator*
Thomas, Patricia Grafton *secondary school educator*
Toadvin-Bester, Josephine Vesella *academic administrator, educator*
Weinblatt, Charles Samuel *university administrator, employment consultant*

University Heights
Travis, Frederick Francis *academic administrator, historian*

Vandalia
Schaefer, Sandra Ellen *secondary education educator*

Warren
Shively, Elaine Marie *university official*

Washington Court House
Fichthorn, Fonda Gay *principal*

Waterford
Montgomery, Gretchen Golzé *secondary education educator*

Wauseon
McNulty, Roberta Jo *educational administrator*

West Chester
Capps, Dennis William *secondary school educator*
Hume, Dean Bradley *secondary education educator, writer*

West Milton
Bowers, Carlton LeRoy *secondary school educator*

Westerville
Carter, Harold Lloyd *secondary education educator*
Corlette, Elizabeth Ann *primary education educator*
Davis, Joseph Lloyd *educational administrator, consultant*
Husarik, Ernest Alfred *educational administrator*
Lattimore, Joy Powell *preschool administrator*

Wilberforce
Hitchcock, Kim Anita *education educator*

Willoughby
Lillich, Alice Louise *retired secondary education educator*

Wilmington
Pohl, Daniel Martin *college administrator*

Wooster
Childers, Susan Lynn Bohn *special education educator, administrator, human resources and transition specialist*
Shepherd, Mary Anne *elementary education educator*

Worthington
Harvey, Wayne Evan *secondary education educator, administrator*

Yellow Springs
Guskin, Alan E. *university president*
Weibl, Richard A. *educational researcher*

Youngstown
Cochran, Leslie Herschel *university administrator*
Loch, John Robert *educational administrator*
Peterson, Gil *university director*
Zitto, Richard Joseph *physics educator*
Zorn, Robert Lynn *education educator*

Zanesville
Jones, Marlene Wiseman *elementary education educator, reading specialist*

PENNSYLVANIA

State College
Mills, Rilla Dean *university administrator, consultant*

SOUTH CAROLINA

Hilton Head Island
Mulhollan, Paige Elliott *academic administrator emeritus*

SOUTH DAKOTA

Brookings
Wagner, Robert Todd *university president, sociology educator*

Dell Rapids
Wehde, Roger Allan *secondary education educator*

Freeman
Senner, Robert William *secondary education educator*

Kadoka
Stout, Maye Alma *educator*

Lemmon
Grey Eagle, Sandra Lee *special education educator*

Midland
Christensen, Richard L. *school system administrator*

Mitchell
Schilling, Katherine Lee Tracy *retired principal*

North Sioux City
Rasmussen, Jerry William *secondary school educator*

Rapid City
Loomer, Gerald Earl *secondary school science educator*

Sioux Falls
Gulson, DeLoris Anne *reading specialist*
Huseboe, Doris Louise *educator, arts consultant*
Johnson, Thomas Floyd *college president, educator*
O'Brien, Cheryl Ann Marie *educator*
Olson, Gary Duane *academic administrator, history educator*
Wagoner, Ralph Howard *academic administrator, educator*

Vermillion
Milton, Leonharda Lynn *elementary and secondary school educator*

Winner
Hansen, Sandra Kay *head librarian*

TENNESSEE

Jefferson
Pickard, Mary Jean *education educator*

TEXAS

Sweetwater
Sibbet, Lorraine Alberta *academic administrator*

UTAH

Provo
Stanford, Melvin Joseph *retired dean, educator*

WISCONSIN

Adams
Beaver, Robert Allen *school system administrator*

Algoma
Oshefsky, Carol Ann *retired elementary education educator*

Antioch
Bryant, Christopher Alan *elementary education educator*

Appleton
Warch, Richard *academic administrator*

Athelstane
Outcalt, David Lewis *academic administrator, mathematician, educator*

Bear Creek
Lorge, Charn Teresa Maria *elementary education educator, real estate agent*

Beloit
Ferrall, Victor Eugene, Jr. *college administrator, lawyer*
Husby, Anita Kay *educational administrator*
Miller, Janet Louise *education educator, consultant*

Brookfield
Gradeless, Donald Eugene *secondary education educator*

Cedarburg
Mielke, Jon Alan *elementary school administrator*

Clayton
Kuntz, Karen Frances *preschool education educator*

Coleman
Widmer, Mark Steven *school administrator*

Columbus
Schellin, Patricia Marie Biddle *educator*

Cross Plains
Rodenschmit, Helen Juliana *elementary education educator*

De Pere
Riley, Margaret *academic administrator*

Dodgeville
Doyle, Lauretta Darice *secondary educator*

Eagle River
Farrell, Lenore Emma *elementary education educator, guidance counselor*

Eau Claire
Brill, Donald Maxim *educator, writer, researcher*
Dahle, Johannes Upton *academic administrator*
Reiter, Bonnie Jean *training and development educator*
Stanton, Sandra Sunquist *school counselor, consultant, educator*
Weissenburger, Fred Elmer *school system administrator*

Elkhorn
Reinke, Doris Marie *retired elementary education educator*

Fond Du Lac
Brown, Nancy McIntire *academic administrator*
Fett, Patricia Diane *elementary education educator*

Glidden
Palecek, Sandra Marie *reading education specialist*

Green Bay
Laughlin, Margaret Ann *education educator*

Hales Corners
Michalski, (Żurowski) Wacław *adult education educator*

Hartland
Nelson, Katherine MacTaggart *educator*

Hayward
Herder, Harry Joseph, Jr. *retired educator*

Kenosha
Campbell, F(enton) Gregory *college administrator, historian*
Cobb, Clayton Leigh *academic advisor*
Levis, Richard George *middle school educator*
Tacki, Bernadette Susan *principal*
Zuhlke, Marybeth *elementary school curriculum consultant, educator*

La Crosse
Beyers, Catherine Meyer *media specialist*
Davis, Laurie Lee *special education educator*
Geyer, Sidna Priest *secondary and business education educator*
Kuipers, Judith L. *academic administrator*

Ladysmith
Macaruso, Victor Maurice *academic administrator*

Madison
Bell/Jackson, Marianne Jeanne *elementary education educator*
Hanna, Donald Eugene *academic administrator*
Johnson, Anthony Colbert *assistant dean, educator*
Lyall, Katharine C(ulbert) *academic administrator, economics educator*
Montello, Raphael Randolph *vocational school educator, culinary executive*
Nagy, Joanne Elizabeth Berg *associate dean university*
Odden, Allan Robert *education educator*
Paris, Kathleen Anne *educational consultant*
Prieve, E. Arthur *arts administration educator*
Robinson, Christopher Sean *counselor, educator*
Weiss, Mareda Ruth *dean*
Wunsch, Marie Ann *provost, vice chancellor*

Manitowoc
Pohlmann, Patty Lou *college official*

Menasha
Dewing, Denis Eugene *school counselor*
Gorsalitz, Jeannine Liane *elementary school educator*

Menomonee Falls
Hinnrichs-Dahms, Holly Beth *middle school educator*

Mequon
Dohmen, Mary Holgate *retired primary school educator*

Milwaukee
Armstrong, Leona May Bottrell *counselor*
Arora, Swarnjit Singh *university administrator, economics educator*
Benson, Moses, Jr. *military education specialist*
Bovée, Warren Gilles *retired journalism educator*
Collins, James Troy, Jr. *academic administrator*
Czarnezki, Mary Ann *women's studies educator*
DiUlio, Albert Joseph *university president, priest*
Doehr-Blanck, Denise Louise *special education educator*
Forseth, Lynn Marie *college administrator*
Frank, Kristy Louise *English educator*
Hansen, John Herbert *university administrator, accountant*
Lietz, Jeremy Jon *educational administrator, writer*
Patel, Minnie Hariprasad *educator*
Raynor, John Patrick *university administrator*
Read, Sister Joel *academic administrator*
Sankovitz, James Leo *development director, lobbyist*
Schroeder, John H. *university chancellor*
Spann, Wilma Nadene *educational administrator*
Thomas, Robert Michael *special education educator*

Mukwonago
Vick, Rod Ryan *secondary education educator, writer*

Oak Creek
Lesjak, Lisa Mary *secondary school administrator*

Omro
Turner, Mildred Edith *day care owner*

Oshkosh
Kerrigan, John E. *academic administrator*

Racine
Bedford, Emmett Gruner *retired professor*
DeRango, Mary Laura Keul *service occupation careers counselor*
Rodrigues-Pavao, Antonio *vocal music teacher*

Rhinelander
Mussehl, Allan Arthur *program director*

Richland Center
Thompson, Dorothy Denise *university administrator*

Ripon
Talbot, John Dudley *college administrator*

River Falls
Thibodeau, Gary A. *academic administrator*

Sheboygan
Johnson, Benjamin Leibold *former education training and management analyst*
Ladiges, Lori Jean *learning disabilities specialist*
Striggow, Keith Gregory *education educator, provost*

Stoddard
Hollenbeck, Sue J. *elementary education educator*

Superior
Davidson, Donald W. *education educator*

Thiensville
Williams, Maxine Eleanor *retired elementary education educator*

Three Lakes
Bauknecht, Barbara Belle *educator*

Twin Lakes
Fleischer, John Richard *retired secondary education educator*

Verona
Hoffmeister, Ann Elizabeth *elementary education educator*

Wausau
Hart, Sharon Yvonne *academic adminstrator*

Wautoma
Sholar, Margerie Eleanor *elementary education educator*

Whitewater
Busse, Eileen E. *special education educator*
Greenhill, H. Gaylon *academic administrator*

Wisconsin Rapids
Olson-Hellerud, Linda Kathryn *elementary education educator*

CANADA

MANITOBA

Winnipeg
Stalker, Jacqueline D'Aoust *academic administrator, educator*

ONTARIO

Toronto
Somerville, William H. *academic administrator*

LIBERIA

Monrovia
Johnson, Larry Robert *education educator*

ADDRESS UNPUBLISHED

Adcock, Rebecca Leigh *educator*
Alves, Elizabeth Martha Hagerty *elementary education educator*
Apps, Jerold Willard *adult education educator*
Arends, Mark W. *educator*
Audley, Barbara Marie *adult education educator, university administrator*
Banjac, Joyce Annette *entrepreneur, business educator*
Barber, Kimberly Lisanby *elementary education educator*
Bare, Lois Kieffaber *college director*
Barnard, Ann Watson *retired academic administrator, educator, writer*
Bavin, Lynda Ann *tutor, mentor*
Becker, Walter Heinrich *vocational educator, planner*
Bernstein, Eva Gould *retired elementary education educator, reading specialist*
Bibbs, Lona Carol *educational program administrator*
Bickett, Richard Joseph *retired elementary school principal, elementary education educator*
Bixler, Sandra Diane *elementary education educator*
Bohling-Philippi, Vicki Dee *family educator*
Boyd, Richard Lyn *secondary school educator*
Caldwell, Carl Howard *dean*
Callahan, Jean Leslie *educator, artist*
Cline, Linda Jean *reading educator*
Coleman, Gary William *elementary education educator*
Conover, Nancy Anderson *secondary school counselor*
Cooler, Thecla Behrens *university administrator, international advisor*
Copeland, Henry Jefferson, Jr. *former college president*
Dow, Jean Louise *school system business administrator*
Dresbach, Mary Louise *state higher education administrator*
Duff, John Bernard *college president, former city official*
Dunn, Helen Elizabeth *retired secondary school educator*
Elmen, Gary Warren *principal*
Esterline, Brenda Lee *elementary school educator, travel advisor*
Euler, Russell Nelson *mathematics educator, researcher*
Evans, Geraldine Ann *academic administrator*
Falk, Marshall Allen *retired university dean, physician*
Fenton, Marjorie *university official, consultant*
Fessler, Patricia Lou *library and media coordinator*
Filchock, Ethel *education educator, poet*
Folz, Kathleen Louise *elementary education educator*
Fonne, Hiram A. *dean*
Frey, Margo Walther *career counselor, columnist*
Frey, Stacey Jane *elementary education educator*
Gamsky, Neal Richard *university administrator, psychology educator*
Gardner, Thomas Joseph *vocational educator*
Gilzow, H(omer) Floyd, Jr. *educational administrator*
Gleue, Lorine Anna *elementary education educator*
Glower, Donald Duane *university executive, mechanical engineer*
Gordon, Audrey Kramen *university administrator*
Gordon, John Siesel *art college administrator, sculptor*
Gowen, Nancy Adele *vocational education educator, consultant*
Groat, Pamela Ferne *school librarian*
Grove, Myrna Jean *elementary education educator*
Haeberle, Rosamond Pauline *retired educator*
Hammer, Joyce Mae *gifted and talented education educator*
Hampton, Dorian Sherard *clinical educator*
Hansen, Cherry Ann *special education educator*
Hardin, Clifford Morris *retired university chancellor, cabinet member*
Hartman, Marie Suzanne *special education educator*
Hasselmo, Nils *university official, linguistics educator*
Hawkins, Jacquelyn *elementary and secondary education educator*
Hedges, Norma Ann *retired secondary education educator*
Hildreth, William Bartley *public administration educator*
Hoff, Kathryn Susan *technology educator, consultant*
Housinger, Warren Donald *retired secondary education educator*
Jacobs, Linda Rotroff *elementary school educator*
Jacobs-Ciranni, Mary Lauralee *elementary education educator*
Jakubauskas, Edward Benedict *college president*
Johnson, Monica Lynn *elementary education educator*
Johnston, John Wayne *educational administrator*
Keim, William Alan *retired educator*
Keller, Jami Ann *special education educator*
Koleson, Donald Ralph *retired college dean, educator*
Koveleski, Kathryn Delane *retired special education educator*
Krebill, Lorrie Leabo *secondary education educator*
Kryzak, Linda Ann *principal*
Kutrieh, Ahmad Ramez *educator*
Lange, Douglas Keith *university administrator*
Lantz, Joanne Baldwin *academic administrator emeritus*
LaRose, Michael H. *secondary education educator, coach*
Leistner, Mary Edna *retired secondary education educator*
LeSage, Janet Billings *special education educator*
Loparo, Charles A., Sr. *educator*
Lovell, Mary Ann *secondary education educator*
Lyon, John Joseph *liberal arts and education educator, administrator, translator*
Marx, Hazel Ruth *retired primaary school educator*
Mascia-Strickler, Martha *special education educator*
Mathews-Graham, Carla *English language educator*
Maurer, Beverly Bennett *school administrator*
McIntosh, Carolyn Meade *retired educational administrator*
McIntrye, Geraldine K. *training center administrator*
Mergenovich, Shirley Ann *educator*
Mets, Lisa Ann *academic administrator*
Monson, David Carl *school superintendent, farmer, state legislator*
Morgan, Rhelda Elnola *secondary school educator*
Mullins, Connie Rae *school board executive*
Murphy, Jeanette Carol *education educator*

Newman, Barbara Mae *retired special education educator*
Nienhouse, Laurence Jay *secondary education educator*
Nondorf, Janice Kathryn *special education educator*
North, Anita *secondary education educator*
Norton, Mary Leta *educator*
Oden, Jean Phifer *special education educator*
O'Reilly, Rosann Tagliaferro *computer educator*
Papazian, Rosalie Marie *elementary education educator*
Parish, Charles Theron *guidance counselor*
Park, John Thornton *academic administrator*
Patterson, Janice Lavelle *academic administrator*
Perreault, Laura Cecile *retired educator, volunteer*
Preusser, Joseph William *academic administrator*
Raphtis, Athena Ellen *elementary school teacher*
Rasmussen, Donna Ilene Lewis *instructional technologist*
Revor, Barbara Kay *secondary school educator*
Robbins, Frances Elaine *educational administrator*
Robertson, Mary Virginia *retired elementary education educator*
Rossetti, Rosemarie *teacher educator, writer, book publisher*
Rost, Marcia Verlene *secondary educator*
Schlesinger, Carole Lynn *elementary education educator*
Scollard, Diane Louise *retired elementary school educator*
Seeber, William Thaden *retired university development director*
Sherman, Richard H. *education educator*
Singerman, Dona Fatibeno *reading specialist*
Smith, Evan Shreeve *university official*
Smith, Patricia J. *educational consultant*
Sonnenschein, Hugo Freund *academic administrator, economics educator*
Speer, Max Michael *special education educator*
Stuckey, Helenjean Lauterbach *counselor educator*
Sullivan, Faith H. *elementary education educator, writer*
Thomas, Carolyn Harper *elementary educator*
Thottupuram, Kurian Cherian *priest, college director, educator*
Titkemeier, Deloy Allen *secondary education educator*
Vandevender, Barbara Jewell *elementary education educator, farmer*
VandeWalle, Don Michael *educator, researcher*
Van Middendorp, Judy E.S. *integrated studies consultant*
Van Sickle, Barbara Ann *special education educator*
Van Wagner, Nancy Lee *retired educator*
Vorous, Patricia Ann Marie *elementary school educator*
Wagner, Helen Adeene *elementary education educator*
Warner, Judith Kay *elementary education educator*
Weimer, Gary W. *academic administrator, consultant*
Widman, Elizabeth Ann *educator*
Willard, Timothy J. *higher education executive, consultant*
Winegar, Lucia Spencer *retired secondary school administrator*
Worthen, John Edward *academic administrator*
Wrzesinski, Elizabeth Jane *university official*
Young, Margaret Anne *elementary educator*

ENGINEERING

UNITED STATES

ARKANSAS

Paragould
Sheridan, Mark William *mechanical engineer, strategic planner*

FLORIDA

Fort Myers
Callanan, Kathleen Joan *retired electrical engineer*
Sechrist, Chalmers Franklin, Jr. *electrical engineering educator*

Longboat Key
Schroeder, Robert Louis *engineering executive*

Tellevast
McGuire, Mark Alan *chemical engineer*

GEORGIA

Marietta
Henke, Steven John *engineering executive*

Savannah
Herbel, LeRoy Alec, Jr. *telecommunications engineer*

ILLINOIS

Abbott Park
Geist, Jill Marie *medical writer*
Pak, Henry H. *biomedical engineer, researcher*

Argonne
Deitrich, Lawrence Walter *mechanical engineer, nuclear engineer*
Haupt, H. James *mechanical design engineer*
Kaun, Thomas David *electrochemical engineer, inventor*
Miller, Shelby Alexander *chemical engineer, educator*
Noonan, John Robert *electrical engineer, material science engineer*

Arlington Heights
Wolfe, Carl Dean *electrical engineer*

Aurora
Dodd, Stephen Cowl *chemical engineer*
Richard, David A. *engineering manager*

Berwyn
De Lerno, Manuel Joseph *electrical engineer*

Buffalo Grove
Kaplan, Mitchell Philip *consulting engineer, marketing executive*
Parker, James John *engineering and marketing manager*

Burbank
Oldendorf, Lawrence Edward *engineering executive*

Carbondale
Lindsey, Jefferson Franklin, III *electrical engineering technology educator*

Carol Stream
Darling, Lawrence Dean *engineering computing executive*
Hampe, William Carl *information services administrator*
Wojtanek, Guy Andrew *mechanical engineer*

Carthage
Erbes, John Robert *engineering executive*

Champaign
Korst, Helmut Hans *mechanical engineer, educator*
Kruger, William Arnold *consulting civil engineer*
May, Linda Karen Cardiff *safety engineer, nurse*
Sundy, George Joseph, Jr. *engineering executive*

Chicago
Agarwal, Gyan Chand *engineering educator*
Aieleszuk, Jan *project engineer*
Akhtar, Saleem *electrical engineer, consultant*
Alexander, Eugene J. *medical imaging systems designer, research enginee*
Alukal, Varghese George *metallurgical engineer*
Banerjee, Prashant *industrial engineering educator*
Blanchard, James Arthur *engineer and computer systems specialist*
Capouch, Edward Arthur *electrical engineer*
Chen, Wai-Kai *electrical engineering and computer science educator, consultant*
Chung, Paul Myungha *mechanical engineer, educator*
Datta, Rathin *chemical engineer*
Dix, Rollin C(umming) *mechanical engineering educator, consultant*
Gerstner, Robert William *structural engineering educator, consultant*
Jaramillo, Carlos Alberto *civil engineer*
Johnson, Ronald Henry *engineer, consultant*
Kim, H. J. (Shaun Kim) *engineering company executive*
Kirstein, Joe Walter *design engineer*
Krishnamachari, Sadagopa Iyengar *mechanical engineer, consultant*
Kudrna, Frank Louis, Jr. *civil engineer, consultant*
Linden, Henry Robert *chemical engineering research executive*
McGuire, Anthony Bartholomew *engineering executive*
Mc Inturf, Faith Mary *engineering company executive, thoroughbred harness racing executive*
McMillan, Hugh Hopkins *environmental engineer*
Minneste, Viktor, Jr. *retired electrical company executive*
Munoz, Mario Alejandro *civil engineer, consultant*
Mustafa, Ali Syed *structural engineer, consultant*
Nickel, Melvin Edwin *metallurgical engineer*
Price, Bridgette Denise *industrial engineer*
Price, Edward Francis *civil engineer*
Ratner, Leah W. *mechanical engineer, researcher*
Rikoski, Richard Anthony *engineering executive, electrical engineer*
Russo, Gilberto *engineering educator*
Sarro, Thomas Lee *software engineer, consultant*
Saxena, Satish Chandra *chemical engineering educator*
Sresty, Guggilam Chalamaiah *environmental engineer*
Stecich, John Patrick *structural engineer*
Stoller, Patricia Sypher *structural engineer*
Westfall, Wayne Lynn *chemical engineer*
Wong, Thomas Tang Yum *engineering educator*

Chicago Heights
Foushi, John Anthony *cost engineer*

Crest Hill
Cizek, David John *sales engineer, small business owner*

Crystal Lake
Hornby, Robert Ray *mechanical engineer*

De Kalb
Bow, Sing Tze *engineer, educator*
He, Lili *electrical engineering educator, researcher*

Decatur
Graf, Karl Rockwell *nuclear engineer*
Ray, Michael D. *design engineer*
Stoa, Terry A. *chemical engineer*

Des Plaines
Atallah, Sami *chemical engineer*
Pasternak, Jan *chief engineer*
Ripp, Bryan Jerome *geological engineer*
Segar, Floyd *engineering manager*

Dixon
Jungk, Thomas Richard *civil engineer*

Downers Grove
Bogett, William R. *accident reconstructionist and safety engineer*
Fay, Peter Carlyle *mechanical engineer*
Rawal, Darshan Lal *civil, structural engineer, consultant*
Stample, James M. *plant engineer*
Thomas, George E. *engineering executive*

Dunlap
Hanard, Marcel Roger, II *research engineer*
Reinsma, Harold Lawrence *design consultant, engineer*

East Moline
Taylor, Byron Keith *industrial engineer*

Elgin
Iliadis, Nick *mechanical engineer*
Koepke, Donald Herbert *retired mechanical engineer and real estate professional*

Elk Grove Village
Guido, Frank *engineer*
Tullio, John J. *electrical engineer*

Elmhurst
Burton, Darrell Irvin *engineering executive*
Eck, Bernard John *engineer*
Ghosh, Kanchan *electrical engineer, researcher*

Evanston
Arenson, Donald Lewis *consulting company executive*
Bazant, Zdenek Pavel *structural engineering educator, scientist, consultant*
Bobco, William David, Jr. *consulting engineering company executive*
Johnson, Richard Ned *mechanical engineer, research executive*
Pao, Lucy Ya *electrical engineering and computer science educat*
Pourkermani, Mahmood *electrical engineer, consultant*
Shah, Surendra Poonamchand *engineering educator, researcher*
Vrbancic, John Emerick *engineering consultant*

Fairview Heights
Sharp, William Charles *systems engineer*

Franklin Park
Miller, Stanley Manfred *systems engineer*

Freeport
Clemmons, James H. *engineering executive*

Galesburg
Page, Lloyd E. *civil engineer*

Geneva
Richard, John C. *design engineer*

Glen Carbon
Glenn, Russell David *electrical engineer*
Strang, William M. *electrical engineer*

Glenview
Decastell, William E. *mechanical engineer, consultant*
Logani, Kulbhushan Lal *civil and structural engineer*
Salata, Wayne Frank *engineering executive*

Grayslake
Spencer, Clyde David *civil engineer, land surveyor*

Gurnee
Theis, Peter Frank *engineering executive, inventor*

Highland
Sudholt, Bryan F. *electronic engineer*

Highland Park
Lewin, Mitchell Joseph *die casting engineer*

Hoffman Estates
Murarka, Narayan P. *electronics engineer, engineering executive*

Itasca
Adams, Paula *mechanical engineer*
Cormican, Terry D. *electrical engineer*
Gibson, Robert Reed *electrical engineer*
Kolodziej, Bert Kasimir *mechanical engineer*
Mitchell, Frank R. *electrical engineer*
Mockus, Joseph Frank *electrical engineer*

Joliet
Tilos, Gregorio Samayo *electrical engineer, educator*

Kankakee
Dodson, Carl Edward *nuclear engineer, real estate agent, executive, minister*

Lake Bluff
Cooley, Jack Lee *engineering manager*
Fortuna, William Frank *architect, architectural engineer*

Lake Forest
Bell, Charles Eugene, Jr. *industrial engineer*
Smith, Sidney Talbert *biomedical engineer*

Lake Zurich
Bukala, Alexander E. *engineering administrator*

Lanark
Quatman, Robert J. *manufacturing engineer*

Lemont
Goldman, Arthur Joseph *research and development executive*

Libertyville
Lynn, Michael Robert *chemical engineer*

Lincolnshire
Kotynek, George Roy *mechanical engineer, educator, marketing executive*

Lisle
Baker, Mark Christopher *computer engineer*

Lombard
Pischl, John Paul *electrical engineer*
Schneider, Alexander William *reliability engineer*

Marengo
Donahue, Michael Peter *manufacturing engineer*

Marion
Tarlton, Michael Ray *civil engineer, youth minister*
Wittenborn, Vernon Duane *civil engineer*

Marshall
Cork, Donald Burl *electrical engineer*

Mattoon
Simonelli, Michael Tarquin *chemical engineer*

Mc Henry
Glaw, John P. *manufacturing engineer*

Melrose Park
Maksymowicz, Wesley *design engineer*
Tulach, John R. *mechanical engineer*

Moline
Malicki, Gregg Hillard *engineer*
Manske, Bradley William *computer engineer*
Wiley, Jack Cleveland *mechanical engineer*

Morton Grove
Giberman, Alexander *engineering director*

Mount Prospect
Avila, Arthur Julian *metallurgical engineer*
Eich, Peter M. *engineering executive*
Junkel, Eric Franz *engineering executive*

Mount Vernon
Knight, Brenda Lee *quality engineer*

Naperville
Craigo, Gordon Earl *engineer*
Koeppe, Eugene Charles, Jr. *electrical engineer*
Peters, Boyd Leon *agricultural engineer*
Prasad, Ram A. *communications systems engineer*
Symuleski, Richard Aloysius *chemical engineer*
Vora, Manu Kishandas *chemical engineer, quality consultant*

Niles
Obermann, George *engineering executive*

North Chicago
Chu, Alexander Hang-Torng *chemical engineer*

Northbrook
Empen, Dan R. *electrical engineer*
Polsky, Michael Peter *mechanical engineer*
Whitman, Robert Leslie *acoustic and optic engineer*

Oak Brook
Degerstrom, James Marvin *engineering manager*
Sands, M. Dale *engineering industry executive*
Wallace, Ralph Eugene *automotive and mechanical engineer*

Oak Forest
Kogut, Kenneth Joseph *consulting engineer*

Oak Park
Relwani, Nirmalkumar Murlidhar (Nick Relwani) *mechanical engineer*
Staunton, John Joseph Jameson *electrical engineer*

Olympia Fields
Licht, Charles A. *mechanical engineer, consultant*

Park Forest
Williams, Jack Raymond *civil engineer*

Peoria
Dempsey, Gary Lee *electrical and computer engineering educator*
Kroll, Dennis Edwards *industrial engineering educator*
Miller, Robin J. *computer engineer*
Polanin, W. Richard *engineering educator*

Prophetstown
Sanders, Gary Glenn *electronics engineer, consultant*

Rantoul
Henry, Richard W. *mechanical engineer*
Valencia, Rogelio Pasco *electronics engineer*

Reddick
Brunner, Eldon John *mechanical engineer, consultant*

Rock Island
Asadi, Asad *mechanical engineer, educator*

Rockford
Bried, Lynndon Herman *manufacturing engineer*
Cunningham, Patrick Jay *laboratory engineer*
Eley, John Duane *electrical engineer, consultant*
Eliason, Jon Tate *electrical engineer*
Shepler, John Edward *engineering executive*

Rockton
Wright, Greg Alan August *mechanical engineer*

Rolling Meadows
Gallagher, David Alden *research engineer*
Pezl, John Joseph *engineer*

Roscoe
Davis, Donald L. *electrical engineer*
Jacobs, Richard Dearborn *consulting engineer company executive*

Round Lake
Bennett, Cynthia Ann Forsythe *software engineer*

Sauget
Baltz, Richard Arthur *chemical engineer*

Schaumburg
Birzer, Richard *engineer*
Dahn, Carl James *aerospace engineer*

Skokie
Adaska, Wayne Scott *geotechnical engineer*

South Beloit
Rovelstad, Andrew *mechanical engineer*

Springfield
Ballenger, Hurley René *electrical engineer*

Busch, William H. *engineer*
Chen, Eden Hsien-chang *engineering consultant*
Jagodzinski, Ronald Edward *mechanical engineer, consultant*
Lyons, J. Rolland *civil engineer*
Newton, Bill Edward *electrical engineering executive*
Summer, Nancy L. *electrical engineer*
Walker, Trevor Joe *computer network engineer*

Urbana
Axford, Roy Arthur *nuclear engineering educator*
Beck, Paul Adams *metallurgist, educator*
Davis, Wayne Joseph *engineering educator*
Eden, James Gary *electrical engineering and physics educator, researcher*
Hirschi, Michael Carl *agricultural engineering educator*
Hummel, John William *agricultural engineer*
Larson, Carl Shipley *engineering educator, consultant*
Olver, Elwood Forrest *retired agricultural engineering educator*
Phillips, William Robert *fluid dynamics educator*
Sauer, Peter William *electrical engineering educator*
Wert, Charles Allen *metallurgical and mining engineering educator*

Vernon Hills
Barrett, Frederick Charles *engineering executive*

Waukegan
Evangelisti, Robert *environmental engineer*
Srinivasa, Venkataramaniah *engineer*

West Chicago
Kieft, Gerald Nelson *mechanical engineer*

Westchester
Zlatin, Larion Y. *mechanical engineer*

Wheaton
Bryant, Paul Everett *civil engineer, city engineer*

Wheeling
Ditthardt, Alfred Robert *electronics engineer*
Soltys, Andrzej *industrial engineer*

Wilmette
Muhlenbruch, Carl W. *civil engineer*

Wood Dale
Smith, Michael William *biomedical engineer, consultant*
Van Allman, Don Thomas *engineering executive*

Wood River
Stevens, Robert Edward *engineering company executive*

Worth
Walkowicz, Ted H. *manager special engineering*

INDIANA

Albion
Lytle, James Robert *product design engineer*

Anderson
Lasley, Douglas E. *engineering executive*
Medema, Jeffrey S. *mechanical engineer*

Auburn
Dietrich, Ronald G. *electrical engineer*
Kummer, Marty E. *mechanical engineer*

Bargersville
Pinney, Jon D. *manufacturing engineer*

Berne
Grube, Allen D. *mechanical engineer*
Pollard, Phil Earl *electrical engineer*

Bloomington
Dawson, James Richard *fire and safety engineer*
Hall, Todd Anthony *research and development engineer*
Kinzler, Stephen Boyd *software engineer*

Buck Creek
Blettner, James Donald *engineering company executive*

Carmel
Monical, Robert Duane *consulting structural engineer*
Ong, James Shaujen *mechanical engineer*

Clarksville
Spurgeon, Wesley C. *material handling administrator*

Columbus
Doell, James F. *electrical engineer*
Kubo, Isoroku *mechanical engineer*
Uhlmansiek, Chris J. *automotive engineer*
Wolber, William George *retired instrument engineer*

Connersville
Stanton, William Taylor *manufacturing engineer*

Crane
Waggoner, Susan Marie *electronics engineer*

Dyer
Brouwer, John J. *engineer*

Elkhart
McCarty, Richard Joseph *consulting engineer*

Evansville
Hartsaw, William O. *mechanical engineering educator*
Veach, Darrell Alves *civil engineer, consultant*

Fort Wayne
Alam, Mohammad Showkat-Ul *engineering educator*
Ensley, Tom Michael *manufacturing engineer*
Hindle, Larry *manufacturing engineer*
Huffman, Jim D. *industrial engineer*
Lendl, Bill *mechanical engineer*
Lyons, Jerry Lee *mechanical engineer*
Thorn, Scott Aron *mechanical engineer*
Weatherford, George Edward *civil engineer*
Wilson, Ken *electrical engineer*

Franklin
Van-Breemen, Bertram *optical engineer*

Gary
Swan, Peter Michael *engineering executive*

Goshen
Heap, James Clarence *retired mechanical engineer*
Van Diepenbos, Mark A. *draftsman*

Greensburg
Blasdel, Beth L. *plant and engineering manager*
Heidlage, Jeffery Paul *manufacturing engineer*
Liang, Ching (Qing) *engineering manager*

Hagerstown
Vanderbilt, Vern Crowin, Jr. *consulting engineer*

Hamilton
Overby, Kenneth Wayne *design engineer*

Hammond
Neff, Gregory Pall *manufacturing engineering educator, consultant*
Pierson, Edward Samuel *engineering educator, consultant*

Huntington
Stanley, Michael Fritz *production engineer*

Indianapolis
Arps, David Foster *electronics engineer*
Bancroft, Randy Cecil *electrical engineer*
Battle, Joe David *engineer*
Collier, David English *electrical engineer, consultant*
Cones, Van Buren *electronics engineer, consultant*
Dillon, Howard Burton *civil engineer*
Duvanenko, Victor J. *electronic engineer*
Evans, Richard James *mechanical engineer*
Fer, Ahmet F. *electrical engineer, educator*
Gable, Robert William, Jr. *aerospace engineer*
Goloschokin, Alexander Isaac *electrical engineer*
Groenert, Charles R. *architectural engineer, executive*
Harris, Bernard Leslie *mechanical engineer*
Holmes, John Steven, II *electrical engineer*
Larsen, Wayne David *engineer*
Owen, Keith Lynn *communications engineer*
Sullivan, Charles Bronson *microelectronic researcher, engineer*
Vlach, Jeffrey Allen *environmental specialist*

Kendallville
Kondas, Shawn James *design engineer*

Kokomo
Coady, Michael Gary *engineering supervisor*
Fivecoate, Kevin *engineering company executive*
Gorski, Chris *engineering consultant*
Hahn, Sangman *mechanical engineer*
Kobus, Joseph M. *mechanical engineer*
Nadian, Behrdooz *mechanical engineer*
Nierste, Joseph Paul *software engineer*
O'Hair, Michael Thomas *electrical engineering educator, administrator*
Schneck, Todd M. *manufacturing engineer*

Madison
Nichols, Ryan J. *engineer*

Middlebury
Siegel, Harvey Robert *engineering and product development executive*

Mishawaka
Volk, John M. *electrical engineer*

Muncie
Seymour, Richard Deming *technology educator*

New Albany
Kretzer, Donald E. *manufacturing engineer*
O'Connor, Terrence Patrick *engineering educator*

Newburgh
Briggs, Leslie Ray *mechanical engineer*
Feldbusch, Michael F. *engineering company executive*

Noblesville
Hawkins, Terry D. *chief engineer*
Selby, Ronald Jay *electrical engineer*

Notre Dame
Bauer, Peter Heinz *engineering educator*
Merz, James Logan *electrical engineering and materials educator, researcher*
Raven, Francis Harvey *mechanical engineering educator*
Sain, Michael Kent *electrical engineering educator*

Owensville
King, Carl William *electrical engineer*

Peru
Einselen, Kenneth Lee *civil engineer*
Little, Lewis H. *electrical engineer*
McMinn, William Lowell, Jr. *engineer*

Plainfield
Sermersheim, J. Scott *manufacturing engineer*

Princeton
Gardner, Joseph Henry *engineer*
Mullins, Richard Austin *chemical engineer*

Rochester
Beller, Doug *engineering manager*

Salem
Heckert, Charles Edwin *industrial engineer*

Sellersburg
Fancher, Hershel E. *development engineer*

Seymour
Schroeder, Nicholas John *engineer*

Shelbyville
Walton, Frank T. *engineering executive*

Sheridan
Barnes, Earnest E. *engineering executive*

South Bend
Bloom, David L. *tool and die designer*
Brown, Jeffrey Sherman *electrical engineer*
Chodzinsky, Daniel *design engineer*
Jorgensen, Robert William *manufacturing engineer*
Remis, Steven Joseph *robotics engineer*
Ross, Donald T. *designer*
Swadener, John Rea *product development engineer*
Walls, Larry E. *design engineer*

Terre Haute
Malooley, David Joseph *electronics and computer technology educator*
Waite, Ruth Irene *electrical and computer engineering educator*
Wheelock, Larry Arthur *engineer, consultant*

Warsaw
Bradt, Rexford Hale *chemical engineer*

West Lafayette
Barany, James Walter *industrial engineering educator*
Cooper, James Albert, Jr. *electrical engineering educator*
Friedlaender, Fritz Josef *electrical engineering educator*
Grace, Richard Edward *engineering educator*
Greenkorn, Robert Albert *chemical engineering educator*
Harr, Milton Edward *civil engineering professor, engineering consultant*
Hayes, John Marion *civil engineer*
Incropera, Frank Paul *mechanical engineering educator*
Lin, Pen-Min *electrical engineer, educator*
Phillips, Terry LeMoine *electrical engineer*
Ramadhyani, Satish *mechanical engineering educator*
Skelton, Robert Eugene *aeronautics and astronautics educator*
Stevenson, Warren Howard *mechanical engineering educator*
Viskanta, Raymond *mechanical engineering educator*

IOWA

Amana
Herndon, Steven G. *design engineer*
Ryan, Richard Kirk *mechanical engineer*

Ames
Buchele, Wesley Fisher *retired agricultural engineering educator*
Huston, Jeffrey Charles *mechanical engineer, educator*
Mischke, Charles Russell *mechanical engineering educator*
Nichols, Jerry L. *production engineer*

Ankeny
Brus, Wayne O. *engineer*

Armstrong
Johnson, William M. *manuracturing engineer*

Bettendorf
Heyderman, Arthur Jerome *engineer, civilian military employee*

Burlington
Sealine, Ron L. *chief engineer*

Carlisle
Ernst, Timothy George *electrical engineer*

Cedar Falls
Johnson, Curtis Scott *engineer*

Cedar Rapids
Blanck, Lorraine Theresa *industrial engineer*
Eulberg, Greg A. *design engineer*
Gillis, Keith A. *process engineer*
Kerska, Steve J. *mechanical engineer*
LeCaptain, David A. *electrical engineer*
Lewis, Daniel Edward *computer company executive, systems engineer*
Preston, Kim K. *electrical-mechanical designer*
Sliney, James Gilmore, Jr. *laser electro-optic engineer, educator*
Smith, Bruce Vaughan *electrical engineer*
Stockert, Terry J. *electrical engineer*
Thomas, Douglas Alan *engineering manager*
Urich, Joseph John *electrical engineer*
Webb, Ronald C. *engineering manager*

Clarion
Hagie, Alan B. *electrical design engineer*

Corydon
Burgher, Norm *electronic engineer*

Council Bluffs
Fletcher, Martin Edward *electrical engineer, computer specialist*

Cresco
Andersen, Thomas Burton *engineer*

Davenport
Albertson, K. Thomas *environmental affairs executive*
Bartlett, Peter Greenough *engineering company executive*
Mulich, Steve Francis *safety engineer*
Sandry, Karla Kay Foreman *industrial engineering educator*

Des Moines
Israni, Kim *civil engineer*
Kruse, Larry George *mechanical engineer*
Riekenberg, Warren Glenn *civil engineer*
Veldkamp, Brent M. *engineering executive*

Dubuque
Henn, John I. *civil engineer*
Hiemcke, Christoph *engineering educator*
Musgrave, Scott Allen *mechanical engineer*
Wattonville, Jason D. *agricultural engineer*

Eldridge
Hamann, James *manufacturing engineer*

Fort Dodge
Fletchall, Lyle R. *civil engineer*

Grimes
Boelman, Kim Brian *electrical design engineer*
McIntosh, Ricky *electrical design engineer*

Ida Grove
Ellis, Travis Kyle *research and development project leader*
Homan, James D. *engineering systems administrator*
Johnson, Jeff D. *research and development engineer*

Iowa City
Chen, Lea D. *engineering educator, researcher*
Kusiak, Andrew *manufacturing engineer, educator*
Lakes, Roderic Stephen *biomedical engineering educator*
Odgaard, Anders Jacob *civil and environmental engineer, educator*
Park, Joon Bu *biomedical engineer, researcher, educator*
Robinson, John Paul *engineering educator, consultant*
Schnoor, Jerald Lee *environmental engineering educator*
Schuchert, Bart O. *product engineering manager*

Keokuk
Walljasper, Dave Leroy *fender engineer*

Laurens
Samuelson, Don S. *engineering manager*

Manchester
Andersen, Brian R. *plant engineer*

Marshalltown
Sheeler, John Briggs *retired chemical engineering educator*

Mason City
Davis, Harlan R. *design engineer*
Davison, Warren Gates *civil engineer*

Monticello
Mauritz, Forrest F. *engineering manager*

Muscatine
Brewer, Donaldee *mechanical engineer*
Stanley, Richard Holt *consulting engineer*
Thomopulos, Gregs G. *consulting engineering company executive*

Onawa
Virtue, Jack Down *engineer, consultant*

Orange City
Hancock, Albert Sidney, Jr. *engineering executive*

Ottumwa
Jordan, Mark A. *agricultural engineer*

Pella
Schroder, Paul D. *mechanical engineer*

Peosta
Decker, Randy J. *machine company executive*

Red Oak
Heideman, Dean Glen, Jr. *electronic engineer*

Sioux City
Burris, Merle Hershal, Jr. *home inspector*
Corbin, Mark R. *project engineer*

Union
Swegle, David B. *engineering executive*

Waterloo
Coburn, Dwight D. *mechnical designer*
Eagles, Derek M. *project engineer*
Felland, Richard A. *electrical design engineer*
Toppin, Scott A. *agricultural engineer*

Webster City
Kadakia, Pratish *mechanical engineer*
Walker, Dewayne Fred *design engineer*

KANSAS

Assaria
Clark, Stanley Ralph *agricultural engineer*
Jones, Randy S. *engineering executive*

Blue Rapids
Grauer, Douglas Dale *civil engineer*

Bushton
Hoelscher, Darrel G. *engineering executive*

Coffeyville
Crosby, Donald P. *mechanical engineer*
Shannon, James Neil *educator*

Conway Springs
Thompson, Donald Eugene *industrial engineer*

De Soto
Volkers, Burton Jay *electrical engineer*

Dodge City
Tuxhorn, Gary L. *mechanical design engineer*

Emporia
Comstock, Robert J. *mechanical draftsman*
Woods, Warren Chip *civil engineer*

Hesston
Pecenka, Craig D. *engineer*

Hutchinson
Munger, Harold Hawley, II *city engineer*

Independence
Barbi, Josef Walter *engineering, manufacturing and export companies executive*

Junction City
Olson, Walter L. *agricultural engineer*

Kansas City
Huslig, Bill *engineer*
Morrow, Brent *mechanical engineer*
Wempe, Eric T. *design engineer*

Lawrence
Haugh, Dan Anthony *mechanical engineer*
McCabe, Steven Lee *structural engineer*
Nordheden, Karen Jean *electrical engineering educator, researcher*
Roberts, James Arnold, Jr. *engineering educator, electrical engineer*
Sandberg, Richard A. *manufacturing engineer*

Leavenworth
Baltzer, Kimberly Lenore *civil engineer, consultant*
Hamilton, Mark Alan *electrical engineer*
Rogers, Frederick Carl *network engineer*

Lenexa
Bozarth, Philip Howard *mechanical engineer*

Lorraine
Wesseler, David *agricultural engineer*

Manhattan
Dillman, Norman Gregg *electronics engineering educator*
Huang, Chi-Lung (Dominic) *mechanical engineer, educator*
Manges, Harry Leo *agricultural engineer*
Russell, Eugene Robert, Sr. *engineering educator, administrator*

Moundridge
Franz, Raymond Andrew *electronic engineer*

Neodesha
Plisek, Don *design engineer*

New Century
Avise, Donald Lee *product engineering executive*

Olathe
Galewski, Michael H. *mechanical designer*
Kimmer, Brian K. *engineering buyer*

Ottawa
Howell, Donald J. *engineer*

Overland Park
Campbell, Kenneth Ray *mechanical engineer*
Dunn, Robert Sigler *engineering executive*
Georgiana, John Thomas *electrical engineer*
Kling, John Robert *mechanical engineer*
Watson, David Bruce *civil, structural engineer*

Riverton
Elsten, Stan *mechanical engineer*

Sabetha
Eilert, Butch Allen *mechanical engineer*

Salina
Nowak, Thomas *engineering company executive*

Shawnee Mission
Bartlett, Roger Danforth *engineering executive*
Cassidy, John Lemont *engineering executive*
Raney, Charles C. *electrical engineer*

Tipton
Eilert, Mark Anthony *agricultural engineer*

Topeka
Frantzen, Jeffrey Alan *civil engineer*

Wichita
Biok, Aspi K. *mechanical engineer*
Hansen, Ole Viggo *chemical engineer*
Hendrich, Thomas J. *mechanical engineer*
Jarvis, Ron *manufacturing engineer*
Johnson, Larry M. *mechanical designer*
Mc Kee, George Moffitt, Jr. *civil engineer, consultant*
Paarmann, Larry Dean *electrical engineering educator*
Stuerke, Kenneth W. *electrical engineer*
Woodson, Shawn Harold *aerospace company executive*

MASSACHUSETTS

Foxboro
Niemoller, Arthur B. *electrical engineer*

MICHIGAN

Ann Arbor
Akcasu, Ahmet Ziyaeddin *nuclear engineer, educator*
Assanis, Dennis N. (Dionissios Assanis) *mechanical engineering educator*
Atasi, Khalil Ziad *engineering executive*
Cao, Xiang-Dong *mechanical engineer*
Dow, William Gould *electrical engineer, educator*
Faeth, Gerard Michael *aerospace engineering educator, researcher*
Greenwood, Donald Theodore *retired aerospace engineering educator*
Gullick, Richard Warren *environmental engineer, scientist*
Harvey, James Raymond *electrical engineer*
Kauffman, Charles William *aerospace engineer*
Larrowe, Vernon Lodge *electrical engineer*
Powell, Kenneth Grant *aerospace engineering educator*
Schumaker, Dennis J. *nuclear engineer*
Schwank, Johannes Walter *chemical engineering educator*
Sheen, Dan Roger *research engineer*
Torno, Randall C. *engineering executive*
Yang, Ralph Tzu-Bow *chemical engineer*
Yih, Chia-Shun *fluid mechanics educator*

Auburn Hills
Matuska, Frank M. *project manager*
Meier, Robert Joseph, Jr. *software engineer*

Bad Axe
Rochefort, Jack Leeland *engineering executive*

Benton Harbor
Ranger, Dee Bruce *engineering manager*

Beverly Hills
Haggerty, John Richard *civil engineer*

Bloomfield Hills
Hartmus, John A. *systems engineer*
Lilly, Gerald Edward *engineering executive*
Morrell, Wayne Markley *computer engineer*

Brighton
David, Ronald E. *mechanical engineer, consultant*
Olesko, Ron *engineering manager*

Calumet
Taivalkoski, Bruce D. *electronics engineer*

Canton
Kendall, Laurel Ann *geotechnical engineer*
Olsen, Gary Alvin *design engineer*

Chesterfield
Tollon, Wayne *engineering manager*

Clark Lake
Werner, Christian Thor *retired engineer, consultant*

Clinton Township
Parker, Jerry L. *mechanical engineer*

Commerce Township
Wilkinson, Alfred E. *engineering executive*

Dearborn
Larson, Gerald Lewis *electrical engineer*
Luettgen, Michael John *engineer*
Nikiforuk, Michael *product engineer, educator*
Olson, Richard Gottlieb *nuclear engineer*
Sun, Jing *electrical engineering educator*
Thomasma, Timothy Dale *industrial engineer, educator*
Wu, Hai *mechanical engineer*

Detroit
Begnoche, R. Terry *environmental engineer*
Hamade, Thomas Ali *chemical engineering educator*
Herrick, Nicholas Jay, Jr. *electrical engineer*
Kline, Kenneth Alan *mechanical engineering educator*
Putatunda, Susil Kumar *metallurgy educator*
Putchakayala, Hari Babu *engineering company executive*
Rothe, Erhard William *engineering educator*
Varran, Mike J. *engineering executive*

East Lansing
Cloud, Gary Lee *engineering educator*
Schlueter, Robert Anthony *electrical engineer, educator*

Eastport
Tomlinson, James Lawrence *mechanical engineer*

Erie
Beers, Robert B. *project manager*
Shaffer, Steve J. *control engineer manager*

Farmington
Bieman, Leonard H. *director vision engineering*
Bliss, George N. *chief engineer*

Farmington Hills
Erzen, Deborah Anne *materials engineer*
Harding, Rick Peter *environmental engineering executive*
Khairallah, Farid *engineering manager*

Fenton
Moore, Stephen Frederick *manufacturing engineer*

Ferndale
Pate, Charlie D. *electrical engineer*

Flat Rock
McGuire, Timothy James *refrigeration technician*

Flint
Krul, Michael Paul *electrical engineer*

Franklin
Roy, Ranjit Kumar *mechanical engineer*

Galesburg
Becker, Lanson *engineering executive*

Garden City
Boote, Terry J. *engineering manager*

Grand Blanc
Yonker, John F. *engineering executive*

Grand Rapids
Brown, Steven Michael *engineering physicist, acoustician*
Fennema, Leonard K. *engineer, design consultant*
Fleischmann, Shirley Tina *mechanical engineer, educator*
Hammond, Thomas *quality engineer*
Kadzban, Douglas Walter *civil engineer*

Grass Lake
Garver, Frederick Merrill *industrial engineering executive*

Grosse Pointe
Tecos, George P. *engineering executive*

Houghton
Goel, Ashok Kumar *electrical engineering educator*
Horvath, Ralph Steve *electrical engineering educator*
Pelc, Karol I. *engineering management educator, researcher*

Kalamazoo
Arnett, Steven J. *engineering manager*
Engelmann, Paul Victor *plastics engineering educator*
Kakabaker, Kenneth Graham *mechanical engineer*
Smith, Troy D. *engineering manager*

Lansing
Cadwallader, Carl Eugene *automotive manufacturing engineer*
Kleven, Jeffrey A. *research and development manager*

Lincoln
Busse, Wilbur Edward *retired engineer*
Huff, David Neil *engineering manager*

Livonia
Duffy, James Joseph *engineer*
Nowicki, David Michael *manufacturing engineer*
Rahman, Ahmed Assem *principal engineer, staff stress analyst*

Madison Heights
Brumfield, Steven Jack *business executive*
Charnitsky, Gary A. *engineer*

Marysville
Sprotberry, Steven J. *product designer*

Mason
Toekes, Barna *chemical engineer, polymer consultant*

Memphis
Akred, Ronald J. *design engineer*
Tucker, Ray *facilities engineer*
Wilson, Thomas *draftsman*

Midland
Meister, Bernard John *chemical engineer*
Porchia, Joseph *chemical engineer, researcher*
Seiler, Wallace Urban *chemical engineer*

Milford
Larson, Kevin Scott *electrical engineer*

New Buffalo
Cosgrove, Jim *plant manager, product liability consultant*

Niles
Fung, Kwok K. *electronic engineer, research manager*

North Branch
Stevenson, James Laraway *communications engineer, consulting*

Oak Park
Johnston, Timothy Sidney *computer engineer*

Owosso
Garn, Glenn *engineering manager*

Plymouth
Clark, Kenneth William *mechanical engineer*
Grannan, William Stephen *safety engineer, consultant*

Pontiac
Danielewicz, Claudia Anne *quality assurance engineer*
Van Den Boom, Wayne Jerome *industrial engineer*

Rochester
Suits, Mike A. *engineering executive*

Rochester Hills
Anand, Yogindra Nath *civil engineer*
Bailey, Richard R. *technology development executive, consultant*
McConnell, George Alan *electrical engineer*

Romulus
Lang, Kristopher Douglas *electrical engineer*
Willey, Kevin Charles *systems engineer*

Royal Oak
Smith, John William Hugh *civil engineer*

Saginaw
Moore, Dick *controls engineering manager*

Saint Clair Shores
Carlson, Ken H. *engineer*

Saint Ignace
Hampton, Glen Richard *environmental engineer*

Saint Joseph
Castenson, Roger R. *agricultural engineer, association executive*

Saline
Damato, Ralph James *systems engineer*
Ferris, Joseph Edward *electrical engineer*

Shelby Township
Bell, Brian *manufacturing engineer*

South Haven
Collins, James Gregory *civil engineering company executive*
Kriner, Richard Wellington *civil engineer*

South Lyon
Guthrie, Michael Steele *magnetic circuit design engineer*

Southfield
Beaudette, Robert Lee *transportation and logistics consultant*
Bedoun, Eddie Amad *electrical engineer*
Gleichman, John Alan *safety and loss control executive*

Sterling Heights
Burke, Thomas Joseph *civil engineer*
Mitchell, Ernst Kern *security systems company executive*

Troy
Ashtiani, Cyrus Nakhaii *electrical engineer, automotive executive*
Bautz, Jeffrey Emerson *mechanical engineer, educator, researcher*
Drebus, John Richard *systems engineer*
Helmle, Ralph Peter *computer systems developer, manager*
Kaminski, Jerome Michael *instructional technologist*
Koehn, E. Brian *systems engineer*
Lehman, Jeffrey John *multi-media engineer*
Waller, David T. *engineering company executive*

Utica
Dietz, Richard Alan *engineer*

Warren
Gallopoulos, Nicholas Efstratios *chemical engineer*
Hotra, Mike A. *maintenance engineer*
Keating, Daniel Bernard *field service engineer*
Lequesne, Bruno Patrice Bernard *research engineer*
Nagy, Louis Leonard *engineering executive, researcher*
Schwing, Richard Charles *chemical engineer*
Shea, Rex Tungsheng *research engineer, educator*

Weidman
De Lorenzo, Orindo Arturo (Dino) *director of engineering*

Wixom
Vorce, Timothy C. *systems engineer*

Ypsilanti
Lou, Zheng (David) *mechanical engineer, biomedical engineer*
Shilander, Jim R. *mechanical engineer*

MINNESOTA

Aitkin
Prickett, Gordon Odin *mining, mineral and energy engineer*

Anoka
Kita, Terry J. *mechanical engineer*

Benson
Krohn, Martin L. *manufacturing engineer*

Bloomington
Beckwith, Larry Edward *mechanical engineer*
Norling, Irwin Denison *retired measurement specialist, photographer*
Varecka, Charles P. *engineering executive*

Burnsville
Lai, Juey Hong *chemical engineer*
Manson, Carey Marc *mechanical engineer*

Chaska
Nicklaus, Matt P. *manufacturing engineer*

Duluth
Ringsred, John Norman *electronics educator*

Eden Prairie
Higgins, Robert Arthur *electrical engineer, educator, consultant*

Edina
Pichler, James Michael *computer engineer*

Elk River
Larsen, Dennis D. *design engineer, business executive*

Fairmont
Bielfelt, Terry James *manufacturing engineer*
Wasmund, Michael Charles *aerospace engineering company administrator*

Fridley
Tsuchiya, Ken *computer engineer*

Glenwood
Daniels, Dan Lee *aeronautical engineer*

Ham Lake
Hatteberg, Donald G. *electrical engineer*

Harris
Buisman, V. Wayne *safety engineer*

Hopkins
Cook, Russell Elbert, Jr. *electrical engineer*
Hansen, Carl G. *electrical engineer*
Madsen, Michael J. *mechanical engineer*

Hutchinson
Krishnamoorthi, Viswanathan *materials engineer*
Mitchell, Robert Howard *quality engineer*

Lakeville
Rotstein, Gustavo Ariel *electrical engineer*

Merrifield
Johnson, Gregory R. *design engineer*

Minneapolis
Bachmeier, Brian Anthony *electrical engineer*
Culter, John Dougherty *chemical engineer*
Duquette, David William *engineering consultant*
Eckert, Ernst R. G. *mechanical engineering educator*
Exe, David Allen *electrical engineer*
Goldstein, Richard Jay *mechanical engineer, educator*
Hawkinson, Thomas Edwin *environmental and occupational health engineer*
Hawley, Sandra Sue *electrical engineer*
Hillstrom, Thomas Peter *engineering executive*
Hogan, Andrew J. *controls engineer, educator*
Lemberg, Steven Floyd *electrical engineer*
Liu, Benjamin Young-hwai *engineering educator*
Parhi, Keshab Kumar *electrical engineering educator*
Pfender, Emil *mechanical engineering educator*
Porter, William L. *electrical engineer*
Schultz, Arnold J., Jr. *linguistic programmer and designer*
Sheikh, Suneel Ismail *aerospace engineer, researcher*
Svard, Trygve N. *electrical engineer*
Tennyson, Joseph Alan *engineering executive*
Weisberg, Leonard R. *retired research and engineering executive*

Minnetonka
Bellus, Peter A. *engineer*
Bibeau, Dennis I. *electrical engineer*
Johnson, Lennart Ingemar *materials engineering consultant*

Montevideo
Liebl, Dale Joseph *manufacturing engineer*

New Prague
Kostecka, Dave J. *manufacturing engineer*

North Branch
Jones, David Richard *die designer, purchasing administrator*

Oakdale
Holm, Leo Jerome *agricultural engineer, public speaker*

Owatonna
Douglas, Daryl D. *mechanical and design engineer*

Plymouth
Peterson, Donn Neal *forensic engineer*
Quinn, Richard Kendall *environmental engineer*
Speak, Thomas John *software engineer*
Stein, Gary Aleck *electrical engineer*

Rochester
Huffine, Coy Lee *retired chemical engineer, consultant*
O'Hare, Daniel John *electrical engineer*
Rentschler, Alvin Eugene *mechanical engineer*
Rust, Robert C. *electonics engineer*
Steiner, Jeffery Allen *project engineer, executive*

Roseville
Galle, Edward Louis *retired food processing research engineer*

Saint Cloud
Weiszhaar, Douglas James *civil engineer*

Saint Paul
Bissen, Dale M. *electronics engineer*
Bondow, Bruce A. *electrical engineer*
Boyle, Bradley Charles *civil engineer*
Bragg, Richard Christopher *electrical design engineer*
Foley, Deborah Ann *civil engineer*
Goodell, John Dewitte *electromechanical engineer*
Lampert, Leonard Franklin *mechanical engineer*
Myren, David James *aeronautical engineer*
Ng, Lewis Yok-Hoi *civil engineer*
Pepitone, Vito C. *design engineer*
Saniti, Daniel Joseph *electronics engineer*
Seaver, Albert Edward *engineer*
Stein, Larry Arden *electrical engineer*

Sauk Rapids
Kaiser, Tim Michael *mechanical engineer*

Warroad
Gouin, Warner Peter *project engineer*

Waseca
Strayer, Brett Allen *mechanical engineer*

MISSOURI

Ava
Murray, Delbert Milton *manufacturing engineer*

Ballwin
Schroy, Jerry Michael *chemical engineer*

Belton
Woodcock, Richard L. *engineer executive*

Boonville
West, Robert Allan *engineer*

Bridgeton
Moll, Joseph Eugene *chemical engineer, chemical company executive*
Stettes, Gregory G. *mechanical engineer*

Carterville
Perry, Michael Moore *electrical engineer*

Chesterfield
Abell, Donald Eugene *retired engineer, consultant*
Kurth, Terry Lee *mechanical engineer*
Langenfield, David Allen *electrical engineer*
Pund, Marvin Louis *optical engineering consultant*

Columbia
Anderson, Jack W. *manufacturing engineer*
Surdin, Dennis R. *laboratory technician*
Viswanath, Dabir Srikantiah *chemical engineer*

Fenton
Ditch, Kevin Jesse *design engineer*

Florissant
Burtness, David Jeffrey *electrical engineer*
Tomazi, George Donald *retired electrical engineer*
Ziemer, John Robert *software engineer*

Fulton
Rose, David James *electrical engineer*

Hazelwood
Bruns, Billy Lee *electrical engineer, consultant*
Johann, Chris Joseph *electronics engineer*
Lindstrom, Lance Alan *electrical engineer*
Livits, Maria *mechanical engineer*

High Ridge
Huffman, John P. *mechanical engineer*

Independence
Lartey, Viktor Amugi *design engineer*

Joplin
Enslow, Roger Demetri *electrical engineer*
Foraker, David Kenneth, III *chemical engineer*
Harvey, Tim W. *program manager, engineer*
Silvey, Ronald L. *project engineer*

Kansas City
Davis, F(rancis) Keith *civil engineer*
Green, Frank Earl *civil engineer*
Kelly, Eugene *engineer*
Skinner, Willis Dean *consulting engineering company executive*
Stewart, Albert Elisha *safety engineer, industrial hygienist*

Kirksville
Davison, Walter Sears, Jr. *civil engineer*

Lebanon
Allison, James Edward *design engineer*

Lees Summit
Buhr, Craig Allen *geotechnical engineer*
Gilmore, Rodney Scott *electrical engineer*
Puglisi, Philip James *electrical engineer*

Maryland Heights
Goldfarb, Marvin Al *retired civil engineer*

Moberly
Tayon, Jeffrey Earl *engineering and design executive*

O'Fallon
Reichle, Paul D. *tool designer*

Rolla
Dagli, Cihan Hayreddin *engineering educator*
Duchek, Michael Gerard *mechanical engineer*
Finaish, Fathi Ali *aeronautical engineering educator*
Moss, Randy Hays *electrical engineering educator*
Numbere, Daopu Thompson *petroleum engineer, educator*
Sarchet, Bernard Reginald *retired chemical engineering educator*
Sheffield, John William *mechanical engineering educator*

Saint Ann
Buchner, Daniel Richard *electrical engineer, defense contractor*

Saint James
Taggart, Gary J. *electrical engineer*

Saint Joseph
Johnson, Marvin Melrose *industrial engineer, consultant*
Yan, Hong-Cheng *electrical engineering educator*

Saint Louis
Agee, Daniel David *mechanical engineer*
Antonacci, Anthony Eugene *food corporation engineer*
Brown, James W. *mechanical engineer*
Collins, Marie Ann *civil engineer*
Commean, Paul Kevin *electrical engineer*
Cosner, Raymond Robert *aeronautical engineer*
Cotter, Jeffrey Gene *tool designer*
Dabbagh, Mahmoud *electrical engineer*
Damon, Bill L. *manufacturing engineer*
Erickson, Robert Anders *optical engineer, physicist*
Goldstein, Julius Lester *biomedical engineer, consultant*
Gould, Phillip Louis *civil engineering educator, consultant*
Grimes, Mark Parker *research and development engineer*
Hahn, James Henry *engineering educator*
Karl, Randall Gregory *electrical engineer*
Krisher, Albert Sherman *chemical engineer*
Moss, Steven C. *electrical engineer*
Muller, Marcel W(ettstein) *electrical engineering educator*
Orton, George Frederick *aerospace engineer*
Richardson, Thomas Hampton *design consulting engineer*
Riley, David Ray *aeronautical engineer*
Rogers, John Russell *manufacturing company executive, engineer*
Saranita, Tom Vito *electrical engineer*
Scheer, Robert P. *mechanical engineer*
Scheller, Jim *mechanical engineer*
Shrauner, Barbara Wayne Abraham *electrical engineering educator*
Speiser, James Warren *electrical engineer, computer systems consultant*
Suess, Patricia Ann *software systems consultant*
Tharp, Edward Leon *civil engineer, consultant*
Ursch, Richard Wayne *electrical engineer*
Wilfred, Ernest Prabhakar *electrical engineer*

Saint Peters
Pirooz, Saeed *chemical engineer, researcher*

Springfield
Smith, Terry Davis *quality engineer*
Stogsdill, Frank Jo *design engineer*

Warrensburg
Marshall, Robert Logan *safety engineer, educator*

Wright City
Ruwwe, William Otto *retired automotive engineer*

NEBRASKA

Beatrice
Crumrine, John C. *mechanical engineer*

Brownsville
Fidler, Charles Robert *electrical engineer*

Columbus
Brockhaus, Donald *engineer*
Campbell, Royce Michael *agricultural engineer*
Goettsche, Jim J. *manufacturing engineer*
Hendricks, Stephen E. *mechanical engineer*

Fort Calhoun
Clemens, Richard Paul, Jr. *electrical engineer*

Gering
Anderson, Larry Lynn *mechanical engineer*

Grand Island
Beck, Steven Roy *design engineer*

Gurley
Egging, Don A. *mechanical engineer*

Lexington
Stombaugh, Jay A. *manufacturing engineer, consultant*

Lincoln
Allington, Robert William *instrument company executive*
Bauer, Mark Timothy *electrical engineer*
Johnson, Redge *electrical engineer, company executive*
Kollars, James Robert *electronics technician*
Lenzen, Laura Elaine *civil engineer*
McClellen, Burnell Homer *engineer, military officer*
Mills, Craig J. *chemical engineer*
Reuter, Ken *systems engineer*
Ullman, Frank Gordon *electrical engineering educator*
Voelker, Robert Heth *electrical engineering educator*

Omaha
Coufal, Charles Francis *electrical engineer*
Coy, William Raymond *civil engineer*
Hines, Eric D.(Ric) *environmental engineer, tennis professional*
Kelpe, Paul Robert *engineer, consultant*
McCloskey, John *environmental engineer*
Nelson, Mark Edward *civil engineer*
Nielson, Jeffrey D. *mechanical engineer*
Tunnicliff, David George *civil engineer*
Zerbs, Stephen Taylor *telecommunications development engineer*

Scottsbluff
Palmer, Thomas Watson *mechanical engineer*

Waverly
Brown, Rick Robert *mechanical engineer*

NORTH DAKOTA

Bismarck
Carmichael, Virgil Wesly *mining, civil and geological engineer, former coal company executive*
Goodin, David Lynn *power systems engineering*

Fargo
Li, Kam Wu *mechanical engineer, educator*
Smith, Donald Arthur *electrical engineer, educator*

OHIO

Akron
Bauman, Aaron A. *project engineer*
Brewer, Daniel F. *engineer*
Dwenger, Thomas Andrew *engineer*
Erickson, Richard Lee *engineering executive*
Frank, Joachim Rheinhard *engineer*
Green, Calvin *electrical engineer*
Kimble, Al E. *engineering executive*
Laslo, Douglas L. *electrical engineer, power company administrator*
Miller, Irving Franklin *chemical engineering educator, academic administrator*
Sancaktar, Erol *engineering educator*
Soska, Geary Victor *robotics consultant*
Sutherland, Jeffrey W. *electrical engineer*
Symens, Ronald Edwin *electrical engineer, consultant*

Alliance
Kitto, John Buck, Jr. *mechanical engineer*
Mohn, Walter Rosing *metallurgical engineer, researcher*
Southards, William Thomas *mechanical engineer*

Amherst
Hill, Duane C. *manufacturing engineer*
Myers, Larry Steven *senior designer*

Ashland
King, James Michael *process engineer*

Ashville
Van Meter, Eroc J. *mechanical engineer*

Athens
Chen, Hollis Ching *electrical engineering and computer science educator*

Mokari, Mohammed Ebrahim *electrical engineer*

Barberton
Blackburn, Michael D. *design engineer*
Gold, Michael *materials engineer*

Batavia
Bower, Kenneth Francis *electrical engineer*
Palazzolo, Daniel P. *mechanical engineer*

Beavercreek
Glaze, Tim Leon *electronics engineer*

Bellevue
Palm, Randy B. *mechanical engineer*

Blacklick
Tyrone, Tomlinson *designer*

Blue Ash
Keller, John Francis, II *industrial engineer*

Bowling Green
Dunlavy, Bruce Merritt *environmental engineering executive*
Ferrenberg, William A. *mechanical engineer*

Bremen
King, Roger Edward *manufacturing engineer*

Broadview Heights
Barth, Charles Fredrik *aerospace engineer*

Brookfield
Lucarell, William R. *electrical engineer*

Brunswick
Rohlik, Harold Edward *engineer*

Bryan
Derks, Irvin L. *engineering executive*
Fast, Kelly *design engineer*
Meloche, Joseph Lawrence *mechanical engineer*

Bucyrus
Heydinger, Theodore S. *design engineer*

Canal Fulton
Butorac, Thomas F. *electrical engineer*

Canton
Ceroke, Clarence John *engineer, consultant*
Cross, Delbert Ray *electronic systems engineer*
Haney, Sean T. *mechanical engineer*
Harlan, Jerry Wallace *electrical engineer*
Hostetler, John D. *systems engineer*
Klover, John Morgan *mechanical engineer, consultant*
Mannella, Larry *manufacturing engineer*
Pedoto, Gerald Joseph *supplier quality engineer*
Rosenbaum, Joel Aaron *electrical engineer, consultant*

Centerville
Jackson, Nicole Renée *mechanical engineer*

Chagrin Falls
Gilding, Ronald Edwin *electrical engineer*
Kovalski, Ray J. *chemical engineer, consultant*

Chardon
Donovan, Robert J. *electrical engineer*

Chillicothe
Rounsley, Robert Richard *chemical engineer, educator*

Cincinnati
Anderson, William Edward *electrical engineer*
Arantes, José Carlos *industrial engineer, educator*
Benzing, Bruce M. *mechanical engineer*
Bluestein, Paul Harold *management engineer*
Bostian, Harry Edward *chemical engineer*
Braun, Michael D. *electrical engineer*
Brown, Harold *aerospace engineer*
Brown, Timothy Clark *engineer*
Burke, Robert R. *electrical engineer*
Cahay, Marc Michel *electrical engineer, educator*
Casson, Charles R. *engineer*
Curry, Wilbur *mechanical engineer*
Davis, Deborah Leah *quality systems engineer*
Dicola, Vincent C. *industrial engineer*
Fried, Joel Robert *chemical engineering educator*
Gray, John F. *mechanical engineer*
Harrison, Herm L. *electrical engineer*
Hersman, Ferd William *retired engineer*
Hesse, David A. *electrical engineer*
Hoehn, Keith E. *mechanical engineer*
Hohnstein, Dean Harlan *mechanical engineer*
Ireland, Lance W. *mechanical engineer*
Isaacs, S. Ted *engineering executive*
Johnson, K(enneth) O(dell) *aerospace engineer*
Jones, Michael Allen *mechanical engineering supervisor*
Kehew, William James *environmental, quality assurance engineering manager*
McCalmont, Paul E. *engineering analysis supervisor*
Miller, Tom C. *mechanical engineer*
Nawalaniec, Christopher Joseph *mechanical engineer*
Neumeier, Lorraine *mechanical engineer*
Ohearen, John Robert *mechanical engineer*
Pancheri, Eugene Joseph *chemical engineer*
Quiogue, Honesto D. *mechanical engineer*
Redlinger, Samuel Edward *chemical engineering consultant*
Roush, Edward *mechanical engineer*
Salmon, Stuart Clive *manufacturing engineer*
Salyers, Perry A. *electronic design engineer*
Steinmetz, Thomas Scott *electrical engineer*
Sterling, Harry Joseph, Jr. *environmental engineer*
Suprock, David M. *mechanical engineer*
Taylor, William Robert *engineer*
Toftner, Richard Orville *engineering executive*
Yelton, Steven John *electronics educator*

Cleveland
Amicarelli, Robert B. *mechanical engineer*
Arata, Louis Kenneth *computer engineer*
Barna, Kenneth James *design engineer*
Barnard, John Kent *engineering executive*

Bickford, James Allan *electrical engineer, consultant*
Burns, James F. *communications engineer*
Ceccoli, Anthony J. *mechanical design engineer*
Ciavarelli, Matt D. *engineering executive*
Crout, Charles John *engineering company executive*
D'Agati, John R. *mechanical engineer*
Dulc, James M. *application engineer*
Feichtinger, Josef *engineer*
Fortunato, Joseph M. *electrical engineering executive*
Gach, Martin G. *electronic design engineer, software engineer*
Germano, Carmen Peter *retired piezoelectric engineer, consultant*
Grodell, Frederick Charles, III *electrical engineer*
Harkins, Richard Wesley *marine engineer, naval architect*
Huff, Michael Allan *electrical engineering educator*
Hulsman, Art J. *aeronautical engineer*
Izatt, Joseph Adam *biomedical engineering researcher*
Kwan, Cho-Fai *chemical engineer*
Lapossy, Kenneth A. *machine engineer*
Lazzara, Joseph J. *project engineer*
Lingafelter, Thomas W. *mechanical engineer*
Lockhart, Robert Frederick *electrical engineer*
Lu, James J., Sr. *electrical engineer*
Madden, James Desmond *forensic engineer*
Mangla, Kishan C. *systems engineer*
McCaul, Joseph Patrick *chemical engineer*
McWhorter, John Francis *manufacturing engineer*
Moyer, John L. *electrical designer, control engineer*
Noebe, Ronald Dean *materials research engineer*
Ono, Cheryl Eiko *senior controls engineer*
Palagyi, James J. *electrical engineer*
Petry, David P. *mechanical engineer*
Pisaneschi, Fred W. *project engineer*
Pretlow, Theresa Pace *biomedical educator, researcher*
Rischar, Charles M. *electrical engineer*
Roesch, Mark Alan *design engineer*
Rolan, Bret Robert *electrical engineer*
Sargent, Noel Boyd *electrical engineer*
Shoemaker, James Michael *aerospace engineer, researcher*
Sidaway, Bruce A. *mechanical engineer*
Sullivan, David P. *electrical engineer*
Trefts, Albert Sharpe *mechanical engineer, consultant*
Trojan, Tom J. *mechanical engineer*
Walters, Michael S. *mechanical engineer*
Wehrle, David S. *engineer*
Weppler, Robert Charles *electrical engineer*
Wessel, Dennis James *mechanical engineering administrator*
Yurko, Joseph Andrew *chemical engineer*

Columbiana
Kyle, Craig Howard *mechanical engineer*

Columbus
Alexander, Kathryn E. *mechanical engineer*
Barcus, William Arthur *manufacturing engineer*
Barnes, David *engineering executive*
Brackman, Edward Dennis *engineer*
Brodkey, Robert Stanley *chemical engineering educator*
Chovan, John David *biomedical engineer*
Creager, Gary S. *transportation engineer*
Dudley, Ronn J. *engineering manager*
Ensminger, Dale *mechanical engineer, electrical engineer*
Fletcher, Thomas Lincoln *electrical engineer*
Gozon, Jozsef Stephan *engineering educator*
Grant, Michael Peter *electrical engineer*
Hadipriono, Fabian Christy *engineering educator, researcher*
Humble, Jimmy Logan *engineer*
Jackson, Curtis Maitland *metallurgical engineer*
Jacox, John William *mechanical engineer, consultant*
Joodi, Pirooz *engineer*
Joseph, Martin F. *chemical engineer*
Keaney, William Regis *engineering and construction services executive, consultant*
Lee, Robert *electrical engineering educator*
Leissa, Arthur William *mechanical engineering educator*
Loomis, James Prentice *aeronautical engineer*
Mitchell, David Andrew *electrical engineer*
Moore, Donald Paul *retired electrical engineer*
Nindra, Beant Singh *electrical engineer*
O'Brien, Jeff J. *engineer*
Ozkan, Umit Sivrioglu *chemical engineering educator*
Pugh, Michael A. *mechanical engineering associate*
Rich, Joseph William *engineering educator, consultant*
Segulja, Danny D. *manufacturing engineer*
Smith, J.W. *mechanical engineer*
Thompson, James Kenneth *mechanical engineer*
Zapp, Robert Louis *electronic test engineer*

Concord
Lenardic, Kenneth Ralph *systems architect, consultant*

Coshocton
Larsen, L. Vernon *retired chemical engineer*

Crestline
Gordon, Ronald F. *mechanical engineer*
Kelly, Joseph Benjamin *ceramic engineer*

Dayton
Buckholtz, Kenneth Robert *electrical engineer*
Campbell, Dane H. *applications engineer*
Carson, Richard McKee *chemical engineer*
Cooper, Thomas David *metallurgical engineer, consultant*
Elrod, William Corbin *aerospace engineering educator*
Gentry, Frank D. *electrical engineer*
Houpis, Constantine Harry *electrical engineering educator*
Hudson, Arthur Cleve *electronics engineer*
Kaye, Christopher James *project engineer*
Kazimierczuk, Marian Kazimierz *electrical engineer, educator*
Mitchell, Philip Michael *aerospace engineer, consultant*
Novotney, Norman Edward *electrical engineer*
Nutt, Ambrose Benjamin *aerospace engineer*
Pasala, Krishna Murthy *electrical engineering educator*
Peck, Charles N. *mechanical engineer*
Rawlins, David D. *automotive engineer*
Sandhu, Sarwan Singh *chemical engineering educator, researcher*

Smith, Steven Antonio *engineer*
Takahashi, Fumiaki *research mechanical engineer*
Tracy, Noel Adams *non destructive evaluation engineer*
Yu-Lee, Reginald Tomas *engineering educator*

Defiance
Higbea, Jerold Carl *electrical engineer*

Dublin
Bauer, Arthur Adolph *metallurgical engineer*
Frank, Thomas Paul *medical equipment manufacturing company executive*
Savarda, Raymond Richard *engineering consultant*

East Liberty
Baik-Kromalic, Sue S. *metallurgical engineer*

Elyria
Thur, Mike Adam, Sr. *product design engineer*

Euclid
Hoffa, Michael D. *electrical engineer*

Fairborn
Conklin, Robert Eugene *electronics engineer*

Fairport Harbor
Kirchner, James William *retired electrical engineer*

Findlay
Mefford, Darrell *physicist, engineer*

Fostoria
Moore, David Joseph *design engineer*

Fredericktown
Bostic, James H. *design engineer*

Galion
Radel, William Harold *design engineer*

Gates Mills
Enyedy, Gustav, Jr. *chemical engineer*

Georgetown
Beasley, James George *civil engineer*

Germantown
Huss, David L. *mechanical engineer*

Gibsonburg
Niswander, Irvin F. (Bud) *manufacturing engineer*
Reineck, Henry A. *drafting engineer*

Greenville
Caldwell, Kenneth Carson *manufacturing engineering executive*
Vorst, Gerry D. *agricultural engineer*

Hamilton
Buelsing, Jeff *mechanical engineer*
Hester, Steven S. *mechanical engineer*
Lis, Matthew J. *mechanical engineer*

Harrison
Bryant, William *mechanical engineer*

Heath
Halifax, Robert William *manufacturing engineer*

Hilliard
Smith, David Bern *electronic design engineer*

Holland
Yammine, Michael Riad *electrical engineering*

Holmesville
Sechrist, Robert Earl *industrial engineer*

Hudson
Sprankel, William Albert *project engineer*

Jackson
Everett, Bill D. *electrical engineer*

Kent
Anderson, William John, II *engineering and business management consultant*
McCauley, Daniel F. *electrical engineer*

Kenton
Buroker, Daniel Jack *engineer*

Kettering
Toerner, David Paul *architectural engineer*

Lancaster
Meyer, Wilbur L. *manufacturing engineer*

Lebanon
Wical, Gregg Thomas *mechanical engineer*

Logan
Carmean, Jerry Richard *broadcast engineer*

Loveland
Anderson, Roy Alan *chemical engineer*
Berchtold, Merrill E. *engineering executive, retired*

Mansfield
Biber, Allan *mechanical engineer*
Hussaini, Akbar Syed *mechanical engineer*
Rose, Derek J. *mechanical engineer*
Steinman, Charles Hunter *electrical engineer*
Swaisgood, Bruce William *mechanical engineer*

Marietta
Chase, Robert William *petroleum engineering educator, consultant*
Sushka, Theodore Wilson *civil engineer, county engineer*

Marion
Tozzer, Jack Carl *civil engineer, surveyor*

Mason
Howard, Arlan J. *design engineer*
Russo, Michael John *manufacturing engineer, manufacturing company executive*
Toft, Brian *mechanical engineer*
Wallenhorst, Thomas *electrical engineer*

Maumee
Hood, Ronald Lee *electrical engineer*
Stender, Mark V. *electrical engineer*

Mayfield Heights
Grants, Valdis *engineering manager*

Medina
Kenat, Thomas Arthur *chemical engineer, consultant*

Mentor
Zaker, Gregory Allen *electronics engineer*

Metamora
Cella, A. F. *chief engineer*
Gembolis, Don *manufacturing engineer*

Miamisburg
Booth, James Albert *engineer*
Gehres, Clint Edwin *mechanical engineer*

Miamitown
Roth, John E. *mechanical engineer*

Middletown
Hoendorf, Raymond *mechanical engineer*
Newby, John Robert *metallurgical engineer*
Selmensberger, James *design engineer*
Smyth, William *machine designer*

Milford
Ferguson, Scott *mechanical engineer*
Mastrorocco, Kevin Samuel *mechanical engineer*
Mathis, James Bennett *engineer*
Rangan, Ravi Mangalam *mechanical engineer*

Millersport
Roehner, Phil G. *engineer*

Minerva
Connell, John M. *mechanical engineer*

Minster
Klein, Robert Emil *electrical engineer*

Monroeville
Hedrick, Thomas Richard, Sr. *engineering executive*

Montpelier
Robinson, Michael A. *mechanical engineer*

Mount Vernon
Buchwald, Kurt A. *mechanical engineer*
Elmore, Jeffrey Michael *engineering consultant*

New Philadelphia
McAfee, Rod Dale *electrical engineer*

Newark
Miller, David Gibbs *electrical contractor*
Myntti, Bill W. *electrical engineer*

North Canton
Esmaili, Mahyar *mechanical engineer*
Lute, Richard Calvin, Jr. *mechanical design engineer*
Maurer, Edgar A. *mechanical engineer*

Norwich
Ely, Wayne Harrison *broadcast engineer*

Orrville
Hartman, Steve Eugene *civil engineer*

Ostrander
Smith, Rick A. *mechanical engineer, consultant*

Peninsula
Gentsch, Ted P. *project engineer*

Perrysburg
Brinker, Gary D. *engineering executive*
Fintel, Eric D. *electrical engineer*

Piqua
Milby, Douglas K. *electrical engineer*

Powell
Adeli, Hojjat *engineer, educator, computer scientist*

Salem
Barkley, Fred L. *mechanical engineer*
Rhuetan, Charles W. *mechanical engineer*

Sandusky
Nainee, Rajan *manufacturing engineer*
Randall, Sharon Ann *mechanical engineer*

Shelby
Moore Moif, Florian Howard *electronics engineer*

Sidney
Legge, John Christopher *mechanical engineer*
Naculich, Paul A. *mechanical engineer*

Solon
Durst, Alan R. *mechanical engineer*
Li, Biyue *mechanical engineer*
Veinerman, Elliot *chemical process engineer*

South Lebanon
Nead, Thomas (Edward) *electrical engineer*

Spencer
Crump, Gwyn Norman *engineer*

Springfield
Barber, Hugh Philip *engineering executive*
Schneider, Mark P. *design engineer*
Ward, Richard Eugene *civil engineering technician*

Swanton
Borochin, Eugene *mechanical engineer*

Tiffin
Eagle, Curtis William *civil engineer*
Huss, Philip F. *electrical engineer*
Loy, Robert E. *mechanical engineer*

Tipp City
Glassmeyer, James Milton *aerospace, computer, and electronics engineer*
McKenzie, Terry P. *systems engineer*

Toledo
Adams, Paul Stuart *corporate ergonomist*
Beat, Andrew James *mechanical engineer*
Colony, David Carl *civil engineering educator*
Heldt, Brian Patrick *systems engineer*
Hoffman, Paul Juian *mechanical engineer*
Kropchuk, Thomas A. *electrical engineer*
Nycz, Joseph Donald *engineer*
Schultz, Warren Robert *manufacturing administrator*
Wandover, George *engineering consultant*
Wolff, Edwin Ray *construction engineer*

Troy
Frock, Jeff L. *mechanical design engineer*
Stover, P. E. *standards engineer*

Utica
Blue, Nelson Clayton *civil engineer*

Warren
Angelo, Brian Gene *electrical engineer*
Boehm, Michael J. *electrical engineer*
Bousfield, James Eustace *industrial engineer*
Dippolito, Daniel F. *electrical engineer*
Keyser, Geogre J. *industrial engineer*
Krivanek, Louis *electrical engineer*
Osiniak, Randall C. *mechanical design engineer*
Patrone, Joseph S. *project engineer*
Shar, Brian Dominic *product engineer*
Small, William L. *electrical engineer*
Vaughn, Arthur L. *electrical engineer*

West Chester
Brown, Don G. *mechanical engineer*
Lyons, Dan A. *computer engineer*
Zimmerman, Dean Arthur *polymer engineer*

Westerville
Kahle, Glenn J. *design engineer*
Kaplan, Yakov *mechanical design engineer*

Westlake
Huff, Ronald Garland *mechanical engineer*

Willoughby
McHugh, Joseph Edward *motion control device application engineer*

Wooster
Lacey, Daniel S. *mechanical engineer*
Turner, Glenn *fluid power specialist*

Worthington
Giannamore, David Michael *electronics engineer*

Wright Patterson AFB
Chelette, Tamara Lynne *biomedical engineer*
D'Azzo, John Joachim *electrical engineer, educator*
Frederick, Ronald David *aerospace engineer*
Most, Marvin Conrad *electrical engineer*
Raeth, Peter George *computer engineer, research scientist, consultant*
Wallace, Robert Luther, II *engineer*

Yorktown
Rigling, Richard Vaughn *sales engineer*

Youngstown
Dolasinski, Steven George *manufacturing engineer*
Kenner, Marilyn Sferra *civil engineer*
Lacivita, Michael John *safety engineer*
Mossman, Robert Gillis, IV *civil and environmental engineer*

Zanesville
Camp, Loren Clinton *county engineer*

SOUTH DAKOTA

Aberdeen
Lacher, Jerome Francis *highway engineer*
Pulfrey, Roy Allan *environmental engineer*

Brookings
De Boer, Darrell Wayne *agricultural engineer*

Colman
Miller, Charles Kent *electrical engineer*

Madison
Lewis, Eric D. *mechanical engineer*

North Sioux City
Lego, Daniel Lee *systems integration engineer*

Pierre
Hyde, Dean Arnold *civil engineer*
Micheel, Donald Earl *construction engineer, therapist*
Templeton, Barbara Ann *civil engineering technologist*

Rapid City
Gowen, Richard Joseph *electrical engineering educator, academic administrator*
Klock, Steven Wayne *engineering executive*
Lefevre, Donald Keith *electrical engineer*
Ramakrishnan, Venkataswamy *civil engineer, educator*

TENNESSEE

Vonore
Lownsdale, Gary Richard *mechanical engineer*

VIRGINIA

Arlington
Arndt, Roger Edward Anthony *hydraulic engineer, educator*

Blacksburg
Batra, Romesh Chander *engineering mechanics educator, researcher*

Hampton
Bartels, Robert Edwin *aerospace engineer*

WISCONSIN

Antigo
Fischer, Kevin J. *service engineer*

Appleton
Heraly, Thomas P. *electrical engineer*
Mayer, Mark E. *engineering executive*
Mims, Albert *safety consultant, executive, educator*

Baileys Harbor
Jacobs, Peter James *electrical engineer*

Beaver Dam
Smelcer, Glen Ernest *mechanical engineer*

Beloit
Traeger, Norman *mechanical engineer*

Brookfield
Brozek, Jeffrey Michael *research engineer*
Curfman, Floyd Edwin *engineering educator*
Thomas, John *mechanical engineer, research and development*

Butler
Hinke, Patrick T. *mechanical engineer*
Rothering, Larry P. *mechanical engineer*

Cudahy
Woodin, Charles P. *engineering director*

Eau Claire
Cheney, David Willi *engineering company executive*

Fond Du Lac
Birschbach, John Peter *manufacturing engineer*
Navis, Glen Edward *industrial engineer*

Franksville
Marz, Michael Blase *electrical engineer*

Genoa
Parkyn, John Duwane *nuclear engineer*

Germantown
Klowak, Marvin B. *mechanical engineer*

Grafton
Luisier, Dennis Lee *engineer design specialist*
Tharman, Mark Richard *quality control technician*
Weber, Stephen Alex *computer-aided designer*

Green Bay
Liemmen, Steve Jay *engineering manager*

Hales Corners
Waltz, Richard W. *electrical engineer*

Hartford
Carlson, Brent James *engineering designer*

Horicon
Johnson, Steven Harold *engineer*
Kettler, Daniel James *manufacturing engineer*

Janesville
Hyzer, James Bandt *forensic engineer, consultant*
Reindl, Rhinehart *applications engineer*

Kohler
Ten Hoven, James Alan *project analyst*

Lake Geneva
Lee, Kevin *registered professional engineer*

Lake Mills
Elliott, Bruce R. *electronics engineer*

Lodi
Francke, Melvin L. *electrical designer*

Madison
Bird, Robert Byron *chemical engineering educator, author*
Dietmeyer, Donald Leo *electrical engineer*
Forster, Peter *electrical engineer*
Green, Robert Douglas *engineer*
Higgins, Thomas James *electrical and computer engineering educator*
Schick, Paul Walter *project engineer*
Sitzman, Jerry Clayton *consulting electrical engineer*
Skiles, James Jean *electrical and computer engineering educator*

Mauston
Benesh, James L. *manufacturing engineer*

Menomonee Falls
Aggarwal, Rattan *electrical engineer*
Beck, Edward Thomas *electrical engineer*
Biehl, Francis Walter *consulting engineer*
Brook, Daniel T. *mechanical engineer*
Hubacek, James T. *developement engineer*
Walterman, Scott A. *mechanical engineer*

Middleton
Schneider, Robert Steven *electrical engineer, educator*

Milwaukee
Albrecht, Chris Evan *mechanical engineer*
Bacon, John Stuart *biochemical engineer*
Bolda, Daniel J. *electrical engineer*
Bub, Alexander David *acoustical engineer*
Christensen, Erik Regnar *engineering educator, researcher*
Falbo, Jeffrey F. *electrical engineer*
Fournelle, Raymond Albert *engineering educator*
Frank, Lowell C. *mechanical engineer*
Graef, Luther William *civil engineer*
Hintz, Michael K. *engineer*
Huegel, William Mortimer *retired civil engineer*
Hutchinson, James A. *engineer*
Ishii, Thomas Koryu *electrical engineering educator*
Kao, Leslie M. *developement engineer*
Krzysztof, Samborski *engineer*
Marciniak, David Buster *engineer, consultant*
Meyer, Michael A. *mechanical engineer*
Mwakisunga, Charles G. *mechanical engineer*
Niederjohn, Russell James *electrical and computer engineering educator*
Reese, Robert J. *engineer*
Reza, Ali M. *electrical engineering educator*
Satula, Keith O. *electrical engineer*
Schuman, LeRoy *mechanical engineer*
Schunck, Richard A. *research engineer*
Serdan, Mark I. *design engineer*
Slichter, D.J. *electrical engineer*
Violet, Ron J. *electrical engineer*
Von Stockhausen, Ron J. *mechanical designer*
Wilsdon, Thomas Arthur *product development engineer, administrator*
Winsey, Greg James *project engineer*
Wojtak, Roger C. *electrical engineer*

Neenah
Franke, Maripat Kemps *chemical engineer*

New Berlin
Borton, Alan Wayne *electrical engineer*

New Holstein
Leu, James G. *project engineer*

Oregon
Ritland, Donald Marvin *environmental engineer*

Platteville
Drury, David Michael *electrical engineer, educator*

Pleasant Prairie
Zell, Blair Paul *systems engineer*

Pound
Nelson, Loren Elwan *engineering administrator*

Racine
Mantey, Paul *electrical engineer*
Sabee, Janet M. *mechanical engineer*
Sikora, Larry Arthur *mechanical engineer*
Stephens, James Linton *mechanical engineer*

Ripon
Meshinesh, Khader *mechanical engineer*

Rothschild
Drew, Richard Allen *electrical and instrument engineer*

Saint Croix Falls
Rimmereide, Arne M. *engineering executive*

Sheboygan
Aldag, Jerome Marvin *mechanical engineer, executive*

Sheboygan Falls
Trowbridge, Jeff *plant engineer*

Slinger
Styve, Orloff Wendell, Jr. *electrical engineer*

Somerset
Johnston, Sherwood A. *engineering executive*

Spooner
Frey, Paul Howard *chemical engineer*

Stoughton
Mehl, Scott Andrew *quality assurance engineer*

Sussex
Dantzman, Gregory Peter *design engineer*

Two Rivers
Hennessy, Felicia Plesic *nuclear engineer*

Watertown
Cech, Joseph Harold *chemical engineer*
Weymer, Patrick Timothy *mechanical engineer*

Waukesha
Barteleme, Vincent P. *design engineer*
Bauer, Kurt W. *civil engineer*
Brunner, Charlotte Marie *civil engineer*
Garasimowicz, Gregory Alexander *mechanical engineer*
Korthas, Kevin John *industrial engineer*
Parkinson, Dwight Clarence *electrical engineer*
Qudeimat, Isam A. *mechanical engineer*

Wausau
Nikolai, Christopher Mark *electronic engineer*
Snuffer, Daniel Haden *process engineer*

West Allis
Storch, John Gary *biomedical engineer*

Windsor
Westly, Kenneth *engineering manager*

Wisconsin Rapids
Lampert, Leonard Lee *consulting engineer, land surveyor*

CANADA

MANITOBA

Anola
de Nevers, Roy Olaf *retired aerospace company executive*

Winnipeg
Christie, Fred Atherton *aerospace engineer*
Fielding, Ronald Roy *aeronautical engineer*

ADDRESS UNPUBLISHED

Abitz, Anthony John *test systems engineer, musician*
Abrams, Max *engineering executive*
Ahrens, Joyce A. *mechanical engineer*
Amos, James A. *electrical engineer*
Arnst, Mike *mechanical design engineer*
Baker, Robin Neil *CAD operator*
Barrett, Alfred H. *electrical engineer*
Barron, D. Douglas *engineering executive*
Bartholomew, Donald Dekle *engineering executive, inventor*
Behrens, Marc *electrical engineer*
Bergthold, Richard Lee *engineering administrator*
Bernstein, Neil Sanford *mechanical engineer, consultant*
Bitsch, Richard *electrical engineer*
Biven, James R. *mechanical engineer*
Blau, Andrew P. *project engineer*
Blum, Michael *aerospace engineer*
Bogner, James M. *electrical engineer*
Bollinger, Robert B. *process engineer*
Bosetti, Eugene R. *supervising engineer*
Brilliant, Howard Michael *aeronautical engineer*
Carter, Richard Glen *engineering development manager*
Casperson, Paul G. *mechanical designer*
Chandler, Edward William *communications systems engineer*
Chew, Weng Cho *engineering educator*
Clayborn, Christin Lynn *engineer*
Clifford, Michael *electrical engineer*
Corkill, Duane *electrical, mechanical engineer*
Cressman, Karl *mechanical engineer*
Cuffe, Stafford Sigesmund *automotive engineer, consultant*
Depiante, Eduardo Victor *nuclear engineer*
Ditzler, Jeffrey L. *plastics engineer*
Dombeck, Wayne Leslie *product designer*
Dombrowski, Frank R. *manufacturing engineer*
Drajeske, Mark Howard *aeronautical engineer, software engineer*
Dunham, Michael D. *design engineer*
Edmundson, Charles Wayne *mechanical engineer, communications executive*
Emery, John A. *electrical engineer*
Feske, Jeff E. *tooling engineer*
Francis, Richard T. *electrical engineer*
Fujii, Samuel Toshimi *engineering manager*
Goetz, Robert J. *chemical engineer*
Goldberger, Arthur Earl, Jr. *industrial engineer, executive*
Gudin, Casimir Contsantine *electrical engineer*
Guiliano, Gary *mechanical engineer*
Haines, David L. *electrical engineer*
Harrison, Kevin D. *design engineer*
Harrison, Larry Edgar *electrical engineer*
Harrison, William J. *engineering manager*
Hawthorne, Steven C. *design engineer*
Hensley, Jerry Robert *manufacturing engineer*
Herrmann, John W. *engineer*
Hersh, David B. *engineer*
Hines, Brian A. *electrical engineer*
Holdren, Richard Lyell *engineering executive*
Hutnick, Victor *engineering consultant*
Inniger, Dean Lee *structural engineer*
Jenner, Bill Edwin *computer engineer*
Kalata, Richard Neil (Rick) *design engineer*
Kemnitz, William F. *retired electrical engineer*
Kent, Jeffrey C. *electrical engineer*
Khodor, Leonid *mechanical engineer*
Klein, Frank *mechanical engineer*
Knapp, Gary Lee *quality engineer*
Kopp, John J. *engineer*
Langley, Greg A. *mechanical engineer*
Laxpati, Sharad Ranjitlal *electrical engineering educator*
LeMarbe, Edward Stanley *engineering manager, engineer*
Lenman, Tomas Stig *engineer*
Lentz, Mark Steven *mechanical engineer*
Li, Yao-En *chemical engineer*
Lindblad, Scott A. *engineer*
Loughran, Robert P. *electrical engineer*
Loy, Richard Franklin *civil engineer*
Lund, Karl S. *engineer*
Lynch, Tony A. *mechanical engineer*
MacDonald, Mike J. *mechanical design engineer*
Martin, Lee *mechanical engineer*
Massmann, Robert *mechanical engineer*
Matus, Mark Thomas *industrial engineer*
Michael, Brian P. *mechanical engineer*
Miu, Richard A *engineer*
Moehr, John E. *electrical engineer*
Moring, Walter G. *product engineer*
Myers, Todd R. *project engineer*
Neher, Leslie Irwin *engineer, former air force officer*
Newton, Sean Richard *electrical engineer*
Nyquist, Gerald Warren *engineering consultant*
Ortiz-Quiñones, Carlos Ruben *electronics engineer, educator*
Pfeffer, Scott M. *communications archtiect*
Pierce, Robert Raymond *materials engineer, consultant*
Porter, Warren M(atthew) *electrical engineer*
Prees, Pat T. *industrial designer*
Przybylowski, Thad M. *engineering manager*
Rahman, Sami Ur *environmental engineer*
Ramaswami, Devabhaktuni *chemical engineer*
Rector, William David *civil engineer*
Reed, Scott E. *civil engineer*
Rhoades, Gene J. *software engineering director*
Riley, Thomas M. *engineer*
Rogers, Douglas Gordon *design engineer*
Rogo, Kathleen *safety engineer*
Rolewicz, Robert John *estimating engineer*
Rutstein, Alexander *engineering consultant*
Rutz, Stephen L. *design draftsman*
Sagar, Percy K. *mechanical engineer*
Salee, Joseph Claude *electrical engineering educator*
Schell, Allan Carter *retired electrical engineer*
Schieffer, James Michael *electrical engineer*
Schmidt, Danny R. *engineering designer*
Schoenecker, Martin J. *design engineer*
Schroeder, Hans *retired electrical engineering educator*
Schroeder, Kory Dean *electrical engineer*
Scott, Susannah C. *transportation engineering consultant*
Seidel, Wolfgang *design engineer*
Sherman, Frank William *engineer*
Sherman, James LeRoy *engineering manager*
Skorupa, Chris *mechanical engineer*
Sloggy, John Edward *engineering executive*
Slotkowski, Kenneth George *electronics engineer*
Spelson, Nicholas James *engineering executive, retired*
Stanevich, Kenneth William *staff engineer*
Stock, Sidney R. *systems engineer*
Sullivan, Roger John *radar engineer, researcher*
Swartzel, Stan J. *electrical engineer*
Todd, Steven M. *mechanical engineer*
Towslee, Arthur C. *electrical engineer*
Tran, Nang Tri *electrical engineer, physicist*
Treinavicz, Kathryn Mary *software engineer*
Veroski, Joseph Damian *electrical engineer*
Wall, John H. *electrical engineer*
Weingarten, Joseph Leonard *aerospace engineer*
Werner, Gary M., Jr. (Gerhard) *manager systems engineering*
West, Gene A. *electrical engineer*
Wilkinson, Todd Thomas *project engineer*
Wilson, Janice L. *hydraulic engineer*
Wise, Kevin Andrew *aerospace engineer*
Wright, David L. *electrical design engineer*
Yankaitis, Michael James *manufacturing engineer*
Yoder, John-David Samuel *mechanical engineer*

FINANCE: BANKING SERVICES. *See also* **FINANCE: INVESTMENT SERVICES.**

UNITED STATES

COLORADO

Boulder
Martin, Phillip Dwight *banking consulting company executive, mayor*

CONNECTICUT

Greenwich
Massey, James L. *investment banker*

ILLINOIS

Alton
Bailey, Susan Carol *commercial banking executive*

Aurora
Cassiday, Donald Marion *banker*

Champaign
Selby, Barbara Kenaga *bank executive*

Chicago
Baker, Walter, III *bank executive*
Bartter, Brit Jeffrey *investment banker*
Bobins, Norman R. *banker*
Bolger, David P. *bank executive*
Ciesielski, Thomas Gregory *bank executive*
De Leonardis, Nicholas John *banker*
Fellingham, Warren Luther, Jr. *banker*
Flusser, Jonathan Scott, Sr. *commercial banker*
Franke, Richard James *investment banker*
Griffiths, Robert Pennell *banker*
Hart, Pamela Heim *banker*
Haydock, Walter James *banker*
Heldring, Ernst M. *bank executive*
Istock, Verne George *banker*
Kinzie, Raymond Wyant *banker, lawyer*
Klebba, Raymond Allen *property manager*
Morgan, Howard Campbell *banker*
Obrecht, Kenneth William *banker*
O'Connell, Harold Patrick, Jr. *banker*
Pritchard, Peter Hugh Anson *banker*
Roberts, Theodore Harris *banker*
Schroeder, Charles Edgar *banker, investment management executive*
Seifert, Achim G. *commercial real estate lender*
Thomas, Richard Lee *banker*
Vitale, David J. *banker*
Vitale, Gerald Lee *credit union executive*

Deerfield
Bagley, Thomas Steven *private equity investor*
Melton, Edward Joseph *commercial banker*

Dundee
Weck, Kristin Willa *savings bank executive*

Elgin
Mogler, Robert Wayne *banker*

Evanston
Scholten, Menno Nico *mortgage banker*

Hinsdale
Hodge, Ernest Vance *banker*

Lake Forest
Keller, Peter Joseph *investment banker*
Ross, Robert Evan *bank executive*

Mattoon
Spitz, Timothy Joe *banker*

Northbrook
Keehn, Silas *retired bank executive*

Rockford
Luter, Novella Marie *credit union administrator*

Springfield
Boss, Edward Herman, Jr. *banker, economist, fiscal advisor*

Sublette
Faber, Curtis W. *banker*

Washington
Blumenshine, Mahlon *banker*

INDIANA

Evansville
McCutchan, William Mark *banker*

Fort Wayne
Beck, Richard Eugene, Jr. *bank officer, educator, reserve police officer,*
Shaffer, Paul E. *retired banker*

Indianapolis
Barnette, Joseph D., Jr. *bank holding company executive*
Bowling, Nancy Jeanne *bank executive*
Miller, Thomas Milton *banker*

Mishawaka
Herman, William John *banker*

Muncie
Sursa, Charles David *banker*

IOWA

Cedar Rapids
Nebergall, Donald Charles *investment consultant*
Wax, Nadine Virginia *retired banker*

Des Moines
Edwards, Richard Alan *banker*

Estherville
Dunn, Frank (Francis Michael Dunn) *banker*

Holstein
German, Kristi Lynn *bank officer, small business owner*

Worthington
Dunkel, Nancy Ann *banker*

KANSAS

Overland Park
Dore, James Francis *financial services executive*

Pratt
Loomis, Howard Krey *banker*

Roeland Park
Morgan, Bruce Blake *banker, economist*

Tonganoxie
Torneden, Connie Jean *bank executive*

Topeka
Johnson, Arnold William *mortgage company executive*

Wichita
Aleshire, Richard Joe *banker*

MICHIGAN

Ann Arbor
Guzman, Laura A. *mortgage company executive*

Birmingham
Carducci, Jack A. *investment banker*

Bloomfield Hills
Davis-Cartey, Catherine Bernice *bank executive*

Detroit
Fisher, Charles Thomas, III *banker*
Ransom, Kevin Renard Dortch *investment banker*

Farmington Hills
Ebert, Douglas Edmund *banker*
Mylod, Robert Joseph *banker*

Holland
Jellison, James Logan, II *banker*

Kalamazoo
Cole, William R. *bank executive*
Spears, Richard R. *bank executive*

MINNESOTA

Duluth
Madich, Bernadine Marie Hoff *savings and loan executive*

Minneapolis
Grundhofer, John F. *banking executive*

Northfield
Talen, William Claire *bank executive, financial consultant*

Saint Paul
Rothmeier, Steven George *merchant banker, investment manager*

MISSOURI

Joplin
McReynolds, Allen, Jr. *investment company executive*

Kansas City
Baum, Jonathan Edward *investment banker*
Brown, Richard Harris *financial executive*
Green, Jerry Howard *investment banker*

Liberty
Prather, R. William, III *banking executive*

Maryland Heights
Bell, Wilson Townsend *banker*

Moberly
Bankhead, Charla Marie *bank officer*

Saint Louis
Davis, James Harold *banker*
Flannagan, William Marvin, Jr. *banker*
Hayes, Samuel Banks, III *banking company executive*
Jacobsen, Thomas H(erbert) *banker*
James, William W. *banker*

Springfield
Archibald, Charles Arnold *holding company executive*
McCartney, N.L. *investment banker*
Nathan, Charles Harold *banking software executive*

NEBRASKA

Lincoln
Lundstrom, Gilbert Gene *banker, lawyer*

Omaha
Harvey, Jack K. *holding company executive*

NEW YORK

New York
Kearney, Michael John *banker*

NORTH DAKOTA

Dickinson
Hann, Alan Frederick *banker*

OHIO

Ashtabula
Cortright, Helen Rae *banker*

Avon Lake
Leuth, Ann T. *bank executive*

Centerburg
Bumpus, Terry Keith *bank officer*

Cincinnati
Cassidy, Samuel M. *banker*

Cleveland
Daberko, David A. *banker*
Koch, Charles Joseph *banker*
Powers, Richard Daniel *bank executive*
Robertson, William Richard *banker, holding company executive*
Schutter, David John *banker*
Siefers, Robert George *banker*

Columbus
Glaser, Gary A. *bank executive*
Hahn, Tanya K. *investment banker*
Herrmann, Arthur Dominey *banker*
Hoskins, W. Lee *banker*
McNennamin, Michael J. *bank executive*
Silveous, C(harles) Daniel *mortgage company executive, financial consultant*

Dublin
Gores, Gary Gene *credit union executive*

Mayfield Heights
Briner, Joseph Lee *banker*

Miamisburg
Tozer, Theodore William *mortgage company executive*

Newark
Manning, Ronald Lee *banker*

Toledo
Kunze, Ralph Carl *savings and loan executive*
Nitschke, Shaun Michael *bank professional*

SOUTH CAROLINA

Columbia
Budry, John Francis *mortgage banker, investment real estate broker*

SOUTH DAKOTA

Centerville
Thomson, John Wanamaker *bank executive*

Freeman
Waltner, John Randolph *banker*

Rapid City
Undlin, Charles Thomas *banker*

VIRGINIA

Fairfax
McCabe, Gary Franke *bank hospitality manager*

WISCONSIN

Hales Corners
Ripp, Don J. *mortgage banker*

Kenosha
Seitz, Florian Charles *retired banker*

Madison
Buffo, William Joseph *mortgage company executive, consultant*

Milwaukee
Bauer, Chris Michael *banker*
Randall, William Louis *banker*

Viroqua
Kuehn, Arnold E. *bank executive*

WYOMING

Cheyenne
Knight, Robert Edward *banker*

ADDRESS UNPUBLISHED

Bird, Phillip Craig *mortgage company executive*
Doughan, Thomas Bruce *banker*
Elsten, Cate *financial consultant*
Fellingham, David Andrew *retired mortgage banker*
Germanotta, Jeffrey Steven *investment banker*
Gibbons, Michael Eugene *investment banker*
Gilbertson, Jill Stensland *banker*
Greer, K. Gordon *banker*
Hayes, Mary Phyllis *savings and loan association executive*
Johnson, Lloyd Peter *retired banker*
Love, Jeffrey William *commercial banker*
Meyer, Henry Lewis, III *banker*
Missman, Jeffrey Stephan *bank executive*
Northenor, D(oris) Jean *banker, senior vice president*
Pendleton, Barbara Jean *retired banker*
Reuber, Grant Louis *banking insurance company executive*
Sweet, Philip W. K., Jr. *former banker*
Viskanta, Tadas Edmund *bank officer, investment analyst*

FINANCE: FINANCIAL SERVICES

UNITED STATES

ILLINOIS

Alton
Compton, Roger Paul *financial consultant*

Arlington Heights
Bender, Robert Keith *actuary*
Johnson, Calvin Stewart *tax accountant*

Aurora
Charbauski, Colleen Anne *accountant*
Luken, Ronald Leigh *consultant*
Suchomel, Jeffrey Raymond *accountant, business consultant*

Barrington
Allen, William C. *financial consultant*
Knitter, Gene H. *financial consultant*
Koehl, Camille Joan *accountant*

Belleville
Brechnitz, Jan G. *investment consultant*
Fietsam, Robert Charles *accountant*

Bloomington
Duitsman, Steven R. *financial consultant*
Hines, Timothy Charles *financial consultant*

Bolingbrook
Katsianis, John Nick *financial executive*

Buffalo Grove
Leonetti, Michael Edward *financial planner*

Cahokia
Healy, Steven Michael *accountant, city official*

Champaign
Ryan, Edward Joseph *accountant*
Spice, Dennis Dean *international marketing and business consultant*

Charleston
Cooper, George Kile *business educator*
Garrett, Norman Anthony *business education educator*

Chicago
Alonzi, Loreto Peter *finance executive*
Baniak, Sheila Mary *accountant*
Barrington, Rodney Craig *financial executive*
Bell, Jason Cameron *accountant*
Bloom, Eric Andrew *financial services company executive*
Brennan, William J. *information industry financial executive*
Britten, James Leo, Sr. *assessor*
Bukowski, Daniel Joseph *portfolio manager*
Bush, Crystal Reed *financial planner*
Butler, Robin C. *financial consultant*
Carlson, Richard Gregory *accountant*
Chapman, Alger Baldwin *finance executive, lawyer*
Chlebowski, John Francis, Jr. *financial executive*
Cohen, Bruce Robert *finance company executive*
Dubey, Stephen Arthur *accountant*
Dunn, J. Terrance *financial company executive, consultant*
Fragola, Teresa T. (Terry) *financial consultant*
Friend, Robert Nathan *financial counselor, economist, market technician*
Goldin, Martin Bruce *financial executive, consultant*
Hanna, James Leanord *financial consultant*
Hansen, Claire V. *financial executive*
Hicks, Cadmus Metcalf, Jr. *financial analyst*
Hill, Clarence E. *auditor*
Kamin, Kay Hodes *financial planner, lawyer, entrepreneur, educator*
Kelly, Patrick S. *accountant*
Kierscht, Charles M. *financial company executive*
Kuntz, Mary M. Kohls *corporate treasurer*
Kurish, James Brian *municipal debt management executive*
Larkridge, Theodore Kenneth *financial manager*
Lindskog, Norbert F. *business and health administration educator, consultant*
Lyman, Arthur Joseph *financial executive*
Masek, Barry Michael *accountant*
Miller, Merton Howard *finance educator*
Milne, Robert David *investment management company executive*
Mizel, Gerald M. *financial company executive*
Nelson, Thomas George *consulting actuary*
Nitterhouse, Denise *accountant, business educator, consultant*
Perlmutter, Norman *finance company executive*
Potterton, John Paul *financial executive*
Steagall, M. Susan *management services executive*
Sullivan, Bernard James *accountant*
Truitt, Kevin *revenue administrator, investment adviser*
Velisaris, Chris Nicholas *financial analyst*
Waite, Darvin Danny *accountant*
Ward, James Frank *pension fund administrator*
Weigand, Robert Eugene *university educator*
Wing, John Adams *financial services executive*

Chicago Heights
Weissman, James K. *tax specialist*

Crestwood
Cowie, Norman Edwin *credit manager*

Crystal Lake
Haas, Jonathan Stuart *financial company executive*
Holmgren, Kim James *financial planner*
Okeson, Thomas L. *financial company executive*

Decatur
Dehner, Phil Michael *financial consultant*

Deerfield
Beasley, Carlton M. *investment advisor*
Chromizky, William Rudolph *accountant*
Fulrath, Andrew Wesley *financial planner, charitable gift planner*
Heiman, Marvin Stewart *financial services company executive*
Serwy, Robert Anthony *accountant*
Shepherd, Lewis Edward *portfolio manager*

Des Plaines
Koller, Marita Ann *accountant*
Malone, Daniel Lee *controller*

Dolton
Lucas, Patricia Lynn *financial executive*

East Peoria
Ewing, Donna Marie *business educator*

Edwardsville
King, Thomas Ellwood *accountant, educator*

Effingham
Davis, Charles F. *financial consultant*

Elgin
Wiese, Dorothy Jean *business educator*

Elmhurst
Catalano, Gerald *accountant, oil company executive*

Evanston
Cassell, Frank Hyde *business educator*
Caywood, Clarke Lawrence *marketing educator, public relations executive*
Jacobs, Donald P. *banking and finance educator*

Franklin Park
Pospisil, Frederick John *financial services*

Gays
Finley, Gary Roger *financial company executive*

Geneva
Young, Jack Allison *financial executive*

Glen Ellyn
Drafke, Michael Walter *business educator, consultant*
Grundy, Roy Rawsthorne *marketing educator*
Rasins, James William *auditor*

Glencoe
McDonald, Bruce A. *financial consultant*
Pimley, Kim Jensen *financial training consultant*

Glenview
Fields, Eric J. *financial advisor*
Joseph, Jeff *investment advisor*
Mack, Stephen W. *financial planner*

Gurnee
Fay, Laura Elizabeth *financial analyst*

Hoffman Estates
Ramunno, Thomas Paul *financial consultant*

Homewood
Brunst-May, Lois *accounting & association management firm executive*
Mc Neill, Carmen Mary *business broker*

Joliet
Colonna, William Mark *accountant*

Lake Zurich
Webb, Robert Donald, Jr. *financial executive*

Libertyville
Feit, Michael *controller*

Lincolnshire
Koufis, John Theodore *accountant*

Macomb
Bauerly, Ronald John *marketing educator*

Mc Henry
Jones, H. W. Kasey *financial planning executive, author, lecturer*

Moline
Allen, Leonard Brown *tax manager*
Bullock, Judy Roeske *human resources executive, certified public accountant*
Campbell, James E. *financial consultant*

Mount Prospect
Lewis, Dennis Frank *financial executive*

Mundelein
Howell, Raymond Gary *financial executive*

North Riverside
Borow, Randy *accountant*

Northbrook
Afterman, Allan B. *accountant, educator, researcher, consultant*
Ames, Jane Irene *corporate controller*
Caldwell, Lyndall S. *financial advisor*
Driscoll, Diane Duffey *financial consultant*
Feeney, William S. *financial advisor*
Feibel, Frederick Arthur *financial consultant*
Green, Kevin H. *financial consultant, lawyer*
Hammersley, Marshall Lester *financial consultant*
Hill, Thomas Clarke, IX *accountant, systems specialist*
Levitt, Paul A. *financial consultant*
Mandel, Karyl Lynn *accountant*
Roehl, Kathleen Ann *financial executive*

Northfield
Consola, Mary Frances *actuary, consultant*
Seaman, Jerome Francis *actuary*

Oak Brook
Ghilarducci, August Christopher *financial and business consultant*

Oak Park
Van Wyk, Betty Vicha *financial planner, township clerk*

Oakbrook Terrace
Keller, Dennis James *management educator*

Okawville
Schmale, Allen Lee *financial services company executive*

Palatine
Field, Robert Steven *investment advisor*
Mackey, Charles Ralph *benefits firm executive*
Morales, John Rueda *corporate accounting executive*
Spinner, Lee Louis *accountant*

Park Ridge
Babjak, Richard Steven, Jr. *financial counselor*

Peoria
Cluskey, Gerald Robert *accounting educator*
Jones, Russell Ted *financial consultant*
Kelly, John Leo *finance company executive*

Quincy
Ballance, John D. *financial associate*
Butterfield, Todd Wendall *financial consultant*
Caufield, Thomas J. *financial planner*
Fross, Lyndell Ray *financial consultant*
Mallory, Troy L. *accountant*

Riverside
Perkins, William H., Jr. *finance company executive*

Riverwoods
Lipinski, Mary J. *financial advisor*

Rockford
Albert, Christine Lynnette *accountant*
Albert, Janyce Louise *business educator, banker*
Morrissey, John Francis *accountant*
Schmerse, Traci Jo *financial services company executive*
Zaksheske, Mark Richard *treasurer*

Roselle
Schoeld, Constance Jerrine *financial planner*

Rosemont
Macioch, James Edward *investment consultant, financial planner*

Schaumburg
Folisi, Joseph Charles *accountant*
Shelffo, Julie Ann *accountant*

Schiller Park
Newby, Thomas Paul *accountant*

Scott AFB
Mustard, Mary Carolyn *financial executive*

Skokie
Forman, Linda Helaine *accountant*
Lang, Louis I. (07) *state legislator, lawyer*

Springfield
Donkin, James Richard *internal auditor*
Fleck, Debborah K. *financial consultant*
Fraser, Stanley Charles *credit union executive*
Nixon, David W. *financial services executive, business analyst*
Reents, Ray Edward *banking and stock consultant*
Travis, Lawrence Allan *accountant*

Sugar Grove
Norris, Blanche Lee *business consultant, educator*

Tinley Park
Baillie-David, Sonja Kirsteen *controller*
Bettenhausen, Brad Lee *treasurer, auditor*

Tuscola
Kirchhoff, Michael Kent *economic development executive*

University Park
Fischer, Bruce Douglas *business educator, management consultant*

Urbana
Williamson, John Maurice *accountant*

Villa Park
Tang, George Chickchee *investment executive*

Westchester
Jones, Margaret L. *finance company executive*
Simoneau, Daniel Robert *accountant, watercolorist, educator*

Wheaton
Surz, Ronald Joseph *financial consultant*

INDIANA

Bloomington
Brown, David Paul *finance educator*
Hustad, Thomas Pegg *marketing educator*
Perkins, William Clyde *business educator*
Swanson, Robert Mclean *retired business educator*

Carmel
Niehaus, James William *accountant*

Danville
Wean, Blanche McNeely *accountant*

Elkhart
High, Ron L. *treasurer manufacturing company*
Holtz, Daniel Alexander *financial consultant*
Hornell, Charles A. *financial consultant*

Fishers
Harper, Paige Ann James *consultant*

Fort Wayne
Arnold, Daniel Douglas *financial consultant*
Biddinger, David Lee *financial consultant*
Bryan, Jeffrey J. *financial consultant*
Gregory, Samuel Bailey, Jr. *financial advisor, financial planner*
Jacobs, Jerry L. *investment advisor*
Johnson, Kirk *financial consultant*
LaPan, Karl Roger *finance and administration executive*
Sipe, Roger Wayne *accountant, consultant*

Franklin
Link, E.G. (Jay) (Jay Link) *corporate executive, financial consultant*

Indianapolis
Beuter, Richard William *accountant*
Braham, Delphine Doris *government accountant*
Carey, Edward Marshel, Jr. *accounting company executive*
Carlock, Mahlon Waldo *financial consultant, former high school administrator*
Carlson, Richard L. *financial consultant*
Cooke, Brian F. *financial advisor*
Cooke, John David *financial advisor*
Fetsch, Michael Francis *financial consultant*
Gutermuth, Scott Alan *accountant, pharmaceutical company executive*
Isaac, Stanley Eugene *accountant*
Kaufman, Barton Lowell *financial services company executive*
Kelley, Joseph R. *financial consultant*
Kellison, Donna Louise George *accountant, educator*
Kissling, Richard Eugene, II *accountant*
Laughlin, James David *public finance executive, consultant*
Ley, Linda Sue *employee benefits company executive*
Mathioudakis, Michael Robert *life insurance and estate planning executive*
Mitchell, Kieron Breon *financial analyst*
Townsend, James Douglas *accountant*
Vaughn, James Michael *controller*
Weingardt, John W. *accountant*
Winemiller, James D. *accountant*
Wood, Margaret A. *accountant*

Kokomo
Harris, Val Edward *financial consultant*

Logansport
Denham, Bradley C. *financial counselor*

Merrillville
Gingerich, James A. *financial consultant*
Kline, Paul Edward *financial consultant*

Muncie
Ball, Virginia B. *investor*

Notre Dame
Reilly, Frank Kelly *business educator*
Shannon, William Norman, III *marketing and international business educator, food service executive*
Vecchio, Robert Peter *business management educator*

Rensselaer
Slaby, Frank *financial executive*

Richmond
Turcotte, Todd Wayne *controller*

South Bend
Bindley, Albin, IV *financial consultant*
Bissell, William W. *financial consultant*
Fred, Michael E. *financial consultant*
Higginbotham, Mark L. *financial consultant*
Junker, David A. *financial advisor*
Kull, Stephen R. *financial advisor*
Wrenn, Walter Bruce *marketing educator, consultant*

Spencer
Pashley, Eugene W., Jr. *financial services company executive*

Terre Haute
Jeffers, Thomas Lee *accountant*

Valparaiso
Trenchard, Kenneth Robert *auditor*

Vincennes
Cutshall, Rex Ralph *management and accounting educator, administrator*

IOWA

Adel
Hougham, Norman Russell *controller*

Ames
Cowan, Arnold Richard *finance educator, researcher*

Ankeny
Boelens, Patricia Ann *accountant, nurse*
Metheny, Jan Walter *business manager, chief financial officer*

Burlington
Hendrichsen, Larry L. *financial executive*

Cedar Rapids
Fiala, Paul G. *financial consultant*
Johnson, Deborah K. *investment advisor*
Speicher, Gary Dean *financial planner*

Davenport
Brocka, M. Suzanne *controller*
Sylvester, Terry Lee *controller, business administrator, school system administrator*

Des Moines
Hollensbe, Ronda Lee *accounting educator*
Houseworth, Louise *administrator*
Smith, Daniel Walker *financial services company executive*

Fonda
Tamm, Eleanor Ruth *retired accountant*

Iowa City
Brawner, Gene E. *financial executive*

Johnston
Morris, Hubert Andrew *auditor*

Keokuk
Atterberg, Douglas Keith *financial planner*

Newton
Richardson, Tod David *financial planner, educator*

Sioux City
Fedders, Don D. *accounting executive*
Pynn, Kathleen Ann *accounting manager*

West Des Moines
Sather, Everett Norman *accountant*
Smith, Jeffrey Howard *accountant*

KANSAS

Ellis
Langley, Eileen Enola *accountant*

Kansas City
Globoke, Joseph Raymond *accountant*

Leavenworth
Karr, James Barry *financial programmer*

Lenexa
Berggren, Terry K. *financial executive*

Manhattan
Gillispie, Harold Leon *tax consultant*

Olathe
Stullken, Ida Marie *auditing clerk*

Overland Park
Bailey, James C. *financial consultant*
Buchanan, William Murray *consulting actuary*
Carey, Jerald Raymond *investment advisor*
Zinke, Michael Duane *finance and accountancy manager*

Salina
Johnson, Verna Mae *accounting educator*

Shawnee Mission
Byrum, Judith Miriam *accountant*
Ferrari, Michael David *financial planner, investment advisor*
Hechler, Robert Lee *financial services company executive*
Stevens, James Hervey, Jr. *financial advisor*

Topeka
Kimbrough, Barbara E. *investment consultant*
McCandless, Barbara J. *auditor*
Miller, Gary Allen *financial planner*
Reser, Elizabeth May *bookkeeper*

Westwood
Ketter, James Patrick *accountant*

Wichita
Greenlee, Michael Larry *tax specialist*

MICHIGAN

Ada
Mathews, George Meprathu *accounting executive*

Adrian
Mohr, Karen *accounting executive*

Allendale
Veazey, Richard Edward *accounting educator*

Ann Arbor
Elger, William Robert, Jr. *accountant*

Arcadia
Ogilvie, Bruce Campbell *financial consultant*

Battle Creek
Jagner, Ronald Paul *financial administrator, consultant*

Big Rapids
Ditmar, Ronald L., Jr. *financial company executive*

Bingham Farms
Bondie, Richard Anthony *financial executive*

Birmingham
Buczak, Douglas Chester *financial advisor, lawyer*
McCuen, John Joachim *financial company executive*

Bloomfield Hills
Cooper, John Arnold *financial analyst*
Forrester, Alan McKay *capital company executive*
McCollum, Timothy A. *financial planner*

Dearborn
Jeffries Ashford, Alecia *accounting analyst*

Detroit
Adams, William Johnston *financial and tax consultant*
Albrecht, John T. *financial executive*
Fettig, Jason L. *financial planner*
Graham, Dean C. *financial consultant*
Guilfoyle, James Joseph *financial executive, accountant*
Harrison, Beatrice Marie Binion *business educator, small business owner*
Kramer, Willard George, Jr. *retired accountant*
LaMoreaux, David Albert *benefit plans administrator*

Farmington
Lore, Mary J. *accountant*

Farmington Hills
Drexler, Mary Sanford *financial executive*
Helppie, Charles Everett, III *financial consultant*
Michlin, Arnold Sidney *finance executive*

Grand Haven
Fortino, John F. *financial consultant*

Grand Rapids
Balfour, Danny Lee *public administration educator, consultant*
Bootsma, Greg D. *financial consultant*
Burch, David B. *financial consultant*
Bylsma, Scott A. *financial consultant*
Ecker, Scott S. *financial consultant*
Falk, Wanda E. *financial advisor*
Fuger, Theodore Hall, Jr. *investment analyst*
Hanson, George Eric *financial planner*
Heckler, Timothy A. *financial advisor*
Johnson, Alan E. *financial consultant*
Knipping, Ronald L. *financial advisor*
Lanning, Randall R. *financial consultant*
Liszewski, Jeffrey S. *financial consultant*
Molenbeek, Robert Gerrit *accountant, realtor*
Thauer, Edwin William, Jr. *financial services executive*

Grandville
Howell, Matthew D. *pension manager*

Houghton
Goltz, Sonia May *management educator*

Hudsonville
Bonzelaar, Gregory Scott *accountant*

Iron Mountain
Knop, Philip Henry *finance executive*

Ishpeming
Bell, Sue A. *financial services company executive*

Jackson
Hildreth, Patricia Yvonne *accounting executive*
Keppeler, Alexis Eric *senior benefits consultant*
Lavin, Roxanna Marie *finance executive*

Kalamazoo
Collins, Dana Jon *financial executive*
Taskey, Roger L. *financial company executive*
Wolf, Richard Alan *investment executive*

Zhang, Charles Cheng *financial planner*

Lansing
Brasic, Gregory Lee *financial administrator*

Lathrup Village
Kunz, James William *systems consultant*

Marquette
Camerius, James Walter *marketing educator, corporate researcher*
Thompson, Joel Edward *accounting educator*

Monroe
Mlocek, Sister Frances Angeline *financial executive*

Muskegon
Brown, Jack Edward *investment counselor*
Busler, Michael Britt *financial manager*
Delong, Donald Reed *accountant*
Erickson, Timothy C. *financial advisor*

Novi
Kerrigan, Walter W., II *financial planner*

Port Huron
Ragle, George Ann *accountant*

Portland
Rich, Joseph John *accountant*

Reading
Drake, B. Max *finance executive*

Rochester
Bazaz, Mohammed S. *accounting educator*

Saginaw
Kern, Franklin Lorenz *auditor*
Prud'homme, Cindy Jo *controller*

Saline
Love, John C. *finance company executive*

Southfield
Boyce, Daniel Hobbs *financial planning company executive*
Golden, Steve M. *financial consultant*
Maben, Burton Freeman *financial planner, analyst*

Sylvan Lake
Wood, Barbara Ann *financial executive*

Traverse City
Bruno, James David *financial consultant*
DiMercurio, Peter N. *financial consultant*
Gillen, John E. *financial manager*
LaCourse, Barbara J. *financial advisor*

Troy
Augustin, Kathryn Mary *financial advisor*
Hull, Duane G. *financial planner*
Lewakowski, Deborah Marguerita *accountant*
Pott, Sandra Kay *finance company executive*

Warren
Manning, Susan Harriet Hinman *procurement analyst*

MINNESOTA

Bloomington
Baker, Terry J. *financial advisor*
Chadwick, John Edwin *financial counselor and planner*
Hanson, Gary Lee *financial company executive*

Eagan
Sletner, Barbara Marie *credit professional*

Edina
Anderson, Todd Peter *financial consultant*
Anderson, Veronica L. *financial consultant*
Chaffee, Richard J., Jr. *financial planner*
Eckerline, Peter Edward *financial consultant*

Excelsior
Fazio, Faye Elizabeth *financial planner*
Hugh, Gregory Joseph *finance company executive*

Lino Lakes
Madsen, Philip Dana *development consultant*

Mankato
Janavaras, Basil John *university business educator, consultant*
Schreier, Bradley *finance company executive*

Maple Grove
Whitman, Andrew Franklin *management educator, insurance-legal consultant*

Maple Lake
Pohlman, Carlyle George *retired accountant*

Minneapolis
Anderson, Richard E. *financial advisor*
Boedigheimer, Scott Michael *accountant*
Childers, Terry Lee *marketing educator, consultant*
Eskew, Wayne R. *portfolio manager*
Gustafon, Deborah *financial services company executive*
Johnson, Steven Craig *financial company executive*
Jones, Norman M. *finance executive*
Kleine, David Matthew *investment advisor*
Lumpkins, Robert L. *business executive*
Miller, Donald Muxlow *accountant, administrator*
Montgomery, Andrew Stuart *financial advisor*
Montgomery, Henry Irving *financial planner*
Petersen, Douglas Arndt *financial development consultant*
Roberts, Beverly Randolph *accountant*
Skorich, Arlene Rita Mae *labor union bookkeeper*
Sorbo, Allen Jon *actuary, consultant*
Sorteberg, Kenneth Warren *executive accountant*
Stein, Paul Clinton *financial planner*
Stifter, Gerard Edward *accountant*

Nevis
Stibbe, Austin Jule *accountant*

New Brighton
Lund, James Bernard *financial advisor*

Plymouth
Hauser, Elloyd *finance company executive*

Saint Paul
Brink, John William *financial corporation executive*
Bry, Jeffrey Allen *auditor*
Dresbach, David Philip *financial consultant, educator*

Wayzata
Jacobson, Anna Sue *finance company executive*

Woodbury
Bretz, Kelly Jean Rydel *actuary*

MISSOURI

Blue Springs
Gimmarro, Steven Paul *financial planning executive*

Branson
Cahill, Arthur Ripley *financial executive*

Cape Girardeau
Farrington, Thomas Richard *financial executive, investment advisor*

Chesterfield
Bartmess, Joseph Pell *financial consultant*
Campbell, John W. *financial consultant*
DeLuca, Peter R. *financial planner*
Graham, James R. *financial planner*
Henry, Roy Monroe *financial planner*
Johnson, Andrew P. *financial consultant*
Kieffer, Robert Paul *financial planner*
Kieffer, Thomas A. *financial executive*
Kopsky, Matt E. *investment advisor*

Clayton
Domke, Gary Edward *securities company executive*

Columbia
Cunningham, Billie M. *accounting educator*
Stockglausner, William George *accountant*

Des Peres
Patton, Ray Baker *financial consultant, real estate broker*

Florissant
Schneider, Thomas Patrick *financial planner*

Hazelwood
Kostecki, Mary Ann *financial tax consultant, small business consultant*

Independence
Roberts, Diana Kaye *accountant*

Jefferson City
Kelly, Margaret Blake *accountant, state official*
Liese, Christopher A. *benefits and financial consulting company owner, state legislator*

Kansas City
Boysen, Melicent Pearl *finance company executive*
Dechart, Daniel W. *financial consultant*
De Lurgio, Stephen Anthony *management educator*
Emery, Larry C. *financial executive*
Garrison, Larry Richard *accounting educator*
Karlin, James Edward *accountant, tax specialist*
Klatt, John Harold *auditor*
Lashley, Jeffrey R. *financial consultant*
Lock, Robert Joseph *accountant*
McSpadden, William A. *financial systems executive*
Oppenheimer, Charles K(enneth), Jr. *financial executive, consultant*
Rozell, Joseph Gerard *accountant*
Shaw, Richard David *marketing and management educator*
Stringham, Evelyn L. *financial services executive*
Turner, Vernita *accountant*
Ward, Todd Pope *consultant*
Zindel, Jon Walter *financial services consultant*

Marshall
Todd, Kathy A. *finance company executive*

Moberly
Ornburn, Kristee Jean *accountant*

Neosho
Weber, Margaret Laura Jane *accountant*

Poplar Bluff
Ruhl, Helena Mae *business educator*

Raytown
Johnson, Sondra Lea *accountant*

Saint Louis
Arthur, Charles Gemmell, IV *accountant*
Badalamenti, Anthony *financial planner*
Bloemer, Rosemary Celeste *bookkeeper*
Brockhaus, Robert Herold, Sr. *business educator, consultant*
Burch, Stephen Kenneth *financial services company executive, real estate investor*
Chilton, Kenneth Wayne *business research director, writer*
Crider, Robert Agustine *international financier, law enforcement official*
Dickey, R. Kevin *financial planner, consultant*
Dillon, Thomas Ray *financial planner*
Driscoll, Charles Francis *financial services company executive, investment adviser*
Gunn, Russell Clifton *financial services company executive*
Harris, Eugene Whitney *financial company executive*
Hewitt, Thomas Edward *financial executive*
Hoke, James Richard *finance executive, management consultant*
Horwitz, William J. *treasurer*
Locher, Duane *controller*
Middeke, Richard Joseph *accountant*
O'Donnell, Mark Joseph *accountant*
Osborn, John David *credit union executive*
Parsons, Daniel Charles *accountant*
Schmidt, Clarence Anton *financial consultant*
Seibert, Earl Henry, Jr. *financial planner, lecturer*
Sharkey, Kathleen *accountant*
Tei, Takuri *accountant*
Wildhaber, Michael Rene *accountant*
Winter, Richard Lawrence *financial and health care management and consulting company executive*

Saint Peters
Brown, Debra Lynn *financial analyst, accountant, consultant*

Springfield
Brown, John J. *financial services company executive*
Gruener, Jennifer Lee *accountant*
Johansen, Herman John *financial consultant*

Unionville
Sparks, (Lloyd) Melvin *appraiser*

Warrensburg
Schwepker, Charles Henry, Jr. *marketing educator*

Whitewater
Gast, Linda Kay *accountant, financial executive*

NEBRASKA

Fremont
Lansworth, Karen Anne *bookkeeper*

Hastings
Nelson, Ricky Eugene *financial executive*

Lincoln
Digman, Lester Aloysius *management educator*
Foy, Edward Donald *investment advisor*
Lienemann, Delmar Arthur, Sr. *accountant, real estate developer*

Omaha
Andreski, Raymond John *financial planner*
Feltz, Todd A. *financial planner*
Murphy-Barstow, Holly Ann *financial consultant*
Nigh, Jay Jackson Casey *investment analyst*
Roscoe, Charlotte Marie *accountant*
Simons, Diana Lee *counselor clerk specialist*

Sidney
Person, Gary Charles *economic development administrator*

NEVADA

Henderson
Spiering, Nancy Jean *accounting executive*

NEW YORK

Geneva
Zammit, John P. *financial planner*

New York
Petru, Suzanne Mitton *health care finance executive*

NORTH DAKOTA

Bismarck
Hawkinson, Don *financial consultant*

Fargo
Ness, Gary Gene *accountant*
Risher, Stephan Olaf *investment officer*

Grand Forks
Wambsganss, Jacob Roy *accounting educator, small business consultant*

Minot
Dick, Robert Michael *financial planner*
Guttormson, Mark Steven *financial planner*
Kontos-Roberts, Nita Rae *finance specialist*

OHIO

Akron
Moore, Walter Emil, Jr. *financial planner*
Rapp, Larry P. *financial advisor*

Athens
Miller, Peggy McLaren *management educator*
Patterson, Harlan Ray *finance educator*
Rakes, Ganas Kaye *finance and banking educator*

Avon Lake
Kray, Elaine Louise *auditor*

Blue Ash
Bookbinder, Keith J. *financial planner*

Brunswick
Reed, Jane Garson *accounting educator, consultant*

Chagrin Falls
Morse, A(lbert) Reynolds *corporate executive*

Cincinnati
Bachman, Frank A. *financial advisor*
Black, David deLaine *investment consultant*
Brokaw, Kathryn Louise Zimmer *municipal finance administrator*
Camma, Philip *accountant*
Conaton, Michael Joseph *financial service executive*
De Ran, Susan Louise *financial consultant*
Dougherty, Charlotte Anne *financial planner, insurance and securities representative*
Ertle, William Justin *manufacturing company financial executive*
Felty, Donald, Sr. *financial advisor*
Green, Scott W. *financial advisor*
Gyuro, Paula Candice *financial planner*
Hammond Black, Meryl Jean *accountant*
Jeckell, William Wilson *retired financial executive and journalist*
Liebschutz, David H. *business consultant*
Nelson, Mary Ellen Dickson *actuary*
Peters, Ann Louise *accounting manager*
Siekmann, Donald Charles *accountant*
Walker, Michael Claude *finance educator*
Williamson, Vikki Lyn *financial executive*
Wurtz, Carl Joseph *financial company executive, management consultant*

Cleveland
Bindernagel, Jackie Marie *finance executive*
Chester, Russell Gilbert, Jr. *accountant, auditor*
Cizmadia, David Paul *financial consultant*
Conley, Michelle Diane *investment consultant*
Dealoia, Michael Christian *financial analyst, researcher*
Gelfand, Ivan *investment advisor*
Hisrich, Robert Dale *business educator*
Kawa, Nancy Ann *accountant*
Kennard, Lawrence Paul *financial planner*
Lammers, Max P. *financial company executive*
Manley, David Thomas *employment benefit plan administration company executive*
Mann, Benjamin Howard *information management company executive*
Noetzel, Arthur Jerome *business administration educator, management consultant*
Pierson, Marilyn Ehle *financial planner*
Siegler, Lawrence Noah *financial consultant*
Skolnik, David Erwin *financial analyst*
Thomas, Richard Stephen *financial executive*

Columbus
Alspach, Dave D. *financial consultant*
Amatos, Barbara Hansen *accounting executive*
Barnes, Steven Lee *certified public accountant*
Dalton, Tom K. *financial advisor*
Duncan, James Stacy *accountant, community college administrator*
Eaton, Michael Christopher *accounting technician*
Fidler, Carol Ann *accountant*
Griggs, John Robert *financial and consumer credit services executive*
Kreager, Eileen Davis *administrative consultant*
Leong, G. Keong *operations management educator*
Ruhlin, Peggy Miller *investment adviser, financial planner*

Concord
Spiek, John Robert, Jr. *accountant*

Cuyahoga Falls
Hessler, William Gerhard *tax consultant*

Dayton
Brown, Samuel, Jr. *accountant*
Dittoe, Robert Bradley *account executive*
McCutcheon, Holly Marie *accountant*
Singhvi, Surendra Singh *finance and strategy consultant*
Walden, James William *accountant, educator*
Wilson, Robert M. *financial executive*

Dublin
Barnes, James L. *financial consultant*
Hartwell, Mack David *financial consultant*
Heneman, Robert Lloyd *management educator*
Jackson, Tricia A. *financial planner*
Sestina, John E. *financial planner*

East Liverpool
Gailey, Joan Dale *business management educator*

Fremont
Recktenwald, Fred William *financial executive*

Greenville
Franz, Daniel Thomas *financial planner*

Harrison
Kocher, Juanita Fay *retired auditor*

Hudson
Ashcroft, Richard Carter *controller*
Nye, Eric *financial services company executive*

Kettering
Hartmann, Richard Paul *accountant*

Mansfield
Haldar, Frances Louise *business educator, accountant, treasurer*
Shah, James M. *actuarial consultant*

Marietta
Aebi, Imogene McDonough *business educator*

Middletown
Miller, Roger L. *financial planner*

Niles
Gorcheff, Nick A. *controller*

North Olmsted
Brady, Michael Cameron *investment consultant*
McCafferty, Owen Edward *accountant, dental-veterinary practice consultant*

Oxford
Leonard, Joseph Wesley *business educator*
Snavely, William Brant *management educator and consultant*

Painesville
Clement, Daniel Roy, III *accountant, assistant nurse, small business owner*

Pepper Pike
Cohn, Barry L. *financial executive*
Hudec, Patrick J. *financial advisor*

Perrysburg
Barbe, Betty Catherine *financial analyst*

Powell
Robison, Barbara Jane *tax accountant*

Rayland
Midei, Richard Allen *financial services executive, entrepreneur*

Sandusky
Duttera, Brian Cleve *financial consultant and sales manager*
Ruthsatz, Randall A. *accountant*

Seaman
Thomas, Kuddy Scott *auditor*

Shaker Heights
Donnem, Sarah Lund *financial analyst, non-profit and political organization consultant*

Steubenville
White, Vicki Lee *bank service representative*

Sylvania
Sampson, Wesley Claude *auditor*

Toledo
Dwyer, Deborah Jean *management educator*
Hong, Paul Chongkun *management and accounting educator*
Mancinotti, Craig John *financial executive*
Rao, Subbanarasimhiah *management educator*
Shoffer, Jeffrey David *financial planner*

Warren
Platthy, Terrance Lee *accountant*
Robbins, Robert Marvin *accountant*

Westerville
Burke, Sheila Jane *financial advisor*
Hodges, Nathan Eldon, Jr. *professional investor*

Westlake
Fetterolf, Charles E. *account executive*

Whitehall
Turns, Mark G. *account clerk payment processor*

Wickliffe
Hanzak, Janice Chrisman *accountant*

Willoughby
Trennel, Lawrence William *accountant*

Wilmington
Hodapp, Larry Frank *accountant*

Youngstown
Grimm, Richard Charles *marketing and finance educator, researcher*

Zanesville
Alexander, Andrew James *financial analyst*

SOUTH DAKOTA

Burbank
Simmons, Joseph Thomas *accountant, educator*

Lead
Aberle, James Robert *accounting executive*

Platte
Pennington, Beverly Melcher *financial services company executive*

Sioux Falls
Brandt, David Dean *accountant, financial planner*

WISCONSIN

Appleton
Fisher, Robert Warren *accountant*
Totzke, James Richard *accounting and information systems administrator*
Vielehr, Byron Coveney *mutual fund executive*

Baraboo
Smith, Walter DeLos *accountant, professional speaker*

Beloit
Rodeman, Frederick Ernest *accountant*

Brookfield
Breu, George *accountant*
Lascari, Nicholas Stephen *finance company executive*

De Pere
Rueden, Henry Anthony *accountant*

Delafield
Huss, William Lee *accountant*

Eau Claire
Husby, Jean Ann *marketing educator, consultant*

Fort Atkinson
Folberg, Donald Moon *financial consultant*

Green Bay
Krusic, Raymond J. *financial consultant*
Van Beek, Dianne Margaret *marketing educator*

Hales Corners
Rombs, Vincent Joseph *retired accountant, lawyer*

Kenosha
Terrill, Ivan Dale *accounting educator*

La Crosse
Kastantin, Joseph Thomas *accounting educator*
Schmocker, Kenneth Ernest *financial planner, underwriter*

Madison
Barley, Barbara Ann *accountant*
Brachman, Richard John, II *financial services consultant*
Eisler, Millard Marcus *financial executive*
Googins, Louise Paulson *financial planner*
Haynes, Marilyn Mae *accountant, educator*
Kneebone, Beverly *tax preparer*
Rahn, Donald L. *accountant*
Reuschlein, Robert William *accountant, researcher*

Mequon
Berry, William Martin *financial consultant*

Milwaukee
Einhorn, Stephen Edward *mergers and acquisitions executive, consultant, investment banker*
Ertel, Gary Arthur *accountant*
Fieldbinder, A. Christine *accountant, educator*
Greene, Charles W. *financial advisor*
Kueh, Thomas M. *financial consultant*
Panenka, James Brian Joseph *financial company executive*
Pleggenkuhle, Lavern Ross *business educator*
Upton, Richard Lewis *advertising agency executive*

Minocqua
Pickert, Robert Walter *accountant*

New Richmond
Counter, James A. *financial planner*

Oconomowoc
Kneiser, Richard John *accountant*

Oshkosh
Huddleston, Kenneth Fred *business education educator*

Pewaukee
Ollhoff, Barbara Jean *marketing educator*
Tessmann, Cary Annette *controller*

Waupun
Wendt, Thomas Gene *controller*

West Bend
Dixon, James Wallace *financial marketing consultant*

ADDRESS UNPUBLISHED

Allen, Anna Marie *financial executive*
Aloisio, Maria Theresa *tax accountant*
Armbrecht, Michael Ray *accountant*
Atwood, William L. *cost analyst, tax consultant*
Austin, Harvey B. *financial consultant*
Banker, William G. *financial consultant*
Beller, Luanne Evelyn *accountant*
Benedek, John Joseph *accountant, city official*
Berger, Michael E. *financial consultant*
Blausey, Jeanne Martha *accountant, financial systems analyst*
Bochnak, Mary Louise *financial consultant*
Campbell, Alice Shaw *retired accountant, poet*
Chambers, James S. *financial consultant*
Chapman, Steven G. *portfolio manager*
Claspill, James Louis *finance company executive*
Cline, Linda Blair *accountant*
Dangel, Steven R. *financial executive*
Daniels, Michael Raymond *accountant*
Davis, Aimee J. *financial consultant*
Davis, Deborah Cecilia *auditor*
Davis, Grant M. *investment consultant*
Davis, William R. *financial planner, stockbroker*
Dean, Michael L. *business administration educator*
Denn, Cyril Joseph *insurance career agent*
Dunn, Leonard E. *financial executive*
England, James Wesley *accountant*
Eubank, George B. *financial consultant*
Farrall, Harold John *retired accountant*
Faulkner, John C. *mathematics and data management consultant*
Fey, Suzanne Jane *management consultant*
Filan, John B. *finance company executive*
Folz, Carol Ann *financial analyst*
Foote, Thomas Lyn *financial consultant*
Fredrickson, Sharon Wong *accountant*
Gehrke, Karen Marie *accountant*
Gerhart, Paul F. *business educator*
Gilbert, Richard A. *investment consultant*
Giljohann, Peter T. *finance company executive*
Healy, John Christopher *tax specialist*
Hofman, John Erwin *accountant*
Huneke, Wayne Robert *insurance company financial executive*
Kenney, T. Michael *financial consultant*
Kienol, Mark Steven *accountant*
Kiesel, William R. *financial consultant*
Klos, John Walter *fire protection services financial officer*
Lebos, Richard Jesse *accountant, law student*
Leffel, John H. *financial consultant*
Markel, Frank Lewis, Jr. *retired actuary*
May, Phyllis Jean *financial executive*
McNamara, David Joseph *financial and tax planning executive*
Miller, Doris Mayhill *accountant*
Mohr, James LeGrand *accountant*
Murphy, Sharon L. *financial company executive*
Oathout, Brenda Halm *auditor*
Osborn, Kenneth Louis *financial executive*
Peruzzo, Albert Louis *actuary, accountant*
Powless, David Griffin *accountant*
Ravens, Robert Allen *financial services company executive*
Reinhard, Norman Arthur *accountant*
Ritchey, Paul Andrew *accountant*
Ryan, Kenneth Robert, Jr. *accountant, stockbroker*
Ryan, Leo Vincent *business educator*
Scott, John Carl *educator*
Seprodi, Judith Catherine *accounting administrator*
Spainhour, (Dallas) Kyle *international division controller*
Stegner, Lynn Nadene *treasurer*
Stewart, Robert Alvin *auditor*
Wallis, Lloyd Randall *accountant*
Weiser, Irving *financial services company executive*
Wright, Judith Rae *retired accountant*

FINANCE: INSURANCE

UNITED STATES

ILLINOIS

Addison
Priz, Edward John *worker's compensation consultant*

Apple River
Ingram, Terrence Neale *insurance agent*

Barrington
Petramale, Donald Leslie *insurance company executive*

Bloomington
Ooms, J(ames) Wesley *insurance company executive*
Rust, Edward Barry, Jr. *insurance company executive, lawyer*

Champaign
Peterson, Roger Lyman *insurance company executive*
Venezia, John Carl *insurance company executive*
Wills, Bart Francis *insurance company executive*

Chatham
Clark, Larry Dale *insurance company executive*

Chicago
Averill, Barry William *health insurance company executive*
Ballard, Daniel Joseph *risk manager*
Bennett, Donald Charles, Jr. *insurance and finance executive*
Chang, Yi-Cheng *insurance agent*
Docktor-Smith, Mary Ann *employee benefits consultant*
Ebel, James V. *adjusting company executive*
Fitzgerald, Daniel Peter *insurance company executive*
Goddard, Linda Ann *insurance company official*
Kapetansky, Glenn *insurance company executive*
Karlin, Gary Lee *insurance executive*
Kendrick, William Monroe *insurance company executive*
Lishka, Edward Joseph *insurance underwriter*
Morris, Lester A. *insurance company executive*
Parcells, Frederick R. *product management*
Parks, Corrine Frances *insurance agency owner*
Preble, Robert Curtis, Jr. *insurance executive*
Schwartz, Linda Evelyn *insurance executive*
Tyree, James C. *insurance company executive*
Zucaro, Aldo Charles *insurance company executive*

Decatur
Mesnard, Darrell Dean, Sr. *insurance agent*
Strong, John David *insurance company executive*

Elk Grove Village
Paliganoff, David James *insurance executive, consultant*

Evanston
Peponis, Harold Arthur *insurance agent, broker*

Fairfield
Smith, Terry G. *insurance sales professional*

Flora
McVay, W. Weldon *insurance agent, farmer*

Freeport
Pascoe, E(dward) Rudy *insurance sales executive*

Geneva
Hamilton, Robert Appleby, Jr. *insurance company executive*

Highland Park
Nathan, Robert Burton *life insurance agent*

Hinsdale
Denton, Ray Douglas *insurance company executive*

Island Lake
Vucovich, Donn Timothy *insurance executive*

Jacksonville
Radcliffe, Jeffery Ellis *insurance agent*

Lake Forest
Brown, Cameron *insurance company consultant*
Butler, William Joseph, Jr. *insurance broker, lawyer*

Lincolnwood
Gopon, Leon Michael *insurance company executive*

Long Grove
Evans, Marvin Paul *insurance operations administrator*
Mathis, David B. *insurance company executive*

Moline
Middleton, Marc Stephen *corporate insurance specialist*

Normal
Sherman, Mark A. *insurance company executive*

Oak Lawn
Howard, Philip Martin *insurance agent*

Orland Park
Schultz, Barbara Marie *insurance company executive*

Peoria
Leu, Robert W. *retired insurance company executive, consultant*

Schaumburg
Golberg, Larry *insurance company executive*

Villa Park
Anderson, Stephen Francis *insurance company executive*

INDIANA

Batesville
Vonderheide, Richard Scott *insurance executive*

Crawfordsville
McCormick, Michael Del *business executive*

Crown Point
Seward, John Edward, Jr. *insurance company executive*

Fort Wayne
DeTore, Arthur William *insurance company executive*
Ivancic, Chris *insurance executive*
Lupke, Duane Eugene *insurance company executive*
Racine, Mark Allen *insurance claims representative*
Rolland, Ian McKenzie *insurance executive*
Steiner, Paul Andrew *retired insurance executive*
West, Thomas Meade *financial services strategic consultant*

Frankfort
Doan, Joe Coapstick *insurance agency executive*

Greenwood
Daniel, Michael Edwin *insurance agency executive*
Schoettle, Frederick John *insurance company executive*

Indianapolis
Funk, James William, Jr. *insurance agency administrator, business owner*
Gaunce, Michael Paul *insurance company executive*
Henderson, Bruce Wingrove *insurance executive*

Jasper
Fleck, Albert Henry, Jr. *insurance agency executive*

Kokomo
Deyo, Richard Arthur *insurance agent, investment officer*

Lafayette
Whitsel, Robert Malcolm *retired insurance company executive*

Leo
Worman, Richard W. *insurance company executive, state senator*

Merrillville
Collie, John, Jr. *insurance agent*

Michigan City
Eriksson, James Ernest *insurance agency executive*

Monticello
Haskins, Perry Glen *insurance company executive*

Muncie
Olinger, Wayne William *insurance agent*

Rensselaer
Smith, Michael Dale *insurance agency executive*

Schererville
Jarrett, Alexis *insurance professional*

Valparaiso
Messer, Allen *insurance consultant, trainer, educator*

IOWA

Cedar Falls
Wessels, Jon J. *insurance executive*

Cedar Rapids
Mitchell, Beverly Ann Bales *agency owner, women's rights advocate*

Council Bluffs
Johnson, Michael Randy *insurance company executive*

Des Moines
Ehlert, Paul Edward *insurance company representative*
Gagne, Patricia C. *insurance company executive*
Hurd, G. David *insurance company executive*
Richards, Roy Clark *insurance company executive*

West Des Moines
Bobenhouse, Nellie Yates *insurance company executive*

KANSAS

Garden City
Durr, Edward E. *insurance agent*

Manhattan
Ball, Louis Alvin *insurance company executive*

Overland Park
Shipman, David Norval *healthcare consultant*

Shawnee Mission
Beets, F. Lee *retired insurance company executive*
Eaton, Karl F(rancis) *insurance executive, consultant*
Hames, Gary Lawrence *insurance company executive*
Lakin, Scott Bradley *insurance agent*
Young, Larry Joe *insurance agent*

Wichita
Henry, Cecil James, Jr. *insurance sales broker*

MICHIGAN

Detroit
Beider, Andrew Michael *insurance agent*

Grand Rapids
Sommers, Dana Eugene *insurance agency executive*

Kalamazoo
Curry, John Patrick *insurance company executive, management consultant*

Lansing
Billard, William Thomas *insurance company executive*

Port Huron
Haynes, Marcia Margaret *insurance agent*

Redford
Hemminger, Allen Edward *retired insurance consultant*

Troy
Stein, Paul Lloyd *insurance company executive*

MINNESOTA

Arden Hills
Van Houten, James Forester *insurance company executive*

Eden Prairie
Lidstrom, Carl Francis *risk management consultant*

Hibbing
Pustovar, Paul Thomas *insurance agency owner*

Ivanhoe
Hoversten, Ellsworth Gary *insurance executive, producer*

Madison Lake
Huntley, Kennes Calvin *insurance educator*

Minneapolis
Anton, Frank Leland *insurance company executive*
Eitingon, Daniel Benjamin *insurance executive*
Keets, John David, Jr. *insurance company executive*
Konieczny, Sharon Louise *insurance company executive*
Lyson, Hal Curtis *investigator*
Stiles, Donald Alan *insurance company executive*
Thompson, Leonard Allen *insurance sales and marketing specialist, consultant*

Monticello
Peterson, Bradley Eugene *insurance agent*

Saint Paul
Hubbs, Ronald M. *retired insurance company executive*
Oswald, Eva Sue Aden *insurance executive*

MISSOURI

Blue Springs
Hanke, Karl William, III *insurance company executive*

Bridgeton
Wills, John Clifton *insurance agent*

Dexter
Smith, Judy Ann *insurance broker*

Grant City
Hull, Robert Dale *insurance agent, investment executive*

Grover
Crist, Lewis Roger *insurance company executive*

Kahoka
Huffman, Robert Merle *insurance company executive*

Kansas City
Bradshaw, William David *insurance company executive*
Dolan, Thomas Patrick *insurance company executive*
Fulton-Martinez, Kathleen *insurance company official*
Hiebert, Donald Lee *insurance company executive*
Nordman, Eric Charles *insurance regulatory specialist*
Yates, Dan Charles *insurance company official*

Saint Charles
Causey, Earl Wayne *insurance company executive*

Saint Louis
Cramer, Michael William *insurance executive*
Duff, Janet Marie *insurance company executive*
Haberstroh, Richard David *insurance agent*
Hogan, Michael Ray *insurance company executive*
Kohlmeier, Steven Bruce *insurance company professional*
LeBlanc, Michael Stephen *insurance and risk executive*
Meyersick, Sharon Kay *insurance administrator, nurse*
Powers, Pierce William, Jr. *insurance specialist*
Tracy, Thomas William *insurance company field manager*

NEBRASKA

Alliance
Langford, Charles Wesley *insurance agent*

Beatrice
Maurstad, David Ingolf *insurance agency executive*

Lincoln
Ferneau, Thomas E. *insurance consultant*
Tyner, Neal Edward *retired insurance company executive*

North Platte
Carlson, Randy Eugene *insurance executive*

Omaha
Jetter, Arthur Carl, Jr. *insurance company executive*
Skutt, Thomas James *insurance company executive*
Strevey, Guy Donald *insurance company executive*
Weekly, John William *insurance company executive*

NEW YORK

New York
Sherrill, H. Virgil *securities company executive*

NORTH DAKOTA

Grand Forks
Wogaman, George Elsworth *insurance executive, financial consultant*

OHIO

Akron
Arnett, James Edward *retired insurance company executive, retired secondary school educator*

Bedford
Moore, Dianne J. Hall *insurance claims administrator*

Canton
Bower, Ronald Edward *insurance agency owner*
Schauer, Thomas Alfred *insurance company executive*
Schuring, J. Kirk *insurance company executive*

Cincinnati
Eden, Norman Nachum *insurance agent*
Helton, William Stokely, Jr. *insurance executive*
Hitch, Robert Landis *insurance company executive*
Puthoff, Francis Urban *insurance salesman*

Cleveland
Dorman, Mark Joseph *financial services agent*
Massie, Samuel Proctor (Trei), III *insurance company executive*
Shepard, Ivan Albert *securities and insurance broker*

Columbus
Bosworth, Jeffrey Willson *insurance company manager, computer systems specialist*
Carlson, Larry Vernon *insurance company executive*
Denman, Mark A. *mortgage protection insurance company official*
Duryee, Harold Taylor *insurance executive*
Frenzer, Peter Frederick *insurance company executive*
Hauck-Fugitt, Christine Claire Kraus *insurance executive*
Neckermann, Peter Josef *insurance company executive*
Thomas, Ned Albert *insurance agent*
Trevethan, Arthur H. *insurance company executive*

Dayton
Olt, John Edward *insurance agent*

Dublin
Power, Thomas Edward *insurance brokers, consultant*

Geneva
Foote, David Ward, Jr. *insurance agency executive*

Hamilton
Marcum, Joseph LaRue *insurance company executive*

Hilliard
Weller, Charles Weston *insurance executive*

Hudson
Applegate, Randall Glenn *insurance executive*

Loveland
Ruwe, William *insurance executive*

Maumee
Oakes, Frank Leslie, Jr. *insurance agency executive*
Rees, Erica Sue *insurance company executive*

Newark
Dawson, Thomas Thiel *insurance company executive*

Springfield
Sproles, Kenneth Ray *insurance agent*

Steubenville
Yost, Robert Byron *insurance company executive*

Youngstown
Carlomagno, Stephen Guido *insurance company executive*
Tierno, Edward Gregory *insurance company executive*

Zanesville
Vandegriff, Thomas Herman *employee benefits consultant*

PENNSYLVANIA

Philadelphia
O'Connor, John Joseph *insurance company executive*

SOUTH DAKOTA

Aberdeen
Stoia, Viorel G. *life underwriter*

Mitchell
Widman, Paul Joseph *insurance agent*

Sioux Falls
Staebell, Ronald Thomas *life insurance agent*
Watson, John Cecil *insurance company executive*

Watertown
Brinkman, Elmer Paul *insurance sales agent, county commissioner*

WISCONSIN

Appleton
Van Eron, Kevin J. *insurance company executive*

Brookfield
Payne, Howard James *insurance company executive*
Trytek, David Douglas *insurance company executive*

Hartland
Price, Paul S. *insurance agency executive*

Madison
Rudolph, Stephen P. *insurance company executive*
Sayles, William W. *insurance company executive*
Sims, Terre Lynn *insurance company executive*

Milwaukee
Heckendorf, Allen Harvey *insurance agency official*

Stevens Point
Dougherty, Daniel Allan *insurance claims manager*

Waukesha
Konig, Kenneth William *insurance agent*

Wausau
Baumgardt, Arden Charles *insurance company executive*

ADDRESS UNPUBLISHED

Alpert, Ann Sharon *insurance claims examiner*
Beckman, Melissa Ann *insurance account executive*
Buck, Earl Wayne *insurance investigator, private detective*
Datcher, Jewell Antoinette *health insurance company consultant*
Gundelfinger, Ralph Mellow *retired insurance company executive*
Hatcher, James R. *insurance executive*
Hibner, Rae A. *insurance company official, nurse*
Hugley, Betty Jean *retired insurance analyst, poet*
Jackson, Jennifer Claire *marine underwriter*
Kanter, Jerome Jacob *insurance company executive*
Knittel, Diane Lynne *insurance marketing executive*
Lawrence, Robert G. *insurance company executive*
Laybourn, Hale *insurance company executive*
Mathews, Robert Earl, II *insurance company executive*
Olsen, George Edward *retired insurance executive*
Redel, Thomas Gregory *insurance regulatory executive, state official*
Reynolds, John Francis *insurance company executive*
Wendt, Elizabeth Warczak *retired insurance company executive*

FINANCE: INVESTMENT SERVICES

UNITED STATES

CALIFORNIA

San Francisco
Gund, George, III *financier, professional sports team executive*

ILLINOIS

Alton
Brueggeman, Timothy Alan *investment broker*
Coughlin, Fred R. *securities executive*
Hunter, David W. *stockbroker*

Arlington Heights
Eriksen, Peter Bendtsen *investment company executive*

Barrington
Ballentine, William Andrew *stockbroker*
Kroll, Stephanie J. *stockbroker*

Belleville
Carden, Robert A. *stockbroker*
Doty, Robert J. *account executive*
Hatley, William Patrick *investment executive*
Krichoff, Benjamin Jeffery *investment broker*
Langenhorst, Vicky L. *securities trader/dealer*
Waller, Kelly Sue *investment broker*

Bloomington
Glover, Rob W. *stockbroker*
Hish, Don R. *stockbroker, financial planner*

Carbondale
Ketter, Kim A. *investment company executive*

Carmi
Holland, Gary V. *investment broker*
Kleinschmidt, Randy Fred *investment broker*

Centralia
Agee, David E. *stockbroker*
Barrow, Roger G. *securities company executive*

Champaign
Buller, Gary W. *investment broker*
Dillavou, John G. *stockbroker, former educator*
Teterycz, Barbara Ann *entrepreneur, advertising executive*

Chicago
Barnello, Michael David *investment company executive*
Brodsky, William J. *futures options exchange executive*
Buckle, Frederick Tarifero *international holding company executive, political and business intelligence analyst*
Curley, James R. *stockbroker*
Gallucci, John P. *stockbroker*
Gelber, Brian *commodities trader*
Granato, Gregory A. *stockbroker*
Greenberg, Steve *brokerage house executive*
Harris, Ronald William *commodities trader*
Hickey, Jerome Edward *investment company executive*
Hickey, Thomas M. *stockbroker*
Karr, Kenneth John *insurance broker executive*
Kelly, Arthur Lloyd *management and investment company executive*
Kirsch, Jeffrey Scott *securities executive*
Kuhn, Ryan Anthony *media investment banker, investor*
Lawlor, William James, III *brokerage house executive*
Lawson, Matthew S. *securities industry executive*
Livingston, Homer J., Jr. *stock exchange executive*
Luthringshausen, Wayne *brokerage house executive*
O'Brien, Brien Michael *investment firm executive*
Patzke, Frank Thomas *investment advisor*
Reece, Beth Pauley *commodities broker*
Rosenthal, Leslie *brokerage house executive*
Stead, James Joseph, Jr. *securities company executive*
Stevens, Paul G., Jr. *brokerage house executive*
Tharin, James Cotter, Jr. *entrepreneur*
Thornton, Colleen Bridget *investment management executive*
Towson, Thomas D. *securities trader*
Underwood, Robert Leigh *venture capitalist*
Weiner, Gerald Arne *stockbroker*
Zeid, Paula Klein *metals broker*

Collinsville
Keppner, Larry E. *stockbroker*

Decatur
Damery, D. Rodney *commodities and stockbroker, farmer*
Halbach, Michael J. *stockbroker*
Harrington, William Richard *investment broker*
Livasy, James Richard *investment broker*

Deerfield
Almiro, Jack J. *stockbroker*
Bradley, Claiborne Sheldon *stockbroker*
Campbell, S. Jack *investment banker*
Esposito, Steven F. *securities company executive*
How, Philip Harrison *stockbroker*
Howell, George Bedell *equity investing and managing executive*

Du Quoin
Britton, Duncan A. *stockbroker*

Effingham
Davis, Stephen S. *stockbroker*

Elgin
Freeman, Corwin Stuart, Jr. *investment adviser*

Glenview
Cohen, Randall B. *stockbroker*
Hurni, Jerry A. *stockbroker*

Gurnee
Guccione, Joyce E. *securities company executive*

Jacksonville
Bordenkircher, John J. *investment represenative*
Lansden, Michael H. *stockbroker*

Jerseyville
Hardin, Paul G. *broker*

Lake Forest
Carlucci, Marian Elaine *investment company executive*

Matteson
Kirkland, Gwendolyn Vickye *investment broker, financial planner*

Moline
Farrell, Richard F. *investment company executive*

Mount Vernon
Baker, Sherry L. *investment broker*
Hornung, George Leonard *stockbroker*
Jones, Cynthia L. *investment broker*

Northbrook
Dixon, Wesley Moon, Jr. *venture capital executive*

Oak Brook
Kelly, Donald Philip *entrepreneur*

Palos Hills
Johnson, Audrey Ann *options trader, stockbroker*

Peoria
Erickson, Mark H. *stockbroker*
Houlihan, Steven J. *stockbroker*

Princeton
Massey, Todd A. *investment banker, consultant*
Schultz, Robert Vernon *entrepreneur*

Quincy
Bunch, R. Diana *stockbroker*
Citro, James Collins *investment executive*
Conover, Phillip Glen *investment broker*
Cutrone, Thomas A. *investment broker*
Dorsey, Gilberta A. *investment broker, trust specialist*
Glanzman, Joyce C. *investment broker*
Gorrell, Larry W. *stockbroker*

River Forest
Wirsching, Charles Philipp, Jr. *brokerage house executive, investor*

Riverwoods
Jawor, John David *stockbroker*
Krinker, Ronald Scott *stockbroker*

Rochester
Chase, Theodore Taylor *securities trader*

Rockford
Jacobson, Phil D. *investment advisor*

Salem
Dwyer, William T. *investment broker*

Skokie
Apolinski, Casey Stanley *stockbroker*
Borenstein, Howard A. *stockbroker*
Christopoulos, George T. *investment representative*
Dillon, Michael C. *stockbroker*
Forlow, David *stockbroker*

Springfield
Kreh Beil, Julie E. *investment broker*
Newtson, Richard Evan *stockbroker*

Wheaton
Back, Robert Wyatt *investment executive, pharmaceutical company executive consultant*

Wheeling
Saranow, Mitchell Harris *investment banker, business executive*

Willow Springs
Jashel, Larry Steven (L. Steven Rose) *entrepreneur, consultant*

Wilmette
Ryan, Michael *investment management consultant*

INDIANA

Batesville
Bessler, Electa L. *securities company executive, councilwoman*

Bloomington
Bullock, David L. *stockbroker*
Jones, Richard A. *stock broker*

Columbus
Schroer, Laurie Ann *investment broker*

Elkhart
Gore, Alvin E. *stockbroker*
Hayes, Randy E. *stockbroker*
Herbster, Steven L. *stockbroker*

Evansville
Brill, Alan Richard *entrepreneur*
Capshaw, Charles W. *investment company executive*
Justice, Phillip Howard *securities broker*

Fort Wayne
Barua, Jayanta Lal *stockbroker*
Brown, Carl E. *stockbroker*
Delton, Mark *investment company executive*
Detwiler, Susan Margaret *information brokerage executive*
Duncan, Stephen C. *stockbroker*
Gibson, Tim G. *investment broker*
Haberly, H. Paul, Jr. *investment broker*
Henry, Michael L. *stockbroker, lawyer*
Howard, Mark A. *stockbroker*
Inglesias, Byron F. *investment officer*

Greensburg
Moore, Albert Lawrence *investment company executive, investment broker*

Indianapolis
Arnold, Stuart W. *account executive*
Baker, R. Kent *entrepreneur*
Bosway, Michael E. *securities broker*
Davis, Diane E. *securities company official*
Eberg, H. Richard *investment banker and broker*
Frost, Brian E. *stockbroker*
Holland, George Frank, II *investment company executive*
King, Kay Sue *investment company executive*
Marks, Marie Schulz *investment service president*
Price, Thomas Allan *entrepreneur*
Reuter, John Robert, Jr. *investment company executive*
Stayton, Michael Bruce *financial entrepreneur, corporate professional*

Jasper
Backer, Marcella L. *investment broker*

Kokomo
Faulkner, Anita L. *stock brokerage executive*

Lafayette
Keck, Joe D. *stockbroker*

Logansport
Denham, Janet *investment broker*

Merrillville
Ennes, Mark Raymond *financial consultant*

Reitmeister, Noel William *financial planner, investment and insurance broker, author, consultant, columnist, television host and producer, educator*

Munster
Bielfeldt, Dennis C. *investment broker*

New Albany
Lobeck, David R. *investment broker*

South Bend
Blasko, Monica Lee *investment company executive*
Coriden, John P. *investment broker*
Coussens, Frank J. *investment company executive*
Deahl, F. Richard *stockbroker*
Draskovits, James F. *investment broker*
Farron, John R. *stockbroker*
Graham, David B., Jr. *stockbroker*
Gyopos, Robert William *stockbroker*
Kobek, Kenneth A. *stockbroker*

Terre Haute
Gerrish, Wakefield E. *investment broker*

IOWA

Altoona
Gilbert, Michael D. *stockbroker*

Ames
Divine, Thomas L. *stockbroker*
Flynn, Carolyn *investment executive*
Gardner, Colleen *investment company executive*

Atlantic
Allen, Michael D. *investment broker*

Cedar Rapids
Brisben, Joseph D. *investment broker*
Clark, Mark A. *stockbroker*
Dinucci, Joseph V. *stockbroker*
Fehlberg, Brenda *investment company manager*
Kocher, Ken A. *stockbroker*

Dubuque
Curl, William Donald *securities dealer*

Iowa City
Courtney, Darrel Gene *investment executive*
Ellerhoff, Roger Dale *securities company executive*
Emerson, Richard Donald *investment broker*

Sioux City
Brower, Wade Michael *stockbroker*
Munzinger, Judith Montgomery *investment executive*

Spencer
Franker, Stephen Grant *investment executive*

West Des Moines
Shoafstall, Earl Fred *entrepreneur, consultant*

KANSAS

Arkansas City
Bedell, S. Clark *stockbroker*
Lewman, Sandra Kay *stockbroker*

De Soto
Wilson, Darrell Glenn *investment banker, software developer*

Leawood
Duggan, Jerry C. *investment banker*

Overland Park
Babcock, Scott V. *stockbroker*
Cordry, Jim A. *investment broker*

Pittsburg
Dobrauc, Antone John, Jr. *securities company official*
Ison, John D. *investment representative*

Pratt
Clontz, Nita M. Barnes *stockbroker*

Shawnee Mission
Pappas, Sharon K. *investment company executive*
Tucker, Keith A. *investment company executive*
Wirkkula, George L. *investment company executive*

Topeka
Baldwin, James Gordon *stockbroker*
Beeman, Terry *stockbroker*
Campbell, Dennis G. *investment advisor*
Cooper, Robert G. *investment executive*
Fleenor, Gary Bryce *brokerage executive, councilman*
Hummer, Terry G. *stockbroker*
Jacquinot, Terry J. *stockbroker*

Wichita
Ade, Larry B. *investment executive*
Banowetz, Arleen Frances *entrepreneur, educator*
Barker, Brent Clark *stockbroker*
Barry, Donald Lee *investment broker*
Boyd, Steven R. *stockbroker*
Engels, Kevin J. *securities company official*
Giffin, Jason S. *investment broker*
Holladay, Eric Dan *stockbroker*
Hukle, James R. *stockbroker*

MICHIGAN

Adrian
Hofflander, Tim G. *stockbroker*

Berkley
Gill, Wilfred George *financial executive*

Birmingham
Sallen, Marvin Seymour *investment company executive*

Bloomfield Hills
Berzac, Cary J. *investment broker, educator*

Detroit
Cooley, James Lumbert *stockbroker*
Flanagan, Dan M. *manager, broker*
Griffin, Patrick J. *bonds sales professional*
Jennings, Joseph N. *stockbroker*
Martin, John Gustin *investment banker*

East Lansing
Tegge, Frank Allen *stock brokerage company executive*

Farmington Hills
Ellmann, Sheila Frenkel *investment company executive*

Fremont
Karsten, Brian S. *investment broker*

Grand Rapids
Alsover, William C. *securities company executive*
Andersen, Bernard M. *stock broker*
Anderson, Chris George *stockbroker*
Balbach, Benjamin S. *stockbroker*
Barney, Eileen K. *stockbroker*
Bauman, Kenneth A. *investment company executive*
Beesley, Donald E. *securities company executive*
Bennett, Chuck William *stockbroker*
Berg, Donald W. *investment company executive*
Bowman, Stephen D. *stockbroker*
Braun, Michael P. *stockbroker*
Bykerk, G. Patrick *stockbroker*
Deal, Daniel E. *stockbroker*
Farquharson, John S. *investment broker*
Freeburg, Amy L. *stockbroker*
Fuger, John A. *stockbroker*
Glanville, Joyce M. *stockbroker*
Graf, Michael F. *stockbroker*
Griswold, Daniel R. *investment company executive*
Haan, Stephen M. *investment broker*
Hampton, Michael R. *investment company executive*
Huisingh, Roger J. *securities trader*
Karpinski, Donald G. *stockbroker*
Kars, Richard Y. *stockbroker*
Kosten, Donald L. *investment broker*
Long, Timothy J. *money manager*

Grosse Pointe
Carnal, Chris D. *stockbroker*

Holland
Bishop, Marc W. *investment broker*
Bosko, Lee Douglas *investment representative*
Clark, Kevin H. *stockbroker*
Finkler, Joseph M. *investment broker*
Hekman, James L. *stockbroker*
Kiss, Stephen P. *investment broker*
Wasylkowski, Steve Eugene *brokerage house executive*

Jackson
Long, John P. *broker*

Marquette
Bradley, Stuart Collins *investment representative*

Muskegon
Anderson, Thomas J. *investment advisor*
Boven, David L. *investment company executive*
Buchweitz, John E. *stockbroker*
Cramer, David Warren *investment banker*
Kendall, Robert E. *investment executive*
La Croix, Alphonse T. *entrepreneur*

Negaunee
Rigdon, Glenn Joseph *real estate appraiser, real estate broker*

Petoskey
Farley, David E. *stockbroker*

Southfield
Eldon, Laura P. *stockbroker*

Traverse City
Batcha, Jay P. *investments broker*
Bensley, Barbara L. *investment broker*
Bonnocini, Paul M. *stockbroker*
Corbett, William Arnold *securities broker, writer*
Hirt, Glenn C. *investment broker*
Kartsimas, James M. *investment broker, veterinarian*

West Bloomfield
Mamut, Mary Catherine *retired entrepreneur*

Zeeland
Barry, James Ronald *account executive*

MINNESOTA

Bloomington
Ascher, Chris J. *stockbroker*
Benson, John Brady *investment company executive*
Brown, Jason R. *stockbroker*
Carlson, Gary L. *stockbroker*
Connor, Daniel G. *stockbroker*
Dunn, Jeffrey W. *stockbroker*
Elvendahl, Susan J. *stockbroker*
Follese, Carolyn J. *stockbroker*
Gill, Chuck S. *stockbroker*
Griffiths, Thomas M. *stockbroker*

Edina
Brown, Gordon A. *financial stockbroker*
Dickey, William A. *stockbroker*
Gisselquist, Joel M. *stockbroker*
Hamlin, Robert J. *stockbroker*
McKee, Glenn Allen *business owner*

Excelsior
Fazio, Anthony Lee *investment company executive*

Minneapolis
Appel, John C. *investment company executive*
Fauth, John J. *venture capitalist*
Kvaale, Thomas Paul *investment company executive*
Lindau, James H. *grain exchange executive*
Lindau, Philip *commodities trader*
Piper, Addison Lewis *securities executive*
Rahn, Noel P. *investment company executive*
Schreck, Robert *commodities trader*
Sit, Eugene C. *investment executive*

Waubun
Christensen, Marvin Nelson *venture capitalist*

MISSOURI

Bowling Green
Galloway, Daniel Lee *investment executive*

Camdenton
Sallee, Frank *securities and investment executive*

Chesterfield
Barresi, Frank M. *investment broker*
Berg, Richard C. *stockbroker*
Castiglioni, Debra Marie *stockbroker*
Gerdin, Barry F., Jr. *stockbroker*
Hardy, James E. *stockbroker*
Hicks, Tadd D. *investment broker*
Kingsbury, James D. *stockbroker*

Fenton
Hombs, Charlton D. *stockbroker*

Florissant
Croak, John H. *investment representative*

Independence
Schondelmeyer, Brent Lee *communications consultant*

Jefferson City
Beatty, Grover Douglas *stockbroker*
Fischer, Gustav Fred *stockbroker*
Gue, Charles Sylvester, Jr. *stockbroker*

Joplin
Herrin, Christy L. *investment representative*

Kansas City
Acuff, Todd W. *stockbroker*
Braude, Michael *commodity exchange executive*
Cao, John *investment executive*
De Vries, Robert John *investment banker*
Kennedy, Arthur J., II *stockbroker*
Kraft, Lorena *investment executive*
Stowers, James Evans, Jr. *investment company executive*

Lees Summit
Korschot, Benjamin Calvin *investment executive*

Maryland Heights
Finnegan, Frank Roman *investment broker*
Friedewald, Robert A. *securities broker*
Kahn, Gene *stockbroker*

Neosho
Berghoetter, Anthony C. *stockbroker*

Rogersville
Harms, Nancy Isabel Fitch *entrepreneur*

Saint Louis
Abernathy, Randy E. *stockbroker*
Barnhart, Bruce A., Jr. *stockbroker*
Bianco, Joseph Peter *securities salesperson*
Billingsly, Z. Dwight *investment consultant, city assessor aide, financial analyst*
Brown, Morton Lindon *securities company executive*
Byrne, Thomas H. *investment broker*
Clark, C. Phillip, III *investment broker*
Coleman, James J., Jr. *investment company executive*
Jackson, Gayle Pendleton White *venture capitalist, international energy specialist*
Newton, George Addison *investment banker, lawyer*
Taylor, Gregory F. *securities broker*
Walker, George Herbert, III *investment banking company executive, lawyer*

Trenton
Bennett, Rodger W. *stockbroker*

Washington
Hirschl, Richard C. *investment broker*
Laboube, Dean R. *stockbroker*

West Plains
Kimberling, Paul Leroy *brokerage executive*

NEBRASKA

Lincoln
Knox, Arthur Lloyd *investor*

Omaha
Johnson, Richard Walter *investment executive*

NORTH DAKOTA

Fargo
Collins, Jay Michael *stockbroker*
Hepper, Calvin Dean *stockbroker*
Holland, Paul V. *stockbroker*
Kappes, Ken J. *stockbroker*
Tallman, Robert Hall *investment company executive*

Grand Forks
Bjerk, Keith A. *stock brokerage executive, home builder*

OHIO

Alliance
Rodman, David Lawrence *investment counselor*

Barberton
Chase, Rex B. *stockbroker*

Bowling Green
Callecod, Joan D. *stockbroker, accountant, auditor*

Chagrin Falls
Rowe, Mae Irene *investment company executive*

Cincinnati
Anning, Robert Doan Hopkins *brokerage company executive*
Assaley, Lewis A. *investment company executive*
Clark, Jeffery D. *stockbroker*
Durket, Mark J. *stockbroker, educator*
Gillette, Kenneth E. *stockbroker*
Greenwald, Jeffrey S. *stockbroker*
Hard, Carol Dubovick *investment company executive*
Hawkins, Wendell E. *stockbroker, educator*
Heile, John David *stockbroker*
Laffoon, Peter G. *investment company executive*
Leugers, Thomas C. *investment executive*
Rensing, Robert Francis *independent investor, consultant*

Cleveland
Adamo, Joseph J. *securities analyst*
Brooks, Joseph W. *stockbroker*
Carter, Kevin Anthony *securities company executive*
Dettelbach, John A. *investment company executive*
Dill, Douglas Arthur *investment counselor*
Hunt, H. Ty *stockbroker*
Jack, Donald M., Jr. *broker*
Killius, Richard W. *stockbroker*
La Gattuta, John A. *stockbroker*
Lane, Alfred L. *brokerage executive*
O'Donnell, Thomas Michael *brokerage firm executive*
Summers, William B. *brokerage house executive*
Swetland, David Wightman *investment company executive*
Tatman, Edward J. *entrepreneur, engineer*
Watterson, Thomas Batchelor *investment executive*

Columbus
Beetham, Chris D. *stockbroker*
Breymaier, Christine A. *investment company executive*
Charters, Michael G. *securities company executive*
Coffman, Curtis M. *securities company official*
Evans, Cindy L. *investment company official*
Hamre, Gary Leslie William *entrepreneur*
Hatfield, Stuart A. *stockbroker*
Kirk, Courtlandt Blaine *bond trader*
Pointer, Peter Leon *investment executive*
Smith, Ronald Louis *stockbroker*

Dublin
Ault, Susan L. *securities broker*
Carter, Marilyn Peterson *securities trader/dealer*

Kent
Kline, Vicki Ann *investment consultant*

Martins Ferry
Gracey, Robert William *account executive, minister*

Medina
Hyde, Robert T. *investment banker*

Newark
Butterfield, Kimberle Rae *account executive*

Pepper Pike
Burke, Pamela de Windt *securities executive*
Crew, J. Burner *stockbroker*
Dougherty, Peter P. *securities company executive*
Gendler, Alan M. *stock brokerage executive*
Koehler, Donald R. *stockbroker*
Shin, William Dong Moon *brokerage house executive*

Pomeroy
Edwards, John David *investment executive*

Powell
Jobes-Platt, Patricia A. *stockbroker*

Westlake
Balson, Chris P. *stockbroker, financial planner*
Barker, Keith Rene *investment banker*

SOUTH DAKOTA

Sioux Falls
Jarabek, Dennis Joseph *brokerage executive*

Yankton
Ibarole, Wayne R. *stockbroker*

WISCONSIN

Baraboo
Borota, Timothy Douglas *stockbroker*

Beaver Dam
Hemling, Calvin L. *stockbroker*
Killingsworth, Mark M. *investment broker*

Green Bay
Bartol, Jon R. *stockbroker*

Madison
Bergren, Linda Jean *stockbroker*
Fasanella, John J. *investment executive*
LaFleur, Dan Lee *stockbroker*
Laufman, Mark David *securities company official*

Manitowoc
Kletzien, William Martin *investment company executive*
Kroening, Nathan G. *investment officer*

Milwaukee
Berglund, Kim Anne *investment company executive*
Bloom, James Edward *commodity trading and financial executive*
Fish, James M. *investment broker*
Heinen, Neil A. *stockbroker*
Kenney, Susan C. *stockbroker*
Klein, Fred A. *stockbroker*
Leonard, Randal Lee *stockbroker*
Leroy, Joseph F. *investment broker*
Lewenauer, John Benjamin *investment broker*
Linn, Thomas M. *investment broker*
Lubar, Sheldon Bernard *venture capitalist*

Oak Creek
Giblin, Louis *stockbroker*

River Falls
Jackson, Nathaniel Richard *investment broker*

Sparta
Bisinger, Jerry H. *investment representative*

Sturgeon Bay
Kulish, John S. *stockbroker*

Zenda
Sills, William Henry, III *investment banker*

WYOMING

Cowley
Henderson, James Harold *entrepreneur, business executive, financial planner*

CANADA

MANITOBA

Winnipeg
Mauro, Arthur V. *investment executive, university chancellor*

ADDRESS UNPUBLISHED

Ammerman, Charles R. *stockbroker*
Apel-Brueggeman, Myrna L. *entrepreneur*
Beck, Donald W. *stockbroker*
Benson, Robert S. *investment broker*
Bern, Scott E. *stockbroker*
Blankenburg, Phillip B. *investment broker*
Boyer, Richard Wakefield *stockbroker*
Brown, John Charles *stockbroker*
Campbell, Ryan D. *account executive*
Curtis, Sarah E. C. *securities sales associate*
DeVries, Richard Boyd *entrepreneur*
Dillon, Hugh J. *stockbroker*
Dormeier, Buff P. *investment professional*
Emmett, Rita *professional speaker*
Ernst, Randy F. *stockbroker*
Farley, John E. *stockbroker*
Fruitt, Tracy L. *stockbroker*
Glenn, Michael T. *investment company executive*
Grimaldi, Jack *investment company official*
Gronner, Mark I. *investment consultant*
Harper, Oliver William, III *investment company executive, consultant*
Harris, Brian M. *broker*
Harris, Joyce D. *stockbroker*
Hender, Eric Marshall *securities company executive*
Higgins, James Scott *investment officer*
Hitz, Duane Everett *brokerage executive*
Hollansky, Bert Voyta *stock brokerage executive*
Hopper, Patrick M. *securities trader*
Johnson, James I. *stockbroker*
Jones, Polly S. *investment company executive*
Keane, Stephen E. *securities company official*
Knaus, Thomas James *investments executive*
Knoblach, James Michael *entrepreneur*
Krug, R. Bernard *stock and commodities broker*
Laine, Art C. *stockbroker*
Rhoads, Patricia Mary (Gruenewald) *securities consultant*

FINANCE: REAL ESTATE

UNITED STATES

ILLINOIS

Addison
Kachiroubas, Christopher *assessor, real estate appraiser*

Bolingbrook
Gorte, Paul Michael *land use planner*

Champaign
Eades, David Cluthe *real estate developer*

Chicago
Balanoff, Clement *real estate agent*
Barnett, Edgar Allan *real estate executive*
Berger, Miles Lee *land economist*
Bluhm, Neil Gary *real estate company executive*
Bohn, Charlotte Galitz *real estate executive*
Campbell, Gavin Elliott *real estate investor and developer*
Cohen, Marvin Richard *real estate management executive*
Daley, Vincent Raymond, Jr. *real estate executive, consultant*
Daly, Patrick F. *real estate executive, architect*
Eubanks-Pope, Sharon G. *real estate entrepreneur*
Field, Karen Ann *real estate broker*
Friedman, Stephen Belais *real estate development consultant*
Galowich, Ronald Howard *real estate investment executive, venture capitalist*
Gerhold, Peter Karl *real estate executive*
Good, Sheldon Fred *realtor*
Hayes, Jacqueline Crement *real estate broker and developer*
Hollander, Elizabeth Russell *urban planner*
Jenkins, Walter Donald *real estate executive*
Levy, Arnold S(tuart) *real estate company executive*
Marciniak, Claudia Noelle *real estate company executive*
Messinger, Susan Francesca *city planner*
Miller, Harold Louis *real estate developer*
Pappas, Philip James *real estate company executive*
Persky, Seymour Howard *real estate development and management executive*
Pollock, Leslie Stuart *city planning consultant*
Rubenstein, Eric Davis *real estate executive*
Schwab, James Charles *urban planner*
Sen, Ashish Kumar *urban planner, educator*
Shields, Patrick Thomas, Jr. *property manager*
Stauber, Joel Vincent *urban planner, architect*
Stein, Paula Jean Anne Barton *hotel real estate consultant*
Strobeck, Charles LeRoy *real estate executive*
Thornber, Judy Paulene *real estate developer, consultant, lawyer*
Utigard, Philip Richard *real estate executive*
Wagener, Donna Lynn *real estate company official*

Deerfield
Sandborg, Verie *environmentalist*

Dundee
Ulakovich, Ronald Stephen *real estate developer*

Evanston
Thiel, Ruth Eleanor *real estate broker*

Fairview Heights
Haas, Marilyn Ann *real estate broker*

Gurnee
O'Leary, Timothy Francis *real estate developer*

Hinsdale
Hausmann, John Edmund *real estate executive, mayor*

Hoffman Estates
Koplin, Mark A. *urban planner, architect*

La Grange
Nalepa, Jim *real estate investor*

Lake Forest
Barker, Barbara *real estate professional*

Long Grove
Van Der Bosch, Susan Hartnett *real estate broker*

Macomb
Maguire, Dave *real estate manager*

Manhattan
Eyrich, Robert Paul *real estate appraiser*

Morton
Schrock, J(oseph) Byron *real estate broker*

Mount Prospect
Herman, Chloe Anna *real estate broker*

Murphysboro
Williams, Gale R. *realtor*

Naperville
Sahler, Christy Lee *real estate manager*

Northfield
Kleinman, Burton Howard *real estate investor*

O'Fallon
Cecil, Dorcas Ann *property management executive*

Oswego
Stephens, Steve Arnold *real estate broker*

Ottawa
Breipohl, Walter Eugene *real estate broker*

Peoria
Rushford, Eloise Johnson *land manager*

Rockford
Hart, Jay Albert Charles *real estate broker*

Saint Charles
McGowan, David Allen *real estate broker*
Urhausen, James Nicholas *real estate developer, construction executive*

Schaumburg
Barrett, Jeffrey Scott *real estate company executive*
Dabareiner, Thomas John *transportation planner*
Pande, Ronald G. *realtor*

Sycamore
Adrian, Joanne Doris *realtor*

Urbana
Blair, Lachlan Ferguson *urban planner, educator*
Hubbard, David Fred *real estate broker*

Washington
Brownfield, William Harry *real estate appraiser*

Waukegan
Gutman, Ruth Louise *real estate broker*

Wilmette
Eigel, Christopher John *real estate executive*

Winnetka
McGarry, Anne Pritchard *real estate salesman*

INDIANA

Bloomington
Lybrook, Tim C. *business executive, real estate executive*
Oswalt, Aria Lucinda *real estate broker*

Carmel
McCool, Richard Bunch *real estate developer*

Dubois
Klawitter, Robert Louis *environmentalist*

Elkhart
Vite, Frank Anthony *realtor*

Evansville
Matthews, C(harles) David *real estate appraiser, consultant*

Fishers
Posha, D. Richard *real estate developer, home builder, designer*

Fort Wayne
Hirschy, Gordon Harold *real estate agent, auctioneer*
O'Brien, Wayne Edward *planner*

Frankfort
Goar, James Vernon, Jr. *real estate broker*

Greenwood
Watkins, Michael James *real estate broker*

Hammond
DeVaney, Cynthia Ann *real estate broker, educator*

Indianapolis
Beckmann, Robert Dean, Jr. *real estate broker*
Borns, Robert Aaron *real estate developer*
Mullen, Thomas Edgar *real estate consultant*
Rees, Michael Joseph *real estate agency executive*
Richards, Neil Stephen *real estate executive*

Jeffersonville
McMichael, Jeane Casey *real estate corporation executive, educator*
Reisert, Charles Edward, Jr. *real estate executive*

Kokomo
Adams, Robert Joe *real estate dealer, farmer*

La Porte
McCann, Sheila Kay *landman*

Lafayette
Landrum, Thomas Lowell *real estate agent, resale shop owner*
Shook, James Creighton *real estate executive*

Montpelier
Neff, Kenneth D. *realtor*

Muncie
Hibbs, Clyde W. *retired environmental sciences educator, consultant*
Segedy, James A. *urban planning educator*

Newburgh
Tierney, Gordon Paul *real estate broker, genealogist*

Terre Haute
Perry, Eston Lee *real estate and equipment leasing company executive*

IOWA

Ames
Wendell, Barbara Taylor *retired real estate agent*

Cedar Rapids
Knepper, Eugene Arthur *real estate professional*

Des Moines
Campbell, Lesley Ann *environmental coordinator*

Iowa City
Edberg, Jeffrey Scott *real estate broker, marketing professional*

Saint Anthony
Kurtz, Carl Paul *conservationist, writer*

Spencer
Lemke, Alan James *environmental specialist*

Waterloo
Martin, Valentina Kuchynka *real estate company executive, consultant*

West Des Moines
McHughes, Brian Andrew *commercial real estate executive*

KANSAS

Dwight
Strom, Elwood Malcolm *soil and water conservationist, consultant*

El Dorado
Clymer, David Hoisington *real estate broker*

Emporia
Jurgens, Leonard John *retired range conservationist*

Kansas City
Rodewald, James Michael *real estate company executive*

Lawrence
Strauss, Eric James *urban planning educator, lawyer, consultant*

Leavenworth
Shehorn, Henry Wayne *real estate developer*

Liberal
Holmes, Carl Dean *state representative, landowner*

Mission
Langworthy, Asher Clinton, Jr. *real estate company executive*

Overland Park
McChesney, Samuel Parker, III *real estate executive*

Prairie Village
Taylor, Ralph Orien, Jr. *real estate developer*

Shawnee Mission
Blair, Clay C. *real estate developer*

Westwood
Buckner, William Claiborne *real estate broker*

Wichita
Forrest, Melba June *real estate broker, appraiser, educator*
Ohlson, Sara Faye *real estate executive*

MICHIGAN

Ann Arbor
Clark, Thomas B., Sr. *real estate broker*
Feldt, Allan Gunnar *retired urban planner, educator*
Richardson, Barbara Connell *transportation research scientist, consultant*
Surovell, Edward David *real estate company executive*
Wood, William J. *real estate consultant*

Berkley
Arroyo, Rodney Lee *city planning and transportation consultant*

Detroit
Hagood, Henry Barksdale *real estate developer*
Topey, Ishmael Aloysius *urban planner*

East Lansing
Hamlin, Roger Eugene *urban planning educator, economic and financial analyst*

Fenton
Manuel, Dennis Lee *real estate broker*

Grand Rapids
Bliek, Eldon Maurice *real estate company officer, consultant*
Higgins, James Joseph *environmental consultant*
Ripperger, Kathryn Lodal *real estate broker*
Van Dellen, Chester, Jr. *environmental consultant, real estate appraiser*

Grosse Pointe
Dunlap, Connie Sue Zimmerman *real estate professional*

Kalamazoo
Hambley, Delbert Eugene *real estate developer*
Mann, Gregory Lee *real estate appraiser, tax tribunal referee*
Taborn, Jeannette Ann *real estate investor*

Lansing
Tipton, James Alva *real estate agent, farmer*

Lapeer
Hodge, Douglas Kern *property appraiser, consultant*

Rogers City
Heidemann, Mary Ann *community planner*

Royal Oak
Halso, Robert *real estate company executive*

Somerset Center
Maxson, John Eugene *land surveyor*

South Lyon
Gooch, Nancy Jane *realtor, mortgage executive*

Southfield
Beron, Gail Laskey *real estate analyst, consultant, appraiser*
Colton, Victor Robert *real estate developer, investor,*

Traverse City
Lindenau, Judith Wood *real estate professional*
McCafferty, John Martin *real estate executive, commodities trader*

White Lake
Clyburn, Luther Linn *real estate broker, appraiser*

Williamston
Fouty, Marvin Francis *land surveyor, land developer, real estate broker*

MINNESOTA

Aitkin
Morton, Craig Richard *real estate investor*

Coon Rapids
Elvig, Merrywayne *real estate manager*

Minneapolis
Bolan, Richard Stuart *urban planner, educator, researcher*
Fine, William Irwin *real estate developer*
Kreiser, Frank David *real estate executive*
Maciej, James Valentine *commercial real estate consultant*
Stuebner, James Cloyd *real estate developer, contractor*
Vergin, Timothy Lynn *commercial real estate appraiser and broker*
Walker, Walter Willard *real estate and investments executive*

Minnetonka
Brauer, Donald George *land developer, planning consultant, engineer*

Rochester
Gilbertson, Steven E(dward) Satyaki *real estate broker, guidance counselor*

Saint Louis Park
Nath, Mahendra *real estate investor*

Saint Paul
Holmes, Gary S. *real estate developer*

Sauk Rapids
Schupp, Keith Lowell *general contractor*

Woodbury
Hopkins, Linda Kay *intellectual property consultant*

MISSOURI

Bolivar
Hillman, Carol Elizabeth *real estate broker*

Dunnegan
Harman, Mike *real estate broker, small business owner*

Holden
Martin, Laura Belle *real estate and farm land manager, retired educator*

Joplin
Buttram, James Alan *commercial real estate agent*
Harvey, Irene Delores *real estate professional*

Lake Saint Louis
Royal, William Henry *real estate developer, architect*

Saint Clair
Hickinbotham, Letha Belle *real estate broker, business owner*

Saint Joseph
Rachow, Sharon Dianne *realtor*
Robertson, John Bernard *real estate professional*

Saint Louis
Anderson, Wallace *real estate executive*
Marking, T(heodore) Joseph, Jr. *transportation and urban planner*
Shuter, Adrienne Joan *real estate broker*

Springfield
Condellone, Trent Peter *real estate developer*

Stockton
Jackson, Betty L. Deason *real estate developer*

West County
Carr, Carolyn Kehlor *realtor, fund raiser*

NEBRASKA

Kimball
Eastman, Nathan LeRoy *realtor, appraiser*

Norfolk
Wozniak, Richard Michael, Sr. *city and regional planner*

North Platte
Harris, James Melvin *real estate appraiser*

Omaha
Gallagher, Paula Marie *real estate appraiser*
Vann, Howard D. *real estate executive*

NORTH DAKOTA

Bismarck
Christianson, James Duane *real estate developer*

Grafton
Tallackson, Harvey Dean *real estate and insurance salesman*

OHIO

Akron
Peavy, Homer Louis, Jr. *real estate executive, accountant*

Athens
Dvorak, Jane Ann *property management executive*

Canton
Jackson, David Lee *real estate executive*
Wolanin, John Charles *realtor*

Chesterland
Grimm, Glenn Alan *real estate company executive, consultant*

Cincinnati
Dietz, Rowland Ernest *real estate manager*
Dunigan, Dennis Wayne *real estate executive*
Levine, Steven Alan *real estate appraiser, environmental consultant*
Morrison, Emily *property manager*
Schuler, Robert Leo *appraiser, consultant*
Shenk, Richard Lawrence *real estate developer, photographer, artist*
Steelman, John Robert *real estate broker, entrepreneur*
Winchell, Margaret Webster St. Clair *realtor*

Cleveland
Adler, Thomas William *real estate executive*
Markos, Chris *real estate company executive*

Columbus
Laurien, Philip Clark *city planner, consultant*
McCurdy, Kurt Basquin *real estate corporation officer*
Merwin, Harmon Turner *retired regional planner*
Pyatt, Leo Anthony *real estate broker*

Concord
Conway, Neil James, III *land title company executive, lawyer, writer*

Dayton
Frydman, Paul *real estate broker and developer*
Gammell, Wayne William *title company executive*
Miles, Alfred Lee *real estate broker, educator*
Stout, Donald Everett *real estate developer, environmental preservationist*

Elyria
Stefanik, Janet Ruth *realtor*

Gahanna
Lucas, Juanita Glassco *realtor, systems analyst*

Gates Mills
Schanfarber, Richard Carl *real estate broker*

Hudson
Stec, John Zygmunt *real estate executive*

Jefferson
Gibbs, Arland LaVerne *real estate agent*

Lodi
Berry, Beverly A. *real estate investment executive*

Mentor
Owens, Elizabeth D. *environmentalist*

Middleburg Heights
Hazlett, Paul Edward *realtor, information systems executive*

Mount Vernon
Meharry, Ronald Lee *real estate investor, inn keeper*

North Canton
Grady, Joseph Patrick *real estate professional*

Parma
Verba, Betty Lou *real estate executive*

Rocky River
Slaby, Lillian Frances *home finance counselor, real estate professional*

Salem
Barcey, Harold Edward Dean (Hal Barcey) *real estate counselor*

South Euclid
Adler, Naomi Samuel *real estate counselor*

Toledo
Batt, Nick *property and investment executive*

Youngstown
Camacci, Michael A. *commercial real estate broker, development consultant*

TEXAS

Dallas
Shore, Caron Dean *commercial real estate executive*

WISCONSIN

Appleton
Brehm, William Allen, Jr. *urban planner*
Law, Michael Lieber *real estate agency executive*

Ashland
Partridge, Ernest DeAlton *environmental philosopher, educator*

Brookfield
Malloy, James Joseph *real estate manager*

Cambridge
Stevens, Chester Wayne *real estate executive*

Eau Claire
Feldt, Robert Junior *retired conservationist*

Greenfield
von Riemer, David Wilhelm Karl (General) *retired real estate representative, author*

Hartland
Genrich, Judith Ann *real estate executive*

La Crosse
Dedo, Dorothy Junell Turner *real estate company executive, civic worker*

Madison
Evans, Donald LeRoy *real estate company executive*
Pinto, John Salvadore *real estate broker*
Rouze, Jeffrey Alan *real estate executive*

Mequon
Ryan, Mary Nell H. *training consultant*

Milwaukee
Machulak, Edward Leon *real estate, mining and advertising company executive*

Plymouth
Arbuckle, Marjorie Ann *real estate sales associate*

Wausau
Prey, Yvonne Mary *real estate broker*

Wauwatosa
Jasiorkowski, Robert Lee *real estate broker, computer consultant*

CANADA

ONTARIO

London
Pearson, Norman *urban and regional planner, administrator, academic and planning consultant, writer*

ADDRESS UNPUBLISHED

Browne, Aldis Jerome, Jr. *real estate broker*
Dendrinos, Dimitrios Spyros *urban planning educator*
Gasper, Ruth Eileen *real estate executive*
Huber, James Damian *rental real estate owner*
Johnson, Kay Durbahn *real estate manager, consultant*
Kopis, F. Jan *real estate broker*
Manji, Kurbanali Mohamed *real estate company executive, architect*
Miller, Esther Scobie Powers *real estate appraiser, professional watercolorist*
O'Leary, Timothy Michael *real estate corporation officer*
Osmycki, Daniel A. *commercial real estate broker, consultant*
Poetter, Bruce E. *real estate executive*
Raether, Edward W. *appraising company executive, valuation consultant*
Rhodes, Helen Mary *real estate broker, educator*
Root, Jonathan Burch *environmental specialist*
Simon, Melvin *real estate developer, professional basketball executive*
Votava, Thomas Anthony *real estate and insurance professional*

GOVERNMENT: AGENCY ADMINISTRATION

UNITED STATES

FLORIDA

Fort Lauderdale
Etling, Terry Douglas *state agency administrator*

ILLINOIS

Bloomington
Elston, Thomas Lee *firefighter, emergency medical technician*
Small, Debra Jean *public service professional*

Chicago
Abadinsky, Howard *criminal justice educator*
Anderson, Douglas Charles *juvenile probation administrator*
Dudzik, Ted Edward *law enforcement official*
Frampton, Richard Keith *state agency administrator, finance specialist*
Jibben, Laura Ann *state agency administrator*
Lucas, Leonard L. *deputy sheriff, poet and storyteller*
McGee, Patrick Edgar *postal service clerk*
Murnane, Edward David *state agency association administrator*
Orozco, Raymond E. *fire protective services official*
Van Pelt, Robert Irving *firefighter*
Vega, Steve *probation officer, poet*
Wayman, David Anthony *state agency administrator*

Danville
Lary, Peter Paul *probation officer, alderman*

Decatur
Erlanson, Deborah McFarlin *state program administrator*

Des Plaines
McNamee, James Michael *police officer*

Downers Grove
Hasen-Sinz, Susan Katherine *state agency administrator, actress*
Ruffolo, Paul Gregory *police officer, educator*

Jerseyville
Girard, G. Tanner *state environmental officer*

Lemont
Metta, David Keith *government official*

Maywood
Farley, Robert Hugh *police detective, child abuse consultant*

North Riverside
Kuratko, Brian D. *police officer, funeral director*

Northlake
Haack, Richard Wilson *retired police officer*

Oak Brook
Garrigan, William Henry, III *firefighter, paramedic*

Oak Park
Schwerdtner, Frederick Howard *retired police commander, lawyer*

Olympia Fields
Somer, Thomas Joseph (TJ Somer) *police officer, lawyer*

Palatine
Hellyer, Timothy Michael *protective services officer*

Palos Heights
Krupowicz, Thomas Edward *retired police officer, fingerprint consultant*

Rock Island
Hanson, Dudley Modahl *federal agency administrator, civil engineer*

Springfield
Adams, Juanita Kay (Nita Adams) *public service administrator*
Flanders, Raymond Alan *governmental health agency administrator*
Hall, William Glenn *state government administrator*
Hughes, Kevin E. *state trooper, emergency medical technician*
Rose, Nelson Henry *state government administrator*
Schroeder, Joyce Katherine *research analyst*
Tylman, Stanley George, Jr. *state agency administrator, educator, analyst*
Walker, (Gale) Richard *state agency staff*
Wells, Randy Lee *policy analyst*

Toulon
Taylor, Robert Miles *police chief*

INDIANA

Carmel
Etter, John Phillip *police officer*

Indianapolis
Bates, John Robert *government agency administrator*
Cohen, Edward Lawrence *state agency administrator*
Fryer, Robert Samuel *state agency administrator, consultant*
Gerdes, Ralph Donald *fire safety consultant*
Harden, Mary Louise *human resources management specialist*
Roush, Phillip Henry *state official*

Knightstown
Cameron, Ron D. *law enforcement retired, security head*

Lowell
Reed, Gerald Wilfred *protective services official*

South Bend
Shock, David Harry *police officer*

Valparaiso
Bucy, Michael Ray *firefighter*

IOWA

Ackley
Hoodjer, Kimberly Kay *state agency administrator*

Davenport
Wilson, Frances Edna *protective services official*

Des Moines
Cherry, Linda Lea *deputy United States marshal*
Cooper, Wayne Allen *state government administrator*
Eason, Alphonso Lee *state agency administrator*
Knight, Robert Vernon *state agency administrator*

KANSAS

Colby
Finley, Philip Bruce *retired state adjutant general*

Gardner
Francis, Kenneth Allen *protective services official*

Oswego
Brand, Grover Junior *retired state agricultural official*

Topeka
Webb, Marvin Russell *former state agency director*

Wichita
Bryan, James Timothy *state trooper*
Etter, Gregg Wayne, Sr. *police officer, educator*

MASSACHUSETTS

Boston
Whitburn, Gerald *state agency administrator*

MICHIGAN

Allegan
Carlson, Donald A. *retired protective services official*

Ann Arbor
Dane, Wilmer Ray *fire chief*
Schmitt, Mary Elizabeth *postal supervisor*

Battle Creek
Squires, Gordon Wayne *federal agency executive*

Belding
Mason, Donald Roger *protective services official, city official*

Dearborn
Jones, Radford Wedgewood *security manager*

Detroit
Budny, James Charles *federal agency administrator*
Forbes-Richardson, Helen Hilda *state agency administrator*
Moss, Leslie Otha *justice administrator*
Ryan, Earl M. *public affairs analyst*

East Lansing
Christian, Kenneth Edward *security administration educator*
Montgomery, James Huey *state government administrator, consultant*

Hastings
Sarver, Jerry P. *protective services official*

Lanse
Butler, Patricia *protective services official*

Lansing
Brook, Susan G. *state agency administrator, horse farmer*

New Haven
Shaw, Charles Rusanda *government investigator*

Traverse City
Jensen, John Gordon, Jr. *police officer*

MINNESOTA

Bloomington
Campbell, Mark Alan *federal agency administrator*

Eden Prairie
Wyman, Paul K. *human resources consultant*

Minneapolis
Aanerud, Melvin Bernard *government agency administrator*
Jackson, Alex Maurice *protective services official, comedian*

New Hope
Oberreuter, John Edward *police inspector*

Saint Paul
Mercer, John Whitty *state agency executive*

MISSOURI

Diamond
Gilman, Terry Ray *state agency administrator*

Jefferson City
Forbis, Bryan Lester *state agency administrator*
Hemeyer, John Clark *protection services official*
Karll, Jo Ann *state agency administrator, lawyer*
Mears, Sandra A. *state agency administrator, lawyer, educator*
Orr, Samuel Joseph *state agency administrator*
Peeno, Larry Noyle *state agency administrator, consultant*
Reiter, Elaine Mary *state agency administrator*
Rost, David Edward *state official*
Ryan, Ronald Lee *highway patrolman*
Tackett, Natalie Jane *state administrator*
Vadner, Gregory A. *state agency administrator*
Waters, Stephen Russell *state agency administrator*

Joplin
Roper, Chris L. *public safety director*

Kansas City
McLendon, Jesse Lawrence *protective services official*
Parker, Dennis Gene *former sheriff, karate instructor*
Walker, Thomas H. *federal agency administrator*

Lambert Airport
Griggs, Leonard LeRoy, Jr. *federal agency administrator*

Lees Summit
Joiner, Larry J. *retired police chief*

Liberty
Orth-Aikmus, Gail Marie *police chief*

Saint Louis
Senter, Karolyn Elizabeth *protection services officer*
Talcott, Wesley Conrad *internal revenue agent*

Springfield
Green, David Ferrell *law enforcement official*
Gruhn, Robert Stephen *parole officer*
Luttrull, Shirley JoAnn *protective services official*

NEBRASKA

Lincoln
Lea, Eleanor Lucille *retired state agency administrator*

Omaha
Humphries, Roger Lee *postal service administrator*

NORTH CAROLINA

Asheville
Roberts, Bill Glen *retired fire chief, investor, consultant*

NORTH DAKOTA

Bismarck
Hagen, Bruce *state agency administrator*
Vogel, Sarah *state agency administrator, lawyer*

OHIO

Berlin
Christner, David Lee *utilities executive*

Centerville
Baver, Roy Lane *retired protection services official, consultant*

Cleveland
Jettke, Harry Jerome *retired government official*

Columbus
Adrian, Richard Robert *detective*
Anderson, John Robert *state agency administrator*
Barner, Bruce Monroe *state agency administrator*
Bianco, Don Christopher *civil servant*
Carr, Clay Bryan, Jr. *federal civil service manager*
Gerhardstein, Samuel Edward *state agency administrator*
Graves, William Joseph *state agency administrator*
Lambowitz, Sheila *state agency administrator*
McInturff, Floyd M. *retired state agency administrator*
Metzler, Eric Harold *state agency administrator*
Ray, Frank David *government agency official*
Seifarth, Mark Evan *state agency administrator*
Somerville, Deborah Marie-Margaret *state agency administrator*
Taylor, Calvin Lee *public administrator*
Thompson, James W., Jr. *state official*

Cuyahoga Falls
Shane, Sandra Kuli *postal service administrator*

Dayton
Sweeney, James Lee *retired government official*

Eaton
Ferriell, Peter Paul *federal agency administrator*

Grove City
DuCharme, Thomas Andrew *fire protection specialist, educator*

Logan
Baker, Wilbur Francis *retired state agency administrator*

Loveland
Espelage, Howard John *police chief*

Montpelier
Deckrosh, Hazen Douglas *retired state agency educator and administrator*

Olmsted Falls
Kiessling, Ronald Frederick *retired federal government executive*

Reynoldsburg
D'Onofrio, Peter Joseph *protective services official, educator*

Warren
Catlin, William Arthur *police chief*

Zanesville
O'Sullivan, Christine *executive director social service agency*
Provance, Terrance Lester *administrator*

SOUTH DAKOTA

Rapid City
Hennies, Thomas Lee *protective services official*

TEXAS

Cedar Hill
Sundstrom, Richard Carl *police analyst, writer*

WISCONSIN

Madison
Lavigna, Robert John *state governement executive*
Schaefer, Robert John *state agency administrator*

Mequon
Wray, Gail Miller *environmentalist, government agency administrator*

Milwaukee
Agostini, Stephen Joseph *city budget director*
Arreola, Philip *police officer*
Czysz, David Eugene *law enforcement professional*
Erdmann, August *protective services official*

Neenah
Lauson, James Garfield, II *retired fire captain, county supervisor*

New Richmond
Cooper, Lee Mollin *fire training specialist*

ADDRESS UNPUBLISHED

Andrews, Eleanor De Ling *state education consultant*
Archer, Linda L. *disability specialist*
Barrie, Lee John *address management systems specialist*
Bergman, John H. *fire department administrator*
Dobmeyer, Douglas Charles *media and social issues executive*
Harder, Robert Clarence *state official*
Hedrick, Basil Calvin *state agency administrator, ethnohistorian, educator, museum and multicultural institutions consultant*
Johnson, Elizabeth *probation officer*
Larkin, Robert Lee *protection services official*
Manos, George P. *state agency administrator*
Sandahl, David Gordon *correctional administrator, consultant, educator*
Sobczak, Darlene Marie *police officer*
Stadlman, Rebecca Murphy *federal agency administrator*
Torregrosa, Hector Luis, Jr. *state agency adjudicator*

GOVERNMENT: EXECUTIVE ADMINISTRATION

UNITED STATES

CALIFORNIA

Mission Viejo
Stroder, Barbara G. *federal agency auditor, consultant*

DISTRICT OF COLUMBIA

Washington
Brachman, Judith Y. *federal official*
Shalala, Donna Edna *federal official, political scientist, educator, university chancellor*
Withrow, Mary Ellen *treasurer of United States*

ILLINOIS

Arlington Heights
Kanouse, Andrew Robert *government official*

Aroma Park
Conrad, Roberta *municipal official, tax consultant*

Athens
Doellman, Anthony T. *state official*

Charleston
McDermand, Douglas David *county official*

Chicago
Bishop, Oliver Richard *state official*
Cherry, Robert Steven, III *municipal agency administrator*
Chun, Shinae *state official*
Cullerton, John James *state senator, lawyer*
Holowinski, John Joseph *state executive*
Inman, David Richard *municipal official*
Levi, Edward Hirsch *former attorney general, university president emeritus*
MacLennan, John Duncan *state official*
Olson, Roy Arthur *government official*
Phillips, Alice Elizabeth *government relations professional*
Pofelski, Mark A. *city purchasing manager, computer service owner*
Topinka, Judy Baar *state official*
Trapikas, Bruno Peter *city government administrator*

De Kalb
Hoyt, Marguerite *city official*
Nicklas, F. William *city official*

Edwardsville
Shimkus, John Mondy *county treasurer*

Elk Grove Village
Yiannias, Nancy Magas *municipal official*

Freeport
Weis, Richard C. *mayor*

Joliet
O'Connell, James Joseph *port official*

Kankakee
Erickson, Clark Erwin *lawyer, author*

Lake Zurich
Dixon, John Fulton *village manager*

Libertyville
Powell, Delmer Henry, Jr. *county official*

Monmouth
Rutledge, Janet Marie *county clerk and recorder*

Morrison
Gallagher, John Robert, Jr. *county official*

Northbrook
Goldberg, Marshall Robert *former diplomat, former tax administrator*

Oak Brook
Bushy, Karen Marie *municipal official*

Oak Park
Replogle, Arthur Seeds *community development executive*

Peoria
Bradshaw, Mary Fenton *government executive secretary*
Dougherty, John A. *county official*

Pontiac
Ruff, Melissa Bredeman *county official*

Quincy
Points, Roy Wilson *municipal official*

Rock Island
Esslinger, Marilyn Ann *city clerk*

Rockford
Howard, Karen Ann *village official*

Springfield
Edgar, Jim *governor*
Gamble, Douglas Irvin *state official, educator*
Grismore Cowles, Mary *government executive*
Holtzee, Jon B. *program specialist*
Kustra, Robert W. (Bob Kustra) *state official, educator*
Lindley, Maralee Irwin *county official, consultant, speaker*
Malany, Le Grand Lynn *attorney general, lawyer, engineer, bank executive*
Mucciante, Mary F. *state official*
Ryan, James E. *attorney general*
Schoeffel, Steven Scot *policy analyst*

Urbana
Prussing, Laurel Lunt *state official, economist*
Satterthwaite, Tod *mayor*

Waukegan
Choinoski, Richard Denis *financial executive*

Westchester
Crois, John Henry *local government official*

Wheaton
Jacklin, William Thomas *county official, educator*

Wilmette
Leach, David Clark, Jr. *municipal administrator*

Woodstock
Andersen, Larry Michael *county government official*

Zion
Leable, Philip F. *township highway commissioner*

INDIANA

Carmel
Quayle, J(ames) Danforth *former vice president United States, entrepreneur*

Fishers
Christie, Walter Scott *retired state official*

Fort Wayne
Helmke, (Walter) Paul, Jr. *mayor, lawyer*
Lee, Timothy Earl *international agency executive, paralegal*

Gary
Spires, Roberta Lynn *court clerk*

Goshen
Bates, David Allen *municipal administrator*

Indianapolis
Bayh, Evan *governor*
Carter, Pamela Lynn *state attorney general*
Cohen, Edward *state official*
Goldsmith, Stephen *mayor*
Husk, Donald Estel *retired state official*
Mannweiler, Paul S. *state legislator*
O'Bannon, Frank Lewis *state official, lawyer*
Smith, Stan *state official*
Whitaker, Charles *state official*
Zeller, Kenneth J. *state official*

North Vernon
Goldsmith, Mark Sargent *urban conservation specialist*

Shelbyville
Zerr, Frank Michael *city clerk, treasurer*

South Bend
Farrand, Rollin Elvin *county engineer, civil engineer, consultant*
Stancati, John F. *municipal official*

IOWA

Burlington
Worden, Douglas James *city official*

Council Bluffs
Boone, Dorothy Mae *county official*

Des Moines
Baxter, Elaine *state government official*
Bertelli, Monty Ray *state official*
Branstad, Terry Edward *governor, lawyer*
Corning, Joy Cole *state official*
Fitzgerald, Michael Lee *state official*
Miller, Thomas J. *state attorney general*
Schaffner, John T. *state government administrator*

George
Hueser, Roberta Jean *city official*

Humboldt
Pyle, Dennis Lee *city administrator*

Keosauqua
Finney, Jon Philip *county auditor*

Muscatine
Boka, Steven Wayne *building and zoning administrator*
Casstevens, David Paul *city administrator*

Steamboat Rock
Taylor, Ray *state senator*

Windsor Heights
Bunkers, Douglas Frederick *city administrator*

KANSAS

Clearwater
Crews, David Terence *federal employee*

Garden City
Talley, Bonnie Eileen *city official*

Kansas City
Hollenbeck, Marynell *municipal government official*

Kinsley
Carlson, Mary Isabel (Maribel Carlson) *county treasurer*

Larned
Reece, Marshall Philip *state official*

Leavenworth
Kansteiner, Beau Kent *municipal official*

Mc Pherson
Steffes, Don Clarence *state senator*

Overland Park
Jekel, Joseph Frank *government official*

Shawnee Mission
Bortko, Edward Joseph *municipal official, retired utilities executive*

Topeka
Carlson, E. Dean *state official*
Gordon, Thelma Hunter *state official*
Graves, William Preston *governor*
Simmons, Chuck *state official*
Stovall, Carla Jo *state official, lawyer*
Thompson, Sally Engstrom *state official*
Thornburgh, Ron E. *state official*

Wichita
Allen-Bouska, Rebecca Auk *county official*
Wieland, Katherine Colleen *government official*

MICHIGAN

Ann Arbor
Cole, Elsa Kircher *lawyer*

Detroit
Archer, Dennis Wayne *mayor, lawyer*
Farrell-Donaldson, Marie Delois *municipal official*
Piper, Paul Joseph *municipal administrator*
Rosner, Bernard *assistant attorney general*

Dowagiac
Palenick, James Michael *city manager*

East Lansing
Sawyer-Koch, Barbara Jo *government executive*

Grand Rapids
Delabbio, Daryl Joseph *county administrator*
Logie, John Hoult *mayor, lawyer*
Sak, Michael Gerard *county government official*

Howell
Wagoner, William Douglas *public administrator, urban/regional planner*

Iron Mountain
Rogina, Joseph Frank *city assessor, zoning administrator*

Kalamazoo
Lam, Nicholas Brian *municipal purchaser*

Lansing
Binsfeld, Connie Berube *lieutenant governor*
Callen, Ronald Corlette *commissioner, state*
Kelley, Frank Joseph *state attorney general*
Leatherwood, Larry L. *state transportation executive*
McGinnis, Kenneth L. *state official*
Miller, Candice S. *state official*
Muchmore, Dennis C. *governmental affairs consultant*
Roberts, Douglas B. *state official*
Welke, Robert A. *state official*

Marquette
Forrester, Rosemary Wellington *regional senatorial representative*

Mount Clemens
Kolakowski, Diana Jean *county commissioner*

Muskegon
Kuhn, Robert Herman *city and county official, engineer*
Roy, Paul Emile, Jr. *county official*

Negaunee
Friggens, Thomas George *state official, historian*

Paw Paw
Dorr, Orrin Joseph *county drain commissioner, farmer*

Redford
Heldenbrand, Marilyn Louise *township governmental official*

Saint Clair Shores
Weis, Lawrence Frederick *city official*

Southfield
Rubinstein, David A. *city official*

Sterling Heights
Pappageorge, John *state official*

Warren
Bonkowski, Ronald Lawrence *mayor*

West Bloomfield
Ho, Leo Chi Chien *Chinese government official*

MINNESOTA

Breckenridge
Laken, Neoma Ann *retired county recorder*

Detroit Lakes
Fundingsland, Lynn Omar *county official*

Fergus Falls
Hanan, Michael Clark *administrator*

Fridley
Flora, John Gerald *director public works, city engineer*

Grand Rapids
Lauber, Darrell Howard *retired county land commissioner*
Whitehorn, Kenneth Lee *county official*

Hills
Erickson, Wendell O. *county commissioner, educator*

Hugo
Museus, Robert Allen *city manager*

Maplewood
Dawson, Craig William *city official*

Minneapolis
Blackstad, Larry Roger *county official*
Fellner, Michael Joseph *government executive, educator*
Rietow, Dottie Miller *government and public relations consultant*

Moorhead
Sinner, George Albert *former state governor, farmer, corporate executive*

Saint Cloud
Hemze, David J. *county official*

Saint Paul
Benson, Joanne *lieutenant governor of Minnesota*
Carlson, Arne Helge *governor*
Denn, James N. *commissioner*
Growe, Joan Anderson *state official*
Humphrey, Hubert Horatio, III *state attorney general*
McGrath, Michael Alan *state government officer*
Megard, Roberta Ann (Bobbi Megard) *city official*
Sanda, Kris(ta Linnea) *state commissioner*

MISSOURI

Benton
Heckemeyer, Anthony Joseph *circuit court judge*

Cape Girardeau
Muser, Daniel Donald *city official*

Chesterfield
Geisel, Michael Oliver *city official*
Roberts, Kyna R. *lobbyist*

Columbia
Shawver, Stanley Walter *county planner*

Independence
Nelson, Brent Lynn *city auditor*

Jefferson City
Bickel, Marvin Dean *printing director state house of representatives*
Blunt, Roy D. *state official*
Carnahan, Mel *governor, lawyer*
Holden, Bob *state official*
Maxwell, Joe *state senator*
Moriarty, Judith Kay Spry *state official*
Myers, Victoria Christina *state official*
Nixon, Jeremiah W. (Jay Nixon) *state attorney general*
Saunders, John L. *state official*
Wilson, Roger B. *lieutenant governor, school administrator*

Kansas City
Anderson, Lorna Kathryn *government official*
Cleaver, Emanuel, II *mayor, minister*
Moore, Donald Lynn *economic planner*
Price, Charles H., II *former ambassador*
Steele, Kathleen Frances *federal official*
Thomas, Gordon Jerome *retired municipal official*

Rolla
Allison, Sandy Diane *public administrator*

Saint Joseph
Kelly, Glenda Marie *former mayor*

Saint Louis
Osterloh, Everett William *county official*
Schou, Charlene Mae *federal goverment official, consultant*

Springfield
Harris, Robert Frank *federal official*

University City
Head, Moses M. *municipal official*

NEBRASKA

Grand Island
Abernethy, Irene Margaret *county official*
Mason, Doris Ann *county official*

Lincoln
Beermann, Allen J. *former state official*
Hasselbalch, Marilyn Jean *state official*
Heineman, David *state official*
Johnson, Cindy Coble *councilwoman, marketing executive*
Moore, Scott *state official*
Moul, Maxine Burnett *state official*
Nelson, E. Benjamin *governor*
Rockey, Dawn E. *state treasurer*
Stenberg, Donald B. *state attorney general*

North Bend
Johnson, Lowell C. *state commissioner*

North Platte
Hawks, James Wade *county highway superintendent, county surveyor*

O'Neill
Hill, Warren Herbert *government official*

Omaha
Dunn, Paul Levi *city official*

NORTH DAKOTA

Bismarck
Gilmore, Kathi *state treasurer*
Hanson, Robert Eugene *state official*
Heitkamp, Heidi *state attorney general*
Jaeger, Alvin A. (Al Jaeger) *secretary of state*
Lydeen, Jerry Bruce *state official*
Myrdal, Rosemarie Caryle *state official, former state legislator*
Pomeroy, Glenn *state insurance commissioner*
Schafer, Edward T. *governor*

Fargo
Spaeth, Nicholas John *lawyer, former state attorney general*

Grand Forks
Glassheim, Eliot Alan *grants officer*

Mandan
Paul, Jack Davis *retired state official, addictions consultant*

Minot
Turner, Jane Ann *federal agent*

OHIO

Akron
Plusquellic, Donald L. *mayor*
Schrader, Helen Maye *retired municipal worker*

Cincinnati
Brown, Stuart G. *city administrator*

Cleveland
Everett, Ronald Emerson *government official*
George, Thomas John *municipal official*
Smercina, Charles Joseph *mayor, accountant*
White, Michael Reed *mayor*

Columbus
Garcia, John Gilbert *state legislator*
Hollister, Nancy *state official*
Kelly, Martin Joseph *state official*
Montgomery, Betty D. *state official, former state legislator*
Schultz, Charles Edward *state official*
Smith, Toni Colette *government official, social worker*
Taft, Bob *state official*
Ventresca, Joseph Anthony *energy coordinator*
Voinovich, George V. *governor*

Concord
English, Laura Jane *zoning coordinator*

Dayton
Lashley, William Bartholomew *county official*
Nelson, Morton *county health commissioner*
Young, Joyce C. *municipal official*

Delaware
Stanfill, Brian Eugene *county official*

Dublin
Felger, Ralph William *educator, retired military officer*

Eaton
Brubaker, Edwin Silvanus *local government consultant*

Fairborn
Hunter, Henry Birdsall *municipal official*

Grove City
McCoy, Kirk Jay *human resources and public affairs manager*

Hamilton
Kramer, Benjamin Robert *sheriff's deputy*

Lakewood
Cain, Madeline Ann *mayor*

Mansfield
Olson, Edward Warren *county official*
Prater, Willis Richard *county government agency official*

Piqua
Patrizio, Frank, Jr. *city manager*

Portsmouth
Davis, Donald W. *government official*

Powell
Schutz, Robert J. *municipal government official*

Ravenna
Ganocy, Carl Paul *city manager*

Sandusky
Link, Frank Albert *retired city manager*

University Heights
Rothschild, Beryl Elaine *mayor*

Wilmington
Hackney, Howard Smith *retired county official*

SOUTH DAKOTA

Aberdeen
Johnson, George Robert *retired government official*

Pierre
Barnett, Mark William *state attorney general*
Harding, G. Homer *former state official*
Hazeltine, Joyce *state official*
Hillard, Carole *state official*
Janklow, William John *governor*
Moser, Jeffery Richard *state official*

Rapid City
Strand, Neal Arnold *county government official*

TEXAS

Houston
Bush, George Herbert Walker *former President of the United States*

WISCONSIN

Alma
Torgerson, Linda Marie *city clerk, librarian*

Ashland
Smith, Jane Schneberger *retired city administrator*

Fort Atkinson
Dochnahl, Mark Edward *municipal government official*

Hartland
Stamsta, Duane Robert *commissioner*

Juneau
Carpenter, David Erwin *county planner*
Titus, David Kenneth *county official*

Madison
Doyle, James E(dward) *state attorney general*
La Follette, Douglas J. *secretary of state*
Mack, Kirbie Lyn *municipal official*
Malinowski, Dennis Edmund *government consultant*
McCallum, Scott *state official*
Thompson, Tommy George *governor*
Tracy, Alan Thomas *government official*
Voight, Jack C. *state official*
Zobel, Robert Leonard *state government official*

Milwaukee
Ament, F. Thomas *county government official*
Bischoff, Janet E. *city government business analyst*
Brady, Michael Joseph *municipal official*
Norquist, John Olof *mayor*

Sheboygan
Billings, Steven Allen *municipal official*

Superior
Axt, Randolph William *volunteer municipal officer*

Wautoma
Benz, John Charles *county clerk*

Whitewater
Malewicki, Debra Suzanne *state official, educator*

MILITARY ADDRESSES OF THE UNITED STATES

PACIFIC

APO
Mondale, Joan Adams *wife of former vice president of U.S.*

CANADA

MANITOBA

Winnipeg
Enns, Harry John *state official*
Filmon, Gary Albert *Canadian provincial premier, civil engineer*

ONTARIO

London
Gosnell, Thomas Charles *former mayor*

ADDRESS UNPUBLISHED

Anderson, Glen Robert *federal official*
Austin, Richard H. *retired state official*
Bauer, Gerard Joseph *municipal administrator*
Burgess, John Norman *veterans service officer*
Camera, Charles Vincent *city administrator*
Crawford, Andrea Steen *village official*
Engler, John *governor*
Fraser, Donald MacKay *former mayor, former congressman, educator*
Isabell, David Thomas *retired city administrator*
McBee, Robert Levi *retired federal government official, writer, consultant*
Mitchelson, Bonnie Elizabeth *Canadian politician, nurse*
Mondale, Walter Frederick *former vice president of United States, diplomat, lawyer*
Rice, Richard Campbell *retired state official, retired army officer*
Robak, Kim M. *state official*
Ryan, George H. *state government official, pharmacist*
Zachery-Hopkins, Donna S. *government tax examiner*

GOVERNMENT: LEGISLATIVE ADMINISTRATION

UNITED STATES

ARKANSAS

North Little Rock
Sloan, Tom *state legislator*

CALIFORNIA

San Francisco
Brown, Timothy N. *state legislator*

DISTRICT OF COLUMBIA

Washington
Abraham, Spencer *senator*
Ashcroft, John David *senator*
Barrett, Thomas M. *congressman*
Barrett, William E. *congressman*
Bereuter, Douglas Kent *congressman*
Boehner, John A. *congressman*
Bond, Christopher Samuel (Kit Bond) *senator, lawyer*
Bonior, David Edward *congressman*
Brown, Sherrod *congressman, former state official*
Burton, Danny Lee *congressman*
Buyer, Steve E. *congressman, lawyer*
Camp, Dave *congressman*
Clay, William Lacy *congressman*
Coats, Daniel Ray *senator*
Collins, Barbara-Rose *congresswoman*
Collins, Cardiss *congresswoman*
Conrad, Kent *senator*
Conyers, John, Jr. *congressman*
Costello, Jerry F., Jr. *congressman, former county official*
Crane, Philip Miller *congressman*
Danner, Patsy Ann (Mrs. C. M. Meyer) *congresswoman*
Daschle, Thomas Andrew *senator*
Dingell, John David, Jr. *congressman*
Dole, Robert J. *senator*
Dorgan, Byron Leslie *senator*
Durbin, Richard Joseph *congressman*
Evans, Lane *congressman*
Ewing, Thomas William *congressman, lawyer*
Exon, J(ohn) James *senator*
Fawell, Harris W. *congressman*
Feingold, Russell Dana *U.S. senator*
Flanagan, Michael Patrick *congressman, lawyer*
Frahm, Sheila *senator, lieutenant governor, former state legislator*
Ganske, J. Greg *congressman, plastic surgeon*
Gephardt, Richard Andrew *congressman*
Gillmor, Paul E. *congressman, lawyer*
Glenn, John Herschel, Jr. *senator*
Grams, Rodney D. *senator, former congressman*
Grassley, Charles Ernest *senator*
Gunderson, Steve Craig *congressman*
Gutierrez, Luis V. *congressman, elementary education educator*
Hall, Tony P. *congressman*
Hamilton, Lee Herbert *congressman*
Hancock, Mel *congressman*
Harkin, Thomas Richard *senator*
Hastert, (J.) Dennis *congressman*
Hobson, David Lee *congressman, lawyer*
Hoekstra, Peter *congressman, manufacturing executive*
Hostettler, John N. *congressman*
Hyde, Henry John *congressman*
Jacobs, Andrew, Jr. *congressman*
Johnson, Timothy Peter *congressman*
Kaptur, Marcia Carolyn *congresswoman*
Kasich, John R. *congressman*
Kassebaum, Nancy Landon *senator*
Kerrey, Bob (J. Robert Kerrey) *senator*
Kildee, Dale Edward *congressman*
Knollenberg, Joseph (Joe Knollenberg) *congressman*
Kohl, Herbert *senator, professional sports team owner*
Leach, James Albert Smith *congressman*
Levin, Carl *senator*
Levin, Sander M. *congressman*
Lightfoot, James Ross *congressman*
Lipinski, William Oliver *congressman*
Lugar, Richard Green *senator*
Manzullo, Donald A *congressman, lawyer*
McCarthy, Karen P. *congresswoman, former state representative*
McIntosh, David M. *congressman*
Metzenbaum, Howard Morton *former U.S. senator*
Minge, David *congressman, lawyer, law educator*
Moseley-Braun, Carol *senator*
Oberstar, James L. *congressman*
Obey, David Ross *congressman*
Petri, Thomas Evert *congressman*
Pomeroy, Earl R. *congressman, former state insurance commissioner*
Porter, John Edward *congressman*
Portman, Rob *congressman*
Poshard, Glenn W. *congressman*
Pressler, Larry *senator*
Ramstad, Jim *congressman, lawyer*
Regula, Ralph *congressman, lawyer*
Roberts, Charles Patrick *congressman*
Roemer, Timothy J. *congressman*
Rush, Bobby L. *congressman*
Sabo, Martin Olav *congressman*
Sawyer, Thomas C. *congressman*
Sensenbrenner, Frank James, Jr. *congressman, lawyer*
Simon, Paul *senator, educator, author*
Skelton, Isaac Newton, IV (Ike Skelton) *congressman*
Souder, Mark Edward *congressman*
Stokes, Louis *congressman*
Talent, James M. *congressman, lawyer*
Traficant, James A., Jr. *congressman*
Upton, Frederick Stephen *congressman*
Vento, Bruce Frank *congressman*
Visclosky, Peter John *congressman, lawyer*
Volkmer, Harold L. *congressman*
Wellstone, Paul *senator*
Yates, Sidney Richard *congressman, lawyer*

ILLINOIS

Ashmore
Weaver, Michael L. *state legislator*

Aurora
Lauzen, Chris *state legislator*

Belleville
Holbrook, Thomas *state legislator*

Bloomington
Brady, William E. *state legislator*
Maitland, John W., Jr. *state legislator*

Blue Mound
Noland, N. Duane *state legislator*

Bradley
Novak, John Philip *state legislator*

Breese
Granberg, Kurt *state legislator, lawyer*

Buffalo Grove
Clayton, Verna Lewis *state legislator*

Calumet City
Fantin, Arline Marie *state legislator*

Canton
Smith, Michael Kent *state legislator*

Carbondale
Bost, Mike *state legislator*

Champaign
Winkel, Richard J. *state legislator*

Chicago
Berman, Arthur Leonard *state senator*
Bugielski, Robert Joseph *state legislator*
Del Valle, Miguel *state legislator*
Dudycz, Walter W. *state legislator*
Dunea, Mary Mills *governor's aide*
Farley, Bruce A. *state legislator*
Feigenholtz, Sara *state legislator*
Frias, Rafael *state legislator*
Garcia, Jesus G. *state legislator*
Giles, Calvin Lamont *state legislator*
Hendon, Ricky *state legislator*
Jones, Emil, Jr. *state senator*
Kaszak, Nancy *state legislator, lawyer*
Kenner, Howard A. *state legislator*
Kotlarz, Joseph S. *state legislator, lawyer*
Laurino, William J. *state legislator*
Martinez, Benjamin A. *state legislator*
McAuliffe, Roger P. *state legislator, police officer*
Molaro, Robert S *state legislator, lawyer*
Moore, Joseph Arthur *alderman, lawyer*
Pugh, Coy *state legislator*
Santiago, Miguel A. *state legislator*
Shaw, William *state legislator*
Stroger, Todd H. *state legislator*
Turner, Arthur L. *state legislator*
Williams, Jackson Taylor *legislative director, lawyer*

Chrisman
Woodyard, Harry *state legislator*

Christopher
Rea, James F. *state senator*

Collinsville
Hoffman, Jay C. *state legislator*

Crystal Lake
Klemm, Richard O. *state legislator*
Skinner, Calvin L., Jr. *state legislator*

Danville
Black, William B. *state legislator*

Du Quoin
Dunn, Ralph *state legislator*

East Moline
Boland, Michael Joseph *state legislator*
Jacobs, Denny *state legislator*

East Saint Louis
Clayborne, James F. *state legislator*
Younge, Wyvetter Hoover *state legislator*

Eldorado
Phelps, David D. *state legislator*

Elgin
Hoeft, Douglas L. *state legislator*
Rauschenberger, Steven J. *state legislator*

Elmhurst
Cronin, Dan *state legislator*

Elmwood Park
Saviano, Angelo *state legislator*

Evanston
Schoenberg, Jeffrey M. *state legislator*

Galesburg
Hawkinson, Carl E. *state legislator*

Geneseo
Sieben, Todd *state legislator*

Gilson
Moffitt, Donald L. *state legislator*

Glen Ellyn
Persico, Vincent Anthony *state legislator*

Greenville
Watson, Frank Charles *state legislator*

Hillside
Turner, John W. *state legislator*

Hoffman Estates
Parke, Terry R. *state legislator*

Jerseyville
Ryder, Tom *state legislator*

Joliet
McGuire, John C. *state legislator*

La Grange
Lyons, Eileen *state legislator*
Raica, Robert M. *state legislator*

Lake Bluff
Barkhausen, David N. *state legislator*
Lachner, Thomas F. *state legislator*

Lake Forest
Frederick, Virginia Fiester *state legislator*

Lansing
Balthis, Bill W. *state legislator*

Lemont
Hassert, Brent *state legislator*

Lincoln
Madigan, Robert A. *state legislator*

Long Grove
Peterson, William E. *state legislator*

Macomb
Myers, Richard P. *state legislator*

Marion
Woolard, Larry *state legislator*

Markham
Murphy, Harold *state legislator*

Maywood
Moore, Eugene *state legislator*

Mokena
Sangmeister, George Edward *congressman, lawyer*

Morton
Ackerman, John C. *state legislator*

Mount Vernon
Jones, John O. *state legislator*
O'Daniel, William L. *state legislator*

Mount Zion
Curry, Julie A. *state legislator*

Mundelein
Salvi, Al *state legislator*

Naperville
Cowlishaw, Mary Lou *state legislator*
Piper, Carol Adeline *councilman*

Nashville
Deering, Terry William *state legislator*

New Lenox
Wennlund, Larry *state legislator*

Northbrook
Parker, Kathleen K. *state legislator*

Northfield
Stern, Grace Mary *former state legislator*

O'Fallon
Stephens, Ronald Earl *state legislator*

Palatine
Fitzgerald, Peter Gosselin *state senator, lawyer*
Pedersen, Bernard Edwin *state legislator*

Palos Heights
O'Connor, Jack *state legislator*

Palos Park
O'Malley, Patrick J. *state legislator*

Peoria
Leitch, David R. *state legislator*

Plainfield
Petka, Ed *state legislator*

Pontiac
Rutherford, Dan *state legislator*

Quincy
Tenhouse, Art *state representative, farmer*

Rock Falls
Mitchell, Gerald L. *state legislator*

Rock Island
Brunsvold, Joel Dean *state legislator, educator*

Rockford
Syverson, Dave *state legislator*

Spring Valley
Mautino, Frank J. *state legislator*

Springfield
Biggins, Robert A. *state legislator*
Blagojevich, Rod R. *state legislator*
Boozell, Mark Eldon *state legislative affairs executive*
Burke, Daniel J. *state legislator*
Capparelli, Ralph C. *state legislator*
Carroll, Howard William *state senator, lawyer*
Currie, Barbara Flynn *state legislator*
Daniels, Lee Albert *state legislator*
Dart, Thomas J. *state legislator*
Davis, Monique D. (Deon Davis) *state legislator*
DeAngelis, Aldo A. *state senator*
Deuchler, Suzanne Louise *state legislator*
Donahue, Laura Kent *state senator*
Erwin, Judy *state legislator*
Flowers, Mary E. *state legislator*
Geo-Karis, Adeline Jay *state senator*
Hasara, Karen A. *state legislator*
Hughes, Ann *state legislator*
Johnson, Thomas Lee *state legislator*
Jones, Lovana S. *state legislator*
Jones, Shirley M. *state legislator*
Krause, Carolyn H. *state legislator, lawyer*
Madigan, Michael Joseph *state legislator*
Mahar, William F., Jr. *state legislator*
Moore, Andrea S. *state legislator*
Murphy, Maureen *state legislator*
Pankau, Carole *state legislator*
Philip, James (Pate Philip) *state senator*
Ronen, Carol *state legislator*
Severns, Penny L. *state legislator*
Smith, Margaret *state legislator*
Welch, Patrick Daniel *state senator*
Zickus, Anne *state legislator*

Steger
Ciarlo, Flora L. *state legislator*

Stockton
Lawfer, I. Ronald *state legislator*

Sycamore
Burzynski, James Bradley *state legislator*
Wirsing, David A. *state legislator*

Urbana
Johnson, Timothy Vincent *state legislator*

Westchester
Durkin, James B. *state legislator*
Walsh, Thomas James *state senator*

Wheaton
Fawell, Beverly Jean *state legislator*
Roskam, Peter James *state legislator, lawyer*

Wood River
Davis, Steve *state legislator*

Yorkville
Cross, Thomas H. *state legislator*

INDIANA

Anderson
Webber, Rolland Lloyd *state legislator*

Attica
Harrison, Joseph William *state senator*

Auburn
Kruse, Dennis K. *state legislator*

Bloomington
Bales, Jerry F. *state legislator*
Kruzan, Mark R. *state legislator*
Sinks, John R., Jr. *state legislator*

Bremen
Adams, Kent J. *state legislator*

Brownsburg
Turpin, Samuel R. *state legislator*

Charlestown
Lewis, James A. *state legislator*

Chesterton
Ayres, Ralph D. *state legislator*

Columbus
Garton, Robert Dean *state senator*
Hayes, Robert E. *state legislator*

Connersville
Robbins, Stephen A. *state legislator*

Covington
Grubb, Floyd Dale *state legislator*

Crown Point
Conlon, James Charles *state legislator*

Depauw
Robertson, Paul Joseph *state legislator*

East Chicago
Harris, Earl L. *state legislator*

Elkhart
Mock, Dean R. *state legislator*

Evansville
Avery, Dennis T. *state legislator*
Hays, J. Jefferson *state legislator*
Lutz, Larry Edward *state legislator*
O'Day, Joseph *state legislator*
Server, Gregory Dale *state legislator, guidance counselor*

Fort Wayne
Alderman, Robert K. *state legislator*
Goeglein, Gloria J. *state legislator*
Moses, Winfield C., Jr. *state legislator*
Wyss, Thomas John *state senator*

Frankfort
Davis, James Lloyd *state legislator*

French Lick
Denbo, Jerry L. *state legislator*

Gary
Borst, Lawrence Marion *state legislator*
Brown, Charlie *state representative*

Goshen
Warner, Philip T. *state legislator*

Granger
Dvorak, Michael A. *state legislator*
Zakas, Joseph C. *state legislator*

Greenfield
Gulling, Nick *state legislator*

Griffith
Villalpando, Jesse Michael *state legislator*

Hammond
Mrvan, Frank, Jr. *state legislator*
Tabaczynski, Ron *state legislator*

Huntington
Stephan, Daniel L. *state legislator*

Indianapolis
Antich, Rose Ann *state legislator*
Barnes, Vanessa Summers *state legislator*
Becker, Vaneta G. *state representative*
Behning, Robert W. *state legislator*
Bodiker, Richard William, Sr. *state legislator*
Bosma, Brian Charles *state legislator*
Brinkman, Joyce Elaine *state legislator*
Budak, Mary Kay *state legislator*
Carson, Julia M. *state legislator*
Clark, James Murray *state legislator*
Crawford, William A. *state legislator*
Dickinson, Mae *state legislator*
Engle, Barbara Louise *state legislator*
Frizzell, David Nason *state legislator*
Howard, Glenn L. *state legislator*
Hume, Lindel O. *state legislator*
Johnson, Steven R. *state legislator*
Keeler, John S. *state legislator*
Leising, Jean *state legislator*
Leuck, Claire M. *state legislator*
Miller, Patricia Louise *state legislator, nurse*
Porter, Gregory W. *state legislator*
Richardson, Kathy Kreag *state legislator*
Scholer, Sue Wyant *state legislator*
Willing, Katherine *state legislator*
Wilson, Esther Marie *state legislator*
Young, R. Michael *state legislator*

Jeffersonville
Bottorff, James *state legislator*

Lagrange
Meeks, Robert L. *state legislator*
Sturtz, W. Dale *state legislator*

Logansport
Weatherwax, Thomas K. *state legislator*

Macy
Friend, William C. *state legislator*

Madison
Lytle, Mark L. *state legislator*

Martinsville
Bray, Richard D. *state legislator*

Merrillville
Dobis, Chester F. *state legislator*

Michigan City
Alevizos, Thomas James *state representative, lawyer*

Milltown
Young, Richard D. *state legislator*

Mishawaka
Fry, Craig R. *state legislator*

Muncie
Munson, Bruce N. *state legislator*

Munster
Fesko, Timothy *state legislator*

New Albany
Cochran, William C. *state legislator*

New Castle
Kinser, Douglas M. *state legislator*

Noblesville
Kenley, Howard *state legislator*

North Manchester
Ruppel, William J. *state legislator*

Plymouth
Cook, Gary L. *state legislator*

Princeton
McConnell, Richard L. *state legislator*

Redkey
Liggett, Ronald David *state legislator*

Selma
Craycraft, Allie V., Jr. *state legislator*

Seymour
Bailey, William W. *state legislator, realtor*

South Bend
Bauer, Burnett Patrick *state legislator*
Hunt, Douglas A. *state legislator*
Kromkowski, Thomas S. *state legislator*

Terre Haute
Hellmann, Robert F. *lawyer, state legislator*

Uniondale
Espich, Jeffrey K. *state legislator*

Valparaiso
Alexa, William E. *state legislator*

West Lafayette
Gery, Michael E. *state legislator*

Winona Lake
Wolkins, David A. *state legislator*

Winslow
Hume, Donald E. *state legislator*

IOWA

Cedar Rapids
Chapman, Kathleen Halloran *state legislator, lawyer*
Running, Richard V. *state legislator, college official*

Davis City
Boswell, Leonard L. *state senator*

Des Moines
Buhr, Florence D. *county official*
Cochran, Dale M. *state legislator*
Deluhery, Patrick John *state senator*
Drake, Richard Francis *state senator*
Freeman, Mary Louise *state senator*
Garman, Teresa Agnes *state legislator*
Grubbs, Steven Eric *state representative*
Grundberg, Betty *state legislator, property manager*
Lundby, Mary A. *state legislator*
Murphy, Patrick Joseph *state representative*
Pate, Paul Danny *state senator, business executive, entrepreneur*
Rittmer, Sheldon *senator, farmer*
Schrader, David F. *congressman*
Szymoniak, Elaine Eisfelder *state senator*

Johnston
Churchill, Steven Wayne *state legislator, fund-raising consultant*

Ottumwa
Moreland, Michael Joseph *state representative*

Saint Ansgar
Koenigs, Deo Aloysius *state representative*

Sioux City
Andersen, Leonard Christian *former state legislator, real estate investor*

Storm Lake
Eddie, Russell James *state legislator, sales executive*

KANSAS

Ames
Freeborn, Joann Lee *state legislator*

Arkansas City
Shriver, Joseph Duane *state legislator*

Atchison
Henry, Gerald T. *state legislator*

Baileyville
Larkin, Bruce F. *state legislator*

Baldwin City
Tanner, Ralph M. *state legislator*

Baxter Springs
Shallenburger, Tim *state legislator*

Bendena
Weiland, Galen Franklin *state legislator*

Bonner Springs
Cox, Ray L. *state legislator*
Ramirez, Alfred *state legislator*

Brookville
Kejr, Joseph *state legislator*

Cheney
Thimesch, Daniel J. *state legislator*

Coffeyville
Garner, Jim D. *state legislator, lawyer*

Colby
Gooch, U. L. *state legislator*

Coldwater
McKinney, Dennis *state legislator*

Derby
Myers, Don V. *state legislator*

Dodge City
Smith, Don C. *state legislator*

El Dorado
Mason, William G. *state legislator*

Emporia
Lowther, James E. *state legislator*

Erie
Reinhardt, Richard R. *state legislator*

Fort Scott
Howell, Andrew *state legislator*

Garden City
Heinemann, David J. *state legislator*

Goessel
Goossen, Duane *state legislator*

Haddam
Hardenburger, Janice *state legislator*

Harper
Alldritt, Richard *state legislator*

Hays
Gross, Delbert L. *state legislator*
Moran, Jerry *state legislator*

Healy
Jennison, Robin L. *state legislator*

Herington
Weber, Shari *state legislator*

Holton
Hutchins, Becky J. *state legislator*

Hutchinson
Kerr, David Mills *state legislator*
O'Neal, Michael Ralph *state legislator, lawyer*

Ingalls
Neufeld, Melvin J. *state legislator*

Johnson
Shore, Eugene L. *state legislator*

Kansas City
Dillon, Herman G. *state legislator*
Edlund, Richard J. *state legislator*
Haley, David *state legislator*
Henderson, Broderick *state legislator*
Long, Jim *state legislator*
Spangler, Douglas Frank *state legislator*
Wisdom, Billie Joe *state legislator*

Lakin
Hayzlett, Gary K. *state legislator*

Lamont
Luthi, Ray *state legislator*

Lawrence
Ballard, Barbara W. *state legislator*
Winter, Winton Allen, Jr. *state senator, lawyer*

Leavenworth
Graeber, Clyde D. *state legislator*

Lenexa
Haulmark, Gary *state legislator*
Parkinson, Mark Vincent *state legislator, lawyer*

Leon
King, Kenneth R. *state legislator*

Liberal
Geringer, Gerald Gene *state legislator*

Little River
Wempe, Jack *state legislator*

Louisburg
Vickrey, Jene *state legislator*

Manhattan
Glasscock, Kenton *state legislator*

Mc Pherson
Crabb, Delbert Elmo *state legislator*
Nichols, Richard Dale *former congressman, banker*

Mission
Tomlinson, Robert (Bob Tomlinson) *state legislator*

Neodesha
Chronister, Rochelle Beach *state legislator*

Newton
Boston, Garry *state legislator*
Downey, Christine *state legislator*

Olathe
Burke, Paul E., Jr. *state senator, business consultant, public government affairs*
O'Connor, Kay *state legislator*
Toplikar, John M. *state legislator*

Osage City
Humerickhouse, Joe D. *state legislator*

Osawatomie
Walker, Doug *state legislator*

Oswego
Correll, Vernon W. *state legislator*

Overland Park
Kline, Phillip D. *state legislator, lawyer*
Merritt, Garry A. *state legislator*
Wilson, Dennis M. *state legislator*

Palmer
Lloyd, Steve *state legislator*

Parsons
Brady, William Robert *state legislator*

Pittsburg
Martin, Phil *state legislator*
McKechnie, Ed *state legislator*

Prairie Village
Langworthy, Audrey Hansen *state legislator*
Nichols, Thomas Britt *state legislator*

Pretty Prairie
Krehbiel, Robert *state legislator*

Salina
Horst, Deena Louise *state legislator*

Shawnee Mission
Bogina, August, Jr. *state senator*
Lane, Al *state legislator*

Stafford
Minor, Melvin G. *state legislator*

Topeka
Allen, Barbara *state legislator*
Benlon, Lisa L. *state legislator*
Bradley, Thomas *state legislator*
Cornfield, Darlene *state legislator*
Dawson, Carol *state legislator*
Flower, Joann *state legislator*
Gilbert, Ruby *state legislator*
Goodwin, Greta Hall *state legislator*
Hensley, Anthony *state legislator*
Hochhauser, Sheila *state legislator*
Kirk, Nancy A. *state legislator, nursing home administrator*
Lawrence, Barbara *state legislator*
Mays, M. Douglas *state legislator, financial consultant*
McClure, Laura *state legislator*
Nichols, Richard (Rocky Nichols) *state legislator*
Packer, Greg A. *state legislator*
Papay, Lillian D. *state legislator*
Pauls, Janice L. *state legislator*
Pettey, Patricia Higgins *state legislator*
Powers, Bruce Theodore *state legislator*
Praeger, Sandy *state legislator*
Reynolds, Marian K. *state legislator*
Ruff, L. Candy *state legislator*
Salisbury, Alicia Laing *state legislator*
Samuelson, Ellen Banman *state legislator*
Sebelius, Kathleen Gilligan *insurance commissioner*
Standifer, Sabrina *state legislator*
Tillotson, Carolyn *state legislator*
Toelkes, Dixie E. *state legislator*
Wagle, Susan *state legislator, small business owner*
Wagnon, Joan *former state legislator, association executive*
Welshimer, Gwen R. *state legislator, real estate broker, appraiser, tax consultant*

Towanda
Corbin, David R. *state legislator*

Troy
Sallee, Don *state legislator*

Wamego
Pugh, Edward W. *state legislator*

Washington
Bryant, William M. *state legislator*

Wichita
Dean, George R. *state legislator*
Donovan, Leslie D., Sr. *state legislator*
Feleciano, Paul, Jr. *state legislator*
Helgerson, Henry *state legislator*
Landwehr, Brenda *state legislator, financial executive*
Mayans, Carlos *state legislator*
Ott, Belva Joleen *state legislator*
Pottorff, Jo Ann *state legislator*
Powell, Anthony J. *state legislator, lawyer*
Rutledge, Joel R. *state legislator, small business owner*
Sawyer, Michael Thomas *state legislator, accountant*
Swenson, Dale *state legislator*
Wells, Jonathan *state legislator*

MICHIGAN

Adrian
Berryman, James *state legislator*

Ann Arbor
Brater, Elizabeth *state legislator*

Augusta
Gilmer, Donald H. *state legislator*

Battle Creek
Bush, Eric Thomas *state legislator*

Bay City
Barcia, James A. *congressman*
Gougeon, Joel *state legislator*

Birmingham
Bouchard, Michael J. *state legislator*

Bloomfield Hills
Jamian, John *state legislator*

Brant
Goschka, Michael John *state legislator*

Clio
Cherry, John D., Jr. *state legislator*

Detroit
Bennane, Michael J. *state legislator*
Hertel, Curtis *state legislator*
Hood, Morris *state legislator*
Leland, Burton *state legislator*
O'Brien, Michael J. *state legislator*
Saunders, Nelson W. *state legislator*
Wallace, Theodore Calvin *state legislator*
Young, Joseph Floyd, Jr. *state legislator*

Drummond Island
Gagliardi, Pat *state legislator*

Elwell
Randall, Gary Lee *state legislator*

Escanaba
Anthony, David *state legislator*

Flint
Clack, Floyd *state legislator*
Conroy, Joe *state legislator*
Emerson, Robert *state legislator*

Fremont
Llewellyn, John T. *state legislator*

Grand Ledge
Fitzgerald, Frank Moore *state legislator*

Grand Rapids
Byl, William *state legislator*
DeLange, Walter L. *state legislator*
Ehlers, Vernon James *congressman*

Grandville
Voorhees, Harold J., Sr. *state legislator*

Grayling
Lowe, Allen *state legislator*

Hesperia
Bobier, Bill *state legislator*

Holland
Dalman, Jessie Fiesselmann *state legislator*
Hillegonds, Paul *state legislator*

Holt
Brewer, Lingg *state legislator*

Hudsonville
Van Regenmorter, William *state legislator*

Huntington Woods
Gubow, David M. *state legislator*

Ironwood
Koivisto, Don *state legislator*

Jackson
Griffin, Michael J. *state legislator*

Kalamazoo
Brown, Mary Carney *former state representative*

Kawkawlin
Wetters, Howard *state legislator*

Lake Orion
Dunaskiss, Mat J. *state legislator*

Lansing
Agee, James G. *state legislator*
Bennett, Loren *state legislator*
Berman, Maxine *state legislator*
Bodem, Beverly A. *state legislator*
Bullard, Willis Clare, Jr. *state legislator*
Byrum, Dianne *state legislator*
Cisky, Jon Ayres *state senator*
Crissman, Penny M. *state legislator*
Cropsey, Alan Lee *state legislator, lawyer*
Curtis, Candace A. *state legislator*
DeGrow, Dan L. *state legislator*
DeHart, Eileen *state legislator*
Dingell, Christopher Dennis *state legislator*
Dobronski, Agnes Marie *state legislator*
Dolan, Jan Clark *state legislator*
Emmons, Joanne *state senator*
Geake, Raymond Robert *state senator*
Geiger, Terry *state legislator*
Green, Mike *state legislator*
Hammerstrom, Beverly Swoish *state representative*
Hanley, Michael Joseph *state legislator*
Hart, George Zaven *state legislator*
Hoffman, Philip Edward *state senator*
Jellema, Jon *state legislator*
Johnson, Shirley *state legislator*
Kaza, Greg John *state representative, economist*
Kelly, Thomas *state legislator*
Kilpatrick, Carolyn Cheeks *state legislator, educator*
LaForge, Edward *state legislator*
Law, Gerald H. *state legislator*
Letarte, Clyde *state legislator*
McManus, George Alvin, Jr. *state senator, cherry farmer*
Murphy, Raymond *state legislator*
North, Walter *state legislator*
Parks, Mary *state legislator*
Perricone, Charles *state legislator*
Pitoniak, Gregory Edward *state representative*
Posthumus, Richard Earl *state senator, farmer*
Price, Hubert *state legislator*
Prusi, Michael *state legislator*
Ryan, James Rogers *state legislator*
Schroer, Mary *state legislator*
Schuette, Bill *state senator*
Schwarz, John J.H. *state senator, surgeon*
Scott, Martha G. *state legislator*
Sikkema, Kenneth R. *state legislator*
Smith, Virgil Clark *state legislator*
Stallworth, Alma Grace *state legislator*
Varga, Ilona *state legislator*
Vaughn, Jackie, III *state legislator*
Whyman, Deborah *state legislator*
Wilk, Kenny A. *state legislator*
Yokich, Tracey A. *state legislator*

Lincoln Park
DeMars, Robert A. *state legislator*

Litchfield
Nye, Michael Earl *state legislator*

Lowell
Horton, Jack *state legislator*

Madison Heights
Freeman, John F. *state legislator*

Marysville
London, Terry *state legislator*

Mc Bain
Gernaat, John *state legislator*

Midland
McNutt, James *state legislator*

Montrose
Hill, Sandra J. *state legislator*

Mount Clemens
Rocca, Sue *state legislator*

Muskegon
Baade, Paul T. *state legislator*

New Baltimore
DeBerussaert, Kenneth Joseph *state legislator*

Newport
Owen, Lynn *state legislator*

Ortonville
Middleton, Thomas F. *state legislator*

Paw Paw
Middaugh, James (Mike) *state legislator*

Portage
Shugars, Dale L. *state legislator*

Rochester
Peters, Gary Charles *state senator, lawyer, educator*

Roseville
Ciaramitaro, Nick *state legislator*

Saint Joseph
Brackenridge, Robert L. *state legislator*
Gast, Harry T., Jr. *state legislator*

Sawyer
Gnodtke, Carl F. *state legislator*

Shelby Township
Jaye, Dave *state legislator*

Spring Lake
Stille, Leon E. *state legislator*

Sturgis
Oxender, Glenn S. *state legislator*

Tipton
Walberg, Timothy Lee *state legislator*

Trenton
Porreca, Vincent Joe *state legislator*

Utica
Carl, Doug *state legislator*

Warren
Miller, Arthur J., Jr. *state legislator*
Olshove, Dennis *state legislator*
Weeks, Lloyd F. *state legislator*

West Branch
Alley, Tom *state legislator*

White Lake
Galloway, David N. *state legislator*

Williamston
Gustafson, Dan *state legislator*

Wyandotte
Palamara, Joseph *state legislator*

Ypsilanti
Profit, Kirk A. *state legislator*

MINNESOTA

Albert Lea
Kraus, Ron *state legislator*

Anoka
Weaver, Charlie *state legislator*

Austin
Leighton, Robert Joseph *state legislator*

Bemidji
Johnson, Bob *state legislator, social worker*

Big Lake
Olson, Mark *state legislator*

Bird Island
Cooper, Roger *state legislator*

Bloomington
Knight, Kevin *state legislator*
Mahon, Mark P. *state legislator*
Riveness, Phillip J. *state legislator*

Brainerd
Samuelson, Donald B. *state legislator*

Bricelyn
Beckman, Tracy *state legislator*

Buffalo
Ourada, Mark *state legislator*

Burnsville
McElroy, Dan *state legislator*
Morrison, Constance Faith *state legislator, realtor*
Wolf, Ken *state legislator*

Caledonia
Johnson, Virgil Joel *state legislator, farmer*

Cass Lake
Finn, Harold R. *state legislator*

Chanhassen
Workman, Tom *state legislator*

Chisholm
Janezich, Jerry R. *state legislator, small business owner*

Chokio
Berg, Charles A. *state legislator*

Circle Pines
Delmont, Mike *state legislator*

Cook
Johnson, Douglas J. *state legislator, secondary education counselor*

Corcoran
Lindner, Arlon *state legislator*

Crookston
Lieder, Bernard L. *state legislator, civil engineer*

Dakota
Morse, Steven *state legislator, farmer*

Dassel
Ness, Robert *state legislator, education consultant*

Duluth
Huntley, Thomas *state legislator, science educator*
Solon, Sam George *state legislator*

Eagan
Pawlenty, Tim *state legislator*

Eden Prairie
Paulsen, Erik *state legislator*

Edina
Terwilliger, Roy W. *state legislator*

Erskine
Moe, Roger Deane *state legislator, secondary education educator*

Forest Lake
Swenson, Douglas *state legislator*

Fosston
Olson, Edgar *state legislator*

Fulda
Winter, Theodore *state legislator*

Glyndon
Langseth, Keith *state legislator, farmer*

Granada
Hugoson, Gene *state legislator, farmer*

Hastings
Dempsey, Jerry *state legislator*

Hawley
Dauner, Marvin K. *state legislator*

Hopkins
Kelley, Steve *state legislator, lawyer*

Isanti
Rostbert, Jim *state legislator*

Ivanhoe
Mulder, Richard Dean *state legislator*

Lake City
Osskopp, Mike *state legislator*

Lakeland
Larsen, Peg *state legislator*

Long Prairie
Otremba, Ken *state legislator*

Lynd
Girard, Jim *state legislator*

Madison
Peterson, Doug *state legislator*

Mankato
Dorn, John *state legislator*

Maple Grove
Anderson, Bruce *state legislator*
Limmer, Warren E. *state legislator, real estate broker*

Minneapolis
Belanger, William V., Jr. *state legislator*
Erhardt, Ron *state legislator*
Kroening, Carl W. *state legislator, public school principal*
Merriam, Gene *state legislator, accountant*
Oliver, Edward Carl *state senator, retired investment executive*
Pogemiller, Lawrence J. *state legislator*
Reichgott Junge, Ember D. *state legislator, lawyer*

Moorhead
Goodno, Kevin P. *state legislator*

New Brighton
Pellow, Dick *state legislator*

Newport
Marko, Sharon *state legislator*

Owatonna
Day, Richard H. *state legislator*

Park Rapids
Kinkel, Anthony G. *state legislator, educator*

Paynesville
Bertram, Joe, Sr. *state legislator*

Plymouth
Van Dellen, H. Todd *state legislator*

Preston
Davids, Gregory M. *state legislator*
Scheevel, Kenrie James *state legislator*

Prior Lake
Johnston, Terry D. *state legislator, insurance agent*

Redwood Falls
Vickerman, Barb *state legislator*

Rosemount
Ozment, Dennis Dean *state legislator*

Rush City
Jennings, Loren G. *state legislator, business owner*

Saint Cloud
Opatz, Joe *state legislator*

Saint Joseph
Dehler, Steve *state legislator*

Saint Paul
Abrams, Ronald Lawrence *state legislator*
Anderson, Ellen Ruth *state senator*
Anderson, Irvin Neal *state legislator*
Bettermann, Hilda *state legislator*
Betzold, Donald Richard *state senator*
Brown, Chuck *state legislator*
Carlson, Lyndon Richard Selvig *state legislator, educator*
Clark, Karen *state legislator*
Cohen, Richard J. *state senator*
Farrell, Jim *state legislator*
Frederickson, Dennis Russel *senator, farmer*
Frerichs, Donald L. *state legislator*
Garcia, Edwina *state legislator*
Greenfield, Lee *state legislator*
Greiling, Mindy *state legislator*
Hanson, Paula E. *state legislator*
Hasskamp, Kris *state legislator*
Haukoos, Melvin Robert *state representative*
Hausman, Alice *state legislator*
Jaros, Mike *state legislator, administrative assistant*
Jefferson, Richard H. *state legislator*
Johnson, Alice M. *state legislator*
Kahn, Phyllis *state legislator*
Kelly, Randy C. *state legislator*
Kelso, Becky *state legislator*
Kiscaden, Sheila M. *state legislator*
Kleis, David *state legislator*
Kramer, Don *state legislator*
Krentz, Jane *state legislator, elementary education educator*
Krinkie, Philip B. *state legislator, business executive*
Larson, Cal *state legislator, real estate and insurance broker*
Leppik, Margaret White *state legislator*
Lesewski, Arlene *state legislator, insurance agent*
Lessard, Robert Bernard *state legislator, recreational facility executive*
Lourey, Becky J. *state legislator*
Luther, Darlene *state legislator*
Macklin, William Edward *state legislator, lawyer*
Mariani, Carlos *state legislator*
McCollum, Betty *state legislator*
McGuire, Mary Jo *state legislator*
Milbert, Robert P. *state legislator*
Molnau, Carol *state legislator*
Mondale, Theodore Adams *state senator*
Munger, Willard *state legislator*
Murphy, Mary C. *state legislator*
Murphy, Steven Leslie *state senator, utilities company official*
Novak, Steven G. *state legislator*
Olson, Gen *state legislator*
Onnen, Tony *state legislator*
Orenstein, Howard *state legislator*
Orfield, Myron Willard, Jr. *state legislator, educator*
Osthoff, Tom *state legislator*
Perlt, Walter E. *state legislator*
Rest, Ann H. *state legislator*
Rhodes, Jim *state legislator*
Rice, James I. *state legislator*
Robertson, Martha Rappaport *state senator, consultant*
Runbeck, Linda C. *state legislator*
Sarna, John J. *state legislator*
Seagren, Alice *state legislator*
Skoglund, Wesley John *state legislator*
Solberg, Loren Albin *state legislator, secondary education educator*
Spear, Allan Henry *state senator, historian, educator*
Tompkins, Eileen *state legislator*
Trimble, Steve *state legislator*
Wejcman, Linda *state legislator*
Wenzel, Stephen G. *state legislator*
Werner, Edward George *research consultant state legislature*
Wiener, Deanna *state legislator*

Saint Peter
Ostrom, Don *state legislator, political science educator*

South Saint Paul
Metzen, James P. *state legislator, banker*

Staples
Sams, Dallas C. *state legislator*

Stillwater
Holsten, Mark *state legislator*
Laidig, Gary W. *state legislator*

Sturgeon Lake
Chmielewski, Florian *state legislator*

Thief River Falls
Stumpf, LeRoy A. *state legislator*

Tracy
Vickerman, Jim *state legislator*

Virginia
Rukavina, Tom *state legislator*

Walters
Kalis, Henry J. *state legislator, farmer*

Waseca
Worke, Gary D. *state legislator*

White Bear Lake
Chandler, Kevin *state legislator*
Mares, Harry *state legislator*

Willmar
Johnson, Dean Elton *state legislator, Lutheran pastor*

Winona
Pelowski, Gene P., Jr. *state legislator*

Woodbury
Price, Leonard Russell (Len Price) *state legislator*

MISSOURI

Ashland
Pauley, Jim G. *state legislator*

Ballwin
Loudon, John *state legislator*

Barnhart
McKenna, William P. *state legislator*

Blue Springs
Ross, Carson *state legislator*

Bonne Terre
Ward, Robert D. *state legislator*

Bridgeton
O'Connor, Patrick J. *state legislator*

California
Rohrbach, Larry *state legislator*

Caruthersville
Prost, Donald *state legislator*

Chesterfield
Hale, David Clovis *former state representative*

Chillicothe
Whiteside, Dale *state legislator*

Concordia
Oetting, David D. *state legislator*

De Soto
Sheldon, Norman E. *state legislator*

Edgar Springs
McBride, Jerry E. *state legislator*

Eldon
Steen, Don *state legislator*

Eminence
Staples, Danny Lew *state senator*

Festus
Stoll, Steve *state legislator*

Florissant
Schneider, John Durbin *state legislator*
Stokan, Lana *state legislator*

Gallatin
Tate, Phil *state legislator*

Gerald
Froelker, Jim *state legislator*

Greenfield
Marshall, William G. *state legislator*

Half Way
Legan, Kenneth *state legislator, farmer*

Hannibal
Clayton, Robert Morrison, III *state legislator*

Harrisonville
Hartzler, Vicky *state legislator*

High Ridge
Alter, William *state legislator*

Holts Summit
Triplett, Robert Joseph *state research analyst*

Huggins
Lybyer, Mike Joseph *state legislator, farmer*

Independence
Franklin, Richard *state representative*

Jefferson
Richardson, Mark *state legislator*
Westfall, Morris *state legislator*

Jefferson City
Backer, Gracia Yancey *state legislator*
Bland, Mary Graves *state legislator*
Bray, Joan *state legislator*
Brown, Harriet *state legislator*
Carter, Paula J. *state legislator*
Caskey, Harold Leroy *state senator*
Clay, William Lacy, Jr. *state legislator*
Cooper, Bonnie Sue *state legislator*
Davis, Dorathea *state legislator*
Days, Rita Denise *state legislator*
Donovan, Laurie B. *state legislator*
Edwards, Marilyn *state legislator*
Farmer, Nancy *state legislator*
Farnen, Ted William *state legislator*
Goode, Wayne *state senator, corporate executive*
Griesheimer, John Elmer *state representative*
Hagan-Harrell, Mary M. *state legislator*
Kasten, Mary Alice C. *state legislator*
Kauffman, Sandra Daley *state legislator*
Linton, William Carl *state legislator*
Luetkenhaus, William Joseph *state legislator*
Lumpe, Sheila *state legislator*
Mays, Carol Jean *state legislator*
McClelland, Emma L. *state legislator*
Montgomery, James V. *state legislator*
Morgan, Annette N. *state legislator*
Murray, Connie Wible *state legislator*
Ostmann, Cindy *state legislator*
Pouche, Fredrick, Jr. *state legislator*
Reynolds, David L. *state legislator*
Ridgeway, Luann *state legislator*
Robirds, Estel *state legislator*
Sallee, Mary Lou *state legislator*
Scheve, May E. *state legislator*
Secrest, Patricia K. *state legislator*
Shear, S. Sue *state legislator*
Sims, Betty *state legislator*
Treppler, Irene Esther *state senator*
Vogel, Carl M. *state legislator*
Wieland, Paul Joseph *state legislator*
Wiggins, Harry *state senator, lawyer*
Williams, Deleta *state legislator*
Williams, Marilyn *state legislator*
Witt, Gary Dean *state legislator*

Joplin
Burton, Gary L. *state legislator*
Surface, Chuck L. *state legislator*

Kansas City
Boucher, Bill *state legislator*
Curls, Phillip B. *state legislator*
Daniels, Fletcher *state legislator*
DePasco, Ronnie Nick *state legislator*
McLuckie, Steve *state legislator*
Quick, Edward E. *state legislator*
Rizzo, Henry *state legislator*
Skaggs, Bill *state legislator*
Thompson, Vernon *state legislator*
Van Zandt, Tim *state legislator*

Kennett
Thomason, Larry *state legislator*

Laddonia
Leake, Sam *state legislator, farmer*

Lebanon
Long, Elizabeth L. *state legislator, small business owner*
Russell, John Thomas *state legislator*

Lees Summit
Kenney, William Patrick *state legislator*

Lemay
Treadway, Joseph L. *state legislator*

Liberty
Canuteson, Greg *state legislator*

Louisiana
Smith, Philip G. *state legislator*

Lowry City
Scott, Delbert Lee *state legislator*

Marshall
Marshall, Thomas W. *state legislator*

Maryville
Barnett, Rex *state legislator*

Memphis
Sears, Jim *state legislator*

Neosho
Marble, Gary *state legislator*

New Cambria
Wiggins, Gary *state legislator*

New Madrid
Copeland, Fred E. *state legislator*

Nixa
Kreider, Jim *state legislator, farmer*

Perryville
Naeger, Patrick A. *state legislator*

Potosi
Crump, Wayne F. *state legislator*

Reeds Spring
Childers, L. Doyle *state legislator*

Richland
Mitchell, James W. *state legislator*

Saint Ann
Foley, James M. *state legislator*

Saint Charles
Ehlmann, Steven E. *state legislator*

Saint Joseph
Shields, Charles W. *state legislator*

Saint Louis
Akin, W. Todd *state legislator*
Auer, Ron *state legislator*
Banks, J.B. *state legislator*
Danforth, John Claggett *senator, lawyer, clergyman*
Dougherty, J. Patrick *state legislator*
Flotron, Francis E. *state legislator*
Ford, Louis H. *state legislator*
Goward, Russell *state legislator*
Hand, Raymond W. *state legislator*
Levin, David L. *state legislator*
May, Brian Henry *state legislator*
Mueller, Walt *state legislator*
Murphy, Jim *state legislator*
Murrey, Dana L. *state legislator*
O'Neill, Matt *state legislator*
O'Toole, James *state legislator*
Ribaudo, Anthony D. *state legislator*
Scott, John E. *state legislator*
Shelton, O. L. *state legislator*
Troupe, Charles Quincy *state legislator*

Saint Peters
Chrismer, Rich *state legislator*
Kissell, Don R. *state legislator*

Salem
Fiebelman, Kenneth Franklin *state representative*

Sedalia
Mathewson, James L. *state legislator*

Springfield
Schilling, Mike *state legislator*
Wannenmacher, Philip *state legislator*
Wooten, Charles (Chuck) *state legislator*

Summersville
Koller, Don *state legislator*

Union
Overschmidt, Francis S. *state legislator*

Unionville
Summers, Don *state legislator*

Versailles
Pryor, Chuck *state legislator*

Warrenton
Nordwald, Charles *state legislator*

Webb City
Elliott, Mark T. *state legislator*

West Plains
Garnett, Jess *state legislator*

NEBRASKA

Hebron
Coordsen, George *state legislator*

Lincoln
Avery, Michael T. *state legislator*
Bernard-Stevens, David F. *state legislator*
Beutler, Christopher John *state legislator*
Bohlke, Ardyce *state legislator*
Bromm, Curt *state legislator*
Chambers, Ernest *state legislator*
Cudaback, Jim D. *state legislator*
Elmer, W. Owen *state legislator*
Engel, L. Patrick *state legislator*
Fisher, Dan *state legislator, bank executive*
Hall, Timothy *state legislator*
Hartnett, D. Paul *state legislator*
Janssen, Ramon E. *state legislator*
Johnson-McKenzie, Janis *state legislator*
Jones, James E. *state legislator*
Kristensen, Douglas Allan *state legislator*
Landis, David Morrison *state legislator*
Lynch, Daniel C. *state legislator*
Marsh, Frank (Irving) *former state official*
Pirsch, Carol McBride *state senator, community relations manager*
Robak, Jennie *state legislator*
Robinson, C.N. (Bud) *state legislator*
Schellpeper, Stan *state legislator*
Schimek, DiAnna Ruth Rebman *state legislator*
Schmitt, Jerry *state legislator*
Vrtiska, Floyd P. *state legislator*
Warner, Jerome *state legislator*
Wesely, Donald Raymond *state senator*
Wickersham, William R. *state legislator*
Will, Eric John *state senator*

Malcolm
Hudkins, Carol L. *state legislator*

Omaha
Lindsay, John C. *state legislator*
Witek, Kate *state senator, trucking company executive*

Papillion
Withem, Ronald E. *state senator, trade association executive*

Plattsmouth
Wehrbein, Roger Ralph *state senator*

NORTH DAKOTA

Arnegard
Drovdal, David (Skip) *state legislator*

Ashley
Kretschmar, William Edward *state legislator, lawyer*

Bismarck
Boucher, Merle *state legislator*
Clark, Tony *state legislator*
DeWitz, Loren *state legislator*
Freborg, Layton W. *state legislator*
Gulleson, Pam *state legislator*
Henegar, Dale L. *state legislator*
Holm, Ruth E. *state legislator*
Keiser, George J. *state legislator*
Kelsch, RaeAnn *state legislator*
Kringstad, Edroy *state legislator*
Martinson, Robert William *state legislator*
Mutzenberger, Marv *state legislator*
Nelson, Carolyn *state legislator*
Oban, Bill *state legislator*
Olson, Alice *state legislator*

Price, Clara Sue *state legislator*
Robinson, Larry J. *state legislator*
Rydell, Catherine M. *state legislator*
Schobinger, Randy Arthur *state legislator*
Stenehjem, Bob *state legislator*
Tennefos, Jens Junior *state legislator*
Walker, Bruce F. *state legislator*
Watne, Darlene Claire *state legislator*

Blanchard
Aarsvold, Ole *state legislator*

Bottineau
Sveen, Gerald O. *state legislator*

Bowman
Bowman, Bill *state legislator*
Kempenich, Keith *state legislator*

Braddock
Naaden, Pete *state legislator*

Carrington
Howard, John *state legislator*

Casselton
Dalrymple, Jack *state legislator*
Nelson, Gary J. *state legislator*

Center
Mahoney, John *state legislator*

Cleveland
Retzer, Elmer R. *state legislator*
Wanzek, Terry M. *state legislator*

Cooperstown
Hagle, Andrew J. *state legislator*

Crosby
Andrist, John M. *state senator*

Devils Lake
Kunkel, Richard W. *state legislator*

Dickinson
Goetz, William G. *state legislator*
Wald, Francis John *state legislator*
Wardner, Rich *state legislator*

Douglas
Delzer, Jeff W. *state legislator*

Drake
Sitz, Mark *state legislator*

Dunn Center
Brown, Grant C. *state legislator*

Edgeley
Schimke, Dennis J. *state legislator*

Fargo
Austin, Dan *state legislator*
Berg, Rick Alan *state legislator, real estate investor*
Bernstein, LeRoy G. *state legislator*
Christopherson, Christine Young *state legislator*
Dorso, John *state legislator*
Gorman, Stephen Thomas *state legislator*
Mathern, Tim *state senator, social worker*
Sandvig, Sally *state legislator*
Soukup, Al *state legislator*

Fessenden
Streibel, Bryce *state senator*

Finley
Laughlin, Bruce *state legislator*

Fullerton
Kelsh, Jerome *state legislator*

Grafton
Gorder, William E. *state legislator*

Grand Forks
Aubyn, Rod *state legislator*
Christenson, Linda *state legislator*
Clayburgh, Richard Scott *state legislator*
Delmore, Lois M. *state legislator*
DeMers, Judy Lee *state legislator, university dean*
Holmberg, Raymon E. *state legislator*
Kliniske, Amy N. *state legislator*
Nottestad, Darrell *state legislator*
Poolman, Jim *state legislator*
Stenehjem, Wayne Kevin *state senator, lawyer*
Svedjan, Ken *state legislator*

Hankinson
Heitkamp, Joel C. *state legislator*

Hazen
Christmann, Randel Darvin *state legislator*
Galvin, Pat G. *state legislator*

Jamestown
Hanson, Lyle *state legislator*
Kroeber, Joe *state legislator*
Nething, David E. *state legislator*

Kenmare
Froseth, Glen *state legislator*

Langdon
Sand, Harvey *state legislator*

Lansford
O'Connell, David Paul *state legislator*

Larimore
Mutch, Duane *state legislator*
Shide, Don *state legislator*

Leonard
Belter, Wesley R. *state legislator*

Lidgerwood
Grumbo, Howard *state legislator*

Linton
Freier, Tom D. *state legislator*

Lisbon
Huether, Robert *state legislator*

Maddock
Schmidt, Arlo E. *state legislator*

Makoti
Dobrinski, Everett *state legislator*

Mandan
Boehm, James *state legislator*
Coats, James O. *state legislator*

Mayville
Kaldor, Lee *state legislator*
Lindaas, Elroy Neil *state legislator*

Minnewaukan
Johnson, Dennis E. *state legislator*

Minot
Haugland, Brynhild *retired state legislator, farmer*
Mickelson, Stacey *state legislator*
Redlin, Rolland W. *state legislator*
Timm, Mike *state legislator*
Wentz, Janet Marie *state legislator*

Mott
Kerzman, James A. *state legislator*

New Salem
Bateman, Rocklin (Rocky) *state legislator*

Northwood
Lloyd, Ed *state legislator*

Palermo
Kinnoin, Meyer D. *state legislator*
Nichols, Ronald *state legislator*

Ray
Torgerson, Jim *state legislator*

Reeder
Jacobs, Leonard J. *state legislator*

Riverdale
Henegar, Kit *state legislator*

Rolla
Wilkie, Gerry L. *state legislator*

Rugby
Solberg, Ken *state legislator*

Tioga
Skarphol, Robert J. *state legislator*

Towner
Gunter, G. Jane *state legislator*

Valley City
Sabby, Leland *state legislator*

Wahpeton
Hausauer, Roy *state legislator*
Thane, Russell T. *state legislator*

Warwick
Langley, Byron *state legislator*

West Fargo
Lee, Judy *state legislator*

Williston
Byerly, Rex R. *state legislator*
Yockim, James Craig *state senator, oil and gas executive*

OHIO

Akron
Sykes, Vernon L. *state legislator*

Andover
Boggs, Ross A., Jr. *state legislator, dairy farmer*

Barberton
Sutton, Betty *state legislator*

Bellaire
Cera, Jack *state legislator*

Bourneville
Shoemaker, Michael C. *state legislator*

Bowling Green
Gardner, Randall *state legislator, realtor*

Canfield
Gerberry, Ronald V. *state legislator*

Cedarville
DeWine, R. Michael *U.S. Senator, lawyer*

Cincinnati
Blessing, Louis W., Jr. *state legislator, lawyer*
Finan, Richard H. *state senator, lawyer*
Winkler, Cheryl J. *state legislator*

Cleveland
Colonna, Rocco J. *state legislator*
Johnson, Jeffrey D. *state legislator*
Korn, Candy Lee *legislative staff member*
Pringle, Barbara Carroll *state legislator*
Suster, Ronald *state legislator*
Sweeney, Patrick A. *state legislator*
Whalen, Vermel M. *state legislator*

Columbus
Abel, Mary *state legislator*
Beatty, Otto, Jr. *state legislator, lawyer*
Benjamin, Ann Womer *state legislator*
Britton, Sam *state legislator*
Burch, Robert L. *state senator, lawyer*
Carnes, James Edward *state legislator*
Davidson, Jo Ann *state legislator*
Dix, Nancy *state senator*
Doty, Karen M. *state legislator, lawyer*
Espy, Ben *state senator, lawyer*
Furney, Linda Jeanne *state legislator*
Gillmor, Karen Lako *state legislator, strategic planner*
Grendell, Diane V. *state legislator, lawyer, nurse*
Hodges, Richard *state legislator*
Kearns, Merle Grace *state senator*
Krebs, Eugene Kehm, II *state legislator*
Lawrence, Joan W. *state legislator*
Lewis, Lloyd Edward, Jr. *state legislator*
Long, Jan Michael *state legislator*
Lucas, June H. *state legislator*
Martin, Alan Robert *legislative staff member*
McLin, Rhine Lana *state senator, funeral service executive, educator*
Mead, Priscilla *state legislator*
Mottley, James Donald *state legislator, lawyer*
Oelslager, W. Scott *state legislator*
Opfer, Darrell Williams *state representative, educator*
Padgett, Joy *state legislator*
Perz, Sally *state legislator*
Prentiss, C.J. *state legislator*
Schafrath, Richard P. *state legislator*
Sheerer, Judy B. *state legislator*
Thomas, E.J. *state legislator*
Tiberi, Pat *state legislator*
Vesper, Rose *state legislator*
Worner, Jennifer Kathryn *legislative liaison*

Dayton
Corbin, Robert L. *state legislator*
Reid, Marilyn Joanne *state legislator, lawyer*
Roberts, Thomas Michael *state legislator*

Delphos
Thompson, William Edward *state legislator*

Elyria
Bender, John R. *state legislator*

Galloway
Watts, Eugene J. *state legislator*

Girard
Latell, Anthony, Jr. *state legislator*

Goshen
Terwilleger, George E. *state legislator*

Greenville
Buchy, Jim *state legislator, packing company executive*

Hamilton
Fox, Michael *state legislator, underwriting consultant*

Hillsboro
Snyder, Harry Cooper *retired state senator*

Kettering
Horn, Charles F. *state senator, lawyer, electrical engineer*

Lima
Cupp, Robert Richard *state senator, attorney*

Manchester
White, Doug *state legislator*

Milford
Bateman, Samuel T. *state legislator, insurance agency executive*

Norwalk
Taylor, William *state legislator*

Perry
Sines, Raymond E. *state legislator*

Rock Creek
Boggs, Robert J. *state senator*

Rushsylvania
Core, Edward K. *state legislator, farmer*

Sharon Vine
Van Vyven, Dale Nulsen *state legislator*

Toledo
Greenwood, Tim *state legislator, lawyer*

Wapakoneta
Brading, Charles Richard *state representative*

Warren
Verich, Michael Gregory *state legislator*

Willowick
Troy, Daniel Patrick *state legislator*

Wooster
Amstutz, Ronald *state legislator*

SOUTH DAKOTA

Aberdeen
Schaunaman, Craig D. *state legislator*
Waltman, Alfred A. *state legislator*
Weigel, Lucinda Mae *legislative staff member*

Armour
Putnam, J. E. (Jim) *state legislator*

Avon
Van Gerpen, Edward E. *state legislator*

Baltic
Wagner, Michael Dickman *state representative*

Belle Fourche
Letellier, Roy *state legislator*

Brandon
Brooks, Roger *state legislator*
Hunt, Roger *state legislator*

Brookings
Brown, Arnold M. *state legislator*
Roe, Robert A. *state legislator*

Buffalo
Johnson, William J. *state legislator*

Burke
Cerny, William F. *state legislator*

Claire City
Gleason, David *state legislator*

Claremont
Cutler, Steve Keith *state legislator*

Columbia
Dennert, H. Paul *state legislator*

Cottonwood
Gabriel, Larry E. *state legislator*

Crooks
Anderson, Mark *state legislator*

Custer
Emery, James W. *state legislator*

De Smet
Bierschbach, Doug *state legislator*

Gettysburg
Schreiber, Lola F. *state legislator*

Hayti
Frederick, Randall Davis *state legislator*

Holabird
Nemec, Nicholas *state legislator*

Houghton
Herseth, Ralph Lars *state legislator*

Huron
Haley, Pat *state legislator*
Volesky, Ron James *state legislator*

Iroquois
Flowers, Charles E. *state legislator*

Madison
Belatti, Richard G. *state legislator*
Kringen, Dale Eldon *state legislator, trasportation executive*
Lange, Gerald F. *state legislator*

Mission
Lucas, Larry James *state legislator*

Mitchell
Matthews, Dan *state legislator*
Olson, Mel *state legislator*

Mobridge
Bender, Darrell G. *state legislator*

Pierre
Barker, Linda K. *state legislator*
Everist, Barbara *state legislator*
Fiegen, Kristie K. *state legislator*
Kundert, Alice E. *retired state legislator*
Monroe, Jeff *state legislator*
Nicolay, Janice *state legislator*
Pederson, Gordon Roy *state legislator, retired military officer*
Rounds, M. Michael *state legislator*

Pine Ridge
Hagen, Richard E. (Dick) *state legislator*

Prairie City
Wishard, Della Mae *state legislator*

Rapid City
Hagg, Rexford A. *state legislator*
Napoli, William Bill *state legislator*
Sears, John D. *state legislator*
Shoener, Jerry J. *state legislator*
Whiting, Fred C. *state legislator*

Rosebud
Valandra, Paul *state legislator*

Scotland
Kloucek, Frank John *state legislator*

Sherman
Rogen, Mark Endre *state senator, farmer*

Sioux Falls
Dunn, Rebecca Jo *state legislator*
Munson, David Roy *state legislator*
Paisley, Keith Watkins *state senator, small business owner*
Richter, Mitch *state legislator*
Wick, Hal Gerard *state legislator*

Spearfish
Jorgensen, Kay Susan *state legislator*
Krautschun, Harvey C. *state legislator*

Strandburg
Weber, Robert R. *state legislator*

Sturgis
McNenny, Kenneth G. *state legislator*

Vermillion
Reedy, John J. (Joe) *state legislator*

Volga
Negstad, Richard B. *state legislator*

Wanblee
Porch, Roger A. *state legislator*

Watertown
Ries, Thomas G. (Torchy) *state legislator*
Thompson, Jim D. *state legislator*

Webster
Olson, Maurice Alan *state legislator*
Schoenbeck, Lee *state legislator*

Wessington
Duxbury, Robert Neil *state legislator*

Wessington Springs
Morford-Burg, JoAnn *state senator, investment company executive*

Wood
Koskan, John M. *state legislator*

Yankton
Hunhoff, Bernie P. *state legislator*
Moore, Garry A. *state legislator*
Munson, Donald E. *state legislator*

WISCONSIN

Albany
Powers, Mike *state legislator*

Antigo
Ourada, Thomas D. *state legislator*

Bear Creek
Lorge, William D. *state legislator, farmer, real estate broker*

Beloit
Weeden, Timothy L. *state legislator*

Berlin
Olsen, Luther S. *state legislator*

Black River Falls
Musser, Terry M. *state legislator*

Cambria
Hahn, Eugene Herman *state legislator*

De Pere
Lasee, Alan J. *state legislator*
Lasse, Frank G. *state legislator*

Eastman
Johnsrud, DuWayne *state legislator*

Eau Claire
Kreibich, Robin G. *state legislator*

Eland
Breske, Roger M. *state legislator*

Fennimore
Brandemuehl, David A. *state legislator*

Florence
Seratti, Lorraine M. *state legislator*

Fond Du Lac
Dobyns, John *state legislator*

Forest Junction
Ott, Alvin R. *state legislator*

Fort Atkinson
Ward, David W. *state legislator*

Green Bay
Cowles, Robert L. *state legislator*
Kelso, Carol *state legislator*
Ryba, John J. *state legislator*

Hartford
Lehman, Michael A. *state legislator*

Hartland
Vrakas, Daniel P. *state legislator*

Janesville
Wood, Wayne W. *state legislator*

Juneau
Fitzgerald, Scott *state legislator*
Goetsch, Robert George *state legislator*

Kaukauna
Vander Loop, William N. *state legislator*

Kenosha
Andrea, Joseph F. *state legislator*
Kreuser, James E. *state legislator*
Wirch, Robert W. *state legislator*

Kohler
Potter, Calvin J. *state legislator*

La Crosse
Meyer, Mark *state legislator*

Ladysmith
Reynolds, Martin L. *state legislator*

Loganville
Albers, Sheryl Kay *state legislator*

Luck
Dueholm, Robert M. *state legislator*

Luxemberg
Hutchison, Dave *state legislator*

Madison
Baldwin, Tammy *state legislator*
Barish, Lawrence Stephen *nonpartisan legislative staff administrator*
Black, Spencer *state legislator*
Brancel, Ben *state assemblymen*
Burke, Brian B. *state senator, lawyer*
Chvala, Charles Joseph *state legislator*
Darling, Alberta Statkus *state legislator, marketing executive, former art museum executive*
Farrow, Margaret Ann *state legislator*
Gronemus, Barbara *state legislator*
Huelsman, Joanne B. *state legislator*
Klug, Scott Leo *congressman*
Krug, Shirley *state legislator*
Krusick, Margaret Ann *state legislator*
Kunicki, Walter Joseph *state legislator*
Moen, Rodney Charles *state senator, retired naval officer*
Moore, Gwendolynne *state legislator*
Notestein, Barbara *state legislator*
Panzer, Mary E. *state legislator*
Plache, Kimberly Marie *state legislator*
Plomdon, David S. *state legislator*
Porter, Cloyd Allen *state representative*
Risser, Fred A. *state senator*
Robson, Judith Biros *state legislator*
Rosenzweig, Peggy A. *state legislator*
Rude, Brian David *state legislator*
Rutkowski, James Anthony *state legislator*
Schneiders, Lolita *state legislator*
Schultz, Dale Walter *state legislator*
Swoboda, Lary Joseph *state legislator*
Travis, David M. *state legislator*
Turner, Robert Lloyd *state legislator*
Walker, Scott Kevin *state legislator*
Williams, Annette Polly *state legislator*
Wineke, Joseph Steven *state legislator*
Young, Rebecca Mary Conrad *state legislator*

Manitowoc
Ziegelbauer, Robert F. *state legislator*

Mc Farland
Hanson, Doris J. *state legislator*

Menomonie
Baldus, Alvin J. *state legislator*
Clausing, Alice *state legislator*

Milwaukee
Bell, Jeanette Lois *state legislator*
Carpenter, Timothy W. *state legislator*
Coggs, G. Spencer *state legislator*
Cullen, David A. *state legislator*
George, Gary Raymond *state senator*
Morris-Tatum, Johnnie *state legislator*
Potter, Rosemary *state legislator*
Riley, Antonio *state legislator*
Wasserman, Sheldon A. *state legislator*
Young, Leon D. *state legislator*

Minocqua
Handrick, Joseph W. *state legislator*

Mosinee
Springer, Thomas J. *state legislator*

Mount Horeb
Skindrud, Rick *state legislator*

Mukwonago
Adelman, Lynn S. *state legislator*

Neenah
Ellis, Michael G. *state legislator*

New Berlin
Lazich, Mary A. *state legislator*

Oconomowoc
Foti, Steven M. *state legislator*

Onalaska
Huebsch, Michael D. *state legislator*

Oshkosh
Klusman, Judith *state legislator*
Owens, Carol *state legislator*
Underheim, Gregg *state legislator*

Peshtigo
Gard, John *state legislator*

Pittsville
Hasenohrl, Donald W. *state legislator*

Poplar
Jauch, Robert *state legislator*

Port Washington
Hoven, Tim *state legislator*

Pulaski
Drzewiecki, Gary Francis *state legislator*

Racine
Ladwig, Bonnie L. *state legislator*
Petak, George *state legislator*

Rice Lake
Hubler, Mary *state legislator*

Schofield
Decker, Russell S. *state legislator*

Shawano
Ainsworth, John H. *state legislator*

Sheboygan
Baumgart, James Raymond *state legislator*

South Milwaukee
Grobschmidt, Richard A. *state legislator*

Stevens Point
Murat, William M. *state legislator*

Superior
Boyle, Frank James *state legislator*

Thorp
Zukowski, Robert K. *state legislator*

Waterford
Gunderson, Scott L. *state legislator*

Waukesha
Jensen, Scott R. *state legislator*

Wausau
Huber, Gregory B. *state legislator*

West Bend
Grothman, Glenn *state legislator*

Whitewater
Coleman, Charles W. *state legislator*
Nass, Stephen L. *state legislator*

Wisconsin Rapids
Schneider, Marlin Dale *state legislator*

ADDRESS UNPUBLISHED

Aker, Alan D. *state legislator*
Anderson, Bob *state legislator, business executive*
Aurand, Clay *state legislator*
Bakk, Thomas *state legislator*
Ballard, Charlie *state legislator*
Ballou, John Dennis *state legislator*
Barnes, James A. *state legislator*
Bartelsmeyer, Linda *state legislator*
Becker, John J. *state legislator*
Beggs, Carol Edward *state legislator*
Bennett, Jon *state legislator*
Bishop, David T. *state legislator*
Boatright, Matt *state legislator*
Bock, Peter Ernest *state legislator*
Bogue, Eric H. *state legislator, lawyer*
Bonner, Dennis *state legislator*
Boudreau, Lynda *state legislator*
Boyd, Barbara *state legislator*
Bradley, Fran *state legislator*
Breaux, Billie J. *state legislator*
Broach, David *state legislator*
Broderick, B. Michael *state legislator, banker*
Broecker, Sherry *state legislator*
Brosz, Don *state legislator, retired educator*
Brown, Pam *state legislator*
Brown, Richard E. *state legislator*
Buck, James Russell *state legislator*
Burton, Woody *state legislator*
Carlson, Alan H. *state legislator*
Carpenter, Dorothy Fulton *former state legislator*
Charlton, Betty Jo *retired state legislator*
Churchill, Robert Wilson *state legislator, lawyer*
Cierpiot, Connie *state legislator*
Clemens, Deb Fischer *state legislator, nursing administrator*
Commers, Tim *state legislator*
Crum, Joe Clay *state legislator*
Daggett, Roxann *state legislator*
Damschroder, Rex *state legislator*
Daniel, Lloyd *state legislator*
Davis, Kay *state legislator*
DeLeo, James A. *state legislator*
DeMersseman, Michael *state legislator, lawyer*
Doderer, Minnette Frerichs *state legislator*
Drake, Robert Alan *state legislator, animal nutritionist, mayor*
Duncan, Cleo *state legislator*
Duniphan, J. P. *state legislator, small business owner*
Edmonds, John *state legislator*
Eidsness, Pat *state legislator*
Entenza, Matt *state legislator*
Enz, Catherine S. *state legislator*
Evans, Brent *state legislator*
Farmer, Mike *state legislator*
Feuerborn, Bill *state legislator*
Findley, Troy Ray *state legislator*
Finseth, Tim *state legislator*
Fitzgerald, Carol E. *state legislator*
Fitzwater, Rodger L. *state legislator*
Flora, Vaughn Leonard *state legislator*
Ford, Jack *state legislator*
Foster, Bill I. *state legislator*
Franklin, Clifford *state legislator*
Freese, Stephen J. *state legislator*
Gaskill, Sam *state legislator*
Gilmore, Phyllis *state legislator*
Graham, James *state legislator*
Grant, Jill *state legislator*
Gratz, William W. *state legislator*
Graves, Sam *state legislator*
Green, Timothy P. *state legislator*
Grindberg, Tony *state legislator*
Haas, Bill *state legislator*
Hackbarth, Tom *state legislator*
Hagan, Robert F. *state legislator*
Haines, Joseph E. *state legislator*
Halverson, Harold Wendell *state legislator*
Harder, Elaine Rene *state legislator*
Harlan, Timothy *state legislator*
Harrington, Nancy *state legislator*
Harris, Bill *state legislator*
Hartke, Charles A. *state legislator*
Hartley, David *state legislator*
Hartzler, Ed *state legislator*
Hassard, Helena *state legislator*
Healy, William James *state legislator*
Heffley, Irene M. *state legislator*
Hegeman, Daniel Jay *state legislator*
Hendrickson, Carl H. *state legislator*
Hickey, John Joseph *state legislator*
Hohulin, Martin *state legislator*
Honigman, David *state legislator*
Hood, Ron *state legislator*
Hoppe, Thomas J. *state legislator*
Hosmer, Craig *state legislator*
Hottinger, Jay *state legislator*
House, Ted *state legislator*
Howard, Janet C. *state legislator*
Howard, Jerry Thomas *state legislator*
Howerton, Jim *state legislator*
Hutmacher, James K. *state senator, water drilling contractor*
Jacob, Ken *state legislator*
Jacobs, Joel *state legislator, business educator*
Jacobson, Jeff *state legislator*
James, Troy Lee *state legislator*
Jensen, Jim *state legislator*
Johnson, Bruce *state legislator*
Johnson, Sidney *state legislator*
Johnson, Tom *state legislator*
Jordan, Jim *state legislator*
Kasputis, Edward *state legislator*
Kaufert, Dean R. *state legislator*
Keeven, Ron *state legislator*
Kimmel, John E. *state legislator*
Kinder, Peter *state legislator*
Klein, Matthew M. *state legislator*
Kleven, Marguerite *state senator*
Klumb, Jason O. *state legislator*
Koppendrayer, LeRoy J. *state legislator, farmer*
Koziura, Joseph F. *state legislator*
Kredit, Kenneth E. *state legislator, automobile dealership executive*
Krupinski, Jerry W. *state legislator*
Kubik, Jack L. *state legislator*
Kucinich, Dennis J. *state legislator*
Kukuk, Alvin H. *state legislator*
LaFave, John *state legislator*
LaFleur, Mitchell C. *state senator, lawyer*
Lambert, Sally Rideout *state legislator*
Landske, Dorothy Suzanne *state senator*
Larson, Donn C. *state senator*
Lee, Roger *state representative, farmer, small business owner*
Logan, Sean D. *state legislator*
Lograsso, Don *state legislator, lawyer*
Lohr, David L. *state legislator*
Luebbers, Jerome F. *state legislator*
Madden, Cheryl Beth *state legislator*
Mallory, Mark L. *state legislator, librarian*
Marty, John *state senator, writer*
Mathieu, Thomas C. *state legislator*
Matzke, Gerald E. *state legislator*
McClain, Richard Wagner *state legislator*
McCoy, Matthew William *state official, human resource manager*
Meshel, Harry *state senator, political party official*
Metzger, Kerry R. *state legislator*
Mollenkamp, Gayle L. *state legislator*
Morris, Candace L. *state legislator*
Morris, Stephen R. *state legislator*
Murphy, Michael B. *state legislator*
Myers, Jon D. *state legislator*
Nein, Scott R. *state legislator*
Netzley, Robert E. *state legislator*
Ogg, William L. *state legislator*
Olman, Lynn *state legislator*
Padfield, Jon R. *state legislator*
Poe, Raymond *state legislator*
Pond, Phyllis Joan *state legislator*
Pryce, Deborah D. *congresswoman*
Ranson, Pat *state legislator*
Rogers, Mike *state legislator*
Roth, Toby *congressman*
Salerno, Amy *state legislator*
Saltsman, Donald L. *state legislator*
Sawyer, Frank S. *state legislator*
Schroek, Ed *state legislator*
Schuck, William *state legislator*
Schumacher, Leslie *state legislator, artist*
Schwab, David *state legislator*
Shadid, George P. *state legislator*
Simoneau, Wayne Anthony *state legislator*
Smith, Alma Wheeler *state legislator*
Sombart, Paul C. *state legislator*
Spangler, Stephen Alan *state legislator*
Stallings, Henry *state legislator*
Steele, Brent E. *state legislator*
Steil, Glenn *state legislator*
Stenehjem, Allan *state legislator*
Stevens, Dan *state legislator*
Stevenson, Dan Charles *state legislator*
Stuhr, Elaine *state legislator*
Swenson, Howard *state legislator, farmer*
Sykora, Barbara Zwach *state legislator*
Tavares, Charleta B. *state legislator*
Tesanovich, Paul *state legislator*
Thompson, Lynn *state legislator*
Thoreson, Laurel *state legislator*
Tuma, John *state legislator, lawyer*
Tunheim, James Ronald *state legislator, farmer*
Turner, Paul Eric *state legislator*
Twyla, Roman *state legislator*
Van Engen, Thomas Lee *state legislator*
Vanleer, James G. *state legislator*
Vaughn, Edward *state legislator*
Viverito, Louis S. *state legislator*
Vukovich, Joseph John *state legislator, lawyer*
Wachtman, Lynn R. *state legislator*
Wait, Ronald A. *state legislator*
Waterman, John M. *state legislator*
Weston, James Randall *state legislator*
Wilder, Michael O. *state legislator*
Willard, Karen *state legislator*
Winters, David Forrest *state legislator*
Womacks, Martha A. *state legislator*
Yoh, Donna (Dee) *state legislator*
Young, Dean A. *state legislator*
Zabrock, Edward Joseph *state legislator*

HEALTHCARE: DENTISTRY

UNITED STATES

ILLINOIS

Batavia
Bicknell, Brian Keith *dentist*

Berwyn
Lee, Stephen Sheng-hao *dentist*

Chicago
Abt, Sylvia Hedy *dentist*
Barr, Sanford Lee *dentist*
Glenner, Richard Allen *dentist, dental historian*
Horowitz, Fred L. *dentist, administrator, consultant*
Jackson, Gregory Wayne *orthodontist*
Santangelo, Mario Vincent *dental association executive, educator*
Shimoda, Thomas Edward *dentist, lawyer*

Elburn
Willey, James Lee *dentist*

Geneva
Kallstrom, Charles Clark *dentist*
Lazzara, Dennis Joseph *orthodontist*

Highland Park
Margolis, Fred Sheldon *pediatric dentist, educator*

Hinsdale
Mele, Joanne Theresa *dentist*

Jacksonville
Loughary, Thomas Michael *dentist*

Kenilworth
Edson, Wayne E. *dentist, consultant*

La Grange
Morelli, Anthony Frank *pediatric dentist*

Lake Forest
Counsell, Lee Albert *dentist*
Jones, Gordon Kempton *dentist*

Mount Vernon
Stephen, Richard Joseph *oral and maxillofacial surgeon*

Northbrook
Williams, David Allan *dentist, educator*

Roselle
Kao, William Chishon *dentist*

Schaumburg
Colvard, Michael David *periodontist, oral medicine and laser surgery specialist*
Shulkin, Neil Howard *dentist*
Uditsky, Daniel Nathan *dentist*

Springfield
Koertner, Camille Kay *dental hygienist*

INDIANA

Anderson
Stohler, Michael Joe *dentist*

Elkhart
Bryan, Norman E. *dentist*

Evansville
Raibley, Parvin Rudolph *dentist*

Gary
Stephens, Paul Alfred *dentist*

Indianapolis
Behner, Elton Dale *dentist*
Patel, Raj-Rajendra Ambalal *dentist, clinical geneticist*
Roberts, Wilbur Eugene *dental educator, research scientist*
Tolliver, Kevin Paul *dentist*

New Albany
Johnson, John Edwin *orthodontist*

Terre Haute
Roshel, John Albert, Jr. *orthodontist*

IOWA

Ankeny
Weigel, Ollie J. *dentist, former mayor*

Des Moines
Fuller, Steven Craig *dentist*

Iowa City
Ogesen, Robert Bruce *dentist*
Ruprecht, Axel *oral and maxillofacial radiologist*

KANSAS

Hays
Wagner, Paul Dean *oral and maxillofacial surgeon*

Kansas City
Boraz, Robert Alan *dentist, surgery and pediatrics educator*
Burnett, Rita Marline *dentist*

Leavenworth
Kittle, Paul Edwin *pediatric dentist*

Liberal
Yount, Kim Allen *dentist*

Topeka
Fyler, Carl John *dentist*
Stroud, Herschel Leon *dentist*

Wellington
Willis, Robert Addison *dentist*

MICHIGAN

Ann Arbor
Ash, Major McKinley, Jr. *dentist, educator*
Reese, James W. *orthodontist*

Bay City
Pearsall, Harry James *dentist*

Grand Rapids
Bander, Thomas Samuel *dentist*
Zietz, Lonny E. *oral and maxillofacial surgeon*

Greenville
Sorensen, Nels Peter, Jr. *dentist*

Midland
Thompson, Seth Charles *retired oral and maxillofacial surgeon*

Warren
Woehrlen, Arthur Edward, Jr. *dentist*

MINNESOTA

Alexandria
Monahan, Edward Joseph, III *orthodontist*

Byron
Nolting, Frederick William *dentist*

Cottage Grove
Weingartner, Gerard John *dentist*

Duluth
Kramer, Alex John *dentist*

Edina
Adzick, Shirley Rae *dentist*

Kenyon
Jacobson, Lloyd Eldred *retired dentist*

Mankato
Dumke, Melvin Philip *dentist*

Minneapolis
Geistfeld, Ronald Elwood *dental educator*

Saint Louis Park
Weisman, Herbert Neal *dentist, financial planner*

MISSOURI

Chesterfield
Biebel, Curt Fred, Jr. *dentist*

Hazelwood
Stuart, Gordon Edgar *dentist*

Kansas City
Burk, Norman *oral surgeon*

Richmond
Fawks, Steven W. *dentist*

Saint Louis
Dalin, Jeffrey Brian *dentist*
Isselhard, Donald Edward *dentist*
Osborn, Mark Eliot *dentist*
Schmidt, Gunter *dentist*

NEBRASKA

Fremont
Callaway, Richard Earl *dentist*
Roesch, Robert Eugene *dentist*

Hastings
McPherson, Robert Eugene *dentist*

Lincoln
Chisholm, George Nickolaus *dentist*

Omaha
Triolo, Peter T. *dental researcher, educator*
Zaiman, K. Robert *dentist*

NORTH DAKOTA

Williston
Bekkedahl, Brad Douglas *dentist*

OHIO

Cleveland
Goodman, Donald Joseph *dentist*
Montgomery, Gary *dentist*
Neuger, Sanford *orthodontics educator*
Robertson, Edward Neil *dentist*

Columbus
Buchsieb, Walter Charles *orthodontist*
Jolly, Daniel Ehs *dental educator*
Patrick, George Milton *dentist*
Stevenson, Robert Benjamin, III *prosthodontist, writer*

Cuyahoga Falls
Barsan, Robert Blake *dentist*

Euclid
Curran, James Francis *dentist*

Fairfield
Cutter, John Michael *dentist*

Hilliard
Relle, Attila Tibor *dentist, geriodontist*

Hubbard
Rose, Ernst *dentist*

Lancaster
Burns, Glenn Richard *dentist*

Milford
Egbert, Randall H. *dentist, financial consultant*

North Royalton
Iacobelli, Mark Anthony *dentist*

Norwalk
Heidelberg, Helen Susan Hatvani *dentist*

Uniontown
Naugle, Robert Paul *dentist*

Willoughby
Stern, Michael David *dentist*

SOUTH DAKOTA

Howard
Hattervig, Robin Lynn *dentist*

Martin
Gunner, Lawrence George *dentist*

Rapid City
Donhiser, William James *pediatric dentist*
Ray, Charles Joseph *dentist*

WISCONSIN

Beloit
Green, Harold Daniel *dentist*

Green Bay
Martens, Donald Mathias *orthodontist*
Swetlik, William Philip *orthodontist*

Madison
Wanek, Ronald Melvin *orthodontist*

Milwaukee
Bogdon, Glendon Joseph *orthodontist*
Scrabeck, Jon Gilmen *dental eductor*
Ziegler, Charles Louis *retired dentist*

Racine
Sikora, Suzanne Marie *dentist*

Wausau
Derwinski, Dennis Anthony *dentist*
Prehn, Donald Frederick *dentist*

ADDRESS UNPUBLISHED

Hoffman, Jerry Irwin *dental educator*
McHugh, Earl Stephen *dentist*
Paris, David Andrew *dentist*
Tiersky, Terri S. *dentist, lawyer*
Torok, John Anthony, III *dentist, financial analyst, portfolio manager*

HEALTHCARE: HEALTH SERVICES

UNITED STATES

ARIZONA

Tucson
Erickson, Whitney Jaye *critical care nurse*

FLORIDA

Bradenton
Forgus, Ronald Henry *psychology educator*

HAWAII

Honolulu
Bergholz, George Frederick *activity therapist*

ILLINOIS

Abbott Park
Hecker, Lawrence Harris *industrial hygienist*

Alsip
Woodson, Donna Marie *physical therapist, Franciscan sister*

Alton
Edmiston, Delores P. *nurse*
Forsee, Sherri Dayle *intensive care nurse*
Waller, Arlou Gill *retired mental health specialist*

Argonne
Masek, Mark Joseph *laboratory administrator*

Arlington Heights
Kennedy, Sandra Anne *physical therapist*
Lewin, Pearl Goldman *psychologist*

Aurora
Johnson, Therese Marie Browne *admissions counselor*

Barrington
Dick, Patricia A. *counselor*
Schaefer, Mary Ann *health facility administrator, consultant*
Williamson-Stoutenburg, Jane Sue *nurse practitioner*

Bartlett
Brandys, Vincent Walter, Jr. *optometrist, consultant*

Bedford Park
Spiegel-Hopkins, Phyllis Marie *psychotherapist*

Belleville
Baer, Scott E. *social worker*
Richerson, Paula Kay *hospice nurse, school nurse*

Bellwood
McCullough-Wiggins, Lydia Statoria *pharmacist, consultant*
Tolan, Mary C. *pediatric nurse practitioner, educator*

Bensenville
Pippin, James Rex *health care company executive, educator*

Berwyn
Sedlak, Richard *naturopath, physical therapist*

Bloomington
Dickson, Robert Frank *nursing home executive*
Markwood, Alan Jeffrey *health association administrator*

Blue Island
King, John (Jack) *human services administrator*

Bolingbrook
Price, Theodora Hadzisteliou *individual and family therapist*

Burr Ridge
Hatch, Edward William (Ted Hatch) *health care executive*

Carbondale
Buckley, John Joseph, Jr. *health care executive*
Bukonda, Ngoyi K. Zacharie *health care management educator*
Firestein, Beth Ann *psychologist*
Tinsley, Diane Johnson *psychologist, educator*

Carterville
Miller, Thomas Michael *physical therapist, educator*

Carthage
Moore, Richard Alan *optometrist*

Champaign
Andresen, Graciela Vazquez *clinical psychologist*
Banich, Marie Therese *neuropsychologist*
Gerth, Sharon Ann *adult health nurse, educator*
Hogan, Robert Kevin *rehabilitation services professional*
Kelly, Gay Anne *social worker, educator*
Leung, Paul *psychologist, rehabilitation educator*
Schiro-Geist, Chrisann *rehabilitation counselor*
Tracey, Terence John *psychology educator*

Chester
Beal, Wanda Elnora *psychologist, writer*

Chicago
Ansfield, Richard Morry *home health services executive*
Anthony-Perez, Bobbie Cotton Murphy *psychology educator, researcher*
Arekapudi, Kumar Vijaya Vasantha *sanitarian, real estate agent*
Balla, (Ferenc) Bulcsu *hospital manager, clinical engineer*
Beser, Roberta Ruth (Bobbie Beser) *physical therapy company executive*
Betz, Ronald Philip *pharmacist*
Cairns, Lindsey Elizabeth *health and human services administrator, planner*
Carney, Jean Kathryn *psychologist*
Champion, Martin R. *health facility administrator, consultant*
Ciosek, Nancy Carol *dietitian, educator*
Cohn, Anne Harris *health planner, health science association administrator*
Conlon, Patrick C. *health facility administrator, nurse educator*
Crawford, Jean Andre *clinical therapist*
D'Andrea, Deborah Dawn *nursing consultant, critical care nurse*
Davis, Danny K. *healthcare consultant, educator*
Deppe, Andrew DeNyse *health care systems planner*
Dickerson, Martha Ann *health facility administrator*
di Menza, Salvatore *psychologist*
Dougherty, Janet Kay *ambulatory surgery and recovery room nurse*
Dudek, Felicia Anne *rehabilitation counselor*
Falconer, Judith Ann *occupational therapist, educator*
Feldman, Edwin *health care executive, internist, cardiologist*
Gervais, Vickii *midwife*
Giannopoulos, Joanne *pharmacist, consultant*
Goldsmith, Ethel Frank *medical social worker*
Grossman, Lisa Robbin *clinical psychologist, lawyer*
Hartman, David Elliott *psychologist*
Hedegard, James Meredith *psychology educator, researcher*
Hirsch, Syrola Ruth *gerontology rehabilitation nurse*
Hudik, Martin Francis *hospital administrator, educator*
Jackson, Donald Ernest *health facility administrator*
Johnson, Karla J. *counselor*
Kay, Richard M. *physician assistant*
Keating, Pamela Joan *nurse anesthetist*
Kremer, Michael John *nurse anesthetist*
Lessick, Mira Lee *nursing educator*
Ling, Kathryn Wrolstad *health association administrator*
Lopez, Jacqueline *dance therapist*
Mack, William Joseph *psychotherapist, rehabilitation specialist*
Mackel-Rice, Gwendolyn Rosetta *social worker, foundation program officer*
McGinn, Patricia Ferris *professional counselor*
Mecklenburg, Gary Alan *hospital executive*
Moretti, Robert James *psychologist, educator*
Mugnaini, Enrico *biobehavioral sciences and psychology educator, researcher, consultant*
Muñoz, Romeo Solano *audio visual curator, educator*
Muthuswamy, Petham Padayatchi *pulmonary medicine and critical care specialist*
Nehring, Wendy Marie *pediatrics nurse*
Olson, Walter Steven *psychologist, educator*
Osowiec, Darlene Ann *clinical psychologist, educator, consultant*
Pesavento, Mari Jo *physical therapist*
Pisciotta, Vivian Virginia *psychotherapist*

Pray, Merle Evelyn *nurse psychotherapist, educator*
Preisler, Harvey D. *medical facility administrator, medical educator*
Rahman, Desirée *healthcare administrator*
Raich, Susan Elizabeth *kinesiotherapist, educator*
Reed, Vastina Kathryn (Tina Reed) *child psychotherapist*
Reilly, Joan Rita *nurse practitioner, educator, school nurse*
Rogalski, Carol Jean *clinical psychologist, educator*
Rothman, Jerry Jay *health facility administrator*
Russell, Lillian *medical, surgical nurse*
Sanders, Jacquelyn Seevak *psychologist, educator*
Schwartz, Eliezer Lazar *psychologist, educator*
Simons, Helen *school psychologist, psychotherapist*
Sladen, Bernard Jacob *psychologist*
Smart, Kathryn Alene *rehabilitation nurse*
Stepanski, Edward Jerome *psychologist*
Stratton, Julius Augustus *psychologist, consultant*
Surgi, Elizabeth Benson *veterinarian*
Tipp, Karen Lynn Wagner *school psychologist*
Tolan, Patrick Henry *psychology educator*
Treger, Harvey *social work educator*
Weiss, Susan Christine *nuclear medicine-radiation technologist, educator*
Zelko, Frank Anthony *neuropsychologist, educator*
Zoloto, Jerrold Albert *psychologist, consultant*

Collinsville
Fortae, Mary Ann *hospice nurse*

Danville
Pfeifer, Eugene *clinical pharmacist, nursing home consultant*

Darien
Klassek, Christine Paulette *behavioral scientist*

Decatur
Halsema, Barbara Ann *geriatrics nurse*
Litchfield, Jean Anne *nurse*
Stone, Timothy Donald, Jr. *health care executive*

Deerfield
Halpin, Mary Elizabeth *psychologist*
Hicks, Judith Eileen *nursing administrator*

Delavan
Alexander, Greta Belle *parapsychologist*

Des Plaines
D'Anca, John Arthur *psychotherapist, educator*
Herter, Joyce Mae *registered nurse*
Nighorn, Sharon Kay *nurse educator, psychotherapist*

Dixon
Belcher-Redebaugh-Levi, Caroline Louise *nursing home administrator, nurse*
Edelson, David *hospital administrator*
Heitzler, Becky Virginia *clinical psychologist*

Dolton
Nidetz, Myron Philip *health care delivery systems consultant, medical administrator, educator*

Downers Grove
DiFilippo, Judith Muraida *rehabilitation nurse*
Dire, Jeffrey Michael *mariage and family therapist, pastoral counselor*
Feeney, Don Joseph, Jr. *psychologist*
Gioioso, Joseph Vincent *psychologist*
Soder-Alderfer, Kay Christie *counseling administrator*
Stitnizky, John Louis *health facilities and hospital services professional*

Dunlap
Hanard, Patricia Ann *clinical nurse specialist*

Dupo
Gallamore, Betty Lou *nurse*

East Peoria
Potter, Jack Arthur *optometrist*

Edwardsville
Adkerson, Donya Lynn *clinical counselor*
Svoboda, Donna Lee *neonatal nurse*

Effingham
Shetler, Christopher David *chiropractor*

Elgin
Sekhon, Jasmeet M. *psychologist*

Elk Grove Village
Mogielski, Phyllis Ann *health association administrator, psychotherapist*

Elmhurst
Dallas, Daniel George *social worker*

Evanston
Cheatham, Mary Ann *auditory physiologist, educator, researcher*
Eagly, Alice Hendrickson *social psychology educator*
Eisen, Marlene Ruth *psychologist, educator*
Haimowitz, Morris Loeb *social psychologist*
Koenigsberg, Judith Z. Nulman *clinical psychologist*
Mineka, Susan *psychology educator*
Pewick, Harold Eugene *social worker*
Sweet, Jerry James *clinical psychologist*
Thompson, Leigh Lassiter *psychologist, educator*
White, Sylvia Frances *gerontology home care nurse, consultant*

Evergreen Park
Allison, Ellen Magdalen *critical care nurse*

Flossmoor
Thompson, Carolyn Wynelle *psychologist, behavioral healthcare executive*

Freeport
Goers, Sarajane *community education nurse*
Hasting, Sharon Ruth *pediatric nurse*
Todd, Jeffrey Warren *public health administrator*
Weaver, Michael Glenn *pharmacist*

Galèna
Alexander, Barbara Leah Shapiro *clinical social worker*

Galesburg
McAndrew, Francis Thomas *psychology educator*
Taylor, Debora Dianne *home health nurse*

Geneva
Abts, Gwyneth Hartmann *dietitian*

Gillespie
Rogers, Patricia G. *nursing administrator*

Glen Ellyn
Kaleba, Richard Joseph *healthcare consultant*
Shekleton, Maureen E. *respiratory nurse, educator*

Glenview
Coulson, Elizabeth Anne *physical therapy educator*

Grand Ridge
Goodchild, Rosina Ann *community health nurse*

Granite City
Barnett, Melinda Montgomery *counselor, psychology educator*
Washington, Marilyn Garrison *health care educator*

Grayslake
Carey, David Arthur *physical therapist*
Hassett, Jacquelyn Ann *retired nurse*

Gurnee
Joy, Marilyn D. *nurse*

Harrisburg
Endsley, Jane Ruth *nursing educator*
Rushing, Philip Dale *retired social worker*

Hazel Crest
Clements-Sarber, Mary Kathy *rehabilitation nurse*
Kaumeyer, Gregory Walter *physical therapist, athletic trainer*

Hillsboro
Herrmann, Jane Marie *physical therapist*

Hillsdale
Frels, Lois Marian Parnell (Mrs. Calvin Edwin Frels) *nursing educator, consultant, researcher*

Hines
Cummings, Joan E. *health facility administrator, educator*

Hinsdale
Burton, Glendean Mae *maternal child health consultant, educator*
Grossman, Kenneth Cedric *health facility director*
Migliorino, Caroline Milano *nursing consultant*

Hoffman Estates
Baldwin, Helaine Rae *clinical psychologist*

Ina
Shaw, Patricia Marie *home care nurse*

Irvington
Van Cleve, Sandra Rose *retired nursing educator*

Joliet
Cochran, Mary Ann *nurse educator*
Dastych, Diane Sue *critical care nurse*
Lynch, Priscilla A. *nursing educator, therapist*
Stewart, Franklin David *social worker*
Vandevender, Deborah Ann *critical care nurse*

Kampsville
Schumann, Alice Melcher *medical technologist, educator, sheep farmer*

Kankakee
Schroeder, David Harold *health care facility executive*

La Grange
Mazzuca, Robin Lynn *nurse, paramedic*
Rogala, Richard Edward *psychologist*

Lake Forest
Murphy, D. Evan *consulting psychologist*

Libertyville
Glenn, Claudia Ann *physical therapist*
Mikaelian, Marisa Gederian *physical therapist, business owner*

Lisle
Weis, Timothy Charles *healthcare executive, consultant*

Lombard
Beideman, Ronald Paul *chiropractor, college dean*

Madison
Holt, Dorothy Jean *critical care nurse*

Manteno
Balgeman, Richard Vernon *radiology administrator, alcoholism counselor*

Mapleton
Hayes, Debra Troxell *family nurse practitioner*

Maryville
Dalton, Patricia Joyce *medical technologist*
Stark, Patricia Ann *psychologist, educator*

Maywood
Cannon, Valerie Lynn *medical laboratory professional*
Walker, Edwin Hockaday, IV *alcohol and drug abuse services professional*

Mc Cook
Cullen-Benson, Scott Paul *employee assistance professional*

Mc Henry
Duel, Ward Calvin *health care consultant*

Midlothian
Sawatski, Sheila Marie *cardio-thoracic nurse*

Morton
Kelly, Norma Ruth *nursing educator, medical surgical nurse*

Mount Prospect
Bertch, Karen Elizabeth *pharmacist, educator*

Mount Sterling
Kropp, Nancy Ann *public health nurse*

Mount Vernon
Gibbons, Larry V. *laboratory director*

Naperville
Anderson, Deborah Kay *physical therapist*
Cunningham, Patrick Joseph, III *therapist*
Monyak, Wendell Peter *pharmacist*
Poole, Brenda Lynne *post-anesthesia nurse*

Niles
Silverman, Harry Mark *physical therapist*

North Riverside
Galluppi, Thomas Lawrence *healthcare executive*

Northbrook
Bryant, James Hamilton, III *health care executive*
Kahn, Sandra S. *psychotherapist*
Metres, Philip John, Jr. *psychologist*
Noeth, Carolyn Frances *speech and language pathologist*
Rudnick, Ellen Ava *health care executive*

Oak Brook
Bower, Barbara Jean *nurse*
Noel, Tallulah Ann *healthcare industry executive*
Schultz, Karen Rose *clinical social worker, author, publisher, speaker*

Oak Lawn
Massura, Eileen Kathleen *family therapist*

Oak Park
Goold, Florence Wilson *occupational therapist*
Strauss, Jeffrey Lewis *healthcare executive*

Oakbrook Terrace
Juneau, Sharyn S. *healthcare administrator*

Okawville
Pomeroy, Bruce Marcel *critical care nurse, educator*

Olney
Heth, Diana Sue *therapist*
Knox, Elisabeth Ann *nurse, educator*

Olympia Fields
Haley, David Alan *preferred provider organization executive*

Onarga
Wilken, Caroline Doane *critical care, emergency, recovery room, and medical/surgical nurse*

Orland Park
McCoy, Henrika *social worker*

Palatine
Benzies, Bonnie Jeanne *clinical and industrial psychologist*

Park Forest
Steinmetz, Jon David *mental health executive, psychologist*

Park Ridge
Emanuel, Brian Patrick *sanitarian*
Horton, Betty Joan *anesthesia nurse, organization administrator*
Vaal, Joseph John, Jr. *psychologist*

Pekin
Goodale, JoAnn Olson *rehabilitation nurse*

Peoria
Bussone, Frank Joseph *health association administrator, television broadcaster*
Lutz, Sandra Jeaniene *family nurse practitioner*
McCollum, Jean Hubble *medical assistant*
Vyverberg, Robert William *mental health facility administrator*
Zehr, Eric Wayne *healthcare administrator*

Peru
Lane, Patricia Peyton *nursing consultant*
Powell, Robert Charles *marriage and family counselor*

Philo
Martin, Earl Dean *physical therapist*

Quincy
Kewney, Rhonda Kathryn *mental health service professional*
Little, Harold Eugene *physical therapist*

River Forest
McGuire, Timothy Joseph *physical therapist, video consultant*

Rock Island
Hartsock, Jane Marie *nurse, educator*

Rockford
Cohen, Phyllis Joanne *nurse*
Ege, Scott Charles *physical therapist*
Erickson, Margaret Ann *physical therapist*
L'Heureux, Dennis Paul *chief health system information officer*
McFalls, Jacquelyn Kay *obstetrics nurse*
Mc Nelly, Frederick Wright, Jr. *psychologist*
Nettleton, Maryanne *veterinarian*
Price, Forest Walter *clinical social worker*

Rockton
Muldowney, Kerry Phillip *psychologist, sociologist, educator*

Rolling Meadows
Saporta, Jack *psychologist, educator*

Rosemont
Shou, Sharon Louise Wikoff *rehabilitation counselor*

Saint Charles
Carpenter, Mary Laure *hospital administrator*

Savoy
Ridgway, Marcella Davies *veterinarian*

Schaumburg
Catlin, Susan Lynn *alcohol and drug abuse psychotherapist*
Rovin, Adrienne Lee *school social worker*
Wenzel, Ann Marie Price *women's health nurse*

Skokie
Damon, Christopher Andrew *health association executive, lawyer*
Reisinger, James John *psychologist, educator*
Schecter, Jerry Sherwin *psychologist*
Villalon, Dalisay Manuel *nurse, real estate broker*
Yogev, Sara *psychologist*

Smithfield
Corsaw, Ardith *geriatrics nurse, administrator*

South Holland
Poprick, Mary Ann *psychologist*

Sparta
Sais, Richard Jon *physical therapist*

Springfield
Campbell, Kathleen Charlotte Murphey *audiology educator and researcher*
Indermark, Ellen Ann *therapist*
Koester, Jeffrey Allen *physical therapist*
Mazzotti, Richard Rene *pharmacist*
O'Connor, Sister Gertrude Theresa *clinical nurse specialist in surgery and anesthesia*
O'Connor, Timothy Lewis *health science association administrator*
Stratton, Richard LeRoy *optometrist, educator*

Sterling
Finney, Thomas D. *chiropractor*
Pignatelli, Ermenia R. *retired physical therapist*

Sycamore
Patten, Maurine Diane *psychologist*

University Park
Leftwich, Robert Eugene *oncological nursing educator*

Urbana
Beasley, Val Richard *veterinarian educator*
Freehill-Davis, Therese Rose *physical therapist*
Haschek-Hock, Wanda Maria *veterinary pathologist, toxicologist, educator, researcher*
Himens, Mary Kathryn *psychotherapist, consultant*

Vandalia
Denning, Melinda Sue *nurse*

Villa Park
Wunderman, Lorna Ellen *healthcare strategic planner, biostatistician*

Virginia
Sudbrink, Becky L. *medical, surgical nurse*

Watseka
Giglio, Nicki Sue *critical care nurse, administrator*

Waukegan
Dahl, Marilyn Gail *psychotherapist, nurse*
Hennessy, Margaret Barrett *health care executive*

Westmont
McConnell, Patricia Ann *health facility administrator*

Westville
Hammer, John Henry, II *hospital administrator*

Wheaton
Koenigsmark, Joyce Elyn Sladek *women's health nurse*

Wilmette
Marcus, Jacqueline Brasnick *nutritionist*
Randolph, Lillian Larson *medical association executive*

Winnetka
Dailey, Mary *counselor, educator*
VanBremen, Lee *medical association executive*

Wood Dale
Rothert, Cathy Cotton *physical therapist*
Thompson, John Henry *consulting executive*

Wood River
Cox, Mary Linda *maintenance industry executive*

INDIANA

Anderson
Whitaker, Audie Dale *hospital laboratory medical technologist*

Bloomington
Fraker, Anne Turner *research consultant*
Goss, David Arthur *optometry educator, researcher*
Karkut, Richard Theodore *clinical psychologist*
Kohr, Roland Ellsworth *retired hospital administrator*
Morrison, Dennis Patrick *psychologist*

Bluffton
Habegger, Cynthia A. *nursing administrator*

Brownsburg
Weddell, Linda Anne *speech and language pathologist*

Chesterton
Cuttill, Raymond Francis, Jr. *psychologist*

Clinton
Shew, Rose Jean *nurse*

Columbus
Harney, Joyce Ann *nursing educator, administrator*

Crawfordsville
Michal, Philip Quentin *veterinarian, mayor*

Crown Point
Villarruel, Mayola Lara *medical surgical nurse, administrator*

Evansville
Cox, Vande Lee *critical care nurse*
Dice, Jeffrey Niles *health care administrator*
Kuric, Judi Lynn Popplewell *clinical nurse specialist, consultant*
Lichlyter, Sharon M. *nurse*
Offerman, Ann Gudkese *rehabilitation nurse*
Ragsdale, Rex H. *health facility administrator, physician*
Tank, Robert T. *physical therapist*
Will, Jane Anne *psychologist*
Witte, Jeffrey Robert *physical therapist assistant*
Young Lively, Sandra Lee *nurse*

Fishers
Chojnacki, Paul Ervin *pharmacist, pharmaceutical company official*

Fort Wayne
Brackett-Burgette, Eileen Yann *healthcare administrator*
Frantz, Dean Leslie *psychotherapist*
Gross, Kelly Lynn *physical therapist assistant, aerobics instructor*
Kennedy, Elizabeth *health facility administrator*
King, Alice Mae *occupational health nurse*
Marsden, David Lawrence *psychiatric technician, writer*
Meyer, Brenda Sue *critical care and home health nurse*
Miller, Diane Kay *nursing educator*
O'Connell, Kathleen LeClear *nursing educator*

Gary
Bennett, Richard Carl *social worker*
Hull, Grafton Hazard, Jr. *social work educator*

Goshen
Gongwer, Judith Marlene Beck *obstetrical nurse*
Stiver, James Frederick *pharmacist, health physicist, administrator, scientist*

Hagerstown
Elkins, Sharon Patricia *nursing educator*

Hope
Golden, Eloise Elizabeth *community health nurse*

Huntingburg
Tretter, Theresa Lynn *physical therapist*

Huntington
Sowash, Becky Maria *physical therapist*

Indianapolis
Brady, Mary Sue *nutrition and dietetics educator*
Bramwell, Marvel Lynnette *nurse, social worker*
Brashear, Diane Lee *marital and sex therapist*
Buhner, Byron Bevis *health science facility administrator*
Clark, Pamela Kay *school counselor*
Crisp, Cheryl Lee *pediatric rehabilitation nurse*
Dieterlen, Paul Leroy *veterinarian*
Duffy, Kathleen May *retired community health nurse*
Featherstonaugh, Henry Gordon *psychologist*
Fox, Donald Lee *mental health counselor, consultant*
Haddad, Freddie Duke, Jr. *hospital development administrator*
Handel, David Jonathan *health care administrator*
Henry, Thomas W. *physical therapist*
Ingersoll, Gail Laura *nursing administrator, nursing educator, nursing researcher*
Jahnke, Pamella Emrick *emergency nurse*
Kildsig, Nancy Evaline *consultant pharmacist*
McWilliams, Cynthia Lynn *public health nurse*
Moelhman, Amy Jo *social worker*
Moon, Cindi A. *critical care nurse*
Mull, Theresa Diane *physical therapist*
Newton, Pynkerton Dion *chiropractor*
Rae, Judith *individual, couple and family therapist*
Rhodes Rowley, Mary Louise *school psychologist*
Richardson, Mildred Tourtillott *psychologist*
Riegsecker, Marvin Dean *pharmacist, state senator*
Savage, Audrey C. *psychotherapist*
Treylinek, Donna Marie *physical therapist*
Vetere, Colleen Marie *nurse*
Wagner, Marion Kathryn *social work educator*
Watt, John Hayden *pharmacist*

Jeffersonville
Rhodes, Betty Fleming *rehabilitation services professional, nurse*

Kokomo
Coppock, Janet Elaine *mental health nurse*

Lafayette
Fleming, Marianne Helen *physical therapist*
Nelson, Teri Lynn *social worker*
Thomas, Cynthia Elizabeth *advanced practice nurse*

Lawrenceburg
Taylor, Donna Bloyd *vocational rehabilitation consultant*

Linden
Eutsler, Therese Anne *physical therapist*

Linton
Wathen, Karen Denise *home health care nurse*

Madison
Flotemersch, Janet Sylvia *dietician*

Marengo
Dittmer, Sharon Juanita *prison nurse*

Marion
Harwood, Virginia Ann *retired nursing educator*
Wiseman, C. Marvin (Marv Wiseman) *marriage and family therapist*

Merrillville
Byers, Susannah Antoinette *nurse practitioner*

Michigan City
Brown, Arnold *physical therapy consultant*

Mishawaka
Erdel, Sally Elizabeth *nurse*
Goebel, Richard Alan *veterinarian*
Neuhoff, Kathleen Toepp *veterinarian, podiatrist*

Muncie
Church, Jay Kay *psychologist, educator*
Irvine, Phyllis Eleanor Kuhnle *nursing educator, administrator*
Siela, Debra Lynne *pulmonary nurse specialist*

Munster
Palmer, Marcia Ann *healthcare management consultant, pharmacist*

New Albany
Kost, Malinda Lenz *home health nurse*

New Castle
Walburn, John Clifford *mental health services professional*

Newburgh
Roberts, Mary Lynn *pediatrics mental health nurse*

North Manchester
Seward, Steven Le Mar *optometrist*

Pendleton
Grider, Kathy Jill *medical record professional*

Portland
Countryman, Ellen Witt *hospital administrator*

Princeton
Robb, Kimberly Kay *critical care nurse, medical/surgical nurse, infant immunization nurse, nursing administrator*

Richmond
Bowles, Frank William, Jr. *health facility administrator*

Shelbyville
Mitton, Michael Paul *nurse anesthesist*

South Bend
Bella, Eugene Alan *health systems company official*
Burzynski, Thomas F. *hospice administrator*
Edwards, Scott Brian *health facility administrator*
Przybylski, Diane Joan *women's health nurse*
Szigeti, Michelle Marie *critical care nurse*

Terre Haute
Coe, Michual William *physical therapist*
Green, Sally Jane *surgical nurse*
Hightower, Jeanne Jackson *nursing administrator*
Moan, Jodi Ann *rehabilitation services professional and camp director*

Valparaiso
Carr, Wiley Nelson *hospital administrator*
Veatch, Jean Louise Corty *telemetry nurse*
White, Linda Sue *cardiology technician*

Vincennes
Templin, Jill L. *physical therapist assistant*

West Lafayette
Forsyth, Dale Marvin *animal nutritionist, educator*
Haworth, Debra Eloise Dill *physical therapist*
Lewis, Hugh B. *veterinary medicine educator*
Schweickert, Richard Justus *psychologist, educator*
Vandergraff, Donna Jean *dietitian*

Westville
Muha-Ronneau, Carol *medical surgical nurse, critical care nurse*

Whiting
Kalina, Christine Marie *occupational health nurse*

Winchester
Tanner, Judith Ann *retired speech-language pathologist*

IOWA

Altoona
Brown, Linda Diane *women's health nurse*

Ames
Ahrens, Franklin Alfred *veterinary pharmacology educator*
Hanisch, Kathy Ann *psychologist*
Ross, Richard Francis *veterinarian, microbiologist, educator*
Wegner, Waldo Wilbert *retirement community and health care facility executive*

Ankeny
Duffy, Pamela Ann *physical therapist*

Bettendorf
Hanson, Ronald Tilford *mental health counselor, psychotherapist, pastor*
Mosby, John Singleton, Jr. *clinical administrator, educator, consultant*

Burlington
Cowles, Rollin James, III *public health administrator*

Cedar Falls
Gilgen, Albert Rudolph *psychologist, educator*
Higgins, Barbara Lorene *school psychologist*

Cedar Rapids
Steil, Michelle Dianne Dunagan *nurse*
Thomas, Margaret Catherine *physical therapist, educator*
Ziese, Nancylee Hanson *social worker*

Charles City
Schober, William Rudolph (Bud) *retired physical therapist*

Colfax
Ramsden, Mary Catherine *substance abuse specialist*

Council Bluffs
Hopp, Dennis William *physical therapist*
Lane, Carol Elaine *nurse*

Danbury
Teut, Kandi L. *emergency medical technician*

Davenport
Lampe, Katherine Evelyn *physical therapist, educator*

Des Moines
Demorest, Allan Frederick *retired psychologist*
Goldsmith, Janet Jane *pediatric nurse practitioner*
Graziano, Charles Dominic *pharmacist*
Gross, Mary Elizabeth *pharmacy manager, educator*
Hall, Donald Vincent *social worker*
Kramer, Mary Elizabeth *health services executive, state legislator*
Lund, Doris Hibbs *retired dietitian*
Reitinger, Thomas Anthony *hospital administrator*
Wallace, Samuel Taylor *hospital administrator*

Donnellson
Lowenberg, Lorraine Lynette *psychiatric and mental health nurse*

Dubuque
Brundage, Victoria Conlin *past psychotherapist, social worker*
Chara, Paul John *psychology educator*

Forest City
Steiger, Sherry Hansen *author, lecturer, counselor*
Vammen, James Oliver *human services administrator*

Glenwood
Campbell, William Edward *state hospital school administrator*

Greene
Landers, Patricia Elaine *nursing supervisor*

Grinnell
Gibson, Janet Marie *psychology educator*

Hawarden
Berreth, Michelle Renée *medical surgical nurse*

Independence
Hammer, Robert Eugene *psychologist*

Indianola
Hutchinson, Eleanor Louise *nursing administrator*

Iowa City
Berg, Mary Jaylene *pharmacy educator, researcher*
Colloton, John William *university health care executive*
Crowley, Ann M. *nutrition educator*
Nathan, Peter E. *psychologist, educator*
Wurster, Dale Erwin *pharmacy educator, university dean*

Jesup
Loeb, DeAnn Jean *nurse*

Knoxville
Chang, Theodore Chien-Hsin *psychologist*
Joslyn, Wallace Danforth *psychologist*
Ribar, Dixie Lee *nursing administrator*
Taylor, Mary Kay *geriatrics nurse*

Lake Mills
Thompson, Jeannine Lucille *community health nurse*

Marion
Noyes, Richard Francis *optometrist*

Marshalltown
Engesser, Karen Lynne Sharp *physical therapist*

Mason City
Davenport, Mary Erickson *physical therapist, swim coach*
Rosenberg, Dale Norman *psychology educator*
Walderbach, Kurt Michael *physical therapist*

Mount Pleasant
Smith, Mary Lou Braun *psychiatric-mental health nurse*

New London
Shores, Robert Phelps *pharmacist, business owner*

Osage
Christensen, Pamela Karen *pediatric nurse*

Oskaloosa
Gleason, Carol Ann *mental health nurse, educator*

Perry
Thomsen, Pamela Dee *long-term care education director*

Shenandoah
Hanna, Suzanne Louise *nurse*

Waterloo
Nielsen, Gail Ann *radiologic technologist*

West Des Moines
Gregg, Gina Kay *crisis care manager behavioral health*
Zimmerman, Jo Ann *health services and educational consultant, former lieutenant governor*

KANSAS

Abilene
Gattshall, Wanda G. *physical therapist assistant*

Atchison
Hackman, Edward Martin *hospital administrator*

Beloit
Kopsa, Gregory Joe *school psychologist*

Bonner Springs
Elliott-Watson, Doris Jean *psychiatric, mental health and gerontological nurse educator*

Colby
Downing, Maureen K. *nurse*
Morrison, James Frank *optometrist, state legislator*

Concordia
Johnson, Dorothy Phyllis *counselor, art therapist*

Dodge City
Briggs, Ada Jane *emergency nurse*
Williamson, Glenna Sue *physical therapist*

El Dorado
Edwards, Alisyn Arden *psychologist*

Fort Riley
Buchanan, Mary Ella *nurse*
Terry, Allan Keith *pharmacist, military officer*

Garden City
Japp, Nyla F. *infection control services administrator*
Schmidt, Patricia Ann *geriatrics nurse*

Goddard
Picotte, Susan Gaynel *geriatrics nurse, nursing educator, rehabilitation nurse*

Great Bend
Cavanaugh, Jean *medical secretary*

Hays
Curl, Eileen Deges *nursing educator*

Hutchinson
Bellamy, Joan Elizabeth *psychologist, consultant*

Kansas City
Boal, Marcia Anne Riley *clinical social worker, administrator*
Gilliland, Marcia Ann *nurse clinician, infection control specialist*
Shafer, Randall William *home health nurse*
Ternus, Jean Ann *nursing educator*

Larned
Davis, Mary Elizabeth *speech pathologist, educator, counselor*

Lawrence
Brehm, Jack Williams *social psychologist, educator*
Chambers, Donald Everard *social worker, educator*
Cohen, Valerie M. *physical therapist*
Frick, John William *health industry executive*
Loudon, Karen Lee *physical therapist*
Mc Coin, John Mack *social worker*
Searles, Lynn Marie *nurse*

Leavenworth
Andersen, Steve Richard *health care executive*

Leawood
Tonkens, Rebecca A. *maternal women's health nurse*

Lenexa
Koontz, Eva Isabelle *medical technologist*

Liberal
Doze, Carla Sue LaRue *critical care geriatrics nurse*

Manhattan
Pence, John Thomas *dietitian*

Mc Pherson
Fisher-Ross, Lisa Lynn *physical therapist*

Newton
Westerhaus, Catherine K. *social worker*

North Newton
Schroeder, Gregg LeRoy *critical care nurse*

Olathe
Jones, Robert Lyle *emergency medical services leader, educator*

Koch, Cory Lee *chiropractor*
Kolich, Cynthia Louise *emergency nurse*

Overland Park
FitzGerald, Thomas Joe *psychologist*
Pracht, Drenda Kay *psychologist*
Reeves-Dudley, Beverly Jayne *nurse anesthetist*

Riverton
Rose, Terri Kaye *obstetrical gynecological nurse practitioner, nurse midwife*

Saint John
Robinson, Alexander Jacob *clinical psychologist*

Salina
Maxwell, Evelyn Mae *whole health educator and consultant*

Shawnee
Douglass, Carol Suzanne *counselor*
Ray, Darrell W. *psychologist*

Shawnee Mission
Asher, Donna Thompson *psychiatric-mental health nurse*
Breen, Katherine Anne *speech and language pathologist*
Diehl, Nancy Elizabeth *physical therapist*
Endlich, Leatrice Ann *therapist*
Jones, George Humphrey *retired healthcare executive, hospital facilities and communications consultant*
Roosa, Jan Bertorotta *clinical psychologist*

Stilwell
Adams, Gary D. *physical therapist*

Topeka
Bartlett, Alice Brand *psychotherapist, educator, dean, researcher*
Calo-Iloreta, Maria Delia *nursing educator*
Cook, Marjorie Ellen Lind *nursing administrator*
Hancock, Doris Colleen *critical care nurse*
Lyon, Joanne B. *psychologist*
McMahon, Phyllis Oliver *physical therapist*
Varner, Charleen LaVerne McClanahan (Mrs. Robert B. Varner) *nutritionist, educator, administrator, dietitian*
Waters, Harold Arthur *veterinarian*

Wellington
Winn, Robert Cheever *rehabilitation services professional*

Wheaton
Willis, Joan Ellen *nurse*

Wichita
Clark, Susan Matthews *psychologist*
Dorr, Stephanie Tilden *psychologist*
Fields, Renee Christine *outpatient mental health therapist*
Healy, Patricia Colleen *social worker*
Johnson, Mary Lucille *nurse*
Sauder, Neil Eugene *critical care nurse*
Sundgren, Ann Christine *physical therapist*

Winfield
Hall, Lydia Jane *geriatrics nurse*
Laws, Carolyn Marie Roderick *medical surgical nurse, pediatrics nurse*
Schul, Bill Dean *psychological administrator, author*

KENTUCKY

Louisville
Fuller, Lee Dennison *nursing educator, therapist*
Yen, Yi-Mei *clinic nurse*

MASSACHUSETTS

Cambridge
Collins, Allan Meakin *cognitive scientist, psychologist, educator*

MICHIGAN

Albion
Hood, Terry Bryant *social worker, consultant*

Allen Park
Kirby, Dorothy Manville *social worker*
Rainey, Christine Rose *pharmacist, company executive*

Ann Arbor
Behling, Charles Frederick *psychology educator*
Bishop, Elizabeth Shreve *psychologist*
Brown-Chappell, Betty L. *social worker, educator*
Clark, Noreen Morrison *behavioral science educator, researcher*
Feingold, Eugene Neil *health services management and policy educator*
Gage, Lois Waite *nursing educator*
Gaston, Hugh Philip *marriage counselor, educator*
Gordon, Jesse Emmanuel *retired psychology educator*
Jackson, James Sidney *psychology educator*
Kennedy, Meri Beth *women's health nurse*
Manis, Melvin *psychologist, educator*
Mowbray, Carol Beatrice Thiessen *mental health researcher, social work educator*
Rogers, Laura Susan *nursing case management*
Shatz, Marilyn Joyce *psychologist*
Stevenson, Harold William *psychology educator*
Valenstein, Elliot Spiro *psychology educator*
Williams, Reg Arthur *nursing educator, software programmer*
Woronoff, Israel *retired psychology educator*
Zucker, Robert A(lpert) *psychologist*

Auburn Hills
Utley, Rose *nursing educator and researcher*

Battle Creek
Andert, Jeffrey Norman *clinical psychologist*
Cady, Patricia Ann *physical therapist assistant*
Davanzo, John Charles *emergency medical services educator*
Ross, M. Joanna *physical therapist*
Simmons, Barbara Jayne *physical therapist assistant*

Bay City
Coughlin, Mary Lynn *physical therapist*

Belleville
Bryant, James Patrick *medical technologist*

Bellevue
Shaw, Jannétte Sue *mental health nurse*

Benton Harbor
Alsbro, Donald Edgar *health educator*

Berrien Springs
Carlson, Gerhard Frederick *school psychologist*

Big Rapids
Burkholder, Gary Stephen *mental health nursing educator*
Uniacke, C(harles) Allyn *optometry educator, consultant*
Weinlander, Max Martin *retired psychologist*

Bingham Farms
Cheyne, Valorie E. *psychologist*

Birmingham
Denes, Michel Janet *physical therapist, consultant in rehabilitation*

Bloomfield Hills
Cowan, David Michael *neuropsychologist*
Millsap, Barbara Ann *clinical social worker*

Bloomingdale
Richter, Naomi Bernice *mental health nurse*

Brighton
Lamson, Evonne Viola *counselor, computer software company executive, consultant, pastor, Christian education administrator*
Mike, Edward Joseph *psychologist, consultant*

Caro
Mielke, Susan Kay *mental health nurse*

Centreville
Schwartz, Karon Stitt *nursing educator*

Cheboygan
Wise, Michael Stephen *hospice director*

Conklin
Kelly, Josephine Kaye *social worker*

Dearborn
Anderson, Linda Lee *oncology nurse*
Peacock, Inez W. *physical therapist*
Suchy, Susanne N. *nursing educator*
Waldecker, Thomas Raymond *social worker*

Detroit
Banks, Lois Michelle *nurse*
Berke, Amy Turner *health science association administrator*
Birdsong, Emil Ardell *psychologist*
Cantoni, Louis Joseph *psychologist, poet, sculptor*
Dooley, John Anthony *clinical psychologist, pain center director*
Felton, Patricia Ann *nurse, hospital administrator*
Good, Nancy Susan *health system administrator*
Hernandez, Wanda Grace *rehabilitation counselor, sales manager*
Jackson, Yvonne Denise *physical therapist*
Jirovec, Ronald Louis *social work educator*
Savoy, Suzanne Marie *critical care nurse*
Sugrue, Mary Sharon *epidemiology nurse*
Watson, Debraha Kafi *respiratory therapist*
Wesley, Ruby LaVerne *nursing educator, administrator, researcher*
Wesselmann, Glenn Allen *hospital executive*

East Lansing
Carleton, Carla Lou *theriogenologist, educator*
Karon, Bertram Paul *psychologist, educator*
Majors, Richard George *psychology educator*
McKinley, Camille Dombrowski *psychologist*
Overton, Sarita Rosa *psychologist*
Schemmel, Rachel Anne *food science and human nutrition educator, researcher*

Farmington
Cooper, Elaine Janice *physical therapist*

Farmington Hills
Abrams, Roberta Busky *hospital administrator, nurse*
McNamara, Ann Dowd *medical technologist*
Sobczak, Judy Marie *clinical psychologist*

Flint
McAlindon, Mary Naomi *healthcare information administrator*
Millon, Delecta Gay *nursing educator*
Speck, Hilda *retired social services administrator*
Woodman, Ellen Armstrong *nurse educator*

Franklin
DeBrincat, Susan Jeanne *nutritionist*
Sax, Mary Randolph *speech pathologist*

Fraser
Heilman, Kathryn *nurse, consultant*

Fruitport
Anderson, Frances Swem *nuclear medical technologist*

Grand Blanc
Reen, Terry Peter *social worker*

Grand Haven
Parmelee, Walker Michael *psychologist*

Grand Rapids
Critelli, Paul Joseph *psychologist*
Gemmell-Akalis, Bonni Jean *psychotherapist*
Kooistra, William Henry *clinical psychologist*
Kramer, Carol Gertrude *marriage and family counselor*
Laufer, Charles Davis *clinical psychologist*
MacDonald, David Richard *industrial psychologist*
Tafelski, Michael Dennis *psychologist*
Vander Goot, Mary Elizabeth *psychologist, educator*

Grosse Pointe
Linclau, Denise Marie *nursing administrator*

Harbor Springs
Bley, Margalo Anne *social worker*

Hastings
Adrounie, V. Harry *public health administrator, scientist, educator, environmentalist*

Hillman
Clay, Margaret Leone *community psychologist, consultant*

Houghton Lake
Marra, Samuel Patrick *retired pharmacist, small business owner*

Kalamazoo
Bennett, Arlie Joyce *clinical social worker*
Campbell, Raymond W. *surgical nurse*
Fenn, William Hartley *health care administrator*
Fredericks, Sharon Kay *nurses aide*
Loudermelt, Laura Alene *mental health nurse*
Maurer, Edward Lance *chiropractor, radiologist*
Walcott, Delores Deborah *psychologist, educator*
Wilson, Ronald J. *marriage and family therapist, educator*

Lake Orion
Tomaszewski, Kathleen Bernadette *social worker, educator*

Lansing
Heater, William Henderson *psychology educator*
Weidenbruch, Anna Mae *nurse*

Lincoln Park
Russell, Harriet Shaw *social worker*
Van Antwerp, George B. *human services administrator*

Livonia
Juenemann, Julie Ann *psychologist, educator*
McCoy, Joenne Rae *psychiatric clinic administrator*

Madison Heights
Wilson, Mary Louise *psychiatric nurse*

Marquette
Poindexter, Kathleen A. Krause *nursing educator, critical care nurse*

Mason
Frappier, Cara Munshaw *school social worker*
Ribby, Alice Marie *nurse*

Middleville
Miller, Stephen Bryan *social worker, marriage counselor*

Midland
Black, Jacinth Baublitz *clinical social worker*
Fogus, Kathleen Marie *nurse*
Taylor, Ann Siegrist *psychologist*
Zimostrad, Scott William *psychologist*

Muskegon
Mercer, Betty Deborah *electrologist, poet, writer, proofreader*

Niles
Fatum, Sandra Kaye *nurse*

Novi
Crane, Patricia Sue *probation services administrator, social worker*

Oakland
Spitsbergen, Dorothy May *children's healthcare specialist*

Okemos
Wolfe, Gail Sommers *veterinarian*

Otsego
Hearns, Patricia A. *nurse practitioner*

Petoskey
Umscheid, Christine *medical surgical and oncological nurse*

Plainwell
Ortiz-Button, Olga *social worker*

Portage
Yoder-Gagnon, Pamala S. *orthopedic nurse*

Richmond
White, Jeffery *emergency medical services executive*

Rochester
Jackson, A(ase) Osa Littrup *physical therapy educator*
Tunnecliffe, Daniel Lee *respiratory care administrator*

Royal Oak
Klosinski, Deanna Dupree *medical laboratory sciences educator*
Larson, Jean Ann *hospital administrator*
Myers, Kenneth Ellis *hospital administrator*

Saginaw
Bosco, Jay William *optometrist*
Shackelford, Martin Robert *social worker*

Saint Clair Shores
Neal-Vittiglio, Cynthia Karen *clinical psychologist*

Saint Joseph
Paden, Carolyn Eileen Belknap *dietitian*

Southfield
French, Diane Lynn *health facility administrator*
Griffin, Deborah Joyce *psychiatric-mental health nurse*
Krieger, Linda Annette *intensive care nurse*
Wagner, Muriel Ginsberg *nutrition therapist*

Sparta
Wallace, Kimberlee Belle *pharmacy educator, consultant*

Spring Arbor
Richard, Lyle Elmore *retired school social worker, consultant*

Spring Lake
Grable, R(eginald) Harold *psychologist*

Three Oaks
Jasper, Doris J. Berry *nurse*

Troy
Ireland, Delores W. (Dolly Ireland) *post-anesthesia nurse*
Potts, Anthony Vincent *optometrist, orthokeratologist*
Taber, Frances Kathryn *geriatrics nurse, administrator*
White, James, Jr. *psychiatric, mental health nurse, consultant*

University Center
May, Margrethe *allied health educator*

Warren
Bishai, Yousef B. *medical administrator*
McDonald, James Michael *employee counselor*

Wayland
Potts, Carol Jean Fox *geriatrics nurse, quality assurance coordinator*

West Bloomfield
Dvorkin, Louis *neuropsychologist*
Romero, Josefino Tabernilla *nurse anesthetist*
Sugintas, Nora Maria *veterinarian, scientist, medical company executive*

Westland
Gaipa, Nancy Christine *pharmacist*
Shaw, Randy Lee *human services administrator*

White Cloud
McCormick, James Hall *social services administrator*

Ypsilanti
Cantrell, Linda Maxine *counselor*
deSouza, Joan Melanie *psychologist*
English, Phyllis Jean *clinical psychologist*
Holland, Joy *health care facility executive*
Voight, Nancy Lee (Mrs. Jay Van Hoven) *counseling psychologist*
Westman, Alida Spaans *psychology educator*
Wilson, Lorraine M. *medical and surgical nurse, nursing educator*

Zeeland
Mast, Mae Jerene *nurse*

MINNESOTA

Bemidji
Christenson, Eileen Elaine *geriatrics nurse*

Blue Earth
Heetland, Dawn Michele *physical therapist*

Brainerd
McTernan, Ann Cibuzar *adult nurse practitioner*

Brooklyn Park
Frank, Paul Wilbur *social worker*

Cambridge
Lahr, John William *optometrist*
Werner, Glenn Allen *psychologist, administrator*

Duluth
Hoffman, Richard George *psychologist*
Larsen, Kathleen Mary *dietitian, program administrator*
Maypole, Donald Eugene *social work educator*
Murphy, Camille Suzanne *nurse*
Rodne, Kjell John *healthcare administrator*
Saari, Kathryn Celeste *public health nurse*
Taylor, Cecelia Monat *mental health nurse*

Eden Prairie
Faibisch, Loren *psychologist*

Edina
Pollock, Tony Joe *nurse consultant*

Fairmont
Hillestad, Donna Dawn *nurse*

Farmington
Davis, Alice Bernice Storlie *physical therapist*

Grand Rapids
Wood, Marlene Ann *nursing administrator*

Hastings
Blackie, Spencer David *physical therapist, administrator*

Lake Park
Offerdahl, Jack Albert *respiratory therapy administrator*

Lilydale
Kilbourne, Barbara Jean *health and human services consultant*

Mankato
Erickson-Weerts, Sally Annette *dietetics educator*
Heupel, Carol Collins *community health and womens health nurse educator*

Maple Grove
Manthei, Robin Dickey *research technician*

Maplewood
Charmoli, Margaret Charity *psychologist*

Minneapolis
Anderson, Geraldine Louise *laboratory scientist*
Barrada, Amr *psychotherapist*
Bartell, Scott Eugene *psychotherapist, social worker*
Budd, Elaine *social worker*
Dahl, Gerald LuVern *psychotherapist, educator, consultant, writer*
Durdahl, Carol Lavaun *psychiatric nurse*
Ettinger, M(artha) Jeanne *retired nurse*
Hesse, Bruce Edward *family therapist, social worker*
Jeffrey-Smith, Lilli Ann *biofeedback specialist, educator, administrator*
Johnston, Holly Watkins *medical surgical nurse*
Kennon, Rozmond Herron *physical therapist*
Keyes, Lea Rae *healthcare and case management consultant*
Kozberg, Steven Freed *psychologist*
Latts, Sander Morris *psychology educator, counselor*
Marks, Florence Carlin Elliott *nursing informaticist*
Miller, Susan Kay *nursing administrator*
Nightingale, Edmund Joseph *clinical psychologist, educator*
Remmel, Rory Patrick *pharmacy educator*
Russell, Michael Erwin *industrial hygienist*
Russomondo-Morehead, Annette Marie *disabled children's facility administrator, child advocate*
Schwartz, Howard Wyn *health facility administrator*
Smayling, Lyda Mozella *speech pathologist*
Stoikes, Mary Eloise *pharmacy researcher*
Toscano, James Vincent *medical institute administration*
Travis, Marlene O. *healthcare management executive*
Walker, Elva Mae Dawson *health consultant*
Wiener, Daniel Norman *psychologist*
Will, Thomas Eric *psychologist*
Zimmerman, Shirley Lee *family social science educator, researcher*

Moorhead
Ritz, Eugene Frederick *therapist*
Zarrett, Mary Ann *mental health professional, educator, consultant*

Morris
Dee, Scott Allen *veterinarian*

Mound
Rosdahl, Caroline Bunker *nurse, educator, author*

Palisade
Kilde, Sandra Jean *nurse anesthetist, educator, consultant*

Park Rapids
Johnson, Mark Alan *psychologist*

Plymouth
Barden, Robert Christopher *psychologist, educator, lawyer*
DiGiovanna, Joseph W., Jr. *physical therapist*

Prior Lake
O'Brochta-Woodward, Ruby Catherine *orthopedic nurse*

Rochester
Busho, Elizabeth Mary *nurse, consultant, educator*
Closson, Bonnie Leigh *rehabilitation clinical nurse*
Flaaten, Ruby Cheryl *nurse manager*
Robinson, Celia Sue *physical therapist*
Zackery, Robert Thompson *health facility administrator*

Saint Cloud
Goodrie, JoAnn Ilene *human services administrator*
Holthaus, Thomas Anthony *hospital administrator*

Saint Louis Park
Schlutter, Lois Cochrane *psychologist*

Saint Paul
Carruthers, Claudelle Ann *occupational and physical therapist*
Chatfield, Ruth Christina *nurse, researcher*
D'Aurora, James Joseph *psychologist, consultant*
Hillenbrand, Anna M. *health care information manager*
Meissner, Ann Loring *psychologist, educator*
Phelan, Phyllis White *psychologist*
Schoenberg, Marlene Cohen *speech pathologist*
Stewart, David Dickson *psychologist*
Stoll, John Henry *psychologist, theologian*
Victor, Lorraine Carol *critical care nurse*

Saint Peter
Thayer, Edna Louise *medical facility administrator, nurse*

Sebeka
Hansen, Marion Joyce *nursing administrator*

Two Harbors
Carlson, Brian Jay *health facility executive*

Vergas
Joyce, Michael Daniel *personal resource management therapist and consultant, neurolearning therapist*

White Bear Lake
Williams, Julie Belle *psychiatric social worker*

Windom
Temlitz, Sylvia (Sylvia Haas) *gerontology nurse, educator*

Winnebago
Murphy, James C. *rehabilitation services professional*

Winona
Gundry, Jo Ann *mental health services professional*
Holm, Joy Alice *psychology educator, art educator, artist, goldsmith*

Woodbury
Simmons, Lawrence William *health care company executive*

MISSOURI

Ballwin
Meiner, Sue Ellen Thompson *gerontologist, nursing educator and researcher*

Belton
Scott, Mildred Hope *nurse*

Bolivar
Brewer, Richard Lynn *psychology educator*
Brown, Autry *psychology educator, clergyman*

Brashear
Howard, Alda Beverly *medical surgical nurse*

Bridgeton
Perry, Gloria Burgess *retired nursing educator*

Canton
Glover, Albert Downing *retired veterinarian*

Cape Girardeau
Nicholson, Gerald Lee *medical facilities administrator*
Steele, Diana Marie *nurse*

Chesterfield
Eltz, Robert Walter *bioprocess technologist*

Clayton
Laster, Atlas, Jr. *psychologist*
McCann-Turner, Robin Lee *child, adolescent analyst*
Orimenko, Martin Paul *chiropractor*

Columbia
Altomari, Mark G. *clinical psychologist*
Anderson, Carla Lee *psychologist*
Beckwith, Catherine S. *veterinarian*
Brinegar, Elizabeth Anne *critical care nurse, educator*
Constantinescu, Gheorghe M. *veterinarian*
Kiesler, Charles Adolphus *psychologist, academic administrator*
Kilgore, Randall Freeman *healthcare administrator*
Morehouse, Lawrence Glen *veterinarian, emeritus professor*
Taylor, Ronald Dean *psychologist, educator*

Crystal City
Sita, Michael John *pharmacist, educator*

Festus
Fakes, Mary E. A. *nurse*

Florissant
Hines, William Elvis *health facility executive, family physician*
Robinson, Patricia Elaine *women's health nurse practitioner*

Fulton
Garrett, Marilyn Ruth *nurse*

Grandin
Wallace, Louise Margaret *clinical coordinator*

Hallsville
Rowles, Joanne Ruth *adult nurse practitioner*

Hannibal
Buxman, Karyn Lynn *nurse*
Nix, Tammy Michelle *medical records administrator*

Harrisonville
Hoffman, John Korbut *physical therapist, consultant*

Imperial
Hughes, Barbara Bradford *nurse*

Independence
Miller, Karen Lynn *clinical social worker*
Norris, Ruth Ann *social worker*
Vigen, Kathryn L. Voss *nursing administrator, educator*

Jefferson City
Hasler Doggett, Stacy Lynn *mental health counselor*
Vieweg, Bruce Wayne *mental health researcher*
Wilks, R(alph) Kenneth, Jr. *government planner*

Joplin
Burr, Jackie Ann *nursing educator*
Gartner, Jessie Lee *emergency nurse*
Houser, Betty Jo *mental health nurse*
Joyce, Christie Lynne *medical surgical nurse*
Klaus, Arleen Elizabeth *rehabilitation nurse*

Kansas City
Amsden, Lucia Landon *therapist, consultant*
Anderson, Cynthia Lynn *medical, surgical nurse*
Bagstad, Kristin Kim *nurse specialist, pediatric nurse practitioner*
Bodenstab, Johnna Lynn *nursing educator*
Butler, Alice Claire *rehabilitation nurse*
Christophersen, Edward Rea *child psychologist*
Colaizzi, Joseph John *homeless services professional, clergyman*
Coon, Saundra Kay *home health nurse, small business owner*
Dexheimer, Kathryn Elaine *adult day care and health promotion executive*
Eddy, Charles Alan *chiropractor*
Gibson, Patricia Ann *health care administrator*
Jackson, Vicki Rae *adult nurse pracititioner*
Johnston, Thomas Patrick *pharmaceutics educator*
Kendall, Earnest James *mental health nurse*
Kingsley, James Gordon *healthcare executive*
Lehmkuhl, Margie Mae *family practice nurse*
Murphy, Mary Kathryn *industrial hygienist*
Myers, Jolynne *cardiovascular nurse educator*
Patterson, Janice Pauline *community and geriatrics health nurse*
Samuel, Robert Thompson *optometrist*
Smith, Robert Francis *psychologist, consultant, account representative*
Steffens, John Howard *cytotechnologist*
Stolov, Jerry Franklin *healthcare executive*
Tunley, Naomi Louise *retired nurse administrator*
Weinman, Steven Alan *emergency nurse, researcher, writer, educator*
Wilson, Dianne Carol *nurse*
Wilson, Susan Bernadette *psychologist*
Winitz, Harris *pyschology educator*
Wooden, Julie *critical care nurse*

Kirksville
French, Michael Francis *non-profit education agency administrator*
Gamm, Carol Amy *counselor*

Kirkwood
Clark, Carl Arthur *retired psychology educator, researcher*

Lebanon
Caplinger, Patricia E. *family nurse practitioner*

Louisiana
Morrow, Mary Jane *critical care nurse*

Marble Hill
Stewart, David Mack *childbirth educator, seismologist, author*

Marshfield
Gloe, Donna *critical care nurse*

Maryland Heights
Veenhuis, Mark Edward *optometrist*

Mexico
Hudson, Harold Don *veterinarian*

Nevada
Studer, Patricia S. *psychologist*

New Haven
Roth, Nancy Louise *former nurse, veterinarian*

O'Fallon
Gross, Stanley Merhl *chiropractor*

Pacific
Fitts, Thomas Allen *emergency nurse*

Saint Charles
Eggleston, Harry *optometrist*

Saint Joseph
Boor, Myron Vernon *psychologist, educator*
Kiekhaefer, Ruth Heins *healthcare executive*

Saint Louis
Allen, Linda Graves *hospital administrator*
Arnold, Kathleen Mary *nursing administrator, educator*
Asbed, Mona H. *healthcare administrator, university coordinator*
Bell, Laura Jeane *retired nurse*
Brownstein, Gloria *physical therapist*
Broyles, Gladys Benites *psychologist, hypnotherapist, counselor*
Bryan, Jean Marie Wehmueller *nurse*
Cacchione, Patrick Joseph *health association executive*
Clark, Gary Daniel *nurse anesthetist, educator*
Clark, Jeanenne Frances *community health nurse specialist*
Coger, Rick *health science facility administrator, educator*
Drucker, Barry Jules *environmental health specialist*
Farrell, John Timothy *hospital administrator*
Fementira, Diomedes Calio *geriatrics nurse*
Finan, John *health facility administrator*
Finger, Stanley *psychology educator*
Friedman, Bruce Howard *psychologist, researcher*
Greenwalt, Mary Susan *counselor*
Harper, Joan Diane *obstetric nurse*
Heffern, Debbi Marie *dietitian*
Henroid, Carol Lynn *nursing educator*
Herzfeld-Kimbrough, Ciby *mental health educator*
Hughes, Tricia Emily *nurse*
Jobe, Muriel Ida *medical technologist, educator*
Jones, Ronald Vance *health science association administrator*
Kaufhold, Lauren Ward *health facility administrator, physical therapist*
Kiser, Karen Maureen *medical technologist, educator*
Klahr, Margaret Carol Declue *nursing administrator, nurse*
LaBruyere, Thomas Edward *health facility administrator*
Molloff, Florence Jeanine *speech and language therapist*
O'Brien, Kathleen Ann *health association executive, educator*
Pope, Annie *health association administrator, planning consultant*
Reeves, Judith Ann *critical care nurse*
Rhodes, Marlene Rutherford *counseling educator, educational consultant*
Richards, Diana Lyn *psychologist*
Rieger, Donna Marie *critical care nurse, educator, consultant*
Rubin, Joanne Leslie *psychologist*
Schoenhard, William Charles, Jr. *health care executive*
Smith, Arthur E. *psychologist, educator*
Spalt, Stella Mickey *medical nurse, nursing educator*
Swanson, Robert Martin *medical center administrator, ordained priest*
Wood, Michael Allen *health care executive*
York, Linda Nattkemper *clinical nurse specialist*

Savannah
Testerman, Opal Mae *home services administrator*

Sparta
Madore, Joyce Louise *gerontology nurse*

Springfield
Adams, Lynn *speech-language pathologist, educator*
Carroll, Marsha Gail *critical care emergency nurse*
Dowdy, Linda Katherine *psychiatric and geriatric nurse*
Lutz, David John *psychology educator*
Roper, Donna Louise *ambulatory services director*
Westphal, Leonard Wyrick *health care executive, consultant*

Steelville
Hagemeier, Juanita Elizabeth *human services administrator*

Stoutland
Sample, Dan *alcohol and drug prevention professional*

Sunset Hills
Stahl, Deborah Ann *clinical psychologist*

Troy
Rhoads, Harvey Donald *chiropractor*

Unionville
Moss, Lisa Ann *critical care nurse*

Washington
Fitts, Janet Sue *trauma nurse coordinator, emergency room nurse, paramedic educator*

Wentzville
Everett, Garrett *veterinary clinic executive*

West Plains
Foulk, Dorothy Margaret *nurse*

NEBRASKA

Bellevue
Kayne, Jon Barry *industrial psychologist*

Fremont
Hawks, Jane Esther Hokanson *nursing educator*
Winans, Anna Jane *dietitian*

Gothenburg
Carr, Marcella Irene *medical surgical nurse*

Grand Island
Wolfe, Margaret Ethel (Vance) *nurse*

Grant
Olson, Ernestine Lee *nurse*

Holdrege
Kennedy-Reed, Cheryl Lynn *nurse, family case manager*

Hoskins
Stambaugh, Peggy Gene *mental health nurse*

Kearney
Osterhoudt, Cora Lavine Shults *mental health and medical/surgical nurse*
Quadhamer, Bettee Colleen *oncological nurse, educator*

Lincoln
Dierks, Merton Lyle *veterinarian*
Donkin, Scott William *chiropractor*
Hruska, Ronald John, Jr. *physical therapy and rehabilitation administrator*
Moshman, David Stewart *educational psychology educator*
Rogge, Mary Ellen *pharmacist*
Sullivan, George Finley *athletic trainer, physical therapist*

Nacy
Johnson, Darlene Ann *nurse*

North Platte
Wilcox, Beverly Joan *school nurse*

Omaha
Brick, Shirley Jean *rehabilitation nurse*
Christensen, Mari Alice *nursing auditor, medicolegal analyst, consultant*
Cote, John Joseph *medical student*
Fritz, Jacquelynn *medical surgical nurse*
Gutierrez, Pamela Jean Holbrook *nurse, clinical perfusionist*
Hachten, Richard Arthur, II *health system administrator*
Johnson, Christine Ann *nurse*
Karst, Gregory Mark *physical therapist, educator*
Landis, George Harvey *psychotherapist*
Leininger, Madeleine Monica *nurse, anthropologist, administrator, consultant, editor*
O'Connell, Kathleen M. *pediatric, medical-surgical, psychiatric nurse*
Penka, Eloise Marie *physical therapist*
Rottmann, Leon Harry *psychologist, educator*
Swanson, Darlene Marie Carlson *speech therapist, educator, speaker, writer*

Papillion
Hull, Joanne Petersen *health facility administrator*

Plattsmouth
Morris, Barbara Katherine *renal, cardiac, vascular nurse*

Ralston
Coffey, Douglas Wayne *mental health nurse*

South Sioux City
Graves, Maureen Ann *counselor*

Valley
Koons, Shirley Ann *dietitian*

Winnebago
Hobus, Ruth Nold *nursing educator and administrator*

NEW JERSEY

Mount Laurel
Weisbrot, Marvin Myron *retired health care administrator, consultant*

NEW YORK

Clarence
Waks, Amir *medical equipment development manager*

NORTH DAKOTA

Bismarck
Bosch, Donna *home health nurse administrator*
Hildebrand, Connie Marie *social worker*
Oldenburger, Norma Jane *medical surgical nurse*
Stauffacher, Trudy Sharron *hospice coordinator*

Bottineau
Tonneson, Irene Marie *nurse, nutritionist*

Dickinson
Kessel, Lloyd R. *acute care nursing director, educator*
Townsend, Richard Blezard *clinical psychologist*

Fargo
Haakenson, Philip Niel *pharmacist, educator*
Nickel, Janet Marlene Milton *geriatrics nurse*
Revell, Dorothy Evangeline Tompkins *dietitian*

Grand Forks
Blecha, Clarence Orville *physical therapist, retired*

Jamestown
Klose, Patsy Mae Ellen *nursing educator*

Manvel
Wilhelmi, Sandra G. *health facility administrator*

OHIO

Akron
Baker, Rose Ann Urdiales *pediatric and mental health nurse*
Coz, Mary Kathleen *respiratory therapist*
Franck, Ardath Amond *psychologist*
Gill Thompson, Norma N. *home healthcare executive*
Hughes, Karen Sue *geriatrics nurse*
Sinacore, Janie Mariol *surgical nurse*
Sonnhalter, Carolyn Therese *physical therapist, consultant*
Talbott, Karen Lee *home health care administrator*
West, Michael Alan *hospital administrator*

Ashtabula
Briggs, Frances Elaine *nursing adminstrator*
Hornbeck, Harold Douglas *psychotherapist*
Poncar, Patricia Jane *nursing educator*
Ranck, Sandra Ann *nurse*

Bay Village
Stanbery, Robert Charles *veterinarian*

Beachwood
Cosner, Thurston Lawrence *retired psychology educator, psychologist*

Berea
Anders, Claudia Dee *occupational therapist*
Mickley, G. Andrew *retired air force officer, psychologist, neuroscientist, educator,*

Bowling Green
Oppliger, Pearl Laviolette *alcohol and drug abuse services professional*

Brecksville
Terbanc, Barbara Joyce *chemical abuse administrator*

Burton
McIntee, Terri Lee *disability advocate*

Cambridge
Todd, Carol Ann *geriatrics nurse*

Canton
Crossland, Ann Elizabeth *psychotherapist*
Dent, Roger Eugene *psychometrist*
Neutzling, Virginia Ruth *healthcare company executive*
Schmucker, Ruby Elvy Ladrach *nursing educator*
Smithkey, John, III *public health nurse, consultant*

Centerville
Cooper-Servaites, Pamela Sue *nursing administrator*

Chagrin Falls
Downing, Cynthia Hurst *therapist, addiction and abuse specialist*

Chillicothe
Smith, Ralph Edward *psychology assistant*
Stump, Earl Spencer *psychologist*

Cincinnati
Bradley, Sister Myra James *health science facility executive*
Cross, Joan Elaine *nurse, insurance company representative*
Donahoe-Fillmore, Betsy Kay *physical therapist*
Gee, Phyllis Ann *critical care nurse*
Geoppinger, James Carl *pharmacist*
Gleser, Goldine Cohnberg *psychologist*
Jenkins, Marilyn Elizabeth *pediatric burn nurse, administrator*
Lamb, Mary Angela *hospital patient educator, nurse*
Lippincott, Jonathan Ramsay *healthcare executive*
Mason, Mark Alan *physical therapist*
Mazzella, Patricia Anne *public health nurse*
McGlothlin, James Duayne *research industrial hygienist, ergonomist*
Morganroth, Patricia Ann *nursing educator*
Prettyman, Paula Marie *critical care nurse, home infusion nurse*
Rosenthal, Susan Leslie *psychologist*
Sacco, Mary Kathleen *nurse*
Schwab, Maureen Dolan *nursing educator*
Stinson, Mary Florence *nursing educator*
Theuerling, Andrew William *staff nurse*
Wales, M. Elizabeth *psychologist*
Wells, Melanie Gail *pediatric physical therapist, educator*
Zierolf, Mary Louise *nurse anesthetist*

Cleveland
Balale, Amelia *physical therapist*
Barrat-Gordon, Rene *social worker*
Bate, Brian R. *psychologist*
Boswell, Nathalie Spence *speech pathologist*
Boyle, Kammer *management psychologist*
Cartier, Charles Ernest *alcohol and drug abuse services professional*
Coleman, Stephen Robert *psychology educator*
Davidson, James Wilson *clinical psychologist*
Deal, William Thomas *school psychologist*
Dylag, Helen Marie *healthcare administrator*
Ferraro, Charles Domenic *psychologist, educator*
Giesser, Nancy Lynne *nursing educator*
Gorski Croissant, Kathleen *occupational therapist*
Hansler, Stephen Paul *social worker*
Hulme, Mary Ann K. *women's health nurse, administrator*
Kohn, Mary Louise Beatrice *nurse*
Kovnat, Karel Debra *psychologist*
Krumhansl, Bernice Rosemary *physical therapist*
Langlois, Esther *marital and family therapist, psychotherapist*
Mantzell, Betty Lou *school health administrator*
Myers, Eddie Earl *clinical psychologist*
O'Brien, Margaret Ann *obstetrics nurse, community health nurse*
Phipps, Wilma J. *nursing educator, author*
Schmidt, Patricia Jean *medical lab technician*
Schrott, Norman *clinical social worker*
Spottsville, Sharon Ann *counselor*
Stokes, Roberta Anne *clinical nurse specialist, manager*
Waters, Gwendolyn *human services administrator*
Whitman, Gayle Ruth *nursing administrator, educator*

Columbus
Becker, Ralph Leonard *psychologist*
Beckholt, Alice *public health nurse*
Borelli, George Louis *psychologist*
Buerki, Robert Armin *pharmacy educator*
Covault, LLoyd R., Jr. *hospital administrator, psychiatrist*
Cuddihy, June Tuck *pediatrics nurse*
Dolder, Angela Marie *physical therapist, educator*
Green, Mary Eloise *nutrition and food management educator*
Hartman, James Robert *public health sanitarian*
Lawson, Debra Lee *physical therapist*
Leland, Henry *psychology educator*
Lince, John Alan *pharmacist*
Macintosh, Betty Arlene *state community services administrator*
Mirtallo, Jay Matthew *pharmacist, educator*
Newman, Barbara Miller *psychologist, educator*
Newman, Philip Robert *psychologist*
Nucklos, Shirley *medical administrator, consultant*
Peppe, Kathryn Kluss *pediatrics nurse, educator*
Pitzer, Martha Seares *nursing educator*
Roberts, Joetta Karen *nursing administrator*
Rowland, Robert Charles *clinical psychotherapist, writer, researcher*
Ryan, Mike *health association administrator*
Schommer, Jon Clifford *pharmaceutical administration educator*
Shaw, Larry A. *health facility administrator*
Shoop, L. Jane *nurse*
Tosino, Clair Gerard *nursing administrator*
Walker, Jewel Lee *health facility administrator, consultant*
Warren, Barbara Jones *nursing researcher, educator*
Weale, John Joseph *veterinarian*
Yinger, Mary Ann *neonatology nurse*
Young, James William *health science association administrator*

Copley
Smith, Joan H. *women's health nurse, educator*

Dayton
Croyle, Barbara Ann *health care management executive*
Cunningham, Sarah Margaret *orthopedics nurse*
Davenport, Nyra J. *social work administrator*
Fridrick, M. Rogene *gerontology educator, retired social worker*
Hatton, Cary *counselor, mental health advocate/ educator*
Jones, Reginald Lorrin *clinical psychologist, consultant*
Kline, Bruce Edward *clinical psychologist*
Kuntz, Kenneth Joseph *psychologist, educator*
Lentz, Linda Kay *school psychologist, learning disability educator*
Mallett, Susan Marie *nurse*
Miller, Tamara Dedra *psychologist*
O'Malley, Patricia *critical care nurse*
Powers, Juanita Carpenter *mental retardation and developmental disability nurse*
Stoeckle, Mary L. *critical care nurse, nursing educator*
Versic, Linda Joan *nurse educator, research company executive*
Wall, Jeffrey Lynn *intravenous nurse, educator*
Williams, Michael Alan *psychologist*

Delaware
Carlton, Robert L. *clinical psychologist*

Dublin
McGloshen, Thomas Hilton, Jr. *marriage and family therapist*

Elyria
Yates, Vivian Marie *nurse educator*

Fairborn
Leffler, Carole Elizabeth *mental health nurse, women's health nurse*

Fairfield
Goodman, Myrna Marcia *school nurse*

Fairlawn
Kurzweil, Alan Dennis *social worker, marriage and family therapist, consultant*

Findlay
George, Deborah Ann *physical therapist, educator*
Peters, Carol Ann Dudycha *counselor*
Peters, Milton Eugene *educational psychologist*
Reamsnyder, Margaret Elizabeth *nurse*
Stephani, Nancy Jean *social worker, journalist*

Franklin
Barker, Donald J. *health facility administrator*
Withrow, Sheila Kay *school nurse*

Galion
Barr, Dixie Lou *geriatrics nurse*
Sutton, Peggy Rose *critical care nurse*

Gallipolis
Boone, Richard Ray *psychologist, naval officer*

Galloway
Schneider, Jeanne Anne *nursing educator*

Girard
Rose, James Scott *audiologist, hearing technology consultant*

Grafton
Palekar, Indira S. *psychologist, physical therapist*

Grove City
Haskins, Kristen Elizabeth *psychologist*
Schlanser, Theresa Dianne *speech-language pathologist*

Hamilton
Erbe, Janet Sue *medical surgical, orthopedics and pediatrics nurse*
Johnson, Pauline Benge *nurse, anesthetist*
McCluskey, Anita *technician*

Highland Heights
Taylor, Theresa Evereth *registered nurse, artist*

Hinckley
Sprungl, Katherine Louise *nurse*

Holland
Fortener, Roger Gerard *rehabilitation services professional*

Kent
Adamle, Kathleen Nora Duffy *oncological nurse*
Kerr, Dianne Lynne *health educator*

Kettering
Altick, Virna Lizette *nurse*

Lancaster
Eckert, Winfield Scott *health science association administrator*
Rowles, Arlene Beverly *geriatric social program administrator*
Rusk, Karla Marie *critical care nurse, research coordinator*

Lebanon
Osborne, Quinton Albert *psychiatric social worker*

Lima
Ball, Elizabeth Suzette *home health care-coronary care nurse*
Miller, Roy Raymond *optician, ocularist*
Palmer, Arthur Eugene *nursing home administrator*
Sweeney, Nancy L. *psychiatric nurse*
Traunero, Debra Ann *social worker*

Lisbon
Grzebieniak, John Francis *psychologist*

Lorain
Harris, Alberta O. Armstrong *critical care nurse, administrator*
Paige, Diane Louise *physical therapist*
Shimandle, Sharon Anne *critical care nurse*

Lyndhurst
Dellas, Marie C. *retired psychology educator and consultant*

Mansfield
Reese, Wina Harner *speech pathologist, consultant*

Mantua
Miller, Kimberly Clarke *human services manager*

Marietta
Krivchenia, Megan Liller *clinical counselor*

Marion
Klingel, Patti Jean *health facility administrator*

Mason
Clements, Michael Craig *health services consulting executive, retired renal dialysis technician*

Massillon
Franklin, Mary Rose *women's health nurse*

Maumee
Jurrus, Kathleen Sue *post-anesthesia care nurse*
Mohler, Terence John *psychologist*

Mc Comb
Ewing, Mary Eileen *radiologic technologist*

Medina
Calhoun, Lyla Lea *clinical social worker, consultant*

Mentor
Smith, Paul Martin *physical therapist, athletic trainer*

Middleburg Heights
Hartman, Lenore Anne *physical therapist*

Middletown
Gilmore, June Ellen *psychologist*
Gordon, Sandy Gale Combs *medical surgical nurse, community health nurse*
Redding, Barbara J. *nursing administrator, occupational health nurse*
Whitt, Linda L. *health facility administrator*

Mount Gilead
Cline, Paul Anderson *health facilities adminstrator*

Napoleon
Butler, Debra Sue *physical therapist*

Navarre
McBride, Vickie Darlene *geriatrics nurse*

New Philadelphia
Knight, Debra Ann Mizer *mental health services professional*
Zinkon, Lana Sue *occupational health nurse*

North Canton
Pittman, Ann Broad *physical therapist*
Tomin, Robin Karen *medical surgical nurse*

North Royalton
Michak, Helen Barbara *nurse, educator*

Owensville
Seifert, Caroline Hamilton *community health nurse, school nurse*

Painesville
Lemr, James Charles *geriatrics nurse*
Lemr, Sandra J. *geriatrics nurse, administrator*

Perrysburg
Murdock, Nanci C. *women's health nurse*

Portsmouth
Hughes, Michael Joseph *counselor, psychologist*
Ward, Patricia Elaine *geriatrics nurse*

Powell
Manchester, Carol Ann Freshwater *psychologist*

Ravenna
Profio, Janice Carol *critical care nurse*

Reynoldsburg
McNew, Frances Wilkins *nursing administrator*
Odor, Richard Lane *mental health administrator, psychologist*

Richmond
Pollock, Sandra Ann *physical therapist*

Richmond Heights
Richman, Jeffery Alan *veterinarian*

Saint Clairsville
Sidon, Claudia Marie *psychiatry, mental health nursing educator*
Zavacky, Lynette Michele *women's health nurse*

Salem
Bernstein, Jeffrey Alan *pharmacist, mathematician, computer scientist*
Moss, Susan *nurse, retail store owner*

Sandusky
Freehling, Harold George, Jr. *respiratory therapist, consultant*
Miller, William Paul *psychologist*
Riedy, Virginia Kathleen *nursing educator*
Round, Alice Faye Bruce *school psychologist*

Shaker Heights
Candee, Benjamin LeRoy, Jr. *retired psychologist, educator*

Sidney
Scharenberg, Sandra Lee *nurse*

South Euclid
Rosner, Robin Lisa Ziskind *mental health technologist*

Spencer
Snyder, Teresa Ann *medical surgical nurse*

Springfield
Crandall, Neal H. *substance abuse counselor*
Hrinko, Daniel Dean *clinical counselor*

Stow
Pickton, Thomas Emil *psychologist*

Sylvania
Verhesen, Anna Maria Hubertina *counselor*

Tiffin
Groce, Joan Alice *retired social services professional*
Moncher, Daniel Joseph *hospital executive, accountant*

Toledo
Kuhlman, Kimberly Ann *clinical dietician*

Pisano, Cynthia Kay *clinical therapist*
Riseley, Martha Suzannah Heater (Mrs. Charles Riseley) *psychologist, educator*
Sheridan, Sinclair *healthcare administrator*
Walters, Gwendolyn Mae (Wallace) *nursing educator, clinical specialist*
Wintersmith, Deborah Sue *drug abuse services professional*

Troy
Enright, Georgann McGee *mental health nurse*
Szoke, Joseph Louis *psychologist, mental health facility administrator*

University Heights
Bloch, Andrea Lynn *physical therapist*

Valley View
Van Kirk, Robert John *nursing case manager, educator*

Van Wert
Greve, Diana Lee *community health nurse*

Vandaba
Sullenbarger, Peggy Ann *nurse manager, rehabilitation consultant*

Vandalia
Davis, Pamela J. *nursing educator*

Wadsworth
Pipitone, Phyllis L. *psychologist, educator, author*

Warren
Gianakos, Patricia Ann *social worker*
VanAuker, Lana Lee *recreational therapist, educator*

Waverly
Kroth, Jeannie Mae *pediatrics nurse*

Westerville
Conley, Sarah Ann *health facility administrator*
Stevenson, Joanne S. *older adults care provider, educator, researcher*
Strapp, Naomi Ann *women's health nurse*
Williams, John Michael *physical therapist, sports medicine educator*
Wisniewski, Sheila Louise *physical therapist*

Westlake
Lehman, Priscilla Lillian *nurse, medical education programs distributing company executive*

Wooster
Albright, Mindy Sue *college health and geriatrics nurse*
O'Neill, Erin Leigh *physical therapist*

Worthington
Bernhagen, Lillian Flickinger *school health consultant*
Bilderback, George Garrison, III *human services manager*
Rinehart, I. Lynn *clinical counselor*
Rummell, Helen Mary *critical care and pediatrics nurse*

Xenia
Blanton, Linda Gayle *counselor, former educator*

Youngstown
Burns, Jon Perry *healthcare administrator*
Lazarus, M. Karen *executive director*
Valenta, Janet Anne *substance abuse professional*

OREGON

Dayton
Rudisill, John Richard *clinical psychologist, educator*

PENNSYLVANIA

Conneaut Lake
Starn, Barbara Jean *nursing administrator*

SOUTH DAKOTA

Aberdeen
Hedges, Mark Stephen *clinical psychologist*

Brookings
Phelps, Brady Justin *psychology educator, editor, author*
Steinley, Lori Anderson *physical therapist*

Canton
Perkinson, Robert Ronald *psychologist consultant*

Chamberlain
Gregg, Robert Lee *pharmacist*

Dakota Dunes
Tronvold, Linda Jean *occupational therapist*

Hot Springs
Fellows, Dale Russell *physical therapist, consultant*

Lead
Fuller, Jacqualyn Gist *speech language clinician*

North Sioux City
Grant, Judith Iversen *family health nurse, nursing administrator*

Sioux Falls
Buseman, Kathleen Anne *ophthalmology nurse*
Fogas, Bruce Scott *psychologist, educator*
Gibson, Sheri Jo *clinical nurse specialist, family nurse practitioner*
Koepsell, Pamela Ann *neonatal nurse*
Nygaard, Lance Corey *nurse, data processing consultant*
Richards, LaClaire Lissetta Jones (Mrs. George A. Richards) *social worker*
Sadler, James Bertram *psychologist, clergyman*
Williams, W. Vail *psychologist*

Vermillion
Lavelle, Ellen *educational psychologist*

Winner
Galbraith, Ruth Ellen *family nurse, patient care coordinator*

Yankton
Kamback, Marvin Carl *psychologist*
Sokol, Dennis Allen *hospital administrator*

TEXAS

Fort Hood
Carter, Arlene Mae *psychiatric nurse*

Temple
Morrison, Gary Brent *hospital administrator*

VIRGINIA

Arlington
Hollander, Doris Ann *psychologist, consultant, businesswoman, author*

WISCONSIN

Algoma
Langevin, Peggy Ann *physical therapist, rehabilitation director*

Appleton
Reichard, Chrystal Jean *physical therapist*

Baldwin
Gleason, Linda Mary *geriatrics nurse*

Bear Creek
Schleicher, Susan L. *critical care nurse*

Beldenville
Mullenax, Charles Howard *veterinarian, researcher*

Beloit
Sweet, Shirley Marie *psychology and social studies educator, consultant*
White, Lawrence Todd *psychology educator*

Brodhead
Heise, Wendy Sue Pinnow *veterinarian*

Brookfield
Bielke, Patricia Anne *psychologist*
Zander, Gaillienne Glashow *psychologist*

Cedarburg
Taken, Maureen M. *pediatric oncology nurse*

Chippewa Falls
Copeland, Christine Susan *therapist*

De Pere
Finder-Stone, Patricia Ann *registered nurse, nursing educator*
Hardy, Raymond Reed *psychology educator*
Ngo, Paul Yen Ly *psychology educator*

Eau Claire
Gautsch, Kay Anne *physical therapist*

Franklin
DeMeulenaere, Christopher John *physical therapist*

Germantown
Brantly, Laura J. *physical therapist*

Green Bay
Butler, Robert Andrews *clinical psychologist*
Chlubna, David John *psychotherapist*
Dykes, Kathryn A. *community health nurse, educator, administrator*
Hillesheim, Mark Thomas *physical therapist*
Mervilde, Michael John *clinical social worker*
Rotherham-Whipp, Cheryl Kay *mental heal administrator*

Janesville
McDonald, Susan B. *psychologist*

Jefferson
Reese, Norma Carol *psychologist*

Kenosha
Cassiday, Karen Lynn *psychologist*

La Crosse
Davies, George James *physical therapist, educator*
Day, Celesta *nursing educator, religion educator*
Gyllander, Nikki K. *human services administrator*
Meisch, Janene Kay *women's health nurse*
Oyster, Carol Kathleen *psychology educator*

Madison
Berven, Norman Lee *counselor, psychologist, educator*
Corcoran, Mary Alice *medical surgical nurse, educator*
Derzon, Gordon M. *hospital administrator*
Dunham, Michael Herman *human services agency executive*
Gavin, Mary Jane *medical, surgical nurse*
Kunz, Jeffrey Robert Melius *health care executive, educator*
Maersch, Nancy Kay *laboratory manager*
Rather, Marsha Lee *nurse educator*
Strezlec, John Allen *social worker*
Szymanski, Edna Mora *rehabilitation psychology and special education educator*

Manitowoc
Cumming, Marion F. *forensic consultant*

Marshfield
Bennington, Jerry William *medical technologist, technical consultant*
David, Barbara Marie *medical, surgical nurse*
Hensch, Shirley Anne *psychology educator*
Martin, Debbie Mary Krecklow *critical care nurse*

Menasha
Mahnke, Kurt Luther *psychotherapist, clergyman*

Menomonee Falls
Bespalec, Dale Anthony *clinical psychologist*
Griswold, Paul Michael *clinical psychologist, consultant*

Milwaukee
Bartels, Jean Ellen *nursing educator*
Cohn, Lucile *psychotherapist, nurse*
Coogan, Frank Neil *health and social services administrator*
Erdman, Pamela Ann *occupational therapist*
Grochowski, Mary Ann *psychotherapist*
Heim, Kathryn Marie *psychiatric nurse, author*
Humber, Wilbur James *psychologist*
Kett, Kathleen Marie *nurse midwife, maternal nurse, consultant*
King, Guadalupe Vasquez *psychology and social work educator*
Kloth, Rachell Darden *herbalist*
LaMalfa, Joachim Jack *clinical psychologist*
Malnory, Margaret Ellen *perinatal clinical nurse specialist, nurse researcher*
Mancuso, Joseph Edward *medical psychotherapist*
Marzano, Mary Kay *physical therapist*
Olston, Mary Kay *school psychologist*
Quereshi, Mohammed Younus *psychology educator, consultant*
Rooney, Carol Bruns *dietitian*
Schmahl, Stephanie Helene *school social worker*
Shields, James Richard *alcohol and drug counselor, consultant*
Warren, Richard M. *experimental psychologist, educator*
Wells, Carolyn Cressy *social work educator*
Winston, Maxine Spears *social worker*
Wright, Diana Krenzel *client support supervisor, computer consultant*

Minong
Moore, Anne K. *medical surgical nurse*

Monroe
Lehman, Rebecca Ann *physical therapist*

Mosinee
Remus, Denise Rae *nurse researcher*

New Berlin
Dude, Mary Ann *women's health nurse, medical paralegal*
Marsh, Clare Teitgen *retired school psychologist*
Nelson, Kay Ellen *speech and language pathologist*
Winkler, Dolores Eugenia *retired hospital administrator*

Oconomowoc
Prestash, Randy John *optometrist*

Onalaska
Doweiko, Jeanette Marie *orientation and mobility specialist, educator*
Kunes, Steven Marshall *health science association administrator*

Oshkosh
McDonald, Sylvia Eichner *neuro-rehabilitation clinical nurse specialist*

Plymouth
Woythal, Constance Lee *psychologist*

Racine
Fouse, Sarah Virginia *geriatrics nurse*
Sullivan, Caroline Elizabeth *nursing educator*

Rhinelander
Keuer, Jean Eleanore *physical therapist*
Van Brunt, Marcia Adele *social worker*

Sauk City
Busack, Gary Lee *managed care adminstrator*

Seymour
Johnson, Andrew Paul *veterinarian*

Spooner
Schaeffer, Brenda Mae *psychologist, author*

Sturgeon Bay
Cecil, Frances (Frances Vander Myde) *nursing administrator, medical surgical nurse, hotel executive*

Suamico
Farrell, Jeremiah Louis *retired psychologist*
Roddan, Ray Gene *chiropractor*

Tomah
Hillman, Lin (Linda Lou Hillman) *nursing administrator*

Watertown
Degnitz, Dorothy Elsie *nurse*
Leitzke, Jacque Herbert *psychologist, corporate executive*

Waukesha
Ellefson, Karen Ann *physical therapist*
Rather, Shari Anne *social worker*
Williams, Paul Leon *psychologist*

Wausau
Ament, Richard Rand *psychologist*
Burtch, Susan Marie *physical therapist, administrator*
Peterson, Virginia Beth *counselor*

Wauwatosa
Janzen, Norine Madelyn Quinlan *medical technologist*
Lucey, Paula Ann *health facility administrator*
Marzinski, Lynn Rose *oncological nurse*

West Allis
Heer, Laurie Ann *physical therapist, educational consultant*

TERRITORIES OF THE UNITED STATES

PUERTO RICO

San Juan
de Snyder, Soami Santiago *audiologist*

CANADA

ONTARIO

Windsor
Auld, Frank *psychologist, educator*

ADDRESS UNPUBLISHED

Abdoo, Raymond Thomas *preventive health consultant*
Adler, Anne Herzberg *counseling psychologist*
Allen, Leatrice Delorice *psychologist*
Anaple, Elsie Mae *medical, surgical and geriatrics nurse*
Anderson, Lois D. *nursing administrator, mental health nurse*
Anderson, Nancy Jane *medical nurse*
Angus, Robert Carlyle, Jr. *health facility administrator*
Barker, Mary Katherine *retired nurse*
Barnhouse, Lillian May Palmer *retired medical surgical nurse, researcher, civic worker*
Barrett, Marilyn Woody *nursing administrator, educator, business consultant*
Battani, Nancy Lee *rehabilitation nurse*
Bay, Susan Louise *critical care nurse*
Bell, Dorothy Frances *nurse, educator*
Bell, Susan Jane *nurse*
Bernardelli, Kathy Louise *critical care nurse*
Betsinger, Peggy Ann *oncological nurse*
Biegel, David Eli *social worker, educator*
Binder, Madeline Dotti *counselor*
Black, Paul D. *health facility administrator*
Blackburn, Pamela M. *medical surgical nurse*
Blair, Margaret Baylor (Meg Schoolfield) *emergency nurse*
Blue, Anita Fae *nurse*
Blunck, Klaire Darlene *nurse*
Boekholder, Theresa Marie *geriatrics nurse*
Bonneson, Mary Elisabeth *psychotherapist*
Borg, Ruth I. *in-home nursing care provider*
Bougalis, Katherine G. *medical surgical nurse, educator*
Briggs, Janet Marie Louise *nurse practitioner*
Buckley, Gail Geary *health administrator*
Burroughs, Pamela Gayle *critical care nurse*
Byers, Jo Ann *pharmacist*
Byrd, Lorenda Sue *nursing administrator*
Canjar, Patricia McWade *psychologist*
Carroll, Jean Gayton *healthcare industry consultant*
Castle, Janice Morris *healthcare management consultant*
Castor, Christina Pelayo *critical care nurse*
Clauser, Angela Frances *medical surgical, pediatrics and geriatrics nurse*
Colosimo, Mary Lynn Sukurs *psychology educator*
Cooper, Signe Skott *retired nurse educator*
Cooper-Lewter, Nicholas Charles *psychotherapist, educator, minister*
Cozort, Amber Lynne *nurse*
Crider, Ruth Lee *community health nurse, nursing administrator*
Damon, Cindy Irene *nurse*
Daniels, Kurt R. *speech and language pathologist*
Day, Anne White *retired registered nurse*
Dell, Thomas Charles *nurse anesthetist*
Dennis, Marcia Lynn *speech and language pathologist*
DeStaffany, Sandra Russell *childbirth educator, author*
Didich, Jan *hospice consultant*
Dixon, Marguerite Anderson *retired nursing educator*
Dodds, Brenda Kay *nurse*
Donnelly-Kempf, Moira Ann *nursing administrator*
Dressel, Irene Emma Ringwald *alcoholism and family therapist*
Eberley, Kelly Ann *physical therapist*
Elliott-Zahorik, Bonnie *nurse, administrator*
Elsea, Sandra Jeanne *community health nurse, clinical specialist*
Essex, Wanda Elizabeth *speech and language pathologist*
Fennema, Betty Jane *nurse*
Ferrari, Linda Joy *nurse*
Fitzpatrick, William Allen *pharmacist*
Frohlichstein, Alan *retinal angiographer*
Gaeta-Harper, Theresa *psychotherapist*
Garber, Sheldon *hospital executive*
Gildenblatt, Roslyn Warshofsky *nursing administrator*
Girvin-Quirk, Susan *nursing administrator*
Glynn, Natalie Jo *physical therapist, athletic trainer, emergency medical technician*
Gonzalez, William G. *hospital administrator, educator*
Gorman, Karen Machmer *optometric physician*
Grimes, Marilyn Jane Larsen *nursing administrator*
Grotheer-Ridings, Patricia *nurse*
Guthrie, Diana Fern *nursing educator*
Hakes, Wanda Faye *retired nursing educator*
Hallberg, Gay Robb *clinical psychologist*
Helfrich, Wauneta Meyne *retired school social worker*

Herkner, Bernadette Kay *occupational health nurse*
Herrin, Frances Sudomier *retired volunteer social worker*
Hoagland, Leora M. *emergency nurse*
Hoffer, Alma Jeanne *nursing educator*
Holmes, Kathryn Louise *medical technologist*
Hooper, Marcia Sarita *pediatric critical care nurse*
Howell, Gail A. *critical care nurse, educator*
Howeth, Diane Kathryn *mental health nurse*
Huibregtse, Jayne Lynnor *medical surgical nurse*
Hyde, Roderick Michael *medical technician*
Isaacs, Kenneth S(idney) *psychoanalyst, educator*
Jackson, M. Dorothy *medical surgical nurse, researcher*
John, Gerald Warren *pharmacist, educator*
Johnson, Beth Ann *pediatric nurse, gerontology nurse*
Kahanovsky, Luis *physical therapist*
Kapitan, Mary L. *retired nursing administrator, educator*
Kaye, Jennifer Lynn *healthcare executive*
King, Dorothy Jackson *psychologist, marriage-family counselor, therapist*
Kison, Carol *nursing educator, critical care nurse*
Klinetob, Carson Wayne *physical therapist*
Kono, Jean E. *nursing educator*
Kostere, Kim Martin *psychologist*
Kowalski, Lucy Ann *retired nurse, educator*
Lake, Gail Ann *women's health nurse, administrator*
Leslie, Cynthia *mental health nurse*
Lindgren, Kermit Lyle *nurse*
Link, Deborah Ann *nurse*
Magafas, Diania Lee *geriatrics nurse consultant, administrator*
Manhal-Baugus, Monique *counselor*
Martin, Cheri Christian *health services administrator*
Mathews, Mary Beth *nursing educator*
Matis, Bonnie Leah *health care administrator*
Maxwell, Kimberly Ann *critical care nurse*
McCormick, Kathleen Marie *medical surgical nurse*
McDougal, Marie Patricia *English and psychology educator*
McGill, Karleen A. *occupational health nurse*
McGrew, Patricia Ann *geriatrics nurse*
Mich, Connie Rita *mental health nurse, educator*
Milewski, Barbara Anne *pediatrics nurse, neonatal intensive care nurse*
Mitchell, Donald E. *rehabilitation counselor, transition counselor*
Mitchell, Vernice Virginia *nurse, poet, author*
Moliere, Jeffrey Michael *cardio-pulmonary administrator*
Moore, Mary Johnson *women's and children's health nurse*
Morey, Sharon Lynn *psychotherapist, mediator*
Morris, Melanie Marie *nurse*
Mruk, Christopher J. *psychologist, educator*
Nash, Janet Rae *geriatrics nurse*
Nolde, Shari Ann *pediatrics, critical care nurse*
Norris, Debra Lynn *physical therapist assistant*
Novak, Donald F. *physical therapist*
Nowak, Chester Joseph *optometrist*
Palombo, Joseph *clinical social worker*
Parsons, Donald, Jr. *critical care nurse*
Pearson, Barbara Lee *social worker*
Peat, Wanda Jean *critical care nurse*
Penke, Cynthia Marie *critical care nurse*
Pieper, Martha Heineman *psychotherapist*
Prettyman-Baker, Sheila *pediatrics, neonatal nurse*
Price, Janis *medical center administrator*
Primus, Mary Jane Davis *social worker, author*
Pritchett, Allen Monroe *healthcare administrator*
Prominski, Eileen Alice *school nurse, educator*
Przybylski, Sandra Marie *speech pathologist*
Ramsey, Sandra Lynn *psychotherapist*
Rickel, Annette Urso *psychology educator*
Riester, Becky J. *orthopedics and neurology nurse*
Robins, Arthur Joseph *social work and psychiatry educator*
Rouw, Carla Sue Roberts *medical nurse*
Rutland, Myrtle Pauline *mental health nurse*
Sanders, Martha J. Morgan *nurse*
Schamburg, Tracy Marie *professional counselor*
Scheiderer, Phyllis Jackson *nursing administrator*
Scott, Amy Annette Holloway *nursing educator*
Seaver, Frank Alexander, III *retired medical center administrator*
Silverman, Ellen *speech and language pathologist*
Simons, R. Kaye *healthcare administrator*
Somes, Joan Marie *emergency nurse*
Sonderegger, Theo Brown *psychology educator*
Staker, George V. *vocational rehabilitation coordinator*
Stear, Cindy Ann *clinical psychologist*
Steiner, Karen Ruth *physician's assistant*
Stevens, Kathleen M. *nurse*
Stewart, Barbara Lynne *geriatrics nursing educator*
Stohlman, Connie Suzanne *obstetrical gynecological nurse*
Such, Mary Jane *nurse, service executive*
Svoboda, Janice June *nurse*
Talbott, Mary Ann *critical care nurse*
Tanner, Teresa L. *medical nurse*
Teitsma, Jack A. *psychologist*
Thomas, Donna Johns *former hospital administrator*
Thompson, Geneva Florence *medical technologist, cytotechnologist*
Thomson, James Adolph *medical group practice administrator*
Thrasher, Rose Marie *critical care and community health nurse*
Timmons, Barbara Alice *geriatrics nurse*
Tinner, Franziska Paula *social worker, artist, designer, educator*
Tobin, Ilona Lines *psychologist, marriage and family counselor, consultant*
Tourtillott, Eleanor Alice *nurse, educational consultant*
VanDemark, Michelle Volin *critical care, neuroscience nurse*
Wademan, Patsy Ann *psychiatric, geriatrics nurse*
Wallschlaeger, Josephine Ingeborg *mental health nurse*
Walston, Lola Inge *dietitian*
Wegener, Kristy Ann *medical surgical nurse, homecare nurse*
Weiner, Esther Riza *clinical psychologist*
Westlie, Margaret Anne *nurse, writer*
Whaley-Buckel, Marnie *social service administrator*
Wieber, David John *physical therapist, athletic trainer, business owner*
Wilson, Francis Marion *public health services officer*
Winkler, Margaret Ann *geriatrics nurse, nursing administrator*
Wyatt, Rose Marie *clinical social worker*
Younger, Betty Nichols *social worker*

HEALTHCARE: MEDICINE

UNITED STATES

ARIZONA

Scottsdale
Nadler, Henry Louis *pediatrician, geneticist, medical educator*

CALIFORNIA

Los Angeles
Barnett, Margaret Edwina *nephrologist, researcher*

Orange
Funahashi, Akira *physician, educator*

FLORIDA

Miami
Ozar, Milton Bernard *urologist*

ILLINOIS

Abbott Park
Bush, Eugene Nyle *pharmacologist, research scientist*

Alton
Kisabeth, Tim Charles *obstetrician, gynecologist*

Arlington Heights
DeDonato, Donald Michael *obstetrician/ gynecologist*
Shetty, Mulki Radhakrishna *oncologist, consultant*

Aurora
Ball, William James *pediatrician*

Barrington
Murad, Tariq *surgical pathologist*

Belleville
Samson, Carla Elaine *family practice physician*

Berwyn
Galinsky, Dennis Lee *radiation oncologist, educator*
Misurec, Rudolf *physician, surgeon*

Bloomington
Trefzger, Richard Charles *surgeon*

Blue Island
Roman, Alan Marshall *general and peripheral vascular surgeon*

Carbondale
Crouse, James Lyle *physician*

Carol Stream
Mains, Douglas Benjamin *orthopaedic surgeon*
Pokornowski, Ronald Felix *internist*
Schmerold, Wilfried Lothar *dermatologist*

Centralia
Qureshi, Shamim *psychiatrist*

Champaign
Risken, Jared Cleveland *physician*
Traugott, Arthur Richard *physician*

Chicago
Anderson, William Gilchrist *physician, surgeon, educator*
Arnsdorf, Morton Frank *cardiologist, educator*
Beaty, Harry Nelson *internist, educator, university dean*
Beigl, William *physician, naturopath, hypnotist, acupuncturist, consultant*
Berendi, Erlinda Bayaua *surgeon*
Bhargava, Hemendra Nath *pharmacologist, educator*
Boren, Stephen Darwin *medical director*
Chatterton, Robert Treat, Jr. *reproductive endocrinology educator*
Chmell, Samuel Jay *orthopedic surgeon*
Coe, Fredric L. *physician, educator, researcher*
Collings, Gilbeart Hooper, Jr. *physician*
Coopersmith, Bernard Ira *obstetrician, gynecologist, educator*
Curry, Raymond Howard *physician*
Datta, Syamal Kumar *medical educator, researcher*
Deorio, Anthony Joseph *surgeon*
Evans, R. Mark *pharmacologist*
Eybel, Carl Eugene *cardiologist*
Feingold, Daniel Leon *anesthesiologist*
Feldman, Harris Joseph *radiologist, educator*
Freitag, Frederick Gerald *osteopathic physician*
Gevitz, Norman Jan *medical historian, educator*
Gladstone, Lee *psychiatrist, addictionist*
Goldberg, Edward Jay *orthopaedic surgeon*
Grimes, Hugh Gavin *physician*
Hart, Cecil William Joseph *otolaryngologist, head and neck surgeon*
Hefter, Gilbert Morris *psychiatrist*
Heller, Richard Elliot *retired surgeon, physician*
Hendrix, Ronald Wayne *physician, radiologist*
Huggins, Charles Brenton *surgical educator*
Jilhewar, Ashok *gastroenterologist*
Johnson, Timothy Patrick *health researcher*
Kaminski, Edward Jozef *pathologist, toxicologist educator*
Katz, Robert Stephen *rheumatologist, educator*
Kornel, Ludwig *medical educator, physician, scientist*
Kozlowski, James Michael *urology and surgery educator*
Leestma, Jan Edward *neuropathologist, medical director*
Loomis, Salora Dale *psychiatrist*
Lopez, Carolyn Catherine *physician*
Lourwood, David Lee, Jr. *pharmacotherapist, educator*
Lumpkin, John Robert *public health physician, state official*
McCurdy, David B. *healthcare ethics consultant, educator*
McDonald, Larry William *neuropathologist educator*
McGaghie, William Craig *medical educator*
McLawhon, Ronald William *pathology educator, biochemist*
Mesulam, Marsel *neurologist, educator*
Moore, Vernon John, Jr. *pediatrician, lawyer, medical consultant*
Musa, Mahmoud Nimir *psychiatry educator*
Naclerio, Robert M. *otolaryngologist, educator*
Nicholas, John Jeffrey *physiatrist, educator*
Oryshkevich, Roman Sviatoslav *physician, physiatrist, dentist, educator*
Osiyoye, Adekunle *obstetrician, gynecologist, educator*
Page, John Arthur *professional association executive, educator*
Plioplys, Audrius Vaclovas *neurologist, researcher*
Rhone, Douglas Pierce *pathologist, educator*
Rodos, Joseph Jerry *osteopathic physician, educator*
Rossi, Ennio C. *internist, educator*
Rotman, Carlos Alberto *obstetrician, gynecologist*
Sandlow, Leslie Jordan *physician, educator*
Schlessinger, Nathan *psychoanalyst*
Serratto-Benvenuto, Maria *pediatric cardiologist*
Silins, Astrida Ilga *retired anesthesiologist*
Singh, Manmohan *orthopedic surgeon, educator*
Socol, Michael Lee *obstetrician, gynecologist, educator*
Swerdlow, Martin Abraham *physician, pathologist, educator*
Taraszkiewicz, Waldemar *physician*
Taswell, Howard Filmore *pathologist, blood bank specialist, educator*
Tedesco, Susan Mary *pharmacy technician*
Thomas, Leona Marlene *health information educator*
Tomita, Tadanori *neurosurgeon*
Trakas, Demetrius Alexander *psychiatrist*
Vargish, Thomas *surgery educator*
Vasa, Rohitkumar Bhupatrai *pediatrician, neonatologist*
Von Roenn, Kelvin Alexander *neurosurgeon*
Weisberg, Seymour William *physician*
Weldon-Linne, C. Michael *pathologist, microbiologist*
Widell, Thomas Alan *emergency physician*
Wied, George Ludwig *physician*
Williams, Philip Copelain *obstetrician, gynecologist*
Winer, Jerome Allen *psychoanalyst, educator*
Yarkony, Gary Michael *physician, researcher*

Darien
Gardner, Howard Garry *pediatrician, educator*

De Kalb
Papaeliou, Louis *occupational medicine physician*

Decatur
Sweet, Arthur *orthopedist*

Des Plaines
Tenczar, Alan J. *podiatrist, pharmacist*

Dixon
Polascik, Mary Ann *ophthalmologist*

Elk Grove Village
Durkee, Timothy James *physician*
Herrerias, Carla Trevette *epidemiologist, manager*

Elmhurst
Fornatto, Elio Joseph *otolaryngologist, educator*

Evanston
Adelson, Bernard Henry *physician*
Chessick, Richard D. *psychiatrist*
Lambert, Mary Pulliam *neurobiologist*
Langsley, Donald Gene *psychiatrist, medical board executive*
Quintanilla, Antonio Paulet *physician, educator*
Sprang, Milton LeRoy *obstetrician, gynecologist, educator*
Takahashi, Joseph S. *neuroscientist*

Freeport
Phillips, Spencer Kleckner *retired surgeon*

Glen Ellyn
Agruss, Neil Stuart *cardiologist*
Hoffman, Michael Charles *otolaryngologist*
Temple, Donald *allergist, dermatologist*

Glencoe
Allinson, Carl *radiologist*
Milloy, Frank Joseph, Jr. *surgeon*

Glendale Heights
Pimental, Patricia Ann *neuropsychologist, consulting company executive, author*

Glenview
Brockman, David Dean *psychoanalyst, psychiatrist*

Greenville
Hall, Tracy Lynn *physician*

Harvey
Heilicser, Bernard Jay *emergency physician*

Hazel Crest
Prentice, Robert Craig *cardiologist*

Hinsdale
Collins, Charles Patrick *emergency physician*
Doege, Theodore Charles *retired physician*
Kazan, Robert Peter *neurosurgeon*

Jacksonville
Hartman, Robert Ray *retired physician, medical consultant*

La Grange
Vyborny, Carl Joseph *radiologist*

La Salle
Fesco, Edward J. *surgeon*

Lake Bluff
Kelly, Daniel John *physician*

Lake Forest
Salter, Edwin Carroll *physician*

Lansing
McKeown, Mary Elizabeth *educational administrator, medical office manager*

Long Grove
Dajani, Esam Zapher *pharmacologist*

Marshall
Mitchell, George Trice *physician*

Mattoon
Maris, Charles Robert *surgeon, otolaryngologist*

Maywood
Littooy, Fred Nelson *peripheral vascular surgeon*
Newman, Barry Marc *pediatric surgeon*
Samarel, Allen Mark *physician, biochemistry and cell biology educator*
Winship, Daniel Holcomb *medicine educator, university dean*

Moline
Arnell, Paula Ann Youngberg *pathologist*
Arnell, Richard Anthony *radiologist*
Banas, John Stanley *obstetrician, gynecologist*

Mount Vernon
Feather, Lisa Kay *physician assistant*

Naperville
Schwab, Paul Josiah *psychiatrist, educator*

Niles
Bianchi, Robert George *retired pharmacologist*

Normal
Cooley, William Emory, Jr. *radiologist*

North Chicago
Kim, Yoon Berm *immunologist, educator*
Wiesner, Dallas Charles *immunologist, researcher*

Oak Forest
Lee, David Chang *physician*

Oak Lawn
Oyama, Joseph Hikaru *internist, nephrologist*
Rathi, Manohar Lal *pediatrician, neonatologist*

Oak Park
Biek, Richard William *physician*
Brackett, Edward Boone, III *orthopedic surgeon*
Schultz, Bryan Christopher *dermatologist, educator*
Valinsky, Mark Steven *podiatrist*

Olney
Edwards, Ian Keith *obstetrician, gynecologist*

Olympia Fields
Kasimos, John Nicholas *pathologist*
Webster, Douglas Peter *emergency physician*

Park Ridge
Grover, John Wagner *physician*
Kitt, Walter *psychiatrist*
Krohn, Jonathan Stuart *anesthesiologist*
Levett, James Michael *cardiothoracic surgeon*
Oserman, Stuart *internist*
Weinberg, Milton, Jr. *cardiovascular-thoracic surgeon*

Pekin
Podzimek-Kotysan, Jana *surgeon*

Peoria
Bartlett, Gerald Lloyd *pathologist, medical educator, researcher*
Bayless, Romaine Belle *physician, educator*
Meriden, Terry *physician*
Pugh, Margaret Jeanne *nurse practitioner*
Traina, Jeffrey Francis *orthopedic surgeon*

River Grove
Hillert, Gloria Bonnin *anatomist, educator*

Rock Island
Forlini, Frank John, Jr. *cardiologist*

Rockford
Baptist, Errol Christopher *pediatrician, educator*
Nora, Richard Ernest *hematologist, oncologist, educator*

Silvis
Rhee, Yang Ho *radiologist*

Springfield
Agich, George John *medical educator*
Feldman, Bruce Alan *psychiatrist*
Fortin, Claude Jean *neurologist*
Parker, Robert Rudolph *podiatrist*
Stone, Stephen Paul *dermatologist*
Trapp, Robert Greig *rheumatologist*
Zaricznyj, Basilius *orthopedic surgeon*

Urbana
Anastasio, Thomas Joseph *neuroscientist, educator, researcher*
Kaufman, Jerome Benzion *neurosurgeon*
O'Morchoe, Charles Christopher Creagh *administrator, anatomical sciences educator*

Villa Park
Becker, Robert Jerome *allergist, health care consultant*

West Chicago
Blumhagen, Jeanne Bourland *pediatrician, emergency physician*

Wheaton
Bogdonoff, Maurice Lambert *physician*

Wilmette
Springer, Harry Aaron *surgeon*

INDIANA

Anderson
King, Charles Ross *physician*

Avilla
Sneary, Max Eugene *retired physician*

Bloomington
Henshel, Diane S. W. *neuroscientist, educator*

Danville
Ochsner, Edward Conner *diagnostic radiologist*

Evansville
Cady, Louis Byron *psychiatrist*
Doepker, J(ohn) Frederick, Jr. *plastic surgeon*
Wayne, Lisle, II *plastic surgeon*

Fort Wayne
Brandt, William Edward *surgeon, consultant*
Donesa, Antonio Braganza *neurosurgeon*
Lambertson, Larry Hall *psychiatrist*
Richardson, Joseph Hill *physician, medical educator*

Goshen
Swanson, Raymond E. *pathologist*

Greenfield
Andrews, Ronald Keith *physician*

Greenwood
Atkins, Clayton H. *family physician, epidemiologist, educator*

Hammond
Steen, Lowell Harrison *physician*

Hobart
Mason, Earl James, Jr. *pathologist, educator*

Huntington
Weston, Roy B. *anesthesiologist*

Indianapolis
Albrecht, Willard Harold *retired medical educator*
Allen, Stephen D(ean) *pathologist, microbiologist*
Alley, Thomas William *physician*
Aufiero, Thomas Xavier *cardiothoracic surgeon*
Bonaventura, Leo Mark *gynecologist*
Bowman, Elizabeth Sue *psychiatrist, educator*
Braddom, Randall L. *physician, medical educator*
Braunstein, Ethan Malcolm *skeletal radiologist, paleopathologist*
Bruns, Robert Frederick, Jr. *pharmacologist*
Campbell, Judith Lowe *child psychiatrist*
Chernish, Stanley Michael *physician*
Cleary, Robert Emmet *gynecologist, infertility specialist*
Conant, Steven George *psychiatrist*
Connell, Kathryn McQuown *medical educator*
Daly, Walter Joseph *physician, educator*
Elkins, James Paul *physician*
Fisch, Charles *physician, educator*
Galvin, Matthew Reppert *psychiatry educator*
Geisler, Hans Emanuel *gynecologic oncologist*
Henderson, Joseph Marvin *gastroenterologist*
Hill, Beverly Ellen *health sciences educator*
Holden, Robert Watson *radiologist, educator, university dean*
Johnson, Stephen Michael *ophthalmologist*
Lahiri, Debomoy Kumar *molecular neurobiologist, educator*
Manders, Karl Lee *neurosurgeon*
McGarvey, William K. *otolaryngologist, surgeon*
Merritt, Doris Honig *pediatrics educator*
Miyamoto, Richard Takashi *otolaryngologist*
Nasser, William Kaleel *cardiologist*
Ross, Edward *cardiologist*
Schmetzer, Alan David *psychiatrist*
Tavel, Morton Edward *physician*
Taylor, Doris Denice *physician, entrepreneur*
Winters, Peter L. *dermatologist*
Woolling, Kenneth Rau *internist*
Yune, Heun Yung *radiologist, educator*

Lafayette
Frey, Harley Harrison, Jr. *anesthesiologist*

Marion
Kucera, Keith Edward *physician*

Michigan City
Nasr, Suhayl Joseph *psychiatrist*

Muncie
Triplett, Douglas Arnold *pathologist*

Nappanee
Borger, Michael Hinton Ivers *osteopathic physician, educator*

New Albany
Chowhan, Naveed Mahfooz *oncologist*

New Castle
Schubert, Esther Virginia *psychiatrist, physician*

Newburgh
Dully, Frank Edward, Jr. *physician, educator*

Rensselaer
Ahler, Kenneth James *physician*

Scottsburg
Kho, Eusebio *surgeon*

South Bend
Feferman, Martin Earl *neurosurgeon*
Kelly, James Patrick *cardiothoracic surgeon*
Moore-Riesbeck, Susan *osteopathic physician*

Valparaiso
Kobak, Alfred Julian, Jr. *obstetrician, gynecologist*

Walton
Chu, Johnson Chin Sheng *physician*

West Lafayette
Rutledge, Charles Ozwin *pharmacologist, educator*

Williamsport
Hart, James Harlan *retired emergency medicine physician*

Zionsville
Heck, David Alan *orthopaedic surgery educator, mechanical engineering educator*

IOWA

Cedar Rapids
Kramer, Leslie *dermatologist*
Spoden, James Edward *otolaryngologist*

Cherokee
Taylor, Samuel Douglas *psychiatrist*

Clinton
Woodman, Grey Musgrave *psychiatrist*

Davenport
Arnold, David Alan *surgeon*
Habak, Philip Antoine *cardiologist*
Rohlf, Paul Leon *urologist*

Des Moines
Denhart, Charles Ford *physician*
Dorner, Douglas Bloom *vascular surgeon, educator*
Ely, Lawrence Orlo *retired surgeon*
Koslow, Alan R. *cardiovascular surgeon*
Pandeya, Nirmalendu Kumar *plastic surgeon, flight surgeon, military officer*
Peters, Carl H. *insurance physician*
Rodgers, Louis Dean *surgeon*
Severson, Wayne Larson *retired physician*
Shingledecker, Leon G. *podiatrist*
Thoman, Mark Edward *pediatrician*
Zagoren, Allen Jeffrey *surgeon*

Emmetsburg
Coffey, James Leo *semi-retired pediatrician, family practitioner*

Fort Dodge
DeLucca, Leopoldo Eloy *otolaryngologist, head and neck surgeon*

Fort Madison
McGee, John Edward *retired gynecologist*

Iowa City
Andreasen, Nancy Coover *psychiatrist, educator*
Bale, James Franklin, Jr. *pediatric neurologist*
Cooper, Reginald Rudyard *orthopedic surgeon, educator*
Ehrenhaft, Johann Leo *surgeon*
Gantz, Bruce Jay *otolaryngologist, educator*
Gergis, Samir Danial *anesthesiologist, educator*
Hammond, Harold Logan *pathology educator, oral and maxillofacial pathologist*
Kasik, John Edward *medical educator*
Kelch, Robert Paul *pediatric endocrinologist*
Lang, Elvira Valentina *radiologist, educator*
Richerson, Hal Bates *physician, internist, allergist, immunologist, educator*
Scott-Conner, Carol Elizabeth Hoffman *surgeon, educator*
Tomanek, Robert J. *anatomy educator*
Williamson, Harold E. *pharmacologist, educator*

Marshalltown
Cassidy, Eugene Patrick *pathologist*

Sioux City
Spellman, George Geneser, Sr. *internist*
Vaught, Richard Loren *urologist*

West Burlington
Daft, William Stanley *physician*

West Des Moines
Ceilley, Roger I. *dermatologist, oncologist, educator*

Winterset
de Regnier, Kevin Vincent *osteopath*

KANSAS

Dodge City
Amawi, Mohammad Sa'di *surgeon*

Hutchinson
Bos, Norman Calvin *retired orthopaedic surgeon*
Graves, Kathryn Louise *dermatologist*

Kansas City
Arakawa, Kasumi *physician, educator*
Bartholome, William Gibson *pediatrician, educator*
Beatty, Robert Michael *neurosurgeon*
Chapman, Albert Lee *anatomy educator, university dean*
Cowley, Benjamin Dollar *nephrologist, molecular biologist*
Holmes, Frederick Franklin *medical educator, physician, researcher*
Mathews, Paul Joseph *allied health educator*
Mathewson, Hugh Spalding *anesthesiologist, educator*
Norris, Charley William *otolaryngologist, educator*
Suzuki, Tsuneo *molecular immunologist*

Leavenworth
Sanders, James Edward *family practice physician*

Leawood
Magee, Thomas Henry *medical doctor, medical educator*

Lenexa
Crater, Timothy Andrews *medical student*

Mission
Thomas, Christopher Yancey, III *surgeon, educator*

Olathe
O'Brien, Daniel Joseph *pharmacologist, toxicologist*

Overland Park
Landry, Mark Edward *podiatrist, researcher*

Prairie Village
Smith, Elizabeth Barker *psychiatrist*

Rose Hill
Chapman, Randell Barkley *family and emergency physician, medical educator*

Salina
Richards, Jon Frederick *physician*

Shawnee
Lanman, Robert Charles *pharmacology and toxicology educator*

Shawnee Mission
Dockhorn, Robert John *physician, educator*
Emmott, David Fielding *physician, urologist*
Hartzler, Geoffrey Oliver *retired cardiologist*
Price, James Gordon *physician*
Sternberg, David Edward *psychiatrist*

Topeka
Johns, William Howard *psychiatrist, neurologist*

Wichita
Cummings, Richard J. *otologist*
Haynes, Deborah Gene *physician*
Moore, Dennis Frederic *physician*

MICHIGAN

Adrian
Haddad, Inad *physician*

Ann Arbor
Aldrich, Michael Sherman *neurologist, educator*
Barksdale, Charles Madsen *psychoneuroendocrinologist*
Baumann, Gregory William *physician, consultant*
Bole, Giles G. *physician, researcher, medical educator*
Brenner, Dean Elliott *medical oncology and pharmacology educator*
Burke, Robert Harry *surgeon, educator*
Coran, Arnold Gerald *pediatric surgeon, educator*
Doyle, Constance Talcott Johnston *physician, educator*
Gilman, Sid *neurologist*
Greenberg, Harry Seth *neurologist, educator*
Humes, H(arvey) David *nephrologist, educator*
Johnston, Carolyn M. *gynecologist, oncologist*
Kimbrough, William Walter, III *psychiatrist*
Kronfol, Ziad Anis *psychiatrist, educator*
Langa, Kenneth A. *physician*
Oesterling, Joseph Edwin *urologic surgeon*
Pierce, Lori J. *physician, educator*
Pitt, Bertram *cardiologist, educator, consultant*
Roberts, James Allen *gynecologic oncologist*
Robinson, Terry Earl *neuroscience and psychology educator*
Rosenberg, Jack Michael *emergency physician*
Smith, David John, Jr. *plastic surgeon*
Sugar, Jonathan Akiba *child psychiatrist*
Tandon, Rajiv *psychiatrist, educator*
Thompson, George Richard *rheumatologist, educator*
Watson, Andrew Samuel *psychiatry and law educator*

Battle Creek
Johnson, Melvin Henry, Jr. *physician*

Bay City
Nicholson, William Noel *clinical neuropsychologist*

Berrien Springs
Kootsey, Joseph Mailen *physiology and computer science educator, administrator*

Birmingham
Caldwell, John Rankin *internist*

Bloomfield Hills
Cohen, Alberto *cardiologist*
David, Murphy Samuel *physician*
Floyd, William Sanford *gynecology and obstetrics educator*
Rosenfeld, Joel *ophthalmologist, lawyer*
Wydra, Frank Thomas *healthcare executive*

Dearborn
Coburn, Ronald Murray *ophthalmic surgeon, researcher*

Detroit
Amirikia, Hassan *obstetrician-gynecologist*
Balon, Richard *psychiatrist, educator*
Beninson, Joseph *dermatologist*
Blain, Alexander, III *surgeon, educator*
Cerny, Joseph Charles *urologist, educator*
Cohen, Max Mark *surgeon*
Ditmars, Donald Melick, Jr. *plastic surgeon*
Goodman, Morris *anatomy educator*
Hay, Rick Vance *nuclear medicine physician*
Iverson, Robert Louis, Jr. *internist, physician, intensive care administrator, medical educator*
Kaplan, Randy Kaye *podiatrist*
Krull, Edward Alexander *dermatologist*
Levine, Donald Paul *infectious disease specialist*
Lindblad, William John *pharmacologist*
Lisak, Robert Philip *physician, researcher, educator*
Lupulescu, Aurel Peter *medical educator, researcher, physician*
Maiese, Kenneth *neurologist*
Marrazzi, Mary Ann *pharmacologist, pharmacology educator*
Mayes, Maureen Davidica *physician, educator*
McCarroll, Kathleen Ann *radiologist, educator*
Moghissi, Kamran S. *obstetrician/gynecologist, educator*
Ofenstein, John Patrick *pediatrics educator*
Saravolatz, Louis Donald *epidemiologist, physician educator*
Schaffler, Mitchell Barry *research scientist, anatomist, educator*
Sokol, Robert James *obstetrician/gynecologist, educator*
Stein, Paul David *cardiologist*
Szilagy, Eric Joseph *surgeon*
Warbasse, Lawrence Hill, III *physician, educator*

East Lansing
Beckmeyer, Henry Ernest *anesthesiologist, medical educator*
Drukker, Bruce H(ighstone) *obstetrics and gynecology educator*
Gulick, Peter Gregory *medical educator*
Huntington, Mark Kenneth *physician, microbiologist*
Pysh, Joseph John *neurologist*
Sauer, Harold John *physician, educator*
Waite, Donald Eugene *medical educator, consultant*
Werner, Arnold *psychiatrist*

Escanaba
Cooper, Janelle Lunette *neurologist, educator*

Farmington Hills
Breiner, Sander James *psychiatry educator, psychoanalyst*
Emara, Mohamed Amin *immunologist*
Feldstein, Richard *psychiatrist*
Gordon, Craig Jeffrey *oncologist, educator*

Flint
Himes, George Elliott *pathologist*
Johnson, Gary Keith *pediatrician*
Mueller, Willys Francis, Jr. *pathologist*
Nagaraju, Marigowda *gastroenterologist*

Grand Blanc
Wasfie, Tarik Jawad *surgeon, educator*

Grand Rapids
Feenstra, Laurence Henry *physician*
Glessner, James Roger *retired orthopedic surgeon*
Ruffini, Richard John *family systems psychiatry and behavioral medicine clinician, educator*
Tiberio, Angela Rose C. *physician*
Truthan, Charles Edwin *physician*

Grandville
Meyer, Judith Louise *obstetrician-gynecologist*

Grosse Pointe
Sphire, Raymond Daniel *anesthesiologist*

Jenison
Cronick-Leonard, Anne Bertha *retired psychiatrist*

Kalamazoo
Corrigan, Mark H.N. *psychopharmacology director*
Green, Phillip Michael *neurologist, gerontologist*
Oleen-Burkey, MerriKay Adelle *research epidemiologist, educator, pharmacist*
Peisner, David Balfour *medical educator*

Lansing
Flory, Clyde Reuben, Jr. *physician, clinical immunologist*
Miller, Ronald Carl *dermatologist, educator*

Livonia
Pittaway, Kenneth Stanley *physician*

Madison Heights
Rochen, Donald Michael *osteopathic physician*

Mancelona
Whelan, Joseph L. *neurologist*

Midland
Hood, James *internist, consultant*
Sadek, Salah Eldine *pathologist, consultant*
Snyder, Robert Lee *anesthesiologist*

Newberry
Summersett, Kenneth George *psychiatric social worker, educator*

Northville
Abbasi, Tariq Afzal *psychiatrist, educator*

Novi
Pitts, Kenneth Ernest *psychiatrist, educator*

Oak Park
Borovoy, Marc Allen *podiatrist*

Okemos
Gillespie, Gary Don *physician*

Otsego
Berneis, Kenneth Stanley *physician, educator*

Perry
Behm, John Robert *physician*

Pontiac
Bautista, Marieta Pascual *psychiatrist*
Dragovic, Ljubisa Jovan *medical examiner, consultant*

Redford
Bahr, Sheila Kay *physician*

Rochester Hills
Badalament, Robert Anthony *urologic oncologist*
Bartunek, James Scott *psychiatrist*

Rockford
Posthuma, Albert Elwood *surgeon*

Royal Oak
Freij, Bishara Joudeh *pediatrician, consultant*
Whittington, Jeremiah *physician*
Wilner, Freeman Marvin *hematologist, oncologist*

Saginaw
Lier, Nancy Jean *medical educator, administrator*
Lovy, Andrew *osteopathic physician, psychiatrist*
Michalak, Michael Vincent *physician assistant*

Saint Clair Shores
Petz, Thomas Joseph *internist*
Walker, Frank Banghart *pathologist*

Saint Joseph
Ahmad, Anwar *radiologist*

Southfield
Ganesh, Orekonde *physician*
Giles, Conrad Leslie *ophthalmic surgeon*
Green, Henry Leonard *physician*
Hammel, Ernest Martin *medical educator, academic administrator*
O'Hara, John Paul, III *orthopaedic surgeon*
Rosenzweig, Norman *psychiatry educator*
Stunz, John Henry, Jr. *physician*
Zubroff, Leonard Saul *surgeon*

Three Rivers
Reiff, James Stanley *addictions physician, psychiatric physician, osteopathic physician, surgeon*

Trenton
Holloway, H(arry) Rex, Jr. *osteopath*

Troy
Golusin, Millard R. *obstetrician/gynecologist*

Warren
Ryan, Jack *physician, hospital corporation executive*
Yakes, Barbara Lee *occupational and preventive medicine physician, former nurse*

West Bloomfield
Alter, John *otolaryngologist, facial cosmetic surgeon, educator*

Ypsilanti
Flaum, Morris Aaron *hematologist, oncologist*
Hildebrandt, H(enry) M(ark) *pediatrician*

MINNESOTA

Apple Valley
Doyle, O'Brien John, Jr. *emergency medical services consultant, lobbyist*

Crosslake
Kettleson, David Noel *retired orthopaedic surgeon, timber manager*

Duluth
Aufderheide, Arthur Carl *pathologist*
Camenga, David LeRoy *neurologist, educator*
Sargent, William Winston *anesthesiologist*

Fairmont
Zemke, Robert Lowell *family practice physician*

Fridley
Scott, Jack Charles *dermatologist, educator*

Hopkins
Atkin, Howard Barth *physician*

Minneapolis
Boudreau, Robert James *nuclear medicine physician, researcher*
Breningstall, Galen Natley *physician*
Brown, Mark Leslie *biomedical scientist*
Chou, Shelley Nien-chun *neurosurgeon, university official, educator*
Dunn, David Lewis *surgeon, researcher*
Filice, Gregory Alan *physician*
From, Arthur Harvey Leigh *cardiologist, educator*
Gebhard, Roger Lee *medical educator, researcher*
Gumnit, Robert Jerome *healthcare executive, epilepsy researcher*
Hakim, Ali Aiman *urologist*
Halikas, James Anastasio *medical educator, psychiatrist*
Holter, Arlen Rolf *cardiothoracic surgeon*
Lee, James Travis, Jr. *surgeon*
Lentz, Richard David *psychiatrist*
Loh, Horace H. *pharmacology educator*
Luepker, Russell Vincent *epidemiology educator*
Malmquist, Carl Phillip *psychiatrist*
Murray, Charles LeRoy *medical oncologist*
Paparella, Michael M. *otolaryngologist*
Peterson, Douglas Arthur *physician*
Phibbs, Clifford Matthew *surgeon, educator*
Quie, Paul Gerhardt *physician, educator*
Rhame, Frank Scorgie *physician, educator*
Stenwick, Michael William *internist, geriatric medicine consultant*
Swaiman, Kenneth Fred *pediatric neurologist, educator*
Uckun, Fatih *research scientist, pediatric medicine educator*
Weir, Edward Kenneth *cardiologist*
Zimmerman, Cheryl Lea *pharmacy educator*

Moose Lake
Christensen, Raymond Gordon *physician*

Owatonna
Heslep, Grant Daniel *ophthalmologist*

Plymouth
Berlinger, Norman Thomas *physician, author*

Rochester
Adjei, Alex Asiedu *internist, oncologist, pharmacologist*
Altchuler, Steven Ira *psychiatry consultant, researcher*
Hagler, Donald Joseph *pediatric cardiologist*
Lagerlund, Terrence Daniel *neurologist*
Malek, Reza Said *urological surgeon*
O'Connell, Edward John *pediatrician*
Pittelkow, Mark Robert *physician, dermatology educator, researcher*
Riggs, Byron Lawrence, Jr. *physician, educator*
Rogers, Roy Steele, III *dermatology educator, dean*
Tuono, Albert Joseph *physician*
Waller, Robert Rex *ophthalmologist, educator, foundation executive*

Saint Cloud
Gruys, Robert Irving *physician, surgeon*
Olson, Barbara Ford *physician*

Saint Louis Park
Engstrom, Frederick William *psychiatrist*

Saint Paul
Baisch, Steven Dale *pediatric intensivist*
Brown, David Robert *pharmacologist*
Crabb, Kenneth Wayne *obstetrician, gynecologist*
Nordlie, Paul Edward *physician, pathologist*
Widin, Gregory Peter *biomedical development administrator*

Stillwater
Asch, Susan McClellan *pediatrician*

Willmar
Vander Aarde, Stanley Bernard *retired otolaryngologist*

MISSOURI

Belton
Lombardo, Richard James *emergency physician*

Branson
Dieterle, Brian Dave *internist*

Cape Girardeau
Duda, Zenon Michael *podiatrist*
Jung, Christopher Harold *otolaryngologist*
Thorpe, William Parr *orthopaedic surgeon*

Chesterfield
Keller, Joseph C. *physician*

Columbia
Bauer, John Harry *physician*
Bryant, Lester R. *surgeon, educator*
Cunningham, Milamari Antoinella *anesthesiologist*
Friedman, Gary Seth *physician, educator*
Heimburger, Elizabeth Morgan *psychiatrist*
Hess, Leonard Wayne *obstetrician gynecologist, perinatologist*
Long, Edwin Tutt *surgeon*
See, William Mitchel (W. Mike See) *cardiovascular and thoracic surgeon*
Southwick, Christopher Lyn *anesthesiologist*

Florissant
Schwarze, Robert Francis *osteopath, dermatologist*

Fredericktown
Raksakulthai, Vinai *obstetrician, gynecologist*

Gravois Mills
Dunn, Floyd Emryl *psychiatrist, neurologist, consultant*

Independence
Accardo, Phillip Louis *osteopath*

Jefferson City
Giffen, Lawrence Everett, Sr. *family physician, anesthesiologist, historian*
Page, Scott Lee *medical association administrator*

Joplin
Estep, Dennis Alan *occupational medicine physician*
Habermann, James Herbert *retired pathologist*
River, George Lambert *hematologist, oncologist*
Singleton, Marvin Ayers *otolaryngologist, senator*

Kansas City
Blim, Richard Don *pediatrician*
Crayton, Billy Gene *physician*
Crockett, James Edwin *physician, educator*
Dixon, George David *radiologist*
Ellfeldt, Howard James *orthopedic surgeon*
Grayson, Paula S. *biofeedback clinician, mental health nurse*
Hamilton, James Joseph *orthopedic surgeon, educator*
Huston, Kent Allen *rheumatologist*
Hyde, Lawrence Layton (Fred Hyde) *ophthalmologist*
Rowland, James Leonard *family practice physician, surgeon, homeopathic physician*
Schoolman, Arnold *neurological surgeon*
Strain, Herbert Arthur, III *plastic surgeon*
Truog, William Edward, III *pediatrician, educator, researcher*
Winship, Myron Jay *physician, microbiologist*

Kirksville
Kuchera, Michael Louis *osteopathic educator*
Lockwood, Michael Dacre *osteopath*

Osage Beach
East, Mark David *physician*

Poplar Bluff
Lotuaco, Luisa Go *pathologist*
Piland, Donald Spencer *internist*

Saint Charles
Dieterich, Russell Burks *obstetrician/gynecologist*
Schneider, Thomas Aquinas *surgeon, educator*

Saint Joseph
Kirila, Carol Elizabeth *osteopathic physician*

Saint Louis
Anderhub, Beth Marie *medical educator*
Babu, Satram R. *geriatric medical educator, researcher*
Barner, Hendrick Boyer *cardiovascular surgeon*
Blaine, G. James, III *electronic radiology administrator, educator*
Colten, Harvey Radin *pediatrician, educator*
Cryer, Philip Eugene *medical educator, scientist, endocrinologist*
Evens, Ronald Gene *radiologist, medical center administrator*
Fischbein, Lewis Conrad *internist*
Hanley, Thomas Patrick *obstetrician, gynecologist*
Hay, Donald Peter *psychiatrist, educator*
Heiken, Jay Paul *physician*
Holtz, Alan Steffen, Sr. *surgeon*
Hsu, Chung Yi *neurologist*
Ikeda, Shigemasa *anesthesiologist*
Kaiser, Fran Elizabeth *endocrinologist, gerontologist*
Kang, Juan *pathologist*
Lagunoff, David *physician, educator*
Ley, Timothy James *hematologist, molecular biologist*
Luther, George Aubrey *orthopedic surgeon*
Malik, Azfar Mohammed *psychiatrist, medical administrator*
Mantovani, John Francis *neurologist, educator*
McFadden, James Frederick, Jr. *surgeon*
Mendelson, David Frey *neurology educator*
Morales-Galarreta, Julio *psychiatrist, child psychoanalyst*
Morley, John Edward *physician*
Nielsen, Carl Helge *anesthesiologist*
North, Carol Sue *psychiatrist, educator*
Onken, Henry Dralle *plastic surgeon*
Peck, William Arno *physician, educator*
Perry, Deborah Vey *senior clinical research associate*
Pohl, David L. *diagnostic radiologist*
Reh, Thomas Edward *radiologist, educator*
Siegel, Barry Alan *nuclear radiologist*
Silverberg, Alan Bernard *endocrinology educator*
Ulett, George Andrew *psychiatrist*
Walz, Bruce James *radiation oncologist*
Wedner, H. James *physician, researcher*
Winn, Hung Nguyen *obstetrician, gynecologist, maternal-fetal medicine physician*

Saint Peters
Sanchez, Guadalupe *dermatologist*

Springfield
Climer, Beth Jane *health information technology coodinator, educator*
Jones, Doug E. *healthcare researcher, real estate broker, oil company owner*
McCorcle, Marcus Duane *obstetrician, gynecologist*

Sullivan
Scott, Ronald Hubert *geriatrics physician, surgeon*

University City
Shen, Jerome Tseng Yung *pediatrician*

Weatherby Lake
Arsenovic, Alexander *physician*

NEBRASKA

Grand Island
Bosley, Warren Guy *pediatrician*

Hemingford
Ruffing, John Jacob, Jr. *family practice physician*

Kearney
De Los Angeles, Reynaldo Adrillana *psychiatrist, consultant*

Lincoln
Hirai, Denitsu *surgeon*
Koszewski, Bohdan Julius *internist, medical educator*
Metz, Philip Steven *surgeon, educator*
Weaver, Arthur Lawrence *physician*

Norfolk
Bartholow, George William *psychiatrist*

Omaha
Bittner, Marvin Joel *physician, educator*
Bylund, David Bruce *pharmacologist, educator*
Camras, Carl Bruce *ophthalmologist, educator*
Casey, Murray Joseph *physician, educator*
Hansl, Nikolaus Rudolf *neuropharmacologist*
Harned, Roger Kent *radiology educator*
Hartman, Herbert Arthur, Jr. *oncologist*
Korbitz, Bernard Carl *retired oncologist, hematologist, educator, consultant*
Mellion, Morris Bernard *physician, educator*
Miller, Daniel Martin *surgeon, oncologist*
Nairn, Roderick *immunologist, biochemist, educator*
Neibel, Oliver Joseph, Jr. *medical services executive*
Oberst, Byron Bay *pediatrician, consultant*
Smith, John Wallace *surgeon, educator*
Ward, Vernon Graves *internist*
Weaver, Arthur Adolph *physician*

NEVADA

Las Vegas
Yin, Raymond Wah *radiologist*

NEW YORK

Buffalo
Nair, Madhavan Puthiya Veethil *immunologist, nutritionist, consultant*

NORTH DAKOTA

Bismarck
Hook, William Franklin *radiologist*

Fargo
Politoff, Alberto Lifschitz *neurologist, neurobiologist*
Ratnasamy, D.M. Daniel *physician*

Minot
Couldwell, William Tupper *neurosurgeon*

Minot AFB
Contiguglia, Joseph Justin *preventive medicine physician, internist*

Williston
Adducci, Joseph Edward *obstetrician, gynecologist*
Anderson, Wayne Lee *surgeon*

OHIO

Ada
Elliott, Robert Betzel *physician*

Akron
Alexander, Thomas Stern *immunologist*
Griffin, Max Eugene *pediatrician*
Kastelic, Joseph Ernest *pediatrician*
Kraus, Henry *retired physician, educator*
LoIudice, Thomas Anthony *gastroenterologist, researcher*
Parker, Michael George *plastic surgeon*
Waickman, Francis Joseph *physician*

Arcanum
Heise, Jesse L. *family practice physician*

Ashtabula
Brace, John Michael *osteopathic physician, otolaryngologist*

Athens
Chila, Anthony George *osteopathic educator*
Colvin, Robert Alan *neurobiology educator*
Hasemeier, Eric Francis *osteopathic physician, educator*
Hedges, Richard H. *epidemiologist, lawyer*

Beachwood
Mayers, Douglas Bruce *anesthesiologist, medical director*
Morris, Jeffrey Selman *orthopedic surgeon*
White, Eugene A. *physician, neuroradiologist*

Canal Winchester
Burrier, Gail Warren *physician*

Canton
Gordon, Irving Martin *osteopathic physician*
Maioriello, Richard Patrick *otolaryngologist*
Nadas, John Adalbert *psychiatrist*
Sicard, Guillermo Rafael *dermatologist*
Vaughn, Lisa Dawn *family physician, educator*

Cincinnati
Alexander, James Wesley *surgeon, educator*
Bower, Robert Hewitt *surgeon, educator, researcher*
Breneman, Debra Lynn *dermatologist, educator*
Cavanaugh, Paul Francis, Jr. *biochemical pharmacologist*
Chin, NeeOo Wong *reproductive endocrinologist*
Cole, Theodore John *osteopathic physician*
Crawford, Alvin Howell *pediatrician, orthopedist*
Deets, Carol Anne *health science educator*
Fisher, Edward Joseph, Jr. *psychiatrist*
Fody, Edward Paul *pathologist*
Forristal, Thomas Joseph *pediatrician*
Grad, Edward Alphonse *family practice physician*
Handwerger, Stuart *pediatrics educator*
Heaton, Charles Lloyd *dermatologist, educator*
Hillard, Paula Janine *physician, educator*
Kitzmiller, Karl William *dermatologist*
Maltz, Robert *surgeon*
Matthews, Norman Eakes *obstetrician, gynecologist, medical director*
Meese, Ernest Harold *thoracic and cardiovascular surgeon*
Nash, J. Frank *pharmacologist, toxicologist*
Sherman, Kenneth Eliot *medicine educator, researcher*
Simon, David Leo *physician*
Walters, Nancy Lu *medical services educator*
Wilmott, Robert William *pediatrician, educator*
Wright, Creighton Bolter *cardiovascular surgeon, educator*

Cleveland
Baker, Mark Early *radiology educator*
Baker, Saul Phillip *geriatrician, cardiologist, internist*
Berggren, Jean Frances Reddell *psychiatrist, educator*
Bloser, Dieter *radiologist*
Boswell, Mark Vance *physician*
Brody, Robert *dermatologist, educator*
Brouhard, Ben Herman *pediatric nephrologist*
Cohen, Alan R. *neurosurgeon*
Cowan, Dale Harvey *internist, lawyer*
Denko, Joanne D. *psychiatrist, writer*
Elmets, Craig Allan *dermatologist*
Ewing-Wilson, Deborah Louise *neurologist*
Friedland, Robert Paul *medical researcher, neurologist, educator*
Friedman, Ernest Harvey *physician, psychiatrist*
Gurd, Alan R. *surgeon*
Harding, Clifford Vincent, III *pathologist, cell biologist, immunologist*
Headrick, Linda Ann *physician, educator*
Holzbach, Raymond Thomas *gastroenterologist, author, educator*
Hoogwerf, Byron James *physician*
Jacobs, Ernest Christopher *physician*
Jacobucci, Nicola Joseph *family physician, educator*
Kramer, John Robert, Jr. *cardiologist, researcher*
Mc Henry, Martin Christopher *physician, educator*
Muzic, Raymond Frank, Jr. *radiology educator, biomedical engineering educator*
Nieder, Michael Louis *pediatrician*
Perry, George *neuroscience researcher*
Pomeranz, Jerome Raphael *dermatologist*
Reydman, Melvin Maxwell *thoracic surgeon*
Robbins, Frederick Chapman *physician, medical school dean emeritus*
Ruff, Robert Louis *neurologist, physiology researcher*
Schwartz, Richard Abram *psychiatrist*
Solomon, Glen David *physician, researcher*
Stafford, Arthur Charles *medical association administrator*
Stanton-Hicks, Michael D'Arcy *anesthesiologist, educator*
Wish, Jay Barry *nephrologist, specialist*

Columbus
Barth, Rolf Frederick *pathologist, educator*
Burkhart, John A *physiatrist, educator*
Burkman, Allan Maurice *pharmacology educator*
Epstein, Avrom David *physician, ophthalmologist*

Essig, Garth Fredric *obstetrician gynecologist, medical educator*
Flood, Joseph *physician, educator*
Ford, Constance Elaine *electroneurodiagnostic technician*
Fryczkowski, Andrzej Witold *ophthalmologist, educator, business executive*
Furste, Wesley Leonard, II *surgeon, educator*
Gaeuman, John Victor *physician, educator*
Goodman, Hubert Thorman *psychiatrist, consultant*
Haque, Malika Hakim *pediatrician*
Hilliard, Kirk Loveland, Jr. *osteopathic physician, educator*
Hom, Theresa Maria *osteopathic physician*
Kaplan, Paul Elias *physiatrist, educator*
Lander, Ruth A. *medical group and association administrator*
Lim, Shun Ping *cardiologist*
Litvak, Ronald *psychiatrist*
Long, Sarah Elizabeth Brackney *physician*
Mortensen, Mary Ellen *pediatrician, educator, medical administrator*
Speicher, Carl Eugene *pathologist*
Stephens, Sheryl Lynne *family practice physician*
Stern, Stephen Lewis *psychiatry educator*
Svendsen, Dale Phillip *psychiatrist, health care administrator, educator*
Tzagournis, Manuel *physician, educator, university administrator*
Zipf, William Byron *pediatric endocrinologist, educator*

Cortland
Kulper, Benjamin Jacob *physician*

Dayton
Arn, Kenneth Dale *physician, city official*
Bullock, John David *ophthalmic surgeon*
Hewes, Robert Charles *radiologist*
Kay, Jerald *child psychiatry educator, researcher*
Lechner, George William *surgeon*
Mossman, Douglas *psychiatrist, educator*
Ruegsegger, Donald Ray, Jr. *radiological physicist, educator*
Steele, Jack Ellwood *surgeon, medical researcher*
Van Niman, Cynthia Marie *family physician, artist*

Dover
Harrold, Leslie Stuart *pathologist*

Elyria
Kuchynski, Marie *physician*

Euclid
Convery, Patrick George *orthopedic surgeon*

Findlay
Sierra, Edward *physician*

Gallipolis
Clarke, Oscar Withers *physician*

Hamilton
Brandabur, Joseph Hubert *pathologist*

Holland
Sippo, Arthur Carmine *occupational medicine physician*

Jefferson
Macklin, Martin Rodbell *psychiatrist*

Lakewood
Adams, Henry George *radiologist*

Lebanon
Holtkamp, Dorsey Emil *medical research scientist*

Lima
Wangler, Mark Adrian *anesthesiologist*

Mansfield
Bogart, Keith Charles *neurologist*
Capaldo, Guy *obstetrician, gynecologist*
Houston, William Robert Montgomery *ophthalmic surgeon*

Marietta
Tipton, Jon Paul *allergist*

Massillon
McClain, Richard Eugene *osteopath*

Medina
Noreika, Joseph Casimir *ophthalmologist*

New Middletown
Hertel, Jay Alan *physician*

New Philadelphia
Wolf, Joan Mangon *health occupations instructor, nursing educator*

Norwalk
Burrell, Joel Brion *neuroimmunologist, researcher, clinician*
Gutowicz, Matthew Francis, Jr. *radiologist*
Holman, William Baker *surgeon, coroner*

Oberlin
Hamilton, Duane Lee *health care executive*

Oregon
Culver, Robert Elroy *osteopathic physician*

Pepper Pike
Angerman, Neil Stanley *medical consultant*

Reynoldsburg
Schneir, Steven Richard *psychiatrist*

Rocky River
Castele, Theodore John *radiologist*

Rootstown
Gerson, Lowell Walter *epidemiologist, educator*
Westerman, Philip William *biomedical researcher, medical educator*

Ross
Neu, Suzanne Marie *toxicologic pathologist*

Shaker Heights
Boyd, Arthur Bernette, Jr. *surgeon, clergyman, beverage company executive*
Riff, Emmanuel Raphael *internist*

Springfield
Kurian, Pius *physician*
Wood, Dirk Gregory *surgeon, physician*

Sylvania
Shanahan, Robert E. *plastic surgeon*

Tipp City
Dallura, Sal Anthony *physician*

Toledo
Barrett, Michael John *anesthesiologist*
Durzinsky, Dennis Steven *cardiothoracic surgeon, educator*
Ferguson-Rayport, Shirley Martha *psychiatrist, educator*
Horner, James Michael *pediatric endocrinologist*
Lassiter, Anthony T. *neurology*
Martin, Donald Creagh *surgeon*
Martin, John Thomas *physician, author, educator*
Mulrow, Patrick Joseph *medical educator*
Rubin, Allan Maier *physician, surgeon*
Sadd, John Roswell *plastic surgeon*
Shermis, Robin Barry *radiologist*
Thombre, Melanie Susan *child psychiatrist*
Zrull, Joel Peter *psychiatry educator*

Uniontown
Krabill, Robert Elmer *osteopathic physician*

Warren
Rizer, Franklin Morris *physician, otolarynogologist*

Willoughby
Pazirandeh, Mahmood *rheumatologist, consultant*
Steinberg, Joel *physician, psychiatrist*

Worthington
Karolin, Stella Helene *psychiatrist*

Youngstown
Barr, Richard Gary *radiologist, chemist*
Buckley, John Joseph *obstetrician, gynecologist*
Butterworth, Jane Rogers Fitch *physician*
Walton, Ralph Gerald *psychiatrist, educator*

Zanesville
Kopf, George Michael *ophthalmologist*
Ray, John Walker *otolaryngologist, educator, broadcast commentator*

SOUTH DAKOTA

Aberdeen
Vidoloff, John Clarence *physiatrist*

Gregory
Greineder, Juergen Kurt *surgeon*

Rapid City
Dhillon, Robin K. J. S. *cardiac, thoracic and vascular surgeon*
Phillips, Gary L. *rehabilitation specialist*

Sioux Falls
Gregg, John Bailey *surgery educator, researcher*
Zawada, Edward Thaddeus, Jr. *physician, educator*

TEXAS

Houston
Baldwin, John Charles *surgeon, researcher*

WISCONSIN

Baraboo
Flygt, Thomas Rex *internist*

Beloit
Druckrey, Gerald Richard *ophthalmologist*

Brookfield
Kamsler, Milton A., Jr. *internist*

East Troy
Fidler, Alan Bandelin *retired physician*

Eau Claire
Murray, Michael John *psychiatrist*
Swenson, Richard Alan *physician educator*

Green Bay
Lacey, James Vincent *physician*
Soeter, John Randolph *cardiothoracic surgeon*
von Heimburg, Roger Lyle *surgeon*

Janesville
Gianitsos, Anestis Nicholas *surgeon*

La Crosse
Dalton, Ruth Margaret *retired pathologist*
Edland, Robert William *radiation oncology educator*
Lindesmith, Larry Alan *physician, administrator*
Romeyn, Richard Loren *orthopedic surgeon*
Silva, Paul Douglas *reproductive endocrinologist*
Songsiridej, Vanee *physician*
Waite, Lawrence Wesley *osteopathic physician*

Madison
Albert, Daniel Myron *ophthalmologist, educator*
Atkinson, Richard Lee, Jr. *internal medicine educator*
Budzak, Kathryn Sue (Mrs. Arthur Budzak) *physician*
Farrell, Philip M. *physician, educator, researcher*
Hetsko, Cyril Michael *physician*
Julian, Thomas Michael *medical educator, gynecologic surgeon*
Klein, Marjorie Hanson *psychiatry educator*
Marton, Laurence Jay *clinical pathologist, educator, researcher*
Merlis, Anthony Logan *neuroradiologist*
Miller, Michael Michel *physician, addiction medicine clinician, health facility administrator, educator*
Nordby, Eugene Jorgen *orthopedic surgeon*
Potter, Van Rensselaer *cancer researcher, author*
Robins, H(enry) Ian *medical oncologist*
Takahashi, Lorey K. *psychiatry educator, scientist*
Urban, Frank Henry *retired dermatologist, state legislator*

Manitowoc
Dickens, Robert Allen *psychiatrist*
Trader, Joseph Edgar *orthopedic surgeon*

Marshfield
Kelman, Donald Brian *neurosurgeon*

Milwaukee
Bhore, Jay Narayan *psychiatrist*
Chambers, LaRoyce Francis *obstetrician, gynecologist*
Chan, Carlyle Hung-lun *psychiatrist, educator*
Daniel, Alan *internist, cardiologist*
Dhamee, M(ohammed) Saeed *anesthesiology educator*
Feinsilver, Donald Lee *psychiatry educator*
Goldstein, Paul H(enry) *ophthalmologist, educator*
Gonnering, Russell Stephen *ophthalmic plastic surgeon*
Hoffman, William Kenneth *retired obstetrician, gynecologist*
Howards, Lawrence Allen *anesthesiologist*
Huizenga, Bernard Andrew *orthopedic surgeon*
Kloehn, Ralph Anthony *plastic surgeon*
Kortebein, Stuart Rowland *orthopedic surgeon*
Krausen, Anthony Sharnik *surgeon*
Libnoch, Joseph Anthony *physician, educator*
Meyer, Jon Keith *psychiatrist, psychoanalyst, educator*
Namdari, Bahram *surgeon*
Soergel, Konrad Hermann *physician*
Truitt, Robert Lindell *immunologist, researcher, pediatrics educator*
Zwicke, Dianne Lynn *internist, cardiologist, educator*

Neenah
Zimmerman, Delano Elmer *physician*

Nekoosa
Thompson, John Edward *physician, surgeon*

Platteville
Snyder, Virginia Lea *anatomist, educator*

Rhinelander
Norden, Leo George *internist*

River Falls
Dohnalek, Donald Wenceslaus *radiologist*

Sheboygan
Golubski, Joseph Frank *pathologist, physician*
Gore, Donald Ray *orthopedic surgeon*

Verona
Kieser, Randall John *family practice, addiction medicine and emergency medicine physician*

Viroqua
Andrew, Mark Henry *surgeon*

West Bend
Gardner, Robert Joseph *general and thoracic surgeon*

CANADA

MANITOBA

Winnipeg
Odim, Jonah *cardiac surgeon, educator*

ONTARIO

Sault Sainte Marie
Luus, George Aarne *physician*

Windsor
Ferguson, John Duncan *medical researcher*

ADDRESS UNPUBLISHED

Barlow, John Leslie Robert *physician*
Becker, Bruce Carl, II *physician, educator*
Bernath, Otto Nicolaus *physician*
Billion, John Joseph *orthopedic surgeon, state representative*
Bird, Harrie Waldo, Jr. *psychiatrist, educator*
Brandell, Jerrold R. *psychotherapist, educator*
Brasseur, James Walter *physician assistant, health care administrator*
Braun, Robert Alexander *retired psychiatrist*
Bree, Alanna Flath *medical researcher*
Bukar, Margaret Witty *physician assistant, healthcare administrator, civic leader*
Calhoun, William *research pharmacologist*
Cherenzia, Bradley James *radiologist*
Clayton, Bruce David *pharmacology educator*
Commito, Richard William *podiatrist*
Cropper, Rebecca Lynn *radiological engineer*
Diaz-Franco, Carlos *surgeon, anatomist, anesthesiologist*
Doolin, Paul F. *radiologist*
Dunaway, Frank Rosser, III *emergency physician*
Engel-Arieli, Susan Lee *physician*
Erickson, Curtis Allen *physician*
Faris, James Vannoy *cardiology educator, hospital executive*
Ferstenfeld, Julian Erwin *internist, educator*
Fox, William Richard *retired physician*
Gable, Karen Elaine *health occupations educator*
Galvez, Angel *physician*
Goldman, Jack Leslie *health professions educator*
Greenberg, Stephen Robert *retired pathology educator*
Hecht, Harold Arthur *orchidologist, chiropractor*
Humbert, James Ronald *pediatrician, educator*
Jenkins, James William *osteopath*
Johnson, David Grant *emergency physician*
Keye, William Richard, Jr. *physician, educator*
Kraybill, William Gress, Jr. *oncologist, educator*
Krizan, Kelly Joe *physician*
Lang, Ernst Frederick *radiologist*
Lindburg, Daytha Eileen *physician assistant*
Linz, Anthony James *osteopathic physician, consultant, educator*
Mallin, Sanford Richard *medical science educator*
Miller, Harry Johnson *hematology educator, oncologist*
Patel, Malini *psychiatrist*
Peterson, Thomas Hull *physician*
Polsinelli, Jerry *osteopathic obstetrician and gynecologist*
Powell, Kenneth Alger *physician*
Pratt, George Byington, III *pediatric radiologist*
Rusoff, Maurice Boris *retired physician*
Rutecki, Gregory William *physician, educator*
St. Cyr, John Albert, II *cardiovascular and thoracic surgeon*
Saneto, Russell Patrick *pediatrician, neurobiologist*
Schmid, Lynette Sue *child and adolescent psychiatrist*
Shapero, James Allen *psychiatrist*
Sherman, Joseph Owen *pediatric surgeon*
Sholiton, Marilyn Cohen *psychiatrist*
Socolofsky, Martha Ann *physician*
Stoken, Jacqueline Marie *physician*
Thompson, Joseph Warren *physician*
Uribe, Victor M. *psychiatrist, educator*
Walenga, Jeanine Marie *medical educator, researcher*
Weiner, Gershon Ralph *physician*

HUMANITIES: LIBERAL STUDIES

UNITED STATES

ILLINOIS

Aurora
Heinz, John Warren *historian, artist, photographer*

Barrington
Fromm, Harold *English language educator*

Carbondale
Abrate, Jayne Elyse *language educator*
Detwiler, Donald Scaife *historian, educator*
Gilbert, Glenn Gordon *linguistics educator*
Hahn, Lewis Edwin *philosopher, retired educator*
O'Day, Edward Joseph, Jr. *history educator*
Timpe, Eugene Frank *German language and literature educator*
Williams, Tony (John) *English educator*

Champaign
Lynn, John Albert *history educator*

Charleston
Buck, Rosemary A. *linguistics educator*
Waldrep, Christopher Reef *historian*

Chicago
Bartscherer, Thomas L. *scholar*
Belmonte, Frances Rose *pastoral studies educator*
Berk, Harlan Joseph *numismatist, writer, antiquarian*
Bouson, Brooks *English educator*
Bruegmann, Robert *architectural historian, educator*
Burd, William A. *numismatist*
Caron, Elisabeth *humanities educator, translator*
Crone, Anna Lisa *Russian literature educator*
Dorwick, Keith *educator*
Ehre, Milton *Slavic languages and literature educator*
Gardaphe, Fred Louis *English language educator*
Garrigan, Kristine Ottesen *English literature educator*
Gray, Hanna Holborn *history educator*
Grove, Helen Harriet *historian, artist*
Hansen, Miriam Bratu *English language educator*
Holli, Melvin George *history educator*
Ingham, Norman William *Russian literature educator, genealogist*
Kaster, Robert Andrew *classics educator*
Krokar, James Paul *history educator*
Ladenson, Robert Franklin *philosophy educator*
Librett, Jeffrey Scott *foreign language educator, researcher*
Long, John Hamilton *historian, editor*
McCaffrey, Lawrence John *historian, educator*
Meltzer, Sharon Bittenson *English language and humanities educator*
Miller, Angela Perez *bilingual and special education educator*
Mullins, Maire Elizabeth *English language educator*
Pestureau, Pierre Gilbert *literature educator, literary critic, editor*
Peterson, Paul Edward *economist*
Ramirez, Susan Elizabeth *Latin-American history educator*
Roeder, George Holzshu *history educator, writer*
Rosenwein, Barbara H. *history educator*
Sewell, William Hamilton, Jr. *historian*
Todd, Mary Ludwig *history educator*
Trela, D. J. *English language and literature educator, academic administrator*
Vanek, Elizabeth-Anne *English language and spirituality educator, minister*
Weil, Vivian *philosophy educator*
Weiner, Lynn Yvette *history educator*
Wendell, David V. *historian, public relations consultant*
Wexman, Virginia Wright *English language educator*

De Kalb
Bradley, John Michael *English language educator, writer*
Kern, Stephen Roger *history educator*

Kipperman, Mark *English language educator*
Posadas, Barbara Mercedes *history educator*

Decatur
Jacobs, Jo Ellen *philosophy educator*

Deerfield
Williams, Clifford Emmett *philosophy educator*

Des Plaines
Krupa, John Henry *English language educator*

Dorsey
Hinkle, Jo Ann *English language educator*

Evanston
Buchbinder-Green, Barbara Joyce *art and architectural historian*
Clayson, Susan Hollis *art historian, educator*
Dipple, Elizabeth Dorothea *language professional, English educator*
Packer, James Earnest *classics educator*
Petry, Carl Forbes *history educator*
Ver Steeg, Clarence Lester *historian, educator*
Wallace, Robert Weldon *classicist, educator*
Weil, Irwin *Slavic languages and literature educator*

Galesburg
Baylor, Elisabeth Anne *retired foreign language educator*

Jacksonville
Davis, James Edward *historian, educator*

Kankakee
Paul, James Francis *humanities and social science educator*

Lake Forest
Cowler, Rosemary Elizabeth *English educator, college administrator*
Zilversmit, Arthur *history educator*

Lebanon
Halfond, Irwin *history educator*

Macomb
Hallwas, John Edward *English language educator*
Leonard, Virginia W. *history educator, writer, researcher*
Spencer, Donald Spurgeon *historian, academic administrator*

Monmouth
Barnes-Bruce, Mary Hanford *English language educator*
Sienkewicz, Thomas Jerome *classics educator*

Mount Prospect
Stamper, James M. *retired English language educator*

Naperville
Lebeau, Bernard Pierre *history and foreign language educator*

Normal
Freed, John Beckmann *history educator*
Harris, Victoria Frenkel *English language educator*

Palatine
Hull, Elizabeth Anne *English language educator*
Smith, Frank Edmund *English educator*

Palos Heights
Higgins, Francis Edward *history educator*

Peoria
Ballowe, James *English educator, author*
Brune, Lester Hugo *American history educator*

River Grove
ZeLeVas, Sharon Rose *art history educator, lawyer*

Rockford
Carlson, Allan Constantine *historian*
Sylvester, Nancy Katherine *speech educator, management consultant*

Roscoe
Radke, Linda Kaye *foreign language educator*

Salem
Whitten, Doris Jean *professional speaker*

University Park
Purdy, Michael Waite *speech and communications educator*

Urbana
Barrett, James Robert *history educator, writer*
Davidson, Fred *education educator*
Douglas, George Halsey *writer, educator*
Fisher, Ralph Talcott, Jr. *historian, educator*
Littlefield, Daniel Curtis *history educator*
Manning, Sylvia *English studies educator*
Nichols, John Alden *history educator*
Nugent, B.A. *executive director, professor*
Smarr, Janet Levarie *comparative literature educator*
Watts, Emily Stipes *English language educator*

INDIANA

Ashley
Griggs, Karen *university educator, technical writer*

Bloomington
Anderson, Judith Helena *English language educator*
Behr, Susanna Marie *language professional, music educator*
Bernhardt-Kabisch, Ernest Karl-Heinz *English and comparative literature educator*
Buelow, George John *musicologist, educator*
Eoyang, Eugene Chen *comparative literature educator*
Geduld, Harry Maurice *humanities educator*
Hanson, Karen *philosopher, educator*
Hertz, David Michael *literature educator*
Kleinbauer, W. Eugene *art history educator*
Leach, Eleanor Winsor *classical studies educator*
Mathiesen, Thomas James *musicology educator*
Moody-Adams, Michele Marcia *philosophy educator*
Ransel, David Lorimer *history educator*
Walbridge, John *foreign language educator*

Centerville
Wendeln, Darlene Doris *English language educator*

Chesterton
Hoy, Suellen *historian*

Evansville
Bigham, Darrel Eugene *history educator*

Fort Wayne
Manheim, Werner *language educator*

Gary
Sheldon, Mark Peter *philosophy educator*

Greencastle
Evans, Arthur Bruce *Romance languages educator*
Ramsey-Rodriguez, Susan Kay *language educator, librarian*

Hanover
Curtis, George Martin, III *history educator*

Indianapolis
Anderson, David Louis *history educator*
Davis, Kenneth Wayne *English language educator, business communication consultant*
Geib, George Winthrop *history educator*
Krasean, Thomas Karl *historian*
Mason, Thomas Alexander *historian*

Jeffersonville
Kramer, Carl Edward *historian, urban planner*

Lafayette
Williams, Vernon J., Jr. *historian, educator, writer*

Marion
Elder, Marjorie Jeanne *English language educator*

Muncie
Davis, Kenneth Morton *artist, art historian, educator*
Ferguson, Ronald Joseph *historian, educator*
Gilman, Donald W., Jr. *French language educator*
King, Adele Cockshoot *French language educator*
Koumoulides, John (Thomas) Anastasios *historian, educator*
Stanley, Margaret Dureta Sexton *retired speech therapist*

Munster
Barrow, Geoffrey Ridley *Spanish language educator*

New Albany
Lliteras, Margarita *Spanish educator*

Notre Dame
Appleby, R(obert) Scott *history educator*
Delaney, Cornelius Francis *philosophy educator*
Dolan, Jay Patrick *history educator*
Douthwaite, Julia Viglione *French literature educator*
McInerny, Ralph Matthew *philosophy educator, author*

Oakland City
Harper, Margaret Earl *English language educator*

Richmond
Hamm, Thomas Douglas *archivist, history educator*
Kakutani, Akiko *Japanese language and linguistics educator*

Terre Haute
Brennan, Matthew Cannon *English literature educator, poet*
Looser, Devoney Kay *English educator*
Shoemaker, Rebecca Shepherd *history educator*
Swindell, Warren C. *humanities educator*
Weixlmann, Joseph Norman, Jr. *English educator, dean*

Valparaiso
Startt, James Dill *history educator*

Vincennes
Nossett, Paula Marie *English language educator*

West Lafayette
Adler, Thomas Peter *English language educator, university official*
Caracciolo, Enrique Ernesto *foreign language educator*
Covey, William Bennett, Jr. *English language and literature educator*
Flory, Wendy Stallard *English language educator*
Leitch, Vincent Barry *literary studies educator*
Mork, Gordon Robert *historian, educator*
Ross, Charles Stanley *English educator*
Splawn, P. Jane *English language educator*

IOWA

Ames
Dial, Denise Lorraine *historian*
Dial, Eleanore Maxwell *foreign language educator*
Pope, Christie Farnham *historian*

Avoca
Hardisty, William Lee *English language educator*

Cedar Falls
Basom, Ann Marie *Russian language and literature educator*
Cawelti, G. Scott *English language educator*
Clohesy, William Warren *philosophy educator*
Ward, Robert Jackson *American literature educator*

Clinton
Lowe, William Curtis *historian*

Davenport
Luzkow, Jack Lawrence *history educator, writer, consultant*
Stauff, Jon William *history educator*

Decorah
Gibbs, Virginia Gayle *Spanish language and literature educator*
Kath, Ruth Robert *foreign language educator*

Des Moines
Lewis, Virginia Lorraine *German language educator, musician*
Marty, Myron August *historian, educator*
Woods, Elsworth Peter *educator, dean, retired*

Iowa City
Alexander, Robert Lester *art historian, educator*
Ash, Mitchell Graham *history educator*
Desmond, Jane C. *fine arts educator*
Dettmer, Helena R. *classics educator*
Donadey, Anne *comparative literature and women's studies educator*
Folsom, Lowell Edwin *English language educator*
Hale, Charles Adams *history educator*
Hawley, Ellis Wayne *historian, educator*
Solbrig, Ingeborg Hildegard *German literature educator, author*

Lamoni
Wight, Darlene *retired speech educator*

Le Mars
Mayes, Jean Marie Keally *global education and foreign language educator*

Marshalltown
Colbert, Thomas Burnell *history and literature educator*

Waterloo
Bierwirth, Henry Christian *history educator*

KANSAS

Chanute
Dillard, Dean Innes *English language educator*

Fort Leavenworth
Epstein, Robert Morris *history educator*

Goddard
Criss, Darlene June *English language educator*

Great Bend
Gunn, Mary Elizabeth *retired English language educator*

Kansas City
Reitz, Charles Edward *philosophy educator*

Lawrence
Boyd, Beverly *English literature educator*
Brundage, James Arthur *historian, educator*
Cateforis, David Christos *art history educator*
Conrad, Joseph Lawrence *Slavic language educator*
Eldredge, Charles Child, III *art history educator*
Kuntz, Dieter Kurt *history educator, researcher, translator*
Pultz, John Francisco *art historian, curator*
Saeed, Mohammed *Islamic historian, eqyptologist, educator*
Schoeck, Richard J(oseph) *English and humanities scholar*
Worster, Donald Eugene *history educator*

Leawood
Graham, John Thomas *history educator*

Manhattan
Higham, Robin *historian, editor, publisher*

Ottawa
Tyler, Priscilla *retired English language and education educator*

Shawnee Mission
Mohr, Ellen G. *English language educator*

Topeka
Everett, William Arlie *musicology educator*
Haury, David Arthur *historical administrator*

University Of Kansas
Freeman, Bryant C. *foreign language educator*

KENTUCKY

Alvaton
Porterfield, Nolan *English language educator, writer*

Louisville
Ford, Gordon Buell, Jr. *English language, linguistics, and medieval studies educator, author, retired hospital industry financial management executive*

MICHIGAN

Allendale
Goode, James Francis *history educator*

Alma
Hoefel, Roseanne Louise *English language educator*

Ann Arbor
Anderson, Elizabeth Secor *philosopher, educator*
Aparicio, Frances Rivera *Romance languages educator*
Brandt, Richard Booker *former philosophy educator*
Morris, Phyllis Sutton *philosophy educator*

Berrien Springs
Markovic, John Jovan *modern European historian, educator*

Big Rapids
Mehler, Barry Alan *humanities educator, journalist, consultant*

Birmingham
Pilling, Patricia Leslie *oral historian, anthropologist*
Snyder, Nancy Margaret *translator, language services company executive*

Bloomfield Hills
Gossett, Kathryn Myers *language professional, educator*
Starkman, Betty Provizer *genealogist, writer, educator*

Cedarville
Pittman, Philip McMillan *historian*

Dearborn
Baumgarten, Elias *philosopher, educator*

Detroit
Beard, Michael Carl *linguist, educator*
Brown, Thomas *history educator*
Bukowczyk, John Joseph *history educator, consultant, writer, lecturer*
Hatzichronoglou, Helen (Lena Hatzichronoglou) *Greek language and literature educator*
Kibler, Louis *Romance languages educator*
Kostuch, Dorothy Ann *art history educator*
Rashid, Harun Ur *philosopher, educational administrator*
Richmond, Marsha Leigh *science historian*
Stivale, Charles Joseph *French language and literature educator*
Strozier, Robert Manning, II *retired English literature educator*
VanBurkleo, Sandra Frances *history educator*
Wojtas, Thomas Gerard *art historian, consultant*

East Lansing
Anderson, David Daniel *retired humanities educator, writer, editor*
Bresnahan, Roger Jiang *humanities educator, researcher*
Cooper, David Dale *American studies educator*
Dean, Thomas Keith *English and American studies educator*
Engel, Bernard Francis *humanities educator*
Grimes, Margaret Whitehurst *medievalist, educator*
Hudson, Mutsuko Endo *Japanese language educator*
Kronegger, Maria Elisabeth *French and comparative literature educator*
McCracken, Charles James *philosophy educator*
Paananen, Victor Niles *English educator*
Roberts, Nora Ruth *English educator*
Snow, Joseph Thomas *language educator*

Escanaba
Howard, Alan Charles *retired English language educator*

Flint
Rendleman, Danny Lee *English language educator*
Scharchburg, Richard P. *history educator, automotive history writer*
Schroeder, Michael Jay *history educator*

Grand Rapids
Hoekema, David Andrew *philosophy educator, academic administrator*
Mellema, Gregory Frank *philosophy educator*
Romanowski, William David *cultural historian, writer*
Zuidervaart, Lambert Paul *philosophy educator*

Grosse Pointe
Peters, Thomas Robert *English language educator, writer*

Grosse Pointe Park
Stronski, Anna Maria Niedźwiedzka *language professional*

Holland
Quimby, Robert Sherman *retired humanities educator*

Houghton
Seely, Bruce Edsall *historian, educator*

Jackson
Feldmann, Judith G. *language professional, educator*

Kalamazoo
Davidson, Clifford Oscar *humanities educator*
Dybek, Stuart *English educator, writer*
Jones, Leander Corbin *educator, media specialist*
Ruoff, Cynthia Osowiec *foreign language educator*
Wilson, Benjamin Calvin *Black American studies educator*

Lansing
Harvey, Joanne H. *genealogist*

Livonia
Holtzman, Roberta Lee *French and Spanish language educator*

Marquette
Thundy, Zacharias Pontian *modern language educator*

Midland
Seiler, Charlotte Woody *retired English language educator*
Servinski, Sarah Jane (Jeroue) *language arts educator*

Monroe
Roberti, Mary Teresa *retired English language educator*

Mount Pleasant
Apter, Ronnie Susan *English educator, translator*

Portage
Stohrer, Philip Charles *media specialist*

Rochester
Arrathoon, Leigh Adelaide *medievalist, editor, writer*
Barnard, John *history educator*
Benson, Linda Kay *Modern China and Inner Asia educator, researcher*
Finucane, Ronald Charles *history educator*
Garcia, Wilma Thackston *English language and literature educator*
Horning, Alice Silverberg *rhetoric and linguistics educator*
Wawro, Geoffrey Dwight Winslow *history educator*
Wood, Susan Elliott *art history educator*

Saint Joseph
Keller, Diane Marie *English language educator, school media specialist*

Southfield
Papazian, Dennis Richard *history educator, political commentator*

Sterling Heights
Ice, Orva Lee, Jr. *history educator*

University Center
Gonzalez, Judyth L. Betz *speech communication educator*

Walled Lake
Rood, Judith Mendelsohn *historian*

Warren
Kintner, Hallie Joanne *demographer*

Ypsilanti
Cere, Ronald Carl *languages educator, consultant, researcher*
Norton, Jody (John Douglas Norton) *English language educator*

MINNESOTA

Bemidji
Bonner, Helen Ward *English language and literature educator*
Evans, Deanna Genelle *English language educator*

Collegeville
Vann, Theresa Mary *historian*

Coon Rapids
Carlson, Linda Marie *language arts educator, consultant*

Duluth
Fetzer, James Henry *philosopher, educator*

Mankato
Chinea-Serrano, Jorge Luis *ethnic studies educator*
Wicker, Nancy Lynn *art history educator*

Marshall
Amato, Joseph A. *history educator*

Minneapolis
Bashiri, Iraj *Central Asian studies educator*
Evans, Sara Margaret *history educator*
Garciagodoy, Juanita *Mexican studies educator*
Jahn, Gary Robert *foreign language educator*
Monson, Dianne Lynn *literacy educator*
Pesklo, Christopher Richard (Peskiluoma) *history educator*
Seidel, Robert Wayne *science historian, educator, institute administrator*
Vecoli, Rudolph John *history educator*

Moorhead
Chan, Henry Yun Shing *history educator*
Coomber, James Elwood *English language educator*
Mason, David James *English language educator*

Morris
Ahern, Wilbert Harrell *history educator, academic administrator*

Northfield
Clark, Clifford Edward, Jr. *history educator*
Soule, George Alan *literature educator*
Ulmer, Anne Close *foreign language educator*
Wilkie, Nancy Clausen *classics and archaeology educator*
Zelliot, Eleanor Mae *history educator*

Red Lake Falls
Proechel, Glen Fred *foreign language educator, minister*

Saint Cloud
Hofsommer, Donovan Lowell *history educator*
Van Buren, Phyllis Eileen *Spanish and German language educator*

Saint Paul
Davis, Joy Lee *English language educator*
Fridley, Russell William *historian*
Miller, Leslie Adrienne *English language educator, poet*
Murray, Peter Bryant *English language educator*
Sherry, Richard James *English language educator*
Webster, Susan Verdi *art history educator*

Winona
Adickes, Sandra Elaine *English language educator, writer*

MISSOURI

Canton
Kane, Carolyn *language professional, writer*

Columbia
Barabtarlo, Gennady Alexis *foreign literature and language educator, writer*
Biers, William Richard *classical studies educator*
Camargo, Martin Joseph *English literature educator*
Cunningham, Noble E., Jr. *history educator, writer*
Curtis, James Malcolm *Russian language educator*
Foley, John Miles *English language and classical studies educator*
Fulweiler, Howard Wells *language professional*
Montuori, Deborah Jane *English language educator*
Nauert, Charles Garfield *history educator*
Northup, Beverly A. Baker *pricipal chief*
Thiher, O. Allen *foreign language professional, educator*
Wallach, Barbara Price *classicist, educator*

Florissant
Ashhurst, Anna Wayne *foreign language educator*

Jefferson City
Loschky, Helen Morris *retired English literature educator*

Joplin
Harder, Henry Louis *literature educator*
Laas, Virginia Jeans *historian*
Sale, Sara Lee *history educator*
Saltzman, Arthur Michael *English language educator*
Schmidt, Karl Joseph *historian, educator*

Kansas City
Ehrlich, George *retired art history educator, researcher*
Feagin, Susan Louise *philosophy educator*
Ford, Jean Elizabeth *former English language educator*
Hix, Harvey Lee *philosophy educator*
Johnson, W. Lloyd *baseball historian, consultant*
Oldani, Louis Joseph *literature educator*

Kirksville
Bartter, Martha Ann *English language educator*
Orel, Sara Elinor *art history educator, archaeologist*

Marshall
Gruber, Loren Charles *English language educator, writer*

Rolla
Allison, Sandy *genealogist, appraiser, political consultant*

Saint Louis
Barry, Bert *language educator*
Berthoff, Rowland Tappan *historian, educator*
Boyd, Robert Cotton *English language educator*
Carroll, Joseph Clelburn *English educator*
Czosnyka, Helena Julia *humanities educator*
Gibson, Roger Fletcher, Jr. *philosopher, educator*
Howard, John Sebastian *English educator*
May, Larry *philosophy educator*
Rava, Susan Roudebush *French language and literature educator*
Sand, Gregory William *history educator, researcher*
Suelflow, August Robert *historian, educator, archivist*
Tierney, James Edward *literature educator*
Ullian, Joseph Silbert *philosophy educator*
Weninger, Robert Karl *foreign literature educator*
Westerfield, Donald Lee *economics educator*
Wolfe, Peter *educator, author*
Wu, Nelson Ikon *art history educator, author, artist*
Zlatic, Thomas David *English literature educator*

Springfield
Miller, Worth Robert *history educator*

Union
Harvey, Robert Gene *English language educator*

Warrensburg
McClure, Arthur Frederick, II *history educator, archivist*
Robbins, Dorothy Ann *foreign language educator*
Yates, Robert Allen *English language educator*

NEBRASKA

Hastings
McEwen, Larry Burdette *retired English and theater arts educator, author*

Kearney
Benzel, Kathryn Nowicki *English language educator*
Coram, Colleen Ann (O'Brien) *Spanish language educator*
Davis, Roger Paul *history educator*
Sullwold, Corliss Kay *history educator*
Umland, Samuel Joseph *English language educator*

Lincoln
Leinieks, Valdis *classicist, educator*

Omaha
Carrigan, JoAnn *history educator*
Okhamafe, Imafedia *English literature and philosophy educator*
Skau, Michael W. *English educator*

NEW MEXICO

Albuquerque
Frings, Manfred Servatius *philosophy educator*

NEW YORK

Schenectady
Murphy, William Michael *literature educator, biographer*

NORTH DAKOTA

Bismarck
Newborg, Gerald Gordon *historical agency administrator*

Fargo
Danbom, David Byers *history educator*
Peet, Howard David *English language and literature educator*

Grand Forks
Caldwell, Mary Ellen *English language educator*
Donaldson, Sandra Marie *English educator*

Mayville
Brunsdale, Mitzi Louisa Mallarian *English language educator, book critic*

Minot
Andreasen, Bethany Jayne *history educator*
Paulson, Suzanne Morrow *English educator*

OHIO

Akron
Baranowski, Shelley Osmun *history educator*
Clinefelter, Ruth Elizabeth Wright *historian, educator*
Ducharme, Howard Maurice *philosopher, educator*
Zangrando, Robert Lewis *historian educator*

Alliance
Saffell, John Edgar *retired history educator*

Athens
Allaire, Gloria Kaun *Italian language educator*
Booth, Alan Rundlett *history educator*
Chojna, Wojtek *philosophy educator*
Dombrowski, Paul Matthew *English educator*
Holt, Mara Dawn *English educator*
Mosley, Albert G. *philosophy educator*
Pach, Chester Joseph, Jr. *history educator*
Perdreau, Cornelia Ruth Whitener (Connie Perdreau) *English as a second language educator, international exchange specialist*
Whealey, Lois Deimel *humanities scholar*

Bowling Green
Lavezzi, John Charles *art history educator, archaeologist*

Canton
Horvath, Brooke Kenton *English language educator*

Chagrin Falls
Rawski, Conrad H(enry) *humanities educator, medievalist*

Chesapeake
Eldridge, Carrie Woodard *history researcher, teacher, consultant*

Cincinnati
Aber, John Irwin *humanities educator, researcher, fiction writer*
Alexander, John Kurt *history educator*
Chard, Leslie Frank, II *English language educator*
Ciani, Alfred Joseph *language professional, dean*
Einbinder, Susan Leslie *literature educator, rabbi*
Foster, Nancy Bushnell *genealogist*
Harris-Cline, Diane *history and classical archaeology educator*
Heilman, Christine Weber *language educator*
Kamesar, Adam *literature educator*
Levine, Bruce Carlan *history educator*
Mills, Carl Rhett *linguist, educator*
Peterson, Gale Eugene *historian*
Shapiro, Herbert *history educator*
Williams, Leslie Ann *art historian*

Cleveland
Anderson, David Gaskill, Jr. *Spanish language educator*
Benseler, David Price *foreign language educator*
Haddad, Gladys Marylin *American studies educator, author, consultant*
Hinze, Klaus-Peter Wilhelm *language educator*
Shorrock, William Irwin *history educator, academic administrator*
Ubbelohde, Carl William *history educator*
Velasco, Esda Nury *speech and language professional*
Weinberg, Helen Arnstein *American art and literature educator*
Woollacott, Angela Mary *historian*
Yin, Philippa Brown *Spanish language and literature educator*
Zupancic, Anthony *English and communication educator*

Columbus
Anderson, Harald Jens *classical studies and languages educator*
Beyerchen, Alan Duane *historian*
Brittin, Marie Eleanor *communications, psychology, speech and hearing science educator*
King, John Norman *English language educator, researcher*
Lake, Barbara Joyce *history and literature educator*
Moulton, Joy Wade *genealogist, writer*
Newman, Michael J. *linguistic educator*
Roche, Mark William *German language educator*
Verzar, Christine Beatrice *art historian, educator*

Concord
Ulsenheimer, Dean *English language educator*

Dayton
Bednarek, Janet Rose *history educator*
Jenkins, Fred William *librarian*
Peñas-Bermejo, Francisco Javier *Spanish language educator*
Romaguera, Enrique *foreign language educator, corporate interpreter*

Deshler
Myers, Christy Colwell *historian, retail merchandiser*

Dublin
McGary, Daria L. *foreign languages educator*

Findlay
Kern, Gilbert Richard *history educator*

Huron
Ruble, Ronald Merlin *humanities and theater communications educator*

Kent
Apseloff, Marilyn Fain *English educator*
Hassler, Donald Mackey, II *English language educator, writer*
Jameson, John Robert *historian, researcher, educator*
Mandia, Patricia Marie *English language and literature educator, writer*
Miller, Terry Ellis *ethnomusicologist*
Rubin, Mark Richard *foreign languages administrator, educator*
Worobec, Christine Diane *history educator*
Wright, Sue Ellen *translator, educator*
Wunderlin, Clarence Edward, Jr. *historian, editor*
Zornow, William Frank *historian, educator*

Logan
Conner, Leland Lavon *Indian lorist*

Medina
Brown, Kathryn Lisbeth *secondary education educator*
Paladino, Lyn A *retired English educator*

Mentor
Sondey, Margaret Ellen *historian, educator*

Niles
Darlington, Oscar Gilpin *historian, educator*

Norwich
King, Lauren Alfred *English language educator*

Oxford
Cayton, Mary Kupiec *historian, educator*
Fahey, David Michael *history educator*
Luce, Stanford Leonard *retired French language and literature educator*
Yamauchi, Edwin Masao *history educator*

Painesville
Nugent, Robert Leon *modern languages educator, librarian*

Parma Heights
Cook, Jeanne G. *historian, genealogist*

Portsmouth
Mirabello, Mark Linden *history educator*

Rio Grande
Doubleday, James Frank *English language educator*
Wilson, Samuel Joseph *historian, educator*

Steubenville
Russell, Henry Michael Woodrow *university educator*

Toledo
Lora, Ronald Gene *history educator*
Smith, Robert Freeman *history educator*
Wikander, Matthew Hays *English language educator*
Wright, Lee Alfred *language educator*

Van Wert
Schweikle, Paul Douglas *genealogist*

Warren
Hourigan, Maureen Marmion *English educator*
Yoke, Carl Bernard *English language educator, critic*

Westerville
Chaney, Norman Richard *English studies educator*

Wilberforce
Marcum, Bradley Dale *English educator*
Schlesinger, Keith Robert *historian, educator*

SOUTH DAKOTA

Brookings
Sweeney, Jerry Kent *history educator*

Rapid City
Day, Michael Joseph *English educator*

Sioux Falls
Carlson Aronson, Marilyn A. *English language educator*
Huseboe, Arthur Robert *American literature educator*
Staggers, Kermit LeMoyne, II *history and political science educator*

Vermillion
Wilson, Norma Clark *English language educator*

TEXAS

College Station
Berger, Harris Merle *ethnomusicologist, educator*

WISCONSIN

Appleton
Breunig, Charles *historian, educator*
Chaney, William Albert *historian, educator*
Doeringer, Franklin M. *historian, educator*
Herscher, Susan Kay *English language educator*

Ashland
Shifferd, Kent Drummond *history educator*

Beloit
Rosenwald, John *humanities educator*

De Pere
Abel, Donald Clement *philosophy educator*
Zahorski, Kenneth James *English language educator, college administrator*

Dodgeville
Kavaloski, Vincent *philosophy educator*

Endeavor
LaFountain, Leslie Joseph *language educator*

Fond Du Lac
Kraus, Michael John *English language and literature educator*

Franklin
Lindsey-Hito, Lois Ellen *Spanish language educator, artist*

Iola
Rulau, Russell *numismatist, consultant*

Janesville
Kinnaman, Theodore Dwight *music educator*

La Crosse
Buffton, Deborah Darlene *history educator*
Pemberton, William Erwin *historian, educator*
Rausch, Joan Mary *art historian*

Lodi
Schereck, William John *retired historian, consultant*

Madison
Bush, Sargent, Jr. *English language educator*
Cassidy, Frederic Gomes *humanities educator*
Chapman, Robin Smith *psycholinguist, educator*
Gordon, Linda *history educator*
Hatheway, Jay *history educator*
Ihde, Aaron John *history of science educator emeritus*
Lessick-Xiao, Anne Elsie *foreign language educator*
Mallon, Florencia Elizabeth *history educator*
Paynter, Mary *English literature educator*
Perkins, Merle Lester *French language educator*
Schoville, Keith N. *Hebrew and Semitic studies educator*
Sealts, Merton Miller, Jr. *English language educator*
Shaw, Joseph Thomas *Slavic languages educator*
Singer, Marcus George *philosopher, educator*

Menomonie
Wallen, Martha Louise *foreign language educator*

Milwaukee
Backes, Nancy Constance *language educator*
Bates, Milton J. *English language educator*
Blaeser, Kimberly Marie *English and comparative literature educator*
Buck, David Douglas *historian*
Camilli, Priscilla Constance *art history educator, curator*
Gauger, Michael Thomas *historian, editor*
Greene, Victor Robert *history educator*
Hay, Robert Pettus *history educator*
Healy, David Frank *history educator*
Horsman, Reginald *history educator*
Kainz, Howard Paul *philosophy educator*
Maguire, Daniel Charles *ethics educator*
Swanson, Roy Arthur *classicist, educator*
Theis, Peter George *retired classics educator*
Wainwright, William Judson *philosophy educator*
Waldbaum, Jane Cohn *art history educator*

Oshkosh
Pontynen, Arthur John *art historian, educator*

Platteville
Branson, Stephanie Rita *English language educator, literary critic*

Ripon
Lowry, Eddie Rountree, Jr. *classical studies educator*

River Falls
Smith, Clyde Curry *historian, educator*

Sparta
Reisinger, Joy Ann *genealogist*

Stevens Point
De Smet, Imogene Lorrainne Marie *classicist, educator*

Superior
Mershart, Ronald Valere *history educator*

Watertown
Wallman, Charles James *historian*

Waukesha
Dukes, Jack Richard *history educator*
Rozga, Margaret *English language educator*

Whitewater
Burrows, Robert Nelson *American and English literature educator*
Wedin, Carolyn E. *English educator*

ADDRESS UNPUBLISHED

Aulie, Richard Paul *science history educator*
Boyd, Adeline Smith *art history educator*
Brown, James Montgomery *retired English language and literature educator, academic administrator*
Cassidy, Mary Joan *historian, consultant*
Chambers, Marjorie Bell *historian*
Cooper-Lewter, Marcia Jean *fine arts educator, administrative assistant*
Cowan-Ricks, Carrel *historical archaeologist*
Czach, Marie *art historian*
DeLong, Lea Rosson *art historian*
Dosé, Frederick Philip, Jr. *art historian, art and antiques appraiser, consultant, liquidator*
Dzuback, Mary Ann *historian, educator*
Friedman, Victor Allen *linguist, eduator*
Gilb, Corinne Lathrop *history educator*
Gutke, Jeffrey Alan *Spanish language educator*
Johnston, Allan James *English language educator*
Kellogg, Dennis Lee *history educator, consultant*
Kramer, Dale Vernon *English language educator*
Lamb, Lois Jean *English educator*
Lawrence, James Rolland *retired history educator*
Leder, Cyril Martin *retired English language educator*
Levine, Phyllis *English language educator*
Martin, John William *educator, antiquarian bookseller*
McKinsey, Thomas Michael *philosopher, educator*
Nochman, Lois Wood Kivi (Mrs. Marvin Nochman) *educator*
Petuchowski, Elizabeth Rita *German language and literature educator*
Richardson, Michael Barrett *history educator*
Saha, Santosh C. *history educator*
van der Marck, Jan *art historian*
Wind, Barry *art history educator*
Winter, Thomas *history educator*

HUMANITIES: LIBRARIES

UNITED STATES

CONNECTICUT

Westport
Hutchison, Kevin Don *librarian, writer*

ILLINOIS

Aurora
Christiansen, Raymond Stephan *librarian, educator*

Bensenville
Rodriguez, Jill Holopigian *library director*

Bloomington
Olson, Rue Eileen *librarian*

Carbondale
Werlich, David Patrick *history educator*

Carol Stream
O'Dell, Lynn Marie Luegge (Mrs. Norman D. O'Dell) *librarian*

Carterville
Ubel, James Andrew *library director*

Cary
McNulty, Diane Rose *library director*

Caseyville
LeBlanc, Diana L. *librarian*

Champaign
Scheetz, George Henry *library director*

Chicago
Barnum, Sally J. *librarian*
Butta, Deena Celeste *librarian*
Gerdes, Neil Wayne *library director*
Guss, Emily Renee *librarian*
Hanrath, Linda Carol *librarian, archivist*
Miletich, Ivo *library and information scientist, bibliographer, educator, linguist, literature research specialist*
Muellner, John Phillip *librarian, educator*
Park, Chung Il *librarian*
Siarny, William Donald *librarian, archivist*
Van Cura, Joyce Bennett *librarian*
Vondruska, Eloise Marie *librarian*

De Kalb
Studwell, William Emmett *librarian, writer*

Deerfield
Fry, Roy H(enry) *librarian, educator*

Dwight
Rumbles, John Bryce *library director*

Elk Grove Village
West, Mark Allen *librarian, educator*

Evanston
Ney, Neal John *library director*

Galva
Ericson, Constance Marie *library director, elementary educator*

Glenview
Blegen, John Clifford *library administrator*

Highland Park
Greenfield, Jane Weiss *library director*

Jacksonville
Gallas, Martin Hans *librarian*

Kansas
Bennett, Charlotte Anne *library director, educator*

Lake Bluff
Weinstock, Grace Evangeline *librarian, retired educator*

Lake Forest
Miller, Arthur Hawks, Jr. *librarian, consultant*

Mc Henry
Burger, Janette Marie *librarian*
Tepe, Ann Silcott *library services professional*

Moline
Moran, Thomas J. *public library director*

Mount Olive
Thimsen, Janice Loretta *librarian*

Naperville
Tucker, Beverly Sowers *information specialist*

Niles
Czarnecki, Cary John *librarian*

Park Forest
Flynn, Barbara Lee *librarian*

Park Ridge
McCully, William Craig *library administrator*

Peoria
Grewell, Johanne H. Fairs *high school library media specialist*

Prospect Heights
Rozanski, Barbara Ann *administrative librarian*

River Forest
Marco, Guy Anthony *librarian, educator*

River Grove
Padgitt, Dorothy Angelos *library director*

Rockford
Rosenfeld, Joel Charles *librarian*

Roselle
Lueder, Dianne Carol *library director*

Saint Joseph
McKinney, Susan Dawn *librarian*

Schaumburg
Adrianopoli, Barbara Catherine *librarian*

Springfield
Coss, John Edward *archivist*
Sorensen, Mark Wayne *archivist, historical researcher*

Stonington
Moma, Nancy Mae *librarian*

Summit
Dudek, Edward Frances *library administrator*

Sycamore
Young, Arthur Price *librarian, educator*

Tremont
Opem, John David *library manager*

Urbana
Choldin, Marianna Tax *librarian, educator*
Schlipf, Frederick Allen *library administrator*
Schmidt, Diane Carol *librarian*

Wheaton
Weimer, Ferne Lauraine *librarian*

Wilmette
Kona, Martha Mistina *librarian, freelance information consultant*

Woodridge
Brown, Mary Sue *library administrator*

INDIANA

Albion
Shultz, Linda Joyce *library director*

Auburn
Mountz, Louise Carson Smith *retired librarian*

Bluffton
Elliott, Barbara Jean *librarian*

Carmel
Fuchs, John Michael *librarian*

Columbia City
Scank, Janet Marie *librarian*

Elkhart
Doellman, Michael Anthony *librarian*

Evansville
Hager, Gregory Michael *library director*
Louden, William Frank *librarian*

Fort Wayne
Krull, Jeffrey Robert *library director*

Hobart
Christianson, Elin Ballantyne *librarian, civic worker*

Indianapolis
Baldwin, James Allen *librarian, researcher*
Gnat, Raymond Earl *librarian*
McKowen, Dorothy Keeton *librarian*
Oldham, Phyllis Virginia Kidd *retired librarian*
Tucker, Dennis Carl *library executive*

Lafayette
Robinson, Joel Martin *library director*
VanHandel, Ralph Anthony *librarian*

Lake Village
Martin, Mary Kaylene *librarian*

Lebanon
Miner, Fern Pippenger *librarian*

Mishawaka
Eisen, David John *librarian*

Muncie
Schaefer, Patricia *librarian*
Yeamans, George Thomas *librarian, educator*

Nashville
Oliger, Yvonne Chinn *librarian*

Owensville
Callis, Peggy *library director*

Peru
Wagner, Charles Alan *librarian*

Plymouth
Sherwood, Lillian Anna *librarian, retired*

Portland
Clamme, Rosalie Ann *library director*

Shelbyville
Short, Ann Marie Herold *library director*

West Lafayette
Collins, Mary Ellen Kennedy *librarian, educator*
Markee, Katherine Madigan *librarian, educator*
Mobley, Emily Ruth *library dean, educator*

IOWA

Ames
Hill, Fay Gish *librarian*

Bennett
Seligman, Colette Arlene *library director*

Camanche
Rittmer, Elaine Heneke *library media specialist*

Carlisle
Berning, Robert William *librarian*

Cedar Rapids
Armitage, Thomas Edward *library director*

Davenport
Block, Marylaine *librarian*
Runge, Kay Kretschmar *library director*

Decorah
Kalsow, Kathryn Ellen *library clerk*

Indianola
Dyer, Cynthia Myers *library director*

Iowa City
Green, Deborah Parkhurst *librarian*
Woods, Lawrence Alan *librarian*

Jesup
Lellig, Cynthia *public library director*

Le Mars
Morris, Susan Marie *librarian*

Mallard
Kacmarynski, Nancy C. *librarian, nurse*

Marion
Kling, Susan Schaefer *librarian*
Renter, Lois Irene Hutson *librarian*

Rembrandt
Reiling, Carolyn Rae *library director*

West Bend
Wuebker, Colleen Marie *librarian*

West Branch
Dennis, (Mary) Ruth *retired librarian*
Walch, Timothy George *library administrator*

KANSAS

Atchison
Donaldson, Virginia Lee *librarian*

Chanute
Willis, Susan Jeanette *library director*

Cimarron
Crotts, Carolyn Pearl *school librarian*

Clay Center
Martin, JoAnne Luther *library director*

Enterprise
Wickman, John Edward *librarian, historian*

Goodland
Warren, Janet Elaine *librarian*

Iola
Carswell, Roger L. *library director*

Kinsley
Craft, Beverly Jo *library director*

Liberal
Bachman, Neal Kenyon *librarian*

Manhattan
Fisher, Julia Kathleen *library media specialist*

Parsons
Rabig, Anthony John *librarian*

Saint John
Padilla, Sue Ann *librarian*

Saint Marys
Dobbins, Freda J. *librarian*

Topeka
Marvin, James Conway *librarian, consultant*

Towanda
Van Buskirk, Janet Louise *library director*

Wakefield
Morice, Sandra Kay *librarian*

Wichita
Rademacher, Richard Joseph *librarian*

MICHIGAN

Adrian
Dombrowski, Mark Anthony *librarian*
Fosbender, Jule Joann *librarian*

Allendale
Schichtel, Barbara Nan *college library administrator*

Ann Arbor
Hodel, Mary Anne *library director*
Williams, John Troy *librarian, educator*

Auburn Hills
Williams, Calvin *librarian, consultant*

Berrien Springs
Waller, Elaine Louise *retired music materials librarian*

Comstock
Kasson, Shirley A. *library administrator*

Detroit
Cooper, Donna Ruth *corporate librarian*
Curtis, Jean Trawick *library director*
Mehaffey, Karen Rae *library director*
Powell, Ronald Rowe *library science educator*

Flint
Corser, Maureen Slagg *librarian, media specialist*

Freeland
Wilder, Della Juanita *librarian, secondary education educator*

Highland Park
Ndenga, Lucy Viola *librarian*

Holland
Wagenaar, Larry John *archivist*

Kalamazoo
Carlson, Andrew Raymond *archivist*
De Vries, David John *reference assistant*
Grotzinger, Laurel Ann *university librarian*

Lake Linden
Johnson, Kathleen Carlton *librarian*

Lansing
Johnson, Jeffrey *deputy state librarian*
Needham, George *librarian*

Marlette
Degelbeck, Gretchen May *library director*

Menominee
Roark, Barbara Ann *librarian*

Monroe
Conable, Gordon M. *library director*

Montague
Gundy-Reed, Frances Darnell *librarian, healthcare manager*

Owosso
Arvin, Charles Stanford *librarian*

Plymouth
Berry, Charlene Helen *librarian, musician*
deBear, Richard Stephen *library planning consultant*

Port Huron
Wu, Harry Pao-Tung *librarian*

Redford
Paffhausen, Frederick John *librarian*

Rochester
Ring, Daniel F(rank) *reference librarian*

Southfield
Cocozzoli, Gary Richard *library director*

Warren
Maxson, Nancy M. *librarian*

Wyandotte
Wallace, Barbara Rae *library director*

MINNESOTA

Adrian
Vaselaar, Meredith Stanton *librarian*

Burnsville
Grovender, Gladys Lovern *archivist consultant*

Hancock
Shaw, Dorothy Ruth *library director, social worker*

Hibbing
von Lang, Frederick William *librarian, genealogist*

Mankato
Christenson, John Donald *library director, consultant*

Minneapolis
Hathaway, Edward William *librarian*
Mabry, Celia Elaine Hales *librarian*
Ostrem, Walter Martin *librarian, educator, consultant*
Wik, Jean Marie (Jean Marie Beck) *librarian, media specialist*

Pine River
O'Brien, Marlys Carol Howe *library director*

Saint Cloud
Peterson, Patricia Elizabeth *library network administrator, educator*

Saint Paul
Davenport, John B(rian) *librarian, archivist*
Fogerty, James Edward *archivist, state official*

Shoreview
Roos, Marianne Louise *library director*

Thief River Falls
Jauquet-Kalinoski, Barbara *library director*

Winona
Sullivan, Kathryn Ann *librarian, educator*

MISSOURI

Blue Springs
Nelson, Freda Nell Hein *librarian*

Brentwood
O'Neill, Kathryn J. *librarian, educator*

Columbia
Almony, Robert Allen, Jr. *librarian, businessman*
DeWeese, June LaFollette *librarian*

Independence
Ferguson, John Wayne, Sr. *librarian*
Johnson, Niel Melvin *archivist, historian*

Jefferson City
Winn, Kenneth Hugh *archivist, historian*

Kansas City
Bradbury, Daniel Joseph *library administrator*
Irvine, Robert Keith *librarian*
Jones, C. Lee *librarian, consultant*
Pedram, Marilyn Beth *reference librarian*
Sherby, Louise Sharon *librarian*

Lake Lotawana
Zobrist, Benedict Karl *library director, historian*

Nevada
Hizer, Marlene Brown *library director*

Norborne
Wightman, Doris Stephenson *library director, city collector*

Saint Charles
Bock, Angela Marie *librarian*

Saint Louis
Gaertner, Donell J. *library director*
Holt, Glen Edward *library administrator*
Lauenstein, Ann Gail *librarian*
Recklein, Linda Sue *library administrator*

Springfield
Bohnenkamper, Katherine Elizabeth *library science educator*
Curtis, Carol Edith *library director*

Washington
Witt, Carolyn M. *library director, educator*

NEBRASKA

Omaha
Bailey, Ella Jane *academic librarian*
Gardner, Evelyn Mae *librarian*
LaCroix, Michael John *librarian*
Larson, Carole Allis *library and information scientist, educator*
Tollman, Thomas Andrew *librarian*

Rushville
Plantz, Christine Marie *librarian, union officer*

York
Schulz, Stanley Dean *library director*

NORTH DAKOTA

Cooperstown
Tanner-Bendickson, Michelle Karalynn *librarian*

Devils Lake
Chattin, James William *library director*

Grand Forks
Renick, Paul Rodney *library media director, educator*

Hillsboro
Gill, Bernard Ives *librarian*

Minot
Caley, Diane Lee *library administrator*

Valley City
Fischer, Mary Elizabeth *library director*

OHIO

Ada
Parkhill, Miriam May *retired librarian*

Akron
Allan, Ann Gould *library science educator*
Schlup, Leonard C. *librarian, researcher, writer, historian*
Tierney, Catherine Marie *librarian*

Ashtabula
Balog, Rita Jean *librarian*

Bedford
Parch, Grace Dolores *librarian*

Bellaire
Kniesner, John Thomas *librarian*

Berea
Dial, David Emory *library director*

Bowling Green
Edwards, Ronald Gary *librarian, historical researcher*

Bucyrus
Herold, Jeffrey Roy Martin *library director*

Cincinnati
Abate, Anne Katherine *librarian, consultant*
Bestehorn, Ute Wiltrud *retired librarian*
Zafren, Herbert Cecil *librarian, educator*

Cleveland
Clifford, Naomi *librarian*
Goldberg, Kenneth Paul *information specialist*
Mason, Marilyn Gell *library administrator, writer, consultant*
Smythe Zâjc, M. Catherine *research librarian, administrator*

Columbus
Black, Larry David *library director*
Hunter, James Jerome *library director*
Klee, Andrew Martin *library assistant*
Meredith, Meri Hill *reference librarian*

Cuyahoga Falls
Bender, John Charles *library director*

Dayton
Coulton, Martha Jean Glasscoe (Mrs. Martin J. Coulton) *library consultant*
Wallach, John S(idney) *library administrator*

Delaware
Brulotte, Richard *librarian*
Schlichting, Catherine Fletcher Nicholson *librarian, educator*

Eaton
Kendall, Susan Haines *library director*

Findlay
Dudley, Durand Stowell *librarian*

Harrison
Everett, Karen J. *librarian*

Lyndhurst
Packer, Diana *reference librarian*

Martins Ferry
Storck, John W.P. *librarian*

Medina
Matthews, Gertrude Ann Urch *retired librarian, writer*

Miamisburg
Yakura, Thelma Pauline *retired library director, consultant, writer*

Middletown
Schaefer, Patricia Ann *retired librarian*

Niles
Yancura, Ann Joyce *library director*

Oberlin
Greenberg, Eva Mueller *librarian*

Pomeroy
Powers, Ruth Eileen *library director*

Portsmouth
Cook, Charles Terrence *library director, consultant*

Shaker Heights
Long, Karen Draut *librarian*

Steubenville
Hall, Alan Craig *library director*

Westerville
Armentrout, Mary Ellen *librarian*

Youngstown
Trucksis, Theresa A. *library director*

PENNSYLVANIA

Villanova
Mullins, James Lee *library director*

SOUTH DAKOTA

Sioux Falls
Dertien, James LeRoy *librarian*
Thompson, Ronelle Kay Hildebrandt *library director*

Timber Lake
Salzer, Margaret Mae *librarian*

TEXAS

College Station
Wilson, Don Whitman *archivist, historian*

Pasadena
Schroeder, Joanne Frances *librarian*

WISCONSIN

Eau Claire
Mitchell, Milton Edward *librarian*

Fremont
Sallee, Lynn Kant *library director*

Hartland
Kosinsky, Barbara Timm *librarian*

La Crosse
Hill, Edwin Lee *librarian*

Madison
Scherdin, Mary Jane Liskovec *librarian, information professional, researcher*

Mequon
Sedgwick, Alice Jane *librarian*

Milwaukee
Herrera, Alberto, Jr. *librarian*
Huston, Kathleen Marie *library administrator*
Jameson, Patricia Madoline *science librarian*
Valance, Marsha Jeanne *library director, story teller*

Oshkosh
Blake, Frank Burgay *librarian, writer*
Jones, Norma Louise *librarian, educator*

Platteville
Freymiller, Mary Jean *archives curator*

Waupun
Norman, Steve Ronald *librarian*

Wausau
Eldred, Heather Ann *librarian*

West Allis
Wasick, Mary Ann *librarian*

Wisconsin Rapids
McCabe, Ronald Brian *library director*

CANADA

ONTARIO

Thunder Bay
Harrison, Karen Ann *library director*

ADDRESS UNPUBLISHED

Diehl, Carol Lou *library director, retired, library consultant*
Ernst, Gordon Emery, Jr. *librarian*
Estes, Elaine Rose Graham *retired librarian*
Gauthier, Mary Elizabeth *librarian, researcher, secondary education educator*
Hatcher, Marie Theresa *librarian*
Klatt, Melvin John *library consultant*
Knight, Margaret L. *librarian, educator*
Ricketts, Sondra Lou *librarian*
Schlather, Mary Agnes *librarian*
Scoles, Clyde Sheldon *library director*
Somers, Joseph Moore *retired librarian*
Trenery, Mary Ellen *librarian*
Worley, Michael Preston *art historian*
Zang, Debra Jean *librarian*

HUMANITIES: MUSEUMS

UNITED STATES

ALABAMA

Anniston
Quick, Edward Raymond *museum director, educator*

ILLINOIS

Chicago
Balzekas, Stanley, Jr. *museum director*
Boyd, Willard Lee *museum administrator, educator, lawyer, professor*
Consey, Kevin Edward *museum administrator*
Edelstein, Teri J. *museum administrator, educator*
Heltne, Paul Gregory *museum executive*
Kahn, James Steven *museum director*
Kramer, Roberta M. *antiques dealer*
Wilson, Karen Lee *museum director*
Wood, James Nowell *museum director and executive*

Mahomet
Kennedy, Cheryl Lynn *museum director*

Peoria
Morris, John David *museum fundraiser*

Schaumburg
Darling, Sharon Sandling *museum director*

Springfield
Leary, Richard Lee *museum curator*
Mc Millan, R(obert) Bruce *museum executive, anthropologist*

INDIANA

Evansville
Streetman, John William, III *museum official*

Goshen
Morris, Robert Julian, Jr. *art gallery owner*

Indianapolis
Gantz, Richard Alan *museum administrator*

IOWA

Davenport
Bradley, William Steven *art museum director*

Iowa City
Prokopoff, Stephen Stephen *art museum director, educator*

Muscatine
Green, Linda Lou *museum curator, educator*

KANSAS

Lawrence
Norris, Andrea Spaulding *art museum director*

Leavenworth
Holt, Robert Anthony *museum administrator*

Manhattan
Walker, Kathrine L. *museum educational administrator, educator*

MICHIGAN

Bingham Farms
Bostick, William Allison *museum administrator*

Dearborn
Skramstad, Harold Kenneth, Jr. *museum administrator, consultant*

Detroit
Edwards, Esther G. *museum administrator, former record, film and entertainment company executive*
Parrish, Maurice Drue *museum executive*
Sachs, Samuel, II *museum director*

East Lansing
Taylor, Jane Lundeen *curator*

Grand Rapids
Chester, Timothy J. *museum director*
Tomlinson, Gary Earl *museum curator*

Grosse Pointe Shores
Devine, Maureen Elizabeth *curator*

MINNESOTA

Rochester
Merrell, Ed, Jr. *historical society administrator*

Saint Paul
Czarniecki, Myron James, III *art museum director, cultural planner*
Peterson, James Lincoln *museum executive*

MISSOURI

Columbia
McVicker, Mary Ellen Harshbarger *museum director, art history educator*

Kansas City
Cattelino, Ronald E. *art education administrator*
Johnson, William Arthur *gallery representative, historian*
Ucko, David Alan *museum director*
Wilson, Marc Fraser *art museum administrator and curator*

Saint Louis
Burke, James Donald *museum administrator*
Crandell, Dwight Samuel *museum executive*
Ketner, Joseph Dale *museum director, art historian*

Springfield
Berger, Jerry Allen *museum director*

NEBRASKA

Kearney
Lund, Virginia Llego *museum director, curator, chemistry educator*

OHIO

Canton
Brown, Jeffrey Douglas *historic preservation administrator*

Cincinnati
Avril, Ellen Bowdre *art museum curator, art historian, educator*
Brown, Daniel *independent art consultant, critic, writer*
Kohnen, Nancy Stone *museum director*
Lehman, Otto Israel H.M. *curator emeritus, educator*
Rogers, Millard Foster, Jr. *retired art museum director*

Cleveland
Bergman, Robert Paul *museum administrator, art historian, educator, lecturer*
Taylor, J(ocelyn) Mary *museum administrator, zoologist, educator*
Thurmer, Robert *art gallery director*
Turner, Evan Hopkins *retired art museum director*
Ward, William Edward *museum exhibition designer*

Dayton
Nyerges, Alexander Lee *museum director*

Toledo
Steadman, David Wilton *museum official*

Wilberforce
Courtney, Vernon S. *museum administrator*

PENNSYLVANIA

Wyndmoor
Wint, Dennis Michael *museum director*

SOUTH DAKOTA

Keystone
Wenk, Daniel N. *landmark site administrator*

Mitchell
Sellars, James Allen *landmark director*

Vermillion
Larson, André Pierre *museum director*

VIRGINIA

Williamsburg
Kelm, Bonnie G. *art museum director, educator*

WISCONSIN

Baraboo
Parkinson, Greg Thomas *museum director*

Kenosha
Pollei, Dane F. *historical society executive*

Madison
Fleischman, Stephen *art center director*

Milwaukee
Biller, Geraldine Pollack *curator*

Sheboygan
Kohler, Ruth DeYoung *arts center executive*

CANADA

MANITOBA

Winnipeg
Wrigley, Robert Ernest *museum director, ecologist*

JAPAN

Miyazaki
Meyer, Ruth Krueger *museum administrator, educator, art historian*

ADDRESS UNPUBLISHED

Cook, Alexander Burns *museum curator, artist, educator*
Danoff, I. Michael *art center director, writer, educator*
Dodenhoff, Helen Jean *curator, archivist*
Matney, Malinda Mae *housing director*
Nold, Carl Richard *state historic parks and museums administrator*
Stearns, Robert Leland *curator*

INDUSTRY: MANUFACTURING. *See also* FINANCE: FINANCIAL SERVICES.

UNITED STATES

ALABAMA

Selma
Meeks, Clayton Brewster *automotive industry executive*

ARIZONA

Cave Creek
Waggoner, Daniel LeRoy *hobby industry executive*

CALIFORNIA

Los Angeles
Triplett, Eric *fashion coordinator*

Torrance
Hershberger, Jerry Richard *automotive executive*

FLORIDA

Naples
Williams, Edson Poe *retired automotive company executive*

Saint Petersburg
Wechsler, Sergio *automotive executive, consultant*

ILLINOIS

Abbott Park
Burnham, Duane Lee *pharmaceutical company executive*
Hodgson, Thomas Richard *health care company executive*

Addison
Brunken, Gerald Walter, Sr. *manufacturing company executive*

Alton
Crook, Emil Albert *construction company executive*
Walker, Jonathan Alan *steelworker*

Antioch
Strang, Charles Daniel *marine engine manufacturing company executive*

Arlington Heights
Lafferty, Peter William *product specialist*

Aurora
Belcher, La Jeune *automotive parts company executive*

Bartonville
Graves, Carol Kenney *construction company executive*

Belvidere
Britt, Ronald Leroy *manufacturing company executive*
Keller, Harold William *chemical company executive*
Taylor, Owen Edwin *manufacturing manager*

Bloomingdale
Pedicini, Louis James *manufacturing company executive*
Wolande, Charles Sanford *corporate executive*

Bloomington
Eviston, Mitchell D. *agricultural products company executive*

Broadview
Pang, Joshua Keun-Uk *trade company executive*

Buffalo Grove
D'Souza, Austin *manufacturing executive*
Simes, Stephen Mark *pharmaceutical products executive*
Wigodner, Byron I. *pharmaceutical executive*

Chester
Welge, Donald Edward *food manufacturing executive*

Chicago
Barber, Edward Bruce *medical products executive*
Bergere, Carleton Mallory *contractor*
Bryan, John Henry *food and consumer products company executive*
Clarke, Richard Stewart *security company executive*
Drexler, Richard Allan *manufacturing company executive*
Gandurski, Ronald Edward *manufacturing executive*
Gidwitz, Gerald *hair care company executive*
Gidwitz, Ronald J. *personal care products company executive*
Gordon, Ellen Rubin *candy company executive*
Hoppert, Gloria Jean *food products executive*
Klein, Richard Temple, Jr. *hand tool manufacturing executive*
Lichten, Nancy G. *chemical company executive*
Lockwood, Frank James *manufacturing company executive*
Malott, Robert Harvey *manufacturing company executive*
Marcuse, Manfred Joachim *paper products executive*
McMillan, James *popcorn company executive*
Moore, John Ronald *manufacturing executive*
Polydoris, Nicholas George *electronics executive*
Schwartz, Charles Phineas, Jr. *replacement auto parts company executive, lawyer*
Signorile, Eugene Robert *business executive, product designer*
Smerling, David Warren *manufacturing executive*
Smithburg, William Dean *food manufacturing company executive*
Stone, Roger Warren *container company executive*
Stotler, Edith Ann *grain company executive*
Tannenberg, Dieter E. A. *manufacturing company executive*
Venit, William Bennett *electrical products company executive, consultant*
Victorine, John William *card company executive*
Wechter, Clari Ann *paint manufacturing company executive*
Wellington, Robert Hall *manufacturing company executive*
Yapoujian, Nerses Nick *manufacturing executive*
Zimny, Robert Walter *metal processing executive*
Zuern, Rosemary Lucile *manufacturing executive, treasurer*

Chicago Heights
Ball, Jason Joseph *plant manager*

Crystal Lake
Althoff, J(ames) L. *construction company executive*
Pearson, Louise Mary *retired manufacturing company executive*
Pearson, Nels Kenneth *retired manufacturing company executive*

De Kalb
Brickner, Bruce *food products executive*
Kahn, Jan Edward *manufacturing company executive*

Decatur
King, Michael Layton *agricultural products executive*

Deerfield
Graham, William B. *pharmaceutical company executive*
Heiar, Kurt Francis *health industry executive*
Kushner, Jeffrey L. *manufacturing company executive*
Loucks, Vernon R., Jr. *healthcare products and services company executive*
Wolf, Andrew *food manufacturing company executive*

Des Plaines
Cassidy, James Mark *construction company executive*
Runge, Lawrence Dean *automotive company executive*

Dunlap
Leetz, John Richard *health care executive*

Elgin
Gwillim, Russell Adams *manufacturing company executive*
Wilson, Robert Byron *manufacturing executive*

Elk Grove Village
Nadig, Gerald George *manufacturing executive*

Evanston
Seidner, Allen Paul *food products executive, computer consultant*

Forest Park
Thomas, Alan *candy company executive*

Genoa
Naden, Vernon Dewitt *manufacturing executive*

Glen Ellyn
Bressler, Joshua Drew *construction executive*
Cvengros, Joseph Michael *manufacturing company executive*

Glencoe
Silver, Ralph David *distilling company director*

Glendale Heights
Koford, Stuart Keith *electronics executive*

Glenview
Habasevich, Robert Allan *healthcare executive*
Maryfield, John Arthur *manufacturing company executive*
Nichols, John Doane *diversified manufacturing corporation executive*
Sherman, Elaine C. *gourmet foods company executive, educator*

Grayslake
Johnson, Margaret H *welding company executive*

Hampshire
Villars, Horace Sumner *food company executive, marketing professional*

Highland Park
Singer, Norman Sol *food products executive, inventor*

Island Lake
Benson, John Earl *construction executive*

Itasca
Fowler, Jack W. *printing company executive*
Venere, Al H. *manufacturing company executive*

La Fox
Jackson, William Cole *manufacturing executive*

La Grange
Hubert, Jean-Luc *chemicals executive*

Lake Bluff
Albrecht, Edward Daniel *metals manufacturing company executive*
Wacker, Frederick Glade, Jr. *manufacturing company executive*

Lake Forest
Brown, Sharon Gail *company executive, consultant*
Reichert, Jack Frank *manufacturing company executive*
Yaconetti, Dianne Mary *business executive*

Lake Villa
Anderson, Milton Andrew *chemical executive*

Lemont
Dillon, Phillip Michael *construction company executive*

Libertyville
Baske, C. Alan *manufacturing company executive*

Lincolnshire
Conatser, John Edward *health care services executive, accountant*
Ferreira, Jo Ann Jeanette Chanoux *consumer electonics manufacturing executive*

Lisle
McCammack, Mike *business executive*

Long Grove
Liuzzi, Robert C. *chemical company executive*

Lyons
Edwards, Russell J. *manufacturing executive*

Mason City
Ainsworth, Thomas C. *seed company executive*

Melrose Park
Gihl, Nicholas T. *company executive*

Mendota
Hume, Horace Delbert *manufacturing company executive*

Mokena
Maiotti, Dennis Paul *manufacturing company executive*

Moline
Becherer, Hans Walter *agricultural equipment manufacturing executive*
Groteluschen, Ralph D. *manufacturing company executive*
Hanson, Robert Arthur *retired agricultural equipment executive*
Stowe, David Henry, Jr. *agricultural and industrial equipment company executive*

Monee
Marvin, Richard Walter *company executive*

Mount Prospect
Kolpak, Douglas Edward *inventory planning supervisor*

Naperville
McConaghy, George Aloysius *chemistry research manager*

Normal
Forhart, Dennis James *automotive executive*

Northbrook
Campbell, Ronald Bruce *clothing company executive*
Schmidt, Arthur Irwin *steel fabricating company executive*

Northfield
Morrison, Robert Scheck *food processing company executive*
Stepan, Frank Quinn *chemical company executive*

Oak Brook
Bouchard, James Paul *steel manufacturing sales executive*

Oak Park
Douglas, Kenneth Jay *food products executive*
Kraus, Albert Andrew, Jr. *retired medical supply company executive*

Palatine
Comerford, Joseph Francis *manufacturing executive*
Fairleigh, Kenneth Fisher, Jr. *electrical manufacturing company executive*
Ford, Quentin K. *manufacturing company executive*

Peoria
Avendano, Noel Jerome *computerized machinist, inventor*
Fites, Donald Vester *tractor company executive*
Vaughan, David John *distribution company executive*

Prospect Heights
Byrne, Michael Joseph *business executive*

Quincy
Taylor, Maurice, Jr. *manufacturing company executive*
Walters, Tom Frederick *manufacturing company official*

Richton Park
Mueller, George Bernard *contracting company executive*

Ringwood
Stresen-Reuter, Frederick Arthur, II *metal fabricating company executive*

Rock Falls
Bippus, David Paul *manufacturing company executive*

Rockford
Gloyd, Lawrence Eugene *diversified manufacturing company executive*
Horst, Bruce Everett *manufacturing company executive*
Kimball, Donald Robert *food company executive*

Rolling Meadows
Cash, Alan Sherwin *electronics assembly specialist*
Johnson, John Andrew *construction executive*

Romeoville
DePaul, John Phil *construction company executive, firefighter*

Round Lake
Johnston, William David *health care company executive*

Schaumburg
Bales, Edward Wagner *manufacturing executive*
Buchanan, Richard Kent *electronics company executive*
Sanderman, Maurice *construction company executive*
Titus, Arthur Leroy *construction executive*

Skokie
Anders, Robert Joseph *pharmaceutical company executive*
Green, David *manufacturing company executive*

South Elgin
Burdett, George Craig *plastics industry executive*

South Holland
Morgan, Arthur Thomas *steel company executive*

Spring Valley
Dzierzynski, Harold Thomas *automotive executive*

Springfield
Janssen, Daniel Joe *roofing manufacturer field advisor, consultant*

Sterling
Conway, John Paul *retired steel executive*
Gurnitz, Robert Ned *steel industry company executive*

Streator
Williams, Jeffry Cephas *business executive*

Sullivan
Earl, Frank D. *manufacturing company executive*

Tinley Park
Leeson, Janet Caroline Tollefson *cake specialties company executive*

Vernon Hills
Small, Marvin Burton *retired industrial chemicals company executive*

Villa Park
Miczuga, Mark Norbert *metal products executive*

Waukegan
Cherry, Peter Ballard *electrical products corporation executive*
Gockley, Barbara Jean *corporate professional*

Westmont
Gottlander, Robert Jan Lars *dental company executive*

Wheaton
Spedale, Vincent John *manufacturing executive*

Wheeling
Keats, Glenn Arthur *manufacturing company executive*

Wilmette
Egloff, Fred Robert *manufacturers representative, writer, historian*

Winnetka
Wood, Leonard Earle, III *managed health care executive*

Wood Dale
Knodell, Robert James *manufacturing company executive*
Kram, Guenther Reinhard *manufacturing executive*

Woodridge
Stall, Alan David *packaging company executive*

INDIANA

Anderson
Hart, John Marcus *electronics company executive*
Pianki, Francis Owen *manufacturing executive educator*

Angola
Young, James E. *company executive*

Berne
Sprunger, Donald J. *construction executive*

Bloomington
Haeberle, William Leroy *corporate director, business educator, entrepreneur*

Brownstown
Robertson, Joseph Edmond *grain processing company executive*

Butler
Leach, Gregory J. *metal products company executive*
Longardner, Craig Theodor *manufacturing executive*

Carmel
Shoup, Charles Samuel, Jr. *chemicals and materials executive*

Chesterfield
Burkett, Gordon R. *manufacturing executive*

Chesterton
Bilheimer, Robert William *metal processing company executive*
Petyo, Michael Edward *construction company owner*

Columbus
Baker, James Kendrick *auto parts manufacturing company executive*
Hartley, James Michaelis *aerospace systems, printing and hardwood products manufacturing executive*
Henderson, James Alan *engine company executive*
Kendall, James William *manufacturing company executive*
Naylor, Jim C. *engine manufacturing company executive*
Neal, Dennis R. *manufacturing executive*

East Chicago
Rakoczy, Jacob David *steel machining and fabricating executive*

Elkhart
Corson, Thomas Harold *manufacturing company executive*
Decio, Arthur Julius *manufacturing company executive*
Hill, Thomas Stewart *electronics executive, consultant, engineer*
Holtz, Glenn Edward *band instrument manufacturing executive*
Kerich, James Patrick *manufacturing company executive*
Kloska, Ronald Frank *manufacturing company executive*
Mathias, Margaret Grossman *manufacturing company executive, leasing company executive*

Evansville
Berry, Phillip Reid *flexible staffing executive*

Fairland
Lewchanin, Jacqueline *manufacturing company executive*

Fairmount
Boswell, Larry Ray *electronics company executive*

Fishers
Snyder, Gary Laine *electronics company project leader*

Fort Wayne
Alexander, William Mark *imaging company executive*
Collins, Linda Lou Powell *contract manager*
Neuenschwander, Thomas Ray *industrial automation company executive*

Gary
Washington, Wilma Jeanne *business executive*

Granger
Miller, Callix Edwin *manufacturing executive, consultant*

Indianapolis
Bindley, William Edward *pharmaceutical executive*
Gilmore, Michael Clinton *health services executive*
Harmon, Tim James *construction executive*
Hoch, John S. *chemicals executive, engineering executive*
Justice, Brady Richmond, Jr. *medical services executive*
Kirkham, James Alvin *manufacturing executive*
Lacy, Andre Balz *industrial executive*
Lundgren, Ralph Edward *foundation officer*
Mc Farland, H. Richard *food company executive*
McKee, Susan Park *meeting planner, writer*
Mortensen, Stanley John *automotive executive*
Powdrill, Gary Leo *production operations manager*
Reilly, Peter C. *chemical company executive*
Riggs, Anna Claire *metals servicing company executive*
Risdon, Michael Paul *manufacturing executive*
Step, Eugene Lee *retired pharmaceutical company executive*
Stewart, Paul Arthur *pharmaceutical company executive*
Swanson, David Heath *agricultural company executive*
Welch, John Francis *violin and viola manufacturing company executive*

Kokomo
McIndoo, Walter Rolla *electronics executive*

Loogootee
Burcham, Eva Helen (Pat Burcham) *electronics technician*

Mishawaka
Silver, Neil Marvin *manufacturing executive*

Munster
Luerssen, Frank Wonson *retired steel company executive*

Nashville
Stackhouse, David William, Jr. *retired furniture systems installation contractor*

South Bend
Allen, Wayde P. *manufacturing executive*
Hohulin, Mark E. *electronics specialist, drafting educator*

Valparaiso
Deardorff, John Milton, Jr. *camera manufacturing executive*

Warsaw
Creighton, W. Edward *food products executive*
Frederick, John *food products executive*

West Lafayette
St. John, Charles Virgil *retired pharmaceutical company executive*

IOWA

Birmingham
Goudy, James Joseph Ralph *electronics executive, educator*

Cedar Falls
Goldsmith, Michael R. *tool design supervisor*

Cedar Rapids
Jain, Rakesh *division manager of electrical product company*

Council Bluffs
Stoner, Leonard D. *novelty company executive*

Davenport
Caffery, John Patrick *lumber company salesman, retired, city alderman*
Ernster, R. Gene *manufacturing manager*
Hartman, Robert J. *aluminum company executive*

Denver
Schumacher, Marvin W. *manufacturing exective*

Des Moines
Hall, Mari *agricultural company executive*
Tuel, Larry LeRoy *construction finance executive*

Dubuque
Bertsch, Frank Henry *furniture manufacturing company executive*
Crahan, Jack Bertsch *manufacturing company executive*
McDonald, Robert Delos *manufacturing company executive*
Tully, Thomas Alois *building materials executive, consultant, educator*

Fairfield
Schaefer, Jimmie Wayne, Jr. *agricultural company executive*

Fort Dodge
Tursso, Dennis Joseph *business executive*

George
Winter, Dale G. *manufacturing executive*

Grinnell
Ashing, Robert W. *manufacturing company executive*

Houghton
Gollhofer, David Lee *manufacuturng executive*

Humboldt
Dodgen, John N. *manufacturing executive*

Iowa Falls
Jensen, Bill H. *production manager*

Jesup
Michels, Adam W. *shop foreman*

Keokuk
Harmon, Roy *plant manager gear company*

Laurens
Hong, Peter Lee *manufacturing executive*

Marion
Starr, David Evan *corporate executive*

Marshalltown
Foote, Sherrill Lynne *retired manufacturing company technician*

Muscatine
Howe, Stanley Merrill *manufacturing company executive*

Newton
Ward, Dean Morris *appliance manufacturing executive*

Pella
Slagter, Keith Eugene *manufacturing company executive*

Sioux City
Frankl, Donald T. *company president*
Lafferty, Craig T. *manufacturing executive*

Waterloo
Thom, Kelsey C. *engineering manager, manufacturing executive*

Webster City
Johnson, Douglas Eugene *manufacturing executive*

KANSAS

Beloit
Brinker, Lee J. *manufacturing company executive*

Hesston
Tryber, Thomas Anthony, Jr. *manufacturing company executive*

Kansas City
Baker, Clarence Albert, Sr. *structural steel construction company executive*
Chalberg-Plunkett, Sherri Linell *construction executive*
Olofson, Tom William *electronics executive*

Lecompton
Baranski, Dennis Anthony *diversified corporation executive*

Lenexa
Ascher, James John *pharmaceutical executive*
Barr, William Crawford *manufacturing company executive*

Olathe
Naegele, Eugene Alexander *electronics company executive*

Overland Park
Derr, Lee E. *chemical company executive*

Parsons
Palmieri, Guy Joseph *manufacturing executive, retired military officer*

Salina
Garrett, David L. *manufacturing company executive*

Scott City
Duff, Craig *agricultural products executive*

Shawnee
Padgett, David Ramon *manufacturing executive*

Shawnee Mission
Ball, Darrell Wayne *construction company executive, consultant*
Smith, DeLancey Allan *retired business executive*

Sunderland, Robert *cement company executive*

Wamego
Evans, Robert A. *manufacturing company executive*

Wichita
Basto, La Donna Joan *business administrator*
Eby, Martin Keller, Jr. *construction company executive*
Johnson, George Taylor *manufacturing executive*
Jonsson, Skuli *construction company executive*
Meyer, Russel William, Jr. *aircraft company executive*
Nienke, Steven A. *construction company executive*
Rosson, Dennis McKinley *manufacturing company executive*
Sinn, James Micheal *manufacturing executive*
Tullis, Dean James *voice products company executive*
Winters, Steve G. *business executive*

KENTUCKY

Lexington
Runcie, John Fryer *manufacturing company executive*

MICHIGAN

Ann Arbor
Larime, Michael Wall *manufacturing executive*
McGovern, Judy Ann *food products executive*
Oliver, Marguerite Bertoni *food service executive*
Stitley, James Walter, Jr. *food manufacturing executive*

Auburn Hills
Eaton, Robert James *automotive company executive*
Feldhouse, Lynn Alexandra *corporate philanthropist*

Battle Creek
Langbo, Arnold Gordon *food company executive*
McKay, Eugene Henry, Jr. *food company executive*

Bay City
Greve, Lucius, II *metals company executive*
Raddatz, John D. *manufacturing executive*

Benton Harbor
Whitwam, David Ray *appliance manufacturing company executive*

Bloomfield Hills
Burgess, Robert K. *construction company executive*
Leonard, Michael A. *automotive executive*
Maxwell, Jack Erwin *manufacturing company executive*

Bridgman
Jenkins, Brien Lee *manufacturing supervisor*

Center Line
Johnson, John Jay *automotive company administrator*

Dearborn
Baughman, Jennifer Jane *automotive executive*
Carter, Robert Lee *automotive company program manager*
Ford, William Clay *automotive company executive*
Hilton, David B. *automotive design stylist*
Sagan, John *former automobile company executive*
Trotman, Alexander J. *automobile manufacturing company executive*

Detroit
Hanson, David Bigelow *construction company executive, engineer*
Kiss, Istvan L. *manufacturing executive*
Raden, Louis *tape and label corporation executive*
Rines, John Randolph *automotive company executive*
Schwartz, Barry M. *iron and metal company executive*
Simon, Paul Jerome *holding company executive, accountant*
Smith, John Francis, Jr. *automobile company executive*
Stella, Frank Dante *food service and dining equipment executive*

East Lansing
Garrison, Charles Eugene *automotive executive*

Escanaba
Brayak, Thomas Lee *concrete and gravel company executive*

Farmington Hills
Houser, Charles William *automotive company executive*
Mackey, Robert Joseph *business executive*

Ferndale
Cole, Gretchen Bornor *distribution and service executive*

Flint
Acton, David L(awrence) *automobile company executive*
Goodstein, Sanders Abraham *scrap iron company executive*

Fraser
Beardslee, Daniel Bain *venture capitalist, educator*
Fisher, Erman Caldwell *corporate executive*

Galesburg
Lawrence, John Warren *business and broadcasting executive*

Grand Haven
Patterson, Doug J. *printing company executive*

Grand Rapids
Helder, Bruce Alan *metal products executive*
Parsh, Phillip J. *manufacturing executive*
Van Andel, Betty Jean *retired direct selling company executive*

Grosse Pointe
Ford, John Battice, III *business executive*
Mc Bride, Robert Dana *steel company executive*

Harbor Springs
Judge, John Emmet *manufacturing company marketing executive*

Highland Park
Haselwood, James Edward *automotive company executive*

Holland
Van Huis, Philip J. *manufacturing executive*

Jackson
Dullock, Scott Anthony *manufacturing executive*
Kelly, Robert Vincent, Jr. *metal company executive*

Kalamazoo
Dykstra, David Allen *corporate executive*
Hite, Judson Cary *retired pharmaceutical company executive*
Jones, Eugene Gordon *pharmaceutical company executive*
Vescovi, Selvi *pharmaceutical company executive*
Wilson, James Rodney *air equipment company executive*

Laingsburg
Scripter, Frank C. *manufacturing company executive*

Lansing
Anderton, James Franklin, IV *holdings company executive*

Marshall
Schubel, Dian *construction company manager*

Midland
Birdsall, Arthur Anthony *chemical executive*
Cuthbert, Robert Lowell *product specialist*
Lentz, Charles Wesley *retired chemical industry executive, consultant*
Popoff, Frank Peter *chemical company executive*
Tabor, Theodore Emmett *chemical company research manager*
Weiler, Scott Michael *machine tool manufacturing company executive*

New Hudson
Rochelle, Robert Edwin *product manager*

Oak Park
Brann, Donald Treasurer *manufacturing executive*
Gluklick, Edward *construction executive*
Moilanen, Thomas Alfred *construction equipment distributor*

Oxford
Brotzke, Gerald F. *manufacturing company executive*

Plymouth
Merrill, Kenneth Coleman *retired automobile company executive*
Navarre, Robert Ward *manufacturing company executive*
Vlcek, Donald Joseph, Jr. *food distribution company executive, consultant*

Pontiac
Stryker, James William *automotive executive, former military officer*

Port Huron
Hills, Randolph Allen *contractor*

Portage
Riesenberger, John Richard *pharmaceutical company executive*

Redford
Hirschberg, Paul D. *manufacturing executive*

Reed City
Murnik, James Michael *corporate executive*

Rochester
Rossio, Richard Dominic *automobile company executive*

Rochester Hills
Darnell, Gerald Thomas *automotive industry executive*
Gouldey, Glenn Charles *manufacturing company executive*

Romulus
Gulda, Edward James *automotive executive*
Scannell, Thomas John *cold metal forming company executive*

Roseville
Meli, David *program manager*

Saint Clair Shores
Heasel, John Frederick *office automations specialist*

Saint Joseph
De Long, Dale Ray *chemicals executive*
King, George Raleigh *manufacturing company executive*

Saranac
Herbrucks, Marilyn *food products executive*
Herbrucks, Stephen *food products executive*

Shelby
Hegg, Scott W. *executive manufacturing company*

Shelby Township
Wheeler, Wilmot Fitch, III *automotive industry executive*

Southfield
Way, Kenneth L. *seat company executive*
Wernecke, Heinz *die cast manufacturer, mechanical engineer*

Sparta
Fairchild, Henry Brant, III *manufacturing executive*

Sterling Heights
Brzoska, Michael Jerome *industrial manufacturing corporation executive*
Edens, Rudi R. *manufacturing engineer, administrator*

Taylor
Lyon, Wayne Barton *manufacturing company executive*
Manoogian, Richard Alexander *manufacturing company executive*

Tecumseh
Herrick, Kenneth Gilbert *manufacturing company executive*
Herrick, Todd W. *manufacturing company executive*

Troy
D'Annunzio, John Anthony *construction executive, technology consultant*
Fielder, James B. *industrial paint company executive*
Grewell, Judith Lynn *automotive executive*
Karlowski, Richard Martin *reliability engineer*
Lianning, Darrel W. *managing consultant*
Martin, Raymond Bruce *plumbing equipment manufacturing company executive*
Reickert, Erick Arthur *automotive executive*
Serafyn, Alexander Jaroslav *automotive executive, retired*
Smith, Wayne Arthur *export company executive*

Warren
Foxworth, John Edwin, Jr. *automotive executive, philatelist*
Ponka, Lawrence John *automotive executive*
Stark, Jay Irwin *automotive company executive*

Waterford
Broughton, Beverly Jane *construction executive*

Zeeland
Ruch, Richard Hurley *manufacturing company executive*

MINNESOTA

Austin
Anderson, Jeffrey Lynn *stone company executive*
Knowlton, Richard L. *food and meat processing company executive*

Avon
Haniland, Jeffrey S. *instrument company executive*

Bloomington
Powell, Ralph Edwin *manufacturing company executive*

Detroit Lakes
Super, William Alan *manufacturing executive*

Duluth
Whitney, Gwin Richard *brick distribution company executive*

Eagan
Clemens, T. Pat *manufacturing company executive*

Minneapolis
Anderson, Davin Charles *business representative, labor consultant*
Atwater, Horace Brewster, Jr. *retired food company executive*
Bazany, Le Roy Francis *manufacturing company executive, controller*
Bean, Atherton *food company executive*
Bell, David Curtis *manufacturing company executive*
Book, William Joseph *manufacturing executive*
Carlson, Curtis LeRoy *corporate executive*
Eames, Earl Ward, Jr. *management educator, development specialist*
Gherty, John E. *food products and agricultural products company executive*
Hale, Roger Loucks *manufacturing company executive*
Morris, Richard Jeffery *plastic extrusion company executive*
Paulu, Frances Brown *international center administrator*
Pederson, Jon Russell *construction equipment company owner*
Samuelson, Leonard W., Jr. *construction executive*
Sullivan, Austin Padraic, Jr. *diversified food company executive*
Willig, Leslie August *photography equipment manufacturing company executive*

Minnetonka
Osterberg, Thomas Karl *construction company executive*

Morris
Wilcox, Jeffrey Scott *instrument company executive*

Osseo
Spencer, Dale A. *medical products executive*

Prior Lake
Reese, Edward W. *medical products executive*

Richfield
McGraw, Vincent DePaul *manufacturing executive*

Rochester
Carlson, Roger Allan *manufacturing company executive, accountant*
Mayr, James Jerome *fertilizer company executive*

Saint Paul
Andersen, Elmer Lee *manufacturing and publishing executive, former governor of Minnesota*
Brullo, Robert Angelo *chemical company executive*
Burd, Francis John *packaging executive*
Ferkingstad, Susanne M. *cosmetics executive*
Grieve, Pierson MacDonald *specialty chemicals and services company executive*
Swanson, Thomas Richard *manufacturing, supply chain and systems executive*

Savage
Bean, Glen Atherton *entrepreneur*

Wayzata
Swanson, Donald Frederick *retired food company executive*

Willmar
Huisinga, Theodore *food products executive*

Winona
Dickinson, Wilfred Arthur *construction executive*

Woodbury
Hilker, Marcus Dudley, Jr. *manufacturing executive*

MISSOURI

Annada
Gibson, Gregory James *elementary school custodian*

Ballwin
Cuba, Robert Gregory *customer technical support administrator*

Barnhart
Miloscia, Steve *cement company foreman*

Blue Springs
Robbins, Kenneth E. *manufacturing company executive*

Boonville
Gehm, David Eugene *construction and environmental management executive*

Cape Girardeau
Lorenz, Ronald Theodore *manufacturing executive*

Carthage
Franklin, Joseph Earl *furniture and bedding components company executive*

Chesterfield
Biggerstaff, Randy Lee *medical products executive, sports medicine rehabilitation consultant*
Cornelsen, Paul Frederick *manufacturing and engineering company executive*
Morris, Richard Louis *healthcare company executive*

Clayton
Buechler, Bradley Bruce *plastic processing company executive, accountant*

Cottleville
Dowdy, John *company executive*

Fenton
Dinkins, Thomas Allen, III *construction equipment company executive*
Frank, Robert Thomas *sporting goods manufacturing company executive*
Marik, Karen L. *manufacturing company executive*
McDowell, George Edward *manufacturing executive*

Fulton
Backer, William Earnest *food products executive*

Green Ridge
Boarman, Marjorie Ruth *manufacturing company executive, consultant*

Hannibal
Coleman, Gloria Jean *chemical manufacturing company professional*

Hazelwood
Verebelyi, Ernest Raymond *manufacturing company executive*

Hermann
Oncken, Harold W. *machine service company executive*

Kansas City
Adams, James Robert *medical organization sales professional*
Bartlett, Paul Dana, Jr. *agribusiness executive*
Bobe, Henry Dale *pharmaceutical executive*
Eide, Eugene Gerhard *tool and die company executive*
Hebenstreit, James Bryant *agricultural products executive, bank and venture capital executive*
Johnson, Richard Dean *pharmaceutical consultant, educator*
Robinson, Chuck Frank *dairy company executive*
Stout, Edward Irvin *medical manufacturing company executive*
Strohmeier, Karl Wilhelm *pharmaceutical industry executive*
VanAuken, Alan Bradley *greeting card company executive*

Maryland Heights
Schultz, Daniel Joseph *manufacturing executive, writer*

Neosho
Mailes, Kim(ber Dean) *automotive executive*

North Kansas City
Karp, Daniel Joseph *manufacturing executive*

Osage Beach
Martin, Gary J. *retired manufacturing executive, mayor*

Ozark
Goosey, Thomas H. *packaging technician*

Raymore
Heller, John L., II *food products executive*

Saint Charles
Brahmbhatt, Sudhirkumar *chemical company executive*
Pundmann, Ed John, Jr. *automotive company executive*

Saint Joseph
Rauth, John Francis *construction executive*

Saint Louis
Abelov, Stephen Lawrence *uniform clothing company executive, consultant*
Ball, Kenneth Leon *manufacturing company executive, organizational development consultant*
Brubaker, James Clark *construction executive*
Busch, August Adolphus, III *brewery executive*
Cohen, Millard Stuart *diversified manufacturing company executive*
Davis, Christopher Kevin *equipment company executive*
Gomes, Edward Clayton, Jr. *construction company executive*
Harrington, Michael Francis *paper and packaging company executive*
Henderson, Stephen John *chemical company executive*
Henry, Deborah Jane *construction executive*
Homeyer, August Henry *former chemical company executive*
Hyland, Steven E. *business administrator*
Jasso, Paul J. *manufacturing company executive*
Jones, Robert E. *company executive*
Knight, Charles Field *electrical equipment manufacturing company executive*
Mahoney, Richard John *manufacturing company executive*
McCarthy, Michael M. *construction executive*
McDonnell, John Finney *aerospace and aircraft manufacturing company executive*
McGuinness, Barbara Sue *food products executive*
McKenna, William John *textile products executive*
Peters, Ronnie D. *steel executive, labor analyst*
Randolph, Joe Wayne *machine manufacturing executive*
Stiritz, William P. *food company executive*
Sutton, John Martin *industrial food broker, consultant*
Wallis, Michael Van *manufacturing manager*

Shelbina
Maisel, Darrell Keith *manufacturing executive*

Springfield
Codutti, Jerry Luis *steel manufacturing executive*
Deatz, George B. *automotive industry executive*
Kinnaird, Angus G. *machinist*
McCrea, Steve C. *automotive executive*
McQueary, Fred M. *pharmaceutical executive*
Parmenter, Lonnie LeRoy *dairy products executive*
Stern, Roy Dalton *manufacturing financial executive*

Stockton
Hammons, R. Dwain *food products executive*

Sullivan
Penn, Ronald Hulen *manufacturing executive*

Wentzville
Wilgus, John William *company executive*

NEBRASKA

Beemer
Reis, Donald C. *manufacturing executive*

Blair
Wickstrom, Lawrence Lee *manfuacturing company executive, consultant*

Columbus
Keller, Harry Allan *electronics technician*

Dakota City
Broyhill, Roy Franklin *manufacturing executive*
Peterson, Robert L. *meat processing executive*

Falls City
Herbster, Marty L. *manufacturing company executive*

Fremont
Pratt, Michael Anthony, Sr. *manufacturing executive*
Williams, Michael K. *agricultural production educator*

Grand Island
White, Gary R. *automotive executive*

Lincoln
Barzydlo, Arnold James *electronics technician*

Omaha
Barth, Tami Sue *food products company executive*
Brown, Bob Oliver *retired manufacturing company executive*
Fletcher, Philip B. *food products company executive*
Graham, Donald D. *manufacturing executive*
Ho, David Kim Hong *professional studies educator*
Jugel, Richard Dennis *corporate executive, management consultant*
Millard, Ken M. *automotive executive*
Nickelson, Willis F. *agricultural products executive*
Seaton, Scott B. *construction company executive*

Superior
Sheets, Stanley Stuart *retired construction company executive*

NEVADA

Las Vegas
Bennett, Bruce W. *construction company executive, civil engineer*

NEW JERSEY

New Providence
Schacht, Henry Brewer *manufacturing executive*

NEW YORK

New York
Daniels, Doria Lynn *manufacturing executive*

NORTH DAKOTA

Bismarck
Jefferson, Daniel *manufacturing executive*

Dickinson
Lupo, Barbara Jane *cosmetics specialist*

Fargo
Ommodt, Donald Henry *dairy company executive*

Grand Forks
Gjovig, Bruce Quentin *manufacturing consultant*

West Fargo
Krueger, Mike *agricultural products executive*

OHIO

Akron
Gault, Stanley Carleton *manufacturing company executive*
Reynolds, A. William *manufacturing company executive*
Turner, Frank Robin *tire manufacturing executive*

Archbold
Brown, William Morgan *manufacturing executive*

Ashtabula
Mako, William Lawrence *manufacturing executive*
Smiley, Peter C. *manufacturing executive*

Baltic
Hershberger, Daniel D. *executive*

Bay Village
Lowry, Bob Bill *manufacturers executive*

Beachwood
Weatherhead, Albert John, III *business executive*

Beavercreek
Davis, Marvin Ralph *business executive*

Bedford
Toomey, William Shenberger *wire manufacturing company executive*

Big Prairie
Wharton, Melanie L. *business executive*

Blacklick
Lawrence, Ralph Waldo *manufacturing company executive*

Bratenahl
Jones, Trevor Owen *automobile supply company executive, management consultant*

Brecksville
Usalis, George Jerome *metal processing executive*

Brookville
Juhl, Daniel Leo *manufacturing and marketing firm executive*

Cambridge
Prouty, Butch H. *maintenance supervisor*

Canfield
Kostelic, Thomas Patrick *manufacturing executive*

Canton
Ewing, David Charles *automobile dealership executive*
Karabasz, Felix Francois *engineering and manufacturing company executive*
Toot, Joseph F., Jr. *bearing manufacturing company executive*

Chagrin Falls
Heckman, Henry Trevennen Shick *steel company executive*
Smith, Craig Richey *machinery executive*

Chardon
Gray, James Patrick *business executive, consultant*
Jones, Sandra *electronics executive*

Cincinnati
Ackermann, Russell Albert *manufacturing company executive*
Anderson, Jerry William, Jr. *technical and business consulting executive, educator*
Benson, Stephen Harold *automotive executive*
Elguezabal, Luis Emilio *food distribution company executive*
Epp, Mary Elizabeth *technologies consultant*
Farrell, Robert W. *manufacturing company executive*
Fluke, William Albert *pharmaceutical company safety manager, engineer*
Geier, James Aylward Develin *manufacturing company executive*
Hayes, Helen *electronics company executive*
Light, Theodore Blaine, Jr. *chemical company executive*
Maisel, Michael *clothing executive*
Merritt, Jimmie Alco *chemical company executive, sales and marketing*
Pichler, Joseph Anton *food products executive*
Ruthman, Thomas Robert *manufacturing executive*
Shepherd, Elsbeth Weichsel *manufacturing consultant*
Smittle, Nelson Dean *electronics executive*
Sottile, Benjamin Joseph *greeting card company executive*
Walker, Ronald F. *corporate executive*
Wilson, Frederic Sandford *pharmaceutical company executive*

Cleveland
Bissett, Barbara Anne *steel distribution company executive*
Bollenbacher, Herbert Kenneth *steel company official*
Bredt, Charles Franklin *lumber and timber executive*
Centa, William James *manufacturing executive*
Chintella, George M. *manufacturing company executive*
Coleman, George Michael *chemical company executive*
Decker, John William *steel company executive*
Gorman, Joseph Tolle *corporate executive*
Hamilton, William Milton *manufacturing executive*
Hill, Howard George *product developer*
Ivy, Conway Gayle *paint company executive*
Kay, Albert Joseph *textile executive*
Kerwin, Kenneth Hills, II *technology and management consultant, electronic systems and electro-optics specialist*
Mac Laren, David Sergeant *manufacturing corporation executive, inventor*
Martinek, Frank Joseph *chemical company executive*
Morgan, Stanley Leins *pharmaceutical company executive, consultant*
Mullally, Pierce Harry *retired steel company executive*
Parker, Patrick Streeter *manufacturing executive*
Petro, David W. *electronics product manager*
Reid, James Sims, Jr. *automobile parts manufacturer*
Smith, Carl Edwin *electronics company executive*
Studniarz, Robert Anthony *manufacturing executive*
Tracht, Allen Eric *electronics executive*
Unger, Paul A. *packaging executive*
Van Aken, William J. *construction executive*
Yanosko, Raymond Anthony *retired educator, game company executive*

Clyde
Steffanni, Brett A. *business manager*

Columbus
Alban, Roger Charles *construction equipment distribution executive*
Anderson, Kerrii B. *construction company executive*
Byrnes, R. John *food packaging company executive*
Corns, Marvin A. *corporate executive*
Evans, Daniel E. *sausage manufacturing and restaurant chain company executive*
Gardner, Robert Meade *building contractor*
Jones, Danny Clyde *healthcare products executive*
Klages, John William *automotive parts company executive*
Schottenstein, Irving E. *construction company executive*

Conneaut
Markley, Lynn McMaster *rubber and plastics company executive*

Coshocton
Voss, Michael J. *product manager electronics company*
Weber, Michael James *retail executive*

Dayton
Ashton, Elizabeth Ann *information industry manager*
Bartoszek, Joseph Edward *environmental specialist*
Bertelson, Robert Calvin *chemical company executive, research chemist*
Harlan, Norman Ralph *construction executive*
Haynes, Gerald Wayne *aerospace manufacturing administrator*
Ladehoff, Leo William *metal products manufacturing executive*
Mason, Steven Charles *forest products company executive*
Shuey, John Henry *diversified products company executive*
Stanforth, Steven Richard *electronics executive, accountant, consultant*
Wilks, Stephen L. *manufacturing company executive*

Delphos
Carder, Charles E. *retired machine operator, writer*

Dublin
Borror, Donald A. *construction company executive*
Borror, Douglas G. *construction company executive*
Schoenfelder, John Robert *pharmaceutical executive*

Elyria
Rehm, John Edwin *manufacturing company executive*
Teets, Jim *manufcturing executive*

Englewood
Piercey, James W. *tool manufacturing company executive*

Fort Jennings
Miller, John R. *construction company executive*

Fremont
Wadsworth, Thomas P. *manufacturing manager*

Hamilton
Antenen, Ann Marie *restoration executive, consultant*

Independence
Nance, James Clifton *company executive*

Jackson Center
Thompson, Wade Francis Bruce *manufacturing company executive*

Lancaster
Sulick, Robert John *general contractor*

Logan
Good, Timothy Jay *medical equipment services company executive*

Lorain
Bado, Kenneth Steve *automotive company administrator*
Lowry, Kevin M. *manufacturing executive*
Offengenden, Anatoly A. *manufacturing company executive*

Madison
Headley, William A. *manufacturing company executive*

Mansfield
Anderson, William Roy *machinist specialist*
Clous, James M. *electrical equipment company executive, engineer*
Green, Robert F. *automotive company executive*
Hooker, James Todd *manufacturing executive*

Maple Heights
Uwagie-Ero, Peter Efosa *publishing executive*

Marietta
Shoaf, Bruce Allen *instrument engineer*

Marysville
Agin, Dennis Michael *aircraft manufacturer, orthodontist educator*

Mayfield Heights
Rankin, Alfred Marshall, Jr. *business executive*

Mentor
Zamecnik, Paul Arthur *medical device manufacturing company executive*

Miamisburg
Mariotti, John Louis *plastics and rubber manufacturing company executive*
Northrop, Stuart Johnston *manufacturing company executive*

Milan
Henry, Joseph Patrick *chemical company executive*

Milford
Donahue, John Lawrence, Jr. *paper company executive*
Greene, Ford C. *health care products executive*
Russell, Stephen James *health care products executive*

New Matamoras
Creighton, Dean F. *manufacturing company executive*

New Philadelphia
Mears, Orum Glenn, III *automotive executive*

Perrysburg
King, John Joseph *manufacturing company executive*

Piqua
Frigge, Thomas Richard *food products executive*

Salem
Collins, Vernon E. (Rick Collins) *manufacturing company executive*

Shadyside
Knight, Willard *manufacturing executive*

Springboro
Wiener, Morry *food broker executive*

Springfield
King, Charles Homer *manufacturing executive*

Stow
Horsfall, Bruce D. *marking products manufacturer*
Kamm, Christian Philip *manufacturing company executive*

Sugar Grove
Bonner, Herbert Dwight *construction management educator*

Tipp City
Panayirci, Sharon Lorraine *textiles executive, design engineer*
Tighe-Moore, Barbara Jeanne *electronics executive*

Toledo
Brooks, Kenneth John *electrical estimator, music engineer*
Lanigan, Robert J. *packaging company executive*
Morcott, Southwood J. *automotive parts manufacturing company executive*
Reins, Ralph Erich *automated service company executive*
Stopper, Herbert *electronics company executive, research educator*
Susor, Donald J. *testing and support administrator*
Zander, Sidney G. *manufacturing executive*

Twinsburg
Novak, Harry R. *manufacturing company executive*

Urbana
Moorshead, John Earl *porcelain manufacturing executive*

Vermilion
Eisermann, Eckehard Hermann *corporate executive*

Warren
Alli, Richard James, Sr. *manufacturing executive*
Thompson, Eric Thomas *manufacturing company executive*

Wellington
Pruitt, Russell Clyde *manufacturing executive*

West Alexandria
Scoville, George Richard *adhesive company product manager*

West Chester
Hooven, Michael Dawson *medical products executive, engineer*
Rishel, James Burton *manufacturing executive*

Westerville
George, Randy W. *executive, manager*
Murch, Everett Lloyd *manufacturing executive*

Wheelersburg
Hulse, Dexter Curtis *manufacturing executive*

Willoughby
Polsinelli, Anthony Renato *manufacturing company executive*
Wolfe, Arthur Llewellyn *chemical executive*

Wooster
Basford, James Orlando *container manufacturing company executive*

Worthington
McConnell, John *manufacturing executive*
Toeniskoetter, Richard Henry *chemicals executive*

Youngstown
Byrd, Ellis Charles *automotive executive*
Marks, Esther L. *metals company executive*
Powers, Paul J. *manufacturing company executive*

OREGON

Portland
McKennon, Keith Robert *chemical company executive*

PENNSYLVANIA

Lower Gwynedd
Torok, Raymond Patrick *aluminum company executive*

SOUTH DAKOTA

Sioux Falls
Christensen, David Allen *manufacturing company executive*

WISCONSIN

Amery
Nelson, Gene F. *manufacturing executive*

Appleton
Boldt, Oscar Charles *construction company executive*
Grayson, David S. *paper company executive*
Nelson, Jeffrey Owen *manufacturing executive*
Rankin, Arthur David *paper company executive*
Spiegelberg, Harry Lester *retired paper products company executive*

Brookfield
Grove, Richard Charles *power tool company executive*

Clear Lake
Glover, James Todd *manufacturing company executive*

Fort Atkinson
Jones, Alan Porter, Jr. *food manufacturing executive*

Grafton
Geisenheimer, Norman Kenneth *sales, marketing, manufacturing executive*

Green Bay
Burton, Robert A. *transmission manufacturing company executive*
Fisk, Dwight Rodney *paper company executive*

Hartford
Greis, Gordon P. *tool and die maker*

Janesville
Ryan, Donald Patrick *contractor*

Kenosha
Infusino, Achille Francis *construction company executive*
Steigerwaldt, Donna Wolf *clothing manufacturing company executive*

Madison
Brockert, David Joseph *food products executive*
Frautschi, Walter Albert *contract and publications printing company executive*
Klodt, Gerald Joseph *office products executive*
Marshall, Linda Rae *cosmetics company executive*
Neyer, Jim V. *product development manager*
Rogers, Al R. *design and development administrator*
Will, James Arthur *pharmaceutical executive, educator*

Marion
Simpson, Vinson Raleigh *manufacturing company executive*

Marshfield
Manicke, Michael Don *automobile service owner*
Reigel, James L. *manufacturing executive*

Mequon
Dohmen, Frederick Hoeger *retired wholesale drug company executive*

Merrill
Taylor, Richard L. *manufacturing company executive*

Middleton
Cook, Charles F. *food industry consultant executive*

Milwaukee
Albrinck, James Louis *manufacturing company executive*
Castlebury, Guy A. *engineering executive*
D'Angelo, Richard Arthur *medical systems company executive*
Jacobs, Burleigh Edmund *foundry executive*
Keyes, James Henry *manufacturing company executive*
Kowalski, David W. *manufacturing executive*
Maynard, John M. *manufacturing executive*
McCoy, Lawrence Edward *paper company executive*
Nims, Dick K. *designer*
Parker, Charles Walter, Jr. *consultant, retired equipment company executive*
Wolff, Thomas William *manufacturing executive*
Zanow, Leroy *manufacturing company technician*

Oak Creek
Walker, Willie Mark *electronics engineering executive*

Oconomowoc
Roessler, David A. *manufacturing executive*

Oshkosh
Drebus, Richard William *pharmaceutical company executive*

Pewaukee
Piper, Douglas *manufacturing company executive*

Racine
Henley, Joseph Oliver *manufacturing company executive*
Johnson, Samuel Curtis *wax company executive*
Quella, Daniel C. *manufacturing company executive*
Titzkowski, Ervin E. *manufacturing company executive*

Saint Francis
Makowski-Jester, Susan *pharmaceuticals company administrator*

Schofield
Boettcher, Phil G. *industrial service executive*

Sussex
Losee, John Frederick, Jr. *manufacturing executive*

Waterloo
Leader, Christopher Robert *manufacturing executive*

Watertown
Peebles, Allene Kay *manufactured housing company executive*

Whitewater
Mattrisch, Dan D. *product designer*

CANADA

MANITOBA

Winnipeg
MacKenzie, George Allan *diversified company executive*

SINGAPORE

Singapore
De Kruif, William Raymond *electronics executive, electrical engineer*

ADDRESS UNPUBLISHED

Abella, Joseph Francisco *electronics company executive*
Alig, Frank Douglas Stalnaker *construction company executive*
Andreas, Dwayne Orville *business executive*
Aschauer, Charles Joseph, Jr. *corporate director, former company executive*
Banis, Robert Joseph *pharmaceutical company executive, educator*
Behm, Ken W. *manufacturing executive*
Beutler, Arthur Julius *manufacturing company executive*
Black, Douglas D. *lumber company executive*
Blackfan, Cyrus Linton *specialty chemicals company executive*
Bosch, John Albert *manufacturing executive, consultant*
Bryan, Joan Marie *consumer products executive*
Cammack, William Roger, Jr. *chemical company executive*
Cech, Donald *project manager*
Coffey, Dennis James *technology consultant*
Cushing, Ralph Harvey *chemical company executive*
Davis, Darrell L. *automotive executive*
Emrich, Jeffrey Pauling *food products executive*
Fisher, Mark Robert *industrial sales and management executive*
Ford, Jerry Lee *service company executive*
Friedman, Richard Lee *lumberyard owner*
Funk, Howard G. *research and development consultant*
Galligan, Frank Daniel *automotive executive*
Garrison, Paul Cornell *retired office products company executive*
Gates, Martina Marie *food products company executive*
Gifford, John Irving *retired agricultural equipment company executive*
Grabner, Caren Sue *food service manager*
Graff, Richard Thomas *manufacturing executive*
Hare, LeRoy, Jr. *pharmaceutical company executive*
Heckel, John Louis (Jack Heckel) *aerospace company executive*
Heit, Ivan *packaging equipment company executive*
Jackson, Fields Lee, Jr. *healthcare manufacturing executive*
Jacobs, Jeffrey Lyndon *food products executive*
Johnson, Marlene M. *furniture company executive*
Kostka, Janice Ellen *automotive wholesale company administrator*
Kramer, Paul A. *manufacturing executive*
Krise, Patricia Love *automotive industry executive*
Kwapich, Steve E. *manufacturing administrator*
Landon, Robert Gray *retired manufacturing company executive*
MacCormack, Lawrence Lee *chemicals marketing executive*
Massingill, John Lee, Jr. *research director*
Matasovic, Marilyn Estelle *business executive*
Mathias, Mark Robert *chemical company executive*
McKernan, Leo Joseph *manufacturing company executive*
Millard, Charles Phillip *manufacturing company executive*
Murphy, Daniel Patrick *database developer*
Noe, Elnora (Ellie Noe) *retired chemical company executive*
Nugent, Daniel Eugene *business executive*
Oster, Lewis Henry *manufacturing executive, engineering consultant*
Owens, Boyd Erdice *manufacturing executive, educator*
Patel, Pravin *manufacturing executive*
Peters, Daniel J. *manufacturing executive*
Peters, Robert Allen *retired drug company executive*
Pingle, Richard C. *project manager*
Rescorla, Charles Laverne *manufacturing executive*
Robertson, Melvina *construction company executive*
Schram, Brian T. *drafting supervisor*
Schultz, Robert J. *retired automobile company executive*
Seagle, Dennis Alan *chemicals executive, chemical engineer*
Sharkey, Leonard Arthur *automobile company executive*
Silver, George *metal trading and processing company executive*
Simon, Michael Paul *general contractor, realtor*
Simon, Robert Michael *manufacturing company executive*
Simpson, Jack Benjamin *medical technologist, business executive*
Studebaker, Glenn Wayne *steel company executive*
Swisher, Phillip M. *company executive*
Taylor, Randall William *quality assurance administrator*
Vette, John Lyle, III *manufacturing specialist*
Ward, James K. *engineering administrator*
Wasson, James Walter *aircraft manufacturing company executive*
Witcher, Daniel Dougherty *retired pharmaceutical company executive*
Wollert, Gerald Dale *retired food company executive, investor*
Woloshen, Jeffery Lawrence *automobile executive, consultant, accountant*
Ying, John L. *manufacturing executive*
Zehnder, Frederick John *retired automotive executive*

INDUSTRY: SERVICE

UNITED STATES

ARIZONA

Scottsdale
Donnelly, Charles Francis *management consultant, lawyer*

CALIFORNIA

San Diego
Charlson, David Harvey *executive search company professional*

CONNECTICUT

Wilton
Pethley, Lowell Sherman *management consultant*

FLORIDA

Fort Lauderdale
DiCarlo, David Lawrence *facilities maintenance professional*

Naples
Pancero, Jack Blocher *restaurant executive*

Saint Petersburg
Lau, Michele Denise *advertising consultant, sales trainer, television personality*

GEORGIA

Atlanta
Yarnell, Jeffrey Alan *regional credit executive*

ILLINOIS

Addison
McDonald, David Eugene *package car driver*

Antioch
Dahl, Laurel Jean *human services administrator*
Patel, Naresh J. *management consultant*

Arlington Heights
Gabrielsen, Carol Ann *employment consulting company executive*
Pollin, Pierre Louis *executive chef*
Spohr, Frederick Stephen *sales professional*
Ulrich, Gladys Marjorie *printing company executive*
Vautier, John M. *sales executive*
Wittmeyer, Ronald F. *managing partner*

Aurora
Hopp, Nancy Smith *marketing executive*

Bannockburn
Friedlander, Daniel Simon *public relations executive*

Barrington
Groesch, John William, Jr. *marketing research consultant*
Mathis, Jack David *advertising executive*
Merrell, Richard G. *executive recruitment company official*
Mullins, Terri A. *executive*
Ross, Frank Howard, III *management consultant*
Wilson, Harold H. *executive*

Bartlett
Miller, Kevin D. *security executive*
Robinson, Lois Hart *retired public relations executive*

Batavia
Mann, Phillip Lynn *data processing company executive*

Belleville
Brauer, Drew Sean *sales executive*
Detsch, Donald D. *business executive*

Bloomingdale
Raiss, Sarah Elizabeth *consulting firm executive*

Bloomington
Barnes, Don A. *business executive*

Blue Island
Friedrich, Charles William *corporate executive*

Bolingbrook
Willadsen, Michael Chris *marketing professional, sales executive*

Bridgeview
Poe-Jackson, Gertie LaVerne *sales executive*

Brookfield
Solatka, Matt Francis *laboratory executive*

Buffalo Grove
Ayres, John T. *marketing manager*
Myer, Paul Joseph *hotel company executive*
Pohlman, William John *advertising executive*
Schlesser, Jerleen Ethel *information systems executive*
Zanevsky, Andrew *computer consulting company executive*

Burr Ridge
Loch, Randall L. *sales executive*
Marcus, Steven Eric *sales executive, musician*
Whitmer, Melvin Howard *technician, educator*

Calumet City
Kovach, Joseph William *management consultant, psychologist, educator*

Capron
Gadke, Karen *biomedical communications and clinical research consultant*

Carbondale
Mabus, Catherine Adam *adminstrative assistant*
Molfese, Victoria J. *research administrator*
Rushing, Michele Renee *academic budget analyst, administrator*
Vance, David Alvin *management educator*

Carmi
Edwards, Judith Elizabeth *advertising executive*

Carol Stream
Byrd, Randall Duane *sales engineer, project manager, actor*
Fisher, Robert Sylvester, Jr. *corporate executive*
Siska, Richard Stanly *marketing professional*

Cary
Lee, Catherine M. *business owner, educator*

Centralia
Robinson, Gary Ray *sales professional*

Champaign
Aniello, Anthony Joseph *information system executive*
Knox, Charles Milton *purchasing agent, consultant*
Murphy, William Michael *public relations executive*
Sheehan, Robert Merrill, Jr. *executive director*
Tobeck, Deborah Anne *information systems specialist*

Chicago
Adolf, Mary McGinley *promotion and advertising executive*
Amatangelo, Nicholas S. *financial printing company executive*
Anderson, Carol Jean *information systems executive*
Armour, John M. *management company executive*
Arrington, Michael Browne *travel management company executive*
Ashkin, Rajasperi Maliapen *marketing executive*
Ashkin, Ronald Evan *international executive*
Bacevicius, John Anthony, V (John Bace) *communications executive*
Baldwin, M(ary) Karen *marketing professional, editor*
Bane, Bradley Lewis *marketing account executive*
Bariff, Martin Louis *information systems educator, consultant*
Barnard, James H. *technical service representative*

Barron, Roberta *human resources management consultant*
Baumberger, Steven Bruce *management consultant*
Bayer, Gary Richard *advertising executive*
Becker, Robert Allen *data processing executive*
Bernatowicz, Frank Allen *management consultant, expert witness*
Bike, William Stanley *fundraiser, writer*
Blair, Howard S. *business executive*
Brandt, William Arthur, Jr. *consulting executive*
Brenner, Stephen Mark *marketing professional*
Brillson, Catherine Graf *marketing professional*
Brown, Margaret Ann *international human resources executive*
Burman, Diane Berger *organization development consultant*
Burrell, Thomas J. *marketing communication executive*
Carrott, Gregory T. *management consultant*
Cary, Arlene D. *retired hotel company sales executive*
Castorino, Sue *communications executive*
Chaiyabhat, Win *risk control professional*
Chorengel, Bernd *international hotel corporation executive*
Choyke, Phyllis May Ford (Mrs. Arthur Davis Choyke, Jr.) *management executive, editor, poet*
Chung, Dean I. *business executive, marketing professional*
Claypoole, Robert Edwin *distribution service company executive*
Clyne, Michael Andrew *political consultant*
Conidi, Daniel Joseph *private investigation agency executive*
Corbett, Frank Joseph *advertising executive*
Donovan, John Vincent *consulting company executive*
Dwyer, Dennis D. *information technology executive*
Eckstein, Norman R. *management consultant*
Edelman, Daniel Joseph *public relations executive*
Eng, Joshua *business executive*
Fassnacht, Debra Kerr *communications executive*
Fisher, John James *advertising executive*
Fisher, Lawrence Edgar *market research executive, anthropologist*
Fizdale, Richard *advertising agency executive*
Flanagan, Joseph Patrick *advertising executive*
Foley, Sara Kay *public relations executive*
Foster, Hattie A. *business executive*
Fulgoni, Gian Marc *market research company executive*
Gall, Betty Bluebaum *office services executive*
Garbaczewski, Daniel Frank *restaurateur*
Gardner, Jolene S. *resource center director*
Garrick, George R. *marketing professional*
Gauthier, Jim *marketing executive*
Givray, Henry Steven *association management services executive*
Goldring, Norman Max *advertising executive*
Gordon, Howard Lyon *advertising and marketing executive*
Graf, Judith Ann *communications executive*
Grant, Paul Bernard *industrial relations educator*
Green, RuthAnn *marketing and management consultant*
Hansen, Carl R. *management consultant*
Harkna, Eric *advertising executive*
Heidrick, Gardner Wilson *management consultant*
Heinecken, Martin Theodore (Ted Heinecken) *publishers sales representation company executive*
Higgens, William John, III *sales executive*
Hirn, Robert William *data processing company executive*
Hochhalter, Gordon Ray *advertising executive*
Hofmann, Phillip J. *business executive*
Hofrichter, David Alan *management consultant*
Hollander, Adrian Willoughby *accounting software company executive*
Holzer, Edwin *advertising executive*
Houchins, Wiley Jack *marketing professional*
Jakala, Chester *business executive*
James-Strand, Nancy Kay Leabhard *advertising executive*
Johns, Alexander B. *company executive*
Johnson, Shirley Elaine *management consultant*
Johnson, William K. *sales executive*
Johnson, William Lloyd *training specialist, retired*
Johnston, Sheryl L. *communications executive*
Kepler, James Alan *communications executive*
Kimball, Edward Martin *data processing consultant*
Kipper, Barbara Levy *corporate executive*
Koch, Carole Jackson *human resources executive*
Kruper, John Gerald (Jack Kruper) *sales and marketing executive*
Kuczmarski, Susan Smith *management consulting company executive*
Labs, Donald Herbert *marketing professional*
Larson, Paul William *public relations executive*
Lehman, George Morgan *food sales executive*
Lesly, Philip *public relations counsel*
Lessack, Edina *communications company executive*
Levin, Diane *public relations consultant, antiques reporter*
Lewin, Stanton Morris *advertising executive*
Liffner, Gloria *food products executive*
Lord, Suzanne Molinet *advertising executive*
Lotz, Edward L., Jr. *sales and marketing professional*
Lynch, William Thomas, Jr. *advertising agency executive*
Mahaffey, John Christopher *association executive*
Marin, Vincent Arul *infosystems executive*
Marks, Gary A. *business executive*
Mason, Bruce *advertising agency executive*
McCallister, Richard Anthony *business consulting company executive*
McConnell, E. Hoy, II *advertising executive*
McTigue, Patrick J. *advertising executive, publishing executive*
Mendelsohn, Zehavah Whitney *data processing executive*
Miller, Bernard J., III *advertising executive*
Miller, Bernard Joseph, Jr. *advertising executive*
Mitchell, Lee Mark *communications executive, investment fund manager, lawyer*
Niedner, Kathryn Ellen *commerical lender*
Pantschak, Vera *public relations executive*
Peterson, James Burdell *management consultant*
Phillips, Scott Allen *public relations professional*
Podlesny, Laura Ann *public relations executive*
Poluchowicz, Roxolana Sofia *information systems executive*
Posner, Kathy Robin *communications executive*
Prosperi, David Philip *public relations executive*
Rabin, Joseph Harry *marketing research company executive*
Rappaport, Cyril M. *personnel administrator*
Ratcliffe, James Maxwell *corporate relations executive*
Reggio, Vito Anthony *management consultant*
Reilly, Robert Frederick *valuation consultant*
Ritter, Doris Standring *human resources professional*
Rozran, Jack Louis *courier service executive*
Rydholm, Ralph Williams *advertising agency executive*
Saul, Bradley Scott *communications, advertising and entertainment executive*
Schindler, Judi(th Kay) *public relations executive, marketing consultant*
Schneider, Wesley Clair *marketing communications company executive*
Scobie, Craig K. *computer company executive*
Seebert, Kathleen Anne *international sales and marketing executive*
Seifert, Timothy Michael *infosystems specialist*
Senior, Richard John Lane *textile rental service executive*
Shields, Valerie Lynne *public relations professional*
Sive, Rebecca Anne *public affairs company executive*
Small, Bruce W. *sales and marketing executive*
Soto, Ramona *training specialist*
Steinberg, Lois Saxelby *marketing executive*
Stern, Carl William, Jr. *management consultant*
Stone, James Howard *management consultant*
Streeto, Joseph Michael *catering company official*
Sunshine, Ron Leon *executive search consultant*
Thomas, Frank *human resources executive, educator*
Tillesen, Scott Robert *gypsum company financial executive*
Tranfaglia, Christina Marie *marketing executive*
Trout, Calvin Daniel *marketing executive*
Vahlberg, Vivian Eleanor *philanthropist*
Varchetta, Felix R. *advertising agency executive*
Wang, Gung H. *management consultant*
Weaver, Donna Rae *company executive*
Weeks, Robert Earl *advertising executive*
Wells, Byron Keith *sales executive*
Work, Mitchell Robert *healthcare marketing professional*
Wright, Patricia Donovan *communications executive*
Zasadil, Jeanne *management consultant*
Zimmermann, David Scott *advertising sales executive*

Chicago Heights
Dowden, Craig Phillips *human resources executive*

Clarendon Hills
Mathisen-Reid, Rhoda Sharon *international communications consultant*

Crystal Lake
Dorwen, Franz F. *administrator*
Halperin, Richard George *data processing executive*

Danville
Fisher, Ted Alan *director of information services, consultant*

Decatur
Blake, William Henry *credit and public relations consultant*
Bluhm, Myron Dean *sales professional*
Bornstein, Jeffrey Victor *marketing executive*
Ferguson, Steven Mark *business analyst*
Fletcher, David J. *medical clinic administrator*
Heisler, Harold Reinhart *management consultant*

Deerfield
Berman-Hammer, Susan *public relations executive*
Kinzelberg, Harvey *leasing company executive*
Nelson, Richard Lawrence *public relations executive*
Warady, Joel David *consumer products company executive*

Des Plaines
Mattison, Robert Myron *consultant, author, researcher*
Mortimer, Lawrence Patrick *sales executive*
Pinchok, Nicholas Christopher *sales representative*
Scheuerman, David Elmer *sales executive*
Small, Richard Donald *travel company executive*

Downers Grove
Beres, Michael John *project manager*
Brady, Catherine Rawson *software company executive*
Lulay, Gail C. *human resources and corporative outplacement executive, consultant*

East Saint Louis
Lindsley, James Bruce *sales and marketing executive*

Edwardsville
Dietrich, Suzanne Claire *instructional designer*

Elburn
Brown, Roger William *manufacturer's representative, real estate developer*
Hansen, H. Jack *management consultant*

Elk Grove Village
Morehead, John Woodson *management consultant*
Morrison, Joseph Francis, Jr. *communications company executive*
Podmokly, Patricia Gayle *typesetting company professional*
Pruim, Fred James *food service consultant*

Elmhurst
Chitwood, Lera Catherine *marketing information professional*
Grippando, Mark *information systems specialist*

Evanston
Crook, Stephen Richard *sales and marketing management consultant*
Durst, Gary Michael *management trainer, speaker*
Goodyear, Julie Ann *marketing and fundraising specialist*
Jelinek, Richard Carl *hospital management consultant company executive, educator*
Kathrein, Michael Lee *leasing company executive, real estate company executive*
Keith, Thomas Warren, Jr. *marketing executive*
Miller, Deborah Jean *computer training and document consultant*
Neuschel, Robert Percy *educator, former management consultant*
O'Keefe, Patricia Rigg *public relations professional*
Rolfe, Michael N. *management consulting firm executive*
Spaeth, Mary Shepard *marketing communications executive*

Evergreen Park
Lucas, Shirley Agnes Hoyt *management executive*
Nelson, Mary Bertha *public relations executive*

Frankfort
Dennis, Peter Ray *environmental corporate executive*
Hall, Paul James, Jr. *sales executive*

Franklin Park
Gemignani, Robert Baldo *marketing director*
Rizzo, Geraldine Josephine *private investigations company official*

Gilberts
Schwan, John J. *sales executive*

Glen Ellyn
Conti, Paul Louis *management consulting company executive*
Hoffman, Joan Bentley *public relations consultant*
Warakomski, Alphonse Walter Joseph, Jr. *sales executive*

Glencoe
Chung, Alison Li *information systems specialist*
Cole, Kathleen Ann *advertising agency executive, retired social worker*
Joseph, Donald Louis *management consultant*
Russ, Edmond Vincent, Jr. *marketing professional*

Glenview
Lacy, Herman Edgar *management consultant*
Riley, John Richard *travel agency owner*

Gurnee
Deterding, Diana Margaret *advertising agency executive*
Peterson, Sally Lu *communications executive*

Highland Park
Fishman, Arnold Lawrence *direct marketing consultant, publisher*
Harris, James Howard *marketing executive*
Harris, Thomas L. *public relations executive*
Herbert, Edward Franklin *public relations executive*

Hinsdale
Lewis, Ronald Loren *health care executive*
Nelson, Robert Eddinger *management and development consultant*
Raney, David Elliot *data processing consultant*
Zaccone, Suzanne Maria *sales executive*
Zahn, Andrew Joseph *food company executive*

Hoffman Estates
Goulet, Kevin *marketing professional*

Homewood
McGarvey, Scott Allen *marketing professional, consultant, educator*
Murray, William J. *marketing executive*

Hudson
Mills, Lois Jean *company executive, former legislative aide, former education educator*

Itasca
Wheeler, Douglas Walter *executive*

Kankakee
Kanouse, Donald Lee *wastewater treatment executive*
Patton, Robert Lee *sales executive*

Kewanee
Smith, Michelle M. *marketing executive*

La Grange
Gable, John Starrett *marketing professional*

Lake Bluff
Lasecki, Robert Richard *management consultant*

Lake Forest
Bradley, Kim Alexandra *sales and marketing specialist*
Davidson, Richard Alan *data communications company executive*
Lambert, Carol A. *executive search consultant*

Lake Zurich
Schmitz, Shirley Gertrude *marketing and sales executive*

Libertyville
Huff, Gayle Compton *advertising agency executive*
Ransom, Margaret Palmquist *public relations executive*

Lincolnshire
Hebda, Lawrence John *data processing executive, consultant*

Lindenhurst
Coleman, Troy Lee *computer company executive*

Lisle
Kirkland, Gerry Paul *sales executive*
Kubo, Gary Michael *advertising executive*
Smith, Sydney David *data processing executive*

Lombard
Burdett, James Richard *golf products innovator*
Peretti, Marilyn Gay Woerner *human services professional*

Long Grove
Frisbie, Marlene Ann *business executive*

Macomb
Merrill, Frank Wayne *mail order sales executive*

Mattoon
Skinlo, Michelle Elaine *data entry clerk*

Mc Henry
Sheft, Mark David *market analyst, consultant, product manager*

Melrose Park
Diamond, Susan Zee *management consultant*

Mendota
Lauer, Edward Michael *management consultant*

Moline
Durham, Charles Joseph *management consultant*

Momence
Thompson, Sally Gail *journalist, educator, executive secretary*

Monee
Huffman, Phyllis V. *administrative assistant*

Morton Grove
Goldberg, Bob *management information systems director, consultant*

Mount Prospect
Gerlitz, Curtis Neal *business executive*
Parker, Allan Leslie *marketing executive*
Pulsifer, Edgar Darling *leasing service and sales executive*

Mount Vernon
McDonald, W. R. *employee benefits consultant, developer*

Mundelein
Lustenader, Barbara Diane *human resources executive*

Naperville
Holscher, Todd Timothy Scott *sales and marketing professional*
Hudetz, Frank C(larence) *printing, packaging company executive*
Jones, Stanley Conroy *communications company executive*
Modery, Richard Gillman *marketing and sales executive*
Pagano, Jon Alain *data processing consultant*
Riede, Ronald Frederick, Jr. *business professional*
Sass, Walter J. *marketing professional*

Niles
Kozanecki, Robert Francis *business executive, educator*
Wilson, Janis Kay *marketing executive*

Normal
Evans, John Thomas *logistics manager*

Northbrook
Cirolia, Donna Mary *government relations executive*
Lovell, Evan McCulloch *international development group manager*
Marshall, Irl Houston, Jr. *residential and commercial cleaning company executive*
Milligan, Robert Lee, Jr. *computer company executive*
Ross, Debra Benita *marketing executive*
Schultz, Gregory *company executive*
Smith, Michael Morgan *management consultant*
Sudbrink, Jane Marie *sales and marketing executive*
Tiffen, Norman Herbert *franchise executive, consultant*
Wajer, Ronald Edward *management consultant*
Winn, Jill Kanaga Kline *management executive*
Ziemann, Edward Frances *food service company executive, sales and marketing professional*

Northfield
Handwerker, Sy *public relations executive*
Larson, Donald Harold *information systems executive*
Mudd, Michael Sidney *public relations executive*

O'Fallon
Hangsleben, John William *personnel specialist*

Oak Brook
Garrett, Eugene Amussen *retired marketing professional*
Haried, James Andrew *business development executive*
Michelsen, John Ernest *software service company executive*
Neely, John Douglas *information services consultant*
Porter, Donald Richard *training specialist, teacher*

Oak Lawn
Gordon, Edward Earl *management consultant*

Oak Park
Andre, L. Aumund *management consultant*
Burke, Thomas John *communications executive*
Durkin, Kevin Thomas *retired marketing professional*
Plummer, Kenneth Alexander *communications company executive*

Olympia Fields
Gartrell, Richard Blair *travel marketing association executive*

Orland Park
Leonard, Robert Dougherty *communications company executive*

Palatine
Claassen, W(alter) Marshall *employment company executive*
Compton, David Bruce *international management consultant*
McMinn, Virginia Ann *human resources consulting company executive*
Medin, Lowell Ansgard *security company executive*

Park Ridge
Irvine, William Kennedy *marketing consultant*

Peoria
Browder, Charles Barclay *sales executive*
Buchko, Aaron Anthony *management educator*
Crosby, Gilbert M. *business analyst*
Errion, Jack G. *marketing professional*
Waldo, Christine B. *marketing promotions specialist*

Peru
Duro, Marcia Culp *temporary employment agency official*

Plainfield
Chase, Maria Elaine Garoufalis *publishing company executive*

Poplar Grove
Friedrich, Rose Marie *travel agency executive*

Quincy
Adams, Beejay (Meredith Elisabeth Jane J. Adams) *sales executive*
Kallner, Norman Gust *management information systems manager*
Nagel, Shirley Ann *executive secretary*
Schanafelt, Ted Keith *sales engineering executive*
Wasylik, Kenneth Edward *business development manager*

River Forest
Hamper, Robert Joseph *marketing executive*
Sanford, Ruth Eileen *data processing company administrator*

Riverwoods
Needham, Daniel Ryan *marketing professional*

Rochelle
Blomquist-Stanbery, Ruth Ellen *computer services company owner, elementary education educator*

Rock Island
Mack, Doris Ann *data processing systems supervisor*

Rockford
Anderson, Max Elliot *television and film production company executive*
Duck, Vaughn Michael *software company executive*
Gossell, Terry Rae *advertising agency executive, small business owner*
Liebovich, Samuel David *warehouse executive*
Webeck, Alfred Stanley *management consultant, financial analyst*

Rolling Meadows
Crawford, George David *credit, collections executive*
Otharsson, Hans Bernhard *software company executive*
Podgorski, Robert Paul *human resources executive*
Sturmon, Patricia Montgomery *public relations executive*

Romeoville
Diemand, Kim Eugene *human resources executive*

Roselle
Friedlander, Patricia Ann *marketing executive*
Levulis, Raymond John *management consultant*

Rosemont
Myers, Michael Charles *marketing executive*
Stabler, Nancy Rae *infosystems specialist*

Saint Charles
Adkins, Fred J. *business director*
McGuire, John W., Sr. *advertising executive, marketing professional, author*
Walls, Thomas Francis *management consultant*

Saint Joseph
Motsinger, Linda Susan Baumgardner *commercial printing firm owner*

Savoy
Grother, David Michael *computer company executive*

Schaumburg
Griffin, Sheila MB *electronics marketing executive*
Hill, Raymond Joseph *packaging company executive*
Kosinski, Richard Andrew *public relations executive*
Kuchta, John Albert *food service manager*
Stabej, Rudolph John *computer consultant*

Skokie
Finkel, Bernard *public relations, communications and association management consultant*
Haben, John William *funeral director*
Seeder, Richard Owen *infosystems specialist*
White, William James *information management and services company executive*

South Holland
Powell, Joyce King *administrative assistant*

Springfield
Ansell, Oscar William, Jr. *data systems manager*
Soliwon, Lothar Ernst *marketing professional*
Stone, Lisa Jane *data processing executive*
Stroh, Raymond Eugene *personnel executive*
Weinhoeft, John Joseph *data processing executive*

Tinley Park
Dietrich, James J., Jr. *freight company executive, consultant*

Urbana
Sandage, Elizabeth Anthea *retired market research executive*

Vernon Hills
Powers, Anthony Richard, Jr. *educational sales professional*

Warrenville
Boersma, Mark *data processing executive*

Wasco
Marsiglio, Lorrie (Dolores Walters Marsiglio) *public relations and marketing executive*

Waukegan
Rose, William *retired business executive*

Wayne
Evans, Charlotte Mortimer *communications consultant, writer*

Westchester
Anderson, Carol Lee *communications executive*

Westmont
Newpher, James Alfred, Jr. *management consultant*

Wheaton
Andrews-Keenan, Patricia J. *public relations executive*
Gioia, Angelo Joseph *marketing executive, underwriter*
Holman, James Lewis *financial and management consultant*
Jett, Charles Cranston *management consultant*
Mellott, Robert Vernon *advertising executive*
Pietrus, Carol Lynn *corporation executive*
Sitarz, Darrell Edwin *company executive*
Swanson, Kathryn Ann *communications executive*

Wheeling
Bernberg, Michael Nathan *consulting company executive*
Jassin, Lawrence Evan *sales professional*
Marcus, Joyce Lynn *marketing executive*

Willow Springs
Davenport, Carl A. *marketing professional*
Styrsky, Dennis Martan *company executive*

Wilmette
Blair, Virginia Ann *public relations executive*
Boyer, Kevin Gary *marketing professional*
Cutler, Norman Barry *funeral service executive*

Winnetka
Duran, F. R. Rick *management consultant*

Wood Dale
Andrews, Carolyn P. *quality assurance professional*
Grau, Thomas Paul *marketing executive*
O'Brien, Carol Jean *municipal parks administrator*
Sorensen, Jimmy Louis *management consultant*

Woodridge
Zucchero, Rocco *communications specialist*

Worth
Bilder, James Gerard *marketing manager*

INDIANA

Auburn
Kempf, Jane Elmira *marketing executive*

Bloomington
Brown, Robert Samuel *administrative assistant*
Burns, Dave *business executive*
Kitzmiller, Greg Louis *marketing educator, strategic consultant, conference speaker*

Boggstown
Gray, Carlos Gibson *restaurateur, seedsman, entertainer, producer*

Carmel
Cunningham, Karen Lee *marketing professional*

Columbus
Kirkpatrick, Robert Hugh *communications executive*
Tucker, Thomas Randall *public relations executive*
Yount, David B. *business executive*

East Chicago
Crum, James Francis *waste recycling company executive*

Elkhart
Chism, James Arthur *information systems executive, business consultant*
Cogan, Doloris Coulter *public relations executive*
Pedler, Suzanne Phyllis *sales professional, recruiter*
Speas, Charles Stuart *personnel director*

Evansville
Fisher, Philip Clyde *business administration educator*
Hall, Carol Lynn *purchasing agent*
Hampel, Robert Edward *advertising executive*
Myers, John Eldridge *quality assurance professional*
Smythe, Thomas *advertising executive*
Weinzapfel, Jonathan *public relations executive, congressional aide*

Fishers
Poffenberger, David John *plant manager*

Fort Wayne
Books, Joy Ann *human resource professional*
Bowman, John Ezra *human resources executive*
Clancy, Terrence Patrick *food service executive*
Kern, Patricia Joan *media specialist*
Waters, Wayne Arthur *conference and travel service agency executive*

Fremont
Greim, Jeffrey B. *company executive*

Granger
Golden, Russell L. *plant superintendent*

Hagerstown
Leach, Matthew James *informations systems specialist*

Hammond
Feldman, Lori Strauss *marketing educator*

Hobart
Harrigan, Richard George *salesperson*

Indianapolis
Boggs, John Steven *sales and development executive*
Boner, Donald Leslie *information systems executive*
Campbell, Patti Susan *public relations professional*
Carr, William H(enry) A. *public relations executive, author*
Cummins, Gregory Edward *sales and marketing specialist*
Dafoe, Christopher Randy *marketing, healthcare education professional*
Damin, David E. *technology integration company executive*
Dedert, Steven Ray *marketing professional, consultant*
Eldridge, Gary Lynn *personnel director, emergency medical technician*
Elliott, Lora Louise *training executive*
Estka, Robert J. *marketing executive*
Fleming, Margaret Ann *marketing executive*
Franklin, Ronald Vincent *technology company executive*
Fulgenzi, Benjamin *computer software executive, consultant, marketing professional*
Green, James Murney *software products executive*
Henselmeier, Sandra Nadine *training and development consulting firm executive*
Kirksey, Robert Frederick *company executive*
Knutson, Roger Craig *marketing and sales professional, inventor*
Krueger, Alan Douglas *communications company executive*
Lamkin, E(ugene) Henry, Jr. *internist, medical management executive*
Landis, Larry Seabrook *marketing and communications consultant*
MacDonald, Gary Bruce *communications executive*
Menchhofer, Robert Henry *sales professional*
Meyer, Fred William, Jr. *memorial parks executive*
Morris, Greg James *advertising executive*
Neville, Robert P. *executive*
Nyhart, Eldon Howard *employee benefits consultant, lawyer*
Phelps, Carrie Lynn *public relations executive*
Quiring, Patti Lee *human resource consulting company executive*
Rati, Robert Dean *data processing executive*
Reinhardt, Kenneth G(erald) *manufacturer's representative*
Strong, Steven Philip *account executive, consultant, optician*
Taylor, James Harry, II *management consultant*
Thompson, Roland *marketing professional*
York-Beriault, Ann Jane *advertising executive*
Zickler, Leonard Louis *exhibit company executive*

Jasper
Goodness, Richard Grayson *sales executive*

Kokomo
Rivers, Lawrence Alan *marketing professional*

Kurtz
Barnard, Marcus *machinist, poet, writer*

Lafayette
Lane, Brian M. *management executive*
Thomas, Gerald Wayne *marketing professional*

Marion
Hall, Charles Adams *infosystems specialist*

Monroeville
Ray, Annette D. *business executive*

Muncie
Barber, Earl Eugene *consulting firm executive*
Huffman, Patricia Ann *sales executive*
Kuratko, Donald F. *business management educator, consultant*
Norris, Tracy Hopkins *retired public relations executive*

New Albany
Graf, Marjorie Ann *advertising executive*
Howie, Allen D. *marketing executive*

New Carlisle
Jacobs, Cindee Ann *service executive*

Newburgh
Babcock, Carol Beth *postal carrier*
Burch, William R. *business executive*

Noblesville
Young, Frederic Hisgin *information systems executive, data processing consultant*

Notre Dame
Crant, James Michael *business educator*

Schererville
Hetrick, Greg Andrew *sales executive*

South Bend
Agbetsiafa, Douglas Kofi *financial and management consultant*
Anderson, Carolyn Joyce *business development executive*
Carney, Susan Margaret *marketing professional*
Goodhew, Howard Ralph, Jr. *wholesale executive*
Lawson, Joyce J. *control clerk, assistant purchasing agent*
Murphy, William Host *sales executive*

Terre Haute
Sawtelle, Edward Stephen *human resources executive*

Valparaiso
Taylor, Kenard Lyle, Jr. *director training*

Wabash
Flott, Leslie William *quality control professional*
Scales, Richard Lewis *sales representative*

West Lafayette
Lovejoy, Stephen B. *environmental policy analyst*

Westfield
Farrell, Daniel George *safety administrator*

Zionsville
Borgo, John L. *marketing executive*

IOWA

Ames
Harmsen, Leroy John *business executive*
Werbel, James David *management educator*

Ankeny
Rivers, Donald Lee *marketing professional*

Arnolds Park
Ritzer, Karen Rae *executive secretary, office administrator*

Atlantic
Simmons, Patricia Ann *employment services manager*
Smith, Darryl D. *business executive*

Cedar Falls
Beck, Darin Eric *family business owner*
Durst, Mark P. *maintenance administrator*

Cedar Rapids
Baker, Frank C. (Buzz Baker) *advertising executive*
Breuer Baculis, Diana Ruth *community relations executive, business owner*
Richardson, Robert Edward *data processing analyst*
Stolte, Larry Gene *marketing executive, former computer and publishing company executive*
Vanderpool, Ward Melvin *management and marketing consultant*

Cherokee
Simonsen, Robert Alan *marketing executive*

Clinton
Baker, Gilbert Jens *management consultant*

Cumming
Landauer, Charles D. *business executive*

Davenport
Foersterling, Jay *consultant*
Holliday, Robert James *purchasing agent, county government official*
Johnson, Sandra Kay *marketing professional*
McMunn, Alan Stuart *business executive, artist*
Young, Kenneth D. *company executive*

Des Moines
Doerring, Fredrick Lorenz *retired engine service company executive*
Dolich, Ira J. *marketing educator, business consultant*
Donohue, John James *management analyst*
Hunt, Dixie Louise *career counselor*
Trentmann, Janet Holt *corporate human resources consultant*
Youngblood, James Robert *information systems executive*

Earlham
Crosbie, Rowena Gladys *management consultant*

Fort Dodge
Faiferlick, Justin Michael *computer services company owner*

George
Symens, Maxine Tanner *restaurant owner*

Hiawatha
Robertson, Florence Winkler *advertising and public relations agency executive*

Humboldt
Hill, Dale A. *packaging manager*

Iowa City
Breese, Thomas Robert *investigative firm executive, investor*
Lytle, Gene E. *marketing executive*

Plainfield
Lynes, James William, Sr. *communications company executive*

Sioux City
Crouch, Harlan Everett *business executive*
Salem, Stephen John *employment agency administrator*

Storm Lake
Rodeen, John K. *business executive*

West Des Moines
Pyle, Anthony L. *sales executive*
Stafford, James Duard *advertising executive*

KANSAS

Basehor
Feagles, Gerald Franklin *marketing executive*
Franklin, Shirley Marie *marketing consultant*

Colby
Brewer, Martha M. *hotel executive*

Emporia
O'Reilly, Hugh Joseph *restaurant executive*

Gardner
Brown, Shirley Jean *funeral home director, owner*

Great Bend
McLaughlin, Deborah Ann *public relations and marketing executive*

Junction City
Werts, Merrill Harmon *management consultant*

Lawrence
Kemp, William Bradley MacLaren *marketing and development director*

Leavenworth
Haag, Donald Richard *director facilities and services*

Leawood
Majure, Oliver Davis *marketing professional*

Lenexa
Huff, David Charles *retired sales executive*

Manhattan
Streeter, John Willis *information systems manager*
Younger, Robert Joseph *human resource management specialist*

Mission
Johnson, Sharon Denise *office administrator, treasurer*

Olathe
Bruski, Paul Steven *marketing executive*

Overbrook
Dale, Kenneth Ray *computer executive*

Overland Park
Ferwerda, Jan Annette *direct marketing consultant*
Haas, Kelley Weyforth *marketing and communications company executive*
Jump, Linda Gail *personnel executive*
Paiva, Joseph Vincent Roshan *software integration company executive*
Poole, David LaRue *management consultant*
Schunck, James Richard *business executive*
Thares, Laura A. *personnel director*

Pittsburg
Box, Thomas Morgan *management consultant, educator*

Salina
Ryan, Stephen Collister *funeral director*

Shawnee Mission
Grady, William Earl *marketing executive*
Herring, Raymond Mark *strategic planning and organizational development*
Matthews, Lori *data processing executive, accountant*
Schowengerdt, Donald Eugene *management consultant*
Sparrow, Larry Clinton *marketing executive*

Topeka
Franklin, Benjamin Barnum *dinner club executive*
Karnes, Jan Arla *marketing executive*
Phillips, David Lee *data processing executive*
Randall, Elizabeth Ellen *press clippings company executive*
Vidricksen, Ben Eugene *food service executive, state legislator*
Volpert, Mary Katherine *administrative assistant, revenue specialist*

Westwood
Israelite, Aaron *marketing professional*

Wichita
Chan, Heng-Beng *restaurant manager, wholesale business owner*
DiGiacomo, Robert James *purchasing and merchandising professional*
George, David Bruce *hotel executive*
Herr, Peter Helmut Friederich *sales executive*
Hinson, Tammi Marie *retail executive*
Lahti, Richard Ivar *quality improvement administrator*
Menefee, Frederick Lewis *advertising executive*
Moldenhauer, Kenneth Lee *training executive*
Payne, David Michael *public policy group executive*
Stewart, Jeffrey K. *quality improvement manager*

KENTUCKY

Florence
Osborne, Gayla Marlene *sales executive*

Louisville
Robinson, Louis Hill *international sales manager*

MASSACHUSETTS

North Chatham
Ress, Charles William *management consultant*

MICHIGAN

Allegan
Drozd, Phyllis Ann *business owner*

Alpena
Werner, David J. *personnel administrator*

Ann Arbor
Agno, John G. *management consultant*
Cunningham, Cheryl M. *business executive*
Gutowski, Anthony Louis *marketing consultant*
Hartley, Terry L. *management consultant*
Horton, William David, Jr. *survivability analyst*
Lindberg, Pamela Jan *lithography company executive*
Lindsay, June Campbell McKee *communications executive*
Pritts, Bradley Arthur, Jr. *management systems consultant*
Quiroz, Peter B. *marketing executive*
Simon, Neil Jerome *consulting company executive*
Smeltzer, Penelope Sue *marketing professional*
Spencer, Mark Edward *management consultant*
Sprandel, Dennis Steuart *management consulting company executive*
Wharton, John James, Jr. *management consultant, physicist*

Battle Creek
Harinck, John Gordon *sales executive, hydraulics engineer*
Harper, John Vincent *management consultant*

Berkley
Meyer, Ronald J. *business executive*
Munro, Roderick Anthony *quality assurance professional, human performance technologist*

Bingham Farms
Laverdiere, Vicki L. *business executive*

Birmingham
McCarthy, Alice Ross *communications executive*

Bloomfield Hills
Mills, Peter Richard *advertising executive*
Ward, Richard C. *advertising executive*

Brighton
Peterson, Paul Edward *sales executive*
Veno, Glen Corey *management consultant*

Cadillac
Krafve, Allen Horton *management consultant*
Welliver, Rose M. *healthcare information company executive*

Canton
Cullen, Chad C. *business executive*
Tyson, Mary P. *marketing professional*

Clinton Township
Bricker, Gerald Wayne *marketing executive*

Dearborn
Leach, Jeffrey Dale *information systems support specialist*
McDaniel, Lauralyn *marketing professional*
Streeter, Victor John *information systems educator*
Ward, Maria Frances *community relations manager*

Dearborn Heights
Darin, Frank Victor John *management consultant*

Detroit
Baetzel, Tracey Alene *information systems professional*
Bukhari, Aftab Ali *computer company executive*
Dittman, Mark Allen *environmental safety officer*
Fauls, Thomas J. *machinery executive*
Go, Robert A. *management consultant*
Linne, John R. *institutional salesperson*
McCracken, Caron Francis *computer company executive, consultant*
McCracken, Ina *business executive*
Monroe, Loren E. *business executive*
Pierce, Acquanetta *business executive*
Totzke, Christopher N. *supervisor supplier quality*
Warfield, Robert N. *management executive*
Zoubareff, Olga Katarina (Kathy Bareoff) *accounting administrative assistant*

Dexter
Lundy, Richard Bruce *computer system company*

Dowagiac
Singleton, Donna Marie *travel agency executive*

East Detroit
Weber, Jack Bernarr *sales executive*

Erie
Betts, Nora Linden *kennel owner*

Farmington
Woodruff, Jane *sales executive*

Farmington Hills
Frederick, Raymond Joseph *sales engineering executive*
Martz, Donald S. *environmental services administrator*
Ravani, Kirit T. *environmental engineering company executive*

Fenton
Demars, Karen *marketing professional*

Ferndale
Morris, Joan Taube *personnel administrator*

Flint
Evens, Mary Ruth *tool room supervisor*

Franklin
Abel Horowitz, Michelle Susan *advertising executive*
Vanderlaan, Richard B. *marketing company executive*

Fraser
Bailey, Cheryl *consulting company executive*

Garden City
Bajaria, Hans Jamnadas *engineering and management consultant*

Gaylord
Ryan, Michael J. *marketing professional*
Weiss, Debra S. *customer service officer*

Grand Blanc
Arends, David Charles *data processing administrator, educator*

Grand Haven
Sellon, Jennifer Parker *marketing professional*

Grand Rapids
Becker, Robert Joseph *database consultant, computer science specialist, database software developer and educator*
Hahn, H. Michael *advertising executive*
Hakala, Judyth Ann *data processing executive*
Hobbs, Robert S. *executive*
Kranz, Kenneth Louis, Jr. *human resources company executive, entrepreneur*
Messner, James W. *advertising executive*
Oldewurtel, F. Keith *maintenance service company executive*
Quinn, Thomas *advertising executive*
Rich, Craig Robert *marketing professional, city councilman*
Schwartz, Garry Albert *advertising executive*
Scott, Richard Lynn *data processing executive*
Spidell, Daniel M., Jr. *business executive*

Grandville
Gotshall, Mark Edward *employee assistance executive*

Grosse Pointe
Coe, John William *management consultant*

Haslett
Whalen, Patricia Therese *marketing professional*

Highland
Thomas, Christopher Sean *information technologies developer*

Holland
Eckel, Hal *information systems specialist*
Whitmore, Andrew *business owner, sales professional*

Huntington Woods
Alexander, Ralph B(ernard) *business executive, physicist*

Ionia
Jensen, Michael J. *food service administrator*

Jackson
Demeter, Nancy Ford *cultural resources management specialist*
Mahar, Shannon Neal *sales executive*
Osborn, Janet Lynn *information systems executive*
Schwinn, David Ronald *management consultant*

Kalamazoo
Adams, Patricia Lee Minckler *program administrator*
DeVries, Beverly Mae *research recruitment specialist*
Hodges, Karla Vineyard *organization development consultant*
Segal, Joyce Trager *communications director*
Tracy, Joel Dean *marketing researcher*

Lansing
Harri, Tammy Ann *data processing executive*
Hilbert, Virginia Lois *computer consultant and training executive*
Johnson, David Lee *management educator*
Lowe, William Daniel *automotive company research executive, consultant*
Waymire, David Dean *public affairs consultant*

Livonia
Schram, Joseph H. *retired sales executive*

Madison Heights
Dinda, Michael W. *business executive*

Marquette
Earle, Mary Margaret *marketing executive*
Pesola, William Ernest *restaurant executive*

Marysville
Hansen, Randall Lee *business executive*

Mattawan
Lough, Rick Leo *sales and marketing professional*

Midland
Hall, David McKenzie *marketing and management educator*
Lindley, Nancy Long *marketing professional*
Schram, Geraldine Moore *security consultant*

Mount Clemens
Rosinski, Robert J. *consultant company executive*

Muskegon
Tyson, John David, Jr. *public and investor relations executive*

Northville
Ingersoll, Donald Paul *management consultant*
Peterson, Hans C. *business executive*

Oak Park
Rosenfeld, Martin Jerome *executive recruiter, educator*

Oxford
Hubbard, John Morris *golf course executive*

Plymouth
Luter, Terri Lee *human resources consulting company executive*
Preece, Nancy Ann *quality professional*
Steavens, Alan D. *customer service administrator*
Taylor, Mark Alan *engineering and consulting firm executive*
Varga, Carolyn Ann *computer company executive*

Port Austin
Davis, Frederick Athie *management executive*

Rapid City
Hefty, Duane Seymore *management consultant*

Reed City
Devendorf, Louise Marie *promoter, writer*

Rochester
Flynn, Raymond Regis *press company executive*

Rochester Hills
Pfister, Karl Anton *industrial company executive*

Roscommon
Lone, Rita Joan *retired linen service manager*

Royal Oak
O'Mara, Marilyn Mae *communications executive*

Saginaw
Jernigan, Alvin, Jr. *automobile sales executive*

Saint Ignace
Dodson, Bruce J. *funeral director*

Saline
Kausek, Albert Joseph *quality consultant, educator, former naval officer*
Low, Louise Anderson *consulting company executive*
Phillips, Ronald C. *personnel company executive*

Saranac
LaVean, Michael Gilbert *advertising agency executive, political consultant*

South Haven
Dunsmore, Allison Rosina Tippman *marketing executive*

Southfield
Amladi, Prasad Ganesh *management consulting executive, health care consultant, researcher*
Bahadur, B. N. *business executive*
Barnett, Marilyn *advertising agency executive*
Cleary, Mark W. *business executive*
Corcoran, James Albert *firefighter*
Harris, Stanley Francis *management educator, consultant*
Hart, Joseph Kirwin *advertising executive*
Howard, Michael Joseph *communications executive, real estate developer*
Jackson, William Gene *computer company executive*
Kalter, Alan *advertising agency executive*
Koch, Albert Acheson *management consultant*
Lawrence, Jon Edward *sales executive*
Lundquist, Virginia Areta *public affairs executive*
Martin, Tripp *quality assurance professional*
McLaughlin, Stanley A., Jr. *travel company executive*
Moore, Thomas James, III *data processing executive*
Nobles, James L. *marketing and sales executive*
Romanoff, Stanley M., Jr. *human resource specialist*
Rossi, Helen Garland Woolfenden *administrative secretary*
Smith, Donald C. *business executive*
Smith, Nancy Hohendorf *sales and marketing executive*

Spring Lake
Johnson, Robert Dale *information systems consultant*

Sturgis
Bibb, James Richard *sales executive*

Traverse City
Coates, Caroline M. *marketing administrator*

Troy
Baker, Ernest Waldo, Jr. *advertising executive*
Buttler, Jewell Ann *public relations executive*
Corr, Robert Mark *computer company executive*
Hill, Richard A. *advertising executive*
Hillman, Robert Kent *sales representative*
Ives, H. William *retired pest control company executive*
Muir, Jim R. *business executive*
Nikoui, Hossein Reza *quality assurance professional*
Ranney, Richard William *electronic data systems company official*
Wilson, Duane Isaac *executive search consultant*
Yasenka, Debra Ann *software consulting company executive*

Walled Lake
Gillespie, J. Martin *sales and distribution company executive*

Warren
Belles, Christine Fugiel *office administration educator*
Smith, Mark Steven *sales manager*
Wallace, Jack Harold *employee development specialist, educator*

West Bloomfield
Bunt, Marion Adams *retired administrative secretary/coordinator*
Husband, William Swire *computer industry executive*

Whitmore Lake
Stanny, Gary *infosystems specialist, rocket scientist*

Wyandotte
Coulter, Christopher Jay *industrial professional*

Ypsilanti
Edwards, Elizabeth A. *marketing educator*
Kettenstock, Richard Edward *computer software and consulting company owner*
Peterson, Roger Andrew *marketing educator*
Riley-Davis, Shirley Merle *advertising agency executive, marketing consultant, writer*
Weber, Patricia Louise Braden *marketing educator*

Zeeland
Wincel, Jeffrey P. *material management professional*

MINNESOTA

Afton
Fitzgerald, James Alfred, Jr. *sales and strategy consultant*

Apple Valley
Kettle, Sally Anne *consulting company executive, educator*

Austin
Budd, Jim *communications manager*
Maschka, Dennis Lee *parks and recreation director*

Biwabik
Monti, Robert Keith *resort executive*

Bloomington
Brummer, Mary D. *administrative assistant*
Schwartz, Robert Charles *communications and business consultant*

Brooklyn Park
Myers Blood, Susan Kay Gunness *marketing professional*
Sipley, Nancy E. Young *career development trainer, writer, consultant*

Burnsville
Lane, Gary Barton *quality assurance professional*
Ringquist, Lynn Anne *micrographics company executive*

Chanhassen
Fish, Gary Wayne *computer company executive, consultant*

Chaska
Cohen, Cheryl Diane Durda *communications executive*

Crookston
Holbrook, Don Allen *economic development professional*

Duluth
Bailey, Charles William *management consultant, researcher*

Eden Prairie
Carlson, Kenneth George *data processing executive*
Cervilla, Constance Marlene *marketing consultant*
Everett, Wayne *marketing consultant*
Schlick, Thomas Leroy *marketing executive*

Edina
Hunt, David Claude *sales and marketing executive*
Wurdeman, Lew Edward *data processing corporation consultant*

Hopkins
Anderson, David *business executive*
Burbank, John Thorn *contract cleaning executive*
DiGiovanni, Larry Joseph *human resources executive*

Lake Crystal
Pawlitschek, Donald Paul *business consultant*

Lake Elmo
Schraut, Sherry Jo *marketing executive*

Le Roy
Erickson, Larry Alvin *electronics sales and marketing executive*

Mankato
Wang, Vincent Tsan-Leun *food service executive*

Marshall
Selbo, Ray Gordon *training director*

Mendota Heights
Newman, Donald John *marketing executive*

Minneapolis
Adams, Kristi Kay *association executive*
Armagost, Elsa Gafvert *retired computer industry communications consultant*
Bergeson, James *advertising executive*
Brooks, Phillip *advertising executive*
Carliner, Saul A. *communications executive*
Carlson, Daniel Erik *market research executive*
Collins, Susan J. *management services company*
Cox, David Carson *media company executive*
Czeswik, Frederick Randall *human resources executive, consultant*
Driscoll, Jennifer Kay *public relations executive*
Dunlap, William DeWayne, Jr. *advertising agency executive*
Egan, Patrick Dennis *organizational development consultant*
Engelman, Wayne *advertising executive*
Fallon, Patrick R. *advertising executive*
Ferner, David Charles *non-profit management and development consultant*
Firestone, Jon *advertising executive*
Floren, David D. *advertising executive*
Fredrickson, Lola Jean *communications company executive*
Guerrero-Anderson, Esperanza *management consultant*
Harlan, Thomas N. *marketing executive*
Hartwell, John Mowry *marketing and sales consultant*
Healton, Bruce Carney *data processing executive*
Hesslund, Bradley Harry *program manager*
Hietala, Allan *advertising executive*
Leavitt, Victoria Seyferth *marketing professional*
Levin, Myles Jeffrey *marketing and sales executive*
Lewis, Stephen A *management executive*
Loucks, Steven R. *environmental management executive*
Lynch, Leland T. *advertising executive*
Miller, Daniel G. *corporate executive*
Nelson, Kirk Richard *telecommunications executive*
Olson, Clifford Larry *management consultant, entrepreneur*
Olson, Lynnette Gail *personnel executive*
Owens, Scott Andrew *sales executive*
Perlman, Lawrence *business executive*
Petersen, Maureen Jeanette Miller *management information consultant, former nurse*
Pigozzi, Robert J. *marketing executive*
Platt, Ann *animal care company executive*
Polsfuss, Craig Lyle *management consultant, psychologist, social worker*
Quiel, David Earl *information management professional*
Reilly, Brian J. *executive*
Russell, Armida Mendez *management consultant*
Schulman, Tammy Beth *communications executive*
Schultz, Louis Edwin *management consultant*
Stubbs, Jan Didra *retired travel industry executive, travel writer*
Sullivan, Michael Patrick *food service executive*
Swenson, Faye Lorene *executive management development firm*
Thompsen, Joyce Ann *organizational consultant*
Toren, Brian Keith *futures and research executive*
Weyl, Tom F. *advertising executive*
Willhite, Lee A. *human resources administrator*
Young, Philip Gilmer *policy analyst*
Yourzak, Robert Joseph *management consultant, engineer, educator*
Zeman, Michael *advertising executive*
Zimmerman, Susan G. *sales executive*
Zimmermann, Robert Laurence *marketing professional*
Zoberi, Nadim Bin-Asad *management consultant*

Minnetonka
Cross, Bonham E(lwood) *retired newspaper account executive*
Forteau, Edwin Brian *marketing advisor to small businesses*
Goldstein, Marc L. *water purification company administrator*
Herzog, Ann Elizabeth *marketing and advertising consultant*
Kostka, Ronald Wayne *marketing consultant*
List, Charles Edward *management and organization development consultant*
Schmidt, Russel Alan, II *sales executive*

Owatonna
Joachim, James Michael *computer information systems educator*

Plymouth
Stenulson, Sonya Helen *advertising executive*

Prior Lake
Davis, James Lee *business executive*
Hatcher, Thomas Fountain *management consultant, publisher*

Rochester
Ricklefs, Karen Lee *quality assurance consultant*
Ricklefs, Merlin John *quality and performance improvement consultant*

Saint Cloud
Oleksey, Vicky Joyce *business owner*
Van Nostrand, Catharine Marie Herr *human resources development executive, writer*

Saint Joseph
Sands, Gene Cameron *public relations executive, educator*

Saint Paul
Brandt, Peter A. *company executive*
Briggs, Robert Henry *infosystems specialist*
Christ, Sandra Louise *customer service representative*
Gang, Stuart Worthington *advertising and public relations company executive*
James, Nicholas *corporate executive*
Lendt, Harold Hanford *manufacturing representative*
Olson, Scott *company executive*
Peters, Deborah Lynn *management consultant*

Savage
Luth, James Curtis *systems consultant*

Victoria
Courtney, Eugene Whitmal *computer company executive*

Virginia
Slocum, Rosemarie R. *physician management search consultant*

Wayzata
Schoen, Charles Judd *service executive*
Waldera, Wayne Eugene *crisis management specialist*

Willmar
Norling, Rayburn *food service executive*

Winona
Barger, Ralph Thomas *consulting executive*

MISSOURI

Ballwin
Reiss, Kenneth William *computer services company executive, educator*

Bolivar
Heitz-Peek, Tamera *public relations executive*

Bridgeton
Campbell, Anita Joyce *computer company executive*

Cape Girardeau
Smallwood, Glenn Walter, Jr. *utility marketing management executive*

Carthage
Frerer, Ronald Kent *customer service representative, owner*

Chesterfield
Henderson, Michael Dean *electrical engineer*
Johnston, Gary *consulting company executive*
Kellis, Randal Anthony *sales executive*
Tyler, William Howard, Jr. *advertising executive, educator*

Columbia
Arnold, Linda Gayle *human resources executive*
Mikrut, John Joseph, Jr. *labor arbitrator, educator*
Parfet, John Richard *business development specialist*
Pfeffer, Walter Louis, II *sales executive, columnist*
Rutter, Elizabeth Jane *consulting firm executive*

De Soto
DeFranco, Anthony *sales representative*

Drexel
Tobler, William Jennings, III *farrier*

Earth City
Selzle, Kurt Ander *sales executive*

Excelsior Springs
Loomis, Robert Arthur *sales executive*

Fenton
Langley, Brad Scott *travel company executive*

Florissant
Kelly, James Joseph *printing company executive*
Wagner, Mary Ann *human resources executive*

Golden City
Howard, Joanne Frances *marketing executive, funeral director, extended care coordinator*

Hazelwood
Dougherty, Thomas *information services executive*

Hillsboro
Cline, Donald Alan *management consultant*

Independence
Booz, Gretchen Arlene *marketing executive*
Shook, Jerry L. *company executive*
Yarrington, Hollis Roger *communications administrator, editor*

Jefferson City
Richter, Ewald Arthur *public relations counselor*

Kansas City
Arbuckle, Philip Wayne *travel company executive*
Baker, Ronald Phillip *service company executive*
Barger, Richard B. *communications consultant*
Bernstein, Robert *advertising executive*
Brenneman, Jon E. *marketing executive*
Camden, David George *sales executive*
Click, Marianne Jane *credit manager*
Crawford, Linda D. *data company executive*
Davison, Dean *public relations executive*
DeLay, William Raymond *communications executive*
Dillingham, John Allen *marketing professional*
Ebbitts, Mark Hobart *travel service professional*
Evans, Margaret Ann *human resources administrator, business owner*
Grafing, Keith Gerhart *marketing representative, consultant*
Hockaday, Irvine O., Jr. *greeting card company executive*
Hoover, Diane E. *business executive*
James, Claudia Ann *business educator and trainer, motivational speaker*
Krause, Heather Dawn *data processing executive*
Markus, Joel Seth *data processing management executive*
Mastin, Timothy Jay *public relations professional*
McClure, Mary Virginia *consumer products company executive*
Murdock, Phelps Dubois, Jr. *marketing consultant*
Paulsen, Elizabeth Robertson *public relations manager*
Peterson, Douglas Eugene *sales executive*
Price, Charlton Reed *management consultant*
Smiley, David Bruce *administrative director*
Smith, Mark Maurice *marketing professional*
Stowers, James, III *data processing company executive*
Tramposh, Anne Katherine *industrial services executive*
Wei, William L. *marketing professional, consultant*
Wiggins, Laurence Eugene *sales executive*

Kirkwood
Koestering, Ernest John, Jr. *semi-retired engineering and marketing consultant*

Labadie
Grothaus, Pamela Sue *marketing professional*

Lebanon
Massey, Ellen Frances Gray *language educator*

Lees Summit
Williams, Kenneth Eugene *advertising specialist*

Lexington
Cosper, Andrea Verbie *management consultant*

Liberty
Eakes, Linda M. *telecommunications executive, consultant*
McCaslin, WC *products and packaging executive*

Nixa
Aduddle, Larry Steven *marketing and sales executive, consultant*

Parkville
Jacobs, Carl Eugene *printing company official*

Saint Charles
Deraps, Larry *customer service representative*
Gross, Charles Robert *personnel executive, legislator, appraiser*
Nickisch, Willard Wayne *funeral director*
Price, Gary Robert *postal worker, broadcaster*

Saint Joseph
Frogge, William Francis *retired communications company executive*
Huff, David Richard *funeral home executive*

Saint Louis
Baczenas, Patrick J. *public relations professional*
Bicklein, John P. *resource specialist*
Bir, Michelle Marie *sales executive*
Breslauer, Suzanne Eisen *public relations consultant*
Coblitz, David Barry *chief technical specialist*
Cooper, Robert James *purchasing consultant*
Dommermuth, William P. *marketing consultant, educator*
Elliott, Susan Spoehrer *information technology executive*
Farrell, Kathleen Ellen *marketing, public relations executive*
Field, Gilbert Vern *information systems manager*
Gers, Harvey *marketing professional*
Giovanni, Robert William *sales executive*
Harrington, Kenneth Alan *communication company executive*
Hasler, Alexander *advertising executive, consultant*
Heck, Debra Upchurch *information technology professional*
Hollingsworth, Gary Mayes *Internet access provider company*
Johnson, Eric Carl *software company executive*
Jones, Ronald Woodbridge *human resources specialist, small business owner*
Kell-Sutton, Jenifer Ann *public relations executive*
Khoury, George Gilbert *printing company executive, baseball association executive*
Kochan, Robert Joseph *advertising executive*
Kupper, Bruce David *advertising executive*
Lucking, Peter Stephen *marketing consultant, industrial engineering consultant*
Malnassy, Louis Sturges *public relations counselor*
McCaslin, Teresa Eve *human resources executive*
Miller, Theresa Ann *management consultant*
Pignolet, Keith Glenn *executive*
Royse, Lynne Ellen *marketing professional*
Ruhnke, William Paul *management executive*
Schnuck, Scott C. *grocery store executive*
Scholin, Ray Albert *printing company executive*
Smith, Kenard Eugene *marketing professional*
Smith, Patricia Newell *training and development manager*
Taylor, Dennis Del *marketing executive*
Tunney, Greg Alan *sales executive*
Van Luven, William Robert *management consultant*
Ward, Richard Compton *management consultant*
Wassell, Loren W. *public affairs administrator, writer*
Weaver, Charles Lyndell, Jr. *marketing and management facility administrator*
Weaver, William Clair, Jr. (Mike Weaver) *human resources development executive*
Yoder, Susan Fischer *tourist agency executive*

Saint Peters
Greene, Christopher William *marketing professional*

Sainte Genevieve
Ward, Michael James *sales executive*

Savannah
Lyle, Mary Kay *order buying company executive*

Springfield
Cooper, J. Michael *advertising executive*
Hignite, Michael Anthony *computer information systems educator, researcher, writer*
Mitchell, John David *public relations executive*
Noble, Robert B. *advertising executive*
Ruda, Neil Michael *data processing executive, minister*
Turnage, Juleen Holderby *public relations executive*

Warrensburg
Harmon, Harry Alan *marketing educator*

Washington
Dawson, Larry Ross *transportation marketing professional*

NEBRASKA

Bellevue
Nicholsen, James Therman *computer company executive*

Lincoln
Andelt, Dan Allen *welding technician*
Borgmann, Connie Sue *advertising and public relations executive*
Brownson, E. Ramona Lidstone Brady *secretary*
Chesnin, Leon *waste management and utilization consultant*
Fleharty, Mary Sue *communication specialist*
Hoppe, John Leslie *business executive*
Jones, Matthew Leon *sales and acquisition specialist*
Podolske, Diane Lynne *management consultant*
Preister, Donald George *greeting card manufacturer, state senator*
Wagenaar, Doreen Dawn *marketing professional*

Omaha
Baumann, Mark H. *business executive*
Bean, Kimberly Sue *information system specialist*
Eggers, James Wesley *executive search consultant*
Lietzen, John Hervy *human resources executive, health agency volunteer*
Meyers, Louisa Ann *business and communications consultant*
Prange, Cedric William *management consultant*
Purcell, Kevin John *business executive*
Scobba, Judy *credit collections executive*
Sickinger, Timothy *advertising executive*
Smart, Denise Torvik *marketing educator*
Thiebauth, Bruce Edward *advertising executive*
Visser, Jennifer Lynne *sales executive*

Papillion
Scott, Raymond Gerald *management executive*

Western
Harrington, Larry Thomas *industrial professional*

Wolbach
Jacobson, Eugene E. *industrial professional*

NEW JERSEY

Berkeley Heights
Christenson, Charles Duane *sales executive*

NEW YORK

Rochester
DeWoody, Geary Michael *marketing professional*

NORTH CAROLINA

Kure Beach
Schutta, James T. *quality assurance executive*

NORTH DAKOTA

Bismarck
Ellingson, Julie Ann Schaff *public relations professional*
Palmer, Richard Joseph *communications director*

Dickinson
Mitzel, Richard J. *management consultant, purchasing manager*

Edinburg
Melsted, Marcella H. *retired administrative assistant, civic worker*

Grand Forks
Zahrly, Janice Honea *management educator*

Mandan
Heick, Leon Joseph *data processing executive*

Minot
Watson, Lynn R. *executive*

Turtle Lake
Grosz, Albert Mick *sales executive*

OHIO

Akron
Brule, Thomas Raymond *franchise executive, lawyer*
Gilpatric, Lawrence *hospitality management educator*
Hawes, Jon Michael *sales and marketing educator*
Jasso, William Gattis *public relations executive*
McCormick, William Edward *environmental consultant*
Meeker, David Anthony *public relations executive*
Pearsall, Lucille J. *company executive*
Rohrbough, Linda Jandecka *computer center administrator*
Walker, Debra May *marketing professional*
Wilfong, Brenda A. *telecommunications executive*
Zeno, Jo Ann *sales executive*

Ashland
Seabolt, Clarence *management executive*

Barberton
Romano, David *company executive*

Bay Village
Berger, James (Hank) *business broker*

Beachwood
Seelbach, William Robert *management executive*

Beaver Creek
Riley, David Richard *management consultant, retired military officer*

Bedford
Prosen, Michael A. *company executive*

Belmont
Perkins, Catherine Ann *corporate executive*

Berea
Caldwell, Jessie J. *quality assurance specialist*
Davidson, Marsha Eileen *communications executive*

Boardman
Komar, Jerry J. *management consulting executive*

Broadview Heights
Sternlieb, Lawrence Jay *marketing professional*

Brunswick
Kovacs, Diane Kaye *internet training consultant*

Canton
Criswell, John *business executive*
Haas, Suzanne Newhouse *management consultant, human resources specialist*
Smith, Donald Roy *public relations professional*

Chagrin Falls
Church, Irene Zaboly *personnel services company executive*
Eastburn, Richard A. *consulting firm executive*
Jue, Richard *food service executive*
Kuby, Barbara Eleanor *personnel executive, management consultant*

Cincinnati
Artzt, Edwin Lewis *consumer products company executive*
Baxter, Susan Johnson *medical sales consultant*
Carl, Aloysius Jerome *business executive*
Carraher, Charles Jacob, Jr. *professional speaker*
Castro, Daniel R. *telecommunications administrator*
Comisar, Chris Farah-Lynn *advertising executive*
Doyle, William Jay, II *business consultant*
Faust, Mark Joseph *management consultant, speaker, trainer*
Freshwater, Paul Ross *consumer goods company executive*
Hernandez, Gloria J. *consulting company executive*
Howe, John Kingman *manufacturing, sales and marketing executive*
Hunter, Michael P. *information systems professional*
Jantzen, Gordon John *human resources specialist*
Kay, Peter Steven *business consultant*
Klein, Charles Henle *lithographing company executive*
Lange, Scott Leslie *communications company executive, voice professional*
Levy, Sam Malcolm *advertising executive*
Lollar, Robert Miller *management consultant*
Million, Kenneth Rhea *management consultant*
Moore, John Edward *marketing professional, freelance writer*
Musser, Margaret Morris *marketing professional*
Pape, Jerry Lee *public relations specialist, retired naval officer*
Pauly, Sanford Dickson *sales professional*
Rose, Michael R. *consulting company executive*
Scherer, Anita (Anita Stock) *advertising executive*
Semple, Harry D. *business executive*
Sherman, John Kingsley *retired industrial sales executive*
Sommer, Scott William *control systems integrator manager*
Stout, Mark Orren *marketing professional*
Strauss, James Lester *investment sales executive, accountant*
Tucker, Michael J. *product marketing manager*
Waits, Gary Lee *sales manager*
Wehling, Robert Louis *household products company executive*
Youkilis, Tom Fishel *purchasing agent*

Circleville
Droste, Jean Rasmusen *educational consultant*

Cleveland
Arnold, David Paul *sales professional*
Baunach, Bruce Nelson *marketing professional*
Benghiat, Russell *advertising agency executive*
Birrer, Holli Ileen *public relations executive*
Byron, Rita Ellen Cooney *travel executive, publisher, real estate agent, civic leader, photojournalist, writer*
Cargile, Michael Edward *advertising agency executive*
Day, Charles Roger *public relations manager, journalist*
Day, Phyllis Arlene *marketing professional*
Dunbar, Mary Asmundson *communications executive, investor and public relations consultant*
Eichhorn, Bradford Reese *management consultant*
Frisman, Roger Lawrence *industrial sales executive*
Gibans, Nina Freedlander *special projects director*
Gombert, Richard William *information systems professional*
Graham, John W. *advertising executive*
Gund, Gordon *advertising executive*
Hanlon, Diane Wiemer *administrative assistant*
Hastie, Ronald Leslie *sales executive*
Henry, Edward Frank *computer accounting service executive*
Iredell, Robert, IV *advertising executive*
Kay, Leslie *public relations consultant, journalist*
Kenny, Raymond Patrick *greeting card company executive*
Kiernozek, Ted. J. *marketing professional*
Kleiman, Berenice Elkin *company executive*
Kuendig, William Norman, II *management consultant, actuarial consultant*
Luce, Priscilla Mark *public affairs executive*
Mainardi, Cesare Roberto Giovanni *management consultant*
McCracken, Michael Dale *customer services representative*
Meyer, Robert Paul *quality assurance executive, consultant, foundation executive*
Monroy, Thomas Gerald *management consulting executive, educator*
Moore, Thomas Earl *public relations executive*
Morin, Patrick Joyce *advertising executive*
Myatt, G. *company executive*
Nygard, Andrew Charles *management consultant*
Olland, Cherie Wallace *marketing professional*
Olson, Barry Gay *advertising executive, creative director*
Perry, Chris Nicholas *advertising executive*
Rhodes, Jacqueline Yvonne *marketing executive*
Roop, James John *public relations executive*
Ruggere, Dennis Joseph *computer company executive*
Smith, Bonnie Beatrice *corporate communications executive*
Stashower, David L. *advertising executive*
Stauffacher, Albert Herbert *resource company executive*
Sudow, Thomas Nisan *marketing services company executive, broadcaster*
Thomas, John Edward *financial services marketing executive*
Wyse, Lois *advertising executive, author*
Wyse, Marc A. *advertising agency executive*

Columbiana
Garrett, Paul William *retired management executive*

Columbus
Alspach, Donn E. *management company executive*
Case, Russell P. *company executive*
Chapman, John William, Jr. *marketing executive*
Colyer, Richard Allen *business executive*
Cooke, Anne E. *administrative assistant*
Cotter, Patricia Ewing *human resource specialist*
Crawford, David Mark *public relations executive*
Hamilton, Randall L. *personnel administrator*
Hrusovsky, John Joseph, II *systems consulting manager*
Jackson, Gregory Stuart *information systems specialist*
Keller, Kenneth Christen *advertising executive*
Kupper, Jeff G. *company executive*
McClain, Thomas E. *communications executive*
Piersante, Denise *marketing executive*
Rieck, James Dean *copywriter, creative consultant*
Schoedinger, David Stanton *funeral director*
Slutsky, Jeff L. *marketing executive*
Spencer, Betty K. *marketing professional*
Sullivan, Ernest Lee *human resources director*
Taylor, Celianna Isley *information systems specialist*
Turner, James F. *business executive*
Tway, Stephen Edward *marketing communications executive, consultant*
Zapp, David Edwin *infosystems specialist, investment consultant*

Coshocton
Harris, Jim R. *business executive*

Dayton
Biar, Jeffery Ken *data processing executive*
Bruns, Pamela Jane *marketing and public relations consultant*
Cole, John A. *service management electronic publishing*
Corbet, Donald Lee *audio company executive, technical systems educator*
Fulton, Darrell Nelson *information systems specialist*
Gasper, David Anthony *computer software executive*
Maher, Frank Aloysius *research and development executive, psychologist*
Schnier, David Christian *marketing executive, author*
See, Alan Jeffery *marketing executive*
Strawbridge, Jesse Ronald *management consultant*
Tobin, Christopher Ward *computer consulting firm executive*
Turner, Robert Sullivan *consulting company executive*
Vander Wiel, Kenneth Carlton *computer services company executive*
Whalen, Robert James *business consultant*

Doylestown
Frase, Charles Frederick *marketing professional*

Dublin
Bastoky, Bruce Michael *human resources executive*
Crawford, Carl Wallace *corporate communications executive*
Evans, Anton Nelson (Tony Evans) *marketing communications executive*
Fink, Thomas Edward *cosmetologist, manager*
O'Brien, Patrick Augustine *business executive*
Tray, Maria A. *business executive*

Elyria
Kattas, Paula Louise *purchasing agent*
Kuznik, Susan Marie *management consultant*
Patton, Thomas James *sales and marketing executive*
Schrott, Janet Ann *human resources specialist, consultant*

Fairlawn
Koch, William Joseph *public relations executive*

Fairport Harbor
Martin, David Robert *purchasing agent, business owner*

Fayetteville
Spence, Joseph Patrick *advertising executive*

Findlay
Panasy, Craig W. *sales and marketing professional*

Fostoria
Basel, Margaret Mary *management consultant*
Howard, Kathleen *computer company executive*

Gahanna
Myers, Phillip Fenton *financial services and technology company executive*

Gates Mills
Abbott, James Samuel *marketing executive*

Germantown
Lansaw, Charles Ray *sales industry executive*

Hamilton
Ferng, Douglas Ming-Haw *infosystems executive*
Weber, Jeffrey William *public affairs professional*

Heath
Gregorich, Penny Denise *production procurement analyst*
Richards, Donald Lee *custodian*

Hilliard
Reid, Bruce Eugene *video executive*

Hudson
Barlow, Franklin Sackett *sales executive, consultant*
Bell, Harry Edward *quality consulting company executive*
Howard, Brian Robert *buyer*
Little, Stephen John *computer company executive*
Marcantonio, Arthur *quality assurance executive*

Independence
Luciano, Gwendolyn Kaye *planning specialist, utility rates administrator*

Jackson
Rodgers, Robert Allen *computer company executive, consultant*

Kent
Bissler, Richard Thomas *mortician*
Stevenson, Thomas Herbert *management consultant, writer*

Lewis Center
Clay, Franklin Delano *advertising executive*

London
Pritt, Judith Kay *service executive, nurse*

Lorain
White, Christopher W. *sales professional*

Louisville
Anderson, Kim Elizabeth *health and fitness organization executive*

Loveland
Carl, Angela Reeves *strategic planning consultant, trainer*
Dalambakis, Christopher A. *sales executive, systems market manager*

Lucasville
Herron, Ned Talbert *marketing professional*

Mansfield
Pesec, David John *data systems executive*

Maple Heights
Sargent, Liz Elaine (Elizabeth Sargent) *safety consulting executive*

Marion
Fassler, Crystal G. *marketing consultant*

Maumee
Nowak, Patricia Rose *advertising executive*
Sacksteder, Thomas M. *sales executive*

Mayfield Heights
Wodoslawsky, Theodore Steven *advertising executive*

Miamisburg
Suarez, Patrick Joseph *technology company executive*

Middletown
Horsley, Teri Lynne *advertising sales representative*
Turpin, Richard E. *sales executive*

Monclova
Chartier, Charles Adrian *sales executive*

New Philadelphia
Rolelli, Cam C. *business executive*

Niles
Travaglini, Raymond Dominic *corporate executive*

North Olmsted
Galysh, Robert Alan *information systems analyst*

North Royalton
Darby, L.E. Jack *public services and properties administrator*

Oberlin
Merleno, Toni Autumn *personnel executive*

Oxford
Dawley, Donald Lee *information systems educator*
Yen, David Chi-Chung *management information systems educator*

Painesville
Christ, Vincent B. *retired sales executive*

Perrysburg
Kovacik, Neal Stephen *hotel and restaurant executive*

Pickerington
Good, Arthur James *business executive*

Piqua
Szczurek, Thomas Eugene *marketing executive*

Powell
Reed, Constance Louise *materials management and purchasing consultant*
Reed, James Wesley *sales and marketing executive*

Shade
Cuckler, Tad *consultant*

Strongsville
Solymossy, Emeric *management consultant, engineer*

Sylvania
Isaac, Bina Susan *data processing executive*
Ring, Herbert Everett *management executive*
Rothschild, Cheryl Lynn *marketing executive*

Tipp City
Taylor, Robert Homer *quality assurance professional, pilot*

Toledo
Block, Allan James *communications executive*
Carpenter, John Edward *marketing professional*
Cummings, Erwin Karl *data processing executive*
Foster, Stephen V. *sales executive*
Kimble, James A. *management consultant, accountant*
Kummerle, Herman Frederick *environmental consulting firm executive*
Sanderson, David Alan *training and development administrator*
Tabor, Randall Arden *sales executive*

Uniontown
Laney, Richard Bryant *marketing executive*

University Heights
Loeffler, Robert Henry *media relations manager*

Urbana
Schulte, Gary Rodger *consumer products company executive*

Warren
Di Liello, Salvatore *data processing executive, educator*
Howard, David A. *marketing professional*
Sandberg, John Alden *quality control professional*
Westman, Robert Allan *management consultant*

Waterville
White, Harry E. *company executive, retired*

West Chester
Dickens, Jacqueline B. *management systems executive*
Neiheisel, Thomas Henry *marketing research consultant*

Westerville
Kerner, Joseph Frank, Jr. *management consultant, educator*
McNeal, Palmer Craig *governmental consultant*

Westlake
Conway, Robert G. *office manager*
Whitehouse, John Harlan, Jr. *systems software consultant, diagnostician*

Wickliffe
Suva, Suzanne *personnel relations executive, consultant, educator*

Wilberforce
Anene, John Odiaka *hospitality industry educator*

Willoughby
Kuhel, James Joseph *information systems analyst*

Wooster
Schmitt, Wolfgang Rudolf *consumer products executive*

Worthington
Kiefer, Richard Lawrence *sales representative*

Wright Patterson AFB
Caudill, Tom Holden *logistics director*

Wyoming
Cooley, William Edward *regulatory affairs manager*

Xenia
Nutter, Zoe Dell Lantis *retired public relations executive*
Vance, Debbie Dee *marketing executive*

Yellow Springs
Schulsinger, Michael Alan *data processing executive*

Youngstown
Fisher, Merle A. *advertising executive*
Forbush, Albert H. *company owner*
Rice, Les J. *company executive*
Spero, Leslie Wayne *linen service and distribution company executive*
Wolf, Margaret Louise *sales support information administrator, marketing*

Zanesville
Young, Dale *business manager*

SOUTH CAROLINA

Hilton Head Island
Coble, Paul Ishler *advertising agency executive*

SOUTH DAKOTA

Beresford
Arends, Wendell Leonard *apartment manager*

Brookings
Ellman, June Christine *research consultant*
Swiden, Ladell Ray *travel company executive*

Deadwood
Nelson, Thomas Roy *hotel executive*

Eagle Butte
Nordvold, Homer Blaine *cattle ranch manager*

Hot Springs
Shaw, Bruce Lloyd *restaurant manager*

Lead
Akrop, Paul Gregory *ski area administrator*

Sioux Falls
Peterson, William Gene *public affairs executive*
Taplett, Lloyd Melvin *human resources management consultant*
Weeks, M. J. *international management consultant*

Spearfish
Redfern, Richard Robert *management consultant, geologist*

Wall
Estes, Douglas Lee *motel owner*

TEXAS

Plano
Havens, Charnell Thomas *management consultant*

UTAH

Park City
Ebbs, George Heberling, Jr. *management consulting company executive*

VIRGINIA

Fairfax
Johns, Michael Douglas *public policy analyst, consultant, writer*

WEST VIRGINIA

Wellsburg
Wellman, Gerald Edwin, Jr. *safety and fire inspector*

WISCONSIN

Appleton
Goldgar, Corinne Hartman *marketing coordinator*
Kolka, Julie Ann *public relations executive*
Petinga, Charles Michael *business executive*

Barron
Gleichert, Gregg Charles *human resources executive*

Brookfield
Bader, Ronald L. *advertising executive*
Gaertig, Janet L. *marketing professional*
Geremia, Frank V. *computer company executive*
Reckner, Jerald *marketing executive*
Saam, Robert Harry *human resources consultant*
Vorpahl, Jeff *computer company executive*
Wacker, Thomas J. *management executive, outplacement cousultant*

Clear Lake
Barnhill, Jean Elizabeth *office manager, personnel officer*

Darien
Miller, Malcolm Henry *manufacturing sales executive, real estate developer*

Eau Claire
Leary, Robin Janell *administrative secretary, county government official*

Elm Grove
Chandler, Kensal R. *executive*
Fowler, Dean Robert *business consultant*

Fontana
Johnson, George William *resource manager*
Read, C(arlyle) Dean, Jr. *consultant*

Green Bay
Crowley, Elizabeth Marlene *management consultant*
Kotalik, George *marketing executive*
Wilson, Charles Douglas *public affairs executive*

Greendale
Tucker, William Thomas, III *computer software company executive*

Greenfield
Rozwick, Donald Joseph *recycling company executive*

Hartford
Vander Pas, William T. *sales executive*

Hudson
Anderson, David Gary *senior account executive*

Jackson
Best, Jeffrey Dean *electronics technician*

Janesville
Kuelz, Sherry Lee *computer professional*

La Crosse
Ruyle, Kim Ernest *training and software development executive*
Wilson, Kathryn Terese *food service director*

Madison
Beyer, Jane Magdalyn *governmental management consultant*
Cleary, Sue Allene Shorney *communication executive*
Ellstrom-Calder, Annette *marketing manager, clinical medicine educator*
Gullikson, Angela Kathleen *quality management analyst*
Gunter, Randel Harlan *advertising agency executive*
Kryn, Randall Lee *public relations executive*
Meyers, Matthew Frank *advertising executive*
Olscheske, Thomas John *information systems specialist, researcher*
Scheidler, James Edward *physicians services company executive*
Stites, Susan Kay *human resources consultant*

Maiden Rock
Tinney, Dee Melvin *marketing executive, consultant*

Menasha
Montalbano, Daniel Clarence *jeweler*
Vetter, James Lou *international marketing executive*

Menomonee Falls
Holmes, Jeffrey H. *business executive*
Sayles, Ronald Lyle *computer executive*

Menomonie
Lyon, Barbara Weber *marketing professional*

Mequon
Miller, Scott Joseph *software executive*

Middleton
Senn, Richard Allan *environmental safety professional*

Milwaukee
Balbach, George Charles *technology company executive*
Behrendt, Mary Ann Weber *marketing consultant*
Bergmann, Linda J. *marketing professional*
Bremner, Joseph P. *management consultant*
Constable, John *advertising executive*
Foran, David John *public relations consultant*
Kahlor, Robert A(rnold) *communications company executive*
Kanning, Eugene H. *food service company executive*
Kath, Randy James *management information services*
King, William Stewart, II *public relations executive*
Laughlin, Steven L. *advertising executive*
McBride, Genevieve Gardner *public relations educator, author*
Peck, Julie Ellen Walsh *consultant*
Roozen, Mary Louise *public relations executive*
Shapiro, Robert Donald *management consultant*
Teuschler, Michael Alexander *computer company executive, consultant*
Tomfohrde, Mitchell Gerald *management consultant*
Wolf, Ronald Clarence *information systems manager*

Minocqua
Beltz, George Allen *retired company executive*

Neenah
Underhill, Robert Alan *consumer products company executive*

New Berlin
Bartelak, Chris *vice president*
Birchbauer, Michael A. *business executive*
Peck, Curtiss Steven *organization development consultant*
Weinzierl, Thomas Allen *data processing and data communications manager*

New Glarus
Wilcox, Winton Wilfred, Jr. *computer specialist, consultant*

Oak Creek
Harris, R(ichard) Steven *data processing executive, consultant, educator*

Pleasant Prairie
Pinter, Diann *business executive*

Pound
Pillath, Richard James *purchasing consultant*

Racine
Boyle, Glen A. *business executive*
Klein, Gabriella Sonja *communications executive*
McGehee, Bryan Keith *information systems manager, systems analyst*
Strobl, Rudolf *business strategist*
Wiechers, James David *data processing executive, electronic data processing auditor*

Rice Lake
Slack, Fred Paul *global industrial sales executive*

Ripon
McDonald, Jay Briggs *sales executive*

Rochester
Betterman, Karen *travel management consultant*

Sheboygan Falls
Wiegand, Kenneth Allan *marketing professional*

Shorewood
Fraser, John G. *marketing professional*

Stevens Point
Clucas, John M. *company executive*
Leafgren, Frederick Alden *human relations consultant*

Sussex
Dewey, Craig Douglas *operations executive*

Thiensville
Dickow, James Fred *management consultant*

Viroqua
Gass, Kenneth Christian *communications executive*

Waterford
Karraker, Louis Rendleman *retired corporate executive*

Waukesha
Dralle, Lambert R. *paper merchant owner*

Waunakee
Berthelsen, John Robert *printing company executive*

Wausau
Rosenberg, James Donald *public relations executive*

West Allis
Armstrong, Rebecca Sue *customer service representative*

Wisconsin Rapids
Knuteson, Miles Gene *advertising executive*

ENGLAND

Coventry
Monberg, Jay Peter *management consultant*

ADDRESS UNPUBLISHED

Allen, Leilani Eleanor *data processing executive*
Andrews, James MacArthur *sales executive*
Archer, Amy T. *marketing professional*
Axelrod, Leonard *management consultant*
Balder, James Ellsworth *infosystems specialist*
Baur, Bob *company executive*
Beall, Ware Thompson, Jr. (Tom Beall) *industrial sales and marketing executive*
Bennett, Terry Allen *technical services consultant*
Borsick, Marlin Lester *data processing executive*
Bouldin, Heidi G. *company executive*
Bovich, Edward Philip *marketing educator, consultant*
Bowman-Randall, Gayle Darlene *equal employment specialist, writer*
Brereton, Charlaine Phyllis *company administrator*
Brittain, David Lawrence *marketing executive*
Brodrick, Nancy Ann *human resources specialist*
Brown, Donna Kay *executive*
Bufka, John Andrew *sales executive*
Bundalo, Milan Richard *management consultant*
Byrd, Robert Ray *computer science educator*
Capobianco, Ernest R. *advertising executive*
Cargo, Rebecca R. *office manager, dairy farmer*
Carney, Larry Brady *telecommunications manager, accountant*
Carter, Mary Nash (Mary Carter Edgington) *advertising executive*
Cervelli, Thomas R. *business executive*
Cobane, Joseph L. *retired manufactures agent*
Collins, Mary Ellen *human resources executive*
Corson, James Allen *business official*
Craig, Elizabeth Louise *management consultant*
Curran, Brad D. *electrical technician*
Czerak, Gerald Stephen *marketing professional*
Darany, George Thomas *advertising and transportation company executive*
Davis, Wayne Pitman *public relations specialist*
Dekorsi, Ann Elizabeth *public relations professional*
De Metz, Della Christine *executive, writer, social consultant*
Denney, Lucinda Ann *relocation services executive*
Depke, Nancy Gallagher *marketing professional*
Donovan, James Robert *business equipment company executive*
Duncan, Louis D. *building and safety director*
Durbin, (Margaret) Rosamond *marketing executive*
Engels, Thomas Joseph *sales executive*
England, Christopher Matthew *marketing information analyst*
Feinberg, Glenda Joyce *restaurant chain executive*
Finder, Kenneth A. *director of business development*
Fischer, Andrew *mechanical designer*
Fischmar, Richard Mayer *resort executive, financial consultant*
Fitzpatrick, Sean Kevin *advertising agency executive*
Ford, E(mma) Jane *public relations executive*
Frank, Debra Wilson *retail manager and trainer*
Friedlander, Joseph David *environmental administrator, ecologist*
Garfield, Nancy Ellen *marketing and advertising professional*
Gehrke, Joan Smith *public relations director*
Gennick, Jonathan George *information systems consultant*
Giancola, Dennis James *marketing professional*
Gleason, Darlene Harriette *retired personnel director*
Golden, Brian Michael *marketing executive*
Gower, Cindy Elaine *electronic technician*
Grassi, Nick J. *business executive*
Griffith, Vaughn A. *program manager farm machinery company*
Hall, Hansel Crimiel *communications executive*
Hamm, Vernon Louis, Jr. *management and financial consultant*
Hardy, Richard Evan *human service professional, consultant*
Harris, David Philip *crisis management executive*
Harrison, Steven W. *business executive*
Hawkins, Lawrence Charles *management consultant, educator*
Heindel, Lee Edward *software marketing manager, consultant, researcher*
Hersher, Richard Donald *management consultant*
Hesselberg, Gerri Sue (Gitel Sarah) *sales executive*
Hicks, Cheryl Lee *executive*
Hite, Elinor Kirkland *oil company human resources manager*
Jacobson, Elliott Roy *political and public relations consultant, film production advisor, writer, actor*
Jenkins, Anthony Curtis *sales executive*
Jenson, Kathy LaVon *marketing director*
Johnson, Mary Theresa *marketing professional*
Johnson, Richard Jerome *computer company executive*
Johnston, Charles Bruce *computerized certification/ license testing company executive*
Jones, Kristi Lynne *business consultant*
Jurs, Addie Poole *marketing professional, publishing executive*
Kampmeier, Curtis Neil *management consultant*
Kendzior, Robert Joseph *marketing executive*
Kidd, Debra Jean *communications executive*
King, Carol A. *business executive*
Koprivica, Dorothy Mary *management consultant, real estate and insurance broker*
Kornokovich, Ron J. *marketing research company executive*
Kreer, Irene Overman *association and meeting management executive*
Kuster, Charles R. *communications executive*
Larson, Marian Gertrude *catalog sales company executive*
Leaman, David Charles *management consultant*
Lewandowski, Michalene Maria *human service consultant, lecturer*
Libby, Gary A. *sales executive*
Luttner, Edward F. *consulting company executive*
Maddy, Coleen *quality assurance professional*
Makepeace, Darryl Lee *consulting company executive*
McGrath, Lee Upton *school rings and yearbooks company executive*
McGuire, Nora E. *account executive*
McKernan, John B. *sales executive*
McKown, Richard Dale *sales and marketing executive*
McLennan, Robert Gordon *management company executive*
Meade, Patricia Sue *marketing professional*
Meis, Nancy Ruth *marketing and development executive*
Meyers, Karen Hopkins *management consultant*
Mikiewicz, Anna Daniella *marketing and sales representative*
Milligan, Amanda Leigh *marketing executive, editor*
Mouzakes-Siler, Helen Harriet (Elena Mouzakes-Siler) *retired executive secretary, lyric soloist*
Nixon, Curtis D. *marketing executive*
Norris, William C. *retired computer systems executive*
Opperman, Danny Gene *packaging professional, consultant*
Ottenwess, J. Lea *data processing executive*
Ouseley, William Norman *security services consultant*
Pardo, Robert Edward *software marketing and development executive*
Parker, Lee Fischer *sales executive*
Patton, Mark Edward *consultant, educator*
Pearson, David J. *electronic design manager*
Perry, Richard Joel *information systems professional*
Phillips, Leo D. *business executive*
Pieper, Jeffrey Robert *sales executive*
Pierce, Lisa Margaret *lecturer, product and market development manager*
Pitt, Gavin Alexander *management consultant, publishing executive*
Poulsen, Fern Sue *special events and public relations consultant*
Pressman, Thane Andrew *consumer products executive*
Ptashkin, Barry Irwin *management consultant*
Rairdin, Craig Allen *software company executive, software developer*
Ranshaw, Jane Ellen *training consultant*
Rhem, Launy Frederique *marketing communication executive*
Rice, Douglas Chapman *management consultant*
Rice, Kenneth Lloyd *environmental services executive, educator*
Scherer, Christian MacArthur *marketing consultant*
Schmutz, Charles Reid *university foundation executive*
Schrenk, Lorenz Philip *human resources executive*
Serocky, William Howard *retired sales professional*
Shapiro, Richard Charles *sales and marketing executive*
Shepp, Connie Ann *information systems specialist*
Shimandle, Francis Edward *advertising executive, writer, illustrator*
Sincoff, Michael Z. *human resources and marketing professional*
Sisbarro, Thomas A. *business executive*
Slegman, Betty Harvey *publicist*
Smith, Paul W. *information systems professional*

Smithburg, Donald Rowan *hospital executive*
Striglis, Dimos *company executive*
Sullivan, Sarah Louise *management and technology consultant*
Swanson, William Russell *marketing professional*
Swift, Dolores Monica Marcinkevich *public relations executive*
Thiede, Janet Lynn *marketing executive*
Thomas, Susan *business executive*
Toirac, S(eth) Thomas *information systems executive, consultant*
Verdier, Quentin Roosevelt *human resources consultant*
Wallace, Shawn Patrick *sales professional*
Warlick, Dennis P. *company executive*
Warrene, Kevin Charles *sales executive*
Wasinger, Kristi Lynn *marketing professional, advertising consultant*
Weber, Jeffery A. *advertising executive*
Weinberg, Robert L. *management consultant*
Weismantel, Gregory Nelson *management consultant and software executive*
Weispfenning, John Thomas *communications educator*
Wikarski, Nancy Susan *information technology consultant*
Wilde, William James *printing company executive*
Williams, Ross Arnold *computer systems engineer*
Wittenberg, Merle Eugene *management consultant*
Wustenberg, Wendy Wiberg *public affairs specialist, consultant*
Yaeger, Therese Francis *management consultant*
Zacks, JoEllen *public affairs executive*

INDUSTRY: TRADE

UNITED STATES

ILLINOIS

Atwood
Hadden, Phillip Gregory *retail business owner*

Auburn
Burtle, Debra Ann *needlework and gift shop owner*

Bloomingdale
Pelant, Barney Frank *international business consulting executive*

Cary
Love, Michael Jonathan *retail company executive*

Champaign
Flora, Kent Allen *small business owner*
Levy, Ronald T. *liquor wholesale distributor*

Chicago
Beck, Robert Lee *bookstore owner*
Brennan, Edward A. *merchandising, insurance and real estate executive*
Cohen, Alan David *packaging company executive*
Fillicaro, Barbara Jean *business owner, consultant*
Gilbert, Samuel Lawrence *business owner*
McSherry, James Francis *small business owner, management consultant*
Morrow, James David *business owner*
Nemirow, Joel Alan *small business executive, psychotherapist*
Piccirilli, Robert James, Jr. *small business owner*

Chicago Heights
Carpenter, Kenneth Russell *international trading executive*
Miller, Trudy Joyce *retail executive, publisher*

Danville
Brumaghim, Paul *small business owner*

Decatur
Bradshaw, Billy Dean *retail executive*
Cain, Richard Duane *small business owner*

Deerfield
Tomaino, Joseph Carmine *retail executive, retired postal inspector*
Walgreen, Charles Rudolph, III *retail store executive*

Downers Grove
Conley, Diana Mae *computer sales and service franchise owner*

Elgin
Amour, Jan'ette Alice *pet center owner*

Elk Grove Village
Naker, Mary Leslie *export transportation company executive*

Glenview
Schulman, Alan Michael *small business owner*

Gurnee
Hedrick, Geary Dean *small business owner*

Highland Park
Ritzlin, George *rare book and map dealer*

Hinsdale
Bradna, Joanne Justice *manufacturer's representative*

Hoffman Estates
Beitler, Stephen Seth *retail company executive*
Kwan, Mary P. *retail company executive*

Morton Grove
McKenna, Andrew James *paper distribution and printing company executive, baseball club executive*

Mundelein
Bernardi, James Edward *retail executive, real estate investor and developer*

Naperville
Carroll, Ellen Therese *small business owner*

Northbrook
Hochmuth, Edward Christian *retail executive, tax consultant*

Oak Park
Spartz, Alice Anne Lenore *retired retail executive*
Spaulding, Daniel Alexander *small business owner*

Olney
Potter, David Lynn *retail executive*

Palatine
Cesario, Robert Charles *franchise executive, consultant*

Pana
Hubbartt, Morris W., Jr. *retail executive*

Park Ridge
Ciulla, William James *import export company executive*
Hall, Joan B. *small business owner*

Rockford
Kitzman, Scott Alan *retail lumber company executive*

Schaumburg
Gardner, Russell Roosevelt *small business owner*

Wauconda
Wood, Leslie Ann *retail administrator*

Wheeling
Hestad, Bjorn Mark *metal distributing company executive*
Ochsner, Othon Henry, II *importer, restaurant critic*

Wilmette
Hansen, Todd Randall *small business owner, educator*

Winnetka
Person, Paula (Mrs. P. Barry Person) *social skills organization executive, entrepreneur*
Weldon, Theodore Tefft, Jr. *retail company executive*

INDIANA

Anderson
Lutz, L. Jack *retail executive, congressman*

Bicknell
Risley, Gregory Byron *furniture company executive, interior designer*

Carmel
Cushman, Kenneth Dean *business owner*

Elkhart
Drexler, Rudy Matthew, Jr. *professional law enforcement work dog trainer*

Evansville
Blesch, K(athy) Suzann *small business owner*

Fort Wayne
Cast, Anita Hursh *small business owner*
Cummings, William Robert, Jr. *business executive*
Laurie, John Alan *commercial floor company executive*

Indianapolis
Chiki, Frank T. *small business owner*
Fredrickson, William Robert *trading company executive*
Johnson, Margaret Douglas *retail executive*
Nugent, Johnny Wesley *tractor company executive, state senator*
Seitz, Melvin Christian, Jr. *distributing company executive*
Seneff, Smiley Howard *business owner*
Strong, Herbert E., Jr. *plumbing supply distributing company executive*

New Albany
Conway, William Frederick, Sr. *business founder*

Oakland City
Harper, Gary Lee *small business owner, educator*

South Bend
Fisher, Carl A *hardware store owner*

Valparaiso
Mosco, Scott M. *retail business owner*

Warsaw
Kaufman, Ethan Allen *retired business owner*

Winamac
Hildebrandt, Greg Alan *small business owner*

IOWA

Cedar Rapids
Baldwin, George Koehler *retail executive*

Cherokee
Powell, Carol Christine *restaurant owner*

Davenport
Black, Stephen P. *small business owner*

Garner
Denney, Roger W. *small business owner*

Independence
Temeyer, Todd John *pizza company executive*

Marshalltown
Shawstad, Raymond Vernon *business owner, retired computer specialist*

Orange City
Korver, Gerry R(ozeboom) *purchasing executive*

West Des Moines
Tice, Patricia Kaye *therapist, entrepreneur, educator, trainer*

KANSAS

Auburn
Barr, Ginger *business owner, former state legislator*

Emporia
Lilburn, Monte Wayne *retail executive*

Great Bend
Straub, Larry Gene *business executive*

Manhattan
Marten, Dennis Lee *retail executive, financial planner*

Mission
Marley, Anne Harder *small business owner*

Olathe
Cordell, Steven Mark *small business owner*

Osawatomie
Jimenez, Bettie Eileen *retired small business owner*

Overland Park
Wekenborg, Connie Louise *retail administrator*

Wichita
Moore, Peggy Sue *corporation financial executive*
Trombold, Walter Stevenson *supply company executive*

Winfield
Lewis, Ellen Miller (Lin Lewis) *business owner, educator*

MICHIGAN

Bad Axe
Sullivan, James Gerald *business owner, postal letter carrier*

Battle Creek
Hazel, James R. C., Jr. *small business owner, civic volunteer*

Bloomfield Hills
Robinson, Jack Albert *retail drug stores executive*

Dearborn
Younis, Mahmoud Rachid *business owner, electrical engineer*

Detroit
Hessler, Scott Asher *retail executive*

Farmington Hills
Pargoff, Robert Michael *small business owner*

Grand Ledge
Dodge, Michael Lee *small business owner*

Grand Rapids
DeLapa, Judith Anne *business owner*
Morin, William Raymond *bookstore chain executive*
Sage, Pamela Kay *small business owner*
Trist, James E. *small business owner, manufacturing engineer*

Harbor Beach
Falkenberg, Mary Elaine *small business owner*

Hartford
Birmele, Raymond Elsworth *small business owner*

Houghton Lake
Manley, Janet Zeegers *retired small business owner*

Ishpeming
Johnson, Joe Carl *small business owner*

Kalamazoo
Mc Carty, Theodore Milson *business executive*

Midland
Huntress, Betty Ann *former music store proprietor, educator*
Wilson, Otis Garfield *appliance dealership executive, commissioner*

Naubinway
Beaudoin, Robert Lawrence *small business owner*

Oscoda
Shackleton, Mary Jane *small business owner*

Paw Paw
Warner, James John *small business owner*

Saint Clair Shores
Seppala, Katherine Seaman (Mrs. Leslie W. Seppala) *retail company executive*

Saint Joseph
McCoy, Richard James *jeweler, real estate developer, broker*

Saugatuck
Breed, Eileen Judith *small business owner*

South Haven
Giesler, Robert Alvin *small business owner*

Southfield
Primo, Joan Erwina *retail and real estate consulting business owner*
Toffolo, Dennis Ray *retail executive*

Troy
Burken, Ruth Marie *retail company executive*
Materne, David *software and distribution company executive*
Nordyke, Harry Randall *company president, business owner*
Strome, Stephen *distribution company executive*

Waterford
Landmesser, Harold Leon *tool distributor consultant*
Lang, Catherine Lou *small business owner*

MINNESOTA

Brooklyn Park
Ulferts, Leon Ronald *trade company executive*

Clear Lake
Boelz, Thomas Leonard *furniture retail executive*

Elk River
Napue, O'Dell Christell *small business owner*

Grand Rapids
Crane, Faye *small business owner*

Hopkins
Beeler, Donald Daryl *retail executive*

Long Lake
Lurton, H. William *retired retail executive*

Minneapolis
Henschel, John Peter *import export company executive*
Mammel, Russell Norman *retired food distribution company executive*
Ruff, Dureen Anne *small business owner, operater*
Wright, Michael William *wholesale distribution, retailing executive*

Saint Paul
Hart, Myrna Jean *art gallery and gift shop owner*

Stillwater
Schmidt, Lynn Marie Lammer *business owner*

Walker
Collins, Thomas William *caterer, consultant*
Doughty, Anthony Rutgers *small business owner*

MISSOURI

Aurora
Goodman, Nancy Jane *small business owner*

Buffalo
Louderback, Kevin Wayne *business owner*

Eureka
Ramos, Vivian Eleanor *development and administrative consultant*

Hazelwood
Bogle, JoeAnn Rose *florist*

Independence
Lundy, Sadie Allen *small business owner*

Kansas City
Allen, Norman Lynn *retail buyer*
Benjamin, Janice Yukon *small business owner*
Stueck, William Noble *small business owner*

Mexico
Robinson, Kristine Danelle *small business owner*

Moberly
Kinder, David C. *small business owner*

Neosho
Moore, Gary Ray *small business owner*

Richmond
Nordsieck, Karen Ann *custom design company owner*

Saint Louis
Fish, Michele Loyd *retailer*
Hartenbach, Stephen Charles *small business owner*
Newman, Andrew Edison *restaurant executive*
Schaffner, John Albert *retail merchandising executive, designer*
Schnuck, Craig D. *grocery stores company executive*
Van Dover, Donald *small business owner, consultant*

Sibley
Morrow, Elizabeth *business owner, sculptress, museum association administrator, educator*

Warsaw
Martinez, Penny Carol *small business owner*

Waynesville
Carlson, David Wayne *software company executive*

NEBRASKA

Ashland
Williams, Glen E. *small business owner*

Gothenburg
Stevens, Douglas R. *business owner*

Lexington
Bailey, William Alvin *retail executive, artist*

Lincoln
Rawley, Ann Keyser *small business owner, picture framer*

Omaha
Gibbs, Linda Ann *bookstore manager*

Sidney
Randolph, Warren Edwin *small business owner*

NEW YORK

New York
Miles, Charlene *small business owner*

OHIO

Akron
West, Hugh Brian *business owner*

Alliance
Schafer, Michael Shawn *small business owner*

Ashland
Finnerty, Madeline Frances *consulting firm owner*

Bellevue
Davenport, Thomas Herbert *small business owner*

Chesterland
Aster, Ruth Marie Rhydderch *business owner*

Cincinnati
Arnett, Louise Eva *information records management executive*
Lauck, A. Victoria *small business owner, volunteer*
Price, Thomas Emile *investment company executive*
Woods, Donald DeWayne *advertising materials designer/manufacturer*

Cleveland
Hinkle, Anita Louise *export-import specialist, educator*
Knisely Bonk, Helen *corporate customs broker*

Columbus
Callander, Kay Eileen Paisley *business owner, retired gifted talented education educator, writer*
Coe, Linda Marlene Wolfe *marketing development, photographer*
Hollis-Allbritton, Cheryl Dawn *retail paper supply store executive*
Pasholk, Paul Douglas *retail executive*
Prehm, John Thomas, Jr. *retired retail executive*
Traver, Noel Allen *small business owner, creative director*

Dayton
Gray, Edman Lowell *metal distribution company executive*
Jenefsky, Jack *wholesale company executive*
Poling, Douglas Emmett *small business owner*

Galion
Butterfield, James T. *small business owner*

Garfield Heights
Polachek-Liptak, Michelle *agency executive*

Hilliard
Keyes, James Lyman, Jr. *diesel engines distributor company owner*

Hudson
Duchon, Roseann Marie *business owner, consultant*

Lima
Fisher, Glenn Duane *small business executive*

Loveland
Piklo, Charlene Lorraine *retail professional*

Madison
Biscotti, Matthew Louis *landscape nursery wholesaler, publisher*

Mansfield
Benham, Lelia *small business owner, social/political activist*
Yoder, Harold Elias *small business owner*

Middletown
Kay, Patricia Kremer *business owner*

North Canton
Belden, Karen Scheiring *shop owner, realtor*

Reynoldsburg
Edelman, Ann Brook *small business owner, writer*
Osterman, Frederic J. *retail executive*

Strongsville
Nekola, Louis William *utility line clearance executive*

Twinsburg
Proctor, Stanley Matthew *business owner*

University Heights
Hile, Duane L. *small business owner*

Westerville
Goh, Anthony Li-Shing *business owner, consultant*

Willoughby
Oldham, Lea Leever *business owner, author*

Youngstown
Catoline, Pauline Dessie *small business owner*
Gottron, Francis Robert, III *small business owner*

SOUTH DAKOTA

Rapid City
Fischer, Robert Keith *retail company executive*

VERMONT

Danby
Rudy, Kathleen Vermeulen *small business owner*

WISCONSIN

Green Bay
Dickman, Craig Steven *retail, distribution-consulting company executive*

Hartford
Gilbert, Bruce Frederic *small business owner*

Hurley
Nicholls, Thomas Maurice *business owner*

Kenosha
Lalgee, John Christopher *export company executive*

Madison
Cunningham, Donald Otto *business owner*
Fahien, Rose Marian *small business owner*
Uselmann, Catherine Rose (Kit Uselmann) *small business owner, network marketer, behavioral researcher, financial independence consultant*

Middleton
Griswold, Greg *small business owner*

Milwaukee
Corporon, Charles Edward *employment agency owner*
Papas, George Nick *bakery company executive*
Rosenberg, John Alan (Jack Rosenberg) *business owner*

Sturgeon Bay
Wallestad, Philip Weston *retired business owner*

ADDRESS UNPUBLISHED

Aved, Barry *retail executive, consultant*
Bogart, Carol Lynn *small business owner, freelance reporter, video producer, radio personality*
Cacciolfi, William Peter, Jr. *small business owner, expolorer*
Davis, Jane Strauss *business owner*
Evans, Robert George, Jr. *retail and mail order executive*
Goldstein, Alfred George *retail and consumer products executive*
Green, Joseph H. *small business owner*
Huvaere, Richard Floyd *auto dealer*
Jones, Brian Matthew *private investigator, small business owner*
King, S(anford) MacCallum *business owner, consultant*
Kuhn, Josephine M. Keller *interior decorating business owner*
LaFlamme, William Robert *technical consultant*
Lee, Benny Y. C. *import and export company executive*
Lueke, Donna Mae *national retail company manager*
McIntosh, Calvin Eugene *retired small business owner*
Melnikoff, Sarah Ann *gem importer, jewelry designer*
Monette, Louis Gayle *small business owner, consultant, writer*
Peterson, Levi K. *machine shop owner*
Richardson, Michael Tyler *small business owner, engineer*
Ring, Victoria A. *small business owner*
Roggelin, Joel M. *business owner*
Sewell, Phyllis Shapiro *retail chain executive*
Stroda, Jurgen H. *owner small business*
Thayer, Richard Lee *small business owner*
Trutter, John Thomas *consulting company executive*
Wos, Carol Elaine *small business owner*

INDUSTRY: TRANSPORTATION

UNITED STATES

COLORADO

Colorado Springs
Freeman, J.P. Hawk *underwater exploration, security and transportation executive, educator*

ILLINOIS

AMF Ohare
Kalcevic, Timothy Francis *airline pilot, educator*

Argonne
Saricks, Christopher Lee *transportation analyst*

Arlington Heights
Hudson, Ronald Morgan *aviation planner*

Calumet City
Pals, Timothy Ray *transportation and marketing executive*

Chicago
Apelbaum, Phyllis L. *delivery messenger service executive*
Barriger, John Walker, IV *transportation executive*
Batory, Ronald Louis *transportation executive*
Coles, Lorraine McClellan *vehicle maintenance analyst*
McCarthy, John Carroll *transportation company executive*
Mosena, David R. *transportation executive*
Reed, John Shedd *former railway executive*

Geneva
Unterman, Eugene Rex *aviation sales and manufacturing company executive*

Glen Ellyn
Logan, Henry Vincent *transportation executive*

Hinsdale
Schoenbeck, Paul John *transportation executive*

Lake Zurich
Dickinson, Daniel Oliver *aviation executive*

Maple Park
Gage, Kenneth Donald *railroad electronics technician, publisher, singer*

Maywood
Christopher, Alexander George *transportation company executive*

Riverdale
Szabo, Joseph Clark *labor lobbyist*

Riverside
Fiorito, Richard Joseph *trucking executive*

Rock Island
Wallen, Richard Lee *transportation executive*

Rosemont
Robie, Michael Henry *airport services executive*

INDIANA

Elkhart
Miller, Philip William *airport executive*

Fishers
Ruzbasan, Anthony *distribution executive*

Fort Wayne
Goshorn, Larry Frederick *aerospace industry administrator, consultant*

Indianapolis
Orcutt, Daniel C. *airport terminal executive*
Roberts, David *airport executive*

Lawrenceburg
Dickey, Julia Edwards *aviation consultant*

Noblesville
Morrison, Joseph Young *transportation consultant*

KANSAS

Olathe
Gramza, Richard L. *transportation executive*

Shawnee Mission
Henson, Paul Harry *transportation executive*

Wichita
Bell, Baillis F. *airport terminal executive*
Branscum, Christine Maria *delivery service executive*
Cheesman, John Michael *aeronautics company administrator, civic leader*

MICHIGAN

Bloomfield Hills
Beaubien, Richard Fromm *transportation executive*

Dearborn
Boulos, Edward Nashed *transportation specialist*
Clark, Nathan Stewart, Jr. *rail transportation company executive*

Detroit
Braun, Robert C. *airport executive*

Flat Rock
Wright, Arthur Franklin *transportation executive, municipal official*

Grand Rapids
Gresley, Stephen Clark *aerospace executive*

Sterling Heights
Weed, Melvin L. *retired railroad conductor, small business owner*

Warren
Morelli, William Annibale, Sr. *aerospace manufacturing company executive*

MINNESOTA

Cannon Falls
Lindquist, Everett Carlton *retired air traffic controller*

Duluth
Woodbury, Peter Michael *airline pilot*

Saint Paul
Anderson, Tim *airport terminal executive*
Bowell, William David, Sr. *cruise and excursion company executive*
Brown, John Allin *test pilot educator*
Ellingson, Lynn Marie *flight attendant*
McDowell, Daniel Quince, Jr. *airline executive, state transportation technician, aeronautic coordinator, state aviation planner*

MISSOURI

Kansas City
Baisden, Eleanor Marguerite *airline compensation executive*
Hardy, David G. *transportation executive*
Malecki, David Michael *airport manager*
Solomon, John Davis *aviation executive*
Wallis, Elizabeth Susan *air traffic control specialist*

Liberty
Bodine, Ronald Jesse *pilot*

Richmond
Miller, Valerie Lynn *transportation executive*

Saint Louis
Harmon, Lonnie Gale *aerospace company business manager*
Heinz, Michael Harold *aerospace executive*

Springfield
Mertz, Fred J. *transportation executive*

NEBRASKA

Omaha
Handwerker, A. M. *retired transportation executive*

NEW MEXICO

Santa Fe
Swartz, William John *transportation resources company executive/retired*

NORTH DAKOTA

Maddock
Lee, Jason Howard *pilot*

OHIO

Cincinnati
Murphy, Eugene F. *aerospace, communications and electronics executive*

Cleveland
Hill, Robert John *aviation executive*
Sheehan, Stephen D. *airport commissioner*

Columbus
Burk, Ronald Lee *traffic safety professional*
Hedrick, Larry Willis *airport executive*
Hooper, Kelley Rae *delivery service executive*

Dayton
Goetz, Michael Blaine *aircraft company executive*

Mentor
Zonneville, Robert E. *trucking company executive*

Middletown
Dodd, Leon Powell, Jr. *aerospace executive*

Oberlin
Williams, Eleanor Joyce *government air traffic control specialist*

Painesville
Luhta, Caroline Naumann *airport manager, flight educator*

Piqua
Disbrow, Michael Ray *aerospace supplier company executive*

Rocky River
Shively, Daniel Jerome *retired transportation executive*

Toledo
Hummer, Thomas Michael *transportation executive*

Wilmington
Benson, Janet Elizabeth *transportation finance executive*

Xenia
Bigelow, Daniel James *aerospace executive*

SOUTH DAKOTA

Sioux Falls
Messerli, Gary Robert *air terminal executive*
Smith, Murray Thomas *transportation company executive*

TEXAS

Round Rock
Aadnesen, Christopher *railroad company executive, consultant*

WISCONSIN

Brillion
Shreve, Allison Anne *former air traffic control specialist*

Manawa
Cummings, Jerre D. *transportation manager*

Menasha
Kollath, David Michael *corporate traffic rate specialist*

Milwaukee
Bateman, C. Barry *airport terminal executive*
Warren, Kenneth John *transit system executive*

Neenah
O'Connor, William Cody *retired transportation executive, consultant*

Oshkosh
Schoenrock, Tracy Allen *airline pilot, securities trader*

Racine
Ihde, Craig Allen *aerial specialists executive*

Stoughton
Armstrong, Richard D. *transportation executive*

Waukesha
Bolte, Richard Alan *transportation executive*

Waupaca
Schoofs, Gerald Joseph *pilot*

ADDRESS UNPUBLISHED

Bramlett, Lonnie L., Jr. *airline towing company executive*
Foss, Charles R. *transportation specialist*
Gehr, Thomas Yeats, Jr. *railway executive*
Lewis, Martin Edward *shipping company executive, foreign government concessionary*
Morse, Leon William *traffic, physical distribution and transportation management executive, consultant*
Mulqueen, Scott Charles *transportation executive*
Orsbon, Benjamin Thomas *transportation planner*
Schmidt, Carl Anthony *locomotive engineer*
Valine, Delmar Edmond, Sr. *corporate executive*
Wheeler, Paul Leonard *retired transportation executive*
White, John Abiathar *pilot, consultant*

INDUSTRY: UTILITIES, ENERGY, RESOURCES

UNITED STATES

CALIFORNIA

Salinas
Todd, Gayle Louise *telecommunications executive*

ILLINOIS

Arlington Heights
Moore, Edwin H. *electric metering company executive*

Byron
Oneil, Susan Jean *media specialist*

Chicago
Batlivala, Robert Bomi D. *oil company executive, economics educator*
Brooker, Thomas Kimball *oil company executive*
Fuller, Harry Laurance *oil company executive*
Kaye, Richard William *utility company executive*
Lowrie, William G. *oil company executive*
Morrow, Richard Martin *retired oil company executive*
O'Connor, James John *utility company executive*
Rucker, Dennis Morton Arthur *telecommunications executive*
Skinner, Samuel Knox *utilities executive, lawyer*
Tata, Prakasam Bala Surya *utilities research coordinator*
Terry, Richard Edward *public utility holding company executive*

Clinton
Lyon, Michael William *utility company executive*

Darien
Zitny, Russell James *telecommunications executive*

Decatur
Dreyer, Alec Gilbert *independent power producer*
Hoffman, Paul Ernest *utility executive*

Elmhurst
John, Richard C. *integrated petroleum company executive*

Geneva
Pershing, Robert George *retired telecommunications company executive*

Hinsdale
Brandt, John Ashworth *fuel company executive*

Homewood
Pierce, Shelby Crawford *oil consultant*

Lake Bluff
Marino, William Francis *telecommunications industry executive, consultant*

Lemont
Fumagalli, Mark Leonard *oil company executive*

Lisle
Tylutki, Joseph John *telecommunications industry executive*

Naperville
Meyers, Michael Neal *telecommunications industry executive*
Yoakam, Marvin C. *telephone company executive*

Northbrook
Demaree, David Harry *utilities executive*

Orland Park
English, Floyd Leroy *telecommunications company executive*

Peoria
DuBois, Mark Benjamin *utilities executive*
Sheehan, Michael Gilbert *utilities executive*
Viets, Robert O. *utilities executive*

Robinson
Legg, Ronald Otis *oil company executive*

Rolling Meadows
Stamos, Peter *telecommunications executive*

Skokie
Mulder, Donald R. *telecommunications executive*

INDIANA

Brownsburg
Diasio, Richard Leonard *power transmission executive, sports facility executive*

Chesterton
Waugh, Joanna *electric utility employee*

Evansville
Cameron, James Gregory *utility executive, government official*

Fort Wayne
Zielke, William Arthur *telecommunications company executive*

Frankfort
Stonehill, Lloyd Herschel *gas company executive, mechanical engineer*

Greensburg
Schilling, Don Russell *electric utility executive*

Hammond
Kovacs, Joseph Anton, III *utility contract specialist*
Lynn, Robert William *gas and electric utility official*
Schroer, Edmund Armin *utility company executive*

Indianapolis
Dyer, Robert Theodore *power producer executive*
Krueger, Betty Jane *telecommunications company executive*
Lindemann, Donald Lee *utility executive*
Meier, David Timothy *utility company specialist*
Todd, Zane Grey *retired utilities executive*

Jeffersonville
Barnes, Lahna Harris *water treatment company owner*

Munster
Fishel, James Dean *telecommunications executive*

Newburgh
McGavic, Judy L. *coal company official*

Plainfield
Odor, David Lee *utility official*

KANSAS

Baxter Springs
Blaylock, Jim L. *gas industry business executive*

Council Grove
Coffin, Bertha Louise *telephone company executive*

Eskridge
Taylor, Russell Benton *mining executive*

Great Bend
Combs, M. Jay *utilities executive*

Independence
Swearingen, Harold Lyndon *oil company executive*

Shawnee Mission
Corneil, Hampton Gaskill *oil company executive*

Stilwell
Keith, Dale Martin *utilities management consultant*

Topeka
Spencer, William Edwin *telephone company executive, engineer*

Wichita
Koch, Charles de Ganahl *oil industry executive*

MICHIGAN

Birmingham
Harter, Roger Karr *retired telephone compnany official*

Covert
Biffer, James Lewis *nuclear training manager*

Detroit
Earley, Anthony Francis, Jr. *utilities company executive, lawyer*
Garberding, Larry Gilbert *utilities companies executive*
Glancy, Alfred Robinson, III *public utility company executive*

East Detroit
Cattaneo, Michael S. *heating and cooling company executive*

Monroe
Bauman, Joseph Wesley *steel company executive*

Shelby Township
Fillbrook, Thomas George *telephone company executive*

Southfield
Hubbard, Z(onia) Dianne *telephone company official*

Traverse City
Howard, Charles P. *drilling company executive*

MINNESOTA

Edina
Adams, John Charles *electrical industry executive*

Fergus Falls
Uggerud, Ward Lee *electric utility company executive*

Henning
Parker, Ronald Bruce *telecommunications executive*

Minneapolis
Andersen, Harry Edward *oil equipment company executive*
Heaney, William Matthew *electric power industry executive*
Johnston, Kerry Alan *oil and gas company executive*

Saint Louis Park
Graf, Melvin William *telecommunications executive*

MISSOURI

Kansas City
Smith, Richard Conrad, Jr. *telecommunications company executive*

Liberty
Ferrell, James Edwin *energy company executive*

Saint Charles
Rodrigues, Daniel A. *electronics company executive*

Saint Louis
Lundy, Dale Allen *telecommunications company administrator*

Springfield
Boehm, Robert Kenneth *telecommunications consultant*

Warrensburg
Collett, Randal Ray *telecommunications administrator*

NORTH DAKOTA

Bismarck
Schuchart, John Albert, Jr. *utility company executive*

Grand Forks
Christianson, Floyd Kenneth *retired oil company executive*

Minot
Tollefson, Ben C. *retired utility sales manager*

Williston
Heninger, Kurt Allen *oil field service executive*

OHIO

Akron
Staines, Michael Laurence *oil and gas production executive*
Swank, David Brian *telecommunications industry executive*
Yeager, David LeRoy *utility company executive*

Canton
Stage, Richard Lee *consultant, retired utilities executive*

Cincinnati
Campbell, Cheryl Nichols *telecommunications company executive*
Kupferle, Arthur Trommer *telecommunications executive*
Rogers, James Eugene *electric and gas utility executive*

Cleveland
Ayers, Richard Wayne *electrical company official*
Moore, Michael Thomas *mining executive*

Columbus
Brown, Wyatt W. *utilities executive*
Falcone, Charles Anthony *electric utility executive*
Jones, James Henry *utility company executive*
Schafer, William Harry *electric power industry administrator*
Smerek, William John *communications executive, electrical engineer*

Dayton
Forster, Peter Hans *utility company executive*

Perrysburg
Williamson, John Pritchard *utility executive*

Westlake
Connelly, John James *retired oil company technical specialist*

SOUTH DAKOTA

Huron
Wilkens, Robert Allen *utilities executive, electrical engineer*

Lead
Mitchell, Steven Thomas *mine superintendent*

Pierre
Dunn, James Bernard *mining company executive, state legislator*

Rapid City
Lien, Bruce Hawkins *minerals and oil company executive*

UTAH

Price
Barker, Gary Leland *mining company executive*

WISCONSIN

Beloit
Obligato, Mary F. *electrical power executive*

Milwaukee
McKenzie, Carolyn Caldwell (Carrie) *telecommunications executive*
Schrader, Thomas F. *utilities executive*

Tomah
Johnson, Linda Arlene *petroleum transporter*

West Allis
Lempke, Michael Wayne *water department executive*

ADDRESS UNPUBLISHED

Anderson, James Donald *mining company executive*
Carmichael, R. Marc *gas company executive*
Flom, Edward Lewis *retired oil company official*
French, Jay Michael *oil company financial analyst, consultant*
Greer, Carl Crawford *petroleum company executive*
Harward, Gary John *retired utility company executive*
Humke, Ramon L. *utility executive*
Mc Carthy, Walter John, Jr. *retired utility executive*
Reynolds, Jack W. *retired utility company executive*
Rinn, Victoria Sue *telecommunications industry executive*
Rogers, Justin Towner, Jr. *retired utility company executive*
Schneider, Mark Steven *telecommunications company executive*
Skala, Gary Dennis *electric and gas utilities executive management consultant*
Tower, Michael J. *management consultant*
White, Willis Sheridan, Jr. *retired utilities company executive*

LAW: JUDICIAL ADMINISTRATION

UNITED STATES

ILLINOIS

Belleville
Stevens, C. Glenn *judge*

Benton
Foreman, James Louis *retired judge*

Chicago
Andersen, Wayne R. *federal judge*
Aspen, Marvin Edward *federal judge*
Bauer, William Joseph *federal judge*
Bilandic, Michael A. *state supreme court justice, former mayor*
Bowman, George Arthur, Jr. *judge*
Fairchild, Thomas E. *federal judge*
Freeman, Charles E. *state supreme court judge*
Kanne, Michael Stephen *federal judge*
Leinenweber, Harry D. *federal judge*
McMorrow, Mary Ann G. *judge*
Moran, James Byron *federal judge*
Pell, Wilbur Frank, Jr. *federal judge*
Rovner, Ilana Kara Diamond *federal judge*

East Saint Louis
Beatty, William Louis *federal judge*

Elgin
Kirkland, Alfred Younges, Sr. *federal judge*

Greenville
DeLaurenti, John Lewis *judge*

Oregon
Moore, John L. *judge*

Pekin
Heiple, James Dee *state supreme court justice*

Peoria
Holdridge, William Ernest *justice*
McCuskey, Michael Patrick *judge*
Mihm, Michael Martin *federal judge*
Morgan, Robert Dale *federal judge*

Pittsfield
Burrows, Cecil J. *judge, lawyer*

Quincy
Schuering, Mark Allen *judge, educator*

Springfield
Miller, Benjamin K. *state supreme court justice*
Mills, Richard Henry *federal judge*
Wood, Harlington, Jr. *federal judge*

INDIANA

Boonville
Campbell, Edward Adolph *judge, electrical engineer*

Evansville
Capshaw, Tommie Dean *judge*

Fort Wayne
Lee, William Charles *judge*

Indianapolis
DeBruler, Roger O. *state supreme court justice*
Dickson, Brent E. *state supreme court justice*
Dillin, S. Hugh *federal judge*
Givan, Richard Martin *state supreme court justice, retired*
Shepard, Randall Terry *judge*

Jasper
Songer, Hugo Charles *judge*

Jeffersonville
Barthold, Clementine B. *retired judge*

Kokomo
Stein, Eleanor Bankoff *judge*

Lagrange
Brown, George E. *judge, educator*

South Bend
Grant, Robert Allen *federal judge*
Manion, Daniel Anthony *federal judge*
Ripple, Kenneth Francis *federal judge*

IOWA

Cedar Rapids
Carter, James H. *state supreme court justice*
Hansen, David Rasmussen *federal judge*

Des Moines
Andreasen, James Hallis *state supreme court judge*
Harris, K. David *justice*
Larson, Jerry L. *state supreme court justice*
McGiverin, Arthur A. *state supreme court justice*
Neuman, Linda Kinney *state supreme court justice*
Snell, Bruce M., Jr. *state supreme court justice*
Stuart, William Corwin *federal judge*
Wolle, Charles Robert *federal judge*

Iowa City
Schultz, Louis William *judge*

Sioux City
O'Brien, Donald Eugene *federal judge*

KANSAS

Kansas City
O'Connor, Earl Eugene *federal judge*
Vratil, Kathryn Hoefer *federal judge*

Lawrence
Tacha, Deanell Reece *federal judge*

Leavenworth
Stanley, Arthur Jehu, Jr. *federal judge*

Manhattan
Mershon, Jerry Lewis *judge*

Olathe
Chipman, Marion Walter *judge*

Saint John
Bennington, Barry Allan *judge*

Topeka
Allegrucci, Donald Lee *state supreme court justice*
Crow, Sam Alfred *federal judge*
Davis, Robert Edward *judge*
Holmes, Richard Winn *retired state supreme court justice, lawyer*
Miller, Robert Haskins *retired state chief justice*
Rogers, Richard Dean *federal judge*
Saffels, Dale Emerson *federal judge*
Six, Fred N. *state supreme court justice*

Wichita
Brown, Wesley Ernest *federal judge*
Theis, Frank Gordon *federal judge*

MICHIGAN

Ada
Engel, Albert Joseph *federal judge*

Bloomfield Hills
Kaufman, Ira Gladstone *judge*

Detroit
Cooley, Wendy *judge, lawyer*
Duggan, Patrick James *federal judge*
Edmunds, Nancy Garlock *federal judge*
Feikens, John *federal judge*
Friedman, Bernard Alvin *federal judge*
Gadola, Paul V. *federal judge*
Gilmore, Horace Weldon *federal judge*
Hackett, Barbara (Kloka) *federal judge*
Lloyd, Leona Loretta *judge*
Lombard, Arthur J. *judge*
Rosen, Gerald Ellis *federal judge*
Taylor, Anna Diggs *federal judge*

Grand Rapids
Bell, Robert Holmes *federal judge*
Brenneman, Hugh Warren, Jr. *judge*
Gibson, Benjamin F. *federal judge*
Hillman, Douglas Woodruff *federal judge*
Miles, Wendell A. *federal judge*
Quist, Gordon Jay *federal judge*

Kalamazoo
Enslen, Richard Alan *federal judge*

Lansing
Brickley, James H. *state supreme court justice*
Cavanagh, Michael Francis *state supreme court justice*
Hollenshead, Robert Earl *judge*
McKeague, David William *district judge*

Paw Paw
Buhl, William Christian *circuit court judge*

Saint Clair Shores
Stanczyk, Benjamin Conrad *judge*

MINNESOTA

Duluth
McNulty, Patrick James *magistrate*

Minneapolis
Doty, David Singleton *federal judge*
Knight, Jeanne Ellen *judge*
MacLaughlin, Harry Hunter *federal judge*
Murphy, Diana E. *federal judge*

Saint Paul
Alsop, Donald Douglas *federal judge*
Coyne, Mary Jeanne *state supreme court justice*
Keith, Alexander Macdonald *state supreme court chief justice*
Kyle, Richard House *federal judge*
Page, Alan Cedric *judge*
Renner, Robert George *federal judge*
Tomljanovich, Esther M. *judge*

MISSOURI

Ballwin
Hungate, William Leonard *retired federal judge, former congressman*

Bonne Terre
Brauer, Robert E. *retired bankruptcy judge*

Chesterfield
McAllister, Robert Dale *judge*

Clayton
Weinstock, Kenneth Martin *judge*

Jefferson City
Benton, W. Duane *judge*
Holstein, John Charles *state supreme court chief justice*

Kansas City
Berrey, Robert Wilson, III *judge, lawyer*
Bowman, Pasco Middleton, II *federal judge*
Gibson, Floyd Robert *federal judge*
Gibson, John Robert *federal judge*
Stevens, Joseph Edward, Jr. *federal judge*
Wright, Scott Olin *federal judge*

Kennett
Rhew, Perry James *judge*

Moberly
Blackmar, Charles Blakey *state supreme court justice*

Saint Louis
Hamilton, Jean Constance *judge*
Limbaugh, Stephen Nathaniel *federal judge*
Litz, Arthur *retired judge*
McMillian, Theodore *federal judge*

Springfield
Clark, Russell Gentry *federal judge*

West Plains
Dunlap, David Houston *judge*

NEBRASKA

Lincoln
Beam, Clarence Arlen *federal judge*
Caporale, D. Nick *state supreme court justice*
Fahrnbruch, Dale E. *state supreme court justice*
Hastings, William Charles *retired state supreme court chief justice*
Kopf, Richard G. *federal judge*
Urbom, Warren Keith *federal judge*

Omaha
Cambridge, William G. *federal judge*
Grant, John Thomas *retired state supreme court justice*
Shanahan, Thomas M. *judge*
Strom, Lyle Elmer *federal judge*

NORTH DAKOTA

Bismarck
Conmy, Patrick A. *federal judge*
Meschke, Herbert Leonard *state supreme court justice*
Neumann, William Allen *judge*
Sandstrom, Dale Vernon *state supreme court judge*
VandeWalle, Gerald Wayne *state supreme court chief justice*
Van Sickle, Bruce Marion *federal judge*

Grand Forks
Smith, Kirk Berton *judge*

New Rockford
Bekken, James Malcolm *district judge*

OHIO

Akron
Bell, Samuel H. *federal judge*
Contie, Leroy John, Jr. *federal judge*

Chillicothe
Radcliffe, Gerald Eugene *judge*

Cincinnati
Allen, Michael Kurt *municipal court judge*
Murdock, Norman Anthony *judge*
Nelson, David Aldrich *federal judge*
O'Connor, John Paul *judge*
Painter, Mark Philip *judge*
Weber, Herman Jacob *federal judge*

Circleville
Ammer, William *retired judge*

Cleveland
Aldrich, Ann *federal judge*
Locher, Ralph Sidney *retired state supreme court justice*
Matia, Paul Ramon *federal judge*

Columbus
Holschuh, John David *federal judge*
Norris, Alan Eugene *federal judge*
Pfeifer, Paul E. *state supreme court justice*
Resnick, Alice Robie *state supreme court justice*
Smith, George Curtis *judge*
Sweeney, Asher William *state supreme court justice*

Dayton
Fain, Mike *judge*
Foley, Patrick J. *judge*

Lucasville
Reno, Ottie Wayne *former judge*

Marietta
Taylor, John Kemper *trial judge, retired*

Medina
Batchelder, Alice M. *federal judge*

Newark
Steiner, Russell A. *lawyer, judge*

Sandusky
Lucal, Martha Jane *judge*

Toledo
Potter, John William *federal judge*

SOUTH DAKOTA

Pierre
Miller, Robert Arthur *state supreme court chief justice*
Sabers, Richard Wayne *state supreme court justice*

Sioux Falls
Severson, Glen Arthur *circuit court judge*

WISCONSIN

Madison
Crabb, Barbara Brandriff *federal judge*
Deininger, David George *judge*
Heffernan, Nathan Stewart *retired state supreme court chief justice*
Wilcox, Jon P. *justice*

Milwaukee
Randa, Rudolph Thomas *judge*

CANADA

MANITOBA

Winnipeg
Hewak, Benjamin *chief justice*

ADDRESS UNPUBLISHED

Brickner, Paul *administrative law judge*
Callow, William Grant *retired state supreme court justice*
Griffin, Robert Paul *former state supreme court justice and US senator*
Lay, Donald Pomeroy *federal judge*
Logan, James Kenneth *federal judge*
Ross, Donald Roe *federal judge*
Stamos, John James *judge*

LAW: LAW PRACTICE AND ADMINISTRATION

UNITED STATES

CALIFORNIA

Loma Linda
Seheult, Malcolm McDonald Richardson *lawyer*

Palo Alto
Miller, Robert Hugh *lawyer*

Rancho Mirage
Reuben, Don Harold *lawyer*

DISTRICT OF COLUMBIA

Washington
Durnil, Gordon Kay *lawyer, diplomat, arbitrator, political party official*
Hoagland, Peter Jackson *lawyer, former congressman*
Jackson, Jesse, Jr. *lawyer*

FLORIDA

Oldsmar
Hirschman, Sherman Joseph *lawyer, educator*

ILLINOIS

Abbott Park
Brock, Charles Marquis *lawyer*
Pope, Lawrence S. *lawyer*

Arlington Heights
Biestek, John Paul *lawyer*

Aurora
Lowe, Ralph Edward *lawyer*

Barrington
Curielli, John Peter *lawyer*
Tobin, Dennis Michael *lawyer*
White, Jeffrey Paul *lawyer*

Belleville
Boyle, Richard Edward *lawyer*
Heiligenstein, Christian E. *lawyer*
James, Ernest Wilbur *lawyer*

Bloomington
Bragg, Michael Ellis *lawyer, insurance company executive*

Carbondale
Adams, Jill Elaine *legal educator*
Kionka, Edward James *lawyer*
Lesar, Hiram Henry *lawyer, educator*
Schroeder, William Arthur *law educator*

Champaign
Miller, Harold Arthur *lawyer*
Nowak, John E. *law educator*
Rawles, Edward Hugh *lawyer*

Chicago
Anagnost, Themis John *lawyer*
Auerbach, Marshall Jay *lawyer*
Baer, John Richard Frederick *lawyer*
Bailey, Robert Short *lawyer*
Baker, Bruce Jay *lawyer*
Baker, James Edward Sproul *retired lawyer*
Barnard, Morton John *lawyer*
Becker, Theodore Michaelson *lawyer*
Bernard, Frank Charles *lawyer*
Birmingham, William Joseph *lawyer*
Blount, Michael Eugene *lawyer*
Blume, Paul Chiappe *lawyer*
Bobbitt, Ronald Albert *lawyer*
Bockelman, John Richard *lawyer*
Bodine, Laurence *lawyer, editor, marketer*
Boland, Edmund P. *lawyer*
Bolaños, Anita Marie *lawyer*
Bower, Glen Landis *lawyer*
Bridewell, David Alexander *lawyer*
Brown, Alan Crawford *lawyer*
Burgdoerfer, Jerry *lawyer*
Burkey, Lee Melville *lawyer*
Bussman, Donald Herbert *lawyer*
Carroll, Christopher Steven *lawyer*
Chaviano, Hugo *lawyer*
Chudzinski, Mark Adam *lawyer*
Clark, David Keith *lawyer, real estate developer*
Coduti, Philip James *legal association admininstration*
Collins, Michael R. *lawyer, business executive*
Conviser, Richard James *law educator, lawyer, publications company executive*
Cressey, Bryan Charles *lawyer*
Crossan, John Robert *lawyer*
Davis, Muller *lawyer*
DeLaRosa, Denise Maria *legal administrator*
Dillard, Kirk Whitfield *lawyer, state senator*
Dilling, Kirkpatrick Wallwick *lawyer*
Dockterman, Michael *lawyer*
Doyle, Francis Robert *law librarian, law educator*
Dropkin, Allen Hodes *lawyer*
Early, Bert Hylton *lawyer, legal search consultant*
Eggert, Russell Raymond *lawyer*
Ettinger, Joseph Alan *lawyer*
Faier, James Michael *lawyer*
Farber, Bernard John *lawyer*
Fazio, Peter Victor, Jr. *lawyer*
Fein, Roger Gary *lawyer*
Felsenthal, Steven Altus *lawyer*
Field, Robert Edward *lawyer*
Fina, Paul Joseph *lawyer*
Finke, Thomas Seddon *lawyer*
Fitzpatrick, Christine Morris *legal administrator, former television executive*
Flynn, Peter Anthony *lawyer*
Gail, Sanford R. *lawyer*
Garber, Samuel Baugh *lawyer, retail company executive*
Geiman, J. Robert *lawyer*
Geraldson, Raymond I., Jr. *lawyer*
Gertz, Elmer *lawyer, author, educator*
Gilkes, Arthur Gwyer *lawyer*
Glieberman, Herbert Allen *lawyer*
Goldgar, Arnold Benjamin *lawyer*
Goodman, Gary Alan *lawyer*
Gotfryd, William Ted *lawyer*
Greenburg, Barry Howard *lawyer*
Griffith, Donald Kendall *lawyer*
Griffith, James David *lawyer*
Gutstein, Solomon *lawyer*
Hablutzel, Philip Norman *law educator*
Hamblet, Michael Jon *lawyer, city official, former state official*

Harvitt, Adrianne Stanley *lawyer*
Heldrich, Gerard Charles, Jr. *lawyer*
Heller, Stanley J. *lawyer, physician, educator*
Helmholz, R(ichard) H(enry) *law educator*
Hilliard, David Craig *lawyer*
Hofer, Roy Ellis *lawyer*
Hoff, John Scott *lawyer*
Holleb, Marshall Maynard *lawyer*
Homburger, Thomas Charles *lawyer*
Horwitz, Clifford Wolf *lawyer*
Hughes, Steven Jay *lawyer*
Hunt, Lawrence Halley, Jr. *lawyer*
Jacover, Jerold Alan *lawyer*
Julius, Norman B. *lawyer*
Kanter, Burton Wallace *lawyer*
Kaplan, Jared *lawyer*
Karnes, Evan Burton, II *lawyer*
Karu, Gilda M(all) *lawyer, government official*
Katz, Avrum Sidney *lawyer*
King, Michael Howard *lawyer*
Knox, James Marshall *lawyer*
Kozak, John W. *lawyer*
Krakowski, Richard John *lawyer, public relations executive*
Kroll, Jeffrey Joseph *lawyer*
Learner, Howard Alan *lawyer*
Levin, Charles Edward *lawyer*
Leyhane, Francis John, III *lawyer*
Lifton, Fred Bernard *lawyer*
Lindgren, Karin Johanna *lawyer*
Long, Kevin Jay *medicolegal consultant*
Lourie, Alexander *lawyer*
Mackey, Benjamin Franklin, Jr. *lawyer, consultant*
Maher, David Willard *lawyer*
Mansfield, Karen Lee *lawyer*
Matanky, Robert William *lawyer*
McCrohon, Craig *lawyer*
Meyer, J. Theodore *lawyer*
Moltz, Marshall Jerome *lawyer*
Monarch, Joel R. *lawyer*
Montgomery, Charles Barry *lawyer*
Moran, John Thomas, Jr. *lawyer*
Nelson, Richard David *lawyer*
Neumeier, Matthew Michael *lawyer*
Nora, Gerald Ernest *lawyer*
Pallasch, B. Michael *lawyer*
Palmer, Robert Towne *lawyer*
Pattishall, Beverly Wyckliffe *lawyer*
Pavalon, Eugene Irving *lawyer*
Pelton, Russell Meredith, Jr. *lawyer*
Phelps, Paul Michael *lawyer*
Piper, Jonathan Bicknell *lawyer*
Pitt, George *lawyer*
Pritikin, James B. *lawyer, employee benefits consultant*
Prochnow, Herbert Victor, Jr. *lawyer*
Proctor, Edward George *lawyer*
Reum, James Michael *lawyer*
Richman, John Marshall *lawyer, business executive*
Rieger, Mitchell Sheridan *lawyer*
Rizzo, Ronald Stephen *lawyer*
Robinson, Theodore Curtis, Jr. *lawyer*
Rubin, E(rwin) Leonard *lawyer*
Ryan, Robert Collins *lawyer*
Sachnoff, Lowell *lawyer*
Saunders, George Lawton, Jr. *lawyer*
Saunders, Lonna Jeanne *lawyer, newscaster, talk show host*
Schmidt, Wayne Walter *legal association executive*
Schneider, Bryan A. *lawyer*
Schoonhoven, Ray James *retired lawyer*
Schuyler, Daniel Merrick *lawyer, educator*
Scott, Theodore R. *lawyer*
Seamons, Quinton Frank *lawyer*
Sennet, Charles Joseph *lawyer*
Siegel, Howard Jerome *lawyer*
Sigal, Michael Stephen *lawyer*
Silets, Harvey Marvin *lawyer*
Simon, Seymour *lawyer, former state supreme court justice*
Skilling, Raymond Inwood *lawyer*
Smedinghoff, Thomas J. *lawyer*
Smith, Arthur B(everly), Jr. *lawyer*
Staab, Michael Joseph *lawyer*
Stack, Paul Francis *lawyer*
Stoll, John Robert *lawyer, educator*
Timmer, Stephen Blaine *lawyer*
Torshen, Jerome Harold *lawyer*
Truskowski, John Budd *lawyer*
Tucker, Bowen Hayward *lawyer*
Vainisi, Jerome Robert *lawyer, former professional football executive*
Wald, Bruce Lewis *lawyer*
Wascher, James Degen *lawyer*
Watts, Dey Wadsworth *retired lawyer*
Weinberger, Seth Jay *lawyer*
Wilson, Clarence Sylvester, Jr. *lawyer, educator*
Witwer, Samuel Weiler, Jr. *lawyer*
Wolf, Neal Lloyd *lawyer*
Wood, Allison Lorraine *lawyer*
York, John C(hristopher) *lawyer*
Young, Keith Lawrence *lawyer*
Zanger, Larry Martin *lawyer, partner*

Collinsville
Tognarelli, Richard Lee *lawyer*

Countryside
Peasley, Louis Carl *lawyer, law educator*

Crystal Lake
Bishop, James Francis *lawyer*
Knox, Susan Marie *paralegal*

Danville
Blan, Kennith William, Jr. *lawyer*

Decatur
Dunn, John Francis *lawyer, state representative*

Deerfield
Bartlett, Robert William *lawyer, publishing executive*
Gash, Lauren Beth *lawyer, state legislator*
Hoffman, John Harry *lawyer, accountant*
Torf, Philip R. *lawyer, pharmacist*

Des Plaines
Davis, Larry Allen *lawyer*
Jacobs, William Russell, II *lawyer*
Malloy, Kathleen Sharon *lawyer*
May, Frank Brendan, Jr. *lawyer*

Downers Grove
Siedlecki, Nancy Therese *lawyer, funeral director*

Edwardsville
Carlson, Jon Gordon *lawyer*
Crowder, Barbara Lynn *lawyer*

Elmhurst
Berry, James Frederick *lawyer, biology educator*

Elmwood Park
Spina, Anthony Ferdinand *lawyer*

Evanston
Polzin, John Theodore *lawyer*
Salem, Richard Allen *mediator*
Van Demark, Ruth Elaine *lawyer*
Warshaw, Roberta Sue *lawyer, financial specialist*

Genoa
Cromley, Jon Lowell *lawyer*

Glen Ellyn
Barrett, Carolyn Hernly *paralegal*
Hudson, Dennis Lee *lawyer, retired government official, arbitrator, educator*

Glencoe
Cascino, Anthony Elmo, Jr. *lawyer, insurance executive*

Highland Park
Venus, Susan M. *legal assistant, director corporate pro bono program*

Hinsdale
Bennett, Margaret Airola *lawyer*
Farrug, Eugene Joseph, Sr. *lawyer*
Sheehan, Dennis William, Sr. *lawyer*

Hoopeston
Manion, Paul Thomas *lawyer*

Lake Forest
Palmer, Ann Therese Darin *lawyer*

Lansing
Hill, Philip *retired lawyer*

Lewistown
Davis, William C., Jr. *lawyer*

Lincolnshire
Prasil, Linda Ann *lawyer, writer*

Lisle
High, Suzanne Irene *lawyer*

Lombard
Willis, Douglas Alan *lawyer*

Marengo
Franks, Herbert Hoover *lawyer*

Marion
Powless, Kenneth Barnett *lawyer*

Mattoon
Horsley, Jack Everett *lawyer, author*

Moline
Moens, Thomas Odin *lawyer, computer consultant*

Monmouth
Flinn, Charles Gallagher *lawyer*

Morton Grove
Russ, Cary *lawyer, federal agency administrator*

Naperville
Horan, Janet K. *lawyer*

North Aurora
Cole, Sarah *law enforcement librarian*

Northbrook
Rotchford, Patricia Kathleen *lawyer*
Sernett, Richard Patrick *lawyer*

Northfield
Baker, Louis W. *lawyer*

Oak Brook
Bishop, Linda Dilene *lawyer, small business owner*
La Petina, Gary Michael *lawyer*
Meadors, Gayle Marleen *lawyer*
Oldfield, E. Lawrence *lawyer*

Oak Brook Mall
Botti, Aldo E. *lawyer*

Oak Park
Sengpiehl, Paul Marvin *lawyer, former state official*

Oakbrook Terrace
O'Brien, Walter Joseph, II *lawyer*

Ottawa
Kaschak, Lawrence Michael *lawyer*

Paris
Lolie, Allan F., Jr. *lawyer*

Park Ridge
Hegarty, Mary Frances *lawyer*
O'Meara, John F. *lawyer*

Peoria
Jagiella, Diana Mary *lawyer*

Princeton
Johnson, Watts Carey *lawyer*

Prospect Heights
Leopold, Mark F. *lawyer*

Rock Island
Heiple, Jonathan James *lawyer*
Lousberg, Peter Herman *lawyer*
Wallace, Franklin Sherwood *lawyer*

Rockford
Johnson, Thomas Stuart *lawyer*
Logli, Paul Albert *lawyer*
Scott, Douglas Patrick *lawyer, state representative*
Van Vleet, William Benjamin *retired lawyer, life insurance company executive*

Schaumburg
Collins, James Francis *lawyer, financial consultant*
Gardner, Caryn Sue *lawyer*
Stockley, Darleen J. *lawyer*

Shorewood
Charlier, Patricia Ann *lawyer*

Skokie
Smith, Mark Steven *lawyer*

Springfield
Collins, Barbara Ballin *lawyer*
Kerr, Gary Enrico *lawyer, educator*
Klingler, Gwendolyn Walbolt *lawyer, alderman*
Mc Gary, Thomas Hugh *lawyer*
Morse, Saul Julian *lawyer*
Mulligan, Rosemary Elizabeth *paralegal*
Reed, Robert Phillip *lawyer*
Sgro, Gregory Peter *lawyer*

Streator
Harrison, Frank Joseph *lawyer*

Urbana
Moore, David Robert *lawyer*

Villa Park
Fenech, Joseph C. *lawyer*

Warrenville
McGurn, George William *lawyer*

Waukegan
Clarke, Lewis Douglas *lawyer*

Westchester
Washburn, John James *lawyer, financial services company executive*

Western Springs
Hanson, Heidi Elizabeth *lawyer*

Westmont
Biggert, Judith Borg *lawyer, state representative*

Wheaton
Fawell, Jeffrey Bruce *lawyer*
Roberts, Keith Edward, Sr. *lawyer*

Wilmette
Atkinson, Jeff John Frederick *lawyer, educator, writer*
Lieberman, Eugene *lawyer*
Musicus, Raphael J. *lawyer, accountant*

Winnetka
Denkewalter, Kim Richard *lawyer*

Winthrop Harbor
Getz, James Edward *legal association administrator*

INDIANA

Beech Grove
Brown, Richard Lawrence *lawyer*

Bloomington
Daw-Schmidt, Kenneth Glenn *law professor*
Shreve, Gene Russell *law educator*

Carmel
Foster, Michael Thomas *lawyer*

Columbus
Harrison, Patrick Woods *lawyer*

Crown Point
Sendak, Theodore Lorraine *lawyer*

Danville
Baldwin, Jeffrey Kenton *lawyer, educator*

Elkhart
Andrews, Ruth Klassen *mediator, consultant*

Evansville
Clouse, John Daniel *lawyer*
Miller, Daniel Raymond *prosecutor*

Fort Wayne
Fink, Thomas Michael *lawyer*
Lebamoff, Ivan Argire *lawyer*
Shoaff, Thomas Mitchell *lawyer*

Hammond
Diamond, Eugene Christopher *lawyer, hospital administrator*
Kohl, Jacquelyn Marie *lawyer*

Hartford City
Ford, David Clayton *lawyer, Indiana state senator*

Indianapolis
Cox, Paul Noel *law educator*
Ewbank, Thomas Peters *lawyer, retired banker*
Funk, David Albert *law educator*
Gray, Mark William *lawyer*
Holt, John Manly *retired corporate lawyer*
Kappes, Philip Spangler *lawyer*
Kirtley, David E. *lawyer*
Koeller, Robert Marion *lawyer*
Lamkin, Martha Dampf *lawyer*
Lisher, John Leonard *lawyer*
McCarthy, Kevin Bart *lawyer*
Padgett, Gregory Lee *lawyer*
Page-Caraher, Denise *mediator, arbitrator*
Patrick, William Bradshaw *lawyer*
Price, John Richard *lawyer*
Quayle, Marilyn Tucker *lawyer, wife of former vice president of United States*
Reynolds, Robert Hugh *lawyer*
Russell, David Williams *lawyer*
Schlegel, Fred Eugene *lawyer*
Stieff, John Joseph *legislative attorney, educator*
Thompson, Bradley Merrill *lawyer*
Townsend, Earl Cunningham, Jr. *lawyer, writer*
Vandivier, Blair Robert *lawyer*
Wellnitz, Craig Otto *lawyer, English language educator*
Yeager, Joseph Heizer, Jr. *lawyer*

Jeffersonville
Pettyjohn, Shirley Ellis *lawyer, real estate executive*

Kokomo
Maugans, John Conrad *lawyer*

Lafayette
O'Callaghan, Patti Louise *court program administrator*

Merrillville
Kinney, Richard Gordon *lawyer, educator*

Muncie
Kelly, Eric Damian *lawyer, educator*
Rankin, Joseph Walter *lawyer*

New Albany
Kraft, John A. *lawyer*

Peru
Loy, William Alexander *lawyer*

Seelyville
Pease, Edward Allan *lawyer, former state legislator, university official*

Seymour
Gill, W(alter) Brent *lawyer*

Shelbyville
Lisher, James Richard *lawyer*

South Bend
Carrington, Michael Davis *criminal justice administrator, educator*
Deahl, Warren Anthony *lawyer*
Knepp, Virginia Lee Hahn *legal assistant*
Reinke, William John *lawyer*

Unionville
Franklin, Frederick Russell *retired legal association executive*

Valparaiso
Koeppen, Raymond Bradley *lawyer*

Vincennes
Emison, Ewing Rabb, Jr. *lawyer*

IOWA

Atlantic
Van Ginkel, James Carol *lawyer*

Cedar Rapids
Rings, Randall Eugene *lawyer*
Wilson, Robert Foster *lawyer*

Charles City
Mc Cartney, Ralph Farnham *lawyer*

Council Bluffs
Hamilton, Darrin Tod *city prosecutor*

Des Moines
Brown, Paul Edmondson *lawyer*
Dahl, Harry Waldemar *lawyer*
Doyle, Richard Henry, IV *lawyer*
Fisher, Thomas George *lawyer, retired media company executive*
Gotsdiner, Murray Bennett *lawyer*
Hicks, Janet Brooks *lawyer*
Koehn, William James *lawyer*
Lawyer, Vivian Jury *lawyer*
Peddicord, Roland Dale *lawyer*

Dubuque
Ernst, Daniel Pearson *lawyer*
Hammer, David Lindley *lawyer, author*

Iowa City
Bonfield, Arthur Earl *lawyer, educator*
Downer, Robert Nelson *lawyer*
Wing, Adrien Katherine *law educator*

Keokuk
Hoffman, James Paul *lawyer, hypnotist*

Mason City
Winston, Harold Ronald *lawyer*

Mount Pleasant
Vance, Michael Charles *lawyer*

Sioux City
Madsen, George Frank *lawyer*
Nymann, P. L. *lawyer*

Windsor Heights
Belin, David William *lawyer*

Winfield
Carty, John Wesley *lawyer*

KANSAS

Beloit
Conroy, Thomas Hyde *lawyer*

Fort Riley
Clarke, Michael Robert *lawyer, educator*

Iola
Toland, Clyde William *lawyer*
Toland, John Robert *lawyer*

Lawrence
Goetz, Raymond *law educator, labor arbitrator*
Murray, Thomas Veatch *lawyer*

Leawood
Snyder, Willard Breidenthal *lawyer*

Lyons
Hodgson, Arthur Clay *lawyer*

Olathe
Eichholz, Mark Joseph *lawyer*
Haskin, J. Michael *lawyer*
Lowe, Roy Goins *lawyer*
Snowbarger, Vincent Keith *lawyer, state representative*

Onaga
Stallard, Wayne Minor *lawyer*

Overland Park
Gaar, Norman Edward *lawyer, former state senator*
Sampson, William Roth *lawyer*
Short, Joel Bradley *lawyer, consultant, software publisher*
Smith, Daniel Lynn *lawyer*
Stanton, Roger D. *lawyer*
Waxse, David John *lawyer*

Shawnee Mission
Bond, Richard Lee *lawyer, state senator*
Leffel, Russell Calvin *lawyer*
Sparks, Billy Schley *lawyer*

Topeka
Albrecht, Shari Feist *administrative law hearing officer*
Caro, Melanie Darleen *lawyer*
Hejtmanek, Danton Charles *lawyer*

Wamego
Lang, John Ernest *lawyer*

Wichita
Arabia, Paul *lawyer*
Ayres, Ted Dean *lawyer, academic counsel*
Homolka, C(alvin) Dean, II *lawyer*
Stinson, Dale Bernard *lawyer*

MICHIGAN

Adrian
Kralick, Richard Louis *lawyer*

Ann Arbor
Allen, Layman Edward *law educator, research scientist*
Browder, Olin Lorraine *legal educator*
Cole, Roland Jay *lawyer*
Joscelyn, Kent Buckley *lawyer, research scientist*
Kamisar, Yale *lawyer, educator*
Muraski, Anthony Augustus *lawyer*
Stein, Eric *retired law educator*
Vining, (George) Joseph *law educator*

Battle Creek
Baldwin, Susan Olin *lawyer*

Bay City
Greve, Guy Robert *lawyer*

Berkley
Linkner, Monica Farris *lawyer*

Bingham Farms
Fershtman, Julie Ilene *lawyer*

Birmingham
Morganroth, Fred *lawyer*

Bloomfield Hills
Janover, Robert H. *lawyer*
Kasischke, Louis Walter *lawyer*
Meyer, George Herbert *lawyer*
Pappas, Edward Harvey *lawyer*
Stewart, Bernard Francis *lawyer*
Vocht, Michelle Elise *lawyer*
Weinstein, William Joseph *lawyer*
Yamin, Joseph Francis *lawyer*

Dearborn
Gardner, Gary Edward *lawyer*
O'Neill, Ann Renee *lawyer, metallurgical engineer*
Payne, John B(urton) *lawyer*

Detroit
Adamany, David Walter *law and political science educator*
Andreoff, Christopher Andon *lawyer*
Babcock, Charles Witten, Jr. *lawyer*
Charla, Leonard Francis *lawyer*
Dunn, William Bradley *lawyer*
Kahn, Mark Leo *arbitrator, educator*
Krsul, John Aloysius, Jr. *lawyer*
Lawrence, John Kidder *lawyer*
Longhofer, Ronald Stephen *lawyer*
Mamat, Frank Trustick *lawyer*
McKim, Samuel John, III *lawyer*
Miller, George DeWitt, Jr. *lawyer*
Nix, Robert Royal, II *lawyer*
Richardson, Ralph Herman *lawyer*
Rooney, Scott William *lawyer*
Santo, Ronald Joseph *lawyer*
Saxton, William Marvin *lawyer*
Seabrooks, Nettie Harris *government executive*
Sedler, Robert Allen *law educator*
Skutt, Richard Michael *lawyer*
Thelen, Bruce Cyril *lawyer*
Thoms, David Moore *lawyer*
Walle, James Paul *lawyer*
Zuckerman, Richard Engle *lawyer, law educator*

East Lansing
Dobson, Tracy Anne *law educator*
Hackett, Wesley Phelps, Jr. *lawyer*

Farmington
Alexander, James Max *lawyer*

Farmington Hills
Haliw, Andrew Jerome, III *lawyer, engineer*
Maloney, Vincent John *lawyer, social worker, psychotherapist*
Tobin, Bruce Howard *lawyer*

Flint
Burns, Avon Lorraine *law educator*
Hart, Clifford Harvey *lawyer*

Grand Rapids
Davis, Henry Barnard, Jr. *lawyer*
Kara, Paul Mark *lawyer*
Mc Callum, Charles Edward *lawyer*
Mears, Patrick Edward *lawyer*
Rinck, James Richard *lawyer*
Scholler, Thomas Peter *lawyer*
Schroder, Barry Charles *lawyer*
Smoke, Richard Edwin *lawyer, investment adviser*

Grosse Pointe
Centner, Charles William *law educator*

Harper Woods
Eaman, Frank Dwight *lawyer*

Highland
Powers, Dennis Norbert *lawyer*

Holland
Moritz, John Reid *lawyer*
Murphy, Max Ray *lawyer*

Ishpeming
Steward, James Brian *lawyer, pharmacist*

Jackson
Crawley, Richard Alan *arbitrator, mediator*

Kalamazoo
Hilboldt, James Sonnemann *lawyer, investment advisor*

Lansing
Ayadi, Naida Anita *retired legislative assistant*
Bretz, Ronald James *lawyer*
Ewert, Quentin Albert *lawyer, consultant*
Falk, Allan *lawyer*
Kritselis, William Nicholas *lawyer*
Marvin, David Edward Shreve *lawyer*
Rooney, John Philip *law educator*
White, David Dwayne *government tax lawyer*
Wyszynski, James Edward, Jr. *lawyer, state government*

Lincoln Park
Zelenak, Edward Michael *lawyer, musician*

Menominee
Anuta, Michael Joseph *lawyer*

Muskegon
Van Leuven, Robert Joseph *lawyer*

Newport
Hensley, Jeffrey Allen *nuclear security*

Northville
Hariri, V. M. *arbitrator, mediator, lawyer, educator*
Leavitt, Martin Jack *lawyer*
Walker, Jonathan Lee *lawyer*

Okemos
Olmsted, Ann Garver *lawyer*

Petoskey
Smith, Wayne Richard *lawyer*

Plymouth
Morgan, Donald Crane *lawyer*

Pontiac
Grantham, Pamela Maas *prosecutor*

Port Huron
Bostwick, Cynthia *lawyer*

Saginaw
Zanot, Craig Allen *lawyer*

Saint Clair Shores
Shehan, Wayne Charles *lawyer*

Saint Joseph
Gleiss, Henry Weston *lawyer*

Southfield
Baughman, Leonora Knoblock *lawyer*
Hotelling, Harold *law and economics educator*
Kippert, Robert John, Jr. *lawyer*
May, Alan Alfred *lawyer*
McClow, Roger James *lawyer*
Morganroth, Mayer *lawyer*
Thurswell, Gerald Elliott *lawyer*

Troy
Chapman, Conrad Daniel *lawyer*
Franklin, Bruce Walter *lawyer*

MINNESOTA

Anoka
Foley, Leo Thomas *lawyer*
Hicken, Jeffrey Price *lawyer*

Benson
Wilcox, Donald Alan *lawyer*

Bloomington
Maffei, Rocco John *lawyer*
Ramos, Frederick *lawyer*

Burnsville
Knutson, David Lee *lawyer, state senator*

Cokato
James, Thomas Barry *lawyer*

Duluth
Burns, Richard Ramsey *lawyer*

Eagan
Angle, Margaret Susan *lawyer*

Golden Valley
Hagglund, Clarance Edward *lawyer, publishing company owner*

Hallock
Malm, Roger Charles *lawyer*

Luverne
Vander Kooi, Benjamin, Jr. *lawyer*

Mankato
Hottinger, John Creighton *state legislator, lawyer*

Minneapolis
Allers, Marlene Elaine *legal administrator*
Barnard, Allen Donald *lawyer*
Brand, Steve Aaron *lawyer*
Clary, Bradley Grayson *lawyer, educator*
Corwin, Gregg Marlowe *lawyer*
Dalglish, Lucy Ann *lawyer*
Erstad, Leon Robert *lawyer*
Hasselquist, Maynard Burton *lawyer*
Johnson, Paul Owen *lawyer*
Lennes, John Burr, Jr. *lawyer*
McGuire, Timothy James *lawyer, county and state official*
Meshbesher, Ronald I. *lawyer*
Mooty, John William *lawyer*
Neff, Fred Leonard *lawyer*
Radmer, Michael John *lawyer, educator*
Ranum, Jane Barnhardt *lawyer*
Reister, Raymond Alex *retired lawyer*
Schnobrich, Roger William *lawyer*
Sortland, Paul Allan *lawyer*
Stein, Bob *lawyer*
Tigue, Randall Davis Bryant *lawyer*
Ventres, Judith Martin *lawyer*
Walters, Joe Aldrich *lawyer*
Wildung, Wendy Jo *lawyer*

Moorhead
Miller, Keith Lloyd *lawyer*

Pipestone
Scott, William Paul *lawyer*

Rochester
Orwoll, Gregg S. K. *lawyer*

Saint Cloud
Lalor, Edward David Darrell *labor and employment arbitrator, lawyer*

Saint Louis Park
Rothenberg, Elliot Calvin *lawyer, writer*
Underland-Rosow, Vicki Louise *mediator, publishing executive*

Saint Paul
Carruthers, Philip Charles *lawyer*
Chester, Stephanie Ann *lawyer, banker*
Claybourne, Frank *lawyer*
Daly, Joseph Leo *law educator*
Failinger, Marie Anita *law educator, editor*
Frey, Robert Mark *lawyer*
Halva, Allen Keith *legal publications consultant*
Hanson, Bruce Eugene *lawyer*
Kigin, Thomas John *lawyer, broadcast executive*
Micallef, Joseph Stephen *lawyer*
Nemo, Anthony James *lawyer*
Popovich, Peter Stephen *lawyer, former state supreme court chief justice*
Sippel, William Leroy *lawyer*
Smith, Steve C. *lawyer, state legislator*
Wattson, Peter Strand *lawyer*

South Saint Paul
Pugh, Thomas Wilfred *lawyer*

Wayzata
Reutiman, Robert William, Jr. *lawyer*

Willmar
Thompson, Joe E. *lawyer*

Worthington
Erickson, Margaret Kathryn *lawyer*

MISSOURI

Ballwin
Banton, Stephen Chandler *lawyer*

Cape Girardeau
McManaman, Kenneth Charles *lawyer*

Cassville
Melton, Emory Leon *lawyer, state legislator, publisher*

Clayton
Belz, Mark *lawyer*
Klarich, David John *lawyer, state senator*
Lasater, John Robert *lawyer*

Columbia
Hulshof, Kenny *public defender, prosecutor, state assistant attorney general*
Moore, Mitchell Jay *lawyer, law educator*
Parrigin, Elizabeth Ellington *lawyer*
Welliver, Warren Dee *lawyer, retired state supreme court justice*

Green City
Sayre, Jeffrey Don *lawyer*

Hannibal
Welch, Joseph Daniel *lawyer*

Independence
Cady, Elwyn Loomis, Jr. *medicolegal consultant, educator*
Lashley, Curtis Dale *lawyer*

Jefferson City
Gaw, Robert Steven *lawyer, state representative*
Graham, Christopher *lawyer*

Joplin
Guillory, Jeffery Michael *lawyer*

Kansas City
Ayers, Jeffrey David *lawyer*
Bailey, Kristen *legal assistant*
Ball, Owen Keith, Jr. *lawyer*
Beckett, Theodore Charles *lawyer*
Beckett, Theodore Cornwall *lawyer*
Bevan, Robert Lewis *lawyer*
Borel, Steven James *lawyer*
Bradshaw, Jean Paul, II *lawyer*
Davis, Gardiner B. *lawyer*
Frantze, David W. *lawyer*
Gaines, Robert Darryl *lawyer, food services executive*
Gibson, George Edward *retired lawyer*
Gorman, Gerald Warner *lawyer*
Graham, Harold Steven *lawyer*
Helder, Jan Pleasant, Jr. *lawyer*
Hoskins, William Keller *lawyer, pharmaceutical company executive*
Howes, Brian Thomas *lawyer*
Langworthy, Robert Burton *lawyer*
Lolli, Don R(ay) *lawyer*
Lotven, Howard Lee *lawyer*
Loudon, Donald Hoover *lawyer*
McGovern, Dianne *legal administrator*
McKinney, Janet Kay *law librarian*
McLarney, Charles Patrick *lawyer*
Molzen, Christopher John *lawyer*
Moore, Stephen James *lawyer*
Mordy, James Calvin *lawyer*
Pemberton, Bradley Powell *lawyer*
Readey, B(artley) John, III *lawyer*
Sader, Neil Steven *lawyer*
Scarritt, Richard Winn *lawyer*
Setzler, Edward Allan *lawyer*
Shay, David E. *lawyer*
Vleisides, Gregory William *lawyer*
Wyrsch, James Robert *lawyer, educator, author*
Ziegenhorn, Eric Howard *lawyer, legal writer*

Kirkwood
Gibbons, Michael Randolph *lawyer*
Sweeney, Robert Kevin *lawyer*

Lees Summit
Hall, Glenn Allen *lawyer, state representative*

Marshall
Peterson, William Allen *lawyer*

Saint Charles
Duggan, Lester W. *lawyer, insurance claims manager*

Saint Louis
Attanasio, John Baptist *law educator*
Barken, Bernard Allen *lawyer*
Beatty, Conny Davinroy *lawyer*
Brown, Paul Sherman *lawyer*
Carr, Arthur Garnsey, III *lawyer*
Chestnut, Kathi Lynne *lawyer*
Crebs, P(aul) Terence *lawyer*
DeWoskin, Alan Ellis *lawyer*
Donohue, Carroll John *lawyer*
Fricke, Thomas Freeland *lawyer*
Green, Marsha Lynn *legal assistant*
Hetlage, Robert Owen *lawyer*
Hunt, Jeffrey Brian *lawyer*
Komen, Leonard *lawyer*
Lowenhaupt, Charles Abraham *lawyer*
Lucchesi, Lionel Louis *lawyer*
Mandelker, Daniel Robert *law educator*
Marino, Charles Joseph *arbitrator*
Mc Daniel, James Edwin *lawyer*
Moore, McPherson Dorsett *lawyer*
Peper, Christian Baird *lawyer*
Perotti, Rose Norma *lawyer*
Preuss, Ronald Stephen *lawyer, educator*
Schmidtlein, Mary Virginia *lawyer*
Schnuck, Terry Edward *lawyer*
Schoene, Kathleen Snyder *lawyer*
Schwabe, John Bennett, II *lawyer*
Sestric, Anthony James *lawyer*
Sherby, Kathleen Reilly *lawyer*
Sneeringer, Stephen Geddes *lawyer*
Walsh, Joseph Leo, III *lawyer*
Wang, Hengtao (Hank T. Wang) *lawyer*
Welch, David William *lawyer*
Williams, Theodore Joseph, Jr. *lawyer*
Wines, Lawrence Eugene *lawyer, corporate executive*
Winning, John Patrick *lawyer*

Springfield
Carlson, Thomas Joseph *lawyer, real estate developer, former mayor*
Penninger, William Holt, Jr. *lawyer*
Roberts, Patrick Kent *lawyer*
Starnes, James Wright *lawyer*

Stockton
Hammons, Brian Kent *lawyer, business executive*

NEBRASKA

Grand Island
Busick, Denzel Rex *lawyer*

Kearney
Munro, Robert Allan lawyer

Lincoln
Brown, Vincent D. lawyer
Green, George Harold, Jr. lawyer, consultant, researcher
Hewitt, James Watt lawyer
Swihart, Fred Jacob lawyer

Madison
Moyer, George Hamilton, Jr. lawyer

Omaha
Barmettler, Joseph John lawyer
Brashear, Kermit Allen, II lawyer
Bredar, Marcia Ann lawyer
Gaines, Tyler Belt lawyer
Hamann, Deryl Frederick lawyer, bank executive
Larson, David Allen law educator
Niemann, Nicholas Kent lawyer
Pollak, Oliver Burt lawyer, educator, writer
Proud, Richard French lawyer, teacher, writer
Riley, William Jay lawyer
Schmidt, Kathleen Marie lawyer

NEW JERSEY

Lyndhurst
Watson, Stephen Allison, III lawyer

NEW YORK

Dobbs Ferry
Ryon, Mortimer lawyer

NORTH DAKOTA

Bismarck
Olson, John Michael lawyer
Walstad, John Michael lawyer, code revisor
Zuger, William Peter lawyer

Grand Forks
Anderson, Damon Ernest lawyer
Cilz, Douglas Arthur lawyer
Rolshoven, Ross William legal investigator, art photographer

OHIO

Akron
Holloway, Donald Phillip lawyer
Lombardi, Frederick McKean lawyer
Ong, John Doyle lawyer
Ruport, Scott Hendricks lawyer

Alliance
Ahonen, Robert M. law educator

Amherst
Knull, Ralph Erhard Carl lawyer

Batavia
Rosenhoffer, Chris lawyer

Bedford
Baldassari, Jeffrey John lawyer

Bucyrus
Neff, Robert Clark lawyer

Canton
Davila, Edwin lawyer
Lindamood, John Beyer lawyer

Cincinnati
Bissinger, Mark Christian lawyer
Case, Douglas Manning lawyer
Chesley, Stanley Morris lawyer
Dehner, Joseph Julnes lawyer
Denham, Patricia Eileen Keller law librarian
Finkelmeier, Philip Renner law librarian, lawyer
Hardy, William Robinson lawyer
Hill, Thomas Clark lawyer
Hoffheimer, Daniel Joseph lawyer
Hopper, George lawyer
Lindberg, Charles David lawyer
Mann, David Scott lawyer
McClain, William Andrew lawyer
Meyers, Pamela Sue lawyer
Nelson, Frederick Dickson lawyer
Stanton, Jeanne Frances lawyer
Vogel, Cedric Wakelee lawyer
Weseli, Roger William lawyer

Cleveland
Band, Jordan Clifford lawyer
Baughman, R(obert) Patrick lawyer
Baxter, Howard H. lawyer
Blackford, Jason Collier lawyer
Boyko, Christopher Allan lawyer, judge
Buzzelli, Laurence Francis lawyer
Collin, Thomas James lawyer
Coyle, Martin Adolphus, Jr. lawyer
Drinko, John Deaver lawyer
Feliciano, Santiago, Jr. lawyer
Garvey, Mary Anne lawyer
Giles, Homer Wayne lawyer
Goldfarb, Bernard Sanford lawyer
Grady, Francis Xavier lawyer
Hoke, Susan Candice law educator
Kirner, Paul Timothy lawyer
Leavitt, Jeffrey Stuart lawyer
Legenza, Richard Andrew lawyer
Morhard, Albert J. lawyer
Oberdank, Lawrence Mark lawyer, arbitrator
Parkes, Wright C. corporate lawyer
Pearlman, Samuel Segel lawyer
Podboy, Alvin Michael, Jr. lawyer, law library director
Ruf, H(arold) William, Jr. lawyer, corporation executive
Sawyer, Raymond Terry lawyer
Sicherman, Marvin Allen lawyer
Skulina, Thomas Raymond lawyer
Spero, Keith Erwin lawyer
Szaller, James Francis lawyer
Waldeck, John Walter, Jr. lawyer
Watson, Richard Thomas lawyer
Weller, Charles David lawyer
White, Paul Dunbar lawyer

Columbus
Ayers, James Cordon lawyer
Baranowski, Edwin Michael lawyer, writer
Brown, Roy Eldridge lawyer
Celebrezze, Anthony J., Jr. lawyer
Diroll, David John lawyer
Farrar, Elizabeth Turrell lawyer
Finegold, Jordan assistant attorney general
Frasier, Ralph Kennedy lawyer, banker
Hutson, Jeffrey Woodward lawyer
Koblentz, Robert Alan lawyer
Kuehnle, Kenton Lee lawyer
La Cour, Louis Bernard lawyer
Larzelere, Kathy Lynn paralegal
Maloon, Jerry L. lawyer, physician, medicolegal consultant
Maynard, Robert Howell lawyer
Mentel, Michael Christopher lawyer
Morgan, Dennis Richard lawyer
O'Reilly, Michael Joseph lawyer, real estate investor
Owsiany, David J. lawyer, lobbyist
Petro, James Michael lawyer, politician
Ray, Frank Allen lawyer
Seward, Jeffrey James lawyer, protective services official, educator, administrator
Sully, Ira Bennett lawyer
Thompson, Harold Lee lawyer
Treneff, Craig Paul lawyer
Tripp, Thomas Neal lawyer, political consultant
Whipps, Edward Franklin lawyer
Workman, Thomas Eldon lawyer
Yeazel, Keith Arthur lawyer

Dayton
Conway, Mark Allyn lawyer
Hartmann, Charles John, Jr. law educator
McSwiney, Charles Ronald lawyer
Vaughn, Noel Wyandt lawyer

Dublin
Powell, Ernestine Breisch retired lawyer
Root, William Keith lawyer

Howard
Lee, William Johnson lawyer

Independence
McLaren, Richard Wellington, Jr. lawyer

Kent
Nome, William Andreas lawyer

Lakewood
Isabella, Joseph Noel lawyer

Newark
Hostetter, James William lawyer

North Royalton
Jungeberg, Thomas Donald lawyer

Oregon
St. Clair, Donald David lawyer

Painesville
Callender, James Sutton, Jr. lawyer

Steubenville
Adulewicz, Casimir T. lawyer, court magistrate

Toledo
Anspach, Robert Michael lawyer
Baker, Richard Southworth lawyer
Boesel, Milton Charles, Jr. lawyer, business executive
Brown, Charles Earl lawyer
Calcamuggio, Larry Glenn lawyer
Chilton, Bradley Stewart criminal justice educator
Esch, Raymond Gates lawyer
Jackson, Reginald Sherman, Jr. lawyer, educator
Tuschman, James Marshall lawyer
Webb, Thomas Irwin, Jr. lawyer

West Chester
Sims, Victor Dwayne lawyer

West Union
Young, Vernon Lewis lawyer

Westerville
Lancione, Bernard Gabe lawyer

Wooster
Kennedy, Charles Allen lawyer

Xenia
Chappars, Timothy Stephen lawyer

Youngstown
Ausnehmer, John Edward lawyer
Carlin, Clair Myron lawyer
Hill, Thomas Allen lawyer
Malkoff, Solomon lawyer

SOUTH CAROLINA

Sheldon
Goss, Richard Henry lawyer

SOUTH DAKOTA

Dakota Dunes
Putney, Mark William lawyer, utility executive

Fort Pierre
Johnson, Julie Marie lawyer/lobbyist

Parker
Zimmer, John Herman lawyer

Sioux Falls
Hanson, Monte Ray lawyer

Spearfish
Hood, Earl James lawyer, state legislator

WISCONSIN

Baraboo
Liebman, Todd Justin lawyer
Roney Drennan, Beth Horton lawyer

Deerfield
Pappas, David Christopher lawyer

Elkhorn
Sweet, Lowell Elwin lawyer

La Crosse
Schroth, John Henry associate lawyer

Little Chute
Cornett, Paul Michael, Sr. lawyer

Madison
Barnick, Helen retired judicial clerk
Bauman, Susan Joan Mayer lawyer
Hildebrand, Daniel Walter lawyer
McCallum, Laurie Riach lawyer, state government
Murphy, Robert Brady Lawrence lawyer
Pritchard, Michael Gregg legal services director, lawyer
Roberson, Linda lawyer
Taylor, Thomas Hugh lawyer

Milwaukee
Bruce, Peter Wayne lawyer, insurance company executive
Croak, Francis R. lawyer
Donahue, John Edward lawyer
Friedman, James Dennis lawyer
Groethe, Reed lawyer
Habush, Robert Lee lawyer
Keane, Steven Edward lawyer
Kircher, John Joseph law educator
Knoll, Robert R. lawyer, county government official
Krueger, Neil L. lawyer, judge
LaBudde, Roy Christian lawyer
Leitner, Mark Matthew lawyer
Levit, William Harold, Jr. lawyer
Martin, Quinn William lawyer
Melin, Robert Arthur lawyer
Mulcahy, Charles Chambers lawyer, educator
Paige, Norma lawyer, corporate executive
Peckerman, Bruce Martin lawyer
Sanfilippo, Jon Walter lawyer
Stomma, Peter Christopher lawyer
Terschan, Frank Robert lawyer
Williams, Clay Rule lawyer

Monroe
Kittelsen, Rodney Olin lawyer

Oshkosh
Wilde, William Richard lawyer

Racine
Swanson, Robert Lee lawyer

Rhinelander
Saari, John William, Jr. lawyer

Sun Prairie
Berkenstadt, James Allan lawyer

Waukesha
Duff, Marc Charles state legislator

Wausau
Drengler, William Allan John lawyer

ADDRESS UNPUBLISHED

Anderson, Geoffrey Allen retired lawyer
Anderson, Stephen Dale lawyer
Baker, Donald lawyer
Beeman, John Sanders lawyer
Bergstrom, Terry Lee research analyst
Bleiweis, Jeffrey I. lawyer
Bruckner, John Joseph patent lawyer, materials engineer
Buechel, William Benjamin retired lawyer
Coleman, Robert Lee retired lawyer
Colombo, Frederick J. lawyer
Dart, Stephen Howard lawyer, insurance company executive
Douglas, Robert Lee lawyer
Emert, Timothy Ray lawyer
Fiala, David Marcus lawyer
Fowler, Douglas Todd lawyer
Gleason, Gerald Wayne lawyer
Gore, David Lee lawyer
Hajek, Robert J., Sr. lawyer, real estate broker, commodities broker, nursing home owner
Henry, DeLysle Leon lawyer
Hoffman, Alan Craig lawyer, consultant
Knot, Alvan Paul lawyer
Krutter, Forrest Nathan lawyer
Lea, Lorenzo Bates lawyer
Lungren, John Howard law educator, oil and gas consultant, author
Mason, James W. lawyer, state legislator
McFarland, Robert Edwin lawyer
McManus, Martin Joseph lawyer, priest
McShane, Lawrence Edward paralegal advocate
Miller, Frank William legal educator
Mondul, Donald David lawyer
Myhand, Wanda Reshel paralegal, legal assistant
Nugent, Shane Vincent lawyer
Pawlik, James David lawyer, historian
Peters, R. Jonathan lawyer, chemical company executive
Pogue, Richard Welch lawyer
Reeder, Robert Harry retired lawyer
Reminger, Richard Thomas lawyer
Rock, Richard Rand lawyer, former state senator
Rodenberg-Roberts, Mary Patricia advocacy services administrator
Rodenburg, Clifton Glenn lawyer
Saliterman, Richard Arlen lawyer, educator
Shelton, Samuel Terrance court administrator
Shook, Ann Jones lawyer
Sladek, Martha J. lawyer
Smith, Lauren Ashley lawyer, journalist, clergyman, physicist
Stough, Charles Daniel lawyer
Struif, L. James lawyer
Torgerson, Larry Keith lawyer
Waaler, Jack lawyer
Walner, Robert Joel lawyer
Wright, Lisa Ann legal assistant

MEDICINE. *See* HEALTHCARE: MEDICINE.

MILITARY

UNITED STATES

DISTRICT OF COLUMBIA

Washington
O'Reilly, Kenneth William military officer

ILLINOIS

Deerfield
Weber, Milan George retired military officer, management consultant

Great Lakes
Gaston, Mack Charles naval officer

Lemont
Herriford, Robert Levi, Sr. army officer

O'Fallon
Teepell, David G. U.S. airforce firefighter

INDIANA

Fort Harrison
Dowden, Russell H., Jr. career officer

Indianapolis
Davis, Larry Michael military officer, health-care consultant

Nashville
Kylander, Chester R. retired civilian military employee

West Lafayette
Bryan, Leslie Aulls, Jr. military officer, university professor

IOWA

Iowa City
Mikelson, John David career officer

Johnston
Schultz, Roger C. career officer

KANSAS

Fort Leavenworth
Schneider, James Joseph military theory educator, consultant

MICHIGAN

Ann Arbor
Ploger, Robert Riis retired military officer, engineer

Plymouth
Brown, Bruce Harding naval officer

MISSOURI

Florissant
Reese, Alferd George retired army civilian logistics specialist

Jefferson City
Patterson, William Glenn, II military officer

Willow Springs
Spence, Wayne Jay naval aviation officer

NEBRASKA

Lincoln
Heng, Stanley Mark military officer

Offutt AFB
Goebel, David Maxwell career officer
Plyler, Conrad A. military officer
Sturgeon, Marty Roger career military officer

Omaha
Fowler, Stephen Eugene retired military officer, human resources executive
Marsh, Clayton Edward retired army officer, information systems specialist

OHIO

Beavercreek
Bouchard, Philippe Ovide *career officer*

Columbus
Garrison, Lawrence Duane *air force officer*
Smith, Alan Bronson, Jr. *military officer, farm executive*

Steubenville
Phillips, Ronda Jo *non-commissioned military officer*

Wright Patterson AFB
Kirkman, William H. *air force officer*

WISCONSIN

Madison
Slack, Jerald David *adjutant general of Wisconsin, civil engineer*

Racine
Kosobucki, John Edmund *career officer*

MILITARY ADDRESSES OF THE UNITED STATES

PACIFIC

APO
Moser, Gregg Anthony *career officer*

ADDRESS UNPUBLISHED

Beauchamp, Thomas Evan *retired military officer*
Fisher, Thomas Scott *career officer, broadcasting network operations officer*
Walz, Robert DeHaven *retired military officer, teacher*

RELIGION

UNITED STATES

ARIZONA

Oro Valley
Tinker, Robert Eugene *minister, educational consultant*

DISTRICT OF COLUMBIA

Washington
Hicks, Sherman Gregory *pastor*

ILLINOIS

Bartlett
Robinson, Jack F(ay) *clergyman*

Belleville
Wittenbrink, Boniface Leo *priest*

Bloomington
Dees, David P. *retired minister*
Gerike, Ernest Luther *clergyman*
Levin, Paul Joseph *evangelist*

Chicago
Anderson, Philip Vernon *pastor*
Barbour, Claude Marie *minister*
Berman, Howard Allen *rabbi*
Bernardin, Joseph Louis Cardinal *archbishop, university chancellor*
Betz, Hans Dieter *theology educator*
Black, Robert Durward *television producer*
Burhoe, Ralph Wendell *religion and science educator*
Burton, Laurel Arthur *educator, minister*
Butler, Steven King *pastor*
Duecker, Robert Sheldon *bishop*
French, William Cullen *theology educator*
Griswold, Frank Tracy, III *bishop*
Hefner, Philip James *theologian*
Howard, John Hazel, Jr. *pastor, counselor*
Hunt, John Stephen *inference reader, spiritual counselor*
James, Marie Moody *clergywoman, musician, vocal music educator*
Nelson, Paul Raymond *church executive, minister*
Nordquist, Sandralee Rahn *lay worker*
Novak, Francis Alphonsus *religious organization executive, priest*
Rowe, Donald Francis *priest, secondary educator, administrator*
Sagarin, James Leon *rabbi, author, editor*
Schupp, Ronald Irving *clergyman, civil rights leader*
Sherwin, Byron Lee *religion educator, college official*
Shumpert, Everett Drayden *minister*

Danville
Wren, Morris Lee *minister*

Darien
Sieracki, Aloysius Alfred *religious organization administrator*

Decatur
Porter, Darrell Carter *evangelist*

Deerfield
Russell, William Ray *clergyman*

Elgin
Ziegler, Earl Keller *minister*

Evanston
Chandler, Daniel Ross *religious studies educator, minister, writer*

Frankfort
Huff, John David *church administrator*

Geneva
Bakken, Howard Norman *music educator, church musician*

Jacksonville
Springsted, Eric Osmon *minister, philosophy and religion educator*

Kenilworth
Bowen, Gilbert Willard *minister*

Knoxville
Clark, Michel Desere *clergyman*

Lebanon
Stanley, Christopher Dennis *religious studies educator*

Lombard
Cosgrove, Charles Henry *theology educator*

Melrose Park
Zúñiga, José Guadalupe *minister*

Moline
Johnson, Mary Lou *lay worker*

Naperville
Landwehr, Arthur John *minister*

Oak Park
Gerson, Gary Stanford *rabbi*
Hallstrand, Sarah Laymon *denomination executive*

Palos Heights
Lin, Jimmy Tai-on *minister*

Peoria
Meyer, John Charles *religious studies educator*

Riverside
Marty, Martin Emil *religion educator, editor*

Rock Island
Swartz, Michael Allen *minister*

Rockford
Hasley, Ronald K. *bishop*

Springfield
Clingan, Donald Frank *retired clergyman*
Ryan, Daniel Leo *bishop*
Shotwell, Malcolm Green *minister*

Urbana
Hoffman, Valerie Jon *religion educator*
Swartz, Paul Frederick *clergyman*

Warrenville
Morris, Vincent Edwin *religious association administrator*

Wheaton
Deyneka, Peter, Jr. *religious organization executive*
Pappas, Barbara E. *Biblical studies educator, author*
Roth, Vanessa L. *religious organization administrator*

INDIANA

Anderson
Massey, James Earl *clergyman, educator*

Auburn
Haiflich, Stevan Richard *minister*

Bunker Hill
Granger, Philip Richard *minister*

Clarksville
Borton, Jerry Lee *head religious order*

Dillsboro
Hallett, Robert Steven *minister, church fund raising executive*

Elkhart
Roth, Willard Edward *clergyman*

Evansville
Hoy, George Philip *clergyman, food bank executive*

Fort Wayne
Bower, Michael L. *clergyman*
Fry, Charles George *theologian, educator*
Mann, David William *minister*
Mather, George Ross *clergy member*
Olson, Keith Raymond *clergyman*

Greencastle
Batto, Bernard Frank *religious studies educator*
Lamar, Martha Lee *chaplain*

Greenwood
Duewel, Wesley Luelf *religious organization executive*

Highland
Willhoit, Jim *minister*

Huntington
Seilhamer, Ray A. *bishop*

Indianapolis
Bates, Gerald Earl *bishop*
Brannon, Ronald Roy *minister*
Castle, Howard Blaine *religious organization administrator*
Cherry, C. Conrad *religious studies educator, author*
Kempski, Ralph Aloisius *bishop*
Plaster, George Francis *Roman Catholic priest*

Kokomo
Ungerer, Walter John *minister*

Notre Dame
Malloy, Edward Aloysius *priest, university administrator, educator*
White, James Floyd *theology educator*

Petersburg
McKown, Leslie Henry *minister*

Plainfield
Hay, John Franklin *church administrator*

Rochester
Merrill, Arthur Lewis *retired theology educator*

Veedersburg
Marshall, Carolyn Ann M. *church official, consultant*

Warsaw
Boggs, John Robert, Jr. *minister, writer*

Winona Lake
Anders, Max Eugene *author, speaker*

IOWA

Amana
Setzer, Kirk *religious leader*

Centerville
Strube, Christopher William *pastor*

Davenport
McCart, Marian Longacre *minister*
McDaniel, George William *priest*
O'Keefe, Gerald Francis *bishop, retired*

Des Moines
Epting, C. Christopher *bishop*

Dubuque
Hanus, Jerome *archbishop*

Iowa City
Bozeman, Theodore D. *religion educator*

West Des Moines
Holderness, Susan Rutherford *religious organization administrator, at-risk educator*

KANSAS

Augusta
Box, Robert Allen *minister*

Garden City
Garrione, Robert Michael *clergy member*
Sharp, Charles Eugene *minister*

Goodland
Ross, Chester Wheeler *retired clergyman, consultant*

Hutchinson
Cowell, Bill *minister*

Kansas City
Wheeler, David Lee *theology educator*

Leavenworth
Buselt, Clara Irene *religious organization administrator*

Olathe
Mixer, Ronald Wayne *minister*

Prairie Village
LeMert, Harold Warner, Jr. *minister*

Shawnee Mission
Haggard, Forrest Deloss *minister*
Olsen, Stanley Severn *minister*

Topeka
Cowling, Randal Keith *minister*
Johnson, Ian Bruce *minister, legal assistant*

Wichita
Armstrong, Hart Reid *minister, editor, publisher*
Eastburn, Jeannette Rose *religious publishing executive*

MARYLAND

Perryville
Fischer, James Adrian *clergyman*

MICHIGAN

Adrian
Boley, Robert William *clergyman, educator*

Ann Arbor
Cambers, Philip William *music minister, music educator, pastor*
Hess, Bartlett Leonard *clergyman*

Berrien Springs
Andreasen, Niels-Erik Albinus *religious educator*
Johnston, Robert Morris *religious studies educator*
Mattingly, Keith Edward *clergyman, educator*

Clarkston
Keough, James Gillman, Jr. *minister*

Dearborn
Priest, Ruth Emily *music minister, choir director, composer arranger*

Detroit
Maida, Adam Joseph *cardinal*
Mc Gehee, H(arry) Coleman, Jr. *bishop*
Murray, David *pastor, social worker*
Pittelko, Roger Dean *clergyman*

East Lansing
Graham, William Fred *religious studies educator*
Shaw, Robert Eugene *minister, administrator*

Flint
Bettendorf, James Bernard *minister, church association administrator*
McClanahan, Connie Dea *pastoral minister*
Meissner, Suzanne Banks *pastoral associate*

Fort Gratiot
Salt, Alfred Lewis *priest*

Gaylord
Cooney, Patrick Ronald *bishop*
Harwood, Jon Carl *minister*

Grand Rapids
Babcock, Wendell Keith *religion educator*
Bolt, John *theology educator*
Hofman, Leonard John *minister*

Grass Lake
Popp, Nathaniel *bishop*

Holland
Hesselink, I(ra) John, Jr. *theology educator*

Kalamazoo
Falk, Nancy Ellen Auer *religion educator*

Lansing
Dinolfo, Paul Carmen *religious organization administrator*
Wozencraft, Sharon Anne *minister*

Livonia
Haggard, Joan Claire *church musician, piano instructor, accompanist*
Hess, Margaret Johnston *religious writer, educator*

Marquette
Skogman, Dale R. *bishop*

Midland
Clarkson, William Morris *children's pastor*

Montague
Sirotko, Theodore Francis *priest, retired military officer*

Pinckney
Hernandez, Ramon Robert *clergyman, librarian*

Redford
Slowinski, Thomas Frank *priest*

Southgate
Walker, Billy Cummins *minister, evangelist*

Traverse City
Burton, Betty June *minister, pastor*

Vassar
Lindner, Scott-Eric *minister*

MINNESOTA

Alexandria
Hultstrand, Donald Maynard *bishop*

Anoka
Mattsson-Boze, Daniel Winston *missionary*

Austin
Alcorn, Wallace Arthur *minister*

Bloomington
Brokke, Catherine Juliet *mission executive*

Brooklyn Center
Payne, Homer Lemuel *retired religious institution administrator*

Collegeville
Wagner, Mary Anthony *theology educator, writer, editor*

Crookston
Stadtfeld, Richard Louis *church administrator*

Elk River
Ebner, Frank Henry *chaplain*

Elysian
Jibben, Jeffrey John *minister*

Glencoe
Van Gorp, Gary Wayne *clergyman*

Golden Valley
Sortland, Allan Berdette *pastor*

Houston
Culver, Robert Duncan *religious educator*

Little Falls
Zirbes, Mary Kenneth *social justice ministry coordinator*

Minneapolis
Anderson, Robert Marshall *bishop*
Bare, James Randolph *minister*
Brown, Laurence David *retired bishop*
Cedar, Paul Arnold *church executive, minister*
Ferm, Lois Roughan *religious organization administrator*
Miller, William Alvin *clergyman, author*
Olson, David Wendell *bishop*

Minnetonka
Parker, Robert Chauncey Humphrey *clergyman, publishing executive, psychic*

New Ulm
Lucker, Raymond Alphonse *bishop*

Park Rapids
Bervig, V. Arleen Haaland *clergyperson, music teacher*

Rochester
Nycklemoe, Glenn Winston *bishop*

Saint Paul
Jaberg, Eugene Carl *theology educator, administrator*
Penchansky, David *religious studies educator*
Roach, John Robert *retired archbishop*

Saint Peter
Bunge, Marcia JoAnn *religious studies educator*

Sherburn
Schaffer, Harwood David *minister*

Stillwater
Hagstrom, Alan John *religious association administrator*

Willmar
Crute, Beverly Jean *minister*

Winona
Dill, Ellen Renée *minister*

Woodbury
Zabel, Lyndon Roy *minister*

MISSOURI

Ballwin
Ackerson, Charles Stanley *minister, social worker*

Branson West
Todd, Cecil William *ministry director*

Bridgeton
Asma, Lawrence Francis *priest*

Chesterfield
Heathcock, John Edwin *clergyman*

Clayton
Splinter, John Paul *clergy member, minister*

Dittmer
Miller, Bertin *priest, social administrator*

Hannibal
Bergen, Martha Steagall *religious educator*

Hazelwood
Sciscoe, Jason William *clergy member*

Jefferson City
Kelley, Patrick Michael *minister, state legislator*
Wazir, Tadar Jihad *chaplain, small business owner*

Kansas City
Boland, Raymond James *bishop*
Bredeck, Martin James *clergyman, theology educator*
Johnson, Robert Edward *theology educator*
Juarez, Martin *priest*
Morgan, Dennis Brent *minister, psychologist*
Palmer, Gary Charles *university lecturer*
Vogel, Arthur Anton *clergyman*
Whitney, Donald Stephen *pastor, writer*

Laddonia
Scheffler, Lewis Francis *pastor, educator, research scientist*

Perryville
Shelby, Charles Francis *priest, fundraising executive*

Saint Joseph
Mockabee, M(arion) Eugene *minister*

Saint Louis
Anderson, Vinton Randolph *bishop*
Bennett, Renée Hotard *theology educator*
Berg, Jean Stewart *consultant*
Doggett, John Nelson, Jr. *clergyman*
Gaulke, Earl H. *religious publisher and editor, clergyman*
Nafzger, Samuel Henry *pastor*
Nance, Earl Edward, Jr. *clergyman, educational administrator*
Prenzlow, Elmer John-Charles, Jr. *minister*
Tolliver, David Joseph *clergyman*
Voelz, James William *theology educator, pastor*
Weber, Gloria Richie *minister, retired state representative*

Springfield
Frey, Neal *religious educator*
Grams, Betty Jane *minister, educator, writer*

Sugar Creek
Rhodes, Oran Wayne *religious educator*

West Alton
Bottens, Ronald Gene *minister*

NEBRASKA

Grand Island
Zichek, Melvin Eddie *retired clergyman, educator*

Lincoln
Davis, Daniel Joseph, Sr. *religious organization executive, pastor*
Leach, Norman Edward *minister*

Omaha
Gnirk, Lloyd Allen *clergyman, educational administrator*
Hofer, Lonnie Joe *evangelist*
Norwich McLennan, Jamie Lou *clergywoman, writer*
Zuerlein, Damian Joseph *priest*

Ord
Peterson, John Edward *minister*

NORTH DAKOTA

Bismarck
Lardy, Sister Susan Marie *prioress*

Fargo
Foss, Richard John *bishop*
Helgeland, John Allen *religion educator*

Minot
Yarger, LeRoy Allen *minister*

OHIO

Ashland
Watson, JoAnn Ford *theology educator*

Athens
Wellman, Billy Lee *pastor*

Bluffton
Naylor, Ruth Eileen Bundy *clergyperson*

Canton
Boulton, Edwin Charles *retired bishop*
Watson, Duane Frederick *religious studies educator*

Chagrin Falls
Pickett, Arthur William, Jr. *minister*

Chesterland
Ruble, Bernard Roy *minister, labor relations consultant*

Cincinnati
Anderson, Joan Balyeat *religion educator, minister*
Linsey, Nathaniel L. *bishop*
Pilarczyk, Daniel Edward *archbishop*

Cleveland
Abrams, Sylvia Fleck *religious studies educator*
Knull, Erhard *minister*
Olcott, Thomas W. *clergyman*
Sherry, Paul Henry *minister, religious organization administrator*

Dayton
Griffin, Paul R. *religious studies educator*
Pyle, Paul William *religious studies educator*
Tilley, Terrence William *religious studies educator*

Delaware
Tannehill, Robert Cooper *theology educator*
Twesigye, Emmanuel Kalenzi *theology educator, clergy member*

Dublin
Baker, Mary Evelyn *church librarian, retired academic librarian*

Gambier
Rhodes, Royal William *religion educator*

Jackson
Hilfiger, Gary William *clergyman*

Kettering
Nuzzi, Ronald James *priest, educator*

Mansfield
Allison, Dennis Ray *minister*

New Albany
Brown, Michael Richard *minister*

Newcomerstown
George, Gary Mark *pastor*

Oxford
Williams, Peter William *religion educator*

Parma
Moskal, Robert M. *bishop*

Sandusky
Maher, Terry Marina *religious organization administrator*

Steubenville
Rushmore, Louis Everette *evangelist*

Struthers
Sugden, Richard Lee *pastor*

Toledo
White, Polly Sears *religious organization administrator*

Worthington
Craig, Judith *bishop*

Youngstown
Corbin, Brian Roland *religious human services administrator*

PENNSYLVANIA

Mechanicsburg
Schmid, Thomas Henderson *clergyman*

SOUTH DAKOTA

Florence
Waite, Robert Allan *clergyman*

Sioux Falls
Cowles, Ronald Eugene *church administrator*
Dudley, Paul V. *bishop*

Watertown
Witcher, Gary Royal *minister, educator*

TEXAS

Austin
Worthing, Carol Marie *minister*

WISCONSIN

Eau Claire
Wantland, William Charles *bishop, lawyer*

Green Bay
Geisendorfer, James Vernon *author*

La Crosse
Paul, John Joseph *bishop*

Ladysmith
Swansen, Anita C. *educator*

Manitowoc
Plank, William Brandt *minister*

Middleton
McDermott, Molly *lay minister*

Milwaukee
Braun, Warren D. *church administrator, social activist*
Enright-Sidney, Catherine *chaplin*
Hirsch, June Schaut *chaplain*
Kolanko, John Raymond *priest*
Lifschutz, Emanuel Lewis *clergy member*
Radke, Dale Lee *religious organization administrator, deacon, editor, pastor*
Weakland, Rembert G. *archbishop*

Waupun
Bausch, Michael George *clergyman*

CANADA

MANITOBA

Churchill
Rouleau, Reynald *bishop*

Saint Boniface
Hacault, Antoine Joseph Leon *archbishop*

The Pas
Sutton, Peter Alfred *archbishop*

Winnipeg
Hermaniuk, Maxim *retired archbishop*

ONTARIO

Kitchener
Huras, William David *bishop*

London
Sherlock, John Michael *bishop*

Saint Catharines
O'Mara, John Aloysius *bishop*

Timmins
Cazabon, Gilles *bishop*

Waterloo
Grimes, Ronald L. *religion educator*

Windsor
Whitney, Barry Lyn *religious studies educator*

NAMIBIA

Ondangwa
Haertel, Charles Wayne *minister*

ADDRESS UNPUBLISHED

Barker, Verlyn Lloyd *retired minister, educator*
Barnes, Rosemary Lois *minister*
Carlson, Guy Raymond *retired minister, religious organization administrator*
Cascino, Donna Kay *religious organization administrator*
Chilstrom, Herbert Walfred *bishop*
Christopher, Sharon A. Brown *bishop*
Eitrheim, Norman Duane *bishop*
Griffin, James Anthony *bishop*
Handy, William Talbot, Jr. *bishop*
Hansen, Wendell Jay *clergyman, gospel broadcaster*
Hill, Paul Mark *clergyman*
Holle, Reginald Henry *retired bishop*
Jewel, Julie Stephanie *clergy member, minister*
John, K. K. (John Kuruvilla Kaiyalethe) *minister*
Johnson, Jeffrey Ferrell *pastor*
Jones, William Augustus, Jr. *retired bishop*
Kucera, Daniel William *retired bishop*
Lee, Mordecai *religious agency administrator*
Lucas, Bert Albert *pastor, social services administator, consultant*
Malewski, Jennifer Jean *clergy member*
Malone, James William *retired bishop*
Marshall, Peter E. *pastor*
Melvin, Billy Alfred *clergyman*
Mischke, Carl Herbert *religious association executive, retired*
Nottingham, William Jesse *church mission executive, minister*
Nygren, E(llis) Herbert *theology educator*
Povish, Kenneth Joseph *retired bishop*
Rose, Robert John *bishop*
Shultz, Retha Mills *retired missionary*
Sisco, Roger D. *minister, marriage and family therapist*
Smalley, William Edward *bishop*
Tanquary, Oliver Leo *minister*
Walker, Donald Robert, Jr. *minister*

SCIENCE: LIFE SCIENCE

UNITED STATES

DISTRICT OF COLUMBIA

Washington
Moss, Thomas Henry *science association administrator*

ILLINOIS

Belleville
Steffen, Alan Leslie *entomologist*

Bridgeview
Frampton, Elon Wilson *microbiologist*

Brookfield
Pawley, Ray Lynn *zoological park herpetology curator*
Rabb, George Bernard *zoologist*

Carbondale
Brandon, Ronald Arthur *zoology educator*
Burr, Brooks Milo *zoology educator*
Middleton, Beth Ann *wetland ecology educator*
Minckler, Leon Sherwood *forestry and conservation educator, author*

Champaign
Ridlen, Samuel Franklin *agriculture educator*
Thurber, Dale King *ornithologist, ecologist and wildlife biologist*
Warren, Steven Dean *ecologist, researcher*

Charleston
Brewer, Paul Alan *biologist*

Chicago
Brodie, Mark Stanley *electrophysiologist, pharmacologist*
Cohn, Stanley Alan *cell biology educator*
Dhaliwal, Amrik Singh *biology educator*
Fuchs, Elaine V. *molecular biologist, educator*
Fukui, Yoshio *biology educator*
Hershkovitz, Philip *zoologist*
Holland, Louis Edward, II *virologist*
Klegerman, Melvin Earl *microbiologist, educator*
Longnecker, Richard Mayne *molecular virologist*
Miller, Patrick William *research administrator, educator*
Ritter, Mary Catherine *research scientist*
Roizman, Bernard *virologist, educator*
Straus, Helen Lorna Puttkammer *biologist, educator*
Taylor, Connie Maria *science educator*
Zhao, Yuqi *molecular geneticist, educator*

Danville
Campbell, Marilyn F. *association executive, author*
Craig, Hurshel Eugene *agronomist*

De Kalb
Waters, Gary L. *poultry scientist*

Decatur
Harris, Donald Wayne *research scientist*

Des Plaines
Lee, Bernard Shing-Shu *research company executive*

Dundee
Burger, George Vanderkarr *wildlife ecologist, researcher*

Edwardsville
Brugam, Richard Blair *biology educator*

Evanston
Altkorn, Robert Ira *research scientist*
Chiou, Wen-An *science educator, researcher*
Menco, Bernard *biologist*
Ruggero, Mario Alfredo *physiologist, educator*

Great Lakes
Simonson, Lloyd Grant *microbiologist*

Harvey
Liem, Khian Kioe *medical entomologist*

Havana
Sparks, Richard Edward *aquatic ecologist*

Lemont
Schlenker, Robert Alison *environment, safety and health administrator*

Libertyville
Munson, Norma Frances *biologist, ecologist, nutritionist, educator*

Lisle
Davis, Gregory Thomas *marine surveyor*
Ware, George Henry *botanist*

Lombard
Velardo, Joseph Thomas *molecular biology and endocrinology educator*

Moline
Martin, Dorothy Regina *biology educator*
Thomas, Jeanette Anne *biology educator*

Mundelein
Ma, Jianneng *microbiologist, researcher*
Newman, Linnaea Rose *horticulturist*

Normal
Corbett, Gail Ann *plant ecologist, educator*

North Chicago
Mandecki, Wlodek *molecular biologist*

Northbrook
Glabe, Elmer Frederick *food scientist*

Oak Park
Walter, James Smiley *physiologist, researcher*

Park Forest
Brandon, Calvin Cornelius *biology educator*

Peoria
Wicklow, Donald Thomas *mycologist*

Rock Island
Dziadyk, Bohdan *botany and ecology educator*

Round Lake
Burhop, Kenneth Eugene *physiologist, researcher*

Schaumburg
Parker, Norman W. *chief corporate scientist*

Skokie
Arieti, David Franklin *environmental scientist, educator*

Springfield
Henebry, Michael Stevens *toxicologist*
Kleen, Vernon Melvin *avian ecologist*

Stonington
Garwood, Douglas Leon *agricultural scientist*

Urbana
Dziuk, Philip John *animal scientist educator*
Feng, Albert S. *science educator, researcher*
Greenough, William Tallant *psychobiologist, educator*
Hixon, James Edward *physiology educator*
Horwitz, Alan Fredrick *cell and molecular biology educator and researcher*
Mustain, Brian Clark *plant consultant*
Nanney, David Ledbetter *genetics educator*
Rolfe, Gary Lavelle *forestry educator*
Sonka, Steven T. *agricultural economics educator, consultant*
Spahr, Sidney Louis *agricultural research and education*
Whitt, Dixie Dailey *microbiology educator*
Wolfe, Ralph Stoner *microbiology educator*

Watseka
Neumann, Frederick Lloyd *plant breeder*

INDIANA

Bloomington
Andersen, Hans Oliver *science and environmental education educator*
DeVoe, Robert Donald *visual physiologist*
Hammel, Harold Theodore *physiology and biophysics educator, researcher*

Chesterton
Wiemann, Marion Russell, Jr. (Baron of Camster) *biologist, microscopist*

Evansville
Brenneman, James Alden *biology educator*

Goshen
Jacobs, Merle Emmor *zoology educator, researcher*

Greensburg
Ricke, David Louis *agricultural and environmental consultant*

Henryville
Stump, Donald Wayne *forester, real estate broker*

Hobart
Seeley, Mark *agronomist*

Indianapolis
Daily, William Allen *retired microbiologist*
Durflinger, Elizabeth Ward *retired zoology educator and university dean*
Hodes, Marion Edward *genetics educator, physician*
Maass-Moreno, Roberto *physiologist, educator, engineer.*
Rothe, Carl Frederick *physiologist, biomedical engineer*
Waltz, Robert Dean *entomologist, state agency administrator*

Lafayette
Achgill, Ralph Kenneth *retired research scientist*
Eads, Thomas Martin *food scientist educator*

Morgantown
Bradway, Keith Emerson *research scientist, retired*

Muncie
Chandler, Paul Michael *ethnoecologist*
Gadziola, Jean Zeun *microbiologist, database coordinator*
Henzlik, Raymond Eugene *zoophysiologist, educator*

New Albany
Baker, Claude Douglas *biology educator, researcher*

Notre Dame
Fraser, Malcolm James, Jr. *biological sciences educator*
Lamberti, Gary Anthony *biology educator*

South Bend
McLinden, James Hugh *molecular biologist*

Tipton
Hoffbeck, Loren John *research agronomist*

West Lafayette
Chaney, William Reynolds *forestry and natural resources educator*
Goodwin, Stephen Bruce *plant pathologist*
Goonewardene, Hilary Felix *retired entomology professor, consultant*
Huber, Don Morgan *plant pathologist, educator*
Hunt, Michael O'Leary *wood science and engineering educator*
Le Master, Dennis Clyde *forest economics and policy educator*
Loesch-Fries, Loretta Sue *virology educator*
Norton, Lloyd Darrell *research soil scientist*
Pak, William Louis *biologist, researcher, educator*
Sharma, Hari Chand *geneticist, researcher*
White, Joe Lloyd *soil scientist, educator*

IOWA

Ames
Anderson, Lloyd Lee *animal science educator*
Bremner, John McColl *agronomy and biochemistry educator*
Brenner, David McCaskie *botanist*
Hatfield, Jerry Lee *plant physiologist, biometeorologist*
Imsande, John David *geneticist, researcher, educator*
Karlen, Douglas Lawrence *soil scientist*
Keeney, Dennis Raymond *soil science educator*
Mertins, James Walter *entomologist*
Paau, Alan Shiukee *industrial microbiologist, administrator*
Swan, James Byron *agronomy educator, soil scientist*
Swenson, Ruth Wildman *cell biologist, educator*
Youngs, Curtis R. *animal science educator*

Boone
Tanner, Richard Thomas *environmental studies educator*

Cambridge
Frederick, Lloyd Randall *soil microbiologist*

Cedar Falls
Wilson, Nixon Albert *biologist, educator*

Cedar Rapids
Dvorak, Clarence Allen *microbiologist*

Eldora
Kerns, Steve *geneticist*

Grinnell
Campbell, David George *ecologist, researcher*
Hatcher, Edward Luverne *agriculturalist*

Iowa City
Milkman, Roger Dawson *genetics educator, molecular evolution researcher*
Wagner, Brett Alan *biologist*

Storm Lake
Klepper, Robert Rush *plant physiologist*

Waterloo
Kimm, Robert George *animal science educator*

Webster City
Ivers, Drew Russell *geneticist, plant breeder*

West Union
Roath, William Wesley *retired research agronomist*

KANSAS

Emporia
Schrock, John Richard *biology educator*

Garden City
Sloderbeck, Phillip Eugene *entomologist*
Witt, Merle Dean *agronomist*

Kansas City
Cardozo, Luis Eduardo *physiologist*

Kiowa
Conrad, Melvin Louis *biology educator*

Lawrence
Armitage, Kenneth Barclay *biology educator, ecologist*
Byers, George William *retired entomology educator*
Lane, Meredith Anne *botany educator, museum curator*
Lichtwardt, Robert William *mycologist*
Shankel, Delbert Merrill *microbiology and biology educator*

Manhattan
Davis, Linda Wiles *biology educator*
Ham, George Eldon *soil microbiologist, educator*
Hart, Renee Ann *food microbiologist, researcher*
Havlin, John Leroy *soil scientist, educator*
Kaufman, Donald Wayne *research ecologist*
Kaufman, Glennis Ann *research ecologist, biologist, educator*
Robel, Robert Joseph *environmental biology educator*
Wright, Emmett Lee *science educator*

Newton
Platt, Dwight Rich *biology educator*
Schmidt, Richard Heinrich *taxidermist, educator*

Topeka
Boyer, Don Raymond *biology educator*
Karr, Gerald Lee *agricultural economist, state senator*

MICHIGAN

Albion
Stowell, Ewell Addison *botany educator, forestry consultant*

Alpena
Davis, Jefferson Bates *microbiologist, consultant*

Ann Arbor
Cantrall, Irving J(ames) *entomologist, educator*
Hawkins, Joseph Elmer, Jr. *retired acoustic physiologist, educator*
Kerppola, Tom Klaus William *research scientist, educator*
Landrum, Peter Franklin *environmental toxicologist*
Lowe, John Burton *molecular biology educator, pathologist*
Martin, Michael McCulloch *biology and chemistry educator*
Miller, Robert Rush *retired biology educator*
Neidhardt, Frederick Carl *microbiologist*
Richardson, Rudy James *toxicology and neurosciences educator*
Saunders, Thomas Lee *molecular biologist*
Savageau, Michael Antonio *microbiology and immunology educator*
Stoermer, Eugene Filmore *biologist, educator*
Whitehouse, Frank, Jr. *microbiologist*

Big Rapids
Murnik, Mary Rengo *biology educator*

Dearborn
Heady, Judith Emily *biology educator*
Narula, Chaitanya Kumar *research scientist*

Detroit
Bhalla, Deepak Kumar *cell biologist, toxicologist, educator*
Gala, Richard Robert *physiology educator*
Graves, James Francis *microbiologist, educator*
Krawetz, Stephen Andrew *molecular biology and genetics educator*
Lerner, Stephen Alexander *microbiologist, physician, educator*

East Lansing
Barman, Susan Marie *physiologist*
Epperson, Bryan Keith *geneticist, educator*
Fried, Jeremy Steven *forester, educator*
Knobloch, Irving William *author, retired biology educator*
Taggart, Ralph Enos *botany and geology educator*
Trosko, James Edward *research radiation geneticist*
Wehling, Wayne F. *entomologist*

Farmington Hills
Dragun, James *soil chemist*

Grand Rapids
Petkus, Alan Francis *microbiologist*

Highland Park
Crittenden, Mary Lynne *science educator*

Houghton
Peterson, Rolf Olin *ecology educator*

Kalamazoo
Kominek, Leo Aloysius *retired microbiologist, psychologist*
Tsai, Ti-Dao *electrophysiologist*
Wood, Linda Susan *molecular biologist, researcher*

Lansing
Carlotti, Ronald John *food scientist*
Hull, Christopher Neil *state agency biologist*
Parlor, Karen Wettlin *microbiologist*

Manchester
Murray, Betty Jean Kafka *plant physiologist, researcher*

Marquette
Riipi, Linda Ruth *biology educator*

Midland
Davidson, John Hunter *agriculturist*
Morgan, Roger John *research scientist*

Mount Pleasant
Novitski, Charles Edward *biology educator*

Okemos
Chou, Ching-Chung *physiology and medical educator*

Saginaw
Faubel, Gerald Lee *agronomist, golf course superintendent*

University Center
Pelzer, Charles Francis *molecular geneticist, biology educator, cancer researcher*

MINNESOTA

Bemidji
Boertje, Stanley Benjamin *retired zoology educator*

Falcon Heights
Aiken, Roger George *energy systems research analyst, educator*

Mapleton
John, Hugo Herman *natural resources educator*

Minneapolis
Evans, Robert Leonard *mathematical physiologist, educator*
Gorham, Eville *ecologist, biogeochemist*
Gudmundson, Barbara Rohrke *ecologist*
Gusek, Todd Walter *food scientist*
Huang, Victor Tsangmin *food scientist, researcher*
Moore, Marjorie Ann *physical therapist educator*
Sammak, Paul Joseph *cell biologist, pharmacologist*
Scott, Rebecca Andrews *biology educator*
Serstock, Doris Shay *retired microbiologist, educator, civic worker*
Shecterle, Linda Marie *biologist*
Sothern, Robert B. *chronobiologist*

Moorhead
Gee, Robert LeRoy *agriculturist, dairy farmer*

Park Rapids
Tonn, Robert James *entomologist*

Roseville
Thompson, Roy Lloyd *agronomist*

Saint Cloud
Kirick, Daniel John *agronomist*

Saint Louis Park
Frestedt, Joy Louise *cytogeneticist and molecular biologist*

Saint Paul
Bowyer, James Louis *forester educator*
Bushnell, William Rodgers *agricultural research scientist*
Chiang, Huai Chang *entomologist, educator*
Dienhart, Charlotte Marie *retired anatomy and cell biology educator*
Elling, Laddie Joe *agronomist, educator*
Emeagwali, Dale Brown *molecular biologist*
Heuer, Marvin Arthur *research and industry consultant*
Hueg, William Frederick *agronomy educator, dairy owner*
Kommedahl, Thor *plant pathology educator*
Munson, Robert Dean *agronomist, soil scientist*
Newman, Raymond Melvin *biologist, educator*
Roy, Robert Russell *toxicologist*
Rubenstein, Irwin *molecular biologist, educator*
Stadelmann, Eduard Joseph *plant physiologist, educator*
Wendt, Hans W(erner) *life scientist, educator*
White, Michael Ernest *animal scientist*
Zeyen, Richard John *plant pathology educator*

Winona
Essar, David William *biology professor*

MISSOURI

Columbia
Blevins, Dale Glenn *agronomy educator*
Brown, Olen Ray *medical microbiology research educator*
Buchanan, Bryant W. *research biologist*
Donald, William Waldie *agronomist*
Novacky, Anton Jan *plant pathologist, educator*
Wildhaber, Mark Lee *fish ecologist, ecotoxicologist*

Greenwood
Klaus, Suzanne Lynne *horticulturist, production specialist*

Hazelwood
Hemming, Bruce Clark *microbiologist*

Jefferson City
Bachant, Joseph Peter *biologist*
Kuebler, Barbara Campbell *science educator*

Kansas City
Hagsten, Ib *animal scientist, educator*
Stern, Daniel Henry *ecologist*

Maryville
Fairchild, Johanne Windle *biology and horticulture educator*

Puxico
Fredrickson, Leigh Harry *wetland ecologist, educator*

Saint Joseph
Ellis, William Ray *soil scientist, agronomist researcher*

Saint Louis
Bird, Matthew Alexius *horticulturist, consultant*
Bolla, Robert Irving *biology educator*
Croat, Thomas Bernard *botanical curator*
Curran, Michael Walter *management scientist*
De Buhr, Larry Eugene *director of education botanical gardens*
Diener, Jean Brock *science educator, author*
Feir, Dorothy Jean *entomologist, physiologist, educator*
Graham, Donald James *food technologist*
Hoessle, Charles Herman *zoo director*
Kohl, Daniel Howard *plant biologist*
Liu, Maw-Shung *physiologist, dentist*
Osdoby, Philip Arnold *biologist, educator*
Whittemore, Alan Thomas *plant taxonomist*
Zhuo, Min *neurobiology educator*

Springfield
Bond, Lora *retired biology educator*

Union
Murrie, William Stephen *science educator*

Windyville
Condron, Barbara O'Guinn *metaphysics educator, school administrator, publisher*

NEBRASKA

Gering
Weihing, John Lawson *plant pathologist, state senator*

Lincoln
Cordes, Sam Meade *agricultural economist*
Dickerson, Gordon Edwin *animal geneticist, biologist*
Genoways, Hugh Howard *systematic biologist, educator*
Leininger, Lester Norman *agronomist, consultant*
Massengale, Martin Andrew *agronomist, university president*

Omaha
Andrews, Richard Vincent *physiologist, educator*
Fawcett, James Davidson *herpetologist, educator*

NEW JERSEY

Camden
Thomas, Terra L. *human services institute executive, psychologist*

NORTH DAKOTA

Fargo
Cross, Harold Zane *agronomist, educator*
Scoby, Donald R. *environmental biologist*
Smith, Glenn Sanborn *plant breeder, university administrator*
Terbizan, Donna Jean *physiology educator*

Lisbon
Taylor, Ardis *science educator*

OHIO

Ada
Hoagstrom, Carl William *biology educator*

Ashland
Rueger, Daniel Scott *horticulture educator*

Ashtabula
Lane, Roger Lee *zoology educator, researcher*

Cincinnati
Gonzalez, Sister Paula *futurist, educator, environmentalist*
LaBarbera, Andrew Richard *reproductive biologist*
Loper, John Carey *molecular genetics and environmental toxicology, research scientist, educator*
Morelli-Schroth, Paula A. *biologist*
Rubin, David C. *biology educator, association administrator*
Saal, Howard Max *clinical geneticist, pediatrician, educator*
Wang, Richard Liqun *molecular biologist*

Cleveland
Brummet, Shauna Renea *molecular biologist*
Gwatkin, Ralph Buchanan Lloyd *biologist*

Columbus
Cohen, Robert Alan *agricultural administrator, educator*
Conway, Tyrrell *molecular microbiologist*
Culver, David Alan *aquatic ecology educator*
Long, John Frederick *veterinary pathobiology educator*
Menkedick, John Richard *research scientist*
Widell, Larry Richard *plant ecologist*

Dayton
Bigley, Nancy Jane *microbiology educator*
Byczkowski, Janusz Zbigniew *toxicologist*
Runkle, James Reade *ecology educator, researcher*

Dublin
Toomey, John Christopher *biologist, research scientist*

East Liverpool
Fowler, Elizabeth Ann *occupational therapist*

Kent
Cooperrider, Tom Smith *botanist*
Dutta, Hirian Moyee *biologist, educator*

Laurelville
Knoop, Paul Eugene, Jr. *naturalist, educator*

Mansfield
Bradley, Joan Ellen *biology educator*

Newark
Greenstein, Julius Sidney *zoology educator*
Owen, Ferris Sydney *farmer, international development administrator*

Oxford
Francko, David Alex *botany educator, administrator, researcher*
Haley-Oliphant, Ann Elizabeth *science educator*
Miller, Harvey Alfred *botanist, educator*
Risser, Paul Gillan *botanist, academic administrator*
Woodworth, Mary Esther *microbiology educator, consultant*

Painesville
Treichel, Mary Jane *mathematics and science educator*

Pepper Pike
Sunshine, Irving *toxicologist*

Reynoldsburg
Richardson, Deanna Ruth *microbiologist*

Rootstown
Docherty, John Joseph *microbiologist*

Springfield
Bank, Harvey L. *biologist*
Hobbs, Horton Holcombe, III *biology educator*
Ryu, Kyoo-Hai Lee *physiologist*

Tiffin
Heikes, Keith *science administrator*

Toledo
Mayfield, Harold Ford *biology educator*
Thomas, Lewis Edward *laboratory executive, retired petroleum company executive*

West Chester
Geis, Philip Anthony *microbiologist*

Westerville
Lorenz, Richard Carl *biologist*

Wilberforce
Okunade, Samuel Adekunle *science educator*
Pickering, Ed Richard *biology educator*

Wooster
Herr, Leonard Jay *plant pathologist*
Rings, Roy Wilson *entomologist, consultant*
Van Keuren, Robert Wilford *retired agronomy educator, researcher*

SOUTH DAKOTA

Clear Lake
Begalka, Timothy Paul *horticulturist*

TENNESSEE

Maryville
Hall, Marion Trufant *botany educator, arboretum director*

WISCONSIN

Appleton
Anjur, Sowmya Sriram *research scientist, educator*

Ashland
Verch, Richard Lee *biology educator*

Bayfield
Gallinat, Michael Paul *fisheries biologist*

Brown Deer
Bennett, William Neal *forensic toxicologist, researcher*

Fond Du Lac
Hayes, Elizabeth Lamb *biology educaotr*

Kewaunee
Keneklis, Theodore Peter *research scientist, trainer*

La Crosse
Dooley, J. Gordon *food scientist*

Madison
Barnes, Robert F. *agronomist*
Cassens, Robert Gene *food scientist*
Clifton, Kelly Hardenbrook *biology educator*
Daie, Jaleh *researcher, science educator, academic administrator*
Evert, Ray Franklin *botany educator*
Graham, James Miller *physiology researcher*
Greenspan, Daniel S. *molecular biologist*
Hearn, John Patrick *biologist, educator*
Jeffries, Thomas William *microbiologist*
Oaks, John Adams *cell biologist, parasitologist*
Ris, Hans *zoologist, educator*
Schatten, Gerald Phillip *cell biologist, reproductive biologist, educator*
Schatz, Paul Frederick *laboratory director*
Sunde, Milton Lester *retired poultry science educator*
Zerbe, John Irwin *forest products technologist, researcher*

Milwaukee
Bast, Rose Ann *biology educator*
Cairney, Kathryn Jane *economic development specialist*
Risch, Richard William *horticultural manager*
Salamun, Peter J(oseph) *botanist, consultant*
Saryan, Leon Aram *biochemical toxicologist*

Muskego
Gillespie, JoAnn Marie *ecologist, educator*

Neenah
Proctor, Nick Hobert *toxicologist, pharmacologist*

Platteville
Duewer, Raymond *horticulturist*

Rhinelander
Dickson, Richard Eugene *plant physiologist*

Richland Center
Scholl, Jesse Myron *retired agronomy educator*

Ripon
Light, Douglas Bruce *biologist, educator*

River Falls
Hustig, Charles Harold *scientific administrator*

Sheboygan
Marr, Kathleen Mary *biologist, educator*

Stevens Point
Bowers, Frank Dana *botany educator*
Boyce, Mark Stephen *ecology educator*

CANADA

MANITOBA

Winnipeg
Saunders, John Kenneth *research scientist*
Sinha, Ranendra Nath *ecologist, stress management consultant*

ADDRESS UNPUBLISHED

Argabright, Melvin Scott *retired conservation agronomist*
Bird, Thomas Joseph *retired microbiologist, environmental consultant*
Blomberg, Goran Ernst Daniel *biologist*
Burdett, Barbra Elaine *biology educator*
DeRoo, Sally A. *biology and geology educator*
Deslauriers, Marie Roxanne Lorraine *research scientist*
DeVriendt, David Mark *crop adviser, agronomist*
Dubowsky, Sondra *zoologist*
Duewer, Elizabeth Ann *biology educator*
Engel, Leslie Carroll *cell and molecular biologist, researcher*
Florence, Paul Smith *agronomist, business owner*
Forbes, Milton Lester *biology educator, writer*
Frizzell, Linda Diane Bane *exercise physiologist*
Gossling, Jennifer *microbiologist*
Hynes, John Thomas *food scientist*
Jacobs, Hyde Spencer *soil chemistry educator*
Johnson, Brenda Kay *biology educator*
Johnson, Ray O. *research scientist*
Lacey, Howard Raymond *food technologist*
Merrill, Michelle C. *science educator, health educator*
Proft Cink, Cecilia Jo *animal scientist*
Schuh, Joseph Francis *weed scientist*
Smith, Philip Luther *molecular geneticist*
Spiess, Eliot Bruce *biologist, educator*
Wiatr, Christopher L. *microbiologist*
Wilson, Douglas R. *science foundation executive*
Yamoor, Mohammed Younis *livestock and agricultural development consultant*

SCIENCE: MATHEMATICS AND COMPUTER SCIENCE

UNITED STATES

ILLINOIS

Argonne
Milosavljevic, Aleksandar Dušan *computer scientist*

Arlington Heights
Shenefiel, Chris Allen *software engineering administrator, educator*

Aurora
Moses, Robert Kenneth *computer technician*

Barrington
Hansen, William Anthony *computer educator*

Belleville
Shepherd, Byrd *systems analyst*

Bellwood
Beauchamp, Jann A. *information scientist, educator*

Bloomington
Prescott, Richard Paul, Jr. *computer company consultant*

Carbondale
Wallis, Walter Denis *mathematician, researcher*

Champaign
Catlett, Charles E. *computer center administrator, network researcher*

Chicago
Beat, Gregory J. *technology facility administrator*
Friedman, Arnold Edward *computer scientist*
Fry, Jonathan Bradford *software engineer*
Fry, Philip Michael *business student*
Gogola, Frank Xavier, Jr *information technology executive, consultant*
Gomer, Anne Olah *mathematics educator*
Hanson, Floyd Bliss *applied mathematician, computational scientist, mathematical biologist*
Kirkpatrick, Anne Saunders *systems analyst*
Larson, Nancy Celeste *computer systems manager*
Lumpkin, Beatrice *mathematics educator*
MacLane, Saunders *mathematician, educator*
Nadathur, Gopalan *computer science educator*
Polyak, Stephen T. *systems consultant*
Prellwitz, Grant Alan *software developer*
Reifenrath, Todd Francis *software developer*
Tantry, Subhash Belman *computer consultant*
Tier, Charles *applied mathematics educator*
Wolf, Margaret A. *computer programmer*

Crescent City
Paris, Michael Anthony *mathematics educator*

Danville
Arnold, Scott Gregory *computer information systems specialist*

De Kalb
Blair, William David *mathematics educator*
Sigwart, Charles Dallas *computer scientist, educator*
Torok, Stephen *information science educator, writer, historian*
Van Meer, Gretchen Leah *engineering educator*

Des Plaines
Drezdzon, William Lawrence *mathematics educator*

Elk Grove Village
Fowler, Carol Helen *acquisitions consultant*

Evanston
Benson, John Allen *mathematics educator*
Chen, Gui-Qiang *mathematician, educator, researcher*

Godfrey
McDaniels, John Louis *retired mathematics educator*

Grayslake
Dulmes, Steven Lee *computer science educator*

Hanover Park
Krull, Dennis Keith *computer programmer, market analyst*

Hinsdale
Butler, Margaret Kampschaefer *retired computer scientist*

Hoffman Estates
Ritter, David Allen *computer science consultant*

Itasca
Ayedun, Kehinde Peter *information systems executive*
Kerr, Wayne Nelson *data processing professional*

Lake in the Hills
Ferino, Christopher Kenneth *computer information scientist*

Lake Zurich
Teeters, Joseph Lee *mathematician, consultant*

Lansing
Criswell, Scott Lee, Jr. *computer automation consultant*

Libertyville
Shipshock, Michael Donald *engineer*

Lisle
Payne, Craig William *information scientist, educator*
Townsley-Kulich, Lisa Gail *mathematics educator*

Lombard
Royster, Darryl *computer programmer and analyst*

Mahomet
Blevins, Jack Louis *hardware and software development consultant*

Malta
Schwendau, Mark Steven *computer graphics educator*

Maywood
Baldwin, Allan Oliver *information scientist, higher education executive*

Melrose Park
Zemaitis, Consuelo Irene *mathematics educator*

Mendon
Donley, Sarah Lynn *computer programmer/analyst*

Moline
Larson, Richard James *computer network systems executive*
Meacham, Jeffrey Wayne *computer programmer*
White, Reginald Wesley *computer educator*

Morton
Grisham, George Robert *mathematics educator*

Naperville
Buntrock, Robert E. *information consultant, organic chemist*
Mitchell, Alton Jay *software engineer*

Niles
Michael, Michael Shlemon *programmer analyst*

Normal
Eggan, Lawrence Carl *math and computer science educator*
Jones, Graham Alfred *mathematics educator*
Otto, Albert Dean *mathematics educator*
Rariden, Robert Lee *information scientist, educator*

Oak Brook
Fogle, Denise Marie *computer consultant*

Palatine
Bender, Virginia Best *computer science educator*

Peoria
Haverhals, John S. *mathematics educator*
Lawler, Glenn Bruce *computer software executive*
McGaughey, Albert Wayne *retired mathematics educator*

Rockford
Frang, Jerry Lee *mathematics educator*

Rolling Meadows
Matson, Peggy Kepuraitis *software engineer*

Rosemont
Haworth, Steven John *software quality specialist*

Schaumburg
Ford, Gary Henry *computer engineer*
Nichols, Greg Mark *systems analyst*

Skokie
Woodford, Mark M. *laboratory automation specialist, computer system project administrator*

Springfield
Curran, Michael D. *computer consultant*
Kwon, Ojoung *computer scientist, educator, consultant*
Lorenzi, John Charles *computer analyst, musician*
Vetter, William Max *government information technology administrator*

Urbana
Brand, Stephen *research associate*
Nahrstedt, Klara *computer science educator*
Paley, Hiram *mathematician*
Riahi, Daniel Nourollah *mathematics educator, researcher*
Vardy, Alexander *mathematician, engineer*
Williams, Martha Ethelyn *information science educator*

Villa Park
Belchak, Frank Robert *computer technologist*
Fosdick, Howard *computer scientist*

Westchester
Pavelka, Elaine Blanche *mathematics educator*

Wheaton
Mayer, Donna Marie *management information systems manager*

INDIANA

Anderson
Harbron, Thomas Richard *computer science educator*

Bloomington
Puri, Madan Lal *mathematics educator*

Crown Point
Leskow, Olive *retired mathematics educator*

East Chicago
Brezene, George S. *systems analyst*

Elwood
Dawson, James Buchanan *computer consulting firm executive*

Fort Wayne
Everill, Richard Harold *computer information scientist*

Gary
Kini, Ranjan Bailur *management information systems educator*

Hammond
Yackel, James William *mathematician, academic administrator*

Hobart
Richards, Michael S. *programmer*

Indianapolis
Bauer-Tomich, Faith E. *programmer, analyst*
Caraher, Michael Edward *systems analyst*
Cliff, Johnnie Marie *mathematics and chemistry educator*
Martindale, Larry Richard *computer services company consultant*
McDonell, Edwin Douglas *information systems executive, consultant, writer*
Nontell, Steven Earl *systems analyst*
Roberts, Dale Burton *systems analyst*
Watt, Jeffrey Xavier *mathematics sciences educator, researcher*
Zheng, Lisa Liqing *computer programmer*

Kokomo
Ray, Tuhin *computer engineer*

La Porte
Shreve, Michael Gerald *computer consultant*

Lafayette
de Branges de Bourcia, Louis *mathematics educator*

Muncie
Leitze, Annette Emily Ricks *mathematics educator*
Yff, Peter *mathematics educator*

Notre Dame
Bass, Steven Craig *computer science educator*
Borelli, Mario *mathematics educator, program director*
Chen, Danny Ziyi *computer scientist, educator*

Saint John
Smith, Terry Lynn *information scientist*

South Bend
Williams, Lynn Roy *mathematics and statistics educator, consultant*

West Lafayette
Fuller, William Richard *mathematics educator*
Kane, Robert B. *mathematics educator, academic dean*
Spafford, Eugene Howard *computer science educator, consultant, author*

Westville
Schwingendorf, Keith Eugene *mathematician, educator, researcher*

Woodburn
Hoot, Marvin Jay *computer consultant*

IOWA

Ames
Brearley, Harrington Cooper, Jr. *computer science educator*
Dahiya, Rajbir Singh *mathematics educator, researcher*
David, Herbert Aron *statistics educator*

Cedar Rapids
O'Connor, Francis Gerald *computer systems management executive*

Center Junction
Antons, Pauline Marie *mathematics educator*

Chariton
Mikesell, Jason Lee *programmer analyst*

Grinnell
Adelberg, Arnold Melvin *mathematics educator, researcher*
Ferguson, Pamela Anderson *mathematics educator, educational administrator*

Hiawatha
Ashbacher, Charles David *computer programmer, educator, mathematician*

Iowa City
Harris, Gregory *computer scientist, researcher*
Johnson, Eugene Walter *mathematics editor*
Park, June Sung *information systems educator*
Potra, Florian Alexander *mathematics educator*
Strohmer, Gerhard Otto *mathematics educator*

Marion
Stover, Donald Rae *software engineering executive, retired*

Sioux City
Steinhaus, Carolyn Pinkerton *computer science educator*

Waverly
Brunkhorst, Robert John *computer programmer, analyst*

KANSAS

Derby
Custine, Christopher G. *computer programmer*

Haysville
Canup, Larry Dale *data systems specialist*

Lawrence
Gay, Aleda Susan *mathematician, educator*
Himmelberg, Charles John, III *mathematics educator, researcher*

Manhattan
Unger, Elizabeth Ann *computer science educator, dean*

Shawnee
Segale, John P. *computer system administrator*

Shawnee Mission
Isberg, Larry Alger *software professional*

Topeka
Foust, Thomas A. *information scientist, minister*

Wichita
Aelmore, Donald K. *systems engineer*
Hostetler, John Jay *systems consultant*
Riffel, Teresa Lynn *systems analyst, consultant*
Wright, Peggy Ann *artificial intelligence specialist*

MICHIGAN

Allendale
Jorgensen, Paul C. *computer scientist, educator*

Ann Arbor
Beutler, Frederick Joseph *information scientist*
Brucken, Nancy Elizabeth *systems analyst*
Fields, Matthew H. *composer, educator, computer programmer*
Gehring, Frederick William *mathematician, educator*
Gilmore, Helen Carol *computer specialist, executive*
Jacquez, Geoffrey Mark *biomedical software company executive*
Krieg, Laurence John *computer educator*
Krieg, Martha Fessler *software engineer*
Lewis, Donald John *mathematics educator*
McGill, Michael John *computer/information scientist*
Patt, Yale Nance *computer science educator*
Song, Renming *mathematics educator, researcher*

Belleville
Meyer, Thomas J. *mathematics educator*

Bellevue
Hamel, Louis Reginald *systems analysis consultant*

Bloomfield Hills
Graff, Robert Alan *computer consultant*

Dearborn
Brown, James Ward *mathematician, educator, author*
Saenz, Gilbert *computer programmer and analyst, poet*

Detroit
Conrad, Michael Earl *computer scientist, researcher*
Grosky, William Irvin *computer science educator*

East Lansing
Cheng, Betty Hsiao-Chih *computer science educator, researcher*
Mc Coy, Thomas LaRue *mathematician, educator*

Farmington Hills
Karniotis, Steven Paul *computer scientist*

Flint
Casadonte, Michael John *computer technician*
D'Souza, Harry J. *mathematics educator*

Grand Junction
May, Bryce Jon *computer consultant*

Grand Rapids
DeMaagd, Gerald Robert *data security consultant*
Timpe, Michael Wayne *systems analyst*

Grosse Pointe
Williford, Edward Allan, III *software consultant*

Houghton
Hicks, Darrell Lee *applied and computational mathematician, educator, consultant*

Ironwood
Tincher, John Evan *timber company executive, consultant*

Kalamazoo
Campbell, Bonnie Jo *mathematics educator*
Hsieh, Philip Po-Fang *mathematics educator*
Johnson, Steven Frederick *computer software developer, internet service*

Novi
Chow, Chi-Ming *retired mathematics educator*

Plymouth
Huang, Charles *software engineer*

Rochester
Wang, Stuart Sui-Sheng *mathematics educator*

Rochester Hills
Graves, Vashti Sylvia *computer analyst, consultant*

Saginaw
Mader, William Steven *systems analyst, operations specialist*

Southfield
Arlinghaus, William Charles *mathematics educator*
Ferguson, Roger Clark *computer science educator*
Raghavan, Srikant *educator, operations management specialist*

Troy
Bennett, Pamela Gale *computer scientist, knowledge engineer*
Miller, Hugh Thomas *computer consultant*

Warren
Bley, Ann *program analyst*
Ginsberg, Myron *computer scientist*

West Bloomfield
Miller, Nancy Ellen *computer consultant*

Whitmore Lake
Carr, Doleen *computer and environmental specialist, consultant*

Ypsilanti
Buckeye, Donald Andrew *mathematics educator*
Gledhill, Roger Clayton *statistician, engineer, mathematician, educator*
Janardan, Konanur Gundappasetty *mathematics and statistics educator*

MINNESOTA

Brooklyn Park
Krautkremer, James J. *information scientist*

Crystal
Torgerson, Thomas Wayne *software developer*

Excelsior
Henke, Janice Carine *educational software developer and marketer*

Golden Valley
Savitt, Steven Lee *computer scientist*

Inver Grove Heights
Evans, Roger Lynwood *scientist, patent liaison*

Luverne
Jelken, James Franklin *computer programmer*

Mankato
Mericle, Robert Bruce *mathematics educator*

Maple Grove
Birr, Larry Gale *software systems designer*

Minneapolis
Du, Ding-Zhu *mathematician, educator*
Garfield, Joan Barbara *statistics educator*
Gini, Maria Luigia *computer science educator*
Nitsche, Johannes Carl Christian *mathematics educator*
Papanikolopoulos, Nikolaos Panagiotis *computer science educator*
Smith, Michael Lawrence *computer company executive, consultant*

Moorhead
Heuer, Gerald Arthur *mathematician, educator*

New Brighton
Shier, Gloria Bulan *mathematics educator*

Roseville
Rhodes, Suzanne Ruth *computer specialist, property administrator*

Saint Cloud
Gilbride, Kathleen Sue *business analyst*
Julstrom, Bryant Arthur *computer science educator*

Saint Paul
Christiano, Mary Helen *systems analyst*
McClure, Alvin Bruce *computer programmer and analyst*
Meyer, John Jay *computer systems analyst*
Ritschel, James Allan *computer research specialist*
Schlieckert, Mary Jean *software development professional*

Spring Lake Park
Powell, Christopher Robert *systems programmer, computer scientist*

Winona
Gardiner, Ormsin Sornmoonpin *mathematics educator, physicist, electrical engineer*

MISSOURI

Columbia
Beem, John Kelly *mathematician, educator*
Renner, Paul Eric *systems analyst, consultant*

Creve Coeur
Weidlick, Michael Joseph *information systems specialist*

Gladstone
Wetzel, Karl H. *computer programmer*

Grain Valley
Hounschell, John Charles *software engineering manager and programmer*

Kansas City
Medhi, Deepankar *computer science educator*
Noe, James Kirby *computer consultant*
Peake, Candice K. Loper *data processing professional*
Schroeder, Shari *software analyst*

Marshall
Hedrick, James Chris *research and development specialist*

Maryville
King, Terry Lee *statistician, mathematician*

Rolla
Zobrist, George Winston *computer scientist, educator*

Saint Charles
Peek, Gary Edwin *computer consultant, skydiving instructor, author*

Saint Louis
Battle, Gregory *operations research analyst*
Coerver, Elizabeth Ann *data base consultant*
Fineberg, Charles M. *computer engineer*
Gielow, Thomas Christopher *software engineer*
Gund, Christopher Michael *computer scientist*
Key, Marcella Ann *computer information specialist*
Klein, Joseph Vincent *computer systems analyst*
Raeuchle, John Steven *computer analyst*
Sabharwal, Chaman Lal *computer science educator*
Ungacta, Malissa Sumagaysay *software engineer*

Springfield
Cale, John Wesley *software engineer*
Robertson, Ruth Ann *systems analyst, engineer*

NEBRASKA

Falls City
Koso, Mic D. *computer programmer, mechanical engineer*

Grand Island
Broadwell, Tonja JoAnn *computer analyst*

Omaha
Chen, Zhengxin *computer scientist*
Hayek, Linda Marie *mathematics educator*
Nissen, Bart Alan *systems analyst*

Scottsbluff
Herbel, Alvin *computer specialist*

NEVADA

Henderson
Jackson, Robert Loring *science and mathematics educator, academic administrator*

NORTH CAROLINA

Swansboro
Mullikin, Thomas Wilson *mathematics educator*

NORTH DAKOTA

Grand Forks
Uherka, David Jerome *mathematics educator*

Jamestown
Woodle, Robert M. *mathematics educator*

OHIO

Akron
Anderson, Eric Charles *computer systems analyst, programmer*
Hollis, William Frederick *information scientist*
Powell, Robert Eugene *computer operator*

Wortham, James Calvin *retired mathematics educator*

Beavercreek
Hoffman, Lawrence Wayne *software engineer, systems consultant*

Beechwood
Lange, Frederick Edward, Jr. *computer information systems architect*

Bowling Green
Newman, Elsie Louise *mathematics educator*

Canton
Barb, Cynthia Marie *mathematics educator*

Chagrin Falls
Schneider, Judith Lynn *mathematics educator*

Cincinnati
Flick, Thomas Michael *mathematics educator, educational administrator*
Nissel, Mark Edward *software engineer*
Pierce, Patricia Ann *software engineer, consultant*
Wenz, Thomas William *computer services executive, government administrator*
Zimov, Bruce Steven *software engineer*

Cleveland
Babula, Maria *software engineer*
Ellis, Brenda Lee *mathematician, computer scientist, consultant, educator*
Hacker, Steven D. *information systems consultant*
Schumann, Mark Wolfgang *computer programmer, consultant*
Waren, Allan David *computer information scientist, educator*
Wild, Stephen Lloyd *computer scientist*

Columbus
Dull, Clifford John *religious groups analyst*
Gartner, Daniel Lee *computer information executive*
Jain, Raj *educator*
Josephson, John Richard *computer scientist*
March, Lee Anthony *computer specialist*
Rakowski, Marek *mathematician, engineer, educator*
Roeder, Rebecca Emily *software engineer*
Sharrock, Anita Kay *computer specialist*
Wyman, Bostwick Frampton *mathematics educator*
Yagel, Roni *computer science educator, consultant*
Zweben, Stuart Harvey *information scientist, educator*

Dayton
Grubbs, Paulette Denise *information engineer*
Jehn, Betty L. (Betty L. James) *retired computer science educator*
Jehn, Lawrence Andrew *computer science educator*
Khalimsky, Efim *mathematics and computer science educator*
McCracken, Charles *mathematician, educator*
Pan, Yi *computer science educator*
Rucker, Richard Sim *information systems executive*
Tseng, Jack C. *systems analyst*

Defiance
Mirchandaney, Arjan Sobhraj *mathematics educator*

Fairborn
Monnin, Frank Joseph *retired program analyst*

Hamilton
Fein, Thomas Paul *software support specialist*

Highland Heights
Burke, Thomas Joseph *software engineer*

Hudson
Pawlicki, Eleanor Genevieve *information specialist*

Independence
Wise, Lawrence Allen *computer analyst*

Kent
Fridy, John Albert *mathematics educator*
Varga, Richard Steven *mathematics educator*

Mansfield
Gregory, Thomas Bradford *mathematics educator*

Marysville
Martin, Barbara Lee *computer programmer, analyst*

Milford
Saxena, Rajiv *software engineer*

Moreland Hills
Sedlock, Michael Eugene *information systems executive*

Newark
Myntti, Jon Nicholas *software engineer*
Perera, Vicumpriya Sriyantha *mathematics educator*

North Olmsted
Pingatore, Sam Robert *systems analyst, consultant, business executive*

Norton
Henderson, Russ G. *data processing consultant*

Oberlin
Colley, Susan Jane *mathematician, educator*

Oxford
Patton, Jon Michael *research consultant, decision science educator*

Pickerington
Blackman, Edwin Jackson *software engineer*

Portsmouth
Hamilton, Virginia Mae *mathematics educator, consultant*

Ravenna
Wagner, Jon A. *computer programmer*

Richmond Heights
Williams, Gilbert Thomas *systems engineer, consultant*

Saint Henry
Thompson, Robert Douglas *computer science educator, consultant*

Toledo
Weber, William Braman, Jr. *mathematician, educator*
Williams, Debra Arneice *computer engineer*

Upper Sandusky
Baker, Harrison Scott *computer consultant*

Westerville
Miller, Charles *business management research and measurements consultant*
Yantis, Richard Perry *mathematics educator, consultant*

Wright Patterson AFB
Mandrell, Gene Douglas *logistician*
Tamburino, Louis Anthony *computer scientist, researcher*

Xenia
Fussichen, Kenneth *computer scientist*

TEXAS

San Antonio
Phinazee, Henry Charles *systems analyst, educator*

WISCONSIN

Eau Claire
Schoen, Carl Patrick *mathematics educator*
Suresh, Nalina *mathematics educator*

Franklin
Bui, Ty Van *computer programmer, systems analyst*

Greenfield
Ouimet, Bernard *programmer*

La Crosse
Matchett, Andrew James *mathematics educator*

Madison
Brauer, Fred Günther *mathematics educator*
Buchholz, Mary *computer systems administrator*
de Boor, Carl *mathematician*
Draper, Norman Richard *statistician, educator*
Finton, David Jon *computer scientist*
Hickman, James Charles *business and statistics educator, business school dean*
Schroeder, John Lorren *computer programmer*
Shea, Daniel Francis *mathematician, educator*

Milwaukee
Anderson, Alfred Jerry *biostatistician*
Heinzelman, Edward George *computer scientist*

Richland Center
Sriskandarajah, Jeganathan *mathematics educator*

Whitewater
Verma, Krishnanand *mathematics educator, researcher, administrator, consultant*

ADDRESS UNPUBLISHED

Altheide, Phyllis Sage *computer scientist, software engineer*
Ancheta, Caesar Paul *software developer*
Andalafte, Edward Ziegler *mathematics educator*
Bharath, Ramachandran *decision sciences educator*
Bloch, Anthony Michael *mathematician, educator*
Bonacina, Maria Paola *computer science educator*
Bowlby, Richard Eric *retired computer systems analyst*
Carey, Joseph Richard *mathematics educator*
Downey, Deoborah Ann *systems specialist*
Enck, John *computer analyst*
Franklin, Marcia Ruth *information systems professional*
Graham, Parker Lee, II *computer systems manager*
Harris, Shari Lea *mathematics educator*
Hawk, Carole Lynn *insurance company executive*
Heinicke, Peter Hart *computer consultant*
Houlette, Forrest Thomas *computer trainer, software consultant, writer*
Jaw, Andrew Chung-Shiang *software analyst*
Juister, Barbara Joyce *retired mathematics educator*
Olsen, Paul Gary *computer operator*
Pollock, Karen Anne *computer analyst*
Reumann, Velma Rose *mathematician*
Sobottka, Fred Herman *systems analyst*
Spellmire, Sandra Marie *systems analyst, programmer*
Stevens, William Alan *computer consultant*
Stuart, Sandra Joyce *computer information scientist*
Tan, Hui Qian *computer science and civil engineering educator*
Warman, Richard Stanley *retired statistician*
Wilson, James P. *computer consultant*

SCIENCE: PHYSICAL SCIENCE

UNITED STATES

CALIFORNIA

Pasadena
Gurnis, Michael Christopher *geological sciences educator*

San Diego
Rhee, Heasoon Arzberger *research chemist*

Santa Barbara
Einhorn, Martin B. *physics educator*

ILLINOIS

Abbott Park
Chu, Daniel Tim Wo *pharmaceutical researcher*
Figard, Steve David *biochemist*
Jeng, Tzyy-Wen *biochemist*
Porter, William Robert *chemist*

Argonne
Berger, Edmond Louis *theoretical physicist*
DeVolpi, Alexander *physicist*
Frost, Brian Reginald Thomas *materials scientist*
Green, David William *chemist, educator*
Murdoch, Bruce Thomas *health physicist*
Price, Lawrence Edward *physicist*
Rosenberg, Richard Allan *research chemist*
Sabau, Carmen Sybile *chemist*

Beech Grove
Murray, Kenneth Malcolm, Jr. *physicist*

Bellwood
Gregory, Vance Peter, Jr. *chemist*

Bloomington
Wilson, Raymond Gale *physics educator*

Buffalo Grove
Eachus, Alan Campbell *chemist*

Cahokia
Viehland, Larry Alan *chemist, educator*

Carbondale
Horsley, Doc *meteorologist*
Smith, Gerard Vinton *chemistry educator*
Tao, Rongjia *physicist, educator*

Champaign
Bauer, Robert Alan *engineering geologist*
Cartwright, Keros *hydrogeologist, researcher*
Simmons, Ralph Oliver *physics educator*

Charleston
Buchanan, David Hamilton *chemistry educator*
Jorstad, Robert Bernard *geologist, educator*

Chicago
Bonham, Russell Aubrey *chemistry educator*
Carlson, Eric Dungan *astronomer*
Cronin, James Watson *physicist, educator*
Epstein, Wolfgang *biochemist, educator*
Farnsworth, Wells Eugene *biochemist, educator*
Gislason, Eric Arni *chemistry educator*
Halpern, Jack *chemist, educator*
Hildebrand, Roger Henry *astrophysicist, physicist*
Iqbal, Zafar Mohd *cancer researcher, biochemist, pharmacologist, toxicologist, consultant*
Jackson, Patricia Anne *environmental executive*
Jain, Nemi Chand *chemist, coating scientist, educator*
Johnson, Porter Wear *physics educator*
Krawetz, Arthur Altshuler *chemist, science administrator*
Lederman, Leon Max *physicist, educator*
Ledvina, Christopher Thomas *geologist, educator*
Moore, Paul Brian *geophysical sciences educator*
Norris, James Rufus, Jr. *chemist, educator*
Robbins, Kenneth Carl *biochemist*
Runkle, Robert Scott *environmental company executive*
Schramm, David Norman *astrophysicist, educator*
Sibener, Steven Jay *chemistry educator*
Trenary, Michael *chemistry educator*
Truran, James Wellington, Jr. *astrophysicist*
Van Ostenburg, Donald Ora *physics educator*
Winston, Roland *physicist, educator*
Wozniak, Wayne Theodore *physical chemist*
Xu, Charlie Yuping *geochemist*
Zhao, Meishan *chemical physics educator, researcher*

Clarendon Hills
Kemmer, Frank Nelson *consulting water chemist and engineer*

Clinton
Wood, Susanne Griffiths *environmental chemist, microbiologist*

De Kalb
Rosenmann, Daniel *physicist, educator*
Sill, Larry Robert *physics educator*

Des Plaines
Wei, Lester Yeehow *research chemist*

Downers Grove
Atoji, Masao *physical chemist*
Schlenk, Fritz *retired biochemistry educator*
Young, Donald Edward *retired physicist, science company executive*

Elmhurst
Betinis, Emanuel James *physics and mathematics educator*

Evanston
Basolo, Fred *chemistry educator*
Burwell, Robert Lemmon, Jr. *chemist, educator*
Freeman, Arthur J. *physics educator*
Katsnelson, Esfir Z. *physicist*
Klotz, Irving Myron *chemist, educator*
Letsinger, Robert Lewis *chemistry educator*
Meshii, Masahiro *materials science educator*
Sachtler, Wolfgang Max Hugo *chemistry educator*
Seidman, David N(athaniel) *materials science and engineering educator*
Shriver, Duward Felix *chemistry educator, researcher, consultant*
Vaynman, Semyon *materials scientist*

Flossmoor
Kumar, Sudhir *biochemistry and neurology educator, researcher*

Glen Ellyn
Curry, Bill Perry *physicist, consultant*
Mooring, F. Paul *physics editor*

Glencoe
Surgi, Marion Rene *chemist*

Glenview
Savic, Stanley Dimitrius *physicist*

Hoffman Estates
Schulz, Michael John *fire and explosion analyst, consultant*

Homewood
Parker, Eugene Newman *retired physicist, educator*

Kankakee
Hanson, John Elbert *chemistry educator*

Lemont
Davids, Cary Nathan *physicist, researcher*
Erck, Robert Alan *metallurgist, researcher*
Geesaman, Donald Franklin *physicist*
Lin, Yuh Meei *natural product chemist*
Matheson, Max Smith *physical chemical researcher*

Lombard
McCoy, Jeanie Shearer *analytical chemist, consultant*

Marseilles
Van Horn, John Kenneth *health physicist, consultant*

Maywood
McDonald, Hugh Joseph *biochemist*

Mount Carmel
Fornoff, Frank J(unior) *retired chemistry educator, consultant*

Naperville
Dixon, William Gordon, Jr. *geologist*
Hensley, Albert Lloyd, Jr. *research chemist, technical consultant*
Kaduk, James Albert *crystallographer*
Sellers, Gregory Jude *physicist*
Sherren, Anne Terry *chemistry educator*

Normal
Bunting, Roger Kent *chemistry educator, business owner*
Lash, Timothy David *chemistry educator, researcher*
Young, Robert Donald *physicist, educator*

North Chicago
Carney, Ronald Eugene *chemist*
Walters, D. Eric *biochemistry educator*

North Riverside
Gorody, Anthony Wagner *geologist, geochemist, consultant*

O'Fallon
Bjerkaas, Carlton Lee *technology services company senior scientist*
Jenner, William Alexander *meteorologist, educator*

Olney
Horrall, Kenneth Bruce *geophysicist, geologist, researcher, consultant*

Peoria
Bagby, Marvin Orville *chemist*
Chamberlain, Joseph Miles *retired astronomer, educator*
Cunningham, Raymond Leo *research chemist*
Gardner, Harold Wayne *research biochemist*
King, Jerry Wayne *research chemist*
Rankin, John Carter *consulting chemist*
Saha, Badal Chandra *biochemist*

Rock Island
Christoffel, Kurt Matthew *chemistry educator*

Rockford
Sorensen, Keld *biochemist*
Walhout, Justine Simon *chemistry educator*
Yu, Fu-Li *biochemistry educator, cancer researcher*

Springfield
Gallina, Charles Onofrio *nuclear scientist*

Urbana
Drickamer, Harry George *retired chemistry educator*
Dunn, Floyd *biophysicist, bioengineer, educator*
Fermanian, Thomas Walter *turfgrass scientist, educator*
Govindjee *biophysics and biology educator*
Hiltibran, Robert Comegys *biochemistry educator*
Hsui, Albert T. *geophysicist, educator*
Jonas, Jiri *chemistry educator*
Mihalas, Dimitri Manuel *astronomer, educator*
Salamon, Myron Ben *physicist, educator*
Snyder, Lewis Emil *astrophysicist*
Weber, Nicholas Noel *physicist, researcher*
Wuebbles, Donald James *atmospheric scientist*

Villa Park
Domsky, Irving Isaac *chemist*

Wheaton
Haddock, Gerald Hugh *geology educator*

INDIANA

Anderson
Gay, David Earl *experimental chemist*

Bloomington
Chisholm, Malcolm Harold *chemistry educator*
Foster, Mark Gardner *retired physicist, educator*
Macfarlane, Malcolm Harris *physics educator*
Robeson, Scott Michael *climatologist*

Elkhart
Kuo, Charles Chang-Yun *materials science engineer*

Evansville
Hankins, Marie Garner *chemistry educator*

Greenfield
Myerholtz, Ralph W., Jr. *retired chemical company executive, research chemist*

Greenwood
Hamill, Robert L. *biochemical research advisor*

Hammond
Ammeraal, Robert Neal *biochemist*
Longas, Maria Oliva *chemistry educator, researcher*
Vojcak, Edward Daniel *metallurgist*

Indianapolis
Belagaje, Rama M. *molecular biologist*
Hackler, Ronald Ervin *chemist*
Han, Xianming Lance *physicist*
Kleschick, William Anthony, III *research chemist*
Leonard, Jack E. *environmental company executive*
Liu, Pingyu *physicist, educator*
Long, Eric Charles *biochemist*
Mason, Douglas Michael *environmental scientist*
Porter, Herschel Donovan *organic chemist*
Termine, John David *biochemist*
Wolt, Jeffrey Duaine *environmental chemist, researcher*

Lafayette
Krockover, Gerald Howard *science educator*
Moder, Kenneth Philip *chemist*
Porile, Norbert Thomas *chemistry educator*

Mishawaka
Braunsdorf, James Allen *physics educator*

Muncie
Harris, Joseph McAllister *chemist*

Notre Dame
Berry, Henry Gordon *physicist, educator*
Garg, Umesh *physicist, educator*
Marshalek, Eugene Richard *physics educator*
Trozzolo, Anthony Marion *chemistry educator*

Schererville
Kadlec, John Woodrow *chemical industry manager*

Speedway
Crandell, Jodie Leigh *environmental specialist*

Terre Haute
O'Sullivan, Mary Colette *chemistry educator*

West Lafayette
Bray, Ralph *physics educator*
Brown, Herbert Charles *chemistry educator*
Cramer, William Anthony *biochemistry and biophysics researcher, educator*
Crane, Frederick Loring *biochemistry educator*
Grant, Edward Robert *chemistry educator*
Lipschutz, Michael Elazar *chemistry educator, consultant, researcher*
Miller, David Harry *physics educator*
Overhauser, Albert Warner *physicist*

IOWA

Ames
Barnes, Richard George *physicist, educator*
Charlesworth, Paul *research chemist, educator*
Corbett, John Dudley *chemistry educator*
Finnemore, Douglas Kirby *physics educator*
Gschneidner, Karl Albert, Jr. *metallurgist, educator, editor, consultant*
Lynch, David William *physicist, educator*
McCallum, Ralph William *materials scientist*
Olson, James Allen *biochemist, educator*
Ruedenberg, Klaus *theoretical chemist, educator*
Seifert, Karl E. *geology educator*
Young, Bing-Lin *physics educator and researcher*

Cedar Rapids
Klosterbuer, James Albert *environmental specialist*

Fayette
Olson, Erik Richard *chemistry educator*

Grinnell
Cunningham, Charles Ernest *physics educator*

Iowa City
Conway, Thomas William *biochemist, educator*
Goodridge, Alan Gardner *research biochemist, educator*
Gurnett, Donald Alfred *physics educator*
Norbeck, Edwin, Jr. *physics educator*

Sioux Center
Maatman, Russell Wayne *retired chemistry educator*

Waverly
Newbrough, Stacey Ann Snyder *environmental educator*

KANSAS

Emporia
Aber, Susan Ward *earth science educator*

Fort Scott
Caple, Sharon *chemistry educator*

Hays
Millhollen, Gary Lloyd *geology educator*

Kansas City
Grisolia, Santiago *biochemistry educator*

Lawrence
Alexander, Jose *organic chemist*
Ammar, Raymond George *physicist, educator*
Cutler, Bruce *electron microscopist*
Eagleman, Joe R. *meteorologist, educator*
Harmony, Marlin Dale *chemistry educator*
Prosser, Francis Ware, Jr. *physics educator*
Rich, Paul Martin *environmental studies educator, biologist*
Whittemore, Donald Osgood *geochemist, hydrogeochemistry educator*

Lebanon
Colwell, John Edwin *retired aerospace scientist*

Manhattan
Hedgcoth, Charles *biochemistry educator, researcher*
Sherwood, Peter Miles Anson *chemistry educator*

Merriam
Fought, Lorianne *chemist*

North Newton
Quiring, Frank Stanley *chemist, educator*

Pittsburg
Foresman, James Buckey *geologist, geochemist, industrial hygienist*

Shawnee Mission
Nuzman, Carl Edward *hydrologist*

Topeka
Barton, Janice Sweeny *chemistry educator*
Foerster, Kent *environmental scientist*

Wichita
Agarwal, Ramesh Kumar *aeronautical scientist, researcher, educator*
Cowdery, Robert Douglas *consulting geologist*
Howell, Orvie Leon *geologist*

MICHIGAN

Ann Arbor
Agranoff, Bernard William *biochemist, educator*
Atzmon, Michael *materials scientist*
Becchetti, Frederick Daniel *physicist, educator*
Beyer, Robert Edward *retired biochemist, educator*
Blurton, Keith Frederick *chemist*
Connor, David Thomas *chemist*
Cordes, Eugene Harold *pharmacy and chemistry educator*
Crary, Selden Bronson *physicist*
DeWitt, Sheila Hobbs *research director*
Haddock, Fred T. *astronomer, educator*
Hagel, William Carl *metallurgical consultant*
Hillegas, William Joseph *materials scientist*
Jones, Lawrence William *educator, physicist*
Massey, Vincent *biochemist, educator*
Olson, Ronald A. *parks and recreation administrator*
Pearson, William Hardy *chemistry educator*
Smith, Richard Harding *analytical biochemist*
Woo, Peter Wing Kee *organic chemist*

Cross Village
Stowe, Robert Allen *catalytic and chemical technology consultant*

Dearborn
Brailsford, Alan David *physicist*
Reeve, Lorraine Ellen *biochemist, researcher*
Ryntz, Rose Ann *chemist*

Detroit
Beres, William Philip *physics educator*
Gupta, Suraj Narayan *physicist, educator*
Johnson, Carl Randolph *chemist, educator*
Wierzbicki, Jacek Gabriel *physicist, researcher*

East Lansing
Brown, Boyd Alex *physicist, educator*
Harrison, Michael Jay *physicist, educator*
Kaplan, Thomas Abraham *physics educator*
Miller, Patricia Palmer *environmental professional*
Preiss, Jack *biochemistry educator*
Tolbert, Nathan Edward *biochemistry educator, plant science researcher*
Yussouff, Mohammed *physicist, educator*

Farmington
Theodore, Ares Nicholas *research chemist*

Farmington Hills
Hodjat, Yahya *metallurgist*
Raczkowski, Waldemar Tadeusz *medical research biochemist, analyst, consultant*

Ferndale
Pence, Leland Hadley *organic chemist*

Flint
Cox, Mary E. *physics and engineering educator, consultant*
Hagler, Alvin Russell *physicist, educator*

Grand Rapids
Kottke, John William *meteorologist*

Houghton
Bates, Dallas Kelvin *chemistry educator*

Kalamazoo
Chou, Kuo-Chen *biophysical chemist*
Fisher, Jed Freeman *chemist*
Greenfield, John Charles *bio-organic chemist*
Kaiser, David Gilbert *chemist*
Mowery, Mark Roth *chemist*
Theis, Don Layne *research chemist*

Lansing
Bitondo, Michael Leonard *pollution control professional*

Madison Heights
Chapman, Gilbert Bryant *physicist*

Marquette
Regis, Robert Stephen *geology educator*

Midland
Bailey, Robert Earl *environmental chemist, researcher*
Dreyfuss, Patricia *chemist, researcher*
Hahn, Stephen Frank *polymer chemist*
Homan, Gary Rex *chemist*
Leng, Marguerite Lambert *regulatory consultant, biochemist*
Loboda, Mark Jon *physicist*
Speier, John Leo, Jr. *retired chemist*
Stenger, Vernon Arthur *analytical chemist, consultant*
Stull, Daniel Richard *retired research thermochemist, educator, consultant*

Okemos
Prouty, Chilton Eaton *geologist, educator*

Rochester
Garfinkle, David *physics educator*

Saginaw
VanHouten, Jacob Wesley *environmental manager, educator, trainer*

Three Rivers
Boyer, Nicodemus Elijah *organic-polymer chemist, consultant*

Warren
Deak, Charles Karol *chemist*
Heremans, Joseph Pierre *physicist*
Lambert, David *physicist*
Schwartz, Shirley E. *chemist*
Tibbetts, Gary George *research physicist*
Vaz, Nuno Artur *physicist*

Ypsilanti
Snyder, Donald Mark *research chemist*

MINNESOTA

Austin
Brown, Rhoderick Edmiston *biochemistry researcher, educator*

Brainerd
Vig, Pradeep Kumar *geophysics educator*

Lake Elmo
Vivona, Daniel Nicholas *chemist*

Minneapolis
Arnett, Carroll D. *chemistry educator*
Berg, Stanton Oneal *firearms and ballistics consultant*
Carr, Charles William *biochemist, emeritus educator*
Carr, Robert Wilson, Jr. *chemistry educator*
Kreevoy, Maurice Mordecai *retired chemistry educator*
Stuewer, Roger Harry *physics historian*
Valls, Oriol Tomas *physicist*
Wood, Wellington Gibson, III *biochemistry educator*

Northfield
Buchwald, Caryl Edward *geology educator, environmental consultant, educational consultant*

Plymouth
Morgan, Robert Anthony *optical physicist, research scientist*

Saint Paul
Alm, Roger Russell *chemist*
Clapp, C(harles) Edward *research chemist, soil biochemistry educator*
Formo, Jerome Lionel *chemist*
Hobbs, Howard Cory *geologist*
Lee, Charles C. *physicist*
Mikkelson, Raymond Charles *physics educator*
Perry, James Alfred *environmental scientist, consultant, educator, administrator*
Reeves, Ann Holt *conservationist*

Saint Peter
Fuller, Richard Milton *physics educator*

White Bear Lake
Holmen, Reynold Emanuel *chemist*

MISSOURI

Cape Girardeau
Hathaway, Ruth Ann *chemist*

Columbia
Bryan, David Alan *physicist, researcher, engineer*
Johns, Williams Davis, Jr. *geologist, educator*
Kuntz, Robert Roy *chemistry educator*
Unklesbay, Athel Glyde *geologist, educator*
Yelon, William B. *physicist, researcher*

Creve Coeur
Bockserman, Robert Julian *chemist*

Jefferson City
Coen, Larry Paul *geologist, environmental manager*

Kansas City
Ching, Wai Yim *physics educator, researcher*
Dias, Jerry Ray *chemistry educator*
Gier, Audra May Calhoon *environmental chemist*
Grosskreutz, Joseph Charles *physicist, engineering researcher, educator*
Hasan, Syed Eqbal *environmental geologist, educator*
Wickham-St. Germain, Margaret Edna *mass spectrometrist*

Kirksville
Baughman, Russell George *chemical educator, researcher*
Festa, Roger Reginald *chemist, educator*

Maryland Heights
Chinn, Rex Arlyn *chemist*

Rolla
Gregg, Jay Mason *geology educator*
Hale, Edward Boyd *physics educator, scientist*
Hatheway, Allen Wayne *geological engineer, educator*
Leventis, Nicholas *chemistry educator, consultant*
Shrestha, Bijaya *nuclear scientist*
Van De Mark, Michael Roy *chemistry educator*
Vineyard, Jerry D. *geologist*

Saint Louis
Brannigan, Lawrence Harlan *chemist, educator*
Diuguid, Lincoln Isaiah *chemist*
Haacke, E(wart) Mark *physicist, consultant*
Henry, Phillip Michael *physicist, development engineer*
Hobbs, Charles Floyd *research chemist*
Holtzer, Marilyn Emerson *physical chemist, educator*
Hughes, Michael Scott *physicist*
Maywood, Paul Stanley *geologist, educator*
Melchiorre, Erik Baldwin *geochemist, educator*
Soper, Donald Arthur *geologist*
Sterling, David A. *environmental and occupational health science educator*
Taber, Donald Charles *chemist*
Wasson, Richard Lee *organic chemistry consultant*
Wrighton, Mark Stephen *chemistry educator*
Zienty, Ferdinand Benjamin *chemical company research executive, consultant*

Springfield
Criswell, Charles Harrison *analytical chemist, environmental and forensic consultant, executive*
Whitaker, Robert John *physics educator*

NEBRASKA

Chadron
Swanson, Jack Lee *chemistry educator*

Fremont
Carlson, Gary Albert *earth science educator*

Kearney
Blickensderfer, Peter William *analytical chemist, retired chemistry educator*

Lincoln
Carlson, Michael Paul *analytical chemist, toxicologist*
Fabrikant, Ilya Iosifovich *physics educator*
Lindsley-Griffin, Nancy *geologist, educator*
Sellmyer, David Julian *physicist, educator*
Starace, Anthony Francis *theoretical atomic physicist*
Yoder, Bruce Alan *chemist*

Omaha
Becker, David Joseph *geologist*
Clowe, Curtis James *environmental chemist*
Wilkins, Daniel Chaim *physicist, educator*
Zepf, Thomas Herman *physics educator, researcher*

NORTH CAROLINA

Charleston
Hayes, Peter Charles *research chemist*

NORTH DAKOTA

Bismarck
Loken, Lance Gabriel *geologist, soil scientist*

Fargo
Burton, Michael Thomas *earth science educator*

Minot
Clausen, Eric N. *earth science educator, university program director*

OHIO

Ada
Smith, Stuart Allan *groundwater scientist, consultant, educator*

Akron
Cheng, Stephen Zheng Di *chemistry educator, polymeric material researcher*
Frederick, John Edgar *chemistry educator*
Halasa, Adel F. *chemist*
Rader, Charles Phillip *chemist*
Wiff, Donald Ray *polymer physicist, manager, researcher*

Alliance
Murdoch, Arthur Roy *chemistry educator*

Archbold
Bergman, Jerry Rae *science educator*

Bowling Green
Mundschau, Michael Victor *chemist*
Neckers, Douglas Carlyle *chemistry educator*

Brecksville
Farkas, Julius *chemist*

Cincinnati
Clarson, Stephen John *chemistry educator, university dean*
Devitt, John William *physicist*
Heineman, William Richard *chemistry educator*
Kawahara, Fred Katsumi *research chemist*
Kupper, Philip Lloyd *chemist*
McLean, Larry R. *biochemist*
Meal, Larie *chemistry educator, researcher, consultant*
Menyhert, Stephan *retired chemist*
Stricklin, Rebecca Ellen *chemistry educator*
Thomas, Craig Eugene *biochemist*

Circleville
Barkley, John Richard *physicist*

Cleveland
Bidelman, William Pendry *astronomer, educator*
Blackwell, John *polymers scientist, educator*

Falzone, Anthony Joseph *research physicist*
Heuer, Arthur Harold *material science and engineering educator*
Koenig, Jack L. *chemist, educator*
Kowalski, Kenneth Lawrence *physicist, educator*
Myers, Ronald Eugene *chemist, consultant*
Singham, Mano *physicist*
Smith, Mark Anthony *biochemist, educator*
Wolff, Gunther Arthur *physical chemist*

Cleveland Heights
Dannley, Ralph Lawrence *retired chemistry educator*

Columbus
Adelson, Edward *physicist, musician, lecturer*
Chiu, Ing-Ming *biochemistry educator*
Hausman, Hershel Judah *physicist, researcher*
Leonelli, Joseph *laser remote sensing expert and executive*
Lott, John Alfred *chemist, educator*
Miller, Terry Alan *chemistry educator*
Moody, J(ohn) William *natural resources executive*
Reese, Douglas Wayne *geologist*
Relle, Ferenc Matyas *chemist*
Sayre, Richard Thomas *biochemist, plant molecular biologist*
Schenz, Anne Filer *product research and development supervisor, educator*
Schenz, Timothy William *chemist*
Slonim, Arnold Robert *biochemist, physiologist*
Steigman, Gary *physics and astronomy educator*
Voss, Anne Coble *nutritional biochemist*
Wojcicki, Andrew Adalbert *chemist, educator*

Dayton
Chuck, Leon *materials scientist*
Cook, Lois Anna *chemistry educator*
Emrick, Donald Day *chemist, consultant*
Fang, Zhaoqiang *research physicist*
Hall, Byron Carlyle, Jr. *physics educator, philosopher, researcher*
Hangartner, Thomas Niklaus *medical physicist, educator*
Janning, John Louis *research scientist, consultant*
Loughran, Gerard Andrew *chemistry consultant, polymer scientist*
Mehta, Rajendra *chemist, researcher, administrator*
Spicer, John Austin *physicist*

Delaware
Dillman, Lowell Thomas *physics educator*

Doylestown
Galehouse, Daniel Christian *physicist, researcher*

Dublin
Castillo, Allan Paul *metallurgist*

Euclid
Zelle, Joseph Frank *radio engineer, physics and electronics educator*

Fairborn
Workman, John Mitchell *chemist*

Granville
Bork, Kennard Baker *geology educator*

Grove City
Keyser, E. Glen *nutritional biochemist*

Hamilton
Gatton, Carl Grover *environmental technologist*

Kent
Duffy, Norman Vincent *chemistry educator*

Manchester
McCluskey, Matthew Clair *physical chemist*

Miamisburg
Taylor, William Leroy *physical chemist*

Norwalk
Germann, Richard Paul *pharmaceutical company chemist, executive*

Oberlin
Carlton, Terry Scott *chemist, educator*

Plain City
Throckmorton, Peter Eugene *organic chemist, consultant*

Rocky River
Dabrowski, Elizabeth Marie *chemistry educator*

Sheffield Lake
Friend, Helen Margaret *chemist*

Sylvania
Erhardt, Paul William *medicinal chemist*

Toledo
James, Philip B. *physicist, educator*

Twinsburg
Mohr, Eileen Theresa *environmental geologist*
Vickers, David S. *physicist*

Warren
Zimmerman, Doris Lucile *chemist*

Wickliffe
Dunn, Horton, Jr. *organic chemist*
Kornbrekke, Ralph Erik *colloid chemist*

Wright Patterson AFB
Garscadden, Alan *physicist*

Yellow Springs
Taylor, Charles Emery *physics educator*

SOUTH DAKOTA

Rapid City
Bunkers, Matthew John *meteorologist*

TEXAS

Austin
Felthouse, Timothy Roy *research chemist*

VIRGINIA

Alexandria
Krieger, Robert Henry, Jr. *remote sensing specialist*

WISCONSIN

Appleton
Van den Akker, Johannes Archibald *physicist*

Green Bay
Sell, Nancy Jean *chemistry, physics and engineering educator*

Kenosha
Goss, George Robert *chemist*
Schneider, Allan Frank *geology educator and researcher*

Madison
Brown, Philip Edward *geology educator*
Burris, Robert Harza *biochemist, educator*
Casey, Martha Link *chemist*
Cassinelli, Joseph Patrick *astronomy educator*
Chilton, Jeffrey Ethan *physicist, researcher*
Cox, Michael Matthew *biochemist*
Craney, Terrance Lee *physics educator*
Dahl, Lawrence Frederick *chemistry educator*
Deutsch, Harold Francis *biochemist, researcher, educator*
Ellis, Arthur Baron *chemist, educator*
Hokin, Lowell Edward *biochemist, educator*
Kaczmarek, Kurt Alan *scientist*
Kraushaar, William Lester *physicist, educator*
Lagally, Max Gunter *physics educator*
March, Robert Herbert *physicist, writer*
McVoy, Kirk Warren *physicist, educator*
Morton, Stephen Dana *chemist*
Scherer, Victor Richard *physicist, computer specialist, musician*
Sih, Charles John *pharmaceutical chemistry educator*
Siitari, David William *materials scientist, consultant*
Smith, Wesley Harold *physics educator*
Stearns, Charles Richard *meteorologist, educator, farmer*
Wendt, Christopher Harold *physicist*
West, Robert Culbertson *chemistry educator*
Zimmerman, Howard Elliot *chemist, educator*

Milwaukee
Baker, John Edward *cardiac biochemist, educator*
Dittman, Richard Henry *physics educator*
Jache, Albert William *retired chemistry educator, scientist*
Lachance, David Jospeh *geologist*
Lamelas, Francisco J. *physicist, educator*
Mallmann, Alexander James *physics educator, researcher*
Nakamoto, Kazuo *chemistry educator*
Reid, Scott Allen *chemistry educator*
Runquist, Alfonse William *chemist*
Salcedo, Rodolfo Nacino *environmental scientist*

Racine
Tweet, Orlando A. *retired industrial chemist*

Waukesha
Bruning, David Hall *astronomer*

CANADA

MANITOBA

Winnipeg
Kanfer, Julian Norman *biochemist, educator*
Smith, Ian Cormack Palmer *biophysicist*

ONTARIO

Windsor
Jones, William Ernest *chemistry educator*

ADDRESS UNPUBLISHED

Berry, Richard Stephen *chemist*
Catacosinos, Paul Anthony *geologist, educator, researcher*
Cummin, Alfred S(amuel) *retired chemist*
Doane, William McKee *chemist, researcher*
Feist, William Charles *consultant*
Gustafson, David Harold *retired research chemist*
Lakshman, Mahesh Kumar *chemist*
Lakshminarayanan, Vasudevan *physiological optics scientist*
Masters, Bruce Allen *biostratographer, micropaleontologist*
Nash, John Joseph *secondary education educator*
Ngai, Ka-Leung *biochemist, researcher*
Nyquist, Richard Allen *vibrational spectroscopist*
Rauscher, Elizabeth Ann *physics educator, researcher*
Riew, Changkiu Keith *materials scientist, polymer chemist*
Schmidt, Edward G. *astronomer*
Shipley, Anna Frances *human environmental sciences educator*
Strobel, Rudolf Gottfried Karl *biochemist*
Topper, Robert Quinn *theoretical chemist*
Warshawsky, Isidore *physicist, consultant*
Westendorf, Robert George *chemist*

Wilson, Kenneth Geddes *physics research administrator, educator*

SOCIAL SCIENCE

UNITED STATES

CALIFORNIA

Los Angeles
Harberger, Arnold Carl *economist, educator*

ILLINOIS

Canton
Chandler, Theresa Lyne *sociology educator*

Carbondale
Derge, David Richard *political science educator*

Champaign
Crandall, Lee Alden *medical sociologist, educator*
Kanet, Roger Edward *political science educator, university administrator*
Nagel, Stuart Samuel *political science educator, lawyer*

Chicago
Becker, Gary Stanley *economist, educator*
Berg, Evelynne Marie *geography educator*
Blaut, James Morris *geography educator*
Block, Carolyn Rebecca *criminologist, researcher*
Chaloupka, Frank Joseph *economics educator*
Coase, Ronald Harry *economics educator*
Fogel, Robert William *economist, educator, historian*
Fox, Sharon Elizabeth *political scientist, educator, researcher*
Gardiner, John Andrew *political science educator*
Goldstein, Margaret Hardy *political scientist*
Hamada, Robert S(eiji) *economist, educator*
Harris, Chauncy Dennison *geographer, educator*
Hebel, Doris A. *astrologer*
Irwin, Douglas Alexander *economics educator*
Johnson, Janet Helen *Egyptology educator*
Kupper, John Douglas *political consultant*
Larson, Allan Louis *political scientist, educator, lay church worker*
Lipson, Charles Henry *political scientist*
Lyons, Arthur *economist*
Lyttle, Bradford Janes *political scientist*
Madden, Bartley Joseph *economist*
Mahler, Vincent A. *political science educator*
Malik, Raymond Howard *economist, scientist, corporate executive, inventor, educator*
Plassmeyer, Susan Anne *public policy analyst*
Rampersad, Peggy A. Snellings *sociologist*
Riepe, Mark William *economic consultant*
Rudolph, Susanne Hoeber *political and social science educator*
Schloss, Nathan *economist*
Schultz, Theodore William *retired economist, educator*
Tromanhauser, Edward Downer *criminologist and political science educator*
Warner, (Robert) Stephen *sociologist, educator*

De Kalb
Arnhart, Larry Eugene *political science educator*
Gherity, James Arthur *economics educator*
Guest, Buddy Ross *geography educator*
Martellaro, Joseph Alexander *economics educator*

Edwardsville
Browne, Dallas *anthropology educator*
Farley, John Edward *sociologist, educator, researcher*
Virgo, John Michael *economist, researcher, educator*

Evanston
Bienen, Henry Samuel *political science educator, university executive*
Brown, James Allison *anthropology educator*
Gordon, Robert James *economics educator*
Jacob, Herbert *political science educator*
Page, Benjamin Ingrim *political science educator, researcher*
Walsh, Joseph *policy analyst, educator, social worker*

Glen Ellyn
Frateschi, Lawrence Jan *economist, statistician, educator*

Heyworth
Martin, William E. *agricultural economist, educator*

Jacksonville
Judd, Laurence Cecil *sociology and Asian studies educator, consultant*

Joliet
Holmgren, Myron Roger *social sciences educator*
Struckhoff, David Raymond *sociology educator*

Macomb
Burchard, Max Norman *sociology educator*
Karim, Muhammad Bazlul *international studies educator*
Walzer, Norman Charles *economics educator*

Naperville
Galvan, Mary Theresa *economics and business educator*

Normal
Lind, Nancy Susan *political science educator*
Owen, Virginia Lee *economist educator*

Rock Island
Kivisto, Peter John *sociologist*

Rockford
Longhenry, John Charles *social studies educator, human resources specialis*

Romeoville
Houlihan, James William *criminal justice educator*

Schaumburg
Handler, Douglas Perry *economist*

Urbana
Baer, Werner *economist, educator*
Carmen, Ira Harris *political scientist, educator*
Cloutier, Martin *agricultural economist, researcher*
Dovring, Folke *land economics educator, consultant*
Emerson, Thomas Eugene *anthropology educator*
Lie, John Jaehoon *sociology educator*
Linowes, David Francis *political economist, educator, corporate executive*
Merritt, Richard Lawrence *political scientist, educator*
Rich, Robert F. *political sciences educator, academic administrator*
Salamon, Sonya *anthropology educator*

Vienna
Jones, Bennie Ray *sociologist, draftsman*

INDIANA

Bloomington
Diamant, Alfred *political science educator*
Hart, Jeffrey Allen *political scientist, educator*
Jumper, Roy Eulliss *political science educator*
O'Meara, Patrick O. *political science educator*
Wicker, Elmus Rogers *economics educator*

Carmel
Nardi, Michael Angelo *public policy consultant*

Evansville
Barber, Charles Turner *political science educator*

Greencastle
Sahu, Sunil Kumar *political science educator*

Indianapolis
Erickson, Judith Bowen *sociologist*
Fredland, Richard Alan *political science educator*
Krauss, John Landers *public policy and urban affairs consultant*
Labsvirs, Janis *economist, educator*
Mason, David Stewart *political science educator*

Lafayette
Melson, Robert Frank *political science educator*

Mishawaka
Conrad, Donald Lewis *sociology educator, clergyman*

Muncie
Meyer, Fred Albert, Jr. *political science educator*

New Albany
Wolf, Thomas Phillip *political science educator, consultant*

Notre Dame
Tenorio, Rafael Alberto *economics educator, researcher*
Weigert, Andrew Joseph *sociology educator*

South Bend
Apostolides, Anthony Demetrios *economist, educator*
Hamburg, Roger Phillip *political science and public affairs educator*
Lewis, John Menzies *political science educator*

Terre Haute
Conyers, James E. *sociology educator*
Dando, William Arthur *geography and geology educator*
Perry, Glenn Earl *political science educator*

West Lafayette
Anderson, James George *sociologist, educator*
Martin, Marshall Allen *agricultural economist*
Masters, William Alan *agricultural economist*
Wilson, Franklin Leondus, III *political science educator*

IOWA

Ames
Gradwohl, David Mayer *anthropology educator*
Meier, Robert Frank *sociology educator*
Quirmbach, Herman Charles *economics educator*

Cedar Falls
Brown, Kenneth Hackman *economics educator*

Decorah
Leake, Richard Scott *economics and management educator, tennis coach*
Wangsness, Wayne Roger *economics educator*

Des Moines
Dhussa, Ramesh Chandra *geography educator*

Iowa City
Ciochon, Russell Lynn *paleoanthropologist*
De Puma, Richard Daniel *classical archaeology educator*
Pogue, Thomas Franklin *economics educator, consultant*

Mount Vernon
Allin, Craig Willard *political science educator*

Sioux City
Lafferty, Nancy Ann *sociology educator*

West Des Moines
Wright, Roy Dean *sociologist, educator, association executive*

KANSAS

Kansas City
Beisecker, Analee Elizabeth *medical sociology educator, researcher*

Lawrence
Heller, Francis H(oward) *law and political science educator emeritus*
Osterkamp, Lynn Bowie *gerontologist, consultant, social worker*
Swann, Michael M. *geographer, educator*
Yetman, Norman Roger *sociology educator*

Manhattan
Ambrosius, Margery Marzahn *political scientist, educator*
Babcock, Michael Ward *economics educator*
Ottenheimer, Harriet Joseph *anthropologist, educator*
Parish, Thomas Scanlan *human development educator*
Thomas, Lloyd Brewster *economics educator*
White, Stephen Edward *geography educator*

Overland Park
Burger, Henry G. *anthropologist, vocabulary scientist, publisher*

Pittsburg
Behlar, Patricia Ann *political science educator*

Shawnee Mission
Gaar, Marilyn Audrey Wiegraffe *political science educator*

Topeka
Jervis, David Thompson *political science educator*

Wichita
Lawless, Robert *anthropologist, educator*
Sheffield, James Franklin, Jr. *political science educator*
Skaggs, Jimmy M. *economics educator*

MASSACHUSETTS

Boston
Carfora, John Michael *economics and political science educator*

Cambridge
Mansbridge, Jane Jebb *political scientist, educator*

MICHIGAN

Ann Arbor
Arlinghaus, Sandra Judith Lach *mathematical geographer, educator*
Courant, Paul Noah *economist, educator*
Freedman, Ronald *sociology educator*
Jacobson, Harold Karan *political science educator, researcher*
Kelly, Raymond Case *anthropology educator*
Kingdon, John Wells *political science educator*
Kmenta, Jan *economics educator*
Lieberthal, Kenneth Guy *political science educator*
Mackie-Mason, Jeffrey King *economics educator*
Mc Cracken, Paul Winston *economist, business educator*
Sarri, Rosemary Conzemius Alcuin *sociology and social work educator*
Smith, Bennett Holly *biological anthropologist*
Smith, Dean Gordon *economist, educator*
Whallon, Robert Edward *anthropology educator*
Williams, Melvin Donald *anthropologist, educator*

Berrien Springs
Storfjell, Johan Bjornar *archaeology educator*
Young, John Wesley *political science educator*

Big Rapids
Ball, Richard Everett *sociology educator*
Santer, Richard Arthur *geography educator*

Dearborn
Rosenthal, Marilynn Mae *medical sociology educator*
Smith, John William *political scientist*

Detroit
Baba, Marietta Lynn *business anthropologist*
Ferguson, Tamara *clinical sociologist*
Kaplan, Bernice Antoville *anthropologist, educator*
Weiss, Mark Lawrence *anthropology educator*

East Lansing
Boyer, Kenneth Duncan *economics educator*
Busch, Lawrence Michael *sociologist, researcher*
Kallen, David Johnson *clinical sociologist, educator*
Kestenbaum, Lawrence *political science educator*
Kreinin, Mordechai Eliahu *economics educator*
Manderscheid, Lester Vincent *agricultural economics educator*
Manning, Peter Kirby *sociology educator*
Obst, Norman Philip *economist, educator*
Woodbury, Stephen Abbott *economics educator*

Holland
Holmes, Jack Edward *political science educator*

Houghton
Solomon, Barry David *geography and environmental policy educator*

Kalamazoo
Buskirk, Phyllis Richardson *retired economist*
Butterfield, Jim *political science educator*
Isaak, Alan Charles *political science educator*
Markle, Gerald Elliott *sociology educator*

Lansing
Ballbach, Philip Thornton *political consultant*
Halsey, John Robert *archaeologist*

Marquette
Spady, Dale Roland *sociology educator*
West, Krista Ann *political science educator*

Mount Pleasant
Baugh, Joyce A. *political science educator*
Croll, Robert Frederick *economist, educator*
Grabinski, C. Joanne *gerontologist, educator*

Rochester
Casstevens, Thomas William *political science educator*
Gregory, Karl Dwight *economist, educator, consultant*

Rochester Hills
Schrimsher, Kandace Pearson *sociology educator, researcher*

Sault Sainte Marie
Johnson, Gary Robert *political scientist, editor*
Ward, William Scott, II *economic development specialist*

University Center
Hoerneman, Calvin A., Jr. *economics educator*

Ypsilanti
Blackwell, Thomas T. *leadership educator, consultant*
Henry, Stuart Dennis *criminology educator*

MINNESOTA

Burnsville
Hiller, Joan Vitek *sociologist*

Collegeville
Finn, Daniel Rush *economics and theology educator, former dean*
Prevost, Gary Francis *government educator, researcher, writer*

Duluth
Mulholland, Susan Collins *archaeologist, researcher*

Forest Lake
Marchese, Ronald Thomas *ancient history and archaeology educator*

Grand Marais
Hattery, Robert Wilber *political science educator*

Minneapolis
Ali, Mohammed *economics educator*
Broadbent, Jeffrey Praed *sociology educator*
Chipman, John Somerset *economist, educator*
Davis, Gordon Bitter *business educator*
Erickson, W(alter) Bruce *business and economics educator, entrepreneur*
Gray, Charles Melvin *economist, educator, consultant*
Gray, Virginia Hickman *political science educator*
Johnson, Badri Nahvi *sociology educator, real estate business owner*
Noonan, Norma Lina Corigliano *political science educator*
Ohanian, Lee Edward *economist, consultant*
Scoville, James Griffin *economics educator*
Weisbrod, Rita Roffers *sociologist, educator*

Moorhead
Trainor, John Felix *retired economics educator*

North Branch
Honadle, George Holmes *social sciences educator*

Northfield
Lewis, Stephen Richmond, Jr. *economist, academic administrator*
Schier, Steven Edward *political science educator, political consultant*

Saint Cloud
Frank, Stephen Ira *political science educator*
Reha, Rose Krivisky *retired business educator*

Saint Joseph
Bye, Lynn Ellen *social work educator*

Saint Paul
Rosenblatt, Paul Conrad *family educator*

MISSOURI

Cape Girardeau
Berg, Donald James *sociologist, educator*

Columbia
Breimyer, Harold Frederick *agricultural economist*
Campbell, Rex *sociology educator*
Hardy, Richard J. *political scientist, educator*
Hopkins, Jill D. *anthropologist, educator*
Lubensky, Earl Henry *anthropologist, archaeologist*
Salter, Christopher Lord *geography educator*
Spier, Robert Forest Gayton *anthropologist, educator*
Tillema, Herbert Kendall *political science educator*
Yesilada, Birol Ali *political science educator*

Half Way
Graves, Jerrell Loren *demographic studies researcher*

Jefferson City
Farnen, Mark Edward *economic development specialist*
Kammerdiener, Randall Robert *political operative*

Kansas City
Cayton, John Charles *criminalist, forensic scientist*
Gamer, Robert Emanuel *political science educator*
Weiner, Stuart Earl *economist*

Kirksville
Graber, Robert Bates *anthropologist*

Point Lookout
Quiko, Eduard *political science educator, consultant*

Saint Charles
Pruett, Helen Gorham *home economist*
Scupin, Raymond Urban *anthropology educator*

Saint Clair
Gullet, Leon Estle *retired cartographer*

Saint Joseph
Hamzaee, Reza Gholi *economics educator*

Saint Louis
Givens, Douglas Randall *archaeologist, educator*
Hooyman, Thomas Gerand *medical ethicist, consultant*
Pittman, David Joshua *sociologist, educator, researcher, consultant*
Vago, Steven *sociology educator, consultant, writer*
Welch, Patrick James *economics educator, author, consultant*
Williams, Mary Alice Baldwin *retired home economist, volunteer consultant*
Winkler, Anne E. *economics educator*
Witherspoon, William *investment economist*
Wolford, John Brenton *anthropologist, educator*
Woodward, Robert Simpson, IV *economics educator*
Worseck, Raymond Adams *economist*

Springfield
Beerline, Kurt Alan *sociology educator*
Van Cleave, William Robert *international relations educator*

Warrensburg
Waite, James LeRoy *political science and geography educator*
Young, James V. *political science educator*

NEBRASKA

Harrison
Knudson, Ruthann *environmental consultant*

Kearney
Anderson, Patricia Ann *home economics educator, family and consumer sciences educator*
Glazier, Stephen Davey *anthropologist, theologian*

Lincoln
Peterson, Wallace Carroll, Sr. *economics educator*

Mc Cook
Larson, Elizabeth Ann *family and consumer sciences educator*

Omaha
Brugler, Alan Robert *economic analyst*
Mueller, Keith John *political science educator*
Rousseau, Mark Owen *sociologist*
Wise, Kenneth Lloyd *political science, international studies educator*

NORTH DAKOTA

Grand Forks
Kweit, Robert William *political science, public administration educator*

OHIO

Akron
Feltey, Kathryn Margaret *sociology educator*
Noble, Allen George *geography and planning educator*
Pendleton, Brian Franklin *sociology educator, former college dean*

Athens
Koshal, Rajindar Kumar *economics educator*

Berea
Miller, Dennis Dixon *economics educator*

Bowling Green
Goza, Franklin William *sociology educator*

Chagrin Falls
Malone, Laurence Adams *economist, consultant*

Cincinnati
Margolis, Michael Stephen *political scientist*
Stevie, Richard George *economist*
Thomas, Norman Carl *political science educator*
Waltzer, Herbert *political science educator*

Cleveland
Beall, Cynthia *anthropologist, educator*
Bonutti, Karl Borromeo *retired economics educator*
Burke, John Francis, Jr. *economist*
Carter, John Dale *organizational development executive*

Columbus
Brown, Lawrence Alan *geography educator*
Camboni, Silvana Maria *resources sociologist*
Epstein, Erwin Howard *sociology and education educator*
Hunt, Fern Ensminger *retired home economics educator, researcher*
Lobao, Linda Mary *sociologist, educator*
Miranda, Mario Javier *economics educator*
Towner, Carolyn H. *political scientist*

Dayton
Karns, Margaret Padelford *political science educator*

Gambier
Clor, Harry M. *political scientist, educator*

Granville
Buker, Eloise Ann *political science educator*

Hamilton
New, Rosetta Holbrock *home economics educator, nutrition consultant*

Kent
Feinberg, Richard *anthropologist, educator*
Robyn, Richard Courtney *political scientist*

Oxford
Barilleaux, Ryan J. *politcal science educator*

Shaker Heights
Daroff, William C. *political consultant, public poli[cy] analyst*

Toledo
Attoh, Samuel Aryeetey *geographer, educator, planner*
Bardis, Panos Demetrios *sociologist, social philosopher, historian, author, editor, poet, educator*
Heintz, Carolinea Cabaniss *retired home economic[s] educator*
Jan, George Pokung *political science educator*

Waterford
Riley, Nancy Mae *retired vocational home economics educator*

Youngstown
Binning, William Charles *political scientist, educat[or]*
Dulberger, Reid Edward *economic development executive*

SOUTH DAKOTA

Brookings
Gilbert, Howard Alden *economics educator*
Gritzner, Charles Frederick *geography educator*
Janssen, Larry Leonard *economics educator, researcher*
Napton, Darrell Eugene *geography educator*
Wagner, Mary Kathryn *sociology educator, forme[r] state legislator*

Fort Thompson
Godfrey, Joyzelle Effie *economic development and small business consultant*

Sioux Falls
Weiland, Richard Paul *political scientist*

Vermillion
Clem, Alan Leland *political scientist*

TEXAS

Irving
Thomas, Cynthia Gail *public policy research executive*

WISCONSIN

Appleton
Adenwalla, Minoo *political science educator*

Beloit
Kreider, Leonard Emil *economics educator*

Eau Claire
Davidson, John Kenneth, Sr. *sociologist, educator, researcher, author, consultant*

La Crosse
Heim, Joseph Peter *political science educator*

Madison
Canon, David Theodore *political science educator*
Haller, Archibald Orben *sociologist, educator*
Olmstead, Clarence Walter *geography educator, retired*
Salomon, Frank Loewen *anthropology educator*
Taylor, Fannie Turnbull *social education and arts administration educator*
Whitehead, Neil Lancelot *anthropologist*
Wolfe, Barbara L. *economics educator, researcher*

Menasha
Brey, James Arnold *geography and geology educa[tor]*

Milwaukee
Baumann, Carol Edler *political science educator*
Bibby, John Franklin *political science educator, writer*
Chowdhury, Abdur Rahim *economics educator*
Metz, Donald Lehman *sociology educator*
Mitchell, George Allen *public policy consultant*
Nardin, Terry *political science educator*

Platteville
Fatzinger, Dale Roger *geographer, educator*
Waters, Thomas Alfred *political science educator*

Superior
Ball, Michael Ray *sociologist, educator*

WYOMING

Laramie
Shogren, Jason Fredrick *economics educator*

ADDRESS UNPUBLISHED

Bambrick, James Joseph *labor economist, labor relations executive*
Blank, Rebecca Margaret *economist*
Brewer, Rose Marie *sociologist, educator*
Dale, Stephen Glenn *political science educator*
Dalessio, Stewart *criminology educator*
Drummond, Dorothy Weitz *geography education consultant, educator, author*
Gonzalez, Sergio Antonio *economist*
Greeley, Andrew Moran *sociologist, author*
Green, Donald Edward *sociology educator*
Holleb, Doris B. *urban planner, economist*

Houseman, Gerald L. *political science educator, writer*
Kofmehl, Kenneth Theodore *political science educator*
Kohn, Walter Samuel Gerst *political scientist, educator*
Lucas, Wayne Lee *sociologist, educator*
Marini, Margaret Mooney *social sciences educator*
McCutcheon, Ronald Eugene *social studies educator*
Reynolds, Nancy Hubbard *sociology educator*
Spencer, Milton Harry *economics and finance educator*
Stinson, Thomas Franklin *economist, educator*
Weil, Rolf Alfred *economist, university president emeritus*